Mickelson Clarified Lexicordance
of the New Testament

"What You Need to Know"

See page iv.

See page iv for such details as:

- "Yeu" is the plural form of "you."
- There are special punctuation and quotation marks.
- *Italics* and Superscript have special meaning.
- Certain proper names, such as "AbRaham," have special treatment.

The fullness of the *Hebraic-Koine* Greek is expressed in English using these and other communication techniques. It is a clarity never before attained in any translation.

This is so important, this notice precedes the Title Page itself.

Also by **Jonathan K. Mickelson**

(NT Reader Editions (4th Edition) - ***(English text only)***:

*MCT **Reader** New Testament, Mickelson Clarified*

available in Standard (9.5pt), Large (12pt), Podium (15pt) print, and **TRI-COLUMN** (9.5pt)

New Testament, intermediate formats (4th Edition) ***with context numbers***:

*Mickelson Clarified **Scholar** New Testament, MCT* (in Standard and Large print)

New Testament Resources (4th Edition) ***with context numbers***:

*Mickelson Clarified **Dictionary** of New Testament Greek, MCT* *

*Mickelson Clarified **Concordance** of the New Testament, MCT* *

*Mickelson Clarified **Interlinear** New Testament, MCT* (with Greek text)

*MCT **English Index** of the New Testament, Mickelson Clarified*

*(especially designed for the Scholar, Professor, Interlinear, and MCT English Index)

New Testament, **advanced** resources (4th Edition) ***with context numbers***:

*Mickelson Clarified **Professor** New Testament, MCT* (with morphology)

*Mickelson Clarified **Lexicordance** of the New Testament, MCT* (with morphology)

Old Testament, available formats (2nd Edition):

*MCT **Reader** Old Testament, Mickelson Clarified*

available in Standard (9.5pt), Large (12pt), Podium (15pt) print, and **TRI-COLUMN** (9.5pt)

*Mickelson Clarified **Scholar** Old Testament, MCT* (in Standard and Large print)

Old Testament Resources (2nd Edition):

*Mickelson Clarified **Dictionary** of Old Testament Hebrew, MCT* *

*Mickelson Clarified **Concordance** of the Old Testament, MCT* *

*Mickelson Clarified **Interlinear** Old Testament, MCT* (with Hebrew text)

*MCT **English Index** of the Old Testament, Mickelson Clarified*

Septuagint / Octuagint® Resources (1st Edition):

*MCT **Octuagint® Interlinear** Greek Old Testament, Mickelson Clarified*
[a more careful and precise Greek translation of the Hebrew Text, while preserving certain critically distinct vocabulary from the Septuagint. The Septuagint itself is lacking the proper consistency and quality deserving of the Holy Scriptures of Yahweh.]

Hebrew New Testament Resources (1st Edition):

*MCT **Brit Chadashah Interlinear** Hebrew New Testament, Mickelson Clarified*
[a clarified and more precise Hebrew translation of the *Hebraic-Koine* Greek New Testament, with critically distinct vocabulary reconciled from the Hebrew Old Testament and the above-mentioned Octuagint®. To date, not one Hebrew New Testament fully preserves the quality of vocabulary contained in the Holy Scriptures of Yahweh.]

Mickelson Clarified Lexicordance of the New Testament, MCT®

An advanced concordance by word, context and morphology

in the Literary Reading Order©

A precise English concordance to the *Hebraic-Koine* Greek of the Clarified Textus Receptus (the 1550 Stephanus-2019 Mickelson), presented with Strong's Numbers and the complete use of the Mickelson Context Numbers© and enhanced morphology.

FOURTH EDITION:
PROCLAIMER SERIES

Editor, Translator and Lexicographer

יהונתן במשיח ברמיכאל

Jonathan Kristen Mickelson

Kennesaw, Georgia 30152

Mickelson Clarified Lexicordance of the New Testament, MCT®

An advanced concordance by word, context and morphology in the Literary Reading Order

(file vS4.285 – May, 2019)

mctbible.org | plowshare.net | octuagint.org
livingsonpress.com | plowsharemission.com

Library of Congress Cataloging in Publication Data

Mickelson, Jonathan K

Mickelson Clarified Lexicordance of the New Testament, MCT: An advanced concordance by word, context and morphology in the Literary Reading Order /
Jonathan K. Mickelson. – Fourth Edition: Proclaimer Series

ISBN 978-1-60922-034-1

1. Bible. N.T.—Concordances—English.

Library of Congress Control Number: 2019901744

This edition printed on acid-free paper.

Edited by Jonathan K. Mickelson | Typeset by Jonathan K. Mickelson | Cover Design and Artwork by Jonathan K. Mickelson

Acknowledgments

The Men of God in my life: Friends, Pastors, Elders
for your help and continued labors in bringing me toward increasing maturity in Christ – admonishing, correcting, and encouraging me in Love. Thank you for your patience, long-suffering and perseverance.

"What a joy to have stood in the crossroads, having asked for the ancient pathways, and then with the passage of time, to have found the request granted."

J. K. Mickelson

Complete Acknowledgment

The Messiah, Yeshua – Jesus, the Anointed One

For taking pity on my soul, for paying my debt on the Cross and thus purchasing my pardon. For rising from the Dead and securing Eternal Life for those who trust on Him. For His Redeeming Work in my life, and for His calling, equipping, and provision. For inscribing His laws on our hearts and minds. For revelation after revelation and insight upon insight. For the trustworthy expectation of Resurrection unto Eternal Life in Him. For His Love, pure and true.

Far beyond mere words... Thank you.

The Greek New Testament text referenced:

Mickelson Clarified Greek New Testament of the 1550 Stephanus-2019 Mickelson

(2019 Clarified Textus Receptus)

A *Hebraic-Koine* Greek text with Strong's numbers, Mickelson's context numbers and morphology.

vS4.285 – May 4, 2019 – Jonathan K. Mickelson

Based on the Stephanus 1550 Greek New Testament by Erasmus
(also known as the *Textus Receptus*)
v2.04 – July 23, 2005 – Jonathan K. Mickelson
v2.03 – June 10, 2003 – Received via Mark O'Farrell (UTF-8 with accents)
v2.00 – Original (with morphology) – Maurice A. Robinson and William G. Pierpont

Dedication

To you, the one seeking to know the God of AbRaham, of YiTsaq and of Jacob, and seeking to know His Word with greater clarity.

*YiTsaq (Isaac)

Thinking of you at great length caused me to realize that it was both necessary and worth all the sacrifices to bring this work to the light of day.

I take my stand with my predecessors to prevent the linguistic erosion and distortion that seek to obscure God's Word, and I stand to hold fast the Holy Scriptures and preserve their meaning, clarity, and instruction - to preserve their truth for my English-speaking brethren in Christ, and for the generations to follow.

May our heavenly Father open your eyes beyond all that I have seen and known in His Holy Word. May you be strengthened; may you choose to follow Him wholeheartedly, not in the manner of my generation who loved the praise of men; but rather, keep seeking praise from Yahweh, the God of Israel, the Redeemer of the wayward Remnant through His Son, Jesus the Anointed-One.

You must repent, and you must trust upon Jesus alone for forgiveness and Eternal Life.

This Jesus died on the Cross for our moral failings and rose from the dead to secure our Redemption.
Through trust in Jesus for Forgiveness and Salvation, one is reconciled to God our Heavenly Father.
(And thus you fulfill the will of the Father).

And having trusted in Jesus, you must be immersed in water, into Jesus Anointed–
in order to be buried together with him in his death–
that is, to be "congenitally fused together in the resemblance of his death"
and thus also awakened together in his resurrection. (Romans 6:3-11)

There is no other Gospel or Good News from Yahweh than this.

J. K. Mickelson

(An overview of Yahweh and Man)

THE OLD TESTAMENT:

THE TESTIMONY OF YAHWEH – יְהוָה

OF ACCOUNTABILITY, CUSTODIAL SALVATION, AND KINSMAN REDEMPTION

(His personal involvement with Man, but especially with his own distinct People whom he personally ransomed: IsraEL, and those who are grafted in by the Trust)

FROM CREATION AND THE FIRST ADAM

TO THE DELUGE AND NOACH– AND A PROMISE

TO THE CALLING FORTH
AND THE TRUST OF ABRAHAM
TO YAHWEH'S **UNILATERAL COVENANT**
WITH HIM, AND THE SON OF PROMISE, YITSAQ

TO JACOB AND HIS SONS,
THE TWELVE TRIBES OF ISRAEL
AND THEIR SOJOURNING IN EGYPT
(WITH A PROMISE)
TO THE PASSOVER

FROM MOSES AND THE COVENANT OF TORAH-LAW
TO JOSHUA AND THE LAND OF ISRAEL

TO THE JUDGES AND A DECLINE INTO LAWLESSNESS

TO BOAZ AND RUTH
TO THE KINGDOM OF ISRAEL
TO YAHWEH'S PROMISE TO KING DAVID

TO THE DIVIDED KINGDOM
AND CONSTANT OFFENSES AGAINST YAHWEH
TO THE DEPORTATION OF NORTHERN ISRAEL
AND ITS REPOPULATION WITH FOREIGNERS

TO PROPHETS PROCLAIMING ACCOUNTABILITY
UNTO YAHWEH AND THE TORAH-LAW
TO THE DEPORTATION OF SOUTHERN JUDAH

FROM BABYLON TO
THE RETURN OF JUDAH
AND THE INTEGRITY
AND THE TRIALS
OF DANIEL, EZRA, AND NEHEMIAH

AND THEN MORE OFFENSES BY JUDAH
WITH ACCOUNTABILITY

AND THROUGHOUT IT ALL...
THE RELATIONSHIPS, THE BLESSINGS, THE COMPASSION AND HEARTACHE,
THE CALLING TO REPENTANCE, THE STERN ACCOUNTABILITY, AND THE RESCUE...

THERE IS THE PROCLAMATION THAT A SAVIOR SHALL COME,
THE ANOINTED-ONE OF YAHWEH
And he did, and he already established...

THE PROMISED "BRAND-NEW COVENANT"	בְּרִית חֲדָשָׁה "BRIT CHADASHAH"

THE NEW TESTAMENT:

THE TESTIMONY OF YAHWEH – יְהוָה

OF ACCOUNTABILITY, CUSTODIAL SALVATION, AND KINSMAN REDEMPTION

(His personal involvement with Man, but especially with his own distinct People whom he personally ransomed: IsraEL, and those who are grafted in by the Trust)

FROM YESHUA יֵשׁוּעַ TO THE PRESENT...	**SO HEAR THIS AND KNOW...**
Forgiveness, reconciliation, and peace with God, with Custodial Salvation and the Expectation of Glory and the Promise of Eternal Life, first **for the Jew**, and also **for the Gentile**, for those who trust in Anointed-One.	We are all accountable to Yahweh of Hosts. And we shall ALL come before him to give an account, either standing as Kinsman-Redeemed by him, or falling down as already condemned by him. And Anointed-One has already made both Jew and Gentile into One brand-new man, fellow-citizens of God's *heavenly* kingdom, for those who trust in him and are Kinsman-Redeemed.

J. K. Mickelson

Table of Contents

Preface

As a completed work (99.9932%), the *Mickelson Clarified Translation*® (MCT)® of the New Testament has reconciled the English vocabulary with the Greek vocabulary of the Hebraic New Testament Scripture (see the *Mickelson Clarified Dictionary of New Testament Greek* for details on the companion MCT N.T. dictionary). This effort distinctly and consistently accounts for the various concepts, contexts, and abstract uses of the Hebraic use of Koine Greek words. This allows for a more accurate correlation and comprehension of God's Scripture. The companion Greek dictionary documents and defines these distinctions in English.

This unique set of Scriptural Greek vocabulary was spoken by Hebrew contemporaries 2,000 years ago who wrote the biblical text within a 50-year time frame. The Biblical Greek vocabulary largely held the same meaning for each of the writers. I truly trust that the biblical writers, under the influence of the Holy Spirit, chose their words and meant them. The English vocabulary used in this translation preserves the distinctions between similar Greek words. For example, the English words "strength, power, force, might, and authority" have specific meanings and weight, and they are used to express the corresponding Greek words and their derivatives only. This holds true in the companion dictionary as well. This interaction between translation and definition refines the efforts of both, and demands a far higher level of textual, linguistic, and literary accountability than previously adhered to.

The Greek words are defined with discrete English word forms and are used in context, distinctly and consistently, within this translation and the companion dictionary. Because of this, one can learn how and when the Greek words were used by the writers and can more appropriately correlate Scriptural instruction and concepts.

What is the Result?

In regard to this special purpose lexicological concordance ("lexicordance"), the result is a *Biblical Hebraic Greek* to *Modern Biblical English* concordance that correlates and references Greek words and Hebraic concepts that are easily researched by the Modern English speaker (***if*** one is well-knowledgeable of Greek morphology).

- - - - -

In all that has been accomplished in Lord, this task has been undertaken and completed in an understated manner so that each of you may explore God's Holy Scriptures in peace. It will take many years to comprehend all that has been accomplished on your behalf. "Beloved, I·well-wish *to·God* concerning all·things, *such·as for* you to·prosper and to·be·healthy·and·sound, just·as your soul prospers."

(3 John 1:2 MCT)

Your fellow disciple and brother in Jesus,
Jonathan K. Mickelson
יהונתן במשיח ברמיכאל

p.s. Our family name "Mickelson" is pronounced Mahy-kuhl-suhn /ˈmaɪkəlsən/, same as "Michaelson."

Key Tenets of the Mickelson Clarified Translation

- **Bring** the English-speaking **person to the Word of God**, not the Word of God to the English-speaking person (that is, not bringing the Word to someone's mindset or bent, but bringing someone to the Word).
- Preserve the Concept actually being conveyed by the author regardless of all personal, linguistic, structural, or stylistic preferences. Simply render what it says, nothing more, nothing less.
- Again, preserve the Concept, then, with all strength and reason, **preserve the Construct** (verb to verb, noun to noun).
- **Do not transliterate.** Use common English, and **fully render the concept in English.** (e.g. "ambassador" for *apostle*, "Material Wealth" for *Mammon*, "stage-acting hypocrite" instead of merely *hypocrite*, etc.)
- Strive for **Word Consistency within the Given Context.** (e.g. consistent use of "man/husband/menfolk" and "woman/wife/womenfolk" in the given context.)
- **Document the Contexts** in which each word is used (now completed for the New Testament).
- As far as is reasonable, **match each Greek word or phrase** to a unique English word or phrase.
- **Do not undermine a Greek word or concept** by assigning it a single English word: use an English phrase as often and liberally as needed for proper expression.
- **Keep it simple**, easy to read, and easy to comprehend.
- **Do not dumb it down.** If an explicit Greek concept requires a college level word, use it or consider an appropriate, succinct, but accurate phrase.
- Preserving the Concept supersedes all secondary tenets when they conflict with this goal.

This is God's Word. It will verify itself. It will ring true, for it is living, and it is true.

Now arriving at this portion of my journey, I affirm and intimately confirm firsthand that God's Word does verify itself, it does ring true and clear.

— "The Plowman" (J. K. Mickelson)

(one laboring hard for an upright harvest to the Lord from among the The Land— through trust in Jesus Anointed, also being accompanied by the good works which He prepared beforehand for us to mature in and excel in, and to graciously receive reward in such providential blessings as these).

What You Need to Know

Second Person Plural – Yeu

In this translation, the plural form of you is spelled "yeu." The original English plural form was "ye," which has fallen out of use. The very nature of this translation required the distinction between singular and plural use of the second person "you." This solution was prayerfully sought and evaluated over two years. The plural form is consistently used on all occurrences: yeu, yeur, yeurs, and yeurselves. Pronounced "yewa" (yeu) and "yewer" (yeur).

Plural examples: "when yeu pray... according to yeur trust... all things are yeurs... store up for yeurselves treasures in heaven." Remember: you=Only one (singular), yeu=Everyone (plural).

A synopsis of God's Word

by J. K. Mickelson

Now these things have been written, that yeu may trust that Jesus is the Anointed-One, the Son of God; and that trusting, yeu may have life-above in his name. For it is the will of the Father that anyone observing the Son and trusting on him may have eternal life-above, and be raised up at the last day. (see John 20:31 and John 6:40).

- This fulfills the will of God, our Heavenly Father.

Love one another. Just as Jesus loved yeu, yeu also should love one another. For the one loving the other has completely fulfilled Torah-Law, which is completely fulfilled in one saying: You shall love your neighbor as yourself. Also, bring forth fruit that lasts. (John 13:34, John 13:8, Romans 13:10, Galatians 5:14, John 15:16)

- This fulfills the will of the Son.

Keep yourself unstained from the world. Do not be little children in the understanding, but mature. For solid food is for the mature, their senses having been trained through habit toward having discernment of both good and bad; unto works of service, for edification of the body of Anointed-One till they should all come into the oneness of the trust, and of the full discernment of the Son of God, to a perfect man, to the measure of the stature of the fullness of Anointed-One. (searching out these Scriptures is your assignment)

- The Redeemed of Jesus need to grow up together into maturity.

Middle Dot – The Interpunct

Modern English often requires several English words to convey the depth and richness that is expressed succinctly by one biblical Greek word. To clearly show that a set of English words is representing one Greek word, the Interpunct (or middle dot) is used between each of the English words. Thus, the two Greek words "ἐδόξαζον θεόν" are rendered as "they·were·glorifying God."

Italics and Superscript

Italicized words are used to express thoughts in English that are implied by the Greek but not explicitly expressed in the Greek text. Example: The harvest *is* large. ("*is*" is implied in Greek, but must be supplied in English).

Although superscript is seldom used, it is employed to convey an associated, intrinsic understanding of a word that is typically inseparable, thus stronger than mere implication. Examples are: the Adversary-Accuser seeks whom he may devour, the Anointed-One has come to give us life-above (i.e. Zoe, not Bios).

The Dagger Symbol – †

The dagger (cross-like symbol) is used to denote special Biblical words whose meanings have markedly greater distinction and significance than English allows. In short, usage of the words "man" and “life” in the English language greatly over-simplify and obscure these varied and resplendent concepts. The dagger is used for two words and one derivative: Man·of·clay† (ἄνθρωπος – ánthrōpôs, אָדָם – ‘ạdạm̱), which differs from the generic use of “man,” and life† (ζωή – zōḗ), which differs from “natural life” or biology (βίος – bíôs). See G0444, G2222, G5363, and H0120 in the Greek and Hebrew Dictionaries. Note that ἄνθρωπος (anthropos) differs in usage from ἀνδρος/ἀνήρ (andros/aner), all of which are typically translated simply as “man” (along with the generic derived use of “man” with certain adjectives), despite the various depths of meaning.

Rhetorical Questions

The rhetorical question is preceded by this punctuation “¿!”. It denotes that the next phrase or sentence is rhetorical in nature, and it may appear in mid-sentence before such a phrase. Most often, this is indicated in the actual *Hebraic-Koine* Greek text by the rhetorical use of the Greek negation “μή” typically meaning “no, or not.” The symbol “¿!” may be vocalized as the questioning sound “hmm?” in order to indicate to the hearer that the following is rhetorical.

Verbs – Shall, Will, Should & May.

In this translation, “shall” always denotes future tense, and “will” is used with other verbs that express determination. “Should” and “may” are subjunctive and are used based on context. The thought, “You should do this” differs from “You may do this.” Thus, context is the determining factor for which is used in a given instance.

Capitalization of Proper Nouns

Many proper nouns in the New Testament are names combined from two or more words. When this occurs with a Hebrew name, the starting letter of secondary words is in small caps. This benefits both the learner and the scholar. Such examples of this capitalization are: IsraEl, AbRaham, JeruSalem, and EliJah.

Quotation Marks

Mickelson Clarified Translation utilizes special quotation marks to offset Old Testament quotations. With unprecedented clarity, quotes from the Septuagint or the Hebraic text are discernible, along with instances where quotations are actually paraphrased. Old Testament quotes begin and end with angle bracket quotation marks such as: ‹Quoted Text›. Standard English quotation rules apply for alternating nested quote marks: ‹“I told him, ‘Yes!’”›

Legend: ‹“ = found in Hebrew and Septuagint with identical meaning.

‹" = found only in Septuagint; Hebrew has different meaning.

‹≈ = paraphrased; not a direct quote from either the Hebrew or Septuagint.

Original Note from James Strong

“Owing to changes in the enumeration while in progress, there were no words left for numbers 2717 and 3203-3302, which were therefore silently dropped out of the vocabulary and references as redundant. This will occasion no practical mistake or inconvenience.”

J. K. Mickelson: If James Strong had only known that computers were coming...

Mickelson's Reference & Context Numbers

Aside from the simpler MCT Reader formats, the Mickelson Reference and Context Numbers are used both in the *Mickelson Clarified Translation* (MCT), with its various published formats, and in the *Mickelson Clarified Dictionary of New Testament Greek.* The Mickelson Reference Numbers are completely compatible with, and based on, the Strong's numbers, but they are expanded in scope and detail, and they contain an initial letter as a language indicator.

The Context Numbers are decimal numbers appended to the Mickelson's Reference Numbers to indicate the context of the word. For example, "G1135" refers to the Greek word "γυνή" (gune) which means woman or wife, based on context. The context for woman is "G1135.1," and the context for wife is "G1135.2." The companion dictionary defines all these context numbers.

Each instance of the various contexts is clarified by hand and not by a computer process. Research is augmented by specialized custom software, but it is impossible for a program to accurately translate God's written Word, let alone discern the various social, cultural, historical, spiritual, natural, or linguistic contexts.

How To Use The Mickelson Reference & Context Numbers

The Mickelson Clarified Scholar, Clarified Professor, and Clarified Interlinear formats include these reference numbers (with context) under each English word. This makes looking up dictionary and concordance entries quick and precise.

Biblical Abbreviations

NT – New Testament
OT – Old Testament
Mt – Matthew
Mk – Mark
Lk – Luke
Jn – John
Ac – Acts
Rm – Romans
1Co – 1 Corinthians
2Co – 2 Corinthians
Gal – Galatians
Eph – Ephesians
Php – Philippians
Col – Colossians
1Th – 1 Thessalonicans
2Th – 2 Thessalonicans
1Ti – 1 Timothy
2Ti – 2 Timothy
Tit – Titus
Phm – Philemon
Heb – Hebrews
Jac – Jacob (*James*)
1Pe – 1 Peter
2Pe – 2 Peter
1Jn – 1 John
2Jn – 2 John
3Jn – 3 John
Jude – Jude
Rv – Revelation

Lexicordance Section

This New Testament Lexicordance shows all the Greek word occurrences expressed in English by the *Mickelson Clarified Translation* (both explicit and implied), as well as the sixteen expressed Hebrew words (which are contextually implied by their Old Testament references).

Sorting Order

The word usage list is sorted by Strong's Number, Mickelson's Context Number, Parsing Information (special order described below), the Literary Reading Order (LRO), and the word's placement within a verse. Implied English words (italicized) have an 'E' preceding the Mickelson/Strong's number and are sorted immediately following the explicit usage listing [e.g. "*EG1135.1*" (*woman*) follows after all the explicit listings for "G1135.1" (woman), but *before* "G1135.2" (wife)].

Special Parsing Order (morphology)

The Parsing listings, occurring per context, are sorted as follows (see entry G0040 for an example):

Verbs – Tense (future/present/past/special), Voice, Mood, then the same as Nouns. (Note: Voice and Mood are sorted, but only alphabetically according to the English letter as listed in the *Parsing Key* on the next page).

Tense: **F**uture (**2F**uture), **P**resent, **I**mperfect, **A**orist (**2A**orist), pe**R**fect (**2**pe**R**fect), p**L**uperfect (**2**p**L**uperfect), **X** (adverbial imperative)

Nouns (Pronouns, Adjectives, and Articles) – Case (by general proximity), Number, Gender,

Case: **N**ominative, **V**ocative, **A**ccusative, **D**ative, **G**enitive

Number: **S**ingular, **P**lural

Gender: **M**asculine, **F**eminine, **N**euter

Exclusions

The following Greek words are listed in summary usage form only; the listing of each occurrence is excluded from the concordance:

G0846 αὐτός - self
G1161 δέ - but
G1519 εἰς - into
G1526 εἰσί - they are
G1565 ἐκεῖνος - that one
G1691 ἐμέ - me
G1698 ἐμοί - to me
G1700 ἐμοῦ - of me, my
G1722 ἔν - in
G2071 ἔσομαι - shall be
G2228 ἤ - or
G2248 ἡμᾶς - us
G2249 ἡμεῖς - we
G2254 ἡμῖν - to us
G2257 ἡμῶν - of us, our
G2258 ἦν - it was
G2443 ἵνα - that
G2532 καί - and
G3165 μέ - me
G3326 μετά - with
G3361 μή - not
G3427 μή - to me
G3450 μοῦ - of me, my
G3588 ὁ, ἡ, τό - the
G3748 ὅστις - that
G3754 ὅτι - that
G3756 οὐ, οὐκ, οὐχ-no, not
G4571 σέ - you
G4671 σοί - to you
G4675 σοῦ - of you
G4771 σύ - you
G5209 ὑμᾶς - yeu
G5210 ὑμεῖς - yeu
G5213 ὑμῖν - to yeu
G5216 ὑμῶν - of yeu

Mickelson's Morphology / Parsing Key

(not used in the Clarified NT Reader or NT Scholar editions. See MCT NT Scribe, Interlinear, Concordance)

Morphology is the part of speech for a word (noun, verb, adjective, etc) along with the specific information of how it is being used in a given sentence (singular, plural, present tense, past tense, etc). Morphology is vitally important in translating one language into another.

UNDECLINED FORMS:

A-NUI = Indeclinable NUmeral (Adjective)
ADV = ADVerb or adverb and particle combined (indeclinable). Also: ARAM-N, ARAM-V
CONJ = CONJunction or conjunctive particle
COND = CONDitional particle or conjunction
INJ = INterJection
PRT = PaRTicle, disjunctive particle
PREP = PREPosition
N-LI = Indeclinable Letter (Noun)
N-OI = Indeclinable Noun of Other type
N-PRI = Indeclinable Noun.
N/P-PRI = Indeclinable PRoper Noun.

ARAM = ARAMaic transliterated word
HEB = HEBrew transliterated word (indeclinable)
NEG = Negative particle (general negation)
NEG-V = Verb Negation (i.e. not writing)
NEG-N = Noun Negation (i.e. not pencils)
NEG-ADJ = Adjective Negation (i.e. not yellow)
NEG-ADV = Adverb Negation (i.e. not quickly)
NEG-VC = Verbal Clause Negation
NEG-CONJ = Conjunction Negation (i.e. lest)
NEG-PREP = Preposition Negation (i.e. not by bread)
NEG-EMPH = Emphasized Negation (No, I will not)
NEG-RHET = Precedes a rhetorical question (¿!)

DECLINED FORMS: All follow the order: prefix-case-number-gender-(suffix)

Prefixes:
N = Noun (common)
N/P = Noun/Person
N/L = Noun/Location
N/G = Noun/Grouping
A = Adjective (common)
A/L = Adjective/Location
A/G = Adjective/Grouping
T = definite article
P:R = Relative pronoun
P:C = reCiprocal pronoun
P:D = Demonstrative pronoun
P:K = correlative pronoun
P:I = Interrogative pronoun
P:X = indefinite pronoun
P:Q = correlative or interrogative pronoun
P:F = reFlexive pronoun (person 1,2,3 added)
P:S = poSsessive pronoun (person 1,2,3 added)
P:P = Personal pronoun (person 1,2,3 added)
(Note: 1st and 2nd personal pronouns have no gender)

Cases (5-case system only):
N = Nominative (subject)
V = Vocative
G = Genitive
D = Dative
A = Accusative (direct object)

Number:
S = Singular
P = Plural

Gender:
M = Masculine
F = Feminine
N = Neuter

Suffixes:
S = Superlative (used only with adjectives and some adverbs)
C = Comparative (used only with adjectives and some adverbs)
ABB = ABBreviated form (used only with various numerals)
I = Interrogative
N = Negative (used only with particles as PRT-N)
C = Contracted form, or two words merged by crasis
ATT = ATTic Greek form
P = Particle attached (with relative pronoun)

REGARDING THE '@' AT SYMBOL:

When the morphology ends with an '@' AT SYMBOL, it indicates that the 'alternate' English word form is intentionally different from the Greek morphology in order to preserve the original concept or context when expressed in English. While rare in the MCT, this is occasionally due to inappropriate innuendo or connotations that some phrases have among English speakers. Other causes are for subject-verb agreement, or when a particular Greek verb tense doesn't make sense when expressed verbatim in English. The '@' AT SYMBOL lets the skilled reader know that the alternate English word form is intentional for proper comprehension in standard English.

The '@' is not required in the MCT when 'alternate' English word forms do occur, but it is considered a scholarly courtesy for those who will carefully examine and scrutinize the translation.

VERB-RELATED FORMS:
All Greek verbs are listed in one of three various forms:

1) V-tense-voice-mood
2) V-tense-voice-mood-person-number
3) V-tense-voice-mood-case-number-gender

Tense:
P = Present
I = Imperfect
F = Future
2F = Second Future
A = Aorist
2A = Second Aorist
R = peRfect
2R = Second peRfect
L = pLuperfect
2L = Second pLuperfect
X = no tense stated (adverbial imperative)

Voice:
A = Active
P = Passive
M = Middle
E = Either middle or passive
D = middle Deponent
O = passive depOnent
N = middle or passive depoNent
Q = impersonal active
X = no voice stated

Mood:
I = Indicative
(declaration of fact- reality)
M = iMperative
(command- potential reality)
S = Subjunctive
(contingency-potentially possible)
O = Optative
(possibility-conceivably possible)
N = iNfinitive
P = Participle
R = impeRative-sense participle

Person:
1 = First person
2 = Second person
3 = Third person

Number:
S = Singular
P = Plural

Gender:
M = Masculine
F = Feminine
N = Neuter

Cases (5-case system only):
N = Nominative
V = Vocative
G = Genitive
D = Dative
A = Accusative

Extra:
-M = Middle significance
-C = Contracted form
-T = Transitive
-A = Aeolic
-ATT = Attic
-AP = Apocopated form
-IRR = Irregular or Impure form

Morphology / Parsing Examples

Matthew 14:25b

Jesus	N/P-NSM	Proper Noun / Person – Nominative Singular Masculine
went	V-2AAI-3S	Verb – 2nd Aorist Active Indicative – 3rd Person Singular
toward	PREP	Preposition
them	P:P-APM	Pronoun : Personal – Accusative Plural Masculine
walking	V-PAP-NSM	Verb – Present Active Participle – Nominative Singular Masculine
upon	PREP	Preposition
the	T-GSF	Article – Genitive Singular Feminine
sea	N-GSF	Noun – Genitive Singular Feminine

A small sampling of verb morphology

He walks	V-PAI	Verb – Present Active Indicative
He walked	V-AAI	Verb – Aorist Active Indicative
He has walked	V-RAI	Verb – Perfect Active Indicative
He has been walking	V-RPP	Verb – Perfect Passive Participle
He shall walk	V-FAI	Verb – Future Active Indicative
He shall be walking	V-FPP	Verb – Future Passive Participle
He may walk *(or not)*	V-PAS	Verb – Present Active Subjunctive

A CONTEXTUAL, LEXICOLOGICAL CONCORDANCE OF

THE NEW TESTAMENT:

THE TESTIMONY OF YAHWEH – יְהוָה

THE PROMISED
"BRAND-NEW COVENANT"

בְּרִית חֲדָשָׁה
"BRIT CHADASHAH"

Implied NT Hebrew Words (12x)

H0410 אֵל ʻe̱l *n-m.* (2x)
Roots:H0352 Compare:H7706 See:H0430 H0433 xLangEquiv:G2316 xLangAlso:G2241
EH0410 (2x)
Rv 4:8 holy, holy *is* Yahweh, *El Shaddai* God Almighty,
Rv 21:22 in it, for Yahweh, *El Shaddai* God Almighty, and

H0762 אֲרָמִית ʻăra̱mıyth *adv.* (4x)
Συριστί Syristí
Roots:H0761 Compare:H5682-1 H6163 xLangEquiv:G4947-6 xLangAlso:G1446 G1444
EH0762 (4x)
Jn 20:16 ·turned·back·around, says·to·him *in·Aramaic*,
Ac 4:36 (which, when·being·interpreted *from·Aramaic*, is
Mk 5:41 which, when·being·interpreted *from·Aramaic*, is
Mk 15:34 Which, when·being·interpreted *from·Aramaic*, is

H1350 גָּאַל ǥa̱ʻal *v.* (1x)
Compare:H6299 H4899 H5337 H5358 See:H1353 H1346-1 H3008 xLangEquiv:G0059 G1805 xLangAlso:G4773 G5546 G0070-3
EH1350.5 (1x)
Rm 11:26 "*The Kinsman·Redeemer* shall·come from·out

H2022 הַר ha̱r *n-m.* (1x)
Roots:H2042 Compare:H1389 H5550 See:H2023 H2024 H2039 H3093 xLangEquiv:G3735
EH2022 (1x)
Rv 16:16 HarMeGiddon *(Mountain of·Great·Crowding)*.

H2598 חֲנֻכָּה cHănu̱kah *n-f.* (1x)
Roots:H2596 Compare:H2282 xLangEquiv:A2597 G1456 xLangAlso:G1457-1
EH2598.2 (1x)
Jn 10:22 ·Renovations *(also called Chanukkah)* occurred in

H4023 מְגִדּוֹ mĕgiḏô *n/l.* (1x)
מְגִדּוֹן mĕgiḏôn [Zechariah 12]
Roots:H1413 See:H0012 H2037-1 xLangAlso:G0717
EH4023 (1x)
Rv 16:16 HarMeGiddon *(Mountain of·Great·Crowding)*.

H5251 נֵס neç *n-m.* (1x)
Roots:H5264 Compare:H0226 H6161
EH5251 (1x)
Jn 3:14 Moses elevated the serpent *upon a·sign·pole* in the

H5921 עַל ʻal *prep.* (1x)
Roots:H5920 xLangEquiv:A5922 xLangAlso:G1909 G5228
EH5921 (1x)
Jn 3:14 Moses elevated the serpent *upon* a·sign·pole in the

H6163 עֲרָבִי ʻăra̱ḇıy *adj/g.* (1x)
עַרְבִי ʻar·ḇıy
עֲרָבִית ʻăra̱ḇıyth [the language]
Roots:H6152 Compare:H0762 H5682-1 xLangAlso:G1446 G1444
EH6163.2 (1x)
Ac 13:8 name is·interpreted *from·Arabic*), stood·opposed·to

H7706 שַׁדַּי śhaḏay *n/p.* (2x)
σαδδαΐ saddaï [Greek transliteration]
Roots:H7703 Compare:H0410 See:H5996 xLangEquiv:G3841 G4522-2
EH7706 (2x)
Rv 4:8 holy *is* Yahweh, *El Shaddai* God Almighty, the·one
Rv 21:22 in it, for Yahweh, *El Shaddai* God Almighty, and

H7941 שֵׁכָר śhekar *n-m.* (1x)
Roots:H7937 Compare:H3196 xLangEquiv:G4608 G3182-1 xLangAlso:G4965
EH7941.1 (1x)
Jn 4:5 being·referred·to·as Sychar *(or·intoxicating)*, near·by

Αα - Alpha

G0001 α a *n.* (4x)
ἄν án [before a vowel]
א a [Hebrew first letter]
Roots:H0000-1 Compare:G0427 G0260 G5598
G0001.1 N-LI A (4x)
Rv 1:8 "I AM the Alpha and the Omega, beginning and end,"
Rv 1:11 "I AM the Alpha and the Omega, the First and the
Rv 21:6 I AM the Alpha and the Omega, the beginning and
Rv 22:13 I AM the Alpha and the Omega, beginning and end

G0002 Ἀαρών Aarṓn *n/p.* (5x)
אַהֲרֹן ʻahărōn [Hebrew]
Roots:H0175 See:G3475 G3198 G2474
G0002.2 N/P-PRI Ἀαρών (5x)
Lk 1:5 *was* from·among the daughters of·Aaron, and her
Ac 7:40 declaring to·Aaron, 'Make for·us gods which
Heb 5:4 ·called·forth by God, even exactly·as Aaron *was*.
Heb 7:11 ·related according·to the assigned·order of·Aaron?
Heb 9:4 urn having the manna, and Aaron's staff (the·one

G0003 Ἀβαδδών Abaddṓn *n/p.* (1x)
אֲבַדּוֹן ʻăḇaḏôn [Hebrew]
Roots:H0011 Compare:G0623
G0003.2 N/P-PRI Ἀβαδδών (1x)
Rv 9:11 *is* Abaddon *(meaning·Total·Destroyer)*, and in the

G0004 ἀ•βαρής abarḗs *adj.* (1x)
Roots:G0001 G0922
G0004.2 A-ASM ἀβαρῆ (1x)
2Co 11:9 ·kept my·own·self from·being·burdensome to·yeu,

G0005 Ἀββᾶ Abbâ *n/p.* (3x)
אַב ʻaḇ [Aramaic noun]
Roots:A0002 xLangEquiv:H0001 G3962
G0005 N/P-PRI Ἀββᾶ (3x)
Gal 4:6 Son into yeur hearts, yelling·out, "Abba, Father!"
Mk 14:36 And he·was·saying, "Abba, Father, all·things *are*
Rm 8:15 ·as·sons, by which we·yell·out, "Abba, Father!"

G0006 Ἄβελ Ábêl *n/p.* (4x)
הֶבֶל heḇel [Hebrew]
Roots:H1893
G0006.2 N/P-PRI Ἄβελ (4x)
Lk 11:51 from the blood of·Abel until the blood of·
Heb 11:4 By·trust, Abel offered to·God a·much·better
Heb 12:24 ·better·things— contrary·to *that·of* Abel.
Mt 23:35 earth, from the blood of·Abel the righteous, unto

G0007 Ἀβ•ιά Abiá *n/p.* (3x)
אֲבִיָּה ʻăḇıyah [Hebrew]
Roots:H0029 xLangAlso:H0281
G0007.5 N/P-PRI Ἀβιά (2x)
Mt 1:7 and RehoboAm begot AbiYah, and AbiYah begot
Mt 1:7 RehoboAm begot AbiYah, and AbiYah begot Asa.
G0007.10 N/P-PRI Ἀβιά (1x)
Lk 1:5 *was* from·among *the* daily·rotation of·AbiJah. And

G0008 Ἀβι•άθαρ Abiáthar *n/p.* (1x)
אֶבְיָתָר ʻeḇyathar [Hebrew]
Roots:H0054
G0008.2 N/P-PRI Ἀβιάθαρ (1x)
Mk 2:26 of·God in·the·days of·AbiAthar the high·priest and

G0009 Ἀβιληνή Abilēnḗ *n/l.* (1x)
xLangAlso:H0058
G0009.2 N/L-GSF Ἀβιληνῆς (1x)
Lk 3:1 with·Lysanias being·the·ruling·tetrarch of·Abilene)—

G0010 Ἀβι•ούδ Abihôúd *n/p.* (2x)
אֲבִיהוּד ʻăḇıyhûd [Hebrew]
Roots:H0031 Compare:G1664
G0010.2 N/P-PRI Ἀβιούδ (2x)
Mt 1:13 Then ZerubBabel begot AbiHud, and AbiHud begot
Mt 1:13 begot AbiHud, and AbiHud begot ElYaQim, and

G0011 Ἀβ•ραάμ Abraám *n/p.* (77x)
אַבְרָהָם ʻaḇra̱ham [Hebrew]
Roots:H0085
G0011.2 N/P-PRI Ἀβραάμ (73x)
Jn 8:33 ·answered him, "We·are AbRaham's offspring†, and
Jn 8:37 ·know that yeu·are AbRaham's offspring†, but·yet
Jn 8:39 and declared to·him, "AbRaham is our father.
Jn 8:39 ·them, "If yeu·were AbRaham's children, yeu·would
Jn 8:39 children, yeu·would do the works of·AbRaham.
Jn 8:40 I·heard personally·from God. AbRaham did·not do
Jn 8:52 that you·have a·demon. AbRaham is·dead, and the
Jn 8:53 you·yourself greater·than our father AbRaham, who
Jn 8:56 "Yeur father AbRaham leaped·for·joy that he·
Jn 8:57 ·of·age, and have·you·clearly·seen AbRaham?"
Jn 8:58 I·say to·yeu, prior·to AbRaham coming·to·be, I
Lk 1:55 to·AbRaham and to·his offspring† into the coming·
Lk 1:73 an·oath which he·swore to our father AbRaham,
Lk 3:8 yeurselves, 'We·have AbRaham *for·our* father.' For
Lk 3:8 ·out of·these stones to·awaken children to·AbRaham.
Lk 3:34 *son* of·YiTsaq, *son* of·AbRaham, *son* of·Terach,
Lk 13:16 this·one, being a·daughter of·AbRaham, whom the
Lk 13:28 whenever yeu·should·gaze·upon AbRaham, YiTsaq
Lk 16:22 ·away by the angels to AbRaham's bosom. But the
Lk 16:23 he·clearly·sees AbRaham from a·distance, and
Lk 16:24 declared, 'Father AbRaham, show·mercy on·me,
Lk 16:25 "But AbRaham declared, 'Child, recall·to·mind
Lk 16:29 AbRaham says to·him, 'They·have Moses and the
Lk 16:30 'No·indeed, father AbRaham! But·yet if someone
Lk 19:9 ·indeed he·himself also is a·son of·AbRaham.
Lk 20:37 Yahweh, "the God of·AbRaham, and the God of·
Ac 3:13 "The God of·AbRaham, and of·YiTsaq, and of·
Ac 3:25 unto our fathers, saying to AbRaham, "And in·
Ac 7:2 ·visible to·our father AbRaham while·he·was·still in
Ac 7:16 in the tomb that AbRaham's *son Jacob* purchased
Ac 7:17 ·drawing·near which God swore to·AbRaham, the
Ac 7:32 of·your fathers, the God of·AbRaham, and the God
Ac 13:26 brothers, the·Sons of·AbRaham by·birth, and
Heb 2:16 — but·rather he·grabs·hold 'of·AbRaham's Seed.'
Heb 6:13 For God, after·promising to·AbRaham, since he·
Heb 7:1 meeting·up with·AbRaham returning·back from the
Heb 7:2 to·whom also AbRaham distributed a·tenth *part*
Heb 7:4 to·whom even the patriarch AbRaham gave a·tenth
Heb 7:5 ·come·forth from·among the loins of·AbRaham.
Heb 7:6 them has·received·tithes from·AbRaham, and he·
Heb 7:9 ·one receiving tithes, has·tithed through AbRaham,
Heb 11:8 By·trust, AbRaham, being·called to·go·forth into
Heb 11:17 By·trust, AbRaham, when·being·tried, had·
Gal 3:6 *It·is of·trust* just·as with·AbRaham, *who* "trusted
Gal 3:7 ·out of·trust, the·same are the·Sons of·AbRaham.
Gal 3:8 announced·the·good·news·in·advance to·AbRaham,
Gal 3:9 are·blessed together with·the·trusting of·AbRaham.
Gal 3:14 ·that the·blessing of·AbRaham may·come·to·be for
Gal 3:16 the promises were·uttered to·AbRaham and to·his
Gal 3:18 *the inheritance* to·AbRaham through promise.
Gal 3:29 then·by·inference, yeu·are of·AbRaham's Seed and
Gal 4:22 For it·has·been·written, that AbRaham had two
Mt 1:1 Anointed, *the* Son of·David, *the* son of·AbRaham.
Mt 1:2 AbRaham begot YiTsaq, and YiTsaq begot Jacob, and
Mt 1:17 generations·of·offspring from AbRaham until David
Mt 3:9 yeurselves, 'We·have AbRaham *for·our* father.' For
Mt 3:9 ·out of·these stones to·awaken children to·AbRaham.
Mt 8:11 ·shall·recline·at·the·table with AbRaham, YiTsaq,
Mt 22:32 "I AM the God of·AbRaham, and the God of·
Mk 12:26 "I·myself *am* the God of·AbRaham, and the God
Rm 4:1 what shall·we·state *for* AbRaham our father to·
Rm 4:2 if AbRaham was·regarded·as·righteous as·a·result
Rm 4:3 Scripture say? "And AbRaham trusted in·Yahweh,
Rm 4:9 trust was·reckoned to·AbRaham for righteousness.'
Rm 4:12 in the uncircumcised trust of·our father AbRaham.
Rm 4:13 *is* not through Torah-Law to·AbRaham or to·his
Rm 4:16 ·one *who·is* birthed·from·out of·AbRaham's trust,
Rm 9:7 because they·are offspring† of·AbRaham, *are* they·

Rm 11:1 an·Israelite, from·among AbRaham's offspring†,
Jac 2:21 AbRaham our father, was·it·not as·a·result of·works
Jac 2:23 saying, "'And AbRaham trusted in·Yahweh, and it·
1Pe 3:6 *who* listened·to·and·obeyed AbRaham, calling him
2Co 11:22 Are·they *the* offspring† of·AbRaham? So·*am*·I.

EG0011.2 (4x)

Lk 16:31 "But *AbRaham* declared to·him, 'If they·do·not
Ac 7:8 And in·this·manner, *AbRaham* begot YiTsaq and
Rm 4:18 *AbRaham*, contrary·to expectation, trusted on an·
Rm 4:20 ·to the promise of·God, *AbRaham* did·not hesitate

G0012 ἄ•βυσσος ábyssôs *n.* (9x)

Roots:G0001 G1037 Compare:G5421 See:G5020 G5421 xLangAlso:H8415 H4688 H6683 H7338 H4113

G0012.2 N-ASF ἄβυσσον (3x)

Lk 8:31 ·not order them to·go·off into the bottomless·pit.
Rm 10:7 "Who shall·descend into the bottomless·pit?""
Rv 20:3 and cast him into the bottomless·pit, and shut him

G0012.2 N-GSF ἀβύσσου (6x)

Rv 9:1 the key of·the well of·the bottomless·pit·*(the·Abyss)*.
Rv 9:2 And he·opened·up the well of·the bottomless·pit, and
Rv 9:11 them— the angel of·the bottomless·pit. *The* name
Rv 11:7 from·out of·the bottomless·pit) shall·make war with
Rv 17:8 ·about to·ascend from·out of·the bottomless·pit, and
Rv 20:1 having the key of·the bottomless·pit and a·great

G0013 Ἄγαβος Ágabôs *n/p.* (2x)

חָגָב CHagab [Hebrew]

Roots:H2285 Compare:G0200

G0013.2 N/P-NSM Ἄγαβος (2x)

Ac 11:28 them by·the·name·of Agabus, after·standing·up,
Ac 21:10 prophet came·down from Judea, Agabus by·name.

G0014 ἀγαθο•εργέω agathôêrgéō *v.* (1x)

Roots:G0018 G2041

G0014 V-PAN ἀγαθοεργεῖν (1x)

1Ti 6:18 *them* to·do·beneficially·good·work, to·be·wealthy

G0015 ἀγαθο•ποιέω agathôpôiéō *v.* (11x)

Roots:G0017

G0015 V-PAM-2P ἀγαθοποιεῖτε (1x)

Lk 6:35 yeur enemies, and beneficially·do·good, and lend,

G0015 V-PAP-APM ἀγαθοποιοῦντας (3x)

Lk 6:33 ·good for·the·ones beneficially·doing·good to·yeu,
1Pe 2:15 will of·God, *by* beneficially·doing·good, to·muzzle
1Pe 3:17 to·suffer *for* beneficially·doing·good·things, than

G0015 V-PAP-NSM ἀγαθοποιῶν (2x)

Ac 14:17 ·witness, by·beneficially·doing·good, giving us
3Jn 1:11 The·one beneficially·doing·good is from·out of·

G0015 V-PAP-NPF ἀγαθοποιοῦσαι (1x)

1Pe 3:6 children, while·beneficially·doing·good and not

G0015 V-PAP-NPM ἀγαθοποιοῦντες (1x)

1Pe 2:20 when suffering for·beneficially·doing·good, this *is*

G0015 V-PAS-2P ἀγαθοποιῆτε (1x)

Lk 6:33 And if yeu·should·beneficially·do·good for·the·ones

G0015 V-AAN ἀγαθοποιῆσαι (2x)

Lk 6:9 ·Sabbaths: to·beneficially·do·good or to·do·bad, to·
Mk 3:4 "Is·it·proper to·beneficially·do·good on·the various·

G0016 ἀγαθο•ποιΐα agathôpôiḯa *n.* (1x)

Roots:G0017

G0016 N-DSF ἀγαθοποιΐα (1x)

1Pe 4:19 their·own souls *to·him* in beneficial·well·doing, as

G0017 ἀγαθο•ποιός agathôpôiós *adj.* (1x)

Roots:G0018 G4160

G0017.2 A-GPM ἀγαθοποιῶν (1x)

1Pe 2:14 and *for the* high·praise of·beneficially·good·doers.

G0018 ἀγαθός agathós *adj.* (103x)

Compare:G2570 G5623 G2556 G4190 See:G0019 G0017 G0016 G0018-1 G0018-2 G0018-3

G0018.1 A-NSM ἀγαθός (10x)

Jn 7:12 ·were·saying, "He·is a·beneficially·good·man," but
Lk 6:45 "The beneficially·good man·of·clay†, from·out of·
Lk 18:19 ·good? No·one·at·all *is* beneficially·good, except
Lk 23:50 inherently·being a·beneficially·good man and
Ac 11:24 because he·was a·beneficially·good man and full
Mt 12:35 The beneficially·good man·of·clay† from·out of·
Mt 19:17 *There·is* no·one·at·all beneficially·good except one
Mt 20:15 eye evil, because I·myself am beneficially·good?'
Mk 10:18 ·*is* no·one·at·all beneficially·good except one,
Eph 4:29 *let·it·be* some beneficially·good *conversation*,

G0018.1 A-NSF ἀγαθή (2x)

Rm 7:12 *is* holy, righteous, and beneficially·good.
Jac 1:17 Every beneficially·good act·of·giving and every

G0018.1 A-NSN ἀγαθόν (5x)

Jn 1:46 *for* anything beneficially·good to·be from·out of·
Mt 7:17 ·this·manner, every beneficially·good tree produces
Mt 7:18 A·beneficially·good tree is·not able to·produce evil
Rm 7:13 So·then, the beneficially·good, has·it·become
Rm 12:2 what *is* the beneficially·good, most·satisfying, and

G0018.1 A-NPN ἀγαθά (1x)

Rm 3:8 in·order·that the beneficially·good·things may·come.

G0018.1 A-VSM ἀγαθέ (6x)

Lk 18:18 ·of him, saying, "Beneficially·good Mentor, what
Lk 19:17 to·him, 'Well·done, you·beneficially·good slave!
Mt 19:16 him declared, "O·beneficially·good Mentor, what
Mt 25:21 'Well·done, O·beneficially·good and trustworthy
Mt 25:23 'Well·done, O·beneficially·good and trustworthy
Mk 10:17 was·inquiring·of him, "Beneficially·good Mentor,

G0018.1 A-ASM ἀγαθόν (3x)

Lk 18:19 ·refer·to me *as* beneficially·good? No·one·at·all *is*
Mt 19:17 ·do you·refer·to me *as* beneficially·good? *There·is*
Mk 10:18 ·do you·refer·to me *as* beneficially·good? *There·is*

G0018.1 A-ASF ἀγαθήν (8x)

Lk 8:8 "And other *seed* fell on the beneficially·good soil, and
Lk 10:42 and Mary selected the beneficially·good portion,
1Pe 3:16 having a·beneficially·good conscience— in·order·
1Pe 3:16 ·maligning yeur beneficially·good behavior in
1Th 3:6 yeu·have a·beneficially·good remembrance of·us
2Th 2:16 consoling and a·beneficially·good expectation in
Tit 2:10 but·rather indicating all beneficially·good trust, in·
1Ti 1:19 holding trust and a·beneficially·good conscience.

G0018.1 A-ASN ἀγαθόν (22x)

Lk 6:45 heart, brings·forth the beneficially·good. And the
Gal 6:10 we·should·work the beneficially·good toward all,
Mt 19:16 what beneficially·good·thing should·I·do in·order·
Rm 2:10 the·one who·is·working the beneficially·good, both
Rm 7:18 my flesh) dwells no beneficially·good·thing; for to·
Rm 7:19 *it·is* not *the* beneficially·good·thing which I·want
Rm 9:11 ·even practicing anything beneficially·good or bad,
Rm 13:3 the authority? Do the beneficially·good·thing, and
Rm 13:4 of·God to·you in the beneficially·good·thing. But if
Rm 16:19 ·to the·thing *which·is* beneficially·good and *to·be*
Php 1:6 ·one already·beginning a·beneficially·good work in
1Pe 3:11 wrong and do *the* beneficially·good·thing; seek
1Th 5:15 ·rather always pursue the beneficially·good, both
Tit 1:16 particularly·for every beneficially·good work.
Tit 3:1 ready particularly·for every beneficially·good work,
2Co 5:10 he·practiced— whether beneficially·good or bad.
2Co 9:8 yeu·may·abound to every beneficially·good work.
Eph 4:28 working the beneficially·good with·his hands, in·
Eph 6:8 beneficially·good·thing each·man should·do, this
2Ti 2:21 ·made·ready for every beneficially·good work.
2Ti 3:17 ·equipped toward all beneficially·good works.
3Jn 1:11 the bad, but·rather the beneficially·good. The·one

G0018.1 A-APM ἀγαθούς (2x)

Mt 5:45 over evil·ones and beneficially·good·ones, and he·
Mt 22:10 both *the* evil and *the* beneficially·good. And the

G0018.1 A-APF ἀγαθάς (2x)

1Pe 3:10 and to·see beneficially·good days must·restrain his
Tit 2:5 ·clean, housekeepers, beneficially·good, *and* being·

G0018.1 A-APN ἀγαθά (10x)

Jn 5:29 the·ones already·doing the beneficially·good, into
Lk 11:13 ·know·how to·give beneficially·good gifts to·yeur
Lk 12:18 all my produce and my beneficially·good·things.
Lk 12:19 many beneficially·good·things being·laid·out for
Lk 16:25 ·receive·in·full your beneficially·good·things, and
Mt 7:11 ·know·how to·give beneficially·good gifts to·yeur
Mt 7:11 heavens, give beneficially·good·things to·the·ones
Mt 12:34 ·yeu·able to·speak beneficially·good·things? For
Mt 12:35 heart casts·forth the beneficially·good·things, and
Rm 10:15 ·good·news of·the beneficially·good·things …"

G0018.1 A-DSF ἀγαθῇ (2x)

Lk 8:15 with a·morally·good and beneficially·good heart,
Ac 23:1 in·all beneficially·good conscience before·God

G0018.1 A-DSN ἀγαθῷ (6x)

Heb 13:21 yeu unto every beneficially·good work in·order
Rm 12:9 being·tightly·joined to·the beneficially·good—
Rm 12:21 overcome the bad with the beneficially·good.
2Th 2:17 ·establish yeu in every beneficially·good word and
Col 1:10 bearing·fruit in every beneficially·good work and
1Ti 5:10 ·followed·through in·every beneficially·good work)

G0018.1 A-DPM ἀγαθοῖς (1x)

1Pe 2:18 merely to·the beneficially·good·ones and fair·ones,

G0018.1 A-DPN ἀγαθοῖς (2x)

Gal 6:6 with·the·one tutoring in all beneficially·good·things.
Eph 2:10 Anointed-One Jesus for beneficially·good works,

G0018.1 A-GSM ἀγαθοῦ (3x)

Lk 6:45 from·out of·the beneficially·good treasure of·his
Mt 12:35 from·out of·the beneficially·good treasure of·his
Rm 5:7 perhaps over the beneficially·good·man, someone

G0018.1 A-GSF ἀγαθῆς (2x)

1Pe 3:21 an·inquiry of·a·beneficially·good conscience
1Ti 1:5 ·a·pure heart, and of·a·beneficially·good conscience,

G0018.1 A-GSN ἀγαθοῦ (4x)

Rm 2:7 ·to a·patient·endurance of·beneficially·good work,
Rm 7:13 in·me through the beneficially·good, in·order·that
1Pe 3:13 attentive·imitators of·the beneficially·good?
Phm 1:6 of·every beneficially·good·thing among yeu in

G0018.1 A-GPM ἀγαθῶν (2x)

Lk 1:53 those·being·hungry with·beneficially·good·things,
Jac 3:17 ·full of·mercy and of·beneficially·good fruits,

G0018.1 A-GPN ἀγαθῶν (5x)

Ac 9:36 She·herself was full of·beneficially·good works and
Heb 9:11 impending beneficially·good·things, came·directly
Heb 10:1 of·the impending beneficially·good *activities* (not
Rm 13:3 not *a·cause·of* fear for·the beneficially·good works,
1Ti 2:10 but·rather through beneficially·good works (which

G0018.2 A-ASN ἀγαθόν (3x)

Rm 8:28 work·together to good·benefit for·the·ones being
Rm 14:16 do·not·let yeur good·benefit be·reviled.
Rm 15:2 ·*conscience* for his good·benefit unto edification.

EG0018.2 (1x)

Rm 14:22 retain *the good·benefit* for·yourself *just* in·the·

G0018.3 A-NSN ἀγαθόν (1x)

Phm 1:14 your beneficially·good·response should·not be as

G0019 ἀγαθωσύνη agathōsýnē *n.* (4x)

Roots:G0018 See:G0018-1 G0018-2 G0018-3

G0019 N-NSF ἀγαθωσύνη (1x)

Gal 5:22 kindness, beneficial·goodness, trust,

G0019 N-DSF ἀγαθωσύνῃ (1x)

Eph 5:9 Spirit *is* in all beneficial·goodness and righteousness

G0019 N-GSF ἀγαθωσύνης (2x)

Rm 15:14 exceedingly·full of·beneficial·goodness, having·
2Th 1:11 good·purpose of·*his*·beneficial·goodness and work

G0020 ἀγαλλίασις agallíasis *n.* (5x)

Roots:G0021 See:G0019-1 xLangAlso:H8342

G0020.1 N-NSF ἀγαλλίασις (1x)

Lk 1:14 ·you shall·be joy and exuberant·leaping·of·joy, and

G0020.1 N-DSF ἀγαλλιάσει (2x)

Lk 1:44 ·about in my womb in an·exuberant·leaping·of·joy.
Jud 1:24 of·his glory with an·exuberant·leaping·of·joy,

G0020.2 N-DSF ἀγαλλιάσει (1x)

Ac 2:46 in exuberant·celebration and simplicity of·heart,

G0020.3 N-GSF ἀγαλλιάσεως (1x)

Heb 1:9 ·*the* oil of·exuberant·joy above·and·beyond your

G0021 ἀγ•αλλιάω agalliáō *v.* (11x)

Roots:G0022-1 G0242 Compare:G4640 See:G0020 G0019-1 xLangAlso:H1523 H5937 H5539

G0021.1 V-PNI-2P ἀγαλλιᾶσθε (2x)

1Pe 1:6 In this yeu·leap·for·joy, *although* being·grieved a·
1Pe 1:8 *him*, yeu·leap·for·joy with·joy quite·unspeakable,

G0021.1 V-PNM-2P ἀγαλλιᾶσθε (1x)
Mt 5:12 "Rejoice and leap·for·joy, because yeur payment·of·
G0021.1 V-PNP-NPM ἀγαλλιώμενοι (1x)
1Pe 4:13 of·his glory, yeu·may·be·joyful, leaping·for·joy.
G0021.1 V-PNS-1P ἀγαλλιώμεθα (1x)
Rv 19:7 We·should·rejoice, and should·leap·for·joy, and
G0021.1 V-AAI-3S ἠγαλλίασεν (1x)
Lk 1:47 and my spirit leaped·for·joy in God my Savior.
G0021.1 V-ADI-3S ἠγαλλιάσατο (4x)
Jn 8:56 father AbRaham leaped·for·joy that he·should·see
Lk 10:21 that·same hour, Jesus leaped·for·joy in·the Spirit
Ac 2:26 ·merry, and my tongue leaped·for·joy, and yet even
Ac 16:34 and leaped·for·joy, with·the·whole·household
G0021.1 V-AON ἀγαλλιασθῆναι (1x)
Jn 5:35 wanted just·for a·short·while to·leap·for·joy in his

G0022 ἄ•γαμος ágamôs *n.* (4x)
Roots:G0001 G1062 Compare:G3933 G3494-1
G0022 N-NSM ἄγαμος (1x)
1Co 7:32 The unmarried·man is·anxious·about the·things
G0022 N-NSF ἄγαμος (2x)
1Co 7:11 if she·is·separated, she·must·remain unmarried, or
1Co 7:34 The unmarried·woman is·anxious·about the·things
G0022 N-DPM ἀγάμοις (1x)
1Co 7:8 But I·say to·the unmarried and to·the widows, it·is

G0023 ἀγαν•ακτέω aganaktéō *v.* (7x)
Roots:G0022-1 G0886-1 See:G0043
G0023.2 V-PAN ἀγανακτεῖν (1x)
Mk 10:41 began to·be·greatly·displeased concerning Jakob
G0023.2 V-PAP-NSM ἀγανακτῶν (1x)
Lk 13:14 answering, being·greatly·displeased because Jesus
G0023.2 V-PAP-NPM ἀγανακτοῦντες (1x)
Mk 14:4 some being·greatly·displeased alongside themselves
G0023.2 V-AAI-3S ἠγανάκτησεν (1x)
Mk 10:14 *this*, Jesus was·greatly·displeased and declared to·
G0023.2 V-AAI-3P ἠγανάκτησαν (3x)
Mt 20:24 the ten were·greatly·displeased concerning the
Mt 21:15 the scribes were·greatly·displeased after·seeing the
Mt 26:8 *this*, his disciples are·greatly·displeased, saying,

G0024 ἀγαν•άκτησις aganáktēsis *n.* (1x)
Roots:G0023
G0024 N-ASF ἀγανάκτησιν (1x)
2Co 7:11 moreover, *what* great·displeasure, moreover,

G0025 ἀγαπάω agapáō *v.* (142x)
Roots:G0022-1 Compare:G5368 G2037-1 See:G0026 G0027 G0026-1
xLangEquiv:H0160 xLangAlso:H5689
G0025.1 V-FAI-1S ἀγαπήσω (1x)
Jn 14:21 my Father, and I·myself shall·love him and shall·
G0025.1 V-FAI-2S ἀγαπήσεις (10x)
Lk 10:27 he·declared, "“You·shall·love Yahweh your God
Gal 5:14 in·the·one, "You·shall·love your neighbor as
Mt 5:43 it·was·uttered, "You·shall·love your neighbor and
Mt 19:19 ' and "You·shall·love your neighbor as yourself
Mt 22:37 to·him, "“You·shall·love Yahweh your God with
Mt 22:39 like it, "You·shall·love your neighbor as yourself.
Mk 12:30 And you·shall·love Yahweh your God from·out
Mk 12:31 like it, "You·shall·love your neighbor as yourself
Rm 13:9 explicitly, "You·shall·love your neighbor as
Jac 2:8 ·to the Scripture, "You·shall·love your neighbor as
G0025.1 V-FAI-3S ἀγαπήσει (4x)
Jn 14:23 And my Father shall·love him, and we·shall·come
Lk 7:42 declare *to·me*, which of·them shall·love him more?
Lk 16:13 he·shall·hate the one and shall·love the other, or
Mt 6:24 either he·shall·hate the one and shall·love the other,
G0025.1 V-FPI-3S ἀγαπηθήσεται (1x)
Jn 14:21 And the·one loving me shall·be·loved by my Father
G0025.1 V-PAI-1S-C ἀγαπῶ (5x)
Jn 14:31 ·that the world may·know that I·love the Father,
2Co 11:11 Why? Because I·do·not love yeu?
1Jn 4:20 If someone should·declare, "I·love God," and he·
2Jn 1:1 her children— whom I·myself do·love in truth, and
3Jn 1:1 well-beloved Gaius, whom I·myself do·love in truth.
G0025.1 V-PAI-1P ἀγαπῶμεν (3x)
1Jn 3:14 into Life-above, because we·love the brothers. The·
1Jn 5:2 By this we·know that we·love the children of·God,
1Jn 5:2 children of·God, whenever we·love God and should·
G0025.1 V-PAI-2S ἀγαπᾷς (2x)
Jn 21:15 *son* of·Jonah, do·you·love me more·than these·
Jn 21:16 "Simon, *son* of·Jonah, do·you·love me?
G0025.1 V-PAI-2P ἀγαπᾶτε (3x)
Lk 6:32 "So·then if yeu·love the·ones loving yeu, what·kind·
Lk 11:43 Pharisees! Because yeu·love the first·row·seat in
1Pe 1:8 whom not having·seen, yeu·love— in whom, not
G0025.1 V-PAI-3S ἀγαπᾷ (8x)
Jn 3:35 The Father loves the Son and has·given all·things
Jn 10:17 On·account·of that, the Father loves me, because I·
Lk 7:5 for he·loves our nation, and he·himself built the
Lk 7:47 to·whom little is·forgiven, *the same* loves little."
Heb 12:6 whom Yahweh loves, he·correctively·disciplines,
1Co 8:3 But if anyone loves God, the·same has·been·
2Co 9:7 out of·compulsion, for 'God loves a·cheerful giver.'
Eph 5:28 The·one loving his wife loves himself.
G0025.1 V-PAI-3P ἀγαπῶσιν (1x)
Lk 6:32 the morally·disqualified·ones love the·ones loving
G0025.1 V-PAM-2P ἀγαπᾶτε (7x)
Lk 6:27 to·the·ones hearing: "Love yeur enemies, do good
Lk 6:35 "So·even·more, love yeur enemies, and
Mt 5:44 But I·myself say to·yeu, love yeur enemies, bless
1Pe 2:17 Honor all·men. Love the brotherhood. Reverently·
Eph 5:25 the husbands: Yeu·must·love yeur·own wives,
Col 3:19 *Now* the husbands: Yeu·must·love the wives, and
1Jn 2:15 Do·not love the world, nor·even the·things in the
G0025.1 V-PAM-3S ἀγαπάτω (1x)
Eph 5:33 each one in·that·manner) must·love his·own wife
G0025.1 V-PAN ἀγαπᾶν (8x)
Mk 12:33 And to·love him from·out of·all the·heart, and
Mk 12:33 of·all the·strength, and to·love one's neighbor as
Rm 13:8 not·even·one·thing, except to·love one·another, for
1Pe 3:10 For "the·one wanting to·love life-above and to·see
1Th 4:9 are instructed·by·God to love one·another.
Eph 5:28 the husbands are·obligated to·love their·own wives
1Jn 4:11 we·ourselves also are·indebted to·love one·another.
1Jn 4:20 ·seen, in·what·way is·he·able to·love God whom
G0025.1 V-PAP-APM ἀγαπῶντας (3x)
Lk 6:32 "So·then if yeu·love the·ones loving yeu, what·kind·
Lk 6:32 morally·disqualified·ones love the·ones loving them.
Mt 5:46 "For if yeu·should·love the·ones loving yeu, what
G0025.1 V-PAP-DPM ἀγαπῶσιν (4x)
Rm 8:28 we·personally·know that, for·the·ones loving God,
Jac 1:12 which the Lord promised to·the·ones loving him.
Jac 2:5 kingdom which he·promised to·the·ones loving him?
1Co 2:9 God made·ready for·the·ones presently·loving him.
G0025.1 V-PAP-GPM ἀγαπώντων (1x)
Eph 6:24 Grace *be* with all the·ones loving our Lord Jesus
G0025.1 V-PAP-NSM ἀγαπῶν (14x)
Jn 14:21 them, that is the·one presently·loving me. And the·
Jn 14:21 me. And the·one loving me shall·be·loved by my
Jn 14:24 "The·one not presently·loving me does·not
Rm 13:8 ·love one·another, for the·one loving the other has·
2Co 12:15 ·though the·more·abundantly *I·am* loving yeu, *the*
Eph 5:28 as their·own bodies. The·one loving his wife loves
1Jn 2:10 The·one loving his brother abides in the light, and
1Jn 3:10 ·out of·God, also the·one not loving his brother.
1Jn 3:14 brothers. The·one not presently·loving the brother
1Jn 4:7 and any one presently·loving has·been·born from·out
1Jn 4:8 The·one not presently·loving does·not already·know
1Jn 4:20 a·liar, for the·one not loving his brother whom he·
1Jn 4:21 from him, that the·one loving God should·love his
1Jn 5:1 from·out of·God; and every one loving *God*, the·one
G0025.1 V-PAS-1P ἀγαπῶμεν (7x)
1Jn 3:11 *the* beginning, that we·should·love one·another,
1Jn 3:18 My dear·children, we·should·not love in·word,
1Jn 3:23 and we·should·presently·love one·another, just·as
1Jn 4:7 Beloved, we·should·love one·another, because the
1Jn 4:12 ever·at·any·time. If we·should·love one·another,
1Jn 4:19 We·ourselves should·love him, because he·himself
2Jn 1:5 *the* beginning, that we·should·love one·another.
G0025.1 V-PAS-2P ἀγαπᾶτε (5x)
Jn 13:34 to·yeu, that yeu·should·love one·another just·as I·
Jn 13:34 ·that even yeu·yeurselves should·love one·another.
Jn 14:15 "If yeu·should·love me, observantly·keep my
Jn 15:12 commandment, that yeu·should·love one·another,
Jn 15:17 yeu, in·order·that yeu·may·love one·another.
G0025.1 V-PAS-3S ἀγαπᾷ (4x)
Jn 14:23 "If anyone should·love me, he·shall·observantly·
1Jn 2:15 in the world. If any·man should·love the world, the
1Jn 4:21 that the·one loving God should·love his brother also
1Jn 5:1 the·one begetting, should·love also the·one having·
G0025.1 V-PPI-1S ἀγαπῶμαι (1x)
2Co 12:15 ·abundantly *I·am* loving yeu, *the* less I·am·loved.
G0025.1 V-IAI-2P ἠγαπᾶτε (2x)
Jn 8:42 was yeur Father, yeu·would love me, for I·myself
Jn 14:28 to yeu.' If yeu·were·loving me, yeu·would rejoice
G0025.1 V-IAI-3S ἠγάπα (5x)
Jn 11:5 And Jesus loved Martha, also her sister, and Lazarus.
Jn 13:23 bosom was one of·his disciples whom Jesus loved.
Jn 19:26 disciple standing·nearby whom he·loved, he·says
Jn 21:7 that disciple whom Jesus loved says to·Peter, "It·is
Jn 21:20 *them* (*the·one* whom Jesus loved, who also sat·back
G0025.1 V-AAI-1S ἠγάπησα (5x)
Jn 13:34 yeu·should·love one·another just·as I·loved yeu, in·
Jn 15:9 the Father loved me, so·also·I loved yeu. Abide in
Jn 15:12 yeu·should·love one·another, just·as I·loved yeu.
Rm 9:13 it·has·been·written, "“Jacob I·loved, but Esau I·
Rv 3:9 and *that* they·should·know that I·myself loved you.
G0025.1 V-AAI-1P ἠγαπήσαμεν (1x)
1Jn 4:10 love: not that we·ourselves loved God, but·rather
G0025.1 V-AAI-2S ἠγάπησας (5x)
Jn 17:23 dispatched me, and *that* you·loved them, just·as
Jn 17:23 and *that* you·loved them, just·as you·loved me.
Jn 17:24 you·gave to·me because you·did·love me before *the*
Jn 17:26 ·that the love with·which you·loved me may·be in
Heb 1:9 You·loved righteousness and hated lawlessness.
G0025.1 V-AAI-3S ἠγάπησεν (12x)
Jn 3:16 For in·this·manner, God loved the world, such·that
Jn 13:1 the·ones in the world, he·loved them to *the* end.
Jn 15:9 "Just·as the Father loved me, so·also·I loved yeu.
Lk 7:47 have·been·forgiven, because she·loved much. "But
Mk 10:21 after·looking·clearly·upon him, loved him and
2Pe 2:15 *son* of·Beor who loved a·payment·of·service for·
Eph 2:4 on·account·of his large love with·which he·loved us,
Eph 5:2 just·as the Anointed-One also loved us and handed
Eph 5:25 also loved the entire·Called·Out·Citizenry and
1Jn 4:10 but·rather that he·himself loved us and dispatched
1Jn 4:11 if in·this·manner, God loved us, we·ourselves also
1Jn 4:19 should·love him, because he·himself first loved us.
G0025.1 V-AAI-3P ἠγάπησαν (3x)
Jn 3:19 and the men·of·clay† loved the darkness rather than
Jn 12:43 for they·loved the glory of·the men·of·clay† more·
Rv 12:11 testimony; and they·did·not love their souls even·
G0025.1 V-AAM-2P ἀγαπήσατε (1x)
1Pe 1:22 ·hypocrisy, yeu·must·love one·another from·out
G0025.1 V-AAP-DSM ἀγαπήσαντι (1x)
Rv 1:5 of·the earth— the·one loving us and already·bathing
G0025.1 V-AAP-GSM ἀγαπήσαντος (2x)
Gal 2:20 of·the Son of·God, the·one loving me, and already·
Rm 8:37 ·gain·a·decisive·victory through the·one loving us.
G0025.1 V-AAP-NSM ἀγαπήσας (3x)
Jn 13:1 to the Father, already·loving his·own, the·ones in
2Th 2:16 even our Father, the·one loving us, and already·
2Ti 4:10 for Demas forsook me, loving the present age, and
G0025.1 V-AAS-2P ἀγαπήσητε (1x)
Mt 5:46 "For if yeu·should·love the·ones loving yeu, what
G0025.1 V-RAP-DPM ἠγαπηκόσιν (1x)
2Ti 4:8 ·all the·ones having·loved his conspicuous·appearing
G0025.2 V-RPP-ASF ἠγαπημένην (3x)
Rm 9:25 and *call·her* 'Having·Been·Loved,' who·was·not
Rm 9:25 ·Been·Loved,' who·was·not having·been·loved."
Rv 20:9 ·the holy·ones and the City having·been·loved. And

G0025.2 V-RPP-DSM ἠγαπημένῳ (1x)

Eph 1:6 ·favored us in the·one having·been·loved,

G0025.2 V-RPP-NPM ἠγαπημένοι (3x)

1Th 1:4 having·seen, O·brothers having·been·loved by God,
2Th 2:13 yeu (O·brothers having·been·loved by *the* Lord),
Col 3:12 of·God (holy and having·been·loved), dress·

G0026 ἀγάπη agápē *n.* (119x)

Roots:G0025 Compare:G2064-3 See:G0026-1
xLangEquiv:H0160

G0026.1 N-NSF ἀγάπη (36x)

Jn 17:26 — "in·order·that the love with·which you·loved me
Gal 5:22 But the fruit of·the Spirit is love, joy, peace,
Mt 24:12 the Lawlessness, the love of·the many shall·be·
Rm 5:5 because the love of·God has·been·poured·forth in
Rm 12:9 The Love *must·be* without·hypocrisy, utterly·
Rm 13:10 Love works no wrong to·the neighbor.
Rm 13:10 ·the neighbor. Accordingly, love *is* Torah-Law's
Jud 1:2 mercy, and peace, and love be·multiplied to·yeu.
Php 1:9 this I·pray, that yeur love may·abound yet more and
1Pe 4:8 "because love shall·cover·and·bury·over a·full·
2Th 1:3 grows·exceedingly, and the love of·each one of·yeu
1Co 8:1 The knowledge puffs·up, but the Love edifies.
1Co 13:4 The Love is·long-suffering *and* is·beneficially·kind
1Co 13:4 ·kind. The Love does·not jealously·desire. The
1Co 13:4 does·not jealously·desire. The Love does·not brag.
1Co 13:8 The Love never·at·any·time falls·short. But if·also
1Co 13:13 Trust, Expectation, *and* Love; but *the* greater
1Co 13:13 *and* Love; but *the* greater of·these *is* the Love.
1Co 16:24 My love *be* with yeu all in Anointed-One Jesus.
2Co 5:14 For the love of·the Anointed-One constrains us,
2Co 13:14 Jesus Anointed, and the love of·God, and the
Eph 6:23 *be* to·the brothers, and love with trust from Father
1Ti 1:5 end·purpose of·the charge is love out of·a·pure heart,
1Jn 2:5 the love of·God has·been·made·completely·mature.
1Jn 2:15 should·love the world, the love of·the Father is not
1Jn 3:17 him, how·does the love of·God presently·abide in
1Jn 4:7 one·another, because the love is birthed·from·out of·
1Jn 4:8 does·not already·know God, because God is love.
1Jn 4:9 In this, the love of·God is·made·apparent among us,
1Jn 4:10 In this, is the love: not that we·ourselves loved God
1Jn 4:12 his love is having·been·made·completely·mature in
1Jn 4:16 God is love; and the·one abiding in the Love abides
1Jn 4:17 In this, the Love with us has·been·fully·completed,
1Jn 4:18 but·rather the completely·mature love casts out the
1Jn 5:3 For this is the love of·God, that we·should·
2Jn 1:6 And this is the Love, that we·should·walk according·

G0026.1 N-ASF ἀγάπην (33x)

Jn 5:42 that yeu·do·not have the love of·God in yeurselves.
Jn 13:35 to·me, if yeu·should·have love for one·another."
Jn 15:13 "A·love greater·than this, has not·even·one·man,
Lk 11:42 the tribunal·justice and the love of·God. It·is·
Rm 5:8 But God demonstrates his love toward us, how·that
Rm 14:15 *your* food, no·longer do·you·walk in love. Do·not
Php 2:2 ·thing, having the same love, contemplating the one
1Pe 4:8 all, *continue* having earnest love among yeurselves,
2Pe 1:7 and along·with *yeur* brotherly·affection, Love.
1Th 3:6 ·good·news to·us of·yeur trust and love, and that
2Th 2:10 because these did·not accept the love of·the truth,
2Th 3:5 fully·direct yeur hearts into the love of·God and into
1Co 13:1 and should·not have love, I·have·become *as* a·
1Co 13:2 and should·not have love, I·am nothing·at·all.
1Co 13:3 and should·not have love, it·benefits not·even·
1Co 14:1 Pursue the Love, and zealously·desire the spiritual
2Co 2:4 but·rather that yeu·may·know the love which I·have
2Co 2:8 Therefore I·implore yeu to·ratify *yeur* love for him.
Eph 1:15 the Lord Jesus and *of* the love for all the holy·ones,
Eph 2:4 on·account·of his large love with·which he·loved
Eph 3:19 knowledge of·the love of·the Anointed-One— in·
Col 1:4 in Anointed-One Jesus and *of·yeur* love, the·one for
Col 1:8 ·one also making·plain to·us yeur love in *the* Spirit.
Col 3:14 these·things, *dress·yeurselves·with* the love, which
Phm 1:5 hearing of·your love and trust which you·have
Phm 1:9 rather on·account·of the love, I·implore *you*, *I* Paul,
1Ti 6:11 devout·reverence, trust, love, patient·endurance,
2Ti 2:22 but pursue righteousness, trust, love, peace, with
1Jn 3:1 See, what·manner·of love the Father has·given to·us
1Jn 3:16 By this we·have·known the love *of·God*, because
1Jn 4:16 have·known and have·trusted the Love that God has
Rv 2:4 I·have *this* against you, that you·left your first love.
Rv 2:19 ·know your works (also the love, and the service,

G0026.1 N-DSF ἀγάπῃ (28x)

Jn 15:9 Abide in my love.
Jn 15:10 yeu·shall·abide in my love, just·as I·myself have·
Jn 15:10 my Father's commandments and abide in his love.
Jud 1:21 purposefully·keep yeurselves in God's love, *yeu*
1Th 3:12 ·more and abound in·the love toward one·another
1Th 5:13 them abundantly with love above·and·beyond, on·
Tit 2:2 in·the trust, in·the love, in·the patient·endurance;
1Co 4:21 yeu with a·rod or with love, also in·a·spirit of·
1Co 16:14 In love, all of·yeu, BE!
2Co 6:6 by Holy Spirit, by love without·hypocrisy,
2Co 8:7 *being* among us) in·the love, *see* that yeu·should·
Eph 1:4 ·blemish directly·in·the·sight of·him— in love,
Eph 3:17 ·been·rooted and having·been·founded in love—
Eph 4:2 long-suffering, bearing·with one·another in love,
Eph 4:15 But being·truthful in love, we·should·grow·up *in*
Eph 4:16 ·growth of·the Body for its·own edification in love.
Eph 5:2 and walk in love, just·as the Anointed-One also
Col 2:2 may·be·comforted, being·knit·together in love, and
Phm 1:7 gratitude and comfort in your love, because the
1Ti 2:15 ·continue in trust and love and renewed·holiness
1Ti 4:12 in word, in conduct, in love, in spirit, in trust, *and*
2Ti 1:13 ·from me, in trust and love, the·one *that·is* in
2Ti 3:10 *my* long-suffering, *my* love, *my* patient·endurance,
1Jn 4:16 and the·one abiding in the Love abides in God,
1Jn 4:18 There·is not fear in the Love, but·rather the
1Jn 4:18 has·not been·made·completely·mature in the Love.
2Jn 1:3 Anointed, the Son of·the Father, in truth and love.
3Jn 1:6 of·your love in·the·sight of·a·convened·Called·Out·

G0026.1 N-GSF ἀγάπης (18x)

Heb 6:10 work and *yeur* wearisome·labor of·love, which
Heb 10:24 ·another to a·keen·provoking of·love and good
Gal 5:6 ·rather trust which·is·itself·operating through love.
Gal 5:13 But·rather through the love, be·slaves to·one·
Rm 8:35 shall·separate us from the love of·the Anointed-One
Rm 8:39 shall·be·able to·separate us from the love of·God in
Rm 15:30 and on·account·of the love of·the Spirit, to·
Php 1:17 the *others fully·proclaim* out of·love, having·seen
Php 2:1 if any personal·consolation of·love, if any
1Pe 5:14 Greet·yeu one·another with a·kiss of·love. Peace
1Th 1:3 trust, and the wearisome·labor of·the love, and the
1Th 5:8 *the* full·chest·armor of·trust and love, and *with·the*
2Co 8:8 and to·test·and·prove the genuineness of·yeur love.
2Co 8:24 them the indicator of·yeur love and of·our boasting
2Co 13:11 ·peaceful; and the God of·love and peace shall·be
Col 1:13 *us* into the kingdom of·the Son of·his love,
1Ti 1:14 ·above·and·beyond with trust and love, the·one in
2Ti 1:7 but·rather of·power, and of·love, and of·a·sound·

EG0026.1 (3x)

Rm 12:15 *Love is* to·rejoice with those·rejoicing, and to·
Rm 12:17 *Love is* giving·back to·not·even·one·man wrong
Rm 12:19 *Love is* not avenging yeurselves, dearly·beloved,

G0026.2 N-DPF ἀγάπαις (1x)

Jud 1:12 at yeur love·feasts, presently·indulging·themselves·

G0027 ἀγαπητός agapētós *adj.* (62x)

Roots:G0025 Compare:G5384 G2064-3 G2064-1

G0027.1 A-NSM ἀγαπητός (12x)

Lk 3:22 "You·yourself are my beloved Son; in you I·take·
Lk 9:35 "This is my beloved Son. Listen·to him!"
Mt 3:17 "This is my beloved Son, in whom I·take·delight.
Mt 12:18 whom I·decidedly·chose, my beloved, in whom
Mt 17:5 "This is my beloved Son, in whom I·take·delight.
Mk 1:11 "You·yourself are my beloved Son, in whom I·
Mk 9:7 "This is my beloved Son. Listen·to him.
2Pe 1:17 "This is my beloved Son, in whom I·myself take·
2Pe 3:15 — just·as also our beloved brother Paul wrote to·
Eph 6:21 to·yeu all·things. *He·is* the beloved brother and
Col 4:7 against me. *He·is* a·beloved brother, a·trustworthy
Col 4:14 Luke, the beloved practitioner·of·healing, and

G0027.1 A-NPM ἀγαπητοί (2x)

Rm 11:28 the Selection, *they·are* beloved on·account·of the
1Ti 6:2 they·are ones·that·trust and *are* beloved, the·ones

G0027.1 A-NPN ἀγαπητά (2x)

1Co 4:14 but·rather, as my beloved children, I·admonish
Eph 5:1 attentive·imitators of·God, as beloved children,

G0027.1 A-VSM ἀγαπητέ (3x)

3Jn 1:2 Beloved·man, I·well-wish *to·God* concerning all·
3Jn 1:5 Beloved·man, trustworthily do·you·do whatever
3Jn 1:11 Beloved·man, do·not attentively·imitate the bad,

G0027.1 A-VPM ἀγαπητοί (19x)

Heb 6:9 But beloved, we·have·been·persuaded concerning
Jac 1:16 Do·not be·deceived, my beloved brothers.
Jac 1:19 As·such, my beloved brothers, every man·of·clay†
Jac 2:5 Listen, my beloved brothers, ¿! is·it·not God *that*
Jud 1:3 Beloved, while·making all diligence to·write to·yeu
Jud 1:17 But yeu, beloved, recall·to·mind the utterances,
Jud 1:20 But yeu, beloved, building·up yeurselves in·yeur
Php 2:12 As·such, my beloved, just·as yeu·listened·and·
1Pe 4:12 Beloved, do·not be·strangely·surprised at the fiery·
2Pe 3:1 This second letter, beloved, even·now I·write to·yeu
2Pe 3:8 ·thing, do·not be·oblivious, O·yeu beloved, that "
2Pe 3:14 Therefore, *yeu* beloved, while·intently·awaiting
2Pe 3:17 Accordingly, O·yeu beloved, while·foreknowing
1Co 15:58 As·such, my beloved brothers, become
1Jn 3:2 Beloved, now we·are children of·God, and it·is·not·
1Jn 3:21 Beloved, if our heart should·not incriminate us, *then*
1Jn 4:1 Beloved, do·not trust every spirit, but·rather test·and·
1Jn 4:7 Beloved, we·should·love one·another, because the
1Jn 4:11 Beloved, if in·this·manner, God loved us, we·

G0027.1 A-ASM ἀγαπητόν (2x)

Lk 20:13 should·I·do? I·shall·send my beloved son. *It·is*
Phm 1:16 above a·slave, a·brother beloved, especially to·me

G0027.1 A-ASN ἀγαπητόν (1x)

1Co 4:17 to·yeu TimoThy, who is my beloved child, and

G0027.1 A-DSM ἀγαπητῷ (1x)

Col 4:9 the trustworthy and beloved brother, who is from·

G0027.1 A-DSF ἀγαπητῇ (1x)

Phm 1:2 and to·the beloved Apphia, and ArchIppus our

G0027.1 A-DPM ἀγαπητοῖς (2x)

Ac 15:25 to yeu together with·our beloved BarNabas and
Rm 1:7 ·ones being in Rome, beloved of·God, called·forth

G0027.2 A-NPM ἀγαπητοί (1x)

1Th 2:8 souls, on·account·that yeu·have·become dear to·us.

G0027.2 A-GSM ἀγαπητοῦ (1x)

Col 1:7 *it* from EpAphras, our dear fellow·slave, who is a·

G0027.3 A-NPM ἀγαπητοί (1x)

Php 4:1 my brothers (dearly·beloved and greatly·yearned·for

G0027.3 A-VPM ἀγαπητοί (6x)

Rm 12:19 avenging yeurselves, dearly·beloved, but·rather
Php 4:1 ·manner stand·fast in *the* Lord, *my* dearly·beloved.
1Pe 2:11 Dearly·beloved, I·implore *yeu* as sojourners and
1Co 10:14 Therefore·indeed, my dearly·beloved, flee from
2Co 7:1 these promises, dearly·beloved, we·should·purify
2Co 12:19 but *we·do* all·things, dearly·beloved, on·behalf

G0027.3 A-DSM ἀγαπητῷ (2x)

Phm 1:1 To·Philemon our dearly·beloved and coworker,
2Ti 1:2 To·TimoThy, a·dearly·beloved child. Grace, mercy,

G0027.4 A-ASM ἀγαπητόν (4x)

Mk 12:6 one son, his well-beloved, he·dispatched him also
Rm 16:5 Greet my well-beloved Epaenetus, who is a·
Rm 16:8 Greet my well-beloved Amplias in *the* Lord.
Rm 16:9 in Anointed-One, and my well-beloved Stachys.

G0027.4 A-ASF ἀγαπητήν (1x)

Rm 16:12 Greet the well-beloved Persis, who repeatedly

G0027.4 A-DSM ἀγαπητῷ (1x)

3Jn 1:1 The Elder. To·the well-beloved Gaius, whom I·

G0028 Ἄγαρ Ágar *n/p.* (2x)
Ἅγαρ Hágar
הָגָר hagar [Hebrew]
Roots:H1904

G0028 N/P-PRI Ἄγαρ (2x)
Gal 4:24 bearing·children for slavery, which is Hagar.
Gal 4:25 For *this* Hagar is Mount Sinai in Arabia, and

G0029 ἀγγαρεύω angarêúō *v.* (3x)
Compare:G0315 xLangAlso:A0104

G0029.2 V-FAI-3S ἀγγαρεύσει (1x)
Mt 5:41 whoever shall·press·and·impose·upon you *to·head·*

G0029.2 V-PAI-3P ἀγγαρεύουσιν (1x)
Mk 15:21 And they·pressed·and·imposed·upon a·certain·

G0029.2 V-AAI-3P ἠγγάρευσαν (1x)
Mt 27:32 *and* they·pressed·and·imposed·upon this·man that

G0030 ἀγγεῖον angêîon *n.* (2x)
Compare:G0043 G0044 G0045 G4632 See:G3582 G2765 G4632 G5473 xLangAlso:H3627

G0030 N-APN ἀγγεῖα (1x)
Mt 13:48 they·collected the good into containers but cast out

G0030 N-DPN ἀγγείοις (1x)
Mt 25:4 prudent took oil in their containers with their lamps.

G0031 ἀγγελία angêlía *n.* (1x)
Roots:G0032 See:G2098

G0031.1 N-NSF ἀγγελία (1x)
1Jn 3:11 Because this is the message that yeu·heard from *the*

G0032 ἄγγελος ángêlôs *n.* (188x)
Compare:G0034 G4587-1 G5502 G5501-4 See:G0071 G0031 G2098 G1804 G2605 xLangEquiv:H4397 A4398 xLangAlso:H0430

G0032.1 N-ASM ἄγγελον (3x)
Lk 7:27 I·myself dispatch my messenger before your
Mt 11:10 I·myself dispatch my messenger before your
Mk 1:2 I·myself dispatch my messenger before your

G0032.1 N-APM ἀγγέλους (2x)
Lk 9:52 and he·dispatched messengers before his personal·
Jac 2:25 ·receiving the messengers and casting *them·* forth

G0032.1 N-GPM ἀγγέλων (1x)
Lk 7:24 And with·the messengers of·John going·off, *Jesus*

G0032.2 N-NSM ἄγγελος (55x)
Jn 5:4 ·to a·certain·season, an·angel was·descending on the
Jn 12:29 Others were·saying, "An·angel has·spoken to·him.
Lk 1:11 ·made·visible to·him an·angel of·Yahweh standing
Lk 1:13 But the angel declared to him, "Do·not be·afraid,
Lk 1:19 And answering, the angel declared to·him, "I·
Lk 1:26 sixth lunar·month, the angel GabriEl was·dispatched
Lk 1:28 toward her, the angel declared, "Be·of·good·cheer,
Lk 1:30 And the angel declared to·her, "Do·not be·afraid,
Lk 1:35 And answering, the angel declared to·her, "Holy
Lk 1:38 And the angel went·away from her.
Lk 2:9 And behold, Yahweh's angel stood·over them, and
Lk 2:10 And the angel declared to·them, "Do·not be·afraid,
Lk 22:43 ·was·made·visible to·him an·angel from heaven,
Ac 5:19 But an·angel of·Yahweh, *coming* through the night,
Ac 7:30 ·fulfilled, an·angel of·Yahweh was·made·visible to·
Ac 8:26 And the·angel of·Yahweh spoke to PhilIppe, saying,
Ac 10:7 And as·soon·as the angel (the·one speaking to·
Ac 12:7 And behold, an·angel of·Yahweh stood·over *him*,
Ac 12:8 And the angel declared to him, "Gird·yourself·
Ac 12:10 and immediately the angel withdrew from him.
Ac 12:15 But they·were·saying, "It·is his angel."
Ac 12:23 And at·once, an·angel of·Yahweh smote him,
Ac 23:9 but if a·spirit or an·angel spoke to·him, we·should·
Ac 27:23 there·stood·by me this night an·angel of·God, of·
Gal 1:8 even if we·ourselves or an·angel from·out of·heaven
Mt 1:20 these·things, behold, an·angel of·Yahweh
Mt 1:24 did as the angel of·Yahweh specifically·assigned
Mt 2:13 ·departing, behold, an·angel of·Yahweh appears to·
Mt 2:19 completely·dying, behold, an·angel of·Yahweh
Mt 28:2 earthquake. For Yahweh's angel, after·descending
Mt 28:5 And responding, the angel declared to·the women,
Rv 8:3 And another angel came and stood·still at the
Rv 8:5 And the angel has·taken the censer·for·frankincense,
Rv 8:7 The first angel sounded, and there·happened hail and
Rv 8:8 And the second angel sounded, and *something* as a·
Rv 8:10 And the third angel sounded, and there·fell a·great
Rv 8:12 And the fourth angel sounded, and the third·part of·
Rv 9:1 And the fifth angel sounded, and I·saw a·star having·
Rv 9:13 And the sixth angel sounded, and I·heard one voice
Rv 10:5 And the angel which I·saw standing upon the sea
Rv 11:15 And the seventh angel sounded, and there·became
Rv 14:8 And there·followed another angel, saying,
Rv 14:9 And a·third angel followed them, saying with a·loud
Rv 14:15 And another angel came·forth out of·the Temple,
Rv 14:17 And another angel came·forth out of·the Temple,
Rv 14:18 And another angel came·forth out·from the
Rv 14:19 And the angel cast his sickle into the earth, and
Rv 16:3 And the second angel poured·out his vial into the
Rv 16:4 And the third angel poured·out his vial into the
Rv 16:8 And the fourth angel poured·out his vial upon the
Rv 16:10 And the fifth angel poured·out his vial upon the
Rv 16:12 And the sixth angel poured·out his vial upon the
Rv 16:17 And the seventh angel poured·out his vial into the
Rv 17:7 And the angel declared to·me, "Why did·you·
Rv 18:21 And one strong angel took·up a·stone as a·great

G0032.2 N-NPM ἄγγελοι (23x)
Lk 2:15 it·happened, after the angels went·away from them
Heb 1:6 "" And fall·prostrate to·him, all angels of·God!""
Mt 4:11 him, and behold, angels came·alongside and were·
Mt 13:39 ·completion of·the age, and the reapers are angels.
Mt 13:49 of·the age. The angels shall·come·forth and shall·
Mt 18:10 any *matter·of·consequence*, their angels in *the*
Mt 22:30 but·rather they·are as God's angels in heaven.
Mt 24:36 ·knows, not·even the angels of·the heavens, except
Mt 25:31 glory, and all the holy angels with him, then he·
Mk 1:13 wild·beasts, and the angels were·attending to·him.
Mk 12:25 ·in·marriage, but·rather are as angels, the·ones in
Mk 13:32 personally·knows, not·even the angels, the·ones
Rm 8:38 death, nor life†, nor angels, nor principalities, nor
1Pe 1:12 — which·things angels long to·stoop·near·and·peer
2Pe 2:11 whereas angels, being greater·in strength and power
Rv 1:20 the seven stars are angels of·the seven Called·Out·
Rv 7:11 And all the angels stood in·a·circle·around the
Rv 8:6 And the seven angels having the seven trumpets made
Rv 9:15 And the four angels were·loosened, the·ones having·
Rv 12:7 MiChaEl and his angels waged·war against the
Rv 12:7 and the Dragon (and his angels) waged·war,
Rv 12:9 the earth, and his angels were·cast·out with him.
Rv 15:6 And the seven angels came·forth from·out of·the

G0032.2 N-ASM ἄγγελον (18x)
Lk 1:18 Then ZacharIas declared to the angel, "How shall·I·
Lk 1:34 Then Mariam declared to the angel, "How shall this
Ac 10:3 of·the day, an·angel of·God entering *this·realm*
Ac 11:13 to·us how he·saw the angel in his house, being·
Ac 12:11 truly that Yahweh dispatched his angel forth and
Ac 23:8 a·resurrection, *also* not·even an·angel nor a·spirit,
Gal 4:14 but·rather accepted me as an·angel of·God, *even*
2Co 11:14 himself is·disguised as an·angel of·light.
Rv 5:2 a·strong angel officially·proclaiming with·a·loud
Rv 7:2 And I·saw another angel ascending from *the* eastern
Rv 10:1 And I·saw another strong angel descending from·out
Rv 10:9 And I·went·aside to·the angel, saying to·him, "Give
Rv 14:6 And I·saw another angel who·is·flying in *the*
Rv 18:1 these·things I·saw an·angel descending from·out of·
Rv 19:17 And I·saw one angel standing in the sun; and he·
Rv 20:1 And I·saw an·angel descending from·out of·the
Rv 22:6 prophets, dispatched his angel to·show to·his slaves
Rv 22:16 Jesus, sent my angel to·testify to·yeu these·things

G0032.2 N-APM ἀγγέλους (17x)
Jn 1:51 and 'the angels of·God ascending and descending'
Jn 20:12 and she·observes two angels in white sitting·down,
Heb 1:7 in·fact, he·says unto the angels, "*This·is* the·one
Heb 1:7 "'*This·is* the·one making his angels spirits and his
Heb 2:9 ·been·made·lesser than *the* angels on·account·of the
Heb 13:2 this some are·hosting angels, being·oblivious *of·it*.
Mt 13:41 Son of·Clay·Man† shall·dispatch his angels, and
Mt 24:31 And he·shall·dispatch his angels with a·great
Mk 13:27 ·dispatch his angels and shall·completely·gather
Jud 1:6 Also the angels, not observantly·keeping their·own
1Co 6:3 ·know that we·shall·judge angels? How·much·more
1Co 11:10 authority on her head on·account·of the angels.
Rv 7:1 after these·things, I·saw four angels standing on the
Rv 8:2 And I·saw the seven angels who stand in·the·sight of·
Rv 9:14 "Loosen the four angels, the·ones having·been·
Rv 15:1 great and marvelous, seven angels having the last
Rv 21:12 twelve gates, and twelve angels upon the gates,

G0032.2 N-DSM ἀγγέλῳ (9x)
Lk 2:13 suddenly together with·the angel, there·came·to·be
Rv 2:1 "To·the angel of·the Called·Out·citizenry of·Ephesus
Rv 2:8 "And to·the angel of·the Called·Out·citizenry in·
Rv 2:12 "And to·the angel of·the Called·Out·citizenry in
Rv 2:18 "And to·the angel of·the Called·Out·citizenry in
Rv 3:1 "And to·the angel of·the Called·Out·citizenry in
Rv 3:7 "And to·the angel of·the Called·Out·citizenry in
Rv 3:14 "And to·the angel of·the Called·Out·citizenry of·
Rv 9:14 saying to·the sixth angel who was·holding the

G0032.2 N-DPM ἀγγέλοις (9x)
Lk 4:10 "He·shall·command his angels concerning you, to·
Heb 2:5 For *it·is* not to·angels *that* he·subjugated the
Mt 4:6 "He·shall·command his angels concerning you,"
Mt 25:41 ·been·made·ready for·the Slanderer and his angels.
1Co 4:9 to·the world, to·angels, and to·men·of·clay†.
1Ti 3:16 is·gazed·upon by·angels, is·officially·proclaimed
Rv 7:2 ·out with·a·loud voice to·the four angels, to·whom it
Rv 15:7 living·beings gave to·the seven angels seven golden
Rv 16:1 Temple saying to·the seven angels, "Head·on·out

G0032.2 N-GSM ἀγγέλου (15x)
Lk 2:21 *name* being·called·forth by the angel prior·to him
Ac 6:15 ·Sanhedrin saw his face as·if *it·was* an·angel's face.
Ac 7:35 a·ransomer by *the* hand of·*the*·angel, the·one being·
Ac 7:38 wilderness, *along* with the angel, the·one speaking
Ac 10:22 ·instructed by a·holy angel to·send·for you into his
Ac 12:9 that the·thing happening through the angel was true,
Rv 1:1 And dispatching through his angel, he·signified *it* to·
Rv 8:4 in·the·sight of·God from·out of·the angel's hand.
Rv 8:13 And I·saw and heard an angel flying in mid-heaven,
Rv 10:7 of·the sound of·the seventh angel, whenever he·
Rv 10:8 ·been·opened·up in the hand of·*the*·angel, the·one
Rv 10:10 the tiny·official·scroll out of·the angel's hand and
Rv 16:5 And I·heard the angel of·the waters saying, "You·
Rv 21:17 of·a·man·of·clay†, which is *that* of·an·angel.
Rv 22:8 before the feet of·the angel, the·one showing me

G0032.2 N-GPM ἀγγέλων (30x)
Lk 9:26 and *that* of·the Father, and of·the holy angels.
Lk 12:8 shall·affirm him by·name before the angels of·God.
Lk 12:9 ·be·utterly·denied in·the·sight of·the angels of·God.
Lk 15:10 joy occurs in·the·sight of·the angels of·God over
Lk 16:22 him to·be·carried·away by the angels to AbRaham's
Lk 24:23 they·had·clearly·seen a·vision of·angels who say
Ac 7:53 Torah-Law as an·institution of·angels and did·not
Heb 1:4 significantly·better·than the angels, by·as·much·as
Heb 1:5 to·which of·the angels did·he·declare at·any·time,
Heb 1:13 to which of·the angels has·he·declared at·any·time,
Heb 2:2 the word being·spoken through angels was steadfast,
Heb 2:16 *of·the fundamental·nature* of·angels— but·rather
Heb 12:22 and to·a·myriad·tens·of·thousands of·angels,
Gal 3:19 being·thoroughly·assigned through angels in *the*
Mt 16:27 the glory of·his Father with his angels, and then
Mt 26:53 ·present to·me more than twelve legions of·angels?
Mk 8:38 in the glory of·his Father with the holy angels."
1Pe 3:22 right·hand of·God, with·angels and authorities and
2Pe 2:4 did·not spare morally·failing angels, but·rather after·
2Th 1:7 YeShua from heaven with *the* angels of·his power;
1Co 13:1 of·the men·of·clay† and of·the angels, and should·
Col 2:18 and in·a·religion of·the angels, one·intruding·into
1Ti 5:21 and of·the Selected angels, that you·should·
Rv 3:5 ·sight of·my Father, and in·the·sight of·his angels.
Rv 5:11 and I·heard *the* voice of·many angels all·around the

Rv 8:13 of·the trumpet of·the three angels, the·ones about to·
Rv 14:10 sulfur in·the·sight of·the holy angels, and in·the·
Rv 15:8 ·blows of·the seven angels should·be·completed.
Rv 17:1 one from·among the seven angels, of·the·one having
Rv 21:9 to me one of·the seven angels (of·the·ones having
EG0032.2 (3x)
Jn 20:13 And those *angels* say to·her, "Woman, why do·
Jud 1:7 As *in* like manner to·these *angels*, Sodom and
Rv 19:9 Then *the angel* says to·me, "Write, 'Supremely·
G0032.3 N-NSM ἄγγελος (1x)
2Co 12:7 flesh, a·messenger of·*The*·Adversary in·order·that
G0032.3 N-ASM ἄγγελον (1x)
Rv 9:11 a·king over them— the angel of·the bottomless·pit.
G0032.6 N-APM ἀγγέλους (1x)
Heb 2:7 *the* supreme·angels; you·did·victoriously·crown him

G0033 ἄγε ágê *v.* (2x)
Roots:G0071
G0033.2 V-PAM-2S ἄγε (2x)
Jac 4:13 Come·on now, the·ones saying, "Today or
Jac 5:1 Come·on now, Wealthy·Men! Weep, howling over

G0034 ἀγέλη agélē *n.* (8x)
Roots:G0071 Compare:G0032 G4168
xLangEquiv:H5739
G0034.2 N-NSF ἀγέλη (6x)
Lk 8:32 Now there·was a·herd there of·a·significant·number
Lk 8:33 the pigs, and the herd impulsively·dashed down the
Mt 8:30 ·was at·a·distance from them a·herd of·many pigs
Mt 8:32 behold, the entire herd of·pigs impulsively·dashed
Mk 5:11 ·of the mountains, a·great herd of·pigs being·fed.
Mk 5:13 the pigs, and the herd impulsively·dashed down the
G0034.2 N-ASF ἀγέλην (2x)
Mt 8:31 freely·permit us to·go·away into the herd of·pigs."
Mt 8:32 ·forth, they·went·off into the herd of·pigs. And

G0035 ἀ•γενεα•λόγητος agênêalógētôs *adj.* (1x)
Roots:G0001 G1075
G0035 A-NSM ἀγενεαλόγητος (1x)
Heb 7:3 ·father, without·mother, without·lineage, having

G0036 ἀ•γενής agênếs *adj.* (1x)
Roots:G0001 G1085 Compare:G2104
G0036.3 A-APN ἀγενῆ (1x)
1Co 1:28 And God selected the bastardly·things of·the world

G0037 ἁγιάζω hagiázō *v.* (29x)
Roots:G0040 Compare:G0048 G2508 G2511
See:G0037-1 G0038-1
xLangEquiv:H6942
G0037.1 V-PAI-1S ἁγιάζω (1x)
Jn 17:19 my·own·self holy in·order·that they·themselves
G0037.1 V-PAI-3S ἁγιάζει (1x)
Heb 9:13 having·been·defiled, makes·one·holy just·for the
G0037.1 V-PAP-NSN ἁγιάζον (1x)
Mt 23:19 Sacrifice·Altar, the·one making the present holy?
G0037.1 V-PAP-NSM ἁγιάζων (2x)
Heb 2:11 For both the·one making·holy and the·ones being·
Mt 23:17 or the Temple, the·one making the gold holy?
G0037.1 V-PPI-3S ἁγιάζεται (1x)
1Ti 4:5 for it·is·made·holy through God's Redemptive-word
G0037.1 V-PPP-APM ἁγιαζομένους (1x)
Heb 10:14 into perpetuity the·ones being·made·holy.
G0037.1 V-PPP-NPM ἁγιαζόμενοι (1x)
Heb 2:11 making·holy and the·ones being·made·holy *are* all
G0037.1 V-AAI-3S ἡγίασεν (1x)
Jn 10:36 *yet* whom the Father made·holy and dispatched into
G0037.1 V-AAM-2S ἁγίασον (1x)
Jn 17:17 "Make them holy in your truth.
G0037.1 V-AAM-2P ἁγιάσατε (1x)
1Pe 3:15 But make Yahweh God holy in yeur hearts.
G0037.1 V-AAO-3S ἁγιάσαι (1x)
1Th 5:23 make yeu·yeurselves holy, absolutely·perfect. And
G0037.1 V-AAS-3S ἁγιάσῃ (2x)
Heb 13:12 YeShua also, that he·may·make·holy the People
Eph 5:26 in·order·that he·may·cleanse·and·make·*her*·holy,
G0037.1 V-API-2P ἡγιάσθητε (1x)
1Co 6:11 ·are·fully·bathed, but·rather yeu·are·made·holy,
G0037.1 V-API-3S ἡγιάσθη (1x)
Heb 10:29 covenant (by which he·was·made·holy) *to·be* a·
G0037.1 V-APM-3S ἁγιασθήτω (3x)
Lk 11:2 your name, let·it·be·made·holy! Your kingdom
Mt 6:9 ·one in the heavens, your name, let·it·be·made·holy!
Rv 22:11 and the·one *being* holy, let·him·be·holy still."
G0037.1 V-RPI-3S ἡγίασται (2x)
1Co 7:14 non-trusting husband has·been·made·holy by the
1Co 7:14 the non-trusting wife has·been·made·holy by the
G0037.1 V-RPP-DPM ἡγιασμένοις (4x)
Ac 20:32 among all the·ones having·been·made·holy.
Ac 26:18 among the·ones having·been·made·holy by·a·trust,
Jud 1:1 having·been·made·holy and having·been·fully·kept
1Co 1:2 — ones·having·been·made·holy in Anointed-One
G0037.1 V-RPP-NSN ἡγιασμένον (1x)
2Ti 2:21 a·vessel unto honor, having·been·made·holy, and
G0037.1 V-RPP-NSF ἡγιασμένη (1x)
Rm 15:16 well·acceptable, having·been·made·holy by Holy
G0037.1 V-RPP-NPM ἡγιασμένοι (2x)
Jn 17:19 also may·be having·been·made·holy in truth.
Heb 10:10 ·are the·ones having·been·made·holy through the

G0038 ἁγιασμός hagiasmós *n.* (10x)
Roots:G0037 Compare:G2413 G3742 See:G0041
G0042
G0038.2 N-NSM ἁγιασμός (2x)
1Th 4:3 is God's will, yeur renewed·holiness: for·yeu to·
1Co 1:30 also righteousness, renewed·holiness, and full·
G0038.2 N-ASM ἁγιασμόν (3x)
Heb 12:14 all *men*, also the renewed·holiness, apart·from
Rm 6:19 *as* slaves to·Righteousness unto renewed·holiness.
Rm 6:22 yeu·have yeur fruit unto renewed·holiness, and at·
G0038.2 N-DSM ἁγιασμῷ (5x)
1Pe 1:2 of·Father God, by a·renewed·holiness of·Spirit— to
1Th 4:4 *earthenware* vessel in renewed·holiness and honor,
1Th 4:7 toward impurity, but·rather into renewed·holiness.
2Th 2:13 yeu for Salvation in renewed·holiness of·Spirit and
1Ti 2:15 and love and renewed·holiness with self-control.

G0039 ἅγιον hágiôn *adj.* (11x)
Roots:G0040 Compare:G2411 G3485 See:G0037-1
G0038-1
xLangEquiv:H6944 xLangAlso:H4720
G0039.1 A-GPN ἁγίων (1x)
Heb 8:2 a·public·servant of·the holy·things and of·the true
G0039.2 A-NSF ἁγία (1x)
Heb 9:2 bread, which is·referred·to·as *the* Holy·Place.
G0039.2 A-NSN ἅγιον (1x)
Heb 9:1 ·ministry *to·God*, and·also the worldly holy·place.
G0039.2 A-APN ἅγια (1x)
Heb 9:24 did·not enter into holy·places made·by·hands,
G0039.4 A-NSF ἁγία (1x)
Heb 9:3 the·one being·referred·to·as *the* Holy of·Holies,
G0039.4 A-APN ἅγια (3x)
Heb 9:12 into the Holy·of·Holies upon·one·occasion·only,
Heb 9:25 high·priest enters into the Holy·of·Holies each year
Heb 13:11 is·carried into the Holy·of·Holies through the
G0039.4 A-GPN ἁγίων (3x)
Heb 9:3 the·one being·referred·to·as *the* Holy of·Holies,
Heb 9:8 *that* the way of·the Holy·of·Holies *was* not·yet to·
Heb 10:19 ·speech upon the entrance of·the Holy·of·Holies

G0040 ἅγιος hágiôs *adj.* (231x)
Roots:G0060-2 Compare:G2413 G0053 G3741
See:G0038-1 G0038
xLangEquiv:H6918
G0040.1 A-NSM ἅγιος (9x)
Rm 7:12 As·such, in·fact, the Torah-Law *is* holy, and the
1Pe 1:16 "Yeu·must·be holy, because I AM holy."
1Co 3:17 For the temple of·God is holy, which *temple* yeu·
Rv 4:8 day and night, saying, "Holy, holy, holy *is* Yahweh,
Rv 4:8 and night, saying, "Holy, holy, holy *is* Yahweh, *El*
Rv 4:8 "Holy, holy, holy *is* Yahweh, *El Shaddai* God
Rv 6:10 How·long, Master, the Holy and the Truthful·One,
Rv 20:6 Supremely·blessed and holy *is* the·one having part
Rv 22:11 still; and the·one *being* holy, let·him·be·holy still.
G0040.1 A-NSF ἁγία (6x)
Ac 7:33 feet, for the place in which you·stand is holy soil.'
Rm 7:12 holy, and the commandment *is* holy, righteous, and
Rm 11:16 *of·dough offered as·a* firstfruit *is* holy, the *whole*
Rm 11:16 And if the root *is* holy, so *are* the branches.
1Co 7:34 of·the Lord in·order·that she·may·be holy, both in·
Eph 5:27 that she·should·be holy and without·blemish.
G0040.1 A-NSN ἅγιον (22x)
Jn 7:39 were·about to·receive, for Holy Spirit was not·yet
Jn 14:26 the Companion/Intercessor, *who·is* the Holy Spirit,
Lk 1:35 angel declared to·her, "Holy Spirit shall·come upon
Lk 1:35 the *child*, being·born holy, shall·be·called God's
Lk 3:22 and the Holy Spirit descended in·a·bodily shape like
Lk 12:12 "For the Holy Spirit shall·instruct yeu in the same
Ac 1:16 ·fulfilled, which the Holy Spirit previously·declared
Ac 10:44 speaking these utterances, the Holy Spirit fell upon
Ac 11:15 as I began to·speak, the Holy Spirit fell upon them
Ac 13:2 Lord, and·also fasting, the Holy Spirit declared,
Ac 19:2 we·did·not·even hear whether there·is a·Holy Spirit.
Ac 19:6 his hands on·them, the Holy Spirit came upon them,
Ac 20:23 other·than that the Holy Spirit thoroughly·testifies
Ac 20:28 among which the Holy Spirit has·placed yeu *to·be*
Ac 21:11 "Thus says the Holy Spirit, 'in·this·manner the
Ac 28:25 utterance, "The Holy Spirit spoke well through
Heb 3:7 Therefore, just·as the Holy Spirit says, "'Today if
Heb 10:15 And *of·this*, the Holy Spirit also testifies to·us,
Mk 13:11 ·yeurselves speaking, but·rather the Holy Spirit.
1Pe 2:5 a·spiritual house, a·holy priesthood to·carry·up
1Pe 2:9 kindred, a·royal priesthood, a·holy nation, a·
1Jn 5:7 the Word, and the Holy Spirit. And these three are
G0040.1 A-NPM ἅγιοι (5x)
Mt 25:31 in his glory, and all the holy angels with him, then
1Pe 1:15 Also yeu·yeurselves must·become holy in all *yeur*
1Pe 1:16 it·has·been·written, "Yeu·must·be holy, because I
Col 3:12 Selected-Ones of·God (holy and having·been·loved
Rv 18:20 her, O·Heaven, and the holy ambassadors and the
G0040.1 A-NPF ἅγιαι (1x)
1Pe 3:5 in·this·manner in·times·past, the holy wives also
G0040.1 A-NPN ἅγια (1x)
1Co 7:14 yeur children are impure, but now they·are holy.
G0040.1 A-VSM ἅγιε (1x)
Jn 17:11 do·come to you. "Holy Father, guard by your·own
G0040.1 A-VPM ἅγιοι (1x)
Heb 3:1 From·which·cause, O·holy brothers (*yeu*
G0040.1 A-ASM ἅγιον (6x)
Ac 3:14 "But yeu denied the Holy and Righteous·One, and
Ac 4:27 ·together against your holy servant·boy Jesus whom
Ac 21:28 ·Courtyard and has·defiled this holy place."
Mk 6:20 ·seen *that* he was·a·righteous and holy man, and he·
1Pe 1:15 already·calling yeu forth, *who·is* holy. Also yeu·
Eph 2:21 ·fitly·framed·together, grows into a·holy temple in
G0040.1 A-ASF ἁγίαν (6x)
Mt 4:5 personally·takes him up into the Holy City and sets
Mt 27:53 ·death, they·entered into the Holy City and were·
Rm 12:1 *as* a·living sacrifice, holy *and* most·satisfying to·
Rv 11:2 And they·shall·trample the Holy City forty two
Rv 21:2 John, saw the HOLY CITY, brand-new JeruSalem,
Rv 21:10 the Great CITY, the Holy JeruSalem, descending
G0040.1 A-ASN ἅγιον (19x)
Jn 20:22 Then he·says to·them, "Receive Holy Spirit!
Lk 1:49 did magnificent·things for·me, and holy *is* his name
Lk 2:23 a·primal·womb shall·be·called holy to·Yahweh"'—
Lk 2:25 the·consoling of·IsraEl. And Holy Spirit was upon
Lk 11:13 out of·heaven, shall·give Holy Spirit to·the·ones
Lk 12:10 to·the·one reviling against the Holy Spirit, it·shall·
Ac 5:3 your heart for·you to·lie to·the Holy Spirit, and to·
Ac 5:32 and so·also *is* the Holy Spirit, whom God gave to·
Ac 8:15 concerning them, that they·may·receive Holy Spirit.
Ac 8:17 on them, and they·were·receiving Holy Spirit.
Ac 8:18 after·distinctly·viewing that the Holy Spirit is·given
Ac 8:19 ·should·lay *my* hands, he·may·receive Holy Spirit."
Ac 10:47 *these* who received the Holy Spirit just·as we·
Ac 15:8 to·them, giving to·them the Holy Spirit, even just·

Ac 19:2 them, "Did·yeu·receive Holy Spirit after·trusting?
Mt 7:6 ·should·not give the·thing *which·is* holy to·the dogs,
Mk 3:29 should·revile against the Holy Spirit does·not have
1Th 4:8 the·one also already·giving to us his Holy Spirit.
Eph 4:30 And do·not grieve the Holy Spirit of·God, by

G0040.1 A-APM ἁγίους (2x)
Eph 1:4 conception for·us to·be holy and without·blemish
Col 1:22 death, to·present yeu holy and without·blemish and

G0040.1 A-DSM ἁγίῳ (1x)
Mt 24:15 the prophet, standing in *the* holy place," (the·one

G0040.1 A-DSF ἁγίᾳ (1x)
2Ti 1:9 saving us and calling·*us*·forth with·a·holy calling,

G0040.1 A-DSF-S ἁγιωτάτῃ (1x)
Jud 1:20 building·up yeurselves in·yeur holy trust, *yeu*

G0040.1 A-DSN ἁγίῳ (24x)
Jn 1:33 him, the·same is the·one immersing in Holy Spirit.'
Lk 3:16 He·himself shall·immerse yeu in Holy Spirit and in·
Ac 1:5 but yeu shall·be·immersed in Holy Spirit after not
Ac 7:51 yeu always do·violently·oppose the Holy Spirit. As
Ac 10:38 *who·was* from Natsareth with·Holy Spirit and
Ac 11:16 ·water, but yeu shall·be·immersed in Holy Spirit.'
Ac 15:28 For it·seemed·good to·the Holy Spirit, and to·us,
Mt 3:11 He·himself shall·immerse yeu in Holy Spirit and in·
Mk 1:8 but he·himself shall·immerse yeu in Holy Spirit."
Mk 12:36 For David himself declared by the Holy Spirit,
Rm 9:1 conscience jointly·testifying with·me in Holy Spirit,
Rm 14:17 righteousness, peace, and joy in Holy Spirit.
Rm 15:16 having·been·made·holy by Holy Spirit.
Rm 16:16 Greet one·another with a·holy kiss. The Called·
Jud 1:20 holy trust, *yeu* who·are·praying by Holy Spirit,
1Pe 1:12 to·yeu, with Holy Spirit already·being·dispatched
2Pe 1:18 ·being together with·him on the holy mountain.
1Th 1:5 also in power and in Holy Spirit and with much
1Th 5:26 Greet all the brothers with a·holy kiss.
1Co 12:3 "Jesus *is* Lord," except by Holy Spirit.
1Co 16:20 Greet one·another with a·holy kiss.
2Co 6:6 long-suffering, by kindness, by Holy Spirit, by love
2Co 13:12 Greet one·another with a·holy kiss.
Eph 1:13 ·officially·sealed with·the Holy Spirit of·the

G0040.1 A-DPM ἁγίοις (3x)
1Th 5:27 ·the letter to·be·read·aloud to·all the holy brothers.
Eph 3:5 as it·is now revealed to·his holy ambassadors and
Col 1:2 To·the·ones in Colossae, holy and trustworthy

G0040.1 A-DPF ἁγίαις (2x)
Rm 1:2 through his prophets in *the* Holy Scriptures
2Pe 3:11 ·for yeu to·subsist in *all* holy conduct and devout·

G0040.1 A-GSM ἁγίου (3x)
Ac 4:30 through the name of·your holy servant·boy, Jesus.
Ac 6:13 reviling utterances against this holy place and
Ac 10:22 was·divinely·instructed by a·holy angel to·send·for

G0040.1 A-GSF ἁγίας (3x)
Lk 1:72 our fathers, and to·be·mindful of·his holy covenant;
2Pe 2:21 ·out the holy commandment being·handed·down
Rv 22:19 life-above, and from·out of·the HOLY CITY, and

G0040.1 A-GSN ἁγίου (39x)
Lk 1:15 ·drink, and he·shall·be·filled with·Holy Spirit, yet·
Lk 1:41 womb, and ElisSabeth was·filled with·Holy Spirit.
Lk 1:67 his father Zacharias was·filled with·Holy Spirit and
Lk 2:26 ·message to·him by the Holy Spirit *that he·was* not
Lk 4:1 And Jesus, full of·Holy Spirit, returned·back from
Ac 1:2 after·giving·commands through Holy Spirit to·the
Ac 1:8 ·receive power, with·the Holy Spirit coming·upon
Ac 2:4 And absolutely·all were·filled with·Holy Spirit, and
Ac 2:33 the Promise of·the Holy Spirit personally·from the
Ac 2:38 ·receive the voluntary·present of·the Holy Spirit.
Ac 4:8 Then Peter, being·filled with·Holy Spirit, declared to
Ac 4:31 and absolutely·all were·filled with·Holy Spirit, and
Ac 6:3 seven men being·attested·to, full of·Holy Spirit and
Ac 6:5 a·man full of·trust and of·Holy Spirit, and·also
Ac 7:55 *Stephen*, inherently·being full of·Holy Spirit, after·
Ac 9:17 ·your·sight and may·be·filled with·Holy Spirit."
Ac 9:31 in·the exhortation·and·comfort of·the Holy Spirit,
Ac 10:45 ·present of·the Holy Spirit has·been·poured·forth,
Ac 11:24 ·beneficially·good man and full of·Holy Spirit and
Ac 13:4 after·being·sent·forth by the Holy Spirit, these·men
Ac 13:9 Paul), being·filled with·Holy Spirit and gazing·
Ac 13:52 ·completely·filled with·joy and with·Holy Spirit.
Ac 16:6 ·were·being·forbidden by the Holy Spirit to·speak
Heb 2:4 ·of miracles and with·distributions of·Holy Spirit,
Heb 6:4 ·present, and becoming participants of·Holy Spirit,
Heb 9:8 with·the Holy Spirit making·plain this·thing: *that*
Mt 1:18 in a·pregnancy birthed·from·out of·Holy Spirit.
Mt 1:20 ·conceived in her is birthed·from·out of·Holy Spirit.
Mt 12:32 should·declare against the Holy Spirit, it·shall·not
Mt 28:19 Father, and of·the Son, and of·the Holy Spirit,
Rm 5:5 ·forth in our hearts through Holy Spirit, the·one
Rm 15:13 in the Expectation by *the* power of·Holy Spirit.
2Pe 1:21 while·being·carried·along by *the* Holy Spirit,
1Th 1:6 ·with much tribulation *and* with joy of·Holy Spirit,
Tit 3:5 a·bath of·regeneration and a·renewing of·Holy Spirit,
1Co 2:13 but·rather with instructions of·Holy Spirit,
1Co 6:19 yeur body is a·temple of·the Holy Spirit *who·is* in
2Co 13:14 and the fellowship of·the Holy Spirit, *be* with
2Ti 1:14 you·must·vigilantly·keep through Holy Spirit, the·

G0040.1 A-GPM ἁγίων (7x)
Lk 1:70 through *the* mouth of·his holy prophets, the·ones
Lk 9:26 and *that* of·the Father, and of·the holy angels.
Ac 3:21 through *the* mouth of·all his holy prophets since *the*
Mk 8:38 in the glory of·his Father with the holy angels."
2Pe 3:2 having·been·already·stated by the holy prophets and
Rv 14:10 fire and sulfur in·the·sight of·the holy angels, and
Rv 22:6 And Yahweh, God of·the holy prophets, dispatched

EG0040.1 (2x)
Mt 12:31 but the revilement of·the *Holy* Spirit shall·not be·
Rm 11:16 the *whole* lump·of·dough *is* also *holy*. And if the

G0040.2 A-NSM ἅγιος (3x)
Lk 4:34 you *and* who you·are, the Holy·One of·God."
Mk 1:24 ·know you, who you·are, the Holy·One of·God."
Rv 3:7 'These·things says the Holy·One, the Truthful·One,

G0040.2 A-NPM ἅγιοι (4x)
Php 4:22 All the holy·ones greet yeu, especially the·ones
2Pe 1:21 Spirit, men·of·clay† (the holy·ones in·God) spoke.
1Co 6:2 personally·know that the holy·ones shall·judge the
2Co 13:13 All the holy·ones greet yeu.

G0040.2 A-ASM ἅγιον (1x)
Php 4:21 Greet every holy·one in Anointed-One Jesus.

G0040.2 A-APM ἁγίους (10x)
Ac 9:32 Peter to·come·down also to the holy·ones, the·ones
Ac 9:41 and hollering·out·for the holy·ones and the widows
Heb 13:24 among·yeu, and all the holy·ones. The·ones from
Rm 16:15 and all the holy·ones together with·them.
1Co 16:1 the·one for the holy·ones, just·as I·thoroughly·
2Co 8:4 ·*us* the fellowship of·the service to the holy·ones.
2Co 9:1 the service to·the holy·ones, it·is superfluous for·me
Eph 1:15 the Lord Jesus and *of* the love for all the holy·ones,
Col 1:4 Jesus and *of·yeur* love, the·one for all the holy·ones
Phm 1:5 toward the Lord Jesus and for all the holy·ones,

G0040.2 A-DPM ἁγίοις (17x)
Ac 9:13 wrongs he·did to·your holy·ones at JeruSalem.
Heb 6:10 ·attending to·the holy·ones and still·attending *to*·
Rm 1:7 beloved of·God, called·forth *as* holy·ones. Grace to·
Rm 15:25 ·traverse to JeruSalem, attending to·the holy·ones.
Rm 15:31 may·become well·acceptable to·the holy·ones,
Jud 1:3 ·being·handed·down only·once to·the holy·ones.
Php 1:1 To·all the holy·ones in Anointed-One Jesus, to·the·
2Th 1:10 ·should·come to·be·glorified in his holy·ones, and
1Co 1:2 Jesus, called·forth *to·be* holy·ones, together with·all
1Co 16:15 themselves for service to·the holy·ones),
2Co 1:1 together with·all the holy·ones, the·ones being in
Eph 1:1 God's will. To·the holy·ones being in Ephesus, and
Eph 1:18 of·the glory of·his inheritance in the holy·ones,
Eph 3:18 to·grasp together with·all the holy·ones what *is* the
Eph 5:3 among yeu, just·as is·befitting·for holy·ones,
Col 1:26 now·in·fact is·made·apparent to·his holy·ones—
Rv 11:18 the prophets, and·also to·the holy·ones, and to·the·

G0040.2 A-DPF ἁγίαις (1x)
Jud 1:14 with a·myriad·tens·of·thousands of·his holy·ones,

G0040.2 A-GSM ἁγίου (1x)
1Jn 2:20 do·have an·anointing from the Holy·One, and yeu·

G0040.2 A-GPM ἁγίων (29x)
Ac 26:10 of·the holy·ones I·myself permanently·shut·up in·
Mt 27:52 and many bodies of·holy·ones (the·ones having·
Rm 8:27 ·intercession over *the* holy·ones according·to *the*
Rm 12:13 needs of·the holy·ones, by·sharing·with·others,
Rm 15:26 for the helplessly·poor of·the holy·ones, the·ones
Rm 16:2 in *the* Lord, as·is·worthy of·the holy·ones, and *that*
1Th 3:13 ·our Lord YeShua Anointed with all his holy·ones.
1Co 6:1 ·ones, and not·indeed before the holy·ones?
1Co 14:33 ·Called·Out·assemblies of·the holy·ones.
2Co 9:12 ·particular the lackings of·the holy·ones, but·rather
Eph 2:19 *yeu·are* fellow-citizens with·the holy·ones and *are*
Eph 3:8 ·one *who·is* less·than·the·least of·all holy·ones, this
Eph 4:12 ·development of·the holy·ones unto a·work of·
Eph 6:18 even with·petition concerning all the holy·ones—
Col 1:12 of·the allotted·heritage of·the holy·ones in the light.
Phm 1:7 ·affections of·the holy·ones have·been·refreshed,
1Ti 5:10 ·strangers, if she·washed *the* holy·ones' feet, if she·
Rv 5:8 ·incense, which are the prayers of·the holy·ones.
Rv 8:3 ·give *it* with·the prayers of·all the holy·ones upon the
Rv 8:4 ·*came* with·the prayers of·the holy·ones, ascended in·
Rv 13:7 ·it 'to·make war with the holy·ones, and to·conquer
Rv 13:10 patient·endurance and the trust of·the holy·ones.
Rv 14:12 Here is a·patient·endurance of·the holy·ones. Here
Rv 15:3 and true *are* your ways, the King of·the holy·ones.
Rv 16:6 they·poured·out *the* blood of·holy·ones and prophets
Rv 17:6 from·out of·the blood of·the holy·ones, and from·
Rv 18:24 *the* blood of·prophets, and of·holy·ones, and of·all
Rv 19:8 the fine·linen is the righteous·acts of·the holy·ones).
Rv 20:9 ·surrounded the garrison of·the holy·ones and the

G0041 ἁγιότης hagiótēs *n.* (1x)
Roots:G0040 Compare:G0047 G3742 See:G0038 G0042

G0041.1 N-GSF ἁγιότητος (1x)
Heb 12:10 in·order·for *us* to·partake of·his holiness.

G0042 ἁγιωσύνη hagiōsýnē *n.* (3x)
Roots:G0040 Compare:G3742 G2413 See:G0041 G0038

G0042.1 N-ASF ἁγιωσύνην (1x)
2Co 7:1 further·finishing devoted·holiness in a·reverent·fear·

G0042.1 N-DSF ἁγιωσύνῃ (1x)
1Th 3:13 hearts blameless in devoted·holiness before God,

G0042.1 N-GSF ἁγιωσύνης (1x)
Rm 1:4 according·to a·spirit of·devoted·holiness, from·out

G0043 ἀγκάλη ankálē *n.* (1x)
Roots:G0044-1 Compare:G1119 See:G0044 G0045 G0030

G0043 N-APF ἀγκάλας (1x)
Lk 2:28 ·himself accepted him into his arms and blessed God

G0044 ἄγκιστρον ánkistrôn *n.* (1x)
Roots:G0044-1 Compare:G0043 G0044-2 G0045 G0030

G0044 N-ASN ἄγκιστρον (1x)
Mt 17:27 to the sea, cast a·hook and take·up the first fish

G0045 ἄγκυρα ánkyra *n.* (4x)
Roots:G0044-1 Compare:G0043 G0044 G0030

G0045 N-ASF ἄγκυραν (1x)
Heb 6:19 *Expectation* we·have as an·anchor of·the soul, both

G0045 N-APF ἀγκύρας (3x)
Ac 27:29 places, after·flinging four anchors out of·*the*·stern,
Ac 27:30 intending to·extend anchors out of·*the*·bow,
Ac 27:40 entirely·removing the anchors, they·were·letting

G0046 ἄ•γναφος ágnaphôs *adj.* (2x)
Roots:G0001 G1102

G0046.1 A-GSN ἀγνάφου (2x)
Mt 9:16 ·one·man throws a·patch of·unprocessed cloth onto
Mk 2:21 ·one·man sews a·patch of·unprocessed cloth on an·

G0047 ἁγνεία hagnêía *n.* (2x)
Roots:G0053 Compare:G0041 G0042 G0038 G3742 G2514
G0047.2 N-DSF ἁγνείᾳ (2x)
1Ti 4:12 in love, in spirit, in trust, *and* in moral·cleanliness.
1Ti 5:2 ·women as sisters, with all moral·cleanliness.

G0048 ἁγνίζω hagnízō *v.* (7x)
Roots:G0053 Compare:G2511 G2508 G0037 See:G0049 G0850-3 xLangEquiv:H5352 xLangAlso:H2891 H5144 H6942 H2398 H2141
G0048.1 V-PAI-3S ἁγνίζει (1x)
1Jn 3:3 this Expectation in him cleanses himself, just·as that·
G0048.1 V-AAM-2P ἁγνίσατε (1x)
Jac 4:8 *yeu* morally·disqualified, and cleanse *yeur* hearts,
G0048.1 V-RAP-NPM ἡγνικότες (1x)
1Pe 1:22 *As·such*, having·cleansed yeur souls in the
G0048.2 V-AAS-3P ἁγνίσωσιν (1x)
Jn 11:55 in·order·that they·should·ceremonially·cleanse.
G0048.2 V-APM-2S ἁγνίσθητι (1x)
Ac 21:24 be·ceremonially·cleansed together with·them, and
G0048.2 V-APP-NSM ἁγνισθείς (1x)
Ac 21:26 *and* being·ceremonially·cleansed together with·
G0048.2 V-RPP-ASM ἡγνισμένον (1x)
Ac 24:18 ·*doing*, having·been·ceremonially·cleansed in the

G0049 ἁγνισμός hagnismṓs *n.* (1x)
Roots:G0048 G2469-1
G0049.2 N-GSM ἁγνισμοῦ (1x)
Ac 21:26 of·the days of·ceremonial·cleansing *would·be*, at

G0050 ἀ•γνοέω agnôéō *v.* (22x)
Roots:G0001 G3539 See:G0051 G0052
G0050.1 V-PAI-2P ἀγνοεῖτε (2x)
Rm 6:3 Or do·yeu·not·know, that as·many·as are·immersed
Rm 7:1 Or do·yeu·not·know, O·brothers (for I·speak to·the·
G0050.1 V-PAP-NSM ἀγνοῶν (1x)
Rm 2:4 and long-suffering, not·knowing that the kindness
G0050.1 V-PAP-NPM ἀγνοοῦντες (1x)
Ac 17:23 yeu·show·devout·reverence while·not·knowing, I·
G0050.1 V-AAP-NPM ἀγνοήσαντες (1x)
Ac 13:27 and their rulers, not·knowing this·man nor·even
G0050.2 V-PAI-1P ἀγνοοῦμεν (1x)
2Co 2:11 for we·are·not ignorant of·his mental·schemes.
G0050.2 V-PAI-3P ἀγνοοῦσιν (1x)
2Pe 2:12 ·reviling in matters·of·which they·are·ignorant),
G0050.2 V-PAN ἀγνοεῖν (6x)
Rm 1:13 Now I·do·not want yeu to·be·ignorant, brothers,
Rm 11:25 for·yeu, brothers, to·be·ignorant of·this mystery,
1Th 4:13 Now I·do·not want yeu to·be·ignorant, brothers,
1Co 10:1 I·do·not want yeu to·be·ignorant that all our
1Co 12:1 brothers, I·do·not want yeu to·be·ignorant.
2Co 1:8 For we·do·not want yeu to·be·ignorant, brothers,
G0050.2 V-PAP-DPM ἀγνοοῦσιν (1x)
Heb 5:2 with·the·ones being·ignorant and being·led·astray,
G0050.2 V-PAP-NSM ἀγνοῶν (1x)
1Ti 1:13 because I·did *it* ignorantly in a·lack·of·trust.
G0050.2 V-PAP-NPM ἀγνοοῦντες (1x)
Rm 10:3 For being·ignorant of·God's righteousness, and
G0050.3 V-IAI-3P ἠγνόουν (2x)
Lk 9:45 But they·were·not·understanding this utterance, and
Mk 9:32 But they·were·not·understanding the utterance and
G0050.4 V-PAI-3S ἀγνοεῖ (1x)
1Co 14:38 But if any·man is·ignoring *this*, let·him·be·
G0050.4 V-PAM-3S ἀγνοείτω (1x)
1Co 14:38 if any·man is·ignoring *this*, let·him·be·ignored.
G0050.5 V-PPP-NSM ἀγνοούμενος (1x)
Gal 1:22 and I·was being·unknown by·the face to·the
G0050.5 V-PPP-NPM ἀγνοούμενοι (1x)
2Co 6:9 as being·unknown and·yet being·recognized, as

G0051 ἀ•γνόημα agnôēma *n.* (1x)
Roots:G0050 Compare:G0190-6 See:G0052
G0051.2 N-GPN ἀγνοημάτων (1x)
Heb 9:7 and *on·behalf* of·the ignorant·errors of·the People,

G0052 ἄ•γνοια ágnôia *n.* (4x)
Roots:G0050 Compare:G0190-6 See:G0051
G0052.1 N-ASF ἄγνοιαν (2x)
Ac 3:17 ·inflicted *the killing* according·to ignorance, just·as
Eph 4:18 life-above of·God through the ignorance existing in
G0052.1 N-DSF ἀγνοίᾳ (1x)
1Pe 1:14 to·the previous longings in yeur ignorance,
G0052.1 N-GSF ἀγνοίας (1x)
Ac 17:30 ·overlooking the times of·ignorance, God now

G0053 ἁγνός hagnṓs *adj.* (8x)
Roots:G0060-2 Compare:G0040 G0172 G0283 G2513 See:G0047 G0048 xLangAlso:H5355
G0053.2 A-NSM ἁγνός (1x)
1Jn 3:3 cleanses himself, just·as that·one is morally·clean.
G0053.2 A-NSF ἁγνή (1x)
Jac 3:17 is first, in·fact, morally·clean, then peaceable, fair
G0053.2 A-NPN ἁγνά (1x)
Php 4:8 ·things·as *are* morally·clean, as·many·things·as *are*
G0053.2 A-ASM ἁγνόν (1x)
1Ti 5:22 moral·failures. Fully·keep yourself morally·clean!
G0053.2 A-ASF ἁγνήν (2x)
1Pe 3:2 after·beholding yeur morally·clean behavior *coupled*
2Co 11:2 to·present *yeu as* a·morally·clean virgin to·the
G0053.2 A-APM ἁγνούς (1x)
2Co 7:11 yeurselves to·be morally·clean in the matter·of·
G0053.2 A-APF ἁγνάς (1x)
Tit 2:5 *sexually·and*·morally·clean, housekeepers,

G0054 ἁγνότης hagnṓtēs *n.* (1x)
Roots:G0053
G0054.1 N-DSF ἁγνότητι (1x)
2Co 6:6 by cleanness, by knowledge, by long-suffering, by

G0055 ἁγνῶς hagnôs *adv.* (1x)
Roots:G0053
G0055.2 ADV ἁγνῶς (1x)
Php 1:16 not with·cleanness·of·motive, imagining *also* to·

G0056 ἀ•γνωσία agnōsía *n.* (2x)
Roots:G0001 G1108
G0056.1 N-ASF ἀγνωσίαν (1x)
1Pe 2:15 to·muzzle the ignorance of·impetuous men·of·clay†
G0056.2 N-ASF ἀγνωσίαν (1x)
1Co 15:34 morally·fail; for some are ignorant of·God. I·say

G0057 ἄ•γνωστος ágnōstôs *adj.* (1x)
Roots:G0001 G1110 Compare:G0261
G0057.1 A-DSM ἀγνώστῳ (1x)
Ac 17:23 had·been·inscribed, 'TO·AN·UNKNOWN GOD.'

G0058 ἀγορά agôrá *n.* (11x)
See:G0060 G1453
G0058.2 N-ASF ἀγοράν (1x)
Ac 16:19 ·*them*·along into the marketplace·forum toward the
G0058.2 N-DSF ἀγορᾷ (3x)
Lk 7:32 sitting·down in a·marketplace and hollering·out to·
Ac 17:17 and·also in the marketplace each and·every day
Mt 20:3 he·saw others standing idle in the marketplace.
G0058.2 N-DPF ἀγοραῖς (6x)
Lk 11:43 gatherings, and the greetings in the marketplaces.
Lk 20:46 being·fond·of greetings in the marketplaces, and
Mt 11:16 sitting·down in marketplaces and hollering·out to·
Mt 23:7 the greetings in the marketplaces, and to·be·called
Mk 6:56 the sick in the marketplaces and were·imploring
Mk 12:38 ·robes, and *wanting* greetings in the marketplaces,
G0058.2 N-GSF ἀγορᾶς (1x)
Mk 7:4 And *when they·come* from a·marketplace, unless

G0059 ἀγοράζω agôrázō *v.* (31x)
Roots:G0058 Compare:G3084 G0070-4 G5608 G4046 See:G0058-1 G1805 xLangAlso:H1350
G0059.2 V-FAI-1P ἀγοράσομεν (1x)
Jn 6:5 "From·what·source shall·we·buy bread in·order·that
G0059.2 V-PAI-3S ἀγοράζει (2x)
Mt 13:44 sells all (as·much·as he·has) and buys that field.
Rv 18:11 her, because not·even·one·man buys their cargo
G0059.2 V-PAP-APM ἀγοράζοντας (3x)
Lk 19:45 ·began to·cast·out the·ones selling and buying in it,
Mt 21:12 all the·ones selling and buying in the Sanctuary·
Mk 11:15 to·cast·out the·ones selling and buying in the
G0059.2 V-PAP-NPM ἀγοράζοντες (1x)
1Co 7:30 as not rejoicing; and the·ones buying, as not fully·
G0059.2 V-IAI-3P ἠγόραζον (1x)
Lk 17:28 ·drinking, they·were·buying, they·were·selling,
G0059.2 V-AAI-1S ἠγόρασα (2x)
Lk 14:18 first declared to·him, 'I·bought a·plot·of·land, and
Lk 14:19 another declared, 'I·bought five yoked·teams of·
G0059.2 V-AAI-3S ἠγόρασεν (1x)
Mt 13:46 all (as·much·as he·was·holding) and bought it.
G0059.2 V-AAI-3P ἠγόρασαν (2x)
Mt 27:7 ·the·same *pieces·of·silver*, they·bought the potter's
Mk 16:1 of·*little*·Jacob) and Salome bought aromatic·spices,
G0059.2 V-AAM-2S ἀγόρασον (1x)
Jn 13:29 Jesus says to·him, "Buy *those·things* that we·have
G0059.2 V-AAM-2P ἀγοράσατε (1x)
Mt 25:9 the·ones selling *oil* and buy *some* for·yeurselves.'
G0059.2 V-AAM-3S ἀγορασάτω (1x)
Lk 22:36 a·dagger, let·him·sell his garment and buy *one*.
G0059.2 V-AAN ἀγοράσαι (3x)
Mt 25:10 And with·them going·off to·buy *oil*, the
Rv 3:18 ·give·counsel to·you to·buy personally·from me
Rv 13:17 ·that not anyone should·be·able to·buy or to·sell,
G0059.2 V-AAP-NSM ἀγοράσας (1x)
Mk 15:46 And after·buying a·linen·cloth and lowering *Jesus*
G0059.2 V-AAS-1P ἀγοράσωμεν (2x)
Lk 9:13 after·traversing, we·ourselves should·buy food for
Mk 6:37 ·going·off, should·we·buy two·hundred denarii
G0059.2 V-AAS-3P ἀγοράσωσιν (3x)
Jn 4:8 city in·order·that they·may·buy provisions·of·food).
Mt 14:15 the villages, they·may·buy food for·themselves."
Mk 6:36 and villages, they·should·buy bread for·themselves
G0059.4 V-AAI-2S ἠγόρασας (1x)
Rv 5:9 ·slaughtered, and you·kinsman·redeemed us to·God
G0059.4 V-AAP-ASM ἀγοράσαντα (1x)
2Pe 2:1 Master, the·one already·kinsman·redeeming them,
G0059.4 V-API-2P ἠγοράσθητε (2x)
1Co 6:20 For yeu·are·kinsman·redeemed with·a·price. Now·
1Co 7:23 Yeu·are·kinsman·redeemed with·a·price. Do·not
G0059.4 V-API-3P ἠγοράσθησαν (1x)
Rv 14:4 These were·kinsman·redeemed from among·the
G0059.4 V-RPP-NPM ἠγορασμένοι (1x)
Rv 14:3 the·ones having·been·kinsman·redeemed from the

G0060 ἀγοραῖος agôraîôs *adj.* (2x)
Roots:G0058
G0060.2 A-NPM ἀγοραῖοι (1x)
Ac 19:38 ·man, *the* public·courts are·holding·open·sessions,
G0060.4 A-GPM ἀγοραίων (1x)
Ac 17:5 certain evil men of·the riffraff and raising·a·mob,

G0061 ἄγρα ágra *n.* (2x)
Roots:G0071
G0061.1 N-ASF ἄγραν (1x)
Lk 5:4 ·off into the deep and lower yeur nets for a·catch."
G0061.1 N-DSF ἄγρᾳ (1x)
Lk 5:9 together with·him) over the catch of·the fish which

G0062 ἀ•γράμματος agrámmatôs *adj.* (1x)
Roots:G0001 G1121 Compare:G0261
G0062.3 A-NPM ἀγράμματοι (1x)
Ac 4:13 grasping that they·were uneducated and untrained

G0063 ἀγρ•αυλέω agrauléō *v.* (1x)
Roots:G0068 G0832 See:G0833
G0063 V-PAP-NPM ἀγραυλοῦντες (1x)
Lk 2:8 region, camping·in·the·field and vigilantly·keeping

G0064 ἀγρεύω agrêúō *v.* (1x)
Roots:G0061
G0064.2 V-AAS-3P ἀγρεύσωσιν (1x)
Mk 12:13 in·order·that they·should·entrap him in·*his*·words

G0065 ἀγρι•έλαιος agriélaiôs *n.* (2x)
Roots:G0066 G1636
G0065.1 N-NSF ἀγριέλαιος (1x)
Rm 11:17 being a·wild·olive·tree, were·grafted·in among

G0065.1 N-GSF ἀγριελαίου (1x)
Rm 11:24 from·among an·olive·tree·which·is·wild nature,

G0066 ἄγριος ágriôs *adj.* (3x)
Roots:G0068
G0066.1 A-NSN ἄγριον (1x)
Mt 3:4 and his nourishment was locusts and wild honey.
G0066.1 A-NPN ἄγρια (1x)
Jud 1:13 wild breaking·waves of·the·sea presently·foaming·
G0066.1 A-ASN ἄγριον (1x)
Mk 1:6 his loins, and *was* eating locusts and wild honey.

G0067 Ἀγρ•ίππας Agríppas *n/p.* (12x)
Roots:G0066 G2462 Compare:G2264 See:G0745 G2266
G0067.2 N/P-NSM Ἀγρίππας (5x)
Ac 25:13 days already·elapsing, King AgrIppa and BerNiki
Ac 25:22 Then AgrIppa replied to Festus, "I·resolve also to·
Ac 26:1 Then AgrIppa replied to Paul, "It·is·freely·
Ac 26:28 But AgrIppa replied to Paul, "In *such* a·brief·
Ac 26:32 Then AgrIppa replied to·Festus, "This man·of·
G0067.2 N/P-VSM Ἀγρίππα (6x)
Ac 25:24 then disclosed, "King AgrIppa, and all the men
Ac 25:26 especially before you, O·King AgrIppa, that, after·
Ac 26:2 myself supremely·blessed, King AgrIppa, *for* I·am·
Ac 26:7 O·King AgrIppa, I·am·called·to·account by the
Ac 26:19 "By·which *cause*, O·King AgrIppa, I·did·not
Ac 26:27 King AgrIppa, do·you·trust the prophets?
G0067.2 N/P-GSM Ἀγρίππα (1x)
Ac 25:23 ·then on·the·next·day, with·AgrIppa and BerNiki

G0068 ἀγρός agrós *n.* (36x)
Roots:G0071 Compare:G5564 G1409-1 G5208 G3977-1 xLangAlso:H7704 A1251
G0068.1 -- (1x)
Lk 17:36 *men* shall·be in the field; one shall·be·personally·
G0068.1 N-NSM ἀγρός (3x)
Mt 13:38 Now the field is the world, and the good seed,
Mt 27:8 Therefore that field is·called *AqelDama*, "Field of·
Mt 27:8 field is·called *AqelDama*, "Field of·Blood", even·
G0068.1 N-ASM ἀγρόν (4x)
Mt 13:44 sells all (as·much·as he·has) and buys that field.
Mt 27:7 they·bought the potter's field as a·burial·place for·
Mt 27:10 same *pieces·of·silver* for the potter's field, just·as
Mk 13:16 And the·one being in the field must·not return to
G0068.1 N-APM ἀγρούς (1x)
Lk 15:15 and *the citizen* sent him into his fields to·feed pigs.
G0068.1 N-DSM ἀγρῷ (9x)
Lk 12:28 today being in the field, and tomorrow being·cast
Lk 15:25 his older son was in a·field, and as he·was·going·
Lk 17:31 likewise, the·one in the field must·not return to
Mt 13:24 to·a·man·of·clay† sowing good seed in his field.
Mt 13:27 sow good seed in your field? So·then, from·what·
Mt 13:31 after·taking, a·man·of·clay† sowed in his field),
Mt 13:44 like treasure having·been·hidden in a·field, which
Mt 24:18 And the·one in the field must·not return *to the·*
Mt 24:40 Then two shall·be in the field; the one is·
G0068.1 N-GSM ἀγροῦ (4x)
Lk 17:7 *to·him* as·he·comes·in from·out of·the field, 'After·
Mt 6:28 Carefully·note the lilies of·the field, how they·grow;
Mt 6:30 ·manner enrobes the grass of·the field, today being
Mt 13:36 to·us the parable of·the darnel·weeds of·the field."
G0068.2 N-ASM ἀγρόν (1x)
Mk 16:12 as·they·were·traversing into *the* countryside.
G0068.2 N-APM ἀγρούς (5x)
Lk 8:34 they·announced *it* in the city and in the countrysides.
Lk 9:12 villages and the countrysides, they·should·lodge and
Mk 5:14 the city and in the countrysides. And they·went·out
Mk 6:36 ·off into the encircling countrysides and villages,
Mk 6:56 or cities, or countrysides, they·were·laying the
G0068.2 N-GSM ἀγροῦ (2x)
Lk 23:26 who·was·coming *in* from *the* countryside, Simon,
Mk 15:21 coming from *the* countryside (the father of·
G0068.3 N-ASM ἀγρόν (1x)
Mt 22:5 ·away, in·fact, one to his·own farm, and *another* to
G0068.4 N-ASM ἀγρόν (1x)
Lk 14:18 to·him, 'I·bought a·plot·of·land, and I·have dire·
G0068.4 N-APM ἀγρούς (3x)
Mt 19:29 wife or children or plots·of·land, for·the·cause·of
Mk 10:29 or wife or children or plots·of·land, for·my cause
Mk 10:30 and mothers and children and plots·of·land, with
G0068.4 N-GSM ἀγροῦ (1x)
Ac 4:37 by·himself on·a·plot·of·land. After·selling *it*, he·

G0069 ἀγρ•υπνέω agrypnéō *v.* (4x)
Roots:G0001 G5258 See:G0070
G0069.2 V-PAI-3P ἀγρυπνοῦσιν (1x)
Heb 13:17 for they·themselves stay·alert on·behalf of·yeur
G0069.2 V-PAM-2P ἀγρυπνεῖτε (2x)
Lk 21:36 "Accordingly, stay·alert, petitioning in every
Mk 13:33 "Look·out, stay·alert and pray, for yeu·do·not
G0069.2 V-PAP-NPM ἀγρυπνοῦντες (1x)
Eph 6:18 in this same *Spirit*, presently·staying·alert with all

G0070 ἀ•γρυπνία agrypnía *n.* (2x)
Roots:G0069
G0070.1 N-DPF ἀγρυπνίαις (2x)
2Co 6:5 in wearisome·labors, in sleeplessness, in fastings,
2Co 11:27 and travail, in sleeplessness many·times, in

G0071 ἄγω ágō *v.* (71x)
Compare:G5342 G1643 See:G4013 G5217
G0071.1 V-PAI-3S ἄγει (1x)
Rm 2:4 that the kindness of·God leads you to repentance?
G0071.1 V-PAI-3P ἄγουσιν (1x)
Jn 18:28 In·due·course, they·led Jesus from Caiaphas to the
G0071.1 V-PPI-2P ἄγεσθε (1x)
Gal 5:18 But if yeu·are·led by·Spirit, yeu·are not under
G0071.1 V-PPI-3P ἄγονται (1x)
Rm 8:14 For as·many·as are·led by·God's Spirit, these are
G0071.1 V-PPP-APN ἀγόμενα (1x)
2Ti 3:6 being·led·away with·a·diversity·of longings,
G0071.1 V-IPI-2P ἤγεσθε (1x)
1Co 12:2 being·led·away, even·as yeu·were·led toward the
G0071.1 V-IPI-3S ἤγετο (1x)
Lk 4:1 ·back from the Jordan and was·led by the Spirit into
G0071.1 V-IPI-3P ἤγοντο (1x)
Lk 23:32 *who·were* criminals, were·led together with·him
G0071.1 V-2AAI-3S ἤγαγεν (1x)
Lk 23:1 absolutely·all the multitude of·them led him to Pilate
G0071.1 V-2AAI-3P ἤγαγον (1x)
Lk 22:54 And arresting him, they·led *him* and brought him
G0071.1 V-2AAN ἀγαγεῖν (1x)
Jn 10:16 ·pen. It·is·mandatory·for me to·lead these·also, and
G0071.2 V-FAI-3S ἄξει (1x)
1Th 4:14 ·manner also God shall·bring together with·him
G0071.2 V-FAP-NSM ἄξων (1x)
Ac 22:5 traversed into Damascus, bringing the·ones being
G0071.2 V-FPI-2P ἀχθήσεσθε (1x)
Mt 10:18 Also yeu·shall·be·brought before governors and
G0071.2 V-PAI-1S ἄγω (1x)
Jn 19:4 says to·them, "See, I·bring him outside to·yeu, in·
G0071.2 V-PAI-3P ἄγουσιν (2x)
Jn 8:3 the scribes and the Pharisees brought to him a·wife
Jn 9:13 They·brought *the* same·man to the Pharisees, the·one
G0071.2 V-PAM-2S ἄγε (1x)
2Ti 4:11 Taking·up *John*·Mark, bring·him with you, for he·
G0071.2 V-PAN ἄγειν (1x)
Ac 23:10 *the* midst of·them, and to·bring *him* into the
G0071.2 V-PAP-NPM ἄγοντες (1x)
Ac 21:16 went·together along·with us, bringing with *them* a·
G0071.2 V-PPN ἄγεσθαι (2x)
Ac 21:34 ·commandingly·ordered him to·be·brought into the
Ac 22:24 commandingly·ordered him to·be·brought into the
G0071.2 V-PPP-APM ἀγομένους (1x)
Lk 21:12 gatherings and prisons, being·brought before kings
G0071.2 V-2AAI-2P ἠγάγετε (2x)
Jn 7:45 declared to·them, "Why·did yeu·not bring him?
Ac 19:37 For yeu·brought these men *here*, *who·are* neither
G0071.2 V-2AAI-3S ἤγαγεν (8x)
Jn 1:42 And he·brought him to Jesus.
Jn 19:13 ·hearing this saying, Pilate brought Jesus outside,
Lk 4:9 Then he·brought him to JeruSalem, and he·set him on
Lk 10:34 him upon his·own beast, he·brought him to an·inn
Ac 5:26 along·with the assistants, brought them, *but* not
Ac 9:27 But BarNabas, grabbing him, brought *him* to the
Ac 11:26 And after·finding him, he·brought him to Antioch.
Ac 23:18 personally·taking him, brought *him* to the
G0071.2 V-2AAI-3P ἤγαγον (10x)
Lk 4:40 ·many·as were sick, everyone brought them to him,
Lk 19:35 And they·brought it to Jesus, and flinging their·
Ac 6:12 together·they·seized him and brought *him* to the
Ac 17:15 the·ones transporting Paul brought him as·far·as·to
Ac 17:19 ·him, they·brought·him to Mars'·Hill·*(also·called·*
Ac 18:12 against·Paul. And they·brought him to the Bema·
Ac 20:12 And they·brought the boy *home* being·alive, and
Ac 23:31 taking·up Paul, they·brought *him* through the
Mt 21:7 brought the donkey and the colt, and they·put their
Mk 11:7 And they·brought the colt to Jesus, and they·threw
G0071.2 V-2AAM-2P ἀγάγετε (4x)
Lk 19:27 me to·reign over them, bring *them* here, and fully·
Lk 19:30 Loosing it, bring *it here*.
Mt 21:2 Loosening *them*, bring *them* to·me.
Mk 11:2 Loosening him, bring *him*.
G0071.2 V-2AAN ἀγαγεῖν (2x)
Ac 17:5 of·Jason, they·were·seeking to·bring them into the
Ac 23:18 ·prisoner, asked *me* to·bring this young·man to
G0071.2 V-2AAP-ASM ἀγαγόντα (1x)
Heb 2:10 whom all·things *exist*), in·bringing many sons to
G0071.2 V-2AAP-NPM ἀγαγόντες (1x)
Ac 5:27 And bringing them, they·set *them* in the joint·
G0071.2 V-2AAS-3S ἀγάγῃ (2x)
Ac 9:2 or women, he·may·bring·them having·been·bound to
Ac 9:21 in·order·that he·may·bring them having·been·bound
G0071.2 V-2AAS-3P ἀγάγωσιν (1x)
Mk 13:11 "But whenever they·should·bring *yeu for·judgment*
G0071.2 V-API-3S ἤχθη (1x)
Ac 25:23 ·ordering *that* Paul be·brought·forth,
G0071.2 V-APN ἀχθῆναι (4x)
Lk 18:40 commandingly·ordered him to·be·brought to him,
Ac 5:21 to the dungeon to·have *the ambassadors* brought.
Ac 25:6 commandingly·ordered *for* Paul to·be·brought.
Ac 25:17 ·ordered the man to·be·brought·forth.
G0071.3 V-2AAI-3P ἤγαγον (1x)
Lk 4:29 him forth outside of·the city and drove him unto the
G0071.3 V-API-3S ἤχθη (1x)
Ac 8:32 ·aloud was this, "' He·was·driven as a·sheep to *the*
G0071.4 V-PAS-1P ἄγωμεν (7x)
Jn 11:7 to·the disciples, "We·should·head·out into Judea
Jn 11:15 yeu·may·trust; but·yet we·should·head·out to him.
Jn 11:16 "We·ourselves should·head·out also in·order·that
Jn 14:31 "Be·awake, we·should·head·out from·here.
Mt 26:46 Be·awake! We·should·head·out. Behold, the·one
Mk 1:38 he·says to·them, "We·should·head·out into the
Mk 14:42 Be·awake! We·should·head·out. Behold, the·one
G0071.6 V-PAI-3S ἄγει (1x)
Lk 24:21 with·all these·things, today marks this third day
G0071.6 V-PPP-GPM ἀγομένων (1x)
Mt 14:6 ·AntiPas' birthdays being·marked with·ceremony, the
G0071.7 V-PPI-3P ἄγονται (1x)
Ac 19:38 *the* public·courts are·holding·open·sessions, and

G0072 ἀγωγή agōgḗ *n.* (1x)
Roots:G0071
G0072 N-DSF ἀγωγῇ (1x)
2Ti 3:10 my instruction, *my* upbringing, *my* determined·

G0073 ἀγών agṓn *n.* (8x)
Roots:G0071 Compare:G0119 G3163 G1408 See:G0075
G0073.2 N-ASM ἀγῶνα (2x)
1Ti 6:12 Be·striving·in the good striving of·the trust, grab·
2Ti 4:7 I·have·strived·in the good striving; I·have·finished
G0073.2 N-DSM ἀγῶνι (1x)
1Th 2:2 to yeu the good·news of·God with much striving.
EG0073.2 (1x)

1Co 15:32 If according·to *the striving·of* men·of·clay†, I·
G0073.3 N-ASM ἀγῶνα (1x)
Heb 12:1 the strenuous·race being·laid·out·before us—
G0073.4 N-ASM ἀγῶνα (2x)
Php 1:30 the same strenuous·struggle such·as yeu·saw in me,
Col 2:1 what·a·huge strenuous·struggle I·have concerning
EG0073.5 (1x)
Rm 9:16 on·the·one running *for·it·as·a·prize*, but·rather on·

G0074 ἀγωνία agōnía *n.* (1x)
Roots:G0073
G0074.2 N-DSF ἀγωνίᾳ (1x)
Lk 22:44 And being in a·strenuous·agony, he·was·praying

G0075 ἀγωνίζομαι agōnízômai *v.* (7x)
Roots:G0073 Compare:G3164 G1264
G0075.1 V-PNM-2S ἀγωνίζου (1x)
1Ti 6:12 Be·striving·in the good striving of·the trust, grab·
G0075.1 V-PNM-2P ἀγωνίζεσθε (1x)
Lk 13:24 "Strive to·enter through the obstructed·and·narrow
G0075.1 V-PNP-NSM ἀγωνιζόμενος (2x)
Col 1:29 ·thing also I·labor·hard, striving according·to his
Col 4:12 greets yeu, always striving on·yeur behalf in the
G0075.1 V-RNI-1S ἠγώνισμαι (1x)
2Ti 4:7 I·have·strived·in the good striving; I·have·finished
G0075.2 V-PNP-NSM ἀγωνιζόμενος (1x)
1Co 9:25 And everyone striving·for·a·prize exercises· in·all·
G0075.3 V-INI-3P ἠγωνίζοντο (1x)
Jn 18:36 then·would strenuously·struggle in·order·that I·

G0076 Ἀδάμ Adám *n/p.* (9x)
אָדָם 'ạdạm [Hebrew]
Roots:H0121 Compare:G0444 See:G2424
G0076.3 N/P-PRI Ἀδάμ (8x)
Lk 3:38 of·Enosh, *son* of·Sheth, *son* of·Adam, *son* of·God.
Rm 5:14 already·reigned from Adam so·far·as·unto Moses,
Rm 5:14 ·failing after the resemblance of·Adam's violation,
Jud 1:14 also, *the* seventh from Adam, prophesied of·these,
1Co 15:22 For just·as all within Adam die, even in·this·
1Co 15:45 "The first man·of·clay†, Adam, came·into·being
1Ti 2:13 For Adam was·molded first, then Eve.
1Ti 2:14 And Adam was·not deluded, but the woman, being·
G0076.4 N/P-PRI Ἀδάμ (1x)
1Co 15:45 " The last Adam *came·into·being* as a·spirit,

G0077 ἀ•δάπανος adápanôs *adj.* (1x)
Roots:G0001 G1160
G0077.2 A-ASN ἀδάπανον (1x)
1Co 9:18 of·the Anointed-One without·charge, in·order not

G0078 Ἀδδί Addí *n/p.* (1x)
עַדִּי 'ădıy
xLangAlso:H5716
G0078.2 N/P-PRI Ἀδδί (1x)
Lk 3:28 *son* of·Malki, *son* of·Addi, *son* of·Qosam, *son* of·

G0079 ἀ•δελφή adêlphḗ *n.* (25x)
Roots:G0080 Compare:G4921-4 See:G3384
xLangEquiv:H0269 xLangAlso:H2994
G0079.1 N-NSF ἀδελφή (4x)
Jn 11:39 Martha, the sister of·the·one having·died, says to·
Jn 19:25 his mother, his mother's sister (Miryam the *wife*
Lk 10:39 And this·woman had a·sister called Mary, who,
Lk 10:40 ·not matter to·you that my sister abandoned me to·
G0079.1 N-NPF ἀδελφαί (3x)
Jn 11:3 In·due·course, his sisters dispatched to him, saying,
Mt 13:56 and·also his sisters, are·they not all indeed
Mk 6:3 Simon? And are not his sisters here alongside us?
G0079.1 N-ASF ἀδελφήν (3x)
Jn 11:5 Jesus loved Martha, also her sister, and Lazarus.
Jn 11:28 ·off and hollered·out·for Mary her sister, privately
Rm 16:15 Julia, Nereus, and his sister, and Olympas, and
G0079.1 N-APF ἀδελφάς (3x)
Lk 14:26 and brothers, and sisters, and yet his·own soul
Mt 19:29 left homes or brothers or sisters or father or mother
Mk 10:29 left home or brothers or sisters or father or mother
G0079.1 N-GSF ἀδελφῆς (2x)
Jn 11:1 ·among the village of·Mary and her sister Martha.
Ac 23:16 And the son of·Paul's sister, coming·directly after·
EG0079.1 (1x)
Jn 11:29 As·soon·as that *sister* heard *it*, she·is·roused swiftly
G0079.2 N-NSF ἀδελφή (4x)
Mt 12:50 *the* same is my brother, and sister, and mother.
Mk 3:35 this·one is my brother, and my sister, and mother.
Jac 2:15 But if a·brother or sister should·subsist *being* naked
1Co 7:15 The brother or the sister has·not been·enslaved in
G0079.2 N-ASF ἀδελφήν (2x)
Rm 16:1 to·yeu Phoebe, our sister, being an·attendant of·the
1Co 9:5 privilege to·lead·about a·wife (a·sister *in·the Trust*)
G0079.2 N-APF ἀδελφάς (2x)
Mk 10:30 homes and brothers and sisters and mothers and
1Ti 5:2 as mothers, younger·women as sisters, with all
G0079.2 N-GSF ἀδελφῆς (1x)
2Jn 1:13 The children of·your Selected sister greet you

G0080 ἀ•δελφός adêlphós *n.* (352x)
Roots:G0001 Compare:G0079 G3962 See:G0081
xLangEquiv:H0251 A0252
G0080.1 N-NSM ἀδελφός (19x)
Jn 1:40 Andrew, Simon Peter's brother, was one from·
Jn 6:8 Andrew, Simon Peter's brother, says to·him,
Jn 11:2 feet with·her hair, whose brother Lazarus was·sick).
Jn 11:21 if you·were here, my brother would not have·died.
Jn 11:23 Jesus says to·her, "Your brother shall·rise·up."
Jn 11:32 if you·were here, my brother would not have·died.
Lk 15:27 ·declared to·him, 'Your brother comes *home*! And
Lk 15:32 to·be·glad, because this your brother was dead and
Lk 20:28 ·us, if any·man's brother should·die while·having
Lk 20:28 ·die childless, that his brother should·take his wife
Mt 10:2 ·as Peter) and Andrew his brother; Jakob (the·one
Mt 10:2 Jakob (the·one of·Zebedee) and John his brother;
Mt 10:21 "And brother shall·hand·over brother to death, and
Mt 22:24 children, his brother shall·dutifully·marry his wife
Mk 6:3 son of·Mariam, and a·brother of·*little*·Jacob, Joses,
Mk 12:19 for·us that if any·man's brother should·die, and
Mk 12:19 children, that his brother should·take his wife and
Mk 13:12 "Now brother shall·hand·over brother to death,
Jud 1:1 a·slave of·YeShua Anointed and a·brother of·Jacob.
G0080.1 N-NPM ἀδελφοί (17x)
Jn 2:12 and his mother, and his brothers, and his disciples),
Jn 7:3 Accordingly, his brothers declared to him, "Walk·on
Jn 7:5 For neither were his brothers trusting in him.
Jn 7:10 But *just* as·soon·as his brothers walked·up, then he·
Lk 8:19 *his* mother and his brothers came·directly toward
Lk 8:20 "Your mother and your brothers stand outside,
Lk 20:29 "Now·then, there·were seven brothers. And the
Mt 12:46 behold, his mother and brothers stood outside,
Mt 12:47 your mother and your brothers stand outside,
Mt 12:48 "Who is my mother? And who are my brothers?"
Mt 13:55 ·*bitterly·rebellious*)? And his brothers, *little*·Jacob,
Mt 22:25 "Now there·were with us seven brothers, and the
Mk 3:31 In·due·course, his brothers and his mother come
Mk 3:32 your mother and your brothers seek·for you outside.
Mk 3:33 "Who is my mother, or my brothers?"
Mk 12:20 "Now·there·were seven brothers, and the first·one
1Co 9:5 ambassadors, and *as* the brothers of·the Lord, and
G0080.1 N-ASM ἀδελφόν (14x)
Jn 1:41 *Andrew* first finds his·own brother Simon and says
Lk 6:14 Peter), and Andrew his brother, Jakob and John,
Ac 12:2 And he·executed Jakob, the brother of·John, with·a·
Gal 1:19 ambassadors, except Jacob, the Lord's brother.
Mt 4:18 Peter) and Andrew his brother, casting a·cast·net
Mt 4:21 of·Zebedee) and John his brother, in the sailboat
Mt 10:21 "And brother shall·hand·over brother to death, and
Mt 17:1 and Jakob and John his brother, and he·brings them
Mk 1:16 he·saw Simon and his brother Andrew casting a·
Mk 1:19 (the·one of·Zebedee) and his brother John, and
Mk 3:17 of·Zebedee) and John the brother of·Jakob, also
Mk 5:37 except Peter, Jakob, and John the brother of·Jakob.
Mk 13:12 "Now brother shall·hand·over brother to death,
1Jn 3:12 Evil·One and slaughtered his brother. And for·what
G0080.1 N-APM ἀδελφούς (10x)
Lk 14:12 friends, nor·even your brothers, nor·even your
Lk 14:26 wife, and children, and brothers, and sisters, and
Lk 16:28 for I·have five brothers; *send him* so·that he·may·
Lk 18:29 that left home, or parents, or brothers, or wife, or
Mt 1:2 begot Jacob, and Jacob begot Judah and his brothers.
Mt 1:11 JosIah begot YeKonYah and his brothers, upon *the*
Mt 4:18 of·Galilee, YeShua saw two brothers, Simon (the·
Mt 4:21 from·there, he·saw two other brothers, Jakob (the·
Mt 19:29 everyone who left homes or brothers or sisters or
Mk 10:29 ·even·one that left home or brothers or sisters or
G0080.1 N-DSM ἀδελφῷ (5x)
Lk 12:13 "Mentor, declare for·my brother to·divide the
Lk 20:28 and should·fully·raise·up offspring† to·his brother.
Mt 22:24 wife and shall·raise·up offspring† to·his brother.
Mt 22:25 having offspring†, he·left his wife to·his brother.
Mk 12:19 should·fully·raise·up offspring† for·his brother.
G0080.1 N-DPM ἀδελφοῖς (2x)
Ac 1:14 of·Jesus, and·also together with·his brothers.
Ac 7:13 ·time, Joseph was·made·known to·his brothers, and
G0080.1 N-GSM ἀδελφοῦ (7x)
Jn 11:19 ·personally·console them concerning their brother.
Lk 3:1 with·his brother Philippus·II being·the·ruling·tetrarch
Lk 3:19 HerOdias (the wife of·his brother Philippus) and
Mt 14:3 ·of HerOdias, the wife of·Philippus, his brother.
Mk 6:17 the wife of·his brother Philippus, because he·
Mk 6:18 ·is·not proper for·you to·have your brother's wife."
1Jn 3:12 evil, and the·ones of·his brother *were* righteous.
G0080.1 N-GPM ἀδελφῶν (1x)
Lk 21:16 ·over both by parents, and brothers, and kinsmen,
EG0080.1 (1x)
Ac 7:14 Then dispatching *his brothers*, 'Joseph summarily·
G0080.2 N-NSM ἀδελφός (24x)
Lk 17:3 "But if your brother should·morally·fail against you,
Mt 5:23 ·recall·to·mind that your brother has anything
Mt 12:50 heavens, *the* same is my brother, and sister, and
Mt 18:15 "But if your brother should·morally·fail against
Mt 18:21 ·many·times shall my brother morally·fail against
Mk 3:35 will of·God, this·one is my brother, and my sister,
Rm 14:15 But if your brother is·grieved through *your* food,
Rm 14:21 ·even *anything* by which your brother stumbles, or
Rm 16:23 greets yeu, *as* also *does* Quartus, the brother.
Jac 1:9 So let the brother of·the low·estate boast in his high·
Jac 2:15 But if a·brother or sister should·subsist *being* naked
2Pe 3:15 just·as also our beloved brother Paul wrote to·yeu
1Co 1:1 through God's will, and SosThenes *our* brother.
1Co 5:11 ·man being·named a·brother should·actually·be a·
1Co 6:6 But·yet brother goes·to·court·to·be·judged against
1Co 7:12 the Lord— if any brother has a·non-trusting wife,
1Co 7:15 he·must·be·separated. The brother or the sister
1Co 8:11 shall the weak brother completely·perish, on·
2Co 1:1 will, and TimoThy *our* brother. To·the Called·Out·
Eph 6:21 *He·is* the beloved brother and trustworthy attendant
Col 1:1 through God's will, and TimoThy *our* brother.
Col 4:7 me. *He·is* a·beloved brother, a·trustworthy attendant
Phm 1:1 Anointed, and TimoThy *our* brother. To·Philemon
Rv 1:9 I, John, also yeur brother and partner·together in the
G0080.2 N-NPM ἀδελφοί (21x)
Lk 8:21 "My mother and my brothers are these, the·ones
Ac 9:30 after·realizing *it*, the brothers brought him down to
Ac 11:1 the ambassadors and the brothers, the·ones being in
Ac 11:12 Moreover, these six brothers also came together
Ac 15:23 the elders, and the brothers, to·*our*·brothers, the·
Ac 17:10 And immediately the brothers sent·forth both Paul
Ac 17:14 immediately the brothers dispatched·forth Paul to·
Ac 18:27 into Achaia, the brothers wrote, encouraging the
Ac 21:17 to JeruSalem, the brothers accepted us quite·
Ac 28:15 From·there, the brothers, upon·hearing the·things
Gal 1:2 and all the brothers together with·me. To·the Called·
Mt 12:49 "Behold my mother and my brothers!
Mt 23:8 *that·is* the Anointed-One, and yeu all are brothers.
Mk 3:34 "See, my mother and my brothers!
Php 4:21 Jesus. The brothers together with·me greet yeu.

1Co 16:20 All the brothers greet yeu. Greet one·another with
2Co 8:23 ·to yeu, or·if our brothers *be·inquired·of, they·are*
2Co 11:9 *was* lacking to·me, the brothers coming from
1Ti 6:2 *them*, because they·are brothers; but·rather more, be·
2Ti 4:21 and Linus, and Claudia, and all the brothers.
Rv 6:11 and their brothers shall·be·completely·fulfilled, the·
G0080.2 N-VSM ἀδελφέ (6x)
Lk 6:42 ·able to·say to·your brother, 'Brother, allow *that* I·
Ac 9:17 on him, he·declared, "Brother Saul, the Lord, Jesus
Ac 21:20 "Do·you·observe, brother, how·many tens·of·
Ac 22:13 *me*, he·declared to·me, 'Brother Saul, look·up!'
Phm 1:7 holy·ones have·been·refreshed, brother, through
Phm 1:20 Yes, brother, may I·myself derive·profit·from you
G0080.2 N-VPM ἀδελφοί (98x)
Ac 1:16 "Men, brothers, it·was·mandatory·for this Scripture
Ac 6:3 Now·then, brothers, inspect from·among yeurselves
Ac 15:7 to them, "Men, brothers, yeu·yeurselves are·fully·
Ac 15:13 answered, saying, "Men, brothers, listen·to me.
Ac 20:32 at·the·present, brothers, I·place·the·direct·care·of
Heb 3:1 From·which·cause, O·holy brothers (*yeu*
Heb 3:12 Look·out, brothers, lest there·shall·be in any of·
Heb 10:19 Accordingly brothers, by the blood of·YeShua,
Heb 13:22 And I·implore yeu, brothers, bear·with the word
Gal 1:11 But I·make·known to·yeu, brothers, that the good·
Gal 3:15 Brothers, I·relate *this matter* according·to a·man·
Gal 4:12 Brothers, I·petition yeu, be as I·myself *am*, because
Gal 4:28 Now we·ourselves, brothers, according·to YiTsaq,
Gal 4:31 So, brothers, we·are not children of·a·maidservant,
Gal 5:11 And I·myself, brothers, if I·still officially·proclaim
Gal 5:13 For, brothers, yeu·yeurselves are·called·forth to
Gal 6:1 Brothers, even though a·man·of·clay† should·be·
Gal 6:18 Brothers, the grace of·our Lord YeShua Anointed
Rm 1:13 want yeu to·be·ignorant, brothers, that many·times
Rm 7:1 Or do·yeu·not·know, O·brothers (for I·speak to·
Rm 7:4 As·such, my brothers, yeu·yeurselves also were·put·
Rm 8:12 So accordingly brothers, we·are under·an·
Rm 10:1 Brothers, in·fact my heart's good·purpose and
Rm 11:25 I·do·not want for·yeu, brothers, to·be·ignorant of·
Rm 12:1 Accordingly, I·implore yeu, brothers, through the
Rm 15:14 ·persuaded concerning yeu, my brothers, that yeu
Rm 15:15 But with·more·daring·boldness, brothers, I·wrote
Rm 15:30 Now I·implore yeu, brothers, on·account·of our
Rm 16:17 Now I·implore yeu, brothers, to·keep·a·watch·of
Jac 1:2 My brothers, resolutely·consider·it all joy whenever
Jac 1:16 Do·not be·deceived, my beloved brothers.
Jac 1:19 As·such, my beloved brothers, every man·of·clay†
Jac 2:1 My brothers, do·not hold the trust of·our Lord
Jac 2:5 Listen, my beloved brothers, ¿!·is·it·not God *that*
Jac 2:14 *is* the advantage, my brothers, though someone
Jac 3:1 My brothers, not many *of·yeu should* become
Jac 3:10 cursing. My brothers, it·is·not kindly·needed·for
Jac 3:12 ¿!·Is a·fig·tree able, my brothers, to·produce olives
Jac 4:11 ·not speak·against one·another, brothers. The·one
Jac 5:7 Accordingly, be·patient brothers, until the returning·
Jac 5:9 groan against one·another, brothers, lest yeu·should·
Jac 5:10 Take *for* an·explicit·example, my brothers, the ill·
Jac 5:12 But above all·things, my brothers, do·not swear,
Jac 5:19 Brothers, if anyone among yeu should·be·led·astray
Php 1:12 I·am·resolved for·yeu to·know, brothers, that the·
Php 3:1 One·thing remaining, my brothers: Rejoice in *the*
Php 3:13 Brothers, I·myself do·not reckon my·own·self to·
Php 3:17 Become co-imitators of·me, brothers, and keep·a·
Php 4:1 As·such, my brothers (dearly·beloved and greatly·
Php 4:8 One·thing remaining, brothers: As·many·things·as
2Pe 1:10 Therefore, brothers, all·the·more quickly·endeavor
1Th 1:4 having·seen, O·brothers having·been·loved by God,
1Th 2:1 For yeu·yeurselves personally·know, brothers, that
1Th 2:9 For yeu·remember, brothers, our wearisome·labor
1Th 2:14 For yeu, brothers, did·become attentive·imitators
1Th 2:17 we·ourselves brothers, being·grievously·removed
1Th 3:7 On·account·of that, brothers, in all our tribulation
1Th 4:1 one·thing remaining, brothers: We·ask·of yeu and
1Th 4:10 But we·implore yeu, brothers, to·abound more·
1Th 4:13 want yeu to·be·ignorant, brothers, concerning the·
1Th 5:1 times and the seasons, brothers, yeu·have no need
1Th 5:4 But yeu, brothers, are not in darkness, in·order·that
1Th 5:12 So we·ask·of yeu, brothers, to·personally·know
1Th 5:14 Now we·exhort yeu, brothers, admonish the
1Th 5:25 Brothers, pray concerning us.
2Th 1:3 to·God always concerning yeu, brothers, just·as it·is
2Th 2:1 Now we·ask·of yeu, brothers, on·behalf·of·the
2Th 2:13 concerning yeu (O·brothers having·been·loved by
2Th 2:15 So accordingly, brothers, stand·fast and securely·
2Th 3:1 One·thing remaining, brothers: Pray concerning us
2Th 3:6 Now we·charge yeu, brothers, in our Lord's name,
2Th 3:13 But yeu, brothers, yeu·should·not be·cowardly in·
1Co 1:10 Now I·implore yeu, brothers, through the name of·
1Co 1:11 to·me concerning yeu, my brothers, by the·ones *of*
1Co 1:26 look·at yeur calling·forth, brothers: how·that not
1Co 2:1 And·I, brothers, already·coming to yeu, came not
1Co 3:1 And I·myself, brothers, am·not able to·speak to·yeu
1Co 4:6 these·things, brothers, I·portrayed·as·an·example
1Co 7:24 in that·*state*·which he·is·called·forth, brothers, in
1Co 7:29 But this I·disclose, brothers, *that* the season *is*
1Co 10:1 Now, brothers, I·do·not want yeu to·be·ignorant
1Co 11:2 Now I·applaud yeu, brothers, that yeu·have·been·
1Co 11:33 ·such, my brothers, as·yeu·are·coming·together
1Co 12:1 the spiritual *bestowments*, brothers, I·do·not want
1Co 14:6 So right·now, brothers, if I·should·come to yeu
1Co 14:20 Brothers, be not little·children in·the
1Co 14:26 how is·it *to·be*, brothers? Whenever yeu·should·
1Co 14:39 As·such, brothers, be·zealous to·prophesy, and
1Co 15:1 Moreover, brothers, I·make·known to·yeu the
1Co 15:50 Now this I·disclose, brothers, that flesh and
1Co 15:58 As·such, my beloved brothers, become
1Co 16:15 I·implore yeu, brothers, (yeu·personally·know
2Co 1:8 ·do·not want yeu to·be·ignorant, brothers, over our
2Co 8:1 Now brothers, we·make·known to·yeu the grace of·
2Co 13:11 Finally, brothers, be·glad. Be·completely·
Eph 6:10 one·thing remaining: My brothers, be·enabled in
1Jn 2:7 Brothers, I·write no brand-new commandment to·yeu
1Jn 3:13 Do·not marvel, my brothers, if the world hates yeu.
G0080.2 N-ASM ἀδελφόν (27x)
Heb 13:23 Yeu·know *that·our* brother TimoThy *is* having·
Mt 18:15 he·should·listen·to you, you·gained your brother.
Rm 14:10 ·do you·yourself unduly·judge your brother? Or
Rm 14:10 why·do you·yourself utterly·disdain your brother?
Jac 4:11 brother and judging his brother, he·speaks·against
Php 2:25 to yeu EpAphroditus, my brother, coworker, and
1Th 3:2 and we·sent TimoThy, our brother, and attendant of·
1Th 4:6 to·overstep and to·swindle his brother in the matter·
2Th 3:15 an·enemy, but·rather admonish *him* as a·brother.
1Co 8:13 if food entices my brother unto·moral·failure, *then*
1Co 8:13 I·should·cause·the·moral·failure·of my brother.
2Co 2:13 not to·find Titus, my brother. But·rather, orderly·
2Co 8:18 we·sent·together with him the brother, whose high·
2Co 8:22 we·sent·together with·them our brother, whom we·
2Co 12:18 ·dispatched·*him*·together·with the brother. ¿!·Did
Phm 1:16 but·rather above a·slave, a·brother beloved,
1Jn 2:9 in the light, and hating his brother, is in the darkness
1Jn 2:10 The·one loving his brother abides in the light, and
1Jn 2:11 But the·one hating his brother is in the darkness,
1Jn 3:10 ·out·of·God, also the·one not loving his brother.
1Jn 3:14 The·one not presently·loving the brother abides in
1Jn 3:15 one presently·hating his brother is a·man-killer†.
1Jn 3:17 should·presently·observe his brother having need,
1Jn 4:20 God," and he·should·hate his brother, he·is a·liar,
1Jn 4:20 not loving his brother whom he·has·clearly·seen,
1Jn 4:21 the·one loving God should·love his brother also.
1Jn 5:16 ·see his brother morally·failing a·moral·failure
G0080.2 N-APM ἀδελφούς (26x)
Jn 20:17 But you·traverse to my brothers and declare to·them
Jn 21:23 this saying went·forth among the brothers, "This
Lk 22:32 return, you·must·firmly·establish your brothers."
Ac 15:1 from Judea were·instructing the brothers, *saying*,
Ac 15:32 themselves, exhorted the brothers through much
Ac 15:36 returning, we·should·visit our brothers in every
Ac 16:40 And seeing the brothers, they·comforted them and
Ac 17:6 they·were·dragging Jason and certain brothers to the
Ac 21:7 and after·greeting the brothers, we·abided with
Ac 22:5 accepted letters to the brothers and traversed into
Ac 28:14 where finding brothers, we·were·exhorted to·stay·
Heb 2:11 *the Initiator* is·not ashamed to·call them brothers,
Mt 5:47 And if yeu·should·greet yeur brothers merely, what·
Mk 10:30 in this season, homes and brothers and sisters and
Rm 16:14 Hermes, and the brothers together with·them.
1Th 4:10 yeu·do this toward all the brothers, the·ones in all
1Th 5:26 Greet all the brothers with a·holy kiss.
1Co 6:8 and rob, and these·things *yeu·do to·yeur* brothers.
1Co 8:12 ·failing in·this·manner toward the brothers, and
2Co 9:3 So I·sent the brothers, lest our boasting on·yeur
2Co 9:5 *it* necessary to·exhort the brothers, that they·should·
Col 4:15 Greet the brothers in LaoDicea, and *greet* Nymphas
1Ti 5:1 *him* as a·father, *likewise* younger·men as brothers,
1Jn 3:14 because we·love the brothers. The·one not
3Jn 1:5 *good·deed* you·may·work for the brothers and for the
3Jn 1:10 he·himself welcomely·receive the brothers, and he·
G0080.2 N-DSM ἀδελφῷ (8x)
Lk 6:42 how are·you·able to·say to·your brother, 'Brother,
Mt 5:22 being·angry with·his brother for·no·reason shall·be
Mt 5:22 Now whoever should·declare to·his brother, 'Raqa·
Mt 5:24 First be·thoroughly·reconciled to·your brother, and
Mt 7:4 Or how shall·you·declare to·your brother, 'Give·way
Mt 18:35 ·of yeu·should·forgive his brother their trespasses
Rm 14:13 a·stumbling·block or a·trap in·a·brother's *way*.
Col 4:9 the trustworthy and beloved brother, who is from·
G0080.2 N-DPM ἀδελφοῖς (15x)
Ac 11:29 to·send service to the brothers, the·ones residing in
Ac 12:17 these·things to·Jacob, and to·the brothers." And
Ac 15:3 And they·were·causing great joy for·all the brothers.
Ac 15:22 who·officially·are·leading among the brothers,
Ac 15:23 and the brothers, to·*our*·brothers, the·ones in
Ac 18:18 ·taking·leave·of the brothers, was·sailing·away
Heb 2:12 I·shall·announce your name to·my brothers. In *the*
Heb 2:17 fully all·things to·the brothers to·become·like *them*
Mt 28:10 announce to·my brothers that they·should·go·off
Rm 8:29 ·for his *Son* to·be firstborn among many brothers.
1Th 5:27 ·the letter to·be·read·aloud to·all the holy brothers.
1Co 15:6 ·of five·hundred brothers upon·one·occasion·only,
Eph 6:23 Peace *be* to·the brothers, and love with trust from
Col 1:2 holy and trustworthy brothers in Anointed-One.
1Ti 4:6 ·hazard·of these·things to·the brothers, you·shall·be
G0080.2 N-GSM ἀδελφοῦ (10x)
Lk 6:41 speck·of·dust, the·one in your brother's eye, but do·
Lk 6:42 ·out the speck·of·dust, the·one in your brother's eye.
Mt 7:3 speck·of·dust, the·one in your brother's eye, but do·
Mt 7:5 the speck·of·dust from·out·of·your brother's eye.
Jac 4:11 The·one speaking·against *his* brother and judging
1Pe 5:12 Silvanus (the trustworthy brother as·how I·reckon *it*
2Th 3:6 from every brother walking in·a·disorderly·manner
1Co 6:5 ·be·able to·discern up *the* middle for·his brothers?
1Co 6:6 goes·to·court·to·be·judged against a·brother, and
1Co 16:12 Now concerning *our* brother Apollos, I repeatedly
G0080.2 N-GPM ἀδελφῶν (15x)
Ac 10:23 ·them, and some of·the brothers from Joppa went·
Ac 14:2 the souls of·the Gentiles against the brothers.
Ac 15:33 with peace from the brothers *to·return* to the
Ac 15:40 ·handed·to·the grace of·God by the brothers.
Ac 16:2 *disciple* was·attested·to by the brothers in Lystra and
Mt 20:24 ·greatly·displeased concerning the two brothers.
Mt 25:40 to·one of·the least of·these my brothers, yeu·did *it*
Php 1:14 And many·more of·the brothers in *the* Lord,
1Co 16:11 me, for I·am·waiting·for him with the brothers.
1Co 16:12 ·come to yeu with the brothers, yet entirely, it·
1Jn 3:16 ·lay·down *our·own* souls on·behalf·of·the brothers.
3Jn 1:3 I·rejoiced very·much, with·*the*·brothers coming and
Rv 12:10 the legal·accuser·of·our brothers is·cast·down, the·
Rv 19:10 your fellow·slave, and of·your brothers having the
Rv 22:9 fellow·slave, and of·your brothers the prophets, and

EG0080.2 (5x)
Ac 15:32 *in·kind*, and they·reaffirmed *the* brothers.
Mt 25:45 of·the least of·these *my* brothers, yeu·did·not·even
Rm 14:20 a·stumbling·block *to·his* brother on·account·of *his*
Tit 3:14 And our *brothers* must·learn also to·conduct good
1Co 9:19 I·may·gain *all* the more brothers *in·Anointed-One*.
G0080.3 N-NPM ἀδελφοί (1x)
Ac 7:26 Men, yeu·yourselves are brothers; for·what·purpose
G0080.3 N-VPM ἀδελφοί (12x)
Ac 2:29 "Men, brothers, it·is·being·proper to·declare to yeu
Ac 2:37 ·ambassadors, "Men, brothers, what shall·we·do?
Ac 3:17 "And now, brothers, I·have·seen that yeu·inflicted
Ac 7:2 *Stephen* replied, "Men, brothers and fathers, listen:
Ac 13:15 saying, "Men, brothers, if there·is within you a·
Ac 13:26 "Men, brothers, the·Sons of·AbRaham by·birth,
Ac 13:38 "Now·then, men, brothers, be·it known to·yeu
Ac 22:1 "Men, brothers and fathers, hear my defense *which*
Ac 23:1 "Men, brothers, I·myself have·been·living·as·a·
Ac 23:5 "I·had·not seen, brothers, that he·is *the* designated·
Ac 23:6 ·of·Sanhedrin, "Men, brothers, I·myself am a·
Ac 28:17 "Men, brothers, I·myself, having·committed not·
G0080.3 N-ASM ἀδελφόν (1x)
Heb 8:11 his neighbor, and each·man his brother, saying,
G0080.3 N-APM ἀδελφούς (3x)
Ac 7:23 upon his heart to·visit his brothers, the Sons of·
Ac 7:25 ·was·assuming *for* his brothers to·comprehend that
Heb 7:5 that·is, of·their brothers, even·though having·
G0080.3 N-GPM ἀδελφῶν (4x)
Ac 3:22 a·Prophet unto·yeu from·among yeur brothers, as
Ac 7:37 a·prophet to·yeu from·among yeur brothers, as *he*·
Ac 28:21 any of·the brothers arriving·publicly announced or
Rm 9:3 the Anointed-One on·behalf of·my brothers, my

G0081 ἀ•δελφότης adêlphótēs *n.* (2x)
Roots:G0080
G0081.2 N-ASF ἀδελφότητα (1x)
1Pe 2:17 all·men. Love the brotherhood. Reverently·fear
G0081.2 N-DSF ἀδελφότητι (1x)
1Pe 5:9 ·be·further·finished in·yeur brotherhood *while·still* in

G0082 ἄ•δηλος ádēlôs *adj.* (2x)
Roots:G0001 G1212
G0082.2 A-NPN ἄδηλα (1x)
Lk 11:44 as the chamber·tombs, the indistinct·ones, and the
G0082.2 A-ASF ἄδηλον (1x)
1Co 14:8 if·ever a·trumpet should·give an·indistinct sound,

G0083 ἀ•δηλότης adēlótēs *n.* (1x)
Roots:G0082 See:G0084
G0083 N-DSF ἀδηλότητι (1x)
1Ti 6:17 ·their·expectations upon *the* uncertainty of·wealth,

G0084 ἀ•δήλως adḗlōs *adv.* (1x)
Roots:G0082 See:G0083
G0084 ADV ἀδήλως (1x)
1Co 9:26 *but* not as uncertainly; in·this·manner I·do·box,

G0085 ἀδημονέω adēmônéō *v.* (3x)
Compare:G3600
G0085 V-PAN ἀδημονεῖν (2x)
Mt 26:37 to·be·grieved and to·be·intensely·distressed.
Mk 14:33 ·be·utterly·amazed and to·be·intensely·distressed.
G0085 V-PAP-NSM ἀδημονῶν (1x)
Php 2:26 all, and being·intensely·distressed, on·account·that

G0086 ᾅ•δης hádēs *n/l.* (12x)
Roots:G0001 G1492 Compare:G2288 G2978-1 G1067 See:G2737 G5020 xLangEquiv:H7585 xLangAlso:H0953
G0086.2 N/L-DSM ᾅδῃ (1x)
Lk 16:23 And in Hades, after·lifting·up his eyes while·
G0086.2 N/L-GSM ᾅδου (4x)
Lk 10:15 heaven, you·shall·be·driven·down unto Hades.
Ac 2:27 forsake my soul in Hades, neither shall·you·give
Ac 2:31 ʿwas·not left·behind in Hades, neither did·his flesh
Mt 11:23 the heaven, shall·be·driven·down unto Hades!
EG0086.2 (1x)
2Pe 2:4 ·Tartarus *(the deepest dungeon of·Hades)*, he·handed
G0086.3 N/P-NSM ᾅδης (3x)
Rv 6:8 it, his name *is* Death, and Hades followed with him.
Rv 20:13 and Death and Hades gave·forth the dead·ones in
Rv 20:14 And Death and Hades were·cast into the Lake of·
G0086.3 N/P-VSM ᾅδη (1x)
1Co 15:55 *is* your painful·sting? O·Hades, where *is* your
G0086.3 N/P-GSM ᾅδου (2x)
Mt 16:18 and Hades' gates shall·not overpower it.
Rv 1:18 ·Amen; and I·have the keys of·Hades and of·Death.

G0087 ἀ•διά•κριτος adiákritôs *adj.* (1x)
Roots:G0001 G1252
G0087.2 A-NSF ἀδιάκριτος (1x)
Jac 3:17 without·discrimination and without·hypocrisy.

G0088 ἀ•διά•λειπτος adiálêiptôs *adj.* (2x)
Roots:G0001 G1223 G3007 Compare:G0413 G3973 See:G0089 G1587
G0088.1 A-NSF ἀδιάλειπτος (1x)
Rm 9:2 grief is a·great and unceasing distress in·my heart.
G0088.2 A-ASF ἀδιάλειπτον (1x)
2Ti 1:3 , how without·ceasing I·have a·reminder

G0089 ἀ•δια•λείπτως adialêíptōs *adv.* (4x)
Roots:G0088
G0089.1 ADV ἀδιαλείπτως (4x)
Rm 1:9 of·his Son, how unceasingly I·make mention of·yeu
1Th 1:3 unceasingly remembering yeu before our God and
1Th 2:13 give·thanks to·God unceasingly, because after·
1Th 5:17 Pray unceasingly.

G0090 ἀ•δια•φθορία adiaphthôría *n.* (1x)
Roots:G0001 G1311 Compare:G0861
G0090.2 N-ASF ἀδιαφθορίαν (1x)
Tit 2:7 *showing* undecaying·purity, impeccable·integrity·

G0091 ἀ•δικέω adikéō *v.* (27x)
Roots:G0094 Compare:G2559
G0091.1 V-PAP-NSM ἀδικῶν (1x)
Rv 22:11 The·one being·unrighteous, let·him·be·unrighteous
G0091.1 V-AAM-3S ἀδικησάτω (1x)
Rv 22:11 being·unrighteous, let·him·be·unrighteous still;
G0091.3 V-PAI-1S ἀδικῶ (1x)
Mt 20:13 I·do·not·do you wrong. Did·you·not·indeed
G0091.3 V-PAI-2P ἀδικεῖτε (2x)
Ac 7:26 for·what·purpose do·yeu·wrong one·another?
1Co 6:8 But·rather, yeu·yourselves do·wrong and rob, and
G0091.3 V-PAP-NSM ἀδικῶν (2x)
Ac 7:27 But the·one morally·wronging the neighbor shoved
Col 3:25 But the·one doing·wrong shall·subsequently·obtain
G0091.3 V-PPI-2P ἀδικεῖσθε (1x)
1Co 6:7 why not·indeed *let* yeurselves·be·wronged? Rather,
G0091.3 V-PPP-ASM ἀδικούμενον (1x)
Ac 7:24 someone being·wronged, he·forcefully·defended *his*
G0091.3 V-AAI-1S ἠδίκησα (1x)
Ac 25:10 ·for me to·be·judged. I·wronged not·even·one *of*
G0091.3 V-AAI-1P ἠδικήσαμεν (1x)
2Co 7:2 us *in·yeur hearts*; we·wronged no·one·at·all, we·
G0091.3 V-AAI-3S ἠδίκησεν (2x)
Col 3:25 ·obtain that·for·which he·did·wrong, and there·is
Phm 1:18 So if he·wronged you, or owes *you* anything,
G0091.3 V-AAP-GSM ἀδικήσαντος (1x)
2Co 7:12 *it·was* not because·of the·one doing·wrong, nor
G0091.3 V-APP-GSM ἀδικηθέντος (1x)
2Co 7:12 because·of the·one being·done·wrong, but·rather
G0091.4 V-PAI-3P ἀδικοῦσιν (1x)
Rv 9:19 having heads, and they·do·bring·harm with them.
G0091.4 V-AAI-2P ἠδικήσατε (1x)
Gal 4:12 as yeu *are*. Not·at·all did·yeu·bring·harm·to me.
G0091.4 V-AAN ἀδικῆσαι (4x)
Rv 7:2 to·whom it was·given to·bring·harm·to the earth and
Rv 9:10 authority *was* to·bring·harm·to the men·of·clay†
Rv 11:5 if any·man should·determine to·bring·harm·to them,
Rv 11:5 if any·man should·determine to·bring·harm·to them,
G0091.4 V-AAS-2S ἀδικήσῃς (1x)
Rv 6:6 ·denarius; and you·should·not bring·harm·to the oil
G0091.4 V-AAS-2P ἀδικήσητε (1x)
Rv 7:3 saying, "Yeu·may·not bring·harm·to the earth,
G0091.4 V-AAS-3S ἀδικήσῃ (1x)
Lk 10:19 ·one·thing, no, it·should·not bring·harm·to yeu.
G0091.4 V-AAS-3P ἀδικήσωσιν (1x)
Rv 9:4 that they·should·not bring·harm·to the vegetation of·
G0091.5 V-APS-3S ἀδικηθῇ (1x)
Rv 2:11 he·may·not be·brought·to·harm as·a·result of·the
G0091.6 V-PAI-1S ἀδικῶ (1x)
Ac 25:11 For if in·fact, I·am·a·harmful·offender, or have·

G0092 ἀ•δίκημα adíkēma *n.* (3x)
Roots:G0091 Compare:G2556 G3900
G0092 N-NSN ἀδίκημα (1x)
Ac 18:14 in·fact, if it·were some wrong·doing or an·evil,
G0092 N-ASN ἀδίκημα (1x)
Ac 24:20 ·them·declare if they·found any wrong·doing in me
G0092 N-APN ἀδικήματα (1x)
Rv 18:5 heaven,ˮ and God remembered her wrong·doings.

G0093 ἀ•δικία adikía *n.* (25x)
Roots:G0094 Compare:G0266 G1294
G0093.1 N-NSF ἀδικία (4x)
Jn 7:18 the·same·man is true, and unrighteousness is not in
Rm 3:5 "But if our unrighteousness commends God's
Rm 9:14 ·we·state? ¿!·Is·there unrighteousness with God?
1Jn 5:17 All unrighteousness is moral·failure, and there·is
G0093.1 N-ASF ἀδικίαν (1x)
Rm 1:18 and *all* unrighteousness of·men·of·clay† (the·ones
G0093.1 N-DSF ἀδικίᾳ (4x)
Rm 1:18 ·ones holding·down the truth by unrighteousness);
Rm 1:29 ·filled with·all unrighteousness, sexual·immorality,
Rm 2:8 ·persuaded by·the unrighteousness, *he·shall·render*
2Th 2:12 but·rather taking·delight in the unrighteousness.
G0093.1 N-DPF ἀδικίαις (1x)
Heb 8:12 favorably·forgiving to·their unrighteousness, and
G0093.1 N-GSF ἀδικίας (9x)
Lk 13:27 from me, all *yeu* workmen of·unrighteousness.'
Ac 8:23 of·bitterness and a·joint·bond of·unrighteousness."
Rm 6:13 *as* instruments of·unrighteousness to·Moral·Failure,
Jac 3:6 *it·is* the world of·unrighteousness. In·this·manner,
2Pe 2:13 a·payment·of·service for·unrighteousness, *as·those*
2Pe 2:15 loved a·payment·of·service for·unrighteousness.
2Th 2:10 with all the delusion of·unrighteousness in the·ones
2Ti 2:19 must·withdraw from unrighteousness."
1Jn 1:9 and should·purify us from all unrighteousness.
G0093.2 N-GSF ἀδικίας (1x)
Lk 16:9 of·the unrighteous·establishment, in·order·that,
G0093.3 N-ASF ἀδικίαν (1x)
2Co 12:13 of·yeu? Graciously·forgive me this injustice.
G0093.3 N-DSF ἀδικίᾳ (1x)
1Co 13:6 It·does·not rejoice over the injustice, but it·
G0093.3 N-GSF ἀδικίας (1x)
Ac 1:18 out of·the payment·of·service for·the injustice; and
G0093.4 N-GSF ἀδικίας (2x)
Lk 16:8 "And the lord applauded the unjust estate·manager,
Lk 18:6 "Hear what the unjust judge says.

G0094 ἄ•δικος ádikôs *adj.* (14x)
Roots:G0001 G1349 See:G0095
G0094.1 A-NSM ἄδικος (4x)
Lk 16:10 And the·one *being* unrighteous with very·little is
Lk 16:10 with very·little is also unrighteous with much.
Heb 6:10 For God *is* not unrighteous to·forget yeur work and
Rm 3:5 "¿!·Is·not God unrighteous, the·one bringing·on
G0094.1 A-NPM ἄδικοι (2x)
Lk 18:11 ·greedy·men, unrighteous·men, adulterers, or even
1Co 6:9 ·know that unrighteous·men shall·not inherit God's
G0094.1 A-APM ἀδίκους (2x)
Mt 5:45 ·rain on righteous·ones and unrighteous·ones.
2Pe 2:9 ·trials, and to·reserve unrighteous·men to a·day of·
G0094.1 A-DSN ἀδίκῳ (1x)
Lk 16:11 trustworthy with the unrighteous material·wealth,
G0094.1 A-GPM ἀδίκων (3x)
Ac 24:15 both of·righteous·ones and unrighteous·ones.
1Pe 3:18 ·one on·behalf of·unrighteous·ones, in·order·that

1Co 6:1 ·court·to·be·judged before the unrighteous·ones, and
EG0094.1 (2x)
2Pe 2:14 *unrighteous* souls having eyes exceedingly·full of·
1Co 6:4 do·yeu·seat these *unrighteous·ones as·judges*, the·

G0095 ἀ•δίκως adíkōs *adv.* (1x)
Roots:G0094
G0095 ADV ἀδίκως (1x)
1Pe 2:19 *toward* God undergoes grief, suffering unjustly.

G0096 ἀ•δόκιμος adókimôs *adj.* (8x)
Roots:G0001 G1384 Compare:G0268 G2556
G0096.2 A-NSM ἀδόκιμος (2x)
Heb 6:8 'thorns and spear·thistles' *is* disqualified, and *is*
1Co 9:27 to·others, I·myself should·become disqualified.
G0096.2 A-NPM ἀδόκιμοι (5x)
Tit 1:16 obstinate, and disqualified particularly·for every
2Co 13:5 is in yeu, except·that yeu·are disqualified?
2Co 13:6 ·shall·know that we·ourselves are not disqualified.
2Co 13:7 *that* we·ourselves may·be as·though disqualified.
2Ti 3:8 ·been·fully·corrupted, disqualified concerning the
G0096.2 A-ASM ἀδόκιμον (1x)
Rm 1:28 God handed them over to a·disqualified mind, to·do

G0097 ἄ•δολος ádolôs *adj.* (1x)
Roots:G0001 G1388
G0097.2 A-ASN ἄδολον (1x)
1Pe 2:2 *of·the* Redemptive-word, *which·is* free·from·guile, in·

G0098 Ἀδραμυττηνός Adramyttēnós *adj/g.* (1x)
G0098.1 A/G-DSN Ἀδραμυττηνῷ (1x)
Ac 27:2 ·upon a·sailing·ship of·Adramyttium, we·launched,

G0099 Ἀδρίας Adrías *n/l.* (1x)
G0099 N/L-DSM Ἀδρίᾳ (1x)
Ac 27:27 ·thoroughly·tossed·about along the Adriatic·Sea, in

G0100 ἁδρότης hadrótēs *n.* (1x)
Compare:G4050 G4051
G0100.3 N-DSF ἁδρότητι (1x)
2Co 8:20 in this bountiful·benevolence being·attended·to by

G0101 ἀ•δυνατέω adynatéō *v.* (2x)
Roots:G0102
G0101.2 V-FAI-3S ἀδυνατήσει (2x)
Lk 1:37 directly·from God shall·not be·impossible."
Mt 17:20 And nothing·at·all shall·be·impossible for·yeu.

G0102 ἀ•δύνατος adýnatôs *adj.* (11x)
Roots:G0001 G1415 Compare:G0418
G0102.1 A-GPM ἀδυνάτων (1x)
Rm 15:1 ·of·conscience of·the·ones *that·are* unable, and not
G0102.2 A-NSM ἀδύνατος (1x)
Ac 14:8 *there·was* a·certain man disabled in·his feet who·
G0102.3 A-NSN ἀδύνατον (7x)
Heb 6:4 For *it·is* impossible for·the·ones after once being·
Heb 6:18 in which *it·was* impossible for·God to·lie, we·may·
Heb 10:4 For *it·is* impossible *for·the* blood of·bulls and of·
Heb 11:6 ·from trust, *it·is* impossible to·fully·satisfy *him*.
Mt 19:26 "With men·of·clay† this is impossible, but with
Mk 10:27 "With men·of·clay† *it·is* impossible, but·yet not
Rm 8:3 For the·thing *which·is* impossible of·the Torah-Law,
G0102.3 A-NPN ἀδύνατα (1x)
Lk 18:27 The·things *which·are* impossible with men·of·clay†
EG0102.3 (1x)
Heb 6:6 *it·is impossible* to·reinstate·and·renew·them again to

G0103 ᾄδω ádō *v.* (6x)
Compare:G5214 G5567 See:G5603
xLangEquiv:H7891
G0103 V-PAI-3P ᾄδουσιν (3x)
Rv 5:9 And they·sing a·brand-new song, saying, "You·are
Rv 14:3 And they·do·sing, as *singing* a·brand-new song in·
Rv 15:3 And they·sing the song of·Moses, a·slave of·God,
G0103 V-PAP-NPM ᾄδοντες (2x)
Eph 5:19 and spiritual songs, singing and making·melody
Col 3:16 and spiritual songs, singing with grace in yeur
EG0103 (1x)
Rv 14:3 And they·do·sing, as *singing* a·brand-new song in·

G0104 ἀεί aeî *adv.* (8x)
Compare:G3842 G1539 See:G0126 G0104-1
G0104.1 ADV ἀεί (7x)
Ac 7:51 and ears, yeu always do·violently·oppose the Holy
Heb 3:10 and declared, 'Always, they·are·led·astray in·
1Pe 3:15 And *be* ready always to *present a·gracious* defense
2Pe 1:12 ·quietly·remind yeu always concerning these·things
Tit 1:12 declared, "Cretans *are* always liars, wicked wild·
2Co 4:11 For we·ourselves always, the·ones living, are·
2Co 6:10 as being·grieved yet always rejoicing, as
G0104.2 ADV ἀεί (1x)
Mk 15:8 ·*him to·do* just·as he·was·doing regularly for·them.

G0105 ἀετός aētós *n.* (4x)
Compare:G0207 G0230-1 G1135-3 See:G0109
xLangEquiv:H5404 A5403
G0105 N-NPM ἀετοί (2x)
Lk 17:37 *is*, there the eagles shall·be·gathered·together."
Mt 24:28 ·be, there the eagles shall·be·gathered·together.
G0105 N-DSM ἀετῷ (1x)
Rv 4:7 and the fourth living·being *is* like a·flying eagle.
G0105 N-GSM ἀετοῦ (1x)
Rv 12:14 two wings of·the great eagle were·given that she·

G0106 ἄ•ζυμος ázymôs *adj.* (13x)
Roots:G0001 G2219 Compare:G0740 G2570-2
See:G3957
xLangEquiv:H4682
G0106.1 A-NPM ἄζυμοι (1x)
1Co 5:7 ·of·dough, just·as *indeed* yeu·are unleavened. For
EG0106.1 (4x)
Lk 22:19 And after·taking *unleavened* bread *and giving*·
Mt 26:26 were·eating, after·taking the *unleavened* bread
Mk 14:22 were·eating, after·taking *the unleavened* bread
1Co 11:23 he·was·handed·over, took *unleavened* bread,
G0106.3 A-NPN ἄζυμα (1x)
Mk 14:1 ·*of* the Passover and the Unleavened·Bread. And
G0106.3 A-DPN ἀζύμοις (1x)
1Co 5:8 but·rather with Unleavened·Bread of·sincerity and
G0106.3 A-GPN ἀζύμων (6x)
Lk 22:1 ·Feast of·the Unleavened·Bread was·drawing·near,
Lk 22:7 the day of·the *Sacred·Feast·of* Unleavened·Bread, in
Ac 12:3 the days *of·the Sacred·Feast* of·Unleavened·Bread,
Ac 20:6 days of·the *Sacred·Feast·of* Unleavened·Bread, and
Mt 26:17 *day* of·the *Sacred·Feast·of* Unleavened·Bread, the
Mk 14:12 of·the *Sacred·Feast·of* Unleavened·Bread, when

G0107 Ἀζώρ Azṓr *n/p.* (2x)
Ἀσζούρ Aszoúr [formal spelling]
xLangAlso:H5809
G0107.2 N/P-PRI Ἀζώρ (2x)
Mt 1:13 AbiHud begot ElYaQim, and ElYaQim begot Azzur.
Mt 1:14 Now Azzur begot Tsadoq, and Tsadoq begot Achim,

G0108 Ἄζωτος Ázōtôs *n/l.* (1x)
אַשְׁדּוֹד 'ashdôd [Hebrew]
Ἀσεδώδ Asêdṓd [Septuagint]
Ἐσδώδ Êsdṓd [Septuagint]
Ἐσδώθ Êsdṓth [Septuagint]
Ἄζωτον Ázōtôn [Septuagint]
Ἀζώτῳ Azṓtō [Septuagint]
Ἀζώτου Azṓtôu [Septuagint]
Roots:H0795
G0108.2 N/L-ASF Ἄζωτον (1x)
Ac 8:40 But Philippe was·found in Ashdod, and going·

G0109 ἀήρ aḗr *n.* (7x)
Roots:G0108-2 Compare:G5594 G3772 See:G1005
G0822
G0109.1 N-NSM ἀήρ (1x)
Rv 9:2 and the sun and the air were·darkened from·out of·the
G0109.1 N-ASM ἀέρα (5x)
Ac 22:23 ·off the garments, and casting dust into the air,
1Th 4:17 ·and·meet the Lord in *the* air. And in·this·manner,
1Co 9:26 in·this·manner I·do·box, *but* not as thrashing air.
1Co 14:9 ·spoken? For yeu·shall·be speaking into *thin* air.
Rv 16:17 ·out his vial into the air, and there·came·forth a·
G0109.1 N-GSM ἀέρος (1x)
Eph 2:2 ·to the prince of·the authority of·the air, of·the spirit

G0110 ἀ•θανασία athanasía *n.* (3x)
Roots:G0001 G2288 Compare:G2349 G0270-2
G0110.1 N-ASF ἀθανασίαν (3x)
1Co 15:53 *for* this mortal to·dress·itself·with immortality.
1Co 15:54 mortal should·dress·itself·with immortality, then
1Ti 6:16 the only·one having immortality, dwelling *in*

G0111 ἀ•θέμιτος athémitôs *adj.* (2x)
Roots:G0001 G5087 Compare:G0459 G0946 G0113
G2557 G2556
G0111.2 A-NSN ἀθέμιτον (1x)
Ac 10:28 it·is a·statutory·offense for·a·man that·is·a·Jew to·
G0111.3 A-DPF ἀθεμίτοις (1x)
1Pe 4:3 drinking·parties, and shamefully·illicit idolatries,

G0112 ἄ•θεος áthêôs *adj.* (1x)
Roots:G0001 G2316
G0112 A-NPM ἄθεοι (1x)
Eph 2:12 ·of·Resurrection, and without·God in the world.

G0113 ἄ•θεσμος áthêsmôs *adj.* (2x)
Roots:G0001 G2330-3 Compare:G0459 G0111
G2556 See:G2330-3
G0113.2 A-GPM ἀθέσμων (2x)
2Pe 2:7 the behavior of·the unscrupulous·men in debauchery
2Pe 3:17 of·the unscrupulous·men, yeu·should·fall·from

G0114 ἀ•θετέω athêtéō *v.* (16x)
Roots:G0001 G5087 Compare:G0593 G0579 G0659
G0554
G0114.1 V-PAI-1S-C ἀθετῶ (1x)
Gal 2:21 "I·do·not set·aside the grace of·God, for if
G0114.1 V-PAI-2P ἀθετεῖτε (1x)
Mk 7:9 Clearly·full·well do·yeu·set·aside the commandment
G0114.1 V-PAI-3S ἀθετεῖ (1x)
Gal 3:15 not·even·one·man sets·it·aside or adds·stipulations
G0114.1 V-AAI-3P ἠθέτησαν (1x)
1Ti 5:12 ·held·in judgment, because they·set·aside the first
G0114.1 V-AAP-NSM ἀθετήσας (1x)
Heb 10:28 Anyone setting·aside Moses' Torah-Law died
G0114.2 V-PAI-3S ἀθετεῖ (3x)
Lk 10:16 and the·one ignoring yeu ignores me; and the·one
Lk 10:16 the·one ignoring me ignores the·one dispatching
1Th 4:8 *it·is* not a·man·of·clay† *that* he·ignores, but·rather
G0114.2 V-PAI-3P ἀθετοῦσιν (1x)
Jud 1:8 contaminate flesh, ignore sovereign·lordship, and
G0114.2 V-PAP-NSM ἀθετῶν (4x)
Jn 12:48 "The·one presently·ignoring me and not receiving
Lk 10:16 listens·to me; and the·one ignoring yeu ignores me
Lk 10:16 me; and the·one ignoring me ignores the·one
1Th 4:8 the·one presently·ignoring *this calling·forth, it·is*
G0114.2 V-AAI-3P ἠθέτησαν (1x)
Lk 7:30 and the experts·in·Torah-Law refused the counsel
G0114.3 V-AAN ἀθετῆσαι (1x)
Mk 6:26 ·at·the·meal, he·did·not want to·refuse her.
G0114.4 V-FAI-1S ἀθετήσω (1x)
1Co 1:19 of·the wise and shall·invalidate the discernment of·

G0115 ἀ•θέτησις athétēsis *n.* (2x)
Roots:G0114
G0115 N-NSF ἀθέτησις (1x)
Heb 7:18 ·fact, a·cancellation of·a·preceding commandment
G0115 N-ASF ἀθέτησιν (1x)
Heb 9:26 for a·cancellation of·moral·failure through the

G0116 Ἀθῆναι Athē̂nai *n/l.* (4x)
G0116.2 N/L-DPF Ἀθήναις (2x)
Ac 17:16 while·Paul was·waiting·for them at Athens, his
1Th 3:1 we·took·delight to·be·left·behind in Athens alone,
G0116.2 N/L-GPF Ἀθηνῶν (2x)
Ac 17:15 Paul brought him as·far·as to Athens. And they·
Ac 18:1 came to Corinth, being·deported out of·Athens,

G0117 Ἀθηναῖος Athēnaîôs *adj/g.* (2x)
Roots:G0116
G0117.1 A/G-NPM Ἀθηναῖοι (1x)
Ac 17:21 (Now all Athenians and the foreigners temporarily·

G0117.1 A/G-VPM Ἀθηναῖοι (1x)
Ac 17:22 replied, "Men, Athenians, I·observe how in all·

G0118 ἀθλέω athlḗō *v.* (2x)

G0118 V-PAS-3S ἀθλῇ (1x)
2Ti 2:5 if someone should·contend *in·athletic·competition,*

G0118 V-AAS-3S ἀθλήσῃ (1x)
2Ti 2:5 ·crowned unless he·should·contend legitimately.

G0119 ἄθλησις áthlēsis *n.* (1x)
Roots:G0118 Compare:G0073 G3823

G0119.2 N-ASF ἄθλησιν (1x)
Heb 10:32 ·endured a·large struggle of·afflictions—

G0120 ἀ•θυμέω athyméō *v.* (1x)
Roots:G0001 G2372 Compare:G1573

G0120.2 V-PAS-3P ἀθυμῶσιν (1x)
Col 3:21 ·irritate yeur children, lest they·should·be·dejected.

G0121 ἄ•θῳος áthōos *adj.* (2x)
Roots:G0001 G5087 Compare:G0172 G0273 G0298 See:G0121-1

G0121.2 A-ASN ἀθῷον (1x)
Mt 27:4 ·failed in·handing·over blood *that·is* without·fault."

G0121.3 A-NSM ἀθῷος (1x)
Mt 27:24 saying, "I·am blameless of the blood of·this

G0122 αἴγειος aígêios *adj.* (1x)
Compare:G2055 G2056 G5131 xLangAlso:H5795

G0122 A-DPN αἰγείοις (1x)
Heb 11:37 in sheepskins *and* in wild·goat hides, being·

G0123 αἰγι•αλός aigialós *n.* (7x)
Roots:G0251 Compare:G5491

G0123 N-ASM αἰγιαλόν (6x)
Jn 21:4 ·dawn, Jesus stood·still upon the shore; however, the
Ac 21:5 And bowing the knees on the shore, we·prayed.
Ac 27:39 ·fully·observing a·certain bay having a·shore, into
Ac 27:40 ·wind, they·were·bearing·down toward the shore.
Mt 13:2 ·down *there*; and all the crowd stood on the shore.
Mt 13:48 after·hauling *it* to the shore and sitting·down,

EG0123 (1x)
Ac 27:13 they·were·sailing·near Crete, very·close·to *shore*.

G0124 Αἰγύπτιος Aigýptiôs *adj/g.* (5x)
מִצְרִי mitsriy [Hebrew]
Roots:G0125
xLangEquiv:H4713

G0124.1 A/G-NSM Αἰγύπτιος (1x)
Ac 21:38 you·yourself not then the Egyptian, *the·one* before

G0124.1 A/G-NPM Αἰγύπτιοι (1x)
Heb 11:29 parched·ground, of·which the Egyptians (taking

G0124.1 A/G-ASM Αἰγύπτιον (2x)
Ac 7:24 ·down·in·labored·anguish, smiting the Egyptian.
Ac 7:28 me, as you·executed the Egyptian yesterday?

G0124.1 A/G-GPM Αἰγυπτίων (1x)
Ac 7:22 ·disciplined in·all *the* wisdom of·the·Egyptians, and

G0125 Αἴγυπτος Aígyptôs *n/l.* (24x)
מִצְרַיִם mitsrayim [Hebrew]
See:G0124
xLangEquiv:H4714

G0125 N/L-NSF Αἴγυπτος (1x)
Rv 11:8 spiritually is·called Sodom and Egypt, where also

G0125 N/L-ASF Αἴγυπτον (9x)
Ac 2:10 *in* Phrygia and PamPhylia, *in* Egypt and *in* the parts
Ac 7:9 ·jealous, sold Joseph away into Egypt. But God was
Ac 7:10 ·established him, governing over Egypt and all his
Ac 7:15 So Jacob walked·down into Egypt, and he·
Ac 7:34 come·over·here, I·shall·dispatch you into Egypt."
Ac 7:39 in·their hearts, they·turned·back·around to Egypt,
Heb 11:27 By·trust, he·forsook Egypt (not fearing the rage
Mt 2:13 his mother, and flee into Egypt, and be there until I·
Mt 2:14 and his mother by·night and departed into Egypt.

G0125 N/L-DSF Αἰγύπτῳ (6x)
Ac 7:12 after·hearing·of there·being grain in Egypt, Jacob
Ac 7:17 the People grew and were·multiplied in Egypt,
Ac 7:34 of·my People *who·are* in Egypt, and I·heard their
Ac 13:17 in the Sojourning in *the* land of·Egypt, and with a·
Heb 11:26 *than* the treasures in Egypt, for he·was·intently·
Mt 2:19 ·to a·vision·in·a·dream) appears to·Joseph in Egypt,

G0125 N/L-GSF Αἰγύπτου (8x)
Ac 7:10 ·the·direct·presence of·Pharaoh king of·Egypt, and
Ac 7:11 a·famine over all the land of·Egypt and Kenaan, and
Ac 7:36 wonders and signs in *the* land of·Egypt, and in *the*
Ac 7:40 who brought us out of·*the*·land of·Egypt, we·do·not
Heb 3:16 ·*so* after·coming·forth out of·Egypt through Moses
Heb 8:9 to·lead them out of·*the*·land of·Egypt, because they·
Mt 2:15 saying, "From·out of·Egypt I·called·forth my son.
Jud 1:5 after·*first*·saving a·People out of·Egypt's land, the

G0126 ἀΐδιος aḯdiôs *adj.* (2x)
Roots:G0104 Compare:G0166 G0104-1

G0126.1 A-NSM ἀΐδιος (1x)
Rm 1:20 ·clearly·seen, both his supra-eternal power and

G0126.2 A-DPM ἀϊδίοις (1x)
Jud 1:6 he·has·reserved *them* in·supra-lasting bonds under

G0127 α•ἰδώς aidṓs *n.* (2x)
Roots:G0001 G1492

G0127.2 N-GSF αἰδοῦς (2x)
Heb 12:28 with modesty·of·conduct and devotion,
1Ti 2:9 ·apparel with modesty·of·conduct and self-control.

G0128 Αἰθί•οψ Aithíôps *n/g.* (2x)
כּוּשׁ kûsh [Hebrew]
Roots:G3700
xLangEquiv:H3568

G0128.1 N/G-GPM Αἰθιόπων (1x)
Ac 8:27 of·Candace, the queen of·the·Ethiopians, who was

G0128.2 N/G-NSM Αἰθίοψ (1x)
Ac 8:27 and behold, *there·was* a·man of·Ethiopia, a·eunuch,

G0129 αἷμα haîma *n.* (102x)
xLangEquiv:H1818

G0129.1 N-NSN αἷμα (22x)
Jn 6:55 is a·full·meal, and my blood truly is a·full·drink.
Jn 19:34 ·tip·of·a·lance, and straight·away blood and water
Lk 11:50 in·order·that the blood of·all the prophets, the
Ac 18:6 to them, "Yeur blood *be* upon yeur own·heads; I·
Ac 22:20 And when the blood of·your martyr Stephen was·
Heb 9:13 For if the blood of·bulls and of·adult·male·goats
Heb 9:14 ·much more shall the blood of·the Anointed-One,
Heb 9:20 "This *is* the blood of·the covenant which God
Heb 10:4 For *it·is* impossible *for·the* blood of·bulls and of·
Heb 13:11 of·these animals, whose blood is·carried into the
Mt 16:17 because flesh and blood did·not reveal *this* to·you
Mt 23:35 all *the* righteous blood being·poured·out upon the
Mt 26:28 for this is my blood, the·one of·the brand-new
Mt 27:25 all the people declared, "His blood *be* on us and on
Mk 14:24 "This is my blood, the·one of·the brand-new
1Co 15:50 that flesh and blood is·not able to·inherit God's
1Jn 1:7 with one·another, and the blood of·Jesus Anointed,
1Jn 5:8 and the water, and the blood. And the three are in
Rv 8:8 the sea, and the third·part of·the sea became blood;
Rv 14:20 outside the City, and blood came·forth out of·the
Rv 16:3 the sea, and it·became as blood of·a·dead·man. And
Rv 16:4 the wellsprings of·waters, and they·became blood.

G0129.1 N-ASN αἷμα (21x)
Jn 6:53 ·Man†, and should·drink his blood, yeu·do·not have
Jn 6:54 flesh, and drinking my blood, has eternal life-above,
Jn 6:56 my flesh, and drinking my blood, abides in me, and·
Lk 13:1 the Galileans, whose blood Pilate mixed with their
Ac 2:19 on the earth down·below: blood and fire and vapor
Ac 2:20 into darkness and the moon into blood, prior·to the
Ac 5:28 yeu·resolve to·bring the blood of·this man·of·clay†
Ac 21:25 the·thing sacrificed·to·an·idol, *from* blood, *from* a·
Heb 9:19 the People, after·taking the blood of·calves and of·
Heb 10:29 resolutely·considering the blood of·the covenant
Mt 27:4 ·failed in·handing·over blood *that·is* without·fault."
Rm 3:15 "Their feet *are* swift to·pour·out blood.
Eph 6:12 ·our wrestling specifically·against blood and flesh,
Rv 6:10 judge and avenge our blood on the·ones residing on
Rv 6:12 made·of·hair, and the moon became as blood,
Rv 11:6 the waters to·turn them into blood, and to·smite the
Rv 12:11 overcame him through the blood of·the Lamb, and
Rv 16:6 Because they·poured·out *the* blood of·holy·ones and
Rv 16:6 prophets, and you·gave them blood to·drink, for
Rv 18:24 "And in her was·found *the* blood of·prophets, and
Rv 19:2 and he·avenged the blood of·his slaves *poured·out*

G0129.1 N-DSN αἵματι (20x)
Lk 22:20 *is* the brand-new covenant in my blood, the *blood*
Heb 9:21 the Tabernacle also with·the blood, and all the
Heb 9:22 ·to the Torah-Law, are·purified with blood. And
Heb 9:25 ·of·Holies each year with another·*animal's* blood.
Heb 10:19 brothers, by the blood of·YeShua, having
Heb 12:24 to·sprinkled blood speaking significantly·better·
Heb 13:20 of·the sheep by an·eternal blood covenant)—
Gal 1:16 I·did·not immediately confer with·flesh and blood,
Mt 23:30 be partners with·them in the blood of·the prophets.
Rm 3:25 through the trust in his blood (as an·indicator of·his
Rm 5:9 being·regarded·as·righteous by his blood, so·much
1Pe 1:19 but·rather *it·was* with·precious blood, as of·a·
1Co 11:25 is the brand-new covenant in my blood. Do this,
Eph 2:13 are·made near by the blood of·the Anointed-One.
1Jn 5:6 but·rather by the water and the blood. And the Spirit
Rv 1:5 us *clean* from our moral·failures in his·own blood.
Rv 5:9 us to·God by your blood— from·out of·every tribe,
Rv 7:14 ·whitened their long·robes in the blood of·the Lamb.
Rv 8:7 hail and fire having·been·mixed with·blood, and
Rv 19:13 ·with a·garment having·been·dipped in·blood, and

G0129.1 N-GSN αἵματος (35x)
Lk 8:43 And a·woman being with a·flow of·blood for twelve
Lk 8:44 garment, and at·once her flow of·blood stood·still.
Lk 11:51 from the blood of·Abel until the blood of·
Lk 11:51 blood of·Abel until the blood of·ZecharYah, the·
Lk 22:44 became like clots of·blood dropping·down upon
Ac 1:19 AqelDama, that·is, an·open·field of·blood.)
Ac 15:20 and *from* the strangled·animal, and *from* the blood.
Ac 15:29 ·things·sacrificed·to·idols, and from·blood, and
Ac 17:26 Also, from·out·of·one blood he·made every nation
Ac 20:26 that I·myself *am* pure from the blood of·all *men*.
Ac 20:28 which he·himself·acquired through his·own blood.
Heb 2:14 ·a·common·fellowship of·flesh and blood, also he·
Heb 9:7 alone, *but* not apart·from blood, which he·offered
Heb 9:12 ·not through blood of·adult·male·goats and calves,
Heb 9:12 but he·entered through his·own blood into the
Heb 9:18 *covenant* has·been·inaugurated apart·from blood.
Heb 11:28 the pouring·out·and·application of·the blood, lest
Heb 12:4 as·far·as·unto *sweating* blood did·yeu·fully·resist,
Heb 13:12 ·holy the People through his·own blood, suffered
Mt 23:35 the earth, from the blood of·Abel the righteous,
Mt 23:35 ·Abel the righteous, unto the blood of·ZecharYah,
Mt 27:6 the Temple·Treasury, since it·is *the* price of·blood."
Mt 27:8 is·called *AqelDama*, "Field of·Blood", even·unto
Mt 27:24 I·am blameless of the blood of·this righteous·man.
Mk 5:25 woman being with a·flow of·blood *for* twelve years,
Mk 5:29 the well of·her blood was·dried·up, and she·knew
1Pe 1:2 ·attentive·obedience and a·sprinkling of·the·blood
1Co 10:16 fellowship of·the blood of·the Anointed-One?
1Co 11:27 ·be held·liable of·the body and blood of·the Lord.
Eph 1:7 the ransom·in·full through his blood— the pardon
Col 1:14 the ransom·in·full through his blood, the pardon of·
Col 1:20 ·making·peace through the blood of *Anointed-One's*
1Jn 5:6 is the·one coming through water and blood, Jesus the
Rv 17:6 ·drunk from·out·of·the blood of·the holy·ones, and
Rv 17:6 and from·out·of·the blood of·the martyrs of·Jesus.

G0129.1 N-GPN αἱμάτων (1x)
Jn 1:13 who are·born, not from·out of·blood, nor from·out

EG0129.1 (3x)
Lk 11:50 the prophets, the *blood* being·poured·out from *the*
Lk 22:20 in my blood, the *blood* being·poured·out on·yeur
1Pe 1:19 and without·stain, *the·blood* of·Anointed-One.

G0130 αἱματ•εκ•χυσία haimatêkchysía *n.* (1x)
Roots:G0129 G1632

G0130 N-GSF αἱματεκχυσίας (1x)
Heb 9:22 And apart·from a·pouring·out·of·blood, there·is no

G0131 αἱμο•ρρέω haimôrrhéō *v.* (1x)
Roots:G0129 G4482
G0131.2 V-PAP-NSF αἱμορροοῦσα (1x)
Mt 9:20 *badly·ill*, discharging·a·flow·of·blood *for* twelve

G0132 Αἰνέας Ainéas *n/p.* (2x)
G0132 N/P-VSM Αἰνέα (1x)
Ac 9:34 And Peter declared to·him, "Aeneas, Jesus the
G0132 N/P-ASM Αἰνέαν (1x)
Ac 9:33 he·found a·certain man·of·clay†, Aeneas by·name,

G0133 αἴνεσις aínêsis *n.* (1x)
Roots:G0134 See:G1868
G0133.1 N-GSF αἰνέσεως (1x)
Heb 13:15 ·carry·up a·sacrifice of·praise to·God continually,

G0134 αἰνέω ainéō *v.* (10x)
Roots:G0136 Compare:G0239 G2988 See:G0133 G1868 xLangAlso:H3034 H1984
G0134 V-PAN αἰνεῖν (1x)
Lk 19:37 began rejoicing, praising God with·a·loud voice
G0134 V-PAP-GPM αἰνούντων (1x)
Lk 2:13 a·multitude of·*the*·heavenly host praising God and
G0134 V-PAP-NPM αἰνοῦντες (2x)
Lk 2:20 returned, glorifying and praising God over all·the·
Lk 24:53 in the Sanctuary·Atrium, praising and blessing
G0134.3 V-FAI-1S αἰνέσω (1x)
Heb 2:12 of·*the*·gathering, I·shall·splendidly·praise you."
G0134.3 V-PAM-2P αἰνεῖτε (2x)
Rm 15:11 And again, "Splendidly·praise Yahweh, all the
Rv 19:5 throne, saying, "Splendidly·praise our God, all·yeu
G0134.3 V-PAP-ASM αἰνοῦντα (1x)
Ac 3:9 saw him walking·along and splendidly·praising God.
G0134.3 V-PAP-NSM αἰνῶν (1x)
Ac 3:8 ·along and leaping and splendidly·praising God.
G0134.3 V-PAP-NPM αἰνοῦντες (1x)
Ac 2:47 splendidly·praising God, and having grace alongside

G0135 αἴνιγμα aínigma *n.* (1x)
Roots:G0136 xLangAlso:H2420
G0135.4 N-DSN αἰνίγματι (1x)
1Co 13:12 a·reflected·image with an·obscured·view, but

G0136 αἶνος aînôs *n.* (2x)
Compare:G1868 See:G0133 xLangAlso:H5797
G0136.3 N-ASM αἶνον (2x)
Lk 18:43 all the people seeing *it*, gave strong·praise to·God.
Mt 21:16 sucklings you·completely·formed strong·praise"?

G0137 Αἰνών Ainṓn *n/l.* (1x)
עַיִן 'ayin [Hebrew]
Roots:H5869
xLangEquiv:A5870
G0137.3 N/L-PRI Αἰνών (1x)
Jn 3:23 also was immersing in Ainon near to·Salim because

G0138 αἱρέομαι hairéômai *v.* (3x)
ἕλλομαι héllômai
[a cognate form, which is otherwise obsolete]
Compare:G1209 G1586 G2983 G4977 See:G0142 G0141 G0234-1 G0830
G0138.2 V-FMI-1S αἱρήσομαι (1x)
Php 1:22 Even·so, I·do·not really·know what I·shall·choose.
G0138.2 V-2AMI-3S εἵλετο (1x)
2Th 2:13 from *the* beginning, God chose yeu for Salvation
G0138.2 V-2AMP-NSM ἑλόμενος (1x)
Heb 11:25 choosing rather to·be·maltreated·together with·

G0139 αἵρεσις haírêsis *n.* (9x)
Roots:G0138 Compare:G4978 G0592
G0139.4 N-NPF αἱρέσεις (1x)
1Co 11:19 ·for *there* also to·be factions among yeu, in·order·
G0139.5 N-ASF αἵρεσιν (1x)
Ac 24:14 Way which they·say *is* a·sect, in·this·manner I·
G0139.5 N-GSF αἱρέσεως (2x)
Ac 24:5 *being* a·champion of·the sect of·the Natsarethans,
Ac 28:22 for in·fact, as·concerning this sect, it·is known to·
G0139.6 N-NSF αἵρεσις (1x)
Ac 5:17 with·him (being the denomination of·the Sadducees)
G0139.6 N-ASF αἵρεσιν (1x)
Ac 26:5 ·to the most·strict denomination of·our religion, I·
G0139.6 N-GSF αἱρέσεως (1x)
Ac 15:5 certain·men from the denomination of·the Pharisees
G0139.7 N-NPF αἱρέσεις (1x)
Gal 5:20 dissensions, factions·and·denominations,
G0139.7 N-APF αἱρέσεις (1x)
2Pe 2:1 shall·privately·introduce factions·and·denominations

G0140 αἱρετίζω hairetízō *v.* (1x)
Roots:G0138 Compare:G2309 See:G0141
G0140.2 V-AAI-1S ᾑρέτισα (1x)
Mt 12:18 my servant·boy, whom I·decidedly·chose, my

G0141 αἱρετικός hairêtikós *adj.* (1x)
Roots:G0138 Compare:G0140 G4978 G0830
G0141 A-ASM αἱρετικόν (1x)
Tit 3:10 a·man·of·clay† that·is·divisively·selective after a·

G0142 αἴρω aírō *v.* (103x)
Compare:G0941 G1308 See:G1869 G0733-1 xLangAlso:H5375
G0142.1 V-FAI-3P ἀροῦσιν (2x)
Lk 4:11 and "They·shall·lift you upon *their* palms, lest·at·
Mt 4:6 you," and "They·shall·lift you upon *their* palms,
G0142.1 V-AAI-3S ἦρεν (2x)
Jn 11:41 And Jesus lifted the eyes upward and declared,
Rv 10:5 upon the sea and upon the earth lifted his hand to the
G0142.1 V-AAI-3P ἦραν (2x)
Lk 17:13 and they·themselves lifted·*up* *their* voices, saying,
Ac 4:24 after·hearing *it*, they·lifted·*up* their·voice toward
G0142.1 V-AAS-3S ἄρῃ (1x)
Mt 27:32 ·upon this·man that he·should·lift·*up* his cross.
G0142.2 V-FAI-3P ἀροῦσιν (1x)
Mk 16:18 "they·shall·take·up serpents; and·if they·should·
G0142.2 V-PAI-2S αἴρεις (1x)
Lk 19:21 man·of·clay†. You·take·up what you·did·not lay·
G0142.2 V-PAM-2P αἴρετε (1x)
Lk 9:3 to them, "Take·up not·even·one·thing for the journey
G0142.2 V-PAP-NSM αἴρων (1x)
Lk 19:22 man·of·clay†, taking·up what I·did·not lay·down,
G0142.2 V-PAS-3P αἴρωσιν (1x)
Mk 6:8 them that they·should·take·up not·even·one·thing for
G0142.2 V-AAI-2P ἤρατε (2x)
Mk 8:19 wicker·baskets full of·fragments did·yeu·take·up?"
Mk 8:20 completely·full of·fragments did·yeu·take·up?"
G0142.2 V-AAI-3S ἦρεν (2x)
Jn 5:9 was healthy·and·sound. And he·took·up his mat and
Rv 18:21 And one strong angel took·up a·stone as a·great
G0142.2 V-AAI-3P ἦραν (5x)
Jn 8:59 So·then they·took·up stones in·order·that they·may·
Mt 14:20 ·full. And they·took·up the remaining·excess of·
Mt 15:37 ·full. And they·took·up seven woven·baskets full
Mk 6:43 And they·took·up twelve wicker·baskets full of·
Mk 8:8 ·full. And they·took·up an·abundance of·fragments,
G0142.2 V-AAM-2S ἆρον (8x)
Jn 5:8 to·him, "Be·awakened, take·up your mat and walk.
Jn 5:11 that·man declared to·me, 'Take·up your mat and
Jn 5:12 the·one declaring to·you, 'Take·up your mat and
Mt 9:6 "Upon·being·awakened, take·up your simple·couch
Mt 17:27 to the sea, cast a·hook and take·up the first fish
Mt 20:14 Take·up the·thing *that·is* yours and head·on·out.
Mk 2:9 'Be·awakened, and take·up your mat and walk'?
Mk 2:11 to·you, be·awakened, and take·up your mat, and
G0142.2 V-AAM-2P ἄρατε (1x)
Mt 11:29 Take·up my yoke upon yeu, and learn from me,
G0142.2 V-AAM-3S ἀράτω (4x)
Lk 9:23 he·must·utterly·deny himself and take·up his cross
Lk 22:36 the·one having a·pouch, let·him·take·it·up, and
Mt 16:24 he·must·utterly·deny himself, take·up his cross,
Mk 8:34 let·him·utterly·deny himself, and take·up his cross,
G0142.2 V-AAN ἆραι (2x)
Jn 5:10 It·is·not proper for·you to·take·up *your* mat."
Mk 13:16 to the·things left·behind to·take·up his garment.
G0142.2 V-AAP-NSM ἄρας (6x)
Lk 5:24 to·you, be·awakened, and taking·up your pallet,
Lk 5:25 ·sight of·them, taking·up what he·was·laying·down
Ac 21:11 And after·coming to us and taking·up Paul's belt,
Mk 2:12 he·is·awakened, and after·taking·up the mat, he·
Mk 10:21 And come·over·here! Upon·taking·up the cross,
1Co 6:15 Now·then, after·taking·up the members of·
G0142.2 V-AAP-NPM ἄραντες (1x)
Ac 27:17 Which after·taking·*it*·up, they·used emergency·
G0142.2 V-AAS-2S ἄρῃς (1x)
Jn 17:15 "I·do·not ask that you·should·take them up out·
G0142.2 V-AAS-3S ἄρῃ (1x)
Mk 15:21 Rufus), in·order·that he·should·take·up his cross.
G0142.2 V-API-3S ἤρθη (2x)
Lk 9:17 And the remaining·excess taken·up by·them *was*
Ac 20:9 down from the third·story and was·taken·up dead.
G0142.3 V-FAI-1S ἀρῶ (1x)
Jn 20:15 where you·laid him, and·I shall·take him away."
G0142.3 V-FAI-3P ἀροῦσιν (1x)
Jn 11:48 Romans shall·come and shall·take·away both our
G0142.3 V-FPI-3S ἀρθήσεται (6x)
Lk 8:18 from him shall·be·taken·away even that·which he·
Lk 19:26 even what he·has shall·be·taken·away from him).
Mt 13:12 that·which he·has shall·be·taken·away from him.
Mt 21:43 the kingdom of·God shall·be·taken·away from yeu
Mt 25:29 that·which he·has shall·be·taken·away from him).
Mk 4:25 that·which he·has shall·be·taken·away from him."
G0142.3 V-PAI-3S αἴρει (8x)
Jn 10:18 "Not·even·one·man takes it away from me, but·
Jn 15:2 bearing fruit, *the* same he·takes·away; and any *vine*·
Jn 16:22 and not·even·one·man takes·away yeur joy from
Lk 8:12 Slanderer, and he·takes·away the Redemptive-word
Lk 11:22 *him forcefully*, he·takes·away his whole·armor in
Mt 9:16 for *when·shrunk*, it·takes·away its complete·fullness
Mk 2:21 *when·shrunk*, takes·away its complete·fullness
Mk 4:15 and he·takes·away the Redemptive-word, the·one
G0142.3 V-PAM-2S αἶρε (3x)
Lk 23:18 ·screamed·out, saying, "Away·with this·man, and
Ac 21:36 were·following, yelling·out, "Take him away."
Ac 22:22 voices, saying, "Away·with such·a·man from the
G0142.3 V-PAP-GSM αἴροντος (2x)
Lk 6:29 and of·the·one taking·away your outer·garment,
Lk 6:30 you, and of·the·one taking·away your things, do·not
G0142.3 V-PAP-NSM αἴρων (1x)
Jn 1:29 of·God, the·one taking·away the moral·failure of·the
G0142.3 V-PPI-3S αἴρεται (1x)
Ac 8:33 Because his life† is·taken·away from the earth."
G0142.3 V-AAI-2P ἤρατε (1x)
Lk 11:52 ·in·Torah-Law! Because yeu·took·away the key
G0142.3 V-AAI-3S ἦρεν (2x)
Jn 19:38 So he·came and took·away the body of·Jesus.
Mt 24:39 came, and took·away absolutely·all·of·them. "In·
G0142.3 V-AAI-3P ἦραν (5x)
Jn 11:41 So·then they·took·away the stone *from the place*
Jn 20:2 she·says to·them, "They·took·away the Lord from·
Jn 20:13 ·says to·them, "Because they·took·away my Lord,
Mt 14:12 after·coming·alongside, took·away the body and
Mk 6:29 *of·it*, they·came and took·away his corpse and laid
G0142.3 V-AAM-2S ἆρον (2x)
Jn 19:15 they·yelled·out, "Take·*him*·away, take·*him*·away,
Jn 19:15 ·out, "Take·*him*·away, take·*him*·away, crucify him
G0142.3 V-AAM-2P ἄρατε (5x)
Jn 2:16 the doves, "Take·away these·things from·here. Do·
Jn 11:39 Jesus says, "Take·away the stone." Martha, the
Lk 19:24 to·the·ones standing·nearby, 'Take·away the mina
Mt 22:13 him hand and foot, take him away and cast·*him*·
Mt 25:28 So·then, take·away the talant·of·silver from him
G0142.3 V-AAN ἆραι (4x)
Lk 17:31 the home, must·not walk·down to·take them away;
Mt 24:17 must·not walk·down to·take·away anything out of·
Mt 24:18 *to the·things* left·behind to·take·away his garments.
Mk 13:15 nor·even enter *it*, to·take·away anything out·of·his
G0142.3 V-AAS-3S ἄρῃ (3x)
Jn 19:38 asked·of Pilate that he·may·take·away the body

Mk 15:24 upon them, *as·to* who should·take·away what.
1Jn 3:5 in·order·that he·should·take·away our moral·failures,
G0142.3 V-API-3S ἤρθη (1x)
Ac 8:33 humiliation, his verdict was·taken·away. And who
G0142.3 V-APM-2S ἄρθητι (2x)
Mt 21:21 to·this mountain, 'Be·taken·away and be·you·cast
Mk 11:23 to·this mountain, 'Be·taken·away, and be·you·
G0142.3 V-APS-3P ἀρθῶσιν (1x)
Jn 19:31 ·broken·apart, and *that* they·should·be·taken·away.
G0142.3 V-RAI-3S ἦρκεν (1x)
Col 2:14 ·opposed to·us), and he·has·taken it away out of·
G0142.3 V-RPP-ASM ἠρμένον (1x)
Jn 20:1 the stone having·been·taken·away from·among the
EG0142.3 (1x)
Lk 6:29 ·not prevent *him from* taking·away *your* inner·tunic
G0142.5 V-PAI-2S αἴρεις (1x)
Jn 10:24 "How·long are·you·keeping our soul in·suspense?
G0142.6 V-AAP-NPM ἄραντες (1x)
Ac 27:13 after·taking·up·anchor, they·were·sailing·near
G0142.8 V-APM-3S ἀρθήτω (1x)
Eph 4:31 yelling, and revilement, be·expunged from yeu,
G0142.9 V-PPP-ASM αἰρόμενον (1x)
Mk 2:3 bringing a·paralyzed·man being·carried by four·men.

G0143 αἰσθάνομαι aisthánômai *v.* (1x)
Compare:G1492 G3539 G4920 G1252 See:G0144 G0145
G0143.1 V-2ADS-3P αἴσθωνται (1x)
Lk 9:45 them, in·order·that they·should·not perceive it. And

G0144 αἴσθησις aísthēsis *n.* (1x)
Roots:G0143 Compare:G1922 G2924 See:G0145
G0144.2 N-DSF αἰσθήσει (1x)
Php 1:9 ·and·full·knowledge and with·all keen·perception,

G0145 αἰσθητήριον aisthētḗriôn *n.* (1x)
Roots:G0143 See:G0144 G0145-1
G0145.2 N-APN αἰσθητήρια (1x)
Heb 5:14 *their* abilities·of·perception having·been·trained

G0146 αἰσχρο•κερδής aischrôkêrdḗs *adj.* (3x)
Roots:G0150 G2771 See:G0147
G0146 A-ASM αἰσχροκερδῆ (2x)
Tit 1:7 ·near·wine, not a·violent·man, not of·shameful·gain,
1Ti 3:3 not a·violent·man, not of·shameful·gain, but·rather
G0146 A-APM αἰσχροκερδεῖς (1x)
1Ti 3:8 giving·heed to·much wine, not of·shameful·gain,

G0147 αἰσχρο•κερδῶς aischrôkêrdō̂s *adv.* (1x)
Roots:G0146
G0147 ADV αἰσχροκερδῶς (1x)
1Pe 5:2 voluntarily; nor·even for·shameful·gain, but·rather

G0148 αἰσχρο•λογία aischrôlôgía *n.* (1x)
Roots:G0150 G3056 Compare:G3473 See:G0151
G0148 N-ASF αἰσχρολογίαν (1x)
Col 3:8 *and* shameful·conversation from·out of·yeur mouth.

G0149 αἰσχρόν aischrṓn *adj.* (2x)
Roots:G0150
G0149 A-NSN αἰσχρόν (2x)
1Co 14:35 home. For it·is shameful for·women to·speak in
Eph 5:12 For it·is shameful even to·refer·to the·things

G0150 αἰσχρός aischrṓs *adj.* (2x)
Compare:G0153 See:G0146 G0149 G0151
G0150.1 A-NSN αἰσχρόν (1x)
1Co 11:6 but if *it·is* shameful for·a·woman to·be·shorn or
G0150.1 A-GSN αἰσχροῦ (1x)
Tit 1:11 through·gracious·sounding·words for·shameful gain.

G0151 αἰσχρότης aischrṓtēs *n.* (1x)
Roots:G0150 See:G0148
G0151 N-NSF αἰσχρότης (1x)
Eph 5:4 *nor* even an·obscenity, or foolish·conversation, or

G0152 αἰσχύνη aischýnē *n.* (6x)
Roots:G0153 Compare:G1791 G0819 xLangAlso:H1322
G0152 N-NSF αἰσχύνη (1x)
Rv 3:18 and *that* the shame of·your nakedness may·not be·
G0152 N-APF αἰσχύνας (1x)
Jud 1:13 ·foaming·upon their·own shame, erratic·wandering
G0152 N-DSF αἰσχύνῃ (1x)
Php 3:19 *whose* glory *is* in their shame. *These are* the·ones
G0152 N-GSF αἰσχύνης (3x)
Lk 14:9 you·should·begin with shame to·fully·hold·onto the
Heb 12:2 him, patiently·endured a·cross of·shame, despising
2Co 4:2 we·have·renounced the hidden·things of·shame, not

G0153 αἰσχύνομαι aischýnômai *v.* (5x)
Compare:G1788 See:G1870 G2617 xLangEquiv:H0954
G0153.2 V-FPI-1S αἰσχυνθήσομαι (2x)
Php 1:20 not·even·one·thing shall·I·be·ashamed, but·rather
2Co 10:8 not for yeur demolition), I·shall·not be·ashamed,
G0153.2 V-PEI-1S αἰσχύνομαι (1x)
Lk 16:3 ·strength to·dig; I·am·ashamed to·ask·for·charity.
G0153.2 V-PPM-3S αἰσχυνέσθω (1x)
1Pe 4:16 ·of·Anointed-One, do·not let·him·be·ashamed, but
G0153.2 V-APS-1P αἰσχυνθῶμεν (1x)
1Jn 2:28 ·of·speech, and may·not be·ashamed before him at

G0154 αἰτέω aitéō *v.* (71x)
Compare:G2065 G1905 G4441 G1833 G1567 See:G0155 G0155-1 G0156 xLangAlso:H7592
G0154.1 V-FAI-3S αἰτήσει (2x)
Lk 11:11 among·yeu, *if* the son shall·request bread, ¿! shall·
1Jn 5:16 *which·is* not unto death, he·shall·request, and *God*
G0154.1 V-FAI-3P αἰτήσουσιν (1x)
Lk 12:48 ·of much, from·him they·shall·request much·more.
G0154.1 V-FMI-1S αἰτήσομαι (1x)
Mk 6:24 to·her mother, "What shall·I·request?" And she·
G0154.1 V-FMI-2P αἰτήσεσθε (2x)
Jn 15:7 should·abide in yeu, yeu·shall·request whatever yeu·
Jn 16:26 "At that day, yeu·shall·request in my name, and I·
G0154.1 V-PAI-2S αἰτεῖς (1x)
Jn 4:9 being a·Jew, request *some* to·drink personally·from
G0154.1 V-PAI-2P αἰτεῖτε (1x)
Jac 4:3 Yeu·request and do·not receive on·account·that yeu·
G0154.1 V-PAI-3P αἰτοῦσιν (1x)
1Co 1:22 And whereas Jews request a·sign, and·also Greeks
G0154.1 V-PAM-2P αἰτεῖτε (3x)
Jn 16:24 in my name. "Request, and yeu·shall·receive, in·
Lk 11:9 "And·I·myself say to·yeu, request, and it·shall·be·
Mt 7:7 "Request, and it·shall·be·given yeu; seek, and yeu·
G0154.1 V-PAM-3S αἰτείτω (2x)
Jac 1:5 of·wisdom, let·him·request personally·from God,
Jac 1:6 But let·him·request in trust, hesitating *for* not·even·
G0154.1 V-PAN αἰτεῖν (1x)
Ac 3:2 ·and·Elegant, to·request the merciful·act·of·charity
G0154.1 V-PAP-DSM αἰτοῦντι (3x)
Lk 6:30 But give to·every one requesting·of you, and of·the·
Mt 5:42 "Give to·the·one requesting·of you, and you·should·
1Pe 3:15 defense to·every·man requesting·of yeu a·reason
G0154.1 V-PAP-DPM αἰτοῦσιν (2x)
Lk 11:13 ·give Holy Spirit to·the·ones requesting·of him?
Mt 7:11 ·good·things to·the·ones requesting·of him?
G0154.1 V-PAP-NSF αἰτοῦσα (1x)
Mt 20:20 *to·him* and requesting something personally·from
G0154.1 V-PAP-NSM αἰτῶν (2x)
Lk 11:10 "For everyone, the·one requesting receives, and
Mt 7:8 For any one requesting receives; and the·one seeking
G0154.1 V-PAS-1P αἰτῶμεν (1x)
1Jn 3:22 And whatever·thing we·may·request, we·receive
G0154.1 V-PMI-1S αἰτοῦμαι (1x)
Eph 3:13 Therefore, I·request *yeu* not to·be·despondent in
G0154.1 V-PMI-1P αἰτούμεθα (1x)
Eph 3:20 us, those·things·which we·request or have·in·mind
G0154.1 V-PMI-2P αἰτεῖσθε (4x)
Mt 20:22 ·know what yeu·are·requesting. Are·yeu·able to·
Mk 10:38 ·know what yeu·are·requesting. Are·yeu·able to·
Mk 11:24 ·things·as yeu·would request as·yeu·are·praying,
Jac 4:3 do·not receive on·account·that yeu·request wrongly,
G0154.1 V-PMN αἰτεῖσθαι (2x)
Mk 15:8 upon·shouting·out, began to·request *for·him to·do*
Jac 4:2 yeu·do·not have, on·account *that* yeu do·not request.
G0154.1 V-PMP-NPM αἰτούμενοι (4x)
Lk 23:23 ·loud voices, requesting·for him to·be·crucified.
Ac 25:3 requesting an·influential·favor against *Paul*, that he·
Ac 25:15 ·it·clear *that* they·are·requesting justice against
Col 1:9 cease praying on·yeur behalf and requesting that—
G0154.1 V-PMS-1P αἰτώμεθα (2x)
1Jn 5:14 him, that if we·should·request anything according·
1Jn 5:15 ·thing we·might request, we·personally·know that
G0154.1 V-IMI-3P ᾐτοῦντο (3x)
Lk 23:25 and murder, whom they·requested. But he·handed
Ac 12:20 over the king's bedroom, they·requested peace, on·
Mk 15:6 ·prisoner, whom·specifically they·requested.
G0154.1 V-AAI-2S ᾔτησας (1x)
Jn 4:10 to·drink,' you would·have requested·of him, and
G0154.1 V-AAI-2P ᾐτήσατε (1x)
Jn 16:24 yeu·did·not request not·even·one·thing in my
G0154.1 V-AAM-2S αἴτησον (1x)
Mk 6:22 to·the young·girl, "Request·of me whatever you·
G0154.1 V-AAN αἰτῆσαι (1x)
Mt 6:8 yeu·yeurselves have the *need* to·request·of him.
G0154.1 V-AAP-NSM αἰτήσας (2x)
Lk 1:63 And requesting a·writing·tablet, he·wrote, saying,
Ac 16:29 So requesting lights, he·rushed·in, and being
G0154.1 V-AAS-1P αἰτήσωμεν (1x)
Mk 10:35 ·should·do for·us whatever we·should·request."
G0154.1 V-AAS-2S αἰτήσῃς (1x)
Mk 6:23 "Whatever you·should·request of·me, I·shall·give
G0154.1 V-AAS-2P αἰτήσητε (5x)
Jn 14:13 And anything that yeu·should·request in my name,
Jn 14:14 If yeu·should·request something in my name, I·
Jn 15:16 ·that whatever yeu·should·request·of the Father in
Jn 16:23 as·many·things·as yeu·would request·of the Father
Mt 21:22 And all·things, as·much·as yeu·may·request in the
G0154.1 V-AAS-3S αἰτήσῃ (3x)
Lk 11:12 Or also, if he·should·request an·egg, ¿! shall·he·
Mt 7:9 who if his son should·request bread, ¿! shall·hand
Mt 7:10 And if he·should·request a·fish, ¿! shall·hand him a·
G0154.1 V-AMI-2P ᾐτήσασθε (1x)
Ac 3:14 Holy and Righteous·One, and requested a·man, a·
G0154.1 V-AMI-3S ᾐτήσατο (6x)
Lk 23:52 after·coming·alongside Pilate, requested the body
Ac 7:46 of·God and requested to·find a·suitable·Tabernacle
Ac 9:2 he·requested personally·from him letters for
Mt 27:58 upon·coming·alongside Pilate, requested the body
Mk 6:25 with haste to the king, she·requested *it*, saying, "I·
Mk 15:43 he·went·in to Pilate and requested the body of·
G0154.1 V-AMI-3P ᾐτήσαντο (2x)
Ac 13:21 And·from·there, they·requested a·king, and God
Ac 13:28 *in·him, yet still* they·requested·of Pilate for·him to·
G0154.1 V-AMS-2S αἰτήσῃ (1x)
Jn 11:22 that as·much·as you·should·request·of God, God
G0154.1 V-AMS-3S αἰτήσηται (1x)
Mt 14:7 he·affirmed to·give her whatever she·may·request.
G0154.1 V-AMS-3P αἰτήσωνται (2x)
Mt 18:19 that they·may·request, it·shall·happen for·them
Mt 27:20 the crowds that they·should·request BarAbbas and
G0154.1 V-RAI-1P ᾐτήκαμεν (1x)
1Jn 5:15 ·things *that* we·have·requested personally·from him

G0155 αἴτημα aítēma *n.* (3x)
Compare:G1783 See:G0154 G0156
G0155.1 N-NSN αἴτημα (1x)
Lk 23:24 rendered·judgment *for* their request to·be·done.
G0155.1 N-APN αἰτήματα (2x)
Php 4:6 with thanksgiving) *these* requests of·yeurs, make·
1Jn 5:15 we·personally·know that we·have the requests,

G0156 αἰτία aitía *n.* (21x)
Compare:G3056 See:G0158 G0154 G0155
EG0156 (1x)
2Co 11:21 *this* according·to *the implied·charge·of* dishonor,
G0156.1 N-ASF αἰτίαν (11x)
Lk 8:47 on·account·of what cause she·laid·hold of·him, and
Ac 13:28 after·finding not·even·one cause of·death *in·him*,

Ac 22:24 what cause they·were·exclaiming in·this·manner
Ac 28:18 not subsisting even·one cause for·death within me.
Ac 28:20 on·account·of this cause, I·personally·called·for
Heb 2:11 *Father*. On·account·of which cause, *YeShua the*
Mt 19:3 to·divorce his wife for·each and·every cause?"
Mt 27:37 his head, they·placed the cause of·his *execution*,
Tit 1:13 is true. On·account·of which cause, reprove them
2Ti 1:6 ·account·of which cause I·remind·and·admonish you
2Ti 1:12 On·account·of which cause also I·suffer these·

G0156.1 N-GSF αἰτίας (1x)
Mk 15:26 ·was the inscription for·the cause of·his *execution*

G0156.2 N-NSF αἰτία (1x)
Ac 10:21 What *is* the motivation on·account·of which yeu·

G0156.3 N-ASF αἰτίαν (1x)
Ac 25:18 ·up not·even·one accusation of·such·things *as* I·

G0156.4 N-NSF αἰτία (1x)
Mt 19:10 to·him, "If the legal·charge of·the man·of·clay† is

G0156.4 N-ASF αἰτίαν (1x)
Ac 23:28 to·know the legal·charge on·account·of which

G0156.4 N-GSF αἰτίας (1x)
Ac 25:27 not also to·signify the legal·charge *laid* against him

G0156.5 N-ASF αἰτίαν (3x)
Jn 18:38 "I·myself find in him not·even·one fault.
Jn 19:4 yeu·may·know that I·find not·even·one fault in him."
Jn 19:6 and crucify *him*, for I·myself find no fault in him."

G0157 αἰτίαμα aitíama *n.* (1x)

Roots:G0156

G0157.2 N-APN αἰτιάματα (1x)
Ac 25:7 bringing many burdensome complaints against Paul,

G0158 αἴτιον aítiôn *adj.* (3x)

Roots:G0159 Compare:G0156

G0158.1 A-ASN αἴτιον (1x)
Lk 23:22 commit? I·found not·even·one cause for·death in

G0158.2 A-ASN αἴτιον (2x)
Lk 23:4 "I·find not·even·one fault in this man·of·clay†.
Lk 23:14 of·yeu, found not·even·one fault in this man·of·

G0159 αἴτιος aítiôs *adj.* (2x)

Compare:G0158 G0747 See:G0154 G0155 G0156

G0159.1 A-GSN αἰτίου (1x)
Ac 19:40 ·inherently·being not·even·one cause about which

G0159.2 A-NSM αἴτιος (1x)
Heb 5:9 he·became *the* initiating·cause of·eternal Salvation

G0160 αἰ·φνίδιος aiphnídiôs *adj.* (2x)

Roots:G0001 G5316 Compare:G1810 G1819 See:G0869

G0160.1 A-NSM αἰφνίδιος (2x)
Lk 21:34 *lest* that day should·stand·over yeu unexpected.
1Th 5:3 then an·unexpected savage·termination assaults

G0161 αἰχμ·αλωσία aichmalōsía *n.* (3x)

Roots:G0164 Compare:G0258-1 See:G0162 G0163

G0161 N-ASF αἰχμαλωσίαν (3x)
Eph 4:8 ·high, by·war, ·he·captured war·captivity·*itself*, and
Rv 13:10 ·together *another into* war·captivity, *he·himself*
Rv 13:10 *he·himself also* heads into war·captivity. If any·

G0162 αἰχμ·αλωτεύω aichmalōtêúō *v.* (2x)

Roots:G0164 Compare:G0163 See:G0161

G0162.1 V-AAI-3S ᾐχμαλώτευσεν (1x)
Eph 4:8 on·high, by·war, ·he·captured war·captivity·*itself*,

G0162.2 V-PAP-NPM αἰχμαλωτεύοντες (1x)
2Ti 3:6 and capturing·by·deceit the silly·lesser·women

G0163 αἰχμ·αλωτίζω aichmalōtízō *v.* (3x)

Roots:G0164 Compare:G0162 See:G0161

G0163.4 V-FPI-3P αἰχμαλωτισθήσονται (1x)
Lk 21:24 and they·shall·be·made·prisoners·of·war into all

G0163.4 V-PAP-ASM αἰχμαλωτίζοντα (1x)
Rm 7:23 of·my mind and making·a·war·prisoner *of* me to·

G0163.4 V-PAP-NPM αἰχμαλωτίζοντες (1x)
2Co 10:5 of·God, and making·prisoners·of·war *of* every

G0164 αἰχμ·άλωτος aichmálōtôs *n.* (1x)

Roots:G0160-1 G0259 Compare:G1198 G1202 See:G0163 G0161 G4869

G0164.2 N-DPM αἰχμαλώτοις (1x)
Lk 4:18 liberty to·subdued·captives and recovery·of·sight to·

G0165 αἰών aiṓn *n.* (131x)

Compare:G5550 G2540 G1074 See:G0104 G0166 xLangAlso:H5769 H5703

G0165.1 N-ASM αἰῶνα (2x)
Heb 1:8 throne, O·God, *is* to the age of·ages; a·scepter of·
2Pe 2:17 ·shroud of·darkness has·been·reserved for an·age.

G0165.1 N-GSM αἰῶνος (6x)
Mt 13:39 harvest is *the* entire·completion of·the age, and the
Mt 13:40 shall·it·be at the entire·completion of·this age.
Mt 13:49 ·be at the entire·completion of·the age. The angels
Mt 24:3 and of·the entire·completion of·the age?"
Mt 28:20 even·unto the entire·completion of·the age." So·
Eph 3:21 all the generations of·the age of·ages. So·be·it,·

EG0165.1 (3x)
1Ti 4:8 promise of·life-above for·the present *age*, and for·the
1Ti 4:8 for·the present *age*, and for·the *age* about·to·come."
1Ti 6:19 foundation for the impending *age*, in·order·that

G0165.2 N-APM αἰῶνας (29x)
Heb 1:2 of·all·things, through whom also he·made the ages.
Heb 11:3 the ages to·have·been·completely·formed by·an·
Heb 13:21 *be* the glory to the ages of·ages. So·be·it,·Amen.
Gal 1:5 *be* the glory to the ages of·ages. So·be·it,·Amen.
Mt 6:13 and the glory, into the ages. So·be·it,·Amen.'
Rm 1:25 ·*one* who is blessed into the ages. So·be·it,·Amen).
Rm 9:5 God over all, blessed into the ages. So·be·it,·Amen.
Rm 11:36 To·him *be* glory into the ages. So·be·it,·Amen.
Jud 1:25 both now and into all the ages. So·be·it,·Amen.
Php 4:20 *be* glory into the ages of·ages. So·be·it,·Amen.
1Pe 4:11 and the might into the ages of·ages. So·be·it,·Amen
1Pe 5:11 and the might into the ages of·ages. So·be·it,·Amen
2Co 11:31 the·one being blessed to the ages, he·has·seen that
1Ti 1:17 honor and glory to the ages of·ages. So·be·it,·Amen
2Ti 4:18 *be* glory into the ages of·ages. So·be·it,·Amen.
Rv 1:6 and the might into the ages of·ages. So·be·it,·Amen.
Rv 1:18 I·am living into the ages of·ages, So·be·it,·Amen;
Rv 4:9 on the throne, the·one living into the ages of·ages,
Rv 4:10 to·the·one living into the ages of·ages and cast their
Rv 5:13 and the glory and the might, into the ages of·ages!"
Rv 5:14 fell·prostrate to·the·one·living into the ages of·ages.
Rv 7:12 *be* to·our God into the ages of·ages. So·be·it,·Amen.
Rv 10:6 he·swore by the·one living into the ages of·ages ('
Rv 11:15 and he·shall·reign into the ages of·ages."
Rv 14:11 of·their torment ascends into ages of·ages, and the·
Rv 15:7 Rage of·God, the·one living into the ages of·ages.
Rv 19:3 And her smoke ascends into the ages of·ages!"
Rv 20:10 ·be·tormented day and night into the ages of·ages.
Rv 22:5 them, and they·shall·reign into the ages of·ages.

G0165.2 N-GSM αἰῶνος (1x)
Heb 1:8 *is* to the age of·ages; a·scepter of·straightness *is* the

G0165.2 N-GPM αἰώνων (27x)
Heb 9:26 of·the ages, he·has·been·made·apparent for a·
Heb 13:21 *be* the glory to the ages of·ages. So·be·it,·Amen.
Gal 1:5 *be* the glory to the ages of·ages. So·be·it,·Amen.
Php 4:20 *be* glory into the ages of·ages. So·be·it,·Amen.
1Pe 4:11 the might into the ages of·ages. So·be·it,·Amen.
1Pe 5:11 the might into the ages of·ages. So·be·it,·Amen.
1Co 2:7 God predetermined before the ages to our glory,
1Co 10:11 for whom the ends of·the ages are·attained.
Eph 3:11 *the* determined·purpose of·the ages which he·made
Eph 3:21 the generations of·the age of·ages. So·be·it,·Amen.
1Ti 1:17 Now to·the King of·the ages, incorruptible,
1Ti 1:17 and glory to the ages of·ages. So·be·it,·Amen.
2Ti 4:18 *be* glory into the ages of·ages. So·be·it,·Amen.
Rv 1:6 and the might into the ages of·ages. So·be·it,·Amen.
Rv 1:18 I·am living into the ages of·ages, So·be·it,·Amen;
Rv 4:9 on the throne, the·one living into the ages of·ages,
Rv 4:10 to·the·one living into the ages of·ages and cast their
Rv 5:13 and the glory and the might, into the ages of·ages!"
Rv 5:14 fell·prostrate to·the·one·living into the ages of·ages.
Rv 7:12 to·our God into the ages of·ages. So·be·it,·Amen."
Rv 10:6 by the·one living into the ages of·ages ('who
Rv 11:15 and he·shall·reign into the ages of·ages."
Rv 14:11 torment ascends into ages of·ages, and the·ones
Rv 15:7 Rage of·God, the·one living into the ages of·ages.
Rv 19:3 And her smoke ascends into the ages of·ages!"
Rv 20:10 ·be·tormented day and night into the ages of·ages.
Rv 22:5 them, and they·shall·reign into the ages of·ages.

G0165.3 N-GSM αἰῶνος (3x)
Jn 9:32 "*Even* from·among of·the beginning·age, it·is·not
Ac 3:21 of·all his holy prophets since *the* beginning·age.
Ac 15:18 to·God are all his works from the·beginning·age.

G0165.4 N-GSM αἰῶνος (1x)
Lk 1:70 of·his holy prophets, the·ones from a·prior·age,

G0165.4 N-GPM αἰώνων (2x)
Eph 3:9 having·been·hidden·away from the prior·ages in God
Col 1:26 ·been·hidden·away from the prior·ages and from the

G0165.5 N-ASM αἰῶνα (2x)
Eph 2:2 ·walked according·to the present·age of·this world,
2Ti 4:10 me, loving the present age, and he·departed to

G0165.5 N-DSM αἰῶνι (6x)
Mt 12:32 him, neither in this present·age, nor in the·one
Rm 12:2 do·not be·conformed to·this present·age, but·rather
Tit 2:12 and with·devout·reverence in the present age,
1Co 3:18 to·be wise in this present·age, let·him·become a·
Eph 1:21 not merely in this present·age, but·rather also in
1Ti 6:17 wealthy·ones in the present age not to·be·arrogant

G0165.5 N-GSM αἰῶνος (11x)
Lk 16:8 the Sons of·this present·age are more·prudent—
Lk 20:34 "The descendants of·this present·age marry and are·
Gal 1:4 us out from·among the evil age currently·standing,
Mt 13:22 and·yet the anxiety of·this present·age and the
Mk 4:19 yet the anxieties of·this present·age— and the
1Co 1:20 Where *is the* disputer of·this present·age? Did God
1Co 2:6 and not *the* wisdom of·this present·age, nor of·the
1Co 2:6 nor of·the rulers of·this present·age, the·ones being·
1Co 2:8 ·one of·the rulers of·this present·age has·known, for
2Co 4:4 whom the god of·this present·age blinded the mental·
Eph 6:12 ·powers of·the darkness of·this present·age, *and*

G0165.6 N-ASM αἰῶνα (29x)
Jn 4:14 he·should·not thirst into the coming·age, but·rather
Jn 6:51 bread, he·shall·live into the coming·age, and also the
Jn 6:58 chewing this bread shall·live into the coming·age."
Jn 8:35 ·*remain* in the home into the coming·age, *but* the Son
Jn 8:35 *but* the Son continues·*to·remain* into the coming·age.
Jn 8:51 he·should·not observe death into the coming·age."
Jn 8:52 no, he·shall·not taste of·death into the coming·age.'
Jn 10:28 ·not completely·perish into the coming·age, and
Jn 11:26 should·not die to·the coming·age. Do·you·trust this
Jn 12:34 the Anointed-One abides to·the coming·age, and
Jn 13:8 my feet *even* to·the coming·age." Jesus answered him,
Jn 14:16 that he·may·abide with yeu into the coming·age,
Lk 1:55 and to·his offspring† into the coming·age, just·as he·
Heb 5:6 ·offers·a·sacrifice to the coming·age according·to the
Heb 6:20 High·Priest for the coming·age according·to the
Heb 7:17 ·a·sacrifice to the coming·age according·to the
Heb 7:21 You *are* a·priest to the coming·age according·to the
Heb 7:24 ·of him continuing to the coming·age, has the
Heb 7:28 ·been·made·completely·mature to the coming·age.
Mt 21:19 come out·from you unto the coming·age." And at·
Mk 3:29 have pardon into the coming·age, but·rather he·is
Mk 11:14 fruit from·out·of you unto the coming·age." And
Jud 1:13 deep·murky·shroud of·darkness into the coming·age.
1Pe 1:23 *which·is* living and abiding to the coming·age—
1Pe 1:25 of·Yahweh endures to·the coming·age."' And this is
1Co 8:13 eat meat unto the coming·age, lest I·should·cause·
2Co 9:9 his righteousness remains into the coming·age."'
1Jn 2:17 doing the will of·God abides into the coming·age.
2Jn 1:2 in us and *which* shall·be with us to the coming·age.

G0165.6 N-APM αἰῶνας (3x)
Lk 1:33 the house of·Jacob into the coming·ages, and of·his
Heb 13:8 yesterday, and today, and into the coming·ages.
Rm 16:27 Jesus Anointed into the coming·ages. So·be·it,·

G0165.6 N-DSM αἰῶνι (2x)
Lk 18:30 season, and in the coming age, eternal life-above.
Mk 10:30 and in the coming age, eternal life-above.

G0165.6 N-DPM αἰῶσιν (1x)
Eph 2:7 he·may·indicate in the upcoming ages the surpassing
G0165.6 N-GSM αἰῶνος (3x)
Lk 20:35 ·fully·worthy to·obtain that coming·age and the
Heb 6:5 *the* miraculous·powers of·*the*·age about·to·come,
2Pe 3:18 and to *the* day of·*the*·coming·age. So·be·it,·Amen.

G0166 αἰώνιος aiṓniôs *adj.* (71x)
Roots:G0165 Compare:G0126 G0104-1
xLangAlso:H5769
G0166.1 A-NSF αἰώνιος (4x)
Jn 12:50 ·know that his commandment is eternal life-above.
Jn 17:3 "And this is the eternal life-above, that they·may·
Rm 6:23 gracious·bestowment of·God *is* eternal life-above in
1Jn 5:20 This is the true God and the eternal life-above.
G0166.1 A-NSN αἰώνιον (1x)
1Ti 6:16 ·whom *be* honor and might eternal. So·be·it,·Amen.
G0166.1 A-NPN αἰώνια (1x)
2Co 4:18 but the·things not being·looked·upon *are* eternal.
G0166.1 A-ASM αἰώνιον (1x)
2Th 1:9 ·pay justice with·an·eternal savage·termination from
G0166.1 A-ASF αἰώνιον (40x)
Jn 3:15 ·perish, but·rather should·have eternal life-above.
Jn 3:16 ·perish, but·rather should·have eternal life-above.
Jn 3:36 trusting in the Son has eternal life-above, and the·one
Jn 4:14 of·water springing·up into eternal life-above."
Jn 4:36 ·together fruit into life-above eternal, in·order·that
Jn 5:24 the·one sending me has eternal life-above, and he·
Jn 5:39 yeu·yeurselves presume to·have eternal life-above by
Jn 6:27 for·the full·meal enduring into eternal life-above,
Jn 6:40 trusting in him, may·have eternal life-above, and I·
Jn 6:47 to·yeu, the·one trusting in me has eternal life-above.
Jn 6:54 and drinking my blood, has eternal life-above, and I·
Jn 10:28 And·I give to·them eternal life-above. And no, they·
Jn 12:25 world shall·vigilantly·keep it unto life-above eternal.
Jn 17:2 flesh, in·order·that he·may·give eternal life-above to
Lk 10:25 what should·I·do to·inherit eternal life-above?
Lk 18:18 should·I·be·doing to·inherit eternal life-above?
Lk 18:30 season, and in the coming age, eternal life-above."
Ac 13:48 ·as were having·been·assigned to eternal life-above)
Heb 9:12 finding·in·himself an·eternal ransoming *for·us*.
Gal 6:8 the Spirit, shall·reap eternal life-above from·out of·
Mt 19:16 ·I·do in·order·that I·may·have eternal life-above?
Mt 19:29 ·times·over and shall·inherit eternal life-above.
Mt 25:46 shall·go·away into eternal tormenting·punishment,
Mt 25:46 but the righteous into life-above eternal."
Mk 10:17 should·I·do that I·may·inherit eternal life-above?
Mk 10:30 and in the coming age, eternal life-above.
Rm 2:7 ·incorruptibility, *he·shall·render* eternal life-above.
Rm 5:21 through righteousness to eternal life-above through
Rm 6:22 ·holiness, and at·the end, *unto* eternal life-above.
Jud 1:21 ·our Lord YeShua Anointed unto eternal life-above.
1Pe 5:10 us forth into his eternal glory by Anointed-One
2Pe 1:11 abundantly to·yeu into the eternal kingdom of·our
2Th 2:16 us, and already·giving *us* eternal consoling and a·
2Co 5:1 a·home not·made·by·human·hand, eternal in the
1Ti 1:16 ·the·ones about to·trust on him to life-above eternal.
1Jn 1:2 and announce to·yeu the eternal life-above, which
1Jn 2:25 did·already·promise to·us: the eternal life-above.
1Jn 3:15 man-killer† does not have eternal life-above abiding
1Jn 5:11 that God gave to·us eternal life-above, and this
1Jn 5:13 life-above *that* yeu·have *is* eternal, and in·order·that
G0166.1 A-ASN αἰώνιον (4x)
Mt 18:8 hands or two feet *and* to·be·cast into the eternal fire.
Mt 25:41 having·been·cursed, into the eternal fire, the·one
2Co 4:17 unto phenomenal" eternal weight of·glory,
Rv 14:6 having *the* eternal good·news to·proclaim to·the·
G0166.1 A-APF αἰωνίους (1x)
Lk 16:9 they·may·accept yeu into the eternal tabernacles.
G0166.1 A-DPM αἰωνίοις (1x)
Rm 16:25 having·been·intentionally·silent from·time eternal,
G0166.1 A-GSM αἰωνίου (1x)
Rm 16:26 ·to a·full·appointment of·the eternal God, with *the*
G0166.1 A-GSF αἰωνίου (11x)
Jn 6:68 ·we·go? You·have utterances of·eternal life-above.
Ac 13:46 yeurselves not worthy of·the eternal life-above,
Heb 5:9 *the* initiating·cause of·eternal Salvation to·all the·
Heb 9:15 may·receive the promise of·the eternal inheritance.
Heb 13:20 of·the sheep by an·eternal blood covenant)—
Mk 3:29 he·is held·liable of·eternal Tribunal·judgment."
Tit 1:2 *and* in *the* Expectation of·eternal life-above, which
Tit 3:7 according·to an·Expectation of·eternal life-above.
1Ti 6:12 of·the trust, grab·hold of·the eternal life-above, to
1Ti 6:19 ·that they·may·grab·hold of·the eternal life-above.
2Ti 2:10 the·one in Anointed-One Jesus with eternal glory.
G0166.1 A-GSN αἰωνίου (3x)
Heb 6:2 ·resurrection of·the·dead, and of·eternal judgment.
Heb 9:14 who through *the* eternal Spirit offered himself
Jud 1:7 ·example, undergoing a·justice of·eternal fire.
G0166.1 A-GPM αἰωνίων (2x)
Tit 1:2 without·falsehood) promised before time eternal,
2Ti 1:9 in *the* Anointed-One, Jesus— before time eternal—
G0166.2 A-ASM αἰώνιον (1x)
Phm 1:15 in·order·that you·completely·have him eternally,

G0167 ἀ•καθ•αρσία akatharsía *n.* (10x)
Roots:G0169 Compare:G4507 G3393
xLangEquiv:H2932
G0167.1 N-NSF ἀκαθαρσία (2x)
Gal 5:19 adultery, sexual·immorality, impurity, debauchery,
Eph 5:3 sexual·immorality, and·also any impurity or greed,
G0167.1 N-ASF ἀκαθαρσίαν (2x)
Rm 1:24 handed them over to impurity among the longings
Col 3:5 earth: sexual·immorality, impurity, burning·passion
G0167.1 N-DSF ἀκαθαρσίᾳ (3x)
Rm 6:19 yeur members *as* slaves to·the impurity and to·the
1Th 4:7 did·not call us forth toward impurity, but·rather into
2Co 12:21 concerning the impurity and sexual·immorality
G0167.1 N-GSF ἀκαθαρσίας (3x)
Mt 23:27 ·overflow of·dead *men's* bones and of·all impurity.
1Th 2:3 ·out of·deceit, nor from·out of·impurity, nor in
Eph 4:19 into an·occupation of·all impurity with greediness

G0168 ἀ•καθ•άρτης akathártēs *n.* (1x)
Roots:G0169 Compare:G4509
G0168 N-GSF ἀκαθάρτητος (1x)
Rv 17:4 and impurity of·her sexual·immorality.

G0169 ἀ•κάθ•αρτος akáthartôs *adj.* (30x)
Roots:G0001 G2508 Compare:G4508 G0952 G0462 G2839 G3393
xLangEquiv:H2933 xLangAlso:H2930
G0169.1 A-NSM ἀκάθαρτος (1x)
Eph 5:5 sexually·immoral·person, or impure·person, or
G0169.1 A-NSN ἀκάθαρτον (4x)
Lk 11:24 "Whenever the impure spirit should·go·forth from
Mt 12:43 "Now whenever the impure spirit should·come·out
Mk 1:26 And the impure spirit, after·convulsing him and
Mk 5:8 *Jesus* was·saying to·him, "Impure spirit, come·forth
G0169.1 A-NPN ἀκάθαρτα (3x)
Mk 3:11 And the impure spirits, whenever one·was·
Mk 5:13 And after·coming·out, the impure spirits entered
1Co 7:14 otherwise yeur children are impure, but now they·
G0169.1 A-ASM ἀκάθαρτον (1x)
Ac 10:28 not·even·one man·of·clay† *as* defiled or impure.
G0169.1 A-ASN ἀκάθαρτον (4x)
Ac 10:14 ·time have·I·eaten anything defiled or impure."
Ac 11:8 ·time did anything defiled or impure enter into my
Mk 3:30 they·were·saying, "He·has an·impure spirit."
Mk 7:25 whose young·daughter was·having an·impure spirit,
G0169.1 A-APN ἀκάθαρτα (2x)
Ac 8:7 For impure spirits, crying·out with·a·loud voice,
Rv 16:13 And I·saw three impure spirits like frogs *come* out
G0169.1 A-DSN ἀκαθάρτῳ (5x)
Lk 8:29 For he·was·charging the impure spirit to·come·forth
Lk 9:42 And Jesus reprimanded the impure spirit and healed
Mk 1:23 there·was a·man·of·clay† with an·impure spirit,
Mk 5:2 ·tombs a·man·of·clay† with an·impure spirit,
Mk 9:25 *them*, he·reprimanded the impure spirit, saying to·
G0169.1 A-DPN ἀκαθάρτοις (2x)
Lk 4:36 and power he·orders the impure spirits, and they·
Mk 1:27 ·to authority he·orders even the impure spirits, and
G0169.1 A-GSN ἀκαθάρτου (4x)
Lk 4:33 a·man·of·clay† having a·spirit of·an·impure demon,
2Co 6:17 "≈and do·not lay·hold of·impurity,≈" and·I shall·
Rv 18:2 of·demons, and a·prison of·every impure spirit, and
Rv 18:2 a·prison·cell of·every impure and intensely·hated
G0169.1 A-GPN ἀκαθάρτων (4x)
Lk 6:18 also the·ones being·harassed by impure spirits. And
Ac 5:16 sick and *those* being·harassed by impure spirits. *And*
Mt 10:1 he·gave to·them authority *over* impure spirits, such·
Mk 6:7 he·was·giving them authority *over* the impure spirits.

G0170 ἀ•καιρέομαι akairéômai *v.* (1x)
Roots:G0001 G2540 See:G0171
G0170.3 V-INI-2P ἠκαιρεῖσθε (1x)
Php 4:10 ·concerned, but yeu·were·without·opportunity.

G0171 ἀ•καίρως akaírōs *adv.* (1x)
Roots:G0001 G2540 Compare:G2122 See:G0170
G0171.3 ADV ἀκαίρως (1x)
2Ti 4:2 when·convenient *and* when·inconvenient! Reprove,

G0172 ἄ•κακος ákakôs *adj.* (2x)
Roots:G0001 G2556 Compare:G0121 G0273 G0298
xLangAlso:H5355 H6612
G0172.2 A-NSM ἄκακος (1x)
Heb 7:26 *who·is* divinely·holy, innocent, uncontaminated,
G0172.2 A-GPM ἀκάκων (1x)
Rm 16:18 ·thoroughly·delude the hearts of·the innocent.)

G0173 ἄκανθα ákantha *n.* (14x)
Roots:G0187-1 Compare:G4647 G5146 G0920-1
See:G0188 G0174
xLangEquiv:H6975 xLangAlso:H1863 H8068
G0173 N-NPF ἄκανθαι (3x)
Lk 8:7 and the thorns, being·sprung·up·together·with·it,
Mt 13:7 thorns, and the thorns sprung·up and utterly·choked
Mk 4:7 the thorns, and the thorns sprung·up and altogether·
G0173 N-APF ἀκάνθας (6x)
Lk 8:14 the *seed* falling among the thorns, these are the·ones
Heb 6:8 *the soil* bearing·forth 'thorns and spear·thistles' *is*
Mt 13:7 And others fell among the thorns, and the thorns
Mt 13:22 ·with·seed among the thorns, this·person is the·one
Mk 4:7 And some fell into the thorns, and the thorns sprung·
Mk 4:18 ·are being·permeated·with·seed among the thorns:
G0173 N-GPF ἀκανθῶν (5x)
Jn 19:2 ·braiding a·victor's·crown out of·thorns, they·put *it*
Lk 6:44 For not from·out of·thorns do·men·collect figs, nor
Lk 8:7 *seed* fell in *the* midst of·the thorns; and the thorns,
Mt 7:16 ·Do men·collect a·cluster·of·grapes from thorns, or
Mt 27:29 ·braiding a·victor's·crown out of·thorns, they·put *it*

G0174 ἀκάνθινος akánthinôs *adj.* (2x)
Roots:G0173
G0174 A-ASM ἀκάνθινον (2x)
Jn 19:5 ·forth outside bearing the thorny victor's·crown and
Mk 15:17 And after·braiding a·thorny victor's·crown, it·is·

G0175 ἄ•καρπος ákarpôs *adj.* (8x)
Roots:G0001 G2590
G0175.1 A-NPN ἄκαρπα (1x)
Jud 1:12 late·autumn trees without·fruit, already·dying·off
G0175.2 A-NSM ἄκαρπος (3x)
Mt 13:22 the Redemptive-word, and he·becomes unfruitful.
Mk 4:19 the Redemptive-word, and it·becomes unfruitful.
1Co 14:14 spirit prays, but my understanding is unfruitful.
G0175.2 A-NPM ἄκαρποι (1x)
Tit 3:14 ·occasions, in·order·that they·may·not be unfruitful.
G0175.2 A-APM ἀκάρπους (1x)
2Pe 1:8 *to·be* neither idle nor unfruitful in the recognition·
G0175.2 A-DPN ἀκάρποις (1x)
Eph 5:11 ·together with·the unfruitful works of·the darkness,
EG0175.2 (1x)
Jn 15:6 ·is·already·cast out as the *unfruitful* vine·sprout and

G0176 ἀ•κατα•γνώστος akatagnṓstôs *adj.* (1x)
Roots:G0001 G2607
G0176 A-ASM ἀκατάγνωστον (1x)

Tit 2:8 reasoning *that·is* faultless in·order·that the·one from·

G0177 ἀ•κατα•κάλυπτος akatakályptôs *adj.* (2x)
Roots:G0001 G2619 Compare:G0343

G0177.2 A-ASF ἀκατακάλυπτον (1x)
1Co 11:13 ·for a·woman to·pray to·God not·fully·veiled?

G0177.2 A-DSF ἀκατακαλύπτῳ (1x)
1Co 11:5 with·her head not·fully·veiled puts·to·shame her

G0178 ἀ•κατά•κριτος akatákritôs *adj.* (2x)
Roots:G0001 G2632

G0178.2 A-ASM ἀκατάκριτον (1x)
Ac 22:25 ·of·clay† *who·is* a·Roman and uncondemned?"

G0178.2 A-APM ἀκατακρίτους (1x)
Ac 16:37 publicly thrashing us uncondemned men·of·clay†,

G0179 ἀ•κατά•λυτος akatálytôs *adj.* (1x)
Roots:G0001 G2647

G0179.1 A-GSF ἀκαταλύτου (1x)
Heb 7:16 ·to a·power of·an·indestructible life-above).

G0180 ἀ•κατά•παυστος akatápaustôs *adj.* (1x)
Roots:G0001 G2664

G0180 A-APM ἀκαταπαύστους (1x)
2Pe 2:14 and not·fully·refraining from·moral·failure, while·

G0181 ἀ•κατα•στασία akatastasía *n.* (5x)
Roots:G0182 Compare:G5478-1

G0181.1 N-NSF ἀκαταστασία (1x)
Jac 3:16 *is*, there *is* instability and every mediocre activity.

G0181.2 N-NPF ἀκαταστασίαι (1x)
2Co 12:20 whisperings, puffed·up·minds, *and* chaos.

G0181.2 N-APF ἀκαταστασίας (1x)
Lk 21:9 yeu·should·hear·of wars and chaos, yeu·should·not

G0181.2 N-DPF ἀκαταστασίαις (1x)
2Co 6:5 in imprisonments, in chaos, in wearisome·labors,

G0181.2 N-GSF ἀκαταστασίας (1x)
1Co 14:33 God is not *the God* of·chaos, but·rather of·peace,

G0182 ἀ•κατά•στατος akatástatôs *adj.* (1x)
Roots:G0001 G2686-6 See:G0181

G0182.1 A-NSM ἀκατάστατος (1x)
Jac 1:8 vacillating·in·his·soul *is* completely·unstable in all

G0183 ἀ•κατά•σχετος akatáschêtôs *adj.* (1x)
Roots:G0001 G2722

G0183 A-NSN ἀκατάσχετον (1x)
Jac 3:8 to·tame the tongue. *It·is* unrestrainable, bad, *and*

G0184 Ἀκελ•δαμά Akêldamá *n/l.* (2x)
Ἀκελ•δαμά Aqêldamá [Greek, Octuagint]
Roots:H2506 H1818

G0184.2 N/L-PRI Ἀκελδαμά (1x)
Ac 1:19 ·called in·their own language, AqelDama, that·is,

EG0184.2 (1x)
Mt 27:8 Therefore that field is·called *AqelDama*, "Field of·

G0185 ἀ•κέραιος akéraiôs *adj.* (3x)
Roots:G0001 G2767

G0185.2 A-NPM ἀκέραιοι (2x)
Mt 10:16 prudent as the serpents and untainted as the doves.
Php 2:15 ·that yeu·may·be blameless and untainted, children

G0185.2 A-APM ἀκεραίους (1x)
Rm 16:19 ·good and *to·be* untainted in·regard·to the bad.

G0186 ἀ•κλινής aklinḗs *adj.* (1x)
Roots:G0001 G2827 Compare:G1365 See:G2828

G0186.2 A-ASF ἀκλινῆ (1x)
Heb 10:23 of·the Expectation without·slouching (for

G0187 ἀκμάζω akmázō *v.* (1x)
Roots:G0187-1 Compare:G4134 See:G0188

G0187.2 V-AAI-3P ἤκμασαν (1x)
Rv 14:18 earth, because her clusters·of·grapes are·ripe."

G0188 ἀκμήν akmḗn *n.* (1x)
Roots:G0187-1 See:G0206 G0173

G0188 N-ASF ἀκμήν (1x)
Mt 15:16 yeu also still·at·this·point without·comprehension?

G0189 ἀκοή akôḗ *n.* (24x)
Roots:G0191 Compare:G5345 See:G3775

G0189.1 N-NSF ἀκοή (2x)
Rm 10:17 of·hearing, and the hearing through an·utterance
1Co 12:17 If *the* whole *body is* hearing, where·is the sense·

G0189.1 N-APF ἀκοάς (1x)
Lk 7:1 all his utterances in the hearing of·the people, he·

G0189.1 N-DSF ἀκοῇ (5x)
Jn 12:38 who trusted *that·which* we·ourselves heard? And to·
Ac 28:26 and declare, "With·hearing, yeu·shall·hear, and
Mt 13:14 the·one saying, "Hearing yeu·shall·hear, and no,
Rm 10:16 who trusted *that·which* we·ourselves heard?"
2Pe 2:8 (for in·looking·upon and in·hearing *these deeds*, the

G0189.1 N-DPF ἀκοαῖς (1x)
Heb 5:11 ·have·become bastardly·slothful with·the hearing.

G0189.1 N-GSF ἀκοῆς (5x)
Heb 4:2 ·yet the Redemptive-word *through* hearing did·not
Gal 3:2 of·Torah-Law, or as·a·result of·a·hearing of·trust?
Gal 3:5 of·Torah-Law, or as·a·result of·a·hearing of·trust?
Rm 10:17 the trust *comes* as·a·result of·hearing, and the
1Th 2:13 God's Redemptive-word of·hearing directly·from us,

G0189.2 N-APF ἀκοάς (2x)
Mt 24:6 ·shall·happen to·hear·of wars and rumors of·wars.
Mk 13:7 yeu·should·hear·of wars and rumors of·wars, do·

G0189.3 N-NSF ἀκοή (2x)
Mt 4:24 And his fame went·off into all Syria.
Mk 1:28 And straight·away his fame went·forth unto all the

G0189.3 N-ASF ἀκοήν (1x)
Mt 14:1 ·AntiPas the tetrarch heard of·the fame of·YeShua

G0189.4 N-NSF ἀκοή (1x)
1Co 12:17 *is* an·eye, where·is the sense·of·hearing placed?

G0189.5 N-NPF ἀκοαί (1x)
Mk 7:35 immediately his ears were·thoroughly·opened·up,

G0189.5 N-ASF ἀκοήν (1x)
2Ti 4:3 ·up instructors for·themselves, those·tickling the ear;

G0189.5 N-APF ἀκοάς (1x)
Ac 17:20 certain strange·things to our ears. Accordingly, we·

G0189.6 N-ASF ἀκοήν (1x)
2Ti 4:4 ·shall·turn the inner·sense·of·hearing away·from the

G0190 ἀ•κολουθέω akôlouthéō *v.* (92x)
Roots:G0001

G0190.4 V-FAI-1S ἀκολουθήσω (3x)
Lk 9:57 to him, "Lord, I·shall·follow you wherever you·
Lk 9:61 also declared, "Lord, I·shall·follow you, but first,
Mt 8:19 to·him, "Mentor, I·shall·follow you wherever you·

G0190.4 V-FAI-2S ἀκολουθήσεις (1x)
Jn 13:36 ·follow me now, but you·shall·follow me later·on."

G0190.4 V-PAI-3S ἀκολουθεῖ (7x)
Jn 10:4 them, and the sheep follow him, because they·
Lk 9:49 ·forbade him, because he·does·not follow with us."
Mt 10:38 does·not take his cross and follow right·behind me,
Mk 9:38 in·your name, one·who does·not follow us, and
Mk 9:38 we·forbade him, because he·does·not follow us."
Rv 6:8 name *is* Death, and Hades followed with him. And
Rv 14:13 ·labors, and their works follow with them."

G0190.4 V-PAI-3P ἀκολουθοῦσιν (1x)
Jn 10:27 my voice, and·I know them, and they·follow me.

G0190.4 V-PAI-3P@ ἀκολουθοῦσιν (1x)
Mk 6:1 his·own fatherland, and his disciples followed him.

G0190.4 V-PAM-2S ἀκολούθει (12x)
Jn 1:43 and he·finds Philip and says to·him, "Follow me."
Jn 21:19 after·declaring this, he·says to·him, "Follow me."
Jn 21:22 what·is·that to you? You·yourself follow me."
Lk 5:27 And he·declared to·him, "Follow me."
Lk 9:59 And he·declared to another, "Follow me." But the·
Lk 18:22 And come·over·here! Follow me!"
Ac 12:8 "Cast your·garment around you and follow me."
Mt 8:22 YeShua declared to·him, "Follow me, and allow the
Mt 9:9 And he·says to·him, "Follow me." And rising·up, he·
Mt 19:21 And come·over·here! Follow me!"
Mk 2:14 tax·booth, and he·says to·him, "Follow me." And
Mk 10:21 Upon·taking·up the cross, follow me!"

G0190.4 V-PAM-3S ἀκολουθείτω (4x)
Jn 12:26 any·man should·attend to·me, let·him·follow me;
Lk 9:23 and take·up his cross each day, and·then follow me.
Mt 16:24 ·deny himself, take·up his cross, and follow me.
Mk 8:34 himself, and take·up his cross, and follow me.

G0190.4 V-PAP-ASM ἀκολουθοῦντα (1x)
Jn 21:20 Peter looks·at the disciple following *them* (*the·one*

G0190.4 V-PAP-APM ἀκολουθοῦντας (1x)
Jn 1:38 ·around and distinctly·viewing them following, says

G0190.4 V-PAP-DSM ἀκολουθοῦντι (1x)
Lk 7:9 ·around, he·declared to·the crowd following him, "I·

G0190.4 V-PAP-DPM ἀκολουθοῦσιν (1x)
Mt 8:10 he·marveled and declared to·the·ones following,

G0190.4 V-PAP-GSF ἀκολουθούσης (1x)
1Co 10:4 ·out of·that·spiritual Solid·Rock following *them*,

G0190.4 V-PAP-NSM ἀκολουθῶν (2x)
Jn 8:12 the light of·the world. The·one following me, no he·
Jn 20:6 So·then, Simon Peter comes following him, and he·

G0190.4 V-PAP-NPM ἀκολουθοῦντες (4x)
Mt 21:9 preceding and the·ones following, were·yelling·out,
Mk 10:32 And·yet while·following, they·were·afraid. And
Mk 11:9 preceding and the·ones following were·yelling·out,
Rv 14:4 These are the·ones following the Lamb wherever he·

G0190.4 V-IAI-3S ἠκολούθει (12x)
Jn 6:2 And a·large crowd was·following him, because they·
Jn 18:15 And Simon Peter was·following Jesus, and *so was*
Lk 18:43 he·received·his·sight and was·following him,
Lk 22:54 Now Peter was·following at·a·distance.
Lk 23:27 And there·was·following him a·large multitude of·
Ac 12:9 And going·out, he·was·following him and had·not
Ac 21:36 multitude of·the people were·following, yelling·out
Mt 26:58 But Peter was·following him from a·distance up·to
Mk 5:24 him, and a·large crowd was·following him, and
Mk 10:52 ·received·his·sight and was·following Jesus along
Mk 14:51 ·also a·certain young·man was·following him *with*
Rv 19:14 the armies in the heaven were·following him upon

G0190.4 V-IAI-3P ἠκολούθουν (1x)
Mk 15:41 when he·was in Galilee, were·following him, and

G0190.4 V-AAI-1P ἠκολουθήσαμεν (3x)
Lk 18:28 "Behold, we·ourselves left all and followed you."
Mt 19:27 we·ourselves left all and followed you. What then
Mk 10:28 "Behold, we·ourselves left all and followed you."

G0190.4 V-AAI-3S ἠκολούθησεν (8x)
Lk 5:28 ·behind absolutely·all, rising·up, he·followed him.
Mt 9:9 And rising·up, he·followed him.
Mt 9:19 And being·roused, YeShua followed him, and *so*·
Mt 20:29 ·forth from Jericho, a·large crowd followed him.
Mk 2:14 And rising·up, he·followed him.
Mk 14:54 But Peter followed him from a·distance, as·far·as
Rv 14:8 And there·followed another angel, saying,
Rv 14:9 And a·third angel followed them, saying with a·loud

G0190.4 V-AAI-3P ἠκολούθησαν (21x)
Jn 1:37 heard him speaking, and they·followed Jesus.
Jn 11:31 quickly and went·out, they·followed her, saying,
Lk 5:11 ·ground, leaving absolutely·all, they·followed him.
Lk 9:11 the crowds, after·knowing *it*, followed him. And
Lk 22:39 And his disciples also followed him.
Ac 13:43 ·reverent converts·to·Judaism followed Paul and
Mt 4:20 immediately, leaving the nets, they·followed him.
Mt 4:22 the sailboat and their father, they·followed him.
Mt 4:25 And large crowds followed him from Galilee and
Mt 8:1 from the mountain, large crowds followed him.
Mt 8:23 into the sailboat, his disciples followed him.
Mt 9:27 from·there, two blind·men followed him, yelling·
Mt 12:15 And large crowds followed him, and he·both·
Mt 14:13 *of·this*, the crowds followed him on·foot from the
Mt 19:2 And large crowds followed him, and he·both·
Mt 20:34 their eyes received·sight, and they·followed him.
Mt 27:55 from a·distance, who followed YeShua from
Mk 1:18 leaving their nets, they·followed him.
Mk 2:15 For there·were many, and they·followed him.
Mk 3:7 a·large multitude from Galilee followed him, and·
Rv 18:5 because "her moral·failures followed even·up·to the

G0190.4 V-AAM-2P ἀκολουθήσατε (2x)
Lk 22:10 of·water shall·meet·up with·yeu; follow him into
Mk 14:13 ·water shall·approach·and·meet yeu. Follow him.

G0190.4 V-AAN ἀκολουθῆσαι (2x)
Jn 13:36 I·head·on·out, you·are·not able to·follow me now,

Jn 13:37 why am·I·not able to·follow you at·this·moment?
G0190.4 V-AAP-GPM ἀκολουθησάντων (1x)
Jn 1:40 from·among the two of·the·ones following him and
G0190.4 V-AAP-NPM ἀκολουθήσαντες (1x)
Mt 19:28 to·yeu, that yeu, the·ones following me, in The
G0190.4 V-AAS-3P ἀκολουθήσωσιν (1x)
Jn 10:5 no, they·should·not follow, but·rather shall·flee

G0191 ἀκούω akôúō *v.* (437x)
Compare:G5219 G4920
xLangEquiv:H8085 A8086

G0191.1 V-FAI-2P ἀκούσετε (2x)
Ac 28:26 declare, "With·hearing, yeu·shall·hear, and no,
Mt 13:14 the·one saying, "Hearing yeu·shall·hear, and no,
G0191.1 V-FAI-3S ἀκούσει (1x)
Mt 12:19 ·yell·out, nor·even·shall any·man hear his voice in
G0191.1 V-FAI-3P ἀκούσουσιν (2x)
Jn 10:16 to·lead these·also, and they·shall·hear my voice,
Rm 10:14 how shall·they·hear apart·from one·officially·
G0191.1 V-FDI-1P ἀκουσόμεθα (1x)
Ac 17:32 And they·declared, "We·shall·hear you again
G0191.1 V-FDI-2S ἀκούσῃ (1x)
Ac 25:22 tomorrow," he·replied, "You·shall·hear him."
G0191.1 V-FDI-2P ἀκούσεσθε (1x)
Ac 3:22 as myself; him yeu·shall·hear in all·things,'' "as·
G0191.1 V-FDI-3P ἀκούσονται (4x)
Jn 5:25 is, when the dead·ones shall·hear the voice of·the
Jn 5:28 the·ones in the chamber·tombs shall·hear his voice.
Ac 21:22 ·together, for they·shall·hear that you·have·come.
Ac 28:28 to·the Gentiles, and they·shall·hear it."
G0191.1 V-FPI-3S ἀκουσθήσεται (1x)
Lk 12:3 in the darkness, they·shall·be·heard in the light; and
G0191.1 V-PAI-1S ἀκούω (5x)
Jn 5:30 ·one·thing of my·own·self. Just·as I·hear, I·judge.
Lk 9:9 is this, concerning whom I·myself hear such·things?
Lk 16:2 'What *is* this I·hear concerning you?
1Co 11:18 Called·Out·citizenry, I·hear *for* severing·schisms
3Jn 1:4 ·greater·than these·things, that I·hear·of my children
G0191.1 V-PAI-1P ἀκούομεν (3x)
Ac 2:8 And how·do we·ourselves each hear our own·distinct
Ac 2:11 Cretans and Arabians— we·hear them speaking in·
2Th 3:11 For we·hear *that there·are* some walking among
G0191.1 V-PAI-2S ἀκούεις (4x)
Jn 3:8 blows where it·wants, and you·hear the sound of·it,
Jn 11:42 had·personally·known that you·hear me always,
Mt 21:16 they·declared to·him, "Do·you·hear what these
Mt 27:13 "Do·you·not hear how·many·things they·testify·
G0191.1 V-PAI-2P ἀκούετε (11x)
Jn 8:47 that, yeu·yeurselves do·not hear *them* because yeu·
Jn 14:24 But the Redemptive-word which yeu·hear is not mine
Lk 10:24 and to·hear the·things·which yeu·hear, and did·
Ac 2:33 ·forth this, which yeu now look·upon and hear.
Ac 19:26 Also, yeu·hear and observe that not merely at·
Gal 4:21 under Torah-Law, do·yeu·not hear the Torah-Law?
Mt 10:27 declare in the light; and what yeu·hear in the ear,
Mt 11:4 to·John those·things·which yeu·hear and look·upon:
Mt 13:17 and to·hear *the·things* which yeu·hear, and did·not
Mk 8:18 look? And having ears, do·yeu·not hear?' "And
Php 1:30 such·as yeu·saw in me, and now hear *to·be* in me.
G0191.1 V-PAI-3S ἀκούει (12x)
Jn 8:47 being birthed·from·out of·God hears the utterances
Jn 9:31 that God does·not hear those·full·of·moral·failure,
Jn 9:31 ·of·God, and should·do his will, this·man he·hears.
Jn 10:3 opens·up, and the sheep hear his voice, and he·calls·
Mt 7:24 "Accordingly, anyone that hears these sayings of·
Mt 13:16 they·look·upon, and yeur ears, because they·hear.
2Co 12:6 me *to·be*, or *above* what he·hears from·out of·me.
1Jn 4:5 from·among the world, and the world hears them.
1Jn 4:6 The·one presently·knowing God hears us. Whoever
1Jn 4:6 not birthed·from·out of·God does·not hear us. As·a·
1Jn 5:14 anything according·to his will, he·hears us.
1Jn 5:15 And if we·personally·know that he·hears us,
G0191.1 V-PAI-3P ἀκούουσιν (5x)
Lk 7:22 lepers are·purified, deaf·men hear, dead·men are·
Lk 16:31 to·him, 'If they·do·not hear Moses and the
Mt 11:5 lepers are·purified and deaf·men hear, dead·men
Mt 13:13 and hearing, they·do·not hear, neither do·they·
Mk 4:20 soil: the·same·which hear the Redemptive-word,
G0191.1 V-PAM-2P ἀκούετε (1x)
Mt 15:10 he·declared to·them, "Hear and comprehend!
G0191.1 V-PAM-3S ἀκουέτω (8x)
Lk 8:8 "The·one having ears to·hear, let·him·hear."
Lk 14:35 "The·one having ears to·hear, let·him·hear."
Mt 11:15 "The·one having ears to·hear, let·him·hear.
Mt 13:9 The·one having ears to·hear, let·him·hear."
Mt 13:43 "The·one having ears to·hear, let·him·hear.
Mk 4:9 "The·one having ears to·hear, let·him·hear."
Mk 4:23 "If any·man has ears to·hear, let·him·hear."
Mk 7:16 If any·man has ears to·hear, let·him·hear."
G0191.1 V-PAN ἀκούειν (23x)
Jn 6:60 "This is a·hard saying; who is·able to·hear it?
Jn 8:43 because yeu·are·not able to·hear my Redemptive-word
Jn 9:27 ·did·not listen. Why·do yeu·want to·hear *it* again?
Lk 5:1 crowd pressing·upon him to·hear the Redemptive-word
Lk 5:15 and large crowds came·together to·hear *him*, and
Lk 8:8 "The·one having ears to·hear, let·him·hear."
Lk 14:35 "The·one having ears to·hear, let·him·hear."
Lk 15:1 ·disqualified were drawing·near to·him to·hear him.
Lk 21:38 ·going to him in the Sanctuary·Atrium to·hear him.
Lk 23:8 ·while on·account·of hearing many·things about him
Ac 8:6 by Philippe in their hearing and·also looking·upon the
Ac 17:21 *attempting* to·say or to·hear something brand-new).
Mt 11:15 "The·one having ears to·hear, let·him·hear.
Mt 13:9 The·one having ears to·hear, let·him·hear."
Mt 13:43 "The·one having ears to·hear, let·him·hear.
Mt 24:6 And yeu·shall·happen to·hear·of wars and rumors
Mk 4:9 "The·one having ears to·hear, let·him·hear."
Mk 4:23 "If any·man has ears to·hear, let·him·hear."
Mk 4:33 to·them, just·as they·were·able to·hear *it*.
Mk 7:16 If any·man has ears to·hear, let·him·hear."
Mk 7:37 He·makes both the deaf to·hear and the mute to·
Rm 11:8 and ears *for·them* not to·hear unto the present day.
Rv 9:20 are·able to·look·about, nor to·hear, nor to·walk;'
G0191.1 V-PAP-APM ἀκούοντας (5x)
Ac 5:5 ·fear came upon all the·ones hearing these·things.
Ac 5:11 and upon all the·ones hearing these·things.
Ac 10:44 fell upon all the·ones hearing the Redemptive-word.
Ac 17:8 the rulers·of·the·city *that·were* hearing these·things.
Ac 26:29 but·rather also all the·ones hearing me this·day,
G0191.1 V-PAP-DSM ἀκούοντι (1x)
Rv 22:18 For I·jointly·testify to·everyone hearing the words
G0191.1 V-PAP-DPM ἀκούουσιν (2x)
Lk 6:27 But·rather I·say to·yeu, to·the·ones hearing: "Love
Eph 4:29 ·order·that it·may·give grace to·the·ones hearing *it*.
G0191.1 V-PAP-GSM ἀκούοντος (2x)
Lk 20:45 And in·the·hearing of·all the people, he·declared
Mt 13:19 "*Concerning* anyone hearing the Redemptive-word
G0191.1 V-PAP-GPM ἀκουόντων (2x)
Lk 19:11 And with·them hearing these·things, augmenting *it*,
2Ti 2:14 ·overturning·catastrophic·ruin of·the·ones hearing.
G0191.1 V-PAP-NSM ἀκούων (11x)
Jn 5:24 to·yeu, the·one hearing my Redemptive-word and
Lk 6:47 ·is·coming toward me, both hearing my sayings and
Lk 19:48 ·all the people were·very·attentive to·hear him,
Ac 5:5 And upon·hearing these words, Ananias fell·down
Mt 7:26 "And everyone hearing these sayings of·mine, and
Mt 13:20 this·person is the·one hearing the Redemptive-word
Mt 13:22 this·person is the·one hearing the Redemptive-word
Mt 13:23 this·person is the·one hearing the Redemptive-word
Phm 1:5 hearing of·your love and trust which you·have
Rv 22:8 the·one looking·upon these·things and hearing *them*.
Rv 22:17 And the·one hearing, let·him·declare, "Come!"
G0191.1 V-PAP-NPN ἀκούοντα (1x)
Ac 13:48 And upon·hearing *this*, the Gentiles were·rejoicing
G0191.1 V-PAP-NPM ἀκούοντες (16x)
Lk 2:47 And all the·ones hearing him were·astonished at his
Lk 4:28 And hearing these·things, everyone in the gathering
Lk 8:10 look·upon, and hearing they·may·not comprehend.''
Lk 8:12 ·by the roadway are the·ones hearing. Then comes
Lk 8:21 are these, the·ones hearing the Redemptive-word of·
Lk 11:28 ·blessed *are* the·ones hearing the Redemptive-word
Ac 7:54 And upon·hearing these·things, they·were·
Ac 9:7 ·silence, in·fact hearing the sound·of·the·voice, but
Ac 9:21 But all the·ones hearing *him* were·astonished and
Ac 18:8 many of·the Corinthians hearing *Paul* were·trusting,
Gal 1:23 But they·were hearing merely, "The·one
Mt 13:13 they·do·not look, and hearing, they·do·not hear,
Mk 4:12 and should·not see, and hearing they·may·hear, and
Mk 4:18 these *are* the·ones hearing the Redemptive-word,
Mk 6:2 gathering, and many hearing *him* were·astounded,
Rv 1:3 the·one reading·aloud and the·ones hearing the words
G0191.1 V-PAS-3P ἀκούωσιν (1x)
Mk 4:12 see, and hearing they·may·hear, and should·not
G0191.1 V-PPI-3S ἀκούεται (1x)
1Co 5:1 It·is·heard all·over *that there·is* sexual·immorality
G0191.1 V-IAI-3S ἤκουεν (3x)
Ac 14:9 The·same·man was·hearing Paul speaking, who
Mk 6:20 many·things, yet was·hearing him with·pleasure.
Mk 12:37 the large crowd was·hearing him with·pleasure.
G0191.1 V-IAI-3P ἤκουον (4x)
Lk 16:14 fond·of·money, also were·hearing all these·things,
Ac 2:6 because each one was·hearing them speaking in·his·
Ac 10:46 for they·were·hearing them speaking in·bestowed·
Mk 6:55 being badly·ill, *to* wherever they·were·hearing,
G0191.1 V-AAI-1S ἤκουσα (34x)
Jn 8:26 these·things which I·heard personally·from him."
Jn 8:40 to·yeu the truth, which I·heard personally·from God.
Jn 15:15 because all·things that I·heard personally·from my
Ac 7:34 *who·are* in Egypt, and I·heard their groaning,' 'and
Ac 11:7 And I·heard a·voice saying to·me, 'Peter, after·
Ac 22:7 to the hard·ground and heard a·voice saying to·me,
Ac 26:14 ·down upon the earth, I·heard a·voice speaking to
Rv 1:10 on the Lord's day and heard right·behind me a·great
Rv 4:1 and the first voice which I·heard *was* as a·trumpet
Rv 5:11 And I·saw, and I·heard *the* voice of·many angels
Rv 5:13 all the·ones in them, I·heard saying, "To·the·one
Rv 6:1 the official·seals, and I·heard one from·among the
Rv 6:3 the second official·seal, I·heard the second living·
Rv 6:5 the third official·seal, I·heard the third living·being
Rv 6:6 And I·heard a·voice in *the* midst of·the four living·
Rv 6:7 ·up the fourth official·seal, I·heard *the* voice of·the
Rv 7:4 And I·heard the number of·the·ones having·been·
Rv 8:13 And I·saw and heard an angel flying in mid-heaven,
Rv 9:13 angel sounded, and I·heard one voice from·among
Rv 9:16 *two·hundred million)*, and I·heard the number of·
Rv 10:4 I·was·about to·write. And I·heard a·voice from·out
Rv 10:8 And the voice which I·heard from·out of·the heaven
Rv 12:10 And I·heard a·loud voice saying in the heaven,
Rv 14:2 And I·heard a·voice from·out of·the heaven, as a·
Rv 14:2 of·a·great thunder. And I·heard a·sound of·harpists
Rv 14:13 And I·heard a·voice from·out of·the heaven saying
Rv 16:1 And I·heard a·great voice from·out of·the Temple
Rv 16:5 And I·heard the angel of·the waters saying, "You·
Rv 16:7 And I·heard another from·among the Sacrifice·Altar
Rv 18:4 And I·heard another voice from·out of·the heaven,
Rv 19:1 And after these·things, I·heard a·great voice of·a·
Rv 19:6 And I·heard as a·voice of·a·large crowd, and as a·
Rv 21:3 And I·heard a·great voice from·out of·the heaven
Rv 22:8 hearing *them*. And when I·heard and looked, I·fell·
G0191.1 V-AAI-1P ἠκούσαμεν (10x)
Jn 12:34 him, "We·ourselves heard from·out of·the
Lk 4:23 yourself. As·many·things·as we·heard happening in
Lk 22:71 testimony? For we·ourselves heard *it* from his·own
Ac 4:20 not to·speak the·things·which we·saw and heard."
Ac 15:24 Since·now *that* we·heard that certain·men going·
Ac 19:2 "But·yet, we·did·not·even hear whether there·is a·
Ac 21:12 And as·soon·as we·heard these·things, both we·
Mk 14:58 "We·ourselves heard him saying, 'I·myself shall·
2Pe 1:18 And·also we·ourselves heard this voice being·
Col 1:9 (since that day *when* we·heard *of·it*) do·not cease

G0191.1 V-AAI-2S ἤκουσας (5x)
Jn 11:41 "Father, I·give·thanks to·you that you·heard me.
Ac 22:15 ·of·clay† of·what you·have·clearly·seen and heard.
2Ti 1:13 which you·heard personally·from me, in trust and
2Ti 2:2 And the·things·which you·heard personally·from me
Rv 3:3 by·what·means you·have·received and heard, so·then
G0191.1 V-AAI-2P ἠκούσατε (24x)
Jn 14:28 "Yeu·heard that I·myself declared to·yeu, 'I·head·
Lk 7:22 report to·John what·things yeu·saw and heard, that
Ac 1:4 Promise of·the Father, which yeu·heard from·me.
Gal 1:13 For yeu·heard of·my former manner·of·life in
Mt 5:21 "Yeu·heard that it·was·uttered to·the ancient·ones,
Mt 5:27 "Yeu·heard that it·was·uttered to·the ancient·ones,
Mt 5:33 "Again, yeu·heard that it·was·uttered to·the
Mt 5:38 "Yeu·heard that it·was·uttered, "An·eye for an·eye
Mt 5:43 "Yeu·heard that it·was·uttered, "You·shall·love
Mt 26:65 See, now yeu·heard his revilement of·God.
Mk 14:64 Yeu·heard the revilement of·God! How·does it·
Jac 5:11 ·enduring. Yeu·heard of·the patient·endurance of·
Php 2:26 on·account·that yeu·heard that he·was·sick.
Php 4:9 and personally·received, and heard, and saw in me,
Eph 3:2 since·indeed yeu·already·heard of·the estate·
Eph 4:21 if·indeed yeu·heard him and are·instructed by him
Col 1:6 in yeu since that day yeu·heard *it* and recognized the
Col 1:23 of·the good·news which yeu·heard (the·one
1Jn 2:7 is the word which yeu·heard from *the* beginning.
1Jn 2:18 hour. And just·as yeu·heard that the Adversary·of·
1Jn 2:24 in yeu, that·which yeu already·heard from *the*
1Jn 2:24 If that·which yeu·already·heard from *the*
1Jn 3:11 is the message that yeu·heard from *the* beginning,
2Jn 1:6 is the commandment, that just·as yeu·heard from *the*
G0191.1 V-AAI-3S ἤκουσεν (17x)
Jn 3:32 And what he·has·clearly·seen and heard, that·thing
Jn 9:35 Jesus heard that they·cast him forth outside.
Jn 11:6 Now·then, as·soon·as he·heard that he·was·sick, in·
Jn 11:20 Martha, as·soon·as she·heard that Jesus was·
Jn 11:29 As·soon·as that *sister* heard *it*, she·is·roused swiftly
Jn 12:18 ·met him, because they·heard him to·have·done
Jn 19:8 Now·then, when Pilate heard this saying, he·was all·
Lk 1:41 it·happened, as·soon·as ElisSabeth heard the greeting
Lk 9:7 Now HerOd·AntiPas the tetrarch heard all the·things
Lk 15:25 to·the home *and* heard instrumental·music and
Ac 8:30 ·toward *him*, PhilIppe heard him reading·aloud
Ac 9:4 upon the earth, he·heard a·voice saying to·him,
Ac 24:24 sent·for Paul, and he·heard him concerning the
Mt 14:1 HerOd·AntiPas the tetrarch heard of·the fame of·
Mk 6:14 And King HerOd·AntiPas heard *of·him*, for his name
1Co 2:9 ·not see, and ear did·not hear, and it·did·not ascend
2Co 12:4 into Paradise, and heard inexpressible utterances,
G0191.1 V-AAI-3P ἤκουσαν (18x)
Jn 1:37 And the two disciples heard him speaking, and they·
Jn 4:1 Lord knew that the Pharisees *had* heard *it said* that
Jn 7:32 The Pharisees heard the crowd grumbling these·
Jn 9:40 *some* from·among the Pharisees heard these·things,
Jn 10:8 and robbers, but·yet the sheep did·not hear them.
Lk 1:58 ·neighbors and her kinsfolk heard that Yahweh was·
Lk 2:20 God over all·the·things that they·heard and saw,
Lk 10:24 the·things·which yeu·hear, and did·not hear *them*."
Ac 5:24 ·Estate and the chief·priests heard these words, they·
Ac 11:1 the·ones being in Judea, heard that the Gentiles also
Ac 22:9 alarmed, but they·did·not *distinctly*·hear the voice
Ac 28:27 and their ears hardly heard, and they·fully·shut
Mt 13:15 and their ears hardly heard, and they·fully·shut
Mt 13:17 *the·things* which yeu·hear, and did·not hear *them*.
Mk 11:18 the scribes and the chief·priests heard *it* and were·
Rm 10:14 ·they·trust *him* of·whom they·did·not hear? And
Rm 10:18 I·say, ¿!·Did they·not hear? As·a·matter·of·fact,
Rv 11:12 And they·heard a·great voice from·out of·the
G0191.1 V-AAM-2P ἀκούσατε (5x)
Lk 18:6 the Lord declared, "Hear what the unjust judge says.
Ac 2:22 "Men, Israelites, hear these words: Jesus of·
Ac 22:1 brothers and fathers, hear my defense *which I·*
Mt 13:18 "Now·then, yeu·yeurselves hear the parable of·
Mt 21:33 "Hear another parable. "There·was a·certain man·
G0191.1 V-AAM-3S ἀκουσάτω (8x)
Rv 2:7 'The·one having an·ear, let·him·hear what the Spirit
Rv 2:11 The·one having an·ear, let·him·hear what the Spirit
Rv 2:17 The·one having an·ear, let·him·hear what the Spirit
Rv 2:29 The·one having an·ear, let·him·hear what the Spirit
Rv 3:6 'The·one having an·ear, let·him·hear what the Spirit
Rv 3:13 The·one having an·ear, let·him·hear what the Spirit
Rv 3:22 The·one having an·ear, let·him·hear what the Spirit
Rv 13:9 If any·man has an·ear, let·him·hear.
G0191.1 V-AAM-3P ἀκουσάτωσαν (1x)
Lk 16:29 Moses and the prophets. Let·them·hear them.'
G0191.1 V-AAN ἀκοῦσαι (17x)
Lk 6:17 and Tsidon, who came to·hear him and to·be·healed
Lk 10:24 see *them*, and to·hear the·things·which yeu·hear,
Lk 11:31 of·the utmost·parts of·the earth to·hear the wisdom
Ac 10:22 his house, and to·hear utterances personally·from
Ac 10:33 of·God. We·are·present to·hear all the·things
Ac 13:7 and Saul, sought to·hear the Redemptive-word of·
Ac 13:44 did·gather·together to·hear the Redemptive-word of·
Ac 15:7 us *for* the Gentiles to·hear the Redemptive-word of·
Ac 19:10 ·ones residing·in Asia to·hear the Redemptive-word
Ac 22:14 the Righteous·One, and to·hear *his* voice from·out
Ac 24:4 you in·your·own fairness to·hear of·us concisely.
Ac 25:22 "I·resolve also to·hear the man·of·clay† myself.
Ac 26:3 Therefore, I·petition you to·hear me patiently.
Ac 28:22 we·consider·it·appropriate to·hear personally·from
Mt 12:42 of·the utmost·parts of·the earth to·hear the wisdom
Mt 13:17 see *them*, and to·hear *the·things* which yeu·hear,
Jac 1:19 every man·of·clay† must·be swift to·hear, slow to·
G0191.1 V-AAP-DPM ἀκούσασιν (1x)
Heb 4:2 ·together with·the Trust within·the·ones hearing *it*.
G0191.1 V-AAP-GPM ἀκουσάντων (3x)
Jn 1:40 him and already·hearing directly·from John.
Ac 4:4 But many of·the·ones hearing the Redemptive-word
Heb 2:3 ·confirmed to us by the·ones already·hearing *him*,
G0191.1 V-AAP-NSF ἀκούσασα (2x)
Mk 5:27 After·hearing about Jesus *and* already·coming in
Mk 7:25 For after·hearing about him, a·woman whose
G0191.1 V-AAP-NSM ἀκούσας (36x)
Jn 4:47 This·man, after·hearing that Jesus comes from·out
Jn 6:45 Accordingly, every·man hearing and learning
Jn 11:4 But Jesus, hearing *that*, declared, "This sickness is
Jn 12:29 the·one standing·by and hearing *it*, was·saying,
Jn 19:13 Accordingly, after·hearing this saying, Pilate
Jn 21:7 Now·then, after·hearing that it·was the Lord,
Lk 6:49 "But the·one hearing and not doing, is like a·man·
Lk 7:3 And after·hearing about Jesus, he·dispatched elders
Lk 7:9 Now after·hearing these·things, Jesus marveled·at
Lk 7:29 And upon·hearing *this*, all the people already·being·
Lk 8:50 But Jesus hearing *it*, answered him, saying, "Do·not
Lk 14:15 reclining·together·at·the·meal hearing these·things,
Lk 18:22 But Jesus, hearing these·things, declared to·him,
Lk 18:23 And after·hearing these·things, he·became
Lk 18:36 And hearing a·crowd traversing·through, he·
Lk 23:6 But Pilate, after·hearing "Galilee," inquired
Ac 7:12 But after·hearing·of there·being grain in Egypt,
Ac 22:26 And *upon* the centurion hearing *that*, coming·
Ac 23:16 sister, coming·directly after·hearing of·the ambush
Ac 24:22 And Felix, after·hearing these·things *and* having·
Mt 2:3 But upon·hearing *this*, King HerOd·the·Great was·
Mt 2:22 But upon·hearing that ArcheLaos reigns in Judea in·
Mt 4:12 Now after·hearing that John was·handed·over *into*
Mt 8:10 And upon·YeShua hearing *this*, he·marveled and
Mt 9:12 But after·hearing *that*, YeShua declared to·them,
Mt 11:2 Now John, after·hearing in the dungeon *of* the
Mt 14:13 And upon·hearing *it*, YeShua departed from·there
Mt 19:22 But after·hearing the saying, the young·man went·
Mt 22:7 "But upon·hearing *this*, the king was·angry, and
Mk 2:17 And after·hearing *that*, Jesus says to·them, "The·
Mk 5:36 But immediately upon·hearing the word being·
Mk 6:16 But HerOd·AntiPas, after·hearing *of·him*, he·
Mk 6:20 ·was·closely·guarding him. And after·hearing him,
Mk 10:47 And after·hearing that it·was Jesus of·Natsareth,
Mk 12:28 And after·hearing of·them questioning·and·
Eph 1:15 ·of that, I·also, after·hearing·of the trust *which·is*
G0191.1 V-AAP-NPM ἀκούσαντες (49x)
Jn 6:60 many from·among his disciples, upon·hearing *this*,
Jn 7:40 So·then after·hearing the saying, many from·among
Jn 8:9 And after·hearing *this*, and being·convicted by *their·*
Jn 12:12 the feast *in·BethAny*) upon·hearing that Jesus was·
Lk 1:66 and all the·ones hearing *them* laid·*them*·up in their
Lk 2:18 And all the·ones hearing *it* marveled concerning the·
Lk 8:14 these are the·ones hearing, yet while·traversing,
Lk 8:15 ·good heart, who after·hearing the Redemptive-word,
Lk 18:26 And upon·hearing *this*, they·declared, "Who then
Lk 20:16 And hearing *this*, they·declared, "May·it·never
Ac 2:37 Now hearing *this*, they·were·fully·jabbed in·the
Ac 4:24 And after·hearing *it*, they·lifted·*up* their·voice
Ac 5:21 And after·hearing *this*, they·entered into the
Ac 5:33 And upon·hearing *this*, they·were·thoroughly·irate
Ac 8:14 in JeruSalem, after·hearing that Samaria had·
Ac 9:38 *was* near to·Joppa, *and* after·hearing that Peter was
Ac 11:18 And after·hearing these·things, they·kept·still, and
Ac 14:14 BarNabas and Paul, after·hearing *of·this and*
Ac 16:38 and they·were·afraid after·hearing that they·were
Ac 17:32 ·fact, after·hearing of·a·resurrection of·dead·men,
Ac 18:26 in the gathering. But after·hearing him, Aquila and
Ac 19:5 And after·hearing *this*, they·were·immersed into the
Ac 19:28 And after·hearing *these·things*, they·were·
Ac 21:20 And after·hearing *these·things*, they·were·
Ac 22:2 (And upon·hearing that he·was·addressing them in·
Ac 28:15 the brothers, upon·hearing the·things about us,
Heb 3:16 For after·hearing, some did·directly·provoke, but·
Heb 12:19 ·utterances, of·which the·ones hearing shunned *it*
Mt 12:24 But upon·hearing *this*, the Pharisees declared,
Mt 14:13 place in private. And after·hearing *of·this*, the
Mt 15:12 ·seen how the Pharisees, after·hearing *this* saying,
Mt 17:6 And upon·hearing *it*, the disciples fell on their faces
Mt 19:25 And upon·hearing *this*, his disciples were
Mt 20:24 And after·hearing *of·this*, the ten were·greatly·
Mt 20:30 the roadway. After·hearing that YeShua passes·by,
Mt 21:45 And after·hearing his parables, the chief·priests
Mt 22:22 And upon·hearing *these words*, they·marveled, and
Mt 22:33 And hearing *this*, the crowds were·astounded at his
Mt 22:34 against him, after·hearing that he·muzzled the
Mt 27:47 of·the·ones standing there, after·hearing *that*,
Mk 3:8 — after·hearing what·many·things he·was·doing, a·
Mk 3:21 the·ones near *of·kin·to* him, hearing *of·it*, went·out
Mk 6:29 And with·his disciples hearing *of·it*, they·came and
Mk 10:41 And after·hearing *of·this*, the ten began to·be·
Mk 14:11 And after·hearing *this*, they·were·glad and
Mk 15:35 of·the·ones standing·nearby, after·hearing *that*,
Mk 16:11 And·those *in·mourning*, hearing that he·lives and
Eph 1:13 ·*expectation*, after·hearing the Redemptive-word of·
Col 1:4 after·hearing *both* of·yeur trust in Anointed-One
G0191.1 V-AAS-1S ἀκούσω (1x)
Php 1:27 being·absent, I·may·hear the·things concerning
G0191.1 V-AAS-2P ἀκούσητε (5x)
Lk 21:9 "But whenever yeu·should·hear·of wars and chaos,
Heb 3:7 Spirit says, "Today if yeu·should·hear his voice,
Heb 3:15 "Today, if yeu·should·hear his voice, yeu·should·
Heb 4:7 "Today, if yeu·should·hear his voice, yeu·should·
Mk 13:7 And whenever yeu·should·hear·of wars and rumors
G0191.1 V-AAS-3S ἀκούσῃ (8x)
Jn 7:51 ·of·clay†, unless it·should·hear directly·from him
Jn 12:47 "And if someone should·hear my utterances and
Jn 16:13 but·rather as·many·things·as he·should·hear, *that*
Ac 3:23 *that* every soul who would not hear that prophet,'
Mt 10:14 accept yeu or·should·not·even hear yeur words,
Mt 18:16 But if he·should·not hear *you*, *then* personally·take
2Ti 4:17 and *that* all the Gentiles may·hear. And·thus I·was·
Rv 3:20 and knock. If anyone should·hear my voice and
G0191.1 V-AAS-3P ἀκούσωσιν (6x)
Lk 8:13 the solid·rock, whenever they·should·hear, *are*
Ac 28:27 ·see with·the eyes, and should·hear with·the ears,

Mt 13:15 ·see with·the eyes, and should·hear with·the ears,
Mk 4:15 is·sown: and whenever they·should·hear, the
Mk 4:16 whenever they·should·hear the Redemptive-word,
Mk 6:11 accept yeu, or·should·not·even hear yeu, as·yeu·
G0191.1 V-API-3S ἠκούσθη (4x)
Jn 9:32 ·the beginning·age, it·is·not been·heard that any·man
Ac 11:22 the account concerning them was·heard among the
Mt 2:18 "'A·voice was·heard in Ramah— a·woeful·wailing
Mk 2:1 after *some* days, and it·was·heard that he·was in·a·
G0191.1 V-APP-DPN ἀκουσθεῖσιν (1x)
Heb 2:1 ·heed to·the·things being·heard, lest·at·any·time we·
G0191.1 V-APS-3S ἀκουσθῇ (4x)
Mt 28:14 And if this should·be·heard by the governor, we·
Rv 18:22 no, should·not be·heard any·longer in you.
Rv 18:22 no, should·not be·heard any·longer in you;
Rv 18:23 no, should·not·ever be·heard any·longer in you—
G0191.1 V-2RAI-1S ἀκήκοα (1x)
Ac 9:13 "Lord, I·have·heard of many·things concerning
G0191.1 V-2RAI-1P-ATT ἀκηκόαμεν (6x)
Jn 4:42 ·of your speech, for we·have·heard *him* ourselves,
Ac 6:11 men to·say, "We·have·heard him speaking reviling
Ac 6:14 For we·have·heard him saying that this Jesus of·
1Jn 1:1 beginning, which we·have·heard, which we·have·
1Jn 1:3 we·have·clearly·seen and have·heard, we·announce
1Jn 1:5 is the announcement which we·have·heard from him
G0191.1 V-2RAI-2P-ATT ἀκηκόατε (2x)
Jn 5:37 concerning me. Not·even yeu·have·heard his voice
1Jn 4:3 of·which yeu·have·heard that it·is·come, and now is
G0191.1 V-2RAI-3P-ATT ἀκηκόασιν (1x)
Rm 15:21 and those·that have·not heard shall·comprehend.
G0191.1 V-2RAP-APM-ATT ἀκηκοότας (1x)
Jn 18:21 me? Inquire·of the·ones having·heard what I·spoke
G0191.2 V-FDI-2P ἀκούσεσθε (1x)
Ac 7:37 brothers, as *he·did* myself; yeu·shall·listen·to him.'
G0191.2 V-PAI-2P ἀκούετε (1x)
Jn 10:20 and is·raving·mad; why·do yeu·listen·to him?
G0191.2 V-PAI-3S ἀκούει (3x)
Jn 10:27 "My sheep listen·to my voice, and·I know them,
Jn 18:37 birthed·from·out of·the truth listens·to my voice."
Lk 10:16 "The·one listening·to yeu listens·to me; and the·
G0191.2 V-PAM-2S ἄκουε (1x)
Mk 12:29 the commandments *is*, "Listen, O·IsraEl: Yahweh
G0191.2 V-PAM-2P ἀκούετε (5x)
Lk 9:35 "This is my beloved Son. Listen·to him!"
Mt 17:5 Son, in whom I·take·delight. Listen·to him!"
Mk 4:3 "Listen! Behold, the·one sowing went·forth to·sow.
Mk 7:14 he·was·saying to·them, "Listen·to me, everyone,
Mk 9:7 "This is my beloved Son. Listen·to him."
G0191.2 V-PAN ἀκούειν (1x)
Ac 4:19 it·is right in·the·sight of·God to·listen·to yeu rather
G0191.2 V-PAP-ASM ἀκούοντα (1x)
Lk 2:46 midst of·the instructors, both listening·to them and
G0191.2 V-PAP-APM ἀκούοντας (1x)
1Ti 4:16 ·save both yourself and the·ones listening·to you.
G0191.2 V-PAP-NSM ἀκούων (2x)
Jn 3:29 the·one standing and listening·for him, rejoices
Lk 10:16 "The·one listening·to yeu listens·to me; and the·
G0191.2 V-IAI-3S ἤκουεν (2x)
Lk 10:39 feet, also was·listening·to his Redemptive-word.
Ac 16:14 And a·certain·woman was·listening, a·woman by·
G0191.2 V-IAI-3P ἤκουον (3x)
Ac 15:12 stayed·silent and were·listening·to BarNabas and
Ac 22:22 And they·were·listening·to him even·until this
Mk 11:14 And his disciples were·listening.
G0191.2 V-AAI-2P ἠκούσατε (1x)
Jn 9:27 even·now, and yeu·did·not listen. Why·do yeu·want
G0191.2 V-AAM-2P ἀκούσατε (4x)
Ac 7:2 "Men, brothers and fathers, listen: "The God of·
Ac 13:16 and the·ones reverently·fearing God, listen.
Ac 15:13 "Men, brothers, listen·to me.
Jac 2:5 Listen, my beloved brothers, ¿!·is·it·not God *that*
G0191.2 V-AAP-NPM ἀκούσαντες (1x)
Mt 2:9 And after·listening·to the king, they·traversed.
G0191.2 V-AAS-3S ἀκούσῃ (1x)
Mt 18:15 him alone. If he·should·listen·to you, you·gained
G0191.3 V-PAI-2P ἀκούετε (2x)
Lk 8:18 ·for how *well* yeu·listen·with·comprehension, for
Mk 4:24 ·for how *well* yeu·listen·with·comprehension. By
G0191.3 V-PAI-3S ἀκούει (1x)
1Co 14:2 not·even·one·man listens·with·comprehension, but
G0191.3 V-PAP-DPM ἀκούουσιν (1x)
Mk 4:24 the·ones listening·with·comprehension, it·shall·be·
G0191.3 V-AAP-NPM ἀκούσαντες (1x)
Jn 5:25 the·ones listening·with·comprehension shall·live.

G0192 ἀ•κρασία akrasía *n.* (2x)
Roots:G0193 Compare:G1466 G4997
G0192.1 N-ASF ἀκρασίαν (1x)
1Co 7:5 tempt yeu on·account·of yeur lack·of·self-restraint.
G0192.1 N-GSF ἀκρασίας (1x)
Mt 23:25 out of·extortion and from·a·lack·of·self-restraint.

G0193 ἀ•κρατής akratḗs *adj.* (1x)
Roots:G0001 G2904 Compare:G1468 G4998
G0193.2 A-NPM ἀκρατεῖς (1x)
2Ti 3:3 ·men, slanderers, without·self-restraint, savages,

G0194 ἄ•κρατος ákratôs *adj.* (1x)
Roots:G0001 G2767
G0194 A-GSM ἀκράτου (1x)
Rv 14:10 having·been·blended·and·poured undiluted into the

G0195 ἀκρίβεια akríbêia *n.* (1x)
Roots:G0197-1 See:G0196
G0195.2 N-ASF ἀκρίβειαν (1x)
Ac 22:3 ·to *the* precise·manner of·*the*·Oral-law of·this

G0196 ἀκριβέστατος akribéstatôs *adj.* (1x)
Roots:G0197-1 See:G0197 G0198 G0199
G0196.2 A-ASF-S ἀκριβεστάτην (1x)
Ac 26:5 according·to the most·strict denomination of·our

G0197 ἀκριβέστερον akribéstêrôn *adv.* (4x)
Roots:G0197-1 See:G0196 G0198 G0199
G0197 ADV-C ἀκριβέστερον (4x)
Ac 18:26 explained to·him the Way of·God more·precisely.
Ac 23:15 *something* more·precisely concerning him; and we·
Ac 23:20 to·inquire more·precisely *about* something
Ac 24:22 *and* having·seen more·precisely concerning The

G0198 ἀκριβόω akribóō *v.* (2x)
Roots:G0197-1 Compare:G1231 G4441 See:G0196 G0197 G0199
G0198.2 V-AAI-3S ἠκρίβωσεν (2x)
Mt 2:7 precisely·ascertained personally·from them the time
Mt 2:16 which he·precisely·ascertained personally·from the

G0199 ἀκριβῶς akribō̂s *adv.* (5x)
Roots:G0197-1 Compare:G0206 G2509 See:G0196 G0197 G0198
G0199.1 ADV ἀκριβῶς (2x)
Mt 2:8 verify·*it*·by·inquiring precisely concerning the little·
Eph 5:15 look·out *then for* precisely how yeu·walk, not as
G0199.2 ADV ἀκριβῶς (3x)
Lk 1:3 ·closely·followed all·things accurately from·the·start,
Ac 18:25 was·instructing accurately the·things concerning
1Th 5:2 yeu·yearselves personally·know accurately that the

G0200 ἀκρίς akrís *n.* (4x)
Roots:G0206 Compare:G0013 See:G0188 xLangEquiv:H0697 xLangAlso:H2285 H5556
G0200 N-NPF ἀκρίδες (2x)
Mt 3:4 and his nourishment was locusts and wild honey.
Rv 9:3 ·out of·the smoke there·came·forth locusts upon the
G0200 N-APF ἀκρίδας (1x)
Mk 1:6 his loins, and *was* eating locusts and wild honey.
G0200 N-GPF ἀκρίδων (1x)
Rv 9:7 And the semblances of·the locusts *were* like horses

G0201 ἀκροατήριον akrôatḗriôn *n.* (1x)
Roots:G0202
G0201.2 N-ASN ἀκροατήριον (1x)
Ac 25:23 entering into the formal·hearing·chamber, together

G0202 ἀκροατής akrôatḗs *n.* (4x)
Roots:G0191
G0202 N-NSM ἀκροατής (2x)
Jac 1:23 Because if any is a·hearer of·*the*·Redemptive-word,
Jac 1:25 this·man being not a·forgetful hearer, but·rather a·
G0202 N-NPM ἀκροαταί (2x)
Rm 2:13 For *it·is* not the hearers of·the Torah-Law *that·are*
Jac 1:22 and not merely hearers, defrauding yeur·own·

G0203 ἀκρο•βυστία akrôbystía *n.* (20x)
עָרְלָה ʿọrlạh [Hebrew]
Roots:G0206 Compare:G4061 See:G2192 xLangEquiv:H6190
G0203.2 N-NSF ἀκροβυστία (1x)
Rm 2:26 If the·one uncircumcised should·vigilantly·keep the
G0203.2 N-ASF ἀκροβυστίαν (1x)
Ac 11:3 ·entered·in alongside men being uncircumcised, and
G0203.2 N-DSF ἀκροβυστίᾳ (1x)
Rm 4:12 the *righteousness* in the uncircumcised trust of·our
G0203.3 N-NSF ἀκροβυστία (7x)
Gal 5:6 circumcision nor uncircumcision has·any strength,
Gal 6:15 circumcision nor uncircumcision has·any strength,
Rm 2:25 your circumcision has·become uncircumcision.
Rm 2:26 Torah-Law, his uncircumcision, shall·it·not·indeed
Rm 2:27 ·from·out of·natural uncircumcision *indeed* judge
1Co 7:19 ·at·all, and the uncircumcision is nothing·at·all,
Col 3:11 Jew, circumcision and uncircumcision, Barbarian,
G0203.3 N-DSF ἀκροβυστίᾳ (5x)
Rm 4:10 being in circumcision, or in uncircumcision? Not in
Rm 4:10 Not in circumcision, but·rather in uncircumcision.
Rm 4:11 *reckoned while·still* in the uncircumcision, in·order·
1Co 7:18 *that* is·called·forth in uncircumcision, must·not be·
Col 2:13 the trespasses and the uncircumcision of·yeur flesh,
G0203.3 N-GSF ἀκροβυστίας (1x)
Rm 4:11 *God* through *the state·of* uncircumcision, in·order·
G0203.4 N-NSF ἀκροβυστία (1x)
Eph 2:11 being·referred·to·as *the* Uncircumcision by the·one
G0203.4 N-ASF ἀκροβυστίαν (2x)
Rm 3:30 ·result of·trust and *the* Uncircumcision through the
Rm 4:9 *only*, or upon the Uncircumcision also?
G0203.4 N-GSF ἀκροβυστίας (1x)
Gal 2:7 of·the Uncircumcision had·been·entrusted *to·me*,

G0204 ἀκρο•γωνιαῖος akrôgōniaîôs *adj.* (2x)
Roots:G0206 G1137
G0204.2 A-ASM ἀκρογωνιαῖον (1x)
1Pe 2:6 I·lay in Tsiyon a·chief·corner stone, Selected, *being*
G0204.2 A-GSM ἀκρογωνιαίου (1x)
Eph 2:20 Anointed himself being *the* chief·corner *stone*,

G0205 ἀκρο•θίνιον akrôthíniôn *n.* (1x)
Roots:G0206 Compare:G4307-2
G0205.2 N-GPN ἀκροθινίων (1x)
Heb 7:4 gave a·tenth from·among the best·of·the·plunder.

G0206 ἄκρον ákrôn *n.* (6x)
Compare:G0197-1 See:G0188 G0199 G0206-1
G0206.2 N-ASN ἄκρον (2x)
Lk 16:24 in·order·that he·may·dip the tip of·his finger in·
Heb 11:21 and he·leaned·prostrate upon the tip of·his staff.
G0206.3 N-GSN ἄκρου (2x)
Mk 13:27 from *the* uttermost·part of·earth as·far·as·to *the*
Mk 13:27 of·earth as·far·as·to *the* uttermost·part of·heaven.
G0206.3 N-GPN ἄκρων (2x)
Mt 24:31 from *the* uttermost·parts of·*the*·heavens unto *the*
Mt 24:31 of·*the*·heavens unto *the* uttermost·parts thereof.

G0207 Ἀκύλας Akýlas *n/p.* (6x)
Compare:G0105 See:G4252 G4251
G0207.2 N/P-NSM Ἀκύλας (3x)
Ac 18:18 and Little·Prisca and Aquila *were* together with·
Ac 18:26 But after·hearing him, Aquila and Little·Prisca
1Co 16:19 of·Asia greet yeu. Aquila and Little·Prisca greet
G0207.2 N/P-ASM Ἀκύλαν (3x)
Ac 18:2 a·certain Jew by·the·name·of Aquila (of·Pontus by·
Rm 16:3 Greet Little·Prisca and Aquila, my coworkers in
2Ti 4:19 Greet Prisca and Aquila, and the household of·

G0208 ἀ•κυρόω akyrṓō *v.* (3x)
Roots:G0001 G2964
G0208 V-PAI-3S ἀκυροῖ (1x)
Gal 3:17 does·not invalidate a·unilateral·covenant having·
G0208 V-PAP-NPM ἀκυροῦντες (1x)
Mk 7:13 invalidating the Holy-word of·God by·yeur Oral·
G0208 V-AAI-2P ἠκυρώσατε (1x)
Mt 15:6 And·thus, yeu·invalidate the commandment of·

G0209 ἀ•κωλύτως akōlýtōs *adv.* (1x)
Roots:G0001 G2967
G0209.2 ADV ἀκωλύτως (1x)
Ac 28:31 — with all clarity·of·speech, without·hindrance.

G0210 ἄ•κων ákōn *adj.* (1x)
Roots:G0001 G1635
G0210.2 A-NSM ἄκων (1x)
1Co 9:17 but *even* if involuntarily, an·estate·management

G0211 ἀλάβαστρον alábastrôn *n.* (4x)
G0211.1 N-ASN ἀλάβαστρον (4x)
Lk 7:37 after·subsequently·obtaining an·alabaster·flask of·
Mt 26:7 having an·alabaster·flask of·deeply·valuable
Mk 14:3 having an·alabaster·flask of·extremely·expensive
Mk 14:3 And upon·shattering the alabaster·flask, she·poured

G0212 ἀλαζονεία alazônêía *n.* (2x)
Roots:G0213
G0212.1 N-NSF ἀλαζονεία (1x)
1Jn 2:16 of·the eyes, and the bragging of·natural·life, is not
G0212.1 N-DPF ἀλαζονείαις (1x)
Jac 4:16 But now yeu·boast in yeur bragging. All such

G0213 ἀλαζών alazṓn *n.* (2x)
See:G0212
G0213 N-NPM ἀλαζόνες (1x)
2Ti 3:2 fond·of·money, braggers, haughty, revilers,
G0213 N-APM ἀλαζόνας (1x)
Rm 1:30 ·God, abusively·insolent, haughty, braggers, *and*

G0214 ἀλαλάζω alalázō *v.* (2x)
Compare:G3649 G2360 See:G0213-2
G0214.2 V-PAP-APM ἀλαλάζοντας (1x)
Mk 5:38 *people* weeping and clamoring repeatedly.
G0214.3 V-PAP-NSN ἀλαλάζον (1x)
1Co 13:1 a·reverberating bronze·gong or a·clanging cymbal.

G0215 ἀ•λάλητος alálētôs *adj.* (1x)
Roots:G0001 G2980 Compare:G0412 G0411 G0731
G0215 A-DPM ἀλαλήτοις (1x)
Rm 8:26 on·our behalf with·groanings unspeakable.

G0216 ἄ•λαλος álalôs *adj.* (3x)
Roots:G0001 G2980 Compare:G1769 G2974 G3424
xLangAlso:H0483
G0216.2 A-NSN ἄλαλον (1x)
Mk 9:25 "Spirit, the·one mute and deaf, I·myself order you,
G0216.2 A-ASN ἄλαλον (1x)
Mk 9:17 I·brought to you my son, having a·mute spirit,
G0216.2 A-APM ἀλάλους (1x)
Mk 7:37 both the deaf to·hear and the mute to·speak."

G0217 ἅλας hálas *n.* (8x)
Roots:G0251
G0217.1 N-NSN ἅλας (6x)
Lk 14:34 "Salt *is* good, but if the salt should·become·bland,
Lk 14:34 good, but if the salt should·become·bland, in what·
Mt 5:13 "Yeu·yeurselves are the salt of·the earth, but if the
Mt 5:13 earth, but if the salt should·become·bland, in what·
Mk 9:50 Salt *is* good, but if the salt should·become unsalty,
Mk 9:50 *is* good, but if the salt should·become unsalty, with
G0217.1 N-ASN ἅλας (1x)
Mk 9:50 shall·yeu·season it? "Have salt in yeurselves, and
G0217.1 N-DSN ἅλατι (1x)
Col 4:6 *to·be* with grace having·been·seasoned with·salt, *and*

G0218 ἀ•λείφω alêíphō *v.* (9x)
Roots:G0001 G3045 Compare:G3462 G5548 G1472
xLangEquiv:H5480
G0218 V-IAI-3S ἤλειφεν (1x)
Lk 7:38 ·kissing his feet and was·rubbing·on the ointment.
G0218 V-IAI-3P ἤλειφον (1x)
Mk 6:13 ·oil, they·were·rubbing·oil·on many that·were·
G0218 V-AAI-2S ἤλειψας (1x)
Lk 7:46 "With·olive·oil, you·did·not rub·oil·on my head,
G0218 V-AAI-3S ἤλειψεν (2x)
Jn 12:3 of·authentic spikenard, Mary rubbed·oil·on the feet
Lk 7:46 head, but she·herself rubbed·oil·on my feet with·
G0218 V-AAP-NSF ἀλείψασα (1x)
Jn 11:2 *that* Mary, the·one rubbing·oil·on the Lord with·
G0218 V-AAP-NPM ἀλείψαντες (1x)
Jac 5:14 ·pray over him, rubbing·oil·on him with·olive·oil
G0218 V-AAS-3P ἀλείψωσιν (1x)
Mk 16:1 after·going *to·him*, they·may·rub·*them*·on him.
G0218 V-AMM-2S ἄλειψαι (1x)
Mt 6:17 "But you, when·fasting, rub·oil·on your head and

G0219 ἀλεκτορο•φωνία alêktôrôphōnía *n.* (1x)
Roots:G0220 G5456 Compare:G3317 G4404
G0219.1 N-GSF ἀλεκτοροφωνίας (1x)
Mk 13:35 or at·midnight, or at·rooster-crow, or at·the·

G0220 ἀλέκτωρ aléktōr *n.* (12x)
Compare:G3733 See:G0223
xLangEquiv:H8650-1
G0220 N-NSM ἀλέκτωρ (7x)
Jn 13:38 most·certainly, I·say to·you, a·rooster, no, shall·
Jn 18:27 denied *it* again, and immediately a·rooster crowed.
Lk 22:34 "I·say to·you, Peter, a·rooster, no, it·shall·not
Lk 22:60 ·once, with·him still speaking, the rooster crowed.
Mt 26:74 And immediately a·rooster crowed.
Mk 14:68 entryway·of·the·courtyard, and a·rooster crowed.
Mk 14:72 And for a·second·time, a·rooster crowed. And
G0220 N-ASM ἀλέκτορα (5x)
Lk 22:61 "Prior·to a·rooster crowing, you·shall·utterly·
Mt 26:34 in·this night, prior·to a·rooster crowing, you·shall·
Mt 26:75 "Prior·to a·rooster crowing, you·shall·utterly·
Mk 14:30 this night, prior·to a·rooster crowing twice, you·
Mk 14:72 to·him, "Prior·to a·rooster crowing twice, you·

G0221 Ἀλεξ•ανδρεύς Alêxandrêús *n/g.* (2x)
Compare:G0222 G0223
G0221.1 N/G-GPM Ἀλεξανδρέων (1x)
Ac 6:9 with Cyrenians and Alexandrians, and the·ones from
G0221.2 N/G-NSM Ἀλεξανδρεύς (1x)
Ac 18:24 (Apollos by·name, of·AlexAndria by·birth), an·

G0222 Ἀλεξ•ανδρῖνος Alêxandrînôs *adj/g.* (2x)
Compare:G0221 G0223
G0222.2 A/G-ASN Ἀλεξανδρῖνον (1x)
Ac 27:6 upon·finding a·sailing·ship of·AlexAndria sailing
G0222.2 A/G-DSN Ἀλεξανδρίνῳ (1x)
Ac 28:11 in a·sailing·ship of·AlexAndria with·a·figurehead

G0223 Ἀλέξ•ανδρος Aléxandrôs *n/p.* (6x)
Roots:G0435 See:G0220
G0223.2 N/P-NSM Ἀλέξανδρος (3x)
Ac 19:33 him forward. And AlexAnder, motioning with·his
1Ti 1:20 of·whom are Hymenaeus and AlexAnder, whom I·
2Ti 4:14 AlexAnder, the coppersmith, pointedly·did me
G0223.2 N/P-ASM Ἀλέξανδρον (2x)
Ac 4:6 and Caiaphas and YoChanan and AlexAnder, and as·
Ac 19:33 But they·pressed AlexAnder forward out of·the
G0223.2 N/P-GSM Ἀλεξάνδρου (1x)
Mk 15:21 countryside (the father of·AlexAnder and Rufus),

G0224 ἄλευρον áleurôn *n.* (2x)
Compare:G4585 See:G0229
xLangEquiv:H7058 xLangAlso:H5560
G0224 N-GSN ἀλεύρου (2x)
Lk 13:21 into three seah·measures of·flour, until all was·
Mt 13:33 *it* into three seah·measures of·flour, until all was·

G0225 ἀ•λήθεια alḗthêia *n.* (112x)
Roots:G0227 xLangAlso:H0571
G0225.2 N-NSF ἀλήθεια (14x)
Jn 1:17 the grace and the truth came·to·be through Jesus
Jn 8:32 ·know the truth, and the truth shall·set yeu free.
Jn 8:44 truth, because there·is not truth in him. Whenever
Jn 14:6 "I AM the way, and the truth, and the life-above.
Jn 17:17 Your Redemptive-word is truth.
Jn 18:38 says to·him, "What is truth?" And after·declaring
Gal 2:5 subjection, in·order·that the truth of·the good·news
Rm 3:7 if by my lie, the truth of·God abounded to his glory,
2Co 7:14 *we·made* before Titus) has·now·become truth.
2Co 11:10 *The* truth of·Anointed-One is in me, *such* that this
Eph 4:21 and are·instructed by him (just·as truth is in Jesus)
1Jn 1:8 we·deceive ourselves, and the truth is not in us.
1Jn 2:4 commandments is a·liar, and the truth is not in him.
1Jn 5:6 is the·one testifying, because the Spirit is the truth.
G0225.2 N-ASF ἀλήθειαν (23x)
Jn 3:21 But the·one doing the truth comes to the light, in·
Jn 8:32 and yeu·shall·know the truth, and the truth shall·set
Jn 8:40 ·clay† that has·spoken to·yeu the truth, which I·heard
Jn 8:45 "And because I·myself say the truth, yeu·do·not trust
Jn 8:46 And if·what I·say *is the* truth, why·do yeu·yeurselves
Jn 16:7 ·myself say to·yeu the truth; it·is·more·advantageous
Jn 16:13 he·shall·guide yeu into all the truth. "For he·shall·
Gal 2:14 walk·uprightly toward the truth of·the good·news,
Mk 5:33 ·down·before him and declared to·him all the truth.
Rm 1:18 the·ones holding·down the truth by unrighteousness
Rm 1:25 who exchanged the truth of·God with the lie, and
Rm 2:2 of·God is according·to truth against the·ones
Rm 9:1 I·say *the* truth in Anointed-One, I·do·not lie, with·
Tit 1:14 ·of·clay† that·are·turning·them·away·from the truth.
2Co 12:6 be impetuous, for I·shall·declare truth. But I·am·
Eph 4:25 "Each·man must·speak truth with his neighbor,"
1Ti 2:7 — (I·relate *the* truth in Anointed-One *and* do·not lie)
1Ti 4:3 ·the·ones trusting and having·fully·known the truth.
2Ti 2:18 who missed·the·mark concerning the truth, saying
1Jn 1:6 in the darkness, we·do·lie, and do·not do the truth.
1Jn 2:21 yeu·do·not personally·know the truth, but·rather
2Jn 1:1 but·rather also all the·ones having·known the truth,
2Jn 1:2 on·account·of the truth abiding in us and *which* shall·
G0225.2 N-DSF ἀληθείᾳ (30x)
Jn 4:23 to·the Father in spirit and in·truth, for even the
Jn 4:24 ·*before* him to·fall·prostrate in spirit and in·truth."
Jn 5:33 ·for John, and he·has·testified to·the truth.
Jn 8:44 and he·does·not stand in the truth, because there·is
Jn 17:17 them holy in your truth. Your Redemptive-word is
Jn 17:19 also may·be having·been·made·holy in truth.
Jn 18:37 in·order·that I·may·testify to·the truth. Everyone
Gal 3:1 yeu to·not be·persuaded by·the truth, *before* whose
Gal 5:7 ·path *such·for* yeu to·not be·persuaded by·the truth?
Mt 22:16 ·instruct the Way of·God in truth, and it·does·not
Rm 2:8 being·obstinate to·the Truth and are·being·persuaded
Php 1:18 whether in·pretense or in·truth, Anointed-One is·
2Pe 1:12 having·been·firmly·established in the present truth.
2Th 2:12 the·ones not trusting the truth, but·rather taking·
1Co 13:6 injustice, but it·rejoices·together with·the truth.
2Co 7:14 as we·spoke all·things to·yeu in truth, even in·this·
Eph 5:9 all beneficial·goodness and righteousness and truth),
Eph 6:14 ·girding yeur·own loins with truth, and dressing·
Col 1:6 ·heard *it* and recognized the grace of·God in truth—
1Ti 2:7 lie)— an·instructor of·Gentiles in trust and truth.
2Ti 3:8 these also stand·opposed·to the truth, men·of·clay†
1Jn 3:18 nor·even in·tongue, but·rather in·deed and in·truth.
2Jn 1:1 — whom I·myself do·love in truth, and not I·myself
2Jn 1:3 Anointed, the Son of·the Father, in truth and love.
2Jn 1:4 children *those* walking in truth, just·as we·received
3Jn 1:1 well-beloved Gaius, whom I·myself do·love in truth.
3Jn 1:3 coming and testifying of·your truth, just·as you walk
3Jn 1:3 testifying of·your truth, just·as you walk in truth.
3Jn 1:4 ·things, that I·hear·of my children walking in truth.
3Jn 1:8 in·order·that we·may·be coworkers with·the truth.
G0225.2 N-GSF ἀληθείας (43x)
Jn 1:14 directly·from *the* Father), full of·grace and truth.
Jn 14:17 the Spirit of·Truth, whom the world is·not able to·
Jn 15:26 the Father, the Spirit of·Truth, who proceeds·forth
Jn 16:13 that·one, the Spirit of·Truth, should·come, he·
Jn 18:37 being birthed·from·out·of the truth listens·to my
Lk 4:25 "But I·say to·yeu in truth, many widows were in
Lk 20:21 ·rather *that* you·instruct the Way of·God in truth.
Lk 22:59 ·asserting, saying, "In truth, this·man also was

Ac 4:27 "For in truth, they·were·gathered·together against
Ac 10:34 mouth, declared, "In truth, I·grasp that God is not
Ac 26:25 utterances of·truth and·also with·a·sound·mind.
Heb 10:26 receiving the recognition of·the truth, no·longer
Mk 12:14 the Way of·God in truth. Is·it·proper to·give a·
Mk 12:32 clearly·full·well did·you·declare in truth, because
Rm 2:20 ·the absolute·knowledge and of·the truth within the
Rm 15:8 ·Circumcision on·behalf of·God's truth, in·order to·
Jac 1:18 he·bred us by·the·Redemptive-word of·truth, for us
Jac 3:14 do·not boast·over and utter·lies against the truth.
Jac 5:19 among yeu should·be·led·astray from the truth, and
1Pe 1:22 in the attentive·obedience of·the truth through *the*
2Pe 2:2 ·account·of whom, the way of·truth shall·be·reviled.
2Th 2:10 did·not accept the love of·the truth, such·for them
2Th 2:13 in renewed·holiness of·Spirit and in·trust of·truth,
Tit 1:1 and *for·the* recognition of·truth (the·one according·to
1Co 5:8 with Unleavened·Bread of·sincerity and truth.
2Co 4:2 by·the manifestation of·the truth, commending
2Co 6:7 by *the* Redemptive-word of·truth, by God's power,
2Co 13:8 able *to·do* anything against the truth, but·rather on·
2Co 13:8 against the truth, but·rather on·behalf of·the truth.
Eph 1:13 after·hearing the Redemptive-word of·the truth, the
Eph 4:24 righteousness and in·divine·holiness of·the truth).
Col 1:5 in the Redemptive-word of·the truth of·the good·news,
1Ti 2:4 ·be·saved and to·come to a·full·knowledge of·truth.
1Ti 3:15 ·the·living God, a·pillar and a·support of·the truth.
1Ti 6:5 *their* minds also having·been·robbed of·the truth—
2Ti 2:15 rightly·dissecting the Redemptive-word of·truth.
2Ti 2:25 to·them repentance for *the* recognition of·truth,
2Ti 3:7 ·even being·able to·come to a·recognition of·truth.
2Ti 4:4 away·from the truth and shall·be·turned·aside to the
1Jn 2:21 and that any lie is not birthed·from·out of·the truth.
1Jn 3:19 ·are birthed·from·out of·the truth and shall·reassure
1Jn 4:6 of·this, we·know the spirit of·truth and the spirit of·
3Jn 1:12 ·to by all·men, and by the truth itself. And also,

EG0225.2 (2x)

Jn 16:15 of·me, *the Spirit of·Truth* shall·receive and shall·
2Th 2:11 an·effective deviation *from·truth* in·order·for them

G0226 ἀ•ληθεύω alēthêúō *v.* (2x)

Roots:G0227

G0226.2 V-PAP-NSM ἀληθεύων (1x)

Gal 4:16 have·I·become yeur enemy, being·truthful to·yeu?

G0226.2 V-PAP-NPM ἀληθεύοντες (1x)

Eph 4:15 But being·truthful in love, we·should·grow·up *in*

G0227 ἀ•ληθής alēthḗs *adj.* (26x)

Roots:G0001 G2990 See:G0228

EG0227 (1x)

Ac 24:9 professing these·things to·hold *true* in·this·manner.

G0227.2 A-NSM ἀληθής (6x)

Jn 3:33 testimony did·stamp·his·own·seal that God is true.
Jn 7:18 him, the·same·man is true, and unrighteousness is
Jn 8:26 But·yet the·one sending me is true, and·I say to the
Mt 22:16 "Mentor, we·have·seen that you·are true, and *that*
Mk 12:14 we·personally·know that you·are true, and *that* it·
Rm 3:4 And let God be true, but every man·of·clay† a·liar;

G0227.2 A-NSF ἀληθής (5x)

Jn 8:14 my testimony is true, because I·personally·know
Jn 8:16 should·judge, my verdict is true, because I·am not
Jn 21:24 and we·personally·know that his testimony is true.
Tit 1:13 This testimony is true. On·account·of which cause,
3Jn 1:12 ·*of* yeu·personally·know that our testimony is true.

G0227.2 A-NSN ἀληθές (2x)

Ac 12:9 through the angel was true, but he·was·supposing
1Jn 2:27 yeu concerning all·things (and is true, and is not a·

G0227.2 A-NPM ἀληθεῖς (1x)

2Co 6:8 and good·reputation, as impostors and·yet true,

G0227.2 A-NPN ἀληθῆ (2x)

Jn 10:41 ·as John declared concerning this·man were true."
Php 4:8 As·many·things·as are true, as·many·things·as *are*

G0227.2 A-ASF ἀληθῆ (1x)

1Pe 5:12 further·testifying this to·be *the* true grace of·God in

G0227.2 A-ASN ἀληθές (2x)

Jn 4:18 This·thing you·have·declared *is* true."
1Jn 2:8 I·do·write to·yeu, which is true in him and in yeu,

G0227.2 A-APN ἀληθῆ (1x)

Jn 19:35 ·knows that *what* he·says *is* true, in·order·that yeu

G0227.2 A-GSF ἀληθοῦς (1x)

2Pe 2:22 it·has·befallen them *according·to* the true proverb,

G0227.3 A-NSF ἀληθής (4x)

Jn 5:31 my·own·self, my testimony is not legally·valid.
Jn 5:32 which he·testifies concerning me is legally·valid.
Jn 8:13 yourself; your testimony is not legally·valid."
Jn 8:17 the testimony of·two men·of·clay† is legally·valid.

G0228 ἀ•ληθινός alēthinós *adj.* (27x)

Roots:G0227 Compare:G4101 xLangAlso:H0571

G0228.1 A-NSM ἀληθινός (2x)

Rv 3:7 says the Holy·One, the Truthful·One, "The·one
Rv 6:10 the Holy and the Truthful·One, do·you·not judge

G0228.2 A-NSM ἀληθινός (5x)

Jn 4:37 For in this *case*, the saying is true, 'One is the·one
Jn 7:28 the·one sending me is true, whom yeu·yeurselves do·
1Jn 5:20 This is the true God and the eternal life-above.
Rv 3:14 ·the·Amen, the trustworthy and true witness, the
Rv 19:11 it *was* being·called Trustworthy and True, and in

G0228.2 A-NSF ἀληθινή (2x)

Jn 15:1 "I AM the true vine, and my Father is the farmer.
Jn 19:35 and his testimony is true; this·one·also personally·

G0228.2 A-NSN ἀληθινόν (2x)

Jn 1:9 *This* was the true Light which illuminates every child·
1Jn 2:8 is·passing·away, and the true Light even·now

G0228.2 A-NPM ἀληθινοί (4x)

Jn 4:23 the true ones·that·fall·prostrate shall·fall·prostrate to·
Rv 19:9 "These are the true sayings of·God."
Rv 21:5 because these words are true and trustworthy."
Rv 22:6 "These words *are* trustworthy and true." And

G0228.2 A-NPF ἀληθιναί (3x)

Rv 15:3 God Almighty. Righteous and true *are* your ways,
Rv 16:7 O·Yahweh, God Almighty, true and righteous *are*
Rv 19:2 Because true and righteous *are* his verdicts; because

G0228.2 A-ASM ἀληθινόν (3x)

Jn 6:32 my Father gives yeu the true bread from·out of·the
Jn 17:3 they·may·know you, the only true God, and Jesus
1Jn 5:20 that we·should·know the·one *who·is* true, and we·

G0228.2 A-ASN ἀληθινόν (1x)

Lk 16:11 ·wealth, who shall·entrust to·yeu the true *wealth*?

G0228.2 A-DSM ἀληθινῷ (2x)

1Th 1:9 the idols, to·be·slaves to·the·living and true God,
1Jn 5:20 and we·are in the·one *who·is* true, in his Son Jesus

G0228.2 A-GSF ἀληθινῆς (2x)

Heb 8:2 ·the holy·things and of·the true Tabernacle, which
Heb 10:22 we·should·come·alongside with a·true heart in

G0228.2 A-GPN ἀληθινῶν (1x)

Heb 9:24 *the* corresponding·patterns of·the true, but·rather

G0229 ἀλήθω alḗthō *v.* (2x)

Compare:G3039 G5149 See:G0224

G0229 V-PAP-NPF ἀλήθουσαι (2x)

Lk 17:35 Two *women* shall·be grinding in·unison; one shall·
Mt 24:41 Two *women shall·be* grinding at the mill-house;

G0230 ἀ•ληθῶς alēthō̂s *adv.* (21x)

Roots:G0227

G0230 ADV ἀληθῶς (21x)

Jn 1:47 him, "See! Truly an·Israelite in whom there·is no
Jn 4:42 we·personally·know that this is truly the Savior of·
Jn 6:14 were·saying, "This is truly the Prophet, the·one
Jn 6:55 For my flesh truly is a·full·meal, and my blood truly
Jn 6:55 is a·full·meal, and my blood truly is a·full·drink.
Jn 7:26 Perhaps the rulers truly do·know that this truly is the
Jn 7:26 truly do·know that this truly is the Anointed-One.
Jn 7:40 the crowd were·saying, "Truly this is the Prophet.
Jn 8:31 in my Redemptive-word, yeu·are truly my disciples;
Jn 17:8 received *them*; and they·knew truly that I·came·forth
Lk 9:27 "But I·say to·yeu truly, there·are some of·the·ones
Lk 12:44 Truly I·say to·yeu, that he·shall·fully·establish him
Lk 21:3 And he·declared, "Truly I·say to·yeu, that this
Ac 12:11 "Now I·personally·know truly that Yahweh
Mt 14:33 to·him, saying, "Truly you·are God's Son.
Mt 26:73 ·by declared to·Peter, "Truly you·yourself are also
Mt 27:54 tremendously, saying, "Truly this was God's Son.
Mk 14:70 again to·Peter, "Truly you·are from·among them,
Mk 15:39 ·last, he·declared, "Truly this man·of·clay† was
1Th 2:13 ·men·of·clay†, but·rather just·as it·is truly, God's
1Jn 2:5 his Redemptive-word, in him truly the love of·God

G0231 ἁλιεύς haliêús *n.* (5x)

Roots:G0251 Compare:G0293-1 See:G0232 xLangEquiv:H1771 xLangAlso:H1728

G0231.2 N-APM ἁλιεῖς (2x)

Mt 4:19 me, and I·shall·make yeu fishers of·men·of·clay†!"
Mk 1:17 ·shall·cause yeu to·become fishers of·men·of·clay†.

G0231.3 N-NPM ἁλιεῖς (3x)

Lk 5:2 from them, the fishermen rinsed·off the nets.
Mt 4:18 a·cast·net into the sea, for they·were fishermen.
Mk 1:16 a·cast·net into the sea, for they·were fishermen.

G0232 ἁλιεύω haliêúō *v.* (1x)

Roots:G0231 xLangAlso:H1770

G0232.2 V-PAN ἁλιεύειν (1x)

Jn 21:3 says to·them, "I·head·on·out to·fish." They·say to·

G0233 ἁλίζω halízō *v.* (3x)

Roots:G0251

G0233 V-FPI-3S ἁλισθήσεται (3x)

Mt 5:13 ·bland, in what·manner shall·it·be·salted? To not·
Mk 9:49 "For everyone shall·be·salted with·fire, and every
Mk 9:49 ·fire, and every sacrifice shall·be·salted with·salt.

G0234 ἀλίσγεμα alísgêma *n.* (1x)

Roots:G0233-2 Compare:G2839 G3393 G3470 G4696 G4507 See:G2840

G0234.1 N-GPN ἀλισγημάτων (1x)

Ac 15:20 for·them to·abstain from the pollutions of·the idols,

G0235 ἀλλά allá *conj.* (638x)

Roots:G0243 Compare:G2228 G3123

G0235.1 CONJ ἀλλ᾽ (5x)

Mk 4:22 become hidden·away, other·than that it·may·come
Mk 9:8 no·longer not·even·one·man, other·than Jesus alone
1Co 3:5 and who *is* Apollos, other than attendants through
2Co 1:13 ·write no other·things to·yeu, other than what yeu·
2Co 2:5 *it·is* not me *that* he·has·grieved (other·than in part),

G0235.2 CONJ ἀλλ᾽ (470x)

Jn 1:8 that Light, but·rather *he·was·dispatched* in·order·that
Jn 1:13 ·*the*·will of·man, but·rather birthed·from·out of·God.
Jn 3:15 completely·perish, but·rather should·have eternal
Jn 3:16 completely·perish, but·rather should·have eternal
Jn 3:17 ·judge the world, but·rather in·order·that the world
Jn 3:28 am not the Anointed-One,' but·rather that 'I·am
Jn 3:36 shall·not gaze·upon life-above, but·rather the wrath
Jn 4:2 himself was·not immersing, but·rather his disciples),
Jn 4:14 thirst into the coming·age, but·rather the water that I·
Jn 5:22 not·even·one·man, but·rather he·has·given all the
Jn 5:24 ·judgment, but·rather has·walked·on out·from the
Jn 5:30 ·not seek my·own will, but·rather the Father's will,
Jn 5:34 from a·man·of·clay†, but·rather I·say these·things
Jn 5:42 but·rather I·have·known yeu, that yeu·do·not have
Jn 6:22 into the small·boat, but·rather *that* his disciples
Jn 6:26 ·saw miraculous·signs, but·rather because yeu·ate
Jn 6:27 ·is·completely·perishing, but·rather for·the full·meal
Jn 6:32 from·out of·the heaven, but·rather my Father gives
Jn 6:36 But·rather I·declared to·yeu, also yeu·have·clearly·
Jn 6:38 I·may·do my·own will, but·rather the will of·the·
Jn 6:39 ·*is, the sheep pen*), but·rather shall·raise it up at the
Jn 7:10 the Sacred·Feast, not openly, but·rather as in secret.
Jn 7:12 were·saying, "No, but·rather he·deceives the crowd.
Jn 7:16 is not mine, but·rather *from* the·one sending me.
Jn 7:22 it·is from·out of·Moses, but·rather from·out of·the
Jn 7:24 according·to *mere*·appearance, but·rather judge the
Jn 7:28 come of·my·own·self, but·rather the·one sending me
Jn 7:49 But·rather this crowd, the·one not knowing the
Jn 8:12 ·about in the darkness, but·rather shall·have the light
Jn 8:16 because I·am not alone, but·rather *it·is* I·myself and
Jn 8:28 ·one·thing of·my·own·self; but·rather just·as my

Jn 8:42 have·I·come of my·own·self, but·rather that *God*
Jn 8:49 do·not have a·demon, but·rather I·deeply·honor my
Jn 8:55 a·liar like yeurselves. But·rather I·have·seen him,
Jn 9:3 nor his parents, but·rather in·order·that the works of·
Jn 9:31 those·full·of·moral·failure, but·rather if any·man
Jn 10:1 sheep, but·rather walking·up from·some·other·way,
Jn 10:5 they·should·not follow, but·rather shall·flee from
Jn 10:18 it away from me, but·rather I·myself lay it down of
Jn 10:33 work, but·rather concerning a·revilement of·God.
Jn 11:4 is not toward death, but·rather on·behalf·of·the glory
Jn 11:30 come into the village, but·rather was in the place
Jn 11:51 declare this from his·own·self, but·rather being *the*
Jn 11:52 of·the nation merely, but·rather in·order·that also
Jn 11:54 the Judeans, but·rather went·away from·there to
Jn 12:6 the helplessly·poor, but·rather because he·was a·
Jn 12:9 Jesus merely, but·rather in·order·that they·may·see
Jn 12:16 these·things at·the first, but·rather when Jesus was·
Jn 12:27 out of·this hour?' But·rather on·account·of this, I·
Jn 12:30 not on·account·of me, but·rather on·account·of yeu
Jn 12:44 does·not trust in me, but·rather in the·one sending
Jn 12:47 the world, but·rather in·order·that I·may·save the
Jn 12:49 speak from·out·of·my·own·self. But·rather Father
Jn 13:9 not my feet merely, but·rather also my hands and
Jn 14:24 yeu·hear is not mine, but·rather *that* of·*the*·Father,
Jn 14:31 But·rather, in·order·that the world may·know that I·
Jn 15:16 *that* selected me, but·rather I·myself selected yeu
Jn 15:19 from·among the world, but·rather I·myself selected
Jn 16:4 "But·rather these·things have·I·spoken to·yeu, that
Jn 16:6 But·rather because I·have·spoken these·things to·yeu
Jn 16:13 speak from himself, but·rather as·many·things·as
Jn 16:25 but·rather I·shall·announce·in·detail to·yeu with·
Jn 17:9 world *that* I·ask, but·rather concerning those·whom
Jn 17:15 ·among the world, but·rather that you·should·guard
Jn 17:20 ·men merely do·I·ask, but·rather also concerning
Jn 18:28 ·be·contaminated, but·rather that they·may·eat the
Jn 18:40 "Not this·one, but·rather BarAbbas." And
Jn 19:21 of·the Jews,' but·rather that this·man declared, 'I·
Jn 19:24 but·rather we·should·determine·by·lot concerning
Jn 19:34 But·rather one of·the soldiers jabbed his side with·
Jn 20:7 strips·of·linen, but·rather having·been·swathed in
Jn 20:27 And do·not be·distrusting, but·rather trusting."
Jn 21:8 from the dry·ground, but·rather about two·hundred
Jn 21:23 to·him that he·does·not die, but·rather, "If I·
Lk 1:60 "No·indeed! But·rather, he·shall·be·called John.
Lk 4:4 not upon bread alone, but·rather upon every utterance
Lk 5:14 *it* not·even·to·one·man, "But·rather going·off, show
Lk 5:31 ·a·practitioner·of·healing, but·rather the·ones being
Lk 5:32 ·men, but·rather morally·disqualified·men to
Lk 5:38 "But·rather fresh·new wine *is only* fit·to·be·cast into
Lk 6:27 "But·rather I·say to·yeu, to·the·ones hearing: "Love
Lk 7:7 to·come to you, but·rather declare with·a·word, and
Lk 7:25 But·rather what have·yeu·gone·forth to·see?
Lk 7:26 "But·rather what have·yeu·gone·forth to·see?
Lk 8:16 places *it* beneath a·couch, but·rather he·puts *it* on a·
Lk 8:27 ·not abiding in *any* home, but·rather in the tombs.
Lk 8:52 She·did·not die, but·rather she·sleeps."
Lk 9:56 *the* souls of·men·of·clay†, but·rather to·save *them*."
Lk 11:4 us into a·proof·trial, but·rather snatch us away·from
Lk 11:33 the measuring·basket, but·rather *places it* on the
Lk 11:42 "But·rather, woe to·yeu, Pharisees! Because yeu·
Lk 12:51 to·yeu, no·indeed, but·rather thorough·division.
Lk 14:10 "But·rather whenever you·should·be·called·forth,
Lk 14:13 "But·rather whenever you·should·make a·reception
Lk 17:8 But·rather shall·he·not·indeed declare to·him,
Lk 18:13 eyes to the heaven, but·rather was·beating at his
Lk 20:21 ·appearance *of·any*, but·rather *that* you·instruct the
Lk 20:38 not a·God of·dead·men, but·rather of·living·men,
Lk 22:26 in·this·manner. "But·rather the·one greater among
Lk 22:42 nevertheless not my will, but·rather yours be·done.
Lk 24:6 He·is not here, but·rather is·awakened. Recall·to·
Ac 1:4 but·rather to·patiently·wait·around for·the Promise
Ac 1:8 But·rather yeu·shall·receive power, with·the Holy
Ac 2:16 But·rather this is the·thing having·been·declared
Ac 4:32 of·his holdings to·be his·own; but·rather for·them,
Ac 5:4 You·did·not lie to·men·of·clay†, but·rather to·God."
Ac 7:39 ·obedient, but·rather shoved·*him*·from·themselves,
Ac 10:35 but·rather in every nation, the·one who·is·
Ac 10:41 but·rather to·witnesses having·been·elected·
Ac 13:25 I·myself am not *he*. But·rather, behold, there·
Ac 15:11 But·rather we·trust through the grace of·*the*·Lord
Ac 15:20 but·rather to·communicate·by·letter to·them, for·
Ac 16:37 For no *way*, but·rather coming *here* themselves,
Ac 18:9 "Do·not be·afraid, but·rather speak, and you·
Ac 18:21 But·rather he·orderly·took·leave·of them,
Ac 21:13 not merely to·be·bound, but·rather also to·die at
Ac 21:24 it·is nothing·at·all. But·rather *that* you·yourself
Ac 26:20 But·rather announcing first to·the·ones in
Ac 26:25 Festus, but·rather I·clearly·enunciate utterances
Ac 26:29 *that* not merely you, but·rather also all the·ones
Heb 2:16 ·*nature* of·angels— but·rather he·grabs·hold ·of·
Heb 3:13 But·rather exhort one·another each and·every day,
Heb 5:4 take the honor, but·rather *it·is* the·one being·called·
Heb 5:5 ·be·made a·high·priest, but·rather the·one speaking
Heb 7:16 commandment, but·rather according·to a·power
Heb 9:24 ·patterns of·the true, but·rather into the heaven
Heb 10:3 But·rather in those *sacrifices*, a·reminder·again *is*·
Heb 10:25 a·habit of·some, but·rather exhorting *one·another*
Heb 10:39 ·back to total·destruction, but·rather of·a·trust to
Heb 11:13 receiving the promises, but·rather seeing them
Heb 12:11 ·not seem to·be joyous, but·rather grievous. But
Heb 12:22 But·rather yeu·have·come·alongside Mount
Heb 12:26 not merely the earth, but·rather also the heaven.
Heb 13:14 continuing city, but·rather we·seek·for the·one
Gal 1:1 through a·man·of·clay†, but·rather through YeShua
Gal 1:12 was·I·instructed, but·rather *I·personally·received it*
Gal 1:17 before me, but·rather I·went·aside into Arabia, and
Gal 2:7 But·rather on·the·contrary, after·seeing that the
Gal 2:14 But·rather, when I·saw that they·did·not walk·
Gal 3:12 is not as·a·result·of·trust, but·rather, "'The man·
Gal 3:16 as upon many *offspring*†, but·rather as upon one,
Gal 3:22 But·rather the Scripture jointly·confined all·things
Gal 4:2 but·rather is under executive·guardians and estate·
Gal 4:7 you·are no·longer a·slave, but·rather a·son; and if
Gal 4:14 nor did·yeu·spit·*me*·out, but·rather accepted me
Gal 4:17 ·moral·good, but·rather they·determine to·exclude
Gal 4:23 But·rather in·fact, the·one birthed·from·out·of·the
Gal 4:31 of·a·maidservant, but·rather of·the free·woman.
Gal 5:6 strength, but·rather trust which·is·itself·operating
Gal 5:13 ·occasion to·the flesh. But·rather through the love,
Gal 6:15 has·any strength, but·rather *it·is* a·brand-new
Mt 4:4 upon bread alone, but·rather upon every utterance
Mt 5:15 it under the measuring·basket, but·rather on the
Mt 5:17 come to·demolish, but·rather to·completely·fulfill.
Mt 5:39 ·to the evil·person, but·rather whoever shall·slap
Mt 6:13 carry us into a·proof·trial, but·rather snatch us away
Mt 6:18 ·of·clay† *to·be* fasting, but·rather to·your Father,
Mt 7:21 kingdom of·the heavens, but·rather the·one doing
Mt 8:4 ·declare *this* to·no·one. But·rather head·on·out, show
Mt 8:8 under my roof, but·rather merely declare a·word, and
Mt 9:12 ·a·practitioner·of·healing, but·rather the·ones being
Mt 9:13 ·ones, but·rather morally·disqualified·ones to
Mt 9:17 ·destroyed. But·rather they·cast fresh·new wine into
Mt 9:24 the young·girl did·not die, but·rather she·sleeps."
Mt 10:20 not the·ones speaking, but·rather the Spirit of·yeur
Mt 10:34 I·did·not come to·cast peace, but·rather a·dagger.
Mt 11:8 But·rather what·did yeu·go·forth to·see?
Mt 11:9 But·rather what·did yeu·go·forth to·see?
Mt 13:21 root in himself, but·rather he·is just·for·a·season,
Mt 15:11 ·of·clay†, but·rather the·thing proceeding·forth out
Mt 16:12 of the leaven of·bread, but·rather of the instruction
Mt 16:17 did·not reveal *this* to·you, but·rather my Father,
Mt 16:23 the·things of·God, but·rather the·things of·the
Mt 18:22 up·to seven·times, but·rather up·to seventy·times
Mt 18:30 And he·was·not willing, but·rather going·off, he·
Mt 19:6 ·such, they·are no·longer two, but·rather one flesh.
Mt 19:11 but·rather those·to·whom it·has·been·given.
Mt 20:23 mine to·give, but·rather *it·shall·be·given to·them*
Mt 20:26 be in·this·manner among yeu, but·rather whoever
Mt 20:28 ·not come to·be·attended·to, but·rather to·attend,
Mt 22:30 ·given·away·in·marriage, but·rather they·are as
Mt 22:32 the God of·dead·men, but·rather of·living·men."
Mt 26:39 not as I·myself will, but·rather as you *will*.
Mk 1:44 to·not·even·one·man. But·rather head·on·out,
Mk 1:45 ·enter openly into a·city, but·rather was outside in
Mk 2:17 ·a·practitioner·of·healing, but·rather the·ones being
Mk 2:17 ·men, but·rather morally·disqualified·men to
Mk 2:22 ·completely·destroyed. "But·rather fresh·new wine
Mk 3:26 able to·remain·established, but·rather has an·end.
Mk 3:29 into the coming·age, but·rather he·is·held·liable·of·
Mk 4:17 in themselves, but·rather they·are just·for·a·season.
Mk 5:19 Jesus did·not allow him, but·rather says to·him,
Mk 5:39 The little·child is·not dead, but·rather she·sleeps."
Mk 6:9 but·rather having·been·shod with·sandals *only*, and
Mk 7:5 Oral·tradition of·the elders, but·rather eat the bread
Mk 7:15 ·defile him, but·rather the·things proceeding·forth
Mk 7:19 ·not traverse into his heart, but·rather into the belly,
Mk 8:33 the·things of·God, but·rather the·things of·the
Mk 9:37 not me he·accepts, but·rather the·one dispatching
Mk 10:8 ·such, they·are no·longer two, but·rather one flesh.
Mk 10:40 mine to·give, but·rather *it·shall·be·given to·them*
Mk 10:43 be in·this·manner among yeu, but·rather whoever
Mk 10:45 ·not come to·be·attended·to, but·rather to·attend,
Mk 11:23 in his heart, but·rather should·trust that the·
Mk 11:32 But·rather if we·should·declare, 'From·out·of·
Mk 12:14 of·men·of·clay†, but·rather instruct the Way of·
Mk 12:25 marry nor are·given·in·marriage, but·rather are as
Mk 12:27 God of·dead·men, but·rather a·God of·living·men
Mk 13:7 ·for *such·things* to·happen, but·rather the end *is*
Mk 13:11 nor·even premeditate, but·rather whatever
Mk 13:11 not yeu·yeurselves speaking, but·rather the Holy
Mk 14:36 not what I·myself will, but·rather what you *will*.
Rm 1:21 ·thanks, but·rather they·already·became·futile in
Rm 1:32 do *the* same, but·rather also give·glad·consent to·
Rm 2:13 righteous personally·before God, but·rather, the
Rm 2:29 But·rather, the·one *vigilantly·keeping* in private, *he*·
Rm 2:29 ·out of·men·of·clay†, but·rather from·out·of·God.
Rm 3:27 No·indeed, but·rather on·account·of a·Law of·
Rm 3:31 May·it·never happen! But·rather, we·establish
Rm 4:4 according·to grace, but·rather according·to the debt.
Rm 4:10 Not in circumcision, but·rather in uncircumcision.
Rm 4:12 *the* Circumcision merely, but·rather yet to·the·ones
Rm 4:13 ·be *the* heir of·the world), but·rather *is* through a·
Rm 4:16 ·the Torah-Law merely, but·rather also to·the·one
Rm 4:20 with·a lack·of·trust, but·rather was·enabled by·the
Rm 4:24 but·rather also on·account·of us, to·whom it·is·
Rm 5:3 And not merely *so*, but·rather also we·boast in the
Rm 5:11 not merely *so*, but·rather we·also are·boasting in
Rm 6:13 ·Failure, but·rather yeu·must·present yeurselves to·
Rm 6:14 ·are not under Torah-Law, but·rather under grace.
Rm 6:15 ·are not under Torah-Law, but·rather under grace?
Rm 7:13 May·it·never happen! But·rather Moral·Failure, in·
Rm 7:15 which I·want *to·do*, but·rather I·do that·thing
Rm 7:17 that·performs it, but·rather the·one dwelling in me,
Rm 7:19 *that* I·do, but·rather a·bad·thing which I·do·not
Rm 7:20 that·performs it, but·rather the·one dwelling in me,
Rm 8:1 not according·to flesh, but·rather according·to Spirit
Rm 8:4 not according·to flesh, but·rather according·to Spirit
Rm 8:9 yeu are not in flesh, but·rather in Spirit, if·perhaps
Rm 8:15 again to fear, but·rather yeu·received a·Spirit of·
Rm 8:20 futility, not voluntarily, but·rather through the·one
Rm 8:23 merely *the creation*, but·rather we·ourselves also,
Rm 8:26 ·to·what is·necessary, but·rather the Spirit himself
Rm 8:32 ·not spare his·own Son, but·rather handed him over
Rm 8:37 But·rather, in all these·things we·gain·a·decisive·
Rm 9:7 *are* they·all *his* children. But·rather "In YiTsaq,
Rm 9:8 *that·are* children of·God, but·rather the children of·
Rm 9:11 ·a·result of·works, but·rather as·a·result of·the·one
Rm 9:16 ·one running *for·it·as·a·prize*, but·rather on·God,
Rm 9:32 not as·a·result of·trust, but·rather as·though *it·were*

Rm 11:4 But·rather what says the response·of·Yahweh to·
Rm 11:11 May·it·never happen! But·rather, through·their
Rm 11:18 *that* bears the root, but·rather the root *that bears*
Rm 11:20 Do·not·be arrogant, but·rather be·afraid.
Rm 12:2 present·age, but·rather be·metamorphosed by·the
Rm 12:3 *himself,* but·rather *for·him* to·contemplate
Rm 12:16 but·rather leading·yeurselves·together with·the
Rm 12:19 dearly·beloved, but·rather yeu·must·give place
Rm 12:21 by the bad, but·rather overcome the bad with the
Rm 13:3 ·good works, but·rather for·the bad·ones. But do·
Rm 13:5 ·of the wrath, but·rather also on·account·of the
Rm 13:14 But·rather dress·yeurselves·with the Lord Jesus
Rm 14:13 one·another, but·rather yeu·must·judge this all·
Rm 14:17 feeding and drinking, but·rather righteousness,
Rm 15:3 did·not accommodate himself, but·rather, just·as it·
Rm 15:21 But·rather just·as it·has·been·written, "To·whom
Rm 16:4 only I·myself give·thanks, but·rather also all the
Rm 16:18 Jesus Anointed, but·rather to·their·own belly.
Jac 1:25 not a·forgetful hearer, but·rather a·doer of·the·work
Jac 1:26 not bridling his tongue, but·rather deluding his·own
Jac 3:15 ·is·coming·down from·above, but·rather *is* earthly,
Jac 4:11 law, you·are not a·doer of·law, but·rather a·judge.
Jud 1:6 principality, but·rather leaving·behind their·own
Jud 1:9 ·up a·verdict of·revilement, but·rather declared, "
Php 1:20 ·one·thing shall·I·be·ashamed, but·rather with all
Php 1:29 to·trust in him, but·rather also to·suffer on·behalf
Php 2:3 self-conceit, but·rather in·the humbleness·of·mind
Php 2:4 of·his·own things *only,* but·rather each·man also
Php 2:12 my presence merely, but·rather now so·much more
Php 2:27 and not on·him merely, but·rather on·me also, lest
Php 3:9 ·out of·Torah-Law), but·rather the·one through a·
Php 4:6 ·about not·even·one·thing, but·rather in everything
Php 4:17 ·seek the gift, but·rather I·anxiously·seek the fruit,
1Pe 1:15 but·rather, *conforming* according·to the·one
1Pe 1:19 but·rather *it·was* with·precious blood, as of·a·
1Pe 1:23 ·seed, but·rather of·an·incorruptible *sowing·of·seed*
1Pe 2:16 a·cover-up for·the depravity, but·rather *behave* as
1Pe 2:18 ·good·ones and fair·ones, but·rather also to·the
1Pe 2:20 ·patiently? But·rather if yeu·shall·bear·it·patiently
1Pe 3:4 but·rather *according·to* the hidden man·of·clay† of·
1Pe 3:21 ·filth, but·rather an·inquiry of·a·beneficially·good
1Pe 4:2 ·longings of·men·of·clay†, but·rather to·God's will.
1Pe 4:13 But·rather rejoice, according·to·what *portion* yeu·
1Pe 5:2 not compulsorily, but·rather voluntarily; nor·even
1Pe 5:2 ·gain, but·rather with·a·cheerful·eagerness;
1Pe 5:3 ·by·allotment, but·rather being model·examples to·
2Pe 1:16 Anointed. But·rather yeu·were·being beholders of·
2Pe 1:21 ·times·past. But·rather, while·being·carried·along
2Pe 2:4 ·failing angels, but·rather after·incarcerating *them*
2Pe 2:5 *the* ancient world, but·rather vigilantly·kept Noach,
2Pe 3:9 tardiness, but·rather is·long-suffering toward us, not
2Pe 3:9 ·be·destroyed, but·rather for·all to·have·room for
1Th 1:5 yeu in word merely, but·rather also in power and in
1Th 1:8 in Macedonia and Achaia, but·rather also in every
1Th 2:2 But·rather even after·previously·suffering, and
1Th 2:4 But·rather just·as we·have·been·tested·and·proven
1Th 2:4 as satisfying men·of·clay†, but·rather God, the·one
1Th 2:7 But·rather we·were pleasantly·engageable in *the*
1Th 2:8 good·news of·God merely, but·rather also our·own
1Th 2:13 *as* a·word of·men·of·clay†, but·rather just·as it·is
1Th 4:7 toward impurity, but·rather into renewed·holiness.
1Th 4:8 a·man·of·clay† *that* he·ignores, but·rather God, the·
1Th 5:6 *do* the rest, but·rather we·should·keep·alert and
1Th 5:9 us for Wrath, but·rather for acquisition of·Salvation
1Th 5:15 wrong to·any *man;* but·rather always pursue the
2Th 2:12 trusting the truth, but·rather taking·delight in the
2Th 3:8 ·from anyone's bread, but·rather were·working in
2Th 3:9 ·not have authority, but·rather that we·should·give
2Th 3:11 ·one·bit, but·rather who·are·meddling·busybodies.
2Th 3:15 *him* not as an·enemy, but·rather admonish *him* as
Tit 1:8 but·rather hospitable, fond·of·doing·beneficially·
Tit 1:15 not·even·one·thing *is* pure, but·rather even their
Tit 2:10 *and* not pilfering, but·rather indicating all

Tit 3:5 we·ourselves did), but·rather he·saved us according·
1Co 1:17 to·immerse, but·rather to·proclaim·the·good·news,
1Co 1:27 But·rather God selected the foolish·things of·the
1Co 2:4 of·mankind's† wisdom, but·rather in demonstration
1Co 2:5 in *the* wisdom of·men·of·clay†, but·rather in God's
1Co 2:7 But·rather we·speak God's wisdom in a·Mystery,
1Co 2:9 But·rather just·as it·has·been·written, "Eye did·not
1Co 2:12 *that* we·ourselves received, but·rather the Spirit,
1Co 2:13 ·mankind's† wisdom, but·rather with instructions
1Co 3:1 as to·spiritual·ones, but·rather as to·fleshly·ones, as
1Co 3:7 nor the·one watering, but·rather God, the·one
1Co 4:14 yeu do·I·write these·things, but·rather, as my
1Co 4:19 ·ones having·been·puffed·up, but·rather the power
1Co 4:20 of·God *is* not in word, but·rather in power.
1Co 5:8 or of·evil, but·rather with Unleavened·Bread of·
1Co 6:8 But·rather, yeu·yeurselves do·wrong and rob, and
1Co 6:11 these·things, but·rather yeu·are·fully·bathed, but·
1Co 6:11 ·are·fully·bathed, but·rather yeu·are·made·holy,
1Co 6:11 ·holy, but·rather yeu·are·regarded·as·righteous in
1Co 6:13 for·the sexual·immorality, but·rather for·the Lord,
1Co 7:4 ·control·over her·own body, but·rather the husband.
1Co 7:4 have·control·over his·own body, but·rather the wife
1Co 7:10 I·charge, *yet* not I·myself, but·rather the Lord, a·
1Co 7:19 is nothing·at·all, but·rather *what·matters is* a·
1Co 7:35 a·noose upon·yeu, but·rather *I·speak* pertaining·to
1Co 9:12 this privilege, but·rather we·quietly·bear all·things
1Co 9:27 But·rather I·knock·down my body and bring·*it*·
1Co 10:13 what yeu·are·able, but·rather together with·the
1Co 10:20 *No,* but·rather *I·reply* that those·things *which* the
1Co 10:24 no·man seek his·own, but·rather each·man the
1Co 10:29 not·indeed your·own, but·rather of·the other,
1Co 10:33 my·own advantage, but·rather the *advantage* of·
1Co 11:8 from·out of·woman, but·rather woman from·out
1Co 11:9 ·of the woman, but·rather woman on·account·of
1Co 11:17 not for the significantly·better, but·rather for the
1Co 12:14 the Body is not one member, but·rather many.
1Co 12:22 But·rather, so·much more *those* members of·the
1Co 12:25 in the Body, but·rather *that* the members should·
1Co 14:2 speaks not to·men·of·clay†, but·rather to·God. For
1Co 14:20 contemplations, but·rather be·as·infants in·the
1Co 14:22 ·ones trusting, but·rather to·the non-trusting·ones
1Co 14:22 non-trusting·ones, but·rather for·the·ones trusting
1Co 14:33 is not *the God* of·chaos, but·rather of·peace, as in
1Co 14:34 ·them to·speak, but·rather to·submit·themselves,
1Co 15:10 me, was not empty. But·rather, I·labored·hard,
1Co 15:10 all; but not I·myself but·rather the Grace of·God,
1Co 15:37 the body that·shall·be, but·rather a·bare kernel,
1Co 15:39 not the same flesh, but·rather in·fact *there·is* one
1Co 15:46 the spiritual *was* not first, but·rather the soulish,
2Co 1:9 ·reliance upon ourselves, but·rather upon God (the·
2Co 1:12 not with fleshly wisdom, but·rather by God's grace
2Co 1:19 "No," but·rather in him has·become "Yes.
2Co 1:24 we·lord·over yeur trust, but·rather are coworkers
2Co 2:4 ·should·be·grieved, but·rather that yeu·may·know
2Co 2:13 my brother. But·rather, orderly·taking·leave·of
2Co 2:17 Redemptive·word of·God. But·rather, as from·out
2Co 3:3 not with·ink, but·rather with·*the*·Spirit of·the·living
2Co 3:3 not on tablets of·stone, but·rather on fleshy tablets
2Co 3:5 as from·among ourselves, but·rather our sufficiency
2Co 3:6 — not of·letter, but·rather of·Spirit, for the letter
2Co 3:14 But·rather, their mental·dispositions were·
2Co 4:2 But·rather, we·have·renounced the hidden·things of·
2Co 4:2 of·God with·guile, but·rather by·the manifestation
2Co 4:5 ·officially·proclaim, but·rather Anointed-One Jesus
2Co 4:16 we·are·not cowardly. But·rather even though our
2Co 4:18 ·looked·upon, but·rather of·the·*internal*·things not
2Co 5:4 but·rather to·fully·dress·ourselves in·order·that the
2Co 5:12 ourselves to·yeu, but·rather *we·are* giving yeu an·
2Co 5:15 to·themselves, but·rather to·the·one already·dying
2Co 6:4 But·rather in everything, *we·are* presently·
2Co 7:5 at·all, but·rather *we·are* being·hard-pressed on
2Co 7:7 and not by his arrival merely, but·rather also by the
2Co 7:9 yeu·were·grieved, but·rather that yeu·were·grieved

2Co 7:12 being·done·wrong, but·rather because·of yeur
2Co 7:14 I·am·not put·to·shame; but·rather as we·spoke
2Co 8:5 not just·as we·expected, but·rather first they·gave
2Co 8:8 ·assigned·authority, but·rather on·account·of the
2Co 8:10 not merely to·do, but·rather also *were·eager* to·be·
2Co 8:13 ·*be* tribulation for·yeu. But·rather out of·equality,
2Co 8:19 *that*— but·rather also after·him·being·elected by
2Co 8:21 ·the·sight of·*the*·Lord, but·rather also in·the·sight
2Co 9:12 lackings of·the holy·ones, but·rather *it·is* excelling
2Co 10:4 *are* not fleshly, but·rather powerful in·God to *the*
2Co 10:12 themselves. But·rather those unduly·measuring
2Co 10:13 ·beyond·measure, but·rather according·to the
2Co 10:18 *that* is verifiably·approved, but·rather whom the
2Co 11:17 ·not speak according·to *the* Lord, but·rather as in
2Co 12:14 I·do·not seek yeur things, but·rather yeu; for the
2Co 12:14 to·store·up for·the parents, but·rather the parents
2Co 13:3 weak toward yeu, but·rather is·powerful in yeu.
2Co 13:7 verifiably·approved, but·rather that yeu·yeurselves
2Co 13:8 against the truth, but·rather on·behalf of·the truth.
Eph 1:21 in this present·age, but·rather also in·the·one about·
Eph 2:19 and sojourners, but·rather *yeu·are* fellow-citizens
Eph 4:29 from·out of·yeur mouth, but·rather *let·it·be* some
Eph 5:15 how yeu·walk, not as unwise, but·rather as wise,
Eph 5:17 ·ones, but·rather ones·comprehending what the
Eph 5:18 ·lifestyle, but·rather be·completely·filled in Spirit
Eph 5:27 or any such·thing, but·rather that she·should·be
Eph 5:29 his·own flesh, but·rather he·entirely·nourishes and
Eph 6:4 children, but·rather entirely·nurture·and·rear them
Eph 6:6 eyeservice as men-pleasers†, but·rather as slaves of·
Eph 6:12 blood and flesh, but·rather: specifically·against the
Col 3:11 slave *or* free, but·rather Anointed-One *is* all, and
Col 3:22 as men-pleasers†, but·rather with fidelity of·heart,
Phm 1:14 as according·to a·compulsion, but·rather *be* fully
Phm 1:16 no·longer as a·slave, but·rather above a·slave, a·
1Ti 2:10 but·rather through beneficially·good works (which
1Ti 2:12 ·of·authority·over a·man, but·rather *she·is* to·be in
1Ti 3:3 ·man, not of·shameful·gain, but·rather fair, not·
1Ti 4:12 your youth, but·rather become a·model·example
1Ti 5:1 ·not chastise an·older·man, but·rather exhort *him* as
1Ti 5:13 and not merely idle, but·rather gossipers also and
1Ti 5:23 No·longer drink·water·only, but·rather use a·little
1Ti 6:2 because they·are brothers; but·rather more, be·slaves
1Ti 6:17 *the* uncertainty of·wealth, but·rather in the living
2Ti 1:7 give us a·spirit of·timidity, but·rather of·power, and
2Ti 1:8 but·rather you·must·endure·hardship·together in·
2Ti 1:9 ·to our works, but·rather according·to his·own
2Ti 1:17 But·rather, coming·to·be in Rome, he·sought·for
2Ti 2:20 made·of·gold and of·silver, but·rather also of·wood
2Ti 2:24 to·quarrel, but·rather to·be pleasantly·engageable
2Ti 4:3 ·and·sound instruction. But·rather, according·to
2Ti 4:8 And not to·me merely, but·rather also to·all the·ones
2Ti 4:16 ·publicly·together with·me, but·rather all *men*
1Jn 2:2 concerning ours merely, but·rather also concerning
1Jn 2:7 to·yeu, but·rather an·old commandment which yeu·
1Jn 2:16 ·out of·the Father, but·rather is birthed·from·out of·
1Jn 2:19 have·continued with us. But·rather *they·went·out,*
1Jn 2:21 truth, but·rather because yeu·do·personally·know it
1Jn 2:27 anyone should·instruct yeu, but·rather as the same
1Jn 3:18 nor·even in·tongue, but·rather in·deed and in·
1Jn 4:1 trust every spirit, but·rather test·and·prove the spirits
1Jn 4:10 we·ourselves loved God, but·rather that he·himself
1Jn 4:18 in the Love, but·rather the completely·mature love
1Jn 5:6 not by the water merely, but·rather by the water and
1Jn 5:18 ·fail, but·rather the·one already·being·begotten
2Jn 1:1 and not I·myself only, but·rather also all the·ones
2Jn 1:5 to·you, but·rather that·which we·were·having from
2Jn 1:8 ·worked, but·rather that·we·may·fully·receive a·full
2Jn 1:12 ·of·paper and ink, but·rather I·expect to·come to
3Jn 1:11 ·imitate the bad, but·rather the beneficially·good.
Rv 2:9 Jews and are not, but·rather *are* a·gathering of·the
Rv 3:9 to·be Jews and are not, but·rather do·lie), behold, I·
Rv 9:5 kill them, but·rather that they·should·be·tormented
Rv 10:7 But·rather in the days of·the sound of·the seventh

Rv 20:6 ·not have authority, but·rather they·shall·be priests
EG0235.2 (2x)
Lk 14:35 nor·even for manure, *but·rather* men·cast it out.
Mt 16:11 not concerning bread, *but·rather* to·beware of the
G0235.3 CONJ ἀλλ᾽ (128x)
Jn 1:31 but·yet in·order·that he·should·be·made·apparent
Jn 1:33 ·not personally·known him, but·yet the·one sending
Jn 3:8 the sound of·it, but·yet you·have·not seen from·what·
Jn 4:23 "But·yet an·hour comes, and now is, when the true
Jn 6:9 and two small·broiled·fish, but·yet what are these·
Jn 6:64 "But·yet there·are some from·among yeu that do·not
Jn 7:27 But·yet we·personally·know this·man, *and* from·
Jn 7:44 to·apprehend him, but·yet not·even·one·man threw
Jn 8:26 to·judge concerning yeu. But·yet the·one sending
Jn 8:37 ·are AbRaham's offspring†, but·yet yeu·seek to·kill
Jn 10:8 are Thieves and robbers, but·yet the sheep did·not
Jn 10:26 But·yet yeu·yeurselves do·not trust, for yeu·are not
Jn 11:11 Lazarus has·been·laid·to·rest. But·yet I·traverse,
Jn 11:15 ·that yeu·may·trust; but·yet we·should·head·out to
Jn 11:22 But·yet I·personally·know, even now, that as·much·
Jn 11:42 that you·hear me always, but·yet on·account·of the
Jn 12:42 trusted in him. But·yet on·account·of the Pharisees
Jn 13:10 And yeu are pure, but·yet not·indeed all *of·yeu*.
Jn 13:18 ·know whom I·selected, but·yet in·order·that the
Jn 15:21 "But·yet all these·things shall·they·do to·yeu on·
Jn 15:25 "But·yet *this·happened*, in·order·that the word may·
Jn 16:7 "But·yet I·myself say to·yeu the truth; it·is·more·
Jn 16:12 many·things to·say to·yeu, but·yet yeu·are·not able
Jn 16:20 and yeu shall·be·grieved, but·yet yeur grief shall·
Jn 16:25 ·spoken to·yeu in proverbs. But·yet an·hour comes,
Jn 16:33 yeu·have tribulation, but·yet be·of·good·courage;
Lk 13:3 I·say to·yeu, no·indeed, but·yet, unless yeu·should·
Lk 13:5 I·say to·yeu, no·indeed, but·yet, unless yeu·should·
Lk 16:30 father AbRaham! But·yet if someone should·
Lk 22:36 Then he·declared to·them, "But·yet now, the·one
Lk 22:53 yeur hands against me. "But·yet this is yeur hour,
Ac 4:17 But·yet, in·order·that it·may·not disseminate any·
Ac 5:13 to·tightly·join·himself to·them, but·yet the people
Ac 7:48 "But·yet the Most·High does·not reside in temples
Ac 19:2 ·declared to him, "But·yet, we·did·not·even hear
Ac 19:26 merely at·Ephesus, but·yet almost throughout·all
Ac 19:27 of·coming into discredit, but·yet also *for* the
Ac 20:24 But·yet not·even·one word causes *me concern*,
Ac 26:16 'But·yet rise·up and stand·still upon your feet, for
Ac 27:10 and of·the sailing·ship, but·yet also of·our souls.
Heb 3:16 some did·directly·provoke, but·yet not all the·
Heb 4:2 ·as they·also *had·been*, but·yet the Redemptive-word
Gal 1:8 But·yet even if we·ourselves or an·angel from·out
Gal 2:3 But·yet not·even Titus (the·one together with·me
Gal 4:30 But·yet what·does the Scripture say?
Gal 6:13 vigilantly·keep Torah-Law, but·yet they·want yeu
Mt 9:18 ·died at·this·moment, but·yet coming *with·me*, you·
Mt 17:12 they·did·not recognize him, but·yet they·did to
Mt 21:21 to·the fig·tree, but·yet also·if yeu·should·declare
Mt 24:6 ·for all *these·things* to·happen, but·still the end is
Mt 27:24 *·them* benefits nothing·at·all, but·yet rather *that* a·
Mk 5:26 ·bit *of·it* being·beneficial, but·yet *with·her* coming
Mk 9:13 "But·yet I·say to·yeu that indeed EliJah has·come,
Mk 9:22 ·completely·destroy him, but·yet if you·are·able *to·*
Mk 10:27 men·of·clay† *it·is* impossible, but·yet not with
Mk 13:20 flesh would be·saved; but·yet on·account·of the
Mk 14:28 "But·yet after *it·is* the *hour* for·me to·be·awakened
Mk 14:29 ·be·tripped·up·and·fall·away, but·yet not I·myself
Mk 14:36 this cup away·from me. But·yet not what I·myself
Mk 14:49 ·hold·of me. "But·yet in·order·that the Scriptures
Rm 4:2 of·works, he·has a·boast, but·yet not toward God.
Rm 5:14 But·yet Death already·reigned from Adam so·far·
Rm 5:15 *is* also in·this·manner (but·yet not as the trespass).
Rm 7:7 May·it·never happen! But·yet, I·did·not know
Rm 9:24 from·among Jews merely, but·yet also from·among
Rm 10:2 they·have a·zeal of·God, but·yet not according·to
Rm 10:8 But·yet what·does it·say?
Rm 10:16 But·yet not all listened·to·and·obeyed the good·
Rm 10:18 But·yet I·say, ¿!·Did they·not hear?
Rm 10:19 But·yet I·say, ¿!·Did IsraEl not know?
Rm 14:20 all·things *are* pure, but·yet *it·is* morally·wrong
Jac 2:18 But·yet, someone shall·declare, "You have trust,
Php 2:7 but·yet he·emptied himself, taking·hold·of *the*
Php 2:27 ·sick almost to·death, but·yet God showed·mercy
Php 3:7 But·yet, what·things that·were gains to·me, these·
1Pe 2:25 sheep being·led·astray, but·yet are now returned
1Pe 3:14 But·yet even·though yeu·may·actually·suffer on·
1Co 3:6 Apollos watered, but·yet God was·growing.
1Co 4:4 not·even·one·thing against·myself, but·yet not by
1Co 4:15 ·teachers in Anointed-One, but·yet *yeu·have* not
1Co 6:6 But·yet brother goes·to·court·to·be·judged against
1Co 6:12 All·things are·proper for·me, but·yet not all·things
1Co 6:12 are·proper for·me, but·yet I·myself shall·not be·
1Co 7:7 to·be also as myself. But·yet each·man has his·own
1Co 7:21 ·it·matter not to·you, but·yet if·also you·are·able
1Co 8:6 but·yet to·us *there·is but* one God, the Father (from·
1Co 8:7 But·yet, the absolute·knowledge *of·this* is not in
1Co 9:2 not an·ambassador to·others, but·yet still I·am to·
1Co 9:12 *participate* more? But·yet we·did·not use this
1Co 9:21 ·Torah-Law to·God, but·yet *I·am* lawfully·subject
1Co 10:5 But·yet with the majority of·them, God did·not
1Co 10:23 ·things are·proper for·me, but·yet not all·things
1Co 10:23 ·things are·proper for·me, but·yet not all·things
1Co 12:24 no *such* need, but·yet God blended·together the
1Co 14:17 you give·thanks well, but·yet the other is·not
1Co 14:19 But·yet in a·convened·Called·Out·assembly, I·
1Co 15:35 But·yet someone shall·declare, "How·are the
1Co 15:40 and terrestrial bodies, but·yet in·fact the glory of·
2Co 1:9 But·yet we, in ourselves, have·had the judicial·
2Co 3:15 But·yet unto the·present·day, whenever Moses is·
2Co 4:8 every·side, but·yet not being·narrowly·constricted;
2Co 4:8 being·at·a·loss, but·yet not being·at·an·utter·loss;
2Co 4:9 being·persecuted, but·yet not being·forsaken;
2Co 4:9 ·cast·down, but·yet not being·completely·destroyed
2Co 4:16 is·thoroughly·decaying·away, but·yet the inward
2Co 5:16 according·to flesh, yet now we·know *him* no·
2Co 7:6 But·yet God, the·one comforting the·ones *that·are*
2Co 11:1 in·the impulsiveness *of·boasting*, but·yet even·so,
2Co 11:6 *I·am* untrained in·the discourse, yet *it·is* not *so* in·
2Co 12:16 impose·a·burden·on yeu. But·yet *yeu·reckon that*
2Co 13:4 as·a·result of·weakness, yet he·lives as·a·result of·
2Co 13:4 are·weak in him, yet we·shall·live together with·
Eph 5:4 not being·appropriate), but·yet rather *share* an·
Col 2:5 I·am·absent in·the flesh, but·yet I·am together with·
1Ti 1:13 ·insolent·man. But·yet I·was·shown·mercy,
1Ti 1:16 But·yet on·account·of this, I·was·shown·mercy in·
1Ti 6:4 ·with not·one·thing, but·yet sickly·harping·on about
2Ti 1:12 I·suffer these·things. But·yet I·am·not ashamed,
2Ti 2:9 as·far·as·unto bonds, but·yet the Redemptive-word
1Jn 2:19 ·went·out from·among us, but·yet they·were not
3Jn 1:9 to·the Called·Out·citizenry, but·yet DioTrephes, the·
3Jn 1:13 many·things to·write, but·yet I·do·not want to·
Rv 2:4 'But·yet I·have *this* against you, that you·left your
Rv 2:6 But·yet you·have this, that you·hate the deeds of·the
Rv 2:14 'But·yet I·have a·few·things against you, because
Rv 2:20 'But·yet I·have a·few·things against you, because
Rv 10:9 ·make your belly bitter, but·yet it·shall·be in your
Rv 17:12 a·kingdom, but·yet they·do·receive authority as
G0235.4 CONJ ἀλλ᾽ (33x)
Jn 5:18 the Sabbath— moreover he·was·saying also *that*
Jn 13:10 ·than to·wash the feet. Moreover, he·is altogether
Jn 16:2 yeu cut·off·from·the·gatherings. Moreover, an·hour
Lk 12:7 Moreover, even the hairs of·yeur head all have·
Lk 16:21 from the wealthy·man's table. Moreover, even the
Lk 21:9 ·things to·occur first. "Moreover, the end does·not
Lk 23:15 "Moreover, neither·did HerOd·AntiPas, for I·sent
Lk 24:21 intending to·ransom IsraEl. Moreover together
Lk 24:22 Moreover *still*, certain women also from·among us
Ac 10:20 Moreover, after·rising·up, walk·down and traverse
Gal 4:8 Moreover in·fact, when not having·seen God, yeu·
Gal 4:29 Moreover, just·as then, the·one being·born
Mk 13:24 "Moreover in those Days, after that
Mk 16:7 Moreover, head·on·out! Declare to·his disciples and
Rm 6:5 resemblance of·his death, moreover we·shall·be also
Rm 9:10 And not merely *this*. Moreover with·Rebeqah also,
Php 1:18 in this I·do·rejoice. Moreover also, I·shall·rejoice.
Php 2:17 Moreover, even if I·am·poured·forth·as·a·devotion
Php 3:8 Moreover, as·a·matter·of·fact, also— I·resolutely·
1Co 3:2 ·not·yet able *to·bear it*. Moreover neither yet now
1Co 4:3 by mankind's† daylight. Moreover, I·scrutinize not·
1Co 15:46 Moreover, the spiritual *was* not first, but·rather
2Co 2:17 ·out·of·sincerity, moreover as birthed·from·out·of·
2Co 7:11 it·did·accomplish in·yeu, moreover, *what*
2Co 7:11 *what* exoneration·of·yeurselves, moreover, *what*
2Co 7:11 *what* great·displeasure, moreover, *what* alarm,
2Co 7:11 *what* alarm, moreover, *what* great·yearning,
2Co 7:11 *what* great·yearning, moreover, *what* zeal,
2Co 7:11 moreover, *what* zeal, moreover, *what* vindication!
2Co 8:7 Moreover, just·as yeu·abound in everything, in·trust
2Co 11:6 ·the absolute·knowledge; moreover in everything,
Eph 5:24 Moreover, just·as the entire·Called·Out·Citizenry
2Ti 3:9 Moreover, they·shall·not continually·advance any·

G0236 ἀλλάσσω allássō *v.* (6x)
Roots:G0243 Compare:G3345 G3346 G3339
G0236 V-FAI-3S ἀλλάξει (1x)
Ac 6:14 ·demolish this place and shall·change the customs
G0236 V-2FPI-1P ἀλλαγησόμεθα (2x)
1Co 15:51 all be·laid·to·rest, but we·shall all be·changed,
1Co 15:52 and we·ourselves shall·be·changed.
G0236 V-2FPI-3P ἀλλαγήσονται (1x)
Heb 1:12 up, and they·shall·be·changed, but you·yourself
G0236 V-AAI-3P ἤλλαξαν (1x)
Rm 1:23 and they·did·change the glory of·the incorruptible
G0236 V-AAN ἀλλάξαι (1x)
Gal 4:20 yeu at·this·moment and to·change my tone, because

G0237 ἀλλαχό•θεν allachóthen *adv.* (1x)
Roots:G0243
G0237 ADV ἀλλαχόθεν (1x)
Jn 10:1 ·rather walking·up from·some·other·way, that·one is

G0238 ἀλλ•ηγορέω allēgōréō *v.* (1x)
Roots:G0243 Compare:G3850 G3942 See:G0058
G0238.2 V-PPP-NPN ἀλληγορούμενα (1x)
Gal 4:24 Which·things are being·an·allegory, for these are

G0239 ἀλληλού•ϊα allēlôúïa *heb.* (4x)
הַלְלוּ יָהּ halᵉlû yah̲ [Hebrew]
Roots:H1984 H3050 Compare:G0134 See:G0281
xLangEquiv:H1984-1 xLangAlso:H8416
G0239.2 HEB ἀλληλούϊα (4x)
Rv 19:1 "Splendidly·praise·Yahweh,·HalleluYah! The
Rv 19:3 "Splendidly·praise·Yahweh,·HalleluYah! And her
Rv 19:4 ·Amen! Splendidly·praise·Yahweh,·HalleluYah!"
Rv 19:6 "Splendidly·praise·Yahweh,·HalleluYah! Because

G0240 ἀλλήλων allēlōn *p:c.* (100x)
Roots:G0243 See:G3326 G4314
G0240.1 P:C-APM ἀλλήλους (67x)
Jn 4:33 the disciples were·saying among one·another, "¿!·
Jn 6:52 Judeans were·quarreling among one·another, saying,
Jn 13:22 were·looking to one·another, being·at·a·loss
Jn 13:34 that yeu·should·love one·another just·as I·loved
Jn 13:34 ·that even yeu·yeurselves should·love one·another.
Jn 15:12 that yeu·should·love one·another, just·as I·loved
Jn 15:17 yeu, in·order·that yeu·may·love one·another.
Jn 16:17 his disciples declared among one·another, "What is
Jn 19:24 Accordingly, they·declared among one·another,
Lk 2:15 the shepherds, declared to one·another, "Now·then,
Lk 4:36 ·were·speaking·together among one·another, saying,
Lk 6:11 ·conferring alongside one·another what they·might
Lk 8:25 they·marveled, saying among one·another, "What
Lk 12:1 such·that they·trampled·down one·another, *Jesus*
Lk 24:14 ·conversing alongside one·another concerning all
Lk 24:17 ·and·forth to one·another while·walking·along, and
Lk 24:32 And they·declared to one·another, "Was not·
Ac 2:7 and were·marveling, saying among one·another,

Ac 4:15 they·rigorously·conferred among one·another,
Ac 7:26 for·what·purpose do·yeu·wrong one·another?'
Ac 21:6 And after·embracing one·another, we·embarked into
Ac 26:31 they·were·speaking among one·another, saying,
Ac 28:4 hand, they·were·saying among one·another, "This
Ac 28:25 among one·another, they·dismissed·themselves,
Heb 10:24 we·should·fully·observe one·another to·a·keen·
Gal 5:15 if yeu·bite and devour one·another, look·out *that*
Gal 5:26 ·men, challenging one·another, envying one·
Mt 24:10 ·and·fall·away, and shall·hand one·another over,
Mt 24:10 one·another over, and shall·hate one·another.
Mk 4:41 ·awe, and they·were·saying to one·another, "Who
Mk 8:16 they·were·deliberating among one·another, saying,
Mk 9:34 they·discussed among one·another who *would·be*
Mk 15:31 were·saying among one·another with the scribes,
Rm 1:27 in their lust toward one·another; males with males
Rm 12:10 *by·showing* family·affection to·one·another; in·
Rm 12:10 ·the honor, by·showing·deference·to one·another;
Rm 12:16 the same·thing for one·another; contemplating not
Rm 13:8 not·even·one·thing, except to·love one·another, for
Rm 14:13 should·we·unduly·judge one·another, but·rather
Rm 14:19 of·peace and the·things edifying to one·another.
Rm 15:7 yeu·must·each·receive one·another, just·as also the
Rm 15:14 who·are·being·able also to·admonish one·another.
Rm 16:16 Greet one·another with a·holy kiss.
Php 2:3 resolutely·considering one·another as·excelling·
1Pe 1:22 yeu·must·love one·another from·out of·a·pure
1Pe 4:9 *Be* hospitable to one·another without grumbling.
1Pe 5:14 Greet·yeu one·another with a·kiss of·love.
1Th 3:12 abound in·the love toward one·another and toward
1Th 4:9 are instructed·by·God to love one·another.
1Th 4:18 As·such, comfort one·another with these words.
1Th 5:11 Therefore yeu·must·comfort one·another, and
1Th 5:15 the beneficially·good, both for one·another, and to
2Th 1:3 one of·yeu all, toward one·another, increases·more,
Tit 3:3 malice and envy, detestable·men hating one·another.
1Co 7:5 Do·not deprive one·another, except·that *which*
1Co 11:33 ·together in·order to·eat, wait·for one·another.
1Co 16:20 greet yeu. Greet one·another with a·holy kiss.
2Co 13:12 Greet one·another with a·holy kiss.
Eph 4:32 And become kind to one·another, tender-hearted,
Col 3:9 lie to one·another, after·having·already·stripped·off
1Jn 3:11 *the* beginning, that we·should·love one·another,
1Jn 3:23 and we·should·presently·love one·another, just·as
1Jn 4:7 Beloved, we·should·love one·another, because the
1Jn 4:11 we·ourselves also are·indebted to·love one·another.
1Jn 4:12 If we·should·love one·another, God abides in us,
2Jn 1:5 *the* beginning, that we·should·love one·another.
Rv 6:4 and that they·should·slaughter one·another. And

G0240.1 P:C-DPM ἀλλήλοις (11x)
Jn 13:35 to·me, if yeu·should·have love for one·another."
Lk 7:32 a·marketplace and hollering·out to·one·another, and
Ac 19:38 proconsuls; let·them·call one·another to·account.
Gal 5:13 ·rather through the love, be·slaves to·one·another.
Gal 5:26 challenging one·another, envying one·another.
Mk 9:50 in yeurselves, and be·peaceful with one·another."
Rm 15:5 among one·another according·to Anointed-One
Jac 5:16 ·confess *yeur* trespasses to·one·another, and
1Pe 5:5 *of·yeu*, being·submitted to·one·another, put·on·the·
Eph 5:21 being·submitted to·one·another in·a·reverent·fear·
Rv 11:10 ·shall·send presents to·one·another because these

G0240.1 P:C-DPN ἀλλήλοις (1x)
Gal 5:17 are·fully·set·opposed to·one·another, in·order·that

G0240.1 P:C-GPM ἀλλήλων (18x)
Jn 5:44 receiving glory personally·from one·another, yet
Jn 6:43 "Do·not grumble with one·another.
Jn 11:56 Jesus and were·saying among one·another, "What·
Jn 13:14 are·obligated to·wash one·another's feet.
Jn 16:19 ·yeu·seek among one·another concerning this·thing
Lk 23:12 HerOd·AntiPas became friends with one·another, for
Ac 15:39 them to·be·utterly·separated from one·another; and
Gal 5:15 ·out *that* yeu·may·not be·consumed by one·another.
Gal 6:2 Bear the burdens of·one·another, and in·this·manner
Rm 2:15 else exonerating·themselves between one·another,
Rm 12:5 and each one the members of·one·another.
Jac 4:11 Do·not speak·against one·another, brothers. The·
Jac 5:9 Do·not groan against one·another, brothers, lest yeu·
Jac 5:16 and well-wish *to·God* on·behalf of·one·another, that
Eph 4:2 long-suffering, bearing·with one·another in love,
Eph 4:25 ' because we·are members of·one·another.
Col 3:13 bearing·with one·another, and being·graciously·
1Jn 1:7 light, we·have fellowship with one·another, and the

G0240.1 P:C-GPN ἀλλήλων (2x)
Mt 25:32 ·shall·distinctly·separate them one from another,
1Co 12:25 should·be·anxious the same over one·another.

G0240.2 P:C-DPM ἀλλήλοις (1x)
Rm 1:12 ·together among yeu through the mutual trust, both

G0241 ἀλλο•γενής allogênḗs *adj.* (1x)

Roots:G0243 G1085 Compare:G0915 G3927 G1484 G1854 G3581 G3941

G0241.3 A-NSM ἀλλογενής (1x)
Lk 17:18 glory to·God, *none* except this resident·alien."

G0242 ἅλλομαι hállomai *v.* (3x)

Compare:G1814 G4640 See:G0021 xLangEquiv:H1801 xLangAlso:H5539

G0242.1 V-PNP-NSM ἁλλόμενος (1x)
Ac 3:8 walking·along and leaping and splendidly·praising

G0242.1 V-INI-3S ἥλλετο (1x)
Ac 14:10 on your feet." And he·was·leaping and walking.

G0242.2 V-PNP-GSN ἁλλομένου (1x)
Jn 4:14 him a·wellspring of·water springing·up into eternal

G0243 ἄλλος állôs *adj.* (165x)

Compare:G2087 G3739 See:G0245

G0243.ª A-ASN ἄλλο (1x)
Gal 5:10 ·shall·contemplate not·even·one·bit otherwise, but

G0243.1 A-NSM ἄλλος (15x)
Jn 4:37 is the·one sowing, and another *is* the·one reaping.
Jn 5:7 I·myself am·coming, another steps·down before me.
Jn 5:32 There·is another, the·one testifying concerning me,
Jn 5:43 ·not receive me. If another should·come in his·own
Jn 18:15 Jesus, and *so was* another disciple. But that disciple
Jn 21:18 ·stretch·out your hands, and another shall·gird you,
Mk 12:32 one God, and there·is not another besides him."
Mk 14:19 "Is·it I·myself?" And another, "Is·it I·myself?
1Co 3:10 ·have·laid a·foundation, and another builds·upon *it*
Rv 6:4 And there·came·forth another horse *that·was* fiery·
Rv 8:3 And another angel came and stood·still at the
Rv 14:8 And there·followed another angel, saying,
Rv 14:15 And another angel came·forth out of·the Temple,
Rv 14:17 And another angel came·forth out of·the Temple,
Rv 14:18 And another angel came·forth out·from the

G0243.1 A-NSF ἄλλη (6x)
Mt 26:71 ·out to the gate·*area*, another *servant·girl* saw him
1Co 15:39 ·*of* flesh of·men·of·clay†, another flesh of·beasts,
1Co 15:39 another flesh of·beasts, another of·fish, and
1Co 15:39 of·beasts, another of·fish, and another of·birds.
1Co 15:41 glory of·*the*·sun, and another glory of·*the*·moon,
1Co 15:41 glory of·*the*·moon, and another glory of·*the*·stars

G0243.1 A-NSN ἄλλο (4x)
Ac 19:32 a·certain·thing, *and some* another·thing, for the
Gal 1:7 which is not *actually* another *good·news at·all*.
Rv 12:3 And another sign was·made·visible in the heaven;
Rv 20:12 ·up. And another official·scroll was·opened·up,

G0243.1 A-ASM ἄλλον (12x)
Jn 14:16 he·shall·give yeu another Companion/Intercessor,
Lk 7:19 ·is·coming? Or should·we·intently·await another?"
Lk 7:20 ·is·coming? Or should·we·intently·await another?'"
Ac 2:12 ·perplexed, saying one to another, "What·is this·
Mk 12:4 And again he·dispatched another slave to them, and
Mk 12:5 And again he·dispatched another, and·this·one·also
Mk 14:58 three days I·shall·build another not·made·by·hand.
1Co 3:11 ·one·man is·able to·lay another foundation than
2Co 11:4 ·is·coming does·officially·proclaim another Jesus,
Rv 7:2 And I·saw another angel ascending from *the* eastern
Rv 10:1 And I·saw another strong angel descending from·out
Rv 14:6 And I·saw another angel who·is·flying in *the*

G0243.1 A-ASF ἄλλην (7x)
Mt 13:24 Another parable he·put·forth·directly to·them,
Mt 13:31 Another parable he·put·forth·directly to·them,
Mt 13:33 Another parable he·spoke to·them: "The kingdom
Mt 19:9 and should·marry another, does·commit·adultery.
Mt 21:33 "Hear another parable. "There·was a·certain man·
Mk 10:11 should·marry another commits·adultery against
Rv 18:4 And I·heard another voice from·out of·the heaven,

G0243.1 A-ASN ἄλλο (3x)
Ac 21:34 a·certain·thing, *and some* another·thing among the
Rv 13:11 And I·saw another Fiendish·Beast ascending out
Rv 15:1 And I·saw another sign in the heaven, great and

G0243.1 A-APN ἄλλα (5x)
Mt 25:16 same, and produced another five talants·of·silver.
Mt 25:17 ·*received* the two, he also gained another two.
Mt 25:20 ·of·silver brought another five talants·of·silver,
Mt 25:20 See, I·gained another five talants·of·silver upon
Mt 25:22 See, I·gained another two talants·of·silver upon

G0243.1 A-DSM ἄλλῳ (10x)
Lk 7:8 and he·traverses; and to·another, 'Come,' and he·
Mt 8:9 and he·traverses; and to·another, 'Come,' and he·
Mk 10:12 and should·be·married to·another, she·commits·
1Co 12:8 of·wisdom, but to·another a·word of·knowledge
1Co 12:9 same Spirit, but to·another, gracious·bestowments
1Co 12:10 and to·another, operations of·miracles, to·another
1Co 12:10 operations of·miracles, to·another prophecy, to·
1Co 12:10 prophecy, to·another discerning of·spirits, but to·
1Co 12:10 of·bestowed·tongues, and to·another, translation
1Co 14:30 should·be·revealed to·another sitting·down, the

G0243.1 A-GSM ἄλλου (1x)
Rv 16:7 And I·heard another from·among the Sacrifice·Altar

G0243.1 A-GSF ἄλλης (3x)
Heb 4:8 ·spoken after these·things concerning another day.
Mt 2:12 into their·own country through another way.
1Co 10:29 unduly·judged by another *man's* conscience?

G0243.2 A-NSM ἄλλος (7x)
Jn 15:24 the works which not·even·one other·man has·done,
Jn 18:16 In·due·course, the other disciple, who was known
Jn 20:3 Accordingly, Peter and the other disciple went·forth,
Jn 20:4 at·the·same·time, yet the other disciple more·swiftly
Jn 20:8 Then accordingly, the other disciple entered also,
Php 3:4 If any other·man presumes *a·reason* to·have·
Rv 17:10 and the one is, *and* the other did·not·yet come; and

G0243.2 A-NSF ἄλλη (6x)
Lk 6:10 was·restored as·healthy·and·sound as the other.
Mt 12:13 it·was·restored as·healthy·and·sound as the other.
Mt 27:61 Magdalene, and the other Miryam, sitting·down
Mt 28:1 Mariam Magdalene and the other Mariam came to·
Mk 3:5 hand was·restored as·healthy·and·sound as the other.
Mk 12:31 ' There·is no other commandment greater·than

G0243.2 A-NSN ἄλλο (2x)
Jn 6:22 ·seeing that there·had·been no other small·boat there
Mk 4:5 But other *seed* fell upon the rocky·ground, where it·

G0243.2 A-NPM ἄλλοι (23x)
Jn 4:38 have·not labored·hard. Others have·labored·hard,
Jn 7:12 a·beneficially·good·man," but others were·saying,
Jn 7:41 Others were·saying, "This is the Anointed-One.
Jn 7:41 But others were·saying, "For ¿! ·is·it from·out of·
Jn 9:9 "This is·he." But others *were·saying*, "He·is like him
Jn 9:16 ·keep the Sabbath." Others were·saying, "How·is
Jn 10:21 Others were·saying, "These·things are not the
Jn 12:29 thunder *that* has·occurred." Others were·saying,
Jn 18:34 ·you say this·thing, or did·others declare·it to·you
Jn 20:25 So the other disciples were·saying to·him, "We·
Jn 21:2 the *sons* of·Zebedee, and two others from·among his
Jn 21:8 And the other disciples came in·the small·boat,
Lk 9:19 "John the Immerser, but others *say* EliJah, and
Lk 9:19 others *say* EliJah, and others *say* that some prophet
Heb 11:35 And others were·torturously·beaten·to·death, not
Mt 16:14 *say* John the Immerser, and others *say* EliJah, but
Mt 21:8 in the roadway, and others were·chopping branches
Mk 6:15 Others were·saying, "It·is EliJah.
Mk 6:15 "It·is EliJah." And others were·saying, "It·is a·

Mk 8:28 some *say*, EliJah, and others, one of·the prophets.
Mk 11:8 the roadway, and others were·chopping limbs out
1Co 9:12 If others participate in·*this*·privilege among·yeu,
1Co 14:29 speak two or three, and *let* the others discern.
G0243.2 A-NPF ἄλλαι (1x)
Mk 15:41 ; and·also many other·women, the·ones walking·
G0243.2 A-NPN ἄλλα (7x)
Jn 6:23 Now other small·boats came out·from Tiberias near
Jn 21:25 And there·are also many other·things, as·much·as
Mt 13:5 But other *seeds* fell upon the rocky·places, where it·
Mt 13:7 And others fell among the thorns, and the thorns
Mt 13:8 But others fell on the soil, the good·one, and were·
Mk 4:36 in the sailboat. And other small·boats were also
Mk 7:4 many other·things which they·personally·received
G0243.2 A-ASM ἄλλον (3x)
Jn 20:2 to Simon Peter and to the other disciple whom Jesus
Jac 5:12 nor by·the earth, nor by·any other oath. But yeur
1Co 1:16 I·do·not personally·know if I·immersed any other.)
G0243.2 A-ASF ἄλλην (3x)
Lk 6:29 on the cheek, hold·forth the other *cheek* also, and of
Mt 5:39 on your right cheek, turn·back to·him the other also.
Mt 10:23 this city, flee into the other, for certainly I·say to·
G0243.2 A-ASN ἄλλο (1x)
Rv 2:24 as they·say), I·shall·cast upon yeu no other burden.
G0243.2 A-APM ἄλλους (12x)
Jn 19:18 they·crucified him, and·also two others with him,
Lk 23:35 saying, "He·saved others, let·him·save himself—
Ac 15:2 and BarNabas, and certain others from·among them,
Mt 4:21 from·there, he·saw two other brothers, Jakob (the·
Mt 20:3 the third hour, he·saw others standing idle in the
Mt 20:6 eleventh hour, he·found others standing idle and
Mt 21:36 Again, he·dispatched other slaves more·than at·the
Mt 22:4 "Again, he·dispatched other slaves, saying,
Mt 27:42 "He·saved others, *yet* he·is·not able to·save himself
Mk 12:5 ·also they·killed, and·then many others (in·fact,
Mk 15:31 the scribes, "He·saved others; himself, he·is·not
1Co 14:19 ·order·that *by·my·voice* I·may·inform others also,
G0243.2 A-APF ἄλλας (1x)
2Co 11:8 I·despoiled other Called·Out·citizenries, taking
G0243.2 A-APN ἄλλα (4x)
Jn 10:16 And I·have other sheep which are not from·among
Jn 20:30 Jesus also did many other signs in·the·sight of·his
Mk 7:8 cups, and many other such similar·things do·yeu·do.
2Co 1:13 For we·write no other·things to·yeu, other than
G0243.2 A-DSM ἄλλῳ (1x)
Ac 4:12 Salvation is not in not·even·one other. For there·is
G0243.2 A-DPM ἄλλοις (6x)
Lk 20:16 and he·shall·give the vineyard to·others." And
Mt 21:41 he·shall·lease the vineyard to·other tenant·farmers,
Mk 12:9 ·farmers and shall·give the vineyard to·others.
1Co 9:2 If I·am not an·ambassador to·others, but·yet still I·
1Co 9:27 after·officially·proclaiming to·others, I·myself
2Co 8:13 For I·do·not *mean* that others *should·have* ease,
G0243.2 A-GSM ἄλλου (1x)
Jn 19:32 *the·legs* of·the other one being·crucified·together
G0243.2 A-GPM ἄλλων (3x)
Lk 5:29 a·large crowd of·tax·collectors and others that were
Lk 9:8 that EliJah appeared, and by·others that one of·the
1Th 2:6 neither from yeu nor from others, *though* being·able
EG0243.2 (3x)
Lk 12:48 and to·whom *others* place·the·direct·care·of much
Lk 19:36 traversing, *other disciples* were·spreading·out their
Php 1:17 But the *others fully·proclaim* out of·love, having·
G0243.3 A-NSM ἄλλος (2x)
Jn 4:37 *case*, the saying is true, 'One is the·one sowing, and
Ac 2:12 were·thoroughly·perplexed, saying one to another,
G0243.3 A-NSF ἄλλη (2x)
1Co 15:39 but·rather in·fact *there·is* one *kind·of* flesh of·
1Co 15:41 *There·is* one glory of·*the*·sun, and another glory
G0243.4 A-NSN ἄλλο (2x)
Mk 4:7 And some fell into the thorns, and the thorns sprung·
Mk 4:8 And some fell into the good soil and was·giving fruit
G0243.4 A-NPM ἄλλοι (4x)
Jn 9:9 Some were·saying, "This is·he.
Ac 19:32 ·due·course, some were·yelling·out a·certain·thing
Ac 21:34 And some were·crying·out a·certain·thing, *and*
Mk 8:28 "John the Immerser, but some *say*, EliJah, and
EG0243.4 (3x)
Ac 19:32 ·out a·certain·thing, *and some* another·thing, for
Ac 21:34 a·certain·thing, *and some* another·thing among the
Mt 16:14 And they·declared, "In·fact, *some say* John the
G0243.5 A-NSM ἄλλος (1x)
Lk 22:59 one hour, someone else was·strongly·asserting,

G0244 ἀλλοτρι•επί•σκοπος allôtriêpískôpôs *n.* (1x)
Roots:G0245 G1985 Compare:G4021
G0244.2 N-NSM ἀλλοτριοεπίσκοπος (1x)
1Pe 4:15 as one·interloping·in·civic·matters·as·an·overseer.

G0245 ἀλλότριος allótriôs *adj.* (14x)
Roots:G0243 Compare:G3581 G1687 See:G0526 G0244
G0245.1 A-ASM ἀλλότριον (2x)
Rm 14:4 unduly·judging another·man's household·servant?
Rm 15:20 lest I·should·build upon another·man's foundation.
G0245.1 A-DSM ἀλλοτρίῳ (2x)
Lk 16:12 trustworthy with another·man's *material·wealth*,
2Co 10:16 ·*us* to·boast by another·man's standard *of·service*
G0245.2 A-DSN ἀλλοτρίῳ (1x)
Heb 9:25 ·of·Holies each year with another·*animal's* blood.
G0245.2 A-DPM ἀλλοτρίοις (1x)
2Co 10:15 *that·is*, in other·men's wearisome·labors, but
G0245.2 A-DPF ἀλλοτρίαις (1x)
1Ti 5:22 quickly, nor·even share in·others' moral·failures.
G0245.2 A-GPM ἀλλοτρίων (2x)
Mt 17:25 ·tribute? From their·own sons or from the others?"
Mt 17:26 Peter says to·him, "From the others." YeShua was·
G0245.7 A-ASF ἀλλοτρίαν (1x)
Heb 11:9 land of·promise as *in* an·estranged·foreign *land*,
G0245.7 A-DSF ἀλλοτρίᾳ (1x)
Ac 7:6 shall·be a·sojourner in an·estranged·foreign land, and
G0245.7 A-GPM ἀλλοτρίων (1x)
Heb 11:34 in battle, routed estranged·foreign garrisons.
G0245.8 A-DSM ἀλλοτρίῳ (1x)
Jn 10:5 And an·interloper, no, they·should·not follow, but·
G0245.8 A-GPM ἀλλοτρίων (1x)
Jn 10:5 ·do·not personally·know the voice of·interlopers."

G0246 ἀλλό•φυλος allóphylôs *adj.* (1x)
Roots:G0243 G5443 See:G5502-5 xLangAlso:H6430
G0246.1 A-DSM ἀλλοφύλῳ (1x)
Ac 10:28 to·come·alongside one·of·a·different·ethnic·tribe,

G0247 ἄλλως állōs *adv.* (1x)
Roots:G0243 Compare:G2088
G0247 ADV ἄλλως (1x)
1Ti 5:25 and the *good works* being otherwise, are·not able

G0248 ἀλοάω alôáō *v.* (3x)
Roots:G1507 See:G0257
G0248 V-PAP-ASM ἀλοῶντα (2x)
1Co 9:9 ·shall·not muzzle an·ox *that·is* treading·out·grain."
1Ti 5:18 ·shall·not muzzle an·ox *that·is* treading·out·grain,"
G0248 V-PAP-NSM ἀλοῶν (1x)
1Co 9:10 the·one *that·is* treading·out·grain in expectation to·

G0249 ἄ•λογος álôgôs *adj.* (3x)
Roots:G0001 G3056
G0249.1 A-NPN ἄλογα (2x)
Jud 1:10 ·acquainted·with naturally (as irrational animals), in
2Pe 2:12 (as natural, irrational animals, having·been·born
G0249.2 A-NSN ἄλογον (1x)
Ac 25:27 to·me unreasonable to·send a·chained·prisoner,

G0250 ἀλόη alóē *n.* (1x)
xLangAlso:H0174
G0250 N-GSF ἀλόης (1x)
Jn 19:39 bringing a·mixture of·myrrh and aloeswood, about

G0251 ἅλς háls *n.* (1x)
Compare:G2281 See:G0217 G0252 G0358 xLangEquiv:H4417
G0251 N-DSM ἁλί (1x)
Mk 9:49 ·fire, and every sacrifice shall·be·salted with·salt.

G0252 ἁλυκός halykós *adj.* (1x)
Roots:G0251 See:G0358
G0252.2 A-ASN ἁλυκόν (1x)
Jac 3:12 wellspring *is·able* to·produce *both* salt water and

G0253 ἀ•λυπότερος alypótêrôs *adj.* (1x)
Roots:G0001 G3077
G0253 A-NSM-C ἀλυπότερος (1x)
Php 2:28 yeu·may·rejoice, and·*that*·I may·be less·grieved.

G0254 ἅλυσις hálysis *n.* (11x)
Compare:G1199 G3976 G4577
G0254 N-NPF ἁλύσεις (1x)
Ac 12:7 And his chains fell·away from·among his hands.
G0254 N-ASF ἅλυσιν (3x)
Ac 28:20 of·IsraEl *that* I·am·entirely·bound·with this chain."
2Ti 1:16 me, and he·was·not ashamed of·my chain.
Rv 20:1 of·the bottomless·pit and a·great chain in his hand.
G0254 N-APF ἁλύσεις (1x)
Mk 5:4 the chains to·have·been·thoroughly·drawn·apart by
G0254 N-DSF ἁλύσει (1x)
Eph 6:20 of·which I·am·an·elder·spokesman in a·chain, that
G0254 N-DPF ἁλύσεσιν (5x)
Lk 8:29 him. And he·was·fettered with·chains, even being·
Ac 12:6 soldiers, having·been·bound with·two chains, and
Ac 21:33 *him* to·be·bound with·two chains, and·then he·
Mk 5:3 ·man was·able to·bind him, not·even with·chains,
Mk 5:4 to·have·been·bound with·shackles and chains, and

G0255 ἀ•λυσι•τελής alysitêlḗs *adj.* (1x)
Roots:G0001 G3081 Compare:G0888 G0512
G0255.2 A-NSN ἀλυσιτελές (1x)
Heb 13:17 ·heavily, for that *is* not·a·better·end for·yeu.

G0256 Ἀλφαῖος Alphaîôs *n/p.* (8x)
חֶלֶף cнêlêph [Ancient Hebrew]
Roots:H2501
G0256.2 N/P-GSM Ἀλφαίου (5x)
Lk 6:15 Thomas, Jakob (the·one of·Alphaeus), and Simon,
Ac 1:13 and MattHew); (Jakob *son* of·Alphaeus, Simon the
Mt 10:3 ·*Alphaeus*); Jakob (the·one of·Alphaeus) and *Judas*
Mk 2:14 *called MattHew* (the·one of·Alphaeus) sitting·down
Mk 3:18 and Jakob (the·one of·Alphaeus), and *Judas called*
EG0256.2 (3x)
Lk 6:15 MattHew *of·Alphaeus* and Thomas, Jakob (the·one
Mt 10:3 the tax·collector *(the·one of·Alphaeus)*; Jakob (the·
Mk 3:18 and BarTholomew, and MattHew *of·Alphaeus*, and

G0257 ἅλων hálōn *n.* (2x)
Roots:G1507 Compare:G4621 G4987-2 xLangEquiv:H1637
G0257.1 N-ASF ἅλωνα (2x)
Lk 3:17 ·purify his threshing·floor and shall·gather·together
Mt 3:12 he·shall·thoroughly·purify his threshing·floor, and

G0258 ἀλώπηξ alṓpēx *n.* (3x)
G0258.1 N-NPF ἀλώπεκες (2x)
Lk 9:58 declared to·him, "The foxes have burrows, and the
Mt 8:20 YeShua says to·him, "The foxes have burrows, and
G0258.1 N-DSF ἀλώπεκι (1x)
Lk 13:32 "Traversing, yeu·declare to·that fox, 'Behold, I·

G0259 ἅλωσις hálōsis *n.* (1x)
Roots:G0234-1 Compare:G0161 See:G0258-1 G0164 G0355
G0259 N-ASF ἅλωσιν (1x)
2Pe 2:12 having·been·born into capture and corruption,

G0260 ἅμα háma *adv.* (10x)
Compare:G3674 See:G0001
G0260 ADV ἅμα (10x)
Ac 24:26 But also at·the·same·time, *he·was* expecting that
Ac 27:40 into the sea, *while* at·the·same·time slackening the
Mt 13:29 ·uproot the wheat at·the·same·time with·them.

Mt 20:1 who went·out at·the·same·time as·dawn to·hire
Rm 3:12 ·away. At·the·same·time, they·are·made·useless;
1Th 4:17 shall·be·snatched·up at·the·same·time together
1Th 5:10 we·should·live at·the·same·time together with·him.
Col 4:3 at·the·same·time praying also concerning us, that
Phm 1:22 But at·the·same·time make·ready for·me also
1Ti 5:13 And also at·the·same·time, they·learn *to·be* idle,

G0261 ἀ•μαθής amathḗs *adj.* (1x)
Roots:G0001 G3129 Compare:G0057 G0062

G0261 A-NPM ἀμαθεῖς (1x)
2Pe 3:16 — which *the* unlearned and unstable distort, as

G0262 ἀ•μαράντινος amarántinôs *adj.* (1x)
Roots:G0263

G0262.2 A-ASM ἀμαράντινον (1x)
1Pe 5:4 ·obtain the undiminishable victor's·crown of·glory.

G0263 ἀ•μάραντος amárantôs *adj.* (1x)
Roots:G0001 G3133 Compare:G2827 See:G0260 G0262

G0263.2 A-ASF ἀμάραντον (1x)
1Pe 1:4 and shrivel-proof inheritance having·been·reserved

G0264 ἀ•μαρτάνω amartánō *v.* (43x)
ἀ•μαρτάνω hamartánō [traditional]
Roots:G0001 G3313 Compare:G0795 G4587 G0703 See:G0265 G0266 G0268 G4258 G1814-2 G2177-1 G1262-1

G0264.1 V-FAI-1P ἁμαρτήσομεν (1x)
Rm 6:15 So·then, what? Shall·we·morally·fail, because we·

G0264.1 V-FAI-3S ἁμαρτήσει (1x)
Mt 18:21 ·times shall my brother morally·fail against me,

G0264.1 V-PAI-2P ἁμαρτάνετε (1x)
1Co 8:12 conscience, yeu·morally·fail toward Anointed-One

G0264.1 V-PAI-3S ἁμαρτάνει (6x)
Tit 3:11 ·as·this has·been·subverted and morally·fails, being
1Co 6:18 committing·sexual·immorality morally·fails his·
1Co 7:36 he·does·not morally·fail; let·*the·couple*·marry.
1Jn 3:6 one abiding in him does·not morally·fail. Any one
1Jn 3:8 because the Slanderer morally·fails from *the*
1Jn 5:18 ·been·born from·out of·God does·not morally·fail,

G0264.1 V-PAM-2S ἁμάρτανε (2x)
Jn 5:14 ·become healthy·and·sound; morally·fail no·longer,
Jn 8:11 Traverse, and morally·fail no·longer!"

G0264.1 V-PAM-2P ἁμαρτάνετε (2x)
1Co 15:34 as·is·right, and do·not morally·fail; for some are
Eph 4:26 Be·angry, but do·not morally·fail!" Do·not·let the

G0264.1 V-PAN ἁμαρτάνειν (1x)
1Jn 3:9 And he·is·not able to·morally·fail, because he·has·

G0264.1 V-PAP-ASM ἁμαρτάνοντα (1x)
1Jn 5:16 his brother morally·failing a·moral·failure *which·is*

G0264.1 V-PAP-APM ἁμαρτάνοντας (1x)
1Ti 5:20 ·reprove the·ones morally·failing in·order·that the

G0264.1 V-PAP-DPM ἁμαρτάνουσιν (1x)
1Jn 5:16 (*that·is*, to·the·ones morally·failing not unto death).

G0264.1 V-PAP-GPM ἁμαρτανόντων (1x)
Heb 10:26 *if* we·ourselves go·on·morally·failing voluntarily

G0264.1 V-PAP-NSM ἁμαρτάνων (1x)
1Jn 3:6 ·fail. Any one morally·failing has·not clearly·seen

G0264.1 V-PAP-NPM ἁμαρτάνοντες (2x)
1Pe 2:20 yeu·are·being·buffeted for·morally·failing, yeu·
1Co 8:12 But by·morally·failing in·this·manner toward the

G0264.1 V-2AAI-1S ἥμαρτον (4x)
Lk 15:18 ·him, "Father, I·morally·failed against the heaven,
Lk 15:21 ·him, 'Father, I·morally·failed against the heaven
Ac 25:8 ·even against Caesar, did·I·morally·fail *in* anything.
Mt 27:4 saying, "I·morally·failed in·handing·over blood

G0264.1 V-2AAI-2S ἥμαρτες (1x)
1Co 7:28 if you·should·marry, you·did·not morally·fail; and

G0264.1 V-2AAI-3S ἥμαρτεν (3x)
Jn 9:2 "Rabbi, who morally·failed, this·man or his parents,
Jn 9:3 answered, "Neither this·man morally·failed, nor his
1Co 7:28 virgin should·marry, she·did·not morally·fail. But

G0264.1 V-2AAI-3P ἥμαρτον (4x)
Rm 2:12 as·many·as did·morally·fail without·Torah-Law
Rm 2:12 And as·many·as did·morally·fail with Torah-Law
Rm 3:23 For all morally·failed and are·destitute of·the glory
Rm 5:12 ·clay† upon this·very *point*: *that* all morally·failed.

G0264.1 V-AAP-APM ἁμαρτήσαντας (1x)
Rm 5:14 even over the·ones not morally·failing after the

G0264.1 V-AAP-DPM ἁμαρτήσασιν (1x)
Heb 3:17 *Was·it* not·indeed the·ones morally·failing, whose

G0264.1 V-AAP-GSM ἁμαρτήσαντος (1x)
Rm 5:16 not as through one already·morally·failing. For in·

G0264.1 V-AAP-GPM ἁμαρτησάντων (1x)
2Pe 2:4 — did·not spare morally·failing angels, but·rather

G0264.1 V-2AAS-2P ἁμάρτητε (1x)
1Jn 2:1 to·yeu, in·order·that yeu·should·not morally·fail.

G0264.1 V-2AAS-3S ἁμάρτῃ (3x)
Lk 17:3 "But if your brother should·morally·fail against you,
Lk 17:4 And if he·should·morally·fail against you seven·
1Jn 2:1 And if anyone should·morally·fail, we·have a·

G0264.1 V-AAS-3S ἁμαρτήσῃ (1x)
Mt 18:15 But if your brother should·morally·fail against you,

G0264.1 V-RAI-1P ἡμαρτήκαμεν (1x)
1Jn 1:10 ·declare that we·have·not morally·failed, we·make

G0265 ἀ•μάρτημα amártēma *n.* (4x)
ἀ•μάρτημα hamártēma [traditional]
Roots:G0264 See:G0266 G0268

G0265.3 N-NSN ἁμάρτημα (1x)
1Co 6:18 Flee the sexual·immorality. Every moral·failing,

G0265.3 N-NPN ἁμαρτήματα (2x)
Mk 3:28 that all the moral·failings shall·be·forgiven the
Mk 4:12 and *their* moral·failings should·be·forgiven them."

G0265.3 N-GPN ἁμαρτημάτων (1x)
Rm 3:25 of·the moral·failings having·already·occurred)—

G0266 ἀ•μαρτία amartía *n.* (176x)
ἀ•μαρτία hamartía [traditional]
חַטָּאָה cнaṭa'ah [Hebrew]
חַטָּאת cнaṭa'th [plural]
Roots:G0264 Compare:G0093 G0703 G4586 See:G0265 G0268
xLangEquiv:H2403 A2408 xLangAlso:H5771

G0266.3 N-NSF ἁμαρτία (16x)
Jn 9:41 Accordingly, yeur moral·failure remains.
Mt 12:31 to·yeu, all·manner·of moral·failure and revilement
Rm 5:13 even·until *the* Torah-Law, moral·failure was in *the*
Rm 5:13 in *the* world, but moral·failure is·not imputed *with·*
Rm 6:14 For moral·failure shall·not lord·over yeu, for yeu·
Rm 7:7 *Is* the Torah-Law moral·failure? May·it·never
Rm 7:8 For apart·from Torah-Law, moral·failure *was* dead.
Rm 7:13 ·be·shown *to·be* moral·failure, is·accomplishing
Rm 14:23 that *is* not from·out of·trust is moral·failure.
Jac 1:15 and with·the moral·failure being·consummated, it·
Jac 4:17 to·do and not doing *it*, to·him it·is moral·failure.
1Jn 3:4 ·of·the·Royal-Law, and the moral·failure is the
1Jn 3:5 our moral·failures, and in him is not moral·failure.
1Jn 5:16 unto death). There·is moral·failure unto death; not
1Jn 5:17 All unrighteousness is moral·failure, and there·is
1Jn 5:17 is moral·failure, and there·is moral·failure not unto

G0266.3 N-NPF ἁμαρτίαι (12x)
Lk 5:20 ·clay†, your moral·failures have·been·forgiven you.
Lk 5:23 'Your moral·failures have·been·forgiven you,' or
Lk 7:47 ·you, her many moral·failures have·been·forgiven,
Lk 7:48 to·her, "Your moral·failures have·been·forgiven."
Mt 9:2 Your moral·failures have·been·forgiven you."
Mt 9:5 'Your moral·failures have·been·forgiven you?
Mk 2:5 "Child, your moral·failures have·been·forgiven you.
Mk 2:9 ·man, 'The moral·failures have·been·forgiven you,'
Rm 4:7 whose moral·failures are·fully·covered·over·and·.
1Ti 5:24 The moral·failures of·some men·of·clay† are
1Jn 2:12 because the moral·failures have·been·forgiven yeu
Rv 18:5 because "her moral·failures followed even·up·to the

G0266.3 N-ASF ἁμαρτίαν (23x)
Jn 1:29 the·one taking·away the moral·failure of·the world!
Jn 8:34 any one committing the moral·failure is a·slave of·
Jn 9:41 blind, yeu·would not have moral·failure. But now
Jn 15:22 to·them, they·were·not having moral·failure, but
Jn 15:24 has·done, they·would·not have moral·failure. But
Jn 19:11 me over to·you has a·greater moral·failure."
Ac 7:60 ·not establish this moral·failure against·them." And
Heb 12:1 hindrance and the readily·besetting moral·failure—
Heb 12:4 ·struggling specifically·against the moral·failure.
Gal 3:22 all·things under moral·failure in·order·that, as·a·
Rm 3:9 both Jews and Greeks, all to·be under moral·failure.
Rm 4:8 Yahweh, no, should·not reckon moral·failure."
Rm 8:10 the body *is* dead through moral·failure. Now the
Jac 1:15 it·reproduces·and·births moral·failure, and with·
Jac 2:9 ·partiality, yeu·work moral·failure, being·convicted
1Pe 2:22 "Who did·not commit moral·failure, neither was
2Co 5:21 the·one not knowing moral·failure made *himself* a·
2Co 11:7 Or did·I·commit a·moral·failure in·humbling my·
1Jn 1:8 that we·do·not have moral·failure, we·deceive
1Jn 3:4 Any one committing the moral·failure also commits
1Jn 3:8 ·one committing the moral·failure is birthed·from·out
1Jn 3:9 ·out of·God does·not commit moral·failure, because
1Jn 5:16 brother morally·failing a·moral·failure *which·is* not

G0266.3 N-APF ἁμαρτίας (23x)
Jn 20:23 Any·of·those·whose moral·failures yeu·should·,
Lk 5:21 Who is·able to·forgive moral·failures, except God
Lk 5:24 authority upon the earth to·forgive moral·failures,"
Lk 7:49 "Who is this that also forgives moral·failures?"
Lk 11:4 And forgive us our moral·failures, for we also
Ac 3:19 in·order·for yeur moral·failures to·be·rubbed·out,
Ac 22:16 fully·bathe·away your moral·failures, calling·upon
Heb 2:17 ·atonement·for the moral·failures of·the People.
Heb 9:28 only·once 'to·carry·up moral·failures for the many
Heb 10:4 and of·adult·male·goats to·remove moral·failures.
Heb 10:11 ·time is·able to·entirely·remove moral·failures.
Mt 3:6 the Jordan, explicitly·confessing their moral·failures.
Mt 9:6 has authority on the earth to·forgive moral·failures,"
Mk 1:5 River, explicitly·confessing their moral·failures.
Mk 2:7 Who is·able to·forgive moral·failures, except one
Mk 2:10 on the earth to·forgive moral·failures—" *then* he·
Rm 11:27 'whenever I·should·remove their moral·failures.'
Jac 5:15 ·be having·committed moral·failures, they·shall·be·
1Pe 2:24 himself carried·up our moral·failures in·his·own
1Th 2:16 *the complete·fullness·of* their moral·failures. So, the
1Jn 1:9 If we·should·confess our moral·failures, he·is
1Jn 1:9 that he·should·forgive us the moral·failures, and
1Jn 3:5 ·that he·should·take·away our moral·failures, and in

G0266.3 N-DSF ἁμαρτίᾳ (2x)
Jn 8:21 and shall·die in yeur moral·failures. Where I·myself
Rm 6:6 no·longer *for* us to·be·a·slave to·the moral·failure.

G0266.3 N-DPF ἁμαρτίαις (9x)
Jn 8:24 that yeu·shall·die in yeur moral·failures. For unless
Jn 8:24 that I AM, yeu·shall·die in yeur moral·failures."
Jn 9:34 ·yourself were·born altogether in moral·failures, and
1Pe 2:24 ·pronounced·dead to·the moral·failures) should·live
1Co 15:17 *is* futile— yeu·are still in yeur moral·failures.
Eph 2:1 dead in·the trespasses and in·the moral·failures,
1Ti 5:22 nor·even share in·others' moral·failures. Fully·keep
2Ti 3:6 having·been·stacked·high with·moral·failures, being·
Rv 18:4 ·may·not share·together in·her moral·failures, and

G0266.3 N-GSF ἁμαρτίας (19x)
Jn 8:46 yeu convicts me concerning moral·failure? And if·
Jn 15:22 ·not have a·pretense concerning their moral·failure.
Jn 16:8 shall·convict the world concerning moral·failure, and
Jn 16:9 Concerning moral·failure, in·fact because they·did·
Heb 4:15 *to·us*, *yet* completely·apart·from moral·failure.
Heb 9:26 for a·cancellation of·moral·failure through the
Heb 10:6 even concerning moral·failure, you·did·not take·
Heb 10:8 even concerning moral·failure, you·did·not want,
Heb 10:18 no·longer an·offering concerning moral·failure.
Heb 11:25 full·enjoyment of·moral·failure just·for·a·season,
Heb 13:11 concerning moral·failure, are·completely·burned
Gal 2:17 an·attendant of·moral·failure? May·it·never happen
Rm 3:20 Torah-Law *is the* recognition of·moral·failure.
Rm 6:6 the body of·moral·failure may·be·fully·rendered·,
Rm 6:16 ·obey, indeed·whether of·moral·failure to death, or
Rm 8:3 flesh and concerning moral·failure, condemned

1Pe 4:1 in flesh has·been·restrained from·moral·failure,
2Pe 2:14 and not·fully·refraining from·moral·failure, while·
1Jn 1:7 his Son, purifies us from all moral·failure.
G0266.3 N-GPF ἁμαρτιῶν (33x)
Lk 1:77 to·his People unto a·pardon of·their moral·failures,
Lk 3:3 of·repentance unto a·pardon of·moral·failures.
Lk 24:47 and pardon of·moral·failures to·be·officially· in his
Ac 2:38 of·Jesus Anointed for pardon of·moral·failures, and
Ac 5:31 repentance to·IsraEl and pardon of·moral·failures.
Ac 10:43 *is* to·receive pardon of·moral·failures through his
Ac 13:38 pardon of·moral·failures is·being·fully·proclaimed
Ac 26:18 pardon of·moral·failures and an·allotted·heritage
Heb 1:3 purification of·our moral·failures through himself,
Heb 5:1 presents and sacrifices on·behalf of·moral·failures,
Heb 5:3 to·offer *sacrifices* on·behalf of·moral·failures.
Heb 7:27 first on·behalf of·their·own moral·failures, *and*
Heb 8:12 and *concerning* their moral·failures and their
Heb 10:2 further a·moral·consciousness of·moral·failures?
Heb 10:3 ·again *is·made* of·moral·failures each year.
Heb 10:12 on·behalf of·moral·failures into perpetuity, sat·
Heb 10:17 "and of·their moral·failures and of·their
Heb 10:26 ·remaining a·sacrifice concerning moral·failures,
Gal 1:4 giving himself on·behalf of·our moral·failures, that
Mt 1:21 shall·save his People from their moral·failures."
Mt 26:28 ·out concerning many for pardon of·moral·failures.
Mk 1:4 of·repentance unto a·pardon of·moral·failures.
Rm 7:5 the intense·cravings of·the moral·failures, the·ones
Jac 5:20 ·cover·and·bury·over a·multitude of·moral·failures.
1Pe 3:18 ·once concerning moral·failures, a·righteous·one
1Pe 4:8 ·and·bury·over a·full·multitude of·moral·failures."
2Pe 1:9 of·the purification from·his former moral·failures.
1Co 15:3 on·behalf of·our moral·failures according·to the
Col 1:14 through his blood, the pardon of·moral·failures.
Col 2:11 ·off from·the body the moral·failures of·the flesh
1Jn 2:2 *the* atonement concerning our moral·failures, and not
1Jn 4:10 *to·be the* atonement concerning our moral·failures.
Rv 1:5 us *clean* from our moral·failures in his·own blood.
EG0266.3 (2x)
Jn 20:23 *and* whose *moral·failures* yeu·should·securely·hold,
1Jn 2:2 also concerning *the moral·failures·of* the whole
G0266.4 N-ASF ἁμαρτίαν (1x)
2Co 5:21 made *himself* a·reparation·for·moral·failure on·
G0266.4 N-GSF ἁμαρτίας (1x)
Heb 9:28 ·time (·apart·from a·reparation·for·moral·failure),
G0266.6 N-NSF ἁμαρτία (5x)
Rm 7:8 But Moral·Failure, taking impromptu·occasion
Rm 7:9 coming, Moral·Failure came·alive·again, and I·
Rm 7:11 For Moral·Failure, taking impromptu·occasion
Rm 7:13 happen! But·rather Moral·Failure, in·order·that it·
Rm 7:13 ·good, in·order·that Moral·Failure, through the
G0266.6 N-ASF ἁμαρτίαν (2x)
Rm 7:7 But·yet, I·did·not know Moral·Failure, except
Rm 7:14 fleshly, having·been·sold·off under Moral·Failure.
G0266.6 N-DSF ἁμαρτίᾳ (4x)
Rm 6:1 Shall·we·continue·on in·Moral·Failure in·order·that
Rm 6:2 We·are·those·who died to·Moral·Failure; how
Rm 6:10 ·died to·the Moral·Failure upon·one·occasion·only,
Rm 6:11 to·be in·fact dead to·the Moral·Failure, but alive to·
G0266.6 N-GSF ἁμαρτίας (3x)
Heb 3:13 through·the·delusional·nature of·Moral·Failure.
Rm 6:7 has·been·regarded·as·innocent of the Moral·Failure.
2Th 2:3 the Clay·Man† of·Moral·Failure should·be·revealed,
G0266.6 N/P-NSF ἁμαρτία (7x)
Rm 5:12 one man·of·clay†, Moral·Failure entered into the
Rm 5:20 But where Moral·Failure increased·more, Grace
Rm 5:21 in·order·that just·as Moral·Failure reigned in Death
Rm 6:12 *each·one·of* you·must·not·let Moral·Failure reign in
Rm 7:17 but·rather the·one dwelling in me, Moral·Failure.
Rm 7:20 but·rather the·one dwelling in me, Moral·Failure.
1Co 15:56 the painful·sting of·Death *is* Moral·Failure, and
G0266.6 N/P-ASF ἁμαρτίαν (1x)
Rm 8:3 moral·failure, condemned Moral·Failure in the flesh
G0266.6 N/P-DSF ἁμαρτίᾳ (1x)
Rm 6:13 of·unrighteousness to·Moral·Failure, but·rather
G0266.6 N/P-GSF ἁμαρτίας (11x)
Jn 8:34 the moral·failure is a·slave of·Moral·Failure.
Rm 5:12 the world and Death through Moral·Failure, also in·
Rm 6:17 *formerly* yeu·were *the* slaves of·Moral·Failure, but
Rm 6:18 ·free from Moral·Failure, yeu·are·already·enslaved
Rm 6:20 when yeu·were slaves of·Moral·Failure, yeu·were
Rm 6:22 from Moral·Failure and already·being·enslaved to·
Rm 6:23 For the wages of·Moral·Failure *is* death, but the
Rm 7:23 *of* me to·the Law of·Moral·Failure, the·one being in
Rm 7:25 but with·the flesh, *a·slave* to·Moral·Failure's Law.
Rm 8:2 me free from the Law of·Moral·Failure and Death.
1Co 15:56 ·Failure, and the power of·Moral·Failure *is* the
G0266.7 N-GSF ἁμαρτίας (1x)
Rm 8:3 Son in *the* resemblance of·morally·failing flesh and

G0267 ἀ•μάρτυρος amártyrôs *adj.* (1x)
Roots:G0001 G3144
G0267 A-ASM ἀμάρτυρον (1x)
Ac 14:17 himself without·witness, by·beneficially·doing·

G0268 ἁ•μαρτωλός amartōlós *adj.* (47x)
ἁ•μαρτωλός hamartōlós [traditional]
Roots:G0264 Compare:G0096 See:G0265 G0266 xLangAlso:H2400
G0268.2 A-NSM ἁμαρτωλός (2x)
Rm 3:7 why am I·also still judged as morally·disqualified?"
1Pe 4:18 ·appear the irreverent and morally·disqualified?"
G0268.2 A-NPM ἁμαρτωλοί (11x)
Lk 6:32 For even the morally·disqualified·ones love the·ones
Lk 6:33 ·yeu? For even the morally·disqualified·ones do the
Lk 6:34 yeu? For the morally·disqualified also lend to·*the*·
Lk 13:2 became morally·disqualified above·and·beyond all
Lk 15:1 and the morally·disqualified were drawing·near to·
Gal 2:15 and not from·among morally·disqualified Gentiles.
Gal 2:17 are·found morally·disqualified, would·this·then·
Mt 9:10 and morally·disqualified·men *were* coming. They·
Mk 2:15 and morally·disqualified·men also reclined·
Rm 5:19 are·fully·established *as* morally·disqualified, also
Jud 1:15 *and* morally·disqualified·men spoke against him.
G0268.2 A-VPM ἁμαρτωλοί (1x)
Jac 4:8 *yeur* hands, *yeu* morally·disqualified, and cleanse
G0268.2 A-ASM ἁμαρτωλόν (1x)
Jac 5:20 turning·back·around a·morally·disqualified·man of·
G0268.2 A-APM ἁμαρτωλούς (5x)
Lk 5:32 but·rather morally·disqualified·men to repentance."
Lk 15:2 ·man welcomes morally·disqualified·men and eats·
Mt 9:13 but·rather morally·disqualified·ones to repentance.
Mk 2:17 but·rather morally·disqualified·men to repentance.
1Ti 1:15 world to·save morally·disqualified·ones, of·whom
G0268.2 A-DSM ἁμαρτωλῷ (4x)
Lk 15:7 over one morally·disqualified·man repenting, rather·
Lk 15:10 ·God over one morally·disqualified·man repenting.
Lk 18:13 ·forgiving·toward me, the morally·disqualified.'
Lk 19:7 to·lodge with a·man *who·is* morally·disqualified!"
G0268.2 A-DSF ἁμαρτωλῷ (1x)
Mk 8:38 (*known·as* the adulteress and morally·disqualified),
G0268.2 A-DPM ἁμαρτωλοῖς (2x)
Lk 6:34 also lend to·*the*·morally·disqualified, in·order·that
1Ti 1:9 ·irreverent·ones and for·morally·disqualified·ones,
G0268.2 A-GPM ἁμαρτωλῶν (11x)
Lk 5:30 with tax·collectors and morally·disqualified·men?"
Lk 7:34 of·tax·collectors and morally·disqualified·men!'
Lk 24:7 into *the* hands of·morally·disqualified men·of·clay†,
Heb 7:26 ·separated from the morally·disqualified·men, and
Heb 12:3 by the morally·disqualified·men against himself,
Mt 9:11 the tax·collectors and morally·disqualified·men?"
Mt 11:19 of·tax·collectors and morally·disqualified·men.'
Mt 26:45 ·over into *the* hands of·morally·disqualified·men.
Mk 2:16 and morally·disqualified·men, were·saying to·his
Mk 2:16 the tax·collectors and morally·disqualified·men?"
Mk 14:41 ·over into the hands of·morally·disqualified·men.
G0268.3 A-NSM ἁμαρτωλός (4x)
Jn 9:16 "How·is a·man·of·clay†, full·of·moral·failure, able
Jn 9:24 that this man·of·clay† is full·of·moral·failure."
Jn 9:25 "Whether he·is full·of·moral·failure, I·do·not
Lk 5:8 me, because I·am a·man full·of·moral·failure, Lord."
G0268.3 A-NSF ἁμαρτωλός (3x)
Lk 7:37 city who was full·of·moral·failure, when·realizing
Lk 7:39 ·hold of·him, because she·is full·of·moral·failure."
Rm 7:13 ·become most exceedingly full·of·moral·failure.
G0268.3 A-GPM ἁμαρτωλῶν (2x)
Jn 9:31 does·not hear those·full·of·moral·failure, but·rather
Rm 5:8 with·us being full·of·moral·failure, Anointed-One

G0269 ἄ•μαχος ámachôs *adj.* (2x)
Roots:G0001 G3163
G0269 A-ASM ἄμαχον (1x)
1Ti 3:3 fair, not·quarrelsome, without·fondness·of·money,
G0269 A-APM ἀμάχους (1x)
Tit 3:2 to·revile no·man, to·be not·quarrelsome, *but* fair,

G0270 ἀμάω amáō *v.* (1x)
Roots:G0260 Compare:G4816 G2325
G0270.2 V-AAP-GPM ἀμησάντων (1x)
Jac 5:4 mowing·and·bundling·up yeur wide·open·fields,

G0271 ἀ•μέθυστος améthystôs *n.* (1x)
Roots:G0001 G3184
G0271 N-NSF ἀμέθυστος (1x)
Rv 21:20 deep·blue·hyacinth; the twelfth, amethyst.

G0272 ἀ•μελέω amêléō *v.* (5x)
Roots:G0001 G3199 Compare:G3865 G3928 G1950
G0272.1 V-FAI-1S ἀμελήσω (1x)
2Pe 1:12 Therefore I·shall·not neglect to·quietly·remind yeu
G0272.1 V-PAM-2S ἀμέλει (1x)
1Ti 4:14 Do·not neglect the gracious·bestowment in you,
G0272.1 V-AAI-1S ἠμέλησα (1x)
Heb 8:9 in my covenant, and·I neglected them,' says
G0272.1 V-AAP-NPM ἀμελήσαντες (2x)
Heb 2:3 utterly·escape after·neglecting so·vast a·Salvation?
Mt 22:5 But neglecting *his call*, they·went·away, in·fact, one

G0273 ἄ•μεμπτος áměmptôs *adj.* (6x)
Roots:G0001 G3201 Compare:G0121 G0298 G0172 See:G0299
G0273.1 A-NSM ἄμεμπτος (1x)
Php 3:6 (the·one in *the* Torah-Law), becoming blameless.
G0273.1 A-NPM ἄμεμπτοι (2x)
Lk 1:6 in·the·sight of·God, traversing blamelessly in all the
Php 2:15 in·order·that yeu·may·be blameless and untainted,
G0273.1 A-APF ἀμέμπτους (1x)
1Th 3:13 ·establish yeur hearts blameless in devoted·holiness
G0273.2 A-NSF ἄμεμπτος (1x)
Heb 8:7 For if that first *covenant* was faultless, then no place
EG0273.2 (1x)
Rm 2:13 ·before God, but·rather, the *faultless* doers of·the

G0274 ἀ•μέμπτως amémptōs *adv.* (2x)
Roots:G0273
G0274 ADV ἀμέμπτως (2x)
1Th 2:10 righteously and blamelessly, we·behaved·ourselves
1Th 5:23 soul, and body be·fully·kept blamelessly unto the

G0275 ἀ•μέριμνος amérimnôs *adj.* (2x)
Roots:G0001 G3308
G0275 A-APM ἀμερίμνους (2x)
Mt 28:14 him, and shall·make yeu *secure* without·anxiety."
1Co 7:32 But I·want you to·be without·anxiety. The

G0276 ἀ•μετά•θετος amêtáthêtôs *adj.* (2x)
Roots:G0001 G3346
G0276.1 A-GPN ἀμεταθέτων (1x)
Heb 6:18 ·of two unalterable matters·of·consequence in
G0276.2 A-ASN ἀμετάθετον (1x)
Heb 6:17 of·promise the unalterable·nature of·his counsel,

G0277 ἀ•μετα•κίνητος amêtakínētôs *adj.* (1x)
Roots:G0001 G3334 Compare:G0761 G0276 G0804 G1476
G0277.1 A-NPM ἀμετακίνητοι (1x)
1Co 15:58 immovably·steadfast, unstirrable·from *the Trust*,

G0278 ἀ•μετα•μέλητος amêtamélētôs *adj.* (2x)
Roots:G0001 G3338 See:G3341
G0278.1 A-NPN ἀμεταμέλητα (1x)

Rm 11:29 and the calling of·God *are* without·regret.

G0278.1 A-ASF ἀμεταμέλητον (1x)

2Co 7:10 repentance unto Salvation without·regret, but the

G0279 ἀ•μετα•νόητος amêtanóētôs *adj.* (1x)

Roots:G0001 G3340

G0279 A-ASF ἀμετανόητον (1x)

Rm 2:5 your hardness and *your* unrepentant heart, you·store·

G0280 ἄ•μετρος ámêtrôs *adj.* (2x)

Roots:G0001 G3358 See:G3357

G0280.3 A-APN ἄμετρα (2x)

2Co 10:13 boast in the things·beyond·measure, but·rather

2Co 10:15 the things·beyond·measure *that* we·are·boasting,

G0281 ἀμήν amḗn *heb.* (151x)

אָמֵן 'ạmẹn [Hebrew]

Roots:H0543 Compare:G1096 See:G0239

G0281.2 HEB ἀμήν (76x)

Jn 1:51 Then he·says to·him, "Certainly, most·certainly, I·

Jn 3:3 and declared to·him, "Certainly, most·certainly, I·say

Jn 3:5 Jesus answered, "Certainly, most·certainly, I·say to·

Jn 3:11 "Certainly, most·certainly, I·say to·you, we·speak

Jn 5:19 declared to·them, "Certainly, most·certainly, I·say

Jn 5:24 "Certainly, most·certainly, I·say to·yeu, the·one

Jn 5:25 "Certainly, most·certainly, I·say to·yeu, an·hour is·

Jn 6:26 them and declared, "Certainly, most·certainly, I·say

Jn 6:32 Jesus declared to·them, "Certainly, most·certainly, I·

Jn 6:47 "Certainly, most·certainly, I·say to·yeu, the·one

Jn 6:53 declared to·them, "Certainly, most·certainly, I·say

Jn 8:34 Jesus answered them, "Certainly, most·certainly, I·

Jn 8:51 "Certainly, most·certainly, I·say to·yeu, if anyone

Jn 8:58 Jesus declared to·them, "Certainly, most·certainly, I·

Jn 10:1 "Certainly, most·certainly, I·say to·yeu, the·one not

Jn 10:7 to·them again, "Certainly, most·certainly, I·say to·

Jn 12:24 "Certainly, most·certainly, I·say to·yeu, unless the

Jn 13:16 "Certainly, most·certainly, I·say to·yeu, a·slave is

Jn 13:20 "Certainly, most·certainly, I·say to·yeu, the·one

Jn 13:21 and declared, "Certainly, most·certainly, I·say to·

Jn 13:38 soul on·behalf of·me? Certainly, most·certainly, I·

Jn 14:12 "Certainly, most·certainly, I·say to·yeu, the·one

Jn 16:20 "Certainly, most·certainly, I·say to·yeu, that yeu

Jn 16:23 me not·even·one·thing. "Certainly, most·certainly,

Jn 21:18 "Certainly, most·certainly, I·say to·you, when you·

Lk 4:24 Then he·declared, "Certainly I·say to·yeu, that not·

Lk 12:37 shall·find keeping·alert. Certainly I·say to·yeu,

Lk 13:35 is·left to·yeu desolate. And certainly I·say to·yeu,

Lk 18:17 Certainly I·say to·yeu, whoever, if he·should·not

Lk 18:29 And he·declared to·them, "Certainly I·say to·yeu,

Lk 21:32 "Certainly I·say to·yeu, this generation·of·

Lk 23:43 Jesus declared to·him, "Certainly I·say to·you,

Mt 5:18 "For certainly I·say to·yeu, until the heaven and the

Mt 5:26 Certainly I·say to·you, no, you·should·not come·

Mt 6:2 by the men·of·clay†. Certainly I·say to·yeu, they·

Mt 6:5 ·apparent to·the men·of·clay†. Certainly I·say to·yeu

Mt 6:16 men·of·clay† *to·be* fasting. Certainly I·say to·yeu

Mt 8:10 to·the·ones following, "Certainly I·say to·yeu, not·

Mt 10:15 Certainly I·say to·yeu, it·shall·be more·tolerable

Mt 10:23 flee into the other, for certainly I·say to·yeu, no,

Mt 10:42 merely in a·disciple's name, certainly I·say to·yeu,

Mt 11:11 "Certainly I·say to·yeu, among those·born of·

Mt 13:17 For certainly I·say to·yeu, that many prophets and

Mt 16:28 "Certainly I·say to·yeu, there·are some of·the·ones

Mt 17:20 ·of yeur lack·of·trust. For certainly I·say to·yeu, if

Mt 18:3 and declared, "Certainly I·say to·yeu, unless yeu·

Mt 18:13 he·should·happen to·find it, certainly I·say to·yeu,

Mt 18:18 "Certainly I·say to·yeu, as·many·things·as yeu·

Mt 19:23 to·his disciples, "Certainly I·say to·yeu that *it·is*

Mt 19:28 YeShua declared to·them, "Certainly I·say to·yeu,

Mt 21:21 YeShua declared to·them, "Certainly I·say to·yeu,

Mt 21:31 YeShua says to·them, "Certainly I·say to·yeu that

Mt 23:36 "Certainly I·say to·yeu, all these·things shall·come

Mt 24:2 look·for all these·things. Certainly I·say to·yeu, no,

Mt 24:34 "Certainly I·say to·yeu, *that* this generation·of·

Mt 24:47 Certainly I·say to·yeu, that he·shall·fully·establish

Mt 25:12 answering, he·declared, 'Certainly I·say to·yeu, I·

Mt 25:40 shall·declare to·them, 'Certainly I·say to·yeu, in

Mt 25:45 ·answer them, saying, 'Certainly I·say to·yeu, in

Mt 26:13 "Certainly I·say to·yeu, wherever this good·news

Mt 26:21 were·eating, he·declared, "Certainly I·say to·yeu,

Mt 26:34 YeShua replied to·him, "Certainly I·say to·you,

Mk 3:28 "Certainly I·say to·yeu, that all the moral·failings

Mk 6:11 a·testimony against·them. Certainly I·say to·yeu,

Mk 8:12 generation seek·for a·sign? Certainly I·say to·yeu,

Mk 9:1 And he·was·saying to·them, "Certainly I·say to·yeu,

Mk 9:41 yeu·are of·Anointed-One, certainly I·say to·yeu, no

Mk 10:15 Certainly I·say to·yeu, whoever, if he·should·not

Mk 10:29 Jesus declared, "Certainly I·say to·yeu, there·is

Mk 11:23 For certainly I·say to·yeu that whoever should·

Mk 12:43 he·says to·them, "Certainly I·say to·yeu, that

Mk 13:30 "Certainly I·say to·yeu, that this generation·of·

Mk 14:9 Certainly I·say to·yeu, wherever this good·news

Mk 14:18 Jesus declared, "Certainly I·say to·yeu, that one

Mk 14:25 "Certainly I·say to·yeu, no, I·should·not drink

Mk 14:30 Jesus says to·him, "Certainly I·say to·you, that

G0281.3 HEB ἀμήν (25x)

Jn 1:51 to·him, "Certainly, most·certainly, I·say to·yeu,

Jn 3:3 to·him, "Certainly, most·certainly, I·say to·you,

Jn 3:5 answered, "Certainly, most·certainly, I·say to·you,

Jn 3:11 "Certainly, most·certainly, I·say to·you, we·speak

Jn 5:19 to·them, "Certainly, most·certainly, I·say to·yeu,

Jn 5:24 "Certainly, most·certainly, I·say to·yeu, the·one

Jn 5:25 "Certainly, most·certainly, I·say to·yeu, an·hour is·

Jn 6:26 declared, "Certainly, most·certainly, I·say to·yeu,

Jn 6:32 to·them, "Certainly, most·certainly, I·say to·yeu,

Jn 6:47 "Certainly, most·certainly, I·say to·yeu, the·one

Jn 6:53 to·them, "Certainly, most·certainly, I·say to·yeu,

Jn 8:34 them, "Certainly, most·certainly, I·say to·yeu that

Jn 8:51 "Certainly, most·certainly, I·say to·yeu, if anyone

Jn 8:58 to·them, "Certainly, most·certainly, I·say to·yeu,

Jn 10:1 "Certainly, most·certainly, I·say to·yeu, the·one not

Jn 10:7 again, "Certainly, most·certainly, I·say to·yeu, I

Jn 12:24 "Certainly, most·certainly, I·say to·yeu, unless the

Jn 13:16 "Certainly, most·certainly, I·say to·yeu, a·slave is

Jn 13:20 "Certainly, most·certainly, I·say to·yeu, the·one

Jn 13:21 "Certainly, most·certainly, I·say to·yeu that one

Jn 13:38 of·me? Certainly, most·certainly, I·say to·you, a·

Jn 14:12 "Certainly, most·certainly, I·say to·yeu, the·one

Jn 16:20 "Certainly, most·certainly, I·say to·yeu, that yeu

Jn 16:23 "Certainly, most·certainly, I·say to·yeu, as·many·

Jn 21:18 "Certainly, most·certainly, I·say to·you, when you·

G0281.4 HEB ἀμήν (35x)

Jn 21:25 the official·scrolls being·written. So·be·it,·Amen.

Lk 24:53 praising and blessing God. So·be·it,·Amen.

Heb 13:21 *be* the glory to the ages of·ages. So·be·it,·Amen.

Gal 1:5 *be* the glory to the ages of·ages. So·be·it,·Amen.

Mt 6:13 and the glory, into the ages. So·be·it,·Amen.'

Mt 28:20 entire·completion of·the age." So·be·it,·Amen.

Mk 16:20 the signs following·afterward. So·be·it,·Amen)].

Rm 1:25 ·*one* who is blessed into the ages. So·be·it,·Amen).

Rm 9:5 God over all, blessed into the ages. So·be·it,·Amen.

Rm 11:36 To·him *be* glory into the ages. So·be·it,·Amen.

Rm 15:33 the God of·Peace *be* with yeu all. So·be·it,·Amen.

Rm 16:24 Jesus Anointed *be* with yeu all. So·be·it,·Amen.

Jud 1:25 both now and into all the ages. So·be·it,·Amen.

Php 4:20 *be* glory into the ages of·ages. So·be·it,·Amen.

1Pe 4:11 the might into the ages of·ages. So·be·it,·Amen.

1Pe 5:11 the might into the ages of·ages. So·be·it,·Amen.

1Pe 5:14 ·ones in Anointed-One YeShua. So·be·it,·Amen.

2Pe 3:18 and to *the* day of·*the*·coming·age. So·be·it,·Amen.

1Co 14:16 untrained declare the "So·be·it,·Amen" at your

2Co 1:20 in him *is* the "So·be·it,·Amen" for·God unto glory

Eph 3:21 generations of·the age of·ages. So·be·it,·Amen.

1Ti 1:17 and glory to the ages of·ages. So·be·it,·Amen.

1Ti 6:16 *be* honor and might eternal. So·be·it,·Amen.

2Ti 4:18 *be* glory into the ages of·ages. So·be·it,·Amen.

1Jn 5:21 ·keep yeurselves from the idols. So·be·it,·Amen.

2Jn 1:13 sister greet you *personally*. So·be·it,·Amen.

Rv 1:6 and the might into the ages of·ages. So·be·it,·Amen.

Rv 1:7 ' Yes, So·be·it,·Amen.

Rv 1:18 into the ages of·ages, So·be·it,·Amen; and I·have

Rv 5:14 living·beings were·saying, "So·be·it,·Amen." And

Rv 7:12 saying, "So·be·it,·Amen! The blessing, and the

Rv 7:12 to·our God into the ages of·ages. So·be·it,·Amen."

Rv 19:4 "So·be·it,·Amen! Splendidly·praise·Yahweh,·

Rv 22:20 I·come swiftly." So·be·it,·Amen. Yes, come,

Rv 22:21 Jesus Anointed *be* with yeu all. So·be·it,·Amen.

G0281.4 PREP ἀμήν (14x)

Heb 13:25 The grace *be* with yeu all. So·be·it,·Amen.

Gal 6:18 Anointed *be* with yeur spirit. So·be·it,·Amen.

Rm 16:27 Anointed into the coming·ages. So·be·it,·Amen.

Php 4:23 Jesus Anointed *be* with yeu all. So·be·it,·Amen.

1Th 5:28 YeShua Anointed *be* with yeu. So·be·it,·Amen.

2Th 3:18 YeShua Anointed *be* with yeu all. So·be·it,·Amen.

Tit 3:15 The grace *be* with yeu all. So·be·it,·Amen.

1Co 16:24 yeu all in Anointed-One Jesus. So·be·it,·Amen.

2Co 13:14 ·the Holy Spirit, *be* with yeu all. So·be·it,·Amen.

Eph 6:24 Anointed with incorruptibility. So·be·it,·Amen.

Col 4:18 The Grace *be* with yeu. So·be·it,·Amen.

Phm 1:25 Anointed *be* with yeur spirit. So·be·it,·Amen.

1Ti 6:21 Grace *be* with you. So·be·it,·Amen.

2Ti 4:22 Grace *be* with yeu. So·be·it,·Amen.

G0281.5 HEB ἀμήν (1x)

Rv 3:14 'These·things says the Sure·One,·the·Amen, the

G0282 ἀ•μήτωρ amḗtōr *adj.* (1x)

Roots:G0001 G3384 Compare:G3737 See:G0540

G0282 A-NSM ἀμήτωρ (1x)

Heb 7:3 ·*is* without·father, without·mother, without·lineage,

G0283 ἀ•μίαντος amíantôs *adj.* (4x)

Roots:G0001 G3392 Compare:G0053 G2513 See:G3393

G0283.1 A-NSM ἀμίαντος (1x)

Heb 7:26 innocent, uncontaminated, having·been·separated

G0283.1 A-NSF ἀμίαντος (2x)

Heb 13:4 and the bed *that·is* uncontaminated— but God

Jac 1:27 Father— pure and uncontaminated religion is this:

G0283.1 A-ASF ἀμίαντον (1x)

1Pe 1:4 an·incorruptible, uncontaminated and shrivel-proof

G0284 Ἀμι•ναδάβ Aminadáb *n/p.* (3x)

עַמִּינָדָב 'ạmîynạdạb [Hebrew]

Roots:H5992

G0284.2 N/P-PRI Ἀμιναδάβ (3x)

Lk 3:33 *son* of·AmmiNadab, *son* of·Ram, *son* of·Chetsron,

Mt 1:4 Now Ram begot AmmiNadab, and AmmiNadab begot

Mt 1:4 AmmiNadab, and AmmiNadab begot Nachshon, and

G0285 ἄμμος ámmôs *n.* (5x)

Roots:G0260 Compare:G4950 xLangEquiv:H2344

G0285 N-NSF ἄμμος (3x)

Heb 11:12 and as the innumerable sand beside the shoreline

Rm 9:27 Sons of·IsraEl may·be as the sand of·the sea, the

Rv 20:8 the number of·whom *is* as the sand of·the sea.

G0285 N-ASF ἄμμον (2x)

Mt 7:26 to·a·foolish man, who built his home upon the sand.

Rv 13:1 And I·settled upon the sand of·the sea, and I·saw a·

G0286 ἀμνός amnṓs *n.* (5x)

Compare:G0721 G4478 G0285-1 See:G3957 xLangEquiv:H3532 xLangAlso:H7353

G0286 N-NSM ἀμνός (3x)

Jn 1:29 he·says, "See the Sacrificial·Lamb of·God, the·one

Jn 1:36 ·along, he·says, "See the Sacrificial·Lamb of·God!"

Ac 8:32 butchering; and as a·sacrificial·lamb *is* voiceless in·

G0286 N-GSM ἀμνοῦ (1x)

1Pe 1:19 blood, as of·a·sacrificial·lamb without·blemish and

EG0286 (1x)

1Pe 1:20 In·fact, *a·sacrificial·lamb*, with·him·having·been·

G0287 ἀμοιβή amôibḗ *n.* (1x)

G0287 N-APF ἀμοιβάς (1x)

1Ti 5:4 and to·give·back compensations to·their·forebears,

G0288 ἄμπ•ελος ámpêlôs *n.* (8x)
Roots:G0297 G0257 Compare:G1666-1 See:G0290
xLangEquiv:H1612 xLangAlso:H3754
G0288 N-NSF ἄμπελος (3x)
Jn 15:1 "I AM the true vine, and my Father is the farmer.
Jn 15:5 "I AM the vine, yeu *are* the vine·sprouts.
Jac 3:12 my brothers, to·produce olives? Or a·vine, figs?
G0288 N-ASF ἄμπελον (1x)
Rv 14:19 and collected·for·vintage the vine of·the earth,
G0288 N-DSF ἀμπέλῳ (1x)
Jn 15:4 unless it·should·abide in the vine, in·this·manner,
G0288 N-GSF ἀμπέλου (3x)
Lk 22:18 drink of the produce of·the vine, until such·time the
Mt 26:29 ·on from·out of·this produce of·the vine, until that
Mk 14:25 from·out of·the produce of·the vine, until that day
G0289 ἀμπελο•υργός ampêlôurgós *adj.* (1x)
Roots:G0288 G2041 Compare:G1092 G2780
xLangEquiv:H3755
G0289.2 A-ASM ἀμπελουργόν (1x)
Lk 13:7 "So he·declared to the vinedresser, 'Behold, *for*
G0290 ἀμπελών ampêlṓn *n.* (23x)
Roots:G0288 Compare:G1638 G4808-1 G2779
xLangEquiv:H3754
G0290 N-ASM ἀμπελῶνα (11x)
Lk 20:9 "A·certain man·of·clay† planted a·vineyard and
Lk 20:16 and he·shall·give the vineyard to·others." And
Mt 20:1 ·time as·dawn to·hire workmen into his vineyard.
Mt 20:2 *for* the day, he·dispatched them into his vineyard.
Mt 20:4 also head·on·out into the vineyard, and whatever
Mt 20:7 yeu·yeurselves head·on·out into the vineyard, and
Mt 21:33 who "planted a·vineyard and placed a·hedge
Mt 21:41 he·shall·lease the vineyard to·other tenant·farmers,
Mk 12:1 "A·certain·man·of·clay† "planted a·vineyard, and
Mk 12:9 ·farmers and shall·give the vineyard to·others.
1Co 9:7 ·own wages? Who plants a·vineyard, and does·not
G0290 N-DSM ἀμπελῶνι (2x)
Lk 13:6 a·fig·tree having·been·planted in his vineyard, and
Mt 21:28 Work today in my vineyard.'
G0290 N-GSM ἀμπελῶνος (10x)
Lk 20:10 ·should·give him of the fruit of·the vineyard. "But
Lk 20:13 "Then the owner of·the vineyard declared, 'What
Lk 20:15 him forth outside of·the vineyard, they·killed *him*.
Lk 20:15 what shall the owner of·the vineyard do to·them?
Mt 20:8 the owner of·the vineyard says to·his executive·
Mt 21:39 ·cast·*him*·forth outside of·the vineyard and killed
Mt 21:40 whenever the owner of·the vineyard should·come,
Mk 12:2 the tenant·farmers of the fruit of·the vineyard.
Mk 12:8 *him* and cast·*him*·forth outside of·the vineyard.
Mk 12:9 "So·then, what·shall the owner of·the vineyard do?
G0291 Ἀμπλίας Amplías *n/p.* (1x)
G0291.2 N/P-ASM Ἀμπλίαν (1x)
Rm 16:8 Greet my well-beloved Amplias in *the* Lord.
G0292 ἀμύνομαι amýnômai *v.* (1x)
G0292.3 V-ADI-3S ἠμύνατο (1x)
Ac 7:24 being·wronged, he·forcefully·defended *his fellow*
G0293 ἀμφί•βληστρον amphíblēstrôn *n.* (2x)
Roots:G0297 G0906 Compare:G1350 G4522
See:G0293-1
xLangEquiv:H2764 xLangAlso:H4365
G0293 N-ASN ἀμφίβληστρον (2x)
Mt 4:18 Andrew his brother, casting a·cast·net into the sea,
Mk 1:16 his brother Andrew casting a·cast·net into the sea,
G0294 ἀμφι•έννυμι amphiénnymi *v.* (7x)
Roots:G0297 Compare:G1746 G1902 G2439
See:G2066
G0294 V-PAI-3S ἀμφιέννυσιν (2x)
Lk 12:28 "So if God in·this·manner enrobes the grass, today
Mt 6:30 And if God in·this·manner enrobes the grass of·the
G0294 V-RPP-ASM ἠμφιεσμένον (2x)
Lk 7:25 to·see? A·man·of·clay† having·been·enrobed in soft
Mt 11:8 ·see? A·man·of·clay† having·been·enrobed in soft
EG0294 (2x)
Lk 12:28 an·oven, how·much more *shall·he·enrobe* yeu, O·
Mt 6:30 ¿!·*shall·he* not much more *enrobe* yeu, O·yeu·of·
EG0294.- (1x)
Mt 6:30 being·cast into an·oven, ¿!·*shall·he* not much more
G0295 Ἀμφί•πολις Amphípôlis *n/l.* (1x)
Roots:G0297 G4172
G0295.2 N/L-ASF Ἀμφίπολιν (1x)
Ac 17:1 after·traveling·through AmphiPolis and Apollonia,
G0296 ἄμφ•οδον ámphôdôn *n.* (1x)
Roots:G0297 G3598
G0296 N-GSN ἀμφόδου (1x)
Mk 11:4 the door at the fork·in·the·road, and they·loose him.
G0297 ἀμφότερος amphṓtêrôs *adj.* (14x)
G0297 A-NPM ἀμφότεροι (7x)
Lk 1:6 And they·were both righteous in·the·sight of·God,
Lk 1:7 was barren, and both were having·well-advanced in
Lk 5:38 into brand-new wineskins, and both are·preserved.
Lk 6:39 *the* blind? Shall·they·not·indeed both fall into a·pit?
Ac 8:38 to·stand·still. And they·both walked·down into the
Mt 15:14 should·guide a·blind·man, both shall·fall into a·pit
Eph 2:18 Because through him, the both *of·us* have the
G0297 A-APM ἀμφοτέρους (1x)
Eph 2:16 *that* he·may·utterly·reconcile the both to·God in
G0297 A-APN ἀμφότερα (5x)
Lk 5:7 And they·came and filled both the sailboats, such·for
Ac 23:8 nor a·spirit, but *the* Pharisees affirm both·things.
Mt 9:17 into brand-new wineskins, and both are·preserved."
Mt 13:30 Allow both to·be·grown·together so·long·as·unto
Eph 2:14 peace, the·one already·making the both one, and
G0297 A-DPM ἀμφοτέροις (1x)
Lk 7:42 to·repay, he·graciously·forgave them·both. So·then
G0298 ἀ•μώμητος amṓmētôs *adj.* (2x)
Roots:G0001 G3469 Compare:G0273 G0423 G4587
G0298 A-NPM ἀμώμητοι (1x)
2Pe 3:14 by·him in peace, without·stain and irreproachable.
G0298 A-NPN ἀμώμητα (1x)
Php 2:15 children of·God, irreproachable, in·the·midst of·
G0299 ἄ•μωμος ámōmôs *adj.* (7x)
Roots:G0001 G3470 Compare:G0784 G0298
See:G0273
G0299.1 A-NSF ἄμωμος (1x)
Eph 5:27 that she·should·be holy and without·blemish.
G0299.1 A-NPM ἄμωμοι (1x)
Rv 14:5 for they·are without·blemish in·the·sight of·the
G0299.1 A-ASM ἄμωμον (1x)
Heb 9:14 Spirit offered himself without·blemish to·God,
G0299.1 A-APM ἀμώμους (3x)
Jud 1:24 *yeu* without·blemish directly·in·the·sight of·his
Eph 1:4 and without·blemish directly·in·the·sight of·him—
Col 1:22 and without·blemish and without·any·charge·of·
G0299.1 A-GSM ἀμώμου (1x)
1Pe 1:19 of·a·sacrificial·lamb without·blemish and without·
G0300 Ἀμών Amṓn *n/p.* (2x)
אָמוֹן ʻạmôṇ [Hebrew]
Roots:H0526
G0300.3 N/P-PRI Ἀμών (2x)
Mt 1:10 MaNasseh, and MaNasseh begot Amon, and Amon
Mt 1:10 MaNasseh begot Amon, and Amon begot JosIah.
G0301 Ἀμώς Amṓs *n/p.* (1x)
Ἀμώτς Amṓts [Greek, Octuagint]
אָמוֹץ ʻạmôtṣ [Hebrew]
Roots:H0531
G0301 N/P-PRI Ἀμώτς (1x)
Lk 3:25 *son* of·MattathIas, *son* of·Amots, *son* of·Nachum,
G0302 ἄν án *prt.* (77x)
Compare:G1437
G0302.ª PRT ἄν (4x)
Ac 5:24 ·perplexed about them as·to what would·come of·
Heb 8:7 *covenant* was faultless, then no place would·be·
Mt 23:3 whatever as·much·as they·should·declare to·yeu
2Co 10:9 I·may·not seem as if *I·intended* to·utterly·frighten
G0302.1 PRT ἄν (5x)
Jn 16:23 to·yeu, as·many·things·as yeu·would request·of·the
Ac 3:22 ' "as·many·things·as he·would speak to·yeu.
Mk 3:28 revilements, as·many·things·as they·would revile.
Mk 6:56 wherever he·was·traversing, whether into villages,
1Th 2:7 a·nurturing·mother would cherishingly·brood·over
G0302.2 PRT ἄν (54x)
Jn 4:10 *some* to·drink,' you would·have requested·of him,
Jn 4:10 requested·of him, and he·would·have given you
Jn 5:46 ·trusting in·Moses, yeu·would be·trusting in·me, for
Jn 8:19 me, also yeu·would have·personally·known my
Jn 8:39 "If yeu·were AbRaham's children, yeu·would do the
Jn 8:42 "If God was yeur Father, yeu·would love me, for I·
Jn 9:41 If yeu·were blind, yeu·would not have moral·failure.
Jn 11:21 if you·were here, my brother would not have·died.
Jn 11:32 if you·were here, my brother would not have·died."
Jn 14:2 abodes, but·if·not, I·would·have declared *that* to·
Jn 14:7 "If yeu·had·known me, yeu·would·have known my
Jn 14:28 If yeu·were·loving me, yeu·would rejoice that I·
Jn 15:19 the world would affectionately·favor its·own, but
Jn 18:30 was not a·criminal, we·would not have·handed him
Jn 18:36 assistants then·would strenuously·struggle in·order·
Lk 7:39 ·man were a·prophet, he·would·be knowing who
Lk 9:26 "For whoever would be·ashamed·of me and my
Lk 10:13 in yeu, long·ago they·would·have repented,
Lk 12:39 the thief would·come, he·would·have kept·alert,
Lk 12:39 ·have kept·alert, and would not have·allowed his
Lk 17:6 in the sea,' and it·would listen·to·and·obey yeu.
Ac 2:39 ·as Yahweh our God would call·forth·unto·himself."
Ac 3:23 it·shall·be *that* every soul who would not hear that
Ac 18:14 ·to reason, O Jews, I·would have·put·up·with yeu.
Ac 26:29 And Paul declared, "I·would well-wish to·God,
Heb 4:8 gave them complete·rest, he·would not have·spoken
Heb 8:4 he·were on earth, he·would not·even be a·priest·
Heb 10:2 Otherwise, ¿!·would·they not have·ceased being·
Heb 11:15 they·came·out, they·would have·had opportunity
Gal 1:10 yet I·was·appeasing men·of·clay†, I·would not be
Gal 3:21 the righteousness really would be·as·a·result of·
Gal 4:15 yeur own·eyes, yeu·would have·given·them to·me.
Mt 11:21 and Tsidon, long·ago they·would·have repented in
Mt 11:23 in Sodom, it·would·have remained as·long·as·unto
Mt 12:7 sacrifice,'' yeu·would not have·pronounced·guilty
Mt 18:6 whoever would entice·or·cause·the·moral·failure·of
Mt 23:30 the days of·our fathers, we·would not be partners
Mt 24:22 not any flesh would be·saved *to·continue living*;
Mt 24:43 the thief comes, he·would·have kept·alert and
Mt 24:43 he·would·have kept·alert and would not·have let
Mk 8:38 "For whoever would be·ashamed·of me and of·my
Mk 9:42 whoever would entice·or·cause·the·moral·failure·of
Mk 11:24 as·many·things·as yeu·would request as·yeu·are·
Mk 13:20 Days, not any flesh would be·saved; but·yet on·
Rm 9:15 ·mercy on·whom I·would show·gracious·mercy,
Rm 9:15 ·pity on·whom I·would compassionately·show·pity.
Rm 9:29 offspring† for·us, we·would·have become as
Rm 9:29 as Sodom, and would be·likened as Gomorrah.
Rm 10:13 For "'all who would call·upon the name of·*the*·
Jac 4:4 whoever would be·definitely·willing to·be a·friend
1Co 2:8 if they·knew *it*, they·would·have not crucified the
1Co 11:31 ourselves *properly*, we·would not be·judged.
1Jn 2:19 from·among us, they·would have·continued with
Rv 13:15 should·make as·many·as would not fall·prostrate
G0302.3 PRT ἄν (10x)
Jn 2:5 to·the attendants, "Whatever he·might say to·yeu, do
Lk 1:62 father, *for* what he·might actually·want him to·be·
Lk 6:11 alongside one·another what they·might do to·Jesus.
Lk 17:6 ·kernel of·mustard·seed *does*, yeu·might say to·this
Lk 19:23 ·coming, I·myself might·have reclaimed my·own
Gal 5:17 ·not do these·things which yeu·might want *to·do*.
Mt 22:9 ·the roadways, and as·many·as yeu·might find, call·
Mt 25:27 I·myself might be·subsequently·obtaining my·own
1Co 7:5 *which* might·be as·a·result of·a·mutual·agreement
1Jn 5:15 he·hears us, whatever·thing we·might request, we·
G0302.4 PRT ἄν (2x)
Lk 10:35 of·him. And whatever you·might spend·further,

Ac 8:31 "For how·is·it *that* I·might be·able *to·know* them,
G0302.5 PRT ἄν (2x)
Ac 2:45 to·all, according·to any·particular need someone
Ac 4:35 ·man, according·to any·particular need someone
G0303 ἀνά aná *prep.* (15x)
See:G0507 G0303-1
G0303.ª PREP ἀνά (2x)
Mk 6:40 they·sat·back·to·eat in·rows, rows by a·hundred,
Mk 6:40 ·eat in·rows, rows by a·hundred, and by fifty *deep*.
G0303.1 PREP ἀνά (3x)
Lk 10:1 also, and he·dispatched them up by·twos before his
Mt 13:25 and sowed *poisonous* darnel·weeds up *in·the* midst
1Co 6:5 one that shall·be·able to·discern up *the* middle for·
G0303.2 PREP ἀναμέσον (1x)
Rv 7:17 because the Lamb, the·one amidst the throne, shall·
G0303.3 PREP ἀνά (1x)
Rv 21:21 gates *were* twelve pearls; again, each one of·the
G0303.4 PREP ἀνά (7x)
Jn 2:6 ·room·for two or three ten·gallon·measures apiece.
Lk 9:3 neither money; neither to·have two tunics apiece.
Lk 9:14 ·recline·back *by* fifty apiece *in·each* reclined·group."
Mt 20:9 about the eleventh hour received a·denarius apiece.
Mt 20:10 yet they also received *the* same, a·denarius apiece.
1Co 14:27 most three·men, and a·portion apiece, and one
Rv 4:8 was·having six wings apiece overflowing of·eyes,
G0303.6 PREP ἀνά (1x)
Mk 7:31 to the Sea of·Galilee, through *the* midst of·the
G0304 ἀνα•βαθμός anabathmós *n.* (2x)
Roots:G0305 Compare:G0898 G2824-2 xLangAlso:H4609
G0304.2 N-APM ἀναβαθμούς (1x)
Ac 21:35 And when he·came to the stairs, *the need* befell
G0304.2 N-GPM ἀναβαθμῶν (1x)
Ac 21:40 while·standing on the stairs, motioned with·his
G0305 ἀνα•βαίνω anabaínō *v.* (82x)
Roots:G0303 G0901-3 Compare:G1631 See:G4320 G0306-1
G0305.1 V-PAI-1S ἀναβαίνω (1x)
Jn 7:8 this Sacred·Feast. I·myself do·not·yet walk·up to this
G0305.1 V-PAI-1P ἀναβαίνομεν (3x)
Lk 18:31 them, "Behold, we·walk·up to JeruSalem, and all
Mt 20:18 "Behold, we·walk·up to JeruSalem, and the Son
Mk 10:33 *saying*, "Behold, we·walk·up to JeruSalem, and
G0305.1 V-PAI-3S ἀναβαίνει (1x)
Mk 3:13 Then *Jesus* walks·up upon the mountain, and he·
G0305.1 V-PAN ἀναβαίνειν (3x)
Ac 15:2 others from·among them, to·walk·up to JeruSalem
Ac 21:4 ·Paul through the Spirit not to·walk·up to JeruSalem.
Ac 21:12 were·imploring him not to·walk·up to JeruSalem.
G0305.1 V-PAP-GPM ἀναβαινόντων (1x)
Jn 12:20 the·ones walking·up in·order·that they·may·fall·
G0305.1 V-PAP-NSM ἀναβαίνων (4x)
Jn 10:1 sheep, but·rather walking·up from·some·other·way,
Lk 19:28 *Jesus* traversed·on ahead, walking·up to JeruSalem
Mt 20:17 And while·walking·up toward JeruSalem, YeShua
Mk 1:10 And immediately walking·up from the water, he·
G0305.1 V-PAP-NPM ἀναβαίνοντες (1x)
Mk 10:32 on the roadway, walking·up toward JeruSalem,
G0305.1 V-IAI-1P ἀνεβαίνομεν (1x)
Ac 21:15 ·belongings, we·were·walking·up to JeruSalem.
G0305.1 V-IAI-3P ἀνέβαινον (1x)
Ac 3:1 Now Peter and John were·walking·up in·unison into
G0305.1 V-2AAI-1S ἀνέβην (3x)
Ac 24:11 days for·me since I·walked·up to JeruSalem to·fall·
Gal 2:1 after fourteen years, I·walked·up again to JeruSalem
Gal 2:2 And I·walked·up according·to a·revelation, and set·
G0305.1 V-2AAI-3S ἀνέβη (14x)
Jn 2:13 near·at·hand, and Jesus walked·up to JeruSalem.
Jn 5:1 of·the Judeans, and Jesus walked·up to JeruSalem.
Jn 7:10 walked·up, then he·himself walked·up also to the
Jn 7:14 the Sacred·Feast *of·Booths*, Jesus walked·up into the
Jn 21:11 Simon Peter walked·up and drew the net upon the
Lk 2:4 And Joseph also walked·up from Galilee, out of·*the*·
Lk 9:28 John, and Jakob, he·walked·up upon the mountain
Ac 10:9 ·near to·the city, Peter walked·up upon the rooftop
Ac 11:2 Now when Peter walked·up to JeruSalem, the·ones
Ac 25:1 into·the province, Festus walked·up from Caesarea
Mt 3:16 ·immersed, YeShua walked·up straight·away from
Mt 5:1 seeing the crowds, he·walked·up upon the mountain.
Mt 14:23 ·dismissing the crowds, he·walked·up upon the
Mk 6:51 And he·walked·up toward them into the sailboat,
G0305.1 V-2AAI-3P ἀνέβησαν (7x)
Jn 7:10 But *just* as·soon·as his brothers walked·up, then he·
Jn 11:55 And many walked·up out of·the region to
Jn 21:3 *And* they·went·forth and walked·up into the
Lk 18:10 "Two men·of·clay† walked·up to the Sanctuary·
Ac 1:13 And when they·entered, they·walked·up into the
Ac 8:39 And when they·walked·up out of·the water,
Rv 20:9 And they·walked·up on the breadth of·the earth, and
G0305.1 V-2AAM-2S-AP ἀνάβα (1x)
Rv 4:1 with me, saying, "Walk·up here, and I·shall·show
G0305.1 V-2AAM-2P ἀνάβητε (2x)
Jn 7:8 Yeu·yeurselves walk·up to this Sacred·Feast.
Rv 11:12 ·the heaven saying to·them, "Walk·up here." And
G0305.1 V-2AAP-GPM ἀναβάντων (1x)
Lk 2:42 twelve years·of·age, after·walking·up with·them to
G0305.1 V-2AAP-NSM ἀναβάς (4x)
Ac 18:22 to Caesarea, *then* walking·up *to·JeruSalem* and
Ac 20:11 Then after·walking·up and breaking bread, and
Ac 25:9 Paul, he·declared, "Will·you walk·up to JeruSalem,
Mt 15:29 ·to the Sea of·Galilee. Then walking·up upon the
G0305.1 V-2AAP-NPM ἀναβάντες (1x)
Lk 5:19 on·account·of the crowd, walking·up on the rooftop
EG0305.1 (1x)
Ac 25:3 that he·may·send·for him *to·walk·up* to JeruSalem,
G0305.2 V-FDI-3S ἀναβήσεται (1x)
Rm 10:6 in your heart, "Who shall·ascend into heaven?
G0305.2 V-PAI-1S ἀναβαίνω (1x)
Jn 20:17 and declare to·them, 'I·ascend to my Father *who·is*
G0305.2 V-PAI-3S ἀναβαίνει (2x)
Rv 14:11 the smoke of·their torment ascends into ages of·
Rv 19:3 And her smoke ascends into the ages of·ages!"
G0305.2 V-PAI-3P ἀναβαίνουσιν (1x)
Lk 24:38 And why·do debates ascend in yeur hearts?
G0305.2 V-PAN ἀναβαίνειν (1x)
Rv 17:8 is not. And it·is·about to·ascend from·out of·the
G0305.2 V-PAP-ASN ἀναβαῖνον (2x)
Rv 13:1 and I·saw a·Daemonic·Beast ascending out of·the
Rv 13:11 I·saw another Fiendish·Beast ascending out of·the
G0305.2 V-PAP-ASM ἀναβαίνοντα (1x)
Jn 6:62 the Son of·Clay·Man† ascending to·where he·was
G0305.2 V-PAP-APM ἀναβαίνοντας (1x)
Jn 1:51 'the angels of·God ascending and descending' upon
G0305.2 V-PAP-NSN ἀναβαῖνον (1x)
Rv 11:7 Abysmal·Beast (the·one ascending from·out of·the
G0305.2 V-2AAI-3S ἀνέβη (7x)
Ac 2:34 "For David did·not ascend into the heavens, but he·
Ac 7:23 ·completely·fulfilled in·him, it·ascended upon his
Ac 21:31 him, news ascended to·the regiment·commander
1Co 2:9 did·not hear, and it·did·not ascend upon *the* heart
Eph 4:9 (Now, "He·ascended:" what is·it except that also
Rv 8:4 of·the holy·ones, ascended in·the·sight of·God from·
Rv 9:2 of·the bottomless·pit, and there·ascended smoke out
G0305.2 V-2AAI-3P ἀνέβησαν (2x)
Ac 10:4 and your merciful·acts ascended for a·memorial in·
Rv 11:12 "Walk·up here." And they·ascended to the heaven
G0305.2 V-2AAP-ASM ἀναβάντα (2x)
Mt 17:27 and take·up the first fish ascending *on·the line*, and
Rv 7:2 And I·saw another angel ascending from *the* eastern
G0305.2 V-2AAP-NSM ἀναβάς (2x)
Eph 4:8 Therefore he·says, "After·ascending on·high, by·
Eph 4:10 is himself also the·one ascending high·above all the
G0305.2 V-RAI-1S ἀναβέβηκα (1x)
Jn 20:17 of·me, for I·have·not·yet ascended to my Father.
G0305.2 V-RAI-3S ἀναβέβηκεν (1x)
Jn 3:13 "And not·even·one·man has·ascended into the
G0305.3 V-2AAI-3S ἀνέβη (1x)
Lk 19:4 ·on ahead, he·climbed·up upon a·mulberry-fig·tree
G0305.3 V-2AAP-ASM ἀναβάντα (1x)
Ac 8:31 Philippe that·he·would·climb·up to·sit·down
G0305.4 V-PAI-3S ἀναβαίνει (1x)
Mk 4:32 it·should·be·sown, it·springs·up and becomes
G0305.4 V-PAP-ASM ἀναβαίνοντα (1x)
Mk 4:8 was·giving fruit, springing·up and growing·more,
G0305.4 V-2AAI-3P ἀνέβησαν (2x)
Mt 13:7 and the thorns sprung·up and utterly·choked them.
Mk 4:7 and the thorns sprung·up and altogether·choked it,
G0306 ἀνα•βάλλομαι anabállômai *v.* (1x)
Roots:G0303 G0906
G0306.2 V-2AMI-3S ἀνεβάλετο (1x)
Ac 24:22 concerning The Way, he·deferred them, declaring,
G0307 ἀνα•βιβάζω anabibázō *v.* (1x)
Roots:G0303 G0973-1 See:G1688
G0307.2 V-AAP-NPM ἀναβιβάσαντες (1x)
Mt 13:48 when it·was·completely·filled, after·hauling *it* to
G0308 ἀνα•βλέπω anablépō *v.* (26x)
Roots:G0303 G0991 Compare:G2601-2 See:G0309
G0308.1 V-AAI-1S ἀνέβλεψα (1x)
Ac 22:13 And·I, in·the same hour, looked·up at him.
G0308.1 V-AAM-2S ἀνάβλεψον (1x)
Ac 22:13 'Brother Saul, look·up!' And·I, in·the same hour,
G0308.1 V-AAP-NSM ἀναβλέψας (7x)
Lk 9:16 ·bread and the two fish, looking·up to the heaven,
Lk 19:5 Jesus came to the place, looking·up, he·saw him,
Lk 21:1 And looking·up, he·saw the wealthy·men casting
Mt 14:19 ·bread and the two fish, looking·up to the heaven,
Mk 6:41 ·bread and the two fish, looking·up to the heaven,
Mk 7:34 and upon·looking·up to the heaven, he·sighed·
Mk 8:24 And looking·up, he·was·saying, "I·look·upon the
G0308.1 V-AAP-NPF ἀναβλέψασαι (1x)
Mk 16:4 And upon·looking·up, they·observed that the stone
G0308.3 V-PAI-3P ἀναβλέπουσιν (2x)
Lk 7:22 that 'the·blind receive·their·sight, lame·men walk,
Mt 11:5 blind·men receive·their·sight and lame·men walk,
G0308.3 V-AAI-1S ἀνέβλεψα (1x)
Jn 9:11 And after·going·off and washing, I·received·sight."
G0308.3 V-AAI-3S ἀνέβλεψεν (5x)
Jn 9:15 were·asking·of him how he·received·his·sight. So
Jn 9:18 that he·was blind and received·his·sight, until such·
Lk 18:43 at·once, he·received·his·sight and was·following
Ac 9:18 from his eyes. And he·received·sight at·once. And
Mk 10:52 And immediately he·received·his·sight and was·
G0308.3 V-AAI-3P ἀνέβλεψαν (1x)
Mt 20:34 and immediately their eyes received·sight, and
G0308.3 V-AAM-2S ἀνάβλεψον (1x)
Lk 18:42 declared to·him, "Receive·your·sight. Your trust
G0308.3 V-AAN ἀναβλέψαι (1x)
Mk 8:25 eyes and made him to·receive·sight, and he·was·
G0308.3 V-AAP-GSM ἀναβλέψαντος (1x)
Jn 9:18 ·out·for the parents of·the·one receiving·his·sight.
G0308.3 V-AAS-1S ἀναβλέψω (2x)
Lk 18:41 "Lord, that I·may·receive·my·sight."
Mk 10:51 "Rabboni, that I·may·receive·my·sight."
G0308.3 V-AAS-2S ἀναβλέψῃς (1x)
Ac 9:17 ·such·a·manner·so·that you·may·receive·your·sight
G0308.3 V-AAS-3S ἀναβλέψῃ (1x)
Ac 9:12 in·such·a·manner·so·that he·may·receive·his·sight."
G0309 ἀνά•βλεψις anáblêpsis *n.* (1x)
Roots:G0308
G0309.3 N-ASF ἀνάβλεψιν (1x)
Lk 4:18 ·captives and recovery·of·sight to·the·blind, to·set·
G0310 ἀνα•βοάω anabôáō *v.* (3x)
Roots:G0303 G0994 Compare:G0994 G2905
G0310 V-AAI-3S ἀνεβόησεν (2x)
Lk 9:38 behold, a·man of the crowd shouted·out, saying,
Mt 27:46 ninth hour YeShua shouted·out with·a·loud voice,
G0310 V-AAP-NSM ἀναβοήσας (1x)
Mk 15:8 And the crowd, upon·shouting·out, began to·

G0311 ἀνα•βολή anabolḗ *n.* (1x)
Roots:G0306
G0311.3 N-ASF ἀναβολὴν (1x)
Ac 25:17 not·even·one postponement on·the next·day), after·

G0312 ἀν•αγγέλλω anangéllō *v.* (18x)
Roots:G0303 G0032 Compare:G0518
G0312.1 V-FAI-1S ἀναγγελῶ (1x)
Jn 16:25 but·rather I·shall·announce·in·detail to·yeu with·
G0312.1 V-FAI-3S ἀναγγελεῖ (4x)
Jn 4:25 ·come, he·shall·announce·in·detail to·us all·things."
Jn 16:13 and he·shall·announce·in·detail to·yeu the·things
Jn 16:14 ·shall·receive and shall·announce·in·detail to·yeu.
Jn 16:15 shall·receive and shall·announce·in·detail to·yeu.
G0312.1 V-PAI-1P ἀναγγέλλομεν (1x)
1Jn 1:5 ·have·heard from him and announce·in·detail to·yeu,
G0312.1 V-AAN ἀναγγεῖλαι (1x)
Ac 20:20 ·*yeu*, but·instead have·announced·in·detail to·yeu,
G0312.2 V-PAP-NSM ἀναγγέλλων (1x)
2Co 7:7 in yeu, when·he·reported·in·detail to·us yeur great·
G0312.2 V-PAP-NPM ἀναγγέλλοντες (1x)
Ac 19:18 explicitly·confessing and reporting their practices
G0312.2 V-AAI-3S ἀνήγγειλεν (1x)
Jn 5:15 ·clay† went·off and reported·in·detail to·the Judeans
G0312.2 V-AAI-3P ἀνήγγειλαν (3x)
Ac 14:27 they·reported·in·detail what·many·things *that*
Ac 15:4 and they·reported·in·detail what·many·things *that*
Ac 16:38 the enforcement·officers reported·in·detail these
G0312.2 V-AAM-2S ἀνάγγειλον (1x)
Mk 5:19 and report·in·detail to·them what·many·things
G0312.2 V-AAN ἀναγγεῖλαι (1x)
Ac 20:27 I·shrink·back *as* not to·report·in·detail to·yeu all
G0312.2 V-2API-3S ἀνηγγέλη (2x)
Rm 15:21 ·whom it·is·not reported·in·detail concerning him,
1Pe 1:12 which are now reported·in·detail to·yeu through
G0312.3 V-AAI-3P ἀνήγγειλαν (1x)
Mk 5:14 the pigs fled and gave·a·detailed·report in the city

G0313 ἀνα•γεννάω anagênnáō *v.* (2x)
Roots:G0303 G1080
G0313.1 V-AAP-NSM ἀναγεννήσας (1x)
1Pe 1:3 according·to his large mercy begetting us again—
G0313.2 V-RPP-NPM ἀναγεγεννημένοι (1x)
1Pe 1:23 having·been·born·again, not [birthed]·from·out of·a·

G0314 ἀνα•γινώσκω anaginṓskō *v.* (33x)
Roots:G0303 G1097 xLangAlso:H7121 A7123
G0314.2 V-PAI-2S ἀναγινώσκεις (1x)
Ac 8:30 ·so, *that* you·know what·things you·read·aloud?"
G0314.2 V-PAI-2P ἀναγινώσκετε (1x)
2Co 1:13 other than what yeu·currently·read·aloud or also
G0314.2 V-PAP-GSM ἀναγινώσκοντος (1x)
Ac 8:30 *him*, Philippe heard him reading·aloud Isaiah the
G0314.2 V-PAP-NSM ἀναγινώσκων (1x)
Rv 1:3 ·blessed *are both* the·one reading·aloud and the·ones
G0314.2 V-PAP-NPM ἀναγινώσκοντες (1x)
Eph 3:4 ·to which, upon·reading·*it*·aloud, yeu·are·able to·
G0314.2 V-PPI-3S ἀναγινώσκεται (1x)
2Co 3:15 ·day, whenever Moses is·read·aloud, a·veil is·laid·
G0314.2 V-PPP-APF ἀναγινωσκομένας (1x)
Ac 13:27 (the·ones being·read·aloud each and·every Sabbath
G0314.2 V-PPP-NSF ἀναγινωσκομένη (1x)
2Co 3:2 hearts, being·known and being·read·aloud by all
G0314.2 V-PPP-NSM ἀναγινωσκόμενος (1x)
Ac 15:21 ·proclaiming him, being·read·aloud in the
G0314.2 V-IAI-3S ἀνεγίνωσκεν (2x)
Ac 8:28 in his chariot, and he·was·reading·aloud Isaiah the
Ac 8:32 ·the Scripture which he·was·reading·aloud was this,
G0314.2 V-2AAI-2P ἀνέγνωτε (10x)
Lk 6:3 "Did·yeu·not·even read·aloud this·thing that David
Mt 12:3 to·them, "Did·yeu·not read·aloud what David did,
Mt 12:5 Or did·yeu·not read·aloud in the Torah-Law, that
Mt 19:4 to·them, "Did·yeu·not read·aloud that the·one
Mt 21:16 "Yes! Have·yeu·not·even·at·any·time read·aloud,
Mt 21:42 "Did·yeu·not·even·at·any·time read·aloud in the
Mt 22:31 did·yeu·not read·aloud of·the·thing being·uttered
Mk 2:25 "Did·yeu·not·even·at·any·time read·aloud what
Mk 12:10 "Did·yeu·not·even read·aloud this Scripture?
Mk 12:26 they·are·awakened, did·yeu·not read·aloud in the
G0314.2 V-2AAI-3P ἀνέγνωσαν (1x)
Jn 19:20 many of·the Judeans read·aloud this title because
G0314.2 V-2AAN ἀναγνῶναι (2x)
Lk 4:16 the day of·Sabbath, and he·stood·up to·read·aloud.
Rv 5:4 to·open·up and to·read·aloud the official·scroll,
G0314.2 V-2AAP-NSM ἀναγνούς (1x)
Ac 23:34 And after·reading·aloud *the letter*, the governor
G0314.2 V-2AAP-NPM ἀναγνόντες (1x)
Ac 15:31 And reading·*it*·aloud, they·rejoiced over the
G0314.2 V-2AAS-2P ἀναγνῶτε (1x)
Col 4:16 and that yeu also should·read·aloud the *letter* from·
G0314.2 V-APN ἀναγνωσθῆναι (1x)
1Th 5:27 ·the Lord for·the letter to·be·read·aloud to·all the
G0314.2 V-APS-3S ἀναγνωσθῇ (2x)
Col 4:16 the letter should·be·read·aloud directly·to yeu,
Col 4:16 yeu, cause that it·should·be·read·aloud also in the
G0314.3 V-PAI-2S ἀναγινώσκεις (1x)
Lk 10:26 ·written in the Torah-Law? How·do you·read *it*?
G0314.3 V-PAP-NSM ἀναγινώσκων (2x)
Mt 24:15 place," (the·one reading, he·must·understand),
Mk 13:14 mandatory" (the·one reading must·understand),

G0315 ἀν•αγκάζω anankázō *v.* (9x)
Roots:G0318 Compare:G0029 G3784 See:G0316 G0317
G0315.2 V-PAI-2S ἀναγκάζεις (1x)
Gal 2:14 not as·a·Jew, why do·you·compel the Gentiles to·
G0315.2 V-PAI-3P ἀναγκάζουσιν (1x)
Gal 6:12 the·flesh, these·men compel yeu to·be·circumcised
G0315.2 V-IAI-1S ἠνάγκαζον (1x)
Ac 26:11 all the gatherings, I·was·compelling *them* to·revile
G0315.2 V-AAI-2P ἠναγκάσατε (1x)
2Co 12:11 impetuous in·boasting! Yeu compelled me, for I·
G0315.2 V-AAI-3S ἠνάγκασεν (2x)
Mt 14:22 And immediately, YeShua compelled his disciples
Mk 6:45 And immediately he·compelled his disciples to·
G0315.2 V-AAM-2S ἀνάγκασον (1x)
Lk 14:23 and hedges, and compel *them* to·come·in, that my
G0315.2 V-API-1S ἠναγκάσθην (1x)
Ac 28:19 *this*, I·was·compelled to·appeal·to Caesar, though
G0315.2 V-API-3S ἠναγκάσθη (1x)
Gal 2:3 being a·Greek) was·compelled to·be·circumcised.

G0316 ἀν•αγκαῖος anankaîos *adj.* (8x)
Roots:G0318 Compare:G1163
G0316.1 A-NSN ἀναγκαῖον (2x)
Ac 13:46 "It·was necessary for·the [Redemptive]-word of·God
Heb 8:3 by·which *pattern*, *it·is* necessary *for* this·man to·
G0316.1 A-NSN-C ἀναγκαιότερον (1x)
Php 1:24 ·on in the flesh *is* necessary on·account·of yeu.
G0316.1 A-NPN ἀναγκαῖα (1x)
1Co 12:22 to·inherently·be more·feeble, are necessary.
G0316.1 A-ASN ἀναγκαῖον (2x)
Php 2:25 Now I·resolutely·considered *it* necessary to·send to
2Co 9:5 I·resolutely·considered *it* necessary to·exhort the
G0316.1 A-APF ἀναγκαίας (1x)
Tit 3:14 good works for the necessary needful·occasions, in·
G0316.2 A-APM ἀναγκαίους (1x)
Ac 10:24 ·together his kinsmen and very·close friends.

G0317 ἀν•αγκαστῶς anankastō̂s *adv.* (1x)
Roots:G0315
G0317 ADV ἀναγκαστῶς (1x)
1Pe 5:2 ·overseeing *it*— not compulsorily, but·rather

G0318 ἀν•άγκη anánkē *n.* (19x)
Roots:G0303 G0043 Compare:G3601 See:G0315 G0316 G0317
G0318.1 N-NSF ἀνάγκη (5x)
Heb 9:16 a·last·will·and·covenant, *it·is* a·necessity *for* death
Heb 9:23 Accordingly, *it·was* a·necessity *for* the·things (in·
Mt 18:7 ·traps, for it·is a·necessity *for* scandalous·traps to·
Rm 13:5 Therefore *it·is* a·necessity to·submit·oneself, not
1Co 9:16 not a·boast·to·me, for necessity is·laid·upon me;
G0318.1 N-ASF ἀνάγκην (5x)
Lk 23:17 Now by·necessity, he·was·having to·fully·release
Heb 7:27 who does·not have a·necessity each day, just·as the
Jud 1:3 common Salvation, I·had necessity to·write to·yeu,
1Co 7:26 on·account·of the currently·standing necessity, that
1Co 7:37 in the heart, not having *financial* necessity, but has
G0318.1 N-DPF ἀνάγκαις (1x)
2Co 6:4 in tribulations, in necessities, in calamities,
G0318.1 N-GSF ἀνάγκης (1x)
Heb 7:12 there·occurs out of·necessity also a·transfer of·
EG0318.1 (1x)
Heb 9:18 by·which *necessity*, not·even the first *covenant*
G0318.2 N-NSF ἀνάγκη (1x)
Lk 21:23 For there·shall·be great dire·need upon the land
G0318.2 N-ASF ἀνάγκην (1x)
Lk 14:18 a·plot·of·land, and I·have dire·need to·go·out and
G0318.2 N-DSF ἀνάγκῃ (1x)
1Th 3:7 all our tribulation and dire·need, we·are·comforted
G0318.2 N-DPF ἀνάγκαις (1x)
2Co 12:10 in mistreatments, in dire·needs, in persecutions,
G0318.3 N-ASF ἀνάγκην (1x)
Phm 1:14 ·not be as·according·to a·compulsion, but·rather *be*
G0318.3 N-GSF ἀνάγκης (1x)
2Co 9:7 not out of·grief nor out of·compulsion, for 'God

G0319 ἀνα•γνωρίζομαι anagnōrízômai *v.* (1x)
Roots:G0303 G1107
G0319 V-API-3S ἀνεγνωρίσθη (1x)
Ac 7:13 ·time, Joseph was·made·known to·his brothers, and

G0320 ἀνά•γνωσις anágnōsis *n.* (3x)
Roots:G0314
G0320 N-ASF ἀνάγνωσιν (1x)
Ac 13:15 But after the reading·aloud of·the Torah-Law and
G0320 N-DSF ἀναγνώσει (2x)
2Co 3:14 being·unveiled upon the reading·aloud of·the old
1Ti 4:13 give·attention to·the reading·aloud *of·Scripture*,

G0321 ἀν•άγω anágō *v.* (24x)
Roots:G0303 G0071 See:G2609
G0321.1 V-2AAI-3P-ATT ἀνήγαγον (2x)
Lk 22:66 and scribes), and they·led him into·their·own
Ac 9:39 ·coming·directly *to·Joppa*, they·led·*him*·up into the
G0321.1 V-API-3S ἀνήχθη (1x)
Mt 4:1 Then YeShua was·led·up into the wilderness by the
G0321.2 V-2AAI-3P-ATT ἀνήγαγον (2x)
Lk 2:22 of·Moses were·fulfilled, they·brought him up to
Ac 7:41 in those days and brought·forth sacrifice to·the idol,
G0321.2 V-2AAN ἀναγαγεῖν (2x)
Ac 12:4 ·watch·over him, being·resolved to·bring him out
Rm 10:7 "=" (that is, to·bring Anointed-One up from·among
G0321.2 V-2AAP-NSM ἀναγαγών (3x)
Lk 4:5 Then the Slanderer, after·bringing him up upon a·
Ac 16:34 Also bringing them up into his house, he·placed·
Heb 13:20 the·one bringing·up from·among dead·men our
G0321.3 V-PPN ἀνάγεσθαι (2x)
Ac 20:3 ·him by the Jews as·he·was·about to·sail into Syria,
Ac 27:21 *such·for·us* not to·be·sailing·away from Crete nor·
G0321.3 V-PPP-DPM ἀναγομένοις (1x)
Ac 28:10 honors. And with·us·making·sail, they·supplied *us*
G0321.3 V-API-1P ἀνήχθημεν (2x)
Ac 20:13 going·onward to the sailing·ship, sailed to Assos,
Ac 28:11 lunar·months, we·sailed·away in a·sailing·ship of·
G0321.3 V-API-3S ἀνήχθη (1x)
Ac 18:21 yeu, God willing." And he·sailed from Ephesus.
G0321.3 V-APN ἀναχθῆναι (2x)
Ac 21:1 *for* us to·be·sailing·away, after·being·drawn·away
Ac 27:12 placed counsel to·sail·away from·there·also, if·
G0321.3 V-APP-NPM ἀναχθέντες (3x)
Ac 13:13 And sailing·away from Paphos, Paul (*and* the·ones
Ac 16:11 Accordingly, sailing from Troas, we·sailed·
Ac 27:4 Sailing·on from·there, we·sailed·leeward·near·to
G0321.4 V-API-1P ἀνήχθημεν (2x)
Ac 21:2 to Phoenicia, once·embarking, we·launched·forth.

Ac 27:2 ·ship of·Adramyttium, we·launched, intending to·
G0321.4 V-API-3P ἀνήχθησαν (1x)
Lk 8:22 other·side of·the lake." And they·launched·forth.

G0322 ἀνα•δείκνυμι anadeîknymi *v.* (2x)
Roots:G0303 G1166 Compare:G1731 See:G0323
G0322.2 V-AAI-3S ἀνέδειξεν (1x)
Lk 10:1 ·things, the Lord expressly·indicated seventy others
G0322.2 V-AAM-2S ἀνάδειξον (1x)
Ac 1:24 ·the·hearts of·all·men, expressly·indicate which one

G0323 ἀνά•δειξις anádeîxis *n.* (1x)
Roots:G0322 Compare:G1732 G0585
G0323.2 N-GSF ἀναδείξεως (1x)
Lk 1:80 until *the* day of·his official·showing to IsraEl.

G0324 ἀνα•δέχομαι anadéchômai *v.* (2x)
Roots:G0303 G1209 Compare:G3579 G4327
G0324.1 V-ADP-NSM ἀναδεξάμενος (1x)
Heb 11:17 and the·one expressly·receiving the promises
G0324.2 V-ADP-NSM ἀναδεξάμενος (1x)
Ac 28:7 ·name·of Poplius who was·warmly·welcoming us.

G0325 ἀνα•δίδωμι anadídōmi *v.* (1x)
Roots:G0303 G1325 Compare:G1929 G0591 G3860
G0325.2 V-2AAP-NPM ἀναδόντες (1x)
Ac 23:33 into Caesarea and hand-delivering the letter to·the

G0326 ἀνα•ζάω anazáō *v.* (5x)
Roots:G0303 G2198
G0326.2 V-AAI-3S ἀνέζησεν (4x)
Lk 15:24 of·mine was dead and came·alive·again; he·was
Lk 15:32 brother was dead and came·alive·again; and he·was
Rm 7:9 coming, Moral·Failure came·alive·again, and I·
Rm 14:9 And he·came·alive·again in·order·that he·may·
G0326.2 V-AAI-3P ἀνέζησαν (1x)
Rv 20:5 rest of·the dead did·not come·alive·again until the

G0327 ἀνα•ζητέω anazētéō *v.* (2x)
Roots:G0303 G2212 See:G1934
G0327 V-IAI-3P ἀνεζήτουν (1x)
Lk 2:44 then they·were·diligently·seeking him among the
G0327 V-AAN ἀναζητῆσαι (1x)
Ac 11:25 went·forth to Tarsus, to·diligently·seek·out Saul.

G0328 ἀνα•ζώννυμι anazṓnnymi *v.* (1x)
Roots:G0303 G2224
G0328.1 V-AMP-NPM ἀναζωσάμενοι (1x)
1Pe 1:13 Therefore girding·up the loins of·yeur innermost·

G0329 ἀνα•ζω•πυρέω anazōpyréō *v.* (1x)
Roots:G0303 G2226 G4442 Compare:G1714
G0329 V-PAN ἀναζωπυρεῖν (1x)
2Ti 1:6 ·admonish you to·rekindle the gracious·bestowment

G0330 ἀνα•θάλλω anathállō *v.* (1x)
Roots:G0303
G0330 V-2AAI-2P ἀνεθάλετε (1x)
Php 4:10 ·earnest·concern over me has·flourished·again, in

G0331 ἀνά•θεμα anáthēma *n.* (7x)
Roots:G0394 Compare:G1944 G2671 G0334
See:G0332 G3134 xLangAlso:H2767
G0331.1 N-DSN ἀναθέματι (1x)
Ac 23:14 "With·an·irrevocable·vow·of·destruction, we·
G0331.2 N-NSN ἀνάθεμα (4x)
Gal 1:8 ·yeu, let·him·be irrevocably·damned·to·destruction.
Gal 1:9 let·him·be irrevocably·damned·to·destruction.
Rm 9:3 to·be irrevocably·damned·to·destruction, *cut·off*
1Co 12:3 "Jesus *is* irrevocably·damned·to·destruction."
G0331.3 N-NSN ἀνάθεμα (1x)
1Co 16:22 let·him·be Anathema MaranAtha *(devoted·to·*
EG0331.3 (1x)
1Co 16:22 MaranAtha *(devoted·to·destruction at·the·Lord's·*.

G0332 ἀνα•θεματίζω anathêmatízō *v.* (4x)
Roots:G0331
G0332.1 V-PAN ἀναθεματίζειν (1x)
Mk 14:71 to·vow·and·bind·*himself*·over·to·destruction and
G0332.1 V-AAI-1P ἀνεθεματίσαμεν (1x)
Ac 23:14 we·vowed·and·bound ourselves over·to·
G0332.1 V-AAI-3P ἀνεθεμάτισαν (2x)
Ac 23:12 vowed·and·bound themselves over·to·destruction,
Ac 23:21 men, who vowed·and·bound themselves over·to·

G0333 ἀνα•θεωρέω anathēōréō *v.* (2x)
Roots:G0303 G2334
G0333 V-PAP-NSM ἀναθεωρῶν (1x)
Ac 17:23 and observing·again yeur objects·of·reverence, I·
G0333 V-PAP-NPM ἀναθεωροῦντες (1x)
Heb 13:7 ·attentively·imitate, observing·again the outcome

G0334 ἀνά•θημα anáthēma *n.* (1x)
Roots:G0394 Compare:G0331
G0334 N-DPN ἀναθήμασιν (1x)
Lk 21:5 with·beautiful stones and vow·offerings, he·declared

G0335 ἀν•α•ίδεια anaídêia *n.* (1x)
Roots:G0001 G0127 Compare:G0427
G0335.2 N-ASF ἀναίδειαν (1x)
Lk 11:8 yet on·account·of his audacity, he·being·awakened

G0336 ἀν•αίρεσις anaírêsis *n.* (5x)
Roots:G0337
G0336 N-DSF ἀναιρέσει (2x)
Ac 8:1 Saul was gladly·consenting to·his execution. And on
Ac 22:20 ·over, also gladly·consenting to·his execution, and
EG0336 (3x)
Ac 12:19 ·ordered *for·them* to·be·led·away *to·execution*.
Mt 27:37 they·placed the cause of·his *execution, which·was*
Mk 15:26 ·the cause of·his *execution* having·been·inscribed,

G0337 ἀν•αιρέω anairéō *v.* (23x)
Roots:G0303 G0138 Compare:G0615 See:G0336
G0337.1 V-2AMI-3S ἀνείλετο (1x)
Ac 7:21 ·put·out, the Pharaoh's daughter took him up and
G0337.3 V-PAI-3S ἀναιρεῖ (1x)
Heb 10:9 O·God."˒ He·eliminates the first in·order·that he·
G0337.3 V-PAN ἀναιρεῖν (1x)
Ac 16:27 his·dagger, he·was·about to·eliminate himself,
G0337.3 V-PPN ἀναιρεῖσθαι (1x)
Ac 23:27 and·also *was* about to·be·eliminated by them, *but*
G0337.3 V-2AAI-3S ἀνεῖλεν (1x)
Mt 2:16 And dispatching *soldiers*, he·eliminated all the boys
G0337.3 V-2AAN ἀνελεῖν (5x)
Ac 5:33 ·irate and were·taking·counsel to·eliminate them.
Ac 9:23 took·counsel·among·themselves to·eliminate him.
Ac 9:29 but they·took·it·upon·themselves to·eliminate him.
Ac 23:15 he shall·draw·near, are ready to·eliminate him."
Ac 25:3 ·they·make an·ambush in the way to·eliminate him.
G0337.3 V-AAS-3P ἀνέλωσιν (3x)
Lk 22:2 scribes were·seeking how they·may·eliminate him,
Ac 9:24 both day and night so·that they·may·eliminate him.
Ac 23:21 nor to·drink until they·should·eliminate him. And
G0337.3 V-API-3S ἀνῃρέθη (1x)
Ac 5:36 ·hundred), who *himself* was·eliminated. And all
G0337.4 V-PAP-GPM ἀναιρούντων (1x)
Ac 22:20 ·over the garments of·the·ones executing him.'
G0337.4 V-PPP-GPM ἀναιρουμένων (1x)
Ac 26:10 ·priests. And with·them being·executed, I·voted a·
G0337.4 V-2AAI-2S ἀνεῖλες (1x)
Ac 7:28 me, as you·executed the Egyptian yesterday?
G0337.4 V-2AAI-2P ἀνείλετε (1x)
Ac 2:23 ·directly·pegging *him to·a·cross*, yeu·executed *him*,
G0337.4 V-2AAI-3S ἀνεῖλεν (1x)
Ac 12:2 And he·executed Jakob, the brother of·John, with·a·
G0337.4 V-2AAI-3P ἀνεῖλον (1x)
Ac 10:39 in JeruSalem— whom they·executed *by* hanging
G0337.4 V-2AAN ἀνελεῖν (1x)
Ac 7:28 ¿!·Do you·yourself want to·execute me, as you·
G0337.4 V-APN ἀναιρεθῆναι (2x)
Lk 23:32 were·led together with·him to·be·executed.
Ac 13:28 they·requested·of Pilate for·him to·be·executed.

G0338 ἀν•αίτιος anaítiôs *adj.* (2x)
Roots:G0001 G0159 See:G0156
G0338 A-NPM ἀναίτιοι (1x)
Mt 12:5 profane the Sabbath, and are without·guilt?
G0338 A-APM ἀναιτίους (1x)
Mt 12:7 not have·pronounced·guilty the·ones without·guilt.

G0339 ἀνα•καθ•ίζω anakathízō *v.* (2x)
Roots:G0303 G2523
G0339.2 V-AAI-3S ἀνεκάθισεν (2x)
Lk 7:15 And the dead·man sat·up and began to·speak.
Ac 9:40 ·up her eyes; and upon·seeing Peter, she·sat·up.

G0340 ἀνα•καινίζω anakainízō *v.* (1x)
Roots:G0303 G2537 Compare:G0341 G0365
G0340 V-PAN ἀνακαινίζειν (1x)
Heb 6:6 *it·is impossible* to·reinstate·and·renew·them again to

G0341 ἀνα•καινόω anakainóō *v.* (2x)
Roots:G0303 G2537 Compare:G0340 G0365
See:G0342 G1877-1
G0341 V-PPI-3S ἀνακαινοῦται (1x)
2Co 4:16 the inward *man·of·clay*† is·being·renewed day by
G0341 V-PPP-ASM ἀνακαινούμενον (1x)
Col 3:10 the·one being·renewed into a·full·knowledge ˓

G0342 ἀνα•καίνωσις anakaínōsis *n.* (2x)
Roots:G0341 Compare:G0605 G1357 G2676 G3824
See:G1456
G0342 N-DSF ἀνακαινώσει (1x)
Rm 12:2 be·metamorphosed by·the renewing of·yeur mind,
G0342 N-GSF ἀνακαινώσεως (1x)
Tit 3:5 a·bath of·regeneration and a·renewing of·Holy Spirit,

G0343 ἀνα•καλύπτω anakalýptō *v.* (2x)
Roots:G0303 G2572 Compare:G0177
G0343 V-PPP-NSN ἀνακαλυπτόμενον (1x)
2Co 3:14 veil remains, not being·unveiled upon the reading·
G0343 V-RPP-DSN ἀνακεκαλυμμένῳ (1x)
2Co 3:18 — with·a·face having·been·unveiled (ourselves·

G0344 ἀνα•κάμπτω anakámptō *v.* (4x)
Roots:G0303 G2578 Compare:G5290 G0390 G1994
G0344.2 V-FAI-1S ἀνακάμψω (1x)
Ac 18:21 in JeruSalem, but I·shall·return·back again to yeu,
G0344.2 V-FAI-3S ἀνακάμψει (1x)
Lk 10:6 ·rest upon it. But·if·not, it·shall·return·back to yeu.
G0344.2 V-AAN ἀνακάμψαι (2x)
Heb 11:15 they·would have·had opportunity to·return·back.
Mt 2:12 ·in·a·dream not to·return·back to HerOd·the·Great,

G0345 ἀνα•κεῖμαι anakêîmai *v.* (14x)
Roots:G0303 G2749 Compare:G0347 G0377
G0345.1 V-PNI-3S ἀνάκειται (1x)
Lk 7:37 ·realizing that he·was·reclining·at·a·meal in the
G0345.1 V-PNP-APM ἀνακειμένους (1x)
Mt 22:11 ·view the·ones reclining·at·the·meal, he·saw a·
G0345.1 V-PNP-DPM ἀνακειμένοις (2x)
Jn 6:11 the disciples to·the·ones reclining·for·the·meal, and
Mk 16:14 to·the eleven, with·them reclining·at·a·meal, and
G0345.1 V-PNP-GSM ἀνακειμένου (2x)
Mt 9:10 while·he is·reclining·at·a·meal in *MattHew's* home,
Mt 26:7 ·down on his head as·he·was·reclining·at·the·meal.
G0345.1 V-PNP-GPM ἀνακειμένων (3x)
Jn 13:28 not·even·one·man who·was·reclining·at·the·meal
Mt 22:10 was·filled with·those·reclining·at·the·meal.
Mk 14:18 And as·they were·reclining·at·the·meal and eating,
G0345.1 V-PNP-NSM ἀνακείμενος (3x)
Jn 13:23 Now reclining·at·the·meal at Jesus' bosom was one
Lk 22:27 *is* greater, the·one reclining·at·the·meal, or the·one
Lk 22:27 *Is·it* not·indeed the·one reclining·at·the·meal? But
G0345.1 V-INI-3S ἀνέκειτο (1x)
Mt 26:20 occurring, he·was·reclined·at·the·meal with the
G0345.2 V-PNP-NSN ἀνακείμενον (1x)
Mk 5:40 ·in where the little·child was reclining·as·a·corpse.

G0346 ἀνα•κεφαλαίομαι anakêphalaiômai *v.* (2x)
Roots:G0303 G2775
G0346.2 V-PPI-3S ἀνακεφαλαιοῦται (1x)
Rm 13:9 any other commandment, it·is·summed·up in this
G0346.3 V-ADN ἀνακεφαλαιώσασθαι (1x)
Eph 1:10 seasons): to·reconsolidate·under·one·head all

G0347 ἀνα•κλίνω anaklínō *v.* (9x)
Roots:G0303 G2827 Compare:G0345 G0377
G0347.2 V-AAI-3S ἀνέκλινεν (1x)
Lk 2:7 son, and swaddled him, and leaned him back in the

G0347.3 V-FAI-3S ἀνακλινεῖ (1x)
Lk 12:37 and shall·make them recline·at·the·table, and
G0347.3 V-AAN ἀνακλῖναι (1x)
Mk 6:39 he·ordered them to·make everyone recline, party *by*
EG0347.3 (1x)
Lk 17:34 in·that night there·shall·be two *reclining* on one
G0347.4 V-FPI-3P ἀνακλιθήσονται (1x)
Mt 8:11 and they·shall·recline·at·the·table with AbRaham,
G0347.4 V-AAI-3P ἀνέκλιναν (1x)
Lk 9:15 ·did *so* in·this·manner, and absolutely·all reclined.
G0347.4 V-APN ἀνακλιθῆναι (1x)
Mt 14:19 ·ordering the crowds to·recline on the grass, and
G0347.5 V-FPI-3P ἀνακλιθήσονται (1x)
Lk 13:29 and south, and shall·recline·at·the·table in the
G0347.5 V-API-3S ἀνεκλίθη (1x)
Lk 7:36 into the Pharisee's home, *Jesus* reclined·at·the·table.

G0348 ἀνα•κόπτω anakóptō *v.* (1x)
Roots:G0303 G2875 Compare:G1465
G0348.3 V-AAI-3S ἀνέκοψεν (1x)
Gal 5:7 ·running well. Who cut·into·yeur·path *such·for* yeu

G0349 ἀνα•κράζω anakrázō *v.* (5x)
Roots:G0303 G2896 xLangAlso:H2199
G0349.1 V-AAI-3S ἀνέκραξεν (2x)
Lk 4:33 demon, and he·screamed·out with·a·loud voice,
Mk 1:23 ·clay† with an·impure spirit, and he·screamed·out,
G0349.1 V-AAI-3P ἀνέκραξαν (2x)
Lk 23:18 And altogether·at·once, they·screamed·out, saying
Mk 6:49 *it* to·be a·phantom, and they·screamed·out.
G0349.1 V-AAP-NSM ἀνακράξας (1x)
Lk 8:28 Jesus, and·then screaming·out, he·fell·down·before

G0350 ἀνα•κρίνω anakrínō *v.* (16x)
Roots:G0303 G2919 Compare:G0426 G1231 G1252 G1381 G4802 See:G1233
G0350.1 V-PAI-1S ἀνακρίνω (1x)
1Co 4:3 Moreover, I·scrutinize not·even my·own·self.
G0350.1 V-PAI-3S ἀνακρίνει (1x)
1Co 2:15 And the spiritual·one scrutinizes, in·fact, all·things,
G0350.1 V-PAP-DPM ἀνακρίνουσιν (1x)
1Co 9:3 My defense to·the·ones scrutinizing me is this:
G0350.1 V-PAP-NSM ἀνακρίνων (1x)
1Co 4:4 ·as·righteous. But the·one scrutinizing me is *the*
G0350.1 V-PAP-NPM ἀνακρίνοντες (3x)
Ac 17:11 with all eagerness, scrutinizing the Scriptures each
1Co 10:25 *it*, scrutinizing not·even·one·thing on·account·of
1Co 10:27 scrutinizing not·even·one·thing on·account·of
G0350.1 V-PPI-1P ἀνακρινόμεθα (1x)
Ac 4:9 if we·ourselves this·day are·scrutinized over *the*
G0350.1 V-PPI-3S ἀνακρίνεται (2x)
1Co 2:15 but he·himself is·scrutinized by not·even·one·man.
1Co 14:24 he·is·convicted by all, he·is·scrutinized by all.
G0350.1 V-AAP-NSM ἀνακρίνας (2x)
Ac 12:19 not finding *him*, *and* after·scrutinizing the sentries,
Ac 24:8 whom you·shall·be·able, after·scrutinizing him, to·
G0350.1 V-APS-1S ἀνακριθῶ (1x)
1Co 4:3 ·small·thing that I·should·be·scrutinized by yeu, or
G0350.2 V-PPI-3S ἀνακρίνεται (1x)
1Co 2:14 to·know *it*, because it·is·investigated spiritually.
G0350.2 V-AAP-NSM ἀνακρίνας (1x)
Lk 23:14 I·myself, after·investigating *him* in·the·sight·of·
G0350.2 V-AAP-NPM ἀνακρίναντες (1x)
Ac 28:18 who, after·investigating me, were·resolving to·

G0351 ἀνά•κρισις anákrisis *n.* (1x)
Roots:G0350
G0351 N-GSF ἀνακρίσεως (1x)
Ac 25:26 that, after·the investigation occurring, I·may·

G0352 ἀνα•κύπτω anakýptō *v.* (4x)
Roots:G0303 G2955 Compare:G1453
G0352.2 V-AAM-2P ἀνακύψατε (1x)
Lk 21:28 to·happen, pull·yourself·up·straight and lift·up
G0352.2 V-AAN ἀνακύψαι (1x)
Lk 13:11 and not being·able to·pull·herself·up·straight to the
G0352.2 V-AAP-NSM ἀνακύψας (2x)
Jn 8:7 ·of him, after·pulling·himself·up·straight, he·declared
Jn 8:10 after·pulling·himself·up·straight and distinctly·

G0353 ἀνα•λαμβάνω analambánō *v.* (13x)
Roots:G0303 G2983 See:G0354
G0353.1 V-2AAI-2P ἀνελάβετε (1x)
Ac 7:43 Also, yeu·took·up the tabernacle of·Molek, and the
G0353.1 V-2AAM-2P ἀναλάβετε (1x)
Eph 6:13 On·account·of that, take·up the whole·armor of·
G0353.1 V-2AAP-NSM ἀναλαβών (1x)
2Ti 4:11 is with me. Taking·up *John*·Mark, bring·him with
G0353.1 V-2AAP-NPM ἀναλαβόντες (2x)
Ac 23:31 ·thoroughly·assigned to·them, taking·up Paul,
Eph 6:16 all·*these*·things, after·taking·up the tall·shield of·
G0353.1 V-API-3S ἀνελήφθη (5x)
Ac 1:2 day when he·was·taken·up, after·giving·commands
Ac 1:22 unto the day that he·was·taken·up from us, *it·is*·
Ac 10:16 ·times, and the vessel was·taken·up again into the
Mk 16:19 the Lord spoke to·them, he·was·taken·up into the
1Ti 3:16 is·trusted *upon* in *the* world, is·taken·up into glory.
G0353.1 V-APP-NSM ἀναληφθείς (1x)
Ac 1:11 ·same Jesus, the·one being·taken·up from yeu into
G0353.3 V-PAN ἀναλαμβάνειν (1x)
Ac 20:13 *while* from·there intending to·take Paul aboard,
G0353.3 V-2AAP-NPM ἀναλαβόντες (1x)
Ac 20:14 ·on with·us at Assos, after·taking him aboard, we·

G0354 ἀνά•ληψις análēpsis *n.* (1x)
Roots:G0353
G0354 N-GSF ἀναλήψεως (1x)
Lk 9:51 ·be·completely·fulfilled for·his being·taken·up, that

G0355 ἀνα•λίσκω analískō *v.* (3x)
Roots:G0303 G0234-1 Compare:G1159 G2618 See:G2654 G4321 G0259
G0355.2 V-FAI-3S ἀναλώσει (1x)
2Th 2:8 whom the Lord shall·consume with·the breath of·
G0355.2 V-AAN ἀναλῶσαι (1x)
Lk 9:54 to·descend from the heaven and to·consume them,
G0355.2 V-APS-2P ἀναλωθῆτε (1x)
Gal 5:15 ·out *that* yeu·may·not be·consumed by one·another.

G0356 ἀνα•λογία analôgía *n.* (1x)
Roots:G0303 G3056
G0356 N-ASF ἀναλογίαν (1x)
Rm 12:6 *then* according·to the proportion of·the trust;

G0357 ἀνα•λογίζομαι analôgízômai *v.* (1x)
Roots:G0356
G0357.1 V-ADM-2P ἀναλογίσασθε (1x)
Heb 12:3 For take·account·again·of the·one having·

G0358 ἄν•αλος análôs *adj.* (1x)
Roots:G0001 G0251 See:G0252
G0358.1 A-NSN ἄναλον (1x)
Mk 9:50 but if the salt should·become unsalty, with what

G0359 ἀνά•λυσις análysis *n.* (1x)
Roots:G0360 Compare:G0867
G0359 N-GSF ἀναλύσεως (1x)
2Ti 4:6 the season of·my bodily·departure has·stood·over *me*

G0360 ἀνα•λύω analýō *v.* (2x)
Roots:G0303 G3089 See:G0359
G0360.2 V-FAI-3S ἀναλύσει (1x)
Lk 12:36 lord when he·shall·break·camp from·among the
G0360.2 V-AAN ἀναλῦσαι (1x)
Php 1:23 having the longing to·break·camp and to·be

G0361 ἀν•α•μάρτητος anamártētôs *adj.* (1x)
Roots:G0001 G0264
G0361.1 A-NSM ἀναμάρτητος (1x)
Jn 8:7 among·yeu *that·is* without·moral·failure, let·him·cast

G0362 ἀνα•μένω anaménō *v.* (1x)
Roots:G0303 G3306 Compare:G4328 G1679 See:G4037
G0362.1 V-PAN ἀναμένειν (1x)
1Th 1:10 and to·patiently·await his Son from·out·of the

G0363 ἀνα•μιμνήσκω anamimnḗskō *v.* (6x)
Roots:G0303 G3403 See:G0364
G0363.1 V-PAI-1S ἀναμιμνήσκω (1x)
2Ti 1:6 which cause I·remind·and·admonish you to·rekindle
G0363.2 V-FAI-3S ἀναμνήσει (1x)
1Co 4:17 ·cause yeu to·recall·to·mind·and·consider my ways
G0363.2 V-PMM-2P ἀναμιμνήσκεσθε (1x)
Heb 10:32 Now recall·to·mind·and·consider the previous
G0363.2 V-PMP-GSM ἀναμιμνησκομένου (1x)
2Co 7:15 with·him·recalling·to·mind·and·considering the
G0363.2 V-AOP-NSM ἀναμνησθείς (1x)
Mk 11:21 And recalling·to·mind·and·considering *it*, Peter
G0363.2 V-API-3S ἀνεμνήσθη (1x)
Mk 14:72 And Peter recalled·to·mind·and·considered the

G0364 ἀνά•μνησις anámnēsis *n.* (4x)
Roots:G0363 Compare:G3417 G5294
G0364.2 N-ASF ἀνάμνησιν (3x)
Lk 22:19 Do this as my continual·reminder."
1Co 11:24 Do this as my continual·reminder."
1Co 11:25 yeu·would·drink *it*, as my continual·reminder."
G0364.3 N-NSF ἀνάμνησις (1x)
Heb 10:3 a·reminder·again *is·made* of·moral·failures each

G0365 ἀνα•νεόω ananêóō *v.* (1x)
Roots:G0303 G3501 Compare:G0340 G0341 G0600 G1357 G1456 G3824 See:G3504-1
G0365 V-PPN ἀνανεοῦσθαι (1x)
Eph 4:23 and *such·for yeu* to·be·rejuvenated in·the spirit of·

G0366 ἀνα•νήφω ananḗphō *v.* (1x)
Roots:G0303 G3525 See:G1594
G0366.2 V-AAS-3P ἀνανήψωσιν (1x)
2Ti 2:26 and *that* they·may·soberly·come·to·their·senses *and*

G0367 Ἀναν•ίας Ananías *n/p.* (13x)
חֲנַנְיָה cнăn̲anyạh [Hebrew]
Roots:H2608 Compare:G0452 See:G4551
G0367.2 N/P-NSM Ἀνανίας (2x)
Ac 5:1 But a·certain man, AnanIas by·name, together with·
Ac 5:5 upon·hearing these words, AnanIas fell·down *and*
G0367.2 N/P-VSM Ἀνανία (1x)
Ac 5:3 But Peter declared, "AnanIas, why *has* the
G0367.3 N/P-NSM Ἀνανίας (4x)
Ac 9:10 disciple at Damascus, AnanIas by·name. And the
Ac 9:13 But AnanIas answered, "Lord, I·have·heard of
Ac 9:17 And AnanIas went·off and entered into the home.
Ac 22:12 "And a·certain AnanIas, a·devoutly·reverent man
G0367.3 N/P-VSM Ἀνανία (1x)
Ac 9:10 to him in a·clear·vision, "O·AnanIas." And he·
G0367.3 N/P-ASM Ἀνανίαν (1x)
Ac 9:12 a·man by·the·name·of AnanIas entering·in and
G0367.4 N/P-NSM Ἀνανίας (2x)
Ac 23:2 designated·high·priest HananIah ordered for·the·ones
Ac 24:1 designated·high·priest HananIah walked·down with
EG0367.4 (2x)
Ac 9:1 ·alongside the designated·high·priest *HananIah*,
Ac 22:5 *to·such*, the designated·high·priest *HananIah* is also

G0368 ἀν•αντί•ρρητος anantírrhētôs *adj.* (1x)
Roots:G0001 G0473 G4483 See:G0369
G0368.2 A-GPM ἀναντιρρήτων (1x)
Ac 19:36 ·then, with·these·things being indisputable, it·is

G0369 ἀν•αντι•ρρήτως anantirrhḗtōs *adv.* (1x)
Roots:G0368
G0369 ADV ἀναντιρρήτως (1x)
Ac 10:29 *to·yeu* without·expressing·opposition. Accordingly,

G0370 ἀν•άξιος anáxiôs *adj.* (1x)
Roots:G0001 G0514
G0370.2 A-NPM ἀνάξιοι (1x)
1Co 6:2 yeu, are·yeu unworthy of·the·smallest arbitrations?

G0371 ἀν•αξίως anaxíōs *adv.* (2x)
Roots:G0370
G0371.3 ADV ἀναξίως (2x)
1Co 11:27 cup of·the Lord in·an·unworthy·manner, shall·be
1Co 11:29 eating and drinking in·an·unworthy·manner, eats

G0372 ἀνά•παυσις anápausis *n.* (5x)
Roots:G0373 Compare:G2663 G4520 xLangEquiv:H6314 xLangAlso:H2014 H7677
G0372.1 N-ASF ἀνάπαυσιν (5x)

Lk 11:24 waterless places, seeking a·rest·break; and not
Mt 11:29 and yeu·shall·find a·rest·break for·yeur souls.
Mt 12:43 waterless places, seeking a·rest·break, and it·does·
Rv 4:8 And they·do·not have a·rest·break day and night,
Rv 14:11 its derived·image do·not have a·rest·break day or

G0373 ἀνα•παύω anapaúō *v.* (12x)
Roots:G0303 G3973 Compare:G2664

G0373.1 V-PMI-3S ἀναπαύεται (1x)
1Pe 4:14 the Spirit of·glory and of·God rests upon yeu. In·

G0373.1 V-PMM-2S ἀναπαύου (1x)
Lk 12:19 being·laid·out for many years. Rest, eat, drink, *and*

G0373.1 V-PMM-2P ἀναπαύεσθε (3x)
Mt 26:45 remaining *moment* and rest·yeurselves? Behold,
Mk 6:31 into a·desolate place, and rest a·little·while!" For
Mk 14:41 and rest·yeurselves? It·is·enough,·no·more! The

G0373.1 V-AMS-3P ἀναπαύσωνται (2x)
Rv 6:11 it·was·uttered to·them that they·should·rest yet *for*
Rv 14:13 "in·order·that they·may·rest from·out of·their

G0373.3 V-FAI-1S ἀναπαύσω (1x)
Mt 11:28 having·been·overloaded, and·I shall·refresh yeu.

G0373.3 V-AAI-3P ἀνέπαυσαν (1x)
1Co 16:18 For they·refreshed my spirit and yeurs.

G0373.3 V-AAM-2S ἀνάπαυσον (1x)
Phm 1:20 you in *the* Lord; refresh my inward·affections in

G0373.3 V-RPI-3S ἀναπέπαυται (2x)
2Co 7:13 because his spirit has·been·refreshed by yeu all.
Phm 1:7 of·the holy·ones have·been·refreshed, brother,

G0374 ἀνα•πείθω anapeíthō *v.* (1x)
Roots:G0303 G3982

G0374.2 V-PAI-3S ἀναπείθει (1x)
Ac 18:13 "This·man persistently·persuades men·of·clay† to·

G0375 ἀνα•πέμπω anapémpō *v.* (4x)
Roots:G0303 G3992

G0375.1 V-AAI-1S ἀνέπεμψα (1x)
Phm 1:12 whom I·sent·back *to·you*. So you·yourself

G0375.1 V-AAI-3S ἀνέπεμψεν (1x)
Lk 23:11 him in·splendid clothing, he·sent him back to·

G0375.2 V-AAI-1S ἀνέπεμψα (1x)
Lk 23:15 ·did HerOd·AntiPas, for I·sent yeu·yeurselves up to

G0375.2 V-AAI-3S ἀνέπεμψεν (1x)
Lk 23:7 ·out of·HerOd·AntiPas' jurisdiction, he·sent him up

G0376 ἀνά•πηρος anápērŏs *adj.* (2x)
Roots:G0303 Compare:G2948 G5560

G0376 A-APM ἀναπήρους (2x)
Lk 14:13 ·poor·ones, totally·maimed·ones, lame·ones,
Lk 14:21 the helplessly·poor, and totally·maimed·ones, and

G0377 ἀνα•πίπτω anapíptō *v.* (11x)
Roots:G0303 G4098 Compare:G0345 G0347

G0377.2 V-2AAI-3S ἀνέπεσεν (2x)
Lk 11:37 And entering·in, *Jesus* sat·back·to·eat.
Lk 22:14 when the hour came, *Jesus* sat·back·to·eat, and the

G0377.2 V-2AAI-3P ἀνέπεσον (2x)
Jn 6:10 Accordingly, the men sat·back·to·eat; the number
Mk 6:40 And they·sat·back·to·eat in·rows, rows by a·

G0377.2 V-AAM-2S ἀνάπεσον (1x)
Lk 14:10 ·forth, after·traversing, sit·back·to·eat in the very·

G0377.2 V-2AAN ἀναπεσεῖν (1x)
Jn 6:10 "Make the men·of·clay† to·sit·back·to·eat." Now

G0377.2 V-AMM-2S ἀνάπεσαι (1x)
Lk 17:7 ·the field, 'After·coming·aside, sit·back·and·eat'?

G0377.3 V-2AAI-3S ἀνέπεσεν (1x)
Jn 21:20 Jesus loved, who also sat·back upon his chest at the

G0377.3 V-2AAN ἀναπεσεῖν (2x)
Mt 15:35 ·ordered the crowds to·sit·back upon the soil.
Mk 8:6 And he·charged the crowd to·sit·back upon the soil.

G0377.3 V-2AAP-NSM ἀναπεσών (1x)
Jn 13:12 took·hold·of his garments, after·sitting·back again,

G0378 ἀνα•πληρόω anaplērŏ́ō *v.* (6x)
Roots:G0303 G4137

G0378.1 V-PPI-3S ἀναπληροῦται (1x)
Mt 13:14 And in them is·utterly·fulfilled the prophecy of·

G0378.1 V-AAM-2P ἀναπληρώσατε (1x)
Gal 6:2 and in·this·manner utterly·fulfill the Law-of-Liberty

G0378.1 V-AAN ἀναπληρῶσαι (1x)
1Th 2:16 at·all·times to·utterly·fulfill *the complete·fullness·*

G0378.2 V-PAP-NSM ἀναπληρῶν (1x)
1Co 14:16 how·shall the·one utterly·occupying the place

G0378.3 V-AAI-3P ἀνεπλήρωσαν (1x)
1Co 16:17 lacking on·yeur *part*, these·men utterly·supplied.

G0378.3 V-AAS-3S ἀναπληρώσῃ (1x)
Php 2:30 in·order·that he·should·utterly·supply yeur lack

G0379 ἀν•απο•λόγητος anapŏlŏ́gētŏs *adj.* (2x)
Roots:G0001 G0626 Compare:G0216 G0094 See:G0627

G0379.3 A-NSM ἀναπολόγητος (1x)
Rm 2:1 presently·judging— you·are without·exoneration, O

G0379.3 A-APM ἀναπολογήτους (1x)
Rm 1:20 ·made— such·for them to·be without·exoneration,

G0380 ἀνα•πτύσσω anaptýssō *v.* (1x)
Roots:G0303 G4428

G0380 V-AAP-NSM ἀναπτύξας (1x)
Lk 4:17 ·handed to·him. And unrolling the official·scroll,

G0381 ἀν•άπτω anáptō *v.* (3x)
Roots:G0303 G0681 xLangAlso:H5400 H1197 H2734 H3341

G0381 V-PAI-3S ἀνάπτει (1x)
Jac 3:5 Behold, a·little fire kindles *something* as·big·as a·

G0381 V-AAP-NPM ἀνάψαντες (1x)
Ac 28:2 way·beyond·the·mark. For kindling a·fire, they·

G0381 V-API-3S ἀνήφθη (1x)
Lk 12:49 ·want, though even·now it·is·already·kindled?

G0382 ἀν•αρίθμητος anaríthmētŏs *adj.* (1x)
Roots:G0001 G0705

G0382.2 A-NSF ἀναρίθμητος (1x)
Heb 11:12 *of·them*, and as the innumerable sand beside the

G0383 ἀνα•σείω anasêíō *v.* (2x)
Roots:G0303 G4579 Compare:G2042 G4531

G0383.3 V-PAI-3S ἀνασείει (1x)
Lk 23:5 saying, "He·incites the people, instructing in all

G0383.3 V-AAI-3P ἀνέσεισαν (1x)
Mk 15:11 But the chief·priests incited the crowd that rather

G0384 ἀνα•σκευάζω anaskêuázō *v.* (1x)
Roots:G0303 G4632 Compare:G0387 G1612 See:G0643

G0384.3 V-PAP-NPM ἀνασκευάζοντες (1x)
Ac 15:24 with·words (dislodging·and·disturbing yeur souls,

G0385 ἀνα•σπάω anaspáō *v.* (2x)
Roots:G0303 G4685

G0385 V-FAI-3S ἀνασπάσει (1x)
Lk 14:5 a·well, and shall·not immediately draw him up on

G0385 V-API-3S ἀνεσπάσθη (1x)
Ac 11:10 and absolutely·all *of·it* was·drawn·up again into

G0386 ἀνά•στασις anástasis *n.* (43x)
Roots:G0450 Compare:G1454 G1815 xLangAlso:H7011-1 H7012

G0386.1 N-ASF ἀνάστασιν (1x)
Lk 2:34 ·out for a·downfall and a·raising·again of·many in

G0386.2 N-NSF ἀνάστασις (6x)
Jn 11:25 "I AM the resurrection and the life-above.
1Co 15:12 yeu say that there·is no resurrection of·dead·men?
1Co 15:13 But if there·is no resurrection of·dead·men, not·
1Co 15:21 a·man·of·clay† *came* resurrection of·dead·men.
1Co 15:42 In·this·manner also *is* the resurrection of·the dead
Rv 20:5 This *is* the First Resurrection. But the rest of·the

G0386.2 N-ASF ἀνάστασιν (11x)
Jn 5:29 beneficially·good, into a·resurrection of·life-above;
Jn 5:29 into a·resurrection of·Final·Tribunal·judgment.
Lk 20:27 *·saying that* there·is not a·resurrection) inquired·of
Ac 4:2 fully·proclaiming in Jesus the resurrection, the·one
Ac 17:18 ·them the·good·news of·Jesus and the resurrection.
Ac 17:32 ·fact, after·hearing of·a·resurrection of·dead·men,
Ac 23:8 say *that* there·is not a·resurrection, *also* not·even
Ac 24:15 there·shall·be a·resurrection of·dead·men, both
Mt 22:23 saying *there·is* not to·be a·resurrection, and they·
Mk 12:18 say *that there·is* not to·be a·resurrection, and they·
2Ti 2:18 saying the resurrection even·now to·have·occurred

G0386.2 N-DSF ἀναστάσει (7x)
Jn 11:24 that he·shall·rise·up in the resurrection at the last
Lk 14:14 ·recompensed at the resurrection of·the righteous."
Lk 20:33 "So·then, in the resurrection, whose wife of·them
Mt 22:28 "So·then, in the resurrection whose wife shall·she·
Mt 22:30 "For in the resurrection, neither do·they·marry nor
Mk 12:23 "So·then in the resurrection, whenever they·
Rv 20:6 having part in the First Resurrection. Over these, the

G0386.2 N-GSF ἀναστάσεως (17x)
Lk 20:35 that coming·age and the resurrection from·out of·the
Lk 20:36 ·Sons of·God, being the·Sons of·the Resurrection.
Ac 1:22 a·witness together with·us of·his resurrection."
Ac 2:31 concerning the resurrection of·the Anointed-One,
Ac 4:33 ·forth the testimonies of·the resurrection of·the Lord
Ac 23:6 *the* Expectation, even *the* resurrection of·dead·men,
Ac 24:21 'Concerning *the* resurrection of·dead·men, I·
Ac 26:23 *·to·be* first of·a·resurrection from·among dead·men
Heb 6:2 ·on of·hands, and of·the·resurrection of·the·dead,
Heb 11:35 their dead from·out of·a·resurrection. And others
Heb 11:35 ·may·obtain a·significantly·better resurrection.
Mt 22:31 "Now concerning the resurrection of·the dead, did·
Rm 1:4 ·holiness, from·out of·a·resurrection of·the·dead;
Rm 6:5 ·be also *in·the resemblance* of·his resurrection—
Php 3:10 him and the power of·his resurrection, even the
1Pe 1:3 through *the* resurrection of·YeShua Anointed from·
1Pe 3:21 — through *the* resurrection of·YeShua Anointed,

EG0386.2 (1x)
Col 2:15 ·declaration *(his Resurrection)*, triumphing·over

G0387 ἀνα•στατόω anastatŏ́ō *v.* (3x)
Roots:G0450 Compare:G0384

G0387.1 V-PAP-NPM ἀναστατοῦντες (1x)
Gal 5:12 they·were·chopped·off, the·ones unsettling yeu.

G0387.2 V-AAP-NPM ἀναστατώσαντες (1x)
Ac 17:6 crying·out, "The·ones upsetting The Land, these·

G0387.3 V-AAP-NSM ἀναστατώσας (1x)
Ac 21:38 these days already·making·an·uprising and leading

G0388 ἀνα•σταυρόω anastaurŏ́ō *v.* (1x)
Roots:G0303 G4717

G0388 V-PAP-APM ἀνασταυροῦντας (1x)
Heb 6:6 *that·is*, presently·re-crucifying for·themselves the

G0389 ἀνα•στενάζω anastênázō *v.* (1x)
Roots:G0303 G4727 Compare:G4727

G0389 V-AAP-NSM ἀναστενάξας (1x)
Mk 8:12 And after·sighing·deeply in·his spirit, he·says,

G0390 ἀνα•στρέφω anastrḗphō *v.* (11x)
Roots:G0303 G4762 Compare:G0654 G1994 G5290 G4291 See:G0391

G0390.ª V-PPP-GPM ἀναστρεφομένων (1x)
Heb 10:33 partners with·the·ones being·used in·this·manner.

G0390.1 V-AAI-3S ἀνέστρεψεν (1x)
Jn 2:15 the moneychangers' money and overturned the tables

G0390.2 V-FAI-1S ἀναστρέψω (1x)
Ac 15:16 After these·things, I·shall·return and shall·rebuild

G0390.2 V-PPP-GPM ἀναστρεφομένων (1x)
Mt 17:22 And upon·them returning into Galilee, YeShua

G0390.2 V-AAP-NPM ἀναστρέψαντες (1x)
Ac 5:22 in the prison·cell. And returning, they·announced *it*

G0390.4 V-PPN ἀναστρέφεσθαι (2x)
Heb 13:18 all·things, willing to·conduct·ourselves morally.
1Ti 3:15 it·is·necessary to·conduct·oneself among God's

G0390.4 V-PPP-APM ἀναστρεφομένους (1x)
2Pe 2:18 ·from the·ones conducting·themselves in error.

G0390.4 V-2API-1P ἀνεστράφημεν (1x)
2Co 1:12 by God's grace), we·conducted·ourselves in the

G0390.4 V-2APM-2P ἀναστράφητε (1x)
1Pe 1:17 work of·each·man, conduct·yeurselves *during* the

G0390.5 V-2API-1P ἀνεστράφημεν (1x)
Eph 2:3 also we all had·our·manner·of·life in·times·past in

G0391 ἀνα•στροφή anastrôphḗ *n.* (15x)
Roots:G0390 Compare:G2688 G0981 G1382

G0391.1 N-ASF ἀναστροφήν (3x)

1Pe 2:12 *Maintain* yeur behavior among the Gentiles, being
1Pe 3:2 ·beholding yeur morally·clean behavior *coupled* with
1Pe 3:16 yeur beneficially·good behavior in Anointed-One.
G0391.1 N-DSF ἀναστροφῇ (1x)
1Pe 1:15 ·yeurselves must·become holy in all *yeur* behavior,
G0391.1 N-GSF ἀναστροφῆς (4x)
Heb 13:7 observing·again the outcome of·*their*·behavior.
Jac 3:13 From·out of·the good behavior, let·him·show his
1Pe 3:1 ·may·be·gained through the behavior of·the wives
2Pe 2:7 ·anguish by the behavior of·the unscrupulous·men in
G0391.2 N-DSF ἀναστροφῇ (1x)
1Ti 4:12 ·the ones·that·trust, in word, in conduct, in love, in
G0391.2 N-DPF ἀναστροφαῖς (1x)
2Pe 3:11 to·subsist in *all* holy conduct and devout·reverence,
EG0391.2 (2x)
Php 3:17 ·as yeu·hold us *as* a·particular·pattern *of·conduct*.
Rv 18:20 decided yeur just·claim as·a·result of·her *conduct*!"
G0391.3 N-ASF ἀναστροφήν (2x)
Gal 1:13 yeu·heard of·my former manner·of·life in Judaism,
Eph 4:22 according·to the previous manner·of·life (the·one
G0391.3 N-GSF ἀναστροφῆς (1x)
1Pe 1:18 futile manner·of·life handed·down·by·your·fathers,

G0392 ἀνα•τάσσομαι anatássômai *v.* (1x)
Roots:G0303 G5021
G0392.2 V-ADN ἀνατάξασθαι (1x)
Lk 1:1 many took·it·upon·themselves to·fully·compose a·

G0393 ἀνα•τέλλω anatéllō *v.* (9x)
Roots:G0303 G5056 See:G1816
G0393.1 V-PAI-3S ἀνατέλλει (1x)
Mt 5:45 in *the* heavens, because he·raises his sun above·the·
G0393.1 V-PAP-ASF ἀνατέλλουσαν (1x)
Lk 12:54 the thick·cloud rising·above·the·horizon from *the*
G0393.1 V-AAI-3S ἀνέτειλεν (2x)
Mt 4:16 upon·them a·light did·rise·above·the·horizon."
Jac 1:11 the sun rose·above·the·horizon together with·the
G0393.1 V-AAP-GSM ἀνατείλαντος (3x)
Mt 13:6 And with·*the*·sun rising·above·the·horizon, it·was·
Mk 4:6 And with·*the*·sun rising·above·the·horizon, it·was·
Mk 16:2 ·tomb with·the sun rising·above·the·horizon.
G0393.1 V-AAS-3S ἀνατείλῃ (1x)
2Pe 1:19 Light·Bearer should·rise·above·the·horizon in yeur
G0393.1 V-RAI-3S ἀνατέταλκεν (1x)
Heb 7:14 our Lord has·risen·above·the·horizon from·among

G0394 ἀνα•τίθεμαι anatíthêmai *v.* (2x)
Roots:G0303 G5087 Compare:G3908
G0394 V-2AMI-1S ἀνεθέμην (1x)
Gal 2:2 according·to a·revelation, and set·forth to·them the
G0394 V-2AMI-3S ἀνέθετο (1x)
Ac 25:14 ·more days, Festus set·forth the·things against

G0395 ἀνα•τολή anatôlê *n.* (10x)
Roots:G0393 Compare:G3720 See:G1424 G1005 G3558 xLangAlso:H6780
G0395.1 N-NSF ἀνατολή (1x)
Lk 1:78 a·light·rising·over·the·horizon from·out of·on·high
G0395.3 N-DSF ἀνατολῇ (2x)
Mt 2:2 For we·saw his star in the east, and we·came to·fall·
Mt 2:9 they·saw in the east was·going·on·ahead·of them,
G0395.3 N-GSF ἀνατολῆς (2x)
Rv 7:2 another angel ascending from *the* eastern sun, having
Rv 21:13 On *the* east *are* three gates; on *the* north *are* three
G0395.3 N-GPF ἀνατολῶν (5x)
Lk 13:29 And they·shall·come from east and west, and from
Mt 2:1 Magian·astrologists from *the* east arrived·publicly in
Mt 8:11 to·yeu that many shall·come from east and west, and
Mt 24:27 comes·forth from *the* east and shines·forth as·far·
Rv 16:12 ·the kings from the eastern sun may·be·made·ready

G0396 ἀνα•τρέπω anatrépō *v.* (2x)
Roots:G0303 G5157 Compare:G1612
G0396.2 V-PAI-3P ἀνατρέπουσιν (2x)
Tit 1:11 ·silence·mouths. Such·men overturn whole houses,
2Ti 2:18 ·now to·have·occurred, and they·overturn the trust

G0397 ἀνα•τρέφω anatréphō *v.* (3x)
Roots:G0303 G5142
G0397.1 V-AMI-3S ἀνεθρέψατο (1x)
Ac 7:21 daughter took him up and nurtured him for her·own
G0397.1 V-2API-3S ἀνετράφη (1x)
Ac 7:20 ·was handsome to·God; *and* he·was·nurtured in his
G0397.2 V-RPP-NSM ἀνατεθραμμένος (1x)
Ac 22:3 *a·city* in·Cilicia, but having·been·reared in this city

G0398 ἀνα•φαίνω anaphaínō *v.* (2x)
Roots:G0303 G5316 Compare:G1166 See:G2014
G0398.3 V-PPN ἀναφαίνεσθαι (1x)
Lk 19:11 ·God is·about to·be·made·totally·apparent at·once.
G0398.4 V-2AAP-NPM ἀναφάναντες (1x)
Ac 21:3 Now after·coming·within·full·sight·of Cyprus and

G0399 ἀνα•φέρω anaphérō *v.* (10x)
Roots:G0303 G5342
G0399.1 V-PAI-3S ἀναφέρει (2x)
Mt 17:1 and John his brother, and he·brings them up upon a·
Mk 9:2 Jakob, and John, and brings them up upon a·high
G0399.2 V-PAN ἀναφέρειν (1x)
Heb 7:27 ·as the high·priests *do*, to·carry·up sacrifices *to·the*
G0399.2 V-PAS-1P ἀναφέρωμεν (1x)
Heb 13:15 ·of him, we·should·carry·up a·sacrifice of·praise
G0399.2 V-IPI-3S ἀνεφέρετο (1x)
Lk 24:51 ·away from them and was·carried·up into the
G0399.2 V-AAI-3S ἀνήνεγκεν (1x)
1Pe 2:24 who himself carried·up our moral·failures in his·
G0399.2 V-2AAN ἀνενεγκεῖν (1x)
Heb 9:28 ·offered only·once 'to·carry·up moral·failures for
G0399.2 V-AAN ἀνενέγκαι (1x)
1Pe 2:5 a·holy priesthood to·carry·up spiritual sacrifices
G0399.2 V-AAP-NSM ἀνενέγκας (2x)
Heb 7:27 this upon·one·occasion·only, carrying·up himself.
Jac 2:21 ·is·regarded·as·righteous, after·carrying·up his son

G0400 ἀνα•φωνέω anaphōnéō *v.* (1x)
Roots:G0303 G5455 See:G2019
G0400 V-AAI-3S ἀνεφώνησεν (1x)
Lk 1:42 And she·exclaimed with·a·loud voice, and declared,

G0401 ἀνά•χυσις anáchysis *n.* (1x)
Roots:G0303 G5502-5 Compare:G0670-3
G0401.3 N-ASF ἀνάχυσιν (1x)
1Pe 4:4 ·*them* into the same sewage of·an·unsaved·lifestyle,

G0402 ἀνα•χωρέω anachōréō *v.* (14x)
Roots:G0303 G5562 Compare:G0672 G4198
G0402 V-PAM-2P ἀναχωρεῖτε (1x)
Mt 9:24 says to·them, "Depart! For the young·girl did·not
G0402 V-AAI-3S ἀνεχώρησεν (9x)
Jn 6:15 they·should·make him king, he·departed again to·a·
Mt 2:14 and his mother by·night and departed into Egypt.
Mt 2:22 ·to a·vision·in·a·dream, he·departed into the
Mt 4:12 ·over *into prison*, YeShua departed for Galilee.
Mt 12:15 And YeShua knowing *it*, departed from·there. And
Mt 14:13 upon·hearing *it*, YeShua departed from·there in a·
Mt 15:21 going·forth from·there, YeShua departed into the
Mt 27:5 ·of·silver at the Temple, he·departed. And going·off
Mk 3:7 And Jesus departed with his disciples to the sea.
G0402 V-AAI-3P ἀνεχώρησαν (1x)
Mt 2:12 to HerOd·the·Great, they·departed into their·own
G0402 V-AAP-GPM ἀναχωρησάντων (1x)
Mt 2:13 And with·them already·departing, behold, an·angel
G0402 V-AAP-NSM ἀναχωρήσας (1x)
Ac 23:19 ·hold of·him by·the hand and departing privately,
G0402 V-AAP-NPM ἀναχωρήσαντες (1x)
Ac 26:31 And after·departing, they·were·speaking among

G0403 ἀνά•ψυξις anápsyxis *n.* (1x)
Roots:G0404
G0403.2 N-GSF ἀναψύξεως (1x)
Ac 3:19 ·out, so·that seasons of·refreshing should·come

G0404 ἀνα•ψύχω anapsýchō *v.* (1x)
Roots:G0303 G5594 See:G0403
G0404.2 V-AAI-3S ἀνέψυξεν (1x)
2Ti 1:16 because many·times he·refreshed me, and he·was·

G0405 ἀνδρα•ποδιστής andrapôdistés *n.* (1x)
Roots:G0435 G4228 xLangAlso:H2327-1
G0405 N-DPM ἀνδραποδισταῖς (1x)
1Ti 1:10 ·who·have·sex·with·men, for·kidnappers, for·liars,

G0406 Ἀνδρέας Andréas *n/p.* (14x)
Roots:G0435
G0406.2 N/P-NSM Ἀνδρέας (6x)
Jn 1:40 Andrew, Simon Peter's brother, was one from·among
Jn 6:8 from·among his disciples, Andrew, Simon Peter's
Jn 12:22 *this* to·Andrew, and again Andrew and PhilIp relay
Ac 1:13 Jakob, John, and Andrew); (PhilIp and Thomas);
Mt 10:2 being·referred·to·as Peter) and Andrew his brother;
Mk 13:3 Jakob, John and Andrew were·inquiring·of him
G0406.2 N/P-ASM Ἀνδρέαν (4x)
Lk 6:14 he·named Peter), and Andrew his brother, Jakob
Mt 4:18 being·referred·to·as Peter) and Andrew his brother,
Mk 1:16 Simon and his brother Andrew casting a·cast·net
Mk 3:18 and Andrew, and PhilIp, and BarTholomew, and
G0406.2 N/P-DSM Ἀνδρέᾳ (1x)
Jn 12:22 PhilIp comes and relays *this* to·Andrew, and again
G0406.2 N/P-GSM Ἀνδρέου (2x)
Jn 1:44 from·among the city of·Andrew and Peter.
Mk 1:29 into the home of·Simon and Andrew, with Jakob
EG0406.2 (1x)
Jn 1:41 This·man *Andrew* first finds his·own brother Simon

G0407 ἀνδρίζομαι andrízômai *v.* (1x)
Roots:G0435 xLangAlso:H0553
G0407.2 V-PNM-2P ἀνδρίζεσθε (1x)
1Co 16:13 ·fast in the trust! " Be·manly! Become·mighty!"

G0408 Ἀνδρό•νικος Andrónikôs *n/p.* (1x)
Roots:G0435 G3534
G0408.2 N/P-ASM Ἀνδρόνικον (1x)
Rm 16:7 Greet AndroNicus and Junianus, my Redeemed·

G0409 ἀνδρο•φόνος andrôphônôs *n.* (1x)
Roots:G0435 G5408 Compare:G0443 G5406 G4607 G3389 See:G0405 G0408
G0409 N-DPM ἀνδροφόνοις (1x)
1Ti 1:9 and thrashers·of·mothers, for·men·of·murder,

G0410 ἀν•έγκλητος anénklētôs *adj.* (5x)
Roots:G0001 G1458 Compare:G0121 G0156 G0273 G0298 G2724 G4587
G0410.1 A-APM ἀνεγκλήτους (1x)
1Co 1:8 unto *the* end, *being* not·called·to·account in the Day
G0410.2 A-NSM ἀνέγκλητος (1x)
Tit 1:6 if any·man is without·any·charge·of·wrong·doing, a·
G0410.2 A-NPM ἀνέγκλητοι (1x)
1Ti 3:10 while·being without·any·charge·of·wrong·doing.
G0410.2 A-ASM ἀνέγκλητον (1x)
Tit 1:7 to·be without·any·charge·of·wrong·doing as an·
G0410.2 A-APM ἀνεγκλήτους (1x)
Col 1:22 and without·any·charge·of·wrong·doing directly·

G0411 ἀν•εκ•διήγητος anêkdiḗgētôs *adj.* (1x)
Roots:G0001 G1555 Compare:G0215 G0731 See:G0412
G0411 A-DSF ἀνεκδιηγήτῳ (1x)
2Co 9:15 *be* to·God for his indescribable voluntary·present!

G0412 ἀν•εκ•λάλητος anêklálētôs *adj.* (1x)
Roots:G0001 G1583 Compare:G0215 See:G0411 G0731
G0412.3 A-DSF ἀνεκλαλήτῳ (1x)
1Pe 1:8 yeu·leap·for·joy with·joy quite·unspeakable, also

G0413 ἀν•έκ•λειπτος anékleiptôs *adj.* (1x)
Roots:G0001 G1587 Compare:G0088 See:G1587
G0413.2 A-ASM ἀνέκλειπτον (1x)
Lk 12:33 *but ones·containing* an·inexhaustible treasure in

G0414 ἀν•εκτότερος anêktótêrôs *adj.* (6x)
Roots:G0430
G0414 A-NSN-C ἀνεκτότερον (6x)
Lk 10:12 to·yeu, that it·shall·be more·tolerable at that Day
Lk 10:14 ·moreover, it·shall·be more·tolerable for·Tyre and
Mt 10:15 it·shall·be more·tolerable for·the·land of·Sodom
Mt 11:22 to·yeu, it·shall·be more·tolerable for·Tyre and

Ββ Γγ Δδ Εε Ζζ Ηη Θθ Ιι Κκ Λλ Μμ Νν Ξξ Οο Ππ Ρρ Σσ Ττ Υυ Φφ Χχ Ψψ Ωω

Mt 11:24 it·shall·be more·tolerable for·the·land of·Sodom in
Mk 6:11 to·yeu, it·shall·be more·tolerable for·Sodom or

G0415 ἀν•ελεήμων anêlêēmōn *adj.* (1x)
Roots:G0001 G1655
G0415 A-APM ἀνελεήμονας (1x)
Rm 1:31 implacable,·truceless·men, *and* unmerciful.

G0416 ἀνεμίζω anêmízō *v.* (1x)
Roots:G0417 Compare:G4154
G0416.2 V-PPP-DSM ἀνεμιζομένῳ (1x)
Jac 1:6 of·a·sea being·driven·by·the·wind and being·tossed·

G0417 ἄνεμος ánêmôs *n.* (32x)
Roots:G0109 Compare:G4151 xLangAlso:H7307
G0417.1 N-NSM ἄνεμος (8x)
Ac 27:14 long after, a·typhoon-like wind slammed against
Mt 14:24 the breaking·waves, for the wind was contrary.
Mt 14:32 embarking into the sailboat, the wind subsided.
Mk 4:39 And the wind subsided, and there·was a·great
Mk 4:41 is this, that even the wind and the sea listen·to·and·
Mk 6:48 in their rowing, for the wind was contrary to·them.
Mk 6:51 into the sailboat, and the wind subsided. And they·
Rv 7:1 of·the earth, in·order·that wind should·not blow on
G0417.1 N-NPM ἄνεμοι (3x)
Mt 7:25 flood·waters came, and the winds blew, and they·
Mt 7:27 flood·waters came, and the winds blew, and they·
Mt 8:27 is this that even the winds and the sea listen·to·and·
G0417.1 N-ASM ἄνεμον (1x)
Mt 14:30 But looking·at the strong wind, he·was·afraid, and
G0417.1 N-APM ἀνέμους (2x)
Ac 27:4 ·to Cyprus, on·account·of the winds being contrary.
Rv 7:1 earth, securely·holding the four winds of·the earth,
G0417.1 N-DSM ἀνέμῳ (4x)
Lk 8:24 ·being·awakened, he·reprimanded the wind and the
Ac 27:15 not being·able to·tack into·the wind, handing *her*
Mk 4:39 ·awakened, he·reprimanded the wind and declared
Eph 4:14 being·carried·about by·every wind of·instruction,
G0417.1 N-DPM ἀνέμοις (2x)
Lk 8:25 Because he·orders even the winds and the water,
Mt 8:26 ·awakened, he·reprimanded the winds and the sea,
G0417.1 N-GSM ἀνέμου (7x)
Jn 6:18 was·thoroughly·roused *due·to* a·great wind blowing.
Lk 7:24 to·distinctly·view? A·reed being·shaken by a·wind?
Lk 8:23 ·asleep. And a·whirling of·wind descended upon
Ac 27:7 adjacent·to Cnidus, *and* with·the wind not letting us
Mt 11:7 to·distinctly·view? A·reed being·shaken by a·wind?
Mk 4:37 And there·happens a·great whirling of·wind, and
Rv 6:13 ·green·figs while·being·shaken by a·great wind.
G0417.1 N-GPM ἀνέμων (4x)
Mt 24:31 Selected-Ones from·among the four winds, from
Mk 13:27 Selected-Ones from·out of·the four winds, from
Jac 3:4 *are* being·driven by harsh winds, *and·yet* they·are·
Jud 1:12 ·water being·carried·about by winds, late·autumn
EG0417.1 (1x)
Ac 27:15 handing *her to·the wind*, we·were·carried·*along*.

G0418 ἀν•έν•δεκτος anéndêktôs *adj.* (1x)
Roots:G0001 G1735 Compare:G0102
G0418.2 A-NSN ἀνένδεκτον (1x)
Lk 17:1 "It·is not·permissible *for* the scandalous·traps not

G0419 ἀν•εξ•ερεύνητος anêxêrêúnētôs *adj.* (1x)
Roots:G0001 G1830
G0419.2 A-NPN ἀνεξερεύνητα (1x)
Rm 11:33 and knowledge of·God! How inexplorable *are* his

G0420 ἀν•εξί•κακος anêxíkakôs *adj.* (1x)
Roots:G0430 G2556
G0420.2 A-ASM ἀνεξίκακον (1x)
2Ti 2:24 to all *men*, instructive, able·to·bear·with·ill·will,

G0421 ἀν•εξ•ιχνίαστος anêxichníastôs *adj.* (2x)
Roots:G0001 G1537 G2487
G0421.2 A-NPF ἀνεξιχνίαστοι (1x)
Rm 11:33 *are* his judgments, and his ways untraceable!
G0421.2 A-ASM ἀνεξιχνίαστον (1x)
Eph 3:8 among the Gentiles the untraceable wealth of·the

G0422 ἀν•επ•αίσχυντος anêpaíschyntôs *adj.* (1x)
Roots:G0001 G1909 G0153
G0422 A-ASM ἀνεπαίσχυντον (1x)
2Ti 2:15 to·God, an·unashamed workman rightly·dissecting

G0423 ἀν•επί•ληπτος anêpílēptôs *adj.* (3x)
Roots:G0001 G1949 Compare:G0298 G4587
G0423.2 A-NPM ἀνεπίληπτοι (1x)
1Ti 5:7 ·that they·may·be above·all·blame·and·suspicion.
G0423.2 A-ASM ἀνεπίληπτον (1x)
1Ti 3:2 to·be above·all·blame·and·suspicion, a·husband of·
G0423.2 A-ASF ἀνεπίληπτον (1x)
1Ti 6:14 unstained, above·all·blame·and·suspicion, *for* so·

G0424 ἀν•έρχομαι anérchômai *v.* (3x)
Roots:G0303 G2064
G0424 V-2AAI-1S ἀνῆλθον (2x)
Gal 1:17 neither did·I·go·up to JeruSalem toward the·ones
Gal 1:18 after three years, I·went·up to JeruSalem to·see·
G0424 V-2AAI-3S ἀνῆλθεν (1x)
Jn 6:3 Then Jesus went·up upon the mountain.

G0425 ἄν•εσις ánêsis *n.* (5x)
Roots:G0447
G0425.1 N-ASF ἄνεσιν (2x)
2Th 1:7 the·ones being·hard-pressed, relaxation with us at
2Co 7:5 our flesh has·had no relaxation at·all, but·rather
G0425.2 N-NSF ἄνεσις (1x)
2Co 8:13 *mean* that others *should·have* ease, and *there·be*
G0425.2 N-ASF ἄνεσιν (2x)
Ac 24:23 Paul, and·also to·hold *him·at* ease, and to·forbid
2Co 2:13 I·did·not have an·ease in·my spirit, *for* me not to·

G0426 ἀν•ετάζω anêtázō *v.* (2x)
Roots:G0303 Compare:G0350 G1381 G4802 See:G1233
G0426 V-PAN ἀνετάζειν (1x)
Ac 22:29 the·ones intending to·interrogate him withdrew
G0426 V-PPN ἀνετάζεσθαι (1x)
Ac 22:24 for·him to·be·interrogated by·scourgings in·order·

G0427 ἄνευ ánêu *prep.* (3x)
Compare:G0001 G0817
G0427 PREP ἄνευ (3x)
Mt 10:29 them shall·fall upon the soil without yeur Father
1Pe 3:1 through the behavior of·the wives without a·word
1Pe 4:9 *Be* hospitable to one·another without grumbling.

G0428 ἀν•εύθετος anêúthêtôs *adj.* (1x)
Roots:G0001 G2111
G0428.2 A-GSM ἀνευθέτου (1x)
Ac 27:12 harbor inherently·being unsuitable, particularly·for

G0429 ἀν•ευρίσκω anêurískō *v.* (2x)
Roots:G0303 G2147
G0429 V-2AAI-3P ἀνεῦρον (1x)
Lk 2:16 ·came with·haste and diligently·found both Mariam
G0429 V-2AAP-NPM ἀνευρόντες (1x)
Ac 21:4 And after·diligently·finding the disciples, we·

G0430 ἀν•έχομαι anéchômai *v.* (15x)
Roots:G0303 G2192
G0430.1 V-FDI-3P ἀνέξονται (1x)
2Ti 4:3 when they·shall·not bear·with the healthy·and·sound
G0430.1 V-PNI-2P ἀνέχεσθε (3x)
2Co 11:1 *of·boasting*, but·yet even·so, bear·with me.
2Co 11:19 For yeu·bear·with the impetuous with·pleasure,
2Co 11:20 For yeu·bear·with·it, if anyone utterly·enslaves
G0430.1 V-PNM-2P ἀνέχεσθε (1x)
Heb 13:22 yeu, brothers, bear·with the word of·exhortation,
G0430.1 V-PNP-NPM ἀνεχόμενοι (2x)
Eph 4:2 with long-suffering, bearing·with one·another in
Col 3:13 bearing·with one·another, and being·graciously·
G0430.1 V-INI-2P ἠνείχεσθε (2x)
2Co 11:1 Oh·that yeu·would·bear·with me a·little·while in·
2Co 11:4 ·accept, yeu·were·bearing·with *him* beautifully.
G0430.2 V-FDI-1S ἀνέξομαι (3x)
Lk 9:41 shall·I·be alongside yeu and shall·put·up·with yeu?
Mt 17:17 ·I·be with yeu? How·long shall·I·put·up·with yeu?
Mk 9:19 alongside yeu? How·long shall·I·put·up·with yeu?
G0430.2 V-2ADI-1S ἠνεσχόμην (1x)
Ac 18:14 ·to reason, O Jews, I·would have·put·up·with yeu.
G0430.3 V-PNI-1P ἀνεχόμεθα (1x)
1Co 4:12 we·bless. Being·persecuted, we·hold·up·*under·it*.
G0430.3 V-PNI-2P ἀνέχεσθε (1x)
2Th 1:4 and tribulations that yeu·hold·up·*under*.

G0431 ἀ•νεψιός anêpsiós *n.* (1x)
Roots:G0001
G0431.2 N-NSM ἀνεψιός (1x)
Col 4:10 yeu, also *John*·Mark (the cousin of·BarNabas,

G0432 ἄνηθον ánēthôn *n.* (1x)
G0432 N-ASN ἄνηθον (1x)
Mt 23:23 ·pay·tithes of·the mint and the dill and the cumin,

G0433 ἀν•ήκω anḗkō *v.* (3x)
Roots:G0303 G2240 Compare:G1832 G4241
G0433.2 V-PAP-NPN ἀνήκοντα (1x)
Eph 5:4 sarcasm (*such* things not being·appropriate), but·yet
G0433.2 V-IAI-3S ἀνῆκεν (1x)
Col 3:18 to·yeur·own husbands, as is·appropriate in *the*
G0433.3 V-PAP-ASN ἀνῆκον (1x)
Phm 1:8 to·order you *to·do* the appropriate·thing,

G0434 ἀν•ήμερος anḗmêrôs *adj.* (1x)
Roots:G0001
G0434 A-NPM ἀνήμεροι (1x)
2Ti 3:3 without·self-restraint, savages, hostile·to·

G0435 ἀνήρ anḗr *n.* (225x)
ἀνδρός andrṓs [middle voice/genitive]
Compare:G0444 G0407 G4213-1 See:G1135 G0405-1
xLangEquiv:H0376 xLangAlso:H0582
G0435.2 N-NSM ἀνήρ (39x)
Jn 1:30 'Right·behind me comes a·man who·has·come·to·be
Lk 5:8 me, because I·am a·man full·of·moral·failure, Lord.
Lk 5:12 one of·the cities, behold, a·man full·of·leprosy; and
Lk 8:27 ·came·and·met him a·certain man from·out of·the
Lk 8:38 Now the man from whom the demons had·come·out
Lk 8:41 And behold, there·came a·man whose name *was*
Lk 9:38 And behold, a·man of·the crowd shouted·out,
Lk 19:2 *there·was* a·man being·called by·the·name·of
Lk 23:50 And behold, a·man, Joseph by·name, a·counselor
Lk 23:50 ·being a·beneficially·good man and righteous.
Lk 24:19 Jesus of·Natsareth, who became a·man, a·prophet
Ac 3:2 And a·certain man inherently·being lame from·out
Ac 5:1 But a·certain man, Ananias by·name, together·with·
Ac 8:9 But a·certain man by·the·name·of Simon was·
Ac 8:27 and behold, *there·was* a·man of·Ethiopia, a·eunuch,
Ac 10:1 Now there·was a·certain man in Caesarea, Cornelius
Ac 10:22 a·righteous man who·is·reverently·fearing God
Ac 10:30 yet behold, a·man stood·still in·the·sight·of·me
Ac 11:24 because he·was a·beneficially·good man and full
Ac 14:8 Lystra, *there·was* a·certain man disabled in·his feet
Ac 16:9 there·was some man of·Macedonia standing and
Ac 18:24 by·birth), an·eloquent man being·powerful in·the
Ac 22:3 "I·myself am in·fact a·man *who·is* a·Jew, having·
Ac 22:12 Ananias, a·devoutly·reverent man according·to·the
Ac 25:14 "There·is a·certain man having·been·left·behind *as*
Rm 4:8 Supremely·blessed *is* a·man to·whom Yahweh, no,
Jac 1:8 A·man vacillating·in·his·soul *is* completely·unstable
Jac 1:12 Supremely·blessed *is* a·man that patiently·endures
Jac 2:2 into yeur gathering a·man *with* a·prominent·gold·ring
Jac 3:2 the·same *is* a·completely·mature man, able also to·
1Co 11:3 and woman's head *is* the man, and Anointed-One's
1Co 11:4 Every man praying or prophesying, having *his*
1Co 11:7 For in·fact a·man is·obligated not to·be·fully·
1Co 11:8 For man is not from·out of·woman, but·rather
1Co 11:9 For also man is·not created on·account·of the
1Co 11:11 Nevertheless, neither *is* man apart·from woman,
1Co 11:12 ·the man, in·this·manner the man *is* also through
1Co 11:14 in·fact, that if a·man should·wear·long·hair, it·is
1Co 13:11 I·have·become a·man, I·have·fully·put·to·rest
G0435.2 N-NPM ἄνδρες (29x)
Jn 6:10 Accordingly, the men sat·back·to·eat; the number

Lk 5:18 And behold, men carrying a·man·of·clay† upon a·
Lk 7:20 And coming·close to him, the men declared, "John
Lk 9:14 For there·were about five·thousand men. And he·
Lk 9:30 behold, two men were·speaking·together with·him,
Lk 11:32 "Men of·Nineveh shall·rise·up in the Final·Tribunal
Lk 17:12 ·and·met him ten leprous men who stood·still
Lk 22:63 And the men, the·ones confining Jesus, were·
Lk 24:4 this, behold, two men stood·over them in clothes
Ac 1:10 behold, two men had·stood·nearby them in white
Ac 2:5 residing in JeruSalem, devout men from every nation
Ac 5:25 "Behold, the men whom yeu·placed in the prison·
Ac 8:2 And devout men went·in·procession·together·to·bury
Ac 8:12 they·were·immersed, both men and women.
Ac 9:7 And the men traveling·together with·him stood in·
Ac 10:17 ·saw, yet behold, the men (the·ones having·been·
Ac 10:19 "Behold, three men seek you.
Ac 11:11 ·this·same·hour, three men were·standing·over *the*
Ac 11:20 some from·among them were men of·Cyprus and
Ac 17:34 But certain men, being·tightly·joined to·him,
Ac 19:7 And there·were about twelve men *in* all.
Ac 20:30 from·among yeu yeurselves, men shall·rise·up,
Ac 21:23 With·us are four men having a·vow upon
Ac 23:21 ·for him *are* more·than forty men, who vowed·and·
Mt 12:41 "Men of·Nineveh shall·rise·up in the Final·Tribunal
Mt 14:21 eating were about five·thousand men, apart·from
Mt 14:35 And once·recognizing him, the men of·that place
Mt 15:38 ·ones eating were four·thousand men, apart·from
Mk 6:44 ·the loaves·of·bread were about five·thousand men.

G0435.2 N-VPM ἄνδρες (29x)

Ac 1:11 who also declared, "Yeu·men of·Galilee, why·do
Ac 1:16 "Men, brothers, it·was·mandatory·for this Scripture
Ac 2:14 clearly·enunciated to·them, "Yeu·men of·Judea and
Ac 2:22 "Men, Israelites, hear these words: Jesus of·
Ac 2:29 "Men, brothers, it·is·being·proper to·declare to yeu
Ac 2:37 and to·the rest of·the·ambassadors, "Men, brothers,
Ac 3:12 answered to the people, "Men, Israelites, why do·
Ac 5:35 to *the joint·council*, "Men, Israelites, take·heed to·
Ac 7:2 And *Stephen* replied, "Men, brothers and fathers,
Ac 7:26 peace, declaring, 'Men, yeu·yeurselves are brothers
Ac 13:15 to them, saying, "Men, brothers, if there·is within
Ac 13:16 ·his hand, declared, "Men, Israelites and the·ones
Ac 13:26 "Men, brothers, the·Sons of·AbRaham by·birth,
Ac 13:38 "Now·then, men, brothers, be·it known to·yeu that
Ac 14:15 and saying, "Men, why·do yeu·do these·things?
Ac 15:7 declared to them, "Men, brothers, yeu·yeurselves
Ac 15:13 answered, saying, "Men, brothers, listen·to me.
Ac 17:22 of·Mars'·Hill, replied, "Men, Athenians, I·observe
Ac 19:25 he·declared, "Men, yeu·are·fully·aware that our
Ac 19:35 the town·clerk replied, "Men, Ephesians, for what
Ac 21:28 while·yelling·out, "Men, Israelites, swiftly·help!
Ac 22:1 "Men, brothers and fathers, hear my defense *which*
Ac 23:1 ·council·of·Sanhedrin, declared, "Men, brothers, I·
Ac 23:6 in the joint·council·of·Sanhedrin, "Men, brothers, I·
Ac 25:24 and all the men being·present·together with·us,
Ac 27:10 saying to·them, "Men, I·observe that the
Ac 27:21 declared, "O Men, in·fact it·was·necessary *for·yeu*
Ac 27:25 "Therefore, men, cheer·up! For I·trust God, that
Ac 28:17 he·was·saying to them, "Men, brothers, I·myself,

G0435.2 N-ASM ἄνδρα (15x)

Lk 1:34 since I·do·not have·intimate·knowledge·of a·man?"
Ac 2:22 of·Natsareth, a·man having·been·exhibited by God
Ac 3:14 Righteous·One, and requested a·man, a·murderer,
Ac 6:5 And they·selected Stephen, a·man full of·trust and
Ac 9:12 in a·clear·vision a·man by·the·name·of AnanIas
Ac 13:21 Saul son of·Qish, a·man from·among *the* tribe of·
Ac 13:22 the *son* of·Jesse, *to·be* a·man according·to my·own
Ac 21:11 at JeruSalem shall·bind the man who owns this belt
Ac 23:27 This man *was* already·being·arrested by the
Ac 23:30 to·my attention against the man, *which·was* about
Ac 24:5 "For after·finding this man *to·be* a·viral·pestilence,
Ac 25:17 ·ordered the man to·be·brought·forth.
Mk 6:20 *that* he was·a·righteous and holy man, and he·was·
1Co 11:9 woman, but·rather woman on·account·of the man.

Eph 4:13 Son of·God, into a·complete man, into a·measure

G0435.2 N-APM ἄνδρας (20x)

Lk 9:32 his glory and the two men, the·ones having·stood·
Ac 6:3 from·among yeurselves seven men being·attested·to,
Ac 6:11 Then they·secretly·induced men to·say, "We·have·
Ac 8:3 *of* the houses *and* dragging·off both men and women,
Ac 9:2 of·The Way, whether being men or women, he·may·
Ac 9:38 the disciples dispatched two men to him, imploring
Ac 10:5 And now send men to Joppa and send·for Simon,
Ac 10:21 Now after·walking·down to the men (the·ones
Ac 11:3 "You·entered·in alongside men being uncircumcised
Ac 11:13 and declaring to·him, 'Dispatch men to Joppa and
Ac 15:22 to·send men being·selected from·among
Ac 15:22 and Silas, men who·officially·are·leading among
Ac 15:25 ·same·determination, to·send selected men to yeu
Ac 17:5 ·taking·to·themselves certain evil men of·the riffraff
Ac 19:37 For yeu·brought these men *here*, *who·are* neither
Ac 21:26 after·personally·taking the men on·the following
Ac 21:38 leading the four·thousand men of·the Assassins out
Ac 22:4 and handing·over into prisons both men and women.
Rm 11:4 I·reserved to·myself seven·thousand men, who did·
1Ti 2:8 Accordingly, I·resolve *for* the men to·pray in every

G0435.2 N-DSM ἀνδρί (12x)

Lk 1:27 ·virgin having·been·espoused to·a·man whose name
Lk 19:7 to·lodge with a·man *who·is* morally·disqualified!"
Ac 10:28 a·statutory·offense for·a·man that·is·a·Jew to·be·
Ac 13:7 Paulus, *who·was* an·intelligent man. This·man,
Ac 17:31 ' by *that* man whom he·specifically·determined,
Ac 25:5 *with·me*, legally·accuse this man, if there·is any
Mt 7:24 I·shall·liken him to·a·prudent man who built his
Mt 7:26 them, shall·be·likened to·a·foolish man, who built
Mk 10:2 him, "Is·it·proper for·a·man to·divorce *his* wife?
Rm 7:3 if she·should·come to·another man with·the husband
Rm 7:3 by·becoming *yoked·together* with·another man.
Jac 1:23 has·directly·resembled a·man fully·observing his

G0435.2 N-DPM ἀνδράσιν (1x)

Ac 25:23 and the most prominent men of·the city, and with·

G0435.2 N-GSM ἀνδρός (11x)

Jn 1:13 nor from·out of·*the*·will of·man, but·rather birthed·
Ac 9:13 of many·things concerning this man, what·many
Ac 11:12 with·me, and we·entered into the man's house.
Jac 1:20 For man's wrath does·not accomplish God's
1Co 11:3 that the head of·every man is the Anointed-One,
1Co 11:7 ·image and glory, but woman is man's glory.
1Co 11:8 of·woman, but·rather woman from·out of·man.
1Co 11:11 neither *is* woman apart·from man, in *the* Lord.
1Co 11:12 woman *is* from·out of·the man, in·this·manner the
1Ti 2:12 to·take·a·stance·of·authority·over a·man, but·rather
1Ti 5:9 sixty years·of·age, having·been a·wife of·one man,

G0435.2 N-GPM ἀνδρῶν (7x)

Lk 11:31 the Final·Tribunal with the men of·this generation,
Lk 14:24 that not·even·one of·those men, the·ones having·
Ac 1:21 it·is·mandatory·of·the men going·together with·us
Ac 4:4 and the number of·the men was about five thousand.
Ac 5:14 ·*citizenry*, multitudes both of·men and of·women)
Ac 5:36 a·number of·men tightly·bonded·themselves, about
Ac 17:12 not a·few of·the dignified Greek women and men.

EG0435.2 (10x)

Jn 6:10 ·to·eat; the number *was* about five·thousand *men*.
Lk 17:36 [(Two *men* shall·be in the field; one shall·be·
Lk 24:5 the face toward the earth, *the men* declared to them,
Mt 16:9 five loaves·of·bread of·the five·thousand *men*, and
Mt 16:10 loaves·of·bread of·the four·thousand *men*, and
Mk 8:9 ·ones eating were about four·thousand *men*, and he·
Mk 8:19 ·of·bread among the five·thousand *men*, how·many
Mk 8:20 ·*of·bread* among the four·thousand *men*, how·many
1Co 7:2 sexual·immoralities, each *man* must·have his·own
1Ti 3:13 For the *men* already·attending well do·acquire for·

G0435.3 N-NSM ἀνήρ (12x)

Jn 4:18 you·have is not your husband. This·thing you·have·
Mt 1:19 Now Joseph her husband, being a·righteous *man* and
Rm 7:2 but if the husband should·die, she·has·been·fully·
Rm 7:3 But if the husband should·die, she·is freed from the

Tit 1:6 ·any·charge·of·wrong·doing, a·husband of·one wife,
1Co 7:3 The husband must·render to·the wife the kind·
1Co 7:4 her·own body, but·rather the husband. And likewise
1Co 7:4 also, the husband does·not have·control·over his·
1Co 7:14 the non-trusting husband has·been·made·holy by
1Co 7:39 over a·lifetime as·long·as her husband lives. But if
1Co 7:39 But if her husband should·be·laid·to·rest·*(that·is,*·,
Eph 5:23 because the husband is head of·the wife, even as

G0435.3 N-NPM ἄνδρες (5x)

1Pe 3:7 *Now* likewise the husbands: *be* dwelling·together
Eph 5:25 *Now* the husbands: Yeu·must·love yeur·own wives
Eph 5:28 In·this·manner, the husbands are·obligated·to·love
Col 3:19 *Now* the husbands: Yeu·must·love the wives, and
1Ti 3:12 Stewards must·be husbands of·one wife, conducting

G0435.3 N-VSM ἄνερ (1x)

1Co 7:16 do·you·personally·know, O·husband, whether

G0435.3 N-ASM ἄνδρα (14x)

Jn 4:16 Head·on·out, holler·out·for your husband, and come
Jn 4:17 and declared, "I·do·not have a·husband." Jesus says
Jn 4:17 "You·declared well, 'I·do·not have a·husband.'
Ac 5:9 the feet of·the·ones burying your husband *are* at the
Ac 5:10 carrying·*her*·out, buried *her* alongside her husband.
Gal 4:27 more children than the·one having the husband."'
Mt 1:16 Jacob begot Joseph the husband of·Mariam, from·
Mk 10:12 should·divorce her husband and should·be·married
1Co 7:2 wife, and each *woman* must·have her·own husband.
1Co 7:11 to·her husband. And a·husband *is* not to·leave *his*
1Co 7:13 a·wife who has a·non-trusting husband also— *if*
1Co 7:16 whether you·shall·save the husband? Or what do·
Eph 5:33 ·that she·should·reverently·fear *her·own* husband.
1Ti 3:2 ·all·blame·and·suspicion, a·husband of·one wife,

G0435.3 N-APM ἄνδρας (1x)

Jn 4:18 For you·have·had five husbands, and now, he·whom

G0435.3 N-DSM ἀνδρί (7x)

Rm 7:2 ·bound by·Torah-Law to·the living husband; but if
1Co 7:3 ·due, and likewise also the wife to·the husband.
1Co 7:11 or she·must·be·reconciled to·her husband. And a·
1Co 7:14 has·been·made·holy by the husband; otherwise
1Co 7:34 world, how she·shall·accommodate the husband.
2Co 11:2 for I·betrothed yeu to·one husband, to·present *yeu*
Rv 21:2 as a·bride having·been·adorned for·her husband.

G0435.3 N-DPM ἀνδράσιν (6x)

1Pe 3:1 be·submitting·yeurselves to·yeur·own husbands,
1Pe 3:5 while·being·in·subjection to·their·own husbands,
Tit 2:5 ·submitted to·their·own husbands in·order·that the
Eph 5:22 ·must·submit·yeurselves to·yeur·own husbands, as
Eph 5:24 also the wives to·their·own husbands in everything.
Col 3:18 ·must·submit·yeurselves to·yeur·own husbands, as

G0435.3 N-GSM ἀνδρός (5x)

Lk 2:36 *a·widow* after·living with a·husband seven years
Lk 16:18 ·divorced from *her* husband commits·adultery.
Rm 7:2 from the *particular* Torah-Law of·the husband.
Rm 7:3 ·come to·another man with·the husband still·living,
1Co 7:10 a·wife *is* not to·be·separated from *her* husband.

G0435.4 N-APM ἄνδρας (1x)

1Co 14:35 they·must·inquire·of their·own menfolk at home

G0436 ἀνθ•ίστημι anthístēmi *v.* (14x)

Roots:G0473 G2476 Compare:G0496 G0498
xLangAlso:H8617

G0436.2 V-2AAM-2P ἀντίστητε (2x)

Jac 4:7 ·yeurselves to·God. Stand·up·against the Slanderer,
1Pe 5:9 whom yeu·must·stand·up·against, solid in·the trust,

G0436.3 V-2AAI-1S ἀντέστην (1x)

Gal 2:11 Peter came to Antioch, I·withstood him in *his* face,

G0436.3 V-2AAN ἀντιστῆναι (2x)

Lk 21:15 be·able to·declare·against nor·even to·withstand.
Eph 6:13 in·order·that yeu·may·be·able to·withstand *them* in

G0436.3 V-RAI-3S ἀνθέστηκεν (1x)

Rm 9:19 ·he·find·fault? For who has·withstood his resolve?

G0436.4 V-PMI-3P ἀνθίστανται (1x)

2Ti 3:8 in·this·manner these also stand·opposed·to the truth

G0436.4 V-IMI-3S ἀνθίστατο (1x)

Ac 13:8 *from·Arabic*), stood·opposed·to them seeking to·

G0436.4 V-2AAI-3P ἀντέστησαν (1x)

2Ti 3:8 as Jannes and Jambres stood·opposed·to Moses, in·

G0436.4 V-2AAN ἀντιστῆναι (2x)

Ac 6:10 ·were·not having·strength to·withstand the wisdom
Mt 5:39 say to·yeu, not to·stand·opposed·to the evil·person,

G0436.4 V-RAI-3S ἀνθέστηκεν (2x)

Rm 13:2 the authority has·stood·opposed·to the institution
2Ti 4:15 for exceedingly he·has·stood·opposed·to our

G0436.4 V-RAP-NPM ἀνθεστηκότες (1x)

Rm 13:2 the·ones having·stood·opposed·to *it* shall·receive

G0437 ἀνθ•ομο•λογέομαι anthômôlôgêômai *v.* (1x)

Roots:G0473 G3670

G0437.2 V-INI-3S ἀνθωμολογεῖτο (1x)

Lk 2:38 responded·likewise·in·affirmation to·Yahweh and

G0438 ἄνθος ánthôs *n.* (4x)

Compare:G2918 xLangAlso:H6731 H5339 H6525

G0438 N-NSN ἄνθος (4x)

Jac 1:10 humiliation, because as a·flower of·grass, he·shall·
Jac 1:11 'it·withered the grass, and its flower fell·away,' and
1Pe 1:24 man·of·clay's† glory *is* as *the* flower of·grass."
1Pe 1:24 grass is·withered, and its flower already·fell·away,

G0439 ἀνθρακιά anthrakiá *n.* (2x)

Roots:G0440

G0439.2 N-ASF ἀνθρακιάν (2x)

Jn 18:18 *there*, having·made a·fire·of·coals because it·was
Jn 21:9 the dry·ground, they·look·upon a·fire·of·coals, and

G0440 ἄνθραξ ánthrax *n.* (1x)

See:G0439 xLangAlso:H1513

G0440.1 N-APM ἄνθρακας (1x)

Rm 12:20 this, you·shall·stack burning·coals of·fire on his

G0441 ἀνθρωπ•άρεσκος anthrōpárêskôs *adj.* (2x)

Roots:G0444 G0700

G0441 A-NPM ἀνθρωπάρεσκοι (2x)

Eph 6:6 according·to eyeservice as men-pleasers†, but·rather
Col 3:22 not with eyeservice as men-pleasers†, but·rather

G0442 ἀνθρ•ώπινος anthrṓpinôs *adj.* (7x)

Roots:G0444

G0442.1 A-NSM ἀνθρώπινος (1x)

1Co 10:13 *that·which is common to* mankind†. But God *is*

G0442.1 A-DSF ἀνθρωπίνῃ (2x)

Jac 3:7 and has·been·tamed by·the nature of·mankind†.
1Pe 2:13 created·governance of·mankind† on·account·of the

G0442.1 A-GSF ἀνθρωπίνης (3x)

1Co 2:4 not with persuasive words of·mankind's† wisdom,
1Co 2:13 not with instructive words of·mankind's† wisdom,
1Co 4:3 by yeu, or by mankind's† daylight. Moreover, I·

G0442.2 A-ASN ἀνθρώπινον (1x)

Rm 6:19 *this* after·the·manner·of·men† on·account·of the

G0443 ἀνθρ•ωπο•κτόνος anthrōpôktônôs *adj.* (3x)

Roots:G0444 G2932-1 Compare:G0409 G5406 See:G0615

G0443 A-NSM ἀνθρωποκτόνος (3x)

Jn 8:44 of·yeur father. That·one was a·man-killer† from *the*
1Jn 3:15 presently·hating his brother is a·man-killer†. And
1Jn 3:15 ·know that any man-killer† does·not have eternal

G0444 ἄνθρ•ωπος ánthrōpôs *n.* (569x)

Roots:G0435 G3700 Compare:G0076 G1027-1 G2349
xLangEquiv:H0120 xLangAlso:H0121

EG0444.2 (1x)

Mt 8:27 saying, "What·manner·of *clay·being* is this that

G0444.3 N-NSM ἄνθρωπος (118x)

Jn 1:6 There·came a·man·of·clay† having·been·dispatched
Jn 2:10 to·him, "Every man·of·clay† first places·out the
Jn 3:1 There·was a·man·of·clay† from·among the Pharisees,
Jn 3:4 says to him, "How·is a·man·of·clay† able to·be·born,
Jn 3:27 and declared, "A·man·of·clay† is·not able to·receive
Jn 4:50 And the man·of·clay† trusted the word that Jesus
Jn 5:5 And a·certain man·of·clay† was there, being in the
Jn 5:9 immediately the man·of·clay† was healthy·and·sound.
Jn 5:12 "Who is the man·of·clay†, the·one declaring to·you,
Jn 5:15 The man·of·clay† went·off and reported·in·detail to·
Jn 7:46 ·time in·this·manner *has* a·man·of·clay† spoken as
Jn 7:46 a·man·of·clay† spoken as *does* this man·of·clay†."
Jn 9:11 "A·man·of·clay† being·referred·to·as Jesus, he·
Jn 9:16 were·saying, "This man·of·clay† is not personally·
Jn 9:16 "How·is a·man·of·clay†, full·of·moral·failure, able
Jn 9:24 ·know that this man·of·clay† is full·of·moral·failure.
Jn 9:30 The man·of·clay† answered and declared to·them,
Jn 10:33 because you, being a·man·of·clay†, make yourself
Jn 11:47 ·do we·do, because this man·of·clay† does many
Jn 11:50 for·us that one man·of·clay† should·die on·behalf
Jn 19:5 "See, the man·of·clay†!"
Lk 2:25 And behold, there·was a·man·of·clay† in JeruSalem
Lk 2:25 Simeon, and the·same man·of·clay† *was* righteous
Lk 4:4 "The man·of·clay† shall·live not upon bread alone,
Lk 4:33 gathering, there·was a·man·of·clay† having a·spirit
Lk 6:6 Yet there·was *a·certain* man·of·clay† there and his
Lk 6:45 "The beneficially·good man·of·clay†, from·out of·
Lk 6:45 And the evil man·of·clay†, from·out of·the evil
Lk 7:8 I·myself am a·man·of·clay† being·assigned under
Lk 7:34 and yeu·say, 'Behold a·man·of·clay†, a·glutton and
Lk 9:25 "For how·is a·man·of·clay† benefited, after·gaining
Lk 10:30 "A·certain man·of·clay† was·walking·down from
Lk 13:19 of·mustard·seed, which a·man·of·clay† took *and*
Lk 14:2 there·was a·certain man·of·clay† before him
Lk 14:16 "A·certain man·of·clay† made a·great supper and
Lk 14:30 saying, 'This man·of·clay† began to·build yet did·
Lk 15:4 "What man·of·clay† from·among yeu, having a·
Lk 15:11 he·declared, "A·certain man·of·clay† had two sons
Lk 16:1 a·certain wealthy man·of·clay† who was·retaining
Lk 16:19 "There·was a·certain wealthy man·of·clay†, and
Lk 19:12 he·declared, "A·man·of·clay†, a·certain nobleman,
Lk 19:21 you·are an·unrelenting man·of·clay†. You·take·up
Lk 19:22 ·myself am an·unrelenting man·of·clay†, taking·up
Lk 20:9 people, "A·certain man·of·clay† planted a·vineyard
Lk 22:10 into the City, a·man·of·clay† bearing a·pitcher of·
Lk 23:6 inquired whether the man·of·clay† was a·Galilean.
Lk 23:47 "Really, this man·of·clay† was a·righteous·man."
Ac 4:22 For the man·of·clay† was more·than forty years·of·
Ac 6:13 saying, "This man·of·clay† does·not cease speaking
Ac 10:26 "Stand·up, *for* also·I myself am a·man·of·clay†."
Ac 19:16 fully·dominating them, the man·of·clay†, whom
Ac 19:35 Ephesians, for what man·of·clay† is·there that
Ac 21:28 This is the man·of·clay† instructing all·men
Ac 21:39 "In·fact, I·myself am a·man·of·clay† *who·is* a·Jew
Ac 22:26 ·about to·do, for this man·of·clay† is a·Roman."
Ac 26:31 "This man·of·clay† practices not·even·one·thing
Ac 26:32 "This man·of·clay† was·able to·have·been·fully·
Ac 28:4 one·another, "This man·of·clay† is entirely a·
Heb 8:2 which Yahweh set·up and not a·man·of·clay†.
Heb 13:6 be·afraid of·what a·man·of·clay† shall·do to·me."
Gal 2:16 that a·man·of·clay† is·not regarded·as·righteous as·
Gal 3:12 ·rather, "The man·of·clay† doing them shall·live
Gal 6:1 even though a·man·of·clay† should·be·overtaken in
Gal 6:7 for whatever a·man·of·clay† should·sow, that also
Mt 4:4 "It·has·been·written, "A·man·of·clay† shall·live not
Mt 7:9 "Or what man·of·clay† is·there from·among yeu, who
Mt 8:9 For even I·myself am a·man·of·clay† under authority,
Mt 11:19 they·say, 'Behold, a·man·of·clay†, a·glutton and
Mt 12:10 And behold, there·was a·man·of·clay† having the
Mt 12:11 "What man·of·clay† shall·there·be from·among
Mt 12:12 by·how·much·does a·man·of·clay† surpass·the· of·
Mt 12:35 beneficially·good man·of·clay† from·out of·the
Mt 12:35 and the evil man·of·clay† from·out of·his evil
Mt 13:28 ·replied to·them, 'A·hostile man·of·clay† did this.'
Mt 13:31 (which after·taking, a·man·of·clay† sowed in his
Mt 13:44 in·a·field, which a·man·of·clay†, after·finding *it*,
Mt 16:26 "For what·is a·man·of·clay† being·benefited, if he·
Mt 16:26 *is·it that* a·man·of·clay† shall·give in·exchange
Mt 19:5 For·this cause a·man·of·clay† shall·leave·behind the
Mt 19:6 yoked·together, a·man·of·clay† must·not separate."
Mt 21:33 ·was a·certain man·of·clay†, a·master·of·the·house
Mt 25:14 *is* just·as a·man·of·clay† journeying·abroad, *who*
Mt 25:24 you that you·are a·hard man·of·clay†, reaping
Mt 26:24 better for·him if that man·of·clay† was·not born."
Mt 27:57 there·came a·wealthy man·of·clay† of Arimathaea,
Mk 1:23 there·was a·man·of·clay† with an·impure spirit,
Mk 3:1 and there·was a·man·of·clay† there having the
Mk 4:26 "*It·is* as though a·man·of·clay† should·cast the
Mk 5:2 ·the chamber·tombs a·man·of·clay† with an·impure
Mk 7:11 say, 'If a·man·of·clay† should·declare to·his father
Mk 8:37 ·is·it *that* a·man·of·clay† shall·give in·exchange
Mk 10:7 ·this cause a·man·of·clay† shall·leave·behind his
Mk 10:9 yoked·together, a·man·of·clay† must·not separate."
Mk 13:34 *is* as a·man·of·clay† taking·a·long·journey·abroad,
Mk 14:13 the City, and a·man·of·clay† bearing a·pitcher of·
Mk 14:21 better for·him if that man·of·clay† was·not born."
Mk 15:39 "Truly this man·of·clay† was a·son of·God.
Rm 3:4 be true, but every man·of·clay† a·liar; just·as it·has·
Rm 6:6 old man·of·clay† is·already·crucified·together *with*·
Rm 7:24 I·myself *am* a·miserable man·of·clay†! Who shall·
Rm 10:5 "The man·of·clay† doing them shall·live by them
Jac 1:7 For that man·of·clay† must·not imagine that he·shall·
Jac 1:19 beloved brothers, every man·of·clay† must·be swift
Jac 2:24 of·works, a·man·of·clay† is·regarded·as·righteous,
Jac 5:17 EliJah was a·man·of·clay† of·like·passions with·us,
Php 2:8 ·a·schematic·layout as a·man·of·clay†, he·humbled
1Pe 3:4 *according·to* the hidden man·of·clay† of·the heart,
1Co 2:14 But a·soulish man·of·clay† does·not accept the·
1Co 4:1 Let a·man·of·clay† reckon us in·this·manner: as
1Co 6:18 provided·that a·man·of·clay† should·commit *it*, is
1Co 11:28 But a·man·of·clay† must·examine·and·verify
1Co 15:45 "The first man·of·clay†, Adam, came·into·
1Co 15:47 The first man·of·clay† *was* from·out of·soil, *as*
1Co 15:47 The second man·of·clay† *is* the Lord from·out
2Co 4:16 our outward man·of·clay† is·thoroughly·decaying·,
Eph 5:31 of·this, a·man·of·clay† shall·leave·behind his
1Ti 2:5 and men·of·clay†: a·man·of·clay†, Anointed-One
Rv 4:7 *is* having the face as a·man·of·clay†, and the fourth

G0444.3 N-NPM ἄνθρωποι (28x)

Jn 3:19 the world, and the men·of·clay† loved the darkness
Jn 6:14 a·miraculous·sign, the men·of·clay† were·saying,
Lk 2:15 heaven, also *that* the men·of·clay†, the shepherds,
Lk 6:22 ·yeu, whenever the men·of·clay† should·hate yeu,
Lk 6:26 whenever all the men·of·clay† should·declare well
Lk 6:31 ·as yeu·want that the men·of·clay† should·do to·yeu,
Lk 11:44 indistinct·ones, and the men·of·clay† walking over
Lk 18:10 "Two men·of·clay† walked·up to the Sanctuary·
Ac 4:13 and untrained men·of·clay†, they·were·marveling;
Ac 14:15 also are men·of·clay† of·like·passions with·yeu,
Ac 16:17 saying, "These men·of·clay† are slaves of·God
Ac 16:20 ·declared, "These men·of·clay†, inherently·being
Heb 6:16 For men·of·clay† in·fact swear by·the·one greater·
Heb 7:8 ·fact, *are* tithes *that* dying men·of·clay† receive, but
Mt 7:12 ·should·want that the men·of·clay† should·do to·yeu
Mt 8:27 But the men·of·clay† marveled, saying, "What·
Mt 12:36 which if the men·of·clay† should·speak *it*, they·
Mt 16:13 saying, "Who·do the men·of·clay† say me to·be—
Mk 8:27 to·them, "Who·do the men·of·clay† say me to·be?
Jud 1:4 For some men·of·clay† crept·into·place·unawares,
2Pe 1:21 by *the* Holy Spirit, men·of·clay† (the holy·ones
2Ti 3:2 For the men·of·clay† shall·be: selfish·and·
2Ti 3:8 stand·opposed·to the truth, men·of·clay† *with* their
2Ti 3:13 But evil men·of·clay† and adept·smooth·talkers
Rv 9:6 in those days, the men·of·clay† shall·seek Death and
Rv 16:9 the men·of·clay† were·burned·by·the·sun with·great
Rv 16:18 ·not happen since the men·of·clay† were upon the
Rv 16:21 men·of·clay†. And the men·of·clay† reviled God

G0444.3 N-VSM ἄνθρωπε (8x)

Lk 5:20 he·declared to·him, "Man·of·clay†, your moral·
Lk 12:14 he·declared to·him, "Man·of·clay†, who fully·
Lk 22:58 And Peter declared, "Man·of·clay†, I·am not!"
Lk 22:60 And Peter declared, "Man·of·clay†, I·do·not
Rm 2:1 you·are without·exoneration, O man·of·clay†! For
Rm 2:3 And do·you·reckon this, O man·of·clay† (the·one
Rm 9:20 As·a·matter·of·fact, O man·of·clay†, who are you·

Jac 2:20 ·you·want to·know, O empty man·of·clay†, that the
G0444.3 N-ASM ἄνθρωπον (56x)
Jn 4:29 "Come·here! See a·man·of·clay† who declared to·
Jn 5:7 "Sir, I·have no man·of·clay†, whenever the water
Jn 7:23 I·made a·whole man·of·clay† healthy·and·sound on
Jn 7:51 ·Does our Oral-law judge the man·of·clay†, unless it·
Jn 8:40 yeu·seek to·kill me, a·man·of·clay† that has·spoken
Jn 9:1 he·saw a·man·of·clay† who·was·blind from·out of·
Jn 9:24 ·time they·hollered·out·for the man·of·clay† that was
Jn 18:14 one man·of·clay† to·be·completely·destroyed on·
Lk 5:18 men carrying a·man·of·clay† upon a·simple·couch
Lk 7:25 to·see? A·man·of·clay† having·been·enrobed in soft
Lk 8:35 to Jesus and found the man·of·clay† from whom the
Lk 18:2 God and not being·respectful·of man·of·clay†.
Lk 18:4 God, and I·am·not respectful·of *any* man·of·clay†,
Lk 23:14 "Yeu·brought this man·of·clay† to·me as one·
Ac 4:14 And looking·upon the man·of·clay†, the·one
Ac 9:33 And there he·found a·certain man·of·clay†, Aeneas
Ac 10:28 to·refer·to not·even·one man·of·clay† *as* defiled or
Ac 22:25 for·yeu to·scourge a·man·of·clay† *who·is* a·Roman
Ac 25:16 ·hand·over any man·of·clay† to total·destruction,
Gal 1:11 by me is not according·to a·man·of·clay†.
Mt 10:35 I·came to·split "a·man·of·clay† against his father,
Mt 11:8 to·see? A·man·of·clay† having·been·enrobed in
Mt 15:11 mouth *that* defiles the man·of·clay†, but·rather the·
Mt 15:11 *indeed*, this·thing defiles the man·of·clay†."
Mt 15:18 heart, and·these·things defile the man·of·clay†.
Mt 15:20 These are the·things defiling the man·of·clay†.
Mt 15:20 hands does·not defile the man·of·clay†."
Mt 22:11 ·the·meal, he·saw a·man·of·clay† there having·not
Mt 26:72 "I·do·not personally·know the man·of·clay†."
Mt 26:74 "I·do·not personally·know the man·of·clay†." And
Mt 27:32 *of·the City*, they·found a·man·of·clay†, a·Cyrenian
Mk 7:15 him, those are the·things defiling the man·of·clay†.
Mk 7:18 from·outside into the man·of·clay† is·not able to·
Mk 7:20 man·of·clay†, that·thing defiles the man·of·clay†.
Mk 7:23 from·inside, and they·defile the man·of·clay†."
Mk 8:36 "For how shall·it·benefit a·man·of·clay†, if he·
Mk 14:71 ·know this man·of·clay† to·whom yeu·refer."
Rm 3:5 *this line of·reasoning* according·to a·man·of·clay†).
Rm 3:28 *that* a·man·of·clay† *is* to·be·regarded·as·righteous
Rm 7:22 of·God according·to the inner man·of·clay†,
1Th 4:8 *·forth*, *it·is* not a·man·of·clay† *that* he·ignores, but·
Tit 3:10 Shun a·man·of·clay† that·is·divisively·selective
1Co 3:3 fleshly, and walk according·to men·of·clay†?
1Co 9:8 ·speak these·things according·to a·man·of·clay†? Or
1Co 15:32 *the striving·of* men·of·clay†, I·fought·with·wild·
2Co 12:2 I·personally·know a·man·of·clay† in
2Co 12:3 And I·personally·know such a·man·of·clay†,
Eph 2:15 in himself into one brand-new man·of·clay†, *thus*
Eph 3:16 ·power through his Spirit in the inner man·of·clay†,
Eph 4:22 to·put·off the old man·of·clay† according·to the
Eph 4:24 ·with the brand-new man·of·clay† (the·one
Col 1:28 admonishing every man·of·clay† and instructing
Col 1:28 ·of·clay† and instructing every man·of·clay† in all
Col 1:28 we·may·present every man·of·clay† complete in
Col 3:9 ·stripped·off the old man·of·clay† together with·his
Rv 9:5 whenever he·should·strike a·man·of·clay†.
G0444.3 N-ASM@ ἄνθρωπον (1x)
Gal 3:15 according·to a·man·of·clay†, that·in·the·same·
G0444.3 N-APM ἀνθρώπους (30x)
Jn 6:10 "Make the men·of·clay† to·sit·back·to·eat." Now
Lk 5:10 ·on, you·shall·be capturing·alive men·of·clay†."
Lk 7:31 shall·I·liken the men·of·clay† of·this generation?
Lk 11:46 ·load·up the men·of·clay† with·oppressive loads,
Lk 13:4 above·and·beyond all men·of·clay† residing in
Ac 16:35 saying, "Fully·release those men·of·clay†."
Ac 16:37 thrashing us uncondemned men·of·clay†, *though*
Ac 18:13 persistently·persuades men·of·clay† to·reverence
Ac 22:15 to all men·of·clay† of·what you·have·clearly·seen
Ac 24:16 ·offense toward God and *toward* the men·of·clay†.
Heb 7:28 fully·establishes men·of·clay† *as* high·priests
Gal 1:10 at·this·moment, do·I·comply·with men·of·clay†, or
Mt 5:19 and should·instruct the men·of·clay† in·this·manner,
Mt 13:25 at the *time for* the men·of·clay† to·sleep, his enemy
Mk 8:24 "I·look·upon the men·of·clay† as how I·clearly·
Rm 5:12 went·through into all men·of·clay† upon this·very
Rm 5:18 all men·of·clay† unto a·verdict·of·condemnation;
Rm 5:18 all men·of·clay† unto an·acquittal·in·righteousness
Jac 3:9 with it, we·curse the men·of·clay†, the·ones having·
1Pe 4:6 in·fact according·to men·of·clay† in·*the*·flesh, but
Tit 3:2 *but* fair, indicating all gentleness to all men·of·clay†.
1Co 7:7 For I·want all men·of·clay† to·be also as myself.
2Co 5:11 fear of·the Lord, we·persuade men·of·clay†. But
1Ti 2:4 who wants all men·of·clay† to·be·saved and to·come
1Ti 6:9 which suck the men·of·clay† down in a·savage·
Rv 9:4 , but·yet only the men·of·clay† who do·not have the
Rv 9:10 to·bring·harm·to the men·of·clay† five lunar·months
Rv 16:2 evil pus·sore to the men·of·clay†, the·ones having
Rv 16:8 to·him to·burn the men·of·clay† with solar·radiation
Rv 16:21 out of·the heaven upon the men·of·clay†. And the
G0444.3 N-DSM ἀνθρώπῳ (27x)
Jn 2:25 ·himself was·knowing what was in the man·of·clay†.
Lk 6:8 And *Jesus* declared to·the man·of·clay†, the·one
Lk 6:10 all, he·declared to·the man·of·clay†, "Stretch·forth
Lk 6:48 "He·is like a·man·of·clay† building a·home, who
Lk 6:49 doing, is like a·man·of·clay† building a·home apart·
Lk 22:22 woe to·that man·of·clay† through whom he·is·
Lk 23:4 "I·find not·even·one fault in this man·of·clay†."
Lk 23:14 in this man·of·clay† according·to those·things·of·
Ac 23:9 not·even·one wrong in this man·of·clay†, but if a·
Gal 5:3 again to·every man·of·clay† being·circumcised, that
Mt 12:13 Then he·says to·the man·of·clay†, "Stretch·out
Mt 13:24 heavens is·likened to·a·man·of·clay† sowing good
Mt 13:45 of·the heavens is like a·man·of·clay†, a·merchant
Mt 13:52 is like a·man·of·clay†, a·master·of·the·house, who
Mt 18:7 woe to·that man·of·clay† through whom the
Mt 18:12 ·happen *that* any man·of·clay† *has* a·hundred
Mt 18:23 of·the heavens is·likened to·a·man·of·clay†, a·king
Mt 19:3 "Is·it·proper for·a·man·of·clay† to·divorce his wife
Mt 20:1 is like a·man·of·clay†, a·master·of·the·house, who
Mt 26:24 but woe to·that man·of·clay† through whom the
Mk 3:3 And *Jesus* says to·the man·of·clay†, the·one having
Mk 3:5 hearts, he·says to·the man·of·clay†, "Stretch·out
Mk 14:21 but woe to·that man·of·clay† through whom the
Rm 14:20 *·is* morally·wrong for·the man·of·clay† *to·partake*,
1Co 7:1 to·me, *it·is* good for·a·man·of·clay† not to·lay·hold
1Co 7:26 good for·a·man·of·clay† to·behave in·this·manner:
2Co 12:4 is·not being·proper for·a·man·of·clay† to·speak.
G0444.3 N-DPM ἀνθρώποις (45x)
Jn 4:28 ·off into the city, and she·says to·the men·of·clay†,
Jn 17:6 apparent to·the men·of·clay† whom you·have·given
Lk 1:25 to·remove my lowly·reproach among men·of·clay†."
Lk 2:14 peace! Among men·of·clay†, a·delightful·purpose
Lk 2:52 personally·before God and men·of·clay†.
Lk 12:36 *·be* like men·of·clay† who·are·awaiting their·own
Lk 16:15 ·esteemed among men·of·clay† is an·abomination
Lk 18:27 *·are* impossible with men·of·clay† are possible
Ac 4:12 ·been·given among the men·of·clay† by which it·is·
Ac 4:16 "What shall·we·do to·these men·of·clay†? For that
Ac 5:4 heart? You·did·not lie to·men·of·clay†, but·rather to·
Ac 5:29 ·comply with·God rather than with·men·of·clay†.
Ac 5:35 to·accomplish concerning these men·of·clay†.
Ac 14:11 toward us being·in·the·likeness of·men·of·clay†."
Ac 15:26 men·of·clay† having·handed·over their souls on·
Ac 17:30 charges all the men·of·clay† everywhere to·repent.
Heb 9:27 ·is·laid·away for·the men·of·clay† to·die only·once
Gal 1:10 God? Or do·I·seek to·appease men·of·clay†? For if
Gal 1:10 For if yet I·was·appeasing men·of·clay†, I·would
Mt 6:5 they·may·be·apparent to·the men·of·clay†. Certainly
Mt 6:14 yeu·should·forgive the men·of·clay† their trespasses
Mt 6:15 ·should·not forgive the men·of·clay† their trespasses
Mt 6:16 ·may·be·appearing to·the men·of·clay† *to·be* fasting
Mt 6:18 ·not be·appearing to·the men·of·clay† *to·be* fasting,
Mt 9:8 God, the·one giving such authority to·men·of·clay†.
Mt 12:31 shall·be·forgiven to·the men·of·clay†, but the
Mt 12:31 Spirit shall·not be·forgiven to·the men·of·clay†.
Mt 19:26 to·them, "With men·of·clay† this is impossible,
Mt 23:5 them to·be·distinctly·viewed by·the men·of·clay†.
Mt 23:28 appear righteous to·the men·of·clay†, but inwardly
Mk 10:27 Jesus says, "With men·of·clay† *it·is* impossible,
Rm 14:18 and verifiably·approved by·the men·of·clay†.
Php 4:5 fairness, let·it·be·known to·all men·of·clay†. The
1Th 2:4 not as satisfying men·of·clay†, but·rather God, the·
1Th 2:15 ·God, even *being* antagonists to·all men·of·clay†
Tit 2:11 ·Salvation, became·apparent to·all men·of·clay†—
Tit 3:8 ·things and profitable·things for·the men·of·clay†.
1Co 3:21 do·not·let·one boast in men·of·clay†, for all·
1Co 4:9 to·the world, to·angels, and to·men·of·clay†.
1Co 14:2 ·tongue speaks not to·men·of·clay†, but·rather to·
1Co 14:3 prophesying speaks to·men·of·clay† *for* edification
Eph 4:8 *·itself*, and gave gifts to·the men·of·clay†.
Eph 6:7 being·slaves to·the Lord and not to·men·of·clay†,
Col 3:23 ·desire as to·the Lord and not to·men·of·clay†,
2Ti 2:2 ·things to·trustworthy men·of·clay† who shall·be
G0444.3 N-GSM ἀνθρώπου (42x)
Jn 2:25 should·testify concerning the man·of·clay†, for he·
Jn 5:27 Tribunal·judgment, because he·is·a·son of·clay†.
Jn 5:34 the testimony not from a·man·of·clay†, but·rather I·
Jn 18:17 from·among the disciples of·this man·of·clay†?"
Jn 18:29 do·yeu·bring against this man·of·clay†?"
Lk 8:29 spirit to·come·forth from the man·of·clay†, for many
Lk 8:33 And after·coming·out of·the man·of·clay†, the
Lk 11:24 should·go·forth from the man·of·clay†, it·goes
Lk 11:26 ·states of·that man·of·clay† become worse·than
Lk 12:16 wealthy man·of·clay† brought·forth·plentifully.
Ac 4:9 *the* good·deed for·the·feeble man·of·clay†— *over* by
Ac 5:28 to·bring the blood of·this man·of·clay† upon us."
Ac 12:22 *It·is* a·voice of·a·god, and not of·a·man·of·clay†."
Ac 17:29 by·*the*·art and *the* cogitation of·a·man·of·clay†.
Ac 25:22 "I·resolve also to·hear the man·of·clay† myself."
Heb 2:6 of·him? Or a·son of·clay†, that you·do·visit him?
Gal 1:1 ·of·clay†, neither through a·man·of·clay†, but·rather
Gal 1:12 personally·received it from a·man·of·clay†, nor
Gal 2:6 *the* personal·appearance of·a·man·of·clay†, for the·
Gal 3:15 a·covenant of·a·man·of·clay† *once* having·been·
Mt 10:36 *the* enemies of·the man·of·clay† *shall·be* his·own
Mt 12:43 should·come·out from the man·of·clay†, it·goes
Mt 12:45 ·states of·that man·of·clay† become worse·than
Mt 19:10 legal·charge of·the man·of·clay† is in·this·manner
Mk 5:8 Impure spirit, come·forth out of·the man·of·clay†.")
Mk 7:15 ·one·thing from·outside of·the man·of·clay†, that
Mk 7:20 proceeding·forth out of·the man·of·clay†, that·thing
Rm 2:9 upon every soul of·a·man·of·clay† performing the
Rm 4:6 ·blessedness of·the man·of·clay† to·whom God
Rm 5:12 just·as through one man·of·clay†, Moral·Failure
Rm 5:15 the grace of·the one man·of·clay†, Jesus Anointed,
Rm 5:19 the inattentive·disregard of·one man·of·clay†, the
Rm 7:1 lords·over the man·of·clay† for·a·span·of time, *that·*
1Pe 1:24 is as grass, and every man·of·clay's† glory *is* as *the*
2Pe 1:21 not by·the·will of·a·man·of·clay† *was* prophecy
2Pe 2:16 with *the* voice of·a·man·of·clay† forbade the
1Co 2:9 upon *the* heart of·a·man·of·clay†, the·things·which
1Co 2:11 ·knows the·things of·the man·of·clay†, except the
1Co 2:11 except the spirit of·the man·of·clay†, the·one in
1Co 15:21 For whereas through a·man·of·clay† *came* the
1Co 15:21 also through a·man·of·clay† *came* resurrection
Rv 21:17 *according·to* a·measure of·a·man·of·clay†, which
G0444.3 N-GPM ἀνθρώπων (100x)
Jn 1:4 and the life-above was the light of·the men·of·clay†.
Jn 5:41 I·do·not receive glory personally·from men·of·clay†,
Jn 8:17 the testimony of·two men·of·clay† is legally·valid.
Jn 12:43 of·the men·of·clay† more·especially indeed·than·
Lk 9:44 to·be·handed·over into *the* hands of·men·of·clay†."
Lk 9:56 ·destroy *the* souls of·men·of·clay†, but·rather to·
Lk 12:8 me by·name before the men·of·clay†, the Son of·
Lk 12:9 of·the men·of·clay† shall·be·utterly·denied in·the·
Lk 16:15 as·righteous in·the·sight of·the men·of·clay†, but
Lk 18:11 just·as the rest of·the men·of·clay† *are*: violently·

Lk 19:30 not·even·one man·of·clay† sat ever·at·any·time.
Lk 20:4 from·out of·heaven, or from·out of·men·of·clay†?"
Lk 20:6 we·should·declare, 'From·out of·men·of·clay†,' all
Lk 21:26 with·men·of·clay† fainting for fear, and for·
Lk 24:7 *the* hands of·morally·disqualified men·of·clay†, and
Ac 4:17 no·longer to·not·even·one man·of·clay† in this
Ac 5:38 Withdraw from these men·of·clay† and let them be
Ac 5:38 ·be birthed·from·out of·men·of·clay†, it·shall·be·
Ac 15:17 ·remnants of·the men·of·clay† may·seek·out the
Ac 17:25 ·upon by *the* hands of·men·of·clay†, *as·though*
Ac 17:26 ·made every nation of·men·of·clay† residing upon
Heb 5:1 from·among men·of·clay† is·fully·established on·
Heb 5:1 on·behalf of·men·of·clay† in·the·things pertaining·
Gal 1:1 — (not from men·of·clay†, neither through a·man·
Mt 4:19 me, and I·shall·make yeu fishers of·men·of·clay†!"
Mt 5:13 out and to·be·trampled·down by the men·of·clay†.
Mt 5:16 radiate·brightly before the men·of·clay†, so·that
Mt 6:1 merciful·act before the men·of·clay†, particularly for·
Mt 6:2 they·may·be·glorified by the men·of·clay†. Certainly
Mt 10:17 But beware of the men·of·clay†, for they·shall·
Mt 10:32 me by·name before the men·of·clay†, I·also shall·
Mt 10:33 should·deny me before the men·of·clay†, him I·
Mt 15:9 *the* religious·requirements of·men·of·clay† *as*
Mt 16:23 ·God, but·rather the·things of·the men·of·clay†."
Mt 17:22 to·be·handed·over into *the* hands of·men·of·clay†.
Mt 19:12 some castrated by the men·of·clay†. And there·are
Mt 21:25 From·out of·heaven or from·out of·men·of·clay†?"
Mt 21:26 if we·should·declare, 'From·out of·men·of·clay†,'
Mt 22:16 ·do·not look to *the* countenance of·men·of·clay†.
Mt 23:4 on the shoulders of·the men·of·clay†, but with·their·
Mt 23:7 and to·be·called by the men·of·clay†, 'Rabbi,
Mt 23:14 kingdom of·the heavens before men·of·clay†! For
Mk 1:17 ·cause yeu to·become fishers of·men·of·clay†."
Mk 3:28 shall·be·forgiven the Sons of·clay†, and·also
Mk 7:7 *the* religious·requirements of·men·of·clay† *as*
Mk 7:8 ·hold·to the Oral·tradition of·men·of·clay†, *such·as*
Mk 7:21 from·out of·the heart of·the men·of·clay†, the
Mk 8:33 of·God, but·rather the·things of·the men·of·clay†."
Mk 9:31 is·handed·over into *the* hands of·men·of·clay†, and
Mk 11:2 ·tied, on which not·even·one man·of·clay† has·sat.
Mk 11:30 of·heaven, or from·out of·men·of·clay†? Answer
Mk 11:32 ·should·declare, 'From·out of·men·of·clay† …'"
Mk 12:14 personal·appearance of·men·of·clay†, but·rather
Rm 1:18 and *all* unrighteousness of·men·of·clay† (the·ones
Rm 2:16 the secrets of·the men·of·clay†. According·to my
Rm 2:29 ·praise *is* not from·out of·men·of·clay†, but·rather
Rm 12:17 ·good·things in·the·sight of·all men·of·clay†,'
Rm 12:18 part, behaving·peacefully with all men·of·clay†.
Jac 3:8 But not·even·one among·clay·men† is·able to·tame
Php 2:7 becoming in *the* resemblance of·men·of·clay†.
1Pe 2:4 having·been·rejected·as·unfit by men·of·clay†, but
1Pe 2:15 ·muzzle the ignorance of·impetuous men·of·clay†.
1Pe 4:2 in flesh to·the·longings of·men·of·clay†, but·rather
2Pe 3:7 and total·destruction of·the irreverent men·of·clay†.
1Th 2:6 nor seeking glory from·among men·of·clay†, neither
1Th 2:13 *it* not *as* a·word of·men·of·clay†, but·rather just·as
2Th 3:2 away·from the absurd and evil men·of·clay†, for not
Tit 1:14 commandments of·men·of·clay† that·are·turning·
1Co 1:25 is wiser·than the *wisdom* of·men·of·clay†, and the
1Co 1:25 ·God is stronger·than the *strength* of·men·of·clay†.
1Co 2:5 ·not be in *the* wisdom of·men·of·clay†, but·rather in
1Co 2:11 what man·of·clay† personally·knows the·things of·
1Co 7:23 Do·not become slaves of·men·of·clay†.
1Co 13:1 bestowed·tongues of·the men·of·clay† and of·the
1Co 15:19 we·are of·all men·of·clay† most·pitied.
1Co 15:39 *there·is* one *kind·of* flesh of·men·of·clay†, another
2Co 3:2 ·known and being·read·aloud by all men·of·clay†,
2Co 4:2 to every man·of·clay's† conscience in·the·sight of·
2Co 8:21 but·rather also in·the·sight of·men·of·clay†.'
Eph 3:5 was·not made·known to·the Sons of·clay†, as it·is
Eph 4:14 by the artful·manipulation of·men·of·clay†, *and* by
Col 2:8 according·to the tradition of·men·of·clay†, *that·is,*
Col 2:22 ·requirements and instructions of·the men·of·clay†.'

1Ti 2:1 ·of·thankfulness to·be·made over all men·of·clay†,
1Ti 2:5 mediator *between* God and men·of·clay†: a·man·of·
1Ti 4:10 who is *the* Savior of·all men·of·clay†, especially of·
1Ti 5:24 of·some men·of·clay† are obvious·beforehand,
1Ti 6:5 of·thoroughly·corrupted men·of·clay†, *their* minds
1Ti 6:16 it·is·not·even possible *for* men·of·clay† to·see), to·
1Jn 5:9 we·receive the testimony of·men·of·clay†, the
Rv 8:11 and many men·of·clay† died as·a·result of·the
Rv 9:7 gold, and their faces *were* as faces of·men·of·clay†.
Rv 9:15 they·should·kill the third·part of·the men·of·clay†.
Rv 9:18 the third·part of·the men·of·clay† were·killed, as·
Rv 9:20 And the rest of·the men·of·clay† who were·not
Rv 11:13 ·killed seven thousand names of·men·of·clay†.
Rv 13:13 to the earth in·the·sight of·the men·of·clay†,
Rv 14:4 ·redeemed from among·the men·of·clay†, *being* a·
Rv 18:13 "and bodies and souls of·men·of·clay†.
Rv 21:3 of·God *is* with the men·of·clay†, and he·shall·

EG0444.3 (7x)

Jn 2:24 ·them, on·account·of him knowing all *men·of·clay†*,
Jn 17:10 and I·have·been·glorified in these *men·of·clay†*.
Ac 17:31 ·forth trust to·all *men·of·clay†* after·raising him up
1Co 9:19 from·among all *men·of·clay†*, I·make·a·slave·of
2Co 4:16 ·yet the inward *man·of·clay†* is·being·renewed day
Col 3:10 ·with the fresh·new *man·of·clay†*, the·one being·
1Ti 5:24 also for·some *men·of·clay†*, they·follow·afterward.

G0444.4 N-NSM ἄνθρωπος (1x)

Mk 2:27 Clay·Man†, not the Clay·Man† on·account·of the

G0444.4 N-ASM ἄνθρωπον (1x)

Mk 2:27 came·to·be on·account·of the Clay·Man†, not the

G0444.4 N-GSM ἀνθρώπου (1x)

Rm 1:23 ·derived·image of·corruptible Clay·Man†, and·also

G0444.5 N-NSM ἄνθρωπος (3x)

Mt 17:14 a·certain·man·of·clay† came·alongside him,
Mt 21:28 suppose? A·certain·man·of·clay† was·having two
Mk 12:1 in parables. "A·certain·man·of·clay† "planted a·

G0444.5 N-ASM ἄνθρωπον (2x)

Mt 9:9 from·there, YeShua saw a·certain·man·of·clay†, *Levi*
Mt 9:32 *men* brought to·him a·certain·man·of·clay†, a·mute

G0444.5 N-DSM ἀνθρώπῳ (1x)

Mt 22:2 heavens is·likened to·a·certain·man·of·clay†, a·king

G0444.5 N-GSM ἀνθρώπου (1x)

Rv 13:18 for it·is a·number of·a·certain·man·of·clay†. And

G0444.6 N-NSM ἄνθρωπος (1x)

2Ti 3:17 in·order·that the clay·man† of·God may·be fully·

G0444.6 N-VSM ἄνθρωπε (1x)

1Ti 6:11 But you, O clay·man† of·God, flee from·these·

G0444.6 N-GSM ἀνθρώπου (2x)

Rv 1:13 a·son of·clay·man†, having·dressed·himself·with a·
Rv 14:14 ·is·sitting·down like a·son of·clay·man†, having on

EG0444.6 (1x)

Rv 13:18 And this *clay·man's†* number *is* Chi·Xi·Stigma,

G0444.7 N-NSM ἄνθρωπος (1x)

Jn 16:21 ·account·of the joy that a·child·of·clay† is·born into

G0444.7 N-ASM ἄνθρωπον (1x)

Jn 1:9 which illuminates every child·of·clay† coming into

G0444.8 N-NSM ἄνθρωπος (1x)

Jn 7:23 If a·man-child·of·clay† receives circumcision on a·

G0444.8 N-ASM ἄνθρωπον (1x)

Jn 7:22 on a·Sabbath, yeu·circumcise a·man-child·of·clay†.

G0444.9 N-GSM ἀνθρώπου (84x)

Jn 1:51 and descending' upon the Son of·Clay·Man†."
Jn 3:13 of·the heaven, the Son of·Clay·Man†, the·one being
Jn 3:14 ·for the Son of·Clay·Man† to·be·elevated *also*,
Jn 6:27 which the Son of·Clay·Man† shall·give to·yeu, for
Jn 6:53 the flesh of·the Son of·Clay·Man†, and should·drink
Jn 6:62 ·observe the Son of·Clay·Man† ascending to·where
Jn 8:28 ·elevate the Son of·Clay·Man†, yeu·shall·know that I
Jn 12:23 that the Son of·Clay·Man† should·be·glorified.
Jn 12:34 ·for the Son of·Clay·Man† to·be·elevated'?
Jn 12:34 "Who is this Son of·Clay·Man†?"
Jn 13:31 "Now the Son of·Clay·Man† is·glorified, and God
Lk 5:24 ·know that the Son of·Clay·Man† has authority upon
Lk 6:5 to·them, "The Son of·Clay·Man† is Lord also of·the

Lk 6:22 name as evil, because·of the Son of·Clay·Man†.
Lk 7:34 The Son of·Clay·Man† has·come eating and
Lk 9:22 ·for the Son of·Clay·Man† to·suffer many·things,
Lk 9:26 the Son of·Clay·Man† shall·be·ashamed·of that·man
Lk 9:44 the Son of·Clay·Man† is·about to·be·handed·over
Lk 9:56 For the Son of·Clay·Man† did·not come to·
Lk 9:58 but the Son of·Clay·Man† does·not have *a·place*
Lk 11:30 ·manner also the Son of·Clay·Man† shall·be to·this
Lk 12:8 ·of·clay†, the Son of·Clay·Man† also shall·affirm
Lk 12:10 against the Son of·Clay·Man†, it·shall·be·forgiven
Lk 12:40 because the Son of·Clay·Man† comes in·that hour
Lk 17:22 one of·the days of·the Son of·Clay·Man†, and yeu·
Lk 17:24 also shall·be the Son of·Clay·Man† in his day.
Lk 17:26 ·it·be also in the days of·the Son of·Clay·Man†.
Lk 17:30 in·that day *when* the Son of·Clay·Man† is·revealed.
Lk 18:8 the Son of·Clay·Man†, upon·coming·*back*, shall·
Lk 18:31 the Son of·Clay·Man† shall·be·finished.
Lk 19:10 For the Son of·Clay·Man† came to·seek and to·
Lk 21:27 'the Son of·Clay·Man† coming in a·thick·cloud'
Lk 21:36 to·be·established before the Son of·Clay·Man†."
Lk 22:22 in·fact, the Son of·Clay·Man† departs according·to
Lk 22:48 ·you·hand·over the Son of·Clay·Man† with·a·kiss?
Lk 22:69 ·on, the Son of·Clay·Man† shall·be sitting·down at
Lk 24:7 ·for the Son of·Clay·Man† to·be·handed·over into
Ac 7:56 ·up, and the Son of·Clay·Man† standing at *the*
Mt 8:20 but the Son of·Clay·Man† does·not have anywhere
Mt 9:6 ·know that the Son of·Clay·Man† has authority on the
Mt 10:23 ·IsraEl, until the Son of·Clay·Man† should·come.
Mt 11:19 The Son of·Clay·Man† came eating and drinking,
Mt 12:8 For the Son of·Clay·Man† is Lord even of·the
Mt 12:32 against the Son of·Clay·Man†, it·shall·be·forgiven
Mt 12:40 ·this·manner the Son of·Clay·Man† shall·be three
Mt 13:37 sowing the good seed is the Son of·Clay·Man†.
Mt 13:41 The Son of·Clay·Man† shall·dispatch his angels,
Mt 16:13 say me to·be— *me*, the Son of·Clay·Man†?"
Mt 16:27 "For the Son of·Clay·Man† is·about to·come in the
Mt 16:28 they·should·see the Son of·Clay·Man† coming in
Mt 17:9 the Son of·Clay·Man† should·rise·up from·among
Mt 17:12 also, the Son of·Clay·Man† is·about to·suffer
Mt 17:22 The Son of·Clay·Man† is·about to·be·handed·over
Mt 18:11 For the Son of·Clay·Man† came to·save the·one
Mt 19:28 whenever the Son of·Clay·Man† should·sit upon
Mt 20:18 the Son of·Clay·Man† shall·be·handed·over to·the
Mt 20:28 just·as the Son of·Clay·Man† did·not come to·be·
Mt 24:27 the returning·Presence of·the Son of·Clay·Man†.
Mt 24:30 sign of·the Son of·Clay·Man† shall·be·apparent in
Mt 24:30 ·gaze·upon 'the Son of·Clay·Man† coming upon
Mt 24:37 the returning·Presence of·the Son of·Clay·Man†.
Mt 24:39 the returning·Presence of·the Son of·Clay·Man†.
Mt 24:44 because the Son of·Clay·Man† comes at·an·hour
Mt 25:13 the hour in which the Son of·Clay·Man† comes.
Mt 25:31 whenever the Son of·Clay·Man† should·come in
Mt 26:2 and·then the Son of·Clay·Man† is·handed·over to·
Mt 26:24 In·fact, the Son of·Clay·Man† heads·on·out just·as
Mt 26:24 whom the Son of·Clay·Man† is·handed·over! It·
Mt 26:45 and the Son of·Clay·Man† is·handed·over into *the*
Mt 26:64 ·upon 'the Son of·Clay·Man† sitting·down at *the*
Mk 2:10 ·know that the Son of·Clay·Man† has authority on
Mk 2:28 As·such, the Son of·Clay·Man† is Lord also of·the
Mk 8:31 ·for the Son of·Clay·Man† to·suffer many·things
Mk 8:38 , the Son of·Clay·Man† also shall·be·ashamed·of
Mk 9:9 the Son of·Clay·Man† should·rise·up from·among
Mk 9:12 ·written concerning the Son of·Clay·Man†, that he·
Mk 9:31 "The Son of·Clay·Man† is·handed·over into *the*
Mk 10:33 the Son of·Clay·Man† shall·be·handed·over to·the
Mk 10:45 For even the Son of·Clay·Man† did·not come to·
Mk 13:26 ·gaze·upon 'the Son of·Clay·Man† coming in
Mk 14:21 In·fact, the Son of·Clay·Man† heads·on·out, just·
Mk 14:21 whom the Son of·Clay·Man† is·handed·over! It·
Mk 14:41 the Son of·Clay·Man† is·handed·over into the
Mk 14:62 ·gaze·upon the Son of·Clay·Man† sitting·down at

EG0444.9 (1x)

Mk 13:34 "*For the Son of·Clay·Man† is* as a·man·of·clay†

G0444.10 N-NSM ἄνθρωπος (1x)
2Th 2:3 the Clay·Man† of·Moral·Failure should·be·revealed,
G0444.13 N-NSM ἄνθρωπος (1x)
Heb 2:6 "What is mortal·man†, that you·are·actively·

G0445 ἀνθ•υπατεύω anthypatêúō *v.* (1x)
Roots:G0446
G0445.2 V-PAP-GSM ἀνθυπατεύοντος (1x)
Ac 18:12 And when·Gallio was·the·proconsul of·Achaia, the

G0446 ἀνθ•ύπατος anthýpatôs *n.* (4x)
Roots:G0473 G5228 See:G0445
G0446.2 N-NSM ἀνθύπατος (1x)
Ac 13:12 the·thing having·happened, the proconsul trusted,
G0446.2 N-NPM ἀνθύπατοι (1x)
Ac 19:38 ·sessions, and there·are proconsuls; let·them·call
G0446.2 N-ASM ἀνθύπατον (1x)
Ac 13:8 to·thoroughly·turn the proconsul away·from the
G0446.2 N-DSM ἀνθυπάτῳ (1x)
Ac 13:7 who was co-opting the proconsul, Sergius Paulus,

G0447 ἀν•ίημι aníēmi *v.* (4x)
Roots:G0303 G2423-1 See:G0425
xLangEquiv:H7503
G0447.3 V-2AAP-NPM ἀνέντες (1x)
Ac 27:40 sea, *while* at·the·same·time slackening the rudder
G0447.3 V-API-3S ἀνέθη (1x)
Ac 16:26 ·opened·up, and everyone's bonds were·slackened.
G0447.4 V-PAP-NPM ἀνιέντες (1x)
Eph 6:9 same·things toward them, giving·up the threatening,
G0447.4 V-2AAS-1S ἀνῶ (1x)
Heb 13:5 "No, I·may·not·ever give·up·on you, nor·even no

G0448 ἀν•ίλεως aníleōs *adj.* (1x)
Roots:G0001 G2436
G0448 A-NSF ἀνίλεως (1x)
Jac 2:13 tribunal·justice without·forgiving·favor *is* for·the·

G0449 ἄ•νιπτος ániptôs *adj.* (3x)
Roots:G0001 G3538
G0449 A-DPM ἀνίπτοις (3x)
Mt 15:20 "But to·eat with·unwashed hands does·not defile
Mk 7:2 that is, with·unwashed *hands*, they·found·fault.
Mk 7:5 but·rather eat the bread with·unwashed hands?

G0450 ἀν•ίστημι anístēmi *v.* (112x)
Roots:G0303 G2476 Compare:G1453 See:G1817
xLangAlso:H6965 A6966
G0450.1 V-2AAI-3S ἀνέστη (3x)
Lk 4:16 the day of·Sabbath, and he·stood·up to·read·aloud.
Lk 8:55 her spirit returned, and she·stood·up at·once, and
Lk 10:25 a·certain expert·in·Torah-Law stood·up, and
G0450.1 V-2AAM-2S ἀνάστηθι (2x)
Ac 10:26 roused him, saying, "Stand·up, *for* also·I myself
Ac 14:10 declared with·a·loud voice, "Stand upright on your
G0450.1 V-2AAP-NSM ἀναστάς (7x)
Ac 1:15 *and* twenty), Peter, after·standing·up, declared,
Ac 5:34 Now standing·up in the joint·council·of·Sanhedrin,
Ac 10:13 "Peter, after·standing·up, make·sacrifice and eat.
Ac 11:7 to·me, 'Peter, after·standing·up, sacrifice and eat.
Ac 11:28 ·the·name·of Agabus, after·standing·up, signified
Ac 13:16 Then Paul, standing·up and motioning with·his
Mk 14:60 the designated·high·priest, after·standing·up in the
G0450.1 V-2AAP-NPM ἀναστάντες (1x)
Mk 14:57 Then after·standing·up, someone was·falsely·
G0450.2 V-FMI-3S ἀναστήσεται (6x)
Jn 11:23 Jesus says to·her, "Your brother shall·rise·up."
Jn 11:24 "I·personally·know that he·shall·rise·up in the
Lk 18:33 And on·the third day, he·shall·rise·up."
Mt 20:19 And on·the third day, he·shall·rise·up."
Mk 9:31 And after·being·killed, he·shall·rise·up on·the third
Mk 10:34 ·kill him, and on·the third day he·shall·rise·up."
G0450.2 V-FMI-3P ἀναστήσονται (4x)
Lk 11:32 "Men of·Nineveh shall·rise·up in the Final·Tribunal
Ac 20:30 yeu yeurselves, men shall·rise·up, speaking
Mt 12:41 "Men of·Nineveh shall·rise·up in the Final·Tribunal
1Th 4:16 the dead·ones in Anointed-One shall·rise·up first.
G0450.2 V-PMI-3S ἀνίσταται (1x)
Heb 7:15 another priest·that·offers·a·sacrifice does·rise·up—
G0450.2 V-PMP-NSM ἀνιστάμενος (1x)
Rm 15:12 and the·one who·is·rising·up to·rule·over Gentiles
G0450.2 V-2AAI-3S ἀνέστη (13x)
Jn 11:31 her, seeing that Mary rose·up quickly and went·out
Lk 9:8 by·others that one of·the ancient prophets rose·up.
Lk 9:19 *say* that some prophet of·the ancient·ones rose·up."
Ac 5:36 before these days, Theudas rose·up, saying himself
Ac 5:37 After this·man, Judas of·Galilee rose·up in the days
Ac 7:18 "another king rose·up, who had·not personally·
Ac 9:34 And immediately he·rose·up.
Ac 26:30 these·things, the king rose·up, and·also the
Mk 3:26 if the Adversary-Accuser rose·up against himself and
Mk 5:42 the young·girl rose·up and was·walking, for she·
Mk 9:27 by·the hand, Jesus awakened him, and he·rose·up.
Rm 14:9 Anointed-One also died and rose·up. And he·came·
1Th 4:14 that YeShua died and rose·up, in·this·manner also
G0450.2 V-2AAI-3P ἀνέστησαν (2x)
Ac 6:9 But there·rose·up certain·men from·among the
1Co 10:7 and to·drink, and they·rose·up to·sexually·play."
G0450.2 V-2AAM-2S ἀνάστηθι (5x)
Ac 8:26 to Philippe, saying, "Rise·up and traverse down *on*
Ac 9:6 the Lord *said* to him, "Rise·up and enter into the city,
Ac 9:34 the Anointed-One heals you. Rise·up and toss·aside
Ac 9:40 he·declared, "Tabitha, rise·up." And she·opened·
Ac 26:16 'But·yet rise·up and stand·still upon your feet, for
G0450.2 V-2AAM-2S-AP ἀνάστα (2x)
Ac 12:7 he·awakened him, saying, "Rise·up in haste." And
Eph 5:14 sleeping, be·awakened and rise·up from·out of·the
G0450.2 V-2AAN ἀναστῆναι (7x)
Jn 20:9 ·for him to·rise·up from·among dead·men.
Lk 24:7 to·be·crucified, and on·the third day to·rise·up.'"
Lk 24:46 to·suffer and to·rise·up from·among dead·men on·
Ac 10:41 with·him after he rose·up from·among dead·men.
Ac 17:3 to·suffer and to·rise·up from·among dead·men, and
Mk 8:31 to·be·killed, and·then after three days to·rise·up.
Mk 9:10 what it·should·mean to·rise·up from·among the
G0450.2 V-2AAP-NSN ἀναστάν (1x)
Lk 23:1 And rising·up, absolutely·all the multitude of·them
G0450.2 V-2AAP-NSF ἀναστᾶσα (2x)
Lk 1:39 And Mariam, rising·up in these days, traversed into
Lk 4:39 her. And at·once rising·up, she·was·attending to·
G0450.2 V-2AAP-NSM ἀναστάς (29x)
Lk 4:38 And rising·up out of·the gathering, he·entered into
Lk 5:25 And at·once, rising·up in·the·sight of·them, taking·
Lk 5:28 ·behind absolutely·all, rising·up, he·followed him.
Lk 6:8 ·still in the middle." And rising·up, he·stood·still.
Lk 11:7 the bed; I·am·not able to·rise·up and·give to·you.'
Lk 11:8 to·yeu, even·though already·rising·up, he·shall·not
Lk 15:18 Rising·up, I·shall·traverse toward my father and
Lk 15:20 "And rising·up, he·came toward his father.
Lk 17:19 And he·declared to·him, "Rising·up, depart. Your
Lk 22:45 And after·rising·up from the prayer *and* coming to
Lk 24:12 But rising·up, Peter ran to the chamber·tomb, and
Ac 5:17 Then the designated·high·priest, rising·up, and all
Ac 8:27 And rising·up, he·traversed, and behold, *there·was*
Ac 9:11 the Lord *said* to him, "Rising·up, traverse on the
Ac 9:18 ·sight at·once. And rising·up, he·was·immersed.
Ac 9:39 And rising·up, Peter went·together with·them.
Ac 10:20 Moreover, after·rising·up, walk·down and traverse
Ac 14:20 surrounding him, after·rising·up, he·entered into
Ac 15:7 ·and·discussion occurring, after·rising·up, Peter
Ac 22:10 declared to me, 'Upon·rising·up, traverse into
Ac 22:16 ·are·about *to·do*? Upon·rising·up, be·immersed,
Mt 9:9 And rising·up, he·followed him.
Mt 26:62 And rising·up, the designated·high·priest declared
Mk 1:35 after·already·rising·up very·early while·still·night,
Mk 2:14 And rising·up, he·followed him.
Mk 7:24 And after·rising·up from·there, he·went·off into the
Mk 10:1 After·rising·up from·there, he·comes into the
Mk 10:50 ·away his outer·garment *and* rising·up, he·came
Mk 16:9 [(Now after·rising·up at·the·watch·of·dawn on·*the*·
G0450.2 V-2AAP-NPM ἀναστάντες (5x)
Lk 4:29 And after·rising·up, they·cast him forth outside of·
Lk 22:46 "Why·do yeu·sleep? Rising·up, be·in·prayer, in·
Lk 24:33 And rising·up the same hour, they·returned·back to
Ac 5:6 And the younger·men, rising·up, tightly·wrapped
Ac 23:9 part, upon·rising·up, they·were·thoroughly·fighting
G0450.2 V-2AAS-3S ἀναστῇ (3x)
Lk 16:31 someone should·rise·up from·among dead·men.'"
Mt 17:9 of·Clay·Man† should·rise·up from·among dead·men
Mk 9:9 of·Clay·Man† should·rise·up from·among dead·men.
G0450.2 V-2AAS-3P ἀναστῶσιν (2x)
Mk 12:23 whenever they·should·rise·up, whose wife shall·
Mk 12:25 whenever they·should·rise·up from·among dead·
G0450.3 V-FAI-1S ἀναστήσω (4x)
Jn 6:39 *the sheep pen),* but·rather shall·raise it up at the last
Jn 6:40 eternal life-above, and I·myself shall·raise him up
Jn 6:44 ·draw him, and I·myself shall·raise him up at·the
Jn 6:54 life-above, and I·myself shall·raise him up at·the last
G0450.3 V-FAI-3S ἀναστήσει (3x)
Ac 3:22 Yahweh yeur God shall·raise·up a·Prophet unto·yeu
Ac 7:37 "Yahweh yeur God shall·raise·up a·prophet to·yeu
Mt 22:24 ·marry his wife and shall·raise·up offspring† to·his
G0450.3 V-FAN ἀναστήσειν (1x)
Ac 2:30 ·to the flesh, he·would·raise·up the Anointed-One
G0450.3 V-PMN ἀνίστασθαι (1x)
Heb 7:11 priest·that·offers·a·sacrifice to·be·raised·up the
G0450.3 V-AAI-3S ἀνέστησεν (4x)
Ac 2:24 whom God raised·up, loosing the pangs of·Death,
Ac 2:32 God raised·up this Jesus, of·which we·ourselves all
Ac 9:41 And giving her a·hand, he·raised her up; and
Ac 13:34 And because he·raised him up from·among dead·
G0450.3 V-AAP-NSM ἀναστήσας (3x)
Ac 3:26 God, after·raising·up his·own servant·boy Jesus,
Ac 13:33 to·us, their children, by·raising·up Jesus; as also
Ac 17:31 ·forth trust to·all *men·of·clay†* after·raising him up

G0451 Ἄννα Ánna *n/p.* (1x)
Ἅννα Hánna [Greek, Octuagint]
חַנָּה cнaṅạh [Hebrew]
Roots:H2584 See:G4826
G0451.3 N/P-NSF Ἄννα (1x)
Lk 2:36 And there·was a·prophetess, Hanna, daughter of·

G0452 Ἄνν•ας Ánnas *n/p.* (5x)
חֲנַנְיָה cнănanyah [Hebrew]
Roots:H2608 Compare:G0367 See:G2533
G0452.2 N/P-NSM Ἄννας (1x)
Jn 18:24 *(Remember that* HannAs dispatched him, having·
G0452.2 N/P-ASM Ἄνναν (2x)
Jn 18:13 they·led him away first to HannAs *the proper high·*
Ac 4:6 *were* in JeruSalem, with HannAs the high·priest and
G0452.2 N/P-GSM Ἄννα (1x)
Lk 3:2 in·the·days of·HannAs and Caiaphas *the* high·priests
EG0452.2 (1x)
Jn 18:13 year. *(And HannAs dispatched the Anointed-One*

G0453 ἀ•νόητος anóētôs *adj.* (6x)
Roots:G0001 G3539 Compare:G3474 G0781 G0878
G0453.1 A-NPM ἀνόητοι (2x)
Gal 3:3 In·this·manner, are·yeu stupid? After·beginning in·
Tit 3:3 For we·ourselves also were once stupid, obstinate,
G0453.1 A-VPM ἀνόητοι (2x)
Lk 24:25 declared to them, "O stupid·ones, and slow in·the
Gal 3:1 O stupid Galatians, who cast·an·evil·eye·on yeu to·
G0453.1 A-APF ἀνοήτους (1x)
1Ti 6:9 a·snare, and *into* many stupid and injurious longings
G0453.1 A-DPM ἀνοήτοις (1x)
Rm 1:14 ·Barbarians, also to·wise·ones and to·stupid·ones.

G0454 ἄ•νοια ánôia *n.* (2x)
Roots:G0001 G3563 Compare:G3472
xLangAlso:H0200
G0454.3 N-NSF ἄνοια (1x)
2Ti 3:9 for their irrational·resentment shall·be obvious to·
G0454.3 N-GSF ἀνοίας (1x)
Lk 6:11 were·filled with·irrational·resentment and were·

G0455 ἀν•οίγω anôígō *v.* (77x)
Roots:G0303 G3608-2
G0455 V-FAI-1S ἀνοίξω (1x)
Mt 13:35 saying, "'I·shall·open·up my mouth in parables;
G0455 V-2FPI-3S ἀνοιγήσεται (4x)
Lk 11:9 ·find; knock, and it·shall·be·opened·up to·yeu.
Lk 11:10 and to·the·one knocking, it·shall·be·opened·up.
Mt 7:7 ·shall·find; knock, and it·shall·be·opened·up to·yeu.
Mt 7:8 finds; and to·the·one knocking it·shall·be·opened·up.
G0455 V-PAI-3S ἀνοίγει (3x)
Jn 10:3 To·him, the doorkeeper opens·up, and the sheep
Ac 8:32 him, in·this·manner he·did·not open·up his mouth.
Rv 3:7 shuts, *who* shuts and not·even·one·man opens·up'":
G0455 V-PAN ἀνοίγειν (2x)
Jn 10:21 ¿! Is a·demon able to·open·up blind eyes?
Ac 18:14 while·Paul was·intending to·open·up his mouth,
G0455 V-PAP-NSM ἀνοίγων (1x)
Rv 3:7 of·David, the·one opening·up and not·even·one·man
G0455 V-AAI-3S ἤνοιξεν (20x)
Jn 9:14 when Jesus made the clay and opened·up his eyes.
Jn 9:17 concerning him, because he·opened·up your eyes."
Jn 9:21 ·not personally·know; or who opened·up his eyes,
Jn 9:26 ·did he·do to·you? How·did he·open·up your eyes?
Jn 9:30 ·what·source he·is, and·yet he·opened·up my eyes.
Jn 9:32 any·man opened·up eyes of·one·having·been·born
Ac 5:19 through the night, opened·up the prison doors; and·
Ac 9:40 rise·up." And she·opened·up her eyes; and upon·
Ac 12:14 Peter's voice, she·did·not open·up the gate due·to
Ac 14:27 with them, and that he·opened·up *the* door of·trust
Rv 6:1 And I·saw when the Lamb opened·up *the* first from·
Rv 6:3 And when he·opened·up the second official·seal, I·
Rv 6:5 And when *the Lamb* opened·up the third official·seal,
Rv 6:7 And when he·opened·up the fourth official·seal, I·
Rv 6:9 And when *the Lamb* opened·up the fifth official·seal,
Rv 6:12 And I·saw when he·opened·up the sixth official·seal
Rv 8:1 And when *the Lamb* opened·up the seventh official·
Rv 9:2 And he·opened·up the well of·the bottomless·pit, and
Rv 12:16 woman, and the earth opened·up her mouth, and
Rv 13:6 And it·opened·up its mouth in revilement toward
G0455 V-AAM-2S ἄνοιξον (2x)
Lk 13:25 'Lord, Lord, open·up to·us,' and answering, he·
Mt 25:11 'Lord, Lord, open·up to·us.'
G0455 V-AAN ἀνοῖξαι (6x)
Ac 26:18 to·open·up their eyes, *and* to·turn·*them*·back·
Rv 5:2 "Who is worthy to·open·up the official·scroll and to·
Rv 5:3 the earth, was·able to·open·up the official·scroll,
Rv 5:4 ·man was·found worthy to·open·up and to·read·aloud
Rv 5:5 ·prevailed *such* to·open·up the official·scroll and to·
Rv 5:9 the official·scroll and to·open·up its official·seals,
G0455 V-AAP-NSM ἀνοίξας (5x)
Jn 11:37 Was·not this·man, the·one opening·up the eyes of·
Ac 8:35 And Philippe, opening·up his mouth and beginning
Ac 10:34 Then Peter, opening·up his mouth, declared, "In
Mt 5:2 And opening·up his mouth, he·was·instructing them,
Mt 17:27 *on·the line*, and upon·opening·up his mouth, you·
G0455 V-AAP-NPM ἀνοίξαντες (3x)
Ac 5:23 the doors. But opening·up, we·found no·one·at·all
Ac 12:16 ·persisting·in knocking. And opening·up *the gate*,
Mt 2:11 to·him. Then after·opening·up their treasures, they·
G0455 V-AAS-3S ἀνοίξῃ (2x)
Col 4:3 us, that God may·open·up to·us a·door for·the
Rv 3:20 should·hear my voice and should·open·up the door,
G0455 V-AAS-3P ἀνοίξωσιν (1x)
Lk 12:36 knocking, they·may·open·up to·him immediately.
G0455 V-2API-3S ἠνοίγη (2x)
Rv 11:19 And the Temple of·God was·opened·up in the
Rv 15:5 of·the Testimony in the heaven is·opened·up.
G0455 V-API-3S ἠνεῴχθη (3x)
Lk 1:64 And his mouth was·opened·up at·once, and his
Ac 12:10 City, which automatically was·opened·up to·them.
Rv 20:12 And another official·scroll was·opened·up, which
G0455 V-API-3P ἠνεῴχθησαν (6x)
Jn 9:10 "How·are your eyes opened·up?"
Ac 16:26 all the doors were·opened·up, and everyone's
Mt 3:16 behold, the heavens were·opened·up to·him, and
Mt 9:30 And their eyes were·opened·up; and Yeshua sternly·
Mt 27:52 and the chamber·tombs are·opened·up, and many
Rv 20:12 of·God, and official·scrolls were·opened·up. And
G0455 V-APN ἀνεῳχθῆναι (1x)
Lk 3:21 ·immersed and praying, the heaven was·opened·up,
G0455 V-APS-3P ἀνοιχθῶσιν (1x)
Mt 20:33 "Lord, that our eyes may·be·opened·up."
G0455 V-2RAI-3S ἀνέῳγεν (2x)
1Co 16:9 a·great and active door has·opened·up to·me, and
2Co 6:11 O·*yeu*·Corinthians, we·have·opened·up our mouth
G0455 V-RPP-ASN ἠνεῳγμένον (2x)
Rv 10:2 hand a·tiny·official·scroll having·been·opened·up.
Rv 10:8 ·scroll, the·one having·been·opened·up in the hand
G0455 V-RPP-ASF ἀνεῳγμένην (1x)
Rv 3:8 I·have·given a·door having·been·opened·up, and
G0455 V-2RPP-ASM ἀνεῳγότα (1x)
Jn 1:51 ·gaze·upon the heaven having·been·opened·up, and
G0455 V-RPP-ASM ἀνεῳγμένον (2x)
Ac 10:11 ·observed the heaven having·been·opened·up, and
Rv 19:11 And I·saw the heaven having·been·opened·up, and
G0455 V-RPP-APF ἀνεῳγμένας (1x)
Ac 16:27 the prison doors having·been·opened·up, drawing
G0455 V-RPP-APM ἀνεῳγμένους (1x)
Ac 7:56 I·observe the heavens having·been·opened·up, and
G0455 V-RPP-GSF ἀνεῳγμένης (1x)
2Co 2:12 (also with·a·door having·been·opened·up to·me by
G0455 V-RPP-GPM ἀνεῳγμένων (1x)
Ac 9:8 eyes having·been·opened·up, he·was·looking·upon
G0455 V-RPP-NSF ἠνεῳγμένη (1x)
Rv 4:1 and behold, a·door having·been·opened·up in the
G0455 V-RPP-NSM ἀνεῳγμένος (1x)
Rm 3:13 throat *is* a·grave having·been·opened·up; with·their

G0456 ἀν•οικοδομέω anôikôdômḗō *v.* (2x)
Roots:G0303 G3618
G0456 V-FAI-1S ἀνοικοδομήσω (2x)
Ac 15:16 I·shall·return and shall·rebuild the tabernacle of·
Ac 15:16 ·fallen·down. And I·shall·rebuild the·things of·it

G0457 ἄν•οιξις ánôixis *n.* (1x)
Roots:G0455
G0457.1 N-DSF ἀνοίξει (1x)
Eph 6:19 to·me, *such·that* with an·opening·up of·my mouth

G0458 ἀ•νομία anômía *n.* (15x)
Roots:G0459 Compare:G3892 G0093 See:G0460 G0457-1 G0457-2 G3551
xLangEquiv:H6588 xLangAlso:H7562 H7564 H5771 H0205
G0458.1 N-ASF ἀνομίαν (1x)
Heb 1:9 You·loved righteousness and hated lawlessness.
G0458.1 N-DSF ἀνομίᾳ (1x)
2Co 6:14 participation has·righteousness with lawlessness?
G0458.1 N-GSF ἀνομίας (2x)
Mt 23:28 ·full of·stage·acting·hypocrisy and lawlessness.
Tit 2:14 'he·may·ransom us from all lawlessness,' and may·
G0458.2 N-NPF ἀνομίαι (1x)
Rm 4:7 *are·they* whose violations·of·law are·forgiven and
G0458.2 N-GPF ἀνομιῶν (2x)
Heb 8:12 their moral·failures and their violations·of·law, no,
Heb 10:17 moral·failures and of·their violations·of·law, no,
G0458.3 N-NSF ἀνομία (1x)
1Jn 3:4 the moral·failure is the violation·of·the·Royal-Law.
G0458.3 N-ASF ἀνομίαν (1x)
1Jn 3:4 also commits the violation·of·the·Royal-Law, and
G0458.4 N-ASF ἀνομίαν (4x)
Mt 7:23 me, the·ones who·are·working the Lawlessness.'
Mt 13:41 and·also the·ones committing the Lawlessness,
Mt 24:12 the·thing to·be·multiplied, the Lawlessness, the
Rm 6:19 to *work* the Lawlessness, in·this·manner now yeu·
G0458.4 N-DSF ἀνομίᾳ (1x)
Rm 6:19 to·the impurity and to·the Lawlessness to *work* the
G0458.4 N-GSF ἀνομίας (1x)
2Th 2:7 the mystery of·the Lawlessness operates even·now.

G0459 ἄ•νομος ánômôs *adj.* (11x)
Roots:G0001 G3551 Compare:G0113 G1482 See:G0458 G0460 G0457-1 G0457-2
xLangAlso:H7564
G0459.2 A-NSM ἄνομος (1x)
2Th 2:8 And then the Lawless·One shall·be·revealed, whom
G0459.2 A-DPM ἀνόμοις (1x)
1Ti 1:9 for·a·righteous·man, but for·lawless·ones and for·
G0459.2 A-GPM ἀνόμων (3x)
Lk 22:37 " And he·was·reckoned among *the* lawless·ones,"
Ac 2:23 given·over, being·taken through lawless hands. *And*
Mk 15:28 "'And he·was·reckoned with lawless·ones.'"
EG0459.2 (1x)
2Th 2:9 *O·the Lawless·One*, whose arrival is according·to an·
G0459.3 A-DPN ἀνόμοις (1x)
2Pe 2:8 *his* righteous soul *over their* unlawful deeds);
G0459.4 A-NSM ἄνομος (2x)
1Co 9:21 *·are* without·Torah-Law, as without·Torah-Law,
1Co 9:21 (not being without·Torah-Law to·God, but·yet *I*·
G0459.4 A-APM ἀνόμους (1x)
1Co 9:21 I·may·gain *the·ones that are* without·Torah-Law.
G0459.4 A-DPM ἀνόμοις (1x)
1Co 9:21 to·the·ones *that·are* without·Torah-Law, as

G0460 ἀ•νόμως anṓmōs *adv.* (2x)
Roots:G0459 See:G0458 G3551
G0460.2 ADV ἀνόμως (2x)
Rm 2:12 ·as did·morally·fail without·Torah-Law also shall·
Rm 2:12 shall·completely·perish without·Torah-Law. And

G0461 ἀν•ορθόω anôrthóō *v.* (3x)
Roots:G0303 G3717 Compare:G0450 G1817 G2476
G0461.2 V-API-3S ἀνωρθώθη (1x)
Lk 13:13 ·her, and at·once she·is·straightened·upright, and
G0461.3 V-FAI-1S ἀνορθώσω (1x)
Ac 15:16 ·foundationally·ruined, and I·shall·raise it upright,
G0461.3 V-AAM-2P ἀνορθώσατε (1x)
Heb 12:12 Therefore raise·upright the limp hands and the

G0462 ἀν•όσιος anósiôs *adj.* (2x)
Roots:G0001 G3741 Compare:G0169
G0462.2 A-NPM ἀνόσιοι (1x)
2Ti 3:2 obstinate to·parents, ungrateful, distinctly·unholy,
G0462.2 A-DPM ἀνοσίοις (1x)
1Ti 1:9 ·disqualified·ones, for·distinctly·unholy·ones and

G0463 ἀν•οχή anôchḗ *n.* (2x)
Roots:G0430 Compare:G3115
G0463.1 N-DSF ἀνοχῇ (1x)
Rm 3:26 with the forbearance of·God toward the·one himself
G0463.1 N-GSF ἀνοχῆς (1x)
Rm 2:4 of·his kindness, forbearance, and long-suffering,

G0464 ἀντ•αγωνίζομαι antagōnízômai *v.* (1x)
Roots:G0473 G0075 Compare:G2610
G0464.1 V-PNP-NPM ἀνταγωνιζόμενοι (1x)
Heb 12:4 strenuously·struggling specifically·against the

G0465 ἀντ•άλλαγμα antállagma *n.* (2x)
Roots:G0473 G0236
G0465.1 N-ASN ἀντάλλαγμα (2x)
Mt 16:26 a·man·of·clay† shall·give in·exchange for·his soul
Mk 8:37 a·man·of·clay† shall·give in·exchange for·his soul?

G0466 ἀντ•ανα•πληρόω antanaplērόō *v.* (1x)
Roots:G0473 G0378
G0466.1 V-PAI-1S ἀνταναπληρῶ (1x)
Col 1:24 on·yeur behalf, and additionally·fill·up the lacking

G0467 ἀντ•απο•δίδωμι antapôdídōmi *v.* (8x)
Roots:G0473 G0591 Compare:G0489 See:G0468 G0469 xLangAlso:H8005
G0467.2 V-FAI-1S ἀνταποδώσω (2x)
Heb 10:30 *belongs* to·me, I·myself shall·recompense,'" says
Rm 12:19 *belongs* to·me; I·myself shall·recompense,'" says
G0467.2 V-FPI-3S ἀνταποδοθήσεται (2x)
Lk 14:14 you. For you shall·be·recompensed at the
Rm 11:35 to·him that it·shall·be·recompensed *back* to·him?
G0467.2 V-2AAN ἀνταποδοῦναι (3x)
Lk 14:14 ·do·not have *that·with·which* to·recompense you.

1Th 3:9 are·we·able to·recompense to·God concerning yeu,
2Th 1:6 with God to·recompense tribulation to·the·ones
EG0467.2 (1x)
2Th 1:7 and *recompensing* to·yeu, the·ones being·

G0468 ἀντ•από•δομα antapódôma *n.* (2x)
Roots:G0467 Compare:G1557 See:G0469
G0468.2 N-ASN ἀνταπόδομα (2x)
Lk 14:12 in·return, and a·recompense may·happen to·you.
Rm 11:9 and into a·trap, and into a·recompense to·them."

G0469 ἀντ•από•δοσις antapódôsis *n.* (1x)
Roots:G0467 Compare:G3405 See:G0468
G0469.2 N-ASF ἀνταπόδοσιν (1x)
Col 3:24 ·receive·in·full the rewarding of·the inheritance, for

G0470 ἀντ•απο•κρίνομαι antapôkrínômai *v.* (2x)
Roots:G0473 G0611
G0470 V-PNP-NSM ἀνταποκρινόμενος (1x)
Rm 9:20 you·yourself, the·one who·is·contradicting God?
G0470 V-AON ἀνταποκριθῆναι (1x)
Lk 14:6 ·not have·strength to·contradict him pertaining·to

G0471 ἀντ•έπω antépō *v.* (2x)
Roots:G0473 G2036
G0471.1 V-2AAN ἀντειπεῖν (2x)
Lk 21:15 be·able to·declare·against nor·even to·withstand.
Ac 4:14 ·having not·even·one·thing to·declare·against *it*.

G0472 ἀντ•έχομαι antéchômai *v.* (4x)
Roots:G0473 G2192
G0472.2 V-FDI-3S ἀνθέξεται (2x)
Lk 16:13 the other, or he·shall·hold·tightly to·one and shall·
Mt 6:24 the other, or·else he·shall·hold·tightly to·one and
G0472.2 V-PNP-ASM ἀντεχόμενον (1x)
Tit 1:9 holding·tightly·to the trustworthy Redemptive-word
G0472.3 V-PNM-2P ἀντέχεσθε (1x)
1Th 5:14 ·encourage the fainthearted, support the weak, be·

G0473 ἀντί antí *prep.* (22x)
See:G0481
G0473.2 PREP ἀντί (4x)
Lk 11:11 Or·if·a·fish, ¿! instead of·a·fish, shall·he·hand
Mt 2:22 ArcheLaos reigns in Judea in·the·stead of·his father
Jac 4:15 Instead, yeu *ought* to·say, "If the Lord should·will,
1Co 11:15 because the hair·of·the·head, instead of·a·mantle,
G0473.3 PREP ἀντί (10x)
Heb 12:16 as Esau, who for one full·meal gave·away his
Mt 5:38 that it·was·uttered, "An·eye for an·eye, and a·tooth
Mt 5:38 "An·eye for an·eye, and a·tooth for a·tooth."
Mt 17:27 ·hold·of that, give *it* to·them for me and you.
Mt 20:28 and to·give his soul *to·be* a·ransom for many."
Mk 10:45 and to·give his soul *to·be* a·ransom for many."
Rm 12:17 ·back to·not·even·one·man wrong for wrong,
1Pe 3:9 not rendering a·wrong for wrong, or a·defamation
1Pe 3:9 for wrong, or a·defamation for defamation, but on·
1Th 5:15 no one should·render wrong for wrong to·any *man*;
G0473.4 PREP ἀντί (7x)
Lk 1:20 that these·things should·occur, because you·did·not
Lk 12:3 Because as·many·things·as yeu·declared in the
Lk 19:44 stone upon stone, because you·did·not know the
Ac 12:23 of·Yahweh smote him, because he·did·not give
Heb 12:2 — who, because of·the joy being·laid·out·before
2Th 2:10 ·are·completely·perishing, because these did·not
Eph 5:31 "'Because of·this, a·man·of·clay† shall·leave·
G0473.5 PREP ἀντί (1x)
Jn 1:16 all received even grace in·addition·to grace.

G0474 ἀντι•βάλλω antibállō *v.* (1x)
Roots:G0473 G0906
G0474.1 V-PAI-2P ἀντιβάλλετε (1x)
Lk 24:17 these that yeu·toss·back·and·forth to one·another

G0475 ἀντι•δια•τίθεμαι antidiatíthêmai *v.* (1x)
Roots:G0473 G1303
G0475.2 V-PMP-APM ἀντιδιατιθεμένους (1x)
2Ti 2:25 who·are·thoroughly·setting·themselves·in·opposition

G0476 ἀντί•δικος antídikôs *n.* (5x)
Roots:G0473 G1349 Compare:G4567 See:G1228
G0476.1 N-NSM ἀντίδικος (2x)
Mt 5:25 lest·at·any·time the legal·adversary should·hand you
1Pe 5:8 Because yeur legal·adversary, Slanderer, strolls·
G0476.1 N-DSM ἀντιδίκῳ (1x)
Mt 5:25 ·settling *terms* with·your legal·adversary swiftly,
G0476.1 N-GSM ἀντιδίκου (2x)
Lk 12:58 ·on·out with your legal·adversary to a·magistrate,
Lk 18:3 'Avenge me of my legal·adversary.'

G0477 ἀντί•θεσις antíthêsis *n.* (1x)
Roots:G0473 G5087
G0477 N-APF ἀντιθέσεις (1x)
1Ti 6:20 and *the* opposing·theories of·the falsely·named

G0478 ἀντι•καθ•ίστημι antikathístēmi *v.* (1x)
Roots:G0473 G2525
G0478.2 V-2AAI-2P ἀντικατέστητε (1x)
Heb 12:4 blood did·yeu·fully·resist, strenuously·struggling

G0479 ἀντι•καλέω antikalĕō *v.* (1x)
Roots:G0473 G2564
G0479 V-AAS-3P ἀντικαλέσωσιν (1x)
Lk 14:12 lest they also should·call·for you in·return, and a·

G0480 ἀντί•κειμαι antíkêimai *v.* (8x)
Roots:G0473 G2749
G0480.2 V-PNI-3S ἀντίκειται (2x)
Gal 5:17 And these are·fully·set·opposed to·one·another,
1Ti 1:10 else fully·set·opposed to·the healthy·and·sound
G0480.2 V-PNP-DSM ἀντικειμένῳ (1x)
1Ti 5:14 for·defamation by·the·one being·fully·set·opposed.
G0480.2 V-PNP-GPM ἀντικειμένων (1x)
Php 1:28 by·the·ones who·are·being·fully·set·opposed—
G0480.2 V-PNP-NSM ἀντικείμενος (1x)
2Th 2:4 the·one who·is·being·fully·set·opposed and 'is·
G0480.2 V-PNP-NPM ἀντικείμενοι (3x)
Lk 13:17 the·ones being·fully·set·opposed to·him were·put·
Lk 21:15 the·ones who·are·fully·set·opposed to·yeu shall·
1Co 16:9 *there·are* many who·are·being·fully·set·opposed.

G0481 ἀντικρύ antikrý *adv.* (1x)
Roots:G0473
G0481 ADV ἀντικρύ (1x)
Ac 20:15 we·arrived the following *day* opposite Chios; and

G0482 ἀντι•λαμβάνομαι antilambánômai *v.* (3x)
Roots:G0473 G2983 Compare:G0997 G3348 G3313
See:G0484
G0482.1 V-PNP-NPM ἀντιλαμβανόμενοι (1x)
1Ti 6:2 the·ones who·are·likewise·taking·hold of·the good·
G0482.2 V-2ADI-3S ἀντελάβετο (1x)
Lk 1:54 "He·helped·and·supported his servant·boy IsraEl,
G0482.3 V-PNN ἀντιλαμβάνεσθαι (1x)
Ac 20:35 it·is·mandatory to·be·helpful·and·supportive of·the

G0483 ἀντι•λέγω antilégō *v.* (10x)
Roots:G0473 G3004 See:G0485
G0483.2 V-PAP-APM ἀντιλέγοντας (1x)
Tit 1:9 instruction and to·convict the·ones contradicting.
G0483.2 V-PAP-GPM ἀντιλεγόντων (1x)
Ac 28:19 But with·the Judeans contradicting *this*, I·was·
G0483.2 V-PAP-NPM ἀντιλέγοντες (1x)
Ac 13:45 being·said by Paul, contradicting and reviling.
G0483.2 V-IAI-3P ἀντέλεγον (1x)
Ac 13:45 and were·contradicting the·things being·said by
G0483.3 V-PAP-ASM ἀντιλέγοντα (1x)
Rm 10:21 a·People being·obstinate and contradictory."
G0483.3 V-PAP-NPM ἀντιλέγοντες (1x)
Lk 20:27 (the·ones being·contradictory *by·saying that* there·
G0483.4 V-PAI-3S ἀντιλέγει (1x)
Jn 19:12 making himself a·king speaks·against Caesar."
G0483.4 V-PPI-3S ἀντιλέγεται (1x)
Ac 28:22 known to·us that everywhere it·is·spoken·against."
G0483.4 V-PPP-ASN ἀντιλεγόμενον (1x)
Lk 2:34 in IsraEl, and for a·sign being·spoken·against,
G0483.5 V-PAP-APM ἀντιλέγοντας (1x)
Tit 2:9 to·be·most·satisfying in all *things*, not sassing·back

G0484 ἀντί•ληψις antílēpsis *n.* (1x)
Roots:G0482
G0484.1 N-APF ἀντιλήψεις (1x)
1Co 12:28 of·healing, supportive·helps, sound·guidance,

G0485 ἀντι•λογία antilôgía *n.* (4x)
Roots:G0483 Compare:G2214 G3859 G4714 G1370
G0485.1 N-GSF ἀντιλογίας (1x)
Heb 7:7 And apart·from any contradiction, the lesser is·
G0485.2 N-ASF ἀντιλογίαν (1x)
Heb 12:3 ·patiently·endured such hostile·grumbling by the
G0485.2 N-DSF ἀντιλογίᾳ (1x)
Jud 1:11 ·perished in·the hostile·grumbling of·Korah.
G0485.3 N-GSF ἀντιλογίας (1x)
Heb 6:16 *is* to·them an·utter·end of·every conflict.

G0486 ἀντι•λοιδορέω antilôidôrĕō *v.* (1x)
Roots:G0473 G3058
G0486 V-IAI-3S ἀντελοιδόρει (1x)
1Pe 2:23 was·not defaming·in·reply; when·suffering, he·

G0487 ἀντί•λυτρον antílytrôn *n.* (1x)
Roots:G0473 G3083
G0487.2 N-ASN ἀντίλυτρον (1x)
1Ti 2:6 himself *as* a·substitutionary·ransom on·behalf·of·all

G0488 ἀντι•μετρέω antimêtrĕō *v.* (2x)
Roots:G0473 G3354
G0488 V-FPI-3S ἀντιμετρηθήσεται (2x)
Lk 6:38 it·shall·be·additionally·measured·back to·yeu."
Mt 7:2 it·shall·be·additionally·measured·back to·yeu.

G0489 ἀντι•μισθία antimisthía *n.* (2x)
Roots:G0473 G3408 Compare:G0467
G0489.3 N-ASF ἀντιμισθίαν (1x)
2Co 6:13 Now for·the same due·reciprocation (I·say *this* as
G0489.4 N-ASF ἀντιμισθίαν (1x)
Rm 1:27 the due·payback which is·mandatory·for their error.

G0490 Ἀντιόχεια Antiôchêia *n/l.* (22x)
See:G0491
G0490.1 N/L-ASF Ἀντιόχειαν (9x)
Ac 11:20 who, after·entering into Antioch, were·speaking to
Ac 11:26 him, he·brought him to Antioch. And it·happened,
Ac 11:27 prophets came·down from JeruSalem to Antioch.
Ac 14:26 And·from·there, they·sailed·off to Antioch, where
Ac 15:22 ·among themselves to Antioch together with·Paul
Ac 15:23 to·*our* brothers, the·ones in Antioch and Syria and
Ac 15:30 after·being·dismissed, they·came to Antioch, and
Ac 18:22 Called·Out·citizenry, he·walked·down to Antioch.
Gal 2:11 But when Peter came to Antioch, I·withstood him
G0490.1 N/L-DSF Ἀντιοχείᾳ (3x)
Ac 11:26 ·imparted·as·a·divine·message in Antioch *that*
Ac 13:1 the Called·Out·citizenry being in Antioch, prophets
Ac 15:35 BarNabas were·lingering in Antioch, instructing
G0490.1 N/L-GSF Ἀντιοχείας (2x)
Ac 11:19 ·to Phoenicia, Cyprus, and Antioch, speaking the
Ac 11:22 BarNabas to·go·throughout as·far·as·to Antioch,
EG0490.1 (1x)
Ac 12:25 returned·back *to·Antioch* from·among JeruSalem
G0490.2 N/L-ASF Ἀντιόχειαν (2x)
Ac 13:14 Perga, came·directly to Antiochia of·Pisidia. And
Ac 14:21 ·back to Lystra, and *to* Iconium, and to·Antiochia,
G0490.2 N/L-DSF Ἀντιοχείᾳ (1x)
2Ti 3:11 — such·as·what happened to·me at Antiochia, at
G0490.2 N/L-GSF Ἀντιοχείας (1x)
Ac 14:19 *certain* Jews came·up from Antiochia and Iconium,
EG0490.2 (3x)
Ac 13:44 all the city *of·Antiochia* did·gather·together to·hear
Ac 13:50 the foremost·men of·the city *of·Antiochia*, and
Ac 14:1 And accordingly *as in·Antiochia*, it·happened the

G0491 Ἀντιοχεύς Antiôchêús *n/g.* (1x)
Roots:G0490
G0491.1 N/G-ASM Ἀντιοχέα (1x)
Ac 6:5 and NicoLaos, a·convert·to·Judaism of·Antioch;

G0492 ἀντι•παρ•έρχομαι antiparérchômai *v.* (2x)
Roots:G0473 G3928
G0492.2 V-2AAI-3S ἀντιπαρῆλθεν (2x)

Αα Ββ Γγ Δδ Εε Ζζ Ηη Θθ Ιι Κκ Λλ Μμ Νν Ξξ Οο Ππ Ρρ Σσ Ττ Υυ Φφ Χχ Ψψ Ωω

Lk 10:31 after·seeing him, he·passed·by·on·the·other·side.
Lk 10:32 and seeing *him*, passed·by·on·the·other·side.

G0493 Ἀντί•πας Antípas *n/p.* (1x)
Roots:G0473 G3962 See:G0494
G0493.2 N/P-NSM Ἀντίπας (1x)
Rv 2:13 in the days in which AntiPas *was* my trustworthy

G0494 Ἀντι•πατρίς Antipatrís *n/l.* (1x)
Roots:G0473 G3962 See:G0493
G0494.2 N/L-ASF Ἀντιπατρίδα (1x)
Ac 23:31 they·brought *him* through the night to AntiPatris.

G0495 ἀντι•πέραν antipéran *adv.* (1x)
Roots:G0473 G4008
G0495 ADV ἀντιπέραν (1x)
Lk 8:26 which is on·the·opposite·side of·Galilee.

G0496 ἀντι•πίπτω antipíptō *v.* (1x)
Roots:G0473 G4098 Compare:G0436 See:G5227
G0496.2 V-PAI-2P ἀντιπίπτετε (1x)
Ac 7:51 and ears, yeu always do·violently·oppose the Holy

G0497 ἀντι•στρατεύομαι antistratêúômai *v.* (1x)
Roots:G0473 G4754 Compare:G4170
G0497.1 V-PNP-ASM ἀντιστρατευόμενον (1x)
Rm 7:23 strategically·warring·against the Royal-Law of·my

G0498 ἀντι•τάσσομαι antitássômai *v.* (5x)
Roots:G0473 G5021 Compare:G0436
G0498 V-PMI-3S ἀντιτάσσεται (3x)
Jac 4:6 " God arranges·himself·against haughty·men, but
Jac 5:6 he·does·not presently·arrange·himself·against yeu.
1Pe 5:5 " God arranges·himself·against haughty·men but
G0498 V-PMP-GPM ἀντιτασσομένων (1x)
Ac 18:6 *the Jews* arranging·themselves·against them and
G0498 V-PMP-NSM ἀντιτασσόμενος (1x)
Rm 13:2 the·one arranging·himself·against the authority

G0499 ἀντί•τυπον antítypôn *adj.* (3x)
Roots:G0473 G5179 See:G5296
G0499.2 A-NSN ἀντίτυπον (1x)
1Pe 3:21 *The* corresponding·pattern, which even now saves
G0499.2 A-APN ἀντίτυπα (1x)
Heb 9:24 *which·are the* corresponding·patterns of·the true,
EG0499.2 (1x)
Heb 8:3 and sacrifices, by·which *pattern, it·is* necessary *for*

G0500 ἀντί•χριστος antíchristôs *n.* (5x)
Roots:G0473 G5547 See:G1136 G3098
G0500.1 N-NSM ἀντίχριστος (2x)
1Jn 2:22 ·one is the adversary·of·the·Anointed-One, the·one
2Jn 1:7 the impostor and the adversary·of·the·Anointed-One.
G0500.1 N-NPM ἀντίχριστοι (1x)
1Jn 2:18 have·become adversaries·of·the·Anointed-One, by·
G0500.2 N-NSM ἀντίχριστος (1x)
1Jn 2:18 that the Adversary·of·the·Anointed-One is·coming,
G0500.2 N-GSM ἀντιχρίστου (1x)
1Jn 4:3 of·the Adversary·of·the·Anointed-One, of·which

G0501 ἀντλέω antlḗō *v.* (4x)
G0501.2 V-PAN ἀντλεῖν (1x)
Jn 4:15 nor·even should·come here to·draw·out *water*."
G0501.2 V-AAM-2P ἀντλήσατε (1x)
Jn 2:8 And he·says to·them, "Draw·*it*·out now and bring *it*
G0501.2 V-AAN ἀντλῆσαι (1x)
Jn 4:7 a·woman from·out of·Samaria to·draw·out water.
G0501.2 V-RAP-NPM ἠντληκότες (1x)
Jn 2:9 (but the attendants having·drawn·out the water had·

G0502 ἄντλημα ántlēma *n.* (1x)
Roots:G0501
G0502.2 N-ASN ἄντλημα (1x)
Jn 4:11 you·have not·even a·bucket·for·drawing·water, and

G0503 ἀντ•οφθαλμέω antôphthalméō *v.* (1x)
Roots:G0473 G3788
G0503.3 V-PAN ἀντοφθαλμεῖν (1x)
Ac 27:15 in·it, and not being·able to·tack into·the wind,

G0504 ἄν•υδρος ánydrôs *adj.* (4x)
Roots:G0001 G5204
G0504.1 A-NPF ἄνυδροι (2x)
Jud 1:12 thick·clouds without·water being·carried·about by
2Pe 2:17 These are wellsprings without·water, thick·clouds
G0504.2 A-GPM ἀνύδρων (2x)
Lk 11:24 the man·of·clay†, it·goes through waterless places,
Mt 12:43 the man·of·clay†, it·goes through waterless places,

G0505 ἀν•υπόκριτος anypókritôs *adj.* (6x)
Roots:G0001 G5272
G0505 A-NSF ἀνυπόκριτος (2x)
Rm 12:9 Love *must·be* without·hypocrisy, utterly·detesting
Jac 3:17 without·discrimination and without·hypocrisy.
G0505 A-ASF ἀνυπόκριτον (1x)
1Pe 1:22 Spirit unto a·brotherly·affection without·hypocrisy,
G0505 A-DSF ἀνυποκρίτῳ (1x)
2Co 6:6 by Holy Spirit, by love without·hypocrisy,
G0505 A-GSF ἀνυποκρίτου (2x)
1Ti 1:5 conscience, and of·a·trust without·hypocrisy—
2Ti 1:5 recollection of·the trust without·hypocrisy in you,

G0506 ἀν•υπό•τακτος anypótaktôs *adj.* (4x)
Roots:G0001 G5293 Compare:G3876
xLangAlso:H4805
G0506.1 A-ASN ἀνυπότακτον (1x)
Heb 2:8 ·even·one·thing did *God* leave unsubjugated to·him.
G0506.2 A-NPM ἀνυπότακτοι (1x)
Tit 1:10 For there·are many insubordinate and idle·talkers
G0506.2 A-DPM ἀνυποτάκτοις (1x)
1Ti 1:9 but for·lawless·ones and for·insubordinate·ones, for·
G0506.3 A-APN ἀνυπότακτα (1x)
Tit 1:6 of·an·unsaved·lifestyle or insubordinations

G0507 ἄνω ánō *adv.* (9x)
Roots:G0303 Compare:G5228 See:G0508 G0509 G0511 G1883
G0507.1 ADV ἄνω (3x)
Jn 11:41 And Jesus lifted the eyes upward and declared,
Heb 12:15 sprouting upward should·firmly·harass *yeu* and
Php 3:14 *it* toward the prize of·the upward calling of·God in
G0507.2 ADV ἄνω (5x)
Jn 8:23 I·myself am birthed·from up·above. Yeu·yeurselves
Ac 2:19 ·give wonders in the heaven up·above and signs on
Gal 4:26 But the JeruSalem up·above is free, which is *the*
Col 3:1 ·the Anointed-One, seek the·things up·above, where
Col 3:2 Contemplate the·things up·above, not the·things
G0507.3 ADV ἄνω (1x)
Jn 2:7 And they·overfilled them until topped·over.

G0508 ἀνώ•γεον anṓgêôn *n.* (2x)
Roots:G0507 G1093 Compare:G5253
G0508.2 N-ASN ἀνώγεον (2x)
Lk 22:12 yeu a·big upper·room having·been·spread·out *for*·
Mk 14:15 yeu a·big upper·room having·been·spread·out *for*·

G0509 ἄνω•θεν ánōthên *adv.* (13x)
Roots:G0507 Compare:G0756 G3825
G0509.1 ADV ἄνωθεν (7x)
Jn 3:3 unless someone should·be·born from·above, he·is·
Jn 3:7 'It·is·necessary·for yeu to·be·born from·above.'
Jn 3:31 "The·one who·is·coming from·above is up·above all.
Jn 19:11 ·been·given to·you from·above. On·account·of that,
Jac 1:17 complete endowment is from·above, descending
Jac 3:15 *that* which·is·coming·down from·above, but·rather
Jac 3:17 But the wisdom *that·is* from·above is first, in·fact,
G0509.2 ADV ἄνωθεν (2x)
Mt 27:51 of·the Temple is·torn in two from top to bottom.
Mk 15:38 of·the Temple was·torn in two from top to bottom.
G0509.3 ADV ἄνωθεν (3x)
Jn 19:23 woven *continuously* from·the·start throughout all
Lk 1:3 ·followed all·things accurately from·the·start, to·write
Ac 26:5 Foreknowing me from·the·start (if they·should·
G0509.4 ADV ἄνωθεν (1x)
Gal 4:9 to·be·slaves, *once* again starting·over·from·the·top?

G0510 ἀνωτερικός anōtêrikós *adj.* (1x)
Roots:G0511
G0510.1 A-APN ἀνωτερικά (1x)
Ac 19:1 ·throughout the uppermost districts *of·Macedonia*,

G0511 ἀνώτερος anṓtêrôs *adj.* (2x)
Roots:G0507 Compare:G5308 G5242 See:G0510
G0511.2 A-ASN ἀνώτερον (1x)
Lk 14:10 'Friend, walk·further·up higher.' Then glory shall·
G0511.3 A-ASN ἀνώτερον (1x)
Heb 10:8 *After* saying above, that "Sacrifice and offering

G0512 ἀν•ωφελής anōphêlḗs *adj.* (2x)
Roots:G0001 G5624 Compare:G0255 G0888
G0512.2 A-NPF ἀνωφελεῖς (1x)
Tit 3:9 for they·are unprofitable and futile·things.
G0512.2 A-ASN ἀνωφελές (1x)
Heb 7:18 on·account·of it *being* weak and unprofitable.

G0513 ἀξίνη axínē *n.* (2x)
Compare:G4486 G4252-2
xLangEquiv:H4621 xLangAlso:H1631
G0513 N-NSF ἀξίνη (2x)
Lk 3:9 "And even·now also, the ax is·laid·out to the root of·
Mt 3:10 "And even·now also, the ax is·laid·out to the root

G0514 ἄξιος áxiôs *adj.* (44x)
Roots:G0071 Compare:G5093
G0514.2 A-NSM ἄξιος (16x)
Jn 1:27 I·myself am not *even* worthy that I·may·loosen his
Lk 7:4 "He·is worthy for·whom this shall·be·personally·
Lk 10:7 the workman is worthy of·his payment·of·service.
Lk 15:19 and am no·longer worthy to·be·called your son;
Lk 15:21 and I·am no·longer worthy to·be·called your son.
Ac 13:25 the shoes of·whose feet I·am not worthy to·loose.'
Heb 11:38 the world was not worthy), being·wanderers in
Mt 10:11 ·by·inquiring who in it is worthy, and·there abide
Mt 10:37 mother over me is not worthy of·me, and the·one
Mt 10:37 son or daughter over me is not worthy of·me.
Mt 10:38 follow right·behind me, he·is not worthy of·me.
1Ti 4:9 *is* the saying and worthy of·all full·acceptance.
Rv 4:11 "You·are worthy, O·Lord, to·receive the glory and
Rv 5:2 voice, "Who is worthy to·open·up the official·scroll
Rv 5:4 not·even·one·man was·found worthy to·open·up and
Rv 5:9 saying, "You·are worthy to·take the official·scroll
G0514.2 A-NSF ἀξία (2x)
Mt 10:13 in·fact the home should·be worthy, *let* yeur peace
Mt 10:13 it, but if it·should·not be worthy, *let* yeur peace
G0514.2 A-NSN ἄξιον (2x)
Lk 23:15 and behold, not·even·one·thing worthy of·death is
Rv 5:12 saying with·a·loud voice, "Worthy is the Lamb
G0514.2 A-NPM ἄξιοι (3x)
Mt 22:8 but the·ones having·been·called were not worthy.
Rm 1:32 ·ones practicing such·things are worthy of·death),
Rv 3:4 ·along with me in white, because they·are worthy.
G0514.2 A-NPN ἄξια (1x)
Rm 8:18 season *are* not worthy *to·be·compared* alongside the
G0514.2 A-ASN ἄξιον (4x)
Ac 23:29 having not·even·one allegation worthy of·death or
Ac 25:11 or have·practiced anything worthy of·death, I·do·
Ac 25:25 ·practiced not·even·one·thing worthy of·death, and
Ac 26:31 practices not·even·one·thing worthy of·death or of·
G0514.2 A-APM ἀξίους (4x)
Lk 3:8 "Now·then, produce fruits worthy of·the repentance,
Ac 13:46 ·judge yeurselves not worthy of·the eternal
Mt 3:8 Now·then, produce fruits worthy of·the repentance.
1Ti 6:1 ·consider their·own masters worthy of·all honor, in·
G0514.2 A-APN ἄξια (1x)
Ac 26:20 God, practicing works worthy of·the repentance.
EG0514.2 (3x)
Jn 6:7 "Two·hundred denarii *worth* of·bread is·not sufficient
Mt 17:27 ·find a·silver·stater·coin *(worth four drachmas)*.
Mk 6:37 ·we·buy two·hundred denarii *worth* of·bread, and
G0514.3 A-NSM ἄξιος (3x)
Mt 10:10 the workman is deserving of·his provision·of·food.
1Ti 1:15 *is* trustworthy and deserving of·all full·acceptance:
1Ti 5:18 workman *is* deserving of·his payment·of·service."
G0514.3 A-NPM ἄξιοι (1x)
Rv 16:6 blood to·drink, for they·are deserving *of·Wrath*."
G0514.3 A-APN ἄξια (1x)

Lk 12:48 but doing things·deserving of·punishing·blows,
G0514.4 A-NSN ἄξιον (2x)
2Th 1:3 yeu, brothers, just·as it·is appropriate, because yeur
1Co 16:4 And if it·should·be appropriate *for* me·also to·
G0514.4 A-APN ἄξια (1x)
Lk 23:41 we·receive·in·full appropriate·*punishment* for·what

G0515 ἀξιόω axiόō *v.* (7x)
Roots:G0514
G0515.1 V-RPI-3S ἠξίωται (1x)
Heb 3:3 this·man has·been·counted·worthy of·more glory
G0515.2 V-FPI-3S ἀξιωθήσεται (1x)
Heb 10:29 shall·he·be·considered·deserving of·a·worse
G0515.2 V-PPM-3P ἀξιούσθωσαν (1x)
1Ti 5:17 well must·be·considered·deserving of·double honor
G0515.2 V-AAI-1S ἠξίωσα (1x)
Lk 7:7 neither did·I·consider my·own·self deserving to·come
G0515.2 V-AAS-3S ἀξιώσῃ (1x)
2Th 1:11 that our God may·consider yeu deserving of·the
G0515.3 V-PAI-1P ἀξιοῦμεν (1x)
Ac 28:22 But we·consider·it·appropriate to·hear personally·
G0515.3 V-IAI-3S ἠξίου (1x)
Ac 15:38 was·not considering·it·appropriate to·personally·

G0516 ἀξίως axíōs *adv.* (6x)
Roots:G0514
G0516.1 ADV ἀξίως (3x)
1Th 2:12 for yeu to·walk worthily of·God, the·one calling
Eph 4:1 implore yeu to·walk worthily of·the calling by·
Col 1:10 *such·for* yeu to·walk worthily of·the Lord into all
G0516.2 ADV ἀξίως (3x)
Rm 16:2 her in *the* Lord, as·is·worthy of·the holy·ones, and
Php 1:27 ·as·a·good·citizen (as·is·worthy of·the good·news
3Jn 1:6 ·onward·on·their·journey, as·is·worthy of·God, *then*

G0517 ἀ•όρατος aὁratôs *adj.* (5x)
Roots:G0001 G3707 Compare:G0852 G0855
G0517 A-NPN ἀόρατα (2x)
Rm 1:20 the invisible·things of·him are·quite·clearly·seen,
Col 1:16 ·ones clearly·visible and the·ones invisible, whether
G0517 A-ASM ἀόρατον (1x)
Heb 11:27 ·endured as one·clearly·seeing the Invisible-One.
G0517 A-DSM ἀοράτῳ (1x)
1Ti 1:17 ·the ages, incorruptible, invisible, to·*the*·only wise
G0517 A-GSM ἀοράτου (1x)
Col 1:15 who is *the* derived·image of·the invisible God, *the*

G0518 ἀπ•αγγέλλω apangéllō *v.* (44x)
Roots:G0575 G0032 Compare:G0312
xLangAlso:H5046
G0518.1 V-FAI-1S ἀπαγγελῶ (1x)
Heb 2:12 *to·Yahweh*, "I·shall·announce your name to·my
G0518.1 V-FAI-3S ἀπαγγελεῖ (1x)
Mt 12:18 him, and he·shall·announce tribunal·justice to·the
G0518.1 V-PAI-1P ἀπαγγέλλομεν (2x)
1Jn 1:2 ·seen *it*, and testify, and announce to·yeu the eternal
1Jn 1:3 ·clearly·seen and have·heard, we·announce to·yeu,
G0518.1 V-PAP-APM ἀπαγγέλλοντας (1x)
Ac 15:27 and Silas, themselves announcing also *to·yeu* the
G0518.1 V-PAP-NSF ἀπαγγέλλουσα (1x)
Jn 20:18 Magdalene came announcing to·the disciples that
G0518.1 V-PAP-NSM ἀπαγγέλλων (2x)
Ac 26:20 But·rather announcing first to·the·ones in
1Co 14:25 ·shall·fall·prostrate to·God, announcing that God
G0518.1 V-AAI-3S ἀπήγγειλεν (8x)
Lk 8:47 falling·down·before him, she·announced to·him, in·
Lk 14:21 ·close, that slave announced these·things to·his
Ac 11:13 And he·announced to·us how he·saw the angel in
Ac 12:14 her joy, but running·in, she·announced, "Peter is·
Ac 16:36 And the prison·warden announced this saying to
Ac 22:26 he·announced to·the regiment·commander, saying
Ac 28:21 brothers arriving·publicly announced or spoken
Mk 16:10 ·one, after·traversing, announced *it* to·the·ones
G0518.1 V-AAI-3P ἀπήγγειλαν (10x)
Jn 4:51 approached·and·met him, and announced *to·him*,
Lk 8:34 they·fled; and going·off, they·announced *it* in the
Lk 8:36 *it*, then·also announced to·them by·what·means the·
Lk 9:36 ·silent, and they·announced to·not·even·one·man in
Lk 18:37 And they·announced to·him that Jesus of·Natsareth
Lk 24:9 the chamber·tomb, they·announced all these·things
Ac 5:22 And returning, they·announced *it*
Mt 8:33 ·off into the city, they·announced all the·things
Mt 28:11 into the City, announced to·the chief·priests
Mk 16:13 And·those·men, going·off, announced *it* to·the
G0518.1 V-AAM-2P ἀπαγγείλατε (4x)
Ac 12:17 he·declared, "Go·announce these·things to·Jacob,
Mt 2:8 whenever yeu·should·find *him*, announce *it* to·me,
Mt 11:4 "Traversing, announce to·John those·things·which
Mt 28:10 ·must·head·on·out *and* announce to·my brothers
G0518.1 V-AAN ἀπαγγεῖλαι (3x)
Ac 23:19 "What is·it that you·have to·announce to·me?
Mt 28:8 and with·great joy, they·ran to·announce *it* to·his
Mt 28:9 And as they·were·traversing to·announce *it* to·his
G0518.1 V-2API-3S ἀπηγγέλη (1x)
Lk 8:20 And it·is·announced to·him, *with·several* saying,
G0518.2 V-PAI-3P ἀπαγγέλλουσιν (1x)
1Th 1:9 For they·themselves report concerning us, what·
G0518.2 V-PAP-NPM ἀπαγγέλλοντες (1x)
Lk 13:1 were·present *who·were* reporting to·him concerning
G0518.2 V-AAI-3S ἀπήγγειλεν (2x)
Ac 5:25 Then coming·close, someone reported to·them,
Ac 23:16 entering into the barracks, he·reported *it* to·Paul.
G0518.2 V-AAI-3P ἀπήγγειλαν (4x)
Lk 7:18 of·John *the Immerser* reported·to him concerning all
Ac 4:23 ·own·company and reported what·many·things *that*
Mt 14:12 And going·*on*, they·reported *it* to·YeShua.
Mk 6:30 alongside Jesus and reported to·him all·things, even
G0518.2 V-AAM-2P ἀπαγγείλατε (1x)
Lk 7:22 "Traversing, report to·John what·things yeu·saw
G0518.2 V-AAN ἀπαγγεῖλαι (1x)
Ac 23:17 for he·has a·certain·thing to·report to·him."

G0519 ἀπ•άγχομαι apánchômai *v.* (1x)
Roots:G0575 See:G0043
G0519.2 V-AMI-3S ἀπήγξατο (1x)
Mt 27:5 And going·off, he·hanged·himself.

G0520 ἀπ•άγω apágō *v.* (16x)
Roots:G0575 G0071
G0520.1 V-PAP-NSF ἀπάγουσα (2x)
Mt 7:13 the way, the·one leading·off to the total·destruction,
Mt 7:14 ·been·pressed·down, the·one leading·off to the
G0520.1 V-2AAM-2S ἄπαγε (1x)
Ac 23:17 Paul was·replying, "Lead this young·man to the
G0520.1 V-2AAP-NSM ἀπαγαγών (1x)
Lk 13:15 feeding·trough, even leading·*him*·off to·watering?
G0520.2 V-PPP-NPM ἀπαγόμενοι (1x)
1Co 12:2 that yeu·were Gentiles being·led·away, even·as
G0520.2 V-2AAI-3S ἀπήγαγεν (1x)
Ac 24:7 with much force, led·*him*·away out of·our hands,
G0520.2 V-2AAI-3P ἀπήγαγον (8x)
Jn 18:13 Then they·led him away first to HannAs *the proper*
Jn 19:16 And they·personally·took Jesus and led·*him*·away.
Lk 23:26 And as they·led him away, upon·grabbing·hold of·
Mt 26:57 ·holding YeShua led·*him*·away to Caiaphas the
Mt 27:2 And binding him, they·led·*him*·away and handed
Mt 27:31 ·own garments. And·then they·led him away to
Mk 14:53 And they·led Jesus away to the designated·high·
Mk 15:16 And the soldiers led him away inside the courtyard
G0520.2 V-2AAM-2P ἀπαγάγετε (1x)
Mk 14:44 Securely·hold him and lead·*him*·away securely."
G0520.2 V-APN ἀπαχθῆναι (1x)
Ac 12:19 ·ordered *for·them* to·be·led·away *to·execution.*

G0521 ἀ•παίδευτος apaídêutôs *adj.* (1x)
Roots:G0001 G3811
G0521.1 A-APF ἀπαιδεύτους (1x)
2Ti 2:23 and uneducated·and·undisciplined speculations,

G0522 ἀπ•αίρω apaírō *v.* (3x)
Roots:G0575 G0142
G0522.1 V-APS-3S ἀπαρθῇ (3x)
Lk 5:35 the bridegroom should·be·lifted·away from them,
Mt 9:15 the bridegroom should·be·lifted·away from them,
Mk 2:20 the bridegroom should·be·lifted·away from them,

G0523 ἀπ•αιτέω apaitéō *v.* (2x)
Roots:G0575 G0154 Compare:G1809
G0523 V-PAI-3P ἀπαιτοῦσιν (1x)
Lk 12:20 This night, they·are·demanding·back your soul
G0523 V-PAM-2S ἀπαίτει (1x)
Lk 6:30 taking·away your things, do·not demand·*them*·back.

G0524 ἀπ•αλγέω apalgéō *v.* (1x)
Roots:G0575
G0524 V-RAP-NPM ἀπηλγηκότες (1x)
Eph 4:19 who, having·become·apathetic, handed themselves

G0525 ἀπ•αλλάσσω apallássō *v.* (3x)
Roots:G0575 G0236 Compare:G0851
G0525.1 V-AAS-3S ἀπαλλάξῃ (1x)
Heb 2:15 and *that* he·may·release them, as·many·as·who
G0525.1 V-RPN ἀπηλλάχθαι (1x)
Lk 12:58 effort on the way to·have·been·released from him,
G0525.2 V-PPN ἀπαλλάσσεσθαι (1x)
Ac 19:12 and *for* the illnesses to·be·removed from them,

G0526 ἀπ•αλλοτριόω apallôtriόō *v.* (3x)
Roots:G0575 G0245 Compare:G3579
G0526.1 V-RPP-APM ἀπηλλοτριωμένους (1x)
Col 1:21 *as·those* having·been·utterly·alienated and enemies
G0526.1 V-RPP-NPM ἀπηλλοτριωμένοι (2x)
Eph 2:12 having·been·utterly·alienated from·the citizenship
Eph 4:18 *while* having·been·utterly·alienated from·the

G0527 ἁπαλός hapalós *adj.* (2x)
Compare:G3120 G4642
G0527 A-NSM ἁπαλός (2x)
Mt 24:32 should·become tender and should·sprout·forth the
Mk 13:28 should·become tender and should·sprout·forth the

G0528 ἀπ•αντάω apantáō *v.* (7x)
Roots:G0575 G0470-2 Compare:G2658 G4876
G5221 See:G0529
G0528 V-FAI-3S ἀπαντήσει (1x)
Mk 14:13 a·pitcher of·water shall·approach·and·meet yeu.
G0528 V-AAI-3S ἀπήντησεν (2x)
Mt 28:9 behold, YeShua approached·and·met them, saying,
Mk 5:2 immediately there·approached·and·met him out of·
G0528 V-AAI-3P ἀπήντησαν (2x)
Jn 4:51 walking·down, his slaves approached·and·met him,
Lk 17:12 ·certain village, there·approached·and·met him ten
G0528 V-AAN ἀπαντῆσαι (2x)
Lk 14:31 ten thousand to·approach·and·meet the·one who·is·
Ac 16:16 of·Pythonic·divination approached·and·met us,

G0529 ἀπ•άντησις apántēsis *n.* (4x)
Roots:G0528 See:G4877 G5222
G0529.2 N-ASF ἀπάντησιν (4x)
Ac 28:15 came·out to approach·and·meet us even·as·far·as
Mt 25:1 went·forth to approach·and·meet the bridegroom.
Mt 25:6 comes! Go·forth to approach·and·meet him!'
1Th 4:17 in *the* thick·clouds to approach·and·meet the Lord

G0530 ἅ•παξ hápax *adv.* (17x)
Roots:G0537 Compare:G4218
G0530.1 ADV ἅπαξ (2x)
Heb 9:7 But into the second *Tabernacle*, once per year, the
2Co 11:25 ·times, I·was·stoned once, I·was·shipwrecked
G0530.2 ADV ἅπαξ (5x)
Heb 6:4 for·the·ones after once being·enlightened, and after·
Heb 10:2 ·ministering, once having·been·purified *so·as* to·
Jud 1:5 ·remind yeu, *due·to* yeu once having·seen this: that
Php 4:16 in ThessaloNica yeu·sent also once and again to my
1Th 2:18 to yeu, in·fact I Paul, also once and again, but the
EG0530.2 (2x)
Heb 6:6 and·then *once* personally·falling·away … *it·is*
Gal 4:9 to·be·slaves, *once* again starting·over·from·the·top?
G0530.3 ADV ἅπαξ (2x)
Heb 12:26 saying, "Yet once·more I·myself do·shake not
Heb 12:27 And the "Yet once·more," makes·plain the
G0530.4 ADV ἅπαξ (5x)

Heb 9:26 But now only·once, at *the* complete·consummation
Heb 9:27 men·of·clay† to·die only·once and·then *to·have* a·
Heb 9:28 the Anointed-One, after·being·offered only·once '
Jud 1:3 already·being·handed·down only·once to·the holy·
1Pe 3:18 also suffered only·once concerning moral·failures,
G0530.5 ADV ἅπαξ (1x)
1Pe 3:20 ·obstinate in·times·past, when at·one·time, the

G0531 ἀ•παρά•βατος aparábatôs *adj.* (1x)
Roots:G0001 G3845
G0531 A-ASF ἀπαράβατον (1x)
Heb 7:24 ·age, has the non-transferable sacred·priesthood,

G0532 ἀ•παρα•σκεύαστος aparaskêuastôs *adj.* (1x)
Roots:G0001 G3903 Compare:G0180-2
G0532 A-APM ἀπαρασκευάστους (1x)
2Co 9:4 and find yeu personally·unprepared, we·ourselves

G0533 ἀπ•α•ρνέομαι aparnêómai *v.* (13x)
Roots:G0575 G0720 Compare:G0550
G0533 V-FDI-1S ἀπαρνήσομαι (2x)
Mt 26:35 with·you, no, I·shall·not utterly·deny you." And·
Mk 14:31 with·you, no, I·shall·not utterly·deny you." And
G0533 V-FDI-2S ἀπαρνήσῃ (7x)
Jn 13:38 crow, until you·shall·utterly·deny me three·times.
Lk 22:34 this·day before you·shall·utterly·deny three·times,
Lk 22:61 crowing, you·shall·utterly·deny me three·times."
Mt 26:34 crowing, you·shall·utterly·deny me three·times."
Mt 26:75 crowing, you·shall·utterly·deny me three·times."
Mk 14:30 twice, you·shall·utterly·deny me three·times."
Mk 14:72 twice, you·shall·utterly·deny me three·times."
G0533 V-FPI-3S ἀπαρνηθήσεται (1x)
Lk 12:9 men·of·clay† shall·be·utterly·denied in·the·sight·of·
G0533 V-ADM-3S ἀπαρνησάσθω (3x)
Lk 9:23 right·behind me, he·must·utterly·deny himself and
Mt 16:24 right·behind me, he·must·utterly·deny himself,
Mk 8:34 right·behind me, let·him·utterly·deny himself, and

G0534 ἀπ•άρτι apárti *adv.* (1x)
Roots:G0575 G0737
G0534 ADV ἀπάρτι (1x)
Rv 14:13 the·ones dying in *the* Lord from·this·moment·on.'"

G0535 ἀπ•αρτισμός apartismós *n.* (1x)
Roots:G0575 G0739 Compare:G5055 See:G0534
G0535 N-ASM ἀπαρτισμόν (1x)
Lk 14:28 the *means* specifically·for *its* full·development?

G0536 ἀπ•αρχή aparchḗ *n.* (8x)
Roots:G0575 G0756
xLangEquiv:H1061 xLangAlso:H7225
G0536.2 N-NSF ἀπαρχή (6x)
Rm 11:16 the *portion of·dough offered as·a* firstfruit *is* holy,
Rm 16:5 Epaenetus, who is a·firstfruit of·Achaia to
1Co 15:20 He·became a·firstfruit of·the·ones having·been·
1Co 15:23 sequence: Anointed-One, a·firstfruit— afterward
1Co 16:15 of·Stephanas, that it·is a·firstfruit of·Achaia, and
Rv 14:4 ·the men·of·clay†, *being* a·firstfruit to·God and to·
G0536.2 N-ASF ἀπαρχήν (2x)
Rm 8:23 ·ourselves also, having the firstfruit of·the Spirit,
Jac 1:18 for us to·be a·certain firstfruit of·his creatures.

G0537 ἅ•πας hápas *adj.* (44x)
Roots:G0001 G3956
G0537.1 A-NSM ἅπας (1x)
Lk 19:48 they·may·do *it*, for absolutely·all the people were·
G0537.1 A-NSN ἅπαν (3x)
Lk 8:37 Then absolutely·all the multitude of·the region·
Lk 19:37 ·the Mount of·Olives, absolutely·all the multitude
Lk 23:1 And rising·up, absolutely·all the multitude of·them
G0537.1 A-NPM ἅπαντες (13x)
Lk 19:7 after·seeing *this*, absolutely·all were·murmuring,
Lk 21:4 For absolutely·all these·men cast from·out·of·their
Ac 2:1 they·were absolutely·all with·the·same·determination
Ac 2:4 And absolutely·all were·filled with·Holy Spirit, and
Ac 2:14 of·Judea and absolutely·all the·ones residing·in
Ac 4:31 ·together; and absolutely·all were·filled with·Holy
Ac 5:12 — (and they·were absolutely·all with·the·same· in
Ac 5:16 ·both·relieved·and·cured, absolutely·all *of·them*.
Ac 6:15 him, absolutely·all the·ones who·were·sitting·down
Ac 16:3 in those places, for absolutely·all had·seen that his
Ac 16:28 ·one·bit·of harm, for we·are absolutely·all here."
Mk 11:32 people, for absolutely·all·men were·holding John,
Jac 3:2 For in·many·things, absolutely·all *of·us* slip·up. If
G0537.1 A-ASM ἅπαντα (2x)
Lk 3:21 Now it·happened, when absolutely·all the people
Mk 16:15 to·them, "Traversing into absolutely·all the world,
G0537.1 A-APM ἅπαντας (9x)
Lk 5:26 And astonishment took·hold·of absolutely·all, and
Lk 7:16 ·fear·and·awe took·hold·of absolutely·all *of·them*,
Lk 9:15 ·did *so* in·this·manner, and absolutely·all reclined.
Lk 17:27 and completely·destroyed absolutely·all·of·them.
Lk 17:29 and completely·destroyed absolutely·all·of·them.
Ac 27:33 was·imploring absolutely·all·of·them to·partake
Mt 24:39 came, and took·away absolutely·all·of·them. "In·
Mk 5:40 casting·out absolutely·all·of·them, he·personally·
Mk 8:25 and looked·clearly·upon absolutely·all·men with·.
G0537.1 A-DPM ἅπασιν (1x)
Lk 3:16 John answered, saying to·absolutely·all *of·them*,
G0537.2 A-NPN ἅπαντα (1x)
Ac 11:10 three·times, and absolutely·all *of·it* was·drawn·up
G0537.2 A-ASM ἅπαντα (1x)
Lk 21:4 ·her destitution cast in·absolutely·all the livelihood
G0537.2 A-ASF ἅπασαν (1x)
Lk 4:6 "To·you I·shall·give absolutely·all this authority and
G0537.2 A-APN ἅπαντα (8x)
Lk 2:39 they·finished absolutely·all the·things according·to
Lk 5:11 dry·ground, leaving absolutely·all, they·followed
Lk 5:28 And leaving·behind absolutely·all, rising·up, he·
Lk 15:13 gathering·together absolutely·all, journeyed·abroad
Ac 10:8 after·recounting·in·detail absolutely·all·*these*·things
Ac 13:29 they·completed absolutely·all the·things having·
Mt 28:11 chief·priests absolutely·all the·things happening.
Eph 6:13 day, and after·accomplishing absolutely·all, *that*
G0537.2 A-GPN ἁπάντων (2x)
Lk 21:12 "But before absolutely·all these·things, they·shall·
Mt 6:32 that yeu·have·need of·absolutely·all these·things.
G0537.3 A-NPN ἅπαντα (1x)
Ac 4:32 it·was *having* absolutely·all·belongings *together in*
G0537.3 A-APN ἅπαντα (1x)
Ac 2:44 they·were·having absolutely·all·belongings shared.

G0538 ἀπατάω apatáō *v.* (4x)
Compare:G4105 G5422 G5574 See:G0539
xLangEquiv:H5377 xLangAlso:H6601
G0538 V-PAM-3S ἀπατάτω (1x)
Eph 5:6 Let not·one·man delude yeu with·empty words, for
G0538 V-PAP-NSM ἀπατῶν (1x)
Jac 1:26 his tongue, but·rather deluding his·own heart, this·
G0538 V-API-3S ἠπατήθη (1x)
1Ti 2:14 And Adam was·not deluded, but the woman, being·
G0538 V-APP-NSF ἀπατηθεῖσα (1x)
1Ti 2:14 but the woman, being·deluded, has·come·to·be in

G0539 ἀπάτη apátē *n.* (8x)
Roots:G0538 Compare:G4106
G0539.1 N-DSF ἀπάτῃ (1x)
2Th 2:10 and with all the delusion of·unrighteousness in the·
G0539.1 N-DPF ἀπάταις (1x)
2Pe 2:13 their delusions while·indulging·themselves·among
G0539.1 N-GSF ἀπάτης (1x)
Col 2:8 ·*of* philosophy and an·empty delusion, according·to
EG0539.1 (1x)
2Th 2:2 to·be·woefully·disturbed *by·any delusion* (neither
G0539.2 N-GSF ἀπάτης (1x)
Eph 4:22 the·one being·corrupted by the delusional longings)
G0539.3 N-NSF ἀπάτη (2x)
Mt 13:22 the delusional·nature of·wealth altogether·choke
Mk 4:19 present·age— and the delusional·nature of·wealth—
G0539.3 N-DSF ἀπάτῃ (1x)
Heb 3:13 should·be·hardened through·the·delusional·nature.

G0540 ἀ•πάτωρ apátōr *adj.* (1x)
Roots:G0001 G3962 Compare:G3737 See:G0282
G0540 A-NSM ἀπάτωρ (1x)
Heb 7:3 *He·is* without·father, without·mother, without·

G0541 ἀπ•αύγασμα apaúgasma *n.* (1x)
Roots:G0575 G0826 See:G1306 G5081
G0541.2 N-NSN ἀπαύγασμα (1x)
Heb 1:3 *Son* (being *the* radiant·offshoot of·*his*·glory and *the*

G0542 ἀπ•είδω apêídō *v.* (1x)
Roots:G0575 G1492
G0542 V-2AAS-1S ἀπίδω (1x)
Php 2:23 as·soon·as I·should·fully·see the·things concerning

G0543 ἀ•πείθεια apêíthêia *n.* (8x)
Roots:G0545 See:G0544
G0543.1 N-GSF ἀπειθείας (4x)
Heb 4:11 ·fall by the same explicit·example of·the obstinate.
Eph 2:2 spirit now operating in the Sons of·the obstinate.
Eph 5:6 wrath of·God comes upon the Sons of·the obstinate.
Col 3:6 the wrath of·God comes on the Sons of·the obstinate,
EG0543.1 (1x)
Heb 4:3 ·as he·has·declared *concerning the obstinate·ones*,
G0543.2 N-ASF ἀπείθειαν (2x)
Heb 4:6 did·not enter on·account·of an·obstinate·attitude,
Rm 11:32 the *peoples* to an·obstinate·attitude, in·order·that
G0543.2 N-DSF ἀπειθείᾳ (1x)
Rm 11:30 ·shown·mercy by·the obstinate·attitude of·these,

G0544 ἀ•πειθέω apêithêō *v.* (16x)
Roots:G0545 See:G0543 xLangAlso:H5637
G0544.2 V-PAI-3P ἀπειθοῦσιν (1x)
1Pe 3:1 also, if some are·obstinate to·the Redemptive-word,
G0544.2 V-PAP-ASM ἀπειθοῦντα (1x)
Rm 10:21 toward a·People being·obstinate and contradictory
G0544.2 V-PAP-DPM ἀπειθοῦσιν (2x)
Rm 2:8 and in·fact, being·obstinate to·the Truth and are·
1Pe 2:7 presently·trusting. But to·those·being·obstinate,
G0544.2 V-PAP-GPM ἀπειθούντων (2x)
Rm 15:31 away·from the·ones being·obstinate in Judea, and
1Pe 4:17 end of·the·ones being·obstinate to·the good·news
G0544.2 V-PAP-NSM ἀπειθῶν (1x)
Jn 3:36 life-above, and the·one being·obstinate to·the Son
G0544.2 V-PAP-NPM ἀπειθοῦντες (3x)
Ac 14:2 *the* Jews, the·ones being·obstinate, roused·up and
Ac 17:5 But being·jealous, the obstinate Jews, even
1Pe 2:8 at·the Redemptive-word, being·obstinate. To which
G0544.2 V-IAI-3P ἠπείθουν (1x)
Ac 19:9 ·hardened and were·being·obstinate, speaking·ill·of
G0544.2 V-AAI-2P ἠπειθήσατε (1x)
Rm 11:30 yeu·yourselves also once were·obstinate to·God,
G0544.2 V-AAI-3P ἠπείθησαν (1x)
Rm 11:31 these now are·obstinate in·order·that by·yeur
G0544.2 V-AAP-DPM ἀπειθήσασιν (3x)
Heb 3:18 ' if·not to·the·ones who·were·being·obstinate?
Heb 11:31 with·the·ones who·were·being·obstinate,
1Pe 3:20 to·those·being·obstinate in·times·past, when at·

G0545 ἀ•πειθής apêithḗs *adj.* (6x)
Roots:G0001 G3982 See:G0544 G0543
G0545.2 A-NSM ἀπειθής (1x)
Ac 26:19 I·did·not become obstinate to·the heavenly vision.
G0545.2 A-NPM ἀπειθεῖς (3x)
Tit 1:16 *him*, being abhorrent, obstinate, and disqualified
Tit 3:3 also were once stupid, obstinate, being·deceived,
2Ti 3:2 haughty, revilers, obstinate to·parents, ungrateful,
G0545.2 A-APM ἀπειθεῖς (2x)
Lk 1:17 ' and *to·turn·back·around the* obstinate·ones by *the*
Rm 1:30 inventors of·bad·things; *being* obstinate to·parents,

G0546 ἀπειλέω apêilêō *v.* (2x)
Compare:G4768 G1690 See:G4324
G0546.3 V-IAI-3S ἠπείλει (1x)
1Pe 2:23 when·suffering, he·was·not threatening, but was·
G0546.3 V-AMS-1P ἀπειλησώμεθα (1x)
Ac 4:17 we·should·most·certainly·threaten them to·speak

G0547 ἀπειλή apêilḗ *n.* (4x)
Roots:G0546
G0547.3 N-ASF ἀπειλήν (1x)
Eph 6:9 them, giving·up the threatening, having·seen that

G0547.3 N-APF ἀπειλάς (1x)
Ac 4:29 take·notice·of their threatenings, and grant·to your
G0547.3 N-DSF ἀπειλῇ (1x)
Ac 4:17 — with·threatening, we·should·most·certainly·
G0547.4 N-GSF ἀπειλῆς (1x)
Ac 9:1 Saul, still seething with·menace and murder against

G0548 ἄπ•ειμι ápêimi *v.* (7x)
Roots:G0575 G1510 Compare:G0549 G1553 See:G0666
G0548.2 V-PXI-1S ἄπειμι (1x)
Col 2:5 For even though I·am·absent in·the flesh, but·yet I·
G0548.2 V-PXP-NSM ἀπών (5x)
Php 1:27 and seeing yeu or·else being·absent, I·may·hear
1Co 5:3 I, in·fact, even·though being·absent in·the body but
2Co 10:1 yeu, but being·absent am·more·bold toward yeu).
2Co 13:2 the second·time even while·being·absent now, I·
2Co 13:10 these·things while·being·absent, in·order·that I·
G0548.2 V-PXP-NPM ἀπόντες (1x)
2Co 10:11 through *our* letters while·being·absent, such *shall·*

G0549 ἄπ•ειμι ápêimi *v.* (1x)
Roots:G0575 G1510-1 Compare:G0548 G0565 See:G1826
G0549 V-IXI-3P ἀπήεσαν (1x)
Ac 17:10 after·coming·directly *there*, went·off into the

G0550 ἀπ•ειπόμην apêipómēn *v.* (1x)
Roots:G0575 G2036 Compare:G0720 G0533
G0550 V-2AMI-1P ἀπειπάμεθα (1x)
2Co 4:2 But·rather, we·have·renounced the hidden·things

G0551 ἀ•πείραστος apêírastôs *adj.* (1x)
Roots:G0001 G3987 See:G3985
G0551.2 A-NSM ἀπείραστος (1x)
Jac 1:13 for God is not·tempted with·moral·wrongs, and

G0552 ἄ•πειρος ápêirôs *adj.* (1x)
Roots:G0001 G3984
G0552 A-NSM ἄπειρος (1x)
Heb 5:13 milk *is* inexperienced with·*the*·Redemptive-word of·

G0553 ἀπ•εκ•δέχομαι apêkdéchômai *v.* (7x)
Roots:G0575 G1551 Compare:G1679
G0553 V-PNI-1P ἀπεκδεχόμεθα (3x)
Gal 5:5 ·Spirit, fully·await an·expectation of·righteousness
Rm 8:25 *then* through patient·endurance we·fully·await *it*.
Php 3:20 out·from which also we·fully·await *the* Savior, *the*
G0553 V-PNI-3S ἀπεκδέχεται (1x)
Rm 8:19 of·the creation fully·awaits the revealing of·the
G0553 V-PNP-APM ἀπεκδεχομένους (1x)
1Co 1:7 ·one gracious·bestowment while·fully·awaiting the
G0553 V-PNP-DPM ἀπεκδεχομένοις (1x)
Heb 9:28 ·visible to·the·ones who·are·fully·awaiting him for
G0553 V-PNP-NPM ἀπεκδεχόμενοι (1x)
Rm 8:23 who·are·fully·awaiting the·adoption·as·sons, *that·*

G0554 ἀπ•εκ•δύομαι apêkdyômai *v.* (2x)
Roots:G0575 G1562 Compare:G0659 G0114 See:G0555
G0554.1 V-ADP-NPM ἀπεκδυσάμενοι (1x)
Col 3:9 ·another, after·having·already·stripped·off the old
G0554.2 V-ADP-NSM ἀπεκδυσάμενος (1x)
Col 2:15 *And* after·utterly·despoiling the principalities and

G0555 ἀπ•έκ•δυσις apékdysis *n.* (1x)
Roots:G0554
G0555 N-DSF ἀπεκδύσει (1x)
Col 2:11 ·by·hand, with the stripping·off from·the body the

G0556 ἀπ•ελαύνω apêlaúnō *v.* (1x)
Roots:G0575 G1643 See:G4900
G0556 V-AAI-3S ἀπήλασεν (1x)
Ac 18:16 And he·drove them away from the Bema·

G0557 ἀπ•ελεγμός apêlêgmós *n.* (1x)
Roots:G0575 G1651
G0557.2 N-ASM ἀπελεγμόν (1x)
Ac 19:27 is·in·danger of·coming into discredit, but·yet also

G0558 ἀπ•ελεύθερος apêlêúthêrôs *n.* (1x)
Roots:G0575 G1658 Compare:G3032
G0558 N-NSM ἀπελεύθερος (1x)
1Co 7:22 a·slave, he·is *the* Lord's freedman, likewise also

G0559 Ἀπελλῆς Apêllễs *n/p.* (1x)
G0559 N/P-ASM Ἀπελλῆν (1x)
Rm 16:10 Greet Apelles, the·one verifiably·approved in

G0560 ἀπ•ελπίζω apêlpízō *v.* (1x)
Roots:G0575 G1679 See:G4276
G0560 V-PAP-NPM ἀπελπίζοντες (1x)
Lk 6:35 and lend, fully·expecting not·even·one·thing—

G0561 ἀπ•έν•αντι apénanti *adv.* (6x)
Roots:G0575 G1725 Compare:G2713
G0561.2 ADV ἀπέναντι (3x)
Ac 3:16 ·man this perfect·soundness fully·in·front of·yeu all.
Mt 21:2 ·traverse into the village fully·in·front of·yeu, and
Mt 27:24 ·off·his·own hands fully·in·front of·the crowd,
G0561.3 ADV ἀπέναντι (2x)
Mt 27:61 other Miryam, sitting·down fully·before the grave.
Rm 3:18 "There·is no fear of·God fully·before their eyes."
G0561.4 ADV ἀπέναντι (1x)
Ac 17:7 practice *things* in·full·opposition to·the decrees of·

G0562 ἀ•πέραντος apêrantôs *adj.* (1x)
Roots:G0001 G4008
G0562.2 A-DPF ἀπεράντοις (1x)
1Ti 1:4 to·give·heed to·myths and to·endless genealogies,

G0563 ἀ•περι•σπάστως apêrispástōs *adv.* (1x)
Roots:G0001 G4048-4
G0563.1 ADV ἀπερισπάστως (1x)
1Co 7:35 ·attending·well to·the Lord without·distraction.

G0564 ἀ•περί•τμητος apêrítmētôs *adj.* (1x)
Roots:G0001 G4059 xLangEquiv:H6189
G0564 A-VPM ἀπερίτμητοι (1x)
Ac 7:51 "Yeu·stiff-necked and uncircumcised in·the heart

G0565 ἀπ•έρχομαι apérchômai *v.* (120x)
ἀπ•έλευθομαι apéleuthômai [middle voice]
ἀπ•έλθω apélthō [active voice]
Roots:G0575 G2064 Compare:G4198 G0549 G0672 G1633 G0863
G0565.1 V-FDI-1P ἀπελευσόμεθα (1x)
Jn 6:68 "Lord, to whom shall·we·go? You·have utterances
G0565.1 V-PNP-GPF ἀπερχομένων (1x)
Mt 25:10 And with·them going·off to·buy *oil*, the
G0565.1 V-2AAI-3S ἀπῆλθεν (30x)
Jn 4:3 he·left Judea and went·off again into Galilee.
Jn 4:28 woman left her water·jar and went·off into the city,
Jn 4:43 the two days, he·went·off from·there and came·forth
Jn 4:47 of·Judea into Galilee, he·went·off toward him and
Jn 5:15 The man·of·clay† went·off and reported·in·detail to·
Jn 6:1 After these·things, Jesus went·off *to·the* other·side of·
Jn 11:28 these·things, she·went·off and hollered·out·for
Jn 12:19 ·thing? See, the world went·off right·behind him."
Lk 1:23 ·service were·fulfilled, *that* he·went·off to his·own
Lk 5:13 And immediately, the leprosy went·off from him.
Lk 5:25 he·was·laying·down on, he·went·off to his·own
Lk 24:12 ·out alone. And·then he·went·off, marveling to
Ac 9:17 And Ananias went·off and entered into the home.
Mt 4:24 And his fame went·off into all Syria.
Mt 9:7 And upon·being·awakened, he·went·off to his house.
Mt 14:25 of·the night, YeShua went·off toward them, '
Mt 16:4 And leaving them behind, he·went·off.
Mt 21:29 But eventually having·regret, he·went·off.
Mt 21:30 'I·myself *will*, sir,' yet he·did·not go·off.
Mt 27:60 to·the door of·the chamber·tomb, he·went·off.
Mk 1:35 ·night, he·went·out and went·off into a·desolate
Mk 1:42 immediately, the leprosy went·off from him, and
Mk 5:20 And he·went·off and began to·officially·herald in
Mk 5:24 So *Jesus* went·off with him, and a·large crowd was·
Mk 6:46 ·orderly·taking·leave·of them, he·went·off to the
Mk 7:24 after·rising·up from·there, he·went·off into the
Mk 8:13 the sailboat again, he·went·off to the other·side *of·*
Mk 14:10 one of·the twelve, went·off to the chief·priests,
Rv 12:17 the woman, and he·went·off to·make war with the
Rv 16:2 And the first went·off and poured·out his vial upon
G0565.1 V-2AAI-3P ἀπῆλθον (16x)
Jn 6:22 but·rather *that* his disciples went·off alone— *they·*
Jn 6:66 many of·his disciples went·off to·the·things left·
Jn 11:46 But some from·among them went·off to the
Jn 18:6 "I AM," they·went·off backwards and fell down·
Jn 20:10 So·then, the disciples went·off again to their·own
Lk 10:30 placing punishing·blows *on·him*, went·off, leaving
Lk 23:33 And when they·went·off to the place, the·one
Lk 24:24 some of·the·ones together with·us went·off to the
Ac 28:29 these·things, the Jews went·off, having a·large
Mt 8:32 And coming·forth, they·went·off into the herd of·
Mt 20:4 ·be right I·shall·give to·yeu.' And they·went·off.
Mt 22:22 they·marveled, and leaving him, they·went·off.
Mk 1:20 the hired·workers, they·went·off right·behind him.
Mk 3:13 ·whom he was·wanting, and they·went·off to him.
Mk 6:32 And they·went·off to a·desolate place in·the
Mk 12:12 So leaving him, they·went·off.
G0565.1 V-2AAN ἀπελθεῖν (6x)
Lk 8:31 ·that he·should·not order them to·go·off into the
Mt 8:18 ·ordered *to·make·ready* to·go·off to the other·side *of·*
Mt 8:21 freely·permit me first to·go·off and to·bury my
Mt 14:16 "They·have no need to·go·off; yeu·yeurselves give
Mt 16:21 that it·is·mandatory·for him to·go·off to JeruSalem,
Mk 9:43 the two hands *and* to·go·off into the Hell·Canyon,
G0565.1 V-2AAP-DSM ἀπελθόντι (1x)
Lk 9:59 "Lord, freely·permit me to·go·off first to·bury my
G0565.1 V-2AAP-GPM ἀπελθόντων (1x)
Lk 7:24 And with·the messengers of·John going·off, *Jesus*
G0565.1 V-2AAP-NSF ἀπελθοῦσα (1x)
Mk 7:30 And after·going·off to her house, she·found the
G0565.1 V-2AAP-NSM ἀπελθών (15x)
Jn 9:11 and wash.' And after·going·off and washing, I·
Jn 12:36 Jesus spoke, and after·going·off, he·was·hidden
Lk 5:14 *it* not·even·to·one·man, "But·rather going·off, show
Lk 9:60 but you·yourself going·off, thoroughly·announce
Lk 22:4 And going·off, he·spoke·together with·the chief·
Ac 5:26 Then after·going·off, the high·warden along·with
Mt 13:46 ·valuable pearl, after·going·off, has·sold·off all
Mt 18:30 he·was·not willing, but·rather going·off, he·cast
Mt 25:18 But going·off, the·one receiving the one *talant·of·*
Mt 25:25 And being·afraid, upon·going·off, I·hid your
Mt 26:42 for a·second·time, after·going·off, he·prayed,
Mt 26:44 And leaving them, going·off again, he·prayed for
Mt 27:5 he·departed. And going·off, he·hanged·himself.
Mk 6:27 to·be·brought. But·then going·off, *HerOd·AntiPas*
Mk 14:39 And again, after·going·off, he·prayed, declaring
G0565.1 V-2AAP-NPF ἀπελθοῦσαι (1x)
Jud 1:7 even going·off to·the·back·*end* of·different flesh,
G0565.1 V-2AAP-NPM ἀπελθόντες (9x)
Lk 8:34 they·fled; and going·off, they·announced *it* in the
Lk 9:12 "Dismiss the crowd, in·order·that going·off into the
Lk 19:32 And going·off, the·ones having·been·dispatched
Lk 22:13 And going·off, they·found *it* just·as he·has·
Mt 8:33 ·ones feeding *them* fled, and going·off into the city,
Mt 14:15 the crowds, in·order·that after·going·off into the
Mk 6:36 Dismiss them in·order·that, after·going·off into the
Mk 6:37 they·say to·him, "Upon·going·off, should·we·buy
Mk 16:13 And·those·men, going·off, announced *it* to·the
G0565.1 V-2AAP-NPM@ ἀπελθόντες (1x)
Mt 13:28 do·you·want *us* to·go·off *so·that* we·may·collect
G0565.1 V-2AAS-2P ἀπέλθητε (2x)
Lk 17:23 *he·is*!' Yeu·should·not go·off *after·them*, nor·even
Mt 10:5 saying, "Yeu·should·not go·off to a·roadway of·
G0565.1 V-LAI-3P ἀπεληλύθεισαν (1x)
Jn 4:8 (for his disciples had·gone·off to·the city in·order·that
G0565.2 V-FDI-3P ἀπελεύσονται (1x)
Mt 25:46 "And these shall·go·away into eternal tormenting·
G0565.2 V-PNS-2S ἀπέρχῃ (2x)
Lk 9:57 I·shall·follow you wherever you·should·go·away."
Mt 8:19 I·shall·follow you wherever you·should·go·away."
G0565.2 V-2AAI-3S ἀπῆλθεν (13x)
Jn 9:7 Accordingly, he·went·away and washed, and he·came
Jn 10:40 And he·went·away again beyond the Jordan into the

Jn 11:54 the Judeans, but·rather went·away from·there to
Lk 1:38 And the angel went·away from her.
Lk 8:39 And he·went·away, officially·proclaiming in the
Ac 10:7 to·Cornelius) went·away, after·hollering·out·for
Mt 13:25 up *in·the* midst of·the wheat, and he·went·away.
Mt 19:22 saying, the young·man went·away being·grieved,
Mk 10:22 at the saying, he·went·away being·grieved, for he·
Rv 9:12 The first woe went·away; behold, there·come two
Rv 11:14 The second woe went·away; behold, the third woe
Rv 18:14 of·the longing of·your soul went·away from you,
Rv 18:14 and the splendid·things went·away from you, and

G0565.2 V-2AAI-3P ἀπῆλθον (4x)
Lk 2:15 after the angels went·away from them into the
Mt 22:5 But neglecting *his call*, they·went·away, in·fact,
Mk 11:4 And they·went·away and found the colt outside
Rv 21:4 any·longer, because the former·things went·away."

G0565.2 V-2AAN ἀπελθεῖν (3x)
Lk 8:37 the Gadarenes asked him to·go·away from them,
Mt 8:31 us out, freely·permit us to·go·away into the herd of·
Mk 5:17 they·began to·implore *Jesus* to·go·away from their

G0565.2 V-2AAS-1S ἀπέλθω (2x)
Jn 16:7 for·yeu that I·myself should·go·away, for if I·should·
Jn 16:7 should·go·away, for if I·should·not go·away, the

G0565.2 V-2AAS-3P ἀπέλθωσιν (1x)
Mt 28:10 to·my brothers that they·should·go·off into Galilee,

G0565.2 V-2RAI-3S ἀπελήλυθεν (1x)
Jac 1:24 he·fully·observed himself and has·gone·away, and

G0565.3 V-FDI-1S ἀπελεύσομαι (1x)
Rm 15:28 to·them this fruit, I·shall·go·aside through yeu

G0565.3 V-2AAI-1S ἀπῆλθον (2x)
Gal 1:17 before me, but·rather I·went·aside into Arabia, and
Rv 10:9 And I·went·aside to the angel, saying to·him, "Give

G0565.3 V-2AAN ἀπελθεῖν (2x)
Ac 4:15 ·ordering them to·go·aside outside of·the joint·
Mt 2:22 ·the·Great, *Joseph* was·afraid to·go·aside there. So

G0565.3 V-2AAP-NSM ἀπελθών (1x)
Mt 26:36 at·this·location, where going·aside, I·should·pray

G0565.3 V-2AAP-NPM ἀπελθόντες (1x)
Mk 14:12 say to·him, "Going·aside, where do·you·want *that*

G0566 ἀπ•έχει apéchêi *v.* (1x)
Roots:G0568 Compare:G2425

G0566.1 V-PAI-3S ἀπέχει (1x)
Mk 14:41 and rest·yeurselves? It·is·enough, no·more! The

G0567 ἀπ•έχομαι apéchômai *v.* (6x)
Roots:G0568 Compare:G4724

G0567.2 V-PMM-2P ἀπέχεσθε (1x)
1Th 5:22 Abstain from every aspect of·evil.

G0567.2 V-PMN ἀπέχεσθαι (5x)
Ac 15:20 ·by·letter to·them, for·them to·abstain from the
Ac 15:29 to·abstain from·things·sacrificed·to·idols, and
1Pe 2:11 and foreign·residents to·abstain·from the fleshly
1Th 4:3 yeur renewed·holiness: for·yeu to·abstain from the
1Ti 4:3 — *and commanding* to·abstain·from foods— which

G0568 ἀπ•έχω apéchō *v.* (11x)
Roots:G0575 G2192

G0568.1 V-PAI-1S ἀπέχω (1x)
Php 4:18 But I·completely·have all and do·abound; I·have·

G0568.1 V-PAI-2S ἀπέχῃς (1x)
Phm 1:15 in·order·that you·completely·have him eternally,

G0568.1 V-PAI-2P ἀπέχετε (1x)
Lk 6:24 Because yeu·completely·have yeur consolation.

G0568.1 V-PAI-3P ἀπέχουσιν (3x)
Mt 6:2 ·yeu, they·completely·have their payment·of·service.
Mt 6:5 ·yeu, they·completely·have their payment·of·service.
Mt 6:16 that they·completely·have their payment·of·service.

G0568.3 V-PAI-3S ἀπέχει (2x)
Mt 15:8 lips, but their heart is·distant, far·away from me.
Mk 7:6 ·*their*·lips, but their heart is·distant, far·away from

G0568.4 V-PAP-ASF ἀπέχουσαν (1x)
Lk 24:13 name Emmaus, being·a·distance from JeruSalem

G0568.5 V-PAP-GSM ἀπέχοντος (2x)
Lk 7:6 even·now, with·him not being·off at·a·distance from
Lk 15:20 But with·him still being·off at·a·distance, his father

G0569 ἀ•πιστέω apistéō *v.* (7x)
Roots:G0571 Compare:G4100 See:G0570

G0569.2 V-PAI-1P ἀπιστοῦμεν (1x)
2Ti 2:13 If we·do·not·trust, that·one still·remains

G0569.2 V-PAP-GPM ἀπιστούντων (1x)
Lk 24:41 And yet not·trusting themselves for the joy and

G0569.2 V-IAI-3P ἠπίστουν (2x)
Lk 24:11 as idle·chatter, and they·were·not·trusting them.
Ac 28:24 ·the·things being·said, but they·were·not·trusting.

G0569.2 V-AAI-3P ἠπίστησαν (2x)
Mk 16:11 ·distinctly·viewed by her, they·did·not·trust *her*.
Rm 3:3 What if some did·not·trust? ¿! Shall their lack·of·

G0569.2 V-AAP-NSM ἀπιστήσας (1x)
Mk 16:16 the·one not·already·trusting shall·be·condemned.

G0570 ἀ•πιστία apistía *n.* (12x)
Roots:G0571 Compare:G4102 See:G0569

G0570.1 N-NSF ἀπιστία (1x)
Rm 3:3 ·trust? ¿! Shall their lack·of·trust fully·nullify the

G0570.1 N-ASF ἀπιστίαν (5x)
Heb 3:19 ·were·not able to·enter·in through a·lack·of·trust.
Mt 13:58 miracles there on·account·of their lack·of·trust.
Mt 17:20 "On·account·of yeur lack·of·trust. For certainly I·
Mk 6:6 he·was·marveling on·account·of their lack·of·trust.
Mk 16:14 *them* for·their lack·of·trust and hardness·of·heart,

G0570.1 N-DSF ἀπιστίᾳ (5x)
Mk 9:24 "Lord, I·trust! Swiftly·help my lack·of·trust!"
Rm 4:20 did·not hesitate with·a lack·of·trust, but·rather was·
Rm 11:20 ·well, by·the lack·of·trust they·were·broken·off,
Rm 11:23 persist in·the lack·of·trust, they·shall·be·grafted·in
1Ti 1:13 because I·did *it* ignorantly in a·lack·of·trust.

G0570.2 N-GSF ἀπιστίας (1x)
Heb 3:12 any of·yeu an·evil heart of·distrust, in withdrawing

G0571 ἄ•πιστος ápistôs *adj.* (23x)
Roots:G0001 G4103 See:G0569 G0570

G0571.1 A-NSM ἄπιστος (1x)
Jn 20:27 And do·not be distrusting, but·rather trusting.

G0571.1 A-NSF ἄπιστος (1x)
Lk 9:41 declared, "O distrusting and perverse generation,

G0571.1 A-VSF ἄπιστος (2x)
Mt 17:17 declared, "O distrusting and perverse generation,
Mk 9:19 him, he·says, "O distrusting generation, how·long

G0571.1 A-GPM ἀπίστων (1x)
Lk 12:46 and shall·lay his portion with the·ones distrusting.

G0571.3 A-NSM ἄπιστος (3x)
1Co 7:14 For the non-trusting husband has·been·made·holy
1Co 7:15 But if the non-trusting·one departs, he·must·be·
1Co 14:24 ·enter·in, a·non-trusting·one or an·untrained·man

G0571.3 A-NSF ἄπιστος (1x)
1Co 7:14 and the non-trusting wife has·been·made·holy by

G0571.3 A-NPM ἄπιστοι (1x)
1Co 14:23 ·enter·in, or non-trusting·ones, shall·they·not

G0571.3 A-ASM ἄπιστον (1x)
1Co 7:13 And a·wife who has a·non-trusting husband also—

G0571.3 A-ASF ἄπιστον (1x)
1Co 7:12 — if any brother has a·non-trusting wife, and she·

G0571.3 A-DPM ἀπίστοις (5x)
Tit 1:15 and *to·the* non-trusting·ones, not·even·one·thing *is*
1Co 14:22 trusting, but·rather to·the non-trusting·ones, but
1Co 14:22 *is* not for·the non-trusting·ones, but·rather for·
2Co 6:14 become disparately·yoked to·non-trusting·ones, for
Rv 21:8 "But timid·ones, and non-trusting·ones, and ones·

G0571.3 A-GSM ἀπίστου (1x)
2Co 6:15 has·one·that·trusts with a·non-trusting·one?

G0571.3 A-GPM ἀπίστων (3x)
1Co 6:6 against a·brother, and that before non-trusting·ones.
1Co 10:27 But if any of·the non-trusting·ones call·for yeu,
2Co 4:4 the mental·perceptions of·the non-trusting·ones,

G0571.4 A-GSM ἀπίστου (1x)
1Ti 5:8 the trust and is worse·than a·non-trusting·heathen.

G0571.7 A-ASM ἄπιστον (1x)
Ac 26:8 Why is·it·judged *to·be* incredible with yeu, that God

G0572 ἁ•πλότης haplótēs *n.* (8x)
Roots:G0573 Compare:G1505 G1618 G0513-1 See:G0574 xLangAlso:H0530 H8537

G0572.3 N-ASF ἁπλότητα (1x)
2Co 9:11 ·enriched in everything to all fidelity, which is·

G0572.3 N-DSF ἁπλότητι (5x)
Rm 12:8 ·one kindly·giving, *kindly·giving* with fidelity; *or*
2Co 1:12 conscience— how·that with fidelity and sincerity
2Co 9:13 and·also in·*yeur*·fidelity of·the common·welfare·
Eph 6:5 ·fear and trembling, with fidelity of·yeur heart, as
Col 3:22 as men-pleasers†, but·rather with fidelity of·heart,

G0572.3 N-GSF ἁπλότητος (2x)
2Co 8:2 poverty abounded to the wealth of·their fidelity—
2Co 11:3 should·be·corrupted from the fidelity, the·one in

G0573 ἁ•πλοῦς haplôûs *adj.* (2x)
Roots:G0001 G4120 See:G0572 G0574

G0573.3 A-NSM ἁπλοῦς (2x)
Lk 11:34 your eye should·be clear·and·focused, your whole
Mt 6:22 if your eye should·be clear·and·focused, your whole

G0574 ἁ•πλῶς haplō̂s *adv.* (1x)
Roots:G0573 G0572 Compare:G0858 G3440

G0574.2 ADV ἁπλῶς (1x)
Jac 1:5 giving to·all with·simplicity·and·fidelity and without

G0575 ἀπό apó *prep.* (674x)
Compare:G1537 See:G3757

G0575.1 PREP ἀπό (2x)
Ac 16:33 of·the night, he·bathed off *their* punishing·blows;
Mt 17:9 And with·them walking·down off the mountain,

G0575.2 PREP ἀπό (523x)
Jn 1:44 Now Philip was from BethSaida, from·among the
Jn 1:45 and·also the prophets: Jesus from Natsareth, the son
Jn 1:51 I·say to·yeu, from this·moment·on, yeu·shall·gaze·
Jn 3:2 we·have·seen that you·have·come from God, *being*
Jn 7:17 ·God, or *whether* I·myself speak from my·own·self.
Jn 7:18 The·man speaking from himself seeks his·own glory,
Jn 7:42 Seed of·David, and from the village of·BethLechem
Jn 8:9 ·forth one·by·one, beginning from the older·men unto
Jn 8:44 That·one was a·man-killer† from *the* beginning, and
Jn 10:5 ·not follow, but·rather shall·flee from him, because
Jn 10:18 "Not·even·one·man takes it away from me, but·
Jn 11:1 sick, *named* Lazarus, from BethAny, from·among
Jn 11:51 And he·did·not declare this from his·own·self, but·
Jn 11:53 So·then, from that day *forth*, they·took·counsel·
Jn 12:21 Philip, the·one from BethSaida of·Galilee, and
Jn 12:36 and after·going·off, he·was·hidden from them.
Jn 13:3 and that he·came·forth from God and was·heading·
Jn 13:19 From this·moment·on, I·relate *it* to·yeu before it·
Jn 14:7 Father also, and from this·moment·on, yeu·do·know
Jn 14:10 speak to·yeu, I·do·not speak from my·own·self, but
Jn 15:27 because yeu·are with me from *the* beginning.
Jn 16:13 "For he·shall·not speak from himself, but·rather as·
Jn 16:22 not·even·one·man takes·away yeur joy from yeu.
Jn 16:30 "By this, we·trust that you·came·forth from God."
Jn 18:28 In·due·course, they·led Jesus from Caiaphas to the
Jn 18:34 Jesus answered him, "From yourself, do·you say
Jn 19:27 "Behold your mother!" And from that hour, the
Jn 19:38 ·things, Joseph (the·one from Arimathaea) being·a·
Jn 21:2 Twin), and NathaniEl from Qanah in·Galilee, and
Jn 21:8 (for they·were not at·a·distance from the dry·ground,
Lk 1:2 (just·as the·ones from *the* beginning handed·*them*·
Lk 1:38 And the angel went·away from her.
Lk 1:48 ' for behold, from now·on all the generations shall·
Lk 1:52 He·demoted powers from *their* thrones and elevated
Lk 1:70 of·his holy prophets, the·ones from a·prior·age,
Lk 2:4 And Joseph also walked·up from Galilee, out of·*the*·
Lk 2:15 after the angels went·away from them into the
Lk 2:36 with a·husband seven years from her virginity,
Lk 2:37 who did·not withdraw from the Sanctuary·Estate,
Lk 3:7 ·any·indication to·yeu to·flee from the impending
Lk 4:1 of·Holy Spirit, returned·back from the Jordan and
Lk 4:13 the Slanderer withdrew from him only·for·a·season
Lk 4:35 him in the midst, came·forth from him, injuring him

Lk 4:42 ·onto him, *such·for·him* not to·depart from them.
Lk 5:2 lake's·edge; then after·disembarking from them, the
Lk 5:3 ·of him to·head·off a·little·way from the dry·ground.
Lk 5:8 knees, saying, "Go·forth from me, because I·am a·
Lk 5:10 "Do·not be·afraid. From now·on, you·shall·be
Lk 5:13 And immediately, the leprosy went·off from him.
Lk 5:35 the bridegroom should·be·lifted·away from them,
Lk 5:36 *the* patch, the·one from the brand-new *garment*,
Lk 6:17 and a·large multitude of·people from all *over* Judea
Lk 7:6 with·him not being·off at·a·distance from the home,
Lk 7:21 he·both·relieved·and·cured many from illnesses,
Lk 8:2 having·been·both·relieved·and·cured from evil spirits
Lk 8:2 being·called Magdalene) from whom had·gone·forth
Lk 8:3 who were·attending to·him from their·own holdings.
Lk 8:12 he·takes·away the Redemptive-word from their hearts
Lk 8:18 should·not have, from him shall·be·taken·away
Lk 8:29 impure spirit to·come·forth from the man·of·clay†,
Lk 8:35 and found the man·of·clay† from whom the demons
Lk 8:37 the Gadarenes asked him to·go·away from them,
Lk 8:38 Now the man from whom the demons had·come·out
Lk 8:46 for I·myself did·know power going·forth from me."
Lk 9:5 accept yeu, while·yeu·are·going·forth from that city,
Lk 9:5 city, jostle·off even the dust from yeur feet for a·
Lk 9:33 with the·*two·men* thoroughly·departing from him,
Lk 9:37 day, with·them coming·down from the mountain, a·
Lk 9:39 and hardly does·it·depart from him, shattering him.
Lk 9:45 and it·was having·been·tightly·veiled from them,
Lk 9:54 we·should·declare fire to·descend from the heaven
Lk 10:21 that you·hid·away these·things from wise and
Lk 10:30 ·of·clay† was·walking·down from JeruSalem to
Lk 10:42 portion, which shall·not be·removed from her."
Lk 11:24 spirit should·go·forth from the man·of·clay†, it·
Lk 11:50 the *blood* being·poured·out from *the* world's
Lk 11:50 may·be·sought·out from this generation,
Lk 11:51 from the blood of·Abel until the blood of·
Lk 12:20 they·are·demanding·back your soul from you.
Lk 12:52 "For from now·on there·shall·be five in one house
Lk 12:54 thick·cloud rising·above·the·horizon from *the* west,
Lk 12:58 on the way to·have·been·released from him, lest
Lk 13:15 his ox or *his* donkey from the feeding·trough, even
Lk 13:16 ·it·not binding·for *her* to·be·loosed from this bond
Lk 13:27 From·what·source are·yeu? Withdraw from me, all
Lk 13:29 And they·shall·come from east and west, and from
Lk 13:29 from east and west, and from north and south, and
Lk 16:3 ·do? Because my lord removes from me the estate·
Lk 16:16 the prophets *were* until John. From then·on, the
Lk 16:18 the·one having·been·divorced from *her* husband
Lk 16:21 ·crumbs, the·ones falling from the wealthy·man's
Lk 16:23 he·clearly·sees AbRaham from a·distance, and
Lk 16:30 if someone should·traverse to them from dead·men,
Lk 17:29 day *when* Lot went·forth from Sodom, it·showered
Lk 17:29 it·showered fire and sulfur from heaven and
Lk 18:34 this utterance was having·been·hidden from them,
Lk 19:24 'Take·away the mina from him, and give *it* to·the·
Lk 19:26 even what he·has shall·be·taken·away from him).
Lk 19:39 And some of·the Pharisees from among·the crowd
Lk 19:42 But now they·are·already·hidden from your eyes.
Lk 21:11 ·be frightening·things and great signs from heaven.
Lk 22:41 And he·himself drew·away from them about a·
Lk 22:42 ·willing to·personally·carry this cup from me …
Lk 22:43 ·was·made·visible to·him an·angel from heaven,
Lk 22:45 And after·rising·up from the prayer *and* coming to
Lk 22:69 From now·on, the Son of·Clay·Man† shall·be
Lk 22:71 For we·ourselves heard *it* from his·own mouth."
Lk 23:5 in all Judea, beginning from Galilee unto here.
Lk 23:26 ·man who·was·coming *in* from *the* countryside,
Lk 23:49 the women following·along with·him from Galilee,
Lk 24:2 having·been·rolled·away from the chamber·tomb.
Lk 24:9 And after·returning·back from the chamber·tomb,
Lk 24:13 being·a·distance from JeruSalem *of·about* sixty
Lk 24:27 And beginning from Moses and all the prophets,
Lk 24:47 name to all the nations, beginning from JeruSalem.
Lk 24:51 them, *that* he·stepped·away from them and was·
Ac 1:4 "*Yeu·are* not to·be·departing from JeruSalem, but·
Ac 1:9 a·thick·cloud received him up from their eyesight.
Ac 1:11 Jesus, the·one being·taken·up from yeu into the
Ac 1:12 they·returned·back to JeruSalem from *the* mount,
Ac 1:22 beginning from the immersion of·John, unto the day
Ac 1:22 unto the day that he·was·taken·up from us, *it·is·*
Ac 2:5 in JeruSalem, devout men from every nation under
Ac 2:17 God, *that* I·shall·pour·forth from my Spirit upon all
Ac 2:18 my female·slaves, I·shall·pour·forth from my Spirit
Ac 2:40 saying, "Save·yeurselves from this warped
Ac 3:19 ·refreshing should·come from *the* personal·presence
Ac 3:24 And even all the prophets from SamuEl and the·ones
Ac 3:26 to·turn·away each·one *of·yeu* from yeur evils."
Ac 5:38 I·say to·yeu: Withdraw from these men·of·clay†
Ac 5:41 in·fact, were·departing from in·front of·the joint·
Ac 6:9 Alexandrians, and the·ones from Cilicia and Asia,
Ac 7:45 Gentiles, whom God thrust·out from *the* face of·our
Ac 8:10 to·this they·all were·giving·heed, from *the* least
Ac 8:26 the roadway, the·one descending from JeruSalem to
Ac 8:33 Because his life† is·taken·away from the earth."'
Ac 8:35 his mouth and beginning from the same Scripture,
Ac 9:3 and·then suddenly a·light from the heaven flashed·
Ac 9:8 And Saul was·roused from the earth, but with·his
Ac 9:18 *something* like scales fell·off from his eyes. And
Ac 10:17 (the·ones having·been·dispatched from Cornelius),
Ac 10:21 having·been·dispatched to him from Cornelius),
Ac 10:23 and some of·the brothers from Joppa went·together
Ac 10:37 in all Judea, beginning from Galilee, after the
Ac 10:38 God anointed Jesus *who·was* from Natsareth with·
Ac 11:11 I·was, having·been·dispatched from Caesarea to
Ac 11:27 days, prophets came·down from JeruSalem to
Ac 12:1 some of·the·ones from the Called·Out·citizenry.
Ac 12:10 and immediately the angel withdrew from him.
Ac 12:19 Then coming·down from Judea to Caesarea,
Ac 13:13 And sailing·away from Paphos, Paul (*and* the·ones
Ac 13:13 in·PamPhylia. And departing from them, John·
Ac 13:14 ·themselves, after·going·throughout from Perga,
Ac 13:23 From this·man's Seed, according·to promise, God
Ac 13:29 him, after·lowering *him* down from the arbor·tree,
Ac 13:31 walking·up·together with·him from Galilee to
Ac 13:39 is·regarded·as·innocent from everything from·
Ac 13:50 and BarNabas and cast them out from their borders.
Ac 14:15 to·yeu to·turn·back·around from these futilities to
Ac 14:19 And *certain* Jews came·up from Antiochia and
Ac 15:1 ·men coming·down from Judea were·instructing the
Ac 15:5 ·fully·rose·up certain·men from the denomination
Ac 15:7 are·fully·acquainted·with how from the·early days,
Ac 15:18 to·God are all his works from the·beginning·age.
Ac 15:19 ·*us* not to·further·harass the·ones from the Gentiles
Ac 15:20 to·them, for·them to·abstain from the pollutions
Ac 15:33 they·were·dismissed with peace from the brothers
Ac 15:38 this·man, the·one withdrawing from them from
Ac 15:38 ·one withdrawing from them from PamPhylia and
Ac 15:39 ·for them to·be·utterly·separated from one·another;
Ac 16:11 Accordingly, sailing from Troas, we·sailed·
Ac 16:18 the name of·Jesus Anointed to·come·out from her."
Ac 17:2 ·having·discussions with·them from the Scriptures,
Ac 17:13 But as·soon·as the Jews from ThessaloNica knew
Ac 17:27 inherently·being not at·a·distance from each one
Ac 18:2 by·birth, recently having·come from Italy with his
Ac 18:5 Silas and TimoThy came·down from Macedonia,
Ac 18:6 I·myself *am* pure. From now·on, I·shall·traverse
Ac 18:16 he·drove them away from the Bema·judgment·seat.
Ac 18:21 And he·sailed from Ephesus.
Ac 19:9 of·the multitude, after·withdrawing from them, he·
Ac 19:12 ·for sweat·towels or aprons from his skin's·surface
Ac 19:12 *for* the illnesses to·be·removed from them, and·
Ac 19:12 and·also *for* the evil spirits to·go·forth from them.
Ac 20:6 And we·ourselves sailed·away from PhilIppi after
Ac 20:9 heavy·sleep, he·fell down from the third·story and
Ac 20:17 And from Miletus, after·sending·word to Ephesus,
Ac 20:18 ·yeurselves are·fully·acquainted, from that first
Ac 20:26 that I·myself *am* pure from the blood of·all *men*.
Ac 21:1 ·sailing·away, after·being·drawn·away from them,
Ac 21:7 ·thoroughly·accomplishing the voyage from Tyre,
Ac 21:10 a·certain prophet came·down from Judea, Agabus
Ac 21:16 And *some* of·the disciples from Caesarea also
Ac 21:27 to·be·entirely·completed, the Jews from Asia,
Ac 22:22 saying, "Away·with such·a·man from the earth,
Ac 22:29 intending to·interrogate him withdrew from him,
Ac 22:30 ·by the Judeans, he·loosed him from the bonds and
Ac 23:21 they·are ready, awaiting the promise from you."
Ac 23:23 they·should·traverse unto Caesarea from *the* third
Ac 23:34 And ascertaining that *he·was* from Cilicia,
Ac 24:18 "But *there·were* certain Jews from Asia,
Ac 25:1 ·the province, Festus walked·up from Caesarea to
Ac 25:7 having·walked·down from JeruSalem stood·around,
Ac 26:18 *and* to·turn·*them*·back·around from darkness to
Ac 27:21 ·*for·us* not to·be·sailing·away from Crete nor·also
Ac 27:44 on some of·the *broken·pieces* from the sailing·ship.
Ac 28:21 anticipate·receiving letters from Judea concerning
Ac 28:23 concerning Jesus, both from the Torah-Law of·
Ac 28:23 ·Moses and the prophets, from dawn until evening.
Heb 3:12 of·distrust, in withdrawing from the·living God.
Heb 4:3 *this* with·the works being·done from *the* world's
Heb 4:4 in the seventh day from all his prescribed·works.
Heb 4:10 also already·fully·ceased from his·own works, just·
Heb 4:10 his·own works, just·as God *did* from his·own.
Heb 5:7 of·death, and *he·was* being·heard from the devotion
Heb 5:8 the attentive·obedience from the·things·which he·
Heb 6:1 *the* foundation— of·repentance from dead works,
Heb 6:7 it·is·cultivated, it·partakes of·blessings from God.
Heb 7:1 ·up with·AbRaham returning·back from the carnage
Heb 7:2 AbRaham distributed a·tenth *part* from all·things.
Heb 7:13 ·to another tribe, from which not·even·one·man
Heb 7:26 having·been·separated from the morally·
Heb 8:11 all shall·personally·know me, from *the* least of·
Heb 9:14 purify yeur conscience from dead works in·order·
Heb 10:22 having·been·sprinkled from an·evil conscience,
Heb 11:12 Therefore, also from one·man, even these *many*
Heb 11:15 of·that *fatherland* from which they·came·out,
Heb 11:34 edge of·*the*·dagger, from weakness were·enabled
Heb 12:15 lest any·man *is·found* falling·short from the grace
Heb 12:25 *imparting·divine·instruction* from *the* heavens,
Heb 13:24 all the holy·ones. The·ones from Italy greet yeu.
Gal 1:1 an·ambassador— (not from men·of·clay†, neither
Gal 1:3 Grace *be* to·yeu and peace from Father God, and
Gal 2:12 For prior·to certain·men coming from Jacob, he·
Gal 3:2 This merely I·want to·learn from yeu, did·yeu·
Gal 4:24 One in·fact *is* from Mount Sinai, bearing·children
Gal 5:4 yeu·are·rendered·fully·nullified from the
Mt 1:17 all the generations·of·offspring from AbRaham until
Mt 1:17 *are* fourteen generations. Then from David until the
Mt 1:17 *are* fourteen generations. And from the Babylonian
Mt 1:21 shall·save his People from their moral·failures."
Mt 1:24 after·being·thoroughly·awakened from the heavy·
Mt 2:1 behold, Magian·astrologists from *the* east arrived·
Mt 2:16 of·its *outermost* borders, from two·years·of·age and
Mt 3:4 was·having his apparel *made* from camel's hair and
Mt 3:7 ·any·indication to·yeu to·flee from the impending
Mt 3:13 ·that·time, YeShua comes·directly from Galilee to
Mt 3:16 YeShua walked·up straight·away from the water.
Mt 4:17 From then·on, YeShua began to·officially·proclaim
Mt 4:25 large crowds followed him from Galilee and *from*
Mt 5:18 ·no·means, should·pass·away from the Torah-Law
Mt 5:29 it out and cast *it* from you, for it·is·advantageous
Mt 5:30 it off and cast *it* from you, for it·is·advantageous
Mt 5:42 ·turning·away the·one wanting to·borrow from you.
Mt 6:13 ·trial, but·rather snatch us away from the Evil·One,
Mt 7:4 *so* I·may·cast·out the speck·of·dust from your eye!'
Mt 7:16 "¿!·Do men·collect a·cluster·of·grapes from thorns,
Mt 7:16 ·of·grapes from thorns, or figs from spear·thistles?
Mt 7:23 'Depart from me, the·ones who·are·working the
Mt 8:1 And upon·walking·down from the mountain, large
Mt 8:11 ·say to·yeu that many shall·come from east and west
Mt 8:30 Now there·was at·a·distance from them a·herd of·

Mt 8:34 *him* that he·should·walk·on from their borders.
Mt 9:15 the bridegroom should·be·lifted·away from them,
Mt 9:16 it·takes·away its complete·fullness from the garment
Mt 9:22 the woman was·made·safe·and·well from that hour.
Mt 11:12 And from the days of·John the Immerser until this·
Mt 11:25 that you·hid·away these·things from wise and
Mt 11:29 yoke upon yeu, and learn from me, because I·am
Mt 12:38 "Mentor, we·want to·see a·sign from you."
Mt 12:43 spirit should·come·out from the man·of·clay†, it·
Mt 13:1 that day, YeShua, after·going·forth from the home,
Mt 13:12 that·which he·has shall·be·taken·away from him.
Mt 13:35 ·forth *things* having·been·hidden from *the* world's
Mt 13:44 *it*, hides *it*. And from the joy of·it, he·heads·on·
Mt 14:2 he·himself is·already·awakened from the dead, and
Mt 14:13 the crowds followed him on·foot from the cities.
Mt 14:26 and they·yelled·out from the fear.
Mt 14:29 And after·stepping·down from the sailboat, Peter
Mt 15:1 and Pharisees from JeruSalem come·alongside
Mt 15:8 lips, but their heart is·distant, far·away from me.
Mt 15:22 behold, a·Kenaanite woman from those borders,
Mt 15:27 For even the puppies eat from the little·crumbs,
Mt 15:27 little·crumbs, the·ones falling from the table of·
Mt 15:28 And her daughter was·healed from that·very hour.
Mt 16:21 From then·on, YeShua began to·show to·his
Mt 16:21 and to·suffer many·things from the elders and
Mt 17:18 and the demon came·out from him. And the boy
Mt 17:18 was·both·relieved·and·cured from that·very hour.
Mt 17:25 you suppose, Simon? From whom·do the kings
Mt 17:25 taxes or a·census·tribute? From their·own sons or
Mt 17:25 ·tribute? From their·own sons or from the others?
Mt 17:26 Peter says to·him, "From the others." YeShua was·
Mt 18:8 chop it off and cast *it* from you. It·is good for·you
Mt 18:9 pluck it out and cast *it* from you. "It·is better for·
Mt 18:35 his brother their trespasses from yeur hearts."
Mt 19:1 these sayings, he·moved·on from Galilee and came
Mt 19:4 that the·one making *them* from *the* beginning
Mt 19:8 yeur wives, but from *the* beginning it·has·not
Mt 20:8 the payment·of·service, beginning from the last
Mt 20:29 And with·them proceeding·forth from Jericho, a·
Mt 21:8 and others were·chopping branches from the trees,
Mt 21:11 the prophet, the·one from Natsareth of·Galilee."
Mt 21:43 kingdom of·God shall·be·taken·away from yeu and
Mt 22:46 dare any·longer to·inquire·of him from that day
Mt 23:33 in·what·way should·yeu·escape from the Tribunal
Mt 23:34 in yeur gatherings and shall·persecute from city to
Mt 23:35 ·out upon the earth, from the blood of·Abel the
Mt 23:39 no, yeu·should·not see me from this·moment·on,
Mt 24:1 YeShua was·departing from the Sanctuary·Atrium,
Mt 24:27 just·as the lightning comes·forth from *the* east and
Mt 24:29 and the stars shall·fall from the heaven, and the
Mt 24:31 the four winds, from *the* uttermost·parts of·*the*·
Mt 24:32 "Now from the fig·tree, yeu·must·learn the parable
Mt 25:28 take·away the talant·of·silver from him and give
Mt 25:29 he·shall·have·an·abundance. But from the·one not
Mt 25:29 that·which he·has shall·be·taken·away from him).
Mt 25:32 he·shall·distinctly·separate them one from another,
Mt 25:32 distinctly·separates the sheep from the young·goats
Mt 25:34 having·been·made·ready for·yeu from *the* world's
Mt 25:41 *the* left·hand, 'Depart from me, the·ones having·
Mt 26:16 And from then·on, he·was·seeking a·good·
Mt 26:29 I·should·not drink from this·moment·on from·out
Mt 26:39 let this cup pass·away from me. Nevertheless not
Mt 26:42 this cup is·not able to·pass·away from me unless I·
Mt 26:47 with daggers and staffs, from the chief·priests and
Mt 26:58 But Peter was·following him from a·distance up·to
Mt 26:64 Moreover I·say to·yeu, from this·moment·on, yeu·
Mt 27:40 If you·are a·son of·God, descend from the cross."
Mt 27:42 of·IsraEl, let·him·descend now from the cross, and
Mt 27:45 Now from *midday*, *the* sixth hour, there·was
Mt 27:51 of·the Temple is·torn in two from top to bottom.
Mt 27:55 women were there observing from a·distance, who
Mt 27:55 who followed YeShua from Galilee, attending to·
Mt 27:64 to·the people, 'He·is·awakened from the dead,'
Mt 28:2 ·alongside, rolled·away the stone from the door and
Mt 28:7 to·his disciples that he·was·awakened from the dead
Mt 28:8 And coming·forth swiftly from the chamber·tomb,
Mk 1:9 in those days *that* Jesus came from Natsareth of·
Mk 1:10 And immediately walking·up from the water, he·
Mk 1:42 immediately, the leprosy went·off from him, and
Mk 2:20 the bridegroom should·be·lifted·away from them,
Mk 3:7 And a·large multitude from Galilee followed him,
Mk 3:7 from Galilee followed him, and·also from Judea,
Mk 3:8 and from JeruSalem, and·then from Edom, and *from*
Mk 3:8 and from JeruSalem, and·then from Edom, and *from*
Mk 3:22 the·ones already·walking·down from JeruSalem,
Mk 4:25 that·which he·has shall·be·taken·away from him."
Mk 5:6 But upon·seeing Jesus from a·distance, he·ran and
Mk 5:17 to·implore *Jesus* to·go·away from their borders.
Mk 5:29 body that she·has·been·healed from the scourge.
Mk 5:35 was·still speaking, one·came from *the house·of* the
Mk 6:33 Then they·ran·together on·foot from all the cities
Mk 7:1 alongside him, after·coming from JeruSalem.
Mk 7:4 And *when they·come* from a·marketplace, unless
Mk 7:6 ·lips, but their heart is·distant, far·away from me.
Mk 7:15 but·rather the·things proceeding·forth from him,
Mk 7:28 beneath the table eat from the young·children's
Mk 7:33 And after·taking him aside from the crowd in
Mk 8:11 personally·from him a·sign from the heaven, trying
Mk 9:9 And with·them walking·down from the mountain,
Mk 10:6 But from creation's beginning, God " made them
Mk 10:46 And as·he is·proceeding·forth from Jericho with
Mk 11:12 next·day, with·them coming·forth from BethAny,
Mk 12:34 "You·are not at·a·distance from the kingdom of·
Mk 13:19 such as has·not happened from *the* beginning of·
Mk 13:27 of·the four winds, from *the* uttermost·part of·earth
Mk 13:28 "Now from the fig·tree, yeu·must·learn the parable
Mk 14:35 possible, the hour may·pass·away from him.
Mk 14:52 the linen·cloth, he·fled from them naked).
Mk 14:54 But Peter followed him from a·distance, as·far·as
Mk 15:21 a·Cyrenian, coming from *the* countryside (the
Mk 15:30 save yourself, and descend from the cross!"
Mk 15:32 of·IsraEl, let·him·descend now from the cross in·
Mk 15:38 of·the Temple was·torn in two from top to bottom.
Mk 15:40 there·were also women observing from a·distance,
Mk 15:45 And after·knowing *it* from the Roman·centurion,
Mk 16:8 ·forth swiftly, they·fled from the chamber·tomb;
Mk 16:9 to·Mariam Magdalene, from whom he·had·cast·out
Rm 1:7 Grace to·yeu and peace from God our Father and *the*
Rm 1:18 For God's wrath is·revealed from heaven against all
Rm 1:20 For from *the* world's creation, the invisible·things
Rm 5:9 so·much more·so we·shall·be·saved from the Wrath
Rm 5:14 Death already·reigned from Adam so·far·as·unto
Rm 6:18 So after·being·set·free from Moral·Failure, yeu·are·
Rm 6:22 ·now, after·being·set·free from Moral·Failure and
Rm 7:2 she·has·been·fully·nullified from the *particular*
Rm 7:3 should·die, she·is freed from the Torah-Law *such*·
Rm 7:6 ·now, we·are·fully·nullified from the Torah-Law,
Rm 8:2 Jesus set me free from the Law of·Moral·Failure and
Rm 8:21 creation itself also shall·be·set·free from the slavery
Rm 8:35 What shall·separate us from the love of·the
Rm 8:39 ·thing shall·be·able to·separate us from the love of·
Rm 9:3 ·to·destruction, *cut·off* from the Anointed-One on·
Rm 11:26 and he·shall·turn·away irreverence from Jacob.
Rm 13:1 For there·is no authority except from God; and the·
Rm 15:19 ·news of·the Anointed-One (from JeruSalem and
Rm 16:17 which yeu learned, and veer·away from them.
Jac 1:17 is from·above, descending from the Father of·lights
Jac 1:27 ·purposefully·keep oneself unstained from the world
Jac 4:7 ·against the Slanderer, and he·shall·flee from yeu.
Jac 5:19 among yeu should·be·led·astray from the truth, and
Jud 1:14 Enoch also, *the* seventh from Adam, prophesied
Php 1:2 *be* to·yeu, and peace, from God our Father and
Php 1:5 yeur fellowship in the good·news from *the* first day
Php 1:28 but of·Salvation for·yeu, and that from God.
Php 4:15 *among·yeu*, when I·went·forth from Macedonia,
1Pe 1:12 Spirit already·being·dispatched from heaven—
1Pe 3:10 days must·restrain his tongue from wrong and his
1Pe 3:11 "'Veer·away from wrong and do *the* beneficially·
2Pe 3:4 ·this·manner *as they·were* from creation's beginning.
1Th 1:1 *be* to·yeu, and peace, from God our Father, and *the*
1Th 1:8 For from yeu, the Redemptive-word of·the Lord has·
1Th 1:9 how yeu·turned·back·around to God from the idols,
1Th 2:6 from·among men·of·clay†, neither from yeu nor
1Th 2:6 neither from yeu nor from others, *though* being·
1Th 2:17 being·grievously·removed from yeu just·for a·
1Th 3:6 at·this·moment, with·TimoThy coming from yeu to
1Th 4:3 for·yeu to·abstain from the sexual·immorality,
1Th 4:16 the Lord himself shall·descend from heaven with
1Th 5:22 Abstain from every aspect of·evil.
2Th 1:2 Grace to·yeu, and peace, from God our Father and
2Th 1:7 revealing of·the Lord YeShua from heaven with *the*
2Th 1:9 savage·termination from *the* personal·presence of·
2Th 1:9 of·the Lord, 'and from the glory of·his strength,'
2Th 2:13 by *the* Lord), because from *the* beginning, God
2Th 3:3 yeu and shall·vigilantly·keep *yeu* from the Evil·One.
2Th 3:6 ·and·withdraw yeurselves from every brother
Tit 1:4 mercy, *and* peace, from Father God and *the* Lord
Tit 2:14 ·order·that 'he·may·ransom us from all lawlessness,'
1Co 1:3 *be* to·yeu, and peace, from God our Father, and
1Co 1:30 Jesus, who is·made to·us wisdom from God, also
1Co 4:5 And then the high·praise from God shall·come·to·be
1Co 6:19 ·*is* in yeu, which yeu·have from God, and yeu·are
1Co 7:10 a·wife *is* not to·be·separated from *her* husband.
1Co 7:27 ·up. Have·you·been·broken·up from a·woman?
1Co 10:14 my dearly·beloved, flee from the idolatry.
1Co 11:23 For I·myself personally·received from the Lord
1Co 14:36 Redemptive-word of·God come·forth from yeu?
2Co 1:2 Grace to·yeu, and peace, from God our Father and
2Co 1:16 and to·come again from Macedonia to yeu, and by
2Co 2:3 grief from them·by·whom it·was·necessary·for me
2Co 3:18 into·the same derived·image from glory to glory,
2Co 3:18 glory to glory, exactly·as from Yahweh's Spirit.
2Co 5:6 we·are·presently·absent·abroad from the Lord—
2Co 5:16 As·such, from now·on, we·ourselves personally·
2Co 7:1 we·should·purify ourselves from all tarnishing of·
2Co 11:3 ·disposition should·be·corrupted from the fidelity,
2Co 11:9 coming from Macedonia utterly·fulfilled·in·
2Co 12:8 ·times in·order·that it·should·withdraw from me.
Eph 1:2 *be* to·yeu, and peace, from God our Father and *our*
Eph 3:9 ·one having·been·hidden·away from the prior·ages in
Eph 4:31 and revilement, be·expunged from yeu, together
Eph 6:23 and love with trust from Father God and *the* Lord
Col 1:2 *be* to·yeu, and peace, from God our Father and *the*
Col 1:7 just·as also yeu·learned *it* from EpAphras, our dear
Col 1:23 *are* not being·stirred·away from the Expectation of·
Col 1:26 ·one having·been·hidden·away from the prior·ages
Col 1:26 ·away from the prior·ages and from the generations,
Col 2:20 together with·Anointed-One from the principles of·
Col 3:24 having·seen that from *the* Lord yeu·shall·receive·
Phm 1:3 Grace to·yeu, and peace, from God our Father and
1Ti 1:2 Grace, mercy, *and* peace from God our Father and
1Ti 3:7 also to·have a·good testimony from the·ones *who·are*
1Ti 6:5 *itself* to·be a·means·of·gain. From such *men*,
1Ti 6:10 ·toward. They·are·utterly·led·astray from the trust,
2Ti 1:2 Grace, mercy, *and* peace, from Father God and
2Ti 1:3 ·God (to·whom I·ritually·minister from *my* forebears
2Ti 2:19 must·withdraw from unrighteousness."
2Ti 2:21 should·entirely·purify himself from these·things,
2Ti 3:15 and that from a·toddler you·have·seen the Sacred
1Jn 1:1 That·which was from *the* beginning, which we·
1Jn 1:5 announcement which we·have·heard from him and
1Jn 1:7 his Son, purifies us from all moral·failure.
1Jn 1:9 and should·purify us from all unrighteousness.
1Jn 2:7 which yeu·were·having from *the* beginning. The old
1Jn 2:7 is the word which yeu·heard from *the* beginning.
1Jn 2:13 yeu·have·known the·one *who·is* from *the* beginning.
1Jn 2:14 yeu·have·known the·one *who·is* from *the* beginning
1Jn 2:20 do·have an·anointing from the Holy·One, and yeu·
1Jn 2:24 that·which yeu already·heard from *the* beginning.

1Jn 2:24 If that·which yeu·already·heard from *the* beginning
1Jn 2:27 already·received from him presently·abides in yeu,
1Jn 3:8 the Slanderer morally·fails from *the* beginning. For
1Jn 3:11 is the message that yeu·heard from *the* beginning,
1Jn 3:17 and should·shut·up his inward·affections from him,
1Jn 4:21 this commandment we·presently·have from him,
1Jn 5:21 ·children, vigilantly·keep yeurselves from the idols
2Jn 1:5 that·which we·were·having from *the* beginning, that
2Jn 1:6 that just·as yeu·heard from *the* beginning, yeu·
3Jn 1:7 ·went·forth, taking not·one·thing from the Gentiles.
Rv 1:4 *be* to·yeu, and peace, from the·one (the·one being,
Rv 1:4 the·one who·is·coming), also from the seven Spirits
Rv 1:5 and from Jesus Anointed, *who·is* the trustworthy
Rv 1:5 and already·bathing us *clean* from our moral·failures
Rv 2:17 I·shall·give to·him to·eat from the hidden manna,
Rv 3:12 the·one descending out·of·the heaven from my God.
Rv 6:4 on it, to·take the peace from the earth, and that they·
Rv 6:16 on us, and hide us from *the* face of·the·one who·is·
Rv 6:16 on the throne, and from the WRATH OF·THE
Rv 7:2 I·saw another angel ascending from *the* eastern sun,
Rv 7:17 And God shall·rub·away every tear from their eyes.'
Rv 9:6 ·shall·long to·die, and Death shall·flee from them.
Rv 13:8 ·the Lamb having·been·slaughtered from *the* world's
Rv 14:3 having·been·kinsman·redeemed from the earth.
Rv 14:4 were·kinsman·redeemed from among·the men·of·
Rv 16:12 ·that the way of·the kings from the eastern sun
Rv 16:17 there·came·forth a·great voice from the Temple of·
Rv 16:17 the Temple of·the heaven, from the throne, saying,
Rv 17:8 the official·scroll of·the life-above from *the* world's
Rv 18:10 standing from a·distance on·account·of the fear of·
Rv 18:14 ·the longing of·your soul went·away from you, and
Rv 18:14 and the splendid·things went·away from you, and
Rv 18:15 ·things, the·ones becoming·wealthy from her,
Rv 18:15 her, shall·stand from a·distance on·account·of the
Rv 18:17 ·many·as work the sea, stood·still from a·distance,
Rv 20:9 And fire descended from God out·of·the heaven and
Rv 20:11 who·is·sitting·down on it, from whose face the
Rv 21:2 brand-new JeruSalem, descending from God out·of·
Rv 21:4 And God shall·rub·away every tear from their eyes.'
Rv 21:10 descending out·of·the heaven from God,
Rv 22:19 if anyone should·remove *anything* from the words
Rv 22:19 God shall·remove his portion from *the* scroll of·the

EG0575.2 (13x)
Jn 7:16 is not mine, but·rather *from* the·one sending me.
Jn 7:42 village of·BethLechem, where David was *from*?"
Jn 11:41 So·then they·took·away the stone *from the place*
Jn 12:17 Now·then, the crowd *from BethAny* was·testifying,
Jn 12:18 that, the crowd *from JeruSalem* also went·and·met
Ac 15:20 of·the idols, and *from* the sexual·immorality, and
Ac 15:20 sexual·immorality, and *from* the strangled·animal,
Ac 15:20 and *from* the strangled·animal, and *from* the blood.
Heb 11:11 an·ovulation of·a·single·seed *from her·ovaries*,
Mt 4:25 followed him from Galilee and *from* DecaPolis, and
Mt 4:25 and *from* DecaPolis, and *from* JeruSalem and Judea,
Mt 4:25 JeruSalem and Judea, and *from* beyond the Jordan.
2Co 5:15 behalf and already·being·awakened *from the dead*.

G0575.3 PREP ἀπό (15x)
Jn 11:18 was near to·JeruSalem, about fifteen stadia away.
Jn 21:8 ·ground, but·rather about two·hundred cubits away).
Lk 11:4 ·trial, but·rather snatch us away·from the Evil·One.'
Ac 13:8 ·thoroughly·turn the proconsul away·from the trust.
Ac 21:21 that you·instruct a·defection away·from Moses *to*
Gal 1:6 yeu·are·transferring away·from the·one calling yeu
Mk 5:34 and be healthy·and·sound away·from your scourge.
Mk 7:17 when he·entered into a·house away·from the crowd,
Mk 14:36 Personally·carry this cup away·from me. But·yet
Rm 15:31 I·may·be·snatched away·from the·ones being·
1Th 1:10 the·one who·is·snatching us away·from the coming
2Th 3:2 ·that we·may·be·snatched away·from the absurd and
2Ti 4:4 ·turn the inner·sense·of·hearing away·from the truth
2Ti 4:18 And the Lord shall·snatch me away·from every evil
Rv 12:14 and half a·season, away·from *the* face of·the

G0575.4 PREP ἀπό (22x)
Jn 5:19 is·not able to·do not·even·one·thing by himself, but·
Lk 7:35 "But Wisdom is·regarded·as·righteous by all her
Lk 9:22 ·things, and to·be·rejected·as·unfit by the elders and
Lk 12:57 yeu·not judge what·is·right even by yeurselves?
Lk 17:25 and to·be·rejected·as·unfit by this generation.
Lk 21:30 ·looking·about, yeu·know by yeur·own·selves that
Lk 24:31 and·then he·himself became unviewable by them.
Ac 2:22 a·man having·been·exhibited by God for yeu with·
Ac 11:19 in·fact, the·ones being·dispersed by the tribulation
Ac 12:20 *needed* to·be·nourished by the royal·territory.
Mt 7:16 By their fruits, yeu·shall·recognize them.
Mt 7:20 Consequently, by their fruits yeu·shall·recognize
Mt 11:19 Wisdom is·regarded·as·righteous by her children."
Mt 27:9 who was·appraised by the·Sons of·IsraEl,
Mk 8:31 ·things and to·be·rejected·as·unfit by the elders,
Rm 15:24 if first I·should·be partly replenished by yeu.
Jac 1:13 must·ever·say, "I·am·tempted by God," for God is
Jac 5:4 ·open·fields, the·one having·been·robbed by yeu, it·
Jud 1:23 even the tunic having·been·stained by the flesh.
2Co 3:5 Not that we·are sufficient by ourselves to·reckon
2Co 7:13 because his spirit has·been·refreshed by yeu all.
Rv 12:6 she·has a·place having·been·made·ready by God,

G0575.5 PREP ἀφ΄ (14x)
Lk 7:45 a·kiss, but she·herself since that *moment* I·entered·
Lk 24:21 marks this third day since these·things were·done.
Ac 3:21 of·all his holy prophets since *the* beginning·age.
Ac 20:18 from that first day since I·walked·over into Asia,
Ac 24:11 more than twelve days for·me since I·walked·up to
Ac 26:4 youth (the·one occurring since beginning in my·own
Heb 9:26 him to·already·suffer many·times since *the* world's
Mt 24:21 such·as has·not been since *the* world's beginning
2Pe 3:4 of·his returning·Presence? For since the fathers are·
2Co 8:10 for·yeu, who since last·year began·previously not
2Co 9:2 Achaia has·been·making·preparation since last·year;
Col 1:6 just·as *it·does* also in yeu since that day yeu·heard *it*
Col 1:9 ·of that, we·ourselves also (since that day *when* we·
Rv 16:18 such·as did·not happen since the men·of·clay†

G0575.6 PREP ἀπό (12x)
Jn 21:6 had·strength to·draw it *back·in* for the multitude of·
Lk 8:43 being with a·flow·of·blood for twelve years, who
Lk 19:3 was, and was·not able·to for the crowd, because he·
Lk 21:26 with·men·of·clay† fainting for fear, and for·
Lk 24:41 And yet not·trusting themselves for the joy and
Gal 2:6 But as·for the·ones seeming to·be something
Mt 28:4 And for fear of·him, the·ones keeping·guard are·
Mk 8:15 "Clearly·see·to·it *that* yeu·look·out for the leaven
Mk 12:38 his instruction, "Look·out for the scribes, the·ones
Rm 15:23 and having a·great·yearning for these·many years
2Co 10:7 let·him·reckon this again for himself; because
Rv 14:20 the horses' bridles, for a·thousand *and* six·hundred

EG0575.6 (4x)
Jn 9:29 God has·spoken to·Moses. But *as·for* this *man*, we·
Mt 9:20 ·*ill*, discharging·a·flow·of·blood *for* twelve years.
Mk 5:25 woman being with a·flow·of·blood *for* twelve years,
Eph 3:6 *The revealing as·for* the Gentiles to·be co-heirs,

G0575.7 PREP ἀφ΄ (6x)
Lk 14:18 "And with one *intent*, they·all began to·excuse·
Lk 15:16 ·longing to·overfill his belly with the carob-pods
Lk 16:21 and longing to·be·stuffed·full with the little·crumbs
Ac 20:9 *and* after·being·weighed·down with heavy·sleep,
1Pe 4:17 *for* the judgment to·begin with the house of·God.
1Pe 4:17 And if *it* first *begins* with us, what *is* the end of·the·

G0575.8 PREP ἀπό (44x)
Jn 5:30 ·not able to·do not·even·one·thing of my·own·self.
Jn 7:28 Yet I·have·not come of my·own·self, but·rather
Jn 8:28 and *that* I·do not·even·one·thing of my·own·self;
Jn 8:42 For neither have·I·come of my·own·self, but·rather
Jn 10:18 ·rather I·myself lay it down of my·own·self. I·have
Jn 15:4 is·not able to·bear fruit of itself unless it·should·
Jn 21:10 says to·them, "Bring of the small·fry which yeu·
Lk 4:41 And demons also were·coming·out of many, yelling·
Lk 5:15 ·both·relieved·and·cured by him of their sicknesses.
Lk 6:13 *to·himself* and was·selecting twelve of them whom
Lk 6:17 came to·hear him and to·be·healed of their illnesses,
Lk 6:29 other *cheek* also, and of the·one taking·away your
Lk 6:30 requesting·of you, and of the·one taking·away your
Lk 8:33 And after·coming·out of the man·of·clay†, the
Lk 9:38 And behold, a·man of the crowd shouted·out,
Lk 11:51 to·yeu, it·shall·be·sought·out of this generation.
Lk 12:1 First·of·all, beware among·yeurselves of the leaven
Lk 12:4 my friends, do·not be·afraid of the·ones killing the
Lk 18:3 to him, saying, 'Avenge me of my legal·adversary.'
Lk 19:26 *more* shall·be·given. But of the·one not having,
Lk 20:10 in·order·that they·should·give him of the fruit of·
Lk 20:46 "Beware of the scribes, the·ones delighting to·
Lk 22:18 No, I·should·not·ever drink of the produce of·the
Lk 23:51 with·their practice; *he·was* of Arimathaea, a·city
Lk 24:42 of·a·broiled fish and *a·piece* of a·honey comb.
Ac 5:2 and he·pilfered *part* of the price, with·his wife also
Ac 5:3 Spirit, and to·pilfer *part* of the price of·the open·field
Ac 8:22 Now·then, repent of this depravity of·yours, and
Ac 9:13 "Lord, I·have·heard of many·things concerning this
Ac 19:13 Then certain of the itinerant Jews, *being* exorcists,
Mt 7:15 "And beware of the false·prophets, who do·come to
Mt 10:17 But beware of the men·of·clay†, for they·shall·
Mt 10:28 And do·not be·afraid of the·ones killing the body,
Mt 16:6 "Clearly·see·to·it also *that* yeu·beware of the leaven
Mt 16:11 bread, *but·rather* to·beware of the leaven of·the
Mt 16:12 he·did·not declare *to·them* to·beware of the leaven
Mt 16:12 leaven of·bread, but·rather of the instruction of·the
Mt 27:21 declared to·them, "Which of the two do·yeu·want
Mt 27:24 saying, "I·am blameless of the blood of·this
Mt 27:57 there·came a·wealthy man·of·clay† of Arimathaea,
Mk 6:43 ·baskets full of·*bread*·fragments and of the fish.
Mk 12:2 ·receive directly·from the tenant·farmers of the fruit
Mk 15:43 Joseph came, the·one of Arimathaea, a·dignified
Rm 6:7 has·been·regarded·as·innocent of the Moral·Failure.

G0575.9 PREP ἀπό (5x)
Rv 6:10 judge and avenge our blood on the·ones residing on
Rv 21:13 On *the* east *are* three gates; on *the* north *are* three
Rv 21:13 On *the* east *are* three gates; on *the* north *are* three
Rv 21:13 on *the* north *are* three gates; on *the* south *are* three
Rv 21:13 *the* south *are* three gates; *and* on *the* west *are* three

G0575.10 PREP ἀπό (5x)
Lk 12:15 ·clearly·see·to·it, and be·vigilant due·to the greed,
Lk 22:45 he·found them being·laid·asleep due·to the grief,
Ac 12:14 she·did·not open·up the gate due·to her joy, but
Ac 22:11 as I·was·not looking·clearly·about due·to the glory
Mt 18:7 "Woe to·the world due·to its scandalous·traps, for

EG0575.10 (1x)
Jn 6:18 the sea was·thoroughly·roused *due·to* a·great wind

G0575.12 PREP ἀπό (5x)
Rm 11:25 ·hardness has·happened to·IsraEl *only* in part, *and*
Rm 15:15 brothers, I·wrote to·yeu in part as once·again·
2Th 2:2 for yeu not quickly to·be·shaken in the mind, nor to·
2Co 1:14 just·as also yeu·already·acknowledged us in part,
2Co 2:5 me *that* he·has·grieved (other·than in part), in·order·

G0575.13 PREP ἀφ΄ (1x)
Lk 13:25 "When·once the master·of·the·house should·be·

G0575.14 PREP ἀπ΄ (1x)
1Jn 2:28 ·of·speech, and may·not be·ashamed before him at

G0575.15 PREP ἀπό (1x)
Ac 10:30 "Four days ago I·was fasting so·far·as·unto this·

G0576 ἀπο•βαίνω apôbaínō *v.* (4x)
Roots:G0575 G0901-3

G0576.1 V-2AAI-3P ἀπέβησαν (1x)
Jn 21:9 So·then, as they·disembarked upon the dry·ground,

G0576.1 V-2AAP-NPM ἀποβάντες (1x)
Lk 5:2 the lake's·edge; then after·disembarking from them,

G0576.2 V-FDI-3S ἀποβήσεται (2x)
Lk 21:13 And it·shall·result to·yeu for a·testimony.
Php 1:19 For I·have·seen that this shall·result in salvation

G0577 ἀπο•βάλλω apôbállō *v.* (2x)
Roots:G0575 G0906 See:G0580 G0579
xLangAlso:H7921

G0577.1 V-2AAP-NSM ἀποβαλών (1x)

Mk 10:50 And after·casting·away his outer·garment *and*
G0577.1 V-2AAS-2P ἀποβάλητε (1x)
Heb 10:35 yeu·should·not cast·away yeur bold·declaration,

G0578 ἀπο•βλέπω apôblépō *v.* (1x)
Roots:G0575 G0991
G0578.2 V-IAI-3S ἀπέβλεπεν (1x)
Heb 11:26 in Egypt, for he·was·intently·looking to the

G0579 ἀπό•βλητος apóblētôs *adj.* (1x)
Roots:G0577 See:G0580
G0579.1 A-NSN ἀπόβλητον (1x)
1Ti 4:4 not·even·one *is to·be* discarded *when* being·received

G0580 ἀπο•βολή apôbolḗ *n.* (2x)
Roots:G0577 Compare:G2209 G1626 See:G0579 xLangAlso:H7921
G0580.1 N-NSF ἀποβολή (1x)
Rm 11:15 For if the casting·away of·them *is* reconciliation
G0580.2 N-NSF ἀποβολή (1x)
Ac 27:22 ·shall·be not·even·one loss of·soul from·among

G0581 ἀπο•γενόμενος apôgênómênôs *v.* (1x)
Roots:G0575 G1096
G0581.3 V-2ADP-NPM ἀπογενόμενοι (1x)
1Pe 2:24 (after·being·legally·pronounced·dead to·the moral·

G0582 ἀπο•γραφή apôgraphḗ *n.* (2x)
Roots:G0583 Compare:G2778
G0582.1 N-NSF ἀπογραφή (1x)
Lk 2:2 (*And* this enrollment first occurred with·Cyrenius
G0582.2 N-GSF ἀπογραφῆς (1x)
Ac 5:37 rose·up in the days of·the census and drew·away a·

G0583 ἀπο•γράφω apôgráphō *v.* (4x)
Roots:G0575 G1125 Compare:G2639
G0583.2 V-PPN ἀπογράφεσθαι (1x)
Lk 2:3 And all traversed to·be·enrolled, each·one into his·
G0583.2 V-RPP-GPM ἀπογεγραμμένων (1x)
Heb 12:23 of·firstborn having·been·enrolled in *the* heavens,
G0583.3 V-PEN ἀπογράφεσθαι (1x)
Lk 2:1 *that* all The Land was·to·be·enrolled·in·a·census.
G0583.3 V-AMN ἀπογράψασθαι (1x)
Lk 2:5 *for·him* to·be·enrolled·in·the·census together with·

G0584 ἀπο•δείκνυμι apôdêíknymi *v.* (4x)
Roots:G0575 G1166 Compare:G1925 G4921 G1731
G0584.2 V-PAP-ASM ἀποδεικνύντα (1x)
2Th 2:4 in the Temple of·God,' exhibiting himself that he·is
G0584.2 V-AAI-3S ἀπέδειξεν (1x)
1Co 4:9 For I·suppose that God exhibited us (the
G0584.2 V-AAN ἀποδεῖξαι (1x)
Ac 25:7 they·were·not having·strength to·exhibit *in·court*,
G0584.2 V-RPP-ASM ἀποδεδειγμένον (1x)
Ac 2:22 of·Natsareth, a·man having·been·exhibited by God

G0585 ἀπό•δειξις apódêixis *n.* (1x)
Roots:G0584 Compare:G1732 G0323 G5039
G0585 N-DSF ἀποδείξει (1x)
1Co 2:4 wisdom, but·rather in demonstration of·Spirit and

G0586 ἀπο•δεκατόω apôdêkatóō *v.* (4x)
Roots:G0575 G1183
G0586.1 V-PAI-1S ἀποδεκατῶ (1x)
Lk 18:12 I·fast twice in·the week, I·tithe all·things, *on* as·
G0586.1 V-PAI-2P ἀποδεκατοῦτε (1x)
Lk 11:42 to·yeu, Pharisees! Because yeu·tithe the mint and
G0586.2 V-PAI-2P ἀποδεκατοῦτε (1x)
Mt 23:23 ·hypocrites! Because yeu·pay·tithes of·the mint
G0586.3 V-PAN ἀποδεκατοῦν (1x)
Heb 7:5 a·commandment to·receive·tithes·of the People

G0587 ἀπό•δεκτος apódêktôs *adj.* (2x)
Roots:G0588 Compare:G1184 See:G0594
G0587 A-NSN ἀπόδεκτον (2x)
1Ti 2:3 this *is* good and fully·acceptable in·the·sight of·God
1Ti 5:4 that is good and fully·acceptable in·the·sight of·God.

G0588 ἀπο•δέχομαι apôdéchômai *v.* (6x)
Roots:G0575 G1209 See:G0587 G0594 G1523 G1926
G0588.1 V-PNI-1P ἀποδεχόμεθα (1x)
Ac 24:3 we·fully·accept *this* with all·manner·of thanksgiving
G0588.1 V-INI-3S ἀπεδέχετο (1x)
Ac 28:30 ·house. And he·was·fully·accepting all the·ones
G0588.1 V-ADI-3S ἀπεδέξατο (1x)
Lk 8:40 returned·back, the crowd fully·accepted him, for
G0588.1 V-ADN ἀποδέξασθαι (1x)
Ac 18:27 the disciples *there* to·fully·accept *Apollos*, who
G0588.1 V-ADP-NPM ἀποδεξάμενοι (1x)
Ac 2:41 in·fact, after·fully·accepting his Redemptive-word
G0588.1 V-API-3P ἀπεδέχθησαν (1x)
Ac 15:4 in JeruSalem, they·were·fully·accepted by the

G0589 ἀπο•δημέω apôdēméō *v.* (6x)
Roots:G0590 Compare:G1927 G3939 G2730
G0589 V-PAP-NSM ἀποδημῶν (1x)
Mt 25:14 *is* just·as a·man·of·clay† journeying·abroad, *who*
G0589 V-AAI-3S ἀπεδήμησεν (5x)
Lk 15:13 absolutely·all, journeyed·abroad into a·distant
Lk 20:9 and·then he·journeyed·abroad for·a·significant time
Mt 21:33 ·leased it to·tenant·farmers and journeyed·abroad.
Mt 25:15 ability, and immediately, he·journeyed·abroad.
Mk 12:1 leased it to·tenant·farmers, and journeyed·abroad.

G0590 ἀπό•δημος apódēmôs *adj.* (1x)
Roots:G0575 G1218 See:G0589
G0590.2 A-NSM ἀπόδημος (1x)
Mk 13:34 *is* as a·man·of·clay† taking·a·long·journey·abroad,

G0591 ἀπο•δίδωμι apôdídōmi *v.* (50x)
Roots:G0575 G1325 Compare:G3860 G0325 G1929 See:G0467
G0591.1 V-2AMI-3S ἀπέδοτο (1x)
Heb 12:16 one full·meal gave·away his rights·as·first-born.
G0591.2 V-FAI-1S ἀποδώσω (2x)
Lk 10:35 I come·back, I·myself shall·give·*it*·back to·you.'
Mt 18:26 me, and I·shall·give·back to·you everything.'
G0591.2 V-FAI-3S ἀποδώσει (4x)
Mt 6:4 ·on in private, shall himself give·back to·you openly.
Mt 6:6 looking·on in private, shall·give·back to·you openly.
Mt 6:18 looking·on in private, shall·give·back to·you openly
Mt 16:27 then 'he·shall·give·back to·each·man according·to
G0591.2 V-FAI-3P ἀποδώσουσιν (1x)
Mt 12:36 *it*, they·shall·give·back an·account concerning it in
G0591.2 V-PAI-1S ἀποδίδωμι (1x)
Lk 19:8 anything *from* any·man, I·give·back *to·him* fourfold
G0591.2 V-PAN ἀποδιδόναι (1x)
1Ti 5:4 and to·give·back compensations to·their·forebears,
G0591.2 V-PAP-NPM ἀποδιδόντες (1x)
Rm 12:17 *Love is* giving·back to·not·even·one·man wrong
G0591.2 V-AAI-3S ἀπέδωκεν (2x)
Lk 9:42 healed the boy, and he·gave him back to·his father.
Rv 18:6 to·her even as she·herself gave·back to·yeu, and
G0591.2 V-2AAM-2P ἀπόδοτε (3x)
Lk 20:25 "Now·then, give·back the·things of·Caesar to·
Mk 12:17 to·them, "Give·back the·things of·Caesar to·
Rv 18:6 "Yeu·must·give·back to·her even as she·herself
G0591.2 V-2AAN ἀποδοῦναι (1x)
Rv 22:12 *is* with me, to·give·back to·each·man as his work
G0591.2 V-2AAO-3S ἀποδῴη (1x)
2Ti 4:14 May the Lord 'give·back to·him according·to his
G0591.2 V-2AAP-NSM ἀποδούς (1x)
Lk 4:20 the official·scroll *and* giving·*it*·back to·the assistant,
G0591.2 V-2AAS-2S ἀποδῷς (1x)
Lk 12:59 even until you·should·give·back the very·last bit.
G0591.2 V-APN ἀποδοθῆναι (1x)
Mt 27:58 commandingly·ordered the body to·be·given·back.
G0591.3 V-FAI-3P ἀποδώσουσιν (1x)
1Pe 4:5 they·who shall·give·forth an·account to·the·one
G0591.3 V-FAP-NPM ἀποδώσοντες (1x)
Heb 13:17 as ones·that·shall·be·giving·forth an·account—
G0591.3 V-IAI-3P ἀπεδίδουν (1x)
Ac 4:33 the ambassadors were·giving·forth the testimonies
G0591.3 V-2AAM-2S ἀπόδος (1x)
Lk 16:2 concerning you? Give·forth an·account of·your
G0591.4 V-FAI-3S ἀποδώσει (1x)
2Ti 4:8 the righteous judge, shall·yield·forth to·me at that
G0591.4 V-PAI-3S ἀποδίδωσιν (1x)
Heb 12:11 But eventually, it·yields·forth a·peaceful fruit of·
G0591.4 V-PAP-ASN ἀποδιδοῦν (1x)
Rv 22:2 twelve *kinds·of* fruits, *and* yielding·forth its fruit
EG0591.4 (2x)
Rm 2:7 ·incorruptibility, *he·shall·render* eternal life-above.
Rm 2:8 by·the unrighteousness, *he·shall·render* Rage and
G0591.5 V-FAI-2S ἀποδώσεις (1x)
Mt 5:33 ·not swear·falsely, but shall·render to·Yahweh your
G0591.5 V-FAI-3S ἀποδώσει (1x)
Rm 2:6 ·himself "'shall·render to·each·man according·to his
G0591.5 V-FAI-3P ἀποδώσουσιν (1x)
Mt 21:41 ·other tenant·farmers, who shall·render to·him the
G0591.5 V-PAM-3S ἀποδιδότω (1x)
1Co 7:3 The husband must·render to·the wife the kind·
G0591.5 V-PAP-NPM ἀποδιδόντες (1x)
1Pe 3:9 not rendering a·wrong for wrong, or a·defamation
G0591.5 V-2AAM-2S ἀπόδος (1x)
Mt 20:8 'Call the workmen and render to·them the payment·
G0591.5 V-2AAM-2P ἀπόδοτε (2x)
Mt 22:21 ·them, "Well·then, render the·things of·Caesar to·
Rm 13:7 Accordingly, render the dues to·all·ones *in*·
G0591.5 V-2AAN ἀποδοῦναι (1x)
Ac 19:40 we·shall·be·able to·render an·account of·this
G0591.5 V-2AAS-3S ἀποδῷ (1x)
1Th 5:15 ·see·to·it *that* no one should·render wrong for
G0591.6 V-FAI-1S ἀποδώσω (1x)
Mt 18:29 ·patient with me, and I·shall·repay you everything.
G0591.6 V-2AAM-2S ἀπόδος (1x)
Mt 18:28 ·strangling *him*, saying, 'Repay me what you·owe
G0591.6 V-2AAN ἀποδοῦναι (2x)
Lk 7:42 having *the ability* to·repay, he·graciously·forgave
Mt 18:25 with·him not having *the ability* to·repay, his lord
G0591.6 V-2AAS-2S ἀποδῷς (1x)
Mt 5:26 from·there until you·should·repay the very·last
G0591.6 V-2AAS-3S ἀποδῷ (2x)
Mt 18:30 prison, until he·should·repay the *amount* being·
Mt 18:34 tormentors, until he·should·repay all the *amount*
G0591.6 V-APN ἀποδοθῆναι (1x)
Mt 18:25 as·much·as he·was·holding, and to·be·repaid.
G0591.7 V-2AMI-3P ἀπέδοντο (1x)
Ac 7:9 the patriarchs, being·jealous, sold Joseph away into
G0591.8 V-2AMI-2P ἀπέδοσθε (1x)
Ac 5:8 "Declare to·me whether yeu·sold·off the open·field

G0592 ἀπο•δι•ορίζω apôdiôrízō *v.* (1x)
Roots:G0575 G1223 G3724 Compare:G1930 See:G1357-1
G0592.2 V-PAP-NPM ἀποδιορίζοντες (1x)
Jud 1:19 are dividing·apart·along·sectarian·or·partisan·lines,

G0593 ἀπο•δοκιμάζω apôdôkimázō *v.* (9x)
Roots:G0575 G1381 Compare:G0683 G1848
G0593.1 V-AAI-3P ἀπεδοκίμασαν (4x)
Lk 20:17 stone which the builders rejected·as·unfit, the·same
Mt 21:42 which the builders rejected·as·unfit, the·same has·
Mk 12:10 which the builders rejected·as·unfit, the·same has·
1Pe 2:7 which the·ones building rejected·as·unfit, this·one
G0593.1 V-API-3S ἀπεδοκιμάσθη (1x)
Heb 12:17 ·inherit the blessing, he·was·rejected·as·unfit, for
G0593.1 V-APN ἀποδοκιμασθῆναι (3x)
Lk 9:22 many·things, and to·be·rejected·as·unfit by the
Lk 17:25 many·things and to·be·rejected·as·unfit by this
Mk 8:31 many·things and to·be·rejected·as·unfit by the
G0593.1 V-RPP-ASM ἀποδεδοκιμασμένον (1x)
1Pe 2:4 ·fact, having·been·rejected·as·unfit by men·of·clay†

G0594 ἀπο•δοχή apôdôchḗ *n.* (2x)
Roots:G0588 Compare:G4356 See:G0587
G0594 N-GSF ἀποδοχῆς (2x)
1Ti 1:15 *is* trustworthy and deserving of·all full·acceptance:
1Ti 4:9 *is* the saying and worthy of·all full·acceptance.

G0595 ἀπό•θεσις apóthêsis *n.* (2x)
Roots:G0659
G0595 N-NSF ἀπόθεσις (2x)
1Pe 3:21 (not *merely* of·flesh *by* a·putting·away of·filth, but·

2Pe 1:14 ·seen that the putting·away of·my bodily·tabernacle

G0596 ἀπο•θήκη apôthḗkē *n.* (6x)

Roots:G0659 Compare:G5009 G2964-4 xLangAlso:H0618 H3965

G0596.2 N-NSF ἀποθήκη (1x)

Lk 12:24 there·is not a·dispensary nor·even a·barn, yet God

G0596.2 N-ASF ἀποθήκην (3x)

Lk 3:17 shall·gather·together the wheat into his barn, but the
Mt 3:12 his wheat into the barn, but he·shall·completely·
Mt 13:30 but gather·together the wheat into my barn.”’”

G0596.2 N-APF ἀποθήκας (2x)

Lk 12:18 ·I·do, I·shall·demolish my barns and shall·build
Mt 6:26 ·reap, nor·even do·they·gather into barns, yet yeur

G0597 ἀπο•θησαυρίζω apôthēsaurízō *v.* (1x)

Roots:G0575 G2343

G0597.2 V-PAP-APM ἀποθησαυρίζοντας (1x)

1Ti 6:19 laying·up·in·store for·themselves a·good

G0598 ἀπο•θλίβω apôthlíbō *v.* (1x)

Roots:G0575 G2346

G0598 V-PAI-3P ἀποθλίβουσιν (1x)

Lk 8:45 the crowds confine you and press·against *you*, and

G0599 ἀπο•θνήσκω apôthnḗskō *v.* (111x)

Roots:G0575 G2348 Compare:G1634 G1606 See:G1727-1 xLangAlso:H4191

G0599 V-FDI-2P ἀποθανεῖσθε (3x)

Jn 8:21 and yeu·shall·seek me and shall·die in yeur moral·
Jn 8:24 I·declared to·yeu that yeu·shall·die in yeur moral·
Jn 8:24 ·trust that I AM, yeu·shall·die in yeur moral·failures

G0599 V-FDI-3S ἀποθανεῖται (1x)

Rm 5:7 over a·righteous·man shall anyone die, for perhaps

G0599 V-PAI-1S ἀποθνήσκω (1x)

1Co 15:31 Each day I·die, as·sure·as *it·is* our boast, which I·

G0599 V-PAI-1P ἀποθνήσκομεν (2x)

Rm 14:8 or·also whether we·should·die, we·die to·the Lord.
1Co 15:32 ·eat and should·drink, for tomorrow we·die.”

G0599 V-PAI-3S ἀποθνήσκει (5x)

Jn 21:23 “This disciple does·not die.” But Jesus did·not
Jn 21:23 ·not declare to·him that he·does·not die, but·rather,
Heb 10:28 Moses' Torah-Law died completely·apart·from
Rm 6:9 dead·men, Anointed-One no·longer dies. Death no·
Rm 14:7 lives to·himself, and not·even·one dies to·himself.

G0599 V-PAI-3P ἀποθνήσκουσιν (1x)

1Co 15:22 just·as all within Adam die, even in·this·manner,

G0599 V-PAN ἀποθνήσκειν (5x)

Jn 4:47 and may·heal his son, for he·was·about to·die.
Jn 11:51 that Jesus was·about to·die on·behalf·of·the nation;
Jn 12:33 signifying what·kind·of death he·was·about to·die.
Jn 18:32 signifying what·kind·of death he·was·about to·die.
Rm 8:13 ·live according·to flesh, yeu·are·about to·die. But

G0599 V-PAP-NSM ἀποθνήσκων (2x)

Heb 11:21 By·trust, Jacob (when·he·was·dying) blessed
Mk 12:20 ·one took a·wife, and·then dying, he·did·not leave

G0599 V-PAP-NPM ἀποθνήσκοντες (3x)

Heb 7:8 in·fact, *are* tithes *that* dying men·of·clay† receive,
2Co 6:9 and·yet being·recognized, as dying and behold—
Rv 14:13 *are* the dead·ones, the·ones dying in *the* Lord

G0599 V-PAS-1P ἀποθνήσκωμεν (2x)

Rm 14:8 Lord; or·also whether we·should·die, we·die to·the
Rm 14:8 ·live, or·also whether we·should·die, we·are the

G0599 V-IAI-3S ἀπέθνησκεν (1x)

Lk 8:42 years·of·age, and she·herself was·dying. But with

G0599 V-2AAI-1S ἀπέθανον (2x)

Gal 2:19 Torah-Law, am·dead to·Torah-Law in·order·that I·
Rm 7:9 Moral·Failure came·alive·again, and I·myself died.

G0599 V-2AAI-1P ἀπεθάνομεν (2x)

Rm 6:2 happen! We·are·those·who died to·Moral·Failure;
Rm 6:8 Now if we·died together with·Anointed-One, we·

G0599 V-2AAI-2P ἀπεθάνετε (2x)

Col 2:20 ·then, if yeu·did·die together with·Anointed-One
Col 3:3 For yeu·already·died, and yeur life·above has·been·

G0599 V-2AAI-3S ἀπέθανεν (32x)

Jn 8:52 that you·have a·demon. AbRaham is·dead, and the
Jn 8:53 our father AbRaham, who is·dead? And the prophets
Jn 11:14 to·them with·clarity·of·speech, “Lazarus is·dead.
Jn 11:32 if you·were here, my brother would not have·died.”
Lk 8:52 Do·not weep. She·did·not die, but·rather she·sleeps.
Lk 8:53 ·down·at him, having·seen that she·did·die.
Lk 16:22 But the wealthy·man died also and was·buried.
Lk 20:29 the first·one, after·taking a·wife, died childless.
Lk 20:30 took the *same* wife, and this·man died childless.
Lk 20:32 So last·of·all, the wife died also.
Gal 2:21 Anointed-One died, offered·freely·for·nothing.”
Mt 9:24 For the young·girl did·not die, but·rather she·sleeps.
Mt 22:27 And last·of·all, the wife died also.
Mk 5:35 saying, “Your daughter is·dead. Why harass the
Mk 5:39 The little·child is·not dead, but·rather she·sleeps.
Mk 9:26 as one·dead— such·for many to·say that he·died.
Mk 12:21 the second took her, and he·died, and neither *did*
Mk 12:22 Last·of·all, the wife died also.
Mk 15:44 ·of him whether he·died long·before·now.
Rm 5:6 Anointed-One died on·behalf·of·irreverent·men
Rm 5:8 ·of·moral·failure, Anointed-One died on·our behalf.
Rm 6:10 For in·that·which he·died, he·died to·the Moral·
Rm 6:10 in·that·which he·died, he·died to·the Moral·Failure
Rm 14:9 ·*purpose* Anointed-One also died and rose·up. And
Rm 14:15 food, on·behalf·of·whom Anointed-One died.
1Th 4:14 For if we·trust that YeShua died and rose·up, in·
1Co 8:11 ·perish, on·account·of whom Anointed-One died?
1Co 15:3 that Anointed-One died on·behalf·of·our moral·
2Co 5:14 this·thing: that if one died on·behalf·of·all, then·
2Co 5:15 Also, he·died on·behalf·of·all in·order·that the·
Rv 8:9 sea, the·ones having souls) died; and the third·part
Rv 16:3 And every living soul in the sea died.

G0599 V-2AAI-3P ἀπέθανον (10x)

Jn 6:49 fathers ate the manna in the wilderness, and died.
Jn 6:58 fathers ate the manna and died. The·one chewing this
Jn 8:53 And the prophets are·dead. Whom·do you·yourself
Lk 20:31 also; they·left·behind no children, and they·died.
Heb 11:13 These all died according·to trust, not receiving the
Heb 11:37 ·half, they·were·tempted, they·died by murder
Mt 8:32 steep·overhang into the sea and died in the waters.
Rm 5:15 of·the one, the many died, so·much more did·
2Co 5:14 died on·behalf·of·all, then·by·inference, all died.
Rv 8:11 and many men·of·clay† died as·a·result·of·the

G0599 V-2AAN ἀποθανεῖν (15x)

Jn 4:49 “Sir, walk·down prior·to my little·child dying.”
Jn 19:7 according·to our Oral-law he·is·due to·die, because
Lk 16:22 *as·such, for* the helpless·beggar to·die, and *for* him
Lk 20:36 For neither are·they·able to·die any·longer, for
Ac 7:4 after his father died, *God* transferred·and·settled him
Ac 9:37 *that* being·sick, she died. And after·bathing her,
Ac 21:13 to·be·bound, but·rather also to·die at JeruSalem
Ac 25:11 worthy·of·death, I·do·not decline to·die. But if
Heb 9:27 for·the men·of·clay† to·die only·once and·then *to*·
Mt 26:35 ·be·necessary·for me to·die together with·you, no,
Rm 5:7 ·good·man, someone also would·dare to·die.
Php 1:21 For me to·live *is* Anointed-One, and to·die *is* gain.
1Co 9:15 for *it·is* good for·me to·die rather than that anyone
Rv 3:2 the·things remaining that are·about to·die, for I·have·
Rv 9:6 ·not find him. And they·shall·long to·die, and Death

G0599 V-2AAP-DSM ἀποθανόντι (1x)

2Co 5:15 but·rather to·the·one already·dying on·their behalf

G0599 V-2AAP-GSM ἀποθανόντος (1x)

1Th 5:10 the·one dying on·our behalf in·order·that, whether

G0599 V-2AAP-NSM ἀποθανών (3x)

Heb 11:4 the·same *trust, although* already·dying, he·himself
Rm 6:7 the·one being·dead has·been·regarded·as·innocent of
Rm 8:34 *It·is* Anointed-One, the·one dying, but·rather also

G0599 V-2AAP-NPN ἀποθανόντα (1x)

Jud 1:12 trees without·fruit, already·dying·off twice,

G0599 V-2AAP-NPM ἀποθανόντες (1x)

Rm 7:6 from the Torah-Law, being·dead *to·that* by that·

G0599 V-2AAS-1P ἀποθάνωμεν (1x)

Jn 11:16 ·head·out also in·order·that we·may·die with him.”

G0599 V-2AAS-3S ἀποθάνῃ (14x)

Jn 6:50 someone may·eat from·out·of it, and may·not die.
Jn 11:25 in me, though he·should·die, yet·shall·he·live.
Jn 11:26 in me, no, should·not die to the coming·age.
Jn 11:37 to·make *it·be* also that this·man should·not die?”
Jn 11:50 that one man·of·clay† should·die on·behalf·of·the
Jn 12:24 falling into the soil, should·die, it abides alone.
Jn 12:24 it abides alone. But if it·should·die, it·bears much
Lk 20:28 any·man's brother should·die while·having a·wife,
Lk 20:28 a·wife, and this·man should·die childless, that his
Mt 22:24 declared, if a·certain·man should·die not having
Mk 12:19 that if any·man's brother should·die, and should·
Rm 7:2 the husband should·die, she·has·been·fully·nullified
Rm 7:3 But if the husband should·die, she·is freed from the
1Co 15:36 you sow is·not giving·life, unless it·should·die.

G0600 ἀπο•καθ•ίστημι apôkathístēmi *v.* (8x)

Roots:G0575 G2525 Compare:G0365 G3824 G2675 See:G0605 xLangAlso:H7725

G0600.1 V-FAI-3S ἀποκαταστήσει (1x)

Mt 17:11 does·come first and shall·reconstitute all·things.

G0600.1 V-PAI-3S ἀποκαθιστά (1x)

Mk 9:12 after·coming first, does·reconstitute all·things.

G0600.2 V-PAI-2S ἀποκαθιστάνεις (1x)

Ac 1:6 do·you at this time restore the kingdom to·IsraEl?

G0600.2 V-API-3S ἀποκατεστάθη (4x)

Lk 6:10 and his hand was·restored as·healthy·and·sound as
Mt 12:13 ·out, and it·was·restored as·healthy·and·sound as
Mk 3:5 and his hand was·restored as·healthy·and·sound as
Mk 8:25 and he·was·restored and looked·clearly·upon

G0600.2 V-APS-2S ἀποκατασταθῶ (1x)

Heb 13:19 this, in·order·that I·may·be·restored to·yeu more·

G0601 ἀπο•καλύπτω apôkalýptō *v.* (27x)

Roots:G0575 G2572 See:G0602

G0601.1 V-FAI-3S ἀποκαλύψει (1x)

Php 3:15 differently, God shall·reveal even this to·yeu.

G0601.1 V-FPI-3S ἀποκαλυφθήσεται (3x)

Lk 12:2 ·altogether·concealed that shall·not be·revealed, nor
Mt 10:26 ·been·concealed, that shall·not be·revealed, and
2Th 2:8 And then the Lawless·One shall·be·revealed, whom

G0601.1 V-PPI-3S ἀποκαλύπτεται (4x)

Lk 17:30 in·that day *when* the Son of·Clay·Man† is·revealed.
Rm 1:17 God's righteousness is·revealed, birthed·from·out
Rm 1:18 For God's wrath is·revealed from heaven against all
1Co 3:13 shall·make·*it*·plain, because it·is·revealed by fire,

G0601.1 V-PPN ἀποκαλύπτεσθαι (1x)

1Pe 5:1 and·also a·partner of·the glory about to·be·revealed.

G0601.1 V-AAI-2S ἀπεκάλυψας (2x)

Lk 10:21 intelligent·men, and you·revealed them to·infants.
Mt 11:25 intelligent·men, and you·revealed them to·infants.

G0601.1 V-AAI-3S ἀπεκάλυψεν (2x)

Mt 16:17 because flesh and blood did·not reveal *this* to·you,
1Co 2:10 But God revealed *them* to·us through his Spirit, for

G0601.1 V-AAN ἀποκαλύψαι (3x)

Lk 10:22 ·whomever the Son should·resolve to·reveal *him*.”
Gal 1:16 to·reveal his Son in me in·order·that I·may·
Mt 11:27 to·whomever the Son should·resolve to·reveal *him*.

G0601.1 V-API-3S ἀπεκαλύφθη (3x)

Jn 12:38 heard? And to·whom is·revealed the arm of·
1Pe 1:12 *And* it·was·revealed to·these·men that *it·was* not
Eph 3:5 as it·is now revealed to·his holy ambassadors and

G0601.1 V-APN ἀποκαλυφθῆναι (4x)

Gal 3:23 in·order·for the impending trust to·be·revealed.
Rm 8:18 alongside the impending glory to·be·revealed in us.
1Pe 1:5 trust for a·Salvation ready to·be·revealed in *the* last
2Th 2:6 ·*him*·down in·order·for him to·be·revealed in his

G0601.1 V-APS-3S ἀποκαλυφθῇ (2x)

2Th 2:3 Clay·Man† of·Moral·Failure should·be·revealed, the
1Co 14:30 *something* should·be·revealed to·another sitting·

G0601.1 V-APS-3P ἀποκαλυφθῶσιν (1x)

Lk 2:35 from·among many hearts should·be·revealed (and

EG0601.1 (1x)

Rm 1:19 *the wrath is·revealed* on·account·that, the·thing

G0602 ἀπο•κάλυψις apôkálypsis *n.* (19x)

Roots:G0601 See:G0601 xLangAlso:H0262

G0602.1 N-ASF ἀποκάλυψιν (3x)

Rm 8:19 ·the creation fully·awaits the revealing of·the Sons
Rm 16:25 (according·to a·revealing of·*the*·Mystery having·
1Co 1:7 while·fully·awaiting the revealing of·our Lord Jesus
G0602.1 N-DSF ἀποκαλύψει (4x)
1Pe 1:7 honor and glory at the·revealing of·YeShua Anointed
1Pe 1:13 to·yeu at *the* revealing of·YeShua Anointed.
1Pe 4:13 so that at the revealing of·his glory, yeu·may·be·
2Th 1:7 with us at the revealing of·the Lord YeShua from
EG0602.1 (1x)
Eph 3:6 *The* *revealing* *as·for* the Gentiles to·be co-heirs,
G0602.2 N-NSF ἀποκάλυψις (1x)
Rv 1:1 *The* Revelation of·Jesus Anointed, which God gave
G0602.2 N-ASF ἀποκάλυψιν (4x)
Lk 2:32 a·light for a·revelation of·Gentiles and *for the* glory
Gal 2:2 And I·walked·up according·to a·revelation, and set·
1Co 14:26 has a·bestowed·tongue, has a·revelation, has a·
Eph 3:3 that according·to a·revelation, he·made·known to·
G0602.2 N-APF ἀποκαλύψεις (1x)
2Co 12:1 I·shall·come to visions and revelations of·*the*·Lord.
G0602.2 N-DSF ἀποκαλύψει (1x)
1Co 14:6 I·should·speak to·yeu either by revelation, or by
G0602.2 N-GSF ἀποκαλύψεως (3x)
Gal 1:12 *it* through a·revelation of·YeShua Anointed.
Rm 2:5 and of·*the*·revelation of·God's righteous·verdict,
Eph 1:17 a·spirit of·wisdom and revelation in recognition of·
G0602.2 N-GPF ἀποκαλύψεων (1x)
2Co 12:7 ·excellence of·the revelations, there·was·given to·

G0603 ἀπο•καρα•δοκία apôkaradôkía *n.* (2x)
Roots:G0575 G1380 Compare:G1680 G1561 xLangEquiv:H7664 xLangAlso:H4723 H8615
G0603 N-NSF ἀποκαραδοκία (1x)
Rm 8:19 For the eager·anticipation of·the creation fully·
G0603 N-ASF ἀποκαραδοκίαν (1x)
Php 1:20 according·to my eager·anticipation and expectation

G0604 ἀπο•κατα•λλάσσω apôkatallássō *v.* (3x)
Roots:G0575 G2644
G0604 V-AAI-3S ἀποκατήλλαξεν (1x)
Col 1:21 by the evil works, so now he·utterly·reconciled
G0604 V-AAN ἀποκαταλλάξαι (1x)
Col 1:20 *he·takes·delight* to·utterly·reconcile through him
G0604 V-AAS-3S ἀποκαταλλάξῃ (1x)
Eph 2:16 and·also *that* he·may·utterly·reconcile the both to·

G0605 ἀπο•κατά•στασις apôkatástasis *n.* (1x)
Roots:G0600 Compare:G0342 G0365 G1357 G2676 G3824 See:G2643
G0605.1 N-GSF ἀποκαταστάσεως (1x)
Ac 3:21 even·until *the* times of·a·reconstitution of·all·things,

G0606 ἀπό•κειμαι apókêimai *v.* (4x)
Roots:G0575 G2749
G0606.1 V-PNI-3S ἀπόκειται (2x)
Heb 9:27 ·to as·much·as it·is·laid·away for·the men·of·clay†
2Ti 4:8 Henceforth, there·is·laid·away for·me the victor's·
G0606.1 V-PNP-ASF ἀποκειμένην (2x)
Lk 19:20 ·holding *for·you*, laying·*it*·away in a·sweat·towel.
Col 1:5 Expectation, the·one being·laid·away for·yeu in the

G0607 ἀπο•κεφαλίζω apôkêphalízō *v.* (4x)
Roots:G0575 G2776
G0607 V-AAI-1S ἀπεκεφάλισα (2x)
Lk 9:9 ·AntiPas declared, "I·myself beheaded John, but who
Mk 6:16 whom I·myself beheaded. He·himself is·already·
G0607 V-AAI-3S ἀπεκεφάλισεν (2x)
Mt 14:10 And after·sending·word, he·beheaded John in the
Mk 6:27 But·then going·off, *HerOd·AntiPas* beheaded him in

G0608 ἀπο•κλείω apôklêíō *v.* (1x)
Roots:G0575 G2808 Compare:G2576
G0608 V-AAS-3S ἀποκλείσῃ (1x)
Lk 13:25 should·be·roused, and should·utterly·shut the door

G0609 ἀπο•κόπτω apôkóptō *v.* (6x)
Roots:G0575 G2875 Compare:G2699
G0609.1 V-FMI-3P ἀποκόψονται (1x)
Gal 5:12 Oh·that even they·were·chopped·off, the·ones
G0609.1 V-AAI-3S ἀπέκοψεν (2x)
Jn 18:10 designated·high·priest, and he·chopped·off his right
Jn 18:26 of·him·whose earlobe Peter chopped·off, says, "¿!·
G0609.1 V-AAI-3P ἀπέκοψαν (1x)
Ac 27:32 Then the soldiers chopped·off the small·ropes of·
G0609.1 V-AAM-2S ἀπόκοψον (2x)
Mk 9:43 So if your hand should·entrap you, chop it off. It·is
Mk 9:45 if your foot should·entrap you, chop it off. It·is

G0610 ἀπό•κριμα apókrima *n.* (1x)
Roots:G0611
G0610.2 N-ASN ἀπόκριμα (1x)
2Co 1:9 have·had the judicial·sentence of·death in·order·that

G0611 ἀπο•κρίνομαι apôkrínômai *v.* (250x)
Roots:G0575 G2919 See:G0612 xLangAlso:H6030
G0611.2 V-AOP-NSM ἀποκριθείς (2x)
Mt 11:25 After·fully·calling·*them*·into·judgment on that
Mt 27:21 And fully·calling·*them*·into·judgment, the
G0611.3 V-FOI-3S ἀποκριθήσεται (1x)
Mt 25:45 Then he·shall·answer them, saying, 'Certainly I·
G0611.3 V-FOI-3P ἀποκριθήσονται (2x)
Mt 25:37 "Then the righteous shall·answer him, saying,
Mt 25:44 "Then they also shall·answer him, saying, 'Lord,
G0611.3 V-PNI-2S ἀποκρίνῃ (4x)
Jn 18:22 declaring, "Do·you·answer the high·priest in·this·
Mt 26:62 declared to·him, "Do·you·answer nothing·at·all?
Mk 14:60 saying, "Do·you·not answer not·even·one·thing?
Mk 15:4 saying, "Do·you·not answer not·even·one·thing?
G0611.3 V-PNI-3S ἀποκρίνεται (1x)
Jn 13:26 Jesus answered, "It·is that·man to·whom I·shall·
G0611.3 V-PNN ἀποκρίνεσθαι (1x)
Col 4:6 to·personally·know how to·answer each individual.
G0611.3 V-ADI-1S ἀπεκρίθην (2x)
Ac 22:8 And I·myself answered, 'Who are·you, Lord?
Ac 25:16 To whom I·answered, 'It·is not *the* manner of·the·
G0611.3 V-ADI-2S ἀπεκρίθης (1x)
Lk 10:28 he·declared to·him, "You·answered uprightly. Do
G0611.3 V-ADI-3S ἀπεκρίθη (92x)
Jn 1:21 ·yourself the Prophet?" And he·answered, "No.
Jn 1:26 John answered them, saying, "I·myself immerse in
Jn 1:48 ·know me?" Jesus answered and declared to·him,
Jn 1:49 NathaniEl answered and says to·him, "Rabbi, you·
Jn 1:50 Jesus answered and declared to·him, "Because I·
Jn 2:19 Jesus answered and declared to·them, "Tear·down
Jn 3:3 Jesus answered and declared to·him, "Certainly,
Jn 3:5 Jesus answered, "Certainly, most·certainly, I·say to·
Jn 3:9 NicoDemus answered and declared to·him, "How·are
Jn 3:10 Jesus answered and declared to·him, "Are you·
Jn 3:27 John answered and declared, "A·man·of·clay† is·not
Jn 4:10 Jesus answered and declared to·her, "If you·had·
Jn 4:13 Jesus answered and declared to·her, "Anyone
Jn 4:17 The woman answered and declared, "I·do·not have
Jn 5:7 The feeble·man answered him, "Sir, I·have no man·
Jn 5:11 He·answered them, "The·one making me healthy·
Jn 5:17 Now Jesus answered them, "My Father works until
Jn 5:19 So·then Jesus answered and declared to·them,
Jn 6:7 PhilIp answered him, "Two·hundred denarii *worth*
Jn 6:26 Jesus answered them and declared, "Certainly, most·
Jn 6:29 Jesus answered and declared to·them, "This is the
Jn 6:43 So Jesus answered and declared to·them, "Do·not
Jn 6:68 Accordingly, Simon Peter answered him, "Lord, to
Jn 6:70 Jesus answered them, "No, *it·is* I·myself *that*
Jn 7:16 Jesus answered them and declared, "My instruction
Jn 7:20 The crowd answered and declared, "You·have a·
Jn 7:21 Jesus answered and declared to·them, "I·did one
Jn 8:14 Jesus answered and declared to·them, "Though I·
Jn 8:19 is your Father?" Jesus answered, "Neither do·yeu·
Jn 8:34 Jesus answered them, "Certainly, most·certainly, I·
Jn 8:49 Jesus answered, "I·myself do·not have a·demon,
Jn 8:54 Jesus answered, "If I·myself glorify my·own·self,
Jn 9:3 Jesus answered, "Neither this·man morally·failed, nor
Jn 9:11 That·man answered and declared, "A·man·of·clay†
Jn 9:25 Accordingly, that·man answered and declared,
Jn 9:27 He·answered them, "I·declared *it* to·yeu even·now,
Jn 9:30 The man·of·clay† answered and declared to·them,
Jn 9:36 That·one answered and declared, "Who is·he, Lord,
Jn 10:25 Jesus answered them, "I·declared *it* to·yeu, and
Jn 10:32 Jesus answered them, "Many good works I·showed
Jn 10:34 Jesus answered them, "Is·it not having·been·
Jn 11:9 Jesus answered, "Are·there not·indeed twelve hours
Jn 12:23 And Jesus answered them, saying, "The hour has·
Jn 12:30 Jesus answered and declared, "This voice has·
Jn 12:34 The crowd answered him, "We·ourselves heard
Jn 13:7 Jesus answered and declared to·him, "What I·myself
Jn 13:8 *even* to the coming·age." Jesus answered him, "If I·
Jn 13:36 you·head·on·out?" Jesus answered him, "Where
Jn 13:38 Jesus answered him, "Shall·you·lay·down your
Jn 14:23 Jesus answered and declared to·him, "If anyone
Jn 16:31 Jesus answered them, "*So* at·this·moment, do·yeu·
Jn 18:8 Jesus answered, "I·declared to·yeu that I AM.
Jn 18:20 Jesus answered him, "I·myself spoke with·
Jn 18:23 Jesus answered him, "If I·spoke wrongly, testify
Jn 18:34 Jesus answered him, "From yourself, do·you say
Jn 18:35 Pilate answered, "¿! Am·I myself a·Jew?
Jn 18:36 Jesus answered, "My kingdom is not from·among
Jn 18:37 are a·king!" Jesus answered, "You·yourself say *it*·
Jn 19:11 Jesus answered, "You·were·not having not·even·
Jn 19:22 Pilate answered, "What I·have·written, I·have·
Jn 20:28 And Thomas answered and declared to·him, "My
Lk 3:16 John answered, saying to·absolutely·all *of·them*,
Lk 4:4 And Jesus answered to him, saying, "It·has·been·
Lk 8:50 But Jesus hearing *it*, answered him, saying, "Do·
Lk 13:15 So·then the Lord answered him and declared, "O·
Lk 17:20 of·God should·come, he·answered them and
Lk 23:9 But *Jesus* answered him not·even·one·thing.
Ac 3:12 And seeing *this*, Peter answered to the people,
Ac 5:8 And Peter answered to·her, "Declare to·me whether
Ac 9:13 But AnanIas answered, "Lord, I·have·heard of
Ac 11:9 But *the* voice answered me for a·second·time from·
Ac 15:13 Jacob *(the half-brother of·Jesus)* answered, saying,
Ac 21:13 But Paul answered, "Why·do yeu·continue
Ac 22:28 And the regiment·commander answered, "I·myself
Ac 24:10 beckoning for·him to·discourse, Paul answered,
Ac 24:25 Felix, becoming alarmed, answered, "Holding it
Ac 25:4 Now·then in·fact, Festus answered *for* Paul to·be·
Ac 25:12 with the council, answered, "You·have·appealed·
Mt 15:23 But he·did·not answer her a·word. And his
Mt 27:12 and the elders, he·answered not·even·one·thing.
Mt 27:14 And he·did·not answer to him not·even one
Mk 3:33 And he·answered them, saying, "Who is my
Mk 5:9 *is* your name?" And he·answered, saying, "My
Mk 7:28 And she·answered and says to·him, "Yes *it·is*, Lord
Mk 9:38 And John answered him, saying, "Mentor, we·saw
Mk 12:28 *and* having·seen that he·answered them well,
Mk 12:29 And Jesus answered him, "*The* foremost of·all the
Mk 12:34 after·seeing that the·same·man answered sensibly,
Mk 14:61 ·keeping·silent and answered not·even·one·thing.
Mk 15:5 Jesus was·no·longer answering not·even·one·thing,
Mk 15:9 So Pilate answered them, saying, "Do·yeu·want
Rv 7:13 one from·among the Elders answered, saying to·me,
G0611.3 V-ADI-3P ἀπεκρίθησαν (20x)
Jn 2:18 Accordingly, the Judeans answered and declared to·
Jn 7:46 The assistants answered, "Never·at·any·time in·this·
Jn 7:47 Then the Pharisees answered them, "¿!·Have even
Jn 7:52 They·answered and declared to·him, "¿! Are you·
Jn 8:33 They·answered him, "We·are AbRaham's offspring†,
Jn 8:39 They·answered and declared to·him, "AbRaham is
Jn 8:48 So·then the Judeans answered and declared to·him,
Jn 9:20 His parents answered them and declared, "We·
Jn 9:34 They·answered and declared to·him, "You·yourself
Jn 10:33 The Judeans answered him, saying, "We·do·not
Jn 18:5 They·answered him, "Jesus of·Natsareth.
Jn 18:30 They·answered and declared to·him, "If this·man
Jn 19:7 The Judeans answered him, "We·ourselves have an·
Jn 19:15 King?" The chief·priests answered, "We·have no
Jn 21:5 ·have anything for·eating?" They·answered him,
Lk 20:7 And they·answered *as* to·not personally·know from·

Mt 12:38 of·the scribes and Pharisees answered, saying,
Mt 25:9 But the prudent answered, saying, '*Not·so*, lest
Mk 8:4 And his disciples answered him, "From·what·source
Mk 8:28 And they·answered, "John the Immerser, but some

G0611.3 V-AOM-2P ἀποκρίθητε (3x)
Lk 22:68 *of·yeu*, no, yeu·may·not answer me, nor should·
Mk 11:29 also one question; so·then answer me, and I·shall·
Mk 11:30 or from·out of·men·of·clay†? Answer me."

G0611.3 V-AON ἀποκριθῆναι (1x)
Mt 22:46 not·even·one·man was·able to·answer him a·word,

G0611.3 V-AOP-NSN ἀποκριθέν (1x)
Ac 19:15 And answering *on·one occasion*, the evil spirit

G0611.3 V-AOP-NSF ἀποκριθεῖσα (1x)
Lk 1:60 And answering, his mother declared, "No·indeed!

G0611.3 V-AOP-NSM ἀποκριθείς (86x)
Lk 1:19 And answering, the angel declared to·him, "I·
Lk 1:35 And answering, the angel declared to·her, "Holy
Lk 3:11 And answering, he·says to·them, "The·one having
Lk 4:8 And answering, Jesus declared to·him, "Get·
Lk 4:12 And answering, Jesus declared to·him, "It·has·
Lk 5:5 And answering, Simon declared to·him, "O·Captain,
Lk 5:22 ·knowing their deliberations, answering, declared to
Lk 5:31 And answering, Jesus declared to them, "The·ones
Lk 7:22 And answering, Jesus declared to·them, "Traversing
Lk 7:40 And answering, Jesus declared to him, "Simon, I·
Lk 7:43 And answering, Simon declared, "I·assume that *it·is*
Lk 8:21 And answering, he·declared to them, "My mother
Lk 9:20 say me to·be?" And answering, Peter declared,
Lk 9:41 And answering, Jesus declared, "O distrusting and
Lk 10:27 And answering, he·declared, "≈You·shall·love
Lk 10:41 And answering, Jesus declared to·her, "Martha,
Lk 11:7 "And answering from·inside, that·man may·declare,
Lk 11:45 Then answering, a·certain·one of·the experts·in·
Lk 13:8 "And answering, he·says to·him, 'Lord, leave it this
Lk 13:14 director·of·the·gathering answering, being·greatly·
Lk 13:25 ·up to·us,' and answering, he·shall·declare to·yeu,
Lk 14:5 And answering toward them, he·declared, "Which
Lk 15:29 But answering *him*, he·declared to·his father,
Lk 19:40 And answering, he·declared to·them, "I·say to·yeu
Lk 20:3 And answering, he·declared to them, "And·I shall·
Lk 20:34 And answering, Jesus declared to·them, "The
Lk 23:3 King of·the Jews?" And answering him, he·replied,
Lk 23:40 But answering, the other *criminal* was·
Lk 24:18 And answering, the individual whose name *was*
Ac 5:29 But answering, Peter and the ambassadors declared,
Ac 8:24 Then answering, Simon declared, "Yeu·yeurselves
Ac 8:34 And answering Philippe, the eunuch declared, "I·
Ac 8:37 heart, it·is·proper." And answering, he·declared,
Ac 25:9 influential·favor with·the Judeans, answering Paul,
Mt 3:15 And answering, YeShua declared to him, "Allow
Mt 4:4 But answering, he·declared, "It·has·been·written,
Mt 8:8 And answering, the centurion was·replying, "Lord, I·
Mt 11:4 And answering, YeShua declared to·them,
Mt 12:39 But answering, he·declared to·them, "An·evil
Mt 12:48 But answering the·one declaring *this* to·him, he·
Mt 13:11 And answering, he·declared to·them, "Because it·
Mt 13:37 And answering, he·declared to·them, "The·one
Mt 14:28 And answering him, Peter declared, "Lord, if it·is·
Mt 15:3 But answering, he·declared to·them, "And why·do
Mt 15:13 But answering, he·declared, "Every plant which
Mt 15:24 Then answering *her*, he·declared, "I·am·not
Mt 15:26 But answering, he·declared, "It·is not good to·take
Mt 15:28 Then answering, YeShua declared to·her, "O
Mt 16:2 Answering, he·declared to·them, "With·early·
Mt 16:16 And answering, Simon Peter declared, "You·
Mt 17:11 And answering, YeShua declared to·them, "In·fact
Mt 17:17 And answering, YeShua declared, "O distrusting
Mt 19:4 And answering, he·declared to·them, "Did·yeu·not
Mt 20:13 But answering one of·them, he·declared,
Mt 20:22 But answering, YeShua declared *to·her sons*,
Mt 21:21 And answering, YeShua declared to·them,
Mt 21:24 And answering, YeShua declared to·them, "I·also
Mt 21:29 But answering, he·declared, 'I·will not.
Mt 21:30 he·declared likewise. And answering, he·declared,
Mt 22:29 And answering, YeShua declared to·them, "Yeu·
Mt 24:4 And answering, YeShua declared to·them, "Look·
Mt 25:12 But answering, he·declared, 'Certainly I·say to·
Mt 25:26 "And answering, his lord declared to·him, 'O·evil
Mt 25:40 And answering, the King shall·declare to·them,
Mt 26:23 And answering, he·declared, "The·one dipping his
Mt 26:25 And answering, Judas (the·one handing him over)
Mt 26:33 And answering, Peter declared to·him, "Even if
Mk 6:37 But answering, *Jesus* declared to·them, "Yeu·
Mk 7:6 And answering, he·declared to·them, "IsaIah
Mk 8:29 say me to·be?" And answering, Peter says to·him,
Mk 9:12 And answering, he·declared to·them, "EliJah, in·
Mk 9:17 And one·man, answering from·among the crowd,
Mk 9:19 But answering him, he·says, "O distrusting
Mk 10:3 And answering, he·declared to·them, "What did·
Mk 10:5 And answering, Jesus declared to·them,
Mk 10:20 And answering, he·declared to·him, "Mentor, all
Mk 10:24 But Jesus, answering again, says to·them,
Mk 10:29 And answering, Jesus declared, "Certainly I·say
Mk 11:22 And answering, Jesus says to·them, "Have God's
Mk 11:29 And answering, Jesus declared to·them, "I·shall·
Mk 11:33 And Jesus answering says to·them, "Neither do
Mk 12:17 And answering, Jesus declared to·them, "Give·
Mk 12:24 And answering, Jesus declared to·them, "*Is·it* not
Mk 13:5 And Jesus answering them began to·say, "Look·out
Mk 14:20 And answering, he·declared to·them, "*It·is* one
Mk 15:2 of·the Jews?" And answering, he·declared to·him,

G0611.3 V-AOP-NPM ἀποκριθέντες (7x)
Lk 9:19 And answering, they·declared, "John the Immerser,
Lk 17:37 And answering, they·say to·him, "Where, Lord?
Lk 20:24 does·it·have?" And answering, they·declared,
Ac 4:19 But answering, Peter and John declared to them,
Mt 21:27 And answering YeShua, they·declared, "We·do·
Mt 26:66 suppose?" And answering, they·declared, "He·is
Mk 11:33 And answering, they·say to·Jesus, "We·do·not

G0611.3 V-AOS-3P ἀποκριθῶσιν (1x)
Mk 14:40 ·known what they·should·answer to·him.

EG0611.3 (1x)
Mk 15:3 ·many·things, *but he·answered not·even·one·thing.*

G0611.4 V-ADI-3S ἀπεκρίθη (1x)
Ac 10:46 Then Peter responded,

G0611.4 V-AOP-NSM ἀποκριθείς (20x)
Lk 6:3 And responding to them, Jesus declared, "Did·yeu·
Lk 9:49 And responding, John declared, "O·Captain, we·
Lk 13:2 And responding, Jesus declared to·them, "Do·yeu·
Lk 14:3 And responding, Jesus declared to the experts·in·
Lk 17:17 And responding, Jesus declared, "Are·not·indeed
Lk 22:51 And responding, Jesus declared, "*Stop!* Yeu·must·
Mt 15:15 Now responding, Peter declared to·him, "Explain
Mt 16:17 And responding, YeShua declared to·him,
Mt 17:4 Now responding *to·this*, Peter declared to·YeShua,
Mt 19:27 Then responding, Peter declared to·him, "Behold,
Mt 22:1 And responding, YeShua declared to·them again by
Mt 26:63 YeShua was·keeping·silent. And responding, the
Mt 27:25 And responding, all the people declared, "His
Mt 28:5 And responding, the angel declared to·the women,
Mk 9:5 Now responding *to·this*, Peter says to·Jesus, "Rabbi,
Mk 10:51 And responding, Jesus says to·him, "What·do
Mk 11:14 And responding, Jesus declared to·it, "May no·
Mk 13:2 And responding, Jesus declared to·him, "Do·you·
Mk 14:48 And responding, Jesus declared to·them, "Did·
Mk 15:12 And responding, Pilate declared again to·them,

G0611.4 V-AOP-NPM ἀποκριθέντες (1x)
Lk 20:39 And responding, certain of·the scribes declared,

G0611.5 V-AOP-NSM ἀποκριθείς (1x)
Mk 12:35 And beginning·to·speak while·instructing in the

G0612 ἀπό•κρισις apókrisis *n.* (6x)
Roots:G0611 Compare:G0627

G0612 N-ASF ἀπόκρισιν (2x)
Jn 1:22 ·that we·may·give an·answer to·the·ones sending us,
Jn 19:9 are you·yourself?" But Jesus gave him no answer.

G0612 N-DSF ἀποκρίσει (1x)
Lk 20:26 And marveling at his answer, they·stayed·silent.

G0612 N-DPF ἀποκρίσεσιν (1x)
Lk 2:47 were·astonished at his comprehension and answers.

EG0612 (2x)
Mt 21:24 which if yeu·should·declare *an·answer* to·me, I·
2Co 5:12 yeu·may·have *an·answer* specifically·for the·ones

G0613 ἀπο•κρύπτω apôkrýptō *v.* (6x)
Roots:G0575 G2928

G0613.1 V-AAI-2S ἀπέκρυψας (2x)
Lk 10:21 and the earth, that you·hid·away these·things from
Mt 11:25 and the earth, that you·hid·away these·things from

G0613.1 V-AAI-3S ἀπέκρυψεν (1x)
Mt 25:18 dug in the earth and hid·away his lord's money.

G0613.1 V-RPP-ASN ἀποκεκρυμμένον (1x)
Col 1:26 the·one having·been·hidden·away from the prior·

G0613.1 V-RPP-ASF ἀποκεκρυμμένην (1x)
1Co 2:7 ·Mystery, the·one having·been·hidden·away, which

G0613.1 V-RPP-GSN ἀποκεκρυμμένου (1x)
Eph 3:9 the·one having·been·hidden·away from the prior·

G0614 ἀπό•κρυφος apókryphôs *adj.* (3x)
Roots:G0613

G0614.1 A-NSN ἀπόκρυφον (2x)
Lk 8:17 apparent; neither *anything* hidden·away, that shall·
Mk 4:22 ·did *anything* become hidden·away, other·than that

G0614.1 A-NPM ἀπόκρυφοι (1x)
Col 2:3 in whom are hidden·away all the treasures of·

G0615 ἀπο•κτείνω apôktêínō *v.* (76x)
Roots:G0575 G2932-1 Compare:G0337 G5407
See:G0443 xLangAlso:H2026 H4191

G0615.1 V-FAI-1S ἀποκτενῶ (1x)
Rv 2:23 And I·shall·kill her children with death; and all the

G0615.1 V-FAI-2P ἀποκτενεῖτε (1x)
Mt 23:34 from·among them yeu·shall·kill and shall·crucify,

G0615.1 V-FAI-3S ἀποκτενεῖ (2x)
Jn 8:22 were·saying, "Is·it·that he·shall·kill himself?
Rv 11:7 them, and shall·conquer them, and shall·kill them.

G0615.1 V-FAI-3P ἀποκτενοῦσιν (6x)
Lk 11:49 them they·shall·kill and shall·relentlessly·persecute
Lk 18:33 And after·flogging *him*, they·shall·kill him. And
Mt 17:23 And they·shall·kill him, and on·the third day he·
Mt 24:9 yeu over for tribulation and shall·kill yeu, and yeu·
Mk 9:31 *the* hands of·men·of·clay†, and they·shall·kill him.
Mk 10:34 and shall·spit·on him, and shall·kill him, and on·

G0615.1 V-PAI-3S ἀποκτενεῖ (2x)
2Co 3:6 but·rather of·Spirit, for the letter kills, but the Spirit
Rv 13:10 into war·captivity. If any·man kills with a·dagger,

G0615.1 V-PAP-GPM ἀποκτεινόντων (2x)
Lk 12:4 do·not be·afraid of·the·ones killing the body, and
Mt 10:28 And do·not be·afraid of·the·ones killing the body,

G0615.1 V-PAP-NSF ἀποκτείνουσα (2x)
Lk 13:34 JeruSalem, the·one killing the prophets and
Mt 23:37 JeruSalem, the·one killing the prophets and

G0615.1 V-PAP-NPM ἀποκτείνοντες (1x)
Mk 12:5 others (in·fact, thrashing some and killing some).

G0615.1 V-PAS-1P ἀποκτείνωμεν (4x)
Lk 20:14 the heir. Come·here! We·should·kill him, that the
Ac 23:14 ·taste not·even·one·thing until we·should·kill Paul.
Mt 21:38 heir. Come·here! We·should·kill him and should·
Mk 12:7 the heir! Come·here! We·should·kill him, and the

G0615.1 V-PAS-3P ἀποκτείνωσιν (8x)
Jn 11:53 ·themselves in·order·that they·should·kill him.
Jn 12:10 ·counsel in·order·that they·may·kill Lazarus also,
Ac 23:12 to·eat nor to·drink until they·should·kill Paul.
Ac 27:42 counsel was that they·should·kill the prisoners,
Mt 26:4 ·hold·of YeShua by·guile, and·then should·kill *him*.
Mk 14:1 ·taking·secure·hold *of·him*, they·may·kill him by
Rv 9:5 to·them it·was·given that they·should·not kill them,
Rv 9:15 year, in·order·that they·should·kill the third·part of·

G0615.1 V-PPN ἀποκτείνεσθαι (1x)
Rv 6:11 ·fulfilled, the·ones about to·be·killed also as they·

G0615.1 V-AAI-2P ἀπεκτείνατε (1x)
Ac 3:15 And yeu·killed the Initiator of·the life-above, whom

G0615.1 V-AAI-3S ἀπέκτεινεν (2x)

Lk 13:4 in Siloam fell and killed them, do·yeu·presume that
Rm 7:11 ·deluded me; and through it, it·killed *me*.
G0615.1 V-AAI-3P ἀπέκτειναν (10x)
Lk 11:47 of·the prophets, and yeur fathers killed them.
Lk 11:48 because they·themselves in·fact killed them, and
Lk 20:15 forth outside of·the vineyard, they·killed *him*.
Ac 7:52 Also they·killed the·ones fully·announcing·
Mt 21:35 they·thrashed, and *one* whom they·killed, and *one*
Mt 21:39 ·*him*·forth outside of·the vineyard and killed *him*.
Mt 22:6 slaves, abusively·mistreated *them* and killed *them*.
Mk 12:5 another, and·this·one·also they·killed, and·then
Mk 12:8 And after·taking·hold·of him, they·killed *him* and
Rm 11:3 "'Yahweh, they·killed your prophets and
G0615.1 V-AAN ἀποκτεῖναι (17x)
Jn 5:16 Jesus, and they·were·seeking to·kill him, because
Jn 5:18 the Judeans were·seeking *all* the·more to·kill him,
Jn 7:1 Judea, because the Judeans were·seeking to·kill him.
Jn 7:19 does the Torah-Law. Why·do yeu·seek to·kill me?
Jn 7:20 "You·have a·demon! Who seeks to·kill you?
Jn 7:25 "Is this not he·whom they·seek to·kill?
Jn 8:37 offspring†, but·yet yeu·seek to·kill me, because my
Jn 8:40 But now yeu·seek to·kill me, a·man·of·clay† that
Jn 18:31 "It·is·not proper for·us to·kill not·even·one·man,"
Lk 12:5 the·one, *that* after the killing, *is* having authority to·
Lk 13:31 ·here, because HerOd·AntiPas wants to·kill you."
Ac 21:31 And as·they·were·seeking to·kill him, news
Mt 10:28 the body, but not being·able to·kill the soul. But
Mt 14:5 And while·wanting to·kill him, he·feared the crowd,
Mk 3:4 ·do·bad? To·save a·soul, or to·kill?" But they·were·
Mk 6:19 ·a·grudge against·him and was·wanting to·kill him,
Rv 6:8 fourth·part of·the earth, to·kill with a·straight·sword,
G0615.1 V-AAP-GPM ἀποκτεινάντων (1x)
1Th 2:15 (even *under* the *Judeans* killing the Lord YeShua
G0615.1 V-AAP-NSM ἀποκτείνας (2x)
Jn 16:2 ·hour is·come that anyone killing yeu might·presume
Eph 2:16 the cross, in himself already·killing the hostility.
G0615.1 V-API-3S ἀπεκτάνθη (1x)
Rv 2:13 martyr, who was·killed closely·among yeu, where
G0615.1 V-API-3P ἀπεκτάνθησαν (4x)
Rv 9:18 ·part of·the men·of·clay† were·killed, as·a·result of·
Rv 9:20 of·the men·of·clay† who were·not killed by these
Rv 11:13 And in the earthquake were·killed seven thousand
Rv 19:21 And the rest were·killed with the straight·sword of·
G0615.1 V-APN ἀποκτανθῆναι (5x)
Lk 9:22 and scribes, and to·be·killed, and to·be·awakened
Mt 16:21 and scribes, and to·be·killed, and to·be·awakened
Mk 8:31 and scribes, and to·be·killed, and·then after three
Rv 11:5 it·is·mandatory·for him to·be·killed in·this·manner.
Rv 13:10 it·is·mandatory·for him to·be·killed with a·dagger
G0615.1 V-APP-NSM ἀποκτανθείς (1x)
Mk 9:31 ·kill him. And after·being·killed, he·shall·rise·up
G0615.1 V-APS-3P ἀποκτανθῶσιν (1x)
Rv 13:15 of·the Daemonic·Beast that they·should·be·killed.
EG0615.1 (1x)
Ac 3:17 that yeu·inflicted *the killing* according·to ignorance,

G0616 ἀπο•κυέω apôkyéō *v.* (2x)
Roots:G0575 G2949
G0616.2 V-PAI-3S ἀποκύει (1x)
Jac 1:15 moral·failure being·consummated, it·breeds death.
G0616.2 V-AAI-3S ἀπεκύησεν (1x)
Jac 1:18 ·own·resolve, he·bred us by·the·Redemptive·word

G0617 ἀπο•κυλίω apôkylíō *v.* (4x)
Roots:G0575 G2947
G0617 V-FAI-3S ἀποκυλίσει (1x)
Mk 16:3 themselves, "Who shall·roll·away for·us the stone
G0617 V-AAI-3S ἀπεκύλισεν (1x)
Mt 28:2 *and* coming·alongside, rolled·away the stone from
G0617 V-RPI-3S ἀποκεκύλισται (1x)
Mk 16:4 ·observed that the stone had·been·rolled·away, for
G0617 V-RPP-ASM ἀποκεκυλισμένον (1x)
Lk 24:2 ·found the stone having·been·rolled·away from the

G0618 ἀπο•λαμβάνω apôlambánō *v.* (12x)
Roots:G0575 G2983
G0618.1 V-PAP-NPM ἀπολαμβάνοντες (1x)
Rm 1:27 ·indecent·act, and fully·receiving in themselves the
G0618.1 V-2AAI-3S ἀπέλαβεν (1x)
Lk 15:27 because he·fully·received him healthy·and·sound.
G0618.1 V-2AAS-1P ἀπολάβωμεν (1x)
2Jn 1:8 but·rather that·we·may·fully·receive a·full payment·
G0618.2 V-FDI-2P ἀπολήψεσθε (1x)
Col 3:24 *the* Lord yeu·shall·receive·in·full the rewarding of·
G0618.2 V-PAI-1P ἀπολαμβάνομεν (1x)
Lk 23:41 for we·receive·in·full appropriate·*punishment* for·
G0618.2 V-2AAI-2S ἀπέλαβες (1x)
Lk 16:25 did·receive·in·full your beneficially·good·things,
G0618.2 V-2AAN ἀπολαβεῖν (1x)
Lk 6:34 whom yeu·expect to·receive·in·full, what·kind·of
G0618.2 V-2AAS-1P ἀπολάβωμεν (1x)
Gal 4:5 that we·may·receive·in·full the adoption·as·sons.
G0618.2 V-2AAS-3S ἀπολάβῃ (1x)
Lk 18:30 who should·not receive·in·full many·times·over in
G0618.2 V-2AAS-3P ἀπολάβωσιν (1x)
Lk 6:34 in·order·that they·may·receive·in·full the equal·
G0618.3 V-PAN ἀπολαμβάνειν (1x)
3Jn 1:8 ·ourselves ought to·fully·receive·and·host such·men,
G0618.4 V-2AMP-NSM ἀπολαβόμενος (1x)
Mk 7:33 And after·taking him aside from the crowd in

G0619 ἀπό•λαυσις apólausis *n.* (2x)
Roots:G0575 G3000-1
G0619 N-ASF ἀπόλαυσιν (2x)
Heb 11:25 to·have full·enjoyment of·moral·failure just·for·a·
1Ti 6:17 to·us abundantly all·things for full·enjoyment).

G0620 ἀπο•λείπω apôleípō *v.* (6x)
Roots:G0575 G3007
G0620.1 V-2AAI-1S ἀπέλιπον (2x)
2Ti 4:13 The cape that I·left·behind at Troas with Carpus, *as*
2Ti 4:20 Trophimus, being·sick, I·left·behind at Miletus.
G0620.1 V-2AAP-APM ἀπολιπόντας (1x)
Jud 1:6 but·rather leaving·behind their·own dwelling·place,
G0620.2 V-PPI-3S ἀπολείπεται (3x)
Heb 4:6 Now·then, since it·is·still·remaining *for* some to·
Heb 4:9 there·is·still·remaining a·Sabbath·Rest for·the
Heb 10:26 no·longer is·there·still·remaining a·sacrifice

G0621 ἀπο•λείχω apôleíchō *v.* (1x)
Roots:G0575
G0621 V-IAI-3P ἀπέλειχον (1x)
Lk 16:21 ·*along and* were·licking·away·at his pus·sores.

G0622 ἀπ•όλλυμι apóllymi *v.* (92x)
Roots:G0575 G3639 Compare:G3089 G0630
See:G0623
G0622.1 V-FAI-1S ἀπολῶ (1x)
1Co 1:19 ·written, "'I·shall·completely·destroy the wisdom
G0622.1 V-FAI-3S ἀπολέσει (3x)
Lk 20:16 and shall·completely·destroy these tenant·farmers,
Mt 21:41 ·him, "He·shall·completely·destroy those bad·men
Mk 12:9 and shall·completely·destroy the tenant·farmers and
G0622.1 V-FAI-3P ἀπολέσουσιν (1x)
Mk 11:18 ·seeking how they·shall·completely·destroy him,
G0622.1 V-FMI-3P ἀπολοῦνται (3x)
Lk 5:37 and the wineskins shall·be·completely·destroyed.
Mt 9:17 wineskins shall·be·completely·destroyed. But·rather
Mk 2:22 and the wineskins shall·be·completely·destroyed.
G0622.1 V-PAM-2S ἀπόλλυε (1x)
Rm 14:15 Do·not completely·destroy that·man with·your
G0622.1 V-PEP-DPM ἀπολλυμένοις (1x)
2Co 4:3 the·ones who·are·being·completely·destroyed,
G0622.1 V-PEP-NPM ἀπολλύμενοι (1x)
2Co 4:9 ·down, but·yet not being·completely·destroyed;
G0622.1 V-AAI-3S ἀπώλεσεν (4x)
Lk 17:27 and completely·destroyed absolutely·all·of·them.
Lk 17:29 and completely·destroyed absolutely·all·of·them.
Mt 22:7 troops, he·completely·destroyed those murderers
Jud 1:5 ·thing *was·that* he·completely·destroyed the·ones not
G0622.1 V-AAN ἀπολέσαι (8x)
Lk 4:34 Did·you·come to·completely·destroy us?
Lk 6:9 to·do·bad, to·save a·soul or to·completely·destroy *it*?
Lk 9:56 ·Man† did·not come to·completely·destroy *the* souls
Lk 19:47 people were·seeking to·completely·destroy him,
Mt 2:13 to·seek the little·child to·completely·destroy him."
Mt 10:28 the·one being·able to·completely·destroy both soul
Mk 1:24 Did·you·come to·completely·destroy us?
Jac 4:12 ·one being·able to·save and to·completely·destroy.
G0622.1 V-AAS-3S ἀπολέσῃ (2x)
Jn 10:10 ·victims, and may·completely·destroy. I·myself
Mk 9:22 in·order·that it·should·completely·destroy him, but·
G0622.1 V-AAS-3P ἀπολέσωσιν (3x)
Mt 12:14 on·specifically·how they·may·completely·destroy.
Mt 27:20 BarAbbas and should·completely·destroy YeShua.
Mk 3:6 on·specifically·how they·should·completely·destroy.
G0622.1 V-2AMI-3S ἀπώλετο (1x)
2Pe 3:6 world at·that·time was·completely·destroyed, being·
G0622.1 V-2AMI-3P ἀπώλοντο (2x)
1Co 10:9 *him*, and they·were·completely·destroyed by the
1Co 10:10 and they·were·completely·destroyed by the
G0622.1 V-2AMN ἀπολέσθαι (2x)
Jn 18:14 man·of·clay† to·be·completely·destroyed on·behalf
2Pe 3:9 for·any to·completely·be·destroyed, but·rather for·
G0622.2 V-FMI-2P ἀπολεῖσθε (2x)
Lk 13:3 ·repent, yeu·shall all likewise completely·perish.
Lk 13:5 ·repent, yeu·shall all likewise completely·perish."
G0622.2 V-2FMI-3S ἀπολεῖται (1x)
1Co 8:11 the weak brother completely·perish, on·account·of
G0622.2 V-FMI-3P ἀπολοῦνται (3x)
Heb 1:11 They·themselves shall·completely·perish, but you·
Mt 26:52 ·of a·dagger shall·completely·perish by a·dagger.
Rm 2:12 also shall·completely·perish without·Torah-Law.
G0622.2 V-PEP-DPM ἀπολλυμένοις (3x)
2Th 2:10 in the·ones who·are·completely·perishing, because
1Co 1:18 to·the·ones who·are·completely·perishing; but to·
2Co 2:15 ·saved, and among the·ones completely·perishing.
G0622.2 V-PMI-1S ἀπόλλυμαι (1x)
Lk 15:17 I·myself am·completely·perishing with·hunger!
G0622.2 V-PMI-1P ἀπολλύμεθα (3x)
Lk 8:24 "Captain, captain, we·are·completely·perishing."
Mt 8:25 "Lord, save us! We·completely·perish."
Mk 4:38 ·it·not matter to·you that we·completely·perish?"
G0622.2 V-PMP-ASF ἀπολλυμένην (1x)
Jn 6:27 full·meal that·is·completely·perishing, but·rather for·
G0622.2 V-PMP-GSN ἀπολλυμένου (1x)
1Pe 1:7 ·than gold *which* is·completely·perishing, even with·
G0622.2 V-2AMI-3S ἀπώλετο (2x)
Ac 5:37 ·behind him. He·also completely·perished. And all
Jac 1:11 the beauty of·its countenance completely·perishes.
G0622.2 V-2AMI-3P ἀπώλοντο (2x)
Jud 1:11 and completely·perished in·the hostile·grumbling
1Co 15:18 ·rest in Anointed-One, they·completely·perished.
G0622.2 V-2AMN ἀπολέσθαι (1x)
Lk 13:33 *that* a·prophet should·completely·perish outside of·
G0622.2 V-2AMP-GSM ἀπολομένου (1x)
Lk 11:51 the·one completely·perishing between the
G0622.2 V-2AMS-3S ἀπόληται (6x)
Jn 3:15 in him should·not completely·perish, but·rather
Jn 3:16 in him should·not completely·perish, but·rather
Jn 11:50 *that* the whole nation should·completely·perish."
Mt 5:29 one of·your members should·completely·perish, and
Mt 5:30 one of·your members should·completely·perish, and
Mt 18:14 one of·these little·ones should·completely·perish.
G0622.2 V-2AMS-3P ἀπόλωνται (1x)
Jn 10:28 And no, they·should·not completely·perish into the
G0622.2 V-2RAP-ASN ἀπολωλός (1x)
Mt 18:11 came to·save the·one having·completely·perished.
G0622.2 V-2RAP-APN ἀπολωλότα (2x)
Mt 10:6 the·ones having·completely·perished of·*the*·house
Mt 15:24 the·ones having·completely·perished of·*the*·house
G0622.2 V-2RAP-NSM ἀπολωλώς (2x)
Lk 15:24 he·was having·completely·perished, and·yet he·

Lk 15:32 and he·was having·completely·perished, and·yet
G0622.3 V-FAI-3S ἀπολέσει (6x)
Jn 12:25 his soul *(and·its·desires)* shall·completely·lose it;
Lk 9:24 to·save his soul's·desire shall·completely·lose it, but
Lk 17:33 to·save his soul's·desire shall·completely·lose it;
Mt 10:39 finding his soul's·desire shall·completely·lose it,
Mt 16:25 to·save his soul's·desire shall·completely·lose it,
Mk 8:35 to·save his soul's·desire shall·completely·lose it, but
G0622.3 V-AAI-1S ἀπώλεσα (2x)
Jn 18:9 to·me, I·did·not completely·lose not·even·one."
Lk 15:9 I·found the drachma which I·completely·lost.'
G0622.3 V-AAP-NSM ἀπολέσας (3x)
Lk 9:25 world but already·completely·losing himself or
Lk 15:4 sheep, that after·completely·losing one from·among
Mt 10:39 it, and the·one completely·losing his soul's·desire,
G0622.3 V-AAS-1S ἀπολέσω (1x)
Jn 6:39 me, that I·should·not completely·lose any *sheep*
G0622.3 V-AAS-1P ἀπολέσωμεν (1x)
2Jn 1:8 we·should·not completely·lose those·things·for· we·
G0622.3 V-AAS-3S ἀπολέσῃ (7x)
Lk 9:24 but whoever should·completely·lose his soul's·desire
Lk 15:8 ·*silver*, if she·should·completely·lose one drachma,
Lk 17:33 whoever should·completely·lose his *soul's·desire*
Mt 10:42 no, he·should·not completely·lose his payment·of·
Mt 16:25 whoever should·completely·lose his soul's·desire,
Mk 8:35 whoever should·completely·lose his soul's·desire
Mk 9:41 no, he·should·not completely·lose his payment·of·
G0622.3 V-2AMI-3S ἀπώλετο (1x)
Jn 17:12 from·among them is·completely·lost except the Son
G0622.3 V-2AMS-3S ἀπόληται (2x)
Jn 6:12 in·order·that not anything may·be·completely·lost."
Lk 21:18 yeur head, no, it·should·not be·completely·lost.
G0622.3 V-2RAP-ASN ἀπολωλός (3x)
Lk 15:4 the·one having·become·completely·lost until he·
Lk 15:6 my sheep, the·one having·become·completely·lost.'
Lk 19:10 and to·save the·one having·been·completely·lost."

G0623 Ἀπ•ολλύων Apôllýōn *n/p.* (1x)
Roots:G0622 Compare:G0003 See:G0684 xLangEquiv:H0011
G0623.2 N/P-NSM Ἀπολλύων (1x)
Rv 9:11 he·has *this* name, Apollyon·*(Total·Destroyer)*.

G0624 Ἀπ•ολλωνία Apôllōnía *n/l.* (1x)
Roots:G0622
G0624.2 N/L-ASF Ἀπολλωνίαν (1x)
Ac 17:1 ·through AmphiPolis and Apollonia, they·came to

G0625 Ἀπ•ολλώς Apôllṓs *n/p.* (11x)
Roots:G0622 See:G0623 G0624
EG0625 (1x)
Ac 18:27 disciples *there* to·fully·accept *Apollos*, who upon·
G0625.2 N/P-NSM Ἀπολλώς (4x)
Ac 18:24 Jew arrived in Ephesus (Apollos by·name, of·
1Co 3:5 is Paul, and who *is* Apollos, other than attendants
1Co 3:6 I·myself planted, Apollos watered, but·yet God
1Co 3:22 Whether Paul, or Apollos, or Kephas·*(called·*
G0625.2 N/P-ASM Ἀπολλώ (3x)
Ac 19:1 Now with Apollos being in Corinth, it·happened
Tit 3:13 the lawyer and Apollos onward·on·their·journey, in·
1Co 4:6 as·to myself and Apollos on·account·of yeu, in·
G0625.2 N/P-GSM Ἀπολλώ (3x)
1Co 1:12 of·Paul," and "I *am* of·Apollos," and "I *am* of·
1Co 3:4 and someone·else, "I *am* of·Apollos," are·yeu not·
1Co 16:12 Now concerning *our* brother Apollos, I repeatedly

G0626 ἀπο•λογέομαι apôlôgéômai *v.* (10x)
Roots:G0575 G3056 See:G0627 G0379
G0626.1 V-PNI-1S ἀπολογοῦμαι (1x)
Ac 24:10 with·cheerful·composure I·give·an·account myself,
G0626.2 V-ADS-2P ἀπολογήσησθε (1x)
Lk 12:11 ·about how or what yeu·should·plead or what yeu·
G0626.2 V-AON ἀπολογηθῆναι (1x)
Lk 21:14 hearts, not to·meditate·beforehand *what* to·plead.
G0626.3 V-PNI-1P ἀπολογούμεθα (1x)
2Co 12:19 ·yeu·suppose that we·make·our·defense to·yeu?
G0626.3 V-PNN ἀπολογεῖσθαι (2x)
Ac 19:33 was·wanting to·make·their·defense to·the·public.
Ac 26:2 *for* I·am·about to·make·my·defense this·day before
G0626.3 V-PNP-GSM ἀπολογουμένου (2x)
Ac 25:8 with·him making·his·defense, *declaring*, "Neither
Ac 26:24 And with *Paul* still·making·his·defense, Festus
G0626.3 V-INI-3S ἀπελογεῖτο (1x)
Ac 26:1 ·stretching·forth his hand, was·making·his·defense:
G0626.4 V-PNP-GPM ἀπολογουμένων (1x)
Rm 2:15 else exonerating·themselves between one·another,

G0627 ἀπο•λογία apôlôgía *n.* (8x)
Roots:G0575 G3056 Compare:G0612 See:G0626 G0379
G0627.2 N-NSF ἀπολογία (1x)
1Co 9:3 My defense to·the·ones scrutinizing me is this:
G0627.2 N-ASF ἀπολογίαν (2x)
Php 1:17 that I·am·laid·out for a·defense of·the good·news.
1Pe 3:15 *a·gracious* defense to·every·man requesting·of yeu
G0627.2 N-DSF ἀπολογίᾳ (2x)
Php 1:7 my bonds and in·the defense and confirmation of·the
2Ti 4:16 At my first defense, not·even·one·man appeared·
G0627.2 N-GSF ἀπολογίας (2x)
Ac 22:1 and fathers, hear my defense *which I·make* now to
Ac 25:16 ·receive a·place to·defend·himself concerning the
G0627.3 N-ASF ἀπολογίαν (1x)
2Co 7:11 *what* exoneration·of·yeurselves, moreover, *what*

G0628 ἀπο•λούω apôlôúō *v.* (2x)
Roots:G0575 G3068 Compare:G3538
G0628.1 V-AMI-2P ἀπελούσασθε (1x)
1Co 6:11 these·things, but·rather yeu·are·fully·bathed, but·
G0628.2 V-AMM-2S ἀπόλουσαι (1x)
Ac 22:16 and fully·bathe·away your moral·failures, calling·

G0629 ἀπο•λύτρωσις apôlýtrōsis *n.* (10x)
Roots:G0575 G3083 Compare:G0628-1 G0859 xLangAlso:H6299 H3724
G0629.1 N-ASF ἀπολύτρωσιν (3x)
Heb 9:15 already·occurring for a·full·ransom (from·the
Eph 1:7 in whom we·have the ransom·in·full through his
Col 1:14 in whom we·have the ransom·in·full through his
G0629.1 N-GSF ἀπολυτρώσεως (1x)
Rm 3:24 by·his grace through the ransom·in·full, the·one in
G0629.3 N-NSF ἀπολύτρωσις (2x)
Lk 21:28 on·account·that yeur full·redemption draws·near."
1Co 1:30 renewed·holiness, and full·redemption,
G0629.3 N-ASF ἀπολύτρωσιν (3x)
Heb 11:35 the blood·bribe in·order·that they·may·obtain a·
Rm 8:23 ·as·sons, *that·is*, the full·redemption of·our body.
Eph 1:14 for a·full·redemption of·the acquired·possession,
G0629.3 N-GSF ἀπολυτρώσεως (1x)
Eph 4:30 ·officially·sealed to *the* day of·full·redemption.

G0630 ἀπο•λύω apôlýō *v.* (69x)
Roots:G0575 G3089 Compare:G0863 G5563 G0622 G1943 G1606 See:G0628-1 xLangAlso:H1644 H8058
G0630.1 V-FAI-1S ἀπολύσω (2x)
Lk 23:16 ·disciplining him, I·shall·fully·release *him*."
Lk 23:22 ·disciplining him, I·shall·fully·release *him*."
G0630.1 V-FPI-2P ἀπολυθήσεσθε (1x)
Lk 6:37 Fully·release, and yeu·shall·be·fully·released.
G0630.1 V-PAM-2P ἀπολύετε (1x)
Lk 6:37 ·not be·pronounced·guilty. Fully·release, and yeu·
G0630.1 V-PAN ἀπολύειν (3x)
Lk 23:17 he·was·having to·fully·release one·man to·them
Ac 3:13 ·Pilate, with·that·one deciding to·fully·release *him*.
Mt 27:15 had·a·custom to·fully·release to·the crowd a
G0630.1 V-IAI-3S ἀπέλυεν (1x)
Mk 15:6 Sacred·Feast, he·was·fully·releasing to·them one
G0630.1 V-AAI-3S ἀπέλυσεν (5x)
Lk 14:4 ·hold *of·him*, he·healed him and fully·released *him*.
Lk 23:25 And he·fully·released to·them the·one having·
Mt 18:27 the lord of·that slave fully·released him and
Mt 27:26 Then he·fully·released BarAbbas to·them, and
Mk 15:15 crowd content, fully·released BarAbbas to·them,
G0630.1 V-AAI-3P ἀπέλυσαν (1x)
Ac 13:3 ·forth hands on·them, they·fully·released *them*.
G0630.1 V-AAM-2S ἀπόλυσον (2x)
Lk 23:18 ·with·this·man, and fully·release to·us BarAbbas!"
Ac 16:35 saying, "Fully·release those men·of·clay†."
G0630.1 V-AAN ἀπολῦσαι (4x)
Jn 19:10 you, and I·have authority to·fully·release you?
Jn 19:12 of·this, Pilate was·seeking to·fully·release him, but
Lk 23:20 Now·then, wanting to·fully·release Jesus, Pilate
Ac 28:18 me, were·resolving to·fully·release *me*, on·
G0630.1 V-AAS-1S ἀπολύσω (5x)
Jn 18:39 for·yeu that I·should·fully·release to·yeu one·man
Jn 18:39 ·yeu·resolve *that* I·should·fully·release to·yeu the
Mt 27:17 ·do yeu·want *that* I·should·fully·release to·yeu?
Mt 27:21 do·yeu·want *that* I·should·fully·release to·yeu?
Mk 15:9 "Do·yeu·want *that* I·should·fully·release to·yeu the
G0630.1 V-AAS-2S ἀπολύσῃς (1x)
Jn 19:12 saying, "If you·should·fully·release this·man, you·
G0630.1 V-AAS-2P ἀπολύσητε (1x)
Lk 22:68 ·not answer me, nor should·yeu·fully·release·*me*.
G0630.1 V-AAS-3S ἀπολύσῃ (1x)
Mk 15:11 rather he·should·fully·release BarAbbas to·them.
G0630.1 V-APP-NPM ἀπολυθέντες (1x)
Ac 4:23 And being·fully·released, they·went to·their·own·
G0630.1 V-APS-2P ἀπολυθῆτε (1x)
Ac 16:36 ·dispatched that yeu·should·be·fully·released. Now
G0630.1 V-RPI-2S ἀπολέλυσαι (1x)
Lk 13:12 you·have·been·fully·released from·your sickness.
G0630.1 V-RPN ἀπολελύσθαι (1x)
Ac 26:32 was·able to·have·been·fully·released, if·he·had·not
G0630.1 V-RPP-ASM ἀπολελυμένον (1x)
Heb 13:23 TimoThy *is* having·been·fully·released, with
G0630.2 V-PAI-2S ἀπολύεις (1x)
Lk 2:29 "Master, now dismiss your slave in peace,
G0630.2 V-IMI-3P ἀπελύοντο (1x)
Ac 28:25 one·another, they·dismissed·themselves, with·Paul
G0630.2 V-AAI-3S ἀπέλυσεν (4x)
Lk 8:38 together with·him, but Jesus dismissed him, saying,
Ac 19:41 ·things, he·dismissed the assembly·of·citizens.
Ac 23:22 the regiment·commander dismissed the young·man
Mk 8:9 about four·thousand *men*, and he·dismissed them.
G0630.2 V-AAI-3P ἀπέλυσαν (3x)
Ac 4:21 ·further·threatening·them, they·dismissed them,
Ac 5:40 in the name of·Jesus, and they·dismissed them.
Ac 17:9 ·from Jason and the rest, they·dismissed them.
G0630.2 V-AAM-2S ἀπόλυσον (4x)
Lk 9:12 declared to·him, "Dismiss the crowd, in·order·that
Mt 14:15 even·now *has* passed·away. Dismiss the crowds,
Mt 15:23 him, saying, "Dismiss her, because she·yells·out
Mk 6:36 Dismiss them in·order·that, after·going·off into the
G0630.2 V-AAN ἀπολῦσαι (2x)
Mt 1:19 ·and·scorn, resolved to·dismiss her privately.
Mt 15:32 and I·do·not want to·dismiss them without·eating,
G0630.2 V-AAP-NSM ἀπολύσας (2x)
Mt 14:23 And after·dismissing the crowds, he·walked·up
Mt 15:39 And after·dismissing the crowds, he·embarked into
G0630.2 V-AAS-1S ἀπολύσω (1x)
Mk 8:3 And if I·should·dismiss them without·eating to·their·
G0630.2 V-AAS-3S ἀπολύσῃ (2x)
Mt 14:22 the other·side, until he·should·dismiss the crowds.
Mk 6:45 until he·himself should·dismiss the crowd.
G0630.2 V-API-3P ἀπελύθησαν (1x)
Ac 15:33 *there* a·time, they·were·dismissed with peace from
G0630.2 V-APP-NPM ἀπολυθέντες (1x)
Ac 15:30 in·fact, after·being·dismissed, they·came to
G0630.6 V-PAP-NSM ἀπολύων (1x)
Lk 16:18 "Anyone divorcing his wife and marrying another
G0630.6 V-AAN ἀπολῦσαι (5x)
Mt 19:3 "Is·it·proper for·a·man·of·clay† to·divorce his wife
Mt 19:7 of·innocence·in·divorcement, and to·divorce her?
Mt 19:8 Moses freely·permitted yeu to·divorce yeur wives,
Mk 10:2 "Is·it·proper for·a·man to·divorce *his* wife?
Mk 10:4 ·in·divorcement, and·then to·divorce *her*."
G0630.6 V-AAS-3S ἀπολύσῃ (5x)

Mt 5:31 'Whoever should·divorce his wife must·give her *a*·
Mt 5:32 say to·yeu, that whoever should·divorce his wife,
Mt 19:9 I·say to·yeu, that whoever should·divorce his wife,
Mk 10:11 to·them, "Whoever should·divorce his wife and
Mk 10:12 And if a·wife should·divorce her husband and
G0630.6 V-RPP-ASF ἀπολελυμένην (3x)
Lk 16:18 marrying the·one having·been·divorced from *her*
Mt 5:32 should·marry her·having·been·divorced commits·.
Mt 19:9 And the *wife* having·been·divorced, upon·marrying,

G0631 ἀπο•μάσσομαι apômássômai *v.* (1x)
Roots:G0575 G3145-1 Compare:G1591
G0631.1 V-PMI-1P ἀπομασσόμεθα (1x)
Lk 10:11 being·stuck to·us, we·do·wipe·*it*·off against·yeu.

G0632 ἀπο•νέμω apônémō *v.* (1x)
Roots:G0575 G3551
G0632 V-PAP-NPM ἀπονέμοντες (1x)
1Pe 3:7 ·a·weaker vessel, while·prescribing honor to·the

G0633 ἀπο•νίπτω apôníptō *v.* (1x)
Roots:G0575 G3538 Compare:G0637
G0633.2 V-AMI-3S ἀπενίψατο (1x)
Mt 27:24 water, he·washed·off·his·own hands fully·in·front

G0634 ἀπο•πίπτω apôpíptō *v.* (1x)
Roots:G0575 G4098
G0634 V-2AAI-3P ἀπέπεσον (1x)
Ac 9:18 *something* like scales fell·off from his eyes.

G0635 ἀπο•πλανάω apôplanáō *v.* (2x)
Roots:G0575 G4105
G0635.1 V-PAN ἀποπλανᾶν (1x)
Mk 13:22 ·give signs and wonders to utterly·lead·astray, if
G0635.1 V-API-3P ἀπεπλανήθησαν (1x)
1Ti 6:10 ·toward. They·are·utterly·led·astray from the trust,

G0636 ἀπο•πλέω apôpléō *v.* (4x)
Roots:G0575 G4126
G0636.1 V-AAI-3P ἀπέπλευσαν (2x)
Ac 13:4 Also from·there, they·sailed·off to Cyprus.
Ac 14:26 And·from·there, they·sailed·off to Antioch, where
G0636.1 V-AAP-NPM ἀποπλεύσαντες (1x)
Ac 20:15 Sailing·off from·there, we·arrived the following
G0636.2 V-PAN ἀποπλεῖν (1x)
Ac 27:1 as·soon·as it·was·decided for us to·set·sail for Italy,

G0637 ἀπο•πλύνω apôplýnō *v.* (1x)
Roots:G0575 G4150 Compare:G0633
G0637 V-AAI-3P ἀπέπλυναν (1x)
Lk 5:2 from them, the fishermen rinsed·off the nets.

G0638 ἀπο•πνίγω apôpnígō *v.* (3x)
Roots:G0575 G4155
G0638.2 V-2API-3S ἀπεπνίγη (1x)
Lk 8:33 ·overhang into the lake and was·utterly·drowned.
G0638.3 V-AAI-3P ἀπέπνιξαν (2x)
Lk 8:7 being·sprung·up·together·with·it, utterly·choked it.
Mt 13:7 and the thorns sprung·up and utterly·choked them.

G0639 ἀ•πορέω apôréō *v.* (4x)
Roots:G0001 G4198 See:G1820
G0639.2 V-PMI-1S ἀποροῦμαι (1x)
Gal 4:20 ·change my tone, because I·am·at·a·loss with yeu.
G0639.2 V-PMP-NSM ἀπορούμενος (1x)
Ac 25:20 And I·myself, being·at·a·loss concerning this
G0639.2 V-PMP-NPM ἀπορούμενοι (2x)
Jn 13:22 to one·another, being·at·a·loss concerning who he·
2Co 4:8 being·narrowly·constricted; being·at·a·loss, but·yet

G0640 ἀ•πορία apôría *n.* (1x)
Roots:G0001 G4198 See:G0639 G1280
G0640 N-DSF ἀπορίᾳ (1x)
Lk 21:25 of·nations, in a·perplexity of·*the*·reverberating and

G0641 ἀπο•ρρίπτω apôrrhíptō *v.* (1x)
Roots:G0575 G4496 Compare:G4495
G0641.2 V-AAP-APM ἀπορρίψαντας (1x)
Ac 27:43 ·able to·swim, after·jumping·far·overboard first,

G0642 ἀπ•ορφανίζω apôrphanízō *v.* (1x)
Roots:G0575 G3737
G0642.2 V-APP-NPM ἀπορφανισθέντες (1x)
1Th 2:17 brothers, being·grievously·removed from yeu just·

G0643 ἀπο•σκευάζω apôskêuázō *v.* (1x)
Roots:G0575 G4632 See:G0384
G0643 V-ADP-NPM ἀποσκευασάμενοι (1x)
Ac 21:15 days, after·packing·up·our·belongings, we·were·

G0644 ἀπο•σκίασμα apôskíasma *n.* (1x)
Roots:G0575 G4639 Compare:G4639
G0644.2 N-NSN ἀποσκίασμα (1x)
Jac 1:17 an·alteration, nor *the* slightest·shadow of·turning.

G0645 ἀπο•σπάω apôspáō *v.* (4x)
Roots:G0575 G4685
G0645.1 V-PAN ἀποσπᾶν (1x)
Ac 20:30 perverse·things, to·draw·away the disciples right·
G0645.1 V-API-3S ἀπεσπάσθη (1x)
Lk 22:41 And he·himself drew·away from them about a·
G0645.1 V-APP-APM ἀποσπασθέντας (1x)
Ac 21:1 ·sailing·away, after·being·drawn·away from them,
G0645.2 V-AAI-3S ἀπέσπασεν (1x)
Mt 26:51 upon·stretching·out his hand, drew·out his dagger.

G0646 ἀπο•στασία apôstasía *n.* (2x)
Roots:G0647 Compare:G1459 G5289 See:G0647-2
G0646.1 N-NSF ἀποστασία (1x)
2Th 2:3 unless there·should·come the Defection first, and
G0646.1 N-ASF ἀποστασίαν (1x)
Ac 21:21 that you·instruct a·defection away·from Moses *to*

G0647 ἀπο•στάσιον apôstásiôn *n.* (3x)
Roots:G0868 Compare:G3080 See:G0646 G0628-1 xLangEquiv:H3748
G0647.3 N-ASN ἀποστάσιον (1x)
Mt 5:31 ·give her *a·document·of* innocence·in·divorcement.'
G0647.3 N-GSN ἀποστασίου (2x)
Mt 19:7 ·give *her* a·document of·innocence·in·divorcement,
Mk 10:4 to·write a·document of·innocence·in·divorcement,

G0648 ἀπο•στεγάζω apôstêgázō *v.* (1x)
Roots:G0575 G4721 Compare:G2572 G2928 G1942
G0648.2 V-AAI-3P ἀπεστέγασαν (1x)
Mk 2:4 on·account·of the crowd, they·pulled·apart the roof

G0649 ἀπο•στέλλω apôstéllō *v.* (136x)
Roots:G0575 G4724 Compare:G3992 G0873 See:G1821 G4882 xLangAlso:H7971 A7972
G0649.1 V-AAN ἀποστεῖλαι (1x)
Lk 4:18 ·of·sight to·the·blind, to·set·apart with freedom
G0649.2 V-FAI-1S ἀποστελῶ (2x)
Lk 11:49 also declared, 'I·shall·dispatch to them prophets
Ac 7:34 now, come·over·here, I·shall·dispatch you into
G0649.2 V-FAI-3S ἀποστελεῖ (5x)
Mt 13:41 The Son of·Clay·Man† shall·dispatch his angels,
Mt 21:3 ·them,' and immediately he·shall·dispatch them."
Mt 24:31 And he·shall·dispatch his angels with a·great
Mk 11:3 And immediately, he·shall·dispatch him here."
Mk 13:27 And at·that·time, he·shall·dispatch his angels and
G0649.2 V-PAI-1S ἀποστέλλω (8x)
Lk 7:27 "Behold, I·myself dispatch my messenger before
Lk 10:3 Behold, I·myself dispatch yeu as adolescent·male·
Lk 24:49 And behold, I·myself dispatch the Promise of·my
Ac 26:17 'to whom now I·dispatch you,
Mt 10:16 "Behold, I·myself dispatch yeu as sheep in *the*
Mt 11:10 "Behold, I·myself dispatch my messenger before
Mt 23:34 ·of that, behold, I·myself dispatch to yeu prophets
Mk 1:2 "Behold, I·myself dispatch my messenger before
G0649.2 V-PAI-3S ἀποστέλλει (3x)
Mk 4:29 ·yielded·up, immediately he·dispatches the sickle,
Mk 11:1 the Mount of·Olives, he·dispatches two of·his
Mk 14:13 And he·dispatches two of·his disciples and says
G0649.2 V-PAI-3P ἀποστέλλουσιν (2x)
Mt 22:16 And they·dispatched their disciples to·him along·
Mk 12:13 And they·dispatched to him some of·the Pharisees
G0649.2 V-PAN ἀποστέλλειν (1x)
Mk 6:7 twelve, and he·began to·dispatch them two by·two.
G0649.2 V-PAS-3S ἀποστέλλῃ (1x)
Mk 3:14 that he·may·dispatch them to·officially·proclaim,
G0649.2 V-PPP-NPN ἀποστελλόμενα (1x)
Heb 1:14 ·serving spirits, being·dispatched into service on·
G0649.2 V-AAI-1S ἀπέστειλα (4x)
Jn 4:38 "I·myself dispatched yeu to·reap *that·for* which yeu·
Jn 17:18 into the world, I·also dispatch them into the world.
Lk 22:35 ·them, "When I·dispatched yeu without·any pouch
2Ti 4:12 And Tychicus I·dispatched to Ephesus.
G0649.2 V-AAI-2S ἀπέστειλας (7x)
Jn 11:42 in·order·that they·may·trust that you dispatched me.
Jn 17:3 God, and Jesus Anointed, whom you·dispatched.
Jn 17:8 you, and they·trusted that you did·dispatch me.
Jn 17:18 "Just·as you·dispatched me into the world, I·also
Jn 17:21 world may·trust that you·yourself dispatched me.
Jn 17:23 world may·know that you·yourself dispatched me,
Jn 17:25 knew you, and these knew that you dispatched me.
G0649.2 V-AAI-3S ἀπέστειλεν (38x)
Jn 3:17 "For God did·not dispatch his Son into the world in·
Jn 3:34 For he·whom God dispatched speaks the utterances
Jn 5:38 because the·same·one whom he·dispatched, him
Jn 6:29 yeu·should·trust in that·one whom he·dispatched."
Jn 6:57 "Just·as the living Father dispatched me, and·I live
Jn 7:29 personally·from him. He·likewise dispatched me."
Jn 8:42 of my·own·self, but·rather that *God* dispatched me.
Jn 10:36 the Father made·holy and dispatched into the world,
Jn 18:24 (*Remember that* HannAs dispatched him, having·
Lk 7:3 after·hearing about Jesus, he·dispatched elders of·the
Lk 9:2 And he·dispatched them to·officially·proclaim the
Lk 9:52 and he·dispatched messengers before his personal·
Lk 10:1 others also, and he·dispatched them up by·twos
Lk 14:17 And he·dispatched his slave at·the hour of·the
Lk 19:29 *the Mount* of·Olives), he·dispatched two of·his
Lk 20:10 "And in due·season, he·dispatched a·slave to the
Lk 22:8 And *Jesus* dispatched Peter and John, declaring,
Ac 3:26 his·own servant·boy Jesus, dispatched him to·yeu
Ac 7:35 ' this·man God dispatched *to·be* a·ruler and a·
Ac 10:8 ·all·*these*·things to·them, he·dispatched them to
Ac 10:36 The Word which *God* dispatched to·the Sons of·
Mt 10:5 These twelve YeShua dispatched, after·charging
Mt 20:2 *for* the day, he·dispatched them into his vineyard.
Mt 21:1 of·Olives), then YeShua dispatched two disciples,
Mt 21:34 of·the fruits drew·near, he·dispatched his slaves to
Mt 21:36 Again, he·dispatched other slaves more·than at·the
Mt 21:37 "But eventually, he·dispatched his son to them,
Mt 22:3 and dispatched his slaves to·call·forth the·ones
Mt 22:4 "Again, he·dispatched other slaves, saying,
Mt 27:19 Bema·judgment·seat, his wife dispatched to him,
Mk 8:26 And he·dispatched him to his house, saying, "You·
Mk 12:2 "And in·due·season, he·dispatched a·slave to the
Mk 12:4 And again he·dispatched another slave to them, and
Mk 12:5 And again he·dispatched another, and·this·one·also
Mk 12:6 son, his well-beloved, he·dispatched him also last
1Co 1:17 For Anointed-One did·not dispatch me to·immerse,
1Jn 4:10 he·himself loved us and dispatched his Son *to·be*
Rv 22:6 of·the holy prophets, dispatched his angel to·show
G0649.2 V-AAI-3P ἀπέστειλαν (14x)
Jn 1:19 the Judeans dispatched priests·that·offer·sacrifices and
Jn 7:32 the chief·priests dispatched assistants in·order·that
Jn 11:3 In·due·course, his sisters dispatched to him, saying,
Lk 19:14 him, and they·dispatched a·delegation right·behind
Lk 20:20 *him*, they·dispatched ambushers pretending
Ac 5:21 of·the Sons of·IsraEl. Then they·dispatched to the
Ac 8:14 Redemptive·word of·God, they·dispatched Peter and
Ac 9:38 in this *city*, the disciples dispatched two men to him
Ac 13:15 the directors·of·the·gathering dispatched to them,
Ac 16:35 court·officers dispatched the enforcement·officers,
Mt 14:35 him, the men of·that place dispatched into all that
Mk 3:31 and standing outside, they·dispatched to him while·
Mk 12:3 they·thrashed him and dispatched *him·back* empty.
Mk 12:4 and dispatched *him·back* having·been·handled·
G0649.2 V-AAM-2S ἀπόστειλον (1x)
Ac 11:13 and declaring to·him, 'Dispatch men to Joppa and
G0649.2 V-AAP-ASM ἀποστείλαντα (4x)
Lk 9:48 ·accept me accepts·him, the·one dispatching me, for
Lk 10:16 ·one ignoring me ignores the·one dispatching me."

Mt 10:40 me accepts the·one already·dispatching me.
Mk 9:37 me he·accepts, but·rather the·one dispatching me."
G0649.2 V-AAP-NSM ἀποστείλας (7x)
Lk 14:32 being yet far·away, dispatching a·delegation, he·
Ac 7:14 Then dispatching *his brothers*, Joseph summarily·
Ac 19:22 So after·dispatching two of·the·ones attending to·
Mt 2:16 was·enraged exceedingly. And dispatching *soldiers*,
Mk 6:17 himself, after·dispatching, took·secure·hold·of
Mk 6:27 And immediately dispatching a·bodyguard, the king
Rv 1:1 ·happen in haste. And dispatching through his angel,
G0649.2 V-AAP-NPM ἀποστείλαντες (1x)
Ac 11:30 Which also they·did, dispatching *it* to the elders
G0649.2 V-AAS-3S ἀποστείλῃ (2x)
Ac 3:20 and *that* he·should·dispatch Jesus Anointed, the·one
Mk 5:10 him much that he·should·not dispatch them outside
G0649.2 V-2API-1S ἀπεστάλην (2x)
Lk 1:19 ·the·sight of·God; and I·am·dispatched to·speak to
Mt 15:24 he·declared, "I·am·not dispatched except to the
G0649.2 V-2API-3S ἀπεστάλη (3x)
Lk 1:26 ·month, the angel GabriEl was·dispatched by God to
Ac 13:26 of·this Salvation is·already·dispatched.
Ac 28:28 of·God is·already·dispatched to·the Gentiles, and
G0649.2 V-2APP-DSN ἀποσταλέντι (1x)
1Pe 1:12 Holy Spirit already·being·dispatched from heaven
G0649.2 V-2APS-3P ἀποσταλῶσιν (1x)
Rm 10:15 ·proclaim, unless they·should·be·dispatched?
G0649.2 V-RAI-1S ἀπέσταλκα (2x)
Ac 10:20 on·account·that I·myself have·dispatched them."
2Co 12:17 any of·them whom I·have·dispatched to yeu?
G0649.2 V-RAI-1P ἀπεστάλκαμεν (1x)
Ac 15:27 "Accordingly, we·have·dispatched Judas and Silas
G0649.2 V-RAI-2P ἀπεστάλκατε (1x)
Jn 5:33 Yeu·yeurselves have·dispatched specifically·for John
G0649.2 V-RAI-3S ἀπέσταλκεν (7x)
Jn 5:36 concerning me, that the Father has·dispatched me.
Jn 20:21 Just·as *my* Father has·dispatched me, even·so·I send
Lk 4:18 ·the·helplessly·poor. He·has·dispatched me to·heal
Lk 7:20 "John the Immerser has·dispatched us to you, saying
Ac 9:17 ·going, has·dispatched me in·such·a·manner·so·that
1Jn 4:9 us, because God has·dispatched his only·begotten
1Jn 4:14 testify that the Father has·dispatched the Son *to·be*
G0649.2 V-RAI-3P ἀπεστάλκασιν (1x)
Ac 16:36 court·officers have·dispatched that yeu·should·be·
G0649.2 V-RPI-1S ἀπέσταλμαι (1x)
Lk 4:43 because I·have·been·dispatched for this·purpose."
G0649.2 V-RPP-APM ἀπεσταλμένους (3x)
Lk 13:34 ·stones·at the·ones having·been·dispatched to you!
Ac 10:21 the men (the·ones having·been·dispatched to him
Mt 23:37 ·stones·at the·ones having·been·dispatched to you!
G0649.2 V-RPP-NSM ἀπεσταλμένος (3x)
Jn 1:6 a·man·of·clay† having·been·dispatched personally·
Jn 3:28 ·rather that 'I·am having·been·dispatched before him
Jn 9:7 ·*Hebrew* is·translated *as* Having·Been·Dispatched).
G0649.2 V-RPP-NPN ἀπεσταλμένα (1x)
Rv 5:6 seven Spirits of·God having·been·dispatched into all
G0649.2 V-RPP-NPM ἀπεσταλμένοι (4x)
Jn 1:24 the·ones having·been·dispatched were from·among
Lk 19:32 ·off, the·ones having·been·dispatched found *it*
Ac 10:17 (the·ones having·been·dispatched from Cornelius),
Ac 11:11 I·was, having·been·dispatched from Caesarea to
EG0649.2 (3x)
Jn 1:8 but·rather *he·was·dispatched* in·order·that he·may·
Jn 18:13 *(And HannAs dispatched the Anointed-One having·*
Ac 15:33 *to·return* to the ambassadors *who·dispatched them.*

G0650 ἀπο•στερέω apôstêréō *v.* (6x)
Roots:G0575 Compare:G4813
G0650.1 V-PAI-2P ἀποστερεῖτε (1x)
1Co 6:8 yeu·yeurselves do·wrong and rob, and these·things
G0650.1 V-PPI-2P ἀποστερεῖσθε (1x)
1Co 6:7 Rather, why not·indeed *let* yeurselves·be·robbed?
G0650.1 V-AAS-2S ἀποστερήσῃς (1x)
Mk 10:19 ·not bear·false·witness," "You·may·not rob,"
G0650.1 V-RPP-GPM ἀπεστερημένων (1x)
1Ti 6:5 *their* minds also having·been·robbed of·the truth—
G0650.1 V-RPP-NSM ἀπεστερημένος (1x)
Jac 5:4 ·open·fields, the·one having·been·robbed by yeu, it·
G0650.2 V-PAM-2P ἀποστερεῖτε (1x)
1Co 7:5 Do·not deprive one·another, except·that *which*

G0651 ἀπο•στολή apôstôlḗ *n.* (4x)
Roots:G0649 Compare:G2011 See:G0652
xLangAlso:H7988-2
G0651.1 N-ASF ἀποστολήν (2x)
Gal 2:8 in·Peter unto a·commission of·the Circumcision,
Rm 1:5 grace and commission for an·attentive·obedience of·
G0651.1 N-GSF ἀποστολῆς (2x)
Ac 1:25 of·this service and commission, from·among which
1Co 9:2 are the official·seal of·my commission in *the* Lord.

G0652 ἀπό•στολος apôstôlôs *n.* (87x)
Roots:G0649 Compare:G2012 See:G0651
xLangEquiv:H7988-1 xLangAlso:H7698-1
G0652.1 N-NPM ἀπόστολοι (1x)
2Co 8:23 *they·are* delegates of·*the*·Called·Out·citizenries
G0652.3 N-NSM ἀπόστολος (18x)
Jn 13:16 lord; neither *is* an·ambassador greater·than the·one
Gal 1:1 Paul, an·ambassador— (not from men·of·clay†,
Rm 1:1 ·forth *to·be* an·ambassador, having·been·specially·
Rm 11:13 ·as I·myself am in·fact an·ambassador of·Gentiles,
1Pe 1:1 Peter, an·ambassador of·YeShua Anointed. To·
2Pe 1:1 a·slave and an·ambassador of·YeShua Anointed.
Tit 1:1 a·slave of·God and an·ambassador of·Jesus Anointed
1Co 1:1 called·forth *to·be* an·ambassador of·Jesus Anointed
1Co 9:1 Am·I not an·ambassador? Am·I not free?
1Co 9:2 If I·am not an·ambassador to·others, but·yet still I·
1Co 15:9 not fit to·be·called an·ambassador, on·account·that
2Co 1:1 Paul, an·ambassador of·Jesus Anointed through
Eph 1:1 Paul, an·ambassador of·Jesus Anointed through
Col 1:1 Paul, an·ambassador of·Jesus Anointed through
1Ti 1:1 Paul, an·ambassador of·Jesus Anointed according·to
1Ti 2:7 *as* an·official·proclaimer and an·ambassador— (I·
2Ti 1:1 Paul, an·ambassador of·Jesus Anointed through
2Ti 1:11 *as* an·official·proclaimer, and an·ambassador, and
G0652.3 N-NPM ἀπόστολοι (15x)
Lk 9:10 And the ambassadors, after·returning·back, gave·an·
Lk 17:5 Then the ambassadors declared to·the Lord, "Add
Lk 22:14 and the twelve ambassadors *did·likewise* together
Ac 4:33 power, the ambassadors were·giving·forth the
Ac 5:29 answering, Peter and the ambassadors declared,
Ac 8:14 Now the ambassadors in JeruSalem, after·hearing
Ac 11:1 And the ambassadors and the brothers, the·ones
Ac 14:14 But the ambassadors, BarNabas and Paul, after·
Ac 15:6 And the ambassadors and the elders gathered·
Ac 15:23 ·own hand: "*From* the ambassadors, the elders,
Mk 6:30 Now the ambassadors gathered·themselves·together
1Th 2:6 to·be a·burden as ambassadors of·Anointed-One.
1Co 9:5 ·as also *do* the rest *of·the* ambassadors, and *as* the
1Co 12:29 Not all *are* ambassadors. Not all *are* prophets.
Rv 18:20 and the holy ambassadors and the prophets,
G0652.3 N-ASM ἀπόστολον (2x)
Heb 3:1 fully·observe the Ambassador and High·Priest of·
Php 2:25 ·soldier (but yeur ambassador and public·servant
G0652.3 N-APM ἀποστόλους (16x)
Lk 6:13 twelve of·them whom also he·named ambassadors.
Lk 11:49 to them prophets and ambassadors, and *some* from·
Lk 24:10 who were·saying these·things to·the ambassadors.
Ac 2:37 to Peter and to·the rest of·the·ambassadors, "Men,
Ac 5:18 their hands upon the ambassadors and placed them
Ac 5:34 ·ordered to·make the ambassadors *stay* outside a
Ac 5:40 after·summoning the ambassadors *and* thrashing
Ac 9:27 *him* to the ambassadors and gave·an·account to·
Ac 15:2 ·walk·up to JeruSalem to the ambassadors and elders
Ac 15:33 *to·return* to the ambassadors *who·dispatched them.*
Gal 1:17 toward the·ones *who·were* ambassadors before me,
1Co 4:9 that God exhibited us (the ambassadors) last, as
1Co 12:28 Called·Out·citizenry: first ambassadors, second
2Co 11:13 ·themselves as ambassadors of·Anointed-One.
Eph 4:11 *is the·one who* gave·forth the ambassadors, and the
Rv 2:2 ·tried the·ones professing to·be ambassadors and are
G0652.3 N-DPM ἀποστόλοις (6x)
Ac 1:2 Holy Spirit to·the ambassadors whom he·selected;
Ac 14:4 and the·one *part was* together with·the ambassadors.
Ac 15:22 Then it·seemed·good to·the ambassadors and the
Rm 16:7 who are of·note among the ambassadors, who also
1Co 15:7 ·upon by·Jacob, *and* then by·all the ambassadors.
Eph 3:5 now revealed to·his holy ambassadors and prophets
G0652.3 N-GSM ἀποστόλου (1x)
2Co 12:12 signs of·an·ambassador were·performed among
G0652.3 N-GPM ἀποστόλων (22x)
Ac 1:26 ·counted·together with the eleven ambassadors.
Ac 2:42 in·the instruction of·the ambassadors and in·the
Ac 2:43 and signs were·done through the ambassadors.
Ac 4:35 ·laying·*them*·down directly·at the ambassadors' feet,
Ac 4:36 ·called BarNabas by the ambassadors (which, when·
Ac 4:37 value and laid *it* directly·at the ambassadors' feet.
Ac 5:2 portion, he·laid *it* directly·at the ambassadors' feet.
Ac 5:12 through the hands of·the ambassadors, many signs
Ac 6:6 ·whom they·set in·the·sight of·the ambassadors, and
Ac 8:1 the ambassadors were·dispersed pervasively·into·all
Ac 8:18 through the laying·on of·the ambassadors' hands,
Ac 15:4 ·citizenry, and *by* the ambassadors and the elders,
Ac 16:4 having·been·decided by the ambassadors and the
Gal 1:19 I·did·not see any·other of·the ambassadors, except
Mt 10:2 And the names of·the twelve ambassadors are these:
Jud 1:17 ·already·stated by the ambassadors of·our Lord
2Pe 3:2 ·*been·already·stated* by·our ambassadors of·the Lord
1Co 15:9 I·myself am the least of·the ambassadors, who am
2Co 11:5 ·fallen·short of·the very highest of·ambassadors.
2Co 12:11 of·the very highest of·ambassadors, even·though
Eph 2:20 the foundation of·the ambassadors and prophets,
Rv 21:14 *the* names of·the twelve ambassadors of·the Lamb.
EG0652.3 (6x)
Ac 5:21 to·the dungeon to·have *the ambassadors* brought.
Ac 5:41 Accordingly, the *ambassadors*, in·fact, were·
Ac 14:5 ·mistreat *the ambassadors* and to·cast·stones·at
Ac 14:6 ·aware·of *it*, *the ambassadors* fled·down to Lystra
Mk 3:14 And he·made twelve *ambassadors*, that they·
1Co 15:11 I·myself or those *ambassadors*, in·this·manner

G0653 ἀπο•στοματίζω apôstômatízō *v.* (1x)
Roots:G0575 G4750
G0653.2 V-PAN ἀποστοματίζειν (1x)
Lk 11:53 him to·speak·off-hand concerning more·things,

G0654 ἀπο•στρέφω apôstréphō *v.* (10x)
Roots:G0575 G4762 Compare:G0665 G1624 G1578
G3868 G1994 See:G0654-1
G0654.1 V-FAI-3S ἀποστρέψει (1x)
Rm 11:26 and he·shall·turn·away irreverence from Jacob.
G0654.1 V-FAI-3P ἀποστρέψουσιν (1x)
2Ti 4:4 in·fact, they·shall·turn the inner·sense·of·hearing
G0654.1 V-PAN ἀποστρέφειν (1x)
Ac 3:26 yeu in this·thing, to·turn·away each·one *of·yeu* from
G0654.1 V-PAP-APM ἀποστρέφοντα (1x)
Lk 23:14 man·of·clay† to·me as one·turning·away the people
G0654.1 V-PMP-GPM ἀποστρεφομένων (1x)
Tit 1:14 of·men·of·clay† that·are·turning·them·away·from
G0654.1 V-PMP-NPM ἀποστρεφόμενοι (1x)
Heb 12:25 the·ones who·are·presently·turning·away·from
G0654.1 V-2API-3P ἀπεστράφησαν (1x)
2Ti 1:15 all the·ones in Asia are·turned·away·from me, of·
G0654.1 V-2APS-2S ἀποστραφῇς (1x)
Mt 5:42 you·should·not be·turning·away the·one wanting to·
G0654.2 V-AAI-3S ἀπέστρεψεν (1x)
Mt 27:3 over, upon·having·regret, returned·back the thirty
G0654.2 V-AAM-2S ἀπόστρεψον (1x)
Mt 26:52 says to·him, "Return·back your dagger into its

G0655 ἀπο•στυγέω apôstygéō *v.* (1x)
Roots:G0575 G4767 Compare:G0948
G0655.1 V-PAP-NPM ἀποστυγοῦντες (1x)
Rm 12:9 ·*be* without·hypocrisy, utterly·detesting the evil,

G0656 ἀπο•συν•άγωγος apôsynágōgôs *adj.* (3x)
Roots:G0575 G4864
G0656.1 A-NSM ἀποσυνάγωγος (1x)
Jn 9:22 he·should·be cut·off·from·the·gathering.
G0656.1 A-NPM ἀποσυνάγωγοι (1x)
Jn 12:42 they·should·not become cut·off·from·the·gathering,
G0656.1 A-APM ἀποσυναγώγους (1x)
Jn 16:2 ·make yeu cut·off·from·the·gatherings. Moreover,

G0657 ἀπο•τάσσομαι apôtássômai *v.* (6x)
Roots:G0575 G5021
G0657.1 V-PMI-3S ἀποτάσσεται (1x)
Lk 14:33 yeu that does·not orderly·take·leave·of all his
G0657.1 V-ADI-3S ἀπετάξατο (1x)
Ac 18:21 But·rather he·orderly·took·leave·of them,
G0657.1 V-AMN ἀποτάξασθαι (1x)
Lk 9:61 freely·permit me to·orderly·take·leave·of the·ones at
G0657.1 V-AMP-NSM ἀποταξάμενος (3x)
Ac 18:18 ·*of* days, after·orderly·taking·leave·of the brothers
Mk 6:46 And after·orderly·taking·leave·of them, he·went·off
2Co 2:13 brother. But·rather, orderly·taking·leave·of them,

G0658 ἀπο•τελέω apôtélĕō *v.* (1x)
Roots:G0575 G5055 Compare:G4931
G0658.2 V-APP-NSF ἀποτελεσθεῖσα (1x)
Jac 1:15 ·the moral·failure being·consummated, it·breeds

G0659 ἀπο•τίθημι apôtíthēmi *v.* (8x)
Roots:G0575 G5087 Compare:G0554 G0114
G0659.1 V-2AMM-2P ἀπόθεσθε (1x)
Col 3:8 yeu·yeurselves also must·put·off all·these things:
G0659.1 V-2AMN ἀποθέσθαι (1x)
Eph 4:22 *such·for* yeu to·put·off the old man·of·clay†
G0659.2 V-2AMP-NPM ἀποθέμενοι (2x)
Jac 1:21 Therefore, putting·away all filthiness and any·
Eph 4:25 Therefore, putting·away the lying, "Each·man
G0659.2 V-2AMS-1P ἀποθώμεθα (1x)
Rm 13:12 Accordingly, we·should·put·away the works of·
G0659.3 V-2AMI-3P ἀπέθεντο (1x)
Ac 7:58 ·at *him*, and the witnesses laid·aside their garments
G0659.3 V-2AMP-NPM ἀποθέμενοι (2x)
Heb 12:1 us— with·us·already·laying·aside every hindrance
1Pe 2:1 Accordingly, with·yeu·laying·aside all malice, and

G0660 ἀπο•τινάσσω apôtinássō *v.* (2x)
Roots:G0575 G5098-2 Compare:G4525 G4579 See:G1621
G0660 V-AAM-2P ἀποτινάξατε (1x)
Lk 9:5 ·are·going·forth from that city, jostle·off even the
G0660 V-AAP-NSM ἀποτινάξας (1x)
Ac 28:5 ·then, in·fact, after·jostling·off the venomous·beast

G0661 ἀπο•τίνω apôtínō *v.* (1x)
Roots:G0575 G5099
G0661 V-FAI-1S ἀποτίσω (1x)
Phm 1:19 by·my·own hand; I·myself shall·fully·pay *it*, not

G0662 ἀπο•τολμάω apôtôlmáō *v.* (1x)
Roots:G0575 G5111 Compare:G3955
G0662.2 V-PAI-3S ἀποτολμᾷ (1x)
Rm 10:20 But Isaiah is·quite·daringly·bold and says, "" I·

G0663 ἀπο•τομία apôtômía *n.* (2x)
Roots:G0664 Compare:G5544 See:G5114
G0663.3 N-ASF ἀποτομίαν (2x)
Rm 11:22 ·kindness and a·severe·cutting-off from·God! In·
Rm 11:22 upon the·ones falling, a·severe·cutting-off, but

G0664 ἀπο•τόμως apôtômōs *adv.* (2x)
Roots:G0575 G5058-2 Compare:G3718 See:G0663 G5114
G0664.3 ADV ἀποτόμως (2x)
Tit 1:13 them with·abrupt·sharpness in·order·that they·may·
2Co 13:10 *yeu* with·abrupt·sharpness while·being·present,

G0665 ἀπο•τρέπω apôtrépō *v.* (1x)
Roots:G0575 G5157 Compare:G3868 G4026 G0654 G1624 G1578
G0665.2 V-PMM-2S ἀποτρέπου (1x)
2Ti 3:5 So·then, turn·yourself·away·and·avoid these *people*!

G0666 ἀπ•ουσία apôusía *n.* (1x)
Roots:G0548
G0666 N-DSF ἀπουσίᾳ (1x)
Php 2:12 now so·much more in my absence), with reverent·

G0667 ἀπο•φέρω apôphérō *v.* (5x)
Roots:G0575 G5342 Compare:G0142 G0941
G0667 V-AAI-3S ἀπήνεγκεν (2x)
Rv 17:3 And he·carried me away in spirit into a·wilderness.
Rv 21:10 And he·carried me away in spirit to a·great and
G0667 V-AAI-3P ἀπήνεγκαν (1x)
Mk 15:1 Jesus, they·carried·*him*·away and handed·*him*·over
G0667 V-2AAN ἀπενεγκεῖν (1x)
1Co 16:3 I·shall·send to·carry yeur gracious·benevolence
G0667 V-APN ἀπενεχθῆναι (1x)
Lk 16:22 ·die, and *for* him to·be·carried·away by the angels

G0668 ἀπο•φεύγω apôphéúgō *v.* (3x)
Roots:G0575 G5343
G0668 V-2AAP-APM ἀποφυγόντας (1x)
2Pe 2:18 really already·escaping·from the·ones conducting·
G0668 V-2AAP-NPM ἀποφυγόντες (2x)
2Pe 1:4 ·divine nature, already·escaping·from the corruption
2Pe 2:20 For if after·escaping·from the contaminations of·

G0669 ἀπο•φθέγγομαι apôphthéngômai *v.* (3x)
Roots:G0575 G5350
G0669 V-PNI-1S ἀποφθέγγομαι (1x)
Ac 26:25 but·rather I·clearly·enunciate utterances of·truth
G0669 V-PNN ἀποφθέγγεσθαι (1x)
Ac 2:4 ·as the Spirit was·giving them to·clearly·enunciate.
G0669 V-ADI-3S ἀπεφθέγξατο (1x)
Ac 2:14 lifted·up his voice and clearly·enunciated to·them,

G0670 ἀπο•φορτίζομαι apôphôrtízômai *v.* (1x)
Roots:G0575 G5412
G0670 V-PNP-NSN ἀποφορτιζόμενον (1x)
Ac 21:3 for the sailing·ship was unloading its cargo there.

G0671 ἀπό•χρησις apóchrēsis *n.* (1x)
Roots:G0575 G5530
G0671 N-DSF ἀποχρήσει (1x)
Col 2:22 all are *subject* to perishing with·usage)— *decrees*

G0672 ἀπο•χωρέω apôchōréō *v.* (3x)
Roots:G0575 G5562 Compare:G0402 G1633
G0672 V-PAI-3S ἀποχωρεῖ (1x)
Lk 9:39 ·with foam, and hardly does·it·depart from him,
G0672 V-PAM-2P ἀποχωρεῖτε (1x)
Mt 7:23 ·time did·I·know yeu! 'Depart from me, the·ones
G0672 V-AAP-NSM ἀποχωρήσας (1x)
Ac 13:13 to Perga in·PamPhylia. And departing from them,

G0673 ἀπο•χωρίζω apôchōrízō *v.* (2x)
Roots:G0575 G5563 Compare:G0873 See:G1316
G0673.1 V-API-3S ἀπεχωρίσθη (1x)
Rv 6:14 heaven was·utterly·separated as an·official·scroll
G0673.1 V-APN ἀποχωρισθῆναι (1x)
Ac 15:39 ·for them to·be·utterly·separated from one·another;

G0674 ἀπο•ψύχω apôpsýchō *v.* (1x)
Roots:G0575 G5594
G0674 V-PAP-GPM ἀποψυχόντων (1x)
Lk 21:26 with·men·of·clay† fainting for fear, and for·

G0675 Ἄππιος Áppiôs *n/p.* (1x)
G0675 N/P-GSM Ἀππίου (1x)
Ac 28:15 us even·as·far·as *the* Forum of·Appius and *the*

G0676 ἀ•πρόσ•ιτος aprósitôs *adj.* (1x)
Roots:G0001 G4314 G2423-1
G0676.2 A-ASN ἀπρόσιτον (1x)
1Ti 6:16 dwelling *in* unapproachable light which no·one·at·

G0677 ἀ•πρόσ•κοπος apróskôpôs *adj.* (3x)
Roots:G0001 G4350
G0677.2 A-NPM ἀπρόσκοποι (1x)
Php 1:10 ·may·be·judged·sincere and without·offense in *the*
G0677.3 A-NPM ἀπρόσκοποι (1x)
1Co 10:32 Become void·of·offense, even to·Jews, also to·
G0677.3 A-ASF ἀπρόσκοπον (1x)
Ac 24:16 a·conscience void·of·offense toward God and

G0678 ἀ•προσ•ωπόλημπτως aprôsōpólēptōs *adv.* (1x)
Roots:G0001 G4383 G2983 Compare:G4381
G0678.3 ADV ἀπροσωπολήπτως (1x)
1Pe 1:17 ·one presently·judging impartially according·to the

G0679 ἄ•πταιστος áptaistôs *adj.* (1x)
Roots:G0001 G4417
G0679.2 A-APM ἀπταίστους (1x)
Jud 1:24 ·vigilantly·keep yeu without·moral·stumblings, and

G0680 ἅπτομαι háptômai *v.* (36x)
Roots:G0681 Compare:G2345 G2902 G2983 G5584 See:G2510 G2133 xLangAlso:H5060
G0680.2 V-PMI-3S ἅπτεται (2x)
Lk 7:39 *is* the woman that lays·hold of·him, because she·is
1Jn 5:18 and the Evil·One does·not lay·hold of·him.
G0680.2 V-PMM-2S ἅπτου (1x)
Jn 20:17 says to·her, "Do·not lay·hold of·me, for I·have·
G0680.2 V-PMM-2P ἅπτεσθε (1x)
2Co 6:17 "and do·not lay·hold of·impurity," and·I shall·
G0680.2 V-PMN ἅπτεσθαι (2x)
Lk 6:19 the entire crowd was·seeking to·lay·hold of·him,
1Co 7:1 good for·a·man·of·clay† not to·lay·hold of·a·wife.
G0680.2 V-PMS-3S ἅπτηται (1x)
Lk 18:15 to·him in·order·that he·may·lay·hold of·them, but
G0680.2 V-INI-3P ἥπτοντο (1x)
Mk 6:56 And as·many·as were·laying·hold of·him, they·
G0680.2 V-ADI-3S ἥψατο (16x)
Lk 5:13 And stretching·out his hand, he·laid·hold of·him,
Lk 7:14 And coming·alongside, he·laid·hold of·the coffin,
Lk 8:44 *him* from·behind, she·laid·hold of·the fringe of·his
Lk 8:46 Jesus declared, "Someone laid·hold of·me, for I·
Lk 8:47 on·account·of what cause she·laid·hold of·him, and
Mt 8:3 stretching·out his hand, laid·hold of·him saying,
Mt 8:15 And he·laid·hold of·her hand, and the fever left her,
Mt 9:20 *YeShua* from·behind, she·laid·hold of·the fringe of·
Mt 9:29 Then he·laid·hold of·their eyes, saying,
Mt 17:7 coming·alongside, YeShua laid·hold of·them and
Mt 20:34 And empathizing, YeShua laid·hold of·their eyes,
Mk 1:41 stretching·out his hand, he·laid·hold of·him and
Mk 5:27 from·behind *him*, she·laid·hold of·his garment.
Mk 5:30 was·saying, "Who laid·hold of·my garments?
Mk 5:31 ·in·around you and say, 'Who laid·hold of·me?
Mk 7:33 ears, and after·spitting, he·laid·hold of·his tongue,
G0680.2 V-ADI-3P ἥψαντο (1x)
Mt 14:36 and as·many·as did·lay·hold *of·it* were·made·
G0680.2 V-AMP-NSM ἁψάμενος (3x)
Lk 8:45 Jesus declared, "Who·is the·one laying·hold of·me?
Lk 8:45 and you·say, 'Who·is the·one laying·hold of·me?
Lk 22:51 even·unto this!" And laying·hold of·his earlobe,
G0680.2 V-AMS-1S ἅψωμαι (2x)
Mt 9:21 "If merely I·should·lay·hold of·his garment, I·
Mk 5:28 "Because if·even I·should·lay·hold of·his garments,
G0680.2 V-AMS-2S ἅψῃ (1x)
Col 2:21 (*such·as* "You·should·not lay·hold·of, nor·even
G0680.2 V-AMS-3S ἅψηται (2x)
Mk 8:22 implore him in·order·that he·may·lay·hold *of·the*
Mk 10:13 ·children to·him, that he·should·lay·hold of·them,
G0680.2 V-AMS-3P ἅψωνται (3x)
Mt 14:36 ·order·that they·may merely lay·hold of·the fringe
Mk 3:10 him in·order·that they·may·lay·hold of·him.
Mk 6:56 him in·order·that they·may·lay·hold *of·him*, if·even

G0681 ἅπτω háptō *v.* (4x)
See:G0680
G0681.2 V-PAI-3S ἅπτει (1x)
Lk 15:8 one drachma, does·not·indeed ignite a·lantern, and
G0681.2 V-AAP-GPM ἁψάντων (1x)
Lk 22:55 And with·them igniting a·fire in *the* midst of·the
G0681.2 V-AAP-NSM ἅψας (2x)
Lk 8:16 "Not·even·one·man, after·igniting a·lantern, covers
Lk 11:33 "Not·even·one·man, after·igniting a·lantern,

G0682 Ἀπφία Apphía *n/p.* (1x)
G0682 N/P-DSF Ἀπφίᾳ (1x)

Phm 1:2 and to·the beloved Apphia, and Archippus our

G0683 ἀπ•ωθέομαι apōthéômai *v.* (6x)
ἀπ•ώθομαι apốthômai
Roots:G0575 Compare:G0593 G1848 G1856 G0906 xLangAlso:H5203

G0683.2 V-PNI-2P ἀπωθεῖσθε (1x)
Ac 13:46 to·yeu, but since·now yeu·shove it away and

G0683.2 V-ADI-3S ἀπώσατο (3x)
Ac 7:27 morally·wronging the neighbor shoved him away,
Rm 11:1 I·say, ¿!·Did God shove·away his People?
Rm 11:2 God did·not shove·away his People which he·

G0683.2 V-ADI-3P ἀπώσαντο (1x)
Ac 7:39 but·rather shoved·*him*·from·themselves, and in·

G0683.2 V-ADP-NPM ἀπωσάμενοι (1x)
1Ti 1:19 some, after·shoving·*it*·away, are·shipwrecked,

G0684 ἀπ•ώλεια apṓlêia *n.* (20x)
Roots:G0622 See:G0623

G0684.1 N-NSF ἀπώλεια (2x)
Php 3:19 whose end *is* total·destruction, whose god *is* the
2Pe 2:3 idle, and their total·destruction does·not nod·off *to*·

G0684.1 N-ASF ἀπώλειαν (10x)
Ac 8:20 be *handed·over* to total·destruction, because you·
Ac 25:16 ·over any man·of·clay† to total·destruction, before
Heb 10:39 ·who·shrinks·back to total·destruction, but·rather
Mt 7:13 the·one leading·off to the total·destruction, and
Rm 9:22 ·been·completely·formed for total·destruction,
2Pe 2:1 bringing·upon themselves abrupt total·destruction.
2Pe 3:16 rest of·Scriptures, to their own total·destruction.
1Ti 6:9 down in a·savage·termination and total·destruction.
Rv 17:8 and to·head·on·out to total·destruction. And the·
Rv 17:11 the seven, and it·heads·on·out to total·destruction.

G0684.1 N-DPF ἀπωλείαις (1x)
2Pe 2:2 ·out their *ways* to·total·destruction, on·account·of

G0684.1 N-GSF ἀπωλείας (5x)
Jn 17:12 except the Son of·Total·Destruction, in·order·that
Php 1:28 in·fact is an·indicator of·total·destruction for·them,
2Pe 2:1 factions·and·denominations of·total·destruction—
2Pe 3:7 ·judgment and total·destruction of·the irreverent
2Th 2:3 should·be·revealed, the Son of·Total·Destruction,

G0684.2 N-NSF ἀπώλεια (2x)
Mt 26:8 "To what·purpose *is* this total·ruin?
Mk 14:4 "Why·has this total·ruin of·the ointment occurred?

G0685 ἀρά ará *n.* (1x)
Roots:G0142 Compare:G4335 See:G0689-1 G2671

G0685.2 N-GSF ἀρᾶς (1x)
Rm 3:14 mouth overflows of·evil·prayer and of·bitterness.

G0686 ἄρα ára *prt.* (33x)
Roots:G0142 Compare:G1352 G5105 See:G1065 G3767 G1487 G0687

G0686.2 PRT ἄρα (12x)
Lk 11:20 I·cast·out the demons, then·by·inference, the
Lk 11:48 "Then·by·inference, yeu·testify and gladly·consent
Heb 12:8 ·become participants), then·by·inference, yeu·are
Gal 2:21 Torah-Law, then·by·inference, Anointed-One died,
Gal 3:29 *are* of·Anointed-One, then·by·inference, yeu·are
Gal 5:11 why·am I·still persecuted? Then·by·inference, the
Mt 12:28 by God's Spirit, then·by·inference, the kingdom
Rm 7:21 By·inference, I·find the law in·the *circumstance*
1Co 5:10 Otherwise, by·inference, yeu·are·obligated to·go·
1Co 15:14 has·not been·awakened, then·by·inference, our
1Co 15:15 awaken, if·perhaps, by·inference, dead·men are·
2Co 5:14 died on·behalf·of all, then·by·inference, all died.

G0686.3 PRT ἄρα (3x)
Ac 8:22 and petition God so·that perhaps the intention of·
Ac 17:27 if perhaps they·might·feel·around·and·about·for
Mk 11:13 *toward it to·see* if perhaps he·shall·find anything

G0686.3 PRT-I ἆρα (1x)
2Co 1:17 ·planning that, ¿!·did perhaps I·use some levity?

G0686.4 PRT ἄρα (7x)
Ac 11:18 ·glorifying God, saying, "So also to·the Gentiles,
Gal 4:31 So, brothers, we·are not children of·a·maidservant,
Mt 17:26 YeShua was·replying to·him, "So the sons are free
Rm 7:25 Anointed our Lord. So accordingly in·fact, with·
Rm 8:12 So accordingly brothers, we·are under·an·
2Th 2:15 So accordingly, brothers, stand·fast and securely·
2Co 7:12 So even·though I·wrote to·yeu, *it·was* not because·

G0686.5 PRT ἄρα (9x)
Heb 4:9 Consequently, there·is·still·remaining a·Sabbath·
Gal 3:7 Consequently, know that the·ones birthed·from·out
Mt 7:20 Consequently, by their fruits yeu·shall·recognize
Rm 5:18 So consequently, as through one trespass, *judgment*
Rm 8:1 Consequently, *there·is* now not·even·one verdict·of·
Rm 9:16 So·then, consequently, *it·depends* not on·the·one
Rm 10:17 Consequently, the trust *comes* as·a·result of·
Rm 14:12 So·then, consequently, each·one of·us shall·give
Eph 2:19 Now·then, consequently, yeu·are no·longer

G0686.6 PRT-I ἆρα (1x)
Ac 12:18 among the soldiers as·to what was·become of·Peter

G0687 ἆρα âra *prt.* (11x)
Roots:G0686

G0687 PRT-I ἆρα (1x)
Ac 8:30 and he·declared, "Then is·it·actually·so, *that* you·

G0687.2 PRT-I ἆρα (9x)
Lk 1:66 hearts, saying, "What then shall this little·child be?
Lk 12:42 Lord declared, "Who then is the trustworthy and
Lk 18:8 upon·coming·*back*, shall·he·find then *such* a·trust
Ac 21:38 Are you·yourself not then the Egyptian, *the·one*
Mt 18:1 YeShua, saying, "Who then is greater in the
Mt 19:25 saying, "Who then is·able to·be·saved?
Mt 19:27 all and followed you. What then shall·be for·us?
Mt 24:45 "Who then is the trustworthy and prudent slave
Mk 4:41 ·saying to one·another, "Who then is this, that even

G0687.3 PRT-I ἆρα (1x)
Gal 2:17 would·this·then·make Anointed-One an·attendant

G0688 Ἀραβία Arabía *n/l.* (2x)
עֲרָב 'ărạb [Hebrew]
Roots:H6152 See:G0690

G0688.2 N/L-ASF Ἀραβίαν (1x)
Gal 1:17 me, but·rather I·went·aside into Arabia, and again

G0688.2 N/L-DSF Ἀραβίᾳ (1x)
Gal 4:25 Hagar is Mount Sinai in Arabia, and corresponds·to

G0689 Ἀράμ Arám *n/p.* (3x)
רָם rạm [Hebrew]
Roots:H7410

G0689.2 N/P-PRI Ἀράμ (3x)
Lk 3:33 *son* of·AmmiNadab, *son* of·Ram, *son* of·Chetsron,
Mt 1:3 and Perets begot Chetsron, and Chetsron begot Ram.
Mt 1:4 Now Ram begot AmmiNadab, and AmmiNadab begot

G0690 Ἄραψ Áraps *n/g.* (1x)
Roots:G0688

G0690.2 N/G-NPM Ἄραβες (1x)
Ac 2:11 Cretans and Arabians— we·hear them speaking in·

G0691 ἀ•ργέω argéō *v.* (1x)
Roots:G0692 See:G2673

G0691.1 V-PAI-3S ἀργεῖ (1x)
2Pe 2:3 for·whom judgment from·long·ago is·not idle, and

G0692 ἀ•ργός argós *adj.* (8x)
Roots:G0001 G2041 See:G0691

G0692.1 A-NSN ἀργόν (1x)
Mt 12:36 I·say to·yeu, that for·every idle utterance, which if

G0692.1 A-NPM ἀργοί (1x)
Mt 20:6 'Why·do yeu·stand here the whole day idle?'

G0692.1 A-NPF ἀργαί (2x)
1Ti 5:13 ·same·time, they·learn *to·be* idle, going·roundabout
1Ti 5:13 homes, and not merely idle, but·rather gossipers

G0692.1 A-APM ἀργούς (3x)
Mt 20:3 he·saw others standing idle in the marketplace.
Mt 20:6 he·found others standing idle and says to·them,
2Pe 1:8 ·fully·establishes *yeu to·be* neither idle nor unfruitful

G0692.2 A-NPF ἀργαί (1x)
Tit 1:12 always liars, wicked wild·beasts, lazy gluttons."

G0693 ἀργύρεος argýrêos *adj.* (3x)
Roots:G0696

G0693 A-NPN ἀργυρᾶ (1x)
2Ti 2:20 vessels made·of·gold and of·silver, but·rather also

G0693 A-APM ἀργυροῦς (1x)
Ac 19:24 a·silversmith making silver temples of·Artemis,

G0693 A-APN ἀργυρᾶ (1x)
Rv 9:20 and 'the idols made·of·gold, silver, bronze, stone,

G0694 ἀργύριον argýriôn *n.* (22x)
Roots:G0696 Compare:G2772 G3546 xLangEquiv:H3701 A3702 xLangAlso:H8255

G0694.1 N-NSN ἀργύριον (1x)
Ac 8:20 to him, "May your silver, together with·you, be

G0694.1 N-ASN ἀργύριον (1x)
Ac 3:6 Then Peter declared, "Silver and gold, it·does·not

G0694.1 N-DSN ἀργυρίῳ (1x)
1Pe 1:18 not with·corruptible·things *such·as* silver or gold

G0694.1 N-GSN ἀργυρίου (1x)
Ac 20:33 "I·longed·for not·even·one·man's silver or gold or

G0694.2 N-ASN ἀργύριον (6x)
Lk 9:3 neither bread, neither money; neither to·have two
Lk 19:23 Why then did·you·not give my money over *to* the
Lk 22:5 and agreed·among·themselves to·give him money.
Mt 25:18 dug in the earth and hid·away his lord's money.
Mt 25:27 ·for you to·cast my money to·the bankers, and *then*
Mk 14:11 ·were·glad and promised to·give money to·him.

G0694.2 N-APN ἀργύρια (2x)
Mt 28:12 ·gave a·significant·sum·of money to·the soldiers,
Mt 28:15 So taking the money, they·did as they·were·

G0694.3 N-ASN ἀργύριον (1x)
Lk 19:15 (*each·one* to·whom he·gave the piece·of·silver), in·

G0694.3 N-APN ἀργύρια (5x)
Mt 26:15 they·settled with·him for·thirty pieces·of·silver.
Mt 27:3 ·back the thirty pieces·of·silver to·the chief·priests
Mt 27:5 And flinging the pieces·of·silver at the Temple, he·
Mt 27:6 chief·priests, taking the pieces·of·silver, declared,
Mt 27:9 "And they·took the thirty pieces·of·silver, the price

G0694.3 N-GSN ἀργυρίου (2x)
Ac 7:16 *Jacob* purchased for·a·price of·silver·pieces near the
Ac 19:19 times·ten·thousand pieces·of·silver *(which·is fifty*

EG0694.3 (2x)
Mt 27:7 from·out·of·the·same *pieces·of·silver*, they·bought
Mt 27:10 and they·gave *the* same *pieces·of·silver* for the

G0695 ἀργυρο•κόπος argyrôkópôs *n.* (1x)
Roots:G0696 G2875

G0695 N-NSM ἀργυροκόπος (1x)
Ac 19:24 ·name·of Demetrius, a·silversmith making silver

G0696 ἄργυρος árgyrôs *n.* (5x)
Compare:G5557 G5475 G4604 G3432-1 G2595-3 See:G0694 xLangAlso:H3701

G0696 N-NSM ἄργυρος (1x)
Jac 5:3 Yeur gold and silver have·been·fully·rusted·down,

G0696 N-ASM ἄργυρον (2x)
Mt 10:9 ·not procure gold, nor·even silver, nor·even copper·
1Co 3:12 this foundation *with* gold, silver, precious stones,

G0696 N-DSM ἀργύρῳ (1x)
Ac 17:29 divine to·be like gold or silver or stone etched by·

G0696 N-GSM ἀργύρου (1x)
Rv 18:12 "cargo of·gold, silver, precious stones, and pearls,

G0697 Ἄρειος Πάγος Árêiôs Págôs *n/l.* (2x)
Roots:G4078 See:G0698

G0697.2 N/L-ASM Ἄρειον (1x)
Ac 17:19 ·him to Mars'·Hill·*(also·called·AreoPagus)*,

G0697.2 N/L-GSM Ἀρείου (1x)
Ac 17:22 being·settled in *the* midst of·Mars'·Hill, replied,

G0698 Ἀρεο•παγίτης Arêôpagítēs *n/g.* (1x)
Roots:G0697

G0698 N/G-NSM Ἀρεοπαγίτης (1x)
Ac 17:34 *was* Dionysius, a·councilman·of·Mars'·Hill, and a·

G0699 ἀρέσκεια aréskêia *n.* (1x)
Roots:G0700

G0699.2 N-ASF ἀρέσκειαν (1x)
Col 1:10 of·the Lord into all willing·compliance: bearing·

G0700 ἀρέσκω arẽskō *v.* (18x)
Roots:G0142 Compare:G3980 G2106 G5562 See:G0699

G0700.1 V-PAN ἀρέσκειν (1x)
Gal 1:10 ·*with* God? Or do·I·seek to·appease men·of·clay†?

G0700.1 V-IAI-1S ἤρεσκον (1x)
Gal 1:10 For if yet I·was·appeasing men·of·clay†, I·would

G0700.2 V-PAN ἀρέσκειν (1x)
Rm 15:1 ·ones *that·are* unable, and not to·satisfy ourselves.

G0700.2 V-PAP-NPM ἀρέσκοντες (1x)
1Th 2:4 we·speak, not as satisfying men·of·clay†, but·rather

G0700.2 V-AAI-3S ἤρεσεν (2x)
Ac 6:5 And the saying was·satisfactory in·the·sight of·the
Mt 14:6 danced in their midst and satisfied HerOd AntiPas.

G0700.2 V-AAN ἀρέσαι (1x)
Rm 8:8 the·ones being in flesh are·not able to·satisfy God.

G0700.2 V-AAP-GSF ἀρεσάσης (1x)
Mk 6:22 ·in and dancing and satisfying HerOd AntiPas and

G0700.3 V-PAN ἀρέσκειν (1x)
1Th 4:1 and to·agreeably·comply with·God in·order·that

G0700.3 V-PAP-GPM ἀρεσκόντων (1x)
1Th 2:15 ·*Judeans are* not agreeably·complying with·God,

G0700.3 V-AAS-3S ἀρέσῃ (1x)
2Ti 2:4 in·order·that he·may·agreeably·comply with·the·one

EG0700.3 (1x)
2Co 10:2 Now I·petition *yeu to·agreeably·comply*, *such·for*

G0700.4 V-PAI-1S ἀρέσκω (1x)
1Co 10:33 Just·as I·also willingly·adapt·for all *men* in·all

G0700.4 V-PAM-3S ἀρεσκέτω (1x)
Rm 15:2 ·one of·us must·willingly·adapt to·his neighbor's

G0700.5 V-FAI-3S ἀρέσει (3x)
1Co 7:32 of·the Lord, how he·shall·accommodate the Lord.
1Co 7:33 of·the world, how he·shall·accommodate his wife.
1Co 7:34 world, how she·shall·accommodate the husband.

G0700.5 V-AAI-3S ἤρεσεν (1x)
Rm 15:3 the Anointed-One did·not accommodate himself,

G0701 ἀρεστός arẽstős *adj.* (4x)
Roots:G0700 See:G2101 G2102

G0701.1 A-NSN ἀρεστόν (2x)
Ac 6:2 declared, "This·is not satisfactory to·us: abandoning
Ac 12:3 And seeing that it·was satisfactory to·the Judeans,

G0701.1 A-APN ἀρεστά (2x)
Jn 8:29 always do the·things *that·are* satisfactory to·him."
1Jn 3:22 the·things *that·are* satisfactory in·the·sight of·him.

G0702 Ἀρέτας Arẽtas *n/p.* (1x)

G0702 N/P-GSM Ἀρέτα (1x)
2Co 11:32 the national·magistrate *under* Aretas the king

G0703 ἀρετή arẽtế *n.* (5x)
Roots:G0142 Compare:G4586 G4587 G0406-1 G0266 See:G0730

G0703.2 N-NSF ἀρετή (1x)
Php 4:8 if *there·is* any courageous·moral·excellence, and if

G0703.2 N-ASF ἀρετήν (1x)
2Pe 1:5 ·with yeur trust: Courageous·Moral·Excellence; and

G0703.2 N-APF ἀρετάς (1x)
1Pe 2:9 ·forth the courageous·moral·excellencies of·the·one

G0703.2 N-DSF ἀρετῇ (1x)
2Pe 1:5 ·with *yeur* courageous·moral·excellence, Knowledge

G0703.2 N-GSF ἀρετῆς (1x)
2Pe 1:3 through glory and courageous·moral·excellence.

G0704 ἀρήν arẽn *n.* (1x)
Roots:G0142 Compare:G0721 G4263 See:G0730

G0704.2 N-APM ἄρνας (1x)
Lk 10:3 dispatch yeu as adolescent·male·lambs in *the* midst

G0705 ἀριθμέω arithmẽō *v.* (3x)
Roots:G0706 Compare:G5585 See:G2674

G0705 V-AAN ἀριθμῆσαι (1x)
Rv 7:9 crowd which not·even·one·man was·able to·number,

G0705 V-RPI-3P ἠρίθμηνται (1x)
Lk 12:7 the hairs of·yeur head all have·been·numbered.

G0705 V-RPP-NPF ἠριθμημέναι (1x)
Mt 10:30 hairs of·yeur head are all having·been·numbered.

G0706 ἀριθμός arithmős *n.* (17x)
Roots:G0142 Compare:G2425 See:G0705 xLangEquiv:H4557

G0706 N-NSM ἀριθμός (9x)
Ac 4:4 trusted, and the number of·the men was about five
Ac 5:36 (to·whom a·number of·men tightly·bonded·
Ac 6:7 ·*in·circulation*; and the number of·the disciples were·
Ac 11:21 them, and a·large number turned·back·around to
Rm 9:27 ·" Although the number of·the Sons of·IsraEl
Rv 9:16 And the number of·troops of·the cavalry *was* twice
Rv 13:18 for it·is a·number of·a·certain·man·of·clay†.
Rv 13:18 And this *clay·man's†* number *is* Chi·Xi·Stigma,
Rv 20:8 together into battle, the number of·whom *is* as the

G0706 N-ASM ἀριθμόν (5x)
Jn 6:10 the men sat·back·to·eat; the number *was* about five·
Rv 7:4 the number of·the·ones having·been·officially·sealed:
Rv 9:16 ·*hundred million)*, and I·heard the number of·them.
Rv 13:17 of·the Daemonic·Beast, or the number of·his name.
Rv 13:18 let·him·calculate the number of·the Daemonic·Beast

G0706 N-DSM ἀριθμῷ (1x)
Ac 16:5 in·the trust and were·abounding in·number each day

G0706 N-GSM ἀριθμοῦ (2x)
Lk 22:3 being from·among the number of·the twelve.
Rv 15:2 *and* out·from·among the number of·its name)—

G0707 Ἀριμαθαία Arimathaía *n/l.* (4x)
רָמָה rạmạh [Hebrew]
Roots:H7414 Compare:G4471

G0707.2 N/L-GSF Ἀριμαθαίας (4x)
Jn 19:38 Joseph (the·one from Arimathaea) being a·disciple
Lk 23:51 ·their practice; *he·was* of Arimathaea, a·city of·the
Mt 27:57 man·of·clay† of Arimathaea, by·the·name·of
Mk 15:43 Joseph came, the·one of Arimathaea, a·dignified

G0708 Ἀρίστ•αρχος Arístarchôs *n/p.* (5x)
Roots:G0142 G0757 See:G0712

G0708.2 N/P-NSM Ἀρίσταρχος (3x)
Ac 20:4 Now already, *both* AristArchus and Secundus of·
Col 4:10 AristArchus, my fellow·prisoner·of·war, greets yeu
Phm 1:24 *John*·Mark, AristArchus, Demas, Luke, *these* my

G0708.2 N/P-ASM Ἀρίσταρχον (1x)
Ac 19:29 ·both Gaius and AristArchus, men·of·Macedonia,

G0708.2 N/P-GSM Ἀριστάρχου (1x)
Ac 27:2 places of·Asia, with·AristArchus (a·Macedonian

G0709 ἀριστάω aristáō *v.* (3x)
Roots:G0712 Compare:G1172 G4885-2

G0709 V-AAI-3P@ ἠρίστησαν (1x)
Jn 21:15 Accordingly, when they·had·dined, Jesus says to·

G0709 V-AAM-2P ἀριστήσατε (1x)
Jn 21:12 to·them, "Come·here! Dine!" And not·even·one

G0709 V-AAS-3S ἀριστήσῃ (1x)
Lk 11:37 in·such·a·manner·so·that he·should·dine next·to

G0710 ἀριστερός aristẽrős *adj.* (3x)
Roots:G0142 Compare:G2176 G1188 See:G0712

G0710.1 A-NSF ἀριστερά (1x)
Mt 6:3 a·merciful·act, do·not·let your left·hand know what

G0710.2 A-GPM ἀριστερῶν (2x)
Lk 23:33 ·fact one at *the* right·hand, and the·other at *the* left.
2Co 6:7 of·righteousness on·the right·hand and on·the·left,

G0711 Ἀριστό•βουλος Aristóbôulôs *n/p.* (1x)
Roots:G0142 G1012 See:G0712

G0711.2 N/P-GSM Ἀριστοβούλου (1x)
Rm 16:10 the·ones from·among AristoBulus' *household*.

G0712 ἄριστον áristôn *n.* (3x)
Roots:G0142 Compare:G1062 G1173 G4224 See:G0730

G0712.2 N-NSN ἄριστον (1x)
Lk 14:12 you·should·make a·luncheon or a·supper, do·not

G0712.2 N-GSN ἀρίστου (1x)
Lk 11:38 ·not first immerse *his hands* before the luncheon.

G0712.3 N-NSN ἄριστον (1x)
Mt 22:4 "Behold, I·made·ready my banquet. My bulls and

G0713 ἀρκετός arkẽtős *adj.* (3x)
Roots:G0714 Compare:G2425

G0713 A-NSM ἀρκετός (1x)
1Pe 4:3 ·by *was* sufficient for·us to·have·accomplished the

G0713 A-NSN ἀρκετόν (2x)
Mt 6:34 ·about the·things of·itself. Sufficient for·the day *is*
Mt 10:25 *It·is* sufficient for·the disciple that he·should·

G0714 ἀρκέω arkẽō *v.* (8x)
Compare:G0713 See:G0142

G0714.3 V-PAI-3S ἀρκεῖ (1x)
Jn 14:8 "Lord, show us the Father, and it·suffices for·us."

G0714.4 V-PAI-3S ἀρκεῖ (1x)
2Co 12:9 to·me, "My grace is·sufficient for·you, for my

G0714.4 V-PAI-3P ἀρκοῦσιν (1x)
Jn 6:7 denarii *worth* of·bread is·not sufficient for·them, that

G0714.4 V-AAS-3S ἀρκέσῃ (1x)
Mt 25:9 '*Not·so*, lest there·should·not be·sufficient *oil* for·us

G0714.5 V-FPI-1P ἀρκεσθησόμεθα (1x)
1Ti 6:8 essential·coverings, with·these we·shall·be·satisfied.

G0714.5 V-PPM-2P ἀρκεῖσθε (1x)
Lk 3:14 ·by·false·charges, and be·satisfied with·yeur wages.

G0714.5 V-PPP-NSM ἀρκούμενος (1x)
3Jn 1:10 And not being·satisfied with these·things, neither

G0714.5 V-PPP-NPM ἀρκούμενοι (1x)
Heb 13:5 being·satisfied with·the·things being·at·hand, for

G0715 ἄρκτος árktôs *n.* (1x)
Roots:G0714 xLangEquiv:H1677 A1678

G0715 N-GSF ἄρκτου (1x)
Rv 13:2 its feet *were* as *the feet* of·a·bear, and its mouth as a·

G0716 ἅρμα hárma *n.* (4x)
Roots:G0142 G0001 Compare:G4480 See:G0719 xLangAlso:H7393 H4818

G0716 N-ASN ἅρμα (1x)
Ac 8:38 he·commandingly·ordered the chariot to·stand·still.

G0716 N-DSN ἅρματι (1x)
Ac 8:29 "Go·alongside and be·tightly·joined to·this chariot."

G0716 N-GSN ἅρματος (1x)
Ac 8:28 and sitting·down in his chariot, and he·was·reading·

G0716 N-GPN ἁρμάτων (1x)
Rv 9:9 wings *was* as the·sound of·chariots, of·many horses

G0717 Ἀρ•μα•γεδδών Armagẽddőn *n/l.* (1x)
Ἀρ•Με•Γιδδών HarMêGiddőn [Greek, Octuagint]
הַר־מְגִדּוֹן HạrMegịdôn [Hebrew]
Roots:H2022 H4023 xLangEquiv:H2037-1

G0717.2 N/L-NSN Ἁρμαγεδδών (1x)
Rv 16:16 being·called HarMeGiddon *(Mountain of·Great·*

G0718 ἁρμόζω harmőzō *v.* (1x)
Roots:G0719 Compare:G3423

G0718.3 V-AMI-1S ἡρμοσάμην (1x)
2Co 11:2 with·a·jealousy of·God, for I·betrothed yeu to·one

G0719 ἁρμός harmős *n.* (1x)
Roots:G0142 G0001 Compare:G0860 G4886 See:G0716

G0719 N-GPM ἁρμῶν (1x)
Heb 4:12 and spirit, and even of·the·joints and marrow, and

G0720 ἀ•ρνέομαι arnẽômai *v.* (31x)
Roots:G0001 G4483 Compare:G0550 G0533

G0720.1 V-PNP-NSM ἀρνούμενος (1x)
1Jn 2:22 if·not the·one who·contradicts·by·saying that Jesus

G0720.2 V-FDI-1S ἀρνήσομαι (1x)
Mt 10:33 the men·of·clay†, him I·also shall·deny before my

G0720.2 V-FDI-3S ἀρνήσεται (1x)
2Ti 2:12 If we·are·denying *him*, he·also shall·be·denying us.

G0720.2 V-PNI-1P ἀρνούμεθα (1x)
2Ti 2:12 "If we·are·denying *him*, he·also shall·be·denying us

G0720.2 V-PNI-3P ἀρνοῦνται (1x)
Tit 1:16 ·seen God, but in·the works they·deny *him*, being

G0720.2 V-PNP-GPM ἀρνουμένων (1x)
Lk 8:45 of·me?" But with·everyone denying *it*, Peter and

G0720.2 V-PNP-NSM ἀρνούμενος (2x)
1Jn 2:22 ·Anointed-One, the·one who·is·denying the Father
1Jn 2:23 Every one who·is·denying the Son does·not·even
G0720.2 V-PNP-NPM ἀρνούμενοι (2x)
Jud 1:4 God into debauchery and denying the only Master,
2Pe 2:1 of·total·destruction— even denying *the* Master, the·
G0720.2 V-INI-3S ἠρνεῖτο (1x)
Mk 14:70 And he·was·denying *it* again. And a·little·while
G0720.2 V-ADI-2S ἠρνήσω (2x)
Rv 2:13 ·securely·hold my name and did·not deny my trust,
Rv 3:8 my Redemptive-word, and did·not deny my name.
G0720.2 V-ADI-2P ἠρνήσασθε (2x)
Ac 3:13 yeu·yeurselves handed·over, and yeu·denied him in
Ac 3:14 "But yeu denied the Holy and Righteous·One, and
G0720.2 V-ADI-3S ἠρνήσατο (7x)
Jn 1:20 And he·affirmed and did·not deny, but he·affirmed,
Jn 18:25 his disciples?" That·man denied *it* and declared,
Jn 18:27 Accordingly, Peter denied *it* again, and
Lk 22:57 But he·denied him, saying, "Woman, I·do·not
Mt 26:70 But he·denied *it* before *them* all, saying, "I·do·not
Mt 26:72 And again he·denied *it* with an·oath, "I·do·not
Mk 14:68 But he·denied *it*, saying, "I·do·not personally·
G0720.2 V-ADN ἀρνήσασθαι (2x)
Ac 4:16 ·in JeruSalem, and we·are·not able to·deny *it*.
2Ti 2:13 trustworthy; he·is·not able to·deny himself."
G0720.2 V-ADP-NSM ἀρνησάμενος (1x)
Lk 12:9 But the·one denying me in·the·sight of·the men·of·
G0720.2 V-ADP-NPM ἀρνησάμενοι (1x)
Tit 2:12 us in·order·that, after·denying the irreverence and
G0720.2 V-ADS-3S ἀρνήσηται (1x)
Mt 10:33 But whoever should·deny me before the men·of·
G0720.2 V-RDI-3S ἤρνηται (1x)
1Ti 5:8 for·the family·members, he·has·denied the trust and
G0720.2 V-RNP-NPM ἠρνημένοι (1x)
2Ti 3:5 of·devout·reverence, but having·denied its power.
G0720.3 V-ADI-3S ἠρνήσατο (1x)
Heb 11:24 full·grown) renounced being·referred·to·as son
G0720.3 V-ADI-3P ἠρνήσαντο (1x)
Ac 7:35 "This Moses whom they·renounced, declaring,

G0721 ἀρνίον arníôn *n.* (33x)
טְלָא ṭᵉlaʾ
Roots:G0704 G2444-3 Compare:G4263 G0286 G0285-1 See:G5008 G3957 xLangEquiv:H2922
G0721.1 N-APN ἀρνία (1x)
Jn 21:15 He·says to·him, "Feed my little·lambs."
G0721.2 N-DSN ἀρνίῳ (1x)
Rv 13:11 ·having two horns like a·young·male·lamb, and it·
G0721.3 N-NSN ἀρνίον (8x)
Rv 5:6 *the* midst of·the Elders, a·Lamb standing as having·
Rv 5:12 "Worthy is the Lamb (the·one having·been·
Rv 6:1 And I·saw when the Lamb opened·up *the* first from·
Rv 7:17 because the Lamb, the·one amidst the throne, shall·
Rv 14:1 I·saw, and behold, a·Lamb standing on the Mount
Rv 17:14 with the Lamb, and the Lamb shall·conquer them,
Rv 21:22 God Almighty, and the Lamb are its Temple.
Rv 21:23 of·God illuminated it, and the Lamb *is* its lantern.
G0721.3 N-DSN ἀρνίῳ (4x)
Rv 5:13 upon the throne and unto·the Lamb, *be* the blessing
Rv 7:10 ·is·sitting·down upon the throne and to·the Lamb!"
Rv 14:4 are the·ones following the Lamb wherever he·may·
Rv 14:4 ·of·clay†, *being* a·firstfruit to·God and to·the Lamb.
G0721.3 N-GSN ἀρνίου (16x)
Rv 5:8 Elders fell·down in·the·sight of·the Lamb, each·one
Rv 6:16 throne, and from the WRATH OF·THE LAMB,
Rv 7:9 in·the·sight of·the Lamb, having·been·arrayed·with
Rv 7:14 ·whitened their long·robes in the blood of·the Lamb.
Rv 12:11 him through the blood of·the Lamb, and through
Rv 13:8 of·the Lamb having·been·slaughtered from *the*
Rv 14:10 of·the holy angels, and in·the·sight of·the Lamb.
Rv 15:3 a·slave of·God, and the song of·the Lamb, saying,
Rv 17:14 These shall·wage·war with the Lamb, and the
Rv 19:7 because the Wedding of·the Lamb did·come and his
Rv 19:9 ·forth to the Wedding Supper of·the Lamb.'" And
Rv 21:9 I·shall·show you the Bride, the Lamb's wife."
Rv 21:14 *the* names of·the twelve ambassadors of·the Lamb.
Rv 21:27 ·been·written in the Lamb's official·scroll of·the
Rv 22:1 ·forth out of·the throne of·God and of·the Lamb.
Rv 22:3 but the throne of·God and of·the Lamb shall·be in it;
EG0721.3 (3x)
Rv 6:5 And when *the Lamb* opened·up the third official·seal,
Rv 6:9 And when *the Lamb* opened·up the fifth official·seal,
Rv 8:1 And when *the Lamb* opened·up the seventh official·

G0722 ἀροτριάω arôtriáō *v.* (3x)
ἀροτριόω arôtrióō [alternate]
Roots:G0723 Compare:G1090 G3504-1 See:G0721-1 G0721-2 G0723-1 xLangAlso:H2790 H5214
G0722 V-PAN ἀροτριᾶν (1x)
1Co 9:10 the·one plowing ought to·plow in expectation, and
G0722 V-PAP-ASM ἀροτριῶντα (1x)
Lk 17:7 ·among yeu having a·slave plowing or shepherding,
G0722 V-PAP-NSM ἀροτριῶν (1x)
1Co 9:10 ·written, because the·one plowing ought to·plow

G0723 ἄροτρον árôtrôn *n.* (1x)
See:G0722 G0723-1 xLangAlso:H0855 H4173
G0723 N-ASN ἄροτρον (1x)
Lk 9:62 upon·throwing his hand to a·plow and *then* looking

G0724 ἁρπαγή harpagḗ *n.* (3x)
Roots:G0726 Compare:G4124 G4811-2 See:G0725
G0724.1 N-ASF ἁρπαγήν (1x)
Heb 10:34 with joy the plundering of·yeur holdings,
G0724.2 N-GSF ἁρπαγῆς (2x)
Lk 11:39 yeur inward·part overflows with·extortion and evil.
Mt 23:25 out of·extortion and from·a·lack·of·self-restraint.

G0725 ἁρπαγμός harpagmós *n.* (1x)
Roots:G0726 Compare:G4661 G4307-2 See:G0724
G0725.2 N-ASM ἁρπαγμόν (1x)
Php 2:6 resolutely·considered it not open·plunder to·be equal

G0726 ἁρπάζω harpázō *v.* (13x)
Roots:G0138 Compare:G1807 G4506 See:G0724 G1283 G0725 G0727
G0726.1 V-PAI-3P ἁρπάζουσιν (1x)
Mt 11:12 is·seized·by·force, and forceful·men seize it.
G0726.1 V-PAN ἁρπάζειν (1x)
Jn 6:15 they·are·about to·come and seize him in·order·that
G0726.1 V-AAN ἁρπάσαι (1x)
Ac 23:10 upon·walking·down, to·seize him from·among
G0726.2 V-FAI-3S ἁρπάσει (1x)
Jn 10:28 and someone shall·not snatch them from·out of·
G0726.2 V-2FPI-1P ἁρπαγησόμεθα (1x)
1Th 4:17 shall·be·snatched·up at·the·same·time together
G0726.2 V-PAI-3S ἁρπάζει (2x)
Jn 10:12 flees; and the wolf snatches them and scatters the
Mt 13:19 *it*, the Evil·One comes and snatches·up the *seed*
G0726.2 V-PAN ἁρπάζειν (1x)
Jn 10:29 and not·even·one is·able to·snatch *them* from·out
G0726.2 V-PAP-NPM ἁρπάζοντες (1x)
Jud 1:23 save with a·fear while·snatching *them* from·out of·
G0726.2 V-AAI-3S ἥρπασεν (1x)
Ac 8:39 water, Yahweh's Spirit snatched Philippe, and the
G0726.2 V-2API-3S ἡρπάγη (1x)
2Co 12:4 how he·was·snatched·up into Paradise, and heard
G0726.2 V-API-3S ἡρπάσθη (1x)
Rv 12:5 of·iron; and her child was·snatched·up to God, and
G0726.2 V-2APP-ASM ἁρπαγέντα (1x)
2Co 12:2 ·knows), such·a·man being·snatched·up unto *the*

G0727 ἅρπαξ hárpax *adj.* (5x)
Roots:G0726 See:G0724 G0725
G0727.1 A-NSM ἅρπαξ (1x)
1Co 5:11 or *is* violently·or·exceedingly·greedy, no, not·even
G0727.1 A-NPM ἅρπαγες (3x)
Lk 18:11 ·clay† *are*: violently·or·exceedingly·greedy·men,
Mt 7:15 but inwardly, they·are violently·greedy wolves.
1Co 6:10 nor violently·or·exceedingly·greedy·men shall·
G0727.1 A-DPM ἅρπαξιν (1x)
1Co 5:10 or ones·who·are·violently·or·exceedingly·greedy,

G0728 ἀρραβών arrhabṓn *n.* (3x)
עֲרָבוֹן ʿărạbôn [Hebrew]
Roots:H6162 Compare:G1862 G3866 G3908
G0728 N-NSM ἀρραβών (1x)
Eph 1:14 who is the earnest·deposit of·our inheritance for
G0728 N-ASM ἀρραβῶνα (2x)
2Co 1:22 ·sealing us and giving the earnest·deposit of·the
2Co 5:5 the·one also giving to·us the earnest·deposit of·the

G0729 ἄ•ρραφος árrhaphôs *adj.* (1x)
Roots:G0001 G4476
G0729.2 A-NSM ἄρραφος (1x)
Jn 19:23 But the inner·tunic was without·seam, as·a·result

G0730 ἄρρην árrhēn *n.* (9x)
ἄρσην ársēn
Roots:G0142 Compare:G2338 See:G0732-1 xLangEquiv:H2145
G0730 N-NSN ἄρσεν (2x)
Lk 2:23 Every male thoroughly·opening·up a·primal·womb
Gal 3:28 nor·even free, there·is·not therein male and female,
G0730 N-NPM ἄρσενες (2x)
Rm 1:27 And likewise also the males, leaving the natural
Rm 1:27 in their lust toward one·another; males with males
G0730 N-ASM ἄρρενα (2x)
Rv 12:5 ·and·birthed a·son, a·male who imminently·intends
Rv 12:13 the woman who reproduced·and·birthed the male.
G0730 N-ASN ἄρσεν (2x)
Mt 19:4 from *the* beginning "made them male and female,"
Mk 10:6 beginning, God " made them male and female."
G0730 N-DPM ἄρσεσιν (1x)
Rm 1:27 one·another; males with males performing the

G0731 ἄ•ρρητος árrhētôs *adj.* (1x)
Roots:G0001 G4490 Compare:G0411 G0215
G0731.2 A-APN ἄρρητα (1x)
2Co 12:4 into Paradise, and heard inexpressible utterances,

G0732 ἄ•ρρωστος árrhōstôs *adj.* (5x)
Roots:G0001 G4517
G0732 A-NPM ἄρρωστοι (1x)
1Co 11:30 many *are* weak and unhealthy among yeu, and a·
G0732 A-APM ἀρρώστους (3x)
Mt 14:14 ·and·cured the unhealthy·ones *among* them.
Mk 6:13 many that·were·unhealthy and were·both·relieving·
Mk 16:18 they·shall·lay *their* hands on unhealthy·ones, and
G0732 A-DPM ἀρρώστοις (1x)
Mk 6:5 upon·a·few unhealthy·ones *whom* he·both·relieved·

G0733 ἀρσενο•κοίτης arsênôkóitēs *n.* (2x)
Roots:G0730 G2845
G0733.1 N-NPM ἀρσενοκοῖται (1x)
1Co 6:9 effeminate·men, nor men·who·have·sex·with·men,
G0733.1 N-DPM ἀρσενοκοίταις (1x)
1Ti 1:10 ·immoral·men, for·men·who·have·sex·with·men,

G0734 Ἀρτεμᾶς Artêmâs *n/p.* (1x)
Roots:G0735 G1435
G0734.2 N/P-ASM Ἀρτεμᾶν (1x)
Tit 3:12 Whenever I·shall·send Artemas to you, or Tychicus,

G0735 Ἄρτεμις Ártêmis *n/p.* (5x)
Roots:G0737 See:G0736
G0735.2 N/P-NSF Ἄρτεμις (2x)
Ac 19:28 ·out, saying, "Great *is* Artemis of·the·Ephesians."
Ac 19:34 yelling·out, "Great *is* Artemis of·the·Ephesians."
G0735.2 N/P-GSF Ἀρτέμιδος (3x)
Ac 19:24 silver temples of·Artemis, personally·furnished no
Ac 19:27 of·the great goddess Artemis to·be·reckoned as
Ac 19:35 temple·custodian of·the great goddess Artemis, and

G0736 ἀρτέμων artêmōn *n.* (1x)
Roots:G0737 Compare:G0740 G0142
G0736.2 N-ASM ἀρτέμονα (1x)
Ac 27:40 and upon·hoisting the topsail to·the blowing·wind

G0737 ἄρτι árti *adv.* (36x)
Roots:G0142 Compare:G0740
G0737.1 ADV ἄρτι (21x)

Jn 9:19 was·born blind? So·then at·this·moment, how does·
Jn 9:25 how·that being blind, at·this·moment, I·look·about.
Jn 13:7 do·not personally·know at·this·moment, but you·
Jn 13:33 to·come,' so·also do·I·say to·yeu at·this·moment.
Jn 13:37 to·follow you at·this·moment? I·shall·lay·down my
Jn 16:12 ·yet yeu·are·not able to·bear·them at·this·moment.
Jn 16:31 answered them, "*So* at·this·moment, do·yeu·trust?
Gal 1:9 ·have·already·stated, so at·this·moment I·say again,
Gal 1:10 For at·this·moment, do·I·comply·with men·of·
Gal 4:20 alongside yeu at·this·moment and to·change my
Mt 3:15 him, "Allow *me* at·this·moment, for in·this·manner
Mt 9:18 just·completely·died at·this·moment, but·yet
Mt 26:53 that I·am·not able at·this·moment to·implore my
1Pe 1:6 being·grieved a·little·bit at·this·moment (though it·
1Pe 1:8 not clearly·seeing at·this·moment but trusting *him*,
1Th 3:6 But at·this·moment, with·TimoThy coming from yeu
2Th 2:7 ·one holding·*him*·down at·this·moment *is·doing so*
1Co 13:12 For at·this·moment, we·look·about through a·
1Co 13:12 face to face. At·this·moment, I·know from·out
1Co 16:7 I·do·not want to·see yeu at·this·moment in route,
Rv 12:10 in the heaven, "At·this·moment did·come the

G0737.2 ADV ἄρτι (6x)
Jn 1:51 to·yeu, from this·moment·on, yeu·shall·gaze·upon
Jn 13:19 From this·moment·on, I·relate *it* to·yeu before it·
Jn 14:7 also, and from this·moment·on, yeu·do·know him,
Mt 23:39 yeu·should·not see me from this·moment·on, until
Mt 26:29 ·not drink from this·moment·on from·out of·this
Mt 26:64 to·yeu, from this·moment·on, yeu·shall·gaze·upon

G0737.3 ADV ἄρτι (8x)
Jn 2:10 ·purposefully·kept the good wine until this·moment."
Jn 5:17 My Father works until this·moment, and·I·also work.
Jn 16:24 Unto this·moment, yeu·did·not request not·even·
Mt 11:12 days of·John the Immerser until this·moment, the
1Co 4:13 an·offscouring of·all·things unto this·moment.
1Co 8:7 *still·accustomed·to* the idol unto this·moment, eat as
1Co 15:6 the majority remain unto this·moment, but some
1Jn 2:9 brother, is in the darkness even·unto this·moment.

G0737.4 ADV ἄρτι (1x)
1Co 4:11 Even·up·to the very·present hour, also we·hunger,

G0738 ἀρτι•γέννητος artigénnētôs *adj.* (1x)
Roots:G0737 G1084

G0738.1 A-NPN ἀρτιγέννητα (1x)
1Pe 2:2 as newborn babies, eagerly·crave the rational milk

G0739 ἄρτιος ártiôs *adj.* (1x)
Roots:G0737 See:G0535

G0739.3 A-NSM ἄρτιος (1x)
2Ti 3:17 may·be fully·developed, having·been·properly·

G0740 ἄρτος ártôs *n.* (102x)
Roots:G0142 Compare:G0106 G1945-5 See:G3957 xLangAlso:H3899 A3900

G0740.1 N-NSM ἄρτος (10x)
Jn 6:33 for the bread of·God is the·one descending from·out
Jn 6:35 "I AM the bread of·life-above. The·one who·is·
Jn 6:41 "I AM the bread, the·one descending out of·the
Jn 6:48 I AM the bread of·the life-above.
Jn 6:50 This is the bread, the·one descending out of·the
Jn 6:51 I AM the living bread, the·one descending out of·the
Jn 6:51 ·age, and also the bread that I·myself shall·give is
Jn 6:58 "This is the bread, the·one descending out of·the
Lk 4:3 declare to·this stone that it·should·become bread."
1Co 10:17 *being* the many, we·are one bread *and* one Body.

G0740.1 N-NPM ἄρτοι (3x)
Jn 6:7 "Two·hundred denarii *worth* of·bread is·not sufficient
Mt 4:3 declare that these stones should·become bread."
Mt 15:33 such·a·vast·quantity·of bread in a·barren·

G0740.1 N-ASM ἄρτον (34x)
Jn 6:23 to·the place where they·ate the bread, with·the Lord
Jn 6:31 "He·gave them bread from·out of·the heaven to·eat
Jn 6:32 has·not given yeu the bread from·out of·the heaven,
Jn 6:32 gives yeu the true bread from·out of·the heaven,
Jn 6:34 "Lord, always give us this bread."
Jn 6:58 The·one chewing this bread shall·live into the
Jn 13:18 "The·one chewing the bread with me lifted·up his
Jn 21:9 ·fish being·set·out laying·upon *it*, and·also bread.
Jn 21:13 Jesus comes and takes the bread and gives *it* to·
Lk 7:33 has·come neither eating bread nor drinking wine,
Lk 9:3 staffs, nor knapsack, neither bread, neither money;
Lk 11:3 'Give us each day our sustaining bread.
Lk 11:11 *if* the son shall·request bread, ¿! shall·he·hand
Lk 14:1 of·the chief Pharisees to·eat bread on·the·Sabbath,
Lk 14:15 "Supremely·blessed *is·he* that shall·eat bread in the
Lk 24:30 with them, after·taking the bread, he·blessed *it*,
Ac 2:46 Sanctuary·Atrium and breaking bread in·each house,
Ac 20:7 having·been·gathered·together to·break bread, Paul
Ac 20:11 Then after·walking·up and breaking bread, and
Ac 27:35 these·things and taking bread, he·gave·thanks to·
Mt 6:11 'Give us this·day our sustaining bread.
Mt 7:9 who if his son should·request bread, ¿! shall·hand
Mt 15:2 wash their hands whenever they·should·eat bread."
Mt 15:26 not good to·take the children's bread and to·cast *it*
Mk 3:20 ·for them not to·be·able so·much·as to·eat bread.
Mk 6:8 No knapsack, no bread, *and* no copper·coinage in
Mk 7:5 but·rather eat the bread with·unwashed hands?
Mk 7:27 not good to·take the children's bread and to·cast *it*
2Th 3:8 ·we·eat personally·from anyone's bread, but·rather
2Th 3:12 while·working, they·should·eat their·own bread.
1Co 10:16 of·the Anointed-One? The bread which we·break
1Co 11:26 as·often·as yeu·should·eat this bread, and should·
1Co 11:27 whoever should·eat this bread or should·drink the
2Co 9:10 to·the·one sowing, and bread for feeding·upon,

G0740.1 N-APM ἄρτους (10x)
Jn 6:5 ·what·source shall·we·buy bread in·order·that these
Mt 16:5 *of·the sea*, his disciples had·forgotten to·take bread.
Mt 16:7 "*It·is* because we·did·not take bread."
Mt 16:8 among yeurselves that yeu·took no bread?
Mk 6:36 villages, they·should·buy bread for·themselves, for
Mk 6:37 two·hundred denarii *worth* of·bread, and should·
Mk 7:2 some of·his disciples eating bread with·defiled hands
Mk 8:14 Now *the disciples* forgot to·take bread, and except
Mk 8:16 "*It·is* because we·do·not have bread."
Mk 8:17 *·is* because yeu·do·not have bread? Do·yeu·not·yet

G0740.1 N-DSM ἄρτῳ (2x)
Lk 4:4 man·of·clay† shall·live not upon bread alone, but·
Mt 4:4 A·man·of·clay† shall·live not upon bread alone, but·

G0740.1 N-GSM ἄρτου (7x)
Jn 6:51 ·man should·eat from·out of·this bread, he·shall·live
Lk 24:35 ·was·known to·them in the breaking of·the bread.
Ac 2:42 and in·the breaking of·the bread, and in·the prayers
Mt 16:11 *this* to·yeu not concerning bread, *but·rather* to·
Mt 16:12 to·beware of·the leaven of·bread, but·rather of·the
1Co 10:17 ·and·belong *by·eating* from·out of·the one bread.
1Co 11:28 let·him·eat from·out of·the bread and drink from·

G0740.1 N-GPM ἄρτων (2x)
Lk 15:17 hired·men have·an·abundance of·bread, and I·
Mk 8:4 be·able to·stuff these·men full with·bread, here in a·

EG0740.1 (1x)
Mt 14:19 and the disciples *gave bread* to·the crowds.

G0740.2 N-NPM ἄρτοι (1x)
Lk 9:13 ·are not more than five loaves·of·bread and two fish,

G0740.2 N-ASM ἄρτον (1x)
Mk 8:14 and except *for* one loaf·of·bread, they·were·not

G0740.2 N-APM ἄρτους (18x)
Jn 6:9 who has five barley loaves·of·bread, and two small·
Jn 6:11 Then Jesus took the loaves·of·bread, and after·
Lk 9:16 And after·taking the five loaves·of·bread and the
Lk 11:5 'Friend, kindly·lend me three loaves·of·bread,
Mt 14:17 *anything* here except five loaves·of·bread and two
Mt 14:19 and upon·taking the five loaves·of·bread and the
Mt 14:19 *bread*, he·gave the loaves·of·bread to·the disciples
Mt 15:34 ·them, "How·many loaves·of·bread do·yeu·have?
Mt 15:36 And after·taking the seven loaves·of·bread and the
Mt 16:9 the five loaves·of·bread of·the five·thousand *men*,
Mt 16:10 the seven loaves·of·bread of·the four·thousand *men*
Mk 6:38 ·them, "How·many loaves·of·bread do·yeu·have?
Mk 6:41 And after·taking the five loaves·of·bread and the
Mk 6:41 he·fully·broke the loaves·of·bread and was·giving
Mk 6:44 the·ones eating of·the loaves·of·bread were about
Mk 8:5 ·of them, "How·many loaves·of·bread do·yeu·have?
Mk 8:6 the seven loaves·of·bread *and* upon·giving·thanks,
Mk 8:19 When I·broke the five loaves·of·bread among the

G0740.2 N-DPM ἄρτοις (1x)
Mk 6:52 comprehend concerning the loaves·of·bread, for

G0740.2 N-GPM ἄρτων (2x)
Jn 6:13 from·out of·the five barley loaves·of·bread, which
Jn 6:26 from·out of·the loaves·of·bread and were·stuffed·full

EG0740.2 (2x)
Mk 8:6 ·giving·thanks, he·broke *the loaves·of·bread*, and
Mk 8:20 when *I·broke* the seven *loaves·of·bread* among the

G0740.3 N-APM ἄρτους (3x)
Lk 6:4 took and ate the Intended·Show bread, which it·is·
Mt 12:4 of·God and ate the Intended·Show bread, which
Mk 2:26 and ate the Intended·Show bread, which it·is·not

G0740.3 N-GPM ἄρτων (1x)
Heb 9:2 and the Intended·Show bread, which is·referred·to·

G0740.4 N-ASM ἄρτον (4x)
Lk 22:19 And after·taking *unleavened* bread *and* giving·
Mt 26:26 after·taking the *unleavened* bread and blessing *it*,
Mk 14:22 after·taking *the unleavened* bread *and* blessing *it*
1Co 11:23 he·was·handed·over, took *unleavened* bread,

G0741 ἀρτύω artýō *v.* (3x)
Roots:G0142

G0741 V-FAI-2P ἀρτύσετε (1x)
Mk 9:50 ·become unsalty, with what shall·yeu·season it?

G0741 V-FPI-3S ἀρτυθήσεται (1x)
Lk 14:34 ·bland, in what·manner shall·it·be·seasoned?

G0741 V-RPP-NSM ἠρτυμένος (1x)
Col 4:6 *is to·be* with grace having·been·seasoned with·salt,

G0742 Ἀρφαξάδ Arphaxád *n/p.* (1x)
אַרְפַּכְשַׁד 'arpakshad [Hebrew]
Roots:H0775 See:G2627

G0742 N/P-PRI Ἀρφαξάδ (1x)
Lk 3:36 *son* of·Qainan, *son* of·Arphaxad, *son* of·Shem, *son*

G0743 ἀρχ•άγγελος archángêlos *n.* (2x)
Roots:G0757 G0032

G0743.1 N-NSM ἀρχάγγελος (1x)
Jud 1:9 Now MiChaEl the chief·angel, when verbally·

G0743.1 N-GSM ἀρχαγγέλου (1x)
1Th 4:16 with battle·cry, with a·chief·angel's voice, and

G0744 ἀρχαῖος archaîos *adj.* (12x)
Roots:G0746

G0744.1 A-NSM ἀρχαῖος (1x)
Rv 12:9 the great Dragon was·cast·out, the original Serpent,

G0744.1 A-ASM ἀρχαῖον (1x)
Rv 20:2 ·held the Dragon, the original Serpent, who is

G0744.2 A-NPN ἀρχαῖα (1x)
2Co 5:17 creation. The ancient·things passed·away; behold,

G0744.2 A-DPM ἀρχαίοις (3x)
Mt 5:21 Yeu·heard that it·was·uttered to·the ancient·ones,
Mt 5:27 Yeu·heard that it·was·uttered to·the ancient·ones,
Mt 5:33 yeu·heard that it·was·uttered to·the ancient·ones,

G0744.2 A-GSM ἀρχαίου (1x)
2Pe 2:5 and *if* he·did·not spare *the* ancient world, but·rather

G0744.2 A-GPM ἀρχαίων (2x)
Lk 9:8 by·others that one of·the ancient prophets rose·up.
Lk 9:19 *say* that some prophet of·the ancient·ones rose·up."

G0744.2 A-GPF ἀρχαίων (1x)
Ac 15:21 For Moses, from·out of·ancient generations, has

G0744.3 A-DSM ἀρχαίῳ (1x)
Ac 21:16 Mnason of·Cyprus, an·early disciple, with·whom

G0744.3 A-GPF ἀρχαίων (1x)
Ac 15:7 are·fully·acquainted·with how from the·early days,

G0745 Ἀρχέ•λαος Archélaôs *n/p.* (1x)
Roots:G0757 G2992 See:G2264 G0067

G0745.2 N/P-NSM Ἀρχέλαος (1x)
Mt 2:22 But upon·hearing that ArcheLaos reigns in Judea in·

G0746 ἀρχή archḗ *n.* (58x)
Roots:G0756 Compare:G0758 xLangAlso:H7225 H8462

G0746.1 N-NSF ἀρχή (7x)
Mt 24:8 But all these *are the* beginning of·birth·pangs.
Mk 1:1 A·beginning of·the good·news of·Jesus Anointed,
Col 1:18 *One himself* who is *the* beginning, *the* firstborn
Rv 1:8 the Alpha and the Omega, beginning and end," says
Rv 3:14 true witness, the beginning of·the creation of·God:
Rv 21:6 Alpha and the Omega, the beginning and the end.
Rv 22:13 the Alpha and the Omega, beginning and end, the

G0746.1 N-NPF ἀρχαί (1x)
Mk 13:8 These *are the* beginnings of·birth·pangs.

G0746.1 N-ASF ἀρχήν (3x)
Jn 8:25 the·same·which I·spoke to·yeu from·the beginning.
Heb 3:14 ·hold·onto the beginning of·the firm·assurance,
Heb 7:3 without·lineage, having neither beginning of·days,

G0746.1 N-APF ἀρχάς (1x)
Heb 1:10 O·Lord, in *the* beginning laid·a·foundation·for the

G0746.1 N-DSF ἀρχῇ (4x)
Jn 1:1 At *the* beginning was the Word, and the Word was
Jn 1:2 The·same was at *the* beginning alongside God.
Ac 11:15 upon them, just·as also upon us at *the* beginning.
Php 4:15 that at *the* beginning of·the good·news *among·yeu*

G0746.1 N-GSF ἀρχῆς (24x)
Jn 6:64 ·known from·among *the* beginning who they·are,
Jn 8:44 was a·man-killer† from *the* beginning, and he·does·
Jn 15:27 because yeu·are with me from *the* beginning.
Jn 16:4 ·not declare to·yeu at *the* beginning, because I·was
Lk 1:2 the·ones from *the* beginning handed·*them*·down to·us
Ac 26:4 youth (the·one occurring since beginning in my·own
Mt 19:4 the·one making *them* from *the* beginning "made
Mt 19:8 but from *the* beginning it·has·not happened in·this·
Mt 24:21 been since *the* world's beginning until the present,
Mk 10:6 But from creation's beginning, God " made them
Mk 13:19 happened from *the* beginning of·creation which
2Pe 3:4 ·manner *as they·were* from creation's beginning."
2Th 2:13 , because from *the* beginning, God chose yeu for
1Jn 1:1 That·which was from *the* beginning, which we·
1Jn 2:7 which yeu·were·having from *the* beginning. The old
1Jn 2:7 is the word which yeu·heard from *the* beginning.
1Jn 2:13 ·known the·one *who·is* from *the* beginning. I·write
1Jn 2:14 the·one *who·is* from *the* beginning. I·already·wrote
1Jn 2:24 yeu already·heard from *the* beginning. If that·which
1Jn 2:24 ·already·heard from *the* beginning should·remain in
1Jn 3:8 the Slanderer morally·fails from *the* beginning. For
1Jn 3:11 that yeu·heard from *the* beginning, that we·should·
2Jn 1:5 that·which we·were·having from *the* beginning, that
2Jn 1:6 ·as yeu·heard from *the* beginning, yeu·should·walk

G0746.2 N-ASF ἀρχήν (1x)
Jn 2:11 Jesus did this initiating of·miraculous·signs in Qanah

G0746.2 N-GSF ἀρχῆς (1x)
Heb 6:1 leaving the initiating Redemptive-word of·the

G0746.3 N-ASF ἀρχήν (1x)
Heb 2:3 after·receiving an·initial *announcement* being·

G0746.3 N-GSF ἀρχῆς (1x)
Heb 5:12 ·which *are* the initial fundamental·principles of·the

G0746.5 N-NPF ἀρχαί (2x)
Rm 8:38 life†, nor angels, nor principalities, nor powers,
Col 1:16 or dominions, or principalities, or authorities.

G0746.5 N-ASF ἀρχήν (2x)
Jud 1:6 ·keeping their·own principality, but·rather leaving·
1Co 15:24 ·fully·render·impotent every principality and all

G0746.5 N-APF ἀρχάς (2x)
Eph 6:12 ·against the principalities, specifically·against the
Col 2:15 after·utterly·despoiling the principalities and the

G0746.5 N-DPF ἀρχαῖς (1x)
Eph 3:10 ·made·known now to·the principalities and to·the

G0746.5 N-GSF ἀρχῆς (2x)
Eph 1:21 high·above all principality and authority, power
Col 2:10 who is the head of·all principality and authority—

G0746.6 N-DSF ἀρχῇ (1x)
Lk 20:20 to·hand him over to·the jurisdiction and authority

G0746.6 N-DPF ἀρχαῖς (1x)
Tit 3:1 to·submit·themselves to·jurisdictions and authorities,

G0746.7 N-APF ἀρχάς (1x)
Lk 12:11 yeu before the gatherings, the magistrates, and the

G0746.9 N-DPF ἀρχαῖς (2x)
Ac 10:11 ·been·tied at·the·four corners and being·sent·down
Ac 11:5 from·out of·the heaven by·four corners, and it·came

G0747 ἀρχ•ηγός archēgós *n.* (5x)
Roots:G0746 G0071 Compare:G0159

G0747.2 N-ASM ἀρχηγόν (4x)
Ac 3:15 And yeu·killed the Initiator of·the life-above, whom
Ac 5:31 God elevated this Initiator *of·the life-above, this*
Heb 2:10 to glory, to·make the Initiator of·their Salvation
Heb 12:2 to YeShua, the Initiator and Complete·Finisher of·

EG0747.2 (1x)
Heb 2:11 cause, *YeShua the Initiator* is·not ashamed to·call

G0748 ἀρχ•ιερατικός archiêratikós *adj.* (1x)
Roots:G0746 G2413 See:G0749

G0748 A-GSN ἀρχιερατικοῦ (1x)
Ac 4:6 ·many·as were from·among *the* high·priest's kindred.

G0749 ἀρχ•ιερεύς archiêrêús *n.* (127x)
Roots:G0746 G2409 See:G0748 G4316 xLangAlso:H3548

G0749.2 N-NPM ἀρχιερεῖς (38x)
Jn 7:32 Pharisees and the chief·priests dispatched assistants
Jn 11:47 Accordingly, the chief·priests and the Pharisees
Jn 11:57 And both the chief·priests and the Pharisees had·
Jn 12:10 But the chief·priests took·counsel in·order·that
Jn 18:35 Your·own nation and the chief·priests handed you
Jn 19:6 Accordingly, when the chief·priests and the
Jn 19:15 King?" The chief·priests answered, "We·have no
Jn 19:21 Accordingly, the chief·priests of·the Judeans were·
Lk 19:47 But the chief·priests and the scribes and the
Lk 20:1 ·the·good·news, the chief·priests and the scribes
Lk 20:19 Then the chief·priests and the scribes in·the same
Lk 22:2 And the chief·priests and the scribes were·seeking
Lk 22:66 ·gathered·together (both chief·priests and scribes),
Lk 23:10 And the chief·priests and the scribes stood, legally·
Lk 24:20 And·also specifically·how the chief·priests and our
Ac 4:23 what·many·things *that* the chief·priests and the
Ac 5:24 Sanctuary·Estate and the chief·priests heard these
Ac 25:15 being at JeruSalem, the chief·priests and the elders
Mt 21:15 But the chief·priests and the scribes were·greatly·
Mt 21:23 ·Atrium while·instructing, the chief·priests and the
Mt 21:45 his parables, the chief·priests and the Pharisees
Mt 26:3 At·that·time, the chief·priests, and the scribes, and
Mt 26:59 Now the chief·priests and the elders and all the
Mt 27:1 ·dawn occurring, all the chief·priests and the elders
Mt 27:6 And the chief·priests, taking the pieces·of·silver,
Mt 27:20 But the chief·priests and the elders persuaded the
Mt 27:41 *him* also, the chief·priests with the scribes and
Mt 27:62 after the preparation·day, the chief·priests and the
Mk 11:18 And the scribes and the chief·priests heard *it* and
Mk 11:27 along the Sanctuary·Atrium, the chief·priests, the
Mk 14:1 And the chief·priests and the scribes were·seeking
Mk 14:53 ·priest, and all the chief·priests and the elders and
Mk 14:55 Now the chief·priests and all the joint·council·of·
Mk 15:1 upon the dawn, the chief·priests, after·making
Mk 15:3 And the chief·priests were·legally·accusing him of·
Mk 15:10 ·knowing that the chief·priests had·handed him
Mk 15:11 But the chief·priests incited the crowd that rather
Mk 15:31 Likewise also, the chief·priests, while·mocking,

G0749.2 N-APM ἀρχιερεῖς (9x)
Jn 7:45 the assistants came to·the chief·priests and Pharisees,
Lk 22:52 Then Jesus declared to·the chief·priests, *the*
Lk 23:4 Then Pilate declared to·the chief·priests and *to* the
Lk 23:13 And after·calling·together the chief·priests, the
Ac 9:21 them having·been·bound to·the chief·priests?"
Ac 22:30 and commandingly·ordered the chief·priests and all
Mt 2:4 after·gathering·together all the chief·priests and *the*
Mt 26:14 Judas IsCariot, upon·traversing to·the chief·priests,
Mk 14:10 went·off to·the chief·priests, in·order·that he·

G0749.2 N-DPM ἀρχιερεῦσιν (6x)
Lk 22:4 he·spoke·together with·the chief·priests and the
Ac 23:14 after·coming·alongside the chief·priests and the
Mt 20:18 ·be·handed·over to·the chief·priests and scribes,
Mt 27:3 the thirty pieces·of·silver to·the chief·priests and the
Mt 28:11 to·the chief·priests absolutely·all the·things
Mk 10:33 ·be·handed·over to·the chief·priests and to·the

G0749.2 N-GSM ἀρχιερέως (1x)
Ac 19:14 the·seven Sons of·Sceva, a·Jewish chief·priest.

G0749.2 N-GPM ἀρχιερέων (11x)
Jn 18:3 assistants from·among the chief·priests and Pharisees
Lk 9:22 ·as·unfit by the elders and chief·priests and scribes,
Lk 23:23 ·them and of·the chief·priests were·overpowering.
Ac 9:14 personally·from the chief·priests to·bind all the·ones
Ac 26:10 authority personally·from the chief·priests. And
Ac 26:12 ·charge personally·from the chief·priests,
Mt 16:21 from the elders and chief·priests and scribes, and
Mt 26:47 and staffs, from the chief·priests and elders of·the
Mt 27:12 he was·legally·accused by the chief·priests and the
Mk 8:31 ·as·unfit by the elders, chief·priests, and scribes,
Mk 14:43 and staffs, directly·from the chief·priests and the

G0749.3 N-NSM ἀρχιερεύς (4x)
Heb 5:1 For every high·priest being·taken from·among men·
Heb 8:3 For every high·priest is·fully·established to·offer
Heb 9:7 once per year, the high·priest *went* alone, *but* not
Heb 9:25 many·times, just·as the high·priest enters into the

G0749.3 N-NPM ἀρχιερεῖς (1x)
Heb 7:27 each day, just·as the high·priests *do*, to·carry·up

G0749.3 N-ASM ἀρχιερέα (4x)
Ac 4:6 with HannAs the high·priest and Caiaphas and
Ac 23:4 declared, "Do·you·defame God's high·priest?"
Heb 4:15 we·do·not have a·high·priest who·is·not being·able
Heb 5:5 glorify himself to·be·made a·high·priest, but·rather

G0749.3 N-APM ἀρχιερεῖς (1x)
Heb 7:28 men·of·clay† *as* high·priests having weakness, but

G0749.3 N-DSM ἀρχιερεῖ (1x)
Jn 18:22 "Do·you·answer the high·priest in·this·manner?

G0749.3 N-GSM ἀρχιερέως (2x)
Heb 13:11 through the high·priest concerning moral·failure,
Mk 2:26 in·the·days of·AbiAthar the high·priest and ate the

G0749.3 N-GPM ἀρχιερέων (1x)
Lk 3:2 ·the·days of·HannAs and Caiaphas *the* high·priests—

EG0749.3 (2x)
Heb 5:7 *a·high·priest*, who in the days of·his flesh, *was*
Heb 7:28 Son *as high·priest*, having·been·made·completely·

G0749.4 N-NSM ἀρχιερεύς (19x)
Jn 11:49 being *the* designated·high·priest that·same year,
Jn 11:51 but·rather being *the* designated·high·priest that year
Jn 18:13 who was *the* designated·high·priest that year. *(And*
Jn 18:19 ·due·course, the designated·high·priest asked Jesus
Ac 5:17 Then the designated·high·priest, rising·up, and all
Ac 5:21 Now the designated·high·priest and the·ones together
Ac 5:27 And the designated·high·priest inquired·of them,
Ac 7:1 Then the designated·high·priest declared, "Are these·
Ac 22:5 As *to·such*, the designated·high·priest *HananIah* is
Ac 23:2 And the designated·high·priest HananIah ordered for·
Ac 23:5 that he·is *the* designated·high·priest, for it·has·been·
Ac 24:1 the designated·high·priest HananIah walked·down
Ac 25:2 Then the designated·high·priest and the foremost of·
Mt 26:62 ·up, the designated·high·priest declared to·him,
Mt 26:63 the designated·high·priest declared to·him,
Mt 26:65 Then the designated·high·priest tore·apart his
Mk 14:60 Then the designated·high·priest, after·standing·up
Mk 14:61 the designated·high·priest was·inquiring·of him,
Mk 14:63 So the designated·high·priest, after·tearing·apart

G0749.4 N-ASM ἀρχιερέα (3x)
Jn 18:24 ·bound, to Caiaphas the designated·high·priest).
Mt 26:57 ·away to Caiaphas the designated·high·priest, where
Mk 14:53 Jesus away to the designated·high·priest, and all the

G0749.4 N-DSM ἀρχιερεῖ (3x)
Jn 18:15 was known to·the designated·high·priest, and he·
Jn 18:16 was known to·the designated·high·priest, went·out
Ac 9:1 ·alongside the designated·high·priest *HananIah*,

G0749.4 N-GSM ἀρχιερέως (11x)

Jn 18:10 struck the slave of·the designated·high·priest, and
Jn 18:15 into the courtyard of·the designated·high·priest.
Jn 18:26 the slaves of·the designated·high·priest, being a·
Lk 22:50 the slave of·the designated·high·priest and removed
Lk 22:54 into the house of·the designated·high·priest. Now
Mt 26:3 in the mansion of·the designated·high·priest, the·one
Mt 26:51 the slave of·the designated·high·priest, he·removed
Mt 26:58 ·to the courtyard of·the designated·high·priest, and
Mk 14:47 the slave of·the designated·high·priest and removed
Mk 14:54 the courtyard of·the designated·high·priest. And he·
Mk 14:66 of·the servant·girls of·the designated·high·priest.

EG0749.4 (2x)

Jn 18:13 to HannAs *the proper high·priest*, for he·was *the*
Jn 18:13 *·bound to·Caiaphas, the designated·high·priest*).

G0749.5 N-NSM ἀρχιερεύς (5x)

Heb 2:17 trustworthy High·Priest in·the·things pertaining·to
Heb 5:10 ·designated by God a·High·Priest "'according·to
Heb 6:20 ·us— YeShua, after·becoming High·Priest for the
Heb 7:26 For such a·High·Priest was·befitting·for us, *who·is*
Heb 9:11 Anointed-One, *the* High·Priest of·the impending

G0749.5 N-ASM ἀρχιερέα (3x)

Heb 3:1 the Ambassador and High·Priest of·our affirmation,
Heb 4:14 having a·great High·Priest, having·gone·through
Heb 8:1 we·do·have such a·High·Priest who is·seated at *the*

G0750 ἀρχι•ποίμην archipôímēn *n.* (1x)

Roots:G0746 G4166 Compare:G4167 G4168

G0750 N-GSM ἀρχιποίμενος (1x)

1Pe 5:4 And with·the chief·Shepherd being·made·apparent,

G0751 Ἄρχ•ιππος Árchippôs *n/p.* (2x)

Roots:G0746 G2462

G0751.2 N/P-DSM Ἀρχίππῳ (2x)

Col 4:17 And declare to·ArchIppus, "Look·out·for the
Phm 1:2 beloved Apphia, and ArchIppus our fellow·soldier,

G0752 ἀρχι•συν•άγωγος archisynágōgôs *n.* (9x)

Roots:G0746 G4864 Compare:G0755 G2519 G2819-2

G0752.1 N-NSM ἀρχισυνάγωγος (2x)

Lk 13:14 And the director·of·the·gathering answering,
Ac 18:8 And Crispus, the director·of·the·gathering, trusted

G0752.1 N-NPM ἀρχισυνάγωγοι (1x)

Ac 13:15 the directors·of·the·gathering dispatched to them,

G0752.1 N-ASM ἀρχισυνάγωγον (1x)

Ac 18:17 SosThenes, the director·of·the·gathering, all the

G0752.1 N-DSM ἀρχισυναγώγῳ (1x)

Mk 5:36 Jesus says to·the director·of·the·gathering, "Do·

G0752.1 N-GSM ἀρχισυναγώγου (3x)

Lk 8:49 *the house·of* the director·of·the·gathering, saying to·
Mk 5:35 *the house·of* the director·of·the·gathering, saying,
Mk 5:38 house of·the director·of·the·gathering and observes

G0752.1 N-GPM ἀρχισυναγώγων (1x)

Mk 5:22 ·comes one of·the directors·of·the·gathering, Jairus

G0753 ἀρχι•τέκτων architéktōn *n.* (1x)

Roots:G0746 G5045 Compare:G5079 G3618
See:G0752-2

G0753.4 N-NSM ἀρχιτέκτων (1x)

1Co 3:10 as a·wise chief·construction·architect, I·have·laid

G0754 ἀρχι•τελώνης architêlṓnēs *n.* (1x)

Roots:G0746 G5057

G0754 N-NSM ἀρχιτελώνης (1x)

Lk 19:2 and *the* same was a·chief·tax·collector, and this·man

G0755 ἀρχι•τρί•κλινος architríklinôs *n.* (3x)

Roots:G0746 G5140 G2827

G0755 N-NSM ἀρχιτρίκλινος (2x)

Jn 2:9 Now as·soon·as the director·of·the·banquet tasted the
Jn 2:9 , the director·of·the·banquet hollered·out·for the

G0755 N-DSM ἀρχιτρικλίνῳ (1x)

Jn 2:8 now and bring *it* to·the director·of·the·banquet." And

G0756 ἄρχομαι árchômai *v.* (85x)

Roots:G0757 Compare:G0509

G0756 V-ADI-3S ἤρξατο (41x)

Jn 13:5 the wash·basin; then he·began to·wash the disciples
Lk 4:21 And he·began to·say to them, "Today, this Scripture
Lk 7:15 And the dead·man sat·up and began to·speak. And
Lk 7:24 of·John going·off, *Jesus* began to·discourse to the
Lk 7:38 *him* while·weeping, she·began to·shower his feet
Lk 9:12 And the day began to·fade. Now the twelve,
Lk 11:29 crowds being·amassed·together, he·began to·say,
Lk 12:1 ·down one·another, *Jesus* began to·say to his
Lk 14:30 'This man·of·clay† began to·build yet did·not
Lk 15:14 that country, and he·himself began to·be·destitute.
Lk 19:45 Sanctuary·Atrium, he·began to·cast·out the·ones
Lk 20:9 Then he·began to·relay this parable to the people,
Ac 1:1 *was* concerning all that Jesus began both to·do and to·
Ac 18:26 And this·man began to·boldly·speak·with·clarity in
Ac 24:2 ·called·for, Tertullus began to·legally·accuse *Paul*,
Ac 27:35 of·them·all, and after·breaking *it*, he·began to·eat.
Mt 4:17 then·on, YeShua began to·officially·proclaim and
Mt 11:7 ·men were·departing, YeShua began to·say to·the
Mt 11:20 Then he·began to·reproach the cities in which the
Mt 16:21 From then·on, YeShua began to·show to·his
Mt 16:22 ·taking him *aside*, began to·reprimand him, saying
Mt 26:37 two Sons of·Zebedee, he·began to·be·grieved and
Mt 26:74 Then he·began to·take·an·irrevocable·vow·of· and
Mk 1:45 upon·going·forth, he·began to·officially·herald *his*
Mk 4:1 Then he·began again to·instruct directly·by the sea.
Mk 5:20 And he·went·off and began to·officially·herald in
Mk 6:2 And with·Sabbath occurring, he·began to·instruct in
Mk 6:7 the twelve, and he·began to·dispatch them two by·
Mk 6:34 a·shepherd,'" and he·began to·instruct them *in*
Mk 8:31 And he·began to·instruct them that it·is·mandatory·
Mk 8:32 ·taking him *aside*, Peter began to·reprimand him.
Mk 10:28 Then Peter began to·say to·him, "Behold, we·
Mk 10:32 again the twelve, he·began to·relate to·them the
Mk 10:47 ·was Jesus of·Natsareth, he·began to·yell·out and
Mk 11:15 the Sanctuary·Atrium, began to·cast·out the·ones
Mk 12:1 And he·began to·relate to·them in parables.
Mk 13:5 And Jesus answering them began to·say, "Look·out
Mk 14:33 and John, and he·began to·be·utterly·amazed and
Mk 14:69 after·seeing him again, began to·say to·the·ones
Mk 14:71 But he·began to·vow·and·bind·*himself*·over·to·
Mk 15:8 upon·shouting·out, began to·request *for·him to·do*

G0756 V-ADI-3P ἤρξαντο (19x)

Lk 5:21 scribes and the Pharisees began to·ponder, saying,
Lk 7:49 reclining·together·at·the·meal began to·say within
Lk 11:53 the scribes and the Pharisees began to·besiege *him*
Lk 14:18 one *intent*, they·all began to·excuse·themselves.
Lk 15:24 ·yet he·is·found.' And they·began to·be·merry.
Lk 19:37 ·all the multitude of·the disciples began rejoicing,
Lk 22:23 And they began to·question·and·discuss among
Lk 23:2 And they·began to·legally·accuse him, saying,
Ac 2:4 ·Holy Spirit, and they·began to·speak·in different
Mt 12:1 ·hungry, they·also began to·pluck heads·of·grain
Mt 26:22 grieved, each·one of·them began to·say to·him,
Mk 2:23 and his disciples began to·make a·pathway,
Mk 5:17 And they·began to·implore *Jesus* to·go·away from
Mk 6:55 surrounding·region, they·began to·carry·about on
Mk 8:11 and began to·mutually·question·and·discuss with·
Mk 10:41 the ten began to·be·greatly·displeased concerning
Mk 14:19 And they·began to·be·grieved and to·say to·him
Mk 14:65 And some began to·spit·on him, and upon·putting·
Mk 15:18 and they·began to·greet him, "*Ah*! Be·well, O·

G0756 V-AMN@ ἄρξασθαι (1x)

Ac 11:15 And as I began to·speak, the Holy Spirit fell upon

EG0756 (1x)

1Pe 4:17 And if *it* first *begins* with us, what *is* the end of·the·

G0756.1 V-FMI-2P ἄρξεσθε (1x)

Lk 13:26 "Then yeu·shall·begin to·say, 'We·ate and drank

G0756.1 V-FMI-3P ἄρξονται (1x)

Lk 23:30 Then shall·they·begin "to·say to·the mountains,

G0756.1 V-PMI-1P ἀρχόμεθα (1x)

2Co 3:1 Do·we·begin again to·commend ourselves?

G0756.1 V-PMP-GPM ἀρχομένων (1x)

Lk 21:28 "And with·these·things beginning to·happen, pull·

G0756.1 V-PMP-NSM ἀρχόμενος (1x)

Lk 3:23 And upon·beginning *his specific·assignment*, Jesus

G0756.1 V-AMN ἄρξασθαι (1x)

1Pe 4:17 the season *for* the judgment to·begin with the house

G0756.1 V-AMP-ASN ἀρξάμενον (1x)

Ac 10:37 occurring in all Judea, beginning from Galilee,

G0756.1 V-AMP-GSM ἀρξαμένου (1x)

Mt 18:24 And with·him beginning to·tally·up, there·was·

G0756.1 V-AMP-NSN ἀρξάμενον (1x)

Lk 24:47 name to all the nations, beginning from JeruSalem.

G0756.1 V-AMP-NSM ἀρξάμενος (6x)

Lk 23:5 instructing in all Judea, beginning from Galilee unto
Lk 24:27 And beginning from Moses and all the prophets,
Ac 1:22 beginning from the immersion of·John, unto the day
Ac 8:35 opening·up his mouth and beginning from the same
Mt 14:30 he·was·afraid, and beginning to·be·plunged·down,
Mt 20:8 to·them the payment·of·service, beginning from the

G0756.1 V-AMP-NPM ἀρξάμενοι (1x)

Jn 8:9 ·were·going·forth one·by·one, beginning from the

G0756.1 V-AMS-2S ἄρξῃ (1x)

Lk 14:9 and then you·should·begin with shame to·fully·

G0756.1 V-AMS-2P ἄρξησθε (2x)

Lk 3:8 repentance, and yeu·should·not begin to·say within
Lk 13:25 the door, and yeu·should·begin to·stand outside

G0756.1 V-AMS-3S ἄρξηται (2x)

Lk 12:45 *back*,' and should·begin to·beat the servant·boys
Mt 24:49 and should·begin to·beat the fellow·slaves and to·

G0756.1 V-AMS-3P ἄρξωνται (1x)

Lk 14:29 all the·ones observing *it* may·begin to·mock him,

G0756.2 V-AMP-NSM ἀρξάμενος (1x)

Ac 11:4 But starting·from·the·beginning, Peter explained·

G0757 ἄρχω árchō *v.* (2x)

See:G0746

G0757.3 V-PAN ἄρχειν (2x)

Mk 10:42 that the·ones presuming to·rule·over the Gentiles
Rm 15:12 the·one who·is·rising·up to·rule·over Gentiles; in

G0758 ἄρχων árchōn *n.* (37x)

Roots:G0757 Compare:G0746

G0758.2 N-GPM ἀρχόντων (1x)

Lk 14:1 ·house of·a·certain·man of·the chief Pharisees to·eat

G0758.3 N-NSM ἄρχων (1x)

Rv 1:5 of·the dead, and the chief·ruler of·the kings of·the

G0758.3 N-GPM ἀρχόντων (1x)

Jn 12:42 many from·among the chief·rulers also trusted in

G0758.4 N-NSM ἄρχων (3x)

Jn 3:1 NicoDemus *was* his name, a·ruler of·the Judeans.
Lk 18:18 And a·certain ruler inquired·of him, saying,
Mt 9:18 to·them, behold, a·ruler, after·coming *to·YeShua*,

G0758.4 N-NPM ἄρχοντες (8x)

Jn 7:26 ·at·all to·him. Perhaps the rulers truly do·know that
Lk 23:35 observing. And the rulers also together with·them
Lk 24:20 the chief·priests and our rulers handed him over to
Ac 3:17 according·to ignorance, just·as also yeur rulers *did*.
Ac 4:26 and the rulers were·gathered·together in·unison
Ac 13:27 JeruSalem, and their rulers, not·knowing this·man
Mt 20:25 "Yeu·have·seen that the rulers of·the Gentiles
Rm 13:3 For the rulers are not *a·cause·of* fear for·the

G0758.4 N-VPM ἄρχοντες (1x)

Ac 4:8 declared to them, "Rulers of·the People, and elders

G0758.4 N-ASM ἄρχοντα (4x)

Ac 7:27 fully·established you *as* ruler and executive·justice
Ac 7:35 fully·established you *as* ruler and executive·justice?
Ac 7:35 ·man God dispatched *to·be* a·ruler and a·ransomer
Ac 23:5 declare *anything* badly of·a·ruler of·your People.'"

G0758.4 N-APM ἄρχοντας (3x)

Lk 23:13 ·together the chief·priests, the rulers, and the
Ac 4:5 the next·day, *that* their rulers and elders and scribes
Ac 16:19 into the marketplace·forum toward the rulers.

G0758.4 N-DPM ἄρχουσιν (1x)

Ac 14:5 together with·their rulers) to·abusively·mistreat *the*

G0758.4 N-GSM ἄρχοντος (1x)

Mt 9:23 upon·coming into the ruler's home and seeing the

G0758.4 N-GPM ἀρχόντων (3x)

Jn 7:48 ¿!·Did any from·among the rulers or from·among the

1Co 2:6 ·this present·age, nor of·the rulers of·this present·age,
1Co 2:8 which not·even·one of·the rulers of·this present·age
G0758.5 N-NSM ἄρχων (3x)
Jn 12:31 of·this world. The prince of·this world shall now
Jn 14:30 much with yeu, for the prince of·this world comes,
Jn 16:11 ·judgment, because the prince of·this world has·
G0758.5 N-ASM ἄρχοντα (1x)
Eph 2:2 world, according·to the prince of·the authority of·
G0758.5 N-DSM ἄρχοντι (4x)
Lk 11:15 ·Master-Of-Dung, *the* prince of·the demons."
Mt 9:34 ·casts·out the demons by the prince of·the demons."
Mt 12:24 ·Master-Of-Dung, *the* prince of·the demons."
Mk 3:22 and "By the prince of·the demons he·casts·out the
G0758.6 N-ASM ἄρχοντα (1x)
Lk 12:58 ·out with your legal·adversary to a·magistrate, give
G0758.7 N-NSM ἄρχων (1x)
Lk 8:41 ·subsisting *as* an·executive·director of·the gathering.

G0759 ἄρωμα árōma *n.* (4x)
Roots:G0142 Compare:G3510-1 G3030 G2368 G2238-2
xLangEquiv:H1314
G0759.2 N-APN ἀρώματα (3x)
Lk 23:56 they·made·ready aromatic·spices and ointments,
Lk 24:1 bringing aromatic·spices which they·made·ready,
Mk 16:1 and Salome bought aromatic·spices, in·order·that
G0759.2 N-GPN ἀρωμάτων (1x)
Jn 19:40 it in·strips·of·linen with the aromatic·spices, just·as

G0760 Ἀσά Asá *n/p.* (2x)
אָסָא 'açạ' [Hebrew]
Roots:H0609
G0760.2 N/P-PRI Ἀσά (2x)
Mt 1:7 RehoboAm begot AbiYah, and AbiYah begot Asa.
Mt 1:8 Now Asa begot JehoShaphat, and JehoShaphat begot

G0761 ἀ•σάλευτος asálêutôs *adj.* (2x)
Roots:G0001 G4531 Compare:G0277 G1476
G0761.2 A-NSF ἀσάλευτος (1x)
Ac 27:41 after·getting·stuck, remained unshakable, but the
G0761.2 A-ASF ἀσάλευτον (1x)
Heb 12:28 personally·receiving an·unshakable kingdom,

G0762 ἄ•σβεστος ásbêstôs *adj.* (4x)
Roots:G0001 G4570
G0762.2 A-ASN ἄσβεστον (2x)
Mk 9:43 into the Hell·Canyon, into the inextinguishable fire,
Mk 9:45 into the Hell·Canyon, into the inextinguishable fire,
G0762.2 A-DSN ἀσβέστῳ (2x)
Lk 3:17 ·shall·completely·burn with·fire inextinguishable."
Mt 3:12 ·burn the chaff with·inextinguishable fire."

G0763 ἀ•σέβεια asébêia *n.* (6x)
Roots:G0765 See:G0764-1
G0763.1 N-ASF ἀσέβειαν (2x)
Rm 1:18 from heaven against all irreverence and *all*
Tit 2:12 in·order·that, after·denying the irreverence and the
G0763.1 N-APF ἀσεβείας (1x)
Rm 11:26 and he·shall·turn·away irreverence from Jacob.
G0763.1 N-GSF ἀσεβείας (1x)
2Ti 2:16 ·continually·advance toward more irreverence.
G0763.2 N-GSF ἀσεβείας (1x)
Jud 1:15 ·them concerning all their irreverent deeds which
G0763.2 N-GPF ἀσεβειῶν (1x)
Jud 1:18 according·to their·own irreverent longings.

G0764 ἀ•σεβέω asêbéō *v.* (2x)
Roots:G0765 Compare:G4576 See:G0764-1
G0764.1 V-AAI-3P ἠσέβησαν (1x)
Jud 1:15 irreverent deeds which they·irreverently·did, and
G0764.2 V-PAN ἀσεβεῖν (1x)
2Pe 2:6 ·example for·those·intending to·be·irreverent;

G0765 ἀ•σεβής asêbḗs *adj.* (10x)
Roots:G0001 G4576 Compare:G2152 See:G0763
G0764
G0765.1 A-NSM ἀσεβής (1x)
1Pe 4:18 shall·appear the irreverent and morally·disqualified
G0765.1 A-NPM ἀσεβεῖς (3x)
Jud 1:4 to this judgment, irreverent·men transferring the
Jud 1:15 all the irreverent·ones among·them concerning all
Jud 1:15 which irreverent *and* morally·disqualified·men
G0765.1 A-ASM ἀσεβῆ (1x)
Rm 4:5 on the·one regarding the irreverent as·righteous, his
G0765.1 A-DPM ἀσεβέσιν (1x)
1Ti 1:9 and for·insubordinate·ones, for·irreverent·ones and
G0765.1 A-GPM ἀσεβῶν (3x)
Rm 5:6 died on·behalf of·irreverent·men (with·us being
2Pe 2:5 ·bringing a·Deluge upon a·world of·irreverent·men;
2Pe 3:7 and total·destruction of·the irreverent men·of·clay†.
EG0765.1 (1x)
Jud 1:8 Likewise also these *irreverent* dreamers, in·fact,

G0766 ἀ•σέλγεια asélgêia *n.* (9x)
Roots:G0001 G4580-1 Compare:G4203 G2064-3
G0766.2 N-NSF ἀσέλγεια (2x)
Gal 5:19 sexual·immorality, impurity, debauchery,
Mk 7:22 ·of·coveting, evils, guile, debauchery, an·evil eye,
G0766.2 N-ASF ἀσέλγειαν (1x)
Jud 1:4 grace of·our God into debauchery and denying the
G0766.2 N-DSF ἀσελγείᾳ (3x)
2Pe 2:7 the behavior of·the unscrupulous·men in debauchery
2Co 12:21 ·immorality and debauchery which they·practiced
Eph 4:19 handed themselves over to·the debauchery, into an·
G0766.2 N-DPF ἀσελγείαις (3x)
Rm 13:13 not in·cohabitations and debaucheries, not in·
1Pe 4:3 — having·traversed in debaucheries, longings,
2Pe 2:18 of·flesh *and* by·debaucheries *that* they·allure the·

G0767 ἄ•σημος ásēmôs *adj.* (1x)
Roots:G0001 G4591
G0767.2 A-GSF ἀσήμου (1x)
Ac 21:39 *a·city* of·Cilicia, a·citizen of·no obscure city. And

G0768 Ἀσήρ Asḗr *n/p.* (2x)
אָשֵׁר 'ạshẹr [Hebrew]
Roots:H0836
G0768.3 N/P-PRI Ἀσήρ (2x)
Lk 2:36 from·among *the* tribe of·Asher, herself having·
Rv 7:6 *the* tribe of·Asher having·been·officially·sealed,

G0769 ἀ•σθένεια asthénêia *n.* (26x)
Roots:G0772 Compare:G3554 G3119 G0771
G0769.1 N-ASF ἀσθένειαν (3x)
Heb 5:2 since he·himself also is·beset·with weakness.
Heb 7:28 men·of·clay† *as* high·priests having weakness, but
Rm 6:19 ·of·men† on·account·of the weakness of·yeur flesh.
G0769.1 N-DSF ἀσθενείᾳ (3x)
1Co 2:3 came·to·be alongside yeu in weakness, and in
1Co 15:43 glory. It·is·sown in weakness; it·is·awakened in
2Co 12:9 my power is·made·fully·complete in weakness."
G0769.1 N-DPF ἀσθενείαις (5x)
Heb 4:15 being·able to·sympathize with·our weaknesses, but
Rm 8:26 ·together·alongside *us* in·our weaknesses, for we·
2Co 12:5 ·self, I·shall·not boast, except in my weaknesses.
2Co 12:9 I·shall·boast in my weaknesses in·order·that the
2Co 12:10 I·purposefully·delight in weaknesses, in
G0769.1 N-GSF ἀσθενείας (3x)
Heb 11:34 of·*the*·dagger, from weakness were·enabled, did·
2Co 11:30 I·shall·boast *about* the·things of·my weakness.
2Co 13:4 though he·is·crucified as·a·result of·weakness, yet
G0769.2 N-NSF ἀσθένεια (1x)
Jn 11:4 *that*, declared, "This sickness is not toward death,
G0769.2 N-ASF ἀσθένειαν (1x)
Gal 4:13 ·personally·know that through sickness of·the flesh,
G0769.2 N-APF ἀσθενείας (3x)
Ac 28:9 rest also, the·ones having sicknesses on the island,
Mt 8:17 "He·himself took our sicknesses, and he·lifted·and·
1Ti 5:23 ·of your stomach and your frequent sicknesses.
G0769.2 N-DSF ἀσθενείᾳ (1x)
Jn 5:5 was there, being in the sickness thirty-eight years.
G0769.2 N-GSF ἀσθενείας (2x)
Lk 13:11 a·woman having a·spirit of·sickness even eighteen
Lk 13:12 you·have·been·fully·released from·your sickness."
G0769.2 N-GPF ἀσθενειῶν (2x)
Lk 5:15 ·both·relieved·and·cured by him of·their sicknesses.
Lk 8:2 ·and·cured from evil spirits and sicknesses: Mariam
EG0769.2 (2x)
Jn 5:6 that he·had·been *in·the sickness* even·now a·long time
Rv 2:22 do·cast her upon a·couch *of·sickness*, and the·ones

G0770 ἀ•σθενέω asthênéō *v.* (36x)
Roots:G0772
G0770.2 V-PAI-1S ἀσθενῶ (1x)
2Co 11:29 Who is·weak, and I·am·not weak? Who is·being·
G0770.2 V-PAI-1P ἀσθενοῦμεν (1x)
2Co 13:4 For we·ourselves also are·weak in him, yet we·
G0770.2 V-PAI-3S ἀσθενεῖ (3x)
Rm 14:21 brother stumbles, or is·enticed, or is·made·weak.
2Co 11:29 Who is·weak, and I·am·not weak?
2Co 13:3 in me, who is·not weak toward yeu, but·rather is·
G0770.2 V-PAP-ASF ἀσθενοῦσαν (1x)
1Co 8:12 and beating their weak conscience, yeu·morally·
G0770.2 V-PAP-ASM ἀσθενοῦντα (1x)
Rm 14:1 ·each·must·receive the·one being·weak in·the trust,
G0770.2 V-PAP-DPM ἀσθενοῦσιν (1x)
1Co 8:9 ·become a·stumbling·block to·the·ones being·weak.
G0770.2 V-PAP-GPM ἀσθενούντων (1x)
Ac 20:35 to·be·helpful·and·supportive of·the weak, and to·
G0770.2 V-PAP-NSM ἀσθενῶν (2x)
Rm 14:2 all·things, but the·one being·weak, eats garden·
1Co 8:11 shall the weak brother completely·perish, on·
G0770.2 V-PAS-1S ἀσθενῶ (1x)
2Co 12:10 for whenever I·may·be·weak, then I·am able.
G0770.2 V-PAS-1P ἀσθενῶμεν (1x)
2Co 13:9 ·glad, whenever we·ourselves should·be·weak, but
G0770.2 V-IAI-3S ἠσθένει (1x)
Rm 8:3 Torah-Law, in that it·was·being·weak through the
G0770.2 V-AAI-1P ἠσθενήσαμεν (1x)
2Co 11:21 that we·ourselves were·*too*·weak *to·do these*
G0770.2 V-AAP-NSM ἀσθενήσας (1x)
Rm 4:19 And not being·weak in·the trust, he·did·not fully·
G0770.3 V-PAI-3S ἀσθενεῖ (3x)
Jn 11:3 "Lord, see, he·whom you·are·fond·of is·sick."
Jn 11:6 as·soon·as he·heard that he·was·sick, in·fact he·
Jac 5:14 *Is* any sick among yeu?
G0770.3 V-PAP-ASM ἀσθενοῦντα (2x)
Lk 7:10 being·sent found the sick slave healthy·and·sound.
2Ti 4:20 but Trophimus, being·sick, I·left·behind at
G0770.3 V-PAP-APM ἀσθενοῦντας (5x)
Lk 4:40 sun sinking·down, as·many·as were sick, everyone
Lk 9:2 the kingdom of·God, and to·heal the·ones being·sick.
Ac 19:12 skin's·surface to·be·brought upon the sick, and *for*
Mt 10:8 Both·relieve·and·cure the·sick; purify lepers;
Mk 6:56 or countrysides, they·were·laying the sick in the
G0770.3 V-PAP-GPM ἀσθενούντων (1x)
Jn 6:2 ·signs which he·was·doing upon the·ones being·sick.
G0770.3 V-PAP-NSM ἀσθενῶν (1x)
Jn 11:1 Now a·certain·man was sick, *named* Lazarus, from
G0770.3 V-IAI-3S ἠσθένει (2x)
Jn 4:46 royal·official, whose son was·sick at CaperNaum.
Jn 11:2 feet with·her hair, whose brother Lazarus was·sick).
G0770.3 V-AAI-1S ἠσθένησα (1x)
Mt 25:36 yeu·arrayed me *with·clothing*. I·was·sick, and yeu·
G0770.3 V-AAI-3S ἠσθένησεν (2x)
Php 2:26 on·account·that yeu·heard that he·was·sick.
Php 2:27 For even he·was·sick almost to·death, but·yet God
G0770.3 V-AAP-ASF ἀσθενήσασαν (1x)
Ac 9:37 it·happened in those days, *that* being·sick, she died.
G0770.4 V-PAP-GPM ἀσθενούντων (1x)
Jn 5:3 multitude of·the·ones being·feeble were·laying·ill—
G0770.4 V-PAP-NSM ἀσθενῶν (1x)
Jn 5:7 The feeble·man answered him, "Sir, I·have no man·

G0771 ἀ•σθένημα asthénēma *n.* (2x)
Roots:G0770 Compare:G0769
G0771.2 N-APN ἀσθενήματα (1x)
Rm 15:1 the weaknesses·of·conscience of·the·ones *that·are*
EG0771.2 (1x)

Rm 15:2 ·adapt·to·his neighbor's weak·conscience for his

G0772 ἀ•σθενής asthênḗs *adj.* (25x)
Roots:G0001 G4598-2 See:G4599

G0772.1 A-GPM ἀσθενῶν (1x)
Rm 5:6 of·irreverent·men (with·us being without·vigor).

G0772.2 A-NSM ἀσθενής (1x)
1Co 9:22 weak, I·became as weak in·order·that I·may·gain

G0772.2 A-NSF ἀσθενής (4x)
Mt 26:41 In·fact, the spirit *is* eager, but the flesh *is* weak."
Mk 14:38 In·fact, the spirit *is* eager, but the flesh *is* weak."
1Co 8:7 and their conscience (being weak) is·tarnished.
2Co 10:10 but his bodily presence *is* weak, and his discourse

G0772.2 A-NSN ἀσθενές (1x)
1Co 1:25 of·men·of·clay†, and the weakness of·God is

G0772.2 A-NPM ἀσθενεῖς (2x)
1Co 4:10 We·ourselves *are* weak, but yeu *are* strong.
1Co 11:30 ·of that, many *are* weak and unhealthy among

G0772.2 A-ASN ἀσθενές (1x)
Heb 7:18 on·account·of it *being* weak and unprofitable.

G0772.2 A-APM ἀσθενεῖς (1x)
1Co 9:22 weak in·order·that I·may·gain the weak. To·every

G0772.2 A-APN ἀσθενῆ (2x)
Gal 4:9 *that* yeu·return again to the weak and pitifully·poor
1Co 1:27 and God selected the weak·things of·the world in·

G0772.2 A-DSN-C ἀσθενεστέρῳ (1x)
1Pe 3:7 according·to knowledge, as with·a·weaker vessel,

G0772.2 A-DPM ἀσθενέσιν (1x)
1Co 9:22 To·the weak, I·became as weak in·order·that I·

G0772.2 A-GSM ἀσθενοῦς (1x)
1Co 8:10 the conscience of·him who·is weak be·reinforced

G0772.2 A-GPM ἀσθενῶν (1x)
1Th 5:14 fainthearted, support the weak, be·patient toward

G0772.3 A-NSM ἀσθενής (1x)
Mt 25:43 ·did·not array me *with·clothing*, sick and in prison,

G0772.3 A-ASM ἀσθενῆ (2x)
Mt 25:39 When did·we·see you sick, or in prison, and came
Mt 25:44 or *being* a·stranger, or naked, or sick, or in prison,

G0772.3 A-APM ἀσθενεῖς (3x)
Lk 10:9 And both·relieve·and·cure the sick in it, and say to·
Ac 5:15 ·for *the people* to·bear·forth the sick in·each·of the
Ac 5:16 JeruSalem, bringing *the* sick and *those* being·

G0772.4 A-NPN-C ἀσθενέστερα (1x)
1Co 12:22 ·ones seeming to·inherently·be more·feeble, are

G0772.4 A-GSM ἀσθενοῦς (1x)
Ac 4:9 over *the* good·deed for·the·feeble man·of·clay†—

G0773 Ἀσία Asía *n/l.* (19x)
See:G0775

G0773.1 N/L-NSF Ἀσία (1x)
Ac 19:27 to·be·demolished, whom all Asia and The Land

G0773.1 N/L-ASF Ἀσίαν (5x)
Ac 2:9 and *in* Judea and Cappadocia, *in* Pontus and Asia,
Ac 19:10 such·for all the·ones residing·in Asia to·hear the
Ac 19:22 Erastus, he·himself held·back in Asia for·a·time.
Ac 20:18 since I·walked·over into Asia, with·what·manner I·
Ac 27:2 ·to the *coastal* places of·Asia, with·AristArchus (a·

G0773.1 N/L-DSF Ἀσίᾳ (6x)
Ac 16:6 Holy Spirit to·speak the Redemptive-word in Asia.
Ac 20:16 happen to·him to·linger·away in Asia. For he·was·
2Co 1:8 the·one happening to·us in Asia, that most
2Ti 1:15 that all the·ones in Asia are·turned·away·from me,
Rv 1:4 Called·Out·citizenries, to·the·ones in Asia. Grace *be*
Rv 1:11 to·the Called·Out·citizenries, to·the·ones in Asia: to

G0773.1 N/L-GSF Ἀσίας (7x)
Ac 6:9 and Asia, mutually·questioning·and·discussing with·
Ac 19:26 but·yet almost throughout·all Asia, this Paul has·
Ac 20:4 And even·as·far·as Asia, SoPater (a·Berean *Jew*),
Ac 21:27 the Jews from Asia, upon·distinctly·viewing him
Ac 24:18 "But *there·were* certain Jews from Asia,
1Pe 1:1 Pontus, Galatia, Cappadocia, Asia, and Bithynia—
1Co 16:19 The Called·Out·citizenries of·Asia greet yeu.

G0774 Ἀσιανός Asianós *n/g.* (1x)
Roots:G0773

G0774.2 N/G-NPM Ἀσιανοί (1x)
Ac 20:4 and *both* Tychicus and Trophimus of·Asia,

G0775 Ἀσι•άρχης Asiárchēs *n/g.* (1x)
Roots:G0773 G0746

G0775 N/G-GPM Ἀσιαρχῶν (1x)
Ac 19:31 And also certain·men of·the chiefs·of·Asia, being

G0776 ἀ•σιτία asitía *n.* (1x)
Roots:G0777 Compare:G3521 G3522

G0776.2 N-GSF ἀσιτίας (1x)
Ac 27:21 a·long·while without·a·bite·of·food, Paul, after·

G0777 ἄ•σιτος ásitos *adj.* (1x)
Roots:G0001 G4621 Compare:G3521 G3522
See:G0776

G0777.2 A-NPM ἄσιτοι (1x)
Ac 27:33 ·*still* ·continue·to·persevere without·a·bite·of·food,

G0778 ἀσκέω askéō *v.* (1x)
Compare:G1128 G1129 G4160 See:G4632

G0778.2 V-PAI-1S-C ἀσκῶ (1x)
Ac 24:16 And in this, I·exert myself: to·have continually a·

G0779 ἀσκός askós *n.* (12x)
See:G0778 G4632

G0779.2 N-NPM ἀσκοί (4x)
Lk 5:37 and the wineskins shall·be·completely·destroyed.
Mt 9:17 But·if·so, the wineskins are·burst, and the wine
Mt 9:17 and the wineskins shall·be·completely·destroyed.
Mk 2:22 and the wineskins shall·be·completely·destroyed.

G0779.2 N-APM ἀσκούς (8x)
Lk 5:37 casts fresh·new wine into old wineskins. But·if·so,
Lk 5:37 the fresh·new wine shall·burst the wineskins, and it
Lk 5:38 *is only* fit·to·be·cast into brand-new wineskins, and
Mt 9:17 ·cast fresh·new wine into old wineskins. But·if·so,
Mt 9:17 fresh·new wine into brand-new wineskins, and both
Mk 2:22 casts fresh·new wine into old wineskins. But·if·so,
Mk 2:22 the fresh·new wine bursts the wineskins, and the
Mk 2:22 *is only* fit·to·be·cast into brand-new wineskins."

G0780 ἀσμένως asménōs *adv.* (2x)
Roots:G2237 See:G2234 G2236

G0780.1 ADV ἀσμένως (1x)
Ac 21:17 the brothers accepted us quite·pleasantly.

G0780.2 ADV ἀσμένως (1x)
Ac 2:41 Redemptive-word with·pleasure, they·were·immersed

G0781 ἄ•σοφος ásôphôs *adj.* (1x)
Roots:G0001 G4680 Compare:G3474 G0878

G0781 A-NPM ἄσοφοι (1x)
Eph 5:15 how yeu·walk, not as unwise, but·rather as wise,

G0782 ἀ•σπάζομαι aspázômai *v.* (63x)
Roots:G0001 G4685 Compare:G1723 G5463 G1968
See:G0783

G0782.1 V-ADP-NSM ἀσπασάμενος (1x)
Ac 20:1 after·summoning the disciples and embracing *them*,

G0782.1 V-ADP-NPM ἀσπασάμενοι (2x)
Ac 21:6 And after·embracing one·another, we·embarked into
Heb 11:13 being·persuaded·of *them*, and embracing *them*,

G0782.2 V-FDP-NPM ἀσπασόμενοι (1x)
Ac 25:13 and BerNiki arrived in Caesarea to·greet Festus.

G0782.2 V-PNI-1S ἀσπάζομαι (1x)
Rm 16:22 the·one writing the letter, greet yeu in *the* Lord.

G0782.2 V-PNI-3S ἀσπάζεται (8x)
Rm 16:23 of·the whole Called·Out·citizenry), greets yeu.
Rm 16:23 the estate·manager of·the city, greets yeu, *as* also
1Pe 5:13 selected·together *with·yeu*, greets yeu, and *so*·
Col 4:10 my fellow·prisoner·of·war, greets yeu, also *John*·
Col 4:12 yeu, a·slave of·Anointed-One, greets yeu, always
Col 4:14 practitioner·of·healing, and Demas, greet yeu.
2Ti 4:21 to·come before winter. EuBulus greets you, and
2Jn 1:13 of·your Selected sister greet you *personally*. So·be·

G0782.2 V-PNI-3P ἀσπάζονται (12x)
Heb 13:24 The·ones from Italy greet yeu.
Rm 16:16 ·Out·citizenries of·the Anointed-One greet yeu.
Rm 16:21 SosiPater, my Redeemed·Kinsmen, greet yeu.
Php 4:21 The brothers together with·me greet yeu.
Php 4:22 All the holy·ones greet yeu, especially the·ones
Tit 3:15 All *that·are* with me greet you. Greet the·ones
1Co 16:19 The Called·Out·citizenries of·Asia greet yeu.
1Co 16:19 Aquila and Little·Prisca greet yeu much in *the*
1Co 16:20 All the brothers greet yeu. Greet one·another with
2Co 13:13 All the holy·ones greet yeu.
Phm 1:23 *These·men* greet you: EpAphras, my fellow·
3Jn 1:14 Peace *be* to·you. The friends greet you. Greet the

G0782.2 V-PNM-2S ἀσπάζου (1x)
3Jn 1:14 The friends greet you. Greet the friends each·by

G0782.2 V-PNN ἀσπάζεσθαι (1x)
Mk 15:18 and they·began to·greet him, "*Ah!* Be·well, O·

G0782.2 V-INI-3P ἠσπάζοντο (1x)
Mk 9:15 and running·toward *him*, they·were·greeting him.

G0782.2 V-ADI-3S ἠσπάσατο (1x)
Lk 1:40 into the house of·ZacharIas and greeted EliSabeth.

G0782.2 V-ADM-2S ἄσπασαι (2x)
Tit 3:15 me greet you. Greet the·ones having·affection·for
2Ti 4:19 Greet Prisca and Aquila, and the household of·

G0782.2 V-ADM-2P ἀσπάσασθε (24x)
Heb 13:24 Greet all the·ones who·are·governing among·yeu,
Mt 10:12 And while·entering into the home, greet it.
Rm 16:3 Greet Little·Prisca and Aquila, my coworkers in
Rm 16:5 in their house. Greet my well-beloved Epaenetus,
Rm 16:6 Greet Maria, who, in·many·ways, labored·hard
Rm 16:7 Greet AndroNicus and Junianus, my Redeemed·
Rm 16:8 Greet my well-beloved Amplias in *the* Lord.
Rm 16:9 Greet Urbanus, our coworker in Anointed-One, and
Rm 16:10 Greet Apelles, the·one verifiably·approved in
Rm 16:10 in Anointed-One. Greet the·ones from·among
Rm 16:11 Greet HerOdion, my Redeemed·Kinsman.
Rm 16:11 Redeemed·Kinsman. Greet the·ones from·among
Rm 16:12 Greet Tryphaena and Tryphosa, the·ones laboring·
Rm 16:12 ·hard in *the* Lord. Greet the well-beloved Persis,
Rm 16:13 Greet Rufus, the One-Selected in *the* Lord, and his
Rm 16:14 Greet ASynkritus, Phlegon, Hermas, PatroBas,
Rm 16:15 Greet PhiloLogus, and Julia, Nereus, and his sister,
Rm 16:16 Greet one·another with a·holy kiss.
Php 4:21 Greet every holy·one in Anointed-One Jesus.
1Pe 5:14 Greet·yeu one·another with a·kiss of·love.
1Th 5:26 Greet all the brothers with a·holy kiss.
1Co 16:20 brothers greet yeu. Greet one·another with a·holy
2Co 13:12 Greet one·another with a·holy kiss.
Col 4:15 Greet the brothers in LaoDicea, and *greet* Nymphas

G0782.2 V-ADP-NSM ἀσπασάμενος (2x)
Ac 18:22 *to·JeruSalem* and greeting the Called·Out·citizenry,
Ac 21:19 And after·greeting them, *Paul* was·recounting·in·

G0782.2 V-ADP-NPM ἀσπασάμενοι (1x)
Ac 21:7 arrived at Ptolemais; and after·greeting the brothers,

G0782.2 V-ADS-2P ἀσπάσησθε (2x)
Lk 10:4 shoes, and yeu·should·greet not·even·one·man in
Mt 5:47 And if yeu·should·greet yeur brothers merely, what·

EG0782.2 (3x)
Mt 5:47 ·indeed even the tax·collectors *greet* in·this·manner?
Rm 16:5 Also *greet* the Called·Out·citizenry *hosted* in their
Col 4:15 brothers in LaoDicea, and *greet* Nymphas and the

G0783 ἀ•σπασμός aspasmós *n.* (10x)
Roots:G0782

G0783.1 N-NSM ἀσπασμός (1x)
Lk 1:29 ·pondering what·manner·of greeting this might·be.

G0783.1 N-ASM ἀσπασμόν (1x)
Lk 1:41 as·soon·as EliSabeth heard the greeting of·Mariam,

G0783.1 N-APM ἀσπασμούς (4x)
Lk 11:43 gatherings, and the greetings in the marketplaces.
Lk 20:46 in long·robes, and being·fond·of greetings in the
Mt 23:7 and the greetings in the marketplaces, and to·be·
Mk 12:38 ·about in long·robes, and *wanting* greetings in the

G0783.1 N-GSM ἀσπασμοῦ (1x)
Lk 1:44 as·soon·as the sound of·your greeting occurred in

G0783.2 N-NSM ἀσπασμός (3x)
2Th 3:17 The salutation of·Paul by·my·own hand, which is
1Co 16:21 The salutation of·Paul by·my·own hand.

Col 4:18 *This·is* the salutation by·my·own hand, Paul:

G0784 ἄ•σπιλος áspilôs *adj.* (4x)
Roots:G0001 G4695 Compare:G0299
G0784.1 A-NPM ἄσπιλοι (1x)
2Pe 3:14 by·him in peace, without·stain and irreproachable.
G0784.1 A-GSM ἀσπίλου (1x)
1Pe 1:19 ·lamb without·blemish and without·stain, *the·blood*
G0784.2 A-ASM ἄσπιλον (1x)
Jac 1:27 *and* to·purposefully·keep oneself unstained from the
G0784.2 A-ASF ἄσπιλον (1x)
1Ti 6:14 the commandment unstained, above·all·blame·and·

G0785 ἀσπίς aspís *n.* (1x)
Compare:G0937-1
xLangEquiv:H6620 xLangAlso:H5919 H4043
G0785.1 N-GPF ἀσπίδων (1x)
Rm 3:13 ' "*The* venom of·asps *is* under their lips.

G0786 ἄ•σπονδος áspôndôs *adj.* (2x)
Roots:G0001 G4689
G0786.3 A-NPM ἄσπονδοι (1x)
2Ti 3:3 ·affection·for·family, implacable,·truceless·men,
G0786.3 A-APM ἀσπόνδους (1x)
Rm 1:31 ·for·family, implacable,·truceless·men, *and*

G0787 ἀσσάριον assáriôn *n.* (2x)
See:G1220 G2835 G3016
G0787.1 N-GSN ἀσσαρίου (1x)
Mt 10:29 two little·sparrows sold for·an·assarion·coin? And
G0787.1 N-GPN ἀσσαρίων (1x)
Lk 12:6 little·sparrows sold for·two assarion·coins? And·yet

G0788 ἆσσον âssôn *adv.* (1x)
Roots:G1451
G0788.2 ADV ἆσσον (1x)
Ac 27:13 they·were·sailing·near Crete, very·close·to *shore*.

G0789 Ἄσσος Ássôs *n/l.* (2x)
G0789 N/L-ASF Ἄσσον (2x)
Ac 20:13 the sailing·ship, sailed to Assos, *while* from·there
Ac 20:14 as he·joined·on with·us at Assos, after·taking him

G0790 ἀ•στατέω astatéō *v.* (1x)
Roots:G0001 G2476
G0790.2 V-PAI-1P ἀστατοῦμεν (1x)
1Co 4:11 and are·buffeted, and are·unsettled·being·homeless;

G0791 ἀστεῖος asteîôs *adj.* (2x)
G0791.2 A-NSM ἀστεῖος (1x)
Ac 7:20 was·born, and he·was handsome to·God; *and* he·
G0791.2 A-ASN ἀστεῖον (1x)
Heb 11:23 ·that they·saw *he·was* a·handsome little·child; and

G0792 ἀστήρ astḗr *n.* (24x)
Roots:G4766 See:G0798
xLangEquiv:H3556
G0792 N-NSM ἀστήρ (4x)
Mt 2:9 And behold, the star which they·saw in the east was·
1Co 15:41 of·*the*·stars, for *one* star varies·from *another* star
Rv 8:10 and there·fell a·great star from·out of·the heaven,
Rv 22:16 the kindred of·David, the star, the·one radiant and
G0792 N-NPM ἀστέρες (5x)
Mt 24:29 her brightness, and the stars shall·fall from the
Mk 13:25 and the stars of·the heaven shall·be falling·away,
Jud 1:13 their·own shame, erratic·wandering stars— for·
Rv 1:20 Lampstands: the seven stars are angels of·the seven
Rv 6:13 and the stars of·the heaven fell to the earth, as *when*
G0792 N-ASM ἀστέρα (4x)
Mt 2:2 of·the Jews? For we·saw his star in the east, and we·
Mt 2:10 Now upon·seeing the star *stationary*, they·rejoiced
Rv 2:28 And I·shall·give him the Early·Morning star.
Rv 9:1 sounded, and I·saw a·star having·fallen from·out of·
G0792 N-APM ἀστέρας (3x)
Rv 1:16 and having in his right hand seven stars. And 'out
Rv 2:1 the·one securely·holding the seven stars in his right·
Rv 3:1 the Spirits of·God and the seven stars: 'I·personally·
G0792 N-GSM ἀστέρος (3x)
Mt 2:7 personally·from them the time of·the appearing star.
1Co 15:41 for *one* star varies·from *another* star in glory.
Rv 8:11 the name of·the star is·referred·to·as Wormwood,
G0792 N-GPM ἀστέρων (5x)
1Co 15:41 ·*the*·moon, and another glory of·*the*·stars, for *one*
Rv 1:20 ·*is* the mystery of·the seven stars which you·saw in
Rv 8:12 and the third·part of·the stars, in·order·that the
Rv 12:1 and upon her head a·victor's·crown of·twelve stars.
Rv 12:4 dragged the third·part of·the stars of·the heaven and

G0793 ἀ•στήρικτος astḗriktôs *adj.* (2x)
Roots:G0001 G4741
G0793.2 A-NPM ἀστήρικτοι (1x)
2Pe 3:16 which *the* unlearned and unstable distort, as *they·do*
G0793.2 A-APF ἀστηρίκτους (1x)
2Pe 2:14 from·moral·failure, while·beguiling unstable souls,

G0794 ἄ•στοργος ástôrgôs *adj.* (2x)
Roots:G0001
G0794.1 A-NPM ἄστοργοι (1x)
2Ti 3:3 without·affection·for·family, implacable,·truceless·
G0794.1 A-APM ἀστόργους (1x)
Rm 1:31 without·affection·for·family, implacable,·

G0795 ἀ•στοχέω astôchéō *v.* (3x)
Roots:G0001 Compare:G0264
G0795.2 V-AAI-3P ἠστόχησαν (2x)
1Ti 6:21 *of·trust*, missed·the·mark concerning the trust.
2Ti 2:18 who missed·the·mark concerning the truth, saying
G0795.2 V-AAP-NPM ἀστοχήσαντες (1x)
1Ti 1:6 ·turned·aside to idle·talk, already·missing·the·mark,

G0796 ἀστραπή astrapḗ *n.* (9x)
Roots:G0797 Compare:G2987 G5458 G2769-2
See:G1823
xLangEquiv:H1300
G0796.1 N-NSF ἀστραπή (3x)
Lk 17:24 For just·as the lightning, the·one flashing from·out
Mt 24:27 For just·as the lightning comes·forth from *the* east
Mt 28:3 His outline·appearance was as lightning, and his
G0796.1 N-NPF ἀστραπαί (4x)
Rv 4:5 from·out of·the throne, lightnings and thunderings
Rv 8:5 and thunderings, and lightnings, and an·earthquake.
Rv 11:19 Temple. And there·occurred lightnings, and voices
Rv 16:18 and thunders, and lightnings. And there·was a·
G0796.1 N-ASF ἀστραπήν (1x)
Lk 10:18 falling as lightning from·out of·heaven.
G0796.2 N-DSF ἀστραπῇ (1x)
Lk 11:36 the radiant·shimmer of·a·lantern may·illuminate

G0797 ἀστράπτω astráptō *v.* (2x)
Roots:G0792 Compare:G0826 See:G0796 G1823
G4015
G0797 V-PAP-DPF ἀστραπτούσαις (1x)
Lk 24:4 stood·over them in clothes flashing·like·lightning.
G0797 V-PAP-NSF ἀστράπτουσα (1x)
Lk 17:24 the lightning, the·one flashing from·out of·the·one

G0798 ἄστρον ástrôn *n.* (4x)
Roots:G0792
G0798.1 N-NPN ἄστρα (1x)
Heb 11:12 just·as the constellations·of·stars of·the sky in·the
G0798.1 N-DPN ἄστροις (1x)
Lk 21:25 moon, and constellations·of·stars. And upon the
G0798.1 N-GPN ἄστρων (1x)
Ac 27:20 sun nor constellations·of·stars appearing over
G0798.2 N-ASN ἄστρον (1x)
Ac 7:43 of·Molek, and the star·constellation of·yeur god

G0799 Ἀ•σύγ•κριτος Asýnkritôs *n/p.* (1x)
Roots:G0001 G4793
G0799.2 N/P-ASM Ἀσύγκριτον (1x)
Rm 16:14 Greet ASynkritus, Phlegon, Hermas, PatroBas,

G0800 ἀ•σύμ•φωνος asýmphōnôs *adj.* (1x)
Roots:G0001 G4859
G0800 A-NPM ἀσύμφωνοι (1x)
Ac 28:25 And being discordant among one·another, they·

G0801 ἀ•σύν•ετος asýnêtôs *adj.* (5x)
Roots:G0001 G4908 Compare:G0878
xLangAlso:H5036
G0801.1 A-NSF ἀσύνετος (1x)
Rm 1:21 their uncomprehending heart was·already·darkened.
G0801.1 A-NPM ἀσύνετοι (2x)
Mt 15:16 yeu also still·at·this·point without·comprehension?
Mk 7:18 also without·comprehension? Do·yeu·not
G0801.1 A-APM ἀσυνέτους (1x)
Rm 1:31 without·comprehension, compact·breakers,
G0801.1 A-DSN ἀσυνέτῳ (1x)
Rm 10:19 yeu with a·nation without·comprehension."'

G0802 ἀ•σύν•θετος asýnthêtôs *adj.* (1x)
Roots:G0001 G4934
G0802.2 A-APM ἀσυνθέτους (1x)
Rm 1:31 compact·breakers, without·affection·for·family,

G0803 ἀ•σφάλεια asphálêia *n.* (3x)
Roots:G0804 See:G0805 G0806
G0803 N-NSF ἀσφάλεια (1x)
1Th 5:3 they·should·say, "Peace and security," then an·
G0803 N-ASF ἀσφάλειαν (1x)
Lk 1:4 ·that you·may·fully·know the security concerning *the*
G0803 N-DSF ἀσφαλείᾳ (1x)
Ac 5:23 dungeon having·been·shut with all security and the

G0804 ἀ•σφαλής asphalḗs *adj.* (6x)
Roots:G0001 See:G0805
G0804.2 A-ASF ἀσφαλῆ (1x)
Heb 6:19 of·the soul, both immovably·sure and steadfast, '
G0804.3 A-NSN ἀσφαλές (1x)
Php 3:1 to·yeu, but for·yeu, *it·is* an·immovable·safeguard.
G0804.4 A-ASN ἀσφαλές (1x)
Ac 25:26 have something absolutely·certain to·write *to·my*
EG0804.4 (1x)
Ac 23:24 Also *be certain* to·provide beasts *for·them* in·order·
G0804.5 A-ASN ἀσφαλές (2x)
Ac 21:34 to·know the absolute·certainty on·account·of the
Ac 22:30 ·resolved to·know the absolute·certainty *as·to* why

G0805 ἀ•σφαλίζω asphalízō *v.* (4x)
Roots:G0804
G0805 V-ADI-3S ἠσφαλίσατο (1x)
Ac 16:24 the innermost prison·cell and secured their feet in
G0805 V-ADI-3P ἠσφαλίσαντο (1x)
Mt 27:66 And traversing, they·secured the grave with the
G0805 V-ADM-2P ἀσφαλίσασθε (1x)
Mt 27:65 Make·*it*·as·secure as yeu·personally·know·how."
G0805 V-APN ἀσφαλισθῆναι (1x)
Mt 27:64 ·order *for* the grave to·be·made·secure until the

G0806 ἀ•σφαλῶς asphalôs *adv.* (3x)
Roots:G0804 See:G0803
G0806 ADV ἀσφαλῶς (3x)
Ac 2:36 all *the* house of·IsraEl must·know securely that God
Ac 16:23 charging the prison·warden to·keep them securely,
Mk 14:44 Securely·hold him and lead·*him*·away securely."

G0807 ἀ•σχημονέω aschēmônéō *v.* (2x)
Roots:G0809 See:G0808
G0807.1 V-PAI-3S ἀσχημονεῖ (1x)
1Co 13:5 does·not behave·improperly, does·not seek its·own
G0807.2 V-PAN ἀσχημονεῖν (1x)
1Co 7:36 *father* deems to·have·improper·etiquette toward his

G0808 ἀ•σχημοσύνη aschēmôsýnē *n.* (2x)
Roots:G0809 Compare:G1132-2 See:G0807
xLangAlso:H6172 H6174 H6181
G0808.2 N-ASF ἀσχημοσύνην (1x)
Rv 16:15 naked, and they·should·look·upon his indecency."
G0808.3 N-ASF ἀσχημοσύνην (1x)
Rm 1:27 males performing the dishonorable,·indecent·act, and

G0809 ἀ•σχήμων aschḗmōn *adj.* (1x)
Roots:G0001 G2192 Compare:G2157 G5611
See:G4976
G0809.4 A-NPN ἀσχήμονα (1x)
1Co 12:23 and our indecent·parts have more·abundant

G0810 ἀ•σωτία asōtía *n.* (3x)
Roots:G0001 G4982 See:G0811
G0810.1 N-NSF ἀσωτία (1x)
Eph 5:18 in which is *the* unsaved·lifestyle, but·rather be·
G0810.1 N-GSF ἀσωτίας (2x)
1Pe 4:4 sewage of·an·unsaved·lifestyle, while·yet·reviling

Tit 1:6 not in legal·accusation of·an·unsaved·lifestyle or

G0811 ἀ•σώτως asṓtōs *adv.* (1x)
Roots:G0001 G4982 See:G0810
G0811.1 ADV ἀσώτως (1x)
Lk 15:13 his substance while·living in·an·unsaved·lifestyle.

G0812 ἀ•τακτέω ataktéō *v.* (1x)
Roots:G0813
G0812.1 V-AAI-1P ἠτακτήσαμεν (1x)
2Th 3:7 us, because we·did·not act·disorderly among yeu.

G0813 ἄ•τακτος átaktôs *adj.* (1x)
Roots:G0001 G5002 See:G0814
G0813.3 A-APM ἀτάκτους (1x)
1Th 5:14 the disorderly·ones, personally·encourage the

G0814 ἀ•τάκτως atáktōs *adv.* (2x)
Roots:G0813
G0814 ADV ἀτάκτως (2x)
2Th 3:6 brother walking in·a·disorderly·manner and not
2Th 3:11 yeu in·a·disorderly·manner, who·are·working not·

G0815 ἄ•τεκνος átêknôs *adj.* (3x)
Roots:G0001 G5043
G0815 A-NSM ἄτεκνος (3x)
Lk 20:28 a·wife, and this·man should·die childless, that his
Lk 20:29 the first·one, after·taking a·wife, died childless.
Lk 20:30 took the *same* wife, and this·man died childless.

G0816 ἀ•τενίζω atênízō *v.* (14x)
Roots:G0001 G5037-1 Compare:G1689 G2657 G0991
G0816 V-PAI-2P ἀτενίζετε (1x)
Ac 3:12 this? Or why·do yeu·gaze·intently at·us, as·though
G0816 V-PAP-NPM ἀτενίζοντες (2x)
Lk 4:20 that·were in the gathering gazing·intently at·him.
Ac 1:10 And as they·were gazing·intently toward the heaven
G0816 V-AAN ἀτενίσαι (2x)
2Co 3:7 of·IsraEl not to·be·able to·gaze·intently into the face
2Co 3:13 the Sons of·IsraEl not gazing·intently for the end,
G0816 V-AAP-NSF ἀτενίσασα (1x)
Lk 22:56 the firelight and after·gazing·intently at·him, a·
G0816 V-AAP-NSM ἀτενίσας (7x)
Ac 3:4 And Peter, gazing·intently upon him together with·
Ac 7:55 full of·Holy Spirit, after·gazing·intently into the
Ac 10:4 And gazing·intently at·him and becoming alarmed,
Ac 11:6 Which gazing·intently upon, I·was·fully·observing,
Ac 13:9 with·Holy Spirit and gazing·intently upon him,
Ac 14:9 Paul speaking, who after·gazing·intently at·him and
Ac 23:1 Paul, after·gazing·intently at·the joint·council·of·
G0816 V-AAP-NPM ἀτενίσαντες (1x)
Ac 6:15 And gazing·intently upon him, absolutely·all the·

G0817 ἄτερ átêr *prep.* (2x)
Compare:G5565 See:G0427
G0817.1 PREP ἄτερ (2x)
Lk 22:6 to·hand him over to·them without·any of·the crowd.
Lk 22:35 "When I·dispatched yeu without·any pouch,

G0818 ἀ•τιμάζω atimázō *v.* (6x)
Roots:G0820
G0818.1 V-PAI-2S ἀτιμάζεις (1x)
Rm 2:23 boast in Torah-Law, do·you·dishonor God through
G0818.1 V-PAI-2P ἀτιμάζετε (1x)
Jn 8:49 I·deeply·honor my Father, and yeu dishonor me.
G0818.1 V-PEN ἀτιμάζεσθαι (1x)
Rm 1:24 of·their·own hearts, to·dishonor their·own bodies
G0818.1 V-AAI-2P ἠτιμάσατε (1x)
Jac 2:6 But yeu·yeurselves dishonored the helplessly·poor.
G0818.2 V-AAP-NPM ἀτιμάσαντες (1x)
Lk 20:11 this·one·also, and dishonorably·treating *him*, they·
G0818.2 V-APN ἀτιμασθῆναι (1x)
Ac 5:41 ·accounted·fully·worthy to·be·dishonorably·treated

G0819 ἀ•τιμία atimía *n.* (7x)
Roots:G0820 Compare:G0152 G1791
G0819.1 N-NSF ἀτιμία (1x)
1Co 11:14 should·wear·long·hair, it·is a·dishonor to·him?
G0819.1 N-ASF ἀτιμίαν (3x)
Rm 9:21 ·fact, one vessel to honor and another to dishonor?
2Co 11:21 ·to *the implied·charge·of* dishonor, as·though that
2Ti 2:20 ·*out* in·fact unto honor, and some unto dishonor.
G0819.1 N-DSF ἀτιμίᾳ (1x)
1Co 15:43 It·is·sown in dishonor; it·is·awakened in glory.
G0819.1 N-GSF ἀτιμίας (1x)
2Co 6:8 through glory and dishonor, through harsh·
G0819.2 N-GSF ἀτιμίας (1x)
Rm 1:26 them over to dishonorable burning·passions, for

G0820 ἄ•τιμος átimôs *adj.* (4x)
Roots:G0001 G5092 See:G0819
G0820.1 A-NSM ἄτιμος (2x)
Mt 13:57 "A·prophet is not without·honor, except in his·own
Mk 6:4 "A·prophet is not without·honor, except in his·own
G0820.2 A-NPM ἄτιμοι (1x)
1Co 4:10 *are* glorious, but we·ourselves *are* dishonored.
G0820.3 A-APN-C ἀτιμότερα (1x)
1Co 12:23 ·we·presume to·be less·honorable, upon·these

G0821 ἀ•τιμόω atimóō *v.* (2x)
Roots:G0820 G0818
G0821 V-RPP-ASM ἠτιμωμένον (1x)
Mk 12:4 *him·back* having·been·handled·dishonorably.
EG0821 (1x)
Mt 21:35 of·his slaves, *handled·them·dishonorably*. In·fact,

G0822 ἀτμίς atmís *n.* (2x)
Roots:G0108-2 See:G0109
G0822 N-NSF ἀτμίς (1x)
Jac 4:14 yeur life†? For it·is a·vapor, one·appearing just·for
G0822 N-ASF ἀτμίδα (1x)
Ac 2:19 down·below: blood and fire and vapor of·smoke.

G0823 ἄ•τομος átômos *adj.* (1x)
Roots:G0001 G5114 Compare:G4743
G0823.3 A-DSN ἀτόμῳ (1x)
1Co 15:52 in an·instant, in a·twinkling of·an·eye, at the last

G0824 ἄ•τοπος átôpôs *adj.* (3x)
Roots:G0001 G5117 Compare:G0092 G2556 G0983 G0807
G0824.1 A-ASN ἄτοπον (1x)
Ac 28:6 not·even·one·thing out·of·place happening to him,
G0824.2 A-ASN ἄτοπον (1x)
Lk 23:41 "But this·man practiced not·even·one·thing amiss."
G0824.3 A-GPM ἀτόπων (1x)
2Th 3:2 we·may·be·snatched away·from the absurd and evil

G0825 Ἀττάλεια Attálêia *n/l.* (1x)
G0825.2 N/L-ASF Ἀττάλειαν (1x)
Ac 14:25 in Perga, they·walked·down into Attalia.

G0826 αὐγάζω augázō *v.* (1x)
Roots:G0827 Compare:G0797 G2989 G5316 See:G0541 G1306 G5081
G0826.1 V-AAN αὐγάσαι (1x)
2Co 4:4 the *ray·of·light* not to·beam·forth·directly on·them,

G0827 αὐγή augḗ *n.* (2x)
Compare:G5457 G4405 G3722 G2246 G1661-2 See:G0826 G1306 G0541
EG0827.1 (1x)
2Co 4:4 such·for the *ray·of·light* not to·beam·forth·directly
G0827.3 N-GSF αὐγῆς (1x)
Ac 20:11 ·this·manner even·unto *the* first·light·of·day, *Paul*

G0828 Αὔγουστος Aúgôustôs *n/p.* (1x)
Compare:G4575
G0828 N/P-GSM Αὐγούστου (1x)
Lk 2:1 ·forth a·decree directly·from Caesar Augustus, *that*

G0829 αὐθ•άδης authádēs *adj.* (2x)
Roots:G0846 G2237
G0829 A-NPM αὐθάδεις (1x)
2Pe 2:10 *They·are* audacious *and* self-pleasing; they·do·not
G0829 A-ASM αὐθάδη (1x)
Tit 1:7 of·God), not self-pleasing, not easily·angered, not

G0830 αὐθ•αίρετος authaírêtos *adj.* (2x)
Roots:G0846 G0140 Compare:G1589 G0141
G0830.1 A-NSM αὐθαίρετος (1x)
2Co 8:17 more·diligent, of·his·own·choice, he·went·forth to
G0830.1 A-NPM αὐθαίρετοι (1x)
2Co 8:3 ·and·beyond *their* power, of·their·own·choice,

G0831 αὐθ•εντέω authêntéō *v.* (1x)
Roots:G0846 Compare:G1850 G2715 G2961
G0831.2 V-PAN αὐθεντεῖν (1x)
1Ti 2:12 *for·her* to·take·a·stance·of·authority·over a·man,

G0832 αὐλέω auléō *v.* (3x)
Roots:G0836
G0832.1 V-PPP-NSN αὐλούμενον (1x)
1Co 14:7 *what tune* is·being·piped or is·being·harped?
G0832.2 V-AAI-1P ηὐλήσαμεν (2x)
Lk 7:32 and saying, 'We·played·flute for·yeu, and yeu·did·
Mt 11:17 and saying, 'We·played·flute for·yeu, and yeu·

G0833 αὐλή aulḗ *n.* (13x)
Roots:G0108-2 Compare:G0980-1 G0933 G1886 G3624 G1430 G1825-1 See:G1886 G4259 G0822 G0109 xLangAlso:H2691 H3957
EG0833 (1x)
Jn 6:39 it *(that·is, the sheep pen)*, but·rather shall·raise it up
G0833.2 N-ASF αὐλήν (1x)
Jn 10:1 through the door into the yard·pen of·the sheep, but·
G0833.2 N-GSF αὐλῆς (1x)
Jn 10:16 not from·among this yard·pen. It·is·mandatory·for
G0833.3 N-ASF αὐλήν (3x)
Jn 18:15 into the courtyard of·the designated·high·priest.
Mk 14:54 to inside the courtyard of·the designated·high·priest
Rv 11:2 But the courtyard, the·one *proceeding* inwardly
G0833.3 N-DSF αὐλῇ (2x)
Mt 26:69 was·sitting·down outside in the courtyard, and one
Mk 14:66 being down·below in the courtyard, *along* comes
G0833.3 N-GSF αὐλῆς (3x)
Lk 22:55 midst of·the courtyard and sitting·down·together,
Mt 26:58 up·to the courtyard of·the designated·high·priest,
Mk 15:16 led him away inside the courtyard, which is *the*
G0833.4 N-ASF αὐλήν (2x)
Lk 11:21 should·keep·watch·over his·own mansion, his
Mt 26:3 ·together in the mansion of·the designated·high·priest

G0834 αὐλητής aulētḗs *n.* (2x)
Roots:G0832
G0834 N-APM αὐλητάς (1x)
Mt 9:23 home and seeing the flute·players and the crowd
G0834 N-GPM αὐλητῶν (1x)
Rv 18:22 ·harpists, and musicians, and of·flute·players, and

G0835 αὐλίζομαι aulízômai *v.* (2x)
Roots:G0833
G0835.2 V-INI-3S ηὐλίζετο (1x)
Lk 21:37 ·forth, he·was·sleeping·out·in·the·open upon the
G0835.2 V-AOI-3S ηὐλίσθη (1x)
Mt 21:17 into BethAny, and there he·slept·out·in·the·open.

G0836 αὐλός aulṓs *n.* (1x)
Roots:G0108-2 Compare:G4947-3 See:G0109 xLangAlso:H2485 H5748 A4953
G0836.2 N-NSM αὐλός (1x)
1Co 14:7 ·things giving sound, whether flute or harp, if it·

G0837 αὐξάνω auxánō *v.* (24x)
Roots:G0849-3 Compare:G4121 G4369
G0837.1 V-PAI-3S αὔξει (4x)
Lk 12:27 "Fully·observe how the lilies grow. They·do·not
Mt 6:28 of·the field, how they·grow; they·do·not labor·hard,
Eph 2:21 being·fitly·framed·together, grows into a·holy
Col 2:19 ·out·of·which all the Body grows·up through the
G0837.1 V-PAM-2P αὐξάνετε (1x)
2Pe 3:18 But grow in grace and in·*the*·knowledge of·our
G0837.1 V-PAP-NSM αὐξάνων (1x)
1Co 3:7 the·one watering, but·rather God, the·one growing.
G0837.1 V-PPP-NPM αὐξανόμενοι (1x)
Col 1:10 beneficially·good work and growing·up into the
G0837.1 V-IAI-3S ηὔξανεν (5x)
Lk 1:80 And the little·child was·growing, and was·
Lk 2:40 little·child was·growing and was·becoming·mighty
Ac 12:24 of·God was·growing and was·multiplied.
Ac 19:20 Lord was·growing and was·exercising·strength.
1Co 3:6 Apollos watered, but·yet God was·growing.

G0837.1 V-AAI-3S ηὔξησεν (2x)
Lk 13:19 into his garden. And it·grew and became a·great
Ac 7:17 to·AbRaham, the People grew and were·multiplied
G0837.1 V-AAS-1P αὐξήσωμεν (1x)
Eph 4:15 being·truthful in love, we·should·grow·up *in* all
G0837.1 V-APS-2P αὐξηθῆτε (1x)
1Pe 2:2 free·from·guile, in·order·that yeu·may·grow by it,
G0837.1 V-APS-3S αὐξηθῇ (1x)
Mt 13:32 ·of·seeds. But whenever it·should·be·grown, it·is
EG0837.1 (2x)
Lk 17:6 "If yeu·were·having trust *that·grows* as a·kernel of·
Mt 17:20 if yeu·should·have trust *that·grows* as a·kernel of·
G0837.2 V-PAP-ASM αὐξάνοντα (1x)
Mk 4:8 fruit, springing·up and growing·more, and it·was·
G0837.2 V-PPP-GSF αὐξανομένης (1x)
2Co 10:15 ·yeur trust being·grown·further) to·be·made·great
G0837.2 V-IAI-3S ηὔξανεν (1x)
Ac 6:7 of·God was·growing·*in·circulation*; and the number
G0837.3 V-PAN αὐξάνειν (1x)
Jn 3:30 It·is·necessary·for that·one to·increasingly·grow, but
G0837.3 V-AAO-3S αὐξήσαι (1x)
2Co 9:10 ·seed, and may·he·increasingly·grow the produce

G0838 αὔξησις aúxēsis *n.* (2x)
Roots:G0837
G0838.2 N-ASF αὔξησιν (2x)
Eph 4:16 ·produces the maturing·growth of·the Body for its·
Col 2:19 ·knit·together with·the maturing·growth of·God.

G0839 αὔριον aúriôn *adv.* (15x)
Roots:G0109 Compare:G2250
xLangEquiv:H5399
G0839.2 ADV αὔριον (1x)
Lk 10:35 going·forth upon the stirring·of·day, casting·forth
G0839.3 ADV αὔριον (12x)
Lk 12:28 in the field, and tomorrow being·cast into an·oven,
Lk 13:32 I·further·finish healing today and tomorrow, and
Lk 13:33 me to·traverse today, and tomorrow, and the *day*
Ac 23:15 ·bring him down to yeu tomorrow, as intending to·
Ac 23:20 that you·should·bring Paul down tomorrow into the
Ac 25:22 "Then tomorrow," he·replied, "You·shall·hear
Mt 6:30 being *here*, and tomorrow being·cast into an·oven,
Mt 6:34 yeu·should·not be·anxious for tomorrow, for
Mt 6:34 for tomorrow shall·be·anxious·about the·things of·
Jac 4:13 "Today or tomorrow we·should·traverse into that
Jac 4:14 ·with the·thing *that shall·happen* tomorrow! For
1Co 15:32 ·eat and should·drink, for tomorrow we·die."
G0839.4 ADV αὔριον (2x)
Ac 4:3 *them* in custody for the next·day, for even·now it·was
Ac 4:5 And it·happened on the next·day, *that* their rulers and

G0840 αὐστηρός austērós *adj.* (2x)
Roots:G0109 Compare:G4642 See:G0857
G0840.1 A-NSM αὐστηρός (2x)
Lk 19:21 you, because you·are an·unrelenting man·of·clay†.
Lk 19:22 that I·myself am an·unrelenting man·of·clay†,

G0841 αὐτ•άρκεια autárkêia *n.* (2x)
Roots:G0842
G0841.1 N-ASF αὐτάρκειαν (1x)
2Co 9:8 yeu, in·order·that having all self-sufficiency in all
G0841.1 N-GSF αὐταρκείας (1x)
1Ti 6:6 Way·of·Devout·Reverence with self-sufficiency is

G0842 αὐτ•άρκης autárkēs *adj.* (1x)
Roots:G0846 G0714 See:G0841
G0842.2 A-NSM αὐτάρκης (1x)
Php 4:11 in whatever·state I·am, to·be self-content *with·that.*

G0843 αὐτο•κατά•κριτος autôkatákritôs *adj.* (1x)
Roots:G0846 G2632
G0843 A-NSM αὐτοκατάκριτος (1x)
Tit 3:11 ·subverted and morally·fails, being self-condemned.

G0844 αὐτό•ματος autômatôs *adj.* (2x)
Roots:G0846 G3145
G0844.3 A-NSF αὐτομάτη (2x)
Ac 12:10 City, which automatically was·opened·up to·them.
Mk 4:28 For the earth automatically bears·fruit; first a·blade,

G0845 αὐτ•όπτης autóptēs *adj.* (1x)
Roots:G0846 G3700 Compare:G2030
G0845.2 A-NPM αὐτόπται (1x)
Lk 1:2 to·us after·becoming eyewitnesses and assistants of·

G0846 αὐτός autós *p:p.* (5842x)
Compare:G0848 G1520 See:G1438 G0109 G1683 G2009-1
(abbreviated listing for G0846)
G0846.ª P:P-GSM αὐτοῦ (2x)
(list for G0846.ª:P:P-GSM excluded)
G0846.ª P:P-GPF αὐτῶν (1x)
(list for G0846.ª:P:P-GPF excluded)
G0846.2 P:P-NSM αὐτός (9x)
(list for G0846.2:P:P-NSM excluded)
G0846.2 P:P-NSF αὐτή (1x)
(list for G0846.2:P:P-NSF excluded)
G0846.2 P:P-NSN αὐτό (6x)
(list for G0846.2:P:P-NSN excluded)
G0846.2 P:P-NPM αὐτοί (2x)
(list for G0846.2:P:P-NPM excluded)
G0846.2 P:P-NPN αὐτά (2x)
(list for G0846.2:P:P-NPN excluded)
G0846.2 P:P-ASM αὐτόν (7x)
(list for G0846.2:P:P-ASM excluded)
G0846.2 P:P-ASF αὐτήν (9x)
(list for G0846.2:P:P-ASF excluded)
G0846.2 P:P-ASN αὐτό (23x)
(list for G0846.2:P:P-ASN excluded)
G0846.2 P:P-APF αὐτάς (1x)
(list for G0846.2:P:P-APF excluded)
G0846.2 P:P-APN αὐτά (8x)
(list for G0846.2:P:P-APN excluded)
G0846.2 P:P-DSM αὐτῷ (4x)
(list for G0846.2:P:P-DSM excluded)
G0846.2 P:P-DSF αὐτῇ (15x)
(list for G0846.2:P:P-DSF excluded)
G0846.2 P:P-DSN αὐτῷ (7x)
(list for G0846.2:P:P-DSN excluded)
G0846.2 P:P-DPF αὐταῖς (2x)
(list for G0846.2:P:P-DPF excluded)
G0846.2 P:P-DPN αὐτοῖς (2x)
(list for G0846.2:P:P-DPN excluded)
G0846.2 P:P-GSM αὐτοῦ (3x)
(list for G0846.2:P:P-GSM excluded)
G0846.2 P:P-GSF αὐτῆς (6x)
(list for G0846.2:P:P-GSF excluded)
G0846.2 P:P-GSN αὐτοῦ (3x)
(list for G0846.2:P:P-GSN excluded)
G0846.2 P:P-GPM αὐτῶν (1x)
(list for G0846.2:P:P-GPM excluded)
G0846.2 P:P-GPF αὐτῶν (1x)
(list for G0846.2:P:P-GPF excluded)
G0846.2 P:P-GPN αὐτῶν (3x)
(list for G0846.2:P:P-GPN excluded)
EG0846.2 (2x)
(list for EG0846.2: excluded)
G0846.3 P:D-NSF αὐτή (21x)
(list for G0846.3:P:D-NSF excluded)
G0846.3 P:P-NSM αὐτός (165x)
(list for G0846.3:P:P-NSM excluded)
G0846.3 P:P-NSF αὐτή (3x)
(list for G0846.3:P:P-NSF excluded)
G0846.3 P:P-NSN αὐτό (4x)
(list for G0846.3:P:P-NSN excluded)
G0846.3 P:P-NPM αὐτοί (75x)
(list for G0846.3:P:P-NPM excluded)
G0846.3 P:P-NPN αὐτά (1x)
(list for G0846.3:P:P-NPN excluded)
G0846.3 P:P-ASM αὐτόν (959x)
(list for G0846.3:P:P-ASM excluded)
G0846.3b P:P-ASM αὐτόν (1x)
(list for G0846.3b:P:P-ASM excluded)
G0846.3 P:P-ASF αὐτήν (123x)
(list for G0846.3:P:P-ASF excluded)
G0846.3 P:P-ASN αὐτό (62x)
(list for G0846.3:P:P-ASN excluded)
G0846.3 P:P-APM αὐτούς (347x)
(list for G0846.3:P:P-APM excluded)
G0846.3 P:P-APF αὐτάς (10x)
(list for G0846.3:P:P-APF excluded)
G0846.3 P:P-APN αὐτά (40x)
(list for G0846.3:P:P-APN excluded)
G0846.3 P:P-APN@ αὐτά (1x)
(list for G0846.3:P:P-APN@ excluded)
G0846.3 P:P-DSM αὐτῷ (842x)
(list for G0846.3:P:P-DSM excluded)
G0846.3 P:P-DSF αὐτῇ (101x)
(list for G0846.3:P:P-DSF excluded)
G0846.3 P:P-DSN αὐτῷ (16x)
(list for G0846.3:P:P-DSN excluded)
G0846.3 P:P-DPM αὐτοῖς (558x)
(list for G0846.3:P:P-DPM excluded)
G0846.3 P:P-DPF αὐταῖς (18x)
(list for G0846.3:P:P-DPF excluded)
G0846.3 P:P-DPN αὐτοῖς (14x)
(list for G0846.3:P:P-DPN excluded)
G0846.3 P:P-GSM αὐτοῦ (337x)
(list for G0846.3:P:P-GSM excluded)
G0846.3a P:P-GSM αὐτοῦ (1x)
(list for G0846.3a:P:P-GSM excluded)
G0846.3 P:P-GSF αὐτῆς (44x)
(list for G0846.3:P:P-GSF excluded)
G0846.3 P:P-GSN αὐτοῦ (40x)
(list for G0846.3:P:P-GSN excluded)
G0846.3 P:P-GPM αὐτῶν (537x)
(list for G0846.3:P:P-GPM excluded)
G0846.3 P:P-GPF αὐτῶν (23x)
(list for G0846.3:P:P-GPF excluded)
G0846.3 P:P-GPN αὐτῶν (21x)
(list for G0846.3:P:P-GPN excluded)
EG0846.3 (82x)
(list for EG0846.3: excluded)
G0846.4 P:P-GSM αὐτοῦ (2x)
(list for G0846.4:P:P-GSM excluded)
G0846.5 P:P-DSM αὐτῷ (2x)
(list for G0846.5:P:P-DSM excluded)
G0846.5 P:P-DPM αὐτοῖς (3x)
(list for G0846.5:P:P-DPM excluded)
G0846.5 P:P-GSM αὐτοῦ (1x)
(list for G0846.5:P:P-GSM excluded)
EG0846.5 (1x)
(list for EG0846.5: excluded)
G0846.6 P:P-DPM αὐτοῖς (1x)
(list for G0846.6:P:P-DPM excluded)
G0846.6 P:P-GPM αὐτῶν (1x)
(list for G0846.6:P:P-GPM excluded)
G0846.7 P:P-ASM αὐτόν (3x)
(list for G0846.7:P:P-ASM excluded)
G0846.7 P:P-ASF αὐτήν (1x)
(list for G0846.7:P:P-ASF excluded)
G0846.7 P:P-DSM αὐτῷ (10x)
(list for G0846.7:P:P-DSM excluded)
G0846.7 P:P-DPM αὐτοῖς (1x)
(list for G0846.7:P:P-DPM excluded)
G0846.7 P:P-GSM αὐτοῦ (1080x)
(list for G0846.7:P:P-GSM excluded)
G0846.7 P:P-GSN αὐτοῦ (3x)
(list for G0846.7:P:P-GSN excluded)
EG0846.7 (28x)
(list for EG0846.7: excluded)
G0846.8 P:P-GSF αὐτῆς (117x)
(list for G0846.8:P:P-GSF excluded)
G0846.8 P:P-GPM αὐτῶν (1x)
(list for G0846.8:P:P-GPM excluded)
G0846.9 P:P-NPM αὐτοί (1x)
(list for G0846.9:P:P-NPM excluded)

G0846.9 P:P-ASM αὐτόν (1x)
(list for G0846.9:P:P-ASM excluded)
G0846.9 P:P-ASN αὐτό (1x)
(list for G0846.9:P:P-ASN excluded)
G0846.9 P:P-APM αὐτούς (2x)
(list for G0846.9:P:P-APM excluded)
G0846.9 P:P-DSF αὐτῇ (1x)
(list for G0846.9:P:P-DSF excluded)
G0846.9 P:P-DSN αὐτῷ (1x)
(list for G0846.9:P:P-DSN excluded)
G0846.9 P:P-DPM αὐτοῖς (1x)
(list for G0846.9:P:P-DPM excluded)
G0846.9 P:P-GSM αὐτοῦ (2x)
(list for G0846.9:P:P-GSM excluded)
G0846.9 P:P-GPN αὐτῶν (1x)
(list for G0846.9:P:P-GPN excluded)
G0846.10 P:P-ASN αὐτό (5x)
(list for G0846.10:P:P-ASN excluded)
G0846.11 P:P-NPM αὐτοί (1x)
(list for G0846.11:P:P-NPM excluded)
G0846.11 P:P-APM αὐτούς (1x)
(list for G0846.11:P:P-APM excluded)
G0846.11 P:P-DPF αὐταῖς (1x)
(list for G0846.11:P:P-DPF excluded)
G0846.11 P:P-GPN αὐτῶν (2x)
(list for G0846.11:P:P-GPN excluded)

G0847 αὐτοῦ autôû *adv.* (6x)
Roots:G0846 Compare:G1786
EG0847 (2x)
Ac 15:33 And after·continuing *there* a·time, they·were·
Ac 18:11 And he·settled *there* a·year and six lunar·months,
G0847.2 ADV αὐτοῦ (3x)
Ac 15:34 ·good to·Silas to·still·stay·over at·this·location.
Ac 21:4 disciples, we·stayed·over at·this·location *for* seven
Mt 26:36 disciples, "Yeu·sit·down at·this·location, where
G0847.3 ADV αὐτοῦ (1x)
Ac 18:19 and·these *two* he·left·behind at·that·location, but

G0848 αὐτοῦ hautôû *p:p.* (2x)
Roots:G1438 Compare:G0846
G0848.2 P:P-GSM αὐτοῦ (1x)
Jn 9:21 He·himself shall·speak concerning himself."
G0848.3 P:F-GPF αὐτῶν (1x)
Rv 9:11 And they·have a·king over them— the angel of·the

G0849 αὐτό•χειρ autóchêir *adj.* (1x)
Roots:G0846 G5495
G0849.2 A-NPM αὐτόχειρες (1x)
Ac 27:19 on·the third *day*, with·our·own·hands, we·flung

G0850 αὐχμηρός auchmērós *adj.* (1x)
Compare:G4652 G4653 See:G0109
G0850.2 A-DSM αὐχμηρῷ (1x)
2Pe 1:19 as to·a·lantern shining·forth in a·murky place—

G0851 ἀφ•αιρέω aphairéō *v.* (10x)
Roots:G0575 G0138 Compare:G0525 G4014
G0851 V-FAI-3S ἀφαιρήσει (1x)
Rv 22:19 of·this prophecy, God shall·remove his portion
G0851 V-FPI-3S ἀφαιρεθήσεται (1x)
Lk 10:42 portion, which shall·not be·removed from her."
G0851 V-PAN ἀφαιρεῖν (1x)
Heb 10:4 and of·adult·male·goats to·remove moral·failures.
G0851 V-PAS-3S ἀφαιρῇ (1x)
Rv 22:19 And if anyone should·remove *anything* from the
G0851 V-PMI-3S ἀφαιρεῖται (1x)
Lk 16:3 should·I·do? Because my lord removes from me the
G0851 V-2AAI-3S ἀφεῖλεν (3x)
Lk 22:50 of·the designated·high·priest and removed his right
Mt 26:51 ·the designated·high·priest, he·removed his earlobe.
Mk 14:47 ·the designated·high·priest and removed his earlobe
G0851 V-2AAN ἀφελεῖν (1x)
Lk 1:25 he·took·notice·of *me*, to·remove my lowly·reproach
G0851 V-2AMS-1S ἀφέλωμαι (1x)
Rm 11:27 ⇒ 'whenever I·should·remove their moral·failures.

G0852 ἀ•φανής aphanḗs *adj.* (1x)
Roots:G0001 G5316 Compare:G0517 G0855
See:G0853
G0852.2 A-NSF ἀφανής (1x)
Heb 4:13 *that·is* not·completely·apparent in·the·sight of·him,

G0853 ἀ•φανίζω aphanízō *v.* (4x)
Roots:G0852 Compare:G1842 See:G0854
xLangAlso:H7843 H8074 H0006
G0853.2 V-PAI-3S ἀφανίζει (2x)
Mt 6:19 where moth and corrosion obliterate, and where
Mt 6:20 neither moth nor corrosion obliterate, and where
G0853.4 V-PPP-NSF ἀφανιζομένη (1x)
Jac 4:14 just·for a·brief·moment and then being·expunged.
G0853.5 V-PAI-3P ἀφανίζουσιν (1x)
Mt 6:16 ·acting·hypocrites, for they·disfigure their faces in·

G0854 ἀ•φανισμός aphanismós *n.* (1x)
Roots:G0853
G0854.1 N-GSM ἀφανισμοῦ (1x)
Heb 8:13 and growing·agedly·old *is* close to·obliteration.

G0855 ἄ•φαντος áphantôs *adj.* (1x)
Roots:G0001 G5316 Compare:G0517 G0852
G0855.2 A-NSM ἄφαντος (1x)
Lk 24:31 and·then he·himself became unviewable by them.

G0856 ἀφ•εδρών aphēdrṓn *n.* (2x)
Roots:G0575 G1476
G0856 N-ASM ἀφεδρῶνα (2x)
Mt 15:17 the belly and·then is·cast·out into an·outhouse?
Mk 7:19 and·then traverses·out into the outhouse, purging all

G0857 ἀ•φειδία aphêidía *n.* (1x)
Roots:G0001 G5339
G0857.3 N-DSF ἀφειδίᾳ (1x)
Col 2:23 and an·unsparingly·harsh·treatment of·body,

G0858 ἀ•φελότης aphēlótēs *n.* (1x)
Roots:G0001 Compare:G0574
G0858.2 N-DSF ἀφελότητι (1x)
Ac 2:46 in exuberant·celebration and simplicity of·heart,

G0859 ἄφ•εσις áphēsis *n.* (15x)
Roots:G0863 Compare:G0628-1 G0629
xLangAlso:H3104 H7964
G0859.2 N-NSF ἄφεσις (3x)
Ac 13:38 ·man, *the* pardon of·moral·failures is·being·fully·
Heb 9:22 ·from a·pouring·out·of·blood, there·is no pardon.
Heb 10:18 And, where *there·is* pardon of·these·things,
G0859.2 N-ASF ἄφεσιν (11x)
Lk 3:3 of·repentance unto a·pardon of·moral·failures.
Lk 24:47 and pardon of·moral·failures to·be·officially·
Ac 2:38 of·Jesus Anointed for pardon of·moral·failures, and
Ac 5:31 repentance to·IsraEl and pardon of·moral·failures.
Ac 10:43 him *is* to·receive pardon of·moral·failures through
Ac 26:18 for·them to·receive pardon of·moral·failures and
Mt 26:28 ·out concerning many for pardon of·moral·failures.
Mk 1:4 of·repentance unto a·pardon of·moral·failures.
Mk 3:29 Holy Spirit does·not have pardon into the coming·
Eph 1:7 his blood— the pardon of·trespasses according·to
Col 1:14 through his blood, the pardon of·moral·failures.
G0859.2 N-DSF ἀφέσει (1x)
Lk 1:77 to·his People unto a·pardon of·their moral·failures,

G0860 ἁφή haphḗ *n.* (2x)
Roots:G0681 Compare:G0719 G4886 See:G0680
G0860.2 N-GSF ἁφῆς (1x)
Eph 4:16 amply·supplying connection·joint, according·to an·
G0860.2 N-GPF ἁφῶν (1x)
Col 2:19 ·up through the connecting·joints and ligaments

G0861 ἀ•φθαρσία aphtharsía *n.* (8x)
Roots:G0862 Compare:G0090
G0861.1 N-ASF ἀφθαρσίαν (4x)
Tit 2:7 ·worthy·of·reverent·respect, incorruptibility,
1Co 15:50 does the corruption inherit the incorruptibility.
1Co 15:53 *being* to·dress·itself·with incorruptibility, and *for*
1Co 15:54 should·dress·itself·with incorruptibility, and this
G0861.1 N-DSF ἀφθαρσίᾳ (2x)
1Co 15:42 in corruption; it·is·awakened in incorruptibility.
Eph 6:24 Anointed with incorruptibility. So·be·it,·Amen.
G0861.2 N-ASF ἀφθαρσίαν (2x)
Rm 2:7 honor, and eternal·incorruptibility, *he·shall·render*
2Ti 1:10 life·above and eternal·incorruptibility through the

G0862 ἄ•φθαρτος áphthartôs *adj.* (7x)
Roots:G0001 G5351
G0862.2 A-NPM ἄφθαρτοι (1x)
1Co 15:52 the dead shall·be·awakened incorruptible, and
G0862.2 A-ASM ἄφθαρτον (1x)
1Co 9:25 ·crown, but we·ourselves an·incorruptible·one.
G0862.2 A-ASF ἄφθαρτον (1x)
1Pe 1:4 into an·incorruptible, uncontaminated and
G0862.2 A-DSM ἀφθάρτῳ (1x)
1Ti 1:17 to·the King of·the ages, incorruptible, invisible, to·
G0862.2 A-DSN ἀφθάρτῳ (1x)
1Pe 3:4 heart, with the incorruptible *garment* of·the calmly·
G0862.2 A-GSM ἀφθάρτου (1x)
Rm 1:23 they·did·change the glory of·the incorruptible God⇒
G0862.2 A-GSF ἀφθάρτου (1x)
1Pe 1:23 ·seed, but·rather of·an·incorruptible *sowing·of·seed*

G0863 ἀφ•ίημι aphíēmi *v.* (146x)
Roots:G0575 G2423-1 Compare:G0630 G1502
G5226 G1634 G1943 G2436 See:G0859 G2433
G5483 xLangAlso:H5545
G0863.1 V-AAI-3S ἀφῆκεν (1x)
Mt 27:50 ·out again with·a·loud voice, sent·away his spirit.
G0863.1 V-2AAP-NSM ἀφείς (2x)
Mt 13:36 Then after·sending·away the crowds, YeShua went
Mk 15:37 And Jesus, after·sending·away *his spirit with* a·
G0863.1 V-2AAP-NPM ἀφέντες (1x)
Mk 4:36 So·then, after·sending·away the crowd, they·
G0863.2 -- (1x)
Lk 17:36 ·be·personally·taken, and the other shall·be·left)]."
G0863.2 V-FAI-1S ἀφήσω (1x)
Jn 14:18 I·shall·not leave yeu orphans. I·do·come alongside
G0863.2 V-FAI-3P ἀφήσουσιν (1x)
Lk 19:44 within you; and they·shall·not leave in you stone
G0863.2 V-FPI-3S ἀφεθήσεται (3x)
Lk 17:34 ·be·personally·taken, and the other shall·be·left.
Lk 17:35 ·be·personally·taken, and the other shall·be·left.
Lk 21:6 ·come in which there·shall·not be·left a·stone upon
G0863.2 V-PAI-1S ἀφίημι (2x)
Jn 14:27 "Peace I·leave with·yeu; my peace I·give to·yeu.
Jn 16:28 into the world. Again, I·leave the world, and
G0863.2 V-PAI-3S ἀφίησιν (2x)
Jn 10:12 ·observes the wolf coming and leaves the sheep and
Mt 4:11 Then the Slanderer leaves him, and behold, angels
G0863.2 V-PAM-3S ἀφιέτω (2x)
1Co 7:12 ·consent to·dwell with him, he·must·not leave her.
1Co 7:13 to·dwell with her, she·must·not leave him.
G0863.2 V-PAN ἀφιέναι (3x)
Lk 11:42 these·things, and not to·leave those·things *undone*.
Mt 23:23 these·things, and not to·leave those·things *undone*.
1Co 7:11 And a·husband *is* not to·leave *his* wife.
G0863.2 V-PPI-3S ἀφίεται (4x)
Lk 13:35 "Behold, yeur house is·left to·yeu desolate. And
Mt 23:38 "Behold, yeur house is·left to·yeu desolate!
Mt 24:40 one is·personally·taken, and the *other* one is·left.
Mt 24:41 one is·personally·taken, and one is·left.
G0863.2 V-AAI-1S ἀφήκαμεν (3x)
Lk 18:28 "Behold, we·ourselves left all and followed you.
Mt 19:27 "Behold, we·ourselves left all and followed you.
Mk 10:28 "Behold, we·ourselves left all and followed you.
G0863.2 V-AAI-2S ἀφῆκας (1x)
Rv 2:4 I·have *this* against you, that you·left your first love.
G0863.2 V-AAI-2P ἀφήκατε (1x)
Mt 23:23 and the cumin, but yeu·left the weightier *matters*
G0863.2 V-AAI-3S ἀφῆκεν (15x)
Jn 4:3 he·left Judea and went·off again into Galilee.
Jn 4:28 So·then, the woman left her water·jar and went·off
Jn 4:52 "Yesterday at·the·seventh hour the fever left him."
Jn 8:29 The Father did·not leave me alone, because I·myself
Lk 4:39 he·reprimanded the fever, and it·left her. And at·

Lk 18:29 ·yeu, there·is not·even·one·man that left home, or
Ac 14:17 ·indeed, he·did·not leave himself without·witness,
Heb 2:8 ·even·one·thing did *God* leave unsubjugated to·him.
Mt 8:15 hand, and the fever left her, and she·was·awakened
Mt 19:29 And everyone who left homes or brothers or sisters
Mt 22:25 ·so not having offspring†, he·left his wife to·his
Mk 1:31 and immediately the fever left her, and she·was·
Mk 10:29 there·is not·even·one that left home or brothers
Mk 12:20 and·then dying, he·did·not leave offspring†.
Mk 12:21 and neither *did* he·himself leave offspring†. And
G0863.2 V-AAI-3P ἀφῆκαν (1x)
Mk 12:22 took her, and they·did·not leave offspring†. Last
G0863.2 V-2AAM-2S ἄφες (6x)
Jn 12:7 Jesus declared, "Leave her *alone*. She·has·
Lk 9:60 declared to·him, "Leave the dead·ones to·bury
Lk 13:8 he·says to·him, 'Lord, leave it this year also, until
Mt 5:24 leave your present there before the Sacrifice·Altar
Mt 5:40 and to·take your inner·tunic, leave him the outer·
Mt 27:49 rest were·saying, "Leave *him·alone*, we·should·
G0863.2 V-2AAM-2P ἄφετε (3x)
Mt 15:14 Leave them. They·are blind guides of·blind·men.
Mk 14:6 And Jesus declared, "Leave her *alone*. Why·do
Mk 15:36 saying, "Let·us·leave *him·alone*; we·should·see
G0863.2 V-2AAP-NSM ἀφείς (4x)
Mt 18:12 ·he·not·indeed traverse, leaving the ninety-nine on
Mt 26:44 And leaving them, going·off again, he·prayed for
Mk 8:13 And leaving them *and* embarking into the sailboat
Mk 13:34 ·a·long·journey·abroad, upon·leaving his home
G0863.2 V-2AAP-NPM ἀφέντες (13x)
Lk 5:11 upon the dry·ground, leaving absolutely·all, they·
Lk 10:30 *on·him*, went·off, leaving *him* more·than half·
Heb 6:1 Therefore leaving the initiating Redemptive-word of·
Mt 4:20 And immediately, leaving the nets, they·followed
Mt 4:22 And immediately, leaving the sailboat and their
Mt 22:22 they·marveled, and leaving him, they·went·off.
Mt 26:56 Then leaving him, all the disciples fled.
Mk 1:18 And immediately, leaving their nets, they·followed
Mk 1:20 ·called them forth, and leaving their father Zebedee
Mk 7:8 For after·leaving the commandment of·God, yeu·
Mk 12:12 specifically·against them. So leaving him, they·
Mk 14:50 Then leaving him, everyone fled.
Rm 1:27 likewise also the males, leaving the natural sexual·
G0863.2 V-2AAS-1P ἀφῶμεν (1x)
Jn 11:48 If we·should·leave him alone in·this·manner, all
G0863.2 V-2AAS-2P ἀφῆτε (1x)
Jn 16:32 to his·own *cares*, and should·leave me alone. And·
G0863.2 V-2AAS-3S ἀφῇ (1x)
Mk 12:19 ·behind a·wife, and should·not leave children, that
G0863.2 V-APS-3S ἀφεθῇ (2x)
Mt 24:2 ·yeu, no, there·should·not be·left here a·stone upon
Mk 13:2 No, there·should·not be·left a·stone upon a·stone
G0863.3 V-FAI-3P ἀφήσουσιν (1x)
Rv 11:9 days, and shall·not allow their corpses to·be·placed
G0863.3 V-PAI-2P ἀφίετε (2x)
Mt 23:14 enter·in, neither do·yeu·allow the·ones entering
Mk 7:12 then yeu·allow him to·no·longer do not·even·one·
G0863.3 V-PAI-3S ἀφίησιν (1x)
Mt 3:15 ·fulfill all righteousness." Then he·allows him.
G0863.3 V-IAI-3S ἤφιεν (2x)
Mk 1:34 demons. And he·was·not allowing the demons to·
Mk 11:16 and he·was·not allowing that anyone should·carry
G0863.3 V-AAI-3S ἀφῆκεν (4x)
Lk 8:51 he·did·not allow not·even·one·person to·enter·in,
Lk 12:39 and would not have·allowed his house to·be·
Mk 5:19 But Jesus did·not allow him, but·rather says to·him,
Mk 5:37 he·did·not allow not·even·one·man to·follow·along
G0863.3 V-AAI-3P ἀφῆκαν (1x)
Mk 11:6 just·as Jesus commanded, and they·allowed them.
G0863.3 V-2AAM-2S ἄφες (4x)
Lk 6:42 brother, 'Brother, allow *that* I·should·cast·out the
Mt 3:15 declared to·him, "Allow *me* at·this·moment, for in·
Mt 8:22 "Follow me, and allow the dead·ones to·bury their·
Mk 7:27 to·her, "First, allow the children to·be·stuffed·full.
G0863.3 V-2AAM-2P ἄφετε (6x)
Jn 11:44 "Loose him, and allow·him to·head·on·out."
Jn 18:8 if yeu·seek me, allow these·men to·head·on·out,"
Lk 18:16 declared, "Allow the little·children to·come to
Mt 13:30 Allow both to·be·grown·together so·long·as·unto
Mt 19:14 But Yeshua declared, "Allow the little·children,
Mk 10:14 declared to·them, "Allow the little·children to·
G0863.4 V-2AAM-2S ἄφες (1x)
Mt 7:4 to·your brother, 'Give·way *so* I·may·cast·out the
G0863.5 V-FAI-1S ἀφήσω (1x)
Mt 18:21 morally·fail against me, and I·shall·forgive him?
G0863.5 V-FAI-2S ἀφήσεις (1x)
Lk 17:4 'I·repent,' you·shall·forgive him."
G0863.5 V-FAI-3S ἀφήσει (3x)
Mt 6:14 yeur heavenly Father also shall·forgive yeu.
Mt 6:15 ·even·shall yeur Father forgive yeur trespasses.
Mk 11:26 ·one in the heavens) shall·forgive yeur trespasses.
G0863.5 V-FPI-3S ἀφεθήσεται (9x)
Lk 12:10 the Son of·Clay·Man†, it·shall·be·forgiven him.
Lk 12:10 against the Holy Spirit, it·shall·not be·forgiven.
Ac 8:22 the intention of·your heart shall·be·forgiven you.
Mt 12:31 revilement shall·be·forgiven to·the men·of·clay†,
Mt 12:31 Spirit shall·not be·forgiven to·the men·of·clay†.
Mt 12:32 the Son of·Clay·Man†, it·shall·be·forgiven him,
Mt 12:32 Holy Spirit, it·shall·not be·forgiven him, neither in
Mk 3:28 that all the moral·failings shall·be·forgiven the Sons
Jac 5:15 moral·failures, they·shall·be·forgiven him.
G0863.5 V-PAI-1P ἀφίεμεν (2x)
Lk 11:4 for we also forgive everyone being·indebted to·us.
Mt 6:12 ·debts, also as we·ourselves forgive our debtors.
G0863.5 V-PAI-2P ἀφίετε (1x)
Mk 11:26 But if yeu·yeurselves do·not forgive, neither yeur
G0863.5 V-PAI-3S ἀφίησιν (1x)
Lk 7:49 "Who is this that also forgives moral·failures?
G0863.5 V-PAM-2P ἀφίετε (1x)
Mk 11:25 anything against anyone, forgive, in·order·that
G0863.5 V-PAN ἀφιέναι (5x)
Lk 5:21 ·of·God? Who is·able to·forgive moral·failures,
Lk 5:24 authority upon the earth to·forgive moral·failures,"
Mt 9:6 has authority on the earth to·forgive moral·failures,"
Mk 2:7 ·of·God? Who is·able to·forgive moral·failures,
Mk 2:10 authority on the earth to·forgive moral·failures—"
G0863.5 V-PPI-3S ἀφίεται (1x)
Lk 7:47 "But to·whom little is·forgiven, *the same* loves little.
G0863.5 V-PPI-3P ἀφίενται (1x)
Jn 20:23 yeu·should·forgive, they·are·forgiven to·them; *and*
G0863.5 V-AAI-1S ἀφῆκα (1x)
Mt 18:32 'Evil slave! I·forgave you all that indebtedness,
G0863.5 V-AAI-3S ἀφῆκεν (1x)
Mt 18:27 slave fully·released him and forgave him the loan.
G0863.5 V-2AAM-2S ἄφες (4x)
Lk 11:4 And forgive us our moral·failures, for we also
Lk 17:3 him; and if he·should·repent, forgive him.
Lk 23:34 was·saying, "Father, forgive them, for they·do·not
Mt 6:12 And forgive us our moral·debts, also as we·
G0863.5 V-2AAS-2P ἀφῆτε (4x)
Jn 20:23 ·whose moral·failures yeu·should·forgive, they·are·
Mt 6:14 "For if yeu·should·forgive the men·of·clay† their
Mt 6:15 But if yeu·should·not forgive the men·of·clay† their
Mt 18:35 unless each·one·of yeu·should·forgive his brother
G0863.5 V-2AAS-3S ἀφῇ (2x)
Mk 11:25 in the heavens) may·forgive yeu your trespasses.
1Jn 1:9 and righteous that he·should·forgive us the moral·
G0863.5 V-API-3P ἀφέθησαν (1x)
Rm 4:7 whose violations·of·law are·forgiven and whose
G0863.5 V-APS-3S ἀφεθῇ (1x)
Mk 4:12 and *their* moral·failings should·be·forgiven them."
G0863.5 V-RPI-3P ἀφέωνται (9x)
Lk 5:20 ·clay†, your moral·failures have·been·forgiven you.
Lk 5:23 'Your moral·failures have·been·forgiven you,' or
Lk 7:47 many moral·failures have·been·forgiven, because
Lk 7:48 to·her, "Your moral·failures have·been·forgiven."
Mt 9:2 Your moral·failures have·been·forgiven you."
Mt 9:5 'Your moral·failures have·been·forgiven you?
Mk 2:5 Child, your moral·failures have·been·forgiven you."
Mk 2:9 ·man, 'The moral·failures have·been·forgiven you,'
1Jn 2:12 moral·failures have·been·forgiven yeu on·account·

G0864 ἀφ•ικνέομαι aphiknéômai *v.* (1x)
Roots:G0575 G2429-1 Compare:G1310 G2185 G2658 G4379 See:G0867 G2425
G0864.4 V-2ADI-3S ἀφίκετο (1x)
Rm 16:19 attentive·obedience is·already·broadcast to all *men*

G0865 ἀ•φιλ•άγαθος aphilágathôs *adj.* (1x)
Roots:G0001 G5358
G0865 A-NPM ἀφιλάγαθοι (1x)
2Ti 3:3 savages, hostile·to·beneficially·good·men,

G0866 ἀ•φιλ•άργυρος aphilárgyrôs *adj.* (2x)
Roots:G0001 G5366
G0866.2 A-NSM ἀφιλάργυρος (1x)
Heb 13:5 *be* without·fondness·of·money, being·satisfied
G0866.2 A-ASM ἀφιλάργυρον (1x)
1Ti 3:3 fair, not·quarrelsome, without·fondness·of·money,

G0867 ἄφ•ιξις áphixis *n.* (1x)
Roots:G0864 Compare:G0359 G0402 G0672 G4198 G1607
G0867.2 N-ASF ἄφιξιν (1x)
Ac 20:29 this, that after my regional·departure, burdensome

G0868 ἀφ•ίστημι aphístēmi *v.* (16x)
Roots:G0575 G2476 Compare:G5298 G4724 See:G0647 G0646
G0868.1 V-FDI-3P ἀποστήσονται (1x)
1Ti 4:1 in later seasons some shall·withdraw·from the trust,
G0868.1 V-PNI-3P ἀφίστανται (1x)
Lk 8:13 and·then in a·season of·proof·trial, they·withdraw.
G0868.1 V-PNM-2S ἀφίστασο (1x)
1Ti 6:5 From such *men*, withdraw·yourself!
G0868.1 V-INI-3S ἀφίστατο (1x)
Lk 2:37 years, who did·not withdraw from the Sanctuary·
G0868.1 V-2AAI-3S ἀπέστη (2x)
Lk 4:13 proof·trial, the Slanderer withdrew from him only·
Ac 12:10 and immediately the angel withdrew from him.
G0868.1 V-2AAI-3P ἀπέστησαν (1x)
Ac 22:29 intending to·interrogate him withdrew from him,
G0868.1 V-2AAM-2P ἀπόστητε (2x)
Lk 13:27 From·what·source are·yeu? Withdraw from me, all
Ac 5:38 the·things I·say to·yeu: Withdraw from these men·
G0868.1 V-2AAM-3S ἀποστήτω (1x)
2Ti 2:19 must·withdraw from unrighteousness."
G0868.1 V-2AAN ἀποστῆναι (1x)
Heb 3:12 heart of·distrust, in withdrawing from the·living
G0868.1 V-2AAP-ASM ἀποστάντα (1x)
Ac 15:38 ·along this·man, the·one withdrawing from them
G0868.1 V-2AAP-NSM ἀποστάς (1x)
Ac 19:9 of·the multitude, after·withdrawing from them, he·
G0868.1 V-2AAS-3S ἀποστῇ (1x)
2Co 12:8 ·times in·order·that it·should·withdraw from me.
EG0868.1 (1x)
Ac 5:39 able to·demolish it; *withdraw*, lest·perhaps yeu·
G0868.2 V-AAI-3S ἀπέστησεν (1x)
Ac 5:37 and drew·away a·significant·number·of people

G0869 ἄ•φνω áphnō *adv.* (3x)
Roots:G0852 Compare:G1810 G1819 See:G0160
G0869.2 ADV ἄφνω (3x)
Ac 2:2 And without·warning, there·came a·reverberating·
Ac 16:26 And without·warning there·was a·great earthquake,
Ac 28:6 ·fever or to·fall·down dead without·warning, but

G0870 ἀ•φόβως aphóbōs *adv.* (4x)
Roots:G0001 G5401
G0870.1 ADV ἀφόβως (4x)
Lk 1:74 enemies) to·ritually·minister to·him without·fear
Jud 1:12 shepherding·and·feeding themselves without·fear.
Php 1:14 ·bold to·speak the Redemptive-word without·fear.
1Co 16:10 ·may·come·to·be alongside yeu without·fear, for

G0871 ἀφ•ομοιόω aphômôiôō *v.* (1x)
Roots:G0575 G3666
G0871.2 V-RPP-NSM ἀφωμοιωμένος (1x)
Heb 7:3 of·life†, but having·been·made·similar to·the Son

G0872 ἀφ•οράω aphôráō *v.* (1x)
Roots:G0575 G3708
G0872.1 V-PAP-NPM ἀφορῶντες (1x)
Heb 12:2 clearly·looking to YeShua, the Initiator and

G0873 ἀφ•ορίζω aphôrízō *v.* (10x)
Roots:G0575 G3724 Compare:G3307 G5563 G0649 G3718 See:G0873-1 G0873-2
G0873.2 V-FAI-3S ἀφοριεῖ (1x)
Mt 25:32 him, and he·shall·distinctly·separate them one
G0873.2 V-FAI-3P-ATT ἀφοριοῦσιν (1x)
Mt 13:49 ·forth and shall·distinctly·separate the evil·ones
G0873.2 V-PAI-3S ἀφορίζει (1x)
Mt 25:32 just·as the shepherd distinctly·separates the sheep
G0873.2 V-AAS-3P ἀφορίσωσιν (1x)
Lk 6:22 whenever they·should·distinctly·separate yeu *from·*
G0873.3 V-IAI-3S ἀφώριζεν (1x)
Gal 2:12 ·back and was·distinctly·detaching himself, fearing
G0873.3 V-AAI-3S ἀφώρισεν (1x)
Ac 19:9 from them, he·distinctly·detached the disciples
G0873.3 V-APM-2P ἀφορίσθητε (1x)
2Co 6:17 *the* midst of·them and be·distinctly·detached,"”
G0873.4 V-AAM-2P ἀφορίσατε (1x)
Ac 13:2 “Now·then, specially·detach for·me both BarNabas
G0873.4 V-AAP-NSM ἀφορίσας (1x)
Gal 1:15 ·delight (the·one specially·detaching me from·out
G0873.4 V-RPP-NSM ἀφωρισμένος (1x)
Rm 1:1 ·ambassador, having·been·specially·detached to *the*

G0874 ἀφ•ορμή aphôrmḗ *n.* (7x)
Roots:G0575 G3729 Compare:G2540
G0874.2 N-ASF ἀφορμήν (7x)
Gal 5:13 in·order·for an·impromptu·occasion to·the flesh.
Rm 7:8 ·Failure, taking impromptu·occasion through the
Rm 7:11 ·Failure, taking impromptu·occasion through the
2Co 5:12 yeu an·impromptu·occasion for·boasting over us,
2Co 11:12 the impromptu·occasion of·the·ones wanting an·
2Co 11:12 ·ones wanting an·impromptu·occasion *to·boast of·*
1Ti 5:14 not·even·one impromptu·occasion for·defamation

G0875 ἀφρίζω aphrízō *v.* (2x)
Roots:G0876
G0875 V-PAI-3S ἀφρίζει (1x)
Mk 9:18 him, and he·foams·at·the·mouth and grates his
G0875 V-PAP-NSM ἀφρίζων (1x)
Mk 9:20 upon the soil, he·was·rolling·about foaming.

G0876 ἀφρός aphrôs *n.* (1x)
See:G0875
G0876 N-GSM ἀφροῦ (1x)
Lk 9:39 and it·convulses him along·with foam, and hardly

G0877 ἀ•φροσύνη aphrôsýnē *n.* (4x)
Roots:G0878 xLangAlso:H5531
G0877.2 N-NSF ἀφροσύνη (1x)
Mk 7:22 eye, revilement, haughtiness, *and* impulsiveness.
G0877.2 N-DSF ἀφροσύνῃ (3x)
2Co 11:1 me a·little·while in·the impulsiveness *of·boasting,*
2Co 11:17 Lord, but·rather as in impulsiveness, in this firm·
2Co 11:21 (I·say *this* in impulsiveness), I·also am·daringly·

G0878 ἄ•φρων áphrōn *adj.* (11x)
Roots:G0001 G5424 Compare:G0781 G3474 G0453 G0801 See:G0877 xLangAlso:H5036
G0878.4 A-NSM ἄφρων (2x)
2Co 12:6 to·boast, I·shall·not be impetuous, for I·shall·
2Co 12:11 I·have·become impetuous in·boasting! Yeu
G0878.4 A-NPM ἄφρονες (1x)
Eph 5:17 ·of this, do·not become impetuous·ones, but·rather
G0878.4 A-VSM ἄφρον (2x)
Lk 12:20 declared to·him, ‘O·impetuous·one! This night,
1Co 15:36 Impetuous·one, that·which you sow is·not giving·
G0878.4 A-VPM ἄφρονες (1x)
Lk 11:40 O·impetuous·ones! ¿!·Did·not the·one making the
G0878.4 A-ASM ἄφρονα (2x)
2Co 11:16 anyone should·suppose me to·be impetuous; but
2Co 11:16 then·also accept me as impetuous in·order·that,
G0878.4 A-GPM ἀφρόνων (3x)
Rm 2:20 an·educator·and·disciplinarian of·impetuous·men,
1Pe 2:15 ·muzzle the ignorance of·impetuous men·of·clay†.
2Co 11:19 For yeu·bear·with the impetuous with·pleasure,

G0879 ἀφ•υπνόω aphypnôō *v.* (1x)
Roots:G0575 G5258
G0879.2 V-AAI-3S ἀφύπνωσεν (1x)
Lk 8:23 But while·they were·sailing, he·fell·asleep. And a·

G0880 ἄ•φωνος áphōnôs *adj.* (4x)
Roots:G0001 G5456 xLangAlso:H0481
G0880.1 A-NSM ἄφωνος (1x)
Ac 8:32 ·lamb *is* voiceless in·the·direct·presence of·the·one
G0880.1 A-NSN ἄφωνον (1x)
2Pe 2:16 a·voiceless female·donkey enunciating with *the*
G0880.1 A-APN ἄφωνα (1x)
1Co 12:2 even·as yeu·were·led toward the voiceless idols.
G0880.2 A-NSN ἄφωνον (1x)
1Co 14:10 and not·even·one of·them *is* without·significance.

G0881 Ἀχάζ Acház *n/p.* (2x)
אָחָז ʼachaz [Hebrew]
Roots:H0271
G0881.2 N/P-PRI Ἀχαζ (2x)
Mt 1:9 YoTham, and YoTham begot Achaz, and Achaz
Mt 1:9 YoTham begot Achaz, and Achaz begot HezekIah.

G0882 Ἀχαΐα Achaḯa *n/l.* (11x)
See:G0883
G0882 N/L-NSF Ἀχαΐα (2x)
Rm 15:26 For Macedonia and Achaia delighted to·make a·
2Co 9:2 that Achaia has·been·making·preparation since
G0882 N/L-ASF Ἀχαΐαν (2x)
Ac 18:27 ·him being·resolved to·go·through into Achaia, the
Ac 19:21 ·going·throughout Macedonia and Achaia, *for·him*
G0882 N/L-DSF Ἀχαΐᾳ (3x)
1Th 1:7 to·all the·ones trusting in Macedonia and Achaia.
1Th 1:8 merely in Macedonia and Achaia, but·rather also in
2Co 1:1 with·all the holy·ones, the·ones being in all Achaia:
G0882 N/L-GSF Ἀχαΐας (4x)
Ac 18:12 And when·Gallio was·the·proconsul of·Achaia, the
Rm 16:5 who is·a·firstfruit of·Achaia to Anointed-One.
1Co 16:15 that it·is·a·firstfruit of·Achaia, and *how* they·
2Co 11:10 ·sealed·up in me within the vicinities of·Achaia.

G0883 Ἀχαϊκός Achaïkôs *n/p.* (1x)
Roots:G0882
G0883.2 N/P-GSM Ἀχαϊκοῦ (1x)
1Co 16:17 ·Stephanas and Fortunatus and Achaicus, because

G0884 ἀ•χάριστος acháristôs *adj.* (2x)
Roots:G0001 G5483
G0884 A-NPM ἀχάριστοι (1x)
2Ti 3:2 obstinate to·parents, ungrateful, distinctly·unholy,
G0884 A-APM ἀχαρίστους (1x)
Lk 6:35 he·himself is kind to·the ungrateful and evil·ones.

G0885 Ἀχείμ Achêím *n/p.* (2x)
xLangAlso:H3199 H3137
G0885 N/P-PRI Ἀχείμ (2x)
Mt 1:14 Tsadoq, and Tsadoq begot Achim, and Achim begot
Mt 1:14 and Tsadoq begot Achim, and Achim begot EliHud.

G0886 ἀ•χειρο•ποίητος achêirôpôíētôs *adj.* (3x)
Roots:G0001 G5499
G0886.1 A-ASM ἀχειροποίητον (1x)
Mk 14:58 days I·shall·build another not·made·by·hand.’”
G0886.1 A-DSF ἀχειροποιήτῳ (1x)
Col 2:11 with·a·circumcision not·made·by·hand, with the
G0886.2 A-ASF ἀχειροποίητον (1x)
2Co 5:1 a·home not·made·by·human·hand, eternal in the

G0887 ἀχλύς achlýs *n.* (1x)
G0887.1 N-NSF ἀχλύς (1x)
Ac 13:11 at·once there·fell upon him dimness·of·sight, then

G0888 ἀ•χρεῖος achrêîôs *adj.* (2x)
Roots:G0001 G5534 Compare:G0512 G0255 G0370 See:G5532
G0888 A-NPM ἀχρεῖοι (1x)
Lk 17:10 also must·say, ‘We·are useless slaves, because we·
G0888 A-ASM ἀχρεῖον (1x)
Mt 25:30 ‘And yeu·cast·out the useless slave into the outer

G0889 α•χρειόω achrêiôō *v.* (1x)
Roots:G0888
G0889 V-API-3P ἠχρειώθησαν (1x)
Rm 3:12 At·the·same·time, they·are·made·useless; there·is

G0890 ἄ•χρηστος áchrēstôs *adj.* (1x)
Roots:G0001 G5543
G0890.1 A-ASM ἄχρηστον (1x)
Phm 1:11 The·one *who* in·times·past *was* not·useful to·you,

G0891 ἄχρι áchri *prep.* (49x)
ἄχρις áchris
Compare:G2193 G3360 See:G0206
G0891.1 PREP ἄχρι (18x)
Lk 1:20 and not being·able to·speak, even·until *the* day that
Lk 17:27 ·given·away·in·marriage, even·until that day *when*
Lk 21:24 being·trampled by Gentiles, even·until *the* seasons
Ac 1:2 even·until *the* day when he·was·taken·up, after·
Ac 3:21 ·for heaven to·accept even·until *the* times of·a·
Ac 7:18 even·until "another king rose·up, who had·not
Ac 22:22 they·were·listening·to him even·until this word,
Gal 4:19 ·birthing·pain again even·until Anointed-One
Mt 24:38 and giving·away·in·marriage, even·until that day
Rm 1:13 yeu (but was·prevented even·until here·and·now),
Rm 5:13 For even·until *the* Torah-Law, moral·failure was in
1Co 11:26 the Lord's death even·until he·should·come.
1Co 15:25 ·for him to·reign, even·until he·should·place all
Rv 2:25 ·have, securely·hold even·until I·should·come.
Rv 7:3 nor the trees, even·until we·should·officially·seal the
Rv 15:8 into the Temple, even·until the seven punishing·
Rv 17:17 to·the Scarlet·Beast, even·until the utterances of·
Rv 20:3 the nations any·longer, even·until the thousand
G0891.2 PREP ἄχρι (13x)
Ac 2:29 buried, and his tomb is with us even·unto this day.
Ac 20:4 And even·as·far·as Asia, SoPater (a·Berean *Jew*),
Ac 20:11 in·this·manner even·unto *the* first·light·of·day,
Ac 22:4 ·*is·I* who persecuted this Way even·unto *their* death,
Ac 26:22 personally·from God, I·stand even·unto this day,
Heb 4:12 thoroughly·penetrating even·unto a·dividing of·
Php 1:5 good·news from *the* first day even·unto the present,
Php 1:6 in yeu shall·further·finish *it* even·unto *the* day of·
2Co 3:14 ·hard·as·stone. For even·unto the·present·day the
2Co 10:13 *of·service* actually·reaching also even·unto yeu.
Rv 2:10 ten days. Become trustworthy even·unto death, and
Rv 2:26 the·one fully·keeping my works even·unto *the* end,
Rv 12:11 and they·did·not love their souls even·unto death.
G0891.3 PREP ἄχρι (8x)
Ac 23:1 ·good conscience before·God even·up·to this day.”
Ac 27:33 And even·until daylight was·about to·occur, Paul
Heb 6:11 ·assurance of·the Expectation, even·up·to *the* end,
Gal 4:2 and estate·managers even·up·to the day·set·forth by·
Rm 8:22 jointly·experiences·birthing·pain even·up·to the
1Co 4:11 Even·up·to the very·present hour, also we·hunger,
Rv 14:20 out of·the winepress, even·up·to the horses' bridles
Rv 18:5 "her moral·failures followed even·up·to the heaven,
G0891.4 PREP ἄχρι (4x)
Ac 11:5 by·four corners, and it·came even·as·far·as me.
Ac 13:6 going·throughout the island, even·as·far·as Paphos,
Ac 28:15 to approach·and·meet us even·as·far·as *the* Forum
2Co 10:14 for we·previously·came even·as·far·as yeu also,
G0891.5 PREP ἄχρις (1x)
Heb 3:13 and·every day, even·for·as·along·as it·is·called
G0891.6 PREP ἄχρις (2x)
Gal 3:19 was·placed·alongside *the promise* only·until the
Rm 11:25 *only* in part, *and* only·until the complete·fullness
G0891.7 PREP ἄχρι (2x)
Lk 4:13 the Slanderer withdrew from him only·for a·season.

Ac 13:11 looking·at the sun— *but* only·for a·season." And

G0891.8 PREP ἄχρις (1x)

Ac 20:6 we·came to them in Troas in·only five days, where

G0892 ἄχυρον áchyrôn *n.* (2x)

Roots:G5502-5 xLangAlso:H8401

G0892 N-ASN ἄχυρον (2x)

Lk 3:17 but the chaff he·shall·completely·burn with·fire

Mt 3:12 ·burn the chaff with·inextinguishable fire."

G0893 ἀ•ψευδής apseudḗs *adj.* (1x)

Roots:G0001 G5579

G0893.1 A-NSM ἀψευδής (1x)

Tit 1:2 which God (the·one without·falsehood) promised

G0894 ἄψινθος ápsinthôs *n.* (2x)

xLangAlso:H3939

G0894.1 N-NSF ἄψινθος (1x)

Rv 8:11 name of·the star is·referred·to·as Wormwood, and

G0894.1 N-ASF ἄψινθον (1x)

Rv 8:11 ·part *of·the waters* become wormwood; and many

G0895 ἄ•ψυχος ápsychôs *adj.* (1x)

Roots:G0001 G5590

G0895.2 A-NPN ἄψυχα (1x)

1Co 14:7 the soulless,·inanimate·things giving sound,

Ββ - Beta

G0896 Βάαλ Báal *n/p.* (1x)

בַּעַל ba'al [Hebrew]

Roots:H1168

G0896.2 N/P-PRI Βάαλ (1x)

Rm 11:4 ·thousand men, who did·not bow a·knee to·Baal."

G0897 Βαβυλών Babylṓn *n/l.* (12x)

בָּבֶל babel [Hebrew]

Roots:H0894 Compare:G2414 G2419 See:G4799 G4172

G0897.2 N/L-NSF Βαβυλών (6x)

Rv 14:8 another angel, saying, "Babylon is·fallen, is·fallen,

Rv 16:19 fell. And Babylon the Great was·recalled·to·mind

Rv 17:5 ·written, MYSTERY, BABYLON THE GREAT,

Rv 18:2 a·great voice, saying, "Babylon the Great is·fallen,

Rv 18:10 woe, the Great City Babylon, the Strong City!

Rv 18:21 the Great City Babylon shall·be·cast·down, and

G0897.2 N/L-DSF Βαβυλῶνι (1x)

1Pe 5:13 *Called·Out·citizenry* in Babylon, selected·together

G0897.2 N/L-GSF Βαβυλῶνος (1x)

Ac 7:43 And I·shall·exile yeu far·beyond Babylon.

G0897.3 N/L-GSF Βαβυλῶνος (4x)

Mt 1:11 his brothers, upon *the time* of·the Babylonian exile.

Mt 1:12 Now after the Babylonian exile, YeKonYah begot

Mt 1:17 from David until the Babylonian exile *are* fourteen

Mt 1:17 And from the Babylonian exile until the

G0898 βαθμός bathmṓs *n.* (1x)

Roots:G0901-3 Compare:G0968 See:G0901 G0899 G4260

G0898.2 N-ASM βαθμόν (1x)

1Ti 3:13 for·themselves good advancement, and·also much

G0899 βάθος báthôs *n.* (9x)

Roots:G0901 Compare:G0901 G3989 xLangAlso:H8415

G0899.1 N-NSN βάθος (3x)

Rm 8:39 nor height, nor depth, nor any other created·thing

Rm 11:33 O *the* depth of·wealth, both of·*the*·wisdom and

Eph 3:18 breadth, and length, and depth, and height *of·it*,

G0899.1 N-ASN βάθος (2x)

Mt 13:5 ·surface, on·account·of it not having depth of·earth.

Mk 4:5 ·surface, on·account·of it·not having depth of·earth.

G0899.1 N-APN βάθη (1x)

Rv 2:24 did·not know "the depths of·the Adversary-Accuser,"

G0899.2 N-ASN βάθος (1x)

Lk 5:4 "Head·off into the deep and lower yeur nets for a·

G0899.2 N-APN βάθη (1x)

1Co 2:10 searches all·things, even, the deep·things of·God.

G0899.2 N-GSN βάθους (1x)

2Co 8:2 of·their joy and their deep down poverty abounded

G0900 βαθύνω bathýnō *v.* (1x)

Roots:G0901

G0900.1 V-AAI-3S ἐβάθυνεν (1x)

Lk 6:48 a·home, who also dug deeply and laid a·foundation

G0901 βαθύς bathýs *adj.* (4x)

Roots:G0898 Compare:G5011 See:G0899 G0900

G0901 A-NSN βαθύ (1x)

Jn 4:11 and the well is deep. So·then from·what·source do·

G0901 A-DSM βαθεῖ (1x)

Ac 20:9 becoming·weighed·down with·a·deep heavy·sleep.

G0901 A-GSM βαθέος (1x)

Lk 24:1 ·the week, with·*the*·sunrise deep *below·the·horizon*,

EG0901 (1x)

Mk 6:40 ·eat in·rows, rows by a·hundred, and by fifty *deep*.

G0902 βαΐον baïôn *n.* (1x)

Roots:G0939 G2444-3 Compare:G2798

G0902 N-APN βαΐα (1x)

Jn 12:13 they·took the boughs of·palm·trees, and went·forth

G0903 Βαλα•άμ Balaám *n/p.* (3x)

בִּלְעָם bil'am [Hebrew]

Roots:H1109 Compare:G2403 See:G5572 xLangAlso:H1086

G0903.2 N/P-PRI Βαλαάμ (3x)

Jud 1:11 ·out the error of·BalaAm for·a·payment·of·service,

2Pe 2:15 following·out the way of·BalaAm *the son* of·Beor

Rv 2:14 ·securely·holding·to the instruction of·BalaAm, who

G0904 Βαλάκ Balák *n/p.* (1x)

Βαλάκ Baláq [Greek, Octuagint]

בָּלָק balaq [Hebrew]

Roots:H1111 xLangAlso:H0011

G0904.2 N/P-PRI Βαλάκ (1x)

Rv 2:14 ·instructing with Balaq·*the·Annihilator* to·cast a·trap

G0905 βαλάντιον balántiôn *n.* (4x)

Roots:G0906 Compare:G2223 G4082

G0905 N-ASN βαλάντιον (2x)

Lk 10:4 Do·not lift·and·carry a·pouch, nor a·knapsack, nor·

Lk 22:36 now, the·one having a·pouch, let·him·take·it·up,

G0905 N-APN βαλάντια (1x)

Lk 12:33 for·yeurselves pouches not becoming·old·and·

G0905 N-GSN βαλαντίου (1x)

Lk 22:35 I·dispatched yeu without·any pouch, knapsack, or

G0906 βάλλω bállō *v.* (127x)

Compare:G4496 G0683 See:G3825-2 G1000 G1002-1 G1002 G0956 G1911

EG0906 (2x)

Col 2:17 *is* the Anointed-One's body *which cast the shadow*.

Rv 20:10 and the Fiendish·False·Prophet *were·cast*, and they·

G0906.1 V-FAI-1S βάλω (1x)

Rv 2:24 as they·say), I·shall·cast upon yeu no other

G0906.1 V-FAI-3P βαλοῦσιν (2x)

Mt 13:42 and they·shall·cast them into the furnace of·the fire

Mt 13:50 and they·shall·cast them into the furnace of·the fire

G0906.1 V-FPI-2S βληθήσῃ (1x)

Mt 5:25 to·the assistant, and you·shall·be·cast into *debtors'*

G0906.1 V-FPI-3S βληθήσεται (1x)

Rv 18:21 the Great City Babylon shall·be·cast·down, and no,

G0906.1 V-PAI-1S βάλλω (1x)

Rv 2:22 'Behold, I·myself do·cast her upon a·couch *of·*

G0906.1 V-PAI-1P βάλλομεν (1x)

Jac 3:3 Behold, we·cast the bits in the horses' mouths

G0906.1 V-PAI-3S βάλλει (6x)

Jn 13:5 After·that, he·casts water into the wash·basin; then

Lk 5:37 "And not·even·one·man casts fresh·new wine into

Mk 2:22 And not·even·one·man casts fresh·new wine into

Mk 12:41 how the crowd cast copper·coinage into the

1Jn 4:18 but·rather the completely·mature love casts out the

Rv 6:13 as *when* a·fig·tree casts its unripe·green·figs while·

G0906.1 V-PAI-3P βάλλουσιν (5x)

Jn 15:6 they·do·gather them together and cast *them* into fire,

Lk 14:35 nor·even for manure, *but·rather* men·cast it out.

Mt 9:17 Neither do·men·cast fresh·new wine into old

Mt 9:17 ·destroyed. But·rather they·cast fresh·new wine into

Rv 4:10 the ages of·ages and cast their victor's·crowns in·

G0906.1 V-PAP-ASF βάλλουσαν (1x)

Lk 21:2 he·saw also a·certain needy widow casting two bits

G0906.1 V-PAP-APM βάλλοντας (3x)

Lk 21:1 he·saw the wealthy·men casting their presents into

Mt 4:18 and Andrew his brother, casting a·cast·net into the

Mk 1:16 and his brother Andrew casting a·cast·net into the

G0906.1 V-PAP-GPM βαλλόντων (1x)

Ac 22:23 flinging·off the garments, and casting dust into the

G0906.1 V-PAP-NPM βάλλοντες (2x)

Mt 27:35 ·divided·up his garments, casting lots in·order·that

Mk 15:24 ·dividing·up his garments, while·casting lots upon

G0906.1 V-PAS-3S βάλλῃ (2x)

Jn 5:7 ·be·troubled, in·order·that he·should·cast me into the

Lk 12:58 and the debt·collection·officer should·cast you into

G0906.1 V-PPI-3S βάλλεται (3x)

Lk 3:9 good fruit is·chopped·down and is·cast into fire."

Mt 3:10 good fruit is·chopped·down and is·cast into fire.

Αα Ββ Γγ Δδ Εε Ζζ Ηη Θθ Ιι Κκ Λλ Μμ Νν Ξξ Οο Ππ Ρρ Σσ Ττ Υυ Φφ Χχ Ψψ Ωω

Mt 7:19 good fruit is·chopped·down and is·cast into fire.
G0906.1 V-PPP-ASM βαλλόμενον (2x)
Lk 12:28 in the field, and tomorrow being·cast into an·oven,
Mt 6:30 being *here*, and tomorrow being·cast into an·oven,
G0906.1 V-PPP-APN βαλλόμενα (1x)
Jn 12:6 ·lifting·out·and·carrying the·things being·cast *in·it*.
G0906.1 V-IAI-3P ἔβαλλον (2x)
Mk 12:41 many that·were·wealthy were·casting·in much.
Mk 14:65 And the assistants were·casting slaps at·him.
G0906.1 V-2AAI-3S ἔβαλεν (19x)
Jn 21:7 (for he·was naked), and he·cast himself into the sea.
Lk 13:19 which a·man·of·clay† took *and* cast into his garden
Lk 21:3 that this helplessly·poor widow cast *in* more·than
Lk 21:4 from·out·of·her destitution cast in·absolutely·all the
Ac 16:24 ·having·received such a·charge, cast them into the
Mt 18:30 but·rather going·off, he·cast him into prison,
Mk 7:33 the crowd in private, *Jesus* cast his fingers into his
Mk 9:22 And many·times it·cast him even into fire and into
Mk 12:42 a·certain helplessly·poor widow cast·in two bits,
Mk 12:44 from·out·of·her destitution cast·in all·things, as·
Rv 8:5 fire of·the Sacrifice·Altar, and cast *it* upon the earth;
Rv 12:4 of·the stars of·the heaven and cast them to the earth.
Rv 12:15 And the Serpent cast out of·his mouth water as a·
Rv 12:16 the flood·water which the Dragon cast out of·his
Rv 14:16 ·sitting·down on the thick·cloud cast·in his sickle
Rv 14:19 And the angel cast his sickle into the earth, and
Rv 14:19 the vine of·the earth, and cast *it* into the great
Rv 18:21 a·stone as a·great millstone, and cast *it* into the sea
Rv 20:3 and cast him into the bottomless·pit, and shut him
G0906.1 V-2AAI-3P ἔβαλον (10x)
Jn 19:24 among·themselves, and they·cast lots upon my
Jn 21:6 Accordingly, they·cast *the net*, and they·no longer
Lk 21:4 For absolutely·all these·men cast from·out·of·their
Lk 23:34 ·dividing·up his garments, they·cast lots.
Ac 16:23 punishing·blows upon·them, they·cast *them* into
Ac 16:37 *though* inherently·being Romans, they·cast *us* into
Mt 13:48 the good into containers but cast out the rotten.
Mt 27:35 among·themselves, and they·cast lots over my
Mk 12:44 For they all cast·in from·out·of·their abundance,
Rv 18:19 "And they·cast loose·dirt on their heads, and were·
G0906.1 V-2AAM-2S βάλε (9x)
Jn 18:11 Jesus declared to·Peter, "Cast your dagger into the
Jn 20:27 And bring your hand, and cast *it* into my side.
Lk 4:9 ·are the Son of·God, cast yourself down from·here.
Mt 4:6 "If you·are *the* Son of·God, cast yourself down. For
Mt 5:29 entraps you, pluck it out and cast *it* from you, for it·
Mt 5:30 entraps you, chop it off and cast *it* from you, for it·
Mt 17:27 after·traversing to the sea, cast a·hook and take·up
Mt 18:8 foot entraps you, chop it off and cast *it* from you.
Mt 18:9 eye entraps you, pluck it out and cast *it* from you.
G0906.1 V-2AAM-2P βάλετε (1x)
Jn 21:6 And he·declared to·them, "Cast the net to the right·
G0906.1 V-2AAM-3S βαλέτω (1x)
Jn 8:7 *that·is* without·moral·failure, let·him·cast the first
G0906.1 V-2AAN βαλεῖν (9x)
Lk 12:49 "I·came to·cast fire upon the earth.
Mt 10:34 ·should·not assume that I·came to·cast peace upon
Mt 10:34 the earth; I·did·not come to·cast peace, but·rather
Mt 15:26 the children's bread and to·cast *it* to·the puppies.
Mt 25:27 it·was·mandatory·for you to·cast my money to·
Mt 27:6 declared, "It·is·not proper to·cast them into the
Mk 7:27 the children's bread and to·cast *it* to·the puppies.
Rv 2:10 the Slanderer is·about to·cast *some* from·among
Rv 2:14 with Balaq·*the·Annihilator* to·cast a·trap in·the·sight
G0906.1 V-2AAP-GPM βαλόντων (1x)
Mk 12:43 has·cast·in more·than all the·ones casting into the
G0906.1 V-2AAP-NSF βαλοῦσα (1x)
Mt 26:12 For she·herself, casting this ointment on my body,
G0906.1 V-2AAS-1S βάλω (3x)
Jn 20:25 nails in his hands, and may·cast my finger into the
Jn 20:25 imprint of·the nails, and may·cast my hand into his
Lk 13:8 I·should·dig around it and should·cast manure *on·it*.
G0906.1 V-2AAS-2P βάλητε (1x)
Mt 7:6 to·the dogs, nor·even should·yeu·cast yeur pearls
G0906.1 V-2AAS-3S βάλῃ (1x)
Mk 4:26 a·man·of·clay† should·cast the scattering·of·seed
G0906.1 V-2AAS-3P βάλωσιν (1x)
Jn 8:59 ·took·up stones in·order·that they·may·cast *them* at
G0906.1 V-API-3S ἐβλήθη (8x)
Jn 15:6 ·not remain in me, he·is·already·cast out as the
Rv 8:7 ·been·mixed with·blood, and they·were·cast into the
Rv 8:8 mountain being·set·ablaze with·fire was·cast into the
Rv 12:9 And the great Dragon was·cast·out, the original
Rv 12:9 all The Land; he·was·cast·out into the earth, and his
Rv 12:13 when the Dragon saw that he·was·cast to the earth,
Rv 20:10 the·one deceiving them, was·cast into the Lake
Rv 20:15 scroll of·the life-above, he·was·cast into the Lake
G0906.1 V-API-3P ἐβλήθησαν (3x)
Rv 12:9 the earth, and his angels were·cast·out with him.
Rv 19:20 The two were·cast, still·living, into the Lake of·the
Rv 20:14 And Death and Hades were·cast into the Lake of·
G0906.1 V-APM-2S βλήθητι (2x)
Mt 21:21 'Be·taken·away and be·you·cast into the sea,' it·
Mk 11:23 'Be·taken·away, and be·you·cast into the sea,'
G0906.1 V-APN βληθῆναι (5x)
Mt 5:13 ·have·strength any·longer, except to·be·cast out and
Mt 18:8 hands or two feet *and* to·be·cast into the eternal fire.
Mt 18:9 having two eyes *and* to·be·cast into the Hell·Canyon
Mk 9:45 having two feet *and* to·be·cast into the Hell·Canyon
Mk 9:47 than having two eyes *and* to·be·cast into the Hell·
G0906.1 V-APP-DSF βληθείσῃ (1x)
Mt 13:47 heavens is like a·dragnet after·being·cast into the
G0906.1 V-APS-3S βληθῇ (2x)
Mt 5:29 your whole body should·be·cast into Hell·Canyon.
Mt 5:30 your whole body should·be·cast into Hell·Canyon.
G0906.1 V-RAI-3S βέβληκεν (1x)
Mk 12:43 helplessly·poor widow has·cast·in more·than all
G0906.1 V-RAP-GSM βεβληκότος (1x)
Jn 13:2 with·the Slanderer even·now having·cast into the
G0906.1 V-RPI-3S βέβληται (2x)
Mt 8:6 "Lord, my servant·boy has·been·cast paralyzed *on a·*
Mk 9:42 his neck, and *that* it·has·been·cast into the sea.
G0906.1 V-RPP-ASF βεβλημένην (2x)
Mt 8:14 *Peter's* mother-in-law having·been·cast *on a·couch*
Mk 7:30 ·out and her daughter having·been·cast upon the
G0906.1 V-RPP-ASM βεβλημένον (2x)
Lk 23:25 ·released to·them the·one having·been·cast into the
Mt 9:2 a·paralyzed·man having·been·cast on a·simple·couch
G0906.1 V-RPP-NSM βεβλημένος (1x)
Lk 23:19 (That·same·man was having·been·cast into prison
G0906.1 V-RPP-NSM@ βεβλημένος (1x)
Jn 3:24 for John had·not·yet been·cast into the prison.
G0906.1 V-LPI-3S ἐβέβλητο (1x)
Lk 16:20 ·name·of Lazarus who had·been·cast alongside his
G0906.2 V-2AAI-3S ἔβαλεν (1x)
Ac 27:14 after, a·typhoon-like wind slammed against *Crete*,

G0907 βαπτίζω baptízō *v.* (80x)

Roots:G0911 Compare:G4472 G2708 See:G0908 G0910
xLangEquiv:H2881

G0907.1 V-PPI-3P βαπτίζονται (1x)
1Co 15:29 Why then are·they·immersed on·behalf·of·the
G0907.1 V-PPP-NPM βαπτιζόμενοι (1x)
1Co 15:29 ·do, the·ones being·immersed on·behalf·of·the
G0907.1 V-AMI-3P ἐβαπτίσαντο (1x)
1Co 10:2 and all were·immersed into Moses in the cloud and
G0907.1 V-AMS-3P βαπτίσωνται (1x)
Mk 7:4 unless they·should·immerse *their hands*, they·do·
G0907.1 V-API-2P ἐβαπτίσθητε (1x)
Ac 19:3 "So·then into what were·yeu·immersed?" And they·
G0907.1 V-API-3S ἐβαπτίσθη (1x)
Lk 11:38 marveled that he·did·not first immerse *his hands*
G0907.3 V-PAI-1S βαπτίζω (3x)
Jn 1:26 them, saying, "I·myself immerse in water, but one·
Lk 3:16 "In·fact, I·myself immerse yeu in·water, but the·one
Mt 3:11 In·fact, I·myself immerse yeu in water for
G0907.3 V-PAI-2S βαπτίζεις (1x)
Jn 1:25 "So·then why·do you·immerse, if you·yourself are
G0907.3 V-PAI-3S βαπτίζει (2x)
Jn 3:26 have·testified, see, the·same·man immerses, and all
Jn 4:1 "Jesus makes and immerses more disciples than John,
G0907.3 V-PAN βαπτίζειν (1x)
Jn 1:33 but·yet the·one sending me to·immerse in water,
G0907.3 V-PAP-NSM βαπτίζων (6x)
Jn 1:28 across the Jordan *River*, where John was immersing.
Jn 1:31 ·of that, I·myself came immersing in the water.
Jn 3:23 And John also was immersing in Ainon near to·
Jn 10:40 place where John was first immersing; and there he·
Mk 1:4 John was immersing in the wilderness and officially·
Mk 6:14 the Immersing·One was·awakened from·among
G0907.3 V-IAI-3S ἐβάπτιζεν (2x)
Jn 3:22 ·awhile there with them and was·immersing.
Jn 4:2 ·indeed Jesus himself was·not immersing, but·rather
G0907.3 V-IPI-3P ἐβαπτίζοντο (3x)
Jn 3:23 And they·came·openly and were·immersed,
Mt 3:6 and they·were·immersed by him in the Jordan,
Mk 1:5 of·JeruSalem, and all were·immersed by him in the
G0907.3 V-AAI-1S ἐβάπτισα (1x)
Mk 1:8 In·fact, I·myself immersed yeu in water, but he·
G0907.3 V-AAI-3S ἐβάπτισεν (3x)
Ac 1:5 Because in·fact, John immersed in·water, but yeu
Ac 11:16 ·was·saying, 'John in·fact immersed in·water, but
Ac 19:4 "In·fact, John did·immerse *with* an·immersion of·
G0907.3 V-API-3S ἐβαπτίσθη (1x)
Mk 1:9 Natsareth of·Galilee and was·immersed by John in
G0907.3 V-APN βαπτισθῆναι (5x)
Lk 3:7 to·the crowds traversing·forth to·be·immersed by him
Lk 3:12 Then tax·collectors also came to·be·immersed, and
Lk 3:21 when absolutely·all the people were·immersed, then
Mt 3:13 the Jordan, directly·to John to·be·immersed by him.
Mt 3:14 "I·myself have need to·be·immersed by you, and
G0907.3 V-APP-GSM βαπτισθέντος (1x)
Lk 3:21 then with·Jesus being·immersed and praying, the
G0907.3 V-APP-NSM βαπτισθείς (1x)
Mt 3:16 And after·being·immersed, YeShua walked·up
G0907.3 V-APP-NPM βαπτισθέντες (2x)
Lk 7:29 people already·being·immersed·in the immersion of·
Lk 7:30 for themselves, not already·being·immersed by him.
G0907.4 V-PAN βαπτίζειν (1x)
1Co 1:17 did·not dispatch me to·immerse, but·rather to·
G0907.4 V-PAP-NPM βαπτίζοντες (1x)
Mt 28:19 disciple all the nations, immersing them in the
G0907.4 V-IPI-3P ἐβαπτίζοντο (2x)
Ac 8:12 name of·Jesus Anointed, they·were·immersed, both
Ac 18:8 *Paul* were·trusting, and they·were·immersed.
G0907.4 V-AAI-1S ἐβάπτισα (4x)
1Co 1:14 to·God that I·immersed not·even·one of·yeu,
1Co 1:15 lest any should·declare that I·immersed in my·own
1Co 1:16 (And I·immersed also the household of·Stephanas.
1Co 1:16 I·do·not personally·know if I·immersed any other
G0907.4 V-AAI-3S ἐβάπτισεν (1x)
Ac 8:38 Philippe and the eunuch. And he·immersed him.
G0907.4 V-AMM-2S βάπτισαι (1x)
Ac 22:16 *to·do*? Upon·rising·up, be·immersed, and fully·
G0907.4 V-API-1P ἐβαπτίσθημεν (2x)
Rm 6:3 ·not·know, that as·many·as are·immersed into Jesus
Rm 6:3 ·immersed into Jesus Anointed are·immersed into his
G0907.4 V-API-2P ἐβαπτίσθητε (2x)
Gal 3:27 For as·many·of·yeu·as are·immersed into *the*
1Co 1:13 on·yeur behalf? Or were·yeu·immersed in the
G0907.4 V-API-3S ἐβαπτίσθη (3x)
Ac 9:18 And rising·up, he·was·immersed.
Ac 16:15 And as·soon·as she·was·immersed, and·also her
Ac 16:33 punishing·blows; and he·was·immersed at·once,
G0907.4 V-API-3P ἐβαπτίσθησαν (2x)
Ac 2:41 with·pleasure, they·were·immersed; and in·that·one
Ac 19:5 And after·hearing *this*, they·were·immersed into the
G0907.4 V-APM-3S βαπτισθήτω (1x)
Ac 2:38 "Repent, and each·one of·yeu be·immersed in the

G0907.4 V-APN βαπτισθῆναι (3x)
Ac 8:36 What prevents me to·be·immersed?"
Ac 10:47 water *such·for* these not to·be·immersed, *these* who
Ac 10:48 ·assigned for·them to·be·immersed in the name of·
G0907.4 V-APP-NSM βαπτισθείς (2x)
Ac 8:13 also trusted. And after·being·immersed, he·was
Mk 16:16 and already·being·immersed shall·be·saved, but
G0907.4 V-RPP-NPM βεβαπτισμένοι (1x)
Ac 8:16 ·subsisting merely having·been·immersed in the
G0907.5 V-FAI-3S βαπτίσει (3x)
Lk 3:16 fit to·loose. He·himself shall·immerse yeu in Holy
Mt 3:11 to·lift·and·carry. He·himself shall·immerse yeu in
Mk 1:8 in water, but he·himself shall·immerse yeu in Holy
G0907.5 V-FPI-2P βαπτισθήσεσθε (2x)
Ac 1:5 in·water, but yeu shall·be·immersed in Holy Spirit
Ac 11:16 in·water, but yeu shall·be·immersed in Holy Spirit
G0907.5 V-PAP-NSM βαπτίζων (1x)
Jn 1:33 him, the·same is the·one immersing in Holy Spirit.
G0907.6 V-FPI-2P βαπτισθήσεσθε (2x)
Mt 20:23 immersion that I·myself shall·be·immersed·in, but
Mk 10:39 I·myself am·immersed, yeu·shall·be·immersed.
G0907.6 V-PPI-1S βαπτίζομαι (4x)
Mt 20:22 that I·myself am·immersed·in, to·be·immersed·in
Mt 20:23 of·my cup and be·immersed·in the immersion that
Mk 10:38 drink·of? And be·immersed·in the immersion that
Mk 10:39 I·myself am·immersed, yeu·shall·be·immersed.
G0907.6 V-APN βαπτισθῆναι (3x)
Lk 12:50 But I·have an·immersion to·be·immersed·in, and
Mt 20:22 I·myself am·immersed·in, to·be·immersed·in *it*?
Mk 10:38 immersion that I·myself *am* to·be·immersed·in?"
G0907.7 V-API-1P ἐβαπτίσθημεν (1x)
1Co 12:13 Spirit we·ourselves were all immersed into one

G0908 βάπτισμα báptisma *n.* (22x)
Roots:G0907
xLangEquiv:H2880-1
G0908.2 N-NSN βάπτισμα (3x)
Lk 20:4 The immersion of·John, was·it from·out·of·heaven,
Mt 21:25 The immersion of·John, from·what·source was·it?
Mk 11:30 The immersion of·John, was *it* from·out·of·heaven
G0908.2 N-ASN βάπτισμα (9x)
Lk 3:3 officially·proclaiming an·immersion of·repentance
Lk 7:29 already·being·immersed·in the immersion of·John
Ac 10:37 Galilee, after the immersion which John officially·
Ac 13:24 *with* an·immersion of·repentance being·officially·
Ac 18:25 ·acquainted·with merely the immersion of·John.
Ac 19:3 And they·declared, "Into John's immersion."
Ac 19:4 John did·immerse *with* an·immersion of·repentance,
Mt 3:7 are·coming to his immersion, *John* declared to·them,
Mk 1:4 officially·proclaiming an·immersion of·repentance
G0908.2 N-GSN βαπτίσματος (1x)
Ac 1:22 beginning from the immersion of·John, unto the day
G0908.3 N-NSN βάπτισμα (2x)
1Pe 3:21 even now saves us, *is* immersion— (not *merely* of·
Eph 4:5 one Lord, one trust, one immersion,
G0908.3 N-DSN βαπτίσματι (1x)
Col 2:12 ·buried·together with·him in the immersion, in
G0908.3 N-GSN βαπτίσματος (1x)
Rm 6:4 ·together with·him through the immersion into Death
G0908.4 N-ASN βάπτισμα (5x)
Lk 12:50 But I·have an·immersion to·be·immersed·in, and
Mt 20:22 to·drink? And the immersion that I·myself am·
Mt 20:23 and be·immersed·in the immersion that I·myself
Mk 10:38 And be·immersed·in the immersion that I·myself
Mk 10:39 ·shall·drink; and in·the immersion that I·myself

G0909 βαπτισμός baptismós *n.* (4x)
Roots:G0907 xLangAlso:H4724
G0909.1 N-APM βαπτισμούς (2x)
Mk 7:4 ·hold, *such·as the* ceremonial·washings of·cups and
Mk 7:8 ·clay†, *such·as the* ceremonial·washings of·pots and
G0909.1 N-DPM βαπτισμοῖς (1x)
Heb 9:10 drinks, and in·various ceremonial·washings, and
G0909.1 N-GPM βαπτισμῶν (1x)
Heb 6:2 of·the·instruction of·ceremonial·washings, and of·

G0910 Βαπτιστής Baptistḗs *n/p.* (15x)
Roots:G0907 See:G2491 G2424 xLangAlso:H1350
EG0910 (1x)
Lk 7:18 the disciples of·John *the Immerser* reported·to him
G0910.2 N/P-NSM Βαπτιστής (4x)
Lk 7:20 declared, "John the Immerser has·dispatched us to
Lk 7:33 "For John the Immerser has·come neither eating
Mt 3:1 days, John the Immerser arrived·publicly, officially·
Mt 14:2 "This is John the Immerser; he·himself is·already·
G0910.2 N/P-ASM Βαπτιστήν (3x)
Lk 9:19 they·declared, "John the Immerser, but others *say*
Mt 16:14 ·fact, *some say* John the Immerser, and others *say*
Mk 8:28 they·answered, "John the Immerser, but some *say*,
G0910.2 N/P-GSM Βαπτιστοῦ (7x)
Lk 7:28 ·one prophet greater·than John the Immerser, but the
Mt 11:11 one·greater·than John the Immerser. But the·one
Mt 11:12 the days of·John the Immerser until this·moment,
Mt 14:8 me here the head of·John the Immerser on a·platter."
Mt 17:13 he·declared to·them concerning John the Immerser.
Mk 6:24 "The head of·John the Immerser."
Mk 6:25 ·hour the head of·John the Immerser on a·platter."

G0911 βάπτω báptō *v.* (3x)
See:G0907
xLangEquiv:H2881
G0911.1 V-AAP-NSM βάψας (1x)
Jn 13:26 ·hand the morsel, *with* I·myself dipping *it*." And
G0911.1 V-AAS-3S βάψῃ (1x)
Lk 16:24 and send Lazarus in·order·that he·may·dip the tip
G0911.1 V-RPP-ASN βεβαμμένον (1x)
Rv 19:13 ·with a·garment having·been·dipped in·blood, and

G0912 Βαρ•αββᾶς Barabbâs *n/p.* (11x)
Roots:A1247 G0005
G0912.2 N/P-NSM Βαραββᾶς (2x)
Jn 18:40 ·rather BarAbbas." And BarAbbas was a·robber.
Mk 15:7 being·referred·to·as BarAbbas, having·been·bound
G0912.2 N/P-ASM Βαραββᾶν (9x)
Jn 18:40 "Not this·one, but·rather BarAbbas." And
Lk 23:18 ·with this·man, and fully·release to·us BarAbbas!"
Mt 27:16 ·referred·to·as BarAbbas·*(meaning·son·of·Abba)*.
Mt 27:17 *that* I·should·fully·release to·yeu? BarAbbas, or
Mt 27:20 that they·should·request BarAbbas and should·
Mt 27:21 to·yeu?" Then they·declared, "BarAbbas."
Mt 27:26 Then he·fully·released BarAbbas to·them, and
Mk 15:11 rather he·should·fully·release BarAbbas to·them.
Mk 15:15 crowd content, fully·released BarAbbas to·them,

G0913 Βαράκ Barák *n/p.* (1x)
Βαράκ Baráq [Greek, Octuagint]
בָּרָק bāraq [Hebrew]
Roots:H1301
G0913.2 N/P-PRI Βαράκ (1x)
Heb 11:32 ·account concerning Gideon, also Baraq, Samson

G0914 Βαραχ•ίας Barachías *n/p.* (1x)
בֶּרֶכְיָה berekyah [Hebrew]
Roots:H1296 See:G2197
G0914.2 N/P-GSM Βαραχίου (1x)
Mt 23:35 of·ZecharYah, descendant of·BerekYah, whom

G0915 βάρβαρος bárbarôs *adj.* (6x)
Compare:G0241 G1484 G1672 G2453 G4658
G0915 A-NSM βάρβαρος (3x)
1Co 14:11 voice, I·shall·be a·barbarian to·the·one speaking,
1Co 14:11 the·one speaking with me *shall·be* a·barbarian.
Col 3:11 and uncircumcision, Barbarian, Scythian, slave *or*
G0915 A-NPM βάρβαροι (2x)
Ac 28:2 And the barbarians were·personally·exhibiting to·us
Ac 28:4 And as·soon·as the barbarians saw the venomous·
G0915 A-DPM βαρβάροις (1x)
Rm 1:14 ·obligation both to·Greeks and to·Barbarians, also

G0916 βαρέω barḗō *v.* (6x)
Roots:G0926
G0916 V-PPM-3S βαρείσθω (1x)
1Ti 5:16 Called·Out·citizenry be·weighed·down, in·order·
G0916 V-PPP-NPM βαρούμενοι (1x)
2Co 5:4 ·tent do·groan, being·weighed·down, whereas we·
G0916 V-API-1P ἐβαρήθημεν (1x)
2Co 1:8 we·were·weighed·down beyond *our·own* ability *to*·
G0916 V-RPP-NPM βεβαρημένοι (3x)
Lk 9:32 were having·been·weighed·down with·heavy·sleep,
Mt 26:43 for their eyes were having·been·weighed·down.
Mk 14:40 their eyes were having·been·weighed·down, and

G0917 βαρέως barḗôs *adv.* (2x)
Roots:G0926
G0917.2 ADV βαρέως (2x)
Ac 28:27 ·thickly·calloused, and their ears hardly heard, and
Mt 13:15 ·thickly·calloused, and their ears hardly heard, and

G0918 Βαρ•θολομαῖος Barthôlômaîôs *n/p.* (4x)
Roots:A1247 H8526
G0918.2 N/P-NSM Βαρθολομαῖος (2x)
Ac 1:13 and Thomas); (BarTholomew and MattHew);
Mt 10:3 Philip and BarTholomew; Thomas and MattHew the
G0918.2 N/P-ASM Βαρθολομαῖον (2x)
Lk 6:14 Jakob and John, and·Philip and BarTholomew,
Mk 3:18 and Philip, and BarTholomew, and MattHew *of*·

G0919 Βαρ•ιησοῦς Bariēsôûs *n/p.* (1x)
Roots:A1247 H3091
G0919.2 N/P-NSM Βαριησοῦς (1x)
Ac 13:6 a·false·prophet, whose name *was* BarJoshua,

G0920 Βαρ•ιωνᾶς Bariōnâs *n/p.* (1x)
Roots:A1247 H3124 See:G2495
G0920.2 N/P-GSM Βάρ Ἰωνᾶ (1x)
Mt 16:17 ·blessed are·you, Simon BarJonah, because flesh

G0921 Βαρ•νάβας Barnábas *n/p.* (29x)
Roots:A1247 A5029 See:G3138
G0921.2 N/P-NSM Βαρνάβας (11x)
Ac 4:36 the·one being·properly·called BarNabas by the
Ac 9:27 But BarNabas, grabbing him, brought *him* to the
Ac 11:25 Then BarNabas went·forth to Tarsus, to·diligently·
Ac 12:25 And BarNabas and Saul returned·back *to·Antioch*
Ac 13:1 and instructors as·follows: BarNabas, Simeon (the·
Ac 13:46 ·with·clarity, Paul and BarNabas declared, "It·
Ac 14:14 But the ambassadors, BarNabas and Paul, after·
Ac 15:35 So Paul and BarNabas were·lingering in Antioch,
Ac 15:37 And BarNabas resolutely·purposed to·personally·
Gal 2:13 such·that BarNabas also was·led·away·together
1Co 9:6 Or *are* only BarNabas and I·myself *excluded*? ¿!·
G0921.2 N/P-ASM Βαρνάβαν (8x)
Ac 11:22 they·dispatched·forth BarNabas to·go·throughout
Ac 13:2 specially·detach for·me both BarNabas and Saul
Ac 13:7 This·man, summoning for·BarNabas and Saul,
Ac 13:50 ·up persecution against Paul and BarNabas and cast
Ac 14:12 In·fact, both they·were·calling BarNabas, Zeus,
Ac 15:2 they·arranged *for* Paul and BarNabas, and certain
Ac 15:36 days, Paul declared to BarNabas, "Now·then
Ac 15:39 one·another; and *for* BarNabas, personally·taking
G0921.2 N/P-DSM Βαρναβᾷ (6x)
Ac 13:43 ·to·Judaism followed Paul and BarNabas, who,
Ac 14:20 he·went·forth together with·BarNabas to Derbe.
Ac 15:2 and BarNabas and with·mutual·questioning·and·
Ac 15:22 Antioch together with·Paul and BarNabas; *namely*,
Ac 15:25 yeu together with·our beloved BarNabas and Paul,
Gal 2:9 they·gave to·me and BarNabas *the* right·hands of·
G0921.2 N/P-GSM Βαρνάβα (4x)
Ac 11:30 the elders through *the* hands of·BarNabas and Saul.
Ac 15:12 ·silent and were·listening·to BarNabas and Paul
Gal 2:1 to JeruSalem with BarNabas, personally·taking·along
Col 4:10 *John*·Mark (the cousin of·BarNabas, concerning

G0922 βάρος bárôs *n.* (7x)
Roots:G0901-3 Compare:G0899 See:G0926 G0939
G0922.1 N-ASN βάρος (1x)
2Co 4:17 unto phenomenal" eternal weight of·glory,
EG0922.1 (1x)
Jn 19:39 about *a·weight* of·a·hundred Roman·pounds.
G0922.2 N-ASN βάρος (3x)
Ac 15:28 not·one·bit·of·a·larger burden besides these·things

Ββ

Mt 20:12 the·ones bearing the burden and the blazing·heat
Rv 2:24 as they·say), I·shall·cast upon yeu no other burden.
G0922.2 N-APN βάρη (1x)
Gal 6:2 Bear the burdens of·one·another, and in·this·manner
G0922.2 N-DSN βάρει (1x)
1Th 2:6 *though* being·able to·be a·burden as ambassadors of·

G0923 Βαρ•σαβᾶς Barsabâs *n/p.* (2x)
Βαρ•τσαβᾶς Bartsabâs [Greek, Octuagint]
Roots:A1247 A6634
G0923.2 N/P-ASM Βαρτσαβᾶν (1x)
Ac 1:23 two, Joseph being·called BarTsabas (who was·
G0923.3 N/P-ASM Βαρσαβᾶν (1x)
Ac 15:22 Judas, the·one being·surnamed BarSabas, and

G0924 Βαρ•τιμαῖος Bartimaîos *n/p.* (1x)
Roots:A1247 H2931
G0924.2 N/P-NSM Βαρτιμαῖος (1x)
Mk 10:46 and a·significant crowd, BarTimaeus the blind (a·

G0925 βαρύνω barýnō *v.* (1x)
Roots:G0926
G0925.1 V-APS-3P βαρυνθῶσιν (1x)
Lk 21:34 hearts should·be·burdened with the·aftermath·of·

G0926 βαρύς barýs *adj.* (6x)
Roots:G0901-3 See:G0922
G0926.1 A-NPF βαρεῖαι (1x)
2Co 10:10 "His letters *are* weighty and strong, but his bodily
G0926.1 A-APN βαρέα (1x)
Mt 23:4 "For they·captively·bind weighty and oppressive
G0926.1 A-APN-C βαρύτερα (1x)
Mt 23:23 cumin, but yeu·left the weightier *matters* of·the
G0926.2 A-NPM βαρεῖς (1x)
Ac 20:29 ·departure, burdensome wolves shall·enter·in
G0926.2 A-NPF βαρεῖαι (1x)
1Jn 5:3 and his commandments are not burdensome.
G0926.2 A-APN βαρέα (1x)
Ac 25:7 also bringing many burdensome complaints against

G0927 βαρύ•τιμος barýtimôs *adj.* (1x)
Roots:G0926 G5092 Compare:G4186
G0927 A-GSN βαρυτίμου (1x)
Mt 26:7 an·alabaster·flask of·deeply·valuable ointment, and

G0928 βασανίζω basanízō *v.* (12x)
Roots:G0931 Compare:G5178 See:G0929 G0930
G0928 V-FPI-3S βασανισθήσεται (1x)
Rv 14:10 of·his Wrath; and he·shall·be·tormented with fire
G0928 V-FPI-3P βασανισθήσονται (1x)
Rv 20:10 *were·cast*, and they·shall·be·tormented day and
G0928 V-PPP-APM βασανιζομένους (1x)
Mk 6:48 And he·saw them being·tormented in their rowing,
G0928 V-PPP-NSN βασανιζόμενον (1x)
Mt 14:24 ·*the*·middle of·the sea, being·tormented under the
G0928 V-PPP-NSF βασανιζομένη (1x)
Rv 12:2 ·birthing·pain and being·tormented to·produce·birth.
G0928 V-PPP-NSM βασανιζόμενος (1x)
Mt 8:6 *on a·couch* at home, dreadfully being·tormented."
G0928 V-IAI-3S ἐβασάνιζεν (1x)
2Pe 2:8 them day by day was·tormenting *his* righteous soul
G0928 V-AAI-3P ἐβασάνισαν (1x)
Rv 11:10 these two prophets tormented the·ones residing on
G0928 V-AAN βασανίσαι (1x)
Mt 8:29 of·God? Did·you·come here to·torment us before
G0928 V-AAS-2S βασανίσῃς (2x)
Lk 8:28 I·petition you *that* you·should·not torment me."
Mk 5:7 ·I·charge you by·God, you·should·not torment me."
G0928 V-APS-3P βασανισθῶσιν (1x)
Rv 9:5 that they·should·be·tormented five lunar·months.

G0929 βασανισμός basanismós *n.* (6x)
Roots:G0928 See:G0930
G0929 N-NSM βασανισμός (2x)
Rv 9:5 five lunar·months. And their torment *was* as *the*
Rv 9:5 torment *was* as *the* torment of·a·scorpion, whenever
G0929 N-ASM βασανισμόν (1x)
Rv 18:7 to·her such·a·vast·quantity·of torment and mourning
G0929 N-GSM βασανισμοῦ (3x)
Rv 14:11 "And the smoke of·their torment ascends into ages
Rv 18:10 on·account·of the fear of·her torment, saying,
Rv 18:15 on·account·of the fear of·her torment, weeping and

G0930 βασανιστής basanistḗs *n.* (1x)
Roots:G0928 Compare:G3644 See:G0929
G0930 N-DPM βασανισταῖς (1x)
Mt 18:34 lord handed him over to·the tormentors, until he·

G0931 βάσανος básanôs *n.* (3x)
Roots:G0901-3 See:G0928 G0939
G0931.4 N-DPF βασάνοις (2x)
Lk 16:23 eyes while·subsisting in torments, he·clearly·sees
Mt 4:24 by·a·diversity·of illnesses and torments, and those·
G0931.4 N-GSF βασάνου (1x)
Lk 16:28 also should·come into this place of·torment.'

G0932 βασιλεία basilêía *n.* (165x)
Roots:G0935 Compare:G2963 See:G0933
xLangAlso:H4410 H4438 H4467
G0932.3 N-NSF βασιλεία (55x)
Jn 18:36 Jesus answered, "My kingdom is not from·among
Jn 18:36 this world. If my kingdom was from·among this
Jn 18:36 So now my kingdom is not from·here.
Lk 6:20 ·poor, because yeurs is the kingdom of·God.
Lk 10:9 to·them, 'The kingdom of·God has·drawn·near to
Lk 10:11 this, that the kingdom of·God has·drawn·near to
Lk 11:2 let·it·be·made·holy! Your kingdom come. Your
Lk 11:17 "Every kingdom being·thoroughly·divided against
Lk 11:18 how shall his kingdom remain·established?
Lk 11:20 ·inference, the kingdom of·God has·already·come
Lk 13:18 "To·what is the kingdom of·God like?
Lk 16:16 then·on, the kingdom of·God is·being·proclaimed,
Lk 17:20 *as·to* when the kingdom of·God should·come, he·
Lk 17:20 declared, "The kingdom of·God does·not come
Lk 17:21 For, behold, the kingdom of·God is on·the·inside
Lk 18:16 forbid them, for of·such is the kingdom of·God.
Lk 19:11 presumed that the kingdom of·God is·about to·be·
Lk 21:10 against nation, and kingdom against kingdom.
Lk 21:31 also know that the kingdom of·God is near·at·hand.
Lk 22:18 until such·time the kingdom of·God should·come.
Mt 3:2 "Yeu·must·repent, for the kingdom of·the heavens
Mt 4:17 Repent, for the kingdom of·the heavens has·drawn·
Mt 5:3 spirit, because theirs is the kingdom of·the heavens.
Mt 5:10 because theirs is the kingdom of·the heavens.
Mt 6:10 Your kingdom come. Your will be·done— as in
Mt 6:13 ·One, because yours is the kingdom, and the power,
Mt 10:7 'The kingdom of·the heavens has·drawn·near.
Mt 11:12 until this·moment, the kingdom of·the heavens is·
Mt 12:25 to·them, "Every kingdom being·divided against
Mt 12:26 ·then, how shall his kingdom remain·established?
Mt 12:28 ·inference, the kingdom of·God has·already·come
Mt 13:24 saying, "The kingdom of·the heavens is·likened
Mt 13:31 saying, "The kingdom of·the heavens is like a·
Mt 13:33 he·spoke to·them: "The kingdom of·the heavens is
Mt 13:44 "Again, the kingdom of·the heavens is like
Mt 13:45 "Again, the kingdom of·the heavens is like a·man·
Mt 13:47 "Again, the kingdom of·the heavens is like a·
Mt 18:23 "On·account·of that, the kingdom of·the heavens
Mt 19:14 to me, for of·such is the kingdom of·the heavens."
Mt 20:1 "For the kingdom of·the heavens is like a·man·of·
Mt 21:43 to·yeu, the kingdom of·God shall·be·taken·away
Mt 22:2 "The kingdom of·the heavens is·likened to·a·
Mt 24:7 against nation, and kingdom against kingdom. And
Mt 25:1 "Then the kingdom of·the heavens shall·be·likened
Mk 1:15 ·fulfilled, and the kingdom of·God has·drawn·near.
Mk 3:24 And if a·kingdom should·be·divided against itself,
Mk 3:24 against itself, that kingdom is·not able to·remain·
Mk 4:26 "In·this·manner is the kingdom of·God: "*It·is* as
Mk 10:14 forbid them, for of·such is the kingdom of·God.
Mk 11:10 Having·been·blessed *is the* kingdom of·our father
Mk 13:8 against nation, and kingdom against kingdom. And
Rm 14:17 For the kingdom of·God is not *about* feeding and
1Co 4:20 For the kingdom of·God *is* not in word, but·rather
Rv 12:10 and the power, and the kingdom of·our God, and
Rv 16:10 and his kingdom became plunged·into·darkness.
G0932.3 N-NPF βασιλεῖαι (1x)
Rv 11:15 saying, "The kingdoms of·the world are·become
G0932.3 N-ASF βασιλείαν (60x)
Jn 3:3 ·above, he·is·not able to·see the kingdom of·God."
Jn 3:5 he·is·not able to·enter into the kingdom of·God.
Lk 4:43 ·the·good·news of·the kingdom of·God to·the other
Lk 8:1 proclaiming·the·good·news of·the kingdom of·God.
Lk 9:2 them to·officially·proclaim the kingdom of·God, and
Lk 9:27 death until they·should·see the kingdom of·God."
Lk 9:60 ·off, thoroughly·announce the kingdom of·God."
Lk 9:62 left·behind, is well-suited for the kingdom of·God."
Lk 12:31 "Moreover, seek the kingdom of·God, and all
Lk 12:32 yeur Father takes·delight to·give yeu the kingdom.
Lk 13:20 "To·what shall·I·liken the kingdom of·God?
Lk 18:17 if he·should·not accept the kingdom of·God as a·
Lk 18:24 the valuables shall·enter into the kingdom of·God!
Lk 18:25 a·wealthy·man to·enter into the kingdom of·God."
Lk 19:12 ·receive for·himself a·kingdom and to·return·back.
Lk 19:15 him coming·back after·receiving the kingdom, that
Lk 21:10 against nation, and kingdom against kingdom.
Lk 22:29 And·I bequeath to·yeu a·kingdom, just·as my
Lk 23:51 who also himself awaited the kingdom of·God.
Ac 1:6 do·you at this time restore the kingdom to·IsraEl?
Ac 14:22 us to·enter into the kingdom of·God through many
Ac 20:25 officially·proclaiming the kingdom of·God, shall·
Ac 28:23 ·thoroughly·testifying·to the kingdom of·God, and·
Ac 28:31 officially·proclaiming the kingdom of·God and
Heb 12:28 ·receiving an·unshakable kingdom, we·may·have
Gal 5:21 such·things shall·not inherit God's kingdom.
Mt 5:20 ·may·not·ever enter into the kingdom of·the heavens
Mt 6:33 But seek·yeu first the kingdom of·God and his
Mt 7:21 shall·enter into the kingdom of·the heavens, but·
Mt 13:52 ·being·discipled into the kingdom of·the heavens is
Mt 18:3 ·should·not enter into the kingdom of·the heavens.
Mt 19:12 on·account·of the kingdom of·the heavens. The·
Mt 19:23 ·man shall·enter into the kingdom of·the heavens.
Mt 19:24 a·wealthy·man to·enter into the kingdom of·God."
Mt 21:31 prostitutes precede yeu into the kingdom of·God.
Mt 23:14 Because yeu·shut·up the kingdom of·the heavens
Mt 24:7 nation, and kingdom against kingdom. And famines
Mt 25:34 the kingdom having·been·made·ready for·yeu from
Mk 4:30 "To·what should·we·liken the kingdom of·God?
Mk 9:1 they·should·see the kingdom of·God having·come in
Mk 9:47 ·you to·enter into the kingdom of·God with·one·eye
Mk 10:15 ·should·not accept the kingdom of·God as·though
Mk 10:23 valuables shall·enter into the kingdom of·God!"
Mk 10:24 in the valuables to·enter into the kingdom of·God!
Mk 10:25 ·a·wealthy·man to·enter into the kingdom of·God.
Mk 13:8 and kingdom against kingdom. And earthquakes
Mk 15:43 also himself was awaiting the kingdom of·God.
2Pe 1:11 to·yeu into the eternal kingdom of·our Lord and
1Th 2:12 ·one calling yeu forth into his kingdom and glory.
1Co 6:9 ·men shall·not inherit God's kingdom? Do·not be·
1Co 6:10 ·greedy·men shall·inherit God's kingdom!
1Co 15:24 ·should·hand·over the kingdom to·the·one *who·is*
1Co 15:50 is·not able to·inherit God's kingdom; neither does
Col 1:13 and relocated *us* into the kingdom of·the Son of·his
Col 4:11 these coworkers for the kingdom of·God *are* the·
2Ti 4:1 ·men at his conspicuous·appearing and his kingdom):
2Ti 4:18 ·and·sound into his heavenly kingdom, to·whom *be*
Rv 17:12 kings who did·not·yet receive a·kingdom, but·yet
Rv 17:17 also to·give their kingdom to·the Scarlet·Beast,
Rv 17:18 City, the·one having a·kingdom over the kings of·
G0932.3 N-APF βασιλείας (3x)
Lk 4:5 showed to·him all the kingdoms of·The Land in a·
Heb 11:33 trust strenuously·subdued kingdoms, worked
Mt 4:8 and shows him all the kingdoms of·the world and
G0932.3 N-DSF βασιλείᾳ (20x)
Lk 7:28 the least·one in the kingdom of·God is greater·than
Lk 13:28 all the prophets in the kingdom of·God, but yeu·
Lk 13:29 shall·recline·at·the·table in the kingdom of·God.
Lk 14:15 *is·he* that shall·eat bread in the kingdom of·God."
Lk 22:16 ·be·completely·fulfilled in the kingdom of·God."

Lk 22:30 ·drink at my table in my kingdom, and may·sit on
Lk 23:42 whenever you·should·come into your kingdom."
Mt 5:19 ·shall·be·called least in the kingdom of·the heavens;
Mt 5:19 shall·be·called great in the kingdom of·the heavens.
Mt 8:11 YiTsaq, and Jacob in the kingdom of·the heavens.
Mt 11:11 ·one *who·is* least in the kingdom of·the heavens is
Mt 13:43 ·forth as the sun in the kingdom of·their Father.
Mt 16:28 the Son of·Clay·Man† coming in his kingdom."
Mt 18:1 "Who then is greater in the kingdom of·the heavens?
Mt 18:4 ·one *who·is* greater in the kingdom of·the heavens.
Mt 20:21 right·hand and one at *your* left, in your kingdom."
Mt 26:29 brand-new with yeu in the kingdom of·my Father."
Mk 14:25 I·may·drink it brand-new in the kingdom of·God."
Eph 5:5 any·inheritance in the kingdom of·the Anointed-One
Rv 1:9 tribulation and in the kingdom and patient·endurance

G0932.3 N-GSF βασιλείας (23x)
Lk 1:33 coming·ages, and of·his kingdom there·shall·be no
Lk 8:10 to·know the mysteries of·the kingdom of·God, but
Lk 9:11 ·speaking to·them concerning the kingdom of·God,
Lk 18:29 or children, for·the·cause·of the kingdom of·God,
Ac 1:3 relating the·things concerning the kingdom of·God.
Ac 8:12 the·things concerning the kingdom of·God and the
Ac 19:8 the·things concerning the kingdom of·God.
Heb 1:8 of·straightness *is* the scepter of·your kingdom.
Mt 4:23 the good·news of·the kingdom, and·also both·
Mt 8:12 But the Sons of·the kingdom shall·be·cast·out into
Mt 9:35 ·proclaiming the good·news of·the kingdom, and
Mt 13:11 ·know the mysteries of·the kingdom of·the heavens
Mt 13:19 the Redemptive-word of·the kingdom yet not
Mt 13:38 these are the Sons of·the kingdom. But the darnel·
Mt 13:41 they·shall·collect from·out of·his kingdom all the
Mt 16:19 to·you the keys of·the kingdom of·the heavens, and
Mt 24:14 of·the kingdom shall·be·officially·proclaimed in
Mk 1:14 the good·news of·the kingdom of·God,
Mk 4:11 to·know the mystery of·the kingdom of·God, but
Mk 6:23 I·shall·give *it* to·you, up·to half of·my kingdom!"
Mk 12:34 ·are not at·a·distance from the kingdom of·God."
Jac 2:5 and *to·be* heirs of·the kingdom which he·promised
2Th 1:5 ·be·accounted·fully·worthy of·the kingdom of·God,

EG0932.3 (3x)
Ac 19:9 discussing *the·things of·the kingdom of·God* each
Mt 25:14 "For *the kingdom of·the heavens is* just·as a·man·
Rv 11:15 of·the world are·become *the kingdoms* of·our Lord

G0933 βασίλειον basíl̂eiôn *adj.* (3x)
Roots:G0934 Compare:G0833 G0980-1 G0919-1
See:G0932

G0933.2 A-DPM βασιλείοις (1x)
Lk 7:25 in·delicate·luxury, are in the royal·palaces.

EG0933.4 (2x)
Lk 1:28 And entering *this·realm* toward her, the angel
Ac 10:3 an·angel of·God entering *this·realm* toward him

G0934 βασίλειος basíl̂eiôs *adj.* (1x)
Roots:G0935 See:G0933

G0934.1 A-NSN βασίλειον (1x)
1Pe 2:9 *are* a·Selected kindred, a·royal priesthood, a·holy

G0935 βασιλεύς basileús *n.* (120x)
Roots:G0939 Compare:G2962 See:G0936 G0938
xLangEquiv:H4428 A4430

G0935 N-NSM βασιλεύς (50x)
Jn 1:49 Son of·God; you·yourself are the King of·IsraEl."
Jn 12:13 ·coming in Yahweh's name,' the King of·IsraEl."
Jn 12:15 "Behold, your King comes *to·you*, sitting·down
Jn 18:33 "Are you·yourself the King of·the Jews?
Jn 18:37 "So·then·indeed, you·yourself are a·king!" Jesus
Jn 18:37 say *it·rightly* because I AM a·king, *for* to this I·
Jn 19:3 Be·well, O·King of·the Jews!" And they·were·
Jn 19:14 and he·says to·the Judeans, "See yeur King!"
Jn 19:19 OF·NATSARETH THE KING OF·THE JEWS."
Jn 19:21 "Do·not write, 'The King of·the Jews,' but·rather
Jn 19:21 that this·man declared, 'I·am King of·the Jews.'"
Lk 14:31 "Or what king, who·is·traversing to·engage·in war
Lk 19:38 Having·been·blessed *is* the King who·is·coming in
Lk 23:3 "Are you·yourself the King of·the Jews?
Lk 23:37 "If you·yourself are the king of·the Jews, save
Lk 23:38 "THIS IS THE KING OF·THE JEWS."
Ac 7:18 even·until another king rose·up, who had·not
Ac 12:1 season, King HerOd·Agrippa violently·threw·forth
Ac 25:13 with·some days already·elapsing, King AgrIppa
Ac 26:26 For the king is·fully·acquainted concerning these·
Ac 26:30 declaring these·things, the king rose·up, and·also
Heb 7:1 For this MalkiTsedeq (King of·Salem, Priest of·God
Heb 7:2 ·translated *from·Hebrew as* "King of·Righteousness,
Heb 7:2 and after·that also "King of·Salem," which is,
Heb 7:2 "King of·Salem," which is, King of·Peace.
Mt 1:6 begot King David, and King David begot Solomon
Mt 2:2 the·one being·reproduced·and·born King of·the Jews
Mt 2:3 ·hearing *this*, King HerOd·the·Great was·troubled, and
Mt 14:9 And the king was·grieved, but on·account·of the
Mt 21:5 "Behold, your King comes to·you, calmly·mild
Mt 22:7 "But upon·hearing *this*, the king was·angry, and
Mt 22:11 "Now the king, after·entering to·distinctly·view
Mt 22:13 "Then the king declared to·the attendants, 'After·
Mt 25:34 "Then the King shall·declare to·the·ones at his
Mt 25:40 And answering, the King shall·declare to·them,
Mt 27:11 "Are you·yourself the King of·the Jews?
Mt 27:29 Be·well, O·King of·the·Jews!"
Mt 27:37 THIS IS YESHUA, THE KING OF·THE JEWS."
Mt 27:42 himself. If he·is King of·IsraEl, let·him·descend
Mk 6:14 And King HerOd·AntiPas heard *of·him*, for his name
Mk 6:22 ·together·at·the·meal, the king declared to·the
Mk 6:26 And the king became exceedingly·grieved, *yet* on·
Mk 6:27 dispatching a·bodyguard, the king ordered for·his
Mk 15:2 "Are you·yourself the King of·the Jews?
Mk 15:26 ·been·inscribed, "THE KING OF·THE JEWS."
Mk 15:32 The Anointed-One, the King of·IsraEl, let·him·
1Ti 6:15 and only Power, the King of·the·ones reigning, and
Rv 15:3 and true *are* your ways, the King of·the holy·ones.
Rv 17:14 he·is Lord of·lords, and King of·kings. And the·
Rv 19:16 the name having·been·written, KING OF·KINGS,

G0935 N-NPM βασιλεῖς (12x)
Lk 10:24 that many prophets and kings wanted to·see the·
Lk 22:25 to·them, "The kings of·the Gentiles lord·over them
Ac 4:26 The kings of·the earth stood·by *ready*, and the rulers
Mt 17:25 Simon? From whom·do the kings of·the earth take
Rv 6:15 And the kings of·the earth, and the greatest·men,
Rv 17:2 with whom the kings of·the earth committed·sexual·
Rv 17:10 And they·are seven kings. The five fell, and the
Rv 17:12 horns which you·saw are ten kings who did·not·yet
Rv 17:12 but·yet they·do·receive authority as kings *for* one
Rv 18:3 of·her sexual·immorality, and the kings of·the earth
Rv 18:9 "And the kings of·the earth, the·ones committing·
Rv 21:24 in its light, and the kings of·the earth bring their

G0935 N-VSM βασιλεῦ (8x)
Ac 25:24 Festus then disclosed, "King AgrIppa, and all the
Ac 25:26 and especially before you, O·King AgrIppa, that,
Ac 26:2 myself supremely·blessed, King AgrIppa, *for* I·am·
Ac 26:7 concerning which expectation, O·King AgrIppa, I·
Ac 26:13 at·mid day, O·king, I·saw in the way a·light from·
Ac 26:19 "By·which *cause*, O·King AgrIppa, I·did·not
Ac 26:27 King AgrIppa, do·you·trust the prophets?
Mk 15:18 Be·well, O·King of·the Jews!"

G0935 N-ASM βασιλέα (15x)
Jn 6:15 ·order·that they·should·make him king, he·departed
Jn 18:39 I·should·fully·release to·yeu the King of·the Jews?
Jn 19:12 making himself a·king speaks·against Caesar."
Jn 19:15 says to·them, "Shall·I·crucify yeur King?" The
Jn 19:15 answered, "We·have no king except Caesar."
Lk 23:2 saying himself to·be *the* Anointed-One, a·King."
Ac 13:21 And·from·there, they·requested a·king, and God
Ac 13:22 he·awakened to·them David as king, for·whom
Ac 17:7 of·Caesar, saying *that* there·is another king, Jesus."
Mt 1:6 Now Jesse begot King David, and King David begot
Mk 6:25 immediately with haste to·the king, she·requested *it*,
Mk 15:9 I·should·fully·release to·yeu the King of·the Jews?
Mk 15:12 *to·the·one* whom yeu·refer·to·as King of·the Jews?
1Pe 2:17 Reverently·fear God. Honor the king.
Rv 9:11 And they·have a·king over them— the angel of·the

G0935 N-APM βασιλεῖς (6x)
Lk 21:12 prisons, being·brought before kings and governors
Mt 10:18 before governors and also kings because·of me, for
Rv 1:6 And he·made us kings and priests·that·offer·a·sacrifice
Rv 5:10 *·be* to·our God kings and priests·that·offer·a·sacrifice,
Rv 16:14 to·traverse·forth to the kings of·the earth and of·
Rv 19:19 the Daemonic·Beast, and the kings of·the earth, and

G0935 N-DSM βασιλεῖ (6x)
Lk 14:31 to·engage·in war against another king, *does* not·
Ac 25:14 ·forth the·things against Paul to·the king, saying,
Mt 18:23 heavens is·likened to·a·man·of·clay†, a·king, who
Mt 22:2 is·likened to·a·certain·man·of·clay†, a·king, who
1Pe 2:13 the Lord, whether to·a·king, as having·superiority,
1Ti 1:17 Now to·the King of·the ages, incorruptible,

G0935 N-DPM βασιλεῦσιν (1x)
Rv 10:11 and nations, and native·tongues, and kings."

G0935 N-GSM βασιλέως (9x)
Lk 1:5 days of·HerOd·the·Great, the king of·Judea, there·was
Ac 7:10 in·the·direct·presence·of Pharaoh king of·Egypt,
Ac 12:20 the·one over the king's bedroom, they·requested
Heb 11:23 and they·were·not afraid of·the king's edict.
Heb 11:27 (not fearing the rage of·the king) for he·mightily·
Mt 2:1 in *the* days of·the king HerOd·the·Great, behold,
Mt 2:9 And after·listening·to the king, they·traversed. And
Mt 5:35 because it·is *the* City of·the superior King.
2Co 11:32 *under* Aretas the king was·dutifully·keeping the

G0935 N-GPM βασιλέων (11x)
Ac 9:15 name in·the·sight of·Gentiles and kings, and·also
Heb 7:1 ·back from the carnage of·the kings, and blessing
Mt 11:8 the soft *garments* are in the houses of·the kings.
Mk 13:9 ·be·set before governors and kings for·my cause,
1Ti 2:2 on·behalf of·kings and all the·ones being in superior·
Rv 1:5 and the chief·ruler of·the kings of·the earth— the·
Rv 16:12 in·order·that the way of·the kings from the eastern
Rv 17:14 ·is Lord of·lords, and King of·kings. And the·ones
Rv 17:18 ·one having a·kingdom over the kings of·the earth.
Rv 19:16 having·been·written, KING OF·KINGS, AND
Rv 19:18 that yeu·may·eat flesh of·kings, and flesh of·

EG0935 (2x)
1Co 4:8 Yeu·reigned *as·kings* completely·apart·from us.
Rv 17:11 even it·itself is an·eighth *king* and is from·among

G0936 βασιλεύω basilêúō *v.* (21x)
Roots:G0935
xLangEquiv:H4427

G0936 V-FAI-1P βασιλεύσομεν (1x)
Rv 5:10 priests·that·offer·a·sacrifice, and we·shall·reign on the

G0936 V-FAI-3S βασιλεύσει (2x)
Lk 1:33 And he·shall·reign over the house of·Jacob into the
Rv 11:15 of·his Anointed-One, and he·shall·reign into the

G0936 V-FAI-3P βασιλεύσουσιν (3x)
Rm 5:17 ·present of·righteousness shall·reign in life·above
Rv 20:6 that·offer·sacrifices, and they·shall·reign with him a·
Rv 22:5 illuminates them, and they·shall·reign into the

G0936 V-PAI-3S βασιλεύει (1x)
Mt 2:22 But upon·hearing that ArcheLaos reigns in Judea in·

G0936 V-PAM-3S βασιλευέτω (1x)
Rm 6:12 *·of* you·must·not·let Moral·Failure reign in yeur

G0936 V-PAN βασιλεύειν (1x)
1Co 15:25 For it·is·mandatory·for him to·reign, even·until

G0936 V-PAP-GPM βασιλευόντων (1x)
1Ti 6:15 Power, the King of·the·ones reigning, and Lord of·

G0936 V-AAI-2S ἐβασίλευσας (1x)
Rv 11:17 you·have·taken your great power and reigned.

G0936 V-AAI-2P ἐβασιλεύσατε (2x)
1Co 4:8 Yeu·reigned *as·kings* completely·apart·from us.
1Co 4:8 it·were·actually·so *that* yeu·did·reign, in·order·that

G0936 V-AAI-3S ἐβασίλευσεν (4x)
Rm 5:14 But·yet Death already·reigned from Adam so·far·
Rm 5:17 one trespass, Death reigned through the one·man,
Rm 5:21 in·order·that just·as Moral·Failure reigned in Death
Rv 19:6 Because Yahweh, God Almighty, reigns.

G0936 V-AAI-3P ἐβασίλευσαν (1x)

Rv 20:4 and they·lived and reigned with Anointed-One the

G0936 V-AAN βασιλεῦσαι (2x)

Lk 19:14 'We·do·not want this·man to·reign over us.'

Lk 19:27 the·ones not wanting me to·reign over them, bring

G0936 V-AAS-3S βασιλεύσῃ (1x)

Rm 5:21 ·manner Grace may·reign through righteousness to

G0937 βασιλικός basilikôs *adj.* (5x)

Roots:G0935

G0937.2 A-ASM βασιλικόν (1x)

Jac 2:8 however, yeu·complete *the* Royal Law according·to

G0937.2 A-ASF βασιλικήν (1x)

Ac 12:21 day, after·dressing·himself in·royal clothing and

G0937.3 A-NSM βασιλικός (2x)

Jn 4:46 And there·was a·certain royal·official, whose son

Jn 4:49 The royal·official says to him, "Sir, walk·down

G0937.4 A-GSF βασιλικῆς (1x)

Ac 12:20 *needed* to·be·nourished by the royal·territory.

G0938 βασίλισσα basílissa *n.* (4x)

Roots:G0936

xLangEquiv:H4436 A4433 xLangAlso:H7694 H4446 H1377

G0938 N-NSF βασίλισσα (3x)

Lk 11:31 "*The* queen of·the·south shall·be·awakened in the

Mt 12:42 *The* queen *of·the* south shall·be·awakened in the

Rv 18:7 in her heart, 'I·sit·down a·queen, and I·am not a·

G0938 N-GSF βασιλίσσης (1x)

Ac 8:27 ·potentate of·Candace, the queen of·the·Ethiopians,

G0939 βάσις básis *n.* (1x)

Roots:G0901-3 Compare:G4228 See:G0922

xLangAlso:H0134

G0939.2 N-NPF βάσεις (1x)

Ac 3:7 And at·once, his feet and ankle·joints were·stabilized

G0940 βασκαίνω baskaínō *v.* (1x)

Roots:G5337-2 Compare:G1839 G3096 See:G5335

G0940.1 V-AAI-3S ἐβάσκανεν (1x)

Gal 3:1 stupid Galatians, who cast·an·evil·eye·on yeu to·not

G0941 βαστάζω bastázō *v.* (28x)

Roots:G0939 Compare:G0142 G0667 G5342

G0941.1 V-FAI-3S βαστάσει (2x)

Gal 5:10 but the·one troubling yeu shall·bear the judgment,

Gal 6:5 For each·man shall·bear his·own load.

G0941.1 V-PAI-1S βαστάζω (1x)

Gal 6:17 ·troubles to·me, for I·myself bear in my body the

G0941.1 V-PAI-2S βαστάζεις (1x)

Rm 11:18 *it·is* not you·yourself *that* bears the root, but·

G0941.1 V-PAI-3S βαστάζει (1x)

Lk 14:27 And whoever does·not bear his cross and come

G0941.1 V-PAM-2P βαστάζετε (1x)

Gal 6:2 Bear the burdens of·one·another, and in·this·manner

G0941.1 V-PAN βαστάζειν (2x)

Jn 16:12 ·yet yeu·are·not able to·bear·them at·this·moment.

Rm 15:1 *to·partake*, ought to·bear *with* the weaknesses·of·

G0941.1 V-PAP-GSN βαστάζοντος (1x)

Rv 17:7 and of·the Scarlet·Beast bearing her, the·one having

G0941.1 V-PAP-NSM βαστάζων (3x)

Jn 19:17 And bearing his·own cross, he·went·forth unto the

Lk 22:10 the City, a·man·of·clay† bearing a·pitcher of·water

Mk 14:13 and a·man·of·clay† bearing a·pitcher of·water

G0941.1 V-PAP-NPM βαστάζοντες (1x)

Lk 7:14 of·the coffin, and the·ones bearing *him* stood·still.

G0941.1 V-AAI-2S ἐβάστασας (1x)

Jn 20:15 "Sir, if you·yourself bore him away, declare to·me

G0941.1 V-AAN βαστάσαι (3x)

Ac 9:15 is my vessel of·Selection to·bear my name in·the·

Ac 15:10 our fathers nor we·ourselves had·strength to·bear?

Rv 2:2 and that you·are·not able to·bear bad·men, and *that*

G0941.1 V-AAP-DPM βαστάσασιν (1x)

Mt 20:12 them equal to·us, the·ones bearing the burden and

G0941.1 V-AAP-NSF βαστάσασα (1x)

Lk 11:27 "Supremely·blessed *is* the womb bearing you, and

EG0941.1 (1x)

Rm 11:18 root, but·rather the root *that* bears you *personally*.

G0941.2 V-PAM-2P βαστάζετε (1x)

Lk 10:4 Do·not lift·and·carry a·pouch, nor a·knapsack, nor·

G0941.2 V-PPN βαστάζεσθαι (1x)

Ac 21:35 *the need* befell him to·be·lifted·and·carried by the

G0941.2 V-IAI-3S ἐβάσταζεν (1x)

Jn 12:6 and was·lifting·out·and·carrying the·things being·

G0941.2 V-IPI-3S ἐβαστάζετο (1x)

Ac 3:2 of·his mother's womb was·lifted·and·carried, whom

G0941.2 V-AAI-2S ἐβάστασας (1x)

Rv 2:3 And you·lifted·and·carried, and you·have patient·

G0941.2 V-AAI-3S ἐβάστασεν (1x)

Mt 8:17 sicknesses, and he·lifted·and·carried the illnesses."

G0941.2 V-AAI-3P ἐβάστασαν (1x)

Jn 10:31 the Judeans lifted·up·and·carried stones again in·

G0941.2 V-AAN βαστάσαι (1x)

Mt 3:11 shoes I·am not fit to·lift·and·carry. He·himself shall·

G0942 βάτος bátôs *n.* (5x)

G0942.1 N-GSM βάτου (1x)

Lk 6:44 nor from·out of·a·bramble·bush do·they·collect a·

G0942.2 N-DSM βάτῳ (1x)

Ac 7:35 ·one being·made·visible to·him in the burning·bush.

G0942.2 N-GSM βάτου (3x)

Lk 20:37 brought·it·to·attention at the burning·bush, *just* as·

Ac 7:30 ·Mount Sinai, in·a·blaze of·fire in·the·burning·bush.

Mk 12:26 how (at the burning·bush) God declared to·him,

G0943 βάτος bátôs *n.* (1x)

בַּת bath [Hebrew]

בַּת bath [Aramaic]

Roots:H1324 Compare:G1115-1 G2884

xLangEquiv:A1325

G0943 N-APM βάτους (1x)

Lk 16:6 And he·declared, 'A·hundred bath·measures of·oil.

G0944 βάτραχος bátrachôs *n.* (1x)

xLangEquiv:H6854

G0944 N-DPM βατράχοις (1x)

Rv 16:13 ·saw three impure spirits like frogs *come* out of·the

G0945 βαττο•λογέω battôlôgéō *v.* (1x)

Roots:G3056

G0945.2 V-AAS-2P βαττολογήσητε (1x)

Mt 6:7 ·should·not talk·repetitively·with·tedious·babblings,

G0946 βδέλυγμα bdélygma *n.* (6x)

Roots:G0948 See:G0947

xLangEquiv:H8441 xLangAlso:H8251

G0946.2 N-NSN βδέλυγμα (1x)

Lk 16:15 ·of·clay† is an·abomination in·the·sight of·God.

G0946.2 N-ASN βδέλυγμα (3x)

Mt 24:15 yeu·should·see " the Abomination of·Desolation,"

Mk 13:14 ·should·see " the Abomination of·Desolation,"

Rv 21:27 defiling or committing an·abomination or a·lie;

G0946.2 N-GPN βδελυγμάτων (2x)

Rv 17:4 her hand overflowing of·abominations and impurity

Rv 17:5 OF·THE ABOMINATIONS OF·THE EARTH.

G0947 βδελυκτός bdêlyktôs *adj.* (1x)

Roots:G0948 See:G0946

G0947.1 A-NPM βδελυκτοί (1x)

Tit 1:16 works they·deny *him*, being abhorrent, obstinate,

G0948 βδελύσσω bdêlýssō *v.* (2x)

Compare:G0655 G3404 See:G0947 G0946

G0948.1 V-PNP-NSM βδελυσσόμενος (1x)

Rm 2:22 ·you·commit·adultery? The·one abhorring the idols

G0948.2 V-RPP-DPM ἐβδελυγμένοις (1x)

Rv 21:8 ·ones, and ones·having·been·abhorrent, and

G0949 βέβαιος bébaiôs *adj.* (9x)

Roots:G0939 Compare:G1476 G4731 G4740

See:G0950 G0973-1

G0949.1 A-NSM βέβαιος (1x)

Heb 2:2 being·spoken through angels was steadfast, and

G0949.1 A-NSF βεβαία (1x)

2Co 1:7 expectation on·yeur behalf *is* steadfast, having·seen

G0949.1 A-ASF βεβαίαν (4x)

Heb 3:6 ·the Expectation *being* steadfast as·long·as·unto *the*

Heb 3:14 firm·assurance, *being* steadfast as·long·as·unto *the*

Heb 6:19 soul, both immovably·sure and steadfast, 'and·

Rm 4:16 in·order·for the promise to·be steadfast to·all the

G0949.2 A-ASM-C βεβαιότερον (1x)

2Pe 1:19 Also, we·have more·firmly the prophetic word, to·

G0949.2 A-ASF βεβαίαν (1x)

2Pe 1:10 yeur calling·forth and Selection firm. For in·doing

G0949.3 A-NSF βεβαία (1x)

Heb 9:17 ·will·and·covenant *is* of·force after men·are·dead,

G0950 βεβαιόω bêbaióō *v.* (8x)

Roots:G0949 Compare:G4732 G2476 G4599 G4741

See:G0951 G1226

G0950.1 V-PPN βεβαιοῦσθαι (1x)

Heb 13:9 good *for* the heart to·be·made·steadfast by·grace,

G0950.1 V-PPP-NPM βεβαιούμενοι (1x)

Col 2:7 ·up in him, and being·made·steadfast in the trust,

G0950.2 V-FAI-3S βεβαιώσει (1x)

1Co 1:8 who also shall·confirm yeu unto *the* end, *being* not·

G0950.2 V-PAP-GSM βεβαιοῦντος (1x)

Mk 16:20 *alongside* and confirming the Redemptive-word

G0950.2 V-PAP-NSM βεβαιῶν (1x)

2Co 1:21 And the·one presently·confirming us together with·

G0950.2 V-AAN βεβαιῶσαι (1x)

Rm 15:8 of·God's truth, in·order to·confirm the promises

G0950.2 V-API-3S ἐβεβαιώθη (2x)

Heb 2:3 through the Lord, it·was·confirmed to us by the·

1Co 1:6 of·the Anointed-One was·confirmed in yeu,

G0951 βεβαίωσις bêbaíōsis *n.* (3x)

Roots:G0950 Compare:G4733

G0951 N-ASF βεβαίωσιν (1x)

Heb 6:16 and the oath for confirmation *is* to·them an·utter·

G0951 N-DSF βεβαιώσει (1x)

Php 1:7 in·the defense and confirmation of·the good·news,

EG0951 (1x)

Heb 6:17 By which *confirmation*, God, being·resolved more·

G0952 βέ•βηλος bébēlôs *adj.* (5x)

Roots:G0939 G0967-1 Compare:G2839 G0169

G5337 See:G0953 G0953-1 xLangAlso:H2455

G0952.3 A-NSM βέβηλος (1x)

Heb 12:16 any sexually·immoral or profane·person as Esau,

G0952.3 A-APM βεβήλους (1x)

1Ti 4:7 So shun the profane and age-old,·senile myths, and

G0952.3 A-APF βεβήλους (2x)

1Ti 6:20 turning·away·from the profane, empty·discussions

2Ti 2:16 But shun the profane *and* empty·discussions, for

G0952.3 A-DPM βεβήλοις (1x)

1Ti 1:9 for·distinctly·unholy·ones and for·profane·ones, for·

G0953 βεβηλόω bêbēlóō *v.* (2x)

Roots:G0952 See:G0953-1

xLangEquiv:H2490 xLangAlso:H1351

G0953.1 V-PAI-3P βεβηλοῦσιν (1x)

Mt 12:5 in the Sanctuary·Courtyard profane the Sabbath, and

G0953.1 V-AAN βεβηλῶσαι (1x)

Ac 24:6 was·attempting to·profane the Sanctuary·Courtyard,

G0954 Βεελ•ζεβούλ Bêêlzêbôúl *n/p.* (7x)

בַּעַל זְבוּב ba'al zᵉbûb [Hebrew (original)]

Roots:H1176

G0954.1 N/P-PRI Βεελζεβούλ (7x)

Lk 11:15 ·out the demons by BaalZebul,·Master-Of-Dung, *the*

Lk 11:18 ·say that I cast·out demons by *the* Master-Of-Dung.

Lk 11:19 And if I·myself by Master-Of-Dung cast·out the

Mt 10:25 ·house, BaalZebul,·Master-Of-Dung, how·much

Mt 12:24 demons, except by BaalZebul,·Master-Of-Dung, *the*

Mt 12:27 And if I·myself, by Master-Of-Dung, cast·out the

Mk 3:22 were·saying "He·has BaalZebul,·Master-Of-Dung,"

G0955 Βελίαλ Bêlíal *n/p.* (1x)

בְּלִיַּעַל bᵉliya'al [Hebrew]

Roots:H1100 Compare:G0096 G2556

G0955.2 N/P-PRI Βελιάρ (1x)

2Co 6:15 alongside Belial·*(the·Worthless·Ruin)*? Or what

G0956 βέλος bélôs *n.* (1x)
Roots:G0906 Compare:G1002 G3057 See:G1002-1 xLangAlso:H2678
G0956.2 N-APN βέλη (1x)
Eph 6:16 to·extinguish all the fiery arrows of·the Evil·One),

G0957 βελτίον bêltíôn *adv.* (1x)
Roots:G0906 See:G0018
G0957 ADV βελτίον (1x)
2Ti 1:18 *to·me* at Ephesus, you·yourself know even·better.

G0958 Βεν•ϊαμίν Bêniamín *n/p.* (4x)
בִּנְיָמִין ḅınyạmıyṇ [Hebrew]
Roots:H1144
G0958.3 N/P-PRI Βενϊαμίν (4x)
Ac 13:21 a·man from·among *the* tribe of·BenJamin, *for* forty
Rm 11:1 AbRaham's offspring†, *from the* tribe of·BenJamin.
Php 3:5 of·IsraEl, *of·the* tribe of·BenJamin, a·Hebrew from·
Rv 7:8 *the* tribe of·BenJamin having·been·officially·sealed,

G0959 Βερ•νίκη Bêrníkē *n/p.* (3x)
Roots:G5342 G3529 Compare:G2131
G0959.2 N/P-NSF Βερνίκη (2x)
Ac 25:13 King AgrIppa and BerNiki arrived in Caesarea
Ac 26:30 and·also the governor, and BerNiki, and the·ones
G0959.2 N/P-GSF Βερνίκης (1x)
Ac 25:23 next·day, with·AgrIppa and BerNiki coming with

G0960 Βέροια Bérôia *n/l.* (2x)
Roots:G4008 See:G0961
G0960 N/L-ASF Βέροιαν (1x)
Ac 17:10 and Silas through the night to Berea— who, after·
G0960 N/L-DSF Βεροίᾳ (1x)
Ac 17:13 of·God also was·fully·proclaimed in Berea by Paul

G0961 Βεροιαῖος Bêrôiaîôs *adj/g.* (2x)
Roots:G0960
G0961.2 A/G-NSM Βεροιαῖος (1x)
Ac 20:4 even·as·far·as Asia, SoPater (a·Berean *Jew*), was·
EG0961.2 (1x)
Ac 17:11 Now these *Berean Jews* were more·noble·than the·

G0962 Βηθ•αβαρά Bēthabará *n/l.* (1x)
Roots:H1004 H5679
G0962.2 N/L-DSF Βηθαβαρά (1x)
Jn 1:28 These·things happened in BethAbara across the

G0963 Βηθ•ανία Bēthanía *n/l.* (13x)
Roots:H1004 Compare:G0967
G0963.2 N/L-NSF Βηθανία (1x)
Jn 11:18 Now BethAny was near to·JeruSalem, about fifteen
G0963.2 N/L-ASF Βηθανίαν (6x)
Jn 12:1 Jesus came to BethAny where Lazarus was, the·one
Lk 19:29 ·near to BethPhage and BethAny alongside the
Lk 24:50 them outside as·far·as to BethAny, and lifting·up
Mt 21:17 ·forth outside of·the City into BethAny, and there
Mk 11:1 to BethPhage and BethAny, alongside the Mount
Mk 11:11 late, he·went·out to BethAny with the twelve.
G0963.2 N/L-DSF Βηθανίᾳ (2x)
Mt 26:6 And with·YeShua coming·to·be in BethAny, in
Mk 14:3 And with·him being in BethAny in the home of·
G0963.2 N/L-GSF Βηθανίας (2x)
Jn 11:1 *named* Lazarus, from BethAny, from·among the
Mk 11:12 ·them coming·forth from BethAny, he·was·hungry
EG0963.2 (2x)
Jn 12:12 coming to the feast *in·BethAny*) upon·hearing that
Jn 12:17 the crowd *from BethAny* was·testifying, the·one

G0964 Βηθ•εσδά Bēthêsdá *n/l.* (1x)
Roots:H1004 H2617
G0964.2 N/L-PRI Βηθεσδά (1x)
Jn 5:2 ·one being·nicknamed BethEsda·*(House·of·Kindness)*.

G0965 Βηθ•λεέμ Bēthlêêm *n/l.* (8x)
בֵּית לֶחֶם ḅeyth lẹcнẹṃ [Hebrew]
Βηθ•λεχέμ Bēthlêchém [Greek, Octuagint]
Roots:H1035
G0965.2 N/L-PRI Βηθλεχέμ (8x)
Jn 7:42 and from the village of·BethLechem, where David
Lk 2:4 of·David (which is·called BethLechem), on·account·
Lk 2:15 ·then, we·should·go·through unto BethLechem, so
Mt 2:1 ·YeShua already·being·born in BethLechem of·Judea,
Mt 2:5 they·declared to·him, "In BethLechem of·Judea. For
Mt 2:6 "But you, O·BethLechem, *in·the* land of·Judah, are
Mt 2:8 And sending them to BethLechem, he·declared,
Mt 2:16 the boys, the·ones in BethLechem and within all of·

G0966 Βηθ•σαϊδά Bēthsaïdá *n/l.* (7x)
Roots:H1004 H6721 xLangAlso:H6719
G0966.2 N/L-PRI Βηθσαϊδά (7x)
Jn 1:44 Now Philip was from BethSaida, from·among the
Jn 12:21 Philip, the·one from BethSaida of·Galilee, and
Lk 9:10 place *belonging·to* the·city being·called BethSaida.
Lk 10:13 Woe to·you, BethSaida! Because if these miracles
Mt 11:21 Woe to·you, BethSaida! Because if the miracles
Mk 6:45 the other·side *of·the sea* toward BethSaida, until he·
Mk 8:22 And he·comes to BethSaida. And they·bring a·

G0967 Βηθ•φαγή Bēthphagḗ *n/l.* (3x)
Roots:H1004 H6291 Compare:G0963
G0967.2 N/L-PRI Βηθφαγή (3x)
Lk 19:29 ·soon·as he·drew·near to BethPhage and BethAny
Mt 21:1 to JeruSalem and came to BethPhage (toward the
Mk 11:1 ·near to JeruSalem, to BethPhage and BethAny,

G0968 βῆμα bē̂ma *n.* (12x)
Roots:G0901-3 Compare:G0898 G2362 G2515 See:G0939
xLangEquiv:H8499 xLangAlso:H4026
G0968.1 N-ASN βῆμα (1x)
Ac 7:5 it, not·even a·foot step, and·yet he·already·promised
G0968.3 N-ASN βῆμα (1x)
Ac 18:12 And they·brought him to the Bema·judgment·seat,
G0968.3 N-DSN βήματι (1x)
Rm 14:10 ·at the Bema·judgment·seat of·the Anointed-One.
G0968.3 N-GSN βήματος (9x)
Jn 19:13 he·sat·down on the Bema·judgment·seat in·a·place
Ac 12:21 upon the Bema·judgment·seat, HerOd·AgrIppa was·
Ac 18:16 he·drove them away from the Bema·judgment·seat.
Ac 18:17 ·beating *him* before the Bema·judgment·seat. And
Ac 25:6 ·sitting·down on the Bema·judgment·seat, *Festus*
Ac 25:10 standing at Caesar's Bema·judgment·seat, where it·
Ac 25:17 the Bema·judgment·seat, I·commandingly·ordered
Mt 27:19 ·seating himself upon the Bema·judgment·seat, his
2Co 5:10 the Bema·judgment·seat of·the Anointed-One in·

G0969 βήρυλλος bḗryllôs *n.* (1x)
G0969.1 N-NSM βήρυλλος (1x)
Rv 21:20 chrysolite; the eighth, beryl; the ninth, topaz; the

G0970 βία bía *n.* (4x)
Compare:G1411 G1849 G2479 G2904 G4598-2 See:G0971 G0972 G0979 G0972-1 G0972-2
xLangEquiv:H2392 xLangAlso:H2428
G0970 N-ASF βίαν (1x)
Ac 21:35 the soldiers on·account·of the force of·the crowd.
G0970 N-GSF βίας (3x)
Ac 5:26 brought them, *but* not with force, for they·feared the
Ac 24:7 after·coming·near with much force, led·*him*·away
Ac 27:41 was·broken by the force of·the breaking·waves.

G0971 βιάζω biázō *v.* (2x)
Roots:G0970 See:G0973 G0979 G0972-1 G2600-1
G0971.2 V-PMI-3S βιάζεται (1x)
Lk 16:16 and everyone forcefully·presses·himself toward it.
G0971.3 V-PPI-3S βιάζεται (1x)
Mt 11:12 the kingdom of·the heavens is·seized·by·force, and

G0972 βίαιος bíaiôs *adj.* (1x)
Roots:G0970 Compare:G4642 G2478 G1415 G2900 See:G0972-2 G0972-1
xLangEquiv:H2389
G0972 A-GSF βιαίας (1x)
Ac 2:2 of·the heaven, just·as of·a·rushing forceful wind, and

G0973 βιαστής biastḗs *n.* (1x)
Roots:G0971
G0973.1 N-NPM βιασταί (1x)
Mt 11:12 is·seized·by·force, and forceful·men seize it.

G0974 βιβλιαρίδιον bibliarídiôn *n.* (4x)
Roots:G0975 G4490-2 xLangAlso:H4039
G0974 N-ASN βιβλαρίδιον (4x)
Rv 10:2 hand a·tiny·official·scroll having·been·opened·up.
Rv 10:8 "Head·on·out! Take the tiny·official·scroll, the·one
Rv 10:9 "Give to·me the tiny·official·scroll." And he·says
Rv 10:10 Then I·took the tiny·official·scroll out of·the

G0975 βιβλίον biblíôn *n.* (34x)
Roots:G0976 G2444-3 Compare:G1992 G3200 G5489 See:G0974 xLangAlso:H5612
G0975.1 N-NSN βιβλίον (3x)
Lk 4:17 And an·official·scroll of·IsaIah the prophet was·
Rv 6:14 ·separated as an·official·scroll being·rolled·up; and
Rv 20:12 ·up. And another official·scroll was·opened·up,
G0975.1 N-NPN βιβλία (1x)
Rv 20:12 ·sight of·God, and official·scrolls were·opened·up.
G0975.1 N-ASN βιβλίον (13x)
Lk 4:17 And unrolling the official·scroll, he·found the place
Lk 4:20 And rolling·up the official·scroll *and* giving·*it*·back
Heb 9:19 he·sprinkled both the official·scroll itself and all
Rv 1:11 you·look·upon, write in an·official·scroll, and send
Rv 5:1 an·official·scroll having·been·written on·*the*·inside
Rv 5:2 is worthy to·open·up the official·scroll and to·loosen
Rv 5:3 was·able to·open·up the official·scroll, neither to·
Rv 5:4 ·open·up and to·read·aloud the official·scroll, neither
Rv 5:5 *such* to·open·up the official·scroll and to·loosen its
Rv 5:7 he·came and has·taken the official·scroll out of·the
Rv 5:8 And when he·took the official·scroll, the four living·
Rv 5:9 ·are worthy to·take the official·scroll and to·open·up
Rv 17:8 been·written in the official·scroll of·the life-above
G0975.1 N-APN βιβλία (2x)
Jn 21:25 to·have·room·for the official·scrolls being·written.
2Ti 4:13 *it·with·you*, and the official·scrolls, *but* especially
G0975.1 N-DSN βιβλίῳ (5x)
Jn 20:30 are not having·been·written in this official·scroll.
Gal 3:10 ·written in the official·scroll of·the Torah-Law to·
Rv 21:27 in the Lamb's official·scroll of·the life-above.
Rv 22:18 ·blows having·been·written in this official·scroll.
Rv 22:19 ·things having·been·written in this official·scroll.
G0975.1 N-DPN βιβλίοις (1x)
Rv 20:12 ·been·written in the official·scrolls, according·to
G0975.1 N-GSN βιβλίου (5x)
Heb 10:7 *the* header of·an·official·scroll it·has·been·written
Rv 22:7 the words of·the prophecy of·this official·scroll."
Rv 22:9 the words of·this official·scroll. Fall·prostrate to·
Rv 22:10 of·the prophecy of·this official·scroll, because the
Rv 22:18 the words of·the prophecy of·this official·scroll, if
EG0975.1 (1x)
Rv 20:12 ·up, which is *the official·scroll* of·the life-above.
G0975.2 N-ASN βιβλίον (2x)
Mt 19:7 ·give *her* a·document of·innocence·in·divorcement,
Mk 10:4 to·write a·document of·innocence·in·divorcement,
EG0975.2 (1x)
Mt 5:31 ·give her *a·document·of* innocence·in·divorcement.'

G0976 βίβλος bíblôs *n.* (13x)
See:G0975 G0974 xLangAlso:A5609
G0976.2 N-APF βίβλους (1x)
Ac 19:19 ·together the scrolls, were·completely·burning
G0976.2 N-DSF βίβλῳ (8x)
Lk 3:4 it·has·been·written in a·scroll of·the·words of·IsaIah
Lk 20:42 And David himself says in a·scroll of·Psalms,
Ac 1:20 "For it·has·been·written in a·scroll of·Psalms, "Let
Ac 7:42 just·as it·has·been·written in a·scroll of·the prophets
Mk 12:26 did·yeu·not read·aloud in the scroll of·Moses, how
Php 4:3 the names of·whom *are* in *the* scroll of·life-above.
Rv 13:8 ·not been·written in the scroll of·life-above of·the
Rv 20:15 having·been·written in the scroll of·the life-above,
G0976.2 N-GSF βίβλου (3x)
Rv 3:5 rub·out his name out of·the scroll of·life-above, but I·
Rv 22:19 from the words of·the·scroll of·this prophecy, God
Rv 22:19 his portion from *the* scroll of·the life-above, and
G0976.3 N-NSF βίβλος (1x)
Mt 1:1 A·record of·*the·paternal* origin *(via·adoption)* of·

G0977 βιβρώσκω bibrṓskō *v.* (1x)
Roots:G1006 Compare:G2068 G5315
G0977.2 V-RAP-DPM βεβρωκόσιν (1x)
Jn 6:13 remained·in·excess by·the·ones having·been·fed.

G0978 Βιθυνία Bithynía *n/l.* (2x)
G0978 N/L-ASF Βιθυνίαν (1x)
Ac 16:7 ·were·attempting to·traverse toward Bithynia, but
G0978 N/L-GSF Βιθυνίας (1x)
1Pe 1:1 Pontus, Galatia, Cappadocia, Asia, and Bithynia—

G0979 βίος bíôs *n.* (11x)
Compare:G2222 G5137 G5446 See:G0970 G0980 G0981 G0982 xLangAlso:H2416 H2416-1
G0979.1 N-ASM βίον (1x)
1Ti 2:2 a·tranquil and intentionally·quiet natural·life in all
G0979.1 N-GSM βίου (4x)
Lk 8:14 wealth and pleasures of·the natural·life, and they·do·
1Pe 4:3 time of·*our*·natural·life already·having·passed·by
2Ti 2:4 business·pursuits of·the natural·life, in·order·that he·
1Jn 2:16 eyes, and the bragging of·natural·life, is not birthed·
G0979.3 N-ASM βίον (6x)
Lk 8:43 all *her* livelihood upon practitioners·of·healing,
Lk 15:12 So he·dispensed the livelihood to·them *both.*
Lk 15:30 the·one devouring your livelihood with prostitutes
Lk 21:4 in·absolutely·all the livelihood that she·was·holding.
Mk 12:44 as·many·as she·was·holding, all her livelihood."
1Jn 3:17 should·have the world's livelihood, and should·

G0980 βιόω biốō *v.* (1x)
Roots:G0979 Compare:G2198 G5446 See:G0981 G0982
G0980 V-AAN βιῶσαι (1x)
1Pe 4:2 in·order no·longer to·live·naturally the remainder·of

G0981 βίωσις bíōsis *n.* (1x)
Roots:G0980 Compare:G0391 See:G0982
G0981.3 N-ASF βίωσιν (1x)
Ac 26:4 ·distinctly·known my way·of·life from·among *my*

G0982 βιωτικός biōtikốs *adj.* (3x)
Roots:G0980 Compare:G4229 G3056 See:G0981
G0982.1 A-DPF βιωτικαῖς (1x)
Lk 21:34 ·anxieties of·things·that·pertain·to·this·natural·life,
G0982.2 A-APN βιωτικά (2x)
1Co 6:3 angels? How·much·more still of·secular·matters?
1Co 6:4 ·have arbitrations of·secular·matters, do·yeu·seat

G0983 βλαβερός blabêrốs *adj.* (1x)
Roots:G0984 Compare:G2556
G0983 A-APF βλαβεράς (1x)
1Ti 6:9 and *into* many stupid and injurious longings, which

G0984 βλάπτω bláptō *v.* (2x)
Compare:G2210 G2559 See:G0983
G0984.2 V-FAI-3S βλάψει (1x)
Mk 16:18 deadly, no, it·shall·not injure them; they·shall·lay
G0984.2 V-AAP-NSN βλάψαν (1x)
Lk 4:35 came·forth from him, injuring him not·one·bit.

G0985 βλαστάνω blastánō *v.* (4x)
Compare:G5453 G1631 G1816 G1816-1 G4261 See:G0986 G1545-2 G0307-1
G0985.1 V-PAS-3S βλαστάνῃ (1x)
Mk 4:27 scattering·of·seed should·germinate and should·be·
G0985.2 V-AAI-3S ἐβλάστησεν (2x)
Mt 13:26 And when the blade blossomed and produced fruit,
Jac 5:18 gave rain, and the earth blossomed·with its fruit.
G0985.2 V-AAP-NSF βλαστήσασα (1x)
Heb 9:4 and Aaron's staff (the·one blossoming), and the

G0986 Βλάστος Blástôs *n/p.* (1x)
Roots:G0985
G0986.2 N/P-ASM Βλάστον (1x)
Ac 12:20 him. And persuading Blastus, the·one over the

G0987 βλασ•φημέω blasphēmếō *v.* (35x)
Roots:G0989 Compare:G3058 See:G0988 xLangEquiv:H1442
G0987.1 V-FPI-3S βλασφημηθήσεται (1x)
2Pe 2:2 ·account·of whom, the way of·truth shall·be·reviled.
G0987.1 V-PAI-3P βλασφημοῦσιν (3x)
Jac 2:7 ¿!·Is·it·not they·themselves *that* revile the beautiful
Jud 1:8 ignore sovereign·lordship, and revile glorious·ones.
Jud 1:10 these·men revile what·many·things they·do·not
G0987.1 V-PAN βλασφημεῖν (2x)
Ac 26:11 gatherings, I·was·compelling *them* to·revile *Jesus*;
Tit 3:2 to·revile no·man, to·be not·quarrelsome, *but* fair,
G0987.1 V-PAP-APM βλασφημοῦντας (1x)
Ac 19:37 ·sanctuaries, nor·even those·reviling yeur goddess.
G0987.1 V-PAP-GPM βλασφημούντων (1x)
Ac 18:6 ·themselves·against them and reviling *Jesus*,
G0987.1 V-PAP-NPM βλασφημοῦντες (5x)
Lk 22:65 they·were·saying many other reviling *things* to him
Ac 13:45 being·said by Paul, contradicting and reviling.
1Pe 4:4 of·an·unsaved·lifestyle, while·yet·reviling *yeu*,
2Pe 2:10 tremble·with·fear while·reviling glorious·ones—
2Pe 2:12 and corruption, while·reviling in matters·of·which
G0987.1 V-PPI-1S βλασφημοῦμαι (1x)
1Co 10:30 why am·I·reviled over that·for·which I·myself
G0987.1 V-PPI-3S βλασφημεῖται (2x)
Rm 2:24 "the name of·God is·reviled among the Gentiles
1Pe 4:14 In·fact, according·to their·part, he·is·reviled; but
G0987.1 V-PPM-3S βλασφημείσθω (1x)
Rm 14:16 do·not·let yeur good·benefit be·reviled.
G0987.1 V-PPP-NPM βλασφημούμενοι (1x)
1Co 4:13 Being·reviled, we·entreat. We·have·now·become
G0987.1 V-PPS-3S βλασφημῆται (2x)
Tit 2:5 the Redemptive·word of·God should·not·be reviled.
1Ti 6:1 name of·God and the instruction may·not be·reviled.
G0987.1 V-IAI-3S ἐβλασφήμει (1x)
Lk 23:39 ·the criminals who·were·hanging was·reviling him,
G0987.1 V-IAI-3P ἐβλασφήμουν (2x)
Mt 27:39 the·ones traversing·directly·by were·reviling him,
Mk 15:29 the·ones traversing·directly·by were·reviling him,
G0987.1 V-AAI-3P ἐβλασφήμησαν (3x)
Rv 16:9 ·great burning·radiation, and they·reviled the name
Rv 16:11 and·also they·reviled the God of·the heaven as·a·
Rv 16:21 And the men·of·clay† reviled God as·a·result of·
G0987.1 V-AAN βλασφημῆσαι (1x)
Rv 13:6 in revilement toward God, to·revile his name, and
G0987.1 V-AAP-DSM βλασφημήσαντι (1x)
Lk 12:10 him. But to·the·one reviling against the Holy Spirit
G0987.1 V-AAS-3P βλασφημήσωσιν (1x)
Mk 3:28 revilements, as·many·things·as they·would revile.
G0987.2 V-PAI-2S βλασφημεῖς (1x)
Jn 10:36 ·*him* yeu·yeurselves say 'You·revile·God,' because
G0987.2 V-PAI-3S βλασφημεῖ (1x)
Mt 9:3 declared within themselves, "This·man reviles·God."
G0987.2 V-PAN βλασφημεῖν (1x)
1Ti 1:20 ·may·be·correctively·disciplined not to·revile·God.
G0987.2 V-AAI-3S ἐβλασφήμησεν (1x)
Mt 26:65 saying, "He·reviled·God! What further need
G0987.2 V-AAS-3S βλασφημήσῃ (1x)
Mk 3:29 But whoever should·revile against the Holy Spirit
G0987.3 V-PPI-1P βλασφημούμεθα (1x)
Rm 3:8 we·do·not *state* (just·as we·are·vilified, and just·as

G0988 βλασ•φημία blasphēmía *n.* (19x)
Roots:G0989 See:G0987 xLangEquiv:H1421
G0988.1 N-NSF βλασφημία (3x)
Mt 12:31 ·failure and revilement shall·be·forgiven to·the
Mk 7:22 debauchery, an·evil eye, revilement, haughtiness,
Eph 4:31 and yelling, and revilement, be·expunged from
G0988.1 N-NPF βλασφημίαι (3x)
Mt 15:19 thefts, false·testimonies, *and* revilements.
Mk 3:28 and·also *concerning* revilements, as·many·things·as
1Ti 6:4 becomes envy, strife, revilements, evil suspicions,
G0988.1 N-ASF βλασφημίαν (3x)
Col 3:8 wrath, rage, malice, revilement, *and* shameful·
Rv 2:9 *I·personally·know* the revilement of·the·ones saying
Rv 13:6 it·opened·up its mouth in revilement toward God,
G0988.1 N-APF βλασφημίας (1x)
Rv 13:5 a·mouth speaking great·things and revilements. And
G0988.1 N-GSF βλασφημίας (3x)
Jud 1:9 dare to·bring·up a·verdict of·revilement, but·rather
Rv 13:1 ·turbans, and upon its heads a·name of·revilement.
Rv 17:3 overflowing of·names of·revilement, having seven
G0988.2 N-NSF βλασφημία (1x)
Mt 12:31 men·of·clay†, but the revilement of·the *Holy* Spirit
G0988.2 N-ASF βλασφημίαν (1x)
Mt 26:65 See, now yeu·heard his revilement·of·God.
G0988.2 N-APF βλασφημίας (2x)
Lk 5:21 is this who speaks revilements·of·God? Who is·able
Mk 2:7 does this·man speak revilements·of·God? Who is·
G0988.2 N-GSF βλασφημίας (2x)
Jn 10:33 but·rather concerning a·revilement·of·God. And
Mk 14:64 Yeu·heard the revilement·of·God! How·does it·

G0989 βλάσ•φημος blásphēmôs *adj.* (5x)
Roots:G0984 G5345 Compare:G3060 G2707 See:G0987 G1426
G0989.1 A-ASF βλάσφημον (1x)
2Pe 2:11 themselves a·reviling verdict personally·before
G0989.1 A-APN βλάσφημα (2x)
Ac 6:11 ·have·heard him speaking reviling utterances against
Ac 6:13 does·not cease speaking reviling utterances against
G0989.2 A-NPM βλάσφημοι (1x)
2Ti 3:2 braggers, haughty, revilers, obstinate to·parents,
G0989.2 A-ASM βλάσφημον (1x)
1Ti 1:13 the·one previously being a·reviler, and a·persecutor,

G0990 βλέμμα blḗmma *n.* (1x)
Roots:G0991 Compare:G2335
G0990.1 N-DSN βλέμματι (1x)
2Pe 2:8 (for in·looking·upon and in·hearing *these deeds*, the

G0991 βλέπω blḗpō *v.* (135x)
Compare:G1492 G3700 G0816 See:G0990 G1227 G1689 G1914 xLangAlso:H6493
G0991.1 V-FAI-2P βλέψετε (2x)
Ac 28:26 comprehend; and looking yeu·shall·look, and no,
Mt 13:14 comprehend; and looking yeu·shall·look, and no,
G0991.1 V-PAI-1S βλέπω (1x)
Rm 7:23 but I·look·at another Law in my members,
G0991.1 V-PAI-1P βλέπομεν (1x)
Heb 3:19 So we·look·at how they·were·not able to·enter·in
G0991.1 V-PAI-2S βλέπεις (6x)
Lk 6:41 "And why do·you·look·at the speck·of·dust, the·one
Mt 7:3 "And why do·you·look·at the speck·of·dust, the·one
Mt 22:16 ·one *man*, for you·do·not look to *the* countenance
Mk 5:31 were·saying to·him, "You·look·at the crowd
Mk 12:14 not·even·one·man, for you·do·not look to *the*
Jac 2:22 Look·at how the trust was·working·together with·
G0991.1 V-PAI-2P βλέπετε (3x)
Mk 8:18 'Having eyes, do·yeu·not look? And having ears,
1Co 1:26 For look·at yeur calling·forth, brothers: how·that
2Co 10:7 Do·yeu·look·at things according·to surface·
G0991.1 V-PAI-3S βλέπει (6x)
Jn 1:29 On·the next·day, John looks·at Jesus, who·is·
Jn 11:9 he·does·not stumble, because he·looks·at the light
Jn 20:1 to the chamber·tomb and looks·at the stone having·
Jn 20:5 ·near·to·peer·in, he·looked·at the strips·of·linen
Jn 21:20 ·turning·himself·about, Peter looks·at the disciple
2Co 12:6 to me above that·which he·looks·upon me *to·be*, or
G0991.1 V-PAI-3P βλέπουσιν (1x)
Mt 13:13 because looking, they·do·not look, and hearing,
G0991.1 V-PAM-2S βλέπε (4x)
Rv 6:1 (as·a·voice of·a·thunder) saying, "Come and look!"
Rv 6:3 the second living·being saying, "Come and look."
Rv 6:5 living·being saying, "Come and look." And I·saw,
Rv 6:7 of·the fourth living·being saying, "Come and look."
G0991.1 V-PAN βλέπειν (1x)
Rv 1:12 And I·turned·about to·look·at the voice that spoke
G0991.1 V-PAP-APM βλέποντας (1x)
Mt 15:31 to·marvel, while·looking·at muted·ones speaking,
G0991.1 V-PAP-NSM βλέπων (4x)
Lk 6:42 *while* you·yourself *are* not looking·at the beam in
Lk 9:62 to·a·plow and *then* looking to·the·things left·behind,
Ac 13:11 and you·shall·be blind, not looking·at the sun—
Mt 14:30 But looking·at the strong wind, he·was·afraid, and

G0991.1 V-PAP-NPM βλέποντες (4x)
Ac 28:26 ·not comprehend; and looking yeu·shall·look, and
Mt 13:13 in parables, because looking, they·do·not look,
Mt 13:14 ·not comprehend; and looking yeu·shall·look, and
Mk 4:12 in·order·that "looking they·may·look, and should·
G0991.1 V-PAS-3P βλέπωσιν (1x)
Mk 4:12 in·order·that "looking they·may·look, and should·
G0991.1 V-IAI-3P ἔβλεπον (1x)
Jn 13:22 the disciples were·looking to one·another, being·
G0991.1 V-AAI-1S ἔβλεψα (1x)
Rv 22:8 And when I·heard and looked, I·fell·down to·fall·
G0991.1 V-AAM-2S βλέψον (1x)
Ac 3:4 him together with·John, declared, "Look upon us."
G0991.2 V-FAI-3P βλέψουσιν (1x)
Rv 11:9 and nations, they·shall·look·upon their corpses
G0991.2 V-PAI-1S βλέπω (2x)
Mk 8:24 he·was·saying, "I·look·upon the men·of·clay† as
2Co 7:8 I·was·regretting *it*, for I·look·upon *it* that the·same
G0991.2 V-PAI-1P βλέπομεν (2x)
Heb 2:9 But we·look·upon Yeshua— the·one *by* a·certain
Rm 8:25 ·await for·what we·do·not look·upon, *then* through
G0991.2 V-PAI-2S βλέπεις (3x)
Lk 7:44 ·replied to·Simon, "Do·you·look·upon this woman?
Mk 13:2 declared to·him, "Do·you·look·upon these great
Rv 1:11 and, "What you·look·upon, write in an·official·
G0991.2 V-PAI-2P βλέπετε (6x)
Lk 10:23 eyes looking·upon the·things·that yeu·look·upon.
Lk 10:24 wanted to·see the·things·which yeu look·upon, and
Ac 2:33 ·forth this, which yeu now look·upon and hear.
Heb 10:25 the·more, as·much·as yeu·look·upon the day
Mt 11:4 to·John those·things·which yeu·hear and look·upon:
Mt 13:17 longed to·see *the·things* which yeu·look·upon, and
G0991.2 V-PAI-3S βλέπει (3x)
Lk 24:12 ·to·peer·in, he·looked·upon the strips·of·linen
Mk 8:23 was·inquiring·of him if he·looked·upon anything.
Rm 8:24 expectantly·awaits that·which also he·looks·upon?
G0991.2 V-PAI-3P βλέπουσιν (3x)
Jn 21:9 upon the dry·ground, they·look·upon a·fire·of·coals,
Mt 13:16 *are* yeur eyes, because they·look·upon, and yeur
Mt 18:10 angels in *the* heavens look·upon the face of·my
G0991.2 V-PAM-2P βλέπετε (1x)
1Co 10:18 Look·upon IsraEl according·to flesh.
G0991.2 V-PAN βλέπειν (5x)
Ac 8:6 hearing and·also looking·upon the miraculous·signs
Ac 12:9 but he·was·supposing to·look·upon a·clear·vision.
Rm 11:8 eyes *for·them* not to·look·upon, and ears *for·them*
Rv 5:3 to·open·up the official·scroll, neither to·look·upon it.
Rv 5:4 ·aloud the official·scroll, neither to·look·upon it.
G0991.2 V-PAP-NSM βλέπων (3x)
Mt 5:28 that everyone looking·upon a·woman specifically
Col 2:5 rejoicing and looking·upon yeur orderly·arrangement
Rv 22:8 I, John, *am* the·one looking·upon these·things and
G0991.2 V-PAP-NPM βλέποντες (4x)
Lk 8:10 in·order·that "looking·upon, they·may·not look·
Lk 10:23 eyes looking·upon the·things·that yeu·look·upon.
Ac 4:14 And looking·upon the man·of·clay†, the·one
Rv 17:8 world's conception, looking·upon the Scarlet·Beast
G0991.2 V-PAS-3S βλέπῃ (1x)
Jn 5:19 but·only what he·should·look·upon the Father
G0991.2 V-PAS-3P βλέπωσιν (3x)
Lk 8:10 "looking·upon, they·may·not look·upon, and
Rv 16:15 naked, and they·should·look·upon his indecency."
Rv 18:9 her, whenever they·should·look·upon the smoke of·
G0991.2 V-PPP-APN βλεπόμενα (2x)
2Co 4:18 the·*external*·things being·looked·upon, but·rather
2Co 4:18 of·the·*internal*·things not being·looked·upon. For
G0991.2 V-PPP-GPN βλεπομένων (2x)
Heb 11:1 *concerning* actions not being·looked·upon.
Heb 11:7 not·even·yet being·looked·upon, being·moved·
G0991.2 V-PPP-NSF βλεπομένη (1x)
Rm 8:24 but an·expectation being·looked·upon is not an·
G0991.2 V-PPP-NPN βλεπόμενα (3x)
Heb 11:3 ·apparent, *that·is*, the·things being·looked·upon.
2Co 4:18 the·things being·looked·upon *are* just·for·a·season,
2Co 4:18 but the·things not being·looked·upon *are* eternal.
G0991.2 V-IAI-3S ἔβλεπεν (1x)
Ac 9:8 ·opened·up, he·was·looking·upon no·one·at·all. And
G0991.3 V-PAP-GPM βλεπόντων (1x)
Ac 1:9 these·things, with·them looking·on, he·was·lifted·up,
G0991.3 V-PAP-NSM βλέπων (3x)
Mt 6:4 And your Father, the·one looking·on in private, shall
Mt 6:6 And your Father, the·one looking·on in private,
Mt 6:18 And your Father, the·one looking·on in private,
G0991.4 V-PAM-2P βλέπετε (1x)
Mt 24:2 declared to·them, "Do·not look·for all these·things.
G0991.5 V-PAI-1S βλέπω (2x)
Jn 9:15 upon my eyes, and I·washed, and I·look·about."
Jn 9:25 ·that being blind, at·this·moment, I·look·about."
G0991.5 V-PAI-1P βλέπομεν (2x)
Jn 9:41 But now yeu·say, 'We·look·about.' Accordingly,
1Co 13:12 we·look·about through a·reflected·image with
G0991.5 V-PAI-3S βλέπει (2x)
Jn 9:19 So·then at·this·moment, how does·he·look·about?"
Jn 9:21 But now by·what·means he·looks·about, we·do·not
G0991.5 V-PAN βλέπειν (4x)
Lk 7:21 he·graciously·bestowed the *ability* to·look·about.
Mt 12:22 and mute·man both to·speak and to·look·about.
Rm 11:10 *such·for·them* not to·look·about, and let their
Rv 9:20 which neither are·able to·look·about, nor to·hear,
G0991.5 V-PAP-APM βλέποντας (1x)
Mt 15:31 walking, and blind·ones looking·about. And they·
G0991.5 V-PAP-NSM βλέπων (2x)
Jn 9:7 ·away and washed, and he·came *back* looking·about.
Ac 9:9 And he·was three days not looking·about, and neither
G0991.5 V-PAP-NPM βλέποντες (2x)
Jn 9:39 and the·ones looking·about may·become blind."
Lk 21:30 ·bud, even·now while·looking·about, yeu·know by
G0991.5 V-PAP-NPM@ βλέποντες (1x)
Jn 9:39 ·ones not *spiritually* looking·about may·look·about,
G0991.5 V-PAS-2S βλέπῃς (1x)
Rv 3:18 on your eyes, in·order·that you·may·look·about.
G0991.5 V-PAS-3P βλέπωσιν (3x)
Jn 9:39 not *spiritually* looking·about may·look·about, and
Lk 8:16 who·are·traversing·in should·look·about·by the light
Lk 11:33 traversing·in may·look·about by·the brightness.
G0991.6 V-PAM-2S βλέπε (1x)
Col 4:17 declare to·Archippus, "Look·out·for the service
G0991.6 V-PAM-2P βλέπετε (22x)
Lk 8:18 "Accordingly, look·out·for how *well* yeu·listen·
Lk 21:8 And he·declared, "Look·out, *that* yeu·may·not be·
Ac 13:40 Accordingly, look·out, lest it·should·come upon
Heb 3:12 Look·out, brothers, lest there·shall·be in any of·
Heb 12:25 Look·out! Yeu·should·not shun the·one speaking.
Gal 5:15 and devour one·another, look·out *that* yeu·may·not
Mt 24:4 declared to·them, "Look·out *that* not anyone
Mk 4:24 he·was·saying to·them, "Look·out·for how *well*
Mk 8:15 "Clearly·see·to·it *that* yeu·look·out for the leaven
Mk 12:38 ·them in his instruction, "Look·out for the scribes,
Mk 13:5 them began to·say, "Look·out lest anyone should·
Mk 13:9 "But yeu·yeurselves look·out·for yeurselves, for
Mk 13:23 But yeu·yeurselves, look·out! Behold, I·have·
Mk 13:33 "Look·out, stay·alert and pray, for yeu·do·not
Php 3:2 Look·out·for the dogs; look·out·for the bad
Php 3:2 Look·out·for the dogs; look·out·for the bad
Php 3:2 bad workmen; look·out·for the mutilation·of·flesh!
1Co 8:9 But look·out! Lest·somehow this privilege·of·yeurs
1Co 16:10 should·come, look·out that he·may·come·to·be
Eph 5:15 Accordingly, look·out *then·for* precisely how yeu·
Col 2:8 Look·out lest any·man shall·be the·one seducing yeu
2Jn 1:8 Look·out·for yeurselves, that we·should·not
G0991.6 V-PAM-3S βλεπέτω (2x)
1Co 3:10 But each·man must·look·out how he·builds·upon
1Co 10:12 to·stand must·look·out lest he·should·fall.
G0991.6 V-PAP-ASM βλέποντα (1x)
Ac 27:12 *which·is* a·harbor of·Crete, looking·out toward *the*

G0992 βλητέος blētĕôs *adj.* (2x)
Roots:G0906
G0992 A-NSN βλητέον (2x)
Lk 5:38 fresh·new wine *is only* fit·to·be·cast into brand-new
Mk 2:22 fresh·new wine *is only* fit·to·be·cast into brand-new

G0993 Βοαν•εργές Bôanêrgĕs *n/p.* (1x)
Roots:A1123 A7266
G0993.2 N/P-PRI Βοανεργές (1x)
Mk 3:17 also on·them he·laid a·name: BoanErges, which is,

G0994 βοάω bôáō *v.* (11x)
Compare:G0310 G2905 G2799 See:G0995
G0994 V-PAP-GSM βοῶντος (4x)
Jn 1:23 *am* "a·voice of·one·crying·out in the wilderness,
Lk 3:4 "A·voice of·one·crying·out in the wilderness,
Mt 3:3 "A·voice of·one·crying·out in the wilderness,
Mk 1:3 "A·voice of·one·crying·out in the wilderness,
G0994 V-PAP-GPM βοώντων (1x)
Lk 18:7 Selected-Ones, the·ones crying·out day and night
G0994 V-PAP-NPN βοῶντα (1x)
Ac 8:7 For impure spirits, crying·out with·a·loud voice,
G0994 V-PAP-NPM βοῶντες (1x)
Ac 17:6 brothers to the rulers·of·the·city, crying·out, "The·
G0994 V-IAI-3P ἐβόων (1x)
Ac 21:34 And some were·crying·out a·certain·thing, *and*
G0994 V-AAI-3S ἐβόησεν (2x)
Lk 18:38 And he·cried·out, saying, "Jesus, O·Son of·David,
Mk 15:34 ·the ninth hour, Jesus cried·out with·a·loud voice,
G0994 V-AAM-2S βόησον (1x)
Gal 4:27 ·and·giving·birth. Burst·forth and cry·out, the·one

G0995 βοή bôē *n.* (1x)
Roots:G0994 Compare:G2805
G0995 N-NPF βοαί (1x)
Jac 5:4 it·yells·out. And the outcries of·the·ones reaping

G0996 βοή•θεια bôēthêia *n.* (2x)
Roots:G0998 Compare:G2202 G4629-2 See:G0997
G0996.1 N-ASF βοήθειαν (1x)
Heb 4:16 mercy and should·find grace for timely swift·help.
G0996.2 N-DPF βοηθείαις (1x)
Ac 27:17 ·*it*·up, they·used emergency·cables, undergirding

G0997 βοη•θέω bôēthĕō *v.* (8x)
Roots:G0998 Compare:G0482 See:G0996
xLangAlso:H5826
G0997.1 V-PAM-2S βοήθει (2x)
Mt 15:25 to·him, saying, "Lord, swiftly·help me."
Mk 9:24 "Lord, I·trust! Swiftly·help my lack·of·trust!"
G0997.1 V-PAM-2P βοηθεῖτε (1x)
Ac 21:28 "Men, Israelites, swiftly·help! This is the·man·of·
G0997.1 V-AAI-1S ἐβοήθησα (1x)
2Co 6:2 in·a·day of·custodial·Salvation I·swiftly·helped you.
G0997.1 V-AAI-3S ἐβοήθησεν (1x)
Rv 12:16 And the earth swiftly·helped the woman, and the
G0997.1 V-AAM-2S βοήθησον (2x)
Ac 16:9 "Crossing into Macedonia, swiftly·help us."
Mk 9:22 something, empathizing over us, swiftly·help us!"
G0997.1 V-AAN βοηθῆσαι (1x)
Heb 2:18 he·is·able to·swiftly·help the·ones being·tried.

G0998 βοη•θός bôēthôs *n.* (1x)
Roots:G0995 See:G0996 G0997
G0998.2 N-NSM βοηθός (1x)
Heb 13:6 "'Yahweh *is* for·me a·swift·helper, and I·shall·not

G0999 βόθυνος bôthynôs *n.* (3x)
Roots:G0900 Compare:G2978-1 xLangAlso:H4718
G0999.1 N-ASM βόθυνον (3x)
Lk 6:39 *the* blind? Shall·they·not·indeed both fall into a·pit?
Mt 12:11 *sheep* should·fall into a·pit on·the various·Sabbaths
Mt 15:14 ·guide a·blind·man, both shall·fall into a·pit."

G1000 βολή bôlē *n.* (1x)
Roots:G0906 See:G1002-1
G1000 N-ASF βολήν (1x)
Lk 22:41 ·away from them about a·stone's cast, and bowing

G1001 βολίζω bôlízō *v.* (2x)
Roots:G1002
G1001.2 V-AAP-NPM βολίσαντες (2x)
Ac 27:28 So after·dropping·the·measuring·line, they·found *it*
Ac 27:28 ·while and dropping·the·measuring·line again,

G1002 βολίς bôlís *n.* (1x)
Roots:G0906 Compare:G0956 G3057 G4577-2
See:G1001
xLangEquiv:H7420
G1002.2 N-DSF βολίδι (1x)
Heb 12:20 ·stones·at, or shall·be·shot·down with·a·javelin."

G1003 Βοόζ Bôốz *n/p.* (3x)
בֹּעַז bô'az [Hebrew]
Roots:H1162 See:G4503 G4477
G1003.2 N/P-PRI Βοόζ (3x)
Lk 3:32 ·Jesse, *son* of·Obed, *son* of·BoAz, *son* of·Salmon,
Mt 1:5 Then Salmon begot BoAz (birthed·from·out of·
Mt 1:5 birthed·from·out of·Rachav), and BoAz begot Obed

G1004 βόρβορος bốrbôrôs *n.* (1x)
Compare:G4081 xLangAlso:H2916
G1004.1 N-GSM βορβόρου (1x)
2Pe 2:22 *keeps·on* bathing·herself in a·wallowing of·muck."

G1005 βορρᾶς bôrrhâs *n.* (2x)
See:G3558 G0395 G1424 xLangAlso:H6828
G1005.2 N-GSM βορρᾶ (2x)
Lk 13:29 east and west, and from north and south, and shall·
Rv 21:13 *are* three gates; on *the* north *are* three gates; on *the*

G1006 βόσκω bốskō *v.* (9x)
Compare:G0977 G4165 See:G1016
G1006.1 V-PAM-2S βόσκε (2x)
Jn 21:15 He·says to·him, "Feed my little·lambs."
Jn 21:17 Jesus says to·him, "Feed my sheep.
G1006.1 V-PAN βόσκειν (1x)
Lk 15:15 and *the citizen* sent him into his fields to·feed pigs.
G1006.1 V-PAP-NPM βόσκοντες (3x)
Lk 8:34 But the·ones feeding *them*, after·seeing the·thing
Mt 8:33 And the·ones feeding *them* fled, and going·off into
Mk 5:14 And the·ones feeding the pigs fled and gave·a·
G1006.1 V-PPP-GPM βοσκομένων (1x)
Lk 8:32 of·a·significant·number of·pigs being·fed on the
G1006.1 V-PPP-NSF βοσκομένη (2x)
Mt 8:30 ·distance from them a·herd of·many pigs being·fed.
Mk 5:11 ·of the mountains, a·great herd of·pigs being·fed.

G1007 Βοσόρ Bôsốr *n/p.* (1x)
בְּעוֹר bᵉ'ôr [Hebrew]
Roots:H1160
G1007.2 N/P-PRI Βοσόρ (1x)
2Pe 2:15 the way of·BalaAm *the son* of·Beor who loved a·

G1008 βοτάνη bôtánē *n.* (1x)
Roots:G1006 Compare:G3001
G1008.2 N-ASF βοτάνην (1x)
Heb 6:7 and producing grain·stalk well-suited for·those on·

G1009 βότρυς bốtrys *n.* (1x)
xLangAlso:H0811 H0812
G1009 N-APM βότρυας (1x)
Rv 14:18 and collect·for·vintage the clusters of·the earth,

G1010 βουλευτής bôulêutḗs *n.* (2x)
Roots:G1011 See:G4825
G1010.2 N-NSM βουλευτής (2x)
Lk 23:50 a·counselor inherently·being a·beneficially·good
Mk 15:43 of Arimathaea, a·dignified counselor who also

G1011 βουλεύω bôulêúō *v.* (8x)
Roots:G1012 Compare:G1260 G1760 G4286 G5426
See:G1010 xLangAlso:H3289
G1011.2 V-PNI-3S βουλεύεται (1x)
Lk 14:31 sit·down first *and* takes·counsel whether he·is able
G1011.2 V-INI-3P ἐβουλεύοντο (1x)
Ac 5:33 ·irate and were·taking·counsel to·eliminate them.
G1011.2 V-ADI-3P ἐβουλεύσαντο (1x)
Jn 12:10 chief·priests took·counsel in·order·that they·may·
G1011.3 V-PNI-1S βουλεύομαι (2x)
2Co 1:17 levity? Or the·things·that I·purpose, do·I·purpose
2Co 1:17 ·that I·purpose, do·I·purpose according·to flesh,
G1011.3 V-ADI-3P ἐβουλεύσαντο (1x)
Ac 27:39 a·shore, into which they·purposed, if it·were·
G1011.4 V-ADI-3S ἐβουλεύσατο (1x)
Ac 15:37 BarNabas resolutely·purposed to·personally·take·
G1011.5 V-PNP-NSM βουλευόμενος (1x)
2Co 1:17 Now·then, in·purposefully·planning that, ¿!·did

G1012 βουλή bôulḗ *n.* (12x)
Roots:G1014 Compare:G1106 G4286 See:G1010
G1011
xLangEquiv:H6098
G1012.2 N-NSF βουλή (3x)
Ac 4:28 hand and your counsel predetermined to·happen.
Ac 5:38 be, because if this counsel or this work should·be
Ac 27:42 And the soldiers' counsel was that they·should·kill
G1012.2 N-ASF βουλήν (4x)
Lk 7:30 ·in·Torah-Law refused the counsel of·God for
Ac 20:27 to·report·in·detail to·yeu all the counsel of·God?
Ac 27:12 placed counsel to·sail·away from·there·also, if·
Eph 1:11 all things according·to the counsel of·his·own will
G1012.2 N-APF βουλάς (1x)
1Co 4:5 and shall·make·apparent the counsels of·the hearts.
G1012.2 N-DSF βουλῇ (3x)
Lk 23:51 ·voted·together with·the counsel and with·their
Ac 2:23 specifically·determined counsel and foreknowledge
Ac 13:36 after·tending to·the counsel of·God in·his·own
G1012.2 N-GSF βουλῆς (1x)
Heb 6:17 the unalterable·nature of·his counsel, ratified *it* by·

G1013 βούλημα bôúlēma *n.* (2x)
Roots:G1014 Compare:G2307 G1106 See:G1012
G1013 N-DSN βουλήματι (1x)
Rm 9:19 ·find·fault? For who has·withstood his resolve?"
G1013 N-GSN βουλήματος (1x)
Ac 27:43 forbade them of·the resolve, and commandingly·

G1014 βούλομαι bôúlômai *v.* (35x)
Compare:G2309 G1962 See:G1013
G1014.1 V-PNI-1S βούλομαι (5x)
Jud 1:5 So I·resolve to·quietly·remind yeu, *due·to* yeu once
Php 1:12 Now I·am·resolved for·yeu to·know, brothers, that
Tit 3:8 these·things, I·resolve for·you to·thoroughly·confirm
1Ti 2:8 Accordingly, I·resolve *for* the men to·pray in every
1Ti 5:14 on·account·of·grace, I·resolve *for* younger
G1014.1 V-PNI-1P βουλόμεθα (1x)
Ac 17:20 our ears. Accordingly, we·resolve to·know what
G1014.1 V-PNI-2P βούλεσθε (2x)
Jn 18:39 So·then, do·yeu·resolve *that* I·should·fully·release
Ac 5:28 with·yeur instruction, and yeu·resolve to·bring the
G1014.1 V-PNI-3S βούλεται (1x)
1Co 12:11 to·each·man individually just·as he·resolves.
G1014.1 V-PNP-GSM βουλομένου (2x)
Ac 18:27 And with·him being·resolved to·go·through into
Ac 19:30 And while·Paul was·resolving to·enter into the
G1014.1 V-PNP-NSM βουλόμενος (4x)
Ac 12:4 ·keep·watch·over him, being·resolved to·bring him
Ac 22:30 On·the next·day, being·resolved to·know the
Ac 23:28 And being·resolved to·know the legal·charge on·
Mk 15:15 So Pilate, being·resolved to·make the crowd
G1014.1 V-PNS-3S βούληται (3x)
Lk 10:22 to·whomever the Son should·resolve to·reveal *him*.
Mt 11:27 to·whomever the Son should·resolve to·reveal *him*.
Jac 3:4 sudden·impulse of·the·one piloting should·resolve.
G1014.1 V-INI-1S ἐβουλόμην (1x)
Ac 25:22 replied to Festus, "I·resolve also to·hear the man·
G1014.1 V-INI-3P ἐβούλοντο (1x)
Ac 28:18 me, were·resolving to·fully·release *me*, on·
G1014.1 V-AOI-3S ἐβουλήθη (1x)
Mt 1:19 ·public·ridicule·and·scorn, resolved to·dismiss her
G1014.1 V-AOP-NSM βουληθείς (1x)
Jac 1:18 Of·his·own·resolve, he·bred us by·the·
EG1014.1 (1x)
1Ti 2:9 In·like·manner also, *I·resolve for* the women to·
G1014.2 V-PNP-APM βουλομένους (1x)
3Jn 1:10 and he·forbids the·ones being·resolved *to·do so*
G1014.2 V-PNP-NSM βουλόμενος (3x)
Ac 27:43 centurion, being·resolved to·thoroughly·save Paul,
Heb 6:17 being·resolved more·abundantly to·fully·exhibit
2Pe 3:9 us, not being·resolved for·any to·completely·be·
G1014.2 V-PNP-NPM βουλόμενοι (1x)
1Ti 6:9 But the·ones being·resolved to·become·wealthy fall
G1014.3 V-PNI-1S βούλομαι (1x)
Ac 18:15 for I·myself am·definitely·not willing to·be judge
G1014.3 V-PNI-2S βούλει (1x)
Lk 22:42 if you·are·definitely·willing to·personally·carry
G1014.3 V-PNO-3S βούλοιτο (1x)
Ac 25:20 whether he·might·be·definitely·willing to·traverse
G1014.3 V-INI-1S ἐβουλόμην (2x)
2Co 1:15 confidence, I·was·definitely·willing to·come to
Phm 1:13 I·myself was·definitely·willing to·fully·retain
G1014.3 V-AOI-1S ἠβουλήθην (1x)
2Jn 1:12 to·yeu *all*, I·am·definitely·not willing *to·do so*
G1014.3 V-AOS-3S βουληθῇ (1x)
Jac 4:4 whoever would be·definitely·willing to·be a·friend

G1015 βουνός bôunốs *n.* (2x)
Compare:G3735 G3714
xLangEquiv:H1389
G1015 N-NSM βουνός (1x)
Lk 3:5 and every mountain and hill shall·be·made·low; and
G1015 N-DPM βουνοῖς (1x)
Lk 23:30 and to·the hills, "Cover us!""

G1016 βοῦς bôûs *n.* (8x)
Roots:G1006
G1016.1 N-NSM βοῦς (1x)
Lk 14:5 of·yeu shall·have a·donkey or an·ox fallen into a·
G1016.1 N-ASM βοῦν (3x)
Lk 13:15 of·yeu on·the Sabbath loosen his ox or *his* donkey
1Co 9:9 ·shall·not muzzle an·ox *that·is* treading·out·grain.""
1Ti 5:18 ·shall·not muzzle an·ox *that·is* treading·out·grain,"
G1016.1 N-APM βόας (2x)
Jn 2:14 ·Atrium, he·found the·ones selling oxen, sheep, and
Jn 2:15 also the sheep and the oxen; and he·poured·out the
G1016.1 N-GPM βοῶν (2x)
Lk 14:19 'I·bought five yoked·teams of·oxen, and I·traverse
1Co 9:9 ' ¿!·Do the oxen matter to·God?

G1017 βραβεῖον brabêîôn *n.* (2x)
See:G1018
G1017.2 N-ASN βραβεῖον (2x)
Php 3:14 I·pursue *it* toward the prize of·the upward calling
1Co 9:24 *that only* one receives the prize? In·this·manner run

G1018 βραβεύω brabêúō *v.* (1x)
See:G1017 G2603
G1018.1 V-PAM-3S βραβευέτω (1x)
Col 3:15 And let the peace of·God arbitrate in yeur hearts,

G1019 βραδύνω bradýnō *v.* (2x)
Roots:G1021 Compare:G5549 G3635
G1019.2 V-PAS-1S βραδύνω (1x)
1Ti 3:15 But if I·should·delay, *I·write* in·order·that you·may·
G1019.3 V-PAI-3S βραδύνει (1x)
2Pe 3:9 The Lord is·not tardy *concerning* the promise, as

G1020 βραδυ•πλοέω bradyplôéō *v.* (1x)
Roots:G1021 G4126
G1020 V-PAP-NPM βραδυπλοοῦντες (1x)
Ac 27:7 And sailing·slowly along for·a·significant·number·

G1021 βραδύς bradýs *adj.* (3x)
See:G1019
G1021.1 A-NSM βραδύς (2x)
Jac 1:19 ·of·clay† must·be swift to·hear, slow to·speak, *and*
Jac 1:19 ·be swift to·hear, slow to·speak, *and* slow to wrath.
G1021.1 A-NPM βραδεῖς (1x)
Lk 24:25 "O stupid·ones, and slow in·the heart to·trust on

G1022 βραδύτης bradýtēs *n.* (1x)
Roots:G1021
G1022 N-ASF βραδύτητα (1x)
2Pe 3:9 some·men resolutely·consider tardiness, but·rather

G1023 βραχίων brachī́ōn *n.* (3x)
Roots:G1024
G1023.1 N-NSM βραχίων (1x)
Jn 12:38 And to·whom is·revealed the arm of·Yahweh?
G1023.1 N-DSM βραχίονι (1x)
Lk 1:51 ·mighty·thing with his arm; he·thoroughly·scattered
G1023.1 N-GSM βραχίονος (1x)
Ac 13:17 ·Egypt, and with a·high arm he·brought them out

G1024 βραχύς brachýs *adj.* (7x)
Compare:G3397 G3641 See:G1023
G1024.2 A-ASN βραχύ (2x)
Lk 22:58 And after a·short·while, someone·else seeing him,
Ac 5:34 to·make the ambassadors *stay* outside a short·while.
G1024.3 A-ASN βραχύ (1x)
Ac 27:28 and after·waiting a·short·while and dropping·the·
G1024.5 A-GPN βραχέων (1x)
Heb 13:22 through concise·passages, I·communicated·by·
G1024.6 A-ASN βραχύ (2x)
Heb 2:7 "*By* a·certain small·degree, you·made him lesser
Heb 2:9 a·certain small·degree having·been·made·lesser than
G1024.7 A-ASN βραχύ (1x)
Jn 6:7 that each·one of·them may·take some small·piece."

G1025 βρέφος bréphōs *n.* (9x)
Compare:G3516
G1025.1 N-NPN βρέφη (1x)
1Pe 2:2 as newborn babies, eagerly·crave the rational milk
G1025.1 N-ASN βρέφος (2x)
Lk 2:12 Yeu·shall·find a·baby having·been·swaddled·*in*,
Lk 2:16 and Joseph, and·also the baby laying·out in the
G1025.1 N-APN βρέφη (2x)
Lk 18:15 ·were also bringing the babies to·him in·order·that
Ac 7:19 *them* put·out·and·expose their baby·boys, such·for
G1025.2 N-NSN βρέφος (2x)
Lk 1:41 of·Mariam, *that* the babe skipped·about in her
Lk 1:44 in my ears, the babe skipped·about in my womb in
EG1025.2 (1x)
1Co 15:8 ·as·if by·the *babe that·was* birthed·from·out·of·a·
G1025.4 N-GSN βρέφους (1x)
2Ti 3:15 and that from a·toddler you·have·seen the Sacred

G1026 βρέχω bréchō *v.* (7x)
Compare:G5205 See:G1028
G1026.2 V-PAN βρέχειν (1x)
Lk 7:38 *him* while·weeping, she·began to·shower his feet
G1026.2 V-PAS-3S βρέχῃ (1x)
Rv 11:6 sky, in·order·that it·should·not shower rain in *the*
G1026.2 V-AAI-3S ἔβρεξεν (2x)
Lk 7:44 my feet, but she·herself showered my feet with·the
Lk 17:29 Lot went·forth from Sodom, it·showered fire and
G1026.3 V-PAI-3S βρέχει (1x)
Mt 5:45 ·good·ones, and he·showers·rain on righteous·ones
G1026.3 V-AAI-3S ἔβρεξεν (1x)
Jac 5:17 to·shower·rain, and it·did·not shower·rain on the
G1026.3 V-AAN βρέξαι (1x)
Jac 5:17 he·prayed in·prayer *for* it·not to·shower·rain, and it·

G1027 βροντή brônté *n.* (12x)
See:G3655
xLangEquiv:H7482 xLangAlso:H1139
G1027 N-NPF βρονταί (7x)
Rv 4:5 of·the throne, lightnings and thunderings and voices
Rv 8:5 there·were voices, and thunderings, and lightnings,
Rv 10:3 he·yelled·out, the Seven Thunders spoke their·own
Rv 10:4 And when the Seven Thunders spoke their·own
Rv 10:4 ·up those·things·which the Seven Thunders spoke,
Rv 11:19 and voices, and thunderings, and an·earthquake,
Rv 16:18 And there·happened voices, and thunders, and
G1027 N-ASF βροντήν (1x)
Jn 12:29 was·saying, "*It·was only* thunder *that* has·occurred.
G1027 N-GSF βροντῆς (3x)
Mk 3:17 a·name: BoanErges, which is, "Sons of·Thunder;"
Rv 6:1 four living·beings (as a·voice of·a·thunder) saying,
Rv 14:2 and as a·voice of·a·great thunder. And I·heard a·
G1027 N-GPF βροντῶν (1x)
Rv 19:6 and as a·voice of·strong thunderings, saying,

G1028 βροχή brôché *n.* (2x)
Roots:G1026 Compare:G5205 G3655 G5494
xLangEquiv:H1653 xLangAlso:H4306
G1028.2 N-NSF βροχή (2x)
Mt 7:25 And the rain·storm descended, and the flood·waters
Mt 7:27 And the rain·storm descended, and the flood·waters

G1029 βρόχος brôchôs *n.* (1x)
Compare:G3803
G1029 N-ASM βρόχον (1x)
1Co 7:35 not that I·may·throw a·noose upon·yeu, but·rather

G1030 βρυγμός brygmós *n.* (7x)
Roots:G1031
G1030 N-NSM βρυγμός (7x)
Lk 13:28 the weeping and the gnashing of·teeth, whenever
Mt 8:12 ·shall·be the weeping and the gnashing of·the teeth."
Mt 13:42 ·shall·be the weeping and the gnashing of·teeth.
Mt 13:50 ·shall·be the weeping and the gnashing of·teeth."
Mt 22:13 ·be the weeping and the gnashing of·the teeth.'
Mt 24:51 ·be the weeping and the gnashing of·the teeth.
Mt 25:30 ·be the weeping and the gnashing of·the teeth.

G1031 βρύχω brýchō *v.* (1x)
See:G1030
G1031 V-IAI-3P ἔβρυχον (1x)
Ac 7:54 to·the heart, and they·were·gnashing *their* teeth at

G1032 βρύω brýō *v.* (1x)
G1032.2 V-PAI-3S βρύει (1x)
Jac 3:11 ¿! ·Does the wellspring gush·forth at the same

G1033 βρῶμα brôma *n.* (18x)
Roots:G0977 Compare:G1035 G1305 G4620 G5160 G5315
G1033.1 N-NSN βρῶμα (3x)
Jn 4:34 Jesus says to·them, "My food is that I·may·do the
1Co 8:8 But food does·not commend us to·God.
1Co 8:13 Therefore·indeed, if food entices my brother unto·
G1033.1 N-NPN βρώματα (1x)
1Co 6:13 The food *is* for·the belly, and the belly *is* for·the
G1033.1 N-ASN βρῶμα (3x)
Rm 14:15 brother is·grieved through *your* food, no·longer
1Co 3:2 I·fed yeu milk and not food, for yeu·were·not·yet
1Co 10:3 And all ate the same spiritual food,
G1033.1 N-APN βρώματα (4x)
Lk 3:11 *any*, and the·one having food must·do likewise."
Lk 9:13 ·traversing, we·ourselves should·buy food for all
Mt 14:15 the villages, they·may·buy food for·themselves."
Mk 7:19 ·out into the outhouse, purging all the food?"
G1033.1 N-DSN βρώματι (1x)
Rm 14:15 ·destroy that·man with·your food, on·behalf·of·
G1033.1 N-DPN βρώμασιν (1x)
1Co 6:13 and the belly *is* for·the food, but God shall·fully·
G1033.1 N-GSN βρώματος (1x)
Rm 14:20 the work of·God for·the·sake·of food. In·fact, all·
G1033.1 N-GPN βρωμάτων (1x)
1Ti 4:3 — *and commanding* to·abstain·from foods— which
EG1033.1 (1x)
Lk 17:8 ·him, 'Make·ready *food* which I·may·eat·for·supper
G1033.2 N-DPN βρώμασιν (2x)
Heb 9:10 *which·stood* merely in ceremonial·foods and drinks
Heb 13:9 ·grace, not by·ceremonial·foods, which·were·not

G1034 βρώσιμος brṓsimôs *adj.* (1x)
Roots:G1035
G1034 A-ASN βρώσιμον (1x)
Lk 24:41 to·them, "Do·yeu·have anything edible here?

G1035 βρῶσις brôsis *n.* (12x)
Roots:G0977 Compare:G1033 G1305 G4620 G5160 G5315 See:G4213 G2447
G1035.1 N-NSF βρῶσις (1x)
Rm 14:17 of·God is·not *about* feeding and drinking, but·
G1035.1 N-ASF βρῶσιν (1x)
2Co 9:10 and bread for feeding·upon, may·he·supply and
G1035.1 N-DSF βρώσει (1x)
Col 2:16 judge yeu *concerning matters* in feeding, or in
G1035.1 N-GSF βρώσεως (1x)
1Co 8:4 the feeding·upon the·things sacrificed·to·idols: We·
G1035.3 N-NSF βρῶσις (1x)
Jn 6:55 For my flesh truly is a·full·meal, and my blood truly
G1035.3 N-ASF βρῶσιν (3x)
Jn 4:32 to·them, "I·myself have a·full·meal to·eat that yeu·
Jn 6:27 not for·the full·meal that·is·completely·perishing,
Jn 6:27 ·perishing, but·rather for·the full·meal enduring into
G1035.3 N-GSF βρώσεως (1x)
Heb 12:16 who for one full·meal gave·away his rights·as·
EG1035.3 (1x)
Mt 24:38 *they·were* chewing *a·full·meal* and drinking,
G1035.5 N-NSF βρῶσις (2x)
Mt 6:19 the earth, where moth and corrosion obliterate, and
Mt 6:20 where neither moth nor corrosion obliterate, and

G1036 βυθίζω bythízō *v.* (2x)
Roots:G1037 Compare:G2670
G1036.1 V-PPN βυθίζεσθαι (1x)
Lk 5:7 filled both the sailboats, such·for them to·be·sinking.
G1036.2 V-PAI-3P βυθίζουσιν (1x)
1Ti 6:9 and injurious longings, which suck the men·of·clay†

G1037 βυθός bythôs *n.* (1x)
Roots:G0899 Compare:G2281 G3989
G1037.2 N-DSM βυθῷ (1x)
2Co 11:25 ·on *for* a·night·and·a·day in the deep·sea.

G1038 βυρσεύς byrsêús *n.* (3x)
G1038 N-DSM βυρσεῖ (2x)
Ac 9:43 ·of days in Joppa with a·certain Simon, a·tanner.
Ac 10:6 with a·certain·man, Simon a·tanner, whose home is
G1038 N-GSM βυρσέως (1x)
Ac 10:32 in *the* home of·Simon, a·tanner, directly·by *the* sea

G1039 βύσσινος byssinôs *adj.* (4x)
Roots:G1040 Compare:G4616
G1039.2 A-NSN βύσσινον (1x)
Rv 19:8 (for the fine·linen is the righteous·acts of·the holy·
G1039.2 A-ASN βύσσινον (3x)
Rv 18:16 the·one having·been·arrayed·with fine·linen, and
Rv 19:8 that she·should·be·arrayed·with fine·linen, pure and
Rv 19:14 having·dressed·themselves·with fine·linen, white

G1040 βύσσος byssôs *n.* (2x)
בּוּץ bûts [Hebrew]
Roots:H0948 Compare:G3043 G2750 G3608 G4616
See:G1039
xLangEquiv:H0948 xLangAlso:H8336
G1040 N-ASF βύσσον (1x)
Lk 16:19 ·wearing a·purple·cloak and fine·linen, splendidly
G1040 N-GSF βύσσου (1x)
Rv 18:12 and pearls, "and of·fine·linen, and purple, silk,

G1041 βωμός bōmós *n.* (1x)
Roots:G0901-3 Compare:G2379 See:G0939
G1041.2 N-ASM βωμόν (1x)
Ac 17:23 objects·of·reverence, I·found a·pedestal on which

Γγ - Gamma

G1042 γαββαθά gabbathá *n.* (1x)
See:G3038 xLangAlso:A1355
G1042.2 N-PRI γαββαθᾶ (1x)
Jn 19:13 but in·Hebrew, *it·is* Gabbatha·*(meaning·the·Knoll)*.

Γγ

G1043 Γαβρι•ήλ Gabriḗl *n/p.* (2x)
גַּבְרִיאֵל g̈abrıy'el [Hebrew]
Roots:H1403 Compare:G3413
G1043.2 N/P-PRI Γαβριήλ (2x)
Lk 1:19 ·him, "I·myself am GabriEl, the·one standing·near
Lk 1:26 lunar·month, the angel GabriEl was·dispatched by

G1044 γάγγραινα gángraina *n.* (1x)
Compare:G3500
G1044 N-NSF γάγγραινα (1x)
2Ti 2:17 their word, as gangrene, shall·have a·susceptible·

G1045 Γάδ Gád *n/p.* (1x)
גָּד g̈ad [Hebrew]
Roots:H1410
G1045.3 N/P-PRI Γάδ (1x)
Rv 7:5 *the* tribe of·Gad having·been·officially·sealed, twelve

G1046 Γαδαρηνός Gadarēnós *adj/g.* (3x)
G1046 A/G-GPM Γαδαρηνῶν (3x)
Lk 8:26 ·down to the region of·the Gadarenes, which is on·
Lk 8:37 of·the region·surrounding the Gadarenes asked him
Mk 5:1 ·side of·the sea, into the region of·the Gadarenes.

G1047 γάζα gáza *n.* (1x)
Compare:G2344 xLangAlso:H1595
G1047 N-GSF γάζης (1x)
Ac 8:27 who was over all her treasury *and* who had·come to

G1048 Γάζα Gáza *n/l.* (1x)
עַזָּה 'ażżah [Hebrew]
Roots:H5804
G1048.2 N/L-ASF Γάζαν (1x)
Ac 8:26 the·one descending from JeruSalem to Gaza." (This

G1049 γαζο•φυλάκιον gazôphylákiôn *n.* (5x)
Roots:G1047 G5438 Compare:G2344
G1049 N-ASN γαζοφυλάκιον (3x)
Lk 21:1 ·men casting their presents into the treasury·room.
Mk 12:41 cast copper·coinage into the treasury·room. And
Mk 12:43 ·than all the·ones casting into the treasury·room.
G1049 N-DSN γαζοφυλακίῳ (1x)
Jn 8:20 Jesus spoke at the treasury·room, while·instructing in
G1049 N-GSN γαζοφυλακίου (1x)
Mk 12:41 ·down directly·opposite the treasury·room, Jesus

G1050 Γάϊος Gáïos *n/p.* (5x)
G1050 N/P-NSM Γαϊος (2x)
Ac 20:4 Secundus of·ThessaloNica, and Gaius of·Derbe, and
Rm 16:23 Gaius, my local·host (and *local·host* of·the whole
G1050 N/P-ASM Γαϊον (2x)
Ac 19:29 And seizing·both Gaius and AristArchus, men·of·
1Co 1:14 not·even·one of·yeu, except Crispus and Gaius,
G1050 N/P-DSM Γαΐω (1x)
3Jn 1:1 To·the well-beloved Gaius, whom I·myself do·love

G1051 γάλα gála *n.* (5x)
See:G0580-1
xLangEquiv:H2461
G1051 N-ASN γάλα (2x)
1Pe 2:2 ·crave the rational milk *of·the Redemptive-word*,
1Co 3:2 I·fed yeu milk and not food, for yeu·were·not·yet
G1051 N-GSN γάλακτος (3x)
Heb 5:12 ·have·become ones·having need of·milk and not
Heb 5:13 participating·by·drinking milk *is* inexperienced
1Co 9:7 and does·not eat from·out of·the milk of·the flock?

G1052 Γαλάτης Galátēs *n/g.* (1x)
Roots:G1053
G1052 N/G-VPM Γαλάται (1x)
Gal 3:1 O stupid Galatians, who cast·an·evil·eye·on yeu to·

G1053 Γαλατία Galatía *n/l.* (4x)
G1053 N/L-ASF Γαλατίαν (1x)
2Ti 4:10 to ThessaloNica, Crescens to Galatia, *and* Titus to
G1053 N/L-GSF Γαλατίας (3x)
Gal 1:2 To·the Called·Out·citizenries of·Galatia.
1Pe 1:1 ·Diaspora *throughout* Pontus, Galatia, Cappadocia,
1Co 16:1 to·the Called·Out·citizenries of·Galatia, even yeu·

G1054 Γαλατικός Galatikós *adj/g.* (2x)
Roots:G1053
G1054 A/G-ASF Γαλατικήν (2x)
Ac 16:6 the country of·Galatia, they·were·being·forbidden
Ac 18:23 ·throughout *the* country of·Galatia and Phrygia in·

G1055 γαλήνη galḗnē *n.* (3x)
G1055 N-NSF γαλήνη (3x)
Lk 8:24 And they·ceased, and there·was calm.
Mt 8:26 the winds and the sea, and there·was a·great calm.
Mk 4:39 the wind subsided, and there·was a·great calm.

G1056 Γαλιλαία Galilaía *n/l.* (66x)
גָּלִילָה g̈alıylah [Hebrew]
Roots:H1551
G1056.2 N/L-VSF Γαλιλαία (1x)
Mt 4:15 beyond the Jordan, O·Galilee of·the Gentiles—
G1056.2 N/L-ASF Γαλιλαίαν (19x)
Jn 1:43 Jesus determined to·go·forth into Galilee, and he·
Jn 4:3 he·left Judea and went·off again into Galilee.
Jn 4:43 he·went·off from·there and came·forth into Galilee,
Jn 4:45 So·then, when he·came into Galilee, the Galileans
Jn 4:47 comes from·out of·Judea into Galilee, he·went·off
Jn 4:54 Jesus did, coming from·out of·Judea into Galilee.
Lk 2:39 they·returned·back into Galilee to their·own city
Lk 4:14 the power of·the Spirit to Galilee, and a·reputation
Lk 23:6 But Pilate, after·hearing "Galilee," inquired whether
Mt 4:12 ·over *into prison*, YeShua departed for Galilee.
Mt 4:23 was·heading·out all around Galilee, instructing in
Mt 26:32 I·shall·go·on·ahead·of yeu into Galilee."
Mt 28:7 he·goes·on·ahead·of yeu into Galilee. There yeu·
Mt 28:10 that they·should·go·off into Galilee, and·there
Mt 28:16 the eleven disciples traversed into Galilee to the
Mk 1:14 Jesus came into Galilee officially·proclaiming the
Mk 1:39 their gatherings among all Galilee and casting·out
Mk 14:28 I·shall·go·on·ahead·of yeu into Galilee."
Mk 16:7 that he·goes·on·ahead·of yeu into Galilee. There
G1056.2 N/L-DSF Γαλιλαίᾳ (5x)
Jn 7:1 ·things, Jesus was·walking in Galilee, for he·was·not
Jn 7:9 these·things to·them, he·remained in Galilee.
Lk 24:6 how he·spoke to·yeu while·still being in Galilee,
Mt 17:22 And upon·them returning into Galilee, YeShua
Mk 15:41 also, when he·was in Galilee, were·following him
G1056.2 N/L-GSF Γαλιλαίας (38x)
Jn 2:1 there·was a·wedding in Qanah of·Galilee, and the
Jn 2:11 of·miraculous·signs in Qanah of·Galilee and made
Jn 4:46 came again into Qanah of·Galilee, where he·made
Jn 6:1 *to·the* other·side of·the Sea of·Galilee, *which·is the*
Jn 7:41 "For ¿! ·is·it from·out of·Galilee *that* the
Jn 7:52 ¿! Are you·yourself also from·out of·Galilee? Search
Jn 7:52 a·prophet has·not been·awakened out of·Galilee."
Jn 12:21 the·one from BethSaida of·Galilee, and were·
Jn 21:2 , and NathaniEl from Qanah in·Galilee, and the *sons*
Lk 1:26 by God to a·city of·Galilee whose name *is* Natsareth
Lk 2:4 Joseph also walked·up from Galilee, out of·*the*·city
Lk 3:1 ·AntiPas being·the·ruling·tetrarch of·Galilee, and
Lk 4:31 ·down to CaperNaum, a·city of·Galilee, and he·was
Lk 4:44 officially·proclaiming in the gatherings of·Galilee.
Lk 5:17 from·out of·every village of·Galilee and Judea, and·
Lk 8:26 which is on·the·opposite·side of·Galilee.
Lk 17:11 went through *the* midst of·Samaria and Galilee.
Lk 23:5 in all Judea, beginning from Galilee unto here."
Lk 23:49 following·along with·him from Galilee, stood at·a·
Lk 23:55 with·him from·out of·Galilee, did·distinctly·view
Ac 9:31 in all of·Judea, Galilee and Samaria were·having
Ac 10:37 in all Judea, beginning from Galilee, after the
Ac 13:31 ·up·together with·him from Galilee to JeruSalem,
Mt 2:22 ·a·dream, he·departed into the districts of·Galilee.
Mt 3:13 YeShua comes·directly from Galilee to the Jordan,
Mt 4:18 while·walking near the Sea of·Galilee, YeShua saw
Mt 4:25 large crowds followed him from Galilee and *from*
Mt 15:29 came near·to the Sea of·Galilee. Then walking·up
Mt 19:1 sayings, he·moved·on from Galilee and came into
Mt 21:11 the prophet, the·one from Natsareth of·Galilee."
Mt 27:55 who followed YeShua from Galilee, attending to·
Mk 1:9 from Natsareth of·Galilee and was·immersed by
Mk 1:16 walking beside the Sea of·Galilee, he·saw Simon
Mk 1:28 went·forth unto all the region·surrounding Galilee.
Mk 3:7 And a·large multitude from Galilee followed him,
Mk 6:21 ·commanders and the foremost·men of·Galilee,
Mk 7:31 he·came to the Sea of·Galilee, through *the* midst
Mk 9:30 they·were·traversing·directly through Galilee, and
EG1056.2 (3x)
Mt 4:13 behind *and* coming *into Galilee*, he·resided in
Mt 8:18 to·go·off to the other·side *of·the Sea* of·Galilee.
Mk 4:35 ·go·through to the other·side *of·the Sea* of·Galilee."

G1057 Γαλιλαῖος Galilaîos *n/g.* (11x)
Roots:G1056
G1057 N/G-NSM Γαλιλαῖος (4x)
Lk 22:59 ·man also was with him, for he·is also a·Galilean."
Lk 23:6 inquired whether the man·of·clay† was a·Galilean.
Ac 5:37 After this·man, Judas of·Galilee rose·up in the days
Mk 14:70 them, for also you·are a·Galilean; even your
G1057 N/G-NPM Γαλιλαῖοι (3x)
Jn 4:45 he·came into Galilee, the Galileans accepted him,
Lk 13:2 that these Galileans became morally·disqualified
Ac 2:7 "Behold, are not all these ones speaking Galileans?
G1057 N/G-VPM Γαλιλαῖοι (1x)
Ac 1:11 declared, "Yeu·men of·Galilee, why·do yeu·still·
G1057 N/G-APM Γαλιλαίους (1x)
Lk 13:2 above·and·beyond all the Galileans, because they·
G1057 N/G-GSM Γαλιλαίου (1x)
Mt 26:69 "You·yourself also were with YeShua of·Galilee."
G1057 N/G-GPM Γαλιλαίων (1x)
Lk 13:1 reporting to·him concerning the Galileans, whose

G1058 Γαλλίων Gallíōn *n/p.* (3x)
G1058 N/P-NSM Γαλλίων (1x)
Ac 18:14 to·open·up his mouth, Gallio declared to the Jews,
G1058 N/P-DSM Γαλλίωνι (1x)
Ac 18:17 ·even·one of·these·things was·mattering to·Gallio.
G1058 N/P-GSM Γαλλίωνος (1x)
Ac 18:12 And when·Gallio was·the·proconsul of·Achaia, the

G1059 Γαμαλι•ήλ Gamaliḗl *n/p.* (2x)
גַּמְלִיאֵל g̈amlıy'el [Hebrew]
Roots:H1583
G1059.2 N/P-PRI Γαμαλιήλ (2x)
Ac 5:34 by·the·name·of GamaliEl, a·teacher·of·Torah-Law,
Ac 22:3 city personally·at the feet of·GamaliEl, *and* having·

G1060 γαμέω gaméō *v.* (30x)
Roots:G1062
G1060 V-PAI-3P γαμοῦσιν (4x)
Lk 20:34 present·age marry and are·given·away·in·marriage.
Lk 20:35 neither marry nor are·given·away·in·marriage.
Mt 22:30 neither do·they·marry nor are·they·given·away·in·
Mk 12:25 they·neither marry nor are·given·in·marriage,
G1060 V-PAM-3P γαμείτωσαν (1x)
1Co 7:36 he·does·not morally·fail; let·*the·couple*·marry.
G1060 V-PAN γαμεῖν (3x)
1Ti 4:3 forbidding to·marry— *and commanding* to·abstain·
1Ti 5:11 ·contrary·to the Anointed-One, they want to·marry,
1Ti 5:14 *for* younger *widows* to·marry, to·bear·children, to·
G1060 V-PAP-NSM γαμῶν (2x)
Lk 16:18 his wife and marrying another commits·adultery,
Lk 16:18 anyone marrying the·one having·been·divorced
G1060 V-PAP-NPM γαμοῦντες (1x)
Mt 24:38 drinking, marrying and giving·away·in·marriage,
G1060 V-IAI-3P ἐγάμουν (1x)
Lk 17:27 they·were·marrying·wives, they·were·being·
G1060 V-AAI-1S ἔγημα (1x)
Lk 14:20 And another declared, 'I·married a·wife, and on·
G1060 V-AAI-3S ἐγάμησεν (1x)

Mk 6:17 of·his brother Philippus, because he·married her.
G1060 V-AAM-3P γαμησάτωσαν (1x)
1Co 7:9 ·do·not have·self-restraint, they·must·marry. For it·
G1060 V-AAN γαμῆσαι (2x)
Mt 19:10 with his wife, it·is·not advantageous to·marry."
1Co 7:9 ·is significantly·better to·marry than to·be·inflamed.
G1060 V-AAP-NSF γαμήσασα (1x)
1Co 7:34 But the·one marrying is·anxious·about the·things
G1060 V-AAP-NSM γαμήσας (3x)
Mt 19:9 ·divorced, upon·marrying, does·commit·adultery."
Mt 22:25 brothers, and the first·one, upon·marrying *a·wife*,
1Co 7:33 But the·one marrying is·anxious·about the·things
G1060 V-AAS-2S γήμῃς (1x)
1Co 7:28 But even if you·should·marry, you·did·not
G1060 V-AAS-3S γήμῃ (4x)
Mt 5:32 should·marry her·having·been·divorced commits·
Mt 19:9 over sexual·immorality, and should·marry another,
Mk 10:11 wife and should·marry another commits·adultery
1Co 7:28 ·fail; and if the virgin should·marry, she·did·not
G1060 V-APN γαμηθῆναι (1x)
1Co 7:39 she·is free to·be·married to·whomever she·wants,
G1060 V-APS-3S γαμηθῇ (1x)
Mk 10:12 her husband and should·be·married to·another,
G1060 V-RAP-DPM γεγαμηκόσιν (1x)
1Co 7:10 And to·the·ones having·married I·charge, *yet* not I·
EG1060 (1x)
1Co 7:6 in concession *concerning becoming married, and*

G1061 γαμίσκω gamískō *v.* (1x)
Roots:G1062 See:G1548 G1547
G1061 V-PPI-3P γαμίσκονται (1x)
Mk 12:25 marry nor are·given·in·marriage, but·rather are as

G1062 γάμος gámôs *n.* (16x)
Compare:G0712 G1173 G1403 xLangAlso:H2861
G1062.1 N-NSM γάμος (5x)
Jn 2:1 third day, there·was a·wedding in Qanah of·Galilee,
Heb 13:4 Highly·valued *is* the wedding in all *cultures*, and
Mt 22:8 to·his slaves, 'In·fact the wedding is ready, but the·
Mt 22:10 the wedding was·filled with·those·reclining·at·the·
Rv 19:7 to·him, because the Wedding of·the Lamb did·
G1062.1 N-ASM γάμον (1x)
Jn 2:2 also was·called·forth to the wedding, and·also his
G1062.1 N-GSM γάμου (3x)
Mt 22:11 having·not dressed·himself·with wedding apparel.
Mt 22:12 did·you·enter here not having wedding apparel?
Rv 19:9 ·been·called·forth to the Wedding Supper of·the
G1062.2 N-APM γάμους (6x)
Lk 14:8 by any *man* to a·wedding·banquet, you·should·not
Mt 22:2 a·king, who made a·wedding·banquet for·his son
Mt 22:3 having·been·called to the wedding·banquet, yet
Mt 22:4 Come·here to the wedding·banquet!"'
Mt 22:9 find, call·*them*·forth to the wedding·banquet.'
Mt 25:10 with him into the wedding·banquet. And the door
G1062.3 N-GPM γάμων (1x)
Lk 12:36 from·among the wedding·banquet, in·order·that

G1063 γάρ gár *conj.* (1065x)
G1063.1 CONJ γάρ (1065x)
Jn 2:25 the man·of·clay†, for he·himself was·knowing what
Jn 3:2 *being* an·instructor, for not·even·one·man is·able to·
Jn 3:16 For in·this·manner, God loved the world, such·that
Jn 3:17 "For God did·not dispatch His Son into the world in·
Jn 3:19 rather than the light, for their deeds were evil.
Jn 3:20 For any one practicing mediocrity hates the light,
Jn 3:24 for John had·not·yet been·cast into the prison.
Jn 3:34 For he·whom God dispatched speaks the utterances
Jn 3:34 the utterances of·God, for *to·him* God does·not give
Jn 4:8 (for his disciples had·gone·off to the city in·order·that
Jn 4:9 a·Samaritan woman?" (for Jews do·not interact with·
Jn 4:18 For you·have·had five husbands, and now, he·whom
Jn 4:23 in spirit and in·truth, for even the Father seeks the·
Jn 4:37 For in this *case*, the saying is true,
Jn 4:42 on·account·of your speech, for we·have·heard *him*
Jn 4:44 for Jesus himself already·testified that, "A·prophet
Jn 4:45 Sacred·Feast *of·Passover*, for they·themselves also
Jn 4:47 and may·heal his son, for he·was·about to·die.
Jn 5:4 For according·to a·certain·season, an angel was·
Jn 5:13 ·known who it·was, for Jesus carefully·slipped·away
Jn 5:19 ·look·upon the Father doing, for whatever that *the*
Jn 5:20 For the Father is·a·friend·to the Son and shows him
Jn 5:21 "For just·as the Father awakens the dead and gives·
Jn 5:22 For not·even·does the Father judge, not·even·one·
Jn 5:26 For just·as the Father has life-above in himself, in·
Jn 5:36 testimony *than·that* of·John, for the works which the
Jn 5:46 For if yeu·were·trusting in·Moses, yeu·would be·
Jn 5:46 yeu·would be·trusting in·me, for that·man wrote
Jn 6:6 trying him, for he·himself had·personally·known
Jn 6:27 of·Clay·Man† shall·give to·yeu, for God the Father
Jn 6:33 for the bread of·God is the·one descending from·out
Jn 6:55 For my flesh truly is a·full·meal, and my blood truly
Jn 6:64 trust." For Jesus had·personally·known from·among
Jn 6:71 *the son* of·Simon, for *it·was* this·man *that* was·
Jn 7:1 was·walking in Galilee, for he·was·not willing to·
Jn 7:4 For *there·is* not·even·one·man *that* does anything in
Jn 7:5 For neither were his brothers trusting in him.
Jn 7:39 him were·about to·receive, for Holy Spirit was not·
Jn 7:41 others were·saying, "For ¿! is·it from·out·of·Galilee
Jn 8:24 in yeur moral·failures. For unless yeu·should·trust
Jn 8:42 yeu·would love me, for I·myself went·forth and
Jn 8:42 have·come out·from God. For neither have·I·come
Jn 9:22 they·feared the Judeans. For the Judeans had·
Jn 9:30 and declared to·them, "For in this is a·marvelous·
Jn 10:26 yeu·yeurselves do·not trust, for yeu·are not from·
Jn 11:39 even·now he·smells·bad, for it·is *the* fourth·day.
Jn 12:8 For yeu always have the helplessly·poor among
Jn 12:43 for they·loved the glory of·the men·of·clay† more·
Jn 12:47 do·not presently·judge him, for I·did·not come in·
Jn 13:11 For he·had·personally·known the·one handing him
Jn 13:13 me Mentor and Lord, and yeu·say well, for I·am.
Jn 13:15 For I·gave an·explicit·example to·yeu in·order·that
Jn 13:29 For some *of·them* were·presuming, since Judas was·
Jn 14:30 shall·I·speak much with yeu, for the prince of·this
Jn 16:7 that I·myself should·go·away, for if I·should·not go·
Jn 16:13 all the truth. "For he·shall·not speak from himself,
Jn 16:27 For the Father himself is·a·friend·to yeu, because
Jn 18:13 *the proper high·priest*, for he·was *the* father-in-law
Jn 19:6 take him and crucify *him*, for I·myself find no fault
Jn 19:31 the cross on the Sabbath (for that Sabbath was the
Jn 19:36 For these·things were·done that the Scripture
Jn 20:9 For not·even·yet had·they·seen the Scripture *which·*
Jn 20:17 Do·not lay·hold of·me, for I·have·not·yet ascended
Jn 21:7 *his* fishing·coat *about·himself* (for he·was naked),
Jn 21:8 the net·of·fish (for they·were not at·a·distance from
Lk 1:15 For he·shall·be great in·the·sight of·Yahweh.
Lk 1:18 shall·I·know this for·certain? For I·myself am an·
Lk 1:30 be·afraid, Mariam, for you found grace personally·
Lk 1:44 For, behold, as·soon·as the sound of·your greeting
Lk 1:48 ·estate of·his female·slave,' for behold, from now·
Lk 1:76 of·the·Most·High, for you·shall·traverse before *the*
Lk 2:10 "Do·not be·afraid, for behold, I·proclaim·good·
Lk 3:8 AbRaham *for·our* father.' For I·say to·yeu that God
Lk 4:8 me, Adversary-Accuser. For it·has·been·written, "
Lk 4:10 For it·has·been·written, "He·shall·command his
Lk 5:9 For amazement enveloped him (and all the·ones
Lk 5:39 immediately wants fresh·new *wine*, for he·says,
Lk 6:23 Rejoice in that day and skip·about, for, behold, yeur
Lk 6:23 *is* large in the heaven, for in the·same·manner, their
Lk 6:26 should·declare well of·yeu! For in the·same·manner
Lk 6:32 ·kind·of grace is·it to·yeu? For even the morally·
Lk 6:33 ·kind·of grace is·it to·yeu? For even the morally·
Lk 6:34 ·of grace is·it yeu? For the morally·disqualified also
Lk 6:38 bosom. "For by·the same standard·of·measurement
Lk 6:43 "For a·good tree is not producing rotten fruit, neither
Lk 6:44 For each tree is·known from·out·of·its·own fruit.
Lk 6:44 from·out·of·its·own fruit. For not from·out·of·
Lk 6:45 the evil. "For from·out·of·the abundance of·the
Lk 6:48 ·strength to·shake it, for it·had·been·founded upon
Lk 7:5 for he·loves our nation, and he·himself built the
Lk 7:6 "Lord, do·not be·harassed. For I·am not fit that you·
Lk 7:8 "For even I·myself am a·man·of·clay† being·assigned
Lk 7:28 "For I·say to·yeu, among those·born of·women
Lk 7:33 "For John the Immerser has·come neither eating
Lk 8:17 "For there·is not *anything* hidden, that shall·not
Lk 8:18 *well* yeu·listen·with·comprehension, for whoever
Lk 8:29 (For he·was·charging the impure spirit to·come·
Lk 8:29 ·forth from the man·of·clay†, for many times it·had·
Lk 8:40 the crowd fully·accepted him, for they·were all
Lk 8:46 "Someone laid·hold of·me, for I·myself did·know
Lk 9:14 For there·were about five·thousand men.
Lk 9:24 For whoever should·want to·save his soul's·desire
Lk 9:25 "For how·is a·man·of·clay† benefited, after·gaining
Lk 9:26 "For whoever would be·ashamed·of me and my
Lk 9:44 into yeur ears— "for the Son of·Clay·Man† is·about
Lk 9:48 ·one dispatching me, for the·one inherently·being
Lk 9:50 "Do·not forbid *him*, for whoever is not against us is
Lk 9:56 For the Son of·Clay·Man† did·not come to·
Lk 10:7 *provided* personally·by them, for the workman is
Lk 10:24 For I·say to·yeu, that many prophets and kings
Lk 11:4 forgive us our moral·failures, for we also forgive
Lk 11:10 "For everyone, the·one requesting receives, and
Lk 11:30 For just·as Jonah was a·sign to·the Ninevites, in·
Lk 12:12 "For the Holy Spirit shall·instruct yeu in the same
Lk 12:30 For all these·things, the nations of·the world seek·
Lk 12:34 "For where yeur treasure is, there also yeur heart
Lk 12:52 "For from now·on there·shall·be five in one house
Lk 12:58 For as you·head·on·out with your legal·adversary
Lk 14:14 to·recompense you. For you shall·be·recompensed
Lk 14:24 'For I·say to·yeu, that not·even·one of·those men,
Lk 14:28 "For which from·among yeu, wanting to·build a·
Lk 16:2 ·your estate·management, for you·shall·not be·able
Lk 16:13 to·be·a·slave to·two lords, for either he·shall·hate
Lk 16:28 for I·have five brothers; *send him* so·that he·may·
Lk 17:21 'Behold, there *it·is*!' For, behold, the kingdom of·
Lk 17:24 For just·as the lightning, the·one flashing from·out
Lk 18:16 and do·not forbid them, for of·such is the kingdom
Lk 18:23 exceedingly·grieved, for he·was tremendously
Lk 18:25 "For it·is easier *for* a·camel to·enter·in through a·
Lk 18:32 For he·shall·be·handed·over to·the Gentiles, and
Lk 19:5 making·haste, drop·down. For today, it·is·
Lk 19:10 For the Son of·Clay·Man† came to·seek and to·
Lk 19:21 For I·was·afraid·of you, because you·are an·
Lk 19:26 "(For I·say to·yeu, that to·any one having, *more*
Lk 19:48 how they·may·do *it*, for absolutely·all the people
Lk 20:6 us to·death, for they·are having·been·persuaded *for*
Lk 20:19 *their* hands on him, for they·knew that he·declared
Lk 20:33 wife of·them does·she·become? For the seven held
Lk 20:36 For neither are·they·able to·die any·longer, for
Lk 20:36 to·die any·longer, for they·are equal·to·the·angels,
Lk 20:38 ·men, but·rather of·living·men, for all live to·him.
Lk 21:4 For absolutely·all these·men cast from·out·of·their
Lk 21:8 *that* yeu·may·not be·deceived, for many shall·come
Lk 21:9 be·terrified, for it·is·mandatory·for these·things to·
Lk 21:15 For I·myself shall·give yeu a·mouth and wisdom,
Lk 21:23 in those Days! For there·shall·be great dire·need
Lk 21:26 which·are·coming·upon The Land, for the powers
Lk 21:35 "For as a·snare it·shall·come upon all the·ones
Lk 22:2 how they·may·eliminate him, for they·feared the
Lk 22:16 For I·say to·yeu that no, I·should·not eat any·
Lk 22:18 For I·say to·yeu: No, I·should·not·ever drink of·the
Lk 22:27 For who *is* greater, the·one reclining·at·the·meal,
Lk 22:37 "For I·say to·yeu, that still it·is·mandatory·for this
Lk 22:37 *the* lawless·ones," for even the·things concerning
Lk 22:59 ·man also was with him, for he·is also a·Galilean.
Lk 22:71 of·any·further testimony? For we·ourselves heard
Lk 23:8 ·AntiPas was·exceedingly·glad, for he·was wanting
Lk 23:12 with one·another, for they·were·previously being
Lk 23:15 ·did HerOd·AntiPas, for I·sent yeu·yeurselves up to
Lk 23:22 he·declared to·them, "For what crime did this·one
Lk 23:34 forgive them, for they·do·not personally·know
Lk 23:41 for we·receive·in·full appropriate·*punishment* for·

Ββ Γγ Δδ Εε Ζζ Ηη Θθ Ιι Κκ Λλ Μμ Νν Ξξ Οο Ππ Ρρ Σσ Ττ Υυ Φφ Χχ Ψψ Ωω

Γγ

Ac 1:20 “For it·has·been·written in a·scroll of·Psalms, “Let
Ac 2:15 For these·men are·not drunk as yeu assume, for it·is
Ac 2:15 are·not drunk as yeu assume, for it·is *but the* third
Ac 2:25 For David says this in·regard·to *his·Lord*, “ I·was·
Ac 2:34 “For David did·not ascend into the heavens, but he·
Ac 2:39 For the promise is for·yeu, and for·yeur children,
Ac 3:22 “For Moses in·fact declared to the fathers,
Ac 4:3 for the next·day, for even·now it·was evening.
Ac 4:12 in not·even·one other. For there·is not·even another
Ac 4:16 shall·we·do to·these men·of·clay†? For that in·fact
Ac 4:20 For we·ourselves are·not able not to·speak the·
Ac 4:22 For the man·of·clay† was more·than forty years·of·
Ac 4:27 “For in truth, they·were·gathered·together against
Ac 4:34 For neither was anyone subsisting among them in·a·
Ac 4:34 them in·a·bind, for as·many·as were·subsisting
Ac 5:26 *but* not with force, for they·feared the people, lest
Ac 5:36 For before these days, Theudas rose·up, saying
Ac 6:14 For we·have·heard him saying that this Jesus of·
Ac 7:33 the shoes from·your feet, for the place in which
Ac 7:40 shall·traverse·before us. *As* for this Moses who
Ac 8:7 For impure spirits, crying·out with·a·loud voice,
Ac 8:16 (For as·of·yet, he·was having·fallen upon not·even·
Ac 8:21 ·chance for·you in this matter, for your heart is not
Ac 8:23 For I·clearly·see you being in a·gall of·bitterness
Ac 8:31 And he·declared, “For how·is·it *that* I·might be·
Ac 8:39 see him any·longer, for he·traversed on·his way
Ac 9:11 a·man·of·Tarsus, Saul by·name. For, behold, he·
Ac 9:16 For I·myself shall·indicate to·him what·many·things
Ac 10:46 for they·were·hearing them speaking in·bestowed·
Ac 13:8 Elymas, the occultist (for so his name is·interpreted
Ac 13:27 For the·ones residing in JeruSalem, and their rulers,
Ac 13:36 “For in·fact David, after·tending to·the counsel of·
Ac 13:47 For in·this·manner it·has·been·commanded to·us
Ac 15:21 For Moses, from·out of·ancient generations, has in·
Ac 15:28 For it·seemed·good to·the Holy Spirit, and to·us,
Ac 16:3 in those places, for absolutely·all had·seen that his
Ac 16:28 not·one·bit·of harm, for we·are absolutely·all here
Ac 16:37 do·they·cast us out privately? For no *way*, but·
Ac 17:20 For you·carry certain strange·things to our ears.
Ac 17:23 For going·throughout and observing·again yeur
Ac 17:28 For in him, we·live and are·stirred and have·
Ac 17:28 ·own poets have·declared, ‘For we·are also *his*
Ac 18:3 them and was·working, for they·were tentmakers *by*
Ac 18:15 ·matter yeurselves, for I·myself am·definitely·not
Ac 18:18 ·shorn his head in Cenchrea, for he·had a·vow.
Ac 18:28 For vigorously, he·was·proving·downright to·the
Ac 19:24 For someone by·the·name·of Demetrius, a·
Ac 19:32 *some* another·thing, for the assembly·of·citizens
Ac 19:35 “Men, Ephesians, for what man·of·clay† is·there
Ac 19:37 For yeu·brought these men *here*, *who·are* neither
Ac 19:40 For we·are·in·danger also to·be·called·to·account
Ac 20:10 “Do·not be·in·a·commotion, for his soul is in him.
Ac 20:13 to·take Paul aboard, for in·this·manner he·was
Ac 20:16 for Paul decided to·sail·directly·by Ephesus, so·
Ac 20:16 to·linger·away in Asia. For he·was·hastening, if it·
Ac 20:27 For ¿!·did I·shrink·back *as* not to·report·in·detail
Ac 20:29 For I·myself personally·know this, that after my
Ac 21:3 and we·moored at Tyre, for the sailing·ship was
Ac 21:13 jointly·crushing my heart? For I·myself am in·a·
Ac 21:22 entirely to·come·together, for they·shall·hear that
Ac 21:29 (For they·were previously·having·clearly·seen
Ac 21:36 For the multitude of·the people were·following,
Ac 22:22 ·man from the earth, for it·is·not befitting for·him
Ac 22:26 what you·are·about to·do, for this man·of·clay† is
Ac 23:5 ·is *the* designated·high·priest, for it·has·been·written,
Ac 23:8 For in·fact, *the* Sadducees say *that* there·is not a·
Ac 23:11 ·courage, Paul. For as you·thoroughly·testified
Ac 23:17 regiment·commander, for he·has a·certain·thing
Ac 23:21 ·not be·persuaded by·them, for from·among them
Ac 24:5 “For after·finding this man *to·be* a·viral·pestilence,
Ac 25:11 For if in·fact, I·am·a·harmful·offender, or have·
Ac 25:27 For it·seems to·me unreasonable to·send a·
Ac 26:16 upon your feet, for I·was·made·visible to·you for

Ac 26:26 For the king is·fully·acquainted concerning these·
Ac 26:26 being·boldly·confident, for I·am·persuaded *for*
Ac 26:26 to·be·hidden from·him; for this·thing was not
Ac 27:22 to·cheer·up. “For there·shall·be not·even·one loss
Ac 27:23 For there·stood·by me this night an·angel of·God,
Ac 27:25 “Therefore, men, cheer·up! For I·trust God, that
Ac 27:34 ·each·take *some* nourishment, for this is·inherently
Ac 27:34 specific·for yeur salvation, for not·even·one hair
Ac 28:2 way·beyond·the·mark. For kindling a·fire, they·
Ac 28:20 to·speak·alongside *with·yeu*, for *it·is* because·of
Ac 28:22 you what·things you·contemplate, for in·fact, as·
Ac 28:27 For the heart of·this People became·thickly·
Heb 1:5 For to·which of·the angels did·he·declare at·any·
Heb 2:2 For if the word being·spoken through angels was
Heb 2:5 For *it·is* not to·angels *that* he·subjugated the
Heb 2:8 his feet.” For in making·subordinate to·him all
Heb 2:10 For it·was·befitting·for *Father God* (on·account·of
Heb 2:11 For both the·one making·holy and the·ones being·
Heb 2:16 For now·then,·as·is·well·known, he·grabs·hold—
Heb 2:18 For in that he·has·suffered, he·himself being·tried,
Heb 3:3 For this·man has·been·counted·worthy of·more
Heb 3:4 For every house is·planned·and·constructed by some
Heb 3:14 For we·have·become partaking·companions of·
Heb 3:16 For after·hearing, some did·directly·provoke, but·
Heb 4:2 For even we·are having·been·brought·the·good·
Heb 4:3 For the·ones trusting do·enter into the complete·rest
Heb 4:4 For somewhere he·has·declared concerning the
Heb 4:8 For if JoShua gave them complete·rest, he·would not
Heb 4:10 For the·one already·entering into his complete·rest,
Heb 4:12 For the Word† of·God *is* living and active, and *he*·
Heb 4:15 For we·do·not have a·high·priest who·is·not being·
Heb 5:1 For every high·priest being·taken from·among men·
Heb 5:12 For even after the time being·due *for·yeu* to·be
Heb 5:13 for anyone *still* participating·by·drinking milk *is*
Heb 5:13 ·Redemptive·word of·righteousness— for he·is *still*
Heb 6:4 For *it·is* impossible for·the·ones after once being·
Heb 6:7 For the soil, after·drinking the rain which·is·coming
Heb 6:10 For God *is* not unrighteous to·forget yeur work and
Heb 6:13 For God, after·promising to·AbRaham, since he·
Heb 6:16 For men·of·clay† in·fact swear by the·one greater·
Heb 7:1 For this MalkiTsedeq (King of·Salem, Priest of·God
Heb 7:10 for he·was yet in the loins of·*his*·father when
Heb 7:11 the Levitical sacred·priesthood, (for under it the
Heb 7:12 For with·the sacred·priesthood being·transferred,
Heb 7:13 For *this other priest*, concerning whom these·
Heb 7:14 For *it·is* obvious·beforehand that our Lord has·
Heb 7:17 For he·testifies, “You *are* a·priest·that·offers·a·
Heb 7:18 For there·is, in·fact, a·cancellation of·a·preceding
Heb 7:19 For the Torah-Law made not·even·one·thing
Heb 7:21 (For in·fact, the priests·that·offer·sacrifices were
Heb 7:26 For such a·High·Priest was·befitting·for us, *who·is*
Heb 7:27 of·the·ones of·the People, for he·did this upon·
Heb 7:28 For the Torah-Law fully·establishes men·of·clay†
Heb 8:3 For every high·priest is·fully·established to·offer
Heb 8:4 For if, in·fact, he·were on earth, he·would not·even
Heb 8:5 the Tabernacle: “For clearly·see·to·it,” he·replies,
Heb 8:7 For if that first *covenant* was faultless, then no place
Heb 8:8 For finding·fault with·them, he·says, “Behold,
Heb 9:2 For a·Tabernacle was·planned·and·constructed; the
Heb 9:13 For if the blood of·bulls and of·adult·male·goats
Heb 9:16 For where *there·is* a·last·will·and·covenant, *it·is* a·
Heb 9:17 For a·last·will·and·covenant *is* of·force after men·
Heb 9:19 For with·every commandment in *the* Torah-Law
Heb 9:24 For the Anointed-One did·not enter into holy·
Heb 10:1 For the Torah-Law, having a·shadow of·the
Heb 10:4 For *it·is* impossible *for·the* blood of·bulls and of·
Heb 10:14 For by·one offering, he·has·made·fully·complete
Heb 10:23 Expectation without·slouching (for trustworthy *is*
Heb 10:26 For *if* we·ourselves go·on·morally·failing
Heb 10:30 For we·personally·know the·one declaring,
Heb 10:34 For even yeu·sympathized with·my bonds, and
Heb 10:36 For yeu·have need of·patient·endurance in·order·
Heb 10:37 “For yet, as·long·as a·little·while, the·one who·

Heb 11:2 For in this, the elders·of·old are·attested·to.
Heb 11:5 ·that God transferred him;” for before his transfer,
Heb 11:6 ·fully·satisfy *him*. For it·is·mandatory·for the·one
Heb 11:10 for he·was·waiting·for the CITY having the
Heb 11:14 For the·ones saying such·things make·it·clear that
Heb 11:16 ·called their God, for he·made·ready a·CITY for·
Heb 11:26 treasures in Egypt, for he·was·intently·looking to
Heb 11:27 rage of·the king) for he·mightily·endured as one·
Heb 11:32 what more should·I·say? For the time shall·be·
Heb 12:3 For take·account·again·of the·one having·
Heb 12:6 For whom Yahweh loves, he·correctively·
Heb 12:7 yeu as *his·own* sons, for what son is·he whom a·
Heb 12:10 For in·fact, they, just·for few days, were·
Heb 12:17 (For yeu·must·have·distinctly·known that even
Heb 12:17 he·was·rejected·as·unfit, for he·found no place
Heb 12:18 For yeu·have·not come·alongside a·mountain
Heb 12:20 (For they·were·not bearing·with·and·upholding
Heb 12:25 shun the·one speaking. For if those·men did·not
Heb 12:29 for even our God *is* a·fully·consuming fire.
Heb 13:2 forget the hospitality·to·strangers, for through this
Heb 13:5 ·things being·at·hand, for he·himself has·declared,
Heb 13:9 and strange·new instructions. For *it·is* good *for* the
Heb 13:11 For the bodies of·these animals, whose blood is·
Heb 13:14 For here we·have no continuing city, but·rather
Heb 13:16 common·welfare·fund, for with·such sacrifices
Heb 13:17 yield·yeurselves— for they·themselves stay·alert
Heb 13:17 and not sighing·heavily, for that *is* not·a·better·
Heb 13:18 Pray concerning us, for we·have·confidence that
Heb 13:22 of·exhortation, for through concise·passages, I·
Gal 1:10 For at·this·moment, do·I·comply·with men·of·
Gal 1:10 Or do·I·seek to·appease men·of·clay†? For if yet I·
Gal 1:12 For I·myself neither personally·received it from a·
Gal 1:13 For yeu·heard of·my former manner·of·life in
Gal 2:6 of·a·man·of·clay†, for the·ones seeming *to·be*
Gal 2:8 (for the·one operating in·Peter unto a·commission
Gal 2:12 For prior·to certain·men coming from Jacob, he·
Gal 2:18 “For if I·build again these·things which I·
Gal 2:19 For I·myself through Torah-Law, am·dead to·
Gal 2:21 set·aside the grace of·God, for if righteousness *is*
Gal 3:10 For as·many·as are birthed·from·out of·works of·
Gal 3:10 they·are under a·curse— for it·has·been·written, “
Gal 3:13 a·curse on·our behalf— for it·has·been·written, “
Gal 3:18 For if the inheritance *is* as·a·result of·Torah-Law,
Gal 3:21 of·God? May·it·never happen! For if the law
Gal 3:26 For yeu·are all the·Sons of·God through the trust in
Gal 3:27 For as·many·of·yeu·as are immersed into *the*
Gal 3:28 ·is·not therein male and female, for yeu are all one
Gal 4:15 ·blessedness yeu *spoke·of*? For I·testify to·yeu that,
Gal 4:22 For it·has·been·written, that AbRaham had two sons
Gal 4:24 Which·things are being·an·allegory, for these are
Gal 4:25 For *this* Hagar is Mount Sinai in Arabia, and
Gal 4:27 For it·has·been·written, “ Be·merry, O·barren·
Gal 4:30 ·out the maidservant and her son, for the son of·the
Gal 5:5 For we·ourselves, by·*the*·Spirit, fully·await an·
Gal 5:6 For in YeShua Anointed, neither circumcision nor
Gal 5:13 For, brothers, yeu·yeurselves are·called·forth to
Gal 5:14 For all the·Torah-Law is·completely·fulfilled in one
Gal 5:17 For the flesh longs against the Spirit, and the Spirit
Gal 6:3 For if any·man supposes·himself to·be something,
Gal 6:5 For each·man shall·bear his·own load.
Gal 6:7 God is·not ridiculed, for whatever a·man·of·clay†
Gal 6:9 *in* doing the good; for in·due season we·shall·reap,
Gal 6:13 For neither·even·do they·themselves, being·
Gal 6:15 For in Anointed-One YeShua, neither circumcision
Gal 6:17 wearisome·troubles to·me, for I·myself bear in my
Mt 1:18 Anointed was in·this·manner. For with·his mother
Mt 1:20 *for* your wife, for the·one already·being·conceived
Mt 1:21 ·*Yahweh·Saves*), for he·himself shall·save his
Mt 2:2 ·and·born King of·the Jews? For we·saw his star in
Mt 2:5 of·Judea. For in·this·manner it·has·been·written
Mt 2:6 the official·leaders of·Judah. For from·out of·you
Mt 2:13 ·declare *it* to·you, for HerOd·the·Great intends to·
Mt 2:20 into *the* land of·IsraEl, for the·ones seeking the

Mt 3:2 saying, "Yeu·must·repent, for the kingdom of·the
Mt 3:3 For this is·he, the·one being·uttered *of* by Isaiah the
Mt 3:9 AbRaham *for·our* father.' For I·say to·yeu that God
Mt 3:15 "Allow *me* at·this·moment, for in·this·manner it·is
Mt 4:6 ·God, cast yourself down. For it·has·been·written,
Mt 4:10 ·out, Adversary-Accuser! For it·has·been·written,
Mt 4:17 to·say, "Repent, for the kingdom of·the heavens
Mt 4:18 a·cast·net into the sea, for they·were fishermen.
Mt 5:12 in the heavens. For in·this·manner they·persecuted
Mt 5:18 "For certainly I·say to·yeu, until the heaven and the
Mt 5:20 "For I·say to·yeu, that unless yeur righteousness
Mt 5:29 cast *it* from you, for it·is·advantageous for·you that
Mt 5:30 cast *it* from you, for it·is·advantageous for·you that
Mt 5:46 "For if yeu·should·love the·ones loving yeu, what
Mt 6:7 the Gentiles *do*, for they·presume that they·shall·be·
Mt 6:8 yeu·should·not be·like them, for yeur Father has·
Mt 6:14 "For if yeu·should·forgive the men·of·clay† their
Mt 6:16 the stage·acting·hypocrites, for they·disfigure their
Mt 6:21 For where yeur treasure is, there also yeur heart
Mt 6:24 to·be·a·slave to·two lords. For either he·shall·hate
Mt 6:32 (For all these·things the Gentiles seek·after) for yeur
Mt 6:32 the Gentiles seek·after) for yeur heavenly Father
Mt 6:34 for tomorrow, for tomorrow shall·be·anxious·about
Mt 7:2 For by whatever standard·of·judgment yeu·unduly·
Mt 7:8 For any one requesting receives; and the·one seeking
Mt 7:12 do even in·this·manner to·them, for this is the
Mt 7:25 yet it·did·not fall, for it·had·been·founded upon the
Mt 7:29 for he·was instructing them as *one* having authority,
Mt 8:9 For even I·myself am a·man·of·clay† under authority,
Mt 9:5 For which is easier?
Mt 9:13 and not sacrifice." For I·did·not come to·call
Mt 9:16 onto an·old garment, for *when·shrunk*, it·takes·
Mt 9:21 for she·was·saying within herself, "If merely I·
Mt 9:24 to·them, "Depart! For the young·girl did·not die,
Mt 10:10 ·even shoes, nor·even a·staff, for the workman is
Mt 10:17 of the men·of·clay†, for they·shall·hand yeu over
Mt 10:19 yeu·should·speak, for it·shall·be·given to·yeu in
Mt 10:20 For yeu·yeurselves are not the·ones speaking, but·
Mt 10:23 flee into the other, for certainly I·say to·yeu, no,
Mt 10:26 do·not fear them. For there·is not·even·one·thing
Mt 10:35 For I·came to·split "a·man·of·clay† against his
Mt 11:10 For this is·he, concerning whom it·has·been·
Mt 11:13 For all the prophets and the Torah-Law prophesied
Mt 11:18 For John came neither eating nor drinking, and
Mt 11:30 For my yoke *is* kind, and my load is lightweight.
Mt 12:8 For the Son of·Clay·Man† is Lord even of·the
Mt 12:33 rotten, and its fruit rotten. For out of·the fruit, the
Mt 12:34 beneficially·good·things? For from·out of·the
Mt 12:37 For from·out of·your words, you·shall·be·
Mt 12:40 For just·as Jonah was three days and three nights in
Mt 12:50 For whoever should·do the will of·my Father, the·
Mt 13:12 For whoever maturely·utilizes·what·he·has, to·him
Mt 13:15 For the heart of·this People became·thickly·
Mt 13:17 For certainly I·say to·yeu, that many prophets and
Mt 14:3 For HerOd·AntiPas, after·taking·secure·hold·of John,
Mt 14:4 For John was·saying to·him, "It·is·not proper for·
Mt 14:24 under the breaking·waves, for the wind was
Mt 15:2 Oral·tradition of·the elders? For they·do·not wash
Mt 15:4 For God commanded, saying, "Deeply·honor your
Mt 15:19 For from·out of·the heart comes·forth evil
Mt 15:27 "Yes *it·is*, Lord. For even the puppies eat from the
Mt 16:2 '*It·shall·be* fine·weather, for the sky is·fiery·red.
Mt 16:3 *There·shall·be* stormy·weather today, for the sky is·
Mt 16:25 For whoever should·want to·save his soul's·desire
Mt 16:26 "For what·is a·man·of·clay† being·benefited, if he·
Mt 16:27 "For the Son of·Clay·Man† is·about to·come in the
Mt 17:15 badly, for he·has·already·fallen many·times into
Mt 17:20 ·account·of yeur lack·of·trust. For certainly I·say
Mt 18:7 due·to its scandalous·traps, for it·is a·necessity *for*
Mt 18:10 one of·these little·ones, for I·say to·yeu that
Mt 18:11 For the Son of·Clay·Man† came to·save the·one
Mt 18:20 "For where two or three are having·been·gathered·
Mt 19:12 For there·are eunuchs, some·who were·born in·
Mt 19:14 them to·come to me, for of·such is the kingdom
Mt 19:22 went·away being·grieved, for he·was holding
Mt 20:1 "For the kingdom of the heavens is like a·man·of·
Mt 20:16 and the first last; for many are called·forth, but
Mt 21:26 ·clay†,' we·fear the crowd, for all hold John as a·
Mt 21:32 For John came to yeu by way of·righteousness, yet
Mt 22:14 "For many are called·forth, but few *are* Selected.
Mt 22:16 concerning not·even·one *man*, for you·do·not look
Mt 22:28 shall·she·be of·the seven? For they·all held her.
Mt 22:30 "For in the resurrection, neither do·they·marry nor
Mt 23:3 do according·to their works. For they·say *it*, and·yet
Mt 23:4 "For they·captively·bind weighty and oppressive
Mt 23:8 'Rabbi,' for one is yeur Preeminent·Leader, *that·is*
Mt 23:9 yeur father upon the earth, for one is yeur Father,
Mt 23:10 ·yeu·be·called preeminent·leaders, for one is yeur
Mt 23:14 before men·of·clay†! For yeu·yeurselves do·not
Mt 23:17 O·fools and blind·men! For which is greater, the
Mt 23:19 O·fools and blind·men! For which *is* greater, the
Mt 23:39 For I·say to·yeu, no, yeu·should·not see me from
Mt 24:5 For many shall·come in my name, saying, 'I AM
Mt 24:6 ·not woefully·disturbed, for it·is·mandatory·for all
Mt 24:7 "For nation shall·be·awakened against nation, and
Mt 24:21 "For then there·shall·be a·Great Tribulation, such·
Mt 24:24 For false·Anointed-Ones shall·be·awakened, and
Mt 24:27 For just·as the lightning comes·forth from *the* east
Mt 24:28 "For wherever the corpse should·be, there the
Mt 24:38 For just·as in the days, the·ones that·were before
Mt 25:14 "For *the kingdom of·the heavens is* just·as a·man·
Mt 25:29 "(For to·everyone maturely·utilizing·what·he·has,
Mt 25:35 For I·was·hungry, and yeu·gave me to·eat.
Mt 25:42 For I·was·hungry, and yeu·did·not give me
Mt 26:9 For this ointment was·able to·be·sold·off for·much,
Mt 26:10 ·troubles to·the woman? For she·worked a·good
Mt 26:11 For yeu always have the helplessly·poor among
Mt 26:12 For she·herself, casting this ointment on my body,
Mt 26:28 for this is my blood, the·one of·the brand-new
Mt 26:31 ·fall·away on this night. For it·has·been·written,
Mt 26:43 he·finds them sleeping again, for their eyes were
Mt 26:52 into its place, for all the·ones taking·hold·of a·
Mt 26:73 are also from·among them, for even your speech
Mt 27:18 For he·had·personally·known that on·account·of
Mt 27:19 that righteous·man, for I·suffered many·things
Mt 27:23 governor was·replying, "For what crime did·he·
Mt 27:43 now, if he·wants him, for he·declared, 'I·am a·
Mt 28:2 ·occurred a·great earthquake. For Yahweh's angel,
Mt 28:5 ·yeurselves do·not be·afraid, for I·have·seen that
Mt 28:6 He·is not here, for he·is·awakened, just·as he·
Mk 1:16 a·cast·net into the sea, for they·were fishermen.
Mk 1:22 at his instruction, for he·was instructing them as
Mk 1:38 ·officially·proclaim there·also. For to this·purpose
Mk 2:15 with·Jesus and his disciples. For there·were many,
Mk 3:10 For he·both·relieved·and·cured many, such·for as·
Mk 3:21 to·take·secure·hold·of him, for they·were·saying,
Mk 3:35 For whoever should·do the will of·God, this·one is
Mk 4:22 For there·is not anything hidden, which should·not
Mk 4:25 "For whoever should·maturely·utilize·what·he·has,
Mk 4:28 For the earth automatically bears·fruit; first a·blade,
Mk 5:8 (For *Jesus* was·saying to·him, "Impure spirit, come·
Mk 5:28 For she·was·saying, "Because if·even I·should·lay·
Mk 5:42 rose·up and was·walking, for she·was of·twelve
Mk 6:14 King HerOd·AntiPas heard *of·him*, for his name was
Mk 6:17 For HerOd·AntiPas himself, after·dispatching, took·
Mk 6:18 For John was·saying to·HerOd·AntiPas, "It·is·not
Mk 6:20 for HerOd·AntiPas was·afraid·of John, having·seen
Mk 6:31 rest a·little·while!" For there·were many coming
Mk 6:36 ·buy bread for·themselves, for they·do·not have
Mk 6:48 being·tormented in their rowing, for the wind was
Mk 6:50 For they·all saw him and were·troubled.
Mk 6:52 for they·did·not comprehend concerning the loaves·
Mk 6:52 concerning the loaves·of·bread, for their heart was
Mk 7:3 For the Pharisees and all the Judeans, unless they·
Mk 7:8 For after·leaving the commandment of·God, yeu·
Mk 7:10 For Moses declared, "Deeply·honor your father
Mk 7:21 For from·inside, from·out of·the heart of·the men·
Mk 7:25 For after·hearing about him, a·woman whose
Mk 7:27 the children to·be·stuffed·full. For it·is not good to·
Mk 7:28 "Yes *it·is*, Lord. For even the puppies beneath the
Mk 8:3 ·be·faint on the way, for some of·them have·come
Mk 8:35 For whoever should·want to·save his soul's·desire
Mk 8:36 "For how shall·it·benefit a·man·of·clay†, if he·
Mk 8:38 "For whoever would be·ashamed·of me and of·my
Mk 9:6 For he·had·not personally·known what he·should·
Mk 9:6 ·speak, for they·were frightened·out·of·their·wits.
Mk 9:31 For he·was·instructing his disciples, and he·was·
Mk 9:34 But they·were·keeping·silent, for along the way
Mk 9:39 "Do·not forbid him, for there·is not·even·one who
Mk 9:40 For whoever is not against yeu is on·behalf of·yeu.
Mk 9:41 For whoever should·give yeu a·cup of·water to·
Mk 9:49 "For everyone shall·be·salted with·fire, and every
Mk 10:14 to me, and do·not forbid them, for of·such is the
Mk 10:22 he·went·away being·grieved, for he·was holding
Mk 10:27 but·yet not with God, for with God all·things are
Mk 10:45 For even the Son of·Clay·Man† did·not come to·
Mk 11:13 nothing·at·all except leaves, for it·was not *the*
Mk 11:18 ·destroy him, for they·were·afraid·of him,
Mk 11:23 For certainly I·say to·yeu that whoever should·
Mk 11:32 the people, for absolutely·all·men were·holding
Mk 12:12 yet they·feared the crowd, for they·knew that he·
Mk 12:14 not·even·one·man, for you·do·not look to *the*
Mk 12:23 wife shall·she·be of·them? For the seven held her
Mk 12:25 "For whenever they·should·rise·up from·among
Mk 12:36 For David himself declared by the Holy Spirit,
Mk 12:44 For they all cast·in from·out of·their abundance,
Mk 13:6 For many shall·come in my name, saying, 'I
Mk 13:7 ·disturbed, for it·is·mandatory·for *such·things* to·
Mk 13:8 "For nation shall·be·awakened against nation, and
Mk 13:9 look·out·for yeurselves, for they·shall·hand yeu
Mk 13:11 that hour, that speak, for it·is not yeu·yeurselves
Mk 13:19 "For those Days shall·be a·Tribulation, such as
Mk 13:22 For false·Anointed-Ones and false·prophets shall·
Mk 13:33 ·alert and pray, for yeu·do·not personally·know
Mk 13:35 keep·alert— for yeu·do·not personally·know
Mk 14:5 For that·thing was·able to·be·sold·off for·upwards·
Mk 14:7 For yeu always have the helplessly·poor among
Mk 14:40 he·found them sleeping again for their eyes were
Mk 14:56 For many were·falsely·testifying against him, and·
Mk 14:70 you·are from·among them, for also you·are a·
Mk 15:10 For he·was·knowing that the chief·priests had·
Mk 15:14 was·saying to·them, "For what crime did·he·
Mk 16:4 had·been·rolled·away, for it·was tremendously
Mk 16:8 ·declare not·even·one·thing, for they·were·afraid)].
Rm 1:9 For God is my witness, to·whom I·ritually·minister
Rm 1:11 For I·greatly·yearn to·see yeu that I·may·kindly·
Rm 1:16 For I·am·not ashamed·of the good·news of·the
Rm 1:16 the good·news of·the Anointed-One, for it·is God's
Rm 1:17 For in this, God's righteousness is·revealed, birthed·
Rm 1:18 For God's wrath is·revealed from heaven against all
Rm 1:19 ·is apparent among them, for God made·*it*·apparent
Rm 1:20 For from *the* world's creation, the invisible·things
Rm 1:26 to dishonorable burning·passions, for even their
Rm 2:1 O man·of·clay†! For in that·which you·judge the
Rm 2:1 other, you·condemn yourself; for the·one judging,
Rm 2:11 For there·is no partiality with God.
Rm 2:12 For as·many·as did·morally·fail without·
Rm 2:13 For *it·is* not the hearers of·the Torah-Law *that·are*
Rm 2:14 (For inasmuch·as Gentiles, the·ones not having
Rm 2:24 For "the name of·God is·reviled among the
Rm 2:25 For in·fact, circumcision benefits if you·should·
Rm 2:28 For *it·is* not the·one with an·outward·appearance *of·*
Rm 3:2 in·each and·every manner. For in·fact, first·of·all,
Rm 3:7 *But the reasoning states*, "For if by my lie, the truth
Rm 3:9 by·no·means, for we·already·legally·charged both
Rm 3:20 in·the·sight of·him,' for through Torah-Law *is the*
Rm 3:22 all the·ones trusting, for there·is no distinction.
Rm 3:23 For all morally·failed and are·destitute of·the glory
Rm 4:2 For if AbRaham was·regarded·as·righteous as·a·

Γγ

Rm 4:3 For what·does the Scripture say?
Rm 4:9 or upon the Uncircumcision also? For we·say that '
Rm 4:13 For the promise *is* not through Torah-Law to·
Rm 4:14 For if the·ones birthed·from·out·of·Torah-Law *are*
Rm 4:15 For the Torah-Law accomplishes wrath (for where
Rm 4:15 Torah-Law accomplishes wrath (for where there·is
Rm 5:6 For yet, according·to due·season, Anointed-One died
Rm 5:7 For scarcely over a·righteous·man shall anyone die,
Rm 5:7 ·man shall anyone die, for perhaps over the
Rm 5:10 For if, while·being enemies, we·are·reconciled to·
Rm 5:13 For even·until *the* Torah-Law, moral·failure was in
Rm 5:15 not as the trespass). For if by·the trespass of·the
Rm 5:16 as through one already·morally·failing. For in·fact,
Rm 5:17 For if by·the one trespass, Death reigned through
Rm 5:19 For just·as through the inattentive·disregard of·one
Rm 6:5 For if we·have·been congenitally·fused·together in·
Rm 6:7 For the·one being·dead has·been·regarded·as·
Rm 6:10 For in·that·which he·died, he·died to·the Moral·
Rm 6:14 For moral·failure shall·not lord·over yeu, for yeu·
Rm 6:14 shall·not lord·over yeu, for yeu·are not under
Rm 6:19 of·yeur flesh. For just·as yeu·presented yeur
Rm 6:20 For when yeu·were slaves of·Moral·Failure, yeu·
Rm 6:21 ·of·which now yeu·are·ashamed? For the end of·
Rm 6:23 For the wages of·Moral·Failure *is* death, but the
Rm 7:1 ·know, O·brothers (for I·speak to·the·ones·knowing
Rm 7:2 For the wife *yoked·together* under·a·husband has·
Rm 7:5 For when we·were in the flesh, the intense·cravings
Rm 7:7 except through Torah-Law, for also I·had·not
Rm 7:8 all·manner·of longing. For apart·from Torah-Law,
Rm 7:11 For Moral·Failure, taking impromptu·occasion
Rm 7:14 For we·personally·know that the Torah-Law is
Rm 7:15 For I·do·not know *why* I·perform that·which *I·do*.
Rm 7:15 that·which *I·do*. For I·do·not practice that·thing
Rm 7:18 For I·personally·know that in me (that·is, in my
Rm 7:18 no beneficially·good·thing; for to·want *to·do the*
Rm 7:19 For *it·is* not *the* beneficially·good·thing which I·
Rm 7:22 For I·also·take·pleasure in·the Torah-Law of·God
Rm 8:2 For the Law-of-Liberty of·the Spirit of·the life-above
Rm 8:3 For the·thing *which·is* impossible of·the Torah-Law,
Rm 8:5 For the·ones being·according·to flesh contemplate
Rm 8:6 For the disposition of·the flesh *is* death, but the
Rm 8:7 *is* hostility toward God, for it·is·not subject to·the
Rm 8:7 to·the Law-of-Liberty of·God, for neither is·it·able
Rm 8:13 For if yeu·live according·to flesh, yeu·are·about to·
Rm 8:14 For as·many·as are·led by·God's Spirit, these are
Rm 8:15 For yeu·did·not receive a·spirit of·slavery again to
Rm 8:18 For I·reckon that the afflictions of·the present
Rm 8:19 For the eager·anticipation of·the creation fully·
Rm 8:20 For the creation was·made·subject to·the futility,
Rm 8:22 For we·personally·know that the entire creation
Rm 8:24 For in·the Expectation, we·are·saved, but an·
Rm 8:24 is not an·expectation, for what man expectantly·
Rm 8:26 in·our weaknesses, for we·do·not personally·know
Rm 8:38 For I·have·been·convinced that neither death, nor
Rm 9:3 For I·myself would·well-wish myself to·be
Rm 9:6 Holy-word of·God has·fallen·short. For not all the·
Rm 9:9 For this *is* the word of·promise, "'According·to this
Rm 9:11 (for *with·the twins* not·yet being·born nor·even
Rm 9:15 For he·says to·Moses, '" I·shall·show·gracious·
Rm 9:17 For the Scripture says to·Pharaoh, "For this same·
Rm 9:19 still does·he·find·fault? For who has·withstood his
Rm 9:28 For *Yahweh is* entirely·completing *the* matter and
Rm 9:32 of·works of·Torah-Law. For they·stumbled at·the
Rm 10:2 For I·testify for·them that they·have a·zeal of·God,
Rm 10:3 For being·ignorant of·God's righteousness, and
Rm 10:4 For Anointed-One *is the* end of·Torah-Law for
Rm 10:5 For Moses describes the righteousness, the·one
Rm 10:10 For with·*the*·heart, one·is·convinced unto
Rm 10:11 For the Scripture says, '" Everyone trusting on
Rm 10:12 For there·is no distinction between Jew and Greek
Rm 10:12 between Jew and Greek— for this same *Lord*
Rm 10:13 For "'all who would call·upon the name of·*the*·
Rm 10:16 ·to·and·obeyed the good·news. For IsaIah says,

Rm 11:1 May·it·never happen! For I·myself also am an·
Rm 11:13 For I·say *this* to·yeu, the Gentiles, in as·much·as
Rm 11:15 For if the casting·away of·them *is* reconciliation
Rm 11:21 For if God did·not spare the fully natural branches,
Rm 11:23 lack·of·trust, they·shall·be·grafted·in, for God is
Rm 11:24 For if you are·already·chopped·off from·among
Rm 11:25 For I·do·not want for·yeu, brothers, to·be·ignorant
Rm 11:29 For the gracious·bestowments and the calling of·
Rm 11:30 For just·as yeu·yeurselves also once were·
Rm 11:32 For God jointly·confined all the *peoples* to an·
Rm 11:34 '" For who knew Yahweh's mind?
Rm 12:3 For through the grace being·given to·me, I·say to·
Rm 12:4 For exactly·as we·have many members in one body
Rm 12:19 to·the wrath *of·God*, for it·has·been·written,
Rm 12:20 ·should·thirst, give him drink; for *by* doing this,
Rm 13:1 to·the·superior authorities. For there·is no authority
Rm 13:3 For the rulers are not *a·cause·of* fear for·the
Rm 13:4 For he·is an·attendant of·God to·you in the
Rm 13:4 bad·thing, be·afraid. For *it·is* not without·reason
Rm 13:4 he·bears the sword, for he·is an·attendant of·God,
Rm 13:6 For on·account·of that, yeu·fully·pay tributes also.
Rm 13:6 yeu·fully·pay tributes also. For they·are God's
Rm 13:8 except to·love one·another, for the·one loving the
Rm 13:9 For, "'You·shall·not commit·adultery.
Rm 13:11 to·be·awakened out·of·heavy·sleep, for now our
Rm 14:3 judge the·one eating, for God purposely·received
Rm 14:4 And, he·shall·be·established, for God is able to·
Rm 14:6 eats unto·*the*·Lord, for to·God he·gives·thanks;
Rm 14:7 For not·even·one·of·us lives to·himself, and not·
Rm 14:8 For both, whether we·should·live, we·live to·the
Rm 14:9 For to this *determined·purpose* Anointed-One also
Rm 14:10 your brother? For we·shall all stand·directly·at
Rm 14:11 For it·has·been·written, "'*As·surely·as* I·myself
Rm 14:17 For the kingdom of·God is not *about* feeding and
Rm 14:18 For the·one being·enslaved in these·things to·the
Rm 15:2 For each·one of·us must·willingly·adapt to·his
Rm 15:3 For even the Anointed-One did·not accommodate
Rm 15:4 For as·many·things·as were·previously·written,
Rm 15:18 For I·shall·not venture to·speak of·any of·such·
Rm 15:24 I·shall·come to yeu, for I·expect to·survey yeu
Rm 15:26 For Macedonia and Achaia delighted to·make a·
Rm 15:27 For they·do·take·delight, and they·are under·an·
Rm 15:27 they·are under·an·obligation for·them. For if the
Rm 16:2 ·may·have·need of·yeu, for she·herself did·become
Rm 16:18 (For such·as·these are·not slaves to·our Lord Jesus
Rm 16:19 For yeur attentive·obedience is·already·broadcast
Jac 1:6 *for* not·even·one·thing. For the·one hesitating has·
Jac 1:7 For that man·of·clay† must·not imagine that he·shall·
Jac 1:11 For the sun rose·above·the·horizon together with·
Jac 1:13 "I·am·tempted by God," for God is not·tempted
Jac 1:20 For man's wrath does·not accomplish God's
Jac 1:24 For he·fully·observed himself and has·gone·away,
Jac 2:2 For if there·should·enter into yeur gathering a·man
Jac 2:10 For whoever shall·observantly·keep the whole
Jac 2:11 For the·one declaring, "'You·may·not commit·
Jac 2:13 For the tribunal·justice without·forgiving·favor *is*
Jac 2:26 For just·as the body apart·from spirit is dead, in·
Jac 3:2 For in·many·things, absolutely·all *of·us* slip·up.
Jac 3:7 For every species of·wild·beasts, also of·birds, and
Jac 3:16 For where jealousy and contention *is*, there *is*
Jac 4:14 *shall·happen* tomorrow! For what·kind·of *essence*
Jac 4:14 ·of *essence is* yeur life†? For it·is a·vapor, one·
Jud 1:4 For some men·of·clay† crept·into·place·unawares,
Php 1:8 For God is my witness, how I·greatly·yearn·after
Php 1:18 For *then* what·does *it·matter*?
Php 1:19 For I·have·seen that this shall·result in salvation
Php 1:21 For me to·live *is* Anointed-One, and to·die *is* gain.
Php 1:23 For I·am·clenched as·a·result of·the two *choices*,
Php 2:5 For contemplate *and set·aim·for* this·thing among
Php 2:13 For it·is God *who·is* the·one operating in yeu both
Php 2:20 For I·have not·even·one·man of·such·kindred·soul,
Php 2:21 For all the·men seek their·own, not the·things·of
Php 2:27 For even he·was·sick almost to·death, but·yet God

Php 3:3 For we·ourselves are the Circumcision, the·ones
Php 3:18 (For many stroll·about, of·whom I·was·saying to·
Php 3:20 For our communal·citizenship inherently·is in *the*
Php 4:11 ·to *a·particular* lacking; for I·myself learned, *that*
1Pe 2:19 For this *is* graciousness, if someone on·account·of
1Pe 2:20 For what·kind·of merit *is·it*, if when yeu·are·being·
1Pe 2:21 For toward this yeu·were·called·forth, because
1Pe 2:25 For yeu·were as sheep being·led·astray, but·yet are
1Pe 3:5 For in·this·manner in·times·past, the holy wives also
1Pe 3:10 For "'the·one wanting to·love life-above and to·see
1Pe 3:17 For *it·is* significantly·better, if the will of·God is·
1Pe 4:3 For the time of·*our*·natural·life already·having·
1Pe 4:6 For to this *end·purpose* was·the·good·news·already·
1Pe 4:15 For do·not·let any of·yeu suffer as a·murderer, or
2Pe 1:8 For *with* these·things subsisting in·yeu and
2Pe 1:9 For in·whom these *qualities* are·not present, he·is
2Pe 1:10 and Selection firm. For in·doing these·things, no,
2Pe 1:11 For in·this·manner, the accessible·entrance shall·
2Pe 1:16 For *it·was* not·by following·out myths having·been·
2Pe 1:17 For he·received personally·from Father God honor
2Pe 1:21 For not by·the·will of·a·man·of·clay† *was*
2Pe 2:4 For if God— did·not spare morally·failing angels,
2Pe 2:8 (for in·looking·upon and in·hearing *these deeds*, the
2Pe 2:18 For when·they·are·enunciating outrageous·things
2Pe 2:19 of·the corruption— for that·by·which someone
2Pe 2:20 For if after·escaping·from the contaminations of·
2Pe 2:21 For it·was significantly·better for·them not to·have·
2Pe 3:4 the promise of·his returning·Presence? For since the
2Pe 3:5 For this is·oblivious·to them (willingly) that by·the
1Th 1:8 For from yeu, the Redemptive-word of·the Lord has·
1Th 1:9 For they·themselves report concerning us, what·
1Th 2:1 For yeu·yeurselves personally·know, brothers, that
1Th 2:3 For our exhortation *was* not birthed·from·out·of·
1Th 2:5 For not·even at·any·time did·we·come with a·word
1Th 2:9 For yeu·remember, brothers, our wearisome·labor
1Th 2:9 ·labor and the travail, for working night and day
1Th 2:14 For yeu, brothers, did·become attentive·imitators
1Th 2:19 For what *is* our expectation, or joy, or victor's·
1Th 2:20 For yeu are our glory and joy.
1Th 3:3 tribulations. For yeu·yeurselves personally·know
1Th 3:4 For even when we·were alongside yeu, we·were·
1Th 3:9 For what thanks are·we·able to·recompense to·God
1Th 4:2 For yeu·personally·know what charges we·gave yeu
1Th 4:3 For this is God's will, yeur renewed·holiness: for·
1Th 4:7 For God did·not call us forth toward impurity, but·
1Th 4:9 need *for·me* to·write to·yeu, for yeu yeurselves are
1Th 4:10 For even yeu·do this toward all the brothers, the·
1Th 4:14 For if we·trust that YeShua died and rose·up, in·
1Th 4:15 For this we·say to·yeu by *the* Lord's word, that we·
1Th 5:2 For yeu·yeurselves personally·know accurately that
1Th 5:3 For whenever they·should·say, "Peace and security,
1Th 5:7 For the·ones falling·asleep, sleep at·night, and the·
1Th 5:18 In everything give·thanks, for this *is* the·will of·
2Th 2:7 For the mystery of·the Lawlessness operates even·
2Th 3:2 absurd and evil men·of·clay†, for not all·men *have*
2Th 3:7 For yeu·yeurselves have·seen how it·is·necessary to·
2Th 3:10 For even when we·were alongside yeu, this we·
2Th 3:11 For we·hear *that there·are* some walking among
Tit 1:7 (for it·is·mandatory·for the overseer to·be without·
Tit 1:10 For there·are many insubordinate and idle·talkers
Tit 2:11 For the grace of·God, the Custodial·Salvation,
Tit 3:3 For we·ourselves also were once stupid, obstinate,
Tit 3:9 and quarrels of·Torah-Law, for they·are unprofitable
Tit 3:12 me to NicoPolis, for I·have·decided to·winter there.
1Co 1:11 For it·was·made·plain to·me concerning yeu, my
1Co 1:17 For Anointed-One did·not dispatch me to·immerse,
1Co 1:18 For the reasoning (the·one of·the cross) is
1Co 1:19 For it·has·been·written, "'I·shall·completely·
1Co 1:21 For whereas (by the wisdom of·God) the world
1Co 1:26 For look·at yeur calling·forth, brothers: how·that
1Co 2:2 For I·decided not to·personally·know anything
1Co 2:8 of·this present·age has·known, for if they·knew *it*,
1Co 2:10 to·us through his Spirit, for the Spirit searches all·

1Co 2:11 For what man·of·clay† personally·knows the·
1Co 2:14 of the Spirit of God, for they·are foolishness to·
1Co 2:16 For "'who knew Yahweh's mind that he·shall·
1Co 3:2 and not food, for yeu·were·not·yet able *to·bear it.*
1Co 3:3 for yeu·are yet fleshly.
1Co 3:3 for yeu·are yet fleshly. For where *there·is* among
1Co 3:4 For whenever someone should·say, "In·fact, I·
1Co 3:9 For we·are coworkers with·God; yeu·are God's
1Co 3:11 For not·even·one·man is·able to·lay another
1Co 3:13 work shall·become apparent, for the day shall·
1Co 3:17 this·one God shall·corrupt. For the temple of·God
1Co 3:19 For the wisdom of·this world is foolishness with
1Co 3:19 is foolishness with God. For it·has·been·written,
1Co 3:21 ·one boast in men·of·clay†, for all·things are yeurs
1Co 4:4 For I·am·conscious·of not·even·one·thing against·
1Co 4:7 For who distinguishes you *one·from·another*?
1Co 4:9 For I·suppose that God exhibited us (the
1Co 4:15 For though yeu·may·have ten·thousand strict·
1Co 4:15 ·*have* not many fathers, for in Anointed-One Jesus
1Co 4:20 For the kingdom of·God *is* not in word, but·rather
1Co 5:3 For I, in·fact, even·though being·absent in·the body
1Co 5:7 yeu·are unleavened. For even Anointed-One, our
1Co 5:12 For what·does·this·have to·do·with·me, to also
1Co 6:16 to·the prostitute is one body? For "the two," he·
1Co 6:20 For yeu·are·kinsman·redeemed with·a·price. Now·
1Co 7:7 For I·want all men·of·clay† to·be also as myself.
1Co 7:9 they·must·marry. For it·is significantly·better to·
1Co 7:14 For the non-trusting husband has·been·made·holy
1Co 7:16 For what do·you·personally·know, O·wife,
1Co 7:22 For the·one being·called·forth in *the* Lord, *though*
1Co 7:31 as not abusing *it* … for the schematic·layout of·this
1Co 8:5 For even if·perhaps they·are being·referred·to·as
1Co 8:8 commend us to·God. For neither if we·should·eat,
1Co 8:10 For if any·man should·see you (the·one having
1Co 9:2 but·yet still I·am to·yeu, for yeu·yeurselves are the
1Co 9:9 For it·has·been·written in the Torah-Law of·Moses,
1Co 9:10 on·account·of us? For on·account·of us it·was·
1Co 9:15 ·done in·this·manner to me, for *it·is* good for·me
1Co 9:16 For though I·should·proclaim·the·good·news, it·is
1Co 9:16 ·is not a·boast to·me, for necessity is·laid·upon me
1Co 9:17 For if I·practice this·thing voluntarily, I·have a·
1Co 9:19 For *though* being free from·among all *men·of·clay†*
1Co 10:4 spiritual drink, for they·were·drinking from·out
1Co 10:5 did·not take·delight, for they·were·struck·down in
1Co 10:17 *and* one Body. For all *of·us* participate·and·
1Co 10:26 For "the Land *is* Yahweh's, and its complete·
1Co 10:28 ·attention, and the conscience, for "the Land *is*
1Co 10:29 but·rather of·the other, for what·reason·is my
1Co 11:5 ·veiled puts·to·shame her head, for it·is one and
1Co 11:6 For if a·woman is·not fully·veiled, also she·must·
1Co 11:7 For in·fact a·man is·obligated not to·be·fully·
1Co 11:8 For man is not from·out·of·woman, but·rather
1Co 11:9 For also man is·not created on·account·of the
1Co 11:12 For just·as the woman *is* from·out·of the man, in·
1Co 11:18 For in·fact first·of·all, as·yeu are·coming·together
1Co 11:19 For it·is·necessary·for *there* also to·be factions
1Co 11:21 For in eating, each·one takes his·own supper
1Co 11:22 *Why*? ¿! For do·yeu·not have homes to·eat and
1Co 11:23 For I·myself personally·received from the Lord
1Co 11:26 For as·often·as yeu·should·eat this bread, and
1Co 11:29 For the·one eating and drinking in·an·unworthy·
1Co 11:31 For if we·were·discerning ourselves *properly*, we·
1Co 12:8 For in·fact to·one is·given through the Spirit a·
1Co 12:12 For exactly·as the body is one and has many
1Co 12:13 For even by one Spirit we·ourselves were all
1Co 12:14 For even the Body is not one member, but·rather
1Co 13:9 For we·know from·out·of·a·portion *of·the whole*,
1Co 13:12 For at·this·moment, we·look·about through a·
1Co 14:2 For the·one speaking in·a·bestowed·tongue speaks
1Co 14:2 to·God. For not·even·one·man listens·with·
1Co 14:5 ·especially that yeu·should·prophesy, for greater *is*
1Co 14:8 For also, if·ever a·trumpet should·give an·
1Co 14:9 the·thing being·spoken? For yeu·shall·be speaking
1Co 14:14 For if I·should·pray in·a·bestowed·tongue, my
1Co 14:17 For in fact, you give·thanks well, but·yet the
1Co 14:31 For yeu·are·able, each one, all to·prophesy, in·
1Co 14:33 For God is not *the God* of·chaos, but·rather of·
1Co 14:34 ·assemblies. For it·has·not been·freely·permitted
1Co 14:35 menfolk at home. For it·is shameful for·women
1Co 15:3 For I·handed·down to·yeu, first-of-all, that·which
1Co 15:9 For I·myself am the least of·the ambassadors, who
1Co 15:16 For if dead·men are·not awakened, not·even
1Co 15:21 For whereas through a·man·of·clay† *came* the
1Co 15:22 For just·as all within Adam die, even in·this·
1Co 15:25 For it·is·mandatory·for him to·reign, even·until
1Co 15:27 For *God* "' subjugated all·things under his feet."'
1Co 15:32 ·eat and should·drink, for tomorrow we·die."'
1Co 15:34 and do·not morally·fail; for some are ignorant
1Co 15:41 and another glory of·*the*·stars, for *one* star varies·
1Co 15:52 at the last trumpet, for it·shall·sound, and the
1Co 15:53 For it·is·necessary·for this corruptible *being* to·
1Co 16:5 Macedonia, for I·am·to·go·throughout Macedonia.
1Co 16:7 For I·do·not want to·see yeu at·this·moment in
1Co 16:9 For a·great and active door has·opened·up to·me,
1Co 16:10 ·be alongside yeu without·fear, for he·works the
1Co 16:11 he·may·come to me, for I·am·waiting·for him
1Co 16:18 For they·refreshed my spirit and yeurs.
2Co 1:8 For we·do·not want yeu to·be·ignorant, brothers,
2Co 1:12 For this is our boasting, the testimony of·our
2Co 1:13 For we·write no other·things to·yeu, other than
2Co 1:19 For the Son of·God, Jesus Anointed, the·one being·
2Co 1:20 For as·many·as *are* God's promises, in him *is* the
2Co 1:24 are coworkers of·yeur joy— for by·the trust, yeu·
2Co 2:2 For if I·myself grieve yeu, then who would·be the·
2Co 2:4 For out·of·much tribulation and anguished·anxiety
2Co 2:9 For to·this *end* also I·wrote, that I·may·know yeur
2Co 2:10 I·myself *do* also. For even if I·myself have·
2Co 2:11 by the Adversary-Accuser, for we·are·not ignorant
2Co 2:17 For we·are not as the many, shortchanging·and·
2Co 3:6 of·letter, but·rather of·Spirit, for the letter kills,
2Co 3:9 For if the service of·the condemnation *had* glory, so·
2Co 3:10 For also the *Service of·Death* having·been·glorified
2Co 3:11 For if the *Service of·Death* is·being·fully·nullified
2Co 3:14 ·hard·as·stone. For even·unto the·present·day the
2Co 4:5 For *it·is* not ourselves *that* we·officially·proclaim,
2Co 4:11 For we·ourselves always, the·ones living, are·
2Co 4:15 For all things *are* on·account·of yeu in·order·that,
2Co 4:17 For our lightweight, momentary tribulation is·
2Co 4:18 ·looked·upon. For the·things being·looked·upon
2Co 5:1 For we·personally·know that if our earthly home of·
2Co 5:2 For even in this we·groan, greatly·yearning to·fully·
2Co 5:4 For even the·ones being in·the bodily·tent do·groan,
2Co 5:7 for we·presently·walk through trust, not through
2Co 5:10 For it·is·mandatory·for every one of·us to·be·
2Co 5:12 For not again do·we·commend ourselves to·yeu,
2Co 5:13 For if we·lost·our·wits, *it·is* for·God; or·if we·are·
2Co 5:14 For the love of·the Anointed-One constrains us,
2Co 5:21 For the·one not knowing moral·failure made
2Co 6:2 for he·says, "'I·favorably·heard you in·an·
2Co 6:14 ·yoked to·non-trusting·ones, for what participation
2Co 6:16 ·God with idols? For yeu·yeurselves are a·temple
2Co 7:3 do·I·say *this*, for I·have·already·stated that yeu·are
2Co 7:5 For even with·us coming into Macedonia, our flesh
2Co 7:8 even·though I·was·regretting *it*, for I·look·upon *it*
2Co 7:9 to repentance, for yeu·were·grieved according·to
2Co 7:10 For the grief according·to God accomplishes
2Co 7:11 For behold this very·same·thing (to·grieve yeu
2Co 8:9 For yeu·know the grace of·our Lord Jesus Anointed,
2Co 8:10 I·give advice, for this is·advantageous for·yeu,
2Co 8:12 For if the eagerness is·set·forth, *it·is* well·
2Co 8:13 For I·do·not *mean* that others *should·have* ease,
2Co 9:1 For, in·fact, concerning the service to the holy·ones,
2Co 9:2 For I·personally·know yeur eagerness, for·which I·
2Co 9:7 out of·grief nor out of·compulsion, for 'God loves
2Co 10:3 For while·strolling·about in *bodily* flesh, we·do·not
2Co 10:4 For the weapons of·our strategic·warfare *are* not
2Co 10:8 For even though I·should·boast somewhat
2Co 10:12 For we·do·not dare to·count·ourselves·among·
2Co 10:14 For *it·is* not as·though we·are·not actually·
2Co 10:14 ourselves, for we·previously·came even as·far·as
2Co 10:18 For *it·is* not that·one commending himself *that* is
2Co 11:2 For I·am·jealous over·yeu with·a·jealousy of·God,
2Co 11:2 ·yeu with·a·jealousy of·God, for I·betrothed yeu
2Co 11:4 For in·fact, if the·one who·is·coming does·
2Co 11:5 For I·reckon not·one·bit to·have·fallen·short of·the
2Co 11:9 of·not·even·one·man. For *that·which was* lacking
2Co 11:13 For such·men·as·these *are* false·ambassadors,
2Co 11:14 ·*is* no marvelous·thing, for the Adversary-Accuser
2Co 11:19 For yeu·bear·with the impetuous with·pleasure,
2Co 11:20 For yeu·bear·with·it, if anyone utterly·enslaves
2Co 12:1 advantageous for·me to·boast, for I·shall·come to
2Co 12:6 For though I·should·want to·boast, I·shall·not be
2Co 12:6 I·shall·not be impetuous, for I·shall·declare truth.
2Co 12:9 grace is·sufficient for·you, for my power is·made·
2Co 12:10 of·Anointed-One, for whenever I·may·be·weak,
2Co 12:11 Yeu compelled me, for I·myself was·due to·be·
2Co 12:11 ·commended by yeu, for *in* not·even·one·thing
2Co 12:13 For what is·it in·which yeu·were·inferior beyond
2Co 12:14 be·a·freeloader of·yeu. For I·do·not seek yeur
2Co 12:14 things, but·rather yeu; for the children are·not
2Co 12:20 For I·fear, lest·somehow after·coming, I·should·
2Co 13:4 For even though he·is·crucified as·a·result of·
2Co 13:4 as·a·result of·God's power. For we·ourselves also
2Co 13:8 For we·are·not able *to·do* anything against the truth
2Co 13:9 For we·are·glad, whenever we·ourselves should·
Eph 2:8 For by·the grace, yeu·are having·been·saved
Eph 2:10 For we·are a·product of·him, already·being·created
Eph 2:14 For he·himself is our peace, the·one already·
Eph 5:5 For yeu·are knowing this·thing, that every sexually·
Eph 5:6 with·empty words, for on·account·of these·things
Eph 5:8 For yeu·were once darkness, but now *yeu·are* light
Eph 5:9 (for the fruit of·the Spirit *is* in all beneficial·
Eph 5:12 For it·is shameful even to·refer·to the·things
Eph 5:13 by the light, for any thing being·made·apparent is
Eph 5:29 For not·even·one·man ever hated his·own flesh,
Eph 6:1 ·and·obey yeur parents in *the* Lord, for this is right.
Col 2:1 For I·want for·yeu to·personally·know what·a·huge
Col 2:5 For even though I·am·absent in·the flesh, but·yet I·
Col 3:3 For yeu·already·died, and yeur life-above has·been·
Col 3:20 the parents according·to all·things, for this is most·
Col 3:24 of·the inheritance, for yeu·are·slaves to·the Lord
Col 4:13 For I·testify for·him, that he·has much zeal over
Phm 1:7 For we·have much gratitude and comfort in your
Phm 1:15 For perhaps on·account·of that, he·departed just·
Phm 1:22 ·me also guest·accommodations, for I·expect that
1Ti 2:3 For this *is* good and fully·acceptable in·the·sight of·
1Ti 2:5 For *there·is* one God, and *there·is* one mediator
1Ti 2:13 For Adam was·molded first, then Eve.
1Ti 3:13 For the *men* already·attending well do·acquire for·
1Ti 4:5 for it·is·made·holy through God's Redemptive-word
1Ti 4:8 "For the *way·of* bodily training is profitable just·for
1Ti 4:10 For to this also we·labor·hard and are·reproached,
1Ti 4:16 persist in·them, for in·doing this you·shall·save
1Ti 5:4 ·back compensations to·their·forebears, for that is
1Ti 5:11 for whenever they·would·live·luxuriously·and·
1Ti 5:15 For even·now some are·turned·aside, *falling·in*
1Ti 5:18 For the Scripture says, "'You·shall·not muzzle an·
1Ti 6:7 For we·carried not·even·one·thing into the world,
1Ti 6:10 For one·root of·all the moral·wrongs is the
2Ti 1:7 For God did·not give us a·spirit of·timidity, but·
2Ti 1:12 ·yet I·am·not ashamed, for I·have·seen in·whom I·
2Ti 2:7 Understand what I·say. For may the Lord give to·
2Ti 2:11 *is* the saying: "For if we·died·together *with·him*,
2Ti 2:16 for they·shall·continually·advance toward more
2Ti 3:2 For the men·of·clay† shall·be: selfish·and·
2Ti 3:6 For from·among these *types* are the·ones
2Ti 3:9 ·advance any·further, for their irrational·resentment
2Ti 4:3 For *the* season shall·be when they·shall·not bear·
2Ti 4:6 For even·now, I·myself am·poured·forth·as·a·

2Ti 4:10 for Demas forsook me, loving the present age, and
2Ti 4:11 bring·him with you, for he·is easily·useful to·me
2Ti 4:15 ·vigilant, for exceedingly he·has·stood·opposed·to
1Jn 2:19 not from·among us; for if they·were from·among
1Jn 4:20 his brother, he·is a·liar, for the·one not loving his
1Jn 5:3 For this is the love of·God, that we·should·
2Jn 1:11 For the·one saying to·him, "Be·well," shares in·his
3Jn 1:3 For I·rejoiced very·much, with·*the*·brothers coming
3Jn 1:7 For on·behalf of·the name, they·went·forth, taking
Rv 1:3 the·things having·been·written in it, for the season *is*
Rv 3:2 that are·about to·die, for I·have·not found your
Rv 9:19 For their authorities are in their mouth *and in their*
Rv 9:19 mouth *and in their tails*, for their tails *were* like
Rv 13:18 number of·the Daemonic·Beast, for it·is a·number
Rv 14:4 are·not tarnished with women, for they·are virgins.
Rv 14:5 was·found no guile, for they·are without·blemish
Rv 16:6 them blood to·drink, for they·are deserving *of*·
Rv 16:14 For they·are spirits of·demons, doing miraculous·
Rv 17:17 "For God gave in their hearts to·do his plan, and
Rv 19:8 ·linen, pure and radiant." (for the fine·linen is the
Rv 19:10 Fall·prostrate to·God, for the testimony of·Jesus is
Rv 21:1 heaven and a·brand-new earth, for the first heaven
Rv 21:22 ·not see a·Temple in it, for Yahweh, *El Shaddai*
Rv 21:23 ·that it·may·shine·forth in it, for the glory of·God
Rv 21:25 may·not be·shut at·day's·end, for night shall·not
Rv 22:9 ·it *that* you·do·not *do·it*; for I·am your fellow·slave,
Rv 22:18 For I·jointly·testify to·everyone hearing the words

G1064 γαστήρ gastḗr *n.* (10x)
Compare:G2836 G4751 G3388 See:G1471
xLangAlso:H0990

G1064.2 N-NPF γαστέρες (1x)
Tit 1:12 always liars, wicked wild·beasts, lazy gluttons."

G1064.4 N-DSF γαστρί (1x)
Lk 1:31 in your·uterus and shall·reproduce·and·birth a·son,

EG1064.4 (1x)
Lk 1:36 is *the* sixth lunar·month *of·pregnancy* for·her (the·

G1064.5 N-DSF γαστρί (7x)
Lk 21:23 to·the·ones being in pregnancy and to·the·ones
Mt 1:18 being in a·pregnancy birthed·from·out of·Holy Spirit
Mt 1:23 shall·be in pregnancy and shall·reproduce·and·birth
Mt 24:19 to·the·ones being in pregnancy and to·the·ones
Mk 13:17 to·the·ones being in pregnancy and to·the·ones
1Th 5:3 the birth·pang, the·one in pregnancy. And no, they·
Rv 12:2 And being in pregnancy, she·yelled·out

G1065 γέ gé *prt.* (7x)

G1065.3 PRT γέ (2x)
Lk 11:8 *him* being his friend, yet on·account·of his audacity,
Lk 18:5 yet on·account·of this widow personally·presenting

G1065.4 PRT γέ (2x)
1Co 6:3 angels? How·much·more still of·secular·matters?
1Co 9:2 an·ambassador to·others, but·yet still I·am to·yeu,

EG1065.4 (1x)
Ac 13:28 of·death *in·him, yet still* they·requested·of Pilate

G1065.5 PRT γέ (2x)
Ac 8:30 he·declared, "Then is·it·actually·so, *that* you·know
1Co 4:8 And oh·that it·were·actually·so *that* yeu·did·reign,

G1066 Γεδεών Gêdêṓn *n/p.* (1x)
גִּדְעוֹן ğid'ôṉ
Roots:H1439

G1066.2 N/P-PRI Γεδεών (1x)
Heb 11:32 me in·giving·an·account concerning Gideon, also

G1067 γέ•εννα gêênna *n/l.* (13x)
Γαϊ Ἐννόμ Gaï Hênnốm [full transliteration]
גֵּיא הִנֹּם ğay' hınốm̱ [Hebrew]
גֵּיהִנֹּם ğeyhınốm̱
Roots:H1516 H2011 Compare:G3041 G0086
See:G5020
xLangEquiv:H1516-1 xLangAlso:H8612 H1522

G1067.3 N-ASF γέενναν (3x)
Mk 9:43 hands *and* to·go·off into the Hell·Canyon, into the
Mk 9:45 feet *and* to·be·cast into the Hell·Canyon, into the
Mk 9:47 eyes *and* to·be·cast into the Hell·Canyon of·fire,

G1067.3 N-GSF γεέννης (3x)
Mt 23:15 ·as·much a·son of·Hell·Canyon as·yeurselves.
Mt 23:33 ·yeu·escape from the Tribunal of·the Hell·Canyon?
Jac 3:6 of·nature, and being·set·aflame by the Hell·Canyon.

G1067.3 N/L-ASF γέενναν (5x)
Lk 12:5 authority to·cast *a·person* into the Hell·Canyon. Yes,
Mt 5:22 shall·be held·liable unto the Hell·Canyon of·fire.
Mt 5:29 your whole body should·be·cast into Hell·Canyon.
Mt 5:30 your whole body should·be·cast into Hell·Canyon.
Mt 18:9 eyes *and* to·be·cast into the Hell·Canyon of·fire.

G1067.3 N/L-DSF γεέννῃ (1x)
Mt 10:28 ·destroy both soul and body in Hell·Canyon.

EG1067.3 (1x)
Mt 5:22 ·be held·liable to·the Tribunal *of·the Hell·Canyon*.

G1068 Γεθ•σημανῆ Gêthsēmanê̄ *n/l.* (2x)
xLangAlso:H1660 H8081

G1068.2 N/L-PRI Γεθσημανῆ (2x)
Mt 26:36 ·open·field being·referred·to·as GethSemane, and
Mk 14:32 of·which the name *is* GethSemane. And *Jesus* says

G1069 γείτων gêítōn *n.* (4x)
Roots:G1093 Compare:G4040 G4139
xLangEquiv:H7934

G1069.1 N-NPM γείτονες (1x)
Jn 9:8 So·then the close·neighbors (and the·ones observing

G1069.1 N-APM γείτονας (2x)
Lk 14:12 kinsmen, nor·even wealthy close·neighbors, lest
Lk 15:6 the friends and the close·neighbors, saying to·them,

G1069.1 N-APF γείτονας (1x)
Lk 15:9 the friends and the close·neighbors saying,

G1070 γελάω gêláō *v.* (2x)
Compare:G3815 See:G1071 G2606
xLangAlso:H6711

G1070 V-FAI-2P γελάσετε (1x)
Lk 6:21 *are* the·ones weeping now, because yeu·shall·laugh.

G1070 V-PAP-NPM γελῶντες (1x)
Lk 6:25 Woe to·yeu, the·ones laughing now! Because yeu·

G1071 γέλως gélōs *n.* (1x)
Roots:G1070 xLangAlso:H7814

G1071 N-NSM γέλως (1x)
Jac 4:9 weep. *Let* yeur laughter be·distorted into mourning,

G1072 γεμίζω gêmízō *v.* (9x)
Roots:G1073

G1072 V-PPN γεμίζεσθαι (1x)
Mk 4:37 the sailboat, such·for it even·now to·be·overfilled.

G1072 V-AAI-3S ἐγέμισεν (1x)
Rv 8:5 censer·for·frankincense, and overfilled it from·out

G1072 V-AAI-3P ἐγέμισαν (2x)
Jn 2:7 with·water." And they·overfilled them until topped·
Jn 6:13 ·together and overfilled twelve wicker·baskets with·

G1072 V-AAM-2P γεμίσατε (1x)
Jn 2:7 says to·them, "Overfill the ceremonial·water·basins

G1072 V-AAN γεμίσαι (1x)
Lk 15:16 And he·was·longing to·overfill his belly with the

G1072 V-AAP-NSM γεμίσας (1x)
Mk 15:36 ·running and overfilling a·sponge of·wine·vinegar

G1072 V-API-3S ἐγεμίσθη (1x)
Rv 15:8 the Temple was·overfilled with·smoke from·among

G1072 V-APS-3S γεμισθῇ (1x)
Lk 14:23 *them* to·come·in, that my house may·be·overfilled.

G1073 γέμω gémō *v.* (11x)
See:G1072

G1073 V-PAI-3S γέμει (2x)
Lk 11:39 but yeur inward·part overflows with·extortion and
Rm 3:14 "Whose mouth overflows of·evil·prayer and of·

G1073 V-PAI-3P γέμουσιν (2x)
Mt 23:25 but from·inside they·overflow out of·extortion
Mt 23:27 but inwardly they·overflow of·dead *men's* bones

G1073 V-PAP-ASN γέμον (2x)
Rv 17:3 demonic·beast, overflowing of·names of·revilement
Rv 17:4 cup in her hand overflowing of·abominations and

G1073 V-PAP-APF γεμούσας (3x)
Rv 5:8 harps and golden vials overflowing with·incense,
Rv 15:7 angels seven golden vials overflowing of·the Rage
Rv 21:9 seven vials, the·ones overflowing of·the seven last

G1073 V-PAP-NPN γέμοντα (2x)
Rv 4:6 *are* four living·beings overflowing of·eyes forward
Rv 4:8 was·having six wings apiece overflowing of·eyes, all·

G1074 γενεά gênêá *n.* (42x)
Roots:G1085 Compare:G4690 G5207 G0165
See:G1081 xLangAlso:H1755 A1859

G1074.1 N-NSF γενεά (3x)
Lk 21:32 I·say to·yeu, this generation·of·offspring, no,
Mt 24:34 I·say to·yeu, *that* this generation·of·offspring, no,
Mk 13:30 I·say to·yeu, that this generation·of·offspring, no,

G1074.1 N-NPF γενεαί (1x)
Mt 1:17 So all the generations·of·offspring from AbRaham

G1074.1 N-ASF γενεάν (1x)
Mt 23:36 shall·come upon this generation·of·offspring.

G1074.1 N-DPF γενεαῖς (1x)
Eph 3:5 other generations·of·offspring was·not made·known

G1074.2 N-NSF γενεά (4x)
Lk 11:29 "This is an·evil generation. It·seeks·for a·sign, and
Mt 12:39 to·them, "An·evil generation (*who·is* also an·
Mt 16:4 An·evil generation (*who·is* also an·adulteress)
Mk 8:12 ·says, "Why·does this generation seek·for a·sign?

G1074.2 N-NPF γενεαί (4x)
Lk 1:48 from now·on all the generations shall·pronounce me
Mt 1:17 until David *are* fourteen generations. Then from
Mt 1:17 the Babylonian exile *are* fourteen generations. And
Mt 1:17 until the Anointed-One *are* fourteen generations.

G1074.2 N-VSF γενεά (3x)
Lk 9:41 "O distrusting and perverse generation, how·long
Mt 17:17 "O distrusting and perverse generation, how·long
Mk 9:19 he·says, "O distrusting generation, how·long shall·

G1074.2 N-ASF γενεάν (2x)
Lk 16:8 the Sons of·the Light in their·own generation.
Mt 11:16 "But to·what shall·I·liken this generation? It·is like

G1074.2 N-APF γενεάς (2x)
Lk 1:50 ·fearing him *unto* generations upon generations.
Eph 3:21 Jesus, unto all the generations of·the age of·ages.

G1074.2 N-DSF γενεᾷ (6x)
Lk 11:30 the Son of·Clay·Man† shall·be to·this generation.
Ac 13:36 of·God in·his·own generation, was·laid·to·rest, and
Heb 3:10 ·vexed with·that generation and declared, 'Always
Mt 12:45 ·manner shall·it·be also to·this evil generation."
Mk 8:12 ·sign shall·*ever*·be·given to·this generation.'"
Mk 8:38 ·my Redemptive·words in this generation (*known·as*

G1074.2 N-DPF γενεαῖς (1x)
Ac 14:16 Who, in the generations having·long·past, gave·

G1074.2 N-GSF γενεᾶς (10x)
Lk 7:31 ·I·liken the men·of·clay† of·this generation? And to·
Lk 11:31 with the men of·this generation, and she·shall·
Lk 11:32 in the Final·Tribunal with this generation, and they·
Lk 11:50 may·be·sought·out from this generation,
Lk 11:51 to·yeu, it·shall·be·sought·out of·this generation.
Lk 17:25 and to·be·rejected·as·unfit by this generation.
Ac 2:40 "Save·yeurselves from this warped generation."
Mt 12:41 ·Tribunal with this generation and shall·condemn it
Mt 12:42 in the Final·Tribunal with this generation, and shall·
Php 2:15 ·midst of·a·warped and perverse generation, among

G1074.2 N-GPF γενεῶν (3x)
Lk 1:50 ·fearing him *unto* generations upon generations.
Ac 15:21 Moses, from·out of·ancient generations, has in·
Col 1:26 prior·ages and from the generations, but now·in·fact

G1074.3 N-ASF γενεάν (1x)
Ac 8:33 ·give·an·account of·his own·offspring? Because his

G1075 γενεα•λογέω gênêalôgéō *v.* (1x)
Roots:G1074 G3056

G1075.2 V-PPP-NSM γενεαλογούμενος (1x)
Heb 7:6 ·one not being·reckoned·by·birth from·among them

G1076 γενεα•λογία gênêalôgía *n.* (2x)
Roots:G1074 G3056 See:G1075
xLangEquiv:H8435

G1076 N-APF γενεαλογίας (1x)

Tit 3:9 But shun foolish speculations, genealogies, strifes,
G1076 N-DPF γενεαλογίαις (1x)
1Ti 1:4 to·give·heed to·myths and to·endless genealogies,

G1077 γενέσια gênésia *n.* (2x)
Roots:G1078
G1077 N-DPN γενεσίοις (1x)
Mk 6:21 a·supper on·his birthday for·his greatest·men and
G1077 N-GPN γενεσίων (1x)
Mt 14:6 with·HerOd·AntiPas' birthdays being·marked with·

G1078 γένεσις gênêsis *n.* (3x)
Roots:G1085 Compare:G5449 See:G1074 G1083
G1078.1 N-GSF γενέσεως (1x)
Mt 1:1 A·record of·*the·paternal* origin *(via·adoption)* of·
G1078.2 N-GSF γενέσεως (1x)
Jac 1:23 ·resembled a·man fully·observing his natural face in
G1078.3 N-GSF γενέσεως (1x)
Jac 3:6 and setting·aflame the regular·course of·nature, and

G1079 γενετή gênêté *n.* (1x)
Roots:G1074 Compare:G1083
G1079 N-GSF γενετῆς (1x)
Jn 9:1 a·man·of·clay† who·was·blind from·out of·*his*·birth.

G1080 γεννάω gênnáō *v.* (100x)
Roots:G1085 Compare:G5088 G1626 G0580
See:G1084
xLangEquiv:H3205
G1080.ª V-FAI-3S γεννήσει (1x)
Lk 1:13 and your wife EliSabeth shall·bear you a·son, and
G1080.ª V-PAI-3P γεννῶσιν (1x)
2Ti 2:23 having·seen that they·give·birth *to* quarrels.
G1080.ª V-PAP-NSF γεννῶσα (1x)
Gal 4:24 *is* from Mount Sinai, bearing·children for slavery,
G1080.ª V-AAI-3S ἐγέννησεν (1x)
Lk 1:57 ·and·give·birth, and she·gave·birth·to a·son.
G1080.ª V-AAI-3P ἐγέννησαν (1x)
Lk 23:29 and *the* wombs that did·not bear, and *the* breasts
G1080.ª V-AAS-3S γεννήσῃ (1x)
Jn 16:21 ·come, but whenever she·may·birth the little·child,
G1080.1 V-AAI-1S ἐγέννησα (2x)
1Co 4:15 Anointed-One Jesus, I·myself begot yeu through
Phm 1:10 my child Onesimus, whom I·begot in my bonds.
G1080.1 V-AAI-3S ἐγέννησεν (41x)
Ac 7:8 And in·this·manner, *AbRaham* begot YiTsaq and
Ac 7:29 in *the* land of·Midian, where he·begot two sons.
Mt 1:2 AbRaham begot YiTsaq, and YiTsaq begot Jacob, and
Mt 1:2 begot YiTsaq, and YiTsaq begot Jacob, and Jacob
Mt 1:2 begot Jacob, and Jacob begot Judah and his brothers.
Mt 1:3 Then Judah begot Perets and Zarach (birthed·from·
Mt 1:3 of·Tamar), and Perets begot Chetsron, and Chetsron
Mt 1:3 and Perets begot Chetsron, and Chetsron begot Ram.
Mt 1:4 Now Ram begot AmmiNadab, and AmmiNadab begot
Mt 1:4 AmmiNadab, and AmmiNadab begot Nachshon, and
Mt 1:4 begot Nachshon, and Nachshon begot Salmon.
Mt 1:5 Then Salmon begot BoAz (birthed·from·out of·
Mt 1:5 of·Rachav), and BoAz begot Obed (birthed·from·out
Mt 1:5 (birthed·from·out of·Ruth), and Obed begot Jesse.
Mt 1:6 Now Jesse begot King David, and King David begot
Mt 1:6 and King David begot Solomon (birthed·from·out
Mt 1:7 Then Solomon begot RehoboAm, and RehoboAm
Mt 1:7 begot RehoboAm, and RehoboAm begot AbiYah, and
Mt 1:7 RehoboAm begot AbiYah, and AbiYah begot Asa.
Mt 1:8 Now Asa begot JehoShaphat, and JehoShaphat begot
Mt 1:8 JehoShaphat, and JehoShaphat begot JehoRam†, and
Mt 1:8 begot JehoRam†, and JehoRam† begot UzzIah.
Mt 1:9 Then UzzIah begot YoTham, and YoTham begot
Mt 1:9 begot YoTham, and YoTham begot Achaz, and
Mt 1:9 YoTham begot Achaz, and Achaz begot HezekIah.
Mt 1:10 Now HezekIah begot MaNasseh, and MaNasseh
Mt 1:10 begot MaNasseh, and MaNasseh begot Amon, and
Mt 1:10 MaNasseh begot Amon, and Amon begot JosIah.
Mt 1:11 Then JosIah begot YeKonYah and his brothers, upon
Mt 1:12 Babylonian exile, YeKonYah begot ShealtiEl, and
Mt 1:12 begot ShealtiEl, and ShealtiEl begot ZerubBabel.
Mt 1:13 Then ZerubBabel begot AbiHud, and AbiHud begot
Mt 1:13 begot AbiHud, and AbiHud begot ElYaQim, and
Mt 1:13 AbiHud begot ElYaQim, and ElYaQim begot Azzur.
Mt 1:14 Now Azzur begot Tsadoq, and Tsadoq begot Achim,
Mt 1:14 begot Tsadoq, and Tsadoq begot Achim, and Achim
Mt 1:14 and Tsadoq begot Achim, and Achim begot EliHud.
Mt 1:15 Then EliHud begot EleAzar, and EleAzar begot
Mt 1:15 begot EleAzar, and EleAzar begot Matthan, and
Mt 1:15 EleAzar begot Matthan, and Matthan begot Jacob.
Mt 1:16 Now Jacob begot Joseph the husband of·Mariam,
G1080.1 V-AAP-ASM γεννήσαντα (1x)
1Jn 5:1 one loving *God*, the·one begetting, should·love also
G1080.1 V-APP-NSM γεννηθείς (1x)
1Jn 5:18 the·one already·being·begotten from·out of·God
G1080.1 V-RAI-1S γεγέννηκα (3x)
Ac 13:33 Today, I·myself have·begotten you.'"
Heb 1:5 Today, I·myself have·begotten you'"?
Heb 5:5 Today, I·myself have·begotten you.'"
G1080.1 V-RPP-ASM γεγεννημένον (1x)
1Jn 5:1 also the·one having·been·begotten from·out of·him.
EG1080.1 (2x)
Ac 7:8 ·the eighth day; and YiTsaq *begot* Jacob; and Jacob
Ac 7:8 *begot* Jacob; and Jacob *begot* the twelve patriarchs.
G1080.2 V-APP-NSN γεννηθέν (1x)
Mt 1:20 wife, for the·one already·being·conceived in her is
G1080.3 V-PPI-3S γεννᾶται (1x)
Mt 2:4 directly·from them where the Anointed-One is·born.
G1080.3 V-PPP-NSN γεννώμενον (1x)
Lk 1:35 also, the *child*, being·born holy, shall·be·called
G1080.3 V-API-1P ἐγεννήθημεν (1x)
Ac 2:8 our own·distinct dialect into which we·were·born?
G1080.3 V-API-2S ἐγεννήθης (1x)
Jn 9:34 to·him, "You·yourself were·born altogether in
G1080.3 V-API-3S ἐγεννήθη (7x)
Jn 9:19 "Is this yeur son, who yeu say was·born blind?
Jn 9:20 ·know that this is our son, and that he·is·born blind.
Jn 16:21 the joy that a·child·of·clay† is·born into the world.
Ac 7:20 "Into which season Moses was·born, and he·was
Mt 1:16 of·Mariam, from·out of·whom was·born YeShua,
Mt 26:24 better for·him if that man·of·clay† was·not born."
Mk 14:21 better for·him if that man·of·clay† was·not born."
G1080.3 V-API-3P ἐγεννήθησαν (3x)
Jn 1:13 who are·born, not from·out of·blood, nor from·out
Heb 11:12 *offspring†* were·born from·him·having·been· *of·*
Mt 19:12 some·who were·born in·this·manner from·out *of·*
G1080.3 V-APN γεννηθῆναι (3x)
Jn 3:4 "How·is a·man·of·clay† able to·be·born, being·an·
Jn 3:4 ·time into the womb of·his mother and to·be·born?"
Jn 3:7 ·you, 'It·is·necessary·for yeu to·be·born from·above.'
G1080.3 V-APP-GSM γεννηθέντος (1x)
Mt 2:1 Now with·YeShua already·being·born in BethLechem
G1080.3 V-APP-GPM γεννηθέντων (1x)
Rm 9:11 *·the twins* not·yet being·born nor·even practicing
G1080.3 V-APP-NSM γεννηθείς (2x)
Heb 11:23 By·trust, Moses (being·born) was·hid three·
Gal 4:29 just·as then, the·one being·born according·to flesh
G1080.3 V-APS-3S γεννηθῇ (3x)
Jn 3:3 to·you, unless someone should·be·born from·above,
Jn 3:5 unless someone should·be·born from·out of·water
Jn 9:2 or his parents, in·order·that he·should·be·born blind?
G1080.3 V-RPI-1S γεγέννημαι (2x)
Jn 18:37 *for* to this I·myself have·been·born. Also to·this I·
Ac 22:28 I·myself, also, *am* having·been·born *a·citizen*."
G1080.3 V-RPI-1P γεγεννήμεθα (1x)
Jn 8:41 have·not been·born out of·sexual·immorality. We·
G1080.3 V-RPI-3S γεγέννηται (5x)
Gal 4:23 ·the maidservant has·been·born according·to flesh,
1Jn 2:29 the righteousness has·been·born from·out of·him.
1Jn 3:9 ·fail, because he·has·been·born from·out of·God.
1Jn 4:7 one presently·loving has·been·born from·out of·God
1Jn 5:1 is the Anointed-One has·been·born from·out of·God;
G1080.3 V-RPP-GSM γεγεννημένου (1x)
Jn 9:32 ·man opened·up eyes of·one·having·been·born blind.
G1080.3 V-RPP-NSN γεγεννημένον (3x)
Jn 3:6 "The·one having·been·born from·out of·the flesh is
Jn 3:6 flesh; and the·one having·been·born from·out of·the
1Jn 5:4 every one having·been·born from·out of·God
G1080.3 V-RPP-NSM γεγεννημένος (4x)
Jn 3:8 is any one having·been·born from·out of·the Spirit.
Ac 22:3 a·man *who·is* a·Jew, having·been·born in Tarsus, *a·*
1Jn 3:9 Any one having·been·born from·out of·God does·not
1Jn 5:18 that any one having·been·born from·out of·God
G1080.3 V-RPP-NPN γεγεννημένα (1x)
2Pe 2:12 irrational animals, having·been·born into capture
EG1080.3 (1x)
Gal 4:29 ·persecuting the·one *being·born* according·to Spirit,

G1081 γέννημα gênnēma *n.* (9x)
Roots:G1080 Compare:G1549 G2039 G0581-1
See:G1074 G4409-4 xLangAlso:H8393
G1081.1 N-VPN γεννήματα (4x)
Lk 3:7 by him, "O·offspring of·vipers, who gave·any·
Mt 3:7 *John* declared to·them, "O·offspring of·vipers, who
Mt 12:34 O·offspring of·vipers, being evil, in·what·way are·
Mt 23:33 O·serpents, O·offspring of·vipers, in·what·way
G1081.2 N-APN γεννήματα (2x)
Lk 12:18 there I·shall·gather·together all my produce and my
2Co 9:10 ·grow the produce of·yeur righteousness,
G1081.2 N-GSN γεννήματος (3x)
Lk 22:18 I·should·not·ever drink of·the produce of·the vine,
Mt 26:29 ·moment·on from·out of·this produce of·the vine,
Mk 14:25 any·longer from·out of·the produce of·the vine,

G1082 Γεννησαρέτ Gênnēsarét *n/l.* (3x)
xLangEquiv:H3672
G1082.2 N/L-PRI Γεννησαρέτ (3x)
Lk 5:1 was standing directly·by the lake of·Gennesaret.
Mt 14:34 ·over, they·came into the land of·Gennesaret.
Mk 6:53 ·came to·the land of·Gennesaret and landed·ashore.

G1083 γέννησις gênnēsis *n.* (2x)
Roots:G1080 Compare:G1079 See:G1078
G1083 N-NSF γέννησις (1x)
Mt 1:18 Now the birth of·YeShua Anointed was in·this·
G1083 N-DSF γεννήσει (1x)
Lk 1:14 ·leaping·of·joy, and many shall·rejoice at his birth.

G1084 γεννητός gênnētós *adj.* (3x)
Roots:G1080 See:G3439
G1084 A-DPM γεννητοῖς (2x)
Lk 7:28 I·say to·yeu, among those·born of·women there·is
Mt 11:11 to·yeu, among those·born of·women there·has·not
EG1084 (1x)
Ac 7:5 him, *even* with·there·not being·a·child *born* to·him.

G1085 γένος gênôs *n.* (22x)
Roots:G1096 Compare:G5449
G1085.1 N-NSN γένος (5x)
Ac 7:13 brothers, and Joseph's kindred became apparent to·
Ac 17:28 'For we·are also *his* kindred.'
Ac 17:29 Accordingly, inherently·being kindred of·God,
1Pe 2:9 But yeu *are* a·Selected kindred, a·royal priesthood,
Rv 22:16 I AM the root and the kindred of·David, the star,
G1085.1 N-ASN γένος (1x)
Ac 7:19 ·shrewd·against our kindred, badly·harmed our
G1085.1 N-DSN γένει (1x)
Gal 1:14 my·own·age among my kindred, inherently·being
G1085.1 N-GSN γένους (3x)
Ac 4:6 ·many·as were from·among *the* high·priest's kindred.
Php 3:5 eight·days·of·age from·among *the* kindred of·IsraEl,
2Co 11:26 dangers from·among *my·own* kindred, dangers
G1085.2 N-NSN γένος (2x)
Mt 17:21 "But this kind does·not depart except by prayer and
Mk 9:29 not·even·one·thing is this kind able to·come·forth,
G1085.2 N-NPN γένη (2x)
1Co 12:10 *thoroughly·differing* kinds of·bestowed·tongues,
1Co 14:10 as·it·may·be, so·many kinds of·voices in *the*
G1085.2 N-APN γένη (1x)
1Co 12:28 *thoroughly·differing* kinds of·bestowed·tongues.
G1085.2 N-GSN γένους (1x)
Mt 13:47 ·together from·among every kind *of·creature*,

Ββ Γγ Δδ Εε Ζζ Ηη Θθ Ιι Κκ Λλ Μμ Νν Ξξ Οο Ππ Ρρ Σσ Ττ Υυ Φφ Χχ Ψψ Ωω

EG1085.2 (1x)

1Co 15:39 in·fact *there·is* one *kind·of* flesh of·men·of·clay†,

G1085.3 N-DSN γένει (4x)

Ac 4:36 ·Consoling), *was* a·Levite *and* of·Cyprus by·birth,
Ac 18:2 by·the·name·of Aquila (of·Pontus by·birth, recently
Ac 18:24 by·name, of·AlexAndria by·birth), an·eloquent
Mk 7:26 was a·Greek, a·Syro-Phoenician by·birth, and she·

G1085.3 N-GSN γένους (1x)

Ac 13:26 brothers, the·Sons of·AbRaham by·birth, and the·

G1086 Γεργεσηνός Gêrgêsēnós *n/g.* (1x)

גִּרְגָּשִׁי ĝır·ĝaśhıy [Hebrew]

Roots:H1622

G1086 N/G-GPM Γεργεσηνῶν (1x)

Mt 8:28 the region of·the Girgashites, there·came·and·met

G1087 γερουσία gêrôusía *n.* (1x)

Roots:G1088 Compare:G4244 xLangAlso:H7869 H2205

G1087.1 N-ASF γερουσίαν (1x)

Ac 5:21 and all the council·of·aged·men of·the Sons of·

G1088 γέρων gérōn *n.* (1x)

Compare:G4246 G1123-1 See:G1094 G1087 G1126 xLangEquiv:H7869 xLangAlso:H2205

G1088 N-NSM γέρων (1x)

Jn 3:4 able to·be·born, being an·agedly·old·man? ¿! Is·he·

G1089 γεύομαι gêúômai *v.* (15x)

Compare:G0977 G2068 G5315 G5176

G1089.1 V-FDI-3S γεύσεται (2x)

Jn 8:52 no, he·shall·not taste of·death into the coming·age.
Lk 14:24 having·been·called·forth, shall·taste my supper.'"

G1089.1 V-FDI-3P γεύσονται (1x)

Lk 9:27 who no, shall·not taste death until they·should·see

G1089.1 V-ADI-2P ἐγεύσασθε (1x)

1Pe 2:3 if·ever "yeu·tasted that Yahweh *is* kind.

G1089.1 V-ADI-3S ἐγεύσατο (1x)

Jn 2:9 as·soon·as the director·of·the·banquet tasted the water

G1089.1 V-ADN γεύσασθαι (1x)

Ac 23:14 over·to·destruction to·taste not·even·one·thing

G1089.1 V-ADP-APM γευσαμένους (2x)

Heb 6:4 being·enlightened, and after·tasting of·the heavenly
Heb 6:5 and after·tasting a·good utterance of·God, and·also

G1089.1 V-ADP-NSM γευσάμενος (1x)

Mt 27:34 ·mixed with gall, and after·tasting *it*, he·was·not

G1089.1 V-ADS-2S γεύσῃ (1x)

Col 2:21 lay·hold·of, nor·even should·you·taste, nor·even

G1089.1 V-ADS-3S γεύσηται (1x)

Heb 2:9 by·the·grace of·God he·should·taste death on·behalf

G1089.1 V-ADS-3P γεύσωνται (2x)

Mt 16:28 here who, no, may·not taste death, until they·
Mk 9:1 here, who, no, should·not taste of·death, until they·

G1089.2 V-ADN γεύσασθαι (1x)

Ac 10:10 ·hungry and was·wanting to·have·a·bite·to·eat, but

G1089.2 V-ADP-NSM γευσάμενος (1x)

Ac 20:11 and after·having·a·bite·to·eat and conversing over

G1090 γεωργέω gêōrgéō *v.* (1x)

Roots:G1092 Compare:G2716 G0722

G1090.1 V-PPI-3S γεωργεῖται (1x)

Heb 6:7 on·account·of whom also it·is·cultivated, it·partakes

G1091 γεώργιον gêōrgiôn *n.* (1x)

Roots:G1092 Compare:G5502-2 xLangAlso:H5657 H7704

G1091 N-NSN γεώργιον (1x)

1Co 3:9 with·God; yeu·are God's cultivated·soil, God's

G1092 γε•ωργός gêōrgós *n.* (19x)

Roots:G1093 G2041 Compare:G0289 G2780 G0721-1 xLangAlso:H0406

G1092.1 N-NSM γεωργός (1x)

Jac 5:7 Behold, the man·that·works·the·soil waits·for the

G1092.1 N-ASM γεωργόν (1x)

2Ti 2:6 the hard·laboring man·that·works·the·soil to·partake

G1092.2 N-NSM γεωργός (1x)

Jn 15:1 I AM the true vine, and my Father is the farmer.

G1092.3 N-NPM γεωργοί (5x)

Lk 20:10 "But the tenant·farmers, after·thrashing him,
Lk 20:14 ·seeing him, the tenant·farmers deliberated among
Mt 21:35 "But the tenant·farmers, after·taking·hold·of·his
Mt 21:38 ·seeing the son, the tenant·farmers declared among
Mk 12:7 "But those tenant·farmers declared among

G1092.3 N-APM γεωργούς (5x)

Lk 20:10 to the tenant·farmers in·order·that they·should·give
Lk 20:16 shall·completely·destroy these tenant·farmers, and
Mt 21:34 his slaves to the tenant·farmers, to·receive its fruits
Mk 12:2 to the tenant·farmers in·order·that he·may·receive
Mk 12:9 ·destroy the tenant·farmers and shall·give the

G1092.3 N-DPM γεωργοῖς (5x)

Lk 20:9 a·vineyard and leased it to·tenant·farmers, and·then
Mt 21:33 " and·then he·leased it to·tenant·farmers and
Mt 21:40 ·come, what shall·he·do to·those tenant·farmers?"
Mt 21:41 ·lease the vineyard to·other tenant·farmers, who
Mk 12:1 ' and leased it to·tenant·farmers, and journeyed·

G1092.3 N-GPM γεωργῶν (1x)

Mk 12:2 ·may·receive directly·from the tenant·farmers of·the

G1093 γῆ gễ *n.* (254x)

Compare:G3625 G5522 G5561 G2889 See:G1049-2 xLangEquiv:H0127 xLangAlso:H0776

G1093.1 N-NSF γῆ (2x)

Ac 7:33 feet, for the place in which you·stand is holy soil.'
Heb 6:7 For the soil, after·drinking the rain which·is·coming

G1093.1 N-ASF γῆν (14x)

Jn 8:6 down, Jesus was·writing with·the finger into the soil.
Jn 8:8 after·stooping down, he·was·writing into the soil.
Jn 12:24 kernel of·wheat, falling into the soil, should·die, it
Lk 8:8 fell on the beneficially·good soil, and once·being·
Lk 13:7 ·purpose·does·it also fully·render the soil useless?
Lk 14:35 It·is neither well-suited for soil, nor·even for
Lk 22:44 like clots of·blood dropping·down upon the soil.
Mt 10:29 them shall·fall upon the soil without yeur Father
Mt 13:8 But others fell on the soil, the good·one, and were·
Mt 13:23 ·with·seed among the good soil, this·person is the·
Mt 15:35 ·ordered the crowds to·sit·back upon the soil.
Mk 4:5 where it·was·not having much soil, and immediately
Mk 4:8 some fell into the good soil and was·giving fruit,
Mk 4:20 ·with·seed among the good soil: the·same·which

G1093.1 N-DSF γῇ (1x)

Lk 8:15 But the *seed* in the good soil, these are *the·ones* with

G1093.1 N-GSF γῆς (5x)

Mk 4:26 should·cast the scattering·of·seed upon the soil,
Mk 8:6 the crowd to·sit·back upon the soil. And after·taking
Mk 9:20 And falling upon the soil, he·was·rolling·about
Mk 14:35 a·little·bit, he·fell on the soil and prayed that, if it·
1Co 15:47 first man·of·clay† *was* from·out of·soil, *as* dusty·

EG1093.1 (1x)

Heb 6:8 But *the soil* bearing·forth 'thorns and spear·thistles'

G1093.2 N-NSF γῆ (17x)

Lk 21:33 "The heaven and the earth shall·pass·away, but my
Ac 7:49 heaven *is* my throne, and the earth *is* my foot stool.
Mt 5:18 until the heaven and the earth should·pass·away, not
Mt 24:35 "The heaven and the earth shall·pass·away, but my
Mt 27:51 And the earth is·shaken, and the solid·rocks are·
Mk 4:28 For the earth automatically bears·fruit; first a·blade,
Mk 13:31 "The heaven and the earth shall·pass·away, but my
Jac 5:18 gave rain, and the earth blossomed·with its fruit.
2Pe 3:5 ·antiquity, and *there·was* an·earth having·consisted,
2Pe 3:7 the heavens and the earth are having·been·stored·up,
2Pe 3:10 ·in·a·blazing·fire; and·also *the* earth (and the
Rv 12:16 And the earth swiftly·helped the woman, and the
Rv 12:16 the woman, and the earth opened·up her mouth,
Rv 14:16 his sickle on the earth, and the earth was·reaped.
Rv 18:1 authority; and the earth was·illuminated as·a·result
Rv 20:11 it, from whose face the earth and the heaven fled·
Rv 21:1 first heaven and the first earth passed·away; and the

G1093.2 N-ASF γῆν (43x)

Lk 6:49 apart·from a·foundation on the earth, which the
Lk 12:49 "I·came to·cast fire upon the earth. Even·so, what·
Lk 16:17 ·for the heaven and the earth to·pass·away, than
Lk 24:5 drooping the face toward the earth, *the men* declared
Ac 4:24 ·one making the heaven, and the earth, and the sea,
Ac 9:4 And falling upon the earth, he·heard a·voice saying
Ac 14:15 'who made the heaven, and the earth, and the sea,
Ac 26:14 of·us already·falling·down upon the earth, I·heard
Heb 1:10 *the* beginning laid·a·foundation·for the earth; and
Heb 12:26 whose *own* voice shook the earth at·that·time. But
Heb 12:26 do·shake not merely the earth, but·rather also the
Mt 5:5 because they·themselves shall·inherit the earth.
Mt 10:34 I·came to·cast peace upon the earth; I·did·not come
Mt 13:5 ·places, where it·was·not having much earth, and
Rm 10:18 ·articulation went·forth into all the earth, and their
Jac 5:12 by·the heaven, nor by·the earth, nor by·any other
2Pe 3:13 'a·Brand-New Heavens and a·Brand-New Earth,' in
Rv 5:6 of·God having·been·dispatched into all the earth.
Rv 6:13 of·the heaven fell to the earth, as *when* a·fig·tree
Rv 7:2 it was·given to·bring·harm·to the earth and the sea,
Rv 7:3 "Yeu·may·not bring·harm·to the earth, neither the sea
Rv 8:5 and cast *it* upon the earth; and there·were voices,
Rv 8:7 and they·were·cast into the earth; and the third·part
Rv 9:1 from·out of·the heaven to the earth. And to·him was·
Rv 9:3 there·came·forth locusts upon the earth, and authority
Rv 10:2 foot upon the sea, and the left *foot* on the earth,
Rv 10:6 the·things in it, and the earth, and the·things in it,
Rv 11:6 and to·smite the earth with·any punishing·blow, as·
Rv 11:18 ·ruin the·ones thoroughly·ruining the earth."
Rv 12:4 heaven and cast them to the earth. And the Dragon
Rv 12:9 Land; he·was·cast·out into the earth, and his angels
Rv 12:12 Woe to·the·ones residing·in the earth and the sea,
Rv 12:13 saw that he·was·cast to the earth, he·persecuted the
Rv 13:12 of·it, and it·makes the earth and the·ones residing
Rv 13:13 of·the heaven to the earth in·the·sight of·the men·
Rv 14:7 'having·made the heaven, and the earth, and sea,'
Rv 14:16 ·cloud cast·in his sickle on the earth, and the earth
Rv 14:19 his sickle into the earth, and collected·for·vintage
Rv 16:1 ·out the vials of·the Rage of·God into the earth."
Rv 16:2 poured·out his vial upon the earth, and it·became a·
Rv 17:2 the·ones residing·in the earth, they·are·made·drunk
Rv 19:2 who was·corrupting the earth with her sexual·
Rv 21:1 a·brand-new heaven and a·brand-new earth, for the

G1093.2 N-DSF γῇ (8x)

Lk 12:51 ·directly to·give peace on the earth? I·say to·yeu,
Mt 5:35 nor by the earth, because it·is his foot stool, nor
Mt 25:18 *talant·of·silver* dug in the earth and hid·away his
Mt 25:25 I·hid your talant·of·silver in the earth. See, you·
Rm 9:17 may·be·thoroughly·announced in all the earth."
1Jn 5:8 three, the·ones testifying on the earth: the Spirit, and
Rv 5:13 the heaven, and on the earth, and beneath the earth,
Rv 13:3 it·was·marveled among the whole earth, *which fell·*

G1093.2 N-GSF γῆς (116x)

Jn 3:31 ·one being birthed·from·out of·the earth is from·out
Jn 3:31 ·out of·the earth is from·out of·the earth, and speaks
Jn 3:31 and speaks from·out of·the earth. The·one who·is·
Jn 12:32 ·be·elevated from·among the earth, I·shall·draw all
Jn 17:4 glorified you on the earth. I·fully·completed the
Lk 2:14 in *the* highest, and on earth, peace! Among men·of·
Lk 5:24 authority upon the earth to·forgive moral·failures,"
Lk 10:21 of·the heaven and the earth, that you·hid·away
Lk 11:2 will be·done, as in heaven, so·also on the earth.
Lk 11:31 ·out of·the utmost·parts of·the earth to·hear the
Lk 12:56 face of·the sky and of·the earth; but how·is·it that·
Lk 18:8 ·*back*, shall·he·find then *such* a·trust on the earth?"
Lk 21:25 And upon the earth *shall·be the* anguished·anxiety
Lk 21:35 who·are·sitting·down on *the* face of·all the earth.
Ac 1:8 and as·far·as·to *the* farthest·part of·the earth."
Ac 2:19 up·above and signs on the earth down·below: blood
Ac 3:25 the paternal·lineages of·the earth shall·be·blessed."
Ac 4:26 The kings of·the earth stood·by *ready*, and the rulers
Ac 8:33 Because his life† is·taken·away from the earth."'
Ac 9:8 And Saul was·roused from the earth, but with·his
Ac 10:11 ·the·four corners and being·sent·down to the earth,
Ac 10:12 four-footed·animals of·the earth were·subsisting,
Ac 11:6 I·saw the four-footed·animals of·the earth, and the
Ac 13:47 ·Salvation unto *the* farthest·part of·the earth.'"

Ac 17:24 inherently·being Lord of·heaven and earth, resides
Ac 17:26 all the face of·the earth, specifically·determining
Ac 22:22 Away·with such·a·man from the earth, for it·is·not
Heb 8:4 if, in·fact, he·were on earth, he·would not·even be
Heb 11:13 foreigners and foreign·residents on the earth.
Heb 11:38 and *in* caves and in·the caverns of·the earth.
Heb 12:25 ·divine·instruction on the earth, so·much more·so
Mt 5:13 "Yeu·yeurselves are the salt of·the earth, but if the
Mt 6:10 will be·done— as in heaven, so·also on the earth.
Mt 6:19 for·yeurselves treasures upon the earth, where moth
Mt 9:6 has authority on the earth to·forgive moral·failures,"
Mt 11:25 of·the heaven and the earth, that you·hid·away
Mt 12:40 three days and three nights in the heart of·the earth.
Mt 12:42 ·out of·the utmost·parts of·the earth to·hear the
Mt 13:5 ·surface, on·account·of it not having depth of·earth.
Mt 16:19 ·bind on the earth shall·be having·been·bound in
Mt 16:19 ·loose on the earth shall·be having·been·loosed in
Mt 17:25 From whom·do the kings of·the earth take taxes or
Mt 18:18 ·bind on the earth shall·be having·been·bound in
Mt 18:18 ·loose on the earth shall·be having·been·loosed in
Mt 18:19 should·mutually·agree on the earth concerning any
Mt 23:9 call *anyone* yeur father upon the earth, for one is
Mt 23:35 blood being·poured·out upon the earth, from the
Mt 24:30 all the tribes of·the earth shall·vividly·lament,' and
Mt 28:18 authority is·given to·me in heaven and upon earth.
Mk 2:10 has authority on the earth to·forgive moral·failures
Mk 4:5 ·surface, on·account·of it·not having depth of·earth.
Mk 4:31 whenever it·should·be·sown in the earth, *is* least
Mk 4:31 least of·all the variety·of·seeds that·are in the earth.
Mk 9:3 such·as a·cloth-fuller on the earth is·not *even* able
Mk 13:27 from *the* uttermost·part of·earth as·far·as·to *the*
Rm 9:28 a·concise·working·of *the* matter upon the earth."
Jac 5:5 Yeu·indulged·in·delicate·luxury on the earth, and
Jac 5:7 fruit of·the earth, suffering·with·long·patience over it
Jac 5:17 it·did·not shower·rain on the earth *for* three years
1Co 8:5 in heaven or upon the earth (just·as there·are many
Eph 1:10 ·things in the heavens and the·things on the earth.
Eph 3:15 ·lineage in *the* heavens and upon earth is·named:
Eph 4:9 first into the lowermost parts of·the earth?
Eph 6:3 ·you, and you·shall·be a·long·time on the earth."
Col 1:16 and the·ones upon the earth, the·ones clearly·visible
Col 1:20 *they·are* the·things upon the earth or the·things in
Col 3:2 the·things up·above, not the·things upon the earth.
Col 3:5 *to* the·things upon the earth: sexual·immorality,
Rv 1:5 chief·ruler of·the kings of·the earth— the·one loving
Rv 1:7 all the tribes of·the earth shall·vividly·lament over
Rv 3:10 The Land, to·try the·ones residing upon the earth.
Rv 5:3 heaven, nor·even upon the earth, nor·even beneath
Rv 5:3 nor·even beneath the earth, was·able to·open·up the
Rv 5:10 ·offer·a·sacrifice, and we·shall·reign on the earth."
Rv 5:13 on the earth, and beneath the earth, and such·as are
Rv 6:4 to·take the peace from the earth, and that they·should·
Rv 6:8 to·them over the fourth·part of·the earth, to·kill with
Rv 6:8 with viral·death, and by the wild·beasts of·the earth.
Rv 6:10 avenge our blood on the·ones residing on the earth?"
Rv 6:15 And the kings of·the earth, and the greatest·men,
Rv 7:1 on the four corners of·the earth, securely·holding the
Rv 7:1 the four winds of·the earth, in·order·that wind
Rv 7:1 ·that wind should·not blow on the earth, nor on the
Rv 8:13 to·the·ones residing on the earth— from·out·of·the
Rv 9:3 to·them, as the scorpions of·the earth have authority.
Rv 9:4 bring·harm·to the vegetation of·the earth (not·even
Rv 10:5 upon the sea and upon the earth lifted his hand to the
Rv 10:8 the·one standing upon the sea and upon the earth."
Rv 11:4 standing in·the·sight of·the God of·the earth.
Rv 11:10 the·ones residing upon the earth shall·rejoice over
Rv 11:10 prophets tormented the·ones residing on the earth.
Rv 13:8 ·ones residing upon the earth shall·fall·prostrate to·it
Rv 13:11 ascending out of·the earth. And it·was·having two
Rv 13:14 the·ones residing on the earth through *the means·of*
Rv 13:14 saying to·the·ones residing on the earth, to·make a·
Rv 14:3 having·been·kinsman·redeemed from the earth.
Rv 14:6 to·the·ones residing on the earth, and to·every
Rv 14:15 because the harvest of·the earth is·dried·up."
Rv 14:18 ·for·vintage the clusters of·the earth, because her
Rv 14:19 collected·for·vintage the vine of·the earth, and cast
Rv 16:14 ·forth to·the kings of·the earth and of·all The Land,
Rv 16:18 the men·of·clay† were upon the earth, so·vast an·
Rv 17:2 the kings of·the earth committed·sexual·immorality.
Rv 17:5 OF·THE ABOMINATIONS OF·THE EARTH.
Rv 17:8 the·ones residing on the earth shall·marvel, whose
Rv 17:18 having a·kingdom over the kings of·the earth."
Rv 18:3 of·the earth committed·sexual·immorality with her,
Rv 18:3 and the merchants of·the earth became·wealthy out
Rv 18:9 "And the kings of·the earth, the·ones committing·
Rv 18:11 And the merchants of·the earth do·weep and mourn
Rv 18:23 were the greatest·men of·the earth, because by
Rv 18:24 the·ones having·been·slaughtered upon the earth."
Rv 19:19 ·Beast, and the kings of·the earth, and their armies
Rv 20:8 in the four corners of·the earth, Gog and Magog, to·
Rv 20:9 ·up on the breadth of·the earth, and they·surrounded
Rv 21:24 and the kings of·the earth bring their glory and

G1093.3 N-ASF γῆν (5x)
Jn 21:9 ·disembarked upon the dry·ground, they·look·upon
Lk 5:11 mooring the sailboats upon the dry·ground, leaving
Lk 8:27 ·forth upon the dry·ground, there·came·and·met him
Ac 27:43 ·far·overboard first, to·get upon the dry·ground.
Ac 27:44 ·all made·it·thoroughly·safe upon the dry·ground.

G1093.3 N-GSF γῆς (6x)
Jn 6:21 sailboat came·to·be upon the dry·ground for which
Jn 21:8 not at·a·distance from the dry·ground, but·rather
Jn 21:11 and drew the net upon the dry·ground, *with·it being*
Lk 5:3 to·head·off a·little·way from the dry·ground. And
Mk 4:1 crowd was·alongside the sea upon the dry·ground.
Mk 6:47 of·the sea, and he *was* alone upon the dry·ground.

G1093.4 N-NSF γῆ (2x)
1Co 10:26 For "the Land *is* Yahweh's, and its complete·
1Co 10:28 conscience, for "the Land *is* Yahweh's, and its

G1093.4 N-VSF γῆ (3x)
Mt 2:6 you, O·BethLechem, *in·the* land of·Judah, are by·no·
Mt 4:15 "O·Land of·Zebulun and land of·Naphtali, *by the*
Mt 4:15 "O·Land of·Zebulun and land of·Naphtali, *by the*

G1093.4 N-ASF γῆν (16x)
Jn 3:22 and his disciples came into the land of·Judea, and he·
Lk 4:25 ·months, as great famine occurred over all the land,
Lk 23:44 ·was a·darkness over all the land until *the* ninth
Ac 7:3 and come·over·here into a·land which I·shall·show
Ac 7:4 transferred·and·settled him into this land in which
Ac 7:11 a·famine over all the land of·Egypt and Kenaan, and
Ac 13:19 he·fully·apportioned their land to·them by·lot.
Ac 27:39 day, they·were·not recognizing the land, but they·
Heb 11:9 By·trust, he·sojourned in the land of·promise as *in*
Mt 2:20 and traverse into *the* land of·IsraEl, for the·ones
Mt 2:21 and his mother and came into *the* land of·IsraEl.
Mt 9:26 of·this *awakening* went·forth into all that land.
Mt 14:34 ·over, they·came into the land of·Gennesaret.
Mt 27:45 ·was darkness over all the land until the·ninth hour.
Mk 6:53 they·came to the land of·Gennesaret and landed·
Mk 15:33 came·to·be over all the land until *the* ninth hour.

G1093.4 N-DSF γῇ (8x)
Ac 7:6 shall·be a·sojourner in an·estranged·foreign land, and
Ac 7:29 and was a·sojourner in *the* land of·Midian, where
Ac 7:36 wonders and signs in *the* land of·Egypt, and in *the*
Ac 13:17 in the Sojourning in *the* land of·Egypt, and with a·
Ac 13:19 ·demolishing seven nations in *the* land of·Kenaan,
Mt 9:31 ·forth, they·widely·promoted it in all that land.
Mt 10:15 ·shall·be more·tolerable for·the·land of·Sodom and
Mt 11:24 it·shall·be more·tolerable for·the·land of·Sodom in

G1093.4 N-GSF γῆς (6x)
Lk 21:23 ·be great dire·need upon the land and WRATH on
Ac 7:3 "Go·forth from·among your land, and from·among
Ac 7:4 coming·forth from·among *the* land of·the·Kaldeans,
Ac 7:40 who brought us out of·*the*·land of·Egypt, we·do·not
Heb 8:9 hand to·lead them out of·*the*·land of·Egypt, because
Jud 1:5 after·*first*·saving a·People out of·Egypt's land, the

EG1093.4 (1x)
Heb 11:9 ·promise as *in* an·estranged·foreign *land*, residing

G1094 γῆρας gễras *n.* (1x)
Compare:G1088
xLangEquiv:H2208 xLangAlso:H7872

G1094 N-DSN γήρᾳ (1x)
Lk 1:36 also having·conceived a·son in her old·age, and this

G1095 γηράσκω gērásko̅ *v.* (2x)
Roots:G1094 Compare:G3820 G4246 See:G1088
G1126

G1095 V-PAP-NSN γηράσκον (1x)
Heb 8:13 ·made·obsolete and growing·agedly·old *is* close to·

G1095 V-AAS-2S γηράσῃς (1x)
Jn 21:18 whenever you·should·grow·agedly·old, you·shall·

G1096 γίνομαι gínômai *v.* (692x)
Compare:G1511 G5225 G0281 See:G1118
xLangEquiv:H1961

G1096.1 V-FDI-3S γενήσεται (1x)
1Co 4:5 high·praise from God shall·come·to·be to·each·man.

G1096.1 V-PNI-3S γίνεται (2x)
Heb 11:6 ·*trust that* he·comes·to·be an·appropriate·rewarder
Mk 11:23 ·which he·says are·coming·to·be; it·shall·be to·

G1096.1 V-2ADI-1S ἐγενόμην (4x)
1Co 2:3 And I·myself came·to·be alongside yeu in weakness
Rv 1:9 ·endurance of·Jesus Anointed, came·to·be in the
Rv 1:10 I·came·to·be in *the* Spirit on the Lord's day and
Rv 4:2 And immediately I·came·to·be in Spirit, and behold,

G1096.1 V-2ADI-3S ἐγένετο (12x)
Jn 1:3 All·things came·to·be through him, and apart·from
Jn 1:3 not·even one·thing came·to·be that has·come·to·be.
Jn 1:10 world, and the world came·to·be through him, yet
Jn 1:17 the grace and the truth came·to·be through Jesus
Jn 6:21 immediately, the sailboat came·to·be upon the dry·
Lk 2:13 angel, there·came·to·be a·multitude of·*the*·heavenly
Lk 4:36 And amazement came·to·be upon everyone, and
Ac 7:31 *it*, *the* voice of·Yahweh came·to·be alongside him,
Mt 21:42 *stone*. This came·to·be directly·from Yahweh, and
Mk 2:27 "The Sabbath came·to·be on·account·of the Clay·
Mk 12:11 This came·to·be directly·from Yahweh, and it·is
Mk 15:33 hour occurring, darkness came·to·be over all the

G1096.1 V-2ADI-3P ἐγένοντο (1x)
2Pe 2:1 But there·came·to·be false·prophets also among the

G1096.1 V-2ADN γενέσθαι (3x)
Jn 8:58 I·say to·yeu, prior·to AbRaham coming·to·be, I AM.
Ac 19:21 "After I come·to·be there, it·is·mandatory·for me
Ac 22:17 Sanctuary·Atrium, *that* I came·to·be in a·trance

G1096.1 V-2ADP-ASM γενόμενον (2x)
Gal 4:4 his Son, coming·to·be birthed·from·out of·a·woman,
Gal 4:4 ·out of·a·woman, coming·to·be under Torah-Law,

G1096.1 V-2ADP-GSM γενομένου (2x)
Mt 26:6 And with·YeShua coming·to·be in BethAny, in
Rm 1:3 the·one coming·to·be birthed·from·out of·David's

G1096.1 V-2ADP-NSM γενόμενος (2x)
Lk 22:40 And coming·to·be at the place, he·declared to·
2Ti 1:17 But·rather, coming·to·be in Rome, he·sought·for

G1096.1 V-2ADP-NPM γενόμενοι (2x)
Ac 13:5 And coming·to·be at Salamis, they·were·fully·
Ac 27:7 and with·difficulty coming·to·be adjacent·to Cnidus,

G1096.1 V-2ADS-3S γένηται (2x)
Gal 3:14 the blessing of·AbRaham may·come·to·be for the
1Co 16:10 look·out that he·may·come·to·be alongside yeu

G1096.1 V-AOI-3S ἐγενήθη (1x)
1Th 1:5 our good·news did·not come·to·be among yeu in

G1096.1 V-2RAI-3S γέγονεν (7x)
Jn 1:3 not·even one·thing came·to·be that has·come·to·be.
Jn 1:15 right·behind me has·come·to·be ahead of·me,
Jn 1:27 right·behind me who has·come·to·be ahead of·me)
Jn 1:30 me comes a·man who has·come·to·be ahead of·me,
Heb 7:16 (who has·come·to·be *a·priest·that·offers·a·sacrifice*,
Rm 11:5 also, there·has·come·to·be a·remnant according·to
1Ti 2:14 being·deluded, has·come·to·be in violation.

G1096.1 V-2RAI-3P γεγόνασιν (1x)
Rm 16:7 who also have·come·to·be in Anointed-One before

G1096.1 V-2RAN γεγονέναι (1x)

Heb 11:3 for the·thing to·have·come·to·be not from·out of·
G1096.1 V-2RAP-APM γεγονότας (1x)
Jac 3:9 the·ones having·come·to·be according·to a·likeness
G1096.2 V-2ADI-3S ἐγένετο (1x)
1Co 15:45 ·of·clay†, Adam, came·into·being as a·living
G1096.2 V-AOI-3S ἐγενήθη (1x)
2Co 3:7 in writing on stones, came·into·being in glory—
EG1096.2 (1x)
1Co 15:45 ⇒ The last Adam *came·into·being* as a·spirit,
G1096.3 V-FDI-2P γενήσεσθε (2x)
Jn 8:33 ·do you·yourself say, 'Yeu·shall·become free·men?
Jn 15:8 and *that* yeu·shall·become my·personal disciples.
G1096.3 V-FDI-3S γενήσεται (4x)
Jn 10:16 voice, and *together* it·shall·become one flock *and*
Jn 16:20 but·yet yeur grief shall·become a·distinct joy.
Lk 8:17 hidden, that shall·not become apparent; neither
1Co 3:13 each·man's work shall·become apparent, for the
G1096.3 V-PNI-3S γίνεται (13x)
Lk 11:26 of·that man·of·clay† become worse·than the first·
Lk 20:33 whose wife of·them does·she·become? For the
Mt 9:16 from the garment, and *the* tear becomes worse.
Mt 12:45 of·that man·of·clay† become worse·than the first·
Mt 13:22 the Redemptive-word, and he·becomes unfruitful.
Mt 13:32 bigger·than the garden·plants and becomes a·tree,
Mk 2:21 ·fullness from·the old, and *the* tear becomes worse.
Mk 4:19 the Redemptive-word, and it·becomes unfruitful.
Mk 4:32 ·sown, it·springs·up and becomes greater·than all
Rm 11:6 otherwise the grace becomes no·longer grace. But
1Co 14:25 the secrets of·his heart become apparent; and in·
1Ti 6:4 ·of·words, from·out of·which becomes envy, strife,
Rv 8:11 and the third·part *of·the waters* become wormwood;
G1096.3 V-PNM-2S γίνου (3x)
1Ti 4:12 youth, but·rather become a·model·example of·the
Rv 2:10 tribulation ten days. Become trustworthy even·unto
Rv 3:2 Become one·keeping·alert, and firmly·establish the·
G1096.3 V-PNM-2P γίνεσθε (18x)
Lk 6:36 "Accordingly, become compassionate, just·as yeur
Lk 12:40 "Accordingly, yeu·yourselves become ready also,
Mt 6:16 ·should·fast, do·not become sullen-looking just·as
Mt 10:16 of·wolves. Accordingly, become prudent as the
Mt 24:44 ·of that, yeu·yourselves become ready also,
Rm 12:16 Do·not become full·of·notions personally·about
Jac 1:22 Now become doers of·*the*·Redemptive-word, and not
Jac 3:1 not many *of·yeu should* become instructors, having·
Php 3:17 Become co-imitators of·me, brothers, and keep·a·
1Co 4:16 I·implore yeu, become attentive·imitators of·me.
1Co 7:23 ·a·price. Do·not become slaves of·men·of·clay†.
1Co 10:32 Become void·of·offense, even to·Jews, also to·
1Co 15:58 beloved brothers, become immovably·steadfast,
2Co 6:14 Yeu·must·not become disparately·yoked to·
Eph 4:32 And become kind to one·another, tender-hearted,
Eph 5:1 Accordingly, become attentive·imitators of·God, as
Eph 5:7 do·not become co-participants with·them.
Eph 5:17 ·account·of this, do·not become impetuous·ones,
G1096.3 V-PNN γίνεσθαι (1x)
1Co 10:20 ·not want yeu to·become partners with·demons.
G1096.3 V-PNS-1P γινώμεθα (2x)
Gal 5:26 We·should·not become self-conceited·men,
2Co 5:21 we·ourselves may·become God's righteousness in
G1096.3 V-2ADI-1S ἐγενόμην (3x)
Ac 26:19 O·King AgrIppa, I·did·not become obstinate to·the
1Co 9:20 And to·the Jews I·became as a·Jew, in·order·that I·
1Co 9:22 To·the weak, I·became as weak in·order·that I·
G1096.3 V-2ADI-2S ἐγένου (2x)
Lk 19:17 ·good slave! Because you·became trustworthy in
Rm 11:17 among them and became a·partner·together of·the
G1096.3 V-2ADI-2P ἐγένεσθε (3x)
Lk 16:11 So·then, if yeu·did·not become trustworthy with
Lk 16:12 And if yeu·did·not become trustworthy with
Jac 2:4 among yeurselves, and are·become judges with·evil
G1096.3 V-2ADI-3S ἐγένετο (37x)
Jn 1:14 And the Word became flesh and encamped among us
Lk 6:49 And the wreckage of·that home became great."
Lk 9:29 the aspect of·his countenance became different, and
Lk 10:21 in·this·manner, it·became a·delightful·purpose
Lk 13:19 And it·grew and became a·great tree, and the birds
Lk 18:23 these·things, he·became exceedingly·grieved, for
Lk 22:44 And his heavy·sweat became like clots of·blood
Lk 22:66 Now as it·became day, the council·of·elders of·the
Lk 24:19 Jesus of·Natsareth, who became a·man, a·prophet
Lk 24:31 him, and·then he·himself became unviewable by
Ac 7:13 and Joseph's kindred became apparent to·Pharaoh.
Ac 9:42 And it·became known in all Joppa, and many trusted
Ac 10:10 And he·became intensely·hungry and was·wanting
Ac 12:18 the soldiers as·to what was·become of·Peter.
Ac 14:5 And as·soon·as there·became a·violent·attempt
Ac 21:1 And as·soon·as it·became *time for* us to·be·sailing·
Heb 5:9 ·completely·mature, he·became *the* initiating·cause
Heb 11:7 the world and became an·heir of·a·righteousness
Mt 11:26 in·this·manner it·became a·delightful·purpose
Mt 17:2 the sun, and his garments became white as the light.
Mk 4:22 neither·did *anything* become hidden·away, other·
Mk 9:3 And his garments became glistening, exceedingly
Mk 9:26 *spirit* came·forth, and he·became as one·dead—
Rm 11:34 Yahweh's mind? Or who became his counselor?"'
1Co 15:20 dead·men. He·became a·firstfruit of·the·ones
2Co 1:18 Redemptive-word toward yeu did·not become "Yes
2Co 1:19 and me), did·not become "Yes" and·then "No,"
Rv 2:8 First and the Last, who became dead and·yet lived:
Rv 6:12 a·great earthquake; and the sun became *as* black as
Rv 6:12 made·of·hair, and the moon became as blood,
Rv 8:8 the sea, and the third·part of·the sea became blood;
Rv 16:2 upon the earth, and it·became a·bad and evil pus·
Rv 16:3 into the sea, and it·became as blood of·a·dead·man.
Rv 16:4 the wellsprings of·waters, and they·became blood.
Rv 16:10 and his kingdom became plunged·into·darkness.
Rv 16:19 And the Great City became three parts, and the
Rv 18:2 is·fallen, and is·become a·residence of·demons,
G1096.3 V-2ADI-3P ἐγένοντο (7x)
Lk 13:2 Galileans became morally·disqualified above·and·
Lk 23:12 both Pilate and HerOd·AntiPas became friends with
Ac 5:36 ·dissolved, and they·became nothing·at·all.
Mt 28:4 keeping·guard are·shaken and became as·if dead.
Rv 11:13 And the rest became alarmed and gave glory to·the
Rv 11:15 angel sounded, and there·became great voices in
Rv 11:15 kingdoms of·the world are·become *the kingdoms*
G1096.3 V-2ADM-3S γενέσθω (1x)
1Co 3:18 wise in this present·age, let·him·become a·fool, in·
G1096.3 V-2ADN γενέσθαι (16x)
Jn 1:12 to·them he·gave privilege to·become children of·God
Jn 9:27 yeu·yourselves also want to·become his disciples?
Ac 1:22 of·these·men *for* one to·become a·witness together
Ac 7:39 fathers did·not want to·become attentively·obedient,
Ac 26:28 do·you·persuade me to·become 'a·Christian,' a·
Ac 26:29 and among *the* large, to·become such as even·I am
Mt 20:26 whoever should·want to·become great among yeu,
Mk 1:17 I·shall·cause yeu to·become fishers of·men·of·clay†
Mk 10:43 whoever should·want to·become great among yeu,
Mk 10:44 whoever of·yeu should·want to·become foremost,
Rm 4:18 in·order·for himself to·become the father of·many
Rm 7:4 *such* for yeu to·become *yoked·together* with·another,
Php 1:13 in *the* Anointed-One to·become apparent to·all in
Php 3:21 *such·for·it* to·become fundamentally·in·nature·like
1Th 1:7 such·for yeu to·become model·examples to·all the·
1Co 7:21 but·yet if·also you·are·able to·become free, use *it*
G1096.3 V-2ADP-ASF γενομένην (1x)
Rm 7:3 ·be an·adulteress by·becoming *yoked·together* with·
G1096.3 V-2ADP-ASM γενόμενον (1x)
Lk 18:24 after·seeing him becoming exceedingly·grieved,
G1096.3 V-2ADP-GSF γενομένης (4x)
Jn 21:4 But even·now with·it·becoming the·break·of·dawn,
Ac 15:2 Now·then, with·it·becoming of·no little controversy
Ac 23:12 And with·it·becoming day, some of·the Judeans,
Mk 6:35 And even·now with·it·becoming a·late hour, his
G1096.3 V-2ADP-GSM γενομένου (1x)
Ac 1:16 Judas (the·one becoming a·guide to·the·ones
G1096.3 V-2ADP-GPF γενομένων (1x)
Lk 24:5 And with·the *women* becoming alarmed and
G1096.3 V-2ADP-NSM γενόμενος (14x)
Ac 4:11 building; *this·is* the·one becoming the·distinct head
Ac 10:4 And gazing·intently at·him and becoming alarmed,
Ac 12:23 the glory to·God. And becoming worm-eaten, he·
Ac 16:27 becoming awake·out·of·*his*·heavy·sleep and
Ac 24:25 *that* shall·be, Felix, becoming alarmed, answered,
Heb 6:20 ·us— YeShua, after·becoming High·Priest for the
Heb 7:26 ·disqualified·men, and becoming higher·than the
Heb 11:24 By·trust, Moses (after·becoming full·grown)
Gal 3:13 curse of·the Torah-Law, becoming a·curse on·our
Mk 6:26 And the king became exceedingly·grieved, *yet* on·
Jac 1:12 ·trial, because after·becoming verifiably·approved,
Php 2:7 *the* fundamental·nature of·a·slave, becoming in *the*
Php 2:8 becoming attentively·obedient as·far·as·unto death,
Php 3:6 (the·one in *the* Torah-Law), becoming blameless.
G1096.3 V-2ADP-NPM γενόμενοι (3x)
Lk 1:2 ·*them*·down to·us after·becoming eyewitnesses and
Lk 24:37 But being·terrified and becoming alarmed, they·
Ac 19:28 *these·things*, they·were·becoming full·of·rage, and
G1096.3 V-2ADS-1S γένωμαι (2x)
1Co 9:23 in·order·that I·may·become a·partner·together of·it
1Co 9:27 to·others, I·myself should·become disqualified.
G1096.3 V-2ADS-1P γενώμεθα (1x)
Tit 3:7 by·his grace, we·should·become heirs according·to
G1096.3 V-2ADS-2P γένησθε (5x)
Heb 6:12 ·that yeu·should·not become bastardly·slothful, but
Mt 5:45 so·that yeu·may·become the·Sons of·yeur Father,
Mt 18:3 ·should·be·turned·back and should·become as the
1Pe 3:13 if yeu·should·become attentive·imitators of·the
2Pe 1:4 through these, yeu·may·become partners of·divine
G1096.3 V-2ADS-3S γένηται (12x)
Lk 4:3 declare to·this stone that it·should·become bread."
Mt 10:25 for·the disciple that he·should·become as his
Mt 23:15 and whenever he·should·become·one, yeu·make
Mt 24:32 whenever its branch should·become tender and
Mk 9:50 but if the salt should·become unsalty, with what
Mk 13:28 whenever its branch should·become tender and
Rm 3:19 world may·become liable·under·justice before·God
Rm 7:13 the commandment, may·become most exceedingly
Rm 15:31 for JeruSalem may·become well·acceptable to·the
1Co 3:18 a·fool, in·order·that he·may·become wise.
1Co 8:9 of·yeurs should·become a·stumbling·block to·the·
Phm 1:6 the fellowship of·your trust may·become active by
G1096.3 V-2ADS-3P γένωνται (4x)
Jn 9:39 and the·ones looking·about may·become blind."
Jn 12:42 they·should·not become cut·off·from·the·gathering,
Mt 4:3 declare that these stones should·become bread."
1Co 11:19 verifiably·approved may·become apparent among
G1096.3 V-AOI-1P ἐγενήθημεν (3x)
Rm 9:29 for·us, we·would·have become as Sodom, and
1Co 4:9 because we·have·now·become a·public·spectacle
1Co 4:13 ·reviled, we·entreat. We·have·now·become as
G1096.3 V-AOI-2P ἐγενήθητε (3x)
1Pe 3:6 *It·is* of·her·whom yeu·did·become children, while·
1Th 1:6 yeu·yourselves did·become attentive·imitators of·us
1Th 2:14 brothers, did·become attentive·imitators of·the
G1096.3 V-AOI-3S ἐγενήθη (6x)
Lk 20:17 ·as·unfit, the·same has·now·become the·distinct
Mt 21:42 ·as·unfit, the·same has·now·become the·distinct
Mk 12:10 ·as·unfit, the·same has·now·become the·distinct
Rm 16:2 for she·herself did·become a·patroness of·many,
1Pe 2:7 ·as·unfit, this·one has·now·become the·distinct
2Co 7:14 *we·made* before Titus) has·now·become truth.
G1096.3 V-AOI-3P ἐγενήθησαν (2x)
Heb 11:34 weakness were·enabled, did·become strong in
Col 4:11 who did·become a·personal·comfort to·me.
G1096.3 V-AOM-2P γενήθητε (1x)
1Pe 1:15 Also yeu·yourselves must·become holy in all *yeur*
G1096.3 V-AOM-3S γενηθήτω (1x)
Ac 1:20 "Let his walled-off·mansion become desolate, and
G1096.3 V-AOP-APM γενηθέντας (1x)

Heb 6:4 ·present, and becoming participants of·Holy Spirit,
G1096.3 V-AOP-NPM γενηθέντες (1x)
Heb 10:33 while·yeu·were·becoming partners with·the·
G1096.3 V-2RAI-1S γέγονα (5x)
Gal 4:16 As·such, have·I·become yeur enemy, being·
1Co 9:22 To·every one, I·have·become all things in·order·
1Co 13:1 ·not have love, I·have·become *as* a·reverberating
1Co 13:11 as an·infant. But when I·have·become a·man, I·
2Co 12:11 I·have·become impetuous in·boasting! Yeu
G1096.3 V-2RAI-1P γεγόναμεν (1x)
Heb 3:14 For we·have·become partaking·companions of·
G1096.3 V-2RAI-2S γέγονας (2x)
Jn 5:14 to·him, "See, you·have·become healthy·and·sound;
Jac 2:11 you·have·become a·transgressor of·Torah-Law.
G1096.3 V-2RAI-2P γεγόνατε (2x)
Heb 5:11 since yeu·have·become bastardly·slothful with·the
Heb 5:12 of·God. And yeu·have·become ones·having need
G1096.3 V-2RAI-3S γέγονεν (9x)
Heb 7:22 YeShua has·become a·surety of·a·significantly·
Gal 3:24 the Torah-Law has·become our strict·elementary·
Rm 2:25 your circumcision has·become uncircumcision.
Rm 7:13 the beneficially·good, has·it·become death to·me?
Jac 2:10 ·up in one *point*, he·has·become held·liable of·all
Jac 5:2 ·rotted, and yeur garments have·become moth-eaten.
1Th 2:1 accessible·entrance to yeu has·not become empty.
2Co 1:19 "No," but·rather in him has·become "Yes."
2Co 5:17 behold, all·things have·become brand-new.
G1096.3 V-2RAI-3S@ γέγονεν (1x)
2Pe 2:20 the final·states have·become worse for·them
G1096.3 V-2RAI-3P γεγόνασιν (2x)
Heb 12:8 ·discipline (of·which all have·become participants)
1Jn 2:18 even now many have·become adversaries·of·the·,
G1096.3 V-2RAN γεγονέναι (1x)
Lk 10:36 to·you to·have·become a·neighbor to·the·one
G1096.3 V-2RAP-NPM γεγονότες (2x)
Heb 7:21 ·sacrifices were having·become *priests* apart·from
Heb 7:23 the·ones having·become priests·that·offer·sacrifices,
G1096.3 V-RPI-2P γεγένησθε (2x)
Ac 7:52 now of·whom, yeu have·become betrayers and
1Th 2:8 souls, on·account·that yeu·have·become dear to·us.
G1096.3 V-RPN γεγενῆσθαι (1x)
Rm 15:8 Anointed to·have·become an·attendant of·*the*·
G1096.3 V-LAI-3S ἐγεγόνει (1x)
Jn 6:17 CaperNaum. And even·now it·had·become dark, and
EG1096.3 (1x)
1Co 7:6 this in concession *concerning* becoming *married*,
G1096.4 V-FDI-3S γενήσεται (2x)
Jn 15:7 yeu·should·determine, and it·shall·happen for·yeu.
Mt 18:19 ·request, it·shall·happen for·them personally·by
G1096.4 V-PNI-3S γίνεται (3x)
Lk 12:54 a·thunderstorm,' and in·this·manner it·happens.
Lk 12:55 'There·shall·be blazing·heat,' and it·happens.
Mk 4:37 And there·happens a·great whirling·of·wind, and
G1096.4 V-PNI-3P γίνονται (1x)
Mk 6:2 that even such miracles happen through his hands?
G1096.4 V-PNN γίνεσθαι (5x)
Lk 21:7 whenever these·things should·be·about to·happen?"
Lk 21:28 beginning to·happen, pull·yourself·up·straight and
Lk 21:36 these·things, the·ones being·about to·happen, and
Ac 26:22 and Moses spoke of·as·being·about to·happen:
1Co 7:36 ·prime and financial·need so happens, let·him·do
G1096.4 V-PNP-ASN γινόμενον (1x)
Ac 28:6 not·even·one·thing out·of·place happening to him,
G1096.4 V-PNP-APN γινόμενα (3x)
Lk 9:7 heard all the·things which·are·happening by him, and
Lk 21:31 yeu·should·see these·things happening, yeu also
Mk 13:29 ·see these·things happening, yeu·must·know that
G1096.4 V-PNP-DPN γινομένοις (1x)
Lk 13:17 all the·glorious·things, the·ones happening by him.
G1096.4 V-PNP-NSN γινόμενον (1x)
Ac 12:9 ·known that the·thing happening through the angel
G1096.4 V-2ADI-3S ἐγένετο (72x)
Jn 1:28 These·things happened in BethAbara across the
Lk 1:8 Now it·happened (with him performing·priestly·
Lk 1:23 And it·happened, as·soon·as the days of·his public·
Lk 1:41 And it·happened, as·soon·as EliSabeth heard the
Lk 1:65 And a·reverent·fear·and·awe happened on all the·
Lk 2:1 And it·happened in those days, *that* there·went·forth
Lk 2:15 And it·happened, after the angels went·away from
Lk 2:46 after three days, it·happened *that* they·found him in
Lk 3:21 Now it·happened, when absolutely·all the people
Lk 5:1 And it·happened, with the crowd pressing·upon him
Lk 5:12 And it·happened with him being in one of·the cities,
Lk 5:17 And it·happened on a·certain day, even while he·
Lk 6:12 And it·happened in those days *that* he·went·forth to
Lk 7:11 And it·happened on the next·day *that* he·was·
Lk 8:1 Now it·happened in the subsequent·order, that he·
Lk 8:22 Now it·happened on one of·the days that he·himself
Lk 8:40 And it·happened, *that*, when Jesus returned·back,
Lk 9:18 And it·happened, in his *usual time* to·be praying
Lk 9:28 And it·happened about eight days after these sayings
Lk 9:33 And it·happened, with the·*two·men* thoroughly·
Lk 9:37 And it·happened, *that* on the next day, with·them
Lk 9:51 And it·happened, among the days to·be·completely·
Lk 9:57 And it·happened to·them, while·traversing along the
Lk 10:38 Now it·happened, with them traversing, that he·
Lk 11:1 Now it·happened, as he·himself was praying in a·
Lk 11:14 and it was mute. And it·happened, with the demon
Lk 11:27 And it·happened, as he was·saying these·things,
Lk 14:1 And it·happened, with him going into a·house of·a·
Lk 16:22 "And it·happened *as·such, for* the helpless·beggar
Lk 17:11 to JeruSalem, it·happened that he·himself went
Lk 17:14 priests·that·offer·sacrifices." And it·happened, with
Lk 18:35 And it·happened, with him drawing·near to Jericho
Lk 19:15 "And it·happened, with him coming·back after·
Lk 19:29 And it·happened, as·soon·as he·drew·near to
Lk 20:1 And it·happened, *that* on one of·those days, with·
Lk 24:4 And it·happened, with them thoroughly·perplexing
Lk 24:15 And it·happened, with them conversing, then
Lk 24:30 And it·happened, with him fully·reclining·back·to·
Lk 24:51 And it·happened, with him blessing them, *that* he·
Ac 4:5 And it·happened on the next·day, *that* their rulers and
Ac 6:1 multiplying, there·happened a·grumbling of·the
Ac 9:32 all *the regions*, it·happened *such·for* Peter to·come·
Ac 9:37 And it·happened in those days, *that* being·sick, she
Ac 9:43 And it·happened *such·for* him to·abide a·significant·
Ac 10:25 And as·soon·as Peter happened to·enter, Cornelius
Ac 11:26 him to Antioch. And it·happened, *such·for* them
Ac 11:28 which even happened in·the·days of·Claudius
Ac 14:1 *as in·Antiochia*, it·happened the same·way in
Ac 16:16 Now *later*, it·happened with·us traversing to
Ac 19:1 Apollos being in Corinth, it·happened *that* Paul,
Ac 19:10 And this happened for·a·span·of two years, such·
Ac 21:5 And when it·happened *for* us to·properly·finish·out
Ac 22:6 around midday, it·happened suddenly from·out of·
Ac 22:17 "And it·happened, with·me returning·back to
Ac 27:44 ·ship. And in·this·manner it·happened *that* they·all
Ac 28:8 And it·happened *that* the father of·Poplius lay·ill,
Ac 28:17 And after three days, it·happened *that* Paul called·
Mt 7:28 And it·happened *that* when YeShua entirely·
Mt 9:10 And it·happened, while·he is·reclining·at·a·meal in
Mt 11:1 And it·happened *that* when YeShua finished
Mt 13:53 And it·happened *that* when YeShua finished these
Mt 19:1 And it·happened *that* when YeShua finished these
Mt 26:1 And it·happened *that* when YeShua finished all
Mk 1:9 And it·happened in those days *that* Jesus came from
Mk 2:15 And it·happened, with him laying·back·to·eat in
Mk 4:4 And it·happened, as he *began* to·sow, that, in·fact,
Mk 5:16 of·how it·happened to·the·one being·possessed·
1Th 3:4 to·be·hard-pressed, even just·as it·happened, and
2Ti 3:11 *my* afflictions— such·as·what happened to·me at
Rv 8:7 first angel sounded, and there·happened hail and fire
Rv 11:13 And in that hour there·happened a·great earthquake
Rv 16:18 earthquake, such·as did·not happen since the men·
G1096.4 V-2ADI-3P ἐγένοντο (4x)
Lk 10:13 Because if these miracles happened in Tyre and
Mt 11:20 large·majority of·his miracles happened, because
Mt 11:23 miracles happening in you had·happened in Sodom
Rv 16:18 And there·happened voices, and thunders, and
G1096.4 V-2ADN γενέσθαι (9x)
Jn 3:9 "How·are these·things able to·happen?"
Jn 13:19 I·relate *it* to·yeu before it·happens in·order·that,
Jn 14:29 *it* to·yeu prior·to *it* happening, in·order·that,
Ac 4:28 hand and your counsel predetermined to·happen.
Mt 24:6 ·mandatory·for all *these·things* to·happen, but·still
Mt 26:54 it·is·mandatory·for *it* to·happen in·this·manner?
Mk 13:7 ·is·mandatory·for *such·things* to·happen, but·rather
Rv 1:1 to·his slaves what is·mandatory to·happen in haste.
Rv 4:1 ·which it·is·mandatory to·happen after these·things."
G1096.4 V-2ADO-3S γένοιτο (16x)
Lk 1:38 of·Yahweh! May·it·happen to·me according·to your
Lk 20:16 *this*, they·declared, "May·it·never happen!"
Gal 2:17 ·attendant of·moral·failure? May·it·never happen!
Gal 3:21 the promises of·God? May·it·never happen! For if
Gal 6:14 But may·it·never happen for·me to·boast, except in
Rm 3:4 May·it·never happen! And let God be true, but every
Rm 3:6 May·it·never happen! Otherwise how·does God
Rm 3:31 through the trust? May·it·never happen! But·rather,
Rm 6:2 May·it·never happen! We·are those·who died to·
Rm 6:15 but·rather under grace? May·it·never happen!
Rm 7:7 the Torah-Law moral·failure? May·it·never happen!
Rm 7:13 death to·me? May·it·never happen! But·rather
Rm 9:14 unrighteousness with God? May·it·never happen!
Rm 11:1 shove·away his People? May·it·never happen! For
Rm 11:11 ·that they·should·fall? May·it·never happen! But·
1Co 6:15 members of·a·prostitute? May·it·never happen!
G1096.4 V-2ADP-ASN γενόμενον (1x)
Lk 23:47 seeing the·thing *that·was* happening, glorified
G1096.4 V-2ADP-APN γενόμενα (6x)
Lk 4:23 ·many·things·as we·heard happening in CaperNaum,
Lk 23:48 observing the·things happening, while·beating
Mt 18:31 after·seeing the·things that·were·happening, were
Mt 18:31 ·clearly·related all the·things that·were·happening.
Mt 27:54 earthquake and the·things happening, they·feared
Mt 28:11 chief·priests absolutely·all the·things happening.
G1096.4 V-2ADP-GSN γενομένου (1x)
Ac 28:9 In·due·course, with·this happening, the rest also,
G1096.4 V-2ADP-GSF γενομένης (4x)
Lk 6:48 solid·rock. And with·a·flash·flood happening, the
Ac 2:6 Now while·this sound was·happening, the multitude
Mk 4:17 or persecution happening on·account·of the
2Co 1:8 our tribulation, the·one happening to·us in Asia,
G1096.4 V-2ADP-NSM γενόμενος (1x)
Lk 10:32 "And likewise a·Levite, happening by the place,
G1096.4 V-2ADP-NPF γενόμεναι (2x)
Lk 10:13 Tyre and Tsidon, the·ones happening in yeu, long·
Mt 11:23 Because if the miracles happening in you had·
G1096.4 V-2ADS-3S γένηται (14x)
Jn 5:14 lest something worse should·happen to·you."
Jn 13:19 ·that, whenever it·should·happen, yeu·may·trust
Jn 14:29 ·that, whenever it·should·happen, yeu·may·trust.
Lk 14:12 in·return, and a·recompense may·happen to·you.
Lk 21:32 no, should·not pass·away, until all should·happen.
Ac 20:16 so·that it·should·not happen to·him to·linger·away
Mt 5:18 ·away from the Torah-Law until all should·happen.
Mt 18:12 "If it·should·happen *that* any man·of·clay† *has* a·
Mt 18:13 And if he·should·happen to·find it, certainly I·say
Mt 24:20 that yeur fleeing should·not happen in·winter, nor·
Mt 24:21 present, neither, no, it·should·not happen *again*.
Mt 24:34 pass·away, until all these·things should·happen.
Mk 13:19 present, and no, it·should·not *ever* happen *again*.
Mk 13:30 so·long·as·until all these·things should·happen.
G1096.4 V-2RAI-3S γέγονεν (14x)
Jn 12:30 "This voice has·happened not on·account·of me,
Jn 14:22 "Lord, how has·it·happened that you intend to·
Lk 14:22 declared, 'Lord, it·has·happened as you·ordered,
Ac 7:40 ·do·not personally·know what has·happened to·him.
Mt 1:22 And all this has·happened, in·order·that it·may·be·
Mt 19:8 *the* beginning it·has·not happened in·this·manner.

Mt 21:4 But all this has·happened in·order·that it·may·be·
Mt 26:56 "But all this has·happened in·order·that the
Mk 5:33 personally·knowing what has·happened in her,
Mk 9:21 a·time has·it·been *that* this has·happened to·him?
Mk 13:19 such as has·not happened from *the* beginning of·
Rm 11:25 *the* stony·hardness has·happened to·IsraEl *only* in
Rv 16:17 from the throne, saying, "It·has·happened!"
Rv 21:6 And he·declared to·me, "It·has·happened! I AM the
G1096.4 V-2RAP-ASN γεγονός (5x)
Lk 8:35 they·went·out to·see what·was·happening. And
Lk 8:56 to·not·even·one·man the·thing having·happened.
Lk 24:12 marveling to himself at·the·thing having·happened.
Ac 5:7 having·seen the·thing having·happened, entered·in.
Ac 13:12 Then after·seeing the·thing having·happened, the
G1096.4 V-2RAP-DSN γεγονότι (1x)
Ac 4:21 ·glorifying God over the·thing having·happened.
G1096.4 V-2RAP-NSN γεγονός (1x)
Mk 5:14 ·out to·see what it·was, the·thing having·happened.
G1096.4 V-RPP-ASN γεγενημένον (1x)
Lk 8:34 after·seeing the·thing having·happened, they·fled;
G1096.4 V-LAI-3S ἐγεγόνει (1x)
Ac 4:22 this miraculous·sign of·healing had·happened.
EG1096.4 (4x)
Jn 15:25 "But·yet *this·happened*, in·order·that the word may·
Rm 11:7 So·then, what *happened*? IsraEl did·not obtain that
Jac 4:14 ·with the·thing *that shall·happen* tomorrow! For
Php 1:12 that the·things *which·happened* against me have·
G1096.5 V-FDI-3S γενήσεται (1x)
1Co 15:54 ·with immortality, then shall·occur the saying,
G1096.5 V-PNI-3S γίνεται (4x)
Lk 15:10 *that such* joy occurs in·the·sight of·the angels of·
Heb 7:12 being·transferred, there·occurs out of·necessity
Mt 26:2 after two days the Passover occurs, and·then the
2Pe 1:20 does·not itself·occur from·a·private explanation.
G1096.5 V-PNN γίνεσθαι (1x)
Ac 27:33 And even·until daylight was·about to·occur, Paul
G1096.5 V-PNP-ASN γινόμενον (1x)
Lk 23:8 to·see some miraculous·sign occurring by him.
G1096.5 V-PNP-APN γινόμενα (1x)
Eph 5:12 ·to the·things which·are·occurring among them
G1096.5 V-PNP-APF γινομένας (1x)
Ac 8:13 ·observing both signs and great miracles occurring.
G1096.5 V-PNP-DSF γινομένῃ (1x)
1Pe 4:12 upon·yeu (occurring specifically·for a·proof·trial
G1096.5 V-PNP-GPN γινομένων (1x)
Ac 24:2 and with·upright·reforms occurring in·this nation
G1096.5 V-2ADI-3S ἐγένετο (22x)
Jn 3:25 there·occurred a·question·and·discussion from·
Jn 6:16 Now as early·evening occurred, his disciples walked·
Jn 10:22 *(also called Chanukkah)* occurred in JeruSalem,
Lk 1:44 ·as the sound of·your greeting occurred in my ears,
Lk 1:59 And it·occurred on the eighth day, *that* they·came
Lk 2:2 first occurred with·Cyrenius being·governor of·Syria)
Lk 2:6 And it·occurred, with them being there, *that* the days
Lk 6:1 And it·occurred on the·first Sabbath after·the·second·
Lk 6:6 And it·occurred also on another Sabbath, *for* him to·
Lk 15:14 spending all *of·it*, there·occurred a·strong famine
Ac 5:12 many signs and wonders occurred among the people
Ac 9:3 the *regular·course·of* traversing, it·occurred *for* him
Ac 10:16 Now this occurred three·times, and the vessel was·
Ac 11:10 And this occurred three·times, and absolutely·all
Ac 15:39 So·then a·sharp·disagreement occurred, such·for
Ac 19:23 in that season, there·occurred no little disturbance
Ac 23:7 speaking that, there·occurred a·controversy *between*
Ac 23:9 And there·occurred a·great *amount·of* yelling.
Mt 8:24 And behold, a·great tempest occurred in the sea,
Mt 28:2 And behold, there·occurred a·great earthquake. For
Mk 2:23 And it·occurred *for* him to·be·traversing·directly
Mk 11:19 early·evening occurred, he·was·traversing·forth
G1096.5 V-2ADI-3P ἐγένοντο (2x)
Mt 11:21 miracles occurring in yeu had·occurred in Tyre and
Rv 11:19 in his Temple. And there·occurred lightnings, and
G1096.5 V-2ADM-3S γενέσθω (1x)
1Co 14:26 All·things must·occur specifically·for edification
G1096.5 V-2ADN γενέσθαι (3x)
Lk 3:22 upon him, and a·voice occurred from·out of·heaven,
Lk 9:36 And with the voice occurring, Jesus was·found alone
Lk 21:9 for it·is·mandatory·for these·things to·occur first.
G1096.5 V-2ADP-ASN γενόμενον (1x)
Ac 10:37 personally·know the utterance occurring in all
G1096.5 V-2ADP-ASF γενομένην (3x)
Lk 23:19 ·account·of a·certain insurrection occurring in the
Ac 13:32 ·the·good·news, the promise occurring toward the
Ac 26:4 *my* youth (the·one occurring since beginning in my·
G1096.5 V-2ADP-APN γενόμενα (1x)
Lk 24:18 and did·not know the·things occurring among her
G1096.5 V-2ADP-GSN γενομένου (2x)
Jn 13:2 And with·supper occurring, with·the Slanderer even·
Mk 6:2 And with·Sabbath occurring, he·began to·instruct in
G1096.5 V-2ADP-GSF γενομένης (24x)
Lk 4:42 And with·day occurring, going·forth, he·traversed
Ac 11:19 by the tribulation, the·one occurring over Stephen,
Ac 12:18 Now with·day occurring, there·was no little
Ac 15:7 mutual·questioning·and·discussion occurring, after·
Ac 16:35 And with·daylight occurring, the court·officers
Ac 21:40 And with·a·large silence occurring, he·addressed
Ac 23:10 So·now with·a·large controversy occurring, the
Ac 25:26 that, after·the investigation occurring, I·may·have
Mt 8:16 And with·early·evening occurring, they·brought to·
Mt 13:21 or with·persecution occurring on·account·of the
Mt 14:15 And with·early·evening occurring, his disciples
Mt 14:23 to·pray, and with·early·evening occurring, he·was
Mt 16:2 to·them, "With·early·evening occurring, yeu·say,
Mt 20:8 "So with·early·evening occurring, the owner of·the
Mt 26:20 with·early·evening occurring, he·was·reclined·at·
Mt 27:1 And with·the·break·of·dawn occurring, all the chief·
Mt 27:57 And with·early·evening occurring, there·came a·
Mk 1:32 And with·early·evening occurring, when the sun
Mk 4:35 same day, with·early·evening occurring, he·says
Mk 6:21 Now with·there·occurring a·day of·happy·occasion,
Mk 6:47 And with·early·evening occurring, the sailboat was
Mk 14:17 And with·early·evening occurring, he·comes with
Mk 15:33 with·*the*·sixth hour occurring, darkness came·to·
Mk 15:42 even·now, with·early·evening occurring, since it·
G1096.5 V-2ADP-GSM γενομένου (1x)
Heb 9:15 with·death already·occurring for a·full·ransom
G1096.5 V-2ADP-NPF γενόμεναι (1x)
Mt 11:21 Because if the miracles occurring in yeu had·
G1096.5 V-2ADS-3S γένηται (2x)
Lk 1:20 *the* day that these·things should·occur, because you·
Mt 26:5 ·day, lest a·commotion should·occur among the
G1096.5 V-2RAI-3S γέγονεν (2x)
Mt 25:6 "And at·the·middle of·night, a·yell has·occurred,
Mk 14:4 "Why·has this total·ruin of·the ointment occurred?
G1096.5 V-2RAN γεγονέναι (1x)
2Ti 2:18 the resurrection even·now to·have·occurred, and
G1096.5 V-2RAN@ γεγονέναι (1x)
Jn 12:29 "*It·was only* thunder *that* has·occurred." Others
G1096.5 V-2RAP-ASN γεγονός (1x)
Lk 2:15 ·see this utterance, the·one having·occurred, which
G1096.5 V-2RAP-NSM γεγονώς (1x)
Gal 3:17 (the·one having·occurred four·hundred and thirty
EG1096.5 (7x)
Lk 21:9 "Moreover, the end does·not *occur* immediately."
Lk 24:35 ·in·detail the·things *that occurred* along the way,
Ac 15:2 with·mutual·questioning·and·discussion *occurring*
Mt 8:33 they·announced all the·things *occurring*, and·also
2Co 9:5 not as·though·some act·of·coveting *was·occurring*.
Col 4:7 ·known to·yeu all the·things *occurring* against me.
Col 4:9 ·known to·yeu all·things, the·ones *occurring* here.
G1096.6 V-PNP-ASM γινόμενον (1x)
Jn 6:19 ·along on the sea and coming near to·the sailboat.
G1096.6 V-2ADI-3S ἐγένετο (18x)
Jn 1:6 There·came a·man·of·clay† having·been·dispatched
Jn 10:35 ·to whom the Holy·word of·God came, and the
Lk 3:2 ·priests— an·utterance of·God came to John the son
Lk 9:34 ·him saying these·things, there·came a·thick·cloud,
Lk 9:35 And there·came a·voice from·out of·the thick·cloud,
Lk 19:9 "Today, Salvation did·come to·this house, because·
Lk 22:14 And when the hour came, *Jesus* sat·back·to·eat,
Ac 2:2 ·warning, there·came a·reverberating·sound from·out
Ac 2:43 And reverent·fear·and·awe came upon·every soul,
Ac 5:5 And great reverent·fear came upon all the·ones
Ac 5:11 And great reverent·fear came upon all the Called·
Ac 10:13 And there·came a·voice to him, *saying*, "Peter,
Ac 19:34 that he·was a·Jew, there·came one voice from·out
Ac 21:30 and the people came running·together. And
Ac 21:35 And when he·came to the stairs, *the need* befell
Ac 27:27 as·soon·as the·fourteenth night was·come, with·us
Mk 1:11 And there·came a·voice from·out of·the heavens,
Rv 12:10 heaven, "At·this·moment did·come the Salvation,
G1096.6 V-2ADO-3S γένοιτο (1x)
Ac 5:24 about them as·to what would·come of·this.
G1096.6 V-2ADP-GPM γενομένων (1x)
Ac 21:17 And with·us coming to JeruSalem, the brothers
G1096.6 V-2ADP-NSM γενόμενος (2x)
Ac 7:38 "This *Moses* is the·one already·coming among the
Ac 12:11 And after·coming to himself, Peter declared,
G1096.6 V-2ADP-NPF γενόμεναι (1x)
Lk 24:22 us astonished us, after·coming at·early·sunrise to
G1096.6 V-2ADS-3S γένηται (4x)
Mt 21:19 "No·longer should fruit come out·from you unto
Rm 7:3 Accordingly, if she·should·come to·another man
2Th 2:7 *is·doing so* until he·should·come out of·*the*·middle.
Col 1:18 ·things he·himself may·come to·be·foremost·of·all,
G1096.6 V-AOI-1P ἐγενήθημεν (1x)
1Th 2:5 For not·even at·any·time did·we·come with a·word
G1096.6 V-2RAI-2S γέγονας (1x)
Jn 6:25 "Rabbi, when did·you·come here?
EG1096.6 (1x)
Ac 21:18 ·entered together with·us *to·come* alongside Jacob;
G1096.7 V-FDI-3S γενήσεται (1x)
Jn 4:14 that I·shall·give him, it·shall·be in him a·wellspring
G1096.7 V-FDP-ASN γενησόμενον (1x)
1Co 15:37 you·sow not the body that·shall·be, but·rather a·
G1096.7 V-PNI-3S γίνεται (2x)
Heb 7:18 For there·is, in·fact, a·cancellation of·a·preceding
Heb 9:22 ·from a·pouring·out·of·blood, there·is no pardon.
G1096.7 V-PNM-2S γίνου (2x)
Jn 20:27 into my side. And do·not be distrusting, but·rather
Lk 19:19 he·declared likewise to·him, 'Be you also over
G1096.7 V-PNM-2P γίνεσθε (6x)
Gal 4:12 Brothers, I·petition yeu, be as I·myself *am*,
1Co 10:7 Yeu·must·not·even be idolaters, just·as *were* some
1Co 11:1 Be attentive·imitators of·me, just·as I·also *am* of·
1Co 14:20 Brothers, be not little·children in·the
1Co 14:20 But in·the contemplations be completely·mature.
Col 3:15 ·forth in one Body; and be expressively·thankful.
G1096.7 V-PNM-3S γινέσθω (2x)
Rm 3:4 And let God be true, but every man·of·clay† a·liar;
1Co 16:14 In love, all of·yeu, BE!
G1096.7 V-PNN γίνεσθαι (2x)
Jac 3:10 kindly·needed·for these·things to·be in·this·manner.
Rv 1:19 the·things·which are·about to·be after these·things.
G1096.7 V-PNP-NPM γινόμενοι (1x)
1Pe 5:3 ·allotment, but·rather being model·examples to·the
G1096.7 V-PNS-1P γινώμεθα (1x)
3Jn 1:8 ·men, in·order·that we·may·be coworkers with·the
G1096.7 V-PNS-3P γίνωνται (1x)
1Co 16:2 ·prosper, lest there·should·be no contributions
G1096.7 V-2ADI-1S ἐγενόμην (2x)
Ac 20:18 into Asia, with·what·manner I·have·been with yeu
Rv 1:18 And *I·AM* the·one living, and was dead; and behold,
G1096.7 V-2ADI-3S ἐγένετο (39x)
Jn 2:1 And on·the third day, there·was a·wedding in Qanah
Jn 5:9 immediately the man·of·clay† was healthy·and·sound.
Jn 7:43 Accordingly, there·was a·severing·schism among
Jn 10:19 Accordingly, there·was a·severing·schism again
Lk 1:5 ·Judea, there·was a·certain priest·that·offers·sacrifices

Lk 2:42 And when he·was twelve years·of·age, after·
Lk 4:25 lunar·months, as great famine occurred over all the
Lk 6:13 And when it·was day, he·hailed his disciples *to·*
Lk 6:16 and Judas IsCariot, who also was a·betrayer.
Lk 8:24 And they·ceased, and there·was calm.
Lk 11:30 For just·as Jonah was a·sign to·the Ninevites, in·
Lk 17:26 "And just·as it·was in the days of·Noach, in·this·
Lk 17:28 "Likewise, *it·shall·be* also as it·was in the days of·
Lk 22:24 And there·was also a·fond·contention among them,
Lk 23:44 sixth hour, and there·was a·darkness over all the
Ac 1:19 And it·was known to·all the·ones residing·in
Ac 5:7 And it·was about an·interval of·three hours, and his
Ac 7:29 fled at this saying, and was a·sojourner in *the* land
Ac 8:1 And on that·very day, there·was a·great persecution
Ac 8:8 And there·was great joy in that city.
Ac 9:19 he·was·strengthened. Now Saul was among the
Ac 16:26 And without·warning there·was a·great earthquake,
Ac 19:17 And this was known to·all the·ones residing·in
Ac 20:37 And everyone was weeping a·long·while. And
Ac 27:39 And when it·was day, they·were·not recognizing
Ac 27:42 And the soldiers' counsel was that they·should·kill
Heb 2:2 the word being·spoken through angels was steadfast,
Mt 8:26 the winds and the sea, and there·was a·great calm.
Mt 27:45 *the* sixth hour, there·was darkness over all the
Mk 1:4 John was immersing in the wilderness and officially·
Mk 4:10 And when he·was alone·by·himself, the·ones in·
Mk 4:39 the wind subsided, and there·was a·great calm.
Mk 6:14 *of·him*, for his name was openly·well·known. And
Mk 9:7 Then there·was a·thick·cloud overshadowing them,
2Ti 3:9 ·be obvious to·all, as it·was also with·these·men.
Rv 6:12 ·seal, and behold, there·was a·great earthquake;
Rv 8:1 the seventh official·seal, there·was silence in the
Rv 12:7 And there·was war in the heaven.
Rv 16:18 and lightnings. And there·was a·great earthquake,

G1096.7 V-2ADI-3P ἐγένοντο (4x)
Lk 13:4 that these·men were delinquent above·and·beyond
Ac 22:9 did·distinctly·view the light and were alarmed, but
Rv 8:5 and cast *it* upon the earth; and there·were voices, and
Rv 16:18 happen since the men·of·clay† were upon the earth,

G1096.7 V-2ADM-2P γένεσθε (1x)
1Pe 1:16 it·has·been·written, "Yeu·must·be holy, because I

G1096.7 V-2ADM-3S γενέσθω (1x)
Lk 22:26 ·one greater among yeu, let·him·be as the younger,

G1096.7 V-2ADN γενέσθαι (3x)
Ac 10:40 on·the third day and gave him to·be manifest,
Ac 20:16 if it·were possible for·him, to·be in JeruSalem *on*
Ac 27:29 *·the·*stern, they·were·well-wishing·for *it* to·be day.

G1096.7 V-2ADP-DPM γενομένοις (2x)
Ac 15:25 ·good to·us, being with·the·same·determination,
Mk 16:10 *·were* with him, to·those·being in·mourning and

G1096.7 V-2ADP-GSM γενομένου (1x)
Ac 25:15 concerning whom, with·me being at JeruSalem,

G1096.7 V-2ADP-NSM γενόμενος (5x)
Lk 22:44 And being in a·strenuous·agony, he·was·praying
Ac 7:32 ' But Moses, being terrified·with·trembling, was·
Ac 16:29 he·rushed·in, and being terrified·with·trembling,
Mk 9:33 ·came to CaperNaum, and once·being in the home,
Jac 1:25 ·continuing *in·it*, this·man being not a·forgetful

G1096.7 V-2ADP-NPM γενόμενοι (1x)
Ac 27:36 they·themselves were all of·a·cheerful·outlook,

G1096.7 V-2ADS-2P γένησθε (2x)
Jn 12:36 light, in·order·that yeu·may·be the·Sons of·Light."
Php 2:15 in·order·that yeu·may·be blameless and untainted,

G1096.7 V-2ADS-3S γένηται (10x)
Jn 9:22 he·should·be cut·off·from·the·gathering.
Lk 20:14 ·should·kill him, that the inheritance may·be ours.'
Heb 2:17 ·become·like *them*, that he·may·be a·merciful and
Mt 23:26 in·order·that their exterior may·be pure also.
Mk 13:18 But pray that yeur fleeing should·not be in·winter.
Rm 15:16 ·up of·the Gentiles may·be well·acceptable,
1Th 3:5 yeu and our wearisome·labor should·be for naught.
2Co 8:14 ·that their abundance also may·be *a·supply* for yeur
2Co 8:14 for yeur lacking, that there·may·be equality.

Eph 6:3 "in·order·that it·may·be well with·you, and you·

G1096.7 V-AOI-1P ἐγενήθημεν (1x)
1Th 2:7 But·rather we·were pleasantly·engageable in *the*

G1096.7 V-AOI-3S ἐγενήθη (2x)
Ac 4:4 and the number of·the men was about five thousand.
1Co 15:10 the·one *bestowed* upon me, was not empty. But·

G1096.7 V-AOI-3P ἐγενήθησαν (1x)
1Co 10:6 Now these·things were our imprinted·examples,

G1096.7 V-AOM-3S γενηθήτω (1x)
Mt 9:29 "According·to yeur trust be·it to·yeu."

G1096.7 V-AOP-NPM γενηθέντες (1x)
2Pe 1:16 But·rather yeu·were·being beholders of·that

G1096.7 V-2RAI-1P γεγόναμεν (1x)
Rm 6:5 if we·have·been congenitally·fused·together in·the

G1096.7 V-2RAI-3S γέγονεν (1x)
Mt 24:21 such·as has·not been since *the* world's beginning

G1096.7 V-2RAP-NSF γεγονυῖα (1x)
1Ti 5:9 ·than sixty years·of·age, having·been a·wife of·one

EG1096.7 (2x)
Ac 8:6 crowds, *being together* with·the·same·determination,
2Co 8:13 *that* yeur abundance *may·be a·supply* for their

G1096.8 V-AOI-1P ἐγενήθημεν (2x)
1Th 1:5 ·know *that* we·behaved·ourselves as·such among
1Th 2:10 blamelessly, we·behaved·ourselves among·yeu,

G1096.9 V-FDI-3S γενήσεται (1x)
Mt 21:21 and be·you·cast into the sea,' it·shall·be·done.

G1096.9 V-PNI-3S γίνεται (1x)
Mk 4:11 *that·are* outside, all·*these*·things are·done in the

G1096.9 V-PNM-3S γινέσθω (1x)
1Co 14:40 *Even·so*, all·things must·be·done decently and in

G1096.9 V-PNN γίνεσθαι (2x)
Ac 4:30 ·signs and wonders to·be·done through the name of·
Ac 14:3 ·signs and wonders to·be·done through their hands).

G1096.9 V-INI-3S ἐγίνετο (1x)
Ac 2:43 and many wonders and signs were·done through the

G1096.9 V-2ADI-3S ἐγένετο (2x)
Jn 19:36 For these·things were·done that the Scripture
Lk 24:21 marks this third day since these·things were·done.

G1096.9 V-2ADM-3S γενέσθω (2x)
Lk 22:42 not my will, but·rather yours be·done."
Ac 21:14 "The will of·the Lord be·done."

G1096.9 V-2ADN γενέσθαι (2x)
Lk 23:24 rendered·judgment *for* their request to·be·done.
Rv 22:6 ·things·*of*·which it·is·mandatory to·be·done in haste

G1096.9 V-2ADS-3S γένηται (2x)
Lk 23:31 *·is* green·with·sap, what should·be·done to the
1Co 9:15 in·order·that it·should·be·done in·this·manner to

G1096.9 V-AOM-3S γενηθήτω (5x)
Lk 11:2 kingdom come. Your will be·done, as in heaven, so·
Mt 6:10 kingdom come. Your will be·done— as in heaven,
Mt 8:13 and as you·trusted, *so* be·it·done to·you." And his
Mt 15:28 *is* your trust! It·is·done for·you as you·wanted.
Mt 26:42 me unless I·should·drink it, your will be·done."

G1096.9 V-AOP-GPN γενηθέντων (1x)
Heb 4:3 *he·declared this* with·the works being·done from *the*

G1096.9 V-2RAI-3S γέγονεν (1x)
Ac 4:16 miraculous·sign has·been·done through them *is*

G1096.10 V-PNI-3S γίνεται (1x)
Mt 27:24 ·yet rather *that* a·commotion is·being·made, taking

G1096.10 V-PNP-NSF γινομένη (1x)
Ac 12:5 earnest prayer over him was being·made to God by

G1096.10 V-PNP-NPM γινόμενοι (1x)
Ac 19:26 saying that the *gods* being·made through hands are

G1096.10 V-INI-3S ἐγίνετο (1x)
Jn 5:4 water was·made healthy·and·sound from·whatever

G1096.10 V-2ADI-1S ἐγενόμην (4x)
Rm 10:20 not seeking me; I·was·made manifest to·the·ones
Eph 3:7 I·was·made a·steward of·this *good·news* according·
Col 1:23 heaven), of·which I, Paul, am·made an·attendant.
Col 1:25 of·which I·myself am·made an·attendant,

G1096.10 V-2ADI-3S ἐγένετο (1x)
Ac 20:3 to·sail into Syria, he·made a·plan to·return·back

G1096.10 V-2ADN γενέσθαι (2x)
Jn 5:6 ·him, "Do·you·want to·be·made healthy·and·sound?
Ac 27:16 ·difficulty we·exercised·strength to·make the skiff

G1096.10 V-2ADP-GSF γενομένης (2x)
Ac 20:3 *But* with·a·plot being·made against·him by the Jews
Ac 26:6 *the* expectation of·the promise being·made by God

G1096.10 V-2ADP-NSM γενόμενος (1x)
Heb 1:4 being·made so·much significantly·better·than the

G1096.10 V-AOI-2P ἐγενήθητε (1x)
Eph 2:13 once being at·a·distance, are·made near by the

G1096.10 V-AOI-3S ἐγενήθη (1x)
1Co 1:30 in Anointed-One Jesus, who is·made to·us wisdom

G1096.10 V-AOM-3S γενηθήτω (1x)
Rm 11:9 "Let their table be·made into a·snare, and into a·

G1096.10 V-AON γενηθῆναι (1x)
Heb 5:5 did·not glorify himself to·be·made a·high·priest,

G1096.10 V-RPP-ASN γεγενημένον (1x)
Jn 2:9 ·the·banquet tasted the water having·been·made wine,

G1096.11 V-2ADP-NSM γενόμενος (1x)
Ac 1:18 for·the injustice; and falling·downhill headfirst, he·

G1097 γινώσκω ginṓskō *v.* (224x)

Compare:G1492 G2467 See:G1108 G1107 G1106 G1110 G1110-1 G1109
xLangEquiv:H3045 A3046

G1097.1 V-FDI-1S γνώσομαι (2x)
Lk 1:18 to the angel, "How shall·I·know this for·certain?
1Co 4:19 Lord should·determine, and I·shall·know, not the

G1097.1 V-FDI-2S γνώσῃ (1x)
Jn 13:7 ·this·moment, but you·shall·know after these·things.

G1097.1 V-FDI-2P γνώσεσθε (5x)
Jn 8:28 the Son of·Clay·Man†, yeu·shall·know that I AM,
Jn 8:32 and yeu·shall·know the truth, and the truth shall·set
Jn 14:20 In that day, yeu shall·know that I·myself *am* in my
Mk 4:13 How·else then shall·yeu·know all the parables?
2Co 13:6 But I·expect that yeu·shall·know that we·ourselves

G1097.1 V-FDI-3S γνώσεται (1x)
Jn 7:17 ·want to·do his will, he·shall·know concerning the

G1097.1 V-FDI-3P γνώσονται (2x)
Jn 13:35 By this, everyone shall·know that yeu·are disciples
Rv 2:23 and all the Called·Out·citizenries shall·know that I

G1097.1 V-FPI-3S γνωσθήσεται (5x)
Lk 8:17 ·away, that shall·not be·known and may·come to *be*
Lk 12:2 be·revealed, nor hidden that shall·not be·known.
Mt 10:26 be·revealed, and hidden, that shall·not be·known.
1Co 14:7 musical·notes, how shall·it·be·known *what tune*
1Co 14:9 word, how shall·it·be·known, the·thing being·

G1097.1 V-PAI-1S γινώσκω (6x)
Jn 10:14 AM the good shepherd, and I·know my *sheep*, and
Jn 10:15 Father knows me, so·even·I know the Father, and
Jn 10:27 listen·to my voice, and·I know them, and they·
Ac 19:15 evil spirit declared, "Jesus I·know, and Paul I·am·
Rm 7:15 For I·do·not know *why* I·perform that·which *I·do*.
1Co 13:12 At·this·moment, I·know from·out of·a·portion,

G1097.1 V-PAI-1P γινώσκομεν (10x)
1Co 13:9 For we·know from·out of·a·portion *of·the whole*,
2Co 5:16 ·to flesh, yet now we·know *him* no·longer *in·this·*
1Jn 2:3 And in this we·do·know that we·have·known him, if
1Jn 2:5 In this, we·do·know that we·are in him.
1Jn 2:18 ·of·the·Anointed-One, by·which we·know that it·is
1Jn 3:19 And by this we·know that we·are birthed·from·out
1Jn 3:24 And by this we·know that he·presently·abides in us,
1Jn 4:6 As·a·result of·this, we·know the spirit of·truth and
1Jn 4:13 By this we·know that we·abide in him, and he·
1Jn 5:2 By this we·know that we·love the children of·God,

G1097.1 V-PAI-2S γινώσκεις (6x)
Jn 1:48 says to·him, "From·what·source do·you·know me?
Jn 3:10 of·IsraEl, and you·do·not know these·things?
Ac 8:30 ·so, *that* you·know what·things you·read·aloud?
Ac 21:37 *·commander* replied, "Do·you·know Greek?
Rm 2:18 and know the will, and examine·and·verify the·
2Ti 1:18 *to·me* at Ephesus, you·yourself know even·better.

G1097.1 V-PAI-2P γινώσκετε (10x)
Jn 8:43 "Why do·yeu·not know my speech?
Jn 14:7 and from this·moment·on, yeu·do·know him, and

Jn 14:17 him. But yeu·yeurselves do·know him, because he·
Lk 21:30 ·looking·about, yeu·know by yeur·own·selves that
Ac 20:34 Now yeu·yeurselves know that these hands tended
Mt 16:3 ·acting·hypocrites, in·fact yeu·know to·discern the
Mt 24:32 ·forth the leaves, yeu·know that the summer *is*
Mk 13:28 ·forth the leaves, yeu·know that the summer is
Php 2:22 But yeu·know the proof·of·him, that as a·child
1Jn 2:29 that he·is righteous, *then* yeu·know that any one

G1097.1 V-PAI-3S γινώσκει (12x)
Jn 7:27 not·even·one·man knows from·what·source he·is."
Jn 10:15 "Just·as the Father knows me, so·even·I know the
Jn 14:17 it·does·not observe him, nor·even knows him. But
Lk 10:22 Father. And not·even·one·man knows who the Son
Lk 12:46 at an·hour when he·does·not know, and shall·cut
Lk 16:15 of·the men·of·clay†, but God knows yeur hearts;
Ac 19:35 ·of·clay† is·there that does·not know *that* the·city
Mt 24:50 *him*, and at an·hour that he·does·not know,
1Co 3:20 again, "Yahweh knows the deliberations of·the
1Jn 3:1 that, the world does·not know us, because it·did·not
1Jn 3:20 is greater·than our heart, and he·knows all·things.
1Jn 4:7 ·born from·out of·God and presently·knows God.

G1097.1 V-PAM-2S γίνωσκε (1x)
2Ti 3:1 But know this, that in *the* last days perilous seasons

G1097.1 V-PAM-2P γινώσκετε (12x)
Jn 13:12 to·them, "Yeu·must·know what I·have·done for·
Jn 15:18 the world hates yeu, yeu·know that it·has·hated me
Lk 10:11 ·*it*·off against·yeu. Moreover, know this, that the
Lk 12:39 "And know this, that if the master·of·the·house
Lk 21:31 ·things happening, yeu also know that the kingdom
Heb 13:23 Yeu·know *that·our* brother TimoThy *is* having·
Gal 3:7 Consequently, know that the·ones birthed·from·out
Mt 24:33 ·see all these·things, yeu·must·know that he·is
Mt 24:43 "But know this, that if the master·of·the·house
Mk 13:29 these·things happening, yeu·must·know that he·is
2Co 8:9 For yeu·know the grace of·our Lord Jesus Anointed,
1Jn 4:2 By this yeu·presently·know the Spirit of·God: every

G1097.1 V-PAM-3S γινωσκέτω (3x)
Ac 2:36 all *the* house of·IsraEl must·know securely that God
Mt 9:30 "Clearly·see·to·it *that* no·one knows *I·did this*."
Jac 5:20 he·must·know that the·one turning·back·around a·

G1097.1 V-PAN γινώσκειν (2x)
Jn 2:24 ·them, on·account·of him knowing all *men·of·clay†*,
Php 1:12 Now I·am·resolved for·yeu to·know, brothers, that

G1097.1 V-PAP-DPM γινώσκουσιν (1x)
Rm 7:1 (for I·speak to·the·ones·knowing Torah-Law), that

G1097.1 V-PAP-NSM γινώσκων (2x)
Jn 7:49 this crowd, the·one not knowing the Oral-law, they·
1Jn 4:6 ·out of·God. The·one presently·knowing God hears

G1097.1 V-PAP-NPM γινώσκοντες (6x)
Heb 10:34 of·yeur holdings, knowing for yeurselves to·have
Rm 6:6 knowing this, that our old man·of·clay† is·already·
Jac 1:3 knowing that the proof·testing of·yeur trust
2Pe 1:20 while·knowing this first, that every prophecy of·
2Pe 3:3 while·knowing this first, that there·shall·come in the
Eph 5:5 For yeu·are knowing this·thing, that every sexually·

G1097.1 V-PAS-1P γινώσκωμεν (1x)
1Jn 5:20 ·insight, that we·should·know the·one *who·is* true,

G1097.1 V-PAS-3S γινώσκῃ (1x)
Jn 17:23 in·order·that the world may·know that you·yourself

G1097.1 V-PAS-3P γινώσκωσιν (1x)
Jn 17:3 is the eternal life-above, that they·may·know you, the

G1097.1 V-PPI-1S γινώσκομαι (1x)
Jn 10:14 and I·know my *sheep*, and am·known by mine.

G1097.1 V-PPI-3S γινώσκεται (2x)
Lk 6:44 For each tree is·known from·out of·its·own fruit.
Mt 12:33 For out of·the fruit, the tree is·known.

G1097.1 V-PPP-NSF γινωσκομένη (1x)
2Co 3:2 in our hearts, being·known and being·read·aloud by

G1097.1 V-IAI-3S ἐγίνωσκεν (3x)
Jn 2:25 man·of·clay†, for he·himself was·knowing what was
Lk 7:39 were a·prophet, he·would·be knowing who and
Mk 15:10 For he·was·knowing that the chief·priests had·

G1097.1 V-IAI-3P ἐγίνωσκον (1x)
Lk 18:34 neither were·they·knowing the·things being·said.

G1097.1 V-2AAI-1S ἔγνων (6x)
Jn 17:25 ·not know you, but I·myself knew you, and these
Lk 8:46 of·me, for I·myself did·know power going·forth
Lk 16:4 I·know what I·shall·do, in·order·that, whenever I·
Mt 7:23 to·them, 'Not·even·at·any·time did·I·know yeu! '
Mt 25:24 declared, 'Lord, I·knew you that you·are a·hard
Rm 7:7 But·yet, I·did·not know Moral·Failure, except

G1097.1 V-2AAI-2S ἔγνως (3x)
Lk 19:42 saying, "If you·knew, even you, at·least in this
Lk 19:44 because you·did·not know the season of·your
Lk 24:18 JeruSalem, and did·not know the·things occurring

G1097.1 V-2AAI-3S ἔγνω (17x)
Jn 1:10 ·to·be through him, yet the world did·not know him.
Jn 4:1 as·soon·as the Lord knew that the Pharisees *had*
Jn 4:53 Accordingly, the father knew that *it·was* at that hour,
Jn 12:9 crowd from·among the Judeans knew that he·was
Jn 13:28 who·was·reclining·at·the·meal knew particularly
Jn 16:19 Now·then, Jesus knew that they·were·wanting to·
Jn 17:25 Father, the world did·not know you, but I·myself
Lk 2:43 And Joseph and his mother did·not know *of·it*.
Mk 5:29 blood was·dried·up, and she·knew in·her body that
Rm 10:19 I·say, ¿!·Did IsraEl not know? First Moses says,
Rm 11:34 '" For who knew Yahweh's mind?
1Co 1:21 world through the wisdom did·not know God, God
1Co 2:16 For "who knew Yahweh's mind that he·shall·
2Ti 2:19 ·seal, '" Yahweh already·knows the·ones being his
1Jn 3:1 does·not know us, because it·did·not know him.
1Jn 4:8 not presently·loving does·not already·know God,
Rv 2:17 which not·even·one·man did·know except the·one

G1097.1 V-2AAI-3P ἔγνωσαν (16x)
Jn 7:26 Perhaps the rulers truly do·know that this truly is the
Jn 8:27 They·did·not know that he·was·saying to·them
Jn 10:6 *Pharisees* did·not know what·*sort·of* things it·was
Jn 12:16 But his disciples did·not know these·things at·the
Jn 16:3 ·do to·yeu, because they·did·not know the Father,
Jn 17:8 received *them*; and they·knew truly that I·came·forth
Jn 17:25 knew you, and these knew that you dispatched me.
Lk 20:19 hands on him, for they·knew that he·declared this
Ac 17:13 ·soon·as the Jews from ThessaloNica knew that the
Heb 3:10 and they·themselves did·not know my ways.'
Mt 21:45 the chief·priests and the Pharisees knew that *it·was*
Mt 24:39 and they·did·not know … until the Deluge came,
Mk 12:12 the crowd, for they·knew that he·declared the
Rm 3:17 And a·way of·peace, they·did·not know."
1Co 2:8 has·known, for if they·knew *it*, they·would·have
Rv 2:24 *of·JeZebel* and who did·not know "the depths of·

G1097.1 V-2AAM-2S γνῶθι (1x)
Heb 8:11 his brother, saying, "Know Yahweh," because all

G1097.1 V-2AAM-2P γνῶτε (1x)
Lk 21:20 ·surrounded by army·camps, then know that her

G1097.1 V-2AAM-3S γνώτω (1x)
Mt 6:3 do·not·let your left·hand know what your right·hand

G1097.1 V-2AAN γνῶναι (16x)
Lk 8:10 "To·yeu it·has·been·given to·know the mysteries
Ac 1:7 "It·is not for·yeu to·know times or seasons which the
Ac 17:19 saying, "Are·we·able to·know what this
Ac 17:20 we·resolve to·know what these·things are·
Ac 21:34 And not being·able to·know the absolute·certainty
Ac 22:14 of·our fathers handpicked you to·know his will,
Ac 22:30 being·resolved to·know the absolute·certainty *as*·
Ac 23:28 And being·resolved to·know the legal·charge on·
Ac 24:11 with·you being·able to·know that there·are not
Mt 13:11 it·has·been·given to·yeu to·know the mysteries of·
Mk 4:11 "It·has·been·given to·yeu to·know the mystery of·
Mk 7:24 he·was·wanting not·even·one·man to·know *it*, but
Jac 2:20 But do·you·want to·know, O empty man·of·clay†,
Php 3:10 *and* to·know him and the power of·his resurrection,
1Th 3:5 no·longer, I·sent·word in·order to·know yeur trust,
1Co 2:14 And he·is·not able to·know *it*, because it·is·

G1097.1 V-2AAP-ASM γνόντα (1x)
2Co 5:21 For the·one not knowing moral·failure made

G1097.1 V-2AAP-NSM γνούς (12x)
Jn 5:6 this·man laying·ill and knowing that he·had·been *in*·
Jn 6:15 So Jesus, knowing that they·are·about to·come and
Lk 12:47 And that slave, the·one knowing his lord's will and
Lk 12:48 And the·one not knowing but doing things·
Ac 23:6 Then Paul, already·knowing that the one part were
Mt 12:15 And YeShua knowing *it*, departed from·there.
Mt 16:8 But YeShua knowing *this*, declared to·them, "O·
Mt 22:18 But YeShua, knowing their evil, declared, "Why·
Mt 26:10 But YeShua, knowing *of·it*, declared to·them,
Mk 8:17 And upon·knowing *it*, Jesus says to·them, "Why·
Mk 15:45 And after·knowing *it* from the Roman·centurion,
Php 2:19 ·in·*my*·soul, after·knowing the·things concerning

G1097.1 V-2AAP-NPM γνόντες (5x)
Lk 9:11 And the crowds, after·knowing *it*, followed him.
Gal 2:9 so·then after·knowing the grace being·given to·me,
Gal 4:9 But now, after·knowing God, or rather being·known
Mk 6:38 ·out and see." And already·knowing, they·say,
Rm 1:21 on·account·that, already·knowing God, they·

G1097.1 V-2AAS-1S γνῶ (1x)
2Co 2:9 I·wrote, that I·may·know yeur proof·of·character,

G1097.1 V-2AAS-2S γνῷς (1x)
Rv 3:3 and no, you·should·not know which hour I·shall·

G1097.1 V-2AAS-2P γνῶτε (4x)
Jn 10:38 trust the works in·order·that yeu·may·know, and
Jn 19:4 to·yeu, in·order·that yeu·may·know that I·find not·
2Co 2:4 ·be·grieved, but·rather that yeu·may·know the love
Eph 6:22 that yeu·may·know the·things concerning us, and

G1097.1 V-2AAS-3S γνῷ (7x)
Jn 7:51 him beforehand, and should·know what *it·is that* he·
Jn 11:57 that if any·man should·know where he·is, he·
Jn 14:31 in·order·that the world may·know that I·love the
Lk 19:15 , in·order·that he·may·know how·much each·man
Mk 5:43 them repeatedly that no·one should·know this, and
Mk 9:30 he·was·not willing that any·man should·know *it*.
Col 4:8 in·order·that he·may·know the·things concerning

G1097.1 V-2AAS-3P γνῶσιν (2x)
Ac 21:24 and *so·that* all may·know how·that, of·which·
Rv 3:9 feet, and *that* they·should·know that I·myself loved

G1097.1 V-API-3S ἐγνώσθη (2x)
Lk 24:35 the way, and how he·was·known to·them in the
Ac 9:24 Now their plot was·known to·Saul. And they·were·

G1097.1 V-APM-3S γνωσθήτω (1x)
Php 4:5 Yeur fairness, let·it·be·known to·all men·of·clay†.

G1097.1 V-APP-NPM γνωσθέντες (1x)
Gal 4:9 after·knowing God, or rather being·known by God,

G1097.1 V-RAI-1S ἔγνωκα (2x)
Jn 5:42 but·rather I·have·known yeu, that yeu·do·not have
1Jn 2:4 The·one saying, "I·have·known him," yet not

G1097.1 V-RAI-1P ἐγνώκαμεν (6x)
Jn 6:69 have·trusted and have·known that you·yourself are
Jn 8:52 to·him, "Now we·have·known that you·have a·
2Co 5:16 if we·have·known Anointed-One according·to
1Jn 2:3 And in this we·do·know that we·have·known him, if
1Jn 3:16 By this we·have·known the love *of·God*, because
1Jn 4:16 And we·ourselves have·known and have·trusted the

G1097.1 V-RAI-2S ἔγνωκας (1x)
Jn 14:9 ·time with yeu, and have·you·not known me, Philip?

G1097.1 V-RAI-2P ἐγνώκατε (4x)
Jn 8:55 "Yet yeu·have·not known him, but I·myself have·
1Jn 2:13 fathers, because yeu·have·known the·one *who·is*
1Jn 2:13 little·children, because yeu·have·known the Father
1Jn 2:14 fathers, because yeu·have·known the·one *who·is*

G1097.1 V-RAI-3S ἔγνωκεν (3x)
1Co 2:8 of·the rulers of·this present·age has·known, for if
1Co 8:2 *from·experience*, he·has·known not·even·one·thing,
1Jn 3:6 has·not clearly·seen him, neither has·known him.

G1097.1 V-RAI-3P ἔγνωκαν (1x)
Jn 17:7 "Now they·have·known that all·things, as·much·as

G1097.1 V-RAP-NPM ἐγνωκότες (1x)
2Jn 1:1 but·rather also all the·ones having·known the truth,

G1097.1 V-LAI-2P ἐγνώκειτε (3x)
Jn 14:7 "If yeu·had·known me, yeu·would·have known my
Jn 14:7 ·had·known me, yeu·would·have known my Father

Mt 12:7 But if yeu·had·known what it·means, “I·want
EG1097.1 (1x)
Ac 8:31 how·is·it *that* I·might be·able *to·know them*, unless
G1097.2 V-PAI-2S γινώσκεις (1x)
Jn 21:17 you·yourself absolutely·know that I·have·affection·
G1097.2 V-2AAN γνῶναι (2x)
1Co 8:2 it·is·necessary *for·one* to·absolutely·know *a·thing*.
Eph 3:19 and to·absolutely·know the surpassing knowledge
G1097.2 V-RPI-3S ἔγνωσται (1x)
1Co 8:3 God, the·same has·been·absolutely·known by him.
G1097.3 V-PAI-1S γινώσκω (1x)
Lk 1:34 since I·do·not have·intimate·knowledge·of a·man?
G1097.3 V-IAI-3S ἐγίνωσκεν (1x)
Mt 1:25 he·was·not having·intimate·knowledge·of her until

G1098 γλεῦκος glêûkôs *n.* (1x)
Compare:G3631 G3690 See:G1099
G1098.2 N-GSN γλεύκους (1x)
Ac 2:13 having·been·excessively·filled with·sweet·wine.”

G1099 γλυκύς glykýs *adj.* (4x)
xLangAlso:H4966
G1099.1 A-NSN γλυκύ (2x)
Rv 10:9 but·yet it·shall·be in your mouth sweet as honey.”
Rv 10:10 it; and it·was in my mouth sweet as honey. And
G1099.2 A-ASN γλυκύ (2x)
Jac 3:11 same narrow·opening *with·both* the fresh *water* and
Jac 3:12 *is·able* to·produce *both* salt water and fresh.

G1100 γλῶσσα glôssa *n.* (50x)
Compare:G1258
xLangEquiv:H3956 xLangAlso:H8193
G1100.1 N-NSF γλῶσσα (7x)
Lk 1:64 was·opened·up at·once, and his tongue *loosed*, and
Ac 2:26 is·made·merry, and my tongue leaped·for·joy, and
Rm 14:11 ·me, and every tongue shall·explicitly·affirm God
Jac 3:5 Even in·this·manner, the tongue is a·small member,
Jac 3:6 And the tongue *is* a·fire; *it·is* the world of·
Jac 3:6 ·this·manner, the tongue is·fully·established among
Php 2:11 and every tongue should·explicitly·affirm that
G1100.1 N-NPF γλῶσσαι (1x)
Ac 2:3 And thoroughly·differing tongues as of·fire were·
G1100.1 N-ASF γλῶσσαν (4x)
Lk 16:24 in·water and may·cool·down my tongue, because I·
Jac 1:26 *yet* not bridling his tongue, but·rather deluding his·
Jac 3:8 among·clay·men† is·able to·tame the tongue. *It·is*
1Pe 3:10 ·good days must·restrain his tongue from wrong
G1100.1 N-APF γλώσσας (1x)
Rv 16:10 And they·gnawed their tongues as·a·result of·the
G1100.1 N-DSF γλώσσῃ (1x)
1Jn 3:18 love in·word, nor·even in·tongue, but·rather in·
G1100.1 N-DPF γλώσσαις (1x)
Rm 3:13 ·up; with·their tongues, they·were·using·guile.”
G1100.1 N-GSF γλώσσης (2x)
Mk 7:33 ears, and after·spitting, he·laid·hold of·his tongue,
Mk 7:35 and the impediment of·his tongue was·loosed, and
G1100.2 N-NPF γλῶσσαι (1x)
Rv 17:15 and crowds, and nations, and native·tongues.
G1100.2 N-ASF γλῶσσαν (2x)
Rv 13:7 to·it over all tribes, and native·tongues, and nations.
Rv 14:6 nation, and tribe, and native·tongue, and people,
G1100.2 N-DPF γλώσσαις (2x)
Ac 2:11 in·our native·tongues the magnificent·things of·God
Rv 10:11 and nations, and native·tongues, and kings.
G1100.2 N-GSF γλώσσης (1x)
Rv 5:9 ·out of·every tribe, and native·tongue, and people,
G1100.2 N-GPF γλωσσῶν (2x)
Rv 7:9 and peoples, and native·tongues, standing in·the·
Rv 11:9 peoples and tribes and native·tongues and nations,
G1100.3 N-NPF γλῶσσαι (2x)
1Co 13:8 if·also bestowed·tongues, they·shall·cease; if·also
1Co 14:22 As·such, the bestowed·tongues are for a·sign, not
G1100.3 N-ASF γλῶσσαν (1x)
1Co 14:26 has an·instruction, has a·bestowed·tongue, has a·
G1100.3 N-DSF γλώσσῃ (6x)
1Co 14:2 the·one speaking in·a·bestowed·tongue speaks not
1Co 14:4 speaking in·a·bestowed·tongue does·edify himself,
1Co 14:13 speaking in·a·bestowed·tongue must·pray that he·
1Co 14:14 For if I·should·pray in·a·bestowed·tongue, my
1Co 14:19 ·than ten·thousand words in a·bestowed·tongue.
1Co 14:27 does·speak in·a·bestowed·tongue, accordingly *let·*
G1100.3 N-DPF γλώσσαις (12x)
Ac 2:4 to·speak·in different bestowed·tongues, just·as the
Ac 10:46 speaking in·bestowed·tongues and magnifying God
Ac 19:6 and they·were·speaking with·bestowed·tongues and
Mk 16:17 they·shall·speak in·brand-new bestowed·tongues;
1Co 12:30 Not all speak in·bestowed·tongues. Not all
1Co 13:1 with·the bestowed·tongues of·the men·of·clay†
1Co 14:5 I·want yeu all to·speak with·bestowed·tongues, but
1Co 14:5 the·one speaking with·bestowed·tongues, except
1Co 14:6 to yeu speaking with·bestowed·tongues, how shall·
1Co 14:18 more·than all of·yeu with·bestowed·tongues.
1Co 14:23 and all should·speak with·bestowed·tongues, and
1Co 14:39 do·not forbid to·speak with·bestowed·tongues.
G1100.3 N-GSF γλώσσης (1x)
1Co 14:9 *are* yeu, through the bestowed·tongue. *For* unless
G1100.3 N-GPF γλωσσῶν (3x)
1Co 12:10 ·*differing* kinds of·bestowed·tongues, and to·
1Co 12:10 and to·another, translation of·bestowed·tongues.
1Co 12:28 *thoroughly·differing* kinds of·bestowed·tongues.

G1101 γλωσσό•κομον glōssókômôn *n.* (2x)
Roots:G1100 G2889 Compare:G4082
G1101.3 N-ASN γλωσσόκομον (2x)
Jn 12:6 and was·holding the money·bag, and was·lifting·
Jn 13:29 since Judas was·holding the money·bag, that Jesus

G1102 γναφεύς gnaphêús *n.* (1x)
G1102 N-NSM γναφεύς (1x)
Mk 9:3 white as snow, such·as a·cloth-fuller on the earth is·

G1103 γνήσιος gnḗsiôs *adj.* (4x)
Roots:G1078 Compare:G4101 G3545 See:G1104
G1077
G1103.1 A-VSM γνήσιε (1x)
Php 4:3 And I·ask·of you also, a·genuine yokefellow, assist
G1103.1 A-DSN γνησίῳ (2x)
Tit 1:4 To·Titus, a·genuine child according·to a·shared trust.
1Ti 1:2 To·TimoThy, a·genuine child in trust.
G1103.2 A-ASN γνήσιον (1x)
2Co 8:8 and to·test·and·prove the genuineness of·yeur love.

G1104 γνησίως gnēsíôs *adv.* (1x)
Roots:G1103
G1104 ADV γνησίως (1x)
Php 2:20 who genuinely shall·be·anxious·about the·things

G1105 γνόφος gnóphôs *n.* (1x)
Compare:G2217 G3509 G3658-1 See:G1104-1
G1105-1 G1105-2
xLangEquiv:H6205
G1105.2 N-DSM γνόφῳ (1x)
Heb 12:18 ·set·ablaze with·fire, nor to·stormy·gloom, and

G1106 γνώμη gnṓmē *n.* (9x)
Roots:G1097 Compare:G1011 G1012 G1013 G1378
G1917 G1962 G4909 See:G1771 G3563
G1106.2 N-ASF γνώμην (3x)
1Co 7:25 But I·give *my* advice, as one·having·been·shown·
1Co 7:40 she·should·remain, according·to my advice; and I·
2Co 8:10 And in this, I·give advice, for this is·advantageous
G1106.3 N-GSF γνώμης (1x)
Phm 1:14 ·one·thing apart·from your input, in·order·that
G1106.4 N-NSF γνώμη (1x)
Ac 20:3 into Syria, he·made a·plan to·return·back through
G1106.4 N-ASF γνώμην (3x)
Rv 17:13 “These have *just* one plan, and they·thoroughly·
Rv 17:17 gave in their hearts to·do his plan, and to·do *just*
Rv 17:17 his plan, and to·do *just* one plan, also to·give their
G1106.4 N-DSF γνώμῃ (1x)
1Co 1:10 ·reformed into the same mind and in the same plan.

G1107 γνωρίζω gnōrízō *v.* (24x)
Roots:G1097
G1107.1 V-FAI-1S γνωρίσω (1x)
Jn 17:26 to·them your name, and shall·make·*it*·known—
G1107.1 V-FAI-3S γνωρίσει (2x)
Eph 6:21 Tychicus shall·make·known to·yeu all·things. *He·*
Col 4:7 Tychicus shall·make·known to·yeu all the·things
G1107.1 V-FAI-3P γνωριοῦσιν (1x)
Col 4:9 yeu. They·shall·make·known to·yeu all·things, the·
G1107.1 V-PAI-1S γνωρίζω (3x)
Gal 1:11 But I·make·known to·yeu, brothers, that the good·
1Co 12:3 Therefore I·make·known to·yeu, that not·even·
1Co 15:1 Moreover, brothers, I·make·known to·yeu the
G1107.1 V-PAI-1P γνωρίζομεν (1x)
2Co 8:1 Now brothers, we·make·known to·yeu the grace of·
G1107.1 V-PPM-3S γνωριζέσθω (1x)
Php 4:6 of·yeurs, make·*them*·be·known directly·to God.
G1107.1 V-AAI-1S ἐγνώρισα (2x)
Jn 15:15 personally·from my Father I·made·known to·yeu.
Jn 17:26 And I·made·known to·them your name, and shall·
G1107.1 V-AAI-1P ἐγνωρίσαμεν (1x)
2Pe 1:16 ·skillfully·devised *that* we·made·known to·yeu the
G1107.1 V-AAI-2S ἐγνώρισας (1x)
Ac 2:28 You·made·known to·me *the* ways of·life-above†;
G1107.1 V-AAI-3S ἐγνώρισεν (2x)
Lk 2:15 ·occurred, which Yahweh made·known to·us.”
Eph 3:3 ·to a·revelation, he·made·known to·me the Mystery
G1107.1 V-AAN γνωρίσαι (3x)
Rm 9:22 to·indicate his wrath and to·make·known his power,
Eph 6:19 ·of·speech, *for·me* to·make·known the Mystery of·
Col 1:27 to·whom God determined to·make·known what *is*
G1107.1 V-AAP-NSM γνωρίσας (1x)
Eph 1:9 already·making·known to·us the Mystery of·his will
G1107.1 V-AAS-3S γνωρίσῃ (1x)
Rm 9:23 also in·order·that he·may·make·known the wealth
G1107.1 V-API-3S ἐγνωρίσθη (1x)
Eph 3:5 ·of·offspring was·not made·known to·the Sons of·
G1107.1 V-APP-GSN γνωρισθέντος (1x)
Rm 16:26 with *the Mystery* already·being·made·known to all
G1107.1 V-APS-3S γνωρισθῇ (1x)
Eph 3:10 wisdom of·God may·be·made·known now to·the
G1107.2 V-PAI-1S γνωρίζω (1x)
Php 1:22 Even·so, I·do·not really·know what I·shall·choose.

G1108 γνῶσις gnôsis *n.* (29x)
Roots:G1097 Compare:G3563 G4907 G1271 G1253
xLangEquiv:H1847
G1108.2 N-NSF γνῶσις (2x)
1Co 8:1 ·all have knowledge. The knowledge puffs·up, but
1Co 13:8 if·also knowledge, it·shall·be·fully·rendered·
G1108.2 N-ASF γνῶσιν (5x)
Lk 1:77 to·give knowledge of·Salvation to·his People unto a·
1Pe 3:7 ·together *with·them* according·to knowledge, as
2Pe 1:5 *yeur* courageous·moral·excellence, Knowledge;
1Co 8:1 ·personally·know that we·all have knowledge. The
1Co 8:10 the·one having knowledge) laying·back·and·eating
G1108.2 N-DSF γνώσει (7x)
2Pe 1:6 and along·with *yeur* knowledge, Self-Restraint; and
2Pe 3:18 grow in grace and in·*the*·knowledge of·our Lord
1Co 1:5 by him, in every word and in·all knowledge—
1Co 8:11 and by your knowledge shall the weak brother
1Co 14:6 by revelation, or by knowledge, or by prophesying
2Co 6:6 by cleanness, by knowledge, by long-suffering, by
2Co 8:7 in·trust, and in·word, and in·knowledge, and in·all
G1108.2 N-GSF γνώσεως (6x)
Rm 11:33 both of·*the*·wisdom and knowledge of·God! How
Rm 15:14 ·filled with·all knowledge, who·are·being·able
1Co 12:8 but to·another a·word of·knowledge by the same
2Co 2:14 ·apparent the aroma of·his knowledge in every
Eph 3:19 ·know the surpassing knowledge of·the love of·the
1Ti 6:20 ·theories of·the falsely·named knowledge—
G1108.3 N-NSF γνῶσις (1x)
1Co 8:7 But·yet, the absolute·knowledge *of·this is* not in
G1108.3 N-ASF γνῶσιν (1x)
1Co 13:2 mysteries and all the absolute·knowledge, and if·
G1108.3 N-DSF γνώσει (1x)
2Co 11:6 *it·is* not *so* in·the absolute·knowledge; moreover in

G1108.3 N-GSF γνώσεως (5x)
Lk 11:52 the key of·the absolute·knowledge. Yeu·yeurselves
Rm 2:20 the formula of·the absolute·knowledge and of·the
Php 3:8 of·the absolute·knowledge of·Anointed-One, Jesus
2Co 4:6 illumination of·the absolute·knowledge of·the glory
2Co 10:5 ·itself·up against the absolute·knowledge of·God,
G1108.4 N-GSF γνώσεως (1x)
Col 2:3 ·away all the treasures of·Wisdom and Knowledge.

G1109 γνώστης gnṓstēs *n.* (1x)
Roots:G1097
G1109 N-ASM γνώστην (1x)
Ac 26:3 especially with·you being an·expert in·all customs

G1110 γνωστός gnōstós *adj.* (15x)
Roots:G1097 See:G1110-1 G1107-1
G1110.1 A-NSM γνωστός (2x)
Jn 18:15 that disciple was known to·the designated·high·priest
Jn 18:16 who was known to·the designated·high·priest,
G1110.1 A-NSN γνωστόν (9x)
Ac 1:19 And it·was known to·all the·ones residing·in
Ac 2:14 ·in JeruSalem, be this known to·yeu and give·ear to·
Ac 4:10 be·it known to·yeu all, and to·all the People of·
Ac 9:42 And it·became known in all Joppa, and many trusted
Ac 13:38 men, brothers, be·it known to·yeu that through
Ac 19:17 And this was known to·all the·ones residing·in
Ac 28:22 this sect, it·is known to·us that everywhere it·is·
Ac 28:28 "Now·then, be·it known to·yeu that the·custodial·
Rm 1:19 on·account·that, the·thing *which·is* known of·God,
G1110.1 A-NPN γνωστά (1x)
Ac 15:18 "Known to·God are all his works from the·
G1110.2 A-NSN γνωστόν (1x)
Ac 4:16 that in·fact a·notable miraculous·sign has·been·done
G1110.3 A-NPM γνωστοί (1x)
Lk 23:49 Now all his acquaintances, and the women
G1110.3 A-DPM γνωστοῖς (1x)
Lk 2:44 among the kinsfolk and among the acquaintances.

G1111 γογγύζω gôngýzō *v.* (8x)
Compare:G1234 See:G1113 xLangAlso:H3885
G1111 V-PAI-3P γογγύζουσιν (1x)
Jn 6:61 in himself that his disciples are·grumbling about this,
G1111 V-PAM-2P γογγύζετε (2x)
Jn 6:43 to·them, "Do·not grumble with one·another.
1Co 10:10 We·must·not·even grumble, just·as some of·them
G1111 V-PAP-GSM γογγύζοντος (1x)
Jn 7:32 heard the crowd grumbling these·things concerning
G1111 V-IAI-3P ἐγόγγυζον (3x)
Jn 6:41 the Judeans were·grumbling concerning him,
Lk 5:30 Pharisees among·them were·grumbling toward his
Mt 20:11 after·receiving *it*, they·were·grumbling against the
G1111 V-AAI-3P ἐγόγγυσαν (1x)
1Co 10:10 just·as some of·them also grumbled, and they·

G1112 γογγυσμός gôngysmós *n.* (4x)
Roots:G1111 See:G1113
xLangEquiv:H8519
G1112 N-NSM γογγυσμός (2x)
Jn 7:12 And there·was much grumbling among the crowds
Ac 6:1 there·happened a·grumbling of·the Hellenistic·Jews
G1112 N-GPM γογγυσμῶν (2x)
Php 2:14 completely·apart·from grumblings and debates,
1Pe 4:9 *Be* hospitable to one·another without grumbling.

G1113 γογγυστής gôngystḗs *n.* (1x)
Roots:G1111 Compare:G3202 See:G1112
G1113 N-NPM γογγυσταί (1x)
Jud 1:16 These are grumblers, malcontented·faultfinders,

G1114 γόης gốēs *n.* (1x)
Compare:G5578 G4108 G2215
G1114.3 N-NPM γόητες (1x)
2Ti 3:13 and adept·smooth·talkers shall·continually·advance

G1115 Γολ•γοθᾶ Gôlgôthâ *n/l.* (3x)
גֻּלְגֹּלֶת gul·góleth [Hebrew]
Roots:H1538
xLangEquiv:G2898
G1115.2 N/L-ASF Γολγοθᾶ (3x)
Jn 19:17 which is·referred·to in·Hebrew *as* GolGotha,
Mt 27:33 to a·place being·referred·to·as GolGotha, that is
Mk 15:22 to *the* place *being·referred·to·as* GolGotha, which,

G1116 Γόμορρα Gómôrrha *n/l.* (5x)
עֲמֹרָה 'ămôrạh [Hebrew]
Roots:H6017 Compare:G4670
G1116.2 N/L-NSF Γόμορρα (2x)
Rm 9:29 as Sodom, and would be·likened as Gomorrah."
Jud 1:7 to·these *angels*, Sodom and Gomorrah and the cities
G1116.2 N/L-DPN Γομόρροις (1x)
Mk 6:11 ·be more·tolerable for·Sodom or Gomorrah in *the*
G1116.2 N/L-GSF Γομόρρας (1x)
2Pe 2:6 and Gomorrah with·an·overturning·catastrophe, he·
G1116.2 N/L-GPN Γομόρρων (1x)
Mt 10:15 for·the·land of·Sodom and Gomorrah in *the* Day

G1117 γόμος gốmôs *n.* (3x)
Roots:G1073
G1117.2 N-ASM γόμον (3x)
Ac 21:3 for the sailing·ship was unloading its cargo there.
Rv 18:11 not·even·one·man buys their cargo any·longer—
Rv 18:12 "cargo of·gold, silver, precious stones, and pearls,

G1118 γονεύς gônêús *n.* (20x)
הוֹרֶה hôrẹh [Hebrew, New Testament]
Roots:G1096 Compare:G3962
xLangEquiv:H1952-2
G1118 N-NPM γονεῖς (8x)
Jn 9:2 this·man or his parents, in·order·that he·should·be·
Jn 9:3 morally·failed, nor his parents, but·rather in·order·
Jn 9:20 His parents answered them and declared, "We·
Jn 9:22 His parents declared these·things, because they·
Jn 9:23 On·account·of that, his parents declared, "He·is of·
Lk 2:41 Now each year his parents traversed to JeruSalem
Lk 8:56 And her parents were·astonished, but he·charged
2Co 12:14 parents, but·rather the parents for·the·children.
G1118 N-APM γονεῖς (5x)
Jn 9:18 *that* they·hollered·out·for the parents of·the·one
Lk 2:27 ·Courtyard. And·when the parents brought in the
Lk 18:29 ·one·man that left home, or parents, or brothers, or
Mt 10:21 children shall·rise·up against parents and shall·put
Mk 13:12 shall·rise·up against *their* parents and shall·put
G1118 N-DPM γονεῦσιν (5x)
Rm 1:30 inventors of·bad·things; *being* obstinate to·parents,
2Co 12:14 obligated to·store·up for·the parents, but·rather
Eph 6:1 the children: Listen·to·and·obey yeur parents in *the*
Col 3:20 ·to·and·obey the parents according·to all·things, for
2Ti 3:2 haughty, revilers, obstinate to·parents, ungrateful,
G1118 N-GPM γονέων (1x)
Lk 21:16 But yeu·shall·be·handed·over both by parents, and
EG1118 (1x)
Lk 2:48 And seeing him, *his parents* were·astounded. And

G1119 γόνυ gốny *n.* (12x)
Compare:G0043 See:G1120 G0044-1
xLangEquiv:H1290
G1119 N-NSN γόνυ (2x)
Rm 14:11 "every knee shall·bow to·me, and every
Php 2:10 at the name of·Jesus, every knee should·bow (of·
G1119 N-ASN γόνυ (1x)
Rm 11:4 ·thousand men, who did·not bow a·knee to·Baal."
G1119 N-APN γόνατα (8x)
Lk 22:41 a·stone's cast, and bowing the knees, he·prayed,
Ac 7:60 And bowing the knees, he·yelled·out with·a·loud
Ac 9:40 forth outside, bowing his knees, he·prayed. And
Ac 20:36 with·him bowing the knees, he·prayed together
Ac 21:5 And bowing the knees on the shore, we·prayed.
Heb 12:12 ·upright the limp hands and the paralyzed knees,
Mk 15:19 bowing their knees, they·were·falling·prostrate to·
Eph 3:14 ·this gracious·cause, I·bow my knees to the Father
G1119 N-DPN γόνασιν (1x)
Lk 5:8 *it*, Simon Peter fell·down·at Jesus' knees, saying,

G1120 γονυ•πετέω gônypêtéō *v.* (4x)
Roots:G1119 G4098 Compare:G5087
G1120 V-PAP-NSM γονυπετῶν (2x)
Mt 17:14 came·alongside him, kneeling·down to·him and
Mk 1:40 imploring him, even kneeling·down·to him and
G1120 V-AAP-NSM γονυπετήσας (1x)
Mk 10:17 after·running·forward and kneeling·down·to him,
G1120 V-AAP-NPM γονυπετήσαντες (1x)
Mt 27:29 in his right·hand, and kneeling·down before him,

G1121 γράμμα grámma *n.* (15x)
Roots:G1125 See:G1124 G1122 xLangAlso:H5612
G1121.1 N-DPN γράμμασιν (1x)
2Co 3:7 ·Death, having·been·engraved in writing on stones,
G1121.2 N-NSN γράμμα (1x)
2Co 3:6 but·rather of·Spirit, for the letter kills, but the
G1121.2 N-APN γράμματα (1x)
Ac 28:21 do·not·even anticipate·receiving letters from Judea
G1121.2 N-DSN γράμματι (1x)
Rm 2:29 in spirit, *and* not in·letter— whose high·praise *is*
G1121.2 N-DPN γράμμασιν (2x)
Lk 23:38 ·been·written over him with·letters in·Greek,
Gal 6:11 Yeu·see with·what·sizable letters I·write to·yeu by·
G1121.2 N-GSN γράμματος (3x)
Rm 2:27 you, the·one through letter and circumcision *being*
Rm 7:6 of·spirit, and not in·oldness of·*the*·letter.
2Co 3:6 of·a·brand-new covenant— not of·letter, but·rather
G1121.3 N-APN γράμματα (2x)
Jn 7:15 this·man personally·know *the Sacred*·Writings, not
2Ti 3:15 a·toddler you·have·seen the Sacred Writings— the·
G1121.3 N-DPN γράμμασιν (1x)
Jn 5:47 if yeu·do·not trust those *Sacred*·Writings, how shall·
G1121.4 N-NPN γράμματα (1x)
Ac 26:24 ·are raving·mad! The many studies do·twist you
G1121.5 N-ASN γράμμα (2x)
Lk 16:6 '*Here*, accept your bill, and sitting·down quickly,
Lk 16:7 '*Here*, accept your bill, and write eighty.

G1122 γραμματεύς grammatêús *n.* (67x)
Roots:G1121
xLangEquiv:H5612-1 xLangAlso:H5608 H7860
G1122.2 N-NSM γραμματεύς (4x)
Mt 8:19 And one scribe coming·alongside, declared to·him,
Mt 13:52 ·of that, every scribe already·being·discipled into
Mk 12:32 And the scribe declared to·him, "Mentor, clearly·
1Co 1:20 *is the* wise? Where *is the* scribe? Where *is the*
G1122.2 N-NPM γραμματεῖς (30x)
Jn 8:3 Then the scribes and the Pharisees brought to him a·
Lk 5:21 And the scribes and the Pharisees began to·ponder,
Lk 5:30 But the scribes and Pharisees among·them were·
Lk 6:7 Now the scribes and the Pharisees were·meticulously·
Lk 11:53 these·things to them, the scribes and the Pharisees
Lk 15:2 And the Pharisees and the scribes were·murmuring,
Lk 19:47 the chief·priests and the scribes and the foremost
Lk 20:1 the chief·priests and the scribes stood·over *him*
Lk 20:19 Then the chief·priests and the scribes in the same
Lk 22:2 the chief·priests and the scribes were·seeking how
Lk 22:66 ·together (both chief·priests and scribes), and they·
Lk 23:10 And the chief·priests and the scribes stood, legally·
Ac 23:9 yelling. And the scribes *that·were* of·the Pharisees
Mt 7:29 them as *one* having authority, and not as the scribes.
Mt 15:1 Then the scribes and Pharisees from JeruSalem
Mt 17:10 "So·then why·do the scribes say that it·is·
Mt 21:15 the scribes were·greatly·displeased after·seeing the
Mt 23:2 saying, "The scribes and the Pharisees sat·down
Mt 26:3 the chief·priests, and the scribes, and the elders of·
Mt 26:57 designated·high·priest, where the scribes and the
Mk 1:22 as one·having authority, and not as the scribes.
Mk 2:16 And the scribes and the Pharisees, upon·seeing him
Mk 3:22 And the scribes, the·ones already·walking·down
Mk 7:5 Then the Pharisees and the scribes inquired·of him,
Mk 9:11 "Why·do the scribes say that it·is·mandatory·for
Mk 11:18 And the scribes and the chief·priests heard *it* and
Mk 11:27 the chief·priests, the scribes, and the elders come
Mk 12:35 "How·do the scribes say that the Anointed-One is
Mk 14:1 the chief·priests and the scribes were·seeking how,
Mk 14:53 the elders and the scribes come·together with·him.
G1122.2 N-VPM γραμματεῖς (8x)

Lk 11:44 "Woe to·yeu, scribes and Pharisees, O·stage·
Mt 23:13 "But woe to·yeu, Scribes and Pharisees, O·stage·
Mt 23:14 "Woe to·yeu, Scribes and Pharisees, O·stage·
Mt 23:15 "Woe to·yeu, Scribes and Pharisees, O·stage·
Mt 23:23 "Woe to·yeu, Scribes and Pharisees, O·stage·
Mt 23:25 "Woe to·yeu, Scribes and Pharisees, O·stage·
Mt 23:27 "Woe to·yeu, Scribes and Pharisees, O·stage·
Mt 23:29 "Woe to·yeu, Scribes and Pharisees, O·stage·

G1122.2 N-APM γραμματεῖς (6x)
Ac 4:5 the next·day, *that* their rulers and elders and scribes
Ac 6:12 the elders, and the scribes. And standing·over *him*,
Mt 2:4 all the chief·priests and *the* scribes of·the people, he·
Mt 23:34 yeu prophets and wise·men and scribes, and *some*
Mk 9:14 and scribes mutually·questioning·and·discussing *a*·
Mk 9:16 Then he·inquired·of the scribes, "What·do yeu·

G1122.2 N-DPM γραμματεῦσιν (2x)
Mt 20:18 ·handed·over to·the chief·priests and scribes, and
Mk 10:33 to·the chief·priests and to·the scribes. And they·

G1122.2 N-GPM γραμματέων (16x)
Lk 9:22 elders and chief·priests and scribes, and to·be·killed,
Lk 20:39 And responding, certain of·the scribes declared,
Lk 20:46 "Beware of the scribes, the·ones delighting to·
Mt 5:20 ·abound more·than *that* of·the scribes and Pharisees,
Mt 9:3 And behold, certain of·the scribes declared within
Mt 12:38 Then some of·the scribes and Pharisees answered,
Mt 16:21 the elders and chief·priests and scribes, and to·be·
Mt 27:41 the chief·priests with the scribes and elders were·
Mk 2:6 Now some of·the scribes were there, sitting·down yet
Mk 7:1 and certain of·the scribes gathered·together alongside
Mk 8:31 elders, chief·priests, and scribes, and to·be·killed,
Mk 12:28 ·together, one of·the scribes, coming·alongside
Mk 12:38 "Look·out for the scribes, the·ones wanting to·
Mk 14:43 the chief·priests and the scribes and the elders.
Mk 15:1 with the elders and scribes and the whole joint·
Mk 15:31 among one·another with the scribes, "He saved

G1122.3 N-NSM γραμματεύς (1x)
Ac 19:35 ·quieting·down the crowd, the town·clerk replied,

G1123 γραπτός graptós *adj.* (1x)
Roots:G1125

G1123 A-ASN γραπτόν (1x)
Rm 2:15 the work of·the Torah-Law written in their hearts,

G1124 γραφή graphḗ *n.* (52x)
Roots:G1125 See:G1121 xLangAlso:H3791

G1124.2 N-NSF γραφή (22x)
Jn 7:38 ·one trusting in me, just·as the Scripture declared,
Jn 7:42 Has·not·indeed the Scripture declared, that the
Jn 10:35 came, and the Scripture is·not able to·be·broken …
Jn 13:18 ·that the Scripture may·be·completely·fulfilled,
Jn 17:12 ·that the Scripture may·be·completely·fulfilled.
Jn 19:24 ·that the Scripture may·be·completely·fulfilled, the·
Jn 19:28 in·order·that the Scripture may·be·fully·completed,
Jn 19:36 that the Scripture should·be·completely·fulfilled,
Jn 19:37 And again another Scripture says, "They·shall·
Lk 4:21 this Scripture has·been·completely·fulfilled in yeur
Gal 3:8 And the Scripture, foreseeing that God regards·as·
Gal 3:22 But·rather the Scripture jointly·confined all·things
Gal 4:30 But·yet what·does the Scripture say?
Mk 15:28 And the Scripture was·completely·fulfilled, the·
Rm 4:3 For what·does the Scripture say?
Rm 9:17 For the Scripture says to·Pharaoh, "For this same·
Rm 10:11 For the Scripture says, " Everyone trusting on
Rm 11:2 ·not personally·know what the Scripture says by
Jac 2:23 And the Scripture is·completely·fulfilled, the·one
Jac 4:5 Or do·yeu·presume that the Scripture says for·naught
1Ti 5:18 For the Scripture says, "You·shall·not muzzle an·
2Ti 3:16 All Scripture *is* breathed·into·and·inspired·by·God,

G1124.2 N-NPF γραφαί (3x)
Mt 26:54 ·should the Scriptures be·completely·fulfilled that
Mt 26:56 in·order·that the Scriptures of·the prophets may·
Mk 14:49 ·that the Scriptures may·be·completely·fulfilled …

G1124.2 N-ASF γραφήν (4x)
Jn 20:9 ·yet had·they·seen the Scripture *which·declared* that
Ac 1:16 ·for this Scripture to·be·completely·fulfilled, which
Mk 12:10 "Did·yeu·not·even read·aloud this Scripture? "A·
Jac 2:8 *the* Royal Law according·to the Scripture, "You·

G1124.2 N-APF γραφάς (9x)
Jn 5:39 "Search the Scriptures, because yeu·yeurselves
Lk 24:32 ·was·thoroughly·opening·up the Scriptures to·us?
Lk 24:45 their understanding to·comprehend the Scriptures.
Ac 17:11 all eagerness, scrutinizing the Scriptures each day,
Mt 22:29 not having·seen the Scriptures, nor·even the
Mk 12:24 *in* not having·seen the Scriptures, nor·even the
2Pe 3:16 as *they·do* also the rest of·Scriptures, to their own
1Co 15:3 of·our moral·failures according·to the Scriptures,
1Co 15:4 on·the third day according·to the Scriptures,

G1124.2 N-DSF γραφῇ (2x)
Jn 2:22 And they·trusted the Scripture and the word which
1Pe 2:6 Therefore also it·is·contained in the Scripture,

G1124.2 N-DPF γραφαῖς (4x)
Lk 24:27 to·them in all the Scriptures the·things concerning
Ac 18:24 an·eloquent man being powerful in the Scriptures.
Mt 21:42 ·even·at·any·time read·aloud in the Scriptures,
Rm 1:2 through his prophets in *the* Holy Scriptures

G1124.2 N-GSF γραφῆς (3x)
Ac 8:32 of·the Scripture which he·was·reading·aloud was
Ac 8:35 from the same Scripture, proclaimed·the·good·news
2Pe 1:20 every prophecy of·Scripture does·not itself·occur

G1124.2 N-GPF γραφῶν (4x)
Ac 17:2 ·having·discussions with·them from the Scriptures,
Ac 18:28 fully·exhibiting through the Scriptures, *for* Jesus
Rm 15:4 ·endurance and the comfort of·the Scriptures.
Rm 16:26 also through prophetic Scriptures, according·to a·

EG1124.2 (1x)
1Ti 4:13 ·attention to·the reading·aloud *of·Scripture*, to·the

G1125 γράφω gráphō *v.* (196x)
See:G1124 G2608-1
xLangEquiv:H3789 A3790 xLangAlso:H2710

G1125.1 V-FAI-1S γράψω (1x)
Rv 3:12 'And I·shall·write upon him the name of·my God,

G1125.1 V-PAI-1S γράφω (16x)
Gal 1:20 (Now the·things·which I·write to·yeu— Behold, in·
2Pe 3:1 letter, beloved, even·now I·write to·yeu, in which I·
2Th 3:17 a·signature in every letter. I·write in·this·manner.
1Co 4:14 Not embarrassing yeu do·I·write these·things, but·
1Co 14:37 ·acknowledge that these·things I·write to·yeu are
2Co 13:2 I·do·write to·the·ones having·already·morally·
2Co 13:10 ·of that, I·write these·things while·being·absent,
1Ti 3:14 These·things I·write to·you, expecting to·come to
1Jn 2:1 ·children, these·things I·write to·yeu, in·order·that
1Jn 2:7 Brothers, I·write no brand-new commandment to·
1Jn 2:8 a·brand-new commandment I·do·write to·yeu,
1Jn 2:12 I·write to·yeu, dear·children, because the moral·
1Jn 2:13 I·write to·yeu, fathers, because yeu·have·known
1Jn 2:13 ·*is* from *the* beginning. I·write to·yeu, young·men,
1Jn 2:13 the Evil·One. I·presently·write to·yeu, little·
2Jn 1:5 not as·though I·wrote a·brand-new commandment

G1125.1 V-PAI-1P γράφομεν (2x)
2Co 1:13 For we·write no other·things to·yeu, other than
1Jn 1:4 And these·things we·write to·yeu, in·order·that our

G1125.1 V-PAM-2S γράφε (1x)
Jn 19:21 were·saying to·Pilate, "Do·not write, 'The King

G1125.1 V-PAN γράφειν (7x)
Jud 1:3 ·making all diligence to·write to·yeu concerning the
Php 3:1 *it·is* not tiresome for·me to·write the same·things to·
1Th 4:9 yeu·have no need *for·me* to·write to·yeu, for yeu
2Co 9:1 holy·ones, it·is superfluous for·me to·write to·yeu.
2Jn 1:12 Having many·things to·write to·yeu *all*, I·am·
3Jn 1:13 I·was·having many·things to·write, but·yet I·do·not
Rv 10:4 their·own voices, I·was·about to·write. And I·heard

G1125.1 V-PPN γράφεσθαι (1x)
1Th 5:1 yeu·have no need *for·me* to·be·writing to·yeu.

G1125.1 V-PPP-APN γραφόμενα (1x)
Jn 21:25 the official·scrolls being·written. So·be·it, Amen.

G1125.1 V-PPS-3S γράφηται (1x)
Jn 21:25 which if each one should·be·written, I·imagine not·

G1125.1 V-IAI-3S ἔγραφεν (2x)
Jn 8:6 ·stooping down, Jesus was·writing with·the finger
Jn 8:8 again after·stooping down, he·was·writing into the

G1125.1 V-AAI-1S ἔγραψα (18x)
Gal 6:11 with·what·sizable letters I·write to·yeu by·my·own
Rm 15:15 ·daring·boldness, brothers, I·wrote to·yeu in part
1Pe 5:12 as·how I·reckon *it*), I·wrote briefly to·yeu—
1Co 5:9 I·wrote to·yeu in the *prior* letter not to·associate·
1Co 5:11 But now·in·fact, I·wrote to·yeu not to·associate·
1Co 9:15 and neither did·I·write these·things in·order·that
2Co 2:3 And I·wrote this same·thing to·yeu, lest coming *to*·
2Co 2:4 anguished·anxiety of·heart I·wrote to·yeu through
2Co 2:9 For to this *end* also I·wrote, that I·may·know yeur
2Co 7:12 So even·though I·wrote to·yeu, *it·was* not because·
Phm 1:19 I, Paul, wrote *this* by·my·own hand; I·myself
Phm 1:21 in·your attentive·obedience, I·wrote to·you,
1Jn 2:14 I·already·wrote to·yeu, fathers, because yeu·have·
1Jn 2:14 *the* beginning. I·already·wrote to·yeu, young·men,
1Jn 2:21 I·did·not write to·yeu because yeu·do·not
1Jn 2:26 These·things I·already·wrote to·yeu concerning the·
1Jn 5:13 These·things I·wrote to·yeu, to·the·ones trusting in
3Jn 1:9 I·wrote to·the Called·Out·citizenry, but·yet

G1125.1 V-AAI-2P ἐγράψατε (1x)
1Co 7:1 concerning the·things·of·which yeu·wrote to·me, *it*·

G1125.1 V-AAI-3S ἔγραψεν (8x)
Jn 1:45 "We·have·found whom Moses wrote *about* in the
Jn 5:46 ·trusting in·me, for that·man wrote concerning me.
Jn 19:19 And Pilate also wrote a·title and placed *it* on the
Lk 1:63 And requesting a·writing·tablet, he·wrote, saying,
Lk 20:28 "Mentor, Moses wrote to·us, if any·man's brother
Mk 10:5 ·to yeur hardness·of·heart, he·wrote yeu this
Mk 12:19 "Mentor, Moses wrote for·us that if any·man's
2Pe 3:15 our beloved brother Paul wrote to·yeu (according·

G1125.1 V-AAI-3P ἔγραψαν (1x)
Ac 18:27 into Achaia, the brothers wrote, encouraging the

G1125.1 V-AAM-2S γράψον (14x)
Lk 16:6 your bill, and sitting·down quickly, write fifty.'
Lk 16:7 '*Here*, accept your bill, and write eighty.'
Rv 1:11 "What you·look·upon, write in an·official·scroll,
Rv 1:19 "Write the·things·which you·saw, and the·things·
Rv 2:1 angel of·the Called·Out·citizenry of·Ephesus write,
Rv 2:8 angel of·the Called·Out·citizenry in·Smyrna write,
Rv 2:12 of·the Called·Out·citizenry in Pergamos write,
Rv 2:18 angel of·the Called·Out·citizenry in Thyatira write,
Rv 3:1 of·the Called·Out·citizenry in Sardis write, 'These·
Rv 3:7 of·the Called·Out·citizenry in PhilAdelphia write,
Rv 3:14 ·the Called·Out·citizenry of·the·LaoDiceans write,
Rv 14:13 heaven saying to·me, "Write, 'Supremely·blessed
Rv 19:9 *angel* says to·me, "Write, 'Supremely·blessed *are*
Rv 21:5 And he·says to·me, "Write, because these words

G1125.1 V-AAN γράψαι (6x)
Lk 1:3 from·the·start, to·write to·you *a·thorough·account*
Ac 25:26 something absolutely·certain to·write *to·my* Lord
Ac 25:26 occurring, I·may·have something to·write.
Mk 10:4 ·permitted *us* to·write a·document of·innocence·in·
Jud 1:3 Salvation, I·had necessity to·write to·yeu, exhorting
3Jn 1:13 but·yet I·do·not want to·write to·you through ink

G1125.1 V-AAP-NSM γράψας (2x)
Jn 21:24 concerning these·things and writing these·things,
Rm 16:22 I, Tertius, the·one writing the letter, greet yeu in

G1125.1 V-AAP-NSM@ γράψας (1x)
Ac 23:25 *And* he·wrote a·letter containing this particular·

G1125.1 V-AAP-NPM γράψαντες (1x)
Ac 15:23 *and who·are* writing *this letter of* these·things

G1125.1 V-AAS-2S γράψῃς (1x)
Rv 10:4 spoke, and you·may·not write these·things."

G1125.1 V-2API-3S ἐγράφη (4x)
Lk 10:20 because yeur names are·already·written in the
Rm 4:23 Now it·was·not written on·account·of him merely,
1Co 9:10 For on·account·of us it·was·written, because the·
1Co 10:11 them, and they·are·written specifically·for our

G1125.1 V-RAI-1S γέγραφα (2x)
Jn 19:22 answered, "What I·have·written, I·have·written."

Αα Ββ Γγ Δδ Εε Ζζ Ηη Θθ Ιι Κκ Λλ Μμ Νν Ξξ Οο Ππ Ρρ Σσ Ττ Υυ Φφ Χχ Ψψ Ωω

Jn 19:22 "What I·have·written, I·have·written."

G1125.1 V-RPI-3S γέγραπται (67x)

Jn 8:17 "But also, it·has·been·written in yeur Torah-Law
Jn 20:31 these·things have·been·written in·order·that yeu·
Lk 2:23 just·as it·has·been·written in Yahweh's Torah-Law,
Lk 3:4 As it·has·been·written in a·scroll of·the·words of·
Lk 4:4 to him, saying, "It·has·been·written, "The man·of·
Lk 4:8 me, Adversary-Accuser. For it·has·been·written, ‹
Lk 4:10 For it·has·been·written, "He·shall·command his
Lk 7:27 This is *he*, concerning whom it·has·been·written, ‹
Lk 10:26 to him, "What has·been·written in the Torah-Law?
Lk 19:46 saying to·them, "It·has·been·written, ‹My house
Lk 24:46 "In·this·manner it·has·been·written, so·also in·
Ac 1:20 "For it·has·been·written in a·scroll of·Psalms, "Let
Ac 7:42 heaven, just·as it·has·been·written in a·scroll of·
Ac 13:33 ·up Jesus; as also it·has·been·written in the second
Ac 15:15 do·mutually·agree, just·as it·has·been·written,
Ac 23:5 *the* designated·high·priest, for it·has·been·written,
Heb 10:7 of·an·official·scroll it·has·been·written concerning
Gal 3:10 they·are under a·curse— for it·has·been·written, ‹
Gal 3:13 a·curse on·our behalf— for it·has·been·written, ‹
Gal 4:22 For it·has·been·written, that AbRaham had two sons
Gal 4:27 For it·has·been·written, "Be·merry, O·barren·
Mt 2:5 For in·this·manner it·has·been·written through the
Mt 4:4 answering, he·declared, "It·has·been·written, "A·
Mt 4:6 cast yourself down. For it·has·been·written, "He·
Mt 4:7 to·him, "Again, it·has·been·written, "You·shall·
Mt 4:10 ·out, Adversary-Accuser! For it·has·been·written, ‹
Mt 11:10 is·he, concerning whom it·has·been·written, ‹
Mt 21:13 and he·says to·them, "It·has·been·written, "My
Mt 26:24 ·on·out just·as it·has·been·written concerning him,
Mt 26:31 on this night. For it·has·been·written, ‹I·shall·
Mk 1:2 As it·has·been·written in the prophets, ‹Behold, I·
Mk 7:6 the stage·acting·hypocrites; as it·has·been·written,
Mk 9:12 "Yet how it·has·been·written concerning the Son
Mk 9:13 ·wanted, just·as it·has·been·written concerning him
Mk 11:17 saying to·them, "Has·it·not been·written, "My
Mk 14:21 ·out, just·as it·has·been·written concerning him,
Mk 14:27 on this night, because it·has·been·written, ‹I·
Rm 1:17 of·trust into trust. Just·as it·has·been·written, ‹
Rm 2:24 on·account·of yeu,› just·as it·has·been·written.
Rm 3:4 man·of·clay† a·liar; just·as it·has·been·written,
Rm 3:10 Just·as it·has·been·written: ‹There·is none
Rm 4:17 (just·as it·has·been·written, "I·have·placed you *as*
Rm 8:36 Just·as it·has·been·written, "For·your cause, we·
Rm 9:13 Just·as it·has·been·written, "Jacob I·loved, but
Rm 9:33 just·as it·has·been·written, ‹Behold, I·lay in
Rm 10:15 ·be·dispatched? Just·as it·has·been·written, ‹
Rm 11:8 just·as it·has·been·written, ‹GOD gave them a·
Rm 11:26 shall·be·saved; just·as it·has·been·written, ‹*The*
Rm 12:19 to·the wrath *of·God*, for it·has·been·written,
Rm 14:11 For it·has·been·written, "‹*As·surely·as* I·myself
Rm 15:3 himself, but·rather, just·as it·has·been·written,
Rm 15:9 ·behalf *of·his* mercy, just·as it·has·been·written,
Rm 15:21 But·rather just·as it·has·been·written, "To·whom
1Pe 1:16 on·account·that it·has·been·written, "Yeu·must·be
1Co 1:19 For it·has·been·written, "I·shall·completely·
1Co 1:31 in·order·that, just·as it·has·been·written, ‹The·
1Co 2:9 But·rather just·as it·has·been·written, ‹Eye did·not
1Co 3:19 foolishness with God. For it·has·been·written,
1Co 4:6 above that·which has·been·written, in·order·that not
1Co 9:9 For it·has·been·written in the Torah-Law of·Moses,
1Co 10:7 *were* some of·them; as it·has·been·written, "The
1Co 14:21 In the Torah-Law it·has·been·written, ‹In other·
1Co 15:45 And in·this·manner it·has·been·written, ‹The
2Co 8:15 Just·as it·has·been·written, ‹The·one did·not
2Co 9:9 Just·as it·has·been·written, "*The·righteous·man*
Rv 13:8 ·it, whose names have·not been·written in the scroll
Rv 17:8 whose names have·not been·written in the official·

G1125.1 V-RPP-ASN γεγραμμένον (7x)

Lk 22:37 ·for this thing having·been·written to·be·finished in
2Co 4:13 trust, according·to the·one having·been·written,
Rv 2:17 name having·been·written which not·even·one·man
Rv 5:1 an·official·scroll having·been·written on·*the*·inside
Rv 14:1 the name of·his Father having·been·written in their
Rv 19:12 a·name having·been·written that not·even·one·man
Rv 19:16 his thigh the name having·been·written, KING OF·

G1125.1 V-RPP-ASF γεγραμμένην (1x)

Mt 27:37 of·his *execution, which·was* having·been·written,

G1125.1 V-RPP-APN γεγραμμένα (4x)

Lk 21:22 ·fulfill all the·things having·been·written.
Lk 24:44 the·things having·been·written concerning me in
Ac 13:29 ·all the·things having·been·written concerning him,
Rv 1:3 ·keeping the·things having·been·written in it, for the

G1125.1 V-RPP-APF γεγραμμένας (1x)

Rv 22:18 the punishing·blows having·been·written in this

G1125.1 V-RPP-DPN γεγραμμένοις (2x)

Ac 24:14 trusting in·all the·things having·been·written in the
Gal 3:10 continue in all the·things having·been·written in the

G1125.1 V-RPP-GPN γεγραμμένων (2x)

Rv 20:12 out of·the·things having·been·written in the
Rv 22:19 and *from* the·things having·been·written in this

G1125.1 V-RPP-NSN γεγραμμένον (10x)

Jn 2:17 recalled·to·mind that it·was having·been·written,
Jn 6:31 the wilderness, just·as it·is having·been·written, ‹
Jn 6:45 "It·is having·been·written in the prophets, ‹And
Jn 10:34 "Is·it not having·been·written in yeur Torah-Law,
Jn 12:14 sat·down on it, just·as it·is having·been·written,
Jn 19:19 *it* on the cross. And having·been·written was,
Jn 19:20 City. And it·was having·been·written in·Hebrew,
Lk 4:17 ·found the place where it·was having·been·written,
Lk 20:17 "So·then, what is this having·been·written, "*The*
Rv 17:5 *was* a·name having·been·written, MYSTERY,

G1125.1 V-RPP-NSF γεγραμμένη (1x)

Lk 23:38 ·inscription also was having·been·written over him

G1125.1 V-RPP-NSM γεγραμμένος (3x)

Jn 15:25 ·fulfilled, the·one having·been·written in their
1Co 15:54 the saying, the·one having·been·written,
Rv 20:15 if anyone is·not found having·been·written in the

G1125.1 V-RPP-NPN γεγραμμένα (3x)

Jn 12:16 ·things were having·been·written concerning him,
Jn 20:30 which are not having·been·written in this official·
Lk 18:31 and all the·things having·been·written through the

G1125.1 V-RPP-NPM γεγραμμένοι (1x)

Rv 21:27 ·*enter* except the·ones having·been·written in the

EG1125.1 (2x)

1Ti 3:15 *I·write* in·order·that you·may·personally·know
Rv 3:12 'And *I·shall·write upon him* my brand-new name.

G1125.2 V-PAI-3S γράφει (1x)

Rm 10:5 For Moses describes the righteousness, the·one

G1126 γρα•ώδης graṓdēs *adj.* (1x)

Roots:G1123-1 G1491 See:G1088

G1126.3 A-APM γραώδεις (1x)

1Ti 4:7 So shun the profane and age-old, senile myths, and

G1127 γρηγορεύω grēgôrêúō *v.* (23x)

Roots:G1453 Compare:G5442 xLangAlso:H8245

G1127.2 V-PAM-2P γρηγορεῖτε (10x)

Ac 20:31 Therefore keep·alert, remembering that for·three·
Mt 24:42 "Accordingly, keep·alert, because yeu·do·not
Mt 25:13 "Accordingly, keep·alert, because yeu·do·not
Mt 26:38 Yeu·remain here and keep·alert with me."
Mt 26:41 Yeu·must·keep·alert and pray, in·order·that yeu·
Mk 13:35 Accordingly, keep·alert— for yeu·do·not
Mk 13:37 "And what I·say to·yeu, I·say to·all. Keep·alert!"
Mk 14:34 Yeu·remain here and keep·alert."
Mk 14:38 Yeu·must·keep·alert and pray, in·order·that yeu·
1Co 16:13 Keep·alert! Stand·fast in the trust! ‹" Be·manly!

G1127.2 V-PAP-APM γρηγοροῦντας (1x)

Lk 12:37 upon·coming, shall·find keeping·alert. Certainly

G1127.2 V-PAP-NSM γρηγορῶν (2x)

Rv 3:2 Become one·keeping·alert, and firmly·establish the·
Rv 16:15 ·blessed *is* the·one keeping·alert and guarding his

G1127.2 V-PAP-NPM γρηγοροῦντες (1x)

Col 4:2 Diligently·continue in·the prayer, keeping·alert in it

G1127.2 V-PAS-1P γρηγορῶμεν (2x)

1Th 5:6 rest, but·rather we·should·keep·alert and should·be·
1Th 5:10 whether we·should·keep·alert or we·should·sleep,

G1127.2 V-PAS-3S γρηγορῇ (1x)

Mk 13:34 the doorkeeper that he·should·keep·alert.

G1127.2 V-AAI-3S ἐγρηγόρησεν (2x)

Lk 12:39 thief would·come, he·would·have kept·alert, and
Mt 24:43 thief comes, he·would·have kept·alert and would

G1127.2 V-AAM-2P γρηγορήσατε (1x)

1Pe 5:8 Be·sober, keep·alert! Because yeur legal·adversary,

G1127.2 V-AAN γρηγορῆσαι (2x)

Mt 26:40 did·yeu·all·not have·strength to·keep·alert with me
Mk 14:37 Did·you·not have·strength to·keep·alert *for* one

G1127.2 V-AAS-2S γρηγορήσῃς (1x)

Rv 3:3 unless you·should·keep·alert, I·shall·come upon you

G1128 γυμνάζω gymnázō *v.* (4x)

Roots:G1131 Compare:G0778 G4160 See:G1129

G1128.2 V-PAM-2S γύμναζε (1x)

1Ti 4:7 age-old,·senile myths, and train yourself *rather* to

G1128.2 V-RPP-ASF γεγυμνασμένην (1x)

2Pe 2:14 a·heart having·been·trained with·acts·of·coveting.

G1128.2 V-RPP-APN γεγυμνασμένα (1x)

Heb 5:14 abilities·of·perception having·been·trained through

G1128.2 V-RPP-DPM γεγυμνασμένοις (1x)

Heb 12:11 for·the·ones having·been·trained through it.

G1129 γυμνασία gymnasía *n.* (1x)

Roots:G1128

G1129.1 N-NSF γυμνασία (1x)

1Ti 4:8 "For the *way·of* bodily training is profitable just·for

G1130 γυμνητεύω gymnētêúō *v.* (1x)

Roots:G1131

G1130.2 V-PAI-1P γυμνητεύομεν (1x)

1Co 4:11 and should·thirst, and go·naked, and are·buffeted

G1131 γυμνός gymnós *adj.* (15x)

See:G1132-1
xLangEquiv:H5903 xLangAlso:H6174

G1131.1 A-NSM γυμνός (6x)

Jn 21:7 fishing·coat *about·himself* (for he·was naked), and
Mt 25:36 naked, and yeu·arrayed me *with·clothing*.
Mt 25:43 yeu·did·not gather me in, naked, and yeu·did·not
Mk 14:52 the linen·cloth, he·fled from them naked).
Rv 3:17 pitiable, helplessly·poor, blind, and naked.
Rv 16:15 garments, lest he·should·walk·along naked, and

G1131.1 A-NPM γυμνοί (2x)

Jac 2:15 or sister should·subsist *being* naked and should·be
2Co 5:3 dressing·ourselves, we·shall·not be·found naked.

G1131.1 A-NPN γυμνά (1x)

Heb 4:13 *are* naked and having·been·vulnerably·exposed to·

G1131.1 A-ASM γυμνόν (2x)

Mt 25:38 and gathered·*you*·in? Or naked, and arrayed *you*
Mt 25:44 thirsting, or *being* a·stranger, or naked, or sick, or

G1131.1 A-ASF γυμνήν (1x)

Rv 17:16 they·shall·make her desolate and naked, and shall·

G1131.1 A-APM γυμνούς (1x)

Ac 19:16 ·out of·that house naked and having·been·wounded

G1131.2 A-GSN γυμνοῦ (1x)

Mk 14:51 having·been·arrayed over *his* nakedness, and the

G1131.3 A-ASM γυμνόν (1x)

1Co 15:37 the body that·shall·be, but·rather a·bare kernel,

G1132 γυμνότης gymnótēs *n.* (3x)

Roots:G1131

G1132 N-NSF γυμνότης (1x)

Rm 8:35 persecution, or famine, or nakedness, or danger, or

G1132 N-DSF γυμνότητι (1x)

2Co 11:27 in fastings many·times, in cold and nakedness.

G1132 N-GSF γυμνότητος (1x)

Rv 3:18 of·your nakedness may·not be·made·apparent. Also,

G1133 γυναικάριον gynaikáriôn *n.* (1x)

Roots:G1135 G2444-3

G1133.2 N-APN γυναικάρια (1x)

2Ti 3:6 the silly·lesser·women having·been·stacked·high

G1134 γυναικεῖος gynaikêîôs *adj.* (1x)
Roots:G1135
G1134 A-DSN γυναικείῳ (1x)
1Pe 3:7 while·prescribing honor to·the feminine as also

G1135 γυνή gynḗ *n.* (235x)
Roots:G1096 Compare:G1133 G0435 See:G1134
xLangEquiv:H0802 A5389
G1135.2 N-NSF γυνή (46x)
Jn 4:7 there·comes a·woman from·out of·Samaria to·draw·
Jn 4:9 Accordingly, the Samaritan woman says to·him,
Jn 4:11 The woman says to·him, "Sir, you·have not·even a·
Jn 4:15 The woman says to him, "Sir, give me this water
Jn 4:17 The woman answered and declared, "I·do·not have
Jn 4:19 The woman says to·him, "Sir, I·observe that you·
Jn 4:25 The woman says to·him, "I·personally·know that
Jn 4:28 So·then, the woman left her water·jar and went·off
Jn 16:21 the woman should·reproduce·and·give·birth, she·
Lk 7:37 And behold, a·woman in the city who was full·of·
Lk 7:39 and what·manner *is* the woman that lays·hold of·him
Lk 8:43 And a·woman being with a·flow of·blood for twelve
Lk 8:47 And the woman, seeing that she·was·not hidden,
Lk 10:38 and a·certain woman by·the·name·of Martha
Lk 11:27 ·things, *that* a·certain woman from·among the
Lk 13:11 And behold, there·was a·woman having a·spirit
Lk 13:21 like leaven, which a·woman took *and* incorporated
Lk 15:8 "Or what woman, having ten drachma·coins·*of*·
Ac 16:14 was·listening, a·woman by·the·name·of Lydia
Ac 17:34 ·Hill, and a·woman by·the·name·of Damaris, and
Mt 9:20 And behold, *there·was* a·woman *badly·ill*,
Mt 9:22 And the woman was·made·safe·and·well from that
Mt 13:33 which upon·taking *it*, a·woman incorporated *it*
Mt 15:22 And behold, a·Kenaanite woman from those
Mt 26:7 ·alongside him a·woman having an·alabaster·flask
Mk 5:25 And *there·was* a·certain woman being with a·flow
Mk 5:33 Then the woman, reverently·fearing and·also
Mk 7:25 after·hearing about him, a·woman whose young·
Mk 7:26 Now the woman was a·Greek, a·Syro-Phoenician
Mk 14:3 there·came a·woman having an·alabaster·flask of·
1Co 11:5 But every woman who·is·praying or prophesying
1Co 11:6 For if a·woman is·not fully·veiled, also she·must·
1Co 11:7 ·image and glory, but woman is man's glory.
1Co 11:8 of·woman, but·rather woman from·out of·man.
1Co 11:9 the woman, but·rather woman on·account·of the
1Co 11:10 ·account·of that, the woman is·obligated to·have
1Co 11:11 ·from woman, neither *is* woman apart·from man,
1Co 11:12 For just·as the woman *is* from·out of·the man, in·
1Co 11:15 But if a·woman should·wear·long·hair, it·is a·
1Ti 2:11 A·woman must·learn in stillness with all subjection.
1Ti 2:14 was·not deluded, but the woman, being·deluded,
Rv 12:1 in the heaven: a·woman having·been·arrayed·with
Rv 12:6 And the woman fled into the wilderness, where she·
Rv 17:4 And the woman *is* the·one having·been·arrayed in·
Rv 17:9 mountains, wherever the woman sits·down on them.
Rv 17:18 "And the woman whom you·saw is the Great City,
G1135.2 N-NPF γυναῖκες (10x)
Lk 8:2 and·also certain women who were having·been·both·
Lk 23:49 and the women following·along with·him from
Lk 23:55 And closely·following, *the* women, also who were
Lk 24:22 Moreover *still*, certain women also from·among us
Lk 24:24 *it* even in·this·manner just·as the women declared,
Ac 8:12 they·were·immersed, both men and women.
Heb 11:35 Women received their dead from·out of·a·
Mt 27:55 Now many women were there observing from a·
Mk 15:40 Now there·were also women observing from a·
1Co 14:34 Yeur women must·stay·silent in the convened·
G1135.2 N-VSF γύναι (8x)
Jn 2:4 says to·her, "Woman, what·does·this·have to·do·
Jn 4:21 Jesus says to·her, "Woman, trust me, because an·
Jn 19:26 he·says to·his mother, "Woman, behold your son!
Jn 20:13 *angels* say to·her, "Woman, why do·you·weep?
Jn 20:15 Jesus says to·her, "Woman, why do·you·weep?
Lk 13:12 to·her, "Woman, you·have·been·fully·released
Lk 22:57 saying, "Woman, I·do·not personally·know him.
Mt 15:28 YeShua declared to·her, "O woman, great *is* your
G1135.2 N-ASF γυναῖκα (12x)
Lk 4:26 *city* Tsarephath of·Tsidon, to a·woman *who was* a·
Lk 7:44 And turning·around toward the woman, he·replied
Lk 7:44 to·Simon, "Do·you·look·upon this woman? "I·
Lk 7:50 And he·declared to the woman, "Your trust has·
Mt 5:28 looking·upon a·woman specifically to·long·for her,
1Co 7:27 ·broken·up from a·woman? Do·not seek a·woman.
1Co 11:9 is·not created on·account·of the woman, but·rather
1Co 11:13 is·it befitting·for a·woman to·pray to·God not·
Rv 2:20 because you·give·leave·for the woman JeZebel,
Rv 12:13 the woman who reproduced·and·birthed the male.
Rv 17:3 And I·saw a·woman who·is·sitting·down upon a·
Rv 17:6 And I·saw the woman getting·drunk from·out of·the
G1135.2 N-APF γυναῖκας (5x)
Ac 8:3 ·off both men and women, he·was·handing·*them*·over
Ac 9:2 whether being men or women, he·may·bring·them
Ac 13:50 personally·stirred·up the women being·reverent
Ac 22:4 and handing·over into prisons both men and women.
1Ti 2:9 also, *I·resolve for* the women to·adorn themselves in
G1135.2 N-DSF γυναικί (8x)
Jn 4:42 Also they·were·saying to·the woman, "No·longer
Mt 26:10 ·present wearisome·troubles to·the woman? For
1Co 7:27 ·you·been·engaged·to·be·married to·a·woman?
1Co 11:6 but if *it·is* shameful for·a·woman to·be·shorn or to·
1Ti 2:12 entrust·an·executive·charge to·a·woman *for·her* to·
Rv 12:14 And to·the woman, two wings of·the great eagle
Rv 12:16 And the earth swiftly·helped the woman, and the
Rv 12:17 the Dragon was·angry toward the woman, and he·
G1135.2 N-DPF γυναιξίν (7x)
Lk 1:28 Having·been·blessed *are* you among women."
Lk 1:42 "Having·been·blessed *are* you among women, and
Ac 1:14 the petition, together with·women and Mariam the
Ac 16:13 ·speaking to·the women coming·together *there*.
Mt 28:5 the angel declared to·the women, "Yeu·yeurselves
1Co 14:35 For it·is shameful for·women to·speak in a·
1Ti 2:10 which is·befitting·for women who·are·making·a· a·
G1135.2 N-GSF γυναικός (13x)
Jn 4:9 personally·from me, being a·Samaritan woman?"
Jn 4:27 that he·was·speaking with a·woman. However, not·
Jn 4:39 on·account·of the saying of·the woman, testifying,
Ac 16:1 a·son of·a·certain Jewish woman (one·that·trusts),
Gal 4:4 ·to·be birthed·from·out of·a·woman, coming·to·be
1Co 7:27 Have·you·been·broken·up from a·woman? Do·not
1Co 11:3 is the Anointed-One, and woman's head *is* the man
1Co 11:8 man is not from·out of·woman, but·rather woman
1Co 11:11 neither *is* man apart·from woman, neither *is*
1Co 11:12 the man *is* also through the woman, but all things
Rv 12:4 Dragon stands in·the·sight of·the woman, the·one
Rv 12:15 ·flood·water right·behind the woman, in·order·that
Rv 17:7 to·you the MYSTERY of·the woman, and of·the
G1135.2 N-GPF γυναικῶν (10x)
Lk 7:28 among those·born of·women there·is not·even·one
Lk 23:27 of·the people, and·also of·women, who also were·
Ac 5:14 multitudes both of·men and of·women)—
Ac 17:4 Greek·men and not a·few of·the foremost women.
Ac 17:12 not a·few of·the dignified Greek women and men.
Mt 11:11 those·born of·women there·has·not been·awakened
Mt 14:21 men, apart·from women and little·children.
Mt 15:38 men, apart·from women and little·children.
Rv 9:8 they·were·having hair as hair of·women, and their
Rv 14:4 who are·not tarnished with women, for they·are
EG1135.2 (13x)
Jn 11:19 alongside the *women* in·company·with Martha and
Jn 19:25 Now *these women* stood near the cross of·Jesus:
Lk 17:35 Two *women* shall·be grinding in·unison; one shall·
Lk 24:5 And with·the *women* becoming alarmed and
Ac 16:14 ·purple·cloth, *a·woman* who·is·reverencing God,
Mt 1:6 birthed·from·out of·the·one *having·been* UrIah's *wife*).
Mt 19:9 ·adultery. And the *wife* having·been·divorced,
Mt 22:25 first·one, upon·marrying *a·wife*, completely·died.
Mt 24:41 Two *women shall·be* grinding at the mill-house;
1Co 7:2 wife, and each *woman* must·have her·own husband.
1Co 11:5 the same as·the *woman* having·been·shaved·bald.
1Ti 2:15 — provided·that *such women* should·continue in
Rv 12:15 this *woman to·be* carried·away·by·the·flood·water.
G1135.3 N-NSF γυνή (28x)
Jn 8:4 "Mentor, this wife was·grabbed·suddenly *while*
Jn 8:9 was·left·behind— and·also the wife standing in *the*
Jn 8:10 "*Ah*, the wife. Where are those·men, your legal·
Lk 1:5 of·AbiJah. And his wife *was* from·among the
Lk 1:13 is·heard, and your wife EliSabeth shall·bear you a·
Lk 1:18 an·old·man, and my wife *is* having·well-advanced
Lk 1:24 after these days, his wife EliSabeth conceived and
Lk 8:3 and Joanna, wife of·Chuza (personal·administrator
Lk 20:32 So last of·all, the wife died also.
Lk 20:33 resurrection, whose wife of·them does·she·become
Ac 5:7 of·three hours, and his wife, not having·seen the·
Mt 22:27 And last of·all, the wife died also.
Mt 22:28 in the resurrection whose wife shall·she·be of·the
Mt 27:19 the Bema·judgment·seat, his wife dispatched to
Mk 10:12 And if a·wife should·divorce her husband and
Mk 12:22 Last of·all, the wife died also.
Mk 12:23 ·should·rise·up, whose wife shall·she·be of·them?
Rm 7:2 For the wife *yoked·together* under·a·husband has·
1Co 7:3 ·due, and likewise also the wife to·the husband.
1Co 7:4 The wife does·not have·control·over her·own body,
1Co 7:4 ·control·over his·own body, but·rather the wife.
1Co 7:13 And a·wife who has a·non-trusting husband also—
1Co 7:14 and the non-trusting wife has·been·made·holy by
1Co 7:34 ·a·distinct·difference *also between* the wife and the
1Co 7:39 A·wife has·been·bound by·Torah-Law over a·
Eph 5:33 himself, and *so·also* the wife *accordingly* (*as·the*
1Ti 5:9 sixty years·of·age, having·been a·wife of·one man,
Rv 19:7 Lamb did·come and his wife did·make herself ready
G1135.3 N-NPF γυναῖκες (5x)
1Pe 3:1 *Now* likewise the wives: be·submitting·yeurselves
1Pe 3:5 in·times·past, the holy wives also were·adorning
Eph 5:22 *Now* the wives: Yeu·must·submit·yeurselves to·
Eph 5:24 ·this·manner also the wives to·their·own husbands
Col 3:18 *Now* the wives: Yeu·must·submit·yeurselves to·
G1135.3 N-VSF γύναι (1x)
1Co 7:16 what do·you·personally·know, O·wife, whether
G1135.3 N-ASF γυναῖκα (43x)
Jn 8:3 brought to him a·wife having·been·grabbed in
Lk 14:20 declared, 'I·married a·wife, and on·account·of that
Lk 14:26 his father, and mother, and wife, and children, and
Lk 16:18 "Anyone divorcing his wife and marrying another
Lk 18:29 parents, or brothers, or wife, or children, for·the·
Lk 20:28 ·man's brother should·die while·having a·wife, and
Lk 20:28 should·take his wife and should·fully·raise·up
Lk 20:29 the first·one, after·taking a·wife, died childless.
Lk 20:30 the second took the *same* wife, and this·man died
Lk 20:33 ·she·become? For the seven held her *for* a·wife."
Ac 18:2 Italy with his wife Little·Prisca·*(that·is,·Priscilla)*,
Mt 1:20 to·personally·take Mariam *for* your wife, for the·one
Mt 1:24 him, and he·personally·took *her for* his wife,
Mt 5:31 'Whoever should·divorce his wife must·give her *a*·
Mt 5:32 should·divorce his wife, personally·aside·from a·
Mt 14:3 on·account·of HerOdias, the wife of·PhilIppus, his
Mt 18:25 him to·be·sold·off, even his wife and children and
Mt 19:3 ·of·clay† to·divorce his wife for·each and·every
Mt 19:9 that whoever should·divorce his wife, except over
Mt 19:29 or father or mother or wife or children or plots·of·
Mt 22:24 shall·dutifully·marry his wife and shall·raise·up
Mt 22:25 having offspring†, he·left his wife to·his brother.
Mk 6:17 on·account·of HerOdias, the wife of·his brother
Mk 6:18 ·is·not proper for·you to·have your brother's wife."
Mk 10:2 "Is·it·proper for·a·man to·divorce *his wife*?"
Mk 10:7 mother, and shall·be·tightly·bonded to·his wife,
Mk 10:11 should·divorce his wife and should·marry another
Mk 10:29 or father or mother or wife or children or plots·of·
Mk 12:19 should·die, and should·leave·behind a·wife, and
Mk 12:19 should·take his wife and should·fully·raise·up
Mk 12:20 and the first·one took a·wife, and·then dying, he·
Mk 12:23 ·be·of·them? For the seven held her *for* a·wife."

Αα Ββ Γγ Δδ Εε Ζζ Ηη Θθ Ιι Κκ Λλ Μμ Νν Ξξ Οο Ππ Ρρ Σσ Ττ Υυ Φφ Χχ Ψψ Ωω

1Co 5:1 such·for someone to·have the father's wife.
1Co 7:2 each *man* must·have his·own wife, and each
1Co 7:10 but·rather the Lord, a·wife *is* not to·be·separated
1Co 7:11 And a·husband *is* not to·leave *his* wife.
1Co 7:12 any brother has a·non-trusting wife, and she·herself
1Co 7:16 O·husband, whether you·shall·save the wife?
1Co 9:5 we·not have privilege to·lead·about a·wife (a·sister
Eph 5:28 The·one loving his wife loves himself.
Eph 5:31 and shall·be·tightly·bonded to his wife, and the
Eph 5:33 ·manner) must·love his·own wife even·as himself,
Rv 21:9 I·shall·show you the Bride, the Lamb's wife."
G1135.3 N-APF γυναῖκας (6x)
Mt 19:8 freely·permitted yeu to·divorce yeur wives, but from
1Co 7:29 … even the·ones having wives should·be as not
Eph 5:25 Yeu·must·love yeur·own wives, just·as the
Eph 5:28 are·obligated to·love their·own wives as their·own
Col 3:19 the husbands: Yeu·must·love the wives, and do·not
1Ti 3:11 *also, the* wives *must·be* morally·worthy·of·reverent·
G1135.3 N-DSF γυναικί (7x)
Lk 2:5 with·Mariam, his espoused wife, being swellingly·
Ac 5:1 together with·Sapphira his wife, sold a·possession,
Ac 24:24 ·arriving·publicly together with·his wife Drusilla
Mt 19:5 mother and shall·be·tightly·bonded to·his wife, and
1Co 7:3 must·render to·the wife the kind·marital·duty being·
1Co 7:14 husband has·been·made·holy by the wife, and the
1Co 7:33 of·the world, how he·shall·accommodate his wife.
G1135.3 N-DPF γυναιξίν (1x)
Ac 21:5 seeing us off (together with·wives and children)
G1135.3 N-GSF γυναικός (10x)
Jn 8:10 ·viewing not·even·one besides the wife, declared to·
Lk 3:19 by him concerning HerOdias (the wife of·his brother
Lk 17:32 "Remember Lot's wife.
Ac 5:2 the price, with·his wife also having·mutually·known
Mt 19:10 ·of·clay† is in·this·manner with his wife, it·is·not
Tit 1:6 ·doing, a·husband of·one wife, having trustworthy
1Co 7:1 good for·a·man·of·clay† not to·lay·hold of·a·wife.
Eph 5:23 the husband is head of·the wife, even as the
1Ti 3:2 ·suspicion, a·husband of·one wife, sober-minded,
1Ti 3:12 Stewards must·be husbands of·one wife, conducting
G1135.3 N-GPF γυναικῶν (1x)
1Pe 3:1 through the behavior of·the wives without a·word
EG1135.3 (1x)
Jn 19:25 his mother's sister (Miryam the *wife* of·Clopas), and

G1136 Γώγ Gṓg *n/p.* (1x)

גּוֹג ĝôg [Hebrew]
Roots:H1463 See:G3098 xLangAlso:H1996
G1136 N/P-PRI Γώγ (1x)
Rv 20:8 four corners of·the earth, Gog and Magog, to·gather

G1137 γωνία gōnía *n.* (9x)

See:G1119
G1137 N-APF γωνίας (1x)
Rv 7:1 four angels standing on the four corners of·the earth,
G1137 N-DSF γωνίᾳ (1x)
Ac 26:26 ·thing was not having·been·practiced in a·corner.
G1137 N-DPF γωνίαις (2x)
Mt 6:5 gatherings and in the corners of·the broad·streets to·
Rv 20:8 the·ones in the four corners of·the earth, Gog and
G1137 N-GSF γωνίας (5x)
Lk 20:17 has·now·become the·distinct head corner *stone*"?
Ac 4:11 the·one becoming the·distinct head corner *stone*."
Mt 21:42 has·now·become the·distinct head corner *stone*.
Mk 12:10 has·now·become the·distinct head corner *stone*.
1Pe 2:7 has·now·become the·distinct head corner *stone*,"

Δδ - Delta

G1138 Δαβίδ Dabíd *n/p.* (59x)

Δαυίδ Dauíd [regional diphthong]
Δαυείδ Dauêíd [later variant]
דָּוִד ḏavid [Hebrew]
Roots:H1732
G1138.2 N/P-PRI Δαβίδ (59x)
Jn 7:42 comes birthed·from·out of·the Seed of·David, and
Jn 7:42 the village of·BethLechem, where David was *from*?
Lk 1:27 Joseph, from·among *the* house of·David. And the
Lk 1:32 shall·give to·him the Throne of·his father David.
Lk 1:69 for·us in the house of·his servant·boy David,
Lk 2:4 into Judea, to *the* city of·David (which is·called
Lk 2:4 from·among *the* house and paternal·lineage of·David,
Lk 2:11 in *the* city of·David, a·Savior is·reproduced·and·
Lk 3:31 *son* of·Mattatha, *son* of·Nathan, *son* of·David,
Lk 6:3 ·aloud this·thing that David did that·one·time·when
Lk 18:38 "Jesus, O·Son of·David, show·mercy on·me.
Lk 18:39 *the* more— "O·Son of·David, show·mercy on·me!
Lk 20:41 ·*for* the Anointed-One to·be David's Son?
Lk 20:42 And David himself says in a·scroll of·Psalms,
Lk 20:44 So·then David calls him 'Lord'; how is·he also his
Ac 1:16 ·declared through David's mouth concerning Judas
Ac 2:25 For David says this in·regard·to *his·Lord*, " I·was·
Ac 2:29 ·of·speech concerning the patriarch David, that also
Ac 2:34 "For David did·not ascend into the heavens, but he·
Ac 4:25 *the* mouth of·your servant·boy David, declaring,
Ac 7:45 *It·was with our fathers* until the days of·David,
Ac 13:22 from·duty, he·awakened to·them David as king,
Ac 13:22 he·declared, "I·found David, the *son* of·Jesse,
Ac 13:34 ·yeu the trustworthy, Divine·Promises of·David."
Ac 13:36 "For in·fact David, after·tending to·the counsel of·
Ac 15:16 and shall·rebuild the tabernacle of·David, the·one
Heb 4:7 "Today," saying *it* by David (after so·vast a·time),
Heb 11:32 and Yiphtach; and also David, SamuEl, and the
Mt 1:1 of·YeShua Anointed, *the* Son of·David, *the* son of·
Mt 1:6 Now Jesse begot King David, and King David begot
Mt 1:6 begot King David, and King David begot Solomon
Mt 1:17 ·offspring from AbRaham until David *are* fourteen
Mt 1:17 generations. Then from David until the Babylonian
Mt 1:20 "Joseph, son of·David, you·should·not be·afraid to·
Mt 9:27 and saying, "O·Son of·David, show·mercy on·us!"
Mt 12:3 "Did·yeu·not read·aloud what David did, when he·
Mt 12:23 "Could this be the Son of·David?"
Mt 15:22 on·me, O·Lord, O·Son of·David; my daughter *is*
Mt 20:30 "Show·mercy on·us, O·Lord, Son of·David."
Mt 20:31 "Show·mercy on·us, O·Lord, Son of·David."
Mt 21:9 "Hosanna to·the Son of·David! "Having·been·
Mt 21:15 "Hosanna to·the Son of·David!"
Mt 22:42 is·he?" They·say to·him, "*The Son* of·David."
Mt 22:43 to·them, "So·then how·does David in Spirit call
Mt 22:45 So·then, if David calls him 'Lord,' how is·he his
Mk 2:25 ·not·even·at·any·time read·aloud what David did,
Mk 10:47 "O·Jesus, the Son of·David, show·mercy on·me.
Mk 10:48 more— "O·Son of·David, show·mercy on·me!"
Mk 11:10 *the* kingdom of·our father David, the·one that·is·
Mk 12:35 say that the Anointed-One is a·Son of·David?
Mk 12:36 For David himself declared by the Holy Spirit,
Mk 12:37 So·then David himself refers·to him *as* 'Lord,' so
Rm 1:3 ·to·be birthed·from·out of·David's Seed according·to
Rm 4:6 exactly·as David also refers·to the supreme·
Rm 11:9 And David says, "Let their table be·made into a·
2Ti 2:8 Jesus Anointed, birthed·from·out of·David's Seed, *is*
Rv 3:7 The·one having the key of·David, the·one opening·up
Rv 5:5 tribe of·Judah (the Root of·David)! He·victoriously·
Rv 22:16 I AM the root and the kindred of·David, the star,

G1139 δαιμονίζομαι daimônízômai *v.* (13x)

Roots:G1142
G1139 V-PNI-3S δαιμονίζεται (1x)
Mt 15:22 my daughter *is* badly possessed·with·a·demon."
G1139 V-PNP-ASM δαιμονιζόμενον (2x)
Mt 9:32 ·of·clay†, a·mute being·possessed·with·a·demon.
Mk 5:15 *formerly* being·possessed·with·demons sitting· and
G1139 V-PNP-APM δαιμονιζομένους (3x)
Mt 4:24 and those·being·possessed·with·demons, and
Mt 8:16 to·him many being·possessed·with·demons, and he·
Mk 1:32 the·ones who·are·being·possessed·with·demons.
G1139 V-PNP-DSM δαιμονιζομένῳ (1x)
Mk 5:16 to·the·one being·possessed·with·demons, and
G1139 V-PNP-GSM δαιμονιζομένου (1x)
Jn 10:21 *of·one* who·is·being·possessed·with·a·demon. ¿!·Is
G1139 V-PNP-GPM δαιμονιζομένων (1x)
Mt 8:33 and·also of·the·ones being·possessed·with·demons.
G1139 V-PNP-NSM δαιμονιζόμενος (1x)
Mt 12:22 one·being·possessed·with·a·demon was·brought
G1139 V-PNP-NPM δαιμονιζόμενοι (1x)
Mt 8:28 two·men being·possessed·with·demons, who·are·
G1139 V-AOP-NSM δαιμονισθείς (2x)
Lk 8:36 the·one being·possessed·with·the·demons was·.
Mk 5:18 the·one having·been·possessed·with·demons was·

G1140 δαιμόνιον daimṓniôn *n.* (61x)

Roots:G1142 See:G1141 xLangAlso:H7700
G1140.1 N-NSN δαιμόνιον (6x)
Jn 10:21 ·with·a·demon. ¿!·Is a·demon able to·open·up
Lk 4:35 And the demon, flinging him in the midst, came·
Lk 9:42 yet coming·alongside, the demon mangled him and
Mt 17:18 *the demon*, and the demon came·out from him.
Mk 7:29 head·on·out. The demon has·come·forth out of·
Mk 7:30 house, she·found the demon having·come·out and
G1140.1 N-NPN δαιμόνια (8x)
Lk 4:41 And demons also were·coming·out of many, yelling·
Lk 8:2 from whom had·gone·forth seven demons,
Lk 8:30 "Legion," because many demons entered into him.
Lk 8:33 of the man·of·clay†, the demons entered into the
Lk 8:35 man·of·clay† from whom the demons had·come·out,
Lk 8:38 whom the demons had·come·out was·petitioning
Lk 10:17 "Lord, even the demons are·subject to·us in your
Jac 2:19 You·do well. The demons also trust *that*, and they·
G1140.1 N-ASN δαιμόνιον (9x)
Jn 7:20 and declared, "You·have a·demon! Who seeks to·
Jn 8:48 you·yourself are a·Samaritan, and have a·demon?"
Jn 8:49 "I·myself do·not have a·demon, but·rather I·deeply·
Jn 8:52 we·have·known that you·have a·demon. AbRaham
Jn 10:20 were·saying, "He·has a·demon and is·raving·mad;
Lk 7:33 nor drinking wine, and yeu·say, 'He·has a·demon.'
Lk 11:14 *afterward, Jesus* was casting·out a·demon, and it
Mt 11:18 nor drinking, and they·say, 'He·has a·demon.'
Mk 7:26 him that he·should·cast·forth the demon out of·her
G1140.1 N-APN δαιμόνια (24x)
Lk 8:27 city, who was·having demons for a·significant·span
Lk 9:1 authority over all the demons, and to·both·relieve·
Lk 9:49 we·saw someone casting·out the demons in your
Lk 11:15 ·Master-Of-Dung, *the* prince of·the demons."
Lk 11:18 "Yeu·say that I cast·out demons by *the*
Lk 11:19 by Master-Of-Dung cast·out the demons, by
Lk 11:20 finger, I·cast·out the demons, then·by·inference,
Lk 13:32 'Behold, I·cast·out demons, and I·further·finish
Mt 7:22 and in·your name cast·out demons, and in·your
Mt 9:34 ·saying, "He·casts·out the demons by the prince of·
Mt 10:8 awaken dead·ones; cast·out demons. Yeu·received
Mt 12:24 "This·man does·not cast·out the demons, except by
Mt 12:27 Master-Of-Dung, cast·out the demons, by whom·
Mt 12:28 But if I·myself cast·out the demons by God's Spirit
Mk 1:34 and he·cast·out many demons. And he·was·not
Mk 1:34 And he·was·not allowing the demons to·speak,
Mk 1:39 among all Galilee and casting·out the demons.
Mk 3:15 ·and·cure the illnesses, and to·cast·out the demons.
Mk 3:22 the prince of·the demons he·casts·out the demons."
Mk 6:13 And they·were·casting·out many demons, and with·
Mk 9:38 we·saw someone casting·out demons in·your name,
Mk 16:9 from whom he·had·cast·out seven demons.
Mk 16:17 name shall·they·cast·out demons; they·shall·speak
Rv 9:20 ·not fall·prostrate *directly·before* the demons, and
G1140.1 N-DPN δαιμονίοις (1x)

1Co 10:20 they·sacrificially·slaughter to·demons, and not
G1140.1 N-GSN δαιμονίου (3x)
Lk 4:33 ·of·clay† having a·spirit of·an·impure demon, and
Lk 11:14 And it·happened, with·the demon going·out, the
Mt 9:33 And with·the demon being·cast·out, the mute spoke,
G1140.1 N-GPN δαιμονίων (8x)
Lk 11:15 ·out the demons by BaalZebul,·Master-Of-Dung, *the*
Mt 9:34 ·casts·out the demons by the prince of·the demons."
Mt 12:24 ·Master-Of-Dung, *the* prince of·the demons."
Mk 3:22 "By the prince of·the demons he·casts·out the
1Co 10:20 ·not want yeu to·become partners with·demons.
1Co 10:21 cup and·also *the* cup of·demons. Yeu·are·not able
1Co 10:21 ·*the*·Lord's table and·also to·*the*·table of·demons.
1Ti 4:1 to·impostrous spirits and to·instructions of·demons,
EG1140.1 (1x)
Mt 17:18 And YeShua reprimanded *the demon*, and the
G1140.2 N-GPN δαιμονίων (1x)
Ac 17:18 ·ardent·proclaimer of·the strange·new demigods."

G1141 δαιμονι•ώδης daimôniṓdēs *adj.* (1x)
Roots:G1140 G1491
G1141 A-NSF δαιμονιώδης (1x)
Jac 3:15 ·above, but·rather *is* earthly, soulish, demonic.

G1142 δαίμων daímōn *n.* (5x)
Compare:G1140 See:G1139
G1142 N-NPM δαίμονες (2x)
Mt 8:31 And the demons were·imploring him, saying, "If
Mk 5:12 And all the demons implored him, saying, "Send us
G1142 N-GSM δαίμονος (1x)
Lk 8:29 he·was·driven by the demon into the wilderness).
G1142 N-GPM δαιμόνων (2x)
Rv 16:14 For they·are spirits of·demons, doing miraculous·
Rv 18:2 and is·become a·residence of·demons, and a·prison

G1143 δάκνω dáknō *v.* (1x)
G1143.1 V-PAI-2P δάκνετε (1x)
Gal 5:15 But if yeu·bite and devour one·another, look·out

G1144 δάκρυ dákry *n.* (11x)
δάκρυον dákryôn
See:G1145
G1144 N-ASN δάκρυον (2x)
Rv 7:17 'And God shall·rub·away every tear from their eyes.
Rv 21:4 'And God shall·rub·away every tear from their eyes.
G1144 N-DPN δάκρυσιν (2x)
Lk 7:38 to·shower his feet with·tears and was·firmly·wiping
Lk 7:44 showered my feet with·the tears and firmly·wiped
G1144 N-GPN δακρύων (7x)
Ac 20:19 humility·of·mind, and with·many tears, and with·
Ac 20:31 admonishing each one, night and day with tears.
Heb 5:7 with a·strong yell and tears toward the·one being·
Heb 12:17 even·though seeking it out with tears.)
Mk 9:24 ·the little·child, yelling·out with tears, was·saying,
2Co 2:4 of·heart I·wrote to·yeu through many tears, not that
2Ti 1:4 (having·been·mindful of·your tears)— while·greatly·

G1145 δακρύω dakrýō *v.* (1x)
Roots:G1144 Compare:G2799 G2354 G3996
xLangAlso:H1830 H1832 H7481
G1145.1 V-AAI-3S ἐδάκρυσεν (1x)
Jn 11:35 Jesus welled·up·with·tears.

G1146 δακτύλιος daktýliôs *n.* (1x)
Roots:G1147 See:G5554 xLangAlso:H2885
G1146.1 N-ASM δακτύλιον (1x)
Lk 15:22 And give *him* a·ring for his hand and shoes for his

G1147 δάκτυλος dáktylôs *n.* (8x)
Roots:G1176 Compare:G0206-1 See:G1146
xLangEquiv:H0676 A0677
G1147 N-ASM δάκτυλον (2x)
Jn 20:25 hands, and may·cast my finger into the imprint of·
Jn 20:27 ·says to·Thomas, "Bring your finger here, and see
G1147 N-APM δακτύλους (1x)
Mk 7:33 in private, *Jesus* cast his fingers into his ears, and
G1147 N-DSM δακτύλῳ (3x)
Jn 8:6 down, Jesus was·writing with·the finger into the soil.
Lk 11:20 "But if with God's finger, I·cast·out the demons,
Mt 23:4 ·of·clay†, but with·their·own fingers, they·are·not
G1147 N-GSM δακτύλου (1x)
Lk 16:24 he·may·dip the tip of·his finger in·water and may·
G1147 N-GPM δακτύλων (1x)
Lk 11:46 do·not reach·for the loads with·one of·yeur fingers.

G1148 Δαλμανουθά Dalmanôuthá *n/l.* (1x)
Compare:G3093
G1148.2 N/L-PRI Δαλμανουθά (1x)
Mk 8:10 disciples, he·came into the parts of·Dalmanutha.

G1149 Δαλματία Dalmatía *n/l.* (1x)
G1149 N/L-ASF Δαλματίαν (1x)
2Ti 4:10 Crescens to Galatia, *and* Titus to Dalmatia.

G1150 δαμάζω damázō *v.* (4x)
See:G1151 G1152
G1150 V-PPI-3S δαμάζεται (1x)
Jac 3:7 of·creatures·in·the·sea, is·tamed and has·been·tamed
G1150 V-AAN δαμάσαι (2x)
Mk 5:4 not·even·one·man was·having·strength to·tame him.
Jac 3:8 ·one among·clay·men† is·able to·tame the tongue. *It*·
G1150 V-RPI-3S δεδάμασται (1x)
Jac 3:7 ·the·sea, is·tamed and has·been·tamed by the nature

G1151 δάμαλις dámalis *n.* (1x)
Roots:G1150
xLangEquiv:H5697 xLangAlso:H6510 H5695
G1151.4 N-GSF δαμάλεως (1x)
Heb 9:13 and of·adult·male·goats (and ashes of·a·red·cow)

G1152 Δάμαρις Dámaris *n/p.* (1x)
Roots:G1150
G1152.2 N/P-NSF Δάμαρις (1x)
Ac 17:34 and a·woman by·the·name·of Damaris, and others

G1153 Δαμασκηνός Damaskēnós *adj/g.* (1x)
Roots:G1154
G1153 A/G-GPM Δαμασκηνῶν (1x)
2Co 11:32 city of·the·Damascenes under·continual·guard,

G1154 Δαμασκός Damaskós *n/l.* (15x)
דַּמֶּשֶׂק ḏaměšeq [Hebrew]
Roots:H1834
G1154.2 N/L-ASF Δαμασκόν (7x)
Ac 9:2 ·from him letters for Damascus pertaining·to the
Ac 9:8 him by·the·hand, they·brought *him* into Damascus.
Ac 22:5 brothers and traversed into Damascus, bringing the·
Ac 22:10 Upon·rising·up, traverse into Damascus, and·there
Ac 22:11 being·together with·me, I·came into Damascus.
Ac 26:12 while·traversing to Damascus with authority and
Gal 1:17 into Arabia, and again returned·back to Damascus.
G1154.2 N/L-DSF Δαμασκῷ (8x)
Ac 9:3 *for* him to·draw·near to·Damascus, and·then
Ac 9:10 there·was a·certain disciple at Damascus, AnanIas
Ac 9:19 was among the disciples at Damascus *for* some days.
Ac 9:22 the·ones residing in Damascus, *by* conclusively·
Ac 9:27 he·boldly·spoke·with·clarity at Damascus in the
Ac 22:6 and drawing·near to·Damascus around midday, it·
Ac 26:20 announcing first to·the·ones in Damascus, and·then
2Co 11:32 In Damascus, the national·magistrate *under*

G1155 δανείζω danêízō *v.* (4x)
Roots:G1156 Compare:G5531 See:G1157
xLangAlso:H3867
G1155.2 V-AMN δανείσασθαι (1x)
Mt 5:42 ·turning·away the·one wanting to·borrow from you.
G1155.3 V-PAI-3P δανείζουσιν (1x)
Lk 6:34 ·disqualified also lend to·*the*·morally·disqualified,
G1155.3 V-PAM-2P δανείζετε (1x)
Lk 6:35 and beneficially·do·good, and lend, fully·expecting
G1155.3 V-PAS-2P δανείζητε (1x)
Lk 6:34 "And if yeu·should·lend *to·them* personally·from

G1156 δάνειον dánêiôn *n.* (1x)
Compare:G5531 See:G1155 G1157 G1325
G1156 N-ASN δάνειον (1x)
Mt 18:27 slave fully·released him and forgave him the loan.

G1157 δανειστής danêistḗs *n.* (1x)
Roots:G1155
G1157 N-DSM δανειστῇ (1x)
Lk 7:41 "There·was a·certain lender *having* two needy·

G1158 Δανι•ήλ Daniḗl *n/p.* (2x)
דָּנִיֵּאל ḏaniyeʼl [Hebrew]
Roots:H1840
xLangEquiv:A1841 xLangAlso:A1096 H1095
G1158.2 N/P-PRI Δανιήλ (2x)
Mt 24:15 ' the·one being·uttered through DaniEl the prophet,
Mk 13:14 ' the·one being·uttered by DaniEl the prophet,

G1159 δαπανάω dapanáō *v.* (5x)
Roots:G1160 Compare:G0355 See:G4325 G1550
G1159.1 V-AAP-NSF δαπανήσασα (1x)
Mk 5:26 many practitioners·of·healing and expending all her
G1159.2 V-FAI-1S δαπανήσω (1x)
2Co 12:15 I·myself shall·cover·the·expense and shall·be·
G1159.2 V-AAM-2S δαπάνησον (1x)
Ac 21:24 with·them, and cover·the·expense for them in·
G1159.3 V-AAP-GSM δαπανήσαντος (1x)
Lk 15:14 And with·him spending all *of·it*, there·occurred a·
G1159.3 V-AAS-2P δαπανήσητε (1x)
Jac 4:3 ·request wrongly, in·order·that yeu·may·spend *it* on

G1160 δαπάνη dapánē *n.* (1x)
See:G0077 G1159
G1160.1 N-ASF δαπάνην (1x)
Lk 14:28 first *and* calculates the expense, whether he·has the

G1161 δέ dé *conj.* (2833x)
Compare:G2532 See:G3303 G1211
xLangAlso:HFC01
(abbreviated listing for G1161)
G1161.ª CONJ δέ (15x)
(list for G1161.ª:CONJ excluded)
G1161.1 CONJ δέ (1276x)
(list for G1161.1:CONJ excluded)
G1161.2 CONJ δέ (1079x)
(list for G1161.2:CONJ excluded)
EG1161.2 (1x)
(list for EG1161.2: excluded)
G1161.3 CONJ δέ (292x)
(list for G1161.3:CONJ excluded)
EG1161.3 (16x)
(list for EG1161.3: excluded)
G1161.4 CONJ δέ (91x)
(list for G1161.4:CONJ excluded)
G1161.5 CONJ δέ (55x)
(list for G1161.5:CONJ excluded)
G1161.7 CONJ δέ (1x)
(list for G1161.7:CONJ excluded)
G1161.8 CONJ δέ (7x)
(list for G1161.8:CONJ excluded)

G1162 δέησις déēsis *n.* (19x)
Roots:G1189 Compare:G1783 G1793 G2428 G4335
G1162.1 N-NSF δέησις (3x)
Lk 1:13 ZacharIas, on·account·that your petition is·heard,
Rm 10:1 my heart's good·purpose and petition to God on·
Jac 5:16 A·petition of·a·righteous·man is·itself·operating *to*
G1162.1 N-ASF δέησιν (2x)
Php 1:4 ·behalf of·yeu all while·making the petition with joy
1Pe 3:12 and his ears *are·open* to their petitions, but *the* face
G1162.1 N-APF δεήσεις (3x)
Lk 5:33 fast frequently, and make petitions, and likewise
Heb 5:7 *was* offering·up both petitions and supplications
1Ti 2:1 Now·then, I·exhort first of·all *for* petitions, prayers,
G1162.1 N-DSF δεήσει (6x)
Ac 1:14 in·the prayer and the petition, together with·women
Php 1:4 always in every petition of·mine on·behalf of·yeu all
Php 4:6 (in·the prayer and in·the petition with thanksgiving)
2Co 1:11 also assisting·together by·the petition on·our behalf
2Co 9:14 And by·their petition on·behalf of·yeu, they·are·
Eph 6:18 perseverance— even with·petition concerning all
G1162.1 N-DPF δεήσεσιν (3x)

Lk 2:37 *to·God* with·fastings and petitions night and day.
1Ti 5:5 and continues·on in·the petitions and in·the prayers
2Ti 1:3 concerning you in my petitions night and day
G1162.1 N-GSF δεήσεως (2x)
Php 1:19 for·me through yeur petition and an·ample·supply
Eph 6:18 all prayer and petition, be·presently·praying in

G1163 δεῖ dêî *v.* (109x)
δεόν dêón
Roots:G1210 Compare:G0316 G5534 G3784 xLangAlso:H6878

G1163.1 V-PQI-3S δεῖ (1x)
Ac 21:22 why is *this*? It·is·binding·for a·multitude entirely
G1163.1 V-IQI-3S ἔδει (1x)
Lk 13:16 years, was·it·not binding·for *her* to·be·loosed from
G1163.2 V-PQI-3S δεῖ (56x)
Jn 3:14 in·this·manner, it·is·mandatory·for the Son of·
Jn 4:20 is the place where it·is·mandatory to·fall·prostrate."
Jn 4:24 and it·is·mandatory·for the·ones falling·prostrate
Jn 9:4 "It·is·mandatory·for me to·be·working the works of·
Jn 10:16 this yard·pen. It·is·mandatory·for me to·lead these·
Jn 12:34 say, 'It·is·mandatory·for the Son of·Clay·Man† to·
Jn 20:9 ·*declared* that it·is·mandatory·for him to·rise·up
Lk 4:43 "It·is·mandatory·for me to·proclaim·the·good·news
Lk 9:22 "It·is·mandatory·for the Son of·Clay·Man† to·
Lk 17:25 "But first, it·is·mandatory·for him to·suffer many·
Lk 21:9 for it·is·mandatory·for these·things to·occur first.
Lk 22:37 I·say to·yeu, that still it·is·mandatory·for this thing
Lk 24:7 saying, 'It·is·mandatory·for the Son of·Clay·Man†
Lk 24:44 "It·is·mandatory·for all·things to·be·completely·
Ac 1:21 "Accordingly, it·is·mandatory of·the men going·
Ac 3:21 Whom in·fact it·is·mandatory·for heaven to·accept
Ac 5:29 "It·is·mandatory to·readily·comply with·God
Ac 9:6 ·be·spoken to·you what is·mandatory·for you to·do."
Ac 9:16 what·many·things it·is·mandatory·for him to·suffer
Ac 15:5 saying, "It·is·mandatory to·circumcise them and
Ac 18:21 declaring, "It·is·mandatory·for me by·all·means
Ac 19:21 I come·to·be there, it·is·mandatory·for me also to·
Ac 20:35 it·is·mandatory to·be·helpful·and·supportive of·
Ac 23:11 in·this·manner it·is·mandatory·for you to·testify
Ac 25:10 ·seat, where it·is·mandatory·for me to·be·judged.
Ac 27:24 Paul. It·is·mandatory·for you to·establish·proof
Heb 11:6 For it·is·mandatory·for the·one who·is·coming·
Mt 16:21 ·his disciples that it·is·mandatory·for him to·go·off
Mt 17:10 scribes say that it·is·mandatory·for EliJah to·come
Mt 24:6 ·disturbed, for it·is·mandatory·for all *these·things*
Mt 26:54 ·fulfilled that *state* it·is·mandatory·for *it* to·happen
Mk 8:31 to·instruct them that it·is·mandatory·for the Son of·
Mk 9:11 scribes say that it·is·mandatory·for EliJah to·come
Mk 13:7 for it·is·mandatory·for *such·things* to·happen, but·
Mk 13:10 "And it·is·mandatory·for the good·news first to·
Mk 13:14 standing where it·is·not mandatory" (the·one
1Th 4:1 us, *remember* how it·is·mandatory·for yeu to·walk
Tit 1:7 (for it·is·mandatory·for the overseer to·be without·
Tit 1:11 of·whom it·is·mandatory to·silence·mouths. Such·
Tit 1:11 are·not mandatory, through·gracious·sounding·words
1Co 15:25 For it·is·mandatory·for him to·reign, even·until
2Co 5:10 For it·is·mandatory·for every one of·us to·be·
Eph 6:20 ·with·clarity as it·is·mandatory·for me to·speak.
Col 4:4 it apparent, as it·is·mandatory·for me to·speak.
1Ti 3:2 Now·then, it·is·mandatory·for the overseer to·be
1Ti 3:7 But it·is·mandatory·for him also to·have a·good
2Ti 2:6 It·is·mandatory·for the hard·laboring man·that·
2Ti 2:24 Now it·is·mandatory·for a·slave of·*the*·Lord not to·
Rv 1:1 to·show to·his slaves what is·mandatory to·happen in
Rv 4:1 you things·which it·is·mandatory to·happen after
Rv 10:11 ·says to·me, "It·is·mandatory·for you to·prophesy
Rv 11:5 ·harm·to them, it·is·mandatory·for him to·be·killed
Rv 13:10 with a·dagger, it·is·mandatory·for him to·be·killed
Rv 17:10 ·should·come, it·is·mandatory·for him to·remain
Rv 20:3 these·things, it·is·mandatory·for him to·be·loosed
Rv 22:6 the·things·*of*·which it·is·mandatory to·be·done in
G1163.2 V-PQN δεῖν (1x)
Lk 18:1 *this·purpose* it·is·to·be·mandatory always to·pray
G1163.2 V-PQP-NSN δέον (1x)
Ac 19:36 it·is being·mandatory·for yeu to·subsist having·
G1163.2 V-IQI-3S ἔδει (11x)
Lk 11:42 the love of·God. It·is·mandatory to·do these·things
Lk 22:7 ·Bread, in which it·was·mandatory·for the Passover
Lk 24:26 Is·it·not·indeed mandatory·for the Anointed-One
Lk 24:46 so·also in·this·manner it·was·mandatory·for the
Ac 1:16 Men, brothers, it·was·mandatory·for this Scripture
Ac 17:3 that it·was·mandatory·for the Anointed-One to·
Heb 9:26 it·was·mandatory·for him to·already·suffer many·
Mt 18:33 Was·it·not mandatory·for you also to·show·mercy
Mt 23:23 the trust. "It·is·mandatory to·do these·things, and
Mt 25:27 Accordingly, it·was·mandatory·for you to·cast my
Rm 1:27 the due·payback which is·mandatory·for their error.
EG1163.2 (2x)
Lk 20:41 ·do they·say *it·is·mandatory·for* the Anointed-One
Ac 1:22 ·taken·up from us, *it·is·mandatory* of·these·men *for*
G1163.3 V-PQI-3S δεῖ (24x)
Jn 3:7 I·declared to·you, 'It·is·necessary·for yeu to·be·born
Jn 3:30 It·is·necessary·for that·one to·increasingly·grow, but
Lk 2:49 Had·yeu·not seen that it·is·necessary·for me to·be
Lk 12:12 yeu in the same hour what is·necessary to·declare."
Lk 13:14 ·are six days in which it·is·necessary to·work.
Lk 13:33 "Nevertheless, it·is·necessary·for me to·traverse
Lk 19:5 For today, it·is·necessary·for me to·abide in your
Ac 4:12 ·of·clay† by which it·is·necessary·for us to·be·saved
Ac 10:6 shall·speak to·you what is·necessary·for you to·do."
Ac 14:22 and how·that "It·is·necessary·for us to·enter into
Ac 16:30 "Sirs, what is·necessary·for me to·do in·order·that
Ac 24:19 of·whom it·is·necessary *for·them* to·be·here before
Ac 27:26 But it·is·necessary·for us to·be·cast·away upon
Heb 2:1 ·of that, it·is·necessary·for us more·abundantly to·
Rm 8:26 ·pray·for according·to·what is·necessary, but·rather
Rm 12:3 ·than what is·necessary to·contemplate *concerning*
2Pe 3:11 what·manner is·necessary·for yeu to·subsist in *all*
2Th 3:7 ·seen how it·is·necessary to·attentively·imitate us,
1Co 8:2 just·as it·is·necessary *for·one* to·absolutely·know
1Co 11:19 For it·is·necessary·for *there* also to·be factions
1Co 15:53 For it·is·necessary·for this corruptible *being* to·
2Co 11:30 If it·is·necessary to·boast, I·shall·boast *about* the·
Col 4:6 ·salt, *and* it·is·necessary·for yeu to·personally·know
1Ti 3:15 how it·is·necessary to·conduct·oneself among
G1163.3 V-PQN δεῖν (2x)
Ac 25:24 *him, that* it·is·not necessary·for him to·live any·
Ac 26:9 presumed *it* to·be·necessary to·practice many·things
G1163.3 V-PQP-APN δέοντα (1x)
1Ti 5:13 speaking things·which are·not being·necessary.
G1163.3 V-PQP-NSN δέον (1x)
1Pe 1:6 ·bit at·this·moment (though it·is being·necessary) in
G1163.3 V-PQS-3S δέῃ (2x)
Mt 26:35 "Though it·should·be·necessary·for me to·die
Mk 14:31 "Even·if it·should·be·necessary·for me to·die·
G1163.3 V-IQI-3S ἔδει (4x)
Jn 4:4 And it·was·necessary·for him to·go through Samaria.
Lk 15:32 But it·is·necessary *for·us* to·be·merry and to·be·
Ac 27:21 in·fact it·was·necessary *for·yeu* to·readily·comply
2Co 2:3 them·by·whom it·was·necessary·for me to·rejoice,
EG1163.3 (2x)
Ac 15:24 saying, '*It·is·necessary* to·be·circumcised and to·
Rm 15:8 Now I·say *it·was·necessary·for* Jesus Anointed to·

G1164 δεῖγμα dêîgma *n.* (1x)
Roots:G1166 See:G1165

G1164.2 N-ASN δεῖγμα (1x)
Jud 1:7 flesh, are·presently·set·forth·as a·public·example,

G1165 δειγματίζω dêigmatízō *v.* (1x)
Roots:G1164

G1165.2 V-AAI-3S ἐδειγμάτισεν (1x)
Col 2:15 he·made·a·public·example *of·them* with a·bold·

G1166 δεικνύω dêiknýō *v.* (31x)
Compare:G0398 G5316 See:G0584 G1925

G1166 V-FAI-1S δείξω (5x)
Ac 7:3 come·over·here into a·land which I·shall·show you."
Jac 2:18 of·your works, and·I shall·show you my trust as·a·
Rv 4:1 Walk·up here, and I·shall·show you things·which it·
Rv 17:1 to·me, "Come·over·here! I·shall·show to·you the
Rv 21:9 "Come·over·here! I·shall·show you the Bride, the
G1166 V-FAI-3S δείξει (4x)
Jn 5:20 that he·himself does, and he·shall·show him works
Lk 22:12 And·that·man shall·show yeu a·big upper·room
Mk 14:15 And he·himself shall·show yeu a·big upper·room
1Ti 6:15 who in·his·own seasons shall·show *he·is* the
G1166 V-PAI-1S δείκνυμι (1x)
1Co 12:31 And yet, I·show to·yeu *the* most surpassingly·
G1166 V-PAI-2S δεικνύεις (1x)
Jn 2:18 "What miraculous·sign do·you·show to·us, *seeing*
G1166 V-PAI-3S δείκνυσιν (2x)
Jn 5:20 is·a·friend·to the Son and shows him all·things that
Mt 4:8 him up to a·very high mountain and shows him all the
G1166 V-PAN δεικνύειν (1x)
Mt 16:21 then·on, YeShua began to·show to·his disciples
G1166 V-PAP-GSM δεικνύοντος (1x)
Rv 22:8 feet of·the angel, the·one showing me these·things.
G1166 V-AAI-1S ἔδειξα (1x)
Jn 10:32 "Many good works I·showed yeu from·out of·my
G1166 V-AAI-3S ἔδειξεν (5x)
Jn 20:20 And after·declaring this, he·showed to·them his
Lk 4:5 him up upon a·high mountain, showed to·him all the
Ac 10:28 ·ethnic·tribe, but God showed to·me to·refer·to
Rv 21:10 and high mountain, and showed me the Great
Rv 22:1 And he·showed me a·pure river of·water of·
G1166 V-AAM-2S δεῖξον (6x)
Jn 14:8 Philip says to·him, "Lord, show us the Father, and
Jn 14:9 ·then how·do you·yourself say, 'Show us the Father'
Lk 5:14 "But·rather going·off, show yourself to·the priest·
Mt 8:4 But·rather head·on·out, show yourself to·the priest·
Mk 1:44 But·rather head·on·out, show yourself to·the priest·
Jac 2:18 and·I have works." Show me your trust as·a·result
G1166 V-AAM-3S δειξάτω (1x)
Jac 3:13 of·the good behavior, let·him·show his works with
G1166 V-AAN δεῖξαι (2x)
Rv 1:1 which God gave·to·him, to·show to·his slaves what
Rv 22:6 dispatched his angel to·show to·his slaves the·
G1166 V-APP-ASM δειχθέντα (1x)
Heb 8:5 particular·pattern, the·one being·shown to·you on

G1167 δειλία dêilía *n.* (1x)
Roots:G1169

G1167.1 N-GSF δειλίας (1x)
2Ti 1:7 did·not give us a·spirit of·timidity, but·rather of·

G1168 δειλιάω dêiliáō *v.* (1x)
Roots:G1167 Compare:G1573

G1168.1 V-PAM-3S δειλιάτω (1x)
Jn 14:27 ·not be·troubled in·yeur heart, nor·even be·timid.

G1169 δειλός dêilós *adj.* (3x)
Compare:G5398 See:G1171 G1174

G1169.1 A-NPM δειλοί (2x)
Mt 8:26 to·them, "Why are·yeu timid, O·yeu·of·little·trust?
Mk 4:40 to·them, "Why are·yeu timid in·this·manner?
G1169.1 A-DPM δειλοῖς (1x)
Rv 21:8 "But timid·ones, and non-trusting·ones, and ones·

G1170 δεῖνα dêîna *adj.* (1x)
Compare:G3778 G5100 See:G1171

G1170.2 A-ASM δεῖνα (1x)
Mt 26:18 into the City to a·particular·man and declare to·him

G1171 δεινῶς dêinôs *adv.* (2x)
See:G1169

G1171 ADV δεινῶς (2x)
Lk 11:53 Pharisees began to·besiege *him* dreadfully, and to·
Mt 8:6 *on a·couch* at home, dreadfully being·tormented."

G1172 δειπνέω dêipnéō *v.* (4x)
Roots:G1173 Compare:G0709 See:G4885-2 G0078-1

G1172 V-FAI-1S δειπνήσω (1x)
Rv 3:20 ·in alongside him, and shall·eat·supper with him,
G1172 V-AAN δειπνῆσαι (2x)
Lk 22:20 Likewise also the cup after eating·supper, saying,

1Co 11:25 *he·took* the cup after eating·supper, saying,

G1172 V-AAS-1S δειπνήσω (1x)

Lk 17:8 'Make·ready *food* which I·may·eat·for·supper, and

G1173 δεῖπνον dêîpnôn *n.* (16x)

Compare:G0712 G1062 See:G1160 G0078-1

G1173.1 N-ASN δεῖπνον (8x)

Jn 12:2 Accordingly, they·made a·supper for·him there, and
Lk 14:12 you·should·make a·luncheon or a·supper, do·not
Lk 14:16 man·of·clay† made a·great supper and called many.
Mk 6:21 HerOd·AntiPas was·making a·supper on·his birthday
1Co 11:20 in·unison, it·is not to·eat *the* Lord's supper.
1Co 11:21 each·one takes his·own supper prior·to *others*;
Rv 19:9 ·called·forth to the Wedding Supper of·the Lamb.'"
Rv 19:17 be·gathered·together for the supper of·the great

G1173.1 N-DSN δείπνῳ (1x)

Jn 21:20 sat·back upon his chest at the supper and declared,

G1173.1 N-GSN δείπνου (4x)

Jn 13:2 And with·supper occurring, with·the Slanderer even·
Jn 13:4 is·roused from·among the supper and lays·aside the
Lk 14:17 at·the hour of·the supper to·declare to·the·ones
Lk 14:24 having·been·called·forth, shall·taste my supper.'"

G1173.2 N-DPN δείπνοις (3x)

Lk 20:46 and foremost·places at the festive·suppers,
Mt 23:6 the foremost·places at the festive·suppers, and the
Mk 12:39 and foremost·places at the festive·suppers.

G1174 δεισι•δαιμονέστερος dêisidaimônéstêrôs *adj.* (1x)

Roots:G1169 G1142

G1174.2a A-APM-C δεισιδαιμονεστέρους (1x)

Ac 17:22 *are* more·filled·with·dreadful·respect for·the· than

G1175 δεισι•δαιμονία dêisidaimônía *n.* (1x)

Roots:G1169 G1142 Compare:G2356 G1479
See:G1174

G1175.2 N-GSF δεισιδαιμονίας (1x)

Ac 25:19 concerning their·own superstitious·religion, and

G1176 δέκα déka *n.* (24x)

xLangEquiv:H6235

G1176.1 N-NUI δέκα (24x)

Lk 14:31 he·is able with ten thousand to·approach·and·meet
Lk 15:8 what woman, having ten drachma·coins·*of·silver*, if
Lk 17:12 there·approached·and·met him ten leprous men
Lk 17:17 Jesus declared, "Are·not·indeed the ten purified?
Lk 19:13 And calling his ten slaves, he·gave ten more·silver·
Lk 19:13 ten slaves, he·gave ten more·silver·minas to·them
Lk 19:16 Lord, your mina actively·earned ten more·minas.'
Lk 19:17 in very·little, be having authority over ten cities.'
Lk 19:24 and give *it* to·the·one having the ten more·minas.'
Lk 19:25 'Lord, he·*already*·has ten more·minas!'
Ac 25:6 among them *for* more than ten days, *and·then*
Mt 20:24 *of·this*, the ten were·greatly·displeased concerning
Mt 25:1 of·the heavens shall·be·likened to·ten virgins, who,
Mt 25:28 and give *it* to·the·one having ten talants·of·silver.'
Mk 10:41 *of·this*, the ten began to·be·greatly·displeased
Rv 2:10 and yeu·shall·have tribulation ten days. Become
Rv 12:3 having seven heads and ten horns, and seven royal·
Rv 13:1 sea, having seven heads and ten horns, and upon its
Rv 13:1 and upon its horns ten royal·turbans, and upon its
Rv 17:3 of·revilement, having seven heads and ten horns.
Rv 17:7 the·one having the seven heads and the ten horns.
Rv 17:12 "And the ten horns which you·saw are ten kings
Rv 17:12 horns which you·saw are ten kings who did·not·yet
Rv 17:16 And the ten horns which you·saw upon the Scarlet·

G1177 δεκα•δύο dêkadýô *n.* (2x)

Roots:G1176 G1417 See:G1427

G1177 N-NUI δεκαδύο (2x)

Ac 19:7 And there·were about twelve men *in* all.
Ac 24:11 there·are not more than twelve days for·me since I·

G1177-3 δεκα•οκτώ dêkaôktố *n.* (3x)

δέκα καί ὀκτώ déka kaí ôktố [full form]

Roots:G1176 G3638 G2532 Compare:G3638-1

G1177-3 N-NUI δέκα καί ὀκτώ (3x)

Lk 13:4 "Or those eighteen, upon whom the tower in Siloam
Lk 13:11 having a·spirit·of·sickness even eighteen years, and
Lk 13:16 bound, behold, eighteen years, was·it·not binding·

G1178 δεκα•πέντε dêkapéntê *n.* (3x)

Roots:G1176 G4002

G1178 N-NUI δεκαπέντε (3x)

Jn 11:18 was near to·JeruSalem, about fifteen stadia away.
Ac 27:28 ·line again, they·found *it to·be* fifteen fathoms.
Gal 1:18 Peter, and I·stayed·over alongside him fifteen days.

G1179 Δεκά•πολις Dêkápôlis *n/l.* (3x)

Roots:G1176 G4172

G1179.2 N/L-DSF Δεκαπόλει (1x)

Mk 5:20 ·herald in the DecaPolis what·many·things Jesus

G1179.2 N/L-GSF Δεκαπόλεως (2x)

Mt 4:25 him from Galilee and *from* DecaPolis, and *from*
Mk 7:31 through *the* midst of·the borders of·DecaPolis.

G1180 δεκα•τέσσαρες dêkatéssarês *n.* (5x)

Roots:G1176 G5064

G1180 N-NPF δεκατέσσαρες (3x)

Mt 1:17 from AbRaham until David *are* fourteen generations.
Mt 1:17 the Babylonian exile *are* fourteen generations. And
Mt 1:17 until the Anointed-One *are* fourteen generations.

G1180 N-GPN δεκατεσσάρων (2x)

Gal 2:1 Then after fourteen years, I·walked·up again to
2Co 12:2 ·man·of·clay† in Anointed-One fourteen years ago

G1181 δεκάτη dêkátē *adj.* (4x)

Roots:G1182 See:G1183

G1181.1 A-ASF δεκάτην (2x)

Heb 7:2 ·whom also AbRaham distributed a·tenth *part* from
Heb 7:4 the patriarch AbRaham gave a·tenth from·among the

G1181.2 A-APF δεκάτας (2x)

Heb 7:8 *and·now*, in·fact, *are* tithes *that* dying men·of·clay†
Heb 7:9 Levi, the·one receiving tithes, has·tithed through

G1182 δέκατος dékatôs *adj.* (3x)

Roots:G1176

G1182 A-NSM δέκατος (1x)

Rv 21:20 beryl; the ninth, topaz; the tenth, chrysoprase; the

G1182 A-NSN δέκατον (1x)

Rv 11:13 earthquake, and the tenth·part of·the City fell.

G1182 N-NSF δεκάτη (1x)

Jn 1:39 day, for it·was *late·afternoon* about *the* tenth hour.

G1183 δεκατόω dêkatốō *v.* (2x)

Roots:G1181

G1183 V-RAI-3S δεδεκάτωκεν (1x)

Heb 7:6 ·among them has·received·tithes from·AbRaham,

G1183 V-RPI-3S δεδεκάτωται (1x)

Heb 7:9 ·one receiving tithes, has·tithed through AbRaham,

G1184 δεκτός dêktós *adj.* (5x)

Roots:G1209 Compare:G1384 See:G0587

G1184.1 A-NSM δεκτός (2x)

Lk 4:24 that not·even·one prophet is acceptable in his·own
Ac 10:35 who·is·working righteousness is acceptable to·him.

G1184.1 A-ASM δεκτόν (1x)

Lk 4:19 to·officially·proclaim an·acceptable Year of·

G1184.1 A-ASF δεκτήν (1x)

Php 4:18 aroma, a·sacrifice acceptable *and* most·satisfying

G1184.1 A-DSM δεκτῷ (1x)

2Co 6:2 "'I·favorably·heard you in·an·acceptable season,

G1185 δελεάζω dêlêázō *v.* (3x)

Roots:G1388 Compare:G1387

G1185.1 V-PPP-NSM δελεαζόμενος (1x)

Jac 1:14 ·forth by his·own longing and being·entrapped.

G1185.2 V-PAI-3P δελεάζουσιν (1x)

2Pe 2:18 *and* by·debaucheries *that* they·allure the·ones really

G1185.3 V-PAP-NPM δελεάζοντες (1x)

2Pe 2:14 from·moral·failure, while·beguiling unstable souls,

G1186 δένδρον déndrôn *n.* (26x)

Compare:G3586 See:G5208
xLangEquiv:A0363 xLangAlso:H6086 A0636

G1186 N-NSN δένδρον (12x)

Lk 3:9 Accordingly, every tree not producing good fruit is·
Lk 6:43 "For a·good tree is not producing rotten fruit, neither
Lk 6:43 fruit, neither *is* a·rotten tree producing good fruit.
Lk 6:44 For each tree is·known from·out·of·its·own fruit.
Mt 3:10 Accordingly, every tree not producing good fruit is·
Mt 7:17 every beneficially·good tree produces good fruit,
Mt 7:17 good fruit, but the rotten tree produces evil fruit.
Mt 7:18 A·beneficially·good tree is·not able to·produce evil
Mt 7:18 fruit, neither *is* a·rotten tree *able* to·produce good
Mt 7:19 Every tree not producing good fruit is·chopped·
Mt 12:33 For out of·the fruit, the tree is·known.
Mt 13:32 the garden·plants and becomes a·tree, such·for the

G1186 N-NPN δένδρα (2x)

Mk 8:24 men·of·clay† as how I·clearly·envision trees, *but*
Jud 1:12 by winds, late·autumn trees without·fruit, already·

G1186 N-ASN δένδρον (5x)

Lk 13:19 And it·grew and became a·great tree, and the birds
Mt 12:33 "Either make the tree good, and its fruit good; or
Mt 12:33 its fruit good; or make the tree rotten, and its fruit
Rv 7:1 the earth, nor on the sea, nor on any tree.
Rv 9:4 (not·even any green·thing nor·even any tree), but·yet

G1186 N-APN δένδρα (2x)

Lk 21:29 "See the fig·tree, and all the trees.
Rv 7:3 neither the sea, nor the trees, even·until we·should·

G1186 N-GPN δένδρων (5x)

Lk 3:9 is·laid·out to the root of·the trees. Accordingly, every
Mt 3:10 ax is·laid·out to the root of·the trees. Accordingly,
Mt 21:8 were·chopping branches from the trees, and they·
Mk 11:8 were·chopping limbs out of·the trees, and they·
Rv 8:7 the third·part of·the trees was·completely·burned·up,

G1187 δεξιο•λάβος dêxiôlábôs *n.* (1x)

Roots:G1188 G2983

G1187.2 N-APM δεξιολάβους (1x)

Ac 23:23 and two·hundred right-handed·spearmen, that they·

G1188 δεξιός dêxiós *adj.* (53x)

Roots:G1209 Compare:G0710
xLangEquiv:H3225

G1188.1 A-NSF δεξιά (1x)

Mt 6:3 your left·hand know what your right·hand is·doing,

G1188.1 A-ASF δεξιάν (2x)

Mt 27:29 and·also a·reed in his right·hand, and kneeling·
Rv 5:1 And I·saw in the right·hand of·the·one sitting·down

G1188.1 A-APF δεξιάς (1x)

Gal 2:9 to·me and BarNabas *the* right·hands of·fellowship,

G1188.1 A-APN δεξιά (1x)

Jn 21:6 Cast the net to the right·hand portions of·the sailboat,

G1188.1 A-DSF δεξιᾷ (11x)

Ac 2:33 ·being·elevated to·the right·hand of·God and·also
Ac 5:31 *this* Savior with·his·own right·hand, to·grant
Heb 1:3 sat·down at *the* right·hand of·the Divine·Majesty
Heb 8:1 who is·seated at *the* right·hand of·the throne of·the
Heb 10:12 perpetuity, sat·down at *the* right·hand of·God.
Heb 12:2 *it*, and sat·down at *the* right·hand of·the throne of·
Rm 8:34 who is even at *the* right·hand of·God, who also
1Pe 3:22 heaven, is at *the* right·hand of·God, with·angels
Eph 1:20 And he·seated *him* at his·own right·hand in the
Col 3:1 is sitting·down at the·right·hand of·God.
Rv 2:1 seven stars in his right·hand, the·one strolling·about

G1188.1 A-GSF δεξιᾶς (2x)

Rv 1:20 stars which you·saw in my right·hand, and the seven
Rv 5:7 ·scroll out of·the right·hand of·the·one sitting·down

G1188.1 A-GPM δεξιῶν (22x)

Lk 20:42 "Sit·down at my right·hand
Lk 22:69 shall·be sitting·down at *the* right·hand of·the power
Lk 23:33 in·fact one at *the* right·hand, and the·other at *the*
Ac 2:25 he·is at my right·hand in·order·that I·should·not be·
Ac 2:34 "Sit·down at my right·hand
Ac 7:55 glory, and Jesus standing at *the* right·hand of·God.
Ac 7:56 of·Clay·Man† standing at *the* right·hand of·God."
Heb 1:13 "'Sit·down at my right·hand, until I·should·lay·out
Mt 20:21 may·sit, one at your right·hand and one at *your* left
Mt 20:23 ·in, but to·sit at my right·hand and at my left is not
Mt 22:44 "Sit·down at my right·hand until I·should·lay·out
Mt 25:33 he·shall·set the sheep at his right·hand, but the
Mt 25:34 shall·declare to·the·ones at his right·hand, 'Come·
Mt 26:64 of·Clay·Man† sitting·down at *the* right·hand' of·the

Mt 27:38 with·him, one at *the* right·hand and one at *the* left.
Mk 10:37 that we·may·sit, one at your right·hand and one at
Mk 10:40 But to·sit at my right·hand and at my left is not
Mk 12:36 "Sit·down at my right·hand until I·should·lay·out
Mk 14:62 ·Man† sitting·down at *the* right·hand of·the power,
Mk 15:27 two robbers: one at his·right·hand, and one at his
Mk 16:19 the heaven and seated at *the* right·hand of·God.
2Co 6:7 of·righteousness on·the right·hand and on·the·left,

G1188.2 A-DPN δεξιοῖς (1x)
Mk 16:5 ·down on the right·side, having·been·arrayed·with

G1188.2 A-GPM δεξιῶν (1x)
Lk 1:11 standing at *the* right·side of·the Sacrifice·Altar of·

G1188.3 A-NSM δεξιός (1x)
Mt 5:29 "So if your right eye entraps you, pluck it out and

G1188.3 A-NSF δεξιά (2x)
Lk 6:6 man·of·clay† there and his right hand was withered.
Mt 5:30 And if your right hand entraps you, chop it off and

G1188.3 A-ASM δεξιόν (1x)
Rv 10:2 And he·placed his right foot upon the sea, and the

G1188.3 A-ASF δεξιάν (2x)
Mt 5:39 shall·slap you on your right cheek, turn·back to·him
Rv 1:17 And he·laid his right hand upon me, saying to·me,

G1188.3 A-ASN δεξιόν (2x)
Jn 18:10 ·priest, and he·chopped·off his right earlobe. And
Lk 22:50 designated·high·priest and removed his right ear.

G1188.3 A-DSF δεξιᾷ (1x)
Rv 1:16 and having in his right hand seven stars.

G1188.3 A-GSF δεξιᾶς (2x)
Ac 3:7 And after·gripping him by·the right hand, he·pulled·
Rv 13:16 ·should·be·given an·etching on their right hand or

G1189 δέομαι dĕômai *v.* (22x)
Roots:G1210 Compare:G4441 G4434 G1793 See:G4326

G1189.2 V-PNI-1S δέομαι (7x)
Lk 8:28 O·Son of·God Most·High? I·petition you *that* you·
Lk 9:38 saying, "Mentor, I·petition you, kindly·look upon
Ac 8:34 the eunuch declared, "I·petition you, concerning
Ac 21:39 ·no obscure city. And I·petition you, freely·permit
Ac 26:3 the·Judeans. Therefore, I·petition you to·hear me
Gal 4:12 Brothers, I·petition yeu, be as I·myself *am*, because
2Co 10:2 Now I·petition *yeu to·agreeably·comply, such·for*

G1189.2 V-PNI-1P δεόμεθα (1x)
2Co 5:20 *yeu* through us. We·petition *yeu* on·behalf of·

G1189.2 V-PNP-NSM δεόμενος (2x)
Ac 10:2 ·acts for·the people and continually petitioning God.
Rm 1:10 in my prayers. Petitioning, if·somehow even·now

G1189.2 V-PNP-NPM δεόμενοι (3x)
Lk 21:36 "Accordingly, stay·alert, petitioning in every
1Th 3:10 ·*are* abundantly petitioning *him* above·and·beyond
2Co 8:4 they·were·petitioning us with much entreaty for·us

G1189.2 V-INI-3S ἐδέετο (1x)
Lk 8:38 the demons had·come·out was·petitioning him to·be

G1189.2 V-AOM-2S δεήθητι (1x)
Ac 8:22 of this depravity of·yours, and petition God so·that

G1189.2 V-AOM-2P δεήθητε (3x)
Lk 10:2 *are* few. Accordingly, petition the Lord of·the
Ac 8:24 declared, "Yeu·yeurselves petition to the Lord on·
Mt 9:38 So·then, petition the Lord of·the harvest, that he·

G1189.2 V-AOP-GPM δεηθέντων (1x)
Ac 4:31 And with·them petitioning, the place was·shaken in

G1189.2 V-API-1S ἐδεήθην (2x)
Lk 9:40 And I·petitioned your disciples in·order·that they·
Lk 22:32 "But I·myself petitioned concerning you, *Simon*,

G1189.2 V-API-3S ἐδεήθη (1x)
Lk 5:12 *and* falling on *his* face, he·petitioned him, saying,

G1190 Δερβαῖος Dêrbaîôs *adj/g.* (1x)
Roots:G1191

G1190.2 A/G-NSM Δερβαῖος (1x)
Ac 20:4 of·ThessaloNica, and Gaius of·Derbe, and TimoThy

G1191 Δέρβη Dĕrbē *n/l.* (3x)

G1191 N/L-ASF Δέρβην (3x)
Ac 14:6 fled·down to Lystra and Derbe, the cities of·
Ac 14:20 he·went·forth together with·BarNabas to Derbe.
Ac 16:1 Then he·arrived in Derbe and Lystra. And behold, a·

G1192 δέρμα dĕrma *n.* (1x)
Roots:G1194 Compare:G5559 See:G1193 xLangAlso:H5785

G1192 N-DPN δέρμασιν (1x)
Heb 11:37 sheepskins *and* in wild·goat hides, being·destitute

G1193 δερμάτινος dêrmátinôs *adj.* (2x)
Roots:G1192

G1193.2 A-ASF δερματίνην (2x)
Mt 3:4 camel's hair and *was·girded·with* a·leather belt around
Mk 1:6 ·with camel's hair and with·a·leather belt around his

G1194 δέρω dĕrō *v.* (15x)
Compare:G3147 G3146 See:G1192

G1194.3 V-2FPI-2P δαρήσεσθε (1x)
Mk 13:9 ·Sanhedrin, and yeu·shall·be·thrashed in gatherings

G1194.3 V-2FPI-3S δαρήσεται (2x)
Lk 12:47 will, shall·be·thrashed with·many *punishing·blows*
Lk 12:48 shall·be·thrashed with·few *punishing·blows*. "So

G1194.3 V-PAI-2S δέρεις (1x)
Jn 18:23 But if *I·spoke* well, why do·you·thrash me?

G1194.3 V-PAI-3S δέρει (1x)
2Co 11:20 exalts·himself, if anyone thrashes yeu to *the* face.

G1194.3 V-PAP-NSM δέρων (2x)
Ac 22:19 was imprisoning and thrashing in·each·of the
1Co 9:26 in·this·manner I·do·box, *but* not as thrashing air.

G1194.3 V-PAP-NPM δέροντες (1x)
Mk 12:5 many others (in·fact, thrashing some and killing

G1194.3 V-AAI-3P ἔδειραν (2x)
Mt 21:35 ·fact, *there·was one* whom they·thrashed, and *one*
Mk 12:3 after·taking·hold·of *him*, they·thrashed him and

G1194.3 V-AAP-NPM δείραντες (4x)
Lk 20:10 "But the tenant·farmers, after·thrashing him,
Lk 20:11 another slave. And thrashing this·one·also, and
Ac 5:40 ·summoning the ambassadors *and* thrashing *them*,
Ac 16:37 "After publicly thrashing us uncondemned men·

G1194.4 V-PAP-NPM δέροντες (1x)
Lk 22:63 Jesus, were·mocking him, verbally·thrashing *him*.

G1195 δεσμεύω dêsmĕúō *v.* (2x)
Roots:G1196 xLangAlso:H0481

G1195.2 V-PAI-3P δεσμεύουσιν (1x)
Mt 23:4 "For they·captively·bind weighty and oppressive

G1195.2 V-PAP-NSM δεσμεύων (1x)
Ac 22:4 *their* death, captively·binding and handing·over into

G1196 δεσμέω dêsmĕō *v.* (1x)
Roots:G1199

G1196.2 V-IPI-3S ἐδεσμεῖτο (1x)
Lk 8:29 ·seized him. And he·was·fettered with·chains, even

G1197 δέσμη dĕsmē *n.* (1x)
Roots:G1196

G1197 N-APF δέσμας (1x)
Mt 13:30 them in bundles specifically to·completely·burn

G1198 δέσμιος dĕsmiôs *n.* (16x)
Roots:G1199 Compare:G1202 G4869 G0164

G1198 N-NSM δέσμιος (7x)
Ac 23:18 me, Paul, the chained·prisoner, asked *me* to·bring
Ac 25:14 ·been·left·behind *as* a·chained·prisoner by Felix,
Ac 28:17 ·over *as* a·chained·prisoner out of·JeruSalem into
Eph 3:1 I, Paul, *am* the chained·prisoner of·Jesus, the
Eph 4:1 ·then, I·myself, the chained·prisoner in *the* Lord,
Phm 1:1 Paul, a·chained·prisoner of·Jesus Anointed, and
Phm 1:9 and now also a·chained·prisoner of·Jesus Anointed.

G1198 N-NPM δέσμιοι (1x)
Ac 16:25 the chained·prisoners were·intently·listening·to

G1198 N-ASM δέσμιον (5x)
Ac 25:27 ·me unreasonable to·send a·chained·prisoner, *and*
Mt 27:15 to·the crowd a chained·prisoner, whomever they·
Mt 27:16 a·notable chained·prisoner, being·referred·to·as
Mk 15:6 to·them one chained·prisoner, whom·specifically
2Ti 1:8 nor·even of·me his chained·prisoner, but·rather

G1198 N-APM δεσμίους (2x)
Ac 16:27 the chained·prisoners to·have·utterly·escaped.
Ac 28:16 ·over the chained·prisoners to·the captain·of·the·

G1198 N-GPM δεσμίων (1x)
Heb 13:3 Keep·in·mind the chained·prisoners, as having·

G1199 δεσμόν dêsmŏn *n.* (20x)
δεσμός dêsmŏs [masculine]
Roots:G1210 Compare:G0254 G3976 G4577

G1199.1 N-NPN δεσμά (2x)
Ac 16:26 ·opened·up, and everyone's bonds were·slackened.
Ac 20:23 ·each city, saying that bonds and tribulations await

G1199.1 N-APM δεσμούς (1x)
Php 1:13 such·for my bonds in *the* Anointed-One to·become

G1199.1 N-APN δεσμά (1x)
Lk 8:29 And tearing·apart the bonds, he·was·driven by the

G1199.1 N-DPM δεσμοῖς (7x)
Heb 10:34 For even yeu·sympathized with·my bonds, and
Jud 1:6 in·supra-lasting bonds under a·deep·murky·shroud
Php 1:7 Both in my bonds and in·the defense and
Php 1:14 Lord, having·confidence by·my bonds, *are* all·the·
Php 1:16 imagining *also* to·bring·on tribulation to·my bonds.
Phm 1:10 my child Onesimus, whom I·begot in my bonds.
Phm 1:13 ·may·attend to·me in the bonds of·the good·news.

G1199.1 N-GSM δεσμοῦ (1x)
Lk 13:16 *her* to·be·loosed from this bond on·the Sabbath day

G1199.1 N-GPM δεσμῶν (7x)
Ac 22:30 him from the bonds and commandingly·ordered the
Ac 23:29 ·even·one allegation worthy of·death or of·bonds.
Ac 26:29 ·I am, *though* personally·aside·from these bonds."
Ac 26:31 not·even·one·thing worthy of·death or of·bonds."
Heb 11:36 and furthermore, of·bonds and imprisonment.
Col 4:18 hand, Paul: Remember my bonds. The Grace *be*
2Ti 2:9 as a·criminal, *even* as·far·as·unto bonds, but·yet the

G1199.2 N-NSM δεσμός (1x)
Mk 7:35 ·opened·up, and the impediment of·his tongue was·

G1200 δεσμο•φύλαξ dêsmôphýlax *n.* (3x)
Roots:G1199 G5441

G1200.2 N-NSM δεσμοφύλαξ (2x)
Ac 16:27 And the prison·warden, becoming awake·out·of·
Ac 16:36 And the prison·warden announced this saying to

G1200.2 N-DSM δεσμοφύλακι (1x)
Ac 16:23 prison, charging the prison·warden to·keep them

G1201 δεσμωτήριον dêsmōtériôn *n.* (6x)
Roots:G1199 G1196

G1201 N-ASN δεσμωτήριον (2x)
Ac 5:21 Then they·dispatched to the dungeon to·have *the*
Ac 5:23 ·fact, we·found the dungeon having·been·shut with

G1201 N-DSN δεσμωτηρίῳ (1x)
Mt 11:2 John, after·hearing in the dungeon *of* the works of·

G1201 N-GSN δεσμωτηρίου (1x)
Ac 16:26 ·for the foundations of·the dungeon to·be·shaken.

EG1201 (2x)
Ac 5:22 assistants, coming·directly *to·the dungeon*, did·not
2Pe 2:4 ·Abyss of·Tartarus *(the deepest dungeon of·Hades)*,

G1202 δεσμώτης dêsmṓtēs *n.* (2x)
Roots:G1199 Compare:G1198 G0164 G4869 See:G1196 G1201

G1202 N-APM δεσμώτας (2x)
Ac 27:1 Paul and certain other prisoners over to·a·centurion,
Ac 27:42 was that they·should·kill the prisoners, lest·any

G1203 δεσ•πότης dêspŏtēs *n.* (10x)
Roots:G1210 G4213-1 Compare:G3617 G2962 G2519 See:G1202-1 G1202-2 xLangEquiv:H1167 xLangAlso:H1168

G1203.1 N-NSM δεσπότης (1x)
Rv 6:10 "How·long, Master, the Holy and the Truthful·One,

G1203.1 N-VSM δέσποτα (2x)
Lk 2:29 "Master, now dismiss your slave in peace,
Ac 4:24 and declared, "Master, you *are* God, 'the·one

G1203.1 N-ASM δεσπότην (2x)
Jud 1:4 debauchery and denying the only Master, God and
2Pe 2:1 even denying *the* Master, the·one already·kinsman·

G1203.1 N-APM δεσπότας (2x)
1Ti 6:1 resolutely·consider their·own masters worthy of·all
1Ti 6:2 And the·ones having masters that·trust·*in·Jesus*, do·

G1203.1 N-DSM δεσπότῃ (1x)
2Ti 2:21 and easily·useful to·the master, *and* having·been·
G1203.1 N-DPM δεσπόταις (2x)
1Pe 2:18 be·submitting·yeurselves to·the masters with all
Tit 2:9 to·submit·themselves to·their·own masters *and* to·be

G1204 δεῦρο dêûrô *adv.* (9x)
See:G1205 xLangAlso:H3212
G1204.2 V-XXM-2S δεῦρο (8x)
Jn 11:43 ·a·loud voice, "Lazarus, come·over·here, outside!"
Lk 18:22 in heaven. And come·over·here! Follow me!"
Ac 7:3 your kinsfolk, and come·over·here into a·land which
Ac 7:34 ' 'And now, come·over·here, I·shall·dispatch you
Mt 19:21 in heaven. And come·over·here! Follow me!"
Mk 10:21 in heaven. And come·over·here! Upon·taking·up
Rv 17:1 saying to·me, "Come·over·here! I·shall·show to·
Rv 21:9 me, saying, "Come·over·here! I·shall·show you the
G1204.3 ADV δεῦρο (1x)
Rm 1:13 (but was·prevented even·until here·and·now), in·

G1205 δεῦ•τε dêûtê *v.* (13x)
Roots:G1204 G1510-1 xLangAlso:H3051
G1205 V-XXM-2P δεῦτε (13x)
Jn 4:29 "Come·here! See a·man·of·clay† who declared to·me
Jn 21:12 Jesus says to·them, "Come·here! Dine!" And not·
Lk 20:14 'This is the heir. Come·here! We·should·kill him,
Mt 4:19 he·says to·them, "Come·here, *fall·in* right·behind
Mt 11:28 "Come·here to me, all the·ones laboring·hard and
Mt 21:38 'This is the heir. Come·here! We·should·kill him
Mt 22:4 all·things *are* ready. Come·here to the wedding·
Mt 25:34 his right·hand, 'Come·here, the·ones having·been·
Mt 28:6 just·as he·declared. Come·here! See the place
Mk 1:17 declared to·them, "Come·here, *fall·in* right·behind
Mk 6:31 he·declared to·them, "Come·here yeu yeurselves
Mk 12:7 'This is the heir! Come·here! We·should·kill him,
Rv 19:17 in mid-heaven, "Come·here! And be·gathered·

G1206 δευτεραῖος dêutêraîôs *adj.* (1x)
Roots:G1208
G1206.2 A-NPM δευτεραῖοι (1x)
Ac 28:13 ·up, we·came on·the·second·day to Puteoli,

G1207 δευτερό•πρωτος dêutêróprōtôs *adj.* (1x)
Roots:G1208 G4413
G1207.3 A-DSN δευτεροπρώτῳ (1x)
Lk 6:1 ·first Sabbath after·the·second·day·of·the·feast *for*

G1208 δεύτερος dêútêrôs *adj.* (44x)
Roots:G1417 xLangAlso:H8145
G1208.1 A-NSM δεύτερος (11x)
Lk 19:18 And the second came, saying, 'Lord, your mina
Lk 20:30 And the second took the *same* wife, and this·man
Mt 22:26 Likewise the second also, and the third, even·unto
Mk 12:21 And the second took her, and he·died, and neither
1Co 15:47 *as* dusty·clay. The second man·of·clay† *is* the
Rv 8:8 And the second angel sounded, and *something* as a·
Rv 16:3 And the second angel poured·out his vial into the
Rv 20:6 Over these, the Second Death does·not have
Rv 20:14 This is the Second Death.
Rv 21:8 with·fire and sulfur, which is *the* Second Death."
Rv 21:19 foundation *was* jasper; the second, sapphire; the
G1208.1 A-NSF δευτέρα (3x)
Mt 22:39 "And *the* second *is* like it, "You·shall·love your
Mk 12:31 And *the* second *is* like it, "You·shall·love your
Rv 11:14 The second woe went·away; behold, the third woe
G1208.1 A-NSN δεύτερον (2x)
Jud 1:5 the second·thing *was·that* he·completely·destroyed
Rv 4:7 like a·lion, and the second living·being *is* like a·calf,
G1208.1 A-ASF δευτέραν (6x)
Ac 12:10 going·through a·first and second watch-station,
Heb 9:7 But into the second *Tabernacle*, once per year, the
2Pe 3:1 This second letter, beloved, even·now I·write to·yeu,
Tit 3:10 ·selective after a·first and second admonition,
2Co 1:15 in·order·that yeu·may·have a·second grace,
Rv 6:3 And when he·opened·up the second official·seal, I·
G1208.1 A-ASN δεύτερον (3x)
Jn 4:54 This *is* again *the* second miraculous·sign *that* Jesus
Heb 9:3 And after the second curtain, *a·second* Tabernacle,
Heb 10:9 the first in·order·that he·may·establish the second.
G1208.1 A-DSM δευτέρῳ (1x)
Ac 13:33 as also it·has·been·written in the second Psalm,
G1208.1 A-DSF δευτέρᾳ (1x)
Lk 12:38 "And if he·should·come in the second watch, or
G1208.1 A-DSN δευτέρῳ (1x)
Mt 21:30 "And coming·alongside the second, he·declared
G1208.1 A-GSM δευτέρου (1x)
Rv 2:11 be·brought·to·harm as·a·result·of·the Second Death.
G1208.1 A-GSF δευτέρας (1x)
Heb 8:7 then no place would·be·sought for·the·second.
G1208.1 A-GSN δευτέρου (1x)
Rv 6:3 official·seal, I·heard the second living·being saying,
G1208.1 ADV δεύτερον (1x)
1Co 12:28 first ambassadors, second prophets, third
EG1208.1 (1x)
Heb 9:3 the second curtain, *a·second* Tabernacle, the·one
G1208.2 A-NSN δεύτερον (1x)
2Co 13:2 ·present the second·time even while·being·absent
G1208.2 A-DSM δευτέρῳ (1x)
Ac 7:13 And at the second·time, Joseph was·made·known
G1208.2 A-GSN δευτέρου (6x)
Jn 9:24 So·then for a·second·time they·hollered·out·for the
Ac 10:15 *spoke* to him again for a·second·time, "What God
Ac 11:9 answered me for a·second·time from·out·of·the
Heb 9:28 ' for a·second·time (completely·apart·from a·
Mt 26:42 Again for a·second·time, after·going·off, he·
Mk 14:72 And for a·second·time, a·rooster crowed.
G1208.2 ADV δεύτερον (3x)
Jn 3:4 ¿! Is·he·able to·enter a·second·time into the womb
Jn 21:16 He·says to·him again a·second·time, "Simon, *son*
Rv 19:3 And a·second·time they·declared, "Splendidly·

G1209 δέχομαι déchômai *v.* (59x)
Compare:G0138 G2983 See:G1184 G0588
G1209.1 V-PNI-3S δέχεται (8x)
Lk 9:48 ·accept this little·child in my name accepts me. And
Lk 9:48 whoever should·accept me accepts·him, the·one
Mt 10:40 "The·one who·is·accepting yeu accepts me, and
Mt 10:40 ·accepting me accepts the·one already·dispatching
Mt 18:5 ·accept one such little·child in my name accepts me.
Mk 9:37 ·children such·as·these in my name accepts me, and
Mk 9:37 me, *it·is* not me he·accepts, but·rather the·one
1Co 2:14 man·of·clay† does·not accept the·things of·the
G1209.1 V-PNI-3P δέχονται (1x)
Lk 8:13 *are those* who with joy accept the Redemptive-word;
G1209.1 V-PNP-NSM δεχόμενος (4x)
Mt 10:40 "The·one who·is·accepting yeu accepts me, and
Mt 10:40 me, and the·one who·is·accepting me accepts the·
Mt 10:41 The·one who·is·accepting a·prophet in a·prophet's
Mt 10:41 ·service; and the·one accepting a·righteous·man in
G1209.1 V-PNS-3P δέχωνται (2x)
Lk 10:8 city yeu·should·enter, and they·should·accept yeu,
Lk 10:10 city yeu·should·enter, and they·do·not accept yeu,
G1209.1 V-ADI-2P ἐδέξασθε (4x)
Gal 4:14 nor did·yeu·spit·*me*·out, but·rather accepted me as
1Th 2:13 of·hearing directly·from us, yeu·did·accept *it* not
2Co 7:15 with reverent·fear and trembling yeu·accepted him.
2Co 11:4 yeu·did·not already·accept, yeu·were·bearing·with
G1209.1 V-ADI-3S ἐδέξατο (3x)
Lk 2:28 then he·himself accepted him into his arms and
Ac 7:38 fathers. *It·is·he* who accepted living eloquent·words
2Co 8:17 Because in·fact, he·accepted the exhortation; but
G1209.1 V-ADI-3P ἐδέξαντο (6x)
Jn 4:45 Galilee, the Galileans accepted him, having·clearly·
Lk 9:53 Yet they·did·not accept him, because his face was *as*
Ac 11:1 that the Gentiles also accepted the Redemptive-word
Ac 17:11 ·*was* these·*Jews*·who accepted the Redemptive-word
Ac 21:17 the brothers accepted us quite·pleasantly.
2Th 2:10 because these did·not accept the love of·the truth,
G1209.1 V-ADM-2S δέξαι (3x)
Lk 16:6 he·declared to·him, '*Here*, accept your bill, and
Lk 16:7 he·says to·him, '*Here*, accept your bill, and write
Ac 7:59 "Lord Jesus, accept my spirit."
G1209.1 V-ADM-2P δέξασθε (4x)
Jac 1:21 ·excess of·depravity, accept with a·calm·mildness
2Co 11:16 but if not, then·also accept me as impetuous in·
Eph 6:17 also accept the helmet of·custodial·Salvation and
Col 4:10 if he·should·come to yeu, accept him),
G1209.1 V-ADN δέξασθαι (4x)
Ac 3:21 it·is·mandatory·for heaven to·accept even·until *the*
Mt 11:14 And if yeu·want to·accept *it*, he·himself is EliJah,
2Co 6:1 we·implore also *for* yeu to·accept the grace of·God
2Co 8:4 entreaty for·us to·accept the gracious·benevolence,
G1209.1 V-ADP-NSF δεξαμένη (1x)
Heb 11:31 who·were·being·obstinate, accepting the spies
G1209.1 V-ADP-NSM δεξάμενος (4x)
Lk 9:11 *it*, followed him. And accepting them, he·was·
Lk 22:17 And after·accepting *the* cup *and* giving·thanks, he·
Ac 22:5 personally·from whom I also accepted letters to the
Php 4:18 ·filled, accepting personally·from EpAphroditus
G1209.1 V-ADP-NPM δεξάμενοι (1x)
1Th 1:6 of·the Lord, after·accepting the Redemptive-word,
G1209.1 V-ADS-3S δέξηται (8x)
Lk 9:48 to·them, "Whoever should·accept this little·child in
Lk 9:48 And whoever should·accept me accepts·him, the·
Lk 18:17 whoever, if he·should·not accept the kingdom of·
Mt 10:14 whoever should·not accept yeu or·should·not·even
Mt 18:5 And whoever should·accept one such little·child in
Mk 9:37 "Whoever should·accept one of·the little·children
Mk 9:37 me, and whoever should·accept me, *it·is* not me he·
Mk 10:15 whoever, if he·should·not accept the kingdom of·
G1209.1 V-ADS-3P δέξωνται (4x)
Lk 9:5 *for* as·many·as should·not accept yeu, while·yeu·are·
Lk 16:4 of·the estate·management, they·may·accept me into
Lk 16:9 yeu·may·cease·living, they·may·accept yeu into the
Mk 6:11 *for* as·many·as should·not accept yeu, or·should·
G1209.1 V-RNI-3S δέδεκται (1x)
Ac 8:14 that Samaria had·accepted the Redemptive-word of·
G1209.2 V-ADI-1P ἐδεξάμεθα (1x)
Ac 28:21 do·not·even anticipate·receiving letters from Judea

G1210 δέω déō *v.* (45x)
Compare:G1195 See:G1163 G1189 G1195
G1210.1 V-FAI-3P δήσουσιν (1x)
Ac 21:11 the Judeans at JeruSalem shall·bind the man who
G1210.1 V-AAI-3S ἔδησεν (4x)
Lk 13:16 whom the Adversary-Accuser bound, behold,
Mt 14:3 after·taking·secure·hold·of John, bound him and
Mk 6:17 took·secure·hold·of John, and he·bound him in the
Rv 20:2 and Adversary-Accuser, and bound him a·thousand
G1210.1 V-AAI-3P ἔδησαν (2x)
Jn 18:12 of·the Judeans arrested Jesus and bound him.
Jn 19:40 the body of·Jesus and bound it in·strips·of·linen
G1210.1 V-AAM-2P δήσατε (1x)
Mt 13:30 the darnel·weeds first and bind them in bundles
G1210.1 V-AAN δῆσαι (2x)
Ac 9:14 personally·from the chief·priests to·bind all the·ones
Mk 5:3 And not·even·one·man was·able to·bind him, not·
G1210.1 V-AAP-NSM δήσας (1x)
Ac 21:11 Paul's belt, and·also binding his·own hands and
G1210.1 V-AAP-NPM δήσαντες (3x)
Mt 22:13 to·the attendants, 'After·binding him hand and
Mt 27:2 And binding him, they·led·*him*·away and handed
Mk 15:1 ·council·of·Sanhedrin, *and* already·binding Jesus,
G1210.1 V-AAS-2S δήσῃς (1x)
Mt 16:19 and whatever you·should·bind on the earth shall·
G1210.1 V-AAS-2P δήσητε (1x)
Mt 18:18 to·yeu, as·many·things·as yeu·should·bind on the
G1210.1 V-AAS-3S δήσῃ (2x)
Mt 12:29 unless first he·should·bind the strong·man?
Mk 3:27 his home, unless he·should·bind the strong·man
G1210.1 V-APN δεθῆναι (2x)
Ac 21:13 ·of·readiness not merely to·be·bound, but·rather
Ac 21:33 ·ordered *him* to·be·bound with·two chains, and·
G1210.1 V-RAP-NSM δεδεκώς (1x)
Ac 22:29 a·Roman, and because he·was having·bound him.

Αα Ββ Γγ Δδ Εε Ζζ Ηη Θθ Ιι Κκ Λλ Μμ Νν Ξξ Οο Ππ Ρρ Σσ Ττ Υυ Φφ Χχ Ψψ Ωω

Δδ

G1210.1 V-RPI-1S δέδεμαι (1x)
Col 4:3 on·account·of which also I·have·been·bound),
G1210.1 V-RPI-3S δέδεται (3x)
Rm 7:2 under·a·husband has·been·bound by·Torah-Law to·
1Co 7:39 A·wife has·been·bound by·Torah-Law over a·
2Ti 2:9 ·yet the Redemptive-word of·God has·not been·bound.
G1210.1 V-RPN δεδέσθαι (1x)
Mk 5:4 many·times to·have·been·bound with·shackles and
G1210.1 V-RPP-ASM δεδεμένον (2x)
Jn 18:24 HannAs dispatched him, having·been·bound, to
Ac 24:27 ·the Judeans, left Paul behind having·been·bound.
G1210.1 V-RPP-APM δεδεμένους (4x)
Ac 9:2 he·may·bring·them having·been·bound to JeruSalem
Ac 9:21 ·that he·may·bring them having·been·bound to the
Ac 22:5 the·ones being there, having·been·bound, to
Rv 9:14 the four angels, the·ones having·been·bound in the
G1210.1 V-RPP-NSN δεδεμένον (1x)
Mt 16:19 on the earth shall·be having·been·bound in the
G1210.1 V-RPP-NSM δεδεμένος (4x)
Jn 11:44 ·died came·forth, having·been·bound hand and foot
Ac 12:6 two soldiers, having·been·bound with·two chains,
Ac 20:22 And now behold, having·been·bound in·the spirit,
Mk 15:7 ·to·as BarAbbas, having·been·bound with the
G1210.1 V-RPP-NPN δεδεμένα (1x)
Mt 18:18 on the earth shall·be having·been·bound in the
EG1210.1 (1x)
Jn 18:13 *the Anointed-One having·been·bound to·Caiaphas,*
G1210.2 V-RPP-ASF δεδεμένην (1x)
Mt 21:2 yeu·shall·find a·donkey having·been·tied·up, and a·
G1210.2 V-RPP-ASM δεδεμένον (4x)
Lk 19:30 ·in, yeu·shall·find a·colt having·been·tied, on
Ac 10:11 linen·sheet having·been·tied at·the·four corners
Mk 11:2 it, yeu·shall·find a·colt having·been·tied, on which
Mk 11:4 the colt outside having·been·tied alongside the door
G1210.3 V-RPI-2S δέδεσαι (1x)
1Co 7:27 Have·you·been·engaged·to·be·married to·a·?

G1211 δή dḗ *prt.* (6x)
See:G1161 xLangAlso:H4994
G1211.1 PRT δή (5x)
Lk 2:15 to one·another, "Now·then, we·should·go·through
Ac 13:2 Spirit declared, "Now·then, specially·detach for·me
Ac 15:36 to BarNabas, "Now·then returning, we·should·visit
1Co 6:20 ·redeemed with·a·price. Now·then, glorify God in
2Co 12:1 Now·then, it·is·not advantageous for·me to·boast,
G1211.2 PRT δή (1x)
Mt 13:23 comprehending *it*, who also·then bears·fruit and

G1212 δῆλος dễlôs *adj.* (4x)
See:G1213
G1212 A-NSN δῆλον (3x)
Gal 3:11 So *it·is* plain that by Torah-Law not·even·one is·
1Co 15:27 ·been·subjugated," *it·is* plain that he·is·excluded,
1Ti 6:7 the world, *and it·is* plain that we·are·not·even able
G1212 A-ASM δῆλον (1x)
Mt 26:73 them, for even your speech makes you plain."

G1213 δηλόω dēlốō *v.* (7x)
Roots:G1212
G1213 V-FAI-3S δηλώσει (1x)
1Co 3:13 for the day shall·make·*it*·plain, because it·is·
G1213 V-PAI-3S δηλοῖ (1x)
Heb 12:27 ·more," makes·plain the transfer·and·removal
G1213 V-PAP-GSN δηλοῦντος (1x)
Heb 9:8 with·the Holy Spirit making·plain this·thing: *that*
G1213 V-IAI-3S ἐδήλου (1x)
1Pe 1:11 in them was·making·plain, when·testifying·
G1213 V-AAI-3S ἐδήλωσεν (1x)
2Pe 1:14 ·as our Lord YeShua Anointed made·plain to·me.
G1213 V-AAP-NSM δηλώσας (1x)
Col 1:8 the·one also making·plain to·us yeur love in *the*
G1213 V-API-3S ἐδηλώθη (1x)
1Co 1:11 For it·was·made·plain to·me concerning yeu, my

G1214 Δημᾶς Dēmâs *n/p.* (3x)
Roots:G1216
G1214 N/P-NSM Δημᾶς (3x)
Col 4:14 beloved practitioner·of·healing, and Demas, greet
Phm 1:24 *John*·Mark, AristArchus, Demas, Luke, *these* my
2Ti 4:10 for Demas forsook me, loving the present age, and

G1215 δημ•ηγορέω dēmēgôréō *v.* (1x)
Roots:G1218 G0058 Compare:G1573-1
G1215.2 V-IAI-3S ἐδημηγόρει (1x)
Ac 12:21 HerOd·Agrippa was·delivering·a·public·address to

G1216 Δημήτριος Dēmḗtriôs *n/p.* (3x)
G1216.2 N/P-NSM Δημήτριος (2x)
Ac 19:24 someone by·the·name·of Demetrius, a·silversmith
Ac 19:38 "Accordingly in·fact, if Demetrius and the
G1216.3 N/P-DSM Δημητρίῳ (1x)
3Jn 1:12 Demetrius has·been·attested·to by all·men, and by

G1217 δημι•ουργός dēmiôurgốs *n.* (1x)
Roots:G1218 G2041 Compare:G2939 G3618 G4160
G1217.3 N-NSM δημιουργός (1x)
Heb 11:10 architectural·designer and civil·engineer *is* God.

G1218 δῆμος dễmôs *n.* (4x)
Roots:G1210 Compare:G2992 G1577 G4866-1
See:G1219
G1218.1 N-NSM δῆμος (1x)
Ac 12:22 And the public was·exclaiming, "*It·is* a·voice of·a·
G1218.1 N-DSM δήμῳ (1x)
Ac 19:33 was·wanting to·make·their·defense to·the public.
G1218.2 N-ASM δῆμον (2x)
Ac 17:5 ·seeking to·bring them into the public·assembly.
Ac 19:30 ·resolving to·enter into the public·assembly, the

G1219 δημόσιος dēmốsiôs *adj.* (5x)
Roots:G1218
G1219.1 A-DSF δημοσίᾳ (1x)
Ac 5:18 the ambassadors and placed them in public custody.
G1219.2 ADV δημοσίᾳ (3x)
Ac 16:37 them, "After publicly thrashing us uncondemned
Ac 18:28 ·downright to·the Jews publicly, fully·exhibiting
Ac 20:20 and have·instructed yeu publicly and in homes,
EG1219.2 (1x)
Jn 7:4 seeks to·be in freeness·of·speech *publicly*. If you·do

G1220 δηνάριον dēnáriôn *n.* (17x)
Compare:G1406 G5007 See:G0787
G1220.1 N-ASN δηνάριον (5x)
Lk 20:24 Fully·exhibit for·me a·denarius. Whose derived·
Mt 20:9 about the eleventh hour received a·denarius apiece.
Mt 20:10 yet they also received *the* same, a·denarius apiece.
Mt 22:19 And they·brought to·him a·denarius.
Mk 12:15 yeu·try me? Bring me a·denarius that I·may·see
G1220.1 N-APN δηνάρια (3x)
Lk 7:41 the one was·owing five·hundred denarii *(about one*
Lk 10:35 stirring·of·day, casting·forth two denarii, he·gave
Mt 18:28 who was·owing him a·hundred denarii, and
G1220.1 N-GSN δηναρίου (4x)
Mt 20:2 the workmen *to·hire them* for a·denarius *for* the day
Mt 20:13 ·indeed mutually·agree with·me for·a·denarius?
Rv 6:6 "A·dry·measure of·wheat for·a·denarius, and three
Rv 6:6 and three dry·measures of·barley for·a·denarius; and
G1220.1 N-GPN δηναρίων (4x)
Jn 6:7 answered him, "Two·hundred denarii *worth* of·bread
Jn 12:5 was·it·not sold·off for·three·hundred denarii and
Mk 6:37 ·off, should·we·buy two·hundred denarii *worth* of·
Mk 14:5 ·sold·off for·upwards·of three·hundred denarii and
EG1220.1 (1x)
Lk 7:41 and the other fifty *denarii (about a·month and a·*

G1221 δή•ποτε dḗpôtê *prt.* (1x)
Roots:G1211 G4218
G1221.2 PRT δήποτε (1x)
Jn 5:4 healthy·and·sound from·whatever ailment by·which

G1222 δή•που dḗpôu *adv.* (1x)
Roots:G1211 G4225
G1222.3 ADV δήπου (1x)
Heb 2:16 For now·then,·as·is·well·known, he·grabs·hold—

G1223 διά diá *prep.* (642x)
δι- di- [shortened prefix]
Compare:G0575 G1537 xLangAlso:H1558
G1223.1 PREP διά (380x)
Jn 1:3 All·things came·to·be through him, and apart·from
Jn 1:7 the Light, in·order·that through him all *men* may·trust
Jn 1:10 and the world came·to·be through him, yet the
Jn 1:17 Because the Torah-Law was·given through Moses,
Jn 1:17 and the truth came·to·be through Jesus Anointed.
Jn 3:17 in·order·that the world through him may·be·saved.
Jn 4:4 And it·was·necessary·for him to·go through Samaria.
Jn 6:57 dispatched me, and·I live through the Father, so the·
Jn 6:57 ·one chewing me, he·likewise shall·live through me.
Jn 8:59 of·the Sanctuary·Atrium going through *the* midst of·
Jn 10:1 to·yeu, the·one not entering·in through the door into
Jn 10:2 "But the·one entering·in through the door is shepherd
Jn 10:9 If someone should·enter·in through me, he·shall·be·
Jn 11:4 ·that the Son of·God may·be·glorified through it."
Jn 14:6 ·even·one comes to the Father, except through me.
Jn 15:3 are trimmed·and·pure through the Redemptive-word
Jn 17:20 ·be·trusting in me through their Redemptive-word—
Lk 1:70 just·as he·spoke through *the* mouth of·his holy
Lk 1:78 through *the* inward·affections of·our God's mercy, in
Lk 4:30 But he·himself, after·going through *the* midst of·
Lk 5:5 "O·Captain, after·laboring·hard all through the night,
Lk 5:19 And not finding through what·kind·of *means* they·
Lk 5:19 they·sent him down through the tiles together with·
Lk 6:1 ·the·feast *for* him to·traverse through the grain·fields,
Lk 8:4 city, *Jesus* declared *the following* through a·parable:
Lk 11:24 the man·of·clay†, it·goes through waterless places,
Lk 13:24 "Strive to·enter through the obstructed·and·narrow
Lk 17:1 to·come, but woe *to·him* through whom they·come!
Lk 17:11 it·happened that he·himself went through *the* midst
Lk 18:25 a·camel to·enter·in through a·tiny·inlet of·a·needle,
Lk 18:31 ·things having·been·written through the prophets
Lk 19:4 because *Jesus* was·about to·go through that *way*.
Lk 22:22 man·of·clay† through whom he·is·handed·over!"
Ac 1:2 ·up, after·giving·commands through Holy Spirit to·
Ac 1:16 Spirit previously·declared through David's mouth
Ac 2:16 is the·thing having·been·declared through JoEl the
Ac 2:22 and signs, which God did through him in *the* midst
Ac 2:23 *was* given·over, being·taken through lawless hands.
Ac 2:43 and signs were·done through the ambassadors.
Ac 3:16 and the trust (the·one through him) gave to·this·
Ac 3:18 God fully·announced·beforehand through *the* mouth
Ac 3:21 of·which God spoke through *the* mouth of·all his
Ac 4:16 miraculous·sign has·been·done through them *is*
Ac 4:25 *You·are* the·one, through *the* mouth of·your
Ac 4:30 ·signs and wonders to·be·done through the name of·
Ac 5:12 Then through the hands of·the ambassadors, many
Ac 5:19 But an·angel of·Yahweh, *coming* through the night,
Ac 7:25 brothers to·comprehend that God, through his hand,
Ac 8:18 the Holy Spirit is·given through the laying·on of·the
Ac 8:20 ·present of·God may·be·procured through valuables.
Ac 9:25 sent·*him*·down *by* lowering *him* through the wall in
Ac 10:36 ·the·good·news of·peace through Jesus Anointed—
Ac 10:43 ·receive pardon of·moral·failures through his name
Ac 11:28 after·standing·up, signified through the Spirit
Ac 11:30 *it* to the elders through *the* hands of·BarNabas and
Ac 12:9 ·known that the·thing happening through the angel
Ac 13:38 be·it known to·yeu that through this·man, *the*
Ac 14:3 ·signs and wonders to·be·done through their hands).
Ac 14:22 into the kingdom of·God through many tribulations
Ac 15:7 of·the good·news through my mouth, and to·trust.
Ac 15:11 But·rather we·trust through the grace of·*the*·Lord
Ac 15:12 and wonders God did through them among the
Ac 15:23 *this letter of* these·things through their·own hand:
Ac 15:27 also *to·yeu* the same·things through *spoken* word.
Ac 15:32 exhorted the brothers through much discourse *in*·
Ac 16:9 ·vision was·made·visible to·Paul through the night:
Ac 17:10 sent·forth both Paul and Silas through the night to
Ac 18:9 the Lord declared to·Paul through a·clear·vision at

Ac 18:27 much, the·ones having·trusted through the grace.
Ac 18:28 publicly, fully·exhibiting through the Scriptures,
Ac 19:11 And·also God, through the hands of·Paul, was·
Ac 19:26 that the *gods* being·made through hands are not
Ac 20:3 he·made a·plan to·return·back through Macedonia.
Ac 20:28 which he·himself·acquired through his·own blood
Ac 21:4 ·same·men were·saying to·Paul through the Spirit
Ac 21:19 God did among the Gentiles through his service.
Ac 23:31 ·up Paul, they·brought *him* through the night to
Ac 28:25 Holy Spirit spoke well through Isaiah the prophet
Heb 1:2 *as* heir of·all·things, through whom also he·made
Heb 1:3 purification of·our moral·failures through himself,
Heb 2:2 For if the word being·spoken through angels was
Heb 2:3 *announcement* being·spoken through the Lord, it·
Heb 2:10 whom all·things *exist* and through whom all·things
Heb 2:10 Salvation completely·mature through afflictions.
Heb 2:14 ·to the same, in·order·that through the death, he·
Heb 2:15 them, as·many·as·who (through fear of·death)
Heb 3:16 after·coming·forth out of·Egypt through Moses.
Heb 3:19 ·were·not able to·enter·in through a·lack·of·trust.
Heb 5:14 having·been·trained through habit toward having
Heb 6:12 ·imitators of·the·ones *who* through trust and
Heb 7:9 ·one receiving tithes, has·tithed through AbRaham,
Heb 7:11 if perfection was through the Levitical sacred·
Heb 7:19 expectation *does*, through which we·draw·near to·
Heb 7:21 with a·swearing·of·oath through the·one saying to
Heb 7:25 ·ones who·are·coming·alongside God through him)
Heb 9:11 ·good·things, came·directly through the greater
Heb 9:12 however·not through blood of·adult·male·goats
Heb 9:12 calves, but he·entered through his·own blood into
Heb 9:14 of·the Anointed-One, who through *the* eternal
Heb 9:26 ·cancellation of·moral·failure through the sacrifice
Heb 10:2 being·offered through the·ones ritually·ministering
Heb 10:10 having·been·made·holy through the offering,
Heb 10:20 which he·inaugurated for·us through the curtain,
Heb 11:4 sacrifice than Qain, through which he·was·attested
Heb 11:4 ·offerings·of·sacrifice; and through the·same *trust*,
Heb 11:7 of·his house; through which he·condemned the
Heb 11:29 the Red Sea as through parched·ground, of·which
Heb 11:33 who through trust strenuously·subdued kingdoms,
Heb 11:39 these, already·being·attested·to through the trust,
Heb 12:1 — we·should·run (through patient·endurance) the
Heb 12:11 for·the·ones having·been·trained through it.
Heb 12:15 should·firmly·harass *yeu* and through this, many
Heb 12:28 grace through which we·may·ritually·minister to·
Heb 13:2 the hospitality·to·strangers, for through this some
Heb 13:11 into the Holy·of·Holies through the high·priest
Heb 13:12 ·make·holy the People through his·own blood,
Heb 13:21 in·the·sight·of·him, through YeShua Anointed—
Heb 13:22 of·exhortation, for through concise·passages, I·
Gal 1:1 from men·of·clay†, neither through a·man·of·clay†,
Gal 1:1 ·man·of·clay†, but·rather through YeShua Anointed
Gal 1:12 *·received it* through a·revelation of·YeShua
Gal 1:15 womb and calling·*me*·forth through his grace)
Gal 2:16 of·Torah-Law, but·only through a·trust of·YeShua
Gal 2:19 For I·myself through Torah-Law, am·dead to·
Gal 2:21 for if righteousness *is* through Torah-Law, then·by·
Gal 3:14 ·receive the promise of·the Spirit through the trust.
Gal 3:18 *the inheritance* to·AbRaham through promise.
Gal 3:19 *was* being·thoroughly·assigned through angels in
Gal 3:26 For yeu·are all the·Sons of·God through the trust in
Gal 4:7 *then* also an·heir of·God through Anointed-One.
Gal 4:13 Yeu·personally·know that through sickness of·the
Gal 4:23 ·out of·the free·woman *was* through the promise.
Gal 5:6 ·rather trust which·is·itself·operating through love.
Gal 5:13 to·the flesh. But·rather through the love, be·slaves
Gal 6:14 of·our Lord YeShua Anointed, through whom *the*
Mt 1:22 ·thing being·uttered by Yahweh through the prophet,
Mt 2:5 ·this·manner it·has·been·written through the prophet,
Mt 2:12 into their·own country through another way.
Mt 2:15 ·thing being·uttered by Yahweh through the prophet,
Mt 2:23 the·thing being·uttered through the prophets, "He·
Mt 4:4 utterance that·is·proceeding·forth through *the* mouth
Mt 4:14 ·fulfilled, the·thing being·uttered through Isaiah the
Mt 7:13 "Yeu·must·enter·in through the obstructed·and·
Mt 7:13 many are the·ones who·are·entering·in through it.
Mt 8:17 ·fulfilled, the·one being·uttered through Isaiah the
Mt 8:28 not to·have·strength to·pass·by through that way.
Mt 12:1 on·the various·Sabbaths through the grain·fields,
Mt 12:17 the·thing being·uttered through Isaiah the prophet
Mt 12:43 the man·of·clay†, it·goes through waterless places,
Mt 13:35 the·thing being·uttered through the prophet,
Mt 15:3 commandment of·God through yeur Oral·tradition?
Mt 15:6 commandment of·God through yeur Oral·tradition.
Mt 18:7 woe to·that man·of·clay† through whom the
Mt 19:24 easier *for* a·camel to·go through *the* tiny·hole of·a·
Mt 21:4 the·thing being·uttered through the prophet, saying,
Mt 24:15 ' the·one being·uttered through DaniEl the
Mt 26:24 but woe to·that man·of·clay† through whom the
Mt 27:9 the·thing being·uttered through Jeremiah the prophet
Mk 2:23 to·be·traversing·directly through the grain·fields on
Mk 6:2 that even such miracles happen through his hands?
Mk 9:30 they·were·traversing·directly through Galilee, and
Mk 10:1 into the borders of·Judea through the other·side of·
Mk 10:25 easier for·a·camel to·enter through the tiny·inlet
Mk 11:16 *any* merchandise through the Sanctuary·Atrium.
Mk 14:21 but woe to·that man·of·clay† through whom the
Mk 15:10 chief·priests had·handed him over through envy.
Mk 16:20 confirming the Redemptive-word through the signs
Rm 1:2 (which he·promised·beforehand through his prophets
Rm 1:5 through whom we·received grace and commission
Rm 1:8 I·give·thanks to·my God through Jesus Anointed
Rm 1:12 ·comforted·together among yeu through the mutual
Rm 2:12 Torah-Law shall·be·judged through Torah-Law.
Rm 2:16 ·to my good·news, *this·is* through Jesus Anointed).
Rm 2:23 do·you·dishonor God through the violation of·the
Rm 2:27 judge you, the·one through letter and circumcision
Rm 3:20 of·him,' for through Torah-Law *is the* recognition
Rm 3:22 And God's righteousness through trust of·Jesus
Rm 3:24 ·present by·his grace through the ransom·in·full,
Rm 3:25 an·atoning·sacrifice·for·favorable·forgiveness through
Rm 3:30 of·trust and *the* Uncircumcision through the trust.
Rm 3:31 ·render·useless *the* Torah-Law through the trust?
Rm 4:11 of·all the·ones trusting *God* through *the state·of*
Rm 4:13 the promise *is* not through Torah-Law to·AbRaham
Rm 4:13 , but·rather *is* through a·righteousness of·trust.
Rm 5:1 we·have peace toward God through our Lord Jesus
Rm 5:2 through whom also we·have the embraceable·access
Rm 5:5 ·been·poured·forth in our hearts through Holy Spirit,
Rm 5:9 ·so we·shall·be·saved from the Wrath through him.
Rm 5:10 we·are·reconciled to·God through the death of·his
Rm 5:11 we·also are·boasting in God through our Lord Jesus
Rm 5:11 our Lord Jesus Anointed, through whom now we·
Rm 5:12 ·of this: *that* just·as through one man·of·clay†,
Rm 5:12 the world and Death through Moral·Failure, also in·
Rm 5:16 *is* not as through one already·morally·failing. For
Rm 5:17 one trespass, Death reigned through the one·man,
Rm 5:17 shall·reign in life-above through the one·man, Jesus
Rm 5:18 So consequently, as through one trespass, *judgment*
Rm 5:18 even in·this·manner, through one righteous·act,
Rm 5:19 For just·as through the inattentive·disregard of·one
Rm 5:19 also in·this·manner through the attentive·obedience
Rm 5:21 ·manner Grace may·reign through righteousness to
Rm 5:21 to eternal life-above through Jesus Anointed our
Rm 6:4 ·buried·together with·him through the immersion
Rm 6:4 ·awakened from·among dead·men through the glory
Rm 7:4 ·put·to·death to·the Torah-Law through the body of·
Rm 7:5 ·the moral·failures, the·ones through the Torah-Law
Rm 7:7 know Moral·Failure, except through Torah-Law, for
Rm 7:8 impromptu·occasion through the commandment,
Rm 7:11 impromptu·occasion through the commandment,
Rm 7:11 thoroughly·deluded me; and through it, it·killed
Rm 7:13 death in·me through the beneficially·good, in·
Rm 7:13 ·that Moral·Failure, through the commandment,
Rm 7:25 I·give·thanks to·God through Jesus Anointed our
Rm 8:3 in that it·was·being·weak through the flesh, God,
Rm 8:10 ·fact, the body *is* dead through moral·failure. Now
Rm 8:10 Now the Spirit *is* life-above through righteousness,
Rm 8:11 ·life-above·to yeur mortal bodies through his Spirit
Rm 8:20 voluntarily, but·rather through the·one subjecting *it*
Rm 8:25 *then* through patient·endurance we·fully·await *it*.
Rm 8:37 we·gain·a·decisive·victory through the·one loving
Rm 10:17 and the hearing through an·utterance of·God.
Rm 11:36 Because from·out·of·him, and through him, and
Rm 12:1 yeu, brothers, through the tender·compassions of·
Rm 12:3 For through the grace being·given to·me, I·say to·
Rm 14:14 that *there·is* nothing·at·all defiled through itself,
Rm 14:15 But if your brother is·grieved through *your* food,
Rm 14:20 ·block *to·his brother* on·account·of *his* eating.
Rm 15:4 the Expectation through the patient·endurance and
Rm 15:18 already·accomplished through me for an·attentive·
Rm 15:28 this fruit, I·shall·go·aside through yeu into Spain.
Rm 15:32 ·come toward yeu with joy through God's will and
Rm 16:18 And through the fine·accommodating·speech and
Rm 16:26 ·apparent— also through prophetic Scriptures,
Rm 16:27 to·him *be* the glory through Jesus Anointed into
Jac 2:12 do: as ones·about to·be·judged through *the* Law of·
Php 1:11 ·righteousness, of·the·ones through Jesus Anointed
Php 1:15 ·proclaim the Anointed-One even through envy and
Php 1:15 and strife, and some also through good·purpose.
Php 1:19 ·result in salvation for·me through yeur petition and
Php 1:20 in my body, whether through life† or through death
Php 1:20 my body, whether through life† or through death.
Php 1:26 may·abound in Jesus Anointed through my arrival
Php 3:7 ·considered a·total·loss through Anointed-One.
Php 3:8 all·things to·be a·total·loss through the superiority
Php 3:9 but·rather the·one through a·trust of·Anointed-One
1Pe 1:3 into a·living Expectation through *the* resurrection of·
1Pe 1:5 ·dutifully·kept by God's power through trust for a·
1Pe 1:7 even with·it·being·tested·and·proven through fire)
1Pe 1:12 to·yeu through the·ones already·proclaiming·the·
1Pe 1:21 (the·ones through him trusting in God, the·one
1Pe 1:22 attentive·obedience of·the truth through *the* Spirit
1Pe 1:23 *sowing·of·seed* through *the* Redemptive-word of·God
1Pe 2:5 well·acceptable to·God through YeShua Anointed.
1Pe 2:14 or to·governors, as being·sent through him, in·fact,
1Pe 3:1 they·may·be·gained through the behavior of·the
1Pe 3:20 eight souls) were·thoroughly·saved through water.
1Pe 3:21 God)— through *the* resurrection of·YeShua
1Pe 4:11 may·be·glorified through YeShua Anointed, to·
1Pe 5:12 Through Silvanus (the trustworthy brother as·how
2Pe 1:3 ·been·endowed to·us, through the recognition of·
2Pe 1:3 of·the·one already·calling us forth through glory and
2Pe 1:4 Through these he·has·endowed to·us the most·
2Pe 1:4 pledges, in·order·that through these, yeu·may·
2Pe 3:5 *being·made* from·out·of·water and through water—
2Pe 3:6 through which the world at·that·time was·
2Pe 3:12 of·the Day of·God— through which *the* heavens,
1Th 3:7 we·are·comforted over yeu through yeur trust.
1Th 4:2 what charges we·gave yeu through the Lord YeShua.
1Th 4:14 ·him the·ones being·laid·to·rest through YeShua.
1Th 5:9 ·rather for acquisition of·Salvation through our Lord
2Th 2:2 *by·any delusion* (neither through spirit, nor through
2Th 2:2 (neither through spirit, nor through word, nor
2Th 2:2 through word, nor through letter as·though through
2Th 2:2 nor through letter as·though through us) as·though
2Th 2:14 which he·called yeu forth through our good·news,
2Th 2:15 yeu·were·instructed, whether through *spoken* word
2Th 2:15 whether through *spoken* word or through our letter.
2Th 3:12 we·charge and exhort through our Lord YeShua
2Th 3:14 listen·to·and·obey our word through this·letter,
Tit 3:5 ·to his mercy, through a·bath of·regeneration and a·
Tit 3:6 ·forth on us abundantly through Jesus Anointed our
1Co 1:1 ·ambassador of·Jesus Anointed through God's will,
1Co 1:9 *is* trustworthy, through whom yeu·are·called·forth
1Co 1:10 I·implore yeu, brothers, through the name of·our
1Co 1:21 of·God) the world through the wisdom did·not
1Co 1:21 God, God took·delight through the foolishness of·
1Co 2:10 But God revealed *them* to·us through his Spirit, for

1Co 3:5 other than attendants through whom yeu·trusted,
1Co 3:15 ·be·saved, but in·this·manner, as through fire.
1Co 4:15 Jesus, I·myself begot yeu through the good·news.
1Co 6:14 shall·fully·awaken us through his·own power.
1Co 8:6 Lord, Jesus Anointed (through whom *are* all·things
1Co 8:6 whom *are* all·things and we·ourselves through him).
1Co 10:1 were under the cloud, and all went through the sea,
1Co 11:12 ·this·manner the man *is* also through the woman,
1Co 12:8 For in·fact to·one is·given through the Spirit a·
1Co 13:12 we·look·about through a·reflected·image with
1Co 14:9 so·also *are* yeu, through the bestowed·tongue.
1Co 14:19 to·speak five words through my understanding,
1Co 15:2 through which also yeu·are·saved, if yeu·fully·
1Co 15:21 For whereas through a·man·of·clay† *came* the
1Co 15:21 the death, also through a·man·of·clay† *came*
1Co 15:57 ·one giving us the victory through our Lord Jesus
1Co 16:3 yeu·should·verifiably·approve through *yeur* letters,
2Co 1:1 ·ambassador of·Jesus Anointed through God's will,
2Co 1:4 in any tribulation, through the comfort with·which
2Co 1:5 our comforting also abounds through Anointed-One.
2Co 1:11 *may·be·bestowed* upon us through many *persons*,
2Co 1:16 and to·go through yeu into Macedonia, and to·
2Co 1:19 ·officially·proclaimed among yeu through us
2Co 1:19 among yeu through us (through Silvanus, TimoThy
2Co 1:20 "So·be·it,·Amen" for·God unto glory through us.
2Co 2:4 ·anxiety of·heart I·wrote to·yeu through many tears,
2Co 2:14 aroma of·his knowledge in every place through us.
2Co 3:4 such confidence we·have through the Anointed-One
2Co 4:14 Jesus shall·awaken us also, through Jesus, and
2Co 4:15 the ever·increasing grace through the many·more
2Co 5:7 for we·presently·walk through trust, not through
2Co 5:7 we·presently·walk through trust, not through sight.
2Co 5:10 ·obtain the·things *done* through the body,
2Co 5:18 ·reconciling us to·himself through Jesus Anointed,
2Co 5:20 as God imploring *yeu* through us. We·petition *yeu*
2Co 6:7 God's power, through the weapons·and·armor of·
2Co 6:8 through glory and dishonor, through harsh·
2Co 6:8 glory and dishonor, through harsh·reputation and
2Co 8:5 to·the Lord and *then* to·us through God's will,
2Co 9:11 is·accomplishing through us an·expression·of·
2Co 9:12 also through many expressions·of·thankfulness to·
2Co 10:1 I·myself do·implore yeu through the gentleness
2Co 10:9 ·*intended* to·utterly·frighten yeu through the letters
2Co 10:11 "Such·as we·are in·word through *our* letters
2Co 11:33 And through a·window, in a·large·basket, I·was·
2Co 11:33 in a·large·basket, I·was·lowered through the wall
2Co 12:17 ¿!·Did I·swindle yeu through any of·them whom
Eph 1:1 an·ambassador of·Jesus Anointed through God's will
Eph 1:5 ·as·sons into himself through Jesus Anointed,
Eph 1:7 whom we·have the ransom·in·full through his blood
Eph 2:8 grace, yeu·are having·been·saved through the trust.
Eph 2:16 the both to·God in one body through the cross, in
Eph 2:18 Because through him, the both *of·us* have the
Eph 3:6 promise in the Anointed-One through the good·news
Eph 3:9 the·one creating all things through Jesus Anointed—
Eph 3:10 the heavenly·places through the entire·Called·Out·
Eph 3:12 ·access with confidence through trust of·him.
Eph 3:16 to·be·made·mighty with·power through his Spirit
Eph 3:17 to·reside in yeur hearts through the trust, having·
Eph 4:16 and is·being·united·together through every amply·
Eph 4:18 from·the life-above of·God through the ignorance
Eph 6:18 Through all prayer and petition, be·presently·
Col 1:1 an·ambassador of·Jesus Anointed through God's will
Col 1:14 we·have the ransom·in·full through his blood, the
Col 1:16 All·things have·been·created through him and for
Col 1:22 in the body of·his flesh through the death, to·
Col 2:8 shall·be the·one seducing yeu through the *use·of*
Col 2:12 ·awakened·together *with·him* through the trust of·
Col 2:19 the Body grows·up through the connecting·joints
Col 3:17 giving·thanks to·the God and Father through him.
Phm 1:7 ·ones have·been·refreshed, brother, through you.
Phm 1:22 for I·expect that through yeur prayers I·shall·be·
1Ti 2:10 but·rather through beneficially·good works (which
1Ti 2:15 she·shall·be·saved through the bearing·of·children
1Ti 4:5 for it·is·made·holy through God's Redemptive-word
1Ti 4:14 which was·given to·you through prophecy, with
2Ti 1:1 an·ambassador of·Jesus Anointed through God's will,
2Ti 1:6 which is in you through the laying·on of·my hands.
2Ti 1:10 now being·made·apparent through the conspicuous·
2Ti 1:10 and eternal·incorruptibility through the good·news,
2Ti 1:14 you·must·vigilantly·keep through Holy Spirit, the·
2Ti 2:2 ·heard personally·from me through many witnesses,
2Ti 3:15 you wise to Salvation through a·trust, the·one in
2Ti 4:17 enabled me, in·order·that through me the official·
1Jn 4:9 the world, in·order·that we·may·live through him.
1Jn 5:6 This is the·one coming through water and blood,
2Jn 1:12 ·not willing *to·do so* through a·sheet·of·paper and
3Jn 1:13 I·do·not want to·write to·you through ink and a·
Rv 1:1 And dispatching through his angel, he·signified *it* to·
Rv 4:11 created all things, and through your will, they·exist
Rv 12:11 they·themselves overcame him through the blood
Rv 12:11 blood of·the Lamb, and through the word of·their
Rv 13:14 residing on the earth through *the means·of* the

G1223.1a PREP δι′ (1x)

Col 1:20 ·*delight* to·utterly·reconcile through him all·things

G1223.1b PREP διά (1x)

Col 1:20 and after·making·peace through the blood of

G1223.1c PREP δι′ (1x)

Col 1:20 him all·things to himself, through *Anointed-One, I·*

EG1223.1 (5x)

Jn 8:59 and in·this·manner, he·was·passing·on *through*.
Jn 9:1 And while·passing·on *through*, he·saw a·man·of·clay†
Heb 4:2 but·yet the Redemptive-word *through* hearing did·
Mt 26:45 "Do·yeu·all·sleep *through* the·one remaining
Mk 14:41 "Do·yeu·all·sleep *through* the·one remaining

G1223.2 PREP διά (8x)

Jn 19:23 *continuously* from·the·start throughout all *of·it*.
Ac 1:3 ·being·gazed·upon by·them throughout forty days,
Ac 9:32 And while·going throughout all *the regions*, it·
Ac 13:49 Lord was·thoroughly·carried throughout the whole
Mt 18:10 to·yeu that throughout any *matter·of·consequence*,
2Th 3:16 himself grant yeu Peace throughout every *matter* at
2Co 8:18 *is* in the good·news throughout all the Called·Out·
Eph 4:6 of·all: the·one over all and throughout all and in yeu

EG1223.2 (1x)

1Pe 1:1 foreign·residents of·*the*·Diaspora *throughout* Pontus,

G1223.3 PREP διά (239x)

Jn 1:31 ·be·made·apparent to·IsraEl, on·account·of that, I·
Jn 2:24 himself to·them, on·account·of him knowing all
Jn 3:29 rejoices with·joy on·account·of the bridegroom's
Jn 4:39 city trusted in him on·account·of the saying of·the
Jn 4:41 And many more trusted on·account·of his·own word.
Jn 4:42 "No·longer do·we·trust on·account·of your speech,
Jn 5:16 And on·account·of that, the Judeans were·
Jn 5:18 Accordingly, on·account·of that, the Judeans were·
Jn 6:65 And he·was·saying, "On·account·of that, I·have·
Jn 7:13 ·of·speech concerning him, on·account·of the fear
Jn 7:22 "On·account·of that Moses has·given to·yeu the
Jn 7:43 ·schism among the crowd on·account·of him.
Jn 8:47 the utterances of·God. On·account·of that, yeu·
Jn 9:23 On·account·of that, his parents declared, "He·is of·
Jn 10:17 "On·account·of that, the Father loves me, because I·
Jn 10:19 among the Judeans on·account·of these sayings.
Jn 10:32 ·out·of·my Father; on·account·of which of·those
Jn 11:15 And I·am·glad on·account·of yeu that I·was not
Jn 11:42 ·hear me always, but·yet on·account·of the crowd,
Jn 12:9 And they·did·not come on·account·of Jesus merely,
Jn 12:11 because on·account·of him, many of·the Judeans
Jn 12:18 On·account·of that, the crowd *from JeruSalem* also
Jn 12:27 ·this hour?' But·rather on·account·of this, I·came
Jn 12:30 This voice has·happened not on·account·of me, but·
Jn 12:30 on·account·of me, but·rather on·account·of yeu.
Jn 12:39 On·account·of that, they·were·not able to·trust,
Jn 12:42 in him. But·yet on·account·of the Pharisees they·
Jn 13:11 handing him over. On·account·of that, he·declared,
Jn 14:11 But·if·not, trust me on·account·of the works
Jn 15:19 yeu from·among the world. On·account·of this, the
Jn 15:21 ·things shall·they·do to·yeu on·account·of my name
Jn 16:15 has, are mine. On·account·of that, I·declared that
Jn 16:21 the tribulation no longer on·account·of the joy that
Jn 19:11 ·given to·you from·above. On·account·of that, the·
Jn 19:38 but having·been·under·cover on·account·of the fear
Jn 19:42 So they·laid Jesus there on·account·of the Judeans
Jn 20:19 having·been·gathered·together on·account·of the
Lk 2:4 is·called BethLechem), on·account·of him being
Lk 5:19 they·may·carry him in on·account·of the crowd,
Lk 8:6 it·withered·away on·account·of *the solid·rock* not
Lk 8:19 ·not able to·encounter him on·account·of the crowd.
Lk 8:47 of·all the people, on·account·of what cause she·
Lk 9:7 ·perplexed, on·account·of *that* it·was·said by some
Lk 11:8 he·shall·not give to·him on·account·of *him* being
Lk 11:8 being his friend, yet on·account·of his audacity, he·
Lk 11:19 yeur sons cast·*them*·out? On·account·of that, they
Lk 11:49 "On·account·of that, the wisdom of·God also
Lk 12:22 to his disciples, "On·account·of that, I·say to·yeu,
Lk 14:20 'I·married a·wife, and on·account·of that, I·am·not
Lk 18:5 yet on·account·of this widow personally·presenting
Lk 19:11 *Jesus* declared a·parable, on·account·of him being
Lk 21:17 ·be being·hated by all on·account·of my name.
Lk 23:8 for a·long·while on·account·of hearing many·things
Lk 23:19 into prison on·account·of a·certain insurrection
Lk 23:25 ·cast into the prison on·account·of insurrection and
Ac 2:26 On·account·of that, my heart is·made·merry, and
Ac 4:2 being·thoroughly·stressed·out on·account·of them
Ac 4:21 ·sternly·punish them on·account·of the people,
Ac 8:11 ·were·giving·heed, on·account·of *that he·continued*
Ac 10:21 *is* the motivation on·account·of which yeu·are·here
Ac 12:20 they·requested peace, on·account·of their country
Ac 16:3 he·circumcised him on·account·of the Jews, the·
Ac 18:2 ·*(that·is,·Priscilla)*, on·account·of Claudius *Caesar*
Ac 18:3 And on·account·of being of·the same·trade, he·was·
Ac 21:34 absolute·certainty on·account·of the commotion,
Ac 21:35 ·and·carried by the soldiers on·account·of the force
Ac 22:24 ·that he·may·realize on·account·of what cause
Ac 23:28 the legal·charge on·account·of which they·were·
Ac 24:2 "While·obtaining much peace on·account·of you,
Ac 24:2 in·this nation on·account·of your providence,
Ac 27:4 ·leeward·near·to Cyprus, on·account·of the winds
Ac 27:9 precarious on·account·of the fast·*Day·of·Atonement*
Ac 28:2 everyone of·us, on·account·of the assaulting rain,
Ac 28:2 ·of the assaulting rain, and on·account·of the cold.
Ac 28:18 to·fully·release *me*, on·account·of there not
Ac 28:20 Accordingly, on·account·of this cause, I·
Heb 1:9 and hated lawlessness. On·account·of that, God,
Heb 1:14 into service on·account·of the·ones about to·inherit
Heb 2:1 On·account·of that, it·is·necessary·for us more·
Heb 2:9 ·lesser than *the* angels on·account·of the affliction
Heb 2:10 *Father God* (on·account·of whom all·things *exist*
Heb 2:11 ·out of·one *Father*. On·account·of which cause,
Heb 4:6 did·not enter on·account·of an·obstinate·attitude,
Heb 5:3 And on·account·of this (just·as concerning the
Heb 6:7 well-suited for·those on·account·of whom also it·is·
Heb 6:18 in·order·that, on·account·of two unalterable
Heb 7:18 ·a·preceding commandment on·account·of it *being*
Heb 7:23 to·personally·continue on·account·of death.
Heb 7:24 But *this·man*, on·account·of him continuing to the
Heb 9:15 And on·account·of this, he·is *the* mediator of·a·
Heb 13:15 Accordingly, on·account·of him, we·should·
Gal 2:4 But *still*, on·account·of the infiltrating, false·
Mt 6:25 "On·account·of that, I·say to·yeu, do·not be·
Mt 10:22 being·hated by all *men* on·account·of my name.
Mt 12:27 yeur sons cast·*them*·out? On·account·of that, they
Mt 12:31 "On·account·of that, I·say to·yeu, all·manner·of
Mt 13:5 it·rose·out·above·the·surface, on·account·of it not
Mt 13:6 it·was·burned·by·the·sun. And on·account·of it not
Mt 13:13 "On·account·of that, I·speak to·them in parables,
Mt 13:21 occurring on·account·of the Redemptive-word,
Mt 13:52 he·declared to·them, "On·account·of that, every
Mt 13:58 miracles there on·account·of their lack·of·trust.

Mt 14:2 from the dead, and on·account·of that, miracles
Mt 14:3 placed *him* in prison on·account·of HerOdias, the
Mt 14:9 king was·grieved, but on·account·of the oath and
Mt 17:20 to·them, "On·account·of yeur lack·of·trust. For
Mt 18:23 "On·account·of that, the kingdom of·the heavens
Mt 19:12 castrated themselves on·account·of the kingdom
Mt 21:43 "On·account·of that, I·say to·yeu, the kingdom of·
Mt 23:13 *prayers*. "On·account·of that, yeu·shall·receive
Mt 23:34 "On·account·of that, behold, I·myself dispatch to
Mt 24:9 ·hated by all the nations on·account·of my name.
Mt 24:12 And on·account·of the·thing to·be·multiplied, the
Mt 24:22 *living*; but on·account·of the Selected-Ones, those
Mt 24:44 On·account·of that, yeu·yeurselves become ready
Mt 27:18 ·known that on·account·of envy they·handed him
Mt 27:19 ·to a·vision·in·a·dream on·account·of him."
Mk 2:4 to·further·draw·near to·him on·account·of the crowd,
Mk 2:27 Sabbath came·to·be on·account·of the Clay·Man†,
Mk 2:27 not the Clay·Man† on·account·of the Sabbath.
Mk 3:9 ·diligently·attend to·him on·account·of the crowd,
Mk 4:5 ·out·above·the·surface, on·account·of it·not having
Mk 4:6 ·by·the·sun, and·then on·account·of it·not having
Mk 4:17 happening on·account·of the Redemptive-word,
Mk 5:4 on·account·of him many·times to·have·been·bound
Mk 6:6 he·was·marveling on·account·of their lack·of·trust.
Mk 6:14 from·among dead·men, and on·account·of that, the
Mk 6:17 him in the prison on·account·of HerOdias, the wife
Mk 6:26 exceedingly·grieved, *yet* on·account·of the oath
Mk 7:29 he·declared to·her, "On·account·of this saying,
Mk 11:24 On·account·of that, I·say to·yeu, all·things, as·
Mk 12:24 "*Is·it* not on·account·of this·thing *that* yeu·are·led·
Mk 13:13 being·hated by all *men* on·account·of my name.
Mk 13:20 ·saved; but·yet on·account·of the Selected-Ones
Rm 1:26 On·account·of that, God handed them over to
Rm 2:24 is·reviled among the Gentiles on·account·of yeu,"
Rm 3:25 ·his righteousness on·account·of the reprieve·from·
Rm 3:27 It·is·excluded. On·account·of what·kind·of law?
Rm 3:27 ·indeed, but·rather on·account·of a·Law of·Trust.
Rm 4:16 On·account·of that, *righteousness is* as·a·result of·
Rm 4:23 Now it·was·not written on·account·of him merely,
Rm 4:24 but·rather also on·account·of us, to·whom it·is·
Rm 4:25 who was·handed·over on·account·of our trespasses,
Rm 4:25 and was·awakened on·account·of our acquittal·in·
Rm 5:12 *a·reconciliation needed* on·account·of this: *that*
Rm 6:19 *this* after·the·manner·of·men† on·account·of the
Rm 11:28 good·news, *they·are* enemies on·account·of yeu,
Rm 11:28 *they·are* beloved on·account·of the patriarchs.
Rm 13:5 ·oneself, not merely on·account·of the wrath, but·
Rm 13:5 wrath, but·rather also on·account·of the conscience
Rm 13:6 For on·account·of that, yeu·fully·pay tributes also.
Rm 15:9 "On·account·of that, I·shall·explicitly·affirm you
Rm 15:15 ·again·reminding yeu, on·account·of the grace
Rm 15:30 yeu, brothers, on·account·of our Lord Jesus
Rm 15:30 Jesus Anointed, and on·account·of the love of·the
Jac 4:2 but yeu·do·not have, on·account *that* yeu do·not
Php 1:7 on·behalf of·all of·yeu, on·account·of having yeu in
Php 1:24 ·on in the flesh *is* necessary on·account·of yeu.
Php 2:30 because on·account·of the work of·Anointed-One,
Php 3:8 on·account·of whom I·suffered·the·damage·and·loss
1Pe 1:20 ·made·apparent in the last times on·account·of yeu
1Pe 2:13 ·governance of·mankind† on·account·of the Lord,
1Pe 2:19 if someone on·account·of conscience *toward* God
1Pe 3:14 ·though yeu·may·actually·suffer on·account·of,
2Pe 2:2 their *ways* to·total·destruction, on·account·of whom,
1Th 1:5 ·ourselves as·such among yeu, on·account·of yeu.
1Th 2:13 On·account·of this also, we·ourselves give·thanks
1Th 3:5 On·account·of this, when·I could·quietly·bear·it no·
1Th 3:7 On·account·of that, brothers, in all our tribulation
1Th 3:9 joy with·which we·rejoice on·account·of yeu before
1Th 5:13 love above·and·beyond, on·account·of their work.
2Th 2:11 And on·account·of this, God shall·send them an·
Tit 1:13 This testimony is true. On·account·of which cause,
1Co 4:6 as·to myself and Apollos on·account·of yeu, in·
1Co 4:10 ·ourselves *are* fools on·account·of Anointed-One,
1Co 4:17 On·account·of that, I·sent to·yeu TimoThy, who is
1Co 7:2 But on·account·of the sexual·immoralities, each
1Co 7:5 tempt yeu on·account·of yeur lack·of·self-restraint.
1Co 7:26 ·be good on·account·of the currently·standing
1Co 8:11 ·perish, on·account·of whom Anointed-One died?
1Co 9:10 Or does·he·say *this* altogether on·account·of us?
1Co 9:10 ·of us? For on·account·of us it·was·written,
1Co 9:23 And this I·do on·account·of the good·news, in·
1Co 10:25 not·even·one·thing on·account·of the conscience.
1Co 10:27 not·even·one·thing on·account·of the conscience.
1Co 10:28 eat on·account·of that·one bringing·it·to·*yeur*·
1Co 11:9 also man is·not created on·account·of the woman,
1Co 11:9 woman, but·rather woman on·account·of the man.
1Co 11:10 On·account·of that, the woman is·obligated to·
1Co 11:10 authority on her head on·account·of the angels.
1Co 11:30 On·account·of that, many *are* weak and unhealthy
2Co 2:10 ·graciously·forgiven *it*), on·account·of yeu *I·did·it*
2Co 3:7 into the face of·Moses on·account·of the glory of·
2Co 3:11 ·*Death* is·being·fully·nullified on·account·of glory,
2Co 4:1 On·account·of that, having this Service *of·the Spirit*,
2Co 4:5 we·ourselves *are* yeur slaves on·account·of Jesus.
2Co 4:11 are·handed·over to death on·account·of Jesus, in·
2Co 4:15 For all things *are* on·account·of yeu in·order·that,
2Co 7:13 On·account·of that, we·have·been·comforted in
2Co 8:8 ·authority, but·rather on·account·of the diligence
2Co 8:9 how·that being wealthy, on·account·of yeu, he·
2Co 9:13 On·account·of the proof of·this service, they·are·
2Co 9:14 ·yearning·for yeu, on·account·of the surpassing
2Co 13:10 On·account·of that, I·write these·things while·
Eph 1:15 On·account·of that, I·also, after·hearing·of the trust
Eph 2:4 wealthy in mercy, on·account·of his large love
Eph 4:18 existing in them, on·account·of the stony·hardness
Eph 5:6 ·empty words, for on·account·of these·things the
Eph 5:17 On·account·of this, do·not become impetuous·ones
Eph 6:13 On·account·of that, take·up the whole·armor of·
Col 1:5 on·account·of the Expectation, the·one being·laid·
Col 1:9 On·account·of that, we·ourselves also (since that
Col 3:6 on·account·of which·things the wrath of·God comes
Col 4:3 of·the Anointed-One on·account·of which also I·
Phm 1:9 rather on·account·of the love, I·implore *you*, *I* Paul,
Phm 1:15 For perhaps on·account·of that, he·departed just·
1Ti 1:16 But·yet on·account·of this, I·was·shown·mercy in·
1Ti 5:23 ·rather use a·little wine on·account·of your stomach
2Ti 1:6 On·account·of which cause I·remind·and·admonish
2Ti 1:12 On·account·of which cause also I·suffer these·
2Ti 2:10 On·account·of that, I·patiently·endure all·things on·
2Ti 2:10 ·endure all·things on·account·of the Selected-Ones
1Jn 2:12 have·been·forgiven yeu on·account·of his name.
1Jn 3:1 ·be·called children of·God. On·account·of that, the
1Jn 4:5 from·out·of·the world, on·account·of that they·speak
2Jn 1:2 on·account·of the truth abiding in us and *which* shall·
3Jn 1:10 On·account·of that, if I·should·come, I·shall·
Rv 1:9 ·called Patmos, on·account·of the Redemptive-word
Rv 1:9 of·God, and on·account·of the testimony of·Jesus
Rv 2:3 and you·have·labored·hard on·account·of my name
Rv 6:9 ·the·ones having·been·slaughtered on·account·of the
Rv 6:9 of·God, and on·account·of the testimony which they·
Rv 7:15 On·account·of that, they·are in·the·sight of·the
Rv 12:12 "On·account·of that, be·merry, the heavens and
Rv 18:8 On·account·of that, her punishing·blows shall·come
Rv 18:10 standing from a·distance on·account·of the fear of·
Rv 18:15 shall·stand from a·distance on·account·of the fear
Rv 20:4 having·been·beheaded on·account·of the testimony
Rv 20:4 of·Jesus and on·account·of the Redemptive-word of·

G1223.4 PREP διά (6x)

Ac 24:17 "And after many·more years, I·came·openly doing
Heb 5:12 For even after the time being·due *for·yeu* to·be
Gal 2:1 Then after fourteen years, I·walked·up again to
Mt 26:61 the Temple of·God and to·build it after three days.'
Mk 2:1 again he·entered into CaperNaum after *some* days,
Mk 14:58 the·one made·by·hand, and after three days I·

G1224 διαβαίνω diabaínō *v.* (3x)

Roots:G1223 G0901-3 Compare:G1330 G1353
xLangEquiv:H5674

G1224.2 V-2AAI-3P διέβησαν (1x)

Heb 11:29 By·trust, they·crossed the Red Sea as through

G1224.2 V-2AAN διαβῆναι (1x)

Lk 16:26 so·that the·ones wanting to·cross from·here to yeu

G1224.2 V-2AAP-NSM διαβάς (1x)

Ac 16:9 him, saying, "Crossing into Macedonia, swiftly·

G1225 διαβάλλω diabállō *v.* (1x)

Roots:G1223 G0906 Compare:G2723 G2635
See:G1228 G1736-1
xLangEquiv:H3960

G1225.2 V-API-3S διεβλήθη (1x)

Lk 16:1 this *estate·manager* was·slandered to·him as·though

G1226 διαβεβαιόομαι diabêbaiôômai *v.* (2x)

Roots:G1223 G0950

G1226.1 V-PNN διαβεβαιοῦσθαι (1x)

Tit 3:8 I·resolve for·you to·thoroughly·confirm *them*, in·

G1226.2 V-PNI-3P διαβεβαιοῦνται (1x)

1Ti 1:7 certain·things·which they·so·thoroughly·affirm.

G1227 διαβλέπω diablépō *v.* (2x)

Roots:G1223 G0991

G1227.2 V-FAI-2S διαβλέψεις (2x)

Lk 6:42 then you·shall·thoroughly·look·about to·cast·out the
Mt 7:5 and then you·shall·thoroughly·look·about to·cast the

G1228 διάβολος diábôlôs *adj.* (38x)

מַלְשִׁין malshiyn [MCT Brit Chadashah]

Roots:G1225 Compare:G4567 G3789 G1404
xLangEquiv:H4457-1 xLangAlso:H7854 H6862

G1228.1 A-NSM διάβολος (1x)

Jn 6:70 the twelve, yet one from·among yeu is a·slanderer."

G1228.1 A-NPM διάβολοι (1x)

2Ti 3:3 implacable, truceless·men, slanderers, without·

G1228.1 A-APF διαβόλους (2x)

Tit 2:3 befitting·of·sacred·women, not slanderers, not
1Ti 3:11 ·worthy·of·reverent·respect, not slanderers, *being*

G1228.2 A-NSM διάβολος (16x)

Lk 4:3 And the Slanderer declared to·him, "If you·are a·son
Lk 4:5 Then the Slanderer, after·bringing him up upon a·
Lk 4:6 And the Slanderer declared to·him, "To·you I·shall·
Lk 4:13 entire proof·trial, the Slanderer withdrew from him
Lk 8:12 Then comes the Slanderer, and he·takes·away the
Mt 4:5 Then the Slanderer personally·takes him up into the
Mt 4:8 Again, the Slanderer personally·takes him up to a·
Mt 4:11 Then the Slanderer leaves him, and behold, angels
Mt 13:39 the·one sowing them, is the Slanderer. The harvest
1Pe 5:8 yeur legal·adversary, Slanderer, strolls·about as a·
1Jn 3:8 Slanderer, because the Slanderer morally·fails from
Rv 2:10 Behold, the Slanderer is·about to·cast *some* from·
Rv 12:9 Serpent, the·one being·called Slanderer and the
Rv 12:12 the sea, because the Slanderer descended to yeu!
Rv 20:2 Serpent, who is Slanderer and Adversary-Accuser,
Rv 20:10 And the Slanderer, the·one deceiving them, was·

G1228.2 A-ASM διάβολον (1x)

Heb 2:14 having the might of·Death, that·is, the Slanderer;

G1228.2 A-DSM διαβόλῳ (4x)

Mt 25:41 having·been·made·ready for·the Slanderer and his
Jac 4:7 to·God. Stand·up·against the Slanderer, and he·
Jud 1:9 ·contending with·the Slanderer (he·was·discussing
Eph 4:27 nor·even give place to·the Slanderer.

G1228.2 A-GSM διαβόλου (13x)

Jn 8:44 are birthed·from·out *of·yeur* father the Slanderer, and
Jn 13:2 occurring, with·the Slanderer even·now having·cast
Lk 4:2 being·tried *for* forty days by the Slanderer. And in
Ac 10:38 ·ones being·dominated by the Slanderer, because
Ac 13:10 all mischief, O·Son of·Slanderer! O·Enemy of·all
Mt 4:1 wilderness by the Spirit to·be·tried by the Slanderer.
Eph 6:11 specifically·against the trickeries of·the Slanderer,
1Ti 3:6 ·fall to an·accusational·judgment of·the Slanderer.
1Ti 3:7 fall into reproach and *into* a·snare of·the Slanderer.
2Ti 2:26 *and escape* out of·the Slanderer's snare, having·
1Jn 3:8 ·failure is birthed·from·out·of·the Slanderer, because

1Jn 3:8 that he·should·tear·down the works of·the Slanderer.
1Jn 3:10 also the children of·the Slanderer. Every one not

G1229 δι•αγγέλλω diangéllō *v.* (3x)
Roots:G1223 G0032
G1229 V-PAM-2S διάγγελλε (1x)
Lk 9:60 going·off, thoroughly·announce the kingdom of·
G1229 V-PAP-NSM διαγγέλλων (1x)
Ac 21:26 ·Courtyard, thoroughly·announcing *when* the
G1229 V-2APS-3S διαγγελῇ (1x)
Rm 9:17 that my name may·be·thoroughly·announced in all

Δδ

G1230 δια•γίνομαι diagínômai *v.* (3x)
Roots:G1223 G1096
G1230 V-2ADP-GSN διαγενομένου (1x)
Mk 16:1 And with·the Sabbath already·elapsing, Mariam
G1230 V-2ADP-GSM διαγενομένου (1x)
Ac 27:9 with·significant·span of·time already·elapsing, and
G1230 V-2ADP-GPF διαγενομένων (1x)
Ac 25:13 Now with·some days already·elapsing, King

G1231 δια•γινώσκω diaginṓskō *v.* (2x)
Roots:G1223 G1097 Compare:G0198 G4441 See:G1233
G1231.2 V-FDI-1S διαγνώσομαι (1x)
Ac 24:22 I·shall·thoroughly·ascertain the·things against yeu
G1231.2 V-PAN διαγινώσκειν (1x)
Ac 23:15 intending to·thoroughly·ascertain *something* more·

G1232 δια•γνωρίζω diagnōrízō *v.* (1x)
Roots:G1223 G1107
G1232.2 V-AAI-3P διεγνώρισαν (1x)
Lk 2:17 they·thoroughly·made·it·known·to·all concerning

G1233 διά•γνωσις diágnōsis *n.* (1x)
Roots:G1231 Compare:G1384
G1233 N-ASF διάγνωσιν (1x)
Ac 25:21 the thorough·examination of·the Revered·Emperor,

G1234 δια•γογγύζω diagôngýzō *v.* (2x)
Roots:G1223 G1111 xLangAlso:H7279
G1234.2 V-IAI-3P διεγόγγυζον (2x)
Lk 15:2 Pharisees and the scribes were·murmuring, saying,
Lk 19:7 ·seeing *this*, absolutely·all were·murmuring, saying,

G1235 δια•γρηγορέω diagrēgôréō *v.* (1x)
Roots:G1223 G1127
G1235 V-AAP-NPM διαγρηγορήσαντες (1x)
Lk 9:32 but upon·being·thoroughly·awakened, they·saw his

G1236 δι•άγω diágō *v.* (2x)
Roots:G1223 G0071
G1236.1 V-PAS-1P διάγωμεν (1x)
1Ti 2:2 in·order·that we·may·thoroughly·lead a·tranquil and
G1236.2 V-PAP-NPM διάγοντες (1x)
Tit 3:3 and pleasures, passing·through·life in malice and

G1237 δια•δέχομαι diadéchômai *v.* (1x)
Roots:G1223 G1209
G1237.1 V-ADP-NPM διαδεξάμενοι (1x)
Ac 7:45 our fathers, after·receiving·it·in·turn, brought·it·in

G1238 διά•δημα diádēma *n.* (3x)
Roots:G1223 G1210 Compare:G4735 xLangEquiv:H6797
G1238 N-NPN διαδήματα (2x)
Rv 12:3 ten horns, and seven royal·turbans upon his heads.
Rv 13:1 and upon its horns ten royal·turbans, and upon its
G1238 N-APN διαδήματα (1x)
Rv 19:12 his head *were* many royal·turbans, having a·name

G1239 δια•δίδωμαι diadídōmai *v.* (5x)
Roots:G1223 G1325 Compare:G1244 G1266 G3307
G1239.1 V-PAI-3P διαδιδώσουσιν (1x)
Rv 17:13 and they·thoroughly·give·forth their·own power
G1239.2 V-PAI-3S διαδίδωσιν (1x)
Lk 11:22 ·had·confided and thoroughly·doles·out his spoils.
G1239.2 V-IPI-3S διεδίδοτο (1x)
Ac 4:35 feet, and it·was·thoroughly·doled·out to·each·man,
G1239.2 V-AAI-3S διέδωκεν (1x)
Jn 6:11 ·thanks, he·thoroughly·doled·*it*·out to·the disciples,
G1239.2 V-2AAM-2S διάδος (1x)
Lk 18:22 and thoroughly·dole·*it*·out to·*the*·helplessly·poor,

G1240 διά•δοχος diádôchôs *n.* (1x)
Roots:G1237
G1240 N-ASM διάδοχον (1x)
Ac 24:27 ·years, Porcius Festus took succession *after* Felix.

G1241 δια•ζώννυμι diazṓnnymi *v.* (3x)
Roots:G1223 G2224
G1241 V-AAI-3S διέζωσεν (1x)
Jn 13:4 And taking a·towel, he·tightly·girded himself.
G1241 V-AMI-3S διεζώσατο (1x)
Jn 21:7 the Lord, Simon Peter tightly·girded *his* fishing·coat
G1241 V-RPP-NSM διεζωσμένος (1x)
Jn 13:5 towel with·which he·was having·been·tightly·girded.

G1242 δια•θήκη diathḗkē *n.* (37x)
Roots:G1303 xLangEquiv:H1285
G1242.2 N-NSF διαθήκη (2x)
Heb 9:16 For where *there·is* a·last·will·and·covenant, *it·is* a·
Heb 9:17 For a·last·will·and·covenant *is* of·force after men·
G1242.3 N-NSF διαθήκη (3x)
Heb 8:10 this *is* the unilateral·covenant that I·shall·enact
Heb 10:16 *is* the unilateral·covenant that I·shall·bequeath
Rm 11:27 this *is* personally my unilateral·covenant to·them,
G1242.3 N-ASF διαθήκην (1x)
Gal 3:17 invalidate a·unilateral·covenant having·been· by
G1242.3 N-GSF διαθήκης (1x)
Ac 3:25 prophets, and of·the unilateral·covenant which God
G1242.4 N-NSF διαθήκη (2x)
Lk 22:20 “This cup *is* the brand-new covenant in my blood,
1Co 11:25 “This cup is the brand-new covenant in my blood.
G1242.4 N-NPF διαθῆκαι (2x)
Gal 4:24 for these are the two covenants. One in·fact *is*
Rm 9:4 the glory, and the covenants, and the enacting·of·
G1242.4 N-ASF διαθήκην (4x)
Ac 7:8 “And he·gave to·him a·covenant of·circumcision.
Heb 8:8 ·consummate a·brand-new covenant with the house
Heb 8:9 Not according·to the covenant that I·made with·their
Gal 3:15 ·same·manner, a·covenant of·a·man·of·clay† *once*
G1242.4 N-DSF διαθήκῃ (2x)
Heb 8:9 did·not continue in my covenant, and·I neglected
Heb 9:15 *that·were* under the first covenant), the·ones
G1242.4 N-GSF διαθήκης (15x)
Lk 1:72 our fathers, and to·be·mindful of·his holy covenant;
Heb 7:22 a·surety of·a·significantly·better covenant.
Heb 8:6 mediator of·a·significantly·better covenant, which
Heb 9:4 of·the covenant having·been·overlaid on·all·sides
Heb 9:4 ·one blossoming), and the tablets of·the covenant.
Heb 9:15 ·is *the* mediator of·a·brand-new covenant, so·that
Heb 9:20 This *is* the blood of·the covenant which God
Heb 10:29 ·considering the blood of·the covenant (by which
Heb 12:24 ·Yeshua, mediator of·a·fresh·new covenant, and
Heb 13:20 of·the sheep by an·eternal blood covenant)—
Mt 26:28 blood, the·one of·the brand-new covenant, the·one
Mk 14:24 the·one of·the brand-new covenant, the·one
2Co 3:6 ·qualified attendants of·a·brand-new covenant— not
2Co 3:14 the reading·aloud of·the old covenant; *it·is the*
Rv 11:19 and the Ark of·his covenant was·made·visible in
G1242.4 N-GPF διαθηκῶν (1x)
Eph 2:12 and foreigners from·the covenants of·the promise,
EG1242.4 (4x)
Heb 8:7 For if that first *covenant* was faultless, then no place
Heb 8:13 he·says, “A·brand-new *covenant*,” he·has·made·
Heb 8:13 ·made·obsolete the first *covenant* *with·the house of·*
Heb 9:18 the first *covenant* has·been·inaugurated apart·from

G1243 δι•αίρεσις diaírêsis *n.* (3x)
Roots:G1244 Compare:G1297-1 xLangAlso:H4256
G1243.2 N-NPF διαιρέσεις (3x)
1Co 12:4 Now there·are varieties of·gracious·bestowments,
1Co 12:5 And there·are varieties of·services, but the same
1Co 12:6 And there·are varieties of·operations, but it·is the

G1244 δι•αιρέω diairéō *v.* (2x)
Roots:G1223 G0138 Compare:G1308 See:G1243
G1244 V-PAP-NSN διαιροῦν (1x)
1Co 12:11 Spirit, dispensing to·each·man individually just·
G1244 V-2AAI-3S διεῖλεν (1x)
Lk 15:12 *for·me*.’ So he·dispensed the livelihood to·them

G1245 δια•καθ•αρίζω diakatharízō *v.* (2x)
Roots:G1223 G2511 xLangAlso:H2891
G1245.1 V-FAI-3S-ATT διακαθαριεῖ (2x)
Lk 3:17 and he·shall·thoroughly·purify his threshing·floor
Mt 3:12 and he·shall·thoroughly·purify his threshing·floor,

G1246 δια•κατ•ελέγχομαι diakatêlénchômai *v.* (1x)
Roots:G1223 G2596 G1651 Compare:G4822
G1246.2 V-INI-3S διακατηλέγχετο (1x)
Ac 18:28 vigorously, he·was·proving·downright to·the Jews

G1247 διακονέω diakônéō *v.* (39x)
Roots:G1249 Compare:G1398 G4332 G3000 G3008 G5256 G2324 See:G1248 xLangEquiv:H8334
G1247.1 V-FAI-3S διακονήσει (1x)
Lk 12:37 ·table, and coming·near, he·shall·attend to·them.
G1247.1 V-PAI-3S διακονεῖ (1x)
1Pe 4:11 of·God; if any·man attends *to·others*, *let·him·be* as
G1247.1 V-PAM-2S διακονεῖ (1x)
Lk 17:8 and after·girding·yourself·about, attend to·me until
G1247.1 V-PAM-3P διακονείτωσαν (1x)
1Ti 3:10 without·any·charge·of·wrong·doing let·them·attend
G1247.1 V-PAN διακονεῖν (2x)
Lk 10:40 ·you that my sister abandoned me to·attend alone?
Ac 6:2 the Redemptive-word of·God to·attend to·meal·tables.
G1247.1 V-PAP-GPM διακονούντων (1x)
Ac 19:22 ·dispatching two of·the·ones attending to·him into
G1247.1 V-PAP-NSM διακονῶν (4x)
Lk 22:26 and the·one governing, as the·one attending.
Lk 22:27 reclining·at·the·meal, or the·one attending? *Is·it*
Lk 22:27 am in *the* midst of·yeu as the·one attending.
Rm 15:25 ·traverse to JeruSalem, attending to·the holy·ones.
G1247.1 V-PAP-NPF διακονοῦσαι (1x)
Mt 27:55 followed YeShua from Galilee, attending to·him.
G1247.1 V-PAP-NPM διακονοῦντες (2x)
Heb 6:10 to·the holy·ones and still·attending *to·them*.
1Pe 4:10 among themselves *let·them·be* attending·to it as
G1247.1 V-PAS-3S διακονῇ (3x)
Jn 12:26 “If any·man should·attend to·me, let·him·follow me
Jn 12:26 And if any·man should·attend to·me, the Father
Phm 1:13 ·that on·your behalf, he·may·attend to·me in the
G1247.1 V-IAI-3S διηκόνει (4x)
Jn 12:2 ·him there, and Martha was·attending *to·them*, but
Lk 4:39 And at·once rising·up, she·was·attending to·them.
Mt 8:15 and she·was·awakened and was·attending to·them.
Mk 1:31 the fever left her, and she·was·attending to·them.
G1247.1 V-IAI-3P διηκόνουν (5x)
Lk 8:3 many others, who were·attending to·him from their·
Mt 4:11 angels came·alongside and were·attending to·him.
Mk 1:13 wild·beasts, and the angels were·attending to·him.
Mk 15:41 were·following him, and were·attending to·him);
1Pe 1:12 but *that* they·were·attending to·us the·same·things
G1247.1 V-AAI-1P διηκονήσαμεν (1x)
Mt 25:44 or sick, or in prison, and did·not attend to·you?
G1247.1 V-AAI-3S διηκόνησεν (1x)
2Ti 1:18 Day; and in·how·many·things he·attended *to·me* at
G1247.1 V-AAN διακονῆσαι (2x)
Mt 20:28 come to·be·attended·to, but·rather to·attend, and
Mk 10:45 come to·be·attended·to, but·rather to·attend, and
G1247.1 V-AAP-NPM διακονήσαντες (2x)
Heb 6:10 for his name, already·attending to·the holy·ones
1Ti 3:13 For the *men* already·attending well do·acquire for·
EG1247.1 (2x)
Mt 26:50 to·him, “O·associate, *attend* to *that* for·which
1Pe 4:11 *let·him·be* as *one·attending* from·out of·strength
G1247.2 V-PPP-DSF διακονουμένῃ (2x)
2Co 8:19 ·benevolence (the·one being·attended·to by us to
2Co 8:20 this bountiful·benevolence being·attended·to by us.
G1247.2 V-APN διακονηθῆναι (2x)
Mt 20:28 ·Man† did·not come to·be·attended·to, but·rather

Mk 10:45 ·Man† did·not come to·be·attended·to, but·rather
G1247.2 V-APP-NSF διακονηθεῖσα (1x)
2Co 3:3 a·letter of·Anointed-One being·attended·to by us,

G1248 διακονία diakônía *n.* (41x)

Roots:G1249 Compare:G3009 G3010 G1755
See:G1247
xLangEquiv:H8335 xLangAlso:H8293

G1248.1 N-ASF διακονίαν (1x)
Lk 10:40 ·distracted concerning much attendance *to·them.*
G1248.1 N-DSF διακονίᾳ (1x)
Rm 12:7 or service, on the attendance *to·others*; or the·one
G1248.2 N-NSF διακονία (7x)
Rm 15:31 and in·order·that my service for JeruSalem may·
2Co 3:7 Now if the Service of·Death, having·been·engraved
2Co 3:8 how·much more shall the Service of·the Spirit be
2Co 3:9 For if the service of·the condemnation *had* glory, so·
2Co 3:9 ·especially *does* the service of·the righteousness
2Co 6:3 in·order·that the Service *of·the Reconciliation*
2Co 9:12 Because the service of·this public·charity, not
G1248.2 N-ASF διακονίαν (15x)
Ac 11:29 *so*, specifically·determined to·send service to the
Ac 12:25 after·completely·fulfilling the service (and·also
Ac 20:24 ·race with joy, and the service, which I·received
Heb 1:14 ·dispatched into service on·account·of the·ones
Rm 11:13 an·ambassador of·Gentiles, I·glorify my service
Rm 12:7 or service, on the attendance *to·others*; or the·one
1Co 16:15 ·arranged themselves for service to·the holy·ones)
2Co 4:1 ·account·of that, having this Service *of·the Spirit*,
2Co 5:18 and giving to·us the Service of·the Reconciliation
2Co 11:8 taking wages *of·them*, specifically·for yeur service.
Col 4:17 ·out·for the service which you·personally·received
1Ti 1:12 me trustworthy, placing·me into service,
2Ti 4:5 ·news·of·redemption, fully·carry·out your service.
2Ti 4:11 with you, for he·is easily·useful to·me for service.
Rv 2:19 (also the love, and the service, and the trust, even
G1248.2 N-DSF διακονίᾳ (2x)
Ac 6:1 were·intentionally·neglected in the daily service.
Ac 6:4 ·the prayer and in·the service of·the Redemptive-word.
G1248.2 N-GSF διακονίας (7x)
Ac 1:17 ·obtained the allotted·portion of·this service."
Ac 1:25 the allotted·portion of·this service and commission,
Ac 21:19 God did among the Gentiles through his service.
2Co 8:4 *upon·us* the fellowship of·the service to the holy·
2Co 9:1 in·fact, concerning the service to the holy·ones, it·
2Co 9:13 ·of the proof of·this service, they·are·glorifying
Eph 4:12 of·the holy·ones unto a·work of·service, unto an·
G1248.2 N-GPF διακονιῶν (1x)
1Co 12:5 And there·are varieties of·services, but the same
EG1248.2 (7x)
2Co 3:7 (the *Service of·Death* presently·being·fully·nullified
2Co 3:10 For also the *Service of·Death* having·been·glorified
2Co 3:10 ·of the surpassing glory *of·the Service of·the Spirit.*
2Co 3:11 For if the *Service of·Death* is·being·fully·nullified
2Co 10:13 to·us, a·measure *of·service* actually·reaching also
2Co 10:15 yeu according·to our standard *of·service*, for a·
2Co 10:16 another·man's standard *of·service* for the·things

G1249 διάκονος diákônôs *n.* (31x)

Compare:G3011 G2819-2 G1377 G3623 See:G1247
G1248
xLangEquiv:H8334

G1249.1 N-NSM διάκονος (14x)
Jn 12:26 I AM, there also my attendant shall·be. And if any·
Gal 2:17 ·make Anointed-One an·attendant of·moral·failure?
Mt 20:26 great among yeu, he·must·be yeur attendant,
Mt 23:11 *who·is* greater among·yeu shall·be yeur attendant.
Mk 9:35 *the same* shall·be last of·all and attendant of·all."
Mk 10:43 ·become great among yeu, shall·be yeur attendant.
Rm 13:4 For he·is an·attendant of·God to·you in the
Rm 13:4 sword, for he·is an·attendant of·God, an·avenger
Eph 6:21 the beloved brother and trustworthy attendant in *the*
Col 1:7 who is a·trustworthy attendant on·yeur behalf of·
Col 1:23 heaven), of·which I, Paul, am·made an·attendant.
Col 1:25 I·myself am·made an·attendant, according·to the
Col 4:7 *is* a·beloved brother, a·trustworthy attendant, and a·
1Ti 4:6 you·shall·be a·good attendant of·Jesus Anointed—
G1249.1 N-NPM διάκονοι (6x)
Jn 2:9 it·was (but the attendants having·drawn·out the water
1Co 3:5 Apollos, other than attendants through whom yeu·
2Co 6:4 ·commending ourselves as attendants of·God: in
2Co 11:15 no great·thing if his attendants also are·disguised
2Co 11:15 also are·disguised as attendants of·righteousness,
2Co 11:23 Are·they attendants of·Anointed-One?
G1249.1 N-ASM διάκονον (2x)
Rm 15:8 to·have·become an·attendant of·*the*·Circumcision
1Th 3:2 our brother, and attendant of·God, and our
G1249.1 N-ASF διάκονον (1x)
Rm 16:1 being an·attendant of·the Called·Out·citizenry,
G1249.1 N-APM διακονούς (2x)
Heb 1:7 his angels spirits and his attendants a·blaze of·fire."
2Co 3:6 us sufficiently·qualified attendants of·a·brand-new
G1249.1 N-DPM διακόνοις (2x)
Jn 2:5 His mother says to·the attendants, "Whatever he·
Mt 22:13 the king declared to·the attendants, 'After·binding
G1249.3 N-NSM διάκονος (1x)
Eph 3:7 I·was·made a·steward of·this *good·news* according·
G1249.3 N-NPM διάκονοι (1x)
1Ti 3:12 Stewards must·be husbands of·one wife, conducting
G1249.3 N-APM διακόνους (1x)
1Ti 3:8 stewards *must·be* morally·worthy·of·reverent·
G1249.3 N-DPM διακόνοις (1x)
Php 1:1 at Philippi, together with·overseers and stewards.

G1250 δι•ακόσιοι diakósiôi *n.* (9x)

Roots:G1364 G1540 xLangAlso:H3967

G1250 N-NPF διακόσιαι (1x)
Ac 27:37 all *told*, we·were two·hundred *and* seventy·six
G1250 N-APM διακοσίους (2x)
Ac 23:23 he·declared, "Make·ready two·hundred soldiers,
Ac 23:23 and two·hundred right-handed·spearmen, that they·
G1250 N-APF διακοσίας (2x)
Rv 11:3 ·shall·prophesy a·thousand two·hundred *and* sixty
Rv 12:6 ·nourish her there a·thousand two·hundred *and* sixty
G1250 N-GPM διακοσίων (1x)
Jn 21:8 ·ground, but·rather about two·hundred cubits away).
G1250 N-GPN διακοσίων (2x)
Jn 6:7 Philip answered him, "Two·hundred denarii *worth*
Mk 6:37 ·going·off, should·we·buy two·hundred denarii
EG1250 (1x)
Rv 9:16 times·ten·thousand *(which·is two·hundred million)*,

G1251 δι•ακούομαι diakôúômai *v.* (1x)

Roots:G1223 G0191

G1251 V-FDI-1S διακούσομαι (1x)
Ac 23:35 he·replied, "I·shall·thoroughly·hear you whenever

G1252 δια•κρίνω diakrínō *v.* (20x)

Roots:G1223 G2919 Compare:G0350 G3307 G3635
G4920 G0118 G4802 G2042 G0426 See:G0087
G1253

G1252.2 V-PAI-3S διακρίνει (1x)
1Co 4:7 For who distinguishes you *one·from·another*?
G1252.3 V-AAI-3S διέκρινεν (1x)
Ac 15:9 he·did·not·even make·one·distinction between both
G1252.4 V-PAM-3P διακρινέτωσαν (1x)
1Co 14:29 speak two or three, and *let* the others discern.
G1252.4 V-PAN διακρίνειν (1x)
Mt 16:3 ·hypocrites, in·fact yeu·know to·discern the face of·
G1252.4 V-PAP-NSM διακρίνων (1x)
1Co 11:29 judgment to·himself, not discerning the Lord's
G1252.4 V-IAI-1P διεκρίνομεν (1x)
1Co 11:31 For if we·were·discerning ourselves *properly*, we·
G1252.4 V-AAN διακρῖναι (1x)
1Co 6:5 Not·even one that shall·be·able to·discern up *the*
EG1252.4 (1x)
Mt 16:3 ·the sky, but are·not able *to·discern* the signs of·the
G1252.5 V-PMP-NPM διακρινόμενοι (1x)
Jud 1:22 show·mercy to·some while·using·discernment.
G1252.6 V-PMP-ASM διακρινόμενον (1x)
Ac 11:12 with·them, hesitating *for* not·even·one·thing.
G1252.6 V-PMP-NSM διακρινόμενος (3x)
Ac 10:20 with·them, hesitating *for* not·even·one·thing, on·
Jac 1:6 ·request in trust, hesitating *for* not·even·one·thing.
Jac 1:6 the·one hesitating has·directly·resembled a·surging·
G1252.6 V-API-3S διεκρίθη (1x)
Rm 4:20 *AbRaham* did·not hesitate with·a lack·of·trust, but·
G1252.6 V-APS-2P διακριθῆτε (1x)
Mt 21:21 ·should·have trust and should·not be·hesitant, not
G1252.6 V-APS-3S διακριθῇ (1x)
Mk 11:23 the sea,' and should·not be·hesitant in his heart,
G1252.8 V-IMI-3P διεκρίνοντο (1x)
Ac 11:2 *the* Circumcision were·discriminating *the matter*
G1252.8 V-API-2P διεκρίθητε (1x)
Jac 2:4 are·yeu·not then discriminating among yeurselves,
G1252.9 V-PMP-NSM διακρινόμενος (1x)
Rm 14:23 And the·one determining *the matter* differently
G1252.10 V-PMP-NSM διακρινόμενος (1x)
Jud 1:9 ·angel, when verbally·contending with·the Slanderer

G1253 διά•κρισις diákrisis *n.* (4x)

Roots:G1252 Compare:G1922 G4678 G4907
xLangAlso:H0998 A0999

G1253.2 N-NPF διακρίσεις (1x)
1Co 12:10 prophecy, to·another discerning of·spirits, but to·
G1253.2 N-ASF διάκρισιν (2x)
Heb 5:14 habit toward having discernment of·both good and
1Co 1:19 shall·invalidate the discernment of·the intelligent."
G1253.3 N-APF διακρίσεις (1x)
Rm 14:1 in·the trust, *though* not into debatable disputations.

G1254 δια•κωλύω diakōlýō *v.* (1x)

Roots:G1223 G2967

G1254 V-IAI-3S διεκώλυεν (1x)
Mt 3:14 But John was·thoroughly·forbidding him, saying,

G1255 δια•λαλέω dialaléō *v.* (2x)

Roots:G1223 G2980

G1255.2 V-IAI-3P διελάλουν (1x)
Lk 6:11 and were·conferring alongside one·another what
G1255.3 V-IPI-3S διελαλεῖτο (1x)
Lk 1:65 And all these utterances were·conveyed among the

G1256 δια•λέγομαι dialégômai *v.* (13x)

Roots:G1223 G3004 See:G1261 G3056

G1256.1 V-PNP-ASM διαλεγόμενον (1x)
Ac 24:12 Sanctuary·Courtyard discussing *anything* alongside
G1256.1 V-PNP-GSM διαλεγομένου (2x)
Ac 20:9 heavy·sleep. With·Paul discussing *matters* over a·
Ac 24:25 But with *Paul* discussing *matters* concerning
G1256.1 V-PNP-NSM διαλεγόμενος (2x)
Ac 19:8 for·a·span·of three lunar·months, discussing (and
Ac 19:9 the disciples *from·them*, discussing *the·things of·the*
G1256.1 V-INI-3S διελέγετο (2x)
Ac 18:4 And he·discussed in the gathering each and·every
Jud 1:9 with·the Slanderer (he·was·discussing about *the*
G1256.1 V-AOI-3P διελέχθησαν (1x)
Mk 9:34 along the way they·discussed among one·another
G1256.2 V-INI-3S διελέγετο (3x)
Ac 17:2 Sabbaths he·was·having·discussions with·them from
Ac 17:17 in·fact, he·was·having·discussions in the gathering
Ac 20:7 bread, Paul was·discussing *matters* with·them,
G1256.2 V-AOI-3S διελέχθη (1x)
Ac 18:19 gathering, was·having·discussions with·the Jews.
G1256.4 V-PNI-3S διαλέγεται (1x)
Heb 12:5 ·the exhortation which thoroughly·relates to·yeu as

G1257 δια•λείπω dialêípō *v.* (1x)

Roots:G1223 G3007 Compare:G1587 G3973
See:G1952

G1257.2 V-2AAI-3S διέλιπεν (1x)
Lk 7:45 I·entered·in, did·not let·up·on earnestly·kissing my

G1258 διά•λεκτος diálêktôs *n.* (6x)

Roots:G1256 Compare:G1100 xLangAlso:H3956
H8193

G1258.2 N-DSF διαλέκτῳ (4x)
Ac 1:19 ·field to·be·called in·their own language, AqelDama,
Ac 21:40 he·addressed *them* in·the Hebrew language, saying,
Ac 22:2 them in·the Hebrew language, they·personally·held

Ac 26:14 to me, and saying in·the Hebrew language, ‘Saul,
G1258.3 N-DSF διαλέκτῳ (2x)
Ac 2:6 ·hearing them speaking in·his·own·distinct dialect.
Ac 2:8 each hear our own·distinct dialect into which we·

G1259 δι•αλλάσσω diallássō *v.* (1x)
Roots:G1223 G0236 Compare:G2132 See:G2644 G0604
G1259.2 V-2APM-2S διαλλάγηθι (1x)
Mt 5:24 ·out. First be·thoroughly·reconciled to·your brother,

G1260 δια•λογίζομαι dialôgízômai *v.* (16x)
Roots:G1223 G3049 Compare:G1011 G1760 G5426 G4820
G1260.1 V-PNI-2P διαλογίζεσθε (3x)
Jn 11:50 nor·even ponder that it·is·more·advantageous for·us
Lk 5:22 to them, “Why·do yeu·ponder in yeur hearts?
Mk 2:8 to·them, “Why·do yeu·ponder these·things in yeur
G1260.1 V-PNI-3P διαλογίζονται (1x)
Mk 2:8 that they·are·pondering *these·things* in·this·manner
G1260.1 V-PNN διαλογίζεσθαι (1x)
Lk 5:21 scribes and the Pharisees began to·ponder, saying,
G1260.1 V-PNP-GPM διαλογιζομένων (1x)
Lk 3:15 ·awaiting, and all·men were·pondering in their
G1260.1 V-PNP-NPM διαλογιζόμενοι (1x)
Mk 2:6 there, sitting·down yet pondering in their hearts,
G1260.1 V-INI-3S διελογίζετο (2x)
Lk 1:29 saying, and was·pondering what·manner·of greeting
Lk 12:17 And he·pondered within himself, saying, ‘What
G1260.2 V-PNI-2P διαλογίζεσθε (2x)
Mt 16:8 ·trust, why·do yeu·deliberate among yeurselves that
Mk 8:17 to·them, “Why·do yeu·deliberate *that it·is* because
G1260.2 V-INI-2P διελογίζεσθε (1x)
Mk 9:33 What·was·it *that* yeu·deliberated among yeurselves
G1260.2 V-INI-3P διελογίζοντο (4x)
Lk 20:14 the tenant·farmers deliberated among themselves,
Mt 16:7 And they·were·deliberating among themselves,
Mt 21:25 And they·were·deliberating closely·among
Mk 8:16 And they·were·deliberating among one·another,

G1261 δια•λογισμός dialôgismós *n.* (14x)
Roots:G1260 Compare:G2214 G2757 G4804
G1261.1 N-NSM διαλογισμός (1x)
Lk 9:46 Then *in·CaperNaum*, a·discussion entered·in among
G1261.1 N-ASM διαλογισμόν (1x)
Lk 9:47 And Jesus, seeing the discussion of·their heart,
G1261.2 N-NPM διαλογισμοί (3x)
Lk 2:35 that *the* deliberations from·among many hearts
Mt 15:19 of·the heart comes·forth evil deliberations, murders
Mk 7:21 ·clay†, the wicked deliberations do·proceed·forth:
G1261.2 N-APM διαλογισμούς (3x)
Lk 5:22 Jesus, fully·knowing their deliberations, answering,
Lk 6:8 he·himself had·personally·known their deliberations.
1Co 3:20 “Yahweh knows the deliberations of·the wise, that
G1261.2 N-DPM διαλογισμοῖς (1x)
Rm 1:21 ·already·became·futile in their deliberations, and
G1261.2 N-GPM διαλογισμῶν (1x)
Jac 2:4 and are·become judges with·evil deliberations?
G1261.3 N-NPM διαλογισμοί (1x)
Lk 24:38 ·been·troubled? And why·do debates ascend in
G1261.3 N-GSM διαλογισμοῦ (1x)
1Ti 2:8 hands, completely·apart·from wrath and debate.
G1261.3 N-GPM διαλογισμῶν (2x)
Rm 14:1 in·the trust, *though* not into debatable disputations.
Php 2:14 completely·apart·from grumblings and debates,

G1262 δια•λύω dialýō *v.* (1x)
Roots:G1223 G3089 Compare:G1287
G1262 V-API-3P διελύθησαν (1x)
Ac 5:36 ·persuaded by·him) were·thoroughly·dissolved, and

G1263 δια•μαρτύρομαι diamartýrômai *v.* (15x)
Roots:G1223 G3140
G1263.1 V-PNI-3S διαμαρτύρεται (1x)
Ac 20:23 the Holy Spirit thoroughly·testifies in·each city,
G1263.1 V-PNP-NSM διαμαρτυρόμενος (3x)
Ac 18:5 ·the spirit *and* was·thoroughly·testifying to·the Jews
Ac 20:21 thoroughly·testifying to·both Jews and Greeks, a·
Ac 28:23 while·thoroughly·testifying·to the kingdom of·
G1263.1 V-PNS-3S διαμαρτύρηται (1x)
Lk 16:28 *him* so·that he·may·thoroughly·testify to·them, lest
G1263.1 V-INI-3S διεμαρτύρετο (1x)
Ac 2:40 he·was·thoroughly·testifying and was·exhorting,
G1263.1 V-ADI-1P διεμαρτυράμεθα (1x)
1Th 4:6 ·previously·declared to·yeu and thoroughly·testified.
G1263.1 V-ADI-2S διεμαρτύρω (1x)
Ac 23:11 For as you·thoroughly·testified concerning me to
G1263.1 V-ADI-3S διεμαρτύρατο (1x)
Heb 2:6 somewhere, someone thoroughly·testified, saying,
G1263.1 V-ADN διαμαρτύρασθαι (2x)
Ac 10:42 to·the people, and to·thoroughly·testify that it·is
Ac 20:24 Lord Jesus, to·thoroughly·testify the good·news
G1263.1 V-ADP-NPM διαμαρτυράμενοι (1x)
Ac 8:25 in·fact, after·thoroughly·testifying and speaking
G1263.2 V-PNI-1S διαμαρτύρομαι (2x)
1Ti 5:21 I·thoroughly·urge *you* in·the·sight of·God, and of·
2Ti 4:1 I·myself thoroughly·urge *you* in·the·sight of·God
G1263.2 V-PNP-NSM διαμαρτυρόμενος (1x)
2Ti 2:14 — while·thoroughly·urging *them* in·the·sight of·the

G1264 δια•μάχομαι diamáchômai *v.* (1x)
Roots:G1223 G3164 Compare:G0075 G0118 G1252
G1264.1 V-INI-3P διεμάχοντο (1x)
Ac 23:9 ·rising·up, they·were·thoroughly·fighting, saying,

G1265 δια•μένω diaménō *v.* (5x)
Roots:G1223 G3306
G1265.1 V-IAI-3S διέμενεν (1x)
Lk 1:22 to·them, yet was·thoroughly·remaining mute.
G1265.2 V-PAI-2S διαμένεις (1x)
Heb 1:11 ·perish, but you·yourself remain·constant; and
G1265.2 V-PAI-3S διαμένει (1x)
2Pe 3:4 ·rest, all·things remain·constant in·this·manner *as*
G1265.2 V-AAS-3S διαμείνῃ (1x)
Gal 2:5 good·news should·remain·constantly alongside yeu.
G1265.2 V-RAP-NPM διαμεμενηκότες (1x)
Lk 22:28 are the·ones having·remained·constantly with me

G1266 δια•μερίζω diamerízō *v.* (15x)
Roots:G1223 G3307 Compare:G1308 G1244
G1266.2 V-FPI-3S διαμερισθήσεται (1x)
Lk 12:53 Father shall·be·thoroughly·divided against son, and
G1266.2 V-PMP-NPM διαμεριζόμενοι (1x)
Lk 23:34 ·do.” And thoroughly·dividing·up his garments,
G1266.2 V-IAI-3P διεμέριζον (1x)
Mk 15:24 they·were·thoroughly·dividing·up his garments,
G1266.2 V-AMI-3P διεμερίσαντο (3x)
Jn 19:24 “‘They·thoroughly·divided·up my garments
Mt 27:35 him, they·thoroughly·divided·up his garments,
Mt 27:35 “‘They·thoroughly·divided·up my garments
G1266.2 V-API-3S διεμερίσθη (1x)
Lk 11:18 Adversary-Accuser is·thoroughly·divided against
G1266.2 V-APP-NSF διαμερισθεῖσα (1x)
Lk 11:17 kingdom being·thoroughly·divided against itself is·
G1266.2 V-RPP-NPM διαμεμερισμένοι (1x)
Lk 12:52 one house having·been·thoroughly·divided, three
EG1266.2 (1x)
Lk 11:17 and a·house *thoroughly·divided* against a·house
G1266.3 V-IAI-3P διεμέριζον (1x)
Ac 2:45 and they·were·thoroughly·distributing them to·all,
G1266.3 V-AAM-2P διαμερίσατε (1x)
Lk 22:17 this, and thoroughly·distribute *it* among·yeurselves
G1266.4 V-PEP-NPF διαμεριζόμεναι (1x)
Ac 2:3 And thoroughly·differing tongues as of·fire were·
EG1266.4 (2x)
1Co 12:10 *thoroughly·differing* kinds of·bestowed·tongues,
1Co 12:28 *and thoroughly·differing* kinds of·bestowed·

G1267 δια•μερισμός diamêrismós *n.* (1x)
Roots:G1266 Compare:G1370 G4978
G1267.1 N-ASM διαμερισμόν (1x)
Lk 12:51 to·yeu, no·indeed, but·rather thorough·division.

G1268 δια•νέμω dianémō *v.* (1x)
Roots:G1223 G3551
G1268.2 V-APS-3S διανεμηθῇ (1x)
Ac 4:17 in·order·that it·may·not disseminate any·further

G1269 δια•νεύω dianêúō *v.* (1x)
Roots:G1223 G3506
G1269 V-PAP-NSM διανεύων (1x)
Lk 1:22 And he·himself was constantly·nodding to·them, yet

G1270 δια•νόημα dianóēma *n.* (1x)
Roots:G1223 G3539 Compare:G1761 G1963 G3540 G5424
G1270.2 N-APN διανοήματα (1x)
Lk 11:17 having·seen their complete·thoughts, declared to·

G1271 διά•νοια diánôia *n.* (13x)
Roots:G1223 G3563 Compare:G4907 G5427 G5590 See:G3510
G1271.2 N-ASF διάνοιαν (2x)
Heb 8:10 my Laws-of-Liberty into their innermost·mind, and
2Pe 3:1 yeur sincere innermost·minds with a·reminder:
G1271.2 N-DSF διανοίᾳ (2x)
Mt 22:37 all your soul, and with all your innermost·mind.”
Col 1:21 and enemies in·*your*·innermost·mind by the evil
G1271.2 N-GSF διανοίας (3x)
Lk 10:27 and from·out of·all your innermost·mind,” and
Mk 12:30 and from·out of·all your innermost·mind, and
1Pe 1:13 ·up the loins of·yeur innermost·mind, being·sober,
G1271.2 N-GPF διανοιῶν (2x)
Heb 10:16 upon their innermost·minds I·shall·inscribe them,
Eph 2:3 ·will of·the flesh and of·the innermost·mind. And
G1271.4 N-DSF διανοίᾳ (1x)
Eph 4:18 with·the innermost·understanding having·been·,
G1271.4 N-GSF διανοίας (1x)
Eph 1:18 of·yeur innermost·understanding having·been·
G1271.5 N-DSF διανοίᾳ (1x)
Lk 1:51 haughty·men in·*the*·innermost·imagination of·their
G1271.6 N-ASF διάνοιαν (1x)
1Jn 5:20 and he·has·given to·us utmost·insight, that we·

G1272 δι•αν•οίγω dianôígō *v.* (8x)
Roots:G1223 G0455
G1272.1 V-PAP-NSN διανοῖγον (1x)
Lk 2:23 male thoroughly·opening·up a·primal·womb shall·
G1272.1 V-PAP-NSM διανοίγων (1x)
Ac 17:3 thoroughly·opening·up and putting·forth·directly
G1272.1 V-IAI-3S διήνοιγεν (1x)
Lk 24:32 as he·was·thoroughly·opening·up the Scriptures to·
G1272.1 V-AAI-3S διήνοιξεν (2x)
Lk 24:45 Then he·thoroughly·opened·up their understanding
Ac 16:14 of·whom the Lord thoroughly·opened·up her heart
G1272.1 V-API-3P διηνοίχθησαν (2x)
Lk 24:31 And their eyes were·thoroughly·opened·up, and
Mk 7:35 his ears were·thoroughly·opened·up, and the
G1272.1 V-APM-2S διανοίχθητι (1x)
Mk 7:34 which is, “Be·thoroughly·opened·up.”

G1273 δια•νυκτερεύω dianyktêrêúō *v.* (1x)
Roots:G1223 G3571
G1273 V-PAP-NSM διανυκτερεύων (1x)
Lk 6:12 he·was staying·up·through·the·night *continuing* in

G1274 δι•ανύω dianýō *v.* (1x)
Roots:G1223
G1274 V-AAP-NPM διανύσαντες (1x)
Ac 21:7 after·thoroughly·accomplishing the voyage from

G1275 δια•παντός diapantós *adv.* (8x)
Roots:G1223 G3956 Compare:G1734-1 xLangEquiv:H8548
G1275 ADV διαπαντός (1x)
Ac 2:25 Yahweh in·the·sight of·me continually, because he·
G1275.2 ADV διαπαντός (6x)
Lk 24:53 And they·were continually in the Sanctuary·Atrium
Ac 10:2 ·acts for·the people and continually petitioning God.
Ac 24:16 to·have continually a·conscience void·of·offense
Heb 9:6 ·offer·sacrifices, in·fact, continually entered into
Heb 13:15 a·sacrifice of·praise to·God continually, that·is, a·

Rm 11:10 let their back continually *be* altogether·bent·over.
G1275.3 ADV διαπαντός (1x)
Mk 5:5 And constantly, night and day, he·was on the

G1276 δια•περάω diapêráō *v.* (6x)
Roots:G1223 G4008 Compare:G1599-1
G1276.1 V-PAS-3P διαπερῶσιν (1x)
Lk 16:26 nor·even may the·ones from·there cross·over to us.
G1276.1 V-AAI-3S διεπέρασεν (1x)
Mt 9:1 into the sailboat, he·crossed·over and came into his·
G1276.1 V-AAP-GSM διαπεράσαντος (1x)
Mk 5:21 And with·Jesus crossing·over again in the sailboat
G1276.1 V-AAP-NPM διαπεράσαντες (2x)
Mt 14:34 And crossing·over, they·came into the land of·
Mk 6:53 And crossing·over, they·came to the land of·
G1276.2 V-PAP-ASN διαπερῶν (1x)
Ac 21:2 after·finding a·sailing·ship sailing·over to Phoenicia

G1277 δια•πλέω diaplêō *v.* (1x)
Roots:G1223 G4126
G1277 V-AAP-NPM διαπλεύσαντες (1x)
Ac 27:5 And after·sailing·through the open·sea adjacent·to

G1278 δια•πονέω diapônêō *v.* (2x)
Roots:G1223 G4188-1 See:G2669 G4190
G1278.2 V-PNP-NPM διαπονούμενοι (1x)
Ac 4:2 being·thoroughly·stressed·out on·account·of them
G1278.2 V-ADP-NSM διαπονηθείς (1x)
Ac 16:18 days. But being·thoroughly·stressed·out, Paul,

G1279 δια•πορεύομαι diapôrêúômai *v.* (5x)
Roots:G1223 G4198
G1279.1 V-PNN διαπορεύεσθαι (1x)
Lk 6:1 ·day·of·the·feast *for* him to·traverse through the
G1279.1 V-PNP-GSM διαπορευομένου (1x)
Lk 18:36 hearing a·crowd traversing·through, he·inquired
G1279.1 V-PNP-NSM διαπορευόμενος (1x)
Rm 15:24 to·survey yeu while·traversing·through, and to·be·
G1279.2 V-INI-3S διεπορεύετο (1x)
Lk 13:22 And *Jesus* was·traversing·throughout each *of·the*
G1279.2 V-INI-3P διεπορεύοντο (1x)
Ac 16:4 And as they·traversed·throughout the cities, they·

G1280 δι•α•πορέω diapôrêō *v.* (5x)
Roots:G1223 G0639 Compare:G4797
G1280 V-PPN διαπορεῖσθαι (1x)
Lk 24:4 with them thoroughly·perplexing about this, behold
G1280 V-IAI-3S διηπόρει (2x)
Lk 9:7 and he·was·thoroughly·perplexed, on·account·of
Ac 10:17 But as Peter was·thoroughly·perplexed in himself
G1280 V-IAI-3P διηπόρουν (2x)
Ac 2:12 ·astonished and were·thoroughly·perplexed, saying
Ac 5:24 words, they·were·thoroughly·perplexed about them

G1281 δια•πραγματεύομαι diapragmatêúômai *v.* (1x)
Roots:G1223 G4231 See:G4231
G1281.2 V-ADI-3S διεπραγματεύσατο (1x)
Lk 19:15 each·man had·thoroughly·accomplished·in·trade.

G1282 δια•πρίω diapríō *v.* (2x)
Roots:G1223 G4249
G1282.3 V-IPI-3P διεπρίοντο (2x)
Ac 5:33 *this*, they·were·thoroughly·irate and were·taking·
Ac 7:54 ·things, they·were·thoroughly·irate to·the heart, and

G1283 δι•αρπάζω diarpázō *v.* (4x)
Roots:G1223 G0726 See:G0724
G1283 V-FAI-3S διαρπάσει (2x)
Mt 12:29 And then he·shall·thoroughly·plunder his home.
Mk 3:27 and then he·shall·thoroughly·plunder his home.
G1283 V-AAN διαρπάσαι (2x)
Mt 12:29 home and to·thoroughly·plunder his belongings,
Mk 3:27 ·is·not able to·thoroughly·plunder the strong·man's

G1284 δια•ρρήσσω diarrhḗssō *v.* (5x)
Roots:G1223 G4486 xLangAlso:H7167
G1284 V-PAP-NSM διαρρήσσων (1x)
Lk 8:29 ·kept in·shackles. And tearing·apart the bonds, he·
G1284 V-IPI-3S διερρήγνυτο (1x)
Lk 5:6 of·fish, and their *one* net was·being·torn·apart.
G1284 V-AAI-3S διέρρηξεν (1x)
Mt 26:65 the designated·high·priest tore·apart his garments,
G1284 V-AAP-NSM διαρρήξας (1x)
Mk 14:63 ·high·priest, after·tearing·apart his·own tunics,
G1284 V-AAP-NPM διαρρήξαντες (1x)
Ac 14:14 ·hearing *of·this and* tearing·apart their garments,

G1285 δια•σαφέω diasaphêō *v.* (1x)
Roots:G1223 See:G4569-3
G1285.2 V-AAI-3P διεσάφησαν (1x)
Mt 18:31 to·their lord, they·clearly·related all the·things

G1286 δια•σείω diasêíō *v.* (1x)
Roots:G1223 G4579 See:G4525
G1286.2 V-AAS-2P διασείσητε (1x)
Lk 3:14 "Yeu·should·violently·shake·and·intimidate not·,

G1287 δια•σκορπίζω diaskôrpízō *v.* (9x)
Roots:G1223 G4650 Compare:G1262 See:G1287-1
G1287.1 V-API-3P διεσκορπίσθησαν (1x)
Ac 5:37 ·convinced by·him) were·thoroughly·dispersed.
G1287.2 V-FPI-3S διασκορπισθήσεται (2x)
Mt 26:31 sheep of·the flock shall·be·thoroughly·scattered.
Mk 14:27 and the sheep shall·be·thoroughly·scattered.
G1287.2 V-AAI-3S διεσκόρπισεν (1x)
Lk 1:51 arm; he·thoroughly·scattered haughty·men in·*the*·
G1287.2 V-RPP-APN διεσκορπισμένα (1x)
Jn 11:52 ·God, the·ones having·been·thoroughly·scattered.
G1287.3 V-AAI-1S διεσκόρπισα (1x)
Mt 25:26 ·together from·where I·did·not winnow·chaff.
G1287.3 V-AAI-2S διεσκόρπισας (1x)
Mt 25:24 ·together from·where you·did·not winnow·chaff.
G1287.4 V-PAP-NSM διασκορπίζων (1x)
Lk 16:1 ·him as·though thoroughly·squandering his holdings
G1287.4 V-AAI-3S διεσκόρπισεν (1x)
Lk 15:13 and there he·thoroughly·squandered his substance

G1288 δια•σπάω diaspáō *v.* (2x)
Roots:G1223 G4685
G1288 V-APS-3S διασπασθῇ (1x)
Ac 23:10 Paul should·be·thoroughly·drawn·apart by them)—
G1288 V-RPN διεσπάσθαι (1x)
Mk 5:4 chains to·have·been·thoroughly·drawn·apart by him,

G1289 δια•σπείρω diaspêírō *v.* (3x)
Roots:G1223 G4687 Compare:G4650 See:G1290 xLangEquiv:H6327
G1289.2 V-API-3P διεσπάρησαν (1x)
Ac 8:1 ambassadors were·dispersed pervasively·into·all the
G1289.2 V-2APP-NPM διασπαρέντες (2x)
Ac 8:4 ·fact, the·ones being·dispersed went·throughout *the*
Ac 11:19 in·fact, the·ones being·dispersed by the tribulation

G1290 δια•σπορά diasporá *n.* (5x)
Roots:G1289
EG1290.1 (1x)
Jn 7:35 into the Diaspora, *the dispersion* among·the Greeks,
G1290.2 N-ASF διασποράν (1x)
Jn 7:35 ¿!·Does he·intend to·traverse into the Diaspora, *the*
G1290.2 N-DSF διασπορᾷ (1x)
Jac 1:1 ·ones in the Diaspora *dispersed·among·the·Gentiles*:
G1290.2 N-GSF διασπορᾶς (1x)
1Pe 1:1 foreign·residents of·*the*·Diaspora *throughout* Pontus,
EG1290.2 (1x)
Jac 1:1 ·ones in the Diaspora *dispersed·among·the·Gentiles*:

G1291 δια•στέλλομαι diastéllômai *v.* (8x)
Roots:G1223 G4724
G1291.1 V-PPP-ASN διαστελλόμενον (1x)
Heb 12:20 the·thing being·thoroughly·set·apart, "If·even a·
G1291.3 V-IMI-3S διεστέλλετο (2x)
Mk 7:36 as·much·as he·himself thoroughly·charged them,
Mk 8:15 And he·thoroughly·charged them, saying, "Clearly·
G1291.3 V-AMI-1P διεστειλάμεθα (1x)
Ac 15:24 ·whom we·did·not thoroughly·charge *such·things*),
G1291.3 V-AMI-3S διεστείλατο (4x)
Mt 16:20 Then he·thoroughly·charged his disciples in·order·
Mk 5:43 And he·thoroughly·charged them repeatedly that
Mk 7:36 And *Jesus* thoroughly·charged them that they·
Mk 9:9 from the mountain, he·thoroughly·charged them that

G1292 δι•άστημα diástēma *n.* (1x)
Roots:G1339
G1292 N-NSN διάστημα (1x)
Ac 5:7 And it·was about an·interval of·three hours, and his

G1293 δια•στολή diastôlḗ *n.* (3x)
Roots:G1291
G1293 N-NSF διαστολή (2x)
Rm 3:22 all the·ones trusting, for there·is no distinction.
Rm 10:12 For there·is no distinction between Jew and Greek
G1293 N-ASF διαστολήν (1x)
1Co 14:7 ·should·not give a·distinction in·the·musical·notes,

G1294 δια•στρέφω diastréphō *v.* (7x)
Roots:G1223 G4762 Compare:G4761 G5351 G1612 See:G1624 G0665 xLangAlso:H5765 H5766
G1294.1 V-AAN διαστρέψαι (1x)
Ac 13:8 ·to them seeking to·thoroughly·turn the proconsul
G1294.3 V-PAP-ASM διαστρέφοντα (1x)
Lk 23:2 "We·found this·man perverting the nation, and
G1294.3 V-PAP-NSM διαστρέφων (1x)
Ac 13:10 shall·you·not cease perverting the straight ways
G1294.4 V-RPP-GSF διεστραμμένης (1x)
Php 2:15 in the·midst of·a·warped and perverse generation,
G1294.4 V-RPP-NSF@ διεστραμμένη (2x)
Lk 9:41 "O distrusting and perverse generation, how·long
Mt 17:17 "O distrusting and perverse generation, how·long
G1294.5 V-RPP-APN διεστραμμένα (1x)
Ac 20:30 ·rise·up, speaking perverse·things, to·draw·away

G1295 δια•σώζω diasṓzō *v.* (8x)
Roots:G1223 G4982
G1295.1 V-AAN διασῶσαι (1x)
Ac 27:43 centurion, being·resolved to·thoroughly·save Paul,
G1295.1 V-AAS-3S διασώσῃ (1x)
Lk 7:3 him to·come that he·may·thoroughly·save his slave.
G1295.1 V-AAS-3P διασώσωσιν (1x)
Ac 23:24 they·should·bring·*him*·thoroughly·safe to Felix
G1295.1 V-API-3P διεσώθησαν (1x)
1Pe 3:20 eight souls) were·thoroughly·saved through water.
G1295.1 V-APN διασωθῆναι (1x)
Ac 27:44 *that* they·all made·it·thoroughly·safe upon the dry·
G1295.1 V-APP-ASM διασωθέντα (1x)
Ac 28:4 after·being·thoroughly·saved from·out of·the sea,
G1295.1 V-APP-NPM διασωθέντες (1x)
Ac 28:1 And being·thoroughly·saved, then they·realized that
G1295.2 V-API-3P διεσώθησαν (1x)
Mt 14:36 ·as did·lay·hold *of·it* were·made·thoroughly·well.

G1296 δια•ταγή diatagḗ *n.* (2x)
Roots:G1299 See:G1297
G1296.2 N-APF διαταγάς (1x)
Ac 7:53 the Torah-Law as an·institution of·angels and did·
G1296.2 N-DSF διαταγῇ (1x)
Rm 13:2 has·stood·opposed·to the institution of·God, and

G1297 διά•ταγμα diátagma *n.* (1x)
Roots:G1299 Compare:G3056 See:G1296 xLangAlso:H1697
G1297.2 N-ASN διάταγμα (1x)
Heb 11:23 and they·were·not afraid of·the king's edict.

G1298 δια•ταράσσω diatarássō *v.* (1x)
Roots:G1223 G5015 Compare:G0387
G1298.2 V-API-3S διεταράχθη (1x)
Lk 1:29 seeing *him*, she·was·thoroughly·troubled over his

G1299 δια•τάσσω diatássō *v.* (16x)
Roots:G1223 G5021 See:G4367 G1297
G1299.1 V-FDI-1S διατάξομαι (1x)
1Co 11:34 I·may·come, I·shall·thoroughly·arrange the rest.
G1299.1 V-AMP-NSM διαταξάμενος (1x)
Ac 24:23 And he·thoroughly·arranged·for the centurion to·
G1299.1 V-RAN διατεταχέναι (1x)
Ac 18:2 *Caesar* having·thoroughly·arranged·for all the Jews
G1299.2 V-PAP-NSM διατάσσων (1x)
Mt 11:1 finished thoroughly·assigning *these·things* to·his
G1299.2 V-PMI-1S διατάσσομαι (1x)

1Co 7:17 And in·this·manner I·thoroughly·assign among all
G1299.2 V-AAI-1S διέταξα (1x)
1Co 16:1 just·as I·thoroughly·assigned to·the Called·Out·
G1299.2 V-AAI-3S διέταξεν (2x)
Lk 8:55 and he·thoroughly·assigned·for *something* to·be·
1Co 9:14 the Lord thoroughly·assigned for·the·ones fully·
G1299.2 V-AMI-1S διεταξάμην (1x)
Tit 1:5 city, as I·myself thoroughly·assigned to·you *with·the*
G1299.2 V-AMI-3S διετάξατο (1x)
Ac 7:44 to·Moses thoroughly·assigned *for·him* to·make it,
G1299.2 V-APP-APN διαταχθέντα (2x)
Lk 17:9 the·things already·being·thoroughly·assigned to·him
Lk 17:10 the·things already·being·thoroughly·assigned to·,
G1299.2 V-2APP-NSM διαταγείς (1x)
Gal 3:19 *was* being·thoroughly·assigned through angels in
G1299.2 V-RPP-ASN διατεταγμένον (2x)
Lk 3:13 directly having·been·thoroughly·assigned to·yeu."
Ac 23:31 *charge* having·been·thoroughly·assigned to·them,
G1299.2 V-RPP-NSM διατεταγμένος (1x)
Ac 20:13 ·manner he·was having·been·thoroughly·assigned,

G1300 δια•τελέω diatêléō *v.* (1x)
Roots:G1223 G5055 Compare:G1961
G1300.2 V-PAI-2P διατελεῖτε (1x)
Ac 27:33 *and·still* yeu·thoroughly·continue·to·persevere,

G1301 δια•τηρέω diatērêō *v.* (2x)
Roots:G1223 G5083 Compare:G1314
G1301.1 V-IAI-3S διετήρει (1x)
Lk 2:51 And his mother was·thoroughly·guarding all these
G1301.3 V-PAP-NPM διατηροῦντες (1x)
Ac 15:29 *if* yeu·thoroughly·keep·guarding yeurselves, yeu·

G1302 δια•τί diatí *prt.* (27x)
Roots:G1223 G5101
G1302.2 PRT-I διατί (27x)
Jn 7:45 declared to·them, "Why·did yeu·not bring him?
Jn 8:43 "Why do·yeu·not know my speech?
Jn 8:46 I·say *is the* truth, why·do yeu·yeurselves not trust
Jn 12:5 "This ointment, why was·it·not sold·off for·three·
Jn 13:37 to·him, "Lord, why am·I·not able to·follow you at·
Lk 5:30 disciples, saying, "Why do·yeu·eat and drink with
Lk 5:33 to him, "Why·is·it·that the disciples of·John fast
Lk 19:23 Why then did·you·not give my money over *to* the
Lk 19:31 any·man should·ask·of yeu, 'Why do·yeu·loose *it*?
Lk 20:5 he·shall·declare, 'So·then why did·yeu·not trust
Lk 24:38 ·been·troubled? And why·do debates ascend in
Ac 5:3 declared, "AnanIas, why *has* the Adversary-Accuser
Mt 9:11 to·his disciples, "Why·does yeur Mentor eat with
Mt 9:14 him, saying, "Why·do we·ourselves and the
Mt 13:10 declared to·him, "Why·do you·speak to·them in
Mt 15:2 "Why·do your disciples walk·contrary·to the Oral·
Mt 15:3 "And why·do yeu·yeurselves walk·contrary·to the
Mt 17:19 disciples declared, "Why·were we·ourselves not
Mt 21:25 ·declare to·us, 'So·then why did·yeu·not trust him
Mk 2:18 say to·him, "Why·is·it·that the disciples of·John
Mk 7:5 scribes inquired·of him, "Why·do your disciples not
Mk 11:31 he·shall·declare, 'So·then why did·yeu·not trust
Rm 9:32 Why? Because *they·pursued it* not as·a·result of·
1Co 6:7 Rather, why not·indeed *let* yeurselves·be·wronged?
1Co 6:7 yeurselves·be·wronged? Rather, why not·indeed *let*
2Co 11:11 Why? Because I·do·not love yeu?
Rv 17:7 the angel declared to·me, "Why did·you·marvel?

G1303 δια•τίθεμαι diatíthêmai *v.* (7x)
Roots:G1223 G5087 Compare:G3549 See:G1242 xLangAlso:H3772
G1303.3 V-PMI-1S διατίθεμαι (1x)
Lk 22:29 And·I bequeath to·yeu a·kingdom, just·as my
G1303.3 V-2AMI-3S διέθετο (2x)
Lk 22:29 a·kingdom, just·as my Father bequeathed to·me,
Ac 3:25 unilateral·covenant which God bequeathed unto our
G1303.3 V-2AMP-GSM διαθεμένου (1x)
Heb 9:16 to·be·carrying·away the·one who·is·bequeathing.
G1303.3 V-2AMP-NSM διαθέμενος (1x)
Heb 9:17 ·time *is·it* in·force when the·one bequeathing lives,
G1303.4 V-FDI-1S διαθήσομαι (2x)
Heb 8:10 ·covenant that I·shall·enact with·the house of·
Heb 10:16 ·covenant that I·shall·bequeath unto them after

G1304 δια•τρίβω diatríbō *v.* (10x)
Roots:G1223 G5147
G1304.2 V-PAP-NPM διατρίβοντες (1x)
Ac 16:12 ·were in that city lingering·awhile·for some days.
G1304.2 V-IAI-3S διέτριβεν (3x)
Jn 3:22 of·Judea, and he·was·lingering·awhile there with
Jn 11:54 Ephraim. And he·was·lingering·awhile there with
Ac 12:19 to Caesarea, *HerOd·Agrippa* was·lingering·awhile.
G1304.2 V-IAI-3P διέτριβον (3x)
Ac 14:28 little time *that* they·were·lingering there together
Ac 15:35 So Paul and BarNabas were·lingering in Antioch,
Ac 25:14 And as they·were·lingering there *for* many·more
G1304.2 V-AAI-1P διετρίψαμεν (1x)
Ac 20:6 in·only five days, where we·lingered seven days.
G1304.2 V-AAI-3P διέτριψαν (1x)
Ac 14:3 Accordingly in·fact, they·lingered a·sufficient time,
G1304.2 V-AAP-NSM διατρίψας (1x)
Ac 25:6 Now after·lingering·awhile among them *for* more

G1305 δια•τροφή diatrôphḗ *n.* (1x)
Roots:G1223 G5142 Compare:G1033 G1035 G4620 G5160 G5315
G1305 N-APF διατροφάς (1x)
1Ti 6:8 And having sufficient·nourishment and *the* essential·

G1306 δι•αυγάζω diaugázō *v.* (1x)
Roots:G1223 G0826
G1306.1 V-AAS-3S διαυγάσῃ (1x)
2Pe 1:19 — until *the* day should·beam·right·through, and *the*

G1307 δια•φανής diaphanḗs *adj.* (1x)
Roots:G1223 G5316
G1307.2 A-NSM διαφανής (1x)
Rv 21:21 CITY *was* pure gold, as nearly·transparent glass.

G1308 δια•φέρω diaphḗrō *v.* (13x)
Roots:G1223 G5342 Compare:G0474 G1266 G0241-2
G1308.a V-PAI-3S διαφέρει (1x)
Gal 2:6 were, it·thoroughly·means not·even·one·thing to·me
G1308.1 V-2AAS-3S διενέγκῃ (1x)
Mk 11:16 that anyone should·carry *any* merchandise through
G1308.2 V-IPI-3S διεφέρετο (1x)
Ac 13:49 of·the Lord was·thoroughly·carried throughout the
G1308.4 V-PPP-GPM διαφερομένων (1x)
Ac 27:27 with·us being·thoroughly·tossed·about along the
G1308.6 V-PAI-3S διαφέρει (2x)
Gal 4:1 an·infant), varies not·even·one·thing from·a·slave,
1Co 15:41 ·*the*·stars, for *one* star varies·from *another* star in
G1308.6 V-PAP-APN διαφέροντα (2x)
Rm 2:18 ·and·verify the·things varying (being·tutored from·
Php 1:10 yeu (*concerning* the·things varying *among·yeu*), in·
G1308.7 V-PAI-2P διαφέρετε (4x)
Lk 12:7 Yeu·surpass·the·value of·many little·sparrows.
Lk 12:24 *do* yeu·yeurselves surpass·the·value of·the birds?
Mt 6:26 yeu·yeurselves *of* more surpassing·value *than* these?
Mt 10:31 yeu·yeurselves surpass·the·value of·many little·
G1308.7 V-PAI-3S διαφέρει (1x)
Mt 12:12 ·does a·man·of·clay† surpass·the·value of·a·sheep?

G1309 δια•φεύγω diaphêúgō *v.* (1x)
Roots:G1223 G5343
G1309 V-2AAO-3S διαφύγοι (1x)
Ac 27:42 lest·any might·thoroughly·escape by·swimming·.

G1310 δια•φημίζω diaphēmízō *v.* (3x)
Roots:G1223 G5345 Compare:G0864
G1310.2 V-PAN διαφημίζειν (1x)
Mk 1:45 often, and to·widely·promote the matter, such·for
G1310.2 V-AAI-3P διεφήμισαν (1x)
Mt 9:31 But upon·going·forth, they·widely·promoted it in
G1310.2 V-API-3S διεφημίσθη (1x)
Mt 28:15 saying is·widely·promoted closely·among Judeans

G1311 δια•φθείρω diaphthêírō *v.* (6x)
Roots:G1223 G5351 Compare:G4595 See:G2704 xLangAlso:H7843
G1311.1 V-RPP-GPM@ διεφθαρμένων (1x)
1Ti 6:5 idle·disputations of·thoroughly·corrupted men·of·,
G1311.2 V-PAI-3S διαφθείρει (1x)
Lk 12:33 draws·near, neither·does moth thoroughly·ruin.
G1311.2 V-PAP-APM διαφθείροντας (1x)
Rv 11:18 ·ruin the·ones thoroughly·ruining the earth."
G1311.2 V-AAN διαφθεῖραι (1x)
Rv 11:18 *for·you* to·thoroughly·ruin the·ones thoroughly·
G1311.2 V-2API-3S διεφθάρη (1x)
Rv 8:9 the third·part of·the ships were·thoroughly·ruined.
G1311.3 V-PPI-3S διαφθείρεται (1x)
2Co 4:16 man·of·clay† is·thoroughly·decaying·away, but·yet

G1312 δια•φθορά diaphthôrá *n.* (6x)
Roots:G1311 xLangAlso:H7845
G1312 N-ASF διαφθοράν (6x)
Ac 2:27 shall·you·give your Divine·Holy·One to·see decay.
Ac 2:31 ·behind in Hades, neither did·his flesh see decay.'
Ac 13:34 intending to·return·back to decay, in·this·manner
Ac 13:35 ·not give your Divine·Holy·One to·see decay.'"
Ac 13:36 and was·laid alongside his fathers and saw decay.
Ac 13:37 But he·whom God awakened did·not see decay.

G1313 διά•φορος diáphôrôs *adj.* (4x)
Roots:G1308 Compare:G4164 G4182
G1313.1 A-APN διάφορα (1x)
Rm 12:6 having various gracious·bestowments according·to
G1313.1 A-DPM διαφόροις (1x)
Heb 9:10 and drinks, and in·various ceremonial·washings,
G1313.2 A-ASN-C διαφορώτερον (1x)
Heb 1:4 ·as he·has·inherited a·more·superb name above·and·
G1313.2 A-GSF-C διαφορωτέρας (1x)
Heb 8:6 he·has·obtained a·more·superb public·service, by·

G1314 δια•φυλάσσω diaphylássō *v.* (1x)
Roots:G1223 G5442 Compare:G1301
G1314 V-AAN διαφυλάξαι (1x)
Lk 4:10 you, to·thoroughly·keep·watch·over you,'

G1315 δια•χειρίζομαι diachêirízômai *v.* (2x)
Roots:G1223 G5495 Compare:G0615
G1315.2 V-AMI-2P διεχειρίσασθε (1x)
Ac 5:30 yeu·yeurselves abusively·manhandled, hanging *him*
G1315.2 V-AMN διαχειρίσασθαι (1x)
Ac 26:21 were·intently·trying to·abusively·manhandle *me*.

G1316 δια•χωρίζομαι diachōrízômai *v.* (1x)
Roots:G1223 G5563 See:G0673
G1316.2 V-PNN διαχωρίζεσθαι (1x)
Lk 9:33 with the·*two·men* thoroughly·departing from him,

G1317 διδακτικός didaktikós *adj.* (2x)
Roots:G1318
G1317 A-ASM διδακτικόν (2x)
1Ti 3:2 self-controlled, orderly, hospitable, instructive,
2Ti 2:24 to all *men*, instructive, able·to·bear·with·ill·will,

G1318 διδακτός didaktós *adj.* (3x)
Roots:G1321 See:G1317
G1318.1 A-DPM διδακτοῖς (1x)
1Co 2:13 ·speak, not with instructive words of·mankind's†
G1318.2 A-NPM διδακτοί (1x)
Jn 6:45 "And they·shall·be all instructed of·Yahweh."
G1318.3 A-DPM διδακτοῖς (1x)
1Co 2:13 wisdom, but·rather with instructions of·Holy Spirit

G1319 διδασκαλία didaskalía *n.* (22x)
Roots:G1320 See:G1322 xLangAlso:H1952-1 H4175
G1319 N-NSF διδασκαλία (1x)
1Ti 6:1 name of·God and the instruction may·not be·reviled.
G1319 N-ASF διδασκαλίαν (3x)
Rm 15:4 for our instruction in·order·that we·may·have the
Tit 2:10 ·adorn *themselves·with* the instruction of·God our
2Ti 3:16 and *is* profitable particularly·for instruction, for
G1319 N-APF διδασκαλίας (3x)
Mt 15:9 ·requirements of·men·of·clay† *as* instructions.'"
Mk 7:7 ·requirements of·men·of·clay† *as* instructions.'

Col 2:22 ·requirements and instructions of·the men·of·clay†.'
G1319 N-DSF διδασκαλίᾳ (10x)
Rm 12:7 *·others*; or the·one instructing, on the instruction;
Tit 1:9 by the healthy·and·sound instruction and to·convict
Tit 2:1 is·suitable·for the healthy·and·sound instruction:
Tit 2:7 ·pattern of·good works in the instruction, *showing*
1Ti 1:10 ·set·opposed to·the healthy·and·sound instruction,
1Ti 4:13 to·the exhortation, *and* to·the instruction.
1Ti 4:16 to·yourself, and·also to·the instruction; persist in·
1Ti 5:17 the·ones laboring·hard in word and instruction.
1Ti 6:3 with·the instruction according·to devout·reverence,
2Ti 3:10 ·yourself have·closely·followed my instruction, *my*
G1319 N-DPF διδασκαλίαις (1x)
1Ti 4:1 to·impostrous spirits and to·instructions of·demons,
G1319 N-GSF διδασκαλίας (3x)
Eph 4:14 ·carried·about by·every wind of·instruction, by the
1Ti 4:6 trust and of·the good instruction, to·which you·have·
2Ti 4:3 ·with the healthy·and·sound instruction. But·rather,
EG1319 (1x)
1Ti 5:21 these *instructions* completely·apart·from prejudice,

G1320 διδάσκαλος didáskalôs *n.* (58x)
Roots:G1321 Compare:G3101 G2819-2 G3011-4 See:G2567 xLangAlso:H4175
G1320.1 N-NSM διδάσκαλος (6x)
Jn 3:2 from God, *being* an·instructor, for not·even·one·man
Jn 3:10 "Are you·yourself the instructor of·IsraEl, and you·
Lk 6:40 ·been·completely·reformed shall·be as his instructor.
Mt 10:25 that he·should·become as his instructor, and the
1Ti 2:7 *and* do·not lie)— an·instructor of·Gentiles in trust
2Ti 1:11 and an·ambassador, and an·instructor of·Gentiles.
G1320.1 N-NPM διδάσκαλοι (4x)
Ac 13:1 in Antioch, prophets and instructors as·follows:
Heb 5:12 time being·due *for·yeu* to·be instructors, *yeu·still*
Jac 3:1 many *of·yeu should* become instructors, having·seen
1Co 12:29 Not all *are* instructors. Not all *are operating·in*
G1320.1 N-ASM διδάσκαλον (3x)
Lk 6:40 "A·disciple is not above his instructor, but everyone
Mt 10:24 is not above the instructor, nor·even a·slave above
Rm 2:20 of·impetuous·men, an·instructor of·infants, having
G1320.1 N-APM διδασκάλους (3x)
1Co 12:28 second prophets, third instructors, after·that *the·*
Eph 4:11 ·redemption, and the shepherds and instructors—
2Ti 4:3 they·shall·further·stack·up instructors for·themselves
G1320.1 N-GPM διδασκάλων (1x)
Lk 2:46 in *the* midst of·the instructors, both listening·to them
G1320.2 N-NSM διδάσκαλος (8x)
Jn 11:28 privately declaring, "The Mentor is·near, and he·
Jn 13:13 "Yeu·yeurselves hail me Mentor and Lord, and yeu·
Jn 13:14 yeur feet *being* Lord and Mentor, then·also yeu·
Lk 22:11 master of·the home, 'The Mentor says to·you,
Mt 9:11 disciples, "Why·does yeur Mentor eat with the tax·
Mt 17:24 and declared, "Yeur mentor, does·he·not fully·pay
Mt 26:18 ·man and declare to·him, 'The Mentor says, "My
Mk 14:14 master·of·the·house, 'The Mentor says, "Where
G1320.2 N-VSM διδάσκαλε (31x)
Jn 1:38 ·being·translated *from Hebrew*, is·to·say Mentor),
Jn 8:4 they·say to·him, "Mentor, this wife was·grabbed·
Jn 20:16 (which is·to·say, "O·my·*great*·Mentor").
Lk 3:12 they·declared to him, "Mentor, what shall·we·do?
Lk 7:40 And he·replies, "Mentor, declare·it."
Lk 9:38 crowd shouted·out, saying, "Mentor, I·petition you,
Lk 10:25 him, he·said, "Mentor, what should·I·do to·inherit
Lk 11:45 ·in·Torah-Law says to·him, "Mentor, *when* saying
Lk 12:13 crowd declared to·him, "Mentor, declare for·my
Lk 18:18 saying, "Beneficially·good Mentor, what should·I·
Lk 19:39 crowd declared to him, "Mentor, reprimand your
Lk 20:21 saying, "Mentor, we·personally·know that you·
Lk 20:28 saying, "Mentor, Moses wrote to·us, if any·man's
Lk 20:39 of·the scribes declared, "Mentor, well declared.
Lk 21:7 saying, "So·then Mentor, when shall these·things
Mt 8:19 declared to·him, "Mentor, I·shall·follow you
Mt 12:38 answered, saying, "Mentor, we·want to·see a·sign
Mt 19:16 him declared, "O·beneficially·good Mentor, what
Mt 22:16 saying, "Mentor, we·have·seen that you·are true,
Mt 22:24 saying, "Mentor, Moses declared, if a·certain·man
Mt 22:36 "Mentor, which·one *is the* great commandment in
Mk 4:38 and say to·him, "Mentor, does·it·not matter to·you
Mk 9:17 the crowd, declared, "Mentor, I·brought to you my
Mk 9:38 him, saying, "Mentor, we·saw someone casting·
Mk 10:17 him, "Beneficially·good Mentor, what should·I·
Mk 10:20 he·declared to·him, "Mentor, all these·things I·
Mk 10:35 to·him, saying, "Mentor, we·want that you·
Mk 12:14 ·say to·him, "Mentor, we·personally·know that
Mk 12:19 "Mentor, Moses wrote for·us that if any·man's
Mk 12:32 declared to·him, "Mentor, clearly·full·well did·
Mk 13:1 says to·him, "Mentor, see what·manner·of stones
G1320.2 N-ASM διδάσκαλον (2x)
Lk 8:49 Your daughter has·died; do·not harass the Mentor."
Mk 5:35 Why harass the Mentor any·longer?

G1321 διδάσκω didáskō *v.* (97x)
Compare:G2727 G3100 G3129 See:G1320 G1317 G1318
G1321.1 V-FAI-3S διδάξει (2x)
Jn 14:26 in my name, that·one shall·instruct yeu *concerning*
Lk 12:12 "For the Holy Spirit shall·instruct yeu in the same
G1321.1 V-PAI-1S διδάσκω (1x)
1Co 4:17 just·as I·instruct everywhere among every Called·
G1321.1 V-PAI-2S διδάσκεις (7x)
Jn 9:34 in moral·failures, and do·you·yourself instruct us?
Lk 20:21 ·know that you·say and instruct uprightly, and do·
Lk 20:21 *of·any*, but·rather *that* you·instruct the Way of·
Ac 21:21 you, that you·instruct a·defection away·from
Mt 22:16 you·are true, and *that* you·instruct the Way of·God
Mk 12:14 of·men·of·clay†, but·rather instruct the Way of·
Rm 2:21 someone·else, do·you·not instruct yourself?
G1321.1 V-PAI-3S διδάσκει (2x)
1Co 11:14 does·not·even the nature itself instruct yeu, in·fact
1Jn 2:27 same anointing presently·instructs yeu concerning
G1321.1 V-PAM-2S δίδασκε (2x)
1Ti 4:11 You·must·charge and instruct these·things.
1Ti 6:2 of·the good·deed. These·things instruct and exhort.
G1321.1 V-PAN διδάσκειν (14x)
Jn 7:35 among·the Greeks, and to·instruct the Greeks?
Lk 6:6 into the gathering and to·instruct. Yet there·was *a·*
Ac 1:1 all that Jesus began both to·do and to·instruct,
Ac 4:2 ·out on·account·of them instructing the people and
Ac 4:18 them not to·enunciate nor·even to·instruct at·all in
Ac 5:28 charge a·charge to·yeu not to·instruct in this name?
Heb 5:12 *yeu·still* have need *for·one* to·instruct yeu again
Mt 11:1 ·on from·there to·instruct and to·officially·proclaim
Mk 4:1 Then he·began again to·instruct directly·by the sea.
Mk 6:2 with·Sabbath occurring, he·began to·instruct in the
Mk 6:34 ' and he·began to·instruct them *in* many·things.
Mk 8:31 And he·began to·instruct them that it·is·mandatory·
1Ti 2:12 ·charge to·a·woman *for·her* to·instruct, nor·even
Rv 2:20 *as* a·prophetess, to·instruct and to·lead·astray my
G1321.1 V-PAP-DSM διδάσκοντι (1x)
Mt 21:23 into the Sanctuary·Atrium while·instructing, the
G1321.1 V-PAP-GSM διδάσκοντος (1x)
Lk 20:1 of·those days, with·him instructing the people in the
G1321.1 V-PAP-NSM διδάσκων (23x)
Jn 6:59 in a·gathering, while·instructing in CaperNaum.
Jn 7:28 ·out in the Sanctuary·Atrium, instructing and saying,
Jn 8:20 spoke at the treasury·room, while·instructing in the
Lk 4:31 ·city of·Galilee, and he·was instructing them on the
Lk 5:17 even while he·himself was instructing, that there·
Lk 13:10 Now he·was instructing in one of·the gatherings on
Lk 13:22 *of·the* cities and villages, instructing and making a·
Lk 19:47 And he·was instructing each day in the Sanctuary·
Lk 21:37 the days, he·was instructing in the Sanctuary·
Lk 23:5 "He·incites the people, instructing in all Judea,
Ac 18:11 six lunar·months, instructing the Redemptive·word
Ac 21:28 is the man·of·clay† instructing all·men everywhere
Ac 28:31 of·God and instructing the·things concerning the
Mt 4:23 all around Galilee, instructing in their gatherings,
Mt 7:29 for he·was instructing them as *one* having authority,
Mt 9:35 cities and the villages, instructing in their gatherings
Mt 26:55 ·down each day alongside yeu instructing in the
Mk 1:22 his instruction, for he·was instructing them as one·
Mk 6:6 ·around·to the encircling villages, while·instructing.
Mk 12:35 And beginning·to·speak while·instructing in the
Mk 14:49 yeu in the Sanctuary·Atrium instructing, and yeu·
Rm 2:21 So·then, the·one instructing someone·else, do·you·
Rm 12:7 *to·others*; or the·one instructing, on the instruction;
G1321.1 V-PAP-NPM διδάσκοντες (7x)
Ac 5:25 in the Sanctuary·Atrium and instructing the people."
Ac 5:42 cease instructing and proclaiming·the·good·news:
Ac 15:35 instructing and proclaiming·the·good·news of·the
Mt 28:20 instructing them to·observantly·keep all·things as·
Tit 1:11 whole houses, instructing things·which are·not
Col 1:28 man·of·clay† and instructing every man·of·clay† in
Col 3:16 in all wisdom, instructing and admonishing
G1321.1 V-PAS-3S διδάσκῃ (1x)
1Jn 2:27 no need that anyone should·instruct yeu, but·rather
G1321.1 V-IAI-3S ἐδίδασκεν (14x)
Jn 7:14 ·up into the Sanctuary·Atrium and was·instructing.
Jn 8:2 And sitting·down, he·was·instructing them.
Lk 4:15 And he·himself was·instructing in their gatherings,
Lk 5:3 And sitting·down, he·was·instructing the crowds
Ac 18:25 ·speaking and was·instructing accurately the·things
Mt 5:2 And opening·up his mouth, he·was·instructing them,
Mt 13:54 his·own fatherland, he·was·instructing them in
Mk 1:21 he·was·instructing on·the various·Sabbaths.
Mk 2:13 alongside him, and he·was·instructing them.
Mk 4:2 And he·was·instructing them many·things by
Mk 9:31 For he·was·instructing his disciples, and he·was·
Mk 10:1 he·had·been·accustomed, he·was·instructing them.
Mk 11:17 And he·was·instructing, saying to·them, "Has·it·
Rv 2:14 who was·instructing with Balaq *the·Annihilator* to·
G1321.1 V-IAI-3P ἐδίδασκον (2x)
Ac 5:21 ·Atrium at the sunrise and were·instructing. Now the
Ac 15:1 ·down from Judea were·instructing the brothers,
G1321.1 V-AAI-1S ἐδίδαξα (1x)
Jn 18:20 world. I·myself always instructed in the gathering
G1321.1 V-AAI-2S ἐδίδαξας (1x)
Lk 13:26 in·the·sight of·you, and you·instructed in our
G1321.1 V-AAI-3S ἐδίδαξεν (3x)
Jn 8:28 but·rather just·as my Father instructed me, I·speak
Lk 11:1 to·pray, just·as John also instructed his disciples."
1Jn 2:27 is·not a·lie, even just·as it·already·instructed yeu),
G1321.1 V-AAI-3P ἐδίδαξαν (1x)
Mk 6:30 they·did, and what·many·things they·instructed.
G1321.1 V-AAM-2S δίδαξον (1x)
Lk 11:1 to him, "Lord, instruct us to·pray, just·as John also
G1321.1 V-AAN διδάξαι (3x)
Ac 11:26 ·Out·citizenry and to·instruct an·ample crowd.
Ac 20:20 ·in·detail to·yeu, and have·instructed yeu publicly
2Ti 2:2 ·clay† who shall·be competent to·instruct others also.
G1321.1 V-AAS-3S διδάξῃ (2x)
Mt 5:19 and should·instruct the men·of·clay† in·this·manner,
Mt 5:19 whoever should·do and should·instruct *them*, the·
G1321.1 V-AAS-3P διδάξωσιν (1x)
Heb 8:11 no, they·should·not *anymore* instruct each·man his
G1321.1 V-API-1S ἐδιδάχθην (1x)
Gal 1:12 a·man·of·clay†, nor was·I·instructed, but·rather *I·*
G1321.1 V-API-2P ἐδιδάχθητε (3x)
2Th 2:15 the traditions which yeu·were·instructed, whether
Eph 4:21 if·indeed yeu·heard him and are·instructed by him
Col 2:7 the trust, just·as yeu·were·instructed, abounding in it
G1321.1 V-API-3P ἐδιδάχθησαν (1x)
Mt 28:15 money, they·did as they·were·instructed. And this
G1321.2 V-PAP-NPM διδάσκοντες (2x)
Mt 15:9 ·reverence me, teaching *the* religious·requirements
Mk 7:7 ·reverence me, teaching *the* religious·requirements

G1322 διδαχή didachḗ *n.* (30x)
Roots:G1321 See:G1319 xLangAlso:H1952-1 H3948 H4148
G1322 N-NSF διδαχή (3x)
Jn 7:16 them and declared, "My instruction is not mine, but·

Ac 17:19 to·know what this brand-new instruction *is, which·*
Mk 1:27 this? What *is* this brand-new instruction? Because
G1322 N-ASF διδαχήν (7x)
Rm 16:17 and the traps contrary·to the instruction which yeu
Tit 1:9 according·to the instruction in·order·that he·may·be
1Co 14:26 has a·psalm, has an·instruction, has a·bestowed·
2Jn 1:10 and does·not bring this instruction, yeu·must·not
Rv 2:14 ones·securely·holding·to the instruction of·BalaAm,
Rv 2:15 ·holding·to the instruction of·the NicoLaitans,
Rv 2:24 (as·many·as do·not have this instruction *of·JeZebel*
G1322 N-DSF διδαχῇ (13x)
Lk 4:32 And they·were·astounded at his instruction, because
Ac 2:42 ·continuing in·the instruction of·the ambassadors
Ac 13:12 being·astounded at the instruction of·the Lord.
Mt 7:28 the crowds were·astounded at his instruction,
Mt 22:33 *this*, the crowds were·astounded at his instruction.
Mk 1:22 And they·were·astounded at his instruction, for he·
Mk 4:2 and in his instruction, he·was·saying to·them,
Mk 11:18 all the crowd was·astounded at his instruction.
Mk 12:38 he·was·saying to·them in his instruction, "Look·
1Co 14:6 knowledge, or by prophesying, or by instruction?
2Ti 4:2 *and* exhort with all long-suffering and instruction!
2Jn 1:9 not abiding in the instruction of·Anointed-One, does·
2Jn 1:9 The·one abiding in the instruction of·Anointed-One,
G1322 N-DPF διδαχαῖς (1x)
Heb 13:9 ·about by·diverse and strange·new instructions. For
G1322 N-GSF διδαχῆς (6x)
Jn 7:17 he·shall·know concerning the instruction, whether
Jn 18:19 his disciples and concerning his instruction.
Ac 5:28 ·filled JeruSalem with·yeur instruction, and yeu·
Heb 6:2 of·the·instruction of·ceremonial·washings, and of·
Mt 16:12 but·rather of the instruction of·the Pharisees and
Rm 6:17 ·heart *to·that* particular·pattern of·instruction which

G1323 δί•δραχμον dídrachmôn *n.* (2x)
Roots:G1364 G1406 Compare:G4715 See:G5069-1
G1323 N-APN δίδραχμα (2x)
Mt 17:24 receiving the two·drachma *tax* came·alongside
Mt 17:24 mentor, does·he·not fully·pay the two·drachmas?"

G1324 Δίδυμος Dídymôs *n/p.* (5x)
Roots:G1364
xLangEquiv:H8380 xLangAlso:G2381
G1324.2 N/P-NSM Δίδυμος (3x)
Jn 11:16 (the·one being·referred·to·as Twin) declared to·the
Jn 20:24 twelve, the·one being·referred·to·as Twin) was not
Jn 21:2 and Thomas (the·one being·referred·to·as Twin), and
EG1324.2 (2x)
Rm 9:10 having a·conception *of·twins* from·out of·one·man
Rm 9:11 (for *with·the* twins not·yet being·born nor·even

G1325 δίδωμι dídōmi *v.* (422x)
See:G1390 G1395 G0593-1
xLangEquiv:H5414 A5415
G1325.1 V-FAI-1S δώσω (22x)
Jn 4:14 ·out of·the water that I·myself shall·give him, no, he·
Jn 4:14 but·rather the water that I·shall·give him, it·shall·be
Jn 6:51 also the bread that I·myself shall·give is my flesh,
Jn 6:51 my flesh, which I·myself shall·give on·behalf of·the
Lk 4:6 to·him, "To·you I·shall·give absolutely·all this
Lk 21:15 For I·myself shall·give yeu a·mouth and wisdom,
Ac 2:19 And I·shall·give wonders in the heaven up·above
Ac 13:34 ·has·declared, "I·shall·give to·yeu the trustworthy
Mt 4:9 to·him, "All these·things I·shall·give to·you, if upon·
Mt 16:19 And I·shall·give to·you the keys of·the kingdom
Mt 20:4 and whatever may·be right I·shall·give to·yeu.' And
Mk 6:22 you·should·want, and I·shall·give *it* to·you."
Mk 6:23 you·should·request of·me, I·shall·give *it* to·you,
Rv 2:7 To·the·one overcoming, I·shall·give to·him to·eat
Rv 2:10 ·unto death, and I·shall·give you a·victor's·crown
Rv 2:17 To·the·one overcoming, I·shall·give to·him to·eat
Rv 2:17 hidden manna, and I·shall·give him a·white pebble,
Rv 2:23 and hearts. And I·shall·give to·each·one of·yeu
Rv 2:26 ·unto *the* end, to·him I·shall·give authority over the
Rv 2:28 And I·shall·give him the Early·Morning star.
Rv 11:3 "And I·shall·give *unto* my two witnesses, and they·

Rv 21:6 and the end. I·myself shall·give to·the·one thirsting
G1325.1 V-FAI-2S δώσεις (2x)
Ac 2:27 neither shall·you·give your Divine·Holy·One to·
Ac 13:35 "You·shall·not give your Divine·Holy·One to·
G1325.1 V-FAI-3S δώσει (16x)
Jn 6:27 which the Son of·Clay·Man† shall·give to·yeu, for
Jn 11:22 ·should·request·of God, God shall·give *it* to·you."
Jn 14:16 ·ask·of the Father, and he·shall·give yeu another
Jn 16:23 ·of the Father in my name, he·shall·give *it* to·yeu.
Lk 1:32 and Yahweh God shall·give to·him the Throne of·
Lk 11:8 ·rising·up, he·shall·not give to·him on·account·of
Lk 11:8 he·being·awakened shall·give him as·much·as he·
Lk 11:13 the·one out of·heaven, shall·give Holy Spirit to·
Lk 16:12 *material·wealth*, who shall·give to·yeu *wealth of*
Lk 20:16 tenant·farmers, and he·shall·give the vineyard to·
Mt 7:11 heavens, give beneficially·good·things to·the·ones
Mt 16:26 *that* a·man·of·clay† shall·give in·exchange for·his
Mk 8:37 *that* a·man·of·clay† shall·give in·exchange for·his
Mk 12:9 the tenant·farmers and shall·give the vineyard to·
Rm 14:12 each·one of·us shall·give account concerning
1Jn 5:16 ·shall·request, and *God* shall·give to·him life-above
G1325.1 V-FAI-3P δώσουσιν (4x)
Lk 6:38 *together*, and overflowing shall·they·give into *the*
Mt 24:24 and false·prophets, and they·shall·give great signs
Mk 13:22 shall·be·awakened and shall·give signs and
Rv 4:9 And whenever the living·beings shall·give glory and
G1325.1 V-FPI-3S δοθήσεται (16x)
Lk 6:38 "Give, and it·shall·be·given to·yeu; good measure,
Lk 8:18 to·him *comprehension* shall·be·given; and whoever
Lk 11:9 say to·yeu, request, and it·shall·be·given yeu; seek,
Lk 11:29 and a·miraculous·sign shall·not be·given to·it,
Lk 19:26 to·any one having, *more* shall·be·given. But of
Ac 24:26 expecting that valuables shall·be·given to·him by
Mt 7:7 "Request, and it·shall·be·given yeu; seek, and yeu·
Mt 10:19 yeu·should·speak, for it·shall·be·given to·yeu in
Mt 12:39 and a·miraculous·sign shall·not be·given to·her,
Mt 13:12 ·what·he·has, to·him *more* shall·be·given, and he·
Mt 16:4 and a·miraculous·sign shall·not be·given to·her,
Mt 21:43 from yeu and shall·be·given to·a·nation producing
Mt 25:29 ·utilizing·what·he·has, *more* shall·be·given, and
Mk 4:25 ·what·he·has, to·him *more* shall·be·given, and
Mk 8:12 'As·if·a·miraculous·sign shall·*ever*·be·given to·this
Jac 1:5 without reproaching, and it·shall·be·given to·him.
G1325.1 V-PAI-1S δίδωμι (10x)
Jn 10:28 And·I give to·them eternal life-above.
Jn 13:34 "A·brand-new commandment I·give to·yeu, that
Jn 14:27 I·leave with·yeu; my peace I·give to·yeu. Not just·
Jn 14:27 the world gives *do* I·myself give to·yeu. Do·not be·
Lk 4:6 ·handed·over to·me, and I·do·give it to·whomever I·
Lk 10:19 Behold, I·give to·yeu the authority, the·one to·
Lk 19:8 the half of·my holdings I·give to·the helplessly·poor
Ac 3:6 but that·thing which I·do·have, I·give to·you. In the
1Co 7:25 ·assignment of·*the*·Lord. But I·give *my* advice, as
2Co 8:10 And in this, I·give advice, for this is·advantageous
G1325.1 V-PAI-3S δίδωσιν (11x)
Jn 3:34 for *to·him* God does·not give the Spirit as·a·result
Jn 6:32 ·the heaven, but·rather my Father gives yeu the true
Jn 6:37 "All that the Father gives me shall·come toward me;
Jn 13:26 dipping the morsel, he·gave *it* to·Judas IsCariot, *the*
Jn 14:27 Not just·as the world gives *do* I·myself give to·yeu.
Jn 21:13 comes and takes the bread and gives *it* to·them, and
Ac 7:25 through his hand, would·give salvation to·them,
Jac 4:6 But he·gives greater grace. Therefore he·says, "' God
Jac 4:6 haughty·men, but gives grace to·humble·men.'"
1Pe 5:5 haughty·men but gives grace to·humble·men.'"
1Co 15:38 but God gives it a·body just·as he·determined,
G1325.1 V-PAM-2S δίδου (3x)
Lk 6:30 But give to·every one requesting·of you, and of the·
Lk 11:3 'Give us each day our sustaining bread.
Mt 5:42 "Give to·the·one requesting·of you, and you·should·
G1325.1 V-PAM-2P δίδοτε (2x)
Lk 6:38 "Give, and it·shall·be·given to·yeu; good measure,
Eph 4:27 nor·even give place to·the Slanderer.

G1325.1 V-PAN διδόναι (7x)
Lk 11:13 personally·know·how to·give beneficially·good
Lk 12:42 over his domestic·staff, to·give *them their* ration·
Lk 23:2 and forbidding *others* to·give tributes to·Caesar,
Ac 20:35 ·is more supremely·blessed to·give than to·receive.
Mt 7:11 personally·know·how to·give beneficially·good gifts
Mt 24:45 over his domestic·staff, to·give them the
1Ti 5:14 ·home, to·give not·even·one impromptu·occasion
G1325.1 V-PAP-DSM διδόντι (2x)
1Co 15:57 thanks *be* to·God, the·one giving us the victory
2Co 8:16 *be* to·God, the·one giving the same earnest·care
G1325.1 V-PAP-GSM διδόντος (2x)
Jac 1:5 the·one giving to·all with·simplicity·and·fidelity
2Th 1:8 in blazing fire, giving retribution to·the·ones not
G1325.1 V-PAP-NSM διδούς (5x)
Jn 6:33 ·out of·the heaven, and giving life-above to·the world
Ac 14:17 ·doing·good, giving us seasons·of·rain from·the·
Ac 17:25 ·a·bind·for anything, with·himself giving life† and
Heb 8:10 says Yahweh, 'giving my Laws-of-Liberty into
Heb 10:16 says Yahweh, giving my Laws-of-Liberty upon
G1325.1 V-PAP-NPN διδόντα (1x)
1Co 14:7 the soulless,·inanimate·things giving sound,
G1325.1 V-PAP-NPM διδόντες (2x)
2Co 5:12 ·rather *we·are* giving yeu an·impromptu·occasion
2Co 6:3 *yeu* while·giving not·one·bit·of an·instance·of·
G1325.1 V-PPI-3S δίδοται (3x)
Ac 8:18 that the Holy Spirit is·given through the laying·on
1Co 12:7 of·the Spirit is·given to·each·man specifically·for
1Co 12:8 For in·fact to·one is·given through the Spirit a·
G1325.1 V-PPP-NSN διδόμενον (1x)
Lk 22:19 is my body, the·one being·given on·yeur behalf.
G1325.1 V-IAI-3S ἐδίδου (9x)
Lk 9:16 and fully·broke *them*, and was·giving *them* to·the
Lk 15:16 yet not·even·one·man was·giving him *anything*.
Ac 2:4 ·as the Spirit was·giving them to·clearly·enunciate.
Mt 13:8 the good·one, and were·giving fruit, in·fact some
Mt 26:26 YeShua broke *it* and was·giving *it* to·the disciples,
Mk 4:8 into the good soil and was·giving fruit, springing·up
Mk 6:7 two by·two. And he·was·giving them authority *over*
Mk 6:41 the loaves·of·bread and was·giving *them* to·his
Mk 8:6 *the loaves·of·bread*, and he·was·giving *them* to·his
G1325.1 V-IAI-3P ἐδίδουν (2x)
Jn 19:3 of·the Jews!" And they·were·giving him slaps.
Mk 15:23 And they·were·giving him wine to·drink having·
G1325.1 V-AAI-1S ἔδωκα (2x)
Jn 13:15 For I·gave an·explicit·example to·yeu in·order·that
Rv 2:21 And I·gave her time in·order·that she·should·repent
G1325.1 V-AAI-1P ἐδώκαμεν (1x)
1Th 4:2 ·personally·know what charges we·gave yeu through
G1325.1 V-AAI-2S ἔδωκας (7x)
Jn 17:2 Just·as *also* you·gave him authority over·all flesh, in·
Jn 17:24 my glory, which you·gave to·me because you·did·
Lk 7:44 I·entered into your home, you·gave·me no water for
Lk 7:45 "You·did·not give me a·kiss, but she·herself since
Lk 15:29 never·at·any·time did·you·give me a·young·goat
Lk 19:23 Why then did·you·not give my money over *to* the
Rv 16:6 and prophets, and you·gave them blood to·drink,
G1325.1 V-AAI-2P ἐδώκατε (3x)
Gal 4:15 yeur own·eyes, yeu·would have·given·them to·me.
Mt 25:35 For I·was·hungry, and yeu·gave me to·eat. I·was·
Mt 25:42 I·was·hungry, and yeu·did·not give me *anything*
G1325.1 V-AAI-3S ἔδωκεν (64x)
Jn 1:12 ·receive him, to·them he·gave privilege to·become
Jn 3:16 the world, such·that he·gave his only·begotten Son,
Jn 4:5 ·by to·the open·field that Jacob gave to·his son Joseph
Jn 4:10 ·of him, and he·would·have given you living water.
Jn 4:12 greater·than our father Jacob, who gave us the well?
Jn 5:26 in himself, in·this·manner, he·gave also to·the Son
Jn 5:27 And he·gave him authority also to·make Tribunal·
Jn 5:36 the works which the Father gave me (in·order·that I·
Jn 6:31 having·been·written, "He·gave them bread from·
Jn 12:49 sending me), he·himself gave me a·commandment
Jn 18:22 ·the assistants standing·nearby gave a·slap to·Jesus,

Jn 19:9 are you·yourself?" But Jesus gave him no answer.
Lk 6:4 ·that·offer·sacrifices, and he·gave also to·the·ones
Lk 7:15 and began to·speak. And he·gave him to·his mother
Lk 9:1 his twelve disciples, he·gave them power and
Lk 10:35 casting·forth two denarii, he·gave *them* to·the
Lk 18:43 all the people seeing *it*, gave strong·praise to·God.
Lk 19:13 his ten slaves, he·gave ten more·silver·minas to·
Lk 19:15 (*each·one* to·whom he·gave the piece·of·silver), in·
Lk 22:19 *and* giving·thanks, he·broke *it* and gave *it* to·them,
Ac 3:16 (the·one through him) gave to·this·same·man this
Ac 5:32 whom God gave to·the·ones readily·complying
Ac 7:5 "But he·did·not give him an·inheritance in it, not·
Ac 7:8 "And he·gave to·him a·covenant of·circumcision.
Ac 7:10 his tribulations, and he·gave him influential·favor
Ac 10:40 on·the third day and gave him to·be manifest,
Ac 11:17 Now·then, since God gave to·them the equally·
Ac 12:23 him, because he·did·not give the glory to·God.
Ac 13:20 ·hundred and fifty years, he·gave *to·them* judges,
Ac 13:21 ·requested a·king, and God gave to·them Saul son
Heb 2:13 and the little·children which God gave to·me."
Heb 7:4 the patriarch AbRaham gave a·tenth from·among the
Mt 10:1 his twelve disciples, he·gave to·them authority *over*
Mt 14:19 after·breaking *bread*, he·gave the loaves·of·bread
Mt 15:36 he·broke *them* and gave *them* to·his disciples, and
Mt 21:23 ·do these·things? And who gave you this authority
Mt 25:15 And in·fact, to·one he·gave five talants·of·silver,
Mt 26:27 the cup and giving·thanks, he·gave *it* to·them,
Mt 26:48 But the·one handing him over gave them a·sign,
Mk 2:26 ·that·offer·sacrifices, and he·gave also to·the·ones
Mk 4:7 ·up and altogether·choked it, and it·gave no fruit.
Mk 6:28 head on a·platter, and he·gave it to·the young·girl,
Mk 6:28 ·girl, and the young·girl gave it to·her mother.
Mk 11:28 these·things? And who gave you this authority in·
Mk 14:22 *it*, Jesus broke *it* and gave *it* to·them, and he·
Mk 14:23 the cup *and* giving·thanks, he·gave *it* to·them.
Rm 11:8 GOD gave them a·spirit of·a·stinging·numbness
Jac 5:18 And he·prayed again, and the sky gave rain, and the
Tit 2:14 who gave himself on·our behalf in·order·that 'he·
1Co 3:5 yeu·trusted, even as the Lord gave to·each·man?
2Co 9:9 dispersed; he·gave to·the working·poor·in·need; his
2Co 10:8 authority, which the Lord gave us for edification
2Co 13:10 authority which the Lord gave me to edification
Eph 1:22 *things* under his feet' and gave him *to·be* head over
Eph 4:8 ·captured war·captivity·*itself*, and gave gifts to·the
2Ti 1:7 For God did·not give us a·spirit of·timidity, but·
1Jn 3:23 ·love one·another, just·as he·already·gave us *this*
1Jn 3:24 ·a·result of·the Spirit whom he·already·gave to·us.
1Jn 5:11 the testimony, that God gave to·us eternal life-above
Rv 1:1 of·Jesus Anointed, which God gave to·him, to·show
Rv 13:2 And the Dragon gave it his power, and his throne,
Rv 13:4 ·*before* the Dragon which gave authority to·the
Rv 15:7 from·among the four living·beings gave to·the seven
Rv 17:17 "For God gave in their hearts to·do his plan, and

G1325.1 V-AAI-3P ἔδωκαν (6x)

Gal 2:9 the·ones seeming to·be pillars, they·gave to·me and
Mt 27:10 and they·gave *the* same *pieces·of·silver* for the
Mt 27:34 they·gave him wine·vinegar to·drink having·been·
Mt 28:12 they·gave a·significant·sum of money to·the
2Co 8:5 but·rather first they·gave their·own·selves to·the
Rv 11:13 the rest became alarmed and gave glory to·the God

G1325.1 V-2AAM-2S δός (14x)

Jn 4:7 Jesus says to·her, "Give me *some* to·drink,"
Jn 4:10 is the·one saying to·you, 'Give me *some* to·drink,'
Jn 4:15 says to him, "Sir, give me this water, in·order·that
Jn 6:34 "Lord, always give us this bread.
Jn 9:24 and they·declared to·him, "Give God glory. We·
Lk 12:58 legal·adversary to a·magistrate, give effort on the
Lk 14:9 ·coming shall·declare to·you, 'Give this·man place,
Lk 15:12 father, 'Father, give me the portion of·substance
Mt 6:11 'Give us this·day our sustaining bread.
Mt 14:8 her mother, she·replied, "Give me here the head of·
Mt 17:27 Taking·hold·of that, give *it* to·them for me and
Mt 19:21 sell your holdings and give to·*the* helplessly·poor,
Mk 10:21 ·as you·have, and give to·the helplessly·poor, and
Rv 10:9 saying to·him, "Give to·me the tiny·official·scroll.

G1325.1 V-2AAM-2P δότε (14x)

Lk 9:13 them, "Yeu·yeurselves give them *something* to·eat.
Lk 11:41 Moreover, yeu·give a·merciful·act·of·charity, one·
Lk 12:33 yeur holdings and give a·merciful·act·of·charity.
Lk 15:22 and dress him. And give *him* a·ring for his hand
Lk 19:24 mina from him, and give *it* to·the·one having the
Ac 8:19 saying, "Give me·also this authority, in·order·that
Mt 10:8 freely·without·charge; give freely·without·charge.
Mt 14:16 to·go·off; yeu·yeurselves give them *something* to·
Mt 25:8 to·the prudent, 'Give to·us from·out·of·yeur oil,
Mt 25:28 the talant·of·silver from him and give *it* to·the·one
Mk 6:37 to·them, "Yeu·yeurselves give them *something* to·
Rm 12:19 ·beloved, but·rather yeu·must·give place to·the
Rv 14:7 "Fear God and give glory to·him, because the hour
Rv 18:7 ·luxury, give to·her such·a·vast·quantity·of torment

G1325.1 V-2AAM-3S δότω (1x)

Mt 5:31 should·divorce his wife must·give her *a·document·of*

G1325.1 V-2AAN δοῦναι (29x)

Jn 6:52 "How·is this·man able to·give us the flesh to·eat?
Lk 1:77 to·give knowledge of·Salvation to·his People unto a·
Lk 2:24 and to·give a·sacrifice according·to the·thing
Lk 11:7 the bed; I·am·not able to·rise·up and·give to·you.'
Lk 12:32 because yeur Father takes·delight to·give yeu the
Lk 12:51 ·yeu·suppose that I·came·directly to·give peace on
Lk 17:18 ·are·not found returning·back to·give glory to·God,
Lk 20:22 Is·it·proper for·us to·give tribute to·Caesar or not?
Lk 22:5 and agreed·among·themselves to·give him money.
Ac 7:5 step, and·yet he·already·promised to·give it to·him
Ac 7:38 who accepted living eloquent·words to·give to·us—
Ac 19:31 they·were·imploring *him* not to·give himself into
Ac 20:32 to·build·yeu·up, and to·give yeu an·inheritance
Mt 14:7 with an·oath, he·affirmed to·give her whatever
Mt 19:7 why·did Moses command *us* to·give *her* a·document
Mt 20:14 'But I·want to·give to·this last·one, even as *I·gave*
Mt 20:23 left is·not mine to·give, but·rather *it·shall·be·given*
Mt 20:28 but·rather to·attend, and to·give his soul *to·be* a·
Mt 22:17 Is·it·proper to·give a·census·tribute to·Caesar or
Mt 26:15 declared, "What·do yeu·want to·give to·me?
Mk 10:40 left is·not mine to·give, but·rather *it·shall·be·given*
Mk 10:45 but·rather to·attend, and to·give his soul *to·be* a·
Mk 12:14 Is·it·proper to·give a·census·tribute to·Caesar or
Mk 14:11 ·were·glad and promised to·give money to·him.
Rv 11:18 and·also *for·you* to·give the payment·of·service
Rv 13:15 And it·was·given to·it to·give breath to·the
Rv 16:9 And they·did·not repent *as* to·give him glory.
Rv 16:19 ·to·mind in·the·sight of·God, to·give to·her the
Rv 17:17 ·do *just* one plan, also to·give their kingdom to·the

G1325.1 V-2AAO-3S δῴη (4x)

2Th 3:16 may the Lord of·Peace himself grant yeu Peace
Eph 1:17 the Father of·Glory, may·give to·yeu a·spirit of·
2Ti 1:16 May the Lord give mercy to·*the*·house of·
2Ti 2:7 For may the Lord give to·you comprehension in all·

G1325.1 V-2AAP-ASM δόντα (3x)

Mt 9:8 they·glorified God, the·one giving such authority to·
1Pe 1:21 him from·among dead·men and giving glory to·him
1Th 4:8 but·rather God, the·one also already·giving to us his

G1325.1 V-2AAP-GSM δόντος (2x)

Gal 1:4 the·one giving himself on·behalf of·our moral·
2Co 5:18 Jesus Anointed, and giving to·us the Service of·the

G1325.1 V-2AAP-NSM δούς (10x)

Lk 20:2 Or who is the·one giving you this authority?
Ac 9:41 And giving her a·hand, he·raised her up; and
Ac 15:8 ·heart, testified to·them, giving to·them the Holy
Mk 13:34 upon·leaving his home and giving authority to·his
Rm 4:20 ·enabled by·the trust, already·giving glory to·God
2Th 2:16 loving us, and already·giving *us* eternal consoling
1Co 12:24 ·together the Body, giving more·abundant honor
2Co 1:22 ·officially·sealing us and giving the earnest·deposit
2Co 5:5 *is* God, the·one also giving to·us the earnest·deposit
1Ti 2:6 the·one giving himself *as* a·substitutionary·ransom

G1325.1 V-2AAS-1P δῶμεν (7x)

Jn 1:22 In·order·that we·may·give an·answer to·the·ones
Mk 6:37 *worth* of·bread, and should·we·give *it* to·them to·
Mk 12:15 Should·we·give, or should·we·not give?
Mk 12:15 Should·we·give, or should·we·not give?" But
2Th 3:9 but·rather that we·should·give ourselves *to·be* a·
1Co 9:12 ·bear all·things, lest we·should·give any hindrance
Rv 19:7 should·leap·for·joy, and should·give glory to·him,

G1325.1 V-2AAS-2S δῷς (1x)

Mk 6:25 ·want that you·should·give me from·this·same·hour

G1325.1 V-2AAS-2P δῶτε (3x)

Mt 7:6 "Yeu·should·not give the·thing *which·is* holy to·the
Jac 2:16 but should·not give to·them the requisite·needs
1Co 14:9 unless yeu·should·give a·clearly·discernible word,

G1325.1 V-2AAS-3S δῷ (6x)

Jn 13:29 ·Feast," or that he·should·give something to·the
Jn 15:16 ·of the Father in my name, he·may·give *it* to·yeu.
1Co 14:7 or harp, if it·should·not give a·distinction in·the
1Co 14:8 if·ever a·trumpet should·give an·indistinct sound,
Eph 4:29 in·order·that it·may·give grace to·the·ones
2Ti 2:25 — if·perhaps God should·give to·them repentance

G1325.1 V-AAS-3S δώσῃ (3x)

Jn 17:2 flesh, in·order·that he·may·give eternal life-above to
Rv 8:3 incense, in·order·that he·should·give *it* with·the
Rv 13:16 ·that to·them they·should·be·given an·etching on

G1325.1 V-2AAS-3P δῶσιν (1x)

Lk 20:10 ·farmers in·order·that they·should·give him of the

G1325.1 V-API-3S ἐδόθη (29x)

Jn 1:17 Because the Torah-Law was·given through Moses,
Jn 12:5 ·hundred denarii and given to·the·helplessly·poor?
Lk 12:48 to·anyone to·whom much is·given, personally·from
Gal 3:21 being·able to·give·life-above was·already·given, the
Mt 14:11 on a·platter and was·given to·the young·girl, and
Mt 28:18 saying, "All authority is·given to·me in heaven
2Co 12:7 revelations, there·was·given to·me a·burly·thorn
Eph 3:8 of·all holy·ones, this grace was·given: to·proclaim
Eph 4:7 But the Grace is·given to·each one of·us according·
1Ti 4:14 in you, which was·given to·you through prophecy,
Rv 6:2 a·bow. And a·victor's·crown was·given to·him, and
Rv 6:4 *that·was* fiery·red. And it·was·given to·him, to·the·
Rv 6:4 one·another. And there·was·given to·him a·great
Rv 6:8 with him. And authority was·given to·them over the
Rv 7:2 angels, to·whom it was·given to·bring·harm·to the
Rv 8:3 ·for·frankincense; and there·was·given to·him much
Rv 9:1 the earth. And to·him was·given the key of·the well
Rv 9:3 the earth, and authority was·given to·them, as the
Rv 9:5 And to·them it·was·given that they·should·not kill
Rv 11:1 And he·gave to·me a·reed like a·rod, saying,
Rv 11:2 ·not measure it, because it·is·given to·the Gentiles.
Rv 13:5 And there·was·given to·it a·mouth speaking great·
Rv 13:5 revilements. And authority was·given to·it to·do
Rv 13:7 And it·was·given to·it 'to·make war with the holy·
Rv 13:7 ' And authority was·given to·it over all tribes, and
Rv 13:14 ·signs which it was·given to·do in·the·sight of·the
Rv 13:15 And it·was·given to·it to·give breath to·the
Rv 16:8 upon the sun, and it·was·given to·him to·burn the
Rv 20:4 upon them, and judgment was·given to·them— and

G1325.1 V-API-3P ἐδόθησαν (3x)

Rv 6:11 white long·robes were·given to·each·one·of·them,
Rv 8:2 of·God; and to·them were·given seven trumpets.
Rv 12:14 of·the great eagle were·given that she·may·fly into

G1325.1 V-APN δοθῆναι (5x)

Lk 8:55 ·assigned·for *something* to·be·given to·her to·eat.
Mt 14:9 he·commandingly·ordered *for·it* to·be·given *her*.
Mt 26:9 for·much, and to·be·given to·*the*·helplessly·poor."
Mk 5:43 and declared *for·something* to·be·given to·her to·eat
Mk 14:5 denarii and to·be·given to·the helplessly·poor·ones

G1325.1 V-APO-3S δοθείη (1x)

Eph 6:19 ·*penetrating* Redemptive-word may·be·given to·me,

G1325.1 V-APP-ASF δοθεῖσαν (8x)

Gal 2:9 so·then after·knowing the grace being·given to·me,
Rm 12:6 according·to the grace being·given to·us, *we·must·*
Rm 15:15 on·account·of the grace being·given to·me by
2Pe 3:15 ·yeu (according·to the wisdom being·given to·him).

1Co 3:10 the grace of·God, the·one being·given to·me, as a·
Eph 3:7 of·God, the·one being·given to·me according·to the
Col 1:25 of·God, the·one being·given to·me for yeu, to·
2Ti 1:9 and grace, the·one already·being·given to·us in *the*
G1325.1 V-APP-DSF δοθείσῃ (1x)
1Co 1:4 grace of·God, the·one already·being·given to·yeu in
G1325.1 V-APP-GSN δοθέντος (1x)
Rm 5:5 Holy Spirit, the·one already·being·given to·us.
G1325.1 V-APP-GSF δοθείσης (2x)
Rm 12:3 For through the grace being·given to·me, I·say to·
Eph 3:2 grace of·God, the·one being·given to·me for yeu:
G1325.1 V-APP-NSF δοθεῖσα (1x)
Mk 6:2 *is* the wisdom, the·one being·given to·him, that even
G1325.1 V-APS-3S δοθῇ (2x)
Gal 3:22 the promise may·be·given to·the·ones trusting.
Mk 13:11 but·rather whatever should·be·given to·yeu in
G1325.1 V-RAI-1S δέδωκα (4x)
Jn 17:8 because I·have·given to·them the utterances which
Jn 17:14 "I·myself have·given them your Redemptive-word,
Jn 17:22 ·have·given to·me I·myself have·given to·them—
Rv 3:8 of·you, I·have·given a·door having·been·opened·up,
G1325.1 V-RAI-2S δέδωκας (12x)
Jn 17:2 eternal life-above to all whom you·have·given to·him.
Jn 17:4 which *likewise* you·have·given to·me in·order·that
Jn 17:6 ·of·clay† whom you·have·given to·me from·among
Jn 17:6 They·were yours, and you·have·given them to·me,
Jn 17:7 that all·things, as·much·as you·have·given to·me,
Jn 17:8 to·them the utterances which you·have·given to·me,
Jn 17:9 concerning those·whom you·have·given to·me,
Jn 17:11 your·own name these whom you·have·given to·me,
Jn 17:12 "I·vigilantly·kept those·that you·have·given to·me,
Jn 17:22 the glory which you·have·given to·me I·myself
Jn 17:24 "Father, those·whom you·have·given to·me, I·want
Jn 18:9 "From·among them whom you·have·given to·me, I·
G1325.1 V-RAI-3S δέδωκεν (12x)
Jn 3:35 Father loves the Son and has·given all·things into his
Jn 5:22 not·even·one·man, but·rather he·has·given all the
Jn 6:32 I·say to·yeu, Moses has·not given yeu the bread
Jn 6:39 any *sheep* which he·has·given me from·among it
Jn 7:19 "¿!·Has·not Moses given yeu the Torah-Law?
Jn 7:22 "On·account·of that Moses has·given to·yeu the
Jn 10:29 "My Father, who has·given *them* to·me, is greater·
Jn 13:3 ·seen that the Father has·given all·things to·him,
Jn 18:11 The cup which the Father has·given me, no, ¿!·
1Jn 3:1 what·manner·of love the Father has·given to·us, that
1Jn 4:13 in us, because he·has·given to·us from·out·of·his
1Jn 5:20 ·God comes, and he·has·given to·us utmost·insight
G1325.1 V-RPI-3S δέδοται (6x)
Lk 8:10 he·declared, "To·yeu it·has·been·given to·know the
Mt 13:11 ·them, "Because it·has·been·given to·yeu to·know
Mt 13:11 ·the heavens, but·to·them, it·has·not been·given.
Mt 19:11 but·rather those·to·whom it·has·been·given.
Mk 4:11 ·saying to·them, "It·has·been·given to·yeu to·know
1Co 11:15 instead·of·a·mantle, has·been·given to·her.
G1325.1 V-RPP-ASF δεδομένην (1x)
2Co 8:1 grace of·God, the·one having·been·given unto the
G1325.1 V-RPP-NSN δεδομένον (4x)
Jn 3:27 unless it·may·be having·been·given to·him from·out
Jn 6:65 it·should·be having·been·given to·him birthed·from·
Jn 19:11 *that* it·was having·been·given to·you from·above.
Ac 4:12 under the heaven having·been·given among the
G1325.1 V-LAI-3S-ATT δεδώκει (1x)
Mk 14:44 him over had·given them a·prearranged·signal,
G1325.1 V-LAI-3P-ATT δεδώκεισαν (1x)
Jn 11:57 and the Pharisees had·given a·commandment, that
EG1325.1 (8x)
Jn 7:39 for Holy Spirit was not·yet *given*, because Jesus was·
Ac 11:17 voluntary·present (as also *he·gave* to·us *who·are*
Ac 15:8 to·them the Holy Spirit, even just·as *he·gave* to·us;
Mt 14:19 and the disciples *gave bread* to·the crowds.
Mt 15:36 ·his disciples, and the disciples *gave* to·the crowd.
Mt 20:14 to·give to·this last·one, even as *I·gave* to·you.
Mt 20:23 but·rather *it·shall·be·given to·them* for·whom it·
Mk 10:40 but·rather *it·shall·be·given to·them* for·whom it·
G1325.2 V-FAI-1S δώσω (1x)
Rv 3:21 the·one overcoming, I·shall·grant *for·him* to·sit
G1325.2 V-PAP-DSM διδόντι (1x)
Ac 14:3 of·his grace and granting miraculous·signs and
G1325.2 V-AAI-3S ἔδωκεν (1x)
Ac 11:18 to·the Gentiles, God granted the repentance unto
G1325.2 V-2AAM-2S δός (2x)
Ac 4:29 ·of their threatenings, and grant·to your slaves *the*
Mk 10:37 they·declared to·him, "Grant to·us that we·may·
G1325.2 V-2AAN δοῦναι (2x)
Lk 1:74 to·grant to·us (after·being·snatched out·of·*the*·hand
Ac 5:31 ·his·own right·hand, to·grant repentance to·IsraEl
G1325.2 V-2AAO-3S δῴη (3x)
Rm 15:5 ·endurance and of·the comfort grant to·yeu the
Eph 3:16 of·his glory, he·may·grant yeu to·be·made·mighty
2Ti 1:18 May the Lord grant to·him to·find mercy
G1325.2 V-API-3S ἐδόθη (1x)
Rv 19:8 to·her was·granted that she·should·be·arrayed·with
EG1325.2 (1x)
Lk 1:43 And from·what·source *is* this *granted* to·me, that the
G1325.3 V-FAI-3S δώσει (2x)
Mt 24:29 and the moon shall·not give·forth her brightness,
Mk 13:24 and the moon shall·not give·forth her brightness,
G1325.3 V-PAI-1S δίδωμι (1x)
Rv 3:9 'Behold, I·give·forth *those* from·among the
G1325.3 V-AAI-3S ἔδωκεν (2x)
Eph 4:11 in·fact, *is the·one who* gave·forth the ambassadors
Rv 20:13 And the Sea gave·forth the dead·ones in her, and
G1325.3 V-AAI-3P ἔδωκαν (2x)
Ac 1:26 And they·gave·forth their lots, and the lot fell upon
Rv 20:13 and Death and Hades gave·forth the dead·ones in

G1326 δι•εγείρω diêgêírō *v.* (7x)
Roots:G1223 G1453 Compare:G1825
G1326.1 V-PAI-1S διεγείρω (1x)
2Pe 3:1 to·yeu, in which I·thoroughly·awaken yeur sincere
G1326.1 V-PAI-3P διεγείρουσιν (1x)
Mk 4:38 the pillow. And they·thoroughly·awaken him and
G1326.1 V-PAN διεγείρειν (1x)
2Pe 1:13 bodily·tabernacle, to·thoroughly·awaken yeu with
G1326.1 V-AAI-3P διήγειραν (1x)
Lk 8:24 ·alongside *him*, they·thoroughly·awakened him,
G1326.1 V-APP-NSM διεγερθείς (2x)
Mt 1:24 Joseph, after·being·thoroughly·awakened from the
Mk 4:39 Then already·being·thoroughly·awakened, he·
G1326.2 V-IPI-3S διηγείρετο (1x)
Jn 6:18 Also, the sea was·thoroughly·roused *due·to* a·great

G1327 δι•έξοδος diéxôdôs *n.* (1x)
Roots:G1223 G1841
G1327.1 N-APF διεξόδους (1x)
Mt 22:9 yeu·traverse to the exit·areas of·the roadways, and

G1328 δι•ερμηνευτής diêrmēnêutḗs *n.* (1x)
Roots:G1329
G1328 N-NSM διερμηνευτής (1x)
1Co 14:28 be one·who·thoroughly·translates, he·must·stay·

G1329 δι•ερμηνεύω diêrmēnêúō *v.* (6x)
Roots:G1223 G2059 Compare:G1956 G3177
See:G1328
G1329.1 V-PAI-3P διερμηνεύουσιν (1x)
1Co 12:30 ·bestowed·tongues. Not all thoroughly·translate.
G1329.1 V-PAM-3S διερμηνευέτω (1x)
1Co 14:27 apiece, and one must·thoroughly·translate.
G1329.1 V-PAS-3S διερμηνεύῃ (2x)
1Co 14:5 excluding·that he·should·thoroughly·translate in·
1Co 14:13 must·pray that he·may·thoroughly·translate.
G1329.2 V-PPP-NSF διερμηνευομένη (1x)
Ac 9:36 who (by·thorough·translation *from·Hebrew*) is·
G1329.3 V-IAI-3S διηρμήνευεν (1x)
Lk 24:27 all the prophets, he·was·expounding to·them in all

G1330 δι•έρχομαι diérchômai *v.* (42x)
Roots:G1223 G2064 Compare:G1224 G1353
G1330.1 V-FDI-3S διελεύσεται (1x)
Lk 2:35 (and a·straight·sword shall·go·through your own
G1330.1 V-INI-3S διήρχετο (1x)
Lk 19:1 And entering, *Jesus* went·through Jericho.
G1330.1 V-2AAI-3S διῆλθεν (1x)
Rm 5:12 also in·this·manner Death went·through into all
G1330.1 V-2AAN διελθεῖν (2x)
Ac 9:38 *him* not to·amble·along in·going·through to them.
Ac 18:27 with·him being·resolved to·go·through into Achaia
G1330.1 V-2AAP-NPM διελθόντες (1x)
Ac 12:10 And going·through a·first and second watch-station
G1330.1 V-2AAS-1P διέλθωμεν (3x)
Lk 2:15 Now·then, we·should·go·through unto BethLechem,
Lk 8:22 to them, "We·should·go·through to the other·side
Mk 4:35 he·says to·them, "We·should·go·through to the
G1330.1 V-2RAP-ASM διεληλυθότα (1x)
Heb 4:14 High·Priest, having·gone·through the heavens,
G1330.2 V-PNI-1S διέρχομαι (1x)
1Co 16:5 Macedonia, for I·am·to·go·throughout Macedonia.
G1330.2 V-PNP-NSM διερχόμενος (3x)
Ac 8:40 ·found in Ashdod, and going·throughout *the region*,
Ac 17:23 For going·throughout and observing·again yeur
Ac 18:23 time, he·went·forth, going·throughout *the* country
G1330.2 V-INI-3S διήρχετο (2x)
Lk 5:15 the word went·throughout even·more concerning
Ac 15:41 And he·went·throughout Syria and Cilicia,
G1330.2 V-INI-3P διήρχοντο (2x)
Lk 9:6 And going·forth, they·went·throughout each·of the
Ac 15:3 they·were·going·throughout Phoenicia and
G1330.2 V-2AAI-1S διῆλθον (1x)
Ac 20:25 whom I·went·throughout officially·proclaiming the
G1330.2 V-2AAI-3S διῆλθον (3x)
Ac 8:4 the·ones being·dispersed went·throughout *the regions*
Ac 10:38 ·same who went·throughout doing·good·deeds and
Ac 11:19 Stephen, went·throughout as·far·as·to Phoenicia,
G1330.2 V-2AAN διελθεῖν (1x)
Ac 11:22 BarNabas to·go·throughout as·far·as·to Antioch,
G1330.2 V-2AAP-ASM διελθόντα (1x)
Ac 19:1 *that* Paul, after·going·throughout the uppermost
G1330.2 V-2AAP-NSM διελθών (2x)
Ac 19:21 spirit, *that* after·going·throughout Macedonia and
Ac 20:2 And after·going·throughout those parts and
G1330.2 V-2AAP-NPM διελθόντες (4x)
Ac 13:6 And going·throughout the island, even·as·far·as
Ac 13:14 ·themselves, after·going·throughout from Perga,
Ac 14:24 And going·throughout Pisidia, they·came to
Ac 16:6 But going·throughout Phrygia and the country of·
G1330.2 V-2AAS-1S διέλθω (1x)
1Co 16:5 yeu, whenever I·should·go·throughout Macedonia,
G1330.3 V-PNI-3S διέρχεται (2x)
Lk 11:24 from the man·of·clay†, it·goes through waterless
Mt 12:43 from the man·of·clay†, it·goes through waterless
G1330.3 V-PNN διέρχεσθαι (2x)
Jn 4:4 And it·was·necessary·for him to·go through Samaria.
Lk 19:4 because *Jesus* was·about to·go through that *way*.
G1330.3 V-PNP-ASM διερχόμενον (1x)
Ac 9:32 And while·going throughout all *the regions*, it·
G1330.3 V-INI-3S διήρχετο (1x)
Lk 17:11 it·happened that he·himself went through *the*
G1330.3 V-2AAI-3S διῆλθον (1x)
1Co 10:1 were under the cloud, and all went through the sea,
G1330.3 V-2AAN διελθεῖν (2x)
Mt 19:24 it·is easier *for* a·camel to·go through *the* tiny·hole
2Co 1:16 and to·go through yeu into Macedonia, and to·
G1330.3 V-2AAP-NSM διελθών (2x)
Jn 8:59 from·out·of·the Sanctuary·Atrium going through *the*
Lk 4:30 But he·himself, after·going through *the* midst of·

G1331 δι•ερωτάω diêrōtáō *v.* (1x)
Roots:G1223 G2065
G1331 V-AAP-NPM διερωτήσαντες (1x)
Ac 10:17 , after·making·a·thorough·inquiry for·Simon's

G1332 δι•ετής diêtḗs *adj.* (1x)
Roots:G1364 G2094
G1332 A-GSM διετοῦς (1x)
Mt 2:16 borders, from two·years·of·age and below,

G1333 δι•ετία diêtía *n.* (2x)
Roots:G1332
G1333 N-ASF διετίαν (1x)
Ac 28:30 And Paul abided a·whole two·years in his·own
G1333 N-GSF διετίας (1x)
Ac 24:27 But having·completely·fulfilled two·years, Porcius

G1334 δι•ηγέομαι diēgḗômai *v.* (8x)
Roots:G1223 G2233
G1334.1 V-FDI-3S διηγήσεται (1x)
Ac 8:33 And who shall·give·an·account of·his own·offspring
G1334.1 V-PNM-2S διηγοῦ (1x)
Lk 8:39 and give·an·account·of what·many·things God did
G1334.1 V-PNP-ASM διηγούμενον (1x)
Heb 11:32 ·for me in·giving·an·account concerning Gideon,
G1334.1 V-ADI-3S διηγήσατο (2x)
Ac 9:27 the ambassadors and gave·an·account to·them how
Ac 12:17 to·stay·silent, he·gave·an·account to·them how the
G1334.1 V-ADI-3P διηγήσαντο (2x)
Lk 9:10 after·returning·back, gave·an·account to *Jesus*
Mk 5:16 the·ones seeing *it* gave·an·account to·them of·how
G1334.1 V-ADS-3P διηγήσωνται (1x)
Mk 9:9 that they·should·give·an·account not·even·to·one·

G1335 δι•ήγεσις diḗgêsis *n.* (2x)
Roots:G1334
G1335 N-ASF διήγησιν (1x)
Lk 1:1 to·fully·compose a·thorough·account concerning the
EG1335 (1x)
Lk 1:3 to·you *a·thorough·account* in·consecutive·order,

G1336 δι•ηνεκής diēnêkḗs *adj.* (4x)
Roots:G1223 G5342 Compare:G1275 G1734-1
See:G1519 G3588
xLangEquiv:H5703
G1336.3 A-ASN διηνεκές (4x)
Heb 7:3 ·abides a·priest·that·offers·a·sacrifice into perpetuity.
Heb 10:1 year into perpetuity) to·make·completely·mature
Heb 10:12 ·behalf of·moral·failures into perpetuity, sat·down
Heb 10:14 into perpetuity the·ones being·made·holy.

G1337 δι•θάλασσος dithálassôs *adj.* (1x)
Roots:G1364 G2281
G1337.2 A-ASM διθάλασσον (1x)
Ac 27:41 a·place where·two·seas·met *producing·a·broad*

G1338 δι•ϊκνέομαι diïknḗômai *v.* (2x)
Roots:G1223 G2425 Compare:G1574 G4044
See:G2185 G0864
G1338.2 V-PNP-NSM διϊκνούμενος (1x)
Heb 4:12 thoroughly·penetrating even·unto a·dividing of·
EG1338.2 (1x)
Eph 6:19 ·my behalf in·order·that *a·thoroughly·penetrating*

G1339 δι•ΐστημι diḯstēmi *v.* (3x)
Roots:G1223 G2476 Compare:G0565 G0548
See:G1292
G1339.2 V-AAP-NPM διαστήσαντες (1x)
Ac 27:28 fathoms; and after·waiting a·short·while and
G1339.3 V-2AAP-GSF διαστάσης (1x)
Lk 22:59 And with·an·interval·of about one hour, someone
G1339.5 V-2AAI-3S διέστη (1x)
Lk 24:51 blessing them, *that* he·stepped·away from them

G1340 δι•ϊσχυρίζομαι diïschyrízômai *v.* (2x)
Roots:G1223 G2478
G1340 V-INI-3S διϊσχυρίζετο (2x)
Lk 22:59 hour, someone else was·strongly·asserting, saying,
Ac 12:15 ·mad!" But she·was·strongly·asserting *for·it* to·be

G1341 δικαιο•κρισία dikaiôkrisía *n.* (1x)
Roots:G1342 G2920 Compare:G2917 See:G1345
G1341 N-GSF δικαιοκρισίας (1x)
Rm 2:5 and of·*the*·revelation of·God's righteous·verdict,

G1342 δίκαιος díkaiôs *adj.* (82x)
Roots:G1349 Compare:G3741 G0040 G0172 G2413
See:G1344
xLangEquiv:H6662
EG1342 (1x)
2Co 9:9 ·written, "*The·righteous·man* dispersed; he·gave
G1342.2 A-NSM δίκαιος (20x)
Lk 2:25 the·same man·of·clay† *was* righteous and devout,
Lk 23:47 "Really, this man·of·clay† was a·righteous·man."
Lk 23:50 ·being a·beneficially·good man and righteous.
Ac 10:22 a·righteous man who·is·reverently·fearing God
Heb 10:38 But the righteous·man shall·live as·a·result of·
Heb 11:4 which he·was·attested to·be righteous, with·God
Gal 3:11 because "the righteous·one shall·live as·a·result
Mt 1:19 Joseph her husband, being a·righteous *man* and not
Rm 1:17 "But the righteous·man shall·live as·a·result of·
Rm 3:10 ·written: "There·is none righteous," "not·even
1Pe 3:18 a·righteous·one on·behalf of·unrighteous·ones, in·
1Pe 4:18 And " If the righteous·man scarcely is·saved,
2Pe 2:8 *these deeds*, the righteous·man residing among them
2Ti 4:8 the Lord, the righteous judge, shall·yield·forth to·me
1Jn 1:9 ·is trustworthy and righteous that he·should·forgive
1Jn 2:29 ·should·personally·know that he·is righteous, *then*
1Jn 3:7 doing the righteousness is righteous, just·as that·one
1Jn 3:7 is righteous, just·as that·one is righteous.
Rv 16:5 waters saying, "You·are righteous, O·Yahweh, the·
Rv 22:11 *being* righteous, let·him·be·regarded·as·righteous
G1342.2 A-NSF δικαία (2x)
Jn 5:30 And my verdict is righteous, because I·do·not seek
Rm 7:12 *is* holy, righteous, and beneficially·good.
G1342.2 A-NSN δίκαιον (3x)
Mt 23:35 may·come all *the* righteous blood being·poured·out
2Pe 2:7 and *if* he·rescued righteous Lot being·worn·down·in·
2Th 1:6 (since *it·is* a·righteous·thing with God to·
G1342.2 A-NPM δίκαιοι (9x)
Lk 1:6 And they·were both righteous in·the·sight of·God,
Lk 18:9 in themselves that they·are righteous, and utterly·
Mt 13:17 many prophets and righteous·men longed to·see
Mt 13:43 Then the righteous shall·brilliantly·radiate·forth as
Mt 23:28 outwardly appear righteous to·the men·of·clay†,
Mt 25:37 "Then the righteous shall·answer him, saying,
Mt 25:46 ·punishment, but the righteous into life·above
Rm 2:13 *that·are* righteous personally·before God, but·rather
Rm 5:19 the many shall·be·fully·established *as* righteous.
G1342.2 A-NPF δίκαιαι (3x)
Rv 15:3 O·Yahweh, God Almighty. Righteous and true *are*
Rv 16:7 God Almighty, true and righteous *are* your verdicts.
Rv 19:2 Because true and righteous *are* his verdicts; because
G1342.2 A-NPN δίκαια (2x)
Php 4:8 as·many·things·as *are* righteous, as·many·things·as
1Jn 3:12 evil, and the·ones of·his brother *were* righteous.
G1342.2 A-VSM δίκαιε (1x)
Jn 17:25 "O·Righteous Father, the world did·not know you,
G1342.2 A-ASM δίκαιον (8x)
Ac 3:14 denied the Holy and Righteous·One, and requested
Ac 22:14 will, and to·see the Righteous·One, and to·hear *his*
Mt 10:41 accepting a·righteous·man in a·righteous·man's
Mk 6:20 having·seen *that* he was·a·righteous and holy man,
Rm 3:26 toward the·one himself being righteous, *which·is*
Jac 5:6 ·guilty *and* murdered the Righteous·One, *yet* he·
Tit 1:8 ·good, self-controlled, righteous, divinely·holy,
1Jn 2:1 the Father, Jesus Anointed, *the* righteous·one.
G1342.2 A-ASF δικαίαν (2x)
Jn 7:24 ·appearance, but·rather judge the righteous verdict."
2Pe 2:8 by day was·tormenting *his* righteous soul *over their*
G1342.2 A-APM δικαίους (6x)
Lk 5:32 I·have·not come to·call righteous·men, but·rather
Lk 20:20 to·be righteous·men in·order·that they·may·grab·
Mt 5:45 ·rain on righteous·ones and unrighteous·ones.
Mt 9:13 For I·did·not come to·call righteous·ones, but·rather
Mk 2:17 I·did·not come to·call righteous·men, but·rather
1Pe 3:12 eyes of·Yahweh *are* upon righteous·men, and his
G1342.2 A-DSM δικαίῳ (2x)
Mt 27:19 "Have·nothing·to·do with that righteous·man, for
1Ti 1:9 that Torah-Law is·not laid·out for·a·righteous·man,
G1342.2 A-DPM δικαίοις (1x)
Lk 15:7 ·than over ninety-nine righteous·men who have no
G1342.2 A-GSM δικαίου (7x)
Ac 7:52 concerning the coming of·the Righteous·One, now
Mt 10:41 ·man in a·righteous·man's name shall·receive a·
Mt 10:41 shall·receive a·righteous·man's payment·of·service
Mt 23:35 from the blood of·Abel the righteous, unto the
Mt 27:24 of the blood of·this righteous·man. Yeu·yeurselves
Rm 5:7 For scarcely over a·righteous·man shall anyone die,
Jac 5:16 A·petition of·a·righteous·man is·itself·operating *to*
G1342.2 A-GSF δικαίας (1x)
2Th 1:5 *This·is* an·indication of·the righteous verdict of·God,
G1342.2 A-GPM δικαίων (6x)
Lk 1:17 thoughtful·insight of·the·righteous·ones— to·make·
Lk 14:14 ·recompensed at the resurrection of·the righteous."
Ac 24:15 both of·righteous·ones and unrighteous·ones.
Heb 12:23 to·spirits of·righteous·men having·been·made·,
Mt 13:49 ·ones from·out of·*the*·midst of·the righteous·ones,
Mt 23:29 and decorate the chamber·tombs of·the righteous,
G1342.3 A-NSN δίκαιον (3x)
Ac 4:19 "Whether it·is right in·the·sight of·God to·listen·to
Php 1:7 just·as it·is right for·me to·contemplate this on·
Eph 6:1 ·and·obey yeur parents in *the* Lord, for this is right.
G1342.3 A-ASN δίκαιον (5x)
Lk 12:57 Now, why·do yeu·not judge what·is·right even by
Mt 20:4 and whatever may·be right I·shall·give to·yeu.'
Mt 20:7 and whatever may·be right, *that* yeu·shall·receive.
2Pe 1:13 And I·do·resolutely·consider·it right, for as·long·as
Col 4:1 ·personally·furnish to·the slaves the right and the

G1343 δικαιοσύνη dikaiôsýnē *n.* (96x)
Roots:G1342 Compare:G2118 See:G1345
xLangAlso:H6664
G1343.2 N-NSF δικαιοσύνη (12x)
Gal 2:21 of·God, for if righteousness *is* through Torah-Law,
Gal 3:21 was·already·given, the righteousness really would
Mt 5:20 unless yeur righteousness should·abound more·than
Rm 1:17 For in this, God's righteousness is·revealed, birthed·
Rm 3:21 ·fact, God's righteousness apart·from Torah-Law
Rm 3:22 And God's righteousness through trust of·Jesus
Rm 10:6 But righteousness, the·one birthed·from·out of·trust,
Rm 14:17 and drinking, but·rather righteousness, peace, and
2Pe 3:13 Earth,' in which righteousness resides.
1Co 1:30 from God, also righteousness, renewed·holiness,
2Co 5:21 ·ourselves may·become God's righteousness in him
2Co 9:9 ·poor·in·need; his righteousness remains into the
G1343.2 N-ASF δικαιοσύνην (35x)
Ac 10:35 and who·is·working righteousness is acceptable to·
Heb 1:9 You·loved righteousness and hated lawlessness.
Heb 11:33 kingdoms, worked righteousness, obtained
Gal 3:6 and it·was·reckoned to·him for righteousness."
Mt 3:15 ·for us to·completely·fulfill all righteousness." Then
Mt 5:6 hungering and thirsting·for the righteousness, because
Mt 6:33 the kingdom of·God and his righteousness, and all
Rm 3:5 unrighteousness commends God's righteousness—"
Rm 4:3 and it·was·reckoned to·him for righteousness."
Rm 4:5 ·righteous, his trust is·reckoned for righteousness—
Rm 4:6 ·whom God reckons righteousness apart·from works,
Rm 4:9 trust was·reckoned to·AbRaham for righteousness.'
Rm 4:11 in·order·for righteousness to·be·reckoned to·them
Rm 4:22 "it·was·reckoned to·him for righteousness."
Rm 6:16 death, or of·attentive·obedience to righteousness.
Rm 8:10 Now the Spirit *is* life·above through righteousness,
Rm 9:30 the·ones not pursuing righteousness, grasped
Rm 9:30 pursuing righteousness, grasped righteousness, the
Rm 9:30 the righteousness birthed·from·out of·trust.
Rm 10:3 For being·ignorant of·God's righteousness, and
Rm 10:3 to·establish their·own righteousness, they·did·not
Rm 10:4 ·Torah-Law for righteousness to·everyone trusting.
Rm 10:5 For Moses describes the righteousness, the·one
Rm 10:10 ·heart, one·is·convinced unto righteousness, and
Jac 1:20 wrath does·not accomplish God's righteousness.

Αα Ββ Γγ Δδ Εε Ζζ Ηη Θθ Ιι Κκ Λλ Μμ Νν Ξξ Οο Ππ Ρρ Σσ Ττ Υυ Φφ Χχ Ψψ Ωω

Jac 2:23 and it·was·reckoned to·him for righteousness.'" And
Php 3:6 ·Out·citizenry; according·to righteousness (the·one
Php 3:9 not having my·own righteousness (the·one from·
Php 3:9 ·Anointed-One (the righteousness from·out of·God
1Pe 3:14 ·suffer on·account·of righteousness, *yeu·are*
1Ti 6:11 and pursue righteousness, devout·reverence, trust,
2Ti 2:22 youthful longings, but pursue righteousness, trust,
1Jn 2:29 one doing the righteousness has·been·born from·out
1Jn 3:7 The·one doing the righteousness is righteous, just·as
1Jn 3:10 Every one not doing righteousness is not birthed·

G1343.2 N-DSF δικαιοσύνῃ (10x)
Lk 1:75 ·holiness and righteousness in·the·sight of·him, all
Ac 17:31 'to·judge The Land by righteousness' by *that* man
Rm 9:28 matter and cutting·*it*·short in righteousness, because
Rm 10:3 submit·themselves to·the righteousness of·God.
2Pe 1:1 trust with·us in *the* righteousness of·our God and
Tit 3:5 (of·the·ones in righteousness which we·ourselves did)
Eph 4:24 ·to God in righteousness and in·divine·holiness of·
Eph 5:9 all beneficial·goodness and righteousness and truth),
2Ti 3:16 education·and·discipline (the·one in righteousness),
Rv 19:11 True, and in righteousness he·judges and wages·

G1343.2 N-DSF-HEB δικαιοσύνῃ (1x)
2Co 6:14 participation has·righteousness with lawlessness?

G1343.2 N-GSF δικαιοσύνης (28x)
Jn 16:8 moral·failure, and concerning righteousness, and
Jn 16:10 and concerning righteousness, because I·head·on·
Ac 24:25 *matters* concerning righteousness, self-restraint,
Heb 5:13 with·*the*·Redemptive-word of·righteousness— for
Heb 11:7 an·heir of·a·righteousness according·to trust.
Heb 12:11 fruit of·righteousness for·the·ones having·been·
Gal 5:5 an·expectation of·righteousness as·a·result of·trust.
Mt 5:10 ·been·persecuted because·of righteousness, because
Mt 21:32 to yeu by way of·righteousness, yet yeu·did·not
Rm 3:25 an·indicator of·his righteousness on·account·of the
Rm 3:26 ·as an·indicator of·his righteousness in the present
Rm 4:11 an·official·seal of·the righteousness of·the trust—
Rm 4:13 , but·rather *is* through a·righteousness of·trust.
Rm 5:17 voluntary·present of·righteousness shall·reign in
Rm 5:21 Grace may·reign through righteousness to eternal
Rm 6:13 members *as* instruments of·righteousness to·God.
Rm 9:31 pursuing a·Torah-Law of·righteousness, did·not
Rm 9:31 already·attain to *the* Torah-Law of·righteousness.
Jac 3:18 And the fruit of·righteousness is·sown in peace by·
Php 1:11 ·filled of·*the*·fruits of·righteousness, of·the·ones
2Pe 2:5 an·official·proclaimer of·righteousness, after·
2Pe 2:21 to·have·recognized the way of·righteousness, than,
2Co 3:9 *does* the service of·the righteousness excel in glory.
2Co 6:7 weapons·and·armor of·righteousness on·the right·
2Co 9:10 ·grow the produce of·yeur righteousness,
2Co 11:15 ·disguised as attendants of·righteousness, whose
Eph 6:14 ·with the full·chest·armor of·righteousness,
2Ti 4:8 for·me the victor's·crown of·righteousness, which the

EG1343.2 (4x)
Rm 4:11 trust— the *righteousness reckoned while·still* in the
Rm 4:12 *that·is*, the *righteousness* in the uncircumcised
Rm 4:16 On·account·of that, *righteousness is* as·a·result of·
Rm 5:18 *the voluntary·present of·righteousness came* upon

G1343.3 N-DSF δικαιοσύνῃ (4x)
Rm 6:18 yeu·are·already·enslaved to·Righteousness.
Rm 6:19 *as* slaves to·Righteousness unto renewed·holiness.
Rm 6:20 yeu·were not·restrained by·Righteousness.
1Pe 2:24 ·the moral·failures) should·live to Righteousness, '

G1343.3 N-GSF δικαιοσύνης (2x)
Ac 13:10 O·Enemy of·all Righteousness, shall·you·not
Heb 7:2 *from·Hebrew as* "King of·Righteousness," and after·

G1344 δικαιόω dikaióō *v.* (40x)
Roots:G1342 Compare:G0121-1 See:G1347
xLangAlso:H5355

G1344.0 V-AAI-3P ἐδικαίωσαν (1x)
Lk 7:29 (even the tax·collectors) regarded God as·righteous.

G1344.1 V-FAI-3S δικαιώσει (1x)
Rm 3:30 ·*among both*, shall·regard *these* as·righteous: *the*

G1344.1 V-FPI-2S δικαιωθήσῃ (1x)
Mt 12:37 words, you·shall·be·regarded·as·righteous, and

G1344.1 V-FPI-3S δικαιωθήσεται (2x)
Gal 2:16 flesh shall·not be·regarded·as·righteous as·a·result
Rm 3:20 'there·shall·not be·regarded·as·righteous any flesh

G1344.1 V-FPI-3P δικαιωθήσονται (1x)
Rm 2:13 of·the Torah-Law shall·be·regarded·as·righteous.

G1344.1 V-PAI-3S δικαιοῖ (1x)
Gal 3:8 foreseeing that God regards·as·righteous the Gentiles

G1344.1 V-PAN δικαιοῦν (1x)
Lk 10:29 the·man, wanting to·regard himself as·righteous,

G1344.1 V-PAP-ASM δικαιοῦντα (2x)
Rm 3:26 *with·God* regarding·as·righteous the·one birthed·
Rm 4:5 on the·one regarding the irreverent as·righteous, his

G1344.1 V-PAP-NSM δικαιῶν (1x)
Rm 8:33 God *is* the·one regarding·as·righteous.

G1344.1 V-PAP-NPM δικαιοῦντες (1x)
Lk 16:15 yeur·own·selves as·righteous in·the·sight of·the

G1344.1 V-PPI-2P δικαιοῦσθε (1x)
Gal 5:4 *And* whoever·of·yeu are·regarded·as·righteous by

G1344.1 V-PPI-3S δικαιοῦται (3x)
Gal 2:16 is·not regarded·as·righteous as·a·result of·works
Gal 3:11 not·even·one is·regarded·as·righteous personally·
Jac 2:24 a·man·of·clay† is·regarded·as·righteous, and not

G1344.1 V-PPN δικαιοῦσθαι (1x)
Rm 3:28 *is* to·be·regarded·as·righteous by·a·trust apart·from

G1344.1 V-PPP-NPM δικαιούμενοι (1x)
Rm 3:24 *now* being·regarded·as·righteous as·a·free·present

G1344.1 V-AAI-3S ἐδικαίωσεν (2x)
Rm 8:30 ·forth, these also he·regarded·as·righteous; and
Rm 8:30 and whom he·regarded·as·righteous, these also he·

G1344.1 V-API-2P ἐδικαιώθητε (1x)
1Co 6:11 but·rather yeu·are·regarded·as·righteous in the

G1344.1 V-API-3S ἐδικαιώθη (6x)
Lk 7:35 "But Wisdom is·regarded·as·righteous by all her
Mt 11:19 But Wisdom is·regarded·as·righteous by her
Rm 4:2 AbRaham was·regarded·as·righteous as·a·result of·
Jac 2:21 *that* he·is·regarded·as·righteous, after·carrying·up
Jac 2:25 was·she·not regarded·as·righteous as·a·result of·
1Ti 3:16 ·apparent in flesh, is·regarded·as·righteous in Spirit

G1344.1 V-APM-3S δικαιωθήτω (1x)
Rv 22:11 righteous, let·him·be·regarded·as·righteous still;

G1344.1 V-APN δικαιωθῆναι (1x)
Gal 2:17 But if (while·seeking to·be·regarded·as·righteous in

G1344.1 V-APP-NPM δικαιωθέντες (3x)
Rm 5:1 already·being·regarded·as·righteous as·a·result of·
Rm 5:9 So·then, now being·regarded·as·righteous by his
Tit 3:7 ·that, after·being·regarded·as·righteous by·his grace,

G1344.1 V-APS-1P δικαιωθῶμεν (2x)
Gal 2:16 in·order·that we·should·be·regarded·as·righteous
Gal 3:24 in·order·that we·may·be·regarded·as·righteous as·

G1344.1 V-APS-2S δικαιωθῇς (1x)
Rm 3:4 '" So·that you·may·be·regarded·as·righteous in your

G1344.1 V-RPI-1S δεδικαίωμαι (1x)
1Co 4:4 not by this have·I·been·regarded·as·righteous. But

G1344.1 V-RPP-NSM δεδικαιωμένος (1x)
Lk 18:14 house having·been·regarded·as·righteous rather·

G1344.2 V-PPI-3S δικαιοῦται (1x)
Ac 13:39 trusting is·regarded·as·innocent from everything

G1344.2 V-APN δικαιωθῆναι (1x)
Ac 13:39 ·were·not able·to be·regarded·as·innocent by the

G1344.2 V-RPI-3S δεδικαίωται (1x)
Rm 6:7 being·dead has·been·regarded·as·innocent of the

G1345 δικαίωμα dikaíōma *n.* (10x)
Roots:G1344 Compare:G1341 G2631 G1654 G3544-1 G4366-2 See:G1343 G1343-1
xLangEquiv:H6666 A6665 xLangAlso:H2708 H2706 H4941

G1345.1 N-NPN δικαιώματα (2x)
Rv 15:4 ' because your righteous·acts are·made·apparent."
Rv 19:8 the fine·linen is the righteous·acts of·the holy·ones).

G1345.1 N-APN δικαιώματα (1x)
Rm 2:26 ·keep the righteous·acts of·the Torah-Law, his

G1345.1 N-GSN δικαιώματος (1x)
Rm 5:18 even in·this·manner, through one righteous·act, *the*

G1345.2 N-ASN δικαίωμα (2x)
Rm 5:16 of·many trespasses unto a·verdict·of·righteousness.
Rm 8:4 the verdict·of·righteousness from·the Torah-Law

G1345.3 N-ASN δικαίωμα (1x)
Rm 1:32 Who, after·recognizing the statute of·God (that

G1345.4 N-APN δικαιώματα (1x)
Heb 9:1 was·having regulations of·ritual·ministry *to·God*,

G1345.4 N-DPN δικαιώμασιν (2x)
Lk 1:6 in all the commandments and regulations of·Yahweh.
Heb 9:10 ceremonial·washings, and in·regulations of·flesh,

G1346 δικαίως dikaíōs *adv.* (5x)
Roots:G1342

G1346.2 ADV δικαίως (3x)
1Th 2:10 ·holy·manner and righteously and blamelessly, we·
Tit 2:12 ·live moderately·with·self-control, righteously, and
1Co 15:34 Awaken·yeurselves·from·stupor as·is·right, and

G1346.3 ADV δικαίως (2x)
Lk 23:41 And we·ourselves in·fact justly, for we·receive·in·
1Pe 2:23 ·handing *his cause* over to·the·one judging justly;

G1347 δικαίωσις dikaíōsis *n.* (2x)
Roots:G1344 Compare:G0121-2 G5586

G1347 N-ASF δικαίωσιν (2x)
Rm 4:25 on·account·of our acquittal·in·righteousness.
Rm 5:18 unto an·acquittal·in·righteousness of·life-above.

G1348 δικαστής dikastḗs *n.* (3x)
Roots:G1349 Compare:G2923 G0758 G4588-1
See:G3312

G1348.1 N-ASF δικαστήν (2x)
Ac 7:27 you *as* ruler and executive·justice over us?
Ac 7:35 you *as* ruler and executive·justice?" this·man God

G1348.3 N-ASF δικαστήν (1x)
Lk 12:14 ·established me *as* estate·executor or distributor

G1349 δίκη díkē *n.* (4x)
Roots:G1166 Compare:G2920 See:G1348 G1342
G0094

G1349.2 N-NSF δίκη (1x)
Ac 28:4 ·saved from·out of·the sea, Justice does·not let *him*

G1349.2 N-ASF δίκην (3x)
Ac 25:15 ·clear *that* they·are·requesting justice against him.
Jud 1:7 ·public·example, undergoing a·justice of·eternal fire
2Th 1:9 shall·pay justice with·an·eternal savage·termination

G1350 δίκτυον díktyôn *n.* (13x)
Compare:G0293 G4522

G1350 N-NSN δίκτυον (2x)
Jn 21:11 ·being so·vast·a·quantity, the net was·not torn.
Lk 5:6 of·fish, and their *one* net was·being·torn·apart.

G1350 N-ASN δίκτυον (4x)
Jn 21:6 to·them, "Cast the net to the right·hand portions of·
Jn 21:8 ·the small·boat, while·dragging the net of·fish (for
Jn 21:11 walked·up and drew the net upon the dry·ground,
Lk 5:5 But at your utterance, I·shall·lower the net."

G1350 N-APN δίκτυα (6x)
Lk 5:2 from them, the fishermen rinsed·off the nets.
Lk 5:4 ·off into the deep and lower yeur nets for a·catch."
Mt 4:20 immediately, leaving the nets, they·followed him.
Mt 4:21 Zebedee, completely·repairing their nets. And he·
Mk 1:18 immediately, leaving their nets, they·followed him.
Mk 1:19 *were* in the sailboat completely·repairing the nets.

EG1350 (1x)
Jn 21:6 Accordingly, they·cast *the net*, and they·no longer

G1351 δί•λογος dílôgôs *adj.* (1x)
Roots:G1364 G3056

G1351.3 A-APM διλόγους (1x)
1Ti 3:8 ·of·reverent·respect, not ambiguous·of·word, not

G1352 δι•ό dió *conj.* (53x)
Roots:G1223 G3739 Compare:G0686 G3767

G1352.1 CONJ διό (51x)
Lk 7:7 Therefore neither did·I·consider my·own·self
Ac 10:29 Therefore, after·being·sent·for, I·came *to·yeu*
Ac 13:35 Therefore he·says also in another *Psalm*, "You·
Ac 15:19 Therefore, I·myself judge *for·us* not to·further·

Ac 20:26 Therefore I·attest to·yeu in the present day, that I·
Ac 20:31 Therefore keep·alert, remembering that for·three·
Ac 24:26 he·may·loose him. Therefore, he·was·sending·for
Ac 25:26 Lord *Nero*. "Therefore I·brought him forth before
Ac 26:3 pervasive·among the·Judeans. Therefore, I·petition
Ac 27:25 "Therefore, men, cheer·up! For I·trust God, that in·
Ac 27:34 Therefore I·implore yeu to·each·take *some*
Heb 3:7 Therefore, just·as the Holy Spirit says, "'Today
Heb 3:10 "'Therefore, I·was·specifically·vexed with·that
Heb 6:1 Therefore leaving the initiating Redemptive·word of·
Heb 10:5 Therefore, he·who·is·entering into the world says,
Heb 11:12 Therefore, also from one·man, even these *many*
Heb 11:16 that·is, a·heavenly·one. Therefore God is·not
Heb 12:12 Therefore raise·upright the limp hands and the
Heb 12:28 Therefore, personally·receiving an·unshakable
Heb 13:12 Therefore YeShua also, that he·may·make·holy
Mt 27:8 Therefore that field is·called *AqelDama*, "Field of·
Rm 1:24 Therefore God also handed them over to impurity
Rm 2:1 Therefore, *for* anyone presently·judging— you·are
Rm 4:22 And therefore "'it·was·reckoned to·him for
Rm 13:5 Therefore *it·is* a·necessity to·submit·oneself, not
Rm 15:7 Therefore yeu·must·each·receive one·another, just·
Jac 1:21 Therefore, putting·away all filthiness and any·
Jac 4:6 But he·gives greater grace. Therefore he·says,
Php 2:9 Therefore God also elevated him above·all·others
1Pe 1:13 Therefore girding·up the loins of·yeur innermost·
1Pe 2:6 Therefore also it·is·contained in the Scripture, "
2Pe 1:10 Therefore, brothers, all·the·more quickly·endeavor
2Pe 1:12 Therefore I·shall·not neglect to·quietly·remind yeu
2Pe 3:14 Therefore, *yeu* beloved, while·intently·awaiting
1Th 2:18 Therefore we·wanted to·come to yeu, in·fact I Paul
1Th 3:1 Therefore, when·we·could·quietly·bear *it* no·longer,
1Th 5:11 Therefore yeu·must·comfort one·another, and
1Co 12:3 Therefore I·make·known to·yeu, that not·even·
2Co 2:8 Therefore I·implore yeu to·ratify *yeur* love for him.
2Co 4:13 "'I·trusted, therefore I·spoke,'" we·ourselves also
2Co 4:13 ' we·ourselves also trust and therefore speak,
2Co 4:16 Therefore, we·are·not cowardly.
2Co 5:9 Therefore we·aspire also, whether being·at·home or
2Co 6:17 "Therefore "yeu·must·come·out from·among *the*
2Co 12:10 Therefore I·purposefully·delight in weaknesses,
Eph 2:11 Therefore remember, that yeu *were* at·one·time the
Eph 3:13 Therefore, I·request *yeu* not to·be·despondent in
Eph 4:8 Therefore he·says, "After·ascending on·high, by·
Eph 4:25 Therefore, putting·away the lying, "'Each·man
Eph 5:14 Therefore he·says, "O·the·one sleeping, be·
Phm 1:8 Therefore, while·having much freeness·of·speech in

G1352.2 CONJ διό (2x)

Lk 1:35 shall·overshadow you. On·account·of·which also,
Rm 15:22 On·account·of·which also, I·was·hindered often

G1353 δι•οδεύω diôdêúō *v.* (2x)

Roots:G1223 G3593 Compare:G1330 G1224
xLangAlso:H5674

G1353 V-IAI-3S διώδευεν (1x)

Lk 8:1 that he·himself was·traveling·throughout each city

G1353 V-AAP-NPM διοδεύσαντες (1x)

Ac 17:1 Now after·traveling·through AmphiPolis and

G1353-1 δί•οδος díôdôs *n.* (3x)

Roots:G1223 G3598 Compare:G5147 G4646 G5163
G0824-2 G4113 G4505 G3938 See:G0306-1
xLangEquiv:H4546

G1353-1.1 N-APF διόδους (3x)

Lk 3:4 of·Yahweh; yeu·must·make his highways straight.
Mt 3:3 of·Yahweh; yeu·must·make his highways straight.'"
Mk 1:3 of·Yahweh; yeu·must·make his highways straight.'

G1354 Διονύσιος Diônýsiôs *n/p.* (1x)

G1354.2 N/P-NSM Διονύσιος (1x)

Ac 17:34 also *was* Dionysius, a·councilman·of·Mars'·Hill,

G1355 δι•ό•περ diópêr *conj.* (3x)

Roots:G1352 G4007

G1355 CONJ διόπερ (3x)

1Co 8:13 Therefore·indeed, if food entices my brother unto·
1Co 10:14 Therefore·indeed, my dearly·beloved, flee from
1Co 14:13 Therefore·indeed, the·one speaking in·a·

G1356 διο•πετής diôpêtḗs *adj.* (1x)

Roots:G2203 G4098

G1356.1 A-GSM διοπετοῦς (1x)

Ac 19:35 and of·the *image* which·fell·down·from·Zeus?

G1357 δι•όρθωσις diórthōsis *n.* (1x)

Roots:G1223 G3717 Compare:G0342 G0365 G0605
G2676 G3824

G1357.1 N-GSF διορθώσεως (1x)

Heb 9:10 ·*them* so·long·as·unto *the* season of·Rectification.

G1358 δι•ορύσσω diôrýssō *v.* (4x)

Roots:G1223 G3736

G1358.2 V-PAI-3P διορύσσουσιν (2x)

Mt 6:19 obliterate, and where thieves break·in and steal.
Mt 6:20 and where thieves do·not break·in nor·even steal.

G1358.2 V-2APN διορυγῆναι (2x)

Lk 12:39 not have·allowed his house to·be·broken·into.
Mt 24:43 and would not·have let his home to·be·broken·into.

G1359 Διόσ•κουροι Dióskôurôi *n/p.* (1x)

Roots:G2203 G2877

G1359 N/P-DPM Διοσκούροις (1x)

Ac 28:11 with·a·figurehead of·the·twin·sons·of·Zeus.

G1360 δι•ότι dióti *conj.* (22x)

Roots:G1223 G3754

G1360 CONJ διότι (22x)

Lk 1:13 be·afraid, Zacharias, on·account·that your petition
Lk 2:7 in the feeding·trough, on·account·that there·was no
Lk 21:28 yeur heads, on·account·that yeur full·redemption
Ac 10:20 ·thing, on·account·that I·myself have·dispatched
Ac 17:31 On·account·that, he·established a·day in which he·
Ac 18:10 on·account·that I AM with you, and not·even·one·
Ac 18:10 to·harm you, on·account·that I·have for·myself
Ac 22:18 of·JeruSalem on·account·that they·shall·not give·
Heb 11:5 he·was·not found, on·account·that God transferred
Heb 11:23 his parents, on·account·that they·saw *he·was* a·
Gal 2:16 of·works of·Torah-Law— on·account·that all flesh
Rm 1:19 *the wrath is·revealed* on·account·that, the·thing
Rm 1:21 on·account·that, already·knowing God, they·neither
Rm 3:20 on·account·that, as·a·result *of·the* deeds of·
Rm 8:7 (on·account·that the disposition of·the flesh *is*
Jac 4:3 do·not receive on·account·that yeu·request wrongly,
Php 2:26 ·distressed, on·account·that yeu·heard that he·was·
1Pe 1:16 on·account·that it·has·been·written, "Yeu·must·be
1Pe 1:24 on·account·that "' All flesh *is* as grass, and every
1Th 2:8 ·own souls, on·account·that yeu·have·become dear
1Th 4:6 matter·of·consequence, on·account·that the Lord *is*
1Co 15:9 an·ambassador, on·account·that I·persecuted the

G1361 Διο•τρεφής Diôtrêphḗs *n/p.* (1x)

Roots:G2203 G5142 Compare:G3531 G2819-2
G5211

G1361.2 N/P-NSM Διοτρεφής (1x)

3Jn 1:9 Called·Out·citizenry, but·yet DioTrephes, the·one

G1362 δι•πλοῦς diplôûs *adj.* (4x)

Roots:G1364 G4119

G1362.1 A-ASM-C διπλότερον (1x)

Mt 23:15 ·make him twice·as·much a·son of·Hell·Canyon

G1362.2 A-ASN διπλοῦν (1x)

Rv 18:6 ·and·poured·out, blend·and·pour·out to·her double.

G1362.2 A-APN διπλᾶ (1x)

Rv 18:6 and double to·her double according·to her works.

G1362.2 A-GSF διπλῆς (1x)

1Ti 5:17 must·be·considered·deserving of·double honor,

G1363 δι•πλόω diplôō *v.* (1x)

Roots:G1362

G1363 V-AAM-2P διπλώσατε (1x)

Rv 18:6 ·herself gave·back to·yeu, and double to·her double

G1364 δίς dís *adv.* (6x)

Roots:G1417 See:G1324

G1364.1 ADV δίς (4x)

Lk 18:12 I·fast twice in·the week, I·tithe all·things, *on* as·
Mk 14:30 ·to·a·rooster crowing twice, you·shall·utterly·deny
Mk 14:72 ·to·a·rooster crowing twice, you·shall·utterly·deny
Jud 1:12 already·dying·off twice, already·being·uprooted,

G1364.2 ADV δίς (2x)

Php 4:16 yeu·sent also once and again to my need.
1Th 2:18 to yeu, in·fact I Paul, also once and again, but the

G1365 διστάζω distázō *v.* (2x)

Roots:G1364

G1365.2 V-AAI-2S ἐδίστασας (1x)

Mt 14:31 "O·you·of·little·trust, why·did you·waver?"

G1365.2 V-AAI-3P ἐδίστασαν (1x)

Mt 28:17 him, they·fell·prostrate to·him, but they·wavered.

G1366 δί•στομος dístômôs *adj.* (3x)

Roots:G1364 G4750

G1366 A-NSM δίστομος (1x)

Rv 1:16 a·sharp double-edged straight·sword is·proceeding·

G1366 A-ASF δίστομον (2x)

Heb 4:12 above·and·beyond any double-edged dagger,
Rv 2:12 ·one having the sharp, double-edged straight·sword:

G1367 δισ•χίλιοι dischíliôi *n.* (1x)

Roots:G1364 G5507

G1367 N-NPM δισχίλιοι (1x)

Mk 5:13 Now there·were about two·thousand *of·them*, and

G1368 δι•ϋλίζω diÿlízō *v.* (1x)

Roots:G1223

G1368 V-PAP-NPM διϋλίζοντες (1x)

Mt 23:24 guides, the·ones thoroughly·filtering·out the gnat,

G1369 διχάζω dicházō *v.* (1x)

Roots:G1364

G1369.1 V-AAN διχάσαι (1x)

Mt 10:35 For I·came to·split "a·man·of·clay† against his

G1370 διχο•στασία dichôstasía *n.* (3x)

Roots:G1364 G4714 Compare:G1267 G4978 G4714

G1370.2 N-NPF διχοστασίαι (2x)

Gal 5:20 dissensions, factions·and·denominations,
1Co 3:3 and strife, and dissensions, are·yeu not·indeed

G1370.2 N-APF διχοστασίας (1x)

Rm 16:17 ·of·the·ones producing the dissensions and the

G1371 διχο•τομέω dichôtômḗō *v.* (2x)

Roots:G1364 G5058-2 Compare:G4249 G3192-1
G3718

G1371.1 V-FAI-3S διχοτομήσει (2x)

Lk 12:46 when he·does·not know, and shall·cut him in·two,
Mt 24:51 and he·shall·cut him in·two and shall·lay his

G1372 διψάω dipsáō *v.* (16x)

Roots:G1373
xLangEquiv:H6770

G1372 V-FAI-3S διψήσει (1x)

Jn 4:13 drinking from·out of·this water shall·thirst again.

G1372 V-FAI-3P διψήσουσιν (1x)

Rv 7:16 any·longer, neither shall·they·thirst any·longer, nor·

G1372 V-PAI-1S-C διψῶ (1x)

Jn 19:28 may·be·fully·completed, says, "I·thirst!"

G1372 V-PAP-ASM διψῶντα (2x)

Mt 25:37 nourished *you*? Or thirsting, and gave·*you*·drink?
Mt 25:44 did·we·see you hungering, or thirsting, or *being* a·

G1372 V-PAP-DSM διψῶντι (1x)

Rv 21:6 shall·give to·the·one thirsting from·out of·the

G1372 V-PAP-NSM διψῶν (1x)

Rv 22:17 And the·one thirsting, let·him·come! And the·one

G1372 V-PAP-NPM διψῶντες (1x)

Mt 5:6 the·ones hungering and thirsting·for the righteousness

G1372 V-PAS-1S διψῶ (1x)

Jn 4:15 this water, in·order·that I·may·not thirst, nor·even

G1372 V-PAS-1P διψῶμεν (1x)

1Co 4:11 also we·hunger, and should·thirst, and go·naked,

G1372 V-PAS-3S διψᾷ (2x)

Jn 7:37 saying, "If any·man should·thirst, let·him·come to
Rm 12:20 ·some·food·for him; if he·should·thirst, give him

G1372 V-AAI-1S ἐδίψησα (2x)

Mt 25:35 yeu·gave me to·eat. I·was·thirsty, and yeu·gave
Mt 25:42 me *anything* to·eat. I·was·thirsty, and yeu·did·not

G1372 V-AAS-3S διψήσῃ (2x)

Jn 4:14 him, no, he·should·not thirst into the coming·age,

Jn 6:35 in me, no, he·should·not <u>thirst</u> ever·at·any·time.

G1373 δίψος dípsôs *n.* (1x)
See:G1372
xLangEquiv:H6772

G1373 N-DSN δίψει (1x)
2Co 11:27 many·times, in hunger and <u>thirst</u>, in fastings

G1374 δί•ψυχος dípsychôs *adj.* (2x)
Roots:G1364 G5590

Δδ

G1374.2 A-NSM δίψυχος (1x)
Jac 1:8 A·man <u>vacillating·in·his·soul</u> *is* completely·unstable
G1374.2 A-VPM δίψυχοι (1x)
Jac 4:8 *yeur* hearts, *yeu who·are* <u>vacillating·in·yeur·souls</u>.

G1375 διωγμός diōgmós *n.* (10x)
Roots:G1377 See:G1376

G1375 N-NSM διωγμός (2x)
Ac 8:1 ·very day, there·was a·great <u>persecution</u> against the
Rm 8:35 tribulation, or calamity, or <u>persecution</u>, or famine,
G1375 N-ASM διωγμόν (1x)
Ac 13:50 and they·roused·up <u>persecution</u> against Paul and
G1375 N-APM διωγμούς (1x)
2Ti 3:11 *and* at Lystra; what <u>persecutions</u> I·underwent, but
G1375 N-DPM διωγμοῖς (3x)
2Th 1:4 trust in all yeur <u>persecutions</u> and tribulations that
2Co 12:10 in dire·needs, in <u>persecutions</u>, in calamities on·
2Ti 3:11 *my* <u>persecutions</u>, *and my* afflictions— such·as·what
G1375 N-GSM διωγμοῦ (2x)
Mt 13:21 or <u>with·persecution</u> occurring on·account·of the
Mk 4:17 ·tribulation or <u>persecution</u> happening on·account·of
G1375 N-GPM διωγμῶν (1x)
Mk 10:30 and plots·of·land, with <u>persecutions</u>, and in the

G1376 διώκτης diṓktēs *n.* (1x)
Roots:G1377 See:G1375

G1376 N-ASM διώκτην (1x)
1Ti 1:13 being a·reviler, and <u>a·persecutor</u>, and an·abusively·

G1377 διώκω diṓkō *v.* (45x)
Compare:G2614 See:G1375 xLangAlso:H7291

G1377.1 V-PAI-1S διώκω (2x)
Php 3:12 ·been·made·completely·mature, but <u>I·pursue</u> *it*, so·
Php 3:14 according·to *that* set·aim, <u>I·pursue</u> *it* toward the
G1377.1 V-PAM-2S δίωκε (2x)
1Ti 6:11 flee from·these·things, and <u>pursue</u> righteousness,
2Ti 2:22 youthful longings, but <u>pursue</u> righteousness, trust,
G1377.1 V-PAM-2P διώκετε (3x)
Heb 12:14 <u>Pursue</u> peace with all *men*, also the renewed·
1Th 5:15 but·rather always <u>pursue</u> the beneficially·good,
1Co 14:1 <u>Pursue</u> the Love, and zealously·desire the spiritual
G1377.1 V-PAP-NSM διώκων (1x)
Rm 9:31 But IsraEl, <u>pursuing</u> a·Torah-Law of·righteousness,
G1377.1 V-PAP-NPN διώκοντα (1x)
Rm 9:30 that Gentiles, the·ones not <u>pursuing</u> righteousness,
G1377.1 V-PAP-NPM διώκοντες (1x)
Rm 12:13 ·sharing·with·others, <u>by·pursuing</u> the hospitality.
G1377.1 V-PAS-1P διώκωμεν (1x)
Rm 14:19 <u>we·should·pursue</u> the·things of·peace and the·
G1377.1 V-AAM-3S διωξάτω (1x)
1Pe 3:11 beneficially·good·thing; seek peace and <u>pursue</u> it.
G1377.1 V-AAS-2P διώξητε (1x)
Lk 17:23 ·off *after·them*, nor·even <u>should·yeu·pursue</u> *them*.
EG1377.1 (1x)
Rm 9:32 Why? Because <u>*they·pursued*</u> *it* not as·a·result of·
G1377.2 V-FAI-2P διώξετε (1x)
Mt 23:34 in yeur gatherings and <u>shall·persecute</u> from city to
G1377.2 V-FAI-3P διώξουσιν (2x)
Jn 15:20 they·persecuted me, <u>they·shall·persecute</u> yeu also.
Lk 21:12 their hands on yeu and <u>shall·persecute</u> *yeu*, handing
G1377.2 V-PAI-2S διώκεις (6x)
Ac 9:4 "Saul, Saul, why·do <u>you·persecute</u> me?
Ac 9:5 Jesus, whom you·yourself <u>persecute</u>. *It·is* hard for·
Ac 22:7 'Saul, Saul, why·do <u>you·persecute</u> me?
Ac 22:8 Jesus of·Natsareth, whom you·yourself <u>persecute</u>.'
Ac 26:14 'Saul, Saul, why·do <u>you·persecute</u> me?
Ac 26:15 ·is·I Myself, Jesus, whom you·yourself <u>persecute</u>.

G1377.2 V-PAP-APM διώκοντας (1x)
Rm 12:14 Bless the·ones <u>persecuting</u> yeu; bless and do·not
G1377.2 V-PAP-GPM διωκόντων (1x)
Mt 5:44 abusively·threatening yeu and <u>persecuting</u> yeu,
G1377.2 V-PAP-NSM διώκων (2x)
Gal 1:23 merely, "The·one <u>persecuting</u> us in·times·past now
Php 3:6 ·to zeal, <u>persecuting</u> the Called·Out·citizenry;
G1377.2 V-PAS-3P διώκωσιν (1x)
Mt 10:23 But whenever <u>they·should·persecute</u> yeu in this
G1377.2 V-AAI-1S ἐδίωξα (2x)
Ac 22:4 "*It·is·I* who <u>persecuted</u> this Way even·unto *their*
1Co 15:9 on·account·that <u>I·persecuted</u> the Called·Out·
G1377.2 V-AAI-3S ἐδίωξεν (1x)
Rv 12:13 ·cast to the earth, <u>he·persecuted</u> the woman who
G1377.2 V-AAI-3P ἐδίωξαν (3x)
Jn 15:20 lord.' If <u>they·persecuted</u> me, they·shall·persecute
Ac 7:52 did yeur fathers not <u>persecute</u>? Also they·killed the·
Mt 5:12 For in·this·manner <u>they·persecuted</u> the prophets,
G1377.2 V-AAS-3P διώξωσιν (1x)
Mt 5:11 *men* should·reproach yeu and <u>should·persecute</u> *yeu*,
G1377.3 V-FPI-3P διωχθήσονται (1x)
2Ti 3:12 in Anointed-One Jesus <u>shall·be·persecuted</u>.
G1377.3 V-PPI-1S διώκομαι (1x)
Gal 5:11 why·am I·still <u>persecuted</u>? Then·by·inference, the
G1377.3 V-PPP-NPM διωκόμενοι (2x)
1Co 4:12 we·bless. <u>Being·persecuted</u>, we·hold·up·*under·it*.
2Co 4:9 <u>being·persecuted</u>, but·yet not being·forsaken; being·
G1377.3 V-PPS-3P διώκωνται (1x)
Gal 6:12 ·that they·should·not <u>be·persecuted</u> for·the cross of·
G1377.3 V-IAI-1S ἐδίωκον (2x)
Ac 26:11 them beyond·excess, <u>I·was·persecuting</u> *them* even
Gal 1:13 exceedingly <u>I·was·persecuting</u> the Called·Out·
G1377.3 V-IAI-3S ἐδίωκεν (1x)
Gal 4:29 ·to flesh <u>was·persecuting</u> the·one *being·born*
G1377.3 V-IAI-3P ἐδίωκον (1x)
Jn 5:16 ·of that, the Judeans <u>were·persecuting</u> Jesus, and
G1377.3 V-RPP-NPM δεδιωγμένοι (1x)
Mt 5:10 *are* the·ones <u>having·been·persecuted</u> because·of

G1378 δόγμα dógma *n.* (6x)
Roots:G1380 Compare:G1106 G1778 G5216-1
See:G1379

G1378.3 N-NSN δόγμα (1x)
Lk 2:1 *that* there·went·forth <u>a·decree</u> directly·from Caesar
G1378.3 N-APN δόγματα (1x)
Ac 16:4 ·down to·them the <u>decrees</u> to·vigilantly·keep, the·
G1378.3 N-DPN δόγμασιν (2x)
Eph 2:15 of·the commandments *contained* in <u>decrees</u>), in·
Col 2:14 against us (the <u>decrees</u> which were sternly·opposed
G1378.3 N-GPN δογμάτων (1x)
Ac 17:7 *things* in·full·opposition to·the <u>decrees</u> of·Caesar,
EG1378.3 (1x)
Col 2:22 to perishing with·usage)— <u>*decrees*</u> according·to '

G1379 δογματίζω dôgmatízō *v.* (1x)
Roots:G1378

G1379.3 V-PPI-2P δογματίζεσθε (1x)
Col 2:20 living in *the* world, <u>are·yeu·subject·to·decrees</u>

G1380 δοκέω dôkéō *v.* (63x)
Compare:G1166 G1209 G2309 G3543 G3049 G5426
G4100 See:G1384 G3861

G1380.1 V-PAI-1S-C δοκῶ (2x)
1Co 4:9 For <u>I·suppose</u> that God exhibited us (the
1Co 7:40 ·to my advice; and <u>I·suppose</u> also to·have God's
G1380.1 V-PAI-2P δοκεῖτε (5x)
Lk 12:40 ·Man† comes in·that hour you·do·not <u>suppose</u>."
Lk 12:51 "<u>Do·yeu·suppose</u> that I·came·directly to·give
Lk 13:2 to·them, "<u>Do·yeu·suppose</u> that these Galileans
Heb 10:29 ·much, <u>do·yeu·suppose</u>, shall·he·be·considered·
2Co 12:19 <u>do·yeu·suppose</u> that we·make·our·defense to·
G1380.1 V-PAI-3S δοκεῖ (9x)
Jn 11:56 "What·do yeu·yeurselves <u>suppose</u>, that no, he·
Gal 6:3 For if any·man <u>supposes·himself</u> to·be something,
Mt 17:25 him, saying, "What·do you <u>suppose</u>, Simon?
Mt 18:12 "What·do yeu·yeurselves <u>suppose</u>? "If·it·should·

Mt 21:28 But what·do yeu <u>suppose</u>? A·certain·man·of·clay†
Mt 22:17 to·us, what·do you <u>suppose</u>? Is·it·proper to·give a·
Mt 22:42 saying, "What·do yeu <u>suppose</u> concerning the
Mt 26:66 What·do yeu·yeurselves <u>suppose</u>?" And answering,
1Co 14:37 If someone <u>supposes·himself</u> to·be a·prophet or
G1380.1 V-PAP-ASN δοκοῦν (1x)
Heb 12:10 ·disciplining *us* according·to their <u>supposing</u>, but
G1380.1 V-IAI-3S ἐδόκει (1x)
Ac 12:9 but <u>he·was·supposing</u> to·look·upon a·clear·vision.
G1380.1 V-IAI-3P ἐδόκουν (1x)
Lk 24:37 alarmed, <u>they·were·supposing</u> to·observe a·spirit.
G1380.1 V-AAI-3P ἔδοξαν (1x)
Mk 6:49 upon the sea, <u>they·supposed</u> *it* to·be a·phantom,
G1380.1 V-AAP-NPM δόξαντες (1x)
Ac 27:13 *and* <u>supposing</u> to·have·taken·secure·hold of·the
G1380.1 V-AAS-3S δόξῃ (1x)
2Co 11:16 Again I·say, not anyone <u>should·suppose</u> me to·be
G1380.2 V-PAI-3S δοκεῖ (7x)
Lk 10:36 of·these three·men <u>seems</u> to·you to·have·become
Ac 17:18 ·*others*? Now <u>he·seems</u> to·be an·ardent·proclaimer
Ac 25:27 For <u>it·seems</u> to·me unreasonable to·send a·
Heb 12:11 ·for the present, does·not <u>seem</u> to·be joyous, but·
Jac 1:26 If any·man among yeu <u>seems</u> to·be religious, *yet* not
1Co 3:18 If any·man among yeu <u>seems</u> to·be wise in this
1Co 11:16 But if any·man <u>seems</u> to·be contentious, we·
G1380.2 V-PAP-GPM δοκούντων (1x)
Gal 2:6 But as·for the·ones <u>seeming</u> to·be something
G1380.2 V-PAP-NPN δοκοῦντα (1x)
1Co 12:22 the·ones <u>seeming</u> to·inherently·be more·feeble,
G1380.2 V-PAP-NPM δοκοῦντες (2x)
Gal 2:6 ·man·of·clay†, for the·ones <u>seeming</u> *to·be something*
Gal 2:9 and John, the·ones <u>seeming</u> to·be pillars, they·gave
G1380.2 V-PAS-3S δοκῇ (1x)
Heb 4:1 ·among yeu <u>should·seem</u> to·have·fallen·short *of·it*.
G1380.2 V-AAI-3S ἔδοξεν (5x)
Lk 1:3 <u>it·seemed</u> *good* to·me·also, having·closely·followed
Ac 15:22 Then <u>it·seemed·good</u> to·the ambassadors and the
Ac 15:25 <u>it·seemed·good</u> to·us, being with·the·same·
Ac 15:28 For <u>it·seemed·good</u> to·the Holy Spirit, and to·us,
Ac 15:34 But <u>it·seemed·good</u> to·Silas to·still·stay·over at·
G1380.2 V-AAS-2S δόξω (1x)
2Co 10:9 in·order·that I·may·not <u>seem</u> as if *I·intended* to·
G1380.3 V-PAI-1S-C δοκῶ (1x)
Lk 17:9 ·being·thoroughly·assigned to·him? <u>I·presume</u> not.
G1380.3 V-PAI-1P δοκοῦμεν (1x)
1Co 12:23 body, <u>which·we·presume</u> to·be less·honorable,
G1380.3 V-PAI-2S δοκεῖς (1x)
Mt 26:53 Or <u>do·you·presume</u> that I·am·not able at·this·
G1380.3 V-PAI-2P δοκεῖτε (4x)
Jn 5:39 because yeu·yeurselves <u>presume</u> to·have eternal
Lk 13:4 fell and killed them, <u>do·yeu·presume</u> that these·men
Mt 24:44 comes at·an·hour which yeu·do·not <u>presume</u>.
Jac 4:5 Or <u>do·yeu·presume</u> that the Scripture says for·naught
G1380.3 V-PAI-3S δοκεῖ (3x)
Lk 8:18 ·taken·away even that·which <u>he·presumes</u> to·have."
Php 3:4 other·man <u>presumes</u> *a·reason* to·have·confidence in
1Co 8:2 if anyone <u>presumes</u> to·personally·know something
G1380.3 V-PAI-3P δοκοῦσιν (1x)
Mt 6:7 *do*, for <u>they·presume</u> that they·shall·be·heard by
G1380.3 V-PAM-2P δοκεῖτε (1x)
Jn 5:45 "Do·not <u>presume</u> that I·myself shall·legally·accuse
G1380.3 V-PAN@ δοκεῖν (1x)
Lk 19:11 and *because* they·themselves <u>presumed</u> that the
G1380.3 V-PAP-NSF δοκοῦσα (1x)
Jn 20:15 That·woman, <u>presuming</u> that he·is the garden·
G1380.3 V-PAP-NSM δοκῶν (1x)
1Co 10:12 ·such, the·one <u>presuming</u> to·stand must·look·out
G1380.3 V-PAP-NPM δοκοῦντες (1x)
Mk 10:42 ·know that the·ones <u>presuming</u> to·rule·over the
G1380.3 V-IAI-3P ἐδόκουν (1x)
Jn 13:29 For some *of·them* <u>were·presuming</u>, since Judas was·
G1380.3 V-AAI-1S ἔδοξα (1x)
Ac 26:9 (within·myself) <u>presumed</u> *it* to·be·necessary to·

G1380.3 V-AAI-3P ἔδοξαν (1x)
Jn 11:13 but those *disciples* presumed that he·says *this*
G1380.3 V-AAS-2P δόξητε (1x)
Mt 3:9 And yeu·should·not presume to·say within yeurselves
G1380.3 V-AAS-3S δόξῃ (1x)
Jn 16:2 killing yeu might·presume to·offer a·ritual·ministry
G1380.4 V-PAI-3S δοκεῖ (1x)
Lk 22:24 *concerning* which of·them is·reputed to·be greater
G1380.5 V-PAP-DPM δοκοῦσιν (1x)
Gal 2:2 to·the·ones being·of·reputation, lest·somehow I·

G1381 δοκιμάζω dôkimázō *v.* (24x)
Roots:G1384 Compare:G0350 G1231 G3985 G1598 See:G0593 G1383 G1233
xLangEquiv:H0974 xLangAlso:H5254
G1381.1 V-FAI-3S δοκιμάσει (1x)
1Co 3:13 and the fire shall·test·and·prove each·man's work
G1381.1 V-PAM-2P δοκιμάζετε (1x)
1Jn 4:1 trust every spirit, but·rather test·and·prove the spirits
G1381.1 V-PAM-3S δοκιμαζέτω (1x)
Gal 6:4 But each·man must·test·and·prove his·own work,
G1381.1 V-PAP-DSM δοκιμάζοντι (1x)
1Th 2:4 ·rather God, the·one testing·and·proving our hearts.
G1381.1 V-PAP-NSM δοκιμάζων (1x)
2Co 8:8 and to·test·and·prove the genuineness of·yeur love.
G1381.1 V-PPM-3P δοκιμαζέσθωσαν (1x)
1Ti 3:10 also these·men must·be·tested·and·proven first;
G1381.1 V-PPP-GSN δοκιμαζομένου (1x)
1Pe 1:7 even with·it·being·tested·and·proven through fire)
G1381.1 V-AAI-1P ἐδοκιμάσαμεν (1x)
2Co 8:22 whom we·tested·and·proved many·times being
G1381.1 V-AAI-3P ἐδοκίμασαν (1x)
Heb 3:9 yeur fathers tried me, tested·and·proved me, and
G1381.1 V-RPI-1P δεδοκιμάσμεθα (1x)
1Th 2:4 just·as we·have·been·tested·and·proven by God to·
EG1381.1 (1x)
1Ti 3:11 wives *must·be* morally·worthy·of·reverent·respect,
G1381.2 V-PAI-3S δοκιμάζει (1x)
Rm 14:22 into·judgment by what he·verifiably·approves.
G1381.2 V-AAS-2P δοκιμάσητε (1x)
1Co 16:3 yeu·should·verifiably·approve through *yeur* letters,
G1381.3 V-PAI-2S δοκιμάζεις (1x)
Rm 2:18 the will, and examine·and·verify the·things varying
G1381.3 V-PAI-2P δοκιμάζετε (1x)
Lk 12:56 ·it that·yeu·do·not examine·and·verify this season?
G1381.3 V-PAM-2P δοκιμάζετε (2x)
1Th 5:21 Examine·and·verify all·things; fully·hold·onto the
2Co 13:5 in the trust. Examine·and·verify yeur·own·selves.
G1381.3 V-PAM-3S δοκιμαζέτω (1x)
1Co 11:28 a·man·of·clay† must·examine·and·verify himself,
G1381.3 V-PAN δοκιμάζειν (3x)
Lk 12:56 yeu·personally·know·how to·examine·and·verify
Rm 12:2 in·order·for yeu to·examine·and·verify what *is* the
Php 1:10 in·order·for·it to·examine·and·verify yeu
G1381.3 V-PAP-NPM δοκιμάζοντες (1x)
Eph 5:10 examining·and·verifying what is most·satisfying
G1381.3 V-AAI-3P ἐδοκίμασαν (1x)
Rm 1:28 ·as they·did·not examine·and·verify God to·hold
G1381.4 V-AAN δοκιμάσαι (1x)
Lk 14:19 ·teams of·oxen, and I·traverse to·test them out. I·

G1382 δοκιμή dôkimḗ *n.* (7x)
Roots:G1384 Compare:G0391 G0981 G2688 G3986 See:G1383 G1381
G1382.1 N-DSF δοκιμῇ (1x)
2Co 8:2 that in a·large proof·test of·tribulation, the
G1382.2 N-ASF δοκιμήν (2x)
Php 2:22 But yeu·know the proof of·him, that as a·child
2Co 13:3 since yeu·seek a·proof of·the Anointed-One
G1382.2 N-GSF δοκιμῆς (1x)
2Co 9:13 On·account·of the proof of·this service, they·are·
G1382.3 N-ASF δοκιμήν (1x)
2Co 2:9 that I·may·know yeur proof·of·character, whether
G1382.4 N-NSF δοκιμή (1x)
Rm 5:4 and the proven·character *fully·cultivates* expectation
G1382.4 N-ASF δοκιμήν (1x)
Rm 5:4 ·endurance *fully·cultivates* proven·character, and the

G1383 δοκίμιον dôkímiôn *n.* (2x)
Roots:G1384 See:G1382
xLangEquiv:H0976
G1383.1 N-NSN δοκίμιον (2x)
Jac 1:3 knowing that the proof·testing of·yeur trust
1Pe 1:7 in·order·that the proof·testing of·yeur trust (*being*

G1384 δόκιμος dôkimôs *adj.* (7x)
Roots:G1209 Compare:G1184 G1233 See:G1381 G1383 G0096
G1384.2 A-NSM δόκιμος (3x)
Rm 14:18 ·God and verifiably·approved by·the men·of·clay†
Jac 1:12 after·becoming verifiably·approved, he·shall·
2Co 10:18 himself *that* is verifiably·approved, but·rather
G1384.2 A-NPM δόκιμοι (2x)
1Co 11:19 ·ones *who·are* verifiably·approved may·become
2Co 13:7 should·appear verifiably·approved, but·rather that
G1384.2 A-ASM δόκιμον (2x)
Rm 16:10 the·one verifiably·approved in Anointed-One.
2Ti 2:15 to·present yourself verifiably·approved to·God, an·

G1385 δοκός dôkôs *n.* (6x)
Roots:G1209 xLangAlso:H6982
G1385.2 N-NSF δοκός (1x)
Mt 7:4 And behold, the beam *is* in your·own eye?
G1385.2 N-ASF δοκόν (5x)
Lk 6:41 but do·not fully·observe the beam, the·one in your·
Lk 6:42 *are* not looking·at the beam in your own·eye?
Lk 6:42 first cast·out the beam from your·own eye, and
Mt 7:3 but do·not fully·observe the beam in your own eye?
Mt 7:5 first cast the beam from·out of·your·own eye, and

G1386 δόλιος dốliôs *adj.* (1x)
Roots:G1388 See:G1387
G1386 A-NPM δόλιοι (1x)
2Co 11:13 workmen full·of·guile, disguising·themselves as

G1387 δολιόω dôliốō *v.* (1x)
Roots:G1386 Compare:G1185 See:G1389
G1387.1 V-IAI-3P ἐδολιοῦσαν (1x)
Rm 3:13 ·up; with·their tongues, they·were·using·guile."

G1388 δόλος dốlôs *n.* (12x)
Compare:G1185 See:G1386 xLangAlso:H4820
G1388.2 N-NSM δόλος (4x)
Jn 1:47 Truly an·Israelite in whom there·is no guile!"
Mk 7:22 acts·of·coveting, evils, guile, debauchery, an·evil
1Pe 2:22 moral·failure, neither was guile found in his mouth
Rv 14:5 And in their mouth was·found no guile, for they·are
G1388.2 N-ASM δόλον (2x)
1Pe 2:1 ·aside all malice, and all guile, and hypocrisies, and
1Pe 3:10 tongue from wrong and his lips not to·speak guile."
G1388.2 N-DSM δόλῳ (4x)
Mt 26:4 ·may·take·secure·hold·of YeShua by·guile, and·then
Mk 14:1 ·secure·hold *of·him*, they·may·kill him by guile.
1Th 2:3 of·deceit, nor from·out of·impurity, nor in guile.
2Co 12:16 shrewdly·cunning, I·took·hold·of yeu with·guile.
G1388.2 N-GSM δόλου (2x)
Ac 13:10 "O *you·are* full of·all guile and all mischief, O·Son
Rm 1:29 ·envy, murder, strife, guile, *and* mischievousness;

G1389 δολόω dôlốō *v.* (1x)
Roots:G1388 Compare:G2585 See:G1387
G1389.1 V-PAP-NPM δολοῦντες (1x)
2Co 4:2 ·cunning nor·even handling the Redemptive-word of·

G1390 δόμα dốma *n.* (4x)
Roots:G1325 Compare:G1435 G5486 See:G1395 G0593-1
xLangEquiv:H4979 xLangAlso:H4991
G1390 N-ASN δόμα (1x)
Php 4:17 Not that I·anxiously·seek the gift, but·rather I·
G1390 N-APN δόματα (3x)
Lk 11:13 to·give beneficially·good gifts to·yeur children,
Mt 7:11 ·how to·give beneficially·good gifts to·yeur children
Eph 4:8 ·captivity *itself*, and gave gifts to·the men·of·clay†.

G1391 δόξα dóxa *n.* (169x)
Roots:G1380 Compare:G2811 G5345 G5092 See:G1741
xLangEquiv:H3519
G1391.2 N-NSF δόξα (38x)
Jn 8:54 glorify my·own·self, my glory is nothing·at·all. It·is
Lk 2:9 and Yahweh's glory radiated·brightly·all·around them
Lk 2:14 "Glory to·God in *the* highest, and on earth, peace!
Lk 14:10 higher.' Then glory shall·be with·you in·the·sight
Lk 19:38 ' Peace in heaven and glory in *the* highest!"
Heb 13:21 — to·whom *be* the glory to the ages of·ages.
Gal 1:5 to·whom *be* the glory to the ages of·ages.
Mt 6:13 and the power, and the glory, into the ages.
Rm 2:10 But glory, honor, and peace, to·every·man, the·one
Rm 9:4 *are* the adoption·as·sons, and the glory, and the
Rm 11:36 To·him *be* glory into the ages.
Rm 16:27 God, to·him *be* the glory through Jesus Anointed
Jud 1:25 God our Savior, *be* glory and majesty, might and
Php 3:19 god *is* the belly, and *whose* glory *is* in their shame.
Php 4:20 to·our God and Father *be* glory into the ages of·
1Pe 1:24 *is* as grass, and every man·of·clay's† glory *is* as *the*
1Pe 4:11 Anointed, to·whom is the glory and the might into
1Pe 5:11 To·him *be* the glory and the might into the ages of·
2Pe 3:18 To·him *be* glory both now and to *the* day of·*the*·
1Th 2:20 For yeu are our glory and joy.
1Co 11:7 ·being God's derived·image and glory, but woman
1Co 11:7 ·image and glory, but woman is man's glory.
1Co 11:15 should·wear·long·hair, it·is a·glory to·her,
1Co 15:40 bodies, but·yet in·fact the glory of·the celestial *is*
1Co 15:41 *There·is* one glory of·*the*·sun, and another glory
1Co 15:41 of·*the*·sun, and another glory of·*the*·moon, and
1Co 15:41 of·*the*·moon, and another glory of·*the*·stars, for
2Co 3:9 the service of·the condemnation *had* glory, so·much
2Co 8:23 ·Out·citizenries *and the* glory of·Anointed-One.
Eph 3:13 in my tribulations over yeu, which is yeur glory.
Eph 3:21 to·him *be* the glory in the entire·Called·Out·
1Ti 1:17 wise God, *be* honor and glory to the ages of·ages.
2Ti 4:18 heavenly kingdom, to·whom *be* glory into the ages
Rv 1:6 To·him *be* the glory and the might into the ages of·
Rv 5:13 blessing and the honor and the glory and the might,
Rv 7:12 The blessing, and the glory, and the wisdom, and
Rv 19:1 The Salvation, and the glory, and the honor, and the
Rv 21:23 ·forth in it, for the glory of·God illuminated it, and
G1391.2 N-ASF δόξαν (58x)
Jn 1:14 us, and we·distinctly·viewed his glory (*the* glory as
Jn 1:14 his glory (*the* glory as of·the·only·begotten directly·
Jn 2:11 Qanah of·Galilee and made his glory apparent. And
Jn 5:41 I·do·not receive glory personally·from men·of·clay†,
Jn 5:44 to·trust, receiving glory personally·from one·another
Jn 5:44 yet yeu·do·not seek the glory, the·one personally·
Jn 7:18 from himself seeks his·own glory, but the·man
Jn 7:18 but the·man seeking the glory of·the·one sending
Jn 8:50 I·myself do·not seek my·own glory; there·is One
Jn 9:24 "Give God glory. We·ourselves personally·know
Jn 11:40 ·trust, you·shall·gaze·upon the glory of·God?
Jn 12:41 these·things when he·saw his glory and spoke
Jn 12:43 for they·loved the glory of·the men·of·clay† more·
Jn 12:43 more·especially indeed·than·even the glory of·God.
Jn 17:22 "And the glory which you·have·given to·me I·
Jn 17:24 in·order·that they·may·observe my glory, which
Lk 2:32 of·Gentiles and *for the* glory of·your People IsraEl.
Lk 4:6 ·all this authority and their glory, because it·has·been·
Lk 9:32 ·thoroughly·awakened, they·saw his glory and the
Lk 17:18 ·are·not found returning·back to·give glory to·God,
Lk 24:26 to·suffer these·things, and to·enter into his glory?"
Ac 7:55 the heaven, he·saw God's glory, and Jesus standing
Ac 12:23 because he·did·not give the glory to·God. And
Heb 2:10 , in·bringing many sons to glory, to·make the
Mt 4:8 him all the kingdoms of·the world and their glory,
Rm 1:23 and "they·did·change the glory of·the incorruptible
Rm 2:7 of·beneficially·good work, seeking glory, honor,
Rm 3:7 truth of·God abounded to his glory, why am I·also
Rm 4:20 ·enabled by·the trust, already·giving glory to·God

Rm 8:18 alongside the impending glory to·be·revealed in us.
Rm 9:23 which he·made·ready·in·advance for glory,
Rm 15:7 purposely·received us into God's glory.
Php 1:11 Anointed, to *the* glory and high·praise of·God.
Php 2:11 Jesus Anointed *is* Lord, to *the* glory of·Father God.
1Pe 1:7 high·praise and honor and glory at the·revealing of·
1Pe 1:21 from·among dead·men and giving glory to·him)—
1Pe 5:10 us forth into his eternal glory by Anointed-One
2Pe 1:17 ·from Father God honor and glory, with·a·voice
1Th 2:6 nor seeking glory from·among men·of·clay†, neither
1Th 2:12 ·one calling yeu forth into his kingdom and glory.
1Co 2:7 God predetermined before the ages to our glory,
1Co 10:31 or anything *that* yeu·do, do all to God's glory.
2Co 1:20 "So·be·it,·Amen" for·God unto glory through us.
2Co 3:7 ·Moses on·account·of the glory of·his countenance
2Co 3:18 ourselves·seeing·and·reflecting the Lord's glory)—
2Co 3:18 derived·image from glory to glory, exactly·as
2Co 4:15 ·thankfulness should·abound to the glory of·God.
2Co 8:19 ·attended·to by us to the glory of·the same Lord,
Rv 4:9 the living·beings shall·give glory and honor and
Rv 4:11 O·Lord, to·receive the glory and the honor and the
Rv 5:12 and strength and honor and glory and blessing!"
Rv 11:13 became alarmed and gave glory to·the God of·the
Rv 14:7 "Fear God and give glory to·him, because the hour
Rv 16:9 And they·did·not repent *as* to·give him glory.
Rv 19:7 should·leap·for·joy, and should·give glory to·him,
Rv 21:11 having the glory of·God (even her brilliance *was*
Rv 21:24 kings of·the earth bring their glory and honor into
Rv 21:26 And they·shall·bring the glory and the honor of·the

G1391.2 N-APF δόξας (3x)

Jud 1:8 ignore sovereign·lordship, and revile glorious·ones.
1Pe 1:11 upon Anointed-One and the glories *to·come* after
2Pe 2:10 tremble·with·fear while·reviling glorious·ones—

G1391.2 N-DSF δόξῃ (20x)

Jn 17:5 with yourself) with·the glory which I·was·having
Lk 9:26 whenever he·should·come in his·own glory, and *that*
Lk 9:31 upon·being·made·visible in glory, were·relating his
Lk 12:27 ·even Solomon in all his glory was·arrayed as one
Heb 2:7 ·did·victoriously·crown him with·glory and honor,
Heb 2:9 having·been·victoriously·crowned with·glory and
Mt 6:29 ·even Solomon, in all his glory, was·arrayed as one
Mt 16:27 is·about to·come in the glory of·his Father with his
Mt 25:31 of·Clay·Man† should·come in his glory, and all the
Mk 8:38 whenever he·should·come in the glory of·his Father
Mk 10:37 right·hand and one at your left, in your glory."
Php 4:19 according·to his wealth in glory in Anointed-One
1Co 15:41 for *one* star varies·from *another* star in glory.
1Co 15:43 in dishonor; it·is·awakened in glory. It·is·sown in
2Co 3:7 on stones, came·into·being in glory— such·for the
2Co 3:8 more shall the Service of·the Spirit be in glory?
2Co 3:9 *does* the service of·the righteousness excel in glory.
2Co 3:11 *is* the·one *of·the Spirit* remaining in glory.
Col 3:4 shall·be·made·apparent together with·him in glory.
1Ti 3:16 is·trusted *upon* in *the* world, is·taken·up into glory.

G1391.2 N-GSF δόξης (49x)

Jn 11:4 but·rather on·behalf of·the glory of·God, in·order·
Lk 21:27 in a·thick·cloud' with power and much glory.
Ac 7:2 "The God of·Glory was·made·visible to·our father
Ac 22:11 looking·clearly·about due·to the glory of·that light,
Heb 1:3 *Son* (being *the* radiant·offshoot of·*his*·glory and *the*
Heb 3:3 has·been·counted·worthy of·more glory than Moses,
Heb 9:5 it *were* kerubim of·glory fully·overshadowing the
Mt 19:28 ·Man† should·sit upon his Throne of·Glory, yeu
Mt 24:30 ·clouds of·the heaven' with power and much glory.
Mt 25:31 him, then he·shall·sit upon his Throne of·Glory.
Mk 13:26 in thick·clouds' with much power and glory.
Rm 3:23 ·failed and are·destitute of·the glory of·God,
Rm 5:2 and we·boast in expectation of·the glory of·God.
Rm 6:4 ·among dead·men through the glory of·the Father,
Rm 8:21 slavery of·corruption into the glorious liberty of·the
Rm 9:23 ·may·make·known the wealth of·his glory upon *the*
Jac 2:1 YeShua Anointed (*the Lord* of·Glory) with partiality.
Jud 1:24 ·sight of·his glory with an·exuberant·leaping·of·joy
Php 3:21 ·in·nature·like the body of·his glory, according·to
1Pe 4:13 at the revealing of·his glory, yeu·may·be·joyful,
1Pe 4:14 because the Spirit of·glory and of·God rests upon
1Pe 5:1 and·also a·partner of·the glory about to·be·revealed
1Pe 5:4 ·obtain the undiminishable victor's·crown of·glory.
2Pe 1:3 through glory and courageous·moral·excellence.
2Pe 1:17 ·carried·forth to·him by the magnificent glory,
2Th 1:9 of·the Lord, 'and from the glory of·his strength,'
2Th 2:14 ·news, for the·acquisition of·the·glory of·our Lord
Tit 2:13 *the* conspicuous·appearing of·the glory of·our great
1Co 2:8 *it*, they·would·have not crucified the Lord of·glory.
2Co 3:10 because·of the surpassing glory *of·the Service of·*
2Co 3:11 ·being·fully·nullified on·account·of glory, so·much
2Co 3:18 into·the same derived·image from glory to glory,
2Co 4:4 the illumination of·the glorious good·news of·the
2Co 4:6 of·the absolute·knowledge of·the glory of·God in
2Co 4:17 unto phenomenal" eternal weight of·glory,
2Co 6:8 through glory and dishonor, through harsh·
Eph 1:6 for a·glorious high·praise of·his grace— in which
Eph 1:12 for a·high·praise of·his glory, *yes us*, the·ones
Eph 1:14 acquired·possession, for a·high·praise of·his glory.
Eph 1:17 Anointed, the Father of·Glory, may·give to·yeu a·
Eph 1:18 what *is* the wealth of·the glory of·his inheritance in
Eph 3:16 according·to the wealth of·his glory, he·may·grant
Col 1:11 according·to the might of·his glory into all patient·
Col 1:27 *is* the wealth of·the glory of·this Mystery among
Col 1:27 is Anointed-One in yeu (the Expectation of·glory),
1Ti 1:11 according·to the glorious good·news of·the
2Ti 2:10 the·one in Anointed-One Jesus with eternal glory.
Rv 15:8 with·smoke from·among the glory of·God and out
Rv 18:1 the earth was·illuminated as·a·result of·his glory.

EG1391.2 (1x)

1Co 15:40 *is* one·kind, and the *glory* of·the terrestrial *is*

G1392 δοξάζω dôxázō *v.* (62x)

Roots:G1391 Compare:G1740 G5091
xLangAlso:H3513

G1392 V-FAI-1S δοξάσω (1x)

Jn 12:28 "Both I·glorified *it*, and I·shall·glorify *it* again."

G1392 V-FAI-3S δοξάσει (4x)

Jn 13:32 in him, God also shall·glorify him in himself, and
Jn 13:32 him in himself, and shall·glorify him straight·away.
Jn 16:14 That·one shall·glorify me, because from·out·of·me,
Jn 21:19 by·what·kind·of death *Peter* shall·glorify God. And

G1392 V-PAI-1S δοξάζω (2x)

Jn 8:54 answered, "If I·myself glorify my·own·self, my
Rm 11:13 an·ambassador of·Gentiles, I·glorify my service

G1392 V-PAM-3S δοξαζέτω (1x)

1Pe 4:16 let·him·be·ashamed, but let·him·glorify God in

G1392 V-PAN δοξάζειν (1x)

Mk 2:12 such·for all to·be·astonished and to·glorify God,

G1392 V-PAP-NSM δοξάζων (4x)

Jn 8:54 ·is my Father *that·is* the·one glorifying me; of·whom
Lk 5:25 on, he·went·off to·his·own house, glorifying God.
Lk 17:15 returned·back with a·loud voice glorifying God,
Lk 18:43 ·his·sight and was·following him, glorifying God.

G1392 V-PAP-NPM δοξάζοντες (2x)

Lk 2:20 the shepherds returned, glorifying and praising God
2Co 9:13 proof of·this service, they·are·glorifying God over

G1392 V-PAS-2P δοξάζητε (1x)

Rm 15:6 *and* with one mouth, yeu·may·glorify the God and

G1392 V-PPI-3S δοξάζεται (2x)

1Pe 4:14 but according·to yeur·part, he·is·glorified.
1Co 12:26 *with·it*; or·if one member is·glorified, all the

G1392 V-PPP-NSM δοξαζόμενος (1x)

Lk 4:15 in their gatherings, being·glorified by all.

G1392 V-PPS-3S δοξάζηται (2x)

1Pe 4:11 in all·things, may·be·glorified through YeShua
2Th 3:1 may·run·unhindered and may·be·glorified, even

G1392 V-IAI-3S ἐδόξαζεν (1x)

Lk 13:13 ·straightened·upright, and she·was·glorifying God.

G1392 V-IAI-3P ἐδόξαζον (7x)

Lk 5:26 absolutely·all, and they·were·glorifying God and
Lk 7:16 ·all *of·them*, and they·were·glorifying God, saying,
Ac 4:21 because all *men* were·glorifying God over the·
Ac 11:18 they·kept·still, and they·were·glorifying God,
Ac 13:48 ·rejoicing and were·glorifying the Redemptive-word
Ac 21:20 *these·things*, they·were·glorifying the Lord. And·
Gal 1:24 And they·were·glorifying God in me.

G1392 V-AAI-1S ἐδόξασα (2x)

Jn 12:28 *saying*, "Both I·glorified *it*, and I·shall·glorify *it*
Jn 17:4 I·myself glorified you on the earth.

G1392 V-AAI-3S ἐδόξασεν (5x)

Lk 23:47 the·thing *that·was* happening, glorified God,
Ac 3:13 of·our fathers,' he·glorified his·own servant·boy,
Heb 5:5 Anointed-One did·not glorify himself to·be·made
Rm 8:30 he·regarded·as·righteous, these also he·glorified.
Rv 18:7 As·much·as she·glorified herself and lived·in·

G1392 V-AAI-3P ἐδόξασαν (3x)

Mt 9:8 *it*, marveled, and they·glorified God, the·one giving
Mt 15:31 ·ones looking·about. And they·glorified the God
Rm 1:21 already·knowing God, they·neither glorified *him* as

G1392 V-AAM-2S δόξασον (3x)

Jn 12:28 Father, glorify your name." Accordingly, there·
Jn 17:1 the hour has·come. Glorify your Son in·order·that
Jn 17:5 "And now, you, O·Father, glorify me (*along* with

G1392 V-AAM-2P δοξάσατε (1x)

1Co 6:20 Now·then, glorify God in yeur body and in yeur

G1392 V-AAN δοξάσαι (1x)

Rm 15:9 *in·order·for* the Gentiles to·glorify God on·behalf

G1392 V-AAS-3S δοξάσῃ (2x)

Jn 17:1 Son in·order·that your Son also may·glorify you.
Rv 15:4 you, O·Yahweh, and should·glorify your name?

G1392 V-AAS-3P δοξάσωσιν (2x)

Mt 5:16 ·see yeur good works and may·glorify yeur Father,
1Pe 2:12 (after·beholding *them*), they·may·glorify God on

G1392 V-API-3S ἐδοξάσθη (6x)

Jn 7:39 not·yet *given*, because Jesus was·not·yet glorified).
Jn 12:16 but·rather when Jesus was·glorified, then they·
Jn 13:31 "Now the Son of·Clay·Man† is·glorified, and God
Jn 13:31 ·Man† is·glorified, and God is·glorified in him.
Jn 13:32 If God is·glorified in him, God also shall·glorify
Jn 15:8 "In this my Father is·glorified, that yeu·may·bear

G1392 V-APS-3S δοξασθῇ (3x)

Jn 11:4 ·that the Son of·God may·be·glorified through it."
Jn 12:23 that the Son of·Clay·Man† should·be·glorified.
Jn 14:13 ·I·do, that the Father may·be·glorified in the Son.

G1392 V-APS-3P δοξασθῶσιν (1x)

Mt 6:2 the avenues, that they·may·be·glorified by the men·

G1392 V-RPI-1S δεδόξασμαι (1x)

Jn 17:10 *are* mine, and I·have·been·glorified in these *men*·

G1392 V-RPI-3S δεδόξασται (1x)

2Co 3:10 ·been·glorified, has·not·even been·glorified in this

G1392 V-RPP-DSF δεδοξασμένῃ (1x)

1Pe 1:8 ·joy quite·unspeakable, also having·been·glorified,

G1392 V-RPP-NSN δεδοξασμένον (1x)

2Co 3:10 *of·Death* having·been·glorified, has·not·even been·

G1393 Δορκάς Dôrkás *n/p.* (2x)

Compare:G5000 See:G1393-1 G1392-2
xLangAlso:H6646

G1393.2 N/P-NSF Δορκάς (2x)

Ac 9:36 is·referred·to·as Dorcas·*(meaning·Gazelle)*. She·
Ac 9:39 outer·garments Dorcas was·making while·she·was·

G1394 δόσις dósis *n.* (2x)

Roots:G1325

G1394.1 N-NSF δόσις (1x)

Jac 1:17 Every beneficially·good act·of·giving and every

G1394.1 N-GSF δόσεως (1x)

Php 4:15 with·me in *the* matter of·giving and of·receiving,

G1395 δότης dótēs *n.* (1x)

Roots:G1325 See:G1390 G0593-1

G1395 N-ASM δότην (1x)

2Co 9:7 out of·compulsion, for 'God loves a·cheerful giver.'

G1396 δουλ•αγωγέω dôulagōgéō *v.* (1x)

Roots:G1401 G0071 Compare:G5293

G1396.2 V-PAI-1S-C δουλαγωγῶ (1x)

1Co 9:27 and bring·it·more·into·subjection, lest·somehow,

G1397 δουλεία dôulêía *n.* (5x)
Roots:G1398 xLangAlso:H5659

G1397.1 N-ASF δουλείαν (1x)
Gal 4:24 Mount Sinai, bearing·children for slavery, which is

G1397.1 N-GSF δουλείας (4x)
Heb 2:15 of·death) were all *their* lifetime held·in slavery.
Gal 5:1 and do·not again be·held·in by·a·yoke of·slavery.
Rm 8:15 For yeu·did·not receive a·spirit of·slavery again to
Rm 8:21 shall·be·set·free from the slavery of·corruption into

G1398 δουλεύω dôulêúō *v.* (25x)
Roots:G1401 Compare:G1659 G1247 See:G1399 G1400 xLangAlso:H5647

G1398.1 V-FAI-3S δουλεύσει (1x)
Rm 9:12 ·her, "The greater shall·be·a·slave to·the lesser."

G1398.1 V-PAI-1S δουλεύω (2x)
Lk 15:29 *these* so·many years I·am·a·slave to·you, and
Rm 7:25 ·the mind, I myself am·a·slave·to God's Royal-Law,

G1398.1 V-PAI-2P δουλεύετε (1x)
Col 3:24 of·the inheritance, for yeu·are·slaves to·the Lord

G1398.1 V-PAI-3P δουλεύουσιν (1x)
Rm 16:18 (For such·as·these are·not slaves to·our Lord Jesus

G1398.1 V-PAM-2P δουλεύετε (1x)
Gal 5:13 ·rather through the love, be·slaves to·one·another.

G1398.1 V-PAM-3P δουλευέτωσαν (1x)
1Ti 6:2 but·rather more, be·slaves *to·them*, because they·

G1398.1 V-PAN δουλεύειν (8x)
Lk 16:13 ·servant is·able to·be·a·slave to·two lords, for
Lk 16:13 other. Yeu·are·not able to·be·a·slave to·God and
Gal 4:9 principles— to·which yeu·want to·be·slaves, *once*
Mt 6:24 "No·one·at·all is·able to·be·a·slave to·two lords.
Mt 6:24 other. You·are·not able to·be·a·slave to·God and
Rm 6:6 no·longer *for* us to·be·a·slave to·the moral·failure.
Rm 7:6 such·for us to·be·slaves in brand-newness of·spirit,
1Th 1:9 from the idols, to·be·slaves to·the·living and true

G1398.1 V-PAP-NSM δουλεύων (1x)
Ac 20:19 being·a·slave to·the Lord with all humility·of·mind

G1398.1 V-PAP-NPM δουλεύοντες (2x)
Tit 3:3 being·deceived, being·slaves to·diverse longings
Eph 6:7 with a·well-minded·intent, being·slaves to·the Lord

G1398.2 V-PAI-3S δουλεύει (1x)
Gal 4:25 at·the present, and is·enslaved with her children.

G1398.2 V-PAP-NSM δουλεύων (1x)
Rm 14:18 For the·one being·enslaved in these·things to·the

G1398.2 V-AAI-2P ἐδουλεύσατε (1x)
Gal 4:8 ·seen God, yeu·were·enslaved to·the·ones who·are

G1398.2 V-AAS-3P δουλεύσωσιν (1x)
Ac 7:7 nation to·whom they·should·be·enslaved, I·myself

G1398.2 V-RAI-1P δεδουλεύκαμεν (1x)
Jn 8:33 ever·at·any·time, have·we·been·enslaved. How·do

G1398.3 V-PAP-NPM δουλεύοντες (1x)
Rm 12:11 ·hot; in·the·proper·season, by·being·subservient;

G1398.3 V-AAI-3S ἐδούλευσεν (1x)
Php 2:22 with·a·father, he·has·been·subservient to·me in·the

G1399 δούλη dôúlē *n.* (3x)
Roots:G1401 Compare:G3610-1 See:G1398 G1400

G1399 N-NSF δούλη (1x)
Lk 1:38 "Behold, the female·slave of·Yahweh! May·it·

G1399 N-APF δούλας (1x)
Ac 2:18 and upon my female·slaves, I·shall·pour·forth from

G1399 N-GSF δούλης (1x)
Lk 1:48 upon the humble·estate of·his female·slave,' for

G1401 δοῦλος dôûlôs *n.* (129x)
Roots:G1210 Compare:G3011 G3610 G1463 G3816 G1658 See:G1398 G1399 G1400 xLangAlso:H5650

G1401.1 A-APN δοῦλα (2x)
Rm 6:19 ·presented yeur members *as* slaves to·the impurity
Rm 6:19 yeur members *as* slaves to·Righteousness unto

G1401.1 N-NSM δοῦλος (35x)
Jn 8:34 the moral·failure is a·slave of·Moral·Failure.
Jn 8:35 And the slave does·not continue *to·remain* in the
Jn 13:16 ·certainly, I·say to·yeu, a·slave is not greater·than
Jn 15:15 slaves, because the slave does·not personally·know
Jn 15:20 declared to·yeu, 'A·slave is not greater·than his
Lk 7:2 Now a·certain centurion's slave, who was dearly·
Lk 12:43 Supremely·blessed *is* that slave, whom his lord,
Lk 12:45 "But if that slave should·declare in his heart, 'My
Lk 12:47 "And that slave, the·one knowing his lord's will
Lk 14:21 coming·close, that slave announced these·things
Lk 14:22 "And the slave declared, 'Lord, it·has·happened as
Gal 1:10 ·of·clay†, I·would not be a·slave of·Anointed-One.
Gal 3:28 Greek, there·is·not therein slave nor·even free,
Gal 4:7 As·such, you·are no·longer a·slave, but·rather a·son
Mt 10:24 the instructor, nor·even a·slave above his lord.
Mt 10:25 ·become as his instructor, and the slave as his lord.
Mt 18:26 ·down, the slave was·falling·prostrate to·him,
Mt 18:28 "But the·same slave, after·going·forth, found one
Mt 20:27 to·be foremost among yeu, he·must·be yeur slave,
Mt 24:45 is the trustworthy and prudent slave whom his lord
Mt 24:46 Supremely·blessed *is* that slave, whom his lord,
Mt 24:48 "But if that bad slave should·declare in his heart,
Mk 10:44 ·want to·become foremost, shall·be slave of·all.
Rm 1:1 Paul, a·slave of·Jesus Anointed, called·forth *to·be*
Jac 1:1 Jacob, a·slave of·God and of·*the*·Lord YeShua
Jud 1:1 Jude, a·slave of·YeShua Anointed and a·brother of·
2Pe 1:1 Shimon Peter, a·slave and an·ambassador of·
Tit 1:1 Paul, a·slave of·God and an·ambassador of·Jesus
1Co 7:21 Are·you·called·forth *being* a·slave? Let·it·matter
1Co 7:22 in *the* Lord, *though being* a·slave, he·is *the* Lord's
1Co 7:22 *though being* free, is slave of·Anointed-One.
Eph 6:8 ·from the Lord, whether *he·be* slave or free.
Col 3:11 Barbarian, Scythian, slave *or* free, but·rather
Col 4:12 the·one from·among yeu, a·slave of·Anointed-One,
Rv 6:15 the powerful·men, and every slave, and every free·

G1401.1 N-NPM δοῦλοι (23x)
Jn 4:51 walking·down, his slaves approached·and·met him,
Jn 18:18 And the slaves and the assistants stood *there*,
Lk 12:37 "Supremely·blessed *are* those slaves, whom the
Lk 12:38 ·this·manner, supremely·blessed are those slaves.
Lk 17:10 'We·are useless slaves, because we·have·done
Ac 16:17 "These men·of·clay† are slaves of·God Most·High,
Mt 13:27 ·alongside, the slaves of·the master·of·the·house
Mt 13:28 Then the slaves declared to·him, 'So do·you·
Mt 22:10 Also those slaves, going·forth into the roadways,
Rm 6:16 ·know that yeu·are slaves to·whom yeu·present
Rm 6:17 that *formerly* yeu·were *the* slaves of·Moral·Failure,
Rm 6:20 For when yeu·were slaves of·Moral·Failure, yeu·
Php 1:1 Paul and TimoThy, slaves of·Jesus Anointed. To·all
1Pe 2:16 ·the depravity, but·rather *behave* as slaves of·God.
2Pe 2:19 inherently·being slaves of·the corruption— for that·
1Co 7:23 ·a·price. Do·not become slaves of·men·of·clay†.
1Co 12:13 Jews or Greeks, whether slave or free; and all
Eph 6:5 *Now* the slaves: Listen·to·and·obey the lords (*the·*
Eph 6:6 but·rather as slaves of·the Anointed-One, doing the
Col 3:22 *Now* the slaves: Yeu·must·listen·to·and·obey in all·
1Ti 6:1 Let as·many slaves as are under a·yoke resolutely·
Rv 19:5 our God, all·yeu his slaves, and the·ones who·are·
Rv 22:3 in it; and his slaves shall·ritually·minister to·him.

G1401.1 N-VSM δοῦλε (6x)
Lk 19:17 'Well·done, you·beneficially·good slave! Because
Lk 19:22 you, O·evil slave. You·had·personally·known that
Mt 18:32 lord says to·him, 'Evil slave! I·forgave you all that
Mt 25:21 ·good and trustworthy slave! You·were trustworthy
Mt 25:23 ·good and trustworthy slave! You·were trustworthy
Mt 25:26 and slothful slave! You·had·personally·known that

G1401.1 N-ASM δοῦλον (18x)
Jn 18:10 it and struck the slave of·the designated·high·priest,
Lk 2:29 Master, now dismiss your slave in peace, according·
Lk 7:3 him to·come that he·may·thoroughly·save his slave.
Lk 7:10 being·sent found the sick slave healthy·and·sound.
Lk 14:17 And he·dispatched his slave at·the hour of·the
Lk 14:23 And the lord declared to the slave, 'Go·out into the
Lk 17:7 ·is·there from·among yeu having a·slave plowing or
Lk 20:10 in due·season, he·dispatched a·slave to the tenant·
Lk 20:11 he·further·proceeded to·send another slave. And
Lk 22:50 them smote the slave of·the designated·high·priest
Mt 25:30 'And yeu·cast·out the useless slave into the outer
Mt 26:51 And smiting the slave of·the designated·high·priest,
Mk 12:2 "And in·due·season, he·dispatched a·slave to the
Mk 12:4 And again he·dispatched another slave to them, and
Mk 14:47 struck the slave of·the designated·high·priest and
Phm 1:16 no·longer as a·slave, but·rather above a·slave, a·
Phm 1:16 as a·slave, but·rather above a·slave, a·brother
2Ti 2:24 Now it·is·mandatory·for a·slave of·*the*·Lord not to·

G1401.1 N-APM δούλους (18x)
Jn 15:15 "No·longer do·I·refer·to yeu *as* slaves, because the
Lk 15:22 But the father declared to his slaves, 'Bring·out the
Lk 19:13 And calling his ten slaves, he·gave ten more·silver·
Lk 19:15 he·declared *for* these slaves to·be·hailed to·him
Ac 2:18 days, upon my male·slaves and upon my female·
Mt 21:34 drew·near, he·dispatched his slaves to the tenant·
Mt 21:35 ·hold of·his slaves, *handled·them·dishonorably*. In·
Mt 21:36 Again, he·dispatched other slaves more·than at·the
Mt 22:3 and dispatched his slaves to·call·forth the·ones
Mt 22:4 "Again, he·dispatched other slaves, saying,
Mt 22:6 ·secure·hold of·his slaves, abusively·mistreated
Mt 25:14 *who* called his·own slaves and handed·over his
Rm 6:16 ·present yeurselves *as* slaves in attentive·obedience
Tit 2:9 *Exhort* slaves to·submit·themselves to·their·own
2Co 4:5 we·ourselves *are* yeur slaves on·account·of Jesus.
Rv 2:20 ·astray my slaves to·commit·sexual·immorality and
Rv 7:3 ·until we·should·officially·seal the slaves of·our God
Rv 13:16 even the free and the slave, in·order·that to·them

G1401.1 N-DSM δούλῳ (6x)
Jn 18:10 right earlobe. And the slave's name was Malchus.
Lk 7:8 and he·comes; and to·my slave, 'Do this,' and he·
Lk 14:21 the master·of·the·house declared to·his slave, 'Go·
Lk 17:9 he·have gratitude *toward* that slave because he·did
Mt 8:9 and he·comes; and to·my slave, 'Do this,' and he·
Rv 1:1 through his angel, he·signified *it* to·his slave John,

G1401.1 N-DPM δούλοις (8x)
Ac 4:29 and grant·to your slaves *the ability* to·speak your
Mt 22:8 "Then he·says to·his slaves, 'In·fact the wedding is
Mk 13:34 and giving authority to·his slaves, and to·each·
Col 4:1 Yeu·must·personally·furnish to·the slaves the right
Rv 1:1 to·him, to·show to·his slaves what is·mandatory to·
Rv 10:7 as he·proclaimed to·his slaves the prophets.
Rv 11:18 the payment·of·service to·your slaves the prophets,
Rv 22:6 to·his slaves the·things·*of*·which it·is·mandatory to·

G1401.1 N-GSM δούλου (6x)
Lk 12:46 the lord of·that slave shall·come in a·day when he·
Gal 4:1 , varies not·even·one·thing from·a·slave, *though*
Mt 18:27 the lord of·that slave fully·released him and
Mt 24:50 the lord of·that slave shall·come on a·day when he·
Php 2:7 ·of *the* fundamental·nature of·a·slave, becoming in
Rv 15:3 ·sing the song of·Moses, a·slave of·God, and the

G1401.1 N-GPM δούλων (5x)
Jn 18:26 from·among the slaves of·the designated·high·priest,
Mt 18:23 wanted to·tally·up an·accounting among his slaves.
Mt 25:19 time, the lord of·those slaves comes and tally·ups
Rv 19:2 he·avenged the blood of·his slaves *poured·out* at her
Rv 19:18 of·all·men, *both* free and slave, both small and

EG1401.1 (2x)
Rm 6:16 *Yeu·are slaves* to·whom yeu·listen·and·obey,
Rm 7:25 but with·the flesh, *a·slave* to·Moral·Failure's Law.

G1402 δουλόω dôulóō *v.* (8x)
Roots:G1401

G1402.1 V-FAI-3P δουλώσουσιν (1x)
Ac 7:6 land, and *that* they·shall·enslave them and shall·

G1402.1 V-API-2P ἐδουλώθητε (1x)
Rm 6:18 yeu·are·already·enslaved to·Righteousness.

G1402.1 V-APP-NPM δουλωθέντες (1x)
Rm 6:22 Moral·Failure and already·being·enslaved to·God,

G1402.1 V-RPI-3S δεδούλωται (2x)
2Pe 2:19 ·been·defeated, even by·this he·has·been·enslaved.
1Co 7:15 or the sister has·not been·enslaved in such·cases,

G1402.1 V-RPP-APF δεδουλωμένας (1x)
Tit 2:3 slanderers, not having·been·enslaved to·much wine,

G1402.1 V-RPP-NPM δεδουλωμένοι (1x)

Αα Ββ Γγ Δδ Εε Ζζ Ηη Θθ Ιι Κκ Λλ Μμ Νν Ξξ Οο Ππ Ρρ Σσ Ττ Υυ Φφ Χχ Ψψ Ωω

Gal 4:3 ·were infants, were having·been·enslaved under the

G1402.2 V-AAI-1S ἐδούλωσα (1x)

1Co 9:19 all *men·of·clay†*, I·make·a·slave·of myself to·all,

G1403 δοχή dôchḗ *n.* (2x)

Roots:G1209 Compare:G1062 G4224
xLangAlso:H4960

G1403 N-ASF δοχήν (2x)

Lk 5:29 And Levi made a·great reception for·him in his·own

Lk 14:13 whenever you·should·make a·reception, call·forth

G1404 δράκων drákōn *n.* (13x)

Compare:G3789 G4567 G4566 G1228
xLangEquiv:H8577

G1404.1 N-NSM δράκων (1x)

Rv 13:11 ·male·lamb, and it·was·speaking as a·dragon.

G1404.2 N-NSM δράκων (8x)

Rv 12:3 and behold a·great fiery·red Dragon, having seven

Rv 12:4 the earth. And the Dragon stands in·the·sight of·the

Rv 12:7 against the Dragon; and the Dragon (and his angels

Rv 12:9 And the great Dragon was·cast·out, the original

Rv 12:13 And when the Dragon saw that he·was·cast to the

Rv 12:16 the flood·water which the Dragon cast out of·his

Rv 12:17 And the Dragon was·angry toward the woman, and

Rv 13:2 as a·mouth of·a·lion. And the Dragon gave it his

G1404.2 N-ASM δράκοντα (2x)

Rv 13:4 ·fell·prostrate *directly·before* the Dragon which gave

Rv 20:2 And he·securely·held the Dragon, the original

G1404.2 N-GSM δράκοντος (2x)

Rv 12:7 his angels waged·war against the Dragon; and the

Rv 16:13 *come* out of·the mouth of·the Dragon, and out of·

G1405 δράσσομαι drássômai *v.* (1x)

Compare:G2638 See:G1404 G1406

G1405.2 V-PNP-NSM δρασσόμενος (1x)

1Co 3:19 "'*He·is* the·one entrapping the wise in their·own

G1406 δραχμή drachmḗ *n.* (5x)

Roots:G1405 Compare:G1220 G3588-2 See:G0787
G1323 G4715 G5069-1
xLangEquiv:H0150 H1871

G1406.1 N-ASF δραχμήν (2x)

Lk 15:8 ·completely·lose one drachma, does·not·indeed

Lk 15:9 I·found the drachma which I·completely·lost.'

EG1406.1 (2x)

Ac 19:19 pieces·of·silver *(which·is fifty thousand drachmas)*.

Mt 17:27 ·stater·coin *(worth four drachmas)*. Taking·hold·of

G1406.2 N-APF δραχμάς (1x)

Lk 15:8 woman, having ten drachma·coins·*of·silver*, if she·

G1407 δρέπανον drépanôn *n.* (8x)

xLangAlso:H4038

G1407.2 N-ASN δρέπανον (8x)

Mk 4:29 immediately he·dispatches the sickle, because the

Rv 14:14 victor's·crown, and in his hand a·sharp sickle.

Rv 14:15 the thick·cloud, "Thrust·in your sickle and reap,

Rv 14:16 on the thick·cloud cast·in his sickle on the earth,

Rv 14:17 in the heaven, he also *was* having a·sharp sickle.

Rv 14:18 yell to·the·one having the sharp sickle, saying,

Rv 14:18 "Thrust·in your sharp sickle and collect·for·vintage

Rv 14:19 And the angel cast his sickle into the earth, and

G1408 δρόμος drômôs *n.* (3x)

Roots:G5143 Compare:G0073 G1240-1
xLangEquiv:H4794 xLangAlso:H4793

G1408.1 N-ASM δρόμον (2x)

Ac 13:25 ·fulfilling his·own running·race, he·was·saying,

Ac 20:24 as·so to·fully·complete my running·race with joy,

G1408.3 N-ASM δρόμον (1x)

2Ti 4:7 I·have·finished the race·course; I·have·fully·kept

G1409 Δρούσιλλα Drôúsilla *n/p.* (1x)

G1409.2 N/P-DSF Δρουσίλλῃ (1x)

Ac 24:24 together with·his wife Drusilla (herself·being a·

G1410 δύναμαι dýnamai *v.* (214x)

Compare:G2480 See:G1411 G1415 G1415-1
xLangAlso:H3201

G1410.1 V-FDI-1P δυνησόμεθα (1x)

Ac 19:40 about which we·shall·be·able to·render an·account

G1410.1 V-FDI-2S δυνήσῃ (2x)

Lk 16:2 for you·shall·not be·able to·manage·the·estate any·

Ac 24:8 ·from whom you·shall·be·able, after·scrutinizing

G1410.1 V-FDI-2P δυνήσεσθε (1x)

Eph 6:16 (with which yeu·shall·be·able to·extinguish all the

G1410.1 V-FDI-3S δυνήσεται (4x)

Mk 8:4 ·source shall·someone be·able to·stuff these·men full

Mk 9:39 name *that* also shall·be·able to·swiftly speak·ill·of

Rm 8:39 any other created·thing shall·be·able to·separate us

1Co 6:5 Not·even one that shall·be·able to·discern up *the*

G1410.1 V-FDI-3P δυνήσονται (1x)

Lk 21:15 to·yeu shall·not be·able to·declare·against nor·even

G1410.1 V-PNI-1S δύναμαι (7x)

Jn 5:30 "I·myself am·not able to·do not·even·one·thing of

Jn 13:37 "Lord, why am·I·not able to·follow you at·this·

Lk 11:7 in the bed; I·am·not able to·rise·up and·give to·you.

Lk 14:20 and on·account·of that, I·am·not able to·come.'

Mt 9:28 to·them, "Do·yeu·trust that I·am·able to·do this?

Mt 26:53 that I·am·not able at·this·moment to·implore my

Mt 26:61 ·man was·disclosing, 'I·am·able to·demolish the

G1410.1 V-PNI-1P δυνάμεθα (9x)

Jn 14:5 so·then how are·we·able to·personally·know the

Ac 4:16 ·in JeruSalem, and we·are·not able to·deny *it*.

Ac 4:20 For we·ourselves are·not able not to·speak the·

Ac 17:19 saying, "Are·we·able to·know what this

Mt 20:22 ·in *it*?" They·say to·him, "We·are·able."

Mk 10:39 And they·declared to·him, "We·are·able." And

1Th 3:9 For what thanks are·we·able to·recompense to·God

2Co 13:8 For we·are·not able *to·do* anything against the truth

1Ti 6:7 *it·is* plain that we·are·not·even able to·carry anything

G1410.1 V-PNI-2S δύνασαι (9x)

Jn 13:36 I·head·on·out, you·are·not able to·follow me now,

Lk 5:12 if you·should·want, you·are·able to·purify me."

Lk 6:42 Or how are·you·able to·say to·your brother,

Mt 5:36 head, because you·are·not able to·make one hair

Mt 8:2 Lord, if you·should·want, you·are·able to·purify me.

Mk 1:40 "If you·should·want, you·are·able to·purify me."

Mk 9:22 him, but·yet if you·are·able *to·do* something,

Mk 9:23 declared to·him, "If you·are·able to·trust, all·things

1Co 7:21 to·you, but·yet if·also you·are·able to·become free

G1410.1 V-PNI-2S-C δύνῃ (1x)

Rv 2:2 and that you·are·not able to·bear bad·men, and *that*

G1410.1 V-PNI-2P δύνασθε (28x)

Jn 5:44 How·are yeu·yeurselves able to·trust, receiving glory

Jn 7:34 I AM, *there* yeu·yeurselves are·not able to·come."

Jn 7:36 I AM, *there* yeu·yeurselves are·not able to·come'?

Jn 8:21 I·myself head·on·out, yeu are·not able to·come."

Jn 8:22 I·myself head·on·out, yeu are·not able to·come.'"

Jn 8:43 speech? *It·is* because yeu·are·not able to·hear my

Jn 13:33 I·myself head·on·out, yeu are·not able to·come,'

Jn 15:5 ·from me, yeu·are·not able to·do not·even·one·thing

Jn 16:12 ·yet yeu·are·not able to·bear them at·this·moment.

Lk 5:34 to them, "¿! Are yeu·able to·make the Sons of·the

Lk 12:26 if yeu·are·not·even able *to·do* that·thing·which·is·

Lk 16:13 the other. Yeu·are·not able to·be·a·slave to·God

Ac 5:39 ·from·out of·God, yeu·are·not able to·demolish it;

Ac 15:1 manner of·Moses, yeu·are·not able to·be·saved."

Ac 27:31 the sailing·ship, yeu are·not able to·be·saved."

Mt 6:24 the other. You·are·not able to·be·a·slave to·God

Mt 12:34 in·what·way are·yeu·able to·speak beneficially·

Mt 16:3 of·the sky, but are·not able *to·discern* the signs of·

Mt 20:22 what yeu·are·requesting. Are·yeu·able to·drink the

Mk 10:38 yeu·are·requesting. Are·yeu·able to·drink the cup

Mk 14:7 whenever yeu·should·want, yeu·are·able to·do well

Jac 4:2 jealously·desire, and·yet yeu·are·not able to·obtain.

1Co 3:2 Moreover neither yet now are·yeu·able,

1Co 10:13 to·be·tried above what yeu·are·able, but·rather

1Co 10:21 Yeu·are·not able to·drink *the* Lord's cup and·also

1Co 10:21 Yeu·are·not able to·participate·and·belong to·*the*·

1Co 14:31 For yeu·are·able, each one, all to·prophesy, in·

Eph 3:4 ·reading·*it*·aloud, yeu·are·able to·understand my

G1410.1 V-PNI-3S δύναται (70x)

Jn 3:2 ·instructor, for not·even·one·man is·able to·do these

Jn 3:3 ·born from·above, he·is·not able to·see the kingdom

Jn 3:4 him, "How·is a·man·of·clay† able to·be·born, being

Jn 3:4 ·agedly·old·man? ¿! Is·he·able to·enter a·second·time

Jn 3:5 of·water and of·Spirit, he·is·not able to·enter into the

Jn 3:9 to·him, "How·are these·things able to·happen?

Jn 3:27 ·of·clay† is·not able to·receive not·even·one·thing,

Jn 5:19 the Son is·not able to·do not·even·one·thing by

Jn 6:44 Not·even·one·man is·able to·come to me, unless the

Jn 6:52 saying, "How·is this·man able to·give us the flesh

Jn 6:60 "This is a·hard saying; who is·able to·hear it?

Jn 6:65 to·yeu that not·even·one·man is·able to·come to me,

Jn 7:7 The world is·not able to·hate yeu, but it·hates me,

Jn 9:4 is·coming, when not·even·one·man is·able to·work.

Jn 9:16 ·man·of·clay†, full·of·moral·failure, able to·do such

Jn 10:21 ·a·demon. ¿!·Is a·demon able to·open·up blind

Jn 10:29 all; and not·even·one is·able to·snatch *them* from·

Jn 10:35 came, and the Scripture is·not able to·be·broken …

Jn 14:17 whom the world is·not able to·receive, because it·

Jn 15:4 Just·as the vine·sprout is·not able to·bear fruit of

Lk 3:8 I·say to·yeu that God is·able from·out of·these stones

Lk 5:21 ·of·God? Who is·able to·forgive moral·failures,

Lk 12:25 ·among yeu by·being·anxious is·able to·add one

Lk 14:26 his·own soul also, he·is·not able to·be my disciple.

Lk 14:27 right·behind me, is·not able to·be my disciple.

Lk 14:33 all his holdings, he·is·not able to·be my disciple.

Lk 16:13 ·one household·servant is·able to·be·a·slave to·two

Lk 18:26 they·declared, "Who then is·able to·be·saved?

Ac 10:47 "Is any·man able to·forbid water *such·for* these not

Ac 25:11 me, no·one·at·all is·able to·gratuitously·hand me

Heb 2:18 being·tried, he·is·able to·swiftly·help the·ones

Heb 7:25 from·which·place he·is·able also to·save·them to

Heb 10:1 , never·at·any·time is·it·able with·the same

Mt 3:9 I·say to·yeu that God is·able from·out of·these stones

Mt 5:14 ·set·out high·upon a·mount is·not able to·be·hidden.

Mt 6:24 "No·one·at·all is·able to·be·a·slave to·two lords.

Mt 6:27 ·among yeu by·being·anxious is·able to·add one

Mt 7:18 A·beneficially·good tree is·not able to·produce evil

Mt 12:29 "Or how·else·is anyone able to·enter into the

Mt 19:25 saying, "Who then is·able to·be·saved?

Mt 26:42 if this cup is·not able to·pass·away from me

Mt 27:42 ·saved others, *yet* he·is·not able to·save himself. If

Mk 2:7 ·of·God? Who is·able to·forgive moral·failures,

Mk 3:24 that kingdom is·not able to·remain·established.

Mk 3:25 itself, that home is·not able to·remain·established.

Mk 3:26 ·been·divided, he·is·not able to·remain·established,

Mk 3:27 One·is·not able to·thoroughly·plunder the strong·

Mk 7:15 that traversing into him is·able to·defile him, but·

Mk 7:18 into the man·of·clay† is·not able to·defile him,

Mk 9:3 a·cloth-fuller on the earth is·not *even* able to·whiten.

Mk 9:29 not·even·one·thing is this kind able to·come·forth,

Mk 10:26 themselves, "Then who is·able to·be·saved?

Mk 15:31 "He·saved others; himself, he·is·not able to·save.

Rm 8:7 Law-of-Liberty of·God, for neither is·it·able *to·be*).

Jac 2:14 have works? ¿! Is the trust not able to·save him?

Jac 3:8 not·even·one among·clay·men† is·able to·tame the

Jac 3:12 ¿!·Is a·fig·tree able, my brothers, to·produce olives?

1Co 2:14 foolishness to·him. And he·is·not able to·know *it*,

1Co 3:11 For not·even·one·man is·able to·lay another

1Co 12:3 And not·even·one·man is·able to·declare, "Jesus

1Co 12:21 And *the* eye is·not able to·declare to·the hand, "I·

1Ti 5:25 being otherwise, are·not able to·be·hidden, *likewise*

1Ti 6:16 sees (*which* it·is·not·even possible *for* men·of·clay†

2Ti 2:13 trustworthy; he·is·not able to·deny himself."

1Jn 3:9 in him. And he·is·not able to·morally·fail, because

1Jn 4:20 ·clearly·seen, in·what·way is·he·able to·love God

Rv 3:8 ·opened·up, and not·even·one·man is·able to·shut it,

Rv 6:17 is·come, and who is·able to·remain·established?

Rv 9:20 and wood, which neither are·able to·look·about, nor

Rv 13:4 Daemonic·Beast? Who is·able to·wage·war against it

G1410.1 V-PNI-3P δύνανται (8x)

Lk 20:36 For neither are·they·able to·die any·longer, for

Ac 24:13 Neither are·they·able to·establish·proof *against* me

Heb 10:11 not·even·at·any·time is·able to·entirely·remove

Mt 9:15 ¿!·Are the Sons of·the bride-chamber able to·mourn,

Mk 2:19 the Sons of·the bride-chamber able to·fast, while
Mk 2:19 among themselves, they·are·not able to·fast.
Rm 8:8 the·ones being in flesh are·not able to·satisfy God.
1Co 15:50 that flesh and blood is·not able to·inherit God's
G1410.1 V-PNN δύνασθαι (8x)
Mk 1:45 such·for *Jesus* no·longer to·be·able to·enter openly
Mk 3:20 such·for them not to·be·able so·much·as to·eat
Mk 4:32 ·for the birds of·the sky to·be·able to·nest under its
Php 3:21 operation *within* himself to·be·able even to·subject
1Co 10:13 the exit·out, for·yeu to·be·able to·bear·under *it*.
2Co 1:4 in·order·for us to·be·able to·comfort the·ones in
2Co 3:7 Sons of·IsraEl not to·be·able to·gaze·intently into
Eph 6:11 yeu to·be·able to·stand·still specifically·against the
G1410.1 V-PNO-1S δυναίμην (1x)
Ac 8:31 "For how·is·it *that* I·might be·able *to·know them*,
G1410.1 V-PNO-3P δύναιντο (1x)
Ac 27:12 ·also, if·somehow they·might·be·able to·arrive at
G1410.1 V-PNP-ASM δυνάμενον (4x)
Heb 4:15 who·is·not being·able to·sympathize with·our
Heb 5:7 yell and tears toward the·one being·able to·save him
Mt 10:28 ·of the·one being·able to·completely·destroy both
Jac 1:21 Redemptive-word, the·one being·able to·save yeur
G1410.1 V-PNP-APN δυνάμενα (2x)
2Ti 3:7 learning, and·yet never·even being·able to·come to
2Ti 3:15 Writings— the·ones being·able to·make you wise
G1410.1 V-PNP-APM δυναμένους (1x)
Ac 27:43 ·ordered the·ones being·able to·swim, after·
G1410.1 V-PNP-DSM δυναμένῳ (4x)
Ac 20:32 of·his grace, the·one being·able to·build·yeu·up,
Rm 16:25 Now to·the·one being·able to·firmly·establish yeu
Jud 1:24 Now to·the·one being·able to·vigilantly·keep yeu
Eph 3:20 to·the·one who·is·being·able, above·and·beyond
G1410.1 V-PNP-GSN δυναμένου (1x)
Ac 27:15 *in·it*, and not being·able to·tack into·the wind,
G1410.1 V-PNP-GSM δυναμένου (1x)
Ac 24:11 with·you being·able to·know that there·are not
G1410.1 V-PNP-GPM δυναμένων (1x)
Mt 10:28 killing the body, but not being·able to·kill the soul.
G1410.1 V-PNP-NSF δυναμένη (1x)
Lk 13:11 and not being·able to·pull·herself·up·straight to
G1410.1 V-PNP-NSM δυνάμενος (6x)
Lk 1:20 keeping·silent, and not being·able to·speak, even·
Ac 21:34 crowd. And not being·able to·know the absolute·
Heb 5:2 *also* being·able to·be·moderate with·the·ones being·
Gal 3:21 law being·able to·give·life-above was·already·given
Mt 19:12 heavens. The·one being·able to·accommodate *it*,
Jac 4:12 one lawmaker, the·one being·able to·save and to·
G1410.1 V-PNP-NPF δυνάμεναι (1x)
Heb 9:9 ·offered, not being·able to·make·completely·mature
G1410.1 V-PNP-NPM δυνάμενοι (3x)
Mk 2:4 Yet not being·able to·further·draw·near to·him on·
Rm 15:14 knowledge, who·are·being·able also to·admonish
1Th 2:6 nor from others, *though* being·able to·be a·burden
G1410.1 V-PNS-3S δύνηται (1x)
Rv 13:17 in·order·that not anyone should·be·able to·buy or
G1410.1 V-PNS-3P δύνωνται (1x)
Lk 16:26 from·here to yeu should·not be·able; nor·even may
G1410.1 V-INI-2P-ATT ἠδύνασθε (1x)
1Co 3:2 and not food, for yeu·were·not·yet able *to·bear it*.
G1410.1 V-INI-3S ἐδύνατο (2x)
Ac 26:32 man·of·clay† was·able to·have·been·fully·released,
Mt 22:46 And not·even·one·man was·able to·answer him a·
G1410.1 V-INI-3S-ATT ἠδύνατο (13x)
Jn 9:33 God, he·would·not be·able to·do not·even·one·thing
Jn 11:37 the eyes of·the blind, able to·make *it·be* also that
Lk 1:22 ·coming·forth, he·was·not able to·speak to·them.
Lk 19:3 who Jesus was, and was·not able·to for the crowd,
Mt 26:9 For this ointment was·able to·be·sold·off for·much,
Mk 5:3 And not·even·one·man was·able to·bind him, not·
Mk 6:5 And he·was·not able to·do there not·even·one
Mk 6:19 and was·wanting to·kill him, but she·was·not able,
Mk 14:5 that·thing was·able to·be·sold·off for·upwards·of
Rv 5:3 beneath the earth, was·able to·open·up the official·

Rv 7:9 crowd which not·even·one·man was·able to·number,
Rv 14:3 Elders; and not·even·one·man was·able to·learn the
Rv 15:8 power. And none·at·all were·able to·enter into the
G1410.1 V-INI-3P-ATT ἠδύναντο (3x)
Jn 12:39 On·account·of that, they·were·not able to·trust,
Lk 8:19 toward him, yet were·not able to·encounter him on·
Mk 4:33 to·them, just·as they·were·able to·hear *it*.
G1410.1 V-ADS-2P δυνηθῆτε (1x)
Eph 6:13 in·order·that yeu·may·be·able to·withstand *them* in
G1410.1 V-AOI-1S-ATT ἠδυνήθην (1x)
1Co 3:1 I·myself, brothers, am·not able to·speak to·yeu as
G1410.1 V-AOI-1P-ATT ἠδυνήθημεν (2x)
Mt 17:19 "Why·were we·ourselves not able to·cast it out?
Mk 9:28 "Why·were we·ourselves not able to·cast it out?
G1410.1 V-AOI-2P-ATT ἠδυνήθητε (1x)
Ac 13:39 yeu·were·not able·to be·regarded·as·innocent by
G1410.1 V-AOI-3S-ATT ἠδυνήθη (1x)
Mk 7:24 ·man to·know *it*, but he·was·not able to·lay·hidden.
G1410.1 V-AOI-3P-ATT ἠδυνήθησαν (3x)
Lk 9:40 they·should·cast him out, yet they·were·not able."
Heb 3:19 ·at how they·were·not able to·enter·in through a·
Mt 17:16 they·were·not able to·cure·or·bring·relief·to him."
EG1410.1 (4x)
Mt 7:18 neither *is* a·rotten tree *able* to·produce good fruit.
Rm 8:31 ·*this* on·our behalf, who *is·able to·be* against us?
Jac 3:12 not·even·one wellspring *is·able* to·produce *both*
Eph 6:13 absolutely·all, *that yeu·may·be·able* to·stand·still.
G1410.2 V-PNI-3S δύναται (3x)
Jn 1:46 declared to·him, "Is·it·possible *for* anything
Lk 6:39 to·them: "Is·it possible·for *the* blind to·guide *the*
Mk 3:23 "How·is·it possible *for·the* Adversary-Accuser to·
G1410.2 V-PNO-3P δύναιντο (1x)
Ac 27:39 which they·purposed, if it·were·possible, to·propel

G1411 δύναμις dýnamis *n.* (125x)

Roots:G1410 Compare:G2904 G0970 G1849 G2479 G4598-2 See:G1415 G1413 xLangAlso:H1369 H3581
G1411.1 N-ASF δύναμιν (2x)
Mt 25:15 to·each·man according·to his·own ability, and
2Co 1:8 ·weighed·down beyond *our·own* ability *to·bear it*,
EG1411.1 (5x)
Lk 7:21 he·graciously·bestowed the *ability* to·look·about.
Lk 7:42 And with·them not having *the ability* to·repay, he·
Ac 4:29 and grant·to your slaves *the ability* to·speak your
Mt 18:25 But with·him not having *the ability* to·repay, his
2Pe 1:15 my exodus, *the ability* to·make recollection of·
G1411.2 N-NSF δύναμις (14x)
Lk 1:35 and *the* power of·the·Most·High shall·overshadow
Lk 5:17 JeruSalem. And the power of·Yahweh was *present*
Lk 6:19 of·him, because power came·forth directly·from
Ac 8:10 "This·man is the great power of·God."
Mt 6:13 yours is the kingdom, and the power, and the glory,
Rm 1:16 for it·is God's power to Salvation to·everyone
Rm 1:20 ·seen, both his supra-eternal power and divinity,
1Co 1:18 to·us who·are·being·saved, it·is the power of·God.
1Co 15:56 Moral·Failure, and the power of·Moral·Failure *is*
2Co 12:9 for·you, for my power is·made·fully·complete in
2Co 12:9 ·that the power of·Anointed-One may·encamp
Rv 7:12 and the honor, and the power, and the strength, *be*
Rv 12:10 the Salvation, and the power, and the kingdom of·
Rv 19:1 the honor, and the power *are* to·Yahweh our God!
G1411.2 N-NPF δυνάμεις (4x)
Lk 21:26 The Land, for the powers of·the heavens shall·be·
Mt 24:29 heaven, and the powers of·the heavens shall·be·
Mk 13:25 shall·be falling·away, and the powers, the·ones in
Rm 8:38 nor principalities, nor powers, nor things·currently·
G1411.2 N-ASF δύναμιν (28x)
Lk 8:46 for I·myself did·know power going·forth from me.
Lk 9:1 disciples, he·gave them power and authority over all
Lk 10:19 and upon all the power of·the enemy; and not·
Lk 24:49 yeu·should·dress·yeurselves·with power from·out
Ac 1:8 But·rather yeu·shall·receive power, with·the Holy
Heb 7:16 according·to a·power of·an·indestructible life-above
Heb 11:34 quenched *the* power of·fire, escaped *the* edge of·

Mt 22:29 ·seen the Scriptures, nor·even the power of·God.
Mk 5:30 immediately in himself the power going·forth out
Mk 12:24 ·seen the Scriptures, nor·even the power of·God?
Rm 9:17 you, that I·may·indicate my power by you, and that
Php 3:10 *and* to·know him and the power of·his resurrection,
2Pe 1:16 ·made·known to·yeu the power and initial·arrival
1Co 1:24 Anointed-One *is* God's power and God's wisdom,
1Co 4:19 ·been·puffed·up, but·rather the power *thereof*.
1Co 14:11 ·know the power·*(the·meaning)* of·the voice, I·
1Co 15:24 every principality and all authority and power.
2Co 8:3 that according·to *their* power, I·testify, even above·
2Co 8:3 above·and·beyond *their* power, of·their·own·choice,
Eph 3:20 *to·do* according·to the power, the·one operating in
2Ti 1:8 in·the good·news according·to God's power;
2Ti 3:5 ·reverence, but having·denied its power. So·then,
Rv 3:8 it, because you·have a·little power, and observantly·
Rv 4:11 and the honor and the power, because you·yourself
Rv 5:12 ·been·slaughtered) to·receive the power and wealth
Rv 11:17 you·have·taken your great power and reigned.
Rv 13:2 And the Dragon gave it his power, and his throne,
Rv 17:13 ·give·forth their·own power and authority to·the
G1411.2 N-DSF δυνάμει (26x)
Lk 1:17 of *Yahweh* in *the* spirit and power of·EliJah, "to·
Lk 4:14 Jesus returned·back in the power of·the Spirit to
Lk 4:36 Because with authority and power he·orders the
Ac 3:12 as·though by·our·own power or devout·reverence
Ac 4:7 they·inquired, "By what·kind·of power, or by what·
Ac 4:33 And with·great power, the ambassadors were·
Ac 10:38 with·Holy Spirit and with·power, the·same who
Mk 9:1 ·see the kingdom of·God having·come in power."
Rm 1:4 ·*be the* Son of·God in power according·to a·spirit of·
Rm 15:13 in the Expectation by *the* power of·Holy Spirit.
Rm 15:19 with power of·signs and wonders, with *the* power
Rm 15:19 and wonders, with *the* power of·God's Spirit,
1Pe 1:5 being·dutifully·kept by God's power through trust
2Pe 2:11 being greater·in strength and power, do·not bring
1Th 1:5 merely, but·rather also in power and in Holy Spirit
2Th 1:11 ·beneficial·goodness and work of·trust in power,
2Th 2:9 of·the Adversary-Accuser with all power and signs
1Co 2:5 wisdom of·men·of·clay†, but·rather in God's power.
1Co 4:20 of·God *is* not in word, but·rather in power.
1Co 5:4 spirit, together with·the power of·our Lord Jesus
1Co 15:43 It·is·sown in weakness; it·is·awakened in power.
2Co 6:7 Redemptive-word of·truth, by God's power, through
Eph 3:16 yeu to·be·made·mighty with·power through his
Col 1:11 being·enabled with all power according·to the
Col 1:29 ·to his operation, the·one operating in me in power.
Rv 1:16 *is* as the sun *that* shines·forth in its power.
G1411.2 N-GSF δυνάμεως (21x)
Lk 21:27 in a·thick·cloud' with power and much glory.
Lk 22:69 ·down at *the* right·hand of·the power of·God."
Ac 6:8 Stephen, full of·trust and power, was·doing great
Heb 1:3 all·things by·the utterance of·his power) who, after·
Mt 24:30 ·clouds of·the heaven' with power and much glory.
Mt 26:64 at *the* right·hand' of·the Power and 'coming upon
Mk 13:26 in thick·clouds' with much power and glory.
Mk 14:62 ·down at *the* right·hand of·the power, and·also '
2Pe 1:3 As with·his divine power, all·things pertaining·to
2Th 1:7 YeShua from heaven with *the* angels of·his power;
1Co 2:4 but·rather in demonstration of·Spirit and of·power,
1Co 6:14 shall·fully·awaken us through his·own power.
2Co 4:7 surpassing·excellence of·the power may·be of·God,
2Co 13:4 yet he·lives as·a·result of·God's power. For we·
2Co 13:4 with·him as·a·result of·God's power for yeu.
Eph 1:19 *is* the surpassing greatness of·his power toward us,
Eph 1:21 all principality and authority, power and dominion,
Eph 3:7 to·me according·to the operation of·his power.
2Ti 1:7 a·spirit of·timidity, but·rather of·power, and of·love,
Rv 15:8 glory of·God and out of·his power. And none·at·all
Rv 18:3 out of·the power of·her voluptuous·luxuries."
G1411.2 N-GPF δυνάμεων (1x)
1Pe 3:22 and powers already·being·made·subject·to·him.
G1411.3 N-APF δυνάμεις (1x)

Δδ

Heb 6:5 *the* miraculous·powers of·*the*·age about·to·come,
G1411.4 N-NPF δυνάμεις (9x)
Lk 10:13 Because if these miracles happened in Tyre and
Mt 11:20 which the large·majority of·his miracles happened,
Mt 11:21 Because if the miracles occurring in yeu had·
Mt 11:23 Because if the miracles happening in you had·
Mt 13:54 ·man *have* this wisdom and·also *do these* miracles?
Mt 14:2 and on·account·of that, miracles operate in him.
Mk 6:2 to·him, that even such miracles happen through his
Mk 6:14 and on·account·of that, the miracles operate in him.
1Co 12:29 Not all *are operating·in* miracles.
G1411.4 N-ASF δύναμιν (3x)
Heb 11:11 Sarah herself received a·miracle for an·ovulation
Mk 6:5 able to·do there not·even·one miracle, except laying
Mk 9:39 there·is not·even·one who shall·do a·miracle in my
G1411.4 N-APF δυνάμεις (6x)
Ac 8:13 ·observing both signs and great miracles occurring.
Ac 19:11 the hands of·Paul, was·doing miracles (*and* not
Gal 3:5 the Spirit to·yeu and operating miracles among yeu,
Mt 7:22 ·out demons, and in·your name do many miracles?'
Mt 13:58 he·did·not do many miracles there on·account·of
1Co 12:28 after·that *the·ones operating·in* miracles, then
G1411.4 N-DPF δυνάμεσιν (3x)
Ac 2:22 by God for yeu with·miracles and wonders and signs
Heb 2:4 with·a·diversity·of miracles and with·distributions
2Co 12:12 by miraculous·signs, and wonders, and miracles.
G1411.4 N-GPF δυνάμεων (2x)
Lk 19:37 voice concerning all *the* miracles that they·saw,
1Co 12:10 and to·another, operations of·miracles, to·another

G1412 δυναμόω dynamóō *v.* (1x)
Roots:G1411
G1412 V-PPP-NPM δυναμούμενοι (1x)
Col 1:11 being·enabled with all power according·to the

G1413 δυνάστης dynástēs *n.* (3x)
Roots:G1410 Compare:G2904
G1413.1 N-NSM δυνάστης (1x)
1Ti 6:15 *·is* the supremely·blessed and only Power, the King
G1413.1 N-APM δυνάστας (1x)
Lk 1:52 He·demoted powers from *their* thrones and elevated
G1413.3 N-NSM δυνάστης (1x)
Ac 8:27 of·Ethiopia, a·eunuch, a·potentate of·Candace, the

G1414 δυνατέω dynatéō *v.* (1x)
Roots:G1415 Compare:G2594 G2480
G1414 V-PAI-3S δυνατεῖ (1x)
2Co 13:3 weak toward yeu, but·rather is·powerful in yeu.

G1415 δυνατός dynatós *adj.* (35x)
Roots:G1410 Compare:G2478 G2900 G0972
See:G1414 G1415-1
G1415.1 A-NSM δυνατός (11x)
Lk 14:31 first *and* takes·counsel whether he·is able with ten
Ac 11:17 , then who *am* I? Was·I able to·prevent God?
Heb 11:19 reckoning that God *was* able to·awaken *him* even
Rm 4:21 what *God* has·promised, *God* was able also to·do.
Rm 11:23 ·grafted·in, for God is able to·engraft them again.
Rm 14:4 ·be·established, for God is able to·establish him.
Jac 3:2 *is* a·completely·mature man, able also to·bridle the
Tit 1:9 in·order·that he·may·be able also to·exhort by the
2Co 9:8 And God *is* able *to·cause* all grace to·abound toward
2Co 12:10 for whenever I·may·be·weak, then I·am able.
2Ti 1:12 ·convinced that he·is able to·vigilantly·keep my
G1415.1 A-NPM δυνατοί (2x)
Ac 25:5 "the·ones among yeu *who·are* able *to·do so*, after·
Rm 15:1 we·ourselves, the·ones *being* able *to·partake*, ought
G1415.2 A-NSN δυνατόν (8x)
Ac 2:24 because·indeed it·was not possible *for·Jesus* to·be·
Ac 20:16 he·was·hastening, if it·were possible for·him, to·
Gal 4:15 ·yeu that, if *it·had·been* possible, digging·out yeur
Mt 24:24 wonders, such·as, if possible, to·deceive even the
Mt 26:39 "O·my Father, if it·is possible, let this cup pass·
Mk 13:22 to utterly·lead·astray, if possible, even the
Mk 14:35 and prayed that, if it·were possible, the hour may·
Rm 12:18 *and* if *it·is* possible, for yeur part, behaving·
G1415.2 A-NPN δυνατά (5x)
Lk 18:27 with men·of·clay† are possible with God."
Mt 19:26 impossible, but with God all·things are possible."
Mk 9:23 to·trust, all·things *are* possible to·the·one trusting."
Mk 10:27 with God, for with God all·things are possible."
Mk 14:36 Father, all·things *are* possible to·you. Personally·
G1415.3 A-NSM δυνατός (4x)
Lk 1:49 "Because the powerful·one did magnificent·things
Lk 24:19 became a·man, a·prophet powerful in deed and
Ac 7:22 of·the·Egyptians, and he·was powerful in words
Ac 18:24 an·eloquent man being powerful in the Scriptures.
G1415.3 A-NPM δυνατοί (3x)
1Co 1:26 ·to flesh, not many *are* powerful, not many *are*
2Co 13:9 but yeu·yeurselves should·be powerful. And this
Rv 6:15 regiment·commanders, and the powerful·men, and
G1415.3 A-NPN δυνατά (1x)
2Co 10:4 *are* not fleshly, but·rather powerful in·God to *the*
G1415.4 A-ASN δυνατόν (1x)
Rm 9:22 his wrath and to·make·known his power, bore with

G1416 δύνω dýnō *v.* (2x)
δῦμι dŷmi
See:G1744
G1416.2 V-PAP-GSM δύνοντος (1x)
Lk 4:40 Now with·the sun sinking·down, as·many·as were
G1416.2 V-2AAI-3S ἔδυ (1x)
Mk 1:32 when the sun sank·down, they·were·bringing to

G1417 δύο dýô *n.* (136x)
G1417.1 -- (1x)
Lk 17:36 [(Two *men* shall·be in the field; one shall·be·
G1417.1 N-NUI δύο (122x)
Jn 1:35 John stood also *with* two from·among his disciples.
Jn 1:37 And the two disciples heard him speaking, and they·
Jn 1:40 was one from·among the two of·the·ones following
Jn 2:6 having·room·for two or three ten·gallon·measures
Jn 4:40 to·abide with them, and he·abided there two days.
Jn 4:43 Now after the two days, he·went·off from·there and
Jn 6:9 barley loaves·of·bread, and two small·broiled·fish,
Jn 8:17 Torah-Law that the testimony of·two men·of·clay† is
Jn 11:6 he·was·sick, in·fact he·remained two days still in *the*
Jn 19:18 they·crucified him, and·also two others with him,
Jn 20:4 But the two·men were·running at·the·same·time, yet
Jn 20:12 and she·observes two angels in white sitting·down,
Jn 21:2 the *sons* of·Zebedee, and two others from·among his
Lk 2:24 of·turtledoves or two of·the·Offspring of·a·dove."
Lk 3:11 "The·one having two tunics must·kindly·give to·
Lk 5:2 Now he·saw two sailboats having·settled directly·by
Lk 7:19 John, summoning a·certain two of·his disciples,
Lk 7:41 ·was a·certain lender *having* two needy·debtors; the
Lk 9:3 neither money; neither to·have two tunics apiece.
Lk 9:13 than five loaves·of·bread and two fish, except·that
Lk 9:16 the five loaves·of·bread and the two fish, looking·up
Lk 9:30 And behold, two men were·speaking·together with·
Lk 9:32 they·saw his glory and the two men, the·ones
Lk 10:35 the stirring·of·day, casting·forth two denarii, he·
Lk 12:6 five little·sparrows sold for·two assarion·coins?
Lk 12:52 ·divided, three against two, and two against three.
Lk 15:11 "A·certain man·of·clay† had two sons.
Lk 17:34 in·that night there·shall·be two *reclining* on one
Lk 17:35 Two *women* shall·be grinding in·unison; one shall·
Lk 18:10 "Two men·of·clay† walked·up to the Sanctuary·
Lk 19:29 of·Olives), he·dispatched two of·his disciples,
Lk 21:2 also a·certain needy widow casting two bits *in* there
Lk 22:38 "Lord, behold, here *are* two daggers." And he·
Lk 23:32 And also two others, *who·were* criminals, were·led
Lk 24:4 about this, behold, two men stood·over them in
Lk 24:13 And behold, two from·among them were
Ac 1:10 departing, behold, two men had·stood·nearby them
Ac 1:23 And they·established two, Joseph being·called
Ac 1:24 which one·from·among these two you·selected
Ac 7:29 in *the* land of·Midian, where he·begot two sons.
Ac 9:38 this *city*, the disciples dispatched two men to him,
Ac 10:7 after·hollering·out·for two of·his household·servants
Ac 12:6 Peter was being·laid·to·sleep between two soldiers,
Ac 19:10 And this happened for·a·span·of two years, such·
Ac 19:22 So after·dispatching two of·the·ones attending to·
Ac 19:34 *present*, for·a·span·of about two hours— yelling·
Ac 23:23 And summoning a·certain two of·the centurions,
Heb 6:18 ·that, on·account·of two unalterable matters·of·
Gal 4:22 ·has·been·written, that AbRaham had two sons, one
Gal 4:24 ·an·allegory, for these are the two covenants. One
Mt 4:18 Sea of·Galilee, YeShua saw two brothers, Simon
Mt 4:21 ·forward from·there, he·saw two other brothers,
Mt 5:41 *to·head·out·for* one mile, head·on·out with him two.
Mt 8:28 ·met him two·men being·possessed·with·demons,
Mt 9:27 passing·on from·there, two blind·men followed him
Mt 10:10 for *yeur* journey, nor·even two tunics, nor·even
Mt 10:29 Are·not·indeed two little·sparrows sold for·an·
Mt 11:2 *and* sending·word by·two of·his disciples,
Mt 14:17 here except five loaves·of·bread and two fish."
Mt 14:19 five loaves·of·bread and the two fish, looking·up to
Mt 18:8 or crippled, rather·than having two hands or two
Mt 18:8 ·than having two hands or two feet *and* to·be·cast
Mt 18:9 with·one·eye, rather·than having two eyes *and* to·
Mt 18:16 personally·take with you one or two more, that "
Mt 18:16 that "at *the* mouth of·two or three witnesses every
Mt 18:19 to·yeu, that if two of·yeu should·mutually·agree
Mt 18:20 "For where two or three are having·been·gathered·
Mt 19:5 to·his wife, and the two shall·be distinctly one flesh
Mt 19:6 As·such, they·are no·longer two, but·rather one
Mt 20:21 "Declare that these two sons of·mine may·sit, one
Mt 20:24 ·greatly·displeased concerning the two brothers.
Mt 20:30 And behold, two blind·men are·sitting·down
Mt 21:1 of·Olives), then YeShua dispatched two disciples,
Mt 21:28 A·certain·man·of·clay† was·having two children,
Mt 21:31 Out of·the two, which one·did the will of·the father
Mt 24:40 Then two shall·be in the field; the one is·
Mt 24:41 Two *women shall·be* grinding at the mill-house;
Mt 25:15 ·of·silver, and to·another two, and to·another one,
Mt 25:17 likewise, the·one *having·received* the two, he also
Mt 25:17 *·received* the two, he also gained another two.
Mt 25:22 also, the·one receiving the two talants·of·silver,
Mt 25:22 Lord, you·handed·over to·me two talants·of·silver.
Mt 25:22 See, I·gained another two talants·of·silver upon
Mt 26:2 "Yeu·personally·know that after two days the
Mt 26:37 *with·him* Peter and the two Sons of·Zebedee, he·
Mt 26:60 eventually, two false·witnesses coming·alongside,
Mt 27:21 "Which of the two do·yeu·want *that* I·should·fully·
Mt 27:38 ·that·time, *there·were* two robbers being·crucified
Mt 27:51 the curtain of·the Temple is·torn in two from top to
Mk 6:7 and he·began to·dispatch them two by·two. And he·
Mk 6:9 and yeu·should·not dress·yeurselves·with two tunics.
Mk 6:38 "Five, and two fish."
Mk 6:41 five loaves·of·bread and the two fish, looking·up to
Mk 6:41 and he·distributed the two fish among·them·all.
Mk 9:43 crippled, than having the two hands *and* to·go·off
Mk 9:45 the life-above, than having two feet *and* to·be·cast
Mk 9:47 with·one·eye, than having two eyes *and* to·be·cast
Mk 10:8 and the two shall·be distinctly one flesh.
Mk 10:8 ' As·such, they·are no·longer two, but·rather one
Mk 11:1 Mount of·Olives, he·dispatches two of·his disciples
Mk 12:42 a·certain helplessly·poor widow cast·in two bits,
Mk 14:1 Now after two days, it·would·be *the Judeans'*
Mk 14:13 And he·dispatches two of·his disciples and says
Mk 15:27 together with·him, they·crucify two robbers: one
Mk 15:38 curtain of·the Temple was·torn in two from top to
Php 1:23 For I·am·clenched as·a·result of·the two *choices*,
1Co 6:16 is one body? For "the two," he·replies, "shall·be
1Co 14:27 ·tongue, accordingly *let·it·be* two or at·the most
1Co 14:29 Now *let* prophets speak two or three, and *let* the
2Co 13:1 "At *the* mouth of·two or three witnesses shall
Eph 2:15 , in·order·that he·should·create the two in himself
Eph 5:31 his wife, and the two shall·be distinctly one flesh.
1Ti 5:19 "except at *the mouth* of·two or three witnesses.
Rv 9:12 went·away; behold, there·come two woes still after
Rv 11:2 ·shall·trample the Holy City forty two lunar·months.

Rv 11:4 These are the two olive·trees and the two Fine·Oil·
Rv 11:4 two olive·trees and the two Fine·Oil·Lampstands
Rv 11:10 ·one·another because these two prophets tormented
Rv 12:14 And to·the woman, two wings of·the great eagle
Rv 13:5 ·given to·it to·do *this for* forty two lunar·months.
Rv 13:11 earth. And it·was·having two horns like a·young·
Rv 19:20 ·its derived·image. The two were·cast, still·living,

G1417.1 N-DPM δυσίν (6x)
Lk 12:52 ·been·thoroughly·divided, three against two, and
Lk 16:13 ·servant is·able to·be·a·slave to·two lords, for
Heb 10:28 ·apart·from compassion upon two or three
Mt 6:24 "No·one·at·all is·able to·be·a·slave to·two lords.
Mk 16:12 he·was·made·apparent to·two·men from·among
Rv 11:3 "And I·shall·give *unto* my two witnesses, and they·

G1417.1 N-DPF δυσίν (3x)
Ac 12:6 two soldiers, having·been·bound with·two chains,
Ac 21:33 ·ordered *him* to·be·bound with·two chains, and·
Mt 22:40 On these two commandments is·hung all the

EG1417.1 (1x)
Ac 18:19 and·these *two* he·left·behind at·that·location, but

G1417.2 N-NUI δύο (1x)
Rv 9:16 cavalry *was* twice ten·thousand times·ten·thousand

G1417.3 N-NUI δύο (2x)
Lk 10:1 also, and he·dispatched them up by·twos before his
Mk 6:7 he·began to·dispatch them two by·two. And he·was·

G1419 δυσ•βάστακτος dysbástaktôs *adj.* (2x)
Roots:G1418 G0941

G1419 A-APN δυσβάστακτα (2x)
Lk 11:46 ·load·up the men·of·clay† with·oppressive loads,
Mt 23:4 ·captively·bind weighty and oppressive loads and

G1420 δυσ•εντερία dysêntêría *n.* (1x)
Roots:G1418 G1787

G1420 N-DSF δυσεντερία (1x)
Ac 28:8 ·clenched with·*recurring*·fevers and dysentery. Paul

G1421 δυσ•ερμήνευτος dysêrmḗnêutôs *adj.* (1x)
Roots:G1418 G2059

G1421.3 A-NSM δυσερμήνευτος (1x)
Heb 5:11 ·us, yet the·explanation·is·difficult to·relay *to·yeu*

G1422 δύσ•κολος dýskôlôs *adj.* (1x)
Roots:G1418 See:G1423

G1422.2 A-NSN δύσκολον (1x)
Mk 10:24 how exceedingly·difficult it·is for·the·ones

G1423 δυσ•κόλως dyskṓlōs *adv.* (3x)
Roots:G1422 See:G1423-1

G1423 ADV δυσκόλως (3x)
Lk 18:24 declared, "How impossibly·difficult *it·is, that*
Mt 19:23 that *it·is* impossibly·difficult *that* a·wealthy·man
Mk 10:23 disciples, "How impossibly·difficult *it·is that* the·

G1424 δυσμή dysmḗ *n.* (5x)
Roots:G1416 See:G0395 G1005 G3558

G1424.2 N-GPF δυσμῶν (5x)
Lk 12:54 ·above·the·horizon from *the* west, immediately
Lk 13:29 And they·shall·come from east and west, and from
Mt 8:11 many shall·come from east and west, and they·shall·
Mt 24:27 shines·forth as·far·as·to *the* west, in·this·manner
Rv 21:13 *are* three gates; *and* on *the* west *are* three gates.

G1425 δυσ•νόητος dysnṓētôs *adj.* (1x)
Roots:G1418 G3539

G1425 A-NPN δυσνόητα (1x)
2Pe 3:16 are some·things *that·are* hard·to·understand—

G1426 δυσ•φημία dysphēmía *n.* (1x)
Roots:G1418 G5345 Compare:G0989 G3059 G0819 See:G2162

G1426.2 N-GSF δυσφημίας (1x)
2Co 6:8 through harsh·reputation and good·reputation, as

G1427 δώ•δεκα dṓdêka *n.* (61x)
Roots:G1417 G1176 Compare:G2395-1 See:G1177

G1427.1 N-NUI δώδεκα (29x)
Jn 6:13 and overfilled twelve wicker·baskets with·fragments
Jn 11:9 "Are·there not·indeed twelve hours of·the daylight?
Lk 2:42 And when he·was twelve years·of·age, after·
Lk 6:13 *to·himself* and was·selecting twelve of them whom
Lk 8:42 ·child, a·daughter of·about twelve years·of·age, and
Lk 8:43 being with a·flow of·blood for twelve years, who
Lk 9:17 *was* twelve wicker·baskets of·*bread*·fragments.
Lk 22:30 ·sit on thrones judging the twelve tribes of·IsraEl."
Ac 7:8 *begot* Jacob; and Jacob *begot* the twelve patriarchs.
Mt 9:20 ·*ill*, discharging·a·flow·of·blood *for* twelve years.
Mt 14:20 of·the fragments— twelve wicker·baskets full.
Mt 19:28 yeu also shall·sit upon twelve thrones, judging the
Mt 19:28 twelve thrones, judging the twelve tribes of·IsraEl.
Mt 26:53 ·present to·me more than twelve legions of·angels?
Mk 3:14 And he·made twelve *ambassadors*, that they·
Mk 5:25 woman being with a·flow of·blood *for* twelve years,
Mk 5:42 was·walking, for she·was of·twelve years·of·age.
Mk 6:43 And they·took·up twelve wicker·baskets full of·
Mk 8:19 did·yeu·take·up?" They·say to·him, "Twelve."
Jac 1:1 YeShua Anointed. To·the twelve tribes, to·the·ones
Rv 12:1 and upon her head a·victor's·crown of·twelve stars.
Rv 21:12 great and high, having twelve gates, and twelve
Rv 21:12 having twelve gates, and twelve angels upon the
Rv 21:12 are *the names* of·the twelve tribes of·the Sons of·
Rv 21:14 wall of·the CITY *is* having twelve foundations, and
Rv 21:16 he·measured the CITY at twelve thousand stadia.
Rv 21:21 And the twelve gates *were* twelve pearls; again,
Rv 21:21 And the twelve gates *were* twelve pearls; again,
Rv 22:2 ·tree of·Life-above, producing twelve *kinds·of* fruits,

G1427.3 N-NUI δώδεκα (31x)
Jn 6:67 So·then Jesus declared to·the twelve, "And *do* yeu·
Jn 6:70 *that* selected yeu, the twelve, yet one from·among
Jn 6:71 to·hand him over, being one from·among the twelve.
Jn 20:24 (one from·among the twelve, the·one being·
Lk 8:1 And the twelve *were* together with·him,
Lk 9:1 And calling·together his twelve disciples, he·gave
Lk 9:12 Now the twelve, coming·alongside, declared to·him,
Lk 18:31 Now personally·taking the twelve, he·declared to
Lk 22:3 being from·among the number of·the twelve.
Lk 22:14 ·to·eat, and the twelve ambassadors *did·likewise*
Lk 22:47 ·to·as Judas, one of·the twelve, went·before them,
Ac 6:2 But the twelve, after·summoning the multitude of·the
Mt 10:1 And summoning his twelve disciples, he·gave to·
Mt 10:2 And the names of·the twelve ambassadors are these:
Mt 10:5 These twelve YeShua dispatched, after·charging
Mt 11:1 ·assigning *these·things* to·his twelve disciples, he·
Mt 20:17 YeShua personally·took the twelve disciples aside
Mt 26:14 Then one of·the twelve, the·one being·referred·to·
Mt 26:20 he·was·reclined·at·the·meal with the twelve.
Mt 26:47 behold, Judas, one of·the twelve, came, and with
Mk 4:10 ·with him (together with·the twelve) asked him
Mk 6:7 Then he·summoned the twelve, and he·began to·
Mk 9:35 ·down, he·hollered·out·for the twelve and says to·
Mk 10:32 And personally·taking again the twelve, he·began
Mk 11:11 late, he·went·out to BethAny with the twelve.
Mk 14:10 Judas IsCariot, one of·the twelve, went·off to the
Mk 14:17 ·evening occurring, he·comes with the twelve.
Mk 14:20 "*It·is* one from·among the twelve, the·one who·is·
Mk 14:43 comes·openly, being one of·the twelve, and with
1Co 15:5 by·Kephas·*(called·Peter)*, then to·the twelve.
Rv 21:14 *are the* names of·the twelve ambassadors of·the

EG1427.3 (1x)
Mk 3:16 And *these are the twelve*: on·Simon, he·laid a·name

G1428 δω•δέκατος dōdékatôs *adj.* (1x)
Roots:G1427

G1428 A-NSM δωδέκατος (1x)
Rv 21:20 deep·blue·hyacinth; the twelfth, amethyst.

G1429 δω•δεκά•φυλον dōdêkáphylôn *n.* (1x)
Roots:G1427 G5443

G1429 N-NSN δωδεκάφυλον (1x)
Ac 26:7 to which *promise* our twelve·tribes, in earnestness,

G1430 δῶμα dō̂ma *n.* (7x)
Roots:G1185-1 Compare:G3624 G0833

G1430.2 N-ASN δῶμα (2x)
Lk 5:19 the crowd, walking·up on the rooftop, they·sent him
Ac 10:9 Peter walked·up upon the rooftop to·pray *at·midday*

G1430.2 N-GSN δώματος (3x)
Lk 17:31 day, whoever shall·be upon the rooftop, with his
Mt 24:17 The·one on the rooftop must·not walk·down to·
Mk 13:15 And the·one on the rooftop must·not walk·down

G1430.2 N-GPN δωμάτων (2x)
Lk 12:3 shall·be·officially·proclaimed upon the rooftops.
Mt 10:27 in the ear, officially·proclaim upon the rooftops.

G1431 δωρεά dōrêá *n.* (12x)
Roots:G1435 Compare:G1390 See:G1433 G1434 G1432

G1431.1 N-NSF δωρεά (2x)
Ac 10:45 the Gentiles, the voluntary·present of·the Holy
Rm 5:15 grace of·God and the voluntary·present by the grace

G1431.1 N-ASF δωρεάν (5x)
Jn 4:10 ·personally·known the voluntary·present of·God, and
Ac 2:38 yeu·shall·receive the voluntary·present of·the Holy
Ac 8:20 *that* the voluntary·present of·God may·be·procured
Ac 11:17 to·them the equally·same voluntary·present (as
Eph 3:7 according·to the voluntary·present of·the grace of·

G1431.1 N-DSF δωρεᾷ (1x)
2Co 9:15 *be* to·God for his indescribable voluntary·present!

G1431.1 N-GSF δωρεᾶς (3x)
Heb 6:4 after·tasting of·the heavenly voluntary·present, and
Rm 5:17 and of·the voluntary·present of·righteousness shall·
Eph 4:7 measure of·the voluntary·present of·Anointed-One.

EG1431.1 (1x)
Rm 5:18 ·act, *the voluntary·present of·righteousness came*

G1432 δωρεάν dōrêán *adv.* (9x)
Roots:G1431 xLangAlso:H2600

G1432.1 ADV δωρεάν (4x)
Rm 3:24 being·regarded·as·righteous as·a·free·present by·
2Th 3:8 Neither as·a·free·present did·we·eat personally·from
Rv 21:6 of·the water of·life-above as·a·free·present.
Rv 22:17 ·him·take the water of·life-above as·a·free·present.

G1432.2 ADV δωρεάν (3x)
Mt 10:8 demons. Yeu·received freely·without·charge; give
Mt 10:8 freely·without·charge; give freely·without·charge.
2Co 11:7 Because freely·without·charge, I·proclaimed to·

G1432.3 ADV δωρεάν (1x)
Gal 2:21 Anointed-One died, offered·freely·for·nothing."

G1432.4 ADV δωρεάν (1x)
Jn 15:25 "They·personally·hated me freely·without·cause."

G1433 δωρέομαι dōrêômai *v.* (3x)
Roots:G1435 Compare:G3936 See:G1434 G1431 G1432

G1433.1 V-ADI-3S ἐδωρήσατο (1x)
Mk 15:45 ·centurion, he·voluntarily·presented the body to·

G1433.2 V-RPI-3S δεδώρηται (1x)
2Pe 1:4 Through these he·has·endowed to·us the most·

G1433.2 V-RPP-GSF δεδωρημένης (1x)
2Pe 1:3 devout·reverence are·having·been·endowed to·us,

G1434 δώρημα dṓrēma *n.* (2x)
Roots:G1433 See:G1431

G1434 N-NSN δώρημα (2x)
Rm 5:16 And the endowment *is* not as through one already·
Jac 1:17 and every complete endowment is from·above,

G1435 δῶρον dō̂rôn *n.* (19x)
Compare:G1390 G2378 G2878 G5486 G5498-1 G1595 See:G1431 G1432 G1433 G1434 G0734 G3564 xLangAlso:H5071 H2065 H7810 H7133

G1435.1 N-NSN δῶρον (2x)
Mt 23:19 which *is* greater, the present or the Sacrifice·Altar,
Eph 2:8 birthed·from·out of·yeurselves; *it·is* God's present.

G1435.1 N-NPN δῶρα (1x)
Heb 9:9 in which both presents and sacrifices were·offered,

G1435.1 N-ASN δῶρον (5x)
Mt 5:23 if you·should·bring your present to the Sacrifice·
Mt 5:24 leave your present there before the Sacrifice·Altar
Mt 5:24 ·your brother, and then coming, offer your present.
Mt 8:4 and offer the present that Moses specifically·
Mt 23:19 Sacrifice·Altar, the·one making the present holy?

G1435.1 N-APN δῶρα (6x)
Lk 21:1 ·saw the wealthy·men casting their presents into the

Heb 5:1 ·order·that he·may·offer both presents and sacrifices
Heb 8:3 ·established·to·offer both presents and sacrifices, by·
Heb 8:4 the·ones offering the presents according·to the
Mt 2:11 treasures, they·brought·forth to·him presents: *being*
Rv 11:10 they·shall·send presents to·one·another because

G1435.1 N-DSN δώρῳ (1x)
Mt 23:18 whoever should·swear by the present, the·one upon

G1435.2 N-NSN δῶρον (2x)
Mt 15:5 ·*be, it·is now* a·voluntary·offering·of·sacrifice,,"
Mk 7:11 is *now* Qorban, a·voluntary·offering·of·sacrifice,"'

G1435.2 N-APN δῶρα (1x)
Lk 21:4 into the voluntary·offerings·of·sacrifice for·God, but

G1435.2 N-DPN δώροις (1x)
Heb 11:4 his voluntary·offerings·of·sacrifice; and through

Εε - Epsilon

G1436 ἔα éa *inj.* (2x)
Roots:G1439

G1436.1 INJ ἔα (2x)
Lk 4:34 saying, "Let·*us*·be! What·does·this·have to·do·
Mk 1:24 saying, "Let·*us*·be! What·does·this·have to·do·

G1437 ἐ•άν êán *cond.* (244x)
Roots:G1487 G0302 See:G3361

G1437.1 COND ἐάν (5x)
Heb 3:6 — provided·that we·should·fully·hold·onto the
Heb 3:14 provided·that we·should·fully·hold·onto the
Jac 2:17 the trust, provided·that it·should·have no works, is
1Co 6:18 provided·that a·man·of·clay† should·commit *it*, is
1Ti 2:15 bearing·of·children— provided·that *such women*

G1437.2 COND ἐάν (212x)
Jn 3:12 trust, how shall·yeu·trust if I·should·declare to·yeu
Jn 5:31 "If I·myself should·testify concerning my·own·self,
Jn 5:43 yeu·do·not receive me. If another should·come in
Jn 6:51 of·the heaven. "If any·man should·eat from·out of·
Jn 6:62 So·then, *what* if yeu·should·observe the Son of·
Jn 7:17 If any·man should·want to·do his will, he·shall·know
Jn 7:37 yelled·out, saying, "If any·man should·thirst, let·
Jn 8:16 And yet if I·myself should·judge, my verdict is true,
Jn 8:31 having·trusted in·him, "If yeu should·continue in
Jn 8:36 So·then, if the Son should·set yeu free, yeu·shall
Jn 8:51 I·say to·yeu, if anyone should·observantly·keep my
Jn 8:52 ·yourself say, 'If someone should·observantly·keep
Jn 8:54 Jesus answered, "If I·myself glorify my·own·self,
Jn 8:55 I·myself have·seen him. And if I·should·declare, 'I·
Jn 9:22 ·themselves even·now that if any·man should·affirm
Jn 9:31 ·full·of·moral·failure, but·rather if any·man may·be
Jn 10:9 "I AM the door. If someone should·enter·in through
Jn 11:9 of·the daylight? If any·man should·walk·along in
Jn 11:10 But if any·man should·walk·along in the night, he·
Jn 11:40 to·you, that, if you·should·trust, you·shall·gaze·
Jn 11:48 If we·should·leave him alone in·this·manner, all
Jn 11:57 a·commandment, that if any·man should·know
Jn 12:24 it abides alone. But if it·should·die, it·bears much
Jn 12:26 "If any·man should·attend to·me, let·him·follow me
Jn 12:26 attendant shall·be. And if any·man should·attend
Jn 12:32 And·I, if I·should·be·elevated from·among the
Jn 12:47 "And if someone should·hear my utterances and
Jn 13:8 Jesus answered him, "If I·should·not wash you,
Jn 13:17 supremely·blessed are·yeu if yeu·should·do them.
Jn 13:35 yeu·are disciples to·me, if yeu·should·have love
Jn 14:3 And if I·should·traverse and should·make·ready a·
Jn 14:14 If yeu·should·request something in my name, I·
Jn 14:15 "If yeu·should·love me, observantly·keep my
Jn 14:23 and declared to·him, "If anyone should·love me,
Jn 15:6 "If someone should·not remain in me, he·is·already·
Jn 15:7 "If yeu·should·abide in me and my utterances
Jn 15:10 "If yeu·should·observantly·keep my
Jn 15:14 are my friends, if yeu·should·do as·much·as I·
Jn 16:7 ·myself should·go·away, for if I·should·not go·away
Jn 16:7 come to yeu; but if I·should·depart, I·shall·send him
Jn 19:12 ·out, saying, "If you·should·fully·release this·man,
Jn 21:22 Jesus says to·him, "If I·should·want him to·remain
Jn 21:23 die, but·rather, "If I·should·want him to·remain
Jn 21:25 ·as Jesus did, which if each one should·be·written,
Lk 4:7 Accordingly, if you should·fall·prostrate in·the·sight
Lk 5:12 saying, "Lord, if you·should·want, you·are·able to·
Lk 6:33 And if yeu·should·beneficially·do·good for·the·ones
Lk 6:34 "And if yeu·should·lend *to·them* personally·from
Lk 10:6 And, in·fact, if a·son·of·peace should·be there,
Lk 11:12 Or also, if he·should·request an·egg, ¿! shall·he·
Lk 12:38 "And if he·should·come in the second watch, or
Lk 12:45 "But if that slave should·declare in his heart, 'My
Lk 14:34 "Salt *is* good, but if the salt should·become·bland,
Lk 15:8 ·coins·*of·silver*, if she·should·completely·lose one
Lk 16:30 AbRaham! But·yet if someone should·traverse to
Lk 17:3 "But if your brother should·morally·fail against you,
Lk 17:3 reprimand him; and if he·should·repent, forgive
Lk 17:4 And if he·should·morally·fail against you seven·
Lk 18:17 I·say to·yeu, whoever, if he·should·not accept the
Lk 19:31 And if any·man should·ask·of·yeu, 'Why do·yeu·
Lk 19:40 "I·say to·yeu that if these should·keep·silent, the
Lk 20:5 saying, "If we·should·declare, 'From·out of·
Lk 20:6 But if we·should·declare, 'From·out of·men·of·
Lk 20:28 Moses wrote to·us, if any·man's brother should·die
Lk 22:67 he·declared to·them, "If I·should·declare *it* to·yeu,
Lk 22:68 And if also I·should·ask *of·yeu*, no, yeu·may·not
Ac 5:38 and let them be, because if this counsel or this work
Ac 26:5 from·the·start (if they·should·determine to·testify),
Heb 3:7 Spirit says, "'Today if yeu·should·hear his voice,
Heb 3:15 it·is·said, "'Today, if yeu·should·hear his voice,
Heb 4:7 ·declared, "'Today, if yeu·should·hear his voice,
Heb 10:38 ·result of·trust, and if he·should·shrink·back, my
Heb 13:23 I·shall·gaze·upon yeu, if he·should·come swiftly.
Gal 1:8 But·yet even if we·ourselves or an·angel from·out
Gal 5:2 I Paul say to·yeu, that if yeu·should·be·circumcised,
Mt 4:9 ·things I·shall·give to·you, if upon·falling·down,
Mt 5:13 salt of·the earth, but if the salt should·become·bland
Mt 5:23 "So·then, if you·should·bring your present to the
Mt 5:46 "For if yeu·should·love the·ones loving yeu, what
Mt 5:47 And if yeu·should·greet yeur brothers merely, what·
Mt 6:14 "For if yeu·should·forgive the men·of·clay† their
Mt 6:15 But if yeu·should·not forgive the men·of·clay† their
Mt 6:22 the eye. Accordingly, if your eye should·be clear·
Mt 6:23 But if your eye should·be evil, your whole body
Mt 7:9 from·among yeu, who if his son should·request bread
Mt 7:10 And if he·should·request a·fish, ¿! shall·hand him a·
Mt 8:2 saying, "Lord, if you·should·want, you·are·able to·
Mt 9:21 within herself, "If merely I·should·lay·hold of·his
Mt 10:13 And if, in·fact the home should·be worthy, *let* yeur
Mt 10:13 peace come upon it, but if it·should·not be worthy,
Mt 11:6 whoever *he·is*, if he·should·not be·tripped·up by
Mt 12:11 shall·have one sheep, that if this *sheep* should·fall
Mt 12:36 idle utterance, which if the men·of·clay† should·
Mt 15:14 of·blind·men. And if a·blind·man should·guide a·
Mt 16:26 ·of·clay† being·benefited, if he·should·gain the
Mt 17:20 For certainly I·say to·yeu, if yeu·should·have trust
Mt 18:12 ·yeurselves suppose? "If it·should·happen *that* any
Mt 18:13 And if he·should·happen to·find it, certainly I·say
Mt 18:15 "But if your brother should·morally·fail against
Mt 18:15 you and him alone. If he·should·listen·to you,
Mt 18:16 But if he·should·not hear *you, then* personally·take
Mt 18:17 And if he·should·disregard them, declare *it* to·the
Mt 18:17 ·Out·assembly, but if also he·should·disregard the
Mt 18:19 I·say to·yeu, that if two of·yeu should·mutually·
Mt 21:3 And if any·man should·declare anything to·yeu,
Mt 21:21 "Certainly I·say to·yeu, if yeu·should·have trust
Mt 21:24 question, which if yeu·should·declare *an·answer*
Mt 21:25 themselves, saying, "If we·should·declare,
Mt 21:26 But if we·should·declare, 'From·out of·men·of·
Mt 22:24 Moses declared, if a·certain·man should·die not
Mt 24:23 "At·that·time, if any·man should·declare to·yeu,
Mt 24:26 "Accordingly, if they·should·declare to·yeu,
Mt 24:48 "But if that bad slave should·declare in his heart,
Mt 28:14 And if this should·be·heard by the governor, we·
Mk 1:40 saying to·him, "If you·should·want, you·are·able
Mk 3:24 And if a·kingdom should·be·divided against itself,
Mk 3:25 And if a·home should·be·divided against itself, that
Mk 7:11 ·yeurselves say, 'If a·man·of·clay† should·declare
Mk 8:3 And if I·should·dismiss them without·eating to their·
Mk 8:36 ·it·benefit a·man·of·clay†, if he·should·gain the
Mk 9:43 "So if your hand should·entrap you, chop it off.
Mk 9:45 And if your foot should·entrap you, chop it off.
Mk 9:47 "And if your eye should·entrap you, cast it out.
Mk 9:50 Salt *is* good, but if the salt should·become unsalty,
Mk 10:12 And if a·wife should·divorce her husband and
Mk 10:15 I·say to·yeu, whoever, if he·should·not accept the
Mk 11:3 And if any·man should·declare to·yeu, 'Why·do
Mk 11:31 themselves, saying, "If we·should·declare,
Mk 11:32 But·rather if we·should·declare, 'From·out of·
Mk 12:19 Moses wrote for·us that if any·man's brother

Mk 13:21 “And at·that·time, if any·man should·declare to·
Mk 14:31 “Even·if it·should·be·necessary·for me to·die·
Rm 2:25 benefits if you·should·practice Torah-Law. But if
Rm 2:25 Torah-Law. But if you·should·be a·transgressor of·
Rm 2:26 Accordingly, if the·one uncircumcised should·
Rm 7:2 to·the living husband; but if the husband should·die,
Rm 7:3 Accordingly, if she·should·come to·another man
Rm 7:3 ·the·public·title·of an·adulteress. But if the husband
Rm 10:9 If you·should·affirm with your mouth, “Jesus *is*
Rm 11:22 ·benevolent·kindness, if you·should·persist in·the
Rm 11:23 And those also, if they·should·not persist in·the
Rm 12:20 Accordingly, “‘If your enemy should·hunger,
Rm 12:20 provide·some·food·for him; if he·should·thirst,
Rm 13:4 beneficially·good·thing. But if you·should·do the
Rm 14:23 differently has·been·condemned if he·should·eat,
Rm 15:24 yeu *from* there·to *Spain*, if first I·should·be partly
Jac 2:2 For if there·should·enter into yeur gathering a·man
Jac 2:15 But if a·brother or sister should·subsist *being* naked
Jac 4:15 yeu *ought* to·say, “If the Lord should·will, then
Jac 5:19 Brothers, if anyone among yeu should·be·led·astray
1Pe 3:13 yeu, if yeu·should·become attentive·imitators of·
1Th 3:8 Because now we·live, if yeu should·stand·fast in *the*
1Co 4:19 to yeu promptly, if the Lord should·determine, and
1Co 5:11 ·with *such·as·these*: if any·man being·named a·
1Co 6:4 Accordingly in·fact, if yeu·should·have arbitrations
1Co 7:8 it·is good·for·them if they·should·remain even·as
1Co 7:11 But even if she·is·separated, she·must·remain
1Co 7:28 But even if you·should·marry, you·did·not
1Co 7:28 you·did·not morally·fail; and if the virgin should·
1Co 7:36 virgin·daughter, if she·should·be past·her·prime
1Co 7:39 husband lives. But if her husband should·be·laid·
1Co 7:40 ·is supremely·blessed if in·this·manner she·should·
1Co 8:8 to·God. For neither if we·should·eat, do·we·excel,
1Co 8:8 ·eat, do·we·excel, nor·even if we·should·not eat,
1Co 8:10 For if any·man should·see you (the·one having
1Co 10:28 But if any·man should·declare to·yeu, “This is
1Co 11:14 yeu, in·fact, that if a·man should·wear·long·hair,
1Co 11:15 But if a·woman should·wear·long·hair, it·is a·
1Co 12:15 If the foot should·declare, “Because I·am not a·
1Co 12:16 And if the ear should·declare, “Because I·am not
1Co 14:6 So right·now, brothers, if I·should·come to yeu
1Co 14:7 flute or harp, if it·should·not give a·distinction in·
1Co 14:11 Now·then, if I·should·not personally·know the
1Co 14:14 For if I·should·pray in·a·bestowed·tongue, my
1Co 14:23 Now·then, if the whole Called·Out·citizenry
1Co 14:24 But if all should·prophesy, and someone should·
1Co 14:28 But if there·should·not be one·who·thoroughly·
1Co 14:30 And if *something* should·be·revealed to·another
1Co 16:4 And if it·should·be appropriate *for* me·also to·
1Co 16:7 alongside yeu, if the Lord should·freely·permit.
1Co 16:10 Now if TimoThy should·come, look·out that he·
2Co 5:1 For we·personally·know that if our earthly home of·
2Co 9:4 Lest·perhaps if *any* Macedonians should·come
2Co 13:2 and to·all the rest— that if I·should·come into the
Col 3:13 ·forgiving to·one·another. If any·man should·hold
Col 4:10 yeu·received commandments; if he·should·come to
1Ti 1:8 that the Torah-Law *is* good, if someone should·use it
1Ti 3:15 But if I·should·delay, *I·write* in·order·that you·may·
2Ti 2:5 But even if someone should·contend *in·athletic·*
2Ti 2:21 Accordingly, if anyone should·entirely·purify
1Jn 1:6 If we·should·declare that we·have fellowship with
1Jn 1:7 But if we·should·walk in the light as he·himself is in
1Jn 1:8 If we·should·declare that we·do·not have moral·
1Jn 1:9 If we·should·confess our moral·failures, he·is
1Jn 1:10 If we·should·declare that we·have·not morally·
1Jn 2:1 ·not morally·fail. And if anyone should·morally·fail,
1Jn 2:3 ·known him, if we·should·observantly·keep his
1Jn 2:15 the·things in the world. If any·man should·love the
1Jn 2:24 *the* beginning. If that·which yeu·already·heard
1Jn 2:29 If yeu·should·personally·know that he·is righteous,
1Jn 3:20 Because if our heart should·incriminate *us*, God is
1Jn 3:21 Beloved, if our heart should·not incriminate us,
1Jn 4:12 ever·at·any·time. If we·should·love one·another,
1Jn 4:20 If someone should·declare, “I·love God,” and he·
1Jn 5:14 toward him, that if we·should·request anything
1Jn 5:15 And if we·personally·know that he·hears us,
1Jn 5:16 If someone should·see his brother morally·failing a·
3Jn 1:10 On·account·of that, if I·should·come, I·shall·
Rv 2:22 into great tribulation, if they·should·not repent out·
Rv 3:20 door and knock. If anyone should·hear my voice
Rv 22:18 of·this official·scroll, if anyone should·place
Rv 22:19 And if anyone should·remove *anything* from the

G1437.3 COND ἐάνπερ (7x)
Ac 9:2 ·to the gatherings, that if·ever he·should·find any
Heb 6:3 this we·shall·do, if·ever God should·freely·permit.
1Co 13:1 If·ever I·should·speak with·the bestowed·tongues
1Co 13:2 And if·ever I·should·have *the gracious·bestowment*
1Co 13:2 absolute·knowledge, and if·ever I·should·have all
1Co 13:3 And if·ever I·should·provide·some·food·for *the*
1Co 14:8 For also, if·ever a·trumpet should·give an·

G1437.4 COND ἐάν (13x)
Lk 16:31 ·be·persuaded, though someone should·rise·up
Ac 13:41 though someone should·give·a·thorough·account
Gal 6:1 even though a·man·of·clay† should·be·overtaken in
Mt 15:5 “Although you·should·have·benefited as·a·result
Mk 4:26 “*It·is* as though a·man·of·clay† should·cast the
Mk 7:11 “Although you·should·have·benefited as·a·result
Rm 9:27 concerning IsraEl, “‘ Although the number of·the
Jac 2:14 my brothers, though someone should·say he·has
1Co 4:15 For though yeu·may·have ten·thousand strict·
1Co 9:16 For though I·should·proclaim·the·good·news, it·is
1Co 13:3 my holdings, and though I·should·hand·over my
2Co 10:8 For even though I·should·boast somewhat
2Co 12:6 For though I·should·want to·boast, I·shall·not be

G1437.5 COND ἐάν (4x)
Rm 14:8 For both, whether we·should·live, we·live to·the
Rm 14:8 to·the Lord; or·also whether we·should·die, we·die
Rm 14:8 Accordingly, both whether we·should·live, or·also
Rm 14:8 we·should·live, or·also whether we·should·die,

G1437.6 COND ἐάν (2x)
1Co 14:16 Otherwise when you·should·bless with·the spirit,
1Jn 3:2 ·know that, when he·should·be·made·apparent, ‘

G1437.7 COND ἐάν (1x)
Rm 15:24 just as·soon·as I·should·traverse for Spain, I·shall·

G1438 ἑαυτοῦ hêautôû *p:f.* (343x)
Roots:G0846

G1438.2 P:F-3APM ἑαυτούς (13x)
Ac 23:14 we·vowed·and·bound ourselves over·to· to·taste
2Th 3:9 we·should·give ourselves *to·be* a·model·example
1Co 11:31 For if we·were·discerning ourselves *properly*, we·
2Co 3:1 ·begin again to·commend ourselves? Yet·not·even
2Co 4:2 of·the truth, commending ourselves to every man·
2Co 4:5 For *it·is* not ourselves *that* we·officially·proclaim,
2Co 4:5 Jesus *the* Lord, and we·ourselves *are* yeur slaves
2Co 5:12 For not again do·we·commend ourselves to·yeu,
2Co 6:4 ·*are* presently·commending ourselves as attendants
2Co 7:1 dearly·beloved, we·should·purify ourselves from all
2Co 10:12 or to·compare ourselves with·some *who·are*
2Co 10:14 to yeu. We·stretch·well·beyond ourselves, for
1Jn 1:8 have moral·failure, we·deceive ourselves, and the

G1438.2 P:F-3DPM ἑαυτοῖς (4x)
Rm 8:23 groan within ourselves, who·are·fully·awaiting the·
Rm 15:1 ·ones *that·are* unable, and not to·satisfy ourselves.
2Co 1:9 But·yet we, in ourselves, have·had the judicial·
2Co 1:9 ·not be having·reliance upon ourselves, but·rather

G1438.2 P:F-3GPM ἑαυτῶν (3x)
Heb 10:25 the complete·gathering of·ourselves, just·as *is* a·
2Co 3:5 we·are sufficient by ourselves to·reckon anything as
2Co 3:5 anything as from·among ourselves, but·rather our

G1438.3 P:F-3GPM ἑαυτῶν (1x)
1Th 2:8 merely, but·rather also our·own souls, on·account·

G1438.4 P:F-3ASM ἑαυτόν (2x)
Gal 5:14 ·one, “‘You·shall·love your neighbor as yourself.’”
Rm 13:9 “‘You·shall·love your neighbor as yourself.’”

G1438.4 P:F-3APF ἑαυτάς (1x)
Lk 23:28 *Yet* moreover, weep over yeurselves and over yeur

G1438.4 P:F-3APM ἑαυτούς (21x)
Lk 16:15 regarding yeur·own·selves as·righteous in·the·sight
Lk 17:14 yeu·must·fully·exhibit yeurselves to·the priests·
Ac 13:46 it away and presently·judge yeurselves not worthy
Ac 15:29 *if* yeu·thoroughly·keep·guarding yeurselves, yeu·
Mk 9:33 ·it *that* yeu·deliberated among yeurselves along the
Mk 13:9 “But yeu·yeurselves look·out·for yeurselves, for
Rm 6:11 must·reckon also yeurselves to·be in·fact dead to·
Rm 6:13 but·rather yeu·must·present yeurselves to·God, as
Rm 6:16 slaves to·whom yeu·present yeurselves *as* slaves in
Rm 12:19 *Love is* not avenging yeurselves, dearly·beloved,
Jac 1:22 not merely hearers, defrauding yeur·own·selves.
Jud 1:20 beloved, building·up yeurselves in·yeur holy trust
Jud 1:21 purposefully·keep yeurselves in God's love, *yeu*
1Pe 4:8 *continue* having earnest love among yeurselves, ‘
2Co 7:11 yeu·demonstrated yeurselves to·be morally·clean
2Co 13:5 Try yeurselves, whether yeu·are in the trust.
2Co 13:5 the trust. Examine·and·verify yeur·own·selves. Or
2Co 13:5 ·yeu·not recognize *for* yeur·own·selves that Jesus
Col 3:16 and admonishing yeurselves in·psalms and hymns
1Jn 5:21 Dear·children, vigilantly·keep yeurselves from the
2Jn 1:8 Look·out·for yeurselves, that we·should·not

G1438.4 P:F-3DPF ἑαυταῖς (1x)
Mt 25:9 the·ones selling *oil* and buy *some* for·yeurselves.’

G1438.4 P:F-3DPM ἑαυτοῖς (20x)
Jn 5:42 that yeu·do·not have the love of·God in yeurselves.
Jn 6:53 his blood, yeu·do·not have life-above in yeurselves.
Lk 3:8 yeu·should·not begin to·say within yeurselves, ‘We·
Lk 12:1 “First·of·all, beware among·yeurselves of the
Lk 12:33 ·of·charity. *Thus* make for·yeurselves pouches not
Lk 16:9 to·yeu: Make friends for·yeurselves from·out·of·the
Lk 17:3 Take·heed to·yeurselves. “But if your brother
Lk 21:34 “And take·heed to·yeurselves, lest·at·any·time yeur
Lk 22:17 and thoroughly·distribute *it* among·yeurselves.
Ac 5:35 Israelites, take·heed to·yeurselves what yeu·intend
Ac 20:28 “So·then take·heed to·yeurselves, and to·the entire
Heb 10:34 holdings, knowing for yeurselves to·have in *the*
Mt 3:9 yeu·should·not presume to·say within yeurselves,
Mt 16:8 ·do yeu·deliberate among yeurselves that yeu·took
Mk 9:50 “Have salt in yeurselves, and be·peaceful with one·
Rm 11:25 ·be full·of·notions personally·about yeurselves:
Rm 12:16 full·of·notions personally·about yeurselves.
Jac 2:4 ·yeu·not then discriminating among yeurselves, and
1Th 5:13 ·of their work. Be·peaceful among yeurselves.
Eph 5:19 speaking to·yeurselves in·psalms and hymns and

G1438.4 P:F-3GSM ἑαυτοῦ (1x)
Jn 18:34 answered him, “From yourself, do·you say this·

G1438.4 P:F-3GPM ἑαυτῶν (5x)
Jn 12:8 have the helplessly·poor among yeurselves. But me,
Lk 12:57 yeu·not judge what·is·right even by yeurselves?
Lk 21:30 ·about, yeu·know by yeur·own·selves that the
Mt 26:11 have the helplessly·poor among yeurselves, but me
Mk 14:7 have the helplessly·poor among yeurselves. And

G1438.5 P:F-3GSM ἑαυτοῦ (1x)
1Co 10:29 I·say, not·indeed your·own, but·rather of·the

G1438.5 P:F-3GPM ἑαυτῶν (3x)
Php 2:12 the *determined·purpose* of·yeur·own Salvation!
1Co 6:19 yeu·have from God, and yeu·are not yeur·own?
Eph 5:25 husbands: Yeu·must·love yeur·own wives, just·as

G1438.6 P:F-3DPM ἑαυτοῖς (1x)
Mt 23:31 ·such, yeu·testify against·yeurselves that yeu·are

G1438.7 P:F-3ASM ἑαυτόν (67x)
Jn 2:24 Jesus himself was·not entrusting himself to·them, on·
Jn 5:18 his·own Father, making himself equal with·God.
Jn 8:22 “Is·it·that he·shall·kill himself? Because he·says,
Jn 11:33 in·the spirit; yet he·troubled himself *to·grieve*,
Jn 13:4 And taking a·towel, he·tightly·girded himself.
Jn 19:7 to·die, because he·made himself *out to·be* God's Son
Jn 21:1 these·things, Jesus made himself apparent again to·
Jn 21:7 (for he·was naked), and he·cast himself into the sea.
Lk 9:23 me, he·must·utterly·deny himself and take·up his
Lk 9:25 but already·completely·losing himself or suffering·
Lk 10:29 the·man, wanting to·regard himself as·righteous,

Lk 11:18 is·thoroughly·divided against himself, how shall
Lk 14:11 the·one elevating himself shall·be·humbled, and
Lk 14:11 and the·one humbling himself shall·be·elevated."
Lk 15:17 "Then coming to himself, he·declared, 'How·
Lk 18:11 was·praying these·things toward himself, 'God,
Lk 18:14 "The·one elevating himself shall·be·humbled, and
Lk 18:14 and the·one humbling himself shall·be·elevated."
Lk 23:2 to·give tributes to·Caesar, saying himself to·be *the*
Lk 23:35 "He·saved others, let·him·save himself— if this·
Lk 24:12 marveling to himself at·the·thing having·happened.
Ac 1:3 also he·established·proof·of himself being·alive after
Ac 5:36 Theudas rose·up, saying himself to·be someone
Ac 8:9 Gentiles of·Samaria, saying himself to·be someone
Ac 14:17 he·did·not leave himself without·witness, by·
Ac 16:27 he·was·about to·eliminate himself, assuming the
Ac 19:31 ·were·imploring *him* not to·give himself into the
Ac 25:4 Caesarea, and *that* he·himself was·about to·depart
Ac 28:16 ·permitted to·abide by himself together with·the
Heb 5:5 did·not glorify himself to·be·made a·high·priest,
Heb 7:27 this upon·one·occasion·only, carrying·up himself.
Heb 9:14 Spirit offered himself without·blemish to·God,
Heb 9:25 in·order·that he·should·offer himself many·times,
Gal 1:4 the·one giving himself on·behalf·of·our moral·
Gal 2:12 ·back and was·distinctly·detaching himself, fearing
Gal 2:20 me, and already·handing himself over on·my
Gal 6:4 then he·shall·have the boasting in himself alone, and
Mt 12:26 he·is·divided against himself. So·then, how shall
Mt 16:24 ·behind me, he·must·utterly·deny himself, take·up
Mt 18:4 whoever should·humble himself as this little·child,
Mt 23:12 any·that shall·elevate himself shall·be·humbled,
Mt 23:12 any·that shall·humble himself shall·be·elevated.
Mt 27:42 *yet* he·is·not able to·save himself. If he·is King
Mk 3:26 rose·up against himself and has·been·divided, he·is·
Mk 5:5 ·out and fully·chopping·at himself with·stones.
Mk 8:34 right·behind me, let·him·utterly·deny himself, and
Mk 12:33 and to·love one's neighbor as himself, is more·than
Mk 15:31 "He·saved others; himself, he·is·not able to·save.
Rm 14:22 *is* the·one not calling himself into·judgment by
Jac 1:24 For he·fully·observed himself and has·gone·away,
Php 2:7 but·yet he·emptied himself, taking·hold·of *the*
Php 2:8 as a·man·of·clay†, he·humbled himself, becoming
2Th 2:4 Temple of·God,' exhibiting himself that he·is God.
Tit 2:14 who gave himself on·our behalf in·order·that 'he·
1Co 3:18 not·even·one·man thoroughly·delude himself. If
1Co 11:28 ·of·clay† must·examine·and·verify himself, and
1Co 14:4 in·a·bestowed·tongue does·edify himself, but the·
2Co 10:18 For *it·is* not that·one commending himself *that* is
Eph 5:2 also loved us and handed himself over on·our behalf,
Eph 5:25 ·Out·Citizenry and handed himself over on·her
Eph 5:28 The·one loving his wife loves himself.
Eph 5:33 must·love his·own wife even·as himself, and *so*·
1Ti 2:6 the·one giving himself *as* a·substitutionary·ransom
2Ti 2:13 trustworthy; he·is·not able to·deny himself."
2Ti 2:21 should·entirely·purify himself from these·things,
1Jn 3:3 Expectation in him cleanses himself, just·as that·one
1Jn 5:18 ·begotten from·out·of·God guards himself, and the

G1438.7 P:F-3DSM ἑαυτῷ (31x)

Jn 5:26 the Father has life-above in himself, in·this·manner,
Jn 5:26 he·gave also to·the Son to·have life-above in himself.
Jn 6:61 But Jesus, having·seen in himself that his disciples
Jn 11:38 Jesus, again being·exasperated in himself, comes to
Jn 13:32 also shall·glorify him in himself, and shall·glorify
Lk 7:39 calling·for him, declared within himself, saying, "If
Lk 9:47 ·hold·of·a·little·child, he·set him near himself
Lk 12:17 And he·pondered within himself, saying, 'What
Lk 12:21 storing·up·treasure for·himself, becoming·wealthy,
Lk 16:3 the estate·manager declared within himself, 'What
Lk 18:4 *appeals*, he·declared within himself, 'Even though
Lk 19:12 country to·receive for·himself a·kingdom and to·
Ac 10:17 was·thoroughly·perplexed in himself *as·to* what
Ac 12:11 And after·coming to himself, Peter declared,
Heb 5:4 And not unto·himself *does* anyone take the honor,
Mt 13:21 he·does·not have root in himself, but·rather he·is

Mk 5:30 recognizing immediately in himself the power
Rm 14:7 For not·even·one of·us lives to·himself, and not·
Rm 14:7 lives to·himself, and not·even·one dies to·himself.
Rm 15:3 did·not accommodate himself, but·rather, just·as it·
Php 3:21 to·be·able even to·subject all things to·himself.
Tit 2:14 lawlessness,' and may·purify to·himself '*his·own*
1Co 11:29 eats and drinks judgment to·himself, not
1Co 14:28 And·thus, he·must·speak to·himself and to·God.
1Co 16:2 ·yeu lay *aside* personally·from himself, storing·up
2Co 5:18 already·reconciling us to·himself through Jesus
2Co 5:19 ·reconciling *the* world to·himself, while·not
2Co 10:7 has·confidence in·himself to·be of·Anointed-One,
Eph 2:15 ·that he·should·create the two in himself into one
Eph 5:27 that he·may·present her to·himself glorious, the
1Jn 5:10 of·God has the testimony in himself; the·one not

G1438.7 P:F-3GSM ἑαυτοῦ (16x)

Jn 5:19 able to·do not·even·one·thing by himself, but·only
Jn 7:18 The·man speaking from himself seeks his·own glory,
Jn 11:51 he·did·not declare this from his·own·self, but·rather
Jn 16:13 "For he·shall·not speak from himself, but·rather as·
Lk 11:26 ·*itself* seven other spirits more·evil·than itself, and
Lk 24:27 in all the Scriptures the·things concerning himself.
Ac 8:34 say this? Concerning himself, or concerning
Heb 1:3 of·our moral·failures through himself, sat·down at
Heb 5:3 in·this·manner also concerning himself), he·is·
Heb 6:13 greater by *which* to·swear, he·swore by himself,
Heb 9:7 which he·offered on·behalf of·himself, and *on*·
Mt 12:45 and personally·takes with himself seven other
Mt 12:45 seven other spirits more·evil·than himself. And
Mk 14:33 Then he·personally·takes with him Peter, Jakob,
Rm 14:12 ·us shall·give account concerning himself to·God.
2Co 10:7 let·him·reckon this again for himself; because just·

EG1438.7 (2x)

Jn 21:1 and he·made *himself* apparent in·this·manner.
Ac 5:36 four·hundred), who *himself* was·eliminated. And

G1438.8 P:F-3ASM ἑαυτόν (1x)

Gal 6:3 being not·even·one·thing, he·deludes his·own mind.

G1438.8 P:F-3GSM ἑαυτοῦ (27x)

Lk 11:21 ·armed, should·keep·watch·over his·own mansion,
Lk 12:47 that slave, the·one knowing his lord's will and not
Lk 13:19 a·man·of·clay† took *and* cast into his garden. And
Lk 14:26 me and does·not considerately·hate his father, and
Lk 14:26 and sisters, and yet his·own soul also, he·is·not
Lk 14:33 that does·not orderly·take·leave·of all his holdings,
Lk 15:5 ·finding *it*, he·puts *it* upon his shoulders, rejoicing.
Lk 15:20 "And rising·up, he·came toward his father. But
Lk 16:5 summoning each one of·his lord's needy·debtors, he·
Lk 19:13 And calling his ten slaves, he·gave ten more·silver·
Gal 6:4 But each·man must·test·and·prove his·own work,
Gal 6:8 Because the·one sowing into his flesh, shall·reap
Rm 4:19 trust, he·did·not fully·observe his·own body, even·
Rm 5:8 But God demonstrates his love toward us, how·that
Rm 8:3 the flesh, God, after·sending his·own Son in *the*
1Th 2:11 , how as a·father *does·for* his children, exhorting
1Th 2:12 ·one calling yeu forth into his kingdom and glory.
1Th 4:4 ·know·how to·possess his·own *earthenware* vessel
2Th 2:6 ·down in·order·for him to·be·revealed in his season.
1Co 7:2 each *man* must·have his·own wife, and each
1Co 7:37 in his heart to·keep·unmarried his virgin·daughter,
1Co 10:24 Let no·man seek his·own, but·rather each·man the
2Co 3:13 *did*, who·was·placing a·veil over his face, *which·is*
Eph 5:28 bodies. The·one loving his wife loves himself.
Eph 5:29 For not·even·one·man ever hated his·own flesh,
Eph 5:33 in·that·manner) must·love his·own wife even·as
Rv 10:7 ·be·finished, as he·proclaimed to·his slaves the

G1438.8 P:F-3GPM ἑαυτῶν (1x)

Php 2:4 ·a·watch, *but* not each·man of·his·own things *only*,

EG1438.8 (2x)

Heb 12:7 God is·bearing·alongside yeu as *his·own* sons, for
Tit 2:14 ·purify to·himself '*his·own* extraordinary People,'

G1438.9 P:F-3ASF ἑαυτήν (4x)

Lk 1:24 conceived and was·entirely·hiding herself *for* five
Rv 2:20 Jezebel, the·one referring·to herself *as* a·prophetess
Rv 18:7 she·glorified herself and lived·in·voluptuous·luxury,
Rv 19:7 did·come and his wife did·make herself ready.

G1438.9 P:F-3DSF ἑαυτῇ (1x)

Mt 9:21 for she·was·saying within herself, "If merely I·

G1438.10 P:F-3DSF ἑαυτῇ (1x)

Ac 7:21 took him up and nurtured him for her·own son.

G1438.10 P:F-3GSF ἑαυτῆς (5x)

Lk 13:34 as a·hen *gathers* her brood under *her* wings, and
Mt 23:37 as a·hen completely·gathers her chicks under her
Mk 5:26 ·healing and expending all her personal belongings
1Th 2:7 would cherishingly·brood·over her·own children.
1Co 11:5 ·her head not·fully·veiled puts·to·shame her head,

EG1438.10 (1x)

Eph 5:33 ·that she·should·reverently·fear *her·own* husband.

G1438.11 P:F-3ASF ἑαυτήν (4x)

Lk 11:17 ·thoroughly·divided against itself is·made·desolate,
Mk 3:24 if a·kingdom should·be·divided against itself, that
Mk 3:25 And if a·home should·be·divided against itself, that
Jac 2:17 ·that it·should·have no works, is dead by itself.

G1438.11 P:F-3ASN ἑαυτό (1x)

Rv 4:8 four living·beings, each one itself, was·having six

G1438.11 P:F-3GSF ἑαυτῆς (3x)

Mt 6:34 ·be·anxious·about the·things of·itself. Sufficient for·
Mt 12:25 being·divided against itself is·made·desolate, and
Mt 12:25 ·divided against itself shall·not remain·established.

G1438.11 P:F-3GSM ἑαυτοῦ (2x)

Jn 15:4 able to·bear fruit of itself unless it·should·abide in
Rm 14:14 *there·is* nothing·at·all defiled through itself, except

G1438.12 P:F-3GSF ἑαυτῆς (1x)

1Co 13:5 behave·improperly, does·not seek its·own, is·not

G1438.12 P:F-3GSM ἑαυτοῦ (1x)

Eph 4:16 ·growth of·the Body for its·own edification in love.

G1438.13 P:F-3APF ἑαυτάς (3x)

Mk 16:3 And they·were·saying among themselves, "Who
1Pe 3:5 holy wives also were·adorning themselves, the·ones
1Ti 2:9 *for* the women to·adorn themselves in orderly, fully·

G1438.13 P:F-3APM ἑαυτούς (30x)

Jn 7:35 the Judeans declared among themselves, "Where·
Jn 11:55 ·that they·should·ceremonially·cleanse themselves.
Jn 12:19 So·then the Pharisees declared among themselves,
Lk 7:30 the counsel of·God for themselves, not already·
Lk 20:5 they·reckoned·together alongside themselves, saying
Lk 20:14 ·farmers deliberated among themselves, saying,
Lk 20:20 pretending themselves to·be righteous·men in·
Lk 22:23 to·question·and·discuss among themselves, which
Lk 23:12 ·previously being in hostility among themselves.
Ac 23:12 vowed·and·bound themselves over·to·destruction,
Ac 23:21 vowed·and·bound themselves over·to·destruction,
Mt 19:12 some·who castrated themselves on·account·of the
Mk 9:10 toward themselves, questioning·and·discussing·
Mk 10:26 beyond·excess, saying among themselves, "Then
Mk 11:31 they·were·reckoning among themselves, saying,
Mk 12:7 those tenant·farmers declared among themselves,
Mk 14:4 being·greatly·displeased alongside themselves, and
Jud 1:12 shepherding·and·feeding themselves without·fear.
1Pe 4:10 among themselves *let·them·be* attending·to it as
1Co 16:15 and *how* they·arranged themselves for service
2Co 8:5 ·rather first they·gave their·own·selves to·the Lord
2Co 10:12 *who·are* commending themselves. But·rather
2Co 10:12 unduly·measuring themselves by themselves, and
2Co 10:12 and comparing themselves to·themselves, do·not
Eph 4:19 ·become·apathetic, handed themselves over to·the
1Ti 6:10 and they·entirely·impaled themselves on·many
Rv 2:9 revilement of·the·ones saying themselves to·be Jews
Rv 3:9 (the·ones saying themselves to·be Jews and are not,
Rv 6:15 and every free·man, hid themselves in the caves and
Rv 8:6 seven trumpets made themselves ready in·order·that

G1438.13 P:F-3DPM ἑαυτοῖς (27x)

Jn 19:24 ·divided·up my garments among·themselves, and
Lk 7:49 ·at·the·meal began to·say within themselves, "Who
Lk 18:9 ones having·confidence in themselves that they·are
Ac 28:29 questioning·and·discussion among themselves.
Heb 6:6 ·*is*, presently·re-crucifying for·themselves the Son

Mt 9:3 of·the scribes declared within themselves, "This·man
Mt 14:15 the villages, they·may·buy food for·themselves."
Mt 16:7 they·were·deliberating among themselves, saying,
Mt 21:25 ·deliberating closely·among themselves, saying,
Mt 21:38 the tenant·farmers declared among themselves,
Mt 27:35 ·divided·up my garments among·themselves, and
Mk 2:8 in·this·manner within themselves, he·declared to·
Mk 4:17 Yet they·do·not have root in themselves, but·rather
Mk 6:36 villages, they·should·buy bread for·themselves, for
Mk 6:51 astonished among themselves beyond excess, and
Rm 1:24 to·dishonor their·own bodies among themselves,
Rm 1:27 and fully·receiving in themselves the due·payback
Rm 2:14 not having Torah-Law are a·law to·themselves,
Rm 13:2 ·to *it* shall·receive judgment for·themselves.
1Pe 1:12 to·these·men that *it·was* not for·themselves, but
2Pe 2:1 bringing·upon themselves abrupt total·destruction.
2Co 5:15 should·no·longer live to·themselves, but·rather to·
2Co 10:12 unduly·measuring themselves by themselves, and
2Co 10:12 and comparing themselves to·themselves, do·not
1Ti 3:13 well do·acquire for·themselves good advancement,
1Ti 6:19 laying·up·in·store for·themselves a·good
2Ti 4:3 ·stack·up instructors for·themselves, those·tickling

G1438.13 P:F-3GPM ἑαυτῶν (8x)
Ac 21:23 ·us are four men having a·vow upon themselves;
Mt 15:30 him, having among themselves *those that·were*
Mt 25:3 lamps, did·not take oil among their·own·selves.
Mk 2:19 the bridegroom among themselves, they·are·not
Mk 8:14 ·not having *any* in the sailboat among themselves.
Mk 9:8 ·even·one·man, other·than Jesus alone with them.
Php 2:3 as·excelling·above·and·beyond their·own·selves.
1Co 6:7 because yeu·hold judgment among them. Rather,

G1438.14 P:F-3APM ἑαυτούς (1x)
Jn 20:10 the disciples went·off again to their·own *homes*.

G1438.14 P:F-3GPM ἑαυτῶν (22x)
Lk 9:60 "Leave the dead·ones to·bury their·own dead, but
Lk 12:36 ·of·clay† who·are·awaiting their·own lord when
Lk 16:8 the Sons of·the Light in their·own generation.
Lk 19:35 to Jesus, and flinging their·own garments upon the
Lk 22:66 ·led him into their·own joint·council·of·Sanhedrin,
Lk 23:48 ·things happening, while·beating their·own chests,
Mt 8:22 and allow the dead·ones to·bury their·own dead."
Mt 21:8 very·large crowd spread·out their·own garments in
Mt 25:3 *were* foolish, upon·taking their·own lamps, did·not
Rm 16:4 who risked their·own necks on·behalf·of·my soul,
Rm 16:18 Jesus Anointed, but·rather to·their·own belly.
Jud 1:6 not observantly·keeping their·own principality, but·
Jud 1:13 ·the·sea presently·foaming·upon their·own shame,
Jud 1:18 according·to their·own irreverent longings.
Php 2:21 For all the·men seek their·own, not the·things·of
1Pe 4:19 must·place·the·direct·care·of their·own souls *to·*
2Th 3:12 while·working, they·should·eat their·own bread.
Eph 5:28 husbands are·obligated·to·love their·own wives as
Eph 5:28 to·love their·own wives as their·own bodies. The·
Rv 10:3 ·out, the Seven Thunders spoke their·own voices.
Rv 10:4 the Seven Thunders spoke their·own voices, I·was·
Rv 17:13 they·thoroughly·give·forth their·own power and

G1438.15 P:F-3APM ἑαυτούς (1x)
Heb 3:13 But·rather exhort one·another each and·every day,

G1438.15 P:F-3DPM ἑαυτοῖς (2x)
Eph 4:32 being·graciously·forgiving to·one·another, also
Col 3:13 and being·graciously·forgiving to·one·another. If

G1438.16 P:F-3ASM ἑαυτόν (1x)
Jac 1:27 *and* to·purposefully·keep oneself unstained from

G1439 ἐάω êáō *v.* (13x)
Compare:G2010 See:G1436

G1439.1 V-FAI-3S ἐάσει (1x)
1Co 10:13 *is* trustworthy, who shall·not let yeu to·be·tried

G1439.1 V-PAM-2P ἐᾶτε (1x)
Lk 22:51 declared, "*Stop!* Yeu·must·let·it·be, even·unto this

G1439.1 V-IAI-3P εἴων (2x)
Ac 19:30 ·assembly, the disciples were·not letting him.
Ac 27:40 ·removing the anchors, they·were·letting *them fall*

G1439.1 V-AAI-3S εἴασεν (3x)
Ac 16:7 toward Bithynia, but the Spirit did·not let them.
Ac 28:4 from·out·of the sea, Justice does·not let *him* live."
Mt 24:43 kept·alert and would not·have let his home to·be·

G1439.1 V-AAI-3P εἴασαν (1x)
Ac 27:32 small·ropes of·the skiff, and they·let her fall·away.

G1439.1 V-AAM-2P ἐάσατε (1x)
Ac 5:38 Withdraw from these men·of·clay† and let them be,

G1439.2 V-PAI-2S ἐᾷς (1x)
Rv 2:20 against you, because you·give·leave·for the woman

G1439.2 V-IAI-3S εἴα (1x)
Lk 4:41 *them*, he·was·not giving·leave·for them to·speak,

G1439.2 V-AAI-3S εἴασεν (1x)
Ac 14:16 having·long·past, gave·leave·for all the nations to·

G1439.2 V-AAP-NPM ἐάσαντες (1x)
Ac 23:32 *in·JeruSalem*, after·giving·leave·for the horsemen

G1440 ἑβδομή•κοντα hêbdômḗkônta *n.* (5x)
Roots:G1442 G1176 See:G1441 G1440-3
xLangEquiv:H7657

G1440.1 N-NUI ἑβδομήκοντα (4x)
Lk 10:1 the Lord expressly·indicated seventy others also,
Lk 10:17 And the seventy returned·back with joy, saying,
Ac 7:14 and all his kinsfolk, in *all*, seventy five souls.
Ac 23:23 two·hundred soldiers, with seventy horsemen and

G1440.2 N-NUI ἑβδομηκονταέξ (1x)
Ac 27:37 *told*, we·were two·hundred *and* seventy·six souls.

G1441 ἑβδομη•κοντάκις hêbdômēkôntákis *adv.* (1x)
Roots:G1440 Compare:G2034 xLangAlso:H7657

G1441.1 ADV ἑβδομηκοντάκις (1x)
Mt 18:22 seven·times, but·rather up·to seventy·times seven.

G1442 ἕβδομος hébdômôs *adj.* (9x)
Roots:G2033
xLangEquiv:H7637

G1442 A-NSM ἕβδομος (4x)
Jud 1:14 Now Enoch also, *the* seventh from Adam,
Rv 11:15 And the seventh angel sounded, and there·became
Rv 16:17 And the seventh angel poured·out his vial into the
Rv 21:20 the sixth, sardius; the seventh, chrysolite; the

G1442 A-ASF ἑβδόμην (2x)
Jn 4:52 to·him, "Yesterday at·the·seventh hour the fever
Rv 8:1 when *the Lamb* opened·up the seventh official·seal,

G1442 A-DSF ἑβδόμῃ (1x)
Heb 4:4 And God fully·rested in the seventh day from all his

G1442 A-GSM ἑβδόμου (1x)
Rv 10:7 days of·the sound of·the seventh angel, whenever

G1442 A-GSF ἑβδόμης (1x)
Heb 4:4 ·declared concerning the seventh *day* in·this·manner

G1443 Ἐβέρ Êbér *n/p.* (1x)
עֵבֶר ʻe̱ḇer [Hebrew]
Roots:H5677

G1443 N/P-PRI Ἔβερ (1x)
Lk 3:35 of·Reu, *son* of·Peleg, *son* of·Eber, *son* of·Shelach,

G1444 Ἑβραϊκός Hêbraïkós *adj/g.* (9x)
Roots:G1443 Compare:G1673 G4515 See:G1446
G1447
xLangEquiv:H5682-1 xLangAlso:H0762 H6163

G1444 A/G-DPN Ἑβραϊκοῖς (1x)
Lk 23:38 in·Greek, Roman·Latin, and Hebrew: "THIS IS

EG1444 (8x)
Jn 1:38 when·being·translated *from Hebrew*, is·to·say
Jn 1:41 which, when·being·interpreted *from·Hebrew*, is the
Jn 1:42 ·rock)," which is·translated *from·Hebrew as* Peter.
Jn 9:7 pool of·Siloam" (which *from·Hebrew* is·translated *as*
Ac 9:36 (by·thorough·translation *from·Hebrew*) is·referred·
Heb 7:2 in·fact, being·translated *from·Hebrew as* "King
Mt 1:23 which, when·being·interpreted *from·Hebrew*, is
Mk 15:22 which, when·being·interpreted *from·Hebrew*, is

G1445 Ἑβραῖος Hêbraîôs *adj/g.* (4x)
Roots:G1443
xLangEquiv:H5680

G1445 A/G-NSM Ἑβραῖος (1x)
Php 3:5 tribe of·BenJamin, a·Hebrew from·among Hebrews;

G1445 A/G-NPM Ἑβραῖοί (1x)
2Co 11:22 Are·they Hebrews? So·*am*·I. Are·they Israelites?

G1445 A/G-APM Ἑβραίους (1x)
Ac 6:1 ·Jews specifically·against the Hebrews, because their

G1445 A/G-GPM Ἑβραίων (1x)
Php 3:5 a·Hebrew from·among Hebrews; according·to

G1446 Ἑβραΐς Hêbraḯs *n/g.* (3x)
Roots:G1443 Compare:G1673 G4515 See:G1444
G1447 xLangAlso:H0762 H6163

G1446 N/G-DSF Ἑβραΐδι (3x)
Ac 21:40 he·addressed *them* in·the Hebrew language,
Ac 22:2 he·was·addressing them in·the Hebrew language,
Ac 26:14 to me, and saying in·the Hebrew language, 'Saul,

G1447 Ἑβραϊστί Hêbraïstí *adv/g.* (6x)
Roots:G1446 Compare:G1676 G4515 G4947-6
See:G1444
xLangEquiv:H5682-1 xLangAlso:H0762

G1447.2 ADV Ἑβραϊστί (6x)
Jn 5:2 ·pool having five colonnades; in·Hebrew, *it·is* the·one
Jn 19:13 ·to·as Stone·Pavement, but in·Hebrew, *it·is*
Jn 19:17 ·Skull, which is·referred·to in·Hebrew *as* GolGotha
Jn 19:20 it·was having·been·written in·Hebrew, in·Greek,
Rv 9:11 for·him in·Hebrew *is* Abaddon·*(meaning·Total·*
Rv 16:16 the·one in·Hebrew being·called HarMeGiddon

G1448 ἐγγίζω êngízō *v.* (43x)
Roots:G1451 Compare:G2020 See:G4331

G1448.2 V-FAI-3S-ATT ἐγγιεῖ (1x)
Jac 4:8 Draw·near to·God, and he·shall·draw·near to·yeu.

G1448.2 V-PAI-1P ἐγγίζομεν (1x)
Heb 7:19 *does*, through which we·draw·near to·God.

G1448.2 V-PAI-3S ἐγγίζει (3x)
Lk 12:33 where no thief draws·near, neither·does moth
Lk 21:28 on·account·that yeur full·redemption draws·near."
Mt 15:8 This People draws·near to·me with·their mouth

G1448.2 V-PAI-3P ἐγγίζουσιν (1x)
Mk 11:1 And when they·drew·near to JeruSalem, to

G1448.2 V-PAN ἐγγίζειν (2x)
Lk 18:35 it·happened, with him drawing·near to Jericho, a·
Ac 9:3 it·occurred *for* him to·draw·near to·Damascus, and·

G1448.2 V-PAP-ASF ἐγγίζουσαν (1x)
Heb 10:25 as·much·as yeu·look·upon the day drawing·near.

G1448.2 V-PAP-DSM ἐγγίζοντι (1x)
Ac 22:6 traversing and drawing·near to·Damascus around

G1448.2 V-PAP-GSM ἐγγίζοντος (1x)
Lk 19:37 And with·him drawing·near, even·now alongside

G1448.2 V-PAP-GPM ἐγγιζόντων (1x)
Ac 10:9 ·along·the·road and drawing·near to·the city, Peter

G1448.2 V-PAP-NPM ἐγγίζοντες (1x)
Lk 15:1 ·disqualified were drawing·near to·him to·hear him.

G1448.2 V-IAI-3S ἤγγιζεν (2x)
Lk 22:1 of·the Unleavened·Bread was·drawing·near, the·one
Ac 7:17 time of·the promise was·drawing·near which God

G1448.2 V-AAI-3S ἤγγισεν (7x)
Lk 7:12 Now as he·drew·near to·the gate of·the city, behold,
Lk 15:25 as he·was·going·*along*, he·drew·near to·the home
Lk 19:29 ·happened, as·soon·as he·drew·near to BethPhage
Lk 19:41 And as he·drew·near, upon·seeing the City, he·
Lk 22:47 ·before them, and he·drew·near to·Jesus to·kiss
Mt 21:34 the season of·the fruits drew·near, he·dispatched
Php 2:30 he·was·drawn·near so·far·as·unto death, ignoring·

G1448.2 V-AAI-3P ἤγγισαν (2x)
Lk 24:28 And they·drew·near to the village, where they·
Mt 21:1 And when they·drew·near to JeruSalem and came to

G1448.2 V-AAM-2P ἐγγίσατε (1x)
Jac 4:8 Draw·near to·God, and he·shall·draw·near to·yeu.

G1448.2 V-AAN ἐγγίσαι (1x)
Ac 23:15 we·ourselves, before he shall·draw·near, are ready

G1448.2 V-AAP-GSM ἐγγίσαντος (1x)
Lk 18:40 him, and with·him drawing·near, *Jesus* inquired·of

G1448.2 V-AAP-NSM ἐγγίσας (2x)
Lk 24:15 Jesus himself, drawing·near, traversed·together
Ac 21:33 Then drawing·near, the regiment·commander

G1448.2 V-RAI-3S ἤγγικεν (14x)
Lk 10:9 'The kingdom of·God has·drawn·near to yeu.'

Lk 10:11 that the kingdom of·God has·drawn·near to yeu.'
Lk 21:8 and, 'The season has·drawn·near.' Accordingly,
Lk 21:20 then know that her " Desolation" has·drawn·near.
Mt 3:2 for the kingdom of·the heavens has·drawn·near."
Mt 4:17 for the kingdom of·the heavens has·drawn·near."
Mt 10:7 'The kingdom of·the heavens has·drawn·near.'
Mt 26:45 Behold, the hour has·drawn·near, and the Son
Mt 26:46 the·one handing me over has·drawn·near."
Mk 1:15 kingdom of·God has·drawn·near. Yeu·must·repent
Mk 14:42 the·one handing me over has·drawn·near."
Rm 13:12 and the day has·drawn·near. Accordingly, we·
Jac 5:8 the returning·Presence of·the Lord has·drawn·near.
1Pe 4:7 But the end of·all·things has·drawn·near.

G1449 ἐγ•γράφω êngráphō *v.* (2x)
Roots:G1722 G1125 Compare:G1795 G5480 See:G1924

G1449 V-RPP-NSF ἐγγεγραμμένη (2x)
2Co 3:2 are our letter having·been·engraved in our hearts,
2Co 3:3 ·to by us, having·been·engraved not with·ink, but·

G1450 ἔγ•γυος éngyôs *adj.* (1x)
Roots:G1722

G1450.2 A-NSM ἔγγυος (1x)
Heb 7:22 has·become a·surety of·a·significantly·better

G1451 ἐγγύς êngýs *adv.* (30x)
Compare:G4890-1 See:G1452 G0043 G4890-1

G1451.1 ADV ἐγγύς (16x)
Jn 3:23 also was immersing in Ainon near to·Salim because
Jn 6:19 on the sea and coming near to·the sailboat. And they·
Jn 6:23 small·boats came out·from Tiberias near to·the place
Jn 11:18 Now BethAny was near to·JeruSalem, about fifteen
Jn 11:54 from·there to the region near the wilderness *and*
Jn 19:20 where Jesus was·crucified was near to·the City.
Lk 19:11 on·account·of him being near to·JeruSalem, and
Ac 1:12 Olive·Orchard, which is near JeruSalem, being a·
Ac 9:38 Now being *as* Lod *was* near to·Joppa, *and* after·
Ac 27:8 Good Harbors, which was near *the* city *of* Lasea *(in·*
Mt 24:32 the leaves, yeu·know that the summer *is* near.
Mt 24:33 yeu·must·know that he·is near upon *the* doors.
Mk 13:28 the leaves, yeu·know that the summer is near.
Mk 13:29 yeu·must·know that he·is near upon *the* doors.
Rm 10:8 it·say? "The utterance is near you, *even* in your
Eph 2:13 being at·a·distance, are·made near by the blood of·

G1451.2 ADV ἐγγύς (12x)
Jn 2:13 the Judeans' Passover was near·at·hand, and Jesus
Jn 6:4 the Sacred·Feast of·the Judeans, was near·at·hand.
Jn 7:2 the *Sacred·Feast* of·Booths, was near·at·hand.
Jn 11:55 Now the Judeans' Passover was near·at·hand. And
Jn 19:42 ·day, because the chamber·tomb was near·at·hand.
Lk 21:30 ·selves that the summer is even·now near·at·hand.
Lk 21:31 also know that the kingdom of·God is near·at·hand.
Mt 26:18 "My season is near·at·hand. I·do the Passover
Php 4:5 The Lord *is* near·at·hand.
Eph 2:17 ·ones at·a·distance, and to·the·ones near·at·hand.'
Rv 1:3 ·been·written in it, for the season *is* near·at·hand.
Rv 22:10 official·scroll, because the season is near·at·hand.

G1451.3 ADV ἐγγύς (2x)
Heb 6:8 ' *is* disqualified, and *is* close to·being·cursed, whose
Heb 8:13 and growing·agedly·old *is* close to·obliteration.

G1452 ἐγγύτερον êngýtêrôn *adv.* (1x)
Roots:G1451

G1452 ADV ἐγγύτερον (1x)
Rm 13:11 now our Salvation *is* nearer than when we·trusted.

G1453 ἐγείρω êgêírō *v.* (141x)
Compare:G0450 G1326 G0386 See:G1454 G1825 G1892 G0058
xLangEquiv:H5782

G1453.1 V-FAI-1S ἐγερῶ (1x)
Jn 2:19 this temple, and in three days I·shall·awaken it."

G1453.1 V-FAI-2S ἐγερεῖς (1x)
Jn 2:20 was·built, and you, in three days, shall·awaken it?

G1453.1 V-FAI-3S ἐγερεῖ (2x)
Jac 5:15 ·fatigued, and the Lord shall·awaken him; and·if
2Co 4:14 awakening the Lord Jesus shall·awaken us also,

G1453.1 V-FPI-3S ἐγερθήσεται (6x)
Lk 11:31 "*The* queen of·the·south shall·be·awakened in the
Lk 21:10 ·them, "Nation shall·be·awakened against nation,
Mt 12:42 *The* queen *of·the* south shall·be·awakened in the
Mt 17:23 and on·the third day he·shall·be·awakened." And
Mt 24:7 "For nation shall·be·awakened against nation, and
Mk 13:8 "For nation shall·be·awakened against nation, and

G1453.1 V-FPI-3P ἐγερθήσονται (4x)
Mt 24:11 false·prophets shall·be·awakened and shall·deceive
Mt 24:24 For false·Anointed-Ones shall·be·awakened, and
Mk 13:22 false·prophets shall·be·awakened and shall·give
1Co 15:52 and the dead shall·be·awakened incorruptible,

G1453.1 V-PAI-3S ἐγείρει (2x)
Jn 5:21 "For just·as the Father awakens the dead and gives·
Ac 26:8 incredible with yeu, that God awakens dead·men?

G1453.1 V-PAM-2P ἐγείρετε (1x)
Mt 10:8 the·sick; purify lepers; awaken dead·ones; cast·out

G1453.1 V-PAN ἐγείρειν (1x)
Heb 11:19 that God *was* able to·awaken *him* even from·

G1453.1 V-PAP-DSM ἐγείροντι (1x)
2Co 1:9 but·rather upon God (the·one awakening the dead).

G1453.1 V-PEM-2S ἐγείρου (1x)
Lk 8:54 ·the hand, hollered·out, saying, "Girl, be·awake."

G1453.1 V-PEM-2P ἐγείρεσθε (3x)
Jn 14:31 in·that·manner. "Be·awake, we·should·head·out
Mt 26:46 Be·awake! We·should·head·out. Behold, the·one
Mk 14:42 Be·awake! We·should·head·out. Behold, the·one

G1453.1 V-PPI-1S ἐγείρομαι (1x)
Mt 27:63 'After three days, I·am·awakened.'

G1453.1 V-PPI-3S ἐγείρεται (4x)
1Co 15:42 in corruption; it·is·awakened in incorruptibility.
1Co 15:43 It·is·sown in dishonor; it·is·awakened in glory.
1Co 15:43 It·is·sown in weakness; it·is·awakened in power.
1Co 15:44 a·soulish body; it·is·awakened a·spiritual body.

G1453.1 V-PPI-3P ἐγείρονται (9x)
Lk 7:22 deaf·men hear, dead·men are·awakened, *and the*
Lk 20:37 Now, *concerning* that the dead are·awakened, even
Mt 11:5 and deaf·men hear, dead·men are·awakened and *the*
Mk 12:26 the dead, that they·are·awakened, did·yeu·not
1Co 15:15 by·inference, dead·men are·not awakened.
1Co 15:16 For if dead·men are·not awakened, not·even
1Co 15:29 of·the dead, if dead·men are·not awakened at·all?
1Co 15:32 to·me, if dead·men are·not awakened? "We·
1Co 15:35 "How·are the dead·men awakened? And in·what·

G1453.1 V-PPS-3S ἐγείρηται (1x)
Mk 4:27 should·sleep, and should·be·awakened night and

G1453.1 V-AAI-3S ἤγειρεν (20x)
Jn 12:1 ·died, whom he·awakened from·among dead·men.
Jn 12:9 also, whom he·awakened from·among dead·men.
Jn 12:17 the chamber·tomb and awakened him from·among
Lk 1:69 "And he·awakened a·horn of·Salvation for·us in the
Ac 3:15 whom God awakened from·among dead·men, to·
Ac 4:10 whom God awakened from·among dead·men, by
Ac 5:30 The God of·our fathers awakened Jesus, whom yeu·
Ac 10:40 This·one, God awakened on·the third day and
Ac 12:7 tapping Peter on·the side, he·awakened him, saying,
Ac 13:22 him from·duty, he·awakened to·them David as
Ac 13:23 ·to promise, God awakened a·Savior for·IsraEl,
Ac 13:30 But God awakened him from·among dead·men—
Ac 13:37 But he·whom God awakened did·not see decay.
Mk 1:31 And coming·alongside, he·awakened her, after·
Mk 9:27 him by·the hand, Jesus awakened him, and he·rose·
Rm 10:9 in your heart that God awakened him from·among
1Th 1:10 whom he·awakened from·among dead·men,
1Co 6:14 God, *who* even awakened the Lord *from·death,*
1Co 15:15 against God that he·awakened the Anointed-One,
1Co 15:15 whom he·did·not awaken, if·perhaps, by·

G1453.1 V-AAI-3P ἤγειραν (1x)
Mt 8:25 And coming·alongside, his disciples awakened him,

G1453.1 V-AAN ἐγεῖραι (2x)
Lk 3:8 ·out of·these stones to·awaken children to·AbRaham.
Mt 3:9 ·out of·these stones to·awaken children to·AbRaham.

G1453.1 V-AAP-ASM ἐγείραντα (2x)
Rm 4:24 trusting on the·one already·awakening Jesus our
1Pe 1:21 in God, the·one awakening him from·among dead·

G1453.1 V-AAP-GSM ἐγείραντος (3x)
Gal 1:1 Father God, the·one awakening him from·among
Rm 8:11 the Spirit of·the·one awakening Jesus from·among
Col 2:12 of·God, the·one already·awakening him from·out

G1453.1 V-AAP-NSM ἐγείρας (3x)
Rm 8:11 in yeu, *then* the·one awakening the Anointed-One
2Co 4:14 having·seen that the·one awakening the Lord Jesus
Eph 1:20 Anointed-One, after·awakening him from·among

G1453.1 V-AMM-2S ἔγειραι (9x)
Jn 5:8 Jesus says to·him, "Be·awakened, take·up your mat
Lk 5:23 you,' or to·declare, 'Be·awakened and walk'?
Lk 5:24 "I·say to·you, be·awakened, and taking·up your
Ac 3:6 ·Jesus Anointed of·Natsareth, be·awakened and walk
Mt 9:5 you?' or to·declare, 'Be·awakened and walk?
Mk 2:9 or to·declare, 'Be·awakened, and take·up your
Mk 2:11 "I·say to·you, be·awakened, and take·up your mat,
Mk 5:41 "Young·girl, I·say to·you, be·awakened!"
Eph 5:14 "O·the·one sleeping, be·awakened and rise·up

G1453.1 V-API-3S ἠγέρθη (16x)
Jn 2:22 when he·was·awakened from·among dead·men, his
Lk 24:6 ·is not here, but·rather is·awakened. Recall·to·mind
Lk 24:34 "The Lord really is·awakened and was·gazed·upon
Mt 8:15 left her, and she·was·awakened and was·attending
Mt 9:25 of·her hand, and the young·girl was·awakened.
Mt 14:2 Immerser; he·himself is·already·awakened from the
Mt 27:52 (the·ones having·been·laid·to·rest) are·awakened.
Mt 27:64 to·the people, 'He·is·awakened from the dead,'
Mt 28:6 ·is not here, for he·is·awakened, just·as he·declared
Mt 28:7 to·his disciples that he·was·awakened from the dead
Mk 2:12 And immediately he·is·awakened, and after·taking·
Mk 6:14 Immersing·One was·awakened from·among dead·
Mk 6:16 He·himself is·already·awakened from·among dead·
Mk 16:6 having·been·crucified. He·was·awakened. He·is
Rm 4:25 trespasses, and was·awakened on·account·of our
Rm 6:4 ·as Anointed-One is·already·awakened from·among

G1453.1 V-API-3P ἠγέρθησαν (1x)
Mt 25:7 Then all those virgins are·awakened, and they·

G1453.1 V-APM-2S ἐγέρθητι (1x)
Lk 7:14 "Young·man, I·say to·you, be·awakened!"

G1453.1 V-APN ἐγερθῆναι (5x)
Lk 9:22 and to·be·killed, and to·be·awakened on·the third
Mt 16:21 and to·be·killed, and to·be·awakened on·the third
Mt 26:32 for·me to·be·awakened, I·shall·go·on·ahead·of yeu
Mk 14:28 for·me to·be·awakened, I·shall·go·on·ahead·of
Rm 13:11 *the* hour for·us to·be·awakened out of·heavy·sleep

G1453.1 V-APP-DSM ἐγερθέντι (2x)
Rm 7:4 the·one already·being·awakened from·among dead·
2Co 5:15 ·their behalf and already·being·awakened *from the*

G1453.1 V-APP-NSM ἐγερθείς (12x)
Jn 21:14 after·being·awakened from·among dead·men.
Lk 8:24 Then upon·being·awakened, he·reprimanded the
Lk 11:8 ·of his audacity, he·being·awakened shall·give him
Mt 2:13 saying, "After·being·awakened, personally·take
Mt 2:14 And after·being·awakened, he·personally·took the
Mt 2:20 saying, "After·being·awakened, personally·take the
Mt 2:21 And after·being·awakened, he·personally·took the
Mt 8:26 Then already·being·awakened, he·reprimanded
Mt 9:6 paralyzed·man), "Upon·being·awakened, take·up
Mt 9:7 And upon·being·awakened, he·went·off to his house.
Rm 6:9 that after·being·awakened from·among dead·men,
Rm 8:34 but rather also, being·awakened, who is even at

G1453.1 V-RPI-3S ἐγήγερται (11x)
Jn 7:52 a·prophet has·not been·awakened out of·Galilee."
Lk 7:16 "A·great prophet has·been·awakened among us;"
Lk 9:7 that John has·been·awakened from·among dead·men,
Mt 11:11 there·has·not been·awakened one·greater·than
1Co 15:4 and that he·has·been·awakened on·the third day
1Co 15:12 that he·has·been·awakened from·among dead·
1Co 15:13 not·even Anointed-One has·been·awakened.
1Co 15:14 has·not been·awakened, then·by·inference, our
1Co 15:16 not·even Anointed-One has·been·awakened.

1Co 15:17 if Anointed-One has·not been·awakened, yeur
1Co 15:20 Anointed-One has·been·awakened from·among
G1453.1 V-RPP-ASM ἐγηγερμένον (2x)
Mk 16:14 distinctly·viewing him having·been·awakened.
2Ti 2:8 *is* having·been·awakened from·among dead·men
G1453.2 V-PPI-3S ἐγείρεται (2x)
Jn 11:29 that *sister* heard *it*, she·is·roused swiftly and goes
Jn 13:4 *he·himself* is·roused from·among the supper and
G1453.2 V-AAI-3S ἤγειρεν (1x)
Ac 10:26 But Peter roused him, saying, "Stand·up, *for* also·I
G1453.2 V-AMM-2S ἐγεῖραι (4x)
Lk 6:8 the withered hand, "Rouse·yourself and stand·still in
Mk 3:3 the withered hand, "Rouse·yourself *forth* into the
Mk 10:49 ·good·courage, rouse·yourself; he·hollers·out·for
Rv 11:1 a·rod, saying, "Rouse·yourself and measure the
G1453.2 V-API-3S ἠγέρθη (1x)
Ac 9:8 And Saul was·roused from the earth, but with·his
G1453.2 V-APM-2P ἐγέρθητε (1x)
Mt 17:7 ·them and declared, "Be·roused·already, and do·not
G1453.2 V-APP-NSM ἐγερθείς (1x)
Mt 9:19 And being·roused, YeShua followed him, and *so·did*
G1453.2 V-APS-3S ἐγερθῇ (1x)
Lk 13:25 the master·of·the·house should·be·roused, and
G1453.4 V-FAI-3S ἐγερεῖ (1x)
Mt 12:11 ·not·indeed take·secure·hold·of it and pull·it·up?
G1453.4 V-AAI-3S ἤγειρεν (1x)
Ac 3:7 by·the right hand, he·pulled·him·up. And at·once,

G1454 ἔγερσις ếgêrsis *n.* (2x)
Roots:G1453 Compare:G0386
G1454.2 N-ASF ἔγερσιν (1x)
Mt 27:53 ·tombs after his awakening·from·death, they·entered
EG1454.2 (1x)
Mt 9:26 the disclosure of·this *awakening* went·forth into all

G1455 ἐγ•κάθ•ετος ênkáthêtôs *adj.* (1x)
Roots:G1722 G2524 Compare:G2685
G1455.2 A-APM ἐγκαθέτους (1x)
Lk 20:20 they·dispatched ambushers pretending themselves

G1456 ἐγ•καίνια ênkaínia *n.* (1x)
Roots:G1722 G2537 Compare:G0106 G4634
See:G0342 G1457 G1457-1
xLangEquiv:H2598 A2597
G1456.5 N-NPN ἐγκαίνια (1x)
Jn 10:22 Now the Feast·of·the·Renovations *(also called*

G1457 ἐγ•καινίζω ênkainízō *v.* (2x)
Roots:G1456 See:G1457-1 xLangAlso:H2596 A2597
G1457 V-AAI-3S ἐνεκαίνισεν (1x)
Heb 10:20 living way which he·inaugurated for·us through
G1457 V-RPI-3S ἐγκεκαίνισται (1x)
Heb 9:18 *covenant* has·been·inaugurated apart·from blood.

G1458 ἐγ•καλέω ênkaléō *v.* (7x)
Roots:G1722 G2564 Compare:G2723 See:G0410
G1458.2 V-FAI-3S ἐγκαλέσει (1x)
Rm 8:33 Who shall·call·to·account against God's
G1458.2 V-PAM-3P ἐγκαλείτωσαν (1x)
Ac 19:38 proconsuls; let·them·call one·another to·account.
G1458.2 V-PPI-1S ἐγκαλοῦμαι (2x)
Ac 26:2 ·the·things for·which I·am·called·to·account by *the*
Ac 26:7 O·King Agrippa, I·am·called·to·account by the
G1458.2 V-PPN ἐγκαλεῖσθαι (1x)
Ac 19:40 also to·be·called·to·account concerning today's
G1458.2 V-PPP-ASM ἐγκαλούμενον (1x)
Ac 23:29 him being·called·to·account concerning issues of·
G1458.2 V-IAI-3P ἐνεκάλουν (1x)
Ac 23:28 ·of which they·were·calling him to·account, I·

G1459 ἐγ•κατα•λείπω ênkatalêípō *v.* (9x)
Roots:G1722 G2641 Compare:G0646 G2641
xLangAlso:H5800
G1459.1 V-2AAI-3S ἐγκατέλιπεν (1x)
Rm 9:29 Yahweh of·Hosts left·behind offspring† for·us, we·
G1459.2 V-FAI-2S ἐγκαταλείψεις (1x)
Ac 2:27 because you·shall·not forsake my soul in Hades,
G1459.2 V-PAP-NPM ἐγκαταλείποντες (1x)
Heb 10:25 not forsaking the complete·gathering of·ourselves
G1459.2 V-PPP-NPM ἐγκαταλειπόμενοι (1x)
2Co 4:9 but·yet not being·forsaken; being·cast·down, but·
G1459.2 V-2AAI-2S ἐγκατέλιπες (2x)
Mt 27:46 my God, for·what·purpose did·you·forsake me?
Mk 15:34 "My God, my God, why did·you·forsake me?
G1459.2 V-2AAI-3S ἐγκατέλιπεν (1x)
2Ti 4:10 for Demas forsook me, loving the present age, and
G1459.2 V-2AAI-3P ἐγκατέλιπον (1x)
2Ti 4:16 with·me, but·rather all *men* forsook me; may·it·not
G1459.2 V-2AAS-1S ἐγκαταλίπω (1x)
Heb 13:5 you, nor·even no, I·may·not·ever forsake you."

G1460 ἐγ•κατ•οικέω ênkatôikéō *v.* (1x)
Roots:G1722 G2730
G1460 V-PAP-NSM ἐγκατοικῶν (1x)
2Pe 2:8 *deeds*, the righteous·man residing among them day

G1461 ἐγ•κεντρίζω ênkêntrízō *v.* (6x)
Roots:G1722 G2759
G1461.1 V-AAN ἐγκεντρίσαι (1x)
Rm 11:23 ·grafted·in, for God is able to·engraft them again.
G1461.2 V-FPI-3P ἐγκεντρισθήσονται (2x)
Rm 11:23 in·the lack·of·trust, they·shall·be·grafted·in, for
Rm 11:24 ·to nature, be·grafted·into their·own olive·tree?
G1461.2 V-API-2S ἐνεκεντρίσθης (2x)
Rm 11:17 a·wild·olive·tree, were·grafted·in among them
Rm 11:24 you·are·already·grafted into a·cultivated·olive·
G1461.2 V-APS-1S ἐγκεντρισθῶ (1x)
Rm 11:19 ·off in·order·that I·myself may·be·grafted·in."

G1462 ἔγ•κλημα ếnklēma *n.* (2x)
Roots:G1458 Compare:G2724
G1462 N-ASN ἔγκλημα (1x)
Ac 23:29 but having not·even·one allegation worthy of·death
G1462 N-GSN ἐγκλήματος (1x)
Ac 25:16 to·defend·himself concerning the allegation.'

G1463 ἐγ•κομβόομαι ênkômbôômai *v.* (1x)
Roots:G1722
G1463.3 V-ADM-2P ἐγκομβώσασθε (1x)
1Pe 5:5 ·another, put·on·the·servant's·work·apron *with* the

G1464 ἐγ•κοπή ênkôpế *n.* (1x)
Roots:G1465
G1464 N-ASF ἐγκοπήν (1x)
1Co 9:12 we·should·give any hindrance to·the good·news

G1465 ἐγ•κόπτω ênkốptō *v.* (3x)
Roots:G1722 G2875 Compare:G0348 G2967
See:G1464
G1465.2 V-IPI-1S ἐνεκοπτόμην (1x)
Rm 15:22 ·of·which also, I·was·hindered often *from* coming
G1465.2 V-AAI-3S ἐνέκοψεν (1x)
1Th 2:18 and again, but the Adversary-Accuser hindered us.
G1465.3 V-PAS-1S ἐγκόπτω (1x)
Ac 24:4 I·should·not·be any·further hindrance upon you, I·

G1466 ἐγ•κράτεια ênkrátêia *n.* (4x)
Roots:G1468 Compare:G0192 G4997
G1466.1 N-NSF ἐγκράτεια (1x)
Gal 5:23 gentleness, *and* self-restraint— against such·things
G1466.1 N-ASF ἐγκράτειαν (1x)
2Pe 1:6 and along·with *yeur* knowledge, Self-Restraint; and
G1466.1 N-DSF ἐγκρατείᾳ (1x)
2Pe 1:6 and along·with *yeur* self-restraint, Patient·Endurance
G1466.1 N-GSF ἐγκρατείας (1x)
Ac 24:25 concerning righteousness, self-restraint, and the

G1467 ἐγ•κρατεύομαι ênkratêúômai *v.* (2x)
Roots:G1468 Compare:G4993
G1467.2 V-PNI-3S ἐγκρατεύεται (1x)
1Co 9:25 striving·for·a·prize exercises·self-restraint in·all·.
G1467.3 V-PNI-3P ἐγκρατεύονται (1x)
1Co 7:9 if they·do·not have·self-restraint, they·must·marry.

G1468 ἐγ•κρατής ênkratếs *adj.* (1x)
Roots:G1722 G2904 Compare:G4998 See:G1466
G1468.2 A-ASM ἐγκρατῆ (1x)
Tit 1:8 righteous, divinely·holy, self-restrained,

G1469 ἐγ•κρίνω ênkrínō *v.* (1x)
Roots:G1722 G2919
G1469 V-AAN ἐγκρῖναι (1x)
2Co 10:12 ·do·not dare to·count·ourselves·among·those, or

G1470 ἐγ•κρύπτω ênkrýptō *v.* (2x)
Roots:G1722 G2928 Compare:G4786
G1470.2 V-AAI-3S ἐνέκρυψεν (2x)
Lk 13:21 which a·woman took *and* incorporated into three
Mt 13:33 upon·taking *it*, a·woman incorporated *it* into three

G1471 ἔγ•κυος ếnkyôs *n.* (1x)
Roots:G1722 G2949 Compare:G1064
G1471.2 N-DSF ἐγκύῳ (1x)
Lk 2:5 his espoused wife, being swellingly·pregnant.

G1472 ἐγ•χρίω ênchríō *v.* (1x)
Roots:G1722 G5548 Compare:G3462 G0218
G1472 V-AAM-2S ἔγχρισον (1x)
Rv 3:18 be·made·apparent. Also, smear eye·salve on your

G1473 ἐγώ êgṓ *p:p.* (370x)
Compare:G1699 G1510 G1683 See:G1691 G1698 G1700 G2248 G2249 G2254 G2257
G1473.1 P:P-1NS ἐγώ (298x)
Jn 1:20 but he·affirmed, "I·myself am not the Anointed-One
Jn 1:23 He·replied, "I·myself *am* a·voice of·one·crying·
Jn 1:26 answered them, saying, "I·myself immerse in water,
Jn 1:27 ·to·be ahead of·me) of·whom I·myself am not *even*
Jn 1:30 This is·he concerning whom I·myself declared,
Jn 1:31 on·account·of that, I·myself came immersing in the
Jn 3:28 testify to·me that I·declared, 'I·myself am not the
Jn 4:14 from·out of·the water that I·myself shall·give him,
Jn 4:32 he·declared to·them, "I·myself have a·full·meal to·
Jn 4:38 "I·myself dispatched yeu to·reap *that·for* which yeu·
Jn 5:7 pool, but while I·myself am·coming, another steps·
Jn 5:30 "I·myself am·not able to·do not·even·one·thing of
Jn 5:31 "If I·myself should·testify concerning my·own·self,
Jn 5:34 But I·myself receive the testimony not from a·man·
Jn 5:36 "But I·myself have the greater testimony *than·that*
Jn 5:36 *are* the same works which I·myself do; it·testifies
Jn 5:43 "I·myself have·come in my Father's name, and yeu·
Jn 5:45 ·not presume that I·myself shall·legally·accuse yeu
Jn 6:40 ·have eternal life-above, and I·myself shall·raise him
Jn 6:44 should·draw him, and I·myself shall·raise him up
Jn 6:51 and also the bread that I·myself shall·give is my flesh
Jn 6:51 my flesh, which I·myself shall·give on·behalf of·the
Jn 6:54 eternal life-above, and I·myself shall·raise him up at·
Jn 6:63 The utterances that I·myself speak to·yeu, *they* are
Jn 6:70 "No, *it·is* I·myself *that* selected yeu, the twelve, yet
Jn 7:7 but it·hates me, because I·myself testify concerning it
Jn 7:8 to this Sacred·Feast. I·myself do·not·yet walk·up to
Jn 7:17 of·God, or *whether* I·myself speak from my·own·
Jn 7:29 But I·myself personally·know him, because I·am
Jn 8:11 to·her, "Not·even·do I·myself condemn you.
Jn 8:14 "Though I·myself may·testify concerning my·own·
Jn 8:15 ·to the flesh; I·myself do·not presently·judge not·
Jn 8:16 And yet if I·myself should·judge, my verdict is true,
Jn 8:16 not alone, but·rather *it·is* I·myself and Father, the·
Jn 8:18 I·myself am one testifying concerning my·own·self,
Jn 8:21 declared again to·them, "I·myself head·on·out, and
Jn 8:21 in yeur moral·failures. Where I·myself head·on·out,
Jn 8:22 Because he·says, 'Where I·myself head·on·out, yeu
Jn 8:23 birthed·from down·below; I·myself am birthed·from
Jn 8:23 are from·among this world; I·myself am not from·
Jn 8:29 me alone, because I·myself always do the·things
Jn 8:38 "I·myself speak that·which I·have·clearly·seen from·
Jn 8:42 love me, for I·myself went·forth and have·come out·
Jn 8:45 "And because I·myself say the truth, yeu·do·not trust
Jn 8:49 Jesus answered, "I·myself do·not have a·demon,
Jn 8:50 And I·myself do·not seek my·own glory; there·is
Jn 8:54 Jesus answered, "If I·myself glorify my·own·self,
Jn 8:55 ·have·not known him, but I·myself have·seen him.
Jn 9:39 "For judgment, I·myself did·come into this world in·
Jn 10:10 ·completely·destroy. I·myself came in·order·that
Jn 10:17 loves me, because I·myself lay·down my soul in·

Jn 10:18 it away from me, but·rather I·myself lay it down of
Jn 10:25 "The works that I·myself do in my Father's name,
Jn 10:30 I·myself and the Father are one.
Jn 10:34 in yeur Torah-Law, "I·myself declared, "Yeu·are
Jn 11:27 Yes, Lord. I·myself have·trusted that you·yourself
Jn 11:42 And I·myself had·personally·known that you·hear
Jn 12:46 "I·myself *being* a·light, have·come into the world,
Jn 12:47 should·not trust, I·myself do·not presently·judge
Jn 12:49 "Because I·myself did·not speak from·out of·my·
Jn 12:50 "Accordingly, whatever I·myself speak, *it·is* just·as
Jn 13:7 declared to·him, "What I·myself do, you·yourself
Jn 13:14 Accordingly, if I·myself washed yeur feet *being*
Jn 13:15 to·yeu in·order·that just·as I·myself did for·yeu,
Jn 13:18 yeu all. I·myself personally·know whom I·selected,
Jn 13:26 I·shall·hand the morsel, *with* I·myself dipping *it*."
Jn 13:33 Judeans, 'Where I·myself head·on·out, yeu are·not
Jn 14:4 ·know to·where *it·is that* I·myself head·on·out, and
Jn 14:10 Do·you·not trust that I·myself *am* in the Father, and
Jn 14:10 "The utterances that I·myself speak to·yeu, I·do·not
Jn 14:11 Trust me that I·myself *am* in the Father, and the
Jn 14:12 me, the works that I·myself do, he·shall·do those·
Jn 14:12 than·these shall·he·do, because I·myself traverse to
Jn 14:14 something in my name, I·myself shall·do *it*.
Jn 14:16 "And I·myself shall·ask·of the Father, and he·shall·
Jn 14:19 observe me. Because I·myself live, yeu·yeurselves
Jn 14:20 day, yeu shall·know that I·myself *am* in my Father,
Jn 14:21 by my Father, and I·myself shall·love him and
Jn 14:27 just·as the world gives *do* I·myself give to·yeu. Do·
Jn 14:28 "Yeu·heard that I·myself declared to·yeu, 'I·head·
Jn 15:10 my love, just·as I·myself have·observantly·kept my
Jn 15:14 if yeu·should·do as·much·as I·myself command yeu
Jn 15:16 selected me, but·rather I·myself selected yeu and
Jn 15:19 the world, but·rather I·myself selected yeu from·
Jn 15:20 Remember the saying that I·myself declared to·yeu,
Jn 15:26 should·come, whom I·myself shall·send to·yeu
Jn 16:4 yeu·may·remember that I·myself declared to·yeu
Jn 16:7 "But·yet I·myself say to·yeu the truth; it·is·more·
Jn 16:7 ·advantageous for·yeu that I·myself should·go·away,
Jn 16:16 ·upon me, because I·myself head·on·out toward the
Jn 16:17 me,' and 'I·myself head·on·out toward the Father'
Jn 16:26 I·do·not say to·yeu that I·myself shall·ask·of the
Jn 16:27 ·trusted that I·myself came·forth personally·from
Jn 16:33 be·of·good·courage; I·myself have·overcome the
Jn 17:4 I·myself glorified you on the earth.
Jn 17:9 "I·myself ask concerning them.
Jn 17:11 are in the world, and I·myself do·come to you.
Jn 17:12 them in the world, I·myself was·guarding them in
Jn 17:14 "I·myself have·given them your Redemptive-word,
Jn 17:14 the world, just·as I·myself am not from·among the
Jn 17:16 the world, just·as I·myself am not from·among the
Jn 17:19 on·behalf of·them, I·myself make my·own·self
Jn 17:22 you·have·given to·me I·myself have·given to·them
Jn 17:23 I·myself in them, and you·yourself in me— "in·
Jn 17:25 did·not know you, but I·myself knew you, and
Jn 18:20 him, "I·myself spoke with·freeness·of·speech to·
Jn 18:20 ·of·speech to·the world. I·myself always instructed
Jn 18:21 these·men personally·know what I·myself declared.
Jn 18:26 ·off, says, "¿!·Did·not I·myself see you in the
Jn 18:35 Pilate answered, "¿! Am·I myself a·Jew?
Jn 18:37 a·king, *for* to this I·myself have·been·born. Also to
Jn 18:38 and he·says to·them, "I·myself find in him not·
Jn 19:6 him and crucify *him*, for I·myself find no fault in
Lk 1:18 this for·certain? For I·myself am an·old·man, and
Lk 1:19 angel declared to·him, "I·myself am GabriEl, the·
Lk 3:16 *of·them*, "In·fact, I·myself immerse yeu in·water,
Lk 7:8 "For even I·myself am a·man·of·clay† being·assigned
Lk 7:27 "Behold, I·myself dispatch my messenger before
Lk 8:46 laid·hold of·me, for I·myself did·know power
Lk 9:9 HerOd·AntiPas declared, "I·myself beheaded John,
Lk 9:9 is this, concerning whom I·myself hear such·things?
Lk 10:3 Head·on·out. Behold, I·myself dispatch yeu as
Lk 10:35 I come·back, I·myself shall·give·*it*·back to·you.'
Lk 11:19 And if I·myself by Master-Of-Dung cast·out the
Lk 15:17 and I·myself am·completely·perishing with·hunger
Lk 19:22 ·personally·known that I·myself am an·unrelenting
Lk 19:23 that at·my·coming, I·myself might·have reclaimed
Lk 20:8 to·them, "Neither *do* I·myself say to·yeu by what·
Lk 21:15 For I·myself shall·give yeu a·mouth and wisdom,
Lk 22:27 the·one reclining·at·the·meal? But I·myself am in
Lk 22:32 "But I·myself petitioned concerning you, *Simon*,
Lk 23:14 and behold, I·myself, after·investigating *him* in·
Lk 24:49 And behold, I·myself dispatch the Promise of·my
Ac 7:7 they·should·be·enslaved, I·myself shall·sheriff,"
Ac 7:32 *saying*, "I·myself *am* the God of·your fathers, the
Ac 9:10 And he·declared, "Behold, I·myself Lord."
Ac 9:16 For I·myself shall·indicate to·him what·many·things
Ac 10:20 on·account·that I·myself have·dispatched them."
Ac 11:5 "I·myself was in *the* city *of* Joppa praying, and in a·
Ac 11:17 Anointed), then who *am* I? Was·I able to·prevent
Ac 13:25 ·do yeu·surmise me to·be? I·myself am not *he*.
Ac 13:33 are my Son. Today, I·myself have·begotten you."
Ac 13:41 be·disconcerted. Because I·myself work a·work in
Ac 15:19 Therefore, I·myself judge *for·us* not to·further·
Ac 17:3 "This Jesus (whom I·myself fully·proclaim to·yeu)
Ac 17:23 ·not·knowing *him*, I·myself fully·proclaim this
Ac 18:6 *be* upon yeur own·heads; I·myself *am* pure. From
Ac 18:15 yeurselves, for I·myself am·definitely·not willing
Ac 20:22 ·been·bound in·the spirit, I·myself traverse to
Ac 20:25 "And now behold, I·myself personally·know that
Ac 20:26 in the present day, that I·myself *am* pure from the
Ac 20:29 For I·myself personally·know this, that after my
Ac 21:13 my heart? For I·myself am in·a·state·of·readiness
Ac 21:39 "In·fact, I·myself am a·man·of·clay† *who·is* a·
Ac 22:3 "I·myself am in·fact a·man *who·is* a·Jew, having·
Ac 22:8 And I·myself answered, 'Who are·you, Lord?
Ac 22:19 are·fully·acquainted that I·myself was imprisoning
Ac 22:21 'Traverse, because I·myself shall·dispatch you
Ac 22:28 ·commander answered, "I·myself, with·a·large
Ac 22:28 And Paul replied, "But I·myself, also, *am* having·
Ac 23:1 I·myself have·been·living·as·a·good·citizen in·all
Ac 23:6 "Men, brothers, I·myself am a·Pharisee, a·son of·a·
Ac 23:6 ·dead·men, *that* I·myself am·called·into·judgment."
Ac 24:21 of·dead·men, I·myself am·called·into·judgment by
Ac 25:18 of·such·things *as* I·myself was·surmising.
Ac 25:20 And I·myself, being·at·a·loss concerning this
Ac 25:25 But I·myself, after·grasping him to·have·practiced
Ac 26:9 "Accordingly in·fact, I·myself (within·myself)
Ac 26:10 holy·ones I·myself permanently·shut·up in·prisons,
Ac 26:15 And I·myself declared, 'Who are·you, Lord?
Ac 28:17 "Men, brothers, I·myself, having·committed not·
Heb 1:5 are my Son. Today, I·myself have·begotten you"?
Heb 1:5 "? And again, "I·myself shall·be his·own distinct
Heb 2:13 again, " I·myself shall·be having·confidence on
Heb 2:13 "Behold, I·myself and the little·children which
Heb 5:5 are my Son. Today, I·myself have·begotten you."
Heb 10:30 *belongs* to·me, I·myself shall·recompense," says
Heb 12:26 "Yet once·more I·myself do·shake not merely
Gal 1:12 For I·myself neither personally·received it from a·
Gal 2:19 For I·myself through Torah-Law, am·dead to·
Gal 2:20 and I·live. No·longer I·myself, but Anointed-One
Gal 4:12 I·petition yeu, be as I·myself *am*, because I·also
Gal 5:10 I·myself do·have·confidence for yeu in *the* Lord,
Gal 5:11 And I·myself, brothers, if I·still officially·proclaim
Gal 6:17 wearisome·troubles to·me, for I·myself bear in my
Mt 3:11 In·fact, I·myself immerse yeu in water for
Mt 3:14 him, saying, "I·myself have need to·be·immersed
Mt 5:22 But I·myself say to·yeu that any one being·angry
Mt 5:28 But I·myself say to·yeu that everyone looking·upon
Mt 5:32 But I·myself say to·yeu, that whoever should·
Mt 5:34 "But I·myself say to·yeu not to·swear at·all: neither
Mt 5:39 But I·myself say to·yeu, not to·stand·opposed·to the
Mt 5:44 But I·myself say to·yeu, love yeur enemies, bless
Mt 8:7 *to·him*, I·myself shall·both·relieve·and·cure him."
Mt 8:9 For even I·myself am a·man·of·clay† under authority,
Mt 10:16 "Behold, I·myself dispatch yeu as sheep in *the*
Mt 11:10 "Behold, I·myself dispatch my messenger before
Mt 12:27 And if I·myself, by Master-Of-Dung, cast·out the
Mt 12:28 But if I·myself cast·out the demons by God's Spirit
Mt 18:33 ·slave, even as I·myself showed·mercy on·you?
Mt 20:15 eye evil, because I·myself am beneficially·good?
Mt 20:22 to·drink the cup that I·myself am·about to·drink?
Mt 20:22 And the immersion that I·myself am·immersed·in,
Mt 20:23 the immersion that I·myself shall·be·immersed·in,
Mt 21:27 to·them, "Neither do I·myself say to·yeu by what·
Mt 21:30 And answering, he·declared, 'I·myself *will*, sir,'
Mt 23:34 ·account·of that, behold, I·myself dispatch to yeu
Mt 25:27 I·myself might be·subsequently·obtaining my·
Mt 26:33 *yet* I·myself not·even·at·any·time shall·be·tripped·
Mt 26:39 Nevertheless not as I·myself will, but·rather as you
Mt 28:20 "And behold, I·myself am with yeu *for* all the days
Mk 1:2 "Behold, I·myself dispatch my messenger before
Mk 1:8 In·fact, I·myself immersed yeu in water, but he·
Mk 6:16 is John, whom I·myself beheaded. He·himself is·
Mk 9:25 the·one mute and deaf, I·myself order you, come·
Mk 10:38 ·yeu·able to·drink the cup that I·myself drink·of?
Mk 10:38 the immersion that I·myself *am* to·be·immersed·in
Mk 10:39 ·fact, the cup that I·myself drink, yeu·shall·drink;
Mk 10:39 and in·the immersion that I·myself am·immersed,
Mk 11:33 to·them, "Neither do I·myself relate to·yeu by
Mk 12:26 ·him, saying, "I·myself *am* the God of·AbRaham
Mk 14:19 to·him one·by·one, "Is·it I·myself?" And another,
Mk 14:19 "Is·it I·myself?" And another, "Is·it I·myself?"
Mk 14:29 ·tripped·up·and·fall·away, but·yet not I·myself."
Mk 14:36 But·yet not what I·myself will, but·rather what
Mk 14:58 saying, 'I·myself shall·demolish this Temple,
Rm 7:9 And I·myself was·living apart·from Torah-Law once
Rm 7:9 Moral·Failure came·alive·again, and I·myself died.
Rm 7:14 the Torah-Law is spiritual, but I·myself am fleshly,
Rm 7:17 right·now, *it·is* no·longer I·myself that·performs it,
Rm 7:20 Now if that·which I·myself do·not want, *if* that·
Rm 7:20 I·do, *it·is* no·longer I·myself that·performs it, but·
Rm 7:24 I·myself *am* a·miserable man·of·clay†! Who shall·
Rm 9:3 For I·myself would·well-wish myself to·be
Rm 10:19 says, "I·myself shall·provoke yeu to·jealousy
Rm 11:1 ·it·never happen! For I·myself also am an·Israelite,
Rm 11:13 Gentiles, in as·much·as I·myself am in·fact an·
Rm 11:19 ·off in·order·that I·myself may·be·grafted·in."
Rm 12:19 *belongs* to·me; I·myself shall·recompense," says
Rm 14:11 ·been·written, "*As·surely·as* I·myself live,' says
Rm 16:4 soul, for·whom not only I·myself give·thanks, but·
Php 3:4 even·though I·myself *was once* also having
Php 3:4 to·have·confidence in flesh, I·myself *have* more:
Php 3:13 Brothers, I·myself do·not reckon my·own·self to·
Php 4:11 ·to *a·particular* lacking; for I·myself learned, *that*
2Pe 1:17 my beloved Son, in whom I·myself take·delight."
Tit 1:3 with·which I·myself am·entrusted according·to a·
Tit 1:5 in·each city, as I·myself thoroughly·assigned to·you
1Co 1:12 of·yeu says, "In·fact, I·myself am of·Paul," and
1Co 2:3 And I·myself came·to·be alongside yeu in weakness
1Co 3:1 And I·myself, brothers, am·not able to·speak to·yeu
1Co 3:4 should·say, "In·fact, I·myself am of·Paul," and
1Co 3:6 I·myself planted, Apollos watered, but·yet God was·
1Co 4:15 for in Anointed-One Jesus, I·myself begot yeu
1Co 6:12 for·me, but·yet I·myself shall·not be·controlled
1Co 7:10 ·married I·charge, *yet* not I·myself, but·rather the
1Co 7:12 But to·the rest I·myself say, not the Lord— if any
1Co 7:28 in·the flesh, but I·myself am·lenient·with yeu.
1Co 9:6 *are* only BarNabas and I·myself *excluded*? ¿!·Do·
1Co 9:15 But I·myself used not·even·one of·these·things,
1Co 9:26 Now·then, in·this·manner I·myself do·run, *but* not
1Co 10:30 if by·gratitude, I·myself participate·neighborly,
1Co 10:30 ·reviled over that·for·which I·myself give·thanks?
1Co 11:23 For I·myself personally·received from the Lord
1Co 15:9 For I·myself am the least of·the ambassadors, who
1Co 15:10 ·them all; but not I·myself but·rather the Grace
1Co 15:11 Accordingly, whether *it·was* I·myself or those
1Co 16:10 ·works the work of·*the*·Lord, as also I·myself *do*.
2Co 1:23 Now I·myself do·call·upon God *for* a·witness upon
2Co 2:2 For if I·myself grieve yeu, then who would·be the·

2Co 2:10 yeu·graciously·forgive anything, I·myself *do* also.
2Co 2:10 even if I·myself have·graciously·forgiven anything
2Co 11:23 I·speak— I·myself *am* above·and·beyond! … in
2Co 11:29 ·failure, and I·myself am·not being·incensed?
2Co 12:11 me, for I·myself was·due to·be·commended by
2Co 12:15 ·pleasure, I·myself shall·cover·the·expense and
2Co 12:16 be·it·so, I·myself did·not impose·a·burden·on
Eph 4:1 Now·then, I·myself, the chained·prisoner in *the*
Eph 5:32 is·a·great mystery, but I·myself do·say *this* in·
Col 1:25 of·which I·myself am·made an·attendant,
Phm 1:13 whom I·myself was·definitely·willing to·fully·
Phm 1:19 *this* by·my·own hand; I·myself shall·fully·pay *it*,
Phm 1:20 brother, may I·myself derive·profit·from you in
1Ti 1:11 ·blessed God, with·which I·myself was·entrusted.
1Ti 1:15 ·disqualified·ones, of·whom I·myself am foremost.
1Ti 2:7 for which I·myself was·placed *as* an·official·
2Ti 1:11 for which I·myself was·placed *as* an·official·
2Ti 4:1 Accordingly, I·myself thoroughly·urge *you* in·the·
2Ti 4:6 even·now, I·myself am·poured·forth·as·a·devotion,
2Jn 1:1 and her children— whom I·myself do·love in truth,
2Jn 1:1 ·love in truth, and not I·myself only, but·rather also
3Jn 1:1 well-beloved Gaius, whom I·myself do·love in truth.
Rv 2:22 'Behold, I·myself do·cast her upon a·couch *of·*
Rv 3:9 and *that* they·should·know that I·myself loved you.
Rv 3:19 ·as I·may·have·affection·for, I·myself reprove and
Rv 5:4 And I·myself was·weeping much, because not·even·
Rv 17:7 Why did·you·marvel? I·myself shall·declare to·you
Rv 21:6 and the end. I·myself shall·give to·the·one thirsting

G1473.2 P:P-1NS ἐγώ (11x)

Jn 4:26 Jesus says to·her, "It·is·I Myself. *Yes*, the·one
Jn 6:20 he·says to·them, "It·is·I Myself. Do·not be·afraid.
Jn 9:9 *But* that·man was·saying, "It·is·I myself."
Ac 9:5 the Lord declared, "It·is·I Myself, Jesus, whom you·
Ac 10:21 "Behold, it·is·I myself whom yeu·seek. What *is*
Ac 22:8 ·declared to·me, 'It·is·I Myself, Jesus of·Natsareth,
Ac 26:15 And he·declared, 'It·is·I Myself, Jesus, whom
Mt 14:27 "Be·of·good·courage, it·is·I Myself! Do·not be·
Mt 26:22 "Lord, is·it·I myself?"
Mt 26:25 "Rabbi, is·it·I myself?" He·says to·him, "You·
Mk 6:50 "Be·of·good·courage! It·is·I Myself. Do·not be·

G1473.3 P:P-1NS ἐγώ (42x)

Jn 6:35 declared to·them, "I AM the bread of·life-above.
Jn 6:41 him, because he·declared, "I AM the bread, the·one
Jn 6:48 I AM the bread of·the life-above.
Jn 6:51 I AM the living bread, the·one descending out of·the
Jn 7:34 ·not find *me*, and where I AM, *there* yeu·yeurselves
Jn 7:36 find *me*? And where I AM, *there* yeu·yeurselves are·
Jn 8:12 again to·them, saying, "I AM the light of·the world.
Jn 8:24 For unless yeu·should·trust that I AM, yeu·shall·die
Jn 8:28 Son of·Clay·Man†, yeu·shall·know that I AM, and
Jn 8:58 to·yeu, prior·to AbRaham coming·to·be, I AM."
Jn 10:7 most·certainly, I·say to·yeu, I AM the door of·the
Jn 10:9 "I AM the door.
Jn 10:11 "I AM the good shepherd.
Jn 10:14 "I AM the good shepherd, and I·know my *sheep*,
Jn 11:25 Jesus declared to·her, "I AM the resurrection and
Jn 12:26 let·him·follow me; and where I AM, there also
Jn 13:19 it·should·happen, yeu·may·trust that I AM.
Jn 14:3 yeu to myself in·order·that where I AM, *there* yeu·
Jn 14:6 Jesus says to·him, "I AM the way, and the truth, and
Jn 15:1 "I AM the true vine, and my Father is the farmer
Jn 15:5 "I AM the vine, yeu *are* the vine·sprouts.
Jn 17:24 ·also may·be with me where I AM, in·order·that
Jn 18:5 Jesus says to·them, "I AM." And even Judas, the·
Jn 18:6 ·as he·declared to·them, "I AM," they·went·off
Jn 18:8 "I·declared to·yeu that I AM. Accordingly, if yeu·
Jn 18:37 "You·yourself say *it·rightly* because I AM a·king,
Lk 21:8 in my name, saying, 'I AM,' and, 'The season has·
Lk 22:70 "Yeu·yeurselves say *it·rightly* because I AM."
Lk 24:39 and my feet, that I AM myself. Verify·by·touching
Ac 18:10 on·account·that I AM with you, and not·even·one·
Mt 22:32 "I AM the God of·AbRaham, and the God of·
Mt 24:5 in my name, saying, 'I AM the Anointed-One,' and
Mk 13:6 in my name, saying, 'I AM *the Anointed-One*,' and
Mk 14:62 And Jesus declared, "I AM, and yeu·shall·gaze·
1Pe 1:16 "Yeu·must·be holy, because I AM holy."
Rv 1:8 "I AM the Alpha and the Omega, beginning and end,
Rv 1:11 saying, "I AM the Alpha and the Omega, the First
Rv 1:17 "Do·not be·afraid; I AM the First and the Last.
Rv 2:23 Called·Out·citizenries shall·know that I AM the·one
Rv 21:6 to·me, "It·has·happened! I AM the Alpha and the
Rv 22:13 I AM the Alpha and the Omega, beginning and end
Rv 22:16 concerning the Called·Out·citizenries. I AM the

G1473.4 P:P-1NS ἐγώ (19x)

Gal 5:2 See, I Paul say to·yeu, that if yeu·should·be·
Rm 7:25 ·fact, with·the mind, I myself am·a·slave·to God's
Rm 15:14 And I myself also have·been·persuaded
Rm 16:22 I, Tertius, the·one writing the letter, greet yeu in
1Th 2:18 ·wanted to·come to yeu, in·fact I Paul, also once
1Co 1:12 I·myself am of·Paul," and "I *am* of·Apollos," and
1Co 1:12 of·Apollos," and "I *am* of·Kephas·*(called·Peter)*,"
1Co 1:12 ·*(called·Peter)*," and "I *am* of·Anointed-One."
1Co 3:4 and someone·else, "I *am* of·Apollos," are·yeu
1Co 5:3 For I, in·fact, even·though being·absent in·the body
2Co 10:1 Now I, Paul, I·myself do·implore yeu through the
2Co 12:13 ·Out·citizenries, except that I myself was·not a·
Eph 3:1 For·this, on·account·of·grace, I, Paul, *am* the
Col 1:23 under the heaven), of·which I, Paul, am·made an·
Phm 1:19 I, Paul, wrote *this* by·my·own hand; I·myself
Rv 1:9 I, John, also yeur brother and partner·together in the
Rv 21:2 And I, John, saw the HOLY CITY, brand-new
Rv 22:8 And I, John, *am* the·one looking·upon these·things
Rv 22:16 "I, Jesus, sent my angel to·testify to·yeu these·

G1474 ἐδαφίζω êdaphízō *v.* (1x)
Roots:G1475 Compare:G2647

G1474 V-FAI-3P-ATT ἐδαφιοῦσιν (1x)

Lk 19:44 they·shall·raze·down·to·the·hard·ground and your

G1475 ἔδαφος édaphôs *n.* (1x)
Roots:G1476 See:G1474 xLangAlso:H7172

G1475.2 N-ASN ἔδαφος (1x)

Ac 22:7 And I·fell to the hard·ground and heard a·voice

G1476 ἑδραῖος hêdraîos *adj.* (3x)
Roots:G1475-3 Compare:G0949 G0277 G4740 G4731 G0761 See:G1475 G1477 G2515 G0856 G1478-1

G1476.2 A-NPM ἑδραῖοι (1x)

Col 1:23 having·been·founded and immovably·settled, and

G1476.3 A-NSM ἑδραῖος (1x)

1Co 7:37 *the·father* who stands immovably·steadfast in the

G1476.3 A-NPM ἑδραῖοι (1x)

1Co 15:58 beloved brothers, become immovably·steadfast,

G1477 ἑδραίωμα hêdraíōma *n.* (1x)
Roots:G1475-3 Compare:G4769 See:G1476

G1477.1 N-NSN ἑδραίωμα (1x)

1Ti 3:15 ·the·living God, a·pillar and a·support of·the truth.

G1478 Ἐζεκ•ίας Êzêkías *n/p.* (2x)
חִזְקִיָּהוּ chizqiyahû
Roots:H2396

G1478.2 N/P-NSM Ἐζεκίας (1x)

Mt 1:10 Now HezekIah begot MaNasseh, and MaNasseh

G1478.2 N/P-ASM Ἐζεκίαν (1x)

Mt 1:9 YoTham begot Achaz, and Achaz begot HezekIah.

G1479 ἐθελο•θρησκεία êthêlôthrēskeía *n.* (1x)
Roots:G2309 G2356

G1479.2 N-DSF ἐθελοθρησκείᾳ (1x)

Col 2:23 a·self-willed·observance·of·ceremonial·religion,

G1480 ἐθίζω êthízō *v.* (1x)
Roots:G1485

G1480.3 V-RPP-ASN εἰθισμένον (1x)

Lk 2:27 ·to the prescribed·custom of·the Torah-Law,

G1481 ἐθν•άρχης êthnárchēs *n.* (1x)
Roots:G1484 G0746 Compare:G2232 G2963 G4588-1

G1481 N-NSM ἐθνάρχης (1x)

2Co 11:32 Damascus, the national·magistrate *under* Aretas

G1482 ἐθνικός êthnikôs *adj.* (2x)
Roots:G1484 Compare:G2451 G1672 See:G0459

G1482.2 A-NSM ἐθνικός (1x)

Mt 18:17 let·him·be to·you just·as the Gentile and the tax·

G1482.2 A-NPM ἐθνικοί (1x)

Mt 6:7 ·with·tedious·babblings, just·as the Gentiles *do*, for

G1483 ἐθνικῶς êthnikôs *adv.* (1x)
Roots:G1482

G1483 ADV ἐθνικῶς (1x)

Gal 2:14 inherently·being a·Jew, live as·a·Gentile and not

G1484 ἔθνος éthnôs *n.* (165x)
Roots:G1486 Compare:G3159-1 G2840-1 See:G1482 xLangEquiv:H1471

G1484.2 N-NPN ἔθνη (17x)

Ac 11:1 in Judea, heard that the Gentiles also accepted the
Ac 13:42 gathering, the Gentiles were·imploring for·these
Ac 13:48 upon·hearing *this*, the Gentiles were·rejoicing and
Ac 15:17 the Lord, even all the Gentiles, upon whom my
Mt 6:32 (For all these·things the Gentiles seek·after) for yeur
Mt 12:21 in his name, Gentiles shall·place·their·expectation.
Rm 2:14 (For inasmuch·as Gentiles, the·ones not having
Rm 9:30 ·state? *In·fact*, that Gentiles, the·ones not pursuing
Rm 15:9 and *in·order·for* the Gentiles to·glorify God on·
Rm 15:11 ·praise Yahweh, all the Gentiles! And applaud
Rm 15:12 in him, Gentiles shall·place·their·expectation."
Rm 15:27 if the Gentiles have·a·common·fellowship in·their
1Th 4:5 ·longing, even exactly·as the Gentiles, the·ones not
1Co 10:20 ·things *which* the Gentiles sacrificially·slaughter,
1Co 12:2 ·have·seen that yeu·were Gentiles being·led·away,
Eph 4:17 to·walk just·as the rest *of·the* Gentiles also walk, in
2Ti 4:17 ·forth and *that* all the Gentiles may·hear. And·thus

G1484.2 N-VPN ἔθνη (1x)

Rm 15:10 ·says, " Be·merry, O·Gentiles, with his People."

G1484.2 N-ASN ἔθνος (1x)

Ac 8:9 ·powers and astonishing the Gentiles of·Samaria,

G1484.2 N-APN ἔθνη (14x)

Ac 10:45 because also upon the Gentiles, the voluntary·
Ac 13:46 behold, we·are·turned·around to·the Gentiles.
Ac 15:7 God selected among us *for* the Gentiles to·hear the
Ac 18:6 From now·on, I·shall·traverse to the Gentiles."
Ac 21:21 *who·are* pervasive·among the Gentiles, saying for·
Ac 22:21 ·dispatch you forth unto *the* Gentiles at·a·distance.'
Gal 2:8 also operated in·me unto the Gentiles),
Gal 2:9 we·ourselves *should·go* to the Gentiles, and they·
Gal 2:14 why do·you·compel the Gentiles to·be·Judaic?
Gal 3:8 ·as·righteous the Gentiles birthed·from·out of·trust,
Gal 3:14 may·come·to·be for the Gentiles in YeShua
Rm 15:16 of·Jesus Anointed to the Gentiles, *as* working·in·
Rm 16:26 already·being·made·known to all the Gentiles—
Eph 3:6 *The revealing as·for* the Gentiles to·be co-heirs,

G1484.2 N-DPN ἔθνεσιν (28x)

Lk 18:32 For he·shall·be·handed·over to·the Gentiles, and
Ac 4:27 Pilate, together with·Gentiles and with·peoples of·
Ac 11:18 "So also to·the Gentiles, God granted the
Ac 14:27 that he·opened·up *the* door of·trust to·the Gentiles.
Ac 15:12 God did through them among the Gentiles.
Ac 21:19 God did among the Gentiles through his service.
Ac 26:20 of·Judea, then·also to·the Gentiles, *for·them* to·
Ac 26:23 ·proclaim light to·the People and to·the Gentiles."
Ac 28:28 of·God is·already·dispatched to·the Gentiles, and
Gal 1:16 I·may·proclaim him among the Gentiles, I·did·not
Gal 2:2 which I·officially·proclaim among the Gentiles, but
Mt 10:18 me, for a·testimony to·them and to·the Gentiles.
Mt 12:18 he·shall·announce tribunal·justice to·the Gentiles.
Mt 20:19 shall·hand him over to·the Gentiles for *them* to·
Mk 10:33 to·death and shall·hand him over to·the Gentiles.
Rm 1:5 of·trust among all the Gentiles concerning his name,
Rm 1:13 also, just·as even·so among the rest *of·the* Gentiles.
Rm 2:24 is·reviled among the Gentiles on·account·of yeu,"
Rm 11:11 the Salvation *is·come* to·the Gentiles, to·provoke
Rm 11:13 I·say *this* to·yeu, the Gentiles, in as·much·as I·
Rm 15:9 ·explicitly·affirm you among Gentiles, *O·Yahweh*,
1Pe 2:12 yeur behavior among the Gentiles, being morally·

1Th 2:16 to·the Gentiles in·order·that they·may·be·saved, in·
1Co 5:1 is·not·even named among the Gentiles, such·for
Eph 3:8 to·proclaim among the Gentiles the untraceable
Col 1:27 glory of·this Mystery among the Gentiles, which is
1Ti 3:16 is·officially·proclaimed among Gentiles, is·trusted
Rv 11:2 because it·is·given to·the Gentiles. And they·shall·
G1484.2 N-GPN ἐθνῶν (38x)
Lk 2:32 a·light for a·revelation of·Gentiles and *for the* glory
Lk 21:24 shall·be being·trampled by Gentiles, even·until *the*
Lk 21:24 seasons of·Gentiles should·be·completely·fulfilled.
Lk 22:25 "The kings of·the Gentiles lord·over them; and the·
Ac 7:45 into the territorial·possession of·the Gentiles, whom
Ac 9:15 to·bear my name in·the·sight of·Gentiles and kings,
Ac 13:47 ·have·placed you to·be a·light for Gentiles, *for* you
Ac 14:2 ·affected the souls of·the Gentiles against the
Ac 14:5 a·violent·attempt (both from·the Gentiles and *the*
Ac 15:3 ·of the turning·back·around of·the Gentiles *to God.*
Ac 15:14 ·first, God visited Gentiles to·take from·among
Ac 15:19 the·ones from the Gentiles turning·back·around to
Ac 15:23 Cilicia, the·ones from·among Gentiles, be·well.
Ac 21:11 ·shall·hand *him* over into *the* hands of·Gentiles.'"
Ac 21:25 "Now concerning the Gentiles having·trusted, we·
Ac 26:17 the People, and *from·among* the Gentiles— 'to
Gal 2:12 he·was·eating·together with the Gentiles. But
Gal 2:15 and not from·among morally·disqualified Gentiles.
Mt 4:15 beyond the Jordan, O·Galilee of·the Gentiles—
Mt 10:5 ·should·not go·off to a·roadway of·Gentiles, and
Mt 20:25 of·the Gentiles exercise·lordship·against them, and
Mk 10:42 ·over the Gentiles exercise·lordship·against them,
Rm 3:29 merely? *Is·he* not·indeed also of·Gentiles? Yes, of·
Rm 3:29 not·indeed also of·Gentiles? Yes, of·Gentiles also,
Rm 9:24 Jews merely, but·yet also from·among Gentiles.
Rm 11:12 deterioration, wealth for·*the*·Gentiles; how·much
Rm 11:13 am in·fact an·ambassador of·Gentiles, I·glorify
Rm 11:25 complete·fullness of·the Gentiles should·enter·in.
Rm 15:12 the·one who·is·rising·up to·rule·over Gentiles; in
Rm 15:16 ·up of·the Gentiles may·be well·acceptable,
Rm 15:18 an·attentive·obedience among·Gentiles, by·word
Rm 16:4 also all the Called·Out·citizenries of·the Gentiles.
1Pe 4:3 ·us to·have·accomplished the will of·the Gentiles—
2Co 11:26 kindred, dangers from·among Gentiles, dangers
Eph 3:1 the Anointed-One, on·behalf of·yeu, the Gentiles,
1Ti 2:7 do·not lie)— an·instructor of·Gentiles in trust and
2Ti 1:11 and an·ambassador, and an·instructor of·Gentiles.
3Jn 1:7 ·went·forth, taking not·one·thing from the Gentiles.
EG1484.2 (1x)
Rm 2:14 in·the Torah-Law, these *Gentiles* not having
G1484.3 N-NSN ἔθνος (6x)
Jn 11:50 not *that* the whole nation should·completely·perish.
Jn 18:35 ·I myself a·Jew? Your·own nation and the·chief·
Lk 21:10 to·them, "Nation shall·be·awakened against nation
Mt 24:7 "For nation shall·be·awakened against nation, and
Mk 13:8 "For nation shall·be·awakened against nation, and
1Pe 2:9 a·royal priesthood, a·holy nation, a·People for an·
G1484.3 N-NPN ἔθνη (11x)
Lk 12:30 all these·things, the nations of·the world seek·after
Ac 4:25 "For·what·purpose·did nations tumultuously·snort·,
Gal 3:8 *saying*, "'In you, all the nations shall·be·blessed.'"
Mt 25:32 all the nations shall·be·gathered·together before
Eph 2:11 that yeu *were* at·one·time the nations among flesh,
Rv 11:18 And the nations are·angered, and your WRATH
Rv 15:4 "all the nations shall·come and shall·fall·prostrate
Rv 17:15 and crowds, and nations, and native·tongues.
Rv 18:3 Because all the nations have·drunk from·out of·the
Rv 18:23 ·poisonous·drugs, all the nations were·led·astray.
Rv 21:24 And the nations, of·the·ones being·saved, shall·
G1484.3 N-ASN ἔθνος (11x)
Jn 11:48 and shall·take·away both our place and nation."
Lk 7:5 for he·loves our nation, and he·himself built the
Lk 21:10 "Nation shall·be·awakened against nation, and
Lk 23:2 "We·found this·man perverting the nation, and
Ac 7:7 And the nation to·whom they·should·be·enslaved, I·
Ac 17:26 he·made every nation of·men·of·clay† residing
Ac 24:17 doing merciful·acts for my nation, and *making*
Mt 24:7 "For nation shall·be·awakened against nation, and
Mk 13:8 "For nation shall·be·awakened against nation, and
Rv 13:7 ·it over all tribes, and native·tongues, and nations.
Rv 14:6 on the earth, and to·every nation, and tribe, and
G1484.3 N-APN ἔθνη (11x)
Lk 21:24 ·be·made·prisoners·of·war into all the nations.
Lk 24:47 in his name to all the nations, beginning from
Ac 13:19 And after·demolishing seven nations in *the* land of·
Ac 14:16 ·leave·for all the nations to·traverse in·their·own
Mt 28:19 disciple all the nations, immersing them in the
Mk 13:10 first to·be·officially·proclaimed to all the nations.
Rv 12:5 ·intends to·shepherd all the nations with a·rod of·
Rv 14:8 because she·has·made all nations drink from·out
Rv 19:15 with it he·should·smite the nations; and he·himself
Rv 20:3 ·that he·should·not deceive the nations any·longer,
Rv 20:8 and shall·go·forth to·deceive the nations, the·ones in
G1484.3 N-DSN ἔθνει (7x)
Ac 10:35 but·rather in every nation, the·one who·is·
Ac 24:2 ·reforms occurring in·this nation on·account·of your
Ac 24:10 a·judge to·this nation, with·cheerful·composure I·
Ac 26:4 since beginning in my·own nation in JeruSalem).
Mt 21:43 yeu and shall·be·given to·a·nation producing the
Rm 10:19 *them that are* not a·nation, *and* I·shall·personally·
Rm 10:19 ·anger yeu with a·nation without·comprehension.
G1484.3 N-DPN ἔθνεσιν (3x)
Mt 24:14 Land for a·testimony to·all the nations, and then
Mk 11:17 ·be·called a·house of·prayer for·all the nations'"?
Rv 10:11 many peoples, and nations, and native·tongues,
G1484.3 N-GSN ἔθνους (7x)
Jn 11:51 that Jesus was·about to·die on·behalf of·the nation;
Jn 11:52 and not on·behalf of·the nation merely, but·rather
Ac 2:5 devout men from every nation under the heaven.
Ac 10:22 being·attested·to by the whole nation of·the Jews,
Ac 28:19 anything *of·which* to·legally·accuse my nation.
Rv 5:9 tribe, and native·tongue, and people, and nation;
Rv 7:9 ·number, *a·crowd* from·among all nations, and tribes,
G1484.3 N-GPN ἐθνῶν (9x)
Lk 21:25 earth *shall·be the* anguished·anxiety of·nations, in
Mt 24:9 ·be being·hated by all the nations on·account·of my
Rm 4:17 "'I·have·placed you *as* a·father of·many nations'").
Rm 4:18 the father of·many nations according·to the·thing
Rv 2:26 end, to·him I·shall·give authority over the nations.
Rv 11:9 native·tongues and nations, they·shall·look·upon
Rv 16:19 three parts, and the cities of·the nations fell. And
Rv 21:26 ·bring the glory and the honor of·the nations into it.
Rv 22:2 for *the* therapeutic·relief·and·cure of·the nations.

G1485 ἔθος éthôs *n.* (12x)
Roots:G1486 Compare:G3544-1 See:G2239 G1484
G1485.1 N-ASN ἔθος (3x)
Lk 1:9 according·to the custom of·the Sanctuary·priesthood,
Lk 2:42 according·to the custom of·the Sacred·Feast
Lk 22:39 Then going·forth according·to his custom, *Jesus*
G1485.1 N-APN ἔθη (2x)
Ac 6:14 place and shall·change the customs which Moses
Ac 16:21 and they·fully·proclaim customs which it·is·not
G1485.1 N-DPN ἔθεσιν (2x)
Ac 21:21 the children, nor·even to·walk after·the customs.
Ac 28:17 People or to·the customs of·our esteemed·fathers,
G1485.1 N-GPN ἐθῶν (1x)
Ac 26:3 with·you being an·expert in·all customs and issues
G1485.2 N-NSN ἔθος (1x)
Heb 10:25 of·ourselves, just·as *is* a·habit of·some, but·
G1485.3 N-NSN ἔθος (2x)
Jn 19:40 just·as is *the* manner for·the Judeans to·prepare·
Ac 25:16 *the* manner of·the·Romans to·gratuitously·hand·
G1485.3 N-DSN ἔθει (1x)
Ac 15:1 yeu·should·be·circumcised in·the manner of·Moses,

G1486 ἔθω éthō *v.* (4x)
See:G1485 G2239
G1486.1 V-LAI-3S εἰώθει (1x)
Mk 10:1 as he·had·been·accustomed, he·was·instructing
G1486.2 V-LAI-3S εἰώθει (1x)
Mt 27:15 the governor had·a·custom to·fully·release to·
G1486.3 V-2RAP-ASN εἰωθός (2x)
Lk 4:16 And according·to his custom, he·entered into the
Ac 17:2 And according·to Paul's custom, he·entered·in

G1487 εἰ êi *cond.* (375x)
See:G1437
G1487.ª COND εἰ (1x)
Jn 8:46 concerning moral·failure? And if·what I·say *is the*
G1487.1 COND εἰ (325x)
Jn 1:25 "So·then why·do you·immerse, if you·yourself are
Jn 3:12 If I·declared to·yeu the earthly·things, and yeu·do·
Jn 4:10 declared to·her, "If you·had·personally·known the
Jn 5:46 For if yeu·were·trusting in·Moses, yeu·would be·
Jn 5:47 But if yeu·do·not trust those *Sacred·*Writings, how
Jn 7:4 in freeness·of·speech *publicly*. If you·do these·things,
Jn 7:23 If a·man-child·of·clay† receives circumcision on a·
Jn 8:19 nor my Father. If yeu·had·personally·known me,
Jn 8:39 says to·them, "If yeu·were AbRaham's children, yeu·
Jn 8:42 Jesus declared to·them, "If God was yeur Father,
Jn 9:41 Jesus declared to·them, "If yeu·were blind, yeu·
Jn 10:24 our soul in·suspense? If you·yourself are the
Jn 10:35 "If he·declared them gods pertaining·to whom the
Jn 10:37 "If I·do·not do the works of·my Father, do·not trust
Jn 10:38 "But if I·do, though yeu·may·not trust me, trust the
Jn 11:12 "Lord, if he·has·been·laid·asleep, he·shall·be·
Jn 11:21 to Jesus, "Lord, if you·were here, my brother
Jn 11:32 saying to·him, "Lord, if you·were here, my brother
Jn 13:14 Accordingly, if I·myself washed yeur feet *being*
Jn 13:17 "If yeu·personally·know these·things, supremely·
Jn 13:32 If God is·glorified in him, God also shall·glorify
Jn 14:7 "If yeu·had·known me, yeu·would·have known my
Jn 14:28 *back* to yeu.' If yeu·were·loving me, yeu·would
Jn 15:18 "If the world hates yeu, yeu·know that it·has·hated
Jn 15:19 "If yeu·were from·among the world, the world
Jn 15:20 greater·than his lord.' If they·persecuted me, they·
Jn 15:20 ·persecute yeu also. If they·observantly·kept my
Jn 15:24 "If I·did·not do among them the works which not·
Jn 18:8 ·yeu that I AM. Accordingly, if yeu·seek me, allow
Jn 18:23 Jesus answered him, "If I·spoke wrongly, testify
Jn 18:23 concerning the wrong. But if *I·spoke* well, why do·
Jn 18:30 and declared to·him, "If this·man was not a·
Jn 18:36 is not from·among this world. If my kingdom was
Jn 20:15 says to·him, "Sir, if you·yourself bore him away,
Lk 4:3 Slanderer declared to·him, "If you·are a·son of·God,
Lk 4:9 And he·declared to·him, "If you·are the Son of·God,
Lk 6:32 "So·then if yeu·love the·ones loving yeu, what·kind·
Lk 7:39 himself, saying, "If this·man were a·prophet, he·
Lk 9:23 to *them* all, "If any·man wants to·come right·behind
Lk 10:13 BethSaida! Because if these miracles happened in
Lk 11:13 "So·then, if yeu, inherently·being evil, personally·
Lk 11:18 But also, if the Adversary-Accuser is·thoroughly·
Lk 11:19 And if I·myself by Master-Of-Dung cast·out the
Lk 11:20 "But if with God's finger, I·cast·out the demons,
Lk 11:36 "Now·then, if your whole body *is* full·of·light, not
Lk 12:26 "So·then, if yeu·are·not·even able *to·do* that·thing·
Lk 12:28 "So if God in·this·manner enrobes the grass, today
Lk 12:39 know this, that if the master·of·the·house had·
Lk 14:26 "If any·man comes to me and does·not
Lk 16:11 So·then, if yeu·did·not become trustworthy with
Lk 16:12 And if yeu·did·not become trustworthy with
Lk 16:31 declared to·him, 'If they·do·not hear Moses and
Lk 17:6 Lord declared, "If yeu·were·having trust *that·grows*
Lk 19:8 ·poor; and if I·extorted·by·false·charges anything
Lk 19:42 saying, "If you·knew, even you, at·least in this
Lk 22:42 if you·are·definitely·willing to·personally·carry
Lk 23:31 "Because if they·do these·things to the arbor·tree
Lk 23:35 others, let·him·save himself— if this·man is the
Lk 23:37 and saying, "If you·yourself are the king of·the
Lk 23:39 was·reviling him, saying, "If you·yourself are the
Ac 4:9 if we·ourselves this·day are·scrutinized over *the*
Ac 5:39 But if it·is birthed·from·out of·God, yeu·are·not able
Ac 8:37 And Philippe declared, "If you·trust from·out of·all

Ac 13:15 "Men, brothers, if there·is within yeu a·word of·
Ac 16:15 *us*, saying, "If yeu·have·judged me to·be
Ac 17:27 if perhaps they·might·feel·around·and·about·for
Ac 18:14 "Accordingly in·fact, if it·were some wrong·doing
Ac 19:38 "Accordingly in·fact, if Demetrius and the
Ac 19:39 "But if yeu·seek anything concerning other·matters
Ac 20:16 For he·was·hastening, if it·were possible for·him,
Ac 23:9 in this man·of·clay†, but if a·spirit or an·angel
Ac 24:19 ·accuse *me*, if they·may·actually·have anything
Ac 24:20 same·men *here*, let·them·declare if they·found any
Ac 25:5 legally·accuse this man, if there·is any *wrong* in
Ac 25:11 For if in·fact, I·am·a·harmful·offender, or have·
Ac 25:11 I·do·not decline to·die. But if there·is no *validity*
Ac 27:39 into which they·purposed, if it·were·possible, to·
Heb 2:2 For if the word being·spoken through angels was
Heb 4:8 For if JoShua gave them complete·rest, he·would not
Heb 7:11 Accordingly in·fact, if perfection was through the
Heb 7:15 it·is excessively fully·obvious, if, according·to the
Heb 8:4 For if, in·fact, he·were on earth, he·would not·even
Heb 8:7 For if that first *covenant* was faultless, then no place
Heb 9:13 For if the blood of·bulls and of·adult·male·goats
Heb 11:15 And in·fact, if they·were·reminiscing of·that
Heb 12:7 If yeu·patiently·endure corrective·discipline, God
Heb 12:8 But if yeu·are completely·apart·from corrective·
Heb 12:25 shun the·one speaking. For if those·men did·not
Gal 1:9 I·say again, if any·man proclaims·a·good·news to·
Gal 1:10 ·appease men·of·clay†? For if yet I·was·appeasing
Gal 2:14 before *them* all, "If you, inherently·being a·Jew,
Gal 2:17 "But if (while·seeking to·be·regarded·as·righteous
Gal 2:18 "For if I·build again these·things which I·
Gal 2:21 the grace of·God, for if righteousness *is* through
Gal 3:18 For if the inheritance *is* as·a·result of·Torah-Law,
Gal 3:21 May·it·never happen! For if the law being·able
Gal 3:29 And if yeu *are* of·Anointed-One, then·by·inference,
Gal 4:7 a·slave, but·rather a·son; and if a·son, *then* also an·
Gal 4:15 For I·testify to·yeu that, if *it·had·been* possible,
Gal 5:11 I·myself, brothers, if I·still officially·proclaim
Gal 5:15 But if yeu·bite and devour one·another, look·out
Gal 5:18 But if yeu·are·led by·Spirit, yeu·are not under
Gal 5:25 If we·live in·Spirit, we·should·conform·and·march·
Gal 6:3 For if any·man supposes·himself to·be something,
Mt 4:3 Tempting·One declared, "If you·are a·son of·God,
Mt 4:6 and he·says to·him, "If you·are *the* Son of·God, cast
Mt 5:29 "So if your right eye entraps you, pluck it out and
Mt 5:30 And if your right hand entraps you, chop it off and
Mt 6:23 shall·be opaquely·dark. So·then, if the light, the·
Mt 6:30 And if God in·this·manner enrobes the grass of·the
Mt 7:11 So·then, if yeu·yeurselves, being evil, personally·
Mt 8:31 were·imploring him, saying, "If you·cast us out,
Mt 10:25 as his lord. If they·called the master·of·the·house,
Mt 11:14 And if yeu·want to·accept *it*, he·himself is EliJah,
Mt 11:21 BethSaida! Because if the miracles occurring in
Mt 11:23 unto Hades! Because if the miracles happening in
Mt 12:7 But if yeu·had·known what it·means, "I·want
Mt 12:26 And if the Adversary-Accuser casts·out the
Mt 12:27 And if I·myself, by Master-Of-Dung, cast·out the
Mt 12:28 But if I·myself cast·out the demons by God's Spirit
Mt 14:28 him, Peter declared, "Lord, if it·is·you yourself,
Mt 16:24 to·his disciples, "If any·man wants to·come right·
Mt 17:4 for·us to·be here. If you·want, we·should·make
Mt 18:8 "So if your hand or your foot entraps you, chop it
Mt 18:9 And if your eye entraps you, pluck it out and cast *it*
Mt 19:10 disciples say to·him, "If the legal·charge of·the
Mt 19:17 except one, God. But if you·want to·enter into the
Mt 19:21 replied to·him, "If you·want to·be complete, head·
Mt 22:45 So·then, if David calls him 'Lord,' how is·he his
Mt 23:30 and say, 'If we·were in the days of·our fathers,
Mt 24:24 and wonders, such·as, if possible, to·deceive even
Mt 24:43 But know this, that if the master·of·the·house had·
Mt 26:24 It·was better for·him if that man·of·clay† was·not
Mt 26:33 to·him, "Even if all·men shall·be·tripped·up by
Mt 26:39 "O·my Father, if it·is possible, let this cup pass·
Mt 26:42 "O·My Father, if this cup is·not able to·pass·away
Mt 27:40 three days, save yourself. If you·are a·son of·God,
Mt 27:42 ·is·not able to·save himself. If he·is King of·IsraEl
Mt 27:43 Let·him·rescue him now, if he·wants him," for he·
Mk 3:26 And if the Adversary-Accuser rose·up against
Mk 4:23 "If any·man has ears to·hear, let·him·hear.
Mk 7:16 If any·man has ears to·hear, let·him·hear.
Mk 8:23 was·inquiring·of him if he·looked·upon anything.
Mk 9:22 ·destroy him, but·yet if you·are·able *to·do*
Mk 9:23 Jesus declared to·him, "If you·are·able to·trust, all·
Mk 9:35 and says to·them, "If any·man wants to·be first, *the*
Mk 9:42 it·is even·much better for·him if a·mill stone be·set
Mk 11:13 he·came *toward it to·see* if perhaps he·shall·find
Mk 11:25 ·fast while·yeu·are·praying, if yeu·have anything
Mk 11:26 But if yeu·yeurselves do·not forgive, neither yeur
Mk 13:22 wonders to utterly·lead·astray, if possible, even
Mk 14:21 It·was better for·him if that man·of·clay† was·not
Mk 14:29 "Even if all shall·be·tripped·up·and·fall·away,
Mk 14:35 on the soil and prayed that, if it·were possible, the
Mk 15:44 And Pilate marveled if, even·now, he·has·died.
Rm 3:3 What if some did·not·trust?
Rm 3:5 "But if our unrighteousness commends God's
Rm 3:7 *But the reasoning states*, "For if by my lie, the truth
Rm 4:2 For if AbRaham was·regarded·as·righteous as·a·
Rm 4:14 For if the·ones birthed·from·out of·Torah-Law *are*
Rm 5:10 For if, while·being enemies, we·are·reconciled to·
Rm 5:15 as the trespass). For if by·the trespass of·the one,
Rm 5:17 For if by·the one trespass, Death reigned through
Rm 6:5 For if we·have·been congenitally·fused·together in·
Rm 6:8 Now if we·died together with·Anointed-One, we·
Rm 7:16 But if I·do that which I·do·not want, I·concur with·
Rm 7:20 Now if that·which I·myself do·not want, *if* that·
Rm 8:9 Spirit dwells in yeu. But if any·man does·not have
Rm 8:10 Now if Anointed-One *is* in yeu, in·fact, the body *is*
Rm 8:11 and if the Spirit of·the·one awakening Jesus from·
Rm 8:13 For if yeu·live according·to flesh, yeu·are·about to·
Rm 8:13 to·die. But if by·*the*·Spirit yeu·put·to·death the
Rm 8:17 and if *we·are* children, then·also *we·are* heirs, heirs
Rm 8:25 But if we·expectantly·await for·what we·do·not
Rm 8:31 ·we·state toward these·things? If God *does·this* on·
Rm 9:22 Now if God, willing to·indicate his wrath and to·
Rm 11:6 And if *it·is* by·grace, *it·is* no·longer as·a·result of·
Rm 11:6 no·longer grace. But if *it·is* as·a·result of·works,
Rm 11:12 Now if their trespass *became* wealth for·*the*·world,
Rm 11:15 For if the casting·away of·them *is* reconciliation
Rm 11:16 Now if the *portion of·dough offered as·a* firstfruit
Rm 11:16 lump·of·dough *is* also *holy*. And if the root *is* holy
Rm 11:17 And if some of·the branches were·broken·off, and
Rm 11:18 the branches. But if you·do·boast·over *them*, *it·is*
Rm 11:21 For if God did·not spare the fully natural branches,
Rm 11:24 For if you are·already·chopped·off from·among
Rm 12:18 *and* if *it·is* possible, for yeur part, behaving·
Rm 13:9 ·not long·for·(or·covet)." And if *there·is* any other
Rm 14:15 But if your brother is·grieved through *your* food,
Rm 15:27 under·an·obligation for·them. For if the Gentiles
Jac 1:5 So, if any of·yeu is·deficient of·wisdom, let·him·
Jac 1:23 Because if any is a·hearer of·*the*·Redemptive-word,
Jac 1:26 If any·man among yeu seems to·be religious, *yet* not
Jac 2:8 If however, yeu·complete *the* Royal Law according·
Jac 2:9 But if yeu·show·partiality, yeu·work moral·failure,
Jac 2:11 murder."' Now if you·shall·not commit·adultery,
Jac 3:2 absolutely·all *of·us* slip·up. If any·man does·not slip·
Jac 3:14 But if yeu·have bitter jealousy and contention in
Jac 4:11 and judges law. But if you·judge law, you·are not
Php 1:22 But if *I·continue·on* to·live in *bodily* flesh, this
Php 2:1 Accordingly, if *there·is* any exhortation in
Php 2:1 in Anointed-One, if any personal·consolation of·
Php 2:1 any personal·consolation of·love, if any fellowship
Php 2:1 if any fellowship of·Spirit, if any inward·affections
Php 2:17 even if I·am·poured·forth·as·a·devotion upon the
Php 3:4 confidence in flesh. If any other·man presumes *a*·
Php 3:15 ·should·contemplate that·thing. And if *in* anything
Php 4:8 ·things·as *are* of·fine·reputation, if *there·is* any
Php 4:8 courageous·moral·excellence, and if *there·is* any
1Pe 1:17 And if yeu·presently·call·upon Father, the·one
1Pe 2:19 For this *is* graciousness, if someone on·account·of
1Pe 2:20 ·kind·of merit *is·it*, if when yeu·are·being·buffeted
1Pe 2:20 But·rather if yeu·shall·bear·it·patiently when
1Pe 3:1 in·order·that also, if some are·obstinate to·the
1Pe 3:17 For *it·is* significantly·better, if the will of·God is·
1Pe 4:11 If any·man speaks *to·others*, *let·him·be* as *one*·
1Pe 4:11 eloquent·words of·God; if any·man attends *to*·
1Pe 4:14 If yeu·are·reproached for *the* name of·
1Pe 4:16 But if *any·man suffers* as "a·Christian," a·Little·
1Pe 4:17 the house of·God. And if *it* first *begins* with us,
1Pe 4:18 And "' If the righteous·man scarcely is·saved,
2Pe 2:4 For if God— did·not spare morally·failing angels,
2Pe 2:20 For if after·escaping·from the contaminations of·
1Th 4:14 For if we·trust that YeShua died and rose·up, in·
2Th 3:10 this we·were·charging yeu, that if anyone does·not
2Th 3:14 Now if anyone does·not listen·to·and·obey our
Tit 1:6 if any·man is without·any·charge·of·wrong·doing, a·
1Co 1:16 I·do·not personally·know if I·immersed any other
1Co 2:8 of·this present·age has·known, for if they·knew *it*,
1Co 3:12 And if any·man builds upon this foundation *with*
1Co 3:14 If any·man's work shall·remain which he·built·
1Co 3:15 If any·man's work shall·be·completely·burned, he·
1Co 3:17 If anyone corrupts the temple of·God, this·one God
1Co 3:18 thoroughly·delude himself. If any·man among yeu
1Co 4:7 you·did·not receive? And if also you·did·receive *it*,
1Co 6:2 shall·judge the world? And if the world is·judged
1Co 7:9 But if they·do·not have self-restraint, they·must·
1Co 7:12 not the Lord— if any brother has a·non-trusting
1Co 7:15 But if the non-trusting·one departs, he·must·be·
1Co 7:36 Now if any *father* deems to·have·improper·
1Co 8:2 And if anyone presumes to·personally·know
1Co 8:3 But if anyone loves God, the·same has·been·
1Co 8:13 Therefore·indeed, if food entices my brother unto·
1Co 9:2 If I·am not an·ambassador to·others, but·yet still I·
1Co 9:11 If we·ourselves sowed to·yeu the spiritual·things,
1Co 9:11 *is·it* a·great·thing if we·ourselves shall·reap yeur
1Co 9:12 If others participate in·*this*·privilege among·yeu,
1Co 9:17 For if I·practice this·thing voluntarily, I·have a·
1Co 9:17 a·payment·of·service, but *even* if involuntarily,
1Co 10:27 But if any of·the non-trusting·ones call·for yeu,
1Co 10:30 Now if by·gratitude, I·myself participate·
1Co 11:6 For if a·woman is·not fully·veiled, also she·must·
1Co 11:6 also she·must·be·shorn, but if *it·is* shameful for·a·
1Co 11:16 But if any·man seems to·be contentious, we·
1Co 11:31 For if we·were·discerning ourselves *properly*, we·
1Co 11:34 And if any·man is·hungry, let·him·eat at home,
1Co 12:17 If the whole body *is* an·eye, where·is the sense·
1Co 12:17 the sense·of·hearing placed? If *the* whole *body is*
1Co 12:19 And if they·were all one member, where·is the
1Co 14:35 And if they·want to·learn anything, they·must·
1Co 14:37 If someone supposes·himself to·be a·prophet or
1Co 14:38 But if any·man is·ignoring *this*, let·him·be·
1Co 15:2 yeu·are·saved, if yeu·fully·hold·onto that·certain
1Co 15:12 Now if Anointed-One is·officially·proclaimed
1Co 15:13 But if there·is no resurrection of·dead·men, not·
1Co 15:14 And if Anointed-One has·not been·awakened,
1Co 15:16 For if dead·men are·not awakened, not·even
1Co 15:17 And if Anointed-One has·not been·awakened,
1Co 15:19 If we·are merely having·placed·our·expectation
1Co 15:29 on·behalf of·the dead, if dead·men are·not
1Co 15:32 If according·to *the striving·of* men·of·clay†, I·
1Co 15:32 what *is* the advantage to·me, if dead·men are·not
1Co 16:22 If any·man does·not have·affection·for the Lord
2Co 2:2 For if I·myself grieve yeu, then who would·be the·
2Co 2:5 But if any·man has·caused·grief, *it·is* not me *that*
2Co 2:10 For even if I·myself have·graciously·forgiven
2Co 3:7 Now if the Service of·Death, having·been·engraved
2Co 3:9 For if the service of·the condemnation *had* glory, so·
2Co 3:11 For if the *Service of·Death* is·being·fully·nullified
2Co 5:14 ·*conclusively*·judging this·thing: that if one died
2Co 5:16 flesh. And even if we·have·known Anointed-One
2Co 5:17 As·such, IF any·man *is* in Anointed-One, *he·is* a·

2Co 7:14 Because if I·have·boasted anything to·him
2Co 8:12 For if the eagerness is·set·forth, *it·is* well·
2Co 10:7 surface·appearance? If any·man has·confidence
2Co 11:4 For in·fact, if the·one who·is·coming does·
2Co 11:15 *it·is* no great·thing if his attendants also are·
2Co 11:16 me to·be impetuous; but if not, then·also accept
2Co 11:20 For yeu·bear·with·it, if anyone utterly·enslaves
2Co 11:20 if anyone utterly·enslaves yeu, if anyone devours
2Co 11:20 if anyone devours *yeu*, if anyone takes *from·yeu*,
2Co 11:20 anyone takes *from·yeu*, if anyone exalts·himself,
2Co 11:20 if anyone exalts·himself, if anyone thrashes yeu
2Co 11:30 If it·is·necessary to·boast, I·shall·boast *about* the·
Col 2:20 Now·then, if yeu·did·die together with·
Col 3:1 if yeu·are·already·awakened·together with·the
Phm 1:17 So·then, if you·hold me *to·be* a·partner,
Phm 1:18 So if he·wronged you, or owes *you* anything,
1Ti 1:10 for·perjurers, and if *there·is* anything else fully·set·
1Ti 3:1 "If any·man longingly·stretches·himself·toward an·
1Ti 3:5 (but if any·man has·not seen·how to·conduct his·
1Ti 5:4 But if any widow has children or grandchildren,
1Ti 5:8 Now if anyone does·not maintain·provision·for his·
1Ti 5:10 by good works (if she·nurtured·and·reared·children,
1Ti 5:10 ·children, if she·hospitably·received·strangers, if
1Ti 5:10 ·hospitably·received·strangers, if she·washed *the*
1Ti 5:10 feet, if she·gave·relief·to those·being·hard-pressed,
1Ti 5:10 *and* if she·diligently·followed·through in·every
1Ti 5:16 If anyone (a·man·that·trusts or a·woman·that·trusts
1Ti 6:3 If any·man instructs·differently and does·not come·
2Ti 2:11 the saying: "For if we·died·together *with·him*, also
2Ti 2:12 If we·patiently·endure, we·also shall·reign·together
2Ti 2:12 ·reign·together *with·him*. "If we·are·denying *him*,
2Ti 2:13 If we·do·not·trust, that·one still·remains
1Jn 2:19 from·among us; for if they·were from·among us,
1Jn 3:13 Do·not marvel, my brothers, if the world hates yeu
1Jn 4:11 Beloved, if in·this·manner, God loved us, we·
2Jn 1:10 If any·man comes to yeu *all*, and does·not bring this
Rv 11:5 And if any·man should·determine to·bring·harm·to
Rv 11:5 their enemies. And if any·man should·determine to·
Rv 13:9 If any·man has an·ear, let·him·hear.
Rv 13:10 If any·man gathers·together *another into* war·
Rv 13:10 heads into war·captivity. If any·man kills with a·
Rv 14:9 voice, "If any·man falls·prostrate *directly·before* the
Rv 20:15 And if anyone is·not found having·been·written in
EG1487.1 (1x)
2Co 11:4 ·officially·proclaim, or *if* yeu·receive another
G1487.2 COND εἰ (23x)
Jn 9:25 and declared, "Whether he·is full·of·moral·failure,
Lk 6:7 him, whether he·shall·both·relieve·and·cure on the
Lk 14:28 calculates the expense, whether he·has the *means*
Lk 14:31 sit·down first *and* takes·counsel whether he·is able
Lk 23:6 "Galilee," inquired whether the man·of·clay† was
Ac 4:19 declared to them, "Whether it·is right in·the·sight
Ac 5:8 "Declare to·me whether yeu·sold·off the open·field
Ac 10:18 hollering·out, they·were·inquiring whether Simon,
Ac 17:11 day, *as·to* whether these·things might·actually·be
Ac 19:2 ·yet, we·did·not·even hear whether there·is a·Holy
Ac 22:27 "Say *it* to·me whether you·yourself are a·Roman!"
Ac 25:20 was·relating·as·to whether he·might·be·definitely·
Mt 26:63 you·should·declare to·us whether you·yourself are
Mt 27:49 *him·alone*, we·should·see whether EliJah comes
Mk 3:2 *as·to* whether he·shall·both·relieve·and·cure him
Mk 15:36 *him·alone*; we·should·see whether EliJah comes
Mk 15:44 ·inquired·of him whether he·died long·before·now
1Co 7:16 ·know, O·wife, whether you·shall·save the
1Co 7:16 ·know, O·husband, whether you·shall·save the
1Co 15:37 kernel, whether it·may·happen·to·be of·wheat or
2Co 2:9 ·of·character, whether yeu·are attentively·obedient
2Co 13:5 Try yeurselves, whether yeu·are in the trust.
1Jn 4:1 test·and·prove the spirits whether they·are from·out
EG1487.2 (1x)
Jn 7:17 ·is from·out of·God, or *whether* I·myself speak from
G1487.3 COND εἰ (4x)
Heb 3:11 my flared·anger, 'As·if they·shall·*ever*·enter into
Heb 4:3 my flared·anger, 'as·if they·shall·*ever*·enter into my
Heb 4:5 again, "'As·if they·shall·*ever*·enter into my
Mk 8:12 ·yeu, 'As·if a·miraculous·sign shall·*ever*·be·given
G1487.4 COND εἰ (9x)
Lk 12:49 ·want, though even·now it·is·already·kindled?
Lk 18:4 himself, 'Even though I·am·not afraid·of God, and
Heb 6:9 ·Salvation, even though we·speak in·this·manner.
1Pe 1:6 ·bit at·this·moment (though it·is being·necessary) in
2Co 4:16 But·rather even though our outward man·of·clay†
2Co 11:6 And even though *I·am* untrained in·the discourse,
2Co 13:4 For even though he·is·crucified as·a·result of·
Col 2:5 For even though I·am·absent in·the flesh, but·yet I·
1Jn 5:9 Though we·receive the testimony of·men·of·clay†,
G1487.5 COND εἰ (5x)
Lk 13:23 "Lord, *is·it so* that the·ones being·saved *are* few?
Lk 17:2 ·a·better·end for·him that a·donkey-sized millstone
Ac 26:8 incredible with yeu, that God awakens dead·men?
Ac 26:23 that the Anointed-One *is·to·be* subjected·to·
Ac 26:23 *is·to·be* subjected·to·suffering, that *he·is·to·be* first
EG1487.5 (1x)
Lk 17:2 around his neck, and *that* it·has·been·flung into the
G1487.6 COND εἰ (3x)
Ac 8:22 and petition God so·that perhaps the intention of·
Rm 11:14 so·that somehow I·may·provoke·to·jealousy *them*
Php 3:12 but I·pursue *it*, so·that also I·may·grasp onto that·
G1487.7 COND εἰ (2x)
Ac 11:17 Now·then, since God gave to·them the equally·
Ac 18:15 But since it·is an·issue concerning a·word and

G1488 εἶ êî *v.* (93x)
Roots:G1510
G1488.1 V-PXI-2S εἶ (91x)
Jn 1:19 ·that they·may·ask·of him, "Who are you·yourself?
Jn 1:21 "So·then, who are you·yourself, EliJah?
Jn 1:21 "I·am not." "Are you·yourself the Prophet?
Jn 1:22 to·him, "Who are·you? In·order·that we·may·give
Jn 1:25 why·do you·immerse, if you·yourself are not the
Jn 1:42 him, declared, "You·yourself are Simon, the son of·
Jn 1:49 "Rabbi, you·yourself are the Son of·God; you·
Jn 1:49 the Son of·God; you·yourself are the King of·IsraEl.
Jn 3:10 declared to·him, "Are you·yourself the instructor of·
Jn 4:12 ¿! Are you·yourself greater·than our father Jacob,
Jn 4:19 "Sir, I·observe that you·yourself are a·prophet.
Jn 6:69 have·known that you·yourself are the Anointed-One,
Jn 7:52 declared to·him, "¿! Are you·yourself also from·out
Jn 8:25 they·were·saying to·him, "Who are you·yourself?
Jn 8:48 not say well that you·yourself are a·Samaritan, and
Jn 8:53 ¿! Are you·yourself greater·than our father AbRaham
Jn 9:28 and declared, "You·yourself are that·man's disciple,
Jn 10:24 in·suspense? If you·yourself are the Anointed-One,
Jn 11:27 have·trusted that you·yourself are the Anointed-One
Jn 18:17 says to·Peter, "Are you·yourself not also from·
Jn 18:25 they·declared to·him, "Are you·yourself not also
Jn 18:33 he·declared to·him, "Are you·yourself the King of·
Jn 18:37 "So·then indeed, you·yourself are a·king!" Jesus
Jn 19:9 says to·Jesus, "From·what·source are you·yourself?
Jn 19:12 ·should·fully·release this·man, you·are not Caesar's
Jn 21:12 ·by·inquiring·of him, "Who are you·yourself?
Lk 3:22 saying, "You·yourself are my beloved Son; in you
Lk 4:3 declared to·him, "If you·are a·son of·God, declare
Lk 4:9 And he·declared to·him, "If you·are the Son of·God,
Lk 4:34 I·personally·know you *and* who you·are, the Holy·
Lk 4:41 saying, "You·yourself are the Anointed-One, the
Lk 7:19 saying, "Are you·yourself the·one who·is·coming?
Lk 7:20 saying, 'Are you·yourself the·one who·is·coming?
Lk 15:31 'Child, you·yourself are always with me, and all
Lk 19:21 you, because you·are an·unrelenting man·of·clay†.
Lk 22:58 ·disclosing, "You·yourself are also from·among
Lk 22:67 "Are you·yourself the Anointed-One?
Lk 22:70 "So·then, you·yourself are the Son of·God?
Lk 23:3 ·of him, saying, "Are you·yourself the King of·the
Lk 23:37 saying, "If you·yourself are the king of·the Jews,
Lk 23:39 saying, "If you·yourself are the Anointed-One,
Lk 23:40 afraid·of God, *seeing* how you·are in the same
Ac 9:5 And he·declared, "Who are·you, Lord?
Ac 13:33 second Psalm, "You·yourself are my Son. Today,
Ac 21:38 Are you·yourself not then the Egyptian, *the·one*
Ac 22:8 And I·myself answered, 'Who are·you, Lord?
Ac 22:27 "Say *it* to·me whether you·yourself are a·Roman!"
Ac 26:15 And I·myself declared, 'Who are·you, Lord?
Heb 1:5 at·any·time, "'You·yourself are my Son. Today, I·
Heb 1:12 ·shall·be·changed, but you·yourself are the same,
Heb 5:5 to him, "'You·yourself are my Son. Today, I·
Gal 4:7 As·such, you·are no·longer a·slave, but·rather a·son
Mt 2:6 *in·the* land of·Judah, are by·no·means least among
Mt 4:3 Tempting·One declared, "If you·are a·son of·God,
Mt 4:6 and he·says to·him, "If you·are *the* Son of·God, cast
Mt 5:25 for·as·long·as such·time *as* you·are on the way
Mt 11:3 declared to·him, "Are you·yourself the·one who·is·
Mt 14:33 to·him, saying, "Truly you·are God's Son."
Mt 16:16 declared, "You·yourself are the Anointed-One, the
Mt 16:17 to·him, "Supremely·blessed are·you, Simon
Mt 16:18 to·you that you·yourself are Peter·*(a·piece·of·rock)*.
Mt 16:23 me, Adversary-Accuser! You·are a·trap to·me,
Mt 22:16 "Mentor, we·have·seen that you·are true, and *that*
Mt 25:24 I·knew you that you·are a·hard man·of·clay†,
Mt 26:63 to·us whether you·yourself are the Anointed-One,
Mt 26:73 "Truly you·yourself are also from·among them,
Mt 27:11 him, saying, "Are you·yourself the King of·the
Mt 27:40 save yourself. If you·are a·son of·God, descend
Mk 1:11 *saying*, "You·yourself are my beloved Son, in
Mk 1:24 I·personally·know you, who you·are, the Holy·One
Mk 3:11 ·out, saying, "You·yourself are the Son of·God.
Mk 8:29 says to·him, "You·yourself are the Anointed-One."
Mk 12:14 "Mentor, we·personally·know that you·are true,
Mk 12:34 declared to·him, "You·are not at·a·distance from
Mk 14:61 him, and he·says to·him, "Are you·yourself the
Mk 14:70 again to·Peter, "Truly you·are from·among them,
Mk 14:70 ·among them, for also you·are a·Galilean; even
Mk 15:2 Pilate inquired·of him, "Are you·yourself the King
Rm 2:1 presently·judging— you·are without·exoneration, O
Rm 9:20 O man·of·clay†, who are you·yourself, the·one
Rm 14:4 Who are you·yourself, the·one unduly·judging
Jac 4:11 But if you·judge law, you·are not a·doer of·law,
Jac 4:12 to·completely·destroy. Who are you·yourself that
Rv 2:9 and the poverty (but you·are wealthy). And *I*·
Rv 3:1 you·have the name that you·live, yet you·are dead.
Rv 3:15 ·know your works, that you·are neither cold nor
Rv 3:16 'In·this·manner *then*, because you·are lukewarm,
Rv 3:17 ·know that you·yourself are the·one miserable,
Rv 4:11 "You·are worthy, O·Lord, to·receive the glory and
Rv 5:9 song, saying, "You·are worthy to·take the official·
Rv 16:5 ·the waters saying, "You·are righteous, O·Yahweh,
G1488.1 V-PXS-2S ᾖς (1x)
Rm 2:25 But if you·should·be a·transgressor of·Torah-Law,
G1488.2 V-PXI-2S εἶ (1x)
Mt 14:28 "Lord, if it·is·you yourself, commandingly·order

G1489 εἴ•γε êígê *cond.* (5x)
Roots:G1487 G1065
G1489.1 COND εἴγε (4x)
Gal 3:4 so·many·things for·no·reason— if·indeed that *it·was*
2Co 5:3 and·then, if·indeed dressing·ourselves, we·shall·not
Eph 4:21 if·indeed yeu·heard him and are·instructed by him
Col 1:23 if·indeed yeu·persist in·the trust, having·been·
G1489.2 COND εἴγε (1x)
Eph 3:2 since·indeed yeu·already·heard of·the estate·

G1490 εἰ δὲ μή êi dè mḗ *conj.* (13x)
εἰ δὲ μή•γε êi dè mḗgê [sometimes]
Roots:G1487 G1161 G3361 G1065
G1490.1 NEG-COND-CONJ εἰ δέ μή (6x)
Jn 14:2 are many abodes, but·if·not, I·would·have declared
Jn 14:11 Father *is* in me. But·if·not, trust me on·account·of
Lk 10:6 shall·rest upon it. But·if·not, it·shall·return·back to
Lk 13:9 ·produce fruit, *good*! But·if·not, you·shall·chop it
Rv 2:5 do the first works; but·if·not, I·come to·you with·
Rv 2:16 'Repent! But·if·not, I·come to·you swiftly, and I·

G1490.2 NEG-COND-CONJ εἰ δέ μήγε (1x)
Lk 14:32 And·if·not, with·the·other being yet far·away,
G1490.3 NEG-COND-CONJ εἰ δέ μήγε (6x)
Lk 5:36 garment upon an·old garment; but·if·so, then the
Lk 5:37 wine into old wineskins. But·if·so, the fresh·new
Mt 6:1 ·viewed by·them. But·if·*yeu·do*·so, yeu·do·not have
Mt 9:17 wine into old wineskins. But·if·so, the wineskins
Mk 2:21 cloth on an·old garment, but·if·so, *then* the
Mk 2:22 wine into old wineskins. But·if·so, the fresh·new

G1491 εἶδος êîdôs *n.* (5x)
Roots:G1492 Compare:G3799 G3444 G3667 G4383 G4976 G5179 G5318 G1085 See:G2397
G1491.1 N-GSN εἴδους (1x)
2Co 5:7 we·presently·walk through trust, not through sight.
G1491.2 N-ASN εἶδος (1x)
Jn 5:37 ever·at·any·time, nor have·clearly·seen his shape.
G1491.2 N-DSN εἴδει (1x)
Lk 3:22 Holy Spirit descended in·a·bodily shape like a·dove
G1491.3 N-NSN εἶδος (1x)
Lk 9:29 him praying, the aspect of·his countenance became
G1491.3 N-GSN εἴδους (1x)
1Th 5:22 Abstain from every aspect of·evil.

G1492 εἴδω êídō *v.* (670x)
Compare:G3700 G0991 G2029 G1097 G2467 See:G0143 G1097 G1921 G2467 G2477 G3708 G4894 xLangAlso:H7200
G1492.1 V-2AAI-1S εἶδον (55x)
Jn 1:48 PhilIp hollered·out·for you, I·saw you being under
Jn 1:50 "Because I·declared to·you, 'I·saw you beneath the
Jn 18:26 says, "¿!·Did·not I·myself see you in the enclosed·
Ac 11:5 and in a·trance I·saw a·clear·vision. A·certain
Ac 11:6 ·fully·observing, and I·saw the four-footed·animals
Ac 26:13 at·mid day, O·king, I·saw in the way a·light from·
Gal 1:19 But I·did·not see any·other of·the ambassadors,
Gal 2:14 But·rather, when I·saw that they·did·not walk·
Rv 1:12 And turning·about, I·saw seven Golden Lampstands
Rv 1:17 And when I·saw him, I·fell toward his feet as dead.
Rv 4:1 After these·things I·saw, and behold, a·door having·
Rv 4:4 And upon the thrones, I·saw the twenty four Elders
Rv 5:1 And I·saw in the right·hand of·the·one sitting·down
Rv 5:2 And I·saw a·strong angel officially·proclaiming with·
Rv 5:6 And I·saw, and behold, in *the* midst of·the throne and
Rv 5:11 And I·saw, and I·heard *the* voice of·many angels all·
Rv 6:1 And I·saw when the Lamb opened·up *the* first from·
Rv 6:2 And I·saw, and behold, a·white horse and the·one
Rv 6:5 "Come and look." And I·saw, and behold, a·black
Rv 6:8 And I·saw, and behold, a·pale horse and the·one
Rv 6:9 the fifth official·seal, I·saw beneath the Sacrifice·
Rv 6:12 And I·saw when he·opened·up the sixth official·seal
Rv 7:1 And after these·things, I·saw four angels standing on
Rv 7:2 And I·saw another angel ascending from *the* eastern
Rv 7:9 After these·things I·saw, and behold, a·large crowd
Rv 8:2 And I·saw the seven angels who stand in·the·sight of·
Rv 8:13 And I·saw and heard an angel flying in mid-heaven,
Rv 9:1 angel sounded, and I·saw a·star having·fallen from·
Rv 9:17 And in·this·manner I·saw the horses in the clear·
Rv 10:1 And I·saw another strong angel descending from·out
Rv 10:5 And the angel which I·saw standing upon the sea
Rv 13:1 of·the sea, and I·saw a·Daemonic·Beast ascending
Rv 13:2 And the Daemonic·Beast which I·saw was like a·
Rv 13:3 And I·saw one of·its heads as·though having·been·
Rv 13:11 And I·saw another Fiendish·Beast ascending out
Rv 14:1 And I·saw, and behold, a·Lamb standing on the
Rv 14:6 And I·saw another angel who·is·flying in *the*
Rv 14:14 And I·saw, and behold, a·white thick·cloud, and
Rv 15:1 And I·saw another sign in the heaven, great and
Rv 15:2 And I·saw *something* as a·transparent, glassy sea
Rv 15:5 And after these·things, I·saw, and behold, the
Rv 16:13 And I·saw three impure spirits like frogs *come* out
Rv 17:3 And I·saw a·woman who·is·sitting·down upon a·
Rv 17:6 And I·saw the woman getting·drunk from·out of·the
Rv 18:1 And after these·things I·saw an·angel descending
Rv 19:11 And I·saw the heaven having·been·opened·up, and
Rv 19:17 And I·saw one angel standing in the sun; and he·
Rv 19:19 And I·saw the Daemonic·Beast, and the kings of·the
Rv 20:1 And I·saw an·angel descending from·out of·the
Rv 20:4 And I·saw thrones, and they·sat upon them, and
Rv 20:11 And I·saw a·Great White Throne, and the·one
Rv 20:12 And I·saw the dead·ones, small and great, standing
Rv 21:1 And I·saw a·brand-new heaven and a·brand-new
Rv 21:2 And I, John, saw the HOLY CITY, brand-new
Rv 21:22 And I·did·not see a·Temple in it, for Yahweh, *El*
G1492.1 V-2AAI-1S@ εἶδον (1x)
Ac 7:34 'Seeing, I·have·surely·seen the harmful·treatment
G1492.1 V-2AAI-1P εἴδομεν (10x)
Lk 5:26 "We·saw things·way·beyond·believable today."
Lk 9:49 "O·Captain, we·saw someone casting·out the
Ac 4:20 not to·speak the·things·which we·saw and heard."
Mt 2:2 ·born King of·the Jews? For we·saw his star in the
Mt 25:37 'Lord, when did·we·see you hungering, and
Mt 25:38 When did·we·see you a·stranger, and gathered·
Mt 25:39 When did·we·see you sick, or in prison, and came
Mt 25:44 'Lord, when did·we·see you hungering, or
Mk 2:12 "Never·at·any·time did·we·see *it* in·this·manner."
Mk 9:38 "Mentor, we·saw someone casting·out demons in·
G1492.1 V-2AAI-2S εἶδες (9x)
Ac 26:16 of·the·things·which you·saw and of·the·things·in·
Rv 1:19 "Write the·things·which you·saw, and the·things·
Rv 1:20 of·the seven stars which you·saw in my right·hand,
Rv 1:20 the seven Lampstands which you·saw are *the* seven
Rv 17:8 *The* Scarlet·Beast that you·saw, it·was and is not.
Rv 17:12 "And the ten horns which you·saw are ten kings
Rv 17:15 "The *Many* Waters which you·saw, where the
Rv 17:16 the ten horns which you·saw upon the Scarlet·Beast
Rv 17:18 "And the woman whom you·saw is the Great City,
G1492.1 V-2AAI-2P εἴδετε (4x)
Jn 6:26 me, not because yeu·saw miraculous·signs, but·
Lk 7:22 report to·John what·things yeu·saw and heard, that
Jac 5:11 ·the patient·endurance of·Job and saw the end·result
Php 4:9 ·received, and heard, and saw in me, practice— and
G1492.1 V-2AAI-3S εἶδεν (45x)
Jn 1:47 Jesus saw NathaniEl coming toward him and says
Jn 6:24 So·then, when the crowd saw that Jesus was not
Jn 8:56 he·should·see my day, and he·saw *it* and was·glad.
Jn 9:1 ·on *through*, he·saw a·man·of·clay† who·was·blind
Jn 11:33 Now as·soon·as Jesus saw her weeping, and the
Jn 12:41 IsaIah declared these·things when he·saw his glory
Jn 20:8 first to·the chamber·tomb. And he·saw and trusted.
Lk 5:2 Now he·saw two sailboats having·settled directly·by
Lk 15:20 being·off at·a·distance, his father saw him, and he·
Lk 19:5 to the place, looking·up, he·saw him, and declared
Lk 21:1 And looking·up, he·saw the wealthy·men casting
Lk 21:2 And he·saw also a·certain needy widow casting two
Ac 2:31 ·behind in Hades, neither did·his flesh see decay.'
Ac 3:9 And all the people saw him walking·along and
Ac 7:55 ·intently into the heaven, he·saw God's glory, and
Ac 8:39 and the eunuch did·not see him any·longer, for he·
Ac 9:12 and he·saw in a·clear·vision a·man by·the·name·of
Ac 9:27 and gave·an·account to·them how *Saul* saw the Lord
Ac 10:3 He·saw openly in a·clear·vision, about *the* ninth
Ac 10:17 *meant·by* the clear·vision which he·saw, yet behold
Ac 11:13 And he·announced to·us how he·saw the angel in
Ac 13:36 and was·laid alongside his fathers and saw decay.
Ac 13:37 But he·whom God awakened did·not see decay.
Ac 16:10 And as·soon·as he·saw the clear·vision,
Mt 3:16 were·opened·up to·him, and he·saw the Spirit of·
Mt 4:16 ·fully·sitting in darkness, they·did·see a·great light.
Mt 4:18 near the Sea of·Galilee, YeShua saw two brothers,
Mt 4:21 And walking·forward from·there, he·saw two other
Mt 8:14 into Peter's home, saw *Peter's* mother-in-law
Mt 9:9 ·on from·there, YeShua saw a·certain·man·of·clay†,
Mt 14:14 And upon·going·forth, YeShua saw a·large crowd,
Mt 20:3 about the third hour, he·saw others standing idle in
Mt 22:11 reclining·at·the·meal, he·saw a·man·of·clay† there
Mt 26:71 gate·*area*, another *servant·girl* saw him and says
Mk 1:10 ·up from the water, he·saw the heavens being·split·
Mk 1:16 beside the Sea of·Galilee, he·saw Simon and his
Mk 1:19 ·forward a·little·way from·there, he·saw Jakob
Mk 2:14 Then passing·on *from·there*, he·saw Levi *called*
Mk 6:34 Jesus, after·coming·ashore, saw a·large crowd,
Mk 6:48 And he·saw them being·tormented in their rowing,
Mk 9:14 to the *other* disciples, he·saw a·large crowd about
1Co 2:9 ·written, "Eye did·not see, and ear did·not hear,
1Ti 6:16 light which no·one·at·all sees (*which* it·is·not·even
Rv 1:2 of·Jesus Anointed, and *to* as·many·things·as he·saw.
Rv 12:13 And when the Dragon saw that he·was·cast to the
G1492.1 V-2AAI-3P εἶδον (24x)
Jn 1:39 They·came and saw where he·abides, and they·
Jn 19:6 chief·priests and the assistants saw him, they·yelled·
Jn 19:33 to Jesus, as·soon·as they·saw him even·now
Lk 2:20 all·the·things that they·heard and saw, just·as it·was·
Lk 2:30 because my eyes saw your custodial·Salvation,
Lk 9:32 ·being·thoroughly·awakened, they·saw his glory
Lk 10:24 yeu look·upon, and did·not see *them*, and to·hear
Lk 19:37 voice concerning all *the* miracles that they·saw,
Lk 24:24 ·as the women declared, but him they·did·not see."
Ac 6:15 ·down in the joint·council·of·Sanhedrin saw his face
Ac 9:35 the·ones residing·in Lod and Sharon saw him, *and*
Ac 12:16 And opening·up *the gate*, they·saw him and were·
Ac 28:4 as·soon·as the barbarians saw the venomous·beast
Heb 3:9 tested·and·proved me, and saw my works *for* forty
Heb 11:23 on·account·that they·saw *he·was* a·handsome
Mt 2:9 And behold, the star which they·saw in the east was·
Mt 13:17 which yeu·look·upon, and did·not see *them*, and
Mt 17:8 lifting·up their eyes, they·saw not·even·one·man,
Mk 6:33 Yet the crowds saw them heading·on·out, and many
Mk 6:50 For they·all saw him and were·troubled.
Mk 9:8 ·all·around, they·saw no·longer not·even·one·man,
Mk 9:9 ·one·man *concerning* what·things they·saw, except
Mk 11:20 ·traversing·directly·by *it*, they·saw the fig·tree
Mk 16:5 ·tomb, they·saw a·young·man sitting·down on the
G1492.1 V-AAM-2S ἴδε (3x)
Jn 1:46 ·Natsareth?" Philip says to·him, "Come and see."
Jn 11:34 "Lord, come and see."
Jn 20:27 "Bring your finger here, and see my hands. And
G1492.1 V-2AAM-2P ἴδετε (11x)
Jn 1:39 He·says to·them, "Come and see." They·came and
Jn 4:29 "Come·here! See a·man·of·clay† who declared to·
Lk 21:29 ·declared to·them a·parable: "See the fig·tree, and
Lk 24:39 See my hands and my feet, that I AM myself.
Lk 24:39 Verify·by·touching me and see, because a·spirit
Ac 13:41 "Yeu·despisers, see, and intently·look, and be·
Gal 6:11 Yeu·see with·what·sizable letters I·write to·yeu by·
Mt 28:6 ·as he·declared. Come·here! See the place where
Mk 6:38 ·of·bread do·yeu·have? Head·on·out and see." And
Php 1:30 the same strenuous·struggle such·as yeu·saw in me,
1Jn 3:1 See, what·manner·of love the Father has·given to·us,
G1492.1 V-2AAN ἰδεῖν (38x)
Jn 3:3 ·above, he·is·not able to·see the kingdom of·God.
Jn 12:21 "Sir, we·want to·see Jesus."
Lk 2:26 Holy Spirit *that he·was* not to·see death before he·
Lk 7:25 what have·yeu·gone·forth to·see? A·man·of·clay†
Lk 7:26 ·rather what have·yeu·gone·forth to·see? A·prophet?
Lk 8:20 your brothers stand outside, wanting to·see you."
Lk 8:35 Then they·went·out to·see what·was·happening.
Lk 9:9 hear such·things?" And he·was·seeking to·see him.
Lk 10:24 and kings wanted to·see the·things·which yeu look·
Lk 14:18 and I·have·dire·need to·go·out and to·see it. I·ask
Lk 17:22 shall·come when yeu·shall·long to·see one of·the
Lk 19:3 And he·was·seeking to·see who Jesus was, and was·
Lk 23:8 for he·was wanting to·see him for a·long·while on·
Lk 23:8 and he·was·expecting to·see some miraculous·sign
Ac 2:27 shall·you·give your Divine·Holy·One to·see decay.
Ac 13:35 ·shall·not give your Divine·Holy·One to·see decay.
Ac 15:6 the elders gathered·together to·see concerning this
Ac 19:21 there, it·is·mandatory·for me also to·see Rome."
Ac 22:14 to·know his will, and to·see the Righteous·One,
Ac 22:18 and saw him saying to·me, 'Make·haste and go·
Ac 28:20 I·personally·called·for yeu, to·see *yeu* and to·

Heb 11:5 was·transferred *such·for* him not to·see death, ≈
Mt 11:8 what·did yeu·go·forth to·see? A·man·of·clay†
Mt 11:9 But·rather what·did yeu·go·forth to·see? A·prophet?
Mt 12:38 "Mentor, we·want to·see a·sign from you.
Mt 13:17 and righteous·men longed to·see *the·things* which
Mt 26:58 he·sat·down with the assistants to·see the end.
Mk 5:14 And they·went·out to·see what it·was, the·thing
Mk 5:32 he·was·looking·all·around to·see the·one doing
Rm 1:11 For I·greatly·yearn to·see yeu that I·may·kindly·
1Pe 3:10 to·love life-above and to·see beneficially·good days
1Th 2:17 ·endeavored the·more·abundantly to·see yeur face
1Th 3:6 of·us always, greatly·yearning to·see us, exactly·as
1Th 3:10 above·and·beyond for this·thing: to·see yeur face,
1Co 16:7 For I·do·not want to·see yeu at·this·moment in
1Ti 6:16 it·is·not·even possible *for* men·of·clay† to·see), to·
2Ti 1:4 — while·greatly·yearning to·see you in·order·that
3Jn 1:14 But I·expect to·see you straight·away, and we·shall·

G1492.1 V-2AAP-NSF ἰδοῦσα (7x)

Jn 11:32 where Jesus was, upon·seeing him, she·fell·down
Lk 1:29 And seeing *him*, she·was·thoroughly·troubled over
Lk 8:47 And the woman, seeing that she·was·not hidden,
Lk 22:56 But after·seeing him sitting·down toward the
Ac 9:40 ·up her eyes; and upon·seeing Peter, she·sat·up.
Mk 14:67 And seeing Peter warming·himself, after·looking·
Mk 14:69 And the servant·girl, after·seeing him again,

G1492.1 V-2AAP-NSM ἰδών (61x)

Jn 5:6 Jesus, seeing this·man laying·ill and knowing that he·
Jn 6:22 ·side of·the sea, after·seeing that there·had·been no
Jn 19:26 Accordingly, Jesus seeing his mother and the
Jn 21:21 Upon·seeing this·man, Peter says to·Jesus, "Lord,
Lk 1:12 And ZacharIas was·troubled after·seeing *him*, and
Lk 5:8 And after·seeing *it*, Simon Peter fell·down·at Jesus
Lk 5:12 full of·leprosy; and after·seeing Jesus *and* falling on
Lk 5:20 And seeing their trust, he·declared to·him, "Man·of·
Lk 7:13 And seeing her, the Lord empathized over her and
Lk 7:39 Now seeing *this*, the Pharisee, the·one calling·for
Lk 8:28 But after·seeing Jesus, and·then screaming·out, he·
Lk 9:47 And Jesus, seeing the discussion of·their heart,
Lk 10:31 that way. And after·seeing him, he·passed·by·on·
Lk 10:32 place, coming and seeing *him*, passed·by·on·the·
Lk 10:33 he *was*. And after·seeing him, he·empathized.
Lk 11:38 And seeing *this*, the Pharisee marveled that he·did·
Lk 13:12 And seeing her, Jesus addressed *her* and declared
Lk 17:14 And upon·seeing *them*, he·declared to·them,
Lk 17:15 one from·among them, seeing that he·was·healed,
Lk 18:24 And Jesus, after·seeing him becoming
Lk 18:43 And all the people seeing *it*, gave strong·praise to·
Lk 19:41 And as he·drew·near, upon·seeing the City, he·
Lk 22:58 after a·short·while, someone·else seeing him, was·
Lk 23:8 Now upon·seeing Jesus, HerOd-AntiPas was·
Lk 23:47 the Roman·centurion, seeing the·thing *that·was*
Ac 3:3 who, after·seeing Peter and John intending to·enter
Ac 3:12 And seeing *this*, Peter answered to the people,
Ac 7:24 And seeing someone being·wronged, he·forcefully·
Ac 7:31 Now upon·seeing *it*, Moses marveled at·the clear·
Ac 7:34 'Seeing, I·have·surely·seen the harmful·treatment
Ac 11:23 who, after·coming·directly and seeing the grace
Ac 12:3 And seeing that it·was satisfactory to·the Judeans,
Ac 13:12 Then after·seeing the·thing having·happened, the
Ac 14:9 after·gazing·intently at·him and seeing that he·has
Ac 16:27 awake·out·of·*his*·heavy·sleep and seeing the prison
Ac 28:15 *the* Three Taverns, which upon·seeing *them*, Paul
Mt 2:16 HerOd-the-Great, after·seeing that he·was·mocked
Mt 3:7 But upon·seeing *that* many of·the Pharisees and
Mt 5:1 And seeing the crowds, he·walked·up upon the
Mt 8:18 And YeShua, seeing large crowds about him, he·
Mt 9:2 ·cast on a·simple·couch. And upon·seeing their trust,
Mt 9:4 And seeing their cogitations, YeShua declared, "For·
Mt 9:22 Then turning·himself·about and seeing her, YeShua
Mt 9:23 into the ruler's home and seeing the flute·players and
Mt 9:36 But after·seeing the crowds, he·empathized
Mt 21:19 And seeing one fig·tree by the roadway, he·came
Mt 27:3 Then after·seeing that *YeShua* was·condemned,
Mt 27:24 And Pilate, after·seeing that *reasoning with·them*
Mk 2:5 And Jesus, after·seeing their trust, says to·the
Mk 5:6 But upon·seeing Jesus from a·distance, he·ran and
Mk 5:22 Jairus by·name. And upon·seeing him, he·falls
Mk 8:33 But turning·himself·about and seeing his disciples,
Mk 9:15 all the crowd, after·seeing him, were·utterly·
Mk 9:20 *the little·child* to him, and upon·seeing *Jesus*,
Mk 9:25 And Jesus, after·seeing that the crowd came·
Mk 10:14 But upon·seeing *this*, Jesus was·greatly·displeased
Mk 11:13 And after·seeing a·fig·tree in·the·distance having
Mk 12:34 And Jesus, after·seeing that the·same·man
Mk 15:39 in·front of·him, after·seeing that in·this·manner,
Php 1:27 ·order·that whether coming and seeing yeu or·else
Rv 17:6 of·the martyrs of·Jesus. And seeing her, I·marveled

G1492.1 V-2AAP-NPM ἰδόντες (40x)

Jn 6:14 So·then, seeing that Jesus did a·miraculous·sign, the
Jn 11:31 and personally·consoling her, seeing that Mary
Jn 20:20 the disciples were·glad after·seeing the Lord.
Jn 20:29 Supremely·blessed *are* the·ones not seeing, and·yet
Lk 2:17 And seeing *it*, they·thoroughly·made·it·known·to·all
Lk 2:48 And seeing him, *his parents* were·astounded.
Lk 8:34 *them*, after·seeing the·thing having·happened, they·
Lk 8:36 Now the·ones seeing *it*, then·also announced to·
Lk 9:54 And after·seeing *this*, his disciples, Jakob and John,
Lk 18:15 of·them, but the disciples seeing *it*, reprimanded
Lk 19:7 And after·seeing *this*, absolutely·all were·
Lk 20:13 *It·is* likely *that* after·seeing this·one, they·shall·be·
Lk 20:14 "But after·seeing him, the tenant·farmers
Lk 22:49 the·ones around him, upon·seeing the·thing *that*
Ac 13:45 But after·seeing the crowds, the Jews were·filled
Ac 14:11 And the crowds, after·seeing what Paul did, they·
Ac 16:19 And with·her lords seeing that the expectation of·
Ac 16:40 *the house·of* Lydia. And seeing the brothers, they·
Ac 21:32 And upon·seeing the regiment·commander and
Heb 11:13 the promises, but·rather seeing them from·afar,
Gal 2:7 But·rather on·the·contrary, after·seeing that the
Mt 2:10 Now upon·seeing the star *stationary*, they·rejoiced
Mt 8:34 meet·up with·YeShua. And after·seeing him, they·
Mt 9:8 But the crowds seeing *it*, marveled, and they·glorified
Mt 9:11 And upon·seeing *it*, the Pharisees declared to·his
Mt 12:2 But the Pharisees seeing *it*, declared to·him,
Mt 14:26 And after·seeing him walking upon the sea, the
Mt 18:31 after·seeing the·things that·were·happening, were
Mt 21:15 the scribes were·greatly·displeased after·seeing the
Mt 21:20 And seeing *this*, the disciples marveled, saying,
Mt 21:32 him, but yeu·yeurselves, after·seeing *this*, did·not
Mt 21:38 "But upon·seeing the son, the tenant·farmers
Mt 26:8 But upon·seeing *this*, his disciples are·greatly·
Mt 27:54 YeShua with him, upon·seeing the earthquake and
Mt 28:17 And upon·seeing him, they·fell·prostrate to·him,
Mk 2:16 and the Pharisees, upon·seeing him eating with the
Mk 5:16 And the·ones seeing *it* gave·an·account to·them of·
Mk 6:49 But after·seeing him walking upon the sea, they·
Mk 7:2 And after·seeing some of·his disciples eating bread
Php 2:28 more·diligently, in·order·that seeing him again,

G1492.1 V-2AAS-1S ἴδω (3x)

Jn 20:25 to·them, "Unless I·may·see the imprint of·the nails
Mk 12:15 ·try me? Bring me a·denarius that I·may·see *it*."
Rv 18:7 not a·widow, and no, I·should·not see mourning.'

G1492.1 V-2AAS-1P ἴδωμεν (5x)

Jn 6:30 do, in·order·that we·may·see and should·trust in·you
Lk 2:15 unto BethLechem, so we·may·see this utterance,
Mt 27:49 "Leave *him·alone*, we·should·see whether EliJah
Mk 15:32 the cross in·order·that we·may·see and may·trust."
Mk 15:36 ·leave *him·alone*; we·should·see whether EliJah

G1492.1 V-2AAS-2S ἴδῃς (1x)

Jn 1:33 'Upon whom you·should·see the Spirit descending,

G1492.1 V-2AAS-2P ἴδητε (12x)

Jn 4:48 him, "Unless yeu·*all*·should·see signs and wonders,
Lk 12:54 "Whenever yeu·should·see the thick·cloud rising·
Lk 13:35 I·say to·yeu, no, yeu·should·not see me, until *the*
Lk 21:20 "And whenever yeu·should·see JeruSalem being·
Lk 21:31 whenever yeu·should·see these·things happening,
Ac 28:26 looking yeu·shall·look, and no, should·not see.
Mt 13:14 yeu·shall·look, and no, yeu·should·not see.
Mt 23:39 no, yeu·should·not see me from this·moment·on,
Mt 24:15 "Accordingly, whenever yeu·should·see " the
Mt 24:33 whenever yeu·should·see all these·things, yeu·
Mk 13:14 "But whenever yeu·should·see " the Abomination
Mk 13:29 whenever yeu·should·see these·things happening,

G1492.1 V-2AAS-3S ἴδῃ (5x)

Jn 8:56 AbRaham leaped·for·joy that he·should·see my day,
Lk 2:26 death before he·should·see Yahweh's Anointed-One.
Lk 19:4 a·mulberry-fig·tree in·order·that he·may·see him,
1Co 8:10 For if any·man should·see you (the·one having
1Jn 5:16 If someone should·see his brother morally·failing a·

G1492.1 V-2AAS-3P ἴδωσιν (9x)

Jn 12:9 but·rather in·order·that they·may·see Lazarus also,
Jn 12:40 in·order·that they·should·not see with·the eyes nor
Lk 9:27 taste death until they·should·see the kingdom of·
Ac 28:27 ·shut their eyes, lest they·should·see with·the eyes,
Mt 5:16 the men·of·clay†, so·that they·may·see yeur good
Mt 13:15 ·shut their eyes, lest they·should·see with·the eyes,
Mt 16:28 death, until they·should·see the Son of·Clay·Man†
Mk 4:12 they·may·look, and should·not see, and hearing
Mk 9:1 of·death, until they·should·see the kingdom of·God

G1492.1 V-RAI-1S οἶδα (10x)

Jn 8:55 ·not known him, but I·myself have·seen him. And if
Jn 8:55 if I·should·declare, 'I·have·not seen him,' I·shall·be
Jn 8:55 ·liar like yeurselves. But·rather I·have·seen him, and
Jn 20:13 my Lord, and I·have·not seen where they·laid him.
Ac 3:17 now, brothers, I·have·seen that yeu·inflicted *the*
Mt 28:5 do·not be·afraid, for I·have·seen that yeu·seek
Rm 15:29 And I·have·seen that, in·coming to yeu, I·shall·
Php 1:19 For I·have·seen that this·shall·result in salvation
Php 1:25 ·this confidence, I·have·seen that I·shall·abide and
2Ti 1:12 ashamed, for I·have·seen in·whom I·have·trusted,

G1492.1 V-RAI-1P οἴδαμεν (6x)

Jn 3:2 "Rabbi, we·have·seen that you·have·come from God
Jn 16:30 Now we·have·seen that you·have·seen all·things,
Jn 20:2 ·tomb, and we·have·not seen where they·laid him.
Mt 22:16 saying, "Mentor, we·have·seen that you·are true,
Rm 2:2 But we·have·seen that the judgment of·God is
1Jn 3:14 We·have·seen that we·ourselves have·walked·on

G1492.1 V-RAI-2S οἶδας (4x)

Jn 3:8 but·yet you·have·not seen from·what·source it·comes
Jn 16:30 Now we·have·seen that you·have·seen all·things,
Mt 15:12 declared to·him, "Have·you·seen how the
2Ti 3:15 and that from a·toddler you·have·seen the Sacred

G1492.1 V-RAI-2P οἴδατε (8x)

Jn 8:14 But yeu have·not seen from·what·source I·come and
Mt 20:25 them, declared, "Yeu·have·seen that the rulers of·
1Th 2:11 Exactly·as yeu·have·seen (each one of·yeu), how
2Th 3:7 For yeu·yeurselves have·seen how it·is·necessary to·
1Co 6:15 Have·yeu·not seen that yeur bodies are members
1Co 6:16 Or have·yeu·not seen that the·one being·tightly·
1Co 9:13 Have·yeu·not seen that the·ones working the
1Co 12:2 Yeu·have·seen that yeu·were Gentiles being·led·

G1492.1 V-RAI-3S οἶδεν (3x)

Mt 6:8 for yeur Father has·seen what·things *are* needed
Mt 6:32 yeur heavenly Father has·seen that yeu·have·need
2Co 11:31 blessed to·the ages, he·has·seen that I·do·not lie.

G1492.1 V-RAI-3P οἴδασιν (1x)

Lk 11:44 ·of·clay† walking over *them* have·not seen *them*."

G1492.1 V-RAN εἰδέναι (2x)

Tit 1:16 They·affirm to·have·seen God, but in·the works
Eph 1:18 ·enlightened— for yeu to·have·seen what is the

G1492.1 V-RAP-APM εἰδότας (1x)

Jud 1:5 ·remind yeu, *due·to* yeu once having·seen this: that

G1492.1 V-RAP-DSM εἰδότι (1x)

Jac 4:17 ·then, *anyone* having·seen *the* morally·good·thing

G1492.1 V-RAP-NSF εἰδυῖα (1x)

Ac 5:7 his wife, not having·seen the·thing having·happened,

G1492.1 V-RAP-NSM εἰδώς (18x)

Jn 6:61 But Jesus, having·seen in himself that his disciples
Jn 13:3 Jesus (having·seen that the Father has·given all·

Jn 18:4 Accordingly, Jesus, having·seen all the·things that·
Jn 19:28 this, Jesus, having·seen that even·now everything
Lk 11:17 he·himself, having·seen their complete·thoughts,
Ac 2:30 inherently·being a·prophet and having·seen that God
Ac 20:22 not having·seen the·things that·shall·befall me
Ac 24:22 ·things *and* having·seen more·precisely concerning
Mt 12:25 And YeShua having·seen their cogitations,
Mk 6:20 ·AntiPas was·afraid·of John, having·seen *that* he
Mk 12:15 But having·seen their stage·acting·hypocrisy,
Mk 12:28 ·alongside *and* having·seen that he·answered them
2Pe 1:14 having·seen that the putting·away of·my bodily·
Tit 3:11 having·seen that the·one such·as·this has·been·
Phm 1:21 I·wrote to·you, having·seen that you·shall·do
1Ti 1:9 while·having·seen this: that Torah-Law is·not laid·
2Ti 2:23 speculations, having·seen that they·give·birth *to*
Rv 12:12 *·is* having great rage, having·seen that he·has *but*

G1492.1 V-RAP-NPM εἰδότες (23x)

Jn 21:12 are you·yourself?" having·seen that it·was the
Lk 8:53 ·down·at him, having·seen that she·did·die.
Gal 2:16 "*As Jews*, having·seen that a·man·of·clay† is·not
Gal 4:8 in·fact, when not having·seen God, yeu·were·
Mt 22:29 Yeu·are·led·astray, not having·seen the Scriptures,
Mk 12:24 ·are·led·astray, *in* not having·seen the Scriptures,
Rm 6:9 having·seen that after·being·awakened from·among
Rm 13:11 And having·seen the season, *know* that even·now,
Jac 3:1 instructors, having·seen that we·shall·receive greater
Php 1:17 out·of·love, having·seen that I·am·laid·out for a·
1Pe 1:8 whom not having·seen, yeu·love— in whom, not
1Pe 1:18 having·seen that *it·was* not with·corruptible·things
1Pe 3:9 a·blessing, having·seen that yeu·were·called·forth
1Pe 5:9 solid in·the trust, having·seen *that* the same
1Th 1:4 having·seen, O·brothers having·been·loved by God,
1Co 15:58 in the work of·the Lord, having·seen that yeur
2Co 1:7 behalf *is* steadfast, having·seen that just·as yeu·are
2Co 4:14 having·seen that the·one awakening the Lord Jesus
2Co 5:11 So·then, having·seen the fear of·the Lord, we·
Eph 6:8 having·seen that whatever beneficially·good·thing
Eph 6:9 giving·up the threatening, having·seen that yeur
Col 3:24 having·seen that from *the* Lord yeu·shall·receive·
Col 4:1 the right and the equality, having·seen that yeu also

G1492.1 V-RAS-1S εἰδῶ (1x)

1Co 13:2 *of* prophecy, and should·have·seen all the

G1492.1 V-LAI-1S ᾔδειν (1x)

Ac 23:5 And Paul replied, "I·had·not seen, brothers, that he·

G1492.1 V-LAI-2P ᾔδειτε (1x)

Lk 2:49 me? Had·yeu·not seen that it·is·necessary·for me

G1492.1 V-LAI-3S ᾔδει (2x)

Jn 2:9 wine, yet had·not seen from·what·source it·was (but
Jn 20:14 *there*, yet she·had·not seen that it·was Jesus.

G1492.1 V-LAI-3P ᾔδεισαν (4x)

Jn 2:9 attendants having·drawn·out the water had·seen), the
Jn 20:9 For not·even·yet had·they·seen the Scripture *which·*
Jn 21:4 however, the disciples had·not seen that it·was Jesus
Ac 16:3 places, for absolutely·all had·seen that his father

EG1492.1 (6x)

Jn 2:18 ·sign do·you·show to·us, *seeing* that you·do these·
Lk 12:55 And whenever *yeu·should·see the* south·wind
Ac 15:36 of·the Lord, *and see* how they·are."
Mk 11:13 he·came *toward it to·see* if perhaps he·shall·find
1Th 3:6 us, exactly·as we·ourselves also *yearn to·see* yeu.
Rv 20:4 ·given to·them— and *I·saw* the souls of·the·ones

G1492.2 V-FAI-3P εἰδήσουσιν (1x)

Heb 8:11 because all shall·personally·know me, from *the*

G1492.2 V-RAI-1S οἶδα (44x)

Jn 4:25 says to·him, "I·personally·know that Messiah is·
Jn 5:32 concerning me, and I·personally·know that the
Jn 7:29 But I·myself personally·know him, because I·am
Jn 8:14 because I·personally·know from·what·source I·came
Jn 8:37 "I·personally·know that yeu·are AbRaham's
Jn 9:12 is this·man?" He·says, "I·do·not personally·know."
Jn 9:25 ·moral·failure, I·do·not personally·know. One·thing
Jn 9:25 ·know. One·thing I·do·personally·know, how·that
Jn 11:22 But·yet I·personally·know, even now, that as·much·
Jn 11:24 to·him, "I·personally·know that he·shall·rise·up in
Jn 12:50 And I·personally·know that his commandment is
Jn 13:18 yeu all. I·myself personally·know whom I·selected,
Lk 4:34 ·completely·destroy us? I·personally·know you *and*
Lk 13:25 to·yeu, 'I·do·not personally·know yeu. From·
Lk 13:27 I·say to·yeu, I·do·not personally·know yeu. From·
Lk 22:57 "Woman, I·do·not personally·know him."
Lk 22:60 I·do·not personally·know what you·are·saying."
Ac 12:11 Peter declared, "Now I·personally·know truly that
Ac 20:25 now behold, I·myself personally·know that yeu all
Ac 20:29 For I·myself personally·know this, that after my
Ac 26:27 the prophets? I·personally·know that you·trust."
Mt 25:12 I·say to·yeu, I·do·not personally·know yeu.'
Mt 26:70 "I·do·not personally·know what you·are·saying."
Mt 26:72 "I·do·not personally·know the man·of·clay†."
Mt 26:74 "I·do·not personally·know the man·of·clay†."
Mk 1:24 to·completely·destroy us? I·personally·know you,
Mk 14:68 *it*, saying, "I·do·not personally·know *him*, neither
Mk 14:71 "I·do·not personally·know this man·of·clay† to·
Rm 7:18 For I·personally·know that in me (that·is, in my
Rm 14:14 I·personally·know, and have·been·convinced by
1Co 1:16 Finally, I·do·not personally·know if I·immersed
2Co 9:2 For I·personally·know yeur eagerness, for·which I·
2Co 12:2 I·personally·know a·man·of·clay† in
2Co 12:2 in body, I·do·not personally·know; or·whether on·
2Co 12:2 of·the body, I·do·not personally·know; God
2Co 12:3 And I·personally·know such a·man·of·clay†,
2Co 12:3 of·the body, I·do·not personally·know, God
Rv 2:2 'I·personally·know your works, and your wearisome·
Rv 2:9 'I·personally·know your works, and the tribulation,
Rv 2:13 'I·personally·know your works, and where you·
Rv 2:19 'I·personally·know your works (also the love, and
Rv 3:1 the seven stars: 'I·personally·know your works, that
Rv 3:8 'I·personally·know your works. Behold, in·the·sight
Rv 3:15 'I·personally·know your works, that you·are neither

G1492.2 V-RAI-1P οἴδαμεν (37x)

Jn 3:11 we·speak that which we·personally·know and testify
Jn 4:22 ·know. We·personally·know *directly·before* whom
Jn 4:42 *him* ourselves, and we·personally·know that this is
Jn 6:42 and mother we·ourselves personally·know? So·then
Jn 7:27 But·yet we·personally·know this·man, *and* from·
Jn 9:20 them and declared, "We·personally·know that this is
Jn 9:21 he·looks·about, we·do·not personally·know; or who
Jn 9:21 we·ourselves do·not personally·know. He·himself
Jn 9:24 God glory. We·ourselves personally·know that this
Jn 9:29 We·ourselves personally·know that God has·spoken
Jn 9:29 we·do·not personally·know from·what·source he·is.
Jn 9:31 Now we·personally·know that God does·not hear
Jn 14:5 "Lord, we·do·not personally·know to·where *it·is*
Jn 16:18 ·while?' We·do·not personally·know what *it·is* he·
Jn 21:24 these·things, and we·personally·know that his
Lk 20:21 "Mentor, we·personally·know that you·say and
Ac 7:40 we·do·not personally·know what has·happened to·
Heb 10:30 For we·personally·know the·one declaring,
Mt 21:27 they·declared, "We·do·not personally·know."
Mk 11:33 they·say to·Jesus, "We·do·not personally·know."
Mk 12:14 "Mentor, we·personally·know that you·are true,
Rm 3:19 But we·personally·know that as·much·as the
Rm 7:14 For we·personally·know that the Torah-Law is
Rm 8:22 For we·personally·know that the entire creation
Rm 8:26 we·do·not personally·know what we·should·pray·
Rm 8:28 And we·personally·know that, for·the·ones loving
1Co 8:1 sacrificed·to·idols: We·personally·know that we·all
1Co 8:4 ·to·idols: We·personally·know that an·idol *is*
2Co 5:1 For we·personally·know that if our earthly home of·
2Co 5:16 ·on, we·ourselves personally·know no·one·at·all
1Ti 1:8 Now we·personally·know that the Torah-Law *is*
1Jn 3:2 what we·shall·be. But we·personally·know that,
1Jn 5:15 And if we·personally·know that he·hears us,
1Jn 5:15 ·might request, we·personally·know that we·have
1Jn 5:18 We·personally·know that any one having·been·born
1Jn 5:19 We·personally·know that we·are birthed·from·out
1Jn 5:20 And we·personally·know that the Son of·God

G1492.2 V-RAI-2S οἶδας (12x)

Jn 13:7 ·yourself do·not personally·know at·this·moment,
Jn 19:10 to·me? Do·you·not personally·know that I·have
Jn 21:15 you·yourself personally·know that I·have·affection·
Jn 21:16 you·yourself personally·know that I·have·affection·
Jn 21:17 "Lord, you·yourself personally·know all·things;
Lk 18:20 You·personally·know the commandments, "You·
Mk 10:19 You·personally·know the commandments, "You·
1Co 7:16 For what do·you·personally·know, O·wife,
1Co 7:16 Or what do·you·personally·know, O·husband,
2Ti 1:15 This you·personally·know, that all the·ones in Asia
Rv 3:17 yet you·do·not personally·know that you·yourself
Rv 7:14 "Sir, you·yourself personally·know." And he·

G1492.2 V-RAI-2P οἴδατε (53x)

Jn 1:26 ·yeu, whom yeu·yeurselves do·not personally·know;
Jn 4:22 yeu·do·not personally·know. We·personally·know
Jn 4:32 that yeu·yeurselves do·not personally·know *about*."
Jn 7:28 and saying, "¿! So·do yeu·personally·know me, and
Jn 7:28 and do·yeu·personally·know from·what·source I·am
Jn 7:28 true, whom yeu·yeurselves do·not personally·know.
Jn 8:19 answered, "Neither do·yeu·personally·know me, nor
Jn 9:30 do·not personally·know from·what·source he·is, and·
Jn 11:49 do·not personally·know not·even·one·thing,
Jn 13:17 "If yeu·personally·know these·things, supremely·
Jn 14:4 And yeu·personally·know to·where *it·is that* I·myself
Jn 14:4 head·on·out, and yeu·personally·know the way."
Lk 9:55 "Yeu·do·not personally·know of·what·manner of·
Ac 2:22 just·as yeu·yeurselves also personally·know—
Ac 3:16 this·man whom yeu·observe and personally·know.
Ac 10:37 "Yeu·yeurselves personally·know the utterance
Gal 4:13 Yeu·personally·know that through sickness of·the
Mt 20:22 *sons*, "Yeu·do·not personally·know what yeu·are·
Mt 24:42 because yeu·do·not personally·know in·which hour
Mt 25:13 because yeu·do·not personally·know the day nor·
Mt 26:2 "Yeu·personally·know that after two days the
Mk 4:13 to·them, "Do·yeu·not personally·know this parable
Mk 10:38 "Yeu·do·not personally·know what yeu·are·
Mk 10:42 says to·them, "Yeu·personally·know that the·ones
Mk 13:33 pray, for yeu·do·not personally·know when the
Mk 13:35 ·alert— for yeu·do·not personally·know when the
Rm 6:16 Do·yeu·not personally·know that yeu·are slaves to·
Rm 11:2 Or do·yeu·not personally·know what the Scripture
Jac 4:4 adulteresses, do·yeu·not personally·know that the
Php 4:15 Now yeu Philippians personally·know also, that at
1Th 1:5 just·as yeu·personally·know *that* we·behaved·
1Th 2:1 For yeu·yeurselves personally·know, brothers, that
1Th 2:2 just·as yeu·personally·know, we·were·boldly·
1Th 2:5 a·word of·flattery (just·as yeu·personally·know), nor
1Th 3:3 yeu·yeurselves personally·know that we·are·laid·out
1Th 3:4 just·as it·happened, and yeu·personally·know *it*.
1Th 4:2 For yeu·personally·know what charges we·gave yeu
1Th 5:2 For yeu·yeurselves personally·know accurately that
2Th 2:6 And now yeu·personally·know the·thing *that·is*
1Co 3:16 Do·yeu·not personally·know that yeu·are a·temple
1Co 5:6 not good. Do·yeu·not personally·know that a·little
1Co 6:2 Do·yeu·not personally·know that the holy·ones
1Co 6:3 Do·yeu·not personally·know that we·shall·judge
1Co 6:9 do·yeu·not personally·know that unrighteous·men
1Co 6:19 Or do·yeu·not personally·know that yeur body is a·
1Co 9:24 Do·yeu·not personally·know that the·ones running
1Co 16:15 brothers, (yeu·personally·know the household of·
1Jn 2:20 the Holy·One, and yeu·personally·know all·things.
1Jn 2:21 ·yeu because yeu·do·not personally·know the truth,
1Jn 2:21 but·rather because yeu·do·personally·know it, and
1Jn 3:5 And yeu·personally·know that that·one was·made·
1Jn 3:15 is a·man-killer†. And yeu·personally·know that any
3Jn 1:12 testify, and *all·of* yeu·personally·know that our

G1492.2 V-RAI-3S οἶδεν (17x)

Jn 7:15 ·does this·man personally·know *the Sacred·*Writings,
Jn 12:35 does·not personally·know where he·is·heading.
Jn 15:15 the slave does·not personally·know what his lord
Jn 19:35 is true; this·one·also personally·knows that *what*
Lk 12:30 yeur Father personally·knows that yeu·have·need

Mt 24:36 and hour no·one·at·all personally·knows, not·even
Mk 4:27 ·to·length, he·himself does·not personally·know.
Mk 13:32 and hour no·one·at·all personally·knows, not·even
Rm 8:27 searching the hearts personally·knows what the
1Co 2:11 man·of·clay† personally·knows the·things of·the
1Co 2:11 ·one *being* personally·knows the·things of·God,
1Co 14:16 ·now he·does·not personally·know what you·say?
2Co 11:11 ·not love yeu? God personally·knows *that I·do.*
2Co 12:2 I·do·not personally·know; God personally·knows),
2Co 12:3 I·do·not personally·know, God personally·knows),
1Jn 2:11 and does·not personally·know where he·is·heading,
Rv 19:12 that not·even·one·man personally·knows, except

G1492.2 V-RAI-3P οἴδασιν (6x)
Jn 10:4 follow him, because they·personally·know his voice.
Jn 10:5 him, because they·do·not personally·know the voice
Jn 15:21 they·do·not personally·know the·one sending me.
Jn 18:21 See, these·men personally·know what I·myself
Lk 23:34 for they·do·not personally·know what they·do."
Jud 1:10 ·many·things they·do·not personally·know. But *in*
G1492.2 V-RAN εἰδέναι (9x)
Jn 14:5 so·then how are·we·able to·personally·know the way
Lk 20:7 *as* to·not personally·know from·what·source *it·was.*
Lk 22:34 *saying that* you·do·not personally·know me."
1Th 5:12 to·personally·know the·ones laboring·hard among
1Co 2:2 I·decided not to·personally·know anything among
1Co 8:2 presumes to·personally·know something *from·*
1Co 11:3 But I·want yeu to·personally·know that the head
Col 2:1 for·yeu to·personally·know what·a·huge strenuous·
Col 4:6 ·for yeu to·personally·know how to·answer each
G1492.2 V-RAP-APM εἰδότας (1x)
2Pe 1:12 *·are already* personally·knowing *these·things* and
G1492.2 V-RAP-DPM εἰδόσιν (1x)
2Th 1:8 to·the·ones not personally·knowing God and to·the·
G1492.2 V-RAP-NSF εἰδυῖα (1x)
Mk 5:33 trembling, personally·knowing what has·happened
G1492.2 V-RAP-NSM εἰδώς (3x)
Jn 13:1 Passover, Jesus, personally·knowing that his hour
Lk 9:33 ·for EliJah," not personally·knowing what he·says.
2Ti 3:14 ·assured·of, having·personally·known from whom
G1492.2 V-RAP-NPN εἰδότα (1x)
1Th 4:5 the Gentiles, the·ones not personally·knowing God;
G1492.2 V-RAP-NPM εἰδότες (2x)
Rm 5:3 ·boast in the tribulations, personally·knowing that:
2Co 5:6 even while·personally·knowing that while·being·at·
G1492.2 V-RAS-1S εἰδῶ (1x)
1Co 14:11 if I·should·not personally·know the power·*(the·*
G1492.2 V-RAS-1P εἰδῶμεν (1x)
1Co 2:12 in·order·that we·may·personally·know the·things
G1492.2 V-RAS-2S εἰδῇς (1x)
1Ti 3:15 in·order·that you·may·personally·know how it·is·
G1492.2 V-RAS-2P εἰδῆτε (6x)
Lk 5:24 But in·order·that yeu·may·personally·know that the
Mt 9:6 But in·order·that yeu·may·personally·know that the
Mk 2:10 But in·order·that yeu·may·personally·know that the
Eph 6:21 yeu·yeurselves may·personally·know the·things
1Jn 2:29 If yeu·should·personally·know that he·is righteous,
1Jn 5:13 in·order·that yeu·may·personally·know that *the*
G1492.2 V-LAI-1S ᾔδειν (4x)
Jn 1:31 And·I had·not personally·known him, but·yet in·
Jn 1:33 And·I had·not personally·known him, but·yet the·
Jn 11:42 And·I·myself had·personally·known that you·hear
Rm 7:7 for also I·had·not personally·known the longing,
G1492.2 V-LAI-2S ᾔδεις (3x)
Jn 4:10 "If you·had·personally·known the voluntary·present
Lk 19:22 slave. You·had·personally·known that I·myself am
Mt 25:26 slave! You·had·personally·known that I·reap
G1492.2 V-LAI-2P ᾔδειτε (2x)
Jn 8:19 my Father. If yeu·had·personally·known me, also
Jn 8:19 also yeu·would have·personally·known my Father."
G1492.2 V-LAI-3S ᾔδει (12x)
Jn 5:13 being·healed had·not personally·known who it·was,
Jn 6:6 he·himself had·personally·known what he·was·about
Jn 6:64 For Jesus had·personally·known from·among *the*
Jn 13:11 For he·had·personally·known the·one handing him
Jn 18:2 him over, also had·personally·known the place,
Lk 6:8 he·himself had·personally·known their deliberations.
Lk 12:39 master·of·the·house had·personally·known in· hour
Ac 7:18 rose·up, who had·not personally·known Joseph.
Ac 12:9 him and had·not personally·known that the·thing
Mt 24:43 the master·of·the·house had·personally·known in·
Mt 27:18 For he·had·personally·known that on·account·of
Mk 9:6 he·had·not personally·known what he·should·speak,
G1492.2 V-LAI-3P ᾔδεισαν (4x)
Lk 4:41 because they·had·personally·known him to·be the
Ac 19:32 majority had·not personally·known for·what cause
Mk 1:34 because they·had·once·personally·known him.
Mk 14:40 they·had·not personally·known what they·should·
EG1492.2 (3x)
Mt 10:29 the soil without yeur Father *personally·knowing.*
1Co 7:17 Except *to·personally·know that* as God imparted to·
Rv 2:9 wealthy). And *I·personally·know* the revilement of·
G1492.3 V-RAI-2P οἴδατε (4x)
Lk 11:13 personally·know·how to·give beneficially·good
Lk 12:56 yeu·personally·know·how to·examine·and·verify
Mt 7:11 personally·know·how to·give beneficially·good
Mt 27:65 Make·*it*·as·secure as yeu·personally·know·how."
G1492.3 V-RAI-3S οἶδεν (1x)
2Pe 2:9 — does·personally·know·how to·snatch devoutly·
G1492.3 V-RAN εἰδέναι (1x)
1Th 4:4 of·yeu to·personally·know·how to·possess his·own
G1492.4 V-RAI-1S οἶδα (2x)
Php 4:12 I·have·seen·how to·be·humbled, and I·have·seen·
Php 4:12 to·be·humbled, and I·have·seen·how to·abound. In
G1492.4 V-RAI-3S οἶδεν (1x)
1Ti 3:5 but if any·man has·not seen·how to·conduct his·own

G1493 εἰδωλεῖον êidōlêîôn *n.* (1x)
Roots:G1497 Compare:G2411 G3485
G1493 N-DSN εἰδωλείῳ (1x)
1Co 8:10 laying·back·and·eating in an·idol's·temple, shall

G1494 εἰδωλό•θυτον êidōlóthytôn *adj.* (10x)
Roots:G1497 G2380
G1494.2 A-NSN εἰδωλόθυτον (3x)
1Co 8:7 this·moment, eat as sacrificing·to·an·idol; and their
1Co 10:19 or that *which·is* sacrificed·to·idols is anything?
1Co 10:28 to·yeu, "This is sacrificed·to·idols," do·not eat
G1494.2 A-ASN εἰδωλόθυτον (1x)
Ac 21:25 *from* the·thing sacrificed·to·an·idol, *from* blood,
G1494.2 A-APN εἰδωλόθυτα (3x)
1Co 8:10 to·eat those·things·which·are·sacrificed·to·idols;
Rv 2:14 *which was* to·eat things·sacrificed·to·idols, and to·
Rv 2:20 ·immorality and to·eat things·sacrificed·to·idols.
G1494.2 A-GPN εἰδωλοθύτων (3x)
Ac 15:29 to·abstain from·things·sacrificed·to·idols, and
1Co 8:1 Now concerning the·things sacrificed·to·idols: We·
1Co 8:4 the feeding·upon the·things sacrificed·to·idols: We·

G1495 εἰδωλο•λατρεία êidōlôlatrêía *n.* (4x)
Roots:G1497 G2999 See:G1496
G1495.2 N-NSF εἰδωλολατρεία (2x)
Gal 5:20 idolatry·*(image·worship)*, making·and·supplying·
Col 3:5 and the covetousness— which is idolatry—
G1495.2 N-DPF εἰδωλολατρείαις (1x)
1Pe 4:3 drinking·parties, and shamefully·illicit idolatries,
G1495.2 N-GSF εἰδωλολατρείας (1x)
1Co 10:14 my dearly·beloved, flee from the idolatry.

G1496 εἰδωλο•λάτρης êidōlôlátrēs *n.* (7x)
Roots:G1497 G3000 See:G1495
G1496 N-NSM εἰδωλολάτρης (2x)
1Co 5:11 ·man, or covetous, or an·idolater, or a·defamer, or
Eph 5:5 greedy·man— which is an·idolater— does·not have
G1496 N-NPM εἰδωλολάτραι (3x)
1Co 6:9 sexually·immoral·men, nor idolaters, nor adulterers,
1Co 10:7 Yeu·must·not·even be idolaters, just·as *were* some
Rv 22:15 and the murderers, and the idolaters, and everyone
G1496 N-DPM εἰδωλολάτραις (2x)
1Co 5:10 ·exceedingly·greedy, or with·idolaters. Otherwise,
Rv 21:8 and makers·of·poisonous·drugs, and idolaters, and

G1497 εἴδωλον êídōlôn *n.* (11x)
Roots:G1491 See:G1493 xLangAlso:H1544
G1497.1 N-NSN εἴδωλον (2x)
1Co 8:4 We·personally·know that an·idol *is* nothing·at·all
1Co 10:19 what do·I·reply? That an·idol is anything, or
G1497.1 N-APN εἴδωλα (3x)
Rm 2:22 the idols, do·you·burglarize·temple·sanctuaries?
1Co 12:2 even·as yeu·were·led toward the voiceless idols.
Rv 9:20 the demons, and 'the idols made·of·gold, silver,
G1497.1 N-DSN εἰδώλῳ (1x)
Ac 7:41 and brought·forth sacrifice to·the idol, and they·
G1497.1 N-GSN εἰδώλου (1x)
1Co 8:7 *still·accustomed·to* the idol unto this·moment, eat as
G1497.1 N-GPN εἰδώλων (4x)
Ac 15:20 ·abstain from the pollutions of·the idols, and *from*
1Th 1:9 to God from the idols, to·be·slaves to·the·living and
2Co 6:16 mutual·compact has·a·temple of·God with idols?
1Jn 5:21 vigilantly·keep yeurselves from the idols. So·be·it,·

G1498 εἴην êíēn *v.* (12x)
εἴη êíē [alternate]
Roots:G1510
G1498.1 V-PXO-3S εἴη (1x)
Ac 8:20 silver, together with·you, be *handed·over* to total·
G1498.2 V-PXO-3S εἴη (9x)
Jn 13:24 to·him to·inquire who it·might·be, concerning the·
Lk 1:29 ·pondering what·manner·of greeting this might·be.
Lk 3:15 if·perhaps he·himself might·be the Anointed-One.
Lk 8:9 him, saying, "What might·be *meant·by* this parable?
Lk 15:26 he·inquired what might·be *meant·by* these·things.
Lk 18:36 ·through, he·inquired what this might·be *about.*
Lk 22:23 ·among them it·might·be intending to·accomplish
Ac 10:17 in himself *as·to* what might·be *meant·by* the clear·
Ac 21:33 he·inquired *of·them* who he·might·be, and what *it·*
G1498.3 V-PXO-2S εἴης (1x)
Rv 3:15 nor fervently·hot. Oh·that you·would·be cold or
G1498.3 V-PXO-3S εἴη (1x)
Lk 9:46 among them *as·to* which of·them would·be greater.

G1499 εἰ καί êi kaí *conj.* (11x)
Roots:G1487 G2532 Compare:G2539
G1499.1 COND εἰ καί (1x)
1Co 7:21 not to·you, but·yet if·also you·are·able to·become
G1499.2 CONJ εἰ καί (1x)
Lk 11:11 ¿! shall·he·hand him a·stone? Or·if a·fish, ¿!
G1499.3 COND εἰ καί (1x)
2Co 4:3 But even·if our good·news is having·been·veiled, it·
G1499.4 COND εἰ καί (7x)
1Pe 3:14 But·yet even·though yeu·may·actually·suffer on·
2Co 7:8 Because even·though I·grieved yeu with the letter, I·
2Co 7:8 ·not regretting *it*, even·though I·was·regretting *it*,
2Co 7:8 letter did·grieve yeu, even·though *it·was* just·for a·
2Co 7:12 So even·though I·wrote to·yeu, *it·was* not because·
2Co 12:11 of·ambassadors, even·though I·am nothing·at·all.
2Co 12:15 souls, even·though the·more·abundantly *I·am*
G1499.4 CONJ εἰ καί (1x)
Lk 11:8 "I·say to·yeu, even·though already·rising·up, he·

G1500 εἰκῇ êikēî *adv.* (7x)
Roots:G1502 Compare:G1432 G3155
G1500.2 ADV εἰκῇ (6x)
Gal 3:4 ·suffer so·many·things for·no·reason— if·indeed
Gal 3:4 for·no·reason— if·indeed that *it·was* for·no·reason?
Gal 4:11 I·have·labored·hard for yeu for·no·reason.
Mt 5:22 with·his brother for·no·reason shall·be·held·liable
1Co 15:2 ·that yeu·trusted for·no·reason *in·particular.*
Col 2:18 clearly·seen, being·puffed·up for·no·reason by his
G1500.3 ADV εἰκῇ (1x)
Rm 13:4 For *it·is* not without·reason *that* he·bears the sword,

G1501 εἴκοσι êíkôsi *n.* (12x)
G1501.1 N-NPM εἴκοσι (8x)
Lk 14:31 who·is·coming against him with twenty thousand?
Ac 1:15 in·unison *of* about a·hundred *and* twenty), Peter,
Ac 27:28 ·line, they·found *it to·be* twenty fathoms; and

Rv 4:4 all·around the throne *were·set·out* twenty four thrones
Rv 4:4 the thrones, I·saw the twenty four Elders sitting·
Rv 4:10 the twenty four Elders shall·fall in·the·sight of·the·
Rv 11:16 And the twenty four Elders, the·ones sitting·down
Rv 19:4 And the twenty four Elders and the four living·

G1501.2 N-NUI εἰκοσιτρεῖς (1x)
1Co 10:8 ·sexual·immorality, and twenty·three thousand fell

G1501.3 N-NUI εἰκοσιτέσσαρες (2x)
Rv 5:8 living·beings and the twenty·four Elders fell·down
Rv 5:14 And the twenty·four Elders fell·down and fell·

G1501.4 N-NUI εἰκοσιπέντε (1x)
Jn 6:19 ·course, having·rowed about twenty·five or thirty

G1502 εἴκω êíkō *v.* (1x)
See:G1500 G5226

G1502 V-AAI-1P εἴξαμεν (1x)
Gal 2:5 just·for an·hour, did·we·yield to·the subjection, in·

G1503 εἴκω êíkō *v.* (2x)
Compare:G3666 See:G1502 G1504
xLangEquiv:H1819 A1821

G1503 V-RAI-3S ἔοικεν (2x)
Jac 1:6 hesitating has·directly·resembled a·surging·wave of·
Jac 1:23 ·doer, this·one has·directly·resembled a·man fully·

G1504 εἰκών êikṓn *n.* (23x)
Roots:G1503 Compare:G3667 G3669 G2072 G5481
G1497 G4610-1 G5179
xLangEquiv:H1823 xLangAlso:H5566

G1504.1 N-NSF εἰκών (6x)
Mt 22:20 to·them, "Whose derived·image and inscription *is*
Mk 12:16 "Whose *is* this derived·image and inscription?
1Co 11:7 head, inherently·being God's derived·image and
2Co 4:4 ·the Anointed-One— who is 'God's derived·image.'
Col 1:15 *Son* who is *the* derived·image of·the invisible God,
Rv 13:15 that also the derived·image of·the Daemonic·Beast

G1504.1 N-ASF εἰκόνα (10x)
Lk 20:24 a·denarius. Whose derived·image and inscription
1Co 15:49 just·as we·have·borne the derived·image of·the
1Co 15:49 we also shall·bear the derived·image of·the
2Co 3:18 into·the same derived·image from glory to glory,
Col 3:10 'according·to *the* derived·image' of·the·one
Rv 13:14 to·make a·derived·image for·the Daemonic·Beast,
Rv 13:15 to·the derived·image of·the Daemonic·Beast that
Rv 14:9 the Daemonic·Beast and its derived·image, and
Rv 14:11 Daemonic·Beast and its derived·image do·not have
Rv 20:4 to·the Daemonic·Beast nor his derived·image, and

G1504.1 N-DSF εἰκόνι (3x)
Rv 13:15 breath to·the derived·image of·the Daemonic·Beast,
Rv 16:2 *upon* the·ones falling·prostrate to·its derived·image.
Rv 19:20 and the·ones falling·prostrate to·its derived·image.

G1504.1 N-GSF εἰκόνος (3x)
Rm 1:23 'a·resemblance of·a·derived·image of·corruptible
Rm 8:29 ·in·nature·like the derived·image of·his Son, in·
Rv 15:2 and out·from·among its derived·image, and out·

G1504.2 N-ASF εἰκόνα (1x)
Heb 10:1 the same *as* a·direct·representation of·the activities

G1505 εἰλι•κρίνεια êilikrínêia *n.* (3x)
Roots:G1506 Compare:G0572 G1618

G1505.2 N-DSF εἰλικρινείᾳ (1x)
2Co 1:12 how·that with fidelity and sincerity before·God

G1505.2 N-GSF εἰλικρινείας (2x)
1Co 5:8 ·rather with Unleavened·Bread of·sincerity and truth
2Co 2:17 But·rather, as from·out of·sincerity, moreover as

G1506 εἰλι•κρινής êilikrinḗs *adj.* (2x)
Roots:G2919 See:G1505

G1506.2 A-NPM εἰλικρινεῖς (1x)
Php 1:10 yeu·may·be judged·sincere and without·offense in

G1506.3 A-ASF εἰλικρινῆ (1x)
2Pe 3:1 ·awaken yeur sincere innermost·minds with a·

G1507 εἰλίσσω hêilíssō *v.* (1x)
Compare:G2947 G2944 See:G1667
xLangAlso:H1556

G1507.2 V-PPP-NSN εἰλισσόμενον (1x)
Rv 6:14 ·separated as an·official·scroll being·rolled·up; and

G1508 εἰ μή êi mḗ *conj.* (89x)
Roots:G1487 G3361

G1508.ª NEG-COND εἰ μή (1x)
Gal 1:7 *good·news at·all*. However, there·are some·men

G1508.1 NEG-COND εἰ μή (4x)
Ac 26:32 ·fully·released, if·he·had·not appealed·to Caesar."
Heb 3:18 ·rest,' if·not to·the·ones who·were·being·obstinate
1Jn 2:22 is the liar, if·not the·one who·contradicts·by·saying
1Jn 5:5 overcoming the world, if·not the·one trusting that

G1508.2 NEG-COND εἰ μή (81x)
Jn 3:13 into the heaven, except the·one descending out of·
Jn 6:22 ·been no other small·boat there except that one into
Jn 6:46 has·clearly·seen the Father, except the·one being
Jn 9:33 Except this·man was personally·from God, he·
Jn 10:10 does·not come, except in·order·that he·may·steal,
Jn 14:6 ·even·one comes to the Father, except through me.
Jn 15:22 "Except *for·that* I·came and I·spoke to·them, they·
Jn 17:12 from·among them is·completely·lost except the Son
Jn 19:11 ·of authority against me, except *that* it·was having·
Jn 19:15 "We·have no king except Caesar."
Lk 4:26 ·one of·them was EliJah sent, except into *the city*
Lk 4:27 ·even·one of·them was·purified, except Naaman the
Lk 5:21 is·able to·forgive moral·failures, except God alone?
Lk 6:4 which it·is·not proper to·eat except alone *for* the
Lk 8:51 allow not·even·one·person to·enter·in, except Peter,
Lk 10:22 knows who the Son is, except the Father, and who
Lk 10:22 and who the Father is, except the Son, and *he* to·
Lk 11:29 shall·not be·given to·it, except the sign of·Jonah
Lk 17:18 ·give glory to·God, *none* except this resident·alien.
Lk 18:19 No·one·at·all *is* beneficially·good, except one:
Ac 11:19 Redemptive·word to·no·one except to·Jews merely.
Ac 21:25 such·thing, except to·vigilantly·keep themselves
Gal 1:19 any·other of·the ambassadors, except Jacob, the
Gal 6:14 ·never happen for·me to·boast, except in the cross
Mt 5:13 ·it·have·strength any·longer, except to·be·cast out
Mt 11:27 ·one·at·all fully·knows the Son, except the Father;
Mt 11:27 anyone fully·know the Father, except the Son, and
Mt 12:4 for·the·ones with him, except only for·the priests·
Mt 12:24 the demons, except by BaalZebul,·Master-Of-Dung,
Mt 12:39 shall·not be·given to·her, except the sign of·Jonah
Mt 13:57 is not without·honor, except in his·own fatherland
Mt 14:17 ·not have *anything* here except five loaves·of·bread
Mt 15:24 "I·am·not dispatched except to·the sheep, the·
Mt 16:4 shall·not be·given to·her, except the sign of·Jonah
Mt 17:8 they·saw not·even·one·man, except YeShua only.
Mt 17:21 "But this kind does·not depart except by prayer and
Mt 19:9 ·divorce his wife, except over sexual·immorality,
Mt 19:17 ·*is* no·one·at·all beneficially·good except one, God
Mt 21:19 not·even·one·thing on it, except merely leaves,
Mt 24:22 And except those Days be·cut·short, not any flesh
Mt 24:36 the angels of·the heavens, except my Father only.
Mk 2:7 is·able to·forgive moral·failures, except one *only*:
Mk 2:26 to·eat except for·the priests·that·offer·sacrifices, and
Mk 5:37 ·one·man to·follow·along with·him, except Peter,
Mk 6:4 is not without·honor, except in his·own fatherland,
Mk 6:5 there not·even·one miracle, except laying his hands
Mk 6:8 *their* journey, *saying*, "… except a·staff merely. No
Mk 8:14 to·take bread, and except *for* one loaf·of·bread,
Mk 9:9 what·things they·saw, except whenever the Son of·
Mk 9:29 this kind able to·come·forth, except by prayer and
Mk 10:18 ·*is* no·one·at·all beneficially·good except one,
Mk 11:13 to it, he·found nothing·at·all except leaves, for it·
Mk 13:20 And except *that* Yahweh cut·short the Days, not
Mk 13:32 heaven, neither the Son, except the Father *only*.
Rm 7:7 ·not know Moral·Failure, except through Torah-Law
Rm 7:7 ·known the longing, except·that the Torah-Law was·
Rm 9:29 has·already·stated, "'Except Yahweh of·Hosts left·
Rm 11:15 *of·them be*, except life·above from·among dead·
Rm 13:1 For there·is no authority except from God; and the·
Rm 13:8 not·even·one·thing, except to·love one·another, for
Rm 14:14 defiled through itself, except to·the·one reckoning
Php 4:15 matter of·giving and of·receiving, except yeu only.
1Co 1:14 I·immersed not·even·one of·yeu, except Crispus
1Co 2:2 anything among yeu, except Jesus Anointed and
1Co 2:11 the·things of·the man·of·clay†, except the spirit
1Co 2:11 ·knows the·things of·God, except the Spirit of·
1Co 7:17 Except *to·personally·know that* as God imparted to·
1Co 10:13 ·proof·trial has·not taken yeu except *that·which is*
1Co 12:3 "Jesus *is* Lord," except by Holy Spirit.
1Co 14:5 except excluding·that he·should·thoroughly·
1Co 15:2 to·yeu, except excluding·that yeu·trusted for·no·
2Co 2:2 making me merry, except the·one being·grieved as·
2Co 12:5 ·self, I·shall·not boast, except in my weaknesses.
2Co 12:13 rest *of·the* Called·Out·citizenries, except that I
Eph 4:9 what is·it except that also he·descended first into
1Ti 5:19 ·from *this standard*: "'except at *the mouth* of·two
Rv 2:17 ·even·one·man did·know except the·one receiving *it*
Rv 13:17 ·able to·buy or to·sell, except the·one having the
Rv 14:3 was·able to·learn the song except the hundred *and*
Rv 19:12 ·one·man personally·knows, except he·himself,
Rv 21:27 *shall·enter* except the·ones having·been·written in

G1508.3 NEG-COND εἰ μή (2x)
1Co 8:4 *there·is* not·even·one other God, yet·not·even one.
2Co 3:1 ourselves? Yet·not·even do·we·have·need, as some

G1508.4 NEG-COND εἰ μή (1x)
Rv 9:4 nor·even any tree), but·yet only the men·of·clay†

G1509 εἰ μή τί êi mḗ tí *conj.* (3x)
Roots:G1508 G5100

G1509.1 COND εἰ μή τί (1x)
2Co 13:5 is in yeu, except·that yeu·are disqualified?

G1509.1 CONJ εἰ μή τί (2x)
Lk 9:13 and two fish, except·that after·traversing, we·
1Co 7:5 deprive one·another, except·that *which* might·be as·

G1510 εἰμί êimí *v.* (141x)
Compare:G1473 G5225 G1510-1 See:G1488 G1498
G1511 G1526 G2070 G2071 G2071-1 G2071-2
G2075 G2076 G2077 G2252 G2258 G2268-1 G0628-1 G2277 G2468 G5600 G5607 xLangAlso:H3068

G1510.1 V-PXI-1S εἰμί (88x)
Jn 1:20 he·affirmed, "I·myself am not the Anointed-One.
Jn 1:21 EliJah?" And he·says, "I·am not." "Are you·
Jn 1:27 ahead of·me) of·whom I·myself am not *even* worthy
Jn 3:28 that I·declared, 'I·myself am not the Anointed-One,'
Jn 3:28 but·rather that 'I·am having·been·dispatched before
Jn 7:28 ·yeu·personally·know from·what·source I·am? Yet I·
Jn 7:29 ·know him, because I·am personally·from him. He·
Jn 7:33 "Yet a·short time am·I with yeu, and·then I·head·on·
Jn 8:16 my verdict is true, because I·am not alone, but·rather
Jn 8:18 I·myself am one testifying concerning my·own·self,
Jn 8:23 down·below; I·myself am birthed·from up·above.
Jn 8:23 ·among this world; I·myself am not from·among this
Jn 9:5 I·should·be in the world, I·am a·light of·the world.
Jn 10:36 ·God,' because I·declared, 'I·am God's Son.'
Jn 13:13 me Mentor and Lord, and yeu·say well, for I·am.
Jn 13:33 "Dear·children, yet a·little·while I·am with yeu.
Jn 14:9 Jesus says to·him, "Am·I so·vast a·time with yeu,
Jn 16:32 should·leave me alone. And·yet I·am not alone,
Jn 17:11 And I·am no longer in the world, but these·men are
Jn 17:14 the world, just·as I·myself am not from·among the
Jn 17:16 the world, just·as I·myself am not from·among the
Jn 18:17 ·this man·of·clay†?" That·man says, "I·am not."
Jn 18:25 That·man denied *it* and declared, "I·am not."
Jn 18:35 Pilate answered, "¿! Am·I myself a·Jew?
Jn 19:21 that this·man declared, 'I·am King of·the Jews.
Lk 1:18 this for·certain? For I·myself am an·old·man, and
Lk 1:19 declared to·him, "I·myself am GabriEl, the·one
Lk 3:16 the strap of·whose shoes I·am not fit to·loose.
Lk 5:8 from me, because I·am a·man full·of·moral·failure,
Lk 7:6 "Lord, do·not be·harassed. For I·am not fit that you·
Lk 7:8 "For even I·myself am a·man·of·clay† being·assigned
Lk 15:19 and am no·longer worthy to·be·called your son;
Lk 15:21 in·the·sight of·you, and I·am no·longer worthy to·
Lk 18:11 'God, I·give·thanks to·you that I·am not just·as the
Lk 19:22 that I·myself am an·unrelenting man·of·clay†,
Lk 22:27 ·one reclining·at·the·meal? But I·myself am in *the*
Lk 22:33 to·him, "Lord, I·am ready to·traverse with you,

Lk 22:58 And Peter declared, "Man·of·clay†, I·am not!"
Ac 10:26 "Stand·up, *for* also·I myself am a·man·of·clay†."
Ac 13:25 yeu·surmise me to·be? I·myself am not *he*. But·
Ac 13:25 the shoes of·whose feet I·am not worthy to·loose.
Ac 21:39 "In·fact, I·myself am a·man·of·clay† *who·is* a·Jew
Ac 22:3 "I·myself am in·fact a·man *who·is* a·Jew, having·
Ac 23:6 "Men, brothers, I·myself am a·Pharisee, a·son of·a·
Ac 25:10 Then Paul declared, "I·am standing at Caesar's
Ac 26:29 to·become such as even·I am, *though* personally·
Ac 27:23 an·angel of·God, of·him·whose I·am and to·whom
Heb 12:21 declared, "I·am frightened·out·of·my·wits and
Mt 3:11 ·than me, whose shoes I·am not fit to·lift·and·carry.
Mt 8:8 was·replying, "Lord, I·am not fit in·order·that you·
Mt 8:9 For even I·myself am a·man·of·clay† under authority,
Mt 11:29 learn from me, because I·am gentle and lowly in·
Mt 18:20 in my name, there am·I in *the* midst of·them.
Mt 20:15 eye evil, because I·myself am beneficially·good?
Mt 27:24 ·the crowd, saying, "I·am blameless of the blood
Mt 27:43 him," for he·declared, 'I·am a·son of·God.'"
Mt 28:20 "And behold, I·myself am with yeu *for* all the days
Mk 1:7 comes right·behind me, of·whom I·am not fit, *even*
Rm 1:14 I·am under·an·obligation both to·Greeks and to·
Rm 7:14 is spiritual, but I·myself am fleshly, having·been·
Rm 11:1 For I·myself also am an·Israelite, from·among
Rm 11:13 in as·much·as I·myself am in·fact an·ambassador
Php 4:11 *that* in whatever·state I·am, to·be self-content
2Pe 1:13 right, for as·long·as I·am in this bodily·tabernacle,
1Co 1:12 "In·fact, I·myself am of·Paul," and "I *am* of·
1Co 3:4 "In·fact, I·myself am of·Paul," and someone·else,
1Co 9:1 Am·I not an·ambassador?
1Co 9:1 Am·I not an·ambassador? Am·I not free?
1Co 9:2 If I·am not an·ambassador to·others, but·yet still I·
1Co 9:2 ·ambassador to·others, but·yet still I·am to·yeu, for
1Co 12:15 foot should·declare, "Because I·am not a·hand, I·
1Co 12:15 I·am not a·hand, I·am not from·among the body,
1Co 12:16 ear should·declare, "Because I·am not an·eye, I·
1Co 12:16 I·am not an·eye, I·am not from·among the body,"
1Co 13:2 and should·not have love, I·am nothing·at·all.
1Co 15:9 For I·myself am the least of·the ambassadors, who
1Co 15:9 of·the ambassadors, who am not fit to·be·called
1Co 15:10 But by·the·grace of·God I·am what I·am, and his
1Co 15:10 But by·the·grace of·God I·am what I·am, and his
2Co 12:10 for whenever I·may·be·weak, then I·am able.
2Co 12:11 of·ambassadors, even·though I·am nothing·at·all.
Col 2:5 in·the flesh, but·yet I·am together with·yeu in·the
1Ti 1:15 ·disqualified·ones, of·whom I·myself am foremost.
Rv 1:18 was dead; and behold, I·am living into the ages of·
Rv 3:17 because you·say, "I·am wealthy. I·have·become·
Rv 18:7 'I·sit·down a·queen, and I·am not a·widow, and no,
Rv 19:10 ·it *that* you·do·not *do·it*. I·am your fellow·slave,
Rv 22:9 ·it *that* you·do·not *do·it*; for I·am your fellow·slave,

G1510.2 V-PXI-1S εἰμί (11x)

Jn 4:26 Jesus says to·her, "It·is·I Myself. *Yes*, the·one
Jn 6:20 But he·says to·them, "It·is·I Myself. Do·not be·
Jn 9:9 *But* that·man was·saying, "It·is·I myself."
Ac 9:5 And the Lord declared, "It·is·I Myself, Jesus, whom
Ac 10:21 declared, "Behold, it·is·I myself whom yeu·seek.
Ac 22:8 And he·declared to me, 'It·is·I Myself, Jesus of·
Ac 26:15 And he·declared, 'It·is·I Myself, Jesus, whom
Mt 14:27 "Be·of·good·courage, it·is·I Myself! Do·not be·
Mt 26:22 "Lord, is·it·I myself?
Mt 26:25 "Rabbi, is·it·I myself?
Mk 6:50 "Be·of·good·courage! It·is·I Myself. Do·not be·

G1510.3 V-PXI-1S εἰμί (42x)

Jn 6:35 declared to·them, "I AM the bread of·life-above.
Jn 6:41 him, because he·declared, "I AM the bread, the·one
Jn 6:48 I AM the bread of·the life-above.
Jn 6:51 I AM the living bread, the·one descending out of·the
Jn 7:34 *me*, and where I AM, *there* yeu·yeurselves are·not
Jn 7:36 *me*? And where I AM, *there* yeu·yeurselves are·not
Jn 8:12 again to·them, saying, "I AM the light of·the world.
Jn 8:24 unless yeu·should·trust that I AM, yeu·shall·die in
Jn 8:28 of·Clay·Man†, yeu·shall·know that I AM, and *that*
Jn 8:58 to·yeu, prior·to AbRaham coming·to·be, I AM."
Jn 10:7 ·certainly, I·say to·yeu, I AM the door of·the sheep.
Jn 10:9 "I AM the door. If someone should·enter·in through
Jn 10:11 "I AM the good shepherd.
Jn 10:14 "I AM the good shepherd, and I·know my *sheep*,
Jn 11:25 declared to·her, "I AM the resurrection and the
Jn 12:26 let·him·follow me; and where I AM, there also my
Jn 13:19 it·should·happen, yeu·may·trust that I AM.
Jn 14:3 yeu to myself in·order·that where I AM, *there* yeu·
Jn 14:6 Jesus says to·him, "I AM the way, and the truth, and
Jn 15:1 "I AM the true vine, and my Father is the farmer.
Jn 15:5 "I AM the vine, yeu *are* the vine·sprouts.
Jn 17:24 ·be with me where I AM, in·order·that they·may·
Jn 18:5 Jesus says to·them, "I AM." And even Judas, the·
Jn 18:6 ·as he·declared to·them, "I AM," they·went·off
Jn 18:8 "I·declared to·yeu that I AM. Accordingly, if yeu·
Jn 18:37 You·yourself say *it·rightly* because I AM a·king, *for*
Lk 21:8 in my name, saying, 'I AM,' and, 'The season has·
Lk 22:70 "Yeu·yeurselves say *it·rightly* because I AM."
Lk 24:39 my feet, that I AM myself. Verify·by·touching me
Ac 18:10 on·account·that I AM with you, and not·even·one·
Mt 22:32 "I AM the God of·AbRaham, and the God of·
Mt 24:5 in my name, saying, 'I AM the Anointed-One,' and
Mk 13:6 name, saying, 'I AM *the Anointed-One*,' and shall·
Mk 14:62 Jesus declared, "I AM, and yeu·shall·gaze·upon
1Pe 1:16 "Yeu·must·be holy, because I AM holy."
Rv 1:8 "I AM the Alpha and the Omega, beginning and end,"
Rv 1:11 saying, "I AM the Alpha and the Omega, the First
Rv 1:17 "Do·not be·afraid; I AM the First and the Last.
Rv 2:23 ·citizenries shall·know that I AM the·one searching
Rv 21:6 "It·has·happened! I AM the Alpha and the Omega,
Rv 22:13 I AM the Alpha and the Omega, beginning and end
Rv 22:16 the Called·Out·citizenries. I AM the root and the

G1511 εἶναι êînai *v.* (130x)

Roots:G1510 Compare:G1096 G5225 See:G2071-1
xLangEquiv:H1961

G1511.1 V-PXN εἶναι (122x)

Jn 1:46 beneficially·good to·be from·out of·Natsareth?
Jn 7:4 when he·himself seeks to·be in freeness·of·speech
Lk 2:4 , on·account·of him being from·among *the* house
Lk 2:6 And it·occurred, with them being there, *that* the days
Lk 2:44 But assuming him to·be in the caravan, they·went a·
Lk 2:49 that it·is·necessary·for me to·be among the·things
Lk 4:41 ·had·personally·known him to·be the Anointed-One.
Lk 5:12 And it·happened with him being in one of·the cities,
Lk 8:38 ·out was·petitioning him to·be together with·him,
Lk 9:18 in his *usual time* to·be praying alone·by·himself,
Lk 9:18 "Who·do the crowds say me to·be?"
Lk 9:20 "And who·do yeu·yeurselves say me to·be?" And
Lk 9:33 "O·Captain, it·is good for·us to·be here, and we·
Lk 11:1 it·happened, as he·himself was praying in a·certain
Lk 11:8 ·not give to·him on·account·of *him* being his friend,
Lk 14:26 his·own soul also, he·is·not able to·be my disciple.
Lk 14:27 right·behind me, is·not able to·be my disciple.
Lk 14:33 all his holdings, he·is·not able to·be my disciple.
Lk 19:11 on·account·of him being near to·JeruSalem, and
Lk 20:6 having·been·persuaded *for* John to·be a·prophet."
Lk 20:20 themselves to·be righteous·men in·order·that they·
Lk 20:41 *for* the Anointed-One to·be David's Son?
Lk 22:24 *concerning* which of·them is·reputed to·be greater.
Lk 23:2 to·Caesar, saying himself to·be *the* Anointed-One,
Ac 2:12 "What·is this·thing actually·supposed to·be?"
Ac 4:32 *for* any of·his holdings to·be his·own; but·rather for·
Ac 5:36 rose·up, saying himself to·be someone (to·whom a·
Ac 8:9 of·Samaria, saying himself to·be someone great;
Ac 8:37 "I·trust Jesus Anointed to·be the Son of·God.
Ac 13:25 'Whom·do yeu·surmise me to·be? I·myself am not
Ac 13:47 "I·have·placed you to·be a·light for Gentiles, *for*
Ac 16:13 where prayer was·accustomed to·be. And sitting·
Ac 16:15 "If yeu·have·judged me to·be trustworthy to·the
Ac 17:7 decrees of·Caesar, saying *that* there·is another king,
Ac 17:18 Now he·seems to·be an·ardent·proclaimer of·the
Ac 17:20 what these·things are·actually·supposed to·be."
Ac 17:29 not to·assume *for* the divine to·be like gold or
Ac 18:3 And on·account·of being of·the same·trade, he·was·
Ac 18:15 ·definitely·not willing to·be judge of·these·things."
Ac 18:28 the Scriptures, *for* Jesus to·be the Anointed-One.
Ac 19:1 Now with Apollos being in Corinth, it·happened
Ac 27:4 ·to Cyprus, on·account·of the winds being contrary.
Ac 28:6 ·their·minds, they·were·saying him to·be a·god.
Heb 5:12 the time being·due *for·yeu* to·be instructors, *yeu·*
Heb 11:4 through which he·was·attested to·be righteous,
Heb 12:11 present, does·not seem to·be joyous, but·rather
Gal 2:6 as·for the·ones seeming to·be something *important*
Gal 2:9 and John, the·ones seeming to·be pillars, they·gave
Gal 4:21 to·me, the·ones wanting to·be under Torah-Law,
Gal 6:3 For if any·man supposes·himself to·be something,
Mt 16:13 "Who·do the men·of·clay† say me to·be— *me*, the
Mt 16:15 "But yeu·yeurselves, who·do yeu·say me to·be?"
Mt 17:4 "Lord, it·is good for·us to·be here. If you·want, we·
Mt 19:21 to·him, "If you·want to·be complete, head·on·out,
Mt 20:27 and whoever should·want to·be foremost among
Mt 22:23 the·ones saying *there·is* not to·be a·resurrection,
Mk 6:49 the sea, they·supposed *it* to·be a·phantom, and
Mk 8:27 "Who·do the men·of·clay† say me to·be?"
Mk 8:29 "But who·do yeu·yeurselves say me to·be?" And
Mk 9:5 "Rabbi, it·is good for·us to·be here. And we·should·
Mk 9:35 "If any·man wants to·be first, *the same* shall·be last
Mk 12:18 who say *that there·is* not to·be a·resurrection, and
Mk 14:64 they all condemned him to·be held·liable of·death.
Rm 1:20 ·made— such·for them to·be without·exoneration,
Rm 1:22 Professing·themselves to·be wise, they·already·
Rm 2:19 within·yourself to·be a·guide of·blind·men, a·light
Rm 3:9 both Jews and Greeks, all to·be under moral·failure.
Rm 3:26 of·God toward the·one himself being righteous,
Rm 4:11 in·order·for him to·be father of·all the·ones
Rm 4:13 Seed (the·one himself to·be *the* heir of·the world),
Rm 4:16 in·order·for the promise to·be steadfast to·all the
Rm 6:11 must·reckon also yeurselves to·be in·fact dead to·
Rm 7:3 *such·for* herself not to·be an·adulteress by·becoming
Rm 8:29 in·order·for his *Son* to·be firstborn among many
Rm 9:3 myself to·be irrevocably·damned·to·destruction, *cut·*
Rm 14:14 to·the·one reckoning something to·be defiled. For·
Rm 15:16 *·assigned* for me to·be a·public·servant of·Jesus
Rm 16:19 yeu, in·fact, to·be wise in·regard·to the·thing
Jac 1:18 of·truth, for us to·be a·certain firstfruit of·his
Jac 1:26 If any·man among yeu seems to·be religious, *yet* not
Jac 4:4 would be·definitely·willing to·be a·friend of·the
Php 1:23 ·break·camp and to·be together with·Anointed-One
Php 2:6 it not open·plunder to·be equal with·God,
Php 3:8 ·consider all·things to·be a·total·loss through the
Php 3:8 ·consider *them* to·be as·things·thrown·to·dogs, in·
Php 4:11 in whatever·state I·am, to·be self-content *with·that*.
1Pe 1:21 — such·for yeur trust and expectation to·be in God.
1Pe 5:12 exhorting and further·testifying this to·be *the* true
1Th 2:6 from others, *though* being·able to·be a·burden as
Tit 1:7 overseer to·be without·any·charge·of·wrong·doing as
Tit 2:2 *for* old·men to·be sober-minded, morally·worthy·of·
Tit 2:4 young·women to·be affectionate·to·their·husbands
Tit 2:9 to·their·own masters *and* to·be most·satisfying in all
Tit 3:1 to·readily·comply, to·be ready particularly·for
Tit 3:2 to·revile no·man, to·be not·quarrelsome, *but* fair,
1Co 3:18 If any·man among yeu seems to·be wise in this
1Co 7:7 For I·want all men·of·clay† to·be also as myself.
1Co 7:25 ·shown·mercy from *the* Lord to·be trustworthy.
1Co 7:32 But I·want yeu to·be without·anxiety. The
1Co 10:6 for us not to·be men·longing·after bad·things,
1Co 11:16 But if any·man seems to·be contentious, we·
1Co 11:19 it·is·necessary·for *there* also to·be factions among
1Co 12:23 body, which·we·presume to·be less·honorable,
1Co 14:37 If someone supposes·himself to·be a·prophet or
2Co 5:9 being·absent·abroad, to·be most·satisfying to·him.
2Co 7:11 ·demonstrated yeurselves to·be morally·clean in
2Co 9:5 *for* the·same to·be ready in·this·manner: as a·
2Co 10:7 has·confidence in·himself to·be of·Anointed-One,
2Co 11:16 not anyone should·suppose me to·be impetuous;

Eph 1:4 before *the* world's conception for·us to·be holy and
Eph 1:12 in·order·for it to·be us, *his Redeemed-Kinsmen*, for
Eph 3:6 *The revealing as·for* the Gentiles to·be co-heirs,
1Ti 1:7 wanting to·be teachers·of·Torah-Law, not
1Ti 2:12 ·over a·man, but·rather *she·is* to·be in stillness.
1Ti 3:2 the overseer to·be above·all·blame·and·suspicion, a·
1Ti 6:5 ·of·Devout·Reverence *itself* to·be a·means·of·gain.
1Ti 6:18 in good deeds, to·be good·at·kind·giving *and*
2Ti 2:24 ·quarrel, but·rather to·be pleasantly·engageable to
1Jn 2:9 The·one saying *himself* to·be in the light, and hating
Rv 2:2 you·tried the·ones professing to·be ambassadors and
Rv 2:9 of·the·ones saying themselves to·be Jews and are not,
Rv 3:9 (the·ones saying themselves to·be Jews and are not,

G1511.1 V-PXN@ εἶναι (2x)
Lk 20:27 *by·saying that* there·is not a·resurrection) inquired·
Ac 23:8 *the* Sadducees say *that* there·is not a·resurrection,

EG1511.1 (2x)
Gal 2:6 for the·ones seeming *to·be something important*—
Rm 4:12 and *in·order·for him to·be* a·father of·circumcision

G1511.2 V-PXN εἶναι (1x)
Jn 17:5 I·was·having with you before the world existed.

EG1511.2 (1x)
1Pe 2:16 *Exist* as free·men, yet not retaining the liberty as a·

G1511.3 V-PXN εἶναι (1x)
1Co 7:26 good for·a·man·of·clay† to·behave in·this·manner:

EG1511.3 (1x)
1Pe 2:16 for·the depravity, but·rather *behave* as slaves of·

G1512 εἴ περ êí pêr *cond.* (6x)
Roots:G1487 G4007

G1512.1 COND εἴπερ (1x)
1Pe 2:3 if·ever "yeu·tasted that Yahweh *is* kind.

G1512.2 COND εἴπερ (3x)
Rm 8:9 but·rather in Spirit, if·perhaps God's Spirit dwells
1Co 8:5 For even if·perhaps they·are being·referred·to·as
1Co 15:15 he·did·not awaken, if·perhaps, by·inference,

G1512.3 COND εἴπερ (2x)
Rm 8:17 ·Anointed-One, since we·suffer·together *with·him*
2Th 1:6 (since *it·is* a·righteous·thing with God to·

G1513 εἴ πως êí pōs *cond.* (3x)
Roots:G1487 G4458

G1513 COND-ADV εἴπως (3x)
Ac 27:12 ·also, if·somehow they·might·be·able to·arrive at
Rm 1:10 prayers. Petitioning, if·somehow even·now at·last
Php 3:11 *in·order·that* if·somehow, I·may·attain to the

G1514 εἰρηνεύω êirēnêúō *v.* (4x)
Roots:G1515 See:G1518

G1514.1 V-PAM-2P εἰρηνεύετε (3x)
Mk 9:50 in yeurselves, and be·peaceful with one·another."
1Th 5:13 ·of their work. Be·peaceful among yeurselves.
2Co 13:11 contemplate the same·thing, be·peaceful; and the

G1514.2 V-PAP-NPM εἰρηνεύοντες (1x)
Rm 12:18 for yeur part, behaving·peacefully with all men·

G1515 εἰρήνη êirḗnē *n.* (92x)
See:G1514 G1518 xLangAlso:H7965 A8001

G1515.1 N-NSF εἰρήνη (40x)
Jn 20:19 And he·says to·them, "Peace *be* to·yeu."
Jn 20:21 declared to·them again, "Peace *be* to·yeu. Just·as
Jn 20:26 And he·declared, "Peace *be* to·yeu."
Lk 2:14 highest, and on earth, peace! Among men·of·clay†,
Lk 10:5 yeu·should·enter, first say, 'Peace to·this house.'
Lk 10:6 should·be there, yeur peace shall·rest upon it.
Lk 19:38 *the* name of·Yahweh!' Peace in heaven and glory
Lk 24:36 of·them, and says to·them, "Peace *be* to·yeu."
Gal 1:3 Grace *be* to·yeu and peace from Father God, and
Gal 5:22 Spirit is love, joy, peace, long-suffering, kindness,
Gal 6:16 ·march·orderly by·this standard, peace *be* upon
Mt 10:13 should·be worthy, *let* yeur peace come upon it, but
Mt 10:13 ·not be worthy, *let* yeur peace be·returned to yeu.
Rm 1:7 Grace to·yeu and peace from God our Father and *the*
Rm 2:10 glory, honor, and peace, to·every·man, the·one
Rm 8:6 the disposition of·the Spirit *is* life-above and peace—
Rm 14:17 but·rather righteousness, peace, and joy in Holy
Jud 1:2 May mercy, and peace, and love be·multiplied to·
Php 1:2 Grace *be* to·yeu, and peace, from God our Father
Php 4:7 And the peace of·God, the·one extending·itself·
1Pe 1:2 May grace and peace be·multiplied to·yeu.
1Pe 5:14 with a·kiss of·love. Peace to·yeu, to·all the·ones in
2Pe 1:2 May grace and peace be·multiplied to·yeu in *the*
1Th 1:1 Grace *be* to·yeu, and peace, from God our Father,
1Th 5:3 For whenever they·should·say, "Peace and security,
2Th 1:2 Grace to·yeu, and peace, from God our Father and
Tit 1:4 Grace, mercy, *and* peace, from Father God and *the*
1Co 1:3 Grace *be* to·yeu, and peace, from God our Father,
2Co 1:2 Grace to·yeu, and peace, from God our Father and
Eph 1:2 Grace *be* to·yeu, and peace, from God our Father
Eph 2:14 For he·himself is our peace, the·one already·
Eph 6:23 Peace *be* to·the brothers, and love with trust from
Col 1:2 Grace *be* to·yeu, and peace, from God our Father
Col 3:15 And let the peace of·God arbitrate in yeur hearts,
Phm 1:3 Grace to·yeu, and peace, from God our Father and
1Ti 1:2 Grace, mercy, *and* peace from God our Father and
2Ti 1:2 Grace, mercy, *and* peace, from Father God and
2Jn 1:3 us, mercy, *and* peace, personally·from Father God,
3Jn 1:14 mouth to mouth. Peace *be* to·you. The friends
Rv 1:4 Grace *be* to·yeu, and peace, from the·one (the·one

G1515.1 N-ASF εἰρήνην (25x)
Jn 14:27 "Peace I·leave with·yeu; my peace I·give to·yeu.
Jn 14:27 "Peace I·leave with·yeu; my peace I·give to·yeu.
Jn 16:33 in·order·that in me yeu·may·have peace. In the
Lk 7:50 "Your trust has·saved you; traverse in peace."
Lk 8:48 trust has·made you safe·and·well; depart in peace."
Lk 12:51 ·suppose that I·came·directly to·give peace on the
Lk 14:32 he·asks·of the *conditions* specifically·for peace.
Lk 19:42 day, the·things pertaining·to your peace! But now
Ac 7:26 and sternly·exhorted them *to·be* at peace, declaring,
Ac 9:31 and Samaria were·having peace, being·edified. And
Ac 10:36 proclaiming·the·good·news of·peace through Jesus
Ac 12:20 bedroom, they·requested peace, on·account·of
Heb 12:14 Pursue peace with all *men*, also the renewed·
Mt 10:34 assume that I·came to·cast peace upon the earth; I·
Mt 10:34 I·did·not come to·cast peace, but·rather a·dagger.
Mk 5:34 you safe·and·well. Head·on·out in peace and be
Rm 5:1 as·a·result of·trust, we·have peace toward God
Rm 10:15 who·are·proclaiming·good·news of·peace, of·the·
Jac 3:18 is·sown in peace by·the·ones making peace.
1Pe 3:11 *the* beneficially·good·thing; seek peace and pursue
2Th 3:16 of·Peace himself grant yeu Peace throughout every
Eph 2:15 one brand-new man·of·clay†, *thus* making peace,
Eph 2:17 coming, he·proclaimed 'peace to·yeu, the·ones at·
2Ti 2:22 trust, love, peace, with the·ones calling·upon the
Rv 6:4 ·sitting·down on it, to·take the peace from the earth,

G1515.1 N-DSF εἰρήνῃ (8x)
Lk 2:29 now dismiss your slave in peace, according·to your
Lk 11:21 ·over his·own mansion, his holdings are at peace.
Ac 16:36 Now accordingly, going·forth, traverse in peace."
Jac 2:16 ·them, "Head·on·out in peace, be·yeu·warmed and
Jac 3:18 ·righteousness is·sown in peace by·the·ones making
2Pe 3:14 to·be·found by·him in peace, without·stain and
1Co 7:15 such·cases, but God has·called us forth in peace.
1Co 16:11 ·his·journey in peace in·order·that he·may·come

G1515.1 N-GSF εἰρήνης (19x)
Lk 1:79 to·fully·direct our feet into *the* way of·peace."
Lk 10:6 And, in·fact, if a·son of·peace should·be there,
Ac 15:33 a·time, they·were·dismissed with peace from the
Ac 24:2 "While·obtaining much peace on·account·of you,
Heb 7:2 "King of·Salem," which is, King of·Peace.
Heb 11:31 ·being·obstinate, accepting the spies with peace.
Heb 13:20 Now *may* the God of·peace, the·one bringing·up
Rm 3:17 And a·way of·peace, they·did·not know.
Rm 14:19 ·should·pursue the·things of·peace and the·things
Rm 15:13 ·fill yeu with·all joy and peace in the·one to·trust,
Rm 15:33 And the God of·Peace *be* with yeu all.
Rm 16:20 And the God of·peace shall·shatter the
Php 4:9 practice— and the God of·peace shall·be with yeu
1Th 5:23 And may the God of·Peace himself make yeu·
2Th 3:16 Now may the Lord of·Peace himself grant yeu
1Co 14:33 *the God* of·chaos, but·rather of·peace, as in all
2Co 13:11 and the God of·love and peace shall·be with yeu.
Eph 4:3 the oneness of·the Spirit in the joint·bond of·peace.
Eph 6:15 in a·state·of·readiness of·the good·news of·peace.

G1516 εἰρηνικός êirēnikós *adj.* (2x)
Roots:G1515

G1516.1 A-ASF εἰρηνικόν (1x)
Heb 12:11 it·yields·forth a·peaceful fruit of·righteousness

G1516.2 A-NSF εἰρηνική (1x)
Jac 3:17 in·fact, morally·clean, then peaceable, fair *and*

G1517 εἰρηνο•ποιέω êirēnôpôiéō *v.* (1x)
Roots:G1518

G1517.1 V-AAP-NSM εἰρηνοποιήσας (1x)
Col 1:20 and after·making·peace through the blood of

G1518 εἰρηνο•ποιός êirēnôpôiós *adj.* (1x)
Roots:G1515 G4160 See:G1517

G1518.2 A-NPM εἰρηνοποιοί (1x)
Mt 5:9 "Supremely·blessed *are* the peacemakers, because

G1519 εἰς êis *prep.* (1746x)
See:G2080 G1519-1
(abbreviated listing for G1519)

EG1519 (3x)
(list for EG1519: excluded)

G1519.1 PREP εἰς (678x)
(list for G1519.1:PREP excluded)

EG1519.1 (2x)
(list for EG1519.1: excluded)

G1519.2 PREP εἰς (436x)
(list for G1519.2:PREP excluded)

EG1519.2 (1x)
(list for EG1519.2: excluded)

G1519.3 PREP εἰς (205x)
(list for G1519.3:PREP excluded)

EG1519.3 (2x)
(list for EG1519.3: excluded)

G1519.4 PREP εἰς (181x)
(list for G1519.4:PREP excluded)

G1519.5 PREP εἰς (33x)
(list for G1519.5:PREP excluded)

EG1519.5 (3x)
(list for EG1519.5: excluded)

G1519.6 PREP εἰς (7x)
(list for G1519.6:PREP excluded)

G1519.7 PREP εἰς (36x)
(list for G1519.7:PREP excluded)

G1519.8 PREP εἰς (21x)
(list for G1519.8:PREP excluded)

G1519.9 PREP εἰς (19x)
(list for G1519.9:PREP excluded)

EG1519.9 (1x)
(list for EG1519.9: excluded)

G1519.10 PREP εἰς (35x)
(list for G1519.10:PREP excluded)

G1519.11 PREP εἰς (40x)
(list for G1519.11:PREP excluded)

EG1519.11 (1x)
(list for EG1519.11: excluded)

G1519.12 PREP εἰς (21x)
(list for G1519.12:PREP excluded)

G1519.13 PREP εἰς (7x)
(list for G1519.13:PREP excluded)

G1519.14 PREP εἰς (14x)
(list for G1519.14:PREP excluded)

G1519-1 εἵς ếís *prep.* (18x)
Roots:G1519
xLangEquiv:HFP5A

G1519-1.2 PREP εἵς (14x)
Jn 16:20 but·yet your grief shall·become a·distinct joy.
Lk 20:17 the·same has·now·become the·distinct head corner
Ac 4:11 *this·is* the·one becoming the·distinct head corner
Heb 1:5 "I·myself shall·be his·own distinct Father, and he·

Heb 1:5 and he·himself shall·be my·own distinct Son"?
Heb 8:10 hearts, and I·shall·be their·own distinct God, and
Heb 8:10 they·themselves shall·be my·own distinct People.
Mt 21:42 the·same has·now·become the·distinct head corner
Mk 12:10 ·same has·now·become the·distinct head corner
1Pe 2:7 this·one has·now·become the·distinct head corner
2Co 6:16 *them*; and I·shall·be their·own distinct God, and
2Co 6:16 they·themselves shall·be my·own distinct People."
2Co 6:18 and "I·shall·be yeur·own distinct Father, and yeu·
2Co 6:18 yeu·yeurselves shall·be my·own distinct sons and

G1519-1.3 PREP εἰς (4x)

Mt 19:5 ·his wife, and the two shall·be distinctly one flesh'"?
Mk 10:8 and the two shall·be distinctly one flesh.'' As·such,
1Co 6:16 two,"' he·replies, "'shall·be distinctly one flesh.'"
Eph 5:31 wife, and the two shall·be distinctly one flesh."

G1520 εἷς hêîs *n.* (276x)

ἕν hén [including the neuter (etc.)]

Compare:G0846 G2398 See:G1527 G3367 G3391 G3762
xLangEquiv:H0259

G1520.1 -- (1x)

Lk 17:36 ·be in the field; one shall·be·personally·taken, and

G1520.1 N-NSM εἷς (94x)

Jn 1:40 Simon Peter's brother, was one from·among the two
Jn 6:8 One from·among his disciples, Andrew, Simon Peter's
Jn 6:70 the twelve, yet one from·among yeu is a·slanderer.
Jn 6:71 to·hand him over, being one from·among the twelve.
Jn 7:50 *Jesus* by·night *and* being one from·among them)
Jn 10:16 it·shall·become one flock *and* one shepherd.
Jn 11:49 And a·certain one from·among them, *named*
Jn 11:50 for·us that one man·of·clay† should·die on·behalf
Jn 12:2 was one of·the·ones reclining·together·at·the·meal
Jn 12:4 So·then one from·among his disciples (Judas
Jn 13:21 I·say to·yeu that one from·among yeu shall·hand
Jn 13:23 at Jesus' bosom was one of·his disciples whom
Jn 18:22 ·him declaring these·things, one of·the assistants
Jn 18:26 One from·among the slaves of·the designated·high·
Jn 19:34 But·rather one of·the soldiers jabbed his side with·
Jn 20:24 But Thomas (one from·among the twelve, the·one
Lk 7:41 two needy·debtors; the one was·owing five·hundred
Lk 9:8 and by·others that one of·the ancient prophets rose·
Lk 17:15 And one from·among them, seeing that he·was·
Lk 17:34 one couch; the one shall·be·personally·taken, and
Lk 18:10 ·Atrium to·pray, the one *being* a·Pharisee and the
Lk 18:19 ·one·at·all *is* beneficially·good, except one: God.
Lk 22:47 ·one being·referred·to·as Judas, one of·the twelve,
Lk 22:50 And a·certain one from·among them smote the
Lk 23:39 And one of·the criminals who·were·hanging was·
Ac 2:6 ·confused, because each one was·hearing them
Ac 4:32 was one. And not·even one was·saying *for* any of·
Ac 11:28 And one from·among them by·the·name·of Agabus
Gal 3:20 is not *a·mediator* of·one *party*, but God is one.
Gal 3:28 for yeu are all one in Anointed-One YeShua.
Mt 8:19 And one scribe coming·alongside, declared to·him,
Mt 18:14 ·of·*his*·will that one of·these little·ones should·
Mt 18:24 to·him, one·man delinquent of·ten·thousand
Mt 19:16 And behold, one coming·alongside him declared,
Mt 19:17 ·*is* no·one·at·all beneficially·good except one, God
Mt 20:21 two sons of·mine may·sit, one at your right·hand
Mt 20:21 ·sit, one at your right·hand and one at *your* left, in
Mt 22:35 And one from·among them, *who·was* an·expert·in·
Mt 23:8 'Rabbi,' for one is yeur Preeminent·Leader, *that·is*
Mt 23:9 father upon the earth, for one is yeur Father, the·one
Mt 23:10 ·yeu·be·called preeminent·leaders, for one is yeur
Mt 24:40 in the field; the one is·personally·taken, and the
Mt 24:40 one is·personally·taken, and the *other* one is·left.
Mt 26:14 Then one of·the twelve, the·one being·referred·to·
Mt 26:21 I·say to·yeu, that one from·among yeu shall·hand
Mt 26:47 speaking, behold, Judas, one of·the twelve, came,
Mt 26:51 And behold, one of·the·ones with YeShua, upon·
Mt 27:38 being·crucified together with·him, one at *the* right·
Mt 27:38 with·him, one at *the* right·hand and one at *the* left.
Mt 27:48 And immediately one from·among them, after·
Mk 2:7 ·able to·forgive moral·failures, except one *only*: God
Mk 5:22 there·comes one of·the directors·of·the·gathering,
Mk 6:15 "It·is a·prophet, or as one of·the prophets."
Mk 9:17 And one·man, answering from·among the crowd,
Mk 10:17 same roadway, one·man, after·running·forward
Mk 10:18 no·one·at·all beneficially·good except one, *that·is*,
Mk 10:37 to·us that we·may·sit, one at your right·hand and
Mk 10:37 ·sit, one at your right·hand and one at your left, in
Mk 12:28 ·and·discussing·together, one of·the scribes,
Mk 12:29 O·IsraEl: Yahweh our God, Yahweh is one.
Mk 12:32 truth, because "there·is one God, and there·is not
Mk 13:1 out of·the Sanctuary·Atrium, one of·his disciples
Mk 14:10 Then Judas IsCariot, one of·the twelve, went·off
Mk 14:18 "Certainly I·say to·yeu, that one from·among yeu,
Mk 14:20 to·them, "*It·is* one from·among the twelve, the·
Mk 14:43 Judas comes·openly, being one of·the twelve,
Mk 14:47 But someone, one of·the·ones standing·nearby,
Mk 15:36 And one·man, after·running and overfilling a·
Rm 3:10 "There·is none righteous," "not·even one."
Rm 3:30 since·indeed *it·is* one God who, *from·among both*,
Rm 12:5 Anointed-One, and each one the members of·one·
Jac 2:19 You·yourself trust that there·is one God. You·do
Jac 4:12 There·is the one lawmaker, the·one being·able to·
1Th 5:11 one·another, and edify one the other, just·as also
1Co 4:6 in·order·that not one *of* yeu·may·be·puffed·up over
1Co 6:5 among yeu? Not·even one that shall·be·able to·
1Co 8:4 *there·is* not·even·one other God, yet·not·even one.
1Co 8:6 but·yet to·us *there·is but* one God, the Father (from·
1Co 8:6 *exist* for him) and one Lord, Jesus Anointed
1Co 9:24 in·fact all run, but *that only* one receives the prize?
1Co 10:17 *being* the many, we·are one bread *and* one Body.
1Co 14:27 apiece, and one must·thoroughly·translate.
2Co 5:14 this·thing: that if one died on·behalf·of·all, then·
Eph 4:5 one Lord, one trust, one immersion,
Eph 4:6 one God and Father of·all: the·one over all and
1Ti 2:5 For *there·is* one God, and *there·is* one mediator
1Ti 2:5 ·*is* one God, and *there·is* one mediator *between* God
Rv 5:5 And one from·among the Elders says to·me, "Do·not
Rv 7:13 Then one from·among the Elders answered, saying
Rv 17:1 And there·came one from·among the seven angels,
Rv 17:10 The five fell, and the one is, *and* the other did·not·
Rv 18:21 And one strong angel took·up a·stone as a·great
Rv 21:9 And there·came to me one of·the seven angels (of·
Rv 21:21 pearls; again, each one of·the gates was *made* out

G1520.1 N-NSN ἕν (43x)

Jn 1:3 apart·from him not·even one·thing came·to·be that
Jn 6:22 other small·boat there except that one into which his
Jn 10:30 I·myself and the Father are one."
Jn 17:11 to·me, in·order·that they·may·be one, just·as we·
Jn 17:21 "in·order·that they·all may·be one, just·as you,
Jn 17:21 "in·order·that they also may·be one in us— "in·
Jn 17:22 — "in·order·that they·may·be one, just·as we·
Jn 17:22 they·may·be one, just·as we·ourselves are one,
Lk 12:6 assarion·coins? And·yet not one from·among them
Ac 23:6 already·knowing that the one part were Sadducees
Mt 5:18 earth should·pass·away, not one iota or one tiny·
Mt 10:29 ·coin? And not one from·among them shall·fall
Mt 18:12 *has* a·hundred sheep, and one from·among them
Mk 4:8 and it·was·bearing *fruit*: one *seed* thirtyfold, and
Mk 4:8 one *seed* thirtyfold, and one *seed* sixtyfold, and one
Mk 4:8 one *seed* sixtyfold, and one *seed* a·hundredfold."
Mk 4:20 ·accept *it*, and bear·fruit: one *seed* thirtyfold, and
Mk 4:20 one *seed* thirtyfold, and one *seed* sixtyfold, and
Mk 4:20 one *seed* sixtyfold, and one *seed* a·hundredfold."
Mk 10:21 and declared to·him, "One·thing you lack, head·
Rm 12:5 we (the many) are one Body in Anointed-One, and
Php 3:13 But in·fact, *there·is* one·thing *that·I·do*: forgetting
2Pe 3:8 But *in* this one·thing, do·not be·oblivious, O·yeu
1Co 3:8 and the·one watering are one, and each·man shall·
1Co 6:16 being·tightly·joined to·the prostitute is one body?
1Co 6:17 ·one being·tightly·joined to·the Lord is one spirit.
1Co 10:17 many, we·are one bread *and* one Body. For all *of*·
1Co 11:5 ·shame her head, for it·is one and the same as·the
1Co 12:11 all these·things operate by·the one and the very·
1Co 12:12 For exactly·as the body is one and has many
1Co 12:12 (being many) are one body, in·this·manner also *is*
1Co 12:14 For even the Body is not one member, but·rather
1Co 12:18 ·placed the members, each one of·them, in the
1Co 12:19 And if they·were all one member, where·is the
1Co 12:20 in·fact *they·are* many members, but one Body.
1Co 12:26 And if one member suffers, all the members
1Co 12:26 ·together *with·it*; or·if one member is·glorified,
Eph 4:4 *There·is* one Body, and one Spirit— just·as also yeu·
Eph 4:4 *There·is* one Body, and one Spirit— just·as also
Eph 4:5 one Lord, one trust, one immersion,
1Jn 5:7 And these three are one.
Rv 4:8 *the* four living·beings, each one itself, was·having
Rv 15:7 And one from·among the four living·beings gave to·

G1520.1 N-ASM ἕνα (46x)

Jn 8:41 out of·sexual·immorality. We·have one Father, God!
Jn 18:14 *for* one man·of·clay† to·be·completely·destroyed
Jn 18:39 that I·should·fully·release to·yeu one·man at the
Jn 20:7 having·been·swathed in one place completely·apart.
Jn 20:12 in white sitting·down, one alongside the head, and
Jn 20:12 one alongside the head, and one alongside the feet,
Lk 12:25 by·being·anxious is·able to·add one half·step to his
Lk 15:19 your son; make me as one of·your hired·men.'"
Lk 15:26 And summoning one of·his servant·boys, he·
Lk 16:5 "And summoning each one of·his lord's needy·
Lk 16:13 for either he·shall·hate the one and shall·love the
Lk 17:2 he·should·cause·the·moral·failure·of one of·these
Lk 20:3 "And·I shall·ask·of yeu one question, and yeu·must·
Lk 23:17 to·fully·release one·man to·them annually·at·this
Ac 1:22 of·these·men *for* one to·become a·witness together
Ac 1:24 expressly·indicate which one from·among these
Ac 2:3 to·them, and it·settled upon each one of·them.
Ac 20:31 I·did·not cease admonishing each one, night and
Ac 23:17 So after·summoning one of·the centurions, Paul
Gal 4:22 had two sons, one birthed·from·out the maidservant,
Gal 4:22 the maidservant, and one birthed·from·out the free·
Mt 6:24 For either he·shall·hate the one and shall·love the
Mt 6:27 yeu by·being·anxious is·able to·add one half·step to
Mt 10:42 whoever should·give to·one of·these little·ones a·
Mt 13:46 who upon·finding one extremely·valuable pearl,
Mt 16:14 *yet* others *say* JeremIah, or one of·the prophets."
Mt 18:6 entice·or·cause·the·moral·failure·of one of·these
Mt 18:16 *then* personally·take with you one or two more,
Mt 18:28 after·going·forth, found one of·his fellow·slaves
Mt 21:24 "I·also shall·ask·of yeu one question, which if yeu·
Mt 23:15 parched·ground to·make one convert·to·Judaism,
Mk 8:14 and except *for* one loaf·of·bread, they·were·not
Mk 8:28 *say*, EliJah, and others, one of·the prophets."
Mk 9:42 entice·or·cause·the·moral·failure·of one of·the
Mk 11:29 "I·shall·inquire·of yeu also one question; so·then
Mk 12:6 "So·then, yet having one son, his well-beloved, he·
Mk 15:6 ·was·fully·releasing to·them one chained·prisoner,
Mk 15:27 they·crucify two robbers: one at his·right·hand,
Mk 15:27 robbers: one at his·right·hand, and one at his left.
Jac 4:13 city, and should·continue there *for* one year, and
1Th 2:11 Exactly·as yeu·have·seen (each one of·yeu), how
1Co 14:31 For yeu·are·able, each one, all to·prophesy, in·
Eph 2:15 two in himself into one brand-new man·of·clay†,
Eph 5:33 ·yeurselves (accordingly each one in·that·manner)
Rv 19:17 And I·saw one angel standing in the sun; and he·
Rv 22:2 ·forth its fruit according·to each one's month. And

G1520.1 N-ASN ἕν (26x)

Jn 7:21 and declared to·them, "I·did one work, and yeu all
Jn 9:25 personally·know. One·thing I·do·personally·know,
Jn 11:52 ·that also he·should·gather·together into one, the
Jn 21:25 did, which if each one should·be·written, I·imagine
Lk 5:3 But embarking into one of·the sailboats, which was
Lk 12:27 in all his glory was·arrayed as one of·these.
Lk 15:4 that after·completely·losing one from·among them,
Lk 18:22 "Yet for·yourself, one·thing remains·left·undone.
Ac 21:19 each and·every one of·those·things·which God did
Ac 28:25 ·themselves, with·Paul declaring one utterance,

Mt 5:29 it·is·advantageous for·you that one of·your members
Mt 5:30 it·is·advantageous for·you that one of·your members
Mt 5:41 ·and·impose·upon you *to·head·out·for* one mile,
Mt 6:29 in all his glory, was·arrayed as one of·these.
Mt 12:11 ·be from·among yeu that shall·have one sheep, that
Mt 18:5 And whoever should·accept one such little·child in
Mt 25:15 two, and to·another one, to·each·man according·to
Mt 25:18 the·one receiving the one *talant·of·silver* dug in
Mt 25:24 the·one having·received the one talant·of·silver,
Mt 27:14 answer to him not·even one utterance, such·for the
Mk 9:37 "Whoever should·accept one of·the little·children
Php 2:2 love, contemplating the one jointly·common·soul.
1Co 12:13 were all immersed into one Body, whether Jews
1Co 12:13 or free; and all are·given·drink into one Spirit.
Eph 2:14 the·one already·making the both one, and already·
1Jn 5:8 And the three are in the one.

G1520.1 N-DSM ἑνί (13x)

Lk 4:40 and laying his hands on·each one of·them, he·both·
Lk 11:46 do·not reach·for the loads with·one of·yeur fingers.
Lk 12:52 five in one house having·been·thoroughly·divided,
Lk 15:7 heaven over one morally·disqualified·man repenting
Lk 15:10 ·God over one morally·disqualified·man repenting.
Lk 15:15 he·tightly·joined·himself to·one of·the citizens of·
Gal 5:14 Torah-Law is·completely·fulfilled in one saying, in
Mt 20:13 But answering one of·them, he·declared,
Mt 25:40 in as·much·as yeu·did *it* to·one of·the least of·these
Mt 25:45 as·much·as yeu·did·not do *it* to·one of·the least of·
Jac 2:10 but shall·slip·up in one *point*, he·has·become held·
2Co 11:2 for I·betrothed yeu to·one husband, to·present *yeu*
Eph 4:7 the Grace is·given to·each one of·us according·to

G1520.1 N-DSN ἑνί (7x)

Rm 12:4 exactly·as we·have many members in one body, but
Rm 15:6 with·the·same·determination *and* with one mouth,
Php 1:27 — that yeu·stand·fast in one spirit, with·one soul
1Co 12:13 For even by one Spirit we·ourselves were all
Eph 2:16 ·reconcile the both to·God in one body through the
Eph 2:18 the embraceable·access to the Father by one Spirit.
Col 3:15 which also yeu·were·called·forth in one Body; and

G1520.1 N-GSM ἑνός (26x)

Lk 16:13 or he·shall·hold·tightly to·one and shall·despise
Ac 17:27 ·being not at·a·distance from each one of·us.
Ac 21:26 should·be·offered on·behalf of·each one of·them.
Heb 2:11 ·made·holy *are* all birthed·from·out of·one *Father*.
Heb 11:12 Therefore, also from one·man, even these *many*
Gal 3:20 the mediator is not *a·mediator* of·one *party*, but
Mt 6:24 or·else he·shall·hold·tightly to·one and shall·despise
Rm 3:12 ·kindness; there·is not so·much·as one."
Rm 5:12 this: *that* just·as through one man·of·clay†, Moral·
Rm 5:15 For if by·the trespass of·the one, the many died, so·
Rm 5:15 ·present by the grace of·the one man·of·clay†, Jesus
Rm 5:16 *is* not as through one already·morally·failing. For
Rm 5:16 the judgment *was* as·a·result of·one *trespass* unto a·
Rm 5:17 For if by·the one trespass, Death reigned through
Rm 5:17 Death reigned through the one·man, *then* so·much
Rm 5:17 in life-above through the one·man, Jesus Anointed.
Rm 5:18 So consequently, as through one trespass, *judgment*
Rm 5:18 even in·this·manner, through one righteous·act, *the*
Rm 5:19 the inattentive·disregard of·one man·of·clay†, the
Rm 5:19 through the attentive·obedience of·the one, the
Rm 9:10 a·conception *of·twins* from·out of·one·man, our
2Th 1:3 and the love of·each one of·yeu all, toward one·
1Co 4:6 ·up over the *other*, *comparing* one against the other.
1Co 10:17 ·and·belong *by·eating* from·out of·the one bread.
1Ti 5:9 sixty years·of·age, having·been a·wife of·one man,
Rv 21:21 one of·the gates was *made* out of·one pearl. And

G1520.1 N-GSN ἑνός (6x)

Lk 10:42 But one·thing is needed, and Mary selected the
Ac 17:26 "Also, from·out of·one blood he·made every
Gal 3:16 many *offspring†*, but·rather as upon one, "And to·
Mt 18:10 *that* yeu·should·not despise one of·these little·ones
1Co 12:12 and all the members of·the one body (being many
Rv 6:1 official·seals, and I·heard one from·among the four

EG1520.1 (4x)

Jn 10:21 utterances *of·one* who·is·being·possessed·with·a·.
Mt 21:35 In·fact, *there·was* *one* whom they·thrashed, and
Mt 21:35 whom they·thrashed, and *one* whom they·killed,
Mt 21:35 they·killed, and *one* whom they·cast·stones·at.

G1520.2 N-NSM εἷς (1x)

Mk 14:51 (But·also a certain young·man was·following him

G1520.2 N-NSN ἕν (1x)

Jn 6:9 "There·is a little·boy here, who has five barley loaves·

G1520.2 N-ASM ἕνα (1x)

Mt 27:15 to·fully·release to·the crowd a chained·prisoner,

G1520.2 N-GSM ἑνός (1x)

Rv 8:13 And I·saw and heard an angel flying in mid-heaven,

G1520.3 N-ASN ἕν (1x)

Jn 17:23 having·been·made·completely·mature in unity—

G1520.4 N-NSM εἷς (1x)

Lk 24:18 And answering, the individual whose name *was*

G1520.4 N-DSM ἑνί (1x)

Col 4:6 to·personally·know how to·answer each individual.

G1520.4 N-GSM ἑνός (1x)

Eph 4:16 ·to an·effective·working of·each individual part in

EG1520.4 (1x)

Mk 4:15 "Now these are the *individuals* directly·by the

G1520.5 N-ASM ἕνα (1x)

1Th 5:11 and edify one the other, just·as also yeu·do.

G1521 εἰσ•άγω êiságō *v.* (10x)

Roots:G1519 G0071

G1521.1 V-PPN εἰσάγεσθαι (1x)

Ac 21:37 And as Paul was·about to·be·brought into the

G1521.1 V-2AAI-3S εἰσήγαγεν (3x)

Jn 18:16 *him* to·the doorkeeper, and she·brought·in Peter.
Ac 21:28 And furthermore, he also brought Greeks into the
Ac 21:29 they·were·assuming that Paul brought into the

G1521.1 V-2AAI-3P εἰσήγαγον (3x)

Lk 22:54 him, they·led *him* and brought him into the house
Ac 7:45 after·receiving·it·in·turn, brought·it·in with JoShua
Ac 9:8 And leading him by·the·hand, they·brought *him* into

G1521.1 V-2AAM-2S εἰσάγαγε (1x)

Lk 14:21 of·the city, and bring·in here the helplessly·poor,

G1521.1 V-2AAN εἰσαγαγεῖν (1x)

Lk 2:27 And·when the parents brought in the little·child

G1521.1 V-2AAS-3S εἰσαγάγῃ (1x)

Heb 1:6 And again, whenever he·should·bring the Firstborn

G1522 εἰσ•ακούω êisakôúō *v.* (5x)

Roots:G1519 G0191

G1522.1 V-FDI-3P εἰσακούσονται (1x)

1Co 14:21 in·this·manner, they·shall·not·even listen·to me,"

G1522.2 V-FPI-3P εἰσακουσθήσονται (1x)

Mt 6:7 for they·presume that they·shall·be·heard by their

G1522.2 V-API-3S εἰσηκούσθη (2x)

Lk 1:13 on·account·that your petition is·heard, and your
Ac 10:31 'Cornelius, your prayer is·heard, and your

G1522.2 V-APP-NSM εἰσακουσθείς (1x)

Heb 5:7 of·death, and *he·was* being·heard from the devotion

G1523 εἰσ•δέχομαι êisdéchômai *v.* (1x)

Roots:G1519 G1209 See:G0588 G1926

G1523.2 V-FDI-1S εἰσδέξομαι (1x)

2Co 6:17 of·impurity," and·I shall·favorably·accept yeu,

G1524 εἴσ•ειμι éisêimi *v.* (4x)

Roots:G1519 G1510-1 Compare:G1525 See:G0549

G1524 V-PXI-3P εἰσίασιν (1x)

Heb 9:6 ·sacrifices, in·fact, continually entered into the first

G1524 V-PXN εἰσιέναι (1x)

Ac 3:3 Peter and John intending to·enter into the Sanctuary·

G1524 V-LAI-3S εἰσῄει (2x)

Ac 21:18 following *day*, Paul had·entered together with·us
Ac 21:26 ·cleansed together with·them, had·entered into the

G1525 εἰσ•έρχομαι êisérchômai *v.* (200x)

Roots:G1519 G2064 Compare:G1524

G1525.1 V-2AAI-3S εἰσῆλθεν (2x)

Ac 1:21 which the Lord Jesus came·in and went·forth among
Rv 11:11 of·life-above from·out of·God came·in upon them,

G1525.1 V-2AAN εἰσελθεῖν (1x)

Lk 14:23 and hedges, and compel *them* to·come·in, that my

G1525.1 V-2AAP-DSM@ εἰσελθόντι (1x)

Lk 17:7 immediately *to·him* as·he·comes·in from·out of·the

G1525.2 V-2AAI-3S εἰσῆλθεν (1x)

Mk 15:43 Being·daringly·bold, he·went·in to Pilate and

G1525.3 V-FDI-1S εἰσελεύσομαι (1x)

Rv 3:20 ·open·up the door, I·shall·enter·in alongside him,

G1525.3 V-FDI-3S εἰσελεύσεται (3x)

Jn 10:9 ·be·saved, and he·shall·enter·in and shall·go·forth,
Mt 7:21 'Lord, Lord,' shall·enter into the kingdom of·the
Mt 19:23 ·difficult *that* a·wealthy·man shall·enter into the

G1525.3 V-FDI-3P εἰσελεύσονται (6x)

Lk 18:24 the·ones holding the valuables shall·enter into the
Ac 20:29 burdensome wolves shall·enter·in among yeu,
Heb 3:11 flared·anger, 'As·if they·shall·*ever*·enter into my
Heb 4:3 my flared·anger, 'as·if they·shall·*ever*·enter into my
Heb 4:5 "'As·if they·shall·*ever*·enter into my complete·rest
Mk 10:23 the·ones having the valuables shall·enter into the

G1525.3 V-FDN εἰσελεύσεσθαι (1x)

Heb 3:18 *that* 'they·were·not to·enter into his complete·rest,'

G1525.3 V-PNI-1P εἰσερχόμεθα (1x)

Heb 4:3 For the·ones trusting do·enter into the complete·rest

G1525.3 V-PNI-2P εἰσέρχεσθε (1x)

Mt 23:14 For yeu·yeurselves do·not enter·in, neither do·yeu·

G1525.3 V-PNI-3S εἰσέρχεται (1x)

Heb 9:25 just·as the high·priest enters into the Holy·of·

G1525.3 V-PNM-3P εἰσερχέσθωσαν (1x)

Lk 21:21 ·ones in the wide·open·fields must·not enter into it.

G1525.3 V-PNP-ASF εἰσερχομένην (1x)

Heb 6:19 steadfast, 'and·also entering into the interior of·

G1525.3 V-PNP-APM εἰσερχομένους (2x)

Lk 11:52 and yeu·forbade the·ones who·were·entering."
Mt 23:14 neither do·yeu·allow the·ones entering to·enter·in.

G1525.3 V-PNP-GSM εἰσερχομένου (1x)

Lk 17:12 And upon·him entering into a·certain village, there·

G1525.3 V-PNP-NSN εἰσερχόμενον (1x)

Mt 15:11 *It·is* not the·thing entering into the mouth *that*

G1525.3 V-PNP-NSM εἰσερχόμενος (3x)

Jn 10:1 ·say to·yeu, the·one not entering·in through the door
Jn 10:2 "But the·one entering·in through the door is shepherd
Heb 10:5 Therefore, he·who·is·entering into the world says,

G1525.3 V-PNP-NPM εἰσερχόμενοι (2x)

Mt 7:13 many are the·ones who·are·entering·in through it.
Mt 10:12 And while·entering into the home, greet it.

G1525.3 V-PNS-2P εἰσέρχησθε (3x)

Lk 10:5 And into whatever home yeu·should·enter, first say,
Lk 10:8 whatever city yeu·should·enter, and they·should·
Lk 10:10 into whatever city yeu·should·enter, and they·do·

G1525.3 V-2AAI-1S εἰσῆλθον (2x)

Lk 7:44 ·look·upon this woman? "I·entered into your home,
Lk 7:45 she·herself since that *moment* I·entered·in, did·not

G1525.3 V-2AAI-1P εἰσήλθομεν (1x)

Ac 11:12 together with·me, and we·entered into the man's

G1525.3 V-2AAI-2S εἰσῆλθες (2x)

Ac 11:3 saying, "You·entered·in alongside men being
Mt 22:12 'O·associate, how did·you·enter here not having

G1525.3 V-2AAI-2P εἰσήλθετε (1x)

Lk 11:52 ·knowledge. Yeu·yeurselves did·not enter, and

G1525.3 V-2AAI-3S εἰσῆλθεν (40x)

Jn 13:27 the Adversary-Accuser entered into that·man. So·
Jn 18:1 into which he·himself entered *along* with his
Jn 18:33 So·then Pilate entered into the Praetorian·hall again
Jn 19:9 and he·entered again into the Praetorian·hall and says
Jn 20:5 ·of·linen laying·out, however, he·did·not enter.
Jn 20:6 following him, and he·entered into the chamber·
Jn 20:8 accordingly, the other disciple entered also, the·one
Lk 1:40 and she·entered into the house of·ZacharIas and
Lk 4:16 And according·to his custom, he·entered into the
Lk 4:38 out of·the gathering, he·entered into Simon's home.
Lk 6:4 how he·entered into the house of·God and took and
Lk 7:1 hearing of·the people, he·entered into CaperNaum.
Lk 8:30 "Legion," because many demons entered into him.
Lk 8:33 the man·of·clay†, the demons entered into the pigs,

Lk 9:46 *in·CaperNaum*, a·discussion entered·in among them
Lk 10:38 traversing, that he·himself entered into a·certain
Lk 17:27 that day *when* Noach entered into the floating·ark,
Lk 19:7 saying, "He·entered to·lodge with a·man *who·is*
Lk 22:3 Then the Adversary-Accuser entered into Judas, the·
Lk 24:29 has·faded." And he·entered·in to·abide together
Ac 3:8 he·was·walking; then he·entered together with·them
Ac 5:7 having·seen the·thing having·happened, entered·in.
Ac 9:17 And AnanIas went·off and entered into the home.
Ac 10:27 ·together with·him, he·entered·in and found many
Ac 11:8 did anything defiled or impure enter into my mouth.
Ac 14:20 him, after·rising·up, he·entered into the city, and
Ac 17:2 ·to Paul's custom, he·entered·in alongside them,
Heb 6:20 where a·forerunner entered on·behalf of·us—
Heb 9:12 and calves, but he·entered through his·own blood
Heb 9:24 the Anointed-One did·not enter into holy·places
Mt 12:4 How he·entered into the house of·God and ate the
Mt 17:25 And when he·entered into the home, YeShua
Mt 21:12 And YeShua entered into the Sanctuary·Estate of·
Mt 24:38 that day *that* Noach entered into the floating·ark,
Mk 2:1 And again he·entered into CaperNaum after *some*
Mk 2:26 How he·entered into the house of·God in·the·days
Mk 3:1 And he·entered again into the gathering, and there·
Mk 7:17 And when he·entered into a·house away·from the
Mk 11:11 And Jesus entered into JeruSalem and into the
Rm 5:12 one man·of·clay†, Moral·Failure entered into the
G1525.3 V-2AAI-3P εἰσῆλθον (11x)
Jn 18:28 And they·themselves did·not enter into the
Lk 9:52 And traversing, they·entered into a·village of·the·
Ac 1:13 And when they·entered, they·walked·up into the
Ac 5:21 And after·hearing *this*, they·entered into the
Ac 10:24 And on·the next·day, they·entered into Caesarea.
Ac 16:40 out of·the prison, they·entered into *the house·of*
Heb 4:6 did·not enter on·account·of an·obstinate·attitude,
Mt 25:10 and the·ones *that·were* ready entered with him into
Mt 27:53 his awakening·from·death, they·entered into the
Mk 5:13 ·out, the impure spirits entered into the pigs, and
2Jn 1:7 Because many impostors entered into the world, the·
G1525.3 V-2AAM-2S εἴσελθε (4x)
Ac 9:6 *said* to him, "Rise·up and enter into the city, and it·
Mt 6:6 whenever you·should·pray, enter into your private·
Mt 25:21 ·establish you over many·things. Enter into the joy
Mt 25:23 ·establish you over many·things. Enter into the joy
G1525.3 V-2AAM-2P εἰσέλθετε (1x)
Mt 7:13 "Yeu·must·enter·in through the obstructed·and·
G1525.3 V-2AAM-3S εἰσελθέτω (1x)
Mk 13:15 into the home, nor·even enter *it*, to·take·away
G1525.3 V-2AAN εἰσελθεῖν (36x)
Jn 3:4 ·old·man? ¿! Is·he·able to·enter a·second·time into
Jn 3:5 and of·Spirit, he·is·not able to·enter into the kingdom
Lk 6:6 another Sabbath, *for* him to·enter into the gathering
Lk 8:32 that he·should·freely·permit them to·enter into those
Lk 8:41 of·Jesus, he·was·imploring him to·enter into his
Lk 8:51 ·not allow not·even·one·person to·enter·in, except
Lk 9:34 with these·things, they·were·afraid to·enter into the
Lk 13:24 "Strive to·enter through the obstructed·and·narrow
Lk 13:24 I·say to·yeu, shall·seek to·enter and shall·not
Lk 15:28 he·was·angry and was·not willing to·enter. So
Lk 18:25 easier *for* a·camel to·enter·in through a·tiny·inlet
Lk 18:25 than *for* a·wealthy·man to·enter into the kingdom
Lk 22:40 *in·order·for yeu* not to·enter into a·proof·trial."
Lk 24:26 to·suffer these·things, and to·enter into his glory?
Ac 10:25 And as·soon·as Peter happened to·enter, Cornelius
Ac 14:1 ·way in Iconium *for* them to·enter into the gathering
Ac 14:22 how·that "It·is·necessary·for us to·enter into the
Ac 19:30 And while·Paul was·resolving to·enter into the
Heb 3:19 ·were·not able to·enter·in through a·lack·of·trust.
Heb 4:1 ·a·promise being·left·behind *for·us* to·enter into his
Heb 4:6 since it·is·still·remaining *for* some to·enter into it,
Heb 4:11 we·should·quickly·endeavor to·enter into that
Mt 12:29 Or how·else·is anyone able to·enter into the strong·
Mt 18:8 It·is good for·you to·enter into the life-above lame or
Mt 18:9 "It·is better for·you to·enter into the life-above with·
Mt 19:17 But if you·want to·enter into the life-above,
Mt 19:24 ·a·needle than *for* a·wealthy·man to·enter into the
Mt 23:14 neither do·yeu·allow the·ones entering to·enter·in.
Mk 1:45 *Jesus* no·longer to·be·able to·enter openly into a·
Mk 9:43 It·is better for·you to·enter into the life-above
Mk 9:45 It·is better for·you to·enter lame into the life-above,
Mk 9:47 It·is better for·you to·enter into the kingdom of·God
Mk 10:24 ·confidence in the valuables to·enter into the
Mk 10:25 "It·is easier for·a·camel to·enter through the tiny·
Mk 10:25 needle, than for·a·wealthy·man to·enter into the
Rv 15:8 And none·at·all were·able to·enter into the Temple,
G1525.3 V-2AAP-ASM εἰσελθόντα (3x)
Ac 9:12 ·man by·the·name·of AnanIas entering·in and laying
Ac 10:3 day, an·angel of·God entering *this·realm* toward
Mk 9:28 And after·entering into a·house, his disciples were·
G1525.3 V-2AAP-DSM εἰσελθόντι (1x)
Mt 8:5 Now as·YeShua was·entering into CaperNaum, a·
G1525.3 V-2AAP-GSF εἰσελθούσης (1x)
Mk 6:22 of·the very·same HerOdias entering·in and dancing
G1525.3 V-2AAP-GSM εἰσελθόντος (1x)
Mt 21:10 And with·him entering into JeruSalem, all the City
G1525.3 V-2AAP-GPM εἰσελθόντων (2x)
Lk 22:10 "Behold, with·yeu entering into the City, a·man·
Ac 25:23 with much pomp and entering into the formal·
G1525.3 V-2AAP-NSF εἰσελθοῦσα (1x)
Mk 6:25 And upon·entering·in immediately with haste to the
G1525.3 V-2AAP-NSM εἰσελθών (20x)
Lk 1:9 ·lot, the·one to·burn·incense after·entering into the
Lk 1:28 And entering *this·realm* toward her, the angel
Lk 7:36 ·eat with him. And entering into the Pharisee's
Lk 8:51 And entering into the home, he·did·not allow not·
Lk 11:37 next·to him. And entering·in, *Jesus* sat·back·to·eat
Lk 19:1 And entering, *Jesus* went·through Jericho.
Lk 19:45 And entering into the Sanctuary·Atrium, he·began
Ac 18:19 but he·himself, after·entering into the gathering,
Ac 19:8 And entering into the gathering, he·was·boldly·
Ac 23:16 after·hearing of·the ambush and entering into the
Ac 28:8 and dysentery. Paul entered·in alongside him, and
Heb 4:10 For the·one already·entering into his complete·rest,
Mt 9:25 was·cast·out, upon·entering, he·took·secure·hold
Mt 22:11 the king, after·entering to·distinctly·view the·ones
Mt 26:58 designated·high·priest, and after·entering inside,
Mk 1:21 And immediately after·entering into the gathering,
Mk 3:27 belongings, not·even·one already·entering into his
Mk 5:39 And after·entering, he·says to·them, "Why are·
Mk 7:24 and Tsidon. And upon·entering into the home, he·
Mk 11:15 And Jesus, after·entering into the Sanctuary·
G1525.3 V-2AAP-NPN εἰσελθόντα (2x)
Lk 11:26 more·evil·than itself, and entering·in, they·reside
Mt 12:45 himself. And *with* them·entering, he·resides there.
G1525.3 V-2AAP-NPF εἰσελθοῦσαι (2x)
Lk 24:3 And entering, they·did·not find the body of·the Lord
Mk 16:5 And upon·entering into the chamber·tomb, they·
G1525.3 V-2AAP-NPM εἰσελθόντες (6x)
Ac 5:10 And the young·men entering, found her dead, and
Ac 11:20 and Cyrene, who, after·entering into Antioch,
Ac 13:14 to Antiochia of·Pisidia. And entering into the
Ac 16:15 *then come·along, and* entering into my house,
Ac 21:8 came to Caesarea. And entering into the house of·
Ac 23:33 These·same·men, after·entering into Caesarea and
G1525.3 V-2AAS-1P εἰσέλθωμεν (1x)
Mk 5:12 into the pigs, in·order·that we·may·enter into them.
G1525.3 V-2AAS-2S εἰσέλθῃς (4x)
Lk 7:6 For I·am not fit that you·should·enter under my roof.
Mt 8:8 I·am not fit in·order·that you·should·enter under my
Mk 8:26 saying, "You·should·not·even enter into the village
Mk 9:25 out of·him, and you·may·enter no·longer into him.
G1525.3 V-2AAS-2P εἰσέλθητε (9x)
Lk 9:4 "And whatever home yeu·should·enter into, there
Lk 22:46 in·order·that yeu·should·not enter into a·proof·trial
Mt 5:20 no, yeu·may·not·ever enter into the kingdom of·
Mt 10:5 of·Gentiles, and yeu·should·not enter into *any* city
Mt 10:11 or village yeu·should·enter, verify·by·inquiring
Mt 18:3 no, yeu·should·not enter into the kingdom of·the
Mt 26:41 in·order·that yeu·may·not enter into a·proof·trial.
Mk 6:10 "In·whatever·place yeu·should·enter into a·home,
Mk 14:38 in·order·that yeu·may·not enter into a·proof·trial.
G1525.3 V-2AAS-3S εἰσέλθῃ (9x)
Jn 10:9 the door. If someone should·enter·in through me,
Lk 18:17 ·God as a·little·child, no, should·not enter into it."
Mk 10:15 ·*is* a·little·child, no, he·should·not enter into it."
Mk 14:14 And wherever he·should·enter, yeu·declare to·the
Rm 11:25 complete·fullness of·the Gentiles should·enter·in.
Jac 2:2 For if there·should·enter into yeur gathering a·man
Jac 2:2 and there·should·enter also a·helpless·beggar in
1Co 14:24 and someone should·enter·in, a·non-trusting·one
Rv 21:27 And no, there·should·not enter into it anyone
G1525.3 V-2AAS-3P εἰσέλθωσιν (2x)
1Co 14:23 ·tongues, and untrained·men should·enter·in, or
Rv 22:14 arbor·tree of·Life-above and may·enter by·the gates
G1525.3 V-2RAI-2P εἰσεληλύθατε (1x)
Jn 4:38 have·labored·hard, and yeu have·entered into their
G1525.3 V-2RAI-3P εἰσεληλύθασιν (1x)
Jac 5:4 the outcries of·the·ones reaping have·entered ·into
EG1525.3 (1x)
Rv 21:27 or a·lie; *none shall·enter* except the·ones having·
EG1525.4 (1x)
Ac 16:15 to·the Lord, *then come·along, and* entering into

G1526 εἰσί êisí *v.* (166x)
εἰσίν êisín
Roots:G1510 Compare:G4960
(abbreviated listing for G1526)
G1526 V-PXI-3P εἰσίν (86x)
(list for G1526:V-PXI-3P excluded)
EG1526 (3x)
(list for EG1526: excluded)
G1526.1 V-PXI-3P εἰσίν (52x)
(list for G1526.1:V-PXI-3P excluded)
G1526.2 V-PXI-3P εἰσίν (25x)
(list for G1526.2:V-PXI-3P excluded)

G1527 εἷς καθ' εἷς hêîs kath' hêîs *adv.* (2x)
Roots:G1520 G2596
G1527.2 ADV εἷς καθ΄ εἷς (2x)
Jn 8:9 they·were·going·forth one·by·one, beginning from
Mk 14:19 to·be·grieved and to·say to·him one·by·one, "Is·it

G1528 εἰσ•καλέω êiskaléō *v.* (1x)
Roots:G1519 G2564
G1528.2 V-ADP-NSM εἰσκαλεσάμενος (1x)
Ac 10:23 So·then inviting them in, *Peter* hosted *them*.

G1529 εἴσ•οδος êísôdôs *n.* (5x)
Roots:G1519 G3598 Compare:G1403 G4318
xLangEquiv:H3996
G1529.2 N-ASF εἴσοδον (1x)
Heb 10:19 ·speech upon the entrance of·the Holy·of·Holies
G1529.2 N-GSF εἰσόδου (1x)
Ac 13:24 prior·to *the* personal·appearance of *Jesus'* entrance.
G1529.4 N-NSF εἴσοδος (1x)
2Pe 1:11 the accessible·entrance shall·be·fully·supplied
G1529.4 N-ASF εἴσοδον (2x)
1Th 1:9 us, what·manner of·accessible·entrance we·have to
1Th 2:1 brothers, that our accessible·entrance to yeu has·not

G1530 εἰσ•πηδάω êispēdáō *v.* (2x)
Roots:G1519
G1530 V-AAI-3S εἰσεπήδησεν (1x)
Ac 16:29 So requesting lights, he·rushed·in, and being
G1530 V-AAI-3P εἰσεπήδησαν (1x)
Ac 14:14 tearing·apart their garments, rushed·in among the

G1531 εἰσ•πορεύομαι êispôrêúômai *v.* (17x)
Roots:G1519 G4198
G1531.1 V-PMP-APM εἰσπορευομένους (1x)
Ac 28:30 ·accepting all the·ones traversing·in toward him,
G1531.1 V-PMP-NSM εἰσπορευόμενος (2x)
Ac 8:3 the Called·Out·citizenry. Traversing·into each *of* the
Ac 9:28 with them while·traversing·in and traversing·out at
G1531.1 V-PNI-3S εἰσπορεύεται (2x)

Lk 22:10 follow him into the home where he·traverses·in.
Mk 5:40 with him, and he·traverses·in where the little·child
G1531.1 V-PNP-NPF εἰσπορευόμεναι (1x)
Mk 4:19 in·which·they·are·traversing— they·altogether·
G1531.1 V-PNP-NPM εἰσπορευόμενοι (3x)
Lk 8:16 the·ones who·are·traversing·in should·look·about·
Lk 11:33 ·that the·ones traversing·in may·look·about by·the
Lk 19:30 *yeu*; in which traversing·in, yeu·shall·find a·colt
G1531.2 V-PNI-3S εἰσπορεύεται (1x)
Mk 7:19 because it·does·not traverse into his heart, but·
G1531.2 V-PNI-3P εἰσπορεύονται (1x)
Mk 1:21 And they·traverse into CaperNaum. And
G1531.2 V-PNP-GPM εἰσπορευομένων (1x)
Ac 3:2 ·charity personally·from the·ones traversing into the
G1531.2 V-PNP-NSN εἰσπορευόμενον (3x)
Mt 15:17 understand that any thing traversing into the mouth
Mk 7:15 of·the man·of·clay†, that traversing into him is·
Mk 7:18 that any thing traversing from·outside into the man·
G1531.2 V-PNP-NPM εἰσπορευόμενοι (1x)
Mk 11:2 ·before yeu, and immediately traversing into it,
G1531.2 V-INI-3S εἰσεπορεύετο (1x)
Mk 6:56 And wherever he·was·traversing, whether into

G1532 εἰσ•τρέχω êistréchō *v.* (1x)
Roots:G1519 G5143
G1532 V-2AAP-NSF εἰσδραμοῦσα (1x)
Ac 12:14 due·to her joy, but running·in, she·announced,

G1533 εἰσ•φέρω êisphérō *v.* (7x)
Roots:G1519 G5342
G1533 V-PAI-2S εἰσφέρεις (1x)
Ac 17:20 For you·carry certain strange·things to our ears.
G1533 V-PPI-3S εἰσφέρεται (1x)
Heb 13:11 animals, whose blood is·carried into the Holy·of·
G1533 V-AAI-1P εἰσηνέγκαμεν (1x)
1Ti 6:7 For we·carried not·even·one·thing into the world,
G1533 V-2AAN εἰσενεγκεῖν (1x)
Lk 5:18 and they·were·seeking *a·way* to·carry him in and
G1533 V-AAS-2S εἰσενέγκῃς (2x)
Lk 11:4 'And may·you·not carry us into a·proof·trial, but·
Mt 6:13 'And may·you·not carry us into a·proof·trial, but·
G1533 V-2AAS-3P εἰσενέγκωσιν (1x)
Lk 5:19 through what·kind·of *means* they·may·carry him in

G1534 εἶτα êîta *adv.* (16x)
See:G1899
G1534.2 ADV εἶτα (1x)
Mk 4:17 ·are just·for·a·season. Afterward, with·tribulation
G1534.3 ADV εἶτα (4x)
Jn 13:5 After·that, he·casts water into the wash·basin; then
Mk 4:28 then a·head·of·grain, after·that, fully·ripe grain in
Mk 8:25 After·that, *Jesus* again laid his hands upon his eyes
1Co 15:24 after·that, the end, whenever he·should·hand·over
G1534.4 ADV εἶτα (10x)
Jn 19:27 Then he·says to·the disciple, "Behold your mother!
Jn 20:27 Then he·says to·Thomas, "Bring your finger here,
Lk 8:12 are the·ones hearing. Then comes the Slanderer, and
Mk 4:28 ·fruit; first a·blade, then a·head·of·grain, after·that
Jac 1:15 Then with·the longing conceiving, it·reproduces·
1Co 12:28 miracles, then gracious·bestowments of·healing,
1Co 15:5 by·Kephas·*(called·Peter)*, then to·the twelve.
1Co 15:7 he·was·gazed·upon by·Jacob, *and* then by·all the
1Ti 2:13 For Adam was·molded first, then Eve.
1Ti 3:10 then while·being without·any·charge·of·wrong·
G1534.5 ADV εἶτα (1x)
Heb 12:9 Furthermore, in·fact, we·had fathers of·our flesh,

G1535 εἴ•τε êítê *conj.* (65x)
Roots:G1487 G5037 Compare:G2228
G1535.1 CONJ εἴτε (24x)
Rm 12:6 *we·must·use them*: if prophecy, *then* according·to
Php 1:18 in·every manner, whether in·pretense or in·truth,
Php 1:20 ·magnified in my body, whether through life† or
Php 1:27 , in·order·that whether coming and seeing yeu or·
1Pe 2:13 on·account·of the Lord, whether to·a·king, as
1Th 5:10 in·order·that, whether we·should·keep·alert or we·
2Th 2:15 yeu·were·instructed, whether through *spoken* word
1Co 3:22 Whether Paul, or Apollos, or Kephas·*(called·Peter)*
1Co 8:5 ·are being·referred·to·as gods, whether in heaven or
1Co 10:31 So·then whether yeu·eat, or drink, or anything
1Co 12:13 immersed into one Body, whether Jews or Greeks
1Co 12:13 whether Jews or Greeks, whether slave or free;
1Co 14:7 ·inanimate·things giving sound, whether flute or
1Co 15:11 Accordingly, whether *it·was* I·myself or those
2Co 1:6 And whether we·are·hard-pressed, *it·is* on·behalf·of·
2Co 1:6 and Salvation, or·whether we·are·comforted, *it·is*
2Co 5:9 Therefore we·aspire also, whether being·at·home or
2Co 5:10 he·practiced— whether beneficially·good or bad.
2Co 12:2 Anointed-One fourteen years ago (whether in body,
2Co 12:2 personally·know; or·whether on·the·outside of·the
2Co 12:3 ·know such a·man·of·clay†, (whether in body, or
Eph 6:8 personally·from the Lord, whether *he·be* slave or
Col 1:16 ·visible and the·ones invisible, whether thrones, or
Col 1:20 *Anointed-One, I·say*, whether *they·are* the·things
G1535.2 CONJ εἴτε (4x)
1Co 13:8 ·time falls·short. But if·also *there·are* prophecies,
1Co 13:8 ·rendered·inoperative; if·also bestowed·tongues,
1Co 13:8 ·tongues, they·shall·cease; if·also knowledge, it·
1Co 14:27 And·if any·man does·speak in·a·bestowed·tongue
G1535.3 CONJ εἴτε (3x)
1Co 12:26 And if one member suffers, all the members
2Co 5:13 For if we·lost·our·wits, *it·is* for·God; or·if we·are·
2Co 8:23 If *any·should·inquire* concerning Titus, *he·is* my
G1535.4 CONJ εἴτε (33x)
Rm 12:7 or service, on the attendance *to·others*; or the·one
Rm 12:7 the attendance *to·others*; or the·one instructing, on
Rm 12:8 or the·one exhorting, on the exhortation; the·one
Php 1:18 in·every manner, whether in·pretense or in·truth,
Php 1:20 my body, whether through life† or through death.
1Pe 2:14 or to·governors, as being·sent through him, in·fact,
1Th 5:10 whether we·should·keep·alert or we·should·sleep,
2Th 2:15 whether through *spoken* word or through our letter
1Co 3:22 Whether Paul, or Apollos, or Kephas·*(called·*
1Co 3:22 Paul, or Apollos, or Kephas·*(called·Peter)*, or *the*
1Co 3:22 Apollos, or Kephas·*(called·Peter)*, or *the* world,
1Co 3:22 ·*Peter)*, or *the* world, or life-above, or death, or
1Co 3:22 world, or life-above, or death, or things·currently·
1Co 3:22 or death, or things·currently·standing, or things·
1Co 3:22 ·currently·standing, or things·about·to·come— all
1Co 8:5 ·to·as gods, whether in heaven or upon the earth
1Co 10:31 So·then whether yeu·eat, or drink, or anything
1Co 10:31 yeu·eat, or drink, or anything *that* yeu·do, do all
1Co 12:13 into one Body, whether Jews or Greeks, whether
1Co 12:13 Jews or Greeks, whether slave or free; and all
1Co 12:26 suffer·together *with·it*; or·if one member is·
1Co 14:7 giving sound, whether flute or harp, if it·should·
1Co 15:11 whether *it·was* I·myself or those *ambassadors*,
2Co 5:9 whether being·at·home or being·absent·abroad, to·
2Co 5:10 he·practiced— whether beneficially·good or bad.
2Co 5:13 *it·is* for·God; or·if we·are·of·sound·mind, *it·is*
2Co 8:23 coworker in·regard·to yeu, or·if our brothers *be·*
2Co 12:3 (whether in body, or on·the·outside of·the body,
Eph 6:8 ·from the Lord, whether *he·be* slave or free.
Col 1:16 ·ones invisible, whether thrones, or dominions, or
Col 1:16 whether thrones, or dominions, or principalities, or
Col 1:16 or dominions, or principalities, or authorities. All·
Col 1:20 ·*are* the·things upon the earth or the·things in the
G1535.5 CONJ εἴτε (1x)
Php 1:27 coming and seeing yeu or·else being·absent, I·may·

G1537 ἐκ êk *prep.* (918x)
ἐξ êx
Compare:G0575 G1223 See:G1622 G1854
G1537.1 PREP ἔκ (131x)
Jn 1:32 ·viewed the Spirit descending out of·heaven like a·
Jn 2:15 And making a·lash out of·small·cords, he·cast·out
Jn 3:13 except the·one descending out of·the heaven, the
Jn 4:12 us the well? Even he·himself drank out of·it, and his
Jn 4:30 Accordingly, they·went·forth out of·the city and
Jn 6:38 because I·have·descended out of·the heaven, not in·
Jn 6:41 the bread, the·one descending out of·the heaven."
Jn 6:42 this·thing, 'I·have·descended out of·the heaven?
Jn 6:50 the bread, the·one descending out of·the heaven, in·
Jn 6:51 living bread, the·one descending out of·the heaven.
Jn 6:58 the bread, the·one descending out of·the heaven. *It·is*
Jn 7:52 a·prophet has·not been·awakened out of·Galilee."
Jn 8:41 have·not been·born out of·sexual·immorality. We·
Jn 9:6 ·on·the·open·ground and made clay out of·the saliva,
Jn 10:39 But he·came·forth out of·their hand.
Jn 11:55 And many walked·up out of·the region to
Jn 12:27 'Father, save me out of·this hour?
Jn 19:2 after·braiding a·victor's·crown out of·thorns, they·
Lk 1:74 to·us (after·being·snatched out of·*the*·hand of·our
Lk 2:4 walked·up from Galilee, out of·*the*·city of·Natsareth,
Lk 4:22 words, the·ones proceeding·forth out of·his mouth.
Lk 4:35 "Be·muzzled! And come·forth out of·him." And the
Lk 4:38 And rising·up out of·the gathering, he·entered into
Lk 11:13 more the Father, the·one out of·heaven, shall·give
Ac 1:18 an·open·field out of·the payment·of·service for·the
Ac 7:40 this Moses who brought us out of·*the*·land of·Egypt,
Ac 8:39 And when they·walked·up out of·the water,
Ac 12:17 how the Lord brought him out of·the prison. And
Ac 13:17 and with a·high arm he·brought them out of·it.
Ac 13:42 And with·the Jews getting out of·the gathering, the
Ac 16:40 And going·forth out of·the prison, they·entered
Ac 18:1 came to Corinth, being·deported out of·Athens,
Ac 18:2 ·for all the Jews to·be·deported out of·Rome). *And*
Ac 19:33 they·pressed AlexAnder forward out of·the crowd,
Ac 22:18 go·forth in haste out of·JeruSalem on·account·that
Ac 24:7 with much force, led·*him*·away out of·our hands,
Ac 27:29 after·flinging four anchors out of·*the*·stern, they·
Ac 27:30 intending to·extend anchors out of·*the*·bow,
Ac 28:3 fire, a·viper, coming·forth out of·the warmth, fully·
Ac 28:17 ·over *as* a·chained·prisoner out of·JeruSalem into
Heb 3:16 *did·so* after·coming·forth out of·Egypt through
Heb 7:12 ·transferred, there·occurs out of·necessity also a·
Heb 8:9 by·my hand to·lead them out of·*the*·land of·Egypt,
Gal 3:13 utterly·kinsman·redeemed us out of·the curse of·the
Mt 12:33 and its fruit rotten. For out of·the fruit, the tree is·
Mt 15:11 ·rather the·thing proceeding·forth out of·the mouth
Mt 15:18 But the·things proceeding·forth out of·the mouth
Mt 21:31 Out of·the two, which one·did the will of·the father
Mt 23:25 but from·inside they·overflow out of·extortion and
Mt 24:17 walk·down to·take·away anything out of·his home.
Mt 26:27 *it* to·them, saying, "Drink out of·it, all *of·yeu*,
Mt 27:29 And after·braiding a·victor's·crown out of·thorns,
Mt 28:2 angel, after·descending out of·heaven *and* coming·
Mk 1:25 "Be·muzzled! And come·forth out of·him."
Mk 1:26 ·out with·a·loud voice, came·forth out of·him.
Mk 1:29 after·coming·forth out of·the gathering, they·went
Mk 5:2 And with·him coming·forth out of·the sailboat,
Mk 5:2 ·approached·and·met him out of·the chamber·tombs
Mk 5:8 "Impure spirit, come·forth out of·the man·of·clay†."
Mk 5:30 in himself the power going·forth out of·him, after·
Mk 6:54 And with·them coming·forth out of·the sailboat,
Mk 7:20 The·thing proceeding·forth out of·the man·of·clay†,
Mk 7:26 he·should·cast·forth the demon out of·her daughter.
Mk 7:29 The demon has·come·forth out of·your daughter."
Mk 9:7 them, and a·voice came out of·the thick·cloud,
Mk 9:25 I·myself order you, come·forth out of·him, and
Mk 11:8 and others were·chopping limbs out of·the trees,
Mk 13:1 as·he was·departing out of·the Sanctuary·Atrium,
Mk 13:15 enter *it*, to·take·away anything out of·his home.
Mk 14:23 And they·all drank out of·it.
Mk 14:31 But he·was·saying out *all the* more vehemently,
Mk 15:39 the·one having·stood·nearby out in·front·of·him,
Mk 15:46 which was·having·been·hewed out of·solid·rock,
Rm 2:8 But to·the·ones *working* out of·being·contentious,
Rm 7:24 Who shall·snatch me out of·this body of·death?
Rm 13:11 hour for·us to·be·awakened out of·heavy·sleep,
Jud 1:5 after·*first*·saving a·People out of·Egypt's land, the
Php 1:16 ·proclaim Anointed-One out of·being·contentious,

Php 1:17 But the *others fully·proclaim* out of·love, having·
1Pe 2:9 ·one already·calling yeu forth out of·darkness into
2Pe 2:9 to·snatch devoutly·reverent·men out of·proof·trials,
2Th 2:7 *is·doing so* until he·should·come out of·*the*·middle.
1Co 5:10 yeu·are·obligated to·go·forth out of·the world.
2Co 2:4 For out of·much tribulation and anguished·anxiety
2Co 4:6 *for* light to·radiate·brightly out of·darkness, who
2Co 8:13 tribulation for·yeu. But·rather out of·equality, now
2Co 9:7 he·is·preinclined in·*his*·heart, not out of·grief nor
2Co 9:7 ·heart, not out of·grief nor out of·compulsion, for ʿ
Eph 6:6 doing the will of·God out of·a·soul's·desire
Col 2:14 , and he·has·taken it away out of·the midst *of·us*,
Col 3:23 ·should·do, be·working *it* out of·a·soul's·desire as
1Ti 1:5 end·purpose of·the charge is love out of·a·pure heart,
2Ti 2:22 the·ones calling·upon the Lord out of·a·pure heart.
2Ti 2:26 ·to·their·senses *and escape* out of·the Slanderer's
2Ti 4:17 And·thus I·was·snatched out of·a·lion's mouth.
3Jn 1:10 casts·*them*·forth out of·the convened·Called·Out·
Rv 1:16 And ʿout of·his mouth, a·sharp double-edged
Rv 2:5 ·haste, and shall·stir your Lampstand out of·its place,
Rv 3:5 no, I·shall·not rub·out his name out of·the scroll of·
Rv 3:12 JeruSalem, the·one descending out of·the heaven
Rv 3:16 ·hot, I·intend to·vomit you out of·my mouth,
Rv 5:7 and has·taken the official·scroll out of·the right·hand
Rv 6:14 mountain and island was·stirred out of·their places.
Rv 7:14 "These are the·ones coming out of·The GREAT
Rv 9:2 ·pit, and there·ascended smoke out of·the well, as
Rv 9:17 as heads of·lions, and out of·their mouths proceeds·
Rv 9:18 ·one which·is·proceeding·forth out of·their mouths.
Rv 10:10 I·took the tiny·official·scroll out of·the angel's
Rv 12:15 And the Serpent cast out of·his mouth water as a·
Rv 12:16 ·water which the Dragon cast out of·his mouth.
Rv 13:1 and I·saw a·Daemonic·Beast ascending out of·the sea
Rv 13:11 another Fiendish·Beast ascending out of·the earth.
Rv 14:15 And another angel came·forth out of·the Temple,
Rv 14:17 And another angel came·forth out of·the Temple,
Rv 14:20 City, and blood came·forth out of·the winepress,
Rv 15:8 from·among the glory of·God and out of·his power.
Rv 16:13 spirits like frogs *come* out of·the mouth of·the
Rv 16:13 mouth of·the Dragon, and out of·the mouth of·the
Rv 16:13 of·the Daemonic·Beast, and out of·the mouth of·the
Rv 16:21 ·*(or·fifty·pounds)*) descends out of·the heaven
Rv 18:3 of·the earth became·wealthy out of·the power of·her
Rv 18:12 every *type·of* vessel *made* out of·*the*·most·precious
Rv 19:5 Then a·voice came·forth out of·the throne, saying,
Rv 19:15 And ʿout of·his mouth proceeds·forth a·sharp
Rv 19:21 the·one which·is·proceeding·forth out of·his mouth
Rv 20:9 And fire descended from God out of·the heaven and
Rv 20:12 are·judged out of·the·things having·been·written in
Rv 21:2 JeruSalem, descending from God out of·the heaven,
Rv 21:10 the Holy JeruSalem, descending out of·the heaven
Rv 21:21 each one of·the gates was *made* out of·one pearl.
Rv 22:1 as crystal, proceeding·forth out of·the throne of·

G1537.2 PREP ἐκ (303x)

Jn 1:13 who are·born, not from·out of·blood, nor from·out
Jn 1:13 from·out of·blood, nor from·out of·*the*·will of·flesh,
Jn 1:13 of·*the*·will of·flesh, nor from·out of·*the*·will of·man,
Jn 1:16 And from·out of·his complete·fullness, we·ourselves
Jn 1:19 and Levites from·out of·JeruSalem in·order·that
Jn 1:46 beneficially·good to·be from·out of·Natsareth?
Jn 3:5 unless someone should·be·born from·out of·water and
Jn 3:6 "The·one having·been·born from·out of·the flesh is
Jn 3:6 and the·one having·been·born from·out of·the Spirit
Jn 3:8 is any one having·been·born from·out of·the Spirit."
Jn 3:27 ·be having·been·given to·him from·out of·the heaven
Jn 3:31 birthed·from·out of·the earth is from·out of·the earth,
Jn 3:31 of·the earth, and speaks from·out of·the earth. The·
Jn 3:31 The·one who·is·coming from·out of·the heaven is
Jn 4:7 ·comes a·woman from·out of·Samaria to·draw·out
Jn 4:13 "Anyone drinking from·out of·this water shall·thirst
Jn 4:14 But whoever should·drink from·out of·the water that
Jn 4:22 because the Salvation is from·out of·the Jews.
Jn 4:47 after·hearing that Jesus comes from·out of·Judea into
Jn 4:54 Jesus did, coming from·out of·Judea into Galilee.
Jn 5:24 but·rather has·walked·on out·from the death into
Jn 6:11 and likewise from·out of·the small·broiled·fish as·
Jn 6:13 wicker·baskets with·fragments from·out of·the five
Jn 6:23 Now other small·boats came out·from Tiberias near
Jn 6:26 because yeu·ate from·out of·the loaves·of·bread and
Jn 6:31 ʿ"He·gave them bread from·out of·the heaven to·eat.
Jn 6:32 has·not given yeu the bread from·out of·the heaven,
Jn 6:32 gives yeu the true bread from·out of·the heaven,
Jn 6:33 of·God is the·one descending from·out of·the heaven
Jn 6:50 in·order·that someone may·eat from·out of·it, and
Jn 6:51 "If any·man should·eat from·out of·this bread, he·
Jn 7:17 the instruction, whether it·is from·out of·God, or
Jn 7:22 (not that it·is from·out of·Moses, but·rather from·out
Jn 7:22 ·out of·Moses, but·rather from·out of·the patriarchs)
Jn 7:38 declared, ʿ"from·out of·his belly shall·flow rivers
Jn 7:41 ·saying, "For ¿!·is·it from·out of·Galilee *that* the
Jn 7:52 "¿! Are you·yourself also from·out of·Galilee?
Jn 8:42 I·myself went·forth and have·come out·from God.
Jn 8:44 a·lie, he·speaks from·out of·his·own *disposition*,
Jn 8:59 and went·forth from·out of·the Sanctuary·Atrium
Jn 9:1 a·man·of·clay† who·was·blind from·out of·*his*·birth.
Jn 10:28 shall·not snatch them from·out of·my hand.
Jn 10:29 ·one is·able to·snatch *them* from·out of·my Father's
Jn 10:32 good works I·showed yeu from·out of·my Father;
Jn 12:3 home was·completely·filled from·out of·the aroma
Jn 12:28 there·came a·voice from·out of·the heaven, *saying*
Jn 12:34 "We·ourselves heard from·out of·the Torah-Law
Jn 12:49 I·myself did·not speak from·out of·my·own·self.
Jn 16:14 shall·glorify me, because from·out of·me, he·shall·
Jn 16:15 ·of that, I·declared that from·out of·me, *the Spirit*
Jn 20:2 ·took·away the Lord from·out of·the chamber·tomb,
Lk 1:78 a·light·rising·over·the·horizon from·out of·on·high
Lk 3:8 to·yeu that God is·able from·out of·these stones to·
Lk 3:22 and a·voice occurred from·out of·heaven, saying,
Lk 5:3 ·was·instructing the crowds from·out of·the sailboat.
Lk 5:17 who were having·come from·out of·every village
Lk 6:42 first cast·out the beam from your·own eye, and
Lk 6:44 For each tree is·known from·out of·its·own fruit.
Lk 6:44 fruit. For not from·out of·thorns do·men·collect figs
Lk 6:44 nor from·out of·a·bramble·bush do·they·collect a·
Lk 6:45 man·of·clay†, from·out of·the beneficially·good
Lk 6:45 the evil man·of·clay†, from·out of·the evil treasure
Lk 6:45 "For from·out of·the abundance of·the heart, his
Lk 8:27 ·and·met him a·certain man from·out of·the city,
Lk 9:35 And there·came a·voice from·out of·the thick·cloud,
Lk 10:7 ·of·service. Do·not walk·on out·from home to home
Lk 10:11 'Even the dust from·out of·yeur·own city, the·one
Lk 10:18 falling as lightning from·out of·heaven.
Lk 10:27 ·shall·love Yahweh your God from·out of·all your
Lk 10:27 of·all your heart, and from·out of·all your soul,
Lk 10:27 of·all your soul, and from·out of·all your strength,
Lk 10:27 your strength, and from·out of·all your innermost·
Lk 11:6 of·mine came·directly to me out·from a·journey, and
Lk 11:16 personally·from him a·sign from·out of·heaven.
Lk 11:31 because she·came from·out of·the utmost·parts
Lk 11:54 to·hunt·for something from·out of·his mouth in·
Lk 12:15 not in·the abundance from·out of·one's holdings
Lk 16:9 for·yeurselves from·out of·the material·wealth of·
Lk 17:7 *to·him* as·he·comes·in from·out of·the field, 'After·
Lk 17:24 the·one flashing from·out of·the·one *part* under
Lk 19:22 he·says to·him, 'From·out of·your·own mouth
Lk 20:4 immersion of·John, was·it from·out of·heaven, or
Lk 20:4 from·out of·heaven, or from·out of·men·of·clay†?
Lk 20:5 "If we·should·declare, 'From·out of·heaven,' he·
Lk 20:6 if we·should·declare, 'From·out of·men·of·clay†,'
Lk 20:35 ·age and the resurrection from·out of·the dead,
Lk 21:4 ·all these·men cast from·out of·their abundance into
Lk 21:4 for·God, but she·herself from·out of·her destitution
Lk 22:16 no, I·should·not eat any·longer from·out of·it until
Lk 23:7 that he·is from·out of·HerOd·AntiPas' jurisdiction,
Lk 23:55 ·come·together with·him from·out of·Galilee, did·
Lk 24:49 ·dress·yeurselves·with power from·out of·on·high.
Ac 2:2 ·came a·reverberating·sound from·out of·the heaven,
Ac 2:30 to·him with·an·oath *that* from·out of·*the*·fruit of·his
Ac 3:2 man inherently·being lame from·out of·his mother's
Ac 8:37 declared, "If you·trust from·out of·all the heart, it·
Ac 11:5 linen·sheet being·sent·down from·out of·the heaven
Ac 11:9 me for a·second·time from·out of·the heaven,
Ac 14:8 inherently·being lame from·out of·his mother's
Ac 15:21 For Moses, from·out of·ancient generations, has
Ac 17:26 "Also, from·out of·one blood he·made every
Ac 19:16 such·for *them* to·utterly·flee from·out of·that house
Ac 19:34 there·came one voice from·out of·all *present*, for·
Ac 22:6 it·happened suddenly from·out of·the heaven *for* a·
Ac 22:14 ·One, and to·hear *his* voice from·out of·his mouth.
Ac 27:30 sailors seeking to·flee out·from the sailing·ship,
Ac 27:34 for not·even·one hair shall·fall out·from yeur head.
Ac 28:4 saw the venomous·beast hanging out·from his hand,
Ac 28:4 after·being·thoroughly·saved from·out of·the sea,
Heb 5:7 the·one being·able to·save him from·out of·death,
Heb 11:3 ·come·to·be not from·out of·things·being·apparent,
Heb 11:35 received their dead from·out of·a·resurrection.
Gal 1:8 or an·angel from·out of·heaven should·proclaim·a·
Gal 1:15 specially·detaching me from·out of·my mother's
Gal 5:8 The persuading *is* not from·out of·the·one calling
Gal 6:8 his flesh, shall·reap corruption from·out of·the flesh;
Gal 6:8 shall·reap eternal life-above from·out of·the Spirit.
Mt 1:16 husband of·Mariam, from·out of·whom was·born
Mt 2:6 of·Judah. For from·out of·you shall·come·forth·one
Mt 2:15 saying, ʿ"From·out of·Egypt I·called·forth my son
Mt 3:9 to·yeu that God is·able from·out of·these stones to·
Mt 3:17 And behold, a·voice from·out of·the heavens,
Mt 7:5 first cast the beam from·out of·your·own eye, and
Mt 7:5 to·cast the speck·of·dust from·out of·your brother's
Mt 8:28 who·are·coming·forth from·out of·the chamber·
Mt 12:34 ·good·things? For from·out of·the abundance of·
Mt 12:35 man·of·clay† from·out of·the beneficially·good
Mt 12:35 and the evil man·of·clay† from·out of·his evil
Mt 12:37 For from·out of·your words, you·shall·be·
Mt 12:37 ·as·righteous, and from·out of·your words, you·
Mt 12:42 it, because she·came from·out of·the utmost·parts
Mt 13:41 and they·shall·collect from·out of·his kingdom all
Mt 13:49 ·separate the evil·ones from·out of·*the*·midst of·the
Mt 15:18 out of·the mouth come·forth from·out of·the heart,
Mt 15:19 For from·out of·the heart comes·forth evil
Mt 16:1 ·exhibit for·them a·sign from·out of·the heaven.
Mt 17:5 And behold, a·voice from·out of·the thick·cloud,
Mt 19:12 ·born in·this·manner from·out *of·their* mother's
Mt 19:20 these·things I·vigilantly·kept from·out of·my youth
Mt 21:16 read·aloud, ʿ" From·out *of·the* mouth of·infants
Mt 21:19 No·longer should fruit come out·from you unto the
Mt 21:25 from·what·source was·it? From·out of·heaven or
Mt 21:25 From·out of·heaven or from·out of·men·of·clay†?
Mt 21:25 "If we·should·declare, 'From·out of·heaven,' he·
Mt 21:26 if we·should·declare, 'From·out of·men·of·clay†,'
Mt 25:8 prudent, 'Give to·us from·out of·yeur oil, because
Mt 26:29 from this·moment·on from·out of·this produce of·
Mt 27:7 consultation, from·out of·the·same *pieces·of·silver*,
Mk 1:11 And there·came a·voice from·out of·the heavens,
Mk 7:21 For from·inside, from·out of·the heart of·the men·
Mk 10:20 ·things I·vigilantly·kept from·out of·my youth."
Mk 11:14 no·one any·longer eat fruit from·out of·you unto
Mk 11:20 ·tree having·been·withered from·out of·*the*·roots.
Mk 11:30 immersion of·John, was *it* from·out of·heaven, or
Mk 11:30 from·out of·heaven, or from·out of·men·of·clay†?
Mk 11:31 "If we·should·declare, 'From·out of·heaven,' he·
Mk 11:32 we·should·declare, 'From·out of·men·of·clay† …
Mk 12:30 ·shall·love Yahweh your God from·out of·all your
Mk 12:30 of·all your heart, and from·out of·all your soul,
Mk 12:30 ·all your soul, and from·out of·all your innermost·
Mk 12:30 your innermost·mind, and from·out of·all your
Mk 12:33 And to·love him from·out of·all the heart, and
Mk 12:33 the heart, and from·out of·all the comprehension,
Mk 12:33 the comprehension, and from·out of·all the soul,
Mk 12:33 of·all the soul, and from·out of·all the strength,

Mk 12:44 For they all cast·in from·out of·their abundance,
Mk 12:44 but she·herself from·out of·her destitution cast·in
Mk 13:27 ·gather his Selected-Ones from·out of·the four
Mk 14:25 ·not drink any·longer from·out of·the produce of·
Rm 1:4 ·holiness, from·out of·a·resurrection of·the·dead;
Rm 2:18 varying (being·tutored from·out of·the Torah-Law).
Rm 2:29 whose high·praise *is* not from·out of·men·of·clay†,
Rm 2:29 ·out of·men·of·clay†, but·rather from·out of·God.
Rm 6:17 yeu·listened·and·obeyed from·out of·*the*·heart *to*·
Rm 9:5 *are* the fathers, and from·out of·whom, according·to
Rm 9:10 having a·conception *of·twins* from·out of·one·man,
Rm 9:21 *over* the clay, from·out of·the same lump·of·clay
Rm 10:5 righteousness, the·one from·out of·the Torah-Law,
Rm 11:26 ·*Redeemer* shall·come from·out of·Tsiyon, the·
Rm 11:36 Because from·out of·him, and through him, and to
Rm 14:23 he·should·eat, because *it·is* not from·out of·trust.
Rm 14:23 anything that *is* not from·out of·trust is moral·
Jac 3:10 From·out of·the same mouth come·forth blessing
Jac 3:13 fully·informed among yeu? From·out of·the good
Jac 5:20 a·morally·disqualified·man from·out of·*the*·error
Jac 5:20 of·his way shall·save a·soul from·out of·death, and·
Jud 1:23 a·fear while·snatching *them* from·out of·the fire,
Php 3:9 righteousness (the·one from·out of·Torah-Law), but·
Php 3:9 (the righteousness from·out of·God *based* upon the
Php 3:20 in *the* heavens, out·from which also we·fully·await
1Pe 1:18 *that* yeu·were·ransomed from·out of·yeur futile
1Pe 1:22 yeu·must·love one·another from·out of·a·pure heart
1Pe 4:11 ·*be* as *one·attending* from·out of·strength which
2Pe 1:18 this voice being·carried·forth from·out of·heaven,
2Pe 2:21 *it*, to·turn·back·around from·out the holy
2Pe 3:5 having·consisted, *being·made* from·out of·water and
1Th 1:10 to·patiently·await his Son from·out of·the heavens,
1Th 2:3 birthed·from·out of·deceit, nor from·out of·impurity,
1Co 2:12 the Spirit, the·one from·out of·God, in·order·that
1Co 7:7 has his·own gracious·bestowment from·out of·God,
1Co 8:6 God, the Father (from·out of·whom *are* all·things
1Co 9:7 a·vineyard, and does·not eat from·out of·its fruit?
1Co 9:7 ·flock, and does·not eat from·out of·the milk of·the
1Co 9:14 the good·news to·live from·out of·the good·news.
1Co 10:4 for they·were·drinking from·out of·that·spiritual
1Co 10:17 ·and·belong *by·eating* from·out of·the one bread.
1Co 11:8 For man is not from·out of·woman, but·rather
1Co 11:8 of·woman, but·rather woman from·out of·man.
1Co 11:12 For just·as the woman *is* from·out of·the man, in·
1Co 11:12 the woman, but all things *are* from·out of·God.
1Co 11:28 in·this·manner let·him·eat from·out of·the bread
1Co 11:28 ·out of·the bread and drink from·out of·the cup.
1Co 13:9 For we·know from·out of·a·portion *of·the whole*,
1Co 13:9 *whole*, and we·prophesy from·out of·a·portion.
1Co 13:10 the·thing from·out of·a·portion shall·be·fully·
1Co 13:12 At·this·moment, I·know from·out of·a·portion,
1Co 15:47 The first man·of·clay† *was* from·out of·soil, *as*
1Co 15:47 man·of·clay† *is* the Lord from·out of·heaven.
2Co 1:10 already·snatched us from·out of·so·vast a·death,
2Co 2:17 But·rather, as from·out of·sincerity, moreover as
2Co 3:5 but·rather our sufficiency *is* from·out of·God,
2Co 4:7 ·the power may·be of·God, and not from·out of·us.
2Co 5:1 should·be·demolished, we·have (from·out of·God)
2Co 5:2 ·with our housing, the·one from·out of·heaven,
2Co 5:18 And all things *are* from·out of·God, the·one
2Co 8:11 *it*— but from·out *of·that·which* yeu·presently·have
2Co 9:2 since last·year; and from·out of·yeur zeal, it·stirred·
2Co 12:6 me *to·be*, or *above* what he·hears from·out of·me.
Eph 3:15 from·out of·whom *the* entire paternal·lineage in *the*
Eph 3:20 ·do above·and·beyond from·out of·an·abundance,
Eph 4:16 from·out of·whom all the Body is·being·fitly·
Eph 4:29 conversation proceed·forth from·out of·yeur mouth
Eph 5:14 be·awakened and rise·up from·out of·the dead,
Eph 5:30 ·are members of·his Body, from·out of·his flesh,
Eph 5:30 from·out of·his flesh, and from·out of·his bones.
Col 1:13 has·already·snatched us from·out of·the authority
Col 1:18 is *the* beginning, *the* firstborn from·out of·the dead,
Col 2:12 ·one already·awakening him from·out of·the dead.
Col 2:19 securely·holding the Head, from·out of·which all
Col 3:8 *and* shameful·conversation from·out of·yeur mouth.
Col 4:16 should·read·aloud the *letter* from·out of·LaoDicea.
1Ti 6:4 ·nuances·of·words, from·out of·which becomes
2Ti 3:11 but the Lord snatched me from·out of·all *of·them*.
1Jn 2:29 the righteousness has·been·born from·out of·him.
1Jn 3:9 Any one having·been·born from·out of·God does·not
1Jn 3:9 ·fail, because he·has·been·born from·out of·God.
1Jn 3:14 we·ourselves have·walked·on out·from Death into
1Jn 4:1 ·prove the spirits whether they·are from·out of·God,
1Jn 4:2 Anointed having·come in flesh is from·out of·God.
1Jn 4:3 having·come in flesh is not from·out of·God. And
1Jn 4:5 They·themselves are from·out of·the world, on·
1Jn 4:7 presently·loving has·been·born from·out of·God and
1Jn 4:13 because he·has·given to·us from·out of·his Spirit.
1Jn 5:1 is the Anointed-One has·been·born from·out of·God;
1Jn 5:1 also the·one having·been·begotten from·out of·him.
1Jn 5:4 one having·been·born from·out of·God overcomes
1Jn 5:18 one having·been·born from·out of·God does·not
1Jn 5:18 already·being·begotten from·out of·God guards
3Jn 1:11 ·one beneficially·doing·good is from·out of·God,
Rv 1:5 witness, *and* the firstborn from·out of·the dead, and
Rv 2:7 I·shall·give to·him to·eat from·out of·the arbor·tree
Rv 3:10 shall·purposefully·keep you from·out of·the hour of·
Rv 4:5 And from·out of·the throne, lightnings and
Rv 5:9 to·God by your blood— from·out of·every tribe, and
Rv 8:4 ascended in·the·sight of·God from·out of·the angel's
Rv 8:5 and overfilled it from·out of·the fire of·the
Rv 8:10 and there·fell a·great star from·out of·the heaven,
Rv 8:13 on the earth— from·out of·the remaining voices of·
Rv 9:1 and I·saw a·star having·fallen from·out of·the heaven
Rv 9:2 and the air were·darkened from·out of·the smoke of·
Rv 9:3 And from·out of·the smoke there·came·forth locusts
Rv 9:21 nor from·out of·their making·and·supplying·of·
Rv 9:21 ·drugs, nor from·out of·their sexual·immorality, nor
Rv 9:21 sexual·immorality, nor from·out of·their thefts.
Rv 10:1 strong angel descending from·out of·the heaven,
Rv 10:4 And I·heard a·voice from·out of·the heaven saying
Rv 10:8 the voice which I·heard from·out of·the heaven *was*
Rv 11:5 them, fire proceeds·forth from·out of·their mouth
Rv 11:7 (the·one ascending from·out of·the bottomless·pit)
Rv 11:11 *the* Spirit of·life-above from·out of·God came·in
Rv 11:12 they·heard a·great voice from·out of·the heaven
Rv 13:13 ·make fire to·descend from·out of·the heaven to
Rv 14:2 And I·heard a·voice from·out of·the heaven, as a·
Rv 14:8 she·has·made all nations drink from·out of·the wine
Rv 14:10 *the* same shall·drink from·out of·the wine of·the
Rv 14:13 And I·heard a·voice from·out of·the heaven saying
Rv 14:13 they·may·rest from·out of·their wearisome·labors,
Rv 14:18 angel came·forth out·from the Sacrifice·Altar,
Rv 15:6 the seven angels came·forth from·out of·the Temple,
Rv 16:1 And I·heard a·great voice from·out of·the Temple
Rv 17:2 earth, they·are·made·drunk from·out of·the wine
Rv 17:6 the woman getting·drunk from·out of·the blood of·
Rv 17:6 of·the holy·ones, and from·out of·the blood of·the
Rv 17:8 it·is·about to·ascend from·out of·the bottomless·pit,
Rv 18:1 I·saw an·angel descending from·out of·the heaven,
Rv 18:3 all the nations have·drunk from·out of·the wine of·
Rv 18:4 And I·heard another voice from·out of·the heaven,
Rv 18:4 ·may·not receive from·out of·her punishing·blows,
Rv 20:1 I·saw an·angel descending from·out of·the heaven,
Rv 20:7 shall·be·loosened from·out of·his prison,
Rv 21:3 And I·heard a·great voice from·out of·the heaven
Rv 21:6 ·give to·the·one thirsting from·out of·the wellspring
Rv 22:19 of·the life-above, and from·out of·the HOLY CITY

G1537.3 PREP ἐκ (301x)

Jn 1:24 ·been·dispatched were from·among the Pharisees.
Jn 1:35 John stood also *with* two from·among his disciples.
Jn 1:40 brother, was one from·among the two of·the·ones
Jn 1:44 Philip was from BethSaida, from·among the city of·
Jn 2:15 ·out everyone from·among the Sanctuary·Atrium,
Jn 2:22 when he·was·awakened from·among dead·men, his
Jn 3:1 There·was a·man·of·clay† from·among the Pharisees,
Jn 3:25 a·question·and·discussion from·among John's
Jn 4:39 And many of·the Samaritans from·among that city
Jn 6:8 One from·among his disciples, Andrew, Simon Peter's
Jn 6:39 *sheep* which he·has·given me from·among it *(that·is*,
Jn 6:60 Accordingly, many from·among his disciples, upon·
Jn 6:64 "But·yet there·are some from·among yeu that do·not
Jn 6:64 had·personally·known from·among *the* beginning
Jn 6:70 the twelve, yet one from·among yeu is a·slanderer.
Jn 6:71 to·hand him over, being one from·among the twelve.
Jn 7:19 And·yet not·even·one from·among yeu does the
Jn 7:25 So·then, some from·among the·men of·JeruSalem
Jn 7:31 And many from·among the crowd trusted in him and
Jn 7:40 the saying, many from·among the crowd were·
Jn 7:44 And some from·among them were·wanting to·
Jn 7:48 ¿!·Did any from·among the rulers or from·among the
Jn 7:48 from·among the rulers or from·among the Pharisees
Jn 7:50 by·night *and* being one from·among them) says to
Jn 8:23 Yeu·yourselves are from·among this world; I·myself
Jn 8:23 this world; I·myself am not from·among this world.
Jn 8:46 Who from·among yeu convicts me concerning
Jn 9:16 So·then some from·among the Pharisees were·saying
Jn 9:32 "*Even* from·among of·the beginning·age, it·is·not
Jn 9:40 And *some* from·among the Pharisees heard these·
Jn 10:16 sheep which are not from·among this yard·pen. It·
Jn 10:20 And many from·among them were·saying, "He·has
Jn 10:26 trust, for yeu·are not from·among my sheep, just·as
Jn 11:1 from BethAny, from·among the village of·Mary
Jn 11:19 And many from·among the Judeans had·come
Jn 11:37 But some from·among them declared, "Was·not
Jn 11:45 So·then many from·among the Judeans, the·ones
Jn 11:46 But some from·among them went·off to the
Jn 11:49 And a·certain one from·among them, *named*
Jn 12:1 ·died, whom he·awakened from·among dead·men.
Jn 12:4 So·then one from·among his disciples (Judas
Jn 12:9 Now·then, a·large crowd from·among the Judeans
Jn 12:9 also, whom he·awakened from·among dead·men.
Jn 12:17 ·out·for Lazarus from·among the chamber·tomb
Jn 12:17 ·tomb and awakened him from·among dead·men.
Jn 12:20 certain Greeks, from·among the·ones walking·up
Jn 12:32 ·I, if I·should·be·elevated from·among the earth, I·
Jn 12:42 ·in·fact, many from·among the chief·rulers also
Jn 13:1 that he·should·walk·on from·among this world to
Jn 13:4 *he·himself* is·roused from·among the supper and
Jn 13:21 I·say to·yeu that one from·among yeu shall·hand
Jn 15:19 "If yeu·were from·among the world, the world
Jn 15:19 but yeu·are not from·among the world, but·rather
Jn 15:19 ·rather I·myself selected yeu from·among the world
Jn 16:5 me, and not·even·one from·among yeu asks·of me,
Jn 16:17 Accordingly, *some* from·among his disciples
Jn 17:6 whom you·have·given to·me from·among the world.
Jn 17:12 not·even·one from·among them is·completely·lost
Jn 17:14 them because they·are not from·among the world,
Jn 17:14 just·as I·myself am not from·among the world.
Jn 17:15 you·should·take them up out·from·among the world
Jn 17:16 "They·are not from·among the world, just·as I·
Jn 17:16 just·as I·myself am not from·among the world.
Jn 18:3 and·also assistants from·among the chief·priests and
Jn 18:9 declared, "From·among them whom you·have·given
Jn 18:17 Are you·yourself not also from·among the disciples
Jn 18:25 Are you·yourself not also from·among his disciples
Jn 18:26 One from·among the slaves of·the designated·high·
Jn 18:36 "My kingdom is not from·among this world. If my
Jn 18:36 If my kingdom was from·among this world, my
Jn 20:1 having·been·taken·away from·among the chamber·
Jn 20:9 ·for him to·rise·up from·among dead·men.
Jn 20:24 But Thomas (one from·among the twelve, the·one
Jn 21:2 ·Zebedee, and two others from·among his disciples.
Jn 21:14 after·being·awakened from·among dead·men.
Lk 1:5 ZacharIas, *who·was* from·among *the* daily·rotation
Lk 1:5 And his wife *was* from·among the daughters of·Aaron
Lk 1:27 name *was* Joseph, from·among *the* house of·David.
Lk 1:71 "Salvation from·among our enemies and from·
Lk 1:71 from·among our enemies and from·among *the* hand

Lk 2:4 on·account·of him being from·among *the* house and
Lk 2:35 that *the* deliberations from·among many hearts
Lk 2:36 daughter of·PhanuEl, from·among *the* tribe of·
Lk 9:7 that John has·been·awakened from·among dead·men,
Lk 11:5 them, "Which from·among yeu shall·have a·friend,
Lk 11:15 But some from·among them declared, "He·casts·
Lk 11:27 *that* a·certain woman from·among the crowd,
Lk 11:49 and *some* from·among them they·shall·kill and
Lk 12:6 And·yet not one from·among them is having·been·
Lk 12:13 And someone from·among the crowd declared to·
Lk 12:25 "And who from·among yeu by·being·anxious is·
Lk 12:36 he·shall·break·camp from·among the wedding·
Lk 14:28 "For which from·among yeu, wanting to·build a·
Lk 14:33 in·this·manner, anyone from·among yeu that does·
Lk 15:4 "What man·of·clay† from·among yeu, having a·
Lk 15:4 that after·completely·losing one from·among them,
Lk 16:31 someone should·rise·up from·among dead·men.'"
Lk 17:7 "Now who·is·there from·among yeu having a·slave
Lk 17:15 And one from·among them, seeing that he·was·
Lk 18:21 ·things I·vigilantly·kept from·among my youth."
Lk 21:16 and they·shall·put·to·death *some* from·among yeu.
Lk 21:18 And·yet a·hair from·among yeur head, no, it·
Lk 22:3 ·surnamed IsCariot, being from·among the number
Lk 22:23 themselves, which from·among them it·might·be
Lk 22:50 And a·certain one from·among them smote the
Lk 22:58 "You·yourself are also from·among them." And
Lk 24:13 And behold, two from·among them were
Lk 24:22 certain women also from·among us astonished us,
Lk 24:46 and to·rise·up from·among dead·men on·the third
Ac 1:24 expressly·indicate which one from·among these two
Ac 1:25 service and commission, from·among which Judas
Ac 3:15 whom God awakened from·among dead·men, to·
Ac 3:22 ·up a·Prophet unto·yeu from·among yeur brothers,
Ac 3:23 ' "shall·be·exterminated from·among the People.
Ac 4:2 the resurrection, the·one from·among dead·men.
Ac 4:6 and as·many·as were from·among *the* high·priest's
Ac 4:10 whom God awakened from·among dead·men, by
Ac 6:3 brothers, inspect from·among yeurselves seven men
Ac 6:9 there·rose·up certain·men from·among the gathering,
Ac 7:3 to him, "Go·forth from·among your land, and from·
Ac 7:3 ·among your land, and from·among your kinsfolk,
Ac 7:4 Then coming·forth from·among *the* land of·the·
Ac 7:10 and snatched him out from·among all his
Ac 7:37 ·up a·prophet to·yeu from·among yeur brothers, as
Ac 10:1 a·centurion from·among a·battalion being·called
Ac 10:41 with·him after he rose·up from·among dead·men.
Ac 10:45 And the·ones from·among *the* Circumcision
Ac 11:2 JeruSalem, the·ones from·among *the* Circumcision
Ac 11:20 And some from·among them were men of·Cyprus
Ac 11:28 And one from·among them by·the·name·of Agabus
Ac 12:7 And his chains fell·away from·among his hands.
Ac 12:11 snatched me out from·among HerOd·AgRippa's hand
Ac 12:25 ·back *to·Antioch* from·among JeruSalem after·
Ac 13:21 Saul son of·Qish, a·man from·among *the* tribe of·
Ac 13:30 But God awakened him from·among dead·men—
Ac 13:34 because he·raised him up from·among dead·men,
Ac 15:2 and certain others from·among them, to·walk·up to
Ac 15:14 visited Gentiles to·take from·among *them* a·People
Ac 15:22 men being·selected from·among themselves to
Ac 15:23 and Cilicia, the·ones from·among Gentiles, be·
Ac 15:24 that certain·men going·out from·among us troubled
Ac 15:29 ·sexual·immorality. From·among which·things *if*
Ac 17:3 to·suffer and to·rise·up from·among dead·men, and
Ac 17:4 And some from·among them were·convinced and
Ac 17:12 in·fact, many from·among them trusted, and·also
Ac 17:31 ·*clay*† after·raising him up from·among dead·men.
Ac 17:33 ·manner, Paul went·forth from·among *the* midst
Ac 20:30 Also from·among yeu yeurselves, men shall·rise·
Ac 21:8 ·news·of·redemption, being from·among the seven)
Ac 23:10 ·down, to·seize him from·among *the* midst of·
Ac 23:21 ·them, for from·among them who·lay·in·wait·for
Ac 24:10 "Being·fully·acquainted from·among many years
Ac 26:4 ·known my way·of·life from·among *my* youth (the·
Ac 26:17 while·snatching you out from·among the People,
Ac 26:23 first of·a·resurrection from·among dead·men *and*
Ac 27:22 ·be not·even·one loss of·soul from·among yeu,
Heb 3:13 lest any from·among yeu should·be·hardened
Heb 4:1 ·be·alarmed, lest any from·among yeu should·seem
Heb 5:1 being·taken from·among men·of·clay† is·fully·
Heb 7:4 gave a·tenth from·among the best·of·the·plunder.
Heb 7:5 And in·fact, the·ones from·among the Sons of·Levi
Heb 7:5 ·though having·come·forth from·among the loins of·
Heb 7:6 not being·reckoned·by·birth from·among them has·
Heb 7:14 has·risen·above·the·horizon from·among Judah,
Heb 11:19 able to·awaken *him* even from·among dead·men,
Heb 13:10 a·Sacrifice·Altar from·among which the·ones
Heb 13:20 the·one bringing·up from·among dead·men our
Gal 1:1 the·one awakening him from·among dead·men),
Gal 1:4 that he·may·snatch us out from·among the evil age
Gal 2:12 fearing the·ones from·among *the* Circumcision.
Gal 2:15 and not from·among morally·disqualified Gentiles
Mt 6:27 And who from·among yeu by·being·anxious is·able
Mt 7:9 "Or what man·of·clay† is·there from·among yeu, who
Mt 10:29 And not one from·among them shall·fall upon
Mt 12:11 man·of·clay† shall·there·be from·among yeu that
Mt 13:47 sea and gathering·together from·among every kind
Mt 13:52 ·of·the·house, who from·among his treasure casts·
Mt 17:9 ·Clay·Man† should·rise·up from·among dead·men."
Mt 18:12 and one from·among them should·be·led·astray,
Mt 22:35 And one from·among them, *who·was* an·expert·in·
Mt 23:34 scribes, and *some* from·among them yeu·shall·kill
Mt 23:34 and *some* from·among them yeu·shall·flog in yeur
Mt 24:31 ·gather his Selected-Ones from·among the four
Mt 25:2 And five *virgins* from·among them were prudent,
Mt 26:21 to·yeu, that one from·among yeu shall·hand me
Mt 26:73 "Truly you·yourself are also from·among them, for
Mt 27:48 And immediately one from·among them, after·
Mt 27:53 And coming·forth from·among the chamber·tombs
Mk 6:14 ·One was·awakened from·among dead·men, and
Mk 6:16 is·already·awakened from·among dead·men."
Mk 7:31 And again, going·forth from·among the borders of·
Mk 9:9 of·Clay·Man† should·rise·up from·among dead·men.
Mk 9:10 it·should·mean to·rise·up from·among the dead.
Mk 9:17 And one·man, answering from·among the crowd,
Mk 12:25 they·should·rise·up from·among dead·men, they·
Mk 14:18 I·say to·yeu, that one from·among yeu, the·one
Mk 14:20 to·them, "*It·is* one from·among the twelve, the·
Mk 14:69 ·nearby, "This·man is from·among them."
Mk 14:70 to·Peter, "Truly you·are from·among them, for
Mk 16:12 ·made·apparent to·two·men from·among them in
Rm 4:12 ·ones *who·are* not from·among *the* Circumcision
Rm 4:24 ·awakening Jesus our Lord from·among dead·men,
Rm 6:4 is·already·awakened from·among dead·men through
Rm 6:9 that after·being·awakened from·among dead·men,
Rm 6:13 as those·that·are·alive from·among dead·men, and
Rm 7:4 already·being·awakened from·among dead·men, in·
Rm 8:11 awakening Jesus from·among dead·men dwells in
Rm 8:11 the Anointed-One from·among dead·men shall also
Rm 9:6 For not all the·ones from·among IsraEl, *are* this
Rm 9:24 he·called·forth— not from·among Jews merely,
Rm 9:24 Jews merely, but·yet also from·among Gentiles.
Rm 10:7 to·bring Anointed-One up from·among dead·men)
Rm 10:9 that God awakened him from·among dead·men,
Rm 11:1 am an·Israelite, from·among AbRaham's offspring†
Rm 11:14 my flesh and may·save some from·among them.
Rm 11:15 *be*, except life-above from·among dead·men?
Rm 11:24 are·already·chopped·off from·among an·olive·
Rm 13:3 you·shall·have high·praise from·among *the* same.
Rm 16:10 the·ones from·among AristoBulus' *household*.
Rm 16:11 Greet the·ones from·among the *household* of·
Jac 2:16 and anyone from·among yeu should·declare to·them
Php 3:5 *at* eight·days·of·age from·among *the* kindred of·
Php 3:5 tribe of·BenJamin, a·Hebrew from·among Hebrews;
Php 4:22 especially the·ones from·among Caesar's household
1Pe 1:3 of·YeShua Anointed from·among dead·men—
1Pe 1:21 the·one awakening him from·among dead·men and
1Th 1:10 whom he·awakened from·among dead·men,
1Th 2:6 nor seeking glory from·among men·of·clay†, neither
Tit 1:10 especially the·ones from·among *the* Circumcision,
Tit 1:12 Someone from·among themselves, a·prophet of·
Tit 2:8 in·order·that the·one from·among *those being*
1Co 5:2 should·be·entirely·expelled from·among *the* midst
1Co 5:13 the evil·person from·among yeurselves in·unison."
1Co 9:13 ·things eat from·among the Sanctuary·Courtyard?
1Co 9:19 For *though* being free from·among all *men·of·clay*†
1Co 12:15 ·am not a·hand, I·am not from·among the body,"
1Co 12:15 this *reasoning*, is·it not from·among the body?
1Co 12:16 I·am not an·eye, I·am not from·among the body,"
1Co 12:16 this *reasoning*, is·it not from·among the body?
1Co 12:27 Body and members from·among a·portion *of·it*,
1Co 15:6 upon·one·occasion·only, from·among whom the
1Co 15:12 he·has·been·awakened from·among dead·men,
1Co 15:20 has·been·awakened from·among dead·men. He·
2Co 3:1 or *of·letters* of·recommendation from·among yeu.
2Co 3:5 to·reckon anything as from·among ourselves, but·
2Co 5:8 ·the·more to·be·absent·abroad from·among the body
2Co 6:17 "yeu·must·come·out from·among *the* midst of·
2Co 11:26 of·robbers, dangers from·among *my·own* kindred,
2Co 11:26 *my·own* kindred, dangers from·among Gentiles,
Eph 1:20 after·awakening him from·among dead·men. And
Col 4:9 brother, who is from·among yeu. They·shall·make·
Col 4:11 *are* the·ones being from·among *the* Circumcision,
Col 4:12 EpAphras, the·one from·among yeu, a·slave of·
2Ti 2:8 *is* having·been·awakened from·among dead·men
2Ti 3:6 For from·among these *types* are the·ones
1Jn 2:19 They·went·out from·among us, but·yet they·were
1Jn 2:19 us, but·yet they·were not from·among us; for if
1Jn 2:19 us; for if they·were from·among us, they·would
1Jn 2:19 ·apparent that they·were not all from·among us.
1Jn 4:5 on·account·of that they·speak from·among the world
2Jn 1:4 ·much that I·have·found from·among your children
Rv 2:10 is·about to·cast *some* from·among yeu into prison
Rv 2:21 ·that she·should·repent out·from·among her sexual·
Rv 2:22 they·should·not repent out·from·among their deeds.
Rv 3:9 Behold, I·give·forth *those* from·among the gathering
Rv 3:18 me gold having·been·refined from·among fire, in·
Rv 5:5 And one from·among the Elders says to·me, "Do·not
Rv 5:5 Lion, the·one being from·among the tribe of·Judah
Rv 6:1 opened·up *the* first from·among the official·seals, and
Rv 6:1 and I·heard one from·among the four living·beings
Rv 7:4 having·been·officially·sealed from·among all *the*
Rv 7:5 From·among *the* tribe of·Judah having·been·
Rv 7:5 twelve thousand. From·among *the* tribe of·ReuBen
Rv 7:5 twelve thousand. From·among *the* tribe of·Gad
Rv 7:6 From·among *the* tribe of·Asher having·been·
Rv 7:6 twelve thousand. From·among *the* tribe of·Naphtali
Rv 7:6 twelve thousand. From·among *the* tribe of·MaNasseh
Rv 7:7 From·among *the* tribe of·Shimon having·been·
Rv 7:7 twelve thousand. From·among *the* tribe of·Levi
Rv 7:7 twelve thousand. From·among *the* tribe of·IsSakar
Rv 7:8 From·among *the* tribe of·Zebulun having·been·
Rv 7:8 twelve thousand. From·among *the* tribe of·Joseph
Rv 7:8 twelve thousand. From·among *the* tribe of·BenJamin
Rv 7:9 ·able to·number, *a·crowd* from·among all nations,
Rv 7:13 Then one from·among the Elders answered, saying
Rv 9:13 and I·heard one voice from·among the four horns
Rv 9:20 did·not·even repent out·from·among the works of·
Rv 9:21 did·they·repent out·from·among their murders, nor
Rv 11:9 And from·among the peoples and tribes and native·
Rv 15:2 overcoming (out·from·among the Daemonic·Beast,
Rv 15:2 ·Beast, and out·from·among its derived·image, and
Rv 15:2 its derived·image, and out·from·among its etching,
Rv 15:2 its etching, *and* out·from·among the number of·its
Rv 15:7 And one from·among the four living·beings gave to·
Rv 15:8 was·overfilled with·smoke from·among the glory
Rv 16:7 And I·heard another from·among the Sacrifice·Altar
Rv 16:11 they·did·not repent out·from·among their deeds.
Rv 17:1 And there·came one from·among the seven angels,
Rv 17:11 is an·eighth *king* and is from·among the seven, and

Rv 18:4 saying: "Come·out from·among her, my People,
Rv 19:21 the fowls were·stuffed·full from·among their flesh.
EG1537.3 (1x)
Ac 26:17 the People, and *from·among* the Gentiles— 'to
G1537.4 PREP ἔκ (1x)
Lk 1:15 with·Holy Spirit, yet·even from·within his mother's
G1537.5 PREP ἔκ (60x)
Jn 1:13 ·*the*·will of·man, but·rather birthed·from·out of·God.
Jn 3:31 all. The·one being birthed·from·out of·the earth is
Jn 6:65 ·been·given to·him birthed·from·out of·my Father."
Jn 7:42 the Anointed-One comes birthed·from·out of·the Seed
Jn 8:23 "Yeu·yeurselves are birthed·from down·below; I·
Jn 8:23 down·below; I·myself am birthed·from up·above.
Jn 8:44 "Yeu·yeurselves are birthed·from·out *of·yeur* father
Jn 8:47 The·one being birthed·from·out of·God hears the
Jn 8:47 *them* because yeu·are not birthed·from·out of·God."
Jn 18:37 truth. Everyone being birthed·from·out of·the truth
Ac 5:38 work should·be birthed·from·out of·men·of·clay†, it·
Ac 5:39 But if it·is birthed·from·out of·God, yeu·are·not able
Ac 23:34 inquired from·which province he·was birthed. And
Heb 2:11 ·made·holy *are* all birthed·from·out of·one *Father*.
Gal 3:7 know that the·ones birthed·from·out of·trust, the·
Gal 3:8 ·as·righteous the Gentiles birthed·from·out of·trust,
Gal 3:9 ·such, the·ones birthed·from·out of·trust are·blessed
Gal 3:10 ·as are birthed·from·out of·works of·Torah-Law,
Gal 4:4 his Son, coming·to·be birthed·from·out of·a·woman,
Gal 4:22 had two sons, one birthed·from·out the maidservant,
Gal 4:22 and one birthed·from·out the free·woman.
Gal 4:23 in·fact, the·one birthed·from·out of·the maidservant
Gal 4:23 but the·one birthed·from·out of·the free·woman
Mt 1:3 begot Perets and Zarach (birthed·from·out of·Tamar),
Mt 1:5 Salmon begot BoAz (birthed·from·out of·Rachav), and
Mt 1:5 and BoAz begot Obed (birthed·from·out of·Ruth), and
Mt 1:6 begot Solomon (birthed·from·out of·the·one *having*·
Mt 1:18 being in·a·pregnancy birthed·from·out of·Holy Spirit
Mt 1:20 ·conceived in her is birthed·from·out of·Holy Spirit.
Mt 5:37 of·these·things is birthed·from·out of·the Evil·One.
Rm 1:3 ·one coming·to·be birthed·from·out of·David's Seed
Rm 1:17 is·revealed, birthed·from·out of·trust into trust.
Rm 2:27 the·one birthed·from·out of·natural uncircumcision
Rm 3:26 the·one birthed·from·out of·a·trust of·Jesus
Rm 4:14 For if the·ones birthed·from·out of·Torah-Law *are*
Rm 4:16 ·the·one *who·is* birthed·from·out of·the Torah-Law
Rm 4:16 ·the·one *who·is* birthed·from·out of·AbRaham's trust
Rm 9:30 the righteousness birthed·from·out of·trust.
Rm 10:6 righteousness, the·one birthed·from·out of·trust,
Jac 4:1 not from·here, birthed·from·out of·yeur pleasures,
1Pe 1:23 not birthed·from·out of·a·corruptible sowing·of·
1Th 2:3 our exhortation *was* not birthed·from·out of·deceit,
1Co 1:30 But *being* birthed·from·out of *God*, yeu are in
2Co 1:11 on·our behalf, birthed·from·out of·many persons,
2Co 2:17 moreover as birthed·from·out of·God *being*
Eph 2:8 And this *is* not birthed·from·out of·yeurselves; *it·is*
Eph 2:9 *This is* not birthed·from·out of·works, in·order·that
2Ti 2:8 Jesus Anointed, birthed·from·out of·David's Seed, *is*
1Jn 2:16 of·natural·life, is not birthed·from·out of·the Father,
1Jn 2:16 Father, but·rather is birthed·from·out of·the world.
1Jn 2:21 and that any lie is not birthed·from·out of·the truth.
1Jn 3:8 the moral·failure is birthed·from·out of·the Slanderer,
1Jn 3:10 doing righteousness is not birthed·from·out of·God,
1Jn 3:12 *did*, who was birthed·from·out of·the Evil·One and
1Jn 3:19 we·know that we·are birthed·from·out of·the truth
1Jn 4:4 Yeu·yeurselves are birthed·from·out of·God, dear·
1Jn 4:6 We·ourselves are birthed·from·out of·God. The·one
1Jn 4:6 Whoever is not birthed·from·out of·God does·not
1Jn 4:7 because the love is birthed·from·out of·God; and any
1Jn 5:19 ·know that we·are birthed·from·out of·God, and the
G1537.6 PREP ἐξ (71x)
Jn 3:34 God does·not give the Spirit as·a·result of·measure.
Jn 4:6 having·become·weary as·a·result of·the road·travel,
Jn 6:66 As·a·result of·this, many of·his disciples went·off to
Jn 19:12 As·a·result of·this, Pilate was·seeking to·fully·
Jn 19:23 ·tunic was without·seam, as·a·result of·it *being*
Ac 19:25 that our prosperity is as·a·result of·this occupation.
Heb 10:38 the righteous·man shall·live as·a·result of·trust,
Gal 2:16 ·not regarded·as·righteous as·a·result of·works of·
Gal 2:16 we·should·be·regarded·as·righteous as·a·result of·
Gal 2:16 and not as·a·result of·works of·Torah-Law— on·
Gal 2:16 ·as·righteous as·a·result of·works of·Torah-Law.
Gal 3:2 ·receive the Spirit as·a·result of·works of·Torah-Law
Gal 3:2 of·Torah-Law, or as·a·result of·a·hearing of·trust?
Gal 3:5 among yeu, *is·it* as·a·result of·works of·Torah-Law,
Gal 3:5 of·Torah-Law, or as·a·result of·a·hearing of·trust?
Gal 3:11 "the righteous·one shall·live as·a·result of·trust."
Gal 3:12 the Torah-Law is not as·a·result of·trust, but·rather,
Gal 3:18 if the inheritance *is* as·a·result of·Torah-Law, *it·is*
Gal 3:18 ·Torah-Law, *it·is* no·longer as·a·result of·promise.
Gal 3:21 really would be as·a·result of·Torah-Law.
Gal 3:22 ·failure in·order·that, as·a·result of·trust in·YeShua
Gal 3:24 we·may·be·regarded·as·righteous as·a·result of·.
Gal 5:5 an·expectation of·righteousness as·a·result of·trust.
Mt 15:5 you·should·have·benefited as·a·result of·me,
Mk 7:11 you·should·have·benefited as·a·result of·me,
Rm 1:17 But the righteous·man shall·live as·a·result of·trust.
Rm 3:20 on·account·that, as·a·result *of·the* deeds of·
Rm 3:30 *the* Circumcision as·a·result of·trust and *the*
Rm 4:2 was·regarded·as·righteous as·a·result of·works, he·
Rm 4:16 that, *righteousness is* as·a·result of·trust, in·order·
Rm 5:1 already·being·regarded·as·righteous as·a·result of·,
Rm 5:16 the judgment *was* as·a·result of·one *trespass* unto
Rm 5:16 ·bestowment *is* as·a·result of·many trespasses unto
Rm 9:11 ·to God's Selection, not as·a·result of·works, but·
Rm 9:11 but·rather as·a·result of·the·one calling·forth),
Rm 9:32 Because *they·pursued it* not as·a·result of·trust, but·
Rm 9:32 ·though *it·were* as·a·result of·works of·Torah-Law.
Rm 10:17 the trust *comes* as·a·result of·hearing, and the
Rm 11:6 *it·is* by·grace, *it·is* no·longer as·a·result of·works,
Rm 11:6 But if *it·is* as·a·result of·works, *then* it·is no·longer
Jac 2:18 Show me your trust as·a·result of·your works,
Jac 2:18 ·I shall·show you my trust as·a·result of·my works.
Jac 2:21 our father, was·it·not as·a·result of·works *that* he·
Jac 2:22 with·his works, and as·a·result of·the works, the
Jac 2:24 Now·then yeu·clearly·see that as·a·result of·works,
Jac 2:24 ·as·righteous, and not as·a·result of·trust merely.
Jac 2:25 ·she·not regarded·as·righteous as·a·result of·works,
Php 1:23 For I·am·clenched as·a·result of·the two *choices*,
1Pe 2:12 yeu as criminals, as·a·result *of·yeur* good works
Tit 3:5 *it·was* not as·a·result of·works (of·the·ones in
1Co 7:5 *which* might·be as·a·result of·a·mutual·agreement
2Co 2:2 except the·one being·grieved as·a·result of·me?
2Co 7:9 ·should·have·suffered·damage·and·loss as·a·result.
2Co 8:7 ·all diligence, and (as·a·result of·yeu *being* among
2Co 13:4 though he·is·crucified as·a·result of·weakness, yet
2Co 13:4 ·weakness, yet he·lives as·a·result of·God's power.
2Co 13:4 ·live together with·him as·a·result of·God's power
1Jn 3:24 he·presently·abides in us, as·a·result of·the Spirit
1Jn 4:6 ·God does·not hear us. As·a·result of·this, we·know
Rv 2:11 ·not be·brought·to·harm as·a·result of·the Second
Rv 8:11 many men·of·clay† died as·a·result of·the waters,
Rv 9:18 ·the men·of·clay† were·killed, as·a·result of·the fire
Rv 9:18 as·a·result of·the fire, and as·a·result of·the smoke,
Rv 9:18 ·a·result of·the smoke, and as·a·result of·the sulfur,
Rv 16:10 their tongues as·a·result of·the continual·anguish,
Rv 16:11 of·the heaven as·a·result of·their continual·anguish
Rv 16:11 continual·anguish and as·a·result of·their pus·sores
Rv 16:21 reviled God as·a·result of·the punishing·blow of·
Rv 18:1 the earth was·illuminated as·a·result of·his glory.
Rv 18:19 sea became·wealthy as·a·result of·her valuableness
Rv 18:20 decided yeur just·claim as·a·result of·her *conduct*!"
G1537.7 PREP ἔκ (35x)
Jn 16:4 these·things I·did·not declare to·yeu at *the* beginning
Lk 1:11 ·him an·angel of·Yahweh standing at *the* right·side
Lk 20:42 declared to·my Lord, "Sit·down at my right·hand
Lk 22:69 ·Clay·Man† shall·be sitting·down at *the* right·hand
Lk 23:33 the criminals, in·fact one at *the* right·hand, and
Lk 23:33 ·fact one at *the* right·hand, and the·other at *the* left.
Ac 2:25 ·me continually, because he·is at my right·hand in·
Ac 2:34 declared to·my Lord, "Sit·down at my right·hand
Ac 7:55 glory, and Jesus standing at *the* right·hand of·God.
Ac 7:56 the Son of·Clay·Man† standing at *the* right·hand of·
Heb 1:13 at·any·time, "'Sit·down at my right·hand, until I·
Mt 20:21 sons of·mine may·sit, one at your right·hand and
Mt 20:21 one at your right·hand and one at *your* left, in your
Mt 20:23 shall·be·immersed·in, but to·sit at my right·hand
Mt 20:23 ·in, but to·sit at my right·hand and at my left is not
Mt 22:44 to·my Lord, "Sit·down at my right·hand until I·
Mt 25:33 in·fact, he·shall·set the sheep at his right·hand, but
Mt 25:33 at his right·hand, but the infantile·goats at *the* left.
Mt 25:34 the King shall·declare to·the·ones at his right·hand,
Mt 25:41 he·shall·declare also to·the·ones at *the* left·hand,
Mt 26:64 Son of·Clay·Man† sitting·down at *the* right·hand'
Mt 27:38 together with·him, one at *the* right·hand and one at
Mt 27:38 with·him, one at *the* right·hand and one at *the* left.
Mk 10:37 to·us that we·may·sit, one at your right·hand and
Mk 10:37 one at your right·hand and one at your left, in your
Mk 10:40 But to·sit at my right·hand and at my left is not
Mk 10:40 But to·sit at my right·hand and at my left is not
Mk 12:36 to·my Lord, "Sit·down at my right·hand until I·
Mk 14:62 Son of·Clay·Man† sitting·down at *the* right·hand
Mk 15:27 ·crucify two robbers: one at his·right·hand, and
Mk 15:27 robbers: one at his·right·hand, and one at his left.
Mk 16:3 shall·roll·away for·us the stone at the door of·the
Mk 16:19 the heaven and seated at *the* right·hand of·God.
Jac 3:11 ¿!·Does the wellspring gush·forth at the same
Rv 19:2 the blood of·his slaves *poured·out* at her hand."
G1537.8 PREP ἔκ (12x)
Jn 9:24 So·then for a·second·time they·hollered·out·for the
Lk 8:27 was·having demons for a·significant·span of·time,
Lk 23:8 wanting to·see him for a·long·while on·account·of
Ac 9:33 by·name, laying·down upon a·mat for eight years,
Ac 10:15 a·voice *spoke* to him again for a·second·time,
Ac 11:9 *the* voice answered me for a·second·time from·out
Heb 9:28 many,' for a·second·time (completely·apart·from
Mt 20:2 with the workmen *to·hire them* for a·denarius *for*
Mt 26:42 Again for a·second·time, after·going·off, he·
Mt 26:44 them, going·off again, he·prayed for a·third·time,
Mk 14:72 And for a·second·time, a·rooster crowed.
Rm 12:18 *and* if *it·is* possible, for yeur part, behaving·
G1537.9 PREP ἔκ (2x)
Jn 17:15 ·should·guard them beyond·reach of·the Evil·One.
Mk 6:51 astonished among themselves beyond excess, and
G1537.10 PREP ἐξ (1x)
2Pe 2:8 residing among them day by day was·tormenting *his*

G1538 ἕκαστος hékastôs *adj.* (83x)

Compare:G2596
G1538.1 A-NSM ἕκαστος (42x)
Jn 6:7 sufficient for·them, that each·one of·them may·take
Jn 7:53 And each·man traversed to his·own house.
Jn 16:32 that yeu·should·be·scattered, each·man to his·own
Lk 2:3 all traversed to·be·enrolled, each·one into his·own
Lk 13:15 ·acting·hypocrite, does·not each·one of·yeu on·the
Ac 2:6 was·greatly·confused, because each one was·hearing
Ac 2:8 And how·do we·ourselves each hear our own·distinct
Ac 2:38 "Repent, and each·one of·yeu be·immersed in the
Ac 11:29 So some of·the disciples, each of·them just·as he·
Heb 8:11 ·not *anymore* instruct each·man his neighbor, and
Heb 8:11 each·man his neighbor, and each·man his brother,
Gal 6:4 But each·man must·test·and·prove his·own work,
Gal 6:5 For each·man shall·bear his·own load.
Mt 18:35 to·yeu, unless each·one·of yeu·should·forgive his
Mt 26:22 tremendously grieved, each·one of·them began to·
Rm 14:5 *to·be alike*. Let each·man be·fully·assured in his·
Rm 14:12 So·then, consequently, each·one of·us shall·give
Rm 15:2 For each·one of·us must·willingly·adapt to·his
Jac 1:14 But each·man is·tempted, being·drawn·forth by his·
Php 2:4 ·keep·a·watch, *but* not each·man of·his·own things
Php 2:4 things *only*, but·rather each·man also the·things of·
1Pe 4:10 Just·as each·man received a·gracious·bestowment,
1Co 1:12 Now I·say this, that each·one of·yeu says, "In·fact

1Co 3:8 are one, and each·man shall·receive his·own
1Co 3:10 builds·upon *it*. But each·man must·look·out how
1Co 7:2 ·of the sexual·immoralities, each *man* must·have
1Co 7:7 as myself. But·yet each·man has his·own gracious·
1Co 7:20 Each·man, in the calling in·which he·was·called·
1Co 7:24 Each·man, in that·*state*·which he·is·called·forth,
1Co 10:24 seek his·own, but·rather each·man the other's
1Co 11:21 For in eating, each·one takes his·own supper
1Co 14:26 yeu·should·come·together, each·one of·yeu has
1Co 15:23 but each in one's·own sequence: Anointed-One, a·
1Co 16:2 first *day* of·the·week, let each·one of·yeu lay *aside*
2Co 5:10 in·order·that each·one may·subsequently·obtain
2Co 9:7 *Let* each·man *sow* just·as he·is·preinclined in·*his*·
Eph 4:25 the lying, "Each·man must·speak truth with his
Eph 5:33 ·yeurselves (accordingly each one in·that·manner)
Eph 6:8 beneficially·good·thing each·man should·do, this
Rv 5:8 ·sight of·the Lamb, each·one *of·the·Elders* having
Rv 20:13 in them. And each·one was·judged according·to
Rv 21:21 twelve pearls; again, each one of·the gates was

G1538.1 A-NSF ἑκάστη (1x)
1Co 7:2 his·own wife, and each *woman* must·have her·own

G1538.1 A-NSN ἕκαστον (2x)
Lk 6:44 For each tree is·known from·out of·its·own fruit.
1Co 12:18 himself·placed the members, each one of·them,

G1538.1 A-ASM ἕκαστον (10x)
Lk 16:5 "And summoning each one of·his lord's needy·
Ac 2:3 to·them, and it·settled upon each one of·them.
Ac 3:26 yeu in this·thing, to·turn·away each·one *of·yeu* from
Ac 20:31 I·did·not cease admonishing each one, night and
Heb 6:11 And we·long·for each·one of·yeu to·indicate the
Heb 11:21 (when·he·was·dying) blessed each of·the Sons
1Th 2:11 Exactly·as yeu·have·seen (each one of·yeu), how
1Th 4:4 for·each·one of·yeu to·personally·know·how to·
1Co 7:17 imparted to·each·man, each·one according·as the
Rv 22:2 yielding·forth its fruit according·to each one's month

G1538.1 A-DSM ἑκάστῳ (17x)
Jn 19:23 made four parts, a·part for·each soldier, and·also
Lk 4:40 and laying his hands on·each one of·them, he·both·
Ac 4:35 feet, and it·was·thoroughly·doled·out to·each·man,
Mt 16:27 'he·shall·give·back to·each·man according·to his
Mt 25:15 to·another one, to·each·man according·to his·own
Mk 13:34 authority to·his slaves, and to·each·man his work,
Rm 2:6 ·himself "shall·render to·each·man according·to his
Rm 12:3 ·as God imparted to·each·man a·measure of·trust.
1Co 3:5 yeu·trusted, even as the Lord gave to·each·man?
1Co 4:5 high·praise from God shall·come·to·be to·each·man.
1Co 7:17 ·*know that* as God imparted to·each·man, each·one
1Co 12:7 ·the Spirit is·given to·each·man specifically·for the
1Co 12:11 dispensing to·each·man individually just·as he·
Eph 4:7 But the Grace is·given to·each one of·us according·
Col 4:6 to·personally·know how to·answer each individual.
Rv 2:23 And I·shall·give to·each·one of·yeu according·to
Rv 22:12 *is* with me, to·give·back to·each·man as his work

G1538.1 A-DSN ἑκάστῳ (1x)
1Co 15:38 ·as he·determined, and to·each variety·of·seed,

G1538.1 A-DPM ἑκάστοις (1x)
Rv 6:11 long·robes were·given to·each·one·of·them, and it·

G1538.1 A-GSM ἑκάστου (6x)
Ac 17:27 ·being not at·a·distance from each one of·us.
Ac 21:26 should·be·offered on·behalf of·each one of·them.
1Pe 1:17 ·to the work of·each·man, conduct·yeurselves
2Th 1:3 ·exceedingly, and the love of·each one of·yeu all,
1Co 3:13 fire shall·test·and·prove each·man's work for·what·
Eph 4:16 ·to an·effective·working of·each individual part in

G1538.1 A-GMS ἑκάστου (1x)
1Co 3:13 each·man's work shall·become apparent, for the

G1538.2 A-ASF ἑκάστην (1x)
Heb 3:13 But·rather exhort one·another each and·every day,

G1538.2 A-ASN ἕκαστον (1x)
Ac 21:19 ·detail each and·every one of·those·things·which

G1539 ἑκάσ•τοτε hêkástôtê *adv.* (1x)
Roots:G1538 G5119 Compare:G3842 G0104

G1539.2 ADV ἑκάστοτε (1x)
2Pe 1:15 ·endeavor for·yeu to·have at·any·time, after my

G1540 ἑκατόν hêkatón *n.* (16x)
Compare:G1542 See:G1250
xLangEquiv:H3967

G1540.1 N-NUI ἑκατόν (12x)
Jn 19:39 about *a·weight* of·a·hundred Roman·pounds.
Jn 21:11 ·full of·big fish (a·hundred *and* fifty·three); and·yet
Lk 15:4 from·among yeu, having a·hundred sheep, that
Lk 16:6 And he·declared, 'A·hundred bath·measures of·oil.
Lk 16:7 And he·declared, 'A·hundred kor·measures of·
Ac 1:15 of·names in·unison *of* about a·hundred *and* twenty),
Mt 18:12 *that* any man·of·clay† *has* a·hundred sheep, and
Mt 18:28 ·slaves who was·owing him a·hundred denarii,
Mk 6:40 ·back·to·eat in·rows, rows by a·hundred, and by
Rv 14:1 Tsiyon, and with him a·hundred *and* forty four
Rv 14:3 to·learn the song except the hundred *and* forty four
Rv 21:17 he·measured its wall, a·hundred *and* forty four

G1540.2 N-NUI ἑκατόν (4x)
Mt 13:8 fruit, in·fact some *seed* a·hundredfold, some *seed*
Mt 13:23 in·fact, some *seed* a·hundredfold, some *seed*
Mk 4:8 one *seed* sixtyfold, and one *seed* a·hundredfold."
Mk 4:20 one *seed* sixtyfold, and one *seed* a·hundredfold."

G1541 ἑκατοντα•έτης hêkatôntaétēs *adj.* (1x)
Roots:G1540 G2094

G1541 A-NSM ἑκατονταέτης (1x)
Rm 4:19 somewhere·near a·hundred·years·of·age, nor the

G1542 ἑκα•τοντα•πλασίων hêkatôntaplasíōn *adj.* (3x)
Roots:G1540 G4111 G4120 Compare:G4179
See:G1542-1

G1542 A-ASM ἑκατονταπλασίονα (1x)
Lk 8:8 ·sprouted, it·produced fruit a·hundred·times·over."

G1542 A-APN ἑκατονταπλασίονα (2x)
Mt 19:29 shall·receive a·hundred·times·over and shall·
Mk 10:30 ·should·not receive a·hundred·times·over now in

G1543 ἑκατοντ•άρχης hêkatôntárchēs *n.* (22x) ἑκατόντ•αρχος hêkatóntarchôs
Roots:G1540 G0757 Compare:G2760 G4757 G4686

G1543.1 N-NSM ἑκατόνταρχος (10x)
Lk 7:6 from the home, the centurion sent friends to him,
Ac 10:1 by·name, a·centurion from·among a·battalion
Ac 10:22 "Cornelius, a·centurion, a·righteous man who·is·
Ac 22:26 And *upon* the centurion hearing *that*, coming·
Ac 27:6 sailing into Italy, the centurion made us embark
Ac 27:11 But the centurion was·convinced by·the pilot and
Ac 27:43 But the centurion, being·resolved to·thoroughly·
Ac 28:16 to Rome, the centurion handed·over the chained·
Mt 8:5 into CaperNaum, a·centurion came·alongside him,
Mt 8:8 And answering, the centurion was·replying, "Lord,

G1543.1 N-ASM ἑκατόνταρχον (1x)
Ac 22:25 Paul declared to the centurion standing·by, "Is·it·

G1543.1 N-APM ἑκατοντάρχους (1x)
Ac 21:32 personally·taking soldiers and centurions. And

G1543.1 N-DSM ἑκατοντάρχῃ (4x)
Ac 24:23 ·arranged·for the centurion to·keep Paul, and·also
Ac 27:1 certain other prisoners over to·a·centurion, Julius
Ac 27:31 Paul declared to·the centurion and to·the soldiers,
Mt 8:13 Then YeShua declared to·the centurion, "Head·on·

G1543.1 N-GSM ἑκατοντάρχου (1x)
Lk 7:2 Now a·certain centurion's slave, who was dearly·

G1543.1 N-GPM ἑκατονταρχῶν (2x)
Ac 23:17 So after·summoning one of·the centurions, Paul
Ac 23:23 a·certain two of·the centurions, he·declared,

EG1543.1 (1x)
Ac 23:18 So·then in·fact, the *centurion*, personally·taking

G1543.2 N-NSM ἑκατόνταρχος (2x)
Lk 23:47 Now the Roman·centurion, seeing the·thing *that*·
Mt 27:54 Now the Roman·centurion and the·ones keeping·

G1544 ἐκ•βάλλω êkbállō *v.* (82x)
Roots:G1537 G0906 xLangAlso:H1644

G1544.1 V-FAI-3P ἐκβαλοῦσιν (1x)
Mk 16:17 "in my name shall·they·cast·out demons; they·

G1544.1 V-FPI-3S ἐκβληθήσεται (1x)
Jn 12:31 prince of·this world shall now be·cast·out outside.

G1544.1 V-FPI-3P ἐκβληθήσονται (1x)
Mt 8:12 Sons of·the kingdom shall·be·cast·out into the outer

G1544.1 V-PAI-1S ἐκβάλλω (5x)
Lk 11:19 if I·myself by Master-Of-Dung cast·out the demons
Lk 11:20 if with God's finger, I·cast·out the demons, then·
Lk 13:32 fox, 'Behold, I·cast·out demons, and I·further·
Mt 12:27 by Master-Of-Dung, cast·out the demons, by
Mt 12:28 But if I·myself cast·out the demons by God's Spirit

G1544.1 V-PAI-2S ἐκβάλλεις (1x)
Mt 8:31 him, saying, "If you·cast us out, freely·permit us

G1544.1 V-PAI-3S ἐκβάλλει (5x)
Lk 11:15 them declared, "He·casts·out the demons by
Mt 9:34 Pharisees were·saying, "He·casts·out the demons
Mt 12:24 declared, "This·man does·not cast·out the demons,
Mt 12:26 Adversary-Accuser casts·out the Adversary-Accuser,
Mk 3:22 the prince of·the demons he·casts·out the demons."

G1544.1 V-PAI-3P ἐκβάλλουσιν (3x)
Lk 11:19 whom·do yeur sons cast·*them*·out? On·account·of
Ac 16:37 into prison. And now do·they·cast us out privately
Mt 12:27 whom·do yeur sons cast·*them*·out? On·account·of

G1544.1 V-PAM-2P ἐκβάλλετε (2x)
Mt 10:8 awaken dead·ones; cast·out demons. Yeu·received
Mt 25:30 'And yeu·cast·out the useless slave into the outer

G1544.1 V-PAN ἐκβάλλειν (5x)
Lk 19:45 ·Atrium, he·began to·cast·out the·ones selling and
Mt 10:1 ·for them to·cast·out and to·both·relieve·and·cure
Mk 3:15 ·and·cure the illnesses, and to·cast·out the demons.
Mk 3:23 Adversary-Accuser to·cast·out Adversary-Accuser?
Mk 11:15 ·Atrium, began to·cast·out the·ones selling and

G1544.1 V-PAN@ ἐκβάλλειν (1x)
Lk 11:18 "Yeu·say that I cast·out demons by *the*

G1544.1 V-PAP-ASM ἐκβάλλοντα (2x)
Lk 9:49 ·Captain, we·saw someone casting·out the demons
Mk 9:38 we·saw someone casting·out demons in·your

G1544.1 V-PAP-NSM ἐκβάλλων (2x)
Lk 11:14 *afterward*, *Jesus* was casting·out a·demon, and it
Mk 1:39 among all Galilee and casting·out the demons.

G1544.1 V-PAS-3P ἐκβάλλωσιν (1x)
Lk 9:40 your disciples in·order·that they·should·cast him out

G1544.1 V-PMP-NPM ἐκβαλλόμενοι (1x)
Ac 27:38 the sailing·ship, *by* casting·out the wheat into the

G1544.1 V-PPI-3S ἐκβάλλεται (1x)
Mt 15:17 into the belly and·then is·cast·out into an·outhouse

G1544.1 V-PPP-APM ἐκβαλλομένους (1x)
Lk 13:28 of·God, but yeu·yeurselves being·cast·out outside.

G1544.1 V-IAI-3P ἐξέβαλλον (1x)
Mk 6:13 And they·were·casting·out many demons, and with·

G1544.1 V-2AAI-1P ἐξεβάλομεν (1x)
Mt 7:22 name, and in·your name cast·out demons, and in·

G1544.1 V-2AAI-3S ἐξέβαλεν (4x)
Jn 2:15 of·small·cords, he·cast·out everyone from·among
Mt 8:16 ·possessed·with·demons, and he·cast·out the spirits
Mt 21:12 Sanctuary·Estate of·God and cast·out all the·ones
Mk 1:34 ·of illnesses, and he·cast·out many demons. And

G1544.1 V-2AAI-3P ἐξέβαλον (2x)
Lk 20:12 But also wounding this·man, they·cast·*him*·out.
Ac 13:50 against Paul and BarNabas and cast them out from

G1544.1 V-2AAM-2S ἔκβαλε (4x)
Lk 6:42 "O·stage·acting·hypocrite, first cast·out the beam
Gal 4:30 Scripture say? "Cast·out the maidservant and her
Mt 7:5 O·stage·acting·hypocrite, first cast the beam from·
Mk 9:47 And if your eye should·entrap you, cast it out. It·is

G1544.1 V-2AAM-2P ἐκβάλετε (1x)
Mt 22:13 take him away and cast·*him*·out into the outer

G1544.1 V-2AAN ἐκβαλεῖν (4x)
Lk 6:42 then you·shall·thoroughly·look·about to·cast·out the
Mt 7:5 you·shall·thoroughly·look·about to·cast the speck·of·
Mt 17:19 "Why·were we·ourselves not able to·cast it out?
Mk 9:28 "Why·were we·ourselves not able to·cast it out?

G1544.1 V-2AAP-NSM ἐκβαλών (2x)
Lk 8:54 And he·himself, after·casting·out everyone outside

Mk 5:40 at·him. But casting·out absolutely·all·of·them, he·
G1544.1 V-2AAP-NPM ἐκβαλόντες (1x)
Ac 7:58 And after·casting·*him*·out outside of·the City, they·
G1544.1 V-2AAS-1S ἐκβάλω (3x)
Jn 6:37 toward me, no, I·should·not cast·out outside,
Lk 6:42 allow *that* I·should·cast·out the speck·of·dust, the·
Mt 7:4 'Give·way *so* I·may·cast·out the speck·of·dust from
G1544.1 V-2AAS-3P ἐκβάλωσιν (2x)
Lk 6:22 should·reproach *yeu*, and should·cast·out yeur name
Mk 9:18 to·your disciples that they·should·cast it out, yet
G1544.1 V-API-3S ἐξεβλήθη (1x)
Mt 9:25 But when the crowd was·cast·out, upon·entering,
G1544.1 V-APP-GSN ἐκβληθέντος (1x)
Mt 9:33 And with·the demon being·cast·out, the mute spoke,
G1544.1 V-LAI-3S ἐκβεβλήκει (1x)
Mk 16:9 from whom he·had·cast·out seven demons.
G1544.2 V-PAI-3S ἐκβάλλει (5x)
Mt 12:35 of·his heart casts·forth the beneficially·good·things
Mt 12:35 from·out of·his evil treasure casts·forth evil·things.
Mt 13:52 who from·among his treasure casts·forth *things*
Mk 1:12 And straight·away the Spirit casts him forth into the
3Jn 1:10 ·resolved *to·do so* and casts·*them*·forth out of·the
G1544.2 V-PAS-3S ἐκβάλλη (2x)
Lk 10:2 ·the harvest, that he·should·cast·forth workmen into
Mk 7:26 ·asking·of him that he·should·cast·forth the demon
G1544.2 V-2AAI-3S ἐξέβαλεν (1x)
Mk 1:43 sternly·warning him, immediately he·cast him forth
G1544.2 V-2AAI-3P ἐξέβαλον (5x)
Jn 9:34 instruct us?" And they·cast him forth outside.
Jn 9:35 Jesus heard that they·cast him forth outside.
Lk 4:29 And after·rising·up, they·cast him forth outside of·
Mt 21:39 ·hold·of him, they·cast·*him*·forth outside of·the
Mk 12:8 they·killed *him* and cast·*him*·forth outside of·the
G1544.2 V-2AAM-2S ἔκβαλε (1x)
Rv 11:2 *toward* the Temple, you·must·cast·forth outside,
G1544.2 V-2AAP-NSF ἐκβαλοῦσα (1x)
Jac 2:25 the messengers and casting·*them*·forth another way?
G1544.2 V-2AAP-NSM ἐκβαλών (2x)
Lk 10:35 upon the stirring·of·day, casting·forth two denarii,
Ac 9:40 But Peter, after·casting everyone forth outside,
G1544.2 V-2AAP-NPM ἐκβαλόντες (1x)
Lk 20:15 So casting him forth outside of·the vineyard, they·
G1544.2 V-2AAS-3S ἐκβάλη (3x)
Jn 10:4 "And whenever he·should·cast·forth his·own sheep,
Mt 9:38 ·the harvest, that he·should·cast·forth workmen into
Mt 12:20 until he·should·cast·forth tribunal·justice into

G1545 ἔκ•βασις êkbasis *n.* (2x)
Roots:G1537 G0901-3 Compare:G0668 G5343 G1628 See:G0939
G1545.2 N-ASF ἔκβασιν (1x)
1Co 10:13 also shall·make the exit·out, for·yeu to·be·able
G1545.3 N-ASF ἔκβασιν (1x)
Heb 13:7 observing·again the outcome of·*their*·behavior.

G1546 ἐκ•βολή êkbôlḗ *n.* (1x)
Roots:G1544
G1546.2 N-ASF ἐκβολήν (1x)
Ac 27:18 *lighten the ship by* throwing·the·cargo·overboard.

G1547 ἐκ•γαμίζω êkgamízō *v.* (5x)
Roots:G1537 G1061 Compare:G1548
G1547 V-PAP-NSM ἐκγαμίζων (2x)
1Co 7:38 even the *father* giving·away·in·marriage does well,
1Co 7:38 not giving·away·in·marriage does significantly·
G1547 V-PAP-NPM ἐκγαμίζοντες (1x)
Mt 24:38 marrying and giving·away·in·marriage, even·until
G1547 V-PPI-3P ἐκγαμίζονται (1x)
Mt 22:30 nor are·they·given·away·in·marriage, but·rather
G1547 V-IPI-3P ἐξεγαμίζοντο (1x)
Lk 17:27 they·were·being·given·away·in·marriage, even·

G1548 ἐκ•γαμίσκω êkgamískō *v.* (2x)
Roots:G1537 G1061 Compare:G1547
G1548 V-PPI-3P ἐκγαμίσκονται (2x)
Lk 20:34 present·age marry and are·given·away·in·marriage.
Lk 20:35 neither marry nor are·given·away·in·marriage.

G1549 ἔκ•γονον êkgônôn *adj.* (1x)
Roots:G1537 G1096 Compare:G1081 G0581-1 xLangAlso:H6631 H4138
G1549.2 A-APN ἔκγονα (1x)
1Ti 5:4 has children or grandchildren, they·must·learn first

G1550 ἐκ•δαπανάω êkdapanáō *v.* (1x)
Roots:G1537 G1159 See:G4325
G1550.2 V-FPI-1S ἐκδαπανηθήσομαι (1x)
2Co 12:15 and shall·be·utterly·spent on·behalf of·yeur souls,

G1551 ἐκ•δέχομαι êkdéchômai *v.* (8x)
Roots:G1537 G1209 Compare:G4327
G1551.2 V-PNI-1S ἐκδέχομαι (1x)
1Co 16:11 ·come to me, for I·am·waiting·for him with the
G1551.2 V-PNI-3S ἐκδέχεται (1x)
Jac 5:7 the man·that·works·the·soil waits·for the precious
G1551.2 V-PNM-2P ἐκδέχεσθε (1x)
1Co 11:33 ·together in·order to·eat, wait·for one·another.
G1551.2 V-PNP-GSM ἐκδεχομένου (1x)
Ac 17:16 Now while·Paul was·waiting·for them at Athens,
G1551.2 V-PNP-GPM ἐκδεχομένων (1x)
Jn 5:3 withered— *all·of·them* waiting·for the stirring of·the
G1551.2 V-PNP-NSM ἐκδεχόμενος (1x)
Heb 10:13 *is still* remaining: waiting·for *the moment* until
G1551.2 V-INI-3S ἐξεδέχετο (2x)
Heb 11:10 for he·was·waiting·for the CITY having the
1Pe 3:20 of·God was·waiting·for *this·moment* in *the* days of·

G1552 ἔκ•δηλος êkdēlôs *adj.* (1x)
Roots:G1537 G1212 See:G2612
G1552 A-NSM ἔκδηλος (1x)
2Ti 3:9 for their irrational·resentment shall·be obvious to·all,

G1553 ἐκ•δημέω êkdēméō *v.* (3x)
Roots:G1537 G1218 Compare:G0548 See:G4898
G1553.2 V-PAI-1P ἐκδημοῦμεν (1x)
2Co 5:6 *indeed*, we·are·presently·absent·abroad from the
G1553.2 V-PAP-NPM ἐκδημοῦντες (1x)
2Co 5:9 being·at·home or being·absent·abroad, to·be most·
G1553.2 V-AAN ἐκδημῆσαι (1x)
2Co 5:8 all·the·more to·be·absent·abroad from·among the

G1554 ἐκ•δίδωμι êkdídōmi *v.* (4x)
Roots:G1537 G1325
G1554.2 V-FDI-3S ἐκδόσεται (1x)
Mt 21:41 bad·men badly, then he·shall·lease the vineyard
G1554.2 V-2AMI-3S ἐξέδοτο (3x)
Lk 20:9 planted a·vineyard and leased it to·tenant·farmers,
Mt 21:33 a·tower," and·then he·leased it to·tenant·farmers
Mk 12:1 built a·tower," and leased it to·tenant·farmers,

G1555 ἐκ•δι•ηγέομαι êkdiēgéômai *v.* (2x)
Roots:G1537 G1223 G2233
G1555.2 V-PNP-NPM ἐκδιηγούμενοι (1x)
Ac 15:3 giving·a·thorough·account·of the turning·back·
G1555.2 V-PNS-3S ἐκδιηγῆται (1x)
Ac 13:41 someone should·give·a·thorough·account to·yeu."

G1556 ἐκ•δικέω êkdikéō *v.* (6x)
Roots:G1558 See:G1557 xLangEquiv:H5358
G1556 V-FAI-1S ἐκδικήσω (1x)
Lk 18:5 *her* wearisome·troubles to·me, I·shall·avenge her,
G1556 V-PAI-2S ἐκδικεῖς (1x)
Rv 6:10 ·One, do·you·not judge and avenge our blood on
G1556 V-PAP-NPM ἐκδικοῦντες (1x)
Rm 12:19 *Love is* not avenging yeurselves, dearly·beloved,
G1556 V-AAI-3S ἐξεδίκησεν (1x)
Rv 19:2 her sexual·immorality, and he·avenged the blood
G1556 V-AAM-2S ἐκδίκησον (1x)
Lk 18:3 to him, saying, 'Avenge me of my legal·adversary.
G1556 V-AAN ἐκδικῆσαι (1x)
2Co 10:6 in readiness to·avenge all inattentive·disregard,

G1557 ἐκ•δίκησις êkdíkēsis *n.* (9x)
Roots:G1556 Compare:G0468 G3709 xLangAlso:H5359
G1557.1 N-NSF ἐκδίκησις (2x)
Heb 10:30 the·one declaring, "'Vengeance *belongs* to·me, I·
Rm 12:19 it·has·been·written, "'Vengeance *belongs* to·me;
G1557.1 N-ASF ἐκδίκησιν (1x)
Ac 7:24 made vengeance for·the·one being·worn·down·in·
G1557.2 N-GSF ἐκδικήσεως (1x)
Lk 21:22 "Because these are Days of·Vengeance, of·the·One
G1557.3 N-ASF ἐκδίκησιν (4x)
Lk 18:7 God make retribution for·his·own Selected-Ones,
Lk 18:8 to·yeu that he·shall·make retribution for·them in
1Pe 2:14 him, in·fact, for retribution to·criminals and *for*
2Th 1:8 in blazing fire, giving retribution to·the·ones not
G1557.4 N-ASF ἐκδίκησιν (1x)
2Co 7:11 *what* zeal, moreover, *what* vindication! In all

G1558 ἔκ•δικος êkdikôs *adj.* (2x)
Roots:G1537 G1349 See:G1556
G1558.2 A-NSM ἔκδικος (2x)
Rm 13:4 an·attendant of·God, an·avenger *to·execute* wrath
1Th 4:6 on·account·that the Lord *is* avenger concerning all

G1559 ἐκ•διώκω êkdiṓkō *v.* (2x)
Roots:G1537 G1377
G1559.2 V-FAI-3P ἐκδιώξουσιν (1x)
Lk 11:49 they·shall·kill and shall·relentlessly·persecute,'
G1559.2 V-AAP-GPM ἐκδιωξάντων (1x)
1Th 2:15 ·own prophets, and relentlessly·persecuting us).

G1560 ἔκ•δοτος êkdôtôs *adj.* (1x)
Roots:G1537 G1325
G1560 A-ASM ἔκδοτον (1x)
Ac 2:23 of·God) *was* given·over, being·taken through

G1561 ἐκ•δοχή êkdôchḗ *n.* (1x)
Roots:G1551 Compare:G1680 G0603
G1561.3 N-NSF ἐκδοχή (1x)
Heb 10:27 frightful apprehension of·Tribunal·judgment and

G1562 ἐκ•δύω êkdýō *v.* (5x)
Roots:G1537 G1416
G1562.2 V-AMN ἐκδύσασθαι (1x)
2Co 5:4 we·do·not want to·undress·ourselves, but·rather to·
G1562.3 V-AAI-3P ἐξέδυσαν (2x)
Mt 27:31 ·had·mocked him, they·stripped the military·cloak
Mk 15:20 they·mocked him, they·stripped the purple·cloak
G1562.3 V-AAP-NPM ἐκδύσαντες (2x)
Lk 10:30 robbers, who also, after·stripping him and placing
Mt 27:28 And after·stripping him, they·placed a·scarlet

G1563 ἐκεῖ êkêî *adv.* (98x)
See:G1565
G1563.1 ADV ἐκεῖ (88x)
Jn 2:1 Qanah of·Galilee, and the mother of·Jesus was there.
Jn 2:6 ·were laying·out there six ceremonial·water·basins of·
Jn 2:12 disciples), and they·remained there not many days.
Jn 3:22 ·Judea, and he·was·lingering·awhile there with them
Jn 3:23 because there·was much water there. And they·came·
Jn 4:6 Now Jacob's well was there. So·then Jesus, having·
Jn 4:40 to·abide with them, and he·abided there two days.
Jn 5:5 And a·certain man·of·clay† was there, being in the
Jn 6:3 the mountain. And there, he·was·sitting·down with
Jn 6:22 there·had·been no other small·boat there except that
Jn 6:24 crowd saw that Jesus was not there, nor his disciples,
Jn 10:40 John was first immersing; and there he·abided.
Jn 10:42 And many trusted in him there.
Jn 11:8 to·stone you, and do·you·head·on·out there again?
Jn 11:15 yeu that I·was not there, in·order·that yeu·may·trust
Jn 11:31 chamber·tomb in·order·that she·may·weep there."
Jn 12:2 they·made a·supper for·him there, and Martha was·
Jn 12:9 Judeans knew that he·was there. And they·did·not
Jn 12:26 and where I AM, there also my attendant shall·be.
Jn 18:2 many·times Jesus did·gather there together with his
Jn 18:3 Pharisees, Judas comes there with searchlights and
Jn 19:42 So they·laid Jesus there on·account·of the Judeans
Lk 2:6 And it·occurred, with them being there, *that* the days
Lk 6:6 Yet there·was *a·certain* man·of·clay† there and his
Lk 8:32 ·was a·herd there of·a·significant·number of·pigs
Lk 9:4 home yeu·should·enter into, there abide, and from·
Lk 10:6 if a·son of·peace should·be there, yeur peace shall·

Lk 11:26 and entering·in, they·reside there. And the final·
Lk 12:18 bigger·ones; and there I·shall·gather·together all
Lk 12:34 where yeur treasure is, there also yeur heart shall·
Lk 15:13 country, and there he·thoroughly·squandered his
Lk 17:21 or, 'Behold, there *it·is*!' For, behold, the
Lk 17:23 or 'Behold, there *he·is*!' Yeu·should·not go·off
Lk 17:37 the body *is*, there the eagles shall·be·gathered·
Lk 21:2 a·certain needy widow casting two bits *in* there.
Lk 22:12 ·been·spread·out *for·guests*. Make·ready there."
Lk 23:33 ·one being·called Skull, there they·crucified him,
Ac 9:33 And there he·found a·certain man·of·clay†, Aeneas
Ac 14:28 *that* they·were·lingering there together with·the
Ac 16:1 a·certain disciple was there, TimoThy by·name, a·
Ac 17:14 Silas and TimoThy were·remaining·behind there.
Ac 19:21 "After I come·to·be there, it·is·mandatory·for me
Ac 25:9 ·up to JeruSalem, there to·be·judged concerning
Ac 25:14 And as they·were·lingering there *for* many·more
Heb 7:8 men·of·clay† receive, but there *and·then, there·was*
Mt 2:13 into Egypt, and be there until I·should·declare *it* to·
Mt 2:15 And he·was there until the demise of·HerOd·the·
Mt 2:22 *Joseph* was·afraid to·go·aside there. So after·
Mt 5:24 leave your present there before the Sacrifice·Altar
Mt 6:21 where yeur treasure is, there also yeur heart shall·be
Mt 12:45 And *with* them·entering, he·resides there. And the
Mt 13:58 ·not do many miracles there on·account·of their
Mt 14:23 with·early·evening occurring, he·was there alone.
Mt 15:29 walking·up upon the mountain, he·sat·down there.
Mt 18:20 ·gathered·together in my name, there am·I in *the*
Mt 19:2 him, and he·both·relieved·and·cured them there.
Mt 21:17 into BethAny, and there he·slept·out·in·the·open.
Mt 22:11 a·man·of·clay† there having·not dressed·himself·
Mt 24:28 the corpse should·be, there the eagles shall·be·
Mt 26:36 where going·aside, I·should·pray *over* there."
Mt 26:71 saw him and says to·the·ones there, "This·one also
Mt 27:36 ·down, they·were·keeping·guard·over him there.
Mt 27:47 Now some of·the·ones standing there, after·hearing
Mt 27:55 Now many women were there observing from a·
Mt 27:61 And there was Mariam Magdalene, and the other
Mt 28:7 yeu into Galilee. There yeu·shall·gaze·upon him.
Mk 1:13 And he·was there in the wilderness forty days,
Mk 2:6 Now some of·the scribes were there, sitting·down yet
Mk 3:1 and there·was a·man·of·clay† there having the
Mk 5:11 Now there·was there, on·the·side·of the mountains,
Mk 6:5 he·was·not able to·do there not·even·one miracle,
Mk 6:10 yeu·should·enter into a·home, there abide until
Mk 6:33 from all the cities and went there before them, and
Mk 6:55 ·ill, *to* wherever they·were·hearing, "There he·is."
Mk 11:5 of·the·ones standing there were·saying to·them,
Mk 13:21 or, 'Behold, there *he·is*!' yeu·should·not trust *it*.
Mk 14:15 *for·guests and* readied. There, make·ready for·us.
Mk 16:7 yeu into Galilee. There yeu·shall·gaze·upon him,
Rm 9:26 my People,' there they·shall·be·called the·Sons
Jac 3:16 jealousy and contention *is*, there *is* instability and
Jac 4:13 that city, and should·continue there *for* one year,
Tit 3:12 me to NicoPolis, for I·have·decided to·winter there.
2Co 3:17 where the Spirit of·Yahweh *is*, there *is* liberty.
Rv 2:14 because you·have there ones·securely·holding·to the
Rv 12:6 ·should·nourish her there a·thousand two·hundred
Rv 12:14 place, where she·is·nourished there a·season, and
Rv 21:25 be·shut at·day's·end, for night shall·not be there.
Rv 22:5 And there·shall·not be night there. Also, they·do·not

G1563.2 ADV ἐκεῖ (3x)
Mt 17:20 mountain, 'Walk·on from·here to·there,' and it·
Rm 15:24 to·be·sent·onward by yeu *from* there·to *Spain*, if
Jac 2:3 ·poor, "You·yourself must·stand·still over·there," or

G1563.3 ADV ἐκεῖ (7x)
Lk 13:28 "*And* there *outside*, there·shall·be the weeping and
Mt 8:12 into the outer darkness, where there·shall·be the
Mt 13:42 the furnace of·the fire, where there·shall·be the
Mt 13:50 the furnace of·the fire, where there·shall·be the
Mt 22:13 into the outer darkness, where there·shall·be the
Mt 24:51 stage·acting·hypocrites, where there·shall·be the
Mt 25:30 outer darkness,' where there·shall·be the weeping

G1564 ἐκεῖ•θεν ěkêîthên *adv.* (28x)
Roots:G1563

G1564.1 ADV ἐκεῖθεν (27x)
Jn 4:43 the two days, he·went·off from·there and came·forth
Jn 11:54 Judeans, but·rather went·away from·there to the
Lk 9:4 ·enter into, there abide, and from·there come·forth.
Lk 12:59 no, you·should·not come·forth from·there, even
Lk 16:26 nor·even may the·ones from·there cross·over to
Ac 13:4 to Seleucia. Also from·there, they·sailed·off to
Ac 16:12 and from·there to Philippi, which is a·foremost city
Ac 18:7 And walking·on from·there, he·came into a·home
Ac 20:13 to Assos, *while* from·there intending to·take Paul
Mt 4:21 And walking·forward from·there, he·saw two other
Mt 5:26 no, you·should·not come·forth from·there until
Mt 9:9 And while·passing·on from·there, YeShua saw a·
Mt 9:27 And with·YeShua passing·on from·there, two blind·
Mt 11:1 disciples, he·walked·on from·there to·instruct and
Mt 12:9 And walking·on from·there, he·went into their
Mt 12:15 And YeShua knowing *it*, departed from·there. And
Mt 13:53 finished these parables, he·moved·on from·there.
Mt 14:13 *it*, YeShua departed from·there in a·sailboat into a·
Mt 15:21 And going·forth from·there, YeShua departed into
Mt 15:29 And walking·on from·there, YeShua came near·to
Mt 19:15 his hands on·them, he·traversed·on from·there.
Mk 1:19 walking·forward a·little·way from·there, he·saw
Mk 6:1 And he·went·out from·there and came into his·own
Mk 6:10 there abide until yeu·should·go·forth from·there.
Mk 6:11 yeu, as·yeu·are·departing from·there, shake·off the
Mk 7:24 And after·rising·up from·there, he·went·off into the
Mk 9:30 And going·forth from·there, they·were·traversing·

EG1564.1 (1x)
Mk 2:14 Then passing·on *from·there*, he·saw Levi *called*

G1565 ἐκεῖνος ěkêînôs *p:d.* (251x)
Roots:G1563 Compare:G5023 See:G3778
(abbreviated listing for G1565)

G1565.1 P:D-NSM ἐκεῖνος (48x)
(list for G1565.1:P:D-NSM excluded)
G1565.1 P:D-NSF ἐκείνη (8x)
(list for G1565.1:P:D-NSF excluded)
G1565.1 P:D-NSN ἐκεῖνο (1x)
(list for G1565.1:P:D-NSN excluded)
G1565.1 P:D-ASM ἐκεῖνον (10x)
(list for G1565.1:P:D-ASM excluded)
G1565.1 P:D-ASF ἐκείνην (10x)
(list for G1565.1:P:D-ASF excluded)
G1565.1 P:D-ASN ἐκεῖνο (1x)
(list for G1565.1:P:D-ASN excluded)
G1565.1 P:D-DSM ἐκείνῳ (11x)
(list for G1565.1:P:D-DSM excluded)
G1565.1 P:D-DSF ἐκείνῃ (29x)
(list for G1565.1:P:D-DSF excluded)
G1565.1 P:D-GSM ἐκείνου (14x)
(list for G1565.1:P:D-GSM excluded)
G1565.1 P:D-GSF ἐκείνης (17x)
(list for G1565.1:P:D-GSF excluded)
G1565.1 P:D-GSN ἐκείνου (2x)
(list for G1565.1:P:D-GSN excluded)
G1565.2 P:D-NSN ἐκεῖνο (1x)
(list for G1565.2:P:D-NSN excluded)
G1565.2 P:D-DSF ἐκείνῃ (3x)
(list for G1565.2:P:D-DSF excluded)
G1565.2 P:D-GSM ἐκείνου (1x)
(list for G1565.2:P:D-GSM excluded)
G1565.2 P:D-GSF ἐκείνης (3x)
(list for G1565.2:P:D-GSF excluded)
G1565.3 P:D-NPM ἐκεῖνοι (16x)
(list for G1565.3:P:D-NPM excluded)
G1565.3 P:D-NPF ἐκεῖναι (5x)
(list for G1565.3:P:D-NPF excluded)
G1565.3 P:D-NPN ἐκεῖνα (1x)
(list for G1565.3:P:D-NPN excluded)
G1565.3 P:D-APM ἐκείνους (4x)
(list for G1565.3:P:D-APM excluded)
G1565.3 P:D-APF ἐκείνας (2x)
(list for G1565.3:P:D-APF excluded)
G1565.3 P:D-APN ἐκεῖνα (1x)
(list for G1565.3:P:D-APN excluded)
G1565.3 P:D-DPM ἐκείνοις (4x)
(list for G1565.3:P:D-DPM excluded)
G1565.3 P:D-DPF ἐκείναις (16x)
(list for G1565.3:P:D-DPF excluded)
G1565.3 P:D-GSM ἐκείνου (1x)
(list for G1565.3:P:D-GSM excluded)
G1565.3 P:D-GPM ἐκείνων (4x)
(list for G1565.3:P:D-GPM excluded)
G1565.3 P:D-GPF ἐκείνων (2x)
(list for G1565.3:P:D-GPF excluded)
G1565.3 P:D-GPN ἐκείνων (1x)
(list for G1565.3:P:D-GPN excluded)
G1565.4 P:D-NSM ἐκεῖνος (5x)
(list for G1565.4:P:D-NSM excluded)
G1565.4 P:D-ASN ἐκεῖνο (2x)
(list for G1565.4:P:D-ASN excluded)
G1565.4 P:D-GSM ἐκείνου (1x)
(list for G1565.4:P:D-GSM excluded)
G1565.5 P:D-APM ἐκείνους (1x)
(list for G1565.5:P:D-APM excluded)
G1565.5 P:D-GPM ἐκείνων (1x)
(list for G1565.5:P:D-GPM excluded)
G1565.6 P:D-NSM ἐκεῖνος (2x)
(list for G1565.6:P:D-NSM excluded)
G1565.6 P:D-NSF ἐκείνη (1x)
(list for G1565.6:P:D-NSF excluded)
G1565.6 P:D-ASM ἐκεῖνον (1x)
(list for G1565.6:P:D-ASM excluded)
G1565.6 P:D-DSF ἐκείνῃ (6x)
(list for G1565.6:P:D-DSF excluded)
G1565.7 P:D-NSM ἐκεῖνος (2x)
(list for G1565.7:P:D-NSM excluded)
G1565.8 P:D-NSM ἐκεῖνος (1x)
(list for G1565.8:P:D-NSM excluded)
G1565.9 P:D-GSM ἐκείνου (3x)
(list for G1565.9:P:D-GSM excluded)
G1565.10 P:D-APM ἐκείνους (2x)
(list for G1565.10:P:D-APM excluded)
G1565.10 P:D-DPM ἐκείνοις (3x)
(list for G1565.10:P:D-DPM excluded)
G1565.10 P:D-GPM ἐκείνων (2x)
(list for G1565.10:P:D-GPM excluded)
G1565.11 P:D-NSM ἐκεῖνος (1x)
(list for G1565.11:P:D-NSM excluded)
G1565.11 P:D-GPM ἐκείνων (1x)
(list for G1565.11:P:D-GPM excluded)

G1566 ἐκεῖσε ěkêîsê *adv.* (2x)
Roots:G1563

G1566 ADV ἐκεῖσε (2x)
Ac 21:3 for the sailing·ship was unloading its cargo there.
Ac 22:5 bringing the·ones being there, having·been·bound,

G1567 ἐκ•ζητέω ěkzētéō *v.* (7x)
Roots:G1537 G2212 Compare:G0154
xLangAlso:H1875

G1567.1 V-FPI-3S ἐκζητηθήσεται (1x)
Lk 11:51 Yes, I·say to·yeu, it·shall·be·sought·out of this
G1567.1 V-PAP-DPM ἐκζητοῦσιν (1x)
Heb 11:6 ·appropriate·rewarder to·the·ones seeking him out
G1567.1 V-PAP-NSM ἐκζητῶν (1x)
Rm 3:11 comprehending; there·is not one seeking·out God.
G1567.1 V-AAI-3P ἐξεζήτησαν (1x)
1Pe 1:10 the prophets sought·*it*·out and diligently·searched
G1567.1 V-AAP-NSM ἐκζητήσας (1x)
Heb 12:17 place for·repentance, even·though seeking it out
G1567.1 V-AAS-3P ἐκζητήσωσιν (1x)
Ac 15:17 of·the men·of·clay† may·seek·out the Lord, even
G1567.1 V-APS-3S ἐκζητηθῇ (1x)
Lk 11:50 world's conception, may·be·sought·out from this

G1568 ἐκ•θαμβέω êkthambéō *v.* (4x)
Roots:G1569 See:G2284
G1568 V-PPM-2P ἐκθαμβεῖσθε (1x)
Mk 16:6 ·them, "Do·not be·utterly·amazed. Yeu·seek Jesus
G1568 V-PPN ἐκθαμβεῖσθαι (1x)
Mk 14:33 and he·began to·be·utterly·amazed and to·be·
G1568 V-API-3S ἐξεθαμβήθη (1x)
Mk 9:15 crowd, after·seeing him, were·utterly·amazed, and
G1568 V-API-3P ἐξεθαμβήθησαν (1x)
Mk 16:5 a·white long·robe, and they·were·utterly·amazed.

G1569 ἔκ•θαμβος ékthambôs *adj.* (1x)
Roots:G1537 G2285 See:G1568
G1569 A-NPM ἔκθαμβοι (1x)
Ac 3:11 being·called Solomon's, *being* utterly·amazed.

G1570 ἔκ•θετος ékthêtôs *adj.* (1x)
Roots:G1537 G5087 Compare:G1620
G1570 A-APN ἔκθετα (1x)
Ac 7:19 to·make *them* put·out·and·expose their baby·boys,

G1571 ἐκ•καθ•αίρω êkkathaírō *v.* (2x)
Roots:G1537 G2508 Compare:G2511
G1571.1 V-AAS-3S ἐκκαθάρῃ (1x)
2Ti 2:21 if anyone should·entirely·purify himself from
G1571.2 V-AAM-2P ἐκκαθάρατε (1x)
1Co 5:7 Accordingly, purge·out the old leaven in·order·that

G1572 ἐκ•καίω êkkaíō *v.* (1x)
Roots:G1537 G2545 xLangAlso:H1197
G1572 V-API-3P ἐξεκαύθησαν (1x)
Rm 1:27 ·intercourse of·the female, are·inflamed in their

G1573 ἐκ•κακέω êkkakéō *v.* (6x)
Roots:G1537 G2556 Compare:G0120 G1590 G1168
G1573.2 V-PAI-1P ἐκκακοῦμεν (2x)
2Co 4:1 just·as we·are·shown·mercy, we·are·not cowardly.
2Co 4:16 Therefore, we·are·not cowardly. But·rather even
G1573.2 V-PAN ἐκκακεῖν (1x)
Lk 18:1 ·mandatory always to·pray and not to·be·cowardly,
G1573.2 V-PAS-1P ἐκκακῶμεν (1x)
Gal 6:9 And we·should·not be·cowardly *in* doing the good;
G1573.2 V-AAS-2P ἐκκακήσητε (1x)
2Th 3:13 yeu·should·not be·cowardly in·well·doing.
G1573.3 V-PAN ἐκκακεῖν (1x)
Eph 3:13 I·request *yeu* not to·be·despondent in my

G1574 ἐκ•κεντέω êkkêntéō *v.* (2x)
Roots:G1537 G2758-1 Compare:G3572 G1338 G4044 See:G2759 xLangAlso:H1856
G1574.2 V-AAI-3P ἐξεκέντησαν (2x)
Jn 19:37 "They·shall·gaze·upon him·whom they·pierced."
Rv 1:7 ·gaze·upon him, and·also they·who pierced him;

G1575 ἐκ•κλάω êkkláō *v.* (4x)
Roots:G1537 G2806
G1575 V-API-3P ἐξεκλάσθησαν (3x)
Rm 11:17 if some of·the branches were·broken·off, and you
Rm 11:19 branches were·broken·off in·order·that I·myself
Rm 11:20 by·the lack·of·trust they·were·broken·off, and
EG1575 (1x)
Ac 27:44 some·men on some of·the *broken·pieces* from the

G1576 ἐκ•κλείω êkklêíō *v.* (3x)
Roots:G1537 G2808
G1576.2 V-AAN ἐκκλεῖσαι (1x)
Gal 4:17 ·rather they·determine to·exclude yeu in·order·that
G1576.2 V-API-3S ἐξεκλείσθη (1x)
Rm 3:27 *is* the boasting? It·is·excluded. On·account·of
EG1576.2 (1x)
1Co 9:6 only BarNabas and I·myself *excluded?* ¿!·Do·we·not

G1577 ἐκ•κλησία êkklēsía *n.* (120x)
מִקְרָאת miqra'ath [Hebrew]
Roots:G1537 G2564 Compare:G1218 G2992 G4177 G4175 G2959-1 G2959-2 G4864 G4866-1 G2819-2 See:G2822 G1573-1 G1577-1 G1826-1 G1577-2 xLangEquiv:H4744-1 xLangAlso:H5712 H6951 H6952 H6116
G1577.2 N-NSF ἐκκλησία (1x)
Ac 19:32 the assembly·of·citizens was having·been·greatly·
G1577.2 N-ASF ἐκκλησίαν (1x)
Ac 19:41 ·things, he·dismissed the assembly·of·citizens.
G1577.2 N-DSF ἐκκλησίᾳ (1x)
Ac 19:39 ·be·fully·settled in the lawful assembly·of·citizens.
G1577.3 N-DSF ἐκκλησίᾳ (1x)
Ac 7:38 already·coming among the called·out·citizenry in
G1577.6 N-NSF ἐκκλησία (2x)
Eph 5:24 ·as the entire·Called·Out·Citizenry is·subject to·the
Col 1:24 Body, which is the entire·Called·Out·Citizenry—
G1577.6 N-ASF ἐκκλησίαν (5x)
Mt 16:18 I·shall·build my entire·Called·Out·Citizenry,
Eph 5:25 loved the entire·Called·Out·Citizenry and handed
Eph 5:27 the entire·Called·Out·Citizenry not having stain,
Eph 5:29 the Lord *does for* the entire·Called·Out·Citizenry,
Eph 5:32 Anointed-One and the entire·Called·Out·Citizenry.
G1577.6 N-DSF ἐκκλησίᾳ (2x)
Eph 1:22 over all *things* in·the entire·Called·Out·Citizenry,
Eph 3:21 *be* the glory in the entire·Called·Out·Citizenry, by
G1577.6 N-GSF ἐκκλησίας (3x)
Eph 3:10 ·places through the entire·Called·Out·Citizenry,
Eph 5:23 *is* head of·the entire·Called·Out·Citizenry. And he·
Col 1:18 of·the Body (the entire·Called·Out·Citizenry); *it·is*
G1577.7 N-NSF ἐκκλησία (4x)
Php 4:15 not·even·one Called·Out·citizenry shared with·me
1Co 14:23 whole Called·Out·citizenry should·come·together
1Ti 3:15 ·which is a·Called·Out·citizenry of·the·living God,
1Ti 5:16 ·not·let the Called·Out·citizenry be·weighed·down,
G1577.7 N-NPF ἐκκλησίαι (8x)
Ac 9:31 Accordingly in·fact, the Called·Out·citizenries in
Ac 16:5 the Called·Out·citizenries were·made·solid in·the
Rm 16:4 also all the Called·Out·citizenries of·the Gentiles.
Rm 16:16 a·holy kiss. The Called·Out·citizenries of·the
1Co 11:16 neither *do* the Called·Out·citizenries of·God.
1Co 16:19 The Called·Out·citizenries of·Asia greet yeu.
Rv 1:20 which you·saw are *the* seven Called·Out·citizenries.
Rv 2:23 and all the Called·Out·citizenries shall·know that I
G1577.7 N-ASF ἐκκλησίαν (11x)
Ac 5:11 came upon all the Called·Out·citizenry, and upon all
Ac 8:1 a·great persecution against the Called·Out·citizenry,
Ac 8:3 ·ravaging the Called·Out·citizenry. Traversing·into
Ac 13:1 ·men among the Called·Out·citizenry being in
Ac 14:23 elders for·each Called·Out·citizenry, after·praying
Ac 14:27 the Called·Out·citizenry, they·reported·in·detail
Ac 18:22 greeting the Called·Out·citizenry, he·walked·down
Ac 20:28 to·shepherd the Called·Out·citizenry of·God,
Gal 1:13 ·persecuting the Called·Out·citizenry of·God and
Php 3:6 persecuting the Called·Out·citizenry; according·to
1Co 15:9 ·that I·persecuted the Called·Out·citizenry of·God.
G1577.7 N-APF ἐκκλησίας (3x)
Ac 15:41 Cilicia, reaffirming the Called·Out·citizenries.
2Co 11:8 I·despoiled other Called·Out·citizenries, taking
2Co 12:13 the rest *of·the* Called·Out·citizenries, except that I
G1577.7 N-DSF ἐκκλησίᾳ (14x)
Ac 2:47 ·saved each day alongside the Called·Out·citizenry.
Ac 11:26 a·whole year among the Called·Out·citizenry and
Ac 15:22 together with·all the Called·Out·citizenry, to·
Heb 12:23 and to·a·Called·Out·citizenry of·firstborn
1Th 1:1 To·the Called·Out·citizenry of·the·ThessaloNicans
2Th 1:1 To·the Called·Out·citizenry of·the·ThessaloNicans
1Co 1:2 To·the Called·Out·citizenry of·God, the·one being
1Co 4:17 everywhere among every Called·Out·citizenry.
1Co 6:4 ·been·utterly·disdained by·the Called·Out·citizenry?
1Co 10:32 ·Greeks, and to·the Called·Out·citizenry of·God.
1Co 11:18 ·together among the Called·Out·citizenry, I·hear
1Co 12:28 God laid·out among the Called·Out·citizenry: first
2Co 1:1 brother. To·the Called·Out·citizenry of·God, the·
3Jn 1:9 I·wrote to·the Called·Out·citizenry, but·yet
G1577.7 N-DPF ἐκκλησίαις (16x)
Gal 1:2 with·me. To·the Called·Out·citizenries of·Galatia.
Gal 1:22 by·the face to·the Called·Out·citizenries of·Judea,
2Th 1:4 in yeu among the Called·Out·citizenries of·God on·
1Co 7:17 ·assign among all the Called·Out·citizenries.
1Co 16:1 ·assigned to·the Called·Out·citizenries of·Galatia,
2Co 8:1 unto the Called·Out·citizenries of·Macedonia,
Rv 1:4 To·the seven Called·Out·citizenries, to·the·ones in
Rv 1:11 and send *it* to·the Called·Out·citizenries, to·the·ones
Rv 2:7 Spirit says to·the Called·Out·citizenries. To·the·one
Rv 2:11 Spirit says to·the Called·Out·citizenries. The·one
Rv 2:17 Spirit says to·the Called·Out·citizenries. To·the·one
Rv 2:29 what the Spirit says to·the Called·Out·citizenries.'"
Rv 3:6 what the Spirit says to·the Called·Out·citizenries.'"
Rv 3:13 what the Spirit says to·the Called·Out·citizenries.'"
Rv 3:22 what the Spirit says to·the Called·Out·citizenries.'"
Rv 22:16 ·things concerning the Called·Out·citizenries. I
G1577.7 N-GSF ἐκκλησίας (19x)
Ac 11:22 the ears of·the Called·Out·citizenry, the·one in
Ac 12:1 some of·the·ones from the Called·Out·citizenry.
Ac 12:5 being·made to God by·the Called·Out·citizenry.
Ac 15:3 by·the Called·Out·citizenry, they·were·going·
Ac 15:4 ·fully·accepted by·the Called·Out·citizenry, and *by*
Ac 20:17 ·called·for the elders of·the Called·Out·citizenry.
Rm 16:1 an·attendant of·the Called·Out·citizenry, the·one in
Rm 16:23 (and *local·host* of·the whole Called·Out·citizenry),
Jac 5:14 ·summon the elders of·the Called·Out·citizenry, and
1Co 11:22 do·yeu·despise the Called·Out·citizenry of·God,
1Co 14:12 toward the edification of·the Called·Out·citizenry.
1Ti 3:5 shall·he·take·care of·a·Called·Out·citizenry of·God?
Rv 2:1 angel of·the Called·Out·citizenry of·Ephesus write,
Rv 2:8 angel of·the Called·Out·citizenry in·Smyrna write,
Rv 2:12 to·the angel of·the Called·Out·citizenry in Pergamos
Rv 2:18 to·the angel of·the Called·Out·citizenry in Thyatira
Rv 3:1 And to·the angel of·the Called·Out·citizenry in Sardis
Rv 3:7 ·the angel of·the Called·Out·citizenry in PhilAdelphia
Rv 3:14 angel of·the Called·Out·citizenry of·the·LaoDiceans
G1577.7 N-GPF ἐκκλησιῶν (5x)
1Th 2:14 ·imitators of·the Called·Out·citizenries of·God,
2Co 8:18 ·news throughout all the Called·Out·citizenries.
2Co 8:23 *·are* delegates of·*the*·Called·Out·citizenries *and the*
2Co 11:28 the anxiety of·all the Called·Out·citizenries.
Rv 1:20 are angels of·the seven Called·Out·citizenries, and
EG1577.7 (5x)
1Pe 5:13 The *Called·Out·citizenry* in Babylon, selected·
1Th 4:12 the·ones outside *the Called·Out·citizenry*, and *that*
1Co 5:12 the·ones outside *the Called·Out·citizenry*? Do yeu·
Col 4:5 outside *the Called·Out·citizenry*, utterly·redeeming
1Ti 3:7 *the Called·Out·citizenry* in·order·that he·should·not
***EG1577.7* N-DSF** (1x)
Ac 5:14 ·alongside *the Called·Out·citizenry*, multitudes both
G1577.8 N-NSF ἐκκλησία (1x)
1Co 14:5 the convened·Called·Out·assembly may·receive
G1577.8 N-ASF ἐκκλησίαν (1x)
1Co 14:4 edifies a·convened·Called·Out·assembly.
G1577.8 N-DSF ἐκκλησίᾳ (5x)
Mt 18:17 declare *it* to·the convened·Called·Out·assembly,
1Co 14:19 in a·convened·Called·Out·assembly, I·determine
1Co 14:28 in a·convened·Called·Out·assembly. And·thus,
1Co 14:35 to·speak in a·convened·Called·Out·assembly.
Col 4:16 the convened·Called·Out·assembly of·LaoDiceans,
G1577.8 N-DPF ἐκκλησίαις (2x)
1Co 14:33 the convened·Called·Out·assemblies of·the holy·
1Co 14:34 in the convened·Called·Out·assemblies. For it·
G1577.8 N-GSF ἐκκλησίας (3x)
Mt 18:17 the convened·Called·Out·assembly, let·him·be to·
3Jn 1:6 in·the·sight of·a·convened·Called·Out·assembly—
3Jn 1:10 ·forth out of·the convened·Called·Out·assembly.
G1577.8 N-GPF ἐκκλησιῶν (2x)
2Co 8:19 by the convened·Called·Out·assemblies *to·be* a·
2Co 8:24 in front of·the convened·Called·Out·assemblies.
G1577.9 N-ASF ἐκκλησίαν (2x)
Rm 16:5 Also *greet* the Called·Out·citizenry *hosted* in their
Col 4:15 Nymphas and the Called·Out·citizenry *hosted* in his
G1577.9 N-DSF ἐκκλησίᾳ (2x)
1Co 16:19 together with·the Called·Out·citizenry *hosted* in
Phm 1:2 ·soldier, and to·the Called·Out·citizenry *hosted* in

G1578 ἐκ•κλίνω êkklínō *v.* (3x)
Roots:G1537 G2827
G1578.2 V-AAI-3P ἐξέκλιναν (1x)
Rm 3:12 They all veered·away. At·the·same·time, they·are·
G1578.2 V-AAM-2P ἐκκλίνατε (1x)
Rm 16:17 which yeu learned, and veer·away from them.
G1578.2 V-AAM-3S ἐκκλινάτω (1x)
1Pe 3:11 "'Veer·away from wrong and do *the* beneficially·

G1579 ἐκ•κολυμβάω êkkôlymbáō *v.* (1x)
Roots:G1537 G2860
G1579 V-AAP-NSM ἐκκολυμβήσας (1x)
Ac 27:42 ·any might·thoroughly·escape by·swimming·away.

G1580 ἐκ•κομίζω êkkômízō *v.* (1x)
Roots:G1537 G2865 Compare:G4792
G1580.2 V-IPI-3S ἐξεκομίζετο (1x)
Lk 7:12 there·was·a·burial·procession·for one·having·died,

G1581 ἐκ•κόπτω êkkóptō *v.* (11x)
Roots:G1537 G2875 Compare:G0663
G1581.1 V-2FPI-2S ἐκκοπήσῃ (1x)
Rm 11:22 you·yourself also shall·be·chopped·off.
G1581.1 V-AAM-2S ἔκκοψον (2x)
Mt 5:30 if your right hand entraps you, chop it off and cast *it*
Mt 18:8 hand or your foot entraps you, chop it off and cast *it*
G1581.1 V-2API-2S ἐξεκόπης (1x)
Rm 11:24 if you are·already·chopped·off from·among an·
G1581.2 V-FAI-2S ἐκκόψεις (1x)
Lk 13:9 *good*! But·if·not, you·shall·chop it down for the·
G1581.2 V-PPI-3S ἐκκόπτεται (3x)
Lk 3:9 not producing good fruit is·chopped·down and is·cast
Mt 3:10 producing good fruit is·chopped·down and is·cast
Mt 7:19 producing good fruit is·chopped·down and is·cast
G1581.2 V-PPN ἐκκόπτεσθαι (1x)
1Pe 3:7 in·order·for yeur prayers not to·be·chopped·down.
G1581.2 V-AAM-2S ἔκκοψον (1x)
Lk 13:7 this fig·tree and find none. Chop it down! For·what·
G1581.2 V-AAS-1S ἐκκόψω (1x)
2Co 11:12 *is* in·order·that I·may·chop·down the impromptu·

G1582 ἐκ•κρέμαμαι êkkrémamai *v.* (1x)
Roots:G1537 G2910
G1582.3 V-IMI-3S ἐξεκρέματο (1x)
Lk 19:48 ·all the people were·very·attentive to·hear him,

G1583 ἐκ•λαλέω êklaléō *v.* (1x)
Roots:G1537 G2980
G1583.2 V-AAN ἐκλαλῆσαι (1x)
Ac 23:22 man, charging *for·him* to·divulge "to·no·one that

G1584 ἐκ•λάμπω êklámpō *v.* (1x)
Roots:G1537 G2989 Compare:G1823 See:G2985 G2986
G1584.1 V-FAI-3P ἐκλάμψουσιν (1x)
Mt 13:43 the righteous shall·brilliantly·radiate·forth as the

G1585 ἐκ•λανθάνομαι êklanthánômai *v.* (1x)
Roots:G1537 G2990 Compare:G1950 G3865
G1585 V-RPI-2P ἐκλέλησθε (1x)
Heb 12:5 And yeu·have·been·utterly·oblivious of·the

G1586 ἐκ•λέγομαι êklégômai *v.* (21x)
Roots:G1537 G3004 Compare:G0138 G5500 See:G1589
G1586.2 V-IMI-3P ἐξελέγοντο (1x)
Lk 14:7 how they·were·selecting the foremost·places, saying
G1586.2 V-AMI-1S ἐξελεξάμην (4x)
Jn 6:70 "No, *it·is* I·myself *that* selected yeu, the twelve, yet
Jn 13:18 I·myself personally·know whom I·selected, but·yet
Jn 15:16 me, but·rather I·myself selected yeu and laterally·
Jn 15:19 but·rather I·myself selected yeu from·among the
G1586.2 V-AMI-2S ἐξελέξω (1x)
Ac 1:24 which one from·among these two you·selected
G1586.2 V-AMI-2P ἐξελέξασθε (1x)
Jn 15:16 "*It·is* not yeu·yeurselves *that* selected me, but·rather
G1586.2 V-AMI-3S ἐξελέξατο (10x)
Lk 10:42 is needed, and Mary selected the beneficially·good
Ac 1:2 Holy Spirit to·the ambassadors whom he·selected;
Ac 13:17 The God of·this People IsraEl selected our fathers,
Ac 15:7 from the·early days, God selected among us *for* the
Mk 13:20 the Selected-Ones whom he·selected, he·cut·short
Jac 2:5 ¿! ·is·it·not God *that* selected the helplessly·poor of·
1Co 1:27 But·rather God selected the foolish·things of·the
1Co 1:27 the wise; and God selected the weak·things of·the
1Co 1:28 And God selected the bastardly·things of·the world
Eph 1:4 just·as he·selected us in him before *the* world's
G1586.2 V-AMI-3P ἐξελέξαντο (1x)
Ac 6:5 entire multitude. And they·selected Stephen, a·man
G1586.2 V-AMP-APM ἐκλεξαμένους (2x)
Ac 15:22 ·send men being·selected from·among themselves
Ac 15:25 ·the·same·determination, to·send selected men to
G1586.2 V-AMP-NSM ἐκλεξάμενος (1x)
Lk 6:13 his disciples *to·himself* and was·selecting twelve of

G1587 ἐκ•λείπω êklêípō *v.* (3x)
Roots:G1537 G3007 Compare:G3973 G1257 See:G0413
G1587.2 V-FAI-3P ἐκλείψουσιν (1x)
Heb 1:12 are the same, and your years shall·not cease.'"
G1587.2 V-PAS-3S ἐκλείπῃ (1x)
Lk 22:32 in·order·that your trust should·not cease, and once
G1587.3 V-2AAS-2P ἐκλίπητε (1x)
Lk 16:9 whenever yeu·may·cease·living, they·may·accept

G1588 ἐκ•λεκτός êklêktós *adj.* (23x)
Roots:G1586 Compare:G0138 G5500 See:G1589 xLangAlso:H0977
G1588.2 A-NSN ἐκλεκτόν (1x)
1Pe 2:9 But yeu *are* a·Selected kindred, a·royal priesthood,
G1588.2 A-NPM ἐκλεκτοί (3x)
Mt 20:16 for many are called·forth, but few *are* Selected."
Mt 22:14 "For many are called·forth, but few *are* Selected."
Rv 17:14 him *are* called·forth, and Selected, and trustworthy
G1588.2 A-ASM ἐκλεκτόν (2x)
1Pe 2:4 by men·of·clay†, but Selected personally·by God,
1Pe 2:6 Tsiyon a·chief·corner stone, Selected, *being* dearly·
G1588.2 A-DSF ἐκλεκτῇ (1x)
2Jn 1:1 The Elder. To·a·Selected lady and her children—
G1588.2 A-DPM ἐκλεκτοῖς (1x)
1Pe 1:1 To·Selected foreign·residents of·*the*·Diaspora
G1588.2 A-GSF ἐκλεκτῆς (1x)
2Jn 1:13 The children of·your Selected sister greet you
G1588.2 A-GPM ἐκλεκτῶν (1x)
1Ti 5:21 Jesus Anointed, and of·the Selected angels, that
G1588.3 A-NSM ἐκλεκτός (1x)
Lk 23:35 is the Anointed-One, the Selected-One of·God."
G1588.4 A-NPM ἐκλεκτοί (1x)
Col 3:12 Accordingly, as Selected-Ones of·God (holy and
G1588.4 A-APM ἐκλεκτούς (7x)
Mt 24:22 but on·account·of the Selected-Ones, those Days
Mt 24:24 if possible, to·deceive even the Selected-Ones.
Mt 24:31 ·gather his Selected-Ones from·among the four
Mk 13:20 ·account·of the Selected-Ones whom he·selected,
Mk 13:22 ·lead·astray, if possible, even the Selected-Ones.
Mk 13:27 ·gather his Selected-Ones from·out of·the four
2Ti 2:10 on·account·of the Selected-Ones in·order·that they
G1588.4 A-GPM ἐκλεκτῶν (3x)
Lk 18:7 God make retribution for·his·own Selected-Ones,
Rm 8:33 shall·call·to·account against God's Selected-Ones?
Tit 1:1 *for·the* trust of·God's Selected-Ones and *for·the*
G1588.5 A-ASM ἐκλεκτόν (1x)
Rm 16:13 Greet Rufus, the One-Selected in *the* Lord, and

G1589 ἐκ•λογή êklôgé *n.* (7x)
Roots:G1586 Compare:G0830 See:G1588
G1589 N-NSF ἐκλογή (1x)
Rm 11:7 ·anxiously·seeks, but the Selection did·obtain *it*,
G1589 N-ASF ἐκλογήν (5x)
Rm 9:11 may·endure according·to God's Selection, not as·a·
Rm 11:5 ·to·be a·remnant according·to a·Selection of·grace.
Rm 11:28 but according·to the Selection, *they·are* beloved
2Pe 1:10 to·make yeur calling·forth and Selection firm. For
1Th 1:4 having·been·loved by God, yeur Selection *by·him*.
G1589 N-GSF ἐκλογῆς (1x)
Ac 9:15 this·man is my vessel of·Selection to·bear my name

G1590 ἐκ•λύω êklýō *v.* (6x)
Roots:G1537 G3089 Compare:G2577 G1573
G1590.2 V-FPI-3P ἐκλυθήσονται (1x)
Mk 8:3 to their·own houses, they·shall·be·faint on the way,
G1590.2 V-PPM-2S ἐκλύου (1x)
Heb 12:5 ·discipline, nor·even be·faint *when* being·reproved
G1590.2 V-PPP-NPM ἐκλυόμενοι (2x)
Heb 12:3 ·should·become·fatigued, being·faint in·yeur souls
Gal 6:9 for in·due season we·shall·reap, not being·faint.
G1590.2 V-APS-3P ἐκλυθῶσιν (1x)
Mt 15:32 without·eating, lest they·should·be·faint on the
G1590.2 V-RPP-NPM ἐκλελυμένοι (1x)
Mt 9:36 them, because they·were having·been·faint, and

G1591 ἐκ•μάσσω êkmássō *v.* (5x)
Roots:G1537 G3145-1 Compare:G0631
G1591.2 V-PAN ἐκμάσσειν (1x)
Jn 13:5 the disciples' feet and to·firmly·wipe *them* with·the
G1591.2 V-IAI-3S ἐξέμασσεν (1x)
Lk 7:38 feet with·tears and was·firmly·wiping *them* with·the
G1591.2 V-AAI-3S ἐξέμαξεν (2x)
Jn 12:3 the feet of·Jesus and firmly·wiped his feet with·her
Lk 7:44 feet with·the tears and firmly·wiped *them* with·the
G1591.2 V-AAP-NSF ἐκμάξασα (1x)
Jn 11:2 Lord with·ointment, and firmly·wiping his feet with·

G1592 ἐκ•μυκτηρίζω êkmyktērízō *v.* (2x)
Roots:G1537 G3456 Compare:G5512 G1702
G1592 V-IAI-3P ἐξεμυκτήριζον (2x)
Lk 16:14 all these·things, and they·were·sneering·at him.
Lk 23:35 also together with·them were·sneering·at *him*,

G1593 ἐκ•νεύω êknêúō *v.* (1x)
Roots:G1537 G3506
G1593.3 V-AAI-3S ἐξένευσεν (1x)
Jn 5:13 for Jesus carefully·slipped·away, with·a·crowd

G1594 ἐκ•νήφω êknéphō *v.* (1x)
Roots:G1537 G3525 See:G0366 xLangAlso:H3364 H6974
G1594 V-AAM-2P ἐκνήψατε (1x)
1Co 15:34 Awaken·yeurselves·from·stupor as·is·right, and

G1595 ἑκούσιον hêkôúsiôn *adj.* (1x)
Roots:G1635 Compare:G1435 xLangAlso:H5071
G1595 A-ASN ἑκούσιον (1x)
Phm 1:14 ·to a·compulsion, but·rather *be* fully voluntary.

G1596 ἑκουσίως hêkôusíōs *adv.* (2x)
Roots:G1635 See:G1595 G0210
G1596 ADV ἑκουσίως (2x)
Heb 10:26 go·on·morally·failing voluntarily after receiving
1Pe 5:2 not compulsorily, but·rather voluntarily; nor·even

G1597 ἔκ•παλαι ékpalai *adv.* (2x)
Roots:G1537 G3819 See:G3820 G3821
G1597.1 ADV ἔκπαλαι (1x)
2Pe 2:3 for·whom judgment from·long·ago is·not idle, and
G1597.3 ADV ἔκπαλαι (1x)
2Pe 3:5 of·God, there·were heavens from·antiquity, and

G1598 ἐκ•πειράζω êkpêirázō *v.* (4x)
Roots:G1537 G3985 Compare:G3987 G1381
G1598 V-FAI-2S ἐκπειράσεις (2x)
Lk 4:12 "You·shall·not thoroughly·try Yahweh your God.
Mt 4:7 "You·shall·not thoroughly·try Yahweh your God.
G1598 V-PAP-NSM ἐκπειράζων (1x)
Lk 10:25 ·Torah-Law stood·up, and thoroughly·trying him,
G1598 V-PAS-1P ἐκπειράζωμεν (1x)
1Co 10:9 Nor·even should·we·thoroughly·try the

G1599 ἐκ•πέμπω êkpémpō *v.* (2x)
Roots:G1537 G3992
G1599 V-AAI-3P ἐξέπεμψαν (1x)
Ac 17:10 And immediately the brothers sent·forth both Paul
G1599 V-APP-NPM ἐκπεμφθέντες (1x)
Ac 13:4 Accordingly in·fact, after·being·sent·forth by the

G1600 ἐκ•πετάννυμι êkpêtánnymi *v.* (1x)
Roots:G1537 G4072 Compare:G1614
G1600.2 V-AAI-1S ἐξεπέτασα (1x)
Rm 10:21 '" The whole day·long I·spread·out my hands

G1601 ἐκ•πίπτω êkpíptō *v.* (13x)
Roots:G1537 G4098
G1601.1 V-AAI-2P ἐξεπέσατε (1x)
Gal 5:4 from the Anointed-One. Yeu·fell·from the grace.
G1601.1 V-2AAS-2P ἐκπέσητε (1x)
2Pe 3:17 yeu·should·fall·from your·own firm·steadfastness.
G1601.1 V-RAI-2S ἐκπέπτωκας (1x)
Rv 2:5 remember from·what·source you·have·fallen, and
G1601.2 V-PAP-NPM ἐκπίπτοντες (1x)
Mk 13:25 stars of·the heaven shall·be falling·away, and the
G1601.2 V-2AAI-3S ἐξέπεσεν (2x)
Jac 1:11 the grass, and its flower fell·away,' and the beauty
1Pe 1:24 grass is·withered, and its flower already·fell·away,
G1601.2 V-2AAI-3P ἐξέπεσον (1x)
Ac 12:7 And his chains fell·away from·among his hands.
G1601.2 V-2AAN ἐκπεσεῖν (1x)
Ac 27:32 small·ropes of·the skiff, and they·let her fall·away.
G1601.2 V-2AAS-3P ἐκπέσωσιν (2x)
Ac 27:17 And, fearing lest they·should·fall into the sand·
Ac 27:29 lest·somehow they·should·fall into rough,·jagged
G1601.3 V-PAI-3S ἐκπίπτει (1x)
1Co 13:8 The Love never·at·any·time falls·short. But if·also
G1601.3 V-RAI-3S ἐκπέπτωκεν (1x)
Rm 9:6 as·though the Holy-word of·God has·fallen·short. For
G1601.4 V-2AAN ἐκπεσεῖν (1x)
Ac 27:26 it·is·necessary·for us to·be·cast·away upon some

G1602 ἐκ•πλέω êkplêō *v.* (3x)
Roots:G1537 G4126
G1602 V-IAI-3S ἐξέπλει (1x)
Ac 18:18 ·of the brothers, was·sailing·away *from·there* into
G1602 V-AAI-1P ἐξεπλεύσαμεν (1x)
Ac 20:6 And we·ourselves sailed·away from Philippi after
G1602 V-AAN ἐκπλεῦσαι (1x)
Ac 15:39 ·taking *John*·Mark, to·sail·away to Cyprus.

G1603 ἐκ•πληρόω êkplērôō *v.* (1x)
Roots:G1537 G4137
G1603 V-RAI-3S ἐκπεπλήρωκεν (1x)
Ac 13:33 because God has·entirely·fulfilled the·same to·us,

G1604 ἐκ•πλήρωσις êkplḗrōsis *n.* (1x)
Roots:G1603
G1604.1 N-ASF ἐκπλήρωσιν (1x)
Ac 21:26 *when* the complete·fulfillment of·the days of·

G1605 ἐκ•πλήσσω êkplḗssō *v.* (13x)
Roots:G1537 G4141 Compare:G1839 G2284
G1605.2 V-PPN ἐκπλήττεσθαι (1x)
Mt 13:54 gathering, as·such·for them to·be·astounded, and
G1605.2 V-PPP-NSM ἐκπλησσόμενος (1x)
Ac 13:12 the proconsul trusted, being·astounded at the
G1605.2 V-IPI-3S ἐξεπλήσσετο (1x)
Mk 11:18 him, because all the crowd was·astounded at his
G1605.2 V-IPI-3P ἐξεπλήσσοντο (9x)
Lk 4:32 And they·were·astounded at his instruction, because
Lk 9:43 And they·all were·astounded at the magnificence of·
Mt 7:28 these sayings, the crowds were·astounded at his
Mt 19:25 his disciples were tremendously astounded, saying,
Mt 22:33 *this*, the crowds were·astounded at his instruction.
Mk 1:22 And they·were·astounded at his instruction, for he·
Mk 6:2 and many hearing *him* were·astounded, saying,
Mk 7:37 And they·were·astounded above·and·beyond·,
Mk 10:26 And they·were·astounded beyond·excess, saying
G1605.2 V-2API-3P ἐξεπλάγησαν (1x)
Lk 2:48 seeing him, *his parents* were·astounded. And his

G1606 ἐκ•πνέω êkpnêō *v.* (3x)
Roots:G1537 G4154 Compare:G5053 G1634
xLangEquiv:H1478
G1606.2 V-AAI-3S ἐξέπνευσεν (3x)
Lk 23:46 after·declaring these·things, he·breathed·his·last.
Mk 15:37 *his spirit with* a·loud voice, breathed·his·last.
Mk 15:39 ·yelling·out, he·breathed·his·last, he·declared,

G1607 ἐκ•πορεύομαι êkpôrêúômai *v.* (34x)
Roots:G1537 G4198 xLangAlso:H4161
G1607.1 V-PNI-3S ἐκπορεύεται (1x)
Mk 7:19 the belly, and·then traverses·out into the outhouse,
G1607.1 V-PNP-NSM ἐκπορευόμενος (1x)
Ac 9:28 while·traversing·in and traversing·out at JeruSalem.
G1607.1 V-INI-3S ἐξεπορεύετο (2x)
Mt 3:5 Then JeruSalem was·traversing·out to him, and all
Mk 1:5 all the region of·Judea was·traversing·out to him,
G1607.2 V-PMP-DPM ἐκπορευομένοις (1x)
Lk 3:7 to·the crowds traversing·forth to·be·immersed by him
G1607.2 V-PNI-3S ἐκπορεύεται (1x)
Mt 17:21 "But this kind does·not depart except by prayer and
G1607.2 V-PNN ἐκπορεύεσθαι (2x)
Ac 25:4 and *that* he·himself was·about to·depart *for·there* in
Rv 16:14 doing miraculous·signs, to·traverse·forth to the
G1607.2 V-PNP-GSM ἐκπορευομένου (1x)
Mk 10:17 And as·he·was·traversing·forth into *the* same
G1607.2 V-PNP-NPM ἐκπορευόμενοι (1x)
Mk 6:11 ·even hear yeu, as·yeu·are·departing from·there,
G1607.2 V-INI-3S ἐξεπορεύετο (1x)
Mk 11:19 occurred, he·was·traversing·forth outside of·the
G1607.3 V-PNP-GSM ἐκπορευομένου (1x)
Mk 13:1 And as·he was·departing out of·the Sanctuary·
G1607.4 V-FDI-3P ἐκπορεύσονται (1x)
Jn 5:29 And they·shall·proceed·forth; the·ones already·doing
G1607.4 V-PMP-DPM ἐκπορευομένοις (1x)
Lk 4:22 words, the·ones proceeding·forth out of·his mouth.
G1607.4 V-PNI-3S ἐκπορεύεται (5x)
Jn 15:26 of·Truth, who proceeds·forth personally·from the
Mk 7:23 All these evil·things proceed·forth from·inside, and
Rv 9:17 and out of·their mouths proceeds·forth fire and
Rv 11:5 ·harm·to them, fire proceeds·forth from·out of·their
Rv 19:15 of·his mouth proceeds·forth a·sharp straight·sword,
G1607.4 V-PNI-3P ἐκπορεύονται (2x)
Mk 7:21 wicked deliberations do·proceed·forth: adulteries,
Rv 4:5 and thunderings and voices proceed·forth; and *there*·
G1607.4 V-PNM-3S ἐκπορευέσθω (1x)
Eph 4:29 rotten conversation proceed·forth from·out of·yeur
G1607.4 V-PNP-ASM ἐκπορευόμενον (1x)
Rv 22:1 radiant as crystal, proceeding·forth out of·the
G1607.4 V-PNP-DSN ἐκπορευομένῳ (1x)
Mt 4:4 every utterance that·is·proceeding·forth through *the*
G1607.4 V-PNP-DSF ἐκπορευομένῃ (1x)
Rv 19:21 the·one which·is·proceeding·forth out of·his
G1607.4 V-PNP-GSN ἐκπορευομένου (1x)
Rv 9:18 the·one which·is·proceeding·forth out of·their
G1607.4 V-PNP-GSM ἐκπορευομένου (1x)
Mk 10:46 And as·he is·proceeding·forth from Jericho with
G1607.4 V-PNP-GPM ἐκπορευομένων (1x)
Mt 20:29 And with·them proceeding·forth from Jericho, a·
G1607.4 V-PNP-NSN ἐκπορευόμενον (2x)
Mt 15:11 but·rather the·thing proceeding·forth out of·the
Mk 7:20 "The·thing proceeding·forth out of·the man·of·
G1607.4 V-PNP-NSF ἐκπορευομένη (1x)
Rv 1:16 double-edged straight·sword is·proceeding·forth,'
G1607.4 V-PNP-NPN ἐκπορευόμενα (2x)
Mt 15:18 But the·things proceeding·forth out of·the mouth
Mk 7:15 but·rather the·things proceeding·forth from him,
G1607.4 V-INI-3S ἐξεπορεύετο (1x)
Lk 4:37 concerning him was·proceeding·forth into every

G1608 ἐκ•πορνεύω êkpôrnêúō *v.* (1x)
Roots:G1537 G4203
G1608 V-AAP-NPF ἐκπορνεύσασαι (1x)
Jud 1:7 them, *in* committing·gross·sexual·immorality, even

G1609 ἐκ•πτύω êkptýō *v.* (1x)
Roots:G1537 G4429 Compare:G1716
G1609.1 V-AAI-2P ἐξεπτύσατε (1x)
Gal 4:14 in my flesh, nor did·yeu·spit·*me*·out, but·rather

G1610 ἐκ•ριζόω êkrizôō *v.* (4x)
Roots:G1537 G4492
G1610 V-FPI-3S ἐκριζωθήσεται (1x)
Mt 15:13 heavenly Father did·not plant shall·be·uprooted.
G1610 V-AAS-2P ἐκριζώσητε (1x)
Mt 13:29 the darnel·weeds, yeu·should·uproot the wheat at·
G1610 V-APM-2S ἐκριζώθητι (1x)
Lk 17:6 say to·this mulberry-fig·tree, 'Be·uprooted, and be·
G1610 V-APP-NPN ἐκριζωθέντα (1x)
Jud 1:12 already·dying·off twice, already·being·uprooted,

G1611 ἔκ•στασις ékstasis *n.* (7x)
Roots:G1839 Compare:G2285 xLangAlso:H8639
G1611.1 N-NSF ἔκστασις (2x)
Lk 5:26 And astonishment took·hold·of absolutely·all, and
Mk 16:8 ·having trembling·of·fear and astonishment. And
G1611.1 N-DSF ἐκστάσει (1x)
Mk 5:42 And they·were·astonished with·great astonishment.
G1611.1 N-GSF ἐκστάσεως (1x)
Ac 3:10 with·amazement and astonishment at the·thing
G1611.2 N-NSF ἔκστασις (1x)
Ac 10:10 ·the·others making·preparation, a·trance fell upon
G1611.2 N-DSF ἐκστάσει (2x)
Ac 11:5 Joppa praying, and in a·trance I·saw a·clear·vision.
Ac 22:17 Sanctuary·Atrium, *that* I came·to·be in a·trance

G1612 ἐκ•στρέφω êkstrêphō *v.* (1x)
Roots:G1537 G4762 Compare:G1294 G0384 G0396
xLangAlso:H5557
G1612.4 V-RPI-3S ἐξέστραπται (1x)
Tit 3:11 such·as·this has·been·subverted and morally·fails,

G1613 ἐκ•ταράσσω êktarássō *v.* (1x)
Roots:G1537 G5015
G1613 V-PAI-3P ἐκταράσσουσιν (1x)
Ac 16:20 ·being Jews, do·exceedingly·trouble our city,

G1614 ἐκ•τείνω êktêínō *v.* (16x)
Roots:G1537 G5037-1 Compare:G1600 G2185
G4385 See:G5239 G1618 G4496 xLangAlso:H5186
G1614.1 V-FAI-2S ἐκτενεῖς (1x)
Jn 21:18 ·grow·agedly·old, you·shall·stretch·out your hands
G1614.1 V-PAN ἐκτείνειν (1x)
Ac 4:30 for you to·stretch·forth your hand for healing, and
G1614.1 V-AAI-2P ἐξετείνατε (1x)
Lk 22:53 ·Atrium, yeu·did·not stretch·forth yeur hands
G1614.1 V-AAI-3S ἐξέτεινεν (2x)
Mt 12:13 your hand." And he·stretched·*it*·out, and it·was·
Mk 3:5 your hand!" And he·stretched·*it*·out, and his hand
G1614.1 V-AAM-2S ἔκτεινον (3x)
Lk 6:10 to·the man·of·clay†, "Stretch·forth your hand." And
Mt 12:13 ·says to·the man·of·clay†, "Stretch·out your hand.
Mk 3:5 he·says to·the man·of·clay†, "Stretch·out your hand!
G1614.1 V-AAP-NSF ἐκτείνας (7x)
Lk 5:13 And stretching·out his hand, he·laid·hold·of·him,
Ac 26:1 Then Paul, after·stretching·forth his hand, was·
Mt 8:3 And YeShua, stretching·out his hand, laid·hold·of·
Mt 12:49 And stretching·forth his hand over his disciples,
Mt 14:31 YeShua, upon·stretching·forth his hand, grabbed·
Mt 26:51 ·ones with YeShua, upon·stretching·out his hand,
Mk 1:41 And Jesus, empathizing, stretching·out his hand,
G1614.2 V-PAN ἐκτείνειν (1x)
Ac 27:30 as·though intending to·extend anchors out of·*the*·

G1615 ἐκ•τελέω êktêlêō *v.* (2x)
Roots:G1537 G5055
G1615 V-AAN ἐκτελέσαι (2x)
Lk 14:29 and not having·strength to·entirely·complete *it*, all
Lk 14:30 yet did·not have·strength to·entirely·complete *it*.'

G1616 ἐκ•τένεια êkténêia *n.* (1x)
Roots:G1618
G1616 N-DSF ἐκτενείᾳ (1x)
Ac 26:7 ·tribes, in earnestness, while·ritually·ministering *to*·

G1617 ἐκ•τενέστερον êktênéstêrôn *adv.* (1x)
Roots:G1618 See:G1619
G1617 ADV ἐκτενέστερον (1x)
Lk 22:44 ·agony, he·was·praying more·earnestly. And his

G1618 ἐκ•τενής êktênés *adj.* (2x)
Roots:G1614 Compare:G0572 G1505 See:G1619
G1618 A-NSF ἐκτενής (1x)
Ac 12:5 in the prison·cell. But earnest prayer over him was
G1618 A-ASF ἐκτενῆ (1x)
1Pe 4:8 all, *continue* having earnest love among yeurselves,

Εε

G1619 ἐκ•τενῶς êktênôs *adv.* (1x)
Roots:G1618 Compare:G4710 See:G1617
G1619 ADV ἐκτενῶς (1x)
1Pe 1:22 one·another from·out of·a·pure heart earnestly—

G1620 ἐκ•τίθημι êktíthēmi *v.* (4x)
Roots:G1537 G5087 Compare:G1570
G1620.1 V-APP-ASM ἐκτεθέντα (1x)
Ac 7:21 And himself being·put·out, the Pharaoh's daughter
G1620.2 V-IMI-3S ἐξετίθετο (2x)
Ac 11:4 Peter explained·himself in·consecutive·order to·
Ac 28:23 to·whom he·was·explaining·himself, while·
G1620.2 V-2AMI-3P ἐξέθεντο (1x)
Ac 18:26 purposely·took him and explained to·him the Way

G1621 ἐκ•τινάσσω êktinássō *v.* (4x)
Roots:G1537 G5098-2 Compare:G4525 G4579 See:G0660
G1621.2 V-AMP-NSM ἐκτιναξάμενος (1x)
Ac 18:6 them and reviling *Jesus*, shaking·out his garments,
G1621.3 V-AAM-2P ἐκτινάξατε (2x)
Mt 10:14 home or that city, shake·off the dust of·yeur feet.
Mk 6:11 ·are·departing from·there, shake·off the loose·dirt
G1621.3 V-AMP-NPM ἐκτιναξάμενοι (1x)
Ac 13:51 But shaking·off the dust of·their feet against them,

G1622 ἐκτός êktós *adv.* (9x)
Roots:G1537 Compare:G1855 G1787
G1622.1 ADV ἐκτός (3x)
1Co 6:18 should·commit *it*, is on·the·outside of·the body;
2Co 12:2 ·know; or·whether on·the·outside of·the body, I·
2Co 12:3 (whether in body, or on·the·outside of·the body, I·
G1622.2 ADV ἐκτός (1x)
Mt 23:26 ·bowl, in·order·that their exterior may·be pure
G1622.3 ADV ἐκτός (1x)
1Co 15:27 *it·is* plain that he·is·excluded, the·one already·
G1622.4 ADV ἐκτός (2x)
1Co 14:5 except excluding·that he·should·thoroughly· in·
1Co 15:2 except excluding·that yeu·trusted for·no·reason
G1622.5 ADV ἐκτός (2x)
Ac 26:22 not·even·one·thing aside·from those·things·which
1Ti 5:19 against an·elder, aside·from *this standard*:

G1623 ἕκτος héktôs *adj.* (14x)
Roots:G1803
G1623 A-NSM ἕκτος (4x)
Lk 1:36 and this is *the* sixth lunar·month *of·pregnancy* for·
Rv 9:13 And the sixth angel sounded, and I·heard one voice
Rv 16:12 And the sixth angel poured·out his vial upon the
Rv 21:20 the fifth, sardonyx; the sixth, sardius; the seventh,
G1623 A-NSF ἕκτη (3x)
Jn 4:6 It·was *midday* about *the* sixth hour, *and*
Jn 19:14 and *it·was midday* about *the* sixth hour, and he·
Lk 23:44 Now it·was *midday* about *the* sixth hour, and
G1623 A-ASF ἕκτην (3x)
Ac 10:9 the rooftop to·pray *at·midday* about *the* sixth hour.
Mt 20:5 Again, going·forth about *the* sixth and ninth hour,
Rv 6:12 I·saw when he·opened·up the sixth official·seal, and
G1623 A-DSM ἕκτῳ (2x)
Lk 1:26 And in the sixth lunar·month, the angel GabriEl was·
Rv 9:14 saying to·the sixth angel who was·holding the
G1623 A-GSF ἕκτης (2x)
Mt 27:45 Now from *midday*, *the* sixth hour, there·was
Mk 15:33 And *at·midday*, with·the·sixth hour occurring,

G1624 ἐκ•τρέπω êktrépō *v.* (5x)
Roots:G1537 G5157 Compare:G0654 G1578
G1624.1 V-2FPI-3P ἐκτραπήσονται (1x)
2Ti 4:4 away·from the truth and shall·be·turned·aside to the
G1624.1 V-2API-3P ἐξετράπησαν (2x)
1Ti 1:6 ·which, some are·already·turned·aside to idle·talk,
1Ti 5:15 For even·now some are·turned·aside, *falling·in*
G1624.1 V-2APS-3S ἐκτραπῇ (1x)
Heb 12:13 lest the lame *limb* should·be·turned·aside, but
G1624.2 V-PMP-NSM ἐκτρεπόμενος (1x)
1Ti 6:20 ·to·your·care, turning·away·from the profane,

G1625 ἐκ•τρέφω êktréphō *v.* (2x)
Roots:G1537 G5142
G1625.1 V-PAI-3S ἐκτρέφει (1x)
Eph 5:29 but·rather he·entirely·nourishes and cherishingly·
G1625.2 V-PAM-2P ἐκτρέφετε (1x)
Eph 6:4 but·rather entirely·nurture·and·rear them in *the*

G1626 ἔκ•τρωμα éktrōma *n.* (1x)
Roots:G1537 G5103-1 Compare:G0580 G1080 G5088 See:G1025 G5134
G1626.3 N-DSN ἐκτρώματι (1x)
1Co 15:8 ·*was* birthed·from·out·of·a·trauma-induced·labor.

G1627 ἐκ•φέρω êkphérō *v.* (7x)
Roots:G1537 G5342 xLangAlso:H3318
G1627.1 V-AAM-2P ἐξενέγκατε (1x)
Lk 15:22 to his slaves, 'Bring·out the most·prestigious long·
G1627.2 V-FAI-3P ἐξοίσουσιν (1x)
Ac 5:9 *are* at the door, and they·shall·carry you out."
G1627.2 V-2AAN ἐξενεγκεῖν (1x)
1Ti 6:7 plain that we·are·not·even able to·carry anything out.
G1627.2 V-AAP-NPM ἐξενέγκαντες (2x)
Ac 5:6 him up, and after·carrying·*him*·out, they·buried *him*.
Ac 5:10 found her dead, and carrying·*her*·out, buried *her*
G1627.3 V-PAN ἐκφέρειν (1x)
Ac 5:15 such·for *the people* to·bear·forth the sick in·each·of
G1627.3 V-PAP-NSF ἐκφέρουσα (1x)
Heb 6:8 But *the soil* bearing·forth 'thorns and spear·thistles'

G1628 ἐκ•φεύγω êkphêúgō *v.* (8x)
Roots:G1537 G5343
G1628.1 V-2AAN ἐκφυγεῖν (1x)
Ac 19:16 them such·for *them* to·utterly·flee from·out of·that
G1628.2 V-FDI-1P ἐκφευξόμεθα (1x)
Heb 2:3 we·ourselves utterly·escape after·neglecting so·vast
G1628.2 V-FDI-2S ἐκφεύξῃ (1x)
Rm 2:3 that you·yourself shall·utterly·escape the judgment
G1628.2 V-2AAI-1S ἐξέφυγον (1x)
2Co 11:33 through the wall and utterly·escaped his hands.
G1628.2 V-2AAN ἐκφυγεῖν (1x)
Lk 21:36 ·may·be·accounted·fully·worthy to·utterly·escape
G1628.2 V-2AAS-3P ἐκφύγωσιν (1x)
1Th 5:3 And no, they·should·not utterly·escape.
G1628.2 V-2RAN ἐκπεφευγέναι (1x)
Ac 16:27 the chained·prisoners to·have·utterly·escaped.
EG1628.2 (1x)
2Ti 2:26 ·soberly·come·to·their·senses *and* escape out of·the

G1629 ἐκ•φοβέω êkphôbéō *v.* (1x)
Roots:G1537 G5399
G1629 V-PAN ἐκφοβεῖν (1x)
2Co 10:9 as if *I·intended* to·utterly·frighten yeu through the

G1630 ἔκ•φοβος ékphôbôs *adj.* (2x)
Roots:G1537 G5401 Compare:G1839 xLangAlso:H3025
G1630 A-NSM ἔκφοβος (1x)
Heb 12:21 "I·am frightened·out·of·my·wits and terrified·
G1630 A-NPM ἔκφοβοι (1x)
Mk 9:6 ·speak, for they·were frightened·out·of·their·wits.

G1631 ἐκ•φύω êkphýō *v.* (3x)
Roots:G1537 G5453 Compare:G0985 G1816 G4261 See:G4854 xLangEquiv:H6779
EG1631.2 (1x)
Lk 2:14 ·of·clay†, a·delightful·purpose *has·sprouted·forth*!"
G1631.3 V-PAS-3S ἐκφύῃ (2x)
Mt 24:32 ·become tender and should·sprout·forth the leaves,
Mk 13:28 ·become tender and should·sprout·forth the leaves,

G1632 ἐκ•χέω êkchéō *v.* (29x)
ἐκ•χύνω êkchýnō [alternate]
Roots:G1537 G5502-5 Compare:G4377-2 G4378 G2708 G2022
G1632.1 V-FPI-3S ἐκχυθήσεται (1x)
Lk 5:37 ·burst the wineskins, and it shall·pour·out, and the
G1632.1 V-PPI-3S ἐκχεῖται (2x)
Mt 9:17 are·burst, and the wine pours·out, and the wineskins
Mk 2:22 the wineskins, and the wine pours·out, and the
G1632.1 V-PPP-NSN ἐκχυνόμενον (5x)
Lk 11:50 the prophets, the *blood* being·poured·out from *the*
Lk 22:20 blood, the *blood* being·poured·out on·yeur behalf.
Mt 23:35 all *the* righteous blood being·poured·out upon the
Mt 26:28 the·one being·poured·out concerning many for
Mk 14:24 the·one being·poured·out concerning many.
G1632.1 V-IPI-3S ἐξεχεῖτο (1x)
Ac 22:20 of·your martyr Stephen was·poured·out, I·myself
G1632.1 V-AAI-3S ἐξέχεεν (8x)
Jn 2:15 and the oxen; and he·poured·out the moneychangers
Rv 16:2 And the first went·off and poured·out his vial upon
Rv 16:3 And the second angel poured·out his vial into the
Rv 16:4 And the third angel poured·out his vial into the
Rv 16:8 And the fourth angel poured·out his vial upon the
Rv 16:10 And the fifth angel poured·out his vial upon the
Rv 16:12 And the sixth angel poured·out his vial upon the
Rv 16:17 And the seventh angel poured·out his vial into the
G1632.1 V-AAI-3P ἐξέχεαν (1x)
Rv 16:6 Because they·poured·out *the* blood of·holy·ones and
G1632.1 V-AAM-2P ἐκχέατε (1x)
Rv 16:1 angels, "Head·on·out and pour·out the vials of·the
G1632.1 V-AAN ἐκχέαι (1x)
Rm 3:15 "Their feet *are* swift to·pour·out blood.
G1632.1 V-API-3S ἐξεχύθη (1x)
Ac 1:18 in·the·middle, and all his intestines poured·out.
G1632.1 V-API-3P ἐξεχύθησαν (1x)
Jud 1:11 way of·Qain, and poured·out the error of·BalaAm
EG1632.1 (1x)
Rv 19:2 the blood of·his slaves *poured·out* at her hand.
G1632.2 V-FAI-1S ἐκχεῶ (2x)
Ac 2:17 says God, *that* I·shall·pour·forth from my Spirit
Ac 2:18 upon my female·slaves, I·shall·pour·forth from my
G1632.2 V-AAI-3S ἐξέχεεν (2x)
Ac 2:33 personally·from the Father, he·poured·forth this,
Tit 3:6 whom he·poured·forth on us abundantly through
G1632.2 V-RPI-3S ἐκκέχυται (2x)
Ac 10:45 ·present of·the Holy Spirit has·been·poured·forth,
Rm 5:5 the love of·God has·been·poured·forth in our hearts

G1633 ἐκ•χωρέω êkchōréō *v.* (1x)
Roots:G1537 G5562 Compare:G0672
G1633.2 V-PAM-3P ἐκχωρείτωσαν (1x)
Lk 21:21 in *the* midst of·it must·depart·beyond·reach; and

G1634 ἐκ•ψύχω êkpsýchō *v.* (3x)
Roots:G1537 G5594 Compare:G2348 G1606
G1634 V-AAI-3S ἐξέψυξεν (3x)
Ac 5:5 words, AnanIas fell·down *and* expired. And great
Ac 5:10 at·once directly·at his feet and expired. And the
Ac 12:23 And becoming worm-eaten, he·expired.

G1635 ἑκών hêkṓn *adj.* (3x)
Compare:G1596 See:G0210 G1595
EG1635.1 (1x)
1Co 9:18 ·of·service: What is *the voluntary practice* for·me?
G1635.2 A-NSM ἑκών (1x)
1Co 9:17 For if I·practice this·thing voluntarily, I·have a·
G1635.2 A-NSF ἑκοῦσα (1x)
Rm 8:20 to·the futility, not voluntarily, but·rather through

G1636 ἐλαία êlaía *n.* (15x)
See:G1637 G1638 G1636-1 xLangEquiv:H2132
G1636.1 N-NPF ἐλαῖαι (1x)
Rv 11:4 These are the two olive·trees and the two Fine·Oil·
G1636.1 N-DSF ἐλαίᾳ (1x)
Rm 11:24 ·to nature, be·grafted·into their·own olive·tree?
G1636.1 N-GSF ἐλαίας (1x)
Rm 11:17 of·the root and the plumpness of·the olive·tree,
G1636.2 N-APF ἐλαίας (1x)
Jac 3:12 able, my brothers, to·produce olives? Or a·vine,
G1636.2 N-GPF ἐλαιῶν (11x)
Jn 8:1 But Jesus traversed to the Mount of·Olives.
Lk 19:29 (the·one being·called *the Mount* of·Olives), he·
Lk 19:37 the descent of·the Mount of·Olives, absolutely·all
Lk 21:37 mount, the·one being·called *the Mount* of·Olives.

Lk 22:39 Jesus traversed to the Mount of·Olives. And his
Mt 21:1 to BethPhage (toward the Mount of·Olives), then
Mt 24:3 sitting·down upon the Mount of·Olives, the disciples
Mt 26:30 ·a·psalm, they·went·out to the Mount of·Olives.
Mk 11:1 alongside the Mount of·Olives, he·dispatches two
Mk 13:3 upon the Mount of·Olives directly·opposite the
Mk 14:26 ·a·psalm, they·went·out to the Mount of·Olives.

G1637 ἔλαιον élaiôn *n.* (14x)
Roots:G1636 See:G1638 xLangAlso:H8081
G1637.1 N-DSN ἐλαίῳ (3x)
Lk 7:46 "With·olive·oil, you·did·not rub·oil·on my head, but
Mk 6:13 and with·olive·oil, they·were·rubbing·oil·on many
Jac 5:14 him, rubbing·oil·on him with·olive·oil in the name
G1637.2 N-ASN ἔλαιον (6x)
Lk 10:34 he·bound·up his wounds, pouring·in oil and wine.
Heb 1:9 you with·the oil of·exuberant·joy above·and·beyond
Mt 25:3 lamps, did·not take oil among their·own·selves.
Mt 25:4 But the prudent took oil in their containers with their
Rv 6:6 and you·should·not bring·harm·to the oil and the
Rv 18:13 "and wine, oil, fine·flour, and wheat, "and
G1637.2 N-GSN ἐλαίου (2x)
Lk 16:6 'A·hundred bath·measures of·oil.' And he·declared
Mt 25:8 'Give to·us from·out of·yeur oil, because our lamps
EG1637.2 (3x)
Mt 25:9 ·so, lest there·should·not be·sufficient oil for·us and
Mt 25:9 rather toward the·ones selling oil and buy some for·
Mt 25:10 And with·them going·off to·buy oil, the

G1638 ἐλαιών êlaiṓn *n.* (1x)
Roots:G1636 Compare:G4808-1 G0290 G2779 See:G1637
G1638.1 N-GSM ἐλαιῶνος (1x)
Ac 1:12 mount, the·one being·called Olive·Orchard, which

G1639 Ἐλαμίτης Êlamítēs *n/g.* (1x)
עֵילָם 'eylam [Hebrew]
עַלְמִי 'almiy [Aramaic]
Roots:H5867 xLangEquiv:A5962
G1639.2 N/G-NPM Ἐλαμῖται (1x)
Ac 2:9 Parthians and Medes and Elamites, and the·ones

G1640 ἐλάσσων êlássōn *adj.* (4x)
ἐλάττων êláttōn
Roots:G1646 Compare:G3187 See:G1641
G1640.1 A-NSN ἔλαττον (1x)
Heb 7:7 ·from any contradiction, the lesser is·blessed by the
G1640.1 A-ASM-C ἐλάσσω (1x)
Jn 2:10 they·should·be·drunk, then the lesser·quality, but
G1640.1 A-DSM ἐλάσσονι (1x)
Rm 9:12 ·her, "The greater shall·be·a·slave to·the lesser.'"
G1640.2 A-NSN ἔλαττον (1x)
1Ti 5:9 be·registered if·she·is not less·than sixty years·of·age

G1641 ἐλαττονέω êlattônéō *v.* (1x)
Roots:G1640 See:G1642
G1641.2 V-AAI-3S ἠλαττόνησεν (1x)
2Co 8:15 much, and the·one did·not decrease·to the less."

G1642 ἐλαττόω êlattóō *v.* (3x)
Roots:G1640 See:G1641
G1642.1 V-AAI-2S ἠλάττωσας (1x)
Heb 2:7 ·certain small·degree, you·made him lesser than the
G1642.1 V-RPP-ASM ἠλαττωμένον (1x)
Heb 2:9 small·degree having·been·made·lesser than the
G1642.2 V-PPN ἐλαττοῦσθαι (1x)
Jn 3:30 ·grow, but for·me to·become·increasingly·less.

G1643 ἐλαύνω êlaúnō *v.* (5x)
Compare:G0071 G3594 See:G0556 G4900 xLangAlso:H5090
G1643.1 V-PPP-NPN ἐλαυνόμενα (1x)
Jac 3:4 being so·vast, and are being·driven by harsh winds,
G1643.1 V-PPP-NPF ἐλαυνόμεναι (1x)
2Pe 2:17 ·water, thick·clouds being·driven by a·whirlwind,
G1643.1 V-IPI-3S ἠλαύνετο (1x)
Lk 8:29 And tearing·apart the bonds, he·was·driven by the
G1643.2 V-PAN ἐλαύνειν (1x)
Mk 6:48 ·saw them being·tormented in their rowing, for the
G1643.2 V-RAP-NPM ἐληλακότες (1x)
Jn 6:19 In·due·course, having·rowed about twenty·five or

G1644 ἐλαφρία êlaphría *n.* (1x)
Roots:G1645
G1644.1 N-DSF ἐλαφρίᾳ (1x)
2Co 1:17 ¿!·did perhaps I·use some levity? Or the·things·

G1645 ἐλαφρός êlaphrṓs *adj.* (2x)
Roots:G1640 See:G1644
G1645.1 A-NSN ἐλαφρόν (2x)
Mt 11:30 For my yoke is kind, and my load is lightweight."
2Co 4:17 For our lightweight, momentary tribulation is·

G1646 ἐλάχιστος êláchistôs *adj.* (13x)
Compare:G3398 See:G1640
G1646.1 A-NSM ἐλάχιστος (2x)
Mt 5:19 ·clay† in·this·manner, he·shall·be·called least in the
1Co 15:9 For I·myself am the least of·the ambassadors, who
G1646.1 A-NSF ἐλαχίστη (1x)
Mt 2:6 of·Judah, are by·no·means least among the official·
G1646.1 A-ASN ἐλάχιστον (1x)
Lk 12:26 ·not·even able to·do that·thing·which·is·least, why
G1646.1 A-DSN ἐλαχίστῳ (2x)
Lk 16:10 "The·one being trustworthy with very·little is also
Lk 16:10 the·one being unrighteous with very·little is also
G1646.1 A-GPM ἐλαχίστων (2x)
Mt 25:40 yeu·did it to·one of·the least of·these my brothers,
Mt 25:45 ·not do it to·one of·the least of·these my brothers,
G1646.1 A-GPF ἐλαχίστων (1x)
Mt 5:19 should·break one of·these least commandments and
G1646.2 A-GPN ἐλαχίστων (1x)
1Co 6:2 yeu, are·yeu unworthy of·the·smallest arbitrations?
G1646.3 A-ASN ἐλάχιστον (1x)
1Co 4:3 it·is a·very·small·thing that I·should·be·scrutinized
G1646.3 A-GSN ἐλαχίστου (1x)
Jac 3:4 and·yet they·are·steered by a·very·small rudder,
G1646.4 A-DSN ἐλαχίστῳ (1x)
Lk 19:17 Because you·became trustworthy in very·little, be

G1647 ἐλαχιστότερος êlachistốtêrôs *adj.* (1x)
Roots:G1646
G1647 A-DSM-C ἐλαχιστοτέρῳ (1x)
Eph 3:8 the·one who·is less·than·the·least of·all holy·ones,

G1648 Ἐλε•άζαρ Êlêázar *n/p.* (2x)
אֶלְעָזָר 'el'azar [Hebrew]
Roots:H0499
G1648.2 N/P-PRI Ἐλεάζαρ (2x)
Mt 1:15 Then EliHud begot EleAzar, and EleAzar begot
Mt 1:15 EliHud begot EleAzar, and EleAzar begot Matthan,

G1649 ἔλεγξις élênxis *n.* (1x)
Roots:G1651 Compare:G1648-1 See:G1650
G1649.2 N-ASF ἔλεγξιν (1x)
2Pe 2:16 But he·had a·reproof of·his·own transgression: a·

G1650 ἔλεγχος élênchôs *n.* (2x)
Roots:G1651 Compare:G1648-1 See:G1649
G1650.1 N-NSM ἔλεγχος (1x)
Heb 11:1 ·awaited, a·conviction concerning actions not
G1650.3 N-ASM ἔλεγχον (1x)
2Ti 3:16 particularly·for instruction, for reproof, for setting·

G1651 ἐλέγχω êlênchō *v.* (17x)
Compare:G2008 See:G1649 G1650 G1326-4 xLangAlso:H3198
G1651.1 V-FAI-3S ἐλέγξει (1x)
Jn 16:8 ·coming to·yeu, that·one shall·convict the world
G1651.1 V-PAI-3S ἐλέγχει (1x)
Jn 8:46 Who from·among yeu convicts me concerning
G1651.1 V-PAN ἐλέγχειν (1x)
Tit 1:9 instruction and to·convict the·ones contradicting.
G1651.1 V-PPI-3S ἐλέγχεται (1x)
1Co 14:24 ·one or an·untrained·man, he·is·convicted by all,
G1651.1 V-PPP-NPM ἐλεγχόμενοι (2x)
Jn 8:9 after·hearing this, and being·convicted by their·own
Jac 2:9 yeu·work moral·failure, being·convicted by the
G1651.2 V-PAM-2P ἐλέγχετε (1x)
Eph 5:11 works of·the darkness, but rather yet refute them.
G1651.2 V-PPP-NPN ἐλεγχόμενα (1x)
Eph 5:13 But all·things being·refuted are·made·apparent by
G1651.2 V-APS-3S ἐλεγχθῇ (1x)
Jn 3:20 toward the light, lest his deeds should·be·refuted.
G1651.4 V-PAI-1S ἐλέγχω (1x)
Rv 3:19 ·for, I·myself reprove and correctively·discipline.
G1651.4 V-PAM-2S ἔλεγχε (3x)
Tit 1:13 which cause, reprove them with·abrupt·sharpness
Tit 2:15 and exhort and reprove with all fully·assigned·
1Ti 5:20 of·all, you·must·reprove the·ones morally·failing
G1651.4 V-PPP-NSM ἐλεγχόμενος (2x)
Lk 3:19 HerOd·AntiPas the tetrarch, being·reproved by him
Heb 12:5 nor·even be·faint when being·reproved by him.
G1651.4 V-AAM-2S ἔλεγξον (2x)
Mt 18:15 you, head·on·out and reprove him between you
2Ti 4:2 and when·inconvenient! Reprove, reprimand, and

G1652 ἐλεεινός êlêêinós *adj.* (2x)
Roots:G1656
G1652 A-NSM ἐλεεινός (1x)
Rv 3:17 are the·one miserable, pitiable, helplessly·poor,
G1652 A-NPM-C ἐλεεινότεροι (1x)
1Co 15:19 we·are of·all men·of·clay† most·pitied.

G1653 ἐλεέω êlêéō *v.* (31x)
Roots:G1656 Compare:G2433 G3627 See:G1655 xLangEquiv:H2616 xLangAlso:H2603 H7355
G1653.1 V-FPI-3P ἐλεηθήσονται (1x)
Mt 5:7 because they·themselves shall·be·shown·mercy.
G1653.1 V-PAI-3S ἐλεεῖ (1x)
Rm 9:18 on·whom he·determines, he·shows·mercy, and on·
G1653.1 V-PAM-2P ἐλεεῖτε (1x)
Jud 1:22 show·mercy to·some while·using·discernment.
G1653.1 V-PAP-NSM ἐλεῶν (1x)
Rm 12:8 diligence; and the·one showing·mercy, doing so
G1653.1 V-AAI-1S ἠλέησα (1x)
Mt 18:33 ·slave, even as I·myself showed·mercy on·you?
G1653.1 V-AAI-3S ἠλέησεν (2x)
Mk 5:19 did for·you, and how he·showed·mercy on·you."
Php 2:27 to·death, but·yet God showed·mercy on·him, and
G1653.1 V-AAM-2S ἐλέησον (11x)
Lk 16:24 'Father AbRaham, show·mercy on·me, and send
Lk 17:13 "Jesus, O·Captain, show·mercy on·us."
Lk 18:38 "Jesus, O·Son of·David, show·mercy on·me."
Lk 18:39 "O·Son of·David, show·mercy on·me!"
Mt 9:27 "O·Son of·David, show·mercy on·us!"
Mt 15:22 to·him, saying, "Show·mercy on·me, O·Lord, O·
Mt 17:15 "Lord, show·mercy on·my son, because he·is·
Mt 20:30 ·yelled·out, saying, "Show·mercy on·us, O·Lord,
Mt 20:31 ·loudly, saying— "Show·mercy on·us, O·Lord,
Mk 10:47 "O·Jesus, the Son of·David, show·mercy on·me."
Mk 10:48 "O·Son of·David, show·mercy on·me!"
G1653.1 V-AAN ἐλεῆσαι (1x)
Mt 18:33 ·for you also to·show·mercy on·your fellow·slave,
G1653.1 V-AAS-3S ἐλεήσῃ (1x)
Rm 11:32 in·order·that he·may·show·mercy to·all the
G1653.1 V-API-1S ἠλεήθην (2x)
1Ti 1:13 ·man. But·yet I·was·shown·mercy, because I·did it
1Ti 1:16 ·account·of this, I·was·shown·mercy in·order·that,
G1653.1 V-API-1P ἠλεήθημεν (1x)
2Co 4:1 ·the Spirit, just·as we·are·shown·mercy, we·are·not
G1653.1 V-API-2P ἠλεήθητε (1x)
Rm 11:30 but now yeu·are·shown·mercy by·the obstinate·
G1653.1 V-APS-3P ἐλεηθῶσιν (1x)
Rm 11:31 they·themselves also should·be·shown·mercy.
G1653.1 V-RPP-NSM ἠλεημένος (1x)
1Co 7:25 advice, as one·having·been·shown·mercy from the
G1653.2 V-FAI-1S ἐλεήσω (1x)
Rm 9:15 '" I·shall·show·gracious·mercy on·whom I·would
G1653.2 V-PAP-GSM ἐλεοῦντος (1x)
Rm 9:16 ·rather on·God, the·one showing·gracious·mercy.
G1653.2 V-PAS-1S ἐλεῶ (1x)
Rm 9:15 ·mercy on·whom I·would show·gracious·mercy,

G1653.3 V-APP-NPM ἐλεηθέντες (1x)
1Pe 2:10 but now being·shown·compassionate·mercy.
G1653.3 V-RPP-NPM ἠλεημένοι (1x)
1Pe 2:10 not having·been·shown·compassionate·mercy, but

G1654 ἐλεημοσύνη êlêēmôsýnē *n.* (14x)
Roots:G1656 Compare:G1345 See:G1655
G1654.2 N-NSF ἐλεημοσύνη (1x)
Mt 6:4 so·that your merciful·act may·be in private.
G1654.2 N-NPF ἐλεημοσύναι (2x)
Ac 10:4 Your prayers and your merciful·acts ascended for a·
Ac 10:31 your merciful·acts were·recalled·to·mind in·the·
G1654.2 N-ASF ἐλεημοσύνην (3x)
Mt 6:1 "Take·heed not to·do yeur merciful·act before the
Mt 6:2 you·should·do a·merciful·act, you·should·not sound·
Mt 6:3 "But as·you are·doing a·merciful·act, do·not·let your
G1654.2 N-APF ἐλεημοσύνας (2x)
Ac 10:2 both doing many merciful·acts for·the people and
Ac 24:17 years, I·came·openly doing merciful·acts for my
G1654.2 N-GPF ἐλεημοσυνῶν (1x)
Ac 9:36 ·good works and merciful·acts which she·was·doing
G1654.3 N-ASF ἐλεημοσύνην (5x)
Lk 11:41 yeu·give a·merciful·act·of·charity, one·being·
Lk 12:33 holdings and give a·merciful·act·of·charity. *Thus*
Ac 3:2 the merciful·act·of·charity personally·from the·ones
Ac 3:3 was·asking to·receive a·merciful·act·of·charity.
Ac 3:10 specifically·for the merciful·act·of·charity at the

G1655 ἐλεήμων êlêēmōn *adj.* (2x)
Roots:G1653 Compare:G5485 See:G1654
xLangAlso:H2623
G1655 A-NSM ἐλεήμων (1x)
Heb 2:17 *them*, that he·may·be a·merciful and trustworthy
G1655 A-NPM ἐλεήμονες (1x)
Mt 5:7 "Supremely·blessed *are* the merciful, because they·

G1656 ἔλεος êlêôs *n.* (28x)
Compare:G5485 G3629-1 See:G1653 G1655 G1652
G1654 G4179-4 xLangAlso:H2617
G1656.1 N-NSM ἔλεος (7x)
Lk 1:50 And his mercy *is* to·the·ones reverently·fearing him
Gal 6:16 peace *be* upon them, and mercy, and upon the
Jud 1:2 May mercy, and peace, and love be·multiplied to·yeu
Tit 1:4 Grace, mercy, *and* peace, from Father God and *the*
1Ti 1:2 Grace, mercy, *and* peace from God our Father and
2Ti 1:2 Grace, mercy, *and* peace, from Father God and
2Jn 1:3 Grace shall·be with us, mercy, *and* peace,
G1656.1 N-NSN ἔλεος (1x)
Jac 2:13 but mercy boasts·triumphantly·over Tribunal·
G1656.1 N-ASM ἔλεον (5x)
Heb 4:16 ·order·that we·may·receive mercy and should·find
Mt 9:13 what it·means, "I·want mercy and not sacrifice.
Mt 12:7 what it·means, "I·want mercy, and not sacrifice,"
Mt 23:23 the tribunal·justice, and the mercy, and the trust.
Tit 3:5 ·rather he·saved us according·to his mercy, through
G1656.1 N-ASN ἔλεος (7x)
Lk 1:58 that Yahweh was·making·great his mercy with her,
Lk 1:72 to·continue *the promised* mercy with our fathers,
Jac 2:13 ·favor *is* for·the·one not doing mercy, but mercy
Jud 1:21 love, *yeu* who·are·awaiting the mercy of·our Lord
1Pe 1:3 the·one according·to his large mercy begetting us
2Ti 1:16 the Lord give mercy to·*the*·house of·OnesiPhorus,
2Ti 1:18 grant to·him to·find mercy personally·from Yahweh
G1656.1 N-DSN ἐλέει (2x)
Rm 11:31 in·order·that by·yeur mercy, they·themselves also
Eph 2:4 But God, being wealthy in mercy, on·account·of his
G1656.1 N-GSN ἐλέους (5x)
Lk 1:54 his servant·boy IsraEl, being·mindful of·*his*·mercy
Lk 1:78 *the* inward·affections of·our God's mercy, in which,
Rm 9:23 glory upon *the* vessels of·mercy, which he·made·
Rm 15:9 to·glorify God on·behalf *of·his* mercy, just·as it·
Jac 3:17 exceedingly·full of·mercy and of·beneficially·good
G1656.2 N-ASN ἔλεος (1x)
Lk 10:37 "The·one continuing the act·of·mercy with him."

G1657 ἐλευθερία êlêuthêría *n.* (13x)
Roots:G1658
xLangEquiv:H1865 xLangAlso:H2668
G1657.1 N-DSF ἐλευθερίᾳ (1x)
Lk 4:18 ·set·apart with freedom those·having·been·crushed,
G1657.2 N-NSF ἐλευθερία (2x)
1Co 10:29 for what·reason·is my liberty unduly·judged by
2Co 3:17 where the Spirit of·Yahweh *is*, there *is* liberty.
G1657.2 N-ASF ἐλευθερίαν (6x)
Lk 4:18 to·officially·proclaim liberty to·subdued·captives
Gal 2:4 ·motives to·spy·out our liberty which we·have in
Gal 5:13 *use* the liberty in·order·for an·impromptu·occasion
Rm 8:21 ·corruption into the glorious liberty of·the children
1Pe 2:16 yet not retaining the liberty as a·cover-up for·the
2Pe 2:19 *false·teachers* who·are·promising liberty to·them,
G1657.2 N-DSF ἐλευθερίᾳ (2x)
Gal 5:1 stand·fast in·the liberty with·which Anointed-One
Gal 5:13 yeu·yeurselves are·called·forth to liberty; merely
G1657.2 N-GSF ἐλευθερίας (2x)
Jac 1:25 into the complete Law of·Liberty, and personally·
Jac 2:12 ·about to·be·judged through *the* Law of·Liberty.

G1658 ἐλεύθερος êlêúthêrôs *adj.* (23x)
Roots:G2064 Compare:G1401 See:G1657
G1658.1 A-NPM ἐλεύθεροι (1x)
Rm 6:20 yeu·were not·restrained by·Righteousness.
G1658.5 A-NSM ἐλεύθερος (8x)
Gal 3:28 there·is·not therein slave nor·even free, there·is·not
1Co 7:21 but·yet if·also you·are·able to·become free, use *it*
1Co 7:22 ·one being·called·forth, *though being* free, is slave
1Co 9:1 an·ambassador? Am·I not free? Have·I·not·indeed
1Co 9:19 For *though* being free from·among all *men·of·clay*†
Eph 6:8 ·from the Lord, whether *he·be* slave or free.
Col 3:11 Scythian, slave *or* free, but·rather Anointed-One
Rv 6:15 every slave, and every free·man, hid themselves in
G1658.5 A-NSF ἐλευθέρα (3x)
Gal 4:26 But the JeruSalem up·above is free, which is *the*
Rm 7:3 But if the husband should·die, she·is freed from the
1Co 7:39 *·deceased)*, she·is free to·be·married to·whomever
G1658.5 A-NPM ἐλεύθεροι (5x)
Jn 8:33 you·yourself say, 'Yeu·shall·become free·men?'"
Jn 8:36 should·set yeu free, yeu·shall really be free·men.
Mt 17:26 "So the sons are free.
1Pe 2:16 *Exist* as free·men, yet not retaining the liberty as a·
1Co 12:13 Greeks, whether slave or free; and all are·given·
G1658.5 A-APM ἐλευθέρους (1x)
Rv 13:16 the helplessly·poor, even the free and the slave, in·
G1658.5 A-GSF ἐλευθέρας (4x)
Gal 4:22 and one birthed·from·out the free·woman.
Gal 4:23 birthed·from·out of·the free·woman *was* through the
Gal 4:30 ·not be·heir with the son of·the free·woman."
Gal 4:31 of·a·maidservant, but·rather of·the free·woman.
G1658.5 A-GPM ἐλευθέρων (1x)
Rv 19:18 and flesh of·all·men, *both* free and slave, both

G1659 ἐλευθερόω êlêuthêrôō *v.* (7x)
Roots:G1658 Compare:G1398
G1659.1 V-FAI-3S ἐλευθερώσει (1x)
Jn 8:32 ·know the truth, and the truth shall·set yeu free."
G1659.1 V-FPI-3S ἐλευθερωθήσεται (1x)
Rm 8:21 the creation itself also shall·be·set·free from the
G1659.1 V-AAI-3S ἠλευθέρωσεν (2x)
Gal 5:1 with·which Anointed-One set us free, and do·not
Rm 8:2 in Anointed-One Jesus set me free from the Law of·
G1659.1 V-AAS-3S ἐλευθερώσῃ (1x)
Jn 8:36 if the Son should·set yeu free, yeu·shall really be
G1659.1 V-APP-NPM ἐλευθερωθέντες (2x)
Rm 6:18 So after·being·set·free from Moral·Failure, yeu·are·
Rm 6:22 even·now, after·being·set·free from Moral·Failure

G1660 ἔλευσις êlêusis *n.* (1x)
Roots:G2064
G1660 N-GSF ἐλεύσεως (1x)
Ac 7:52 concerning the coming of·the Righteous·One, now

G1661 ἐλεφάντινος êlêphántinôs *adj.* (1x)
Compare:G3599 See:G1661-1
xLangEquiv:H8127
G1661.2 A-ASN ἐλεφάντινον (1x)
Rv 18:12 "and every *type·of* ivory vessel, and every *type·of*

G1662 Ἐλ•ιακείμ Êliakêím *n/p.* (3x)
Ἐλ•ιακείμ Êliaqêím [Greek, Octuagint]
אֶלְיָקִים 'ęlyaqıym [Hebrew]
Roots:H0471
G1662.5 N/P-PRI Ἐλιακείμ (2x)
Mt 1:13 AbiHud, and AbiHud begot ElYaQim, and ElYaQim
Mt 1:13 AbiHud begot ElYaQim, and ElYaQim begot Azzur.
G1662.6 N/P-PRI Ἐλιακείμ (1x)
Lk 3:30 *son* of·Yoseph, *son* of·Yonan, *son* of·ElYaQim,

G1663 Ἐλι•έζερ Êliézêr *n/p.* (1x)
אֱלִיעֶזֶר 'ĕlıy'ezer [Hebrew]
Roots:H0461
G1663.2 N/P-PRI Ἐλιέζερ (1x)
Lk 3:29 *son* of·Yose, *son* of·EliEzer, *son* of·JoRim, *son* of·

G1664 Ἐλι•ούδ Êlioúd *n/p.* (2x)
Roots:H0410 H1935 Compare:G0010
xLangAlso:H5989 H0379
G1664.2 N/P-PRI Ἐλιούδ (2x)
Mt 1:14 and Tsadoq begot Achim, and Achim begot EliHud.
Mt 1:15 Then EliHud begot EleAzar, and EleAzar begot

G1665 Ἐλι•σάβετ Êlisábêt *n/p.* (9x)
אֱלִישֶׁבַע 'ĕlıyshęba' [Hebrew]
Roots:H0472
G1665.2 N/P-PRI Ἐλισάβετ (9x)
Lk 1:5 the daughters of·Aaron, and her name *was* EliSabeth.
Lk 1:7 *born* to·them, because·indeed EliSabeth was barren,
Lk 1:13 and your wife EliSabeth shall·bear you a·son, and
Lk 1:24 these days, his wife EliSabeth conceived and was·
Lk 1:36 "And behold, your cousin EliSabeth, she·herself *is*
Lk 1:40 into the house of·ZacharIas and greeted EliSabeth.
Lk 1:41 And it·happened, as·soon·as EliSabeth heard the
Lk 1:41 in her womb, and EliSabeth was·filled with·Holy
Lk 1:57 Now EliSabeth's time was·fulfilled for·her to·

G1666 Ἐλι•σσαῖος Êlissaîôs *n/p.* (1x)
אֱלִישָׁע 'ĕlıysha' [Hebrew]
Roots:H0477
G1666.2 N/P-GSM Ἐλισσαίου (1x)
Lk 4:27 were in IsraEl in·the·days of·EliSha the prophet, yet

G1667 ἑλίσσω hêlíssō *v.* (1x)
Roots:G1507 xLangAlso:H1556
G1667.2 V-FAI-2S ἑλίξεις (1x)
Heb 1:12 And as a·mantle, you·shall·roll them up, and

G1668 ἕλκος hélkôs *n.* (3x)
Roots:G1670 Compare:G4127 G5134 See:G1669
G1668.2 N-NSN ἕλκος (1x)
Rv 16:2 and it·became a·bad and evil pus·sore to the men·of·
G1668.2 N-APN ἕλκη (1x)
Lk 16:21 *·along and* were·licking·away·at his pus·sores.
G1668.2 N-GPN ἑλκῶν (1x)
Rv 16:11 ·anguish and as·a·result of·their pus·sores, and

G1669 ἑλκόω hêlkôō *v.* (1x)
Roots:G1668
G1669.3 V-RPP-NSM ἡλκωμένος (1x)
Lk 16:20 his gate, having·been·afflicted·with·pus·sores,

G1670 ἑλκύω hêlkýō *v.* (8x)
ἕλκω hélkō
Compare:G1667 G4951 G2694 See:G0138
G1670.1 V-FAI-1S ἑλκύσω (1x)
Jn 12:32 from·among the earth, I·shall·draw all *men* toward
G1670.1 V-PAI-3P ἕλκουσιν (1x)
Jac 2:6 yeu, and *the* same *that* draw yeu into arbitrations?
G1670.1 V-IAI-3P εἷλκον (1x)
Ac 21:30 ·hold of·Paul, they·were·drawing him outside of·
G1670.1 V-AAI-3S εἵλκυσεν (2x)
Jn 18:10 having a·dagger, Simon Peter drew it and struck

Jn 21:11 Simon Peter walked·up and drew the net upon the

G1670.1 V-AAN ἑλκύσαι (1x)

Jn 21:6 and they·no longer had·strength to·draw it *back·in*

G1670.1 V-AAS-3S ἑλκύσῃ (1x)

Jn 6:44 (the·one sending me) should·draw him, and I·myself

G1670.2 V-AAI-3P εἵλκυσαν (1x)

Ac 16:19 Paul and Silas, they·drew·*them*·along into the

G1671 Ἑλλάς Hêllás *n/l.* (1x)

Ἑλλάδα Êlláda [Modern Greek]

See:G1672

G1671.1 N/L-ASF Ἑλλάδα (1x)

Ac 20:2 exhorting them often in·word, he·came into Greece,

G1672 Ἕλλην Héllēn *n/g.* (28x)

Roots:G1671 Compare:G1482 G1672 See:G1675 G1674

G1672.1 N/G-NSM Ἕλλην (4x)

Ac 16:3 ·all had·seen that his father inherently·was a·Greek.

Gal 2:3 together with·me being a·Greek) was·compelled to·

Gal 3:28 ·is·not therein Jew nor·even Greek, there·is·not

Col 3:11 where there·is·not therein Greek and Jew,

G1672.1 N/G-NPM Ἕλληνες (4x)

Jn 12:20 And there·were certain Greeks, from·among the·

Ac 18:17 ·of·the·gathering, all the Greeks were·beating *him*

1Co 1:22 Jews request a·sign, and·also Greeks seek wisdom,

1Co 12:13 Body, whether Jews or Greeks, whether slave or

G1672.1 N/G-APM Ἕλληνας (5x)

Jn 7:35 among·the Greeks, and to·instruct the Greeks?

Ac 18:4 Sabbath, and was·persuading Jews and Greeks.

Ac 19:10 of·the Lord Jesus, both Jews and Greeks.

Ac 21:28 he also brought Greeks into the Sanctuary·

Rm 3:9 ·already·legally·charged both Jews and Greeks, all

G1672.1 N/G-DSM Ἕλληνι (2x)

Rm 1:16 trusting, both to·Jew first, and·also to·Greek.

Rm 2:10 ·good, both to·Jew first, then·also to·Greek.

G1672.1 N/G-DPM Ἕλλησιν (6x)

Ac 19:17 to·both Jews and Greeks. And reverent·fear·and·

Ac 20:21 ·testifying to·both Jews and Greeks, a·repentance

Rm 1:14 ·an·obligation both to·Greeks and to·Barbarians,

1Co 1:23 ·offense to·Jews and foolishness to·Greeks.

1Co 1:24 ·forth, to·both Jews and Greeks, Anointed-One *is*

1Co 10:32 even to·Jews, also to·Greeks, and to·the Called·

G1672.1 N/G-GSM Ἕλληνος (3x)

Ac 16:1 (one·that·trusts), but his·father *was* a·Greek.

Rm 2:9 the wrong, of·Jew first, and also of·Greek.

Rm 10:12 no distinction between Jew and Greek— for this

G1672.1 N/G-GPM Ἑλλήνων (3x)

Jn 7:35 *the dispersion* among·the Greeks, and to·instruct

Ac 14:1 multitude both of·Jews and·also of·Greeks to·trust.

Ac 17:4 ·ones who·are·being·reverent Greek·men and not a·

EG1672.1 (1x)

Jn 12:21 Now·then, the·same *Greeks* came·alongside Philip,

G1673 Ἑλληνικός Hêllēnikós *adj/g.* (2x)

Roots:G1672 Compare:G1446 G4515 See:G1676 xLangAlso:H0762 H6163

G1673.1 A/G-DPN Ἑλληνικοῖς (1x)

Lk 23:38 ·been·written over him with·letters in·Greek,

G1673.2 A/G-DSF Ἑλληνικῇ (1x)

Rv 9:11 and in the Greek·language he·has *this* name,

G1674 Ἑλληνίς Hêllēnís *n/g.* (2x)

Roots:G1672

G1674 N/G-NSF Ἑλληνίς (1x)

Mk 7:26 Now the woman was a·Greek, a·Syro-Phoenician

G1674 N/G-GPF Ἑλληνίδων (1x)

Ac 17:12 not a·few of·the dignified Greek women and men.

G1675 Ἑλληνιστής Hêllēnistḗs *n/g.* (3x)

Roots:G1672 See:G1674

G1675.1 N/G-APM Ἑλληνιστάς (2x)

Ac 9:29 ·and·discussing alongside the Hellenistic·Jews, but

Ac 11:20 the Hellenistic·Jews, proclaiming·the·good·news

G1675.1 N/G-GPM Ἑλληνιστῶν (1x)

Ac 6:1 of·the Hellenistic·Jews specifically·against the

G1676 Ἑλληνιστί Hêllēnistí *adv/g.* (2x)

Roots:G1672 Compare:G1447 G4515 G4947-6 See:G1675 G1673

G1676 ADV Ἑλληνιστί (2x)

Jn 19:20 having·been·written in·Hebrew, in·Greek, *and* in·

Ac 21:37 ·*commander* replied, "Do·you·know Greek?

G1677 ἐ•λλογέω êllôgḗō *v.* (2x)

Roots:G1722 G3056

G1677 V-PAM-2S ἐλλόγει (1x)

Phm 1:18 you, or owes *you* anything, impute that to·me;

G1677 V-PPI-3S ἐλλογεῖται (1x)

Rm 5:13 but moral·failure is·not imputed *with·there* being

G1678 Ἐλ•μωδάμ Êlmōdám *n/p.* (1x)

אַלְמוֹדָד ʼalmôdad [Hebrew]

Roots:H0486

G1678 N/P-PRI Ἐλμωδάμ (1x)

Lk 3:28 ·Addi, *son* of·Qosam, *son* of·ElModam, *son* of·Er,

G1679 ἐλπίζω êlpízō *v.* (31x)

Roots:G1680 Compare:G3982 G4037 G0362 G4328 G2172 See:G0560 G4276

G1679.1 V-PAI-1S ἐλπίζω (10x)

Rm 15:24 ·come to yeu, for I·expect to·survey yeu while·

Php 2:19 But I·do·expect, in *the* Lord Jesus, to·send

Php 2:23 Accordingly in·fact, I·expect to·send this·man

1Co 16:7 but *instead*, I·expect to·stay·over some time

2Co 1:13 and I·expect that yeu·shall·acknowledge *this* even

2Co 5:11 and I·expect also to·have·been·made·manifest in

2Co 13:6 But I·expect that yeu·shall·know that we·ourselves

Phm 1:22 guest·accommodations, for I·expect that through

2Jn 1:12 ·paper and ink, but·rather I·expect to·come to yeu,

3Jn 1:14 But I·expect to·see you straight·away, and we·shall·

G1679.1 V-PAI-2P ἐλπίζετε (1x)

Lk 6:34 personally·from whom yeu·expect to·receive·in·full,

G1679.1 V-PAI-3S ἐλπίζει (1x)

Ac 26:7 *to·God* night and day, expect *it* to·fully·come—

G1679.1 V-PAP-NSM ἐλπίζων (2x)

Ac 24:26 at·the·same·time, *he·was* expecting that valuables

1Ti 3:14 These·things I·write to·you, expecting to·come to

G1679.1 V-IAI-1P ἠλπίζομεν (1x)

Lk 24:21 "But we·ourselves were·expecting that he·himself

G1679.1 V-IAI-3S ἤλπιζεν (1x)

Lk 23:8 about him; and he·was·expecting to·see some

G1679.1 V-AAI-1P ἠλπίσαμεν (1x)

2Co 8:5 *they·did*, not just·as we·expected, but·rather first

G1679.2 V-PAI-1P ἐλπίζομεν (1x)

Rm 8:25 But if we·expectantly·await for·what we·do·not

G1679.2 V-PAI-3S ἐλπίζει (2x)

Rm 8:24 for what man expectantly·awaits that·which also

1Co 13:7 trusts all·things, expectantly·awaits all·things,

G1679.2 V-PPP-GPM ἐλπιζομένων (1x)

Heb 11:1 ·assurance of·things·being·expectantly·awaited, a·

G1679.3 V-FAI-3P-ATT ἐλπιοῦσιν (2x)

Mt 12:21 his name, Gentiles shall·place·their·expectation."

Rm 15:12 in him, Gentiles shall·place·their·expectation."

G1679.3 V-PAP-NPF ἐλπίζουσαι (1x)

1Pe 3:5 the·ones placing·their·expectation upon God,

G1679.3 V-AAM-2P ἐλπίσατε (1x)

1Pe 1:13 ·sober, place·yeur·expectation completely upon the

G1679.3 V-RAI-1P ἠλπίκαμεν (2x)

2Co 1:10 in whom we·have·placed·our·expectation that even

1Ti 4:10 because we·have·placed·our·expectation upon the·

G1679.3 V-RAI-2P ἠλπίκατε (1x)

Jn 5:45 whom yeu·yeurselves have·placed·yeur·expectation.

G1679.3 V-RAI-3S ἤλπικεν (1x)

1Ti 5:5 ·left·all·alone, has·placed·her·expectation upon God

G1679.3 V-RAN ἠλπικέναι (1x)

1Ti 6:17 nor·even to·have·placed·their·expectations upon *the*

G1679.3 V-RAP-NPM ἠλπικότες (1x)

1Co 15:19 ·are merely having·placed·our·expectation in this

G1680 ἐλπίς êlpís *n.* (55x)

Compare:G0603 G1561 See:G1679 G0415-1 xLangEquiv:H4723 H8615 xLangAlso:H7664 H8431 H3689 H3690

G1680.1 N-NSF ἐλπίς (5x)

Ac 16:19 lords seeing that the expectation of·their income

Ac 27:20 *us*, all remaining expectation for·us to·be·saved

Rm 8:24 ·saved, but an·expectation being·looked·upon is

Rm 8:24 being·looked·upon is not an·expectation, for what

1Th 2:19 For what *is* our expectation, or joy, or victor's·

G1680.1 N-ASF ἐλπίδα (3x)

Rm 4:18 *AbRaham*, contrary·to expectation, trusted on an·

Rm 5:4 and the proven·character *fully·cultivates* expectation.

2Co 10:15 ·labors, but having an·expectation (with·yeur

G1680.1 N-DSF ἐλπίδι (3x)

Rm 4:18 trusted on an·Expectation in·order·for himself to·

1Co 9:10 plowing ought to·plow in expectation, and the·one

1Co 9:10 ·grain in expectation to·participate·by·eating of·his

G1680.1 N-GSF ἐλπίδος (1x)

1Co 9:10 to·participate·by·eating of·his expectation.

G1680.2 N-NSF ἐλπίς (5x)

Rm 5:5 And the Expectation does·not put·to·shame, because

1Co 13:13 ·things continue: Trust, Expectation, *and* Love;

2Co 1:7 And our expectation on·yeur behalf *is* steadfast,

Eph 1:18 ·seen what is the expectation of·his calling·forth,

Col 1:27 is Anointed-One in yeu (the Expectation of·glory),

G1680.2 N-ASF ἐλπίδα (15x)

Ac 24:15 having an·expectation in God, which these·men

Gal 5:5 fully·await an·expectation of·righteousness as·a·

Rm 15:4 ·that we·may·have the Expectation through the

Php 1:20 ·to my eager·anticipation and expectation: that in

1Pe 1:3 — into a·living Expectation through *the* resurrection

1Pe 1:21 — such·for yeur trust and expectation to·be in God.

1Th 4:13 ·as the rest, the·ones not having an·Expectation.

1Th 5:8 and *with·the* Expectation of·Salvation for·a·helmet.

2Th 2:16 and a·beneficially·good expectation in grace,

Tit 2:13 ·awaiting the supremely·blessed Expectation and

Tit 3:7 heirs according·to an·Expectation of·eternal life-above

2Co 3:12 So·then, having such an·expectation, we·use

Eph 2:12 not having an·Expectation·of·Resurrection, and

Col 1:5 on·account·of the Expectation, the·one being·laid·

1Jn 3:3 And any one having this Expectation in him cleanses

G1680.2 N-DSF ἐλπίδι (9x)

Ac 2:26 yet even my flesh shall·fully·encamp in expectation,

Ac 26:6 being·judged over *the* expectation of·the promise

Rm 5:2 and we·boast in expectation of·the glory of·God.

Rm 8:20 ·rather through the·one subjecting *it* in expectation

Rm 8:24 For in·the Expectation, we·are·saved, but an·

Rm 12:12 in·the Expectation, by·rejoicing; in·the tribulation,

Rm 15:13 for yeu to·abound in the Expectation by *the* power

Tit 1:2 *and* in *the* Expectation of·eternal life-above, which

Eph 4:4 ·are·called·forth in one expectation of·yeur calling

G1680.2 N-GSF ἐλπίδος (13x)

Ac 23:6 ·Pharisee; *it·is* concerning *the* Expectation, even *the*

Ac 26:7 ·come— concerning which expectation, O·King

Ac 28:20 for *it·is* because·of the Expectation of·IsraEl *that* I·

Heb 3:6 and the boasting of·the Expectation *being* steadfast

Heb 6:11 the full·assurance of·the Expectation, even·up·to

Heb 6:18 ·hold of·the Expectation being·laid·out·before *us*.

Heb 7:19 of·a·significantly·better expectation *does*, through

Heb 10:23 of·the Expectation without·slouching (for

Rm 15:13 the God of·the Expectation completely·fill yeu

1Pe 3:15 yeu a·reason concerning the Expectation in yeu—

1Th 1:3 and the patient·endurance of·the Expectation, of·our

Col 1:23 ·away from the Expectation of·the good·news

1Ti 1:1 Savior, and Lord Jesus Anointed, our Expectation.

EG1680.2 (1x)

Heb 6:19 Which *Expectation* we·have as an·anchor of·the

G1681 Ἐλύμας Êlýmas *n/p.* (1x)

Compare:G3097

G1681.2 N/P-NSM Ἐλύμας (1x)

Ac 13:8 But Elymas, the occultist (for so his name is·

Αα Ββ Γγ Δδ Εε Ζζ Ηη Θθ Ιι Κκ Λλ Μμ Νν Ξξ Οο Ππ Ρρ Σσ Ττ Υυ Φφ Χχ Ψψ Ωω

G1682 ἐλωΐ ēlōí *aram.* (2x)
אֱלָהּ 'ĕlah̲ [Aramaic]
Roots:A0426
G1682 ARAM ἐλωΐ (2x)
Mk 15:34 voice, saying, "'Eloi, Eloi, lama shebaq-thani?
Mk 15:34 voice, saying, "'Eloi, Eloi, lama shebaq-thani?

G1683 ἐμ•αυτοῦ ēmautôû *p:f.* (37x)
ἐμ•αυτῷ ēmautȭ [dative case]
ἐμ•αυτόν ēmautőn [accusative case]
Roots:G1700 G0846 Compare:G1691 G1699 G1473
G1683.1 P:F-1ASM ἐμαυτόν (10x)
Jn 8:54 "If I·myself glorify my·own·self, my glory is
Jn 17:19 I·myself make my·own·self holy in·order·that
Lk 7:7 neither did·I·consider my·own·self deserving to·come
Lk 7:8 having soldiers under my·own·self, and I·say to·
Gal 2:18 I·demonstrate my·own·self *to·be* a·transgressor.
Mt 8:9 having soldiers under my·own·self, and I·say to·this
Php 3:13 do·not reckon my·own·self to·have·grasped *it*. But
1Co 4:3 Moreover, I·scrutinize not·even my·own·self.
2Co 11:7 in·humbling my·own·self that yeu·yeurselves may·
2Co 11:9 I·purposefully·kept my·own·self from·being· to·
G1683.1 P:F-1DSM ἐμαυτῷ (1x)
2Co 2:1 But I·decided this for·my·own·self, not again to·
G1683.1 P:F-1GSM ἐμαυτοῦ (12x)
Jn 5:30 to·do not·even·one·thing of my·own·self. Just·as I·
Jn 5:31 I·myself should·testify concerning my·own·self, my
Jn 7:17 ·God, or *whether* I·myself speak from my·own·self.
Jn 7:28 Yet I·have·not come of my·own·self, but·rather the·
Jn 8:14 I·myself may·testify concerning my·own·self, my
Jn 8:18 am one testifying concerning my·own·self, and
Jn 8:28 I·do not·even·one·thing of my·own·self; but·rather
Jn 8:42 For neither have·I·come of my·own·self, but·rather
Jn 10:18 lay it down of my·own·self. I·have authority to·lay
Jn 12:49 did·not speak from·out of·my·own·self. But·rather
Jn 14:10 to·yeu, I·do·not speak from my·own·self, but the
2Co 12:5 ·boast; but on·behalf of·my·own·self, I·shall·not
G1683.2 P:F-1ASM ἐμαυτόν (8x)
Jn 12:32 the earth, I·shall·draw all *men* toward myself."
Jn 14:3 ·personally·receive yeu to myself in·order·that where
Jn 14:21 shall·love him and shall·manifest myself to·him."
Ac 26:2 "I·have·resolutely·considered myself supremely·,
1Co 4:6 I·portrayed·as·an·example as·to myself and Apollos
1Co 7:7 men·of·clay† to·be also as myself. But·yet each·man
1Co 9:19 all *men·of·clay†*, I·make·a·slave·of myself to·all,
Phm 1:13 to·fully·retain alongside myself, in·order·that on·
G1683.2 P:F-1DSM ἐμαυτῷ (4x)
Ac 20:24 ·hold my soul *as* precious to·myself, as·so to·fully·
Ac 26:9 in·fact, I·myself (within·myself) presumed *it* to·be·
Rm 11:4 ·him? "'I·reserved to·myself seven·thousand men,
1Co 4:4 ·of not·even·one·thing against·myself, but·yet not
G1683.2 P:F-1GSM ἐμαυτοῦ (1x)
Ac 24:10 ·composure I·give·an·account concerning myself,
G1683.3 P:F-1GSM ἐμαυτοῦ (1x)
1Co 10:33 *things*, not seeking my·own advantage, but·rather

G1684 ἐμ•βαίνω ēmbaínō *v.* (18x)
Roots:G1722 G0901-3 Compare:G1910
G1684.2 V-2AAI-3S ἐνέβη (2x)
Lk 8:22 of·the days that he·himself embarked into a·sailboat
Mt 15:39 after·dismissing the crowds, he·embarked into the
G1684.2 V-2AAI-3P ἐνέβησαν (2x)
Jn 6:22 one into which his disciples embarked, and that Jesus
Jn 6:24 his disciples, they also embarked into the sailboats
G1684.2 V-2AAN ἐμβῆναι (2x)
Mt 14:22 YeShua compelled his disciples to·embark into the
Mk 6:45 he·compelled his disciples to·embark into the
G1684.2 V-2AAP-ASM ἐμβάντα (2x)
Mt 13:2 to him, such·for him to·embark into the sailboat
Mk 4:1 to him, such·that he *was* embarking into the sailboat
G1684.2 V-2AAP-DSM ἐμβάντι (1x)
Mt 8:23 And embarking into the sailboat, his disciples
G1684.2 V-2AAP-GSM ἐμβάντος (1x)
Mk 5:18 And while *Jesus* was·embarking into the sailboat,
G1684.2 V-2AAP-GPM ἐμβάντων (1x)
Mt 14:32 And with·him embarking into the sailboat, the
G1684.2 V-2AAP-NSM ἐμβάς (5x)
Lk 5:3 But embarking into one of·the sailboats, which was
Lk 8:37 fear. And with·him embarking into the sailboat, he·
Mt 9:1 And after·embarking into the sailboat, he·crossed·
Mk 8:10 And immediately, after·embarking into the sailboat
Mk 8:13 And leaving them *and* embarking into the sailboat
G1684.2 V-2AAP-NPM ἐμβάντες (1x)
Jn 6:17 and after·embarking into the sailboat, they·were·
G1684.3 V-2AAP-NSM ἐμβάς (1x)
Jn 5:4 So·then, the first·one stepping·in after the agitation

G1685 ἐμ•βάλλω ēmbállō *v.* (1x)
Roots:G1722 G0906
G1685.1 V-2AAN ἐμβαλεῖν (1x)
Lk 12:5 killing, *is* having authority to·cast *a·person* into the

G1686 ἐμ•βάπτω ēmbáptō *v.* (3x)
Roots:G1722 G0911
G1686 V-PMP-NSM ἐμβαπτόμενος (1x)
Mk 14:20 the twelve, the·one who·is·dipping with me in the
G1686 V-AAP-NSM ἐμβάψας (2x)
Jn 13:26 dipping *it*." And dipping the morsel, he·gave *it* to·
Mt 26:23 he·declared, "The·one dipping his hand with me

G1687 ἐμ•βατεύω ēmbatéúō *v.* (1x)
Roots:G1722 G0941-1 See:G1684
G1687.2 V-PAP-NSM ἐμβατεύων (1x)
Col 2:18 one·intruding·into those·things·which he·has·not

G1688 ἐμ•βιβάζω ēmbibázō *v.* (1x)
Roots:G1722 G0973-1 See:G4264 G2601
G1688.2 V-AAI-3S ἐνεβίβασεν (1x)
Ac 27:6 into Italy, the centurion made us embark upon it.

G1689 ἐμ•βλέπω ēmblépō *v.* (12x)
Roots:G1722 G0991 Compare:G2657 G0816 See:G1914
G1689.1 V-PAP-NPM ἐμβλέποντες (1x)
Ac 1:11 ·do yeu·still·stand *there* looking·clearly·up into the
G1689.1 V-IAI-3P ἐνέβλεπον (1x)
Ac 22:11 "And as I·was·not looking·clearly·about due·to the
G1689.1 V-AAI-3S ἐνέβλεψεν (2x)
Lk 22:61 turning·around, the Lord looked·clearly·at Peter.
Mk 8:25 and looked·clearly·upon absolutely·all·men with·
G1689.1 V-AAM-2P ἐμβλέψατε (1x)
Mt 6:26 "Look·clearly at the birds of·the sky, because they·
G1689.1 V-AAP-NSF ἐμβλέψασα (1x)
Mk 14:67 warming·himself, after·looking·clearly·at him,
G1689.1 V-AAP-NSM ἐμβλέψας (6x)
Jn 1:36 And after·looking·clearly·upon Jesus walking·along,
Jn 1:42 And Jesus, looking·clearly·upon him, declared,
Lk 20:17 And looking·clearly·upon them, he·declared, "So·
Mt 19:26 But looking·clearly·at *them*, YeShua declared to·
Mk 10:21 And Jesus, after·looking·clearly·upon him, loved
Mk 10:27 And after·looking·clearly·upon them, Jesus says,

G1690 ἐμ•βριμάομαι ēmbrimáômai *v.* (6x)
Roots:G1722 Compare:G0546
EG1690 (1x)
Mk 14:41 he·comes the third·time, and *sternly* says to·them,
G1690.4 V-PNP-NSM ἐμβριμώμενος (1x)
Jn 11:38 Jesus, again being·exasperated in himself, comes
G1690.4 V-INI-3P ἐνεβριμῶντο (1x)
Mk 14:5 ·poor·ones." And they·were·exasperated with·her.
G1690.4 V-ADI-3S ἐνεβριμήσατο (1x)
Jn 11:33 ·together with·her, he·was·exasperated in·the spirit
G1690.5 V-ADI-3S ἐνεβριμήσατο (1x)
Mt 9:30 were·opened·up; and YeShua sternly·warned them,
G1690.5 V-ADP-NSM ἐμβριμησάμενος (1x)
Mk 1:43 And sternly·warning him, immediately he·cast him

G1691 ἐμέ ēmé *p:p.* (88x)
Roots:G3165 Compare:G1683 G1700
(abbreviated listing for G1691)
G1691.1 P:P-1AS ἐμέ (85x)
(list for G1691.1:P:P-1AS excluded)
G1691.3 P:P-1AS ἐμέ (3x)
(list for G1691.3:P:P-1AS excluded)

G1692 ἐμέω ēmêō *v.* (1x)
Compare:G1829 G2044 G4429 G2037-2 See:G1691-1 G1828-1 xLangAlso:H6958 H7006
G1692.2 V-AAN ἐμέσαι (1x)
Rv 3:16 nor fervently·hot, I·intend to·vomit you out of·my

G1693 ἐμ•μαίνομαι ēmmaínômai *v.* (1x)
Roots:G1722 G3105
G1693.2 V-PNP-NSM ἐμμαινόμενος (1x)
Ac 26:11 and·also maniacally·raging·against them beyond·

G1694 Ἐμμανου•ήλ Ēmmanôuēl *n/p.* (1x)
עִמָּנוּאֵל 'imȧnû'el [Hebrew]
Roots:H6005
G1694.2 N/P-PRI Ἐμμανουήλ (1x)
Mt 1:23 and they·shall·call his name ImmanuEl," which,

G1695 Ἐμμαούς Ēmmaôús *n/l.* (1x)
xLangEquiv:H3222
G1695.2 N/L-PRI Ἐμμαούς (1x)
Lk 24:13 a·village with·the name Emmaus, being·a·distance

G1696 ἐμ•μένω ēmménō *v.* (3x)
Roots:G1722 G3306
G1696.2 V-PAI-3S ἐμμένει (1x)
Gal 3:10 *is* everyone that does·not continue in all the·things
G1696.2 V-PAN ἐμμένειν (1x)
Ac 14:22 disciples, exhorting *them* to·continue in·the trust,
G1696.2 V-AAI-3P ἐνέμειναν (1x)
Heb 8:9 because they·themselves did·not continue in my

G1697 Ἐμμόρ Ēmmőr *n/p.* (1x)
חֲמוֹר cHămôr [Hebrew]
Roots:H2544 Compare:G4966
G1697.2 N/P-PRI Ἐμμόρ (1x)
Ac 7:16 of·silver·pieces near the Sons of·Chamor *the father*

G1698 ἐμοί ēmôí *p:p.* (101x)
Roots:G3427
(abbreviated listing for G1698)
G1698.1 P:P-1DS ἐμοί (93x)
(list for G1698.1:P:P-1DS excluded)
EG1698.1 (3x)
(list for EG1698.1: excluded)
G1698.2 P:P-1DS ἐμοί (1x)
(list for G1698.2:P:P-1DS excluded)
G1698.3 P:P-1DS ἐμοί (1x)
(list for G1698.3:P:P-1DS excluded)
G1698.4 P:P-1DS-HEB ἐμοί (3x)
(list for G1698.4:P:P-1DS-HEB excluded)

G1699 ἐμός ēmős *p:s.* (71x)
Roots:G1473 See:G1698 G1700 G1691
G1699.1 P:S-1NSF ἐμή (11x)
Jn 3:29 Accordingly, this (my joy) has·been·completely·
Jn 5:30 Just·as I·hear, I·judge. And my verdict is righteous,
Jn 7:16 them and declared, "My instruction is not mine, but·
Jn 8:16 And yet if I·myself should·judge, my verdict is true,
Jn 15:11 ·I·spoken to·yeu in·order·that my joy may·remain
Jn 15:12 "This is my commandment, that yeu·should·love
Jn 18:36 Jesus answered, "My kingdom is not from·among
Jn 18:36 this world. If my kingdom was from·among this
Jn 18:36 to·the Judeans. So now my kingdom is not from·
1Co 9:3 My defense to·the·ones scrutinizing me is this:
2Co 2:3 having·confidence in yeu all that my joy is *preferred*
G1699.1 P:S-1NSM ἐμός (5x)
Jn 7:6 ·then Jesus says to·them, "My season is·not·yet here,
Jn 7:8 to this Sacred·Feast, because my season has·not·yet
Jn 8:37 to·kill me, because my Redemptive-word does·not
Jn 12:26 where I AM, there also my attendant shall·be. And
2Co 8:23 concerning Titus, *he·is* my partner and coworker
G1699.1 P:S-1NSN ἐμόν (1x)
Jn 4:34 Jesus says to·them, "My food is that I·may·do the
G1699.1 P:S-1NPN ἐμά (2x)
Jn 10:27 "My sheep listen·to my voice, and·I know them,
Jn 17:10 "So·then, all my·things are yours, and your·things
G1699.1 P:S-1ASF ἐμήν (12x)

Jn 8:43 “Why do·yeu·not know my speech?
Jn 8:56 AbRaham leaped·for·joy that he·should·see my day,
Jn 14:27 “Peace I·leave with·yeu; my peace I·give to·yeu.
Jn 17:13 they·may·have my joy having·been·completely·
Jn 17:24 I AM, in·order·that they·may·observe my glory,
Lk 22:19 Do this as my continual·reminder.”
Gal 1:13 For yeu·heard of·my former manner·of·life in
2Pe 1:15 for·yeu to·have at·any·time, after my exodus, *the*
1Co 7:40 she·should·remain, according·to my advice; and I·
1Co 11:24 Do this as my continual·reminder.”
1Co 11:25 yeu·would·drink *it*, as my continual·reminder.”
2Co 1:23 do·call·upon God *for* a·witness upon my soul, that
G1699.1 P:S-1ASM ἐμόν (2x)
Jn 8:43 yeu·are·not able to·hear my Redemptive-word.
Jn 8:51 should·observantly·keep my Redemptive-word, no,
G1699.1 P:S-1ASN ἐμόν (2x)
Mt 18:20 are having·been·gathered·together in my name,
1Co 16:18 For they·refreshed my spirit and yeurs.
G1699.1 P:S-1APF ἐμάς (1x)
Jn 14:15 ·love me, observantly·keep my commandments.
G1699.1 P:S-1APM ἐμούς (3x)
Lk 9:26 would be·ashamed·of me and my Redemptive-words,
Mk 8:38 be·ashamed·of me and of·my Redemptive-words in
Rv 2:20 and to·lead·astray my slaves to·commit·sexual·
G1699.1 P:S-1APN ἐμά (2x)
Jn 10:14 the good shepherd, and I·know my *sheep*, and am·
3Jn 1:4 these·things, that I·hear·of my children walking in
G1699.1 P:S-1DSF ἐμῇ (1x)
Jn 15:9 loved me, so·also·I loved yeu. Abide in my love.
G1699.1 P:S-1DSM ἐμῷ (1x)
Jn 8:31 “If yeu should·continue in my Redemptive-word, yeu·
G1699.1 P:S-1DSN ἐμῷ (2x)
Rm 3:7 “For if by my lie, the truth of·God abounded to his
1Co 11:25 is the brand-new covenant in my blood. Do this,
G1699.1 P:S-1DPN ἐμοῖς (2x)
Jn 5:47 *Sacred*·Writings, how shall·yeu·trust my utterances?
Mt 20:15 ·me to·do whatever I·should·want with my things?
G1699.1 P:S-1GSF ἐμῆς (4x)
Rm 10:1 Brothers, in·fact my heart's good·purpose and
Php 1:26 in Jesus Anointed through my arrival to yeu again.
1Co 9:2 are the official·seal of·my commission in *the* Lord.
2Ti 4:6 the season of·my bodily·departure has·stood·over *me*
G1699.1 P:S-1GPN ἐμῶν (1x)
Jn 10:26 for yeu·are not from·among my sheep, just·as I·
G1699.2 P:S-1NSF ἐμή (1x)
Jn 7:16 “My instruction is not mine, but·rather *from* the·one
G1699.2 P:S-1NSM ἐμός (1x)
Jn 14:24 which yeu·hear is not mine, but·rather *that* of·*the*·
G1699.2 P:S-1NSN ἐμόν (2x)
Mt 20:23 at my left is not mine to·give, but·rather *it·shall·be*·
Mk 10:40 at my left is not mine to·give, but·rather *it·shall*·
G1699.2 P:S-1NPN ἐμά (3x)
Jn 16:15 ·as the Father has, are mine. On·account·of that, I·
Jn 17:10 yours, and your·things *are* mine, and I·have·been·
Lk 15:31 and all the·things *that·are* mine, they·are yours.
G1699.2 P:S-1GPN ἐμῶν (1x)
Jn 10:14 and I·know my *sheep*, and am·known by mine.
G1699.3 P:S-1NPN ἐμά (1x)
Phm 1:12 ·receive him, that·is, my·own inward·affections,
G1699.3 P:S-1ASF ἐμήν (1x)
Php 3:9 in him, not having my·own righteousness (the·one
G1699.3 P:S-1ASN ἐμόν (4x)
Jn 5:30 because I·do·not seek my·own will, but·rather the
Jn 6:38 not in·order·that I·may·do my·own will, but·rather
Mt 25:27 be·subsequently·obtaining my·own together with·
1Co 1:15 should·declare that I·immersed in my·own name.
G1699.3 P:S-1DSF ἐμῇ (5x)
Gal 6:11 ·sizable letters I·write to·yeu by·my·own hand.
2Th 3:17 The salutation of·Paul by·my·own hand, which is
1Co 16:21 The salutation of·Paul by·my·own hand.
Col 4:18 *This·is* the salutation by·my·own hand, Paul:
Phm 1:19 Paul, wrote *this* by·my·own hand; I·myself shall·

G1700 ἐμοῦ êmôû *p:p.* (113x)
Roots:G3450 Compare:G1691 See:G1683
(abbreviated listing for G1700)
G1700.1 P:P-1GS ἐμοῦ (99x)
(list for G1700.1:P:P-1GS excluded)
G1700.2 P:P-1GS ἐμοῦ (13x)
(list for G1700.2:P:P-1GS excluded)
G1700.3 P:P-1GS ἐμοῦ (1x)
(list for G1700.3:P:P-1GS excluded)

G1701 ἐμ•παιγμός êmpaigmŏs *n.* (1x)
Roots:G1702
G1701 N-GPM ἐμπαιγμῶν (1x)
Heb 11:36 received a·trial of·*cruel*·mockings and scourgings

G1702 ἐμ•παίζω êmpaízō *v.* (13x)
Roots:G1722 G3815 Compare:G3456 G2058-1
See:G1701 xLangAlso:H3887
G1702.2 V-FAI-3P ἐμπαίξουσιν (1x)
Mk 10:34 And they·shall·mock him, and shall·flog him, and
G1702.2 V-FPI-3S ἐμπαιχθήσεται (1x)
Lk 18:32 to·the Gentiles, and shall·be·mocked, and shall·be·
G1702.2 V-PAN ἐμπαίζειν (1x)
Lk 14:29 all the·ones observing *it* may·begin to·mock him,
G1702.2 V-PAP-NPM ἐμπαίζοντες (2x)
Mt 27:41 Likewise while·mocking *him* also, the chief·priests
Mk 15:31 the chief·priests, while·mocking, were·saying
G1702.2 V-IAI-3P ἐνέπαιζον (3x)
Lk 22:63 the·ones confining Jesus, were·mocking him,
Lk 23:36 And the soldiers also were·mocking him, coming·
Mt 27:29 ·down before him, they·were·mocking him, saying
G1702.2 V-AAI-3P ἐνέπαιξαν (2x)
Mt 27:31 And when they·had·mocked him, they·stripped the
Mk 15:20 And when they·mocked him, they·stripped the
G1702.2 V-AAN ἐμπαῖξαι (1x)
Mt 20:19 over to·the Gentiles for *them* to·mock, and to·flog,
G1702.2 V-AAP-NSM ἐμπαίξας (1x)
Lk 23:11 ·with his troops), after·mocking *him* and arraying
G1702.2 V-API-3S ἐνεπαίχθη (1x)
Mt 2:16 ·the·Great, after·seeing that he·was·mocked by the

G1703 ἐμ•παίκτης êmpaíktēs *n.* (2x)
Roots:G1702 Compare:G5572
G1703.1 N-NPM ἐμπαῖκται (2x)
Jud 1:18 ·saying to·yeu that there·shall·be mockers in *the*
2Pe 3:3 in the last days mockers, traversing according·to

G1704 ἐμ•περι•πατέω êmpêripatêō *v.* (1x)
Roots:G1722 G4043
G1704.1 V-FAI-1S ἐμπεριπατήσω (1x)
2Co 6:16 ·indwell in them, and shall·stroll·among *them*; and

G1705 ἐμ•πίπλημι êmpíplēmi *v.* (5x)
ἐμ•πλήθω êmpléthō
Roots:G1722 G4130
G1705.2 V-PAP-NSM ἐμπιπλῶν (1x)
Ac 14:17 and fruit-bearing seasons, filling·up our hearts
G1705.2 V-AAI-3S ἐνέπλησεν (1x)
Lk 1:53 He·filled·up those·being·hungry with·beneficially·
G1705.2 V-API-3P ἐνεπλήσθησαν (1x)
Jn 6:12 But as they·are·filled·up, he·says to·his disciples,
G1705.2 V-RPP-NPM ἐμπεπλησμένοι (1x)
Lk 6:25 to·yeu, the·ones having·been·filled·up! Because
G1705.3 V-APS-1S ἐμπλησθῶ (1x)
Rm 15:24 if first I·should·be partly replenished by yeu.

G1706 ἐμ•πίπτω êmpíptō *v.* (11x)
Roots:G1722 G4098
G1706.1 V-FDI-3S ἐμπεσεῖται (1x)
Lk 14:5 ·yeu shall·have a·donkey or an·ox fallen into a·well,
G1706.1 V-PAI-3P ἐμπίπτουσιν (1x)
1Ti 6:9 ·resolved to·become·wealthy fall into a·proof·trial
G1706.1 V-2AAN ἐμπεσεῖν (1x)
Heb 10:31 *It·is* a·frightful·thing to·fall into *the* hands of·the·
G1706.1 V-2AAP-GSM ἐμπεσόντος (1x)
Lk 10:36 ·become a·neighbor to·the·one falling among the
G1706.1 V-2AAS-3S ἐμπέσῃ (3x)
Mt 12:11 that if this *sheep* should·fall into a·pit on·the
1Ti 3:6 being·inflated·with·self-conceit he·should·fall to an·
1Ti 3:7 in·order·that he·should·not fall into reproach and
EG1706.1 (1x)
2Pe 2:10 but especially the·ones *falling·in* right·behind flesh,
EG1706.4 (3x)
Mt 4:19 to·them, “Come·here, *fall·in* right·behind me, and
Mk 1:17 to·them, “Come·here, *fall·in* right·behind me! And
1Ti 5:15 some are·turned·aside, *falling·in* right·behind the

G1707 ἐμ•πλέκω êmplékō *v.* (2x)
Roots:G1722 G4120 See:G1708 G4117
G1707.2 V-PPI-3S ἐμπλέκεται (1x)
2Ti 2:4 who·is·strategically·going·to·war is·entangled with·
G1707.2 V-2APP-NPM ἐμπλακέντες (1x)
2Pe 2:20 once·again are·being·entangled in·these·things *and*

G1708 ἐμ•πλοκή êmplôkḗ *n.* (1x)
Roots:G1707 Compare:G4117
G1708 N-GSF ἐμπλοκῆς (1x)
1Pe 3:3 *that·is* with·an·elaborate·braiding of·hair and a·

G1709 ἐμ•πνέω êmpnéō *v.* (1x)
Roots:G1722 G4154
G1709.2 V-PAP-NSM ἐμπνέων (1x)
Ac 9:1 Now Saul, still seething with·menace and murder

G1710 ἐμ•πορεύομαι êmpôrêúômai *v.* (2x)
Roots:G1722 G4198 Compare:G4122 See:G1711
G1712 G1713
xLangEquiv:H7402
G1710.2 V-ADS-1P ἐμπορευσώμεθα (1x)
Jac 4:13 *for* one year, and should·commercially·trade, and
G1710.3 V-FDI-3P ἐμπορεύσονται (1x)
2Pe 2:3 in greed, they·shall·commercially·exploit yeu with·

G1711 ἐμ•πορία êmpôría *n.* (1x)
Roots:G1713 See:G1712 G1710 xLangAlso:H7402
H4819
G1711.2 N-ASF ἐμπορίαν (1x)
Mt 22:5 farm, and *another* to his commercial·endeavor.

G1712 ἐμ•πόριον êmpôriôn *n.* (1x)
Roots:G1713 See:G1711 G1710 xLangAlso:H7402
G1712.1 N-GSN ἐμπορίου (1x)
Jn 2:16 ·not make my Father's house a·house of·commerce.”

G1713 ἔμ•πορος émpôrôs *n.* (5x)
Roots:G1722 G4198 Compare:G3328-3 See:G1711
G1712 G1710
xLangEquiv:H7404-1 H7402 xLangAlso:H5503
G1713.2 N-NPM ἔμποροι (4x)
Rv 18:3 her, and the merchants of·the earth became·wealthy
Rv 18:11 “And the merchants of·the earth do·weep and
Rv 18:15 “The merchants of·these·things, the·ones
Rv 18:23 — “because your merchants were the greatest·men
G1713.2 N-DSM ἐμπόρῳ (1x)
Mt 13:45 a·man·of·clay†, a·merchant seeking high·quality

G1714 ἐμ•πρήθω êmpréthō *v.* (1x)
Roots:G1722 Compare:G0329 G2545 G4448
G1714 V-AAI-3S ἐνέπρησεν (1x)
Mt 22:7 ·destroyed those murderers and torched their city.

G1715 ἔμ•προσ•θεν émprôsthên *adv.* (48x)
Roots:G1722 G4314 Compare:G1799 G1725 G1726
G1715.2 ADV ἔμπροσθεν (1x)
Rv 4:6 living·beings overflowing of·eyes forward and behind
G1715.3 PREP ἔμπροσθεν (41x)
Jn 3:28 that ‘I·am having·been·dispatched before him.’
Jn 10:4 ·forth his·own sheep, he·traverses before them, and
Jn 12:37 ·done so·many miraculous·signs before them, they·
Lk 5:19 together with·the pallet into the midst before Jesus.
Lk 7:27 who shall·fully·prepare your way before you.”
Lk 10:21 it·became a·delightful·purpose before you.”
Lk 12:8 should·affirm me by·name before the men·of·clay†,
Lk 12:8 also shall·affirm him by·name before the angels of·
Lk 14:2 man·of·clay† before him swollen·with·dropsy.
Lk 19:27 *them* here, and fully·slaughter *them* before me.’”
Lk 21:36 to·happen, and to·be·established before the Son
Ac 18:17 were·beating *him* before the Bema·judgment·seat.
Gal 2:14 ·the good·news, I·declared to·Peter before *them* all,
Mt 5:16 yeur light radiate·brightly before the men·of·clay†,

Mt 5:24 leave your present there before the Sacrifice·Altar
Mt 6:1 not to·do yeur merciful·act before the men·of·clay†,
Mt 6:2 ·act, you·should·not sound·a·trumpet before you,
Mt 7:6 nor·even should·yeu·cast yeur pearls before the pigs,
Mt 10:32 shall·affirm me by·name before the men·of·clay†,
Mt 10:32 I·also shall·affirm him by·name before my Father,
Mt 10:33 whoever should·deny me before the men·of·clay†,
Mt 10:33 ·of·clay†, him I·also shall·deny before my Father,
Mt 11:10 who shall·fully·prepare your way before you.
Mt 11:26 it·became a·delightful·purpose before you.
Mt 17:2 And he·was·metamorphosed before them. And his
Mt 18:14 "In·this·manner, before *the face* of·yeur Father,
Mt 23:14 the kingdom of·the heavens before men·of·clay†!
Mt 25:32 the nations shall·be·gathered·together before him,
Mt 26:70 But he·denied *it* before *them* all, saying, "I·do·not
Mt 27:11 Now YeShua stood·still before the governor. And
Mt 27:29 right·hand, and kneeling·down before him, they·
Mk 1:2 who shall·fully·prepare your way before you.
Mk 9:2 And he·was·metamorphosed before them.
1Th 1:3 unceasingly remembering yeu before our God and
1Th 2:19 ·indeed even yeu, *being* before our Lord YeShua
1Th 3:9 ·which we·rejoice on·account·of yeu before our God
1Th 3:13 hearts blameless in devoted·holiness before God,
2Co 5:10 to·be·made·manifest before the Bema·judgment·
1Jn 3:19 ·the truth and shall·reassure our hearts before him.
Rv 19:10 And I·fell before his feet to·fall·prostrate to·him.
Rv 22:8 looked, I·fell·down to·fall·prostrate before the feet

G1715.4 ADV ἔμπροσθεν (3x)
Lk 19:4 And running·on ahead, he·climbed·up upon a·
Lk 19:28 these·things, *Jesus* traversed·on ahead, walking·up
Php 3:13 and stretching·myself·toward the·things ahead,

G1715.4 PREP ἔμπροσθεν (3x)
Jn 1:15 right·behind me has·come·to·be ahead of·me,
Jn 1:27 right·behind me who has·come·to·be ahead of·me)
Jn 1:30 me comes a·man who has·come·to·be ahead of·me,

G1716 ἐμ•πτύω ĕmptýō *v.* (6x)
Roots:G1722 G4429 Compare:G1609

G1716 V-FAI-3P ἐμπτύσουσιν (1x)
Mk 10:34 and shall·flog him, and shall·spit·on him, and

G1716 V-FPI-3S ἐμπτυσθήσεται (1x)
Lk 18:32 ·be·abusively·mistreated, and shall·be·spat·upon.

G1716 V-PAN ἐμπτύειν (1x)
Mk 14:65 And some began to·spit·on him, and upon·putting·

G1716 V-IAI-3P ἐνέπτυον (1x)
Mk 15:19 his head with·a·reed and were·spitting·on him.

G1716 V-AAI-3P ἐνέπτυσαν (1x)
Mt 26:67 Then they·spat in his face and buffeted him, and

G1716 V-AAP-NPM ἐμπτύσαντες (1x)
Mt 27:30 And after·spitting at him, they·took the reed and

G1717 ἐμ•φανής ĕmphanḗs *adj.* (2x)
Roots:G1722 G5316 See:G5321 G1718

G1717 A-NSM ἐμφανής (1x)
Rm 10:20 seeking me; I·was·made manifest to·the·ones not

G1717 A-ASM ἐμφανῆ (1x)
Ac 10:40 on·the third day and gave him to·be manifest,

G1718 ἐμ•φανίζω ĕmphanízō *v.* (10x)
Roots:G1717 Compare:G0584 G1213 G4591 G5263 G5346 G2727

G1718.1 V-FAI-1S ἐμφανίσω (1x)
Jn 14:21 shall·love him and shall·manifest myself to·him."

G1718.1 V-PAN ἐμφανίζειν (1x)
Jn 14:22 that you·intend to·manifest yourself to·us, and not·

G1718.1 V-API-3P ἐνεφανίσθησαν (1x)
Mt 27:53 into the Holy City and were·manifested to·many.

G1718.1 V-APN ἐμφανισθῆναι (1x)
Heb 9:24 now to·be·manifested in·the personal·presence

G1718.2 V-PAI-3P ἐμφανίζουσιν (1x)
Heb 11:14 saying such·things make·it·clear that they·seek a·

G1718.2 V-AAI-3P ἐνεφάνισαν (2x)
Ac 24:1 *named* Tertullus, who made·it·clear to·the governor
Ac 25:15 ·the Judeans made·it·clear *that* they·are·requesting

G1718.2 V-AAM-2P ἐμφανίσατε (1x)
Ac 23:15 make·it·clear to·the regiment·commander that he·

G1718.3 V-AAI-2S ἐνεφάνισας (1x)
Ac 23:22 "to·no·one that you·made these·things clear to·me.

G1718.3 V-AAI-3P ἐνεφάνισαν (1x)
Ac 25:2 of·the Judeans made·clear to·him *the·things* against

G1719 ἔμ•φοβος ĕmphôbôs *adj.* (6x)
Roots:G1722 G5401

G1719.2 A-NSM ἔμφοβος (2x)
Ac 10:4 ·intently at·him and becoming alarmed, he·declared,
Ac 24:25 shall·be, Felix, becoming alarmed, answered,

G1719.2 A-NPM ἔμφοβοι (3x)
Lk 24:37 and becoming alarmed, they·were·supposing to·
Ac 22:9 ·view the light and were alarmed, but they·did·not
Rv 11:13 And the rest became alarmed and gave glory to·the

G1719.2 A-GPM ἐμφόβων (1x)
Lk 24:5 with·the *women* becoming alarmed and drooping the

G1720 ἐμ•φυσάω ĕmphysáō *v.* (1x)
Roots:G1722 G5445-5 Compare:G4154 xLangAlso:H5301

G1720.3 V-AAI-3S ἐνεφύσησεν (1x)
Jn 20:22 And after·declaring this, he·puffed·on *them*. Then

G1721 ἔμ•φυτος ĕmphytôs *adj.* (1x)
Roots:G1722 G5453

G1721 A-ASM ἔμφυτον (1x)
Jac 1:21 a·calm·mildness the implanted Redemptive-word,

G1722 ἔν ĕn *prep.* (2792x)
ἐγ- ĕg- [alternate prefix]
ἐμ- ĕm- [soft prefix]
Compare:G1519 G1537 G3384 See:G1751 G1762 G1759 G1782 G1787 xLangAlso:HFP20
(abbreviated listing for G1722)

G1722.1 -- (1x)
(list for G1722.1:-- excluded)

G1722.1 PREP ἔν (1981x)
(list for G1722.1:PREP excluded)

EG1722.1 (3x)
(list for EG1722.1: excluded)

G1722.2 PREP ἔν (96x)
(list for G1722.2:PREP excluded)

G1722.3 PREP ἔν (82x)
(list for G1722.3:PREP excluded)

G1722.4 PREP ἔν (186x)
(list for G1722.4:PREP excluded)

G1722.5 PREP ἔν (178x)
(list for G1722.5:PREP excluded)

EG1722.5 (2x)
(list for EG1722.5: excluded)

G1722.6 PREP ἔν (25x)
(list for G1722.6:PREP excluded)

G1722.7 PREP ἔν (160x)
(list for G1722.7:PREP excluded)

G1722.8 PREP ἔν (15x)
(list for G1722.8:PREP excluded)

G1722.9 PREP ἔν (10x)
(list for G1722.9:PREP excluded)

G1722.10 PREP ἔν (14x)
(list for G1722.10:PREP excluded)

G1722.11 PREP ἔν (4x)
(list for G1722.11:PREP excluded)

G1722.12 PREP ἔν (7x)
(list for G1722.12:PREP excluded)

G1722.13 PREP ἔν (2x)
(list for G1722.13:PREP excluded)

G1722.14 PREP ἔν (4x)
(list for G1722.14:PREP excluded)

G1722.15 PREP ἔν (6x)
(list for G1722.15:PREP excluded)

G1722.16 PREP ἔν (6x)
(list for G1722.16:PREP excluded)

G1722.17 PREP ἔν (3x)
(list for G1722.17:PREP excluded)

G1722.19 PREP ἔν (4x)
(list for G1722.19:PREP excluded)

G1722.20 PREP ἔν (1x)
(list for G1722.20:PREP excluded)

G1722.21 PREP ἔν (2x)
(list for G1722.21:PREP excluded)

G1723 ἐν•αγκαλίζομαι ĕnankalízômai *v.* (2x)
Roots:G1722 G0043 Compare:G0782

G1723 V-ADP-NSM ἐναγκαλισάμενος (2x)
Mk 9:36 then taking him in·his·arms, he·declared to·them,
Mk 10:16 And taking them in·his·arms, while·placing his

G1724 ἐν•άλιος ĕnáliôs *adj.* (1x)
Roots:G1722 G0251

G1724.3 A-GPN ἐναλίων (1x)
Jac 3:7 ·things, and of·creatures·in·the·sea, is·tamed and

G1725 ἔν•αντι ĕnanti *adv.* (14x)
Roots:G1722 G0473 Compare:G1715 G1799 See:G1727 G0561 G2713

EG1725 (13x)
Jn 4:22 fall·prostrate *directly·before* whom yeu·do·not
Jn 4:22 We·personally·know *directly·before* whom we·
Jn 4:23 such·as·these falling·prostrate *directly·before* him.
Jn 4:24 falling·prostrate *directly·before* him to·fall·prostrate
Lk 4:8 You·shall·fall·prostrate *directly·before* Yahweh your
Lk 24:52 after·falling·prostrate *directly·before* him,
Mt 4:10 "You·shall·fall·prostrate *directly·before* Yahweh
Rv 9:20 ·should·not fall·prostrate *directly·before* the demons
Rv 13:4 And they·fell·prostrate *directly·before* the Dragon
Rv 13:4 and they·fell·prostrate *directly·before* the Daemonic·
Rv 13:12 they·should·fall·prostrate *directly·before* the first
Rv 14:9 falls·prostrate *directly·before* the Daemonic·Beast
Rv 14:11 falling·prostrate *directly·before* the Daemonic·Beast

G1725.1 ADV ἔναντι (1x)
Lk 1:8 him performing·priestly·duties in·front of·God in the

G1726 ἐν•αντίον ĕnantíôn *adv.* (5x)
Roots:G1727 Compare:G1715 G1799 See:G5121 xLangAlso:H6440

G1726.1 ADV ἐναντίον (1x)
Mk 2:12 the mat, he·went·forth in·front of·them·all, such·

G1726.2 ADV ἐναντίον (3x)
Lk 20:26 ·his utterances in·the·direct·presence of·the people.
Ac 7:10 and wisdom in·the·direct·presence of·Pharaoh king
Ac 8:32 voiceless in·the·direct·presence of·the·one shearing

G1726.3 ADV ἐναντίον (1x)
Lk 24:19 in deed and word directly·before God and all the

G1727 ἐν•αντίος ĕnantíôs *adj.* (8x)
Roots:G1725 Compare:G1715 G1799 See:G5227 G2713 G1726

G1727.1 A-GSF ἐναντίας (1x)
Mk 15:39 the·one having·stood·nearby out in·front of·him,

G1727.2 A-NSM ἐναντίος (2x)
Mt 14:24 the breaking·waves, for the wind was contrary.
Mk 6:48 for the wind was contrary to·them. And about *the*

G1727.2 A-APM ἐναντίους (1x)
Ac 27:4 ·to Cyprus, on·account·of the winds being contrary.

G1727.2 A-APN ἐναντία (1x)
Ac 26:9 ·necessary to·practice many·things contrary to the

G1727.3 A-ASN ἐναντίον (1x)
Ac 28:17 not·even·one·thing antagonistic to·the People or

G1727.3 A-GSF ἐναντίας (1x)
Tit 2:8 *those being* antagonistic may·be·embarrassed, having

G1727.4 A-GPM ἐναντίων (1x)
1Th 2:15 ·God, even *being* antagonists to·all men·of·clay†

G1728 ἐν•άρχομαι ĕnárchômai *v.* (2x)
Roots:G1722 G0756 See:G4278

G1728 V-ADP-NSM ἐναρξάμενος (1x)
Php 1:6 the·one already·beginning a·beneficially·good work

G1728 V-ADP-NPM ἐναρξάμενοι (1x)
Gal 3:3 are·yeu stupid? After·beginning in·*the*·Spirit, are·

G1729 ἐν•δεής ĕndĕēs *adj.* (1x)
Roots:G1722 G1210

G1729 A-NSM ἐνδεής (1x)
Ac 4:34 was anyone subsisting among them in·a·bind, for as·

G1730 ἔν•δειγμα éndêigma *n.* (1x)
Roots:G1731 See:G1732
G1730 N-NSN ἔνδειγμα (1x)
2Th 1:5 *This·is* an·indication of·the righteous verdict of·God,

G1731 ἐν•δείκνυμι êndêíknymi *v.* (12x)
Roots:G1722 G1166 Compare:G0322 G0584 G4921 See:G1732
G1731.1 V-PMI-3P ἐνδείκνυνται (1x)
Rm 2:15 who themselves·indicate the work of·the
G1731.1 V-PMN ἐνδείκνυσθαι (1x)
Heb 6:11 we·long·for each·one of·yeu to·indicate the same
G1731.1 V-PMP-APM ἐνδεικνυμένους (2x)
Tit 2:10 pilfering, but·rather indicating all beneficially·good
Tit 3:2 not·quarrelsome, *but* fair, indicating all gentleness to
G1731.1 V-AMI-2P ἐνεδείξασθε (1x)
Heb 6:10 ·labor of·love, which yeu·have·indicated for his
G1731.1 V-AMM-2P ἐνδείξασθε (1x)
2Co 8:24 Accordingly, indicate for them the indicator of·
G1731.1 V-AMN ἐνδείξασθαι (1x)
Rm 9:22 Now if God, willing to·indicate his wrath and to·
G1731.1 V-AMS-1S ἐνδείξωμαι (1x)
Rm 9:17 ·awakened you, that I·may·indicate my power by
G1731.1 V-AMS-3S ἐνδείξηται (2x)
Eph 2:7 in·order·that he·may·indicate in the upcoming ages
1Ti 1:16 foremost, Jesus Anointed may·indicate the entirety
EG1731.1 (1x)
Eph 2:7 wealth of·his grace, *indicated* in *his* kindness
G1731.2 V-AMI-3S ἐνεδείξατο (1x)
2Ti 4:14 the coppersmith, pointedly·did me much harm.

G1732 ἔν•δειξις éndêixis *n.* (4x)
Roots:G1731 Compare:G0585 G5039 G0323 See:G1730
G1732 N-NSF ἔνδειξις (1x)
Php 1:28 in·fact is an·indicator of·total·destruction for·them,
G1732 N-ASF ἔνδειξιν (3x)
Rm 3:25 his blood (as an·indicator of·his righteousness on·
Rm 3:26 (specifically·as an·indicator of·his righteousness in
2Co 8:24 indicate for them the indicator of·yeur love and

G1733 ἕν•δεκα héndêka *n.* (6x)
Roots:G1520 G1176 See:G1734
G1733 N-NUI ἕνδεκα (6x)
Lk 24:9 ·announced all these·things to·the eleven and to·all
Lk 24:33 ·found the eleven having·been·mustered·together,
Ac 1:26 ·counted·together with the eleven ambassadors.
Ac 2:14 ·being·settled together with·the eleven, lifted·up his
Mt 28:16 Now the eleven disciples traversed into Galilee to
Mk 16:14 he·was·made·apparent to·the eleven, with·them

G1734 ἐν•δέκατος hêndékatôs *adj.* (3x)
Roots:G1733 xLangAlso:H6249
G1734 A-NSM ἐνδέκατος (1x)
Rv 21:20 chrysoprase; the eleventh, deep·blue·hyacinth;
G1734 A-ASF ἐνδεκάτην (2x)
Mt 20:6 "Now going·forth about the eleventh hour, he·
Mt 20:9 the·ones *hired* about the eleventh hour received a·

G1735 ἐν•δέχεται êndéchêtai *v.* (1x)
Roots:G1722 G1209
G1735.2 V-PNI-3S-I ἐνδέχεται (1x)
Lk 13:33 because it·is·not acceptable *that* a·prophet should·

G1736 ἐν•δημέω êndēméō *v.* (3x)
Roots:G1722 G1218
G1736.2 V-PAP-NPM ἐνδημοῦντες (2x)
2Co 5:6 ·knowing that while·being·at·home in the body,
2Co 5:9 also, whether being·at·home or being·absent·abroad
G1736.2 V-AAN ἐνδημῆσαι (1x)
2Co 5:8 ·among the body and to·be·at·home alongside the

G1737 ἐν•διδύσκω êndidýskō *v.* (2x)
Roots:G1746 Compare:G5409
G1737 V-IMI-3S ἐνεδιδύσκετο (2x)
Lk 8:27 ·span of·time, and was·not wearing a·garment, and
Lk 16:19 ·of·clay†, and he·was·wearing a·purple·cloak and

G1738 ἔν•δικος éndikôs *adj.* (2x)
Roots:G1722 G1349
G1738.2 A-NSN ἔνδικον (1x)
Rm 3:8 Of·such·men, the judgment is just.
G1738.2 A-ASF ἔνδικον (1x)
Heb 2:2 ·disregard received a·just reward·for·disservice,

G1739 ἐν•δόμησις êndómēsis *n.* (1x)
Roots:G1722 G1185-1 See:G3619
G1739.2 N-NSF ἐνδόμησις (1x)
Rv 21:18 And the construction of·its wall was *of* jasper.

G1740 ἐν•δοξάζω êndôxázō *v.* (2x)
Roots:G1741 Compare:G1392
G1740.2 V-APN ἐνδοξασθῆναι (1x)
2Th 1:10 whenever he·should·come to·be·glorified in his
G1740.2 V-APS-3S ἐνδοξασθῇ (1x)
2Th 1:12 Lord YeShua Anointed may·be·glorified in yeu,

G1741 ἔν•δοξος éndôxôs *adj.* (4x)
Roots:G1722 G1391 xLangEquiv:H3519
G1741.2 A-NPM ἔνδοξοι (1x)
1Co 4:10 *are* strong. Yeu *are* glorious, but we·ourselves *are*
G1741.2 A-ASF ἔνδοξον (1x)
Eph 5:27 that he·may·present her to·himself glorious, the
G1741.2 A-DSM ἐνδόξῳ (1x)
Lk 7:25 Behold, the·ones in glorious attire, also subsisting
G1741.2 A-DPN ἐνδόξοις (1x)
Lk 13:17 was·rejoicing over all the glorious·things, the·ones

G1742 ἔν•δυμα éndyma *n.* (8x)
Roots:G1746 Compare:G1903 G2440 G2441 G2689 G4018 xLangAlso:H3830
G1742 N-NSN ἔνδυμα (1x)
Mt 28:3 was as lightning, and his apparel white as snow.
G1742 N-ASN ἔνδυμα (3x)
Mt 3:4 same John was·having his apparel *made* from camel's
Mt 22:11 having·not dressed·himself·with wedding apparel.
Mt 22:12 ·you·enter here not having wedding apparel?' And
G1742 N-DPN ἐνδύμασιν (1x)
Mt 7:15 do·come to yeu in sheep's apparel, but inwardly,
G1742 N-GSN ἐνδύματος (3x)
Lk 12:23 and the body *is more·than* the apparel.
Mt 6:25 ·nourishment, and the body *more·than* the apparel?
Mt 6:28 are·yeu·anxious concerning apparel? Carefully·note

G1743 ἐν•δυναμόω êndynamóō *v.* (8x)
Roots:G1722 G1412
G1743 V-PAP-DSM ἐνδυναμοῦντι (1x)
Php 4:13 *to·do* all·things in the·one enabling me, *the*
G1743 V-PPM-2S ἐνδυναμοῦ (1x)
2Ti 2:1 you, my child, be·enabled in the grace, the·one in
G1743 V-PPM-2P ἐνδυναμοῦσθε (1x)
Eph 6:10 remaining: My brothers, be·enabled in *the* Lord
G1743 V-IPI-3S ἐνεδυναμοῦτο (1x)
Ac 9:22 But Saul was·enabled *all* the·more, and was·
G1743 V-AAI-3S ἐνεδυνάμωσεν (1x)
2Ti 4:17 the Lord stood·by me and enabled me, in·order·that
G1743 V-AAP-DSM ἐνδυναμώσαντι (1x)
1Ti 1:12 Jesus our Lord, the·one enabling me. Because he·
G1743 V-API-3S ἐνεδυναμώθη (1x)
Rm 4:20 ·a lack·of·trust, but·rather was·enabled by·the trust
G1743 V-API-3P ἐνεδυναμώθησαν (1x)
Heb 11:34 from weakness were·enabled, did·become strong

G1744 ἐν•δύνω êndýnō *v.* (1x)
Roots:G1722 G1416 Compare:G1746 G2572 G3345 G1525 G2062-1 See:G1737
G1744.4 V-PAP-NPM ἐνδύνοντες (1x)
2Ti 3:6 *types* are the·ones impersonating·their·way into the

G1745 ἔν•δυσις éndysis *n.* (1x)
Roots:G1746
G1745 N-GSF ἐνδύσεως (1x)
1Pe 3:3 ·golden·articles, or of·dressing *with·showy* garments

G1746 ἐν•δύω êndýō *v.* (29x)
Roots:G1722 G1416 Compare:G0294 G2439 G1902 G4060 See:G1737 xLangAlso:H3847
G1746 V-PAI-3P ἐνδύουσιν (1x)
Mk 15:17 And they·dress him with·a·purple·cloak. And
G1746 V-AAI-3P ἐνέδυσαν (2x)
Mt 27:31 ·cloak *from* him and dressed him with·his·own
Mk 15:20 purple·cloak from·him, and dressed him *with* his·
G1746 V-AAM-2P ἐνδύσατε (1x)
Lk 15:22 most·prestigious long·robe, and dress him. And
G1746 V-AMI-2P ἐνεδύσασθε (1x)
Gal 3:27 yeu·did·dress·yeurselves·with *the* Anointed-One.
G1746 V-AMM-2P ἐνδύσασθε (3x)
Rm 13:14 But·rather dress·yeurselves·with the Lord Jesus
Eph 6:11 Dress·yeurselves·with the whole·armor of·God,
Col 3:12 , dress·yeurselves·with compassionate inward·
G1746 V-AMN ἐνδύσασθαι (3x)
1Co 15:53 *being* to·dress·itself·with incorruptibility, and *for*
1Co 15:53 *for* this mortal to·dress·itself·with immortality.
Eph 4:24 and to·dress·yeurselves·with the brand-new man·
G1746 V-AMP-NSM ἐνδυσάμενος (1x)
Ac 12:21 day, after·dressing·himself in·royal clothing and
G1746 V-AMP-NPM ἐνδυσάμενοι (4x)
1Th 5:8 ·sober, dressing·ourselves·with *the* full·chest·armor
2Co 5:3 and·then, if·indeed dressing·ourselves, we·shall·not
Eph 6:14 and dressing·yeurselves·with the full·chest·armor
Col 3:10 and dressing·yeurselves·with the fresh·new *man·of·*
G1746 V-AMS-1P ἐνδυσώμεθα (1x)
Rm 13:12 and we·should·dress·ourselves·with the weapons·
G1746 V-AMS-2P ἐνδύσησθε (4x)
Lk 12:22 body, what yeu·should·dress·yeurselves·with.
Lk 24:49 yeu·should·dress·yeurselves·with power from·out
Mt 6:25 body, with·what yeu·should·dress·yeurselves. Is
Mk 6:9 and yeu·should·not dress·yeurselves·with two tunics.
G1746 V-AMS-3S ἐνδύσηται (2x)
1Co 15:54 *being* should·dress·itself·with incorruptibility,
1Co 15:54 this mortal should·dress·itself·with immortality,
G1746 V-RMP-ASM ἐνδεδυμένον (2x)
Mt 22:11 having·not dressed·himself·with wedding apparel.
Rv 1:13 having·dressed·himself·with a·foot·length·robe,
G1746 V-RMP-NSM ἐνδεδυμένος (1x)
Mk 1:6 John was having·dressed·himself·with camel's hair
G1746 V-RMP-NPM ἐνδεδυμένοι (2x)
Rv 15:6 ·blows, having·dressed·themselves in·pure and
Rv 19:14 horses, having·dressed·themselves·with fine·linen,
EG1746 (1x)
Col 3:14 over all these·things, *dress·yeurselves·with* the love

G1747 ἐν•έδρα ênédra *n.* (1x)
Roots:G1722 G1476 See:G1749
G1747.1 N-ASF ἐνέδραν (1x)
Ac 25:3 to JeruSalem, while·they·make an·ambush in the

G1748 ἐν•εδρεύω ênêdrêúō *v.* (2x)
Roots:G1747
G1748.1 V-PAI-3P ἐνεδρεύουσιν (1x)
Ac 23:21 for from·among them who·lay·in·wait·for him *are*
G1748.1 V-PAP-NPM ἐνεδρεύοντες (1x)
Lk 11:54 laying·in·wait·for him, and seeking to·hunt·for

G1749 ἔν•εδρον énêdrôn *n.* (1x)
Roots:G1747
G1749.1 N-ASN ἔνεδρον (1x)
Ac 23:16 ·directly after·hearing of·the ambush and entering

G1750 ἐν•ειλέω ênêiléō *v.* (1x)
Roots:G1722 G1507 Compare:G1794
G1750 V-AAI-3S ἐνείλησεν (1x)
Mk 15:46 *Jesus* down, *Joseph* tightly·enwrapped him in·the

G1751 ἔν•ειμι énêimi *v.* (1x)
Roots:G1722 G1510 See:G1762
G1751.2 V-PXP-APN ἐνόντα (1x)
Lk 11:41 ·act·of·charity, one·being·within·yeur·means, and

G1752 ἕνεκα hēnêka *adv.* (25x)
ἕνεκεν hēnêkên
εἵνεκεν hêínêkên

G1752.1 ADV ἕνεκεν (1x)
Rm 14:20 demolish the work of·God for·the·sake·of food.
G1752.2 ADV ἕνεκεν (4x)
Lk 4:18 Spirit *is* upon me for·the·cause·of which he·anointed
Lk 18:29 or children, for·the·cause·of the kingdom of·God,
Lk 21:12 kings and governors for·the·cause·of my name.
Mt 19:29 or plots·of·land, for·the·cause·of my name, shall·
G1752.3 ADV εἵνεκεν (10x)
Lk 6:22 name as evil, because·of the Son of·Clay·Man†.
Ac 26:21 "Because·of these·things, the Judeans, upon·
Ac 28:20 *with·yeu*, for *it·is* because·of the Expectation of·
Mt 5:10 having·been·persecuted because·of righteousness,
Mt 5:11 ·of evil utterance against yeu, because·of me.
Mt 10:18 before governors and also kings because·of me, for
2Co 3:10 in this particular·aspect: because·of the surpassing
2Co 7:12 to·yeu, *it·was* not because·of the·one doing·wrong,
2Co 7:12 ·wrong, nor because·of the·one being·done·wrong,
2Co 7:12 ·wrong, but·rather because·of yeur earnest·care
G1752.4 ADV ἕνεκα (10x)
Lk 9:24 ·lose his soul's·desire for·my cause, the·same shall·
Ac 19:32 ·known for·what cause they·had·come·together.
Mt 10:39 ·losing his soul's·desire, for·my cause, shall·find it
Mt 16:25 ·lose his soul's·desire, for·my cause, shall·find it.
Mt 19:5 "For·this cause a·man·of·clay† shall·leave·behind
Mk 8:35 ·lose his soul's·desire for·my cause and *for·that* of·
Mk 10:7 "For·this cause a·man·of·clay† shall·leave·behind
Mk 10:29 or plots·of·land, for·my cause and of·the good·
Mk 13:9 governors and kings for·my cause, for a·testimony
Rm 8:36 "For·your cause, we·are·put·to·death all the day·

G1753 ἐν•έργεια ênérgêia *n.* (9x)
Roots:G1756 See:G1754 G1755
EG1753 (1x)
Jac 5:16 is·itself·operating *to* much *effect*. It·has·strength.
G1753.1 N-ASF ἐνέργειαν (5x)
Php 3:21 glory, according·to the operation *within* himself to·
2Th 2:9 according·to an·operation of·the Adversary-Accuser
Eph 1:19 trusting, according·to the operation of·the strength
Eph 3:7 to·me according·to the operation of·his power.
Col 1:29 ·hard, striving according·to his operation, the·one
G1753.3 N-ASF ἐνέργειαν (1x)
2Th 2:11 shall·send them an·effective deviation *from·truth*
G1753.4 N-ASF ἐνέργειαν (1x)
Eph 4:16 ·joint, according·to an·effective·working of·each
G1753.4 N-GSF ἐνεργείας (1x)
Col 2:12 through the trust of·the effective·work of·God, the·

G1754 ἐν•εργέω ênêrgéō *v.* (23x)
Roots:G1756 See:G1753 G1755
G1754.2 V-PAI-3S ἐνεργεῖ (1x)
1Co 12:11 But all these·things operate by·the one and the
G1754.2 V-PAI-3P ἐνεργοῦσιν (2x)
Mt 14:2 and on·account·of that, miracles operate in him."
Mk 6:14 on·account·of that, the miracles operate in him."
G1754.2 V-PAN ἐνεργεῖν (1x)
Php 2:13 and to·operate on·behalf of·*his*·good·purpose.
G1754.2 V-PAP-GSN ἐνεργοῦντος (1x)
Eph 2:2 air, of·the spirit now operating in the Sons of·the
G1754.2 V-PAP-GSM ἐνεργοῦντος (1x)
Eph 1:11 determined·purpose of·the·one operating all things
G1754.2 V-PAP-NSM ἐνεργῶν (3x)
Gal 3:5 the Spirit to·yeu and operating miracles among yeu,
Php 2:13 For it·is God *who·is* the·one operating in yeu both
1Co 12:6 but it·is the same God, the·one operating all in all.
G1754.2 V-PMI-3S ἐνεργεῖται (3x)
1Th 2:13 God's Redemptive-word, which operates also in yeu,
2Th 2:7 the mystery of·the Lawlessness operates even·now.
2Co 4:12 As·such in·fact, the death operates in us, but the
G1754.2 V-PMP-ASF ἐνεργουμένην (2x)
Eph 3:20 according·to the power, the·one operating in us,
Col 1:29 ·to his operation, the·one operating in me in power.
G1754.2 V-PMP-GSF ἐνεργουμένης (1x)
2Co 1:6 (the·one operating along·with a·patient·endurance
G1754.2 V-PMP-NSF ἐνεργουμένη (2x)
Gal 5:6 ·rather trust which·is·itself·operating through love.
Jac 5:16 of·a·righteous·man is·itself·operating *to* much *effect*
G1754.2 V-IMI-3S ἐνηργεῖτο (1x)
Rm 7:5 through the Torah-Law, did·operate in our members
G1754.2 V-AAI-3S ἐνήργησεν (2x)
Gal 2:8 of·the Circumcision, also operated in·me unto the
Eph 1:20 which he·operated in the Anointed-One, after·
G1754.2 V-AAP-NSM ἐνεργήσας (1x)
Gal 2:8 (for the·one operating in·Peter unto a·commission
EG1754.2 (2x)
1Co 12:28 after·that *the·ones operating·in* miracles, then
1Co 12:29 Not all *are operating·in* miracles.

G1755 ἐν•έργημα ênérgēma *n.* (2x)
Roots:G1754 Compare:G1248 G5486 See:G1753
G1755 N-NPN ἐνεργήματα (1x)
1Co 12:10 and to·another, operations of·miracles, to·another
G1755 N-GPN ἐνεργημάτων (1x)
1Co 12:6 And there·are varieties of·operations, but it·is the

G1756 ἐν•εργής ênêrgḗs *adj.* (3x)
Roots:G1722 G2041 See:G1753 G1754
G1756.1 A-NSM ἐνεργής (1x)
Heb 4:12 of·God *is* living and active, and *he·is* sharper,
G1756.1 A-NSF ἐνεργής (2x)
1Co 16:9 For a·great and active door has·opened·up to·me,
Phm 1:6 fellowship of·your trust may·become active by *the*

G1757 ἐν•ευ•λογέω ênêulôgéō *v.* (2x)
Roots:G1722 G2127
G1757.2 V-FPI-3P ἐνευλογηθήσονται (2x)
Ac 3:25 the paternal·lineages of·the earth shall·be·blessed."
Gal 3:8 *saying*, "'In you, all the nations shall·be·blessed.'"

G1758 ἐν•έχω ênéchō *v.* (3x)
Roots:G1722 G2192 Compare:G1707 G3802 G4624 See:G1777
G1758.1 V-PPM-2P ἐνέχεσθε (1x)
Gal 5:1 and do·not again be·held·in by·a·yoke of·slavery.
G1758.2 V-IAI-3S ἐνεῖχεν (1x)
Mk 6:19 HerOdias was·holding·a·grudge against·him and
G1758.3 V-PAN ἐνέχειν (1x)
Lk 11:53 and the Pharisees began to·besiege *him* dreadfully,

G1759 ἐνθάδε ênthádê *adv.* (8x)
Roots:G1722
G1759.2 ADV ἐνθάδε (8x)
Jn 4:15 thirst, nor·even should·come here to·draw·out *water*
Jn 4:16 ·out, holler·out·for your husband, and come here."
Lk 24:41 "Do·yeu·have anything edible here?"
Ac 10:18 the·one being·surnamed Peter, is·a·guest here.
Ac 16:28 ·one·bit·of harm, for we·are absolutely·all here."
Ac 17:6 The Land, these·men are·presently here also,
Ac 25:17 with·them coming·together here (making not·
Ac 25:24 at JeruSalem, and here, crying·out·against *him*,

G1760 ἐν•θυμέομαι ênthyméômai *v.* (3x)
Roots:G1722 G2372 Compare:G1260 G5426 G4820 See:G1761
G1760.2 V-PNI-2P ἐνθυμεῖσθε (1x)
Mt 9:4 ·purpose·do yeu·yeurselves cogitate evil·things in
G1760.2 V-PNP-GSM ἐνθυμουμένου (1x)
Ac 10:19 But while·Peter was·cogitating about the clear·
G1760.2 V-AOP-GSM ἐνθυμηθέντος (1x)
Mt 1:20 But with·him cogitating these·things, behold, an·

G1761 ἐν•θύμησις ênthýmēsis *n.* (4x)
Roots:G1760 Compare:G1270 G1963 G3540
G1761 N-APF ἐνθυμήσεις (2x)
Mt 9:4 And seeing their cogitations, YeShua declared, "For·
Mt 12:25 YeShua having·seen their cogitations, declared to·
G1761 N-GSF ἐνθυμήσεως (1x)
Ac 17:29 by·*the*·art and *the* cogitation of·a·man·of·clay†.
G1761 N-GPF ἐνθυμήσεων (1x)
Heb 4:12 and *he·is* a·discerner of·the·cogitations and intents

G1762 ἔν•ι êni *v.* (5x)
Roots:G1751
G1762.2 V-PXI-3S ἔνι (5x)
Gal 3:28 There·is·not therein Jew nor·even Greek, there·is·
Gal 3:28 nor·even Greek, there·is·not therein slave nor·even
Gal 3:28 nor·even free, there·is·not therein male and female,
Jac 1:17 — with whom there·is·not therein an·alteration, nor
Col 3:11 where there·is·not therein Greek and Jew,

G1763 ἐνιαυτός êniautós *n.* (14x)
Compare:G2094 xLangAlso:H8141
G1763 N-ASM ἐνιαυτόν (7x)
Ac 11:26 to·be·gathered·together a·whole year among the
Ac 18:11 And he·settled *there* a·year and six lunar·months,
Heb 9:25 the Holy·of·Holies each year with another·*animal's*
Heb 10:1 (which they·offer each year into perpetuity) to·
Heb 10:3 ·again *is·made* of·moral·failures each year.
Jac 4:13 and should·continue there *for* one year, and should·
Rv 9:15 lunar·month, and year, in·order·that they·should·
G1763 N-APM ἐνιαυτούς (2x)
Gal 4:10 days, and lunar·months, and seasons, and years.
Jac 5:17 on the earth *for* three years and six lunar·months.
G1763 N-GSM ἐνιαυτοῦ (4x)
Jn 11:49 *the* designated·high·priest that·same year, declared
Jn 11:51 *the* designated·high·priest that year, he·prophesied
Jn 18:13 who was *the* designated·high·priest that year. *(And*
Heb 9:7 second *Tabernacle*, once per year, the high·priest
G1763.2 N-ASM ἐνιαυτόν (1x)
Lk 4:19 ·officially·proclaim an·acceptable Year of·Yahweh.

G1764 ἐν•ίστημι ênístēmi *v.* (8x)
Roots:G1722 G2476 Compare:G3195
G1764.2 V-RAI-3S ἐνέστηκεν (1x)
2Th 2:2 Anointed-One is·currently·standing *at·the·present*.
G1764.2 V-RAP-ASF ἐνεστῶσαν (1x)
1Co 7:26 on·account·of the currently·standing necessity, that
G1764.2 V-RAP-ASM ἐνεστηκότα (1x)
Heb 9:9 for the season, then·currently·standing, in which
G1764.2 V-RAP-GSM ἐνεστῶτος (1x)
Gal 1:4 ·among the evil age currently·standing, according·to
G1764.2 V-RAP-NPN ἐνεστῶτα (2x)
Rm 8:38 nor powers, nor things·currently·standing, nor
1Co 3:22 or death, or things·currently·standing, or things·
G1764.3 V-FDI-3P ἐνστήσονται (1x)
2Ti 3:1 that in *the* last days perilous seasons shall·settle·in.
EG1764.3 (1x)
2Th 2:3 because *that Day shall·not come·to·stand*, unless

G1765 ἐν•ισχύω ênischýō *v.* (2x)
Roots:G1722 G2480 Compare:G4599
G1765 V-PAP-NSM ἐνισχύων (1x)
Lk 22:43 to·him an·angel from heaven, strengthening him.
G1765 V-AAI-3S ἐνίσχυσεν (1x)
Ac 9:19 ·receiving nourishment, he·was·strengthened. Now

G1766 ἔννατος ênnatôs *adj.* (10x)
Roots:G1767
xLangEquiv:H8671
G1766 A-NSM ἔνατος (1x)
Rv 21:20 the eighth, beryl; the ninth, topaz; the tenth,
G1766 A-ASF ἐννάτην (5x)
Ac 3:1 the *afternoon* hour of·prayer, *being* the ninth *hour*.
Ac 10:3 in a·clear·vision, about *the* ninth hour of·the day,
Ac 10:30 and *midafternoon* at·the ninth hour while·praying
Mt 20:5 going·forth about *the* sixth and ninth hour, he·did
Mt 27:46 And about the ninth hour YeShua shouted·out
G1766 A-DSF ἐννάτῃ (1x)
Mk 15:34 And at·the ninth hour, Jesus cried·out with·a·loud
G1766 A-GSF ἐννάτης (3x)
Lk 23:44 a·darkness over all the land until *the* ninth hour.
Mt 27:45 darkness over all the land until the·ninth hour.
Mk 15:33 came·to·be over all the land until *the* ninth hour.

G1767 ἐννέα ênnéa *n.* (1x)
See:G1766
G1767 N-NUI ἐννέα (1x)
Lk 17:17 the ten purified? But where *are* the *other* nine?

G1768 ἐννενη•κοντα•εννέα ênnenēkôntaênnéa *n.* (4x)
Roots:G1767
G1768 N-NUI ἐννενηκονταεννέα (4x)
Lk 15:4 them, does·not leave·behind the ninety-nine in the
Lk 15:7 rather·than over ninety-nine righteous·men who
Mt 18:12 traverse, leaving the ninety-nine on the mountains,
Mt 18:13 ·same *sheep* than over the ninety-nine, the·ones not

G1769 ἐν•νεός ênneôs *adj.* (1x)
Roots:G1770 Compare:G0216 G2974 G4602 G3424 See:G2981
G1769.4 A-NPM ἐννεοί (1x)
Ac 9:7 ·together with·him stood in·stunned·silence, in·fact

G1770 ἐν•νεύω ênneúō *v.* (1x)
Roots:G1722 G3506 Compare:G4591 See:G1769
G1770.2 V-IAI-3P ἐνένευον (1x)
Lk 1:62 And they·were·making·gestures to·his father, *for*

G1771 ἔν•νοια énnôia *n.* (3x)
Roots:G1722 G3563
G1771.2 N-ASF ἔννοιαν (1x)
1Pe 4:1 must·arm·yeurselves with·the same intent. Because
G1771.2 N-GPF ἐννοιῶν (1x)
Heb 4:12 of·the·cogitations and intents of·the·heart.
EG1771.2 (1x)
Lk 14:18 "And with one *intent*, they·all began to·excuse·

G1772 ἔν•νομος énnômôs *adj.* (2x)
Roots:G1722 G3551
G1772.1 A-DSF ἐννόμῳ (1x)
Ac 19:39 ·be·fully·settled in the lawful assembly·of·citizens.
G1772.2 A-NSM ἔννομος (1x)
1Co 9:21 but·yet *I·am* lawfully·subject to·Anointed-One),

G1773 ἔν•νυχον énnychôn *adv.* (1x)
Roots:G1722 G3571
G1773.2 ADV ἔννυχον (1x)
Mk 1:35 ·rising·up very·early while·still·night, he·went·out

G1774 ἐν•οικέω ênôikéō *v.* (5x)
Roots:G1722 G3611
G1774 V-FAI-1S ἐνοικήσω (1x)
2Co 6:16 God declared, "I·shall·indwell in them, and shall·
G1774 V-PAM-3S ἐνοικείτω (1x)
Col 3:16 of·Anointed-One indwell among yeu abundantly in
G1774 V-PAP-ASN ἐνοικοῦν (1x)
Rm 8:11 bodies through his Spirit indwelling within yeu.
G1774 V-PAP-GSN ἐνοικοῦντος (1x)
2Ti 1:14 through Holy Spirit, the·one indwelling in us.
G1774 V-AAI-3S ἐνῴκησεν (1x)
2Ti 1:5 ·hypocrisy in you, which indwelt first in your

G1775 ἑνότης hênótēs *n.* (2x)
Roots:G1520
G1775.1 N-ASF ἑνότητα (2x)
Eph 4:3 ·endeavoring to·fully·keep the oneness of·the Spirit
Eph 4:13 we·all should·attain unto the oneness of·the trust,

G1776 ἐν•οχλέω ênôchléō *v.* (1x)
Roots:G1722 G3791 See:G3926
G1776.2 V-PAS-3S ἐνοχλῇ (1x)
Heb 12:15 sprouting upward should·firmly·harass *yeu* and

G1777 ἔν•οχος ênôchôs *adj.* (10x)
Roots:G1758 Compare:G1772 G3805 See:G5293
G1777.1 A-NPM ἔνοχοι (1x)
Heb 2:15 of·death) were all *their* lifetime held·in slavery.
G1777.2 A-NSM ἔνοχος (8x)
Mt 5:21 should·murder shall·be held·liable to·the tribunal.
Mt 5:22 for·no·reason shall·be held·liable to·the Tribunal *of*
Mt 5:22 shall·be held·liable to·the joint·council·of·Sanhedrin
Mt 5:22 'You·fool,' shall·be held·liable unto the Hell·
Mt 26:66 they·declared, "He·is held·liable of·death."
Mk 3:29 he·is held·liable of·eternal Tribunal·judgment."
Jac 2:10 he·has·become held·liable of·all *transgressions*.
1Co 11:27 ·manner, shall·be held·liable of·the body and
G1777.2 A-ASM ἔνοχον (1x)
Mk 14:64 they all condemned him to·be held·liable of·death.

G1778 ἔν•ταλμα éntalma *n.* (3x)
Roots:G1781 Compare:G5216-1 G1378 See:G1785 xLangAlso:H6673
G1778.2 N-APN ἐντάλματα (3x)
Mt 15:9 *the* religious·requirements of·men·of·clay† *as*
Mk 7:7 *the* religious·requirements of·men·of·clay† *as*
Col 2:22 ·to ·the religious·requirements and instructions of·

G1779 ἐν•ταφιάζω êntaphiázō *v.* (2x)
Roots:G1722 G5028 See:G1780
G1779.1 V-PAN ἐνταφιάζειν (1x)
Jn 19:40 is *the* manner for·the Judeans to·prepare·for·burial.
G1779.1 V-AAN ἐνταφιάσαι (1x)
Mt 26:12 did *it* specifically·for my preparation·of·burial.

G1780 ἐν•ταφιασμός êntaphiasmós *n.* (2x)
Roots:G1779
G1780 N-ASM ἐνταφιασμόν (1x)
Mk 14:8 ·ointment·to my body for the preparation·for·burial.
G1780 N-GSM ἐνταφιασμοῦ (1x)
Jn 12:7 ·kept it for the day of·my preparation·for·burial.

G1781 ἐν•τέλλομαι êntéllômai *v.* (18x)
Roots:G1722 G5056 Compare:G2004 G2753 G4929 G2720 See:G1785 G1778 xLangEquiv:H6680
G1781 V-FNI-3S ἐντελεῖται (2x)
Lk 4:10 "He·shall·command his angels concerning you, to·
Mt 4:6 ·written, "He·shall·command his angels concerning
G1781 V-PNI-1S ἐντέλλομαι (2x)
Jn 15:14 yeu·should·do as·much·as I·myself command yeu.
Jn 15:17 "These·things I·command yeu, in·order·that yeu·
G1781 V-ADI-1S ἐνετειλάμην (1x)
Mt 28:20 ·keep all·things as·much·as I·commanded yeu.
G1781 V-ADI-3S ἐνετείλατο (10x)
Jn 8:5 Moses commanded for·us to·cast·stones·at such·
Jn 14:31 even just·as the Father commanded me, I·do *it just*
Heb 9:20 covenant which God commanded alongside yeu.
Heb 11:22 ·IsraEl, and he·gave·a·command concerning his
Mt 15:4 For God commanded, saying, "Deeply·honor your
Mt 17:9 off the mountain, YeShua commanded them, saying
Mt 19:7 "So·then why·did Moses command *us* to·give *her* a·
Mk 10:3 to·them, "What did·Moses command yeu?
Mk 11:6 ·declared to·them just·as Jesus commanded, and
Mk 13:34 his work, and·then commanded the doorkeeper
G1781 V-ANP-NSM ἐντειλάμενος (1x)
Ac 1:2 ·was·taken·up, after·giving·commands through Holy
G1781 V-RPI-3S ἐντέταλται (1x)
Ac 13:47 in·this·manner it·has·been·commanded to·us *by*
EG1781 (1x)
1Ti 4:3 to·marry— *and commanding* to·abstain·from foods

G1782 ἐντεῦ•θεν ênteûthên *adv.* (12x)
Roots:G1722 See:G1759
G1782.ª ADV ἐντεῦθεν (1x)
Jn 19:18 others with him, *one* on·each·side and Jesus in·*the*·
G1782.1 ADV ἐντεῦθεν (9x)
Jn 2:16 "Take·away these·things from·here. Do·not make
Jn 7:3 to him, "Walk·on from·here and head·on·out into
Jn 14:31 "Be·awake, we·should·head·out from·here.
Jn 18:36 So now my kingdom is not from·here."
Lk 4:9 ·are the Son of·God, cast yourself down from·here.
Lk 13:31 "Go·out, and depart from·here, because HerOd·
Lk 16:26 so·that the·ones wanting to·cross from·here to yeu
Mt 17:20 to·this mountain, 'Walk·on from·here to·there,'
Jac 4:1 yeu? *Are·they* not from·here, birthed·from·out of·
G1782.2 ADV ἐντεῦθεν (2x)
Rv 22:2 midst of·its broad·street, and on·both sides of·the
Rv 22:2 ·its broad·street, and on·both sides of·the river, *was*

G1783 ἔν•τευξις énteuxis *n.* (2x)
Roots:G1793 Compare:G1162 G2428 G4335
G1783.2 N-GSF ἐντεύξεως (1x)
1Ti 4:5 God's Redemptive-word and an·earnest·request.
G1783.3 N-APF ἐντεύξεις (1x)
1Ti 2:1 petitions, prayers, intercessions, *and* expressions·of·

G1784 ἔν•τιμος éntimôs *adj.* (5x)
Roots:G1722 G5092 Compare:G2158 G5093 G4185 xLangAlso:H3368
G1784.3 A-APM ἐντίμους (1x)
Php 2:29 *the* Lord with all joy, and hold such·men in·honor,
G1784.4 A-NSM-C ἐντιμότερος (1x)
Lk 14:8 ·place, lest a·more·honorable·man·than you may·be
G1784.5 A-NSM ἔντιμος (1x)
Lk 7:2 slave, who was dearly·valued by·him, was·about to·
G1784.5 A-ASM ἔντιμον (2x)
1Pe 2:4 Selected personally·by God, *being* dearly·precious.
1Pe 2:6 stone, Selected, *being* dearly·precious; and the·one

G1785 ἐν•τολή êntôlḗ *n.* (71x)
Roots:G1781 Compare:G2003 See:G1778 xLangEquiv:H4687 xLangAlso:H6673
G1785 N-NSF ἐντολή (14x)
Jn 12:50 I·personally·know that his commandment is eternal
Jn 15:12 "This is my commandment, that yeu·should·love
Mt 22:36 which·one *is the* great commandment in the
Mt 22:38 This is *the* foremost and greatest commandment.
Mk 12:28 ·of him, "Which commandment is foremost of·all
Mk 12:30 your strength." This commandment *is* foremost.
Mk 12:31 There·is no other commandment greater·than these
Rm 7:10 And the commandment, the·one *that* is·found in·me
Rm 7:12 Torah-Law *is* holy, and the commandment *is* holy,
Rm 13:9 *there·is* any other commandment, it·is·summed·up
Eph 6:2 (which is *the* first commandment with a·promise),
1Jn 2:7 *the* beginning. The old commandment is the word
1Jn 3:23 And this is his commandment, that we·should·
2Jn 1:6 This is the commandment, that just·as yeu·heard
G1785 N-NPF ἐντολαί (2x)
1Co 14:37 I·write to·yeu are commandments of·the Lord.
1Jn 5:3 his commandments, and his commandments are not
G1785 N-ASF ἐντολήν (21x)
Jn 10:18 This commandment I·received personally·from
Jn 11:57 and the Pharisees had·given a·commandment, that
Jn 12:49 ·himself gave me a·commandment *concerning* what
Jn 13:34 "A·brand-new commandment I·give to·yeu, that
Lk 15:29 ·at·any·time did·I·neglect your commandment, and
Lk 23:56 *over* the Sabbath according·to the commandment.
Ac 17:15 ·back, taking *with·them* a·commandment to Silas
Heb 7:5 they·have a·commandment to·receive·tithes·of the
Mt 15:3 walk·contrary·to the commandment of·God through
Mt 15:6 yeu·invalidate the commandment of·God through
Mk 7:8 For after·leaving the commandment of·God, yeu·
Mk 7:9 ·set·aside the commandment of·God in·order·that
Mk 10:5 ·of·heart, he·wrote yeu this commandment.
1Ti 6:14 to·observantly·keep the commandment unstained,
1Jn 2:7 I·write no brand-new commandment to·yeu, but·
1Jn 2:7 to·yeu, but·rather an·old commandment which yeu·
1Jn 2:8 ·other·hand, a·brand-new commandment I·do·write
1Jn 3:23 just·as he·already·gave us *this* commandment.
1Jn 4:21 And this commandment we·presently·have from
2Jn 1:4 ·as we·received a·commandment personally·from the
2Jn 1:5 ·though I·wrote a·brand-new commandment to·you,
G1785 N-APF ἐντολάς (18x)
Jn 14:15 ·love me, observantly·keep my commandments.
Jn 14:21 "The·one having my commandments, and
Jn 15:10 ·keep my commandments, yeu·shall·abide in my
Jn 15:10 ·kept my Father's commandments and abide in his
Lk 18:20 You·personally·know the commandments, "You·
Mt 19:17 life-above, observantly·keep the commandments."
Mk 10:19 You·personally·know the commandments, "You·
Col 4:10 concerning whom yeu·received commandments; if
1Jn 2:3 if we·should·observantly·keep his commandments.
1Jn 2:4 not observantly·keeping his commandments is a·liar,
1Jn 3:22 we·observantly·keep his commandments and do
1Jn 3:24 ·keeping his commandments presently·abides in
1Jn 5:2 and should·observantly·keep his commandments.
1Jn 5:3 we·should·observantly·keep his commandments, and
2Jn 1:6 ·should·walk·according·to his commandments. This
Rv 12:17 ·keeping the commandments of·God and having
Rv 14:12 ·keeping the commandments of·God and the trust

Rv 22:14 the·ones doing his commandments, in·order·that it·
G1785 N-DPF ἐντολαῖς (3x)
Lk 1:6 blamelessly in all the commandments and regulations
Mt 22:40 On these two commandments is·hung all the
Tit 1:14 myths and commandments of·men·of·clay† that·are·
G1785 N-GSF ἐντολῆς (9x)
Heb 7:16 ·Torah-Law of·a·fleshly commandment, but·rather
Heb 7:18 of·a·preceding commandment on·account·of it
Heb 9:19 For with·every commandment in *the* Torah-Law
Rm 7:8 ·occasion through the commandment, accomplished
Rm 7:9 once, but with·the commandment coming, Moral·
Rm 7:11 through the commandment, thoroughly·deluded me;
Rm 7:13 ·Failure, through the commandment, may·become
2Pe 2:21 holy commandment being·handed·down to·them.
2Pe 3:2 of·the commandment *having·been·already·stated* by·
G1785 N-GPF ἐντολῶν (4x)
Mt 5:19 of·these least commandments and should·instruct
Mk 12:29 "*The* foremost of·all the commandments *is*,
1Co 7:19 *is* a·proper·observance of·God's commandments.
Eph 2:15 the Torah-Law of·the commandments *contained* in

G1786 ἐν•τόπιος ĕntŏpiŏs *adj.* (1x)
Roots:G1722 G5117 Compare:G0847
G1786.3 A-NPM ἐντόπιοι (1x)
Ac 21:12 and the·ones residing·in·that·place, were·imploring

G1787 ἐντός ĕntŏs *adv.* (2x)
Roots:G1722 Compare:G2081 G1622 See:G1751
G1787.1 ADV ἐντός (1x)
Lk 17:21 the kingdom of·God is on·the·inside of·yeu."
G1787.2 ADV ἐντός (1x)
Mt 23:26 Pharisee, first purify the interior of·the cup and of·

G1788 ἐν•τρέπω ĕntrĕpō *v.* (9x)
Roots:G1722 G5157 Compare:G0153 G2617 G0127 See:G1791 xLangAlso:H2659
G1788.2 V-2FPI-3P ἐντραπήσονται (3x)
Lk 20:13 ·seeing this·one, they·shall·be·respectful·of *him*.'
Mt 21:37 saying, 'They·shall·be·respectful·of my son.'
Mk 12:6 saying, 'They·shall·be·respectful·of my son.'
G1788.2 V-PPI-1S ἐντρέπομαι (1x)
Lk 18:4 God, and I·am·not respectful·of *any* man·of·clay†,
G1788.2 V-PPP-NSM ἐντρεπόμενος (1x)
Lk 18:2 God and not being·respectful·of man·of·clay†.
G1788.2 V-IMI-1P ἐνετρεπόμεθα (1x)
Heb 12:9 and we·were·respectful·to·them. Shall·we not
G1788.3 V-PAP-NSM ἐντρέπων (1x)
1Co 4:14 Not embarrassing yeu do·I·write these·things, but·
G1788.3 V-2APS-3S ἐντραπῇ (2x)
2Th 3:14 ·order·that he·may·be·embarrassed·and·turn·about.
Tit 2:8 *those being* antagonistic may·be·embarrassed, having

G1789 ἐν•τρέφω ĕntrĕphō *v.* (1x)
Roots:G1722 G5142
G1789.2 V-PPP-NSM ἐντρεφόμενος (1x)
1Ti 4:6 Anointed— while·being·nurtured·and·trained·by the

G1790 ἔν•τρομος ĕntrŏmŏs *adj.* (3x)
Roots:G1722 G5156
G1790 A-NSM ἔντρομος (3x)
Ac 7:32 But Moses, being terrified·with·trembling, was·not
Ac 16:29 being terrified·with·trembling, he·fell·down·before
Heb 12:21 ·out·of·my·wits and terrified·with·trembling.")

G1791 ἐν•τροπή ĕntrŏpē *n.* (2x)
Roots:G1788 Compare:G0152 G0819
G1791 N-ASF ἐντροπήν (2x)
1Co 6:5 *this* to yeur·own embarrassment. In·this·manner, is·
1Co 15:34 I·say *this* to yeur·own embarrassment.

G1792 ἐν•τρυφάω ĕntryphaō *v.* (1x)
Roots:G1722 G5171 Compare:G2970 G4910
G1792 V-PAP-NPM ἐντρυφῶντες (1x)
2Pe 2:13 stains and blemishes, luxuriously·indulging in their

G1793 ἐν•τυγχάνω ĕntynchánō *v.* (5x)
Roots:G1722 G5177 Compare:G4336 See:G1783 G5241
G1793.2 V-PAI-3S ἐντυγχάνει (1x)
Rm 11:2 by EliJah? How he·confers with·God against IsraEl
G1793.2 V-2AAI-3P ἐνέτυχον (1x)
Ac 25:24 all the multitude of·the Judeans conferred with·me,
G1793.4 V-PAI-3S ἐντυγχάνει (2x)
Rm 8:27 Spirit *is*, how he·makes·intercession over *the* holy·
Rm 8:34 ·God, who also makes·intercession on·behalf·of·us
G1793.4 V-PAN ἐντυγχάνειν (1x)
Heb 7:25 always living to make·intercession on·their behalf

G1794 ἐν•τυλίσσω ĕntylíssō *v.* (3x)
Roots:G1722 Compare:G1750 See:G1507
G1794.2 V-AAI-3S ἐνετύλιξεν (2x)
Lk 23:53 ·lowering it down, he·swathed it in·a·linen·cloth,
Mt 27:59 the body, Joseph swathed it in·a·pure linen·cloth
G1794.2 V-RPP-ASN ἐντετυλιγμένον (1x)
Jn 20:7 ·of·linen, but·rather having·been·swathed in one

G1795 ἐν•τυπόω ĕntypŏō *v.* (1x)
Roots:G1722 G5179
G1795.2 V-RPP-NSF ἐντετυπωμένη (1x)
2Co 3:7 Service of·Death, having·been·engraved in writing

G1796 ἐν•υβρίζω ĕnybrízō *v.* (1x)
Roots:G1722 G5195
G1796 V-AAP-NSM ἐνυβρίσας (1x)
Heb 10:29 ·thing, and abusively·insulting the Spirit of·

G1797 ἐν•υπνιάζομαι ĕnypniázŏmai *v.* (2x)
Roots:G1798
G1797.1 V-FPI-3P ἐνυπνιασθήσονται (1x)
Ac 2:17 ·visions, and yeur older·men shall·dream dreams.
G1797.2 V-PNP-NPM ἐνυπνιαζόμενοι (1x)
Jud 1:8 Likewise also these *irreverent* dreamers, in·fact,

G1798 ἐν•ύπνιον ĕnýpniŏn *n.* (1x)
Roots:G1722 G5258 Compare:G3677 G3701
G1798 N-APN ἐνύπνια (1x)
Ac 2:17 ·visions, and yeur older·men shall·dream dreams.

G1799 ἐν•ώπιον ĕnṓpiŏn *adv.* (98x)
Roots:G1722 G3700 Compare:G1715 G1725 xLangAlso:H5869
G1799 ADV ἐνώπιον (97x)
Jn 20:30 did many other signs in·the·sight of·his disciples,
Lk 1:6 And they·were both righteous in·the·sight of·God,
Lk 1:15 For he·shall·be great in·the·sight of·Yahweh. And,
Lk 1:17 he·himself shall·go·onward in·the·sight of *Yahweh*
Lk 1:19 GabriEl, the·one standing·near in·the·sight of·God;
Lk 1:75 ·holiness and righteousness in·the·sight of·him, all
Lk 4:7 if you should·fall·prostrate in·the·sight of·me, all
Lk 5:18 to·carry him in and to·lay *him* in·the·sight of *Jesus*.
Lk 5:25 And at·once, rising·up in·the·sight of·them, taking·
Lk 8:47 him, she·announced to·him, in·the·sight of·all the
Lk 12:6 them is having·been·forgotten in·the·sight of·God.
Lk 12:9 the·one denying me in·the·sight of·the men·of·clay†
Lk 12:9 shall·be·utterly·denied in·the·sight of·the angels of·
Lk 13:26 'We·ate and drank in·the·sight of·you, and you·
Lk 14:10 ·be with·you in·the·sight of·the·ones reclining·
Lk 15:10 *that such* joy occurs in·the·sight of·the angels of·
Lk 15:18 ·failed against the heaven, and in·the·sight of·you,
Lk 15:21 against the heaven and in·the·sight of·you, and I·
Lk 16:15 as·righteous in·the·sight of·the men·of·clay†, but
Lk 16:15 ·of·clay† is an·abomination in·the·sight of·God.
Lk 23:14 after·investigating *him* in·the·sight of·yeu, found
Lk 24:11 their utterances appeared in·the·sight of·them as
Lk 24:43 And taking *it*, he·ate in·the·sight of·them.
Ac 2:25 ·keeping Yahweh in·the·sight of·me continually,
Ac 4:10 does this·man stand·nearby in·the·sight of·yeu,
Ac 4:19 "Whether it·is right in·the·sight of·God to·listen·to
Ac 6:5 the saying was·satisfactory in·the·sight of·the entire
Ac 6:6 men·whom they·set in·the·sight of·the ambassadors,
Ac 7:46 who found grace in·the·sight of·God and requested
Ac 8:21 for your heart is not straight in·the·sight of·God.
Ac 9:15 to·bear my name in·the·sight of·Gentiles and kings,
Ac 10:4 ·acts ascended for a·memorial in·the·sight of·God.
Ac 10:30 yet behold, a·man stood·still in·the·sight of·me in
Ac 10:31 ·acts were·recalled·to·mind in·the·sight of·God.
Ac 10:33 we·ourselves *are* all in·the·sight of·God. We·are·
Ac 19:9 ·ill·of The Way in·the·sight of·the multitude, after·
Ac 19:19 ·completely·burning *them* in·the·sight of·all *men*.
Ac 27:35 he·gave·thanks to·God in·the·sight of·them·all,
Heb 4:13 *that·is* not·completely·apparent in·the·sight of·him,
Heb 13:21 which·is·most·satisfying in·the·sight of·him,
Gal 1:20 I·write to·yeu— Behold, in·the·sight of·God, I·do·
Rm 3:20 ·as·righteous any flesh in·the·sight of·him,' for
Rm 12:17 ·in morally·good·things in·the·sight of·all men·of·
Rm 14:22 *good·benefit* for·yourself *just* in·the·sight of·God.
Jac 4:10 Be·humbled in·the·sight of·the Lord, and he·shall·
1Pe 3:4 which is extremely·precious in·the·sight of·God.
1Co 1:29 so·that all flesh may·not boast in·the·sight of·him.
2Co 4:2 man·of·clay's† conscience in·the·sight of·God.
2Co 7:12 ·it to·become·apparent to yeu in·the·sight of·God.
2Co 8:21 not ·merely in·the·sight of·*the*·Lord, but·rather
2Co 8:21 ·Lord, but·rather also in·the·sight of·men·of·clay†.
1Ti 2:3 *is* good and fully·acceptable in·the·sight of·God our
1Ti 5:4 that is good and fully·acceptable in·the·sight of·God.
1Ti 5:20 In·the·sight of·all, you·must·reprove the·ones
1Ti 5:21 I·thoroughly·urge *you* in·the·sight of·God, and of·
1Ti 6:12 the good affirmation in·the·sight of·many witnesses
1Ti 6:13 I·charge you in·the·sight of·God (the·one giving·
2Ti 2:14 ·thoroughly·urging *them* in·the·sight of·the Lord
2Ti 4:1 ·myself thoroughly·urge *you* in·the·sight of·God and
1Jn 3:22 the·things *that·are* satisfactory in·the·sight of·him.
3Jn 1:6 love in·the·sight of·a·convened·Called·Out·assembly
Rv 1:4 the seven Spirits who are in·the·sight of·his throne,
Rv 2:14 ·*Annihilator* to·cast a·trap in·the·sight of·the Sons
Rv 3:2 having·been·completely·fulfilled in·the·sight of·God.
Rv 3:5 ·explicitly·affirm his name in·the·sight of·my Father,
Rv 3:5 ·sight of·my Father, and in·the·sight of·his angels.
Rv 3:8 works. Behold, in·the·sight of·you, I·have·given a·
Rv 3:9 and should·fall·prostrate in·the·sight of·your feet, and
Rv 4:5 of·fire being·set·ablaze in·the·sight of·the throne,
Rv 4:6 And in·the·sight of·the throne *there·is* a·transparent,·
Rv 4:10 Elders shall·fall in·the·sight of·the·one sitting·down
Rv 4:10 cast their victor's·crowns in·the·sight of·the throne,
Rv 5:8 ·four Elders fell·down in·the·sight of·the Lamb, each·
Rv 7:9 native·tongues, standing in·the·sight of·the throne
Rv 7:9 ·the·sight of·the throne and in·the·sight of·the Lamb,
Rv 7:11 they·fell on their faces in·the·sight of·the throne.
Rv 7:15 ·account·of that, they·are in·the·sight of·the throne
Rv 8:2 the seven angels who stand in·the·sight of·God; and
Rv 8:3 Sacrifice·Altar, the·one in·the·sight of·the throne.
Rv 8:4 holy·ones, ascended in·the·sight of·God from·out·of·
Rv 9:13 golden Sacrifice·Altar, the·one in·the·sight of·God,
Rv 11:4 ·Oil·Lampstands standing in·the·sight of·the God
Rv 11:16 the·ones sitting·down in·the·sight of·God on their
Rv 12:4 And the Dragon stands in·the·sight of·the woman,
Rv 12:10 ·one legally·accusing them in·the·sight of·our God
Rv 13:12 of·the first Daemonic·Beast in·the·sight of·it, and it·
Rv 13:13 heaven to·the earth in·the·sight of·the men·of·clay†
Rv 13:14 was·given to·do in·the·sight of·the Daemonic·Beast,
Rv 14:3 *singing* a·brand-new song in·the·sight of·the throne,
Rv 14:3 of·the throne, and in·the·sight of·the four living·
Rv 14:5 they·are without·blemish in·the·sight of·the throne
Rv 14:10 with fire and sulfur in·the·sight of·the holy angels,
Rv 14:10 of·the holy angels, and in·the·sight of·the Lamb.
Rv 15:4 ·come and shall·fall·prostrate in·the·sight of·you,"
Rv 16:19 Great was·recalled·to·mind in·the·sight of·God, to·
Rv 19:20 ·one doing the miraculous·signs in·the·sight of·it,
Rv 20:12 small and great, standing in·the·sight of·God, and
EG1799 (1x)
1Ti 6:13 all things) and *in·the·sight* of·Anointed-One Jesus

G1800 Ἐνώς Ĕnṓs *n/p.* (1x)
אֱנוֹשׁ 'ĕnôsh [Hebrew]
Roots:H0583
G1800.2 N/P-PRI Ἐνώς (1x)
Lk 3:38 *son* of·Enosh, *son* of·Sheth, *son* of·Adam, *son* of·

G1801 ἐν•ωτίζομαι ĕnōtízŏmai *v.* (1x)
Roots:G1722 G3775 xLangEquiv:H0238
G1801.2 V-ADM-2P ἐνωτίσασθε (1x)

Ac 2:14 be this known to·yeu and give·ear to·my utterances.

G1802 Ἐνώχ Ênŏch *n/p.* (3x)

חֲנוֹךְ cнănôk [Hebrew]

Roots:H2585 See:G2627

G1802 N/P-PRI Ἐνώχ (3x)

Lk 3:37 *son* of·MethuShelach, *son* of·Enoch, *son* of·Jared,
Heb 11:5 By·trust, Enoch was·transferred *such·for* him not
Jud 1:14 Now Enoch also, *the* seventh from Adam,

G1803 ἕξ hĕx *n.* (11x)

See:G1623 G1810-1
xLangEquiv:H8337 A8353

G1803 N-NUI ἕξ (11x)

Jn 2:6 laying·out there six ceremonial·water·basins of·stone,
Jn 2:20 Judeans declared, "*In* forty six years, this Temple
Jn 12:1 In·due·course, six days before the Passover, Jesus
Lk 4:25 for·a·span·of three years and six lunar·months, as
Lk 13:14 to·the crowd, "There·are six days in which it·is·
Ac 11:12 Moreover, these six brothers also came together
Ac 18:11 And he·settled *there* a·year and six lunar·months,
Mt 17:1 And after six days, YeShua personally·takes Peter
Mk 9:2 And after six days, Jesus personally·takes Peter,
Jac 5:17 on the earth *for* three years and six lunar·months.
Rv 4:8 one itself, was·having six wings apiece overflowing

G1804 ἐξ•αγγέλλω êxangĕllō *v.* (1x)

Roots:G1537 G0032 See:G2605

G1804 V-AAS-2P ἐξαγγείλητε (1x)

1Pe 2:9 — that yeu·should·proclaim·forth the courageous·

G1805 ἐξ•αγοράζω êxagŏrázō *v.* (5x)

Roots:G1537 G0059 Compare:G3084

G1805.1 V-PMP-NPM ἐξαγοραζόμενοι (2x)

Eph 5:16 utterly·redeeming the season, because the days are
Col 4:5 *Called·Out·citizenry*, utterly·redeeming the season.

G1805.3 V-AAI-3S ἐξηγόρασεν (1x)

Gal 3:13 Anointed-One utterly·kinsman·redeemed us out of·

G1805.3 V-AAS-3S ἐξαγοράσῃ (1x)

Gal 4:5 in·order·that he·may·utterly·kinsman·redeem the·

EG1805.3 (1x)

Gal 3:14 *He·utterly·kinsman·redeemed us* in·order·that the

G1806 ἐξ•άγω êxágō *v.* (13x)

Roots:G1537 G0071

G1806.1 V-PAI-3S ἐξάγει (1x)

Jn 10:3 his·own sheep each·by name and leads them out.

G1806.1 V-PAI-3P ἐξάγουσιν (1x)

Mk 15:20 his·own garments, and led him out in·order·that

G1806.1 V-2AAI-3S ἐξήγαγεν (2x)

Lk 24:50 And he·led them outside as·far·as to BethAny, and
Mk 8:23 blind·man by·the hand, he·led him outside of·the

G1806.1 V-2AAN ἐξαγαγεῖν (1x)

Heb 8:9 ·hold of·them by·my hand to·lead them out of·*the*·

G1806.1 V-2AAP-NSM ἐξαγαγών (2x)

Ac 5:19 ·up the prison doors; and·also leading them out, he·
Ac 21:38 ·making·an·uprising and leading the four·thousand

G1806.1 V-2AAP-NPM ἐξαγαγόντες (1x)

Ac 16:39 and after·leading·*them*·out, they·were·asking *of*·

G1806.2 V-2AAI-3S ἐξήγαγεν (4x)

Ac 7:36 This·man brought them out, after·doing wonders
Ac 7:40 *As* for this Moses who brought us out of·*the*·land of·
Ac 12:17 to·them how the Lord brought him out of·the
Ac 13:17 and with a·high arm he·brought them out of·it.

G1806.2 V-2AAM-3P ἐξαγαγέτωσαν (1x)

Ac 16:37 coming *here* themselves, let·them·bring us out."

G1807 ἐξ•αιρέω êxairĕō *v.* (8x)

Roots:G1537 G0138 Compare:G4506 G0726
xLangEquiv:H5337

G1807.1 V-2AAM-2S ἔξελε (2x)

Mt 5:29 if your right eye entraps you, pluck it out and cast *it*
Mt 18:9 And if your eye entraps you, pluck it out and cast *it*

G1807.2 V-PMP-NSM ἐξαιρούμενος (1x)

Ac 26:17 while·snatching you out from·among the People,

G1807.2 V-2AMI-1S ἐξειλόμην (1x)

Ac 23:27 with·the squad·of·soldiers, I·snatched him out,

G1807.2 V-2AMI-3S ἐξείλετο (2x)

Ac 7:10 and snatched him out from·among all his
Ac 12:11 his angel forth and snatched me out from·among

G1807.2 V-2AMN ἐξελέσθαι (1x)

Ac 7:34 groaning,' 'and I·descended to·snatch them out.' '

G1807.2 V-2AMS-3S ἐξέληται (1x)

Gal 1:4 of·our moral·failures, that he·may·snatch us out

G1808 ἐξ•αίρω êxairō *v.* (2x)

Roots:G1537 G0142

G1808.3 V-FAI-2P ἐξαρεῖτε (1x)

1Co 5:13 "Yeu·shall·entirely·expel the evil·person from·

G1808.3 V-APS-3S ἐξαρθῇ (1x)

1Co 5:2 deed should·be·entirely·expelled from·among *the*

G1809 ἐξ•αιτέω êxaitĕō *v.* (1x)

ἐξ•αιτέομαι êxaitĕômai [middle voice]

Roots:G1537 G0154 Compare:G0523

G1809.2 V-AMI-3S ἐξῃτήσατο (1x)

Lk 22:31 behold, the Adversary-Accuser demanded yeu·*all*,

G1810 ἐξ•αί•φνης êxaiphnēs *adv.* (5x)

Roots:G1537 G0160 Compare:G1819 G0160 G0869

G1810 ADV ἐξαίφνης (5x)

Lk 2:13 And suddenly together with·the angel, there·came·
Lk 9:39 a·spirit takes him, and suddenly he·yells·out; and it·
Ac 9:3 ·near to·Damascus, and·then suddenly a·light from
Ac 22:6 midday, it·happened suddenly from·out of·the
Mk 13:36 lest upon·coming suddenly he·should·find yeu

G1811 ἐξ•α•κολουθέω êxakŏlôuthĕō *v.* (3x)

Roots:G1537 G0190

G1811.1 V-FAI-3P ἐξακολουθήσουσιν (1x)

2Pe 2:2 And many shall·follow·out their *ways* to·total·

G1811.1 V-AAP-NPM ἐξακολουθήσαντες (2x)

2Pe 1:16 not·by following·out myths having·been·skillfully·
2Pe 2:15 way; they·are·led·astray, following·out the way

G1812 ἑξ•ακόσιοι hêxakŏsiôi *n.* (1x)

Roots:G1803 G1540

G1812 N-GPM ἑξακοσίων (1x)

Rv 14:20 bridles, for a·thousand *and* six·hundred stadia.

G1813 ἐξ•α•λείφω êxalêiphō *v.* (5x)

Roots:G1537 G0218 Compare:G5597 G0853 G1625-3

G1813.1 V-FAI-1S ἐξαλείψω (1x)

Rv 3:5 and no, I·shall·not rub·out his name out of·the

G1813.1 V-AAP-NSM ἐξαλείψας (1x)

Col 2:14 after·rubbing·out the handwriting against us (the

G1813.2 V-FAI-3S ἐξαλείψει (2x)

Rv 7:17 'And God shall·rub·away every tear from their eyes.
Rv 21:4 'And God shall·rub·away every tear from their eyes.

G1813.2 V-APN ἐξαλειφθῆναι (1x)

Ac 3:19 ·for yeur moral·failures to·be·rubbed·out, so·that

G1814 ἐξ•άλλομαι êxállômai *v.* (1x)

Roots:G1537 G0242 Compare:G4640 See:G0021

G1814 V-PNP-NSM ἐξαλλόμενος (1x)

Ac 3:8 And upon·leaping·forth, he·stood·still; then he·was·

G1815 ἐξ•ανά•στασις êxanástasis *n.* (1x)

Roots:G1817 Compare:G0386

G1815.2 N-ASF ἐξανάστασιν (1x)

Php 3:11 ·attain to the exceptional·resurrection of·the dead.

G1816 ἐξ•ανα•τέλλω êxanatĕllō *v.* (2x)

Roots:G1537 G0393 Compare:G0985 G1631 G4261 G5453

G1816 V-AAI-3S ἐξανέτειλεν (2x)

Mt 13:5 and immediately it·rose·out·above·the·surface, on·
Mk 4:5 and immediately it·rose·out·above·the·surface, on·

G1817 ἐξ•αν•ίστημι êxanístēmi *v.* (3x)

Roots:G1537 G0450

G1817.1 V-AAS-3S ἐξαναστήσῃ (2x)

Lk 20:28 his wife and should·fully·raise·up offspring† to·his
Mk 12:19 wife and should·fully·raise·up offspring† for·his

G1817.3 V-2AAI-3P ἐξανέστησαν (1x)

Ac 15:5 But there·fully·rose·up certain·men from the

G1818 ἐξ•απατάω êxapatáō *v.* (5x)

Roots:G1537 G0538

G1818 V-PAI-3P ἐξαπατῶσιν (1x)

Rm 16:18 ·blessing, they·thoroughly·delude the hearts of·

G1818 V-PAM-3S ἐξαπατάτω (1x)

1Co 3:18 Let not·even·one·man thoroughly·delude himself.

G1818 V-AAI-3S ἐξηπάτησεν (2x)

Rm 7:11 the commandment, thoroughly·deluded me; and
2Co 11:3 as the Serpent thoroughly·deluded Eve by his

G1818 V-AAS-3S ἐξαπατήσῃ (1x)

2Th 2:3 Yeu·should·not·let anyone thoroughly·delude yeu in

G1819 ἐξ•ά•πινα êxápina *adv.* (1x)

Roots:G1537 G0160 Compare:G1810

G1819 ADV ἐξάπινα (1x)

Mk 9:8 And suddenly, after·looking·all·around, they·saw no·

G1820 ἐξ•α•πορέομαι êxapŏrĕômai *v.* (2x)

Roots:G1537 G0639

G1820.2 V-PNP-NPM ἐξαπορούμενοι (1x)

2Co 4:8 being·at·a·loss, but·yet not being·at·an·utter·loss;

G1820.2 V-APN ἐξαπορηθῆναι (1x)

2Co 1:8 *it*, such·for us to·be·at·an·utter·loss even of·the *will*

G1821 ἐξ•απο•στέλλω êxapŏstĕllō *v.* (11x)

Roots:G1537 G0649 See:G4882

G1821.2 V-FAI-1S ἐξαποστελῶ (1x)

Ac 22:21 because I·myself shall·dispatch you forth unto *the*

G1821.2 V-AAI-3S ἐξαπέστειλεν (5x)

Lk 1:53 those·being·wealthy, he·dispatched·forth empty.
Ac 7:12 in Egypt, Jacob dispatched·forth our fathers first.
Ac 12:11 ·know truly that Yahweh dispatched his angel forth
Gal 4:4 of·time was·come, God dispatched·forth his Son,
Gal 4:6 yeu·are sons, God dispatched·forth the Spirit of·his

G1821.2 V-AAI-3P ἐξαπέστειλαν (5x)

Lk 20:10 after·thrashing him, dispatched·*him*·forth empty.
Lk 20:11 ·treating *him*, they·dispatched·*him*·forth empty.
Ac 9:30 him down to Caesarea and dispatched him forth to
Ac 11:22 And they·dispatched·forth BarNabas to·go·
Ac 17:14 the brothers dispatched·forth Paul to·traverse as

G1822 ἐξ•αρτίζω êxartízō *v.* (2x)

Roots:G1537 G0739

G1822.1 V-AAN ἐξαρτίσαι (1x)

Ac 21:5 it·happened *for* us to·properly·finish·out the days,

G1822.2 V-RPP-NSM ἐξηρτισμένος (1x)

2Ti 3:17 having·been·properly·equipped toward all

G1823 ἐξ•αστράπτω êxastráptō *v.* (1x)

Roots:G1537 G0797 Compare:G1584 G4744 G2989
See:G0796 G4015

G1823.2 V-PAP-NSM ἐξαστράπτων (1x)

Lk 9:29 and his attire *was* white *and* radiantly·shimmering.

G1824 ἐξ•αυτῆς êxautēs *adv.* (6x)

Roots:G1537 G0846 See:G5610

G1824 ADV ἐξαυτῆς (6x)

Ac 10:33 So·then, from·this·same·hour I·sent to you, and
Ac 11:11 "And behold, from·this·same·hour, three men
Ac 21:32 who from·this·same·hour, ran·down to them,
Ac 23:30 Judeans, I·sent *him* from·this·same·hour to you,
Mk 6:25 you·should·give me from·this·same·hour the head
Php 2:23 to·send this·man from·this·same·hour as·soon·as I·

G1825 ἐξ•εγείρω êxêgêirō *v.* (2x)

Roots:G1537 G1453 Compare:G1326
xLangEquiv:H3364

G1825.1 V-FAI-3S ἐξεγερεῖ (1x)

1Co 6:14 also *from·death* shall·fully·awaken us through

G1825.1 V-AAI-1S ἐξήγειρα (1x)

Rm 9:17 same·purpose *for affliction* I·fully·awakened you,

G1826 ἔξ•ειμι ĕxêimi *v.* (5x)

Roots:G1537 G1510-1 Compare:G1831 See:G0549
G0863

G1826.1 V-2AXP-GPM ἐξιόντων (1x)

Ac 13:42 And with·the Jews getting out of·the gathering, the

G1826.2 V-PXN ἐξιέναι (1x)

Ac 27:43 after·jumping·far·overboard first, to·get upon the

EG1826.2 (1x)

Ac 27:44 And the rest *got there*, in·fact, some·men on planks

G1826.3 V-PXN ἐξιέναι (1x)

Ac 20:7 with·them, intending to·go·onward on·the next·day;

G1826.4 V-IXI-3P ἐξῄεσαν (1x)
Ac 17:15 Athens. And they·were·going·back, taking *with*·

G1827 ἐξ•ελέγχω êxelénchō *v.* (1x)
Roots:G1537 G1651

G1827.1 V-AAN ἐξελέγξαι (1x)
Jud 1:15 against all, and to·thoroughly·convict all the

G1828 ἐξ•έλκω êxélkō *v.* (1x)
Roots:G1537 G1670

G1828.1 V-PPP-NSM ἐξελκόμενος (1x)
Jac 1:14 ·man is·tempted, being·drawn·forth by his·own

G1829 ἐξ•έραμα êxérama *n.* (1x)
Roots:G1537 G2037-2 Compare:G1691-1 G4427 G1828-1 xLangAlso:H6892

G1829 N-ASN ἐξέραμα (1x)
2Pe 2:22 ·dog *keeps·on* returning to his·own throw·up,'" and

G1830 ἐξ•ερευνάω êxêreunáō *v.* (1x)
Roots:G1537 G2045 xLangAlso:H2664

G1830.1 V-AAI-3P ἐξηρεύνησαν (1x)
1Pe 1:10 ·out and diligently·searched *for·it* after·prophesying

G1831 ἐξ•έρχομαι êxérchômai *v.* (224x)
Roots:G1537 G2064 Compare:G1826 G4358 xLangAlso:H3318

G1831.1 V-FDI-3S ἐξελεύσεται (1x)
Mt 2:6 of·you shall·come·forth·one who·is·officially·leading
G1831.1 V-FDI-3P ἐξελεύσονται (2x)
Ac 7:7 they·shall·come·forth and shall·ritually·minister to·
Mt 13:49 The angels shall·come·forth and shall·distinctly·
G1831.1 V-PNI-3S ἐξέρχεται (3x)
Mt 15:18 ·forth out of·the mouth come·forth from·out of·the
Mt 24:27 For just·as the lightning comes·forth from *the* east
Jac 3:10 ·out of·the same mouth come·forth blessing and
G1831.1 V-PNI-3P ἐξέρχονται (2x)
Lk 4:36 he·orders the impure spirits, and they·come·out."
Mt 15:19 from·out of·the heart comes·forth evil deliberations
G1831.1 V-PNM-2P ἐξέρχεσθε (1x)
Lk 9:4 ·enter into, there abide, and from·there come·forth.
G1831.1 V-PNP-NPM ἐξερχόμενοι (2x)
Mt 8:28 ·demons, who·are·coming·forth from·out of·the
Mt 27:32 Now as·they·were·coming·out *of·the City*, they·
G1831.1 V-INI-3S ἐξήρχετο (3x)
Lk 4:41 And demons also were·coming·out of many, yelling·
Lk 6:19 ·him, because power came·forth directly·from him
Ac 8:7 ·a·loud voice, were·coming·out of·many of·the·ones
G1831.1 V-2AAI-1S ἐξῆλθον (5x)
Jn 16:27 that I·myself came·forth personally·from God.
Jn 16:28 "I·came·forth personally·from the Father, and have·
Jn 17:8 ·knew truly that I·came·forth personally·from you,
Lk 11:24 ·return·back to my house from·which I·came·out.'
Mt 12:44 ·return into my house from·which I·came·out;' and
G1831.1 V-2AAI-2S ἐξῆλθες (1x)
Jn 16:30 "By this, we·trust that you·came·forth from God."
G1831.1 V-2AAI-2P ἐξήλθετε (2x)
Mt 26:55 crowds, "Did·yeu·come·out as against an·armed·
Mk 14:48 declared to·them, "Did·yeu·come·forth, as against
G1831.1 V-2AAI-3S ἐξῆλθεν (21x)
Jn 4:43 he·went·off from·there and came·forth into Galilee,
Jn 10:39 him. But he·came·forth out of·their hand.
Jn 11:44 the·one having·died came·forth, having·been·bound
Jn 13:3 into his hands, and that he·came·forth from God and
Jn 19:5 So Jesus came·forth outside bearing the thorny
Jn 19:34 and straight·away blood and water came·out.
Lk 4:35 him in the midst, came·forth from him, injuring him
Ac 16:18 ·out from her." And he·came·out the same hour.
Mt 8:34 the entire city came·out to meet·up with·YeShua.
Mt 17:18 *demon*, and the demon came·out from him. And
Mk 1:26 ·out with·a·loud voice, came·forth out of·him.
Mk 9:26 repeatedly, *the spirit* came·forth, and he·became as
1Co 14:36 the Redemptive-word of·God come·forth from you
Rv 6:2 was·given to·him, and he·came·forth conquering, so
Rv 6:4 And there·came·forth another horse *that·was* fiery·
Rv 14:15 And another angel came·forth out of·the Temple,
Rv 14:17 And another angel came·forth out of·the Temple,
Rv 14:18 And another angel came·forth out·from the
Rv 14:20 City, and blood came·forth out of·the winepress,
Rv 16:17 the air, and there·came·forth a·great voice from
Rv 19:5 Then a·voice came·forth out of·the throne, saying,
G1831.1 V-2AAI-3P ἐξῆλθον (5x)
Ac 28:15 ·things about us, came·out to approach·and·meet
Heb 11:15 *fatherland* from which they·came·out, they·would
Mk 8:11 And the Pharisees came·forth and began to·
Rv 9:3 from·out of·the smoke there·came·forth locusts upon
Rv 15:6 And the seven angels came·forth from·out of·the
G1831.1 V-2AAM-2S ἔξελθε (4x)
Lk 4:35 "Be·muzzled! And come·forth out of·him." And the
Mk 1:25 "Be·muzzled! And come·forth out of·him."
Mk 5:8 "Impure spirit, come·forth out of·the man·of·clay†.
Mk 9:25 I·myself order you, come·forth out of·him, and
G1831.1 V-2AAM-2P ἐξέλθετε (2x)
2Co 6:17 "Therefore "yeu·must·come·out from·among *the*
Rv 18:4 heaven, saying: "Come·out from·among her, my
G1831.1 V-2AAN ἐξελθεῖν (3x)
Lk 8:29 ·charging the impure spirit to·come·forth from the
Ac 16:18 the name of·Jesus Anointed to·come·out from her."
Mk 9:29 ·one·thing is this kind able to·come·forth, except by
G1831.1 V-2AAP-DSM ἐξελθόντι (1x)
Mk 5:2 And with·him coming·forth out of·the sailboat,
G1831.1 V-2AAP-GPM ἐξελθόντων (2x)
Mk 6:54 And with·them coming·forth out of·the sailboat,
Mk 11:12 next·day, with·them coming·forth from BethAny,
G1831.1 V-2AAP-NSF ἐξελθοῦσα (2x)
Ac 28:3 the fire, a·viper, coming·forth out of·the warmth,
Mt 15:22 *who*, upon·coming·forth yelled·out to·him,
G1831.1 V-2AAP-NSM ἐξελθών (3x)
Lk 1:22 But after·coming·forth, he·was·not able to·speak to·
Lk 15:28 was·not willing to·enter. So coming·out, his father
Ac 7:4 Then coming·forth from·among *the* land of·the·
G1831.1 V-2AAP-NPN ἐξελθόντα (2x)
Lk 8:33 And after·coming·out of the man·of·clay†, the
Mk 5:13 ·permitted them. And after·coming·out, the impure
G1831.1 V-2AAP-NPF ἐξελθοῦσαι (1x)
Mt 28:8 And coming·forth swiftly from the chamber·tomb,
G1831.1 V-2AAP-NPM ἐξελθόντες (4x)
Heb 3:16 all the·ones *did·so* after·coming·forth out of·Egypt
Mt 8:32 "Head·on·out." And coming·forth, they·went·off
Mt 27:53 And coming·forth from·among the chamber·tombs
Mk 1:29 And immediately, after·coming·forth out of·the
G1831.1 V-2AAS-2S ἐξέλθῃς (2x)
Lk 12:59 no, you·should·not come·forth from·there, even
Mt 5:26 no, you·should·not come·forth from·there until
G1831.1 V-2AAS-3S ἐξέλθῃ (1x)
Mt 12:43 the impure spirit should·come·out from the man·
G1831.1 V-RAI-1S ἐξελήλυθα (1x)
Mk 1:38 For to this·purpose I·have·come·forth."
G1831.1 V-RAI-2P ἐξεληλύθατε (1x)
Lk 22:52 toward him, "Have·yeu·come·out, as against an·
G1831.1 V-RAI-3S ἐξελήλυθεν (1x)
Mk 7:29 ·on·out. The demon has·come·forth out of·your
G1831.1 V-RAP-ASN ἐξεληλυθός (1x)
Mk 7:30 she·found the demon having·come·out and her
G1831.1 V-RAP-APM ἐξεληλυθότας (1x)
Heb 7:5 even·though having·come·forth from·among the
G1831.1 V-LAI-3S ἐξεληλύθει (2x)
Lk 8:35 from whom the demons had·come·out, sitting·down
Lk 8:38 the demons had·come·out was·petitioning him to·be
G1831.2 V-FDI-3S ἐξελεύσεται (2x)
Jn 10:9 and he·shall·enter·in and shall·go·forth, and he·
Rv 20:8 and shall·go·forth to·deceive the nations, the·ones in
G1831.2 V-PNM-2P ἐξέρχεσθε (1x)
Mt 25:6 bridegroom comes! Go·forth to approach·and·meet
G1831.2 V-PNN ἐξέρχεσθαι (1x)
Ac 19:12 and·also *for* the evil spirits to·go·forth from them.
G1831.2 V-PNP-GPM ἐξερχομένων (1x)
Mt 9:32 And with·them going·forth, behold, *men* brought to·
G1831.2 V-PNP-NSM ἐξερχόμενος (1x)
Lk 21:37 upon·going·forth, he·was·sleeping·out·in·the·
G1831.2 V-PNP-NPM ἐξερχόμενοι (3x)
Lk 9:5 ·not accept yeu, while·yeu·are·going·forth from that
Lk 9:6 And going·forth, they·went·throughout each·of the
Mt 10:14 hear yeur words, while·going·forth·from the home
G1831.2 V-PNS-1P ἐξερχώμεθα (1x)
Heb 13:13 Now·then, we·should·go·forth to him outside the
G1831.2 V-INI-3P ἐξήρχοντο (1x)
Jn 8:9 *·own* conscience, they·were·going·forth one·by·one,
G1831.2 V-2AAI-1S ἐξῆλθον (3x)
Jn 8:42 me, for I·myself went·forth and have·come out·from
Php 4:15 *among·yeu*, when I·went·forth from Macedonia,
2Co 2:13 ·leave·of them, I·went·forth into Macedonia.
G1831.2 V-2AAI-1P ἐξήλθομεν (1x)
Ac 16:13 ·the day of·Sabbath, we·went·forth outside of·the
G1831.2 V-2AAI-2P ἐξήλθετε (3x)
Mt 11:7 John, "What·did yeu·go·forth into the wilderness
Mt 11:8 But·rather what·did yeu·go·forth to·see?
Mt 11:9 But·rather what·did yeu·go·forth to·see?
G1831.2 V-2AAI-3S ἐξῆλθεν (45x)
Jn 8:59 but Jesus hid·himself and went·forth from·out of·the
Jn 11:31 Mary rose·up quickly and went·out, they·followed
Jn 13:30 the morsel, that·one went·forth immediately. And
Jn 13:31 When he·went·forth, Jesus says, "Now the Son of·
Jn 18:1 these·things, Jesus went·forth together with·his
Jn 18:16 to·the designated·high·priest, went·out and declared
Jn 18:29 Accordingly, Pilate went·out to them and declared,
Jn 18:38 And after·declaring this, he·went·out again to the
Jn 19:4 Now·then, Pilate went·forth outside again and says
Jn 19:17 bearing his·own cross, he·went·forth unto the *place*
Jn 20:3 and the other disciple went·forth, and they·came to
Jn 21:23 So·then this saying went·forth among the brothers,
Lk 2:1 days, *that* there·went·forth a·decree directly·from
Lk 4:14 Galilee, and a·reputation went·forth concerning him
Lk 5:27 these·things, he·went·forth and distinctly·viewed a·
Lk 6:12 in those days *that* he·went·forth to the mountain to·
Lk 7:17 this saying concerning him went·forth among all
Lk 8:5 "The·one sowing went·out to·sow his scattering·of·
Lk 17:29 but on·that day *when* Lot went·forth from Sodom,
Ac 1:21 the Lord Jesus came·in and went·forth among us,
Ac 10:23 ·the next·day, Peter went·forth together with·them
Ac 11:25 Then BarNabas went·forth to Tarsus, to·diligently·
Ac 14:20 next·day he·went·forth together with·BarNabas to
Ac 15:40 went·forth after·being·directly·handed to·the
Ac 16:19 the expectation of·their income went·out *from·her*,
Ac 17:33 in·this·manner, Paul went·forth from·among *the*
Ac 18:23 *for* some time, he·went·forth, going·throughout
Ac 20:1 and embracing *them*, went·forth to·traverse into
Ac 20:11 even·unto *the* first·light·of·day, *Paul* went·forth.
Heb 11:8 listened·and·obeyed; and he·went·forth, not
Mt 9:26 the disclosure of·this *awakening* went·forth into all
Mt 13:3 "Behold, the·one sowing went·forth to·sow.
Mt 20:1 ·the·house, who went·out at·the·same·time as·dawn
Mt 21:17 leaving them behind, he·went·forth outside of·the
Mk 1:28 And straight·away his fame went·forth unto all the
Mk 1:35 ·early while·still·night, he·went·out and went·off
Mk 2:12 ·up the mat, he·went·forth in·front of·them·all,
Mk 2:13 And he·went·forth again beside the sea, and all the
Mk 4:3 Behold, the·one sowing went·forth to·sow.
Mk 6:1 And he·went·out from·there and came into his·own
Mk 8:27 Then Jesus went·out with his disciples into the
Mk 11:11 ·the hour being late, he·went·out to BethAny with
Mk 14:68 And he·went·forth outside into the entryway·of·
Rm 10:18 "" Their clear·articulation went·forth into all the
2Co 8:17 ·diligent, of·his·own·choice, he·went·forth to yeu.
G1831.2 V-2AAI-3P ἐξῆλθον (13x)
Jn 4:30 Accordingly, they·went·forth out of·the city and
Jn 12:13 boughs of·palm·trees, and went·forth to meet him,
Jn 21:3 with·you." *And* they·went·forth and walked·up into
Lk 8:35 Then they·went·out to·see what·was·happening.
Ac 16:40 the brothers, they·comforted them and went·forth.
Mt 25:1 taking their lamps, went·forth to approach·and·meet
Mt 26:30 And after·singing·a·psalm, they·went·out to the
Mk 3:21 hearing *of·it*, went·out to·take·secure·hold·of him,
Mk 5:14 countrysides. And they·went·out to·see what it·was

Mk 14:16 And his disciples went·forth and came into the
Mk 14:26 And after·singing·a·psalm, they·went·out to the
1Jn 2:19 They·went·out from·among us, but·yet they·were
3Jn 1:7 on·behalf·of·the name, they·went·forth, taking not·
G1831.2 V-2AAM-2S ἔξελθε (6x)
Lk 5:8 Jesus' knees, saying, "Go·forth from me, because I·
Lk 13:31 saying to·him, "Go·out, and depart from·here,
Lk 14:21 declared to·his slave, 'Go·out quickly into the
Lk 14:23 to the slave, 'Go·out into the roadways and hedges
Ac 7:3 declared to him, "Go·forth from·among your land,
Ac 22:18 to·me, 'Make·haste and go·forth in haste out of·
G1831.2 V-2AAN ἐξελθεῖν (7x)
Jn 1:43 next·day, Jesus determined to·go·forth into Galilee,
Lk 14:18 ·land, and I·have dire·need to·go·out and to·see it.
Ac 16:3 Paul wanted this·man to·go·forth together with·him.
Ac 16:10 immediately we·sought to·go·forth into Macedonia
Ac 16:39 they·were·asking *of·them* to·go·out of·the city.
Heb 11:8 AbRaham, being·called to·go·forth into the place
1Co 5:10 ·inference, yeu·are·obligated to·go·forth out of·the
G1831.2 V-2AAP-ASF ἐξελθοῦσαν (2x)
Lk 8:46 for I·myself did·know power going·forth from me.
Mk 5:30 in himself the power going·forth out of·him, after·
G1831.2 V-2AAP-ASM ἐξελθόντα (1x)
Mt 26:71 And with·him going·out to the gate·*area*, another
G1831.2 V-2AAP-DSM ἐξελθόντι (1x)
Lk 8:27 And with·him going·forth upon the dry·ground,
G1831.2 V-2AAP-GSN ἐξελθόντος (1x)
Lk 11:14 it·happened, with·the demon going·out, the mute·
G1831.2 V-2AAP-NSF ἐξελθοῦσα (1x)
Mk 6:24 And after·going·out *of·the room*, she·declared to·
G1831.2 V-2AAP-NSM ἐξελθών (18x)
Jn 18:4 ·were·coming upon him, going·forth, he·declared
Lk 4:42 And with·day occurring, going·forth, he·traversed
Lk 10:35 "And going·forth upon the stirring·of·day, casting·
Lk 22:39 Then going·forth according·to his custom, *Jesus*
Lk 22:62 And Peter, going·forth outside, wept bitterly.
Ac 12:9 And going·out, he·was·following him and had·not
Ac 12:17 ·the brothers." And going·forth, he·traversed into
Mt 13:1 that day, YeShua, after·going·forth from the home,
Mt 14:14 And upon·going·forth, YeShua saw a·large crowd,
Mt 15:21 And going·forth from·there, YeShua departed into
Mt 18:28 "But the·same slave, after·going·forth, found one
Mt 20:3 "And going·forth *midmorning* about the third hour,
Mt 20:5 Again, going·forth about *the* sixth and ninth hour,
Mt 20:6 "Now going·forth about the eleventh hour, he·
Mt 24:1 And going·forth, YeShua was·departing from the
Mt 26:75 three·times." And going·forth outside, he·wept
Mk 1:45 But upon·going·forth, he·began to·officially·herald
Mk 7:31 And again, going·forth from·among the borders of·
G1831.2 V-2AAP-NPF ἐξελθοῦσαι (1x)
Mk 16:8 [(And going·forth swiftly, they·fled from the
G1831.2 V-2AAP-NPM ἐξελθόντες (14x)
Lk 10:10 they·do·not accept yeu, going·out into the same
Ac 12:10 ·up·to·them. And going·forth, they·went·onward
Ac 15:24 ·heard that certain·men going·out from·among us
Ac 16:36 Now accordingly, going·forth, traverse in peace.
Ac 16:40 And going·forth out of·the prison, they·entered
Ac 21:5 ·out the days, upon·going·forth, we·were·traversing
Ac 21:8 the·ones in·company·with Paul, going·forth, came
Mt 9:31 But upon·going·forth, they·widely·promoted it in all
Mt 12:14 But the Pharisees, upon·going·forth, took
Mt 22:10 Also those slaves, going·forth into the roadways,
Mk 3:6 And going·forth, the Pharisees immediately were·
Mk 6:12 Then going·forth, they·were·officially·proclaiming
Mk 9:30 And going·forth from·there, they·were·traversing·
Mk 16:20 And going·forth, those *disciples* officially·
G1831.2 V-2AAS-2P ἐξέλθητε (3x)
Mt 10:11 worthy, and·there abide until yeu·should·go·forth.
Mt 24:26 in the wilderness,' yeu·should·not go·out. *Or*,
Mk 6:10 there abide until yeu·should·go·forth from·there.
G1831.2 V-2AAS-3S ἐξέλθῃ (2x)
Lk 11:24 the impure spirit should·go·forth from the man·of·
Rv 3:12 and no, he·should·not go·forth outside any·longer.

G1831.2 V-RAI-2P ἐξεληλύθατε (3x)
Lk 7:24 "What have·yeu·gone·forth into the wilderness to·
Lk 7:25 But·rather what have·yeu·gone·forth to·see?
Lk 7:26 "But·rather what have·yeu·gone·forth to·see?
G1831.2 V-RAI-3S ἐξελήλυθεν (1x)
1Th 1:8 yeur trust toward God has·gone·forth, such·for us
G1831.2 V-RAI-3P ἐξεληλύθασιν (1x)
1Jn 4:1 because many false·prophets have·gone·out into the
G1831.2 V-LAI-3S ἐξεληλύθει (1x)
Lk 8:2 from whom had·gone·forth seven demons,
EG1831.2 (2x)
Mt 13:4 And when he·himself *went·forth* to·sow, in·fact,
1Jn 2:19 with us. But·rather *they·went·out*, in·order·that
G1831.3 V-2AAP-NSM ἐξελθών (1x)
Mk 6:34 And Jesus, after·coming·ashore, saw a·large crowd

G1832 ἔξ•εστι êxêsti *v.* (32x)
ἐξ•όν êxốn [neuter present participle]
Roots:G1537 G1510 Compare:G0433 G4241 G5534 See:G1849
G1832.1 V-PQI-3S ἔξεστιν (19x)
Jn 5:10 "It·is a·Sabbath. It·is·not proper for·you to·take·up
Jn 18:31 to·him, "It·is·not proper for·us to·kill not·even·
Lk 6:2 "Why·do yeu·do that·which it·is·not proper to·do on
Lk 6:4 bread, which it·is·not proper to·eat except alone *for*
Lk 6:9 yeu. Which·thing is·proper on·the various·Sabbaths:
Ac 8:37 ·trust from·out of·all the heart, it·is·proper." And
Ac 16:21 which it·is·not proper for·us to·personally·accept,
Mt 12:2 disciples do that·which it·is·not proper to·do on a·
Mt 12:12 of·a·sheep? As·such, it·is·proper to·do good on·
Mt 14:4 ·saying to·him, "It·is·not proper for·you to·have her
Mt 20:15 Or is·it·not proper for·me to·do whatever I·should·
Mt 27:6 declared, "It·is·not proper to·cast them into the
Mk 2:24 ·do on the Sabbath·days that·which is·not proper?"
Mk 2:26 bread, which it·is·not proper to·eat except for·the
Mk 6:18 ·AntiPas, "It·is·not proper for·you to·have your
1Co 6:12 All·things are·proper for·me, but·yet not all·things
1Co 6:12 are·advantageous. All·things are·proper for·me,
1Co 10:23 All·things are·proper for·me, but·yet not all·
1Co 10:23 are·advantageous. All·things are·proper for·me,
G1832.1 V-PQP-NSN ἐξόν (3x)
Ac 2:29 "Men, brothers, it·is·being·proper to·declare to yeu
Mt 12:4 which was not being·proper for·him to·eat, neither
2Co 12:4 is·not being·proper for·a·man·of·clay† to·speak.
G1832.2 V-PQI-3S ἔξεστιν (10x)
Lk 14:3 saying, "Is·it·proper to·both·relieve·and·cure on·the
Lk 20:22 Is·it·proper for·us to·give tribute to·Caesar or not?
Ac 21:37 ·commander, "Is·it·proper for·me to·declare
Ac 22:25 standing·by, "Is·it·proper for·yeu to·scourge a·
Mt 12:10 "Is·it·proper to·both·relieve·and·cure on·the
Mt 19:3 to·him, "Is·it·proper for·a·man·of·clay† to·divorce
Mt 22:17 you suppose? Is·it·proper to·give·a·census·tribute
Mk 3:4 to·them, "Is·it·proper to·beneficially·do·good on·the
Mk 10:2 ·of him, "Is·it·proper for·a·man to·divorce *his* wife
Mk 12:14 ·God in truth. Is·it·proper to·give·a·census·tribute

G1833 ἐξ•ετάζω êxêtázō *v.* (3x)
Roots:G1537
G1833.2 V-AAM-2P ἐξετάσατε (2x)
Mt 2:8 verify·*it*·by·inquiring precisely concerning the little·
Mt 10:11 yeu·should·enter, verify·by·inquiring who in it is
G1833.2 V-AAN ἐξετάσαι (1x)
Jn 21:12 disciples was·daring to·verify·by·inquiring·of him,

G1834 ἐξ•ηγέομαι êxēgéômai *v.* (6x)
Roots:G1537 G2233 Compare:G1285 G5419 G1843
G1834.2 V-PNP-GPM ἐξηγουμένων (1x)
Ac 15:12 Paul recounting·in·detail what·many miraculous·
G1834.2 V-INI-3S ἐξηγεῖτο (1x)
Ac 21:19 *Paul* was·recounting·in·detail each·and·every one
G1834.2 V-INI-3P ἐξηγοῦντο (1x)
Lk 24:35 they·themselves recounted·in·detail the·things *that*
G1834.2 V-ADI-3S ἐξηγήσατο (2x)
Jn 1:18 of·the Father, that·one recounted·*him*·in·detail.
Ac 15:14 Shimon *Peter* recounted·in·detail *that* just·as at·

G1834.2 V-ADP-NSM ἐξηγησάμενος (1x)
Ac 10:8 and after·recounting·in·detail absolutely·all·*these*·

G1835 ἑξήκοντα hêxḗkônta *n.* (8x)
See:G1803
xLangEquiv:H8346 A8361
G1835.1 N-NUI ἑξήκοντα (4x)
Lk 24:13 ·a·distance from JeruSalem *of·about* sixty stadia.
1Ti 5:9 *if·she·is* not less·than sixty years·of·age, having·been
Rv 11:3 ·prophesy a·thousand two·hundred *and* sixty days,
Rv 12:6 her there a·thousand two·hundred *and* sixty days.
G1835.2 N-NUI ἑξήκοντα (4x)
Mt 13:8 a·hundredfold, some *seed* sixtyfold, and some *seed*
Mt 13:23 a·hundredfold, some *seed* sixtyfold, and some *seed*
Mk 4:8 *seed* thirtyfold, and one *seed* sixtyfold, and one *seed*
Mk 4:20 thirtyfold, and one *seed* sixtyfold, and one *seed* a·

G1836 ἑξῆς hêxē̂s *adv.* (5x)
Roots:G2192 Compare:G0839 G1887 See:G2517
G1836.1 ADV ἑξῆς (1x)
Lk 9:37 And it·happened, *that* on the next day, with·them
G1836.2 ADV ἑξῆς (4x)
Lk 7:11 it·happened on the next·day *that* he·was·traversing
Ac 21:1 to Cos, and on·the next·day to Rhodes, and·from·
Ac 25:17 not·even·one postponement on·the next·day), after·
Ac 27:18 ·tossed·by·the·storm, the next·day they·did *lighten*

G1837 ἐξ•ηχέομαι êxēchéômai *v.* (1x)
Roots:G1537 G2278
G1837 V-RPI-3S ἐξήχηται (1x)
1Th 1:8 of·the Lord has·been·echoed·forth. Not merely in

G1838 ἕξις héxis *n.* (1x)
Roots:G2192 Compare:G4234
G1838.1 N-ASF ἕξιν (1x)
Heb 5:14 having·been·trained through habit toward having

G1839 ἐξ•ίστημι êxístēmi *v.* (17x)
Roots:G1537 G2476 Compare:G1605 G2296 G2284 G4852-2 G4658-1 See:G1611 xLangAlso:H8074 A8075
G1839.2 V-PAP-NSM ἐξιστῶν (1x)
Ac 8:9 ·dark·occult·powers and astonishing the Gentiles of·
G1839.2 V-PMN ἐξίστασθαι (1x)
Mk 2:12 ·all, such·for all to·be·astonished and to·glorify
G1839.2 V-IMI-3S ἐξίστατο (1x)
Ac 8:13 *And* he·was·astonished upon·observing both signs
G1839.2 V-IMI-3P ἐξίσταντο (6x)
Lk 2:47 And all the·ones hearing him were·astonished at his
Ac 2:7 And they·all were·astonished and were·marveling,
Ac 2:12 all were·astonished and were·thoroughly·perplexed,
Ac 9:21 ·ones hearing *him* were·astonished and were·saying,
Mt 12:23 all the crowds were·astonished and were·saying,
Mk 6:51 And they·were·exceedingly astonished among
G1839.2 V-2AAI-3P ἐξέστησαν (5x)
Lk 8:56 And her parents were·astonished, but he·charged
Lk 24:22 women also from·among us astonished us, after·
Ac 10:45 trusting *in·Jesus* were·astonished, as·many·as
Ac 12:16 ·up *the gate*, they·saw him and were·astonished.
Mk 5:42 And they·were·astonished with·great astonishment
G1839.2 V-RAN ἐξεστακέναι (1x)
Ac 8:11 ·of *that he·continued* to·have·astonished them *for*
G1839.3 V-2AAI-1P ἐξέστημεν (1x)
2Co 5:13 For if we·lost·our·wits, *it·is* for·God; or·if we·are·
G1839.3 V-2AAI-3S ἐξέστη (1x)
Mk 3:21 ·of him, for they·were·saying, "He·lost·his·wits."

G1840 ἐξ•ισχύω êxischýō *v.* (1x)
Roots:G1537 G2480 Compare:G2902 G4599
G1840 V-AAS-2P ἐξισχύσητε (1x)
Eph 3:18 in·order·that yeu·may·have·full·strength to·grasp

G1841 ἔξ•οδος éxôdôs *n.* (3x)
Roots:G1537 G3598 Compare:G4505 See:G1840-3 G1840-4 G1840-5
xLangEquiv:H4161 H3318 xLangAlso:H2351
G1841.1 N-ASF ἔξοδον (2x)
Lk 9:31 glory, were·relating his exodus which he·was·about
2Pe 1:15 to·have at·any·time, after my exodus, *the ability*
G1841.1 N-GSF ἐξόδου (1x)

Heb 11:22 remembered concerning the exodus of·the Sons

G1842 ἐξ•ολοθρεύω êxôlôthrêúō *v.* (1x)
Roots:G1537 G3645 Compare:G0853 G4931 xLangEquiv:H6789 xLangAlso:H3772 H7843

G1842 V-FPI-3S ἐξολοθρευθήσεται (1x)
Ac 3:23 ' "shall·be·exterminated from·among the People.

G1843 ἐξ•ομο•λογέω êxômôlôgéō *v.* (11x)
Roots:G1537 G3670 Compare:G1834 xLangAlso:H3034 H7650

G1843.1 V-FMI-1S ἐξομολογήσομαι (2x)
Rm 15:9 ·of that, I·shall·explicitly·affirm you among
Rv 3:5 of·life-above, but I·shall·explicitly·affirm his name

G1843.1 V-FMI-3S ἐξομολογήσεται (1x)
Rm 14:11 and every tongue shall·explicitly·affirm God.'"

G1843.1 V-PMI-1S ἐξομολογοῦμαι (2x)
Lk 10:21 and declared, "I·explicitly·affirm to·you, O·Father
Mt 11:25 YeShua declared, "I·explicitly·affirm to·you, O·

G1843.1 V-AAI-3S ἐξωμολόγησεν (1x)
Lk 22:6 And he·explicitly·affirmed *it*, and he·was·seeking a·

G1843.1 V-AMS-3S ἐξομολογήσηται (1x)
Php 2:11 every tongue should·explicitly·affirm that Jesus

G1843.2 V-PMM-2P ἐξομολογεῖσθε (1x)
Jac 5:16 Explicitly·confess *yeur* trespasses to·one·another,

G1843.2 V-PMP-NPM ἐξομολογούμενοι (3x)
Ac 19:18 *forward*, explicitly·confessing and reporting their
Mt 3:6 the Jordan, explicitly·confessing their moral·failures.
Mk 1:5 River, explicitly·confessing their moral·failures.

G1844 ἐξ•ορκίζω êxôrkízō *v.* (1x)
Roots:G1537 G3726 Compare:G3726 See:G1845

G1844 V-PAI-1S ἐξορκίζω (1x)
Mt 26:63 to·him, "Under·oath,·I·solemnly·charge you by

G1845 ἐξ•ορκιστής êxôrkistés *n.* (1x)
Roots:G1844

G1845.2 N-GPM ἐξορκιστῶν (1x)
Ac 19:13 Jews, *being* exorcists, took·it·upon·themselves to·

G1846 ἐξ•ορύσσω êxôrýssō *v.* (2x)
Roots:G1537 G3736

G1846.1 V-AAP-NPM ἐξορύξαντες (1x)
Gal 4:15 if *it·had·been* possible, digging·out yeur own·eyes,

G1846.2 V-AAP-NPM ἐξορύξαντες (1x)
Mk 2:4 he·was, and after·digging·through, they·lowered the

G1847 ἐξ•ου•δε•νόω êxôudênóō *v.* (1x)
Roots:G1537 G3762 See:G1848 xLangAlso:H3988

G1847.2 V-APS-3S ἐξουδενωθῇ (1x)
Mk 9:12 ·things and should·be·treated·with·utter·contempt.

G1848 ἐξ•ου•θε•νέω êxôuthênéō *v.* (11x)
Roots:G1847 Compare:G4065 G0593 G4360 xLangEquiv:H3988

G1848.1 V-PAI-2S ἐξουθενεῖς (1x)
Rm 14:10 why·do you·yourself utterly·disdain your brother

G1848.1 V-PAM-2P ἐξουθενεῖτε (1x)
1Th 5:20 Do·not utterly·disdain prophecies.

G1848.1 V-PAM-3S ἐξουθενείτω (1x)
Rm 14:3 The·one eating must·not utterly·disdain the·one not

G1848.1 V-PAP-APM ἐξουθενοῦντας (1x)
Lk 18:9 they·are righteous, and utterly·disdaining the rest.

G1848.1 V-AAI-2P ἐξουθενήσατε (1x)
Gal 4:14 And yeu·did·not utterly·disdain my proof·trial, the·

G1848.1 V-AAP-NSM ἐξουθενήσας (1x)
Lk 23:11 Then utterly·disdaining him, HerOd·AntiPas (along·

G1848.1 V-AAS-3S ἐξουθενήσῃ (1x)
1Co 16:11 not anyone should·utterly·disdain him, but send

G1848.1 V-RPP-APN ἐξουθενημένα (1x)
1Co 1:28 and the·things having·been·utterly·disdained, even

G1848.1 V-RPP-APM ἐξουθενημένους (1x)
1Co 6:4 the·ones having·been·utterly·disdained by the

G1848.1 V-RPP-NSM ἐξουθενημένος (1x)
2Co 10:10 his discourse *is* having·been·utterly·disdained."

G1848.2 V-APP-NSM ἐξουθενηθείς (1x)
Ac 4:11 is "the stone being·disdainfully·rejected by yeu,

G1849 ἐξ•ουσία êxôusía *n.* (105x)
Roots:G1832 Compare:G0970 G1411 G2479 G2904 See:G1850

G1849.1 N-NSF ἐξουσία (9x)
Mt 28:18 saying, "All authority is·given to·me in heaven
Rm 13:1 For there·is no authority except from God; and the·
Jud 1:25 and majesty, might and authority, both now and
Rv 6:8 with him. And authority was·given to·them over the
Rv 9:3 upon the earth, and authority was·given to·them, as
Rv 9:10 tails, and their authority *was* to·bring·harm·to the
Rv 12:10 ·our God, and the authority of·his Anointed-One,
Rv 13:5 and revilements. And authority was·given to·it to·
Rv 13:7 ·conquer them.' And authority was·given to·it over

G1849.1 N-NPF ἐξουσίαι (3x)
Rm 13:1 and the·ones being authorities, they·are having·
Col 1:16 or principalities, or authorities. All·things have·
Rv 9:19 For their authorities are in their mouth *and in their*

G1849.1 N-ASF ἐξουσίαν (51x)
Jn 5:27 And he·gave him authority also to·make Tribunal·
Jn 10:18 of my·own·self. I·have authority to·lay it down,
Jn 10:18 to·lay it down, and I·have authority to·take it again.
Jn 17:2 Just·as *also* you·gave him authority over·all flesh, in·
Jn 19:10 ·know that I·have authority to·crucify you, and I·
Jn 19:10 you, and I·have authority to·fully·release you?
Jn 19:11 having not·even·one·bit·of authority against me,
Lk 4:6 ·you I·shall·give absolutely·all this authority and their
Lk 5:24 the Son of·Clay·Man† has authority upon the earth
Lk 7:8 ·man·of·clay† being·assigned under authority, having
Lk 9:1 he·gave them power and authority over all the
Lk 10:19 I·give to·yeu the authority, the·one to·trample
Lk 12:5 the killing, *is* having authority to·cast *a·person* into
Lk 19:17 in very·little, be having authority over ten cities.
Lk 20:2 Or who is the·one giving you this authority?"
Ac 8:19 "Give me·also this authority, in·order·that on·
Ac 9:14 And here, he·has authority personally·from the
Ac 26:10 in·prisons, receiving authority personally·from the
Mt 7:29 instructing them as *one* having authority, and not as
Mt 8:9 I·myself am a·man·of·clay† under authority, having
Mt 9:6 that the Son of·Clay·Man† has authority on the earth
Mt 9:8 God, the·one giving such authority to·men·of·clay†.
Mt 10:1 disciples, he·gave to·them authority *over* impure
Mt 21:23 these·things? And who gave you this authority?"
Mk 1:22 instructing them as one·having authority, and not as
Mk 1:27 Because according·to authority he·orders even the
Mk 2:10 the Son of·Clay·Man† has authority on the earth to·
Mk 3:15 and to·have authority to·both·relieve·and·cure the
Mk 6:7 And he·was·giving them authority *over* the impure
Mk 11:28 you this authority in·order·that you·should·do
Mk 13:34 his home and giving authority to·his slaves, and
Rm 9:21 Or does·not the potter have authority *over* the clay,
Rm 13:3 do·you·want not to·be·afraid·of the authority? Do
2Th 3:9 Not because we·do·not have authority, but·rather
1Co 7:37 necessity, but has authority concerning his·own
1Co 11:10 the woman is·obligated to·have authority on her
1Co 15:24 every principality and all authority and power.
2Co 13:10 ·present, according·to the authority which the
Rv 2:26 end, to·him I·shall·give authority over the nations.
Rv 9:3 to·them, as the scorpions of·the earth have authority.
Rv 11:6 These have authority to·shut the sky, in·order·that
Rv 11:6 prophecy. And they·have authority over the waters
Rv 13:2 it his power, and his throne, and great authority.
Rv 13:4 Dragon which gave authority to·the Daemonic·Beast,
Rv 13:12 And it·exercises all the authority of·the first
Rv 14:18 the Sacrifice·Altar, having authority over the fire;
Rv 16:9 name of·God— the·one having authority over these
Rv 17:12 but·yet they·do·receive authority as kings *for* one
Rv 17:13 their·own power and authority to·the Scarlet·Beast.
Rv 18:1 of·the heaven, having great authority; and the earth
Rv 20:6 the Second Death does·not have authority, but·rather

G1849.1 N-APF ἐξουσίας (3x)
Lk 12:11 the magistrates, and the authorities, do·not be·
Eph 6:12 ·against the authorities, specifically·against the
Col 2:15 and the authorities, he·made·a·public·example *of*·

G1849.1 N-DSF ἐξουσίᾳ (14x)
Lk 4:32 instruction, because his word was with authority.
Lk 4:36 *is* this! Because with authority and power he·orders
Lk 20:2 by what·kind·of authority do·you·do these·things?
Lk 20:8 to·yeu by what·kind·of authority I·do these·things."
Lk 20:20 to·the jurisdiction and authority of·the governor.
Ac 1:7 seasons which the Father placed in his·own authority.
Ac 5:4 ·was·it *not·indeed* in your·own authority? How *is·it*
Mt 21:23 "By what·kind·of authority do·you·do these·things
Mt 21:24 to·yeu by what·kind·of authority I·do these·things.
Mt 21:27 to·yeu by what·kind·of authority I·do these·things.
Mk 11:28 "By what·kind·of authority do·you·do these·things
Mk 11:29 to·yeu by what·kind·of authority I·do these·things.
Mk 11:33 to·yeu by what·kind·of authority I·do these·things.
Rm 13:2 ·against the authority has·stood·opposed·to the

G1849.1 N-DPF ἐξουσίαις (3x)
Rm 13:1 ·every soul submit·itself to·the·superior authorities.
Tit 3:1 to·jurisdictions and authorities, to·readily·comply, to·
Eph 3:10 to·the principalities and to·the authorities in the

G1849.1 N-GSF ἐξουσίας (7x)
Ac 26:12 Damascus with authority and an·executive·charge
Ac 26:18 and *from* the authority of·the Adversary-Accuser to
2Co 10:8 excessively concerning our authority, which the
Eph 1:21 high·above all principality and authority, power
Eph 2:2 according·to the prince of·the authority of·the air,
Col 1:13 us from·out of·the authority of·darkness and
Col 2:10 who is the head of·all principality and authority—

G1849.1 N-GPF ἐξουσιῶν (1x)
1Pe 3:22 with·angels and authorities and powers already·

EG1849.1 (2x)
Rm 13:7 the dues to·all·ones *in·superior authority*: the
Rv 2:27 I·also have·received *authority* personally·from my

G1849.2 N-NSF ἐξουσία (2x)
1Co 8:9 ·somehow this privilege of·yeurs should·become a·
Rv 22:14 ·order·that it·shall·be their privilege *to·reach* upon

G1849.2 N-ASF ἐξουσίαν (5x)
Jn 1:12 him, to·them he·gave privilege to·become children
Heb 13:10 in·the Tabernacle have no privilege to·eat.
1Co 9:4 ¿!·Do we·not have privilege to·eat and to·drink?
1Co 9:5 ¿!·Do we·not have privilege to·lead·about a·wife
1Co 9:6 *excluded*? ¿!·Do·we·not have privilege to·not work

G1849.2 N-DSF ἐξουσίᾳ (2x)
1Co 9:12 But·yet we·did·not use this privilege, but·rather
1Co 9:18 in·order not to·abuse my privilege in the good·

G1849.2 N-GSF ἐξουσίας (1x)
1Co 9:12 If others participate *in·this·privilege* among·yeu,

G1849.3 N-NSF ἐξουσία (1x)
Lk 22:53 this is yeur hour, and the jurisdiction of·darkness."

G1849.3 N-GSF ἐξουσίας (1x)
Lk 23:7 he·is from·out of·HerOd·AntiPas' jurisdiction, he·sent

G1850 ἐξ•ουσιάζω êxôusiázō *v.* (4x)
Roots:G1849

G1850.1 V-PAI-3S ἐξουσιάζει (2x)
1Co 7:4 The wife does·not have·control·over her·own body,
1Co 7:4 husband does·not have·control·over his·own body,

G1850.1 V-PAP-NPM ἐξουσιάζοντες (1x)
Lk 22:25 and the·ones having·control·over them are·called

G1850.2 V-FPI-1S ἐξουσιασθήσομαι (1x)
1Co 6:12 I·myself shall·not be·controlled under anything.

G1851 ἐξ•οχή êxôché *n.* (1x)
Roots:G1537 G2192

G1851.3 N-ASF ἐξοχήν (1x)
Ac 25:23 regiment·commanders and the most prominent men

G1852 ἐξ•υπνίζω êxypnízō *v.* (1x)
Roots:G1853

G1852 V-AAS-1S ἐξυπνίσω (1x)
Jn 11:11 in·order·that out·of·heavy·sleep,·I·may·wake him.

G1853 ἔξ•υπνος éxypnôs *adj.* (1x)
Roots:G1537 G5258 See:G1852

G1853 A-NSM ἔξυπνος (1x)
Ac 16:27 becoming awake·out·of·*his*·heavy·sleep and seeing

G1854 ἔξω ἔxō *adv.* (66x)
Roots:G1537 Compare:G0245 See:G5318
G1854.1 ADV ἔξω (1x)
2Co 4:16 our outward man·of·clay† is·thoroughly·decaying·
G1854.2 ADV ἔξω (58x)
Jn 6:37 toward me, no, I·should·not cast·out outside,
Jn 9:34 instruct us?" And they·cast him forth outside.
Jn 9:35 heard that they·cast him forth outside. And finding
Jn 11:43 "Lazarus, come·over·here, outside!"
Jn 12:31 prince of·this world shall now be·cast·out outside.
Jn 18:16 But Peter stood outside alongside the door.
Jn 19:4 Now·then, Pilate went·forth outside again and says
Jn 19:4 "See, I·bring him outside to·yeu, in·order·that yeu·
Jn 19:5 So Jesus came·forth outside bearing the thorny
Jn 19:13 Pilate brought Jesus outside, and he·sat·down on
Jn 20:11 But Mariam stood outside toward the chamber·
Lk 1:10 of·the people were praying outside at·the hour of·
Lk 4:29 ·up, they·cast him forth outside of·the city and
Lk 8:20 and your brothers stand outside, wanting to·see you.
Lk 8:54 ·out everyone outside and taking·secure·hold of·her
Lk 13:25 yeu·should·begin to·stand outside and to·knock at·
Lk 13:28 of·God, but yeu·yeurselves being·cast·out outside.
Lk 13:33 should·completely·perish outside of·JeruSalem.
Lk 20:15 So casting him forth outside of·the vineyard, they·
Lk 22:62 And Peter, going·forth outside, wept bitterly.
Lk 24:50 And he·led them outside as·far·as to BethAny, and
Ac 4:15 to·go·aside outside of·the joint·council·of·Sanhedrin
Ac 5:23 and the sentries standing outside before the doors.
Ac 5:34 to·make the ambassadors *stay* outside a short·while.
Ac 7:58 And after·casting·*him*·out outside of·the City, they·
Ac 9:40 after·casting everyone forth outside, bowing his
Ac 14:19 Paul, they·were·dragging *him* outside of·the city
Ac 16:13 day of·Sabbath, we·went·forth outside of·the city
Ac 16:30 And bringing them outside, he·replied, "Sirs, what
Ac 21:5 and children) until *we·were* outside of·the city. And
Ac 21:30 ·drawing him outside of·the Sanctuary·Courtyard,
Heb 13:11 are·completely·burned outside the arrayed·
Heb 13:12 through his·own blood, suffered outside the gate.
Heb 13:13 ·go·forth to him outside the arrayed·encampment,
Mt 12:46 his mother and brothers stood outside, seeking to·
Mt 12:47 and your brothers stand outside, seeking to·speak
Mt 21:17 them behind, he·went·forth outside of·the City
Mt 21:39 him, they·cast·*him*·forth outside of·the vineyard
Mt 26:69 Now Peter was·sitting·down outside in the
Mt 26:75 And going·forth outside, he·wept bitterly.
Mk 1:45 a·city, but·rather was outside in desolate places,
Mk 3:31 *along*, and standing outside, they·dispatched to him
Mk 3:32 mother and your brothers seek·for you outside."
Mk 4:11 to·them, the·ones *that·are* outside, all·*these*·things
Mk 5:10 he·should·not dispatch them outside of·the region.
Mk 8:23 by·the hand, he·led him outside of·the village. And
Mk 11:4 found the colt outside having·been·tied alongside
Mk 11:19 he·was·traversing·forth outside of·the City.
Mk 12:8 *him* and cast·*him*·forth outside of·the vineyard.
Mk 14:68 And he·went·forth outside into the entryway·of·
1Th 4:12 toward the·ones outside *the Called·Out·citizenry*,
1Co 5:12 ·judge the·ones outside *the Called·Out·citizenry*?
1Co 5:13 But the·ones outside, God presently·judges.
Col 4:5 toward the·ones outside *the Called·Out·citizenry*,
Rv 3:12 and no, he·should·not go·forth outside any·longer.
Rv 11:2 the Temple, you·must·cast·forth outside, and you·
Rv 14:20 And the winepress was·trampled outside the City,
Rv 22:15 But outside *are* the dogs, and the·ones utilizing·
EG1854.2 (1x)
Lk 13:28 "*And* there *outside*, there·shall·be the weeping and
G1854.3 ADV ἔξω (5x)
Jn 15:6 remain in me, he·is·already·cast out as the *unfruitful*
Lk 14:35 for manure, *but·rather* men·cast it out. "The·one
Mt 5:13 except to·be·cast out and to·be·trampled·down by
Mt 13:48 the good into containers but cast out the rotten.
1Jn 4:18 the completely·mature love casts out the fear,
G1854.4 ADV ἔξω (1x)
Ac 26:11 *them* even as·far·as to the foreign cities.

G1855 ἔξω•θεν ἔxōthên *adv.* (10x)
Roots:G1854 Compare:G1622 G2081
G1855.2 ADV ἔξωθεν (4x)
Mt 23:27 which in·fact outwardly appear stately·and·elegant,
Mt 23:28 in·fact, yeu also outwardly appear righteous to·the
1Pe 3:3 ·be, not *according·to* the outwardly, *that·is* with·an·
2Co 7:5 ·hard-pressed on every·side. Outwardly *are* quarrels
G1855.3 ADV ἔξωθεν (6x)
Lk 11:39 yeu Pharisees purify the outside of·the cup and the
Lk 11:40 ¿!·Did·not the·one making the outside also make
Mt 23:25 Because yeu·purify the outside of·the cup and of·
Mk 7:15 ·is·not·even·one·thing from·outside of·the man·of·
Mk 7:18 that any thing traversing from·outside into the man·
1Ti 3:7 the·ones *who·are* outside *the Called·Out·citizenry* in·

G1856 ἐξ•ωθέω êxōthéō *v.* (2x)
ἐξ•ώθω êxṓthō
Roots:G1537 Compare:G3992 G0683
G1856.1 V-AAI-3S ἐξῶσεν (1x)
Ac 7:45 of·the Gentiles, whom God thrust·out from *the* face
G1856.3 V-AAN ἐξῶσαι (1x)
Ac 27:39 if·it·were·possible, to·propel the sailing·ship.

G1857 ἐξώτερος êxṓtêrôs *adj.* (3x)
Roots:G1854 xLangAlso:H2435
G1857 A-ASN ἐξώτερον (3x)
Mt 8:12 shall·be·cast·out into the outer darkness, where
Mt 22:13 and cast·*him*·out into the outer darkness, where
Mt 25:30 the useless slave into the outer darkness,' where

G1858 ἑορτάζω hêôrtázō *v.* (1x)
Roots:G1859 xLangAlso:H2287
G1858.1 V-PAS-1P ἑορτάζωμεν (1x)
1Co 5:8 we·should·purposefully·observe·the·sacred·feast,

G1859 ἑορτή hêôrtḗ *n.* (34x)
Compare:G0421-1 G3831 See:G1858
xLangAlso:H2282 H4150
G1859.ª N-NSF ἑορτή (1x)
Jn 5:1 these·things, there·was a·Sacred·Feast of·the Judeans,
G1859.ª N-ASF ἑορτήν (2x)
Jn 11:56 that no, he·may·not come to·the Sacred·Feast?"
Ac 18:21 me by·all·means to·make the Sacred·Feast, the·
G1859.1 N-ASF ἑορτήν (1x)
Jn 12:12 (the·one coming to·the feast *in·BethAny*) upon·
G1859.1 N-DSF ἑορτῇ (2x)
Mt 26:5 "Not on the feast·day, lest a·commotion should·
Mk 14:2 "Not on the feast *day*, lest there·shall·be a·
G1859.3 N-NSF ἑορτή (1x)
Jn 7:2 Now the Judeans' Sacred·Feast, the *Sacred·Feast* of·
G1859.3 N-GSF ἑορτῆς (1x)
Col 2:16 participating of·a·Sacred·Feast or of·a·new·moon
G1859.4 N-NSF ἑορτή (1x)
Jn 6:4 And the Passover, the Sacred·Feast of·the Judeans,
G1859.4 N-ASF ἑορτήν (5x)
Jn 4:45 for they·themselves also went to·the Sacred·Feast.
Jn 13:29 that we·have need·of for the Sacred·Feast," or that
Lk 23:17 one·man to·them annually·at·this Sacred·Feast.
Mt 27:15 Now annually·at·this Sacred·Feast, the governor
Mk 15:6 annually·at·this Sacred·Feast, he·was·fully·releasing
G1859.4 N-DSF ἑορτῇ (4x)
Jn 2:23 the Passover among the Sacred·Feast, many trusted
Jn 4:45 ·did in JeruSalem at·the Sacred·Feast *of·Passover*, for
Jn 12:20 ·that they·may·fall·prostrate at·the Sacred·Feast.
Lk 2:41 for·the *Judeans'* Sacred·Feast of·the Passover.
G1859.4 N-GSF ἑορτῆς (2x)
Jn 13:1 And before the Sacred·Feast of·the Passover, Jesus,
Lk 2:42 according·to the custom of·the Sacred·Feast
EG1859.4 (1x)
Mk 14:1 ·be *the Judeans' Sacred·Feast·of* the Passover and
G1859.5 N-NSF ἑορτή (1x)
Lk 22:1 the *Judeans'* Sacred·Feast of·the Unleavened·Bread
EG1859.5 (5x)
Lk 22:7 the day of·the *Sacred·Feast·of* Unleavened·Bread, in
Ac 12:3 the days *of·the Sacred·Feast* of·Unleavened·Bread,
Ac 20:6 the days of·the *Sacred·Feast·of* Unleavened·Bread,
Mt 26:17 first *day* of·the *Sacred·Feast·of* Unleavened·Bread,
Mk 14:12 first day of·the *Sacred·Feast·of* Unleavened·Bread,
G1859.9 N-ASF ἑορτήν (3x)
Jn 7:8 Yeu·yeurselves walk·up to this Sacred·Feast. I·myself
Jn 7:8 do·not·yet walk·up to this Sacred·Feast, because my
Jn 7:10 walked·up also to the Sacred·Feast, not openly, but·
G1859.9 N-DSF ἑορτῇ (1x)
Jn 7:11 ·seeking him at the Sacred·Feast and were·saying,
G1859.9 N-GSF ἑορτῆς (2x)
Jn 7:14 ·now halfway·through the Sacred·Feast *of·Booths*,
Jn 7:37 on·the great *day* of·the Sacred·Feast *of·Booths*, Jesus
EG1859.9 (1x)
Jn 7:2 Judeans' Sacred·Feast, the *Sacred·Feast* of·Booths,

G1860 ἐπ•αγγελία êpangêlía *n.* (57x)
Roots:G1861
G1860.1 N-NSF ἐπαγγελία (1x)
1Jn 1:5 This then is the announcement which we·have·heard
EG1860.1 (1x)
Heb 2:3 an·initial *announcement* being·spoken through the
G1860.2 N-NSF ἐπαγγελία (6x)
Ac 2:39 For the promise is for·yeu, and for·yeur children,
Gal 3:22 Anointed, the promise may·be·given to·the·ones
Rm 4:13 For the promise *is* not through Torah-Law to·
Rm 4:14 ·void, and the promise has·been·fully·nullified.
2Pe 3:4 "Where is the promise of·his returning·Presence?
1Jn 2:25 And this is the promise that he·himself did·already·
G1860.2 N-NPF ἐπαγγελίαι (3x)
Gal 3:16 Now the promises were·uttered to·AbRaham and
Rm 9:4 and the ritual·ministry *to·God*, and the promises—
2Co 1:20 For as·many·as *are* God's promises, in him *is* the
G1860.2 N-ASF ἐπαγγελίαν (16x)
Lk 24:49 And behold, I·myself dispatch the Promise of·my
Ac 1:4 ·patiently·wait·around for·the Promise of·the Father,
Ac 2:33 of·God and·also receiving the Promise of·the Holy
Ac 13:23 From this·man's Seed, according·to promise, God
Ac 13:32 ·the·good·news, the promise occurring toward the
Ac 23:21 they·are ready, awaiting the promise from you."
Heb 9:15 ·forth may·receive the promise of·the eternal
Heb 10:36 ·God, yeu·may·subsequently·obtain the promise.
Heb 11:39 did·not subsequently·obtain the promise *yet*,
Gal 3:14 ·that we·may·receive the promise of·the Spirit
Gal 3:17 such·for it to·fully·nullify the promise.
Gal 3:29 Seed and *are* heirs according·to promise.
Rm 4:16 grace, in·order·for the promise to·be·steadfast to·
Rm 4:20 And in·regard·to the promise of·God, *AbRaham*
1Ti 4:8 ·for all·things, having promise of·life-above for·the
2Ti 1:1 will, according·to *the* promise of·life-above, the·one
G1860.2 N-APF ἐπαγγελίας (6x)
Heb 6:12 and long-suffering are·inheriting the promises.
Heb 7:6 and he·has·blessed the·one having the promises.
Heb 11:13 not receiving the promises, but·rather seeing
Heb 11:17 ·receiving the promises was·offering·up his only·
Rm 15:8 truth, in·order to·confirm the promises *made* to·the
2Co 7:1 Accordingly, having these promises, dearly·beloved
G1860.2 N-DSF ἐπαγγελίᾳ (1x)
Eph 6:2 ' (which is *the* first commandment with a·promise),
G1860.2 N-DPF ἐπαγγελίαις (1x)
Heb 8:6 has·been·enacted upon significantly·better promises.
G1860.2 N-GSF ἐπαγγελίας (17x)
Ac 7:17 ·as the time of·the promise was·drawing·near which
Ac 26:6 over *the* expectation of·the promise being·made by
Heb 4:1 with·a·promise being·left·behind *for·us* to·enter
Heb 6:15 after·patiently·waiting, he·obtained the promise.
Heb 6:17 to·the heirs of·promise the unalterable·nature of·
Heb 11:9 he·sojourned in the land of·promise as *in* an·
Heb 11:9 and Jacob, the co-heirs of·the same promise,
Gal 3:18 *it·is* no·longer as·a·result of·promise. But God
Gal 3:18 *the inheritance* to·AbRaham through promise.
Gal 4:23 ·out of·the free·woman *was* through the promise.
Gal 4:28 according·to YiTsaq, are children of·promise.
Rm 9:8 ·rather the children of·the promise are·reckoned for
Rm 9:9 For this *is* the word of·promise, "'According·to this
2Pe 3:9 is·not tardy *concerning* the promise, as some·men

Eph 1:13 ·sealed with·the Holy Spirit of·the promise,
Eph 2:12 foreigners from·the covenants of·the promise, not
Eph 3:6 and co-participants of·his promise in the
G1860.2 N-GPF ἐπαγγελιῶν (2x)
Heb 11:33 righteousness, obtained promises, stopped·up *the*
Gal 3:21 *is* the Torah-Law against the promises of·God?
EG1860.2 (3x)
Lk 1:72 to·continue *the promised* mercy with our fathers,
Ac 26:7 to which *promise* our twelve·tribes, in earnestness,
Gal 3:19 was·placed·alongside *the promise* only·until the

G1861 ἐπ•αγγέλλω êpangéllō *v.* (15x)
Roots:G1909 G0032 Compare:G5335
G1861.2 V-PNP-NPM ἐπαγγελλόμενοι (1x)
2Pe 2:19 *false·teachers* who·are·promising liberty to·them,
G1861.2 V-ADI-3S ἐπηγγείλατο (5x)
Ac 7:5 a·foot step, and·yet he·already·promised to·give it
Jac 1:12 which the Lord promised to·the·ones loving him.
Jac 2:5 ·the kingdom which he·promised to·the·ones loving
Tit 1:2 (the·one without·falsehood) promised before time
1Jn 2:25 promise that he·himself did·already·promise to·us:
G1861.2 V-ADP-ASM ἐπαγγειλάμενον (1x)
Heb 11:11 *him* trustworthy, the·one already·promising *it*.
G1861.2 V-ADP-NSM ἐπαγγειλάμενος (2x)
Heb 6:13 For God, after·promising to·AbRaham, since he·
Heb 10:23 ·slouching (for trustworthy *is* the·one promising).
G1861.2 V-ANI-3P ἐπηγγείλαντο (1x)
Mk 14:11 *this*, they·were·glad and promised to·give money
G1861.2 V-RNI-3S ἐπήγγελται (3x)
Heb 12:26 But now he·has·promised, saying, "Yet once·
Gal 3:19 for·whom *the inheritance* has·been·promised. *And*
Rm 4:21 ·assured that, what *God* has·promised, *God* was
G1861.3 V-PNP-DPF ἐπαγγελλομέναις (1x)
1Ti 2:10 ·for women who·are·making·a·profession·of a·).
G1861.3 V-PNP-NPM ἐπαγγελλόμενοι (1x)
1Ti 6:21 which some, who·are·making·a·profession *of·trust*,

G1862 ἐπ•άγγελμα êpángelma *n.* (2x)
Roots:G1861 Compare:G0728 G3866
G1862.2 N-NPN ἐπαγγέλματα (1x)
2Pe 1:4 the most·greatest and precious pledges, in·order·that
G1862.2 N-ASN ἐπάγγελμα (1x)
2Pe 3:13 according·to his pledge, we·intently·await ·a·

G1863 ἐπ•άγω êpágō *v.* (3x)
Roots:G1909 G0071
G1863 V-PAP-NPM ἐπάγοντες (1x)
2Pe 2:1 ·redeeming them, bringing·upon themselves abrupt
G1863 V-2AAN ἐπαγαγεῖν (1x)
Ac 5:28 instruction, and yeu·resolve to·bring the blood of·
G1863 V-AAP-NSM ἐπάξας (1x)
2Pe 2:5 of·righteousness, after·bringing a·Deluge upon a·

G1864 ἐπ•αγωνίζομαι êpagōnízômai *v.* (1x)
Roots:G1909 G0075
G1864 V-PNN ἐπαγωνίζεσθαι (1x)
Jud 1:3 exhorting *yeu* to·strenuously·struggle·for the trust

G1865 ἐπ•αθροίζω êpathrôízō *v.* (1x)
Roots:G1909 G0119-1 Compare:G4816 See:G4867
G1865 V-PPP-GPM ἐπαθροιζομένων (1x)
Lk 11:29 with·the crowds being·amassed·together, he·began

G1866 Ἐπ•αίνετος Êpaínêtôs *n/p.* (1x)
Roots:G1867
G1866.2 N/P-ASM Ἐπαίνετον (1x)
Rm 16:5 Greet my well-beloved Epaenetus, who is a·

G1867 ἐπ•αινέω êpainéō *v.* (6x)
Roots:G1909 G0134 See:G1866
G1867 V-PAI-1S ἐπαινῶ (3x)
1Co 11:2 Now I·applaud yeu, brothers, that yeu·have·been·
1Co 11:17 in·this charging, I·do·not applaud *yeu*, because
1Co 11:22 ·I·applaud yeu in this? I·do·not applaud *yeu*.
G1867 V-AAI-3S ἐπῄνεσεν (1x)
Lk 16:8 "And the lord applauded the unjust estate·manager,
G1867 V-AAM-2P ἐπαινέσατε (1x)
Rm 15:11 all the Gentiles! And applaud him, all the
G1867 V-AAS-1S ἐπαινέσω (1x)
1Co 11:22 should·I·declare to·yeu? Should·I·applaud yeu in

G1868 ἔπ•αινος épainôs *n.* (11x)
Roots:G1909 G0134 Compare:G0136 See:G0133 xLangAlso:H8416
G1868.1 N-NSM ἔπαινος (4x)
Rm 2:29 not in·letter— whose high·praise *is* not from·out
Php 4:8 and if *there·is* any high·praise, take·a·reckoning·of
1Co 4:5 And then the high·praise from God shall·come·to·
2Co 8:18 him the brother, whose high·praise *is* in the good·
G1868.1 N-ASM ἔπαινον (7x)
Rm 13:3 and you·shall·have high·praise from·among *the*
Php 1:11 Anointed, to *the* glory and high·praise of·God.
1Pe 1:7 fire) may·be·found in high·praise and honor and
1Pe 2:14 and *for the* high·praise of·beneficially·good·doers.
Eph 1:6 for a·glorious high·praise of·his grace— in which
Eph 1:12 *Redeemed-Kinsmen*, for a·high·praise of·his glory,
Eph 1:14 acquired·possession, for a·high·praise of·his glory.

G1869 ἐπ•αίρω êpaírō *v.* (19x)
Roots:G1909 G0142 Compare:G5229 G5312 xLangEquiv:H5375 xLangAlso:H7311
G1869.1 V-PAP-APM ἐπαίροντας (1x)
1Ti 2:8 ·pray in every place, lifting·up divinely·holy hands,
G1869.1 V-PMP-ASN ἐπαιρόμενον (1x)
2Co 10:5 elevated·thing *that* is·lifting·itself·up against the
G1869.1 V-AAI-3S ἐπῆρεν (3x)
Jn 13:18 chewing the bread with me lifted·up his heel against
Jn 17:1 Jesus spoke these·things and lifted·up his eyes to the
Ac 2:14 together with·the eleven, lifted·up his voice and
G1869.1 V-AAI-3P ἐπῆραν (2x)
Ac 14:11 ·seeing what Paul did, they·lifted·up their voices,
Ac 22:22 this word, and *then* they·lifted·up their voices,
G1869.1 V-AAM-2P ἐπάρατε (2x)
Jn 4:35 ? Behold, I·say to·yeu, lift·up yeur eyes and
Lk 21:28 pull·yourself·up·straight and lift·up yeur heads,
G1869.1 V-AAN ἐπᾶραι (1x)
Lk 18:13 ·a·distance, was·not willing to·lift·up not·even his
G1869.1 V-AAP-NSF ἐπάρασα (1x)
Lk 11:27 from·among the crowd, lifting·up her·voice,
G1869.1 V-AAP-NSM ἐπάρας (4x)
Jn 6:5 So·then, after·lifting·up the eyes and surveying that a·
Lk 6:20 And lifting·up his eyes to his disciples, he·was·
Lk 16:23 And in Hades, after·lifting·up his eyes while·
Lk 24:50 as·far·as to BethAny, and lifting·up his hands, he·
G1869.1 V-AAP-NPM ἐπάραντες (1x)
Mt 17:8 And lifting·up their eyes, they·saw not·even·one·
G1869.1 V-API-3S ἐπήρθη (1x)
Ac 1:9 with·them looking·on, he·was·lifted·up, and a·
G1869.2 V-AAP-NPM ἐπάραντες (1x)
Ac 27:40 rudder cables, and upon·hoisting the topsail to·the
G1869.3 V-PMI-3S ἐπαίρεται (1x)
2Co 11:20 *from·yeu*, if anyone exalts·himself, if anyone

G1870 ἐπ•αισχύνομαι êpaischýnômai *v.* (11x)
Roots:G1909 G0153
G1870 V-FOI-3S ἐπαισχυνθήσεται (2x)
Lk 9:26 the Son of·Clay·Man† shall·be·ashamed·of that·man
Mk 8:38 Son of·Clay·Man† also shall·be·ashamed·of him,
G1870 V-PNI-1S ἐπαισχύνομαι (2x)
Rm 1:16 For I·am·not ashamed·of the good·news of·the
2Ti 1:12 But·yet I·am·not ashamed, for I·have·seen in·whom
G1870 V-PNI-2P ἐπαισχύνεσθε (1x)
Rm 6:21 those·things·of·which now yeu·are·ashamed? For
G1870 V-PNI-3S ἐπαισχύνεται (2x)
Heb 2:11 *YeShua the Initiator* is·not ashamed to·call them
Heb 11:16 Therefore God is·not ashamed·of them, *or* to·be·
G1870 V-AOS-2S ἐπαισχυνθῇς (1x)
2Ti 1:8 you·should·not be·ashamed·of the testimony of·our
G1870 V-AOS-3S ἐπαισχυνθῇ (2x)
Lk 9:26 "For whoever would be·ashamed·of me and my
Mk 8:38 "For whoever would be·ashamed·of me and of·my
G1870 V-API-3S ἐπῃσχύνθη (1x)
2Ti 1:16 me, and he·was·not ashamed of·my chain.

G1871 ἐπ•αιτέω êpaitéō *v.* (1x)
Roots:G1909 G0154
G1871 V-PAN ἐπαιτεῖν (1x)
Lk 16:3 ·strength to·dig; I·am·ashamed to·ask·for·charity.

G1872 ἐπ•α•κολουθέω êpakôlôuthéō *v.* (5x)
Roots:G1909 G0190
G1872.1 V-PAI-3P ἐπακολουθοῦσιν (1x)
1Ti 5:24 also for·some *men·of·clay*†, they·follow·afterward.
G1872.1 V-PAP-GPN ἐπακολουθούντων (1x)
Mk 16:20 the signs following·afterward. So·be·it,·Amen)].
G1872.1 V-AAS-2P ἐπακολουθήσητε (1x)
1Pe 2:21 ·us in·order·that yeu·should·follow·afterward in·his
EG1872.1 (1x)
1Ti 5:25 able to·be·hidden, *likewise following·afterward*.
G1872.2 V-AAI-3S ἐπηκολούθησεν (1x)
1Ti 5:10 *and* if she·diligently·followed·through in·every

G1873 ἐπ•ακούω êpakôúō *v.* (1x)
Roots:G1909 G0191
G1873 V-AAI-1S ἐπήκουσα (1x)
2Co 6:2 he·says, "'I·favorably·heard you in·an·acceptable

G1874 ἐπ•ακροάομαι êpakrôáômai *v.* (1x)
Roots:G1909 G0202
G1874 V-INI-3P ἐπηκροῶντο (1x)
Ac 16:25 chained·prisoners were·intently·listening·to them.

G1875 ἐπ•άν êpán *conj.* (3x)
Roots:G1909 G0302
G1875 CONJ ἐπάν (3x)
Lk 11:22 "But whenever the·one stronger·than him should·
Lk 11:34 eye. Accordingly, whenever your eye should·be
Mt 2:8 the little·child; and whenever yeu·should·find *him*,

G1876 ἐπ•άν•αγκες êpánankês *adv.* (1x)
Roots:G1909 G0318
G1876 ADV ἐπάναγκες (1x)
Ac 15:28 a·larger burden besides these·things of·necessity:

G1877 ἐπ•αν•άγω êpanágō *v.* (3x)
Roots:G1909 G0321
G1877.2 V-2AAM-2S ἐπανάγαγε (1x)
Lk 5:4 he·declared to Simon, "Head·off into the deep and
G1877.2 V-2AAN ἐπαναγαγεῖν (1x)
Lk 5:3 *Jesus* asked·of him to·head·off a·little·way from the
G1877.3 V-PAP-NSM ἐπανάγων (1x)
Mt 21:18 And heading·back into the City with·the·break·of·

G1878 ἐπ•ανα•μιμνήσκω êpanamimnḗskō *v.* (1x)
Roots:G1909 G0363
G1878 V-PAP-NSM ἐπαναμιμνήσκων (1x)
Rm 15:15 to·yeu in part as once·again·reminding yeu, on·

G1879 ἐπ•ανα•παύομαι êpanapaúômai *v.* (2x)
Roots:G1909 G0373 Compare:G1945
G1879.2 V-FDI-3S ἐπαναπαύσεται (1x)
Lk 10:6 should·be there, yeur peace shall·rest upon it. But·
G1879.3 V-PNI-2S ἐπαναπαύῃ (1x)
Rm 2:17 ·yourself a·Jew, and you·rely·upon the Torah-Law,

G1880 ἐπ•αν•έρχομαι êpanérchômai *v.* (2x)
Roots:G1909 G0424
G1880 V-PNN ἐπανέρχεσθαι (1x)
Lk 10:35 spend·further, when I come·back, I·myself shall·
G1880 V-2AAN ἐπανελθεῖν (1x)
Lk 19:15 with him coming·back after·receiving the

G1881 ἐπ•αν•ίσταμαι êpanístamai *v.* (2x)
Roots:G1909 G0450
G1881.1 V-FDI-3P ἐπαναστήσονται (2x)
Mt 10:21 child, and children shall·rise·up against parents
Mk 13:12 child; and children shall·rise·up against *their*

G1882 ἐπ•αν•όρθωσις êpanórthōsis *n.* (1x)
Roots:G1909 G0461
G1882.1 N-ASF ἐπανόρθωσιν (1x)
2Ti 3:16 for reproof, for setting·straight, *and* for education·

G1883 ἐπ•άνω êpánō *adv.* (20x)
Roots:G1909 G0507
G1883.2 ADV ἐπάνω (1x)
Mt 5:14 ·city that·is·being·set·out high·upon a·mount is·not

G1883.3 ADV ἐπάνω (3x)
Mt 21:7 and they·put their garments up·over them and seated
Mt 21:7 up·over them and seated *him* up·over those.
Mt 27:37 Then up·over his head, they·placed the cause of·his
G1883.4 ADV ἐπάνω (3x)
Jn 3:31 "The·one who·is·coming from·above is up·above all.
Jn 3:31 ·is·coming from·out of·the heaven is up·above all.
Mt 2:9 going·*on* until it·stood·still up·above where the
G1883.5 ADV ἐπάνω (1x)
Mt 28:2 the stone from the door and sat·down on·top of·it.
G1883.6 ADV ἐπάνω (2x)
Mk 14:5 to·be·sold·off for·upwards·of three·hundred denarii
1Co 15:6 he·was·gazed·upon by·upwards·of five·hundred
G1883.7 ADV ἐπάνω (6x)
Lk 10:19 the authority, the·one to·trample upon serpents and
Mt 23:18 by the present, the·one upon it, he·is·obligated.
Mt 23:20 ·Altar, swears by it and by all the·things upon it.
Mt 23:22 ·God and by the·one who·is·sitting·down upon it.
Rv 6:8 horse and the·one who·is·sitting·down upon it, his
Rv 20:3 up, and set·an·official·seal upon him, in·order·that
G1883.8 ADV ἐπάνω (4x)
Lk 4:39 And standing·forward over her, he·reprimanded the
Lk 11:44 and the·men·of·clay† walking over *them* have·not
Lk 19:17 in very·little, be having authority over ten cities.'
Lk 19:19 'Be you also over five cities.'

G1884 ἐπ•αρκέω ēparkéō *v.* (3x)
Roots:G1909 G0714
G1884 V-PAM-3S ἐπαρκείτω (1x)
1Ti 5:16 has solitary·widows, let·them·give·relief to·them,
G1884 V-AAI-3S ἐπήρκεσεν (1x)
1Ti 5:10 feet, if she·gave·relief to·those·being·hard-pressed,
G1884 V-AAS-3S ἐπαρκέσῃ (1x)
1Ti 5:16 in·order·that it·may·give·relief to·the·ones *that·are*

G1885 ἐπ•αρχία ēparchía *n.* (2x)
Roots:G1885-1
G1885.2 N-DSF ἐπαρχίᾳ (1x)
Ac 25:1 days after walking·over into·the province, Festus
G1885.2 N-GSF ἐπαρχίας (1x)
Ac 23:34 inquired from·which province he·was birthed. And

G1886 ἔπ•αυλις épaulis *n.* (1x)
Roots:G1909 G0833 Compare:G1430 G3614 G3624 G2732 G2733 G0833 See:G4259 xLangAlso:H2918 H2691 H1002
G1886 N-NSF ἔπαυλις (1x)
Ac 1:20 "Let his walled-off·mansion become desolate, and

G1887 ἐπ•αύριον ēpaúriôn *adv.* (17x)
Roots:G1909 G0839 Compare:G0839 G1836 See:G2250
G1887 ADV ἐπαύριον (17x)
Jn 1:29 On·the next·day, John looks·at Jesus, who·is·
Jn 1:35 Again, on·the next·day, John stood also *with* two
Jn 1:43 On·the next·day, Jesus determined to·go·forth into
Jn 6:22 On·the next·day, the crowd— the·one standing on·
Jn 12:12 On·the next·day, a·large crowd (the·one coming to
Ac 10:9 On·the next·day, with·those *household·servants*
Ac 10:23 *them.* And on·the next·day, Peter went·forth
Ac 10:24 And on·the next·day, they·entered into Caesarea.
Ac 14:20 city, and on·the next·day he·went·forth together
Ac 20:7 intending to·go·onward on·the next·day; and he·
Ac 21:8 And on·the next·day, the·ones in·company·with
Ac 22:30 On·the next·day, being·resolved to·know the
Ac 23:32 On·the next·day, *the soldiers* returned·back to the
Ac 25:6 to Caesarea, on·the next·day, after·sitting·down on
Ac 25:23 So·then on·the next·day, with·AgrIppa and BerNiki
Mt 27:62 And on·the next·day, which is after the
Mk 11:12 And on·the next·day, with·them coming·forth

G1888 ἐπ•αυτο•φώρῳ ēpautôphṓrō *adv.* (1x)
Roots:G1909 G0846
G1888.2 ADV ἐπαυτοφώρῳ (1x)
Jn 8:4 *while* being·in·adultery, in·the·actual·crime·itself.

G1889 Ἐπ•αφρᾶς Êpaphrâs *n/p.* (3x)
Roots:G1891
G1889.2 N/P-NSM Ἐπαφρᾶς (2x)
Col 4:12 EpAphras, the·one from·among yeu, a·slave of·
Phm 1:23 *These·men* greet you: EpAphras, my fellow·
G1889.2 N/P-GSM Ἐπαφρᾶ (1x)
Col 1:7 just·as also yeu·learned *it* from EpAphras, our dear

G1890 ἐπ•αφρίζω ēpaphrízō *v.* (1x)
Roots:G1909 G0875
G1890.1 V-PAP-NPN ἐπαφρίζοντα (1x)
Jud 1:13 of·the·sea presently·foaming·upon their·own shame

G1891 Ἐπ•αφρόδιτος Êpaphrốditôs *n/p.* (2x)
Roots:G1909 Compare:G1889
G1891.2 N/P-ASM Ἐπαφρόδιτον (1x)
Php 2:25 necessary to·send to yeu EpAphroditus, my brother
G1891.2 N/P-GSM Ἐπαφροδίτου (1x)
Php 4:18 personally·from EpAphroditus the·things *which·*

G1892 ἐπ•εγείρω ēpēgeírō *v.* (2x)
Roots:G1909 G1453 Compare:G2042 xLangAlso:H6965
G1892.1 V-AAI-3P ἐπήγειραν (2x)
Ac 13:50 and they·roused·up persecution against Paul and
Ac 14:2 being·obstinate, roused·up and harmfully·affected

G1893 ἐπ•εί êpeî *conj.* (27x)
Roots:G1909 G1487 Compare:G0575 G1512 See:G1894 G1895 G1897
G1893.2 CONJ ἐπεί (17x)
Jn 13:29 *of·them* were·presuming, since Judas was·holding
Jn 19:31 In·due·course, since it·was preparation·day, in·
Lk 1:34 this be, since I·do·not have·intimate·knowledge·of
Lk 7:1 And since *Jesus* fully·finished all his utterances in the
Heb 2:14 Accordingly, since the little·children have·a·
Heb 4:6 Now·then, since it·is·still·remaining *for* some to·
Heb 5:2 and being·led·astray, since he·himself also is·beset·
Heb 5:11 *to·yeu* since yeu·have·become bastardly·slothful
Heb 6:13 to·AbRaham, since he·was·having no·one·at·all
Heb 9:17 after men·are·dead, since not·at·any·time *is·it* in·
Heb 11:11 of·maturity, since she·resolutely·considered *him*
Mt 18:32 all that indebtedness, since you·implored *of* me.
Mt 27:6 them into the Temple·Treasury, since it·is *the* price
Mk 15:42 ·evening occurring, since it·was preparation·day
1Co 14:12 *with* yeu·yeurselves. Since yeu·are zealots of·
2Co 11:18 Since many boast according·to the flesh, I·also
2Co 13:3 since yeu·seek a·proof of·the Anointed-One
G1893.3 CONJ ἐπεί (10x)
Heb 9:26 Otherwise, it·was·mandatory·for him to·already·
Heb 10:2 Otherwise, ¿! would·they not have·ceased being·
Rm 3:6 May·it·never happen! Otherwise how·does God
Rm 11:6 no·longer as·a·result of·works, otherwise the grace
Rm 11:6 *then* it·is no·longer grace, otherwise the work is
Rm 11:22 benevolent·kindness. Otherwise, you·yourself
1Co 5:10 or with·idolaters. Otherwise, by·inference, yeu·
1Co 7:14 ·holy by the husband; otherwise yeur children are
1Co 14:16 Otherwise when you·should·bless with·the spirit,
1Co 15:29 Otherwise what shall·they·do, the·ones being·

G1894 ἐπ•ει•δή êpeidḗ *conj.* (11x)
Roots:G1893 G1211 See:G1895
G1894.1 CONJ ἐπειδή (6x)
Ac 13:46 to·be·spoken to·yeu, but since·now yeu·shove it
Ac 14:12 Paul, Hermes, since·now he·himself was the·one
Ac 15:24 Since·now *that* we·heard that certain·men going·
Mt 21:46 they·feared the crowds, since·now *the crowds*
Php 2:26 since·now he·was greatly·yearning·for yeu all, and
1Co 14:16 since·now he·does·not personally·know what
G1894.2 CONJ ἐπειδή (1x)
Lk 11:6 since·just·now a·friend of·mine came·directly to·me
G1894.3 CONJ ἐπειδή (4x)
1Co 1:21 For whereas (by the wisdom of·God) the world
1Co 1:22 And whereas Jews request a·sign, and·also Greeks
1Co 15:21 For whereas through a·man·of·clay† *came* the
2Co 5:4 being·weighed·down, whereas we·do·not want to·

G1895 ἐπ•ει•δή•περ êpeidḗpêr *conj.* (1x)
Roots:G1894 G4007 Compare:G1897
G1895 CONJ ἐπειδήπερ (1x)
Lk 1:1 Since·indeed many took·it·upon·themselves to·fully·

G1896 ἐπ•εῖδον êpeîdôn *v.* (2x)
ἔπιδε épidê
[and other moods and persons of the same tense]
Roots:G1492 G1909 Compare:G0991 G4337
G1896 V-2AAI-3S ἐπεῖδεν (1x)
Lk 1:25 in *the* days when he·took·notice·of *me*, to·remove
G1896 V-2AAM-2S ἔπιδε (1x)
Ac 4:29 And at·the present, O·Yahweh, take·notice·of their

G1897 ἐπ•εί•περ êpeípêr *conj.* (1x)
Roots:G1893 G4007 Compare:G1895
G1897 CONJ ἐπείπερ (1x)
Rm 3:30 since·indeed *it·is* one God who, *from·among both*,

G1898 ἐπ•εισ•αγωγή êpeisagōgḗ *n.* (1x)
Roots:G1909 G1521
G1898 N-NSF ἐπεισαγωγή (1x)
Heb 7:19 but *the* superseding·introduction of·a·significantly·

G1899 ἔπ•ειτα épêita *adv.* (17x)
Roots:G1909 G1534
G1899.1 ADV ἔπειτα (2x)
Gal 1:21 Afterward, I·came into the vicinities of·Syria and
1Co 15:23 a·firstfruit— afterward, the·ones of·
EG1899.1 (1x)
Lk 11:14 Now *afterward*, *Jesus* was casting·out a·demon,
G1899.2 ADV ἔπειτα (6x)
Lk 16:7 After·that, he·declared to·another, 'And you, how·
Heb 7:2 King of·Righteousness," and after·that also "King
1Th 4:17 After·that, we·ourselves (the·ones living, the·ones
1Co 12:28 third instructors, after·that *the·ones operating·in*
1Co 15:6 After·that, he·was·gazed·upon by·upwards·of five·
1Co 15:7 After·that, he·was·gazed·upon by·Jacob, *and* then
G1899.3 ADV ἔπειτα (6x)
Jn 11:7 Then after that he·says to·the disciples, "We·should·
Gal 1:18 Then after three years, I·went·up to JeruSalem to·
Gal 2:1 Then after fourteen years, I·walked·up again to
Mk 7:5 Then the Pharisees and the scribes inquired·of him,
Jac 3:17 in·fact, morally·clean, then peaceable, fair *and*
Jac 4:14 just·for a·brief·moment and then being·expunged.
G1899.4 ADV ἔπειτα (2x)
Heb 7:27 ·failures, *and* then·afterward *on·behalf* of·the·ones
1Co 15:46 but·rather the soulish, then·afterward the spiritual

G1900 ἐπ•έκεινα êpêkêina *adv.* (1x)
Roots:G1909 G1565 Compare:G5238 G4008 G5228 xLangAlso:H1973
G1900.3 ADV ἐπέκεινα (1x)
Ac 7:43 And I·shall·exile yeu far·beyond Babylon.⇒

G1901 ἐπ•εκ•τείνομαι êpêktêínômai *v.* (1x)
Roots:G1909 G1614
G1901 V-PMP-NSM ἐπεκτεινόμενος (1x)
Php 3:13 and stretching·myself·toward the·things ahead,

G1902 ἐπ•εν•δύομαι êpêndýômai *v.* (2x)
Roots:G1909 G1746 See:G1903
G1902 V-AMN ἐπενδύσασθαι (2x)
2Co 5:2 greatly·yearning to·fully·dress·ourselves·with our
2Co 5:4 but·rather to·fully·dress·ourselves in·order·that the

G1903 ἐπ•εν•δύτης êpêndýtēs *n.* (1x)
Roots:G1902 Compare:G1742 G2440
G1903.2 N-ASF ἐπενδύτην (1x)
Jn 21:7 Peter tightly·girded *his* fishing·coat *about·himself*

G1904 ἐπ•έρχομαι êpérchômai *v.* (10x)
Roots:G1909 G2064
G1904.1 V-FDI-3S ἐπελεύσεται (2x)
Lk 1:35 to·her, "Holy Spirit shall·come upon you, and *the*
Lk 21:35 "For as·a·snare it·shall·come upon all the·ones
G1904.1 V-PNP-DPF ἐπερχομέναις (1x)
Jac 5:1 over yeur miseries, the·ones coming·upon *yeu*.
G1904.1 V-PNP-DPM ἐπερχομένοις (1x)
Eph 2:7 ·that he·may·indicate in the upcoming ages the
G1904.1 V-PNP-GPM ἐπερχομένων (1x)
Lk 21:26 ·of·the·things which·are·coming·upon The Land,
G1904.1 V-2AAI-3P ἐπῆλθον (1x)
Ac 14:19 And *certain* Jews came·up from Antiochia and

Εε

G1904.1 V-2AAP-GSN ἐπελθόντος (1x)

Ac 1:8 power, with·the Holy Spirit coming·upon yeu, and

G1904.1 V-2AAP-NSM ἐπελθών (1x)

Lk 11:22 ·conquer him after·coming·upon *him forcefully*, he·

G1904.1 V-2AAS-3S ἐπέλθῃ (2x)

Ac 8:24 ·which yeu·have·declared should·come upon me."

Ac 13:40 look·out, lest it·should·come upon yeu, the·thing

G1905 ἐπ•ερωτάω êpêrōtáō *v.* (61x)

Roots:G1909 G2065 Compare:G4441 G0154 xLangAlso:H7592

G1905 V-FAI-1S ἐπερωτήσω (2x)

Lk 6:9 to them, "I·shall·inquire·of yeu. Which·thing is·

Mk 11:29 declared to·them, "I·shall·inquire·of yeu also one

G1905 V-PAI-2S ἐπερωτᾷς (1x)

Jn 18:21 Why·do you·inquire·of me?

G1905 V-PAI-3P ἐπερωτῶσιν (1x)

Mk 7:5 the Pharisees and the scribes inquired·of him, "Why·

G1905 V-PAM-3P ἐπερωτάτωσαν (1x)

1Co 14:35 they·must·inquire·of their·own menfolk at home

G1905 V-PAN ἐπερωτᾶν (1x)

Lk 20:40 were·they·daring to·inquire·of him not·even·one·

G1905 V-PAP-ASM ἐπερωτῶντα (1x)

Lk 2:46 both listening·to them and inquiring·of them.

G1905 V-PAP-DPM ἐπερωτῶσιν (1x)

Rm 10:20 ·made manifest to·the·ones not inquiring·of me."

G1905 V-IAI-3S ἐπηρώτα (8x)

Lk 23:9 And he·was·inquiring·of him with a·significant·

Mk 5:9 And he·was·inquiring·of him, "What *is* your name?

Mk 8:5 And he·was·inquiring·of them, "How·many loaves·

Mk 8:23 hands upon·him, *Jesus* was·inquiring·of him if he·

Mk 8:27 along the way, he·was·inquiring·of his disciples,

Mk 9:33 ·being in the home, he·was·inquiring·of them,

Mk 10:17 and kneeling·down·to him, was·inquiring·of him,

Mk 14:61 the designated·high·priest was·inquiring·of him,

G1905 V-IAI-3P ἐπηρώτων (9x)

Lk 3:10 And the crowds were·inquiring·of him, saying, "So·

Lk 3:14 And army·officers also were·inquiring·of him,

Lk 8:9 And his disciples were·inquiring·of him, saying,

Lk 22:64 his face, and were·inquiring·of him, saying,

Ac 1:6 after·coming·together, they·were·inquiring·of him,

Mk 7:17 his disciples were·inquiring·of him concerning the

Mk 9:11 And they·were·inquiring·of him, saying, "Why·do

Mk 9:28 into a·house, his disciples were·inquiring·of him in

Mk 13:3 John and Andrew were·inquiring·of him privately,

G1905 V-AAI-3S ἐπηρώτησεν (18x)

Jn 18:7 So·then he·inquired·of them again, "Whom·do yeu·

Lk 8:30 And Jesus inquired·of him, saying, "What is your

Lk 9:18 with·him. And he·inquired·of them, saying, "Who·

Lk 18:18 And a·certain ruler inquired·of him, saying,

Lk 18:40 and with·him drawing·near, *Jesus* inquired·of him,

Lk 23:3 And Pilate inquired·of him, saying, "Are you·

Lk 23:6 "Galilee," inquired whether the man·of·clay† was

Ac 5:27 And the designated·high·priest inquired·of them,

Mt 22:35 *who·was* an·expert·in·Torah-Law, inquired·of *him*,

Mt 22:41 ·been·gathered·together, YeShua inquired·of them,

Mt 27:11 And the governor inquired·of him, saying, "Are

Mk 9:16 Then he·inquired·of the scribes, "What·do yeu·

Mk 9:21 And *Jesus* inquired·of his father, "About how·long

Mk 12:28 that he·answered them well, inquired·of him,

Mk 14:60 ·up in the midst, inquired·of Jesus, saying, "Do·

Mk 15:2 And Pilate inquired·of him, "Are you·yourself the

Mk 15:4 And Pilate inquired·of him again, saying, "Do·you·

Mk 15:44 the Roman·centurion, he·inquired·of him whether

G1905 V-AAI-3P ἐπηρώτησαν (10x)

Lk 20:21 And they·inquired·of him, saying, "Mentor, we·

Lk 20:27 *that* there·is not a·resurrection) inquired·of him,

Lk 21:7 And they·inquired·of him, saying, "So·then Mentor,

Mt 12:10 ·may·legally·accuse him, they·inquired·of him,

Mt 16:1 and Sadducees inquired·of him to·fully·exhibit for·

Mt 17:10 And his disciples inquired·of him, saying, "So·

Mt 22:23 not to·be a·resurrection, and they·inquired·of him,

Mk 10:2 to·try him, the Pharisees inquired·of him, "Is·it·

Mk 10:10 in the home, his disciples inquired·of him again

Mk 12:18 not to·be a·resurrection, and they·inquired·of him,

G1905 V-AAM-2S ἐπερώτησον (1x)

Jn 18:21 ·inquire·of me? Inquire·of the·ones having·heard

G1905 V-AAN ἐπερωτῆσαι (3x)

Mt 22:46 ·did anyone dare any·longer to·inquire·of him from

Mk 9:32 the utterance and were·afraid to·inquire·of him.

Mk 12:34 ·one was·daring any·longer to·inquire·of him.

G1905 V-AAP-NSM ἐπερωτήσας (1x)

Ac 23:34 the governor inquired from·which province he·

G1905 V-APP-NSM ἐπερωτηθείς (1x)

Lk 17:20 Now after·being·inquired·of by the Pharisees *as·to*

EG1905 (2x)

2Co 8:23 If *any·should·inquire* concerning Titus, *he·is* my

2Co 8:23 ·to yeu, or·if our brothers *be·inquired·of, they·are*

G1906 ἐπ•ερώτημα êpêrṓtēma *n.* (1x)

Roots:G1905

G1906 N-NSN ἐπερώτημα (1x)

1Pe 3:21 ·filth, but·rather an·inquiry of·a·beneficially·good

G1907 ἐπ•έχω êpéchō *v.* (5x)

Roots:G1909 G2192 Compare:G4337 See:G3563

G1907.2 V-PAP-NPM ἐπέχοντες (1x)

Php 2:16 holding·forward *the* Redemptive-word of·life-above

G1907.4 V-PAM-2S ἔπεχε (1x)

1Ti 4:16 Pay·close·attention to·yourself, and·also to·the

G1907.4 V-PAP-NSM ἐπέχων (1x)

Lk 14:7 paying·close·attention how they·were·selecting the

G1907.4 V-IAI-3S ἐπεῖχεν (1x)

Ac 3:5 And he·was·paying·close·attention to·them,

G1907.5 V-2AAI-3S ἐπέσχεν (1x)

Ac 19:22 and Erastus, he·himself held·back in Asia for·a·

G1908 ἐπ•ηρεάζω êpērêázō *v.* (3x)

Roots:G1909

G1908.1 V-PAP-GPM ἐπηρεαζόντων (2x)

Lk 6:28 on·behalf·of·the·ones abusively·threatening yeu.

Mt 5:44 on·behalf·of·the·ones abusively·threatening yeu and

G1908.2 V-PAP-NPM ἐπηρεάζοντες (1x)

1Pe 3:16 the·ones abusively·maligning yeur beneficially·

G1909 ἐπί êpí *prep.* (885x)

ἐπ- êp- [alternate prefix]

ἐφ- êph- [soft prefix]

Compare:G4314 G5228 See:G0846 xLangAlso:H5921 HFP20

G1909.1 PREP ἐπ΄ (278x)

Jn 1:32 out of·heaven like a·dove, and he·abided upon him.

Jn 1:33 ·one declared to·me, 'Upon whom you·should·see

Jn 1:33 descending, and remaining upon him, the·same is

Jn 1:51 ascending and descending' upon the Son of·Clay·

Jn 3:36 but·rather the wrath of·God does·remain upon him."

Jn 4:27 And his disciples came upon this, and they·marveled

Jn 6:2 ·signs which he·was·doing upon the·ones being·sick.

Jn 6:21 the sailboat came·to·be upon the dry·ground for

Jn 9:15 ·declared to·them, "He·put clay upon my eyes, and

Jn 11:38 it·was a·cave, and a·stone was·resting upon it.

Jn 12:15 comes *to·you*, sitting·down upon a·donkey's colt."

Jn 13:25 Then this·one, falling·back upon Jesus' chest, says

Jn 18:4 ·seen all the·things that·were·coming upon him,

Jn 19:24 ·themselves, and they·cast lots upon my attire." In·

Jn 19:31 the bodies should·not remain upon the cross on the

Jn 20:7 and the sweat·towel that was upon his head, *that* it·

Jn 21:11 walked·up and drew the net upon the dry·ground,

Jn 21:20 Jesus loved, who also sat·back upon his chest at the

Lk 1:12 ·troubled after·seeing *him*, and fear fell upon him.

Lk 1:35 "Holy Spirit shall·come upon you, and *the* power of·

Lk 1:48 Because 'he·kindly·looked upon the humble·estate

Lk 2:25 And Holy Spirit was upon him.

Lk 2:40 And God's grace was upon him.

Lk 3:20 he·added even this upon all *these*·things— that he·

Lk 3:22 in·a·bodily shape like a·dove upon him, and a·voice

Lk 4:4 "The man·of·clay† shall·live not upon bread alone,

Lk 4:4 upon bread alone, but·rather upon every utterance of·

Lk 4:11 "They·shall·lift you upon *their* palms, lest·at·any·

Lk 4:18 Yahweh's Spirit *is* upon me for·the·cause·of which

Lk 4:36 And amazement came·to·be upon everyone, and

Lk 5:11 And mooring the sailboats upon the dry·ground,

Lk 5:18 carrying a·man·of·clay† upon a·simple·couch who

Lk 5:24 Son of·Clay·Man† has authority upon the earth to·

Lk 5:36 *from* a·brand-new garment upon an·old garment;

Lk 6:48 it, for it·had·been·founded upon the solid·rock.

Lk 8:6 "And other *seed* fell upon the solid·rock, and once·

Lk 8:13 "And the·ones upon the solid·rock, whenever they·

Lk 8:27 And with·him going·forth upon the dry·ground,

Lk 9:38 I·petition you, kindly·look upon my son, because

Lk 10:6 ·be there, yeur peace shall·rest upon it. But·if·not,

Lk 10:19 serpents and scorpions, and upon all the power of·

Lk 10:34 And mounting him upon his·own beast, he·brought

Lk 10:35 "And going·forth upon the stirring·of·day, casting·

Lk 11:20 the kingdom of·God has·already·come upon yeu.

Lk 12:3 shall·be·officially·proclaimed upon the rooftops.

Lk 13:4 "Or those eighteen, upon whom the tower in Siloam

Lk 15:5 ·then after·finding *it*, he·puts *it* upon his shoulders,

Lk 15:20 ·then running, he·affectionately·fell upon his neck

Lk 17:31 that day, whoever shall·be upon the rooftop, with

Lk 19:4 he·climbed·up upon a·mulberry-fig·tree in·order·

Lk 19:35 and flinging their·own garments upon the colt,

Lk 19:43 "Because days shall·come upon you, and your

Lk 19:44 and they·shall·not leave in you stone upon stone,

Lk 20:18 "Anyone falling upon that stone shall·be·dashed·

Lk 20:18 shall·be·dashed·to·pieces; but upon whomever it·

Lk 21:6 there·shall·not be·left a·stone upon a·stone that

Lk 21:23 For there·shall·be great dire·need upon the land

Lk 21:25 and constellations·of·stars. And upon the earth

Lk 21:35 For as·a·snare it·shall·come upon all the·ones who·

Lk 22:44 like clots of·blood dropping·down upon the soil.

Lk 23:48 convening·publicly upon that distinct·spectacle,

Lk 24:49 the Promise of·my Father upon yeu, but yeu·

Ac 1:26 and the lot fell upon Matthias. And he·was·fully·

Ac 2:3 to·them, and it·settled upon each one of·them.

Ac 2:17 *that* I·shall·pour·forth from my Spirit upon all flesh,

Ac 2:18 And in those days, upon my male·slaves and upon

Ac 2:18 upon my male·slaves and upon my female·slaves, I·

Ac 4:33 ·the Lord Jesus, and great grace was upon them all.

Ac 5:5 And great reverent·fear came upon all the·ones

Ac 5:11 And great reverent·fear came upon all the Called·

Ac 5:11 all the Called·Out·citizenry, and upon all the·ones

Ac 5:18 and they·threw their hands upon the ambassadors

Ac 5:28 to·bring the blood of·this man·of·clay† upon us."

Ac 7:23 ·fulfilled in·him, it·ascended upon his heart to·visit

Ac 7:57 and impulsively·dashed upon him with·the·same·

Ac 8:16 he·was having·fallen upon not·even·one of·them,

Ac 8:24 ·which yeu·have·declared should·come upon me."

Ac 9:4 And falling upon the earth, he·heard a·voice saying

Ac 9:33 Aeneas by·name, laying·down upon a·mat for eight

Ac 10:9 ·the city, Peter walked·up upon the rooftop to·pray

Ac 10:10 making·preparation, a·trance fell upon him.

Ac 10:44 the Holy Spirit fell upon all the·ones hearing the

Ac 10:45 with·Peter, because also upon the Gentiles, the

Ac 11:15 ·speak, the Holy Spirit fell upon them, just·as also

Ac 11:15 upon them, just·as also upon us at *the* beginning.

Ac 12:21 and sitting·down upon the Bema·judgment·seat,

Ac 13:11 And at·once there·fell upon him dimness·of·sight

Ac 13:40 look·out, lest it·should·come upon yeu, the·thing

Ac 15:10 yeu·try God, to·put a·yoke upon the neck of·the

Ac 15:17 even all the Gentiles, upon whom my name has·

Ac 15:17 whom my name has·been·surnamed upon them,

Ac 17:26 every nation of·men·of·clay† residing upon all the

Ac 18:6 "Yeur blood *be* upon yeur own·heads; I·myself *am*

Ac 19:6 the Holy Spirit came upon them, and they·were·

Ac 19:12 from his skin's·surface to·be·brought upon the sick,

Ac 19:16 And leaping upon them and fully·dominating them,

Ac 19:17 And reverent·fear·and·awe fell upon them all, and

Ac 20:37 And affectionately·falling upon Paul's neck, they·

Ac 21:23 ·us are four men having a·vow upon themselves;

Ac 24:4 I·should·not·be any·further hindrance upon you, I·

Ac 26:16 'But·yet rise·up and stand·still upon your feet, for

Ac 27:43 ·far·overboard first, to·get upon the dry·ground.

Ac 27:44 ·all made·it·thoroughly·safe upon the dry·ground.
Heb 6:7 the rain which·is·coming upon it many·times and
Heb 8:6 has·been·enacted upon significantly·better promises.
Heb 8:10 ·mind, and I·shall·inscribe them upon their hearts,
Heb 10:16 giving my Laws·of·Liberty upon their hearts, and
Heb 10:16 their hearts, and upon their innermost·minds I·
Heb 10:28 completely·apart·from compassion upon two or
Heb 11:21 of·Joseph, and he·leaned·prostrate upon the tip
Gal 3:16 to·the seeds," as upon many *offspring†*, but·rather
Gal 3:16 as upon many *offspring†*, but·rather as upon one,
Gal 6:16 by·this standard, peace *be* upon them, and mercy,
Gal 6:16 them, and mercy, and upon the IsraEl of·God.
Mt 1:11 and his brothers, upon *the time* of·the Babylonian
Mt 3:16 ·God descending like a·dove and coming upon him.
Mt 4:4 "A·man·of·clay† shall·live not upon bread alone,
Mt 4:4 bread alone, but·rather upon every utterance that·is·
Mt 4:6 ' and "They·shall·lift you upon *their* palms, lest·at·
Mt 6:19 ·not store·up for·yeurselves treasures upon the earth,
Mt 7:24 man who built his home upon the solid·rock.
Mt 7:25 fall, for it·had·been·founded upon the solid·rock.
Mt 7:26 to·a·foolish man, who built his home upon the sand.
Mt 9:18 *with·me*, you·must·lay your hand upon her, and she·
Mt 10:13 ·be worthy, *let* yeur peace come upon it, but if it·
Mt 10:27 in the ear, officially·proclaim upon the rooftops.
Mt 10:29 not one from·among them shall·fall upon the soil
Mt 10:34 assume that I·came to·cast peace upon the earth; I·
Mt 11:29 Take·up my yoke upon yeu, and learn from me,
Mt 12:18 I·shall·place my Spirit upon him, and he·shall·
Mt 12:28 the kingdom of·God has·already·come upon yeu.
Mt 13:5 But other *seeds* fell upon the rocky·places, where it·
Mt 14:25 went·off toward them, 'walking upon the sea.'
Mt 14:26 And after·seeing him walking upon the sea, the
Mt 14:28 ·order me to·come to you upon the water."
Mt 14:29 the sailboat, Peter walked upon the water to·go to
Mt 15:35 ·ordered the crowds to·sit·back upon the soil.
Mt 16:18 "But upon this Solid·Rock I·shall·build my
Mt 18:6 millstone should·be·hung upon his neck, and *that*
Mt 19:28 the Son of·Clay·Man† should·sit upon his Throne
Mt 19:28 yeu also shall·sit upon twelve thrones, judging
Mt 21:5 ·mild and having·mounted upon a·donkey even
Mt 23:2 and the Pharisees sat·down upon the seat of·Moses.
Mt 23:9 ·should·not call *anyone* yeur father upon the earth,
Mt 23:35 that upon yeu may·come all *the* righteous blood
Mt 23:35 righteous blood being·poured·out upon the earth,
Mt 23:36 shall·come upon this generation·of·offspring.
Mt 24:2 ·should·not be·left here a·stone upon a·stone that
Mt 24:3 And with·him sitting·down upon the Mount of·
Mt 24:30 Son of·Clay·Man† coming upon the thick·clouds
Mt 24:33 yeu·must·know that he·is near upon *the* doors.
Mt 25:20 I·gained another five talants·of·silver upon them.'
Mt 25:22 I·gained another two talants·of·silver upon them.'
Mt 25:31 him, then he·shall·sit upon his Throne of·Glory.
Mt 26:64 Power and 'coming upon the thick·clouds of·the
Mt 27:19 ·seating himself upon the Bema·judgment·seat, his
Mt 27:29 out of·thorns, they·put *it* upon his head and·also a·
Mt 28:18 authority is·given to·me in heaven and upon earth.
Mk 1:10 and the Spirit like a·dove descending upon him.
Mk 4:1 crowd was alongside the sea upon the dry·ground.
Mk 4:5 But other *seed* fell upon the rocky·ground, where it·
Mk 4:26 should·cast the scattering·of·seed upon the soil,
Mk 6:39 recline, party *by* party, upon the green grass.
Mk 6:47 of·the sea, and he *was* alone upon the dry·ground.
Mk 6:48 he·comes toward them, walking upon the sea, and
Mk 6:49 But after·seeing him walking upon the sea, they·
Mk 7:30 and her daughter having·been·cast upon the couch.
Mk 8:6 And he·charged the crowd to·sit·back upon the soil.
Mk 8:25 *Jesus* again laid his hands upon his eyes and made
Mk 9:20 *the little·child*. And falling upon the soil, he·was·
Mk 10:16 while·placing his hands upon them, he·was·
Mk 11:7 they·threw their garments on·it, and he·sat upon it.
Mk 13:2 there·should·not be·left a·stone upon a·stone that
Mk 13:29 yeu·must·know that he·is near upon *the* doors.
Mk 15:1 And immediately upon the dawn, the chief·priests,
Mk 15:24 his garments, while·casting lots upon them, *as·to*
Rm 2:9 tribulation and calamity, upon every soul of·a·man·
Rm 3:22 Anointed *is* for all and *is* upon all the·ones trusting,
Rm 4:9 *is* this supreme·blessedness upon the Circumcision
Rm 4:9 Circumcision *only*, or upon the Uncircumcision also
Rm 5:12 ·through into all men·of·clay† upon this·very *point*:
Rm 9:23 the wealth of·his glory upon *the* vessels of·mercy,
Rm 9:28 a·concise·working·of *the* matter upon the earth."
Rm 11:22 In·fact, upon the·ones falling, a·severe·cutting-off
Rm 15:3 of·the·ones reproaching you fell upon me."
Rm 15:20 lest I·should·build upon another·man's foundation.
Jac 2:3 *if* yeu·should·kindly·look upon the·one prominently·
Jac 2:7 beautiful name, the·one being·surnamed upon yeu?
Jac 2:21 ·carrying·up his son YiTsaq upon the sacrifice·altar?
Php 1:3 I·give·thanks to·my God upon every mention of·yeu,
Php 2:17 I·am·poured·forth·as·a·devotion upon the sacrifice
Php 2:27 on·me also, lest I·should·have grief upon grief.
Php 3:9 righteousness from·out of·God *based* upon the trust)
1Pe 1:13 place·yeur·expectation completely upon the grace
1Pe 2:24 ·failures in his·own body upon the arbor·tree, in·
1Pe 3:5 the·ones placing·their·expectation upon God,
1Pe 3:12 the eyes of·Yahweh *are* upon righteous·men, and
1Pe 4:14 the Spirit of·glory and of·God rests upon yeu. In·
1Pe 5:7 flinging all yeur anxiety upon him, because it·
1Th 2:16 So, the wrath already·anticipated upon them *is* for
1Co 2:9 and it·did·not ascend upon *the* heart of·a·man·of·
1Co 3:12 And if any·man builds upon this foundation *with*
1Co 8:5 gods, whether in heaven or upon the earth (just·as
1Co 16:17 I·rejoice upon the arrival of·Stephanas and
2Co 1:9 ·that we·may·not be having·reliance upon ourselves,
2Co 1:9 upon ourselves, but·rather upon God (the·one
2Co 1:23 do·call·upon God *for* a·witness upon my soul, that
2Co 3:14 not being·unveiled upon the reading·aloud of·the
2Co 3:15 is·read·aloud, a·veil is·laid·out upon their hearts.
2Co 9:14 ·account·of the surpassing grace of·God upon yeu.
2Co 12:9 the power of·Anointed-One may·encamp upon me.
Eph 2:20 being·built upon the foundation of·the ambassadors
Eph 3:15 ·lineage in *the* heavens and upon earth is·named:
Eph 4:26 ·not·let the sun go·down upon yeur personal·anger,
Eph 5:6 the wrath of·God comes upon the Sons of·the
Col 1:16 the heavens, and the·ones upon the earth, the·ones
Col 1:20 *I·say*, whether *they·are* the·things upon the earth or
Col 3:2 the·things up·above, not the·things upon the earth.
Col 3:5 deaden yeur members *to* the·things upon the earth:
1Ti 4:10 we·have·placed·our·expectation upon the·living
1Ti 5:5 ·all·alone, has·placed·her·expectation upon God,
1Ti 6:17 nor·even to·have·placed·their·expectations upon *the*
Rv 1:17 And he·laid his right hand upon me, saying to·me,
Rv 2:24 as they·say), I·shall·cast upon yeu no other burden.
Rv 3:3 you·should·keep·alert, I·shall·come upon you as a·
Rv 3:3 ·should·not know which hour I·shall·come upon you.
Rv 3:10 ·trial, the·one about to·come upon all The Land, to·
Rv 3:10 The Land, to·try the·ones residing upon the earth.
Rv 3:12 'And I·shall·write upon him the name of·my God,
Rv 4:2 the heaven, and upon the throne is·one·sitting·down.
Rv 4:4 twenty four thrones. And upon the thrones, I·saw the
Rv 5:3 in the heaven, nor·even upon the earth, nor·even
Rv 5:7 right·hand of·the·one sitting·down upon the throne.
Rv 5:13 the earth, and such·as are upon the sea, and all the·
Rv 5:13 "To·the·one who·is·sitting·down upon the throne
Rv 7:10 To·the·one who·is·sitting·down upon the throne
Rv 8:3 of·all the holy·ones upon the golden Sacrifice·Altar,
Rv 8:10 as a·torch, and it·fell upon the third·part of·the
Rv 8:10 of·the rivers, and upon the wellsprings of·waters;
Rv 10:1 a·thick·cloud; and a·rainbow *was* upon his head,
Rv 10:2 And he·placed his right foot upon the sea, and the
Rv 10:5 angel which I·saw standing upon the sea and upon
Rv 10:5 standing upon the sea and upon the earth lifted his
Rv 10:8 of·*the*·angel, the·one standing upon the sea and
Rv 10:8 the·one standing upon the sea and upon the earth."
Rv 11:10 And the·ones residing upon the earth shall·rejoice
Rv 11:11 of·life-above from·out of·God came·in upon them,
Rv 11:11 ·in upon them, and they·stood·still upon their feet,
Rv 11:11 and great fear fell upon the·ones observing them.
Rv 11:16 of·God on their thrones, fell upon their faces, and
Rv 12:1 her feet, and upon her head a·victor's·crown of·
Rv 12:3 ten horns, and seven royal·turbans upon his heads.
Rv 13:1 And I·settled upon the sand of·the sea, and I·saw a·
Rv 13:1 and ten horns, and upon its horns ten royal·turbans,
Rv 13:1 horns ten royal·turbans, and upon its heads a·name
Rv 13:8 And all the·ones residing upon the earth shall·fall·
Rv 13:16 on their right hand or upon their foreheads.
Rv 14:14 a·white thick·cloud, and upon the thick·cloud *one*
Rv 16:2 went·off and poured·out his vial upon the earth, and
Rv 16:8 fourth angel poured·out his vial upon the sun, and it·
Rv 16:10 angel poured·out his vial upon the throne of·the
Rv 16:12 sixth angel poured·out his vial upon the great river
Rv 16:18 since the men·of·clay† were upon the earth, so·vast
Rv 16:21 descends out of·the heaven upon the men·of·clay†.
Rv 17:1 the·one who·is·sitting·down upon the Many
Rv 17:3 who·is·sitting·down upon a·scarlet demonic·beast,
Rv 17:5 And upon her forehead *was* a·name having·been·
Rv 17:16 ten horns which you·saw upon the Scarlet·Beast,
Rv 18:24 the·ones having·been·slaughtered upon the earth."
Rv 19:11 horse and the·one sitting·down upon it *was* being·
Rv 19:14 the heaven were·following him upon white horses,
Rv 19:21 of·the·one who·is·sitting·down upon the horse,
Rv 20:4 and they·sat upon them, and judgment was·given
Rv 20:4 and did·not receive the etching upon their foreheads,
Rv 21:5 And the·one who·is·sitting·down upon the throne
Rv 21:12 gates, and twelve angels upon the gates, and
Rv 22:14 ·be their privilege *to·reach* upon the arbor·tree of·
Rv 22:18 these·things, God shall·place upon him the

EG1909.1 (2x)

Mt 21:5 having·mounted upon a·donkey even *upon* a·colt, a·
Rv 3:12 'And *I·shall·write upon him* my brand-new name.

G1909.2 PREP ἐπ´ (168x)

Jn 4:6 ·travel, was·sitting·down in·this·manner on the well.
Jn 6:19 they·observe Jesus walking·along on the sea and
Jn 7:30 not·even·one·man threw his hand on him, because
Jn 7:44 him, but·yet not·even·one·man threw hands on him.
Jn 12:14 finding a·young·donkey, sat·down on it, just·as it·
Jn 17:4 I·myself glorified you on the earth. I·fully·completed
Jn 19:13 and he·sat·down on the Bema·judgment·seat in a·
Jn 19:19 also wrote a·title and placed *it* on the cross. And
Lk 1:65 a·reverent·fear·and·awe happened on all the·ones
Lk 2:14 to·God in *the* highest, and on earth, peace! Among
Lk 4:9 and he·set him on the topmost·ledge of·the
Lk 4:29 unto the brow of·the mount on which their city had·
Lk 5:12 and after·seeing Jesus *and* falling on *his* face, he·
Lk 5:19 ·account·of the crowd, walking·up on the rooftop,
Lk 5:25 taking·up what he·was·laying·down on, he·went·off
Lk 6:29 "To·the·one pummeling you on the cheek, hold·
Lk 6:48 dug deeply and laid a·foundation on the solid·rock.
Lk 6:49 a·home apart·from a·foundation on the earth, which
Lk 8:8 "And other *seed* fell on the beneficially·good soil, and
Lk 8:16 but·rather he·puts *it* on a·lampstand, in·order·that
Lk 11:2 will be·done, as in heaven, so·also on the earth.
Lk 11:33 but·rather *places it* on the lampstand, in·order·
Lk 17:16 and he·fell·down on *his* face directly·at his feet,
Lk 17:34 night there·shall·be two *reclining* on one couch; the
Lk 18:8 ·*back*, shall·he·find then *such* a·trust on the earth?
Lk 19:30 a·colt having·been·tied, on which not·even·one
Lk 20:19 hour sought to·throw *their* hands on him, for they·
Lk 21:12 they·shall·throw their hands on yeu and shall·
Lk 21:35 upon all the·ones who·are·sitting·down on *the* face
Lk 22:21 of·the·one handing me over *is* with me on the table.
Lk 22:30 my kingdom, and may·sit on thrones judging the
Lk 23:30 "to·say to·the mountains, "Fall on us!" and to·the
Lk 24:25 ·ones, and slow in·the heart to·trust on all that the
Ac 2:19 heaven up·above and signs on the earth down·below
Ac 2:30 ·raise·up the Anointed-One to·sit on his Throne—
Ac 4:5 And it·happened on the next·day, *that* their rulers and
Ac 4:22 was more·than forty years·of·age, on whom this
Ac 5:15 and to·lay *them* on simple·couches and mats, in·
Ac 5:30 ·manhandled, hanging *him* on an·arbor·tree.

Ac 8:17 Then they·were·laying *their* hands on them, and
Ac 9:11 "Rising·up, traverse on the avenue, the·one being·
Ac 9:17 And after·laying his hands on him, he·declared,
Ac 9:42 known in all Joppa, and many trusted on the Lord.
Ac 10:39 whom they·executed *by* hanging on an·arbor·tree.
Ac 11:17 *he·gave* to·us *who·are* already·trusting on the Lord
Ac 14:10 with·a·loud voice, "Stand upright on your feet."
Ac 16:31 And they·declared, "Trust on the Lord Jesus
Ac 21:5 And bowing the knees on the shore, we·prayed.
Ac 21:27 into·an·uproar, and they·threw their hands on him
Ac 21:40 him, Paul, while·standing on the stairs, motioned
Ac 22:19 in·each·of the gatherings, the·ones trusting on you.
Ac 25:6 ·day, after·sitting·down on the Bema·judgment·seat
Ac 25:17 , after·sitting·down on the Bema·judgment·seat,
Ac 27:44 *got there*, in·fact, some·men on planks, and some·
Ac 27:44 on planks, and some·men on some of·the *broken·*
Ac 28:3 of·kindling·sticks and putting *them* on the fire, a·
Heb 2:13 " I·myself shall·be having·confidence on him."
Heb 8:4 For if, in·fact, he·were on earth, he·would not·even
Heb 11:13 foreigners and foreign·residents on the earth.
Heb 12:25 the·one imparting·divine·instruction on the earth,
Gal 3:13 ·accursed *is* any one being·hung on an·arbor·tree.
Mt 4:5 Holy City and sets him on the topmost·ledge of·the
Mt 5:15 the measuring·basket, but·rather on the lampstand,
Mt 5:39 but·rather whoever shall·slap you on your right
Mt 5:45 ·ones, and he·showers·rain on righteous·ones and
Mt 6:10 will be·done— as in heaven, so·also on the earth.
Mt 9:2 ·paralyzed·man having·been·cast on a·simple·couch.
Mt 9:6 the Son of·Clay·Man† has authority on the earth to·
Mt 9:16 a·patch of·unprocessed cloth onto an·old garment,
Mt 13:2 ·down *there*; and all the crowd stood on the shore.
Mt 13:8 But others fell on the soil, the good·one, and were·
Mt 14:8 me here the head of·John the Immerser on a·platter."
Mt 14:11 And his head was·brought on a·platter and was·
Mt 14:19 ·ordering the crowds to·recline on the grass, and
Mt 16:19 and whatever you·should·bind on the earth shall·be
Mt 16:19 and whatever you·should·loose on the earth shall·
Mt 17:6 ·hearing *it*, the disciples fell on their faces and were
Mt 18:12 traverse, leaving the ninety-nine on the mountains,
Mt 18:18 as·many·things·as yeu·should·bind on the earth
Mt 18:18 as·many·things·as yeu·should·loose on the earth
Mt 18:19 if two of·yeu should·mutually·agree on the earth
Mt 21:44 "And the·one falling on this stone shall·be·dashed·
Mt 21:44 stone shall·be·dashed·to·pieces, but on whomever
Mt 23:4 loads and put *them* on the shoulders of·the men·of·
Mt 24:17 The·one on the rooftop must·not walk·down to·
Mt 26:7 ointment, and she·poured·*it*·down on his head as·
Mt 26:12 she·herself, casting this ointment on my body, did
Mt 26:39 And going·onward a·little·bit, he·fell on his face,
Mt 26:50 they·threw their hands on YeShua and securely·
Mt 27:25 "His blood *be* on us and on our children.
Mt 27:25 "His blood *be* on us and on our children."
Mk 2:4 they·lowered the mat on which the paralyzed·man
Mk 2:10 the Son of·Clay·Man† has authority on the earth to·
Mk 2:21 a·patch of·unprocessed cloth on an·old garment,
Mk 4:21 not in·order·that it·should·be·put on the lampstand?
Mk 4:38 was in the stern·of·the·boat, sleeping on the pillow.
Mk 6:25 ·hour the head of·John the Immerser on a·platter."
Mk 6:28 and brought his head on a·platter, and he·gave it to·
Mk 6:55 ·region, they·began to·carry·about on their mats
Mk 9:3 as snow, such·as a·cloth-fuller on the earth is·not
Mk 11:2 a·colt having·been·tied, on which not·even·one
Mk 13:15 And the·one on the rooftop must·not walk·down
Mk 14:35 going·onward a·little·bit, he·fell on the soil and
Mk 14:46 And they·threw their hands on him and securely·
Mk 16:18 they·shall·lay *their* hands on unhealthy·ones, and
Rm 4:5 not working, but trusting on the·one regarding the
Rm 4:18 expectation, trusted on an·Expectation in·order·for
Rm 4:24 — the·ones trusting on the·one already·awakening
Rm 9:33 and any one trusting on him shall·not be·put·to·
Rm 10:11 " Everyone trusting on him shall·not be·put·to·
Rm 12:20 you·shall·stack burning·coals of·fire on his head.
Jac 5:5 Yeu·indulged·in·delicate·luxury on the earth, and
Jac 5:17 ·rain, and it·did·not shower·rain on the earth *for*
Php 3:12 so·that also I·may·grasp onto that·for·which also
1Pe 2:6 dearly·precious; and the·one trusting on him, no,
Tit 3:6 whom he·poured·forth on us abundantly through
1Co 11:10 is·obligated to·have authority on her head on·
1Co 14:25 and in·this·manner falling·down on *his* face, he·
Eph 1:10 ·things in the heavens and the·things on the earth.
Eph 6:3 with·you, and you·shall·be a·long·time on the earth.
Col 3:6 ·things the wrath of·God comes on the Sons of·the
1Ti 1:16 ·example for·the·ones about to·trust on him to
Rv 2:17 ·give him a·white pebble, also on the pebble, a·
Rv 4:4 white garments, and they·had on their heads victor's·
Rv 4:9 thanks to·the·one who·is·sitting·down on the throne,
Rv 4:10 in·the·sight of·the·one sitting·down on the throne,
Rv 5:1 the right·hand of·the·one sitting·down on the throne,
Rv 5:10 ·offer·a·sacrifice, and we·shall·reign on the earth."
Rv 6:2 horse and the·one who·is·sitting·down on it having a·
Rv 6:4 to·him, to·the·one who·is·sitting·down on it, to·take
Rv 6:5 horse and the·one who·is·sitting·down on it having a·
Rv 6:10 avenge our blood on the·ones residing on the earth?
Rv 6:16 and to·the solid·rocks, "Fall on us, and hide us
Rv 6:16 face of·the·one who·is·sitting·down on the throne,
Rv 7:1 I·saw four angels standing on the four corners of·the
Rv 7:1 in·order·that wind should·not blow on the earth, nor
Rv 7:1 should·not blow on the earth, nor on the sea, nor on
Rv 7:1 blow on the earth, nor on the sea, nor on any tree.
Rv 7:11 living·beings, and they·fell on their faces in·the·
Rv 7:15 And the·one who·is·sitting·down on the throne
Rv 7:16 *that* the sunray should·fall on them, nor·even any
Rv 8:13 woe, woe to·the·ones residing on the earth— from·
Rv 9:7 ·been·made·ready for battle; and on their heads *were*
Rv 9:17 ·vision, and the·ones sitting·down on them, having
Rv 10:2 foot upon the sea, and the left *foot* on the earth,
Rv 11:10 prophets tormented the·ones residing on the earth.
Rv 11:16 sitting·down in·the·sight of·God on their thrones,
Rv 13:14 and it·deceives the·ones residing on the earth
Rv 13:14 ·Beast, saying to·the·ones residing on the earth,
Rv 13:16 they·should·be·given an·etching on their right hand
Rv 14:1 and behold, a·Lamb standing on the Mount Tsiyon,
Rv 14:6 ·news to·proclaim to·the·ones residing on the earth,
Rv 14:14 a·son of·clay·man†, having on his head a·golden
Rv 14:15 to·the·one who·is·sitting·down on the thick·cloud,
Rv 14:16 the·one who·is·sitting·down on the thick·cloud
Rv 14:16 the thick·cloud cast·in his sickle on the earth, and
Rv 15:2 name)— standing on the transparent,·glassy sea,
Rv 17:8 And the·ones residing on the earth shall·marvel,
Rv 17:9 mountains, wherever the woman sits·down on them.
Rv 18:19 "And they·cast loose·dirt on their heads, and were·
Rv 19:4 ·God, to·the·one who·is·sitting·down on the throne,
Rv 19:12 *were* as a·blaze of·fire, and on his head *were* many
Rv 19:16 And he·has on the garment and on his thigh the
Rv 19:16 he·has on the garment and on his thigh the name
Rv 19:18 ·horses, and of·the·ones sitting·down on them, and
Rv 19:19 against the·one who·is·sitting·down on the horse,
Rv 20:9 And they·walked·up on the breadth of·the earth, and
Rv 20:11 and the·one who·is·sitting·down on it, from

EG1909.2 (2x)

Mt 8:6 my servant·boy has·been·cast paralyzed *on a·couch* at
Mt 8:14 mother-in-law having·been·cast *on a·couch* and

G1909.3 PREP ἐπί (44x)

Jn 5:2 Now at the Sheep·Gate in JeruSalem, there·is a·pool
Jn 8:7 ·moral·failure, let·him·cast the first stone at her."
Jn 8:59 stones in·order·that they·may·cast *them* at him, but
Jn 21:1 apparent again to·the disciples at the Sea of·Tiberias;
Lk 1:14 ·leaping·of·joy, and many shall·rejoice at his birth.
Lk 2:33 mother were marveling at the·things being·spoken
Lk 2:47 hearing him were·astonished at his comprehension
Lk 4:22 for·him, and they·were·marveling at the gracious
Lk 4:32 And they·were·astounded at his instruction, because
Lk 5:5 we·took nothing·at·all. But at your utterance, I·
Lk 9:43 And they·all were·astounded at the magnificence of·
Lk 20:26 of·the people. And marveling at his answer, they·
Lk 20:37 Moses brought·it·to·attention at the burning·bush,
Lk 22:30 ·order·that yeu·may·eat and may·drink at my table
Lk 22:40 And coming·to·be at the place, he·declared to·
Ac 3:1 ·unison into the Sanctuary·Courtyard at the *afternoon*
Ac 3:10 merciful·act·of·charity at the Stately·and·Elegant
Ac 3:10 and astonishment at the·thing having·befallen him.
Ac 3:12 "Men, Israelites, why do·yeu·marvel at this?
Ac 3:16 And at the trust of·his name, *this·trust* stabilized
Ac 5:9 of·the·ones burying your husband *are* at the door, and
Ac 7:54 heart, and they·were·gnashing *their* teeth at him.
Ac 10:17 for·Simon's home, they·stood·over at the gate.
Ac 10:25 met·up with·him. *And* falling at his feet, he·fell·
Ac 11:11 three men were·standing·over *the gate* at the home
Ac 13:12 trusted, being·astounded at the instruction of·the
Ac 25:10 "I·am standing at Caesar's Bema·judgment·seat,
Heb 9:26 now only·once, at *the* complete·consummation of·
Mt 7:28 the crowds were·astounded at his instruction,
Mt 18:16 or two more, that "at *the* mouth of·two or three
Mt 22:33 *this*, the crowds were·astounded at his instruction.
Mk 1:22 And they·were·astounded at his instruction, for he·
Mk 10:22 And after·glowering at the saying, he·went·away
Mk 10:24 And the disciples were·amazed at his words. But
Mk 11:4 ·been·tied alongside the door at the fork·in·the·road
Mk 11:18 all the crowd was·astounded at his instruction.
Mk 12:17 And they·marveled at him.
Mk 12:26 scroll of·Moses, how (at the burning·bush) God
1Co 14:16 ·be·it,·Amen" at your expression·of·thankfulness
2Co 13:1 I·am·coming to yeu. "At *the* mouth of·two or
1Ti 5:19 *this standard*: "except at *the mouth* of·two or three
Rv 3:20 'Behold, I·stand at the door and knock.
Rv 8:3 angel came and stood·still at the Sacrifice·Altar,
Rv 21:16 he·measured the CITY at twelve thousand stadia.

G1909.4 PREP ἐπί (106x)

Jn 9:6 and he·smeared the clay over the eyes of·the blind·
Lk 1:29 *him*, she·was·thoroughly·troubled over his saying,
Lk 1:33 And he·shall·reign over the house of·Jacob into the
Lk 2:8 vigilantly·keeping the night watches over their flock.
Lk 2:20 glorifying and praising God over all·the·things that
Lk 4:25 ·months, as great famine occurred over all the land,
Lk 5:9 all the·ones together with·him) over the catch of·the
Lk 7:13 her, the Lord empathized over her and declared to·
Lk 9:1 ·gave them power and authority over all the demons,
Lk 9:43 But with·all marveling over all·things which Jesus
Lk 12:14 me *as* estate·executor or distributor over yeu?
Lk 12:42 his lord shall·fully·establish over his domestic·staff
Lk 12:44 ·yeu, that he·shall·fully·establish him over all his
Lk 13:17 all the crowd was·rejoicing over all the glorious·
Lk 15:7 joy in the heaven over one morally·disqualified·man
Lk 15:7 rather·than over ninety-nine righteous·men who
Lk 15:10 angels of·God over one morally·disqualified·man
Lk 19:14 'We·do·not want this·man to·reign over us.'
Lk 19:23 then did·you·not give my money over *to* the bank,
Lk 19:27 the·ones not wanting me to·reign over them, bring
Lk 19:41 ·drew·near, upon·seeing the City, he·wept over it,
Lk 23:28 Daughters of·JeruSalem, do·not weep over me. *Yet*
Lk 23:28 *Yet* moreover, weep over yeurselves and over yeur
Lk 23:28 weep over yeurselves and over yeur children.
Lk 23:38 also was·having·been·written over him with·letters
Lk 23:44 and there·was a·darkness over all the land until
Ac 4:9 this·day are·scrutinized over *the* good·deed for·the·
Ac 4:21 ·glorifying God over the·thing having·happened.
Ac 6:3 whom we·shall·fully·establish over this need.
Ac 7:10 fully·established him, governing over Egypt and all
Ac 7:11 "Now there·came a·famine over all the land of·
Ac 7:27 you *as* ruler and executive·justice over us?
Ac 8:2 and they·made great visceral·lamentation over him.
Ac 8:27 of·the·Ethiopians, who was over all her treasury
Ac 11:19 tribulation, the·one occurring over Stephen, went·
Ac 11:28 there·was·about to·be a·great famine over all The
Ac 12:20 And persuading Blastus, the·one over the king's
Ac 13:31 *Jesus* who was·gazed·upon over many·more days
Ac 15:31 ·*it*·aloud, they·rejoiced over the exhortation.
Ac 16:18 And this she·did over many days. But being·
Ac 17:2 ·in alongside them, and over three Sabbaths he·was·

Ac 19:13 name of·the Lord Jesus over the·ones having the
Ac 20:9 With·Paul discussing *matters* over a·longer·*period*,
Ac 20:11 and conversing over a·long·while in·this·manner
Ac 20:38 being·distressed especially over the words which
Ac 26:6 "And now I·stand being·judged over *the* expectation
Ac 27:20 ·of·stars appearing over many·more days, and
Ac 28:6 but with·them anticipating over a·long·while and
Heb 2:7 and fully·established him over the works of·your
Heb 3:6 but Anointed-One as a·son over his·own house, of·
Heb 10:21 and *having* a·high priest over the house of·God—
Mt 5:45 ·raises his sun above·the·horizon over evil·ones and
Mt 12:49 And stretching·forth his hand over his disciples,
Mt 14:14 a·large crowd, and he·empathized over them, and
Mt 15:32 YeShua declared, "I·empathize over the crowd,
Mt 18:13 to·yeu, he·rejoices more over that·same *sheep* than
Mt 18:13 over that·same *sheep* than over the ninety-nine,
Mt 19:9 his wife, except over sexual·immorality, and
Mt 24:45 his lord fully·established over his domestic·staff,
Mt 24:47 ·yeu, that he·shall·fully·establish him over all his
Mt 25:21 slave! You·were trustworthy over a·few·things, I·
Mt 25:21 I·shall·fully·establish you over many·things.
Mt 25:23 slave! You·were trustworthy over a·few·things, I·
Mt 25:23 I·shall·fully·establish you over many·things.
Mt 27:35 ·themselves, and they·cast lots over my attire."'
Mt 27:45 hour, there·was darkness over all the land until
Mk 3:5 while·being·jointly·grieved over the stony·hardness
Mk 6:34 crowd, and he·empathized over them, because
Mk 8:2 "I·empathize over the crowd, because even·now
Mk 9:22 *to·do* something, empathizing over us, swiftly·help
Mk 14:51 ·cloth having·been·arrayed over *his* nakedness,
Mk 15:33 occurring, darkness came·to·be over all the land
Mk 15:46 ·rock, and he·rolled a·stone over the door of·the
Rm 5:14 so·far·as·unto Moses, even over the·ones not
Rm 9:5 Anointed-One, the·one being God over all, blessed
Rm 16:19 Accordingly, I·rejoice over yeu. But·yet I·want
Jac 5:1 Weep, howling over yeur miseries, the·ones coming·
Jac 5:7 of·the earth, suffering·with·long·patience over it,
Jac 5:14 Called·Out·citizenry, and let·them·pray over him,
1Th 3:7 and dire·need, we·are·comforted over yeu through
1Th 3:9 to·God concerning yeu, over all the joy with·which
2Th 2:4 and 'is·arrogantly·exalting·himself over all *that·is*
1Co 7:39 ·bound by·Torah-Law over a·lifetime as·long·as
1Co 13:6 It·does·not rejoice over the injustice, but it·
2Co 3:13 Moses *did*, who·was·placing a·veil over his face,
2Co 7:13 *all* the·more, we·rejoiced over the joy of·Titus,
2Co 9:13 they·are·glorifying God over the affirmation of·
Eph 4:6 and Father of·all: the·one over all and throughout
Eph 6:16 Over all·*these*·things, after·taking·up the tall·shield
Col 3:14 And over all these·things, *dress·yeurselves·with* the
1Ti 1:18 according·to the preceding prophecies over you,
Rv 1:7 the tribes of·the earth shall·vividly·lament over him.'
Rv 2:26 end, to·him I·shall·give authority over the nations.
Rv 6:8 And authority was·given to·them over the fourth·part
Rv 9:11 And they·have a·king over them— the angel of·the
Rv 10:11 ·for you to·prophesy again over many peoples, and
Rv 11:6 And they·have authority over the waters to·turn
Rv 11:10 upon the earth shall·rejoice over them and shall·be·
Rv 13:7 ' And authority was·given to·it over all tribes, and
Rv 14:18 the Sacrifice·Altar, having authority over the fire;
Rv 16:9 the·one having authority over these punishing·blows
Rv 17:18 the·one having a·kingdom over the kings of·the
Rv 18:9 her, and shall·vividly·lament over her, whenever
Rv 18:11 of·the earth do·weep and mourn over her, because
Rv 18:20 "Be·merry over her, O·Heaven, and the holy
Rv 20:6 in the First Resurrection. Over these, the Second

G1909.5 PREP ἐπί (21x)

Lk 1:17 ·turn fathers' hearts back·around toward *the* children
Lk 18:7 night to him, yet while·being·patient toward them?
Lk 22:52 and *the* elders coming·directly toward him,
Ac 8:26 traverse down *on* the·south·side toward the roadway
Ac 9:35 him, *and* they·turned·back·around toward the Lord.
Ac 16:19 into the marketplace·forum toward the rulers.
Ac 17:14 dispatched·forth Paul to·traverse as toward the sea,
Ac 26:20 to·repent and to·turn·back·around toward God,
Heb 6:1 we·should·be·carrying·on toward the completeness·
Heb 6:1 from dead works, and of·trust toward God,
Mt 18:26 'Lord, be·patient toward me, and I·shall·give·back
Rm 11:22 a·severe·cutting-off, but toward you *personally*,
Php 3:14 ·to *that* set·aim, I·pursue *it* toward the prize of·the
1Th 4:7 God did·not call us forth toward impurity, but·rather
1Co 7:36 to·have·improper·etiquette toward his virgin·
2Co 9:6 and the·one sowing toward beneficial·blessings also
Eph 2:7 *indicated* in *his* kindness toward us in Anointed-One
2Ti 2:14 *for·this·leads* toward an·overturning·catastrophic·
2Ti 2:16 for they·shall·continually·advance toward more
2Ti 3:13 shall·continually·advance toward the more·wicked·
Rv 12:17 And the Dragon was·angry toward the woman, and

EG1909.5 (1x)

Mk 11:13 having leaves, he·came *toward it to·see* if perhaps

G1909.6 PREP ἐπ' (63x)

Jn 6:16 occurred, his disciples walked·down to the sea,
Jn 19:33 But coming to Jesus, as·soon·as they·saw him even·
Lk 1:16 of·the Sons of·IsraEl back·around to Yahweh their
Lk 3:2 — an·utterance of·God came to John the son of·
Lk 6:35 because he·himself is kind to the ungrateful and
Lk 9:62 ·man, upon·throwing his hand to a·plow and *then*
Lk 10:6 But·if·not, it·shall·return·back to yeu.
Lk 10:9 'The kingdom of·God has·drawn·near to yeu.'
Lk 10:11 that the kingdom of·God has·drawn·near to yeu.'
Lk 12:25 is·able to·add one half·step to his span·of·life?
Lk 12:58 ·on·out with your legal·adversary to a·magistrate,
Lk 17:4 ·times in·the day should·turn·back·around to you,
Lk 19:5 And as·soon·as Jesus came to the place, looking·up,
Lk 23:1 ·all the multitude of·them led him to Pilate.
Lk 23:33 And when they·went·off to the place, the·one
Lk 24:1 deep *below·the·horizon*, they·came to the tomb,
Lk 24:12 But rising·up, Peter ran to the chamber·tomb, and
Lk 24:22 after·coming at·early·sunrise to the chamber·tomb
Lk 24:24 together with·us went·off to the chamber·tomb, and
Ac 8:32 '" He·was·driven as a·sheep to *the* butchering; and
Ac 8:36 down the roadway, they·came to some water. And
Ac 9:21 ·bring them having·been·bound to the chief·priests?
Ac 10:11 and a·certain vessel descending to him, as *being*
Ac 10:11 ·the·four corners and being·sent·down to the earth,
Ac 11:21 number turned·back·around to Yahweh trusting *in·*
Ac 12:10 second watch-station, they·came to the iron gate,
Ac 12:12 ·completely·aware, he·came to the home of·Miri,
Ac 14:13 after·bringing bulls and garlands to the gates, he·
Ac 14:15 ·turn·back·around from these futilities to the living
Ac 15:19 from the Gentiles turning·back·around to God,
Ac 17:6 Jason and certain brothers to the rulers·of·the·city,
Ac 17:19 ·him, they·brought·him to Mars'·Hill·*(also·called·*,
Ac 18:12 And they·brought him to the Bema·judgment·seat,
Ac 20:13 we·ourselves, going·onward to the sailing·ship,
Ac 21:32 who from·this·same·hour, ran·down to them,
Ac 21:35 And when he·came to the stairs, *the need* befell
Ac 24:8 ·ordering his legal·accusers to·come to you,
Ac 25:12 ·appealed·to Caesar. To Caesar you·shall·traverse.
Ac 26:18 the authority of·the Adversary-Accuser to God, for·
Heb 12:10 supposing, but he *does·so* to *our* advantage, in·
Gal 4:9 God, how·is·it *that* yeu·return again to the weak and
Gal 5:13 brothers, yeu·yeurselves are·called·forth to liberty;
Mt 3:7 and Sadducees are·coming to his immersion, *John*
Mt 3:13 YeShua comes·directly from Galilee to the Jordan,
Mt 5:23 you·should·bring your present to the Sacrifice·Altar,
Mt 6:27 is·able to·add one half·step to his span·of·life?
Mt 13:48 ·completely·filled, after·hauling *it* to the shore and
Mt 21:19 by the roadway, he·came to it and found not·even·
Mt 22:9 Now·then, yeu·traverse to the exit·areas of·the
Mt 24:16 "then the·ones in Judea must·flee to the mountains.
Mt 26:50 "O·associate, *attend* to *that* for·which you·are·
Mk 5:21 a·large crowd is·already·gathered·together to him,
Mk 6:53 And crossing·over, they·came to the land of·
Mk 11:13 on it. And after·coming to it, he·found nothing·at·
Mk 15:22 Then they·bring him to *the* place *being·referred·to·*
Mk 16:2 *day* of·*the*·week, they·went to the chamber·tomb
1Pe 2:25 but·yet are now returned to the Shepherd and
2Pe 2:22 "'A·dog *keeps·on* returning to his·own throw·up,"'
2Th 2:1 Anointed, and of·our complete·gathering to him,
2Ti 4:4 the truth and shall·be·turned·aside to the myths.
Rv 7:17 them and shall·guide them to living wellsprings of·
Rv 16:14 miraculous·signs, to·traverse·forth to the kings of·
Rv 21:10 he·carried me away in spirit to a·great and high

EG1909.6 (1x)

Ac 15:3 the turning·back·around of·the Gentiles *to God.* And

G1909.7 PREP ἐπί (4x)

Lk 3:2 in·the·days of·HannAs and Caiaphas *the* high·priests
Lk 4:27 many lepers were in IsraEl in·the·days of·EliSha the
Ac 11:28 even happened in·the·days of·Claudius Caesar.
Mk 2:26 into the house of·God in·the·days of·AbiAthar the

G1909.8 PREP ἐπί (7x)

Lk 4:25 the heaven was·shut·up for·a·span·of three years
Ac 19:8 he·was·boldly·speaking·with·clarity for·a·span·of
Ac 19:10 And this happened for·a·span·of two years, such·
Ac 19:34 from·out·of·all *present*, for·a·span·of about two
Heb 11:30 being·surrounded for·a·span·of seven days.
Gal 4:1 I·say *that* the heir, for·a·span·of time (as·long·as
Rm 7:1 lords·over the man·of·clay† for·a·span·of time, *that·*

G1909.9 PREP ἐπί (84x)

Lk 1:47 and my spirit leaped·for·joy in God my Savior.
Lk 4:25 "But I·say to·yeu in truth, many widows were in
Lk 5:27 Levi by·name, sitting·down in the tax·booth. And
Lk 6:17 ·down with them, he·stood·still in a·level place,
Lk 9:48 should·accept this little·child in my name accepts
Lk 9:49 ·saw someone casting·out the demons in your name;
Lk 11:22 ·away his whole·armor in which he·had·confided
Lk 18:9 to certain ones having·confidence in themselves that
Lk 20:21 ·rather *that* you·instruct the Way of·God in truth.
Lk 21:8 ·not be·deceived, for many shall·come in my name,
Lk 22:59 was·strongly·asserting, saying, "In truth, this·man
Lk 24:47 ·failures to·be·officially·proclaimed in his name to
Ac 2:26 yet even my flesh shall·fully·encamp in expectation,
Ac 2:38 each·one of·yeu be·immersed in the name of·Jesus
Ac 3:11 people ran·together toward them in the colonnade
Ac 4:17 ·longer to·not·even·one man·of·clay† in this name."
Ac 4:18 to·enunciate nor·even to·instruct at·all in the name
Ac 4:27 "For in truth, they·were·gathered·together against
Ac 5:28 charge a·charge to·yeu not to·instruct in this name?
Ac 5:40 they·charged *them* not to·speak in the name of·Jesus
Ac 8:28 ·was returning·back and sitting·down in his chariot,
Ac 10:34 his mouth, declared, "In truth, I·grasp that God is
Ac 14:3 time, boldly·speaking·with·clarity in the Lord (the·
Ac 20:9 ·name·of EuTychus was·sitting·down in the window
Heb 1:2 spoke to·us in these last days by *his* Son, whom he·
Heb 9:10 *which·stood* merely in ceremonial·foods and drinks
Mt 2:22 ·hearing that ArcheLaos reigns in Judea in·the·stead
Mt 9:9 ·to·as MattHew, who·is·sitting·down in the tax·booth
Mt 13:14 And in them is·utterly·fulfilled the prophecy of·
Mt 18:5 should·accept one such little·child in my name
Mt 24:5 For many shall·come in my name, saying, 'I AM
Mt 25:40 'Certainly I·say to·yeu, in as·much·as yeu·did *it*
Mt 25:45 'Certainly I·say to·yeu, in as·much·as yeu·did·not
Mt 27:29 *it* upon his head and·also a·reed in his right·hand,
Mt 27:43 "He·has·confidence in God. Let·him·rescue him
Mk 2:14 the·one of·Alphaeus) sitting·down in the tax·booth,
Mk 4:31 which, whenever it·should·be·sown in the earth,
Mk 4:31 least of·all the variety·of·seeds that·are in the earth.
Mk 4:38 And he·himself was in the stern·of·the·boat,
Mk 5:33 personally·knowing what has·happened in her,
Mk 8:4 ·men full with·bread, here in a·barren·wilderness?
Mk 9:37 one of·the little·children such·as·these in my name
Mk 9:39 ·is not·even·one who shall·do a·miracle in my name
Mk 10:24 ·is for·the·ones having·confidence in the valuables
Mk 12:14 instruct the Way of·God in truth. Is·it·proper to·
Mk 12:32 Mentor, clearly·full·well did·you·declare in truth,
Mk 13:6 For many shall·come in my name, saying, 'I AM
Rm 1:10 always in my prayers. Petitioning, if·somehow
Rm 5:2 we·stand, and we·boast in expectation of·the glory
Rm 6:21 were·yeu·having then in those·things·of·which now

Rm 8:20 ·rather through the·one subjecting *it* in expectation
Rm 11:13 to·yeu, the Gentiles, in as·much·as I·myself am
Rm 15:12 who·is·rising·up to·rule·over Gentiles; in him,
Php 4:10 over me has·flourished·again, in which also yeu·
1Pe 1:20 with·him·already·being·made·apparent in the last
2Pe 3:3 this first, that there·shall·come in the last days
1Th 1:2 all of·yeu, making mention of·yeu in our prayers,
1Th 3:7 On·account·of that, brothers, in all our tribulation
Tit 1:2 *and* in *the* Expectation of·eternal life-above, which
1Co 9:10 the·one plowing ought to·plow in expectation, and
1Co 9:10 treading·out·grain in expectation to·participate·by·
2Co 1:4 the·one comforting us in all our tribulation, in·order·
2Co 2:3 ·for me to·rejoice, having·confidence in yeu all that
2Co 7:4 ·above·and·beyond with·the joy in all our tribulation
2Co 7:7 the consoling with·which he·was·comforted in yeu,
2Co 7:13 ·of that, we·have·been·comforted in yeur comfort;
2Co 9:6 ·blessings also shall·reap in beneficial·blessings.
Eph 1:16 of·yeu, making mention of·yeu in my prayers—
Phm 1:4 God, making mention of·you always in my prayers,
Phm 1:7 we·have much gratitude and comfort in your love,
1Jn 3:3 one having this Expectation in him cleanses himself,
Rv 1:20 of·the seven stars which you·saw in my right·hand,
Rv 5:1 And I·saw in the right·hand of·the·one sitting·down
Rv 7:3 ·seal the slaves of·our God in their foreheads."
Rv 9:4 ·not have the official·seal of·God in their foreheads.
Rv 9:14 angels, the·ones having·been·bound in the great
Rv 11:8 And their corpses *shall·lay* in the broad·street of·the
Rv 14:1 of·his Father having·been·written in their foreheads.
Rv 14:9 ·image, and receives *its* etching in his forehead, or
Rv 14:9 receives *its* etching in his forehead, or in his hand,
Rv 17:8 names have·not been·written in the official·scroll
Rv 20:1 of·the bottomless·pit and a·great chain in his hand.
Rv 20:4 upon their foreheads, *nor* even in their hands— and
Rv 22:4 his face, and his name *shall·be* in their foreheads.

G1909.10 PREP ἐπί (2x)

Heb 7:11 sacred·priesthood, (for under it the People had·
Heb 9:15 (from·the violations *that·were* under the first

G1909.11 PREP ἐπί (42x)

Jn 13:18 the bread with me lifted·up his heel against me.'
Lk 9:5 the dust from yeur feet for a·testimony against them."
Lk 11:17 being·thoroughly·divided against itself is·made·
Lk 11:17 a·house *thoroughly·divided* against a·house falls.
Lk 11:18 is·thoroughly·divided against himself, how shall
Lk 12:52 ·been·thoroughly·divided, three against two, and
Lk 12:52 ·divided, three against two, and two against three.
Lk 12:53 Father shall·be·thoroughly·divided against son, and
Lk 12:53 against son, and son against father; mother against
Lk 12:53 son against father; mother against daughter, and
Lk 12:53 against daughter, and daughter against mother;
Lk 12:53 mother; mother-in-law against her daughter-in-law
Lk 12:53 and daughter-in-law against her mother-in-law."
Lk 14:31 ·and·meet the·one who·is·coming against him with
Lk 21:10 "Nation shall·be·awakened against nation, and
Lk 21:10 against nation, and kingdom against kingdom.
Lk 22:52 "Have·yeu·come·out, as against an·armed·robber,
Lk 22:53 yeu·did·not stretch·forth yeur hands against me.
Ac 4:27 they·were·gathered·together against your holy
Ac 8:1 a·great persecution against the Called·Out·citizenry,
Ac 13:11 the Lord's hand *is* against you, and you·shall·be
Ac 13:50 and they·roused·up persecution against Paul and
Ac 13:51 ·off the dust of·their feet against them, they·went
Mt 10:21 and children shall·rise·up against parents and
Mt 12:26 Adversary-Accuser, he·is·divided against himself.
Mt 22:34 But the Pharisees gathered·together against him,
Mt 24:7 "For nation shall·be·awakened against nation, and
Mt 24:7 against nation, and kingdom against kingdom. And
Mt 26:55 Did·yeu·come·out as against an·armed·robber with
Mt 27:27 gathered·together the whole battalion against him.
Mk 3:24 And if a·kingdom should·be·divided against itself,
Mk 3:25 And if a·home should·be·divided against itself, that
Mk 3:26 if the Adversary-Accuser rose·up against himself and
Mk 10:11 ·marry another commits·adultery against her.
Mk 13:8 "For nation shall·be·awakened against nation, and
Mk 13:8 against nation, and kingdom against kingdom. And
Mk 13:12 and children shall·rise·up against *their* parents
Mk 14:48 "Did·yeu·come·forth, as against an·armed·robber,
Rm 1:18 is·revealed from heaven against all irreverence and
Rm 2:2 ·God is according·to truth against the·ones practicing
1Pe 3:12 but *the* face of·Yahweh *is* against those·doing bad.
2Co 10:2 I·reckon to·be·daringly·bold against some— the·

G1909.12 PREP ἐφ' (9x)

Lk 7:44 your home, you·gave·me no water for my feet, but
Lk 18:4 And for a·time, he·did·not want·to.
Ac 15:14 to·take from·among *them* a·People for his name.
Ac 21:24 and cover·the·expense for them in·order·that
Php 1:5 for yeur fellowship in the good·news from *the* first
2Pe 1:13 ·do·resolutely·consider·it right, for as·long·as I·am
1Co 1:4 God always concerning yeu for the grace of·God,
2Co 9:15 Thanks *be* to·God for his indescribable voluntary·
Eph 2:10 in Anointed-One Jesus for beneficially·good works

G1909.13 PREP ἐπί (16x)

Lk 12:11 they·should·bring yeu before the gatherings, the
Lk 21:12 and prisons, being·brought before kings and
Ac 23:30 his legal·accusers also to·say before you the·things
Ac 24:19 it·is·necessary *for·them* to·be·here before you and
Ac 24:20 standing·still before the joint·council·of·Sanhedrin,
Ac 25:9 to·be·judged concerning these·things before me?
Ac 25:26 "Therefore I·brought him forth before yeu, and
Ac 25:26 before yeu, and especially before you, O·King
Ac 26:2 to·make·my·defense this·day before you concerning
Mt 10:18 Also yeu·shall·be·brought before governors and
Mk 13:9 and yeu·shall·be·set before governors and kings
1Co 6:1 go·to·court·to·be·judged before the unrighteous·
1Co 6:1 ·ones, and not·indeed before the holy·ones?
1Co 6:6 against a·brother, and that before non-trusting·ones.
2Co 7:14 boasting (the·one *we·made* before Titus) has·now·
1Ti 6:13 Jesus (the·one testifying before Pontius Pilate the

G1909.14 PREP ἐπ' (8x)

Ac 1:21 the Lord Jesus came·in and went·forth among us,
Mt 13:7 And others fell among the thorns, and the thorns
Mt 13:20 ·one already·being·permeated·with·seed among the
Mt 13:23 ·one already·being·permeated·with·seed among the
Mk 4:16 being·permeated·with·seed among the rocky·places
Mk 4:20 already·being·permeated·with·seed among the good
2Th 1:10 — because our testimony among yeu was·trusted.
Rv 7:15 ·down on the throne shall·encamp among them.

G1909.15 PREP ἐπί (7x)

Ac 28:14 we·were·exhorted to·stay·over with them *for*
Heb 8:8 ·consummate a·brand-new covenant with the house
Heb 8:8 with the house of·IsraEl and with the house of·Judah
Mt 18:29 saying, 'Be·patient with me, and I·shall·repay
Rm 10:19 shall·provoke yeu to·jealousy with *them that are*
Rm 10:19 ·anger yeu with a·nation without·comprehension.
3Jn 1:10 And not being·satisfied with these·things, neither

G1909.16 PREP ἐπί (1x)

Rv 18:17 *ship's* pilot, and all aboard the company of·ships,

G1909.17 PREP ἐπί (11x)

Jn 12:16 ·things were having·been·written concerning him,
Ac 5:35 to·accomplish concerning these men·of·clay†.
Heb 7:13 *this other priest*, concerning whom these·things
Heb 8:1 Now concerning the·things being·said, *this·is the*
Heb 11:4 testifying concerning his voluntary·offerings·of·
Mk 6:52 ·not comprehend concerning the loaves·of·bread,
Mk 9:12 "Yet how it·has·been·written concerning the Son
Mk 9:13 just·as it·has·been·written concerning him."
2Th 3:4 we·have·confidence in *the* Lord concerning yeu, that
2Co 12:21 ·failed and not repenting concerning the impurity
Rv 22:16 these·things concerning the Called·Out·citizenries.

G1909.18 PREP ἐπί (1x)

Lk 16:26 And on·top·of all these·things, between us and yeu

G1909.19 PREP ἐπί (4x)

Lk 1:59 they·were·calling him Zacharias, after the name of·
Lk 15:4 traverse after the·one having·become·completely·
Heb 9:17 ·will·and·covenant *is* of·force after men·are·dead,
Rm 5:14 the·ones not morally·failing after the resemblance

G1909.20 PREP ἐπί (3x)

Mt 21:19 And seeing one fig·tree by the roadway, he·came
Mt 28:14 And if this should·be·heard by the governor, we·
1Co 8:11 and by your knowledge shall the weak brother

G1910 ἐπι•βαίνω êpibaínō *v.* (6x)

Roots:G1909 G0901-3 Compare:G1684 G1913

G1910.2 V-2AAI-1S ἐπέβην (1x)

Ac 20:18 from that first day since I·walked·over into Asia,

G1910.2 V-2AAP-NSM ἐπιβάς (1x)

Ac 25:1 three days after walking·over into·the province,

G1910.3 V-2AAI-1P ἐπέβημεν (1x)

Ac 21:6 after·embracing one·another, we·embarked into the

G1910.3 V-2AAP-NPM ἐπιβάντες (2x)

Ac 21:2 to Phoenicia, once·embarking, we·launched·forth.
Ac 27:2 And after·embarking·upon a·sailing·ship of·

G1910.4 V-RAP-NSM ἐπιβεβηκώς (1x)

Mt 21:5 calmly·mild and having·mounted upon a·donkey

G1911 ἐπι•βάλλω êpibállō *v.* (18x)

Roots:G1909 G0906 Compare:G1977 G0114 G0659 See:G1438

G1911.1 V-FAI-3P ἐπιβαλοῦσιν (1x)

Lk 21:12 ·all these·things, they·shall·throw their hands on

G1911.1 V-PAI-3S ἐπιβάλλει (2x)

Lk 5:36 to them, "Not·even·one·man throws a·patch *from* a·
Mt 9:16 not·even·one·man throws a·patch of·unprocessed

G1911.1 V-2AAI-3S ἐπέβαλεν (3x)

Jn 7:30 him, but not·even·one·man threw his hand on him,
Jn 7:44 him, but·yet not·even·one·man threw hands on him.
Ac 12:1 King HerOd·Agrippa violently·threw·forth his hands

G1911.1 V-2AAI-3P ἐπέβαλον (6x)

Ac 4:3 And they·threw their hands on·them and placed *them*
Ac 5:18 and they·threw their hands upon the ambassadors
Ac 21:27 crowd into·an·uproar, and they·threw their hands
Mt 26:50 Then going·alongside, they·threw their hands on
Mk 11:7 colt to Jesus, and they·threw their garments on·it,
Mk 14:46 And they·threw their hands on him and securely·

G1911.1 V-2AAN ἐπιβαλεῖν (1x)

Lk 20:19 in the same hour sought to·throw *their* hands on

G1911.1 V-2AAP-NSM ἐπιβαλών (1x)

Lk 9:62 "Not·even·one·man, upon·throwing his hand to a·

G1911.1 V-2AAS-1S ἐπιβάλω (1x)

1Co 7:35 advantage; not that I·may·throw a·noose upon·yeu

G1911.2 V-IAI-3S ἐπέβαλλεν (1x)

Mk 4:37 and the breaking·waves were·breaking into the

G1911.3 V-2AAP-NSM ἐπιβαλών (1x)

Mk 14:72 me three·times." And reflecting·upon *it*, he·was·

G1911.4 V-PAP-ASN ἐπιβάλλον (1x)

Lk 15:12 portion of·substance being·stashed·away *for·me*.'

G1912 ἐπι•βαρέω êpibaréō *v.* (3x)

Roots:G1909 G0916

G1912.2 V-PAS-1S ἐπιβαρῶ (1x)

2Co 2:5 , in·order·that I·may·not be·a·burden·upon yeu all.

G1912.2 V-AAN ἐπιβαρῆσαι (2x)

1Th 2:9 day (specifically not to·be·a·burden·upon any of·yeu
2Th 3:8 ·for *us* not to·be·a·burden·upon any of·yeu.

G1913 ἐπι•βιβάζω êpibibázō *v.* (3x)

Roots:G1909 G0973-1 Compare:G1910 See:G0307 G1688

G1913 V-AAI-3P ἐπεβίβασαν (1x)

Lk 19:35 upon the colt, they·mounted Jesus upon *it*.

G1913 V-AAP-NSM ἐπιβιβάσας (1x)

Lk 10:34 ·in oil and wine. And mounting him upon his·own

G1913 V-AAP-NPM ἐπιβιβάσαντες (1x)

Ac 23:24 *for·them* in·order·that after·mounting Paul upon

G1914 ἐπι•βλέπω êpiblépō *v.* (4x)

Roots:G1909 G0991 See:G1689

G1914.1 V-AAM-2P ἐπιβλέψατε (1x)

Ac 13:41 see, and intently·look, and be·disconcerted.

G1914.2 V-AAI-3S ἐπέβλεψεν (1x)

Lk 1:48 Because 'he·kindly·looked upon the humble·estate

G1914.2 V-AAM-2S ἐπίβλεψον (1x)

Lk 9:38 "Mentor, I·petition you, kindly·look upon my son,

G1914.2 V-AAS-2P ἐπιβλέψητε (1x)

Jac 2:3 and *if* yeu·should·kindly·look upon the·one

G1915 ἐπί•βλημα êpíblēma *n.* (6x)
Roots:G1911
G1915 N-ASN ἐπίβλημα (4x)
Lk 5:36 Not·even·one·man throws a·patch *from* a·brand-new
Lk 5:36 makes·a·tear; and·also *the* patch, the·one from the
Mt 9:16 ·even·one·man throws a·patch of·unprocessed cloth
Mk 2:21 ·even·one·man sews a·patch of·unprocessed cloth
EG1915 (2x)
Lk 5:36 then the brand-new *patch* makes·a·tear; and·also
Mk 2:21 *then* the brand-new *patch, when·shrunk,* takes·away

G1916 ἐπι•βοάω êpibóáō *v.* (1x)
Roots:G1909 G0994
G1916 V-PAP-NPM ἐπιβοῶντες (1x)
Ac 25:24 JeruSalem, and here, crying·out·against *him, that*

G1917 ἐπι•βουλή êpiboulḗ *n.* (4x)
Roots:G1909 G1014 Compare:G1106
G1917.2 N-NSF ἐπιβουλή (1x)
Ac 9:24 Now their plot was·known to·Saul. And they·were·
G1917.2 N-DPF ἐπιβουλαῖς (1x)
Ac 20:19 the·ones befalling me by the plots of·the Jews.
G1917.2 N-GSF ἐπιβουλῆς (2x)
Ac 20:3 ·months. *But* with·a·plot being·made against·him
Ac 23:30 Now with·a·plot being·brought to·my attention

G1918 ἐπι•γαμβρεύω êpigambrêúō *v.* (1x)
Roots:G1909 G1062 xLangAlso:H2992
G1918.2 V-FAI-3S ἐπιγαμβρεύσει (1x)
Mt 22:24 children, his brother shall·dutifully·marry his wife

G1919 ἐπί•γειος êpígêiôs *adj.* (7x)
Roots:G1909 G1093
G1919.1 A-NSF ἐπίγειος (2x)
Jac 3:15 ·down from·above, but·rather *is* earthly, soulish,
2Co 5:1 we·personally·know that if our earthly home of·the
G1919.1 A-APN ἐπίγεια (2x)
Jn 3:12 If I·declared to·yeu the earthly·things, and yeu·do·
Php 3:19 *are* the·ones contemplating the earthly·things).
G1919.2 A-NPN ἐπίγεια (1x)
1Co 15:40 also celestial bodies and terrestrial bodies, but·yet
G1919.2 A-GPN ἐπιγείων (2x)
Php 2:10 ·bow (of·celestial·ones, and of·terrestrial·ones, and
1Co 15:40 ·kind, and the *glory* of·the terrestrial *is* another.

G1920 ἐπι•γίνομαι êpigínômai *v.* (1x)
Roots:G1909 G1096
G1920.2 V-2ADP-GSM ἐπιγενομένου (1x)
Ac 28:13 day, with·*the*·south·wind springing·up, we·came

G1921 ἐπι•γινώσκω êpiginṓskō *v.* (42x)
Roots:G1909 G1097 Compare:G1987 G2467 See:G1922
G1921.1 V-FDI-1S ἐπιγνώσομαι (1x)
1Co 13:12 ·portion, but then I·shall·fully·know just·as also
G1921.1 V-PAI-3S ἐπιγινώσκει (2x)
Mt 11:27 my Father, and no·one·at·all fully·knows the Son,
Mt 11:27 nor·even·does anyone fully·know the Father,
G1921.1 V-2AAP-NSM ἐπιγνούς (2x)
Lk 5:22 But Jesus, fully·knowing their deliberations,
Mk 2:8 And Jesus, fully·knowing immediately in·his spirit
G1921.1 V-2AAS-2S ἐπιγνῷς (1x)
Lk 1:4 in·order·that you·may·fully·know the security
G1921.1 V-API-1S ἐπεγνώσθην (1x)
1Co 13:12 I·shall·fully·know just·as also I·am·fully·known.
G1921.1 V-RAP-DPM ἐπεγνωκόσιν (1x)
1Ti 4:3 ·the·ones trusting and having·fully·known the truth.
G1921.2 V-FDI-2P ἐπιγνώσεσθε (2x)
Mt 7:16 By their fruits, yeu·shall·recognize them. "¿!·Do
Mt 7:20 by their fruits yeu·shall·recognize them.
G1921.2 V-PAI-2P ἐπιγινώσκετε (1x)
2Co 13:5 Or do·yeu·not recognize *for* yeur·own·selves that
G1921.2 V-PPP-NPM ἐπιγινωσκόμενοι (1x)
2Co 6:9 as being·unknown and·yet being·recognized, as
G1921.2 V-IAI-3P ἐπεγίνωσκον (3x)
Ac 3:10 And they·were·recognizing that he·himself was the·
Ac 4:13 ·were·marveling; and they·were·recognizing them,
Ac 27:39 it·was day, they·were·not recognizing the land, but
G1921.2 V-2AAI-2P ἐπέγνωτε (1x)
Col 1:6 day yeu·heard *it* and recognized the grace of·God in
G1921.2 V-2AAI-3P ἐπέγνωσαν (3x)
Lk 24:31 ·thoroughly·opened·up, and they·recognized him,
Mt 17:12 even·now, and they·did·not recognize him, but·yet
Mk 6:33 heading·on·out, and many recognized him. Then
G1921.2 V-2AAN ἐπιγνῶναι (2x)
Lk 24:16 ·securely·held, *such·for them* not to·recognize him.
Ac 24:8 after·scrutinizing him, to·recognize concerning all
G1921.2 V-2AAP-DPM ἐπιγνοῦσιν (1x)
2Pe 2:21 of·righteousness, than, after·recognizing *it,* to·
G1921.2 V-2AAP-NSF ἐπιγνοῦσα (1x)
Ac 12:14 And after·recognizing Peter's voice, she·did·not
G1921.2 V-2AAP-NSM ἐπιγνούς (1x)
Mk 5:30 And Jesus, recognizing immediately in himself the
G1921.2 V-2AAP-NPM ἐπιγνόντες (3x)
Mt 14:35 And once·recognizing him, the men of·that place
Mk 6:54 of·the sailboat, immediately, after·recognizing him
Rm 1:32 Who, after·recognizing the statute of·God (that
G1921.2 V-RAN ἐπεγνωκέναι (1x)
2Pe 2:21 ·better for·them not to·have·recognized the way of·
G1921.3 P:P-1GS ἐπιγινώσκεις (1x)
Ac 25:10 even as you·yourself realize better·than·most.
G1921.3 V-2AAI-3P ἐπέγνωσαν (2x)
Lk 1:22 to·them. Then they·realized that he·has·clearly·seen
Ac 28:1 being·thoroughly·saved, then they·realized that the
G1921.3 V-2AAP-GPM ἐπιγνόντων (1x)
Ac 19:34 But after·realizing that he·was a·Jew, there·came
G1921.3 V-2AAP-NSF ἐπιγνοῦσα (1x)
Lk 7:37 when·realizing that he·was·reclining·at·a·meal in
G1921.3 V-2AAP-NSM ἐπιγνούς (2x)
Lk 23:7 And after·realizing that he·is from·out·of·HerOd·
Ac 22:29 also was·afraid after·realizing that he·was a·
G1921.3 V-2AAP-NPM ἐπιγνόντες (1x)
Ac 9:30 But after·realizing *it,* the brothers brought him down
G1921.3 V-2AAS-3S ἐπιγνῷ (1x)
Ac 22:24 in·order·that he·may·realize on·account·of what
G1921.4 V-FDI-2P ἐπιγνώσεσθε (1x)
2Co 1:13 and I·expect that yeu·shall·acknowledge *this* even
G1921.4 V-PAI-2P ἐπιγινώσκετε (1x)
2Co 1:13 yeu·currently·read·aloud or also acknowledge; and
G1921.4 V-PAM-2P ἐπιγινώσκετε (1x)
1Co 16:18 acknowledge the·ones such·as·these.
G1921.4 V-PAM-3S ἐπιγινωσκέτω (1x)
1Co 14:37 spiritual, let·him·acknowledge that these·things
G1921.4 V-2AAI-2P ἐπέγνωτε (1x)
2Co 1:14 just·as also yeu·already·acknowledged us in part,

G1922 ἐπί•γνωσις êpígnōsis *n.* (20x)
Roots:G1921 Compare:G0144 G1253 See:G1108
G1922.1 N-ASF ἐπίγνωσιν (4x)
Col 1:10 and growing·up into the full·knowledge of·God,
Col 2:2 into a·full·knowledge of·the Mystery of·God and
Col 3:10 the·one being·renewed into a·full·knowledge ‘
1Ti 2:4 ·be·saved and to·come to a·full·knowledge of·truth.
G1922.1 N-DSF ἐπιγνώσει (1x)
2Pe 1:2 ·multiplied to·yeu in *the* full·knowledge of·God and
G1922.2 N-NSF ἐπίγνωσις (1x)
Rm 3:20 Torah-Law *is the* recognition of·moral·failure.
G1922.2 N-ASF ἐπίγνωσιν (4x)
Heb 10:26 after receiving the recognition of·the truth, no·
Tit 1:1 Selected-Ones and *for·the* recognition of·truth (the·
2Ti 2:25 to·them repentance for *the* recognition of·truth,
2Ti 3:7 ·even being·able to·come to a·recognition of·truth.
G1922.2 N-DSF ἐπιγνώσει (2x)
Eph 1:17 of·wisdom and revelation in recognition of·him—
Phm 1:6 by *the* recognition of·every beneficially·good·thing
G1922.2 N-GSF ἐπιγνώσεως (1x)
2Pe 1:3 through the recognition of·the·one already·calling
G1922.3 N-ASF ἐπίγνωσιν (2x)
Rm 10:2 not according·to recognition·and·full·knowledge.
Col 1:9 with·the recognition·and·full·knowledge of·his will
G1922.3 N-DSF ἐπιγνώσει (2x)
Rm 1:28 to·hold *him* in recognition·and·full·knowledge, God
Php 1:9 more in recognition·and·full·knowledge and with·all
G1922.3 N-GSF ἐπιγνώσεως (1x)
Eph 4:13 of·the recognition·and·full·knowledge of·the Son
G1922.5 N-ASF ἐπίγνωσιν (1x)
2Pe 1:8 in the recognition·and·acknowledgment of·our Lord
G1922.5 N-DSF ἐπιγνώσει (1x)
2Pe 2:20 by a·recognition·and·acknowledgment of·the Lord

G1923 ἐπι•γραφή êpigraphḗ *n.* (5x)
Roots:G1924
G1923 N-NSF ἐπιγραφή (4x)
Lk 23:38 And an·inscription also was·having·been·written
Mt 22:20 "Whose derived·image and inscription *is* this?
Mk 12:16 *is* this derived·image and inscription?" And they·
Mk 15:26 And this·was the inscription for·the cause of·his
G1923 N-ASF ἐπιγραφήν (1x)
Lk 20:24 Whose derived·image and inscription does·it·have?

G1924 ἐπι•γράφω êpigráphō *v.* (5x)
Roots:G1909 G1125
G1924 V-FAI-1S ἐπιγράψω (2x)
Heb 8:10 innermost·mind, and I·shall·inscribe them upon
Heb 10:16 upon their innermost·minds I·shall·inscribe them,
G1924 V-RPP-APN ἐπιγεγραμμένα (1x)
Rv 21:12 gates, and names having·been·inscribed, which are
G1924 V-RPP-NSF ἐπιγεγραμμένη (1x)
Mk 15:26 cause of·his *execution* having·been·inscribed,
G1924 V-LPI-3S ἐπεγέγραπτο (1x)
Ac 17:23 I·found a·pedestal on which had·been·inscribed,

G1925 ἐπι•δείκνυμι êpidéíknymi *v.* (9x)
Roots:G1909 G1166 Compare:G0584
G1925.2 V-PAP-NSM ἐπιδεικνύς (1x)
Ac 18:28 to·the Jews publicly, fully·exhibiting through the
G1925.2 V-PMP-NPF ἐπιδεικνύμεναι (1x)
Ac 9:39 and fully·exhibiting what·many inner·tunics and
G1925.2 V-AAI-3S ἐπέδειξεν (1x)
Lk 24:40 this·thing, he·fully·exhibited for·them his hands
G1925.2 V-AAM-2P ἐπιδείξατε (3x)
Lk 17:14 yeu·must·fully·exhibit yeurselves to·the priests·
Lk 20:24 Fully·exhibit for·me a·denarius. Whose derived·
Mt 22:19 Fully·exhibit for·me the currency of·the census·
G1925.2 V-AAN ἐπιδεῖξαι (3x)
Heb 6:17 more·abundantly to·fully·exhibit to·the heirs of·
Mt 16:1 inquired·of him to·fully·exhibit for·them a sign
Mt 24:1 disciples came·alongside to·fully·exhibit for·him the

G1926 ἐπι•δέχομαι êpidéchômai *v.* (2x)
Roots:G1909 G1209 See:G0588 G1523
G1926.2 V-PNI-3S ἐπιδέχεται (2x)
3Jn 1:9 among·them, does·not welcomely·receive us.
3Jn 1:10 does he·himself welcomely·receive the brothers,

G1927 ἐπι•δημέω êpidēméō *v.* (2x)
Roots:G1909 G1218 Compare:G2730 G3939 G0589 See:G3927
G1927.2 V-PAP-NPM ἐπιδημοῦντες (2x)
Ac 2:10 and the·ones temporarily·residing·here·from Rome,
Ac 17:21 the foreigners temporarily·residing·there were· for

G1928 ἐπι•δια•τάσσομαι êpidiatássômai *v.* (1x)
Roots:G1909 G1299
G1928.2 V-PNI-3S ἐπιδιατάσσεται (1x)
Gal 3:15 ·one·man sets·it·aside or adds·stipulations *to·it.*

G1929 ἐπι•δίδωμι êpidídōmi *v.* (11x)
Roots:G1909 G1325 Compare:G0325 G0591 G3860
G1929.2 V-FAI-1S ἐπιδώσω (1x)
Jn 13:26 "It·is that·man to·whom I·shall·hand the morsel,
G1929.2 V-FAI-3S ἐπιδώσει (5x)
Lk 11:11 shall·request bread, ¿! shall·he·hand him a·stone?
Lk 11:11 ¿! instead of·a·fish, shall·he·hand him a·serpent?
Lk 11:12 ·request an·egg, ¿! shall·he·hand him a·scorpion?
Mt 7:9 son should·request bread, ¿! shall·hand him a·stone?
Mt 7:10 ·should·request a·fish, ¿! shall·hand him a·serpent?
G1929.2 V-IAI-3S ἐπεδίδου (1x)
Lk 24:30 and after·breaking *it,* he·was·handing *it* to·them.
G1929.2 V-AAI-3P ἐπέδωκαν (1x)
Lk 24:42 And they·handed him a·piece of·a·broiled fish and

G1929.2 V-2AAP-NPM ἐπιδόντες (1x)
Ac 27:15 to·tack into·the wind, handing *her to·the wind*, we·
G1929.2 V-API-3S ἐπεδόθη (1x)
Lk 4:17 ·scroll of·Isaiah the prophet was·handed to·him.
G1929.3 V-AAI-3P ἐπέδωκαν (1x)
Ac 15:30 the multitude, they·hand-delivered the letter.

G1930 ἐπι•δι•ορθόω êpidiôrthóō *v.* (1x)
Roots:G1909 G1356-2 Compare:G0461 G2735 See:G0592
G1930.ª V-AMS-2S ἐπιδιορθώσῃ (1x)
Tit 1:5 in Crete, that you·should·fully·set·in·order the·things

G1931 ἐπι•δύω êpidýō *v.* (1x)
Roots:G1909 G1416
G1931.2 V-PAM-3S ἐπιδυέτω (1x)
Eph 4:26 ' Do·not·let the sun go·down upon yeur personal·

G1932 ἐπι•είκεια êpiêíkêia *n.* (2x)
Roots:G1933
G1932.2 N-DSF ἐπιεικείᾳ (1x)
Ac 24:4 I·implore you in·your·own fairness to·hear of·us
G1932.2 N-GSF ἐπιεικείας (1x)
2Co 10:1 the gentleness and fairness of·Anointed-One (*I*,

G1933 ἐπι•εικής êpiêikḗs *adj.* (5x)
Roots:G1909 G1503 Compare:G2261 G4235 G4236 G4240 G4239
G1933.2 A-NSF ἐπιεικής (1x)
Jac 3:17 ·clean, then peaceable, fair *and* readily·compliant,
G1933.2 A-ASM ἐπιεικῆ (1x)
1Ti 3:3 of·shameful·gain, but·rather fair, not·quarrelsome,
G1933.2 A-APM ἐπιεικεῖς (1x)
Tit 3:2 ·man, to·be not·quarrelsome, *but* fair, indicating all
G1933.2 A-DPM ἐπιεικέσιν (1x)
1Pe 2:18 beneficially·good·ones and fair·ones, but·rather
G1933.3 A-NSN ἐπιεικές (1x)
Php 4:5 Yeur fairness, let·it·be·known to·all men·of·clay†.

G1934 ἐπι•ζητέω êpizētéō *v.* (14x)
Roots:G1909 G2212 See:G0327
G1934.1 V-PAI-1P ἐπιζητοῦμεν (1x)
Heb 13:14 but·rather we·seek·for the·one about·to·come.
G1934.1 V-PAI-2P ἐπιζητεῖτε (1x)
Ac 19:39 "But if yeu·seek anything concerning other·matters
G1934.1 V-PAI-3S ἐπιζητεῖ (6x)
Lk 11:29 "This is an·evil generation. It·seeks·for a·sign, and
Lk 12:30 ·things, the nations of·the world seek·after. "And
Mt 6:32 (For all these·things the Gentiles seek·after) for yeur
Mt 12:39 (*who·is* also an·adulteress) seeks·for a·sign, and a·
Mt 16:4 (*who·is* also an·adulteress) seeks·for a·sign, and a·
Mk 8:12 "Why·does this generation seek·for a·sign?
G1934.1 V-PAI-3P ἐπιζητοῦσιν (1x)
Heb 11:14 ·things make·it·clear that they·seek a·fatherland.
G1934.1 V-AAI-3S ἐπεζήτησεν (1x)
Ac 13:7 for·BarNabas and Saul, sought to·hear the
G1934.1 V-AAP-NSM ἐπιζητήσας (1x)
Ac 12:19 And HerOd·Agrippa, after·seeking·for him and not
G1934.3 V-PAI-1S ἐπιζητῶ (2x)
Php 4:17 Not that I·anxiously·seek the gift, but·rather I·
Php 4:17 ·seek the gift, but·rather I·anxiously·seek the fruit,
G1934.3 V-PAI-3S ἐπιζητεῖ (1x)
Rm 11:7 ·not obtain that which it·still·anxiously·seeks, but

G1935 ἐπι•θανάτιος êpithanátiôs *adj.* (1x)
Roots:G1909 G2288
G1935 A-APM ἐπιθανατίους (1x)
1Co 4:9 last, as doomed·to·death, because we·have·now·

G1936 ἐπί•θεσις êpíthêsis *n.* (4x)
Roots:G2007
G1936.2 N-GSF ἐπιθέσεως (4x)
Ac 8:18 is·given through the laying·on of·the ambassadors
Heb 6:2 of·ceremonial·washings, and of·laying·on of·hands,
1Ti 4:14 prophecy, with *the* laying·on of·the hands of·the
2Ti 1:6 which is in you through the laying·on of·my hands.

G1937 ἐπι•θυμέω êpithyméō *v.* (16x)
Roots:G1909 G2372 Compare:G2442 G1971 G2206 G3715 See:G1939 G1938
G1937.2 V-FAI-2S ἐπιθυμήσεις (2x)
Rm 7:7 was·saying, "'You·shall·not long·for·(or·covet).'"
Rm 13:9 ·false·witness. You·shall·not long·for·(or·covet).'"
G1937.2 V-FAI-2P ἐπιθυμήσετε (1x)
Lk 17:22 "Days shall·come when yeu·shall·long to·see one
G1937.2 V-FAI-3P ἐπιθυμήσουσιν (1x)
Rv 9:6 shall·not find him. And they·shall·long to·die, and
G1937.2 V-PAI-1P ἐπιθυμοῦμεν (1x)
Heb 6:11 And we·long·for each·one of·yeu to·indicate the
G1937.2 V-PAI-2P ἐπιθυμεῖτε (1x)
Jac 4:2 Yeu·long·for and do·not have.
G1937.2 V-PAI-3S ἐπιθυμεῖ (2x)
Gal 5:17 For the flesh longs against the Spirit, and the Spirit
1Ti 3:1 ·assignment·of·oversight, he·longs·for a·good work.
G1937.2 V-PAI-3P ἐπιθυμοῦσιν (1x)
1Pe 1:12 ·things angels long to·stoop·near·and·peer into.
G1937.2 V-PAP-NSM ἐπιθυμῶν (1x)
Lk 16:21 and longing to·be·stuffed·full with the little·crumbs
G1937.2 V-IAI-3S ἐπεθύμει (1x)
Lk 15:16 And he·was·longing to·overfill his belly with the
G1937.2 V-AAI-1S ἐπεθύμησα (2x)
Lk 22:15 "With·longing, I·longed to·eat this Passover with
Ac 20:33 "I·longed·for not·even·one·man's silver or gold or
G1937.2 V-AAI-3P ἐπεθύμησαν (2x)
Mt 13:17 and righteous·men longed to·see *the·things* which
1Co 10:6 ·things, just·as they·also longed·after *such·things*.
G1937.2 V-AAN ἐπιθυμῆσαι (1x)
Mt 5:28 looking·upon a·woman specifically to·long·for her,

G1938 ἐπι•θυμητής êpithymētḗs *n.* (1x)
Roots:G1937 See:G1939
G1938 N-APM ἐπιθυμητάς (1x)
1Co 10:6 for us not to·be men·longing·after bad·things, just·

G1939 ἐπι•θυμία êpithymía *n.* (38x)
Roots:G1937 Compare:G1972 G1974 G3715 G3804 See:G1938
G1939.1 N-NSF ἐπιθυμία (4x)
Jac 1:15 Then with·the longing conceiving, it·reproduces·
1Jn 2:16 all *that·is* in the world, the longing of·the flesh, and
1Jn 2:16 of·the flesh, and the longing of·the eyes, and the
1Jn 2:17 the world passes·away, and its longing, but the·one
G1939.1 N-NPF ἐπιθυμίαι (1x)
Mk 4:19 remaining longings in·which·they·are·traversing—
G1939.1 N-ASF ἐπιθυμίαν (5x)
Gal 5:16 and no, yeu·would·not finish a·longing of·flesh.
Rm 7:7 I·had·not personally·known the longing, except·that
Rm 7:8 accomplished in me all·manner·of longing. For
Php 1:23 two *choices*, having the longing to·break·camp and
Col 3:5 impurity, burning·passion, wrong longing, and the
G1939.1 N-APF ἐπιθυμίας (10x)
Jn 8:44 and yeu·want to·do the longings of·yeur father.
Rm 13:14 do·not make provision for longings of·the flesh.
Jud 1:16 traversing according·to their·own longings. And
Jud 1:18 according·to their·own irreverent longings.
2Pe 3:3 traversing according·to their own longings,
Tit 2:12 and the worldly longings, we·should·live
Eph 4:22 ·one being·corrupted by the delusional longings)—
1Ti 6:9 *into* many stupid and injurious longings, which suck
2Ti 2:22 So flee the youthful longings, but pursue
2Ti 4:3 ·to their·own longings, they·shall·further·stack·up
G1939.1 N-DSF ἐπιθυμίᾳ (4x)
Lk 22:15 to them, "With·longing, I·longed to·eat this
2Pe 1:4 ·from the corruption *caused* by worldly longing.
2Pe 2:10 who·are·traversing in a·contaminating longing,
1Th 2:17 ·abundantly to·see yeur face with much longing.
G1939.1 N-DPF ἐπιθυμίαις (10x)
Gal 5:24 together with·the intense·cravings and the longings.
Rm 1:24 to impurity among the longings of·their·own hearts,
Rm 6:12 ·for *yeu* to·listen·to·and·obey her in its longings.
1Pe 1:14 ·conforming to·the previous longings in yeur
1Pe 4:2 ·of *his* time in flesh to·the·longings of·men·of·clay†,
1Pe 4:3 in debaucheries, longings, excesses·of·wine,
2Pe 2:18 ·things of·futility, *it·is* by longings of·flesh *and* by·
Tit 3:3 being·slaves to·diverse longings and pleasures,
Eph 2:3 ·of·life in·times·past in the longings of·our flesh,
2Ti 3:6 being·led·away with·a·diversity·of longings,
G1939.1 N-GSF ἐπιθυμίας (3x)
Jac 1:14 ·forth by his·own longing and being·entrapped.
1Th 4:5 not in *the* burning·passion of·longing, even exactly·
Rv 18:14 And the juicy·ripe·fruit of·the longing of·your soul
G1939.1 N-GPF ἐπιθυμιῶν (1x)
1Pe 2:11 to·abstain·from the fleshly longings, which

G1940 ἐπι•καθ•ίζω êpikathízō *v.* (1x)
Roots:G1909 G2523
G1940 V-AAI-3S ἐπεκάθισεν (1x)
Mt 21:7 garments up·over them and seated *him* up·over those

G1941 ἐπι•καλέομαι êpikalêômai *v.* (32x)
Roots:G1909 G2564 Compare:G1951 G4316
G1941.1 V-FMI-3P ἐπικαλέσονται (1x)
Rm 10:14 So·then, how shall·they·call·upon *him* in whom
G1941.1 V-PMI-1S ἐπικαλοῦμαι (1x)
2Co 1:23 Now I·myself do·call·upon God *for* a·witness upon
G1941.1 V-PMI-2P ἐπικαλεῖσθε (1x)
1Pe 1:17 And if yeu·presently·call·upon Father, the·one
G1941.1 V-PMP-ASM ἐπικαλούμενον (1x)
Ac 7:59 ·stones·at Stephen while·he·is·calling·upon *the Lord*
G1941.1 V-PMP-APM ἐπικαλουμένους (3x)
Ac 9:14 to·bind all the·ones who·are·calling·upon your name
Ac 9:21 ·ones in JeruSalem who·are·calling·upon this name,
Rm 10:12 ·wealthy to all the·ones who·are·calling·upon him.
G1941.1 V-PMP-DPM ἐπικαλουμένοις (1x)
1Co 1:2 *those* in every place who·are·calling·upon the name
G1941.1 V-PMP-GPM ἐπικαλουμένων (1x)
2Ti 2:22 peace, with the·ones calling·upon the Lord out of·
G1941.1 V-AMP-NSM ἐπικαλεσάμενος (1x)
Ac 22:16 ·away your moral·failures, calling·upon the name
G1941.1 V-AMS-3S ἐπικαλέσηται (2x)
Ac 2:21 *that* anyone who himself·should·call·upon the name
Rm 10:13 "all who would call·upon the name of·*the*·Lord
G1941.2 V-PMI-1S ἐπικαλοῦμαι (1x)
Ac 25:11 ·hand me over to·them. I·appeal·to Caesar."
G1941.2 V-AMN ἐπικαλέσασθαι (1x)
Ac 28:19 *this*, I·was·compelled to·appeal·to Caesar, though
G1941.2 V-AMP-GSM ἐπικαλεσαμένου (2x)
Ac 25:21 "But with·Paul appealing to·be·reserved for the
Ac 25:25 and also with·he·himself appealing this to the
G1941.2 V-RMI-2S ἐπικέκλησαι (1x)
Ac 25:12 answered, "You·have·appealed·to Caesar. To
G1941.2 V-LDI-3S ἐπεκέκλητο (1x)
Ac 26:32 ·fully·released, if·he·had·not appealed·to Caesar."
G1941.3 V-PPN ἐπικαλεῖσθαι (1x)
Heb 11:16 ·of them, *or* to·be·properly·called their God, for
G1941.3 V-APP-NSM ἐπικληθείς (1x)
Ac 4:36 Yosef, the·one being·properly·called BarNabas by
G1941.4 V-PPI-3S ἐπικαλεῖται (2x)
Ac 10:5 Joppa and send·for Simon, who is·surnamed Peter.
Ac 10:32 summarily·call·for Simon, who is·surnamed Peter,
G1941.4 V-PPP-ASM ἐπικαλούμενον (3x)
Lk 22:3 into Judas, the·one being·surnamed IsCariot, being
Ac 11:13 Joppa and send·for Simon being·surnamed Peter,
Ac 15:22 Judas, the·one being·surnamed BarSabas, and
G1941.4 V-PPP-GSM ἐπικαλουμένου (1x)
Ac 12:12 the mother of·John (being·surnamed Mark), where
G1941.4 V-PPP-NSM ἐπικαλούμενος (1x)
Ac 10:18 whether Simon, the·one being·surnamed Peter, is·
G1941.4 V-API-3S ἐπεκλήθη (1x)
Ac 1:23 being·called BarTsabas (who was·surnamed Justus)
G1941.4 V-APP-ASN ἐπικληθέν (1x)
Jac 2:7 beautiful name, the·one being·surnamed upon yeu?
G1941.4 V-APP-ASM ἐπικληθέντα (1x)
Ac 12:25 ·along John, the·one being·surnamed Mark).
G1941.4 V-APP-NSM ἐπικληθείς (1x)
Mt 10:3 Lebbaeus, the·one being·surnamed Thaddaeus;

G1941.4 V-RPI-3S ἐπικέκληται (1x)
Ac 15:17 whom my name has·been·surnamed upon them,

G1942 ἐπι•κάλυμα êpikályma *n.* (1x)
Roots:G1943 Compare:G4392
G1942.3 N-ASN ἐπικάλυμμα (1x)
1Pe 2:16 retaining the liberty as a·cover-up for·the depravity,

G1943 ἐπι•καλύπτω êpikalýptō *v.* (1x)
Roots:G1909 G2572 Compare:G0863 G0630 G2436 See:G1942
G1943.3 V-API-3P ἐπεκαλύφθησαν (1x)
Rm 4:7 moral·failures are·fully·covered·over·and·buried.

G1944 ἐπι•κατ•άρατος êpikatáratôs *adj.* (3x)
Roots:G1943-2 Compare:G0331 xLangEquiv:H0779
G1944.1 A-NSM ἐπικατάρατος (2x)
Gal 3:10 it·has·been·written, "Utterly·accursed *is* everyone
Gal 3:13 it·has·been·written, "Utterly·accursed *is* any one
G1944.1 A-NPM ἐπικατάρατοι (1x)
Jn 7:49 knowing the Oral-law, they·are utterly·accursed."

G1945 ἐπί•κειμαι êpíkêimai *v.* (7x)
Roots:G1909 G2749 Compare:G1879 G2001
G1945.1 V-PNI-3S ἐπίκειται (1x)
1Co 9:16 a·boast to·me, for necessity is·laid·upon me; and
G1945.1 V-PNP-ASN ἐπικείμενον (1x)
Jn 21:9 and a·small·broiled·fish being·set·out laying·upon *it*,
G1945.1 V-PNP-GSM ἐπικειμένου (1x)
Ac 27:20 and with·no little wintry·storm laying·upon *us*, all
G1945.2 V-INI-3S ἐπέκειτο (1x)
Jn 11:38 it·was a·cave, and a·stone was·resting upon it.
G1945.3 V-PNN ἐπικεῖσθαι (1x)
Lk 5:1 with the crowd pressing·upon him to·hear the
G1945.4 V-PNP-NPN ἐπικείμενα (1x)
Heb 9:10 of·flesh, imposed *on·them* so·long·as·unto *the*
G1945.5 V-INI-3P ἐπέκειντο (1x)
Lk 23:23 And they·were·insisting with·loud voices,

G1946 Ἐπι•κούρειος Êpikôúrêiôs *n/g.* (1x)
Compare:G4770 See:G1947
G1946.2 N/G-GPM Ἐπικουρείων (1x)
Ac 17:18 certain philosophers of·the Epicureans and of·the

G1947 ἐπι•κουρία êpikôuría *n.* (1x)
Roots:G1909 G2877 See:G1946
G1947 N-GSF ἐπικουρίας (1x)
Ac 26:22 after·obtaining assistance personally·from God, I·

G1948 ἐπι•κρίνω êpikrínō *v.* (1x)
Roots:G1909 G2919
G1948.1 V-AAI-3S ἐπέκρινεν (1x)
Lk 23:24 And Pilate rendered·judgment *for* their request to·

G1949 ἐπι•λαμβάνομαι êpilambánômai *v.* (19x)
Roots:G1909 G2983 See:G2638
G1949.1 V-PNI-3S ἐπιλαμβάνεται (2x)
Heb 2:16 now·then, as·is·well·known, he·grabs·hold— not
Heb 2:16 ·*nature* of·angels— but·rather he·grabs·hold ·of·
G1949.1 V-2ADI-3S ἐπελάβετο (2x)
Ac 21:33 the regiment·commander grabbed·hold of·him and
Mt 14:31 ·stretching·forth his hand, grabbed·hold of·him,
G1949.1 V-2ADM-2S ἐπιλαβοῦ (1x)
1Ti 6:12 good striving of·the trust, grab·hold of·the eternal
G1949.1 V-2ADN ἐπιλαβέσθαι (1x)
Lk 20:26 ·not have·strength to·grab·hold of·his utterances
G1949.1 V-2ADP-GSM ἐπιλαβομένου (1x)
Heb 8:9 in *the* day after·grabbing·hold of·them by·my hand
G1949.1 V-2ADP-NSM ἐπιλαβόμενος (4x)
Lk 9:47 of·their heart, grabbing·hold of·a·little·child, he·set
Lk 14:4 they·kept·still. And grabbing·hold *of·him*, he·healed
Ac 23:19 ·commander, after·grabbing·hold of·him by·the
Mk 8:23 And after·grabbing·hold of·the blind·man by·the
G1949.1 V-2ADP-NPM ἐπιλαβόμενοι (3x)
Lk 23:26 upon·grabbing·hold of·a·certain·man who·was·
Ac 17:19 And grabbing·hold of·him, they·brought·him to
Ac 21:30 running·together. And grabbing·hold of·Paul,
G1949.1 V-2ADS-3P ἐπιλάβωνται (2x)
Lk 20:20 in·order·that they·may·grab·hold of·his words, in·
1Ti 6:19 in·order·that they·may·grab·hold of·the eternal
G1949.2 V-2ADP-NSM ἐπιλαβόμενος (1x)
Ac 9:27 But BarNabas, grabbing him, brought *him* to the
G1949.2 V-2ADP-NPM ἐπιλαβόμενοι (2x)
Ac 16:19 income went·out *from·her*, after·grabbing Paul and
Ac 18:17 Then, after·grabbing SoSthenes, the director·of·

G1950 ἐπι•λανθάνομαι êpilanthánômai *v.* (8x)
Roots:G1909 G2990 Compare:G1585 G3865 xLangAlso:H7911
G1950.1 V-PNM-2P ἐπιλανθάνεσθε (2x)
Heb 13:2 Do·not forget the hospitality·to·strangers, for
Heb 13:16 But do·not forget the benevolence and common·
G1950.1 V-PNP-NSM ἐπιλανθανόμενος (1x)
Php 3:13 ·thing *that·I·do*: forgetting the·things left·behind
G1950.1 V-2ADI-3S ἐπελάθετο (1x)
Jac 1:24 immediately, he·forgot what·sort·of·man he·was.
G1950.1 V-2ADI-3P ἐπελάθοντο (1x)
Mk 8:14 Now *the disciples* forgot to·take bread, and except
G1950.1 V-2ADI-3P@ ἐπελάθοντο (1x)
Mt 16:5 *of·the sea*, his disciples had·forgotten to·take bread.
G1950.1 V-2ADN ἐπιλαθέσθαι (1x)
Heb 6:10 For God *is* not unrighteous to·forget yeur work and
G1950.1 V-RPP-NSN ἐπιλελησμένον (1x)
Lk 12:6 them is having·been·forgotten in·the·sight·of·God.

G1951 ἐπι•λέγομαι êpilégômai *v.* (2x)
Roots:G1909 G3004 Compare:G1941 G4316
G1951.1 V-PPP-NSF ἐπιλεγομένη (1x)
Jn 5:2 *it·is* the·one being·nicknamed BethEsda·*(House·of·*.
G1951.2 V-AMP-NSM ἐπιλεξάμενος (1x)
Ac 15:40 And Paul, picking Silas, went·forth after·being·

G1952 ἐπι•λείπω êpilêípō *v.* (1x)
Roots:G1909 G3007
G1952.2 V-FAI-3S ἐπιλείψει (1x)
Heb 11:32 time shall·be·totally·deficient·for me in·giving·

G1953 ἐπι•λησμονή êpilēsmônḗ *n.* (1x)
Roots:G1950 Compare:G3024
G1953.1 N-GSF ἐπιλησμονῆς (1x)
Jac 1:25 ·*it*, this·man being not a·forgetful hearer, but·rather

G1954 ἐπί•λοιπος êpílôipôs *adj.* (1x)
Roots:G1909 G3062 xLangAlso:H3499
G1954.2 A-ASM ἐπίλοιπον (1x)
1Pe 4:2 no·longer to·live·naturally the remainder·of *his* time

G1955 ἐπί•λυσις êpílysis *n.* (1x)
Roots:G1956 Compare:G2058
G1955 N-GSF ἐπιλύσεως (1x)
2Pe 1:20 does·not itself·occur from·a·private explanation.

G1956 ἐπι•λύω êpilýō *v.* (2x)
Roots:G1909 G3089 Compare:G1329 G3177 See:G1955
G1956.2 V-FPI-3S ἐπιλυθήσεται (1x)
Ac 19:39 other·matters, it·shall·be·fully·settled in the lawful
G1956.3 V-IAI-3S ἐπέλυεν (1x)
Mk 4:34 But privately, he·was·explaining all·things to·his

G1957 ἐπι•μαρτυρέω êpimartyrêō *v.* (1x)
Roots:G1909 G3140
G1957 V-PAP-NSM ἐπιμαρτυρῶν (1x)
1Pe 5:12 — exhorting and further·testifying this to·be *the*

G1958 ἐπι•μέλεια êpimélêia *n.* (1x)
Roots:G1959
G1958.2 N-GSF ἐπιμελείας (1x)
Ac 27:3 ·traverse to his·friends to·obtain caring·hospitality.

G1959 ἐπι•μελέομαι êpimêlêômai *v.* (3x)
Roots:G1909 G3199 Compare:G3309 See:G1958
G1959 V-FDI-3S ἐπιμελήσεται (1x)
1Ti 3:5 how shall·he·take·care of·a·Called·Out·citizenry of·
G1959 V-AOI-3S ἐπεμελήθη (1x)
Lk 10:34 he·brought him to·an·inn and took·care of·him.
G1959 V-APM-2S ἐπιμελήθητι (1x)
Lk 10:35 and declared to·him, 'Take·care of·him. And

G1960 ἐπι•μελῶς êpimêlôs *adv.* (1x)
Roots:G1959
G1960 ADV ἐπιμελῶς (1x)
Lk 15:8 the home, and seek carefully until such·time *that*

G1961 ἐπι•μένω êpimḗnō *v.* (19x)
Roots:G1909 G3306
G1961.1 V-FAI-1S ἐπιμενῶ (1x)
1Co 16:8 But I·shall·stay·over in Ephesus until the Pentecost
G1961.1 V-PAP-GPM ἐπιμενόντων (1x)
Ac 21:10 And with·us still·staying·over *for* many·more days,
G1961.1 V-AAI-1S ἐπέμεινα (1x)
Gal 1:18 ·interview Peter, and I·stayed·over alongside him
G1961.1 V-AAI-1P ἐπεμείναμεν (2x)
Ac 21:4 the disciples, we·stayed·over at·this·location *for*
Ac 28:12 ·moored at Syracuse, we·stayed·over *for* three
G1961.1 V-AAN ἐπιμεῖναι (4x)
Ac 10:48 Then they·asked him to·stay·over some days.
Ac 15:34 ·good to·Silas to·still·stay·over at·this·location.
Ac 28:14 brothers, we·were·exhorted to·stay·over with them
1Co 16:7 but *instead*, I·expect to·stay·over some time
G1961.2 V-FAI-1P ἐπιμενοῦμεν (1x)
Rm 6:1 Shall·we·continue·on in·Moral·Failure in·order·
G1961.2 V-PAN ἐπιμένειν (2x)
Ac 13:43 were·persuading them to·continue·on in·the grace
Php 1:24 But to·continue·on in the flesh *is* necessary on·
EG1961.2 (1x)
Php 1:22 But if *I·continue·on* to·live in *bodily* flesh, this
G1961.3 V-PAI-2P ἐπιμένετε (1x)
Col 1:23 if·indeed yeu·persist in·the trust, having·been·
G1961.3 V-PAM-2S ἐπίμενε (1x)
1Ti 4:16 and·also to·the instruction; persist in·them, for in·
G1961.3 V-IAI-3S ἐπέμενεν (1x)
Ac 12:16 But Peter was·persisting·in knocking. And
G1961.3 V-IAI-3P ἐπέμενον (1x)
Jn 8:7 But as they·were·persisting·in asking·of him, after·
G1961.3 V-AAS-3S ἐπιμείνῃς (1x)
Rm 11:22 if you·should·persist in·the benevolent·kindness.
G1961.3 V-AAS-3P ἐπιμείνωσιν (1x)
Rm 11:23 also, if they·should·not persist in·the lack·of·trust

G1962 ἐπι•νεύω êpinêúō *v.* (1x)
Roots:G1909 G3506 Compare:G4909 G1014 G1106
G1962.3 V-AAI-3S ἐπένευσεν (1x)
Ac 18:20 a·longer time with them, he·did·not consent.

G1963 ἐπί•νοια êpínôia *n.* (1x)
Roots:G1909 G3563 Compare:G1270 G1761 G3540
G1963.2 N-NSF ἐπίνοια (1x)
Ac 8:22 God so·that perhaps the intention of·your heart

G1964 ἐπι•ορκέω êpiôrkḗō *v.* (1x)
Roots:G1965 Compare:G5260
G1964 V-FAI-2S ἐπιορκήσεις (1x)
Mt 5:33 "You·shall·not swear·falsely, but shall·render to·

G1965 ἐπί•ορκος êpíôrkôs *adj.* (1x)
Roots:G1909 G3727
G1965.2 A-DPM ἐπιόρκοις (1x)
1Ti 1:10 for·kidnappers, for·liars, for·perjurers, and if

G1966 ἐπι•οῦσα êpiôûsa *v.* (5x)
Roots:G1909 G1510-1 See:G2250 G3571
G1966 V-PXP-DSF ἐπιούσῃ (5x)
Ac 7:26 Also the following day, he·made·himself·visible to·
Ac 16:11 to Samos·of·Thrace, also the following *day* to
Ac 20:15 from·there, we·arrived the following *day* opposite
Ac 21:18 And on·the following *day*, Paul had·entered
Ac 23:11 And on·the following night, the Lord, upon·

G1967 ἐπι•ούσιος êpiôúsiôs *adj.* (2x)
Roots:G1909 G1510 Compare:G1966 xLangAlso:H8443
G1967 A-ASM ἐπιούσιον (2x)
Lk 11:3 'Give us each day our sustaining bread.
Mt 6:11 'Give us this·day our sustaining bread.

G1968 ἐπι•πίπτω êpipíptō *v.* (13x)
Roots:G1909 G4098 Compare:G0347 G0726 G0782 G1945 G4843
G1968.1 V-2AAI-3S ἐπέπεσεν (7x)
Lk 1:12 ·troubled after·seeing *him*, and fear fell upon him.
Ac 10:10 ·others making·preparation, a·trance fell upon him

Ac 10:44 utterances, the Holy Spirit fell upon all the·ones
Ac 11:15 to·speak, the Holy Spirit fell upon them, just·as
Ac 13:11 And at·once there·fell upon him dimness·of·sight
Ac 19:17 Greeks. And reverent·fear·and·awe fell upon them
Ac 20:10 And walking·down, Paul fell·upon him, and after·
G1968.1 V-2AAI-3P ἐπέπεσον (1x)
Rm 15:3 of·the·ones reproaching you fell upon me."
G1968.1 V-RAP-NSN ἐπιπεπτωκός (1x)
Ac 8:16 as·of·yet, he·was having·fallen upon not·even·one
G1968.2 V-2AAP-NSM ἐπιπεσών (1x)
Jn 13:25 Then this·one, falling·back upon Jesus' chest, says
G1968.3 V-2AAI-3S ἐπέπεσεν (1x)
Lk 15:20 And·then running, he·affectionately·fell upon his
G1968.3 V-2AAP-NPM ἐπιπεσόντες (1x)
Ac 20:37 ·long·while. And affectionately·falling upon Paul's
G1968.4 V-PAN ἐπιπίπτειν (1x)
Mk 3:10 ·having scourges to·press·toward him in·order·that

G1969 ἐπι•πλήσσω êpiplḗssō *v.* (1x)
Roots:G1909 G4141
xLangEquiv:H3256
G1969.1 V-AAS-2S ἐπιπλήξῃς (1x)
1Ti 5:1 You·should·not chastise an·older·man, but·rather

G1971 ἐπι•ποθέω êpipôthéō *v.* (10x)
Roots:G1909 Compare:G2442 See:G1972 G1973 G1974
G1971.1 V-PAI-1S ἐπιποθῶ (2x)
Rm 1:11 For I·greatly·yearn to·see yeu that I·may·kindly·
Php 1:8 is my witness, how I·greatly·yearn·after yeu all in
G1971.1 V-PAI-3S ἐπιποθεῖ (1x)
Jac 4:5 spirit that resides in us greatly·yearns *even* unto envy
G1971.1 V-PAP-GPM ἐπιποθούντων (1x)
2Co 9:14 ·behalf of·yeu, they·are·greatly·yearning·for yeu,
G1971.1 V-PAP-NSM ἐπιποθῶν (2x)
Php 2:26 since·now he·was greatly·yearning·for yeu all, and
2Ti 1:4 tears)— while·greatly·yearning to·see you in·order·
G1971.1 V-PAP-NPM ἐπιποθοῦντες (2x)
1Th 3:6 of·us always, greatly·yearning to·see us, exactly·as
2Co 5:2 greatly·yearning to·fully·dress·ourselves·with our
EG1971.1 (1x)
1Th 3:6 us, exactly·as we·ourselves also *yearn to·see* yeu.
G1971.2 V-AAM-2P ἐπιποθήσατε (1x)
1Pe 2:2 as newborn babies, eagerly·crave the rational milk

G1972 ἐπι•πόθησις êpipôthēsis *n.* (2x)
Roots:G1971 Compare:G1939 See:G1974 G1973
G1972 N-ASF ἐπιπόθησιν (2x)
2Co 7:7 ·reported·in·detail to·us yeur great·yearning, yeur
2Co 7:11 alarm, moreover, *what* great·yearning, moreover,

G1973 ἐπι•πόθητος êpipóthētôs *adj.* (1x)
Roots:G1971 See:G1972 G1974
G1973 A-NPM ἐπιπόθητοι (1x)
Php 4:1 (dearly·beloved and greatly·yearned·for, my joy and

G1974 ἐπι•ποθία êpipôthía *n.* (1x)
Roots:G1971 Compare:G1939 See:G1972 G1973
G1974.1 N-ASF ἐπιποθίαν (1x)
Rm 15:23 and having a·great·yearning for these·many years

G1975 ἐπι•πορεύομαι êpipôrêúômai *v.* (1x)
Roots:G1909 G4198
G1975 V-PNP-GPM ἐπιπορευομένων (1x)
Lk 8:4 with *others that* were·traversing·onward toward him

G1976 ἐπι•ῤῥάπτω êpirrháptō *v.* (1x)
Roots:G1909 G4476
G1976.2 V-PAI-3S ἐπιρράπτει (1x)
Mk 2:21 not·even·one·man sews a·patch of·unprocessed

G1977 ἐπι•ῤῥίπτω êpirrhíptō *v.* (2x)
Roots:G1909 G4496 Compare:G1911
G1977 V-AAP-NPM ἐπιρρίψαντες (2x)
Lk 19:35 it to Jesus, and flinging their·own garments upon
1Pe 5:7 flinging all yeur anxiety upon him, because it·

G1978 ἐπί•σημος êpísēmôs *adj.* (2x)
Roots:G1909 G4591
G1978.2 A-ASM ἐπίσημον (1x)
Mt 27:16 they·were·holding a·notable chained·prisoner,
G1978.3 A-NPM ἐπίσημοι (1x)
Rm 16:7 ·prisoners·of·war, who are of·note among the

G1979 ἐπι•σιτισμός êpisitismós *n.* (1x)
Roots:G1909 G4621 Compare:G1033 G1035 G1305 G4620 G5160 G5315
xLangEquiv:H6720
G1979 N-ASM ἐπισιτισμόν (1x)
Lk 9:12 ·should·lodge and find provision·of·food, because

G1980 ἐπι•σκέπτομαι êpiskḗptômai *v.* (11x)
Roots:G1909 G4649 Compare:G1983 See:G1984 G1985
xLangEquiv:H6485
G1980.1 V-ADM-2P ἐπισκέψασθε (1x)
Ac 6:3 Now·then, brothers, inspect from·among yeurselves
G1980.2 V-PNI-2S ἐπισκέπτῃ (1x)
Heb 2:6 of·him? Or a·son of·clay†, that you·do·visit him?
G1980.2 V-PNN ἐπισκέπτεσθαι (1x)
Jac 1:27 religion is this: to·visit *the* orphans and widows in
G1980.2 V-ADI-2P ἐπεσκέψασθε (2x)
Mt 25:36 I·was·sick, and yeu·visited me. I·was in prison,
Mt 25:43 sick and in prison, and yeu·did·not visit me.'
G1980.2 V-ADI-3S ἐπεσκέψατο (4x)
Lk 1:68 God of·IsraEl, because he·visited and made a·
Lk 1:78 ·the·horizon from·out of·on·high has·visited us,
Lk 7:16 among us;" and, "God visited his People."
Ac 15:14 just·as at·the·first, God visited Gentiles to·take
G1980.2 V-ADN ἐπισκέψασθαι (1x)
Ac 7:23 it·ascended upon his heart to·visit his brothers, the
G1980.2 V-ADS-1P ἐπισκεψώμεθα (1x)
Ac 15:36 "Now·then returning, we·should·visit our brothers

G1981 ἐπι•σκηνόω êpiskēnóō *v.* (1x)
Roots:G1909 G4637
G1981.1 V-AAS-3S ἐπισκηνώσῃ (1x)
2Co 12:9 the power of·Anointed-One may·encamp upon me.

G1982 ἐπι•σκιάζω êpiskiázō *v.* (5x)
Roots:G1909 G4639 Compare:G4654 See:G2683
G1982.1 V-FAI-3S ἐπισκιάσει (1x)
Lk 1:35 *the* power of·the·Most·High shall·overshadow you.
G1982.1 V-PAP-NSF ἐπισκιάζουσα (1x)
Mk 9:7 Then there·was a·thick·cloud overshadowing them,
G1982.1 V-AAI-3S ἐπεσκίασεν (2x)
Lk 9:34 ·came a·thick·cloud, and it·overshadowed them.
Mt 17:5 a·thick·cloud full·of·light overshadowed them.
G1982.1 V-AAS-3S ἐπισκιάσῃ (1x)
Ac 5:15 if·even his shadow may·overshadow some of·them

G1983 ἐπι•σκοπέω êpiskôpéō *v.* (2x)
Roots:G1909 G4648 Compare:G1980 See:G1984 G1985 xLangAlso:H6485
G1983.1 V-PAP-NPM ἐπισκοποῦντες (2x)
Heb 12:15 *Be* diligently·overseeing: lest any·man *is·found*
1Pe 5:2 ·flock of·God among yeu, diligently·overseeing *it*—

G1984 ἐπι•σκοπή êpiskôpḗ *n.* (4x)
Roots:G1980 See:G1985
xLangEquiv:H6486
G1984.1 N-GSF ἐπισκοπῆς (2x)
Lk 19:44 you·did·not know the season of·your inspection."
1Pe 2:12 *them*), they·may·glorify God on Inspection Day.
G1984.2 N-ASF ἐπισκοπήν (1x)
Ac 1:20 "May·another take his assignment·of·oversight."
G1984.2 N-GSF ἐπισκοπῆς (1x)
1Ti 3:1 ·himself·toward an·assignment·of·oversight, he·

G1985 ἐπί•σκοπος êpískôpôs *n.* (5x)
Roots:G1909 G4649 Compare:G4245 G1988 G2819-2 G4367-1 G2040-2 See:G1983 G1984 G0244
xLangEquiv:H6496 xLangAlso:H6486
G1985.1 N-ASM ἐπίσκοπον (3x)
1Pe 2:25 to the Shepherd and Overseer of·yeur souls.
Tit 1:7 ·for the overseer to·be without·any·charge·of·wrong·
1Ti 3:2 the overseer to·be above·all·blame·and·suspicion, a·
G1985.1 N-APM ἐπισκόπους (1x)
Ac 20:28 Spirit has·placed yeu *to·be* overseers, to·shepherd
G1985.1 N-DPM ἐπισκόποις (1x)
Php 1:1 at PhiIippi, together with·overseers and stewards.

G1986 ἐπι•σπάομαι êpispáômai *v.* (1x)
Roots:G1909 G4685 Compare:G4059 See:G0203
G1986.2 V-PNM-3S ἐπισπάσθω (1x)
1Co 7:18 must·not be·uncircumcised. Any·man *that* is·

G1987 ἐπί•σταμαι êpístamai *v.* (14x)
Roots:G1909 G2476 Compare:G1921 G2186 See:G1990 G3563
G1987.2 V-PNI-2P ἐπίστασθε (1x)
Ac 19:25 "Men, yeu·are·fully·aware that our prosperity is
G1987.3 V-PNI-1S ἐπίσταμαι (2x)
Ac 19:15 I·know, and Paul I·am·fully·acquainted·with, but
Mk 14:68 *him*, neither am·I·fully·acquainted·with what you·
G1987.3 V-PNI-2P ἐπίστασθε (4x)
Ac 10:28 Yeu·yeurselves are·fully·acquainted·with how it·is
Ac 15:7 yeu·yeurselves are·fully·acquainted·with how from
Ac 20:18 "Yeu·yeurselves are·fully·acquainted, from that
Jac 4:14 are·not *even* fully·acquainted·with the·thing *that*
G1987.3 V-PNI-3S ἐπίσταται (1x)
Ac 26:26 king is·fully·acquainted concerning these·things, to
G1987.3 V-PNI-3P ἐπίστανται (2x)
Ac 22:19 they·themselves are·fully·acquainted that I·myself
Jud 1:10 as·many·things·as they·are·fully·acquainted·with
G1987.3 V-PNP-NSM ἐπιστάμενος (4x)
Ac 18:25 *though* being·fully·acquainted·with merely the
Ac 24:10 "Being·fully·acquainted from·among many years
Heb 11:8 not being·fully·acquainted·with where he·was·
1Ti 6:4 ·with·self-conceit while·being·fully·acquainted·with,

G1988 ἐπι•στάτης êpistátēs *n.* (7x)
Roots:G1909 G2476 Compare:G4367-1 G4755 G1985 G2233 G2519
xLangEquiv:H5057
G1988.2 N-VSM ἐπιστάτα (7x)
Lk 5:5 declared to·him, "O·Captain, after·laboring·hard all
Lk 8:24 him, saying, "Captain, captain, we·are·completely·
Lk 8:24 "Captain, captain, we·are·completely·perishing."
Lk 8:45 with him declared, "Captain, the crowds confine
Lk 9:33 declared to Jesus, "O·Captain, it·is good for·us to·
Lk 9:49 John declared, "O·Captain, we·saw someone
Lk 17:13 saying, "Jesus, O·Captain, show·mercy on·us.

G1989 ἐπι•στέλλω êpistéllō *v.* (3x)
Roots:G1909 G4724
G1989.2 V-AAI-1S ἐπέστειλα (1x)
Heb 13:22 ·passages, I·communicated·by·letter to·yeu.
G1989.2 V-AAI-1P ἐπεστείλαμεν (1x)
Ac 21:25 we·ourselves communicated·by·letter, judging
G1989.2 V-AAN ἐπιστεῖλαι (1x)
Ac 15:20 but·rather to·communicate·by·letter to·them, for·

G1990 ἐπι•στήμων êpistḗmōn *adj.* (1x)
Roots:G1987 See:G1989-1
G1990.3 A-NSM ἐπιστήμων (1x)
Jac 3:13 Who *is* wise and fully·informed among yeu?

G1991 ἐπι•στηρίζω êpistērízō *v.* (4x)
Roots:G1909 G4741
G1991.2 V-PAP-NSM ἐπιστηρίζων (2x)
Ac 15:41 and Cilicia, reaffirming the Called·Out·citizenries.
Ac 18:23 Phrygia in·consecutive·order, reaffirming all the
G1991.2 V-PAP-NPM ἐπιστηρίζοντες (1x)
Ac 14:22 reaffirming the souls of·the disciples, exhorting
G1991.2 V-AAI-3P ἐπεστήριξαν (1x)
Ac 15:32 discourse *in·kind*, and they·reaffirmed *the brothers*

G1992 ἐπι•στολή êpistôlḗ *n.* (28x)
Roots:G1989 Compare:G0975 G3200 G5489
xLangEquiv:A0104 H0107
G1992.1 N-NSF ἐπιστολή (4x)
2Co 3:2 ·yeurselves are our letter having·been·engraved in
2Co 3:3 yeu·are a·letter of·Anointed-One being·attended·to
2Co 7:8 I·look·upon *it* that the·same letter did·grieve yeu,
Col 4:16 whenever the letter should·be·read·aloud directly·to
G1992.1 N-NPF ἐπιστολαί (1x)
2Co 10:10 *reckoning* replies, "His letters *are* weighty and
G1992.1 N-ASF ἐπιστολήν (6x)
Ac 15:30 the multitude, they·hand-delivered the letter.
Ac 23:25 *And* he·wrote a·letter containing this particular·

Ac 23:33 and hand-delivering the letter to·the governor, also
Rm 16:22 I, Tertius, the·one writing the letter, greet yeu in
2Pe 3:1 This second letter, beloved, even·now I·write to·yeu,
1Th 5:27 by·the Lord for·the letter to·be·read·aloud to·all

G1992.1 N-APF ἐπιστολάς (2x)
Ac 9:2 ·requested personally·from him letters for Damascus
Ac 22:5 ·from whom I also accepted letters to the brothers

G1992.1 N-DSF ἐπιστολῇ (3x)
2Th 3:17 is a·signature in every letter. I·write in·this·manner
1Co 5:9 ·wrote to·yeu in the *prior* letter not to·associate·with
2Co 7:8 I·grieved yeu with the letter, I·am·not regretting *it*,

G1992.1 N-DPF ἐπιστολαῖς (1x)
2Pe 3:16 ·as *he·does* also in all his letters, speaking in them

G1992.1 N-GSF ἐπιστολῆς (3x)
2Th 2:2 word, nor through letter as·though through us) as·
2Th 2:15 whether through *spoken* word or through our letter.
2Th 3:14 word through this·letter, yeu·must·personally·note

G1992.1 N-GPF ἐπιστολῶν (4x)
1Co 16:3 ·verifiably·approve through *yeur* letters, these I·
2Co 3:1 as some *do*, of·letters of·recommendation to yeu,
2Co 10:9 to·utterly·frighten yeu through the letters.
2Co 10:11 in·word through *our* letters while·being·absent,

EG1992.1 (4x)
Ac 15:23 *and who·are* writing *this letter of* these·things
Ac 23:34 And after·reading·aloud *the letter*, the governor
2Co 3:1 yeu, or *of·letters* of·recommendation from·among
Col 4:16 should·read·aloud the *letter* from·out of·LaoDicea.

G1993 ἐπι•στομίζω êpistômízō *v.* (1x)
Roots:G1909 G4750 Compare:G5392

G1993.2 V-PAN ἐπιστομίζειν (1x)
Tit 1:11 of·whom it·is·mandatory to·silence·mouths. Such·

G1994 ἐπι•στρέφω êpistréphō *v.* (40x)
Roots:G1909 G4762 Compare:G0344 G0390
See:G1995

G1994.1 V-AAI-1S ἐπέστρεψα (1x)
Rv 1:12 And I·turned·about to·look·at the voice that spoke

G1994.1 V-AAP-NSM ἐπιστρέψας (2x)
Ac 16:18 ·out, Paul, even turning·about, declared to·the
Rv 1:12 with me. And turning·about, I·saw seven Golden

G1994.2 V-2APP-NSM ἐπιστραφείς (4x)
Jn 21:20 So after·turning·himself·about, Peter looks·at the
Mt 9:22 Then turning·himself·about and seeing her, YeShua
Mk 5:30 ·forth out of·him, after·turning·himself·about in the
Mk 8:33 But turning·himself·about and seeing his disciples,

G1994.3 V-FAI-3S ἐπιστρέψει (1x)
Lk 1:16 "And he·shall·turn many of·the Sons of·IsraEl back·

G1994.3 V-PAN ἐπιστρέφειν (2x)
Ac 14:15 ·good·news to·yeu to·turn·back·around from these
Ac 26:20 to·repent and to·turn·back·around toward God,

G1994.3 V-PAP-DPM ἐπιστρέφουσιν (1x)
Ac 15:19 from the Gentiles turning·back·around to God,

G1994.3 V-AAI-2P ἐπεστρέψατε (1x)
1Th 1:9 yeu, and how yeu·turned·back·around to God from

G1994.3 V-AAI-3S ἐπέστρεψεν (1x)
Ac 11:21 them, and a·large number turned·back·around to

G1994.3 V-AAI-3P ἐπέστρεψαν (1x)
Ac 9:35 him, *and* they·turned·back·around toward the Lord.

G1994.3 V-AAM-2P ἐπιστρέψατε (1x)
Ac 3:19 yeu·must·repent and turn·back·around, in·order·for

G1994.3 V-AAN ἐπιστρέψαι (3x)
Lk 1:17 of·EliJah, "to·turn fathers' hearts back·around
Ac 26:18 eyes, *and* to·turn·*them*·back·around from darkness
2Pe 2:21 ·recognizing *it*, to·turn·back·around from·out the

G1994.3 V-AAP-NSM ἐπιστρέψας (2x)
Ac 9:40 he·prayed. And turning·back·around to the body,
Jac 5:20 the·one turning·back·around a·morally·disqualified·

G1994.3 V-AAS-3S ἐπιστρέψῃ (3x)
Lk 17:4 ·times in·the day should·turn·back·around to you,
Jac 5:19 truth, and someone should·turn him back·around,
2Co 3:16 whenever one·should·turn·back·around to Yahweh

G1994.3 V-AAS-3P ἐπιστρέψωσιν (3x)
Ac 28:27 with·the heart, and should·turn·back·around, and
Mt 13:15 with·the heart, and should·turn·back·around, and
Mk 4:12 lest·at·any·time they·should·turn·back·around, and

G1994.3 V-2APS-3P ἐπιστραφῶσιν (1x)
Jn 12:40 with·the heart and may·be·turned·back·around, and

EG1994.3 (1x)
Lk 1:17 ' and *to·turn·back·around the* obstinate·ones by *the*

G1994.4 V-FAI-1S ἐπιστρέψω (1x)
Mt 12:44 Then it·says, 'I·shall·return into my house from·

G1994.4 V-PAI-2P ἐπιστρέφετε (1x)
Gal 4:9 by God, how·is·it *that* yeu·return again to the weak

G1994.4 V-AAI-3S ἐπέστρεψεν (1x)
Lk 8:55 And her spirit returned, and she·stood·up at·once,

G1994.4 V-AAI-3P ἐπέστρεψαν (1x)
Lk 2:20 And the shepherds returned, glorifying and praising

G1994.4 V-AAM-3S ἐπιστρεψάτω (3x)
Lk 17:31 in the field must·not return to the·things left·behind
Mt 24:18 in the field must·not return *to the·things* left·behind
Mk 13:16 being in the field must·not return to the·things left·

G1994.4 V-AAP-NSM ἐπιστρέψας (2x)
Lk 22:32 and once you return, you·must·firmly·establish
2Pe 2:22 "'A·dog *keeps·on* returning to his·own throw·up,

G1994.4 V-AAP-NPM ἐπιστρέψαντες (1x)
Ac 15:36 to BarNabas, "Now·then returning, we·should·visit

G1994.4 V-2API-2P ἐπεστράφητε (1x)
1Pe 2:25 but·yet are now returned to the Shepherd and

G1994.4 V-2APM-3S ἐπιστραφήτω (1x)
Mt 10:13 ·not be worthy, *let* yeur peace be·returned to yeu.

G1995 ἐπι•στροφή êpistrôphḗ *n.* (1x)
Roots:G1994 Compare:G0654-1

G1995.2 N-ASF ἐπιστροφήν (1x)
Ac 15:3 ·account·of the turning·back·around of·the Gentiles

G1996 ἐπι•συν•άγω êpisynágō *v.* (7x)
Roots:G1909 G4863 Compare:G4896 G1826-1
See:G1997

G1996.2 V-FAI-3S ἐπισυνάξει (1x)
Mk 13:27 and shall·completely·gather his Selected-Ones

G1996.2 V-FAI-3P ἐπισυνάξουσιν (1x)
Mt 24:31 and they·shall·completely·gather his Selected-Ones

G1996.2 V-PAI-3S ἐπισυνάγει (1x)
Mt 23:37 children as a·hen completely·gathers her chicks

G1996.2 V-2AAN ἐπισυναγαγεῖν (1x)
Mt 23:37 ·times I·wanted to·completely·gather your children

G1996.2 V-AAN ἐπισυνάξαι (1x)
Lk 13:34 ·times I·wanted to·completely·gather your children

G1996.2 V-APP-GPF ἐπισυναχθεισῶν (1x)
Lk 12:1 crowd being·completely·gathered of·the tens·of·

G1996.2 V-RPP-NSF ἐπισυνηγμένη (1x)
Mk 1:33 was having·been·completely·gathered alongside the

G1997 ἐπι•συν•αγωγή êpisynagōgḗ *n.* (2x)
Roots:G1996 Compare:G1577 See:G4864

G1997.1 N-ASF ἐπισυναγωγήν (1x)
Heb 10:25 forsaking the complete·gathering of·ourselves,

G1997.1 N-GSF ἐπισυναγωγῆς (1x)
2Th 2:1 Anointed, and of·our complete·gathering to him,

G1998 ἐπι•συν•τρέχω êpisyntréchō *v.* (1x)
Roots:G1909 G4936

G1998.2 V-PAI-3S ἐπισυντρέχει (1x)
Mk 9:25 that the crowd came·running·together·toward *them*,

G1999 ἐπι•σύ•στασις êpisýstasis *n.* (2x)
Roots:G1909 G4921 Compare:G4945

G1999 N-NSF ἐπισύστασις (1x)
2Co 11:28 *there·is* my·own daily turmoil: the anxiety of·all

G1999 N-ASF ἐπισύστασιν (1x)
Ac 24:12 anyone, or making a·turmoil of·a·crowd, neither in

G2000 ἐπι•σφαλής êpisphalḗs *adj.* (1x)
Roots:G1909

G2000.2 A-GSM ἐπισφαλοῦς (1x)
Ac 27:9 being even·now precarious on·account·of the fast·

G2001 ἐπ•ισχύω êpischýō *v.* (1x)
Roots:G1909 G2480 Compare:G1945

G2001.2 V-IAI-3P ἐπίσχυον (1x)
Lk 23:5 But they·were·strongly·insisting, saying, "He·

G2002 ἐπι•σωρεύω êpisōrêúō *v.* (1x)
Roots:G1909 G4987 Compare:G4987

G2002.1 V-FAI-3P ἐπισωρεύσουσιν (1x)
2Ti 4:3 longings, they·shall·further·stack·up instructors for·

G2003 ἐπι•ταγή êpitagḗ *n.* (7x)
Roots:G2004 Compare:G1849 G1785 See:G4929

G2003.1 N-ASF ἐπιταγήν (2x)
1Co 7:6 *and* not according·to an·authoritative·assignment.
1Co 7:25 ·not have an·authoritative·assignment of·*the*·Lord.

G2003.2 N-ASF ἐπιταγήν (3x)
Rm 16:26 according·to a·full·appointment of·the eternal
Tit 1:3 according·to a·full·appointment of·God our Savior.
1Ti 1:1 according·to a·full·appointment of·God our Savior,

G2003.3 N-ASF ἐπιταγήν (1x)
2Co 8:8 *this* according·to fully·assigned·authority, but·rather

G2003.3 N-GSF ἐπιταγῆς (1x)
Tit 2:15 and reprove with all fully·assigned·authority. Let

G2004 ἐπι•τάσσω êpitássō *v.* (10x)
Roots:G1909 G5021 Compare:G1781 G2753 G4367
See:G2003 G4929

G2004.3 V-PAI-1S ἐπιτάσσω (1x)
Mk 9:25 mute and deaf, I·myself order you, come·forth out

G2004.3 V-PAI-3S ἐπιτάσσει (3x)
Lk 4:36 with authority and power he·orders the impure
Lk 8:25 *man* is this? Because he·orders even the winds and
Mk 1:27 Because according·to authority he·orders even the

G2004.3 V-PAN ἐπιτάσσειν (1x)
Phm 1:8 ·of·speech in Anointed-One to·order you *to·do* the

G2004.3 V-AAI-2S ἐπέταξας (1x)
Lk 14:22 'Lord, it·has·happened as you·ordered, and yet

G2004.3 V-AAI-3S ἐπέταξεν (3x)
Ac 23:2 HananIah ordered for·the·ones standing·nearby him
Mk 6:27 a·bodyguard, the king ordered for·his head to·be·
Mk 6:39 And he·ordered them to·make everyone recline,

G2004.3 V-AAS-3S ἐπιτάξῃ (1x)
Lk 8:31 in·order·that he·should·not order them to·go·off

G2005 ἐπι•τελέω êpitêlêō *v.* (11x)
Roots:G1909 G5055

G2005.1 V-FAI-3S ἐπιτελέσει (1x)
Php 1:6 ·good work in yeu shall·further·finish *it* even·unto

G2005.1 V-PAI-1S ἐπιτελῶ (1x)
Lk 13:32 ·out demons, and I·further·finish healing today

G2005.1 V-PAN ἐπιτελεῖν (1x)
Heb 8:5 when·he·was·about to·further·finish the Tabernacle:

G2005.1 V-PAP-NPM ἐπιτελοῦντες (2x)
Heb 9:6 Tabernacle, further·finishing the ritual·ministries.
2Co 7:1 and spirit, further·finishing devoted·holiness in a·

G2005.1 V-PEI-2P ἐπιτελεῖσθε (1x)
Gal 3:3 ·Spirit, are·yeu·finishing·further now in·*the*·flesh?

G2005.1 V-PPN ἐπιτελεῖσθαι (1x)
1Pe 5:9 *are* to·be·further·finished in·yeur brotherhood *while*·

G2005.1 V-AAM-2P ἐπιτελέσατε (1x)
2Co 8:11 So right·now also, yeu·must·further·finish to·do *it*,

G2005.1 V-AAN ἐπιτελέσαι (1x)
2Co 8:11 *there·may·be the eagerness* to·further·finish *it*—

G2005.1 V-AAP-NSF ἐπιτελέσας (1x)
Rm 15:28 after·further·finishing this *consequential·matter*

G2005.1 V-AAS-3S ἐπιτελέσῃ (1x)
2Co 8:6 in·this·manner he·should·further·finish among yeu

G2006 ἐπ•ιτήδειος êpitḗdêiôs *adj.* (1x)

G2006.3 A-APN ἐπιτήδεια (1x)
Jac 2:16 ·not give to·them the requisite·needs of·the body—

G2007 ἐπι•τίθημι êpitíthēmi *v.* (42x)
Roots:G1909 G5087 See:G1936

G2007.1 V-PAI-3S ἐπιτίθησιν (2x)
Lk 8:16 places *it* beneath a·couch, but·rather he·puts *it* on a·
Lk 15:5 And·then after·finding *it*, he·puts *it* upon his

G2007.1 V-PAI-3P-ATT ἐπιτιθέασιν (1x)
Mt 23:4 weighty and oppressive loads and put *them* on the

G2007.1 V-PMN ἐπιτίθεσθαι (1x)
Ac 15:28 and to·us, to·put on·yeu not·one·bit·of·a·larger

G2007.1 V-AAI-3S ἐπέθηκεν (1x)

Jn 9:15 So he·declared to·them, "He·put clay upon my eyes,
G2007.1 V-AAI-3P ἐπέθηκαν (3x)
Jn 19:2 a·victor's·crown out of·thorns, they·put *it* on·his
Mt 21:7 and the colt, and they·put their garments up·over
Mt 27:29 a·victor's·crown out of·thorns, they·put *it* upon his
G2007.1 V-2AAN ἐπιθεῖναι (1x)
Ac 15:10 why·do yeu·try God, to·put a·yoke upon the neck
G2007.1 V-2AAP-GSM ἐπιθέντος (1x)
Ac 28:3 a·multitude of·kindling·sticks and putting *them* on
G2007.1 V-APS-3S ἐπιτεθῇ (1x)
Mk 4:21 couch, *and* not in·order·that it·should·be·put on the
G2007.2 V-FAI-3S ἐπιθήσει (1x)
Rv 22:18 alongside these·things, God shall·place upon him
G2007.2 V-PAS-3S ἐπιτιθῇ (1x)
Rv 22:18 ·scroll, if anyone should·place *anything additional*
G2007.2 V-AAI-3S ἐπέθηκεν (2x)
Mk 3:16 *twelve*: on·Simon, he·laid a·name "Peter·*(a·piece·*
Mk 3:17 of·Jakob, also on·them he·laid a·name: BoanErges,
G2007.2 V-AAI-3P ἐπέθηκαν (2x)
Lk 23:26 Simon, a·Cyrenian, they·placed the cross on·him
Mt 27:37 up·over his head, they·placed the cause of·his
G2007.2 V-2AAP-NPM ἐπιθέντες (2x)
Lk 10:30 ·stripping him and placing punishing·blows *on·him*,
Ac 16:23 And after·placing many punishing·blows upon·
G2007.3 V-FAI-3P ἐπιθήσουσιν (1x)
Mk 16:18 it·shall·not injure them; they·shall·lay *their* hands
G2007.3 V-IAI-3P ἐπετίθουν (1x)
Ac 8:17 Then they·were·laying *their* hands on them, and
G2007.3 V-AAI-3S ἐπέθηκεν (3x)
Lk 13:13 And he·laid his hands on·her, and at·once she·is·
Mk 8:25 After·that, *Jesus* again laid his hands upon his eyes
Rv 1:17 his feet as dead. And he·laid his right hand upon me
G2007.3 V-2AAM-2S ἐπίθες (1x)
Mt 9:18 but·yet coming *with·me*, you·must·lay your hand
G2007.3 V-2AAP-ASM ἐπιθέντα (1x)
Ac 9:12 ·name·of AnanIas entering·in and laying *his* hand
G2007.3 V-2AAP-GSM ἐπιθέντος (1x)
Ac 19:6 And with·Paul laying his hands on·them, the Holy
G2007.3 V-2AAP-NSM ἐπιθείς (6x)
Lk 4:40 ·of illnesses *being·present*; and laying his hands on·
Ac 9:17 into the home. And after·laying his hands on him,
Ac 28:8 him, and after·praying *and* laying his hands on·him,
Mt 19:15 And after·laying his hands on·them, he·traversed·
Mk 6:5 not·even·one miracle, except laying his hands upon·
Mk 8:23 into his eyes *and* laying his hands upon·him, *Jesus*
G2007.3 V-2AAS-1S ἐπιθῶ (1x)
Ac 8:19 in·order·that on·whomever I·should·lay *my* hands,
G2007.3 V-2AAS-2S ἐπιθῇς (1x)
Mk 5:23 *with·me* in·order·that you·may·lay your hands on·
G2007.3 V-2AAS-3S ἐπιθῇ (2x)
Mt 19:13 ·brought to·him in·order·that he·may·lay his hands
Mk 7:32 ·implore him in·order·that he·should·lay his hand
G2007.4 V-PAM-2S ἐπιτίθει (1x)
1Ti 5:22 Lay·forth hands on·not·one·man quickly, nor·even
G2007.4 V-AAI-3P ἐπέθηκαν (1x)
Ac 6:6 and after·praying, they·laid·forth hands on·them.
G2007.4 V-2AAP-NPM ἐπιθέντες (1x)
Ac 13:3 and praying, and after·laying·forth hands on·them,
G2007.5 V-2AMI-3P ἐπέθεντο (1x)
Ac 28:10 with·us·making·sail, they·supplied *us* the·things
G2007.6 V-FMI-3S ἐπιθήσεται (1x)
Ac 18:10 not·even·one·man shall·put·a·hand on·you to·harm

G2008 ἐπι•τιμάω êpitimáō *v.* (29x)

Roots:G1909 G5091 Compare:G1651 G2967 G3679 See:G2008-1 G2009
G2008.2 V-PAN ἐπιτιμᾶν (2x)
Mt 16:22 ·taking him *aside*, began to·reprimand him, saying
Mk 8:32 ·taking him *aside*, Peter began to·reprimand him.
G2008.2 V-PAP-NSM ἐπιτιμῶν (1x)
Lk 4:41 Son of·God." And reprimanding *them*, he·was·not
G2008.2 V-IAI-3S ἐπετίμα (1x)
Lk 23:40 the other *criminal* was·reprimanding him, saying,
G2008.2 V-IAI-3P ἐπετίμων (3x)
Lk 18:39 the·ones going·on·ahead were·reprimanding him,
Mk 10:13 the disciples were·reprimanding the·ones bringing
Mk 10:48 And many were·reprimanding him that he·should·
G2008.2 V-AAI-3S ἐπετίμησεν (12x)
Lk 4:35 And Jesus reprimanded him, saying, "Be·muzzled!
Lk 4:39 ·forward over her, he·reprimanded the fever, and it·
Lk 8:24 upon·being·awakened, he·reprimanded the wind
Lk 9:42 *him*. And Jesus reprimanded the impure spirit and
Lk 9:55 But turning·around, he·reprimanded them and
Mt 8:26 already·being·awakened, he·reprimanded the winds
Mt 17:18 And YeShua reprimanded *the demon*, and the
Mt 20:31 And the crowd reprimanded them that they·should·
Mk 1:25 And Jesus reprimanded him, saying, "Be·muzzled!
Mk 4:39 ·thoroughly·awakened, he·reprimanded the wind
Mk 8:33 seeing his disciples, he·reprimanded Peter, saying,
Mk 9:25 ·together·toward *them*, he·reprimanded the impure
G2008.2 V-AAI-3P ἐπετίμησαν (2x)
Lk 18:15 but the disciples seeing *it*, reprimanded them.
Mt 19:13 And the disciples reprimanded them.
G2008.2 V-AAM-2S ἐπιτίμησον (3x)
Lk 17:3 should·morally·fail against you, reprimand him; and
Lk 19:39 to him, "Mentor, reprimand your disciples."
2Ti 4:2 *and* when·inconvenient! Reprove, reprimand, *and*
G2008.2 V-AAO-3S ἐπιτιμήσαι (1x)
Jud 1:9 "'May Yahweh reprimand you.'"
G2008.3 V-IAI-3S ἐπετίμα (1x)
Mk 3:12 he·was·stringently·forbidding them in·order·that
G2008.3 V-AAI-3S ἐπετίμησεν (2x)
Mt 12:16 And he·stringently·forbade them in·order·that
Mk 8:30 And he·stringently·forbade them that not·even·to·
G2008.3 V-AAP-NSM ἐπιτιμήσας (1x)
Lk 9:21 So stringently·forbidding them, he·charged *them* to·

G2009 ἐπι•τιμία êpitimía *n.* (1x)

Roots:G1909 G5092 See:G2008
G2009.2 N-NSF ἐπιτιμία (1x)
2Co 2:6 to·such·a·man *is* this public·penalty, the·one

G2009-1 ἐπι•το•αυτό êpitôautó *adv.* (9x) ἐπί τό αὐτό êpí tô autó

Roots:G1909 G0846 G3588 Compare:G1800-1 xLangAlso:H3162
G2009-1.1 ADV ἐπί τό αὐτό (9x)
Lk 17:35 Two *women* shall·be grinding in·unison; one shall·
Ac 1:15 (and it·was a·crowd of·names in·unison *of* about a·
Ac 2:1 absolutely·all with·the·same·determination in·unison.
Ac 2:44 all the·ones trusting were in·unison, and they·were·
Ac 3:1 Peter and John were·walking·up in·unison into the
Ac 4:26 were·gathered·together in·unison against Yahweh
1Co 7:5 and should·come·together in·unison again, in·
1Co 11:20 ·then, as·yeu are·coming·together in·unison, it·is
1Co 14:23 ·citizenry should·come·together in·unison, and all

G2010 ἐπι•τρέπω êpitrépō *v.* (19x)

Roots:G1909 G5157 Compare:G1439 See:G2011 G2012 xLangAlso:H7558
G2010.3 V-PAI-1S ἐπιτρέπω (1x)
1Ti 2:12 I·do·not entrust·an·executive·charge to·a·woman
G2010.5 V-PAS-3S ἐπιτρέπῃ (2x)
Heb 6:3 this we·shall·do, if·ever God should·freely·permit.
1Co 16:7 alongside yeu, if the Lord should·freely·permit.
G2010.5 V-PPI-3S ἐπιτρέπεται (1x)
Ac 26:1 to Paul, "It·is·freely·permitted for·you to·discourse
G2010.5 V-AAI-3S ἐπέτρεψεν (6x)
Jn 19:38 body of·Jesus, and Pilate freely·permitted *him*. So
Lk 8:32 into those *pigs*. And he·freely·permitted them.
Ac 27:3 humanely, Julius freely·permitted *him* to·traverse to
Mt 19:8 ·of·heart *that* Moses freely·permitted yeu to·divorce
Mk 5:13 And immediately Jesus freely·permitted them. And
Mk 10:4 they·declared, "Moses freely·permitted *us* to·write
G2010.5 V-AAM-2S ἐπίτρεψον (5x)
Lk 9:59 declared, "Lord, freely·permit me to·go·off first to·
Lk 9:61 but first, freely·permit me to·orderly·take·leave·of
Ac 21:39 And I·petition you, freely·permit me to·speak to
Mt 8:21 to·him, "Lord, freely·permit me first to·go·off and
Mt 8:31 "If you·cast us out, freely·permit us to·go·away into
G2010.5 V-AAP-GSM ἐπιτρέψαντος (1x)
Ac 21:40 And after·freely·permitting him, Paul, while·
G2010.5 V-AAS-3S ἐπιτρέψῃ (1x)
Lk 8:32 him that he·should·freely·permit them to·enter into
G2010.5 V-API-3S ἐπετράπη (1x)
Ac 28:16 but Paul was·freely·permitted to·abide by himself
G2010.5 V-RPI-3S ἐπιτέτραπται (1x)
1Co 14:34 it·has·not been·freely·permitted for·them to·speak

G2011 ἐπι•τροπή êpitrôpḗ *n.* (1x)

Roots:G2010 Compare:G0651 G4774 See:G2012
G2011.1 N-GSF ἐπιτροπῆς (1x)
Ac 26:12 and an·executive·charge personally·from the chief·

G2012 ἐπί•τροπος êpítrôpôs *n.* (3x)

Roots:G2010 Compare:G0652 G3623 See:G2011
G2012.3 N-DSM ἐπιτρόπῳ (1x)
Mt 20:8 of·the vineyard says to·his executive·manager,
G2012.4 N-APM ἐπιτρόπους (1x)
Gal 4:2 is under executive·guardians and estate·managers
G2012.5 N-GSM ἐπιτρόπου (1x)
Lk 8:3 of·Chuza (personal·administrator of·HerOd·AntiPas),

G2013 ἐπι•τυγχάνω êpitynchánō *v.* (5x)

Roots:G1909 G5177 Compare:G2975 G2865
G2013.2 V-2AAI-2P ἐπέτυχον (1x)
Heb 11:33 worked righteousness, obtained promises,
G2013.2 V-2AAI-3S ἐπέτυχεν (3x)
Heb 6:15 after·patiently·waiting, he·obtained the promise.
Rm 11:7 IsraEl did·not obtain that which it·still·anxiously·
Rm 11:7 ·seeks, but the Selection did·obtain *it*, and the rest
G2013.2 V-2AAN ἐπιτυχεῖν (1x)
Jac 4:2 ·desire, and·yet yeu·are·not able to·obtain. Yeu·fight

G2014 ἐπι•φαίνω êpiphaínō *v.* (4x)

Roots:G1909 G5316 Compare:G2989 See:G0398
G2014.1 V-AAN ἐπιφᾶναι (1x)
Lk 1:79 to·shine·light·upon the·ones who·are·sitting·down
G2014.2 V-PAP-GPN ἐπιφαινόντων (1x)
Ac 27:20 constellations·of·stars appearing over many·more
G2014.2 V-2API-3S ἐπεφάνη (1x)
Tit 3:4 and *his* affection·for·mankind† became·apparent,
G2014.3 V-2API-3S ἐπεφάνη (1x)
Tit 2:11 ·Salvation, became·apparent to·all men·of·clay†—

G2015 ἐπι•φάνεια êpiphánêia *n.* (6x)

Roots:G2016 Compare:G0602 G3952 G5321
G2015.1 N-ASF ἐπιφάνειαν (3x)
Tit 2:13 and *the* conspicuous·appearing of the glory of·our
2Ti 4:1 and dead·men at his conspicuous·appearing and his
2Ti 4:8 the·ones having·loved his conspicuous·appearing.
G2015.1 N-DSF ἐπιφανείᾳ (1x)
2Th 2:8 with·the conspicuous·appearing of·his returning·
G2015.1 N-GSF ἐπιφανείας (2x)
1Ti 6:14 ·as·until the conspicuous·appearing of·our Lord
2Ti 1:10 through the conspicuous·appearing of·our Savior

G2016 ἐπι•φανής êphiphanḗs *adj.* (1x)

Roots:G2014 See:G2015
G2016.1 A-ASF ἐπιφανῆ (1x)
Ac 2:20 the great and conspicuous Day of·Yahweh coming.

G2017 ἐπι•φαύω êpiphaúō *v.* (1x)

Roots:G2014
G2017.2 V-FAI-3S ἐπιφαύσει (1x)
Eph 5:14 and the Anointed-One shall·give·light to·you."

G2018 ἐπι•φέρω êpiphérō *v.* (5x)

Roots:G1909 G5342
G2018.1 V-PAN ἐπιφέρειν (1x)
Php 1:16 imagining *also* to·bring·on tribulation to·my
G2018.1 V-PAP-NSM ἐπιφέρων (1x)
Rm 3:5 God unrighteous, the·one bringing·on the wrath?
G2018.2 V-PPN ἐπιφέρεσθαι (1x)
Ac 19:12 from his skin's·surface to·be·brought upon the sick,
G2018.2 V-IAI-2P ἐπέφερον (1x)
Ac 25:18 ·in, were·bringing·up not·even·one accusation of·
G2018.2 V-2AAN ἐπενεγκεῖν (1x)
Jud 1:9 , did·not dare to·bring·up a·verdict of·revilement,

G2019 ἐπι•φωνέω êpiphōnéō *v.* (3x)
Roots:G1909 G5455 See:G0400
G2019.2 V-IAI-3S ἐπεφώνει (1x)
Ac 12:22 And the public was·exclaiming, "*It·is* a·voice of·a·
G2019.2 V-IAI-3P ἐπεφώνουν (2x)
Lk 23:21 But they·were·exclaiming, saying, "Crucify *him*,
Ac 22:24 cause they·were·exclaiming in·this·manner against

G2020 ἐπι•φώσκω êpiphṓskō *v.* (2x)
Roots:G2017 Compare:G1448
G2020.1 V-PAP-DSF ἐπιφωσκούσῃ (1x)
Mt 28:1 ·joint·Sabbaths, with·it·growing·light toward the
G2020.2 V-IAI-3S ἐπέφωσκεν (1x)
Lk 23:54 ·day, and a·Sabbath was·quickly·drawing·near.

G2021 ἐπι•χειρέω êpichêiréō *v.* (3x)
Roots:G1909 G5495
G2021.2 V-IAI-3P ἐπεχείρουν (1x)
Ac 9:29 but they·took·it·upon·themselves to·eliminate him.
G2021.2 V-AAI-3P ἐπεχείρησαν (2x)
Lk 1:1 many took·it·upon·themselves to·fully·compose a·
Ac 19:13 exorcists, took·it·upon·themselves to·name the

G2022 ἐπι•χέω êpichéō *v.* (1x)
Roots:G1909 G5502-5 Compare:G1632
G2022 V-PAP-NSM ἐπιχέων (1x)
Lk 10:34 he·bound·up his wounds, pouring·in oil and wine

G2023 ἐπι•χορηγέω êpichôrēgéō *v.* (5x)
Roots:G1909 G5524 Compare:G2186-2
G2023.1 V-FPI-3S ἐπιχορηγηθήσεται (1x)
2Pe 1:11 accessible·entrance shall·be·fully·supplied to·yeu
G2023.1 V-PAP-NSM ἐπιχορηγῶν (2x)
Gal 3:5 Now·then, the·one fully·supplying the Spirit to·yeu
2Co 9:10 And the·one fully·supplying seed to·the·one
G2023.1 V-PPP-NSN ἐπιχορηγούμενον (1x)
Col 2:19 and ligaments being·fully·supplied and being·knit·
G2023.1 V-AAM-2P ἐπιχορηγήσατε (1x)
2Pe 1:5 all diligence, yeu·must·fully·supply along·with yeur

G2024 ἐπι•χορηγία êpichôrēgía *n.* (2x)
Roots:G2023 See:G2842
G2024.1 N-GSF ἐπιχορηγίας (1x)
Php 1:19 yeur petition and an·ample·supply of·the Spirit of·
G2024.2 N-GSF ἐπιχορηγίας (1x)
Eph 4:16 through every amply·supplying connection·joint,

G2025 ἐπι•χρίω êpichríō *v.* (2x)
Roots:G1909 G5548
G2025 V-AAI-3S ἐπέχρισεν (2x)
Jn 9:6 out of·the saliva, and he·smeared the clay over the
Jn 9:11 Jesus, he·made clay and smeared·*it*·over my eyes,

G2026 ἐπ•οικο•δομέω êpôikôdôméō *v.* (8x)
Roots:G1909 G3618
G2026 V-PAI-3S ἐποικοδομεῖ (3x)
1Co 3:10 ·laid a·foundation, and another builds·upon *it*. But
1Co 3:10 each·man must·look·out how he·builds·upon *it*.
1Co 3:12 And if any·man builds upon this foundation *with*
G2026 V-PAP-NPM ἐποικοδομοῦντες (1x)
Jud 1:20 yeu, beloved, building·up yeurselves in·yeur holy
G2026 V-PPP-NPM ἐποικοδομούμενοι (1x)
Col 2:7 having·been·rooted and being·built·up in him, and
G2026 V-AAI-3S ἐπῳκοδόμησεν (1x)
1Co 3:14 shall·remain which he·built·upon *the foundation*,
G2026 V-AAN ἐποικοδομῆσαι (1x)
Ac 20:32 grace, the·one being·able to·build·yeu·up, and to·
G2026 V-APP-NPM ἐποικοδομηθέντες (1x)
Eph 2:20 being·built upon the foundation of·the ambassadors

G2027 ἐπ•οκέλλω êpôkéllō *v.* (1x)
Roots:G1909 G3634-7
G2027.2 V-AAI-3P ἐπώκειλαν (1x)
Ac 27:41 *producing a·broad sand·bar*, they·ran the boat

G2028 ἐπ•ονομάζω êpônômázō *v.* (1x)
Roots:G1909 G3687
G2028.4 V-PMI-2S ἐπονομάζῃ (1x)
Rm 2:17 See, you·yourself label·yourself a·Jew, and you·

G2029 ἐπ•οπτεύω êpôptêúō *v.* (2x)
Roots:G2030 Compare:G2400 G1980 G1914 G2334
G2029 V-AAP-NPM ἐποπτεύσαντες (2x)
1Pe 2:12 ·a·result *of·yeur* good works (after·beholding *them*),
1Pe 3:2 (after·beholding yeur morally·clean behavior

G2030 ἐπ•όπτης êpóptēs *n.* (1x)
Roots:G1909 G3700 Compare:G0845 See:G2029
G2030.2 N-NPM ἐπόπται (1x)
2Pe 1:16 yeu·were·being beholders of·that magnificence.

G2031 ἔπος êpôs *n.* (1x)
Roots:G2036
G2031 N-ASN ἔπος (1x)
Heb 7:9 And *so* as to·make a·declaration, even Levi, the·one

G2032 ἐπ•ουράνιος êpôuraniôs *adj.* (20x)
Roots:G1909 G3772
G2032.1 A-NSM ἐπουράνιος (2x)
Mt 18:35 ·manner also, shall my heavenly Father do to·yeu,
1Co 15:48 and as *is* the heavenly·man, such also *shall·be*
G2032.1 A-NPM ἐπουράνιοι (1x)
1Co 15:48 ·man, such also *shall·be* the heavenly·ones.
G2032.1 A-ASF ἐπουράνιον (1x)
2Ti 4:18 ·keep·safe·and·sound into his heavenly kingdom,
G2032.1 A-DSF ἐπουρανίῳ (1x)
Heb 12:22 the·living God's CITY, to·a·heavenly JeruSalem,
G2032.1 A-GSM ἐπουρανίου (1x)
1Co 15:49 ·bear the derived·image of·the heavenly·man.
G2032.1 A-GSF ἐπουρανίου (3x)
Heb 3:1 brothers (*yeu* participants of·a·heavenly calling)
Heb 6:4 and after·tasting of·the heavenly voluntary·present,
Heb 11:16 *fatherland*, that·is, a·heavenly·one. Therefore
G2032.2 A-NPN ἐπουράνια (1x)
1Co 15:40 *There·are* also celestial bodies and terrestrial
G2032.2 A-GPM ἐπουρανίων (1x)
Php 2:10 every knee should·bow (of·celestial·ones, and of·
G2032.2 A-GPN ἐπουρανίων (1x)
1Co 15:40 ·yet in·fact the glory of·the celestial *is* one·kind,
G2032.3 A-APN ἐπουράνια (2x)
Jn 3:12 ·trust if I·should·declare to·yeu the heavenly·things?
Heb 9:23 the heavenly·things themselves with·significantly·
G2032.3 A-DPN ἐπουρανίοις (1x)
Eph 1:3 blessing by the heavenly·things in·Anointed-One,
G2032.3 A-GPN ἐπουρανίων (1x)
Heb 8:5 ·pattern and shadow of·the heavenly·things, just·as
G2032.4 A-DPN ἐπουρανίοις (4x)
Eph 1:20 *him* at his·own right·hand in the heavenly·places,
Eph 2:6 ·together in the heavenly·places in Anointed-One
Eph 3:10 ·the authorities in the heavenly·places through the
Eph 6:12 the spiritual·things of·evil in the heavenly·places.

G2033 ἑπτά hêptá *n.* (85x)
See:G1442 G2034
G2033 N-NUI ἑπτά (85x)
Lk 2:36 after·living with a·husband seven years from her
Lk 8:2 from whom had·gone·forth seven demons,
Lk 11:26 and personally·takes *to·itself* seven other spirits
Lk 20:29 "Now·then, there·were seven brothers. And the
Lk 20:31 her, and in·like·manner, the seven also; they·left·
Lk 20:33 does·she·become? For the seven held her *for* a·
Ac 6:3 from·among yeurselves seven men being·attested·to,
Ac 13:19 And after·demolishing seven nations in *the* land of·
Ac 19:14 ·*were* doing this·thing: the·seven Sons of·Sceva,
Ac 20:6 in·only five days, where we·lingered seven days.
Ac 21:4 we·stayed·over at·this·location *for* seven days;
Ac 21:8 being from·among the seven), we·abided with him.
Ac 21:27 And as·soon·as the seven days were·about to·be·
Ac 28:14 to·stay·over with them *for* seven days. And in·this·
Heb 11:30 being·surrounded for·a·span·of seven days.
Mt 12:45 personally·takes with himself seven other spirits
Mt 15:34 And they·declared, "Seven, and a·few small·fish
Mt 15:36 And after·taking the seven loaves·of·bread and the
Mt 15:37 ·full. And they·took·up seven woven·baskets full
Mt 16:10 Nor·even the seven loaves·of·bread of·the four·
Mt 18:22 ·times, but·rather up·to seventy·times seven.
Mt 22:25 "Now there·were with us seven brothers, and the
Mt 22:26 second also, and the third, even·unto the seventh.
Mt 22:28 whose wife shall·she·be of·the seven? For they·all
Mk 8:5 ·bread do·yeu·have?" And they·declared, "Seven."
Mk 8:6 And after·taking the seven loaves·of·bread *and*
Mk 8:8 ·abundance of·fragments, seven woven·baskets *full*.
Mk 8:20 And when *I·broke* the seven *loaves·of·bread* among
Mk 8:20 did·yeu·take·up?" And they·declared, "Seven."
Mk 12:20 "Now·there·were seven brothers, and the first·one
Mk 12:22 And the seven took her, and they·did·not leave
Mk 12:23 shall·she·be of·them? For the seven held her *for*
Mk 16:9 from whom he·had·cast·out seven demons.
Rv 1:4 John, To·the seven Called·Out·citizenries, to·the·
Rv 1:4 , also from the seven Spirits who are in·the·sight of·
Rv 1:12 And turning·about, I·saw seven Golden Lampstands
Rv 1:13 and in *the* midst of·the seven Lampstands, *one* like
Rv 1:16 and having in his right hand seven stars. And 'out
Rv 1:20 *this·is* the mystery of·the seven stars which you·saw
Rv 1:20 my right·hand, and the seven Golden Lampstands:
Rv 1:20 Golden Lampstands: the seven stars are angels of·
Rv 1:20 stars are angels of·the seven Called·Out·citizenries,
Rv 1:20 ·Out·citizenries, and the seven Lampstands which
Rv 1:20 which you·saw are *the* seven Called·Out·citizenries.
Rv 2:1 says the·one securely·holding the seven stars in his
Rv 2:1 ·about in *the* midst of·the seven Golden Lampstands:
Rv 3:1 having the Spirits of·God and the seven stars: 'I·
Rv 4:5 proceed·forth; and *there·are* seven lamps of·fire
Rv 4:5 of·the throne, which are the seven Spirits of·God.
Rv 5:1 having·been·fully·sealed·up with·seven official·seals.
Rv 5:5 official·scroll and to·loosen its seven official·seals."
Rv 5:6 as having·been·slaughtered, having seven horns and
Rv 5:6 having seven horns and seven eyes which are the
Rv 5:6 eyes which are the seven Spirits of·God having·been·
Rv 8:2 And I·saw the seven angels who stand in·the·sight of·
Rv 8:2 of·God; and to·them were·given seven trumpets.
Rv 8:6 And the seven angels having the seven trumpets made
Rv 8:6 And the seven angels having the seven trumpets made
Rv 10:3 And when he·yelled·out, the Seven Thunders spoke
Rv 10:4 And when the Seven Thunders spoke their·own
Rv 10:4 ·up those·things·which the Seven Thunders spoke,
Rv 11:13 the earthquake were·killed seven thousand names
Rv 12:3 ·great fiery·red Dragon, having seven heads and ten
Rv 12:3 and ten horns, and seven royal·turbans upon his
Rv 13:1 out of·the sea, having seven heads and ten horns,
Rv 15:1 great and marvelous, seven angels having the last
Rv 15:1 seven angels having the last seven punishing·blows,
Rv 15:6 And the seven angels came·forth from·out of·the
Rv 15:6 Temple, having the seven punishing·blows, having·
Rv 15:7 four living·beings gave to·the seven angels seven
Rv 15:7 ·beings gave to·the seven angels seven golden vials
Rv 15:8 even·until the seven punishing·blows of·the seven
Rv 15:8 ·blows of·the seven angels should·be·completed.
Rv 16:1 ·out of·the Temple saying to·the seven angels,
Rv 17:1 there·came one from·among the seven angels, of·
Rv 17:1 angels, of·the·one having the seven vials, and he·
Rv 17:3 of·names of·revilement, having seven heads and ten
Rv 17:7 her, the·one having the seven heads and the ten
Rv 17:9 "The seven heads are seven mountains, wherever the
Rv 17:9 "The seven heads are seven mountains, wherever the
Rv 17:10 And they·are seven kings. The five fell, and the
Rv 17:11 and is from·among the seven, and it·heads·on·out
Rv 21:9 ·came to me one of·the seven angels (of·the·ones
Rv 21:9 angels (of·the·ones having the seven vials, the·ones
Rv 21:9 ·ones overflowing of·the seven last punishing·blows

G2034 ἑπτά•κις hêptákis *adv.* (4x)
Roots:G2033
G2034.1 ADV ἑπτάκις (4x)
Lk 17:4 ·morally·fail against you seven·times in·the day, and
Lk 17:4 in·the day, and seven·times in·the day should·turn·
Mt 18:21 me, and I·shall·forgive him? Up·to seven·times?"
Mt 18:22 say to·you, up·to seven·times, but·rather up·to

G2035 ἑπτακισ•χίλιοι hêptakischíliôi *adj.* (1x)
Roots:G2034 G5507
G2035 A-APM ἑπτακισχιλίους (1x)
Rm 11:4 "'I·reserved to·myself seven·thousand men, who
G2036 ἔπω ěpō *v.* (979x)
εἶπον êipôn [aorist]
Compare:G3004 G5346 G4483 G2980 See:G2031 G2046 xLangAlso:H0559
G2036.1 V-2AAI-1S εἶπον (36x)
Jn 1:15 "This was·he of·whom I·declared, 'The·one who·is·
Jn 1:30 is·he concerning whom I·myself declared, 'Right·
Jn 1:50 declared to·him, "Because I·declared to·you, 'I·saw
Jn 3:7 You·should·not marvel that I·declared to·you, 'It·is·
Jn 3:12 If I·declared to·yeu the earthly·things, and yeu·do·
Jn 3:28 Yeu·yourselves testify to·me that I·declared, 'I·
Jn 6:36 But·rather I·declared to·yeu, also yeu·have·clearly·
Jn 8:24 Accordingly, I·declared to·yeu that yeu·shall·die in
Jn 9:27 He·answered them, "I·declared *it* to·yeu even·now,
Jn 10:25 Jesus answered them, "I·declared *it* to·yeu, and
Jn 10:26 from·among my sheep, just·as I·declared to·yeu.
Jn 10:36 'You·revile·God,' because I·declared, 'I·am God's
Jn 11:40 Jesus says to·her, "Did·I·not declare to·you, that, if
Jn 11:42 the·one having·stood·by, I·declared *it* in·order·that
Jn 13:33 ·seek me, and just·as I·declared to·the Judeans,
Jn 14:2 but·if·not, I·would·have declared *that* to·yeu. I·
Jn 14:26 yeu *concerning* all·things which I·declared to·yeu.
Jn 14:28 "Yeu·heard that I·myself declared to·yeu, 'I·head·
Jn 14:28 me, yeu·would rejoice that I·declared, 'I·traverse
Jn 15:20 the saying that I·myself declared to·yeu, 'A·slave
Jn 16:4 ·remember that I·myself declared to·yeu of·them.
Jn 16:4 And these·things I·did·not declare to·yeu at *the*
Jn 16:15 On·account·of that, I·declared that from·out·of·me,
Jn 16:19 ·another concerning this·thing which I·declared,
Jn 18:8 Jesus answered, "I·declared to·yeu that I AM.
Jn 18:21 ·men personally·know what I·myself declared."
Ac 11:8 But I·declared, 'Not·any·such·thing, Lord, because
Ac 22:10 And I·declared, 'What should·I·do, Lord?
Ac 22:19 "And·I declared, 'Lord, they·themselves are·fully·
Ac 26:15 And I·myself declared, 'Who are·you, Lord?
Heb 3:10 ·vexed with·that generation and declared, 'Always
Heb 10:7 At·that·time I·declared, 'Behold, I·come— on *the*
Gal 2:14 truth of·the good·news, I·declared to·Peter before
Mt 16:11 yeu·do·not understand that·I·declared *this* to·yeu
Mt 28:7 ·shall·gaze·upon him. Behold, I·declared *it* to·yeu.
Mk 9:18 and withers·away. And I·declared to·your disciples
G2036.1 V-AAI-1S εἶπα (1x)
Jn 10:34 Torah-Law, "I·myself declared, "Yeu·are gods""
G2036.1 V-2AAI-2S εἶπας (5x)
Jn 4:17 Jesus says to·her, "You·declared well, 'I·do·not
Lk 20:39 "Mentor, well declared."
Mt 26:25 He·says to·him, "You·yourself declared *it*."
Mt 26:64 says to·him, "You·yourself declared *it*. Moreover
Mk 12:32 "Mentor, clearly·full·well did·you·declare in truth
G2036.1 V-2AAI-2P εἴπατε (1x)
Lk 12:3 Because as·many·things·as yeu·declared in the
G2036.1 V-2AAI-3S εἶπεν (644x)
Jn 1:23 of·Yahweh,"" just·as IsaIah the prophet declared."
Jn 1:33 me to·immerse in water, that·one declared to·me,
Jn 1:42 looking·clearly·upon him, declared, "You·yourself
Jn 1:46 And NathaniEl declared to·him, "Is·it·possible *for*
Jn 1:48 me?" Jesus answered and declared to·him, "Before
Jn 1:50 Jesus answered and declared to·him, "Because I·
Jn 2:16 And he·declared to·the·ones selling the doves,
Jn 2:19 Jesus answered and declared to·them, "Tear·down
Jn 2:22 the Scripture and the word which Jesus declared.
Jn 3:2 came to Jesus by·night and declared to·him, "Rabbi,
Jn 3:3 Jesus answered and declared to·him, "Certainly,
Jn 3:9 NicoDemus answered and declared to·him, "How·are
Jn 3:10 Jesus answered and declared to·him, "Are you·
Jn 3:27 John answered and declared, "A·man·of·clay† is·not
Jn 4:10 Jesus answered and declared to·her, "If you·had·
Jn 4:13 Jesus answered and declared to·her, "Anyone
Jn 4:17 The woman answered and declared, "I·do·not have
Jn 4:27 However, not·even·one·man declared, "What·do
Jn 4:29 See a·man·of·clay† who declared to·me all the·
Jn 4:32 But he·declared to·them, "I·myself have a·full·meal
Jn 4:39 testifying, "He·declared to·me all the·many·things
Jn 4:48 Now·then Jesus declared to him, "Unless yeu·*all*·
Jn 4:50 trusted the word that Jesus declared to·him, and he·
Jn 4:53 at that hour, in which Jesus declared to·him, "Your
Jn 5:11 me healthy·and·sound, that·man declared to·me,
Jn 5:14 in the Sanctuary·Atrium, and he·declared to·him,
Jn 5:19 So·then Jesus answered and declared to·them,
Jn 6:10 And Jesus declared, "Make the men·of·clay† to·sit·
Jn 6:26 Jesus answered them and declared, "Certainly, most·
Jn 6:29 Jesus answered and declared to·them, "This is the
Jn 6:32 Accordingly, Jesus declared to·them, "Certainly,
Jn 6:35 And Jesus declared to·them, "I AM the bread of·
Jn 6:41 ·grumbling concerning him, because he·declared, "I
Jn 6:43 So Jesus answered and declared to·them, "Do·not
Jn 6:53 Accordingly, Jesus declared to·them, "Certainly,
Jn 6:59 He·declared these·things in a·gathering, while·
Jn 6:61 disciples are·grumbling about this, declared to·them,
Jn 6:67 So·then Jesus declared to·the twelve, "And *do* yeu·
Jn 7:16 Jesus answered them and declared, "My instruction
Jn 7:20 The crowd answered and declared, "You·have a·
Jn 7:21 Jesus answered and declared to·them, "I·did one
Jn 7:33 So·then Jesus declared to·them, "Yet a·short time
Jn 7:36 ·*of* saying is this that he·declared, 'Yeu·shall·seek
Jn 7:38 in me, just·as the Scripture declared, "from·out·of·
Jn 7:39 (But he·declared this concerning the Spirit, which
Jn 7:42 Has·not·indeed the Scripture declared, that the
Jn 8:7 after·pulling·himself·up·straight, he·declared to them,
Jn 8:10 not·even·one besides the wife, declared to·her, "*Ah*,
Jn 8:11 She·declared, "Not·even·one, Lord.
Jn 8:11 And Jesus declared to·her, "Not·even·do I·myself
Jn 8:14 Jesus answered and declared to·them, "Though I·
Jn 8:21 In·due·course, Jesus declared again to·them, "I·
Jn 8:23 And he·declared to·them, "Yeu·yourselves are
Jn 8:25 you·yourself?" And Jesus declares to·them, "Even
Jn 8:28 Then accordingly, Jesus declared to·them,
Jn 8:42 Accordingly, Jesus declared to·them, "If God was
Jn 8:58 Jesus declared to·them, "Certainly, most·certainly, I·
Jn 9:7 and he·declared to·him, "Head·on·out, wash in the
Jn 9:11 That·man answered and declared, "A·man·of·clay†
Jn 9:11 smeared·*it*·over my eyes, and he·declared to·me,
Jn 9:15 how he·received·his·sight. So he·declared to·them,
Jn 9:17 And he·declared, "He·is a·prophet!"
Jn 9:25 that·man answered and declared, "Whether he·is
Jn 9:30 The man·of·clay† answered and declared to·them,
Jn 9:35 And finding him, he·declared to·him, "You·
Jn 9:36 That·one answered and declared, "Who is·he, Lord,
Jn 9:37 And Jesus declared to·him, "Even you·have·clearly·
Jn 9:39 Then Jesus declared, "For judgment, I·myself did·
Jn 9:41 Jesus declared to·them, "If yeu·were blind, yeu·
Jn 10:6 Jesus declared this proverb to·them, but those
Jn 10:7 So·then Jesus declared to·them again, "Certainly,
Jn 10:35 "If he·declared them gods pertaining·to whom the
Jn 10:41 as·many·as John declared concerning this·man were
Jn 11:4 But Jesus, hearing *that*, declared, "This sickness is
Jn 11:11 These·things he·declared, and after that he·says to·
Jn 11:14 Jesus declared to·them with·clarity·of·speech,
Jn 11:16 ·to·as Twin) declared to·the fellow·disciples,
Jn 11:21 Then Martha declared to Jesus, "Lord, if you·were
Jn 11:25 Jesus declared to·her, "I AM the resurrection and
Jn 11:34 and he·declared, "Where have·yeu·laid him?
Jn 11:41 Jesus lifted the eyes upward and declared, "Father,
Jn 11:49 ·high·priest that·same year, declared to·them,
Jn 11:51 And he·did·not declare this from his·own·self, but·
Jn 12:6 Now he·declared this, not because it·was·mattering
Jn 12:7 Accordingly, Jesus declared, "Leave her *alone*.
Jn 12:30 Jesus answered and declared, "This voice has·
Jn 12:35 Accordingly, Jesus declared to·them, "Yet a·short
Jn 12:38 may·be·completely·fulfilled, which he·declared,
Jn 12:39 ·not able to·trust, because *as* IsaIah declared again,
Jn 12:41 IsaIah declared these·things when he·saw his glory
Jn 12:44 And Jesus yelled·out and declared, "The·one
Jn 13:7 Jesus answered and declared to·him, "What I·myself
Jn 13:11 On·account·of that, he·declared, "Yeu·are not·
Jn 13:12 after·sitting·back again, he·declared to·them,
Jn 13:21 spirit, and he·testified and declared, "Certainly,
Jn 13:28 knew particularly why he·declared this to·him.
Jn 14:23 Jesus answered and declared to·him, "If anyone
Jn 16:19 ·wanting to·ask him, and he·declared to·them,
Jn 17:1 his eyes to the heaven, and he·declared, "Father, the
Jn 18:4 upon him, going·forth, he·declared to·them,
Jn 18:6 Now·then, as·soon·as he·declared to·them, "I AM,"
Jn 18:9 may·be·completely·fulfilled, which *Jesus* declared,
Jn 18:11 So·then Jesus declared to·Peter, "Cast your dagger
Jn 18:16 ·high·priest, went·out and declared *him* to·the
Jn 18:25 That·man denied *it* and declared, "I·am not.
Jn 18:29 Pilate went·out to them and declared, "What legal·
Jn 18:31 So·then Pilate declared to·them, "Yeu·yourselves
Jn 18:32 ·completely·fulfilled which he·declared, signifying
Jn 18:33 hollered·out·for Jesus. And he·declared to·him,
Jn 18:37 Accordingly, Pilate declared to·him, "So·then·
Jn 19:21 but·rather that this·man declared, 'I·am King of·
Jn 19:30 received the wine·vinegar, he·declared, "It·has·
Jn 20:18 the Lord, and *that* he·declared these·things to·her.
Jn 20:21 Now·then, Jesus declared to·them again, "Peace
Jn 20:25 ·seen the Lord." But he·declared to·them, "Unless
Jn 20:26 the midst *of·them*. And he·declared, "Peace *be* to·
Jn 20:28 And Thomas answered and declared to·him, "My
Jn 21:6 And he·declared to·them, "Cast the net to the right·
Jn 21:17 Peter was·grieved because he·declared to·him the
Jn 21:17 ·have·affection·for me?" And he·declared to·him,
Jn 21:19 This he·declared, signifying by·what·kind·of death
Jn 21:20 his chest at the supper and declared, "Lord, who is
Jn 21:23 But Jesus did·not declare to·him that he·does·not
Lk 1:13 But the angel declared to him, "Do·not be·afraid,
Lk 1:18 Then ZacharIas declared to the angel, "How shall·I·
Lk 1:19 And answering, the angel declared to·him, "I·
Lk 1:28 toward her, the angel declared, "Be·of·good·cheer,
Lk 1:30 And the angel declared to·her, "Do·not be·afraid,
Lk 1:34 Then Mariam declared to the angel, "How shall this
Lk 1:35 And answering, the angel declared to·her, "Holy
Lk 1:38 And Mariam declared, "Behold, the female·slave
Lk 1:42 she·exclaimed with·a·loud voice, and declared,
Lk 1:46 And Mariam declared, "My soul does·magnify
Lk 1:60 And answering, his mother declared, "No·indeed!
Lk 2:10 And the angel declared to·them, "Do·not be·afraid,
Lk 2:28 into his arms and blessed God. And he·declared,
Lk 2:34 blessed them, and he·declared to Mariam his mother
Lk 2:48 And his mother declared to him, "Child, why·did
Lk 2:49 And he·declared to them, "How *is·it* that yeu·were·
Lk 3:13 And he·declared to them, "Exact not·one·bit more·
Lk 3:14 we·ourselves do?" And he·declared to them,
Lk 4:3 And the Slanderer declared to·him, "If you·are a·son
Lk 4:6 And the Slanderer declared to·him, "To·you I·shall·
Lk 4:8 And answering, Jesus declared to·him, "Get·
Lk 4:9 of·the Sanctuary·Estate. And he·declared to·him, "If
Lk 4:12 And answering, Jesus declared to·him, "It·has·
Lk 4:23 And he·declared to them, "Entirely, yeu·shall·
Lk 4:24 Then he·declared, "Certainly I·say to·yeu, that not·
Lk 4:43 And he·declared to them, "It·is·mandatory·for me
Lk 5:4 as·soon·as he·ceased speaking, he·declared to Simon
Lk 5:5 And answering, Simon declared to·him, "O·Captain,
Lk 5:10 And Jesus declared to Simon, "Do·not be·afraid.
Lk 5:20 And seeing their trust, he·declared to·him, "Man·
Lk 5:22 their deliberations, answering, declared to them,
Lk 5:24 (he·declared to·the·one having·been·paralyzed),
Lk 5:27 in the tax·booth. And he·declared to·him, "Follow
Lk 5:31 And answering, Jesus declared to them, "The·ones
Lk 5:34 And he·declared to them, "¿!·Are yeu·able to·make
Lk 6:3 to them, Jesus declared, "Did·yeu·not·even read·
Lk 6:8 And *Jesus* declared to·the man·of·clay†, the·one
Lk 6:9 So·then Jesus declared to them, "I·shall·inquire·of
Lk 6:10 ·upon them all, he·declared to·the·man·of·clay†,
Lk 6:39 And he·declared a·parable to·them: "Is·it possible·

Lk 7:9 And turning·around, he·declared to·the crowd
Lk 7:13 Lord empathized over her and declared to·her, "Do·
Lk 7:14 *him* stood·still. And he·declared, "Young·man, I·
Lk 7:22 And answering, Jesus declared to·them,
Lk 7:31 And the Lord declared, "So·then to·what shall·I·
Lk 7:39 the·one calling·for him, declared within himself,
Lk 7:40 And answering, Jesus declared to him, "Simon, I·
Lk 7:43 And answering, Simon declared, "I·assume that *it*·
Lk 7:43 the more." And he·declared to·him, "You·judged
Lk 7:48 And he·declared to·her, "Your moral·failures have·
Lk 7:50 And he·declared to the woman, "Your trust has·
Lk 8:4 *from* each city, *Jesus* declared *the following* through
Lk 8:10 And he·declared, "To·yeu it·has·been·given to·
Lk 8:21 And answering, he·declared to them, "My mother
Lk 8:22 with his disciples, and he·declared to them, "We·
Lk 8:25 And he·declared to·them, "Where is yeur trust?
Lk 8:28 and with·a·loud voice he·declared, "What·does·
Lk 8:30 "What is your name?" And he·declared, "Legion,"
Lk 8:45 And Jesus declared, "Who·is the·one laying·hold
Lk 8:45 *it*, Peter and the·ones with him declared, "Captain,
Lk 8:46 And Jesus declared, "Someone laid·hold of·me, for
Lk 8:48 And he·declared to·her, "Daughter, be·of·good·
Lk 8:52 vividly·lamenting·over her, but he·declared, "Do·
Lk 9:3 And he·declared to them, "Take·up not·even·one·
Lk 9:9 And HerOd·AntiPas declared, "I·myself beheaded
Lk 9:13 But he·declared to them, "Yeu·yeurselves give
Lk 9:14 five·thousand men. And he·declared to his disciples
Lk 9:20 But he·declared to·them, "And who·do yeu·
Lk 9:20 me to·be?" And answering, Peter declared, "The
Lk 9:33 ·departing from him, *that* Peter declared to Jesus,
Lk 9:41 And answering, Jesus declared, "O distrusting and
Lk 9:43 ·things which Jesus did, he·declared to his disciples,
Lk 9:48 and declared to·them, "Whoever should·accept this
Lk 9:49 And responding, John declared, "O·Captain, we·
Lk 9:50 And Jesus declared to him, "Do·not forbid *him*, for
Lk 9:55 he·reprimanded them and declared, "Yeu·do·not
Lk 9:57 the roadway, *that* a·certain·man declared to him,
Lk 9:58 And Jesus declared to·him, "The foxes have
Lk 9:59 And he·declared to another, "Follow me.
Lk 9:59 But the·man declared, "Lord, freely·permit me to·
Lk 9:60 But Jesus declared to·him, "Leave the dead·ones to·
Lk 9:61 And another also declared, "Lord, I·shall·follow
Lk 9:62 And Jesus declared unto him, "Not·even·one·man,
Lk 10:18 And he·declared to·them, "I·was·observing the
Lk 10:21 Jesus leaped·for·joy in·the Spirit and declared, "I·
Lk 10:22 turning·around toward the disciples, he·declared,
Lk 10:23 *to·be* alongside his disciples, he·declared privately,
Lk 10:26 He·declared to him, "What has·been·written in the
Lk 10:27 And answering, he·declared, "⁽ᵉ⁾You·shall·love
Lk 10:28 And he·declared to·him, "You·answered uprightly.
Lk 10:29 to·regard himself as·righteous, declared to Jesus,
Lk 10:30 taking·up *the question*, Jesus declared, "A·certain
Lk 10:35 *them* to·the innkeeper, and declared to·him,
Lk 10:37 And he·declared, "The·one continuing the act·of·
Lk 10:37 Accordingly, Jesus declared to·him, "Traverse,
Lk 10:40 And standing·over *him*, she·declared, "Lord,
Lk 10:41 And answering, Jesus declared to·her, "Martha,
Lk 11:1 a·certain·one of·his disciples declared to him,
Lk 11:2 And he·declared to·them, "Whenever yeu·should·
Lk 11:5 And he·declared to them, "Which from·among yeu
Lk 11:17 ·seen their complete·thoughts, declared to·them,
Lk 11:27 the crowd, lifting·up her·voice, declared to·him,
Lk 11:28 But he·himself declared, "As·a·matter·of·fact,
Lk 11:39 And the Lord declared to him, "Now yeu Pharisees
Lk 11:46 And *Jesus* declared, "Woe to·yeu also, the experts·
Lk 11:49 the wisdom of·God also declared, 'I·shall·dispatch
Lk 12:13 someone from·among the crowd declared to·him,
Lk 12:14 And he·declared to·him, "Man·of·clay†, who
Lk 12:15 Then he·declared to them, "Yeu·clearly·see·to·it,
Lk 12:16 And he·declared a·parable to them, saying, "The
Lk 12:18 "Then *this·man* declared, 'This shall·I·do, I·shall·
Lk 12:20 "But God declared to·him, 'O·impetuous·one!
Lk 12:22 Then he·declared to his disciples, "On·account·of

Lk 12:41 But Peter declared to·him, "Lord, do·you·say this
Lk 12:42 And the Lord declared, "Who then is the
Lk 13:2 And responding, Jesus declared to·them, "Do·yeu·
Lk 13:7 "So he·declared to the vinedresser, 'Behold, *for*
Lk 13:12 Jesus addressed *her* and declared to·her, "Woman
Lk 13:15 Lord answered him and declared, "O·stage·acting·
Lk 13:20 And again he·declared, "To·what shall·I·liken the
Lk 13:23 Then someone declared to him, "Lord, *is·it so* that
Lk 13:23 being·saved *are* few?" And he·declared to·them,
Lk 13:32 And he·declared to·them, "Traversing, yeu·declare
Lk 14:3 And responding, Jesus declared to the experts·in·
Lk 14:5 And answering toward them, he·declared, "Which
Lk 14:15 ·at·the·meal hearing these·things, declared to·him,
Lk 14:16 Then *Jesus* declared to·him, "A·certain man·of·
Lk 14:18 to·excuse·themselves. The first declared to·him,
Lk 14:19 And another declared, 'I·bought five yoked·teams
Lk 14:20 And another declared, 'I·married a·wife, and on·
Lk 14:21 the master·of·the·house declared to·his slave,
Lk 14:22 "And the slave declared, 'Lord, it·has·happened as
Lk 14:23 And the lord declared to the slave, 'Go·out into the
Lk 14:25 ·him, and turning·around, he·declared to them,
Lk 15:3 And he·declared this parable to them, saying,
Lk 15:11 Then he·declared, "A·certain man·of·clay† had
Lk 15:12 And the younger of·them declared to·the father,
Lk 15:17 Then coming to himself, he·declared, 'How·many
Lk 15:21 "But the son declared to·him, 'Father, I·morally·
Lk 15:22 "But the father declared to his slaves, 'Bring·out
Lk 15:27 And he·declared to·him, 'Your brother comes
Lk 15:29 But answering *him*, he·declared to·his father,
Lk 15:31 "And he·declared to·him, 'Child, you·yourself are
Lk 16:2 And hollering·out·for him, he·declared to·him,
Lk 16:3 "And the estate·manager declared within himself,
Lk 16:6 And he·declared, 'A·hundred bath·measures of·oil.
Lk 16:6 ·measures of·oil.' And he·declared to·him, '*Here*,
Lk 16:7 After·that, he·declared to·another, 'And you, how·
Lk 16:7 ·much·do you·owe?' And he·declared, 'A·hundred
Lk 16:15 And he·declared to·them, "Yeu·yeurselves are the·
Lk 16:24 "And hollering·out, he·himself declared, 'Father
Lk 16:25 "But AbRaham declared, 'Child, recall·to·mind
Lk 16:27 "Then he·declared, 'So·then I·implore·of you,
Lk 16:30 And he·declared, 'No·indeed, father AbRaham!
Lk 16:31 "But *AbRaham* declared to·him, 'If·they·do·not
Lk 17:1 And *Jesus* declared to the disciples, "It·is not·
Lk 17:6 And the Lord declared, "If yeu·were·having trust
Lk 17:14 And upon·seeing *them*, he·declared to·them,
Lk 17:17 And responding, Jesus declared, "Are·not·indeed
Lk 17:19 And he·declared to·him, "Rising·up, depart.
Lk 17:20 ·come, he·answered them and declared, "The
Lk 17:22 Then he·declared to the disciples, "Days shall·
Lk 17:37 Lord?" And he·declared to·them, "Wherever the
Lk 18:4 these *persistent appeals*, he·declared within himself
Lk 18:6 Then the Lord declared, "Hear what the unjust
Lk 18:9 And he·declared also this parable to certain ones
Lk 18:16 But Jesus, summoning them, declared, "Allow
Lk 18:19 And Jesus declared to·him, "Why·do you·refer·to
Lk 18:21 And he·declared, "All these·things I·vigilantly·
Lk 18:22 Jesus, hearing these·things, declared to·him, "Yet
Lk 18:24 him becoming exceedingly·grieved, declared,
Lk 18:27 But he·declared, "The·things *which·are* impossible
Lk 18:28 Then Peter declared, "Behold, we·ourselves left all
Lk 18:29 And he·declared to·them, "Certainly I·say to·yeu,
Lk 18:31 personally·taking the twelve, he·declared to them,
Lk 18:41 I·should·do for·you?" And he·declared, "Lord,
Lk 18:42 And Jesus declared to·him, "Receive·your·sight.
Lk 19:5 looking·up, he·saw him, and declared to him,
Lk 19:8 Zacchaeus, after·being·settled, declared to the Lord
Lk 19:9 And Jesus declared to him, "Today, Salvation did·
Lk 19:11 augmenting *it*, *Jesus* declared a·parable, on·
Lk 19:12 Accordingly, he·declared, "A·man·of·clay†, a·
Lk 19:13 more·silver·minas to·them and declared to them,
Lk 19:15 the kingdom, that he·declared *for* these slaves to·
Lk 19:17 And he·declared to·him, 'Well·done, you·
Lk 19:19 And he·declared likewise to·him, 'Be you also

Lk 19:24 "And he·declared to·the·ones standing·nearby,
Lk 19:32 ·dispatched found *it* just·as he·declared to·them.
Lk 19:40 And answering, he·declared to·them, "I·say to·
Lk 20:3 And answering, he·declared to them, "And·I shall·
Lk 20:8 And Jesus declared to·them, "Neither *do* I·myself
Lk 20:13 "Then the owner of·the vineyard declared, 'What
Lk 20:17 And looking·clearly·upon them, he·declared, "So·
Lk 20:19 on him, for they·knew that he·declared this parable
Lk 20:23 their shrewd·cunning, he·declared to them, "Why·
Lk 20:25 And he·declared to·them, "Now·then, give·back
Lk 20:34 And answering, Jesus declared to·them, "The
Lk 20:41 But he·declared to them, "How·do they·say *it·is*·
Lk 20:42 of·Psalms, "Yahweh declared to·my Lord, "Sit·
Lk 20:45 of·all the people, he·declared to·his disciples,
Lk 21:3 And he·declared, "Truly I·say to·yeu, that this
Lk 21:5 ·beautiful stones and vow·offerings, he·declared,
Lk 21:8 And he·declared, "Look·out, *that* yeu·may·not be·
Lk 21:29 And he·declared to·them a·parable: "See the fig·
Lk 22:10 And he·declared to·them, "Behold, with·yeu
Lk 22:15 And he·declared to them, "With·longing, I·longed
Lk 22:17 *the* cup *and* giving·thanks, he·declared, "Take this
Lk 22:25 And he·declared to·them, "The kings of·the
Lk 22:31 Then the Lord declared, "Simon, Simon, behold,
Lk 22:33 And *Simon* declared to·him, "Lord, I·am ready to·
Lk 22:34 And he·declared, "I·say to·you, Peter, a·rooster,
Lk 22:35 And he·declared to·them, "When I·dispatched yeu
Lk 22:36 Then he·declared to·them, "But·yet now, the·one
Lk 22:38 *are* two daggers." And he·declared to·them, "It·is
Lk 22:40 at the place, he·declared to·them, "Be·in·prayer
Lk 22:46 and he·declared to·them, "Why·do yeu·sleep?
Lk 22:48 But Jesus declared to·him, "Judas, do·you·hand·
Lk 22:51 And responding, Jesus declared, "*Stop!* Yeu·must·
Lk 22:52 Then Jesus declared to the chief·priests, *the*
Lk 22:56 at·him, a·certain servant·girl declared, "This·man
Lk 22:58 And Peter declared, "Man·of·clay†, I·am not!"
Lk 22:60 And Peter declared, "Man·of·clay†, I·do·not
Lk 22:61 the word of·the Lord, how he·declared to·him,
Lk 22:67 And he·declared to·them, "If I·should·declare *it*
Lk 23:4 Then Pilate declared to the chief·priests and *to* the
Lk 23:14 declared to them, "Yeu·brought this man·of·clay†
Lk 23:22 And *for* the third·time, he·declared to them, "For
Lk 23:28 But turning·around toward them, Jesus declared,
Lk 23:43 And Jesus declared to·him, "Certainly I·say to·you
Lk 23:46 ·out with·a·loud voice, Jesus declared, "Father,
Lk 24:17 And he·declared to them, "What sayings *are* these
Lk 24:18 whose name *was* CleoPas declared to him, "*Are*
Lk 24:19 And he·declared to·them, "Like·what?
Lk 24:25 Then he·himself declared to them, "O stupid·ones,
Lk 24:38 And he·declared to·them, "Why are·yeu having·
Lk 24:41 the joy and marveling, he·declared to·them, "Do·
Lk 24:44 And he·declared to·them, "These *are* the words
Lk 24:46 And he·declared to·them, "In·this·manner it·has·
Ac 1:7 And he·declared to them, "It·is not for·yeu to·know
Ac 1:15 *and* twenty), Peter, after·standing·up, declared,
Ac 2:34 he·himself says, "Yahweh declared to·my Lord,
Ac 3:4 upon him together with·John, declared, "Look upon
Ac 3:6 Then Peter declared, "Silver and gold, it·does·not
Ac 3:22 "For Moses in·fact declared to the fathers,
Ac 4:8 being·filled with·Holy Spirit, declared to them,
Ac 5:3 But Peter declared, "AnanIas, why *has* the
Ac 5:8 open·field for·so·much?" And she·declared, "Yes,
Ac 5:9 So Peter declared to her, "How *is·it* that yeu are·
Ac 5:19 doors; and·also leading them out, he·declared,
Ac 5:35 And *then* he·declared to *the joint·council*, "Men,
Ac 7:1 Then the designated·high·priest declared, "Are these·
Ac 7:3 and declared to him, "Go·forth from·among your
Ac 7:7 ·enslaved, I·myself shall·sheriff," declared God, ⁽ᵉ⁾
Ac 7:33 "And Yahweh declared to·him, "Loosen the shoes
Ac 7:56 And he·declared, "Behold, I·observe the heavens
Ac 8:20 But Peter declared to him, "May your silver,
Ac 8:24 Then answering, Simon declared, "Yeu·yeurselves
Ac 8:29 And the Spirit declared to·Philippe, "Go·alongside
Ac 8:30 IsaIah the prophet, and he·declared, "Then is·it·

Ac 8:31 And he·declared, "For how·is·it *that* I·might be·
Ac 8:34 Philippe, the eunuch declared, "I·petition you,
Ac 8:37 And Philippe declared, "If you·trust from·out of·all
Ac 8:37 And answering, he·declared, "I·trust Jesus
Ac 9:5 And he·declared, "Who are·you, Lord?
Ac 9:5 Lord?" And the Lord declared, "It·is·I Myself,
Ac 9:6 trembling and being·amazed, he·declared, "Lord,
Ac 9:10 And the Lord declared to him in a·clear·vision, "O·
Ac 9:10 "O·Ananias." And he·declared, "Behold, I·myself
Ac 9:15 But the Lord declared to him, "Traverse! Because
Ac 9:17 his hands on him, he·declared, "Brother Saul, the
Ac 9:34 And Peter declared to·him, "Aeneas, Jesus the
Ac 9:40 ·back·around to the body, he·declared, "Tabitha,
Ac 10:4 at·him and becoming alarmed, he·declared, "What
Ac 10:4 What is·it, Lord?" And he·declared to·him, "Your
Ac 10:14 But Peter declared, "Not·any·such·thing, Lord,
Ac 10:19 about the clear·vision, the Spirit declared to·him,
Ac 10:21 him from Cornelius), Peter declared, "Behold, it·
Ac 10:34 Peter, opening·up his mouth, declared, "In truth,
Ac 11:12 And the Spirit declared to·me to·go·together with·
Ac 12:8 And the angel declared to him, "Gird·yourself·
Ac 12:11 after·coming to himself, Peter declared, "Now I·
Ac 12:17 out of·the prison. And he·declared, "Go·announce
Ac 13:2 ·also fasting, the Holy Spirit declared, "Now·then,
Ac 13:10 declared, "O *you·are* full of·all guile and all
Ac 13:16 ·up and motioning with·his hand, declared, "Men,
Ac 13:22 for·whom also testifying, he·declared, "I·found
Ac 14:10 *Paul* declared with·a·loud voice, "Stand upright
Ac 15:7 occurring, after·rising·up, Peter declared to them,
Ac 15:36 Now after some days, Paul declared to BarNabas,
Ac 16:18 Paul, even turning·about, declared to·the spirit,
Ac 18:6 shaking·out his garments, he·declared to them,
Ac 18:9 And the Lord declared to·Paul through a·clear·
Ac 18:14 to·open·up his mouth, Gallio declared to the Jews,
Ac 19:2 he·declared to them, "Did·yeu·receive Holy Spirit
Ac 19:3 And he·declared to them, "So·then into what were·
Ac 19:4 Then Paul declared, "In·fact, John did·immerse
Ac 19:15 *occasion*, the evil spirit declared, "Jesus I·know,
Ac 19:25 concerning the *trades* such·as·these, he·declared,
Ac 20:10 ·altogether·enclosing·about *him*, he·declared,
Ac 20:18 ·as they·came·close to him, he·declared to·them,
Ac 20:35 of·the Lord Jesus that he·himself declared, 'It·is
Ac 21:11 his·own hands and feet, he·declared, "Thus says
Ac 21:39 But Paul declared, "In·fact, I·myself am a·man·of·
Ac 22:8 are·you, Lord?' And he·declared to me, 'It·is·I
Ac 22:10 Lord?' And the Lord declared to me, 'Upon·
Ac 22:13 to me and standing·over *me*, he·declared to·me,
Ac 22:14 "And he·declared, 'The God of·our fathers
Ac 22:21 "And he·declared to me, 'Traverse, because I·
Ac 22:25 him with·the straps, Paul declared to the centurion
Ac 22:27 *Paul*, the regiment·commander declared to·him,
Ac 23:1 at·the joint·council·of·Sanhedrin, declared, "Men,
Ac 23:3 Then Paul declared to him, "God is·about to·
Ac 23:11 Lord, upon·standing·over him, declared, "Be·of·
Ac 23:20 And he·declared, "The Judeans agreed·among·
Ac 23:23 two of·the centurions, he·declared, "Make·ready
Ac 25:9 Judeans, answering Paul, he·declared, "Will·you
Ac 25:10 Then Paul declared, "I·am standing at Caesar's
Ac 26:15 are·you, Lord?' And he·declared, 'It·is·I Myself,
Ac 26:29 And Paul declared, "I·would well-wish to·God,
Ac 27:21 ·being·settled in *the* midst of·them, declared, "O
Ac 27:31 Paul declared to·the centurion and to·the soldiers,
Heb 1:5 to·which of·the angels did·he·declare at·any·time,
Heb 12:21 was frightful, *such·that* Moses declared, "I·am
Mt 2:8 them to BethLechem, he·declared, "Upon·traversing,
Mt 3:7 to his immersion, *John* declared to·them, "O·
Mt 3:15 And answering, YeShua declared to him, "Allow
Mt 4:3 ·alongside him, the Tempting·One declared, "If you·
Mt 4:4 But answering, he·declared, "It·has·been·written,
Mt 8:10 he·marveled and declared to·the·ones following,
Mt 8:13 Then YeShua declared to·the centurion, "Head·on·
Mt 8:19 one scribe coming·alongside, declared to·him,
Mt 8:21 And another of·his disciples declared to·him, "Lord
Mt 8:22 But YeShua declared to·him, "Follow me, and
Mt 8:32 And he·declared to·them, "Head·on·out.
Mt 9:2 their trust, YeShua declared to·the paralyzed·man,
Mt 9:4 their cogitations, YeShua declared, "For·what·
Mt 9:12 But after·hearing *that*, YeShua declared to·them,
Mt 9:15 And YeShua declared to·them, "¿!·Are the Sons of·
Mt 9:22 and seeing her, YeShua declared, "Daughter, be·of·
Mt 11:3 declared to·him, "Are you·yourself the·one who·is·
Mt 11:4 And answering, YeShua declared to·them,
Mt 11:25 on that occasion, YeShua declared, "I·explicitly·
Mt 12:3 But he·declared to·them, "Did·yeu·not read·aloud
Mt 12:11 And *YeShua* declared to·them, "What man·of·
Mt 12:25 having·seen their cogitations, declared to·them,
Mt 12:39 But answering, he·declared to·them, "An·evil
Mt 12:47 And someone declared to·him, "Behold, your
Mt 12:48 the·one declaring *this* to·him, he·declared, "Who
Mt 12:49 hand over his disciples, he·declared, "Behold my
Mt 13:11 And answering, he·declared to·them, "Because it·
Mt 13:37 And answering, he·declared to·them, "The·one
Mt 13:52 So he·declared to·them, "On·account·of that,
Mt 13:57 But YeShua declared to·them, "A·prophet is not
Mt 14:2 and declared to·his servant·boys, "This is John the
Mt 14:16 But YeShua declared to·them, "They·have no need
Mt 14:18 But he·declared, "Bring them here to·me.
Mt 14:28 And answering him, Peter declared, "Lord, if it·
Mt 14:29 And he·declared, "Come.
Mt 15:3 But answering, he·declared to·them, "And why·do
Mt 15:10 upon·summoning the crowd, he·declared to·them,
Mt 15:13 But answering, he·declared, "Every plant which
Mt 15:15 Now responding, Peter declared to·him, "Explain
Mt 15:16 Then YeShua declared, "Are yeu also still·at·this·
Mt 15:24 Then answering *her*, he·declared, "I·am·not
Mt 15:26 But answering, he·declared, "It·is not good to·
Mt 15:27 And she·declared, "Yes *it·is*, Lord.
Mt 15:28 Then answering, YeShua declared to·her, "O
Mt 15:32 his disciples, YeShua declared, "I·empathize over
Mt 16:2 Answering, he·declared to·them, "With·early·
Mt 16:6 Then YeShua declared to·them, "Clearly·see·to·it
Mt 16:8 But YeShua knowing *this*, declared to·them, "O·
Mt 16:12 that he·did·not declare *to·them* to·beware of the
Mt 16:16 answering, Simon Peter declared, "You·yourself
Mt 16:17 And responding, YeShua declared to·him,
Mt 16:23 But turning·around, he·declared to·Peter, "Get·
Mt 16:24 Then YeShua declared to·his disciples, "If any·
Mt 17:4 Now responding *to·this*, Peter declared to·YeShua,
Mt 17:7 YeShua laid·hold of·them and declared, "Be·
Mt 17:11 And answering, YeShua declared to·them, "In·
Mt 17:13 comprehended that he·declared to·them concerning
Mt 17:17 And answering, YeShua declared, "O distrusting
Mt 17:20 And YeShua declared to·them, "On·account·of
Mt 17:22 returning into Galilee, YeShua declared to·them,
Mt 18:3 and declared, "Certainly I·say to·yeu, unless yeu·
Mt 18:21 Peter, coming·alongside him, declared, "Lord,
Mt 19:4 And answering, he·declared to·them, "Did·yeu·not
Mt 19:5 and·also declared, "For·this cause a·man·of·clay†
Mt 19:11 But he·declared to·them, "Not all·men have·room·
Mt 19:14 But YeShua declared, "Allow the little·children,
Mt 19:16 behold, one coming·alongside him declared, "O·
Mt 19:17 And *YeShua* declared to·him, "Why·do you·refer·
Mt 19:18 "Which·ones?" And YeShua declared, "'You·
Mt 19:23 And YeShua declared to·his disciples, "Certainly
Mt 19:26 looking·clearly·at *them*, YeShua declared to·them,
Mt 19:27 Then responding, Peter declared to·him, "Behold,
Mt 19:28 And YeShua declared to·them, "Certainly I·say to·
Mt 20:4 And·to·these he·declared, 'Yeu also head·on·out
Mt 20:13 answering one of·them, he·declared, 'Associate,
Mt 20:17 privately by the roadway, and he·declared to·them,
Mt 20:21 And he·declared to·her, "What·do you·want?
Mt 20:22 But answering, YeShua declared *to·her sons*,
Mt 20:25 upon·summoning them, declared, "Yeu·have·
Mt 20:32 YeShua hollered·out·for them and declared,
Mt 21:21 And answering, YeShua declared to·them,
Mt 21:24 And answering, YeShua declared to·them, "I·also
Mt 21:28 coming·alongside the first, he·declared, 'Child,
Mt 21:29 But answering, he·declared, 'I·will not.
Mt 21:30 ·alongside the second, he·declared likewise. And
Mt 21:30 And answering, he·declared, 'I·myself *will*, sir,'
Mt 22:1 And responding, YeShua declared to·them again by
Mt 22:13 "Then the king declared to·the attendants, 'After·
Mt 22:18 knowing their evil, declared, "Why·do yeu·try
Mt 22:24 "Mentor, Moses declared, if a·certain·man should·
Mt 22:29 And answering, YeShua declared to·them, "Yeu·
Mt 22:37 And YeShua declared to·him, "'You·shall·love
Mt 22:44 "Yahweh declared to·my Lord, "Sit·down at my
Mt 24:2 And YeShua declared to·them, "Do·not look·for all
Mt 24:4 And answering, YeShua declared to·them, "Look·
Mt 25:12 But answering, he·declared, 'Certainly I·say to·
Mt 25:22 receiving the two talants·of·silver, declared, 'Lord
Mt 25:24 ·received the one talant·of·silver, declared, 'Lord,
Mt 25:26 "And answering, his lord declared to·him, 'O·evil
Mt 26:1 all these sayings, he·declared to·his disciples,
Mt 26:10 YeShua, knowing *of·it*, declared to·them, "Why·
Mt 26:15 declared, "What·do yeu·want to·give to·me?
Mt 26:18 And he·declared, "Head·on·out into the City to a·
Mt 26:21 And as·they were·eating, he·declared, "Certainly
Mt 26:23 And answering, he·declared, "The·one dipping
Mt 26:25 (the·one handing him over) declared, "Rabbi, is·
Mt 26:26 ·giving *it* to·the disciples, and he·declared, "Take,
Mt 26:33 And answering, Peter declared to·him, "Even if
Mt 26:49 going·toward YeShua, he·declared, "Be·well,
Mt 26:50 And YeShua declared to·him, "O·associate, *attend*
Mt 26:55 In that·same hour, YeShua declared to·the crowds,
Mt 26:62 ·up, the designated·high·priest declared to·him,
Mt 26:63 the designated·high·priest declared to·him,
Mt 27:17 ·been·gathered·together, Pilate declared to·them,
Mt 27:21 ·into·judgment, the governor declared to·them,
Mt 27:25 responding, all the people declared, "His blood *be*
Mt 27:43 if he·wants him," for he·declared, 'I·am a·son
Mt 27:63 that thing the impostor declared *while·he·was* still
Mt 28:5 And responding, the angel declared to·the women,
Mt 28:6 for he·is·awakened, just·as he·declared. Come·here
Mk 1:17 And Jesus declared to·them, "Come·here, *fall·in*
Mk 2:8 ·manner within themselves, he·declared to·them,
Mk 2:19 And Jesus declared to·them, "¿!·Are the Sons of·
Mk 3:9 And he·declared to·his disciples that a·small·boat
Mk 4:39 he·reprimanded the wind and declared to·the sea,
Mk 4:40 And he·declared to·them, "Why are·yeu timid in·
Mk 5:7 yelling·out with·a·loud voice, he·declared, "What·
Mk 5:33 and fell·down·before him and declared to·him all
Mk 5:34 And he·declared to·her, "Daughter, your trust has·
Mk 5:43 ·know this, and declared *for·something* to·be·given
Mk 6:16 ·AntiPas, after·hearing *of·him*, he·declared, "This
Mk 6:22 ·at·the·meal, the king declared to·the young·girl,
Mk 6:24 ·going·out *of·the room*, she·declared to·her mother,
Mk 6:24 "What shall·I·request?" And she·declared, "The
Mk 6:31 And he·declared to·them, "Come·here yeu
Mk 6:37 But answering, *Jesus* declared to·them, "Yeu·
Mk 7:6 And answering, he·declared to·them, "IsaIah
Mk 7:10 For Moses declared, "Deeply·honor your father
Mk 7:27 But Jesus declared to·her, "First, allow the children
Mk 7:29 And he·declared to·her, "On·account·of this saying
Mk 8:7 And upon·blessing *them*, he·declared *to·his disciples*
Mk 8:34 along·with his disciples, *Jesus* declared to·them,
Mk 9:12 And answering, he·declared to·them, "EliJah, in·
Mk 9:17 answering from·among the crowd, declared,
Mk 9:21 to·him?" And he·declared, "From·young·
Mk 9:23 Then Jesus declared to·him, "If you·are·able to·
Mk 9:29 And he·declared to·them, "By not·even·one·thing
Mk 9:36 then taking him in·his·arms, he·declared to·them,
Mk 9:39 But Jesus declared, "Do·not forbid him, for there·is
Mk 10:3 And answering, he·declared to·them, "What did·
Mk 10:5 And answering, Jesus declared to·them,
Mk 10:14 Jesus was·greatly·displeased and declared to·them,
Mk 10:18 And Jesus declared to·him, "Why·do you·refer·to
Mk 10:20 And answering, he·declared to·him, "Mentor, all
Mk 10:21 him, loved him and declared to·him, "One·thing

Mk 10:29 And answering, Jesus declared, "Certainly I·say
Mk 10:36 And he·declared to·them, "What·do yeu·want me
Mk 10:38 But Jesus declared to·them, "Yeu·do·not
Mk 10:39 And Jesus declared to·them, "In·fact, the cup
Mk 10:49 ·still, Jesus declared *to·them* to·holler·out·for him.
Mk 10:51 Then the blind·man declared to·him, "Rabboni
Mk 10:52 And Jesus declared to·him, "Head·on·out, your
Mk 11:14 And responding, Jesus declared to·it, "May no·
Mk 11:29 And answering, Jesus declared to·them, "I·shall·
Mk 12:12 crowd, for they·knew that he·declared the parable
Mk 12:15 their stage·acting·hypocrisy, he·declared to·them,
Mk 12:17 And answering, Jesus declared to·them, "Give·
Mk 12:24 And answering, Jesus declared to·them, "*Is·it* not
Mk 12:26 (at the burning·bush) God declared to·him, saying,
Mk 12:32 And the scribe declared to·him, "Mentor, clearly·
Mk 12:34 ·same·man answered sensibly, declared to·him,
Mk 12:36 For David himself declared by the Holy Spirit,
Mk 12:36 Spirit, "Yahweh declared to·my Lord, "Sit·down
Mk 13:2 And responding, Jesus declared to·him, "Do·you·
Mk 14:6 And Jesus declared, "Leave her *alone*.
Mk 14:16 and they·found *it* just·as he·declared to·them. And
Mk 14:18 ·the·meal and eating, Jesus declared, "Certainly
Mk 14:20 And answering, he·declared to·them, "*It·is* one
Mk 14:22 and gave *it* to·them, and he·declared, "Take, eat!
Mk 14:24 And he·declared to·them, "This is my blood, the·
Mk 14:48 And responding, Jesus declared to·them, "Did·
Mk 14:62 And Jesus declared, "I AM, and yeu·shall·gaze·
Mk 14:72 the utterance which Jesus declared to·him, "Prior·
Mk 15:2 And answering, he·declared to·him, "You·
Mk 15:12 And responding, Pilate declared again to·them,
Mk 15:39 ·yelling·out, he·breathed·his·last, he·declared,
Mk 16:7 ·shall·gaze·upon him, just·as he·declared to·yeu."
Mk 16:15 And he·declared to·them, "Traversing into
Jac 2:11 You·may·not commit·adultery,'" also declared,
Jud 1:9 ·up a·verdict of·revilement, but·rather declared, "
Tit 1:12 a·prophet of·their own, declared, "Cretans *are*
1Co 11:24 ·giving·thanks, he·broke *it* and declared, "Take,
2Co 6:16 ·temple of·the·living God, just·as God declared, "
Rv 7:14 personally·know." And he·declared to·me, "These
Rv 17:7 And the angel declared to·me, "Why did·you·
Rv 21:5 who·is·sitting·down upon the throne declared,
Rv 21:6 And he·declared to·me, "It·has·happened! I AM the
Rv 22:6 And he·declared to·me, "These words *are*

G2036.1 V-2AAI-3P εἶπον (127x)

Jn 1:22 Accordingly, they·declared to·him, "Who are·you?
Jn 1:25 And they·asked·of him and declared to·him, "So·
Jn 1:38 What·do you·seek?" They·declared to·him, "Rabbi
Jn 2:18 the Judeans answered and declared to·him, "What
Jn 2:20 So·then the Judeans declared, "*In* forty six years,
Jn 3:26 And they·came to John and declared to·him, "Rabbi,
Jn 4:52 he·had gotten·better. And they·declared to·him,
Jn 6:25 on·the·other·side of·the sea, they·declared to·him,
Jn 6:28 So·then they·declared to him, "What·do we·do in·
Jn 6:30 Accordingly, they·declared to·him, "So·then what
Jn 6:34 So·then they·declared to him, "Lord, always give us
Jn 6:60 his disciples, upon·hearing *this*, declared, "This is
Jn 7:3 Accordingly, his brothers declared to him, "Walk·on
Jn 7:35 the Judeans declared among themselves, "Where·
Jn 7:45 Pharisees, and those *Pharisees* declared to·them,
Jn 7:52 They·answered and declared to·him, "¿! Are you·
Jn 8:13 Accordingly, the Pharisees declared to·him, "You
Jn 8:39 They·answered and declared to·him, "AbRaham is
Jn 8:41 So·then they·declared to·him, "We·ourselves
Jn 8:48 So·then the Judeans answered and declared to·him,
Jn 8:52 Accordingly, the Judeans declared to·him, "Now
Jn 8:57 Accordingly, the Judeans declared to him, "You·are
Jn 9:12 So·then they·declared to·him, "Where is this·man?
Jn 9:20 His parents answered them and declared, "We·
Jn 9:22 His parents declared these·things, because they·
Jn 9:23 On·account·of that, his parents declared, "He·is of·
Jn 9:24 that was blind, and they·declared to·him, "Give
Jn 9:26 Then they·declared to·him again, "What·did he·do
Jn 9:28 So·then they·defamed him and declared, "You·
Jn 9:34 They·answered and declared to·him, "You·yourself
Jn 9:40 ·ones being with him, and they·declared to·him, "¿!
Jn 11:12 Accordingly, his disciples declared, "Lord, if he·
Jn 11:37 But some from·among them declared, "Was·not
Jn 11:46 to the Pharisees and declared to·them what·things
Jn 12:19 So·then the Pharisees declared among themselves,
Jn 16:17 ·among his disciples declared among one·another,
Jn 18:7 yeu·seek?" And they·declared, "Jesus of·Natsareth.
Jn 18:25 warming·himself. So·then they·declared to·him,
Jn 18:30 They·answered and declared to·him, "If this·man
Jn 18:31 Accordingly, the Judeans declared to·him, "It·is·
Jn 18:34 ·thing, or did·others declare·it to·you concerning
Jn 19:24 Accordingly, they·declared among one·another,
Lk 1:61 And they·declared to her, "There·is not·even·one
Lk 2:15 ·of·clay†, the shepherds, declared to one·another,
Lk 3:12 came to·be·immersed, and they·declared to him,
Lk 5:33 Now they·declared to him, "Why·is·it·that the
Lk 6:2 And some of·the Pharisees declared to·them, "Why·
Lk 7:20 coming·close to him, the men declared, "John the
Lk 9:12 the twelve, coming·alongside, declared to·him,
Lk 9:13 And they·declared, "Among·us there·are not more
Lk 9:19 And answering, they·declared, "John the Immerser,
Lk 9:54 his disciples, Jakob and John, declared, "Lord, do·
Lk 11:15 But some from·among them declared, "He·casts·
Lk 17:5 Then the ambassadors declared to·the Lord, "Add
Lk 18:26 And upon·hearing *this*, they·declared, "Who then
Lk 19:25 And they·declared to·him, 'Lord, he·*already*·has
Lk 19:33 ·loosing the colt, its owners declared to them,
Lk 19:34 And they·declared, "The Lord has need of·it.
Lk 19:39 Pharisees from among·the crowd declared to him,
Lk 20:2 and declared to him, saying, "Declare to·us, by
Lk 20:16 And hearing *this*, they·declared, "May·it·never
Lk 20:24 And answering, they·declared, "Caesar's.
Lk 20:39 certain of·the scribes declared, "Mentor, well
Lk 22:9 And they·declared to·him, "Where do·you·want
Lk 22:35 And they·declared, "Not·even·one·thing.
Lk 22:38 And they·declared, "Lord, behold, here *are* two
Lk 22:49 the·thing *that* shall·be, they·declared to·him,
Lk 22:70 are the Son of·God?" And he·declared to them,
Lk 22:71 And they·declared, "What need do·we·have of·
Lk 24:5 face toward the earth, *the men* declared to them,
Lk 24:19 "Like·what?" And they·declared to·him,
Lk 24:24 in·this·manner just·as the women declared, but him
Lk 24:32 And they·declared to one·another, "Was·not·
Ac 1:11 who also declared, "Yeu·men of·Galilee, why·do
Ac 1:24 And praying, they·declared, "You, O·Lord,
Ac 2:37 ·jabbed in·the heart, and they·declared to Peter and
Ac 4:19 But answering, Peter and John declared to them,
Ac 4:23 *that* the chief·priests and the elders declared to them.
Ac 4:24 God with·the·same·determination, and declared,
Ac 5:29 Peter and the ambassadors declared, "It·is·
Ac 6:2 the multitude of·the disciples, declared, "This·is not
Ac 10:22 And they·declared, "Cornelius, a·centurion, a·
Ac 12:15 And they·declared to her, "You·are·raving·mad!"
Ac 13:46 ·with·clarity, Paul and BarNabas declared, "It·was
Ac 16:20 them to·the court·officers, they·declared, "These
Ac 16:31 And they·declared, "Trust on the Lord Jesus
Ac 17:32 they·were·jeering. And they·declared, "We·
Ac 19:2 Spirit after·trusting?" And they·declared to him,
Ac 19:3 were·yeu·immersed?" And they·declared, "Into
Ac 21:20 the Lord. And·then they·declared to·him, "Do·
Ac 23:4 Now the·ones standing·nearby declared, "Do·you·
Ac 23:14 and the elders, declared, "With·an·irrevocable·
Ac 28:21 And they·declared to him, "We·ourselves do·not·
Mt 2:5 And they·declared to·him, "In BethLechem of·Judea.
Mt 9:3 certain of·the scribes declared within themselves,
Mt 9:11 ·seeing *it*, the Pharisees declared to·his disciples,
Mt 12:2 the Pharisees seeing *it*, declared to·him, "Behold,
Mt 12:24 ·hearing *this*, the Pharisees declared, "This·man
Mt 13:10 coming·alongside, the disciples declared to·him,
Mt 13:27 slaves of·the master·of·the·house declared to·him,
Mt 13:28 Then the slaves declared to·him, 'So do·you·
Mt 15:12 after·coming·alongside, declared to·him, "Have·
Mt 15:34 ·bread do·yeu·have?" And they·declared, "Seven
Mt 16:14 And they·declared, "In·fact, *some say* John the
Mt 17:19 in private, the disciples declared, "Why·were we·
Mt 17:24 *tax* came·alongside Peter and declared, "Yeur
Mt 21:16 and they·declared to·him, "Do·you·hear what
Mt 21:27 And answering YeShua, they·declared, "We·do·
Mt 21:38 the tenant·farmers declared among themselves,
Mt 25:8 And the foolish declared to·the prudent, 'Give to·us
Mt 26:35 And·also, all the disciples declared likewise.
Mt 26:61 declared, "This·man was·disclosing, 'I·am·able
Mt 26:66 And answering, they·declared, "He·is held·
Mt 26:73 ·while, the·ones standing·by declared to·Peter,
Mt 27:4 without·fault." And they·declared, "What·is·that
Mt 27:6 taking the pieces·of·silver, declared, "It·is·not
Mt 27:21 ·release to·yeu?" Then they·declared, "BarAbbas.
Mk 3:32 ·down around him, and they·declared to·him,
Mk 8:5 ·bread do·yeu·have?" And they·declared, "Seven.
Mk 8:20 did·yeu·take·up?" And they·declared, "Seven.
Mk 10:4 And they·declared, "Moses freely·permitted *us* to·
Mk 10:37 Then they·declared to·him, "Grant to·us that we·
Mk 10:39 And they·declared to·him, "We·are·able.
Mk 11:6 And they·declared to·them just·as Jesus
Mk 12:7 those tenant·farmers declared among themselves,
Mk 12:16 and inscription?" And they·declared to·him,
Mk 16:8 to·not·even·one·man did·they·declare not·even·,

G2036.1 V-2AAM-2S εἰπέ (20x)

Jn 10:24 are the Anointed-One, declare *it* to·us with·clarity·
Jn 20:15 bore him away, declare to·me where you·laid him,
Jn 20:17 you·traverse to my brothers and declare to·them,
Lk 4:3 "If you·are a·son of·God, declare to·this stone that it·
Lk 7:7 to·come to you, but·rather declare with·a·word, and
Lk 7:40 And he·replies, "Mentor, declare·it."
Lk 7:42 ·forgave them·both. So·then declare *to·me*, which
Lk 10:40 to·attend alone? So·then declare to·her that she·
Lk 12:13 to·him, "Mentor, declare for·my brother to·divide
Lk 20:2 to him, saying, "Declare to·us, by what·kind·of
Lk 22:67 you·yourself the Anointed-One? Declare to·us."
Ac 5:8 answered to·her, "Declare to·me whether yeu·sold·
Ac 28:26 toward this People, and declare, "With·hearing,
Mt 4:3 "If you·are a·son of·God, declare that these stones
Mt 8:8 my roof, but·rather merely declare a·word, and my
Mt 18:17 And if he·should·disregard them, declare *it* to·the
Mt 20:21 She·says to·him, "Declare that these two sons
Mt 22:17 So·then declare to·us, what·do you suppose?
Mt 24:3 in private, saying, "Declare to·us, when shall these·
Mk 13:4 "Declare to·us, when·shall these·things be?

G2036.1 V-2AAM-2P εἴπατε (13x)

Lk 10:10 ·out into the same broad·streets, yeu·must·declare,
Lk 13:32 to·them, "Traversing, yeu·declare to·that fox,
Lk 20:3 ·of yeu one question, and yeu·must·declare to·me.
Mt 10:27 I·say to·yeu in the darkness, declare in the light;
Mt 21:5 ""Declare·yeu to·the daughter of·Tsiyon," "
Mt 22:4 saying, 'Declare to·the·ones having·been·called,
Mt 26:18 the City to a·particular·man and declare to·him,
Mt 28:7 Then traversing swiftly, declare to·his disciples that
Mt 28:13 saying, "Yeu·must·declare, 'His disciples stole
Mk 11:3 'Why·do yeu·do this?' Yeu·declare 'The Lord has
Mk 14:14 ·enter, yeu·declare to·the·master·of·the·house,
Mk 16:7 Moreover, head·on·out! Declare to·his disciples
Col 4:17 And declare to·ArchIppus, "Look·out·for the

G2036.1 V-2AAM-3S εἰπάτω (1x)

Rv 22:17 And the·one hearing, let·him·declare, "Come!"

G2036.1 V-2AAM-3P εἰπάτωσαν (1x)

Ac 24:20 same·men *here*, let·them·declare if they·found any

G2036.1 V-2AAN εἰπεῖν (16x)

Lk 5:14 charged him to·declare *it* not·even·to·one·man,
Lk 5:23 Which is easier, to·declare, 'Your moral·failures
Lk 5:23 ·been·forgiven you,' or to·declare, 'Be·awakened
Lk 7:40 "Simon, I·have something to·declare to·you." And
Lk 8:56 them to·declare to·not·even·one·man the·thing
Lk 9:21 *them* to·declare not·even·to·one·man this·thing,
Lk 12:12 yeu in the same hour what is·necessary to·declare."
Lk 14:17 supper to·declare to·the·ones having·been·called·

Ac 2:29 brothers, it·is·being·proper to·declare to yeu with
Ac 21:37 "Is·it·proper for·me to·declare something to you?
Mt 9:5 For which is easier? To·declare, 'Your moral·
Mt 9:5 ·been·forgiven you?' or to·declare, 'Be·awakened
Mk 2:9 Which is easier to·declare to·the paralyzed·man,
Mk 2:9 ·been·forgiven you,' or to·declare, 'Be·awakened,
1Co 12:3 And not·even·one·man is·able to·declare, "Jesus
1Co 12:21 And *the* eye is·not able to·declare to·the hand, "I·
G2036.1 V-2AAP-ASM εἰπόντα (3x)
Ac 10:3 *this·realm* toward him and declaring to·him,
Ac 11:13 in his house, being·settled and declaring to·him,
Heb 10:30 For we·personally·know the·one declaring,
G2036.1 V-2AAP-DSM εἰπόντι (1x)
Mt 12:48 But answering the·one declaring *this* to·him, he·
G2036.1 V-2AAP-GSM εἰπόντος (5x)
Jn 18:22 And upon·him declaring these·things, one of·the
Ac 26:30 And with·him declaring these·things, the king rose·
Ac 28:25 ·themselves, with·Paul declaring one utterance,
Ac 28:29 And with·him declaring these·things, the Jews
Mk 1:42 And with·him declaring *this*, immediately, the
G2036.1 V-2AAP-NSF εἰποῦσα (3x)
Jn 11:28 And after·declaring these·things, she·went·off and
Jn 11:28 Mary her sister, privately declaring, "The Mentor
Jn 20:14 And after·declaring these·things, she·is·turned·
G2036.1 V-2AAP-NSM εἰπών (35x)
Jn 5:12 Who is the man·of·clay†, the·one declaring to·you,
Jn 7:9 And after·declaring these·things to·them, he·remained
Jn 9:6 After·declaring these·things, he·spat down·on·the·
Jn 11:43 And after·declaring these·things, he·yelled·out
Jn 13:21 After·declaring these·things, Jesus was·troubled in·
Jn 18:1 After·declaring these·things, Jesus went·forth
Jn 18:22 gave a·slap to·Jesus, declaring, "Do·you·answer
Jn 18:38 truth?" And after·declaring this, he·went·out again
Jn 20:20 And after·declaring this, he·showed to·them his
Jn 20:22 And after·declaring this, he·puffed·on *them*.
Jn 21:19 shall·glorify God. And after·declaring this, he·says
Lk 5:13 his hand, he·laid·hold of·him, declaring, "I·want.
Lk 9:22 declaring, "It·is·mandatory·for the Son of·Clay·
Lk 19:28 And after·declaring these·things, *Jesus* traversed·
Lk 19:30 declaring, "Head·on·out into the village directly·
Lk 22:8 dispatched Peter and John, declaring, "Traversing,
Lk 23:46 '" And after·declaring these·things, he·breathed·
Lk 24:40 And after·declaring this·thing, he·fully·exhibited
Ac 1:9 And after·declaring these·things, with·them looking·
Ac 4:25 mouth of·your servant·boy David, declaring, "For·
Ac 7:26 ·exhorted them *to·be* at peace, declaring, 'Men,
Ac 7:27 the neighbor shoved him away, declaring, "Who
Ac 7:37 "This Moses is the·one declaring to·the Sons of·
Ac 7:60 against·them." And after·declaring this, he·was·
Ac 18:21 ·rather he·orderly·took·leave·of them, declaring,
Ac 19:21 *for·him* to·traverse to JeruSalem, declaring, "After
Ac 19:41 And after·declaring these·things, he·dismissed the
Ac 20:36 And after·declaring these·things, with·him bowing
Ac 22:24 the barracks, declaring for·him to·be·interrogated
Ac 24:22 Way, he·deferred them, declaring, "Whenever
Ac 27:35 And after·declaring these·things and taking bread,
Mt 26:44 he·prayed for a·third·time, declaring the same
Mk 14:39 after·going·off, he·prayed, declaring the same
Jac 2:11 For the·one declaring, "'You·may·not commit·
2Co 4:6 Because God *is* the·one already·declaring *for* light
G2036.1 V-2AAP-NPM εἰπόντες (3x)
Ac 7:35 "This Moses whom they·renounced, declaring,
Ac 7:40 declaring to·Aaron, "Make for·us gods which
Ac 21:14 being·persuaded, we·kept·still, declaring, "The
G2036.1 V-2AAS-1S εἴπω (7x)
Jn 3:12 how shall·yeu·trust if I·should·declare to·yeu the
Jn 8:55 have·seen him. And if I·should·declare, 'I·have·not
Jn 12:27 has·been·troubled, and what should·I·declare?
Jn 12:49 *concerning* what I·should·declare and what I·
Lk 22:67 he·declared to·them, "If I·should·declare *it* to·yeu,
Mt 2:13 and be there until I·should·declare *it* to·you, for
1Co 11:22 ·ones not having? What should·I·declare to·yeu?
G2036.1 V-2AAS-1P εἴπωμεν (10x)
Lk 9:54 do·you·want *that* we·should·declare fire to·descend
Lk 20:5 saying, "If we·should·declare, 'From·out of·heaven
Lk 20:6 But if we·should·declare, 'From·out of·men·of·
Mt 21:25 saying, "If we·should·declare, 'From·out of·
Mt 21:26 But if we·should·declare, 'From·out of·men·of·
Mk 11:31 saying, "If we·should·declare, 'From·out of·
Mk 11:32 But·rather if we·should·declare, 'From·out of·
1Jn 1:6 If we·should·declare that we·have fellowship with
1Jn 1:8 If we·should·declare that we·do·not have moral·
1Jn 1:10 If we·should·declare that we·have·not morally·
G2036.1 V-2AAS-2S εἴπῃς (5x)
Mt 8:4 ·see·to·it *that* you·should·declare *this* to·no·one. But·
Mt 26:63 ·living God, that you·should·declare to·us whether
Mk 1:44 *that* you·should·declare not·even·one·thing to·not·
Mk 8:26 village, nor·even should·you·declare *this* to·anyone
Rm 10:6 *it* in·this·manner, "You·should·not declare in your
G2036.1 V-2AAS-2P εἴπητε (8x)
Lk 12:11 what yeu·should·plead or what yeu·should·declare.
Lk 13:35 *the time* should·come when yeu·should·declare, "
Mt 17:9 saying, "Yeu·should·declare the clear·vision to·
Mt 21:21 but·yet also·if yeu·should·declare to·this mountain,
Mt 21:24 which if yeu·should·declare *an·answer* to·me, I·
Mt 23:39 from this·moment·on, until yeu·should·declare,
Jac 2:3 the splendid clothing, and should·declare to·him,
Jac 2:3 ·place," and should·declare to·the helplessly·poor,
G2036.1 V-2AAS-3S εἴπῃ (24x)
Lk 11:5 to him at·midnight, and should·declare to·him,
Lk 11:7 answering from·inside, that·man may·declare, 'Do·
Lk 12:45 "But if that slave should·declare in his heart, 'My
Lk 14:10 ·for you should·come, he·may·declare to·you,
Mt 5:22 "Now whoever should·declare to·his brother,
Mt 5:22 But whoever should·declare, 'You·fool,' shall·be
Mt 12:32 And whoever should·declare a·word against the
Mt 12:32 him, but whoever should·declare against the Holy
Mt 15:5 say, 'Whoever should·declare to·his father or to·his
Mt 21:3 And if any·man should·declare anything to·yeu,
Mt 24:23 "At·that·time, if any·man should·declare to·yeu,
Mt 24:48 "But if that bad slave should·declare in his heart,
Mk 7:11 'If a·man·of·clay† should·declare to·his father or
Mk 11:3 And if any·man should·declare to·yeu, 'Why·do
Mk 11:23 ·yeu that whoever should·declare to·this mountain,
Mk 11:23 ·be; it·shall·be to·him whatever he·may·declare.
Mk 13:21 at·that·time, if any·man should·declare to·yeu,
Jac 2:16 anyone from·among yeu should·declare to·them,
1Co 1:15 lest any should·declare that I·immersed in my·own
1Co 10:28 But if any·man should·declare to·yeu, "This is
1Co 12:15 If the foot should·declare, "Because I·am not a·
1Co 12:16 And if the ear should·declare, "Because I·am not
1Co 15:27 ' But inasmuch·as *God* should·declare that "all·
1Jn 4:20 If someone should·declare, "I·love God," and he·
G2036.1 V-2AAS-3P εἴπωσιν (7x)
Lk 6:26 all the men·of·clay† should·declare well of·yeu! For
Mt 5:11 and by·lying, should·declare all·manner·of evil
Mt 16:20 in·order·that they·should·declare to·no·one that he·
Mt 23:3 whatever as·much·as they·should·declare to·yeu to·
Mt 24:26 "Accordingly, if they·should·declare to·yeu,
Mt 27:64 should·steal him, and should·declare to·the people
Mk 7:36 that they·should·declare *it* to·not·even·one·man.
EG2036.1 (2x)
Jn 20:9 the Scripture *which·declared* that it·is·mandatory·for
Ac 25:8 with·him making·his·defense, *declaring*, "Neither
G2036.2 V-2AAN εἰπεῖν (1x)
Heb 7:9 And *so* as to·make a·declaration, even Levi, the·one

G2037 Ἔραστος Ěrastôs *n/p.* (3x)
Roots:G2037-1 See:G2064-3
G2037.2 N/P-NSM Ἔραστος (2x)
Rm 16:23 , greets yeu. Erastus, the estate·manager of·the
2Ti 4:20 Erastus remained at Corinth, but Trophimus, being·
G2037.2 N/P-ASM Ἔραστον (1x)
Ac 19:22 into Macedonia, TimoThy and Erastus, he·himself

G2038 ἐργάζομαι ĕrgázômai *v.* (41x)
Roots:G2041 Compare:G2872 G4160 xLangAlso:H5647 H6466
G2038.1 V-PNI-1S ἐργάζομαι (2x)
Jn 5:17 Father works until this·moment, and·I·also work."
Ac 13:41 be·disconcerted. Because I·myself work a·work in
G2038.1 V-PNI-2S ἐργάζῃ (1x)
Jn 6:30 and should·trust in·you? What·thing do·you·work?
G2038.1 V-PNI-2P ἐργάζεσθε (1x)
Jac 2:9 But if yeu·show·partiality, yeu·work moral·failure,
G2038.1 V-PNI-3S ἐργάζεται (3x)
Jn 5:17 them, "My Father works until this·moment, and·I·
Rm 13:10 Love works no wrong to·the neighbor.
1Co 16:10 yeu without·fear, for he·works the work of·*the*·
G2038.1 V-PNI-3P ἐργάζονται (1x)
Rv 18:17 and sailors, and as·many·as work the sea, stood·
G2038.1 V-PNM-2S ἐργάζου (1x)
Mt 21:28 'Child, head·on·out. Work today in my vineyard.
G2038.1 V-PNM-2P ἐργάζεσθε (2x)
Jn 6:27 "Work, *but* not for·the full·meal that·is·completely·
Col 3:23 soever *that* yeu·should·do, be·working *it* out of·a·
G2038.1 V-PNN ἐργάζεσθαι (6x)
Jn 9:4 "It·is·mandatory·for me to·be·working the works of·
Jn 9:4 is·coming, when not·even·one·man is·able to·work.
Lk 13:14 days in which it·is·necessary to·work. Accordingly,
1Th 4:11 yeur·own *tasks*, and to·work·with yeur own hands,
2Th 3:10 if anyone does·not want to·work, nor·even *then*
1Co 9:6 ·we·not have privilege to·not work *an·occupation*?
G2038.1 V-PNP-APM ἐργαζομένους (1x)
2Th 3:11 ·disorderly·manner, who·are·working not·one·bit,
G2038.1 V-PNP-DSM ἐργαζομένῳ (3x)
Rm 2:10 the·one who·is·working the beneficially·good,
Rm 4:4 Now to·the·one working, the payment·of·service is·
Rm 4:5 And·yet to·the·one not working, but trusting on the·
G2038.1 V-PNP-NSM ἐργαζόμενος (2x)
Ac 10:35 ·fearing him and who·is·working righteousness is
Eph 4:28 let·him·labor·hard, working the beneficially·good
G2038.1 V-PNP-NPM ἐργαζόμενοι (6x)
Mt 7:23 me, the·ones who·are·working the Lawlessness."
1Th 2:9 ·labor and the travail, for working night and day
2Th 3:8 bread, but·rather were·working in weariness and
2Th 3:12 ·that with stillness, while·working, they·should·eat
1Co 4:12 and we·labor·hard, working with·our·own hands.
1Co 9:13 ·not seen that the·ones working the sacred·things
G2038.1 V-PNS-1P ἐργαζώμεθα (2x)
Jn 6:28 ·do we·do in·order·that we·may·work the works of·
Gal 6:10 opportunity, we·should·work the beneficially·good
G2038.1 V-INI-3S εἰργάζετο (1x)
Ac 18:3 he·was·abiding with them and was·working, for
G2038.1 V-ADI-1P εἰργασάμεθα (1x)
2Jn 1:8 ·lose those·things·for·which we·worked, but·rather
G2038.1 V-ADI-3S εἰργάσατο (3x)
Mt 25:16 receiving the five talants·of·silver worked with *the*
Mt 26:10 to·the woman? For she·worked a·good deed to me.
Mk 14:6 ·troubles to·her? She·worked a·good work to me.
G2038.1 V-ADI-3P εἰργάσαντο (1x)
Heb 11:33 ·subdued kingdoms, worked righteousness,
G2038.1 V-ADS-2S ἐργάσῃ (1x)
3Jn 1:5 ·you·do whatever *good·deed* you·may·work for the
G2038.1 V-RPP-NPN εἰργασμένα (1x)
Jn 3:21 ·apparent, that they·are having·been·worked in God.
EG2038.1 (2x)
Rm 2:7 In·fact, to·the·ones *working* according·to a·patient·
Rm 2:8 But to·the·ones *working* out of·being·contentious,

G2039 ἐργασία ĕrgasía *n.* (7x)
Roots:G2040 Compare:G5622 G2771 G2526-3 G1081
G2039.1 N-ASF ἐργασίαν (1x)
Lk 12:58 ·adversary to·a·magistrate, give effort on the way
G2039.2 N-ASF ἐργασίαν (1x)
Eph 4:19 ·the debauchery, into an·occupation of·all impurity
G2039.2 N-GSF ἐργασίας (1x)
Ac 19:25 that our prosperity is·as·a·result of·this occupation.

EG2039.2 (1x)
1Co 9:6 ·we·not have privilege to·not work *an·occupation*?
G2039.3 N-ASF ἐργασίαν (2x)
Ac 16:16 lords with·much income by·maniacal·soothsaying.
Ac 19:24 ·furnished no little income for·the craftsmen.
G2039.3 N-GSF ἐργασίας (1x)
Ac 16:19 the expectation of·their income went·out *from·her*,

G2040 ἐργάτης êrgátēs *n.* (16x)

Roots:G2041 See:G2039
G2040.1 N-NSM ἐργάτης (3x)
Lk 10:7 ·by them, for the workman is worthy of·his
Mt 10:10 ·even a·staff, for the workman is deserving of·his
1Ti 5:18 ' and "The workman *is* deserving of·his payment·
G2040.1 N-NPM ἐργάται (4x)
Lk 10:2 *is* large, but the workmen *are* few. Accordingly,
Lk 13:27 from me, all *yeu* workmen of·unrighteousness.'
Mt 9:37 the harvest *is* large, but the workmen *are* few.
2Co 11:13 *are* false·ambassadors, workmen full·of·guile,
G2040.1 N-ASM ἐργάτην (1x)
2Ti 2:15 an·unashamed workman rightly·dissecting the
G2040.1 N-APM ἐργάτας (6x)
Lk 10:2 harvest, that he·should·cast·forth workmen into his
Ac 19:25 these·men, and·also the workmen concerning the
Mt 9:38 harvest, that he·should·cast·forth workmen into his
Mt 20:1 at·the·same·time as·dawn to·hire workmen into his
Mt 20:8 ·manager, 'Call the workmen and render to·them
Php 3:2 look·out·for the bad workmen; look·out·for the
G2040.1 N-GPM ἐργατῶν (2x)
Mt 20:2 ·mutually·agreeing with the workmen *to·hire them*
Jac 5:4 ·service for·the workmen mowing·and·bundling·up

G2041 ἔργον érgôn *n.* (178x)

Compare:G2526-3 G2873 G4161 See:G2040 G2039
xLangAlso:H4399 H4639 H5656
G2041.1 N-NSN ἔργον (10x)
Jn 6:29 "This is the work of·God, that yeu·should·trust in
Ac 5:38 this counsel or this work should·be birthed·from·out
Rm 11:6 grace, otherwise the work is no·longer work.
Rm 11:6 grace, otherwise the work is no·longer work.
1Co 3:13 each·man's work shall·become apparent, for the
1Co 3:13 ·test·and·prove each·man's work for·what·type it·is
1Co 3:14 If any·man's work shall·remain which he·built·
1Co 3:15 If any·man's work shall·be·completely·burned, he·
1Co 9:1 Lord? Are yeu·yeurselves not my work in *the* Lord?
Rv 22:12 to·give·back to·each·man as his work shall·be.
G2041.1 N-NPN ἔργα (13x)
Jn 5:36 *than·that* of·John, for the works which the Father
Jn 5:36 them), *they·are* the same works which I·myself do;
Jn 7:7 I·myself testify concerning it, that its works are evil.
Jn 9:3 ·that the works of·God should·be·made·apparent in
Jn 10:25 "The works that I·myself do in my Father's name,
Ac 15:18 to·God are all his works from the·beginning·age.
Heb 1:10 earth; and the heavens are works of·your hands.
Gal 5:19 But the works of·the flesh are apparent, which are
2Pe 3:10 and·also *the* earth (and the works *that·are* in it)
1Ti 5:25 also, the good works *of·some* are obvious·
1Jn 3:12 ·slaughter him? Because his·own works were evil,
Rv 14:13 wearisome·labors, and their works follow with
Rv 15:3 "Great and marvelous *are* your works, O·Yahweh,
G2041.1 N-ASN ἔργον (28x)
Jn 4:34 sending me, and *that* I·may·fully·complete his work.
Jn 7:21 and declared to·them, "I·did one work, and yeu all
Jn 10:32 ·account·of which of·those works do·yeu·stone me?
Jn 17:4 the earth. I·fully·completed the work, which *likewise*
Ac 13:2 and Saul for the work to·which I·have·summoned
Ac 13:41 Because I·myself work a·work in yeur days, a·
Ac 13:41 work a·work in yeur days, a·work which, no, yeu·
Ac 14:26 for the work which they·completely·fulfilled.
Ac 15:38 and not going·together with·them to the work.
Gal 6:4 each·man must·test·and·prove his·own work, and
Mk 13:34 and to·each·man his work, and·then commanded
Mk 14:6 ·troubles to·her? She·worked a·good work to me.
Rm 2:15 themselves·indicate the work of·the Torah-Law
Rm 14:20 Do·not demolish the work of·God for·the·sake·of
Jac 1:4 patient·endurance have *her* complete work, that yeu·
Php 1:6 already·beginning a·beneficially·good work in yeu
Php 2:30 because on·account·of the work of·Anointed-One,
1Pe 1:17 impartially according·to the work of·each·man,
1Th 5:13 ·beyond, on·account·of their work. Be·peaceful
2Th 1:11 of·*his*·beneficial·goodness and work of·trust in
Tit 1:16 particularly·for every beneficially·good work.
Tit 3:1 ready particularly·for every beneficially·good work,
1Co 16:10 ·fear, for he·works the work of·*the*·Lord, as also
2Co 9:8 yeu·may·abound to every beneficially·good work.
Eph 4:12 of·the holy·ones unto a·work of·service, unto an·
2Ti 2:21 ·made·ready for every beneficially·good work.
2Ti 3:17 ·equipped toward all beneficially·good works.
2Ti 4:5 do *the* work of·a·proclaimer·of·the·good·news·of·,
G2041.1 N-APN ἔργα (42x)
Jn 5:20 and he·shall·show him works greater·than these,
Jn 6:28 we·do in·order·that we·may·work the works of·God?
Jn 7:3 your disciples also may·observe the works that you do
Jn 8:39 children, yeu·would do the works of·AbRaham.
Jn 9:4 ·for me to·be·working the works of·the·one sending
Jn 10:32 them, "Many good works I·showed yeu from·out
Jn 10:37 "If I·do·not do the works of·my Father, do·not trust
Jn 14:10 Father abiding in me, he·himself does the works.
Jn 14:11 ·not, trust me on·account·of the works themselves.
Jn 14:12 the·one trusting in me, the works that I·myself do,
Jn 15:24 ·not do among them the works which not·even·one
Ac 26:20 toward God, practicing works worthy of·the
Heb 2:7 fully·established him over the works of·your hands..
Heb 3:9 ·and·proved me, and saw my works *for* forty years.
Mt 5:16 ·that they·may·see yeur good works and may·glorify
Mt 11:2 the dungeon *of* the works of·the Anointed-One *and*
Mt 23:3 but do·not do according·to their works. For they·say
Mt 23:5 But all their works *that* they·do *are* specifically·for
Rm 13:12 we·should·put·away the works of·darkness, and
Jac 2:14 he·has trust but should·not have works? ¿! Is the
Jac 2:17 provided·that it·should·have no works, is dead by
Jac 2:18 "You have trust, and·I have works." Show me your
Jac 3:13 let·him·show his works with a·calm·mildness of·
2Co 11:15 whose end shall·be according·to their works.
2Ti 1:9 not according·to our works, but·rather according·to
2Ti 4:14 the Lord 'give·back to·him according·to his works,'
1Jn 3:8 that he·should·tear·down the works of·the Slanderer.
Rv 2:2 'I·personally·know your works, and your wearisome·
Rv 2:5 repent, and do the first works; but·if·not, I·come to·
Rv 2:9 'I·personally·know your works, and the tribulation,
Rv 2:13 'I·personally·know your works, and where you·
Rv 2:19 'I·personally·know your works (also the love, and
Rv 2:19 , also *that* your works, even the last·ones *are* more·
Rv 2:23 ·give to·each·one of·yeu according·to yeur works.
Rv 2:26 and the·one fully·keeping my works even·unto *the*
Rv 3:1 'I·personally·know your works, that you·have the
Rv 3:2 your works having·been·completely·fulfilled in·the·
Rv 3:8 'I·personally·know your works. Behold, in·the·sight
Rv 3:15 'I·personally·know your works, that you·are neither
Rv 18:6 double to·her double according·to her works. In the
Rv 20:12 in the official·scrolls, according·to their works.
Rv 20:13 each·one was·judged according·to their works.
G2041.1 N-DSN ἔργῳ (5x)
Heb 13:21 unto every beneficially·good work in·order·to·do
2Th 2:17 yeu in every beneficially·good word and work.
1Co 15:58 *Trust*, always abounding in the work of·the Lord,
Col 1:10 in every beneficially·good work and growing·up
1Ti 5:10 ·through in·every beneficially·good work).
G2041.1 N-DPN ἔργοις (8x)
Jn 10:38 me, trust the works in·order·that yeu·may·know,
Ac 7:41 they·were·merry in the works of·their·own hands.
Jac 2:22 the trust was·working·together with·his works, and
Tit 1:16 to·have·seen God, but in·the works they·deny *him*,
Eph 2:10 Jesus for beneficially·good works, which God
Eph 5:11 ·together with·the unfruitful works of·the darkness,
Col 1:21 in·*your*·innermost·mind by·the evil works, so now
1Ti 5:10 being·attested·to by good works (if she·nurtured·
G2041.1 N-GSN ἔργου (7x)
Jn 10:33 ·not stone you concerning a·good work, but·rather
Heb 6:10 *is* not unrighteous to·forget yeur work and *yeur*
Rm 2:7 ·endurance of·beneficially·good work, seeking glory,
Jac 1:25 hearer, but·rather a·doer of·the·work, this·man
1Th 1:3 our God and Father (*yeur* work of·the trust, and the
1Ti 3:1 ·of·oversight, he·longs·for a·good work."
2Ti 4:18 ·snatch me away·from every evil work. And *me*, he·
G2041.1 N-GPN ἔργων (38x)
Ac 9:36 full of·beneficially·good works and merciful·acts
Heb 4:3 *he·declared this* with·the works being·done from *the*
Heb 4:10 already·fully·ceased from his·own works, just·as
Heb 6:1 — of·repentance from dead works, and of·trust
Heb 9:14 yeur conscience from dead works in·order·for *yeu*
Heb 10:24 to a·keen·provoking of·love and good works,
Gal 2:16 ·as·righteous as·a·result of·works of·Torah-Law,
Gal 2:16 and not as·a·result of·works of·Torah-Law— on·
Gal 2:16 ·as·righteous as·a·result of·works of·Torah-Law.
Gal 3:2 the Spirit as·a·result of·works of·Torah-Law, or as·a·
Gal 3:5 yeu, *is·it* as·a·result of·works of·Torah-Law, or as·a·
Gal 3:10 ·as are birthed·from·out of·works of·Torah-Law,
Rm 3:27 what·kind·of law? The·one of·works? No·indeed,
Rm 3:28 by·a·trust apart·from works of·Torah-Law.
Rm 4:2 ·regarded·as·righteous as·a·result of·works, he·has
Rm 4:6 ·whom God reckons righteousness apart·from works,
Rm 9:11 Selection, not as·a·result of·works, but·rather as·a·
Rm 9:32 ·though *it·were* as·a·result of·works of·Torah-Law.
Rm 11:6 *it·is* no·longer as·a·result of·works, otherwise the
Rm 11:6 But if *it·is* as·a·result of·works, *then* it·is no·longer
Rm 13:3 ·*of* fear for·the beneficially·good works, but·rather
Jac 2:18 me your trust as·a·result of·your works, and·I shall·
Jac 2:18 ·I shall·show you my trust as·a·result of·my works.
Jac 2:20 the trust, completely·apart·from the works, is dead?
Jac 2:21 as·a·result of·works *that* he·is·regarded·as·righteous
Jac 2:22 works, and as·a·result of·the works, the trust is·
Jac 2:24 ·see that as·a·result of·works, a·man·of·clay† is·
Jac 2:25 ·righteous as·a·result of·works, hospitably·receiving
Jac 2:26 also, the trust apart·from the works is dead.
1Pe 2:12 as·a·result *of·yeur* good works (after·beholding
Tit 2:7 ·forth *as* a·particular·pattern of·good works in the
Tit 2:14 People,' *one being* a·zealot of·good works.
Tit 3:5 *it·was* not as·a·result of·works (of·the·ones in
Tit 3:8 ·have·a·considerable·care to·conduct good works.
Tit 3:14 must·learn also to·conduct good works for the
Eph 2:9 *is* not birthed·from·out of·works, in·order·that not
1Ti 2:10 but·rather through beneficially·good works (which
Rv 9:20 repent out·from·among the works of·their hands,
EG2041.1 (2x)
Jn 14:12 ·likewise. And greater *works* than·these shall·he·do
1Ti 5:25 ·beforehand; and the *good works* being otherwise,
G2041.2 N-NPN ἔργα (3x)
Jn 3:19 rather than the light, for their deeds were evil.
Jn 3:20 toward the light, lest his deeds should·be·refuted.
Jn 3:21 light, in·order·that his deeds may·be·made·apparent,
G2041.2 N-ASN ἔργον (2x)
Mt 26:10 to·the woman? For she·worked a·good deed to me.
1Co 5:2 this deed should·be·entirely·expelled from·among
G2041.2 N-APN ἔργα (4x)
Jn 8:41 "Yeu·yeurselves do the deeds of·yeur father." So·
Rm 2:6 "'shall·render to·each·man according·to his deeds."'
3Jn 1:10 I·shall·quietly·recollect his deeds which he·does,
Rv 2:6 this, that you·hate the deeds of·the NicoLaitans,
G2041.2 N-DSN ἔργῳ (5x)
Lk 24:19 a·prophet powerful in deed and word directly·
Rm 15:18 ·obedience among·Gentiles, by·word and deed,
2Co 10:11 such *shall·we·be* also in·deed while·being·present.
Col 3:17 yeu·should·do in word or in deed, *do* all in *the* Lord
1Jn 3:18 nor·even in·tongue, but·rather in·deed and in·truth.
G2041.2 N-DPN ἔργοις (5x)
Lk 11:48 and gladly·consent to·the deeds of·yeur fathers,
Ac 7:22 and he·was powerful in words and in deeds.
2Pe 2:8 *his* righteous soul *over their* unlawful deeds);
1Ti 6:18 ·good·work, to·be·wealthy in good deeds, to·be
2Jn 1:11 "Be·well," shares in·his evil deeds.

G2041.2 N-GSN ἔργου (1x)
Php 1:22 this *continues* a·fruit of·work for·me. Even·so, I·
G2041.2 N-GPN ἔργων (4x)
Rm 3:20 ·that, as·a·result *of·the* deeds of·Torah-Law, ·
Jud 1:15 their irreverent deeds which they·irreverently·did,
Rv 2:22 they·should·not repent out·from·among their deeds.
Rv 16:11 they·did·not repent out·from·among their deeds.
EG2041.2 (1x)
2Pe 2:8 (for in·looking·upon and in·hearing *these deeds*, the

G2042 ἐρεθίζω êrêthízō *v.* (2x)
Roots:G2054 Compare:G1892 G3949 See:G2052
G2042.2 V-AAI-3S ἠρέθισεν (1x)
2Co 9:2 and from·out of·yeur zeal, it·stirred·up many·more.
G2042.3 V-PAM-2P ἐρεθίζετε (1x)
Col 3:21 Yeu·must·not contentiously·irritate yeur children,

G2043 ἐρείδω êrêídō *v.* (1x)
G2043.2 V-AAP-NSF ἐρείσασα (1x)
Ac 27:41 and in·fact, the bow, after·getting·stuck, remained

G2044 ἐρεύγομαι êrêúgômai *v.* (1x)
Compare:G1692 G1829 G0375-2 xLangEquiv:H5042
G2044.1 V-FDI-1S ἐρεύξομαι (1x)
Mt 13:35 I·shall·belch·forth *things* having·been·hidden

G2045 ἐρευνάω êrêunáō *v.* (6x)
Roots:G2046 Compare:G4441 See:G1830
G2045.1 V-PAI-3S ἐρευνᾷ (1x)
1Co 2:10 his Spirit, for the Spirit searches all·things, even,
G2045.1 V-PAM-2P ἐρευνᾶτε (1x)
Jn 5:39 "Search the Scriptures, because yeu·yeurselves
G2045.1 V-PAP-NSM ἐρευνῶν (2x)
Rm 8:27 And the·one searching the hearts personally·knows
Rv 2:23 ·know that I AM the·one searching kidneys and
G2045.1 V-PAP-NPM ἐρευνῶντες (1x)
1Pe 1:11 while·searching for which or what·kind·of season
G2045.1 V-AAM-2S ἐρεύνησον (1x)
Jn 7:52 ·yourself also from·out of·Galilee? Search and see!

G2046 ἔρω érō *v.* (75x)
εἴρηκα êírēka [perfect tense]
Roots:G2036 Compare:G3004 G5346 G2980 See:G4483 G4490 xLangAlso:H0559
G2046.1 V-FAI-1S ἐρῶ (8x)
Lk 12:19 Then I·shall·declare to·my soul, "Soul, you·have
Lk 15:18 toward my father and shall·declare to·him, "Father
Mt 13:30 season of·the harvest, I·shall·declare to·the reapers
Mt 21:24 *an·answer* to·me, I·also shall·declare to·yeu by
Mk 11:29 answer me, and I·shall·declare to·yeu by what·
Php 4:4 Lord always, *and* again I·shall·declare, "Rejoice!"
2Co 12:6 ·not be impetuous, for I·shall·declare truth. But I·
Rv 17:7 did·you·marvel? I·myself shall·declare to·you the
G2046.1 V-FAI-2S ἐρεῖς (4x)
Ac 23:5 ·written, "You·shall·not declare *anything* badly
Mt 7:4 Or how shall·you·declare to·your brother, 'Give·way
Rm 9:19 So·then, you·shall·declare to·me, "Why still does·
Rm 11:19 Accordingly, you·shall·declare, "The branches
G2046.1 V-FAI-2P ἐρεῖτε (5x)
Lk 4:23 them, "Entirely, yeu·shall·declare to·me this adage,
Lk 19:31 *it?*' In·this·manner yeu·shall·declare to·him,
Lk 22:11 And yeu·shall·declare to·the master of·the home,
Mt 17:20 ·seed *does*, yeu·shall·declare to·this mountain,
Mt 21:3 should·declare anything to·yeu, yeu·shall·declare,
G2046.1 V-FAI-3S ἐρεῖ (15x)
Lk 12:10 "And all who shall·declare a·word against the Son
Lk 13:25 and answering, he·shall·declare to·yeu, 'I·do·
Lk 13:27 But he·shall·declare, 'I·say to·yeu, I·do·not
Lk 14:9 you and him, upon·coming shall·declare to·you,
Lk 17:7 shepherding, who shall·declare immediately *to·him*
Lk 17:8 But·rather shall·he·not·indeed declare to·him,
Lk 20:5 'From·out of·heaven,' he·shall·declare, 'So·then
Mt 21:25 'From·out of·heaven,' he·shall·declare to·us,
Mt 25:34 "Then the King shall·declare to·the·ones at his
Mt 25:40 And answering, the King shall·declare to·them,
Mt 25:41 "Then he·shall·declare also to·the·ones at *the* left·
Mk 11:31 'From·out of·heaven,' he·shall·declare, 'So·then
Jac 2:18 But·yet, someone shall·declare, "You have trust,
1Co 14:16 the place of·the untrained declare the "So·be·it,·
1Co 15:35 But·yet someone shall·declare, "How·are the
G2046.1 V-FAI-3P ἐροῦσιν (5x)
Lk 17:21 nor·even shall·they·declare, 'Behold, here *it·is*!' or
Lk 17:23 "And they·shall·declare to·yeu, 'Behold, here *he·is*
Lk 23:29 Days are·coming in which they·shall·declare,
Mt 7:22 Many shall·declare to·me at that Day, 'Lord, Lord,
1Co 14:23 shall·they·not declare that yeu·are·raving·mad?
G2046.1 V-RAI-1S-ATT εἴρηκα (4x)
Jn 6:65 "On·account·of that, I·have·declared to·yeu that not·
Jn 14:29 "And now I·have·declared *it* to·yeu prior·to *it*
Jn 15:15 his lord does; but I·have·declared yeu *to·be* friends,
Rv 7:14 And I·have·declared to·him, "Sir, you·yourself
G2046.1 V-RAI-2S-ATT εἴρηκας (1x)
Jn 4:18 your husband. This·thing you·have·declared *is* true."
G2046.1 V-RAI-2P-ATT εἰρήκατε (1x)
Ac 8:24 of·these·things·which yeu·have·declared should·
G2046.1 V-RAI-3S-ATT εἴρηκεν (9x)
Jn 12:50 *it·is* just·as the Father has·declared to·me; in·this·
Lk 22:13 they·found *it* just·as he·has·declared to·them. And
Ac 13:34 ·back to decay, in·this·manner he·has·declared, "
Heb 1:13 to which of·the angels has·he·declared at·any·time,
Heb 4:3 ·rest— just·as he·has·declared *concerning the*
Heb 4:4 For somewhere he·has·declared concerning the
Heb 10:9 he·has then declared, " Behold, I·come, *I·am* the·
Heb 13:5 being·at·hand, for he·himself has·declared, "No,
2Co 12:9 And he·has·declared to·me, "My grace is·
G2046.1 V-RAI-3P-ATT εἰρήκαν (2x)
Ac 17:28 certain of·yeur very·own poets have·declared, 'For
Rv 19:3 And a·second·time they·declared, "Splendidly·
G2046.1 V-RAP-GSN-ATT εἰρηκότος (1x)
Mt 26:75 of·the utterance *that* YeShua had·declared to·him,
G2046.1 V-RPI-3S εἴρηται (2x)
Lk 4:12 declared to·him, "It·has·been·declared, "You·
Heb 4:7 so·vast a·time), just·as it·has·been·declared,
G2046.1 V-RPP-ASN-ATT εἰρημένον (3x)
Lk 2:24 ·to·the·thing having·been·declared in Yahweh's
Ac 13:40 upon yeu, the·thing having·been·declared in the
Rm 4:18 according·to the·thing having·been·declared, "In·
G2046.1 V-RPP-NSN-ATT εἰρημένον (1x)
Ac 2:16 this is the·thing having·been·declared through JoEl
G2046.1 V-LAI-3S-ATT εἰρήκει (2x)
Jn 11:13 And Jesus had·declared *this* concerning his death,
Ac 20:38 over the words which he·had·declared, that no·
EG2046.1 (1x)
Heb 4:3 ·rest,"" and·yet *he·declared this* with·the works
G2046.2 V-FAI-1P ἐροῦμεν (7x)
Rm 3:5 righteousness—" What shall·we·state? "¿!·Is·not
Rm 4:1 Accordingly, what shall·we·state *for* AbRaham our
Rm 6:1 So·then, what shall·we·state? Shall·we·continue·on
Rm 7:7 So·then, what shall·we·state? *Is* the Torah-Law
Rm 8:31 So·then, what shall·we·state toward these·things?
Rm 9:14 Accordingly, what shall·we·state? ¿!·Is·there
Rm 9:30 So·then, what shall·we·state? *In·fact*, that Gentiles,
G2046.2 V-FAI-3S ἐρεῖ (1x)
Rm 9:20 the·thing molded state to·the·one already·molding
EG2046.2 (3x)
Mt 26:54 ·fulfilled that *state* it·is·mandatory·for *it* to·happen
Rm 3:7 *But the reasoning states*, "For if by my lie, the truth
Rm 3:8 But we·do·not *state* (just·as we·are·vilified, and

G2047 ἐρημία ērēmía *n.* (4x)
Roots:G2048 See:G2049 G2050
G2047.2 N-DSF ἐρημίᾳ (2x)
Mt 15:33 ·quantity·of bread in a·barren·wilderness, such·as
2Co 11:26 a·city, dangers in a·barren·wilderness, dangers at
G2047.2 N-DPF ἐρημίαις (1x)
Heb 11:38 , being·wanderers in barren·wildernesses, and *in*
G2047.2 N-GSF ἐρημίας (1x)
Mk 8:4 ·men full with·bread, here in a·barren·wilderness?"

G2048 ἔρημος érēmôs *adj.* (50x)
Compare:G5561 See:G2047 G2049 G2050 xLangAlso:H4057
G2048.1 A-NSM ἔρημος (4x)
Lk 13:35 yeur house is·left to·yeu desolate. And certainly
Mt 14:15 "The place is desolate, and the hour even·now *has*
Mt 23:38 "Behold, yeur house is·left to·yeu desolate!
Mk 6:35 "The place is desolate, and even·now *it·is* a·late
G2048.1 A-NSF ἔρημος (1x)
Ac 1:20 "Let his walled-off·mansion become desolate, and
G2048.1 A-ASM ἔρημον (6x)
Lk 4:42 going·forth, he·traversed into a·desolate place. And
Lk 9:10 privately into a·desolate place *belonging·to* the·city
Mt 14:13 from·there in a·sailboat into a·desolate place in
Mk 1:35 he·went·out and went·off into a·desolate place, and
Mk 6:31 yeurselves aside privately into a·desolate place, and
Mk 6:32 And they·went·off to a·desolate place in·the
G2048.1 A-DSM ἐρήμῳ (1x)
Lk 9:12 ·of·food, because we·are here in a·desolate place."
G2048.1 A-DPM ἐρήμοις (1x)
Mk 1:45 but·rather was outside in desolate places, and they·
G2048.1 A-GSF ἐρήμου (1x)
Gal 4:27 ·pain, because the desolate·woman has·many more
G2048.2 A-NSF ἔρημος (1x)
Ac 8:26 (This is a·wilderness).
G2048.2 A-ASM ἔρημον (1x)
Rv 17:3 me away in spirit into a·wilderness. And I·saw a·
G2048.2 A-ASF ἔρημον (8x)
Lk 4:1 Jordan and was·led by the Spirit into the wilderness,
Lk 7:24 ·gone·forth into the wilderness to·distinctly·view?
Ac 21:38 men of·the Assassins out into the wilderness?"
Mt 4:1 YeShua was·led·up into the wilderness by the Spirit
Mt 11:7 yeu·go·forth into the wilderness to·distinctly·view?
Mk 1:12 ·away the Spirit casts him forth into the wilderness.
Rv 12:6 the woman fled into the wilderness, where she·has
Rv 12:14 that she·may·fly into the wilderness, into her place,
G2048.2 A-APF ἐρήμους (1x)
Lk 8:29 he·was·driven by the demon into the wilderness).
G2048.2 A-DSF ἐρήμῳ (22x)
Jn 1:23 a·voice of·one·crying·out in the wilderness, "Make·
Jn 3:14 *upon a·sign·pole* in the wilderness, in·this·manner,
Jn 6:31 ate the manna in the wilderness, just·as it·is having·
Jn 6:49 fathers ate the manna in the wilderness, and died.
Lk 3:2 came to John the son of·ZacharIas in the wilderness.
Lk 3:4 A·voice of·one·crying·out in the wilderness, 'Make·
Lk 15:4 the ninety-nine in the wilderness, and·then traverse
Ac 7:30 ·visible to·him in the wilderness of·Mount Sinai, in
Ac 7:36 in *the* Red Sea, and in the wilderness forty years.
Ac 7:38 called·out·citizenry in the wilderness, *along* with
Ac 7:42 respect·offerings *for* forty years in the wilderness?
Ac 7:44 with our fathers in the wilderness, *being* just·as the·
Ac 13:18 he·bore·with their lifestyle in the wilderness.
Heb 3:8 in the day of·the Proof·Trial in the wilderness,
Heb 3:17 ·failing, whose slain·bodies fell in the wilderness?
Mt 3:1 officially·proclaiming in the wilderness of·Judea,
Mt 3:3 A·voice of·one·crying·out in the wilderness, 'Make·
Mt 24:26 'Behold, he·is in the wilderness,' yeu·should·not
Mk 1:3 A·voice of·one·crying·out in the wilderness, 'Make·
Mk 1:4 in the wilderness and officially·proclaiming an·
Mk 1:13 And he·was there in the wilderness forty days,
1Co 10:5 for they·were·struck·down in the wilderness.
G2048.2 A-DPF ἐρήμοις (2x)
Lk 1:80 and was in the wildernesses until *the* day of·his
Lk 5:16 ·retreating into the wildernesses and was·praying.
G2048.2 A-GSF ἐρήμου (1x)
Jn 11:54 to the region near the wilderness *and* into a·city

G2049 ἐρημόω ērēmóō *v.* (5x)
Roots:G2048 See:G2047 G2050 G1830-2 xLangEquiv:H8045 xLangAlso:H8074
G2049.1 V-API-3S ἠρημώθη (2x)
Rv 18:17 in·one hour such·vast wealth is·desolated.' "And
Rv 18:19 Because in·one hour, she·is·desolated.'
G2049.1 V-RPP-ASF@ ἠρημωμένην (1x)

Rv 17:16 and they·shall·make her desolate and naked, and
G2049.2 V-PPI-3S ἐρημοῦται (2x)
Lk 11:17 ·divided against itself is·made·desolate, and a·
Mt 12:25 being·divided against itself is·made·desolate, and

G2050 ἐρήμωσις êrēmōsis *n.* (3x)
Roots:G2049 See:G2047 xLangAlso:H8077
G2050.2 N-NSF ἐρήμωσις (1x)
Lk 21:20 then know that her " Desolation" has·drawn·near.
G2050.2 N-GSF ἐρημώσεως (2x)
Mt 24:15 " the Abomination of·Desolation," the·one being·
Mk 13:14 " the Abomination of·Desolation," the·one being·

G2051 ἐρίζω êrízō *v.* (1x)
Roots:G2054 Compare:G3164
G2051.1 V-FAI-3S ἐρίσει (1x)
Mt 12:19 He·shall·not engage·in·strife, neither shall·he·yell·

G2052 ἐριθεία êrithêía *n.* (7x)
Roots:G2042
G2052.1 N-NSF ἐριθεία (1x)
Jac 3:16 For where jealousy and contention *is*, there *is*
G2052.1 N-NPF ἐριθεῖαι (2x)
Gal 5:20 jealousies, ragings, contentions, dissensions,
2Co 12:20 jealousies, ragings, contentions, backbitings,
G2052.1 N-ASF ἐριθείαν (2x)
Jac 3:14 if yeu·have bitter jealousy and contention in yeur
Php 2:3 *be·done* according·to contention or self-conceit, but·
G2052.2 N-GSF ἐριθείας (2x)
Rm 2:8 to·the·ones *working* out of·being·contentious, and
Php 1:16 Anointed-One out of·being·contentious, not with·

G2053 ἔριον êriôn *n.* (2x)
Compare:G5155 G2359
xLangEquiv:H6785 A6015
G2053 N-NSN ἔριον (1x)
Rv 1:14 and *his* hairs *are* white like wool (*as* white as snow)
G2053 N-GSN ἐρίου (1x)
Heb 9:19 ·goats, with water, scarlet wool, and hyssop, he·

G2054 ἔρις êris *n.* (9x)
Compare:G3163 G5379 See:G2051
G2054.1 N-NSF ἔρις (2x)
1Co 3:3 ·*is* among yeu jealousy, and strife, and dissensions,
1Ti 6:4 ·out of·which becomes envy, strife, revilements, evil
G2054.1 N-NPF ἔρεις (3x)
Gal 5:20 ·of·poisonous·drugs, hostilities, strifes, jealousies,
1Co 1:11 *house* of·Chloe, that there·are strifes among yeu.
2Co 12:20 Lest·somehow *there·be* strifes, jealousies, ragings
G2054.1 N-ASF ἔριν (1x)
Php 1:15 even through envy and strife, and some also
G2054.1 N-APF ἔρεις (1x)
Tit 3:9 speculations, genealogies, strifes, and quarrels of·
G2054.1 N-DSF ἔριδι (1x)
Rm 13:13 and debaucheries, not in·strife and jealousy.
G2054.1 N-GSF ἔριδος (1x)
Rm 1:29 exceedingly·full of·envy, murder, strife, guile, *and*

G2055 ἐρίφιον êriphiôn *n.* (1x)
Roots:G2056 Compare:G0122 G5131
G2055.2 N-APN ἐρίφια (1x)
Mt 25:33 at his right·hand, but the infantile·goats at *the* left.

G2056 ἔριφος êriphôs *n.* (2x)
Roots:G2053 Compare:G0122 G5131 See:G2055
G2056 N-ASM ἔριφον (1x)
Lk 15:29 me a·young·goat in·order·that I·may·be·merry
G2056 N-GPM ἐρίφων (1x)
Mt 25:32 ·separates the sheep from the young·goats.

G2057 Ἑρμᾶς Hêrmâs *n/p.* (1x)
Roots:G2060
G2057 N/P-ASM Ἑρμᾶν (1x)
Rm 16:14 Greet ASynkritus, Phlegon, Hermas, PatroBas,

G2058 ἑρμηνεία hêrmēnêía *n.* (2x)
Roots:G2059 Compare:G1955 See:G2060 G2058-1
G2058 N-NSF ἑρμηνεία (1x)
1Co 12:10 and to·another, translation of·bestowed·tongues.
G2058 N-ASF ἑρμηνείαν (1x)
1Co 14:26 has a·revelation, has a·translation. All·things

G2059 ἑρμηνεύω hêrmēnēúō *v.* (4x)
Roots:G2060 See:G1329 G2058 G2058-1
xLangAlso:H3887 H8638
G2059 V-PPI-3S ἑρμηνεύεται (2x)
Jn 1:42 ·*rock*)," which is·translated *from·Hebrew as* Peter.
Jn 9:7 (which *from·Hebrew* is·translated *as* Having·Been·
G2059 V-PPP-NSN ἑρμηνευόμενον (1x)
Jn 1:38 (which, when·being·translated *from Hebrew*, is·to·
G2059 V-PPP-NSM ἑρμηνευόμενος (1x)
Heb 7:2 First, in·fact, being·translated *from·Hebrew as*

G2060 Ἑρμῆς Hêrmē̂s *n/p.* (2x)
Roots:G2046 See:G2061
G2060.2 N/P-ASM Ἑρμῆν (1x)
Ac 14:12 Zeus, and Paul, Hermes, since·now he·himself
G2060.3 N/P-ASM Ἑρμῆν (1x)
Rm 16:14 Hermas, PatroBas, Hermes, and the brothers

G2061 Ἑρμο•γένης Hêrmôgénēs *n/p.* (1x)
Roots:G2060 G1096
G2061.2 N/P-NSM Ἑρμογένης (1x)
2Ti 1:15 me, of·whom *also* are Phygellus and HermoGenes.

G2062 ἑρπετόν hêrpêtón *n.* (4x)
Roots:G2062-1 xLangAlso:H7431
G2062.1 N-NPN ἑρπετά (1x)
Ac 10:12 the wild·beasts, and the creeping·things, and the
G2062.1 N-APN ἑρπετά (1x)
Ac 11:6 the wild·beasts, and the creeping·things, and the
G2062.1 N-GPN ἑρπετῶν (2x)
Rm 1:23 and four-footed·animals, and creeping·things.'
Jac 3:7 of·birds, and of·creeping·things, and of·creatures·in·

G2063 ἐρυθρός êrythrós *adj.* (2x)
Compare:G2847 G4449 G4450 See:G2281 G2062-3
G2062-2 xLangAlso:H5488
G2063.2 A-ASF ἐρυθράν (1x)
Heb 11:29 By·trust, they·crossed the Red Sea as through
G2063.2 A-DSF ἐρυθρᾷ (1x)
Ac 7:36 in *the* land of·Egypt, and in *the* Red Sea, and in the

G2064 ἔρχομαι ěrchômai *v.* (642x)
ἐλεύθομαι êlêúthômai [middle voice]
ἔλθω élthō [active voice]
Compare:G2658 G2240 G1510-1 See:G0565 G1660
G2064.1 V-FDI-1S ἐλεύσομαι (7x)
Rm 9:9 "“According·to this season I·shall·come, and there·
Rm 15:24 I·should·traverse for Spain, I·shall·come to yeu,
Rm 15:29 ·coming to yeu, I·shall·come in complete·fullness
Php 2:24 in *the* Lord that also I·myself shall·come promptly.
1Co 4:19 But I·shall·come to yeu promptly, if the Lord
1Co 16:5 Now I·shall·come to yeu, whenever I·should·go·
2Co 12:1 for·me to·boast, for I·shall·come to visions and
G2064.1 V-FDI-1P ἐλευσόμεθα (1x)
Jn 14:23 Father shall·love him, and we·shall·come to him,
G2064.1 V-FDI-3S ἐλεύσεται (5x)
Jn 16:7 the Companion/Intercessor shall·not come to yeu;
Lk 20:16 He·shall·come and shall·completely·destroy these
Ac 1:11 yeu into the heaven, shall·come in·this·manner as
Mk 12:9 do? He·shall·come and shall·completely·destroy
1Co 16:12 but he·shall·come whenever he·should·have·
G2064.1 V-FDI-3P ἐλεύσονται (10x)
Jn 11:48 and the Romans shall·come and shall·take·away
Lk 5:35 But days shall·come, and then, whenever the
Lk 17:22 "Days shall·come when yeu·shall·long to·see one
Lk 21:6 which yeu·observe, days shall·come in which there·
Lk 21:8 ·not be·deceived, for many shall·come in my name,
Mt 9:15 is with them? But days shall·come, whenever the
Mt 24:5 For many shall·come in my name, saying, 'I AM
Mk 2:20 But days shall·come, whenever the bridegroom
Mk 13:6 For many shall·come in my name, saying, 'I AM
2Pe 3:3 ·knowing this first, that there·shall·come in the last
G2064.1 V-PNI-1S ἔρχομαι (20x)
Jn 5:7 but while I·myself am·coming, another steps·down
Jn 8:14 have·not seen from·what·source I·come and where I·
Jn 14:3 ·make·ready a·place for·yeu, I·come again and
Jn 14:18 ·not leave yeu orphans. I·do·come alongside yeu.
Jn 14:28 'I·head·on·out, and I·come *back* to yeu.
Jn 17:11 are in the world, and I·myself do·come to you.
Jn 17:13 "And now I·come to you, and these·things I·speak
Jn 21:22 ·want him to·remain until I·come, what·is·that to
Jn 21:23 ·want him to·remain until I·come, what·is·that to
Lk 13:7 Behold, *for* three years, I·come seeking fruit on this
Lk 19:13 them, 'Keep·yourselves·busy until I·come·*back*.'
2Co 13:1 This *is the* third·time I·am·coming to yeu. "At *the*
1Ti 4:13 Until I·come, give·attention to·the reading·aloud *of*·
Rv 2:5 the first works; but·if·not, I·come to·you with·haste,
Rv 2:16 'Repent! But·if·not, I·come to·you swiftly, and I·
Rv 3:11 'Behold, I·come swiftly. Securely·hold that·which
Rv 16:15 "Behold, I·come as a·thief. Supremely·blessed *is*
Rv 22:7 "Behold, I·come swiftly! Supremely·blessed *is* the·
Rv 22:12 "And behold, I·come swiftly, and my payment·of·
Rv 22:20 these·things says, "Yes, I·come swiftly." So·be·
G2064.1 V-PNI-2S ἔρχου (10x)
Jn 1:46 ·Natsareth?" Philip says to·him, "Come and see."
Jn 11:34 him?" They·said to·him, "Lord, come and see."
Lk 7:8 he·traverses; and to·another, 'Come,' and he·comes;
Mt 3:14 by you, and do·you·yourself come to me?
Mt 8:9 he·traverses; and to·another, 'Come,' and he·comes;
Rv 6:1 (as·a·voice of·a·thunder) saying, "Come and look!"
Rv 6:3 the second living·being saying, "Come and look."
Rv 6:5 the third living·being saying, "Come and look." And
Rv 6:7 of·the fourth living·being saying, "Come and look."
Rv 22:20 So·be·it, Amen. Yes, come, Lord Jesus.
G2064.1 V-PNI-3S ἔρχεται (87x)
Jn 1:30 'Right·behind me comes a·man who has·come·to·
Jn 3:8 ·have·not seen from·what·source it·comes or where it·
Jn 3:20 hates the light, and does·not come toward the light,
Jn 3:21 But the·one doing the truth comes to the light, in·
Jn 4:5 In·due·course, he·comes to·a·city of·Samaria being·
Jn 4:7 there·comes a·woman from·out of·Samaria to·draw·
Jn 4:21 trust me, because an·hour is·coming when, neither
Jn 4:23 "But·yet an·hour comes, and now is, when the true
Jn 4:25 "I·personally·know that Messiah is·coming, the·one
Jn 4:35 yet four·lunar·months, and *then* comes the harvest'?
Jn 5:24 and he·does·not come into Tribunal·judgment, but·
Jn 5:25 I·say to·yeu, an·hour is·coming, and now is, when
Jn 5:28 at·that, because an·hour is·coming in which all the·
Jn 6:5 and surveying that a·large crowd is·come toward him,
Jn 6:45 learning personally·from the Father comes to me.
Jn 7:41 from·out of·Galilee *that* the Anointed-One comes?
Jn 7:42 that the Anointed-One comes birthed·from·out of·the
Jn 9:4 it·is day. Night is·coming, when not·even·one·man
Jn 10:10 "The Thief does·not come, except in·order·that he·
Jn 11:20 ·as she·heard that Jesus was·coming, went·and·met
Jn 11:38 again being·exasperated in himself, comes to the
Jn 12:12 upon·hearing that Jesus was·coming to JeruSalem,
Jn 12:15 "Behold, your King comes *to·you*, sitting·down
Jn 12:22 Philip comes and relays *this* to·Andrew, and again
Jn 13:6 So·then he·comes to Simon Peter, and that·one says
Jn 14:6 and the life-above. Not·even·one comes to the Father
Jn 14:30 for the prince of·this world comes, and he·does·not
Jn 16:2 Moreover, an·hour is·come that anyone killing yeu
Jn 16:25 ·yeu in proverbs. But·yet an·hour comes, when no
Jn 16:32 "Behold, an·hour comes, and now has·come that
Jn 18:3 and Pharisees, Judas comes there with searchlights
Jn 20:1 , Mariam Magdalene comes to the chamber·tomb
Jn 20:2 So·then she·runs and comes to Simon Peter and to
Jn 20:6 So·then, Simon Peter comes following him, and he·
Jn 20:18 Mariam Magdalene came announcing to·the
Jn 20:26 doors having·been·shut, Jesus came and stood·still
Jn 21:13 Then Jesus comes and takes the bread and gives *it*
Lk 3:16 but the·one stronger·than me comes, the strap of·
Lk 7:8 'Come,' and he·comes; and to·my slave, 'Do this,'
Lk 8:12 are the·ones hearing. Then comes the Slanderer, and
Lk 8:49 ·yet speaking, there·comes someone directly·from
Lk 12:39 ·which hour the thief would·come, he·would·have
Lk 12:40 because the Son of·Clay·Man† comes in·that hour
Lk 12:54 yeu·say, 'There·comes a·thunderstorm,' and in·
Lk 14:26 "If any·man comes to me and does·not

Lk 14:27 does·not bear his cross and come right·behind me,
Lk 17:1 to·come, but woe *to·him* through whom they·come!
Lk 17:20 *as·to* when the kingdom of·God should·come, he·
Lk 17:20 of·God does·not come with meticulous·observation
Ac 13:25 But·rather, behold, there·comes·one after me, the
Mt 8:9 'Come,' and he·comes; and to·my slave, 'Do this,'
Mt 13:19 *it*, the Evil·One comes and snatches·up the *seed*
Mt 17:11 to·them, "In·fact EliJah does·come first and shall·
Mt 18:7 ·of·clay† through whom the scandalous·trap comes!
Mt 21:5 Behold, your King comes to·you, calmly·mild and
Mt 24:42 personally·know in·which hour yeur Lord comes.
Mt 24:43 *of·the night* the thief comes, he·would·have kept·
Mt 24:44 the Son of·Clay·Man† comes at·an·hour which
Mt 25:6 'Behold, the bridegroom comes! Go·forth to
Mt 25:13 the hour in which the Son of·Clay·Man† comes.
Mt 25:19 the lord of·those slaves comes and tally·ups an·
Mt 26:36 Then YeShua comes with them to an·open·field
Mt 26:40 And he·comes to the disciples and finds them
Mt 26:45 Then he·comes to his disciples and says to·them,
Mt 27:49 we·should·see whether EliJah comes to·save him.
Mk 1:7 "The·one stronger·than me comes right·behind me,
Mk 1:40 And a·leper came to him, imploring him, even
Mk 4:15 ·hear, the Adversary-Accuser comes immediately,
Mk 5:22 And behold, there·comes one of·the directors·of·
Mk 5:38 And he·comes to the house of·the director·of·the·
Mk 6:48 fourth watch of·the night, he·comes toward them,
Mk 8:22 And he·comes to BethSaida. And they·bring a·
Mk 10:1 After·rising·up from·there, he·comes into the
Mk 13:35 the lord of·the home comes, *whether* at·early·
Mk 14:17 with·early·evening occurring, he·comes with the
Mk 14:37 And he·comes and finds them sleeping.
Mk 14:41 And he·comes the third·time, and *sternly* says to·
Mk 14:66 in the courtyard, *along* comes one of·the servant·
Mk 15:36 we·should·see whether EliJah comes to·lower him
1Th 5:2 of·Yahweh, in·this·manner, comes as a·thief at
Eph 5:6 these·things the wrath of·God comes upon the Sons
Col 3:6 which·things the wrath of·God comes on the Sons
1Jn 2:18 Adversary·of·the·Anointed-One is·coming, even
1Jn 4:3 of·which yeu·have·heard that it·is·come, and now is
2Jn 1:10 If any·man comes to yeu *all*, and does·not bring this
Rv 1:7 Behold, 'he·comes with the thick·clouds,' and '
Rv 11:14 went·away; behold, the third woe comes swiftly.

G2064.1 V-PNI-3P ἔρχονται (18x)

Jn 3:26 the·same·man immerses, and all *men* come to him."
Lk 23:29 behold, Days are·coming in which they·shall·
Heb 8:8 'Behold, *the* days come,' says Yahweh, 'and I·
Mt 7:15 of the false·prophets, who do·come to yeu in
Mt 25:11 the rest *of·the* virgins came also, saying, 'Lord,
Mk 2:3 Then *more* come to him, bringing a·paralyzed·man
Mk 2:18 were fasting. And they·come and say to·him,
Mk 3:31 his brothers and his mother come *along*, and
Mk 5:15 And they·come to Jesus and observe the·one
Mk 5:35 As·he was·still speaking, one·came from *the house*·
Mk 10:46 Then they·come into Jericho. And as·he is·
Mk 11:15 And they·come to JeruSalem. And Jesus, after·
Mk 11:27 And they·come again to JeruSalem.
Mk 11:27 the scribes, and the elders come alongside him,
Mk 12:18 Then *the* Sadducees come to him, who say *that*
Mk 14:32 Then they·come to an·open·field of·which the
1Co 15:35 And in·what·kind·of body do·they·come?"
Rv 9:12 woe went·away; behold, there·come two woes still

G2064.1 V-PNM-2P ἔρχεσθε (2x)

Jn 1:39 He·says to·them, "Come and see." They·came and
Lk 14:17 ·ones having·been·called·forth, 'Come, because

G2064.1 V-PNM-3S ἐρχέσθω (1x)

Jn 7:37 "If any·man should·thirst, let·him·come to me and

G2064.1 V-PNN ἔρχεσθαι (9x)

Jn 6:15 knowing that they·are·about to·come and seize him
Lk 10:1 city and place where he·himself was·about to·come.
Lk 12:45 'My lord is·delayed in·coming *back*,' and should·
Lk 18:16 "Allow the little·children to·come to me, and do·
Ac 24:8 ·ordering his legal·accusers to·come to you,
Mt 11:14 *it*, he·himself is EliJah, the·one about to·come.
Mt 16:27 "For the Son of·Clay·Man† is·about to·come in the
Mk 10:14 "Allow the little·children to·come to me, and do·
Rv 3:10 ·the proof·trial, the·one about to·come upon all The

G2064.1 V-PNP-ASN ἐρχόμενον (1x)

Mt 3:16 ·God descending like a·dove and coming upon him.

G2064.1 V-PNP-ASF ἐρχομένην (1x)

Ac 18:21 the Sacred·Feast, the·one coming in JeruSalem,

G2064.1 V-PNP-ASM ἐρχόμενον (15x)

Jn 1:9 illuminates every child·of·clay† coming into the world
Jn 1:29 John looks·at Jesus, who·is·coming toward him,
Jn 1:47 Jesus saw NathaniEl coming toward him and says
Jn 6:37 toward me; and the·one who·is·coming toward me,
Jn 10:12 sheep, he·observes the wolf coming and leaves the
Lk 21:27 'the Son of·Clay·Man† coming in a·thick·cloud'
Ac 19:4 ·should·trust in the·one who·is·coming after him,
Heb 6:7 soil, after·drinking the rain which·is·coming upon it
Mt 16:28 ·should·see the Son of·Clay·Man† coming in his
Mt 24:30 'the Son of·Clay·Man† coming upon the thick·
Mt 26:64 ' of·the Power and 'coming upon the thick·clouds
Mk 13:26 'the Son of·Clay·Man† coming in thick·clouds'
Mk 14:62 and·also 'coming with the thick·clouds of·the
Mk 15:21 Simon, a·Cyrenian, coming from *the* countryside
2Jn 1:7 not affirming Jesus Anointed as·coming in flesh.

G2064.1 V-PNP-APN ἐρχόμενα (2x)

Jn 16:13 ·in·detail to·yeu the·things which·are·coming.
Jn 18:4 ·seen all the·things that·were·coming upon him,

G2064.1 V-PNP-APM ἐρχομένους (1x)

Mt 3:7 of·the Pharisees and Sadducees are·coming to his

G2064.1 V-PNP-DSN ἐρχομένῳ (1x)

Ac 13:44 And on·the coming Sabbath, almost all the city *of*·

G2064.1 V-PNP-DSM ἐρχομένῳ (3x)

Lk 14:31 ·and·meet the·one who·is·coming against him with
Lk 18:30 season, and in the coming age, eternal life-above.
Mk 10:30 with persecutions, and in the coming age, eternal

G2064.1 V-PNP-GSF ἐρχομένης (1x)

1Th 1:10 who·is·snatching us away·from the coming Wrath.

G2064.1 V-PNP-GSM ἐρχομένου (2x)

Lk 23:26 ·hold of·a·certain·man who·was·coming *in* from
1Co 4:18 ·up, as·though *it·is* not me who·is·coming to yeu.

G2064.1 V-PNP-GPM ἐρχομένων (1x)

3Jn 1:3 very·much, with·*the*·brothers coming and testifying

G2064.1 V-PNP-NSF ἐρχομένη (2x)

Lk 18:5 me as an·end·result *of·her·persistently* coming *to·me*.
Mk 11:10 father David, the·one that·is·coming in *the* name

G2064.1 V-PNP-NSM ἐρχόμενος (26x)

Jn 1:15 I·declared, 'The·one who·is·coming right·behind me
Jn 1:27 it·is he (the·one who·is·coming right·behind me who
Jn 3:31 "The·one who·is·coming from·above is up·above all.
Jn 3:31 of·the earth. The·one who·is·coming from·out·of·the
Jn 6:14 the Prophet, the·one who·is·coming into the world.
Jn 6:35 bread of·life-above. The·one who·is·coming to me,
Jn 11:27 Son of·God, the·one who·is·coming into the world.
Jn 12:13 ·blessed *is* the·one who·is·coming in Yahweh's
Lk 6:47 "Any one who·is·coming toward me, both hearing
Lk 7:19 "Are you·yourself the·one who·is·coming? Or
Lk 7:20 'Are you·yourself the·one who·is·coming? Or
Lk 13:35 ·been·blessed *is* the·one who·is·coming in *the*
Lk 19:38 ·been·blessed *is* the King who·is·coming in *the*
Heb 10:37 ·while, the·one who·is·coming shall·come and
Mt 3:11 but the·one who·is·coming right·behind me is
Mt 11:3 "Are you·yourself the·one who·is·coming, or do·
Mt 21:9 ·been·blessed *is* the·one who·is·coming in *the* name
Mt 23:39 ·been·blessed *is* the·one who·is·coming in *the*
Mk 11:9 ·been·blessed *is* the·one who·is·coming in *the* name
Rm 15:29 And I·have·seen that, in·coming to yeu, I·shall·
2Co 11:4 if the·one who·is·coming does·officially·proclaim
2Ti 4:13 with Carpus, *as* you·are·coming, bring *it·with·you*,
Rv 1:4 the·one who·was, and the·one who·is·coming), also
Rv 1:8 who·was, and the·one who·is·coming, the Almighty.
Rv 4:8 and the·one being, and the·one who·is·coming."
Rv 11:17 that·was, and the·one who·is·coming, because

G2064.1 V-PNP-NPM ἐρχόμενοι (4x)

Lk 13:14 to·work. Accordingly, coming on those *days*, be·
Lk 16:21 dogs were·coming·*along and* were·licking·away·at
Mk 6:31 For there·were many coming and heading·on·out,
Rv 7:14 "These are the·ones coming out of·The GREAT

G2064.1 V-PNS-1S ἔρχωμαι (1x)

Jn 4:15 ·not thirst, nor·even should·come here to·draw·out

G2064.1 V-PNS-3S ἔρχηται (2x)

Jn 7:27 the Anointed-One should·come, not·even·one·man
Heb 13:23 I·shall·gaze·upon yeu, if he·should·come swiftly.

G2064.1 V-INI-3S ἤρχετο (3x)

Jn 8:2 ·Atrium, and all the people were·coming to him. And
Lk 18:3 in that city, and she·was·coming to him, saying,
Mk 2:13 and all the crowd was·coming alongside him, and

G2064.1 V-INI-3P ἤρχοντο (4x)

Jn 4:30 ·forth out of·the city and were·coming toward him.
Jn 20:3 disciple went·forth, and they·came to the chamber·
Ac 19:18 ·ones having·trusted were·*now*·coming *forward*,
Mk 1:45 in desolate places, and they·came to him from·

G2064.1 V-2AAI-1S ἦλθον (20x)

Jn 1:31 on·account·of that, I·myself came immersing in the
Jn 8:14 ·know from·what·source I·came and where I·head·
Jn 9:39 "For judgment, I·myself did·come into this world in·
Jn 10:10 I·myself came in·order·that they·may·have
Jn 12:27 But·rather on·account·of this, I·came to this hour.
Jn 12:47 I·did·not come in·order·that I·may·presently·judge
Jn 15:22 "Except *for·that* I·came and I·spoke to·them, they·
Lk 12:49 "I·came to·cast fire upon the earth.
Ac 10:29 ·for, I·came *to·yeu* without·expressing·opposition.
Ac 22:11 being·together with·me, I·came into Damascus.
Gal 1:21 Afterward, I·came into the vicinities of·Syria and
Mt 5:17 "Yeu·should·not assume that I·came to·demolish the
Mt 5:17 the prophets. I·did·not come to·demolish, but·rather
Mt 9:13 ' For I·did·not come to·call righteous·ones, but·
Mt 10:34 "Yeu·should·not assume that I·came to·cast peace
Mt 10:34 upon the earth; I·did·not come to·cast peace, but·
Mt 10:35 For I·came to·split "a·man·of·clay† against his
Mk 2:17 badly·ill. I·did·not come to·call righteous·men,
1Co 2:1 already·coming to yeu, came not according·to
2Co 1:23 that to·spare yeu, I·did·not·yet come to Corinth.

G2064.1 V-2AAI-1P ἤλθομεν (8x)

Ac 20:6 ·*Feast·of* Unleavened·Bread, and we·came to them
Ac 20:14 after·taking him aboard, we·came to Mitylene.
Ac 20:15 the following *day* we·came to Miletus,
Ac 27:8 sailing·near it with·difficulty, we·came to some
Ac 28:13 springing·up, we·came on·the·second·day to
Ac 28:16 And when we·came to Rome, the centurion
Mt 2:2 in the east, and we·came to·fall·prostrate to·him."
Mt 25:39 ·we·see you sick, or in prison, and came to you?

G2064.1 V-2AAI-2S ἦλθες (3x)

Lk 4:34 ·Natsareth? Did·you·come to·completely·destroy us
Mt 8:29 O·Son of·God? Did·you·come here to·torment us
Mk 1:24 Did·you·come to·completely·destroy us?

G2064.1 V-2AAI-2P ἤλθετε (1x)

Mt 25:36 I·was in prison, and yeu·came to me.'

G2064.1 V-2AAI-3S ἦλθεν (91x)

Jn 1:7 The·same came for a·testimony, in·order·that he·may·
Jn 1:11 He·came to his·own, and his·own did·not personally·
Jn 3:2 The·same came to Jesus by·night and declared to·him,
Jn 3:22 Jesus and his disciples came into the land of·Judea,
Jn 4:45 So·then, when he·came into Galilee, the Galileans
Jn 4:46 In·due·course, Jesus came again into Qanah of·
Jn 6:23 Now other small·boats came out·from Tiberias near
Jn 9:7 ·away and washed, and he·came *back* looking·about.
Jn 11:32 So as·soon·as Mary came where Jesus was, upon·
Jn 12:1 before the Passover, Jesus came to BethAny where
Jn 12:28 Accordingly, there·came a·voice from·out of·the
Jn 16:21 ·has grief because her hour is·come, but whenever
Jn 19:38 freely·permitted *him*. So he·came and took·away
Jn 19:39 And NicoDemus came also, the·one coming at·the
Jn 20:4 more·swiftly outran Peter and came first to the
Jn 20:19 fear of·the Judeans, Jesus came and stood·still in
Jn 20:24 ·to·as Twin) was not with them when Jesus came.
Lk 2:27 And he·came by the Spirit into the Sanctuary·
Lk 2:51 he·walked·down with them, and came to Natsareth,

Lk 4:16 Now he·came to Natsareth, where he·was having·
Lk 8:41 And behold, there·came a·man whose name *was*
Lk 8:47 that she·was·not hidden, came trembling; and
Lk 9:56 ·Clay·Man† did·not come to·completely·destroy *the*
Lk 10:33 while·traveling, came adjacent·to *where* he *was*.
Lk 11:31 ·condemn them, because she·came from·out of·the
Lk 13:6 in his vineyard, and he·came seeking fruit on it yet
Lk 15:20 "And rising·up, he·came toward his father.
Lk 15:30 But when this son of·yours came *home*, the·one
Lk 17:27 ·then the Deluge came and completely·destroyed
Lk 19:5 And as·soon·as Jesus came to the place, looking·up,
Lk 19:10 For the Son of·Clay·Man† came to·seek and to·
Lk 19:18 And the second came, saying, 'Lord, your mina
Lk 19:20 "And another came, saying, 'Lord, behold, *here·is*
Lk 22:7 Then came the day of·the *Sacred·Feast·of*
Ac 7:11 "Now there·came a·famine over all the land of·
Ac 11:5 by·four corners, and it·came even·as·far·as me.
Ac 12:12 after·becoming·completely·aware, he·came to the
Ac 18:1 And after these·things, Paul came to Corinth, being·
Ac 18:7 And walking·on from·there, he·came into a·home
Ac 19:6 on·them, the Holy Spirit came upon them, and they·
Ac 20:2 exhorting them often in·word, he·came into Greece,
Gal 2:11 But when Peter came to Antioch, I·withstood him
Gal 4:4 when the complete·fullness of·time was·come, God
Mt 2:21 little·child and his mother and came into *the* land of·
Mt 9:1 sailboat, he·crossed·over and came into his·own city
Mt 11:18 For John came neither eating nor drinking, and
Mt 11:19 The Son of·Clay·Man† came eating and drinking,
Mt 12:42 ·condemn it, because she·came from·out of·the
Mt 13:4 roadway, and the birds came and devoured them.
Mt 13:25 to·sleep, his enemy came and sowed *poisonous*
Mt 15:29 walking·on from·there, YeShua came near·to the
Mt 15:39 into the sailboat and came into the borders of·
Mt 17:12 I·say to·yeu, that EliJah came even·now, and they·
Mt 18:11 For the Son of·Clay·Man† came to·save the·one
Mt 19:1 he·moved·on from Galilee and came into the
Mt 20:28 Son of·Clay·Man† did·not come to·be·attended·to,
Mt 21:19 fig·tree by the roadway, he·came to it and found
Mt 21:32 For John came to yeu by way of·righteousness, yet
Mt 24:39 know … until the Deluge came, and took·away
Mt 25:10 ·off to·buy *oil*, the bridegroom came, and the·ones
Mt 26:47 Judas, one of·the twelve, came, and with him *was*
Mt 27:57 occurring, there·came a·wealthy man·of·clay† of
Mt 28:1 and the other Mariam came to·observe the grave.
Mk 1:9 in those days *that* Jesus came from Natsareth of·
Mk 1:14 ·handed·over *to·prison*, Jesus came into Galilee
Mk 4:4 and the birds of·the sky came and devoured it.
Mk 5:33 has·happened in her, came and fell·down·before
Mk 6:1 And he·went·out from·there and came into his·own
Mk 7:31 borders of·Tyre and Tsidon, he·came to the Sea of·
Mk 8:10 sailboat with his disciples, he·came into the parts
Mk 9:7 them, and a·voice came out of·the thick·cloud,
Mk 9:33 Then he·came to CaperNaum, and once·being in the
Mk 10:45 Son of·Clay·Man† did·not come to·be·attended·to,
Mk 10:50 ·garment *and* rising·up, he·came toward Jesus.
Mk 11:13 in·the·distance having leaves, he·came *toward it*
Mk 14:3 ·back·and·eating, there·came a·woman having an·
Mk 14:41 It·is·enough,·no·more! The hour is·come! Behold,
Mk 15:43 Joseph came, the·one of Arimathaea, a·dignified
Jud 1:14 Yahweh came with a·myriad·tens·of·thousands of·
1Ti 1:15 Anointed-One Jesus came into the world to·save
Rv 5:7 And he·came and has·taken the official·scroll out of·
Rv 6:17 the GREAT DAY of·his WRATH is·come, and who
Rv 8:3 And another angel came and stood·still at the
Rv 11:18 are·angered, and your WRATH came, and·also the
Rv 14:7 hour of·his Tribunal·judgment did·come! And fall·
Rv 14:15 reap, because the hour is·come for·you to·reap,
Rv 17:1 And there·came one from·among the seven angels,
Rv 17:10 *and* the other did·not·yet come; and whenever he·
Rv 18:10 in one hour your Tribunal·judgment came.'
Rv 19:7 the Wedding of·the Lamb did·come and his wife
Rv 21:9 And there·came to me one of·the seven angels (of·

G2064.1 V-2AAI-3P ἦλθον (40x)

Jn 1:39 "Come and see." They·came and saw where he·
Jn 3:26 And they·came to John and declared to·him, "Rabbi,
Jn 4:27 And his disciples came upon this, and they·marveled
Jn 4:40 *just* as·soon·as the Samaritans came toward him,
Jn 6:24 embarked into the sailboats and came to CaperNaum,
Jn 7:45 So·then the assistants came to the chief·priests and
Jn 10:8 All the·many·which came before me are Thieves and
Jn 10:41 And many came to him and were·saying, "John, in·
Jn 12:9 there. And they·did·not come on·account·of Jesus
Jn 19:32 the *Roman* soldiers came and in·fact broke·apart
Jn 21:8 And the other disciples came in·the small·boat,
Lk 1:59 eighth day, *that* they·came to·circumcise the little·
Lk 2:16 And they·came with·haste and diligently·found both
Lk 3:12 Then tax·collectors also came to·be·immersed, and
Lk 4:42 were·seeking him, and they·came unto him and
Lk 5:7 to·assist them. And they·came and filled both the
Lk 6:17 of·Tyre and Tsidon, who came to·hear him and to·
Lk 8:35 to·see what·was·happening. And they·came to Jesus
Lk 24:1 deep *below·the·horizon*, they·came to the tomb,
Lk 24:23 not finding his body, they·came, saying also *that*
Ac 8:36 down the roadway, they·came to some water.
Ac 11:12 these six brothers also came together with·me,
Ac 12:10 and second watch-station, they·came to the iron
Ac 13:13 the·ones in·company·with *him*) came to Perga in·
Ac 14:24 going·throughout Pisidia, they·came to PamPhylia.
Ac 15:30 ·fact, after·being·dismissed, they·came to Antioch
Ac 17:1 and Apollonia, they·came to ThessaloNica where
Ac 17:13 in Berea by Paul, they·came there·also, stirring·up
Ac 21:8 ·with Paul, going·forth, came to Caesarea. And
Gal 2:12 But when they·came, he·was·shrinking·back and
Mt 7:25 descended, and the flood·waters came, and the
Mt 7:27 descended, and the flood·waters came, and the
Mt 14:34 And crossing·over, they·came into the land of·
Mt 21:1 they·drew·near to JeruSalem and came to BethPhage
Mk 3:8 he·was·doing, a·large multitude came to him.
Mk 5:1 And they·came·over to the other·side of·the sea, into
Mk 6:29 disciples hearing *of·it*, they·came and took·away
Mk 6:53 And crossing·over, they·came to the land of·
Mk 14:16 his disciples went·forth and came into the City,
Rv 7:13 ·robes? And from·what·source did·they·come?"

G2064.1 V-2AAM-2S ἐλθέ (4x)

Jn 4:16 ·out, holler·out·for your husband, and come here."
Mt 14:29 And he·declared, "Come." And after·stepping·
Rv 22:17 and the Bride say, "Come!" And the·one hearing,
Rv 22:17 hearing, let·him·declare, "Come!" And the·one

G2064.1 V-2AAM-3S ἐλθέτω (4x)

Lk 11:2 let·it·be·made·holy! Your kingdom come. Your will
Mt 6:10 Your kingdom come. Your will be·done— as in
Mt 10:13 should·be worthy, *let* yeur peace come upon it, but
Rv 22:17 And the·one thirsting, let·him·come! And the·one

G2064.1 V-2AAN ἐλθεῖν (45x)

Jn 5:40 "And yeu·do·not want to·come to me, in·order·that
Jn 6:44 Not·even·one·man is·able to·come to me, unless the
Jn 6:65 to·yeu that not·even·one·man is·able to·come to me,
Jn 7:34 I AM, *there* yeu·yeurselves are·not able to·come."
Jn 7:36 I AM, *there* yeu·yeurselves are·not able to·come'?
Jn 8:21 I·myself head·on·out, yeu are·not able to·come."
Jn 8:22 I·myself head·on·out, yeu are·not able to·come.'"
Jn 13:33 head·on·out, yeu are·not able to·come,' so·also do·
Lk 7:7 did·I·consider my·own·self deserving to·come to you,
Lk 9:23 "If any·man wants to·come right·behind me, he·
Lk 14:20 and on·account·of that, I·am·not able to·come.'
Lk 17:1 *for* the scandalous·traps not to·come, but woe *to·him*
Ac 2:20 the great and conspicuous Day of·Yahweh coming.
Ac 8:40 ·news in·all the cities, until he came to Caesarea.
Ac 19:1 uppermost districts *of·Macedonia*, came to Ephesus.
Ac 19:27 occupation is·in·danger of·coming into discredit,
Ac 22:30 their joint·council·of·Sanhedrin to·come. And·then
Gal 2:12 For prior·to certain·men coming from Jacob, he·
Gal 3:23 the trust *was* to·come, we·were·dutifully·kept under
Mt 13:32 ·for the birds of·the sky to·come and to·nest on its
Mt 14:28 yourself, commandingly·order me to·come to you
Mt 16:24 "If any·man wants to·come right·behind me, he·
Mt 17:10 say that it·is·mandatory·for EliJah to·come first?
Mt 18:7 *for* scandalous·traps to·come! Nevertheless, woe to·
Mt 19:14 and do·not forbid them to·come to me, for of·such
Mt 22:3 ·banquet, yet they·were·not willing to·come.
Mt 24:48 'My lord is·delayed in·coming *back*,'
Mk 8:34 "Whoever wants to·come right·behind me, let·
Mk 9:11 say that it·is·mandatory·for EliJah to·come first?
Rm 1:10 I·shall·prosper by the will of·God to·come to yeu.
Rm 1:13 many·times I·personally·determined to·come to yeu
Rm 15:22 also, I·was·hindered often *from* coming to yeu.
Rm 15:23 ·yearning for these·many years to·come to yeu,
1Th 2:18 Therefore we·wanted to·come to yeu, in·fact I Paul
Tit 3:12 or Tychicus, quickly·endeavor to·come to me to
2Co 1:15 I·was·definitely·willing to·come to yeu
2Co 1:16 yeu into Macedonia, and to·come again from
2Co 2:1 this for·my·own·self, not again to·come to yeu in
2Co 12:14 I·am at·the·ready *for* a·third·time to·come to yeu,
1Ti 2:4 ·clay† to·be·saved and to·come to a·full·knowledge
1Ti 3:14 I·write to·you, expecting to·come to you more·
2Ti 3:7 ·yet never·even being·able to·come to a·recognition
2Ti 4:9 Quickly·endeavor to·come to me promptly,
2Ti 4:21 Quickly·endeavor to·come before winter. EuBulus
2Jn 1:12 and ink, but·rather I·expect to·come to yeu, and to·

G2064.1 V-2AAP-ASM ἐλθόντα (1x)

2Co 12:21 *And* lest, after·coming again, my God may·

G2064.1 V-2AAP-APM ἐλθόντας (1x)

Lk 5:7 other sailboat *that·was* already·coming to·assist them.

G2064.1 V-2AAP-DSM ἐλθόντι (3x)

Mt 8:28 And with·him coming to the other·side into the
Mt 9:28 And after·coming into the home, the blind·men
Mt 21:23 And with·him coming into the Sanctuary·Atrium

G2064.1 V-2AAP-GSF ἐλθούσης (2x)

Gal 3:25 But with·the Trust coming, we·are no·longer under
Rm 7:9 but with·the commandment coming, Moral·Failure

G2064.1 V-2AAP-GSM ἐλθόντος (3x)

Lk 12:36 in·order·that *with·him* coming and knocking, they·
Ac 25:23 ·day, with·AgrIppa and BerNiki coming with much
1Th 3:6 at·this·moment, with·TimoThy coming from yeu to

G2064.1 V-2AAP-GPM ἐλθόντων (3x)

Mt 17:14 And with·them coming to the crowd, a·certain·
Mt 17:24 And with·them coming to CaperNaum, the·ones
2Co 7:5 For even with·us coming into Macedonia, our flesh

G2064.1 V-2AAP-NSN ἐλθόν (1x)

Mt 12:44 I·came·out;' and upon·coming *to·it*, it·finds *it*

G2064.1 V-2AAP-NSF ἐλθοῦσα (5x)

Mt 15:25 But coming *anyway*, she·was·falling·prostrate to·
Mk 5:26 being·beneficial, but·yet *with·her* coming rather to
Mk 5:27 ·hearing about Jesus *and* already·coming in the
Mk 7:25 an·impure spirit, upon·coming, she·fell·down
Mk 12:42 And upon·coming, a·certain helplessly·poor

G2064.1 V-2AAP-NSM ἐλθών (45x)

Jn 4:54 ·sign *that* Jesus did, coming from·out of·Judea into
Jn 7:50 NicoDemus (the·one coming alongside *Jesus* by·
Jn 12:12 ·day, a·large crowd (the·one coming to the feast *in·*
Jn 16:8 "And upon·coming *to·yeu*, that·one shall·convict the
Jn 19:39 came also, the·one coming at·the first to Jesus by·
Jn 20:8 disciple entered also, the·one coming first to the
Lk 7:3 asking him to·come that he·may·thoroughly·save his
Lk 10:32 happening by the place, coming and seeing *him*,
Lk 12:37 whom the lord, upon·coming, shall·find keeping·
Lk 12:43 whom his lord, upon·coming, shall·find doing in·
Lk 14:9 you and him, upon·coming shall·declare to·you,
Lk 15:6 And coming to the house, he·calls·together the
Lk 15:17 "Then coming to himself, he·declared, 'How·
Lk 18:8 of·Clay·Man†, upon·coming·*back*, shall·he·find
Lk 19:23 the bank, that at·my·coming, I·myself might·have
Lk 22:45 ·up from the prayer *and* coming to the disciples,
Ac 21:11 And after·coming to us and taking·up Paul's belt,
Ac 22:13 after·coming to me and standing·over *me*, he·
Mt 2:8 *it* to·me, that upon·coming, I·also may·fall·prostrate
Mt 2:23 And after·coming *there*, he·resided in a·city being·
Mt 4:13 ·leaving Natsareth behind *and* coming *into Galilee*,
Mt 5:24 to·your brother, and then coming, offer your present

Mt 8:2 And behold, a·leper, after·coming *toward·him*, was·
Mt 8:14 And YeShua, upon·coming into Peter's home, saw
Mt 9:18 behold, a·ruler, after·coming *to·YeShua*, was·
Mt 9:18 ·died at·this·moment, but·yet coming *with·me*, you·
Mt 9:23 And YeShua, upon·coming into the ruler's home
Mt 13:54 And coming into his·own fatherland, he·was·
Mt 16:13 And YeShua, upon·coming into the district of·
Mt 24:46 whom his lord, upon·coming, shall·find *him*
Mt 25:27 bankers, and *then* upon·coming, I·myself might
Mt 26:43 And coming, he·finds them sleeping again, for
Mk 5:23 ·final·point·of·death. Come *with·me* in·order·that
Mk 9:12 EliJah, in·fact, after·coming first, does·reconstitute
Mk 9:14 And upon·coming to the *other* disciples, he·saw a·
Mk 11:13 anything on it. And after·coming to it, he·found
Mk 13:36 lest upon·coming suddenly he·should·find yeu
Mk 14:45 And upon·coming *and* immediately going·toward
Php 1:27 , in·order·that whether coming and seeing yeu or·
1Co 2:1 And·I, brothers, already·coming to yeu, came not
2Co 2:3 this same·thing to·yeu, lest coming *to·yeu*, I·should·
2Co 2:12 Now after·coming to Troas for the good·news of·
2Co 12:20 I·fear, lest·somehow after·coming, I·should·find
Eph 2:17 And coming, he·proclaimed 'peace to·yeu, the·
1Jn 5:6 This is the·one coming through water and blood,

G2064.1 V-2AAP-NPM ἐλθόντες (19x)
Jn 11:45 the Judeans, the·ones coming alongside Mary and
Jn 19:33 But coming to Jesus, as·soon·as they·saw him even·
Ac 16:7 Coming adjacent·to Mysia, they·were·attempting to·
Ac 16:37 For no *way*, but·rather coming *here* themselves,
Ac 16:39 And coming, they·implored them, and after·
Mt 2:11 And coming into the home, they·found the little·
Mt 9:10 *were* coming. They·were·reclining·together·at·the·
Mt 14:33 ·ones in the sailboat, after·coming *alongside*, fell·
Mt 16:5 And after·coming to the other·side *of·the sea*, his
Mt 18:31 tremendously grieved, and coming to·their lord,
Mt 20:9 And upon·coming *forward*, the·ones *hired* about the
Mt 20:10 But the first·ones *hired*, upon·coming *forward*,
Mt 27:33 Then coming to a·place being·referred·to·as
Mt 27:64 lest his disciples, coming by·night, should·steal
Mt 28:11 some of·the sentinel·guard, after·coming into the
Mt 28:13 'His disciples stole him, coming by·night with·us
Mk 7:1 alongside him, after·coming from JeruSalem.
Mk 12:14 And upon·coming, they·say to·him, "Mentor, we·
2Co 11:9 to·me, the brothers coming from Macedonia

G2064.1 V-2AAS-1S ἔλθω (7x)
Rm 15:32 in·order·that I·may·come toward yeu with joy
1Co 4:21 What·do yeu·want? Should·I·come toward yeu
1Co 11:34 And as·soon·as I·may·come, I·shall·thoroughly·
1Co 14:6 ·now, brothers, if I·should·come to yeu speaking
1Co 16:2 ·be no contributions whenever I·should·come.
2Co 13:2 the rest— that if I·should·come into the *vicinity*
3Jn 1:10 ·of that, if I·should·come, I·shall·quietly·recollect

G2064.1 V-2AAS-2S ἔλθῃς (1x)
Lk 23:42 me to·mind whenever you·should·come into your

G2064.1 V-2AAS-3S ἔλθῃ (33x)
Jn 4:25 that·one should·come, he·shall·announce·in·detail
Jn 5:43 receive me. If another should·come in his·own name
Jn 7:31 "Whenever the Anointed-One should·come, ¿! shall·
Jn 11:56 that no, he·may·not come to the Sacred·Feast?
Jn 15:26 the Companion/Intercessor should·come, whom I·
Jn 16:4 whenever the hour should·come, yeu·may·remember
Jn 16:13 the Spirit of·Truth, should·come, he·shall·guide
Lk 1:43 that the mother of·my Lord should·come to me?
Lk 8:17 that shall·not be·known and may·come to *be* openly·
Lk 9:26 ·of that·man whenever he·should·come in his·own
Lk 12:38 "And if he·should·come in the second watch, or
Lk 12:38 in the second watch, or should·come in the third
Lk 14:10 ·called·for you should·come, he·may·declare to·
Lk 22:18 until such·time the kingdom of·God should·come."
Gal 3:19 only·until the Seed should·come for·whom *the*
Mt 10:23 ·IsraEl, until the Son of·Clay·Man† should·come.
Mt 21:40 the owner of·the vineyard should·come, what shall·
Mt 23:35 that upon yeu may·come all *the* righteous blood
Mt 25:31 the Son of·Clay·Man† should·come in his glory,
Mk 4:22 hidden·away, other·than that it·may·come to *be*
Mk 8:38 ·ashamed·of him, whenever he·should·come in the
Rm 3:8 ·order·that the beneficially·good·things may·come."
2Th 1:10 whenever he·should·come to·be·glorified in his
2Th 2:3 *·to·stand*, unless there·should·come the Defection
1Co 4:5 season, until the Lord should·come, who also shall·
1Co 11:26 the Lord's death even·until he·should·come.
1Co 13:10 But whenever the complete should·come, then
1Co 16:10 Now if TimoThy should·come, look·out that he·
1Co 16:11 in peace in·order·that he·may·come to me, for I·
1Co 16:12 entreated him in·order·that he·should·come to yeu
1Co 16:12 ·of·*his*·will that he·should·come now, but he·
Col 4:10 commandments; if he·should·come to yeu, accept
Rv 17:10 and whenever he·should·come, it·is·mandatory·for

G2064.1 V-2AAS-3P ἔλθωσιν (4x)
Lk 16:28 lest they·themselves also should·come into this
Ac 3:19 so·that seasons of·refreshing should·come from *the*
Ac 17:15 and TimoThy, that they·should·come to him as
2Co 9:4 if *any* Macedonians should·come together with·me

G2064.1 V-2RAI-1S ἐλήλυθα (7x)
Jn 5:43 "I·myself have·come in my Father's name, and yeu·
Jn 7:28 ·source I·am? Yet I·have·not come of my·own·self,
Jn 8:42 ·from God. For neither have·I·come of my·own·self,
Jn 12:46 "I·myself *being* a·light, have·come into the world,
Jn 16:28 ·from the Father, and have·come into the world.
Jn 18:37 Also to this I·have·come into the world, in·order·
Lk 5:32 I·have·not come to·call righteous·men, but·rather

G2064.1 V-2RAI-2S ἐλήλυθας (2x)
Jn 3:2 "Rabbi, we·have·seen that you·have·come from God,
Ac 21:22 ·together, for they·shall·hear that you·have·come.

G2064.1 V-2RAI-3S ἐλήλυθεν (9x)
Jn 3:19 the verdict, that the Light has·come into the world,
Jn 12:23 saying, "The hour has·come, that the Son of·Clay·
Jn 13:1 personally·knowing that his hour has·come, that he·
Jn 16:32 and now has·come that yeu·should·be·scattered,
Jn 17:1 "Father, the hour has·come. Glorify your Son in·
Lk 7:33 "For John the Immerser has·come neither eating
Lk 7:34 The Son of·Clay·Man† has·come eating and
Mk 9:13 to·yeu that indeed EliJah has·come, and they·did to·
Php 1:12 *which·happened* against me have·come rather for a·

G2064.1 V-2RAP-ASF ἐληλυθυῖαν (1x)
Mk 9:1 ·see the kingdom of·God having·come in power."

G2064.1 V-2RAP-ASM ἐληλυθότα (3x)
Ac 18:2 of·Pontus by·birth, recently having·come from Italy
1Jn 4:2 which affirms Jesus Anointed having·come in flesh
1Jn 4:3 Jesus, the Anointed-One, having·come in flesh is

G2064.1 V-2RAP-NPM ἐληλυθότες (1x)
Lk 5:17 ·down, who were having·come from·out of·every

G2064.1 V-LAI-3S ἐληλύθει (6x)
Jn 6:17 ·had·become dark, and Jesus had·not come to them.
Jn 7:30 his hand on him, because his hour had·not·yet come.
Jn 8:20 him, because his hour had·not·yet come.
Jn 11:30 Now Jesus had·not·yet come into the village, but·
Ac 8:27 her treasury *and* who had·come to JeruSalem to·fall·
Ac 9:21 ·upon this name, and·also had·come here for that

G2064.1 V-LAI-3P ἐληλύθεισαν (1x)
Jn 11:19 from·among the Judeans had·come alongside the

G2064.2 V-PNI-1P ἐρχόμεθα (1x)
Jn 21:3 to·him, "We·ourselves also go together with·you."

G2064.2 V-PNI-3S ἔρχεται (2x)
Jn 11:29 heard *it*, she·is·roused swiftly and goes to him.
Heb 11:8 being·fully·acquainted·with where he·was·going.

G2064.2 V-PNI-3P ἔρχονται (2x)
Mk 3:19 handed him over. Then they·went into a·house.
Mk 16:2 first *day* of·*the*·week, they·went to the chamber·

G2064.2 V-PNP-GSM ἐρχομένου (1x)
Ac 5:15 mats, in·order·that with·Peter going·by, if·even his

G2064.2 V-PNP-NSM ἐρχόμενος (1x)
Lk 15:25 a·field, and as he·was·going·*along*, he·drew·near

G2064.2 V-INI-2S ἤρχου (1x)
Ac 9:17 roadway in·which you·were·going, has·dispatched

G2064.2 V-INI-3P ἤρχοντο (1x)
Jn 6:17 into the sailboat, they·were·going across the sea

G2064.2 V-2AAI-1P ἤλθομεν (2x)
Ac 21:1 ·drawn·away from them, we·went sailing·straight to
Ac 28:14 days. And in·this·manner we·went toward Rome

G2064.2 V-2AAI-3S ἦλθεν (3x)
Lk 3:3 And he·went into all the region·surrounding the
Mt 12:9 And walking·on from·there, he·went into their
Mt 13:36 ·away the crowds, YeShua went *back* into the

G2064.2 V-2AAI-3P ἦλθον (5x)
Jn 4:45 for they·themselves also went to the Sacred·Feast.
Lk 2:44 to·be in the caravan, they·went a·day's journey, then
Ac 4:23 ·fully·released, they·went to their·own·company
Ac 13:51 of·their feet against them, they·went to Iconium.
Mk 1:29 ·forth out of·the gathering, they·went into the home

G2064.2 V-2AAN ἐλθεῖν (2x)
Lk 14:1 And it·happened, with him going into a·house of·a·
Mt 14:29 Peter walked upon the water to·go to YeShua.

G2064.2 V-2AAP-NSN ἐλθόν (1x)
Lk 11:25 And going·forth, it·finds *it* having·been·swept and

G2064.2 V-2AAP-NSM ἐλθών (3x)
Jn 11:17 Now·then, after·going *to·him*, Jesus found him
Mt 2:9 ·going·on·ahead·of them, going·*on* until it·stood·still
Mt 8:7 YeShua says to·him, "After·going *to·him*, I·myself

G2064.2 V-2AAP-NPF ἐλθοῦσαι (1x)
Mk 16:1 aromatic·spices, in·order·that after·going *to·him*,

G2064.2 V-2AAP-NPM ἐλθόντες (1x)
Mt 14:12 and buried it. And going·*on*, they·reported *it* to·

G2064.3 V-PNI-3S ἔρχεται (1x)
Mk 4:21 ·case·that the lantern is·brought *forth* in·order·that

G2065 ἐρωτάω ĕrōtáō *v.* (58x)
Roots:G2046 Compare:G2045 G0154 G3870 G4441

G2065.2 V-FAI-1S ἐρωτήσω (4x)
Jn 14:16 "And I·myself shall·ask·of the Father, and he·shall·
Jn 16:26 ·not say to·yeu that I·myself shall·ask·of the Father
Lk 20:3 to them, "And·I shall·ask·of yeu one question, and
Mt 21:24 to·them, "I·also shall·ask·of yeu one question,

G2065.2 V-FAI-2P ἐρωτήσετε (1x)
Jn 16:23 that day yeu·shall·not ask·of me not·even·one·thing

G2065.2 V-PAI-1S ἐρωτῶ (8x)
Jn 17:9 "I·myself ask concerning them. *It·is* not concerning
Jn 17:9 *It·is* not concerning the world *that* I·ask, but·rather
Jn 17:15 "I·do·not ask that you·should·take them up out·
Jn 17:20 concerning these·men merely do·I·ask, but·rather
Lk 14:18 to·go·out and to·see it. I·ask *that* you have me
Lk 14:19 I·traverse to·test them out. I·ask *that* you have me
Php 4:3 And I·ask·of you also, a·genuine yokefellow, assist
2Jn 1:5 And now I·ask·of you, my·Lady, not as·though I·

G2065.2 V-PAI-1P ἐρωτῶμεν (3x)
1Th 4:1 remaining, brothers: We·ask·of yeu and exhort *yeu*
1Th 5:12 So we·ask·of yeu, brothers, to·personally·know
2Th 2:1 Now we·ask·of yeu, brothers, on·behalf of·the

G2065.2 V-PAI-3S ἐρωτᾷ (2x)
Jn 16:5 me, and not·even·one from·among yeu asks·of me,
Lk 14:32 dispatching a·delegation, he·asks·of the *conditions*

G2065.2 V-PAN ἐρωτᾶν (1x)
Jn 16:19 Jesus knew that they·were·wanting to·ask him, and

G2065.2 V-PAP-GPM ἐρωτώντων (1x)
Ac 18:20 But with·them asking *him* to·abide a·longer time

G2065.2 V-PAP-NSM ἐρωτῶν (1x)
Lk 7:3 of·the Judeans to him, asking him to·come that he·

G2065.2 V-PAP-NPM ἐρωτῶντες (1x)
Jn 8:7 But as they·were·persisting·in asking·of him, after·

G2065.2 V-PAS-3S ἐρωτᾷ (2x)
Jn 16:30 and have no need that any·man should·ask·of you.
Lk 19:31 And if any·man should·ask·of yeu, 'Why do·yeu·

G2065.2 V-IAI-3S ἠρώτα (6x)
Jn 4:47 he·went·off toward him and was·asking·of him that
Lk 7:36 ·certain·one of·the Pharisees was·asking·of him that
Lk 11:37 Pharisee was·asking him in·such·a·manner·so·that
Ac 3:3 was·asking to·receive a·merciful·act·of·charity.
Mt 16:13 of·Caesarea Philippi, was·asking·of his disciples,
Mk 7:26 by·birth, and she·was·asking·of him that he·

G2065.2 V-IAI-3P ἠρώτων (4x)
Jn 4:40 came toward him, they·were·asking him to·abide

Jn 9:15 the Pharisees again also were·asking·of him how he·
Jn 12:21 BethSaida of·Galilee, and were·asking·of him,
Ac 16:39 ·*them*·out, they·were·asking *of·them* to·go·out of·
G2065.2 V-AAI-3S ἠρώτησεν (4x)
Jn 18:19 the designated·high·priest asked Jesus concerning
Jn 19:38 fear of·the Judeans, asked·of Pilate that he·may·
Lk 5:3 was Simon's, *Jesus* asked·of him to·head·off a·little·
Ac 23:18 Paul, the chained·prisoner, asked *me* to·bring this
G2065.2 V-AAI-3P ἠρώτησαν (10x)
Jn 1:21 And they·asked·of him, "So·then, who are you·
Jn 1:25 And they·asked·of him and declared to·him, "So·
Jn 5:12 So·then they·asked·of him, "Who is the man·of·
Jn 9:2 And his disciples asked·of him, saying, "Rabbi, who
Jn 9:19 And they·asked·of them, saying, "Is this yeur son,
Jn 19:31 day), the Judeans asked·of Pilate that their legs
Lk 4:38 ·a·high fever, and they·asked·of him concerning her
Lk 8:37 ·surrounding the Gadarenes asked him to·go·away
Ac 10:48 of·the Lord. Then they·asked him to·stay·over
Mk 4:10 him (together with·the twelve) asked him *about* the
G2065.2 V-AAM-2P ἐρωτήσατε (2x)
Jn 9:21 He·himself is of·mature·age; ask him. He·himself
Jn 9:23 "He·is of·mature·age; ask him."
G2065.2 V-AAN ἐρωτῆσαι (2x)
Lk 9:45 it. And they·were·afraid to·ask him concerning this
Ac 23:20 agreed·among·themselves to·ask·of you that you·
G2065.2 V-AAS-1S ἐρωτήσω (1x)
Lk 22:68 And if also I·should·ask *of·yeu*, no, yeu·may·not
G2065.2 V-AAS-3S ἐρωτήσῃ (1x)
1Jn 5:16 concerning that·thing do·I·say that he·should·ask.
G2065.2 V-AAS-3P ἐρωτήσωσιν (1x)
Jn 1:19 ·out of·JeruSalem in·order·that they·may·ask·of him,
G2065.3 V-PAI-1S ἐρωτῶ (1x)
Lk 16:27 he·declared, 'So·then I·implore·of you, father, that
G2065.3 V-IAI-3P ἠρώτων (2x)
Jn 4:31 the meanwhile, the disciples were·imploring·of him,
Mt 15:23 disciples coming·alongside were·imploring·of him,

G2066 ἐσθής êsthḗs *n.* (11x)

Compare:G2440 See:G0294 G2067
G2066 N-ASF ἐσθῆτα (3x)
Lk 23:11 and arraying him in·splendid clothing, he·sent him
Ac 12:21 ·himself in·royal clothing and sitting·down upon
Jac 2:3 ·one prominently·wearing the splendid clothing, and
G2066 N-DSF ἐσθῆτι (4x)
Ac 1:10 two men had·stood·nearby them in white clothing,
Ac 10:30 stood·still in·the·sight of·me in radiant clothing,
Jac 2:2 *with* a·prominent·gold·ring, in splendid clothing, and
Jac 2:2 ·enter also a·helpless·beggar in filthy clothing,
EG2066 (4x)
Mt 6:31 or, '*with* what *clothing* should·we·be·arrayed?
Mt 25:36 and yeu·arrayed me *with·clothing*. I·was·sick, and
Mt 25:38 ·*you*·in? Or naked, and arrayed *you with·clothing*?
Mt 25:43 and yeu·did·not array me *with·clothing*, sick and

G2067 ἔσθησις ésthēsis *n.* (1x)

Roots:G2066
G2067 N-DPF ἐσθήσεσιν (1x)
Lk 24:4 stood·over them in clothes flashing·like·lightning.

G2068 ἐσθίω êsthíō *v.* (66x)

Compare:G0977 G1089 G2719 G2603-3 See:G5315 xLangEquiv:H0398 A0399
G2068.1 V-PAI-2P ἐσθίετε (2x)
Lk 5:30 saying, "Why do·yeu·eat and drink with tax·
1Co 10:31 So·then whether yeu·eat, or drink, or anything
G2068.1 V-PAI-3S ἐσθίει (10x)
Mt 9:11 "Why·does yeur Mentor eat with the tax·collectors
Mt 15:27 For even the puppies eat from the little·crumbs,
Mk 2:16 disciples, "How·is·it·that he·eats and drinks with
Mk 7:28 the puppies beneath the table eat from the young·
Rm 14:2 but the·one being·weak, eats garden·plants.
Rm 14:6 The·one eating, eats unto·*the*·Lord, for to·God he·
Rm 14:6 eating, unto·*the*·Lord he·does·not eat, and to·God
1Co 9:7 a·vineyard, and does·not eat from·out of·its fruit?
1Co 9:7 a·flock, and does·not eat from·out of·the milk of·
1Co 11:29 drinking in·an·unworthy·manner, eats and drinks
G2068.1 V-PAI-3P ἐσθίουσιν (6x)
Lk 5:33 the·ones of·the Pharisees, but yours eat and drink?
Mk 7:3 rigorously, they·do·not eat, securely·holding·to the
Mk 7:4 ·immerse *their hands*, they·do·not eat. And there·are
Mk 7:5 of·the elders, but·rather eat the bread with·unwashed
1Co 8:7 idol unto this·moment, eat as sacrificing·to·an·idol;
1Co 9:13 working the sacred·things eat from·among the
G2068.1 V-PAM-2P ἐσθίετε (4x)
Lk 10:8 and they·should·accept yeu, eat *such·things as are*
1Co 10:25 being·sold in a·meat·market, eat *it*, scrutinizing
1Co 10:27 to·traverse, eat anything being·placed·before yeu,
1Co 10:28 ·to·idols," do·not eat on·account·of that·one
G2068.1 V-PAM-3S ἐσθιέτω (3x)
2Th 3:10 does·not want to·work, nor·even *then* must·he·eat.
1Co 11:28 and in·this·manner let·him·eat from·out of·the
1Co 11:34 And if any·man is·hungry, let·him·eat at home,
G2068.1 V-PAN ἐσθίειν (6x)
Lk 12:45 and the servant·girls, and to·eat and to·drink and
Ac 27:35 of·them·all, and after·breaking *it*, he·began to·eat.
Mt 12:1 they·also began to·pluck heads·of·grain and to·eat.
Mt 24:49 to·beat the fellow·slaves and to·eat and to·drink
1Co 8:10 to·eat those·things·which·are·sacrificed·to·idols;
1Co 11:22 For do·yeu·not have homes to·eat and to·drink in?
G2068.1 V-PAP-ASM ἐσθίοντα (3x)
Mk 2:16 the Pharisees, upon·seeing him eating with the tax·
Rm 14:3 must·not utterly·disdain the·one not eating; and the·
Rm 14:3 not eating must·not judge the·one eating, for God
G2068.1 V-PAP-APM ἐσθίοντας (1x)
Mk 7:2 some of·his disciples eating bread with·defiled hands
G2068.1 V-PAP-DSM ἐσθίοντι (1x)
Rm 14:20 ·block *to·his brother* on·account·of *his* eating.
G2068.1 V-PAP-GPM ἐσθιόντων (4x)
Mt 26:21 And as·they were·eating, he·declared, "Certainly
Mt 26:26 And as·they were·eating, after·taking the
Mk 14:18 ·they were·reclining·at·the·meal and eating, Jesus
Mk 14:22 And as·they were·eating, after·taking *the*
G2068.1 V-PAP-NSM ἐσθίων (11x)
Lk 7:33 the Immerser has·come neither eating bread nor
Lk 7:34 Son of·Clay·Man† has·come eating and drinking,
Mt 11:18 For John came neither eating nor drinking, and
Mt 11:19 The Son of·Clay·Man† came eating and drinking,
Mk 1:6 his loins, and *was* eating locusts and wild honey.
Mk 14:18 that one from·among yeu, the·one eating with me,
Rm 14:3 The·one eating must·not utterly·disdain the·one not
Rm 14:3 and the·one not eating must·not judge the·one
Rm 14:6 earnestly·regard *it*. The·one eating, eats unto·*the*·
Rm 14:6 and the·one not eating, unto·*the*·Lord he·does·not
1Co 11:29 For the·one eating and drinking in·an·unworthy·
G2068.1 V-PAP-NPM ἐσθίοντες (4x)
Lk 10:7 in the same home, eating and drinking the·things
Mt 14:21 And the·ones eating were about five·thousand men,
Mt 15:38 And the·ones eating were four·thousand men,
1Co 10:18 Are not·indeed the·ones eating of·the sacrifices,
G2068.1 V-PAS-2P ἐσθίητε (2x)
Lk 22:30 in·order·that yeu·may·eat and may·drink at my
1Co 11:26 For as·often·as yeu·should·eat this bread, and
G2068.1 V-PAS-3S ἐσθίῃ (1x)
1Co 11:27 As·such, whoever should·eat this bread or
G2068.1 V-PAS-3P ἐσθίωσιν (2x)
Mt 15:2 wash their hands whenever they·should·eat bread."
2Th 3:12 while·working, they·should·eat their·own bread.
G2068.1 V-IAI-3P ἤσθιον (4x)
Lk 6:1 ·of·grain, and they·were·eating by·rubbing *them* in·
Lk 15:16 carob-pods that the pigs were·eating, yet not·even·
Lk 17:27 They·were·eating, they·were·drinking, they·were·
Lk 17:28 days of·Lot: they·were·eating, they·were·drinking,
EG2068.1 (1x)
1Co 10:17 participate·and·belong *by·eating* from·out of·the
G2068.2 V-PAN ἐσθίειν (1x)
Heb 10:27 ·*is* about 'to·devour the·ones sternly·opposed.'

G2069 Ἐσλί Êslí *n/p.* (1x)

Roots:H0454
G2069 N/P-PRI Ἐσλί (1x)
Lk 3:25 *son* of·Nachum, *son* of·Esli, *son* of·Naggai,

G2070 ἐσμέν êsmén *v.* (53x)

Roots:G1510
G2070.1 V-PXI-1P ἐσμέν (52x)
Jn 8:33 They·answered him, "We·are AbRaham's offspring†,
Jn 9:28 disciple, but we·ourselves are Moses' disciples.
Jn 9:40 ·declared to·him, "¿! Are we·ourselves also blind?
Jn 10:30 I·myself and the Father are one."
Jn 17:22 they·may·be one, just·as we·ourselves are one,
Lk 9:12 find provision·of·food, because we·are here in a·
Lk 17:10 yeu also must·say, 'We·are useless slaves, because
Ac 2:32 this Jesus, of·which we·ourselves all are witnesses.
Ac 3:15 dead·men, to·which we·ourselves are witnesses.
Ac 5:32 And we·ourselves are his witnesses of·these
Ac 10:39 "And we·ourselves are witnesses of·all·the·things
Ac 14:15 ·ourselves also are men·of·clay† of·like·passions
Ac 16:28 not·one·bit·of harm, for we·are absolutely·all here
Ac 17:28 poets have·declared, 'For we·are also *his* kindred.
Ac 23:15 before he shall·draw·near, are ready to·eliminate
Heb 3:6 his·own house, of·whose house are we·ourselves—
Heb 4:2 even we·are having·been·brought·the·good·news,
Heb 10:10 will, we·are the·ones having·been·made·holy
Heb 10:39 we·ourselves are not of·one·who·shrinks·back to
Gal 3:25 with·the Trust coming, we·are no·longer under a·
Gal 4:28 according·to YiTsaq, are children of·promise.
Gal 4:31 So, brothers, we·are not children of·a·maidservant
Mk 5:9 "My name *is* Legion, because we·are many."
Rm 6:15 Shall·we·morally·fail, because we·are not under
Rm 8:12 accordingly brothers, we·are under·an·obligation,
Rm 8:16 ·testifies with·our spirit that we·are children of·God
Rm 12:5 in·this·manner, we (the many) are one Body in
Rm 14:8 or·also whether we·should·die, we·are the Lord's.
Php 3:3 For we·ourselves are the Circumcision, the·ones
1Th 5:5 and the·Sons of·Day. We·are not of·night nor·even
1Co 3:9 For we·are coworkers with·God; yeu·are God's
1Co 10:17 *though being* the many, we·are one bread *and*
1Co 10:22 Lord to·jealousy? ¿! Are·we stronger·than he?
1Co 15:19 If we·are merely having·placed·our·expectation
1Co 15:19 in Anointed-One, we·are of·all men·of·clay†
2Co 1:14 us in part, that we·are yeur boasting, exactly·as
2Co 1:24 yeur trust, but·rather are coworkers of·yeur joy—
2Co 2:15 Because we·are to·God a·sweet·scent of·
2Co 2:17 For we·are not as the many, shortchanging·and·
2Co 3:5 Not that we·are sufficient by ourselves to·reckon
2Co 10:11 this, "Such·as we·are in·word through *our* letters
2Co 13:6 ·shall·know that we·ourselves are not disqualified.
Eph 2:10 For we·are a·product of·him, already·being·created
Eph 4:25 ' because we·are members of·one·another.
Eph 5:30 because we·are members of·his Body, from·out of·
1Jn 2:5 In this, we·do·know that we·are in him.
1Jn 3:2 Beloved, now we·are children of·God, and it·is·not·
1Jn 3:19 by this we·know that we·are birthed·from·out of·the
1Jn 4:6 We·ourselves are birthed·from·out of·God. The·one
1Jn 4:17 just·as that·one is, so·also are we·ourselves in this
1Jn 5:19 ·know that we·are birthed·from·out of·God, and the
1Jn 5:20 the·one *who·is* true, and we·are in the·one *who·is*
G2070.2 V-PXI-1P ἐσμέν (1x)
Ac 17:28 we live and are·stirred and have·existence. As also

G2071 ἔσομαι ésômai *v.* (190x)

ἔσῃ ésēi [2nd person]
ἔσται éstai [3rd person]
ἐσόμεθα êsómêtha [1st plural]
ἔσεσθε ésesthê [2nd plural]
ἔσονται ésôntai [3rd plural]

Roots:G1510 See:G2071-1 G2071-2
(abbreviated listing for G2071)
EG2071 (3x)
(list for EG2071: excluded)
G2071.1 V-FXI-1S ἔσομαι (13x)
(list for G2071.1:V-FXI-1S excluded)
G2071.2 V-FXI-2S ἔσῃ (9x)
(list for G2071.2:V-FXI-2S excluded)

G2071.3 V-FXI-3S ἔσται (120x)
(list for G2071.3:V-FXI-3S excluded)
G2071.4 V-FXI-1P ἐσόμεθα (4x)
(list for G2071.4:V-FXI-1P excluded)
G2071.5 V-FXI-2P ἔσεσθε (10x)
(list for G2071.5:V-FXI-2P excluded)
G2071.6 -- (1x)
(list for G2071.6:-- excluded)
G2071.6 V-FXI-3P ἔσονται (30x)
(list for G2071.6:V-FXI-3P excluded)

G2071-1 ἔσεσθαι ésêsthai *v.* (5x)
Roots:G2071 Compare:G1511 See:G2071-2
G2071-1.1 V-FXN ἔσεσθαι (2x)
Ac 11:28 the Spirit *that* there·was·about to·be a·great famine
Ac 23:30 the man, *which·was* about to·be *carried·out* by the
G2071-1.2 V-FXN ἔσεσθαι (3x)
Ac 24:15 there·shall·be a·resurrection of·dead·men, both
Ac 24:25 and the impending judgment *that* shall·be, Felix,
Ac 27:10 that the impending voyage shall·be with a·battering

G2071-2 ἐσόμενος ěsómênôs *v.* (1x)
ἐσόμενα ěsómêna [plural neuter]
Roots:G2071 Compare:G5607 See:G2071-1
G2071-2.2 V-FXP-ASN ἐσόμενον (1x)
Lk 22:49 upon·seeing the·thing *that* shall·be, they·declared

G2072 ἔσ•οπτρον ésôptrôn *n.* (2x)
Roots:G1519 G3700 Compare:G2734 G5194 G4610-1
G2072.1 N-DSN ἐσόπτρῳ (1x)
Jac 1:23 ·observing his natural face in a·reflected·image.
G2072.1 N-GSN ἐσόπτρου (1x)
1Co 13:12 through a·reflected·image with an·obscured·view,

G2073 ἑσπέρα hêspéra *n.* (3x)
Compare:G3796 G3798 See:G5610
G2073 N-NSF ἑσπέρα (1x)
Ac 4:3 for the next·day, for even·now it·was evening.
G2073 N-ASF ἑσπέραν (1x)
Lk 24:29 with us, because it·is toward evening, and the day
G2073 N-GSF ἑσπέρας (1x)
Ac 28:23 ·Moses and the prophets, from dawn until evening.

G2074 Ἐσρώμ Êsrṓm *n/p.* (3x)
חֶצְרוֹן cHętsrôn [Hebrew]
Roots:H2696
G2074.2 N/P-PRI Ἐσρώμ (3x)
Lk 3:33 *son* of·Ram, *son* of·Chetsron, *son* of·Perets, *son* of·
Mt 1:3 , and Perets begot Chetsron, and Chetsron begot
Mt 1:3 and Perets begot Chetsron, and Chetsron begot Ram.

G2075 ἐστέ ěstě́ *v.* (95x)
Roots:G1510
G2075.1 V-PXI-2P ἐστέ (91x)
Jn 8:23 "Yeu·yeurselves are birthed·from down·below; I·
Jn 8:23 up·above. Yeu·yeurselves are from·among this
Jn 8:31 in my Redemptive-word, yeu·are truly my disciples;
Jn 8:37 ·personally·know that yeu·are AbRaham's offspring†,
Jn 8:44 "Yeu·yeurselves are birthed·from·out *of·yeur* father
Jn 8:47 ·not hear *them* because yeu·are not birthed·from·out
Jn 10:26 do·not trust, for yeu·are not from·among my sheep,
Jn 10:34 "I·myself declared, "Yeu·are gods""?
Jn 13:10 ·is altogether pure. And yeu are pure, but·yet not·
Jn 13:11 ·of that, he·declared, "Yeu·are not·indeed all pure.
Jn 13:17 supremely·blessed are·yeu if yeu·should·do them.
Jn 13:35 everyone shall·know that yeu·are disciples to·me,
Jn 15:3 "Even·now yeu are trimmed·and·pure through the
Jn 15:14 Yeu·yeurselves are my friends, if yeu·should·do as·
Jn 15:19 ·favor its·own, but yeu·are not from·among the
Jn 15:27 yeu also do·testify, because yeu·are with me from
Lk 6:22 "Supremely·blessed are·yeu, whenever the men·of·
Lk 9:55 personally·know of·what·manner of·spirit yeu are.
Lk 11:44 O·stage·acting·hypocrites! Because yeu·are as the
Lk 13:25 personally·know yeu. From·what·source are·yeu?"
Lk 13:27 ·know yeu. From·what·source are·yeu? Withdraw
Lk 16:15 "Yeu·yeurselves are the·ones regarding yeur·
Lk 22:28 "Yeu·yeurselves are the·ones having·remained·
Lk 24:17 while·walking·along, and *why* are·yeu sullen?
Lk 24:38 to·them, "Why are·yeu having·been·troubled?
Lk 24:48 "And yeu·yeurselves are witnesses of·these·things.
Ac 3:25 "Yeu·yeurselves are the·Sons of·the prophets, and
Ac 7:26 'Men, yeu·yeurselves are brothers; for·what·
Ac 19:15 Paul I·am·fully·acquainted·with, but who are yeu?
Ac 22:3 ·being a·zealot of·God, just·as yeu all are this·day.
Heb 12:8 But if yeu·are completely·apart·from corrective·
Heb 12:8 , then·by·inference, yeu·are bastards and not
Gal 3:3 In·this·manner, are·yeu stupid?
Gal 3:26 For yeu·are all the·Sons of·God through the trust in
Gal 3:28 and female, for yeu are all one in Anointed-One
Gal 3:29 then·by·inference, yeu·are of·AbRaham's Seed
Gal 4:6 And because yeu·are sons, God dispatched·forth the
Gal 5:18 But if yeu·are·led by·Spirit, yeu·are not under
Mt 5:11 "Supremely·blessed are·yeu whenever *men* should·
Mt 5:13 "Yeu·yeurselves are the salt of·the earth, but if the
Mt 5:14 "Yeu·yeurselves are the light of·the world.
Mt 8:26 to·them, "Why are·yeu timid, O·yeu·of·little·trust?
Mt 10:20 For yeu·yeurselves are not the·ones speaking, but·
Mt 15:16 YeShua declared, "Are yeu also still·at·this·point
Mt 23:8 *that·is* the Anointed-One, and yeu all are brothers.
Mt 23:28 inwardly yeu·are exceedingly·full of·stage·acting·
Mt 23:31 ·yeurselves that yeu·are the·Sons of·the·ones
Mk 4:40 to·them, "Why are·yeu timid in·this·manner?
Mk 7:18 to·them, "So, are yeu·yeurselves also without·
Mk 9:41 in my name, because yeu·are of·Anointed-One,
Rm 1:6 whom also yeu·yeurselves are *the* called·forth·ones
Rm 6:14 lord·over yeu, for yeu·are not under Torah-Law,
Rm 6:16 ·not personally·know that yeu·are slaves to·whom
Rm 8:9 But yeu are not in flesh, but·rather in Spirit, if·
Rm 15:14 also are exceedingly·full of·beneficial·goodness,
1Th 2:20 For yeu are our glory and joy.
1Th 4:9 for yeu yeurselves are instructed·by·God to love
1Th 5:4 But yeu, brothers, are not in darkness, in·order·that
1Th 5:5 Yeu·yeurselves are all the·Sons of·Light and the·
1Co 1:30 ·from·out of *God*, yeu are in Anointed-One Jesus,
1Co 3:3 for yeu·are yet fleshly. For where *there·is* among
1Co 3:3 strife, and dissensions, are·yeu not·indeed fleshly,
1Co 3:4 "I *am* of·Apollos," are·yeu not·indeed fleshly?
1Co 3:9 coworkers with·God; yeu·are God's cultivated·soil,
1Co 3:16 ·not personally·know that yeu·are a·temple of·God
1Co 3:17 of·God is holy, which *temple* yeu·yeurselves are.
1Co 4:8 Even·now yeu·are having·been·stuffed·full·to·.
1Co 5:2 And yeu are having·been·puffed·up, and did·not·
1Co 5:7 lump·of·dough, just·as *indeed* yeu·are unleavened.
1Co 6:2 is·judged by yeu, are·yeu unworthy of·the·smallest
1Co 6:19 yeu·have from God, and yeu·are not yeur·own?
1Co 9:1 Anointed our Lord? Are yeu·yeurselves not my
1Co 9:2 to·yeu, for yeu·yeurselves are the official·seal of·
1Co 12:27 Now yeu·yeurselves are Anointed-One's Body
1Co 14:12 yeu·yeurselves. Since yeu·are zealots of·spiritual
1Co 15:17 yeur trust *is* futile— yeu·are still in yeur moral·
2Co 1:7 having·seen that just·as yeu·are partners of·the
2Co 2:9 ·character, whether yeu·are attentively·obedient in
2Co 3:2 Yeu·yeurselves are our letter having·been·engraved
2Co 3:3 ·apparent that yeu·are a·letter of·Anointed-One
2Co 6:16 For yeu·yeurselves are a·temple of·the·living
2Co 7:3 for I·have·already·stated that yeu·are in our hearts
2Co 13:5 Try yeurselves, whether yeu·are in the trust.
2Co 13:5 is in yeu, except·that yeu·are disqualified?
Eph 2:5 (by·grace, yeu·are having·been·saved).
Eph 2:8 For by·the grace, yeu·are having·been·saved
Eph 2:19 ·then, consequently, yeu·are no·longer foreigners
Eph 5:5 For yeu·are knowing this·thing, that every sexually·
Col 2:10 And yeu·are in him, having·been·completely·
1Jn 2:14 to·yeu, young·men, because yeu·are strong, and
1Jn 4:4 Yeu·yeurselves are birthed·from·out of·God, dear·
EG2075.1 (3x)
Rm 6:16 in attentive·obedience? *Yeu·are slaves* to·whom
Eph 2:19 but·rather *yeu·are* fellow-citizens with the·holy·
Eph 2:19 ·the holy·ones and *are* family·members of·God,
G2075.2 V-PXI-2P ἐστέ (1x)
Mk 13:11 that speak, for it·is not yeu·yeurselves speaking,

G2076 ἐστί ěstí *v.* (922x)
ἐστίν ěstín
Roots:G1510 Compare:G5225
G2076.1 V-PXI ἐστίν (4x)
Mk 7:2 with·defiled hands, that is, with·unwashed *hands*,
Rm 10:6 heaven?" (that is, to·bring Anointed-One down),
Rm 10:7 ·pit?"" (that is, to·bring Anointed-One up from·
Rm 10:8 in your heart" (that is, the utterance of·the trust
G2076.1 V-PXI-3S ἐστίν (809x)
Jn 1:19 Now this is the testimony of·John, when the Judeans
Jn 1:27 it·is he (the·one who·is·coming right·behind me
Jn 1:30 This is·he concerning whom I·myself declared,
Jn 1:33 upon him, the·same is the·one immersing in Holy
Jn 1:34 and have·testified, that this is the Son of·God.
Jn 1:41 ·interpreted *from·Hebrew*, is the Anointed-One.
Jn 1:47 Truly an·Israelite in whom there·is no guile!"
Jn 3:6 having·been·born from·out of·the flesh is flesh; and
Jn 3:6 ·one having·been·born from·out of·the Spirit is spirit.
Jn 3:8 *So·also*, in·this·manner, is any one having·been·born
Jn 3:19 "And this is the verdict, that the Light has·come into
Jn 3:29 "The·one having the bride is a·bridegroom. But the
Jn 3:31 "The·one who·is·coming from·above is up·above all.
Jn 3:31 being birthed·from·out of·the earth is from·out of·the
Jn 3:31 ·is·coming from·out of·the heaven is up·above all.
Jn 3:33 testimony did·stamp·his·own·seal that God is true.
Jn 4:10 ·present of·God, and who is the·one saying to·you,
Jn 4:11 ·for·drawing·water, and the well is deep. So·then
Jn 4:18 and now, he·whom you·have is not your husband.
Jn 4:20 yeu say, that in JeruSalem is the place where it·is·
Jn 4:22 because the Salvation is from·out of·the Jews.
Jn 4:23 "But·yet an·hour comes, and now is, when the true
Jn 4:34 says to·them, "My food is that I·may·do the will of·
Jn 4:37 For in this *case*, the saying is true, 'One is the·one
Jn 4:37 saying is true, 'One is the·one sowing, and another
Jn 4:42 and we·personally·know that this is truly the Savior
Jn 5:2 Sheep·Gate in JeruSalem, there·is a·pool having five
Jn 5:10 ·been·both·relieved·and·cured, "It·is a·Sabbath. It·
Jn 5:12 they·asked·of him, "Who is the man·of·clay†, the·
Jn 5:25 an·hour is·coming, and now is, when the dead·ones
Jn 5:27 Tribunal·judgment, because he·is a·son of·clay†.
Jn 5:30 And my verdict is righteous, because I·do·not seek
Jn 5:31 my·own·self, my testimony is not legally·valid.
Jn 5:32 There·is another, the·one testifying concerning me,
Jn 5:32 which he·testifies concerning me is legally·valid.
Jn 5:45 the Father. "There·is the·one legally·accusing yeu,
Jn 6:9 "There·is a little·boy here, who has five barley loaves·
Jn 6:14 ·of·clay† were·saying, "This is truly the Prophet,
Jn 6:29 and declared to·them, "This is the work of·God, that
Jn 6:31 in the wilderness, just·as it·is having·been·written, '
Jn 6:33 for the bread of·God is the·one descending from·out
Jn 6:39 "And this is the Father's will, the·one sending me,
Jn 6:40 And this is the will of·the·one sending me, that
Jn 6:42 And they·were·saying, "Is this not Jesus, the son of·
Jn 6:45 "It·is having·been·written in the prophets, "And
Jn 6:50 This is the bread, the·one descending out of·the
Jn 6:51 the bread that I·myself shall·give is my flesh, which
Jn 6:55 For my flesh truly is a·full·meal, and my blood truly
Jn 6:55 is a·full·meal, and my blood truly is a·full·drink.
Jn 6:58 "This is the bread, the·one descending out of·the
Jn 6:60 *this*, declared, "This is a·hard saying; who is·able
Jn 6:63 The Spirit is the·one giving·life·above. The flesh
Jn 6:70 the twelve, yet one from·among yeu is a·slanderer."
Jn 7:6 is·not·yet here, but yeur season is always ready.
Jn 7:11 Sacred·Feast and were·saying, "Where is that·man?
Jn 7:12 they·were·saying, "He·is a·beneficially·good·man,"
Jn 7:16 and declared, "My instruction is not mine, but·rather
Jn 7:17 the instruction, whether it·is from·out of·God, or
Jn 7:18 of·the·one sending him, the·same·man is true, and
Jn 7:18 ·man is true, and unrighteousness is not in him.
Jn 7:22 the circumcision (not that it·is from·out of·Moses,
Jn 7:25 of·JeruSalem were·saying, "Is this not he·whom

Jn 7:26 truly do·know that this truly is the Anointed-One.
Jn 7:27 ·know this·man, *and* from·what·source he·is. Now
Jn 7:27 not·even·one·man knows from·what·source he·is."
Jn 7:28 but·rather the·one sending me is true, whom yeu·
Jn 7:36 What *manner·of* saying is this that he·declared,
Jn 7:40 the crowd were·saying, "Truly this is the Prophet."
Jn 7:41 Others were·saying, "This is the Anointed-One."
Jn 8:13 yourself; your testimony is not legally·valid."
Jn 8:14 my·own·self, my testimony is true, because I·
Jn 8:16 I·myself should·judge, my verdict is true, because I·
Jn 8:17 the testimony of·two men·of·clay† is legally·valid.
Jn 8:19 they·were·saying to·him, "Where is your Father?
Jn 8:26 But·yet the·one sending me is true, and·I say to the
Jn 8:29 And the·one sending me is with me. The Father did·
Jn 8:34 the moral·failure is a·slave of·Moral·Failure.
Jn 8:39 and declared to·him, "AbRaham is our father." Jesus
Jn 8:44 stand in the truth, because there·is not truth in him.
Jn 8:44 of·his·own *disposition*, because he·is a·liar and the
Jn 8:50 seek my·own glory; there·is One presently·seeking
Jn 8:54 glorify my·own·self, my glory is nothing·at·all. It·is
Jn 8:54 my glory is nothing·at·all. It·is my Father *that·is* the·
Jn 8:54 of·whom yeu·yeurselves say that he·is yeur God.
Jn 9:4 of·the·one sending me, for·as·long·as it·is day. Night
Jn 9:8 blind) were·saying, "Is this not the·one who·was·
Jn 9:9 Some were·saying, "This is·he." But others *were·*
Jn 9:9 But others *were·saying*, "He·is like him." *But* that·
Jn 9:12 So·then they·declared to·him, "Where is this·man?
Jn 9:16 "This man·of·clay† is not personally·from God,
Jn 9:17 And he·declared, "He·is a·prophet!"
Jn 9:19 they·asked·of them, saying, "Is this yeur son, who
Jn 9:20 "We·personally·know that this is our son, and that
Jn 9:24 ·know that this man·of·clay† is full·of·moral·failure.
Jn 9:25 declared, "Whether he·is full·of·moral·failure, I·do·
Jn 9:29 we·do·not personally·know from·what·source he·is."
Jn 9:30 "For in this is a·marvelous·thing, that yeu·yeurselves
Jn 9:30 personally·know from·what·source he·is, and·yet he·
Jn 9:36 and declared, "Who is·he, Lord, in·order·that I·may·
Jn 9:37 ·clearly·seen him, and it·is the·same·one speaking
Jn 10:1 ·up from·some·other·way, that·one is a·Thief and a·
Jn 10:2 entering·in through the door is shepherd of·the sheep
Jn 10:13 hired·worker flees, because he·is a·hired·worker,
Jn 10:29 who has·given *them* to·me, is greater·than all; and
Jn 10:34 answered them, "Is·it not having·been·written in
Jn 11:4 declared, "This sickness is not toward death, but·
Jn 11:10 night, he·stumbles, because the light is not in him.
Jn 11:39 even·now he·smells·bad, for it·is *the* fourth·day."
Jn 11:57 where he·is, he·should·bring·it·to·*their*·attention,
Jn 12:14 sat·down on it, just·as it·is having·been·written,
Jn 12:31 "There·is now a·Tribunal·judgment of·this world.
Jn 12:34 to·be·elevated'? "Who is this Son of·Clay·Man†?
Jn 12:35 "Yet a·short time is the light with yeu.
Jn 12:50 ·know that his commandment is eternal life-above.
Jn 13:10 the feet. Moreover, he·is altogether pure. And yeu
Jn 13:16 I·say to·yeu, a·slave is not greater·than his lord;
Jn 13:25 "Lord, who is·it?"
Jn 13:26 Jesus answered, "It·is that·man to·whom I·shall·
Jn 14:10 I·myself *am* in the Father, and the Father is in me?
Jn 14:21 ·keeping them, that is the·one presently·loving me.
Jn 14:24 the Redemptive-word which yeu·hear is not mine,
Jn 14:28 the Father,' because my Father is greater·than me.
Jn 15:1 "I AM the true vine, and my Father is the farmer.
Jn 15:12 "This is my commandment, that yeu·should·love
Jn 15:20 declared to·yeu, 'A·slave is not greater·than his
Jn 16:17 among one·another, "What is this that he·says to·us
Jn 16:18 they·were·saying, "What is this·thing that he·says,
Jn 16:32 ·yet I·am not alone, because the Father is with me.
Jn 17:3 "And this is the eternal life-above, that they·may·
Jn 17:17 holy in your truth. Your Redemptive-word is truth.
Jn 18:36 answered, "My kingdom is not from·among this
Jn 18:36 So now my kingdom is not from·here."
Jn 18:38 Pilate says to·him, "What is truth?
Jn 18:39 "Now it·is a·custom for·yeu that I·should·fully·
Jn 19:35 ·testified, and his testimony is true; this·one·also
Jn 19:40 the aromatic·spices, just·as is *the* manner for·the
Jn 20:15 ·woman, presuming that he·is the garden·keeper,
Jn 20:31 ·that yeu·may·trust that Jesus is the Anointed-One,
Jn 21:7 Jesus loved says to·Peter, "It·is the Lord." Now·then
Jn 21:20 "Lord, who is the·one handing you over?
Jn 21:24 This is the disciple, the·one testifying concerning
Jn 21:24 and we·personally·know that his testimony is true.
Lk 1:36 in her old·age, and this is *the* sixth lunar·month *of·*
Lk 1:61 to her, "There·is not·even·one among your kinsfolk
Lk 1:63 he·wrote, saying, "His name is John." And they·all
Lk 2:11 is·reproduced·and·birthed who is *the* Anointed-One,
Lk 4:22 And·also they·were·saying, "Is not this Joseph's son
Lk 4:24 that not·even·one prophet is acceptable in his·own
Lk 5:21 saying, "Who is this who speaks revilements·of·
Lk 5:23 Which is easier, to·declare, 'Your moral·failures
Lk 5:34 to·fast, while the bridegroom is with them?
Lk 5:39 ·new *wine*, for he·says, 'The old is finer *wine*.'"
Lk 6:5 "The Son of·Clay·Man† is Lord also of·the Sabbath.
Lk 6:20 helplessly·poor, because yeurs is the kingdom of·
Lk 6:32 ·ones loving yeu, what·kind·of grace is·it to·yeu?
Lk 6:33 ·doing·good to·yeu, what·kind·of grace is·it to·yeu?
Lk 6:34 to·receive·in·full, what·kind·of grace is·it yeu?
Lk 6:35 of·the Most·High, because he·himself is kind to the
Lk 6:36 just·as yeur Father also is compassionate.
Lk 6:40 "A·disciple is not above his instructor, but everyone
Lk 6:43 "For a·good tree is not producing rotten fruit, neither
Lk 6:47 doing them, I·shall·indicate to·yeu what he·is like.
Lk 6:48 "He·is like a·man·of·clay† building a·home, who
Lk 6:49 and not doing, is like a·man·of·clay† building a·
Lk 7:4 saying, "He·is worthy for·whom this shall·be·
Lk 7:23 And supremely·blessed is·he who should·not be·
Lk 7:27 This is *he*, concerning whom it·has·been·written, "
Lk 7:28 those·born of·women there·is not·even·one prophet
Lk 7:28 least·one in the kingdom of·God is greater·than he."
Lk 7:39 ·hold of·him, because she·is full·of·moral·failure."
Lk 7:49 within themselves, "Who is this that also forgives
Lk 8:11 "Now the parable is this: The scattering·of·seed is
Lk 8:11 The scattering·of·seed is the Redemptive-word of·
Lk 8:17 "For there·is not *anything* hidden, that shall·not
Lk 8:25 And he·declared to·them, "Where is yeur trust?
Lk 8:25 "What *manner·of man* is this?
Lk 8:26 Gadarenes, which is on·the·opposite·side of·Galilee
Lk 8:30 Jesus inquired·of him, saying, "What is your name?
Lk 9:9 beheaded John, but who is this, concerning whom I·
Lk 9:33 to Jesus, "O·Captain, it·is good for·us to·be here,
Lk 9:35 ·the thick·cloud, saying, "This is my beloved Son.
Lk 9:38 ·look upon my son, because he·is my only·child.
Lk 9:50 "Do·not forbid *him*, for whoever is not against us is
Lk 9:50 for whoever is not against us is on·behalf of·us."
Lk 9:62 to the·things left·behind, is well-suited for the
Lk 10:7 them, for the workman is worthy of·his payment·of·
Lk 10:22 ·even·one·man knows who the Son is, except the
Lk 10:22 the Father, and who the Father is, except the Son,
Lk 10:29 declared to Jesus, "And who is my neighbor?
Lk 10:42 But one·thing is needed, and Mary selected the
Lk 11:23 "The·one not being with me is against me, and the·
Lk 11:29 to·say, "This is an·evil generation. It·seeks·for a·
Lk 11:34 "The lantern of·the body is the eye. Accordingly,
Lk 11:34 ·focused, your whole body is also full·of·light; but
Lk 11:35 *that* the light, the·one in you, is not darkness.
Lk 12:1 of the leaven of·the Pharisees, which is hypocrisy.
Lk 12:2 "For there·is not·even·one·thing having·been·
Lk 12:6 ·among them is having·been·forgotten in·the·sight
Lk 12:15 of·one's holdings *does* anyone's life† itself *exist*."
Lk 12:23 "The soul is more·than the physical·nourishment,
Lk 12:34 "For where yeur treasure is, there also yeur heart
Lk 12:42 declared, "Who then is the trustworthy and prudent
Lk 13:18 he·was·saying, "To·what is the kingdom of·God
Lk 13:19 "It·is like a·kernel of·mustard·seed, which a·man·
Lk 13:21 It·is like leaven, which a·woman took *and*
Lk 14:22 as you·ordered, and yet there·is place *for·more*.'
Lk 14:31 first *and* takes·counsel whether he·is able with ten
Lk 14:35 It·is neither well-suited for soil, nor·even for
Lk 16:10 trustworthy with very·little is also trustworthy with
Lk 16:10 unrighteous with very·little is also unrighteous with
Lk 16:15 among men·of·clay† is an·abomination in·the·sight
Lk 16:17 But it·is easier·for the heaven and the earth to·pass·
Lk 17:1 to the disciples, "It·is not·permissible *for* the
Lk 17:21 the kingdom of·God is on·the·inside of·yeu."
Lk 18:16 forbid them, for of·such is the kingdom of·God.
Lk 18:25 "For it·is easier *for* a·camel to·enter·in through a·
Lk 18:29 I·say to·yeu, there·is not·even·one·man that left
Lk 19:9 because·indeed he·himself also is a·son of·AbRaham
Lk 19:46 ·been·written, "My house is a·house of·prayer,"
Lk 20:2 ·you·do these·things? Or who is the·one giving you
Lk 20:14 themselves, saying, 'This is the heir. Come·here!
Lk 20:17 "So·then, what is this having·been·written, "*The*
Lk 20:38 So he·is not a·God of·dead·men, but·rather of·
Lk 20:44 'Lord'; how is·he also his Son?
Lk 21:30 ·selves that the summer is even·now near·at·hand.
Lk 21:31 also know that the kingdom of·God is near·at·hand.
Lk 22:11 says to·you, "Where is the local·travel·lodge,
Lk 22:19 saying, "This is my body, the·one being·given
Lk 22:38 And he·declared to·them, "It·is sufficient."
Lk 22:53 "But·yet this is yeur hour, and the jurisdiction of·
Lk 22:59 ·man also was with him, for he·is also a·Galilean."
Lk 22:64 "Prophesy, who is the·one striking you?
Lk 23:7 after·realizing that he·is from·out·of·HerOd·AntiPas'
Lk 23:15 worthy of·death is having·been·practiced by·him.
Lk 23:35 ·save himself— if this·man is the Anointed-One,
Lk 23:38 and Hebrew: "THIS IS THE KING OF·THE
Lk 24:6 He·is not here, but·rather is·awakened.
Lk 24:29 "Abide with us, because it·is toward evening, and
Ac 1:7 he·declared to them, "It·is not for·yeu to·know times
Ac 1:12 ·called Olive·Orchard, which is near JeruSalem,
Ac 2:15 drunk as yeu assume, for it·is *but the* third hour of·
Ac 2:16 But·rather this is the·thing having·been·declared
Ac 2:25 of·me continually, because he·is at my right·hand
Ac 2:29 and buried, and his tomb is with us even·unto this
Ac 2:39 For the promise is for·yeu, and for·yeur children,
Ac 4:11 This is "the stone being·disdainfully·rejected by
Ac 4:12 And the Salvation is not in not·even·one other.
Ac 4:12 in not·even·one other. For there·is not·even another
Ac 4:19 to them, "Whether it·is right in·the·sight of·God to·
Ac 4:36 ·interpreted *from·Aramaic*, is Son of·Consoling),
Ac 5:39 But if it·is birthed·from·out·of God, yeu·are·not able
Ac 6:2 disciples, declared, "This·is not satisfactory to·us:
Ac 7:33 feet, for the place in which you·stand is holy soil.'
Ac 7:37 "This Moses is the·one declaring to·the Sons of·
Ac 7:38 "This *Moses* is the·one already·coming among the
Ac 8:10 saying, "This·man is the great power of·God.
Ac 8:21 There·is not a·portion nor·even a·small·chance for·
Ac 8:21 matter, for your heart is not straight in·the·sight of·
Ac 8:26 (This is a·wilderness).
Ac 9:15 "Traverse! Because this·man is my vessel of·
Ac 9:20 in the gatherings, *saying*, "This is the Son of·God!"
Ac 9:21 ·astonished and were·saying, "Is this not the·one
Ac 9:22 conclusively·proving that this is the Anointed-One.
Ac 10:4 becoming alarmed, he·declared, "What is·it, Lord?
Ac 10:6 Simon a·tanner, whose home is directly·by *the* sea.
Ac 10:28 ·with how it·is a·statutory·offense for·a·man that·
Ac 10:34 In truth, I·grasp that God is not one·who·is·partial,
Ac 10:35 who·is·working righteousness is acceptable to·him.
Ac 10:36 through Jesus Anointed— This·one is Lord of·all.
Ac 10:42 and to·thoroughly·testify that it·is he, the·one
Ac 12:15 But they·were·saying, "It·is his angel."
Ac 13:15 "Men, brothers, if there·is within yeu a·word of·
Ac 16:12 ·there to PhilIppi, which is a·foremost city of·the
Ac 17:3 I·myself fully·proclaim to·yeu) is the Anointed-One
Ac 18:15 But since it·is an·issue concerning a·word and
Ac 19:2 we·did·not·even hear whether there·is a·Holy Spirit.
Ac 19:25 ·aware that our prosperity is as·a·result of·this
Ac 19:35 for what man·of·clay† is·there that does·not know
Ac 20:10 Do·not be·in·a·commotion, for his soul is in him."
Ac 20:35 he·himself declared, 'It·is more supremely·blessed
Ac 21:22 Now·then, why is *this*?

Ac 21:28 swiftly·help! This is the man·of·clay† instructing
Ac 22:26 ·about to·do, for this man·of·clay† is a·Roman."
Ac 23:5 seen, brothers, that he·is *the* designated·high·priest,
Ac 23:19 was·inquiring, "What is·it that you·have to·
Ac 25:5 legally·accuse this man, if there·is any *wrong* in
Ac 25:11 decline to·die. But if there·is no *validity* at·all to·
Ac 25:14 saying, "There·is a·certain man having·been·left·
Ac 25:16 To whom I·answered, 'It·is not *the* manner of·the·
Ac 28:4 ·another, "This man·of·clay† is entirely a·murderer,
Ac 28:22 as·concerning this sect, it·is known to·us that
Heb 2:6 saying, "What is mortal·man†, that you·are·
Heb 4:13 And there·is not a·creature *that·is* not·completely·
Heb 5:13 of·righteousness— for he·is *still* an·infant.
Heb 5:14 But the solid nourishment is *for* the completely·
Heb 7:2 "King of·Salem," which is, King of·Peace.
Heb 7:15 And furthermore, it·is excessively fully·obvious, if
Heb 8:6 ·superb public·service, by·as·much·as he·is also *the*
Heb 9:5 concerning which, now is not *the time for·us* to·
Heb 9:15 And on·account·of this, he·is *the* mediator of·a·
Heb 11:1 Now trust is a·firm·assurance of·things·being·
Heb 11:6 ·is·coming·alongside God to·trust that he·is, and
Heb 12:7 sons, for what son is·he whom a·father does·not
Gal 1:7 which is not *actually* another *good·news at·all*.
Gal 1:11 the·one being·proclaimed by me is not according·to
Gal 3:12 And the Torah-Law is not as·a·result of·trust, but·
Gal 3:16 And to·your single·seed," which is Anointed-One.
Gal 3:20 Now the mediator is not *a·mediator* of·one *party*,
Gal 3:20 is not *a·mediator* of·one *party*, but God is one.
Gal 4:1 heir, for·a·span·of time (as·long·as he·is an·infant),
Gal 4:2 but·rather is under executive·guardians and estate·
Gal 4:24 bearing·children for slavery, which is Hagar.
Gal 4:25 For *this* Hagar is Mount Sinai in Arabia, and
Gal 4:26 But the JeruSalem up·above is free, which is *the*
Gal 4:26 up·above is free, which is *the* mother of·us all.
Gal 5:3 ·circumcised, that he·is under·an·obligation to·do all
Gal 5:22 But the fruit of·the Spirit is love, joy, peace,
Gal 5:23 self-restraint— against such·things there·is no law.
Mt 1:20 ·being·conceived in her is birthed·from·out of·Holy
Mt 1:23 when·being·interpreted *from·Hebrew*, is "God
Mt 2:2 "Where is the·one being·reproduced·and·born King
Mt 3:3 For this is·he, the·one being·uttered *of* by IsaIah the
Mt 3:11 who·is·coming right·behind me is stronger·than me,
Mt 3:15 ·moment, for in·this·manner it·is befitting·for us to·
Mt 3:17 ·the heavens, saying, "This is my beloved Son, in
Mt 5:3 in·the spirit, because theirs is the kingdom of·the
Mt 5:10 righteousness, because theirs is the kingdom of·the
Mt 5:34 neither by the heaven, because it·is God's throne,
Mt 5:35 nor by the earth, because it·is his foot stool, nor
Mt 5:35 nor toward JeruSalem, because it·is *the* City of·the
Mt 5:37 in·excess of·these·things is birthed·from·out of·the
Mt 5:48 yeur Father, the·one in the heavens, is complete.
Mt 6:13 the Evil·One, because yours is the kingdom, and the
Mt 6:21 For where yeur treasure is, there also yeur heart
Mt 6:22 "The lantern of·the body is the eye. Accordingly, if
Mt 6:23 light, the·one in you, is darkness, how·dense *is* the
Mt 6:25 yeu·should·dress·yeurselves. Is not·indeed the soul
Mt 7:9 "Or what man·of·clay† is·there from·among yeu, who
Mt 7:12 ·this·manner to·them, for this is the Torah-Law and
Mt 8:27 "What·manner·of *clay·being* is this that even the
Mt 9:5 For which is easier?
Mt 9:15 to·mourn, as·long·as the bridegroom is with them?
Mt 10:10 for the workman is deserving of·his provision·of·
Mt 10:11 verify·by·inquiring who in it is worthy, and·there
Mt 10:24 "A·disciple is not above the instructor, nor·even a·
Mt 10:26 For there·is not·even·one·thing having·been·
Mt 10:37 father or mother over me is not worthy of·me, and
Mt 10:37 son or daughter over me is not worthy of·me.
Mt 10:38 follow right·behind me, he·is not worthy of·me.
Mt 11:6 And he·is supremely·blessed, whoever *he·is*, if he·
Mt 11:10 For this is·he, concerning whom it·has·been·
Mt 11:11 in the kingdom of·the heavens is greater·than he.
Mt 11:14 yeu·want to·accept *it*, he·himself is EliJah, the·one
Mt 11:16 shall·I·liken this generation? It·is like little·boys
Mt 11:30 For my yoke *is* kind, and my load is lightweight."
Mt 12:6 one·greater·than the Sanctuary·Courtyard is here.
Mt 12:8 For the Son of·Clay·Man† is Lord even of·the
Mt 12:30 "The·one not being with me is against me, and the·
Mt 12:48 *this* to·him, he·declared, "Who is my mother?
Mt 12:50 in *the* heavens, *the* same is my brother, and sister,
Mt 13:19 This·person is the·one already·being·permeated·
Mt 13:20 the rocky·places, this·person is the·one hearing the
Mt 13:21 in himself, but·rather he·is just·for·a·season, and
Mt 13:22 the thorns, this·person is the·one hearing the
Mt 13:23 the good soil, this·person is the·one hearing the
Mt 13:31 "The kingdom of·the heavens is like a·kernel of·
Mt 13:32 which in·fact is smaller·than all the variety·of·
Mt 13:32 whenever it·should·be·grown, it·is bigger·than the
Mt 13:33 "The kingdom of·the heavens is like leaven, which
Mt 13:37 sowing the good seed is the Son of·Clay·Man†.
Mt 13:38 Now the field is the world, and the good seed,
Mt 13:39 enemy, the·one sowing them, is the Slanderer.
Mt 13:39 The harvest is *the* entire·completion of·the age, and
Mt 13:44 the kingdom of·the heavens is like treasure having·
Mt 13:45 the kingdom of·the heavens is like a·man·of·clay†,
Mt 13:47 the kingdom of·the heavens is like a·dragnet after·
Mt 13:52 the kingdom of·the heavens is like a·man·of·clay†,
Mt 13:55 ¿!·Is this not the carpenter's son?
Mt 13:57 to·them, "A·prophet is not without·honor, except
Mt 14:2 to·his servant·boys, "This is John the Immerser; he·
Mt 14:15 him, saying, "The place is desolate, and the hour
Mt 14:26 were·troubled, saying, "It·is a·phantom!" and
Mt 15:26 answering, he·declared, "It·is not good to·take the
Mt 16:20 ·declare to·no·one that he·himself is YeShua, the
Mt 17:4 to·YeShua, "Lord, it·is good for·us to·be here.
Mt 17:5 saying, "This is my beloved Son, in whom I·take·
Mt 18:1 saying, "Who then is greater in the kingdom of·the
Mt 18:4 as this little·child, this·one is the·one *who·is* greater
Mt 18:7 due·to its scandalous·traps, for it·is a·necessity *for*
Mt 18:8 and cast *it* from you. It·is good for·you to·enter into
Mt 18:9 *it* from you. "It·is better for·you to·enter into the
Mt 18:14 in *the* heavens, it·is not a·determination·of·*his*·will
Mt 19:10 ·charge of·the man·of·clay† is in·this·manner with
Mt 19:14 to me, for of·such is the kingdom of·the heavens.
Mt 19:24 And again I·say to·yeu, it·is easier *for* a·camel to·
Mt 19:26 "With men·of·clay† this is impossible, but with
Mt 20:1 the kingdom of·the heavens is like a·man·of·clay†,
Mt 20:15 I·should·want with my things? Is your eye evil,
Mt 20:23 at my right·hand and at my left is not mine to·give,
Mt 21:10 all the City was·shaken, saying, "Who is this?
Mt 21:11 crowds were·saying, "This is YeShua the prophet,
Mt 21:38 among themselves, 'This is the heir. Come·here!
Mt 21:42 directly·from Yahweh, and it·is marvelous in our
Mt 22:8 'In·fact the wedding is ready, but the·ones having·
Mt 22:32 God of·Jacob'"? God is not the God of·dead·men,
Mt 22:38 This is *the* foremost and greatest commandment.
Mt 22:42 the Anointed-One? Whose son is·he?" They·say
Mt 22:45 'Lord,' how is·he his Son?
Mt 23:8 'Rabbi,' for one is yeur Preeminent·Leader, *that·is*
Mt 23:9 upon the earth, for one is yeur Father, the·one in the
Mt 23:10 ·leaders, for one is yeur Preeminent·Leader, *that·is*
Mt 23:16 "by the Temple," it·is nothing·at·all, but whoever
Mt 23:17 and blind·men! For which is greater, the gold, or
Mt 23:18 by the Sacrifice·Altar, it·is nothing·at·all, but
Mt 24:6 *these·things* to·happen, but·still the end is not·yet.
Mt 24:26 ·declare to·yeu, 'Behold, he·is in the wilderness,'
Mt 24:33 these·things, yeu·must·know that he·is near upon
Mt 24:45 "Who then is the trustworthy and prudent slave
Mt 26:18 Mentor says, "My season is near·at·hand. I·do the
Mt 26:26 "Take, eat! This is my body."
Mt 26:28 for this is my blood, the·one of·the brand-new
Mt 26:38 ·them, "My soul is exceedingly·grieved unto death
Mt 26:39 "O·my Father, if it·is possible, let this cup pass·
Mt 26:48 "Whomever I·should·kiss, that·is him. Securely·
Mt 26:66 they·declared, "He·is held·liable of·death."
Mt 26:68 ·us, O·Anointed-One, who is the·one striking you
Mt 27:6 the Temple·Treasury, since it·is *the* price of·blood.
Mt 27:33 ·to·as GolGotha, that is being·referred·to·as, *the*
Mt 27:37 having·been·written, "THIS IS YESHUA, THE
Mt 27:42 able to·save himself. If he·is King of·IsraEl, let·
Mt 27:62 on·the next·day, which is after the preparation·day
Mt 28:6 He·is not here, for he·is·awakened, just·as he·
Mk 1:27 ·discuss among themselves, saying, "What is this?
Mk 2:9 Which is easier to·declare to·the paralyzed·man,
Mk 2:19 able to·fast, while the bridegroom is with them?
Mk 2:28 As·such, the Son of·Clay·Man† is Lord also of·the
Mk 3:17 a·name: BoanErges, which is, "Sons of·Thunder;"
Mk 3:29 coming·age, but·rather he·is held·liable of·eternal
Mk 3:33 them, saying, "Who is my mother, or my brothers?
Mk 3:35 ·do the will of·God, this·one is my brother, and my
Mk 4:22 For there·is not anything hidden, which should·not
Mk 4:26 he·was·saying, "In·this·manner is the kingdom of·
Mk 4:41 to one·another, "Who then is this, that even the
Mk 5:41 ·being·interpreted *from·Aramaic*, is "Young·girl,
Mk 6:3 Is this not the carpenter, the son of·Mariam, and a·
Mk 6:4 to·them, "A·prophet is not without·honor, except in
Mk 6:15 Others were·saying, "It·is EliJah." And others
Mk 6:15 And others were·saying, "It·is a·prophet, or as one
Mk 6:16 *of·him*, he·declared, "This is John, whom I·myself
Mk 6:35 say, "The place is desolate, and even·now *it·is* a·
Mk 6:55 ·ill, *to* wherever they·were·hearing, "There he·is."
Mk 7:11 whatever *it·should·be*, that·thing is *now* Qorban,
Mk 7:15 There·is not·even·one·thing from·outside of·the
Mk 7:27 the children to·be·stuffed·full. For it·is not good to·
Mk 7:34 Ephphatha," which is, "Be·thoroughly·opened·up.
Mk 9:5 says to·Jesus, "Rabbi, it·is good for·us to·be here.
Mk 9:7 ·the thick·cloud, saying, "This is my beloved Son.
Mk 9:39 forbid him, for there·is not·even·one who shall·do
Mk 9:40 For whoever is not against yeu is on·behalf of·yeu.
Mk 9:40 For whoever is not against yeu is on·behalf of·yeu.
Mk 9:42 ·ones trusting in me, it·is even·much better for·him
Mk 9:43 you, chop it off. It·is better for·you to·enter into
Mk 9:45 you, chop it off. It·is better for·you to·enter lame
Mk 9:47 you, cast it out. It·is better for·you to·enter into the
Mk 10:14 forbid them, for of·such is the kingdom of·God.
Mk 10:24 exceedingly·difficult it·is for·the·ones having·
Mk 10:25 "It·is easier for·a·camel to·enter through the tiny·
Mk 10:29 "Certainly I·say to·yeu, there·is not·even·one that
Mk 10:40 at my right·hand and at my left is not mine to·give,
Mk 12:7 among themselves, 'This is the heir! Come·here!
Mk 12:11 directly·from Yahweh, and it·is marvelous in our
Mk 12:27 He·is not the God of·dead·men, but·rather a·God
Mk 12:28 him, "Which commandment is foremost of·all?
Mk 12:29 O·IsraEl: Yahweh our God, Yahweh is one.
Mk 12:31 as yourself." There·is no other commandment
Mk 12:32 in truth, because "there·is one God, and there·is
Mk 12:32 there·is one God, and there·is not another besides
Mk 12:33 one's neighbor as himself, is more·than all the
Mk 12:35 say that the Anointed-One is a·Son of·David?
Mk 12:37 'Lord,' so from·what·source is his Son?
Mk 12:42 ·poor widow cast·in two bits, which is a·quadran.
Mk 13:28 the leaves, yeu·know that the summer is near.
Mk 13:29 happening, yeu·must·know that he·is near upon
Mk 13:33 yeu·do·not personally·know when the season is.
Mk 14:14 says, "Where is the local·travel·lodge where I·
Mk 14:22 "Take, eat! This is my body."
Mk 14:24 he·declared to·them, "This is my blood, the·one
Mk 14:34 "My soul is exceedingly·grieved unto death.
Mk 14:44 Whomever I·should·kiss, it·is him. Securely·hold
Mk 14:69 standing·nearby, "This·man is from·among them.
Mk 15:16 inside the courtyard, which is *the* Praetorian·hall.
Mk 15:22 when·being·interpreted *from·Hebrew*, is *the* Place
Mk 15:34 when·being·interpreted *from·Aramaic*, is "My
Mk 15:42 it·was preparation·day (that is, *a·day* before·a·
Mk 16:6 ·been·crucified. He·was·awakened. He·is not here.
Rm 1:9 For God is my witness, to·whom I·ritually·minister
Rm 1:12 that is, to·be·comforted·together among yeu
Rm 1:16 of·the Anointed-One, for it·is God's power to
Rm 1:19 *which·is* known of·God, it·is apparent among them,
Rm 1:25 creating *it* (*the·one* who is blessed into the ages.

Rm 2:2 ·seen that the judgment of·God is according·to truth
Rm 2:11 For there·is no partiality with God.
Rm 2:28 *of·vigilantly·keeping Torah-Law* that·is a·Jew,
Rm 3:8 Of·such·men, the judgment is just.
Rm 3:10 ·as it·has·been·written: "There·is none righteous,"
Rm 3:11 "There·is not one comprehending; there·is not one
Rm 3:11 not one comprehending; there·is not one seeking·
Rm 3:12 ·time, they·are·made·useless; there·is none doing
Rm 3:12 doing benevolent·kindness; there·is not so·much·as
Rm 3:18 "There·is no fear of·God fully·before their eyes.
Rm 3:22 all the·ones trusting, for there·is no distinction.
Rm 4:15 accomplishes wrath (for where there·is no law,
Rm 4:16 ·out of·AbRaham's trust, who is father of·us all
Rm 5:14 of·Adam's violation, who is a·figure of·the·one
Rm 7:3 But if the husband should·die, she·is freed from the
Rm 7:14 we·personally·know that the Torah-Law is spiritual,
Rm 8:9 ·not have Anointed-One's Spirit, this·one is not his.
Rm 8:24 being·looked·upon is not an·expectation, for what
Rm 8:34 also, being·awakened, who is even at *the* right·
Rm 9:2 that my grief is a·great and unceasing distress in·my
Rm 10:1 petition to God on·behalf of·IsraEl is for Salvation.
Rm 10:8 ·does it·say? "The utterance is near you, *even* in
Rm 10:12 For there·is no distinction between Jew and Greek
Rm 11:6 *it·is* as·a·result of·works, *then* it·is no·longer grace,
Rm 11:6 grace, otherwise the work is no·longer work.
Rm 11:23 they·shall·be·grafted·in, for God is able to·engraft
Rm 13:1 authorities. For there·is no authority except from
Rm 13:4 For he·is an·attendant of·God to·you in the
Rm 13:4 he·bears the sword, for he·is an·attendant of·God,
Rm 14:4 he·shall·be·established, for God is able to·establish
Rm 14:17 For the kingdom of·God is not *about* feeding and
Rm 14:23 that *is* not from·out of·trust is moral·failure.
Rm 16:5 Epaenetus, who is a·firstfruit of·Achaia to
Jac 1:13 God," for God is not·tempted with·moral·wrongs,
Jac 1:17 and every complete endowment is from·above,
Jac 1:23 Because if any is a·hearer of·*the*·Redemptive-word,
Jac 1:27 — pure and uncontaminated religion is this: to·visit
Jac 2:17 ·that it·should·have no works, is dead by itself.
Jac 2:19 You·yourself trust that there·is one God. You·do
Jac 2:20 trust, completely·apart·from the works, is dead?
Jac 2:26 the body apart·from spirit is dead, in·this·manner
Jac 2:26 also, the trust apart·from the works is dead.
Jac 3:5 Even in·this·manner, the tongue is a·small member,
Jac 3:15 This wisdom is not *that* which·is·coming·down
Jac 3:17 But the wisdom *that·is* from·above is first, in·fact,
Jac 4:4 that the friendship of·the world is hostility with·God?
Jac 4:12 There·is the one lawmaker, the·one being·able to·
Jac 4:14 *is* yeur life†? For it·is a·vapor, one·appearing just·
Jac 4:16 All such boasting is evil.
Jac 4:17 to·do and not doing *it*, to·him it·is moral·failure.
Jac 5:11 of·Yahweh, that Yahweh is very·empathetic and
Php 1:7 just·as it·is right for·me to·contemplate this on·
Php 1:8 For God is my witness, how I·greatly·yearn·after
Php 1:28 — which in·fact is an·indicator of·total·destruction
Php 2:13 For it·is God *who·is* the·one operating in yeu both
1Pe 1:6 ·bit at·this·moment (though it·is being·necessary) in
1Pe 1:25 ' And this is the utterance, the good·news·already·
1Pe 2:15 Because in·this·manner, it·is the will of·God, *by*
1Pe 3:4 spirit, which is extremely·precious in·the·sight of·
1Pe 3:22 traversing into heaven, is at *the* right·hand of·God
1Pe 4:11 YeShua Anointed, to·whom is the glory and the
2Pe 1:9 these *qualities* are·not present, he·is blind, being·
2Pe 1:14 the putting·away of·my bodily·tabernacle is abrupt,
2Pe 1:17 the magnificent glory, "This is my beloved Son, in
2Pe 3:4 and saying, "Where is the promise of·his returning·
1Th 2:13 of·men·of·clay†, but·rather just·as it·is truly,
1Th 4:3 For this is God's will, yeur renewed·holiness: for·
2Th 1:3 yeu, brothers, just·as it·is appropriate, because yeur
2Th 2:4 Temple of·God,' exhibiting himself that he·is God.
2Th 2:9 ·*One*, whose arrival is according·to an·operation of·
2Th 3:3 But trustworthy is the Lord, who shall·firmly·
2Th 3:17 by·my·own hand, which is a·signature in every
Tit 1:6 if any·man is without·any·charge·of·wrong·doing, a·
Tit 1:13 This testimony is true. On·account·of which cause,
1Co 1:18 (the·one of·the cross) is foolishness, in·fact, to·
1Co 1:18 but to·us who·are·being·saved, it·is the power of·
1Co 1:25 because the foolishness of·God is wiser·than the
1Co 1:25 and the weakness of·God is stronger·than the
1Co 3:5 So·then, who is Paul, and who *is* Apollos, other
1Co 3:7 As·such, neither is the·one planting anything, nor
1Co 3:11 than the·one being·laid·out, which is Jesus the
1Co 3:13 ·and·prove each·man's work for·what·type it·is.
1Co 3:17 For the temple of·God is holy, which *temple* yeu·
1Co 3:19 the wisdom of·this world is foolishness with God.
1Co 3:22 or things·about·to·come— all *of·it* is yeurs,
1Co 4:3 But with·me it·is a·very·small·thing that I·should·
1Co 4:4 But the·one scrutinizing me is *the* Lord.
1Co 4:17 I·sent to·yeu TimoThy, who is my beloved child,
1Co 6:5 In·this·manner, is·there not a·wise·man among
1Co 6:7 in·fact, even·now there·is altogether a·deterioration
1Co 6:16 being·tightly·joined to·the prostitute is one body?
1Co 6:17 ·one being·tightly·joined to·the Lord is one spirit.
1Co 6:18 ·clay† should·commit *it*, is on·the·outside of·the
1Co 6:19 personally·know that yeur body is a·temple of·the
1Co 7:8 unmarried and to·the widows, it·is good for·them if
1Co 7:9 ·must·marry. For it·is significantly·better to·marry
1Co 7:19 The circumcision is nothing·at·all, and the
1Co 7:19 ·all, and the uncircumcision is nothing·at·all, but·
1Co 7:22 *though being* a·slave, he·is *the* Lord's freedman,
1Co 7:22 *though being* free, is slave of·Anointed-One.
1Co 7:29 in·order·that *with* the *time which* is remaining …
1Co 7:39 ·rest·*(that·is,·deceased)*, she·is free to·be·married
1Co 7:40 But she·is supremely·blessed if in·this·manner she·
1Co 9:3 My defense to·the·ones scrutinizing me is this:
1Co 9:16 I·should·proclaim·the·good·news, it·is not a·boast
1Co 9:16 is·laid·upon me; and woe is to·me, unless I·
1Co 9:18 the payment·of·service: What is *the voluntary*
1Co 10:16 which we·bless, is·it not·indeed fellowship of·the
1Co 10:16 bread which we·break, is·it not·indeed fellowship
1Co 10:19 what do·I·reply? That an·idol is anything, or that
1Co 10:19 or that *which·is* sacrificed·to·idols is anything?
1Co 10:28 ·declare to·yeu, "This is sacrificed·to·idols," do·
1Co 11:3 that the head of·every man is the Anointed-One,
1Co 11:5 puts·to·shame her head, for it·is one and the same
1Co 11:7 ·image and glory, but woman is man's glory.
1Co 11:8 For man is not from·out of·woman, but·rather
1Co 11:13 yeurselves in·unison, is·it befitting·for a·woman
1Co 11:14 should·wear·long·hair, it·is a·dishonor to·him?
1Co 11:15 should·wear·long·hair, it·is a·glory to·her,
1Co 11:20 are·coming·together in·unison, it·is not to·eat *the*
1Co 11:24 "Take, eat! This is my body, the·one being·
1Co 11:25 saying, "This cup is the brand-new covenant in
1Co 12:6 ·are varieties of·operations, but it·is the same God,
1Co 12:12 For exactly·as the body is one and has many
1Co 12:14 For even the Body is not one member, but·rather
1Co 12:15 ¿! from this *reasoning*, is·it not from·among the
1Co 12:16 ¿! from this *reasoning*, is·it not from·among the
1Co 14:14 spirit prays, but my understanding is unfruitful.
1Co 14:15 So·then, which is·it? I·shall·pray with·the spirit,
1Co 14:25 to·God, announcing that God is really among yeu
1Co 14:26 Accordingly, how is·it *to·be*, brothers?
1Co 14:33 For God is not *the God* of·chaos, but·rather of·
1Co 14:35 at home. For it·is shameful for·women to·speak
1Co 15:12 among yeu say that there·is no resurrection of·
1Co 15:13 But if there·is no resurrection of·dead·men, not·
1Co 15:44 a·spiritual body. There·is a·soulish body, and
1Co 15:44 ·is a·soulish body, and there·is a·spiritual body.
1Co 15:58 ·seen that yeur wearisome·labor is not empty in
1Co 16:15 of·Stephanas, that it·is a·firstfruit of·Achaia, and
2Co 1:12 For this is our boasting, the testimony of·our
2Co 2:3 in yeu all that my joy is *preferred* by·all of·yeu.
2Co 3:17 Now the Lord is the Spirit, and where the Spirit of·
2Co 4:3 But even·if our good·news is having·been·veiled, it·
2Co 4:3 having·been·veiled, it·is having·been·veiled among
2Co 4:4 of·the Anointed-One— who is 'God's derived·
2Co 9:1 to the holy·ones, it·is superfluous for·me to·write
2Co 9:12 not merely is·it utterly·fulfilling·in·particular the
2Co 10:18 commending himself *that* is verifiably·approved,
2Co 11:10 *The* truth of·Anointed-One is in me, *such* that this
2Co 12:13 For what is·it in·which yeu·were·inferior beyond
2Co 13:5 *for* yeur·own·selves that Jesus Anointed is in yeu,
Eph 1:14 who is the earnest·deposit of·our inheritance for
Eph 1:18 for yeu to·have·seen what is the expectation of·his
Eph 1:23 which is his Body, the complete·fullness of·the·one
Eph 2:14 For he·himself is our peace, the·one already·
Eph 3:13 in my tribulations over yeu, which is yeur glory.
Eph 4:9 "He·ascended:" what is·it except that also he·
Eph 4:10 The·one descending is himself also the·one
Eph 4:15 ·up *in* all things in him who is the head, *namely* the
Eph 4:21 are·instructed by him (just·as truth is in Jesus)—
Eph 5:5 or greedy·man— which is an·idolater— does·not
Eph 5:10 ·and·verifying what is most·satisfying to·the Lord.
Eph 5:12 For it·is shameful even to·refer·to·the·things
Eph 5:13 light, for any thing being·made·apparent is light.
Eph 5:18 with·wine, in which is *the* unsaved·lifestyle, but·
Eph 5:23 because the husband is head of·the wife, even as
Eph 5:23 ·Out·Citizenry. And he·himself is Savior of·the
Eph 5:32 This is a·great mystery, but I·myself do·say *this* in·
Eph 6:1 ·and·obey yeur parents in *the* Lord, for this is right.
Eph 6:2 and mother" (which is *the* first commandment with
Eph 6:9 ·seen that yeur same Lord also is in *the* heavens, and
Eph 6:9 in *the* heavens, and there·is not partiality with him.
Eph 6:12 because it·is not for·our wrestling specifically·
Eph 6:17 dagger of·the Spirit, which is an·utterance of·God.
Col 1:6 all the world. And it·is itself·bearing·fruit, just·as *it*·
Col 1:7 dear fellow·slave, who is a·trustworthy attendant
Col 1:15 *It·is the Son* who is *the* derived·image of·the
Col 1:17 And he·himself is before all·things, and by him all·
Col 1:18 And he·himself is the head of·the Body (the entire·
Col 1:18 ; *it·is Anointed-One himself* who is *the* beginning,
Col 1:24 ·his Body, which is the entire·Called·Out·Citizenry
Col 1:27 among the Gentiles, which is Anointed-One in yeu
Col 2:10 ·completely·fulfilled *in him*, who is the head of·all
Col 3:1 up·above, where Anointed-One is sitting·down at
Col 3:5 and the covetousness— which is idolatry—
Col 3:14 which is a·ligament·*(a·uniting·principle)* of·the
Col 3:20 ·to all·things, for this is most·satisfying to·the Lord
Col 3:25 ·for·which he·did·wrong, and there·is no partiality.
Col 4:9 and beloved brother, who is from·among yeu. They·
1Ti 1:5 the end·purpose of·the charge is love out of·a·pure
1Ti 1:20 of·whom are Hymenaeus and AlexAnder, whom I·
1Ti 3:15 the·same·which is a·Called·Out·citizenry of·the·
1Ti 3:16 And admittedly, great is the Mystery of·the Way·
1Ti 4:8 For the *way·of* bodily training is profitable just·for a·
1Ti 4:8 Way·of·Devout·Reverence is profitable specifically·
1Ti 4:10 upon the·living God, who is *the* Savior of·all men·
1Ti 5:4 to·their·forebears, for that is good and fully·
1Ti 5:8 the trust and is worse·than a·non-trusting·heathen.
1Ti 6:6 with self-sufficiency is a·great means·of·gain.
1Ti 6:10 of·all the moral·wrongs is the fondness·of·money,
2Ti 1:6 ·bestowment of·God, which is in you through the
2Ti 1:12 ·been·convinced that he·is able to·vigilantly·keep
2Ti 2:17 ·body·as·pasture, of·whom is Hymenaeus and
2Ti 4:11 Only Luke is with me. Taking·up *John*·Mark,
2Ti 4:11 ·him with you, for he·is easily·useful to·me for
1Jn 1:5 This then is the announcement which we·have·heard
1Jn 1:5 announce·in·detail to·yeu, that God is light, and in
1Jn 1:5 is light, and in him there·is not darkness, none·at·all.
1Jn 1:7 ·should·walk in the light as he·himself is in the light,
1Jn 1:8 we·deceive ourselves, and the truth is not in us.
1Jn 1:9 ·confess our moral·failures, he·is trustworthy and
1Jn 1:10 him a·liar, and his Redemptive-word is not in us.
1Jn 2:2 And he·himself is *the* atonement concerning our
1Jn 2:4 not observantly·keeping his commandments is a·liar,
1Jn 2:4 commandments is a·liar, and the truth is not in him.
1Jn 2:7 The old commandment is the word which yeu·heard
1Jn 2:8 I·do·write to·yeu, which is true in him and in yeu,
1Jn 2:9 and hating his brother, is in the darkness even·unto
1Jn 2:10 in the light, and there·is no scandalous·trap in him.

1Jn 2:11 But the·one hating his brother is in the darkness,
1Jn 2:15 the world, the love of·the Father is not in him.
1Jn 2:16 the bragging of·natural·life, is not birthed·from·out
1Jn 2:16 of·the Father, but·rather is birthed·from·out of·the
1Jn 2:18 Little·children, it·is *the* last hour.
1Jn 2:18 by·which we·know that it·is *the* last hour.
1Jn 2:21 and that any lie is not birthed·from·out of·the truth.
1Jn 2:22 Who is the liar, if·not the·one who·contradicts·by·
1Jn 2:22 ·one who·contradicts·by·saying that Jesus is not the
1Jn 2:22 This·one is the adversary·of·the·Anointed-One,
1Jn 2:25 And this is the promise that he·himself did·already·
1Jn 2:27 yeu concerning all·things (and is true, and is not a·
1Jn 2:27 all·things (and is true, and is not a·lie, even just·as
1Jn 2:29 If yeu·should·personally·know that he·is righteous,
1Jn 3:2 him, because we·shall·gaze·upon him just·as he·is.'
1Jn 3:3 cleanses himself, just·as that·one is morally·clean.
1Jn 3:4 the moral·failure is the violation·of·the·Royal-Law.
1Jn 3:5 our moral·failures, and in him is not moral·failure.
1Jn 3:7 The·one doing the righteousness is righteous, just·as
1Jn 3:7 is righteous, just·as that·one is righteous.
1Jn 3:8 the moral·failure is birthed·from·out of·the Slanderer,
1Jn 3:10 one not doing righteousness is not birthed·from·out
1Jn 3:11 Because this is the message that yeu·heard from *the*
1Jn 3:15 one presently·hating his brother is a·man-killer†.
1Jn 3:20 ·incriminate *us*, God is greater·than our heart, and
1Jn 3:23 And this is his commandment, that we·should·
1Jn 4:2 Anointed having·come in flesh is from·out of·God.
1Jn 4:3 having·come in flesh is not from·out of·God.
1Jn 4:3 from·out of·God. And that·thing is the *spirit* of·the
1Jn 4:3 ·have·heard that it·is·come, and now is in the world,
1Jn 4:4 ·overcome them, because greater is the·one in yeu,
1Jn 4:6 hears us. Whoever is not birthed·from·out of·God
1Jn 4:7 because the love is birthed·from·out of·God; and any
1Jn 4:8 does·not already·know God, because God is love.
1Jn 4:10 In this, is the love: not that we·ourselves loved God
1Jn 4:12 his love is having·been·made·completely·mature in
1Jn 4:15 Whoever should·affirm that Jesus is the Son of·God
1Jn 4:16 God has in us. God is love; and the·one abiding in
1Jn 4:17 ·judgment, because just·as that·one is, so·also are
1Jn 4:18 There·is not fear in the Love, but·rather the
1Jn 4:20 and he·should·hate his brother, he·is a·liar, for the·
1Jn 5:1 one trusting that Jesus is the Anointed-One has·been·
1Jn 5:3 For this is the love of·God, that we·should·
1Jn 5:4 And this is the victory (the·one overcoming the
1Jn 5:5 Who is the·one overcoming the world, if·not the·one
1Jn 5:5 if·not the·one trusting that Jesus is the Son of·God?
1Jn 5:6 This is the·one coming through water and blood,
1Jn 5:6 And the Spirit is the·one testifying, because the Spirit
1Jn 5:6 is the·one testifying, because the Spirit is the truth.
1Jn 5:9 ·of·clay†, the testimony of·God is greater, because
1Jn 5:9 ·God is greater, because this is the testimony of·God
1Jn 5:11 And this is the testimony, that God gave to·us
1Jn 5:11 eternal life-above, and this life-above is in his Son.
1Jn 5:14 And this is the freeness·of·speech that we·have
1Jn 5:16 not unto death). There·is moral·failure unto death;
1Jn 5:17 All unrighteousness is moral·failure, and there·is
1Jn 5:17 is moral·failure, and there·is moral·failure not unto
1Jn 5:20 in his Son Jesus Anointed. This is the true God and
2Jn 1:6 And this is the Love, that we·should·walk according·
2Jn 1:6 ·to his commandments. This is the commandment,
2Jn 1:7 as·coming in flesh. This is the impostor and the
3Jn 1:11 ·one beneficially·doing·good is from·out of·God,
3Jn 1:12 ·*of* yeu·personally·know that our testimony is true.
Rv 2:7 of·the arbor·tree of·Life-above, which is in *the* midst
Rv 5:2 with·a·loud voice, "Who is worthy to·open·up the
Rv 5:12 with·a·loud voice, "Worthy is the Lamb (the·one
Rv 5:13 And every creature which is in the heaven, and on
Rv 13:10 with·a·dagger. Here is the patient·endurance and
Rv 13:18 Here is the wisdom. The·one having the
Rv 13:18 of·the Daemonic·Beast, for it·is a·number of·a·
Rv 14:12 Here is a·patient·endurance of·the holy·ones.
Rv 17:8 that you·saw, it·was and is not. And it·is·about to·
Rv 17:8 the Scarlet·Beast that was, and is not, and·yet is.
Rv 17:8 the Scarlet·Beast that was, and is not, and·yet is.
Rv 17:10 five fell, and the one is, *and* the other did·not·yet
Rv 17:11 the Scarlet·Beast that was and is not, even it·itself is
Rv 17:11 and is not, even it·itself is an·eighth *king* and is
Rv 17:11 is an·eighth *king* and is from·among the seven, and
Rv 17:14 shall·conquer them, because he·is Lord of·lords,
Rv 17:18 "And the woman whom you·saw is the Great City,
Rv 19:8 (for the fine·linen is the righteous·acts of·the holy·
Rv 19:10 for the testimony of·Jesus is the spirit of·prophecy
Rv 20:2 Dragon, the original Serpent, who is Slanderer and
Rv 20:12 ·scroll was·opened·up, which is *the official·scroll*
Rv 20:14 the Lake of·the Fire. This is the Second Death.
Rv 21:1 earth passed·away; and the Sea, she·is no longer.
Rv 21:8 with·fire and sulfur, which is *the* Second Death.
Rv 21:16 foursquare, and its length is as·vast and as·long·as
Rv 21:17 of·a·man·of·clay†, which is *that* of·an·angel.
Rv 22:10 official·scroll, because the season is near·at·hand.

G2076.1 V-PXI-3S@ ἐστίν (2x)

Mk 9:21 "About how·long a·time has·it·been *that* this has·
2Co 2:2 grieve yeu, then who would·be the·one making me

EG2076.1 (9x)

Lk 11:34 should·be evil, your body *is* also opaquely·dark.
Lk 11:36 if your whole body *is* full·of·light, not having any
Lk 18:24 "How impossibly·difficult *it·is*, *that* the·ones
Mt 13:20 Redemptive-word and straight·away *is* receiving it
Mt 24:32 the leaves, yeu·know that the summer *is* near.
Mk 10:23 "How impossibly·difficult *it·is that* the·ones
Rm 11:6 And if *it·is* by·grace, *it·is* no·longer as·a·result of·
Rm 11:6 if *it·is* by·grace, *it·is* no·longer as·a·result of·works
Rm 11:6 no·longer grace. But if *it·is* as·a·result of·works,

G2076.2 V-PXI-3S ἐστίν (57x)

Jn 3:21 ·apparent, that they·are having·been·worked in God.
Jn 4:35 ·yeurselves say, 'There·are yet four·lunar·months,
Jn 6:9 ·broiled·fish, but·yet what are these·things among so·
Jn 6:63 that I·myself speak to·yeu, *they* are spirit, and *they*
Jn 6:63 speak to·yeu, *they* are spirit, and *they* are life-above.
Jn 7:7 I·myself testify concerning it, that its works are evil.
Jn 10:16 I·have other sheep which are not from·among this
Jn 10:21 were·saying, "These·things are not the utterances
Jn 16:15 ·things·as the Father has, are mine. On·account·of
Jn 17:7 ·as you·have·given to·me, are personally·from you,
Jn 17:10 "So·then, all my·things are yours, and your·things
Jn 20:30 of·his disciples, which are not having·been·written
Jn 21:25 And there·are also many other·things, as·much·as
Lk 11:21 ·over his·own mansion, his holdings are at peace.
Lk 11:41 and behold, *suddenly* all·things are pure for·yeu?
Lk 14:17 'Come, because all·things are even·now ready.'
Lk 18:27 impossible with men·of·clay† are possible with
Lk 20:6 us to·death, for they·are having·been·persuaded *for*
Ac 15:18 "Known to·God are all his works from the·
Ac 19:36 being indisputable, it·is being·mandatory·for yeu
Ac 21:24 ·informed concerning you, it·is nothing·at·all.
Gal 4:24 Which·things are being·an·allegory, for these are
Gal 5:19 But the works of·the flesh are apparent, which are
Gal 5:19 of·the flesh are apparent, which are *these*: adultery,
Mt 10:2 the names of·the twelve ambassadors are these: first,
Mt 15:20 These are the·things defiling the man·of·clay†.
Mt 19:26 impossible, but with God all·things are possible."
Mk 4:31 least of·all the variety·of·seeds that·are in the earth.
Mk 7:4 they·do·not eat. And there·are many other·things
Mk 7:15 ·forth from him, those are the·things defiling the
Mk 10:27 with God, for with God all·things are possible."
Php 4:8 brothers: As·many·things·as are true, as·many·
2Pe 3:16 these·things, in which are some·things *that·are*
Tit 3:8 good works. These·things are the good·things and
1Co 2:14 ·the Spirit of·God, for they·are foolishness to·him.
1Co 3:21 boast in men·of·clay†, for all·things are yeurs.
1Co 6:15 that yeur bodies are members of·Anointed-One?
1Co 6:20 in yeur body and in yeur spirit, which are God's.
1Co 7:14 otherwise yeur children are impure, but now they·
1Co 7:14 yeur children are impure, but now they·are holy.
1Co 12:12 body (being many) are one body, in·this·manner
1Co 12:22 to·inherently·be more·feeble, are necessary.
1Co 14:10 There·are, as·it·may·be, so·many kinds of·voices
2Co 7:15 his inward·affections are more·abundant toward
Col 2:17 which·things are a·shadow of·the·things impending
Col 2:22 which all are *subject* to perishing with·usage)—
Col 2:23 These·very·things are in·fact a·rationalization of·
1Ti 5:25 the good works *of·some* are obvious·beforehand;
2Ti 1:15 me, of·whom *also* are Phygellus and HermoGenes.
2Ti 2:20 But in a·great home there·are not merely vessels
1Jn 3:10 In this the children of·God are apparent, also the
1Jn 4:1 ·prove the spirits whether they·are from·out of·God,
Rv 1:4 the seven Spirits who are in·the·sight of·his throne,
Rv 5:13 beneath the earth, and such·as are upon the sea, and
Rv 21:12 names having·been·inscribed, which are *the names*
Rv 21:16 The length and the breadth and its height are equal.
Rv 21:22 God Almighty, and the Lamb are its Temple.

G2076.2 V-PXI-3S@ ἐστίν (1x)

Lk 15:31 and all the·things *that·are* mine, they·are yours.

EG2076.2 (1x)

Jn 17:10 are yours, and your·things *are* mine, and I·have·

G2076.3 V-PXI-3S ἐστίν (31x)

Jn 2:9 yet had·not seen from·what·source it·was (but the
Jn 2:17 recalled·to·mind that it·was having·been·written,
Jn 5:13 ·healed had·not personally·known who it·was, for
Jn 5:15 reported·in·detail to·the Judeans that it·was Jesus,
Jn 6:24 when the crowd saw that Jesus was not there, nor his
Jn 6:64 not trusting, and who was the·one to·be·handing him
Jn 12:9 ·among the Judeans knew that he·was there. And
Jn 20:14 *there*, yet she·had·not seen that it·was Jesus.
Jn 21:4 the disciples had·not seen that it·was Jesus.
Jn 21:7 Now·then, after·hearing that it·was the Lord,
Jn 21:12 you·yourself?" having·seen that it·was the Lord.
Lk 19:3 he·was·seeking to·see who Jesus was, and was·not
Lk 23:6 inquired whether the man·of·clay† was a·Galilean.
Lk 24:21 were·expecting that he·himself is the·one intending
Ac 9:26 all afraid of·him, not trusting that he·was a·disciple.
Ac 9:38 ·Joppa, *and* after·hearing that Peter was in this *city*,
Ac 12:3 And seeing that it·was satisfactory to·the Judeans,
Ac 12:9 the·thing happening through the angel was true, but
Ac 19:34 But after·realizing that he·was a·Jew, there·came
Ac 21:33 he·might·be, and what *it·was* he·was having·done.
Ac 22:29 was·afraid after·realizing that he·was a·Roman,
Ac 23:6 ·knowing that the one part were Sadducees and the
Ac 23:27 him out, upon·learning that he·was a·Roman.
Ac 23:34 inquired from·which province he·was birthed. And
Ac 26:26 ·him; for this·thing was not having·been·practiced
Mk 2:1 *some* days, and it·was·heard that he·was in a·house.
Mk 5:14 And they·went·out to·see what it·was, the·thing
Mk 10:47 And after·hearing that it·was Jesus of·Natsareth,
Mk 14:35 soil and prayed that, if it·were possible, the hour
Rm 4:21 what *God* has·promised, *God* was able also to·do.
Rv 16:21 because its punishing·blow was tremendously great

G2076.4 V-PXI-3S ἐστίν (2x)

Jn 4:29 ·things I·did! Could this be the Anointed-One?
Mt 12:23 and were·saying, "Could this be the Son of·David?

G2076.5 V-PXI-3S ἐστίν (2x)

Lk 12:24 For·such *creatures*, there·is not a·dispensary nor·
Ac 18:10 you, on·account·that I·have for·myself many

G2076.6 V-PXI-3S ἐστίν (3x)

Mt 9:13 But upon·departing, learn what it·means, "I·want
Mt 12:7 But if yeu·had·known what it·means, "I·want
Mk 9:10 what it·should·mean to·rise·up from·among the

G2076.7 V-PXI-3S ἐστίν (1x)

Ac 21:11 JeruSalem shall·bind the man who owns this belt,

G2077 ἔστω ěstō *v.* (17x)

ἔστωσαν ěstōsan [third person plural]
Roots:G1510 See:G2277 G2468

G2077 V-PXM-3S ἔστω (14x)

Ac 1:20 desolate, and do·not let·there·be one residing in it,"
Ac 2:14 the·ones residing·in JeruSalem, be this known to·
Ac 4:10 be·it known to·yeu all, and to·all the People of·
Ac 13:38 men, brothers, be·it known to·yeu that through
Ac 28:28 "Now·then, be·it known to·yeu that the custodial·

Gal 1:8 ·yeu, let·him·be irrevocably·damned·to·destruction.
Gal 1:9 let·him·be irrevocably·damned·to·destruction.
Mt 5:37 "But yeur word must·be, 'Yes' *for* 'yes' *and* 'No
Mt 18:17 ·Called·Out·assembly, let·him·be to·you just·as
Mt 20:26 great among yeu, he·must·be yeur attendant,
Mt 20:27 to·be foremost among yeu, he·must·be yeur slave,
Jac 1:19 brothers, every man·of·clay† must·be swift to·hear,
1Pe 3:3 whose adorning must·be, not *according·to* the
2Co 12:16 But be·it·so, I·myself did·not impose·a·burden·on
G2077 V-PXM-3P ἔστωσαν (2x)
Lk 12:35 "Yeur loins must·be having·been·girded·about and
1Ti 3:12 Stewards must·be husbands of·one wife, conducting
EG2077 (1x)
Lk 12:36 "And yeu·yeurselves *must·be* like men·of·clay†

G2078 ἔσχατος ěschatôs *adj.* (54x)
Roots:G2192 xLangAlso:H0319
G2078.2 A-NSM ἔσχατος (7x)
Mk 9:35 first, *the same* shall·be last of·all and attendant of·
1Co 15:26 *The* last enemy *that* is·fully·rendered·inert *is*
1Co 15:45 a·living soul." The last Adam *came·into·being* as
Rv 1:11 and the Omega, the First and the Last," and,
Rv 1:17 "Do·not be·afraid; I AM the First and the Last.
Rv 2:8 ·things says the First and the Last, who became dead
Rv 22:13 beginning and end, the First and the Last."
G2078.2 A-NSF ἐσχάτη (4x)
Mt 27:64 dead,' and the last error shall·be worse·than the
Mk 12:22 and they·did·not leave offspring†. Last of·all, the
1Jn 2:18 Little·children, it·is *the* last hour. And just·as yeu·
1Jn 2:18 by·which we·know that it·is *the* last hour.
G2078.2 A-NPM ἔσχατοι (9x)
Lk 13:30 "And behold, there·are last who shall·be first, and
Lk 13:30 shall·be first, and there·are first who shall·be last."
Mt 19:30 "But many *who·are* first shall·be last, and *the* last
Mt 19:30 many *who·are* first shall·be last, and *the* last first.
Mt 20:12 saying, 'These last·ones did one hour, and you·
Mt 20:16 "In·this·manner, the last shall·be first, and the first
Mt 20:16 last shall·be first, and the first last; for many are
Mk 10:31 "But many *who·are* first shall·be last, and the last
Mk 10:31 *who·are* first shall·be last, and the last first."
G2078.2 A-ASM ἔσχατον (2x)
Mk 12:6 well-beloved, he·dispatched him also last to them,
1Co 15:8 And last of·all, he·was·gazed·upon by·me·also,
G2078.2 A-APM ἐσχάτους (1x)
1Co 4:9 us (the ambassadors) last, as doomed·to·death,
G2078.2 A-APF ἐσχάτας (1x)
Rv 15:1 seven angels having the last seven punishing·blows,
G2078.2 A-APN ἔσχατα (1x)
Rv 2:19 your works, even the last·ones *are* more·than the
G2078.2 A-DSM ἐσχάτῳ (3x)
Mt 20:14 'But I·want to·give to·this last·one, even as *I·gave*
Jud 1:18 there·shall·be mockers in *the* last time, who·are·
1Pe 1:5 a·Salvation ready to·be·revealed in *the* last season.
G2078.2 A-DSF ἐσχάτῃ (8x)
Jn 6:39 *pen),* but·rather shall·raise it up at the last Day.
Jn 6:40 and I·myself shall·raise him up at·the last Day."
Jn 6:44 him, and I·myself shall·raise him up at·the last Day.
Jn 6:54 and I·myself shall·raise him up at·the last Day.
Jn 7:37 On the last day, on·the great *day* of·the Sacred·Feast
Jn 11:24 he·shall·rise·up in the resurrection at the last Day."
Jn 12:48 The·same shall·judge him at the last Day.
1Co 15:52 in·a·twinkling·of·an·eye, at the last trumpet, for
G2078.2 A-DPF ἐσχάταις (3x)
Ac 2:17 "'And it·shall·be in the last days, says God, *that* I·
Jac 5:3 Yeu·stored·up·treasure in *the* last days.
2Ti 3:1 this, that in *the* last days perilous seasons shall·
G2078.2 A-GSN ἐσχάτου (1x)
2Pe 3:3 first, that there·shall·come in the last days mockers,
G2078.2 A-GPM ἐσχάτων (3x)
Jn 8:9 from the older·men unto the last·of·them; and Jesus
Mt 20:8 ·of·service, beginning from the last unto the first.
1Pe 1:20 ·made·apparent in the last times on·account·of yeu
G2078.2 A-GPF ἐσχάτων (2x)
Heb 1:2 spoke to·us in these last days by *his* Son, whom he·

Rv 21:9 overflowing of·the seven last punishing·blows), and
G2078.3 A-ASM ἔσχατον (3x)
Lk 14:9 with shame to·fully·hold·onto the very·last place.
Lk 14:10 sit·back·to·eat in the very·last place, in·order·that
Mt 5:26 ·there until you·should·repay the very·last quadran.
G2078.3 A-ASN ἔσχατον (1x)
Lk 12:59 even until you·should·give·back the very·last bit."
G2078.4 A-GSN ἐσχάτου (2x)
Ac 1:8 and as·far·as·to *the* farthest·part of·the earth."
Ac 13:47 ·Salvation unto *the* farthest·part of·the earth.'"
G2078.5 A-NPN ἔσχατα (3x)
Lk 11:26 there. And the final·states of·that man·of·clay†
Mt 12:45 there. And the final·states of·that man·of·clay†
2Pe 2:20 *and* are·defeated, the final·states have·become

G2079 ἐσχάτως êschátōs *adv.* (1x)
Roots:G2078 See:G2192
G2079.2 ADV ἐσχάτως (1x)
Mk 5:23 little·daughter is at·the·final·point·of·death. Come

G2080 ἔσω ěsō *adv.* (8x)
Roots:G1519
G2080.1 ADV ἔσω (6x)
Jn 20:26 again his disciples were inside, and Thomas with
Ac 5:23 But opening·up, we·found no·one·at·all inside."
Mt 26:58 ·high·priest, and after·entering inside, he·sat·down
Mk 14:54 a·distance, as·far·as to inside the courtyard of·the
Mk 15:16 the soldiers led him away inside the courtyard,
1Co 5:12 not·indeed presently·judge the·ones inside?
G2080.2 ADV ἔσω (2x)
Rm 7:22 of·God according·to the inner man·of·clay†,
Eph 3:16 ·power through his Spirit in the inner man·of·clay†,

G2081 ἔσω•θεν ěsōthên *adv.* (14x)
Roots:G2080 Compare:G1787 G1855
G2081.1 ADV ἔσωθεν (5x)
Mt 7:15 in sheep's apparel, but inwardly, they·are violently·
Mt 23:27 ·and·elegant, but inwardly they·overflow of·dead
Mt 23:28 ·of·clay†, but inwardly yeu·are exceedingly·full
2Co 7:5 Outwardly *are* quarrels, inwardly *are* fears.
Rv 4:8 overflowing of·eyes, all·around and inwardly. And
G2081.2 ADV ἔσωθεν (2x)
Lk 11:39 but yeur inward·part overflows with·extortion and
2Co 4:16 but·yet the inward *man·of·clay†* is·being·renewed
G2081.3 ADV ἔσωθεν (7x)
Lk 11:7 "And answering from·inside, that·man may·declare,
Lk 11:40 the·one making the outside also make the inside?
Mt 23:25 serving·bowl, but from·inside they·overflow out
Mk 7:21 For from·inside, from·out of·the heart of·the men·
Mk 7:23 All these evil·things proceed·forth from·inside, and
Rv 5:1 having·been·written on·*the*·inside and on·the·back,
Rv 11:2 courtyard, the·one *proceeding* inwardly *toward* the

G2082 ἐσώτερος êsṓtêrôs *adj.* (2x)
Roots:G2080 xLangAlso:H6442
G2082.1 A-ASN ἐσώτερον (1x)
Heb 6:19 'and·also entering into the interior of·the curtain,'
G2082.2 A-ASF ἐσωτέραν (1x)
Ac 16:24 cast them into the innermost prison·cell and

G2083 ἑταῖρος hêtaîrôs *n.* (4x)
Compare:G0405-1 G3353 G4898 G5384
xLangAlso:H2270
G2083.2 N-VSM ἑταῖρε (3x)
Mt 20:13 of·them, he·declared, 'Associate, I·do·not·do you
Mt 22:12 he·says to·him, 'O·associate, how did·you·enter
Mt 26:50 YeShua declared to·him, "O·associate, *attend* to
G2083.2 N-DPM ἑταίροις (1x)
Mt 11:16 marketplaces and hollering·out to·their associates,

G2084 ἑτερό•γλωσσος hêtêrógl ōssôs *adj.* (1x)
Roots:G2087 G1100
G2084.2 A-DPM ἑτερογλώσσοις (1x)
1Co 14:21 ·written, "In other·tongues and in other lips I·

G2085 ἑτερο•διδασκαλέω hêtêrôdidaskalếō *v.* (2x)
Roots:G2087 G1320
G2085 V-PAI-3S ἑτεροδιδασκαλεῖ (1x)
1Ti 6:3 If any·man instructs·differently and does·not come·

G2085 V-PAN ἑτεροδιδασκαλεῖν (1x)
1Ti 1:3 you·may·charge some not to·instruct·differently,

G2086 ἑτερο•ζυγέω hêtêrôzygếō *v.* (1x)
Roots:G2087 G2218
G2086.2 V-PAP-NPM ἑτεροζυγοῦντες (1x)
2Co 6:14 become disparately·yoked to·non-trusting·ones, for

G2087 ἕτερος hếtêrôs *adj.* (100x)
Compare:G0243 G0245 G3739 See:G2088
xLangAlso:H0312
G2087.1 A-NSM ἕτερος (8x)
Lk 9:61 And another also declared, "Lord, I·shall·follow
Lk 14:19 And another declared, 'I·bought five yoked·teams
Lk 14:20 And another declared, 'I·married a·wife, and on·
Lk 19:20 "And another came, saying, 'Lord, behold, *here·is*
Ac 1:20 in it,' and "May·another take his assignment·of·
Ac 7:18 even·until "another king rose·up, who had·not
Heb 7:15 another priest·that·offers·a·sacrifice does·rise·up—
Mt 8:21 And another of·his disciples declared to·him, "Lord
G2087.1 A-NSF ἑτέρα (2x)
Jn 19:37 And again another Scripture says, "They·shall·
1Co 15:40 ·kind, and the *glory* of·the terrestrial *is* another.
G2087.1 A-NSN ἕτερον (1x)
Ac 4:12 For there·is not·even another name under the heaven
G2087.1 A-ASM ἕτερον (8x)
Lk 9:59 And he·declared to another, "Follow me.
Lk 20:11 And he·further·proceeded to·send another slave.
Ac 12:17 And going·forth, he·traversed into another place.
Ac 17:7 of·Caesar, saying *that* there·is another king, Jesus.
Heb 7:11 *for* another priest·that·offers·a·sacrifice to·be·raised·
Gal 1:19 But I·did·not see any·other of·the ambassadors,
Mt 11:3 ·one who·is·coming, or do·we·anticipate another?"
Rm 7:23 but I·look·at another Law in my members,
G2087.1 A-ASF ἑτέραν (2x)
Lk 9:56 And they·traversed to another village.
Lk 16:18 his wife and marrying another commits·adultery,
G2087.1 A-ASN ἕτερον (3x)
Gal 1:6 *the* grace of·Anointed-One unto another good·news,
2Co 11:4 ·proclaim, or *if* yeu·receive another spirit, which
2Co 11:4 ·did·not already·receive, or another good·news,
G2087.1 A-DSM ἑτέρῳ (7x)
Lk 14:31 ·traversing to·engage·in war against another king,
Lk 16:7 After·that, he·declared to·another, 'And you, how·
Ac 13:35 Therefore he·says also in another *Psalm*, "You·
Heb 5:6 Just·as he·says also in another *passage*, "You *are*
Rm 7:3 if she·should·come to·another man with·the
Rm 7:3 by·becoming *yoked·together* with·another man.
Rm 7:4 yeu to·become *yoked·together* with·another, the·one
G2087.1 A-DSF ἑτέρᾳ (4x)
Ac 20:15 opposite Chios; and with·another *day of·sailing*,
Ac 27:3 And with another *day of·sailing*, we·moored at
Mk 16:12 from·among them in another form while·walking,
Jac 2:25 the messengers and casting·*them*·forth another way?
G2087.1 A-DSN ἑτέρῳ (1x)
Lk 6:6 And it·occurred also on another Sabbath, *for* him to·
G2087.1 A-GSF ἑτέρας (1x)
Heb 7:13 has·participated·with·and·belongs·to another tribe,
G2087.2 -- (1x)
Lk 17:36 ·be·personally·taken, and the other shall·be·left)]."
G2087.2 A-NSM ἕτερος (6x)
Lk 7:41 *year's wages),* and the other fifty *denarii (about a·*
Lk 17:34 ·be·personally·taken, and the other shall·be·left.
Lk 18:10 one *being* a·Pharisee and the other a·tax·collector.
Lk 23:40 answering, the other *criminal* was·reprimanding
1Co 8:4 and that *there·is* not·even·one other God, yet·not·
1Co 14:17 give·thanks well, but·yet the other is·not edified.
G2087.2 A-NSF ἑτέρα (3x)
Lk 17:35 ·be·personally·taken, and the other shall·be·left.
Rm 8:39 depth, nor any other created·thing shall·be·able to·
Rm 13:9 ' And if *there·is* any other commandment, it·is·
G2087.2 A-NSN ἕτερον (4x)
Lk 8:6 "And other *seed* fell upon the solid·rock, and once·
Lk 8:7 "And other *seed* fell in *the* midst of·the thorns; and
Lk 8:8 "And other *seed* fell on the beneficially·good soil, and

Ac 23:6 were Sadducees and the other Pharisees, he·yelled·
G2087.2 A-NPM ἕτεροι (6x)
Lk 11:16 And others, trying *him*, were·seeking personally·
Lk 23:32 And also two others, *who·were* criminals, were·led
Ac 2:13 And while·jeering, others were·saying, "These·
Ac 17:34 ·name·of Damaris, and others together with·them.
Heb 11:36 And others received a·trial of·*cruel*·mockings and
Mt 16:14 others *say* EliJah, but *yet* others *say* JeremIah, or
G2087.2 A-NPF ἕτεραι (1x)
Lk 8:3 and Susanna, and many others, who were·attending
G2087.2 A-ASM ἕτερον (7x)
Lk 16:13 the one and shall·love the other, or he·shall·hold·
Gal 6:4 the boasting in himself alone, and not in the other.
Mt 6:24 one and shall·love the other, or·else he·shall·hold·
Rm 2:1 For in that·which you·judge the other, you·condemn
Rm 13:8 ·one loving the other has·completely·fulfilled *the*
Jac 4:12 Who are you·yourself that unduly·judges the other?
1Co 6:1 ·against the other, go·to·court·to·be·judged before
G2087.2 A-APM ἑτέρους (4x)
Lk 10:1 the Lord expressly·indicated seventy others also, and
Ac 27:1 both Paul and certain other prisoners over to·a·
Mt 15:30 crippled, and many others, and they·quickly·
2Ti 2:2 ·clay† who shall·be competent to·instruct others also.
G2087.2 A-APN ἕτερα (4x)
Lk 3:18 many other·things, he·was·proclaiming·good·news
Lk 11:26 ·takes *to·itself* seven other spirits more·evil·than
Lk 22:65 And they·were·saying many other reviling *things*
Mt 12:45 with himself seven other spirits more·evil·than
G2087.2 A-DSN ἑτέρῳ (1x)
Lk 5:7 to·the·ones in the other sailboat *that·was* already·
G2087.2 A-DPM ἑτέροις (1x)
Ac 2:40 And with·many other words, he·was·thoroughly·
G2087.2 A-DPF ἑτέραις (2x)
Lk 4:43 of·the kingdom of·God to·the other cities also,
Eph 3:5 (which in other generations·of·offspring was·not
G2087.2 A-DPN ἑτέροις (1x)
1Co 14:21 In other·tongues and in other lips I·shall·speak to·
G2087.2 A-GSM ἑτέρου (5x)
Lk 16:13 to·one and shall·despise the other. Yeu·are·not able
Mt 6:24 to·one and shall·despise the other. You·are·not able
1Co 4:6 ·up over the *other*, *comparing* one against the other.
1Co 10:24 his·own, but·rather each·man the other's *good*.
1Co 10:29 your·own, but·rather of·the other, for what·
G2087.2 A-GPM ἑτέρων (3x)
Ac 15:35 of·the Lord, with many others also.
Php 2:4 *only*, but·rather each·man also the·things of·others.
2Co 8:8 the diligence of·others *in·the consequential·matter*
G2087.2 A-GPN ἑτέρων (1x)
Ac 19:39 concerning other·matters, it·shall·be·fully·settled
EG2087.2 (1x)
Heb 7:13 For *this other priest*, concerning whom these·
G2087.3 A-NSM ἕτερος (2x)
Lk 22:58 And after a·short·while, someone·else seeing him,
1Co 3:4 I·myself am of·Paul," and someone·else, "I *am* of·
G2087.3 A-NSN ἕτερον (1x)
1Ti 1:10 and if *there·is* anything else fully·set·opposed to·the
G2087.3 A-ASM ἕτερον (1x)
Rm 2:21 the·one instructing someone·else, do·you·not
G2087.3 A-ASN ἕτερον (1x)
Ac 17:21 for not·even·one·thing, other than *attempting* to·
G2087.3 A-DSM ἑτέρῳ (2x)
1Co 12:9 and to·someone·else, trust by the same Spirit, but
1Co 12:10 ·spirits, but to·someone·else, *thoroughly·differing*
G2087.3 A-GSM ἑτέρου (1x)
Ac 8:34 Concerning himself, or concerning someone else?"
G2087.4 A-NSN ἕτερον (1x)
Lk 9:29 aspect of·his countenance became different, and his
G2087.4 A-DPF ἑτέραις (1x)
Ac 2:4 they·began to·speak·in different bestowed·tongues,
G2087.4 A-GSF ἑτέρας (1x)
Jud 1:7 even going·off to·the·back·*end* of·different flesh,
G2087.5 A-NSF ἑτέρα (1x)
1Co 15:40 ·fact the glory of·the celestial *is* one·kind, and the

G2088 ἑτέρως hêtérōs *adv.* (1x)
Roots:G2087 Compare:G0247
G2088 ADV ἑτέρως (1x)
Php 3:15 if *in* anything yeu·contemplate differently, God

G2089 ἔτι éti *adv.* (101x)
Compare:G3063 See:G2094
G2089.1 ADV ἔτι (36x)
Jn 4:35 say, 'There·are yet four·lunar·months, and *then*
Jn 7:33 Jesus declared to·them, "Yet a·short time am·I with
Jn 12:35 Jesus declared to·them, "Yet a·short time is the
Jn 13:33 "Dear·children, yet a·little·while I·am with yeu.
Jn 14:19 "Yet a·little·while, and the world observes me no
Jn 16:12 "I·have yet many·things to·say to·yeu, but·yet yeu·
Lk 1:15 ·be·filled with·Holy Spirit, yet·even from·within his
Lk 8:49 While·he was·yet speaking, there·comes someone
Lk 9:42 And with·him yet coming·alongside, the demon
Lk 14:22 as you·ordered, and yet there·is place *for·more*.
Lk 14:26 brothers, and sisters, and yet his·own soul also,
Lk 14:32 And·if·not, with·the·other being yet far·away,
Lk 18:22 declared to·him, "Yet for·yourself, one·thing
Lk 22:47 And while·he was·yet speaking, behold a·crowd.
Lk 24:41 And yet not·trusting themselves for the joy and
Ac 2:26 my tongue leaped·for·joy, and yet even my flesh
Ac 10:44 As·Peter was·yet speaking these utterances, the
Heb 7:10 for he·was yet in the loins of·*his*·father when
Heb 10:37 "For yet, as·long·as a·little·while, the·one who·
Heb 11:4 *although* already·dying, he·himself still speaks.
Heb 12:26 saying, "Yet once·more I·myself do·shake not
Heb 12:27 And the "Yet once·more," makes·plain the
Gal 1:10 ·of·clay†? For if yet I·was·appeasing men·of·clay†,
Mt 17:5 While·he was·yet speaking, behold, a·thick·cloud
Mt 19:20 from·out of·my youth, yet what more·do·I·lack?
Mk 12:6 "So·then, yet having one son, his well-beloved, he·
Mk 14:43 And immediately, while·yet speaking of·him,
Rm 5:6 For yet, according·to due·season, Anointed-One died
Rm 5:8 love toward us, how·that yet, with·us being full·of·
Php 1:9 that yeur love may·abound yet more and more in
2Th 2:5 ·not remember, that while·being yet alongside yeu,
1Co 3:2 *to·bear it*. Moreover neither yet now are·yeu·able,
1Co 3:3 for yeu·are yet fleshly. For where *there·is* among
1Co 12:31 gracious·bestowments. And yet, I·show to·yeu
2Co 1:10 ·expectation that even yet he·shall·snatch·*us*·up—
Rv 6:11 ·uttered to·them that they·should·rest yet *for* a·short
G2089.2 ADV ἔτι (21x)
Jn 14:30 "Not any·longer shall·I·speak much with yeu, for
Lk 16:2 ·shall·not be·able to·manage·the·estate any·longer.'
Lk 20:36 For neither are·they·able to·die any·longer, for
Heb 8:12 no, I·should·not recall·to·mind any·longer."
Heb 10:17 no, I·should·not recall·to·mind any·longer."
Mt 5:13 ·purpose does·it·have·strength any·longer, except
Mk 5:35 Why harass the Mentor any·longer?"
Rm 6:2 ·Moral·Failure; how shall·we·live in it any·longer?
Rv 3:12 and no, he·should·not go·forth outside any·longer.
Rv 7:16 They·shall·not hunger any·longer, neither shall·
Rv 7:16 neither shall·they·thirst any·longer, nor·even, no,
Rv 12:8 was their place found any·longer in the heaven.
Rv 18:21 ·down, and no, it·should·not be·found any·longer.
Rv 18:22 no, should·not be·heard any·longer in you. And
Rv 18:22 no, should·not be·found any·longer in you. And
Rv 18:22 no, should·not be·heard any·longer in you;
Rv 18:23 no should·not·ever shine·forth any·longer in you;
Rv 18:23 no, should·not·ever be·heard any·longer in you—
Rv 20:3 ·not deceive the nations any·longer, even·until the
Rv 21:4 ' And Death shall·not be any·longer, neither
Rv 21:4 ·anguish. It·shall·not be any·longer, because the
G2089.3 ADV ἔτι (9x)
Jn 11:54 was·no longer strolling·about with·freeness·of·
Jn 14:19 world observes me no longer, but yeu·yourselves
Jn 16:10 toward my Father, and yeu·observe me no longer;
Jn 16:21 the tribulation no longer on·account·of the joy that
Jn 16:25 comes, when no longer shall·I·speak to·yeu in
Jn 17:11 And I·am no longer in the world, but these·men are
Jn 21:6 *the net*, and they·no longer had·strength to·draw it
Rv 21:1 earth passed·away; and the Sea, she·is no longer.
Rv 22:3 And there·shall·no longer be any irrevocable·vow·
G2089.4 ADV ἔτι (24x)
Jn 20:1 week at·the·watch·of·dawn (while·being still dark),
Lk 15:20 father. But with·him still being·off at·a·distance,
Lk 22:37 I·say to·yeu, that still it·is·mandatory·for this thing
Lk 22:60 And at·once, with·him still speaking, the rooster
Lk 24:6 ·to·mind how he·spoke to·yeu while·still being in
Lk 24:44 I·spoke to yeu, while·still being together with·yeu:
Ac 9:1 Now Saul, still seething with·menace and murder
Ac 18:18 And Paul, still continuing·on *there* a·sufficient
Heb 9:8 with·the first Tabernacle still being standing.
Gal 5:11 brothers, if I·still officially·proclaim circumcision
Gal 5:11 ·proclaim circumcision, why·am I·still persecuted?
Mt 12:46 And with·him still speaking to·the crowds, behold,
Mt 26:47 And with·him still speaking, behold, Judas, one of·
Mt 27:63 the impostor declared *while·he·was* still living,
Mk 5:35 As·he was·still speaking, one·came from *the house*·
Mk 8:17 yeur heart still having·been·petrified·hard·as·stone?
Rm 3:7 why am I·also still judged as morally·disqualified?
Rm 9:19 ·shall·declare to·me, "Why still does·he·find·fault?
1Co 15:17 *is* futile— yeu·are still in yeur moral·failures.
Rv 9:12 behold, there·come two woes still after these·things.
Rv 22:11 ·unrighteous, let·him·be·unrighteous still; and the·
Rv 22:11 the·one being·filthy, let·him·be·filthy still; and
Rv 22:11 let·him·be·regarded·as·righteous still; and the·one
Rv 22:11 and the·one *being* holy, let·him·be·holy still."
G2089.5 ADV ἔτι (3x)
Lk 22:71 "What need do·we·have of·any·further testimony?
Mk 14:63 "What need do·we·have of·any·further witnesses?
Rv 10:6 in it') that there·shall·not be any·further delay.
G2089.6 ADV ἔτι (3x)
Heb 7:11 ·enacted), what further need *was·there for* another
Heb 10:2 ·have not·one·bit further a·moral·consciousness of·
Mt 26:65 "He·reviled·God! What further need have·we of·
G2089.7 ADV ἔτι (3x)
Ac 21:28 and this place. And furthermore, he also brought
Heb 7:15 And furthermore, it·is excessively fully·obvious, if,
Heb 11:36 and scourgings, and furthermore, of·bonds and
G2089.8 ADV ἔτι (2x)
Heb 11:32 And what more should·I·say?
Mt 18:16 personally·take with you one or two more, that

G2090 ἑτοιμάζω hêtôimázō *v.* (41x)
Roots:G2092 Compare:G2680 G3903 See:G2091
xLangAlso:H6437
G2090 V-PAM-2S ἑτοίμαζε (1x)
Phm 1:22 But at·the·same·time make·ready for·me also
G2090 V-AAI-1S ἡτοίμασα (1x)
Mt 22:4 ·been·called, "Behold, I·made·ready my banquet.
G2090 V-AAI-2S ἡτοίμασας (2x)
Lk 2:31 which you·made·ready in front of·all the peoples;
Lk 12:20 shall·be those·things·which you·made·ready?'
G2090 V-AAI-3S ἡτοίμασεν (3x)
Heb 11:16 their God, for he·made·ready a·CITY for·them.
1Co 2:9 God made·ready for·the·ones presently·loving him.
Rv 19:7 did·come and his wife did·make herself ready.
G2090 V-AAI-3P ἡτοίμασαν (6x)
Lk 22:13 to·them. And they·made·ready the Passover.
Lk 23:56 ·back, they·made·ready aromatic·spices and
Lk 24:1 aromatic·spices which they·made·ready, and certain·
Mt 26:19 appointed them, and they·made·ready the Passover
Mk 14:16 to·them. And they·made·ready the Passover.
Rv 8:6 having the seven trumpets made themselves ready in·
G2090 V-AAM-2S ἑτοίμασον (1x)
Lk 17:8 declare to·him, 'Make·ready *food* which I·may·eat·
G2090 V-AAM-2P ἑτοιμάσατε (7x)
Lk 3:4 in the wilderness, 'Make·ready the Way of·Yahweh;
Lk 22:8 "Traversing, make·ready for·us the Passover, that
Lk 22:12 ·been·spread·out *for·guests*. Make·ready there."
Ac 23:23 he·declared, "Make·ready two·hundred soldiers,
Mt 3:3 in the wilderness, 'Make·ready the Way of·Yahweh;
Mk 1:3 in the wilderness, 'Make·ready the Way of·Yahweh;

Mk 14:15 ·*guests and* readied. There, make·ready for·us."
G2090 V-AAN ἑτοιμάσαι (4x)
Jn 14:2 *that* to·yeu. I·traverse to·make·ready a·place for·yeu
Lk 1:17 ·ones— to·make·ready a·People having·been·fully·
Lk 1:76 ·presence of·*the*·Lord to·make·ready his ways;
Lk 9:52 of·the·Samaritans, as·such to·make·ready for·him.
G2090 V-AAP-NSM ἑτοιμάσας (1x)
Lk 12:47 lord's will and not making·ready, nor·even doing
G2090 V-AAS-1S ἑτοιμάσω (1x)
Jn 14:3 ·traverse and should·make·ready a·place for·yeu, I·
G2090 V-AAS-1P ἑτοιμάσωμεν (3x)
Lk 22:9 "Where do·you·want *that* we·should·make·ready?"
Mt 26:17 do·you·want that·we·should·make·ready for·you
Mk 14:12 *that* we·should·make·ready in·order·that you·may·
G2090 V-APS-3S ἑτοιμασθῇ (1x)
Rv 16:12 kings from the eastern sun may·be·made·ready.
G2090 V-RPI-3S ἡτοίμασται (2x)
Mt 20:23 *to·them* for·whom it·has·been·made·ready by my
Mk 10:40 ·*given to·them* for·whom it·has·been·made·ready."
G2090 V-RPP-ASN ἡτοιμασμένον (1x)
Mt 25:41 the·one having·been·made·ready for·the Slanderer
G2090 V-RPP-ASF ἡτοιμασμένην (2x)
Mt 25:34 the kingdom having·been·made·ready for·yeu from
Rv 21:2 of·the heaven, having·been·made·ready as a·bride
G2090 V-RPP-ASM ἡτοιμασμένον (1x)
Rv 12:6 she·has a·place having·been·made·ready by God,
G2090 V-RPP-DPM ἡτοιμασμένοις (1x)
Rv 9:7 *were* like horses having·been·made·ready for battle;
G2090 V-RPP-NSN ἡτοιμασμένον (1x)
2Ti 2:21 ·the master, *and* having·been·made·ready for every
G2090 V-RPP-NPM ἡτοιμασμένοι (1x)
Rv 9:15 ·loosened, the·ones having·been·made·ready for the
EG2090 (1x)
Mt 8:18 he·commandingly·ordered *to·make·ready* to·go·off

G2091 ἑτοιμασία hêtôimasía *n.* (1x)
Roots:G2090
G2091 N-DSF ἑτοιμασίᾳ (1x)
Eph 6:15 ·own feet in a·state·of·readiness of·the good·news

G2092 ἕτοιμος hétôimôs *adj.* (17x)
See:G2093 G2090
G2092.1 A-NSM ἕτοιμος (3x)
Jn 7:6 is·not·yet here, but yeur season is always ready.
Lk 22:33 "Lord, I·am ready to·traverse with you, even unto
Mt 22:8 'In·fact the wedding is ready, but the·ones having·
G2092.1 A-NPM ἕτοιμοι (5x)
Lk 12:40 "Accordingly, yeu·yeurselves become ready also,
Ac 23:15 he shall·draw·near, are ready to·eliminate him."
Ac 23:21 And now they·are ready, awaiting the promise
Mt 24:44 that, yeu·yeurselves become ready also, because
1Pe 3:15 And *be* ready always to *present a·gracious* defense
G2092.1 A-NPF ἕτοιμοι (1x)
Mt 25:10 and the·ones *that·were* ready entered with him
G2092.1 A-NPN ἕτοιμα (2x)
Lk 14:17 'Come, because all·things are even·now ready.'
Mt 22:4 ·sacrificed, and all·things *are* ready. Come·here to
G2092.1 A-ASF ἑτοίμην (2x)
1Pe 1:5 through trust for a·Salvation ready to·be·revealed in
2Co 9:5 *for* the·same to·be ready in·this·manner: as a·
G2092.1 A-APM ἑτοίμους (1x)
Tit 3:1 to·readily·comply, to·be ready particularly·for every
G2092.2 A-ASN ἕτοιμον (1x)
Mk 14:15 ·been·spread·out *for·guests and* readied. There,
G2092.2 A-APN ἕτοιμα (1x)
2Co 10:16 standard *of·service* for the·things *being* readied.
G2092.3 A-DSN ἑτοίμῳ (1x)
2Co 10:6 and having in readiness to·avenge all inattentive·

G2093 ἑτοίμως hêtôímōs *adv.* (3x)
Roots:G2092
G2093.1 ADV ἑτοίμως (1x)
1Pe 4:5 to·the·one having readiness to·judge *the·ones* living
G2093.2 ADV ἑτοίμως (1x)
Ac 21:13 For I·myself am in·a·state·of·readiness not merely
G2093.3 ADV ἑτοίμως (1x)
2Co 12:14 Behold, I·am at·the·ready *for* a·third·time to·

G2094 ἔτος étôs *n.* (49x)
Compare:G1763 G5207 xLangAlso:H8141
G2094.1 N-NPN ἔτη (9x)
Ac 7:36 in *the* Red Sea, and in the wilderness forty years.
Heb 1:12 are the same, and your years shall·not cease."
Mt 9:20 ·*ill*, discharging·a·flow·of·blood *for* twelve years.
Mk 5:25 woman being with a·flow of·blood *for* twelve years,
2Pe 3:8 *is* with *the* Lord as a·thousand years, and a·thousand
2Pe 3:8 a·thousand years, and a·thousand years as one day.
Rv 20:3 even·until the thousand years should·be·completed.
Rv 20:5 ·again until the thousand years should·be·finished.
Rv 20:7 whenever the thousand years should·be·completed,
G2094.1 N-ASN ἔτος (2x)
Lk 2:41 Now each year his parents traversed to JeruSalem
Lk 13:8 'Lord, leave it this year also, until such·time *that* I·
G2094.1 N-APN ἔτη (19x)
Jn 5:5 was there, being in the sickness thirty-eight years.
Lk 2:36 after·living with a·husband seven years from her
Lk 4:25 heaven was·shut·up for·a·span·of three years and six
Lk 12:19 ·good·things being·laid·out for many years. Rest,
Lk 13:7 'Behold, *for* three years, I·come seeking fruit on
Lk 13:11 a·spirit of·sickness even eighteen years, and was
Lk 13:16 behold, eighteen years, was·it·not binding·for *her*
Lk 15:29 'Behold, *these* so·many years I·am·a·slave to·you,
Ac 7:6 them and shall·harm *them* four·hundred years.
Ac 7:42 sacrifices and respect·offerings *for* forty years in the
Ac 13:21 from·among *the* tribe of·BenJamin, *for* forty years.
Ac 19:10 this happened for·a·span·of two years, such·for all
Heb 3:9 ·and·proved me, and saw my works *for* forty years.
Heb 3:17 was·he·specifically·vexed forty years? *Was·it* not·
Gal 1:18 Then after three years, I·went·up to JeruSalem to·
Gal 3:17 ·occurred four·hundred and thirty years after) does·
Rv 20:2 and bound him a·thousand years,
Rv 20:4 and reigned with Anointed-One the thousand years.
Rv 20:6 and they·shall·reign with him a·thousand years.
G2094.1 N-DSN ἔτει (1x)
Lk 3:1 Now in *the* fifteenth year of·the governing·term of·
G2094.1 N-DPN ἔτεσιν (2x)
Jn 2:20 "*In* forty six years, this Temple was·built, and you, in
Ac 13:20 about four·hundred and fifty years, he·gave *to·them*
G2094.1 N-GPN ἐτῶν (9x)
Lk 2:37 *was* a·widow for·about eighty·four years, who did·
Lk 8:43 with a·flow of·blood for twelve years, who after·
Ac 7:30 "And with·forty years being·completely·fulfilled,
Ac 9:33 laying·down upon a·mat for eight years, *and* who
Ac 24:10 ·acquainted from·among many years of·you being
Ac 24:17 "And after many·more years, I·came·openly doing
Gal 2:1 Then after fourteen years, I·walked·up again to
Rm 15:23 a·great·yearning for these·many years to·come to
2Co 12:2 ·of·clay† in Anointed-One fourteen years ago
G2094.2 N-APN ἔτη (1x)
Jn 8:57 "You·are not·yet fifty years·of·age, and have·you·
G2094.2 N-GPN ἐτῶν (6x)
Lk 2:42 when he·was twelve years·of·age, after·walking·up
Lk 3:23 Jesus himself was about thirty years·of·age, being a·
Lk 8:42 a·daughter of·about twelve years·of·age, and she·
Ac 4:22 man·of·clay† was more·than forty years·of·age, on
Mk 5:42 for she·was of·twelve years·of·age. And they·
1Ti 5:9 *if she·is* not less·than sixty years·of·age, having·been

G2095 εὖ êû *adv.* (6x)
See:G0018 G2570
G2095.1 ADV εὖ (3x)
Ac 15:29 yeurselves, yeu·shall·practice well. Farewell."
Mk 14:7 yeu·should·want, yeu·are·able to·do well by·them.
Eph 6:3 "in·order·that it·may·be well with·you, and you·
G2095.2 ADV εὖ (3x)
Lk 19:17 to·him, 'Well·done, you·beneficially·good slave!
Mt 25:21 replied to·him, 'Well·done, O·beneficially·good
Mt 25:23 replied to·him, 'Well·done, O·beneficially·good

G2096 Εὕα Êúa *n/p.* (2x)
Εὕα Hêúa [alternate]
חַוָּה cʜa̱va̱h [Hebrew]
Roots:H2332
G2096.2 N/P-NSF Εὕα (1x)
1Ti 2:13 For Adam was·molded first, then Eve.
G2096.2 N/P-ASF Εὕαν (1x)
2Co 11:3 as the Serpent thoroughly·deluded Eve by his

G2097 εὐ•αγγελίζω êuangêlízō *v.* (55x)
Roots:G2095 G0032 See:G2099 xLangAlso:H1319
G2097.3 V-PMI-1S εὐαγγελίζομαι (1x)
Lk 2:10 for behold, I·proclaim·good·news to·yeu of·great
G2097.3 V-PMI-1P εὐαγγελιζόμεθα (1x)
Ac 13:32 to·yeu, we·ourselves proclaim·the·good·news, the
G2097.3 V-PMI-3S εὐαγγελίζεται (1x)
Gal 1:23 us in·times·past now proclaims·the·good·news, the
G2097.3 V-PMN εὐαγγελίζεσθαι (3x)
Lk 4:18 to·proclaim·the·good·news to·the·helplessly·poor.
Rm 15:20 *I·am* aspiring to·proclaim·the·good·news, *but* not
1Co 1:17 but·rather to·proclaim·the·good·news, not with
G2097.3 V-PMP-DSM εὐαγγελιζομένῳ (1x)
Ac 8:12 ·trusted PhilIppe as·he·was·proclaiming the·things
G2097.3 V-PMP-GSM εὐαγγελιζομένου (1x)
Lk 20:1 ·Atrium and proclaiming·the·good·news, the chief·
G2097.3 V-PMP-GPM εὐαγγελιζομένων (2x)
Rm 10:15 of·the·ones who·are·proclaiming·good·news of·,
Rm 10:15 of·the·ones who·are·proclaiming·good·news of·
G2097.3 V-PMP-NSM εὐαγγελιζόμενος (3x)
Lk 8:1 and proclaiming·the·good·news of·the kingdom of·
Ac 10:36 proclaiming·the·good·news of·peace through
1Co 9:18 that while·proclaiming·the·good·news, I·may·lay·
G2097.3 V-PMP-NPM εὐαγγελιζόμενοι (7x)
Lk 9:6 each·of the villages, proclaiming·the·good·news, and
Ac 5:42 instructing and proclaiming·the·good·news: Jesus *is*
Ac 8:4 *the regions* proclaiming the Redemptive-word.
Ac 11:20 ·Jews, proclaiming·the·good·news of·the Lord
Ac 14:7 And they·were there, proclaiming·the·good·news.
Ac 14:15 proclaiming·the·good·news to·yeu to·turn·back·
Ac 15:35 instructing and proclaiming·the·good·news of·the
G2097.3 V-PMS-1S εὐαγγελίζωμαι (3x)
Gal 1:16 Son in me in·order·that I·may·proclaim him among
1Co 9:16 For though I·should·proclaim·the·good·news, it·is
1Co 9:16 is to·me, unless I·should·proclaim·the·good·news!
G2097.3 V-PPI-3S εὐαγγελίζεται (1x)
Lk 16:16 ·on, the kingdom of·God is·being·proclaimed, and
G2097.3 V-PPI-3P εὐαγγελίζονται (2x)
Lk 7:22 *the* helplessly·poor are·proclaimed·the·good·news.'
Mt 11:5 *the* ·poor are·*hearing*·the·good·news·proclaimed.
G2097.3 V-IMI-3S εὐηγγελίζετο (3x)
Lk 3:18 he·was·proclaiming·good·news to·the people.
Ac 8:40 *the region*, he·proclaimed·the·good·news in·all the
Ac 17:18 he·proclaimed to·them the·good·news of·Jesus and
G2097.3 V-AAI-3S εὐηγγέλισεν (1x)
Rv 10:7 should·be·finished, as he·proclaimed to·his slaves
G2097.3 V-AAN εὐαγγελίσαι (1x)
Rv 14:6 *the* eternal good·news to·proclaim to·the·ones
G2097.3 V-AMI-1S εὐηγγελισάμην (4x)
Gal 4:13 flesh, I·proclaimed·the·good·news to·yeu at·the
1Co 15:1 to·yeu the good·news which I·proclaimed to·yeu,
1Co 15:2 that·certain Redemptive-word I·proclaimed to·yeu,
2Co 11:7 freely·without·charge, I·proclaimed to·yeu the
G2097.3 V-AMI-1P εὐηγγελισάμεθα (1x)
Gal 1:8 ·to that·which we·already·proclaimed to·yeu, let·
G2097.3 V-AMI-3S εὐηγγελίσατο (2x)
Ac 8:35 proclaimed·the·good·news of·Jesus to·him.
Eph 2:17 And coming, he·proclaimed 'peace to·yeu, the·
G2097.3 V-AMI-3P εὐηγγελίσαντο (1x)
Ac 8:25 ·did also proclaim·the·good·news in·many villages
G2097.3 V-AMN εὐαγγελίσασθαι (6x)
Lk 1:19 and to·proclaim·good·news to·you of·these·things.
Lk 4:43 ·for me to·proclaim·the·good·news of·the kingdom
Ac 16:10 ·summoned us to·proclaim·the·good·news to·them.

Rm 1:15 me *is* eager also to·proclaim·the·good·news to·yeu,
2Co 10:16 yeu *for·us* to·proclaim·the·good·news, *and* not
Eph 3:8 grace was·given: to·proclaim among the Gentiles
G2097.3 V-AMP-GSM εὐαγγελισαμένου (1x)
1Th 3:6 even with·he·himself·proclaiming·good·news to·us
G2097.3 V-AMP-GPM εὐαγγελισαμένων (1x)
1Pe 1:12 the·ones already·proclaiming·the·good·news to·yeu
G2097.3 V-AMP-NPM εὐαγγελισάμενοι (1x)
Ac 14:21 And after·proclaiming·the·good·news to·that city
G2097.3 V-API-3S εὐηγγελίσθη (1x)
1Pe 4:6 *end·purpose* was·the·good·news·already·proclaimed
G2097.3 V-APP-ASN εὐαγγελισθέν (1x)
Gal 1:11 the good·news, the·one being·proclaimed by me is
G2097.3 V-APP-NSN εὐαγγελισθέν (1x)
1Pe 1:25 the good·news·already·being·proclaimed to yeu.
G2097.3 V-APP-NPM εὐαγγελισθέντες (1x)
Heb 4:6 previously being·proclaimed·the·good·news did·not
G2097.3 V-RPP-NPM εὐηγγελισμένοι (1x)
Heb 4:2 even we·are having·been·brought·the·good·news,
G2097.4 V-PMI-3S εὐαγγελίζεται (1x)
Gal 1:9 any·man proclaims·a·good·news to·yeu contrary·to
G2097.4 V-PMS-3S εὐαγγελίζηται (1x)
Gal 1:8 ·out·of·heaven should·proclaim·a·good·news to·yeu

G2098 εὐ•αγγέλιον êuangéliôn *n.* (81x)
Roots:G2095 G0032 See:G2097 G0031
xLangAlso:H1319
G2098.2 N-NSN εὐαγγέλιον (6x)
Mt 24:14 And this good·news of·the kingdom shall·be·
Mt 26:13 this good·news should·be·officially·proclaimed in
Mk 13:10 the good·news first to·be·officially·proclaimed to
Mk 14:9 this good·news should·be·officially·proclaimed in
1Th 1:5 Because our good·news did·not come·to·be among
2Co 4:3 But even·if our good·news is having·been·veiled, it·
G2098.2 N-ASN εὐαγγέλιον (35x)
Ac 20:24 to·thoroughly·testify the good·news of·the grace
Gal 1:6 *the* grace of·Anointed-One unto another good·news,
Gal 1:7 to·distort the good·news of·the Anointed-One.
Gal 1:11 ·yeu, brothers, that the good·news, the·one being·
Gal 2:2 to·them the good·news which I·officially·proclaim
Gal 2:7 ·seeing that the good·news of·the Uncircumcision
Mt 4:23 ·proclaiming the good·news of·the kingdom, and·
Mt 9:35 ·proclaiming the good·news of·the kingdom, and
Mk 1:14 ·proclaiming the good·news of·the kingdom of·God
Mk 16:15 officially·proclaim the good·news to·all the
Rm 1:1 ·been·specially·detached to *the* good·news of·God—
Rm 1:16 ashamed·of the good·news of·the Anointed-One,
Rm 2:16 men·of·clay†. According·to my good·news, *this·is*
Rm 11:28 In·fact, according·to the good·news, *they·are*
Rm 15:16 ·in·the·sanctuary·above *for* the good·news of·God,
Rm 15:19 ·fulfilled the good·news of·the Anointed-One
Rm 16:25 ·establish yeu according·to my good·news and the
Php 1:5 for yeur fellowship in the good·news from *the* first
Php 2:22 he·has·been·subservient to·me in the good·news.
1Th 2:2 to·speak to·yeu the good·news of·God with much
1Th 2:4 to·be·entrusted with·the good·news, in·this·manner
1Th 2:8 ·give to·yeu, not the good·news of·God merely,
1Th 2:9 ·officially·proclaimed to·yeu the good·news of·God.
1Co 9:14 fully·proclaiming the good·news to·live from·out
1Co 9:18 I·may·lay·out the good·news of·the Anointed-One
1Co 9:23 I·do on·account·of the good·news, in·order·that I·
1Co 15:1 ·known to·yeu the good·news which I·proclaimed
2Co 2:12 to Troas for the good·news of·the Anointed-One
2Co 9:13 subjection to·the good·news of·Anointed-One, and·
2Co 11:4 already·receive, or another good·news, which yeu·
2Co 11:7 I·proclaimed to·yeu the good·news of·God.
Eph 1:13 of·the truth, the good·news of·yeur Salvation— in
1Ti 1:11 the glorious good·news of·the supremely·blessed
2Ti 2:8 from·among dead·men according·to my good·news,
Rv 14:6 having *the* eternal good·news to·proclaim to·the·
G2098.2 N-DSN εὐαγγελίῳ (12x)
Mk 1:15 Yeu·must·repent and trust in the good·news!"
Rm 1:9 in my spirit in the good·news of·his Son, how
Rm 10:16 not all listened·to·and·obeyed the good·news. For
Php 4:3 struggled·together with·me in the good·news, with
1Pe 4:17 ·ones being·obstinate to·the good·news of·God?
1Th 3:2 our coworker in the good·news of·Anointed-One, in·
2Th 1:8 listening·to·and·obeying the good·news of·our Lord
1Co 9:12 hindrance to·the good·news of·the Anointed-One.
1Co 9:18 ·order not to·abuse my privilege in the good·news.
2Co 8:18 high·praise *is* in the good·news throughout all the
2Co 10:14 *·proclaiming* the good·news of·the Anointed-One.
2Ti 1:8 ·together in·the good·news according·to God's power
G2098.2 N-GSN εὐαγγελίου (24x)
Ac 15:7 the Redemptive-word of·the good·news through my
Gal 2:5 the truth of·the good·news should·remain·constantly
Gal 2:14 toward the truth of·the good·news, I·declared to·
Mk 1:1 A·beginning of·the good·news of·Jesus Anointed,
Mk 8:35 ·my cause and *for·that* of·the good·news, the·same
Mk 10:29 plots·of·land, for·my cause and of·the good·news,
Rm 15:29 of·blessing of·the good·news of·the Anointed-One
Php 1:7 defense and confirmation of·the good·news, yeu all
Php 1:12 for a·continual·advancement of·the good·news,
Php 1:17 that I·am·laid·out for a·defense of·the good·news.
Php 1:27 (as·is·worthy of·the good·news of·Anointed-One),
Php 1:27 struggling·together for·the trust of·the good·news,
Php 4:15 that at *the* beginning of·the good·news *among·yeu*,
2Th 2:14 he·called yeu forth through our good·news, for the·
1Co 4:15 Jesus, I·myself begot yeu through the good·news.
1Co 9:14 the good·news to·live from·out of·the good·news.
2Co 4:4 of·the glorious good·news of·the Anointed-One—
Eph 3:6 in the Anointed-One through the good·news.
Eph 6:15 in a·state·of·readiness of·the good·news of·peace.
Eph 6:19 *·me* to·make·known the Mystery of·the good·news,
Col 1:5 in the Redemptive-word of·the truth of·the good·news,
Col 1:23 the Expectation of·the good·news which yeu·heard
Phm 1:13 ·may·attend to·me in the bonds of·the good·news.
2Ti 1:10 and eternal·incorruptibility through the good·news,
EG2098.2 (4x)
Gal 1:7 which is not *actually* another *good·news at·all.*
Gal 2:7 *to·me*, just·as *the good·news* of·the Circumcision
Eph 3:7 ·made a·steward of·this *good·news* according·to the
Col 1:6 with·the *good·news* being·present among yeu, just·as

G2099 εὐ•αγγελιστής êuangêlistḗs *n.* (3x)
Roots:G2097
xLangEquiv:H4018-1
G2099.2 N-APM εὐαγγελιστάς (1x)
Eph 4:11 the proclaimers·of·the·good·news·of·redemption,
G2099.2 N-GSM εὐαγγελιστοῦ (2x)
Ac 21:8 (the proclaimer·of·the·good·news·of·redemption,
2Ti 4:5 of·a·proclaimer·of·the·good·news·of·redemption,

G2100 εὐ•αρεστέω êuarêstéō *v.* (3x)
Roots:G2101
G2100 V-PPI-3S εὐαρεστεῖται (1x)
Heb 13:16 for with·such sacrifices God is·fully·satisfied.
G2100 V-AAN εὐαρεστῆσαι (1x)
Heb 11:6 trust, *it·is* impossible to·fully·satisfy *him*. For it·is·
G2100 V-RAN εὐηρεστηκέναι (1x)
Heb 11:5 ·been·testified *of·him* to·have·fully·satisfied God.

G2101 εὐ•άρεστος êuárêstôs *adj.* (9x)
Roots:G2095 G0701 See:G2102 G2100
G2101 A-NSM εὐάρεστος (1x)
Rm 14:18 to·the Anointed-One *is* most·satisfying to·God and
G2101 A-NSN εὐάρεστον (3x)
Rm 12:2 what *is* the beneficially·good, most·satisfying, and
Eph 5:10 ·and·verifying what is most·satisfying to·the Lord.
Col 3:20 all·things, for this is most·satisfying to·the Lord.
G2101 A-NPM εὐάρεστοι (1x)
2Co 5:9 being·absent·abroad, to·be most·satisfying to·him.
G2101 A-ASF εὐάρεστον (2x)
Rm 12:1 sacrifice, holy *and* most·satisfying to·God, *which·*
Php 4:18 a·sacrifice acceptable *and* most·satisfying to·God.
G2101 A-ASN εὐάρεστον (1x)
Heb 13:21 the·thing which·is·most·satisfying in·the·sight·of·
G2101 A-APM εὐαρέστους (1x)
Tit 2:9 to·their·own masters *and* to·be most·satisfying in all

G2102 εὐ•αρέστως êuarḗstōs *adv.* (1x)
Roots:G2101
G2102 ADV εὐαρέστως (1x)
Heb 12:28 to·God quite·satisfactorily with modesty·of·

G2103 Εὔ•βουλος Éúbôulôs *n/p.* (1x)
Roots:G2095 G1014
G2103.2 N/P-NSM Εὔβουλος (1x)
2Ti 4:21 to·come before winter. EuBulus greets you, and

G2104 εὐ•γενής êugênḗs *adj.* (3x)
Roots:G2095 G1096 Compare:G0036
G2104.2 A-NPM-C εὐγενέστεροι (1x)
Ac 17:11 *Berean Jews* were more·noble·than the·ones in
G2104.3 A-NSM εὐγενής (1x)
Lk 19:12 "A·man·of·clay†, a·certain nobleman, traversed
G2104.3 A-NPM εὐγενεῖς (1x)
1Co 1:26 not many *are* powerful, not many *are* noblemen.

G2105 εὐ•δία êudía *n.* (1x)
Roots:G2095 G2203
G2105 N-NSF εὐδία (1x)
Mt 16:2 yeu·say, '*It·shall·be* fine·weather, for the sky is·

G2106 εὐ•δοκέω êudôkéō *v.* (22x)
Roots:G2095 G1380 Compare:G0700 G2102 G2309
G4913 See:G2107
G2106.3 V-PAI-1P εὐδοκοῦμεν (1x)
2Co 5:8 even while·we·take·delight *preferring* all·the·more
G2106.3 V-PAI-3S εὐδοκεῖ (1x)
Heb 10:38 ·back, my soul does·not take·delight in him.⇨
G2106.3 V-AAI-1S εὐδόκησα (5x)
Lk 3:22 are my beloved Son; in you I·take·delight."
Mt 3:17 "This is my beloved Son, in whom I·take·delight."
Mt 17:5 beloved Son, in whom I·take·delight. Listen·to him!
Mk 1:11 are my beloved Son, in whom I·take·delight."
2Pe 1:17 my beloved Son, in whom I·myself take·delight."
G2106.3 V-AAI-1P εὐδοκήσαμεν (1x)
1Th 3:1 *it* no·longer, we·took·delight to·be·left·behind in
G2106.3 V-AAI-2S εὐδόκησας (2x)
Heb 10:6 moral·failure, you·did·not take·delight.
Heb 10:8 ·not want, neither did·you·take·delight *in·them*⇨
G2106.3 V-AAI-3S εὐδόκησεν (6x)
Lk 12:32 because yeur Father takes·delight to·give yeu the
Gal 1:15 But when God took·delight (the·one specially·
Mt 12:18 in whom my soul takes·delight. I·shall·place my
1Co 1:21 did·not know God, God took·delight through the
1Co 10:5 of·them, God did·not take·delight, for they·were·
Col 1:19 *of·God Most·High* takes·delight to·reside in him,
G2106.3 V-AAI-3P εὐδόκησαν (2x)
Rm 15:26 and Achaia delighted to·make a·certain common·
Rm 15:27 For they·do·take·delight, and they·are under·an·
G2106.3 V-AAP-NPM εὐδοκήσαντες (1x)
2Th 2:12 trusting the truth, but·rather taking·delight in the
EG2106.3 (1x)
Col 1:20 cross, *now·also he·takes·delight* to·utterly·reconcile
G2106.4 V-IAI-1P εὐδοκοῦμεν (1x)
1Th 2:8 ·for yeu, we·were·delighted to·kindly·give to·yeu,
G2106.5 V-PAI-1S εὐδοκῶ (1x)
2Co 12:10 Therefore I·purposefully·delight in weaknesses,

G2107 εὐ•δοκία êudôkía *n.* (9x)
Roots:G2095 G1380 See:G2106
G2107.2 N-NSF εὐδοκία (1x)
Rm 10:1 in·fact my heart's good·purpose and petition to
G2107.2 N-ASF εὐδοκίαν (4x)
Php 1:15 and strife, and some also through good·purpose.
2Th 1:11 every good·purpose of·*his*·beneficial·goodness and
Eph 1:5 Anointed, according·to the good·purpose of·his will
Eph 1:9 his good·purpose which he·personally·determined
G2107.2 N-GSF εὐδοκίας (1x)
Php 2:13 and to·operate on·behalf of·*his*·good·purpose.
G2107.3 N-NSF εὐδοκία (3x)
Lk 2:14 ·of·clay†, a·delightful·purpose *has·sprouted·forth*!"
Lk 10:21 ·manner, it·became a·delightful·purpose before
Mt 11:26 ·manner it·became a·delightful·purpose before you

G2108 εὐ•εργεσία êuergêsía *n.* (3x)
Roots:G2110 See:G2109
G2108 N-DSF εὐεργεσίᾳ (1x)
Ac 4:9 over *the* good·deed for·the·feeble man·of·clay†—
G2108 N-GSF εὐεργεσίας (1x)
1Ti 6:2 who·are·likewise·taking·hold of·the good·deed.
EG2108 (1x)
3Jn 1:5 do·you·do whatever *good·deed* you·may·work for
G2109 εὐ•εργετέω êuergêtéō *v.* (1x)
Roots:G2110 See:G2108
G2109 V-PAP-NSM εὐεργετῶν (1x)
Ac 10:38 went·throughout doing·good·deeds and healing all
G2110 εὐ•εργέτης êuergétēs *n.* (1x)
Roots:G2095 G2041 See:G2108
G2110.2 N-NPM εὐεργέται (1x)
Lk 22:25 having·control·over them are·called 'benefactors.'
G2111 εὔ•θετος éuthêtôs *adj.* (3x)
Roots:G2095 G5087 See:G0428
G2111.2 A-NSM εὔθετος (1x)
Lk 9:62 to the·things left·behind, is well-suited for the
G2111.2 A-NSN εὔθετον (1x)
Lk 14:35 It·is neither well-suited for soil, nor·even for
G2111.2 A-ASF εὔθετον (1x)
Heb 6:7 grain·stalk well-suited for·those on·account·of
G2112 εὐ•θέως êuthéōs *adv.* (80x)
Roots:G2117 Compare:G3916
G2112.1 ADV εὐθέως (1x)
3Jn 1:14 But I·expect to·see you straight·away, and we·shall·
G2112.2 ADV εὐθέως (79x)
Jn 5:9 And immediately the man·of·clay† was healthy·and·
Jn 6:21 him into the sailboat. And immediately, the sailboat
Jn 13:30 the morsel, that·one went·forth immediately. And
Jn 18:27 denied *it* again, and immediately a·rooster crowed.
Lk 5:13 Be·purified!" And immediately, the leprosy went·
Lk 5:39 drinking old *wine* immediately wants fresh·new
Lk 6:49 burst·directly·against, and immediately it·fell. And
Lk 12:36 knocking, they·may·open·up to·him immediately.
Lk 12:54 ·the·horizon from *the* west, immediately yeu·say,
Lk 14:5 into a·well, and shall·not immediately draw him up
Lk 17:7 shall·declare immediately *to·him* as·he·comes·in
Lk 21:9 "Moreover, the end does·not *occur* immediately."
Ac 9:18 And immediately, *something* like scales fell·off
Ac 9:20 And immediately, he·was·officially·proclaiming the
Ac 9:34 toss·aside your *mat*." And immediately he·rose·up.
Ac 12:10 one alleyway, and immediately the angel withdrew
Ac 16:10 clear·vision, immediately we·sought to·go·forth
Ac 17:10 And immediately the brothers sent·forth both Paul
Ac 17:14 And then immediately the brothers dispatched·
Ac 21:30 Sanctuary·Courtyard, and immediately the doors
Ac 22:29 So·then immediately, the·ones intending to·
Gal 1:16 Gentiles, I·did·not immediately confer with·flesh
Mt 4:20 And immediately, leaving the nets, they·followed
Mt 4:22 And immediately, leaving the sailboat and their
Mt 8:3 Be·purified." And immediately, his leprosy was·
Mt 13:5 and immediately it·rose·out·above·the·surface, on·
Mt 14:22 And immediately, YeShua compelled his disciples
Mt 14:27 But immediately YeShua spoke to·them, saying,
Mt 14:31 And immediately, YeShua, upon·stretching·forth
Mt 20:34 of·their eyes, and immediately their eyes received·
Mt 21:2 of·yeu, and immediately yeu·shall·find a·donkey
Mt 21:3 of·them,' and immediately he·shall·dispatch them.
Mt 24:29 "But immediately after the TRIBULATION of·
Mt 25:15 ability, and immediately, he·journeyed·abroad.
Mt 26:49 And immediately, going·toward YeShua, he·
Mt 26:74 ·of·clay†." And immediately a·rooster crowed.
Mt 27:48 And immediately one from·among them, after·
Mk 1:10 And immediately walking·up from the water, he·
Mk 1:18 And immediately, leaving their nets, they·followed
Mk 1:20 And immediately he·called them forth, and leaving
Mk 1:21 CaperNaum. And immediately after·entering into
Mk 1:29 And immediately, after·coming·forth out·of·the
Mk 1:30 ·with·fever, and immediately they·related *this* to·
Mk 1:31 ·hold·of her hand, and immediately the fever left
Mk 1:42 with·him declaring *this*, immediately, the leprosy
Mk 1:43 And sternly·warning him, immediately he·cast him
Mk 2:2 And immediately, many were·gathered·together,
Mk 2:8 And Jesus, fully·knowing immediately in·his spirit
Mk 2:12 And immediately he·is·awakened, and after·taking·
Mk 3:6 the Pharisees immediately were·making consultation
Mk 4:5 soil, and immediately it·rose·out·above·the·surface,
Mk 4:15 the Adversary-Accuser comes immediately, and he·
Mk 4:16 ·hear the Redemptive-word, immediately receive it
Mk 4:17 immediately they·are·recaptured·into·moral·.
Mk 4:29 ·be·yielded·up, immediately he·dispatches the
Mk 5:2 sailboat, immediately there·approached·and·met him
Mk 5:13 And immediately Jesus freely·permitted them.
Mk 5:29 And immediately, the well of·her blood was·dried·
Mk 5:30 And Jesus, recognizing immediately in himself the
Mk 5:36 But immediately upon·hearing the word being·
Mk 5:42 And immediately, the young·girl rose·up and was·
Mk 6:25 And upon·entering·in immediately with haste to the
Mk 6:27 And immediately dispatching a·bodyguard, the king
Mk 6:45 And immediately he·compelled his disciples to·
Mk 6:50 and were·troubled. And immediately he·spoke with
Mk 6:54 out·of·the sailboat, immediately, after·recognizing
Mk 7:35 And immediately his ears were·thoroughly·opened·
Mk 8:10 And immediately, after·embarking into the sailboat
Mk 9:15 And immediately all the crowd, after·seeing him,
Mk 9:20 him, and upon·seeing *Jesus*, immediately the spirit
Mk 9:24 And immediately the father of·the little·child,
Mk 10:52 And immediately he·received·his·sight and
Mk 11:2 ·before yeu, and immediately traversing into it,
Mk 11:3 of·him.' And immediately, he·shall·dispatch him
Mk 14:43 And immediately, while·yet speaking of·him,
Mk 14:45 upon·coming *and* immediately going·toward him,
Mk 15:1 And immediately upon·the dawn, the chief·priests,
Jac 1:24 and has·gone·away, and immediately, he·forgot
Rv 4:2 And immediately I·came·to·be in Spirit, and behold,
G2113 εὐ•θυ•δρομέω êuthydrômé̄ō *v.* (2x)
Roots:G2117 G1408
G2113.2 V-AAI-1P εὐθυδρομήσαμεν (1x)
Ac 16:11 from Troas, we·sailed·straight to Samos·of·Thrace
G2113.2 V-AAP-NPM εὐθυδρομήσαντες (1x)
Ac 21:1 ·away from them, we·went sailing·straight to Cos,
G2114 εὐ•θυμέω êuthymé̄ō *v.* (3x)
Roots:G2115
G2114.2 V-PAM-2P εὐθυμεῖτε (1x)
Ac 27:25 "Therefore, men, cheer·up! For I·trust God, that
G2114.2 V-PAN εὐθυμεῖν (1x)
Ac 27:22 I·urgently·recommend·for yeu to·cheer·up. "For
G2114.3 V-PAI-3S εὐθυμεῖ (1x)
Jac 5:13 *Is* any in·a·cheerful·mood? Let·him·make·song.
G2115 εὔ•θυμος éuthymôs *adj.* (2x)
Roots:G2095 G2372 Compare:G2431 See:G2114
G2115.3 A-NPM εὔθυμοι (1x)
Ac 27:36 ·themselves were all of·a·cheerful·outlook, and
G2115.4 ADV εὐθυμότερον (1x)
Ac 24:10 with·cheerful·composure I·give·an·account
G2116 εὐ•θύνω êuthýnō *v.* (2x)
Roots:G2117 Compare:G3329
G2116.1 V-AAM-2P εὐθύνατε (1x)
Jn 1:23 ·out in the wilderness, "Make·straight the Way of·
G2116.3 V-PAP-GSM εὐθύνοντος (1x)
Jac 3:4 sudden·impulse of·the·one piloting should·resolve.
G2117 εὐ•θύς êuthýs *adj.* (16x)
Roots:G2095 G5087 Compare:G2112 G3916 G3977 See:G2116 G2118
G2117.1 A-NSF εὐθεῖα (1x)
Ac 8:21 for your heart is not straight in·the·sight·of·God.
G2117.1 A-ASF εὐθεῖαν (3x)
Lk 3:5 winding·paths shall·be *made* into a·straight *path*, and
Ac 9:11 the avenue, the·one being·called Straight, and seek
2Pe 2:15 forsaking the straight way; they·are·led·astray,
G2117.1 A-APF εὐθείας (4x)
Lk 3:4 of·Yahweh; yeu·must·make his highways straight.
Ac 13:10 ·not cease perverting the straight ways of·Yahweh?
Mt 3:3 of·Yahweh; yeu·must·make his highways straight.'
Mk 1:3 ·Yahweh; yeu·must·make his highways straight.'
G2117.4 ADV εὐθύς (8x)
Jn 13:32 him in himself, and shall·glorify him straight·away.
Jn 19:34 ·the·tip·of·a·lance, and straight·away blood and
Jn 21:3 walked·up into the sailboat straight·away. And on
Mt 3:16 YeShua walked·up straight·away from the water.
Mt 13:20 the Redemptive-word and straight·away *is* receiving
Mt 13:21 straight·away he·is·recaptured·into·moral·failure.
Mk 1:12 And straight·away the Spirit casts him forth into the
Mk 1:28 And straight·away his fame went·forth unto all the
G2118 εὐ•θύτης êuthýtēs *n.* (1x)
Roots:G2117 Compare:G1343 See:G2118-1 xLangAlso:H3483
G2118.1 N-GSF εὐθύτητος (1x)
Heb 1:8 age of·ages; a·scepter of·straightness *is* the scepter
G2119 εὐ•καιρέω êukairé̄ō *v.* (3x)
Roots:G2121 See:G2120
G2119.2 V-IAI-3P ηὐκαίρουν (1x)
Mk 6:31 and they·were·not·even having·opportunity to·eat.
G2119.3 V-AAS-3S εὐκαιρήσῃ (1x)
1Co 16:12 ·come whenever he·should·have·opportune·time.
G2119.4 V-IAI-3P εὐκαίρουν (1x)
Ac 17:21 ·residing·there were·spending·their·leisure·time
G2120 εὐ•καιρία êukairía *n.* (2x)
Roots:G2121 See:G2119
G2120 N-ASF εὐκαιρίαν (2x)
Lk 22:6 and he·was·seeking a·good·opportunity to·hand him
Mt 26:16 he·was·seeking a·good·opportunity in·order·that
G2121 εὔ•καιρος éukairôs *adj.* (2x)
Roots:G2095 G2540 Compare:G0433 G0514 See:G2122 G2120 G2119
G2121.2 A-GSF εὐκαίρου (1x)
Mk 6:21 ·there·occurring a·day of·happy·occasion, when
G2121.5 A-ASF εὔκαιρον (1x)
Heb 4:16 mercy and should·find grace for timely swift·help.
G2122 εὐ•καίρως êukaírōs *adv.* (2x)
Roots:G2121 Compare:G0171
G2122.2 ADV εὐκαίρως (1x)
Mk 14:11 ·seeking how he·should·conveniently hand him
G2122.3 ADV εὐκαίρως (1x)
2Ti 4:2 Stand·forward when·convenient *and* when·
G2123 εὐ•κοπώτερος êukôpṓtêrôs *adj.* (7x)
Roots:G2095 G2873
G2123.2 A-NSN-C εὐκοπώτερον (7x)
Lk 5:23 Which is easier, to·declare, 'Your moral·failures
Lk 16:17 But it·is easier·for the heaven and the earth to·pass·
Lk 18:25 "For it·is easier *for* a·camel to·enter·in through a·
Mt 9:5 For which is easier? To·declare, 'Your moral·failures
Mt 19:24 again I·say to·yeu, it·is easier *for* a·camel to·go
Mk 2:9 Which is easier to·declare to·the paralyzed·man,
Mk 10:25 "It·is easier for·a·camel to·enter through the tiny·
G2124 εὐ•λάβεια êulábêia *n.* (2x)
Roots:G2126 Compare:G2317
G2124.2 N-GSF εὐλαβείας (2x)
Heb 5:7 *he·was* being·heard from the devotion *expressed*.
Heb 12:28 with modesty·of·conduct and devotion,
G2125 εὐ•λαβέομαι êulabéômai *v.* (2x)
Roots:G2126 xLangAlso:H2013
G2125.2 V-APP-NSM εὐλαβηθείς (2x)
Ac 23:10 (being·moved·with·apprehension lest Paul should·
Heb 11:7 ·looked·upon, being·moved·with·apprehension,
G2126 εὐ•λαβής êulabés *adj.* (3x)
Roots:G2095 G2983 Compare:G3741 See:G2124 G2125
G2126.3 A-NSM εὐλαβής (1x)
Lk 2:25 man·of·clay† *was* righteous and devout, awaiting
G2126.3 A-NPM εὐλαβεῖς (2x)
Ac 2:5 Jews residing in JeruSalem, devout men from every
Ac 8:2 And devout men went·in·procession·together·to·bury

G2127 εὐ•λογέω êulôgéō *v.* (44x)
Roots:G2095 G3056 Compare:G2551 See:G2128 xLangAlso:H1288 A1289
G2127.2 V-FAI-1S εὐλογήσω (1x)
Heb 6:14 Most assuredly, blessing I·shall·indeed·bless you,
G2127.2 V-PAI-1P εὐλογοῦμεν (3x)
Jac 3:9 With it, we·bless *our* God and Father.
1Co 4:12 Being·defamed, we·bless. Being·persecuted, we·
1Co 10:16 The cup of·blessing which we·bless, is·it not·
G2127.2 V-PAM-2P εὐλογεῖτε (4x)
Lk 6:28 bless the·ones cursing yeu, and pray on·behalf of·
Mt 5:44 love yeur enemies, bless the·ones who·are·cursing
Rm 12:14 Bless the·ones persecuting yeu; bless and do·not
Rm 12:14 the·ones persecuting yeu; bless and do·not curse.
G2127.2 V-PAN εὐλογεῖν (1x)
Lk 24:51 And it·happened, with him blessing them, *that* he·
G2127.2 V-PAP-ASM εὐλογοῦντα (1x)
Ac 3:26 him to·yeu first, blessing yeu in this·thing, to·turn·
G2127.2 V-PAP-NSM εὐλογῶν (2x)
Lk 1:64 tongue *loosed*, and he·was·speaking, blessing God.
Heb 6:14 Most assuredly, blessing I·shall·indeed·bless you,
G2127.2 V-PAP-NPM εὐλογοῦντες (1x)
Lk 24:53 Sanctuary·Atrium, praising and blessing God. So·
G2127.2 V-PPI-3S εὐλογεῖται (1x)
Heb 7:7 contradiction, the lesser is·blessed by the mightier.
G2127.2 V-PPI-3P εὐλογοῦνται (1x)
Gal 3:9 ·from·out of·trust are·blessed together with·the
G2127.2 V-IAI-3S ηὐλόγει (1x)
Mk 10:16 his hands upon them, he·was·blessing them.
G2127.2 V-AAI-3S εὐλόγησεν (9x)
Lk 2:28 him into his arms and blessed God. And he·declared,
Lk 2:34 And Simeon blessed them, and he·declared to
Lk 9:16 looking·up to the heaven, he·blessed them, and
Lk 24:30 after·taking the bread, he·blessed *it*, and after·
Lk 24:50 and lifting·up his hands, he·blessed them.
Heb 11:20 By·trust, YiTsaq blessed Jacob and Esau
Heb 11:21 Jacob (when·he·was·dying) blessed each of·the
Mt 14:19 looking·up to the heaven, he·blessed *it*. And after·
Mk 6:41 looking·up to the heaven, he·blessed *it*. And he·
G2127.2 V-AAP-NSM εὐλογήσας (5x)
Heb 7:1 from the carnage of·the kings, and blessing him;
Mt 26:26 the *unleavened* bread and blessing *it*, YeShua
Mk 8:7 a·few small·fish. And upon·blessing *them*, he·
Mk 14:22 *the unleavened* bread *and* blessing *it*, Jesus broke
Eph 1:3 Jesus Anointed, the·one already·blessing us with
G2127.2 V-AAS-2S εὐλογήσῃς (1x)
1Co 14:16 Otherwise when you·should·bless with·the spirit,
G2127.2 V-RAI-3S εὐλόγηκεν (1x)
Heb 7:6 from·AbRaham, and he·has·blessed the·one having
G2127.2 V-RPP-NSF εὐλογημένη (3x)
Lk 1:28 *is* with you! Having·been·blessed *are* you among
Lk 1:42 and declared, "Having·been·blessed *are* you among
Mk 11:10 Having·been·blessed *is the* kingdom of·our father
G2127.2 V-RPP-NSM εὐλογημένος (7x)
Jn 12:13 "Hosanna! "Having·been·blessed *is* the·one who·
Lk 1:42 among women, and having·been·blessed *is* the fruit
Lk 13:35 "Having·been·blessed *is* the·one who·is·coming
Lk 19:38 saying, "'Having·been·blessed *is* the King who·is·
Mt 21:9 of·David! "Having·been·blessed *is* the·one who·is·
Mt 23:39 ·should·declare, "Having·been·blessed *is* the·one
Mk 11:9 "Having·been·blessed *is* the·one who·is·coming in
G2127.2 V-RPP-NPM εὐλογημένοι (1x)
Mt 25:34 ·here, the·ones having·been·blessed of·my Father!
G2127.4 V-PAP-NPM εὐλογοῦντες (1x)
1Pe 3:9 in·order·that yeu·should·inherit the·active·blessing.

G2128 εὐ•λογητός êulôgētós *adj.* (8x)
Roots:G2127 Compare:G3107 See:G2129 xLangAlso:H1288
G2128 A-NSM εὐλογητός (7x)
Lk 1:68 "Blessed *be* Yahweh, God of·IsraEl, because he·
Rm 1:25 creating *it* (*the·one* who is blessed into the ages.
Rm 9:5 the·one being God over all, blessed into the ages.
1Pe 1:3 Blessed *be* the God and Father of·our Lord YeShua
2Co 1:3 Blessed *be* the God and Father of·our Lord Jesus
2Co 11:31 Jesus Anointed, the·one being blessed to the ages
Eph 1:3 Blessed *be* the God and Father of·our Lord Jesus
G2128 A-GSM εὐλογητοῦ (1x)
Mk 14:61 the Anointed-One, the Son of·the Blessed-One?"

G2129 εὐ•λογία êulôgía *n.* (16x)
Roots:G2127 Compare:G3107 G5542 G3108 See:G2128 G3052 xLangEquiv:H1293
G2129.1 N-NSF εὐλογία (4x)
Gal 3:14 ·that the blessing of·AbRaham may·come·to·be for
Jac 3:10 of·the same mouth come·forth blessing and cursing.
Rv 5:13 unto·the Lamb, *be* the blessing and the honor and
Rv 7:12 "So·be·it,·Amen! The blessing, and the glory, and
G2129.1 N-ASF εὐλογίαν (3x)
Heb 12:17 to·inherit the blessing, he·was·rejected·as·unfit,
1Pe 3:9 but on·the·contrary, a·blessing, having·seen that
Rv 5:12 and strength and honor and glory and blessing!"
G2129.1 N-DSF εὐλογίᾳ (1x)
Eph 1:3 us with every spiritual blessing by the heavenly·
G2129.1 N-GSF εὐλογίας (3x)
Heb 6:7 it·is·cultivated, it·partakes of·blessings from God.
Rm 15:29 in complete·fullness of·blessing of·the good·news
1Co 10:16 The cup of·blessing which we·bless, is·it not·
G2129.2 N-ASF εὐλογίαν (2x)
2Co 9:5 ·rectify yeur beneficial·blessing in·advance, the·one
2Co 9:5 in·this·manner: as a·beneficial·blessing, and not as·
G2129.2 N-DPF εὐλογίαις (2x)
2Co 9:6 sowing toward beneficial·blessings also shall·reap in
2Co 9:6 ·blessings also shall·reap in beneficial·blessings.
G2129.5 N-GSF εὐλογίας (1x)
Rm 16:18 and pleasant·blessing, they·thoroughly·delude the

G2130 εὐ•μετά•δοτος êumêtádôtôs *adj.* (1x)
Roots:G2095 G3330 Compare:G2843
G2130.1 A-APM εὐμεταδότους (1x)
1Ti 6:18 deeds, to·be good·at·kind·giving *and* sociable,

G2131 Εὐ•νίκη Êuníkē *n/p.* (1x)
Roots:G2095 G3529 Compare:G0959 See:G5095 G3090
G2131.2 N/P-DSF Εὐνείκῃ (1x)
2Ti 1:5 Lois and your mother EuNiki, and I·have·been·

G2132 εὐ•νοέω êunôéō *v.* (1x)
Roots:G2095 G3563 Compare:G1259 G2433 G2644 See:G2133
G2132.3 V-PAP-NSM εὐνοῶν (1x)
Mt 5:25 "Be kindly·settling *terms* with·your legal·adversary

G2133 εὔ•νοια éunôia *n.* (2x)
Roots:G2095 G3563 See:G2132
G2133.1 N-GSF εὐνοίας (1x)
Eph 6:7 with a·well-minded·intent, being·slaves to·the Lord
G2133.3 N-ASF εὔνοιαν (1x)
1Co 7:3 ·render to·the wife the kind·marital·duty being·due,

G2134 εὐν•ουχίζω êunôuchízō *v.* (2x)
Roots:G2135
G2134.1 V-AAI-3P εὐνούχισαν (2x)
Mt 19:12 there·are eunuchs, some castrated by the men·of·
Mt 19:12 some·who castrated themselves on·account·of the

G2135 εὐν•οῦχος êunôûchôs *n.* (8x)
Roots:G2192 See:G2134
G2135.1 N-NSM εὐνοῦχος (5x)
Ac 8:27 *there·was* a·man of·Ethiopia, a·eunuch, a·potentate
Ac 8:34 And answering Philippe, the eunuch declared, "I·
Ac 8:36 to some water. And the eunuch disclosed, "Behold,
Ac 8:38 both Philippe and the eunuch. And he·immersed
Ac 8:39 snatched Philippe, and the eunuch did·not see him
G2135.1 N-NPM εὐνοῦχοι (3x)
Mt 19:12 For there·are eunuchs, some·who were·born in·
Mt 19:12 womb. And there·are eunuchs, some castrated by
Mt 19:12 men·of·clay†. And there·are eunuchs, some·who

G2136 Εὐ•οδία Êuôdía *n/p.* (1x)
Roots:G2095 G3598 See:G2137
G2136.2 N/P-ASF Εὐωδιάν (1x)
Php 4:2 I·implore EuOdia and I·implore SynTyche to·

G2137 εὐ•οδόω êuôdóō *v.* (4x)
Roots:G2095 G3598 Compare:G2141 G2112-1
G2137.4 V-FPI-1S εὐοδωθήσομαι (1x)
Rm 1:10 even·now at·last *that* I·shall·prosper by the will of·
G2137.4 V-PPI-3S εὐοδοῦται (1x)
3Jn 1:2 to·be·healthy·and·sound, just·as your soul prospers.
G2137.4 V-PPN εὐοδοῦσθαι (1x)
3Jn 1:2 ·*as for* you to·prosper and to·be·healthy·and·sound,
G2137.4 V-PPS-3S εὐοδῶται (1x)
1Co 16:2 storing·up as he·may·prosper, lest there·should·be

G2138 εὐ•πειθής êupêithḗs *adj.* (1x)
Roots:G2095 G3982
G2138.2 A-NSM εὐπειθής (1x)
Jac 3:17 fair *and* readily·compliant, exceedingly·full of·

G2139 εὐ•περί•στατος êupêrístatôs *adj.* (1x)
Roots:G2095 G4012 G2476 Compare:G4029
G2139.3 A-ASF εὐπερίστατον (1x)
Heb 12:1 hindrance and the readily·besetting moral·failure—

G2140 εὐ•ποιΐα êupôiḯa *n.* (1x)
Roots:G2095 G4160 Compare:G2842
G2140.2 N-GSF εὐποιΐας (1x)
Heb 13:16 forget the benevolence and common·welfare·fund

G2141 εὐ•πορέω êupôréō *v.* (1x)
Roots:G2095 G4197 Compare:G2137 G2112-1 See:G2142
G2141.2 V-INI-3S ηὐπορεῖτο (1x)
Ac 11:29 just·as he·was·having·good·financial·means *to·do*

G2142 εὐ•πορία êupôría *n.* (1x)
Roots:G2095 G4197 Compare:G2137 See:G2141
G2142.2 N-NSF εὐπορία (1x)
Ac 19:25 ·are·fully·aware that our prosperity is as·a·result

G2143 εὐ•πρέπεια êuprépêia *n.* (1x)
Roots:G2095 G4241 Compare:G2566-3 G5611-1 See:G2143-1 xLangAlso:H3308
G2143.2 N-NSF εὐπρέπεια (1x)
Jac 1:11 ' and the beauty of·its countenance completely·

G2144 εὐ•πρόσ•δεκτος êuprósdêktôs *adj.* (5x)
Roots:G2095 G4327
G2144.2 A-NSM εὐπρόσδεκτος (2x)
2Co 6:2 Behold, now *is* the·well·acceptable season! Behold,
2Co 8:12 *it·is* well·acceptable according·to·what someone
G2144.2 A-NSF εὐπρόσδεκτος (2x)
Rm 15:16 may·be well·acceptable, having·been·made·holy
Rm 15:31 may·become well·acceptable to·the holy·ones,
G2144.2 A-APF εὐπροσδέκτους (1x)
1Pe 2:5 spiritual sacrifices well·acceptable to·God through

G2145 εὐ•πρόσ•εδρος êuprósêdrôs *adj.* (1x)
Roots:G2095 G4332
G2145.1 A-ASN εὐπρόσεδρον (1x)
1Co 7:35 *of* sitting·alongside·and·attending·well to·the Lord

G2146 εὐ•προσ•ωπέω êuprôsōpéō *v.* (1x)
Roots:G2095 G4383
G2146.2 V-AAN εὐπροσωπῆσαι (1x)
Gal 6:12 they·want to·project·a·good·appearance in·the·flesh

G2147 εὑρίσκω hêurískō *v.* (181x)
εὕρω hêúrō [primary form]
εὑρέω hêuréō [cognate form]
Compare:G2212
G2147 V-FAI-1P εὑρήσομεν (1x)
Jn 7:35 to·traverse that we·ourselves shall·not find him?
G2147 V-FAI-2S εὑρήσεις (1x)
Mt 17:27 mouth, you·shall·find a·silver·stater·coin *(worth*
G2147 V-FAI-2P εὑρήσετε (10x)
Jn 7:34 Yeu·shall·seek me and shall·not find *me*, and where I
Jn 7:36 'Yeu·shall·seek me and shall·not find *me*?
Jn 21:6 of·the sailboat, and yeu·shall·find." Accordingly,
Lk 2:12 Yeu·shall·find a·baby having·been·swaddled·*in*·
Lk 11:9 ·be·given yeu; seek, and yeu·shall·find; knock, and
Lk 19:30 ·in, yeu·shall·find a·colt having·been·tied, on
Mt 7:7 ·be·given yeu; seek, and yeu·shall·find; knock, and
Mt 11:29 ·the heart, and yeu·shall·find a·rest·break for·yeur

Mt 21:2 immediately yeu·shall·find a·donkey having·been·
Mk 11:2 into it, yeu·shall·find a·colt having·been·tied, on
G2147 V-FAI-3S εὑρήσει (8x)
Jn 10:9 ·in and shall·go·forth, and he·shall·find pasture.
Lk 12:37 the lord, upon·coming, shall·find keeping·alert.
Lk 12:43 upon·coming, shall·find doing in·this·manner.
Lk 18:8 ·Man†, upon·coming *back*, shall·he·find then *such*
Mt 10:39 his soul's·desire, for·my cause, shall·find it.
Mt 16:25 ·lose his soul's·desire, for·my cause, shall·find it.
Mt 24:46 lord, upon·coming, shall·find *him* doing in·this·
Mk 11:13 *it to·see* if perhaps he·shall·find anything on it.
G2147 V-FAI-3P εὑρήσουσιν (1x)
Rv 9:6 ·clay† shall·seek Death and shall·not find him. And
G2147 V-FPI-1P εὑρεθησόμεθα (1x)
2Co 5:3 dressing·ourselves, we·shall·not be·found naked.
G2147 V-PAI-1S εὑρίσκω (7x)
Jn 18:38 ·says to·them, "I·myself find in him not·even·one
Jn 19:4 ·that yeu·may·know that I·find not·even·one fault in
Jn 19:6 and crucify *him*, for I·myself find no fault in him.
Lk 13:7 seeking fruit on this fig·tree and find none. Chop it
Lk 23:4 and *to* the crowds, "I·find not·even·one fault in this
Rm 7:18 to·perform the morally·good·thing, I·do·not find.
Rm 7:21 By·inference, I·find the law in·the *circumstance*
G2147 V-PAI-1P εὑρίσκομεν (1x)
Ac 23:9 ·fighting, saying, "We·find not·even·one wrong in
G2147 V-PAI-3S εὑρίσκει (13x)
Jn 1:41 This·man *Andrew* first finds his·own brother Simon
Jn 1:43 to·go·forth into Galilee, and he·finds PhilIp and says
Jn 1:45 PhilIp finds NathaniEl and says to·him, "We·have·
Jn 5:14 After these·things, Jesus finds him in the Sanctuary·
Lk 11:10 receives, and the·one seeking finds, and to·the·one
Lk 11:25 And going·forth, it·finds *it* having·been·swept and
Ac 10:27 ·entered·in and found many having·come·together.
Mt 7:8 receives; and the·one seeking finds; and to·the·one
Mt 12:43 seeking a·rest·break, and it·does·not find *any*.
Mt 12:44 and upon·coming *to·it*, it·finds *it* being·vacant,
Mt 26:40 he·comes to the disciples and finds them sleeping.
Mt 26:43 And coming, he·finds them sleeping again, for
Mk 14:37 And he·comes and finds them sleeping. And he·
G2147 V-PAP-NSN εὑρίσκον (1x)
Lk 11:24 seeking a·rest·break; and not finding *any*, it·says,
G2147 V-PAP-NPM εὑρίσκοντες (2x)
Ac 4:21 them, finding not·even·one·thing of·how they·
Mt 7:14 to the life-above, and few are the·ones finding it.
G2147 V-PPI-1P εὑρισκόμεθα (1x)
1Co 15:15 And also, we·are·found *to·be* false·witnesses of·
G2147 V-IAI-3P εὕρισκον (3x)
Lk 19:48 yet they·were·not finding how they·may·do *it*, for
Ac 7:11 and our fathers were·not finding sustenance.
Mk 14:55 to·put him to·death, and they·were·not finding *it*.
G2147 V-IPI-3S εὑρίσκετο (1x)
Heb 11:5 "and he·was·not found, on·account·that God
G2147 V-2AAI-1S εὗρον (9x)
Lk 7:9 to·yeu, not·even in IsraEl did·I·find so·vast a·trust."
Lk 15:6 ·together with·me, because I·found my sheep, the·
Lk 15:9 ·together with·me, because I·found the drachma
Lk 23:14 *him* in·the·sight of·yeu, found not·even·one fault
Lk 23:22 did this·one commit? I·found not·even·one cause
Ac 13:22 testifying, he·declared, "I·found David, the *son*
Ac 17:23 yeur objects·of·reverence, I·found a·pedestal on
Ac 23:29 *and* I·found him being·called·to·account
Mt 8:10 to·yeu, not·even in IsraEl did·I·find so·vast a·trust.
G2147 V-2AAI-1P εὕρομεν (3x)
Lk 23:2 saying, "We·found this·man perverting the nation,
Ac 5:23 "In·fact, we·found the dungeon having·been·shut
Ac 5:23 But opening·up, we·found no·one·at·all inside."
G2147 V-2AAI-2S εὗρες (2x)
Lk 1:30 Mariam, for you·found grace personally·before
Rv 2:2 and are not, and you·found them *to·be* false·ones.
G2147 V-2AAI-3S εὗρεν (15x)
Jn 2:14 in the Sanctuary·Atrium, he·found the·ones selling
Jn 11:17 after·going *to·him*, Jesus found him having *been·*
Lk 4:17 And unrolling the official·scroll, he·found the place
Lk 13:6 and he·came seeking fruit on it yet did·not find *any*.
Lk 22:45 to the disciples, he·found them being·laid·asleep
Ac 7:46 who found grace in·the·sight of·God and requested
Ac 9:33 And there he·found a·certain man·of·clay†, Aeneas
Heb 12:17 he·was·rejected·as·unfit, for he·found no place
Mt 18:28 slave, after·going·forth, found one of·his fellow·
Mt 20:6 the eleventh hour, he·found others standing idle
Mt 21:19 he·came to it and found not·even·one·thing on it,
Mk 7:30 to her house, she·found the demon having·come·
Mk 11:13 after·coming to it, he·found nothing·at·all except
Mk 14:40 And upon·returning·back, he·found them sleeping
2Ti 1:17 ·for me more·diligently·than *others*, and found *me*.
G2147 V-2AAI-3P εὗρωσιν (28x)
Lk 2:46 three days, it·happened *that* they·found him in the
Lk 6:7 that they·might·find a·legal·accusation against·him.
Lk 7:10 the house, the·ones being·sent found the sick slave
Lk 8:35 they·came to Jesus and found the man·of·clay† from
Lk 9:12 they·should·lodge and find provision·of·food,
Lk 19:32 the·ones having·been·dispatched found *it* just·as
Lk 22:13 And going·off, they·found *it* just·as he·has·
Lk 24:2 And they·found the stone having·been·rolled·away
Lk 24:3 And entering, they·did·not find the body of·the
Lk 24:24 to the chamber·tomb, and found *it* even in·this·
Lk 24:33 to JeruSalem. And they·found the eleven having·
Ac 5:10 And the young·men entering, found her dead, and
Ac 5:22 ·directly *to·the dungeon*, did·not find them in the
Ac 13:6 even·as·far·as Paphos, they·found a·certain Jewish
Ac 19:19 ·calculated the price of·them and found *it to·be* five
Ac 24:12 And they·did·not·even find me in the Sanctuary·
Ac 24:18 in which·things they·found me *so·doing*, having·
Ac 24:20 let·them·declare if they·found any wrong·doing in
Ac 27:28 ·dropping·the·measuring·line, they·found *it to·be*
Ac 27:28 ·the·measuring·line again, they·found *it to·be*
Mt 2:11 into the home, they·found the little·child with
Mt 22:10 gathered·together all, as·many·as they·found, both
Mt 26:60 yet they·found none. And with·many false·
Mt 26:60 coming·alongside, *still* they·found none. But
Mt 27:32 ·out *of·the City*, they·found a·man·of·clay†, a·
Mk 11:4 And they·went·away and found the colt outside
Mk 14:16 into the City, and they·found *it* just·as he·declared
2Co 9:4 with·me and find yeu personally·unprepared, we·
G2147 V-2AAN εὑρεῖν (4x)
Ac 7:46 and requested to·find a·suitable·Tabernacle for·the
Mt 18:13 And if he·should·happen to·find it, certainly I·say
2Co 2:13 in·my spirit, *for* me not to·find Titus, my brother.
2Ti 1:18 Lord grant to·him to·find mercy personally·from
G2147 V-2AAO-3P εὕροιεν (1x)
Ac 17:27 ·and·about·for him and find·him, though·indeed
G2147 V-2AAP-NSF εὑροῦσα (1x)
Lk 15:9 And·then after·finding *it*, she·calls·together the
G2147 V-2AAP-NSM εὑρών (10x)
Jn 9:35 forth outside. And finding him, he·declared to·him,
Jn 12:14 And Jesus, finding a·young·donkey, sat·down on it
Lk 15:5 And·then after·finding *it*, he·puts *it* upon his
Ac 11:26 And after·finding him, he·brought him to Antioch.
Ac 12:19 after·seeking·for him and not finding *him*, *and*
Ac 19:1 came to Ephesus. And finding some disciples,
Ac 27:6 ·there, upon·finding a·sailing·ship of·AlexAndria
Mt 10:39 The·one finding his soul's·desire shall·completely·
Mt 13:44 which a·man·of·clay†, after·finding *it*, hides *it*.
Mt 13:46 who upon·finding one extremely·valuable pearl,
G2147 V-2AAP-NSM@ εὑρών (1x)
Ac 18:2 and he·found a·certain Jew by·the·name·of Aquila
G2147 V-2AAP-NPF εὑροῦσαι (1x)
Lk 24:23 and not finding his body, they·came, saying also
G2147 V-2AAP-NPM εὑρόντες (9x)
Jn 6:25 Now after·finding him on·the·other·side of·the sea,
Lk 2:45 And not finding him, they·returned·back to
Lk 5:19 And not finding through what·kind·of *means* they·
Ac 13:28 And after·finding not·even·one cause of·death *in·*
Ac 17:6 And not finding them, they·were·dragging Jason and
Ac 21:2 And after·finding a·sailing·ship sailing·over to
Ac 24:5 "For after·finding this man *to·be* a·viral·pestilence,
Ac 28:14 where finding brothers, we·were·exhorted to·stay·
Mk 1:37 And upon·finding him, they·say to·him, "All *men*
G2147 V-2AAS-1S εὕρω (1x)
2Co 12:20 after·coming, I·should·find yeu such·as I·do·not
G2147 V-2AAS-1P εὕρωμεν (1x)
Heb 4:16 we·may·receive mercy and should·find grace for
G2147 V-AAS-2S εὑρήσῃς (1x)
Rv 18:14 and no·longer, no, you·should·not·ever find them.
G2147 V-2AAS-2P εὕρητε (2x)
Mt 2:8 the little·child; and whenever yeu·should·find *him*,
Mt 22:9 and as·many·as yeu·might find, call·*them*·forth to
G2147 V-2AAS-3S εὕρῃ (5x)
Lk 12:38 third watch, and should·find *them* in·this·manner,
Lk 15:4 ·become·completely·lost until he·should·find it?
Lk 15:8 carefully until such·time *that* she·should·find *it*?
Ac 9:2 gatherings, that if·ever he·should·find any *disciples*
Mk 13:36 ·coming suddenly he·should·find yeu sleeping.
G2147 V-2AMP-NSM εὑράμενος (1x)
Heb 9:12 ·only, finding·in·himself an·eternal ransoming *for·*
G2147 V-API-1S εὑρέθην (1x)
Rm 10:20 and says, "' I·was·found by·the·ones not seeking
G2147 V-API-1P εὑρέθημεν (1x)
Gal 2:17 we·ourselves also are·found morally·disqualified,
G2147 V-API-3S εὑρέθη (13x)
Lk 9:36 the voice occurring, Jesus was·found alone. And
Lk 15:24 having·completely·perished, and·yet he·is·found.'
Lk 15:32 having·completely·perished, and·yet he·is·found.'
Ac 8:40 But Philippe was·found in Ashdod, and going·
Mt 1:18 them coming·together, she·was·found being in a·
Rm 7:10 the commandment, the·one *that* is·found in·me for
1Pe 2:22 moral·failure, neither was guile found in his mouth
Rv 5:4 not·even·one·man was·found worthy to·open·up and
Rv 12:8 neither was their place found any·longer in the
Rv 14:5 And in their mouth was·found no guile, for they·are
Rv 18:24 "And in her was·found *the* blood of·prophets, and
Rv 20:11 ·away. And there·is·not found a·place for·them.
Rv 20:15 And if anyone is·not found having·been·written in
G2147 V-API-3P εὑρέθησαν (2x)
Lk 17:18 They·are·not found returning·back to·give glory to·
Rv 16:20 island fled·away, and mountains were·not found.
G2147 V-APN εὑρεθῆναι (1x)
2Pe 3:14 ·things, quickly·endeavor to·be·found by·him in
G2147 V-APP-NSM εὑρεθείς (1x)
Php 2:8 And being·found in·a·schematic·layout as a·man·of·
G2147 V-APS-1S εὑρεθῶ (2x)
Php 3:9 even *that* I·should·be·found in him, not having my·
2Co 12:20 want, and·*that*·I should·be·found by·yeu such·as
G2147 V-APS-2P εὑρεθῆτε (1x)
Ac 5:39 lest·perhaps yeu·should·be·found *to·be* even as·
G2147 V-APS-3S εὑρεθῇ (4x)
1Pe 1:7 ·proven through fire) may·be·found in high·praise
1Co 4:2 that each·man should·be·found trustworthy.
Rv 18:21 ·down, and no, it·should·not be·found any·longer.
Rv 18:22 trade, no, should·not be·found any·longer in you.
G2147 V-APS-3P εὑρεθῶσιν (1x)
2Co 11:12 what they·boast, they·may·be·found *to·be lowly*
G2147 V-RAI-1S εὕρηκα (2x)
2Jn 1:4 very·much that I·have·found from·among your
Rv 3:2 to·die, for I·have·not found your works having·been·
G2147 V-RAI-1P εὑρήκαμεν (2x)
Jn 1:41 and says to·him, "We·have·found the Messiah,"
Jn 1:45 says to·him, "We·have·found whom Moses wrote
G2147 V-RAN εὑρηκέναι (1x)
Rm 4:1 *for* AbRaham our father to·have·found, according·to
EG2147 (3x)
Jn 2:14 doves; and·also *he·found* the exchangers·of·money
Mt 15:33 "From·what·source *should·we·find* for·ourselves
Rm 7:21 to·do the morally·good·thing, *I·find* that the bad·

G2148 Εὐρο•κλύδων Êurôklýdōn *n/p.* (1x)

Roots:G2830
G2148.2 N/T-NSM Εὐροκλύδων (1x)
Ac 27:14 *Crete*, the·one being·called EuroClydon *that·is*,

G2149 εὐρύ•χωρος êurýchōrôs *n.* (1x)
Roots:G5561 Compare:G4116 G5561
G2149 N-NSF εὐρύχωρος (1x)
Mt 7:13 broad *is* the gate, and spacious *is* the way, the·one
G2150 εὐ•σέβεια êusébêia *n.* (15x)
Roots:G2152 See:G2151
G2150.2 N-ASF εὐσέβειαν (6x)
2Pe 1:3 and devout·reverence are·having·been·endowed to·
2Pe 1:6 ·with *yeur* patient·endurance, Devout·Reverence;
Tit 1:1 of·truth (the·one according·to devout·reverence),
1Ti 4:7 myths, and train yourself *rather* to devout·reverence.
1Ti 6:3 with·the instruction according·to devout·reverence,
1Ti 6:11 and pursue righteousness, devout·reverence, trust,
G2150.2 N-DSF εὐσεβείᾳ (3x)
Ac 3:12 ·own power or devout·reverence we·have·made him
2Pe 1:7 ·with *yeur* devout·reverence, Brotherly·Affection;
1Ti 2:2 in all devout·reverence and in·impeccable·integrity·
G2150.2 N-DPF εὐσεβείαις (1x)
2Pe 3:11 to·subsist in *all* holy conduct and devout·reverence,
G2150.2 N-GSF εὐσεβείας (1x)
2Ti 3:5 having a·formula of·devout·reverence, but having·
G2150.3 N-NSF εὐσέβεια (2x)
1Ti 4:8 "but the Way·of·Devout·Reverence is profitable
1Ti 6:6 the Way·of·Devout·Reverence with self-sufficiency
G2150.3 N-ASF εὐσέβειαν (1x)
1Ti 6:5 assuming the Way·of·Devout·Reverence *itself* to·be
G2150.3 N-GSF εὐσεβείας (1x)
1Ti 3:16 is the Mystery of·the Way·of·Devout·Reverence.
G2151 εὐ•σεβέω êusêbêō *v.* (2x)
Roots:G2152 See:G2150
G2151.2 V-PAI-2P εὐσεβεῖτε (1x)
Ac 17:23 *to*·whom yeu·show·devout·reverence while·not·
G2151.2 V-PAN εὐσεβεῖν (1x)
1Ti 5:4 house to·show·devout·reverence and to·give·back
G2152 εὐ•σεβής êusêbḗs *adj.* (4x)
Roots:G2095 G4576 Compare:G0765 See:G2150 G2151
G2152.2 A-NSM εὐσεβής (2x)
Ac 10:2 *a* devoutly·reverent *man* and one·reverently·fearing
Ac 22:12 Ananias, a·devoutly·reverent man according·to the
G2152.2 A-ASM εὐσεβῆ (1x)
Ac 10:7 and a·devoutly·reverent soldier of·the·ones
G2152.2 A-APM εὐσεβεῖς (1x)
2Pe 2:9 to·snatch devoutly·reverent·men out of·proof·trials,
G2153 εὐ•σεβῶς êusêbỗs *adv.* (2x)
Roots:G2152
G2153 ADV εὐσεβῶς (2x)
Tit 2:12 righteously, and with·devout·reverence in the
2Ti 3:12 to·live with·devout·reverence in Anointed-One
G2154 εὔ•σημος êúsēmôs *adj.* (1x)
Roots:G2095 G4591
G2154.2 A-ASM εὔσημον (1x)
1Co 14:9 unless yeu·should·give a·clearly·discernible word,
G2155 εὔ•σπλαγχνος êúsplanchnôs *adj.* (2x)
Roots:G2095 G4698
G2155.2 A-NPM εὔσπλαγχνοι (2x)
1Pe 3:8 ·as·brothers, tender-hearted, thoughtfully·kind—
Eph 4:32 tender-hearted, being·graciously·forgiving to·one·
G2156 εὐ•σχημόνως êuschēmṓnōs *adv.* (3x)
Roots:G2158
G2156 ADV εὐσχημόνως (3x)
Rm 13:13 We·should·walk decently, as in daylight, not in·
1Th 4:12 ·order·that yeu·may·walk decently toward the·ones
1Co 14:40 *Even·so*, all·things must·be·done decently and in
G2157 εὐ•σχημοσύνη êuschēmôsýnē *n.* (1x)
Roots:G2158 Compare:G5611 G0809
G2157 N-ASF εὐσχημοσύνην (1x)
1Co 12:23 our indecent·parts have more·abundant decorum.
G2158 εὐ•σχήμων êuschḗmōn *adj.* (5x)
Roots:G2095 G4976 Compare:G1784 G0820 See:G2156 G2157
G2158.3 A-NSM εὐσχήμων (1x)
Mk 15:43 the·one of Arimathaea, a·dignified counselor who
G2158.3 A-ASN εὔσχημον (1x)
1Co 7:35 *I·speak* pertaining·to *what is* dignified and *of*
G2158.3 A-APM εὐσχήμονας (1x)
Ac 13:50 being·reverent (even the dignified·ones), and·also
G2158.3 A-GPM εὐσχημόνων (1x)
Ac 17:12 and·also not a·few of·the dignified Greek women
G2158.4 A-NPN εὐσχήμονα (1x)
1Co 12:24 Now our decent·parts have no *such* need, but·yet
G2159 εὐ•τόνως êutṓnōs *adv.* (2x)
Roots:G2095 G5037-1 Compare:G0772
G2159.1 ADV εὐτόνως (2x)
Lk 23:10 the scribes stood, legally·accusing him vigorously.
Ac 18:28 For vigorously, he·was·proving·downright to·the
G2160 εὐ•τραπελία êutrapêlía *n.* (1x)
Roots:G2095 G5157
G2160.2 N-NSF εὐτραπελία (1x)
Eph 5:4 or foolish·conversation, or sarcasm (*such* things
G2161 Εὔ•τυχος Êútychôs *n/p.* (1x)
Roots:G2095 G5177
G2161.2 N/P-NSM Εὔτυχος (1x)
Ac 20:9 ·man by·the·name·of EuTychus was·sitting·down in
G2162 εὐ•φημία êuphēmía *n.* (1x)
Roots:G2163 Compare:G1426
G2162.2 N-GSF εὐφημίας (1x)
2Co 6:8 through harsh·reputation and good·reputation, as
G2163 εὔ•φημος êúphēmôs *adj.* (1x)
Roots:G2095 G5345 See:G1262 G0989 G1426
G2163.2 A-NPN εὔφημα (1x)
Php 4:8 as·many·things·as *are* of·fine·reputation, if *there·is*
G2164 εὐ•φορέω êuphôrêō *v.* (1x)
Roots:G2095 G5409
G2164.3 V-AAI-3S εὐφόρησεν (1x)
Lk 12:16 wealthy man·of·clay† brought·forth·plentifully.
G2165 εὐ•φραίνω êuphraínō *v.* (14x)
Roots:G2095 G5424 Compare:G5463 G5059-6 See:G2167
xLangEquiv:H8055 xLangAlso:H8057
G2165.2 V-FPI-3P εὐφρανθήσονται (1x)
Rv 11:10 shall·rejoice over them and shall·be·merry, and
G2165.2 V-PAP-NSM εὐφραίνων (1x)
2Co 2:2 would·be the·one making me merry, except the·one
G2165.2 V-PPM-2S εὐφραίνου (2x)
Lk 12:19 Rest, eat, drink, *and* be·merry.'"
Rv 18:20 "Be·merry over her, O·Heaven, and the holy
G2165.2 V-PPM-2P εὐφραίνεσθε (1x)
Rv 12:12 "On·account·of that, be·merry, the heavens and
G2165.2 V-PPN εὐφραίνεσθαι (1x)
Lk 15:24 And they·began to·be·merry.
G2165.2 V-PPP-NSM εὐφραινόμενος (1x)
Lk 16:19 and fine·linen, splendidly being·merry each day.
G2165.2 V-IPI-3P εὐφραίνοντο (1x)
Ac 7:41 to·the idol, and they·were·merry in the works of·
G2165.2 V-API-3S εὐφράνθη (1x)
Ac 2:26 ·account·of that, my heart is·made·merry, and my
G2165.2 V-APM-2S εὐφράνθητι (1x)
Gal 4:27 it·has·been·written, '" Be·merry, O·barren·woman
G2165.2 V-APM-2P εὐφράνθητε (1x)
Rm 15:10 And again he·says, '" Be·merry, O·Gentiles, with
G2165.2 V-APN εὐφρανθῆναι (1x)
Lk 15:32 it·is·necessary *for·us* to·be·merry and to·be·glad,
G2165.2 V-APS-1S εὐφρανθῶ (1x)
Lk 15:29 ·young·goat in·order·that I·may·be·merry with my
G2165.2 V-APS-1P εὐφρανθῶμεν (1x)
Lk 15:23 And eating *it*, we·should·be·merry!
G2166 Εὐφράτης Êuphrátēs *n/l.* (2x)
פְּרָת pĕrath [Hebrew]
xLangEquiv:H6578
G2166.2 N/L-ASM Εὐφράτην (1x)
Rv 16:12 vial upon the great river EuPhrates, and its water
G2166.2 N/L-DSM Εὐφράτῃ (1x)
Rv 9:14 great river EuPhrates *(that·is, Good·Rushing·River)*."
G2167 εὐ•φροσύνη êuphrôsýnē *n.* (2x)
Roots:G2095 G5424 Compare:G5479 G2431 G2115 G5487-1 See:G2165 xLangAlso:H8057
G2167 N-GSF εὐφροσύνης (2x)
Ac 2:28 ·shall·completely·fill me *full* of·euphoria with your
Ac 14:17 filling·up our hearts with·nurturing and euphoria."
G2168 εὐ•χαριστέω êucharistếō *v.* (39x)
Roots:G2170
G2168.2 V-PAI-1S εὐχαριστῶ (11x)
Jn 11:41 "Father, I·give·thanks to·you that you·heard me.
Lk 18:11 himself, 'God, I·give·thanks to·you that I·am not
Rm 1:8 First in·fact, I·give·thanks to·my God through Jesus
Rm 7:25 I·give·thanks to·God through Jesus Anointed our
Rm 16:4 for·whom not only I·myself give·thanks, but·rather
Php 1:3 I·give·thanks to·my God upon every mention of·yeu,
1Co 1:4 I·give·thanks to·my God always concerning yeu for
1Co 1:14 I·give·thanks to·God that I·immersed not·even·one
1Co 10:30 ·reviled over that·for·which I·myself give·thanks?
1Co 14:18 *In·fact*, I·give·thanks to·my God, speaking more·
Phm 1:4 I·give·thanks to·my God, making mention of·you
G2168.2 V-PAI-1P εὐχαριστοῦμεν (4x)
1Th 1:2 We·give·thanks to·God always concerning all of·
1Th 2:13 also, we·ourselves give·thanks to·God unceasingly
Col 1:3 We·give·thanks to·the God and Father of·our Lord
Rv 11:17 saying, "We·give·thanks to·you, O·Yahweh, God
G2168.2 V-PAI-2S εὐχαριστεῖς (1x)
1Co 14:17 For in·fact, you give·thanks well, but·yet the
G2168.2 V-PAI-3S εὐχαριστεῖ (2x)
Rm 14:6 unto·*the*·Lord, for to·God he·gives·thanks; and
Rm 14:6 ·Lord he·does·not eat, and to·God he·gives·thanks.
G2168.2 V-PAM-2P εὐχαριστεῖτε (1x)
1Th 5:18 In everything give·thanks, for this *is* the·will of·
G2168.2 V-PAN εὐχαριστεῖν (2x)
2Th 1:3 We·are·indebted to·give·thanks to·God always
2Th 2:13 are·indebted to·give·thanks always to·God
G2168.2 V-PAP-NSM εὐχαριστῶν (2x)
Lk 17:16 face directly·at his feet, giving·thanks to·him. And
Eph 1:16 I·do·not cease giving·thanks on·behalf·of·yeu,
G2168.2 V-PAP-NPM εὐχαριστοῦντες (3x)
Eph 5:20 giving·thanks always on·behalf·of·all·things *to·our*
Col 1:12 while·giving·thanks to·the Father: the·one already·
Col 3:17 *the* Lord Jesus' name, giving·thanks to·the God and
G2168.2 V-AAI-3S εὐχαρίστησεν (1x)
Ac 27:35 taking bread, he·gave·thanks to·God in·the·sight
G2168.2 V-AAI-3P εὐχαρίστησαν (1x)
Rm 1:21 *him* as God nor gave·*him*·thanks, but·rather they·
G2168.2 V-AAP-GSM εὐχαριστήσαντος (1x)
Jn 6:23 they·ate the bread, with·the Lord giving·thanks.
G2168.2 V-AAP-NSM εὐχαριστήσας (9x)
Jn 6:11 and after·giving·thanks, he·thoroughly·doled·*it*·out
Lk 22:17 ·accepting *the* cup *and* giving·thanks, he·declared,
Lk 22:19 *unleavened* bread *and* giving·thanks, he·broke *it*
Ac 28:15 *them*, Paul took courage, giving·thanks to·God.
Mt 15:36 and the fish *and* upon·giving·thanks, he·broke
Mt 26:27 after·taking the cup and giving·thanks, he·gave *it*
Mk 8:6 loaves·of·bread *and* upon·giving·thanks, he·broke
Mk 14:23 after·taking the cup *and* giving·thanks, he·gave *it*
1Co 11:24 and after·giving·thanks, he·broke *it* and declared,
G2168.2 V-APS-3S εὐχαριστηθῇ (1x)
2Co 1:11 *such·that* thanks·may·be·given on·our behalf.
G2169 εὐ•χαριστία êucharistía *n.* (15x)
Roots:G2170 See:G2168
G2169.1 N-NSF εὐχαριστία (1x)
Eph 5:4 but·yet rather *share* an·expression·of·thankfulness.
G2169.1 N-ASF εὐχαριστίαν (2x)
2Co 4:15 the expression·of·thankfulness should·abound to
2Co 9:11 through us an·expression·of·thankfulness to·God.
G2169.1 N-APF εὐχαριστίας (1x)
1Ti 2:1 *and* expressions·of·thankfulness to·be·made over
G2169.1 N-DSF εὐχαριστίᾳ (3x)
1Co 14:16 at your expression·of·thankfulness, since·now
Col 2:7 abounding in it in an·expression·of·thankfulness.
Col 4:2 ·alert in it with an·expression·of·thankfulness—

G2169.1 N-GPF εὐχαριστιῶν (1x)
2Co 9:12 through many expressions·of·thankfulness to·God.
G2169.2 N-NSF εὐχαριστία (1x)
Rv 7:12 and the wisdom, and the thanks, and the honor,
G2169.2 N-ASF εὐχαριστίαν (2x)
1Th 3:9 For what thanks are·we·able to·recompense to·God
Rv 4:9 and honor and thanks to·the·one who·is·sitting·down
G2169.3 N-GSF εὐχαριστίας (4x)
Ac 24:3 with all·manner·of thanksgiving both everywhere
Php 4:6 and in·the petition with thanksgiving) *these* requests
1Ti 4:3 for partaking with thanksgiving for·the·ones trusting
1Ti 4:4 discarded *when* being·received with thanksgiving,

G2170 εὐ•χάριστος êucháristôs *adj.* (1x)
Roots:G2095 G5483 See:G2169 G2168
G2170.2 A-NPM εὐχάριστοι (1x)
Col 3:15 ·forth in one Body; and be expressively·thankful.

G2171 εὐχή êuchḗ *n.* (3x)
Roots:G2172 Compare:G4335 xLangAlso:H5088 H5145
G2171.2 N-NSF εὐχή (1x)
Jac 5:15 the desire·expressed·for·his·well-being *along* with·
G2171.3 N-ASF εὐχήν (2x)
Ac 18:18 ·shorn his head in Cenchrea, for he·had a·vow.
Ac 21:23 ·us are four men having a·vow upon themselves;

G2172 εὔχομαι êúchômai *v.* (7x)
Compare:G4336 G4727 See:G0685 G2171
G2172.2 V-PNI-1S εὔχομαι (2x)
2Co 13:7 Now I·well-wish to God for·yeu not to·do not·
3Jn 1:2 Beloved·man, I·well-wish *to·God* concerning all·
G2172.2 V-PNI-1P εὐχόμεθα (1x)
2Co 13:9 And this also we·well-wish, *even* yeur complete·
G2172.2 V-PNM-2P εὔχεσθε (1x)
Jac 5:16 to·one·another, and well-wish *to·God* on·behalf of·
G2172.2 V-INI-1S ηὐχόμην (1x)
Rm 9:3 For I·myself would·well-wish myself to·be
G2172.2 V-INI-3P ηὔχοντο (1x)
Ac 27:29 of·*the*·stern, they·were·well-wishing·for *it* to·be
G2172.2 V-ADO-1S εὐξαίμην (1x)
Ac 26:29 Paul declared, "I·would well-wish to·God, *that* not

G2173 εὔ•χρηστος êúchrēstôs *adj.* (3x)
Roots:G2095 G5543
G2173 A-NSM εὔχρηστος (1x)
2Ti 4:11 with you, for he·is easily·useful to·me for service.
G2173 A-NSN εὔχρηστον (1x)
2Ti 2:21 ·been·made·holy, and easily·useful to·the master,
G2173 A-ASM εὔχρηστον (1x)
Phm 1:11 but just·now *is* easily·useful to·you and to·me,

G2174 εὐ•ψυχέω êupsychéō *v.* (1x)
Roots:G2095 G5590
G2174.1 V-PAS-1S εὐψυχῶ (1x)
Php 2:19 that I·also may·be·well·in·*my*·soul, after·knowing

G2175 εὐ•ωδία êuōdía *n.* (3x)
Roots:G2095 G3605 Compare:G3744 See:G2175-1 xLangAlso:H5207
G2175.2 N-NSF εὐωδία (1x)
2Co 2:15 we·are to·God a·sweet·scent of·Anointed-One,
G2175.3 N-GSF εὐωδίας (2x)
Php 4:18 ·*were·sent* personally·from yeu, a·soothing aroma,
Eph 5:2 and a·sacrifice to·God for a·soothing aroma.

G2176 εὐ•ώνυμος êuṓnymôs *adj.* (10x)
Roots:G2095 G3686 Compare:G0710
G2176.2 A-ASF εὐώνυμον (1x)
Ac 21:3 leaving it behind on·the·left·side, we·were·sailing
G2176.3 A-GPM εὐωνύμων (1x)
Mt 25:41 ·declare also to·the·ones at *the* left·hand, 'Depart
G2176.4 A-ASM εὐώνυμον (1x)
Rv 10:2 foot upon the sea, and the left *foot* on the earth,
G2176.4 A-GPM εὐωνύμων (7x)
Mt 20:21 right·hand and one at *your* left, in your kingdom.
Mt 20:23 at my right·hand and at my left is not mine to·give,
Mt 25:33 at his right·hand, but the infantile·goats at *the* left.
Mt 27:38 with·him, one at *the* right·hand and one at *the* left.
Mk 10:37 your right·hand and one at your left, in your glory.
Mk 10:40 at my right·hand and at my left is not mine to·give,
Mk 15:27 robbers: one at his·right·hand, and one at his left.

G2177 ἐφ•άλλομαι êphállômai *v.* (1x)
Roots:G1909 G0242 xLangAlso:H6743
G2177 V-PNP-NSM ἐφαλλόμενος (1x)
Ac 19:16 And leaping upon them and fully·dominating them,

G2178 ἐφ•άπαξ êphápax *adv.* (5x)
Roots:G1909 G0530
G2178 ADV ἐφάπαξ (5x)
Heb 7:27 he·did this upon·one·occasion·only, carrying·up
Heb 9:12 Holy·of·Holies upon·one·occasion·only, finding·
Heb 10:10 the offering, upon·one·occasion·only, of·the
Rm 6:10 to·the Moral·Failure upon·one·occasion·only, but
1Co 15:6 brothers upon·one·occasion·only, from·among

G2179 Ἐφεσῖνος Êphêsînôs *n/g.* (1x)
Roots:G2181
G2179 N/G-GSF Ἐφεσίνης (1x)
Rv 2:1 angel of·the Called·Out·citizenry of·Ephesus write,

G2180 Ἐφέσιος Êphésiôs *adj/g.* (5x)
Roots:G2181
G2180 A/G-NPM Ἐφέσιοι (1x)
Ac 19:35 replied, "Men, Ephesians, for what man·of·clay†
G2180 A/G-ASM Ἐφέσιον (1x)
Ac 21:29 ·seen Trophimus the Ephesian together with·him in
G2180 A/G-GPM Ἐφεσίων (3x)
Ac 19:28 "Great *is* Artemis of·the·Ephesians."
Ac 19:34 "Great *is* Artemis of·the Ephesians."
Ac 19:35 the·city of·the Ephesians is·being temple·custodian

G2181 Ἔφεσος Éphêsôs *n/l.* (15x)
See:G2179 G2180
G2181 N/L-ASF Ἔφεσον (8x)
Ac 18:19 Now he·arrived in Ephesus, and·these *two* he·left·
Ac 18:24 a·certain Jew arrived in Ephesus (Apollos by·
Ac 19:1 districts *of·Macedonia*, came to Ephesus. And
Ac 19:17 known to·all the·ones residing·in Ephesus, to·both
Ac 20:16 Paul decided to·sail·directly·by Ephesus, so·that it·
Ac 20:17 ·word to Ephesus, he·summarily·called·for the
2Ti 4:12 And Tychicus I·dispatched to Ephesus.
Rv 1:11 to·the·ones in Asia: to Ephesus, and to Smyrna,
G2181 N/L-DSF Ἐφέσῳ (5x)
1Co 15:32 I·fought·with·wild·beasts at Ephesus, what *is* the
1Co 16:8 But I·shall·stay·over in Ephesus until the Pentecost
Eph 1:1 To·the holy·ones being in Ephesus, and to·those·
1Ti 1:3 ·as I·implored you to·continue·on at Ephesus (*even*
2Ti 1:18 ·things he·attended *to·me* at Ephesus, you·yourself
G2181 N/L-GSF Ἐφέσου (2x)
Ac 18:21 And he·sailed from Ephesus.
Ac 19:26 observe that not merely at·Ephesus, but·yet almost

G2182 ἐφ•ευρετής êphêurétēs *n.* (1x)
Roots:G1909 G2147
G2182 N-APM ἐφευρετάς (1x)
Rm 1:30 haughty, braggers, *and* inventors of·bad·things;

G2183 ἐφ•ημερία êphēmería *n.* (2x)
Roots:G2184 xLangAlso:H4931
G2183.2 N-GSF ἐφημερίας (2x)
Lk 1:5 *who·was* from·among *the* daily·rotation of·AbiJah.
Lk 1:8 of·God in the assigned·order of·his daily·rotation)

G2184 ἐφ•ήμερος êphḗmêrôs *adj.* (1x)
Roots:G1909 G2250
G2184.2 A-GSF ἐφημέρου (1x)
Jac 2:15 ·be being·deficient of·the daily provision·of·food,

G2185 ἐφ•ικνέομαι êphiknéômai *v.* (2x)
Roots:G1909 G2429-1 Compare:G2658 G0864 G4379 See:G1338 G0864
G2185.2 V-PNP-NPM ἐφικνούμενοι (1x)
2Co 10:14 as·though we·are·not actually·reaching *even* to
G2185.2 V-2ADN ἐφικέσθαι (1x)
2Co 10:13 *of·service* actually·reaching also even·unto yeu.

G2186 ἐφ•ίστημι êphístēmi *v.* (21x)
Roots:G1909 G2476 See:G1988 G1987 G2721
G2186.1 V-2AAI-3S ἐπέστη (2x)
Lk 2:9 And behold, Yahweh's angel stood·over them, and
Ac 12:7 behold, an·angel of·Yahweh stood·over *him*, and a·
G2186.1 V-2AAI-3P ἐπέστησαν (5x)
Lk 20:1 chief·priests and the scribes stood·over *him* together
Lk 24:4 this, behold, two men stood·over them in clothes
Ac 4:1 Sanctuary·Estate and the Sadducees stood·over them,
Ac 10:17 ·inquiry for·Simon's home, they·stood·over at the
Ac 11:11 ·hour, three men were·standing·over *the gate* at
G2186.1 V-2AAP-NSF ἐπιστᾶσα (2x)
Lk 2:38 And she·herself, standing·over *them* in·the same
Lk 10:40 *to·them*. And standing·over *him*, she·declared,
G2186.1 V-2AAP-NSM ἐπιστάς (3x)
Ac 22:13 after·coming to me and standing·over *me*, he·
Ac 23:11 night, the Lord, upon·standing·over him, declared
Ac 23:27 by them, *but* after·standing·over *him* together
G2186.1 V-2AAP-NPM ἐπιστάντες (1x)
Ac 6:12 the scribes. And standing·over *him*, together·they·
G2186.1 V-2AAS-3S ἐπιστῇ (1x)
Lk 21:34 ·life, and·also *lest* that day should·stand·over yeu
G2186.1 V-RAI-3S ἐφέστηκεν (1x)
2Ti 4:6 season of·my bodily·departure has·stood·over *me*.
G2186.1 V-RAP-NSM ἐφεστώς (1x)
Ac 22:20 I·myself also was having·stood·over, also gladly·
G2186.2 V-2AAM-2S ἐπίστηθι (1x)
2Ti 4:2 Stand·forward when·convenient *and* when·
G2186.2 V-2AAP-NSM ἐπιστάς (1x)
Lk 4:39 And standing·forward over her, he·reprimanded the
G2186.3 V-PMI-3S ἐφίσταται (1x)
1Th 5:3 an·unexpected savage·termination assaults them,
G2186.3 V-2AAP-NPM ἐπιστάντες (1x)
Ac 17:5 ·in the city. And assaulting the home of·Jason, they·
G2186.3 V-RAP-ASM ἐφεστῶτα (1x)
Ac 28:2 of·us, on·account·of the assaulting rain, and on·

G2187 Ἐφραΐμ Êphraḯm *n/l.* (1x)
אֶפְרַיִם ʼephrayim [Hebrew]
Roots:H0669 See:G3128
G2187.6 N/L-PRI Ἐφραΐμ (1x)
Jn 11:54 *and* into a·city being·referred·to·as Ephraim. And

G2188 ἐφφαθά êphphathá *aram.* (1x)
פְּתַח pĕthach [Aramaic]
Roots:A6606
G2188 ARAM ἐφφαθά (1x)
Mk 7:34 ·heavily and says to·him, "Ephphatha," which is,

G2189 ἔχθρα échthra *n.* (6x)
Roots:G2190 Compare:G3411-1 xLangAlso:H0342
G2189.1 N-NSF ἔχθρα (2x)
Rm 8:7 the disposition of·the flesh *is* hostility toward God,
Jac 4:4 that the friendship of·the world is hostility with·God?
G2189.1 N-NPF ἔχθραι (1x)
Gal 5:20 ·supplying·of·poisonous·drugs, hostilities, strifes,
G2189.1 N-ASF ἔχθραν (2x)
Eph 2:15 ·inert in his flesh the hostility (*namely* the
Eph 2:16 the cross, in himself already·killing the hostility.
G2189.1 N-DSF ἔχθρᾳ (1x)
Lk 23:12 ·previously being in hostility among themselves.

G2190 ἐχθρός êchthrós *adj.* (32x)
Compare:G4767 G3404-1 G5227 See:G2189 xLangAlso:H0341
G2190.1 A-NSM ἐχθρός (1x)
Mt 13:28 He·replied to·them, 'A·hostile man·of·clay† did
G2190.3 A-NSM ἐχθρός (6x)
Gal 4:16 ·such, have·I·become yeur enemy, being·truthful
Mt 13:25 men·of·clay† to·sleep, his enemy came and sowed
Mt 13:39 The enemy, the·one sowing them, is·the Slanderer.
Rm 12:20 "'If your enemy should·hunger, provide·some·
Jac 4:4 ·the world is·fully·established·as an·enemy of·God.
1Co 15:26 *The* last enemy *that* is·fully·rendered·inert *is*
G2190.3 A-NPM ἐχθροί (6x)
Lk 19:43 you, and your enemies shall·cast a·palisade around
Heb 10:13 *moment* until his enemies should·be·laid·out *as*
Mt 10:36 and *the* enemies of·the man·of·clay† *shall·be* his·
Rm 5:10 For if, while·being enemies, we·are·reconciled to·

Rm 11:28 good·news, *they·are* enemies on·account·of yeu,
Rv 11:12 the thick·cloud, and their enemies observed them.

G2190.3 A-VSM ἐχθρέ (1x)

Ac 13:10 ·Son of·Slanderer! O·Enemy of·all Righteousness,

G2190.3 A-ASM ἐχθρόν (2x)

Mt 5:43 ·love your neighbor and shall·hate your enemy."
2Th 3:15 resolutely·consider *him* not as an·enemy, but·rather

G2190.3 A-APM ἐχθρούς (13x)

Lk 6:27 hearing: "Love yeur enemies, do good to·the·ones
Lk 6:35 So·even·more, love yeur enemies, and beneficially·
Lk 19:27 'Moreover, those my enemies, the·ones not
Lk 20:43 until I·should·lay·out your enemies *as* your foot
Ac 2:35 until I·should·lay·out your enemies *as* your foot
Heb 1:13 until I·should·lay·out your enemies *as* your foot
Mt 5:44 say to·yeu, love yeur enemies, bless the·ones who·
Mt 22:44 until I·should·lay·out your enemies *as* your foot
Mk 12:36 until I·should·lay·out your enemies *as* your foot
Php 3:18 I·say *that they·are* the enemies of·the cross of·the
1Co 15:25 he·should·place all the enemies under his·own
Col 1:21 ·alienated and enemies in·*your*·innermost·mind by
Rv 11:5 of·their mouth and devours their enemies. And if

G2190.3 A-GSM ἐχθροῦ (1x)

Lk 10:19 all the power of·the enemy; and not·even·one·thing

G2190.3 A-GPM ἐχθρῶν (2x)

Lk 1:71 Salvation from·among our enemies and from·among
Lk 1:74 out of·*the*·hand of·our enemies) to·ritually·minister

G2191 ἔχιδνα échidna *n.* (5x)
xLangAlso:H6848

G2191.1 N-NSF ἔχιδνα (1x)

Ac 28:3 *them* on the fire, a·viper, coming·forth out of·the

G2191.1 N-GPF ἐχιδνῶν (4x)

Lk 3:7 "O·offspring of·vipers, who gave·any·indication to·
Mt 3:7 to·them, "O·offspring of·vipers, who gave·any·
Mt 12:34 O·offspring of·vipers, being evil, in·what·way are·
Mt 23:33 O·serpents, O·offspring of·vipers, in·what·way

G2192 ἔχω échō *v.* (714x)
σχέω schéō
[alternate form, certain tenses only]

G2192.1 V-FAI-2S ἕξεις (4x)

Lk 18:22 ·helplessly·poor, and you·shall·have treasure in
Mt 19:21 helplessly·poor, and you·shall·have treasure in
Mk 10:21 helplessly·poor, and you·shall·have treasure in
Rm 13:3 ·thing, and you·shall·have high·praise from·among

G2192.1 V-FAI-2P ἕξετε (1x)

Rv 2:10 yeu·may·be·tried, and yeu·shall·have tribulation ten

G2192.1 V-FAI-3S ἕξει (5x)

Jn 8:12 in the darkness, but·rather shall·have the light of·the
Lk 11:5 "Which from·among yeu shall·have a·friend, and
Gal 6:4 ·own work, and then he·shall·have the boasting in
Mt 12:11 ·be from·among yeu that shall·have one sheep, that
2Ti 2:17 gangrene, shall·have a·susceptible·body·as·pasture,

G2192.1 V-FAI-3P ἕξουσιν (1x)

1Co 7:28 ·fail. But such·ones shall·have tribulation in·the

G2192.1 V-PAI-1S ἔχω (41x)

Jn 4:17 answered and declared, "I·do·not have a·husband."
Jn 4:17 "You·declared well, 'I·do·not have a·husband.'
Jn 4:32 to·them, "I·myself have a·full·meal to·eat that yeu·
Jn 5:7 him, "Sir, I·have no man·of·clay†, whenever the
Jn 5:36 "But I·myself have the greater testimony *than·that*
Jn 8:26 I·have many·things to·speak and to·judge concerning
Jn 8:49 "I·myself do·not have a·demon, but·rather I·deeply·
Jn 10:16 And I·have other sheep which are not from·among
Jn 10:18 it down of·my·own·self. I·have authority to·lay it
Jn 10:18 to·lay it down, and I·have authority to·take it again.
Jn 16:12 "I·have yet many·things to·say to·yeu, but·yet yeu·
Jn 19:10 personally·know that I·have authority to·crucify
Jn 19:10 to·crucify you, and I·have authority to·fully·release
Lk 7:40 him, "Simon, I·have something to·declare to·you.
Lk 11:6 and I·do·not have that·which I·shall·place·before
Lk 12:17 'What should·I·do, because I·have no place·where
Lk 12:50 But I·have an·immersion to·be·immersed·in, and
Lk 14:18 a·plot·of·land, and I·have dire·need to·go·out and
Lk 16:28 for I·have five brothers; *send him* so·that he·may·
Ac 3:6 ·me, but that·thing which I·do·have, I·give to·you.
Ac 25:26 whom I·do·not have something absolutely·certain
Mt 3:14 saying, "I·myself have need to·be·immersed by
Rm 15:17 Accordingly, I·have a·boast in Jesus Anointed in·
Jac 2:18 "You have trust, and·I have works." Show me your
Php 2:20 For I·have not·even·one·man of·such·kindred·soul,
1Co 7:25 I·do·not have an·authoritative·assignment of·*the*·
1Co 9:17 ·thing voluntarily, I·have a·payment·of·service,
1Co 12:21 to·declare to·the hand, "I·have no need of·you,"
1Co 12:21 the head to·the feet, "I·have no need of·yeu.
1Co 15:31 our boast, which I·have in Anointed-One Jesus
2Co 2:4 ·know the love which I·have more·abundantly for
Col 2:1 ·a·huge strenuous·struggle I·have concerning yeu,
1Ti 1:12 And I·have gratitude to·Anointed-One Jesus our
2Ti 1:3 I·have gratitude to·God (to·whom I·ritually·minister
2Ti 1:3 how without·ceasing I·have a·reminder concerning
3Jn 1:4 I·have no joy even·greater·than these·things, that I·
Rv 1:18 So·be·it,·Amen; and I·have the keys of·Hades and
Rv 2:4 'But·yet I·have *this* against you, that you·left your
Rv 2:14 'But·yet I·have a·few·things against you, because
Rv 2:20 'But·yet I·have a·few·things against you, because
Rv 3:17 ·wealthy and have need of·not·even·one·thing," yet

G2192.1 V-PAI-1P ἔχομεν (46x)

Jn 8:41 ·born out of·sexual·immorality. We·have one Father
Jn 13:29 "Buy *those·things* that we·have need·of for the
Jn 19:7 answered him, "We·ourselves have an·Oral-law, and
Jn 19:15 chief·priests answered, "We·have no king except
Lk 3:8 within yeurselves, 'We·have AbRaham *for·our* father
Lk 22:71 "What need do·we·have of·any·further testimony
Heb 4:15 For we·do·not have a·high·priest who·is·not being·
Heb 6:19 Which *Expectation* we·have as an·anchor of·the
Heb 8:1 *this·is the* summary: we·do·have such a·High·Priest
Heb 13:10 We·have a·Sacrifice·Altar from·among which
Heb 13:14 For here we·have no continuing city, but·rather
Heb 13:18 ·have·confidence that we·have a·good conscience
Gal 2:4 ·spy·out our liberty which we·have in Anointed-One
Gal 6:10 Accordingly, as we·have opportunity, we·should·
Mt 3:9 within yeurselves, 'We·have AbRaham *for·our* father
Mt 14:17 to·him, "We·do·not have *anything* here except
Mt 26:65 What further need have·we of·witnesses?
Mk 8:16 "*It·is* because we·do·not have bread."
Mk 14:63 "What need do·we·have of·any·further witnesses
Rm 5:1 ·righteous as·a·result of·trust, we·have peace toward
Rm 12:4 For exactly·as we·have many members in one body
2Pe 1:19 Also, we·have more·firmly the prophetic word, to·
1Th 1:9 what·manner of·accessible·entrance we·have to you,
2Th 3:9 Not because we·do·not have authority, but·rather
1Co 2:16 ' But we·ourselves have Anointed-One's mind.
1Co 8:1 We·personally·know that we·all have knowledge.
1Co 9:4 ¿!·Do we·not have privilege to·eat and to·drink?
1Co 9:5 ¿!·Do we·not have privilege to·lead·about a·wife
1Co 9:6 *excluded*? ¿!·Do·we·not have privilege to·not work
1Co 11:16 we·ourselves do·not have *any·other* such custom
2Co 3:4 And such confidence we·have through the
2Co 4:7 But we·have this treasure in earthenware vessels, in·
2Co 5:1 ·tent should·be·demolished, we·have (from·out of·
Eph 1:7 in whom we·have the ransom·in·full through his
Eph 2:18 him, the both *of·us* have the embraceable·access to
Eph 3:12 in whom we·have the freeness·of·speech and the
Col 1:14 in whom we·have the ransom·in·full through his
Phm 1:7 For we·have much gratitude and comfort in your
1Jn 1:6 If we·should·declare that we·have fellowship with
1Jn 1:7 is in the light, we·have fellowship with one·another,
1Jn 1:8 we·should·declare that we·do·not have moral·failure,
1Jn 2:1 ·morally·fail, we·have a·Companion/Intercessor
1Jn 3:21 us, *then* we·have freeness·of·speech toward God.
1Jn 4:21 this commandment we·presently·have from him,
1Jn 5:14 is the freeness·of·speech that we·have toward him,
1Jn 5:15 we·personally·know that we·have the requests,

G2192.1 V-PAI-2S ἔχεις (25x)

Jn 4:11 "Sir, you·have not·even a·bucket·for·drawing·water,
Jn 4:11 So·then from·what·source do·you·have the living
Jn 6:68 whom shall·we·go? You·have utterances of·eternal
Jn 7:20 answered and declared, "You·have a·demon! Who
Jn 8:48 you·yourself are a·Samaritan, and have a·demon?
Jn 8:52 "Now we·have·known that you·have a·demon.
Jn 13:8 ·not wash you, you·do·not have a·portion with me.
Jn 16:30 you·have·seen all·things, and have no need that
Lk 12:19 "Soul, you·have many beneficially·good·things
Lk 18:22 Sell all·things, as·many·things·as you·have, and
Ac 23:19 "What is·it that you·have to·announce to·me?
Mt 25:25 ·silver in the earth. See, you·have *what is* yours.
Mk 10:21 head·on·out, sell as·much·as you·have, and give
Rm 14:22 Do·you·yourself have trust?
Jac 2:18 someone shall·declare, "You have trust, and·I have
1Co 4:7 ·*another*? And what·do you·have that you·did·not
Phm 1:5 love and trust which you·have toward the Lord
Rv 2:3 ·lifted·and·carried, and you·have patient·endurance,
Rv 2:6 But·yet you·have this, that you·hate the deeds of·the
Rv 2:14 because you·have there ones·securely·holding·to
Rv 2:15 you·yourself also have ones·securely·holding·to the
Rv 3:1 ·know your works, that you·have the name that you·
Rv 3:4 'You·have a·few names even in Sardis which did·not
Rv 3:8 is·able to·shut it, because you·have a·little power,
Rv 3:11 Securely·hold that·which you·have, in·order·that

G2192.1 V-PAI-2P ἔχετε (41x)

Jn 5:38 And yeu·do·not have his Redemptive-word abiding in
Jn 5:42 ·known yeu, that yeu·do·not have the love of·God in
Jn 6:53 his blood, yeu·do·not have life-above in yeurselves.
Jn 12:8 For yeu always have the helplessly·poor among
Jn 12:8 But me, yeu·have not always."
Jn 12:35 with yeu. Walk for·as·long·as yeu·have the light,
Jn 12:36 For·as·long·as yeu·have the light, trust in the light,
Jn 16:22 yeu·yeurselves in·fact now have grief. But I·shall·
Jn 16:33 In the world, yeu·have tribulation, but·yet be·of·
Jn 21:5 Little·children, ¿! do·yeu·have anything for·eating?
Lk 24:41 ·declared to·them, "Do·yeu·have anything edible
Heb 5:12 to·be instructors, *yeu·still* have need *for·one* to·
Heb 10:36 For yeu·have need of·patient·endurance in·order·
Mt 5:46 payment·of·service do·yeu·have? Do·not·indeed
Mt 6:1 yeu·do·not have a·payment·of·service personally·
Mt 6:8 *are* needed before yeu·yeurselves have the *need* to·
Mt 15:34 "How·many loaves·of·bread do·yeu·have?" And
Mt 26:11 For yeu always have the helplessly·poor among
Mt 26:11 yeurselves, but me, yeu·do·not always have.
Mt 27:65 replied to·them, "Yeu·have a·sentinel·guard.
Mk 4:40 ·this·manner? How·is·it *that* yeu·do·not have trust?
Mk 6:38 ·many loaves·of·bread do·yeu·have? Head·on·out
Mk 8:5 "How·many loaves·of·bread do·yeu·have?" And
Mk 8:17 ·deliberate *that it·is* because yeu·do·not have bread?
Mk 11:25 ·yeu·are·praying, if yeu·have anything against
Mk 14:7 For yeu always have the helplessly·poor among
Mk 14:7 But me, yeu·have not always.
Rm 6:22 already·being·enslaved to·God, yeu·have yeur fruit
Jac 3:14 But if yeu·have bitter jealousy and contention in
Jac 4:2 Yeu·long·for and do·not have. Yeu·murder and
Jac 4:2 and wage·war, but yeu·do·not have, on·account *that*
1Th 3:6 and that yeu·have a·beneficially·good remembrance
1Th 4:9 the brotherly·affection, yeu·have no need *for·me* to·
1Th 5:1 the seasons, brothers, yeu·have no need *for·me* to·
1Co 6:19 *who·is* in yeu, which yeu·have from God, and yeu·
1Co 11:22 *Why*? ¿! For do·yeu·not have homes to·eat and
Col 4:1 having·seen that yeu also have a·Lord in *the*
1Jn 2:20 But yeu·yeurselves do·have an·anointing from the
1Jn 2:27 presently·abides in yeu, and yeu·have no need that
1Jn 5:13 ·know that *the* life-above *that* yeu·have *is* eternal,
Rv 2:25 that·which yeu·presently·have, securely·hold even·

G2192.1 V-PAI-3S ἔχει (91x)

Jn 3:36 The·one trusting in the Son has eternal life-above, and
Jn 4:44 already·testified that, "A·prophet has no honor in
Jn 5:24 trusting the·one sending me has eternal life-above,
Jn 5:26 For just·as the Father has life-above in himself, in·
Jn 6:9 a·little·boy here, who has five barley loaves·of·bread,
Jn 6:47 to·yeu, the·one trusting in me has eternal life-above.
Jn 6:54 and drinking my blood, has eternal life-above, and

Jn 10:20 them were·saying, “He·has a·demon and is·raving·
Jn 12:48 not receiving my utterances, has *this* one presently·
Jn 13:10 “The·one having·been·bathed has no need other·
Jn 14:30 comes, and he·does·not have not·even·one·thing in
Jn 15:13 “A·love greater·than this, has not·even·one·man,
Jn 16:15 ·things, as·many·things·as the Father has, are mine.
Jn 16:21 ·reproduce·and·give·birth, she·has grief because
Jn 19:11 handing me over to·you has a·greater moral·failure.
Lk 5:24 that the Son of·Clay·Man† has authority upon the
Lk 7:33 nor drinking wine, and yeu·say, ‘He·has a·demon.’
Lk 9:58 the Son of·Clay·Man† does·not have *a·place* where
Lk 14:28 calculates the expense, whether he·has the *means*
Lk 17:9 “¿!·Does he·have gratitude *toward* that slave
Lk 19:25 to·him, ‘Lord, he·*already*·has ten more·minas!’
Lk 19:26 even what he·has shall·be·taken·away from him).
Lk 19:31 ‘Because the Lord has need of·it.’”
Lk 19:34 And they·declared, “The Lord has need of·it.”
Lk 20:24 derived·image and inscription does·it·have?” And
Lk 22:37 ’ for even the·things concerning me have an·end.”
Lk 24:39 see, because a·spirit does·not have flesh and bones
Ac 9:14 And here, he·has authority personally·from the
Ac 14:9 at·him and seeing that he·has trust to·be·saved,
Ac 15:21 from·out of·ancient generations, has in·each city
Ac 23:17 ·commander, for he·has a·certain·thing to·report
Heb 3:3 planning·and·constructing the house has more honor
Heb 7:24 to the coming·age, has the non-transferable sacred·
Heb 7:27 who does·not have a·necessity each day, just·as the
Heb 10:35 ·declaration, which has great reward·for·service.
Mt 5:23 ·to·mind that your brother has anything against you,
Mt 8:20 of·Clay·Man† does·not have anywhere he·may·prop
Mt 9:6 ·know that the Son of·Clay·Man† has authority on the
Mt 11:18 nor drinking, and they·say, ‘He·has a·demon.’
Mt 13:12 even that·which he·has shall·be·taken·away from
Mt 13:21 But he·does·not have root in himself, but·rather he·
Mt 13:44 ·out and sells all (as·much·as he·has) and buys that
Mt 21:3 yeu·shall·declare, ‘The Lord has need of·them,’ and
Mt 25:29 even that·which he·has shall·be·taken·away from
Mk 2:10 that the Son of·Clay·Man† has authority on the
Mk 3:22 were·saying “He·has Baalzebul,·Master-Of-Dung,”
Mk 3:26 able to·remain·established, but·rather has an·end.
Mk 3:29 the Holy Spirit does·not have pardon into the
Mk 3:30 they·were·saying, “He·has an·impure spirit.”
Mk 4:23 “If any·man has ears to·hear, let·him·hear.
Mk 4:25 even that·which he·has shall·be·taken·away from
Mk 7:16 If any·man has ears to·hear, let·him·hear.
Mk 11:3 Yeu·declare ‘The Lord has need of·him.’ And
Rm 4:2 ·as·righteous as·a·result of·works, he·has a·boast,
Rm 8:9 But if any·man does·not have Anointed-One's Spirit,
Rm 9:21 Or does·not the potter have authority *over* the clay,
Rm 12:4 but all the members have not the same practice,
1Co 7:7 But·yet each·man has his·own gracious·bestowment
1Co 7:12 Lord— if any brother has a·non-trusting wife, and
1Co 7:13 And a·wife who has a·non-trusting husband also—
1Co 7:37 *financial* necessity, but has authority concerning
1Co 12:12 ·as the body is one and has many members, and
1Co 12:23 our indecent·parts have more·abundant decorum.
1Co 12:24 Now our decent·parts have no *such* need, but·yet
1Co 14:26 ·come·together, each·one of·yeu has a·psalm,
1Co 14:26 of·yeu has a·psalm, has an·instruction, has a·
1Co 14:26 has an·instruction, has a·bestowed·tongue, has
1Co 14:26 has a·bestowed·tongue, has a·revelation, has a·
1Co 14:26 has a·revelation, has a·translation. All·things
2Co 8:12 ·have, not according·to·what he·does·not have.
Eph 5:5 is an·idolater— does·not have any·inheritance in
Col 4:13 For I·testify for·him, that he·has much zeal over
1Ti 5:4 But if any widow has children or grandchildren,
1Ti 5:16 or a·woman·that·trusts) has solitary·widows, let·
1Jn 2:23 ·is·denying the Son does·not·even have the Father.
1Jn 3:15 that any man-killer† does·not have eternal life-above
1Jn 4:16 and have·trusted the Love that God has in us. God
1Jn 4:18 because the fear has a·tormenting·punishment. But
1Jn 5:10 ·one trusting in the Son of·God has the testimony in
1Jn 5:12 The·one having the Son has the life-above; the·one
1Jn 5:12 having the Son of·God does·not have the life-above.
2Jn 1:9 the instruction of·Anointed-One, does·not have God.
2Jn 1:9 instruction of·Anointed-One, this·one has both the
Rv 9:11 and in the Greek·language he·has *this* name,
Rv 12:6 where she·has a·place having·been·made·ready by
Rv 12:12 rage, having·seen that he·has *but* a·brief season.
Rv 13:9 If any·man has an·ear, let·him·hear.
Rv 13:14 for·the Daemonic·Beast, which has the gash by·the
Rv 19:16 And he·has on the garment and on his thigh the
Rv 20:6 the Second Death does·not have authority, but·rather
Rv 21:23 And the CITY has no need of·the sun, neither of·

G2192.1 V-PAI-3P ἔχουσιν (33x)

Jn 2:3 of·Jesus says to him, “They·do·not have wine.”
Jn 15:22 but now they·do·not have a·pretense concerning
Lk 5:31 “The·ones being·healthy·and·sound have no need
Lk 8:13 the Redemptive-word; yet these have no root, who
Lk 9:58 declared to·him, “The foxes have burrows, and the
Lk 14:14 they·do·not have *that·with·which* to·recompense
Lk 15:7 over ninety-nine righteous·men who have no need
Lk 16:29 AbRaham says to·him, ‘They·have Moses and the
Ac 19:38 with·him have a·matter specifically·against any·
Heb 7:5 they·have a·commandment to·receive·tithes·of the
Heb 13:10 ·ministering in·the Tabernacle have no privilege
Mt 8:20 says to·him, “The foxes have burrows, and the birds
Mt 9:12 to·them, “The·ones being·well have no need of·a·
Mt 14:16 declared to·them, “They·have no need to·go·off;
Mt 15:32 days, and they·do·not have *anything* which they·
Mk 2:17 to·them, “The·ones being·well have no need of·a·
Mk 2:19 *For* as·long a·time as they·do·have the bridegroom
Mk 4:17 Yet they·do·not have root in themselves, but·rather
Mk 6:36 for they·do·not have that·which they·may·eat.”
Mk 8:2 three days and do·not have that·which they·may·eat.
Rm 10:2 For I·testify for·them that they·have a·zeal of·God,
1Co 12:30 Not all have gracious·bestowments of·healing.
Rv 2:24 in Thyatira (as·many·as do·not have this instruction
Rv 4:8 And they·do·not have a·rest·break day and night,
Rv 9:3 to·them, as the scorpions of·the earth have authority.
Rv 9:4 the men·of·clay† who do·not have the official·seal
Rv 9:10 And they·have tails like scorpions, and there·were
Rv 9:11 And they·have a·king over them— the angel of·the
Rv 11:6 These have authority to·shut the sky, in·order·that
Rv 11:6 of·their prophecy. And they·have authority over the
Rv 14:11 and its derived·image do·not have a·rest·break day
Rv 17:13 “These have *just* one plan, and they·thoroughly·
Rv 22:5 Also, they·do·not have need of·a·lantern, nor·even

G2192.1 V-PAM-2S ἔχε (2x)

Lk 14:18 I·ask *that* you have me excused.’
Lk 14:19 I·ask *that* you have me excused.’

G2192.1 V-PAM-2P ἔχετε (2x)

Mk 9:50 what shall·yeu·season it? “Have salt in yeurselves,
Mk 11:22 Jesus says to·them, “Have God's *type·of* trust.

G2192.1 V-PAM-3S ἐχέτω (3x)

Jac 1:4 But let the patient·endurance have *her* complete work
1Co 7:2 ·immoralities, each *man* must·have his·own wife,
1Co 7:2 wife, and each *woman* must·have her·own husband.

G2192.1 V-PAN ἔχειν (25x)

Jn 5:26 he·gave also to·the Son to·have life-above in himself
Jn 5:39 yeu·yeurselves presume to·have eternal life-above by
Lk 8:18 ·taken·away even that·which he·presumes to·have.”
Lk 9:3 neither money; neither to·have two tunics apiece.
Ac 24:16 I·exert myself: to·have continually a·conscience
Ac 24:23 to·keep Paul, and·also to·hold *him·at* ease, and to·
Heb 8:3 *it·is* necessary *for* this·man to·have something also
Heb 10:2 ·been·purified *so·as* to·have not·one·bit further a·
Heb 10:34 knowing for yeurselves to·have in *the* heavens a·
Heb 11:25 ·God than to·have full·enjoyment of·moral·failure
Mt 13:5 ·surface, on·account·of it not having depth of·earth.
Mt 13:6 And on·account·of it not having root, it·is·already·
Mt 14:4 “It·is·not proper for·you to·have her.”
Mk 3:15 and to·have authority to·both·relieve·and·cure the
Mk 4:5 ·surface, on·account·of it·not having depth of·earth.
Mk 4:6 ·sun, and·then on·account·of it·not having root, it·
Mk 6:18 “It·is·not proper for·you to·have your brother's wife
Php 1:7 of·all of·yeu, on·account·of having yeu in my heart.
2Pe 1:15 ·quickly·endeavor for·yeu to·have at·any·time,
1Th 1:8 such·for us not to·have need to·speak anything.
1Co 5:1 Gentiles, such·for someone to·have the father's wife
1Co 7:40 advice; and I·suppose also to·have God's Spirit.
1Co 11:10 the woman is·obligated to·have authority on her
2Co 8:11 — but from·out *of·that·which* yeu·presently·have.
1Ti 3:7 ·is·mandatory·for him also to·have a·good testimony

G2192.1 V-PAN@ ἔχειν (1x)

Jac 2:14 though someone should·say he·has trust but

G2192.1 V-PAO-3P ἔχοιεν (1x)

Ac 24:19 if they·may·actually·have anything specifically·

G2192.1 V-PAP-ASN ἔχον (2x)

Rv 13:1 ascending out of·the sea, having seven heads and
Rv 17:3 of·names of·revilement, having seven heads and ten

G2192.1 V-PAP-ASF ἔχουσαν (7x)

Ac 16:16 servant·girl having a·spirit of·Pythonic·divination
Heb 11:10 ·was·waiting·for the CITY having the foundations
Mk 11:13 ·seeing a·fig·tree in·the·distance having leaves,
Eph 5:27 the entire·Called·Out·Citizenry not having stain,
Rv 21:11 having the glory of·God (even her brilliance *was*
Rv 21:12 also having a·wall great and high, having twelve
Rv 21:12 a·wall great and high, having twelve gates, and

G2192.1 V-PAP-ASM ἔχοντα (20x)

Jn 11:17 Jesus found him having *been·laid·to·rest* in the
Lk 12:5 after the killing, *is* having authority to·cast *a·person*
Lk 24:39 flesh and bones, just·as yeu·observe me having.”
Ac 23:18 young·man to you, having something to·speak to·
Ac 23:29 ·their Oral-law, but having not·even·one allegation
Ac 27:39 ·were·fully·observing a·certain bay having a·shore,
Heb 2:14 ·fully·render·impotent the·one having the might of·
Heb 7:6 and he·has·blessed the·one having the promises.
Mk 9:17 I·brought to you my son, having a·mute spirit,
Mk 9:43 the life-above crippled, than having the two hands
Mk 9:45 into the life-above, than having two feet *and* to·be·
Mk 9:47 of·God with·one·eye, than having two eyes *and* to·
Rm 2:20 an·instructor of·infants, having the formula of·the
1Co 8:10 should·see you (the·one having knowledge) laying·
1Ti 3:4 his·own house well, having his·children in
1Jn 3:17 should·presently·observe his brother having need,
Rv 7:2 *the* eastern sun, having an·official·seal of·the·living
Rv 14:6 in *the* mid-heaven, having *the* eternal good·news to·
Rv 18:1 from·out of·the heaven, having great authority; and
Rv 20:1 from·out of·the heaven, having the key of·the

G2192.1 V-PAP-APM ἔχοντας (8x)

Lk 9:11 the·ones having need of·therapeutic·relief·and·cure.
Ac 19:13 ·the Lord Jesus over the·ones having the evil spirits
Heb 7:28 men·of·clay† *as* high·priests having weakness, but
1Co 11:22 and put·to·shame the·ones not having? What
Rv 9:17 sitting·down on them, having full·chest·armor, fiery
Rv 15:1 and marvelous, seven angels having the last seven
Rv 15:2 on the transparent,·glassy sea, having harps of·God.
Rv 16:2 to the men·of·clay†, the·ones having the etching of·

G2192.1 V-PAP-DSF ἐχούσῃ (1x)

1Th 5:3 assaults them, just·as having the birth·pang, the·one

G2192.1 V-PAP-DSM ἔχοντι (9x)

Lk 3:11 tunics must·kindly·give to·the·one not having *any*,
Lk 6:8 to·the man·of·clay†, the·one having the withered
Lk 19:24 and give *it* to·the·one having the ten more·minas.
Lk 19:26 ·yeu, that to·any one having, *more* shall·be·given.
Mt 25:28 and give *it* to·the·one having ten talants·of·silver.’
Mk 3:3 to·the man·of·clay†, the·one having the withered
1Pe 4:5 an·account to·the·one having readiness to·judge *the*·
Eph 4:28 ·*enough* to·kindly·give to·the·one having need.
Rv 14:18 ·out with·a·loud yell to·the·one having the sharp

G2192.1 V-PAP-GSN ἔχοντος (1x)

Rv 17:7 ·Beast bearing her, the·one having the seven heads

G2192.1 V-PAP-GSF ἐχούσης (1x)

Gal 4:27 more children than the·one having the husband.”

G2192.1 V-PAP-GSM ἔχοντος (3x)

Lk 19:26 But of·the·one not having, even what he·has shall·
Mt 18:25 But with·him not having *the ability* to·repay, his
Rv 16:9 name of·God— the·one having authority over these

G2192.1 V-PAP-GPM ἐχόντων (9x)
Lk 7:42 And with·them not having *the ability* to·repay, he·
Lk 12:4 after these·things not having anything much·more
Ac 8:7 were·coming·out of·many of·the·ones having *them*,
Heb 5:14 through habit toward having discernment of·both
Mk 8:1 immense and not having that·which they·may·eat),
Rv 12:17 commandments of·God and having the testimony
Rv 17:1 the seven angels, of·the·one having the seven vials,
Rv 19:10 and of·your brothers having the testimony of·
Rv 21:9 ·the seven angels (of·the·ones having the seven vials
G2192.1 V-PAP-NSN ἔχον (4x)
Lk 11:36 *is* full·of·light, not having any part opaquely·dark,
Rv 4:7 and the third living·being *is* having the face as a·man·
Rv 5:6 as having·been·slaughtered, having seven horns and
Rv 21:14 the wall of·the CITY *is* having twelve foundations,
G2192.1 V-PAP-NSF ἔχουσα (11x)
Jn 5:2 in JeruSalem, there·is a·pool having five colonnades;
Lk 13:11 there·was a·woman having a·spirit of·sickness
Lk 15:8 Or what woman, having ten drachma·coins·*of·silver*
Heb 9:4 having a·golden censer and the Ark of·the covenant
Heb 9:4 in which *was* a·golden urn having the manna, and
Mt 26:7 him a·woman having an·alabaster·flask of·deeply·
Mk 14:3 a·woman having an·alabaster·flask of·extremely·
Rm 9:10 with·Rebeqah also, having a·conception *of·twins*
1Ti 4:8 ·for all·things, having promise of·life-above for·the
Rv 17:4 stones and pearls, *and* having a·golden cup in her
Rv 17:18 the Great City, the·one having a·kingdom over the
G2192.1 V-PAP-NSM ἔχων (74x)
Jn 3:29 "The·one having the bride is a·bridegroom.
Jn 14:21 "The·one having my commandments, and
Jn 18:10 Now·then, having a·dagger, Simon Peter drew it
Lk 3:11 to·them, "The·one having two tunics must·kindly·
Lk 3:11 *any*, and the·one having food must·do likewise.
Lk 4:33 ·was a·man·of·clay† having a·spirit of·an·impure
Lk 7:8 being·assigned under authority, having soldiers under
Lk 8:8 he·was·hollering·out, "The·one having ears to·hear,
Lk 14:35 "The·one having ears to·hear, let·him·hear.
Lk 15:4 ·of·clay† from·among yeu, having a·hundred sheep,
Lk 17:7 ·is·there from·among yeu having a·slave plowing or
Lk 19:17 in very·little, be having authority over ten cities.
Lk 20:28 any·man's brother should·die while·having a·wife,
Lk 22:36 "But·yet now, the·one having a·pouch, let·him·
Lk 22:36 And the·one not having a·dagger, let·him·sell his
Ac 24:15 having an·expectation in God, which these·men
Ac 28:19 Caesar, though not·as having anything *of·which* to·
Heb 7:3 ·mother, without·lineage, having neither beginning
Heb 10:1 For the Torah-Law, having a·shadow of·the
Mt 7:29 he·was instructing them as *one* having authority, and
Mt 8:9 ·man·of·clay† under authority, having soldiers under
Mt 11:15 "The·one having ears to·hear, let·him·hear.
Mt 12:10 behold, there·was a·man·of·clay† having the hand
Mt 13:9 The·one having ears to·hear, let·him·hear.
Mt 13:43 "The·one having ears to·hear, let·him·hear.
Mt 22:12 did·you·enter here not having wedding apparel?
Mt 22:24 if a·certain·man should·die not having children, his
Mt 22:25 completely·died. And·so not having offspring†,
Mk 1:22 for he·was instructing them as one·having authority,
Mk 3:1 there·was a·man·of·clay† there having the withered
Mk 4:9 ·was·saying to·them, "The·one having ears to·hear,
Mk 12:6 "So·then, yet having one son, his well-beloved, he·
Rm 15:23 ·now, no·longer having a·place *to·publicly·work*
Rm 15:23 these vicinities, and having a·great·yearning for
Php 1:23 as·a·result of·the two *choices*, having the longing
Php 3:4 I·myself *was once* also having confidence in flesh.
Php 3:9 ·found in him, not having my·own righteousness
Tit 1:6 a·husband of·one wife, having trustworthy children
Tit 2:8 may·be·embarrassed, having not·even·one mediocre
1Co 6:1 ·yeu, having a·matter·of·consequence specifically·
1Co 7:37 in the heart, not having *financial* necessity, but has
1Co 11:4 praying or prophesying, having *his* head fully·
Phm 1:8 Therefore, while·having much freeness·of·speech
1Ti 6:16 the only·one having immortality, dwelling *in*
2Ti 2:19 foundation of·God stands, having this official·seal,
1Jn 3:3 And any one having this Expectation in him cleanses
1Jn 5:12 The·one having the Son has the life-above; the·one
1Jn 5:12 the life-above; the·one not having the Son of·God
2Jn 1:12 Having many·things to·write to·yeu *all*, I·am·
Rv 1:16 and having in his right hand seven stars.
Rv 2:7 'The·one having an·ear, let·him·hear what the Spirit
Rv 2:11 'The·one having an·ear, let·him·hear what the Spirit
Rv 2:12 'These·things says the·one having the sharp,
Rv 2:17 'The·one having an·ear, let·him·hear what the Spirit
Rv 2:18 the Son of·God, the·one having his eyes as a·blaze
Rv 2:29 'The·one having an·ear, let·him·hear what the Spirit
Rv 3:1 'These·things says the·one having the Spirits of·God
Rv 3:6 'The·one having an·ear, let·him·hear what the Spirit
Rv 3:7 Truthful·One, "'The·one having the key of·David,
Rv 3:13 'The·one having an·ear, let·him·hear what the Spirit
Rv 3:22 'The·one having an·ear, let·him·hear what the Spirit
Rv 6:2 the·one who·is·sitting·down on it having a·bow. And
Rv 6:5 who·is·sitting·down on it having a·balance·scale in
Rv 8:3 ·Altar, having a·golden censer·for·frankincense; and
Rv 12:3 a·great fiery·red Dragon, having seven heads and
Rv 12:12 descended to yeu! *He·is* having great rage, having·
Rv 13:17 or to·sell, except the·one having the etching, or the
Rv 13:18 is the wisdom. The·one having the understanding,
Rv 14:14 ·down like a·son of·clay·man†, having on his head
Rv 14:17 in the heaven, he also *was* having a·sharp sickle.
Rv 14:18 out·from the Sacrifice·Altar, having authority over
Rv 17:9 mind·*(or·understanding)*, the·one having wisdom.
Rv 19:12 royal·turbans, having a·name having·been·written
Rv 20:6 ·blessed and holy *is* the·one having part in the First
G2192.1 V-PAP-NPN ἔχοντα (7x)
Mt 9:36 ·been·flung·about, as sheep not having a·shepherd.
Mt 18:8 lame or crippled, rather·than having two hands or
Mt 18:9 life-above with·one·eye, rather·than having two eyes
Mk 6:34 they·were "'as sheep not having a·shepherd,'" and
Rm 2:14 Gentiles, the·ones not having Torah-Law, should·
Col 2:23 a·rationalization of·wisdom, having within *them* a·
Rv 8:9 (the·ones in the sea, the·ones having souls) died; and
G2192.1 V-PAP-NPF ἔχουσαι (2x)
Rv 9:19 their tails *were* like serpents having heads, and they·
Rv 14:1 *and* forty four thousand, having the name of·his
G2192.1 V-PAP-NPF@ ἔχουσαι (1x)
1Ti 5:12 being·held·in judgment, because they·set·aside the
G2192.1 V-PAP-NPM ἔχοντες (41x)
Ac 2:47 ·praising God, and having grace alongside all the
Ac 21:23 With·us are four men having a·vow upon
Ac 28:9 the rest also, the·ones having sicknesses on the
Ac 28:29 ·off, having a·large questioning·and·discussion
Heb 4:14 So·then having a·great High·Priest, having·gone·
Heb 5:12 And yeu·have·become ones·having need of·milk
Heb 10:19 of·YeShua, having freeness·of·speech upon the
Heb 12:1 we·ourselves, also having so·vast a·cloud of·
Mt 15:30 came·alongside him, having among themselves
Mk 8:18 'Having eyes, do·yeu·not look?
Mk 8:18 do·yeu·not look? And having ears, do·yeu·not
Mk 10:23 ·difficult *it·is that* the·ones having the valuables
Rm 2:14 these *Gentiles* not having Torah-Law are a·law to·
Rm 8:23 but·rather we·ourselves also, having the firstfruit
Rm 12:6 Now having various gracious·bestowments
Jud 1:19 ·or·partisan·lines, soulish, not having *the* Spirit.
Php 1:30 having the same strenuous·struggle such·as yeu·
Php 2:2 ·contemplate the same·thing, having the same love,
1Pe 3:16 having a·beneficially·good conscience— in·order·
1Pe 4:8 And above all, *continue* having earnest love among
2Pe 2:14 *unrighteous souls* having eyes exceedingly·full of·
2Pe 2:14 unstable souls, having a·heart having·been·trained
1Th 4:13 ·as the rest, the·ones not having an·Expectation.
1Co 7:29 … even the·ones having wives should·be as not
1Co 7:29 the·ones having wives should·be as not having *any*;
2Co 3:12 So·then, having such an·expectation, we·use
2Co 4:1 On·account·of that, having this Service *of·the Spirit*
2Co 4:13 Having the same spirit of·the trust, according·to
2Co 6:10 many, as having not·even·one·thing and·yet fully·
2Co 7:1 Accordingly, having these promises, dearly·beloved
2Co 9:8 toward yeu, in·order·that having all self-sufficiency
2Co 10:6 and having in readiness to·avenge all inattentive·
2Co 10:15 wearisome·labors, but having an·expectation
Eph 2:12 promise, not having an·Expectation·of·Resurrection,
1Ti 6:2 And the·ones having masters that·trust·*in·Jesus*, do·
1Ti 6:8 And having sufficient·nourishment and *the* essential·
2Ti 3:5 having a·formula of·devout·reverence, but having·
Rv 5:8 ·the Lamb, each·one *of·the·Elders* having harps and
Rv 8:6 And the seven angels having the seven trumpets made
Rv 15:6 ·forth from·out of·the Temple, having the seven
Rv 18:19 City, in which all the·ones having ships in the sea
G2192.1 V-PAS-1S ἔχω (7x)
Mt 19:16 ·I·do in·order·that I·may·have eternal life-above?
1Co 13:1 angels, and should·not have love, I·have·become
1Co 13:2 And if·ever I·should·have *the gracious·bestowment*
1Co 13:2 ·knowledge, and if·ever I·should·have all the trust,
1Co 13:2 mountains, and should·not have love, I·am
1Co 13:3 I·should·be·set·ablaze, and should·not have love,
2Co 2:3 lest coming *to·yeu*, I·should·have grief from them·
G2192.1 V-PAS-1P ἔχωμεν (5x)
Heb 6:18 for·God to·lie, we·may·have a·strong consoling
Heb 12:28 kingdom, we·may·have grace through which we·
Rm 15:4 in·order·that we·may·have the Expectation through
1Jn 2:28 ·made·apparent, we·may·have clarity·of·speech,
1Jn 4:17 in·order·that we·may·have freeness·of·speech in
G2192.1 V-PAS-2P ἔχητε (12x)
Jn 5:40 ·come to me, in·order·that yeu·may·have life-above.
Jn 13:35 disciples to·me, if yeu·should·have love for one·
Jn 16:33 to·yeu, in·order·that in me yeu·may·have peace. In
Jn 20:31 and that trusting, yeu·may·have life-above in his
Mt 17:20 I·say to·yeu, if yeu·should·have trust *that·grows* as
Mt 21:21 I·say to·yeu, if yeu·should·have trust and should·
1Th 4:12 and *that* yeu·may·have need of·not·one·thing.
1Co 4:15 For though yeu·may·have ten·thousand strict·
1Co 6:4 if yeu·should·have arbitrations of·secular·matters,
2Co 1:15 in·order·that yeu·may·have a·second grace,
2Co 5:12 in·order·that yeu·may·have *an·answer* specifically·
1Jn 1:3 in·order·that yeu also may·have fellowship with us,
G2192.1 V-PAS-3S ἔχῃ (10x)
Jn 3:15 ·perish, but·rather should·have eternal life-above.
Jn 3:16 ·perish, but·rather should·have eternal life-above.
Jn 6:40 and trusting in him, may·have eternal life-above, and
Lk 8:18 for whoever should·have *comprehension*, to·him
Lk 8:18 and whoever should·not have, from him shall·be·
Jac 2:14 should·say he·has trust but should·not have works?
Jac 2:17 the trust, provided·that it·should·have no works, is
2Co 8:12 according·to·what someone may·have, not
Eph 4:28 in·order·that he·may·have *amply·enough* to·kindly·
1Jn 3:17 But whoever should·have the world's livelihood,
G2192.1 V-PAS-3P ἔχωσιν (5x)
Jn 8:6 him in·order·that they·may·have *something* to·legally·
Jn 10:10 came in·order·that they·may·have life-above, and
Jn 10:10 life-above, and that·they·may·have *it* abundantly.
Jn 17:13 in the world, in·order·that they·may·have my joy
1Ti 5:20 in·order·that the rest also may·have reverent·fear.
G2192.1 V-IAI-1S εἶχον (2x)
Jn 17:5 with·the glory which I·was·having with you before
3Jn 1:13 I·was·having many·things to·write, but·yet I·do·not
G2192.1 V-IAI-1P εἴχομεν (2x)
Heb 12:9 Furthermore, in·fact, we·had fathers of·our flesh,
2Jn 1:5 ·you, but·rather that·which we·were·having from *the*
G2192.1 V-IAI-2S εἶχες (1x)
Jn 19:11 "You·were·not having not·even·one·bit·of authority
G2192.1 V-IAI-2P εἴχετε (4x)
Jn 9:41 ·were blind, yeu·would not have moral·failure. But
Lk 17:6 declared, "If yeu·were·having trust *that·grows* as a·
Rm 6:21 Accordingly, what fruit were·yeu·having then in
1Jn 2:7 ·old commandment which yeu·were·having from *the*
G2192.1 V-IAI-3S εἶχεν (18x)
Jn 2:25 and because he·was·having no need that anyone
Lk 8:27 from·out of·the city, who was·having demons for a·
Lk 15:11 ·declared, "A·certain man·of·clay† had two sons.
Lk 23:17 ·necessity, he·was·having to·fully·release one·man

Ac 2:45 ·to any·particular need someone was·having.
Ac 4:35 ·to any·particular need someone was·having.
Ac 18:18 ·shorn his head in Cenchrea, for he·had a·vow.
Heb 6:13 since he·was·having no·one·at·all greater by
Heb 9:1 also was·having regulations of·ritual·ministry *to·*
Mt 3:4 And *this* same John was·having his apparel *made*
Mt 13:5 rocky·places, where it·was·not having much earth,
Mt 21:28 A·certain·man·of·clay† was·having two children,
Mk 4:5 rocky·ground, where it·was·not having much soil,
Mk 5:3 who was·having his residence among the chamber·
Mk 7:25 whose young·daughter was·having an·impure spirit,
Mk 14:8 made·do with·what she·had. She·came·beforehand
Mk 16:8 they·themselves were·having trembling·of·fear and
Rv 13:11 out of·the earth. And it·was·having two horns like

G2192.1 V-IAI-3P εἶχον (13x)
Jn 15:22 to·them, they·were·not having moral·failure, but
Jn 15:24 ·man has·done, they·would·not have moral·failure.
Ac 2:44 and they·were·having absolutely·all·belongings
Ac 4:14 they·were·having not·even·one·thing to·declare·
Ac 9:31 Galilee and Samaria were·having peace, being·
Ac 13:5 of·the Jews, and they·were·having also John·*Mark*
Ac 25:19 "But they·were·having certain issues specifically·
Heb 11:15 they·would have·had opportunity to·return·back.
Mk 3:10 *of·them* as were·having scourges to·press·toward
Mk 8:14 one loaf·of·bread, they·were·not having *any* in the
Rv 4:8 ·beings, each one itself, was·having six wings apiece
Rv 9:8 And they·were·having hair as hair of·women, and
Rv 9:9 And they·were·having full·chest·armor, as full·chest·

G2192.1 V-2AAI-1S ἔσχον (1x)
Jud 1:3 the common Salvation, I·had necessity to·write to·

G2192.1 V-2AAI-3S ἔσχεν (4x)
Jn 4:52 them the hour in which he·had gotten·better. And
Gal 4:22 it·has·been·written, that AbRaham had two sons,
Mk 2:25 what David did, when he·had need and was·hungry
2Pe 2:16 But he·had a·reproof of·his·own transgression: a·

G2192.1 V-2AAI-3P ἔσχον (1x)
Rv 4:4 in white garments, and they·had on their heads

G2192.1 V-2AAS-1S σχῶ (3x)
Ac 25:26 occurring, I·may·have something to·write.
Rm 1:13 ·and·now), in·order·that I·may·have some fruit
Php 2:27 on·me also, lest I·should·have grief upon grief.

G2192.1 V-RAI-1S ἔσχηκα (1x)
2Co 2:13 I·did·not have an·ease in·my spirit, *for* me not to·

G2192.1 V-RAI-1P ἐσχήκαμεν (2x)
Rm 5:2 through whom also we·have the embraceable·access
2Co 1:9 we, in ourselves, have·had the judicial·sentence of·

G2192.1 V-RAI-3S ἔσχηκεν (1x)
2Co 7:5 Macedonia, our flesh has·had no relaxation at·all,

EG2192.1 (5x)
Lk 9:58 and the birds of·the sky *have* nests, but the Son of·
Heb 10:21 and *having* a·high priest over the house of·God—
Mt 8:20 and the birds of·the sky *have* nests, but the Son of·
2Th 3:2 evil men·of·clay†, for not all·men *have* the trust.
2Co 8:13 I·do·not *mean* that others *should·have* ease, and

G2192.2 V-PAI-1S ἔχω (1x)
Ac 20:24 causes *me concern*, neither do·I·hold my soul *as*

G2192.2 V-PAI-2S ἔχεις (2x)
Jn 4:18 and now, he·whom you·have is·not your husband.
Phm 1:17 So·then, if you·hold me *to·be* a·partner,

G2192.2 V-PAI-2P ἔχετε (2x)
Php 3:17 ·ones walking in·this·manner just·as yeu·hold us *as*
1Co 6:7 among yeu, because yeu·hold judgment among

G2192.2 V-PAI-3P ἔχουσιν (1x)
Mt 21:26 we·fear the crowd, for all hold John as a·prophet.

G2192.2 V-PAM-2P ἔχετε (2x)
Jac 2:1 My brothers, do·not hold the trust of·our Lord
Php 2:29 *the* Lord with all joy, and hold such·men in·honor,

G2192.2 V-PAN ἔχειν (3x)
Lk 8:6 on·account·of *the solid·rock* not holding moisture.
Ac 24:9 professing these·things to·hold *true* in·this·manner.
Rm 1:28 ·did·not examine·and·verify God to·hold *him* in

G2192.2 V-PAO-3S ἔχοι (1x)
Ac 25:16 being·legally·accused actually·holds the legal·

G2192.2 V-PAP-ASN ἔχον (1x)
Ac 24:25 alarmed, answered, "Holding it for·now, depart.

G2192.2 V-PAP-APM ἔχοντας (1x)
1Ti 3:9 *but* holding the Mystery of·the trust in a·pure

G2192.2 V-PAP-NSM ἔχων (3x)
Mt 19:22 ·grieved, for he·was holding many possessions.
Mk 10:22 ·grieved, for he·was holding many possessions.
1Ti 1:19 holding trust and a·beneficially·good conscience.

G2192.2 V-PAP-NPM ἔχοντες (1x)
Lk 18:24 *it·is, that* the·ones holding the valuables shall·enter

G2192.2 V-PAS-3S ἔχῃ (1x)
Col 3:13 If any·man should·hold a·fault specifically·against

G2192.2 V-IAI-1S εἶχον (1x)
Lk 19:20 *here·is* your mina which I·was·holding *for·you,*

G2192.2 V-IAI-3S εἶχεν (10x)
Jn 12:6 he·was a·thief, and was·holding the money·bag, and
Jn 13:29 since Judas was·holding the money·bag, that Jesus
Lk 13:6 "A·certain·man was·holding·onto a·fig·tree having·
Lk 21:4 ·absolutely·all the livelihood that she·was·holding."
Mt 13:46 has·sold·off all (as·much·as he·was·holding) and
Mt 18:25 and all·things as·much·as he·was·holding, and to·
Mk 12:44 cast·in all·things, as·many·as she·was·holding, all
Rv 9:14 to·the sixth angel who was·holding the trumpet,
Rv 10:2 And he·was·holding in his hand a·tiny·official·scroll
Rv 21:15 ·one speaking with me was·holding a·golden reed

G2192.2 V-IAI-3P εἶχον (6x)
Mt 14:5 the crowd, because they·were·holding him as a·
Mt 21:46 ·now *the crowds* were·holding him *with·regard* as
Mt 27:16 they·were·holding a·notable chained·prisoner,
Mk 8:7 And they·were·holding a·few small·fish. And upon·
Mk 11:32 people, for absolutely·all·men were·holding John,
Rv 6:9 ·account·of the testimony which they·were·holding.

G2192.2 V-2AAI-2S ἔσχες (1x)
Jn 4:18 For you·have·had five husbands, and now, he·whom

G2192.2 V-2AAI-3P ἔσχον (3x)
Lk 20:33 ·she·become? For the seven held her *for* a·wife.
Mt 22:28 shall·she·be of·the seven? For they·all held her."
Mk 12:23 ·be of·them? For the seven held her *for* a·wife.

G2192.2 V-RAP-ASM ἐσχηκότα (1x)
Mk 5:15 ·mind, the·one *who·was* having·held the legion.

G2192.3 V-FAI-3S ἕξει (1x)
Mt 1:23 Behold, the veiled·virgin shall·be in pregnancy and

G2192.3 V-FAI-3P ἕξουσιν (1x)
Mk 16:18 hands on unhealthy·ones, and they·shall·be well."

G2192.3 V-PAI-1S ἔχω (2x)
Ac 21:13 heart? For I·myself am in·a·state·of·readiness not
2Co 12:14 Behold, I·am at·the·ready *for* a·third·time to·

G2192.3 V-PAI-2S ἔχεις (1x)
Jn 8:57 declared to him, "You·are not·yet fifty years·of·age,

G2192.3 V-PAI-2P ἔχετε (1x)
Mk 8:17 nor·even comprehend? Is yeur heart still having·

G2192.3 V-PAI-3S ἔχει (5x)
Jn 5:6 ·ill and knowing that he·had·been *in·the sickness*
Jn 9:21 ·not personally·know. He·himself is of·mature·age;
Jn 9:23 his parents declared, "He·is of·mature·age; ask him.
Ac 7:1 designated·high·priest declared, "Are these·things so?
Mk 5:23 "My little·daughter is at·the·final·point·of·death.

G2192.3 V-PAI-3S@ ἔχει (1x)
Mt 13:27 So·then, from·what·source are the darnel·weeds?

G2192.3 V-PAI-3P ἔχουσιν (2x)
Ac 15:36 of·the Lord, *and see* how they·are."
1Co 15:34 ·not morally·fail; for some are ignorant of·God.

G2192.3 V-PAN ἔχειν (1x)
Ac 12:15 ·was·strongly·asserting *for·it* to·be in·this·manner.

G2192.3 V-PAO-3S ἔχοι (1x)
Ac 17:11 these·things might·actually·be in·this·manner.

G2192.3 V-PAP-ASN ἔχον (1x)
Ac 1:12 which is near JeruSalem, being a·Sabbath's journey.

G2192.3 V-PAP-APM ἔχοντας (7x)
Ac 11:3 You·entered·in alongside men being uncircumcised,
Mt 4:24 they·brought to·him all the·ones being badly·ill,
Mt 8:16 both·relieved·and·cured all the·ones being badly·ill,
Mt 14:35 and brought to·him all the·ones being badly·ill,
Mk 1:32 ·bringing to him all the·ones being badly·ill, and
Mk 1:34 ·and·cured many being badly·ill with·a·diversity·of
Mk 6:55 ·about on their mats the·ones being badly·ill, *to*

G2192.3 V-PAP-DPF ἐχούσαις (3x)
Lk 21:23 "But woe to·the·ones being in pregnancy and to·
Mt 24:19 "And woe to·the·ones being in pregnancy and to·
Mk 13:17 "And woe to·the·ones being in pregnancy and to·

G2192.3 V-PAP-GSF ἐχούσης (1x)
Heb 9:8 with·the first Tabernacle still being standing.

G2192.3 V-PAP-NSF ἔχουσα (2x)
Mt 1:18 ·together, she·was·found being in·a·pregnancy
Rv 12:2 And being in pregnancy, she·yelled·out

G2192.3 V-PAP-NSM ἔχων (2x)
Jn 5:5 ·certain man·of·clay† was there, being in the sickness
Lk 7:2 ·him, was·about to·completely·die, being badly·ill.

G2192.3 V-PAP-NPN ἔχοντα (1x)
1Ti 5:25 and the *good works* being otherwise, are·not able

G2192.3 V-PAP-NPM ἔχοντες (4x)
Lk 5:31 ·of·healing, but·rather the·ones being badly·ill.
Mt 9:12 ·of·healing, but·rather the·ones being badly·ill.
Mk 2:17 ·of·healing, but·rather the·ones being badly·ill. I·
1Pe 2:12 the Gentiles, being morally·good in·order·that,

G2192.3 V-IAI-3P εἶχον (1x)
Lk 4:40 sun sinking·down, as·many·as were sick, everyone

G2192.4 V-PPP-APF ἐχομένας (1x)
Mk 1:38 "We·should·head·out into the neighboring towns,

G2192.5 V-PPP-APN ἐχόμενα (1x)
Heb 6:9 and *of·the* things·following·in·line with·Salvation,

G2192.6 V-PPP-DSF ἐχομένῃ (3x)
Lk 13:33 tomorrow, and the *day* following, because it·is·not
Ac 20:15 in Trogyllium, the following *day* we·came to
Ac 21:26 ·taking the men on·the following day *and* being·

G2192.7 V-PAM-2S ἔχε (2x)
Rm 14:22 *Then* accordingly, retain *the good·benefit* for·
2Ti 1:13 Retain *the* primary·model of·healthy·and·sound

G2192.7 V-PAP-NPM ἔχοντες (1x)
1Pe 2:16 *Exist* as free·men, yet not retaining the liberty as a·

G2192.7 V-IAI-3S εἶχεν (1x)
Lk 16:1 man·of·clay† who was·retaining an·estate·manager,

G2192.8 V-PAI-3S ἔχει (3x)
Mt 13:12 For whoever maturely·utilizes·what·he·has, to·him
Mt 13:12 does·not maturely·utilize·what·he·has, even that·
Mk 4:25 does·not maturely·utilize·what·he·has, even that·

G2192.8 V-PAP-DSM ἔχοντι (1x)
Mt 25:29 to·everyone maturely·utilizing·what·he·has, *more*

G2192.8 V-PAP-GSM ἔχοντος (1x)
Mt 25:29 the·one not maturely·utilizing·what·he·has, even

G2192.8 V-PAS-3S ἔχῃ (1x)
Mk 4:25 whoever should·maturely·utilize·what·he·has, to·

G2193 ἕως hḗōs *conj.* (140x)

Compare:G0891 G3360

G2193.ª CONJ ἕως (1x)
Ac 21:26 of·ceremonial·cleansing *would·be*, at which *time*

G2193.2 CONJ ἕως (83x)
Jn 2:7 And they·overfilled them until topped·over.
Jn 2:10 ·purposefully·kept the good wine until this·moment."
Jn 5:17 "My Father works until this·moment, and·I·also
Jn 9:18 blind and received·his·sight, until such·time *that*
Jn 13:38 no, shall·not crow, until you·shall·utterly·deny me
Jn 21:22 "If·I·should·want him to·remain until I·come, what·
Jn 21:23 "If·I·should·want him to·remain until I·come, what·
Lk 1:80 and was in·the wildernesses until *the* day of·his
Lk 9:27 no, shall·not taste death until they·should·see the
Lk 11:51 from the blood of·Abel until the blood of·
Lk 12:50 and how am·I·clenched until it·should·be·finished
Lk 12:59 ·forth from·there, even until you·should·give·back
Lk 13:8 it this year also, until such·time *that* I·should·dig
Lk 13:21 seah·measures of·flour, until all was·leavened.
Lk 13:35 no, yeu·should·not see me, until *the time* should·
Lk 15:4 having·become·completely·lost until he·should·find
Lk 15:8 and seek carefully until such·time *that* she·should·
Lk 16:16 Torah-Law and the prophets *were* until John. From
Lk 17:8 ·yourself·about, attend to·me until I·should·eat and

Lk 19:13 them, ‘Keep·yourselves·busy until I·come·*back*.’
Lk 20:43 until I·should·lay·out your enemies *as* your foot
Lk 21:32 no, should·not pass·away, until all should·happen.
Lk 22:16 eat any·longer from·out·of·it until such·time *that* it·
Lk 22:18 produce of·the vine, until such·time the kingdom
Lk 23:44 a·darkness over all the land until *the* ninth hour.
Lk 24:49 of·JeruSalem until yeu·should·dress·yeurselves·
Ac 2:35 until I·should·lay·out your enemies *as* your foot
Ac 7:45 *It·was with our fathers* until the days of·David,
Ac 8:40 ·the·good·news in·all the cities, until he came to
Ac 13:20 he·gave *to·them* judges, until SamuEl the prophet.
Ac 21:5 with·wives and children) until *we·were* outside of·
Ac 23:12 neither to·eat nor to·drink until they·should·kill
Ac 23:14 to·taste not·even·one·thing until we·should·kill
Ac 23:21 to·eat nor to·drink until they·should·eliminate him.
Ac 25:21 ·ordered him to·be·kept until I·may·send him to
Ac 28:23 ·Moses and the prophets, from dawn until evening.
Heb 1:13 my right·hand, until I·should·lay·out your enemies
Heb 10:13 waiting·for *the moment* until his enemies should·
Mt 1:17 ·of·offspring from AbRaham until David *are*
Mt 1:17 Then from David until the Babylonian exile *are*
Mt 1:17 from the Babylonian exile until the Anointed-One
Mt 1:25 ·knowledge·of her until she·reproduced·and·birthed
Mt 2:9 ·ahead·of them, going·*on* until it·stood·still up·above
Mt 2:13 Egypt, and be there until I·should·declare *it* to·you,
Mt 2:15 And he·was there until the demise of·HerOd·the·
Mt 5:18 “For certainly I·say to·yeu, until the heaven and the
Mt 5:18 should·pass·away from the Torah-Law until all
Mt 5:26 ·not come·forth from·there until you·should·repay
Mt 10:11 worthy, and·there abide until yeu·should·go·forth.
Mt 10:23 the cities of·IsraEl, until the Son of·Clay·Man†
Mt 11:12 days of·John the Immerser until this·moment, the
Mt 11:13 prophets and the Torah-Law prophesied until John.
Mt 12:20 he·shall·not quench, until he·should·cast·forth
Mt 13:33 seah·measures of·flour, until all was·leavened.
Mt 14:22 him to the other·side, until he·should·dismiss the
Mt 16:28 no, may·not taste death, until they·should·see the
Mt 17:9 ·declare the clear·vision to·no·man, until the Son
Mt 18:30 he·cast him into prison, until he·should·repay the
Mt 18:34 over to·the tormentors, until he·should·repay all
Mt 22:44 “Sit·down at my right·hand until I·should·lay·out
Mt 23:39 me from this·moment·on, until yeu·should·declare
Mt 24:21 been since *the* world's beginning until the present,
Mt 24:34 no, should·not pass·away, until all these·things
Mt 24:39 and they·did·not know … until the Deluge came,
Mt 26:29 ·this produce of·the vine, until that day whenever
Mt 27:45 darkness over all the land until the·ninth hour.
Mt 27:64 *for* the grave to·be·made·secure until the third day,
Mk 6:10 into a·home, there abide until yeu·should·go·forth
Mk 6:45 toward BethSaida, until he·himself should·dismiss
Mk 9:1 should·not taste of·death, until they·should·see the
Mk 12:36 “Sit·down at my right·hand until I·should·lay·out
Mk 14:25 ·the produce of·the vine, until that day whenever
Mk 14:32 “Yeu·sit·down here, until I·should·pray.”
Mk 15:33 came·to·be over all the land until *the* ninth hour.
Jac 5:7 be·patient brothers, until the returning·Presence of·
Jac 5:7 ·with·long·patience over it, until he·should·receive
2Pe 1:19 in a·murky place— until *the* day should·beam·
2Th 2:7 at·this·moment *is·doing so* until he·should·come out
1Co 4:5 anything before *the* season, until the Lord should·
1Co 16:8 But I·shall·stay·over in Ephesus until the Pentecost
1Ti 4:13 Until I·come, give·attention to·the reading·aloud *of*·
Rv 6:11 yet *for* a·short time, until also their fellow·slaves
Rv 20:5 dead did·not come·alive·again until the thousand

G2193.3 CONJ ἕως (34x)

Jn 8:9 beginning from the older·men unto the last·of·them;
Jn 16:24 Unto this·moment, yeu·did·not request not·even·
Lk 2:15 Now·then, we·should·go·through unto BethLechem,
Lk 4:29 of·the city and drove him unto the brow of·the
Lk 4:42 him, and they·came unto him and were·fully·
Lk 10:15 the·one being·elevated·up unto the heaven, you·
Lk 10:15 the heaven, you·shall·be·driven·down unto Hades.
Lk 22:51 “*Stop!* Yeu·must·let·it·be, even·unto this!” And
Lk 23:5 in all Judea, beginning from Galilee unto here.”
Ac 1:22 from the immersion of·John, unto the day that he·
Ac 8:10 were·giving·heed, from *the* least unto *the* greatest,
Ac 13:47 *to·be* for custodial·Salvation unto *the* farthest·part
Ac 23:23 that they·should·traverse unto Caesarea from *the*
Heb 8:11 from *the* least of·them unto *the* greatest of·them.
Mt 11:23 the·one being·elevated unto the heaven, shall·be·
Mt 11:23 the heaven, shall·be·driven·down unto Hades!
Mt 20:8 ·of·service, beginning from the last unto the first.’
Mt 22:26 second also, and the third, even·unto the seventh.
Mt 23:35 the blood of·Abel the righteous, unto the blood of·
Mt 24:31 ·parts of·*the*·heavens unto *the* uttermost·parts
Mt 26:38 “My soul is exceedingly·grieved unto death. Yeu·
Mt 27:8 “Field of·Blood”, even·unto the present.
Mt 28:20 all the days, even·unto the entire·completion of·
Mk 13:19 of·creation which God created unto the present,
Mk 14:34 “My soul is exceedingly·grieved unto death. Yeu·
Rm 11:8 and ears *for·them* not to·hear unto the present day.
1Co 1:8 who also shall·confirm yeu unto *the* end, *being* not·
1Co 4:13 an·offscouring of·all·things unto this·moment.
1Co 8:7 *still·accustomed·to* the idol unto this·moment, eat as
1Co 15:6 whom the majority remain unto this·moment, but
2Co 1:13 that yeu·shall·acknowledge *this* even unto *the* end,
2Co 3:15 But·yet unto the·present·day, whenever Moses is·
2Co 12:2 , such·a·man being·snatched·up unto *the* third
1Jn 2:9 brother, is in the darkness even·unto this·moment.

G2193.4 CONJ ἕως (5x)

Mt 18:21 me, and I·shall·forgive him? Up·to seven·times?
Mt 18:22 “I·do·not say to·you, up·to seven·times, but·rather
Mt 18:22 seven·times, but·rather up·to seventy·times seven.
Mt 26:58 ·following him from a·distance up·to the courtyard
Mk 6:23 I·shall·give *it* to·you, up·to half of·my kingdom!”

G2193.5 CONJ ἕως (4x)

Jn 9:4 works of·the·one sending me, for·as·long·as it·is day.
Jn 12:35 with yeu. Walk for·as·long·as yeu·have the light,
Jn 12:36 For·as·long·as yeu·have the light, trust in the light,
Mt 5:25 legal·adversary swiftly, for·as·long·as such·time *as*

G2193.7 CONJ ἕως (9x)

Lk 24:50 And he·led them outside as·far·as to BethAny, and
Ac 1:8 and in·Samaria, and as·far·as·to *the* farthest·part of·
Ac 11:19 Stephen, went·throughout as·far·as·to Phoenicia,
Ac 11:22 BarNabas to·go·throughout as·far·as·to Antioch,
Ac 17:15 transporting Paul brought him as·far·as·to Athens.
Ac 26:11 I·was·persecuting *them* even as·far·as to the
Mt 24:27 from *the* east and shines·forth as·far·as·to *the* west,
Mk 13:27 ·part of·earth as·far·as·to *the* uttermost·part of·
Mk 14:54 him from a·distance, as·far·as to inside the

G2193.8 CONJ ἕως (1x)

Rm 3:12 benevolent·kindness; there·is not so·much·as one.

G2193.9 CONJ ἕως (3x)

Ac 9:38 *him* not to·amble·along in·going·through to them.
Mt 27:51 Temple is·torn in two from top to bottom. And the
Mk 15:38 of·the Temple was·torn in two from top to bottom.

Zζ - Zeta

G2194 Ζαβουλών Zabôulṓn *n/l.* (3x)
זְבוּלוּן zëбûlûn̠ [Hebrew]
Roots:H2074

G2194.3 N/L-PRI Ζαβουλών (1x)

Rv 7:8 *the* tribe of·Zebulun having·been·officially·sealed,

G2194.4 N/L-PRI Ζαβουλών (2x)

Mt 4:13 within *the* borders of·Zebulun and Naphtali,
Mt 4:15 “O·Land of·Zebulun and land of·Naphtali, *by the*

G2195 Ζακχαῖος Zakchaîôs *n/p.* (3x)
זַכַּי zak̂ay [Hebrew]
Roots:H2140

G2195 N/P-NSM Ζακχαῖος (2x)

Lk 19:2 ·name·of Zacchaeus·*(meaning·transparently·clean)*,
Lk 19:8 And Zacchaeus, after·being·settled, declared to the

G2195 N/P-VSM Ζακχαῖε (1x)

Lk 19:5 to him, “Zacchaeus, making·haste, drop·down.

G2196 Ζαράχ Zarách *n/p.* (1x)
Ζεράχ Zêrách [transliteration]
זֶרַח zeraçн [Hebrew]
זָרַח zaraçн [alternate]
Roots:H2226

G2196.4 N/P-PRI Ζαράχ (1x)

Mt 1:3 Judah begot Perets and Zarach (birthed·from·out of·

G2197 Ζαχαρ•ίας Zacharías *n/p.* (11x)
זְכַרְיָה zëkaryah
Roots:H2148

G2197.2 N/P-GSM Ζαχαρίου (2x)

Lk 11:51 of·Abel until the blood of·ZecharYah, the·one
Mt 23:35 unto the blood of·ZecharYah, descendant of·

G2197.4 N/P-NSM Ζαχαρίας (4x)

Lk 1:5 ·offers·sacrifices by·the·name·of ZacharIas, *who·was*
Lk 1:12 And ZacharIas was·troubled after·seeing *him*, and
Lk 1:18 Then ZacharIas declared to the angel, “How shall·I·
Lk 1:67 And his father ZacharIas was·filled with·Holy Spirit

G2197.4 N/P-VSM Ζαχαρία (1x)

Lk 1:13 “Do·not be·afraid, ZacharIas, on·account·that your

G2197.4 N/P-ASM Ζαχαρίαν (2x)

Lk 1:21 the people were intently·awaiting ZacharIas, and
Lk 1:59 and they·were·calling him ZacharIas, after the

G2197.4 N/P-GSM Ζαχαρίου (2x)

Lk 1:40 she·entered into the house of·ZacharIas and greeted
Lk 3:2 came to John the son of·ZacharIas in the wilderness.

G2198 ζάω záō *v.* (143x)
Compare:G0980 See:G2222 G1933-2 G5550
xLangAlso:H2421 A2418

G2198.1 V-FAI-1P ζήσομεν (2x)

Heb 12:9 ·subjection to·the Father of·spirits, and shall·live?
Rm 6:2 died to·Moral·Failure; how shall·we·live in it any·

G2198.1 V-FAI-2S ζήσῃ (1x)

Lk 10:28 Do this, and you·shall·live.”

G2198.1 V-FDI-1P ζησόμεθα (1x)

2Co 13:4 in him, yet we·shall·live together with·him as·a·

G2198.1 V-FDI-2P ζήσεσθε (2x)

Jn 14:19 I·myself live, yeu·yeurselves shall·live also.
Rm 8:13 ·to·death the practices of·the body, yeu·shall·live.

G2198.1 V-FDI-3S ζήσεται (13x)

Jn 6:51 from·out·of·this bread, he·shall·live into the coming·
Jn 6:57 ·one chewing me, he·likewise shall·live through me.
Jn 6:58 The·one chewing this bread shall·live into the
Jn 11:25 in me, though he·should·die, yet·shall·he·live.
Lk 4:4 “The man·of·clay† shall·live not upon bread alone,
Heb 10:38 the righteous·man shall·live as·a·result of·trust,
Gal 3:11 “the righteous·one shall·live as·a·result of·trust.”
Gal 3:12 The man·of·clay† doing them shall·live by them.”
Mt 4:4 ·written, “A·man·of·clay† shall·live not upon bread
Mt 9:18 ·must·lay your hand upon her, and she·shall·live.”
Mk 5:23 on·her, so·that she·may·be·saved and shall·live.”
Rm 1:17 But the righteous·man shall·live as·a·result of·trust

Rm 10:5 The man·of·clay† doing them shall·live by them."
G2198.1 V-FDI-3P ζήσονται (1x)
Jn 5:25 the·ones listening·with·comprehension shall·live.
G2198.1 V-PAI-1S ζῶ (6x)
Jn 6:57 Father dispatched me, and·I live through the Father,
Jn 14:19 me. Because I·myself live, yeu·yeurselves shall·
Gal 2:20 ·together with·Anointed-One, and I·live. No·longer
Gal 2:20 And that·which now I·live in flesh, I·live in the
Gal 2:20 ·which now I·live in flesh, I·live in the trust of·the
Rm 14:11 *'As·surely·as* I·myself live,' says Yahweh,⇒
G2198.1 V-PAI-1P ζῶμεν (5x)
Ac 17:28 For in him, we·live and are·stirred and have·
Gal 5:25 If we·live in·Spirit, we·should·conform·and·march·
Rm 14:8 both, whether we·should·live, we·live to·the Lord;
1Th 3:8 Because now we·live, if yeu·should·stand·fast in *the*
2Co 6:9 as dying and behold— we·live, as being·
G2198.1 V-PAI-2S ζῇς (2x)
Gal 2:14 inherently·being a·Jew, live as·a·Gentile and not
Rv 3:1 that you·have the name that you·live, yet you·are
G2198.1 V-PAI-2P ζῆτε (1x)
Rm 8:13 For if yeu·live according·to flesh, yeu·are·about to·
G2198.1 V-PAI-3S ζῇ (13x)
Jn 4:50 "Depart, your son lives." And the man·of·clay†
Jn 4:51 and announced *to·him*, saying, "Your boy lives."
Jn 4:53 declared to·him, "Your son lives." And he·himself
Heb 7:8 *who·is still* being·a·witness because he·lives.
Heb 9:17 ·time *is·it* in·force when the·one bequeathing lives,
Gal 2:20 No·longer I·myself, but Anointed-One lives in me.
Mk 16:11 hearing that he·lives and was·distinctly·viewed
Rm 6:10 ·occasion·only, but in·that·which he·lives, he·lives
Rm 6:10 ·only, but in·that·which he·lives, he·lives to·God.
Rm 7:1 for·a·span·of time, *that·is, for* as·long·as he·lives?
Rm 14:7 For not·even·one of·us lives to·himself, and not·
1Co 7:39 over a·lifetime as·long·as her husband lives. But if
2Co 13:4 of·weakness, yet he·lives as·a·result of·God's
G2198.1 V-PAI-3P ζῶσιν (1x)
Lk 20:38 but·rather of·living·men, for all live to·him."
G2198.1 V-PAN ζῆν (10x)
Lk 24:23 ·vision of·angels who say *that* he·himself *is* living.
Ac 22:22 the earth, for it·is·not befitting·for·him to·live."
Ac 25:24 *that* it·is·not necessary·for him to·live any·longer.
Ac 28:4 from·out of·the sea, Justice does·not let *him* live."
Rm 8:12 *but* not to·the flesh, to·live according·to the flesh.
Php 1:21 For me to·live *is* Anointed-One, and to·die *is* gain.
Php 1:22 But if *I·continue·on* to·live in *bodily* flesh, this
1Co 9:14 ·proclaiming the good·news to·live from·out of·the
2Co 1:8 ·for us to·be·at·an·utter·loss even of·the *will* to·live.
2Ti 3:12 ·ones determining to·live with·devout·reverence in
G2198.1 V-PAP-ASM ζῶντα (1x)
Lk 24:5 "Why among the dead do·yeu·seek the·one living?
G2198.1 V-PAP-APM ζῶντας (1x)
1Pe 4:5 having readiness to·judge *the·ones* living and *the*
G2198.1 V-PAP-DSM ζῶντι (4x)
Rv 4:9 on the throne, the·one living into the ages of·ages,
Rv 4:10 and they·fall·prostrate to·the·one living into the
Rv 5:14 ·down and fell·prostrate to·the·one·living into the
Rv 10:6 and he·swore by the·one living into the ages of·ages
G2198.1 V-PAP-GSM ζῶντος (3x)
Rm 7:3 husband still·living, she·shall·bear·the·public·title·of
1Pe 1:23 of·God, *which·is* living and abiding to·the coming·
Rv 15:7 of·the Rage of·God, the·one living into the ages of·
G2198.1 V-PAP-GPM ζώντων (1x)
Rm 14:9 ·lordship·over both *the* dead and *the* living.
G2198.1 V-PAP-NSF ζῶσα (1x)
1Ti 5:6 presently·living·luxuriously has·died while·she·lives.
G2198.1 V-PAP-NSM ζῶν (7x)
Jn 11:26 And anyone, the·one living and trusting in me, no,
Lk 15:13 his substance while·living in·an·unsaved·lifestyle.
Heb 4:12 For the Word† of·God *is* living and active, and *he·*
Heb 7:25 him), always living to make·intercession on·their
Mt 27:63 impostor declared *while·he·was* still living, 'After
Rv 1:18 And *I·AM* the·one living, and was dead; and behold,
Rv 1:18 dead; and behold, I·am living into the ages of·ages,

G2198.1 V-PAP-NPM ζῶντες (6x)
1Th 4:15 that we·ourselves, the·ones living (the·ones
1Th 4:17 ·that, we·ourselves (the·ones living, the·ones *still*
2Co 4:11 always, the·ones living, are·handed·over to death
2Co 5:15 in·order·that the·ones living should·no·longer live
Col 2:20 of·the world, why, as·though living in *the* world,
Rv 19:20 The two were·cast, still·living, into the Lake of·
G2198.1 V-PAS-1P ζῶμεν (2x)
Rm 14:8 For both, whether we·should·live, we·live to·the
Rm 14:8 Accordingly, both whether we·should·live, or·also
G2198.1 V-PAS-3P ζῶσιν (2x)
1Pe 4:6 in·*the·*flesh, but may·live according·to God in·*the·*
2Co 5:15 ·ones living should·no·longer live to·themselves,
G2198.1 V-IAI-1S ἔζων (1x)
Rm 7:9 And I·myself was·living apart·from Torah-Law once
G2198.1 V-IAI-2P ἐζῆτε (1x)
Col 3:7 also once walked, when yeu·were·living with them.
G2198.1 V-AAI-1S ἔζησα (1x)
Ac 26:5 denomination of·our religion, I·lived a·Pharisee.
G2198.1 V-AAI-3S ἔζησεν (2x)
Rv 2:8 First and the Last, who became dead and·yet lived:
Rv 13:14 which has the gash by·the dagger, and·yet lived.
G2198.1 V-AAI-3P ἔζησαν (1x)
Rv 20:4 in their hands— and they·lived and reigned with
G2198.1 V-AAP-NSF ζήσασα (1x)
Lk 2:36 days, *being a·widow* after·living with a·husband
G2198.1 V-AAS-1S ζήσω (1x)
Gal 2:19 to·Torah-Law in·order·that I·may·live to·God.
G2198.1 V-AAS-1P ζήσωμεν (5x)
Jac 4:15 Lord should·will, then we·should·live, and should·
1Pe 2:24 to·the moral·failures) should·live to Righteousness
1Th 5:10 ·sleep, we·should·live at·the·same·time together
Tit 2:12 we·should·live moderately·with·self-control,
1Jn 4:9 the world, in·order·that we·may·live through him.
EG2198.1 (1x)
Mt 24:22 flesh would be·saved *to·continue living*; but on·
G2198.3 V-PAN ζῆν (1x)
Ac 25:19 ·died, whom Paul was·professing to·be·alive.
G2198.3 V-PAP-ASM ζῶντα (2x)
Ac 1:3 he·established·proof·of himself being·alive after his
Ac 20:12 they·brought the boy *home* being·alive, and they·
G2198.4 V-PAP-ASN ζῶν (2x)
Jn 4:10 ·of him, and he·would·have given you living water."
Jn 4:11 from·what·source do·you·have the living water?
G2198.4 V-PAP-ASF ζῶσαν (4x)
Heb 10:20 (a·freshly·carved and living way which he·
Rm 12:1 to·present yeur bodies *as* a·living sacrifice, holy
1Pe 1:3 us again— into a·living Expectation through *the*
1Co 15:45 Adam, came·into·being as a·living soul.⇒ The
G2198.4 V-PAP-ASM ζῶντα (2x)
Ac 14:15 ·around from these futilities to the living God,
1Pe 2:4 whom yeu·are·coming·alongside, the·living stone,
G2198.4 V-PAP-APN ζῶντα (1x)
Ac 7:38 *It·is·he* who accepted living eloquent·words to·give
G2198.4 V-PAP-APF ζώσας (1x)
Rv 7:17 and shall·guide them to living wellsprings of·waters.
G2198.4 V-PAP-DSM ζῶντι (5x)
Heb 9:14 ·for *yeu* to·ritually·minister to·the·living God?
Rm 7:2 ·been·bound by·Torah-Law to·the living husband;
1Th 1:9 the idols, to·be·slaves to·the·living and true God,
1Ti 4:10 ·have·placed·our·expectation upon the·living God,
1Ti 6:17 of·wealth, but·rather in the living God (the·one
G2198.4 V-PAP-GSN ζῶντος (1x)
Jn 7:38 ·out of·his belly shall·flow rivers of·living water.⇒"
G2198.4 V-PAP-GSM ζῶντος (11x)
Jn 6:69 are the Anointed-One, the Son of·the living God."
Heb 3:12 of·distrust, in withdrawing from the·living God.
Heb 10:31 ·thing to·fall into *the* hands of·the·living God.
Heb 12:22 Mount Tsiyon and the·living God's CITY, to·a·
Mt 16:16 are the Anointed-One, the Son of·the living God."
Mt 26:63 ·oath, I·solemnly·charge you by the·living God,
Rm 9:26 they·shall·be·called the·Sons of·the·living God."⇒
2Co 3:3 ·ink, but·rather with·*the·*Spirit of·the·living God,

2Co 6:16 For yeu·yeurselves are a·temple of·the·living God,
1Ti 3:15 ·which is a·Called·Out·citizenry of·the·living God,
Rv 7:2 sun, having an·official·seal of·the·living God, and
G2198.4 V-PAP-NSF ζῶσα (1x)
Rv 16:3 blood of·a·dead·man. And every living soul in the
G2198.4 V-PAP-NSM ζῶν (2x)
Jn 6:51 I AM the living bread, the·one descending out of·the
Jn 6:57 "Just·as the living Father dispatched me, and·I live
G2198.4 V-PAP-NPM ζῶντες (1x)
1Pe 2:5 And yeu·yeurselves, as living stones, are·built·up,
G2198.5 V-PAP-APM ζῶντας (1x)
2Ti 4:1 (the·one about to·judge living·men and dead·men at
G2198.5 V-PAP-GPM ζώντων (4x)
Lk 20:38 a·God of·dead·men, but·rather of·living·men, for
Ac 10:42 by God *to·be* Judge of·living·men and dead·men.
Mt 22:32 the God of·dead·men, but·rather of·living·men."
Mk 12:27 but·rather a·God of·living·men. Accordingly, yeu
G2198.6 V-PAP-ASF ζῶσαν (1x)
Ac 9:41 holy·ones and the widows, he·presented her alive.
G2198.6 V-PAP-APM ζῶντας (2x)
Rm 6:11 to·the Moral·Failure, but alive to·God in Jesus
Rm 6:13 as those·that·are·alive from·among dead·men, and
G2198.7 V-PAN ζῆν (1x)
Heb 2:15 of·death) were all *their* lifetime held·in slavery.

G2199 Ζεβεδαῖος Zêbêdaîôs *n/p.* (12x)

זַבְדִּי zaḇ·ḏiy [Hebrew]
Roots:H2067
G2199.2 N/P-ASM Ζεβεδαῖον (1x)
Mk 1:20 and leaving their father Zebedee in the sailboat
G2199.2 N/P-GSM Ζεβεδαίου (11x)
Jn 21:2 in·Galilee, and the *sons* of·Zebedee, and two others
Lk 5:10 Jakob and John, the·Sons of·Zebedee, who were
Mt 4:21 brothers, Jakob (the·one of·Zebedee) and John his
Mt 4:21 with their father Zebedee, completely·repairing their
Mt 10:2 brother; Jakob (the·one of·Zebedee) and John his
Mt 20:20 of·the·Sons of·Zebedee came·alongside him, with
Mt 26:37 and the two Sons of·Zebedee, he·began to·be·
Mt 27:56 and Joses, and the mother of·the·Sons of·Zebedee.
Mk 1:19 he·saw Jakob (the·one of·Zebedee) and his brother
Mk 3:17 and Jakob (the·one of·Zebedee) and John the
Mk 10:35 John, the Sons of·Zebedee, approach·close to·him

G2200 ζεστός zêstŏs *adj.* (3x)

Roots:G2204 Compare:G2329 G2330
G2200.4 A-NSM ζεστός (3x)
Rv 3:15 you·are neither cold nor fervently·hot. Oh·that you·
Rv 3:15 Oh·that you·would·be cold or fervently·hot!
Rv 3:16 and neither cold nor fervently·hot, I·intend to·vomit

G2201 ζεῦγος zêûgôs *n.* (2x)

Roots:G2200-1 See:G2218 xLangAlso:H6776
G2201.2 N-APN ζεύγη (1x)
Lk 14:19 declared, 'I·bought five yoked·teams of·oxen, and
G2201.3 N-NSN ζεῦγος (1x)
Lk 2:24 Torah-Law, "a·braced·pair of·turtledoves or two

G2202 ζευκτηρία zêuktēría *n.* (1x)

Roots:G2200-1 Compare:G0996 See:G2218
G2202.2 N-APF ζευκτηρίας (1x)
Ac 27:40 at·the·same·time slackening the rudder cables, and

G2203 Ζεύς Zêús *n/p.* (2x)

Δίς Dís
[oblique cases (probably cognate), otherwise obsolete]
See:G2211 xLangAlso:H3068
G2203.1 N/P-ASM Δία (1x)
Ac 14:12 both they·were·calling BarNabas, Zeus, and Paul,
G2203.1 N/P-GSM Διός (1x)
Ac 14:13 And the priest of·Zeus that·offers·sacrifices, the·one

G2204 ζέω zéō *v.* (2x)

Compare:G2330 See:G2200
G2204.4 V-PAP-NSM ζέων (1x)
Ac 18:25 And being·fervently·hot in·the spirit, he·was·
G2204.4 V-PAP-NPM ζέοντες (1x)

Rm 12:11 in·the spirit, by·being·fervently·hot; in·the

G2205 ζῆλος zē̂lôs *n.* (17x)
Roots:G2204 Compare:G5355 See:G2206 G2205-1 xLangEquiv:H7068

G2205.2 N-NSM ζῆλος (2x)
Jn 2:17 ·been·written, "The zeal of·your house devours me.
2Co 9:2 and from·out of·yeur zeal, it·stirred·up many·more

G2205.2 N-ASM ζῆλον (4x)
Rm 10:2 I·testify for·them that they·have a·zeal of·God, but·
Php 3:6 according·to zeal, persecuting the Called·Out·
2Co 7:11 great·yearning, moreover, *what* zeal, moreover,
Col 4:13 for·him, that he·has much zeal over yeu, and the·

G2205.3 N-ASM ζῆλον (1x)
2Co 7:7 yeur distressing, yeur fervency on·behalf of·me,

G2205.4 N-NSM ζῆλος (2x)
Jac 3:16 For where jealousy and contention *is*, there *is*
1Co 3:3 For where *there·is* among yeu jealousy, and strife,

G2205.4 N-NPM ζῆλοι (2x)
Gal 5:20 hostilities, strifes, jealousies, ragings, contentions
2Co 12:20 ·somehow *there·be* strifes, jealousies, ragings,

G2205.4 N-ASM ζῆλον (1x)
Jac 3:14 But if yeu·have bitter jealousy and contention in

G2205.4 N-DSM ζήλῳ (2x)
Rm 13:13 and debaucheries, not in·strife and jealousy.
2Co 11:2 For I·am·jealous over·yeu with·a·jealousy of·God,

G2205.4 N-GSM ζήλου (2x)
Ac 5:17 of·the Sadducees), they·were·filled with·jealousy,
Ac 13:45 were·filled with·jealousy and were·contradicting

G2205.5 N-NSN ζῆλος (1x)
Heb 10:27 ·judgment and a·fiery indignation, *which·is* about

G2206 ζηλόω zēlóō *v.* (12x)
Roots:G2205 Compare:G1937 G2309 xLangEquiv:H7065

G2206.2 V-PAI-3P ζηλοῦσιν (1x)
Gal 4:17 They·zealously·desire yeu, *but* not for·moral·good,

G2206.2 V-PAM-2P ζηλοῦτε (1x)
1Co 14:1 Pursue the Love, and zealously·desire the spiritual

G2206.2 V-PAS-2P ζηλοῦτε (1x)
Gal 4:17 yeu in·order·that yeu·should·zealously·desire them.

G2206.3 V-PAM-2P ζηλοῦτε (2x)
1Co 12:31 But be·zealous·for the significantly·better
1Co 14:39 As·such, brothers, be·zealous to·prophesy, and

G2206.3 V-PPN ζηλοῦσθαι (1x)
Gal 4:18 But *it·is* good to·be·zealous always in *a* good *thing*,

G2206.3 V-AAM-2S ζήλωσον (1x)
Rv 3:19 Accordingly, be·zealous and repent.

G2206.4 V-PAI-2P ζηλοῦτε (1x)
Jac 4:2 have. Yeu·murder and jealously·desire, and·yet yeu·

G2206.4 V-PAI-3S ζηλοῖ (1x)
1Co 13:4 The Love does·not jealously·desire. The Love

G2206.5 V-PAI-1S ζηλῶ (1x)
2Co 11:2 For I·am·jealous over·yeu with·a·jealousy of·God,

G2206.5 V-AAP-NPM ζηλώσαντες (2x)
Ac 7:9 "And the patriarchs, being·jealous, sold Joseph away
Ac 17:5 But being·jealous, the obstinate Jews, even

G2207 ζηλωτής zēlōtḗs *n.* (7x)
Roots:G2206 Compare:G2581 See:G2208

G2207.1 N-NSM ζηλωτής (2x)
Ac 22:3 esteemed·father, inherently·being a·zealot of·God,
Gal 1:14 ·being more·exceedingly a·zealot of·my forefathers

G2207.1 N-NPM ζηλωταί (2x)
Ac 21:20 they·inherently·are all zealots of·the Torah-Law.
1Co 14:12 Since yeu·are zealots of·spiritual *bestowments*,

G2207.1 N-ASM ζηλωτήν (1x)
Tit 2:14 People,' *one being* a·zealot of·good works.

G2207.2 N-NSM ζηλωτής (1x)
Ac 1:13 *son* of·Alphaeus, Simon the Zealot, and Judas *son*

G2207.2 N-ASM ζηλωτήν (1x)
Lk 6:15 , and Simon, the·one being·called Zealot,

G2209 ζημία zēmía *n.* (4x)
Compare:G0580 See:G2210 G1150 xLangAlso:H5143

G2209.2 N-ASF ζημίαν (1x)
Ac 27:21 Crete nor·also to·gain this battering and damage.

G2209.3 N-GSF ζημίας (1x)
Ac 27:10 with a·battering and much damage·and·loss, not

G2209.4 N-ASF ζημίαν (2x)
Php 3:7 I·have·resolutely·considered a·total·loss through
Php 3:8 ·consider all·things to·be a·total·loss through the

G2210 ζημιόω zēmióō *v.* (6x)
Roots:G2209 Compare:G0984 xLangAlso:A5142

G2210.4 V-FPI-3S ζημιωθήσεται (1x)
1Co 3:15 ·burned, he·shall·suffer·damage·and·loss, but he·

G2210.4 V-API-1S ἐζημιώθην (1x)
Php 3:8 whom I·suffered·the·damage·and·loss of·all·things,

G2210.4 V-APP-NSM ζημιωθείς (1x)
Lk 9:25 ·losing himself or suffering·damage·and·loss?

G2210.4 V-APS-2P ζημιωθῆτε (1x)
2Co 7:9 yeu·should·have·suffered·damage·and·loss as·a·

G2210.4 V-APS-3S ζημιωθῇ (2x)
Mt 16:26 and should·suffer·the·damage·and·loss of·his·own
Mk 8:36 yet should·suffer·the·damage·and·loss of·his·own

G2211 Ζηνᾶς Zēnâs *n/p.* (1x)
Roots:G2203 G1435

G2211.2 N/P-ASM Ζηνᾶν (1x)
Tit 3:13 Diligently send Zenas the lawyer and Apollos

G2212 ζητέω zētéō *v.* (120x)
Compare:G2045 G4441 G2147 See:G0327 G1567 G1934 xLangAlso:H1245

G2212.1 V-FAI-2P ζητήσετε (4x)
Jn 7:34 Yeu·shall·seek me and shall·not find *me*, and where I
Jn 7:36 that he·declared, 'Yeu·shall·seek me and shall·not
Jn 8:21 "I·myself head·on·out, and yeu·shall·seek me and
Jn 13:33 ·little·while I·am with yeu. Yeu·shall·seek me, and

G2212.1 V-FAI-3P ζητήσουσιν (2x)
Lk 13:24 I·say to·yeu, shall·seek to·enter and shall·not
Rv 9:6 days, the men·of·clay† shall·seek Death and shall·

G2212.1 V-FPI-3S ζητηθήσεται (1x)
Lk 12:48 personally·from him much shall·be·sought, and

G2212.1 V-PAI-1S ζητῶ (4x)
Jn 5:30 is righteous, because I·do·not seek my·own will,
Jn 8:50 And I·myself do·not seek my·own glory; there·is
Gal 1:10 ·*with* God? Or do·I·seek to·appease men·of·clay†?
2Co 12:14 For I·do·not seek yeur things, but·rather yeu; for

G2212.1 V-PAI-2S ζητεῖς (2x)
Jn 4:27 ·even·one·man declared, "What·do you·seek?" or,
Jn 20:15 why do·you·weep? Whom·do you·seek?" That·

G2212.1 V-PAI-2P ζητεῖτε (15x)
Jn 1:38 says to·them, "What·do yeu·seek?" They·declared
Jn 5:44 ·from one·another, yet yeu·do·not seek the glory,
Jn 6:26 most·certainly, I·say to·yeu, yeu·seek me, not
Jn 7:19 does the Torah-Law. Why·do yeu·seek to·kill me?
Jn 8:37 AbRaham's offspring†, but·yet yeu·seek to·kill me,
Jn 8:40 But now yeu·seek to·kill me, a·man·of·clay† that
Jn 16:19 to·them, "Do·yeu·seek among one·another
Jn 18:4 ·forth, he·declared to·them, "Whom·do yeu·seek?"
Jn 18:7 ·inquired·of them again, "Whom·do yeu·seek?" And
Jn 18:8 Accordingly, if yeu·seek me, allow these·men to·
Lk 24:5 "Why among the dead do·yeu·seek the·one living?
Ac 10:21 Behold, it·is·I myself whom yeu·seek. What *is* the
Mt 28:5 for I·have·seen that yeu·seek YeShua, the·one
Mk 16:6 "Do·not be·utterly·amazed. Yeu·seek Jesus the
2Co 13:3 since yeu·seek a·proof of·the Anointed-One

G2212.1 V-PAI-3S ζητεῖ (7x)
Jn 4:23 for even the Father seeks the·ones such·as·these
Jn 7:4 in secret when he·himself seeks to·be in freeness·of·
Jn 7:18 The·man speaking from himself seeks his·own glory,
Jn 7:20 "You·have a·demon! Who seeks to·kill you?
Lk 15:8 sweep the home, and seek carefully until such·time
Mt 18:12 the mountains, *and* seek the·one being·led·astray?
1Co 13:5 ·not behave·improperly, does·not seek its·own, is·

G2212.1 V-PAI-3P ζητοῦσιν (7x)
Jn 7:25 "Is this not he·whom they·seek to·kill?
Ac 10:19 "Behold, three men seek you.
Mk 1:37 him, they·say to·him, "All *men* seek·for you."
Mk 3:32 your mother and your brothers seek·for you outside.
Rm 11:3 ·I alone am·all·that·is·left, and they·seek my soul.
Php 2:21 For all the·men seek their·own, not the·things·of
1Co 1:22 Jews request a·sign, and·also Greeks seek wisdom,

G2212.1 V-PAM-2S ζήτει (2x)
1Co 7:27 ·be·married to·a·woman? Do·not seek a·break·up.
1Co 7:27 ·broken·up from a·woman? Do·not seek a·woman.

G2212.1 V-PAM-2P ζητεῖτε (7x)
Lk 11:9 and it·shall·be·given yeu; seek, and yeu·shall·find;
Lk 12:29 yeu·yeurselves, do·not seek what yeu·should·eat,
Lk 12:31 "Moreover, seek the kingdom of·God, and all
Mt 6:33 But seek·yeu first the kingdom of·God and his
Mt 7:7 and it·shall·be·given yeu; seek, and yeu·shall·find;
1Co 14:12 *bestowments*, yeu·must·seek that yeu·may·excel
Col 3:1 with·the Anointed-One, seek the·things up·above,

G2212.1 V-PAM-3S ζητείτω (1x)
1Co 10:24 Let no·man seek his·own, but·rather each·man the

G2212.1 V-PAN ζητεῖν (2x)
Ac 17:27 *for·them* to·seek the Lord, if perhaps they·might·
Mt 2:13 for HerOd·the·Great intends to·seek the little·child

G2212.1 V-PAP-DSM ζητοῦντι (1x)
Mt 13:45 ·of·clay†, a·merchant seeking high·quality pearls,

G2212.1 V-PAP-DPM ζητοῦσιν (2x)
Rm 2:7 of·beneficially·good work, seeking glory, honor,
Rm 10:20 " I·was·found by·the·ones not seeking me; I·was·

G2212.1 V-PAP-GPM ζητούντων (2x)
Ac 21:31 And as·they·were·seeking to·kill him, news
Ac 27:30 But with·the sailors seeking to·flee out·from the

G2212.1 V-PAP-NSN ζητοῦν (2x)
Lk 11:24 through waterless places, seeking a·rest·break; and
Mt 12:43 through waterless places, seeking a·rest·break, and

G2212.1 V-PAP-NSM ζητῶν (9x)
Jn 7:18 glory, but the·man seeking the glory of·the·one
Jn 8:50 glory; there·is One presently·seeking and judging.
Lk 11:10 requesting receives, and the·one seeking finds, and
Lk 13:6 in his vineyard, and he·came seeking fruit on it yet
Lk 13:7 *for* three years, I·come seeking fruit on this fig·tree
Ac 13:8 ·opposed·to them seeking to·thoroughly·turn the
Mt 7:8 requesting receives; and the·one seeking finds; and
1Pe 5:8 as a·roaring lion seeking whom he·may·swallow·up,
1Co 10:33 *men* in·all *things*, not seeking my·own advantage,

G2212.1 V-PAP-NPM ζητοῦντες (11x)
Jn 6:24 sailboats and came to CaperNaum, seeking·for Jesus.
Lk 2:45 him, they·returned·back to JeruSalem, seeking him.
Lk 11:54 ·wait·for him, and seeking to·hunt·for something
Gal 2:17 But if (while·seeking to·be·regarded·as·righteous in
Mt 2:20 of·IsraEl, for the·ones seeking the little·child's soul
Mt 12:46 brothers stood outside, seeking to·speak with·him.
Mt 12:47 brothers stand outside, seeking to·speak with·you.
Mt 21:46 Yet while·seeking to·securely·hold him, they·
Mk 8:11 ·discuss with·him, seeking personally·from him a·
Rm 10:3 righteousness, and seeking to·establish their·own
1Th 2:6 nor seeking glory from·among men·of·clay†, neither

G2212.1 V-PPI-3S ζητεῖται (1x)
1Co 4:2 *with* such·a·thing remaining, it·is·sought in the

G2212.1 V-IAI-1P ἐζητοῦμεν (1x)
Lk 2:48 Behold, your father and·I were·seeking you, being·

G2212.1 V-IAI-2P ἐζητεῖτε (1x)
Lk 2:49 "How *is·it* that yeu·were·seeking me?

G2212.1 V-IAI-3S ἐζήτει (8x)
Jn 19:12 of·this, Pilate was·seeking to·fully·release him, but
Lk 6:19 the entire crowd was·seeking to·lay·hold of·him,
Lk 9:9 hear such·things?" And he·was·seeking to·see him.
Lk 19:3 And he·was·seeking to·see who Jesus was, and was·
Lk 22:6 *it*, and he·was·seeking a·good·opportunity to·hand
Ac 13:11 he·was·seeking others·to·lead·him·by·the·hand.
Mt 26:16 he·was·seeking a·good·opportunity in·order·that
Mk 14:11 And he·was·seeking how he·should·conveniently

G2212.1 V-IAI-3P ἐζήτουν (18x)
Jn 5:16 Jesus, and they·were·seeking to·kill him, because
Jn 5:18 that, the Judeans were·seeking *all* the·more to·kill
Jn 7:1 Judea, because the Judeans were·seeking to·kill him.
Jn 7:30 So·then they·were·seeking to·apprehend him, but
Jn 10:39 they·were·seeking again to·apprehend him.

Jn 11:8 “Rabbi, the Judeans now were·seeking to·stone you,
Jn 11:56 the Sanctuary·Atrium, they·were·seeking Jesus and
Lk 4:42 And the crowds were·seeking him, and they·came
Lk 5:18 ·paralyzed, and they·were·seeking *a·way* to·carry
Lk 11:16 trying *him*, were·seeking personally·from him a·
Lk 19:47 people were·seeking to·completely·destroy him,
Lk 22:2 the scribes were·seeking how they·may·eliminate
Ac 17:5 the home of·Jason, they·were·seeking to·bring them
Mt 26:59 the joint·council·of·Sanhedrin were·seeking false·
Mk 11:18 *it* and were·seeking how they·shall·completely·
Mk 12:12 And they·were·seeking to·take·secure·hold·of him
Mk 14:1 the chief·priests and the scribes were·seeking how,
Mk 14:55 joint·council·of·Sanhedrin were·seeking testimony

G2212.1 V-IPI-3S ἐζητεῖτο (1x)
Heb 8:7 then no place would·be·sought for·the·second.

G2212.1 V-AAI-1P ἐζητήσαμεν (1x)
Ac 16:10 ·vision, immediately we·sought to·go·forth into

G2212.1 V-AAI-3S ἐζήτησεν (1x)
2Ti 1:17 in Rome, he·sought·for me more·diligently·than

G2212.1 V-AAI-3P ἐζήτησαν (1x)
Lk 20:19 in the same hour sought to·throw *their* hands on

G2212.1 V-AAM-2S ζήτησον (1x)
Ac 9:11 ·one being·called Straight, and seek in Judas' home

G2212.1 V-AAM-3S ζητησάτω (1x)
1Pe 3:11 and do *the* beneficially·good·thing; seek peace and

G2212.1 V-AAN ζητῆσαι (1x)
Lk 19:10 the Son of·Clay·Man† came to·seek and to·save

G2212.1 V-AAS-3S ζητήσῃ (1x)
Lk 17:33 “Whoever should·seek to·save his soul's·desire

EG2212.1 (1x)
Jn 6:22 his disciples went·off alone— *they·sought·for him.*

G2212.2 V-IAI-3P ἐζήτουν (1x)
Jn 7:11 Now·then, the Judeans were·seeking him at the

G2213 ζήτημα zḗtēma *n.* (5x)
Roots:G2212 See:G2214 G4804

G2213.2 N-NSN ζήτημα (1x)
Ac 18:15 But since it·is an·issue concerning a·word and

G2213.2 N-APN ζητήματα (1x)
Ac 25:19 ·having certain issues specifically·against him

G2213.2 N-GSN ζητήματος (1x)
Ac 15:2 to the ambassadors and elders concerning this issue.

G2213.2 N-GPN ζητημάτων (2x)
Ac 23:29 ·to·account concerning issues of·their Oral-law,
Ac 26:3 ·all customs and issues *which·are* pervasive·among

G2214 ζήτησις zḗtēsis *n.* (6x)
Roots:G2212 Compare:G1261 G2757 See:G4804 G2213

G2214.2 N-NSF ζήτησις (1x)
Jn 3:25 there·occurred a·question·and·discussion from·

G2214.3 N-ASF ζήτησιν (1x)
Ac 25:20 this disputable·question, was·relating·as·to

G2214.3 N-APF ζητήσεις (1x)
1Ti 6:4 ·on about disputable·questions and quarrels·over·the·

G2214.4 N-APF ζητήσεις (3x)
Tit 3:9 But shun foolish speculations, genealogies, strifes,
1Ti 1:4 which contrarily·present speculations rather than
2Ti 2:23 uneducated·and·undisciplined speculations, having·

G2215 ζιζάνιον zizániôn *n.* (8x)
Compare:G5578 G4108 G1114

G2215.2 N-NPN ζιζάνια (3x)
Mt 13:26 fruit, then the darnel·weeds appeared also.
Mt 13:38 of·the kingdom. But the darnel·weeds are the Sons
Mt 13:40 just·as the darnel·weeds are·collected and are·

G2215.2 N-APN ζιζάνια (4x)
Mt 13:25 came and sowed *poisonous* darnel·weeds up *in·the*
Mt 13:27 So·then, from·what·source are the darnel·weeds?'
Mt 13:29 ·collecting the darnel·weeds, yeu·should·uproot the
Mt 13:30 reapers, “Collect the darnel·weeds first and bind

G2215.2 N-GPN ζιζανίων (1x)
Mt 13:36 to·us the parable of·the darnel·weeds of·the field.”

G2216 Ζοροβάβελ Zôrôbábêl *n/p.* (3x)
Ζερουβάβελ Zêrôubábêl [Greek, Octuagint]
זְרֻבָּבֶל zᵉrubabel [Hebrew]
זְרֻבָּבֶל zᵉrubabel [Aramaic]
Roots:H2216
xLangEquiv:A2217

G2216.2 N/P-PRI Ζοροβάβελ (2x)
Mt 1:12 begot ShealtiEl, and ShealtiEl begot ZerubBabel.
Mt 1:13 Then ZerubBabel begot AbiHud, and AbiHud begot

G2216.3 N/P-PRI Ζοροβάβελ (1x)
Lk 3:27 *son* of·RhesaYah, *son* of·ZorubBabel, *son* of·

G2217 ζόφος zóphôs *n.* (4x)
Compare:G1105 G3509 G4655

G2217.2 N-NSM ζόφος (2x)
Jud 1:13 ·reserved the deep·murky·shroud of·darkness into
2Pe 2:17 the deep·murky·shroud of·darkness has·been·

G2217.2 N-ASM ζόφον (1x)
Jud 1:6 under a·deep·murky·shroud for Tribunal·judgment

G2217.2 N-GSM ζόφου (1x)
2Pe 2:4 into·drag·chains of·a·deep·murky·shroud, having·

G2218 ζυγός zygós *n.* (6x)
Roots:G2200-1 See:G2201 G2202 G2086

G2218.1 N-NSM ζυγός (1x)
Mt 11:30 For my yoke *is* kind, and my load is lightweight.

G2218.1 N-ASM ζυγόν (3x)
Ac 15:10 why·do yeu·try God, to·put a·yoke upon the neck
Mt 11:29 Take·up my yoke upon yeu, and learn from me,
1Ti 6:1 as are under a·yoke resolutely·consider their·own

G2218.1 N-DSM ζυγῷ (1x)
Gal 5:1 and do·not again be·held·in by·a·yoke of·slavery.

G2218.3 N-ASM ζυγόν (1x)
Rv 6:5 ·is·sitting·down on it having a·balance·scale in his

G2219 ζύμη zýmē *n.* (13x)
Roots:G2204 See:G2220 G2220-1
xLangEquiv:H7603 xLangAlso:H2557

G2219.2 N-NSF ζύμη (2x)
Gal 5:9 A·little leaven leavens the whole lump·of·dough.
1Co 5:6 ·not personally·know that a·little leaven leavens the

G2219.2 N-ASF ζύμην (1x)
1Co 5:7 purge·out the old leaven in·order·that yeu·may·be

G2219.2 N-DSF ζύμῃ (4x)
Lk 13:21 It·is like leaven, which a·woman took *and*
Mt 13:33 of·the heavens is like leaven, which upon·taking *it*,
1Co 5:8 ·the·sacred·feast, not with old leaven, nor·even with
1Co 5:8 leaven, nor·even with leaven of·malice or of·evil,

G2219.2 N-GSF ζύμης (6x)
Lk 12:1 among·yeurselves of the leaven of·the Pharisees,
Mt 16:6 *that* yeu·beware of the leaven of·the Pharisees and
Mt 16:11 *but·rather* to·beware of the leaven of·the Pharisees
Mt 16:12 *to·them* to·beware of the leaven of·bread, but·
Mk 8:15 ·it *that* yeu·look·out for the leaven of·the Pharisees
Mk 8:15 of·the Pharisees and of·the leaven of·HerOd·AntiPas.

G2220 ζυμόω zymóō *v.* (4x)
Roots:G2219 See:G2220-1 G2219-1

G2220.1 V-PAI-3S ζυμοῖ (2x)
Gal 5:9 A·little leaven leavens the whole lump·of·dough.
1Co 5:6 ·know that a·little leaven leavens the whole lump·

G2220.1 V-API-3S ἐζυμώθη (2x)
Lk 13:21 seah·measures of·flour, until all was·leavened.”
Mt 13:33 seah·measures of·flour, until all was·leavened.”

G2221 ζωγρέω zōgréō *v.* (2x)
Roots:G2198 G0064 Compare:G0234-1 See:G2226

G2221.2 V-PAP-NSM ζωγρῶν (1x)
Lk 5:10 now·on, you·shall·be capturing·alive men·of·clay†.

G2221.2 V-RPP-NPM ἐζωγρημένοι (1x)
2Ti 2:26 snare, having·been·captured·alive by him at his

G2222 ζωή zōḗ *n.* (135x)
חַי ĥɛy
Roots:G2198 Compare:G0979 G5590
xLangEquiv:H2416-1 xLangAlso:H2416

G2222.1 N-NSF ζωή (4x)
Lk 12:15 of·one's holdings *does* anyone's life† itself exist.”
Ac 8:33 ·offspring? Because his life† is·taken·away from
Rm 8:38 ·convinced that neither death, nor life†, nor angels,
Jac 4:14 For what·kind·of *essence is* yeur life†? For it·is a·

G2222.1 N-DSF ζωῇ (1x)
1Co 15:19 ·our·expectation in this life† in Anointed-One,

G2222.1 N-GSF ζωῆς (4x)
Jn 6:51 ·myself shall·give on·behalf of·the life† of·the world.
Lk 1:75 in·the·sight of·him, all the days of·our life†.
Heb 7:3 of·days, nor end of·life†, but having·been·made·
Php 1:20 my body, whether through life† or through death.

G2222.2 N-NSF ζωή (20x)
Jn 1:4 In him was life-above, and the life-above was the light
Jn 1:4 was life-above, and the life-above was the light of·the
Jn 6:63 speak to·yeu, *they* are spirit, and *they* are life-above.
Jn 11:25 the resurrection and the life-above. The·one trusting
Jn 12:50 ·know that his commandment is eternal life-above.
Jn 14:6 the truth, and the life-above. Not·even·one comes to
Jn 17:3 And this is the eternal life-above, that they·may·know
Rm 6:23 ·bestowment of·God *is* eternal life-above in Jesus
Rm 8:6 the disposition of·the Spirit *is* life-above and peace—
Rm 8:10 Now the Spirit *is* life-above through righteousness,
Rm 11:15 ·*them be*, except life-above from·among dead·men
1Co 3:22 ·Peter), or *the* world, or life-above, or death, or
2Co 4:10 also the life-above of·Jesus may·be·made·apparent
2Co 4:11 ·of Jesus, in·order·that the life-above also of·Jesus
2Co 4:12 the death operates in us, but the life-above in yeu.
Col 3:3 ·died, and yeur life-above has·been·hidden together
Col 3:4 *who·is* our life-above, should·be·made·apparent,
1Jn 1:2 (and the life-above is·made·apparent, and we·have·
1Jn 5:11 eternal life-above, and this life-above is in his Son.
1Jn 5:20 This is the true God and the eternal life-above.

G2222.2 N-ASF ζωήν (59x)
Jn 3:15 ·perish, but·rather should·have eternal life-above.
Jn 3:16 ·perish, but·rather should·have eternal life-above.
Jn 3:36 in the Son has eternal life-above, and the·one being·
Jn 3:36 to·the Son shall·not gaze·upon life-above, but·rather
Jn 4:14 of·water springing·up into eternal life-above.”
Jn 4:36 and gathers·together fruit into life-above eternal, in·
Jn 5:24 sending me has eternal life-above, and he·does·not
Jn 5:24 has·walked·on out·from the death into the life-above.
Jn 5:26 For just·as the Father has life-above in himself, in·
Jn 5:26 he·gave also to·the Son to·have life-above in himself.
Jn 5:39 presume to·have eternal life-above by them. Yet those
Jn 5:40 ·come to me, in·order·that yeu·may·have life-above.
Jn 6:27 full·meal enduring into eternal life-above, which the
Jn 6:33 of·the heaven, and giving life-above to·the world.”
Jn 6:40 in him, may·have eternal life-above, and I·myself
Jn 6:47 to·yeu, the·one trusting in me has eternal life-above.
Jn 6:53 his blood, yeu·do·not have life-above in yeurselves.
Jn 6:54 my blood, has eternal life-above, and I·myself shall·
Jn 10:10 came in·order·that they·may·have life-above, and
Jn 10:28 And·I give to·them eternal life-above. And no, they·
Jn 12:25 world shall·vigilantly·keep it unto life-above eternal.
Jn 17:2 in·order·that he·may·give eternal life-above to all
Jn 20:31 that trusting, yeu·may·have life-above in his name.
Lk 10:25 what should·I·do to·inherit eternal life-above?”
Lk 18:18 should·I·be·doing to·inherit eternal life-above?”
Lk 18:30 season, and in the coming age, eternal life-above.”
Ac 11:18 God granted the repentance unto life-above.”
Ac 13:48 were having·been·assigned to eternal life-above).
Ac 17:25 anything, with·himself giving life† and breath to·
Gal 6:8 Spirit, shall·reap eternal life-above from·out of·the
Mt 7:14 the·one leading·off to the life-above, and few are
Mt 18:8 for·you to·enter into the life-above lame or crippled,
Mt 18:9 for·you to·enter into the life-above with·one·eye,
Mt 19:16 ·I·do in·order·that I·may·have eternal life-above?”
Mt 19:17 ·want to·enter into the life-above, observantly·keep
Mt 19:29 ·times·over and shall·inherit eternal life-above.
Mt 25:46 but the righteous into life-above eternal.”
Mk 9:43 for·you to·enter into the life-above crippled, than
Mk 9:45 ·you to·enter lame into the life-above, than having
Mk 10:17 should·I·do that I·may·inherit eternal life-above?”

Αα Ββ Γγ Δδ Εε Ζζ Ηη Θθ Ιι Κκ Λλ Μμ Νν Ξξ Οο Ππ Ρρ Σσ Ττ Υυ Φφ Χχ Ψψ Ωω

Mk 10:30 and in the coming age, eternal life-above.
Rm 2:7 ·incorruptibility, *he·shall·render* eternal life-above.
Rm 5:21 righteousness to eternal life-above through Jesus
Rm 6:22 ·holiness, and at·the end, *unto* eternal life-above.
Rm 7:10 ·one *that* is·found in·me for life-above, this *resulted*
Jud 1:21 ·our Lord YeShua Anointed unto eternal life-above.
1Pe 3:10 For "'the·one wanting to·love life-above and to·see
2Pe 1:3 ·things pertaining·to life-above and devout·reverence
2Co 2:16 to·some an·aroma of·life-above unto life-above. And
1Ti 1:16 ·the·ones about to·trust on him to life-above eternal.
2Ti 1:10 illuminating life-above and eternal·incorruptibility
1Jn 1:2 announce to·yeu the eternal life-above, which was
1Jn 2:25 did·already·promise to·us: the eternal life-above.
1Jn 3:15 does·not have eternal life-above abiding in him.
1Jn 5:11 that God gave to·us eternal life-above, and this
1Jn 5:12 ·one having the Son has the life-above; the·one not
1Jn 5:12 having the Son of·God does·not have the life-above.
1Jn 5:13 ·personally·know that *the* life-above *that* yeu·have *is*
1Jn 5:16 and *God* shall·give to·him life-above (*that·is*, to·
G2222.2 N-DSF ζωῇ (3x)
Lk 16:25 that you, in your life-above, did·receive·in·full your
Rm 5:10 ·reconciled, we·shall·be·saved by his life-above.
Rm 5:17 ·righteousness shall·reign in life-above through the
G2222.2 N-GSF ζωῆς (42x)
Jn 5:29 ·good, into a·resurrection of·life-above; and the·ones
Jn 6:35 I AM the bread of·life-above. The·one who·is·coming
Jn 6:48 I AM the bread of·the life-above.
Jn 6:68 ·we·go? You·have utterances of·eternal life-above.
Jn 8:12 but·rather shall·have the light of·the life-above."
Ac 2:28 *the* ways of·life-above†; you·shall·completely·fill
Ac 3:15 yeu·killed the Initiator of·the life-above, whom God
Ac 5:20 to·the people all the utterances of·this life-above."
Ac 13:46 not worthy of·the eternal life-above, behold, we·
Heb 7:16 ·to a·power of·an·indestructible life-above).
Rm 5:18 unto an·acquittal·in·righteousness of·life-above.
Rm 6:4 also should·walk in brand-newness of·life-above.
Rm 8:2 of·the Spirit of·the life-above in Anointed-One Jesus
Jac 1:12 ·shall·receive the victor's·crown of·life-above, which
Php 2:16 ·forward *the* Redemptive-word of·life-above— for
Php 4:3 the names of·whom *are* in *the* scroll of·life-above.
1Pe 3:7 *being* co-heirs of·*the*·grace of·life-above, in·order·for
Tit 1:2 in *the* Expectation of·eternal life-above, which God
Tit 3:7 according·to an·Expectation of·eternal life-above.
2Co 2:16 and to·some an·aroma of·life-above unto life-above
2Co 5:4 mortality may·be·swallowed·up by the life-above.
Eph 4:18 ·alienated from·the life-above of·God through the
1Ti 4:8 ·things, having promise of·life-above for·the present
1Ti 6:12 trust, grab·hold of·the eternal life-above, to which
1Ti 6:19 ·that they·may·grab·hold of·the eternal life-above.
2Ti 1:1 according·to *the* promise of·life-above, the·one in
1Jn 1:1 ·by·touch, concerning the Word of·the life-above;
Rv 2:7 to·eat from·out of·the arbor·tree of·Life-above, which
Rv 2:10 I·shall·give you a·victor's·crown of·the life-above.
Rv 3:5 his name out of·the scroll of·life-above, but I·shall·
Rv 11:11 ·half days, *the* Spirit of·life-above from·out of·God
Rv 13:8 been·written in the scroll of·life-above of·the Lamb
Rv 17:8 in the official·scroll of·the life-above from *the*
Rv 20:12 which is *the official·scroll* of·the life-above. And
Rv 20:15 in the scroll of·the life-above, he·was·cast into the
Rv 21:6 of·the water of·life-above as·a·free·present.
Rv 21:27 in the Lamb's official·scroll of·the life-above.
Rv 22:1 me a·pure river of·water of·life-above, radiant as
Rv 22:2 *was the* arbor·tree of·Life-above, producing twelve
Rv 22:14 upon the arbor·tree of·Life-above and may·enter
Rv 22:17 ·him·take the water of·life-above as·a·free·present.
Rv 22:19 from *the* scroll of·the life-above, and from·out of·
G2222.2 N/P-ASF ζωήν (1x)
1Jn 3:14 ·walked·on out·from Death into Life-above, because
EG2222.2 (1x)
Ac 5:31 elevated this Initiator *of·the* life-above, *this* Savior

G2223 ζώνη zṓnē *n.* (8x)
Compare:G0905 G4082 See:G2218 G2224 xLangAlso:H0073
G2223.1 N-ASF ζώνην (1x)
Rv 1:13 ·about·with a·golden band directly·against the
G2223.1 N-APF ζώνας (1x)
Rv 15:6 ·been·girded·about·with golden bands around *their*
G2223.2 N-NSF ζώνη (1x)
Ac 21:11 the man who owns this belt, and they·shall·hand
G2223.2 N-ASF ζώνην (3x)
Ac 21:11 to us and taking·up Paul's belt, and·also binding
Mt 3:4 hair and *was·girded·with* a·leather belt around his
Mk 1:6 camel's hair and with·a·leather belt around his loins,
G2223.3 N-ASF ζώνην (1x)
Mk 6:8 no bread, *and* no copper·coinage in the pouch,
G2223.3 N-APF ζώνας (1x)
Mt 10:9 silver, nor·even copper·coinage in yeur pouches,

G2224 ζώννυμι zṓnnymi *v.* (2x)
Roots:G2223 See:G0328 G1241 G4024
G2224 V-FAI-3S ζώσει (1x)
Jn 21:18 your hands, and another shall·gird you, and shall·
G2224 V-IAI-2S ἐζώννυες (1x)
Jn 21:18 you·were younger, you·were·girding yourself, and

G2225 ζωο•γονέω zōôgônéō *v.* (2x)
Roots:G2198 G1096 See:G2226
G2225.2 V-PPN ζωογονεῖσθαι (1x)
Ac 7:19 their baby·boys, such·for *them* not to·remain·alive.
G2225.3 V-FAI-3S ζωογονήσει (1x)
Lk 17:33 ·completely·lose his *soul's·desire* shall·preserve it.

G2226 ζῶον zōôn *n.* (23x)
Roots:G2198
G2226.1 N-NSN ζῶον (4x)
Rv 4:7 And the first living·being *is* like a·lion, and the
Rv 4:7 like a·lion, and the second living·being *is* like a·calf,
Rv 4:7 a·calf, and the third living·being *is* having the face as
Rv 4:7 ·of·clay†, and the fourth living·being *is* like a·flying
G2226.1 N-NPN ζῶα (6x)
Rv 4:6 throne, *are* four living·beings overflowing of·eyes
Rv 4:8 And *the* four living·beings, each one itself, was·
Rv 4:9 And whenever the living·beings shall·give glory and
Rv 5:8 official·scroll, the four living·beings and the twenty·
Rv 5:14 And the four living·beings were·saying, "So·be·it,·
Rv 19:4 Elders and the four living·beings fell·down and fell·
G2226.1 N-GSN ζώου (3x)
Rv 6:3 ·seal, I·heard the second living·being saying, "Come
Rv 6:5 official·seal, I·heard the third living·being saying,
Rv 6:7 I·heard *the* voice of·the fourth living·being saying,
G2226.1 N-GPN ζώων (7x)
Rv 5:6 of·the throne and of·the four living·beings, and in *the*
Rv 5:11 the throne and the living·beings and the Elders, and
Rv 6:1 one from·among the four living·beings (as a·voice
Rv 6:6 in *the* midst of·the four living·beings saying, "A·dry·
Rv 7:11 the Elders and the four living·beings, and they·fell
Rv 14:3 and in·the·sight of·the four living·beings, and of·the
Rv 15:7 one from·among the four living·beings gave to·the
G2226.2 N-NPN ζῶα (2x)
Jud 1:10 ·acquainted·with naturally (as irrational animals), in
2Pe 2:12 (as natural, irrational animals, having·been·born
G2226.2 N-GPN ζώων (1x)
Heb 13:11 For the bodies of·these animals, whose blood is·

G2227 ζωο•ποιέω zōôpôiéō *v.* (12x)
Roots:G2198 G4160 See:G2222 G2226
G2227.1 V-PAI-3S ζωοποιεῖ (1x)
Jn 5:21 Father awakens the dead and gives·life·to *them*; even
G2227.1 V-PAP-GSM ζωοποιοῦντος (2x)
Rm 4:17 ·trusted (*who·is* the·one giving·life·to the dead·ones
1Ti 6:13 in·the·sight of·God (the·one giving·life·to all things
G2227.1 V-PPI-3S ζωοποιεῖται (1x)
1Co 15:36 that·which you sow is·not giving·life, unless it·
G2227.2 V-FAI-3S ζωοποιήσει (1x)
Rm 8:11 dead·men shall also give·life-above·to yeur mortal
G2227.2 V-FPI-3P ζωοποιηθήσονται (1x)
1Co 15:22 the Anointed-One shall·be·given·life-above,
G2227.2 V-PAI-3S ζωοποιεῖ (2x)
Jn 5:21 in·this·manner the Son gives·life-above·to whom he·
2Co 3:6 for the letter kills, but the Spirit gives·life-above.
G2227.2 V-PAP-ASN ζωοποιοῦν (1x)
1Co 15:45 *came·into·being* as a·spirit, giving·life-above.
G2227.2 V-PAP-NSN ζωοποιοῦν (1x)
Jn 6:63 The Spirit is the·one giving·life-above. The flesh
G2227.2 V-AAN ζωοποιῆσαι (1x)
Gal 3:21 being·able to·give·life-above was·already·given, the
G2227.2 V-APP-NSM ζωοποιηθείς (1x)
1Pe 3:18 in·flesh, but being·given·life-above in·the·Spirit,

Ηη - Eta

G2228 ἤ ē *prt.* (347x)
Compare:G0235 G3123 See:G3588
(abbreviated listing for G2228)
G2228.1 PRT ἤ (290x)
(list for G2228.1:PRT excluded)
G2228.2 PRT ἤ (2x)
(list for G2228.2:PRT excluded)
G2228.3 PRT ἤ (4x)
(list for G2228.3:PRT excluded)
G2228.4 PRT ἤ (39x)
(list for G2228.4:PRT excluded)
G2228.5 PRT ἤ (5x)
(list for G2228.5:PRT excluded)
G2228.6 PRT ἤ (2x)
(list for G2228.6:PRT excluded)
G2228.7 PRT ἤ (5x)
(list for G2228.7:PRT excluded)

G2229 ἦ ē̂ *prt.* (2x)
Roots:G2228 Compare:G3375 See:G3303 G2235 G0281
G2229.2 PRT ἦ (1x)
Heb 6:14 saying, "Most assuredly, blessing I·shall·indeed·
G2229.3 V-PXS-3S ᾖ (1x)
1Co 5:11 a·brother should·actually·be a·sexually·immoral·,

G2230 ἡγεμονεύω hēgêmônêúō *v.* (2x)
Roots:G2232 See:G2231
G2230 V-PAP-GSM ἡγεμονεύοντος (2x)
Lk 2:2 first occurred with·Cyrenius being·governor of·Syria)
Lk 3:1 — (with·Pontius Pilate being·governor of·Judea, and

G2231 ἡγεμονία hēgêmônía *n.* (1x)
Roots:G2232 See:G2230
G2231.2 N-GSF ἡγεμονίας (1x)
Lk 3:1 year of·the governing·term of·Tiberius Caesar—

G2232 ἡγεμών hēgêmṓn *n.* (22x)
סָגָן çagan̲ [Hebrew]
הֶגְמוֹן hegᵉmôn̲ [Hebrew transliteration]
Roots:G2233 Compare:G1481 G2963 G2519 G1988 G4588-1 G1985 See:G2230 G2231 xLangEquiv:H5461 A5460 xLangAlso:H5057
G2232.1 N-DPM ἡγεμόσιν (1x)
Mt 2:6 ·no·means least among the official·leaders of·Judah.
G2232.2 N-NSM ἡγεμών (6x)
Ac 23:34 *letter*, the governor inquired from·which province
Ac 26:30 king rose·up, and·also the governor, and BerNiki,
Mt 27:11 And the governor inquired·of him, saying, "Are
Mt 27:15 ·this Sacred·Feast, the governor had·a·custom to·
Mt 27:21 ·into·judgment, the governor declared to·them,
Mt 27:23 And the governor was·replying, "For what crime
G2232.2 N-ASM ἡγεμόνα (2x)
Ac 23:24 ·bring·*him*·thoroughly·safe to Felix the governor."
Mt 27:14 such·for the governor to·marvel exceedingly.
G2232.2 N-APM ἡγεμόνας (2x)
Lk 21:12 before kings and governors for·the·cause·of my
Mt 10:18 yeu·shall·be·brought before governors and also
G2232.2 N-DSM ἡγεμόνι (4x)
Ac 23:26 Lysias, to·the most·noble governor Felix, be·well.
Ac 23:33 and hand-delivering the letter to·the governor, also
Ac 24:1 who made·it·clear to·the governor *the·things* against
Mt 27:2 and handed him over to·Pontius Pilate the governor.
G2232.2 N-DPM ἡγεμόσιν (1x)
1Pe 2:14 or to·governors, as being·sent through him, in·fact,
G2232.2 N-GSM ἡγεμόνος (5x)
Lk 20:20 to·the jurisdiction and authority of·the governor.
Ac 24:10 Then with·the governor beckoning for·him to·
Mt 27:11 Now YeShua stood·still before the governor. And
Mt 27:27 soldiers of·the governor, after·personally·taking
Mt 28:14 this should·be·heard by the governor, we·ourselves
G2232.2 N-GPM ἡγεμόνων (1x)
Mk 13:9 and yeu·shall·be·set before governors and kings

G2233 ἡγέομαι hēgéômai *v.* (28x)
Roots:G0071 Compare:G1781 G2753 G5426 G1988 See:G2230 G2231 G2232 G2519
G2233.1 V-PNP-APM ἡγουμένους (1x)
Ac 15:22 Silas, men who·officially·are·leading among the
G2233.1 V-PNP-NSM ἡγούμενος (2x)
Ac 14:12 the·one who·was·officially·leading the discourse.
Mt 2:6 shall·come·forth·one who·is·officially·leading, one·
G2233.2 V-PNP-ASM ἡγούμενον (1x)
Ac 7:10 fully·established him, governing over Egypt and all
G2233.2 V-PNP-APM ἡγουμένους (1x)
Heb 13:24 Greet all the·ones who·are·governing among·yeu,
G2233.2 V-PNP-DPM ἡγουμένοις (1x)
Heb 13:17 by·the·ones who·are·governing among·yeu, and
G2233.2 V-PNP-GPM ἡγουμένων (1x)
Heb 13:7 the·ones who·are·governing among·yeu, who
G2233.2 V-PNP-NSM ἡγούμενος (1x)
Lk 22:26 as the younger, and the·one governing, as the·one
G2233.3 V-PNI-1S ἡγοῦμαι (3x)
Php 3:8 also— I·resolutely·consider all·things to·be a·
Php 3:8 of·all·things, and do·resolutely·consider *them* to·be
2Pe 1:13 And I·do·resolutely·consider·it right, for as·long·as
G2233.3 V-PNI-3P ἡγοῦνται (1x)
2Pe 3:9 promise, as some·men resolutely·consider tardiness,
G2233.3 V-PNM-2P ἡγεῖσθε (2x)
2Pe 3:15 And resolutely·consider the long-suffering of·our
2Th 3:15 Even·so, resolutely·consider *him* not as an·enemy,
G2233.3 V-PNM-3P ἡγείσθωσαν (1x)
1Ti 6:1 under a·yoke resolutely·consider their·own masters
G2233.3 V-PNN ἡγεῖσθαι (1x)
1Th 5:13 and to·resolutely·consider them abundantly with
G2233.3 V-PNP-NPM ἡγούμενοι (2x)
Php 2:3 humbleness·of·mind resolutely·considering one· as·
2Pe 2:13 *as·those* who·are·resolutely·considering sensual· in
G2233.3 V-ADI-1S ἡγησάμην (2x)
Php 2:25 Now I·resolutely·considered *it* necessary to·send to
2Co 9:5 Accordingly, I·resolutely·considered *it* necessary
G2233.3 V-ADI-2P ἡγήσασθε (1x)
Jac 1:2 My brothers, resolutely·consider·it all joy whenever
G2233.3 V-ADI-3S ἡγήσατο (3x)
Heb 11:11 since she·resolutely·considered *him* trustworthy,
Php 2:6 ·nature of·God, resolutely·considered it not open·
1Ti 1:12 Because he·resolutely·considered me trustworthy,
G2233.3 V-ADP-NSM ἡγησάμενος (2x)
Heb 10:29 Son of·God, and resolutely·considering the blood
Heb 11:26 resolutely·considering the reproach of·the
G2233.3 V-RNI-1S ἥγημαι (2x)
Ac 26:2 "I·have·resolutely·considered myself supremely·
Php 3:7 these·things I·have·resolutely·considered a·total·loss

G2234 ἡδέως hēdéōs *adv.* (3x)
Roots:G2237 See:G2236 G0780
G2234.2 ADV ἡδέως (3x)
Mk 6:20 many·things, yet was·hearing him with·pleasure.
Mk 12:37 the large crowd was·hearing him with·pleasure.
2Co 11:19 ·with the impetuous with·pleasure, *yeurselves*

G2235 ἤ•δη ḗdē *adv.* (59x)
Roots:G2228 G2229 G1211
G2235 ADV ἤδη (59x)
Jn 3:18 ·one not trusting has·been·judged even·now, because
Jn 4:35 because they·are white even·now unto harvest.
Jn 4:51 And with·him even·now walking·down, his slaves
Jn 5:6 that he·had·been *in·the·sickness* even·now a·long time
Jn 6:17 CaperNaum. And even·now it·had·become dark, and
Jn 7:14 But even·now halfway·through the Sacred·Feast *of·*
Jn 9:22 had·agreed·among·themselves even·now that if·any·
Jn 9:27 "I·declared *it* to·yeu even·now, and yeu·did·not
Jn 11:17 *·to·rest* in the chamber·tomb four days even·now.
Jn 11:39 to·him, "O·Lord, even·now he·smells·bad, for it·is
Jn 13:2 with·the Slanderer even·now having·cast into the
Jn 15:3 "Even·now yeu are trimmed·and·pure through the
Jn 19:28 ·seen that even·now everything has·been·finished,
Jn 19:33 as·soon·as they saw him even·now having·died,
Jn 21:4 But even·now with·it·becoming the·break·of·dawn,
Jn 21:14 This *is* even·now a·third·time *that* Jesus is·made·
Lk 3:9 "And even·now also, the ax is·laid·out to the root of·
Lk 7:6 together with·them. And even·now, with·him not
Lk 11:7 *your* wearisome·troubles to·me. Even·now, the door
Lk 12:49 ·want, though even·now it·is·already·kindled?
Lk 14:17 'Come, because all·things are even·now ready.'
Lk 19:37 with·him drawing·near, even·now alongside the
Lk 21:30 they·should·bud, even·now while·looking·about,
Lk 21:30 ·selves that the summer is even·now near·at·hand.
Ac 4:3 for the next·day, for even·now it·was evening.
Ac 27:9 voyage being even·now precarious on·account·of
Ac 27:9 *·of·Atonement* also even·now to·have·passed·by,
Mt 3:10 "And even·now also, the ax is·laid·out to the root
Mt 5:28 her, committed·adultery with·her even·now in his
Mt 14:15 desolate, and the hour even·now *has* passed·away.
Mt 14:24 But the sailboat was even·now in·*the*·middle of·the
Mt 15:32 because even·now they·continue·on with·me *for*
Mt 17:12 ·yeu, that EliJah came even·now, and they·did·not
Mt 24:32 the parable: "Even·now, whenever its branch
Mk 4:37 the sailboat, such·for it even·now to·be·overfilled.
Mk 6:35 And even·now with·it·becoming a·late hour, his
Mk 6:35 place is·desolate, and even·now *it·is* a·late hour.
Mk 8:2 crowd, because even·now they·continue·on with·me
Mk 11:11 ·around·upon all·things, even·now with·the hour
Mk 13:28 the parable: "Even·now, whenever its branch
Mk 15:42 And even·now, with·early·evening occurring,
Mk 15:44 And Pilate marveled if, even·now, he·has·died.
Rm 1:10 Petitioning, if·somehow even·now at·last *that* I·
Rm 4:19 his·own body, even·now having·been·deadened,
Rm 13:11 ·seen the season, *know* that even·now, this *is the*
Php 3:12 Not that even·now I·took·hold·of *it*, or even·now
Php 3:12 or even·now have·been·made·completely·mature,
Php 4:10 greatly, that even·now at·last yeur·earnest·concern
2Pe 3:1 second letter, beloved, even·now I·write to·yeu, in
2Th 2:7 mystery of·the Lawlessness operates even·now. *It·is*
1Co 4:8 Even·now yeu·are having·been·stuffed·full·to·
1Co 4:8 ·excess. Even·now yeu·became·wealthy! Yeu·
1Co 5:3 but being·present in·the spirit, even·now, as·though
1Co 6:7 Accordingly in·fact, even·now there·is altogether a·
1Ti 5:15 For even·now some are·turned·aside, *falling·in*
2Ti 2:18 saying the resurrection even·now to·have·occurred,
2Ti 4:6 For even·now, I·myself am·poured·forth·as·a·
1Jn 2:8 ·away, and the true Light even·now shines·forth.
1Jn 4:3 that it·is·come, and now is in the world, even·now.

G2236 ἥδιστα hḗdista *adv.* (2x)
Roots:G2234 See:G0780
G2236 ADV ἥδιστα (2x)
2Co 12:9 rather, with·great·pleasure, I·shall·boast in my
2Co 12:15 And with·great·pleasure, I·myself shall·cover·

G2237 ἡδονή hēdônḗ *n.* (5x)
See:G0780 G2234 G4913
G2237.1 N-DPF ἡδοναῖς (2x)
Jac 4:3 in·order·that yeu·may·spend *it* on yeur pleasures.
Tit 3:3 ·diverse longings and pleasures, passing·through·life
G2237.1 N-GPF ἡδονῶν (2x)
Lk 8:14 anxieties and wealth and pleasures of·the natural·life
Jac 4:1 ·here, birthed·from·out·of·yeur pleasures, the·ones
G2237.2 N-ASF ἡδονήν (1x)
2Pe 2:13 who·are·resolutely·considering sensual·pleasure in

G2238 ἡδύ•οσμον hēdýôsmôn *n.* (2x)
Roots:G2234 G3744
G2238 N-ASN ἡδύοσμον (2x)
Lk 11:42 Because yeu·tithe the mint and the rue and all·
Mt 23:23 Because yeu·pay·tithes of·the mint and the dill and

G2239 ἦθος ē̂thôs *n.* (1x)
Roots:G1485 See:G2550
G2239.2 N-APN ἤθη (1x)
1Co 15:33 "Bad influences corrupt fine moral·habits."

G2240 ἥκω hḗkō *v.* (27x)
Compare:G2064 G2658 G0864 See:G2240
G2240 V-FAI-1S ἥξω (2x)
Rv 3:3 unless you·should·keep·alert, I·shall·come upon you

Rv 3:3 ·should·not know which hour I·shall·come upon you.
G2240 V-FAI-3S ἥξει (8x)
Jn 6:37 that the Father gives me shall·come toward me; and
Lk 12:46 the lord of·that slave shall·come in a·day when he·
Heb 10:37 the·one who·is·coming shall·come and shall·not
Mt 23:36 I·say to·yeu, all these·things shall·come upon this
Mt 24:14 to·all the nations, and then the end shall·come.
Mt 24:50 the lord of·that slave shall·come on a·day when he·
Rm 11:26 "*The Kinsman·Redeemer* shall·come from·out of·
2Pe 3:10 But the Day of·*the*·Lord shall·come as a·thief, in a·
G2240 V-FAI-3P ἥξουσιν (5x)
Lk 13:29 And they·shall·come from east and west, and from
Lk 19:43 "Because days shall·come upon you, and your
Mt 8:11 I·say to·yeu that many shall·come from east and
Rv 15:4 all the nations shall·come and shall·fall·prostrate in·
Rv 18:8 ·of that, her punishing·blows shall·come in one day:
G2240 V-PAI-1S ἥκω (3x)
Jn 8:42 for I·myself went·forth and have·come out·from God
Heb 10:7 ·time I·declared, 'Behold, I·come— on *the* header
Heb 10:9 declared, '" Behold, I·come, *I·am* the·one to·do
G2240 V-PAI-3S ἥκει (4x)
Jn 2:4 to·do·with·me and you? My hour has·not·yet come."
Jn 4:47 after·hearing that Jesus comes from·out of·Judea
Lk 15:27 to·him, 'Your brother comes *home*! And your
1Jn 5:20 ·know that the Son of·God comes, and he·has·given
G2240 V-IAI-3P ἦκον (1x)
Ac 28:23 for·him, many·more were·coming alongside him
G2240 V-AAS-1S ἥξω (1x)
Rv 2:25 ·have, securely·hold even·until I·should·come.
G2240 V-AAS-3S ἥξῃ (1x)
Lk 13:35 *the time* should·come when yeu·should·declare, "
G2240 V-AAS-3P ἥξωσιν (1x)
Rv 3:9 them that they·should·come and should·fall·prostrate
G2240 V-RAI-3P ἥκασιν (1x)
Mk 8:3 way, for some of·them have·come *from* a·distance."

G2241 ἠλί ēlí *heb.* (2x)

אֵל 'el [Hebrew]
Roots:H0410
G2241.2 HEB ἠλί (2x)
Mt 27:46 ·loud voice, saying, "'Eli, Eli, lama shebaq-thani?
Mt 27:46 voice, saying, "'Eli, Eli, lama shebaq-thani?

G2242 Ἡλί Hēlí *n/p.* (1x)

עֵלִי 'eliy [Hebrew]
Roots:H5941
G2242.3 N/P-PRI Ἡλί (1x)
Lk 3:23 *being a·grandson of·Mariam's father*, Eli, *who·was*:

G2243 Ἡλ•ίας Hēlías *n/p.* (30x)

אֵלִיָּה 'eliyah [Hebrew]
Roots:H0452
G2243.2 N/P-NSM Ἡλίας (17x)
Jn 1:21 ·then, who are you·yourself, EliJah?" And he·says,
Jn 1:25 not the Anointed-One, nor EliJah, nor the Prophet?
Lk 4:26 yet to not·even·one of·them was EliJah sent, except
Lk 9:8 and by some that EliJah appeared, and by·others that
Lk 9:30 ·together with·him, who were Moses and EliJah—
Lk 9:54 heaven and to·consume them, even as EliJah did?
Mt 11:14 to·accept *it*, he·himself is EliJah, the·one about to·
Mt 17:3 Moses and EliJah were·made·visible to·them,
Mt 17:11 to·them, "In·fact EliJah does·come first and shall·
Mt 17:12 "But I·say to·yeu, that EliJah came even·now, and
Mt 27:49 we·should·see whether EliJah comes to·save him.
Mk 6:15 Others were·saying, "It·is EliJah." And others
Mk 9:4 they·gazed·upon them, EliJah together with·Moses,
Mk 9:12 he·declared to·them, "EliJah, in·fact, after·
Mk 9:13 ·yet I·say to·yeu that indeed EliJah has·come, and
Mk 15:36 we·should·see whether EliJah comes to·lower
Jac 5:17 EliJah was a·man·of·clay† of·like·passions with·us,
G2243.2 N/P-ASM Ἡλίαν (7x)
Lk 9:19 the Immerser, but others *say* EliJah, and others *say*
Mt 16:14 the Immerser, and others *say* EliJah, but *yet* others
Mt 17:10 say that it·is·mandatory·for EliJah to·come first?
Mt 27:47 were·saying, "This·man hollers·out·for EliJah."
Mk 8:28 Immerser, but some *say*, EliJah, and others, one
Mk 9:11 say that it·is·mandatory·for EliJah to·come first?
Mk 15:35 "Behold, he·hollers·out·for EliJah."
G2243.2 N/P-DSM Ἡλίᾳ (4x)
Lk 9:33 one·for Moses, and one·for EliJah," not personally·
Mt 17:4 for·you, and one for·Moses, and one for·EliJah."
Mk 9:5 for·you, and one for·Moses, and one for·EliJah."
Rm 11:2 what the Scripture says by EliJah? How he·confers
G2243.2 N/P-GSM Ἡλίου (2x)
Lk 1:17 *Yahweh* in *the* spirit and power of·EliJah, "to·turn
Lk 4:25 were in IsraEl in the days of·EliJah, when the heaven

G2244 ἡλικία hēlikía *n.* (9x)

See:G2245 G4080 G4915
G2244.1 N-DSF ἡλικίᾳ (1x)
Lk 2:52 ·continually·advancing in·wisdom, maturity, and
G2244.1 N-GSF ἡλικίας (2x)
Heb 11:11 ·after·and·beyond *the* season of·maturity, since
Eph 4:13 into a·measure of·maturity of·the complete·fullness
G2244.2 N-ASF ἡλικίαν (2x)
Jn 9:21 personally·know. He·himself is of·mature·age; ask
Jn 9:23 his parents declared, "He·is of·mature·age; ask him.
G2244.3 N-DSF ἡλικίᾳ (1x)
Lk 19:3 ·to for the crowd, because he·was small of·stature.
EG2244.3 (1x)
Heb 7:8 *and·then, there·was the·one of·stature who·is still*
G2244.4 N-ASF ἡλικίαν (2x)
Lk 12:25 is·able to·add one half·step to his span·of·life?
Mt 6:27 is·able to·add one half·step to his span·of·life?

G2245 ἡλίκος hēlíkôs *adj.* (2x)

Compare:G4080 See:G2244
G2245.1 A-ASF ἡλίκην (1x)
Jac 3:5 a·little fire kindles *something* as·big·as a·forest!
G2245.3 A-ASM ἡλίκον (1x)
Col 2:1 to·personally·know what·a·huge strenuous·struggle

G2246 ἥλιος hḗliôs *n.* (32x)

Roots:G1661-2 Compare:G0827 G3722 See:G0138
xLangEquiv:H8121 A8122
G2246.1 N-NSM ἥλιος (9x)
Lk 23:45 Then the sun was·darkened, and the curtain of·the
Ac 2:20 The sun shall·be·distorted into darkness and the
Mt 24:29 of·those days, the sun shall·be·darkened, and the
Mk 1:32 occurring, when the sun sank·down, they·were·
Mk 13:24 TRIBULATION, the sun shall·be·darkened, and
Jac 1:11 For the sun rose·above·the·horizon together with·
Eph 4:26 ' Do·not·let the sun go·down upon yeur personal·
Rv 6:12 a·great earthquake; and the sun became *as* black as
Rv 9:2 of·a·great furnace, and the sun and the air were·
G2246.1 N-ASM ἥλιον (3x)
Ac 13:11 ·be blind, not looking·at the sun— *but* only·for a·
Mt 5:45 because he·raises his sun above·the·horizon over
Rv 16:8 poured·out his vial upon the sun, and it·was·given
G2246.1 N-DSM ἡλίῳ (2x)
Lk 21:25 "And there·shall·be signs in *the* sun, moon, and
Rv 19:17 one angel standing in the sun; and he·yelled·out
G2246.1 N-GSM ἡλίου (11x)
Lk 4:40 Now with·the sun sinking·down, as·many·as were
Ac 26:13 of·the sun radiating·brightly·all·around me and
Ac 27:20 And with·neither sun nor constellations·of·stars
Mt 13:6 And with·*the*·sun rising·above·the·horizon, it·was·
Mk 4:6 And with·*the*·sun rising·above·the·horizon, it·was·
Mk 16:2 ·tomb with·the sun rising·above·the·horizon.
Rv 7:2 ascending from *the* eastern sun, having an·official·
Rv 8:12 and the third·part of·the sun was·pounded, and the
Rv 16:12 kings from the eastern sun may·be·made·ready.
Rv 21:23 CITY has no need of·the sun, neither of·the moon,
Rv 22:5 need of·a·lantern, nor·even of·sun light, because
G2246.3 N-NSM ἥλιος (4x)
Mt 13:43 shall·brilliantly·radiate·forth as the sun in the
Mt 17:2 And his face radiated·brightly as the sun, and his
Rv 1:16 his appearance *is* as the sun *that* shines·forth in its
Rv 10:1 and his face *was* as the sun, and his feet as pillars
G2246.3 N-ASM ἥλιον (1x)
Rv 12:1 a·woman having·been·arrayed·with the sun, and the
G2246.3 N-GSM ἡλίου (1x)
1Co 15:41 *There·is* one glory of·*the*·sun, and another glory
G2246.4 N-NSM ἥλιος (1x)
Rv 7:16 nor·even, no, *that* the sunray should·fall on them,

G2247 ἧλος hē̂lôs *n.* (2x)

Compare:G4716 G3956-1 See:G2247-1 G4338
G1335-2 G2520-1 xLangAlso:H4548
G2247 N-GPM ἥλων (2x)
Jn 20:25 I·may·see the imprint of·the nails in his hands, and
Jn 20:25 finger into the imprint of·the nails, and may·cast my

G2248 ἡμᾶς hēmâs *p:p.* (188x)

Roots:G1473 See:G2254
(abbreviated listing for G2248)
G2248 P:P-1AP ἡμᾶς (179x)
(list for G2248:P:P-1AP excluded)
EG2248 (9x)
(list for EG2248: excluded)

G2249 ἡμεῖς hēmêîs *p:p.* (126x)

Roots:G1473 See:G2248 G2257
(abbreviated listing for G2249)
G2249 P:P-1NP ἡμεῖς (126x)
(list for G2249:P:P-1NP excluded)

G2250 ἡμέρα hēméra *n.* (399x)

Roots:G2247-2 Compare:G0839 See:G2522 G5610
G1475-3
xLangEquiv:H3117 A3118
G2250.1 N-NSF ἡμέρα (16x)
Jn 9:4 sending me, for·as·long·as it·is day. Night is·coming,
Jn 19:31 (for that Sabbath was the great day), the Judeans
Lk 6:13 And when it·was day, he·hailed his disciples *to*·
Lk 9:12 And the day began to·fade. Now the twelve,
Lk 21:34 ·life, and·also *lest* that day should·stand·over yeu
Lk 22:7 Then came the day of·the *Sacred·Feast·of*
Lk 22:66 Now as it·became day, the council·of·elders of·the
Lk 23:54 And *that* day was preparation·day, and a·Sabbath
Lk 24:29 it·is toward evening, and the day has·faded." And
Ac 27:39 And when it·was day, they·were·not recognizing
2Pe 1:19 — until *the* day should·beam·right·through, and *the*
2Pe 3:8 O·yeu beloved, that "one day *is* with *the* Lord as a·
2Pe 3:8 a·thousand years, and a·thousand years as one day."
1Co 3:13 apparent, for the day shall·make·*it*·plain, because
2Co 6:2 Behold, now *is the* day of·custodial·Salvation!
Rv 8:12 and the day should·not shine·forth for·the third·
G2250.1 N-NPF ἡμέραι (19x)
Lk 1:23 ·happened, as·soon·as the days of·his public·service
Lk 2:6 *that* the days for·her to·reproduce·and·give·birth
Lk 2:21 And when eight days were·fulfilled to·circumcise
Lk 2:22 Now when the days of·her purification according·to
Lk 5:35 But days shall·come, and then, whenever the
Lk 9:28 And it·happened about eight days after these sayings
Lk 13:14 "There·are six days in which it·is·necessary to·
Lk 17:22 disciples, "Days shall·come when yeu·shall·long
Lk 19:43 "Because days shall·come upon you, and your
Lk 21:6 these·things which yeu·observe, days shall·come in
Ac 9:23 ·as a·significant·number·of days were·completely·,
Ac 12:3 Now it·was the days *of·the Sacred·Feast* of·
Ac 21:27 seven days were·about to·be·entirely·completed,
Ac 24:11 there·are not more than twelve days for·me since I·
Heb 8:8 'Behold, *the* days come,' says Yahweh, 'and I·
Mt 9:15 is with·them? But days shall·come, whenever the
Mt 24:37 But just·as *were* the days of·Noach, in·this·manner
Mk 2:20 But days shall·come, whenever the bridegroom
Eph 5:16 ·redeeming the season, because the days are evil.
G2250.1 N-ASF ἡμέραν (55x)
Jn 1:39 and they·abided with him that day, for it·was *late*·
Jn 8:56 leaped·for·joy that he·should·see my day, and he·
Jn 12:7 ·kept it for the day of·my preparation·for·burial.
Lk 2:37 *to·God* with·fastings and petitions night and day.
Lk 9:23 and take·up his cross each day, and·then follow me.
Lk 11:3 'Give us each day our sustaining bread.
Lk 16:19 and fine·linen, splendidly being·merry each day.
Lk 19:47 And he·was instructing each day in the Sanctuary·

Hη

Lk 22:53 With·me being each day with yeu in the Sanctuary·
Lk 24:21 today marks this third day since these·things
Ac 2:1 with the day of·Pentecost to·be·completely·fulfilled,
Ac 2:46 Each day, both while·diligently·continuing with·the·
Ac 2:47 the·ones being·saved each day alongside the Called·
Ac 3:2 whom they·were·laying each day alongside the door
Ac 5:42 And every day in the Sanctuary·Atrium, and in·each
Ac 16:5 ·the trust and were·abounding in·number each day.
Ac 17:11 scrutinizing the Scriptures each day, *as·to* whether
Ac 17:17 marketplace each and·every day alongside the·ones
Ac 17:31 On·account·that, he·established a·day in which he·
Ac 19:9 *of·the kingdom of·God* each day in the school·
Ac 20:16 ·him, to·be in JeruSalem *on* the day of·Pentecost.
Ac 20:31 admonishing each one, night and day with tears.
Ac 21:7 the brothers, we·abided with them one day.
Ac 26:7 ·ritually·ministering *to·God* night and day, expect *it*
Ac 27:29 ·*the*·stern, they·were·well-wishing·for *it* to·be day.
Ac 27:33 "This·day is·the·fourteenth day of·anticipating,
Ac 28:13 And after one day, with·*the*·south·wind springing·
Ac 28:23 And after·arranging a·day for·him, many·more
Heb 3:8 Direct·Provocation, in the day of·the Proof·Trial
Heb 3:13 ·another each and·every day, even·for·as·along·as
Heb 4:7 he·specifically·determined a·certain day, *namely*
Heb 7:27 who does·not have a·necessity each day, just·as the
Heb 10:11 ·sacrifices stands each day publicly·serving and
Heb 10:25 as·much·as yeu·look·upon the day drawing·near.
Mt 20:2 for a·denarius *for* the day, he·dispatched them into
Mt 20:6 'Why·do yeu·stand here the whole day idle?
Mt 25:13 yeu·do·not personally·know the day nor·even the
Mt 26:55 me? I·was·sitting·down each day alongside yeu
Mk 4:27 and should·be·awakened night and day, but how
Mk 14:49 Each day I·was alongside yeu in the Sanctuary·
Rm 14:5 someone judges one·day *to·be* above·and·beyond
Rm 14:5 one·day *to·be* above·and·beyond *another* day, yet
Rm 14:5 yet someone *else* judges every day *to·be alike*. Let
Rm 14:6 ·one earnestly·regarding the day, earnestly·regards
Rm 14:6 ·one not earnestly·regarding the day, unto·*the*·Lord
Php 1:10 and without·offense in *the* day of·Anointed-One,
Php 2:16 a·boast by·me in *the* day of·Anointed-One that I·
2Pe 2:8 righteous·man residing among them day by day was·
2Pe 2:9 ·men to a·day of·Tribunal·judgment to·be·sternly·
2Pe 3:18 now and to *the* day of·*the*·coming·age. So·be·it,·
2Th 3:8 and travail night and day specifically·for *us* not to·
1Co 15:31 Each day I·die, as·sure·as *it·is* our boast, which I·
Eph 4:30 ·officially·sealed to *the* day of·full·redemption.
2Ti 1:12 to·vigilantly·keep my trust·deposit toward that day.
Rv 9:15 ·been·made·ready for the hour, day, lunar·month,

G2250.1 N-APF ἡμέρας (66x)

Jn 2:12 disciples), and they·remained there not many days.
Jn 4:40 to·abide with them, and he·abided there two days.
Jn 4:43 Now after the two days, he·went·off from·there and
Jn 11:6 he·was·sick, in·fact he·remained two days still in *the*
Jn 11:17 ·*to·rest* in the chamber·tomb four days even·now.
Jn 20:26 And after eight days, again his disciples were inside
Lk 1:24 And after these days, his wife EliSabeth conceived
Lk 1:75 in·the·sight of·him, all the days of·our life†.
Lk 2:43 and after·fully·completing the days, *then* at their
Lk 2:46 And after three days, it·happened *that* they·found
Lk 4:2 being·tried *for* forty days by the Slanderer.
Lk 9:51 among the days to·be·completely·fulfilled for·his
Lk 15:13 "And not many days after, the younger son,
Lk 21:37 Now *during* the days, he·was instructing in the
Ac 1:5 ·be·immersed in Holy Spirit after not *too* many days."
Ac 3:24 also fully·announced·beforehand these days.
Ac 9:9 And he·was three days not looking·about, and neither
Ac 9:19 was among the disciples at Damascus *for* some days.
Ac 9:43 him to·abide a·significant·number·of days in Joppa
Ac 10:48 Then they·asked him to·stay·over some days.
Ac 13:31 many·more days by·the·ones walking·up·together
Ac 15:36 Now after some days, Paul declared to BarNabas,
Ac 16:12 ·were in that city lingering·awhile·for some days.
Ac 16:18 this she·did over many days. But being·thoroughly·
Ac 18:18 *number·of* days, after·orderly·taking·leave·of the
Ac 20:6 from Philippi after the days of·the *Sacred·Feast·of*
Ac 20:6 in·only five days, where we·lingered seven days.
Ac 21:4 at·this·location *for* seven days; these·same·men
Ac 21:5 us to·properly·finish·out the days, upon·going·forth,
Ac 21:10 ·us still·staying·over *for* many·more days, a·certain
Ac 21:15 after these days, after·packing·up·our·belongings,
Ac 24:1 And after five days, the designated·high·priest
Ac 24:24 And after some days, after·arriving·publicly
Ac 25:1 Now·then, three days after walking·over into·the
Ac 25:6 *for* more than ten days, *and·then* walking·down to
Ac 25:14 ·were·lingering there *for* many·more days, Festus
Ac 27:20 ·of·stars appearing over many·more days, and
Ac 28:7 He·hosted *us for* three days courteously.
Ac 28:12 at Syracuse, we·stayed·over *for* three days.
Ac 28:14 with them *for* seven days. And in·this·manner we·
Ac 28:17 And after three days, it·happened *that* Paul called·
Heb 8:10 with·the house of·IsraEl after those days,' says
Heb 10:16 unto them after those days, says Yahweh, giving
Heb 10:32 ·to·mind·and·consider the previous days in which
Heb 11:30 being·surrounded for·a·span·of seven days.
Heb 12:10 ·for few days, were·educating·and·disciplining *us*
Gal 1:18 Peter, and I·stayed·over alongside him fifteen days.
Gal 4:10 Yeu·meticulously·keep days, and lunar·months,
Mt 4:2 And after·fasting forty days and forty nights,
Mt 12:40 For just·as Jonah was three days and three nights in
Mt 12:40 the Son of·Clay·Man† shall·be three days and three
Mt 15:32 they·continue·on with·me *for* three days, and they·
Mt 17:1 And after six days, YeShua personally·takes Peter
Mt 26:2 ·personally·know that after two days the Passover
Mt 27:63 still living, 'After three days, I·am·awakened.'
Mt 28:20 am with yeu *for* all the days, even·unto the entire·
Mk 1:13 there in the wilderness forty days, being·tried by the
Mk 8:2 they·continue·on with·me *for* three days and do·not
Mk 8:31 to·be·killed, and·then after three days to·rise·up.
Mk 9:2 And after six days, Jesus personally·takes Peter,
Mk 14:1 Now after two days, it·would·be *the Judeans'*
1Pe 3:10 and to·see beneficially·good days must·restrain his
Rv 11:3 ·hundred *and* sixty days, having·been·arrayed·with
Rv 11:9 their corpses three and a·half days, and shall·not
Rv 11:11 And after the three and a·half days, *the* Spirit of·
Rv 12:6 her there a·thousand two·hundred *and* sixty days.

G2250.1 N-DSF ἡμέρᾳ (62x)

Jn 2:1 And on·the third day, there·was a·wedding in Qanah
Jn 5:9 was·walking, and on the same day was a·Sabbath.
Jn 7:37 On the last day, on·the great *day* of·the Sacred·Feast
Jn 14:20 In that day, yeu shall·know that I·myself *am* in my
Jn 16:23 "And in that day yeu·shall·not ask·of me not·even·
Jn 16:26 "At that day, yeu·shall·request in my name, and I·
Jn 20:19 *almost* early·evening on·that *same* day, the first *day*
Lk 1:59 And it·occurred on the eighth day, *that* they·came
Lk 4:16 into the gathering on the day of·Sabbath, and he·
Lk 6:23 "Rejoice in that day and skip·about, for, behold,
Lk 9:22 to·be·killed, and to·be·awakened on·the third day."
Lk 9:37 *that* on the next day, with·them coming·down from
Lk 12:46 of·that slave shall·come in a·day when he·does·not
Lk 13:14 ·relieved·and·cured, and not on·the Sabbath day."
Lk 13:16 to·be·loosed from this bond on·the Sabbath day?"
Lk 13:31 In the same day, there·came·alongside certain
Lk 14:5 ·not immediately draw him up on the Sabbath day?"
Lk 17:24 also shall·be the Son of·Clay·Man† in his day.
Lk 17:29 but on·that day *when* Lot went·forth from Sodom,
Lk 17:30 In the·same·manner shall·it·be in·that day *when* the
Lk 17:31 "In that day, whoever shall·be upon the rooftop,
Lk 18:33 And on·the third day, he·shall·rise·up."
Lk 19:42 at·least in this your day, the·things pertaining·to
Lk 23:12 And in the same day, both Pilate and HerOd·AntiPas
Lk 24:7 to·be·crucified, and on·the third day to·rise·up.'"
Lk 24:13 were traversing on that·same day to a·village with·
Lk 24:46 to·rise·up from·among dead·men on·the third day.
Ac 2:41 they·were·immersed; and in·that·one day, about
Ac 7:8 and circumcised him on·the eighth day; and YiTsaq
Ac 7:26 Also the following day, he·made·himself·visible to·
Ac 8:1 And on·that·very day, there·was a·great persecution
Ac 10:40 God awakened on·the third day and gave him to·
Ac 12:21 And upon·an·assigned day, after·dressing·himself
Ac 13:14 into the gathering on·the day of·Sabbath, they·sat·
Ac 16:13 Also on·the day of·Sabbath, we·went·forth outside
Ac 20:26 I·attest to·yeu in the present day, that I·myself *am*
Ac 21:26 following day *and* being·ceremonially·cleansed
Heb 4:4 And God fully·rested in the seventh day from all his
Heb 8:9 ·their fathers in *the* day after·grabbing·hold·of·them
Mt 6:34 of·itself. Sufficient for·the day *is* its·own hardship.
Mt 13:1 And in that day, YeShua, after·going·forth from the
Mt 16:21 to·be·killed, and to·be·awakened on·the third day.
Mt 17:23 him, and on·the third day he·shall·be·awakened."
Mt 20:19 And on·the third day, he·shall·rise·up."
Mt 22:23 On the same day, *some* Sadducees came·alongside
Mt 24:50 ·that slave shall·come on a·day when he·does·not
Mk 4:35 And in the same day, with·early·evening occurring,
Mk 9:31 ·being·killed, he·shall·rise·up on·the third day."
Mk 10:34 ·kill him, and on·the third day he·shall·rise·up."
Mk 14:12 Now on·the first day of·the *Sacred·Feast·of*
Jac 5:5 ·nourished yeur hearts, as in a·day of·butchering.
2Th 1:10 at by·all the·ones trusting in that day)— because
1Co 10:8 and twenty·three thousand fell in one day.
1Co 15:4 ·been·awakened on·the third day according·to the
2Co 4:16 inward *man·of·clay†* is·being·renewed day by day.
2Co 4:16 inward *man·of·clay†* is·being·renewed day by day.
2Co 6:2 and in a·day of·custodial·Salvation I·swiftly·helped
Eph 6:13 *them* in the evil day, and after·accomplishing
2Ti 4:8 judge, shall·yield·forth to·me at that day. And not
1Jn 4:17 freeness·of·speech in the day of·Tribunal·judgment,
Rv 1:10 *the* Spirit on the Lord's day and heard right·behind
Rv 18:8 her punishing·blows shall·come in one day: death,

G2250.1 N-DPF ἡμέραις (46x)

Jn 2:19 this temple, and in three days I·shall·awaken it."
Jn 2:20 was·built, and you, in three days, shall·awaken it?
Lk 1:5 In the days of·HerOd·the·Great, the king of·Judea,
Lk 1:7 and both were having·well-advanced in their days.
Lk 1:18 and my wife *is* having·well-advanced in her days."
Lk 1:25 done for·me, in *the* days when he·took·notice·of *me*
Lk 1:39 Mariam, rising·up in these days, traversed into the
Lk 2:1 And it·happened in those days, *that* there·went·forth
Lk 2:36 herself having·well-advanced in many days, *being a·*
Lk 4:2 And in those days, he·did·not eat not·even·one·thing.
Lk 4:25 were in IsraEl in the days of·EliJah, when the heaven
Lk 5:35 ·away from them, they·shall·fast in those days."
Lk 6:12 And it·happened in those days *that* he·went·forth to
Lk 9:36 in those days not·even·one of·those·things·which
Lk 17:26 just·as it·was in the days of·Noach, in·this·manner
Lk 17:26 shall·it·be also in the days of·the Son of·Clay·
Lk 17:28 also as it·was in the days of·Lot: they·were·eating,
Lk 23:7 himself being also at JeruSalem in these days.
Lk 24:18 the·things occurring among her in these days?"
Ac 1:15 And in these days, in *the* midst of·the disciples (and
Ac 2:17 "'And it·shall·be in the last days, says God, *that* I·
Ac 2:18 And in those days, upon my male·slaves and upon
Ac 5:37 of·Galilee rose·up in the days of·the census and
Ac 6:1 And in these days of·the disciples multiplying, there·
Ac 7:41 they·made·a·calf in those days and brought·forth
Ac 9:37 And it·happened in those days, *that* being·sick, she
Ac 11:27 And in those days, prophets came·down from
Ac 13:41 I·myself work a·work in yeur days, a·work which,
Ac 27:7 ·slowly along for·a·significant·number·of days, and
Heb 5:7 *a·high·priest*, who in the days of·his flesh, *was*
Mt 2:1 of·Judea, in *the* days of·the king HerOd·the·Great,
Mt 3:1 Now in those days, John the Immerser arrived·
Mt 23:30 'If we·were in the days of·our fathers, we·would
Mt 24:38 For just·as in the days, the·ones that·were before
Mt 27:40 Temple and building *it* in three days, save yourself.
Mk 1:9 And it·happened in those days *that* Jesus came from
Mk 2:20 from them, and then they·shall·fast in those days.
Mk 8:1 In those days (with·*the*·crowd being immense and
Mk 15:29 the Temple and building *it* in three days,
Jac 5:3 Yeu·stored·up·treasure in *the* last days.
1Pe 3:20 was·waiting·for *this·moment in the* days of·Noach,

2Ti 3:1 that in *the* last days perilous seasons shall·settle·in.
Rv 2:13 my trust, even in the days in which AntiPas *was* my
Rv 9:6 And in those days, the men·of·clay† shall·seek Death
Rv 10:7 But·rather in the days of·the sound of·the seventh
Rv 11:6 ·not shower rain in *the* days of·their prophecy. And

G2250.1 N-GSF ἡμέρας (52x)

Jn 11:53 So·then, from that day *forth*, they·took·counsel·
Lk 1:20 ·able to·speak, even·until *the* day that these·things
Lk 1:80 wildernesses until *the* day of·his official·showing to
Lk 2:44 in the caravan, they·went a·day's journey, then they·
Lk 4:42 And with·day occurring, going·forth, he·traversed
Lk 17:4 against you seven·times in·the day, and seven·times
Lk 17:4 seven·times in·the day should·turn·back·around to
Lk 17:27 ·in·marriage, even·until that day *when* Noach
Lk 18:7 the·ones crying·out day and night to him, yet
Ac 1:2 even·until *the* day when he·was·taken·up, after·
Ac 1:22 of·John, unto the day that he·was·taken·up from us,
Ac 2:15 yeu assume, for it·is *but the* third hour of·the day.
Ac 2:29 buried, and his tomb is with us even·unto this day.
Ac 9:24 ·meticulously·watching the gates both day and night
Ac 10:3 *the* ninth hour of·the day, an·angel of·God entering
Ac 10:30 Cornelius replied, "Four days ago I·was fasting so·
Ac 12:18 Now with·day occurring, there·was no little
Ac 20:18 from that first day since I·walked·over into Asia,
Ac 23:1 ·good conscience before·God even·up·to this day."
Ac 23:12 And with·it·becoming day, some of·the Judeans,
Ac 26:13 at·mid day, O·king, I·saw in the way a·light from·
Ac 26:22 I·stand even·unto this day, being·a·witness to·
Heb 4:8 ·spoken after these·things concerning another day.
Mt 20:12 the burden and the blazing·heat of·the day.'
Mt 22:46 any·longer to·inquire·of him from that day *onward.*
Mt 24:36 "But concerning that day and hour no·one·at·all
Mt 24:38 ·away·in·marriage, even·until that day *that* Noach
Mt 26:29 of·the vine, until that day whenever I·may·drink it
Mt 27:64 grave to·be·made·secure until the third day, lest his
Mk 5:5 And constantly, night and day, he·was on the
Mk 6:21 Now with·there·occurring a·day of·happy·occasion,
Mk 13:32 "But concerning that day and hour no·one·at·all
Mk 14:25 of·the vine, until that day whenever I·may·drink it
Rm 11:8 and ears *for·them* not to·hear unto the present day."
Jud 1:6 ·murky·shroud for Tribunal·judgment of·a·great day.
Php 1:5 good·news from *the* first day even·unto the present,
Php 1:6 ·finish *it* even·unto *the* day of·Jesus Anointed—
2Pe 2:8 residing among them day by day was·tormenting *his*
1Th 2:9 for working night and day (specifically not to·be·
1Th 3:10 Night and day, *we·are* abundantly petitioning *him*
1Th 5:5 the·Sons of·Light and the·Sons of·Day. We·are not
1Th 5:8 But we·ourselves, being of·day, should·be·sober,
Col 1:6 ·as *it·does* also in yeu since that day yeu·heard *it* and
Col 1:9 we·ourselves also (since that day *when* we·heard *of·it*
1Ti 5:5 ·on in·the petitions and in·the prayers night and day.
2Ti 1:3 concerning you in my petitions night and day
Rv 4:8 And they·do·not have a·rest·break day and night,
Rv 7:15 of·God and ritually·minister to·him day and night in
Rv 12:10 them in·the·sight·of our God day and night.
Rv 14:11 ·image do·not have a·rest·break day or night, nor·
Rv 16:14 to the battle of·that great day of·God Almighty.
Rv 20:10 ·*cast*, and they·shall·be·tormented day and night

G2250.1 N-GPF ἡμερῶν (21x)

Jn 12:1 In·due·course, six days before the Passover, Jesus
Lk 5:17 And it·happened on a·certain day, even while he·
Lk 8:22 Now it·happened on one of·the days that he·himself
Lk 17:22 yeu·shall·long to·see one of·the days of·the Son of·
Lk 20:1 *that* on one of·those days, with·him instructing the
Ac 1:3 ·gazed·upon by·them throughout forty days, and·also
Ac 5:36 For before these days, Theudas rose·up, saying
Ac 7:45 *It·was with our fathers* until the days of·David,
Ac 15:7 ·acquainted·with how from the·early days, God
Ac 20:6 them in Troas in·only five days, where we·lingered
Ac 21:26 of·the days of·ceremonial·cleansing *would·be*, at
Ac 21:38 before these days already·making·an·uprising and
Ac 25:13 Now with·some days already·elapsing, King
Heb 1:2 spoke to·us in these last days by *his* Son, whom he·
Heb 7:3 ·lineage, having neither beginning of·days, nor end
Mt 11:12 And from the days of·John the Immerser until this·
Mt 26:61 Temple of·God and to·build it after three days.'"
Mk 2:1 into CaperNaum after *some* days, and it·was·heard
Mk 14:58 and after three days I·shall·build another not·
2Pe 3:3 there·shall·come in the last days mockers, traversing
Rv 2:10 and yeu·shall·have tribulation ten days. Become

EG2250.1 (9x)

Jn 7:37 day, on·the great *day* of·the Sacred·Feast *of·Booths*,
Jn 20:19 on·that *same* day, the first *day* of·the week, and
Lk 13:14 coming on those *days*, be·both·relieved·and·cured
Ac 20:15 we·arrived the following *day* opposite Chios; and
Ac 20:15 Chios; and with·another *day of·sailing*, we·drew·
Ac 20:15 Trogyllium, the following *day* we·came to Miletus
Ac 27:3 And with another *day of·sailing*, we·moored at
Heb 4:4 concerning the seventh *day* in·this·manner, "'And
Mk 14:2 "Not on the feast *day*, lest there·shall·be a·

G2250.2 N-NSF ἡμέρα (1x)

Ac 27:33 And even·until daylight was·about to·occur, Paul

G2250.2 N-DSF ἡμέρᾳ (2x)

Jn 11:9 ·man should·walk·along in the daylight, he·does·not
Rm 13:13 ·walk decently, as in daylight, not in·revelries and

G2250.2 N-GSF ἡμέρας (3x)

Jn 11:9 not·indeed twelve hours of·the daylight? If any·man
Ac 16:35 And with·daylight occurring, the court·officers
1Co 4:3 by yeu, or by mankind's† daylight. Moreover, I·

G2250.3 N-NSF ἡμέρα (1x)

Rm 13:12 ·advanced, and the day has·drawn·near.

G2250.3 N-DSF ἡμέρᾳ (1x)

2Pe 2:13 ·pleasure in the daytime *to·be* a·delicate·luxury.

G2250.4 N-ASF ἡμέραν (2x)

Rm 8:36 ·are·put·to·death all the day·long; we·are·reckoned
Rm 10:21 "' The whole day·long I·spread·out my hands

G2250.5 N-GSF ἡμέρας (1x)

Rv 21:25 its gates may·not be·shut at·day's·end, for night

G2250.6 N-ASF ἡμέραν (1x)

2Co 11:28 ·pressing, *there·is* my·own daily turmoil: the

EG2250.8 (1x)

2Th 2:3 manner, because *that Day shall·not come·to·stand,*

G2250.9 N-NSF ἡμέρα (1x)

2Th 2:2 us) as·though the Day of·the Anointed-One is·

G2250.9 N-DSF ἡμέρᾳ (3x)

1Co 1:8 *being* not·called·to·account in the Day of·our Lord
1Co 5:5 the spirit may·be·saved in the Day of·the Lord Jesus
2Co 1:14 ·as yeu *are* also ours in the Day of·the Lord Jesus.

G2250.10 N-NSF ἡμέρα (2x)

1Th 5:2 personally·know accurately that the Day of·Yahweh,
1Th 5:4 darkness, in·order·that the Day should·grab yeu as

G2250.10 N-ASF ἡμέραν (1x)

Ac 2:20 the great and conspicuous Day of·Yahweh coming.

G2250.11 N-NSF ἡμέρα (1x)

2Pe 3:10 But the Day of·*the*·Lord shall·come as a·thief, in a·

G2250.11 N-ASF ἡμέραν (1x)

2Pe 3:7 for·fire, for a·Day of·Final·Tribunal·judgment and

G2250.11 N-DSF ἡμέρᾳ (12x)

Jn 6:39 *pen),* but·rather shall·raise it up at the last Day.
Jn 6:40 and I·myself shall·raise him up at·the last Day."
Jn 6:44 him, and I·myself shall·raise him up at·the last Day.
Jn 6:54 and I·myself shall·raise him up at·the last Day.
Jn 11:24 he·shall·rise·up in the resurrection at the last Day."
Jn 12:48 The·same shall·judge him at the last Day.
Lk 10:12 it·shall·be more·tolerable at that Day for·Sodom,
Mt 10:15 Gomorrah in *the* Day of·Final·Tribunal·judgment,
Mt 11:22 Tsidon in *the* Day of·Final·Tribunal·judgment than
Mt 11:24 ·Sodom in *the* Day of·Final·Tribunal·judgment than
Mt 12:36 it in *the* Day of·Final·Tribunal·judgment.
Mk 6:11 in *the* Day of·Final·Tribunal·judgment than for·that

G2250.11 N-GSF ἡμέρας (1x)

2Pe 3:12 the imminent·arrival of·the Day of·God— through

G2250.12 N-DSF ἡμέρᾳ (4x)

Mt 7:22 Many shall·declare to·me at that Day, 'Lord, Lord,
Rm 2:16 at a·Day when God judges the secrets of·the men·
1Pe 2:12 *them),* they·may·glorify God on Inspection Day.
2Ti 1:18 personally·from Yahweh in that Day; and in·how·

G2250.13 N-NPF ἡμέραι (5x)

Lk 21:22 "Because these are Days of·Vengeance, of·the·One
Lk 23:29 "Because, behold, Days are·coming in which
Mt 24:22 And except those Days be·cut·short, not any flesh
Mt 24:22 the Selected-Ones, those Days shall·be·cut·short.
Mk 13:19 "For those Days shall·be a·Tribulation, such as

G2250.13 N-APF ἡμέρας (2x)

Mk 13:20 except *that* Yahweh cut·short the Days, not any
Mk 13:20 whom he·selected, he·cut·short the Days.

G2250.13 N-DPF ἡμέραις (4x)

Lk 21:23 and to·the·ones nursing·infants in those Days! For
Mt 24:19 and to·the·ones nursing·infants in those Days!
Mk 13:17 and to·the·ones nursing·infants in those Days!
Mk 13:24 "Moreover in those Days, after that

G2250.14 N-GPF ἡμερῶν (1x)

Mt 24:29 after the TRIBULATION of·those days, the sun

G2250.15 N-NSF ἡμέρα (1x)

Rv 6:17 because the GREAT DAY of·his WRATH is·come,

G2250.16 N-DSF ἡμέρᾳ (1x)

Rm 2:5 ·store·up Wrath for·yourself in a·Day of·Wrath and

G2251 ἡμέτερος hēmétêrôs *p:s.* (9x)

Roots:G2249

G2251 P:S-1NSF ἡμετέρα (1x)

1Jn 1:3 fellowship with us, and our fellowship *is* also with

G2251 P:S-1NPM ἡμέτεροι (1x)

Tit 3:14 And our *brothers* must·learn also to·conduct good

G2251 P:S-1ASF ἡμετέραν (2x)

Rm 15:4 ·previously·written for our instruction in·order·that
1Co 15:31 day I·die, as·sure·as *it·is* our boast, which I·have

G2251 P:S-1ASM ἡμέτερον (1x)

Ac 24:6 and determined to·judge according·to our Oral-law.

G2251 P:S-1DPF ἡμετέραις (1x)

Ac 2:11 — we·hear them speaking in·our native·tongues the

G2251 P:S-1DPM ἡμετέροις (1x)

2Ti 4:15 he·has·stood·opposed·to our Redemptive-words.

G2251 P:S-1GSF ἡμετέρας (1x)

Ac 26:5 ·to the most·strict denomination of·our religion, I·

G2251 P:S-1GPF ἡμετέρων (1x)

1Jn 2:2 ·failures, and not concerning ours merely, but·rather

G2252 ἤμην ḗmēn *v.* (25x)

ἦμεν ễmên [1st plural]

Roots:G2258 See:G2268-1

G2252.1 V-IXI-1S ἤμην (16x)

Jn 11:15 I·am·glad on·account·of yeu that I·was not there,
Jn 16:4 to·yeu at *the* beginning, because I·was with yeu.
Jn 17:12 "When I·was with them in the world, I·myself was·
Ac 10:30 "Four days ago I·was fasting so·far·as·unto this·
Ac 11:5 "I·myself was in *the* city *of* Joppa praying, and in a·
Ac 11:11 at the home where I·was, having·been·dispatched
Ac 11:17 , then who *am* I? Was·I able to·prevent God?
Ac 22:19 ·acquainted that I·myself was imprisoning and
Ac 22:20 ·poured·out, I·myself also was having·stood·over,
Gal 1:10 ·of·clay†, I·would not be a·slave of·Anointed-One.
Gal 1:22 and I·was being·unknown by·the face to·the
Mt 25:35 and yeu·gave me drink. I·was a·stranger, and yeu·
Mt 25:36 ·sick, and yeu·visited me. I·was in prison, and
Mt 25:43 I·was a·stranger, and yeu·did·not gather me in,
Mk 14:49 Each day I·was alongside yeu in the Sanctuary·
1Co 13:11 When I·was an·infant, I·was·speaking as an·

G2252.2 V-IXI-1P ἦμεν (9x)

Ac 16:12 *and* a·colony; and we·were in that city lingering·
Ac 27:37 all *told*, we·were two·hundred *and* seventy·six
Gal 4:3 ·manner, we·ourselves, when we·were infants, were
Gal 4:3 we·were infants, were having·been·enslaved under
Mt 23:30 and say, 'If we·were in the days of·our fathers,
Rm 7:5 For when we·were in the flesh, the intense·cravings
1Th 3:4 For even when we·were alongside yeu, we·were·
2Th 3:10 For even when we·were alongside yeu, this we·
Eph 2:3 innermost·mind. And we·were by·nature children

G2253 ἡμι•θανής hēmithanḗs *adj.* (1x)
Roots:G2255 G2348 Compare:G3498
G2253 A-ASM ἡμιθανῆ (1x)
Lk 10:30 ·*him*, went·off, leaving *him* more·than half·dead.

G2254 ἡμῖν hēmîn *p:p.* (180x)
Roots:G1473 See:G2248
(abbreviated listing for G2254)
G2254.ª P:P-1DP ἡμῖν (1x)
(list for G2254.ª:P:P-1DP excluded)
G2254.1 P:P-1DP ἡμῖν (170x)
(list for G2254.1:P:P-1DP excluded)
EG2254.1 (2x)
(list for EG2254.1: excluded)
G2254.2 P:P-1DP ἡμῖν (4x)
(list for G2254.2:P:P-1DP excluded)
G2254.3 P:P-1DP-HEB ἡμῖν (3x)
(list for G2254.3:P:P-1DP-HEB excluded)

G2255 ἥμισυ hḗmisy *adj.* (5x)
See:G0260
xLangEquiv:H2677
G2255 A-ASN ἥμισυ (3x)
Rv 11:9 ·look·upon their corpses three and a·half days, and
Rv 11:11 And after the three and a·half days, *the* Spirit of·
Rv 12:14 and seasons, and half a·season, away·from *the*
G2255 A-APN ἡμίση (1x)
Lk 19:8 Behold, Lord, the half of·my holdings I·give to·the
G2255 A-GSN ἡμίσους (1x)
Mk 6:23 I·shall·give *it* to·you, up·to half of·my kingdom!"

G2256 ἡμι•ώριον hēmiṓriōn *n.* (1x)
Roots:G2255 G5610
G2256 N-ASN ἡμιώριον (1x)
Rv 8:1 ·was silence in the heaven *for* about half·an·hour.

G2257 ἡμῶν hēmō̂n *p:p.* (420x)
Roots:G1473
(abbreviated listing for G2257)
G2257.1 P:P-1GP ἡμῶν (77x)
(list for G2257.1:P:P-1GP excluded)
EG2257.1 (2x)
(list for EG2257.1: excluded)
G2257.2 P:P-1GP ἡμῶν (319x)
(list for G2257.2:P:P-1GP excluded)
EG2257.2 (9x)
(list for EG2257.2: excluded)
G2257.3 P:P-1GP ἡμῶν (3x)
(list for G2257.3:P:P-1GP excluded)
G2257.4 P:P-1GP ἡμῶν (10x)
(list for G2257.4:P:P-1GP excluded)

G2258 ἦν ē̂n *v.* (430x)
ἦσαν ē̂san [3rd plural]
Roots:G1510 See:G2252 G2268-1
(abbreviated listing for G2258)
G2258.1 V-IXI-3S ἦν (308x)
(list for G2258.1:V-IXI-3S excluded)
G2258.1 V-IXI-3S@ ἦν (1x)
(list for G2258.1:V-IXI-3S@ excluded)
G2258.1 V-IXI-3P ἦσαν (3x)
(list for G2258.1:V-IXI-3P excluded)
EG2258.1 (3x)
(list for EG2258.1: excluded)
G2258.2 V-IXI-1P ἦμεν (1x)
(list for G2258.2:V-IXI-1P excluded)
G2258.2 V-IXI-2S ἦσθα (2x)
(list for G2258.2:V-IXI-2S excluded)
G2258.2 V-IXI-3S ἦν (10x)
(list for G2258.2:V-IXI-3S excluded)
G2258.2 V-IXI-3P ἦσαν (91x)
(list for G2258.2:V-IXI-3P excluded)
G2258.2 V-IXI-3P@ ἦσαν (1x)
(list for G2258.2:V-IXI-3P@ excluded)
EG2258.2 (1x)
(list for EG2258.2: excluded)
G2258.3 V-IXI-3S ἦν (4x)
(list for G2258.3:V-IXI-3S excluded)
G2258.4 V-IXI-1P ἦμεν (1x)
(list for G2258.4:V-IXI-1P excluded)
G2258.4 V-IXI-3S ἦν (2x)
(list for G2258.4:V-IXI-3S excluded)
G2258.5 V-IXI-3S ἦν (1x)
(list for G2258.5:V-IXI-3S excluded)
G2258.6 V-IXI-3P ἦσαν (1x)
(list for G2258.6:V-IXI-3P excluded)

G2259 ἡνίκα hēníka *adv.* (2x)
Compare:G3753
G2259.3 ADV ἡνίκα (2x)
2Co 3:15 the·present·day, whenever Moses is·read·aloud, a·
2Co 3:16 But whenever one·should·turn·back·around to

G2260 ἤ•περ ḗpêr *prt.* (1x)
Roots:G2228 G4007
G2260.2 PRT ἤπερ (1x)
Jn 12:43 ·clay† more·especially indeed·than·even the glory

G2261 ἤπιος ḗpiôs *adj.* (2x)
Roots:G2031
G2261.2 A-NPM ἤπιοι (1x)
1Th 2:7 But·rather we·were pleasantly·engageable in *the*
G2261.2 A-ASM ἤπιον (1x)
2Ti 2:24 but·rather to·be pleasantly·engageable to all *men*,

G2262 Ἤρ Ḗr *n/p.* (1x)
עֵר 'ḙr [Hebrew]
Roots:H6147
G2262.2 N/P-PRI Ἤρ (1x)
Lk 3:28 ·Addi, *son* of·Qosam, *son* of·ElModam, *son* of·Er,

G2263 ἤρεμος ḗrêmôs *adj.* (1x)
Roots:G2048 Compare:G2272
G2263 A-ASM ἤρεμον (1x)
1Ti 2:2 we·may·thoroughly·lead a·tranquil and intentionally·

G2264 Ἡρῴ•δης Hērṓdēs *n/p.* (47x)
Roots:G2267-1 G1491 Compare:G0067 See:G0745 G2266 xLangAlso:H0123
G2264.2 N/P-NSM Ἡρῴδης (4x)
Mt 2:3 ·hearing *this*, King HerOd·the·Great was·troubled,
Mt 2:7 Then HerOd·the·Great, after·privately calling·for the
Mt 2:13 *it* to·you, for HerOd·the·Great intends to·seek the
Mt 2:16 Then HerOd·the·Great, after·seeing that he·was·
G2264.2 N/P-ASM Ἡρῴδην (1x)
Mt 2:12 not to·return·back to HerOd·the·Great, they·departed
G2264.2 N/P-GSM Ἡρῴδου (5x)
Lk 1:5 In the days of·HerOd·the·Great, the king of·Judea,
Mt 2:1 in *the* days of·the king HerOd·the·Great, behold,
Mt 2:15 until the demise of·HerOd·the·Great, in·order·that it·
Mt 2:19 But upon·HerOd·the·Great completely·dying, behold,
Mt 2:22 in·the·stead of·his father HerOd·the·Great, *Joseph*
G2264.3 N/P-NSM Ἡρῴδης (17x)
Lk 3:19 But HerOd·AntiPas the tetrarch, being·reproved by
Lk 3:19 all *the* evils which HerOd·AntiPas committed,
Lk 9:7 Now HerOd·AntiPas the tetrarch heard all the·things
Lk 9:9 And HerOd·AntiPas declared, "I·myself beheaded
Lk 13:31 from·here, because HerOd·AntiPas wants to·kill
Lk 23:8 ·seeing Jesus, HerOd·AntiPas was·exceedingly glad,
Lk 23:11 utterly·disdaining him, HerOd·AntiPas (along·with
Lk 23:12 day, both Pilate and HerOd·AntiPas became friends
Lk 23:15 "Moreover, neither·did HerOd·AntiPas, for I·sent
Ac 4:27 *they·being* both HerOd·AntiPas and Pontius Pilate,
Mt 14:1 In that season, HerOd·AntiPas the tetrarch heard of·
Mt 14:3 For HerOd·AntiPas, after·taking·secure·hold·of John
Mk 6:14 And King HerOd·AntiPas heard *of·him*, for his name
Mk 6:16 But HerOd·AntiPas, after·hearing *of·him*, he·
Mk 6:17 For HerOd·AntiPas himself, after·dispatching, took·
Mk 6:20 for HerOd·AntiPas was·afraid·of John, having·seen
Mk 6:21 when HerOd·AntiPas was·making a·supper on·his
G2264.3 N/P-ASM Ἡρῴδην (1x)
Lk 23:7 he·sent him up to HerOd·AntiPas, himself being
G2264.3 N/P-DSM Ἡρῴδῃ (3x)
Mt 14:6 danced in their midst and satisfied HerOd·AntiPas.
Mk 6:18 For John was·saying to·HerOd·AntiPas, "It·is·not
Mk 6:22 dancing and satisfying HerOd·AntiPas and the·ones
G2264.3 N/P-GSM Ἡρῴδου (6x)
Lk 3:1 and with·HerOd·AntiPas being·the·ruling·tetrarch
Lk 8:3 of·Chuza (personal·administrator of·HerOd·AntiPas),
Lk 23:7 that he·is from·out of·HerOd·AntiPas' jurisdiction,
Ac 13:1 nursed·and·reared·together with·HerOd·AntiPas the
Mt 14:6 But with·HerOd·AntiPas' birthdays being·marked
Mk 8:15 ·the Pharisees and of·the leaven of·HerOd·AntiPas."
EG2264.3 (1x)
Mk 6:27 But·then going·off, *HerOd·AntiPas* beheaded him in
G2264.4 N/P-NSM Ἡρῴδης (5x)
Ac 12:1 King HerOd·AgrIppa violently·threw·forth his
Ac 12:6 And when HerOd·AgrIppa was·intending to·bring
Ac 12:19 And HerOd·AgrIppa, after·seeking·for him and not
Ac 12:20 Now HerOd·AgrIppa was furiously·quarreling with·
Ac 12:21 HerOd·AgrIppa was·delivering·a·public·address to
G2264.4 N/P-GSM Ἡρῴδου (2x)
Ac 12:11 me out from·among HerOd·AgrIppa's hand and
Ac 23:35 ·vigilantly·kept in HerOd·AgrIppa's Praetorian·hall.
EG2264.4 (2x)
Ac 12:4 ·apprehending *Peter*, *HerOd·Agrippa* placed *him* in
Ac 12:19 to Caesarea, *HerOd·AgrIppa* was·lingering·awhile.

G2265 Ἡρω•διανοί Hērōdianoî *n/g.* (3x)
Ἡρω•διανός Hērōdianṓs [singular form]
Roots:G2264 G2389-1
G2265 N/G-GPM Ἡρωδιανῶν (3x)
Mt 22:16 disciples to·him along·with the HerOdians, saying,
Mk 3:6 ·making consultation with the HerOdians against him
Mk 12:13 of·the Pharisees and HerOdians, in·order·that

G2266 Ἡρω•διάς Hērōdiás *n/p.* (6x)
Roots:G2264 See:G0067
G2266.2 N/P-NSF Ἡρωδιάς (1x)
Mk 6:19 But HerOdias was·holding·a·grudge·against·him
G2266.2 N/P-ASF Ἡρωδιάδα (2x)
Mt 14:3 *him* in prison on·account·of HerOdias, the wife of·
Mk 6:17 him in the prison on·account·of HerOdias, the wife
G2266.2 N/P-GSF Ἡρωδιάδος (3x)
Lk 3:19 being·reproved by him concerning HerOdias (the
Mt 14:6 with·ceremony, the daughter of·HerOdias danced in
Mk 6:22 daughter of·the very·same HerOdias entering·in and

G2267 Ἡρω•δίων Hērōdíōn *n/p.* (1x)
Roots:G2264
G2267.2 N/P-ASM Ἡροδίωνα (1x)
Rm 16:11 Greet HerOdion, my Redeemed·Kinsman.

G2268 Ἡσα•ΐας Hēsaïas *n/p.* (21x)
יְשַׁעְיָה yĕsha'yah [Hebrew]
Roots:H3470
G2268.2 N/P-NSM Ἡσαΐας (10x)
Jn 1:23 of·Yahweh,"= just·as IsaIah the prophet declared.
Jn 12:39 ·not able to·trust, because *as* IsaIah declared again,
Jn 12:41 IsaIah declared these·things when he·saw his glory
Mt 15:7 O·stage·acting·hypocrites! IsaIah did·prophesy well
Mk 7:6 to·them, "IsaIah prophesied well concerning yeu, the
Rm 9:27 But IsaIah yells·out concerning IsraEl, '" Although
Rm 9:29 And just·as IsaIah has·already·stated, '"Except
Rm 10:16 ·to·and·obeyed the good·news. For IsaIah says,
Rm 10:20 But IsaIah is·quite·daringly·bold and says, '" I·
Rm 15:12 And again, IsaIah says, '" There·shall·be the root
G2268.2 N/P-ASM Ἡσαΐαν (2x)
Ac 8:28 and he·was·reading·aloud IsaIah the prophet.
Ac 8:30 PhilIppe heard him reading·aloud IsaIah the prophet,
G2268.2 N/P-GSM Ἡσαΐου (9x)
Jn 12:38 in·order·that the saying of·IsaIah the prophet may·
Lk 3:4 ·written in·a·scroll of·the·words of·IsaIah the prophet,
Lk 4:17 And an·official·scroll of·IsaIah the prophet was·
Ac 28:25 Spirit spoke well through IsaIah the prophet to our
Mt 3:3 is·he, the·one being·uttered *of* by IsaIah the prophet,
Mt 4:14 the·thing being·uttered through IsaIah the prophet,
Mt 8:17 the·one being·uttered through IsaIah the prophet,
Mt 12:17 the·thing being·uttered through IsaIah the prophet
Mt 13:14 is·utterly·fulfilled the prophecy of·IsaIah, the·one

G2268-1 ἦς ẽs *v.* (16x)
ἦσθα ẽstha [alternate]
ἦτε ẽtê [2nd plural]
Roots:G2258 See:G2252 G5600
G2268-1.1 V-IXI-2S ἦς (5x)
Jn 11:21 "Lord, if you·were here, my brother would not
Jn 11:32 "Lord, if you·were here, my brother would not
Jn 21:18 I·say to·you, when you·were younger, you·were·
Mt 25:21 and trustworthy slave! You·were trustworthy over
Mt 25:23 and trustworthy slave! You·were trustworthy over
G2268-1.2 V-IXI-2P ἦτε (11x)
Jn 8:39 says to·them, "If yeu·were AbRaham's children, yeu·
Jn 9:41 declared to·them, "If yeu·were blind, yeu·would not
Jn 15:19 "If yeu·were from·among the world, the world
Rm 6:17 *be* gratitude, that *formerly* yeu·were *the* slaves of·
Rm 6:20 For when yeu·were slaves of·Moral·Failure, yeu·
Rm 6:20 ·Failure, yeu·were not·restrained by·Righteousness
1Pe 2:25 For yeu·were as sheep being·led·astray, but·yet are
1Co 6:11 And some *of* yeu·were these·things, but·rather yeu·
1Co 12:2 ·have·seen that yeu·were Gentiles being·led·away,
Eph 2:12 in that season yeu·were apart·from Anointed-One,
Eph 5:8 For yeu·were once darkness, but now *yeu·are* light

G2269 Ἠσαῦ Ēsaû *n/p.* (3x)
עֵשָׂו 'eṣạv [Hebrew]
Roots:H6215 Compare:G2384 See:G2401
G2269.2 N/P-PRI Ἠσαῦ (3x)
Heb 11:20 Jacob and Esau concerning things·to·come.
Heb 12:16 sexually·immoral or profane·person as Esau, who
Rm 9:13 ·been·written, "Jacob I·loved, but Esau I·hated."

G2270 ἡ•συχάζω hēsycházō *v.* (5x)
Roots:G1476 G2192 See:G2272
G2270.1 V-PAN ἡσυχάζειν (1x)
1Th 4:11 and to·aspire to·keep·still, and to·accomplish yeur·
G2270.1 V-AAI-1P ἡσυχάσαμεν (1x)
Ac 21:14 ·him not being·persuaded, we·kept·still, declaring,
G2270.1 V-AAI-3P ἡσύχασαν (3x)
Lk 14:4 And they·kept·still. And grabbing·hold *of·him*, he·
Lk 23:56 and in·fact, they·kept·still *over* the Sabbath
Ac 11:18 And after·hearing these·things, they·kept·still, and

G2271 ἡ•συχία hēsychía *n.* (4x)
Roots:G2272 Compare:G1055 G4602 G4714
G2271.1 N-DSF ἡσυχίᾳ (2x)
1Ti 2:11 A·woman must·learn in stillness with all subjection.
1Ti 2:12 ·over a·man, but·rather *she·is* to·be in stillness.
G2271.1 N-GSF ἡσυχίας (1x)
2Th 3:12 in·order·that with stillness, while·working, they·
G2271.2 N-ASF ἡσυχίαν (1x)
Ac 22:2 language, they·personally·held more still). And he·

G2272 ἡ•σύχιος hēsýchiôs *adj.* (2x)
Roots:G1476 G2192 Compare:G4714 G2263 See:G2271
G2272.3 A-GSN ἡσυχίου (1x)
1Pe 3:4 of·the calmly·mild and quietly·undisturbable spirit,
G2272.4 A-ASM ἡσύχιον (1x)
1Ti 2:2 ·lead a·tranquil and intentionally·quiet natural·life in

G2273 ἤ•τοι ḗtôi *conj.* (1x)
Roots:G2228 G5104
G2273.4 CONJ ἤτοι (1x)
Rm 6:16 ·and·obey, indeed·whether of·moral·failure to

G2274 ἡττάω hēttáō *v.* (3x)
Roots:G2276 Compare:G3528 See:G2275 G2556
G2274.4 V-API-2P ἡττήθητε (1x)
2Co 12:13 what is·it in·which yeu·were·inferior beyond the
G2274.5 V-PNI-3P ἡττῶνται (1x)
2Pe 2:20 ·entangled in·these·things *and* are·defeated, the
G2274.5 V-RNI-3S ἥττηται (1x)
2Pe 2:19 for that·by·which someone has·been·defeated, even

G2275 ἥττημα hḗttēma *n.* (2x)
Roots:G2274 Compare:G3534
G2275.1 N-NSN ἥττημα (2x)
Rm 11:12 for *the*·world, and their deterioration, wealth for·
1Co 6:7 ·now there·is altogether a·deterioration among yeu,

G2276 ἧττον hḗttôn *adj.* (2x)
Roots:G2556 Compare:G5501 See:G2274
G2276.1 A-ASN ἧττον (1x)
1Co 11:17 the significantly·better, but·rather for the worse.
G2276.2 A-ASN ἧττον (1x)
2Co 12:15 ·abundantly *I·am* loving yeu, *the* less I·am·loved.

G2277 ἤτω ḗtō *v.* (2x)
Roots:G1510 See:G2077 G2468
G2277.1 V-PXM-3S ἤτω (1x)
1Co 16:22 Jesus Anointed, let·him·be Anathema MaranAtha
G2277.2 V-PXM-3S ἤτω (1x)
Jac 5:12 "Yes," let·it·be "Yes," and *yeur* "No, No,

G2278 ἠχέω ēchéō *v.* (2x)
Roots:G2279 Compare:G1002-3 xLangAlso:H1949
G2278.2 V-PAP-GSF ἠχούσης (1x)
Lk 21:25 in a·perplexity of·*the*·reverberating and billowing
G2278.2 V-PAP-NSM ἠχῶν (1x)
1Co 13:1 I·have·become *as* a·reverberating bronze·gong or

G2279 ἦχος ẽchôs *n.* (3x)
See:G2278
G2279.2 N-NSM ἦχος (1x)
Ac 2:2 there·came a·reverberating·sound from·out of·the
G2279.3 N-NSM ἦχος (1x)
Lk 4:37 And an·echoing·rumor concerning him was·
G2279.4 N-DSM ἤχῳ (1x)
Heb 12:19 and to·a·reverberating shofar blast, and to·a·

Θθ - Theta

G2280 Θαδδαῖος Thaddaîôs *n/p.* (4x)
See:G3002
G2280.2 N/P-ASM Θαδδαῖον (1x)
Mk 3:18 and *Judas called Lebbaeus* Thaddaeus, and Simon
EG2280.2 (2x)
Jn 14:22 Judas *Thaddaeus*, not IsCariot, says to·him, "Lord,
Ac 1:13 the Zealot, and Judas *son* of·Jacobus *Thaddaeus*).
G2280.3 N/P-NSM Θαδδαῖος (1x)
Mt 10:3 Lebbaeus, the·one being·surnamed Thaddaeus;

G2281 θάλασσα thálassa *n.* (99x)
Roots:G0251 Compare:G3989 G1037 See:G3864 G0086
xLangEquiv:H3220 A3221
G2281.1 N-NSF θάλασσα (4x)
Jn 6:18 Also, the sea was·thoroughly·roused *due·to* a·great
Mt 8:27 even the winds and the sea listen·to·and·obey him!"
Mk 4:41 even the wind and the sea listen·to·and·obey him?
Rv 4:6 of·the throne *there·is* a·transparent,·glassy sea, like
G2281.1 N-ASF θάλασσαν (44x)
Jn 6:16 occurred, his disciples walked·down to the sea,
Jn 21:7 (for he·was naked), and he·cast himself into the sea.
Lk 17:2 and *that* it·has·been·flung into the sea, than that he·
Ac 4:24 and the earth, and the sea, and all the·things in
Ac 10:6 home is directly·by *the* sea. This·man shall·speak
Ac 10:32 *the* home of·Simon, a·tanner, directly·by *the* sea.'
Ac 14:15 and the earth, and the sea, and all the·things in
Ac 17:14 Paul to·traverse as toward the sea, but both Silas
Ac 27:30 the skiff into the sea under·a·pretense as·though
Ac 27:38 sailing·ship, *by* casting·out the wheat into the sea.
Ac 27:40 *them fall* into the sea, *while* at·the·same·time
Heb 11:29 they·crossed the Red Sea as through parched·
Mt 4:18 And while·walking near the Sea of·Galilee, YeShua
Mt 4:18 casting a·cast·net into the sea, for they·were
Mt 8:32 down the steep·overhang into the sea and died in the
Mt 13:1 from the home, was·sitting·down beside the sea.
Mt 13:47 after·being·cast into the sea and gathering·together
Mt 14:26 ·seeing him walking upon the sea, the disciples
Mt 15:29 YeShua came near·to the Sea of·Galilee. Then
Mt 17:27 up, after·traversing to the sea, cast a·hook and
Mt 21:21 and be·you·cast into the sea,' it·shall·be·done.
Mt 23:15 Because yeu·head·round·about the sea and the
Mk 1:16 And walking beside the Sea of·Galilee, he·saw
Mk 2:13 And he·went·forth again beside the sea, and all the
Mk 3:7 departed with his disciples to the sea. And a·large
Mk 4:1 again to·instruct directly·by the sea. And a·large
Mk 4:1 the crowd was alongside the sea upon the dry·ground
Mk 5:13 the steep·overhang into the sea. Now there·were
Mk 5:21 ·together to him, and he·was directly·by the sea.
Mk 7:31 Tsidon, he·came to the Sea of·Galilee, through *the*
Mk 9:42 his neck, and *that* it·has·been·cast into the sea.
Mk 11:23 and be·you·cast into the sea,' and should·not be·
Rv 7:2 it was·given to·bring·harm·to the earth and the sea,
Rv 7:3 bring·harm·to the earth, neither the sea, nor the trees,
Rv 8:8 ·set·ablaze with·fire was·cast into the sea, and the
Rv 10:2 he·placed his right foot upon the sea, and the left
Rv 10:6 and the·things in it, and the sea, and the·things in it'
Rv 12:12 ·ones residing·in the earth and the sea, because the
Rv 14:7 and the earth, and sea,' and wellsprings of·waters!"
Rv 15:2 a·transparent,·glassy sea having·been·mixed with·
Rv 15:2 standing on the transparent,·glassy sea, having harps
Rv 16:3 poured·out his vial into the sea, and it·became as
Rv 18:17 and as·many·as work the sea, stood·still from a·
Rv 18:21 millstone, and cast *it* into the sea, saying, "In·this·
G2281.1 N-DSF θαλάσσῃ (13x)
Lk 17:6 ·uprooted, and be·planted in the sea,' and it·would
Ac 7:36 of·Egypt, and in *the* Red Sea, and in the wilderness
Mt 8:24 a·great tempest occurred in the sea, such·for the
Mt 8:26 ·reprimanded the winds and the sea, and there·was
Mk 1:16 casting a·cast·net into the sea, for they·were
Mk 4:1 into the sailboat to·sit·down along the sea, and all the
Mk 4:39 the wind and declared to·the sea, "Keep·silent,

Mk 5:13 *of·them*, and they·were·drowned in the sea.
1Co 10:2 ·immersed into Moses in the cloud and in the sea.
2Co 11:26 in a·barren·wilderness, dangers at sea, *and in*
Rv 8:9 creatures (the·ones in the sea, the·ones having souls)
Rv 16:3 And every living soul in the sea died.
Rv 18:19 having ships in the sea became·wealthy as·a·result
G2281.1 N-GSF θαλάσσης (29x)
Jn 6:1 went·off *to·the* other·side of·the Sea of·Galilee, *which·*
Jn 6:17 they·were·going across the sea toward CaperNaum.
Jn 6:19 Jesus walking·along on the sea and coming near to·
Jn 6:22 standing on·the·other·side of the sea, after·seeing
Jn 6:25 him on·the·other·side of the sea, they·declared to·
Jn 21:1 again to·the disciples at the Sea of·Tiberias; and he·
Lk 21:25 a·perplexity of·*the*·reverberating and billowing sea,
Ac 28:4 ·being·thoroughly·saved from·out of·the sea, Justice
Heb 11:12 innumerable sand beside the shoreline of·the sea.
Mt 4:15 land of·Naphtali, *by the* roadway of·sea, beyond the
Mt 14:24 ·now in·*the*·middle of·the sea, being·tormented
Mt 14:25 went·off toward them, 'walking upon the sea.'
Mt 18:6 ·be·plunged·down in the open·depth of·the sea.
Mk 5:1 they·came·over to the other·side of·the sea, into the
Mk 6:47 the sailboat was in *the* midst of·the sea, and he *was*
Mk 6:48 them, walking upon the sea, and was·wanting to·
Mk 6:49 ·seeing him walking upon the sea, they·supposed *it*
Rm 9:27 may·be as the sand of·the sea, the small·remnant
Jac 1:6 a·surging·wave of·a·sea being·driven·by·the·wind
Jud 1:13 breaking·waves of·the·sea presently·foaming·upon
1Co 10:1 were under the cloud, and all went through the sea,
Rv 5:13 and such·as are upon the sea, and all the·ones in
Rv 7:1 blow on the earth, nor on the sea, nor on any tree.
Rv 8:8 the sea, and the third·part of·the sea became blood;
Rv 10:5 which I·saw standing upon the sea and upon the
Rv 10:8 the·one standing upon the sea and upon the earth.
Rv 13:1 And I·settled upon the sand of·the sea, and I·saw a·
Rv 13:1 a·Daemonic·Beast ascending out of·the sea, having
Rv 20:8 the number of·whom *is* as the sand of·the sea.
EG2281.1 (7x)
Jn 6:1 of·the Sea of·Galilee, *which·is the Sea* of·Tiberias.
Mt 8:18 to·go·off to the other·side *of·the Sea of·Galilee*.
Mt 16:5 ·coming to the other·side *of·the sea*, his disciples
Mk 4:35 ·go·through to the other·side *of·the Sea of·Galilee*."
Mk 5:21 sailboat to the other·side *of·the sea*, a·large crowd
Mk 6:45 to the other·side *of·the sea* toward BethSaida, until
Mk 8:13 again, he·went·off to the other·side *of·the sea*.
G2281.3 N-NSF θάλασσα (2x)
Rv 20:13 And the Sea gave·forth the dead·ones in her, and
Rv 21:1 earth passed·away; and the Sea, she·is no longer.

G2282 θάλπω thálpō *v.* (2x)
Compare:G0040
G2282.2 V-PAI-3S θάλπει (1x)
Eph 5:29 ·nourishes and cherishingly·broods·over it— just·
G2282.2 V-PAS-3S θάλπῃ (1x)
1Th 2:7 would cherishingly·brood·over her·own children.

G2283 Θάμαρ Thámar *n/p.* (1x)
תָּמָר ṭamar [Hebrew]
Roots:H8559
G2283.2 N/P-PRI Θάμαρ (1x)
Mt 1:3 Perets and Zarach (birthed·from·out of·Tamar), and

G2284 θαμβέω thambéō *v.* (5x)
Roots:G2285 Compare:G1605 G1839 See:G1568 G1569
G2284 V-PAP-NSM θαμβῶν (1x)
Ac 9:6 And trembling and being·amazed, he·declared,
G2284 V-IPI-3P ἐθαμβοῦντο (2x)
Mk 10:24 And the disciples were·amazed at his words.
Mk 10:32 ·ahead·of them, and they·were·amazed. And·yet
G2284 V-API-3P ἐθαμβήθησαν (1x)
Mk 1:27 And they·were all amazed, such·for *them* to·
EG2284 (1x)
Lk 5:10 And likewise also *amazed were* Jakob and John, the·

G2285 θάμβος thámbôs *n.* (3x)
Compare:G1611 See:G2284 G1569
G2285 N-NSN θάμβος (2x)
Lk 4:36 And amazement came·to·be upon everyone, and
Lk 5:9 For amazement enveloped him (and all the·ones
G2285 N-GSN θάμβους (1x)
Ac 3:10 they·were·filled with·amazement and astonishment

G2286 θανάσιμος thanásimôs *adj.* (1x)
Roots:G2288
G2286.1 A-ASN θανάσιμον (1x)
Mk 16:18 and·if they·should·drink something deadly, no,

G2287 θανατή•φορος thanatḗphôrôs *adj.* (1x)
Roots:G2288 G5342
G2287.2 A-GSM θανατηφόρου (1x)
Jac 3:8 bad, *and* exceedingly·full of·deadly venom.

G2288 θάνατος thánatôs *n.* (122x)
Roots:G2348 Compare:G3500 G0086 G3041 G2078 G3061 See:G2286
xLangEquiv:H4194 A4193 xLangAlso:H1698
G2288.1 N-NSM θάνατος (9x)
Rm 6:21 ·are·ashamed? For the end of·those·things *is* death.
Rm 6:23 For the wages of·Moral·Failure *is* death, but the
Rm 7:13 the beneficially·good, has·it·become death to·me?
Rm 8:6 For the disposition of·the flesh *is* death, but the
Rm 8:38 For I·have·been·convinced that neither death, nor
1Co 3:22 or life-above, or death, or things·currently·standing
1Co 15:21 through a·man·of·clay† *came* the death, also
2Co 4:12 As·such in·fact, the death operates in us, but the
Rv 18:8 ·blows shall·come in one day: death, and mourning,
G2288.1 N-ASM θάνατον (22x)
Jn 8:51 no, he·should·not observe death into the coming·age
Jn 11:4 sickness is not toward death, but·rather on·behalf of·
Lk 2:26 *that he·was* not to·see death before he·should·see
Lk 22:33 with you, even unto prison and unto death."
Heb 9:16 a·necessity *for* death to·be·carrying·away the·one
Heb 11:5 was·transferred *such·for* him not to·see death, "
Mt 10:21 brother shall·hand·over brother to death, and father
Mk 13:12 Now brother shall·hand·over brother to death, and
Rm 6:3 into Jesus Anointed are·immersed into his death?
Rm 6:16 indeed·whether of·moral·failure to death, or of·
Rm 7:10 is·found in·me for life-above, this *resulted* in death.
Rm 7:13 ·failure, is·accomplishing death in·me through the
Jac 1:15 moral·failure being·consummated, it·breeds death.
1Co 11:26 the Lord's death even·until he·should·come.
2Co 2:16 *we·are* an·aroma of·death unto death, and to·some
2Co 4:11 are·handed·over to death on·account·of Jesus, in·
2Co 7:10 but the grief of·the world accomplishes death.
1Jn 5:16 ·failure *which·is* not unto death, he·shall·request,
1Jn 5:16 to·the·ones morally·failing not unto death). There·is
1Jn 5:16 There·is moral·failure unto death; not concerning
1Jn 5:17 ·failure, and there·is moral·failure not unto death.
Rv 13:3 as·though having·been·slaughtered to death, and its
G2288.1 N-DSM θανάτῳ (11x)
Jn 12:33 signifying what·kind·of death he·was·about to·die.
Jn 18:32 signifying what·kind·of death he·was·about to·die.
Jn 21:19 signifying by·what·kind·of death *Peter* shall·glorify
Heb 7:23 to·personally·continue on·account·of death.
Mt 15:4 ·of father or mother must·completely·die *the* death."
Mt 20:18 and scribes, and they·shall·condemn him to·death
Mk 7:10 father or mother must·completely·die *the* death."
Mk 10:33 they·shall·condemn him to·death and shall·hand
Php 2:27 For even he·was·sick almost to·death, but·yet God
Php 3:10 becoming·fundamentally·like·him in·his death—
Rv 2:23 And I·shall·kill her children with death; and all the
G2288.1 N-DPM θανάτοις (1x)
2Co 11:23 *and* in *facing various* deaths many·times!
G2288.1 N-GSM θανάτου (43x)
Jn 5:24 but·rather has·walked·on out·from the death into the
Jn 8:52 no, he·shall·not taste of·death into the coming·age.
Jn 11:13 had·declared *this* concerning his death, but those
Lk 1:79 in darkness and shadow of·death, to·fully·direct our
Lk 9:27 who no, shall·not taste death until they·should·see
Lk 23:15 ·thing worthy of·death is having·been·practiced by·
Lk 23:22 I·found not·even·one cause for·death in him.
Lk 24:20 him over to·a·judgment of·death, and crucified him
Ac 13:28 after·finding not·even·one cause of·death *in·him*,
Ac 22:4 this Way even·unto *their* death, captively·binding
Ac 23:29 ·even·one allegation worthy of·death or of·bonds.
Ac 25:11 have·practiced anything worthy of·death, I·do·not
Ac 25:25 ·practiced not·even·one·thing worthy of·death, and
Ac 26:31 not·even·one·thing worthy of·death or of·bonds."
Ac 28:18 not subsisting even·one cause for·death within me.
Heb 2:9 ·grace of·God he·should·taste death on·behalf·of·all.
Heb 2:14 through the death, he·may·fully·render·impotent
Heb 2:14 the·one having the might of·Death, that·is, the
Heb 2:15 as·many·as·who (through fear of·death) were all
Heb 5:7 being·able to·save him from·out of·death, and *he·*
Heb 9:15 covenant, so·that with·death already·occurring for
Mt 4:16 *the* region and shadow of·death, upon·them a·light
Mt 16:28 no, may·not taste death, until they·should·see the
Mt 26:38 is exceedingly·grieved unto death. Yeu·remain
Mt 26:66 they·declared, "He·is held·liable of·death."
Mk 9:1 no, should·not taste of·death, until they·should·see
Mk 14:34 is exceedingly·grieved unto death. Yeu·remain
Mk 14:64 they all condemned him to·be held·liable of·death.
Rm 1:32 practicing such·things are worthy of·death), not
Rm 5:10 ·are·reconciled to·God through the death of·his Son
Rm 6:5 ·together in·the resemblance of·his death, moreover
Rm 7:24 Who shall·snatch me out of·this body of·death?
Jac 5:20 way shall·save a·soul from·out of·death, and·also
Php 1:20 my body, whether through life† or through death.
Php 2:8 attentively·obedient as·far·as·unto death, even of·
Php 2:8 as·far·as·unto death, even of·death on·a·cross.
Php 2:30 ·near so·far·as·unto death, ignoring·the·personal·
2Co 1:9 judicial·sentence of·death in·order·that we·may·not
2Co 1:10 ·snatched us from·out·of·so·vast a·death, and does·
2Co 2:16 to·some *we·are* an·aroma of·death unto death, and
Col 1:22 body of·his flesh through the death, to·present yeu
Rv 2:10 Become trustworthy even·unto death, and I·shall·
Rv 12:11 and they·did·not love their souls even·unto death.
G2288.2 N-ASM θάνατον (1x)
Rm 6:4 through the immersion into Death, in·order·that just·
G2288.2 N/P-NSM θάνατος (12x)
Rm 5:12 into the world and Death through Moral·Failure,
Rm 5:12 also in·this·manner Death went·through into all
Rm 5:14 But·yet Death already·reigned from Adam so·far·
Rm 5:17 if by·the one trespass, Death reigned through the
Rm 6:9 no·longer dies. Death no·longer lords·over him.
1Co 15:26 last enemy *that* is·fully·rendered·inert *is* Death.
1Co 15:54 having·been·written, "Death is·swallowed·up in
Rv 6:8 upon it, his name *is* Death, and Hades followed with
Rv 9:6 And they·shall·long to·die, and Death shall·flee from
Rv 20:13 dead·ones in her, and Death and Hades gave·forth
Rv 20:14 And Death and Hades were·cast into the Lake of·
Rv 21:4 their eyes.' And Death shall·not be any·longer,
G2288.2 N/P-VSM θάνατε (1x)
1Co 15:55 "O·Death, where *is* your painful·sting?
G2288.2 N/P-ASM θάνατον (2x)
2Ti 1:10 in·fact, *the·one* already·fully·nullifying Death, and
Rv 9:6 the men·of·clay† shall·seek Death and shall·not find
G2288.2 N/P-DSM θανάτῳ (3x)
Rm 5:21 just·as Moral·Failure reigned in Death, even in·this·
Rm 7:5 in our members in·order·to·bear·fruit for·Death.
1Jn 3:14 not presently·loving the brother abides in Death.
G2288.2 N/P-GSM θανάτου (7x)
Ac 2:24 loosing the pangs of·Death, because·indeed it·was
Heb 2:9 on·account·of the affliction of·Death, *but·now*
Rm 8:2 me free from the Law of·Moral·Failure and Death.
1Co 15:56 But the painful·sting of·Death *is* Moral·Failure,
2Co 3:7 Now if the Service of·Death, having·been·engraved
1Jn 3:14 have·walked·on out·from Death into Life-above,
Rv 1:18 ·Amen; and I·have the keys of·Hades and of·Death.
EG2288.2 (3x)
2Co 3:7 the *Service of·Death* presently·being·fully·nullified)
2Co 3:10 also the *Service of·Death* having·been·glorified,
2Co 3:11 if the *Service of·Death* is·being·fully·nullified on·

Θθ

G2288.3 N-GSM θανάτου (2x)
Rv 13:3 and its deadly gash was·both·relieved·and·cured.
Rv 13:12 own deadly gash was·both·relieved·and·cured.
G2288.4 N-NSM θάνατος (3x)
Rv 20:6 these, the Second Death does·not have authority,
Rv 20:14 This is the Second Death.
Rv 21:8 with·fire and sulfur, which is *the* Second Death."
G2288.4 N-GSM θανάτου (1x)
Rv 2:11 ·brought·to·harm as·a·result of·the Second Death.'"
G2288.5 N-DSM θανάτῳ (1x)
Rv 6:8 and with hunger, and with viral·death, and by the

G2289 θανατόω thanatóō *v.* (11x)
Roots:G2288 xLangAlso:H4191
G2289 V-FAI-3P θανατώσουσιν (3x)
Lk 21:16 and they·shall·put·to·death *some* from·among yeu
Mt 10:21 ·rise·up against parents and shall·put them to·death
Mk 13:12 against *their* parents and shall·put them to·death.
G2289 V-PAI-2P θανατοῦτε (1x)
Rm 8:13 But if by·*the*·Spirit yeu·put·to·death the practices
G2289 V-PPI-1P θανατούμεθα (1x)
Rm 8:36 "For·your cause, we·are·put·to·death all the day·
G2289 V-PPP-NPM θανατούμενοι (1x)
2Co 6:9 ·correctively·disciplined and not being·put·to·death,
G2289 V-AAN θανατῶσαι (2x)
Mt 27:1 against YeShua such·for him to·be·put·to·death.
Mk 14:55 Jesus in·order to·put him to·death, and they·were·
G2289 V-AAS-3P θανατώσωσιν (1x)
Mt 26:59 against YeShua, that they·may·put him to·death,
G2289 V-API-2P ἐθανατώθητε (1x)
Rm 7:4 ·yeurselves also were·put·to·death to·the Torah-Law
G2289 V-RPP-NSM θανατωθείς (1x)
1Pe 3:18 to·God, in·fact having·been·put·to·death in·flesh,

G2290 θάπτω tháptō *v.* (11x)
Compare:G1580 G2572 G4792 See:G5027 G5028 xLangEquiv:H6912
G2290.2 V-AAI-3P ἔθαψαν (3x)
Ac 5:6 him up, and after·carrying·*him*·out, they·buried *him*.
Ac 5:10 and carrying·*her*·out, buried *her* alongside her
Mt 14:12 ·alongside, took·away the body and buried it. And
G2290.2 V-AAN θάψαι (4x)
Lk 9:59 freely·permit me to·go·off first to·bury my father."
Lk 9:60 "Leave the dead·ones to·bury their·own dead, but
Mt 8:21 ·permit me first to·go·off and to·bury my father."
Mt 8:22 and allow the dead·ones to·bury their·own dead."
G2290.2 V-AAP-GPM θαψάντων (1x)
Ac 5:9 the feet of·the·ones burying your husband *are* at the
G2290.2 V-2API-3S ἐτάφη (3x)
Lk 16:22 But the wealthy·man died also and was·buried.
Ac 2:29 that also he·is·completely·dead and buried, and his
1Co 15:4 and that he·was·buried, and that he·has·been·

G2291 Θάρα Thára *n/p.* (1x)
תֶּרַח ṭeracн [Hebrew]
Roots:H8646
G2291 N/P-PRI Θάρα (1x)
Lk 3:34 *son* of·AbRaham, *son* of·Terach, *son* of·Nachor,

G2292 θαρρέω tharrhéō *v.* (6x)
Roots:G2293 Compare:G5111 G3982 G4006
G2292.1 V-PAI-1P θαρροῦμεν (1x)
2Co 5:8 And we·do·exercise·courage, even while·we·take·
G2292.1 V-PAP-APM θαρροῦντας (1x)
Heb 13:6 Such·for us to·say, while·exercising·courage,
G2292.1 V-PAP-NPM θαρροῦντες (1x)
2Co 5:6 So·then, *we·are* exercising·courage always even
G2292.2 V-PAI-1S-C θαρρῶ (1x)
2Co 7:16 that in everything, I·am·more·encouraged by yeu.
G2292.4 V-PAI-1S-C θαρρῶ (1x)
2Co 10:1 yeu, but being·absent am·more·bold toward yeu).
G2292.4 V-AAN θαρρῆσαι (1x)
2Co 10:2 ·*for me* not to·be·bold when·I·am·present with·the

G2293 θαρσέω tharséō *v.* (8x)
Roots:G2294 See:G2292
G2293.2 V-PAM-2S θάρσει (5x)
Lk 8:48 to·her, "Daughter, be·of·good·courage. Your trust
Ac 23:11 him, declared, "Be·of·good·courage, Paul. For as
Mt 9:2 "Child, be·of·good·courage. Your moral·failures
Mt 9:22 "Daughter, be·of·good·courage; your trust has·
Mk 10:49 to·him, "Be·of·good·courage, rouse·yourself; he·
G2293.2 V-PAM-2P θαρσεῖτε (3x)
Jn 16:33 tribulation, but·yet be·of·good·courage; I·myself
Mt 14:27 saying, "Be·of·good·courage, it·is·I Myself! Do·
Mk 6:50 and he·says to·them, "Be·of·good·courage! It·is·I

G2294 θάρσος thársos *n.* (1x)
Compare:G4006 See:G2293
G2294 N-ASN θάρσος (1x)
Ac 28:15 *them*, Paul took courage, giving·thanks to·God.

G2295 θαῦμα thaûma *n.* (1x)
Roots:G2300 Compare:G5059 See:G2296 G2297 G2298
G2295.1 N-ASN θαῦμα (1x)
Rv 17:6 And seeing her, I·marveled with·great marvel.

G2296 θαυμάζω thaumázō *v.* (45x)
Roots:G2295 Compare:G1839 G2284 See:G2298
G2296.1 V-FDI-3P θαυμάσονται (1x)
Rv 17:8 residing on the earth shall·marvel, whose names
G2296.1 V-PAI-1S θαυμάζω (1x)
Gal 1:6 I·marvel that so quickly yeu·are·transferring away·
G2296.1 V-PAI-2P θαυμάζετε (2x)
Jn 7:21 "I·did one work, and yeu all marvel.
Ac 3:12 "Men, Israelites, why do·yeu·marvel at this?
G2296.1 V-PAM-2P θαυμάζετε (2x)
Jn 5:28 "Do·not marvel at·that, because an·hour is·coming in
1Jn 3:13 Do·not marvel, my brothers, if the world hates yeu.
G2296.1 V-PAN θαυμάζειν (2x)
Mt 27:14 such·for the governor to·marvel exceedingly.
Mk 15:5 not·even·one·thing, such·for Pilate to·marvel.
G2296.1 V-PAP-GPM θαυμαζόντων (2x)
Lk 9:43 But with·all marveling over all·things which Jesus
Lk 24:41 for the joy and marveling, he·declared to·them,
G2296.1 V-PAP-NSM θαυμάζων (1x)
Lk 24:12 And·then he·went·off, marveling to himself at·the·
G2296.1 V-PAP-NPM θαυμάζοντες (1x)
Lk 2:33 and his mother were marveling at the·things being·
G2296.1 V-PAS-2P θαυμάζητε (1x)
Jn 5:20 him works greater·than these, that yeu may·marvel.
G2296.1 V-IAI-3S ἐθαύμαζεν (1x)
Mk 6:6 And he·was·marveling on·account·of their lack·of·
G2296.1 V-IAI-3P ἐθαύμαζον (7x)
Jn 7:15 And the Judeans were·marveling, saying, "How·
Lk 1:21 Zacharias, and they·were·marveling at him *that he*·
Lk 4:22 ·testifying for·him, and they·were·marveling at the
Ac 2:7 they·all were·astonished and were·marveling, saying
Ac 4:13 untrained men·of·clay†, they·were·marveling; and
Mk 5:20 ·things Jesus did for·him, and all were·marveling.
Mk 6:51 beyond excess, and they·were·marveling,
G2296.1 V-AAI-1S ἐθαύμασα (1x)
Rv 17:6 And seeing her, I·marveled with·great marvel.
G2296.1 V-AAI-2S ἐθαύμασας (1x)
Rv 17:7 to·me, "Why did·you·marvel? I·myself shall·
G2296.1 V-AAI-3S ἐθαύμασεν (5x)
Lk 7:9 after·hearing these·things, Jesus marveled·at him.
Lk 11:38 *this*, the Pharisee marveled that he·did·not first
Ac 7:31 upon·seeing *it*, Moses marveled at·the·clear·vision,
Mt 8:10 ·YeShua hearing *this*, he·marveled and declared to·
Mk 15:44 And Pilate marveled if, even·now, he·has·died.
G2296.1 V-AAI-3P ἐθαύμασαν (11x)
Jn 4:27 upon this, and they·marveled that he·was·speaking
Lk 1:63 And they·all marveled.
Lk 2:18 ·ones hearing *it* marveled concerning the·things·that
Lk 8:25 And being·afraid, they·marveled, saying among
Lk 11:14 And the crowds marveled.
Mt 8:27 But the men·of·clay† marveled, saying, "What·
Mt 9:8 the crowds seeing *it*, marveled, and they·glorified
Mt 9:33 the mute spoke, and the crowds marveled, saying,
Mt 21:20 And seeing *this*, the disciples marveled, saying,
Mt 22:22 upon·hearing *these words*, they·marveled, and
Mk 12:17 And they·marveled at him.
G2296.1 V-AAN θαυμάσαι (1x)
Mt 15:31 such·for the crowds to·marvel, while·looking·at
G2296.1 V-AAP-NPM θαυμάσαντες (1x)
Lk 20:26 of·the people. And marveling at his answer, they·
G2296.1 V-AAS-2S θαυμάσῃς (1x)
Jn 3:7 You·should·not marvel that I·declared to·you, 'It·is·
G2296.1 V-API-3S ἐθαυμάσθη (1x)
Rv 13:3 ·and·cured. And it·was·marveled among the whole
G2296.1 V-APN θαυμασθῆναι (1x)
2Th 1:10 in his holy·ones, and to·be·marveled at by·all the·
G2296.2 V-PAP-NPM θαυμάζοντες (1x)
Jud 1:16 while·admiring persons of·profitable·advantage

G2297 θαυμάσιος thaumásiôs *adj.* (1x)
Roots:G2295 Compare:G5059 See:G2298 xLangEquiv:H6382 xLangAlso:H6383
G2297.1 A-APN θαυμάσια (1x)
Mt 21:15 after·seeing the marvelous·things that he·did and·

G2298 θαυμαστός thaumastós *adj.* (7x)
Roots:G2296 Compare:G3167 G2986 See:G2297
G2298.2 A-NSF θαυμαστή (2x)
Mt 21:42 ·from Yahweh, and it·is marvelous in our eyes"?
Mk 12:11 ·from Yahweh, and it·is marvelous in our eyes.
G2298.2 A-NSN θαυμαστόν (2x)
Jn 9:30 "For in this is a·marvelous·thing, that yeu·yeurselves
2Co 11:14 And *this·is* no marvelous·thing, for the
G2298.2 A-NPN θαυμαστά (1x)
Rv 15:3 saying, "Great and marvelous *are* your works, O·
G2298.2 A-ASN θαυμαστόν (2x)
1Pe 2:9 yeu forth out of·darkness into his marvelous light.
Rv 15:1 in the heaven, great and marvelous, seven angels

G2299 θεά thêá *n.* (3x)
Roots:G2316
G2299 N-ASF θεάν (1x)
Ac 19:37 ·sanctuaries, nor·even those·reviling yeur goddess.
G2299 N-GSF θεᾶς (2x)
Ac 19:27 of·the great goddess Artemis to·be·reckoned as
Ac 19:35 temple·custodian of·the great goddess Artemis, and

G2300 θεάομαι thêáômai *v.* (24x)
Compare:G3700 G3708 G1492 G1980 See:G2302 G1097 G2334
G2300.1 V-ADI-1P ἐθεασάμεθα (2x)
Jn 1:14 among us, and we·distinctly·viewed his glory (*the*
1Jn 1:1 with·our eyes, which we·distinctly·viewed, and our
G2300.1 V-ADI-2P ἐθεάσασθε (1x)
Ac 1:11 ·manner as yeu·distinctly·viewed him traversing
G2300.1 V-ADI-3S ἐθεάσατο (1x)
Lk 5:27 he·went·forth and distinctly·viewed a·tax·collector,
G2300.1 V-ADI-3P ἐθεάσαντο (2x)
Lk 23:55 of·Galilee, did·distinctly·view the chamber·tomb
Ac 22:9 with·me, in·fact, did·distinctly·view the light and
G2300.1 V-ADM-2P θεάσασθε (1x)
Jn 4:35 yeur eyes and distinctly·view the wide·open·fields,
G2300.1 V-ADN θεάσασθαι (3x)
Lk 7:24 ·forth into the wilderness to·distinctly·view? A·reed
Mt 11:7 ·forth into the wilderness to·distinctly·view? A·reed
Mt 22:11 after·entering to·distinctly·view the·ones reclining·
G2300.1 V-ADP-DPM θεασαμένοις (1x)
Mk 16:14 trust the·ones distinctly·viewing him having·been·
G2300.1 V-ADP-NSM θεασάμενος (3x)
Jn 1:38 ·around and distinctly·viewing them following, says
Jn 8:10 ·straight and distinctly·viewing not·even·one besides
Ac 8:18 And Simon, after·distinctly·viewing that the Holy
G2300.1 V-ADP-NPM θεασάμενοι (2x)
Jn 11:45 Mary and distinctly·viewing the·things·which Jesus
Ac 21:27 Jews from Asia, upon·distinctly·viewing him in
G2300.1 V-API-3S ἐθεάθη (1x)
Mk 16:11 that he·lives and was·distinctly·viewed by her,
G2300.1 V-APN θεαθῆναι (2x)
Mt 6:1 particularly for·it to·be·distinctly·viewed by·them.
Mt 23:5 them to·be·distinctly·viewed by·the men·of·clay†.
G2300.1 V-RNI-1S τεθέαμαι (1x)
Jn 1:32 saying, "I·have·distinctly·viewed the Spirit

G2300.1 V-RNI-1P τεθεάμεθα (1x)
1Jn 4:14 ·yet we·ourselves have·distinctly·viewed and testify
G2300.1 V-RNI-3S τεθέαται (1x)
1Jn 4:12 Not·even·one·man has·distinctly·viewed God ever·
G2300.2 V-ADN θεάσασθαι (1x)
Rm 15:24 I·expect to·survey yeu while·traversing·through,
G2300.2 V-ADP-NSM θεασάμενος (1x)
Jn 6:5 after·lifting·up the eyes and surveying that a·large

G2301 θεατρίζω thêatrízō *v.* (1x)
Roots:G2302
G2301.2 V-PPP-NPM θεατριζόμενοι (1x)
Heb 10:33 while·yeu·were·being·made·a·public·spectacle

G2302 θέατρον théatrôn *n.* (3x)
Roots:G2300 Compare:G2335 See:G2301
G2302.3 N-ASN θέατρον (2x)
Ac 19:29 ·the·same·determination into the public·theater.
Ac 19:31 *him* not to·give himself into the public·theater.
G2302.4 N-NSN θέατρον (1x)
1Co 4:9 we·have·now·become a·public·spectacle to·the

G2303 θεῖον thêîon *n.* (7x)
Roots:G2304 See:G2306
xLangEquiv:H1614
G2303 N-NSN θεῖον (1x)
Rv 9:17 mouths proceeds·forth fire and smoke and sulfur.
G2303 N-ASN θεῖον (1x)
Lk 17:29 it·showered fire and sulfur from heaven and
G2303 N-DSN θείῳ (3x)
Rv 14:10 ·tormented with fire and sulfur in·the·sight of·the
Rv 19:20 ·the Fire, the·one being·set·ablaze with the sulfur.
Rv 21:8 the·one being·set·ablaze with·fire and sulfur, which
G2303 N-GSN θείου (2x)
Rv 9:18 and as·a·result of·the sulfur, the·one which·is·
Rv 20:10 ·cast into the Lake of·the Fire and sulfur, where the

G2304 θεῖος thêîos *adj.* (3x)
Roots:G2316 See:G2305 G2320
G2304 A-ASN θεῖον (1x)
Ac 17:29 ·ought not to·assume *for* the divine to·be like gold
G2304 A-GSF θείας (2x)
2Pe 1:3 As with·his divine power, all·things pertaining·to
2Pe 1:4 these, yeu·may·become partners of·divine nature,

G2305 θειότης thêiótēs *n.* (1x)
Roots:G2304 See:G2320
G2305 N-NSF θειότης (1x)
Rm 1:20 supra-eternal power and divinity, being·understood

G2306 θει•ώδης thêiṓdēs *adj.* (1x)
Roots:G2303 G1491
G2306 A-APM θειώδεις (1x)
Rv 9:17 like·deep·blue·hyacinth, and sulfurous. And the

G2307 θέλημα thélēma *n.* (64x)
Roots:G2309 Compare:G1013 G5427 See:G2308
G2307.1 N-NSN θέλημα (2x)
Mt 18:14 it·is not a·determination·of·*his*·will that one of·
1Co 16:12 *the* determination·of·*his*·will that he·should·come
G2307.1 N-APN θελήματα (1x)
Eph 2:3 doing the determinations·of·the·will of·the flesh
G2307.2 N-NSN θέλημα (13x)
Jn 6:39 "And this is the Father's will, the·one sending me,
Jn 6:40 And this is the will of·the·one sending me, that
Lk 11:2 Your kingdom come. Your will be·done, as in
Lk 22:42 me … nevertheless not my will, but·rather yours
Ac 21:14 ·still, declaring, "The will of·the Lord be·done.
Mt 6:10 Your kingdom come. Your will be·done— as in
Mt 26:42 me unless I·should·drink it, your will be·done."
Rm 12:2 ·good, most·satisfying, and complete will of·God.
1Pe 2:15 Because in·this·manner, it·is the will of·God, *by*
1Pe 3:17 ·better, if the will of·God is·thus·determined, to·
1Th 4:3 For this is God's will, yeur renewed·holiness: for·
1Th 5:18 for this *is* the·will of·God in Anointed-One
Eph 5:17 ones·comprehending what the will of·the Lord *is*.
G2307.2 N-ASN θέλημα (27x)
Jn 4:34 food is that I·may·do the will of·the·one sending me,
Jn 5:30 because I·do·not seek my·own will, but·rather the
Jn 5:30 will, but·rather the Father's will, the·one sending me
Jn 6:38 not in·order·that I·may·do my·own will, but·rather
Jn 6:38 ·own will, but·rather the will of·the·one sending me.
Jn 7:17 If any·man should·want to·do his will, he·shall·know
Jn 9:31 ·of·God, and should·do his will, this·man he·hears.
Lk 12:47 the·one knowing his lord's will and not making·
Lk 12:47 doing pertaining·to his will, shall·be·thrashed with·
Ac 22:14 handpicked you to·know his will, and to·see the
Heb 10:7 concerning me— to·do your will, O·God.'"
Heb 10:9 I·come, *I·am* the·one to·do your will, O·God."
Heb 10:36 in·order·that, after·doing the will of·God, yeu·
Heb 13:21 ·good work in·order to·do his will, producing in
Gal 1:4 currently·standing, according·to the will of·our God
Mt 7:21 but·rather the·one doing the will of·my Father, the·
Mt 12:50 For whoever should·do the will of·my Father, the·
Mt 21:31 of·the two, which one·did the will of·the father?
Mk 3:35 For whoever should·do the will of·God, this·one is
Rm 2:18 and know the will, and examine·and·verify the·
1Pe 4:3 for·us to·have·accomplished the will of·the Gentiles
1Pe 4:19 ·to the will of·God must·place·the·direct·care·of
Eph 6:6 ·the Anointed-One, doing the will of·God out of·a·
2Ti 2:26 having·been·captured·alive by him at his will.
1Jn 2:17 but the·one doing the will of·God abides into the
1Jn 5:14 ·request anything according·to his will, he·hears us
Rv 4:11 all things, and through your will, they·exist and are·
G2307.2 N-APN θελήματα (1x)
Ac 13:22 ·to my·own heart, who shall·do all my will."
G2307.2 N-DSN θελήματι (6x)
Lk 23:25 But he·handed Jesus over to·their will.
Heb 10:10 By that will, we·are the·ones having·been·made·
Rm 1:10 *that* I·shall·prosper by the will of·God to·come to
1Pe 4:2 ·longings of·men·of·clay†, but·rather to·God's will.
2Pe 1:21 For not by·the·will of·a·man·of·clay† *was*
Col 4:12 ·been·completely·fulfilled in every will of·God.
G2307.2 N-GSN θελήματος (14x)
Jn 1:13 ·out of·blood, nor from·out of·*the*·will of·flesh, nor
Jn 1:13 of·flesh, nor from·out of·*the*·will of·man, but·rather
Rm 15:32 through God's will and may·be·refreshed·together
1Co 1:1 of·Jesus Anointed through God's will, and
1Co 7:37 but has authority concerning his·own will, and has·
2Co 1:1 of·Jesus Anointed through God's will, and TimoThy
2Co 8:5 to·the Lord and *then* to·us through God's will,
Eph 1:1 of·Jesus Anointed through God's will. To·the holy·
Eph 1:5 according·to the good·purpose of·his will,
Eph 1:9 to·us the Mystery of·his will (according·to his
Eph 1:11 things according·to the counsel of·his·own will—
Col 1:1 of·Jesus Anointed through God's will, and TimoThy
Col 1:9 ·the recognition·and·full·knowledge of·his will in all
2Ti 1:1 of·Jesus Anointed through God's will, according·to

G2308 θέλησις thélēsis *n.* (1x)
Roots:G2309 See:G2307
G2308.1 N-ASF θέλησιν (1x)
Heb 2:4 of·Holy Spirit, according·to his·own determination.

G2309 θέλω thélō *v.* (215x)
ἐθέλω êthélō
θελέω thêléō [in certain tenses]
ἐθελέω êthêléō
[also, which are otherwise obsolete]
Roots:G0138 Compare:G0140 G1014 G2106 G3724 G2206 See:G2308 xLangAlso:H2654
EG2309 (1x)
2Pe 3:11 *determine* what·manner is·necessary·for yeu to·
G2309.1 V-PAI-1S θέλω (1x)
1Co 14:19 ·Called·Out·assembly, I·determine to·speak five
G2309.1 V-PAI-3S θέλει (3x)
Rm 9:18 on·whom he·determines, he·shows·mercy, and on·
Rm 9:18 ·mercy, and on·whom he·determines, he·hardens.
1Pe 3:17 if the will of·God is·thus·determined, to·suffer *for*
G2309.1 V-PAI-3P θέλουσιν (1x)
Gal 4:17 ·good, but·rather they·determine to·exclude yeu in·
G2309.1 V-PAN θέλειν (1x)
Php 2:13 operating in yeu both to·determine and to·operate
G2309.1 V-PAP-DSM θέλοντι (1x)
Mt 5:40 the·one determining for·you to·go·to·court·to·be·
G2309.1 V-PAP-NPM θέλοντες (1x)
2Ti 3:12 the·ones determining to·live with·devout·reverence
G2309.1 V-PAS-2P θέλητε (1x)
Jn 15:7 ·shall·request whatever yeu·should·determine, and it·
G2309.1 V-PAS-3S θέλῃ (2x)
Rv 11:5 if any·man should·determine to·bring·harm·to them,
Rv 11:5 if any·man should·determine to·bring·harm·to them,
G2309.1 V-PAS-3P θέλωσιν (1x)
Ac 26:5 from·the·start (if they·should·determine to·testify),
G2309.1 V-AAI-1S ἠθέλησα (1x)
Phm 1:14 But I·determined to·do not·even·one·thing apart·
G2309.1 V-AAI-1P ἠθελήσαμεν (1x)
Ac 24:6 ·hold·of and determined to·judge according·to our
G2309.1 V-AAI-3S ἠθέλησεν (3x)
Jn 1:43 On·the next·day, Jesus determined to·go·forth into
1Co 15:38 gives it a·body just·as he·determined, and to·each
Col 1:27 to·whom God determined to·make·known what *is*
G2309.1 V-AAS-3S θελήσῃ (1x)
1Co 4:19 if the Lord should·determine, and I·shall·know,
G2309.2 V-PAI-1S θέλω (3x)
Mt 21:29 But answering, he·declared, 'I·will not.' But
Mt 26:39 Nevertheless not as I·myself will, but·rather as you
Mk 14:36 But·yet not what I·myself will, but·rather what
G2309.2 V-PAI-2S θέλεις (1x)
Ac 25:9 Paul, he·declared, "Will·you walk·up to JeruSalem,
G2309.2 V-PAI-3S θέλει (1x)
1Co 7:36 so happens, let·him·do what he·will, he·does·not
G2309.2 V-PAI-3P θέλουσιν (1x)
Mt 23:4 fingers, they·are·not willing *even* to·bother·with
G2309.2 V-PAN θέλειν (2x)
2Co 8:10 to·do, but·rather also *were·eager* to·be·willing.
2Co 8:11 ·*was* the eagerness to·be·willing, in·this·manner
G2309.2 V-PAP-GSM θέλοντος (1x)
Ac 18:21 ·back again to yeu, God willing." And he·sailed
G2309.2 V-PAP-NSM θέλων (2x)
Rm 9:22 Now if God, willing to·indicate his wrath and to·
Rv 22:17 let·him·come! And the·one willing, let·him·take
G2309.2 V-PAP-NPM θέλοντες (2x)
Heb 13:18 all·things, willing to·conduct·ourselves morally.
Gal 1:7 troubling yeu and willing to·distort the good·news
G2309.2 V-IAI-3S ἤθελεν (7x)
Jn 7:1 in Galilee, for he·was·not willing to·walk in Judea,
Lk 15:28 "Then he·was·angry and was·not willing to·enter.
Lk 18:13 at·a·distance, was·not willing to·lift·up not·even
Mt 2:18 children. And she·was·not willing to·be·comforted,
Mt 18:30 And he·was·not willing, but·rather going·off, he·
Mt 27:34 and after·tasting *it*, he·was·not willing to·drink *it*.
Mk 9:30 Galilee, and he·was·not willing that any·man
G2309.2 V-IAI-3P ἤθελον (2x)
Jn 6:21 Then they·were·willing to·receive him into the
Mt 22:3 ·banquet, yet they·were·not willing to·come.
G2309.2 V-AAS-3S θελήσῃ (1x)
Jac 4:15 "If the Lord should·will, then we·should·live, and
EG2309.2 (3x)
Mt 21:30 answering, he·declared, 'I·myself *will*, sir,' yet
Mt 26:39 not as I·myself will, but·rather as you *will*."
Mk 14:36 not what I·myself will, but·rather what you *will*."
G2309.4 V-PAI-1S θέλω (31x)
Jn 17:24 ·whom you·have·given to·me, I·want that they·also
Lk 5:13 ·laid·hold of·him, declaring, "I·want. Be·purified!"
Lk 12:49 Even·so, what·do I·*actually*·want, though even·
Gal 3:2 This merely I·want to·learn from yeu, did·yeu·
Mt 8:3 laid·hold of·him saying, "I·want·to. Be·purified."
Mt 9:13 what it·means, "I·want mercy and not sacrifice.
Mt 12:7 ·had·known what it·means, "I·want mercy, and not
Mt 15:32 they·may·eat, and I·do·not want to·dismiss them
Mt 20:14 'But I·want to·give to·this last·one, even as *I·gave*
Mk 1:41 of·him and says to·him, "I·want·to. Be·purified."
Mk 6:25 *it*, saying, "I·want that you·should·give me from·
Rm 1:13 Now I·do·not want yeu to·be·ignorant, brothers,
Rm 7:15 I·do·not practice that·thing which I·want *to·do*, but·

Rm 7:16 if I·do that which I·do·not want, I·concur with·the
Rm 7:19 not *the* beneficially·good·thing which I·want *to·do*,
Rm 7:19 ·rather a·bad·thing which I·do·not want, that·thing
Rm 7:20 if that·which I·myself do·not want, *if* that·thing I·
Rm 11:25 For I·do·not want for·yeu, brothers, to·be·ignorant
Rm 16:19 I·rejoice over yeu. But·yet I·want yeu, in·fact, to·
1Th 4:13 Now I·do·not want yeu to·be·ignorant, brothers,
1Co 7:7 For I·want all men·of·clay† to·be also as myself.
1Co 7:32 But I·want yeu to·be without·anxiety.
1Co 10:1 brothers, I·do·not want yeu to·be·ignorant that all
1Co 10:20 And I·do·not want yeu to·become partners with·
1Co 11:3 But I·want yeu to·personally·know that the head
1Co 12:1 brothers, I·do·not want yeu to·be·ignorant.
1Co 14:5 Now I·want yeu all to·speak with·bestowed·
1Co 16:7 For I·do·not want to·see yeu at·this·moment in
2Co 12:20 ·should·find yeu such·as I·do·not want, and·*that*·I
Col 2:1 For I·want for·yeu to·personally·know what·a·huge
3Jn 1:13 to·write, but·yet I·do·not want to·write to·you

G2309.4 V-PAI-1P θέλομεν (6x)

Jn 12:21 ·of him, saying, "Sir, we·want to·see Jesus."
Lk 19:14 saying, 'We·do·not want this·man to·reign over
Mt 12:38 saying, "Mentor, we·want to·see a·sign from you.
Mk 10:35 "Mentor, we·want that you·should·do for·us
2Co 1:8 For we·do·not want yeu to·be·ignorant, brothers,
2Co 5:4 whereas we·do·not want to·undress·ourselves, but·

G2309.4 V-PAI-2S θέλεις (18x)

Jn 5:6 to·him, "Do·you·want to·be·made healthy·and·sound
Jn 21:18 you, and shall·carry *you* where you·do·not want."
Lk 9:54 "Lord, do·you·want *that* we·should·declare fire to·
Lk 18:41 saying, "What·do you·want *that* I·should·do for·
Lk 22:9 "Where do·you·want *that* we·should·make·ready?
Ac 7:28 ¿!·Do you·yourself want to·execute me, as you·
Ac 9:6 "Lord, what·do you·want me to·do?
Mt 13:28 to·him, 'So do·you·want *us* to·go·off *so·that* we·
Mt 15:28 It·is·done for·you as you·wanted." And her
Mt 17:4 ·us to·be here. If you·want, we·should·make three
Mt 19:17 God. But if you·want to·enter into the life-above,
Mt 19:21 replied to·him, "If you·want to·be complete, head·
Mt 20:21 ·declared to·her, "What·do you·want?" She·says
Mt 26:17 "Where do·you·want that·we·should·make·ready
Mk 10:51 to·him, "What·do you·want *that* I·should·do for·
Mk 14:12 where do·you·want *that* we·should·make·ready
Rm 13:3 bad·ones. But do·you·want not to·be·afraid·of the
Jac 2:20 But do·you·want to·know, O empty man·of·clay†,

G2309.4 V-PAI-2P θέλετε (18x)

Jn 5:40 "And yeu·do·not want to·come to me, in·order·that
Jn 6:67 "And *do* yeu·yeurselves not want to·head·on·out?
Jn 8:44 the Slanderer, and yeu·want to·do the longings of·
Jn 9:27 yeu·did·not listen. Why·do yeu·want to·hear *it* again
Jn 9:27 "¿!·Do yeu·yeurselves also want to·become his
Lk 6:31 "And just·as yeu·want that the men·of·clay† should·
Gal 4:9 ·poor principles— to·which yeu·want to·be·slaves,
Mt 11:14 And if yeu·want to·accept *it*, he·himself is EliJah,
Mt 20:32 declared, "What·do yeu·want *that* I·should·do for·
Mt 26:15 declared, "What·do yeu·want to·give to·me?
Mt 27:17 "Whom·do yeu·want *that* I·should·fully·release
Mt 27:21 of the two do·yeu·want *that* I·should·fully·release
Mk 10:36 to·them, "What·do yeu·want me to·do for·yeu?
Mk 15:9 saying, "Do·yeu·want *that* I·should·fully·release
Mk 15:12 "So·then, what·do yeu·want *that* I·should·do *to*·
1Co 4:21 What·do yeu·want? Should·I·come toward yeu
1Co 10:27 ·ones call·for yeu, and yeu·want to·traverse, eat
2Co 12:20 should·be·found by·yeu such·as yeu·do·not want.

G2309.4 V-PAI-3S θέλει (12x)

Jn 3:8 The breeze blows where it·wants, and you·hear the
Jn 5:21 ·manner the Son gives·life-above·to whom he·wants.
Lk 5:39 old *wine* immediately wants fresh·new *wine*, for he·
Lk 9:23 all, "If any·man wants to·come right·behind me, he·
Lk 13:31 ·here, because HerOd·AntiPas wants to·kill you."
Mt 16:24 "If any·man wants to·come right·behind me, he·
Mt 27:43 Let·him·rescue him now, if he·wants him," for he·
Mk 8:34 to·them, "Whoever wants to·come right·behind me
Mk 9:35 and says to·them, "If any·man wants to·be first, *the*

2Th 3:10 that if anyone does·not want to·work, nor·even
1Co 7:39 free to·be·married to·whomever she·wants, merely
1Ti 2:4 who wants all men·of·clay† to·be·saved and to·come

G2309.4 V-PAI-3P θέλουσιν (4x)

Gal 6:12 As·much·as they·want to·project·a·good· in the·
Gal 6:13 but·yet they·want yeu to·be·circumcised in·order·
1Co 14:35 And if they·want to·learn anything, they·must·
1Ti 5:11 ·contrary·to the Anointed-One, they·want to·marry,

G2309.4 V-PAN θέλειν (1x)

Rm 7:18 no beneficially·good·thing; for to·want *to·do the*

G2309.4 V-PAO-3S θέλοι (1x)

Lk 1:62 *for* what he·might actually·want him to·be·called.

G2309.4 V-PAP-ASM θέλοντα (1x)

Mt 5:42 be·turning·away the·one wanting to·borrow from

G2309.4 V-PAP-DSM θέλοντι (1x)

Rm 7:21 in·the *circumstance where* wanting for·myself to·do

G2309.4 V-PAP-GSM θέλοντος (1x)

Rm 9:16 *it·depends* not on·the·one wanting *it*, nor·even on·

G2309.4 V-PAP-GPM θελόντων (2x)

Mk 12:38 for the scribes, the·ones wanting to·stroll·about in
2Co 11:12 of·the·ones wanting an·impromptu·occasion *to*·

G2309.4 V-PAP-NSM θέλων (11x)

Lk 10:29 But the·man, wanting to·regard himself as·
Lk 14:28 which from·among yeu, wanting to·build a·tower,
Lk 23:8 glad, for he·was wanting to·see him for a·long·
Lk 23:20 Now·then, wanting to·fully·release Jesus, Pilate
Ac 24:27 And Felix, wanting to·store·up influential·favors
Ac 25:9 But Festus, wanting to·store·up influential·favor
Heb 12:17 that even long·afterward, wanting to·inherit the
Mt 1:19 not wanting her to·be·exposed·to·public·ridicule·
Mt 14:5 And while·wanting to·kill him, he·feared the crowd,
1Pe 3:10 For "the·one wanting to·love life-above and to·see
2Co 11:32 under·continual·guard, wanting to·apprehend me.

G2309.4 V-PAP-NPM θέλοντες (4x)

Lk 8:20 your brothers stand outside, wanting to·see you."
Lk 16:26 so·that the·ones wanting to·cross from·here to yeu
Gal 4:21 Say to·me, the·ones wanting to·be under
1Ti 1:7 wanting to·be teachers·of·Torah-Law, not

G2309.4 V-PAS-1S θέλω (4x)

Jn 21:22 says to·him, "If I·should·want him to·remain until
Jn 21:23 but·rather, "If I·should·want him to·remain until
Lk 4:6 to·me, and I·do·give it to·whomever I·should·want.
Mt 20:15 for·me to·do whatever I·should·want with my

G2309.4 V-PAS-2S θέλῃς (4x)

Lk 5:12 "Lord, if you·should·want, you·are·able to·purify
Mt 8:2 "Lord, if you·should·want, you·are·able to·purify me
Mk 1:40 to·him, "If you·should·want, you·are·able to·purify
Mk 6:22 "Request·of me whatever you·should·want, and I·

G2309.4 V-PAS-2P θέλητε (3x)

Gal 5:17 ·not do these·things which yeu·might want *to·do*.
Mt 7:12 all·things, as·much·as yeu·should·want that the
Mk 14:7 And whenever yeu·should·want, yeu·are·able to·

G2309.4 V-PAS-3S θέλῃ (8x)

Jn 7:17 If any·man should·want to·do his will, he·shall·know
Lk 9:24 For whoever should·want to·save his soul's·desire
Mt 16:25 For whoever should·want to·save his soul's·desire
Mt 20:26 but·rather whoever should·want to·become great
Mt 20:27 and whoever should·want to·be foremost among
Mk 8:35 For whoever should·want to·save his soul's·desire
Mk 10:43 but·rather whoever should·want to·become great
Mk 10:44 whoever of·yeu should·want to·become foremost,

G2309.4 V-IAI-1S ἤθελον (1x)

Gal 4:20 I·was·wanting to·be·present alongside yeu at·this·

G2309.4 V-IAI-2S ἤθελες (1x)

Jn 21:18 ·strolling·about wherever you·were·wanting. But

G2309.4 V-IAI-3S ἤθελεν (7x)

Ac 10:10 ·hungry and was·wanting to·have·a·bite·to·eat, but
Ac 14:13 to the gates, he·was·wanting to·sacrifice together
Ac 19:33 hand, was·wanting to·make·their·defense to·the
Mk 3:13 and he·summons those·whom he was·wanting, and
Mk 6:19 ·a·grudge against·him and was·wanting to·kill him,
Mk 6:48 upon the sea, and was·wanting to·pass·by them.
Mk 7:24 home, he·was·wanting not·even·one·man to·know

G2309.4 V-IAI-3P ἤθελον (4x)

Jn 6:11 small·broiled·fish as·much·as they·were·wanting.
Jn 7:44 from·among them were·wanting to·apprehend him,
Jn 16:19 Jesus knew that they·were·wanting to·ask him,
Mt 27:15 a chained·prisoner, whomever they·were·wanting.

G2309.4 V-AAI-1S ἠθέλησα (2x)

Lk 13:34 How·many·times I·wanted to·completely·gather
Mt 23:37 How·many·times I·wanted to·completely·gather

G2309.4 V-AAI-1P ἠθελήσαμεν (1x)

1Th 2:18 Therefore we·wanted to·come to yeu, in·fact I Paul

G2309.4 V-AAI-2S ἠθέλησας (2x)

Heb 10:5 Sacrifice and offering you·did·not want, but you·
Heb 10:8 moral·failure, you·did·not want, neither did·you·

G2309.4 V-AAI-2P ἠθελήσατε (3x)

Jn 5:35 shining·forth, and yeu wanted just·for a·short·while
Lk 13:34 brood under *her* wings, and yeu·did·not want *it*!
Mt 23:37 chicks under her wings, yet yeu·did·not want *it*!

G2309.4 V-AAI-3S ἠθέλησεν (5x)

Lk 18:4 And for a·time, he·did·not want·to. "But after these
Ac 16:3 Paul wanted this·man to·go·forth together with·him.
Mt 18:23 a·king, who wanted to·tally·up an·accounting
Mk 6:26 ·together·at·the·meal, he·did·not want to·refuse her
1Co 12:18 each one of·them, in the Body just·as he·wanted.

G2309.4 V-AAI-3P ἠθέλησαν (4x)

Lk 10:24 prophets and kings wanted to·see the·things·which
Ac 7:39 fathers did·not want to·become attentively·obedient,
Mt 17:12 but·yet they·did to him as·much·as they·wanted.
Mk 9:13 ·did to·him as·many·things·as they·wanted, just·as

G2309.4 V-AAP-APM θελήσαντας (1x)

Lk 19:27 enemies, the·ones not wanting me to·reign over

G2309.4 V-AAS-1S θελήσω (1x)

2Co 12:6 For though I·should·want to·boast, I·shall·not be

G2309.4 V-AAS-3P θελήσωσιν (1x)

Rv 11:6 ·any punishing·blow, as·often·as they·should·want.

EG2309.4 (1x)

1Co 14:5 ·tongues, but *I·want* more·especially that yeu·

G2309.5 V-PAP-APM θέλοντας (1x)

2Pe 3:5 For this is·oblivious·to them (willingly) that by·the

G2309.6 V-PAO-3S θέλοι (3x)

Ac 2:12 "What·is this·thing actually·supposed to·be?
Ac 17:18 this two-bit·peddler actually·supposes to·relate *to*·
Ac 17:20 what these·things are·actually·supposed to·be."

G2309.7 V-PAP-GPM θελόντων (1x)

Lk 20:46 the scribes, the·ones delighting to·stroll·about in

G2309.7 V-PAP-NSM θέλων (1x)

Col 2:18 *such·a* one·delighting in a·rigidly·imposed·

G2310 θεμέλιος thêmélîôs *n.* (17x)

Roots:G5087 Compare:G2602 See:G2311
xLangAlso:H4146

G2310.2 N-NSM θεμέλιος (2x)

2Ti 2:19 ·in·fact, the solid foundation of·God stands, having
Rv 21:19 The first foundation *was* jasper; the second,

G2310.2 N-NPM θεμέλιοι (1x)

Rv 21:19 And the foundations of·the wall of·the CITY *were*

G2310.2 N-ASM θεμέλιον (8x)

Lk 6:48 dug deeply and laid a·foundation on the solid·rock.
Lk 14:29 ·perhaps, with·him laying *the* foundation, and not
Heb 6:1 not laying·down again *the* foundation— of·
Rm 15:20 lest I·should·build upon another·man's foundation.
1Co 3:10 ·architect, I·have·laid a·foundation, and another
1Co 3:11 ·man is·able to·lay another foundation than the·one
1Co 3:12 if any·man builds upon this foundation *with* gold,
1Ti 6:19 ·in·store for·themselves a·good foundation for the

G2310.2 N-APM θεμελίους (2x)

Heb 11:10 the foundations whose architectural·designer and
Rv 21:14 of·the CITY *is* having twelve foundations, and on

G2310.2 N-APN θεμέλια (1x)

Ac 16:26 such·for the foundations of·the dungeon to·be·

G2310.2 N-DSM θεμελίῳ (1x)

Eph 2:20 being·built upon the foundation of·the ambassadors

G2310.2 N-GSM θεμελίου (1x)

Lk 6:49 building a·home apart·from a·foundation on the

EG2310.2 (1x)

1Co 3:14 he·built·upon *the foundation*, he·shall·receive a·

G2311 θεμελιόω thêmêlióō *v.* (6x)
Roots:G2310 Compare:G2598
xLangEquiv:H3245

G2311.1 V-AAI-2S ἐθεμελίωσας (1x)
Heb 1:10 in *the* beginning laid·a·foundation·for the earth;

G2311.1 V-AAO-3S θεμελιώσαι (1x)
1Pe 5:10 ·he·invigorate, may·he·lay·a·foundation *for·yeu.*

G2311.2 V-RPP-NPM τεθεμελιωμένοι (2x)
Eph 3:17 ·been·rooted and having·been·founded in love—
Col 1:23 trust, having·been·founded and immovably·settled,

G2311.2 V-LPI-3S τεθεμελίωτο (2x)
Lk 6:48 to·shake it, for it·had·been·founded upon the solid·
Mt 7:25 yet it·did·not fall, for it·had·been·founded upon the

G2312 θεο•δίδακτος thêôdídaktôs *adj.* (1x)
Roots:G2316 G1321

G2312 A-NPM θεοδίδακτοι (1x)
1Th 4:9 for yeu yeurselves are instructed·by·God to love

G2313 θεο•μαχέω thêômachéō *v.* (1x)
Roots:G2314

G2313 V-PAS-1P θεομαχῶμεν (1x)
Ac 23:9 spoke to·him, we·should·not fight·against·God."

G2314 θεο•μάχος thêômáchôs *adj.* (1x)
Roots:G2316 G3164 See:G2313

G2314 A-NPM θεομάχοι (1x)
Ac 5:39 ·be·found *to·be* even as·men·fighting·against·God."

G2315 θεό•πνευστος thêópnêustôs *adj.* (1x)
Roots:G2316 G4154

G2315.2 A-NSF θεόπνευστος (1x)
2Ti 3:16 Scripture *is* breathed·into·and·inspired·by·God, and

G2316 θεός thêós *n.* (1372x)
ΘΕός ΤΗΈός
[signifies Yahweh in the original]
Compare:G2962-1 See:G2304 G2299 G3588
xLangAlso:H0430 H0410

G2316.1 N-NSM θεός (2x)
Php 3:19 end *is* total·destruction, whose god *is* the belly, and
2Co 4:4 in whom the god of·this present·age blinded the

G2316.1 N-NPM θεοί (5x)
Jn 10:34 "I·myself declared, "Yeu·are gods""?
Ac 14:11 ·of·Lycaonia, "The gods descended toward us
Ac 19:26 the *gods* being·made through hands are not gods.
1Co 8:5 ·perhaps they·are being·referred·to·as gods, whether
1Co 8:5 earth (just·as there·are many gods, and many lords),

G2316.1 N-ASM θεόν (1x)
Ac 28:6 ·their·minds, they·were·saying him to·be a·god.

G2316.1 N-APM θεούς (2x)
Jn 10:35 "If he·declared them gods pertaining·to whom the
Ac 7:40 "Make for·us gods which shall·traverse·before us.

G2316.1 N-DSM θεῷ (1x)
Ac 17:23 had·been·inscribed, 'TO·AN·UNKNOWN GOD.'

G2316.1 N-DPM θεοῖς (1x)
Gal 4:8 to·the·ones who·are not by·nature gods *at·all.*

G2316.1 N-GSM θεοῦ (2x)
Ac 7:43 and the star·constellation of·yeur god Remphan, the
Ac 12:22 was·exclaiming, "*It·is* a·voice of·a·god, and not

EG2316.1 (1x)
Ac 19:26 saying that the *gods* being·made through hands

G2316.2 N-NSM θεός (313x)
Jn 1:1 Word was alongside God, and the Word was God.
Jn 3:2 that you·yourself do unless God should·be with him.
Jn 3:16 For in·this·manner, God loved the world, such·that
Jn 3:17 "For God did·not dispatch his Son into the world in·
Jn 3:33 testimony did·stamp·his·own·seal that God is true.
Jn 3:34 For he·whom God dispatched speaks the utterances
Jn 3:34 utterances of·God, for *to·him* God does·not give the
Jn 4:24 God *is* Spirit, and it·is·mandatory·for the·ones
Jn 6:27 shall·give to·yeu, for God the Father officially·
Jn 8:42 Jesus declared to·them, "If God was yeur Father,
Jn 8:54 of·whom yeu·yeurselves say that he·is yeur God.
Jn 9:29 personally·know that God has·spoken to·Moses. But
Jn 9:31 Now we·personally·know that God does·not hear
Jn 11:22 you·should·request·of God, God shall·give *it* to·
Jn 13:31 of·Clay·Man† is·glorified, and God is·glorified in
Jn 13:32 If God is·glorified in him, God also shall·glorify
Jn 13:32 God is·glorified in him, God also shall·glorify him
Jn 20:28 "My Lord and my God."
Lk 1:32 ·the·Most·High, and Yahweh God shall·give to·him
Lk 1:68 "Blessed *be* Yahweh, God of·IsraEl, because he·
Lk 3:8 For I·say to·yeu that God is·able from·out·of·these
Lk 5:21 is·able to·forgive moral·failures, except God alone?
Lk 7:16 among us;" and, "God visited his People.
Lk 8:39 ·an·account·of what·many·things God did for·you."
Lk 12:20 "But God declared to·him, 'O·impetuous·one!
Lk 12:24 nor·even a·barn, yet God nourishes them. "By·
Lk 12:28 "So if God in·this·manner enrobes the grass, today
Lk 16:15 of·the men·of·clay†, but God knows yeur hearts;
Lk 18:7 And, ¿! shall·not God make retribution for·his·own
Lk 18:11 ·things toward himself, 'God, I·give·thanks to·you
Lk 18:13 saying, 'God, be·favorably·forgiving·toward me,
Lk 18:19 ·one·at·all *is* beneficially·good, except one: God.
Lk 20:38 So he·is not a·God of·dead·men, but·rather of·
Ac 2:17 the last days, says God, *that* I·shall·pour·forth from
Ac 2:22 wonders and signs, which God did through him in
Ac 2:24 whom God raised·up, loosing the pangs of·Death,
Ac 2:30 a·prophet and having·seen that God swore to·him
Ac 2:32 God raised·up this Jesus, of·which we·ourselves all
Ac 2:36 of·IsraEl must·know securely that God made this
Ac 2:39 ·as Yahweh our God would call·forth·unto·himself."
Ac 3:13 "'The God of·AbRaham, and of·YiTsaq, and of·
Ac 3:13 of·YiTsaq, and of·Jacob, the God of·our fathers,'
Ac 3:15 of·the life-above, whom God awakened from·among
Ac 3:18 those·things·which God fully·announced· through
Ac 3:21 of·all·things, of·which God spoke through *the*
Ac 3:22 "Yahweh yeur God shall·raise·up a·Prophet unto·
Ac 3:25 ·the unilateral·covenant which God bequeathed unto
Ac 3:26 God, after·raising·up his·own servant·boy Jesus,
Ac 4:10 yeu crucified, whom God awakened from·among
Ac 4:24 "Master, you *are* God, 'the·one making the heaven
Ac 5:30 The God of·our fathers awakened Jesus, whom yeu·
Ac 5:31 God elevated this Initiator *of·the life-above*, *this*
Ac 5:32 Holy Spirit, whom God gave to·the·ones readily·
Ac 7:2 listen: "The God of·Glory was·made·visible to·our
Ac 7:6 And God spoke in·this·manner, that his "offspring†
Ac 7:7 I·myself shall·sheriff,'' declared God, "And after
Ac 7:9 sold Joseph away into Egypt. But God was with him
Ac 7:17 was·drawing·near which God swore to·AbRaham,
Ac 7:25 *for* his brothers to·comprehend that God, through his
Ac 7:32 "I·myself *am* the God of·your fathers, the God of·
Ac 7:32 God of·your fathers, the God of·AbRaham, and the
Ac 7:32 God of·AbRaham, and the God of·YiTsaq, and the
Ac 7:32 and the God of·YiTsaq, and the God of·Jacob." But
Ac 7:35 executive·justice?" this·man God dispatched *to·be*
Ac 7:37 "Yahweh yeur God shall·raise·up a·prophet to·yeu
Ac 7:42 Then God turned·around and handed them over to·
Ac 7:45 of·the Gentiles, whom God thrust·out from *the* face
Ac 10:15 a·second·time, "What God purified, you·yourself
Ac 10:28 ·of·a·different·ethnic·tribe, but God showed to·me
Ac 10:34 In truth, I·grasp that God is·not one·who·is·partial,
Ac 10:38 how God anointed Jesus *who·was* from Natsareth
Ac 10:38 by the Slanderer, because God was with him.
Ac 10:40 This·one, God awakened on·the third day and
Ac 11:9 of·the heaven, 'That·which God purified, you must·
Ac 11:17 Now·then, since God gave to·them the equally·
Ac 11:18 also to·the Gentiles, God granted the repentance
Ac 13:17 The God of·this People IsraEl selected our fathers,
Ac 13:21 they·requested a·king, and God gave to·them Saul
Ac 13:23 according·to promise, God awakened a·Savior
Ac 13:30 But God awakened him from·among dead·men—
Ac 13:33 because God has·entirely·fulfilled the·same to·us,
Ac 13:37 But he·whom God awakened did·not see decay.
Ac 14:27 ·in·detail what·many·things *that* God did with
Ac 15:4 ·in·detail what·many·things *that* God did with them.
Ac 15:7 how from the·early days, God selected among us
Ac 15:8 And God, the knower·of·the·heart, testified·to·them,
Ac 15:12 miraculous·signs and wonders God did through
Ac 15:14 *that* just·as at·the·first, God visited Gentiles to·
Ac 17:24 God, the·one making the world and all the·things
Ac 17:30 the times of·ignorance, God now charges all the
Ac 19:11 And·also God, through the hands of·Paul, was·
Ac 21:19 ·every one of·those·things·which God did among
Ac 22:14 he·declared, 'The God of·our fathers handpicked
Ac 23:3 declared to him, "God is·about to·pummel you, O·
Ac 26:8 incredible with yeu, that God awakens dead·men?
Ac 27:24 and behold, God has·graciously·given you all
Heb 1:1 long·ago to·the fathers by the prophets, God
Heb 1:8 *he·says*, "'Your throne, O·God, *is* to the age of·
Heb 1:9 On·account·of that, God, your God, anointed you
Heb 1:9 ·of that, God, your God, anointed you *with·the* oil
Heb 2:13 and the little·children which God gave to·me."'
Heb 3:4 the·one planning·and·constructing all·things *is* God.
Heb 4:4 *day* in·this·manner, "'And God fully·rested in the
Heb 4:10 from his·own works, just·as God *did* from his·own
Heb 6:3 this we·shall·do, if·ever God should·freely·permit.
Heb 6:10 For God *is* not unrighteous to·forget yeur work and
Heb 6:13 For God, after·promising to·AbRaham, since he·
Heb 6:17 By which *confirmation*, God, being·resolved more·
Heb 9:20 of·the covenant which God commanded alongside
Heb 10:7 concerning me— to·do your will, O·God.'"
Heb 10:9 the·one to·do your will, O·God." He·eliminates
Heb 11:5 ·not found, on·account·that God transferred him;"
Heb 11:10 architectural·designer and civil·engineer *is* God.
Heb 11:16 ·heavenly·one. Therefore God is·not ashamed·of
Heb 11:16 *or* to·be·properly·called their God, for he·made·
Heb 11:19 reckoning that God *was* able to·awaken *him* even
Heb 12:7 ·discipline, God is·bearing·alongside yeu as *his·*
Heb 12:29 for even our God *is* a·fully·consuming fire.
Heb 13:4 but God presently·judges sexually·immoral·people
Heb 13:16 for with·such sacrifices God is·fully·satisfied.
Heb 13:20 Now *may* the God of·peace, the·one bringing·up
Gal 1:15 But when God took·delight (the·one specially·
Gal 2:6 not·even·one·thing to·me. God does·not receive *the*
Gal 3:8 foreseeing that God regards·as·righteous the
Gal 3:18 of·promise. But God has·graciously·bestowed *the*
Gal 3:20 is·not *a·mediator* of·one *party*, but God is one.
Gal 4:4 of·time was·come, God dispatched·forth his Son,
Gal 4:6 And because yeu·are sons, God dispatched·forth the
Gal 6:7 Do·not be·deceived; God is·not ridiculed, for
Mt 1:23 ·being·interpreted *from·Hebrew*, is "God with us."
Mt 3:9 For I·say to·yeu that God is·able from·out·of·these
Mt 6:30 And if God in·this·manner enrobes the grass of·the
Mt 15:4 For God commanded, saying, "Deeply·honor your
Mt 19:6 Accordingly, what God yoked·together, a·man·of·
Mt 19:17 ·at·all beneficially·good except one, God. But if
Mt 22:32 "I AM the God of·AbRaham, and the God of·
Mt 22:32 God of·AbRaham, and the God of·YiTsaq, and the
Mt 22:32 and the God of·YiTsaq, and the God of·Jacob"?
Mt 22:32 and the God of·Jacob"? God is·not the God of·
Mt 22:32 "? God is·not the God of·dead·men, but·rather of·
Mk 2:7 to·forgive moral·failures, except one *only*: God?"
Mk 10:6 But from creation's beginning, God " made them
Mk 10:9 Accordingly, what God yoked·together, a·man·of·
Mk 10:18 ·at·all beneficially·good except one, *that·is*, God.
Mk 12:26 (at the burning·bush) God declared to·him, saying,
Mk 12:26 "I·myself *am* the God of·AbRaham, and the God
Mk 12:26 God of·AbRaham, and the God of·YiTsaq, and the
Mk 12:26 and the God of·YiTsaq, and the God of·Jacob"?
Mk 12:27 He·is not the God of·dead·men, but·rather a·God
Mk 12:27 of·dead·men, but·rather a·God of·living·men.
Mk 12:29 O·IsraEl: Yahweh our God, Yahweh is one.
Mk 12:32 truth, because "there·is one God, and there·is not
Mk 13:19 *the* beginning of·creation which God created unto
Mk 15:34 ·interpreted *from·Aramaic*, is "My God, my God,
Mk 15:34 "My God, my God, why did·you·forsake me?
Rm 1:9 For God is my witness, to·whom I·ritually·minister
Rm 1:19 among them, for God made·*it*·apparent to·them.
Rm 1:24 Therefore God also handed them over to impurity
Rm 1:26 On·account·of that, God handed them over to

Rm 1:28 recognition·and·full·knowledge, God handed them
Rm 2:16 at a·Day when God judges the secrets of·the men·
Rm 3:4 May·it·never happen! And let God be true, but
Rm 3:5 shall·we·state? "¿!·Is·not God unrighteous, the·one
Rm 3:6 happen! Otherwise how·does God judge the world?
Rm 3:25 whom God personally·determined *to·be* an·atoning·
Rm 3:29 Or *is·he* the God of·Jews merely?
Rm 3:30 since·indeed *it·is* one God who, *from·among both,*
Rm 4:6 man·of·clay† to·whom God reckons righteousness
Rm 5:8 But God demonstrates his love toward us, how·that
Rm 8:3 ·weak through the flesh, God, after·sending his·own
Rm 8:31 toward these·things? If God *does·this* on·our behalf
Rm 8:33 God's Selected-Ones? God *is* the·one regarding·
Rm 9:5 *is* the Anointed-One, the·one being God over all,
Rm 9:22 Now if God, willing to·indicate his wrath and to·
Rm 10:9 in your heart that God awakened him from·among
Rm 11:1 I·say, ¿!·Did God shove·away his People?
Rm 11:2 God did·not shove·away his People which he·
Rm 11:21 For if God did·not spare the fully natural branches,
Rm 11:23 they·shall·be·grafted·in, for God is able to·
Rm 11:32 For God jointly·confined all the *peoples* to an·
Rm 12:3 seeing·as God imparted to·each·man a·measure
Rm 14:3 the·one eating, for God purposely·received him.
Rm 14:4 And, he·shall·be·established, for God is able to·
Rm 15:5 Now may the God of·the patient·endurance and of·
Rm 15:13 Now, may the God of·the Expectation
Rm 15:33 And the God of·Peace *be* with yeu all.
Rm 16:20 And the God of·peace shall·shatter the
Jac 1:13 God," for God is not·tempted with·moral·wrongs,
Jac 2:5 beloved brothers, ¿!·is·it·not God *that* selected the
Jac 2:19 ·yourself trust that there·is one God. You·do well.
Jac 4:6 ·says, "' God arranges·himself·against haughty·men,
Php 1:8 For God is my witness, how I·greatly·yearn·after
Php 2:9 Therefore God also elevated him above·all·others
Php 2:13 For it·is God *who·is* the·one operating in yeu both
Php 2:27 to·death, but·yet God showed·mercy on·him, and
Php 3:15 yeu·contemplate differently, God shall·reveal even
Php 4:9 me, practice— and the God of·peace shall·be with
Php 4:19 And my God shall·completely·fulfill yeur every
1Pe 1:3 Blessed *be* the God and Father of·our Lord YeShua
1Pe 4:11 from·out of·strength which God supplies, in·order·
1Pe 4:11 God supplies, in·order·that God, in all·things,
1Pe 5:5 "' God arranges·himself·against haughty·men but
1Pe 5:10 But the God of·all grace, the·one already·calling us
2Pe 2:4 For if God— did·not spare morally·failing angels,
1Th 2:5 nor with a·pretext for·covetousness (God *is* witness),
1Th 2:10 Yeu *are* witnesses, and God *also*, how in·a·
1Th 3:11 Now may our God and Father himself, and our
1Th 4:7 For God did·not call us forth toward impurity, but·
1Th 4:14 ·up, in·this·manner also God shall·bring together
1Th 5:9 Because God did·not place us for Wrath, but·rather
1Th 5:23 And may the God of·Peace himself make yeu·
2Th 1:11 yeu, that our God may·consider yeu deserving of·
2Th 2:4 Temple of·God,' exhibiting himself that he·is God.
2Th 2:11 And on·account·of this, God shall·send them an·
2Th 2:13 , because from *the* beginning, God chose yeu for
2Th 2:16 Lord YeShua Anointed himself, and God, even our
Tit 1:2 of·eternal life·above, which God (the·one without·
1Co 1:9 God *is* trustworthy, through whom yeu·are·called·
1Co 1:20 present·age? Did God not·indeed make·foolish the
1Co 1:21 did·not know God, God took·delight through the
1Co 1:27 But·rather God selected the foolish·things of·the
1Co 1:27 the wise; and God selected the weak·things of·the
1Co 1:28 And God selected the bastardly·things of·the world
1Co 2:7 ·hidden·away, which God predetermined before the
1Co 2:9 the·things·which God made·ready for·the·ones
1Co 2:10 But God revealed *them* to·us through his Spirit, for
1Co 3:6 Apollos watered, but·yet God was·growing.
1Co 3:7 the·one watering, but·rather God, the·one growing.
1Co 3:17 the temple of·God, this·one God shall·corrupt. For
1Co 4:9 For I·suppose that God exhibited us (the
1Co 5:13 But the·ones outside, God presently·judges. So·
1Co 6:13 food, but God shall·fully·render·inoperative even
1Co 6:14 And God, *who* even awakened the Lord *from·death*
1Co 7:15 in such·cases, but God has·called us forth in peace
1Co 7:17 ·*know that* as God imparted to·each·man, each·one
1Co 8:4 that *there·is* not·even·one other God, yet·not·even
1Co 8:6 but·yet to·us *there·is but* one God, the Father (from·
1Co 10:5 the majority of·them, God did·not take·delight, for
1Co 10:13 *is common to* mankind†. But God *is* trustworthy,
1Co 11:3 head *is* the man, and Anointed-One's head *is* God.
1Co 12:6 but it·is the same God, the·one operating all in all.
1Co 12:18 But even·now, God himself·placed the members,
1Co 12:24 no *such* need, but·yet God blended·together the
1Co 12:28 ·fact, some·of·whom *which* God laid·out among
1Co 14:25 to·God, announcing that God is really among yeu
1Co 14:33 For God is not *the God* of·chaos, but·rather of·
1Co 15:28 all·things in·him, in·order·that God may·be all in
1Co 15:38 but God gives it a·body just·as he·determined,
2Co 1:3 Blessed *be* the God and Father of·our Lord Jesus
2Co 1:3 of·the tender·compassions and God of·all comfort,
2Co 1:18 But God *is* trustworthy, because our
2Co 1:21 and·also already·anointing us, *is* God—
2Co 4:6 Because God *is* the·one already·declaring *for* light
2Co 5:5 for us this very·thing *is* God, the·one also giving to·
2Co 5:19 how that God was in Anointed-One presently·
2Co 6:16 a·temple of·the·living God, just·as God declared,
2Co 6:16 and I·shall·be their·own distinct God, and they·
2Co 7:6 But·yet God, the·one comforting the·ones *that·are*
2Co 9:7 out of·compulsion, for 'God loves a·cheerful giver.
2Co 9:8 And God *is* able *to·cause* all grace to·abound toward
2Co 10:13 the standard measure which God distributed to·us,
2Co 11:11 I·do·not love yeu? God personally·knows *that I·*
2Co 11:31 The God and Father of·our Lord Jesus Anointed,
2Co 12:2 I·do·not personally·know; God personally·knows),
2Co 12:3 I·do·not personally·know, God personally·knows),
2Co 12:21 after·coming again, my God may·humble me
2Co 13:11 be·peaceful; and the God of·love and peace
Eph 1:3 Blessed *be* the God and Father of·our Lord Jesus
Eph 1:17 in·order·that the God of·our Lord Jesus Anointed,
Eph 2:4 But God, being wealthy in mercy, on·account·of his
Eph 2:10 which God made·ready·in·advance in·order·that
Eph 4:6 one God and Father of·all: the·one over all and
Eph 4:32 ·another, also just·as God graciously·forgave yeu
Col 1:27 to·whom God determined to·make·known what *is*
Col 4:3 concerning us, that God may·open·up to·us a·door
1Ti 2:5 For *there·is* one God, and *there·is* one mediator
1Ti 3:16 ·of·Devout·Reverence. God is·made·apparent in
1Ti 4:3 to·abstain·from foods— which God created for
2Ti 1:7 For God did·not give us a·spirit of·timidity, but·
2Ti 2:25 ·opposition— if·perhaps God should·give to·them
1Jn 1:5 and announce·in·detail to·yeu, that God is light, and
1Jn 3:20 should·incriminate *us*, God is greater·than our
1Jn 4:8 does·not already·know God, because God is love.
1Jn 4:9 among us, because God has·dispatched his only·
1Jn 4:11 Beloved, if in·this·manner, God loved us, we·
1Jn 4:12 If we·should·love one·another, God abides in us,
1Jn 4:15 Jesus is the Son of·God, God abides in him, and
1Jn 4:16 and have·trusted the Love that God has in us.
1Jn 4:16 Love that God has in us. God is love; and the·one
1Jn 4:16 abiding in the Love abides in God, and God in him.
1Jn 5:10 in the testimony that God has·testified concerning
1Jn 5:11 this is the testimony, that God gave to·us eternal
1Jn 5:20 This is the true God and the eternal life·above.
Rv 1:1 of·Jesus Anointed, which God gave to·him, to·show
Rv 4:8 holy *is* Yahweh, *El Shaddai* God Almighty, the·one
Rv 7:17 'And God shall·rub·away every tear from their eyes.
Rv 11:17 to·you, O·Yahweh, God Almighty, the·one being,
Rv 15:3 your works, O·Yahweh, God Almighty. Righteous
Rv 16:7 "Yes, O·Yahweh, God Almighty, true and
Rv 17:17 "For God gave in their hearts to·do his plan, and
Rv 18:5 heaven," and God remembered her wrong·doings.
Rv 18:8 because strong *is* Yahweh God, the·one judging
Rv 18:20 the prophets, because God decided yeur just·claim
Rv 19:6 Because Yahweh, God Almighty, reigns.
Rv 21:3 shall·be his Peoples, and God, himself, shall·be
Rv 21:3 himself, shall·be with them, *and be* their God.
Rv 21:4 'And God shall·rub·away every tear from their eyes.
Rv 21:7 I·shall·be his·very·own— *a·distinct* God; and he·
Rv 21:22 for Yahweh, *El Shaddai* God Almighty, and the
Rv 22:5 ·sun light, because Yahweh God illuminates them,
Rv 22:6 And Yahweh, God of·the holy prophets,
Rv 22:18 alongside these·things, God shall·place upon him
Rv 22:19 ·*the*·scroll of·this prophecy, God shall·remove his

G2316.2 N-VSM θεέ (2x)

Mt 27:46 ' That·is *to·say*, "'My God, my God, for·what·
Mt 27:46 "'My God, my God, for·what·purpose did·you·

G2316.2 N-ASM θεόν (149x)

Jn 1:1 and the Word was alongside God, and the Word
Jn 1:2 The·same was at *the* beginning alongside God.
Jn 1:18 ·one·man has·clearly·seen God ever·at·any·time.
Jn 5:18 moreover he·was·saying also *that* God *was* his·own
Jn 8:41 We·have one Father, God!"
Jn 10:33 you, being a·man·of·clay†, make yourself God."
Jn 11:22 that as·much·as you·should·request·of God, God
Jn 13:3 ·forth from God and was·heading·on·out to God),
Jn 14:1 *in* yeur heart. Yeu·trust in God, trust also in me.
Jn 17:3 ·know you, the only true God, and Jesus Anointed,
Jn 20:17 yeur Father, and *to* my God *who·is* also yeur God.
Jn 20:17 Father, and *to* my God *who·is* also yeur God.'"
Jn 21:19 by·what·kind·of death *Peter* shall·glorify God. And
Lk 1:16 Sons of·IsraEl back·around to Yahweh their God.
Lk 1:64 tongue *loosed*, and he·was·speaking, blessing God.
Lk 2:13 of·*the*·heavenly host praising God and saying,
Lk 2:20 glorifying and praising God over all·the·things that
Lk 2:28 him into his arms and blessed God. And he·declared,
Lk 4:8 ·fall·prostrate *directly·before* Yahweh your God," and
Lk 4:12 You·shall·not thoroughly·try Yahweh your God.'"
Lk 5:25 on, he·went·off to his·own house, glorifying God.
Lk 5:26 ·all, and they·were·glorifying God and were·filled
Lk 7:16 ·all *of·them*, and they·were·glorifying God, saying,
Lk 7:29 (even the tax·collectors) regarded God as·righteous.
Lk 10:27 "You·shall·love Yahweh your God from·out of·all
Lk 12:21 ·himself, becoming·wealthy, yet not toward God."
Lk 13:13 ·straightened·upright, and she·was·glorifying God.
Lk 17:15 returned·back with a·loud voice glorifying God,
Lk 18:2 — *one* who·is·not reverently·fearing God and not
Lk 18:4 'Even though I·am·not afraid·of God, and I·am·not
Lk 18:43 and was·following him, glorifying God. And all
Lk 19:37 began rejoicing, praising God with·a·loud voice
Lk 20:37 he·says Yahweh, "the God of·AbRaham, and the
Lk 20:37 God of·AbRaham, and the God of·YiTsaq, and the
Lk 20:37 and the God of·YiTsaq, and the God of·Jacob."
Lk 23:40 "Are·not·even you·yourself afraid·of God, *seeing*
Lk 23:47 ·thing *that·was* happening, glorified God, saying,
Lk 24:53 praising and blessing God. So·be·it,·Amen.
Ac 2:47 splendidly·praising God, and having grace alongside
Ac 3:8 ·along and leaping and splendidly·praising God.
Ac 3:9 saw him walking·along and splendidly·praising God.
Ac 4:21 because all *men* were·glorifying God over the·thing
Ac 4:24 ·voice toward God with·the·same·determination,
Ac 6:11 reviling utterances against Moses and *against* God."
Ac 10:2 and one·reverently·fearing God together with·all his
Ac 10:22 who·is·reverently·fearing God and being·attested·
Ac 10:46 in·bestowed·tongues and magnifying God. Then
Ac 11:17 , then who *am* I? Was·I able to·prevent God?"
Ac 11:18 ·kept·still, and they·were·glorifying God, saying,
Ac 12:5 over him was being·made to God by the Called·Out·
Ac 13:16 and the·ones reverently·fearing God, listen.
Ac 13:26 the·ones among yeu reverently·fearing God, to·yeu
Ac 14:15 from these futilities to the living God, 'who made
Ac 15:10 accordingly, why·do yeu·try God, to·put a·yoke
Ac 15:19 from the Gentiles turning·back·around to God,
Ac 16:14 *a·woman* who·is·reverencing God, of·whom the
Ac 16:25 while·praying, were·singing·praise·to God, and
Ac 18:7 ·name·of Justus, who·is·reverencing God, whose
Ac 18:13 men·of·clay† to·reverence God contrary·to the
Ac 20:21 a·repentance (the·one toward God), and a·trust
Ac 24:15 having an·expectation in God, which these·men

Ac 24:16 void·of·offense toward God and *toward* the men·
Ac 26:18 of·the Adversary-Accuser to God, for·them to·
Ac 26:20 and to·turn·back·around toward God, practicing
Heb 2:17 ·Priest in·the·things pertaining·to God, in·order to·
Heb 5:1 ·clay† in·the·things pertaining·to God, in·order·that
Heb 6:1 from dead works, and of·trust toward God,
Heb 6:18 in which *it·was* impossible for·God to·lie, we·may·
Heb 8:10 and I·shall·be their·own distinct God, and they·
Gal 1:10 men·of·clay†, or *comply·with* God? Or do·I·seek
Gal 1:24 And they·were·glorifying God in me.
Gal 4:8 when not having·seen God, yeu·were·enslaved to·
Gal 4:9 But now, after·knowing God, or rather being·known
Mt 4:7 "'You·shall·not thoroughly·try Yahweh your God.'"
Mt 4:10 ·fall·prostrate *directly·before* Yahweh your God,
Mt 5:8 heart, because they·themselves shall·gaze·upon God.
Mt 9:8 *it*, marveled, and they·glorified God, the·one giving
Mt 15:31 And they·glorified the God of·IsraEl.
Mt 22:37 "'You·shall·love Yahweh your God with all your
Mt 27:43 He·has·confidence in God. Let·him·rescue him
Mk 2:12 ·for all to·be·astonished and to·glorify God, saying,
Mk 5:7 On·oath, I·charge you by·God, you·should·not
Mk 12:30 you·shall·love Yahweh your God from·out·of·all
Rm 1:21 ·account·that, already·knowing God, they·neither
Rm 1:21 ·neither glorified *him* as God nor gave·*him*·thanks,
Rm 1:28 they·did·not examine·and·verify God to·hold *him*
Rm 2:23 in Torah-Law, do·you·dishonor God through the
Rm 3:11 comprehending; there·is not one seeking·out God.
Rm 4:2 of·works, he·has a·boast, but·yet not toward God.
Rm 5:1 ·trust, we·have peace toward God through our Lord
Rm 8:7 of·the flesh *is* hostility toward God, for it·is·not
Rm 8:27 over *the* holy·ones according·to *the will·of* God.
Rm 8:28 that, for·the·ones loving God, all·things work·
Rm 10:1 ·purpose and petition to God on·behalf of·IsraEl is
Rm 15:6 mouth, yeu·may·glorify the God and Father of·our
Rm 15:9 ·*for* the Gentiles to·glorify God on·behalf *of·his*
Rm 15:17 in Jesus Anointed in·the·things pertaining·to God.
Rm 15:30 with·me in the prayers to God on·my behalf,
Jac 3:9 With it, we·bless *our* God and Father. And with it,
Jud 1:4 denying the only Master, God and our Lord YeShua
Php 4:6 of·yeurs, make·*them*·be·known directly·to God.
1Pe 1:21 through him trusting in God, the·one awakening
1Pe 1:21 — such·for yeur trust and expectation to·be in God.
1Pe 2:12 *them*), they·may·glorify God on Inspection Day.
1Pe 2:17 the brotherhood. Reverently·fear God. Honor the
1Pe 3:5 the·ones placing·their·expectation upon God,
1Pe 3:15 But make Yahweh God holy in yeur hearts.
1Pe 3:21 of·a·beneficially·good conscience toward God)—
1Pe 4:6 ·flesh, but may·live according·to God in·*the*·spirit.
1Pe 4:16 ·him·be·ashamed, but let·him·glorify God in this
1Th 1:8 place yeur trust toward God has·gone·forth, such·for
1Th 1:9 and how yeu·turned·back·around to God from the
1Th 4:5 the Gentiles, the·ones not personally·knowing God;
1Th 4:8 ·clay† *that* he·ignores, but·rather God, the·one also
2Th 1:8 ·ones not personally·knowing God and to·the·ones
2Th 2:4 *that·is* being·referred·to·as God or that·is·reverenced
2Th 2:4 ·such·for him to·sit·down as God in the Temple of·
Tit 1:16 They·affirm to·have·seen God, but in·the works
1Co 1:21 the wisdom did·not know God, God took·delight
1Co 6:20 Now·then, glorify God in yeur body and in yeur
1Co 8:3 But if anyone loves God, the·same has·been·
2Co 1:23 Now I·myself do·call·upon God *for* a·witness upon
2Co 3:4 we·have through the Anointed-One toward God.
2Co 7:9 yeu·were·grieved according·to God, in·order·that in
2Co 7:10 grief according·to God accomplishes repentance
2Co 7:11 ·same·thing (to·grieve yeu according·to God), *see*
2Co 9:13 of·this service, they·are·glorifying God over the
2Co 13:7 Now I·well-wish to God for·yeu not to·do not·
Eph 4:24 ·being·created according·to God in righteousness
Col 3:22 with fidelity of·heart, reverently·fearing God.
1Ti 5:5 ·alone, has·placed·her·expectation upon God, and
1Jn 3:21 us, *then* we·have freeness·of·speech toward God.
1Jn 4:6 of·God. The·one presently·knowing God hears us.
1Jn 4:7 ·born from·out·of·God and presently·knows God.
1Jn 4:8 ·loving does·not already·know God, because God is
1Jn 4:10 not that we·ourselves loved God, but·rather that
1Jn 4:12 ·man has·distinctly·viewed God ever·at·any·time. If
1Jn 4:20 should·declare, "I·love God," and he·should·hate
1Jn 4:20 ·what·way is·he·able to·love God whom he·has·not
1Jn 4:21 that the·one loving God should·love his brother
1Jn 5:2 whenever we·love God and should·observantly·keep
2Jn 1:9 of·Anointed-One, does·not have God. The·one
3Jn 1:11 but the·one doing·bad has·not clearly·seen God.
Rv 12:5 and her child was·snatched·up to God, and *to* his
Rv 13:6 ·up its mouth in revilement toward God, to·revile his
Rv 14:7 with a·loud voice, "Fear God and give glory to·him,
Rv 16:11 and·also they·reviled the God of·the heaven as·a·
Rv 16:21 the men·of·clay† reviled God as·a·result·of·the
Rv 19:5 "Splendidly·praise our God, all·yeu his slaves, and

G2316.2 N-DSM θεῷ (158x)

Jn 3:21 that they·are having·been·worked in God."
Jn 5:18 his·own Father, making himself equal with·God.
Jn 9:24 ·declared to·him, "Give God glory. We·ourselves
Jn 16:2 yeu might·presume to·offer a·ritual·ministry to·God.
Lk 1:30 for you·found grace personally·before God.
Lk 1:37 utterance directly·from God shall·not be·impossible.
Lk 1:47 and my spirit leaped·for·joy in God my Savior.
Lk 2:14 "Glory to·God in *the* highest, and on earth, peace!
Lk 2:52 personally·before God and men·of·clay†.
Lk 16:13 able to·be·a·slave to·God and to·Material·Wealth."
Lk 17:18 found returning·back to·give glory to·God, *none*
Lk 18:27 with men·of·clay† are possible with God."
Lk 18:43 all the people seeing *it*, gave strong·praise to·God.
Lk 20:25 ·Caesar to·Caesar, and the·things of·God to·God."
Ac 5:4 You·did·not lie to·men·of·clay†, but·rather to·God."
Ac 5:29 ·mandatory to·readily·comply with·God rather than
Ac 7:20 ·born, and he·was handsome to·God; *and* he·was·
Ac 7:46 to·find a·suitable·Tabernacle for·the God of·Jacob.
Ac 12:23 he·did·not give the glory to·God. And becoming
Ac 15:18 "Known to·God are all his works from the·
Ac 16:34 with·the·whole·household having·trusted in·God.
Ac 20:32 I·place·the·direct·care·of yeu to·God, and to·the
Ac 23:1 ·good conscience before·God even·up·to this day.
Ac 24:14 I·ritually·minister to·God my esteemed·Father,
Ac 26:29 Paul declared, "I·would well-wish to·God, *that* not
Ac 27:25 cheer·up! For I·trust God, that in·this·manner, it·
Ac 27:35 he·gave·thanks to·God in·the·sight·of·them·all,
Ac 28:15 *them*, Paul took courage, giving·thanks to·God.
Heb 7:19 *does*, through which we·draw·near to·God.
Heb 7:25 ·ones who·are·coming·alongside God through him)
Heb 9:14 offered himself without·blemish to·God, purify
Heb 9:14 ·for *yeu* to·ritually·minister to·the·living God?
Heb 11:4 ·trust, Abel offered to·God a·much·better sacrifice
Heb 11:5 ·been·testified *of·him* to·have·fully·satisfied God.
Heb 11:6 the·one who·is·coming·alongside God to·trust that
Heb 12:23 in *the* heavens, and to·God, Judge of·all, and to·
Heb 12:28 we·may·ritually·minister to·God quite· with
Heb 13:15 ·carry·up a·sacrifice of·praise to·God continually,
Gal 2:19 to·Torah-Law in·order·that I·may·live to·God.
Gal 3:11 ·as·righteous personally·before God, because "the
Mt 6:24 able to·be·a·slave to·God and to·Material·Wealth.
Mt 19:26 is impossible, but with God all·things are possible.
Mt 22:21 ·Caesar to·Caesar, and the·things of·God to·God."
Mk 10:27 ·*is* impossible, but·yet not with God, for with God
Mk 10:27 not with God, for with God all·things are possible.
Mk 12:17 to·Caesar, and the·things of·God to·God." And
Rm 1:8 First in·fact, I·give·thanks to·my God through Jesus
Rm 2:11 For there·is no partiality with God.
Rm 2:13 *that·are* righteous personally·before God, but·rather
Rm 2:17 the Torah-Law, and make·your·boast in God,
Rm 3:19 may·become liable·under·justice before·God—
Rm 4:20 ·enabled by·the trust, already·giving glory to·God
Rm 5:10 enemies, we·are·reconciled to·God through the
Rm 5:11 but·rather we·also are·boasting in God through our
Rm 6:10 ·only, but in·that·which he·lives, he·lives to·God.
Rm 6:11 Moral·Failure, but alive to·God in Jesus Anointed
Rm 6:13 but·rather yeu·must·present yeurselves to·God, as
Rm 6:13 members *as* instruments of·righteousness to·God.
Rm 6:17 Now to·God *be* gratitude, that *formerly* yeu·were
Rm 6:22 and already·being·enslaved to·God, yeu·have yeur
Rm 7:4 ·men, in·order·that we·should·bear·fruit for·God.
Rm 7:25 I·give·thanks to·God through Jesus Anointed our
Rm 8:8 the·ones being in flesh are·not able to·satisfy God.
Rm 9:14 ¿!·Is·there unrighteousness with God? May·it·never
Rm 9:20 you·yourself, the·one who·is·contradicting God?
Rm 11:2 EliJah? How he·confers with·God against IsraEl,
Rm 11:30 ·yeurselves also once were·obstinate to·God, but
Rm 12:1 holy *and* most·satisfying to·God, *which·is* yeur
Rm 14:6 eats unto·*the*·Lord, for to·God he·gives·thanks;
Rm 14:6 ·Lord he·does·not eat, and to·God he·gives·thanks.
Rm 14:11 and every tongue shall·explicitly·affirm God.'
Rm 14:12 ·us shall·give account concerning himself to·God.
Rm 14:18 *is* most·satisfying to·God and verifiably·approved
Rm 16:27 to·*the*·only wise God, to·him *be* the glory through
Jac 1:27 Directly·from *our* God and Father— pure and
Jac 4:7 submit·yeurselves to·God. Stand·up·against the
Jac 4:8 Draw·near to·God, and he·shall·draw·near to·yeu.
Jud 1:1 To·the·ones in Father God, having·been·made·holy
Jud 1:25 to·*the*·only wise God our Savior, *be* glory and
Php 1:3 I·give·thanks to·my God upon every mention of·yeu,
Php 2:6 it not open·plunder to·be equal with·God,
Php 3:3 the·ones ritually·ministering to·God in·spirit, and
Php 4:18 a·sacrifice acceptable *and* most·satisfying to·God.
Php 4:20 Now to·our God and Father *be* glory into·the ages
1Pe 2:4 but Selected personally·by God, *being* dearly·
1Pe 2:5 sacrifices well·acceptable to·God through YeShua
1Pe 2:20 ·good, this *is* graciousness personally·before God.
1Pe 3:18 in·order·that he·may·escort us to·God, in·fact
2Pe 1:21 Spirit, men·of·clay† (the holy·ones in·God) spoke.
1Th 1:1 of·the·ThessaloNicans *which·is* in Father God and *in*
1Th 1:2 We·give·thanks to·God always concerning all of·
1Th 1:9 the idols, to·be·slaves to·the·living and true God,
1Th 2:2 we·were·boldly·confident in our God to·speak to
1Th 2:4 as satisfying men·of·clay†, but·rather God, the·one
1Th 2:13 we·ourselves give·thanks to·God unceasingly,
1Th 2:15 *are* not agreeably·complying with·God, even *being*
1Th 3:9 are·we·able to·recompense to·God concerning yeu,
1Th 4:1 to·agreeably·comply with·God in·order·that yeu·
2Th 1:1 ·citizenry of·the·ThessaloNicans in God our Father
2Th 1:3 ·indebted to·give·thanks to·God always concerning
2Th 1:6 ·righteous·thing with God to·recompense tribulation
2Th 2:13 to·give·thanks always to·God concerning yeu (O·
Tit 3:8 having·trusted in·God may·have·a·considerable·care
1Co 1:4 I·give·thanks to·my God always concerning yeu for
1Co 1:14 I·give·thanks to·God that I·immersed not·even·one
1Co 3:19 world is foolishness with God. For it·has·been·
1Co 7:24 brothers, in that·*state* he·must·continue with God.
1Co 8:8 But food does·not commend us to·God. For neither
1Co 9:9 ¿!·Do the oxen matter to·God?
1Co 9:21 (not being without·Torah-Law to·God, but·yet *I·am*
1Co 10:20 ·slaughter to·demons, and not to·God. And I·do·
1Co 11:13 ·for a·woman to·pray to·God not·fully·veiled?
1Co 14:2 not to·men·of·clay†, but·rather to·God. For not·
1Co 14:18 *In·fact*, I·give·thanks to·my God, speaking more·
1Co 14:25 face, he·shall·fall·prostrate to·God, announcing
1Co 14:28 And·thus, he·must·speak to·himself and to·God.
1Co 15:24 the kingdom to·the·one *who·is* God and Father,
1Co 15:57 But thanks *be* to·God, the·one giving us the
2Co 1:9 ourselves, but·rather upon God (the·one awakening
2Co 1:20 the "So·be·it, Amen" for·God unto glory through
2Co 2:14 Now thanks *be* to·God— the·one always causing
2Co 2:15 we·are to·God a·sweet·scent of·Anointed-One,
2Co 5:11 But we·have·been·made·manifest to·God, and I·
2Co 5:13 if we·lost·our·wits, *it·is* for·God; or·if we·are·of·
2Co 5:20 on·behalf of·Anointed-One, be·reconciled to·God!
2Co 8:16 But thanks *be* to·God, the·one giving the same
2Co 9:11 through us an·expression·of·thankfulness to·God.
2Co 9:12 through many expressions·of·thankfulness to·God.
2Co 9:15 Thanks *be* to·God for his indescribable voluntary·
2Co 10:4 *are* not fleshly, but·rather powerful in·God to *the*

Eph 2:16 he·may·utterly·reconcile the both to·God in one
Eph 3:9 ·away from the prior·ages in God, the·one creating
Eph 5:2 an·offering and a·sacrifice to·God for a·soothing
Eph 5:20 on·behalf of·all·things *to·our* God and Father in *the*
Col 1:3 We·give·thanks to·the God and Father of·our Lord
Col 3:3 ·hidden together with·the Anointed-One in God.
Col 3:17 name, giving·thanks to·the God and Father through
Phm 1:4 I·give·thanks to·my God, making mention of·you
1Ti 1:17 invisible, to·*the*·only wise God, *be* honor and
1Ti 4:10 ·placed·our·expectation upon the·living God, who
1Ti 6:17 but·rather in the living God (the·one personally·
2Ti 1:3 I·have gratitude to·God (to·whom I·ritually·minister
2Ti 2:15 yourself verifiably·approved to·God, an·unashamed
1Jn 4:15 of·God, God abides in him, and he·himself in God.
1Jn 4:16 abiding in the Love abides in God, and God in him.
1Jn 5:10 the·one not trusting God has·made *God* himself a·
Rv 1:6 and priests·that·offer·a·sacrifice to·his God and Father.
Rv 5:9 and you·kinsman·redeemed us to·God by your
Rv 5:10 you·made us *to·be* to·our God kings and priests·that·
Rv 7:11 ·sight of·the throne. And they·fell·prostrate to·God,
Rv 7:12 the strength, *be* to·our God into the ages of·ages.
Rv 11:13 alarmed and gave glory to·the God of·the heaven.
Rv 11:16 fell upon their faces, and fell·prostrate to·God,
Rv 14:4 men·of·clay†, *being* a·firstfruit to·God and to·the
Rv 19:1 the honor, and the power *are* to·Yahweh our God!
Rv 19:4 fell·down and fell·prostrate to·God, to·the·one who·
Rv 19:10 testimony of·Jesus. Fall·prostrate to·God, for the
Rv 22:9 words of·this official·scroll. Fall·prostrate to·God."

G2316.2 N-GSM θεοῦ (698x)

Jn 1:6 having·been·dispatched personally·from God. His
Jn 1:12 he·gave privilege to·become children of·God, to·
Jn 1:13 ·*the*·will of·man, but·rather birthed·from·out of·God.
Jn 1:29 "See the Sacrificial·Lamb of·God, the·one taking·
Jn 1:34 and have·testified, that this is the Son of·God."
Jn 1:36 "See the Sacrificial·Lamb of·God!"
Jn 1:49 you·yourself are the Son of·God; you·yourself are
Jn 1:51 and 'the angels of·God ascending and descending'
Jn 3:2 we·have·seen that you·have·come from God, *being*
Jn 3:3 ·above, he·is·not able to·see the kingdom of·God."
Jn 3:5 he·is·not able to·enter into the kingdom of·God.
Jn 3:18 in the name of·the only·begotten Son of·God.
Jn 3:34 dispatched speaks the utterances of·God, for *to·him*
Jn 3:36 but·rather the wrath of·God does·remain upon him.
Jn 4:10 ·personally·known the voluntary·present of·God, and
Jn 5:25 shall·hear the voice of·the Son of·God, and the·ones
Jn 5:42 that yeu·do·not have the love of·God in yeurselves.
Jn 5:44 the glory, the·one personally·from the only God?
Jn 6:28 ·do in·order·that we·may·work the works of·God?"
Jn 6:29 "This is the work of·God, that yeu·should·trust in
Jn 6:33 for the bread of·God is the·one descending from·out
Jn 6:46 except the·one being personally·from God; this·one
Jn 6:69 are the Anointed-One, the Son of·the living God."
Jn 7:17 whether it·is from·out of·God, or *whether* I·myself
Jn 8:40 which I·heard personally·from God. AbRaham did·
Jn 8:42 went·forth and have·come out·from God. For neither
Jn 8:47 The·one being birthed·from·out of·God hears the
Jn 8:47 of·God hears the utterances of·God. On·account·of
Jn 8:47 *them* because yeu·are not birthed·from·out of·God."
Jn 9:3 ·that the works of·God should·be·made·apparent in
Jn 9:16 man·of·clay† is not personally·from God, because
Jn 9:33 this·man was personally·from God, he·would·not be·
Jn 9:35 "You·yourself, do·you·trust in the Son of·God?"
Jn 10:35 pertaining·to whom the Holy-word of·God came,
Jn 10:36 ·God,' because I·declared, 'I·am God's Son.'
Jn 11:4 ·rather on·behalf of·the glory of·God, in·order·that
Jn 11:4 ·order·that the Son of·God may·be·glorified through
Jn 11:27 the Anointed-One, the Son of·God, the·one who·is·
Jn 11:40 ·trust, you·shall·gaze·upon the glory of·God?"
Jn 11:52 one, the children of·God, the·ones having·been·
Jn 12:43 more·especially indeed·than·even the glory of·God.
Jn 13:3 he·came·forth from God and was·heading·on·out to
Jn 16:27 that I·myself came·forth personally·from God.
Jn 16:30 "By this, we·trust that you·came·forth from God."

Jn 19:7 ·die, because he·made himself *out to·be* God's Son."
Jn 20:31 is the Anointed-One, the Son of·God; and that
Lk 1:6 ·were both righteous in·the·sight of·God, traversing
Lk 1:8 him performing·priestly·duties in·front of·God in the
Lk 1:19 the·one standing·near in·the·sight of·God; and I·
Lk 1:26 angel GabriEl was·dispatched by God to a·city of·
Lk 1:35 *child*, being·born holy, shall·be·called God's Son.
Lk 1:78 through *the* inward·affections of·our God's mercy, in
Lk 2:40 ·filled with·wisdom. And God's grace was upon
Lk 3:2 high·priests— an·utterance of·God came to John the
Lk 3:6 flesh shall·gaze·upon the custodial·Salvation of·God.'
Lk 3:38 of·Enosh, *son* of·Sheth, *son* of·Adam, *son* of·God.
Lk 4:3 "If you·are a·son of·God, declare to·this stone that it·
Lk 4:9 "If you·are the Son of·God, cast yourself down from·
Lk 4:34 you *and* who you·are, the Holy·One of·God."
Lk 4:41 are the Anointed-One, the Son of·God." And
Lk 4:43 ·the·good·news of·the kingdom of·God to·the other
Lk 5:1 him to·hear the Redemptive-word of·God, he·himself
Lk 6:4 how he·entered into the house of·God and took and
Lk 6:12 ·through·the·night *continuing* in the prayer of·God.
Lk 6:20 ·poor, because yeurs is the kingdom of·God.
Lk 7:28 least·one in the kingdom of·God is greater·than he.
Lk 7:30 refused the counsel of·God for themselves, not
Lk 8:1 proclaiming·the·good·news of·the kingdom of·God.
Lk 8:10 the mysteries of·the kingdom of·God, but to·the rest,
Lk 8:11 scattering·of·seed is the Redemptive-word of·God.
Lk 8:21 ·ones hearing the Redemptive-word of·God and doing
Lk 8:28 ·with·me and you Jesus, O·Son of·God Most·High?
Lk 9:2 them to·officially·proclaim the kingdom of·God, and
Lk 9:11 to·them concerning the kingdom of·God, and healed
Lk 9:20 Peter declared, "The Anointed-One of·God."
Lk 9:27 death until they·should·see the kingdom of·God."
Lk 9:43 ·all were·astounded at the magnificence of·God. But
Lk 9:60 ·off, thoroughly·announce the kingdom of·God."
Lk 9:62 left·behind, is well-suited for the kingdom of·God."
Lk 10:9 'The kingdom of·God has·drawn·near to yeu.
Lk 10:11 that the kingdom of·God has·drawn·near to yeu.
Lk 11:20 "But if with God's finger, I·cast·out the demons,
Lk 11:20 the kingdom of·God has·already·come upon yeu.
Lk 11:28 the Redemptive-word of·God and vigilantly·keeping
Lk 11:42 ·justice and the love of·God. It·is·mandatory to·do
Lk 11:49 ·account·of that, the wisdom of·God also declared,
Lk 12:6 them is having·been·forgotten in·the·sight of·God.
Lk 12:8 shall·affirm him by·name before the angels of·God.
Lk 12:9 ·be·utterly·denied in·the·sight of·the angels of·God.
Lk 12:31 Moreover, seek the kingdom of·God, and all these·
Lk 13:18 "To·what is the kingdom of·God like?
Lk 13:20 "To·what shall·I·liken the kingdom of·God?
Lk 13:28 all the prophets in the kingdom of·God, but yeu·
Lk 13:29 shall·recline·at·the·table in the kingdom of·God.
Lk 14:15 *is·he* that shall·eat bread in the kingdom of·God."
Lk 15:10 occurs in·the·sight of·the angels of·God over one
Lk 16:15 ·of·clay† is an·abomination in·the·sight of·God.
Lk 16:16 then·on, the kingdom of·God is·being·proclaimed,
Lk 17:20 *as·to* when the kingdom of·God should·come, he·
Lk 17:20 "The kingdom of·God does·not come with
Lk 17:21 behold, the kingdom of·God is on·the·inside of·
Lk 18:16 forbid them, for of·such is the kingdom of·God.
Lk 18:17 ·not accept the kingdom of·God as a·little·child, no
Lk 18:24 the valuables shall·enter into the kingdom of·God!
Lk 18:25 a·wealthy·man to·enter into the kingdom of·God."
Lk 18:29 or children, for·the·cause·of the kingdom of·God,
Lk 19:11 the kingdom of·God is·about to·be·made·totally·
Lk 20:21 ·rather *that* you·instruct the Way of·God in truth.
Lk 20:25 ·Caesar to·Caesar, and the·things of·God to·God."
Lk 20:36 ·angels, and are the·Sons of·God, being the·Sons
Lk 21:4 into the voluntary·offerings·of·sacrifice for·God, but
Lk 21:31 also know that the kingdom of·God is near·at·hand.
Lk 22:16 ·be·completely·fulfilled in the kingdom of·God."
Lk 22:18 until such·time the kingdom of·God should·come."
Lk 22:69 ·down at *the* right·hand of·the power of·God."
Lk 22:70 ·then, you·yourself are the Son of·God?" And he·
Lk 23:35 is the Anointed-One, the Selected-One of·God."

Lk 23:51 who also himself awaited the kingdom of·God.
Lk 24:19 in deed and word directly·before God and all the
Ac 1:3 relating the·things concerning the kingdom of·God.
Ac 2:11 ·our native·tongues the magnificent·things of·God."
Ac 2:22 a·man having·been·exhibited by God for yeu with·
Ac 2:23 counsel and foreknowledge of·God) *was* given·over,
Ac 2:33 to·the right·hand of·God and·also receiving the
Ac 4:19 it·is right in·the·sight of·God to·listen·to yeu rather
Ac 4:19 ·God to·listen·to yeu rather than to·God, yeu·judge.
Ac 4:31 the Redemptive-word of·God with clarity·of·speech.
Ac 5:39 But if it·is birthed·from·out of·God, yeu·are·not able
Ac 6:2 the Redemptive-word of·God to·attend to·meal·tables.
Ac 6:7 Redemptive-word of·God was·growing·*in·circulation*;
Ac 7:46 who found grace in·the·sight of·God and requested
Ac 7:55 into the heaven, he·saw God's glory, and Jesus
Ac 7:55 glory, and Jesus standing at *the* right·hand of·God.
Ac 7:56 of·Clay·Man† standing at *the* right·hand of·God."
Ac 8:10 "This·man is the great power of·God."
Ac 8:12 the·things concerning the kingdom of·God and the
Ac 8:14 the Redemptive-word of·God, they·dispatched Peter
Ac 8:20 voluntary·present of·God may·be·procured through
Ac 8:21 for your heart is not straight in·the·sight of·God.
Ac 8:22 of·yours, and petition God so·that perhaps the
Ac 8:37 "I·trust Jesus Anointed to·be the Son of·God."
Ac 9:20 "This is the Son of·God!"
Ac 10:2 ·acts for·the people and continually petitioning God.
Ac 10:3 of·the day, an·angel of·God entering *this·realm*
Ac 10:4 ·acts ascended for a·memorial in·the·sight of·God.
Ac 10:31 ·acts were·recalled·to·mind in·the·sight of·God.
Ac 10:33 *are* all in·the·sight of·God. We·are·present to·hear
Ac 10:33 having·been·specifically·assigned to·you by God."
Ac 10:41 having·been·elected·beforehand by God, to·us who
Ac 10:42 ·been·specifically·determined by God *to·be* Judge
Ac 11:1 Gentiles also accepted the Redemptive-word of·God.
Ac 11:23 ·directly and seeing the grace of·God, was·glad.
Ac 12:24 But the Redemptive-word of·God was·growing and
Ac 13:5 ·proclaiming the Redemptive-word of·God in the
Ac 13:7 Saul, sought to·hear the Redemptive-word of·God.
Ac 13:36 to·the counsel of·God in·his·own generation, was·
Ac 13:43 them to·continue·on in·the grace of·God.
Ac 13:44 ·together to·hear the Redemptive-word of·God.
Ac 13:46 for·the Redemptive-word of·God first to·be·spoken
Ac 14:22 us to·enter into the kingdom of·God through many
Ac 14:26 ·been·directly·handed to·the grace of·God, for the
Ac 15:40 ·being·directly·handed to·the grace of·God by the
Ac 16:17 "These men·of·clay† are slaves of·God Most·High,
Ac 17:13 Redemptive-word of·God also was·fully·proclaimed
Ac 17:29 inherently·being kindred of·God, we·ought not
Ac 18:11 the Redemptive-word of·God among them.
Ac 18:21 but I·shall·return·back again to yeu, God willing."
Ac 18:26 explained to·him the Way of·God more·precisely.
Ac 19:8 the·things concerning the kingdom of·God.
Ac 20:24 ·testify the good·news of·the grace of·God.
Ac 20:25 ·proclaiming the kingdom of·God, shall·gaze·upon
Ac 20:27 to·report·in·detail to·yeu all the counsel of·God?
Ac 20:28 ·shepherd the Called·Out·citizenry of·God, which
Ac 22:3 ·father, inherently·being a·zealot of·God, just·as
Ac 23:4 declared, "Do·you·defame God's high·priest?
Ac 26:6 of·the promise being·made by God to the fathers,
Ac 26:22 ·obtaining assistance personally·from God, I·stand
Ac 27:23 me this night an·angel of·God, of·him·whose I·am
Ac 28:23 ·testifying·to the kingdom of·God, and·also
Ac 28:28 ·Salvation of·God is·already·dispatched to·the
Ac 28:31 ·proclaiming the kingdom of·God and instructing
Heb 1:6 '" And fall·prostrate to·him, all angels of·God!"'
Heb 2:4 with·God also·further·testifying·jointly, both with·
Heb 2:9 that by·the·grace of·God he·should·taste death on·
Heb 3:12 of·distrust, in withdrawing from the·living God.
Heb 4:9 ·remaining a·Sabbath·Rest for·the People of·God.
Heb 4:12 For the Word† of·God *is* living and active, and *he*·
Heb 4:14 the Son of·God, we·should·take·secure·hold of·
Heb 5:4 ·rather *it·is* the·one being·called·forth by God, even
Heb 5:10 ·specifically·designated by God a·High·Priest

Heb 5:12 ·principles·of·the eloquent·words of·God. And
Heb 6:5 and after·tasting a·good utterance of·God, and·also
Heb 6:6 Son of·God and exposing·*him*·to·public·ridicule·
Heb 6:7 it·is·cultivated, it·partakes of·blessings from God.
Heb 7:1 Priest of·God Most·High that·offers·a·sacrifice) *is*
Heb 7:3 ·been·made·similar to·the Son of·God, he·abides a·
Heb 9:24 in·the personal·presence of·God on·our behalf.
Heb 10:12 perpetuity, sat·down at *the* right·hand of·God.
Heb 10:21 and *having* a·high priest over the house of·God—
Heb 10:29 the·one trampling·down the Son of·God, and
Heb 10:31 ·thing·to·fall into *the* hands of·the·living God.
Heb 10:36 the will of·God, yeu·may·subsequently·obtain the
Heb 11:3 ·completely·formed by·an·utterance of·God, for
Heb 11:4 to·be righteous, with·God testifying concerning
Heb 11:25 ·together with·the People of·God than to·have
Heb 11:40 with·God previously·looking·at something
Heb 12:2 sat·down at *the* right·hand of·the throne of·God.
Heb 12:15 *is·found* falling·short from the grace of·God; lest
Heb 12:22 Mount Tsiyon and the·living God's CITY, to·a·
Heb 13:7 spoke to·yeu the Redemptive-word of·God, whose
Gal 1:1 through YeShua Anointed and Father God, the·one
Gal 1:3 *be* to·yeu and peace from Father God, and *from* our
Gal 1:4 according·to the will of·our God and Father,
Gal 1:13 the Called·Out·citizenry of·God and was·fiercely·
Gal 1:20 to·yeu— Behold, in·the·sight of·God, I·do·not lie.
Gal 2:20 in the trust of·the Son of·God, the·one loving me,
Gal 2:21 "I·do·not set·aside the grace of·God, for if
Gal 3:17 ·been·previously·ratified by God in Anointed-One,
Gal 3:21 against the promises of·God? May·it·never happen!
Gal 3:26 For yeu·are all the·Sons of·God through the trust in
Gal 4:7 *then* also an·heir of·God through Anointed-One.
Gal 4:9 or rather being·known by God, how·is·it *that* yeu·
Gal 4:14 but·rather accepted me as an·angel of·God, *even* as
Gal 5:21 such·things shall·not inherit God's kingdom.
Gal 6:16 them, and mercy, and upon the IsraEl of·God.
Mt 3:16 and he·saw the Spirit of·God descending like a·dove
Mt 4:3 "If you·are a·son of·God, declare that these stones
Mt 4:6 "If you·are *the* Son of·God, cast yourself down.
Mt 5:9 they·themselves shall·be·called the·Sons of·God.
Mt 5:34 neither by the heaven, because it·is God's throne,
Mt 6:33 But seek·yeu first the kingdom of·God and his
Mt 8:29 you, YeShua, O·Son of·God? Did·you·come here
Mt 12:4 How he·entered into the house of·God and ate the
Mt 12:28 cast·out the demons by God's Spirit, then·by·
Mt 12:28 the kingdom of·God has·already·come upon yeu.
Mt 14:33 to·him, saying, "Truly you·are God's Son."
Mt 15:3 ·contrary·to the commandment of·God through yeur
Mt 15:6 ·invalidate the commandment of·God through yeur
Mt 16:16 are the Anointed-One, the Son of·the living God."
Mt 16:23 ·do·not contemplate the·things of·God, but·rather
Mt 19:24 a·wealthy·man to·enter into the kingdom of·God."
Mt 21:12 into the Sanctuary·Estate of·God and cast·out all
Mt 21:31 prostitutes precede yeu into the kingdom of·God.
Mt 21:43 the kingdom of·God shall·be·taken·away from
Mt 22:16 and *that* you·instruct the Way of·God in truth, and
Mt 22:21 ·Caesar to·Caesar, and the·things of·God to·God."
Mt 22:29 ·seen the Scriptures, nor·even the power of·God.
Mt 22:30 but·rather they·are as God's angels in heaven.
Mt 22:31 of·the·thing being·uttered to·yeu by God, saying,
Mt 23:22 swears by the throne of·God and by the·one who·
Mt 26:61 ·able to·demolish the Temple of·God and to·build
Mt 26:63 ·I·solemnly·charge you by the·living God, that
Mt 26:63 ·yourself are the Anointed-One, the Son of·God."
Mt 27:40 If you·are a·son of·God, descend from the cross.
Mt 27:43 him,⇨ for he·declared, 'I·am a·son of·God.'"
Mt 27:54 "Truly this was God's Son."
Mk 1:1 of·the good·news of·Jesus Anointed, God's Son.
Mk 1:14 the good·news of·the kingdom of·God,
Mk 1:15 and the kingdom of·God has·drawn·near. Yeu·
Mk 1:24 ·know you, who you·are, the Holy·One of·God."
Mk 2:26 into the house of·God in·the·days of·AbiAthar the
Mk 3:11 "You·yourself are the Son of·God."
Mk 3:35 whoever should·do the will of·God, this·one is my
Mk 4:11 the mystery of·the kingdom of·God, but·to·them,
Mk 4:26 "In·this·manner is the kingdom of·God: "*It·is* as
Mk 4:30 "To·what should·we·liken the kingdom of·God? Or
Mk 5:7 ·me and you, Jesus, O·Son of·God Most·High?
Mk 7:8 the commandment of·God, yeu·securely·hold·to the
Mk 7:9 the commandment of·God in·order·that yeu·may·
Mk 7:13 the Holy-word of·God by·yeur Oral·tradition, which
Mk 8:33 ·do·not contemplate the·things of·God, but·rather
Mk 9:1 they·should·see the kingdom of·God having·come in
Mk 9:47 to·enter into the kingdom of·God with·one·eye,
Mk 10:14 forbid them, for of·such is the kingdom of·God.
Mk 10:15 ·not accept the kingdom of·God as·though *he·is* a·
Mk 10:23 valuables shall·enter into the kingdom of·God!"
Mk 10:24 in the valuables to·enter into the kingdom of·God!
Mk 10:25 ·wealthy·man to·enter into the kingdom of·God."
Mk 11:22 Jesus says to·them, "Have God's *type·of* trust.
Mk 12:14 but·rather instruct the Way of·God in truth. Is·it·
Mk 12:17 to·Caesar, and the·things of·God to·God." And
Mk 12:24 ·seen the Scriptures, nor·even the power of·God?
Mk 12:34 not at·a·distance from the kingdom of·God." And
Mk 14:25 I·may·drink it brand-new in the kingdom of·God."
Mk 15:39 "Truly this·man·of·clay† was a·son of·God."
Mk 15:43 himself was awaiting the kingdom of·God. Being·
Mk 16:19 the heaven and seated at *the* right·hand of·God.
Rm 1:1 ·been·specially·detached to *the* good·news of·God—
Rm 1:4 ·determined *to·be the* Son of·God in power
Rm 1:7 being in Rome, beloved of·God, called·forth *as*
Rm 1:7 Grace to·yeu and peace from God our Father and *the*
Rm 1:10 I·shall·prosper by the will of·God to·come to yeu.
Rm 1:16 Anointed-One, for it·is God's power to Salvation
Rm 1:17 For in this, God's righteousness is·revealed, birthed·
Rm 1:18 For God's wrath is·revealed from heaven against all
Rm 1:19 the·thing *which·is* known of·God, it·is apparent
Rm 1:23 ·change the glory of·the incorruptible God⇨ into ‘
Rm 1:25 who exchanged the truth of·God with the lie, and
Rm 1:32 after·recognizing the statute of·God (that the·ones
Rm 2:2 ·have·seen that the judgment of·God is according·to
Rm 2:3 ·yourself shall·utterly·escape the judgment of·God?
Rm 2:4 not·knowing that the kindness of·God leads you to
Rm 2:5 and of·*the*·revelation of·God's righteous·verdict,
Rm 2:24 For ⇨the name of·God is·reviled among the
Rm 2:29 ·out·of·men·of·clay†, but·rather from·out of·God.
Rm 3:2 they·are·entrusted·with the eloquent·words of·God.
Rm 3:3 their lack·of·trust fully·nullify the trust of·God?
Rm 3:5 unrighteousness commends God's righteousness—"
Rm 3:7 if by my lie, the truth of·God abounded to his glory,
Rm 3:18 "There·is no fear of·God fully·before their eyes.
Rm 3:21 But now·in·fact, God's righteousness apart·from
Rm 3:22 And God's righteousness through trust of·Jesus
Rm 3:23 ·failed and are·destitute of·the glory of·God,
Rm 3:26 with the forbearance of·God toward the·one himself
Rm 4:17 *And being* directly·before God whom he·trusted
Rm 4:20 And in·regard·to the promise of·God, *AbRaham*
Rm 5:2 and we·boast in expectation of·the glory of·God.
Rm 5:5 because the love of·God has·been·poured·forth in
Rm 5:15 so·much more did·abound the grace of·God and the
Rm 7:22 ·pleasure in·the Torah-Law of·God according·to the
Rm 8:7 for it·is·not subject to·the Law-of-Liberty of·God, for
Rm 8:9 but·rather in Spirit, if·perhaps God's Spirit dwells in
Rm 8:14 For as·many·as are led by·God's Spirit, these are
Rm 8:14 are·led by·God's Spirit, these are the·Sons of·God.
Rm 8:16 with·our spirit that we·are children of·God,
Rm 8:17 ·*are* heirs, heirs in·fact of·God and co-heirs with·
Rm 8:19 fully·awaits the revealing of·the Sons of·God.
Rm 8:21 into the glorious liberty of·the children of·God.
Rm 8:33 shall·call·to·account against God's Selected-Ones?
Rm 8:34 is even at *the* right·hand of·God, who also makes·
Rm 8:39 ·separate us from the love of·God in Anointed-One,
Rm 9:6 not as·though the Holy-word of·God has·fallen·short.
Rm 9:8 of·the flesh *that·are* children of·God, but·rather the
Rm 9:11 ·purpose may·endure according·to God's Selection,
Rm 9:16 *for·it·as·a·prize*, but·rather on·God, the·one
Rm 9:26 they·shall·be·called the·Sons of·the·living God."'
Rm 10:2 for·them that they·have a·zeal of·God, but·yet not
Rm 10:3 For being·ignorant of·God's righteousness, and
Rm 10:3 submit·themselves to·the righteousness of·God.
Rm 10:17 and the hearing through an·utterance of·God.
Rm 11:22 ·kindness and a·severe·cutting-off from·God! In·
Rm 11:29 and the calling of·God *are* without·regret.
Rm 11:33 both of·*the*·wisdom and knowledge of·God! How
Rm 12:1 through the tender·compassions of·God, to·present
Rm 12:2 ·good, most·satisfying, and complete will of·God.
Rm 13:1 there·is no authority except from God; and the·ones
Rm 13:1 authorities, they·are having·been·assigned by God.
Rm 13:2 has·stood·opposed·to the institution of·God, and
Rm 13:4 For he·is an·attendant of·God to·you in the
Rm 13:4 for he·is an·attendant of·God, an·avenger *to*·
Rm 13:6 also. For they·are God's public·servants, diligently·
Rm 14:17 For the kingdom of·God is not *about* feeding and
Rm 14:20 demolish the work of·God for·the·sake·of food.
Rm 14:22 *just* in·the·sight of·God. Supremely·blessed *is* the·
Rm 15:7 purposely·received us into God's glory.
Rm 15:8 of·*the*·Circumcision on·behalf of·God's truth, in·
Rm 15:15 ·account·of the grace being·given to·me by God,
Rm 15:16 ·above *for* the good·news of·God, in·order·that the
Rm 15:19 wonders, with *the* power of·God's Spirit, such·for
Rm 15:32 yeu with joy through God's will and may·be·
Rm 16:26 ·to a·full·appointment of·the eternal God, with *the*
Jac 1:1 Jacob, a·slave of·God and of·*the*·Lord YeShua
Jac 1:5 let·him·request personally·from God, the·one giving
Jac 1:13 must·ever·say, "I·am·tempted by God," for God is
Jac 1:20 wrath does·not accomplish God's righteousness.
Jac 2:23 ' And he·was·called God's "Close·Friend.
Jac 3:9 having·come·to·be according·to a·likeness of·God.
Jac 4:4 of·the world is hostility with·God? Accordingly,
Jac 4:4 ·the world is·fully·established·as an·enemy of·God.
Jud 1:4 transferring the grace of·our God into debauchery
Jud 1:21 purposefully·keep yeurselves in God's love, *yeu*
Php 1:2 to·yeu, and peace, from God our Father and *from*
Php 1:11 Anointed, to *the* glory and high·praise of·God.
Php 1:28 but of·Salvation for·yeu, and that from God.
Php 2:6 fundamental·nature of·God, resolutely·considered it
Php 2:11 Jesus Anointed *is* Lord, to *the* glory of·Father God.
Php 2:15 and untainted, children of·God, irreproachable, in
Php 3:9 (the righteousness from·out of·God *based* upon the
Php 3:14 of·the upward calling of·God in Anointed-One
Php 4:7 And the peace of·God, the·one extending·itself·
1Pe 1:2 according·to *the* foreknowledge of·Father God, by a·
1Pe 1:5 ·ones being·dutifully·kept by God's power through
1Pe 1:23 ·*of·seed* through *the* Redemptive-word of·God,
1Pe 2:10 not a·people, but *are* now God's People, the·ones
1Pe 2:15 it·is the will of·God, *by* beneficially·doing·good,
1Pe 2:16 ·the depravity, but·rather *behave* as slaves of·God.
1Pe 2:19 ·account·of conscience *toward* God undergoes grief
1Pe 3:4 which is extremely·precious in·the·sight of·God.
1Pe 3:17 if the will of·God is·thus·determined, to·suffer *for*
1Pe 3:20 long-suffering of·God was·waiting·for *this·moment*
1Pe 3:22 is at *the* right·hand of·God, with·angels and
1Pe 4:2 ·longings of·men·of·clay†, but·rather to·God's will.
1Pe 4:10 it as good estate·managers of·God's manifold grace.
1Pe 4:11 *let·him·be* as *one·speaking* eloquent·words of·God;
1Pe 4:14 the Spirit of·glory and of·God rests upon yeu.
1Pe 4:17 judgment to·begin with the house of·God. And if *it*
1Pe 4:17 ·ones being·obstinate to·the good·news of·God?
1Pe 4:19 will of·God must·place·the·direct·care·of their·own
1Pe 5:2 Shepherd the little·flock of·God among yeu,
1Pe 5:6 under the mighty hand of·God, in·order·that he·may·
1Pe 5:12 this to·be *the* true grace of·God in which yeu·stand.
2Pe 1:1 in *the* righteousness of·our God and Savior YeShua
2Pe 1:2 to·yeu in *the* full·knowledge of·God and of·YeShua
2Pe 1:17 he·received personally·from Father God honor and
2Pe 3:5 that by·the Word of·God, there·were heavens from·
2Pe 3:12 the imminent·arrival of·the Day of·God— through
1Th 1:1 *be* to·yeu, and peace, from God our Father, and *the*
1Th 1:3 remembering yeu before our God and Father (*yeur*
1Th 1:4 ·seen, O·brothers having·been·loved by God, yeur

1Th 2:2 to yeu the good·news of·God with much striving.
1Th 2:4 ·tested·and·proven by God to·be·entrusted with·the
1Th 2:8 ·yeu, not the good·news of·God merely, but·rather
1Th 2:9 ·officially·proclaimed to yeu the good·news of·God.
1Th 2:12 for yeu to·walk worthily of·God, the·one calling
1Th 2:13 after·personally·receiving God's Redemptive-word
1Th 2:13 just·as it·is truly, God's Redemptive-word, which
1Th 2:14 of·the Called·Out·citizenries of·God, the·ones in
1Th 3:2 our brother, and attendant of·God, and our
1Th 3:9 we·rejoice on·account·of yeu before our God?
1Th 3:13 blameless in devoted·holiness before God, even our
1Th 4:3 For this is God's will, yeur renewed·holiness: for·
1Th 4:16 a·chief·angel's voice, and with God's trumpet, and
1Th 5:18 for this *is* the·will of·God in Anointed-One YeShua
2Th 1:2 to·yeu, and peace, from God our Father and *the*
2Th 1:4 the Called·Out·citizenries of·God on·behalf·of·yeur
2Th 1:5 *·is* an·indication of·the righteous verdict of·God, for
2Th 1:5 ·fully·worthy of·the kingdom of·God, on·behalf·of·
2Th 1:12 according·to the grace of·our God and of·*the*·Lord
2Th 2:4 as God in the Temple of·God,' exhibiting himself
2Th 3:5 yeur hearts into the love of·God and into *the* patient·
Tit 1:1 Paul, a·slave of·God and an·ambassador of·Jesus
Tit 1:1 accordingly *for·the* trust of·God's Selected-Ones and
Tit 1:3 according·to a·full·appointment of·God our Savior.
Tit 1:4 *and* peace, from Father God and *the* Lord Jesus
Tit 1:7 ·of·wrong·doing as an·estate·manager of·God), not
Tit 2:5 the Redemptive-word of·God should·not·be reviled.
Tit 2:10 *themselves·with* the instruction of·God our Savior in
Tit 2:11 For the grace of·God, the Custodial·Salvation,
Tit 2:13 ·appearing of·the glory of·our great God and Savior,
Tit 3:4 But when the kindness of·God our Savior and *his*
1Co 1:1 ·ambassador of·Jesus Anointed through God's will,
1Co 1:2 To·the Called·Out·citizenry of·God, the·one being
1Co 1:3 to·yeu, and peace, from God our Father, and Lord
1Co 1:4 yeu for the grace of·God, the·one already·being·
1Co 1:18 to·us who·are·being·saved, it·is the power of·God.
1Co 1:21 whereas (by the wisdom of·God) the world through
1Co 1:24 Greeks, Anointed-One *is* God's power and God's
1Co 1:24 Anointed-One *is* God's power and God's wisdom,
1Co 1:25 because the foolishness of·God is wiser·than the
1Co 1:25 and the weakness of·God is stronger·than the
1Co 1:30 Jesus, who is·made to·us wisdom from God, also
1Co 2:1 ·fully·proclaiming to·yeu the testimony of·God.
1Co 2:5 wisdom of·men·of·clay†, but·rather in God's power.
1Co 2:7 But·rather we·speak God's wisdom in a·Mystery,
1Co 2:10 searches all·things, even, the deep·things of·God.
1Co 2:11 *being* personally·knows the·things of·God, except
1Co 2:11 the·things of·God, except the Spirit of·God.
1Co 2:12 Spirit, the·one from·out of·God, in·order·that we·
1Co 2:12 ·things being·graciously·bestowed to·us by God.
1Co 2:14 accept the·things of·the Spirit of·God, for they·are
1Co 3:9 For we·are coworkers with·God; yeu·are God's
1Co 3:9 coworkers with·God; yeu·are God's cultivated·soil,
1Co 3:9 yeu·are God's cultivated·soil, God's structure.
1Co 3:10 According·to the grace of·God, the·one being·
1Co 3:16 personally·know that yeu·are a·temple of·God, and
1Co 3:16 of·God, and *that* the Spirit of·God dwells in yeu?
1Co 3:17 If anyone corrupts the temple of·God, this·one God
1Co 3:17 For the temple of·God is holy, which *temple* yeu·
1Co 3:23 of·Anointed-One, and Anointed-One *is* of·God.
1Co 4:1 and estate·managers of·God's mysteries.
1Co 4:5 high·praise from God shall·come·to·be to·each·man.
1Co 4:20 For the kingdom of·God *is* not in word, but·rather
1Co 6:9 unrighteous·men shall·not inherit God's kingdom?
1Co 6:10 ·greedy·men shall·inherit God's kingdom!
1Co 6:11 of·the Lord Jesus, and by the Spirit of·our God.
1Co 6:19 in yeu, which yeu·have from God, and yeu·are not
1Co 6:20 in yeur body and in yeur spirit, which are God's.
1Co 7:7 ·own gracious·bestowment from·out of·God, in·fact,
1Co 7:19 *is* a·proper·observance of·God's commandments.
1Co 7:40 advice; and I·suppose also to·have God's Spirit.
1Co 10:31 or anything *that* yeu·do, do all to God's glory.
1Co 10:32 ·Greeks, and to·the Called·Out·citizenry of·God.
1Co 11:7 his head, inherently·being God's derived·image
1Co 11:12 the woman, but all things *are* from·out of·God.
1Co 11:16 neither *do* the Called·Out·citizenries of·God.
1Co 11:22 ·yeu·despise the Called·Out·citizenry of·God, and
1Co 12:3 not·even·one·man speaking by God's Spirit says,
1Co 14:36 did the Redemptive-word of·God come·forth from
1Co 15:9 ·that I·persecuted the Called·Out·citizenry of·God.
1Co 15:10 But by·the·grace of·God I·am what I·am, and his
1Co 15:10 not I·myself but·rather the Grace of·God, the·one
1Co 15:15 ·are·found *to·be* false·witnesses of·God, because
1Co 15:15 we·testified against God that he·awakened the
1Co 15:34 ·fail; for some are ignorant of·God. I·say *this* to
1Co 15:50 and blood is·not able to·inherit God's kingdom;
2Co 1:1 ·ambassador of·Jesus Anointed through God's will,
2Co 1:1 To·the Called·Out·citizenry of·God, the·one being
2Co 1:2 to·yeu, and peace, from God our Father and *from*
2Co 1:4 with·which we·ourselves are·comforted by God.
2Co 1:12 with fidelity and sincerity before·God (not with
2Co 1:12 fleshly wisdom, but·rather by God's grace), we·
2Co 1:19 For the Son of·God, Jesus Anointed, the·one being·
2Co 1:20 For as·many·as *are* God's promises, in him *is* the
2Co 2:17 ·and·hustling the Redemptive-word of·God. But·
2Co 2:17 birthed·from·out of·God *being* directly·in·the·sight
2Co 2:17 ·God *being* directly·in·the·sight of·God, we·speak
2Co 3:3 but·rather with·*the*·Spirit of·the·living God, not on
2Co 3:5 but·rather our sufficiency *is* from·out of·God,
2Co 4:2 handling the Redemptive-word of·God with·guile,
2Co 4:2 man·of·clay's† conscience in·the·sight of·God.
2Co 4:4 ·the Anointed-One— who is 'God's derived·image.'
2Co 4:6 ·the absolute·knowledge of·the glory of·God in *the*
2Co 4:7 ·excellence of·the power may·be of·God, and not
2Co 4:15 ·thankfulness should·abound to the glory of·God.
2Co 5:1 we·have (from·out of·God) a·structure, a·home
2Co 5:18 all things *are* from·out of·God, the·one already·
2Co 5:20 on·behalf·of·Anointed-One, as God imploring *yeu*
2Co 5:21 we·ourselves may·become God's righteousness in
2Co 6:1 ·implore also *for* yeu to·accept the grace of·God—
2Co 6:4 ·commending ourselves as attendants of·God: in
2Co 6:7 by *the* Redemptive-word of·truth, by God's power,
2Co 6:16 mutual·compact has·a·temple of·God with idols?
2Co 6:16 ·yeurselves are a·temple of·the·living God, just·as
2Co 7:1 devoted·holiness in a·reverent·fear·and·awe of·God.
2Co 7:12 ·it to·become·apparent to yeu in·the·sight of·God.
2Co 8:1 we·make·known to·yeu the grace of·God, the·one
2Co 8:5 to·the Lord and *then* to·us through God's will,
2Co 9:14 ·account·of·the surpassing grace of·God upon yeu.
2Co 10:5 ·up against the absolute·knowledge of·God, and
2Co 11:2 I·am·jealous over·yeu with·a·jealousy of·God, for
2Co 11:7 I·proclaimed to·yeu the good·news of·God.
2Co 12:19 directly·in·the·sight of·God in Anointed-One, but
2Co 13:4 yet he·lives as·a·result of·God's power. For we·
2Co 13:4 together with·him as·a·result of·God's power for
2Co 13:14 Jesus Anointed, and the love of·God, and the
Eph 1:1 ·ambassador of·Jesus Anointed through God's will.
Eph 1:2 *be* to·yeu, and peace, from God our Father and *our*
Eph 2:8 birthed·from·out of·yeurselves; *it·is* God's present.
Eph 2:19 ·the holy·ones and *are* family·members of·God,
Eph 2:22 are·built·together for a·residence of·God in Spirit.
Eph 3:2 ·the estate·management of·the grace of·God, the·one
Eph 3:7 the voluntary·present of·the grace of·God, the·one
Eph 3:10 wisdom of·God may·be·made·known now to·the
Eph 3:19 ·filled to all the complete·fullness of·God.
Eph 4:13 ·and·full·knowledge of·the Son of·God, into a·
Eph 4:18 ·alienated from·the life-above of·God through the
Eph 4:30 do·not grieve the Holy Spirit of·God, by whom
Eph 5:1 Accordingly, become attentive·imitators of·God, as
Eph 5:5 in the kingdom of·the Anointed-One and of·God.
Eph 5:6 ·of these·things the wrath of·God comes upon the
Eph 5:21 to·one·another in a·reverent·fear·and·awe of·God.
Eph 6:6 doing the will of·God out of·a·soul's·desire
Eph 6:11 ·with the whole·armor of·God, particularly·for yeu
Eph 6:13 whole·armor of·God in·order·that yeu·may·be·able
Eph 6:17 dagger of·the Spirit, which is an·utterance of·God.
Eph 6:23 love with trust from Father God and *the* Lord Jesus
Col 1:1 ·ambassador of·Jesus Anointed through God's will,
Col 1:2 *be* to·yeu, and peace, from God our Father and *the*
Col 1:6 ·heard *it* and recognized the grace of·God in truth—
Col 1:10 and growing·up into the full·knowledge of·God,
Col 1:15 who is *the* derived·image of·the invisible God, *the*
Col 1:25 ·to the estate·management of·God, the·one being·
Col 1:25 to·completely·fulfill the Redemptive-word of·God,
Col 2:2 a·full·knowledge of·the Mystery of·God and Father,
Col 2:12 the trust of·the effective·work of·God, the·one
Col 2:19 ·knit·together with·the maturing·growth of·God.
Col 3:1 is sitting·down at the·right·hand of·God.
Col 3:6 ·account·of which·things the wrath of·God comes on
Col 3:12 Accordingly, as Selected-Ones of·God (holy and
Col 3:15 And let the peace of·God arbitrate in yeur hearts,
Col 4:11 coworkers for the kingdom of·God *are* the·ones
Col 4:12 ·been·completely·fulfilled in every will of·God.
Phm 1:3 to·yeu, and peace, from God our Father and *the*
1Ti 1:1 according·to a·full·appointment of·God our Savior,
1Ti 1:2 mercy, *and* peace from God our Father and Jesus
1Ti 1:4 speculations rather than God's estate·management,
1Ti 1:11 ·news of·the supremely·blessed God, with·which I·
1Ti 2:3 and fully·acceptable in·the·sight of·God our Savior,
1Ti 2:5 *there·is* one mediator *between* God and men·of·clay†
1Ti 3:5 ·he·take·care of·a·Called·Out·citizenry of·God?),
1Ti 3:15 ·necessary to·conduct·oneself among God's house,
1Ti 3:15 is a·Called·Out·citizenry of·the·living God, a·pillar
1Ti 4:4 Because every creature of·God *is* good, and not·
1Ti 4:5 it·is·made·holy through God's Redemptive-word and
1Ti 5:4 that is good and fully·acceptable in·the·sight of·God.
1Ti 5:21 I·thoroughly·urge *you* in·the·sight of·God, and of·
1Ti 6:1 in·order·that the name of·God and the instruction
1Ti 6:11 you, O clay·man† of·God, flee from·these·things,
1Ti 6:13 I·charge you in·the·sight of·God (the·one giving·
2Ti 1:1 an·ambassador of·Jesus Anointed through God's will,
2Ti 1:2 peace, from Father God and Anointed-One Jesus our
2Ti 1:6 you to·rekindle the gracious·bestowment of·God,
2Ti 1:8 in·the good·news according·to God's power;
2Ti 2:9 ·yet the Redemptive-word of·God has·not been·bound.
2Ti 2:19 ·in·fact, the solid foundation of·God stands, having
2Ti 3:17 ·that the clay·man† of·God may·be fully·developed,
2Ti 4:1 thoroughly·urge *you* in·the·sight of·God and the
1Jn 2:5 the love of·God has·been·made·completely·mature.
1Jn 2:14 and the Redemptive-word of·God abides in yeu, and
1Jn 2:17 but the·one doing the will of·God abides into the
1Jn 3:1 we·should·be·called children of·God. On·account·of
1Jn 3:2 Beloved, now we·are children of·God, and it·is·not·
1Jn 3:8 *·purpose* the Son of·God was·made·apparent: that
1Jn 3:9 having·been·born from·out of·God does·not commit
1Jn 3:9 ·fail, because he·has·been·born from·out of·God.
1Jn 3:10 In this the children of·God are apparent, also the
1Jn 3:10 righteousness is not birthed·from·out of·God, also
1Jn 3:17 how·does the love of·God presently·abide in him?
1Jn 4:1 spirits whether they·are from·out of·God, because
1Jn 4:2 By this yeu·presently·know the Spirit of·God: every
1Jn 4:2 Anointed having·come in flesh is from·out of·God.
1Jn 4:3 in flesh is not from·out of·God. And that·thing is the
1Jn 4:4 are birthed·from·out of·God, dear·children, and have·
1Jn 4:6 We·ourselves are birthed·from·out of·God. The·one
1Jn 4:6 is not birthed·from·out of·God does·not hear us.
1Jn 4:7 because the love is birthed·from·out of·God; and any
1Jn 4:7 has·been·born from·out of·God and presently·knows
1Jn 4:9 In this, the love of·God is·made·apparent among us,
1Jn 4:15 ·affirm that Jesus is the Son of·God, God abides in
1Jn 5:1 Anointed-One has·been·born from·out of·God; and
1Jn 5:2 that we·love the children of·God, whenever we·love
1Jn 5:3 this is the love of·God, that we·should·observantly·
1Jn 5:4 having·been·born from·out of·God overcomes the
1Jn 5:5 if·not the·one trusting that Jesus is the Son of·God?
1Jn 5:9 of·men·of·clay†, the testimony of·God is greater,
1Jn 5:9 this is the testimony of·God which he·has·testified
1Jn 5:10 ·one trusting in the Son of·God has the testimony in
1Jn 5:12 ·one not having the Son of·God does·not have the

1Jn 5:13 the name of·the Son of·God, in·order·that yeu·may·
1Jn 5:13 ·that yeu·may·trust in the name of the Son of·God.
1Jn 5:18 ·been·born from·out of·God does·not morally·fail,
1Jn 5:18 ·being·begotten from·out of·God guards himself,
1Jn 5:19 ·know that we·are birthed·from·out of·God, and the
1Jn 5:20 we·personally·know that the Son of·God comes,
2Jn 1:3 peace, personally·from Father God, and personally·
3Jn 1:6 ·onward·on·their·journey, as·is·worthy of·God, *then*
3Jn 1:11 beneficially·doing·good is from·out of·God, but
Rv 1:2 who testified·to the Redemptive-word of·God, and *to*
Rv 1:9 on·account·of the Redemptive-word of·God, and on·
Rv 2:7 which is in *the* midst of·the paradise of·God.'"
Rv 2:18 'These·things says the Son of·God, the·one having
Rv 3:1 says the·one having the Spirits of·God and the seven
Rv 3:2 having·been·completely·fulfilled in·the·sight of·God.
Rv 3:12 ·make a·pillar in the Temple of·my God, and no, he·
Rv 3:12 ·write upon him the name of·my God, and the name
Rv 3:12 the name of·the CITY of·my God, the brand-new
Rv 3:12 descending out of·the heaven from my God. 'And *I*·
Rv 3:14 true witness, the beginning of·the creation of·God:
Rv 4:5 of·the throne, which are the seven Spirits of·God.
Rv 5:6 the seven Spirits of·God having·been·dispatched into
Rv 6:9 on·account·of the Redemptive-word of·God, and on·
Rv 7:2 having an·official·seal of·the·living God, and he·
Rv 7:3 ·should·officially·seal the slaves of·our God in their
Rv 7:10 "The Salvation of·our God! To·the·one who·is·
Rv 7:15 ·the·sight of·the throne of·God and ritually·minister
Rv 8:2 angels who stand in·the·sight of·God; and to·them
Rv 8:4 ·ones, ascended in·the·sight of·God from·out of·the
Rv 9:4 ·not have the official·seal of·God in their foreheads.
Rv 9:13 golden Sacrifice·Altar, the·one in·the·sight of·God,
Rv 10:7 even the Mystery of·God should·be·finished, as he·
Rv 11:1 ·yourself and measure the Temple of·God, and the
Rv 11:4 standing in·the·sight of·the God of·the earth.
Rv 11:11 Spirit of·life-above from·out of·God came·in upon
Rv 11:16 the·ones sitting·down in·the·sight of·God on their
Rv 11:19 And the Temple of·God was·opened·up in the
Rv 12:6 ·has a·place having·been·made·ready by God, that
Rv 12:10 and the kingdom of·our God, and the authority of·
Rv 12:10 ·accusing them in·the·sight of·our God day and
Rv 12:17 ·keeping the commandments of·God and having
Rv 14:5 without·blemish in·the·sight of·the throne of·God.
Rv 14:10 of·the wine of·the Rage of·God, the·one having·
Rv 14:12 ·keeping the commandments of·God and the trust
Rv 14:19 cast *it* into the great winepress of·the Rage of·God.
Rv 15:1 because in them the Rage of·God is·completed.
Rv 15:2 on the transparent,·glassy sea, having harps of·God.
Rv 15:3 the song of·Moses, a·slave of·God, and the song
Rv 15:7 vials overflowing of·the Rage of·God, the·one living
Rv 15:8 with·smoke from·among the glory of·God and out
Rv 16:1 pour·out the vials of·the Rage of·God into the earth.
Rv 16:9 and they·reviled the name of·God— the·one having
Rv 16:14 to the battle of·that great day of·God Almighty.
Rv 16:19 was·recalled·to·mind in·the·sight of·God, to·give
Rv 17:17 ·until the utterances of·God should·be·completed.
Rv 19:9 "These are the true sayings of·God."
Rv 19:13 ·blood, and his name is·called The Word of·God.
Rv 19:15 wine of·the Rage and the Wrath of·God Almighty.
Rv 19:17 ·gathered·together for the supper of·the great God,
Rv 20:4 and on·account·of the Redemptive-word of·God, and
Rv 20:6 they·shall·be priests of·God and of·Anointed-One
Rv 20:9 And fire descended from God out of·the heaven and
Rv 20:12 great, standing in·the·sight of·God, and official·
Rv 21:2 JeruSalem, descending from God out of·the heaven,
Rv 21:3 Behold, the Tabernacle of·God *is* with the men·of·
Rv 21:10 descending out of·the heaven from God,
Rv 21:11 having the glory of·God (even her brilliance *was*
Rv 21:23 in it, for the glory of·God illuminated it, and the
Rv 22:1 proceeding·forth out of·the throne of·God and of·the
Rv 22:3 ·destruction, but the throne of·God and of·the Lamb

G2316.2 N/P-GSM θεοῦ (2x)

Rm 6:23 but the gracious·bestowment of·God *is* eternal
Rm 7:25 mind, I myself am·a·slave·to God's Royal-Law, but

EG2316.2 (34x)

Jn 8:42 of my·own·self, but·rather that *God* dispatched me.
Lk 2:37 ritually·ministering *to·God* with·fastings and
Lk 11:51 the Sacrifice·Altar and the house *of·God*. Yes, I·say
Ac 7:4 his father died, *God* transferred·and·settled him into
Ac 10:36 The Word which *God* dispatched to·the Sons of·
Ac 15:3 the turning·back·around of·the Gentiles *to God*. And
Ac 17:23 *him*, I·myself fully·proclaim this *God* to·yeu.
Ac 19:9 *the·things of·the kingdom of·God* each day in the
Ac 26:7 while·ritually·ministering *to·God* night and day,
Heb 2:8 not·even·one·thing did *God* leave unsubjugated to·
Heb 2:10 For it·was·befitting·for *Father God* (on·account·of
Heb 9:1 regulations of·ritual·ministry *to·God*, and·also the
Mt 16:22 him, saying, "*God* be·favorable·to·you, Lord.
Rm 3:26 *Jesus*, and *with·God* regarding·as·righteous the·one
Rm 4:11 father of·all the·ones trusting *God* through *the state*·
Rm 4:21 ·being·fully·assured that, what *God* has·promised,
Rm 4:21 what *God* has·promised, *God* was able also to·do.
Rm 9:4 ·Torah-Law, and the ritual·ministry *to·God*, and the
Rm 12:19 yeu·must·give place to·the wrath *of·God*, for it·
Jac 5:16 and well-wish *to·God* on·behalf of·one·another,
1Co 1:30 But *being* birthed·from·out of *God*, yeu are in
1Co 9:17 an·estate·management *of·the grace of·God* has *still*
1Co 14:33 For God is·not *the God* of·chaos, but·rather of·
1Co 15:27 For *God* '" subjugated all·things under his feet."'
1Co 15:27 ' But inasmuch·as *God* should·declare that "all·
Eph 2:6 And *God* awakened·*us*·together and sat·*us*·down·
Col 1:19 all the complete·fullness *of·God Most·High* takes·
1Jn 3:16 this we·have·known the love *of·God*, because that·
1Jn 3:24 his commandments presently·abides in *God*, and
1Jn 3:24 presently·abides in God, and *God* in him. And by
1Jn 5:1 ·God; and every one loving *God*, the·one begetting,
1Jn 5:10 ·one not trusting God has·made *God* himself a·liar,
1Jn 5:16 death, he·shall·request, and *God* shall·give to·him
3Jn 1:2 ·man, I·well-wish *to·God* concerning all·things,

G2316.4 N-NSM ΘΕός (1x)

Rm 11:8 just·as it·has·been·written, "GOD gave them a·

G2317 θεο•σέβεια thêôsébêia *n.* (1x)

Roots:G2318 Compare:G2124

G2317 N-ASF θεοσέβειαν (1x)

1Ti 2:10 ·are·making·a·profession·of a·reverence·of·God).

G2318 θεο•σεβής thêôsêbḗs *adj.* (1x)

Roots:G2316 G4576

G2318 A-NSM θεοσεβής (1x)

Jn 9:31 but·rather if any·man may·be reverent·of·God, and

G2319 θεο•στυγής thêôstygḗs *adj.* (1x)

Roots:G2316 G4767

G2319 A-APM θεοστυγεῖς (1x)

Rm 1:30 backbiters, detesters·of·God, abusively·insolent,

G2320 θεότης thêótēs *n.* (1x)

Roots:G2316 See:G2305

G2320 N-GSF θεότητος (1x)

Col 2:9 all the complete·fullness of·Godhood resides bodily.

G2321 Θεό•φιλος Thêóphilôs *n/p.* (2x)

Roots:G2316 G5384

G2321.2 N/P-VSM Θεόφιλε (2x)

Lk 1:3 in·consecutive·order, most·noble TheoPhilus,
Ac 1:1 ·fact, the first account I·made, O TheoPhilus, *was*

G2322 θεραπεία thêrapêía *n.* (4x)

Roots:G2323 See:G2324 G2395-1
xLangEquiv:H8644

G2322.2 N-ASF θεραπείαν (1x)

Rv 22:2 for *the* therapeutic·relief·and·cure of·the nations.

G2322.2 N-GSF θεραπείας (1x)

Lk 9:11 the·ones having need of·therapeutic·relief·and·cure.

G2322.3 N-GSF θεραπείας (2x)

Lk 12:42 shall·fully·establish over his domestic·staff, to·give
Mt 24:45 fully·established over his domestic·staff, to·give

G2323 θεραπεύω thêrapêúō *v.* (44x)

Roots:G2330-1 Compare:G2390 See:G2322 G2324
xLangAlso:H7495

G2323.1 V-PPI-3S θεραπεύεται (1x)

Ac 17:25 nor·even is·waited·upon by *the* hands of·men·of·

G2323.3 V-FAI-1S θεραπεύσω (1x)

Mt 8:7 *to·him*, I·myself shall·both·relieve·and·cure him."

G2323.3 V-FAI-3S θεραπεύσει (2x)

Lk 6:7 him, whether he·shall·both·relieve·and·cure on the
Mk 3:2 whether he·shall·both·relieve·and·cure him on·the

G2323.3 V-PAM-2P θεραπεύετε (2x)

Lk 10:9 And both·relieve·and·cure the sick in it, and say to·
Mt 10:8 Both·relieve·and·cure the·sick; purify lepers;

G2323.3 V-PAN θεραπεύειν (5x)

Lk 9:1 the demons, and to·both·relieve·and·cure illnesses.
Lk 14:3 Is·it·proper to·both·relieve·and·cure on·the Sabbath
Mt 10:1 ·cast·out and to·both·relieve·and·cure every illness
Mt 12:10 "Is·it·proper to·both·relieve·and·cure on·the
Mk 3:15 authority to·both·relieve·and·cure the illnesses, and

G2323.3 V-PAP-NSM θεραπεύων (2x)

Mt 4:23 and·also both·relieving·and·curing every illness
Mt 9:35 and both·relieving·and·curing every illness and

G2323.3 V-PAP-NPM θεραπεύοντες (1x)

Lk 9:6 ·news, and both·relieving·and·curing everywhere.

G2323.3 V-PPM-2P θεραπεύεσθε (1x)

Lk 13:14 on those *days*, be·both·relieved·and·cured, and not

G2323.3 V-PPN θεραπεύεσθαι (1x)

Lk 5:15 *him*, and to·be·both·relieved·and·cured by him of

G2323.3 V-IAI-3P ἐθεράπευον (1x)

Mk 6:13 and were·both·relieving·and·curing *them*.

G2323.3 V-IPI-3P ἐθεραπεύοντο (3x)

Lk 6:18 spirits. And they·were·both·relieved·and·cured.
Ac 5:16 the·very·same·ones were·both·relieved·and·cured,
Ac 28:9 ·alongside, and they·were·both·relieved·and·cured;

G2323.3 V-AAI-3S ἐθεράπευσεν (14x)

Lk 4:40 one of·them, he·both·relieved·and·cured them.
Lk 7:21 same hour he·both·relieved·and·cured many from
Lk 13:14 Jesus both·relieved·and·cured on·the Sabbath, was·
Mt 4:24 ·paralyzed. And he·both·relieved·and·cured them.
Mt 8:16 ·a·word and both·relieved·and·cured all the·ones
Mt 12:15 him, and he·both·relieved·and·cured them all.
Mt 12:22 and mute, and he·both·relieved·and·cured him,
Mt 14:14 and he·both·relieved·and·cured the unhealthy·ones
Mt 15:30 of·YeShua. And he·both·relieved·and·cured them,
Mt 19:2 him, and he·both·relieved·and·cured them there.
Mt 21:14 ·Atrium, and he·both·relieved·and·cured them.
Mk 1:34 And he·both·relieved·and·cured many being badly·
Mk 3:10 For he·both·relieved·and·cured many, such·for as·
Mk 6:5 unhealthy·ones *whom* he·both·relieved·and·cured.

G2323.3 V-AAM-2S θεράπευσον (1x)

Lk 4:23 ·of·Healing, bring·both·relief·and·cure·to yourself.

G2323.3 V-API-3S ἐθεραπεύθη (3x)

Mt 17:18 boy was·both·relieved·and·cured from that·very
Rv 13:3 and its deadly gash was·both·relieved·and·cured.
Rv 13:12 own deadly gash was·both·relieved·and·cured.

G2323.3 V-API-3P ἐθεραπεύθησαν (1x)

Ac 8:7 ·paralyzed and lame were·both·relieved·and·cured.

G2323.3 V-RPP-ASM τεθεραπευμένον (1x)

Ac 4:14 the·one having·been·both·relieved·and·cured

G2323.3 V-RPP-DSM τεθεραπευμένῳ (1x)

Jn 5:10 to·the·one having·been·both·relieved·and·cured, "It·

G2323.3 V-RPP-NPF τεθεραπευμέναι (1x)

Lk 8:2 were having·been·both·relieved·and·cured from evil

G2323.4 V-AAN θεραπεῦσαι (1x)

Mt 17:16 they·were·not able to·cure·or·bring·relief·to him."

G2323.4 V-APN θεραπευθῆναι (1x)

Lk 8:43 neither could be·cured·or·brought·relief, by not·

G2324 θεράπων thêrápōn *n.* (1x)

Roots:G2330 Compare:G5256 See:G2322 G2323

G2324.2 N-NSM θεράπων (1x)

Heb 3:5 his house as a·domestic·attendant (for a·testimony

G2325 θερίζω thêrízō *v.* (21x)

Roots:G2330 Compare:G0270 See:G2326 G2327
G2325-1

G2325 V-FAI-1P θερίσομεν (2x)

Gal 6:9 for in·due season we·shall·reap, not being·faint.
1Co 9:11 if we·ourselves shall·reap yeur fleshly·things?

G2325 V-FAI-3S θερίσει (5x)
Gal 6:7 a·man·of·clay† should·sow, that also shall·he·reap.
Gal 6:8 into his flesh, shall·reap corruption from·out·of·the
Gal 6:8 into the Spirit, shall·reap eternal life-above from·out
2Co 9:6 sowing sparingly also shall·reap sparingly, and the·
2Co 9:6 ·blessings also shall·reap in beneficial·blessings.
G2325 V-PAI-1S θερίζω (1x)
Mt 25:26 ·had·personally·known that I·reap where I·did·not
G2325 V-PAI-2S θερίζεις (1x)
Lk 19:21 you·did·not lay·down, and reap what you·did·not
G2325 V-PAI-3P θερίζουσιν (2x)
Lk 12:24 they·do·not sow nor·even do·they·reap. For·such
Mt 6:26 they·do·not sow, neither do·they·reap, nor·even do·
G2325 V-PAN θερίζειν (1x)
Jn 4:38 "I·myself dispatched yeu to·reap *that·for* which yeu·
G2325 V-PAP-NSM θερίζων (5x)
Jn 4:36 "And the·one reaping receives payment·of·service
Jn 4:36 and the·one reaping may·rejoice at·the·same·time.
Jn 4:37 is the·one sowing, and another *is* the·one reaping.'
Lk 19:22 I·did·not lay·down, and reaping what I·did·not
Mt 25:24 a·hard man·of·clay†, reaping where you·did·not
G2325 V-AAM-2S θέρισον (1x)
Rv 14:15 "Thrust·in your sickle and reap, because the hour
G2325 V-AAN θερίσαι (1x)
Rv 14:15 the hour is·come for·you to·reap, because the
G2325 V-AAP-GPM θερισάντων (1x)
Jac 5:4 And the outcries of·the·ones reaping have·entered
G2325 V-API-3S ἐθερίσθη (1x)
Rv 14:16 his sickle on the earth, and the earth was·reaped.

G2326 θερισμός thērismós *n.* (13x)
Roots:G2325 Compare:G5166-2 G0281-1 See:G2327 G2325-1 xLangAlso:H7105
G2326.1 N-NSM θερισμός (6x)
Jn 4:35 yet four·lunar·months, and *then* comes the harvest'?
Lk 10:2 "In·fact, the harvest *is* large, but the workmen *are*
Mt 9:37 "In·fact, the harvest *is* large, but the workmen *are*
Mt 13:39 the Slanderer. The harvest is *the* entire·completion
Mk 4:29 the sickle, because the harvest has·presented *itself*."
Rv 14:15 for·you to·reap, because the harvest of·the earth
G2326.1 N-ASM θερισμόν (3x)
Jn 4:35 because they·are white even·now unto harvest.
Lk 10:2 that he·should·cast·forth workmen into his harvest.
Mt 9:38 that he·should·cast·forth workmen into his harvest."
G2326.1 N-GSM θερισμοῦ (4x)
Lk 10:2 petition the Lord of·the harvest, that he·should·cast·
Mt 9:38 petition the Lord of·the harvest, that he·should·cast·
Mt 13:30 ·grown·together so·long·as·unto the harvest, and in
Mt 13:30 in the season of·the harvest, I·shall·declare to·the

G2327 θεριστής thēristḗs *n.* (2x)
Roots:G2325 See:G2326 G2325-1
G2327 N-NPM θερισταί (1x)
Mt 13:39 ·completion of·the age, and the reapers are angels.
G2327 N-DPM θερισταῖς (1x)
Mt 13:30 harvest, I·shall·declare to·the reapers, "Collect the

G2328 θερμαίνω thērmaínō *v.* (6x)
Roots:G2329 See:G2330
G2328.2 V-PEM-2P θερμαίνεσθε (1x)
Jac 2:16 ·out in peace, be·yeu·warmed and be·stuffed·full,"
G2328.2 V-PMP-ASM θερμαινόμενον (1x)
Mk 14:67 Peter warming·himself, after·looking·clearly·at
G2328.2 V-PMP-NSM θερμαινόμενος (3x)
Jn 18:18 was standing with them, also warming·himself.
Jn 18:25 was standing·by and warming·himself. So·then
Mk 14:54 the assistants and warming·himself alongside the
G2328.2 V-INI-3P ἐθερμαίνοντο (1x)
Jn 18:18 cold, and they·were·warming·themselves. And

G2329 θέρμη thérmē *n.* (1x)
Roots:G2330-1 Compare:G2330 See:G2328 G2329-1 G2328-1
G2329 N-GSF θέρμης (1x)
Ac 28:3 coming·forth out of·the warmth, fully·fastened·onto

G2330 θέρος thérôs *n.* (3x)
Roots:G2330-1 Compare:G2329 G2329-1
G2330.2 N-NSN θέρος (3x)
Lk 21:30 by yeur·own·selves that the summer is even·now
Mt 24:32 the leaves, yeu·know that the summer *is* near.
Mk 13:28 the leaves, yeu·know that the summer is near.

G2331 Θεσσαλο•νικεύς Thêssalônikêús *n/g.* (4x)
Roots:G2332
G2331.1 N/G-GPM Θεσσαλονικέων (2x)
1Th 1:1 Called·Out·citizenry of·the·ThessaloNicans *which·is*
2Th 1:1 Called·Out·citizenry of·the·ThessaloNicans in God
G2331.2 N/G-GSM Θεσσαλονικέως (1x)
Ac 27:2 ·AristArchus (a·Macedonian of·ThessaloNica) being
G2331.2 N/G-GPM Θεσσαλονικέων (1x)
Ac 20:4 AristArchus and Secundus of·ThessaloNica, and

G2332 Θεσσαλο•νίκη Thêssalôníkē *n/l.* (5x)
Roots:G3529 See:G2331 G3109
G2332.2 N/L-ASF Θεσσαλονίκην (2x)
Ac 17:1 Apollonia, they·came to ThessaloNica where the
2Ti 4:10 age, and he·departed to ThessaloNica, Crescens to
G2332.2 N/L-DSF Θεσσαλονίκῃ (2x)
Ac 17:11 more·noble·than the·ones in ThessaloNica— *it·was*
Php 4:16 Because even in ThessaloNica yeu·sent also once
G2332.2 N/L-GSF Θεσσαλονίκης (1x)
Ac 17:13 as·soon·as the Jews from ThessaloNica knew that

G2333 Θευδᾶς Thêudâs *n/p.* (1x)
G2333 N/P-NSM Θευδᾶς (1x)
Ac 5:36 For before these days, Theudas rose·up, saying

G2334 θεωρέω thēōréō *v.* (57x)
Roots:G2300 G3708 Compare:G3700 G1492 See:G2335 G5084 G5083
G2334 V-PAI-1S θεωρῶ (4x)
Jn 4:19 says to·him, "Sir, I·observe that you·yourself are a·
Ac 7:56 "Behold, I·observe the heavens having·been·
Ac 17:22 "Men, Athenians, I·observe how in all·things yeu
Ac 27:10 to·them, "Men, I·observe that the impending
G2334 V-PAI-2S θεωρεῖς (1x)
Ac 21:20 they·declared to·him, "Do·you·observe, brother,
G2334 V-PAI-2P θεωρεῖτε (9x)
Jn 14:19 no longer, but yeu·yeurselves observe me. Because
Jn 16:10 toward my Father, and yeu·observe me no longer;
Jn 16:16 "A·little·while, and yeu·do·not observe me, and
Jn 16:17 'A·little·while, and yeu·do·not observe me, and
Jn 16:19 'A·little·while, and yeu·do·not observe me, and
Lk 21:6 "*As·for* these·things which yeu·observe, days shall·
Lk 24:39 flesh and bones, just·as yeu·observe me having."
Ac 3:16 this·man whom yeu·observe and personally·know.
Ac 19:26 Also, yeu·hear and observe that not merely at·
G2334 V-PAI-3S θεωρεῖ (9x)
Jn 10:12 *even* his·own sheep, he·observes the wolf coming
Jn 12:45 the·one observing me observes the·one sending me.
Jn 14:17 to·receive, because it·does·not observe him, nor·
Jn 14:19 a·little·while, and the world observes me no longer,
Jn 20:6 chamber·tomb. And he·observes the strips·of·linen
Jn 20:12 and she·observes two angels in white sitting·down,
Jn 20:14 left·behind. And she·observes Jesus standing *there*,
Ac 10:11 Then he·observed the heaven having·been·opened·
Mk 5:38 ·of·the·gathering and observes a·commotion,
G2334 V-PAI-3P θεωροῦσιν (3x)
Jn 6:19 thirty stadia, they·observe Jesus walking·along on
Mk 5:15 they·come to Jesus and observe the·one *formerly*
Mk 16:4 And upon·looking·up, they·observed that the stone
G2334 V-PAM-2P θεωρεῖτε (3x)
Jn 12:19 among themselves, "Observe how yeu·do·not
Ac 25:24 being·present·together with·us, observe this·man,
Heb 7:4 Now observe what·stature this·man *was*, to·whom
G2334 V-PAN θεωρεῖν (2x)
Lk 24:37 alarmed, they·were·supposing to·observe a·spirit.
Ac 20:38 no·longer would·they·*be·able* to·observe his face.
G2334 V-PAP-APM θεωροῦντας (1x)
Rv 11:11 and great fear fell upon the·ones observing them.
G2334 V-PAP-DSM θεωροῦντι (1x)
Ac 17:16 ·provoked within himself, upon·observing the city
G2334 V-PAP-GPM θεωρούντων (1x)
Ac 28:6 and observing not·even·one·thing out·of·place
G2334 V-PAP-NSM θεωρῶν (4x)
Jn 6:40 me, that anyone, the·one observing the Son, and
Jn 12:45 And the·one observing me observes the·one
Lk 23:35 And the people stood *there* observing. And the
Ac 8:13 *And* he·was·astonished upon·observing both signs
G2334 V-PAP-NPF θεωροῦσαι (2x)
Mt 27:55 many women were there observing from a·distance
Mk 15:40 there·were also women observing from a·distance,
G2334 V-PAP-NPM θεωροῦντες (6x)
Jn 2:23 in his name, observing his miraculous·signs which
Jn 9:8 ·neighbors (and the·ones observing him previously
Lk 14:29 *it*, all the·ones observing *it* may·begin to·mock
Lk 23:48 distinct·spectacle, observing the·things happening,
Ac 4:13 Now observing the clarity·of·speech of·Peter and
Ac 9:7 the sound·of·the·voice, but observing no·one.
G2334 V-PAS-2P θεωρῆτε (1x)
Jn 6:62 So·then, *what* if yeu·should·observe the Son of·
G2334 V-PAS-3S θεωρῇ (1x)
1Jn 3:17 and should·presently·observe his brother having
G2334 V-PAS-3P θεωρῶσιν (1x)
Jn 17:24 I AM, in·order·that they·may·observe my glory,
G2334 V-IAI-1P ἐθεώρουν (1x)
Lk 10:18 to·them, "I·was·observing the Adversary-Accuser
G2334 V-IAI-3S ἐθεώρει (2x)
Mk 3:11 impure spirits, whenever one·was·observing him,
Mk 12:41 the treasury·room, Jesus was·observing how the
G2334 V-IAI-3P ἐθεώρουν (1x)
Mk 15:47 ·nearby, were·observing *where* he·was·laid.
G2334 V-AAI-3P ἐθεώρησαν (1x)
Rv 11:12 the thick·cloud, and their enemies observed them.
G2334 V-AAN θεωρῆσαι (1x)
Mt 28:1 and the other Mariam came to·observe the grave.
G2334 V-AAS-3S θεωρήσῃ (1x)
Jn 8:51 no, he·should·not observe death into the coming·age
G2334 V-AAS-3P θεωρήσωσιν (1x)
Jn 7:3 that your disciples also may·observe the works that

G2335 θεωρία thēōría *n.* (1x)
Roots:G2334 Compare:G2302 G0990
G2335.2 N-ASF θεωρίαν (1x)
Lk 23:48 ·publicly upon that distinct·spectacle, observing

G2336 θήκη thḗkē *n.* (1x)
Roots:G5087
G2336 N-ASF θήκην (1x)
Jn 18:11 "Cast your dagger into the sheath! The cup which

G2337 θηλάζω thēlázō *v.* (6x)
Roots:G2337-1 See:G2338
G2337.1 V-AAI-2S ἐθήλασας (1x)
Lk 11:27 bearing you, and *the* breasts which nursed *you*."
G2337.1 V-AAI-3P ἐθήλασαν (1x)
Lk 23:29 did·not bear, and *the* breasts which did·not nurse.'
G2337.3 V-PAP-GPM θηλαζόντων (1x)
Mt 21:16 and sucklings you·completely·formed strong·praise
G2337.4 V-PAP-DPF θηλαζούσαις (3x)
Lk 21:23 pregnancy and to·the·ones nursing·infants in those
Mt 24:19 pregnancy and to·the·ones nursing·infants in those
Mk 13:17 pregnancy and to·the·ones nursing·infants in those

G2338 θῆλυς thēlys *adj.* (5x)
Roots:G2337-1 Compare:G0730 See:G2337 G2337-2 xLangEquiv:H5347
G2338 A-NSN θῆλυ (1x)
Gal 3:28 there·is·not therein male and female, for yeu are
G2338 A-NPF θήλειαι (1x)
Rm 1:26 for even their females exchanged the natural
G2338 A-ASN θῆλυ (2x)
Mt 19:4 from *the* beginning "made them male and female,"
Mk 10:6 beginning, God " made them male and female."
G2338 A-GSF θηλείας (1x)
Rm 1:27 sexual·intercourse of·the female, are·inflamed in

G2339 θήρα thḗra *n.* (1x)
See:G2340
G2339.2 N-ASF θήραν (1x)
Rm 11:9 into a·snare, and into a·hunting·pit, and into a·trap,

G2340 θηρεύω thērěúō *v.* (1x)
Roots:G2339
G2340.1 V-AAN θηρεῦσαι (1x)
Lk 11:54 him, and seeking to·hunt·for something from·out

G2341 θηριο•μαχέω thēriômachéō *v.* (1x)
Roots:G2342 G3164
G2341.1 V-AAI-1S ἐθηριομάχησα (1x)
1Co 15:32 ·of·clay†, I·fought·with·wild·beasts at Ephesus,

G2342 θηρίον thēríôn *n.* (46x)
Roots:G2444-3 Compare:G2934 G2447 G1404 G5578 See:G2339
xLangEquiv:H2416 A2423
G2342.1 N-NSN θηρίον (1x)
Heb 12:20 "If·even a·wild·beast should·lay·a·finger·on the
G2342.1 N-NPN θηρία (2x)
Ac 10:12 earth were·subsisting, and the wild·beasts, and the
Tit 1:12 *are* always liars, wicked wild·beasts, lazy gluttons.
G2342.1 N-APN θηρία (1x)
Ac 11:6 of·the earth, and the wild·beasts, and the creeping·
G2342.1 N-GPN θηρίων (3x)
Mk 1:13 And he·was with the wild·beasts, and the angels
Jac 3:7 For every species of·wild·beasts, also of·birds, and
Rv 6:8 with viral·death, and by the wild·beasts of·the earth.
G2342.2 N-ASN θηρίον (2x)
Ac 28:4 barbarians saw the venomous·beast hanging out·from
Ac 28:5 in·fact, after·jostling·off the venomous·beast into the
G2342.3 N-ASN θηρίον (1x)
Rv 17:3 who·is·sitting·down upon a·scarlet demonic·beast,
G2342.4 N-NSN θηρίον (1x)
Rv 11:7 ·finish their testimony, the Abysmal·Beast (the·one
G2342.5 N-NSN θηρίον (3x)
Rv 13:2 And the Daemonic·Beast which I·saw was like a·
Rv 19:20 And the Daemonic·Beast was·apprehended, and
Rv 20:10 sulfur, where the Daemonic·Beast and the Fiendish·
G2342.5 N-ASN θηρίον (6x)
Rv 13:1 sea, and I·saw a·Daemonic·Beast ascending out of·
Rv 13:4 ·prostrate *directly·before* the Daemonic·Beast, saying,
Rv 13:12 *directly·before* the first Daemonic·Beast, whose own
Rv 14:9 ·prostrate *directly·before* the Daemonic·Beast and its
Rv 14:11 *directly·before* the Daemonic·Beast and its derived·
Rv 19:19 And I·saw the Daemonic·Beast, and the kings of·the
G2342.5 N-DSN θηρίῳ (4x)
Rv 13:4 which gave authority to·the Daemonic·Beast, and
Rv 13:4 "Who *is* like the Daemonic·Beast? Who is·able to·
Rv 13:14 a·derived·image for·the Daemonic·Beast, which has
Rv 20:4 did·not fall·prostrate to·the Daemonic·Beast nor his
G2342.5 N-GSN θηρίου (13x)
Rv 13:3 *which·fell·in line* right·behind the Daemonic·Beast.
Rv 13:12 of·the first Daemonic·Beast in·the·sight of·it, and it·
Rv 13:14 to·do in·the·sight of·the Daemonic·Beast, saying to·
Rv 13:15 to·the derived·image of·the Daemonic·Beast, that
Rv 13:15 derived·image of·the Daemonic·Beast should·speak,
Rv 13:15 of·the Daemonic·Beast that they·should·be·killed.
Rv 13:17 or the name of·the Daemonic·Beast, or the number
Rv 13:18 ·calculate the number of·the Daemonic·Beast, for it·
Rv 15:2 (out·from·among the Daemonic·Beast, and out·from·
Rv 16:2 having the etching of·the Daemonic·Beast, and *upon*
Rv 16:10 vial upon the throne of·the Daemonic·Beast, and his
Rv 16:13 out of·the mouth of·the Daemonic·Beast, and out of·
Rv 19:20 receiving the etching of·the Daemonic·Beast, and
G2342.6 N-ASN θηρίον (1x)
Rv 13:11 And I·saw another Fiendish·Beast ascending out
G2342.7 N-NSN θηρίον (2x)
Rv 17:8 *The* Scarlet·Beast that you·saw, it·was and is not.
Rv 17:11 And the Scarlet·Beast that was and is not, even it·
G2342.7 N-ASN θηρίον (2x)
Rv 17:8 conception, looking·upon the Scarlet·Beast that was,
Rv 17:16 which you·saw upon the Scarlet·Beast, these shall·
G2342.7 N-DSN θηρίῳ (2x)
Rv 17:13 their·own power and authority to·the Scarlet·Beast.
Rv 17:17 ·give their kingdom to·the Scarlet·Beast, even·until
G2342.7 N-GSN θηρίου (2x)
Rv 17:7 of·the woman, and of·the Scarlet·Beast bearing her,
Rv 17:12 as kings *for* one hour with the Scarlet·Beast.

G2343 θησαυρίζω thēsaurízō *v.* (8x)
Roots:G2344 Compare:G2698 See:G0597
xLangAlso:H0686
G2343.1 V-PAP-NSM θησαυρίζων (1x)
Lk 12:21 ·manner *is* the·one storing·up·treasure for·himself,
G2343.1 V-AAI-2P ἐθησαυρίσατε (1x)
Jac 5:3 flesh as fire. Yeu·stored·up·treasure in *the* last days.
G2343.2 V-PAI-2S θησαυρίζεις (1x)
Rm 2:5 unrepentant heart, you·store·up Wrath for·yourself
G2343.2 V-PAM-2P θησαυρίζετε (2x)
Mt 6:19 "Do·not store·up for·yeurselves treasures upon the
Mt 6:20 But store·up for·yeurselves treasures in heaven,
G2343.2 V-PAN θησαυρίζειν (1x)
2Co 12:14 are·not obligated to·store·up for·the parents, but·
G2343.2 V-PAP-NSM θησαυρίζων (1x)
1Co 16:2 *aside* personally·from himself, storing·up as he·
G2343.2 V-RPP-NPM τεθησαυρισμένοι (1x)
2Pe 3:7 the earth are having·been·stored·up, being·reserved

G2344 θησαυρός thēsaurós *n.* (18x)
Roots:G5087 Compare:G1047 See:G2343
xLangAlso:H1595
G2344 N-NSM θησαυρός (2x)
Lk 12:34 "For where yeur treasure is, there also yeur heart
Mt 6:21 For where yeur treasure is, there also yeur heart
G2344 N-NPM θησαυροί (1x)
Col 2:3 are hidden·away all the treasures of·Wisdom and
G2344 N-ASM θησαυρόν (5x)
Lk 12:33 *but ones·containing* an·inexhaustible treasure in the
Lk 18:22 ·poor, and you·shall·have treasure in heaven. And
Mt 19:21 ·poor, and you·shall·have treasure in heaven. And
Mk 10:21 ·poor, and you·shall·have treasure in heaven. And
2Co 4:7 But we·have this treasure in earthenware vessels, in·
G2344 N-APM θησαυρούς (3x)
Mt 2:11 after·opening·up their treasures, they·brought·forth
Mt 6:19 "Do·not store·up for·yeurselves treasures upon the
Mt 6:20 But store·up for·yeurselves treasures in heaven,
G2344 N-DSM θησαυρῷ (1x)
Mt 13:44 ·the heavens is like treasure having·been·hidden in
G2344 N-GSM θησαυροῦ (5x)
Lk 6:45 ·out of·the beneficially·good treasure of·his heart,
Lk 6:45 ·of·clay†, from·out of·the evil treasure of·his heart,
Mt 12:35 ·out of·the beneficially·good treasure of·his heart
Mt 12:35 from·out of·his evil treasure casts·forth evil·things.
Mt 13:52 who from·among his treasure casts·forth *things*
G2344 N-GPM θησαυρῶν (1x)
Heb 11:26 *to·be* greater wealth *than* the treasures in Egypt,

G2345 θιγγάνω thingánō *v.* (3x)
Roots:G2345-1 Compare:G0680 G5584
G2345.1 V-2AAS-2S θίγῃς (1x)
Col 2:21 ·you·taste, nor·even should·you·lay·a·finger·on *it*,
G2345.1 V-2AAS-3S θίγῃ (2x)
Heb 11:28 the firstborn should·lay·a·finger·on them.
Heb 12:20 a·wild·beast should·lay·a·finger·on the mountain,

G2346 θλίβω thlíbō *v.* (10x)
Compare:G4085 See:G4918 G5147
G2346.3 V-PAP-DPM θλίβουσιν (1x)
2Th 1:6 tribulation to·the·ones hard-pressing yeu,
G2346.4 V-PPI-1P θλιβόμεθα (1x)
2Co 1:6 And whether we·are·hard-pressed, *it·is* on·behalf of·
G2346.4 V-PPN θλίβεσθαι (1x)
1Th 3:4 to·yeu that we·are·about to·be·hard-pressed, even
G2346.4 V-PPP-DPM θλιβομένοις (2x)
2Th 1:7 to·yeu, the·ones being·hard-pressed, relaxation with
1Ti 5:10 if she·gave·relief to·those·being·hard-pressed, *and*
G2346.4 V-PPP-NPM θλιβόμενοι (3x)
Heb 11:37 ·destitute, being·hard-pressed, being·maltreated,
2Co 4:8 Being·hard-pressed on every·side, but·yet not being·
2Co 7:5 but·rather *we·are* being·hard-pressed on every·side
G2346.5 V-RPP-NSF τεθλιμμένη (1x)
Mt 7:14 and the way having·been·pressed·down, the·one
G2346.6 V-PAS-3P θλίβωσιν (1x)
Mk 3:9 ·of the crowd, lest they·should·press·in·against him.

G2347 θλῖψις thlîpsis *n.* (45x)
Roots:G2346 Compare:G3709 G3804 G1375 G4192 G3986 G4451
xLangEquiv:H6869
G2347.2 N-NSF θλῖψις (5x)
Ac 7:11 and Kenaan, and a·great tribulation, and our fathers
Rm 2:9 tribulation and calamity, upon every soul of·a·man·
Rm 5:3 the tribulation fully·cultivates patient·endurance,
Rm 8:35 of·the Anointed-One? *Shall* tribulation, or calamity
2Co 8:13 ease, and *there·be* tribulation for·yeu. But·rather
G2347.2 N-NPF θλίψεις (1x)
Ac 20:23 city, saying that bonds and tribulations await me.
G2347.2 N-ASF θλῖψιν (8x)
Jn 16:33 In the world, yeu·have tribulation, but·yet be·of·
Mt 24:9 ·shall·hand yeu over for tribulation and shall·kill
Php 1:16 imagining *also* to·bring·on tribulation to·my bonds.
2Th 1:6 to·recompense tribulation to·the·ones hard-pressing
1Co 7:28 But such·ones shall·have tribulation in·the flesh,
Rv 2:9 your works, and the tribulation, and the poverty (but
Rv 2:10 ·be·tried, and yeu·shall·have tribulation ten days.
Rv 2:22 with her into great tribulation, if they·should·not
G2347.2 N-DSF θλίψει (9x)
Rm 12:12 in·the tribulation, by·patiently·enduring; in·the
Jac 1:27 and widows in their tribulation, *and* to·purposefully·
Php 4:14 yeu·did well sharing·together in·my tribulation.
1Th 1:6 along·with much tribulation *and* with joy of·Holy
1Th 3:7 brothers, in all our tribulation and dire·need, we·
2Co 1:4 comforting us in all our tribulation, in·order·for us
2Co 1:4 to·comfort the·ones in any tribulation, through the
2Co 7:4 ·and·beyond with·the joy in all our tribulation.
Rv 1:9 and partner·together in the tribulation and in the
G2347.2 N-DPF θλίψεσιν (6x)
Heb 10:33 both by·reproaches and tribulations, and *in·fact*,
Rm 5:3 also we·boast in the tribulations, personally·knowing
1Th 3:3 to·be·woefully·shaken by these tribulations. For
2Th 1:4 persecutions and tribulations that yeu·hold·up·*under*
2Co 6:4 ·God: in much patient·endurance, in tribulations, in
Eph 3:13 not to·be·despondent in my tribulations over yeu,
G2347.2 N-GSF θλίψεως (8x)
Jn 16:21 little·child, she·remembers the tribulation no longer
Ac 11:19 the·ones being·dispersed by the tribulation, the·one
Mt 13:21 ·a·season, and with·tribulation or with·persecution
Mk 4:17 ·season. Afterward, with·tribulation or persecution
2Co 1:8 brothers, over our tribulation, the·one happening
2Co 2:4 For out of·much tribulation and anguished·anxiety
2Co 4:17 momentary tribulation is·accomplishing for·us
2Co 8:2 that in a·large proof·test of·tribulation, the
G2347.2 N-GPF θλίψεων (3x)
Ac 7:10 him out from·among all his tribulations, and he·gave
Ac 14:22 the kingdom of·God through many tribulations."
Col 1:24 the lacking of·the tribulations of·the Anointed-One
G2347.3 N-NSF θλῖψις (2x)
Mt 24:21 "For then there·shall·be a·Great Tribulation, such·
Mk 13:19 "For those Days shall·be a·Tribulation, such as
G2347.4 N-ASF θλῖψιν (2x)
Mt 24:29 immediately after the TRIBULATION of·those
Mk 13:24 in those Days, after that TRIBULATION, the sun
G2347.4 N-GSF θλίψεως (1x)
Rv 7:14 coming out of·The GREAT TRIBULATION, and

G2348 θνήσκω thnḗskō *v.* (13x)
θάνω thánō
[simpler primary form, used only in certain tenses]
Compare:G1634 G3499 G1606 See:G0599 G2289
G2348 V-RAI-3S τέθνηκεν (3x)
Lk 8:49 to·him, "Your daughter has·died; do·not harass the
Mk 15:44 if, even·now, he·has·died. And summoning the
1Ti 5:6 presently·living·luxuriously has·died while·she·lives.
G2348 V-RAI-3P τεθνήκασιν (1x)

Mt 2:20 the·ones seeking the little·child's soul have·died."

G2348 V-2RAN τεθνάναι (1x)

Ac 14:19 *him* outside of·the city assuming him to·have·died.

G2348 V-RAP-ASM τεθνηκότα (1x)

Jn 19:33 they·saw him even·now having·died, they·did·not

G2348 V-RAP-GSM τεθνηκότος (2x)

Jn 11:39 the sister of·the·one having·died, says to·him, "O·

Ac 25:19 some·man *named* Jesus, having·died, whom Paul

G2348 V-RAP-NSM τεθνηκώς (4x)

Jn 11:41 where the·one having·died was laying·outstretched.

Jn 11:44 And the·one having·died came·forth, having·been·

Jn 12:1 where Lazarus was, the·one having·died, whom he·

Lk 7:12 there·was·a·burial·procession·for one·having·died,

G2348 V-LAI-3S ετεθνηκει (1x)

Jn 11:21 if you·were here, my brother would not have·died.

G2349 θνητός thnētős *adj.* (6x)

Roots:G2348 Compare:G1027-1 G0444 See:G0110

G2349.2 A-NSN θνητόν (2x)

1Co 15:53 *for* this mortal to·dress·itself·with immortality.

1Co 15:54 this mortal should·dress·itself·with immortality,

G2349.2 A-APN θνητά (1x)

Rm 8:11 also give·life·above·to yeur mortal bodies through

G2349.2 A-DSF θνητῇ (1x)

2Co 4:11 should·be·made·apparent in our mortal flesh.

G2349.2 A-DSN θνητῷ (1x)

Rm 6:12 Moral·Failure reign in yeur mortal body, such·for

G2349.3 A-NSN θνητόν (1x)

2Co 5:4 in·order·that the mortality may·be·swallowed·up by

G2350 θορυβέω thôrybéō *v.* (4x)

Roots:G2351

G2350.1 V-IAI-3P ἐθορύβουν (1x)

Ac 17:5 ·a·mob, were·making·a·commotion·in the city. And

G2350.2 V-PPI-2P θορυβεῖσθε (1x)

Mk 5:39 ·them, "Why are·yeu·in·a·commotion and weeping

G2350.2 V-PPM-2P θορυβεῖσθε (1x)

Ac 20:10 he·declared, "Do·not be·in·a·commotion, for his

G2350.2 V-PPP-ASM θορυβούμενον (1x)

Mt 9:23 flute·players and the crowd being·in·a·commotion,

G2351 θόρυβος thórybôs *n.* (7x)

Roots:G2360

G2351.2 N-NSM θόρυβος (3x)

Mt 26:5 feast·day, lest a·commotion should·occur among

Mt 27:24 but·yet rather *that* a·commotion is·being·made,

Mk 14:2 *day*, lest there·shall·be a·commotion of·the people.

G2351.2 N-ASM θόρυβον (3x)

Ac 20:1 Now after the commotion ceased, Paul, after·

Ac 21:34 ·of the commotion, he·commandingly·ordered him

Mk 5:38 ·the·gathering and observes a·commotion, *people*

G2351.2 N-GSM θορύβου (1x)

Ac 24:18 neither with crowd, nor with a·commotion. "But

G2352 θραύω thraúō *v.* (1x)

Compare:G4486 G3089 G2362-3

G2352 V-RPP-APM τεθραυσμένους (1x)

Lk 4:18 ·set·apart with freedom those·having·been·crushed,

G2353 θρέμμα thrémma *n.* (1x)

Roots:G5142 Compare:G2934 G2934-1 xLangAlso:H4806

G2353.2 N-NPN θρέμματα (1x)

Jn 4:12 drank out of·it, and his sons, and his prized·cattle."

G2354 θρηνέω thrēnéō *v.* (4x)

Roots:G2355 Compare:G2799 G1145 G2875 G3427-1 xLangAlso:H6969

G2354 V-FAI-2P θρηνήσετε (1x)

Jn 16:20 that yeu shall·weep and shall·bewail, but the world

G2354 V-IAI-3P ἐθρήνουν (1x)

Lk 23:27 ·vividly·lamenting and were·bewailing·over him.

G2354 V-AAI-1P ἐθρηνήσαμεν (2x)

Lk 7:32 and yeu·did·not dance; we·bewailed for·yeu, and

Mt 11:17 and yeu·did·not dance; we·bewailed for·yeu, and

G2355 θρῆνος thrēnôs *n.* (1x)

Roots:G2360 Compare:G0213-2 G3648-1 G3427-2 G3629-1 G2805 See:G2354 G2354-1 xLangAlso:H7015 H5204

G2355.2 N-NSM θρῆνος (1x)

Mt 2:18 ·heard in Ramah— a·woeful·wailing and weeping

G2356 θρησκεία thrēskêía *n.* (4x)

Roots:G2357 Compare:G1175 See:G1479

G2356.2 N-NSF θρησκεία (2x)

Jac 1:26 deluding his·own heart, this·man's religion *is* futile.

Jac 1:27 Father— pure and uncontaminated religion is this:

G2356.2 N-DSF θρησκείᾳ (1x)

Col 2:18 ·humility·of·mind and in·a·religion of·the angels,

G2356.2 N-GSF θρησκείας (1x)

Ac 26:5 the most·strict denomination of·our religion, I·lived

G2357 θρῆσκος thrēskôs *adj.* (1x)

Roots:G2360 See:G2356

G2357.2 A-NSM θρῆσκος (1x)

Jac 1:26 If any·man among yeu seems to·be religious, *yet* not

G2358 θρι·αμβεύω thriambêúō *v.* (2x)

Roots:G2360 G0680 Compare:G3528 G2620 G0234-1

G2358.2 V-AAP-NSM θριαμβεύσας (1x)

Col 2:15 *(his Resurrection)*, triumphing·over them in it.

G2358.3 V-PAP-DSM θριαμβεύοντι (1x)

2Co 2:14 — the·one always causing us to·triumph in the

G2359 θρίξ thríx *n.* (15x)

τριχός trichős [genitive case]

Compare:G2864 See:G5155 xLangEquiv:H8181 A8177 xLangAlso:H6545

G2359 N-NSF θρίξ (2x)

Lk 21:18 And·yet a·hair from·among yeur head, no, it·

Ac 27:34 salvation, for not·even·one hair shall·fall out·from

G2359 N-NPF τρίχες (3x)

Lk 12:7 Moreover, even the hairs of·yeur head all have·

Mt 10:30 But also the hairs of·yeur head are all having·been·

Rv 1:14 His head and *his* hairs *are* white like wool (*as* white

G2359 N-ASF τρίχα (1x)

Mt 5:36 you·are·not able to·make one hair white or black.

G2359 N-APF τρίχας (3x)

Mk 1:6 ·dressed·himself·with camel's hair and with·a·leather

Rv 9:8 And they·were·having hair as hair of·women, and

Rv 9:8 And they·were·having hair as hair of·women, and

G2359 N-DPF θριξίν (4x)

Jn 11:2 firmly·wiping his feet with·her hair, whose brother

Jn 12:3 and firmly·wiped his feet with·her hair, and the home

Lk 7:38 was·firmly·wiping *them* with·the hairs of·her head,

Lk 7:44 and firmly·wiped *them* with·the hairs of·her head.

G2359 N-GPF τριχῶν (2x)

Mt 3:4 apparel *made* from camel's hair and *was·girded·with*

1Pe 3:3 ·*is* with·an·elaborate·braiding of·hair and a·draping

G2360 θροέω thrôéō *v.* (3x)

Compare:G0214 G3649 G5015 G5182 G4525 See:G2355

G2360.2 V-PPM-2P θροεῖσθε (2x)

Mt 24:6 ·see·to·it *that* yeu·are·not woefully·disturbed, for it·

Mk 13:7 rumors of·wars, do·not be·woefully·disturbed, for

G2360.2 V-PPN θροεῖσθαι (1x)

2Th 2:2 mind, nor to·be·woefully·disturbed *by·any delusion*

G2361 θρόμβος thrómbôs *n.* (1x)

Roots:G5142

G2361 N-NPM θρόμβοι (1x)

Lk 22:44 ·sweat became like clots of·blood dropping·down

G2362 θρόνος thrónôs *n.* (61x)

Roots:G2352-1 Compare:G0968 G2515 G1368-3 xLangEquiv:H3678 A3764

G2362.1 N-NSM θρόνος (6x)

Ac 7:49 "The heaven *is* my throne, and the earth *is* my foot

Heb 1:8 the Son *he·says*, "'Your throne, O·God, *is* to the

Mt 5:34 neither by the heaven, because it·is God's throne,

Rv 2:13 *even* where the throne of·the Adversary-Accuser *is*,

Rv 4:2 ·be in Spirit, and behold, a·throne was·set·out in the

Rv 22:3 ·vow·to·destruction, but the throne of·God and of·

G2362.1 N-NPM θρόνοι (2x)

Col 1:16 the·ones invisible, whether thrones, or dominions,

Rv 4:4 the throne *were·set·out* twenty four thrones. And upon

G2362.1 N-ASM θρόνον (3x)

Rv 12:5 her child was·snatched·up to God, and *to* his throne.

Rv 13:2 it his power, and his throne, and great authority.

Rv 16:10 ·out his vial upon the throne of·the Daemonic·Beast,

G2362.1 N-APM θρόνους (4x)

Mt 19:28 yeu also shall·sit upon twelve thrones, judging the

Rv 4:4 And upon the thrones, I·saw the twenty four Elders

Rv 11:16 in·the·sight of·God on their thrones, fell upon their

Rv 20:4 And I·saw thrones, and they·sat upon them, and

G2362.1 N-DSM θρόνῳ (3x)

Mt 23:22 heaven, swears by the throne of·God and by the·

Rv 3:21 *for·him* to·sit with me on my throne, even·as I·also

Rv 3:21 and did·sit·down with my Father on his throne.

G2362.1 N-GSM θρόνου (35x)

Heb 8:1 *the* right·hand of·the throne of·the Divine·Majesty

Heb 12:2 sat·down at *the* right·hand of·the throne of·God.

Rv 1:4 the seven Spirits who are in·the·sight of·his throne,

Rv 4:2 the heaven, and upon the throne is·one·sitting·down.

Rv 4:3 a·rainbow all·around the throne, in·clear·appearance

Rv 4:4 And all·around the throne *were·set·out* twenty four

Rv 4:5 And from·out of·the throne, lightnings and

Rv 4:5 being·set·ablaze in·the·sight of·the throne, which are

Rv 4:6 ·the·sight of·the throne *there·is* a·transparent,·glassy

Rv 4:6 And in *the* midst of·the throne, and in·a·circle·around

Rv 4:6 throne, and in·a·circle·around the throne, *are* four

Rv 4:9 to·the·one who·is·sitting·down on the throne, the·one

Rv 4:10 of·the·one sitting·down on the throne, and they·fall·

Rv 4:10 victor's·crowns in·the·sight of·the throne, saying,

Rv 5:1 ·the·one sitting·down on the throne, an·official·scroll

Rv 5:6 in *the* midst of·the throne and of·the four living·

Rv 5:7 right·hand of·the·one sitting·down upon the throne.

Rv 5:11 of·many angels all·around the throne and the living·

Rv 5:13 who·is·sitting·down upon the throne and unto·the

Rv 6:16 of·the·one who·is·sitting·down on the throne, and

Rv 7:9 standing in·the·sight of·the throne and in·the·sight

Rv 7:10 ·one who·is·sitting·down upon the throne and to·the

Rv 7:11 angels stood in·a·circle·around the throne and the

Rv 7:11 their faces in·the·sight of·the throne. And they·fell·

Rv 7:15 that, they·are in·the·sight of·the throne of·God and

Rv 7:15 ·is·sitting·down on the throne shall·encamp among

Rv 7:17 the·one amidst the throne, shall·shepherd them and

Rv 8:3 Sacrifice·Altar, the·one in·the·sight of·the throne.

Rv 14:3 a·brand-new song in·the·sight of·the throne, and in·

Rv 14:5 without·blemish in·the·sight of·the throne of·God.

Rv 16:17 Temple of·the heaven, from the throne, saying,

Rv 19:4 to·the·one who·is·sitting·down on the throne, saying

Rv 19:5 Then a·voice came·forth out of·the throne, saying,

Rv 21:5 ·one who·is·sitting·down upon the throne declared,

Rv 22:1 proceeding·forth out of·the throne of·God and of·

G2362.1 N-GPM θρόνων (2x)

Lk 1:52 He·demoted powers from *their* thrones and elevated

Lk 22:30 and may·sit on thrones judging the twelve tribes

G2362.2 N-ASM θρόνον (1x)

Lk 1:32 God shall·give to·him the Throne of·his father

G2362.2 N-GSM θρόνου (3x)

Ac 2:30 ·raise·up the Anointed-One to·sit on his Throne—

Mt 19:28 of·Clay·Man† should·sit upon his Throne of·Glory,

Mt 25:31 him, then he·shall·sit upon his Throne of·Glory.

G2362.3 N-ASM θρόνον (1x)

Rv 20:11 And I·saw a·Great White Throne, and the·one

G2362.4 N-DSM θρόνῳ (1x)

Heb 4:16 with freeness·of·speech to·the Throne of·Grace, in·

G2363 Θυάτειρα Thyátêira *n/l.* (4x)

G2363 N/L-APN Θυάτειρα (1x)

Rv 1:11 and to Pergamos, and to Thyatira, and to Sardis,

G2363 N/L-DPN Θυατείροις (2x)

Rv 2:18 angel of·the Called·Out·citizenry in Thyatira write,

Rv 2:24 ·say, and to·the rest in Thyatira (as·many·as do·not

G2363 N/L-GPN Θυατείρων (1x)

Ac 16:14 from·*the*·city of·Thyatira, a·seller·of·purple·cloth,

G2364 θυγάτηρ thygátēr *n.* (29x)
See:G2365
xLangEquiv:H1323

G2364.1 N-NSF θυγάτηρ (10x)
Lk 2:36 Hanna, daughter of·PhanuEl, from·among *the*
Lk 8:42 to·him an·only·child, a·daughter of·about twelve
Lk 8:49 to·him, "Your daughter has·died; do·not harass the
Lk 12:53 against daughter, and daughter against mother;
Ac 7:21 being·put·out, the Pharaoh's daughter took him up
Mt 9:18 "My daughter just·completely·died at·this·moment,
Mt 14:6 with·ceremony, the daughter of·HerOdias danced in
Mt 15:22 O·Son of·David; my daughter *is* badly possessed·
Mt 15:28 And her daughter was·healed from that·very hour
Mk 5:35 saying, "Your daughter is·dead. Why harass the

G2364.1 N-NPF θυγατέρες (2x)
Ac 2:17 yeur sons and yeur daughters shall·prophesy, and
Ac 21:9 And this·man had daughters, four virgin·daughters

G2364.1 N-VSF θύγατερ (4x)
Jn 12:15 "Do·not be·afraid, O·Daughter of·Tsiyon!"
Lk 8:48 he·declared to·her, "Daughter, be·of·good·courage.
Mt 9:22 YeShua declared, "Daughter, be·of·good·courage;
Mk 5:34 And he·declared to·her, "Daughter, your trust has·

G2364.1 N-VPF θυγατέρες (1x)
Lk 23:28 Jesus declared, "Daughters of·JeruSalem, do·not

G2364.1 N-ASF θυγατέρα (4x)
Lk 13:16 And this·one, being a·daughter of·AbRaham,
Mt 10:35 against his father, a·daughter against her mother,
Mt 10:37 affectionately·favoring son or daughter over me is
Mk 7:30 ·come·out and her daughter having·been·cast upon

G2364.1 N-APF θυγατέρας (1x)
2Co 6:18 shall·be my·own distinct sons and daughters,"

G2364.1 N-DSF θυγατρί (2x)
Lk 12:53 father; mother against daughter, and daughter
Mt 21:5 ""Declare·yeu to·the daughter of·Tsiyon,"

G2364.1 N-GSF θυγατρός (4x)
Heb 11:24 being·referred·to·as son of·Pharaoh's daughter,
Mk 6:22 and·then with·the daughter of·the very·same
Mk 7:26 he·should·cast·forth the demon out of·her daughter.
Mk 7:29 The demon has·come·forth out of·your daughter."

G2364.1 N-GPF θυγατέρων (1x)
Lk 1:5 his wife *was* from·among the daughters of·Aaron, and

G2365 θυγάτριον thygátriôn *n.* (2x)
Roots:G2364

G2365.1 N-NSN θυγάτριον (1x)
Mk 5:23 "My little·daughter is at·the·final·point·of·death.

G2365.2 N-NSN θυγάτριον (1x)
Mk 7:25 whose young·daughter was·having an·impure spirit,

G2366 θύελλα thýêlla *n.* (1x)
Roots:G2380 Compare:G2978 G4578 G5494

G2366 N-DSF θυέλλῃ (1x)
Heb 12:18 ·gloom, and to·darkness, and to·fierce·wind,

G2367 θύϊνος thýïnôs *adj.* (1x)
Roots:G2380

G2367 A-ASN θύϊνον (1x)
Rv 18:12 and scarlet, "and every citron wood, "and every

G2368 θυμίαμα thymíama *n.* (6x)
Roots:G2370 Compare:G3030 G0759 See:G2369
xLangAlso:H7004

G2368.1 N-NPN θυμιάματα (1x)
Rv 8:3 there·was·given to·him much incense, in·order·that

G2368.1 N-APN θυμιάματα (1x)
Rv 18:13 "and·also cinnamon, incense, ointments, and

G2368.1 N-GSN θυμιάματος (2x)
Lk 1:10 people were praying outside at·the hour of·incense.
Lk 1:11 at *the* right·side of·the Sacrifice·Altar of·incense.

G2368.1 N-GPN θυμιαμάτων (2x)
Rv 5:8 and golden vials overflowing with·incense, which are
Rv 8:4 And the smoke of·the incense, *which·came* with·the

G2369 θυμια•στήριον thymiastēriôn *n.* (1x)
Roots:G2370 Compare:G3031 G4444-1 See:G2368
xLangEquiv:H4289

G2369.1 N-ASN θυμιατήριον (1x)
Heb 9:4 having a·golden censer and the Ark of·the covenant

G2370 θυμιάω thymiáō *v.* (1x)
Roots:G2380 See:G2368 G2369

G2370.1 V-AAN θυμιᾶσαι (1x)
Lk 1:9 ·the·lot, the·one to·burn·incense after·entering into

G2371 θυμο•μαχέω thymômachéō *v.* (1x)
Roots:G2372 G3164

G2371.2 V-PAP-NSM θυμομαχῶν (1x)
Ac 12:20 was furiously·quarreling with·them·of·Tyre and

G2372 θυμός thymôs *n.* (18x)
Roots:G2380 Compare:G3709 G3950 G5433 G0192
G3806 G3376-2 See:G2373 G1937 G2115 G3115-1
G3690-2 G4289 G5590
xLangEquiv:H7110 xLangAlso:H0639-1 H2534

G2372.2 N-NSM θυμός (2x)
Rm 2:8 unrighteousness, *he·shall·render* Rage and Wrath,
Eph 4:31 Let all bitterness, and rage, and wrath, and yelling,

G2372.2 N-ASM θυμόν (3x)
Heb 11:27 Egypt (not fearing the rage of·the king) for he·
Col 3:8 all·these things: wrath, rage, malice, revilement,
Rv 12:12 *He·is* having great rage, having·seen that he·has

G2372.2 N-GSM θυμοῦ (4x)
Lk 4:28 everyone in the gathering was·filled with·rage.
Ac 19:28 *these·things*, they·were·becoming full of·rage, and
Rv 14:8 of·the wine of·the rage of·her sexual·immorality."
Rv 18:3 of·the wine of·the rage of·her sexual·immorality,

G2372.3 N-NSM θυμός (1x)
Rv 15:1 because in them the Rage of·God is·completed.

G2372.3 N-GSM θυμοῦ (6x)
Rv 14:10 from·out of·the wine of·the Rage of·God, the·one
Rv 14:19 cast *it* into the great winepress of·the Rage of·God.
Rv 15:7 golden vials overflowing of·the Rage of·God, the·
Rv 16:1 and pour·out the vials of·the Rage of·God into the
Rv 16:19 ·her the cup of·the wine of·the Rage of·his Wrath.
Rv 19:15 winepress of·the wine of·the Rage and the Wrath

G2372.4 N-NPM θυμοί (2x)
Gal 5:20 hostilities, strifes, jealousies, ragings, contentions,
2Co 12:20 *there·be* strifes, jealousies, ragings, contentions,

G2373 θυμόω thymôō *v.* (1x)
Roots:G2372 See:G2373-2
xLangEquiv:H7107 xLangAlso:H2194

G2373 V-API-3S ἐθυμώθη (1x)
Mt 2:16 the Magian·astrologists, was·enraged exceedingly.

G2374 θύρα thýra *n.* (39x)
Compare:G4439 G4440 See:G2377 G2376 G2375
G2376-1 xLangAlso:H6607 H1817

G2374 N-NSF θύρα (6x)
Jn 10:7 ·certainly, I·say to·yeu, I AM the door of·the sheep.
Jn 10:9 "I AM the door. If someone should·enter·in through
Lk 11:7 Even·now, the door has·been·shut, and my little·
Mt 25:10 into the wedding·banquet. And the door was·shut.
1Co 16:9 For a·great and active door has·opened·up to·me,
Rv 4:1 and behold, a·door having·been·opened·up in the

G2374 N-NPF θύραι (2x)
Ac 16:26 And at·once, all the doors were·opened·up, and
Ac 21:30 ·Courtyard, and immediately the doors were·shut.

G2374 N-ASF θύραν (14x)
Lk 13:25 and should·utterly·shut the door, and yeu·should·
Lk 13:25 to·stand outside and to·knock at·the door, saying,
Ac 3:2 day alongside the door of·the Sanctuary·Courtyard,
Ac 12:13 as·Peter *was* knocking *at* the door of·the gate, a·
Ac 14:27 and that he·opened·up *the* door of·trust to·the
Mt 6:6 ·chamber, and after·shutting your door, pray to·your
Mk 1:33 ·been·completely·gathered alongside the door.
Mk 2:2 not·even alongside the door. And he·was·speaking
Mk 11:4 outside having·been·tied alongside the door at the
Mk 15:46 ·rolled a·stone over the door of·the chamber·tomb.
Col 4:3 may·open·up to·us a·door for·the Redemptive·word
Rv 3:8 of·you, I·have·given a·door having·been·opened·up,
Rv 3:20 'Behold, I·stand at the door and knock.
Rv 3:20 voice and should·open·up the door, I·shall·enter·in

G2374 N-APF θύρας (2x)
Ac 5:19 night, opened·up the prison doors; and·also leading
Ac 16:27 seeing the prison doors having·been·opened·up,

G2374 N-DSF θύρᾳ (3x)
Jn 18:16 stood outside alongside the door. In·due·course, the
Ac 5:9 your husband *are* at the door, and they·shall·carry
Mt 27:60 a·great stone to·the door of·the chamber·tomb, he·

G2374 N-DPF θύραις (2x)
Mt 24:33 yeu·must·know that he·is near upon *the* doors.
Mk 13:29 yeu·must·know that he·is near upon *the* doors.

G2374 N-GSF θύρας (6x)
Jn 10:1 not entering·in through the door into the yard·pen of·
Jn 10:2 the·one entering·in through the door is shepherd of·
Ac 12:6 ·guarding the prison·cell, *standing* before the door.
Mt 28:2 ·away the stone from the door and sat·down on·top
Mk 16:3 for·us the stone at the door of·the chamber·tomb?
2Co 2:12 (also with·a·door having·been·opened·up to·me by

G2374 N-GPF θυρῶν (4x)
Jn 20:19 week, and with·the doors having·been·shut where
Jn 20:26 them; *and* with·the doors having·been·shut, Jesus
Ac 5:23 standing outside before the doors. But opening·up,
Jac 5:9 Behold, *the* judge stands before the doors.

G2375 θυρεός thyrêôs *n.* (1x)
Roots:G2374 xLangAlso:H7982 H4043 H6793

G2375 N-ASM θυρεόν (1x)
Eph 6:16 ·things, after·taking·up the tall·shield of·the trust

G2376 θυρίς thyrís *n.* (2x)
Roots:G2374
xLangEquiv:H2474

G2376.2 N-GSF θυρίδος (2x)
Ac 20:9 ·down in the window, becoming·weighed·down
2Co 11:33 And through a·window, in a·large·basket, I·was·

G2377 θυρ•ωρός thyrōrôs *n.* (4x)
Roots:G2374 Compare:G4440-1 G4440
xLangEquiv:H6335-1

G2377.2 N-NSM θυρωρός (1x)
Jn 10:3 To·him, the doorkeeper opens·up, and the sheep

G2377.2 N-NSF θυρωρός (1x)
Jn 18:17 ·then the servant·girl (the doorkeeper) says to·Peter,

G2377.2 N-DSM θυρωρῷ (1x)
Mk 13:34 the doorkeeper that he·should·keep·alert.

G2377.2 N-DSF θυρωρῷ (1x)
Jn 18:16 ·out and declared *him* to·the doorkeeper, and she·

G2378 θυσία thysía *n.* (32x)
Roots:G2380 Compare:G1435 G5498-1 G4376
See:G2379 G2378-2
xLangEquiv:H2077 xLangAlso:H4503

G2378 N-NSF θυσία (2x)
Heb 10:26 is·there·still·remaining a·sacrifice concerning
Mk 9:49 ·fire, and every sacrifice shall·be·salted with·salt.

G2378 N-NPF θυσίαι (1x)
Heb 9:9 which both presents and sacrifices were·offered, not

G2378 N-ASF θυσίαν (12x)
Lk 2:24 and to·give a·sacrifice according·to·the·thing
Ac 7:41 in those days and brought·forth sacrifice to·the idol,
Heb 10:5 world says, " Sacrifice and offering you·did·not
Heb 10:8 saying above, that "Sacrifice and offering and
Heb 10:12 ·offering one sacrifice on·behalf of·moral·failures
Heb 11:4 offered to·God a·much·better sacrifice than Qain,
Heb 13:15 we·should·carry·up a·sacrifice of·praise to·God
Mt 9:13 "I·want mercy and not sacrifice." For I·did·not
Mt 12:7 "I·want mercy, and not sacrifice," yeu·would not
Rm 12:1 ·present yeur bodies *as* a·living sacrifice, holy *and*
Php 4:18 yeu, a·soothing aroma, a·sacrifice acceptable *and*
Eph 5:2 behalf, an·offering and a·sacrifice to·God for a·

G2378 N-APF θυσίας (7x)
Ac 7:42 did·yeu·offer to·me sacrifices and respect·offerings
Heb 5:1 presents and sacrifices on·behalf of·moral·failures,
Heb 7:27 high·priests *do*, to·carry·up sacrifices *to·the altar*,
Heb 8:3 to·offer both presents and sacrifices, by·which
Heb 10:11 offering many·times the same sacrifices, which
1Pe 2:5 ·carry·up spiritual sacrifices well·acceptable to·God
1Co 10:18 not·indeed the·ones eating of·the sacrifices, *also*

G2378 N-DSF θυσίᾳ (1x)
Php 2:17 ·as·a·devotion upon the sacrifice and public·service

G2378 N-DPF θυσίαις (3x)
Heb 9:23 with·significantly·better sacrifices than these.
Heb 10:1 ·time is·it·able with·the same sacrifices (which
Heb 13:16 for with·such sacrifices God is·fully·satisfied.
G2378 N-GSF θυσίας (1x)
Heb 9:26 of·moral·failure through the sacrifice of·himself.
G2378 N-GPF θυσιῶν (2x)
Lk 13:1 whose blood Pilate mixed with their sacrifices.
Mk 12:33 ·than all the burnt·offerings and the sacrifices."
EG2378 (3x)
Heb 5:3 to·offer *sacrifices* on·behalf of·moral·failures.
Heb 9:23 heavens) to·be·purified with·these *sacrifices*, but
Heb 10:3 But·rather in those *sacrifices*, a·reminder·again *is*·

G2379 θυσια•στήριον thysiastḗriôn *n.* (24x)
Roots:G2378
xLangEquiv:H4196 A4056
EG2379 (1x)
Heb 7:27 to·carry·up sacrifices *to·the altar*, first on·behalf
G2379.ª N-ASN θυσιαστήριον (1x)
Rv 11:1 of·God, and the Sacrifice·Altar, and the·ones
G2379.ª N-GSN θυσιαστηρίου (2x)
Rv 14:18 came·forth out·from the Sacrifice·Altar, having
Rv 16:7 another from·among the Sacrifice·Altar saying,
G2379.1 N-ASN θυσιαστήριον (1x)
Jac 2:21 ·up his son YiTsaq upon the sacrifice·altar?
G2379.1 N-APN θυσιαστήρια (1x)
Rm 11:3 ·foundationally·ruined your sacrifice·altars, and·I
G2379.2 N-ASN θυσιαστήριον (2x)
Rv 8:3 and stood·still at the Sacrifice·Altar, having a·golden
Rv 8:3 upon the golden Sacrifice·Altar, the·one in·the·sight
G2379.2 N-GSN θυσιαστηρίου (3x)
Lk 1:11 at *the* right·side of·the Sacrifice·Altar of·incense.
Rv 8:5 it from·out of·the fire of·the Sacrifice·Altar, and cast
Rv 9:13 four horns of·the golden Sacrifice·Altar, the·one in·
G2379.3 N-NSN θυσιαστήριον (1x)
Mt 23:19 the present or the Sacrifice·Altar, the·one making
G2379.3 N-ASN θυσιαστήριον (2x)
Heb 13:10 We·have a·Sacrifice·Altar from·among which
Mt 5:23 your present to the Sacrifice·Altar, and·there you·
G2379.3 N-DSN θυσιαστηρίῳ (5x)
Heb 7:13 ·man has·given·attention at·the Sacrifice·Altar.
Mt 23:18 should·swear by the Sacrifice·Altar, it·is nothing·
Mt 23:20 the·one swearing by the Sacrifice·Altar, swears by
1Co 9:13 to·the Sacrifice·Altar participate·together in·the
1Co 9:13 ·Altar participate·together in·the Sacrifice·Altar?
G2379.3 N-GSN θυσιαστηρίου (5x)
Lk 11:51 ·perishing between the Sacrifice·Altar and the
Mt 5:24 there before the Sacrifice·Altar and head·on·out.
Mt 23:35 and the Sacrifice·Altar *in·the Sanctuary·Courtyard.*
1Co 10:18 sacrifices, *also* partners of·the Sacrifice·Altar?
Rv 6:9 I·saw beneath the Sacrifice·Altar the souls of·the·

G2380 θύω thýō *v.* (14x)
Compare:G4969
xLangEquiv:H2076 A1684
G2380.2 V-PAN θύειν (2x)
Ac 14:13 he·was·wanting to·sacrifice together with·the
Ac 14:18 ·restrained the crowds not to·sacrifice to·them.
G2380.2 V-PPN θύεσθαι (1x)
Lk 22:7 it·was·mandatory·for the Passover to·be·sacrificed.
G2380.2 V-IAI-3P ἔθυον (1x)
Mk 14:12 ·Bread, when they·were·sacrificing the Passover,
G2380.2 V-AAI-2S ἔθυσας (1x)
Lk 15:30 with prostitutes, you·sacrificed for·him the
G2380.2 V-AAI-3S ἔθυσεν (1x)
Lk 15:27 And your father sacrificed the fattened calf,
G2380.2 V-AAM-2S θῦσον (2x)
Ac 10:13 "Peter, after·standing·up, make·sacrifice and eat."
Ac 11:7 'Peter, after·standing·up, sacrifice and eat.'
G2380.2 V-AAM-2P θύσατε (1x)
Lk 15:23 bringing the fattened calf, sacrifice *it*. And eating *it*
G2380.2 V-API-3S ἐτύθη (1x)
1Co 5:7 Passover·lamb, is·already·sacrificed on·our behalf.
G2380.2 V-RPP-NPN τεθυμένα (1x)
Mt 22:4 bulls and fatlings *are* having·been·sacrificed, and
G2380.5 V-PAI-3S θύει (2x)
1Co 10:20 Gentiles sacrificially·slaughter, they·sacrificially·
1Co 10:20 they·sacrificially·slaughter to·demons, and not
G2380.5 V-AAS-3S θύσῃ (1x)
Jn 10:10 ·that he·may·steal, and may·slaughter·victims, and

G2381 Θωμᾶς Thōmâs *n/p.* (12x)
תְּאוֹם ta̧'ôm̱ [Hebrew]
Roots:H8380 Compare:G1324
G2381.2 N/P-NSM Θωμᾶς (8x)
Jn 11:16 So·then Thomas (the·one being·referred·to·as
Jn 14:5 Thomas says to·him, "Lord, we·do·not personally·
Jn 20:24 But Thomas (one from·among the twelve, the·one
Jn 20:26 disciples were inside, and Thomas with them; *and*
Jn 20:28 And Thomas answered and declared to·him, "My
Jn 21:2 Simon Peter, and Thomas (the·one being·referred·
Ac 1:13 Andrew); (Philip and Thomas); (BarTholomew
Mt 10:3 Philip and BarTholomew; Thomas and MattHew the
G2381.2 N/P-VSM Θωμᾶ (1x)
Jn 20:29 says to·him, "Thomas, because you·have·clearly·
G2381.2 N/P-ASM Θωμᾶν (2x)
Lk 6:15 MattHew *of·Alphaeus* and Thomas, Jakob (the·one
Mk 3:18 and MattHew *of·Alphaeus*, and Thomas, and Jakob
G2381.2 N/P-DSM Θωμᾷ (1x)
Jn 20:27 Then he·says to·Thomas, "Bring your finger here,

G2382 θώραξ thṓrax *n.* (5x)
Compare:G4738
xLangEquiv:H8302 H5630
G2382.2 N-ASM θώρακα (2x)
1Th 5:8 dressing·ourselves·with *the* full·chest·armor of·trust
Eph 6:14 ·with the full·chest·armor of·righteousness,
G2382.2 N-APM θώρακας (3x)
Rv 9:9 And they·were·having full·chest·armor, as full·chest·
Rv 9:9 ·having full·chest·armor, as full·chest·armor of·iron;
Rv 9:17 ·down on them, having full·chest·armor, fiery, like·

Iι - Iota

G2383 Ἰάειρος Iáêirôs *n/p.* (2x)
יָאִיר ya̧ʻıyr [Hebrew]
Roots:H2971
G2383.2 N/P-NSM Ἰάειρος (2x)
Lk 8:41 a·man whose name *was* Jairus, and he·himself was·
Mk 5:22 of·the directors·of·the·gathering, Jairus by·name.

G2384 Ἰακώβ Iakṓb *n/p.* (28x)
יַעֲקֹב ya̧ʻăqôb [Hebrew]
Roots:H3290 Compare:G2269 See:G2385
G2384.2 N/P-PRI Ἰακώβ (25x)
Jn 4:5 near·by to·the open·field that Jacob gave to·his son
Jn 4:6 Now Jacob's well was there.
Jn 4:12 you·yourself greater·than our father Jacob, who gave
Lk 1:33 And he·shall·reign over the house of·Jacob into the
Lk 3:34 *son* of·Jacob, *son* of·YiTsaq, *son* of·AbRaham, *son*
Lk 13:28 ·upon AbRaham, YiTsaq, and Jacob, and all the
Lk 20:37 and the God of·YiTsaq, and the God of·Jacob."
Ac 3:13 and of·YiTsaq, and of·Jacob, the God of·our
Ac 7:8 eighth day; and YiTsaq *begot* Jacob; and Jacob *begot*
Ac 7:8 and YiTsaq *begot* Jacob; and Jacob *begot* the twelve
Ac 7:12 grain in Egypt, Jacob dispatched·forth our fathers
Ac 7:14 Joseph summarily·called·for his father Jacob and all
Ac 7:15 So Jacob walked·down into Egypt, and he·
Ac 7:32 God of·YiTsaq, and the God of·Jacob.' But Moses,
Ac 7:46 to·find a·suitable·Tabernacle for·the God of·Jacob.
Heb 11:9 in tents with YiTsaq and Jacob, the co-heirs of·the
Heb 11:20 By·trust, YiTsaq blessed Jacob and Esau
Heb 11:21 By·trust, Jacob (when·he·was·dying) blessed
Mt 1:2 YiTsaq, and YiTsaq begot Jacob, and Jacob begot
Mt 1:2 YiTsaq begot Jacob, and Jacob begot Judah and his
Mt 8:11 AbRaham, YiTsaq, and Jacob in the kingdom of·the
Mt 22:32 and the God of·YiTsaq, and the God of·Jacob"?
Mk 12:26 and the God of·YiTsaq, and the God of·Jacob"?
Rm 9:13 Just·as it·has·been·written, "Jacob I·loved, but
Rm 11:26 and he·shall·turn·away irreverence from Jacob.
EG2384.2 (1x)
Ac 7:16 that AbRaham's *son Jacob* purchased for·a·price of·
G2384.3 N/P-PRI Ἰακώβ (2x)
Mt 1:15 EleAzar begot Matthan, and Matthan begot Jacob.
Mt 1:16 Now Jacob begot Joseph the husband of·Mariam,

G2385 Ἰάκωβος Iákōbôs *n/p.* (43x)
Roots:G2384
G2385.2 N/P-NSM Ἰάκωβος (5x)
Lk 9:54 ·seeing *this*, his disciples, Jakob and John, declared
Ac 1:13 ·to·abide as·follows: (Peter, Jakob, John, and
Mt 10:2 Andrew his brother; Jakob (the·one of·Zebedee)
Mk 10:35 And Jakob and John, the Sons of·Zebedee,
Mk 13:3 the Sanctuary·Estate, Peter, Jakob, John and
G2385.2 N/P-ASM Ἰάκωβον (12x)
Lk 5:10 And likewise also *amazed were* Jakob and John, the·
Lk 6:14 and Andrew his brother, Jakob and John, and·Philip
Lk 8:51 ·person to·enter·in, except Peter, Jakob, and John,
Lk 9:28 Peter, John, and Jakob, he·walked·up upon the
Ac 12:2 And he·executed Jakob, the brother of·John, with·a·
Mt 4:21 ·saw two other brothers, Jakob (the·one of·Zebedee
Mt 17:1 YeShua personally·takes Peter and Jakob and John
Mk 1:19 a·little·way from·there, he·saw Jakob (the·one of·
Mk 3:17 and Jakob (the·one of·Zebedee) and John the
Mk 5:37 ·along with·him, except Peter, Jakob, and John the
Mk 9:2 days, Jesus personally·takes Peter, Jakob, and John,
Mk 14:33 ·personally·takes with him Peter, Jakob, and John,
G2385.2 N/P-GSM Ἰακώβου (4x)
Mk 1:29 home of·Simon and Andrew, with Jakob and John.
Mk 3:17 and John the brother of·Jakob, also on·them he·
Mk 5:37 except Peter, Jakob, and John the brother of·Jakob.
Mk 10:41 ·be·greatly·displeased concerning Jakob and John.
EG2385.2 (1x)
Mt 20:20 him, with her sons *(Jakob and John), and she·was*
G2385.3 N/P-NSM Ἰάκωβος (2x)
Ac 1:13 and MattHew); (Jakob *son* of·Alphaeus, Simon the

Mt 10:3 tax·collector *(the·one of·Alphaeus)*; Jakob (the·one
G2385.3 N/P-ASM Ἰάκωβον (2x)
Lk 6:15 and Thomas, Jakob (the·one of·Alphaeus), and
Mk 3:18 and Thomas, and Jakob (the·one of·Alphaeus),
G2385.4 N/P-NSM Ἰάκωβος (4x)
Ac 15:13 with them staying·silent, Jakob *(the half-brother*
Gal 2:9 the grace being·given to·me, Jakob, Kephas·*(called·*
Mt 13:55 And his brothers, *little·*Jakob, Joses, Simon and
Jac 1:1 Jakob, a·slave of·God and of·*the·*Lord YeShua
G2385.4 N/P-ASM Ἰάκωβον (2x)
Ac 21:18 together with·us *to·come* alongside Jacob; and all
Gal 1:19 ·other of·the ambassadors, except Jacob, the Lord's
G2385.4 N/P-DSM Ἰακώβῳ (2x)
Ac 12:17 "Go·announce these·things to·Jacob, and to·the
1Co 15:7 After·that, he·was·gazed·upon by·Jacob, *and* then
G2385.4 N/P-GSM Ἰακώβου (7x)
Lk 24:10 and Mariam *the mother* of·*little·*Jacob, and the
Gal 2:12 ·men coming from Jacob, he·was·eating·together
Mt 27:56 and Mariam the mother of·*little·*Jacob and Joses,
Mk 6:3 son of·Mariam, and a·brother of·*little·*Jacob, Joses,
Mk 15:40 Mariam (the mother of·little Jacob and of·Joses),
Mk 16:1 and Mariam (the *mother* of·*little·*Jacob) and Salome
Jud 1:1 of·YeShua Anointed and a·brother of·Jacob. To·the·
G2385.5 N/P-GSM Ἰακώβου (2x)
Lk 6:16 *and* Judas *son* of·Jacobus·*Thaddaeus*, and Judas
Ac 1:13 the Zealot, and Judas *son* of·Jacobus *Thaddaeus*).

G2386 ἴαμα íama *n.* (3x)
Roots:G2390 See:G2392
G2386.2 N-GPN ἰαμάτων (3x)
1Co 12:9 ·another, gracious·bestowments of·healing by the
1Co 12:28 gracious·bestowments of·healing, supportive·
1Co 12:30 all have gracious·bestowments of·healing. Not all

G2387 Ἰαμβρῆς Iambrês *n/p.* (1x)
Μαμβρῆς Mambrês [alternate spelling]
Compare:G2389 xLangAlso:H4471
G2387.2 N/P-NSM Ἰαμβρῆς (1x)
2Ti 3:8 Now as Jannes and Jambres stood·opposed·to Moses

G2388 Ἰαννά Ianná *n/p.* (1x)
Roots:H3238
G2388.2 N/P-PRI Ἰαννά (1x)
Lk 3:24 of·Levi, *son* of·Malki, *son* of·Janna, *son* of·Joseph,

G2389 Ἰαννῆς Iannês *n/p.* (1x)
Ἰοανά Iôaná [Greek variant of the Talmud]
Compare:G2387
G2389.2 N/P-NSM Ἰαννῆς (1x)
2Ti 3:8 Now as Jannes and Jambres stood·opposed·to Moses

G2390 ἰάομαι iáômai *v.* (28x)
Compare:G2323 See:G2386 G2392 G2394 G2395-1
xLangAlso:H7495
G2390 V-FPI-3S ἰαθήσεται (2x)
Lk 7:7 with·a·word, and my servant·boy shall·be·healed.
Mt 8:8 declare a·word, and my servant·boy shall·be·healed.
G2390 V-PNI-3S ἰᾶται (1x)
Ac 9:34 Aeneas, Jesus the Anointed-One heals you. Rise·up
G2390 V-PNN ἰᾶσθαι (2x)
Lk 5:17 And the power of·Yahweh was *present* to·heal them.
Lk 9:2 the kingdom of·God, and to·heal the·ones being·sick.
G2390 V-PNP-NSM ἰώμενος (1x)
Ac 10:38 doing·good·deeds and healing all the·ones being·
G2390 V-INI-3S ἰᾶτο (2x)
Lk 6:19 came·forth directly·from him and healed *them* all.
Lk 9:11 kingdom of·God, and healed the·ones having need
G2390 V-ADI-3S ἰάσατο (4x)
Lk 9:42 reprimanded the impure spirit and healed the boy,
Lk 14:4 And grabbing·hold *of·him*, he·healed him and fully·
Lk 22:51 And laying·hold of·his earlobe, he·healed him.
Ac 28:8 *and* laying his hands on·him, he·healed him.
G2390 V-ADN ἰάσασθαι (1x)
Lk 4:18 ·poor. He·has·dispatched me to·heal the·ones *with*
G2390 V-ADS-1S ἰάσωμαι (3x)
Jn 12:40 ·be·turned·back·around, and I·should·heal them."
Ac 28:27 should·turn·back·around, and I·should·heal them."
Mt 13:15 should·turn·back·around, and I·should·heal them.
G2390 V-ADS-3S ἰάσηται (1x)
Jn 4:47 him that he·may·walk·down and may·heal his son,
G2390 V-API-2P ἰάθητε (1x)
1Pe 2:24 thrashed·and·swollen·body yeu·are·already·healed.'
G2390 V-API-3S ἰάθη (4x)
Lk 8:47 ·hold of·him, and how at·once, she·was·healed.
Lk 17:15 them, seeing that he·was·healed, returned·back
Mt 8:13 And his servant·boy was·healed in the *very* same
Mt 15:28 And her daughter was·healed from that·very hour
G2390 V-APN ἰαθῆναι (1x)
Lk 6:17 came·to·hear him and to·be·healed of·their illnesses,
G2390 V-APP-GSM@ ἰαθέντος (1x)
Ac 3:11 lame·man who·was·healed securely·holding Peter
G2390 V-APP-NSM ἰαθείς (1x)
Jn 5:13 And the·one being·healed had·not personally·known
G2390 V-APS-2P ἰάθητε (1x)
Jac 5:16 of·one·another, that yeu·may·be·healed. A·petition
G2390 V-APS-3S ἰαθῇ (1x)
Heb 12:13 but more·especially *so·that* it·may·be·healed.
G2390 V-RPI-3S ἴαται (1x)
Mk 5:29 in·her body that she·has·been·healed from the

G2391 Ἰάρεδ Iárêd *n/p.* (1x)
יֶ֫רֶד yered [Hebrew]
Roots:H3382 See:G2627
G2391 N/P-PRI Ἰαρέδ (1x)
Lk 3:37 *son* of·Enoch, *son* of·Jared, *son* of·MahalalEl, *son*

G2392 ἴασις íasis *n.* (3x)
Roots:G2390 See:G2386 G2395-1
G2392 N-ASF ἴασιν (1x)
Ac 4:30 you to·stretch·forth your hand for healing, and *for*
G2392 N-APF ἰάσεις (1x)
Lk 13:32 demons, and I·further·finish healing today and
G2392 N-GSF ἰάσεως (1x)
Ac 4:22 this miraculous·sign of·healing had·happened.

G2393 ἴασπις íaspis *n.* (4x)
xLangAlso:H3471
G2393 N-NSF ἴασπις (2x)
Rv 21:18 the construction of·its wall was *of* jasper. And the
Rv 21:19 The first foundation *was* jasper; the second,
G2393 N-DSF ἰάσπιδι (2x)
Rv 4:3 was in·clear·appearance like a·jasper and a·sardius
Rv 21:11 *was* like a·precious stone, even·as a·jasper stone,

G2394 Ἰάσων Iásōn *n/p.* (5x)
Roots:G2390
G2394.2 N/P-NSM Ἰάσων (2x)
Ac 17:7 whom Jason has·hospitably·received, and all these·
Rm 16:21 coworker, and·also Lucius, Jason, and SosiPater,
G2394.2 N/P-ASM Ἰάσονα (1x)
Ac 17:6 finding them, they·were·dragging Jason and certain
G2394.2 N/P-GSM Ἰάσονος (2x)
Ac 17:5 assaulting the home of·Jason, they·were·seeking to·
Ac 17:9 the security·bail personally·from Jason and the rest,

G2395 ἰατρός iatrós *n.* (7x)
Roots:G2390 Compare:G2322 G5333
G2395.2 N-NSM ἰατρός (1x)
Col 4:14 Luke, the beloved practitioner·of·healing, and
G2395.2 N-VSM ἰατρέ (1x)
Lk 4:23 'O·Practitioner·of·Healing, bring·both·relief·and·
G2395.2 N-APM ἰατρούς (1x)
Lk 8:43 *her* livelihood upon practitioners·of·healing, neither
G2395.2 N-GSM ἰατροῦ (3x)
Lk 5:31 have no need of·a·practitioner·of·healing, but·rather
Mt 9:12 have no need of·a·practitioner·of·healing, but·rather
Mk 2:17 have no need of·a·practitioner·of·healing, but·rather
G2395.2 N-GPM ἰατρῶν (1x)
Mk 5:26 under many practitioners·of·healing and expending

G2395-1 ιβ iota beta *n.* (12x)
Compare:G1427 See:G4496-1 G5516
G2395-1.2 N-NUI-ABB ιβ (12x)
Rv 7:5 having·been·officially·sealed, twelve thousand.
Rv 7:5 having·been·officially·sealed, twelve thousand.
Rv 7:5 ·Gad having·been·officially·sealed, twelve thousand.
Rv 7:6 having·been·officially·sealed, twelve thousand.
Rv 7:6 having·been·officially·sealed, twelve thousand.
Rv 7:6 having·been·officially·sealed, twelve thousand.
Rv 7:7 having·been·officially·sealed, twelve thousand.
Rv 7:7 having·been·officially·sealed, twelve thousand.
Rv 7:7 having·been·officially·sealed, twelve thousand.
Rv 7:8 having·been·officially·sealed, twelve thousand.
Rv 7:8 having·been·officially·sealed, twelve thousand.
Rv 7:8 having·been·officially·sealed, twelve thousand.

G2396 ἴδε íde *inj.* (28x)
Roots:G1492 See:G2400
G2396 INJ ἴδε (26x)
Jn 1:29 and he·says, "See the Sacrificial·Lamb of·God,
Jn 1:36 ·along, he·says, "See the Sacrificial·Lamb of·God!"
Jn 1:47 and says concerning him, "See! Truly an·Israelite in
Jn 3:26 you·yourself have·testified, see, the·same·man
Jn 5:14 he·declared to·him, "See, you·have·become healthy·
Jn 7:26 But see, he·speaks with·clarity·of·speech, and they·
Jn 11:3 saying, "Lord, see, he·whom you·are·fond·of is·
Jn 11:36 the Judeans were·saying, "See how fond·he·was·of
Jn 12:19 yeu·do·not benefit not·even·one·thing? See, the
Jn 16:29 disciples say to·him, "See, now you·speak with·
Jn 18:21 what I·spoke to·them. See, these·men personally·
Jn 19:4 again and says to·them, "See, I·bring him outside to·
Jn 19:5 And *Pilate* says to·them, "See, the man·of·clay†!"
Jn 19:14 and he·says to·the Judeans, "See yeur King!"
Gal 5:2 See, I Paul say to·yeu, that if yeu·should·be·
Mt 25:20 to·me five talants·of·silver. See, I·gained another
Mt 25:22 to·me two talants·of·silver. See, I·gained another
Mt 25:25 talant·of·silver in the earth. See, you·have *what is*
Mt 26:65 need have·we of·witnesses? See, now yeu·heard
Mk 2:24 were·saying to·him, "See, why·do they·do on the
Mk 3:34 around him, he·says, "See, my mother and my
Mk 11:21 says to·him, "Rabbi, see, the fig·tree which you·
Mk 13:1 to·him, "Mentor, see what·manner·of stones and
Mk 15:4 ·thing? See how·many·things they·testify·against
Mk 16:6 He·is not here. See the place where they·laid him!
Rm 2:17 See, you·yourself label·yourself a·Jew, and you·
G2396 V-AAM-2S ἴδε (2x)
Jn 7:52 ·out of·Galilee? Search and see! Because a·prophet
Rm 11:22 Accordingly, see *both* a·benevolent·kindness and

G2397 ἰδέα idéa *n.* (1x)
Roots:G1492 Compare:G4383 G3799 G4610-1
G1491 See:G1491
G2397.3 N-NSF ἰδέα (1x)
Mt 28:3 His outline·appearance was as lightning, and his

G2398 ἴδιος ídiôs *adj.* (113x)
Compare:G1520 G2977
G2398.1 A-APN ἴδια (1x)
1Th 4:11 to·keep·still, and to·accomplish yeur·own *tasks*,
G2398.1 A-DSM ἰδίῳ (2x)
Lk 6:41 fully·observe the beam, the·one in your·own eye?
1Co 15:23 but each in one's·own sequence: Anointed-One, a·
G2398.1 A-DSF ἰδίᾳ (1x)
Ac 3:12 ·intently at·us, as·though by·our·own power or
G2398.1 A-DPM ἰδίοις (3x)
1Pe 3:1 be·submitting·yeurselves to·yeur·own husbands,
Eph 5:22 Yeu·must·submit·yeurselves to·yeur·own husbands
Col 3:18 Yeu·must·submit·yeurselves to·yeur·own husbands
G2398.1 A-DPF ἰδίαις (1x)
1Co 4:12 and we·labor·hard, working with·our·own hands.
G2398.1 A-GSM ἰδίου (1x)
2Pe 3:17 yeu·should·fall·from your·own firm·steadfastness.
G2398.1 A-GPM ἰδίων (1x)
1Th 2:14 also suffered under yeur·own fellow·countrymen,
G2398.2 A-NSM ἴδιος (1x)
Tit 1:12 themselves, a·prophet of·their own, declared,
G2398.2 A-NPM ἴδιοι (1x)
Jn 1:11 to his·own, and his·own did·not personally·receive
G2398.2 A-NPN ἴδια (1x)
Jn 10:12 over·that·which are not *even* his·own sheep, he·
G2398.2 A-ASM ἴδιον (12x)

Jn 1:41 This·man *Andrew* first finds his·own brother Simon
Jn 5:18 ·saying also *that* God *was* his·own Father, making
Ac 1:25 ·to, *in·order* to·traverse into his·own place."
Ac 4:32 *for* any of·his holdings to·be his·own; but·rather for·
Gal 6:5 For each·man shall·bear his·own load.
Mt 22:5 they·went·away, in·fact, one to his·own farm, and
2Pe 2:22 "'A·dog *keeps·on* returning to his·own throw·up,'"
1Co 3:8 shall·receive his·own payment·of·service according·
1Co 3:8 ·of·service according·to his·own wearisome·labor.
1Co 7:2 wife, and each *woman* must·have her·own husband.
1Co 11:21 in eating, each·one takes his·own supper prior·to
1Ti 5:4 first at·their·own house to·show·devout·reverence

G2398.2 A-ASF ἰδίαν (8x)

Jn 7:18 ·man speaking from himself seeks his·own glory, but
Lk 2:3 traversed to·be·enrolled, each·one into his·own city.
Mt 9:1 ·over and came into his·own city *of·CaperNaum.*
Mt 25:15 one, to·each·man according·to his·own ability,
Rm 10:3 and seeking to·establish their·own righteousness,
2Pe 3:16 rest of·Scriptures, to their own total·destruction.
1Ti 4:2 ·words, their·own conscience having·been·seared
2Ti 1:9 ·rather according·to his·own determined·purpose and

G2398.2 A-ASN ἴδιον (6x)

Jn 15:19 the world would affectionately·favor its·own, but
Lk 10:34 And mounting him upon his·own beast, he·brought
Jud 1:6 but·rather leaving·behind their·own dwelling·place,
1Co 6:18 ·immorality morally·fails against his·own body.
1Co 7:7 ·man has his·own gracious·bestowment from·out of·
1Co 15:38 and to·each variety·of·seed, its·own body.

G2398.2 A-APM ἰδίους (5x)

Jn 13:1 to the Father, already·loving his·own, the·ones in
Mt 25:14 journeying·abroad, *who* called his·own slaves and
1Th 2:15 the Lord YeShua and their·own prophets, and
1Co 14:35 they·must·inquire·of their·own menfolk at home
1Ti 6:1 a·yoke resolutely·consider their·own masters worthy

G2398.2 A-APF ἰδίας (2x)

2Pe 3:3 traversing according·to their own longings,
2Ti 4:3 But·rather, according·to their·own longings, they·

G2398.2 A-APN ἴδια (7x)

Jn 1:11 He·came to his·own, and his·own did·not personally·
Jn 10:3 his voice, and he·calls·forth his·own sheep each·by
Jn 10:4 "And whenever he·should·cast·forth his·own sheep,
Jn 16:32 ·should·be·scattered, each·man to his·own *cares,*
Jn 19:27 that hour, the disciple took her into his·own *home.*
Ac 21:6 and those *disciples* returned·back to their·own *home.*
Mk 15:20 and dressed him *with* his·own garments, and led

G2398.2 A-DSM ἰδίῳ (3x)

Ac 28:30 abided a·whole two·years in his·own hired·house.
Rm 14:4 household·servant? To·his·own lord he·stands·fast
Rm 14:5 Let each·man be·fully·assured in his·own mind.

G2398.2 A-DSF ἰδίᾳ (5x)

Jn 4:44 "A·prophet has no honor in his·own fatherland."
Ac 1:7 seasons which the Father placed in his·own authority.
Ac 1:19 this open·field to·be·called in·their own language,
Ac 13:36 to·the counsel of·God in·his·own generation, was·
Rm 11:24 ·to nature, be·grafted·into their·own olive·tree?

G2398.2 A-DSN ἰδίῳ (1x)

Jn 5:43 If another should·come in his·own name, that·man

G2398.2 A-DPM ἰδίοις (6x)

1Pe 3:5 while·being·in·subjection to·their·own husbands,
Tit 2:5 being·submitted to·their·own husbands in·order·that
Tit 2:9 slaves to·submit·themselves to·their·own masters *and*
1Co 9:7 ·goes·to·war at·any·time with·his·own wages?
Eph 5:24 ·manner also the wives to·their·own husbands in
1Ti 6:15 who in·his·own seasons shall·show *he·is* the

G2398.2 A-DPF ἰδίαις (1x)

1Th 4:11 *tasks,* and to·work·with yeur own hands, just·as

G2398.2 A-GSM ἰδίου (7x)

Lk 6:44 each tree is·known from·out of·its·own fruit. For not
Ac 20:28 which he·himself·acquired through his·own blood.
Heb 9:12 but he·entered through his·own blood into the
Heb 13:12 ·make·holy the People through his·own blood,
Rm 8:32 He·that did·not spare his·own Son, but·rather
1Ti 3:4 one·conducting his·own house well, having his·
1Ti 3:5 ·man has·not seen·how to·conduct his·own house,

G2398.2 A-GSF ἰδίας (3x)

Ac 25:19 him concerning their·own superstitious·religion,
Jac 1:14 being·drawn·forth by his·own longing and being·
2Pe 2:16 But he·had a·reproof of·his·own transgression: a·

G2398.2 A-GSN ἰδίου (3x)

1Co 7:4 The wife does·not have·control·over her·own body,
1Co 7:4 husband does·not have·control·over his·own body,
1Co 7:37 but has authority concerning his·own will, and

G2398.2 A-GPM ἰδίων (3x)

Heb 7:27 *altar,* first on·behalf of·their·own moral·failures,
1Ti 3:12 conducting their·children and their·own houses well
1Ti 5:8 anyone does·not maintain·provision·for his·own, and

G2398.2 A-GPN ἰδίων (2x)

Jn 8:44 a·lie, he·speaks from·out of·his·own *disposition,*
Heb 4:10 his·own works, just·as God *did* from his·own.

G2398.3 A-ASF ἰδίαν (10x)

Gal 2:2 but in private to·the·ones being·of·reputation, lest·
Mt 14:13 into a·desolate place in private. And after·hearing
Mt 14:23 ·up upon the mountain in private to·pray, and with·
Mt 17:1 he·brings them up upon a·high mountain in private.
Mt 17:19 after·coming·alongside YeShua in private, the
Mt 24:3 the disciples came·alongside him in private, saying,
Mk 6:32 ·off to a·desolate place in·the sailboat in private.
Mk 7:33 him aside from the crowd in private, *Jesus* cast his
Mk 9:2 a·high mountain in private, alone·by·themselves.
Mk 9:28 disciples were·inquiring·of him in private, "Why·

G2398.3 A-GSF ἰδίας (1x)

2Pe 1:20 does·not itself·occur from·a·private explanation.

G2398.4 A-ASF ἰδίαν (7x)

Lk 9:10 them, he·quietly·retreated privately into a·desolate
Lk 10:23 his disciples, he·declared privately, "Supremely·
Ac 23:19 by·the hand and departing privately, was·inquiring,
Mt 20:17 the twelve disciples aside privately by the roadway,
Mk 4:34 But privately, he·was·explaining all·things to·his
Mk 6:31 ·here yeu yeurselves aside privately into a·desolate
Mk 13:3 John and Andrew were·inquiring·of him privately,

G2398.5 A-DSF ἰδίᾳ (1x)

1Co 12:11 to·each·man individually just·as he·resolves.

G2398.6 A-APM ἰδίους (1x)

Ac 4:23 they·went to their·own·company and reported

G2398.6 A-GPM ἰδίων (1x)

Ac 24:23 ·forbid not·one of·his own·company to·tend *to·him*

G2398.7 A-DSF ἰδίᾳ (2x)

Ac 2:6 ·hearing them speaking in·his·own·distinct dialect.
Ac 2:8 we·ourselves each hear our own·distinct dialect into

G2398.8 A-DSM ἰδίῳ (1x)

Gal 6:9 doing the good; for in·due season we·shall·reap, not

G2398.8 A-DPM ἰδίοις (2x)

Tit 1:3 but in·due seasons made his Redemptive-word
1Ti 2:6 on·behalf of·all— the testimony in·due seasons,

G2399 ἰδιώτης idiṓtēs *n.* (5x)

Roots:G2398

G2399.1 N-NPM ἰδιῶται (2x)

Ac 4:13 they·were uneducated and untrained men·of·clay†,
1Co 14:23 ·tongues, and untrained·men should·enter·in, or

G2399.1 N-NAM ἰδιώτης (2x)

1Co 14:24 ·one or an·untrained·man, he·is·convicted by all,
2Co 11:6 And even though *I·am* untrained in·the discourse,

G2399.1 N-GSM ἰδιώτου (1x)

1Co 14:16 ·occupying the place of·the untrained declare the

G2400 ἰδού idoú *v.* (213x)

Roots:G1492 Compare:G2029 See:G2396 G2400-1 xLangEquiv:H2005

G2400 V-2AAM-2S ἰδού (213x)

Jn 4:35 *then* comes the harvest'? Behold, I·say to·yeu, lift·
Jn 12:15 "Behold, your King comes *to·you,* sitting·down
Jn 16:32 "Behold, an·hour comes, and now has·come that
Jn 19:26 he·says to·his mother, "Woman, behold your son!"
Jn 19:27 he·says to·the disciple, "Behold your mother!" And
Lk 1:20 And behold, you·shall·be keeping·silent, and not
Lk 1:31 And behold, you·shall·conceive in your·uterus and
Lk 1:36 "And behold, your cousin Elisabeth, she·herself *is*
Lk 1:38 And Mariam declared, "Behold, the female·slave
Lk 1:44 For, behold, as·soon·as the sound of·your greeting
Lk 1:48 of·his female·slave,' for behold, from now·on all
Lk 2:9 And behold, Yahweh's angel stood·over them, and
Lk 2:10 Do·not be·afraid, for behold, I·proclaim·good·news
Lk 2:25 And behold, there·was a·man·of·clay† in JeruSalem,
Lk 2:34 Mariam his mother, "Behold, this *child* is·laid·out
Lk 2:48 ·did you·do us in·this·manner? Behold, your father
Lk 5:12 in one of·the cities, behold, a·man full of·leprosy;
Lk 5:18 And behold, men carrying a·man·of·clay† upon a·
Lk 6:23 skip·about, for, behold, yeur payment·of·service *is*
Lk 7:12 ·the city, behold, there·was·a·burial·procession·for
Lk 7:25 ·been·enrobed in soft garments? Behold, the·ones in
Lk 7:27 it·has·been·written, "Behold, I·myself dispatch my
Lk 7:34 and yeu·say, 'Behold a·man·of·clay†, a·glutton
Lk 7:37 And behold, a·woman in the city who was full·of·
Lk 8:41 And behold, there·came a·man whose name *was*
Lk 9:30 And behold, two men were·speaking·together with·
Lk 9:38 And behold, a·man of the crowd shouted·out, saying
Lk 9:39 And behold, a·spirit takes him, and suddenly he·
Lk 10:3 Head·on·out. Behold, I·myself dispatch yeu as
Lk 10:19 Behold, I·give to·yeu the authority, the·one to·
Lk 10:25 And behold, a·certain expert·in·Torah-Law stood·
Lk 11:31 ·Solomon; and behold, one·of·larger·stature·than
Lk 11:32 of·Jonah; and behold, one·of·larger·stature·than
Lk 11:41 ·being·within·yeur·means, and behold, *suddenly*
Lk 13:7 to the vinedresser, 'Behold, *for* three years, I·come
Lk 13:11 And behold, there·was a·woman having a·spirit of·
Lk 13:16 the Adversary-Accuser bound, behold, eighteen
Lk 13:30 "And behold, there·are last who shall·be first, and
Lk 13:32 ·declare to·that fox, 'Behold, I·cast·out demons,
Lk 13:35 "Behold, yeur house is·left to·yeu desolate.
Lk 14:2 And behold, there·was a·certain man·of·clay† before
Lk 15:29 he·declared to·his father, 'Behold, *these* so·many
Lk 17:21 nor·even shall·they·declare, 'Behold, here *it·is*!' or
Lk 17:21 or, 'Behold, there *it·is*!' For, behold, the kingdom
Lk 17:21 For, behold, the kingdom of·God is on·the·inside
Lk 17:23 And they·shall·declare to·yeu, 'Behold, here *he·is*!
Lk 17:23 or 'Behold, there *he·is*!' Yeu·should·not go·off
Lk 18:28 Then Peter declared, "Behold, we·ourselves left all
Lk 18:31 to them, "Behold, we·walk·up to JeruSalem, and
Lk 19:2 And behold, *there·was* a·man being·called by·the·
Lk 19:8 declared to the Lord, "Behold, Lord, the half of·
Lk 19:20 saying, 'Lord, behold, *here·is* your mina which I·
Lk 22:10 he·declared to·them, "Behold, with·yeu entering
Lk 22:21 "*And* moreover, behold, the hand of·the·one
Lk 22:31 "Simon, Simon, behold, the Adversary-Accuser
Lk 22:38 And they·declared, "Lord, behold, here *are* two
Lk 22:47 while·he was·yet speaking, behold a·crowd. And
Lk 23:14 ·turning·away the people, and behold, I·myself,
Lk 23:15 *·accuse this·man,* and behold, not·even·one·thing
Lk 23:29 "Because, behold, Days are·coming in which they·
Lk 23:50 And behold, a·man, Joseph by·name, a·counselor
Lk 24:4 thoroughly·perplexing about this, behold, two men
Lk 24:13 And behold, two from·among them were traversing
Lk 24:49 And behold, I·myself dispatch the Promise of·my
Ac 1:10 heaven with·him departing, behold, two men had·
Ac 2:7 saying among one·another, "Behold, are not all
Ac 5:9 ·together to·try Yahweh's Spirit? Behold, the feet of·
Ac 5:25 to·them, saying, "Behold, the men whom yeu·
Ac 5:28 this name? And behold, yeu·have·completely·filled
Ac 7:56 And he·declared, "Behold, I·observe the heavens
Ac 8:27 ·up, he·traversed, and behold, *there·was* a·man of·
Ac 8:36 And the eunuch disclosed, "Behold, *here·is* water.
Ac 9:10 And he·declared, "Behold, I·myself Lord.
Ac 9:11 ·of·Tarsus, Saul by·name. For, behold, he·prays,
Ac 10:17 clear·vision which he·saw, yet behold, the men
Ac 10:19 Spirit declared to·him, "Behold, three men seek
Ac 10:21 , Peter declared, "Behold, it·is·I myself whom
Ac 10:30 in my house, yet behold, a·man stood·still in·the·
Ac 11:11 "And behold, from·this·same·hour, three men
Ac 12:7 And behold, an·angel of·Yahweh stood·over *him,*
Ac 13:11 And now behold, the Lord's hand *is* against you,

Ac 13:25 not *he*. But·rather, behold, there·comes·one after
Ac 13:46 eternal life·above, behold, we·are·turned·around to
Ac 16:1 in Derbe and Lystra. And behold, a·certain disciple
Ac 20:22 "And now behold, having·been·bound in·the spirit,
Ac 20:25 "And now behold, I·myself personally·know that
Ac 27:24 to·establish·proof to·Caesar, and behold, God has·
Heb 2:13 ' And again, "'Behold, I·myself and the little·
Heb 8:8 with·them, he·says, "'Behold, *the* days come,'
Heb 10:7 At·that·time I·declared, 'Behold, I·come— on *the*
Heb 10:9 he·has then declared, '" Behold, I·come, *I·am* the·
Gal 1:20 ·things·which I·write to·yeu— Behold, in·the·sight
Mt 1:20 with·him cogitating these·things, behold, an·angel
Mt 1:23 "Behold, the veiled·virgin shall·be in pregnancy
Mt 2:1 king HerOd·the·Great, behold, Magian·astrologists
Mt 2:9 the king, they·traversed. And behold, the star which
Mt 2:13 And with·them already·departing, behold, an·angel
Mt 2:19 ·the·Great completely·dying, behold, an·angel of·
Mt 3:16 from the water. And behold, the heavens were·
Mt 3:17 And behold, a·voice from·out of·the heavens, saying
Mt 4:11 leaves him, and behold, angels came·alongside and
Mt 7:4 ·of·dust from your eye!' And behold, the beam *is* in
Mt 8:2 And behold, a·leper, after·coming *toward·him*, was·
Mt 8:24 And behold, a·great tempest occurred in the sea,
Mt 8:29 And behold, they·yelled·out, saying, "What·does·
Mt 8:32 into the herd of·pigs. And behold, the entire herd
Mt 8:34 And behold, the entire city came·out to meet·up
Mt 9:2 And behold, they·were·bringing to·him a·paralyzed·
Mt 9:3 And behold, certain of·the scribes declared within
Mt 9:10 in *MattHew's* home, *that* behold, even many tax·
Mt 9:18 ·him speaking these·things to·them, behold, a·ruler,
Mt 9:20 And behold, *there·was* a·woman *badly·ill*,
Mt 9:32 And with·them going·forth, behold, *men* brought
Mt 10:16 "Behold, I·myself dispatch yeu as sheep in *the*
Mt 11:8 in soft garments? Behold, the·ones prominently·
Mt 11:10 it·has·been·written, "Behold, I·myself dispatch
Mt 11:19 and they·say, 'Behold, a·man·of·clay†, a·glutton
Mt 12:2 *it*, declared to·him, "Behold, your disciples do that·
Mt 12:10 And behold, there·was a·man·of·clay† having the
Mt 12:18 "Behold my servant·boy, whom I·decidedly·chose
Mt 12:41 of·Jonah; and behold, one·of·larger·stature·than
Mt 12:42 and behold, one·of·a·larger·stature·than Solomon
Mt 12:46 still speaking to·the crowds, behold, his mother
Mt 12:47 someone declared to·him, "Behold, your mother
Mt 12:49 disciples, he·declared, "Behold my mother and
Mt 13:3 saying, "Behold, the·one sowing went·forth to·
Mt 15:22 And behold, a·Kenaanite woman from those
Mt 17:3 And behold, Moses and EliJah were·made·visible
Mt 17:5 While·he was·yet speaking, behold, a·thick·cloud
Mt 17:5 ·of·light overshadowed them. And behold, a·voice
Mt 19:16 And behold, one coming·alongside him declared,
Mt 19:27 Peter declared to·him, "Behold, we·ourselves left
Mt 20:18 "Behold, we·walk·up to JeruSalem, and the Son of·
Mt 20:30 And behold, two blind·men are·sitting·down
Mt 21:5 daughter of·Tsiyon," "Behold, your King comes
Mt 22:4 ·ones having·been·called, "Behold, I·made·ready
Mt 23:34 "On·account·of that, behold, I·myself dispatch to
Mt 23:38 "Behold, yeur house is·left to·yeu desolate!
Mt 24:23 if any·man should·declare to·yeu, 'Behold, here *is*
Mt 24:25 Behold, I·have·already·stated *this* to·yeu.
Mt 24:26 if they·should·declare to·yeu, 'Behold, he·is in the
Mt 24:26 *Or*, 'Behold, *he·is* in the private·chambers,' yeu·
Mt 25:6 a·yell has·occurred, 'Behold, the bridegroom
Mt 26:45 *moment* and rest·yeurselves? Behold, the hour has·
Mt 26:46 Be·awake! We·should·head·out. Behold, the·one
Mt 26:47 And with·him still speaking, behold, Judas, one
Mt 26:51 And behold, one of·the·ones with YeShua, upon·
Mt 27:51 And behold, the curtain of·the Temple is·torn in
Mt 28:2 And behold, there·occurred a·great earthquake.
Mt 28:7 from the dead, and behold, he·goes·on·ahead·of yeu
Mt 28:7 There yeu·shall·gaze·upon him. Behold, I·declared
Mt 28:9 *it* to·his disciples, behold, YeShua approached·and·
Mt 28:11 Now as·they were·traversing, behold, some of·the
Mt 28:20 "And behold, I·myself am with yeu *for* all the days,

Mk 1:2 in the prophets, "Behold, I·myself dispatch my
Mk 3:32 and they·declared to·him, "Behold, your mother
Mk 4:3 "Listen! Behold, the·one sowing went·forth to·sow.
Mk 5:22 And behold, there·comes one of·the directors·of·
Mk 10:28 began to·say to·him, "Behold, we·ourselves left
Mk 10:33 *saying*, "Behold, we·walk·up to JeruSalem, and
Mk 13:21 if any·man should·declare to·yeu, 'Behold, here *is*
Mk 13:21 or, 'Behold, there *he·is*!' yeu·should·not trust *it*.
Mk 13:23 look·out! Behold, I·have·already·stated all·
Mk 14:41 The hour is·come! Behold, the Son of·Clay·Man†
Mk 14:42 Be·awake! We·should·head·out. Behold, the·one
Mk 15:35 were·saying, "Behold, he·hollers·out·for EliJah.
Rm 9:33 just·as it·has·been·written, "Behold, I·lay in
Jac 3:3 Behold, we·cast the bits in the horses' mouths
Jac 3:4 Behold also the sailing·ships, being so·vast, and *are*
Jac 3:5 member, yet it·boasts·greatly. Behold, a·little fire
Jac 5:4 Behold, the payment·of·service for·the workmen
Jac 5:7 of·the Lord. Behold, the man·that·works·the·soil
Jac 5:9 lest yeu·should·be·condemned. Behold, *the* judge
Jac 5:11 Behold, we·pronounce·them supremely·blessed,
Jud 1:14 saying, "Behold, Yahweh came with a·myriad·
1Pe 2:6 in the Scripture, "Behold, I·lay in Tsiyon a·chief·
1Co 15:51 Behold, I·relay to·yeu a·mystery.
2Co 5:17 The ancient·things passed·away; behold, all·things
2Co 6:2 I·swiftly·helped you."' Behold, now *is* the·well·
2Co 6:2 now *is* the·well·acceptable season! Behold, now *is*
2Co 6:9 being·recognized, as dying and behold— we·live,
2Co 7:11 For behold this very·same·thing (to·grieve yeu
2Co 12:14 Behold, I·am at·the·ready *for* a·third·time to·
Rv 1:7 Behold, 'he·comes with the thick·clouds,' and
Rv 1:18 and was·dead; and behold, I·am living into the
Rv 2:10 which·things you·are·about to·suffer. Behold, the
Rv 2:22 'Behold, I·myself do·cast her upon a·couch *of*·
Rv 3:8 'I·personally·know your works. Behold, in·the·sight
Rv 3:9 'Behold, I·give·forth *those* from·among the gathering
Rv 3:9 but·rather do·lie), behold, I·shall·make them that
Rv 3:11 'Behold, I·come swiftly.
Rv 3:20 'Behold, I·stand at the door and knock.
Rv 4:1 these·things I·saw, and behold, a·door having·been·
Rv 4:2 ·to·be in Spirit, and behold, a·throne was·set·out in
Rv 5:5 "Do·not weep. Behold the Lion, the·one being from·
Rv 5:6 And I·saw, and behold, in *the* midst of·the throne
Rv 6:2 And I·saw, and behold, a·white horse and the·one
Rv 6:5 And I·saw, and behold, a·black horse and the·one
Rv 6:8 And I·saw, and behold, a·pale horse and the·one
Rv 6:12 the sixth official·seal, and behold, there·was a·great
Rv 7:9 After these·things I·saw, and behold, a·large crowd
Rv 9:12 The first woe went·away; behold, there·come two
Rv 11:14 The second woe went·away; behold, the third woe
Rv 12:3 in the heaven; and behold a·great fiery·red Dragon,
Rv 14:1 And I·saw, and behold, a·Lamb standing on the
Rv 14:14 And I·saw, and behold, a·white thick·cloud, and
Rv 15:5 these·things, I·saw, and behold, the Temple of·the
Rv 16:15 "Behold, I·come as a·thief.
Rv 19:11 having·been·opened·up, and behold a·white horse
Rv 21:3 ·out of·the heaven saying, "Behold, the Tabernacle
Rv 21:5 the throne declared, "Behold, I·make all·things
Rv 22:7 "Behold, I·come swiftly! Supremely·blessed *is* the·
Rv 22:12 "And behold, I·come swiftly, and my payment·of·

G2401 Ἰδουμαία Idôumaía *n/l.* (1x)
אֱדֹם ʼĕdôm [Hebrew]
Roots:H0123 Compare:G2269
G2401.2 N/L-GSF Ἰδουμαίας (1x)
Mk 3:8 and from JeruSalem, and·then from Edom, and *from*

G2402 ἱδρώς hidrṓs *n.* (1x)
G2402 N-NSM ἱδρώς (1x)
Lk 22:44 more·earnestly. And his heavy·sweat became like

G2403 Ἰε•ζαβήλ Iêzabḗl *n/p.* (2x)
אִיזֶבֶל ʼıyzeḇel [Hebrew]
Roots:H0348 Compare:G0903 See:G5572
G2403.2 N/P-PRI Ἰεζαβήλ (1x)
Rv 2:20 you·give·leave·for the woman JeZebel, the·one
EG2403.2 (1x)
Rv 2:24 have this instruction *of·JeZebel* and who did·not

G2404 Ἱεράπολις Hiêrápôlis *n/l.* (1x)
Roots:G2413 G4172
G2404.2 N/L-DSF Ἱεραπόλει (1x)
Col 4:13 the·ones in LaoDicea, and the·ones in HieraPolis.

G2405 ἱερατεία hiêratêía *n.* (2x)
Roots:G2407 Compare:G2411 See:G2406 G2420
xLangEquiv:H3550
G2405 N-ASF ἱερατείαν (1x)
Heb 7:5 ·Levi receiving the Sanctuary·priesthood, they·have
G2405 N-GSF ἱερατείας (1x)
Lk 1:9 of·the Sanctuary·priesthood, he·clearly·obtained·the·

G2406 ἱεράτευμα hiêráteuma *n.* (2x)
Roots:G2407 Compare:G2418 G2819-2 See:G2405
G2420 xLangAlso:H3550
G2406.3 N-NSN ἱεράτευμα (2x)
1Pe 2:5 house, a·holy priesthood to·carry·up spiritual
1Pe 2:9 a·Selected kindred, a·royal priesthood, a·holy nation

G2407 ἱερατεύω hiêratêúō *v.* (1x)
Roots:G2409 See:G2406 xLangAlso:H3547
G2407.2 V-PAN ἱερατεύειν (1x)
Lk 1:8 (with him performing·priestly·duties in·front·of God

G2408 Ἱερεμ•ίας Hiêrêmías *n/p.* (3x)
Ἱερμε•ΐάς Iêrmêïás [transliteration]
יִרְמְיָה yırmᵉyah [Hebrew]
יִרְמְיָהוּ yırmᵉyahû
Roots:H3414
G2408.7 N/P-ASM Ἱερεμίαν (1x)
Mt 16:14 EliJah, but *yet* others *say* JeremIah, or one of·the
G2408.7 N/P-GSM Ἱερεμίου (2x)
Mt 2:17 the·thing being·uttered by JeremIah the prophet,
Mt 27:9 ·thing being·uttered through JeremIah the prophet,

G2409 ἱερεύς hiêrêús *n.* (35x)
Roots:G2413 See:G0749
xLangEquiv:H3548 A3549
G2409.1 N-NSM ἱερεύς (1x)
Ac 14:13 And the priest of·Zeus that·offers·sacrifices, the·one
G2409.2 N-NSM ἱερεύς (4x)
Lk 1:5 a·certain priest·that·offers·sacrifices by·the·name·of
Lk 10:31 a·certain priest·that·offers·sacrifices was·walking·
Ac 5:24 Now as·soon·as the high priest and the high·warden
Heb 10:11 ·fact, every priest·that·offers·sacrifices stands each
G2409.2 N-NPM ἱερεῖς (6x)
Ac 4:1 to the people, the priests·that·offer·sacrifices and the
Heb 7:21 the priests·that·offer·sacrifices were having·become
Heb 7:23 having·become priests·that·offer·sacrifices, *since*
Heb 9:6 in·this·manner, the priests·that·offer·sacrifices, in·fact
Mt 12:5 ·Sabbaths the priests·that·offer·sacrifices in the
Rv 20:6 but·rather they·shall·be priests of·God and of·
G2409.2 N-APM ἱερεῖς (2x)
Jn 1:19 dispatched priests·that·offer·sacrifices and Levites
Lk 6:4 except alone *for* the priests·that·offer·sacrifices, and he·
G2409.2 N-DSM ἱερεῖ (3x)
Lk 5:14 show yourself to·the priest·that·offers·sacrifices, and
Mt 8:4 show yourself to·the priest·that·offers·sacrifices, and
Mk 1:44 show yourself to·the priest·that·offers·sacrifices, and
G2409.2 N-DPM ἱερεῦσιν (3x)
Lk 17:14 yeurselves to·the priests·that·offer·sacrifices." And it·
Mt 12:4 him, except only for·the priests·that·offer·sacrifices?
Mk 2:26 to·eat except for·the priests·that·offer·sacrifices, and
G2409.2 N-GPM ἱερέων (2x)
Ac 6:7 of·the priests·that·offer·sacrifices were·listening·to· the
Heb 8:4 *that there·are* the priests·that·offer·sacrifices, the·ones
EG2409.2 (1x)
Heb 7:21 having·become *priests* apart·from a·swearing·of·
G2409.3 N-NSM ἱερεύς (7x)
Heb 5:6 "'You *are* a·priest·that·offers·a·sacrifice to·the coming·
Heb 7:1 (King of·Salem, Priest of·God Most·High that·
Heb 7:3 he·abides a·priest·that·offers·a·sacrifice into perpetuity
Heb 7:15 another priest·that·offers·a·sacrifice does·rise·up—

Heb 7:17 "'You *are* a·priest·that·offers·a·sacrifice to the
Heb 7:21 have·regret, 'You *are* a·priest to the coming·age
Heb 8:4 not·even be a·priest·that·offers·a·sacrifice, being *that*
G2409.3 N-ASM ἱερέα (2x)
Heb 7:11 another priest·that·offers·a·sacrifice to·be·raised·up
Heb 10:21 and *having* a·high priest over the house of·God—
G2409.3 N-APM ἱερεῖς (2x)
Rv 1:6 ·made us kings and priests·that·offer·a·sacrifice to·his
Rv 5:10 to·our God kings and priests·that·offer·a·sacrifice, and
EG2409.3 (2x)
Heb 7:13 For *this other priest*, concerning whom these·
Heb 7:16 has·come·to·be *a·priest·that·offers·a·sacrifice*, not

G2410 Ἱεριχώ Hiêrichố *n/l.* (7x)

יְרִיחוֹ yᵉrıycнô [Hebrew]
Roots:H3405
G2410.2 N/L-PRI Ἱεριχώ (7x)
Lk 10:30 was·walking·down from JeruSalem to Jericho, and
Lk 18:35 with him drawing·near to Jericho, a·certain blind·
Lk 19:1 And entering, *Jesus* went·through Jericho.
Heb 11:30 By·trust, the walls of·Jericho fell·down, being·
Mt 20:29 with·them proceeding·forth from Jericho, a·large
Mk 10:46 Then they·come into Jericho. And as·he is·
Mk 10:46 as·he is·proceeding·forth from Jericho with his

G2411 ἱερόν hiêrṓn *n.* (72x)

Roots:G2413 Compare:G0039 G0038-1 G3485 G4638 G1493 See:G2418 G2417 G2416 xLangEquiv:H4720
G2411.2 N-ASN ἱερόν (1x)
Ac 19:27 but·yet also *for* the sanctuary of·the great goddess
G2411.3 N-ASN ἱερόν (1x)
Mt 21:12 entered into the Sanctuary·Estate of·God and cast·
G2411.3 N-GSN ἱεροῦ (8x)
Lk 2:37 from the Sanctuary·Estate, ritually·ministering *to*·
Lk 4:9 on the topmost·ledge of·the Sanctuary·Estate. And
Lk 22:52 *the* wardens of·the Sanctuary·Estate, and *the*
Ac 4:1 and the high·warden of·the Sanctuary·Estate and the
Ac 5:24 and the high·warden of·the Sanctuary·Estate and the
Mt 4:5 him on the topmost·ledge of·the Sanctuary·Estate,
Mt 24:1 for·him the structures of·the Sanctuary·Estate.
Mk 13:3 directly·opposite the Sanctuary·Estate, Peter, Jakob,
G2411.4 N-ASN ἱερόν (8x)
Jn 7:14 ·up into the Sanctuary·Atrium and was·instructing.
Jn 8:2 he·came·directly again into the Sanctuary·Atrium, and
Lk 18:10 ·clay† walked·up to the Sanctuary·Atrium to·pray,
Lk 19:45 And entering into the Sanctuary·Atrium, he·began
Ac 5:21 *this*, they·entered into the Sanctuary·Atrium at the
Mt 21:23 into the Sanctuary·Atrium while·instructing, the
Mk 11:11 JeruSalem and into the Sanctuary·Atrium. And
Mk 11:15 after·entering into the Sanctuary·Atrium, began
G2411.4 N-DSN ἱερῷ (26x)
Jn 2:14 And in the Sanctuary·Atrium, he·found the·ones
Jn 5:14 finds him in the Sanctuary·Atrium, and he·declared
Jn 7:28 Jesus yelled·out in the Sanctuary·Atrium, instructing
Jn 8:20 while·instructing in the Sanctuary·Atrium. And not·
Jn 10:23 was·walking in the Sanctuary·Atrium at Solomon's
Jn 11:56 in the Sanctuary·Atrium, they·were·seeking Jesus
Jn 18:20 gathering and in the Sanctuary·Atrium where the
Lk 19:47 instructing each day in the Sanctuary·Atrium. But
Lk 20:1 in the Sanctuary·Atrium and proclaiming·the·good·
Lk 21:37 he·was instructing in the Sanctuary·Atrium, but
Lk 21:38 ·going to him in the Sanctuary·Atrium to·hear him.
Lk 22:53 day with yeu in the Sanctuary·Atrium, yeu·did·not
Lk 24:53 ·were continually in the Sanctuary·Atrium, praising
Ac 2:46 in the Sanctuary·Atrium and breaking bread in·each
Ac 5:20 ·*in*, speak in the Sanctuary·Atrium to·the people all
Ac 5:25 are standing in the Sanctuary·Atrium and instructing
Ac 5:42 And every day in the Sanctuary·Atrium, and in·each
Ac 22:17 ·me being·in·prayer in the Sanctuary·Atrium, *that* I
Mt 21:12 and buying in the Sanctuary·Atrium, and he·
Mt 21:14 came·alongside him in the Sanctuary·Atrium, and
Mt 21:15 boys yelling·out in the Sanctuary·Atrium, saying,
Mt 26:55 yeu instructing in the Sanctuary·Atrium, and yeu·
Mk 11:15 and buying in the Sanctuary·Atrium, and he·
Mk 11:27 with·him walking along the Sanctuary·Atrium, the
Mk 12:35 while·instructing in the Sanctuary·Atrium, Jesus
Mk 14:49 alongside yeu in the Sanctuary·Atrium instructing,
G2411.4 N-GSN ἱεροῦ (5x)
Jn 2:15 everyone from·among the Sanctuary·Atrium, also the
Jn 8:59 from·out of·the Sanctuary·Atrium going through *the*
Mt 24:1 was·departing from the Sanctuary·Atrium, yet his
Mk 11:16 *any* merchandise through the Sanctuary·Atrium.
Mk 13:1 ·he was·departing out of·the Sanctuary·Atrium, one
G2411.5 N-ASN ἱερόν (10x)
Lk 2:27 the Spirit into the Sanctuary·Courtyard. And·when
Ac 3:1 ·up in·unison into the Sanctuary·Courtyard at the
Ac 3:2 the·ones traversing into the Sanctuary·Courtyard,
Ac 3:3 to·enter into the Sanctuary·Courtyard, was·asking to·
Ac 3:8 ·them into the Sanctuary·Courtyard, walking·along
Ac 21:26 the Sanctuary·Courtyard, thoroughly·announcing
Ac 21:28 into the Sanctuary·Courtyard and has·defiled this
Ac 21:29 that Paul brought into the Sanctuary·Courtyard).
Ac 24:6 to·profane the Sanctuary·Courtyard, whom also we·
Ac 25:8 nor against the Sanctuary·Courtyard, nor·even
G2411.5 N-DSN ἱερῷ (6x)
Lk 2:46 ·found him in the Sanctuary·Courtyard, sitting·down
Ac 21:27 in the Sanctuary·Courtyard, they·were·stirring·up
Ac 24:12 me in the Sanctuary·Courtyard discussing *anything*
Ac 24:18 ·cleansed in the Sanctuary·Courtyard, neither with
Ac 26:21 in the Sanctuary·Courtyard, were·intently·trying
Mt 12:5 ·sacrifices in the Sanctuary·Courtyard profane the
G2411.5 N-GSN ἱεροῦ (6x)
Lk 21:5 saying concerning the Sanctuary·Courtyard, that it·
Ac 3:2 the door of·the Sanctuary·Courtyard, the·one being·
Ac 3:10 ·and·Elegant Gate of·the Sanctuary·Courtyard; and
Ac 21:30 him outside of·the Sanctuary·Courtyard, and
Mt 12:6 one·greater·than the Sanctuary·Courtyard is here.
1Co 9:13 eat from·among the Sanctuary·Courtyard? *And·that*
EG2411.5 (1x)
Mt 23:35 and the Sacrifice·Altar *in·the Sanctuary·Courtyard.*

G2412 ἱερο•πρεπής hiêrôprêpḗs *adj.* (1x)

Roots:G2413 G4241
G2412 A-APF ἱεροπρεπεῖς (1x)
Tit 2:3 *they·be* in a·demeanor befitting·of·sacred·women, not

G2413 ἱερός hiêrṓs *adj.* (2x)

Compare:G0040 G0042 G3741 G1342 G2819-2 See:G2409 G2411 G2406 G2412
G2413 A-APN ἱερά (2x)
1Co 9:13 the·ones working the sacred·things eat from·among
2Ti 3:15 a·toddler you·have·seen the Sacred Writings— the·

G2414 Ἱερο•σόλυμα Hiêrôsólyma *n/l.* (62x)

יְרוּשָׁלַםִ yᵉrûshạlaịm [Hebrew]
יְרוּשְׁלֶם yᵉrûshạlẹm [Aramaic]
Roots:H3389 Compare:G0897 See:G2419 G4172 xLangEquiv:A3390
G2414.2 N/L-NSF Ἱεροσόλυμα (2x)
Mt 2:3 ·the·Great was·troubled, and all JeruSalem with him.
Mt 3:5 Then JeruSalem was·traversing·out to him, and all
G2414.2 N/L-ASF Ἱεροσόλυμα (32x)
Jn 2:13 near·at·hand, and Jesus walked·up to JeruSalem.
Jn 5:1 of·the Judeans, and Jesus walked·up to JeruSalem.
Jn 11:55 out of·the region to JeruSalem before the Passover,
Jn 12:12 upon·hearing that Jesus was·coming to JeruSalem,
Lk 2:22 they·brought him up to JeruSalem to·present *him* to·
Lk 2:42 ·up with·them to JeruSalem according·to the custom
Lk 18:31 "Behold, we·walk·up to JeruSalem, and all the·
Lk 19:28 traversed·on ahead, walking·up to JeruSalem.
Ac 11:2 when Peter walked·up to JeruSalem, the·ones from·
Ac 13:13 them, John·*Mark* returned·back to JeruSalem.
Ac 18:21 the·one coming in JeruSalem, but I·shall·return·
Ac 20:16 possible for·him, to·be in JeruSalem *on* the day of·
Ac 21:17 And with·us coming to JeruSalem, the brothers
Ac 25:1 Festus walked·up from Caesarea to JeruSalem.
Ac 25:9 "Will·you walk·up to JeruSalem, there to·be·judged
Ac 25:15 with·me being at JeruSalem, the chief·priests and
Gal 1:17 neither did·I·go·up to JeruSalem toward the·ones
Gal 1:18 to JeruSalem to·see·and·personally·interview Peter,
Gal 2:1 I·walked·up again to JeruSalem with BarNabas,
Mt 2:1 from *the* east arrived·publicly in JeruSalem,
Mt 5:35 foot stool, nor toward JeruSalem, because it·is *the*
Mt 16:21 ·is·mandatory·for him to·go·off to JeruSalem, and
Mt 20:17 And while·walking·up toward JeruSalem, YeShua
Mt 20:18 "Behold, we·walk·up to JeruSalem, and the Son
Mt 21:1 And when they·drew·near to JeruSalem and came to
Mt 21:10 And with·him entering into JeruSalem, all the City
Mk 10:32 the roadway, walking·up toward JeruSalem, and
Mk 10:33 "Behold, we·walk·up to JeruSalem, and the Son
Mk 11:11 And Jesus entered into JeruSalem and into the
Mk 11:15 And they·come to JeruSalem. And Jesus, after·
Mk 11:27 And they·come again to JeruSalem. And with·him
Mk 15:41 ·ones walking·up·together with·him to JeruSalem.
G2414.2 N/L-DPN Ἱεροσολύμοις (14x)
Jn 2:23 And as·soon·as he·was in JeruSalem at the Passover
Jn 4:20 and yeu say, that in JeruSalem is the place where it·
Jn 4:21 nor·even in JeruSalem, shall·yeu·fall·prostrate to·
Jn 4:45 all·the·things that he·did in JeruSalem at the Sacred·
Jn 5:2 Now at the Sheep·Gate in JeruSalem, there·is a·pool
Jn 10:22 *called Chanukkah)* occurred in JeruSalem, and it·
Lk 23:7 himself being also at JeruSalem in these days.
Ac 8:1 Called·Out·citizenry, the·one in JeruSalem; and all
Ac 8:14 Now the ambassadors in JeruSalem, after·hearing
Ac 11:22 Called·Out·citizenry, the·one in JeruSalem. And
Ac 25:24 conferred with·me, both at JeruSalem, and here,
Ac 26:4 since beginning in my·own nation in JeruSalem).
Ac 26:10 Which·thing also I·did in JeruSalem, and many of·
Ac 26:20 in Damascus, and·then in·JeruSalem and unto all
G2414.2 N/L-GPN Ἱεροσολύμων (11x)
Jn 1:19 from·out of·JeruSalem in·order·that they·may·ask·of
Jn 11:18 Now BethAny was near to·JeruSalem, about fifteen
Ac 1:4 ·*are* not to·be·departing from JeruSalem, but·rather
Ac 11:27 prophets came·down from JeruSalem to Antioch.
Ac 25:7 having·walked·down from JeruSalem stood·around,
Ac 28:17 *as* a·chained·prisoner out of·JeruSalem into the
Mt 4:25 *from* DecaPolis, and *from* JeruSalem and Judea, and
Mt 15:1 Pharisees from JeruSalem come·alongside YeShua
Mk 3:8 and from JeruSalem, and·then from Edom, and *from*
Mk 3:22 ·walking·down from JeruSalem, were·saying "He·
Mk 7:1 alongside him, after·coming from JeruSalem.
EG2414.2 (3x)
Jn 12:18 the crowd *from JeruSalem* also went·and·met him,
Lk 24:14 all these·things having·befallen *in·JeruSalem.*
Rv 11:8 of·the great City *that·is JeruSalem*, which spiritually

G2415 Ἱερο•σολυμίτης Hiêrôsôlymítēs *n/g.* (2x)

Roots:G2414
G2415 N/G-NPM Ἱεροσολυμῖται (1x)
Mk 1:5 him, and·also the *people* of·JeruSalem, and all were·
G2415 N/G-GPM Ἱεροσολυμιτῶν (1x)
Jn 7:25 from·among the·men of·JeruSalem were·saying, "Is

G2416 ἱερο•συλέω hiêrôsyléō *v.* (1x)

Roots:G2417
G2416.2 V-PAI-2S ἱεροσυλεῖς (1x)
Rm 2:22 the idols, do·you·burglarize·temple·sanctuaries?

G2417 ἱερό•συλος hiêrósylôs *adj.* (1x)

Roots:G2411 G4813 Compare:G0952 See:G2416
G2417.2 A-APM ἱεροσύλους (1x)
Ac 19:37 neither despoilers·of·temple·sanctuaries, nor·even

G2418 ἱερο•υργέω hiêrôurgéō *v.* (1x)

Roots:G2411 G2041 Compare:G2406 See:G2411
G2418.2 V-PAP-ASM ἱερουργοῦντα (1x)
Rm 15:16 *as* working·in·the·sanctuary·above *for* the good·

G2419 Ἱερου•σαλήμ Hiêrôusalḗm *n/l.* (85x)

יְרוּשְׁלֶם yᵉrûshạlẹm [Aramaic]
יְרוּשָׁלַםִ yᵉrûshạlaịm [Hebrew]
Roots:A3390 Compare:G0897 See:G2414 G4172 xLangEquiv:H3389
G2419.2 N/L-PRI Ἱερουσαλήμ (81x)
Lk 2:25 there·was·a·man·of·clay† in JeruSalem, whose

Lk 2:38 to·all the·ones awaiting a·ransoming in JeruSalem.
Lk 2:41 his parents traversed to JeruSalem for·the *Judeans'*
Lk 2:43 the boy Jesus remained·behind in JeruSalem. And
Lk 2:45 him, they·returned·back to JeruSalem, seeking him.
Lk 4:9 Then he·brought him to JeruSalem, and he·set him on
Lk 5:17 of·Galilee and Judea, and·also JeruSalem. And the
Lk 6:17 from all *over* Judea and JeruSalem, and from·the
Lk 9:31 he·was·about to·completely·fulfill in JeruSalem.
Lk 9:51 ·himself firmly·set his face to·traverse to JeruSalem,
Lk 9:53 his face was *as* one·who·is·traversing to JeruSalem.
Lk 10:30 was·walking·down from JeruSalem to Jericho, and
Lk 13:4 ·and·beyond all men·of·clay† residing in JeruSalem?
Lk 13:22 and making a·circuitous·route toward JeruSalem.
Lk 13:33 should·completely·perish outside of·JeruSalem.
Lk 13:34 "O·JeruSalem, JeruSalem, the·one killing the
Lk 13:34 "O·JeruSalem, JeruSalem, the·one killing the
Lk 17:11 with him traversing to JeruSalem, it·happened that
Lk 19:11 on·account·of him being near to·JeruSalem, and
Lk 21:20 yeu·should·see JeruSalem being·surrounded by
Lk 21:24 "And JeruSalem shall·be being·trampled by
Lk 23:28 declared, "Daughters of·JeruSalem, do·not weep
Lk 24:13 being·a·distance from JeruSalem *of·about* sixty
Lk 24:18 "*Are* you only sojourning in JeruSalem, and did·not
Lk 24:33 same hour, they·returned·back to JeruSalem. And
Lk 24:47 name to all the nations, beginning from JeruSalem.
Lk 24:49 must·settle in the City of·JeruSalem until yeu·
Lk 24:52 him, returned·back to JeruSalem with great joy.
Ac 1:8 ·shall·be witnesses to·me both in JeruSalem, and in
Ac 1:12 Then they·returned·back to JeruSalem from *the*
Ac 1:12 which is near JeruSalem, being a·Sabbath's journey
Ac 1:19 to·all the·ones residing·in JeruSalem, such·for this
Ac 2:5 there·were Jews residing in JeruSalem, devout men
Ac 2:14 absolutely·all the·ones residing·in JeruSalem, be
Ac 4:6 *were* in JeruSalem, with HannAs the high·priest and
Ac 4:16 apparent to·all the·ones residing·in JeruSalem, and
Ac 5:16 *out* of·the cities all·around JeruSalem, bringing *the*
Ac 5:28 yeu·have·completely·filled JeruSalem with·yeur
Ac 6:7 disciples were·multiplied in JeruSalem tremendously;
Ac 8:25 *and John* returned·back to JeruSalem, they·did also
Ac 8:26 the·one descending from JeruSalem to Gaza."
Ac 8:27 *and* who had·come to JeruSalem to·fall·prostrate.
Ac 9:2 he·may·bring·them having·been·bound to JeruSalem.
Ac 9:13 wrongs he·did to·your holy·ones at JeruSalem.
Ac 9:21 the·ones in JeruSalem who·are·calling·upon this
Ac 9:26 Now after·coming·directly to JeruSalem, Saul was·
Ac 9:28 while·traversing·in and traversing·out at JeruSalem.
Ac 10:39 of·the Judeans and in JeruSalem— whom they·
Ac 12:25 from·among JeruSalem after·completely·fulfilling
Ac 13:27 For the·ones residing in JeruSalem, and their rulers
Ac 13:31 with·him from Galilee to JeruSalem, who are his
Ac 15:2 them, to·walk·up to JeruSalem to the ambassadors
Ac 15:4 ·publicly in JeruSalem, they·were·fully·accepted by
Ac 16:4 ambassadors and the elders, the·ones in JeruSalem.
Ac 19:21 *for·him* to·traverse to JeruSalem, declaring,
Ac 20:22 I·myself traverse to JeruSalem, not having·seen
Ac 21:4 through the Spirit not to·walk·up to JeruSalem.
Ac 21:11 ·manner the Judeans at JeruSalem shall·bind the
Ac 21:12 were·imploring him not to·walk·up to JeruSalem.
Ac 21:13 but·rather also to·die at JeruSalem on·behalf·of the
Ac 21:15 ·belongings, we·were·walking·up to JeruSalem.
Ac 21:31 all JeruSalem has·been·stirred·up·into·an·uproar,
Ac 22:5 to JeruSalem in·order·that they·should·be·punished·
Ac 22:17 with·me returning·back to JeruSalem, even with·
Ac 22:18 out of·JeruSalem on·account·that they·shall·not
Ac 23:11 concerning me to JeruSalem, in·this·manner it·is·
Ac 24:11 since I·walked·up to JeruSalem to·fall·prostrate.
Ac 25:3 ·for him *to·walk·up* to JeruSalem, while·they·make
Ac 25:20 ·willing to·traverse to JeruSalem, and·there to·be·
Heb 12:22 God's CITY, to·a·heavenly JeruSalem, and to·a·
Gal 4:25 and corresponds·to JeruSalem at·the·present, and
Gal 4:26 But the JeruSalem up·above is free, which is *the*
Mt 23:37 "O·JeruSalem, JeruSalem, the·one killing the
Mt 23:37 "O·JeruSalem, JeruSalem, the·one killing the

Mk 11:1 And when they·drew·near to JeruSalem, to
Rm 15:19 (from JeruSalem and around·in·a·circuit to·as·far·
Rm 15:25 right·now, I·traverse to JeruSalem, attending to·
Rm 15:26 ·poor of·the holy·ones, the·ones in JeruSalem.
Rm 15:31 for JeruSalem may·become well·acceptable to·the
1Co 16:3 yeur gracious·benevolence away to JeruSalem.
Rv 21:10 Great CITY, the Holy JeruSalem, descending out

EG2419.2 (2x)

Ac 18:22 *then* walking·up *to·JeruSalem* and greeting the
Ac 23:32 to the barracks *in·JeruSalem*, after·giving·leave·for

G2419.3 N/L-PRI Ἱερουσαλήμ (2x)

Rv 3:12 God, the brand-new JeruSalem, the·one descending
Rv 21:2 HOLY CITY, brand-new JeruSalem, descending

G2420 ἱερωσύνη hiêrōsýnē *n.* (4x)

Roots:G2413 Compare:G2405 G2406 See:G2411
G2418 xLangAlso:H3550

G2420.2 N-ASF ἱερωσύνην (1x)

Heb 7:24 ·age, has the non-transferable sacred·priesthood,

G2420.2 N-GSF ἱερωσύνης (3x)

Heb 7:11 was through the Levitical sacred·priesthood, (for
Heb 7:12 For with·the sacred·priesthood being·transferred,
Heb 7:14 ·even·one·thing concerning a·sacred·priesthood.

G2421 Ἰεσσαί Iêssaí *n/p.* (5x)

יִשַׁי yiśhay [Hebrew]
Roots:H3448

G2421.2 N/P-PRI Ἰεσσαί (5x)

Lk 3:32 *son* of·Jesse, *son* of·Obed, *son* of·BoAz, *son* of·
Ac 13:22 "I·found David, the *son* of·Jesse, *to·be* a·man
Mt 1:5 (birthed·from·out·of·Ruth), and Obed begot Jesse.
Mt 1:6 Now Jesse begot King David, and King David begot
Rm 15:12 " There·shall·be the root of·Jesse, and the·one

G2422 Ἰεφθάε Iêphthaê *n/p.* (1x)

יִפְתָּח yiph·tacH [Hebrew]
Roots:H3316

G2422.2 N/P-PRI Ἰεφθάε (1x)

Heb 11:32 Baraq, Samson, and Yiphtach; and also David,

G2423 Ἰεχον•ίας Iêchônías *n/p.* (2x)

יְכָנְיָה yᵉkon·yah [Hebrew]
Roots:H3204 xLangAlso:H3659

G2423.2 N/P-NSM Ἰεχονίας (1x)

Mt 1:12 the Babylonian exile, YeKonYah begot ShealtiEl,

G2423.2 N/P-ASM Ἰεχονίαν (1x)

Mt 1:11 Then JosIah begot YeKonYah and his brothers,

G2424 Ἰη•σοῦς Iēsôûs *n/p.* (1043x)

יֵשׁוּעַ yeśhûa' [Hebrew, shortened]
יְהוֹשׁוּעַ yᵉhôśhû'a [Hebrew]
יְהוֹשֻׁעַ yᵉhôśhu'a [Hebrew, alternate]
Roots:H3442 See:G0076
xLangEquiv:A3443 xLangAlso:H3091 H3444

G2424.2 N/P-NSM Ἰησοῦς (501x)

Jn 1:38 But Jesus, turning·around and distinctly·viewing
Jn 1:42 him to Jesus. And Jesus, looking·clearly·upon him,
Jn 1:43 On·the next·day, Jesus determined to·go·forth into
Jn 1:47 Jesus saw NathaniEl coming toward him and says
Jn 1:48 do·you·know me?" Jesus answered and declared to·
Jn 1:50 Jesus answered and declared to·him, "Because I·
Jn 2:2 And Jesus also was·called·forth to the wedding, and·
Jn 2:4 Jesus says to·her, "Woman, what·does·this·have to·
Jn 2:7 Jesus says to·them, "Overfill the ceremonial·water·
Jn 2:11 Jesus did this initiating of·miraculous·signs in Qanah
Jn 2:13 was near·at·hand, and Jesus walked·up to JeruSalem
Jn 2:19 Jesus answered and declared to·them, "Tear·down
Jn 2:22 the Scripture and the word which Jesus declared.
Jn 2:24 But Jesus himself was·not entrusting himself to·them
Jn 3:3 Jesus answered and declared to·him, "Certainly,
Jn 3:5 Jesus answered, "Certainly, most·certainly, I·say to·
Jn 3:10 Jesus answered and declared to·him, "Are you·
Jn 3:22 After these·things, Jesus and his disciples came into
Jn 4:1 heard *it said* that "Jesus makes and immerses more
Jn 4:2 (though·indeed Jesus himself was·not immersing, but·

Jn 4:6 was there. So·then Jesus, having·become·weary as·a·
Jn 4:7 of·Samaria to·draw·out water. Jesus says to·her,
Jn 4:10 Jesus answered and declared to·her, "If you·had·
Jn 4:13 Jesus answered and declared to·her, "Anyone
Jn 4:16 Jesus says to·her, "Head·on·out, holler·out·for your
Jn 4:17 I·do·not have a·husband." Jesus says to·her, "You·
Jn 4:21 Jesus says to·her, "Woman, trust me, because an·
Jn 4:26 Jesus says to·her, "It·is·I Myself.
Jn 4:34 Jesus says to·them, "My food is that I·may·do the
Jn 4:44 for Jesus himself already·testified that, "A·prophet
Jn 4:46 In·due·course, Jesus came again into Qanah of·
Jn 4:47 This·man, after·hearing that Jesus comes from·out
Jn 4:48 Now·then Jesus declared to him, "Unless yeu·*all*·
Jn 4:50 Jesus says to·him, "Depart, your son lives.
Jn 4:50 ·of·clay† trusted the word that Jesus declared to·him,
Jn 4:53 *it·was* at that hour, in which Jesus declared to·him,
Jn 4:54 *the* second miraculous·sign *that* Jesus did, coming
Jn 5:1 of·the Judeans, and Jesus walked·up to JeruSalem.
Jn 5:6 Jesus, seeing this·man laying·ill and knowing that he·
Jn 5:8 Jesus says to·him, "Be·awakened, take·up your mat
Jn 5:13 who it·was, for Jesus carefully·slipped·away, with·
Jn 5:14 After these·things, Jesus finds him in the Sanctuary·
Jn 5:15 to·the Judeans that it·was Jesus, the·one making him
Jn 5:17 Now Jesus answered them, "My Father works until
Jn 5:19 So·then Jesus answered and declared to·them,
Jn 6:1 After these·things, Jesus went·off *to·the* other·side of·
Jn 6:3 Then Jesus went·up upon the mountain.
Jn 6:5 crowd is·come toward him, Jesus says to PhilIp,
Jn 6:10 And Jesus declared, "Make the men·of·clay† to·sit·
Jn 6:11 Then Jesus took the loaves·of·bread, and after·
Jn 6:14 So·then, seeing that Jesus did a·miraculous·sign, the
Jn 6:15 So Jesus, knowing that they·are·about to·come and
Jn 6:17 ·now it·had·become dark, and Jesus had·not come to
Jn 6:22 embarked, and that Jesus did·not enter·together
Jn 6:24 when the crowd saw that Jesus was not there, nor
Jn 6:26 Jesus answered them and declared, "Certainly, most·
Jn 6:29 Jesus answered and declared to·them, "This is the
Jn 6:32 Accordingly, Jesus declared to·them, "Certainly,
Jn 6:35 And Jesus declared to·them, "I AM the bread of·
Jn 6:42 "Is this not Jesus, the son of·Joseph, whose father
Jn 6:43 So Jesus answered and declared to·them, "Do·not
Jn 6:53 Accordingly, Jesus declared to·them, "Certainly,
Jn 6:61 But Jesus, having·seen in himself that his disciples
Jn 6:64 For Jesus had·personally·known from·among *the*
Jn 6:67 So·then Jesus declared to·the twelve, "And *do* yeu·
Jn 6:70 Jesus answered them, "No, *it·is* I·myself *that*
Jn 7:1 And after these·things, Jesus was·walking in Galilee,
Jn 7:6 So·then Jesus says to·them, "My season is·not·yet
Jn 7:14 the Sacred·Feast *of·Booths*, Jesus walked·up into the
Jn 7:16 Jesus answered them and declared, "My instruction
Jn 7:21 Jesus answered and declared to·them, "I·did one
Jn 7:28 Accordingly, Jesus yelled·out in the Sanctuary·
Jn 7:33 So·then Jesus declared to·them, "Yet a·short time
Jn 7:37 *day* of·the Sacred·Feast *of·Booths*, Jesus stood and
Jn 7:39 not·yet *given*, because Jesus was·not·yet glorified).
Jn 8:1 But Jesus traversed to the Mount of·Olives.
Jn 8:6 But after·stooping down, Jesus was·writing with·the
Jn 8:9 the last·of·them; and Jesus alone was·left·behind—
Jn 8:10 Then Jesus, after·pulling·himself·up·straight and
Jn 8:11 And Jesus declared to·her, "Not·even·do I·myself
Jn 8:12 In·due·course, Jesus spoke again to·them, saying, "I
Jn 8:14 Jesus answered and declared to·them, "Though I·
Jn 8:19 is your Father?" Jesus answered, "Neither do·yeu·
Jn 8:20 These utterances Jesus spoke at the treasury·room,
Jn 8:21 In·due·course, Jesus declared again to·them, "I·
Jn 8:25 are you·yourself?" And Jesus declares to·them,
Jn 8:28 Then accordingly, Jesus declared to·them,
Jn 8:31 So·then, Jesus was·saying to *those* Judeans, the·ones
Jn 8:34 Jesus answered them, "Certainly, most·certainly, I·
Jn 8:39 "AbRaham is our father." Jesus says to·them, "If
Jn 8:42 Accordingly, Jesus declared to·them, "If God was
Jn 8:49 Jesus answered, "I·myself do·not have a·demon,
Jn 8:54 Jesus answered, "If I·myself glorify my·own·self,

Jn 8:58 Jesus declared to·them, "Certainly, most·certainly, I·
Jn 8:59 *them* at him, but Jesus hid·himself and went·forth
Jn 9:3 Jesus answered, "Neither this·man morally·failed, nor
Jn 9:11 "A·man·of·clay† being·referred·to·as Jesus, he·made
Jn 9:14 And it·was a·Sabbath when Jesus made the clay and
Jn 9:35 Jesus heard that they·cast him forth outside.
Jn 9:37 And Jesus declared to·him, "Even you·have·clearly·
Jn 9:39 Then Jesus declared, "For judgment, I·myself did·
Jn 9:41 Jesus declared to·them, "If yeu·were blind, yeu·
Jn 10:6 Jesus declared this proverb to·them, but those
Jn 10:7 So·then Jesus declared to·them again, "Certainly,
Jn 10:23 And Jesus was·walking in the Sanctuary·Atrium at
Jn 10:25 Jesus answered them, "I·declared *it* to·yeu, and
Jn 10:32 Jesus answered them, "Many good works I·showed
Jn 10:34 Jesus answered them, "Is·it not having·been·
Jn 11:4 But Jesus, hearing *that*, declared, "This sickness is
Jn 11:5 And Jesus loved Martha, also her sister, and Lazarus.
Jn 11:9 Jesus answered, "Are·there not·indeed twelve hours
Jn 11:13 And Jesus had·declared *this* concerning his death,
Jn 11:14 Then accordingly, Jesus declared to·them with·
Jn 11:17 ·then, after·going *to·him*, Jesus found him having
Jn 11:20 as·soon·as she·heard that Jesus was·coming, went·
Jn 11:23 Jesus says to·her, "Your brother shall·rise·up.
Jn 11:25 Jesus declared to·her, "I AM the resurrection and
Jn 11:30 Now Jesus had·not·yet come into the village, but·
Jn 11:32 So as·soon·as Mary came where Jesus was, upon·
Jn 11:33 Now as·soon·as Jesus saw her weeping, and the
Jn 11:35 Jesus welled·up·with·tears.
Jn 11:38 Accordingly, Jesus, again being·exasperated in
Jn 11:39 Jesus says, "Take·away the stone.
Jn 11:40 Jesus says to·her, "Did·I·not declare to·you, that, if
Jn 11:41 was laying·outstretched. And Jesus lifted the eyes
Jn 11:44 ·about with·a·sweat·towel. Jesus says to·them,
Jn 11:45 and distinctly·viewing the·things·which Jesus did,
Jn 11:46 and declared to·them what·things Jesus did.
Jn 11:51 year, he·prophesied that Jesus was·about to·die on·
Jn 11:54 Accordingly, Jesus was·no longer strolling·about
Jn 12:1 six days before the Passover, Jesus came to BethAny
Jn 12:7 Accordingly, Jesus declared, "Leave her *alone*.
Jn 12:12 *in·BethAny*) upon·hearing that Jesus was·coming to
Jn 12:14 And Jesus, finding a·young·donkey, sat·down on it,
Jn 12:16 ·the first, but·rather when Jesus was·glorified, then
Jn 12:23 And Jesus answered them, saying, "The hour has·
Jn 12:30 Jesus answered and declared, "This voice has·
Jn 12:35 Accordingly, Jesus declared to·them, "Yet a·short
Jn 12:36 These·things Jesus spoke, and after·going·off, he·
Jn 12:44 And Jesus yelled·out and declared, "The·one
Jn 13:1 ·Feast of·the Passover, Jesus, personally·knowing
Jn 13:3 Jesus (having·seen that the Father has·given all·
Jn 13:7 Jesus answered and declared to·him, "What I·myself
Jn 13:8 *even* to the coming·age." Jesus answered him, "If I·
Jn 13:10 Jesus says to·him, "The·one having·been·bathed
Jn 13:21 ·declaring these·things, Jesus was·troubled in·the
Jn 13:23 bosom was one of·his disciples whom Jesus loved.
Jn 13:26 Jesus answered, "It·is that·man to·whom I·shall·
Jn 13:27 entered into that·man. So·then Jesus says to·him,
Jn 13:29 was·holding the money·bag, that Jesus says to·him,
Jn 13:31 When he·went·forth, Jesus says, "Now the Son of·
Jn 13:36 where·do you·head·on·out?" Jesus answered him,
Jn 13:38 Jesus answered him, "Shall·you·lay·down your
Jn 14:6 Jesus says to·him, "I AM the way, and the
Jn 14:9 Jesus says to·him, "Am·I so·vast a·time with yeu,
Jn 14:23 Jesus answered and declared to·him, "If anyone
Jn 16:19 Now·then, Jesus knew that they·were·wanting to·
Jn 16:31 Jesus answered them, "*So* at·this·moment, do·yeu·
Jn 17:1 Jesus spoke these·things and lifted·up his eyes to the
Jn 18:1 ·declaring these·things, Jesus went·forth together
Jn 18:2 the place, because many·times Jesus did·gather there
Jn 18:4 Accordingly, Jesus, having·seen all the·things that·
Jn 18:5 "Jesus of·Natsareth." Jesus says to·them, "I AM.
Jn 18:8 Jesus answered, "I·declared to·yeu that I AM.
Jn 18:11 So·then Jesus declared to·Peter, "Cast your dagger
Jn 18:20 Jesus answered him, "I·myself spoke with·
Jn 18:23 Jesus answered him, "If I·spoke wrongly, testify
Jn 18:34 Jesus answered him, "From yourself, do·you say
Jn 18:36 Jesus answered, "My kingdom is not from·among
Jn 18:37 you·yourself are a·king!" Jesus answered, "You·
Jn 19:5 So Jesus came·forth outside bearing the thorny
Jn 19:9 are you·yourself?" But Jesus gave him no answer.
Jn 19:11 Jesus answered, "You·were·not having not·even·
Jn 19:19 ·written was, "JESUS OF·NATSARETH THE
Jn 19:20 because the place where Jesus was·crucified was
Jn 19:26 Accordingly, Jesus seeing his mother and the
Jn 19:28 After this, Jesus, having·seen that even·now
Jn 19:30 Accordingly, when Jesus received the wine·vinegar
Jn 20:2 to the other disciple whom Jesus was·fond·of, and
Jn 20:14 *there*, yet she·had·not seen that it·was Jesus.
Jn 20:15 Jesus says to·her, "Woman, why do·you·weep?
Jn 20:16 Jesus says to·her, "Mariam.
Jn 20:17 Jesus says to·her, "Do·not lay·hold of·me, for I·
Jn 20:19 the fear of·the Judeans, Jesus came and stood·still
Jn 20:21 Now·then, Jesus declared to·them again, "Peace
Jn 20:24 ·to·as Twin) was not with them when Jesus came.
Jn 20:26 with·the doors having·been·shut, Jesus came and
Jn 20:29 Jesus says to·him, "Thomas, because you·have·
Jn 20:30 Now·then in·fact, Jesus also did many other signs
Jn 20:31 ·written in·order·that yeu·may·trust that Jesus is the
Jn 21:1 After these·things, Jesus made himself apparent
Jn 21:4 ·becoming the·break·of·dawn, Jesus stood·still upon
Jn 21:4 the disciples had·not seen that it·was Jesus.
Jn 21:5 So Jesus says to·them, "Little·children, ¿! do·yeu·
Jn 21:7 that disciple whom Jesus loved says to·Peter, "It·is
Jn 21:10 Jesus says to·them, "Bring of·the small·fry which
Jn 21:12 Jesus says to·them, "Come·here! Dine!" And not·
Jn 21:13 Then Jesus comes and takes the bread and gives *it*
Jn 21:14 ·now a·third·time *that* Jesus is·made·apparent to·his
Jn 21:15 when they·had·dined, Jesus says to·Simon Peter,
Jn 21:17 that I·have·affection·for you." Jesus says to·him,
Jn 21:20 following *them* (*the·one* whom Jesus loved, who
Jn 21:22 Jesus says to·him, "If I·should·want him to·remain
Jn 21:23 does·not die." But Jesus did·not declare to·him
Jn 21:25 many other·things, as·much·as Jesus did, which if
Lk 2:21 his name was·called Jesus, the *name* being·called·
Lk 2:43 returning·back, the boy Jesus remained·behind in
Lk 2:52 And Jesus was·continually·advancing in·wisdom,
Lk 3:23 *his specific·assignment*, Jesus himself was about
Lk 4:1 And Jesus, full of·Holy Spirit, returned·back from the
Lk 4:4 And Jesus answered to him, saying, "It·has·been·
Lk 4:8 And answering, Jesus declared to·him, "Get·
Lk 4:12 And answering, Jesus declared to·him, "It·has·
Lk 4:14 And Jesus returned·back in the power of·the Spirit
Lk 4:35 And Jesus reprimanded him, saying, "Be·muzzled!
Lk 5:10 partners with·Simon. And Jesus declared to Simon,
Lk 5:22 But Jesus, fully·knowing their deliberations,
Lk 5:31 And answering, Jesus declared to them, "The·ones
Lk 6:3 And responding to them, Jesus declared, "Did·yeu·
Lk 6:9 So·then Jesus declared to them, "I·shall·inquire·of
Lk 7:6 And Jesus was·traversing together with·them.
Lk 7:9 after·hearing these·things, Jesus marveled·at him.
Lk 7:22 And answering, Jesus declared to·them,
Lk 7:40 And answering, Jesus declared to him, "Simon, I·
Lk 8:30 And Jesus inquired·of him, saying, "What is your
Lk 8:38 to·be together with·him, but Jesus dismissed him,
Lk 8:39 the whole city what·many·things Jesus did for·him.
Lk 8:45 And Jesus declared, "Who·is the·one laying·hold
Lk 8:46 And Jesus declared, "Someone laid·hold of·me, for
Lk 8:50 But Jesus hearing *it*, answered him, saying, "Do·not
Lk 9:36 with the voice occurring, Jesus was·found alone.
Lk 9:41 And answering, Jesus declared, "O distrusting and
Lk 9:42 ·convulsed *him*. And Jesus reprimanded the impure
Lk 9:43 ·all marveling over all·things which Jesus did, he·
Lk 9:47 And Jesus, seeing the discussion of·their heart,
Lk 9:50 And Jesus declared to him, "Do·not forbid *him*, for
Lk 9:58 And Jesus declared to·him, "The foxes have
Lk 9:60 But Jesus declared to·him, "Leave the dead·ones to·
Lk 9:62 And Jesus declared unto him, "Not·even·one·man,
Lk 10:21 In that·same hour, Jesus leaped·for·joy in·the
Lk 10:30 And taking·up *the question*, Jesus declared, "A·
Lk 10:37 Accordingly, Jesus declared to·him, "Traverse,
Lk 10:41 And answering, Jesus declared to·her, "Martha,
Lk 13:2 And responding, Jesus declared to·them, "Do·yeu·
Lk 13:12 And seeing her, Jesus addressed *her* and declared
Lk 13:14 because Jesus both·relieved·and·cured on·the
Lk 14:3 And responding, Jesus declared to the experts·in·
Lk 17:17 And responding, Jesus declared, "Are·not·indeed
Lk 18:16 But Jesus, summoning them, declared, "Allow the
Lk 18:19 And Jesus declared to·him, "Why·do you·refer·to
Lk 18:22 But Jesus, hearing these·things, declared to·him,
Lk 18:24 And Jesus, after·seeing him becoming exceedingly·
Lk 18:37 to·him that Jesus of·Natsareth was·passing·by.
Lk 18:40 being·settled, Jesus commandingly·ordered him
Lk 18:42 And Jesus declared to·him, "Receive·your·sight.
Lk 19:5 And as·soon·as Jesus came to the place, looking·up,
Lk 19:9 And Jesus declared to him, "Today, Salvation did·
Lk 20:8 And Jesus declared to·them, "Neither *do* I·myself
Lk 20:34 And answering, Jesus declared to·them, "The
Lk 22:48 But Jesus declared to·him, "Judas, do·you·hand·
Lk 22:51 And responding, Jesus declared, "*Stop!* Yeu·must·
Lk 22:52 Then Jesus declared to the chief·priests, *the*
Lk 23:28 But turning·around toward them, Jesus declared,
Lk 23:34 Then Jesus was·saying, "Father, forgive them, for
Lk 23:43 And Jesus declared to·him, "Certainly I·say to·you
Lk 23:46 hollering·out with·a·loud voice, Jesus declared,
Lk 24:15 ·and·discussing *these·things*, even Jesus himself,
Lk 24:36 speaking these·things, Jesus himself stood·still in
Ac 1:1 *was* concerning all that Jesus began both to·do and
Ac 1:11 into the heaven? This·same Jesus, the·one being·
Ac 1:21 time in which the Lord Jesus came·in and went·forth
Ac 6:14 saying that this Jesus of·Natsareth shall·demolish
Ac 9:5 "It·is·I Myself, Jesus, whom you·yourself persecute.
Ac 9:17 Saul, the Lord, Jesus, the·one being·made·visible
Ac 9:34 to·him, "Aeneas, Jesus the Anointed-One heals you
Ac 17:3 and *fully·proclaiming*, "This Jesus (whom I·myself
Ac 22:8 'It·is·I Myself, Jesus of·Natsareth, whom you·
Ac 26:15 'It·is·I Myself, Jesus, whom you·yourself
Heb 6:20 on·behalf of·us— YeShua, after·becoming High·
Heb 7:22 ·to so·vast *an·oath*, YeShua has·become a·surety
Heb 13:8 YeShua Anointed *is* the same yesterday, and today,
Heb 13:12 Therefore YeShua also, that he·may·make·holy
Gal 3:1 ·own eyes YeShua Anointed was·previously·written
Mt 1:16 from·out of·whom was·born YeShua, the·one
Mt 3:13 At·that·time, YeShua comes·directly from Galilee
Mt 3:15 And answering, YeShua declared to him, "Allow
Mt 3:16 ·being·immersed, YeShua walked·up straight·away
Mt 4:1 Then YeShua was·led·up into the wilderness by the
Mt 4:7 YeShua was·replying to·him, "Again, it·has·been·
Mt 4:10 Then YeShua says to·him, "Head·on·out,
Mt 4:12 was·handed·over *into prison*, YeShua departed for
Mt 4:17 From then·on, YeShua began to·officially·proclaim
Mt 4:18 near the Sea of·Galilee, YeShua saw two brothers,
Mt 4:23 And YeShua was·heading·out all around Galilee,
Mt 7:28 *that* when YeShua entirely·completed these sayings,
Mt 8:3 And YeShua, stretching·out his hand, laid·hold of·
Mt 8:4 Then YeShua says to·him, "Clearly·see·to·it *that*
Mt 8:7 And YeShua says to·him, "After·going *to·him*, I·
Mt 8:10 And upon·YeShua hearing *this*, he·marveled and
Mt 8:13 Then YeShua declared to·the centurion, "Head·on·
Mt 8:14 And YeShua, upon·coming into Peter's home, saw
Mt 8:18 And YeShua, seeing large crowds about him, he·
Mt 8:20 And YeShua says to·him, "The foxes have burrows,
Mt 8:22 But YeShua declared to·him, "Follow me, and
Mt 9:2 And upon·seeing their trust, YeShua declared to·the
Mt 9:4 And seeing their cogitations, YeShua declared,
Mt 9:9 ·on from·there, YeShua saw a·certain·man·of·clay†,
Mt 9:12 But after·hearing *that*, YeShua declared to·them,
Mt 9:15 And YeShua declared to·them, "¿!·Are the Sons of·
Mt 9:19 And being·roused, YeShua followed him, and *so*·
Mt 9:22 ·himself·about and seeing her, YeShua declared,
Mt 9:23 And YeShua, upon·coming into the ruler's home and

Mt 9:28 came·alongside him. And YeShua says to·them,
Mt 9:30 were·opened·up; and YeShua sternly·warned them,
Mt 9:35 And YeShua was·heading·out all around the cities
Mt 10:5 These twelve YeShua dispatched, after·charging
Mt 11:1 *that* when YeShua finished thoroughly·assigning
Mt 11:4 And answering, YeShua declared to·them,
Mt 11:7 as·these·men were·departing, YeShua began to·say
Mt 11:25 ·judgment on that occasion, YeShua declared, "I·
Mt 12:1 In that season, YeShua traversed on·the various·
Mt 12:15 And YeShua knowing *it*, departed from·there.
Mt 12:25 And YeShua having·seen their cogitations,
Mt 13:1 And in that day, YeShua, after·going·forth from the
Mt 13:34 YeShua spoke all these·things to·the crowds in
Mt 13:36 after·sending·away the crowds, YeShua went *back*
Mt 13:51 YeShua says to·them, "Did·yeu·comprehend all
Mt 13:53 And it·happened *that* when YeShua finished these
Mt 13:57 ·up by him. But YeShua declared to·them, "A·
Mt 14:13 And upon·hearing *it*, YeShua departed from·there
Mt 14:14 And upon·going·forth, YeShua saw a·large crowd,
Mt 14:16 But YeShua declared to·them, "They·have no
Mt 14:22 And immediately, YeShua compelled his disciples
Mt 14:25 watch of·the night, YeShua went·off toward them
Mt 14:27 But immediately YeShua spoke to·them, saying,
Mt 14:31 And immediately, YeShua, upon·stretching·forth
Mt 15:16 Then YeShua declared, "Are yeu also still·at·this·
Mt 15:21 And going·forth from·there, YeShua departed into
Mt 15:28 Then answering, YeShua declared to·her, "O
Mt 15:29 And walking·on from·there, YeShua came near·to
Mt 15:32 after·summoning his disciples, YeShua declared,
Mt 15:34 And YeShua says to·them, "How·many loaves·of·
Mt 16:6 Then YeShua declared to·them, "Clearly·see·to·it
Mt 16:8 But YeShua knowing *this*, declared to·them, "O·
Mt 16:13 And YeShua, upon·coming into the district of·
Mt 16:17 And responding, YeShua declared to·him,
Mt 16:20 ·declare to·no·one that he·himself is YeShua, the
Mt 16:21 From then·on, YeShua began to·show to·his
Mt 16:24 Then YeShua declared to·his disciples, "If any·
Mt 17:1 after six days, YeShua personally·takes Peter and
Mt 17:7 Then coming·alongside, YeShua laid·hold of·them
Mt 17:9 ·down off the mountain, YeShua commanded them,
Mt 17:11 And answering, YeShua declared to·them, "In·
Mt 17:17 And answering, YeShua declared, "O distrusting
Mt 17:18 And YeShua reprimanded *the demon*, and the
Mt 17:20 And YeShua declared to·them, "On·account·of
Mt 17:22 returning into Galilee, YeShua declared to·them,
Mt 17:25 he·entered into the home, YeShua preempted him,
Mt 17:26 From the others." YeShua was·replying to·him,
Mt 18:2 And YeShua, summoning a·little·child, set him in
Mt 18:22 YeShua says to·him, "I·do·not say to·you, up·to
Mt 19:1 And it·happened *that* when YeShua finished these
Mt 19:14 But YeShua declared, "Allow the little·children,
Mt 19:18 "Which·ones?" And YeShua declared, "'You·
Mt 19:21 YeShua replied to·him, "If you·want to·be
Mt 19:23 And YeShua declared to·his disciples, "Certainly
Mt 19:26 looking·clearly·at *them*, YeShua declared to·them,
Mt 19:28 And YeShua declared to·them, "Certainly I·say to·
Mt 20:17 ·up toward JeruSalem, YeShua personally·took the
Mt 20:22 But answering, YeShua declared *to·her sons*,
Mt 20:25 But YeShua, upon·summoning them, declared,
Mt 20:30 After·hearing that YeShua passes·by, they·yelled·
Mt 20:32 after·standing·still, YeShua hollered·out·for them
Mt 20:34 And empathizing, YeShua laid·hold of·their eyes,
Mt 21:1 of·Olives), then YeShua dispatched two disciples,
Mt 21:6 doing just·as YeShua specifically·assigned to·them,
Mt 21:11 were·saying, "This is YeShua the prophet, the·one
Mt 21:12 And YeShua entered into the Sanctuary·Estate of·
Mt 21:16 *boys* are·saying?" And YeShua says to·them,
Mt 21:21 And answering, YeShua declared to·them,
Mt 21:24 And answering, YeShua declared to·them, "I·also
Mt 21:31 "The first·one." YeShua says to·them, "Certainly
Mt 21:42 YeShua says to·them, "Did·yeu·not·even·at·any·
Mt 22:1 And responding, YeShua declared to·them again by
Mt 22:18 But YeShua, knowing their evil, declared, "Why·
Mt 22:29 And answering, YeShua declared to·them, "Yeu·
Mt 22:37 And YeShua declared to·him, "'You·shall·love
Mt 22:41 ·been·gathered·together, YeShua inquired·of them
Mt 23:1 Then YeShua spoke to·the crowds and to·his
Mt 24:1 And going·forth, YeShua was·departing from the
Mt 24:2 And YeShua declared to·them, "Do·not look·for all
Mt 24:4 And answering, YeShua declared to·them, "Look·
Mt 26:1 And it·happened *that* when YeShua finished all
Mt 26:10 But YeShua, knowing *of·it*, declared to·them,
Mt 26:19 And the disciples did as YeShua appointed them,
Mt 26:26 and blessing *it*, YeShua broke *it* and was·giving *it*
Mt 26:31 Then YeShua says to·them, "All yeu shall·be·
Mt 26:34 YeShua replied to·him, "Certainly I·say to·you,
Mt 26:36 Then YeShua comes with them to an·open·field
Mt 26:50 And YeShua declared to·him, "O·associate, *attend*
Mt 26:52 Then YeShua says to·him, "Return·back your
Mt 26:55 In that·same hour, YeShua declared to·the crowds,
Mt 26:63 But YeShua was·keeping·silent. And responding,
Mt 26:64 YeShua says to·him, "You·yourself declared *it*.
Mt 27:11 Now YeShua stood·still before the governor.
Mt 27:11 of·the Jews?" And YeShua was·replying to·him,
Mt 27:37 ·been·written, "THIS IS YESHUA, THE KING
Mt 27:46 the ninth hour YeShua shouted·out with·a·loud
Mt 27:50 But YeShua, after·yelling·out again with·a·loud
Mt 28:9 behold, YeShua approached·and·met them, saying
Mt 28:10 Then YeShua says to·them, "Do·not be·afraid!
Mt 28:16 to the mountain where YeShua assigned them.
Mt 28:18 And coming·alongside, YeShua spoke to·them,
Mk 1:9 in those days *that* Jesus came from Natsareth of·
Mk 1:14 ·being·handed·over *to·prison*, Jesus came into
Mk 1:17 And Jesus declared to·them, "Come·here, *fall·in*
Mk 1:25 And Jesus reprimanded him, saying, "Be·muzzled!
Mk 1:41 And Jesus, empathizing, stretching·out his hand, he·
Mk 2:5 And Jesus, after·seeing their trust, says to·the
Mk 2:8 And Jesus, fully·knowing immediately in·his spirit
Mk 2:17 And after·hearing *that*, Jesus says to·them, "The·
Mk 2:19 And Jesus declared to·them, "¿!·Are the Sons of·
Mk 3:7 And Jesus departed with his disciples to the sea.
Mk 5:13 And immediately Jesus freely·permitted them. And
Mk 5:19 But Jesus did·not allow him, but·rather says to·him,
Mk 5:20 the DecaPolis what·many·things Jesus did for·him,
Mk 5:30 And Jesus, recognizing immediately in himself the
Mk 5:36 the word being·spoken, Jesus says to·the director·
Mk 6:4 But Jesus was·saying to·them, "A·prophet is not
Mk 6:34 And Jesus, after·coming·ashore, saw a·large crowd,
Mk 7:27 But Jesus declared to·her, "First, allow the children
Mk 8:1 after·summoning his disciples, Jesus says to·them,
Mk 8:17 And upon·knowing *it*, Jesus says to·them, "Why·
Mk 8:27 Then Jesus went·out with his disciples into the
Mk 9:2 And after six days, Jesus personally·takes Peter,
Mk 9:23 Then Jesus declared to·him, "If you·are·able to·
Mk 9:25 And Jesus, after·seeing that the crowd came·
Mk 9:27 ·holding him by·the hand, Jesus awakened him,
Mk 9:39 But Jesus declared, "Do·not forbid him, for there·is
Mk 10:5 And answering, Jesus declared to·them,
Mk 10:14 ·seeing *this*, Jesus was·greatly·displeased and
Mk 10:18 And Jesus declared to·him, "Why·do you·refer·to
Mk 10:21 And Jesus, after·looking·clearly·upon him, loved
Mk 10:23 And after·looking·around, Jesus says to·his
Mk 10:24 at his words. But Jesus, answering again, says to·
Mk 10:27 And after·looking·clearly·upon them, Jesus says,
Mk 10:29 And answering, Jesus declared, "Certainly I·say
Mk 10:32 JeruSalem, and Jesus was going·on·ahead·of them
Mk 10:38 But Jesus declared to·them, "Yeu·do·not
Mk 10:39 "We·are·able." And Jesus declared to·them, "In·
Mk 10:42 But Jesus, upon·summoning them, says to·them,
Mk 10:47 And after·hearing that it·was Jesus of·Natsareth,
Mk 10:49 And after·standing·still, Jesus declared *to·them* to·
Mk 10:51 And responding, Jesus says to·him, "What·do
Mk 10:52 And Jesus declared to·him, "Head·on·out, your
Mk 11:6 they·declared to·them just·as Jesus commanded,
Mk 11:11 And Jesus entered into JeruSalem and into the
Mk 11:14 And responding, Jesus declared to·it, "May no·
Mk 11:15 ·come to JeruSalem. And Jesus, after·entering into
Mk 11:22 And answering, Jesus says to·them, "Have God's
Mk 11:29 And answering, Jesus declared to·them, "I·shall·
Mk 11:33 And Jesus answering says to·them, "Neither do
Mk 12:17 And answering, Jesus declared to·them, "Give·
Mk 12:24 And answering, Jesus declared to·them, "*Is·it* not
Mk 12:29 And Jesus answered him, "*The* foremost of·all the
Mk 12:34 And Jesus, after·seeing that the·same·man
Mk 12:35 in the Sanctuary·Atrium, Jesus was·saying,
Mk 12:41 the treasury·room, Jesus was·observing how the
Mk 13:2 And responding, Jesus declared to·him, "Do·you·
Mk 13:5 And Jesus answering them began to·say, "Look·out
Mk 14:6 And Jesus declared, "Leave her *alone*.
Mk 14:18 ·reclining·at·the·meal and eating, Jesus declared,
Mk 14:22 bread *and* blessing *it*, Jesus broke *it* and gave *it*
Mk 14:27 Then Jesus says to·them, "All yeu·shall·be·
Mk 14:30 And Jesus says to·him, "Certainly I·say to·you,
Mk 14:48 And responding, Jesus declared to·them, "Did·
Mk 14:62 And Jesus declared, "I AM, and yeu·shall·gaze·
Mk 14:72 the utterance which Jesus declared to·him, "Prior·
Mk 15:5 But Jesus was·no·longer answering not·even·one·
Mk 15:34 And at·the ninth hour, Jesus cried·out with·a·loud
Mk 15:37 And Jesus, after·sending·away *his spirit with* a·
Php 2:11 should·explicitly·affirm that Jesus Anointed *is* Lord
2Pe 1:14 even just·as our Lord YeShua Anointed made·plain
1Th 3:11 and our Lord YeShua Anointed, fully·direct our
1Th 4:14 For if we·trust that YeShua died and rose·up, in·
2Th 2:16 Now our Lord YeShua Anointed himself, and God,
1Co 3:11 being·laid·out, which is Jesus the Anointed-One.
1Co 8:6 and one Lord, Jesus Anointed (through whom *are*
1Co 11:23 to·yeu, that the Lord Jesus, on·the night in which
2Co 1:19 For the Son of·God, Jesus Anointed, the·one
2Co 13:5 *for* yeur·own·selves that Jesus Anointed is in yeu,
1Ti 1:15 full·acceptance: Anointed-One Jesus came into the
1Ti 1:16 in me foremost, Jesus Anointed may·indicate the
1Ti 2:5 men·of·clay†: a·man·of·clay†, Anointed-One Jesus,
2Ti 4:22 The Lord Jesus Anointed *be* with your spirit.
1Jn 2:22 the·one who·contradicts·by·saying that Jesus is not
1Jn 4:15 Whoever should·affirm that Jesus is the Son of·God
1Jn 5:1 Every one trusting that Jesus is the Anointed-One
1Jn 5:5 if·not the·one trusting that Jesus is the Son of·God?
1Jn 5:6 through water and blood, Jesus the Anointed-One,
Rv 22:16 "I, Jesus, sent my angel to·testify to·yeu these·

G2424.2 N/P-VSM Ἰησοῦ (10x)

Lk 4:34 to·do·with·us and you, O·YeShua of·Natsareth?
Lk 8:28 ·does·this·have to·do·with·me and you Jesus, O·Son
Lk 17:13 voices, saying, "Jesus, O·Captain, show·mercy
Lk 18:38 And he·cried·out, saying, "Jesus, O·Son of·David,
Ac 7:59 even while·saying, "Lord Jesus, accept my spirit.
Mt 8:29 to·do·with·us and you, YeShua, O·Son of·God?
Mk 1:24 to·do·with·us and you, O·YeShua of·Natsareth?
Mk 5:7 ·have to·do·with·me and you, Jesus, O·Son of·God
Mk 10:47 to·yell·out and to·say, "O·Jesus, the Son of·David
Rv 22:20 Yes, come, Lord Jesus.

G2424.2 N/P-ASM Ἰησοῦν (134x)

Jn 1:29 ·the next·day, John looks·at Jesus, who·is·coming
Jn 1:42 And he·brought him to Jesus. And Jesus, looking·
Jn 1:45 and·also the prophets: Jesus from Natsareth, the
Jn 3:2 The·same came to Jesus by·night and declared to·him,
Jn 5:16 the Judeans were·persecuting Jesus, and they·were·
Jn 6:19 stadia, they·observe Jesus walking·along on the sea
Jn 6:24 sailboats and came to CaperNaum, seeking·for Jesus.
Jn 11:21 Then Martha declared to Jesus, "Lord, if you·were
Jn 11:56 ·Atrium, they·were·seeking Jesus and were·saying
Jn 12:9 And they·did·not come on·account·of Jesus merely,
Jn 12:11 were·heading·on·out and were·trusting in Jesus.
Jn 12:21 "Sir, we·want to·see Jesus."
Jn 17:3 the only true God, and Jesus Anointed, whom you·
Jn 18:5 They·answered him, "Jesus of·Natsareth." Jesus
Jn 18:7 ·seek?" And they·declared, "Jesus of·Natsareth."
Jn 18:12 assistants of·the Judeans arrested Jesus and bound
Jn 18:19 the designated·high·priest asked Jesus concerning his
Jn 18:28 In·due·course, they·led Jesus from Caiaphas to the

Jn 18:33 the Praetorian·hall again and hollered·out·for Jesus.
Jn 19:1 Then accordingly, Pilate took Jesus and flogged *him*.
Jn 19:13 this saying, Pilate brought Jesus outside, and he·
Jn 19:16 And they·personally·took Jesus and led·*him*·away.
Jn 19:18 him, *one* on·each·side and Jesus in·*the*·middle.
Jn 19:23 Now·then, when they·crucified Jesus, the soldiers
Jn 19:33 But coming to Jesus, as·soon·as they·saw him even·
Jn 19:39 ·one coming at·the first to Jesus by·night, bringing
Jn 19:42 So they·laid Jesus there on·account·of the Judeans
Jn 20:14 left·behind. And she·observes Jesus standing *there*,
Lk 1:31 ·and·birth a·son, and you·shall·call his name Jesus.
Lk 2:27 the parents brought in the little·child Jesus, to·do
Lk 5:12 full of·leprosy; and after·seeing Jesus *and* falling on
Lk 7:4 And coming·close to Jesus, they·were·imploring him
Lk 7:19 of·his disciples, sent *them* to Jesus, saying, "Are
Lk 8:28 But after·seeing Jesus, and·then screaming·out, he·
Lk 8:35 And they·came to Jesus and found the man·of·clay†
Lk 8:40 it·happened, *that*, when Jesus returned·back, the
Lk 9:33 him, *that* Peter declared to Jesus, "O·Captain, it·is
Lk 10:29 himself as·righteous, declared to Jesus, "And who
Lk 19:3 And he·was·seeking to·see who Jesus was, and was·
Lk 19:35 And they·brought it to Jesus, and flinging their·
Lk 19:35 upon the colt, they·mounted Jesus upon *it*.
Lk 22:63 men, the·ones confining Jesus, were·mocking him,
Lk 23:8 Now upon·seeing Jesus, HerOd-AntiPas was·
Lk 23:20 Now·then, wanting to·fully·release Jesus, Pilate
Lk 23:25 they·requested. But he·handed Jesus over to·their
Ac 1:16 ·one becoming a·guide to·the·ones arresting Jesus),
Ac 2:22 hear these words: Jesus of·Natsareth, a·man
Ac 2:32 God raised·up this Jesus, of·which we·ourselves all
Ac 2:36 that God made this same Jesus, whom yeu crucified,
Ac 3:13 he·glorified his·own servant·boy, Jesus, whom yeu·
Ac 3:20 and *that* he·should·dispatch Jesus Anointed, the·one
Ac 3:26 ·raising·up his·own servant·boy Jesus, dispatched
Ac 4:27 your holy servant·boy Jesus whom you·anointed,
Ac 5:30 The God of·our fathers awakened Jesus, whom yeu·
Ac 5:42 and proclaiming·the·good·news: Jesus *is* the
Ac 7:55 he·saw God's glory, and Jesus standing at *the* right·
Ac 8:35 proclaimed·the·good·news of·Jesus to·him.
Ac 8:37 he·declared, "I·trust Jesus Anointed to·be the Son
Ac 10:38 how God anointed Jesus *who·was* from Natsareth
Ac 11:17 ·*are* already·trusting on the Lord Jesus Anointed),
Ac 11:20 proclaiming·the·good·news of·the Lord Jesus.
Ac 13:23 God awakened a·Savior for·IsraEl, Jesus,
Ac 13:33 their children, by·raising·up Jesus; as also it·has·
Ac 16:31 "Trust on the Lord Jesus Anointed, and you·shall·
Ac 17:7 of·Caesar, saying *that* there·is another king, Jesus."
Ac 17:18 to·them the·good·news of·Jesus and the
Ac 18:5 ·thoroughly·testifying to·the Jews *that* Jesus *is* the
Ac 18:28 the Scriptures, *for* Jesus to·be the Anointed-One.
Ac 19:4 after him, that·is, in the Anointed-One Jesus."
Ac 19:13 "On·oath,·we·charge yeu *by* Jesus whom Paul
Ac 19:15 the evil spirit declared, "Jesus I·know, and Paul I·
Ac 20:21 a·trust (the·one toward our Lord Jesus Anointed).
Heb 2:9 But we·look·upon YeShua— the·one *by* a·certain
Heb 3:1 ·Priest of·our affirmation, Anointed-One YeShua,
Heb 4:14 having·gone·through the heavens, YeShua the Son
Heb 12:2 clearly·looking to YeShua, the Initiator and
Heb 13:20 ·up from·among dead·men our Lord YeShua (the
Gal 2:16 Anointed-One YeShua in·order·that we·should·be·
Gal 4:14 an·angel of·God, *even* as Anointed-One YeShua.
Mt 1:21 ·call his name YeShua·*(meaning·Yahweh·Saves)*,
Mt 1:25 And he·called his name YeShua.
Mt 14:29 Peter walked upon the water to·go to YeShua.
Mt 17:8 they·saw not·even·one·man, except YeShua only.
Mt 26:4 they·may·take·secure·hold·of YeShua by·guile,
Mt 26:50 ·threw their hands on YeShua and securely·held
Mt 26:57 the·ones securely·holding YeShua led·*him*·away to
Mt 27:17 BarAbbas, or YeShua, the·one being·referred·to·
Mt 27:20 BarAbbas and should·completely·destroy YeShua.
Mt 27:22 "So·then what shall·I·do with·YeShua, the·one
Mt 27:26 and after·lashing YeShua, he·handed·*him*·over in·
Mt 27:27 governor, after·personally·taking YeShua into the
Mt 27:54 and the·ones keeping·guard·over YeShua with him
Mt 28:5 for I·have·seen that yeu·seek YeShua, the·one
Mk 5:6 But upon·seeing Jesus from a·distance, he·ran and
Mk 5:15 And they·come to Jesus and observe the·one
Mk 6:30 ·themselves·together alongside Jesus and reported
Mk 9:8 not·even·one·man, other·than Jesus alone with them
Mk 10:50 ·garment *and* rising·up, he·came toward Jesus.
Mk 11:7 And they·brought the colt to Jesus, and they·threw
Mk 14:53 And they·led Jesus away to the designated·high·
Mk 14:60 ·up in the midst, inquired·of Jesus, saying, "Do·
Mk 15:1 *and* already·binding Jesus, they·carried·*him*·away
Mk 15:15 and after·lashing Jesus, he·handed·*him*·over in·
Mk 16:6 be·utterly·amazed. Yeu·seek Jesus the Natsarethan,
Rm 4:24 on the·one already·awakening Jesus our Lord from·
Rm 6:3 ·as are·immersed into Jesus Anointed are·immersed
Rm 8:11 of·the·one awakening Jesus from·among dead·men
Rm 10:9 ·should·affirm with your mouth, "Jesus *is* Lord,"
Rm 13:14 dress·yeurselves·with the Lord Jesus Anointed,
Rm 15:5 one·another according·to Anointed-One Jesus,
Rm 15:8 I·say *it·was·necessary·for* Jesus Anointed to·have·
Jud 1:4 only Master, God and our Lord YeShua Anointed.
Php 3:20 ·fully·await *the* Savior, *the* Lord Jesus Anointed,
1Th 1:10 from·among dead·men, YeShua, the·one who·is·
1Th 2:15 the *Judeans* killing the Lord YeShua and their·own
1Co 2:2 among yeu, except Jesus Anointed and this *Jesus*
1Co 9:1 Have·I·not·indeed clearly·seen Jesus Anointed our
1Co 12:3 says, "Jesus *is* irrevocably·damned·to·destruction.
1Co 12:3 ·even·one·man is·able to·declare, "Jesus *is* Lord,"
1Co 16:22 ·not have·affection·for the Lord Jesus Anointed,
2Co 4:5 ·proclaim, but·rather Anointed-One Jesus *the* Lord,
2Co 4:5 we·ourselves *are* yeur slaves on·account·of Jesus.
2Co 4:11 ·over to death on·account·of Jesus, in·order·that
2Co 4:14 the·one awakening the Lord Jesus shall·awaken us
2Co 11:4 does·officially·proclaim another Jesus, whom we·
Eph 6:24 all the·ones loving our Lord Jesus Anointed with
Col 2:6 ·received the Anointed-One, Jesus the Lord, *so*
Phm 1:5 which you·have toward the Lord Jesus and for all
Phm 1:6 ·good·thing among yeu in Anointed-One Jesus.
2Ti 2:8 Remember *that* Jesus Anointed, birthed·from·out·of·
1Jn 2:1 alongside the Father, Jesus Anointed, *the* righteous·
1Jn 4:2 spirit which affirms Jesus Anointed having·come in
1Jn 4:3 spirit that does·not affirm Jesus, the Anointed-One,
2Jn 1:7 the·ones not affirming Jesus Anointed as·coming in

G2424.2 N/P-DSM Ἰησοῦ (95x)

Jn 1:36 And after·looking·clearly·upon Jesus walking·along,
Jn 1:37 heard him speaking, and they·followed Jesus.
Jn 12:22 and again Andrew and PhilIp relay *it* to·Jesus.
Jn 18:15 And Simon Peter was·following Jesus, and *so was*
Jn 18:15 ·priest, and he·entered·together with·Jesus into the
Jn 18:22 standing·nearby gave a·slap to·Jesus, declaring,
Jn 19:9 the Praetorian·hall and says to·Jesus, "From·what·
Jn 21:21 Upon·seeing this·man, Peter says to·Jesus, "Lord,
Lk 6:11 alongside one·another what they·might do to·Jesus.
Lk 22:47 them, and he·drew·near to·Jesus to·kiss him.
Lk 23:42 And he·was·saying to·Jesus, "Lord, recall me to·
Ac 4:2 people and fully·proclaiming in Jesus the resurrection
Ac 4:13 them, that they·were together with·Jesus.
Heb 12:24 and to·YeShua, mediator of·a·fresh·new covenant
Gal 2:4 we·have in Anointed-One YeShua— in·order·that
Gal 3:14 ·come·to·be for the Gentiles in YeShua Anointed—
Gal 3:26 of·God through the trust in Anointed-One YeShua.
Gal 3:28 for yeu are all one in Anointed-One YeShua.
Gal 5:6 For in YeShua Anointed, neither circumcision nor
Gal 6:15 For in Anointed-One YeShua, neither circumcision
Mt 8:5 Now as·YeShua was·entering into CaperNaum, a·
Mt 8:34 city came·out to meet·up with·YeShua. And after·
Mt 9:10 ·were·reclining·together·at·the·meal with·YeShua
Mt 9:27 And with·YeShua passing·on from·there, two blind·
Mt 14:12 And going·*on*, they·reported *it* to·YeShua.
Mt 15:1 from JeruSalem come·alongside YeShua saying,
Mt 17:4 *to·this*, Peter declared to·YeShua, "Lord, it·is good
Mt 17:19 Then after·coming·alongside YeShua in private,
Mt 18:1 hour, the disciples came·alongside YeShua, saying,
Mt 21:27 And answering YeShua, they·declared, "We·do·
Mt 26:17 the disciples came·alongside YeShua, saying to·
Mt 26:49 immediately, going·toward YeShua, he·declared,
Mt 27:55 a·distance, who followed YeShua from Galilee,
Mt 27:57 who also himself became·a·disciple of·YeShua.
Mk 2:15 reclined·together·at·the·meal with·Jesus and his
Mk 9:4 and they·were speaking·together with·Jesus.
Mk 9:5 Now responding *to·this*, Peter says to·Jesus, "Rabbi,
Mk 10:52 ·his·sight and was·following Jesus along the
Mk 11:33 And answering, they·say to·Jesus, "We·do·not
Rm 3:24 the ransom·in·full, the·one in Jesus Anointed—
Rm 6:11 but alive to·God in Jesus Anointed our Lord.
Rm 6:23 *is* eternal life-above in Jesus Anointed our Lord.
Rm 8:1 for·the·ones in Anointed-One Jesus, *for·the·ones*
Rm 8:2 of·the life-above in Anointed-One Jesus set me free
Rm 8:39 the love of·God in Anointed-One, Jesus our Lord.
Rm 14:14 have·been·convinced by *the* Lord Jesus, that *there*·
Rm 15:17 I·have a·boast in Jesus Anointed in·the·things
Rm 16:3 and Aquila, my coworkers in Anointed-One Jesus,
Rm 16:18 are·not slaves to·our Lord Jesus Anointed, but·
Jud 1:1 and having·been·fully·kept in·YeShua Anointed, *to*·
Php 1:1 the holy·ones in Anointed-One Jesus, to·the·ones
Php 1:26 in me may·abound in Jesus Anointed through my
Php 2:5 yeurselves, which *was* also in Anointed-One Jesus
Php 2:19 I·do·expect, in *the* Lord Jesus, to·send TimoThy
Php 3:3 ·spirit, and boasting in Anointed-One Jesus, and not
Php 3:14 ·the upward calling of·God in Anointed-One Jesus.
Php 4:7 and yeur mental·dispositions in Anointed-One Jesus.
Php 4:19 ·to his wealth in glory in Anointed-One Jesus.
Php 4:21 Greet every holy·one in Anointed-One Jesus. The
1Pe 5:10 eternal glory by Anointed-One YeShua— after·our·
1Pe 5:14 the·ones in Anointed-One YeShua. So·be·it,·Amen.
1Th 1:1 in Father God and *in* Lord YeShua Anointed. Grace
1Th 2:14 in Judea being in Anointed-One YeShua. Because
1Th 4:1 *yeu* by *the* Lord YeShua, just·as yeu·personally·
1Th 5:18 the·will of·God in Anointed-One YeShua for yeu.
2Th 1:1 in God our Father and *the* Lord YeShua Anointed.
1Co 1:2 ·made·holy in Anointed-One Jesus, called·forth *to*·
1Co 1:4 ·one already·being·given to·yeu in Jesus Anointed,
1Co 1:30 yeu are in Anointed-One Jesus, who is·made to·us
1Co 4:15 fathers, for in Anointed-One Jesus, I·myself begot
1Co 15:31 which I·have in Anointed-One Jesus our Lord.
1Co 16:24 yeu all in Anointed-One Jesus. So·be·it,·Amen.
Eph 1:1 and to·those·that·trust in Anointed-One Jesus.
Eph 1:15 pervasive·among yeu in the Lord Jesus and *of* the
Eph 2:6 in the heavenly·places in Anointed-One Jesus,
Eph 2:7 in *his* kindness toward us in Anointed-One Jesus.
Eph 2:10 in Anointed-One Jesus for beneficially·good works
Eph 2:13 right·now in Anointed-One Jesus, yeu·yeurselves,
Eph 3:11 he·made in Anointed-One, Jesus our Lord—
Eph 3:21 ·Out·Citizenry, by Anointed-One Jesus, unto all
Eph 4:21 are·instructed by him (just·as truth is in Jesus)—
Col 1:4 of·yeur trust in Anointed-One Jesus and *of·yeur* love,
Col 1:28 man·of·clay† complete in Anointed-One Jesus—
Phm 1:23 fellow·prisoner·of·war in Anointed-One Jesus,
1Ti 1:12 I·have gratitude to·Anointed-One Jesus our Lord,
1Ti 1:14 with trust and love, the·one in Anointed-One Jesus.
1Ti 3:13 ·clarity in *the* trust, the·one in Anointed-One Jesus.
2Ti 1:1 of·life-above, the·one in Anointed-One Jesus.
2Ti 1:9 to·us in *the* Anointed-One, Jesus— before time
2Ti 1:13 and love, the·one *that·is* in Anointed-One Jesus.
2Ti 2:1 in the grace, the·one in Anointed-One Jesus.
2Ti 2:10 the·one in Anointed-One Jesus with eternal glory.
2Ti 3:12 in Anointed-One Jesus shall·be·persecuted.
2Ti 3:15 through a·trust, the·one in Anointed-One Jesus.
1Jn 5:20 *who·is* true, in his Son Jesus Anointed. This is the

G2424.2 N/P-GSM Ἰησοῦ (232x)

Jn 1:17 and the truth came·to·be through Jesus Anointed.
Jn 2:1 Qanah of·Galilee, and the mother of·Jesus was there.
Jn 2:3 And lacking wine, the mother of·Jesus says to him,
Jn 12:3 rubbed·oil·on the feet of·Jesus and firmly·wiped his
Jn 13:23 Now reclining·at·the·meal at Jesus' bosom was one
Jn 13:25 Then this·one, falling·back upon Jesus' chest, says

Jn 18:32 saying of·Jesus may·be·completely·fulfilled which
Jn 19:25 *women* stood near the cross of·Jesus: *Mariam* his
Jn 19:38 a·disciple of·Jesus but having·been·under·cover on·
Jn 19:38 that he·may·take·away the body of·Jesus, and Pilate
Jn 19:38 So he·came and took·away the body of·Jesus.
Jn 19:40 So·then they·took the body of·Jesus and bound it
Jn 20:12 the feet, where the body of·Jesus was·lain·out.
Lk 3:21 ·immersed, then with·Jesus being·immersed and
Lk 5:8 *it*, Simon Peter fell·down·at Jesus' knees, saying,
Lk 5:19 together with·the pallet into the midst before Jesus.
Lk 7:3 And after·hearing about Jesus, he·dispatched elders
Lk 8:35 directly·at the feet of·Jesus, having·been·attired and
Lk 8:41 directly·at the feet of·Jesus, he·was·imploring him
Lk 10:39 who, sitting·down·near at Jesus' feet, also was·
Lk 23:26 the cross on·him, *for·him* to·carry *it* behind Jesus.
Lk 23:52 ·alongside Pilate, requested the body of·Jesus.
Lk 24:3 they·did·not find the body of·the Lord Jesus.
Lk 24:19 to·him, "Concerning Jesus of·Natsareth, who
Ac 1:14 and Mariam the mother of·Jesus, and·also together
Ac 2:38 in the name of·Jesus Anointed for pardon of·moral·
Ac 3:6 In the name of·Jesus Anointed of·Natsareth, be·
Ac 4:10 that by the name of·Jesus Anointed of·Natsareth,
Ac 4:18 nor·even to·instruct at·all in the name of·Jesus.
Ac 4:30 through the name of·your holy servant·boy, Jesus."
Ac 4:33 of·the resurrection of·the Lord Jesus, and great
Ac 5:40 to·speak in the name of·Jesus, and they·dismissed
Ac 8:12 of·God and the name of·Jesus Anointed, they·were·
Ac 8:16 ·been·immersed in the name of·the Lord Jesus).
Ac 9:27 ·with·clarity at Damascus in the name of·Jesus.
Ac 9:29 in the name of·the Lord Jesus, and also he·was·
Ac 10:36 ·the·good·news of·peace through Jesus Anointed—
Ac 15:11 the grace of·*the*·Lord Jesus Anointed to·be·saved;
Ac 15:26 on·behalf of·the name of·our Lord Jesus Anointed.
Ac 16:18 you in the name of·Jesus Anointed to·come·out
Ac 19:5 ·were·immersed into the name of·the Lord Jesus.
Ac 19:10 the Redemptive-word of·the Lord Jesus, both Jews
Ac 19:13 the name of·the Lord Jesus over the·ones having
Ac 19:17 and the name of·the Lord Jesus was·magnified.
Ac 20:24 ·from the Lord Jesus, to·thoroughly·testify the
Ac 20:35 the words of·the Lord Jesus that he·himself
Ac 21:13 on·behalf of·the name of·the Lord Jesus."
Ac 25:19 concerning some·man *named* Jesus, having·died,
Ac 26:9 ·things contrary to·the name of·Jesus of·Natsareth.
Ac 28:23 and·also persuading them concerning Jesus, both
Ac 28:31 the·things concerning the Lord Jesus Anointed—
Heb 10:10 ·occasion·only, of·the body of·YeShua Anointed.
Heb 10:19 by the blood of·YeShua, having freeness·of·
Heb 13:21 in·the·sight of·him, through YeShua Anointed—
Gal 1:1 ·of·clay†, but·rather through YeShua Anointed and
Gal 1:3 Father God, and *from* our Lord YeShua Anointed,
Gal 1:12 *it* through a·revelation of·YeShua Anointed.
Gal 2:16 but·only through a·trust of·YeShua Anointed, we·
Gal 3:22 ·that, as·a·result of·trust in·YeShua Anointed, the
Gal 6:14 in the cross of·our Lord YeShua Anointed, through
Gal 6:17 bear in my body the marks of·the Lord YeShua.
Gal 6:18 the grace of·our Lord YeShua Anointed *be* with
Mt 1:1 origin *(via·adoption)* of·YeShua Anointed, *the* Son
Mt 1:18 Now the birth of·YeShua Anointed was in·this·
Mt 2:1 Now with·YeShua already·being·born in BethLechem
Mt 14:1 ·AntiPas the tetrarch heard of·the fame of·YeShua
Mt 15:30 them directly·at the feet of·YeShua. And he·both·
Mt 26:6 And with·YeShua coming·to·be in BethAny, in
Mt 26:51 one of·the·ones with YeShua, upon·stretching·out
Mt 26:59 were·seeking false·testimony against YeShua, that
Mt 26:69 "You·yourself also were with YeShua of·Galilee."
Mt 26:71 "This·one also was with YeShua of·Natsareth."
Mt 26:75 of·the utterance *that* YeShua had·declared to·him,
Mt 27:1 took consultation against YeShua such·for him to·
Mt 27:58 Pilate, requested the body of·YeShua. Then Pilate
Mk 1:1 A·beginning of·the good·news of·Jesus Anointed,
Mk 5:21 And with·Jesus crossing·over again in the sailboat
Mk 5:27 After·hearing about Jesus *and* already·coming in
Mk 14:55 ·seeking testimony against Jesus in·order to·put
Mk 14:67 "You also were with Jesus of·Natsareth."
Mk 15:43 ·went·in to Pilate and requested the body of·Jesus.
Rm 1:1 Paul, a·slave of·Jesus Anointed, called·forth *to·be*
Rm 1:4 of·the·dead; *specifically*, Jesus Anointed our Lord,
Rm 1:6 are *the* called·forth·ones of·Jesus Anointed).
Rm 1:7 from God our Father and *the* Lord Jesus Anointed.
Rm 1:8 ·thanks to·my God through Jesus Anointed on·behalf
Rm 2:16 ·to my good·news, *this·is* through Jesus Anointed).
Rm 3:22 righteousness through trust of·Jesus Anointed *is* for
Rm 3:26 birthed·from·out of·a·trust of·Jesus (specifically·as
Rm 5:1 peace toward God through our Lord Jesus Anointed,
Rm 5:11 in God through our Lord Jesus Anointed, through
Rm 5:15 grace of·the one man·of·clay†, Jesus Anointed, to
Rm 5:17 in life-above through the one·man, Jesus Anointed.
Rm 5:21 to eternal life-above through Jesus Anointed our
Rm 7:25 I·give·thanks to·God through Jesus Anointed our
Rm 15:6 the God and Father of·our Lord Jesus Anointed.
Rm 15:16 for me to·be a·public·servant of·Jesus Anointed to
Rm 15:30 on·account·of our Lord Jesus Anointed, and on·
Rm 16:20 The grace of·our Lord Jesus Anointed *be* with yeu.
Rm 16:24 The grace of·our Lord Jesus Anointed *be* with yeu
Rm 16:25 and the official·proclamation of·Jesus Anointed
Rm 16:27 ·him *be* the glory through Jesus Anointed into the
Jac 1:1 a·slave of·God and of·*the*·Lord YeShua Anointed.
Jac 2:1 ·not hold the trust of·our Lord YeShua Anointed (*the*
Jud 1:1 Jude, a·slave of·YeShua Anointed and a·brother of·
Jud 1:17 by the ambassadors of·our Lord YeShua Anointed,
Jud 1:21 the mercy of·our Lord YeShua Anointed unto
Php 1:1 Paul and TimoThy, slaves of·Jesus Anointed. To·all
Php 1:2 from God our Father and *from* Lord Jesus Anointed.
Php 1:6 ·finish *it* even·unto *the* day of·Jesus Anointed—
Php 1:8 ·after yeu all in inward·affections of·Jesus Anointed.
Php 1:11 of·the·ones through Jesus Anointed, to *the* glory
Php 1:19 an·ample·supply of·the Spirit of·Jesus Anointed
Php 2:10 that at the name of·Jesus, every knee should·bow
Php 2:21 ·own, not the·things·of the Anointed-One, Jesus.
Php 3:8 ·knowledge of·Anointed-One, Jesus my Lord— on·
Php 3:12 also I·am·grasped by the Anointed-One Jesus.
Php 4:23 The grace of·our Lord Jesus Anointed *be* with yeu
1Pe 1:1 Peter, an·ambassador of·YeShua Anointed. To·
1Pe 1:2 and a·sprinkling of·the·blood of·YeShua Anointed.
1Pe 1:3 and Father of·our Lord YeShua Anointed, the·one
1Pe 1:3 *the* resurrection of·YeShua Anointed from·among
1Pe 1:7 and glory at the·revealing of·YeShua Anointed—
1Pe 1:13 to·yeu at *the* revealing of·YeShua Anointed.
1Pe 2:5 well·acceptable to·God through YeShua Anointed.
1Pe 3:21 — through *the* resurrection of·YeShua Anointed,
1Pe 4:11 may·be·glorified through YeShua Anointed, to·
2Pe 1:1 a·slave and an·ambassador of·YeShua Anointed.
2Pe 1:1 of·our God and Savior YeShua Anointed.
2Pe 1:2 *the* full·knowledge of·God and of·YeShua our Lord.
2Pe 1:8 ·acknowledgment of·our Lord YeShua Anointed.
2Pe 1:11 kingdom of·our Lord and Savior YeShua Anointed.
2Pe 1:16 and initial·arrival of·our Lord YeShua Anointed.
2Pe 2:20 of·the Lord and Savior YeShua Anointed, and *they*
2Pe 3:18 of·our Lord and Savior YeShua Anointed. To·him
1Th 1:1 God our Father, and *the* Lord YeShua Anointed.
1Th 1:3 of·the Expectation, of·our Lord YeShua Anointed),
1Th 2:19 *being* before our Lord YeShua Anointed at his
1Th 3:13 ·Presence of·our Lord YeShua Anointed with all
1Th 4:2 charges we·gave yeu through the Lord YeShua.
1Th 4:14 ·him the·ones being·laid·to·rest through YeShua.
1Th 5:9 of·Salvation through our Lord YeShua Anointed,
1Th 5:23 returning·Presence of·our Lord YeShua Anointed.
1Th 5:28 The grace of·our Lord YeShua Anointed *be* with
2Th 1:2 God our Father and *the* Lord YeShua Anointed.
2Th 1:7 the revealing of·the Lord YeShua from heaven with
2Th 1:8 the good·news of·our Lord YeShua Anointed,
2Th 1:12 of·our Lord YeShua Anointed may·be·glorified in
2Th 1:12 of·our God and of·*the*·Lord YeShua Anointed.
2Th 2:1 returning·Presence of·our Lord YeShua Anointed,
2Th 2:14 of·the·glory of·our Lord YeShua Anointed.
2Th 3:6 our Lord's name, YeShua Anointed, to·deliberately·
2Th 3:12 and exhort through our Lord YeShua Anointed, in·
2Th 3:18 The grace of·our Lord YeShua Anointed *be* with
Tit 1:1 of·God and an·ambassador of·Jesus Anointed—
Tit 1:4 Father God and *the* Lord Jesus Anointed our Savior.
Tit 2:13 of·our great God and Savior, Jesus Anointed—
Tit 3:6 on us abundantly through Jesus Anointed our Savior,
1Co 1:1 *to·be* an·ambassador of·Jesus Anointed through
1Co 1:2 ·upon the name of·our Lord Jesus Anointed— both
1Co 1:3 from God our Father, and Lord Jesus Anointed.
1Co 1:7 ·awaiting the revealing of·our Lord Jesus Anointed,
1Co 1:8 ·to·account in the Day of·our Lord Jesus Anointed.
1Co 1:9 *the* fellowship of·his Son Jesus Anointed our Lord.
1Co 1:10 the name of·our Lord Jesus Anointed, in·order·that
1Co 5:4 "In the name of·our Lord Jesus Anointed, with·yeu
1Co 5:4 together with·the power of·our Lord Jesus Anointed,
1Co 5:5 spirit may·be·saved in the Day of·the Lord Jesus."
1Co 6:11 in the name of·the Lord Jesus, and by the Spirit of·
1Co 15:57 us the victory through our Lord Jesus Anointed.
1Co 16:23 The grace of·the Lord Jesus Anointed *be* with yeu
2Co 1:1 Paul, an·ambassador of·Jesus Anointed through
2Co 1:2 from God our Father and *from* Lord Jesus Anointed.
2Co 1:3 the God and Father of·our Lord Jesus Anointed, the
2Co 1:14 ·as yeu *are* also ours in the Day of·the Lord Jesus.
2Co 4:6 of·the glory of·God in *the* face of·Jesus Anointed.
2Co 4:10 the mortal·deadness of·the Lord Jesus, that also the
2Co 4:10 the life-above of·Jesus may·be·made·apparent in
2Co 4:11 life-above also of·Jesus should·be·made·apparent in
2Co 4:14 ·awaken us also, through Jesus, and shall·present
2Co 5:18 ·reconciling us to·himself through Jesus Anointed,
2Co 8:9 the grace of·our Lord Jesus Anointed, how·that
2Co 11:31 and Father of·our Lord Jesus Anointed, the·one
2Co 13:14 The grace of·the Lord Jesus Anointed, and the
Eph 1:1 Paul, an·ambassador of·Jesus Anointed through
Eph 1:2 from God our Father and *our* Lord Jesus Anointed.
Eph 1:3 God and Father of·our Lord Jesus Anointed, the·one
Eph 1:5 ·as·sons into himself through Jesus Anointed,
Eph 1:17 ·order·that the God of·our Lord Jesus Anointed, the
Eph 2:20 and prophets, with·Jesus Anointed himself being
Eph 3:1 I, Paul, *am* the chained·prisoner of·Jesus, the
Eph 3:9 the·one creating all things through Jesus Anointed—
Eph 3:14 my knees to the Father of·our Lord Jesus Anointed,
Eph 5:20 and Father in *the* name of·our Lord Jesus Anointed,
Eph 6:23 trust from Father God and *the* Lord Jesus Anointed.
Col 1:1 Paul, an·ambassador of·Jesus Anointed through
Col 1:2 from God our Father and *the* Lord Jesus Anointed.
Col 1:3 God and Father of·our Lord Jesus Anointed, praying
Col 3:17 *do* all in *the* Lord Jesus' name, giving·thanks to·the
Phm 1:1 Paul, a·chained·prisoner of·Jesus Anointed, and
Phm 1:3 from God our Father and *the* Lord Jesus Anointed.
Phm 1:9 and now also a·chained·prisoner of·Jesus Anointed.
Phm 1:25 The grace of·our Lord Jesus Anointed *be* with yeur
1Ti 1:1 Paul, an·ambassador of·Jesus Anointed according·to
1Ti 1:1 of·God our Savior, and Lord Jesus Anointed, our
1Ti 1:2 from God our Father and Jesus Anointed our Lord.
1Ti 4:6 you·shall·be a·good attendant of·Jesus Anointed—
1Ti 5:21 ·the·sight of·God, and of·Lord Jesus Anointed, and
1Ti 6:3 (the·ones of·our Lord Jesus Anointed) and with·the
1Ti 6:13 and *in·the·sight* of·Anointed-One Jesus (the·one
1Ti 6:14 ·appearing of·our Lord Jesus Anointed—
2Ti 1:1 Paul, an·ambassador of·Jesus Anointed through
2Ti 1:2 from Father God and Anointed-One Jesus our Lord.
2Ti 1:10 ·appearing of·our Savior Jesus Anointed, *who·is*, in·
2Ti 2:3 ·hardship as a·good soldier of·Jesus Anointed.
2Ti 4:1 ·sight of·God and the Lord Jesus Anointed (the·one
1Jn 1:3 with the Father, and with his Son Jesus Anointed.
1Jn 1:7 one·another, and the blood of·Jesus Anointed, his
1Jn 3:23 ·trust on·the name of·his Son Jesus Anointed; and
2Jn 1:3 and personally·from *the* Lord Jesus Anointed, the
Rv 1:1 *The* Revelation of·Jesus Anointed, which God gave
Rv 1:2 ·God, and *to* the testimony of·Jesus Anointed, and *to*
Rv 1:5 and from Jesus Anointed, *who·is* the trustworthy
Rv 1:9 kingdom and patient·endurance of·Jesus Anointed,
Rv 1:9 and on·account·of the testimony of·Jesus Anointed.

Rv 12:17 ·God and having the testimony of·Jesus Anointed.
Rv 14:12 the commandments of·God and the trust of·Jesus.
Rv 17:6 of·the blood of·the martyrs of·Jesus. And seeing her,
Rv 19:10 having the testimony of·Jesus. Fall·prostrate to·
Rv 19:10 to·God, for the testimony of·Jesus is the spirit of·
Rv 20:4 ·of the testimony of·Jesus and on·account·of the
Rv 22:21 The grace of·our Lord Jesus Anointed *be* with yeu
EG2424.2 (68x)
Jn 7:50 (the·one coming alongside *Jesus* by·night *and* being
Jn 9:22 ·now that if any·man should·affirm *Jesus to·be the*
Jn 18:9 may·be·completely·fulfilled, which *Jesus* declared,
Lk 5:3 which was Simon's, *Jesus* asked·of him to·head·off
Lk 5:18 to·carry him in and to·lay *him* in·the·sight of *Jesus*.
Lk 6:8 deliberations. And *Jesus* declared to·the man·of·
Lk 7:1 And since *Jesus* fully·finished all his utterances in the
Lk 7:24 of·John going·off, *Jesus* began to·discourse to the
Lk 7:36 into the Pharisee's home, *Jesus* reclined·at·the·table.
Lk 8:4 him *from* each city, *Jesus* declared *the following*
Lk 9:10 gave·an·account to *Jesus* what·many·things they·did
Lk 9:23 Then *Jesus* was·saying to *them* all, "If any·man
Lk 11:14 Now *afterward, Jesus* was casting·out a·demon,
Lk 11:37 Now as *Jesus* was·speaking, a·certain Pharisee
Lk 11:37 And entering·in, *Jesus* sat·back·to·eat.
Lk 11:46 And *Jesus* declared, "Woe to·yeu also, the experts·
Lk 12:1 ·trampled·down one·another, *Jesus* began to·say to
Lk 13:22 And *Jesus* was·traversing·throughout each *of·the*
Lk 14:16 Then *Jesus* declared to·him, "A·certain man·of·
Lk 17:1 And *Jesus* declared to the disciples, "It·is not·
Lk 18:40 and with·him drawing·near, *Jesus* inquired·of him,
Lk 19:1 And entering, *Jesus* went·through Jericho.
Lk 19:4 he·may·see him, because *Jesus* was·about to·go
Lk 19:11 ·things, augmenting *it, Jesus* declared a·parable,
Lk 19:28 ·declaring these·things, *Jesus* traversed·on ahead,
Lk 22:8 And *Jesus* dispatched Peter and John, declaring,
Lk 22:14 when the hour came, *Jesus* sat·back·to·eat, and the
Lk 22:39 according·to his custom, *Jesus* traversed to the
Lk 23:9 But *Jesus* answered him not·even·one·thing.
Ac 1:4 being·huddled·close·together, *Jesus* charged them,
Ac 2:24 it·was not possible *for·Jesus* to·be·securely·held by
Ac 3:16 ·observe and personally·know. *Jesus'* name and the
Ac 11:21 turned·back·around to Yahweh trusting *in·Jesus*.
Ac 13:24 prior·to *the* personal·appearance of *Jesus'* entrance.
Ac 13:31 *Jesus* who was·gazed·upon over many·more days
Ac 15:13 Jacob *(the half-brother of·Jesus)* answered, saying
Ac 18:6 ·against them and reviling *Jesus*, shaking·out his
Ac 18:25 the·things concerning the Lord *Jesus, though*
Ac 26:11 I·was·compelling *them* to·revile *Jesus*; and·also
Heb 2:11 On·account·of which cause, *YeShua the Initiator*
Mt 9:18 after·coming *to·YeShua*, was·falling·prostrate to·
Mt 9:20 After·coming·alongside *YeShua* from·behind, she·
Mt 12:11 And *YeShua* declared to·them, "What man·of·
Mt 16:1 And upon·coming·alongside to·tempt *YeShua*, the
Mt 19:17 And *YeShua* declared to·him, "Why·do you·refer·
Mt 27:3 Then after·seeing that *YeShua* was·condemned,
Mk 1:45 matter, such·for *Jesus* no·longer to·be·able to·enter
Mk 2:27 And *Jesus* was·saying to·them, "The Sabbath
Mk 3:3 And *Jesus* says to·the man·of·clay†, the·one having
Mk 3:13 Then *Jesus* walks·up upon the mountain, and he·
Mk 5:8 (For *Jesus* was·saying to·him, "Impure spirit, come·
Mk 5:17 And they·began to·implore *Jesus* to·go·away from
Mk 5:18 And while *Jesus* was·embarking into the sailboat,
Mk 5:24 So *Jesus* went·off with him, and a·large crowd was·
Mk 6:37 But answering, *Jesus* declared to·them, "Yeu·
Mk 7:33 the crowd in private, *Jesus* cast his fingers into his
Mk 7:36 And *Jesus* thoroughly·charged them that they·
Mk 8:23 his hands upon·him, *Jesus* was·inquiring·of him if
Mk 8:34 along·with his disciples, *Jesus* declared to·them,
Mk 9:20 him, and upon·seeing *Jesus*, immediately the spirit
Mk 9:21 And *Jesus* inquired·of his father, "About how·long
Mk 14:32 *is* GethSemane. And *Jesus* says to·his disciples,
Mk 15:46 ·buying a·linen·cloth and lowering *Jesus* down,
Mk 16:9 on·*the*·first *day* of·*the*·week, *Jesus* did·appear first
Rm 3:24 *yet those trusting in Jesus are now* being·regarded·
Rm 3:26 being righteous, *which·is Jesus*, and *with·God*
Rm 10:12 Greek— for this same *Lord Jesus is* Lord of·all,
1Co 2:2 Anointed and this *Jesus* having·been·crucified.
G2424.3 N/P-NSM Ἰησοῦς (1x)
Heb 4:8 For if JoShua gave them complete·rest, he·would
G2424.3 N/P-GSM Ἰησοῦ (1x)
Ac 7:45 ·it·in·turn, brought·it·in with JoShua into the
G2424.5 N/P-NSM Ἰησοῦς (1x)
Col 4:11 and JeShua (the·one being·referred·to·as Justus).

G2425 ἱκανός hikanós *adj.* (42x)

Roots:G2429-1 Compare:G0566 G0713 See:G2426 G2240 G1338 G2185
G2425.1 A-NPM ἱκανοί (1x)
2Ti 2:2 ·of·clay† who shall·be competent to·instruct others
G2425.2 A-NSM ἱκανός (1x)
2Co 2:16 And who *is* sufficient specifically·for these·things?
G2425.2 A-NSN ἱκανόν (2x)
Lk 22:38 And he·declared to·them, "It·is sufficient."
2Co 2:6 Sufficient to·such·a·man *is* this public·penalty, the·
G2425.2 A-NPM ἱκανοί (1x)
2Co 3:5 Not that we·are sufficient by ourselves to·reckon
G2425.2 A-ASM ἱκανόν (1x)
Ac 14:3 Accordingly in·fact, they·lingered a·sufficient time,
G2425.2 A-APF ἱκανάς (1x)
Ac 18:18 continuing·on *there* a·sufficient *number·of* days,
G2425.3 A-NSM ἱκανός (1x)
Ac 11:24 trust. And an·ample crowd was·placed·alongside
G2425.3 A-ASM ἱκανόν (2x)
Ac 11:26 ·Out·citizenry and to·instruct an·ample crowd.
Ac 19:26 Asia, this Paul has·won·over an·ample crowd *by*
EG2425.3 (1x)
Eph 4:28 he·may·have *amply·enough* to·kindly·give to·the·
G2425.4 A-NSM ἱκανός (6x)
Lk 3:16 of·whose shoes I·am not fit to·loose. He·himself
Lk 7:6 For I·am not fit that you·should·enter under my roof.
Mt 3:11 me, whose shoes I·am not fit to·lift·and·carry. He·
Mt 8:8 "Lord, I·am not fit in·order·that you·should·enter
Mk 1:7 me, of·whom I·am not fit, *even* after·stooping·down,
1Co 15:9 who am not fit to·be·called an·ambassador, on·
G2425.5 A-ASN ἱκανόν (1x)
Mk 15:15 to·make the crowd content, fully·released
G2425.5 A-GPM ἱκανῶν (1x)
Lk 8:32 there of·a·significant·number of·pigs being·fed on
G2425.6 A-NPM ἱκανοί (4x)
Lk 7:11 Nain, and a·significant·number of·his disciples
Ac 12:12 , where a·significant·number were having·been·
Ac 19:19 And a·significant·number of·the·ones practicing
1Co 11:30 yeu, and a·significant·number are·laid·to·rest.
G2425.6 A-NPF ἱκαναί (2x)
Ac 9:23 And as·soon·as a·significant·number·of days were·
Ac 20:8 And there·was a·significant·number·of lamps in the
G2425.6 A-ASM ἱκανόν (1x)
Ac 5:37 drew·away a·significant·number·of people right·
G2425.6 A-APM ἱκανούς (2x)
Lk 20:9 and·then he·journeyed·abroad for·a·significant time.
Ac 14:21 discipling a·significant·number, they·returned·back
G2425.6 A-APF ἱκανάς (1x)
Ac 9:43 ·*for* him to·abide a·significant·number·of days in
G2425.6 A-DPM ἱκανοῖς (1x)
Lk 23:9 ·of him with a·significant·number·of words. But
G2425.6 A-DPF ἱκαναῖς (1x)
Ac 27:7 ·slowly along for·a·significant·number·of days, and
G2425.7 A-NSM ἱκανός (1x)
Lk 7:12 was a·widow. And a·significant crowd of·the city
G2425.7 A-NSN ἱκανόν (1x)
Ac 22:6 ·the heaven *for* a·significant light to·flash·all·around
G2425.7 A-GSM ἱκανοῦ (1x)
Mk 10:46 Jericho with his disciples and a·significant crowd,
G2425.8 A-APN ἱκανά (1x)
Mt 28:12 they·gave a·significant·sum·of money to·the
G2425.9 A-ASN ἱκανόν (1x)
Ac 17:9 after·taking the security·bail personally·from Jason
G2425.10 A-GSM ἱκανοῦ (1x)
Ac 27:9 Now with·significant·span of·time already·elapsing,
G2425.10 A-GPM ἱκανῶν (1x)
Lk 8:27 was·having demons for a·significant·span of·time,
G2425.11 A-DSM ἱκανῷ (1x)
Ac 8:11 ·have·astonished them *for* the longest time with·the
G2425.12 A-NSM ἱκανός (1x)
Ac 20:37 And everyone was weeping a·long·while. And
G2425.12 A-ASN ἱκανόν (1x)
Ac 20:11 over a·long·while in·this·manner even·unto *the*
G2425.12 A-GSM ἱκανοῦ (1x)
Lk 23:8 to·see him for a·long·while on·account·of hearing

G2426 ἱκανότης hikanótēs *n.* (1x)

Roots:G2425
G2426 N-NSF ἱκανότης (1x)
2Co 3:5 ourselves, but·rather our sufficiency *is* from·out of·

G2427 ἱκανόω hikanóō *v.* (2x)

Roots:G2425 Compare:G1606-1
G2427.2 V-AAI-3S ἱκάνωσεν (1x)
2Co 3:6 us sufficiently·qualified attendants of·a·brand-new
G2427.2 V-AAP-DSM ἱκανώσαντι (1x)
Col 1:12 the·one already·sufficiently·qualifying us for the

G2428 ἱκετηρία hikētēría *n.* (1x)

Roots:G2425 Compare:G1783 G1162 G4335
G2428 N-APF ἱκετηρίας (1x)
Heb 5:7 ·up both petitions and supplications with a·strong

G2429 ἱκμάς hikmás *n.* (1x)

G2429 N-ASF ἰκμάδα (1x)
Lk 8:6 on·account·of *the solid·rock* not holding moisture.

G2430 Ἰκόνιον Ikóniôn *n/l.* (6x)

Roots:G1504
G2430.2 N/L-ASN Ἰκόνιον (2x)
Ac 13:51 of·their feet against them, they·went to Iconium.
Ac 14:21 ·back to Lystra, and *to* Iconium, and to·Antiochia,
G2430.2 N/L-DSN Ἰκονίῳ (3x)
Ac 14:1 it·happened the same·way in Iconium *for* them to·
Ac 16:2 ·attested·to by the brothers in Lystra and Iconium.
2Ti 3:11 to·me at Antiochia, at Iconium, *and* at Lystra; what
G2430.2 N/L-GSN Ἰκονίου (1x)
Ac 14:19 came·up from Antiochia and Iconium, and after·

G2431 ἱλαρός hilarós *adj.* (1x)

Roots:G2436 Compare:G2115 G5479 G2167 See:G2432
G2431 A-ASM ἱλαρόν (1x)
2Co 9:7 out of·compulsion, for 'God loves a·cheerful giver.'

G2432 ἱλαρότης hilarótēs *n.* (1x)

Roots:G2431 Compare:G4288 G4290
G2432 N-DSF ἱλαρότητι (1x)
Rm 12:8 ·one showing·mercy, *doing so* with cheerfulness.

G2433 ἱλάσκομαι hiláskômai *v.* (2x)

Roots:G2436 Compare:G1653 G0604 G2644 G0863 See:G2434 G2435 G1837-2 xLangAlso:H5545
G2433.2 V-PPN ἱλάσκεσθαι (1x)
Heb 2:17 in·order to·favorably·make·atonement·for the
G2433.2 V-APM-2S ἱλάσθητι (1x)
Lk 18:13 'God, be·favorably·forgiving·toward me, the

G2434 ἱλασμός hilasmós *n.* (2x)

Roots:G2433 Compare:G2643 See:G2435 G1837-4 xLangAlso:H3725
G2434.2 N-NSM ἱλασμός (1x)
1Jn 2:2 And he·himself is *the* atonement concerning our
G2434.2 N-ASM ἱλασμόν (1x)
1Jn 4:10 his Son *to·be the* atonement concerning our moral·

G2435 ἱλα•στήριον hilastḗriôn *n.* (2x)

Roots:G2433 Compare:G2643 See:G2434 G2379 xLangAlso:H3722 H3725 H3727
G2435.3 N-ASN ἱλαστήριον (1x)
Rm 3:25 *to·be* an·atoning·sacrifice·for·favorable·forgiveness
G2435.4 N-ASN ἱλαστήριον (1x)
Heb 9:5 atonement·seat·(the·seat·of·favorable·forgiveness),

G2436 ἵλεως hílêōs *adj.* (2x)
Roots:G0138 Compare:G0448 G1655 G5483 G1943 See:G2433 xLangAlso:H5545

G2436.3 A-NSM-ATT ἵλεως (1x)
Mt 16:22 him, saying, "*God* be·favorable to·you, Lord.

G2436.5 A-NSM-ATT ἵλεως (1x)
Heb 8:12 Because I·shall·be favorably·forgiving to·their

G2437 Ἰλλυρικόν Illyrikón *n/l.* (1x)

G2437.2 N/L-GSN Ἰλλυρικοῦ (1x)
Rm 15:19 and around·in·a·circuit to·as·far·as Illyricum).

G2438 ἱμάς himás *n.* (4x)
Roots:G0260

G2438.1 N-ASM ἱμάντα (3x)
Jn 1:27 not *even* worthy that I·may·loosen his shoe strap."
Lk 3:16 stronger·than me comes, the strap of·whose shoes I·
Mk 1:7 after·stooping·down, to·loose the strap of·his shoes.

G2438.1 N-DPM ἱμᾶσιν (1x)
Ac 22:25 And as they·prestretched him with·the straps, Paul

G2439 ἱματίζω himatízō *v.* (2x)
Roots:G2440 Compare:G1746 G1902 See:G2441

G2439 V-RPP-ASM ἱματισμένον (2x)
Lk 8:35 having·been·attired and being·of·sound·mind, and
Mk 5:15 and having·been·attired and being·of·sound·mind,

G2440 ἱμάτιον himátiôn *n.* (65x)
Compare:G2066 G1742 G1903 G4158 See:G2439 G2441 xLangAlso:H8071

G2440.1 N-NSN ἱμάτιον (1x)
Heb 1:11 shall·become·old·and·worn·out as *does* a·garment.

G2440.1 N-NPN ἱμάτια (3x)
Mt 17:2 as the sun, and his garments became white as the
Mk 9:3 And his garments became glistening, exceedingly
Jac 5:2 ·rotted, and yeur garments have·become moth-eaten.

G2440.1 N-ASN ἱμάτιον (9x)
Jn 19:2 on·his head and arrayed him *with* a·purple garment,
Jn 19:5 victor's·crown and the purple garment. And *Pilate*
Lk 5:36 a·brand-new garment upon an·old garment; but·if·so
Lk 8:27 ·time, and was·not wearing a·garment, and was·not
Lk 22:36 a·dagger, let·him·sell his garment and buy *one*.
Ac 12:8 he·says to·him, "Cast your·garment around you and
Mk 13:16 to·the·things left·behind to·take·up his garment.
Rv 19:13 having·been·arrayed·with a·garment having·been·
Rv 19:16 And he·has on·the garment and on·his thigh the

G2440.1 N-APN ἱμάτια (26x)
Jn 13:4 the supper and lays·aside the garments. And taking a·
Jn 13:12 and took·hold·of his garments, after·sitting·back
Jn 19:24 ·divided·up my garments among·themselves, and
Lk 19:35 and flinging their·own garments upon the colt,
Lk 19:36 were·spreading·out their garments beneath *him* in
Lk 23:34 thoroughly·dividing·up his garments, they·cast lots
Ac 7:58 witnesses laid·aside their garments directly·at the
Ac 14:14 *of·this and* tearing·apart their garments, rushed·in
Ac 16:22 ·away their garments, commandingly·ordered *for*·
Ac 18:6 *Jesus*, shaking·out his garments, he·declared to
Ac 22:20 ·watch·over the garments of·the·ones executing
Ac 22:23 ·out, and flinging·off the garments, and casting
Mt 21:7 colt, and they·put their garments up·over them and
Mt 21:8 ·large crowd spread·out their·own garments in the
Mt 24:18 *to the·things* left·behind to·take·away his garments.
Mt 26:65 ·high·priest tore·apart his garments, saying, "He·
Mt 27:31 and dressed him with·his·own garments. And·then
Mt 27:35 they·thoroughly·divided·up his garments, casting
Mt 27:35 ·divided·up my garments among·themselves, and
Mk 11:7 Jesus, and they·threw their garments on·it, and he·
Mk 11:8 And many spread·out their garments in the roadway
Mk 15:20 and dressed him *with* his·own garments, and led
Mk 15:24 ·dividing·up his garments, while·casting lots upon
Rv 3:4 which did·not tarnish their garments; and they·shall·
Rv 3:18 ·be·wealthy, and·also white garments, in·order·that
Rv 16:15 keeping·alert and guarding his garments, lest he·

G2440.1 N-DSN ἱματίῳ (2x)
Mt 9:16 of·unprocessed cloth onto an·old garment, for *when*·
Mk 2:21 of·unprocessed cloth on an·old garment, but·if·so,

G2440.1 N-DPN ἱματίοις (4x)
Lk 7:25 having·been·enrobed in soft garments? Behold, the·
Mt 11:8 having·been·enrobed in soft garments? Behold, the·
Rv 3:5 the·same shall·be·arrayed in white garments, and no
Rv 4:4 having·been·arrayed in white garments, and they·

G2440.1 N-GSN ἱματίου (8x)
Lk 5:36 a·patch *from* a·brand-new garment upon an·old
Lk 8:44 she·laid·hold of·the fringe of·his garment, and at·
Mt 9:16 its complete·fullness from the garment, and *the* tear
Mt 9:20 ·behind, she·laid·hold of·the fringe of·his garment,
Mt 9:21 ·hold of·his garment, I·shall·be·made·safe·and·well.
Mt 14:36 lay·hold of·the fringe of·his garment, and as·many·
Mk 5:27 from·behind *him*, she·laid·hold of·his garment.
Mk 6:56 *only* of·the fringe of·his garment. And as·many·as

G2440.1 N-GPN ἱματίων (4x)
Mt 23:5 tefillin and enlarge the fringes of·their garments.
Mk 5:28 of·his garments, I·shall·be·made·safe·and·well."
Mk 5:30 "Who laid·hold of·my garments?"
1Pe 3:3 ·articles, or of·dressing *with·showy* garments,

EG2440.1 (3x)
Lk 5:36 the·one from the brand-new *garment*, does·not
Mt 11:8 ·ones prominently·wearing the soft *garments* are in
1Pe 3:4 with the incorruptible *garment* of·the calmly·mild

G2440.2 N-ASN ἱμάτιον (3x)
Lk 6:29 taking·away your outer·garment, you·should·not
Mt 5:40 your inner·tunic, leave him the outer·garment also.
Mk 10:50 after·casting·away his outer·garment *and* rising·up

G2440.2 N-APN ἱμάτια (2x)
Jn 19:23 the soldiers took his outer·garments and made four
Ac 9:39 inner·tunics and outer·garments Dorcas was·making

G2441 ἱματισμός himatismós *n.* (6x)
Roots:G2439 Compare:G1742 G2440

G2441 N-NSM ἱματισμός (1x)
Lk 9:29 became different, and his attire *was* white *and*

G2441 N-ASM ἱματισμόν (2x)
Jn 19:24 and they·cast lots upon my attire."' In·fact, in·due·
Mt 27:35 ·themselves, and they·cast lots over my attire."'

G2441 N-DSM ἱματισμῷ (2x)
Lk 7:25 Behold, the·ones in glorious attire, also subsisting
1Ti 2:9 or gold, or pearls, or extremely·expensive attire,

G2441 N-GSM ἱματισμοῦ (1x)
Ac 20:33 ·for not·even·one·man's silver or gold or attire.

G2442 ἱμείρομαι himeírômai *v.* (1x)
Compare:G1937 G1971

G2442 V-PMP-NPM ἱμειρόμενοι (1x)
1Th 2:8 In·this·manner, ourselves·yearning·for yeu, we·

G2443 ἵνα hína *conj.* (636x)
Roots:G1438 Compare:G3754 G3704 See:G3363
(abbreviated listing for G2443)

G2443.1 CONJ ἵνα (436x)
(list for G2443.1:CONJ excluded)

EG2443.1 (1x)
(list for EG2443.1: excluded)

G2443.2 CONJ ἵνα (195x)
(list for G2443.2:CONJ excluded)

EG2443.2 (4x)
(list for EG2443.2: excluded)

G2444 ἱνα•τί hinatí *adv.* (6x)
Roots:G2443 G5101

G2444.1 ADV-I ἱνατί (5x)
Lk 13:7 it down! For·what·purpose·does·it also fully·render
Ac 4:25 "For·what·purpose·did nations tumultuously·snort·
Ac 7:26 for·what·purpose do·yeu·wrong one·another?
Mt 9:4 "For·what·purpose·do yeu·yeurselves cogitate evil·
Mt 27:46 my God, for·what·purpose did·you·forsake me?

G2444.2 ADV ἱνατί (1x)
1Co 10:29 ·rather of·the other, for what·reason·is my liberty

G2445 Ἰόππη Ióppē *n/l.* (11x)
יָפוֹ yaphô [Hebrew]
Roots:H3305

G2445.2 N/L-ASF Ἰόππην (4x)
Ac 10:5 And now send men to Joppa and send·for Simon,
Ac 10:8 ·*these*·things to·them, he·dispatched them to Joppa.
Ac 10:32 Now·then, send to Joppa and summarily·call·for
Ac 11:13 'Dispatch men to Joppa and send·for Simon being·

G2445.2 N/L-DSF Ἰόππῃ (4x)
Ac 9:36 Now at Joppa, there·was a·certain female·disciple
Ac 9:38 being *as* Lod *was* near to·Joppa, *and* after·hearing
Ac 9:43 a·significant·number·of days in Joppa with a·certain
Ac 11:5 "I·myself was in *the* city *of* Joppa praying, and in a·

G2445.2 N/L-GSF Ἰόππης (2x)
Ac 9:42 And it·became known in all Joppa, and many trusted
Ac 10:23 of·the brothers from Joppa went·together with·him.

EG2445.2 (1x)
Ac 9:39 After·coming·directly *to·Joppa*, they·led·*him*·up

G2446 Ἰορδάνης Iôrdánēs *n/l.* (15x)
יַרְדֵּן yar·dēn [Hebrew]
Roots:H3383

G2446.2 N/L-ASM Ἰορδάνην (2x)
Mt 3:13 ·directly from Galilee to the Jordan, directly·to John
Mk 1:9 of·Galilee and was·immersed by John in the Jordan.

G2446.2 N/L-DSM Ἰορδάνῃ (2x)
Mt 3:6 by him in the Jordan, explicitly·confessing their
Mk 1:5 by him in the Jordan River, explicitly·confessing

G2446.2 N/L-GSM Ἰορδάνου (11x)
Jn 1:28 in BethAbara across the Jordan *River*, where John
Jn 3:26 with you beyond the Jordan, to·whom you·yourself
Jn 10:40 And he·went·away again beyond the Jordan into the
Lk 3:3 all the region·surrounding the Jordan *River*, officially·
Lk 4:1 Spirit, returned·back from the Jordan and was·led by
Mt 3:5 and all the region·surrounding the Jordan *River*,
Mt 4:15 of·sea, beyond the Jordan, O·Galilee of·the Gentiles
Mt 4:25 JeruSalem and Judea, and *from* beyond the Jordan.
Mt 19:1 came into the borders of·Judea beyond the Jordan.
Mk 3:8 Edom, and *from* beyond the Jordan, and *from* around
Mk 10:1 through the other·side of·the Jordan, and again,

G2447 ἰός iós *n.* (3x)
Roots:G2423-1 G1510-1 Compare:G1035 See:G2342 xLangAlso:H2457

G2447.2 N-NSM ἰός (1x)
Jac 5:3 ·fully·rusted·down, and its rust shall·be testimony

G2447.3 N-NSM ἰός (1x)
Rm 3:13 ' "*The* venom of·asps *is* under their lips.

G2447.3 N-GSM ἰοῦ (1x)
Jac 3:8 bad, *and* exceedingly·full of·deadly venom.

G2448 Ἰουδά Iôudá *n/l.* (7x)
יְהוּדָה yᵉhûdạh
Roots:H3063 H3194 See:G2453

G2448.3 N/G-GSM Ἰούδα (4x)
Heb 7:14 ·the·horizon from·among Judah, in·regard·to
Heb 8:8 the house of·IsraEl and with the house of·Judah.
Rv 5:5 ·one being from·among the tribe of·Judah (the Root
Rv 7:5 *the* tribe of·Judah having·been·officially·sealed,

G2448.4 N/L-GSM Ἰούδα (3x)
Lk 1:39 mountainous·region with haste, into a·city of·Judah,
Mt 2:6 you, O·BethLechem, *in·the* land of·Judah, are by·no·
Mt 2:6 least among the official·leaders of·Judah. For from·

G2449 Ἰουδαία Iôudaía *n/l.* (44x)
Roots:G2453 See:G1093

G2449 A/G-ASF Ἰουδαίαν (1x)
Jn 3:22 came into the land of·Judea, and he·was·lingering·

G2449 N/L-NSF Ἰουδαία (2x)
Mt 3:5 was·traversing·out to him, and all Judea, and all the
Mk 1:5 And all the region of·Judea was·traversing·out to

G2449 N/L-ASF Ἰουδαίαν (7x)
Jn 4:3 he·left Judea and went·off again into Galilee.
Jn 7:3 ·on from·here and head·on·out into Judea, that your
Jn 11:7 disciples, "We·should·head·out into Judea again."
Lk 2:4 out of·*the*·city of·Natsareth, into Judea, *to the* city
Ac 2:9 ·in MesoPotamia and *in* Judea and Cappadocia, *in*
Ac 11:1 the brothers, the·ones being in Judea, heard that the
2Co 1:16 to yeu, and by yeu to·be·sent·onward into Judea.

G2449 N/L-DSF Ἰουδαίᾳ (9x)
Jn 7:1 for he·was·not willing to·walk in Judea, because the

Lk 7:17 him went·forth among all Judea and among all the
Lk 21:21 Then the·ones in Judea must·flee into the
Ac 1:8 in JeruSalem, and in all Judea, and in·Samaria, and
Ac 11:29 service to the brothers, the·ones residing in Judea.
Mt 24:16 "then the·ones in Judea must·flee to the mountains.
Mk 13:14 "then the·ones in Judea must·flee into the
Rm 15:31 away·from the·ones being·obstinate in Judea, and
1Th 2:14 of·God, the·ones in Judea being in Anointed-One

G2449 N/L-GSF Ἰουδαίας (25x)

Jn 4:47 that Jesus comes from·out of·Judea into Galilee, he·
Jn 4:54 Jesus did, coming from·out of·Judea into Galilee.
Lk 1:5 of·HerOd·the·Great, the king of·Judea, there·was a·
Lk 1:65 among the whole mountainous·region of·Judea,
Lk 3:1 — (with·Pontius Pilate being·governor of·Judea, and
Lk 5:17 ·out of·every village of·Galilee and Judea, and·also
Lk 6:17 of·people from all *over* Judea and JeruSalem, and
Lk 23:5 the people, instructing in all Judea, beginning from
Ac 8:1 pervasively·into·all the regions of·Judea and Samaria.
Ac 9:31 Called·Out·citizenries in all of·Judea, Galilee and
Ac 10:37 utterance occurring in all Judea, beginning from
Ac 12:19 Then coming·down from Judea to Caesarea,
Ac 15:1 ·men coming·down from Judea were·instructing the
Ac 21:10 a·certain prophet came·down from Judea, Agabus
Ac 26:20 and unto all the region of·Judea, then·also to·the
Ac 28:21 ·receiving letters from Judea concerning you,
Gal 1:22 to·the Called·Out·citizenries of·Judea, the·ones in
Mt 2:1 already·being·born in BethLechem of·Judea, in *the*
Mt 2:5 to·him, "In BethLechem of·Judea. For in·this·manner
Mt 2:22 that ArcheLaos reigns in Judea in·the·stead of·his
Mt 3:1 officially·proclaiming in the wilderness of·Judea,
Mt 4:25 and *from* JeruSalem and Judea, and *from* beyond
Mt 19:1 came into the borders of·Judea beyond the Jordan.
Mk 3:7 from Galilee followed him, and·also from Judea,
Mk 10:1 he·comes into the borders of·Judea through the

G2450 Ἰουδαΐζω Iôudaḯzō *v/g.* (1x)
Roots:G2453 See:G2454

G2450.1 V/G-PAN Ἰουδαΐζειν (1x)

Gal 2:14 why do·you·compel the Gentiles to·be·Judaic?

G2451 Ἰουδαϊκός Iôudaïkós *adj/g.* (1x)
Roots:G2453 Compare:G1482 G1672 See:G2452

G2451.2 A/G-DPM Ἰουδαϊκοῖς (1x)

Tit 1:14 not giving·heed to·Jewish myths and

G2452 Ἰουδαϊκῶς Iôudaïkō̂s *adv/g.* (1x)
Roots:G2451

G2452.2 ADV Ἰουδαϊκῶς (1x)

Gal 2:14 live as·a·Gentile and not as·a·Jew, why do·you·

G2453 Ἰουδαῖος Iôudaîôs *adj/g.* (207x)
Roots:G2448 See:G2455

G2453.1 A/G-VPM Ἰουδαῖοι (1x)

Ac 2:14 to·them, "Yeu·men of·Judea and absolutely·all the·

G2453.1 A/G-GPM Ἰουδαίων (1x)

Ac 12:11 all the anticipated·evil of·the people of·Judea."

G2453.2 A/G-NPM Ἰουδαῖοι (36x)

Jn 1:19 the Judeans dispatched priests·that·offer·sacrifices and
Jn 2:18 Accordingly, the Judeans answered and declared to·
Jn 2:20 So·then the Judeans declared, "*In* forty six years,
Jn 5:10 Accordingly, the Judeans were·saying to·the·one
Jn 5:16 ·account·of that, the Judeans were·persecuting Jesus
Jn 5:18 on·account·of that, the Judeans were·seeking *all* the·
Jn 6:41 the Judeans were·grumbling concerning him,
Jn 6:52 So·then the Judeans were·quarreling among one·
Jn 7:1 Judea, because the Judeans were·seeking to·kill him.
Jn 7:11 Now·then, the Judeans were·seeking him at the
Jn 7:15 And the Judeans were·marveling, saying, "How·
Jn 7:35 Accordingly, the Judeans declared among
Jn 8:22 So·then the Judeans were·saying, "Is·it·that he·
Jn 8:48 So·then the Judeans answered and declared to·him,
Jn 8:52 Accordingly, the Judeans declared to·him, "Now
Jn 8:57 Accordingly, the Judeans declared to him, "You·are
Jn 9:18 Accordingly, the Judeans did·not trust concerning
Jn 9:22 the Judeans had·agreed·among·themselves even·now
Jn 10:24 So·then the Judeans surrounded him and were·
Jn 10:31 the Judeans lifted·up·and·carried stones again in·
Jn 10:33 The Judeans answered him, saying, "We·do·not
Jn 11:8 "Rabbi, the Judeans now were·seeking to·stone you,
Jn 11:31 So·then the Judeans, the·ones being with her in the
Jn 11:36 So·then the Judeans were·saying, "See how fond·
Jn 18:20 ·Atrium where the Judeans always come·together.
Jn 18:31 Accordingly, the Judeans declared to·him, "It·is·
Jn 19:7 The Judeans answered him, "We·ourselves have an·
Jn 19:12 him, but the Judeans were·yelling·out, saying, "If
Jn 19:31 great day), the Judeans asked·of Pilate that their
Ac 21:11 'in·this·manner the Judeans at JeruSalem shall·
Ac 23:20 "The Judeans agreed·among·themselves to·ask·of
Ac 24:9 And the Judeans also agreed·among·themselves,
Ac 25:7 ·publicly, the Judeans having·walked·down from
Ac 26:4 in·fact, all the Judeans have·distinctly·known my
Ac 26:21 ·of these·things, the Judeans, upon·arresting me in
Mk 7:3 the Pharisees and all the Judeans, unless they·should·

G2453.2 A/G-APM Ἰουδαίους (6x)

Jn 8:31 Jesus was·saying to *those* Judeans, the·ones having·
Jn 9:22 ·things, because they·feared the Judeans. For the
Jn 11:33 and the weeping Judeans coming·together with·her
Jn 18:38 he·went·out again to the Judeans, and he·says to·
Ac 25:10 I·wronged not·even·one *of* the·Judeans, even as
Ac 26:3 *which·are* pervasive·among the·Judeans. Therefore,

G2453.2 A/G-DSF Ἰουδαίᾳ (1x)

Ac 24:24 ·his wife Drusilla (herself·being a·Judean), Felix

G2453.2 A/G-DPM Ἰουδαίοις (12x)

Jn 5:15 ·off and reported·in·detail to·the Judeans that it·was
Jn 10:19 again among the Judeans on·account·of these
Jn 11:54 ·freeness·of·speech among the Judeans, but·rather
Jn 13:33 me, and just·as I·declared to·the Judeans, 'Where
Jn 18:14 ·one jointly·giving·counsel to·the Judeans, how·that
Jn 18:36 I·should·not be·handed·over to·the Judeans. So
Jn 19:14 hour, and he·says to·the Judeans, "See yeur King!
Jn 19:40 is *the* manner for·the Judeans to·prepare·for·burial.
Ac 12:3 satisfactory to·the Judeans, he·further·proceeded to·
Ac 24:27 to·store·up influential·favors with·the Judeans, left
Ac 25:9 ·up influential·favor with·the Judeans, answering
Mt 28:15 closely·among Judeans so·far·as·unto the present·

G2453.2 A/G-GPM Ἰουδαίων (34x)

Jn 2:6 ·to the manner·of·purification of·the Judeans,
Jn 2:13 Now the Judeans' Passover was near·at·hand, and
Jn 3:1 NicoDemus *was* his name, a·ruler of·the Judeans.
Jn 3:25 disciples against *the* Judeans concerning purification.
Jn 5:1 there·was a·Sacred·Feast of·the Judeans, and Jesus
Jn 6:4 the Sacred·Feast of·the Judeans, was near·at·hand.
Jn 7:2 Now the Judeans' Sacred·Feast, the *Sacred·Feast* of·
Jn 7:13 him, on·account·of the fear of·the Judeans.
Jn 11:19 many from·among the Judeans had·come alongside
Jn 11:45 So·then many from·among the Judeans, the·ones
Jn 11:55 Now the Judeans' Passover was near·at·hand.
Jn 12:9 a·large crowd from·among the Judeans knew that he·
Jn 12:11 him, many of·the Judeans were·heading·on·out and
Jn 18:12 and the assistants of·the Judeans arrested Jesus and
Jn 19:20 In·due·course, many of·the Judeans read·aloud this
Jn 19:21 chief·priests of·the Judeans were·saying to·Pilate,
Jn 19:38 on·account·of the fear of·the Judeans, asked·of
Jn 19:42 there on·account·of the Judeans' preparation·day,
Jn 20:19 on·account·of the fear of·the Judeans, Jesus came
Lk 7:3 Jesus, he·dispatched elders of·the Judeans to him,
Lk 23:51 of Arimathaea, a·city of·the Judeans, who also
Ac 10:39 both in the region of·the Judeans and in JeruSalem
Ac 21:20 how·many tens·of·thousands of·Judeans there·are,
Ac 22:30 ·accused personally·by the Judeans, he·loosed him
Ac 23:12 day, some of·the Judeans, making a·secret·mob,
Ac 23:27 already·being·arrested by the Judeans and·also *was*
Ac 23:30 about to·be *carried·out* by the Judeans, I·sent *him*
Ac 25:2 and the foremost of·the Judeans made·clear to·him
Ac 25:15 and the elders of·the Judeans made·it·clear *that*
Ac 25:24 all the multitude of·the Judeans conferred with·me,
Ac 26:2 for·which I·am·called·to·account by *the* Judeans,
Ac 26:7 AgrIppa, I·am·called·to·account by the Judeans.
Ac 28:19 But with·the Judeans contradicting *this*, I·was·
1Th 2:14 just·as they·themselves *suffered* under the Judeans

EG2453.2 (6x)

Lk 2:41 to JeruSalem for·the *Judeans'* Sacred·Feast of·the
Lk 22:1 Now the *Judeans'* Sacred·Feast of·the Unleavened·
Mk 14:1 days, it·would·be *the Judeans' Sacred·Feast·of* the
1Th 2:15 (even *under* the *Judeans* killing the Lord YeShua
1Th 2:15 . And *such·Judeans are* not agreeably·complying
1Th 2:16 *these same Judeans* at·all·times to·utterly·fulfill *the*

G2453.3 A/G-ASM Ἰουδαῖον (1x)

Ac 13:6 ·as Paphos, they·found a·certain Jewish occultist, a·

G2453.3 A/G-GSM Ἰουδαίου (1x)

Ac 19:14 the·seven Sons of·Sceva, a·Jewish chief·priest.

G2453.3 A/G-GSF Ἰουδαίας (1x)

Ac 16:1 by·name, a·son of·a·certain Jewish woman (one·

G2453.4 A/G-NSM Ἰουδαῖος (13x)

Jn 4:9 "How·is·it *that* you, being a·Jew, request *some* to·
Jn 18:35 "¿! Am·I myself a·Jew? Your·own nation and the
Ac 18:24 Now a·certain Jew arrived in Ephesus (Apollos
Ac 19:34 But after·realizing that he·was a·Jew, there·came
Ac 21:39 ·myself am a·man·of·clay† *who·is* a·Jew of·Tarsus,
Ac 22:3 am in·fact a·man *who·is* a·Jew, having·been·born in
Gal 2:14 "If you, inherently·being a·Jew, live as·a·Gentile
Gal 3:28 There·is·not therein Jew nor·even Greek, there·is·
Rm 2:17 See, you·yourself label·yourself a·Jew, and you·
Rm 2:28 *·keeping Torah-Law* that·is a·Jew, neither the·one
Rm 2:29 *vigilantly·keeping* in private, *he·is* a·Jew, and *with*
1Co 9:20 to·the Jews I·became as a·Jew, in·order·that I·may·
Col 3:11 there·is·not therein Greek and Jew, circumcision

G2453.4 A/G-NPM Ἰουδαῖοι (19x)

Jn 4:9 woman?" (for Jews do·not interact with·Samaritans).
Ac 2:5 And there·were Jews residing in JeruSalem, devout
Ac 2:10 ·here·from Rome, also Jews and converts·to·Judaism
Ac 9:23 the Jews took·counsel·among·themselves to·
Ac 13:45 the crowds, the Jews were·filled with·jealousy and
Ac 13:50 But the Jews personally·stirred·up the women
Ac 14:2 But *the* Jews, the·ones being·obstinate, roused·up
Ac 14:19 And *certain* Jews came·up from Antiochia and
Ac 16:20 inherently·being Jews, do·exceedingly·trouble
Ac 17:5 being·jealous, the obstinate Jews, even purposely·
Ac 17:13 But as·soon·as the Jews from ThessaloNica knew
Ac 18:12 the Jews made·a·full·assault with·the·same·
Ac 21:27 to·be·entirely·completed, the Jews from Asia,
Ac 24:18 "But *there·were* certain Jews from Asia,
Ac 28:29 declaring these·things, the Jews went·off, having
Gal 2:13 the rest *of·the* Jews also were·hypocritical·together
Gal 2:15 We·ourselves *are* Jews by·nature, and not from·
1Co 1:22 And whereas Jews request a·sign, and·also Greeks
1Co 12:13 into one Body, whether Jews or Greeks, whether

G2453.4 A/G-VPM Ἰουδαῖοι (1x)

Ac 18:14 according·to reason, O Jews, I·would have·put·up·

G2453.4 A/G-ASM Ἰουδαῖον (1x)

Ac 18:2 and he·found a·certain Jew by·the·name·of Aquila

G2453.4 A/G-APM Ἰουδαίους (11x)

Ac 9:22 and was·confounding the Jews, the·ones residing in
Ac 16:3 he·circumcised him on·account·of the Jews, the·
Ac 18:2 ·arranged·for all the Jews to·be·deported out of·
Ac 18:4 Sabbath, and was·persuading Jews and Greeks.
Ac 18:14 Gallio declared to the Jews, "Accordingly in·fact,
Ac 19:10 of·the Lord Jesus, both Jews and Greeks.
Ac 21:21 Moses *to* all the Jews *who·are* pervasive·among the
Rm 3:9 for we·already·legally·charged both Jews and Greeks
1Co 9:20 a·Jew, in·order·that I·may·gain Jews; to·the·ones
Rv 2:9 of·the·ones saying themselves to·be Jews and are not,
Rv 3:9 (the·ones saying themselves to·be Jews and are not,

G2453.4 A/G-DSM Ἰουδαίῳ (3x)

Ac 10:28 for·a·man that·is·a·Jew to·be·tightly·joined or to·
Rm 1:16 to·everyone trusting, both to·Jew first, and·also to·
Rm 2:10 the beneficially·good, both to·Jew first, then·also

G2453.4 A/G-DPM Ἰουδαίοις (13x)

Ac 11:19 Redemptive·word to·no·one except to·Jews merely.
Ac 14:4 ·one *part* was together with·the Jews, and the·one
Ac 17:17 in the gathering with·the Jews and with·the·ones
Ac 18:5 *and* was·thoroughly·testifying to·the Jews *that* Jesus

Ac 18:19 gathering, was·having·discussions with·the Jews.
Ac 18:28 he·was·proving·downright to·the Jews publicly,
Ac 19:17 residing·in Ephesus, to·both Jews and Greeks.
Ac 20:21 thoroughly·testifying to·both Jews and Greeks, a·
Ac 24:5 stirring controversy among·all the Jews in The Land
1Co 1:23 ·fact a·scandalous·offense to·Jews and foolishness
1Co 1:24 *who·are* called·forth, to·both Jews and Greeks,
1Co 9:20 And to·the Jews I·became as a·Jew, in·order·that I·
1Co 10:32 Become void·of·offense, even to·Jews, also to·
G2453.4 A/G-GSM Ἰουδαίου (3x)
Rm 2:9 ·of·clay† performing the wrong, of·Jew first, and
Rm 3:1 So·then what *is* the Jew's superior·benefit?
Rm 10:12 there·is no distinction between Jew and Greek—
G2453.4 A/G-GPM Ἰουδαίων (38x)
Jn 4:22 because the Salvation is from·out of·the Jews.
Jn 18:33 "Are you·yourself the King of·the Jews?"
Jn 18:39 I·should·fully·release to·yeu the King of·the Jews?"
Jn 19:3 Be·well, O·King of·the Jews!" And they·were·
Jn 19:19 OF·NATSARETH THE KING OF·THE JEWS."
Jn 19:21 'The King of·the Jews,' but·rather that this·man
Jn 19:21 'I·am King of·the Jews.'"
Lk 23:3 "Are you·yourself the King of·the Jews?" And
Lk 23:37 you·yourself are the king of·the Jews, save yourself
Lk 23:38 "THIS IS THE KING OF·THE JEWS."
Ac 10:22 whole nation of·the Jews, was·divinely·instructed
Ac 13:5 in the gatherings of·the Jews, and they·were·having
Ac 13:42 And with·the Jews getting out of·the gathering, the
Ac 13:43 being·let·loose, many of·the Jews and the·ones
Ac 14:1 into the gathering of·the Jews, and in·this·manner
Ac 14:1 a·large multitude both of·Jews and·also of·Greeks
Ac 14:5 from·the Gentiles and *the* Jews together with·their
Ac 17:1 where the gathering·place of·the Jews was.
Ac 17:10 *there*, went·off into the gathering of·the Jews.
Ac 19:13 Then certain of the itinerant Jews, *being* exorcists,
Ac 19:33 of·the crowd, with·the Jews pushing him forward.
Ac 20:3 against·him by the Jews as·he·was·about to·sail into
Ac 20:19 the·ones befalling me by the plots of·the Jews.
Ac 22:12 being·attested·to by all the residing Jews,
Ac 25:8 against the Torah-Law of·the Jews, nor against the
Ac 28:17 the·ones being foremost of·the Jews. And with·
Mt 2:2 being·reproduced·and·born King of·the Jews? For
Mt 27:11 "Are you·yourself the King of·the Jews?" And
Mt 27:29 Be·well, O·King of·the·Jews!"
Mt 27:37 THIS IS YESHUA, THE KING OF·THE JEWS."
Mk 15:2 "Are you·yourself the King of·the Jews?" And
Mk 15:9 I·should·fully·release to·yeu the King of·the Jews?"
Mk 15:12 *the·one* whom yeu·refer·to·as King of·the Jews?"
Mk 15:18 Be·well, O·King of·the Jews!"
Mk 15:26 "THE KING OF·THE JEWS."
Rm 3:29 Or *is·he* the God of·Jews merely?
Rm 9:24 he·called·forth— not from·among Jews merely,
2Co 11:24 Five·times by *the* Jews I·received forty *stripes*
EG2453.4 (5x)
Ac 17:11 Now these *Berean Jews* were more·noble·than the·
Ac 18:6 with *the Jews* arranging·themselves·against them
Ac 20:4 Asia, SoPater (a·Berean *Jew*), was·accompanying
Gal 2:16 "*As Jews*, having·seen that a·man·of·clay† is·not
Rm 3:9 So·then what, are·we *Jews* any·better·off?

G2454 Ἰουδαϊσμός Iôudaïsmṓs *n/g.* (2x)
Roots:G2450
G2454 N/G-DSM Ἰουδαϊσμῷ (2x)
Gal 1:13 of·my former manner·of·life in Judaism, that most
Gal 1:14 ·was·continually·advancing in Judaism above many

G2455 Ἰούδας Iôúdas *n/p.* (40x)
יְהוּדָה yᵉhûdạh [Hebrew]
Roots:H3063 Compare:G2448
G2455.2 N/P-NSM Ἰούδας (1x)
Mt 1:3 Then Judah begot Perets and Zarach (birthed·from·
G2455.2 N/P-ASM Ἰούδαν (1x)
Mt 1:2 begot Jacob, and Jacob begot Judah and his brothers.
G2455.2 N/P-GSM Ἰούδα (1x)
Lk 3:33 *son* of·Chetsron, *son* of·Perets, *son* of·Judah,
G2455.5 N/P-NSM Ἰούδας (14x)
Jn 12:4 from·among his disciples (Judas IsCariot, Simon's
Jn 13:29 were·presuming, since Judas was·holding the
Jn 18:2 And Judas, the·one handing him over, also had·
Jn 18:3 chief·priests and Pharisees, Judas comes there with
Jn 18:5 And even Judas, the·one handing him over, stood
Lk 22:47 And the·one being·referred·to·as Judas, one of·the
Ac 1:25 from·among which Judas walked·contrary·to, *in*·
Mt 10:4 Simon the Zealot, and Judas IsCariot, the·one also
Mt 26:14 the·one being·referred·to·as Judas IsCariot, upon·
Mt 26:25 And answering, Judas (the·one handing him over)
Mt 26:47 still speaking, behold, Judas, one of·the twelve,
Mt 27:3 ·seeing that *YeShua* was·condemned, Judas, the·one
Mk 14:10 Then Judas IsCariot, one of·the twelve, went·off to
Mk 14:43 while·yet speaking of·him, Judas comes·openly,
G2455.5 N/P-VSM Ἰούδα (1x)
Lk 22:48 declared to·him, "Judas, do·you·hand·over the Son
G2455.5 N/P-ASM Ἰούδαν (4x)
Jn 6:71 Now he·was·referring·to Judas IsCariot, *the son* of·
Lk 6:16 *son* of·Jacobus·*Thaddaeus*, and Judas IsCariot, who
Lk 22:3 the Adversary-Accuser entered into Judas, the·one
Mk 3:19 and Judas IsCariot, who also handed him over.
G2455.5 N/P-DSM Ἰούδᾳ (1x)
Jn 13:26 the morsel, he·gave *it* to·Judas IsCariot, *the son* of·
G2455.5 N/P-GSM Ἰούδα (2x)
Jn 13:2 ·now having·cast into the heart of·Judas IsCariot, *son*
Ac 1:16 through David's mouth concerning Judas (the·one
G2455.6 N/P-NSM Ἰούδας (2x)
Mt 13:55 his brothers, *little*·Jacob, Joses, Simon and Jude,
Jud 1:1 Jude, a·slave of·YeShua Anointed and a·brother of·
G2455.6 N/P-GSM Ἰούδα (1x)
Mk 6:3 a·brother of·*little*·Jacob, Joses, Jude, and Simon?
EG2455.6 (2x)
Mt 10:3 (the·one of·Alphaeus) and *Judas called* Lebbaeus,
Mk 3:18 (the·one of·Alphaeus), and *Judas called Lebbaeus*
G2455.7 N/P-NSM Ἰούδας (2x)
Jn 14:22 Judas *Thaddaeus*, not IsCariot, says to·him, "Lord,
Ac 1:13 the Zealot, and Judas *son* of·Jacobus *Thaddaeus*).
G2455.7 N/P-ASM Ἰούδαν (1x)
Lk 6:16 *and* Judas *son* of·Jacobus·*Thaddaeus*, and Judas
G2455.8 N/P-GSM Ἰούδα (1x)
Ac 9:11 and seek in Judas' home for a·man·of·Tarsus, Saul
G2455.9 N/P-NSM Ἰούδας (1x)
Ac 15:32 Both Judas and Silas, being prophets also
G2455.9 N/P-ASM Ἰούδαν (2x)
Ac 15:22 BarNabas; *namely*, Judas, the·one being·surnamed
Ac 15:27 "Accordingly, we·have·dispatched Judas and Silas
G2455.10 N/P-NSM Ἰούδας (1x)
Ac 5:37 After this·man, Judas of·Galilee rose·up in the days
G2455.11 N/P-GSM Ἰούδα (1x)
Lk 3:26 *son* of·Shimei, *son* of·Joseph, *son* of·Jehudah,
G2455.12 N/P-GSM Ἰούδα (1x)
Lk 3:30 *son* of·Shimeon, *son* of·Yehudah, *son* of·Yoseph,

G2456 Ἰουλία Iôulía *n/p.* (1x)
Roots:G2457
G2456 N/P-ASF Ἰουλίαν (1x)
Rm 16:15 Greet PhiloLogus, and Julia, Nereus, and his sister

G2457 Ἰούλιος Iôúliôs *n/p.* (2x)
See:G2456
G2457 N/P-NSM Ἰούλιος (1x)
Ac 27:3 treating Paul humanely, Julius freely·permitted *him*
G2457 N/P-DSM Ἰουλίῳ (1x)
Ac 27:1 other prisoners over to·a·centurion, Julius by·name,

G2458 Ἰουνίας Iôunías *n/p.* (1x)
G2458.2 N/P-ASM Ἰουνίαν (1x)
Rm 16:7 Greet AndroNicus and Junianus, my Redeemed·

G2459 Ἰοῦστος Iôûstôs *n/p.* (3x)
G2459.2 N/P-NSM Ἰοῦστος (1x)
Ac 1:23 BarTsabas (who was·surnamed Justus) and MatthIas.
G2459.3 N/P-GSM Ἰούστου (1x)
Ac 18:7 by·the·name·of Justus, who·is·reverencing God,
G2459.4 N/P-NSM Ἰοῦστος (1x)
Col 4:11 JeShua (the·one being·referred·to·as Justus). Only

G2460 ἱππεύς hippeús *n.* (2x)
Roots:G2462 See:G2461 xLangAlso:H6571
G2460 N-APM ἱππεῖς (2x)
Ac 23:23 soldiers, with seventy horsemen and two·hundred
Ac 23:32 ·giving·leave·for the horsemen to·traverse *onward*

G2461 ἱππικόν hippikón *adj.* (1x)
Roots:G2462 See:G2460
G2461 A-GSN ἱππικοῦ (1x)
Rv 9:16 the number of·troops of·the cavalry *was* twice ten·

G2462 ἵππος híppôs *n.* (16x)
See:G2460 G2461 G2459-1
G2462 N-NSM ἵππος (5x)
Rv 6:2 and behold, a·white horse and the·one who·is·sitting·
Rv 6:4 there·came·forth another horse *that·was* fiery·red.
Rv 6:5 and behold, a·black horse and the·one who·is·sitting·
Rv 6:8 and behold, a·pale horse and the·one who·is·sitting·
Rv 19:11 ·up, and behold a·white horse and the·one sitting·
G2462 N-APM ἵππους (1x)
Rv 9:17 And in·this·manner I·saw the horses in the clear·
G2462 N-DPM ἵπποις (2x)
Rv 9:7 locusts *were* like horses having·been·made·ready for
Rv 19:14 white horses, having·dressed·themselves·with fine·
G2462 N-GSM ἵππου (2x)
Rv 19:19 the·one who·is·sitting·down on the horse, and
Rv 19:21 ·one who·is·sitting·down upon the horse, the·one
G2462 N-GPM ἵππων (6x)
Jac 3:3 the bits in the horses' mouths specifically to·persuade
Rv 9:9 as the·sound of·chariots, of·many horses running to
Rv 9:17 And the heads of·the horses *were* as heads of·lions,
Rv 14:20 ·the winepress, even·up·to the horses' bridles, for
Rv 18:13 "and livestock, sheep, horses, and carriages, "and
Rv 19:18 of·strong·men, and flesh of·horses, and of·the·

G2463 ἶρις îris *n.* (2x)
Roots:G2046
G2463 N-NSF ἶρις (2x)
Rv 4:3 stone, and *there·was* a·rainbow all·around the throne,
Rv 10:1 ·with a·thick·cloud; and a·rainbow *was* upon his

G2464 Ἰσαάκ Isaák *n/p.* (20x)
Ἰτσαάκ Itsaáq [Greek, Octuagint]
יִצְחָק yıtscḥạq [Hebrew]
Roots:H3327
G2464.2 N/P-PRI Ἰσαάκ (20x)
Lk 3:34 *son* of·Jacob, *son* of·YiTsaq, *son* of·AbRaham, *son*
Lk 13:28 yeu·should·gaze·upon AbRaham, YiTsaq, and
Lk 20:37 of·AbRaham, and the God of·YiTsaq, and the God
Ac 3:13 The God of·AbRaham, and of·YiTsaq, and of·Jacob
Ac 7:8 ·manner, *AbRaham* begot YiTsaq and circumcised
Ac 7:8 him on·the eighth day; and YiTsaq *begot* Jacob; and
Ac 7:32 of·AbRaham, and the God of·YiTsaq, and the God
Heb 11:9 *land*, residing in tents with YiTsaq and Jacob, the
Heb 11:17 when·being·tried, had·offered·up YiTsaq, and
Heb 11:18 "'In YiTsaq, a·Seed shall·be·called·forth to·you,
Heb 11:20 By·trust, YiTsaq blessed Jacob and Esau
Gal 4:28 brothers, according·to YiTsaq, are children of·
Mt 1:2 AbRaham begot YiTsaq, and YiTsaq begot Jacob, and
Mt 1:2 AbRaham begot YiTsaq, and YiTsaq begot Jacob,
Mt 8:11 ·recline·at·the·table with AbRaham, YiTsaq, and
Mt 22:32 of·AbRaham, and the God of·YiTsaq, and the God
Mk 12:26 of·AbRaham, and the God of·YiTsaq, and the
Rm 9:7 But·rather "'In YiTsaq, a·Seed shall·be·called·forth
Rm 9:10 *of·twins* from·out of·one·man, our father YiTsaq—
Jac 2:21 after·carrying·up his son YiTsaq upon the

G2465 ἰσ·άγγελος isángêlôs *adj.* (1x)
Roots:G2470 G0032
G2465 A-NPM ἰσάγγελοι (1x)
Lk 20:36 any·longer, for they·are equal·to·the·angels, and

G2466 Ἰσαχάρ Isachár *n/p.* (1x)
יִשָּׂשכָר yıșạșkạr [Hebrew]
Roots:H3485
G2466.3 N/P-PRI Ἰσαχάρ (1x)

Rv 7:7 *the* tribe of·IsSakar having·been·officially·sealed,

G2467 ἴσημι ísēmi *v.* (2x)

Roots:G1492 Compare:G1097 G1987 See:G4894

G2467 V-RAI-3P ἴσασιν (1x)

Ac 26:4 the Judeans have·distinctly·known my way·of·life

G2467 V-RAM-2P ἴστε (1x)

Heb 12:17 (For yeu·must·have·distinctly·known that even

G2468 ἴσθι ísthi *v.* (5x)

Roots:G1510 See:G2077 G2277

G2468 V-PXM-2S ἴσθι (5x)

Lk 19:17 trustworthy in very·little, be having authority over

Mt 2:13 flee into Egypt, and be there until I·should·declare

Mt 5:25 "Be kindly·settling *terms* with·your legal·adversary

Mk 5:34 ·out in peace and be healthy·and·sound away·from

1Ti 4:15 Meditate·upon these·things; be in these·things in·

G2469 Ἰσ•καριώτης Iskariṓtēs *n/g.* (11x)

Roots:H0377 H7152 xLangAlso:H7151

G2469.2 N/G-NSM Ἰσκαριώτης (5x)

Jn 12:4 ·among his disciples (Judas IsCariot, Simon's *son*,

Jn 14:22 Judas *Thaddaeus*, not IsCariot, says to·him, "Lord,

Mt 10:4 the Zealot, and Judas IsCariot, the·one also handing

Mt 26:14 ·referred·to·as Judas IsCariot, upon·traversing to

Mk 14:10 Then Judas IsCariot, one of·the twelve, went·off to

G2469.2 N/G-ASM Ἰσκαριώτην (4x)

Jn 6:71 Now he·was·referring·to Judas IsCariot, *the son* of·

Lk 6:16 *son* of·Jacobus·*Thaddaeus*, and Judas IsCariot, who

Lk 22:3 into Judas, the·one being·surnamed IsCariot, being

Mk 3:19 and Judas IsCariot, who also handed him over.

G2469.2 N/G-DSM Ἰσκαριώτῃ (1x)

Jn 13:26 the morsel, he·gave *it* to·Judas IsCariot, *the son* of·

G2469.2 N/G-GSM Ἰσκαριώτου (1x)

Jn 13:2 ·cast into the heart of·Judas IsCariot, *son* of·Simon,

G2470 ἴσος ísôs *adj.* (8x)

Roots:G1492 Compare:G3664 See:G2471 G2481

G2470.1 A-NPN ἴσα (2x)

Php 2:6 it not open·plunder to·be equal with·God,

Rv 21:16 The length and the breadth and its height are equal.

G2470.1 A-ASM ἴσον (1x)

Jn 5:18 his·own Father, making himself equal with·God.

G2470.1 A-ASF ἴσην (1x)

Ac 11:17 gave to·them the equally·same voluntary·present

G2470.1 A-APM ἴσους (1x)

Mt 20:12 hour, and you·made them equal to·us, the·ones

G2470.1 A-APN ἴσα (1x)

Lk 6:34 ·that they·may·receive·in·full the equal·amount.

G2470.2 A-NSF ἴση (1x)

Mk 14:59 ·manner was their testimony equal·in·substance.

G2470.2 A-NPF ἴσαι (1x)

Mk 14:56 ·yet the testimonies were not equal·in·substance.

G2471 ἰσότης isótēs *n.* (3x)

Roots:G2470 Compare:G3665 G3669 See:G2481

G2471.2 N-NSF ἰσότης (1x)

2Co 8:14 for yeur lacking, that there·may·be equality.

G2471.2 N-ASF ἰσότητα (1x)

Col 4:1 slaves the right and the equality, having·seen that

G2471.2 N-GSF ἰσότητος (1x)

2Co 8:13 for·yeu. But·rather out of·equality, now in *this*

G2472 ἰσό•τιμος isótimôs *adj.* (1x)

Roots:G2470 G5092

G2472 A-ASF ἰσότιμον (1x)

2Pe 1:1 already·clearly·obtaining an·equally·valuable trust

G2473 ἰσό•ψυχος isópsychôs *adj.* (1x)

Roots:G2470 G5590 Compare:G3675 See:G4861

G2473.2 A-ASM ἰσόψυχον (1x)

Php 2:20 ·have not·even·one·man of·such·kindred·soul, who

G2474 Ἰσρα•ήλ Israḗl *n/p.* (71x)

יִשְׂרָאֵל yiśrā'ēl [Hebrew]

Roots:H3478 See:G2475
xLangEquiv:A3479

EG2474.2 (1x)

Heb 8:13 the first *covenant with·the house of·IsraEl*. Now

G2474.3 N/P-PRI Ἰσραήλ (70x)

Jn 1:31 he·should·be·made·apparent to·IsraEl, on·account·of

Jn 1:49 Son of·God; you·yourself are the King of·IsraEl."

Jn 3:10 "Are you·yourself the instructor of·IsraEl, and you·

Jn 12:13 ·coming in Yahweh's name," the King of·IsraEl."

Lk 1:16 ·turn many of·the Sons of·IsraEl back·around to

Lk 1:54 ·supported his servant·boy IsraEl, being·mindful of·

Lk 1:68 *be* Yahweh, God of·IsraEl, because he·visited and

Lk 1:80 until *the* day of·his official·showing to IsraEl.

Lk 2:25 devout, awaiting the·consoling of·IsraEl. And Holy

Lk 2:32 of·Gentiles and *for the* glory of·your People IsraEl."

Lk 2:34 and a·raising·again of·many in IsraEl, and for a·sign

Lk 4:25 many widows were in IsraEl in the days of·EliJah,

Lk 4:27 many lepers were in IsraEl in·the·days of·EliSha the

Lk 7:9 to·yeu, not·even in IsraEl did·I·find so·vast a·trust.

Lk 22:30 ·sit on thrones judging the twelve tribes of·IsraEl."

Lk 24:21 is the·one intending to·ransom IsraEl. Moreover

Ac 1:6 do·you at this time restore the kingdom to·IsraEl?"

Ac 2:36 all *the* house of·IsraEl must·know securely that

Ac 4:8 "Rulers of·the People, and elders of·IsraEl,

Ac 4:10 all, and to·all the People of·IsraEl, that by the name

Ac 4:27 together with·Gentiles and with·peoples of·IsraEl,

Ac 5:21 the council·of·aged·men of·the Sons of·IsraEl. Then

Ac 5:31 right·hand, to·grant repentance to·IsraEl and pardon

Ac 7:23 his heart to·visit his brothers, the Sons of·IsraEl.

Ac 7:37 Moses is the·one declaring to·the Sons of·IsraEl,

Ac 7:42 prophets, "O·house of·IsraEl, ¿! did·yeu·offer to·

Ac 9:15 of·Gentiles and kings, and·also the·Sons of·IsraEl.

Ac 10:36 to·the Sons of·IsraEl, proclaiming·the·good·news

Ac 13:17 The God of·this People IsraEl selected our fathers,

Ac 13:23 promise, God awakened a·Savior for·IsraEl, Jesus,

Ac 13:24 by·John to·all the People of·IsraEl, prior·to *the*

Ac 28:20 the Expectation of·IsraEl *that* I·am·entirely·bound·

Heb 8:8 covenant with the house of·IsraEl and with the

Heb 8:10 I·shall·enact with·the house of·IsraEl after those

Heb 11:22 the exodus of·the Sons of·IsraEl, and he·gave·a·

Gal 6:16 them, and mercy, and upon the IsraEl of·God.

Mt 2:6 one·who shall·shepherd my People IsraEl.""

Mt 2:20 and traverse into *the* land of·IsraEl, for the·ones

Mt 2:21 and his mother and came into *the* land of·IsraEl.

Mt 8:10 to·yeu, not·even in IsraEl did·I·find so·vast a·trust.

Mt 9:33 ·at·any·time did·it·appear in·this·manner in IsraEl."

Mt 10:6 having·completely·perished of·*the*·house of·IsraEl.

Mt 10:23 yeu·may·not finish the cities of·IsraEl, until the

Mt 15:24 ·completely·perished of·*the*·house of·IsraEl."

Mt 15:31 And they·glorified the God of·IsraEl.

Mt 19:28 twelve thrones, judging the twelve tribes of·IsraEl.

Mt 27:9 who was·appraised by the·Sons of·IsraEl,

Mt 27:42 If he·is King of·IsraEl, let·him·descend now from

Mk 12:29 *is*, "Listen, O·IsraEl: Yahweh our God, Yahweh

Mk 15:32 the King of·IsraEl, let·him·descend now from the

Rm 9:6 For not all the·ones from·among IsraEl, *are* this

Rm 9:6 not all the·ones from·among IsraEl, *are* this IsraEl.

Rm 9:27 But IsaIah yells·out concerning IsraEl, " Although

Rm 9:27 the number of·the Sons of·IsraEl may·be as the

Rm 9:31 But IsraEl, pursuing a·Torah-Law of·righteousness,

Rm 10:1 petition to God on·behalf of·IsraEl is for Salvation.

Rm 10:19 But·yet I·say, ¿!·Did IsraEl not know?

Rm 10:21 But to IsraEl he·says, " The whole day·long I·

Rm 11:2 How he·confers with·God against IsraEl, saying,

Rm 11:7 what *happened*? IsraEl did·not obtain that which

Rm 11:25 *the* stony·hardness has·happened to·IsraEl *only* in

Rm 11:26 And in·this·manner all IsraEl shall·be·saved; just·

Php 3:5 ·of·age from·among *the* kindred of·IsraEl, *of·the*

1Co 10:18 Look·upon IsraEl according·to flesh. Are not·

2Co 3:7 such·for the Sons of·IsraEl not to·be·able to·gaze·

2Co 3:13 pertaining·to the Sons of·IsraEl not gazing·intently

Eph 2:12 ·alienated from·the citizenship of·IsraEl, and

Rv 2:14 a·trap in·the·sight of·the Sons of·IsraEl, *which was*

Rv 7:4 from·among all *the* tribes of·the·Sons of·IsraEl.

Rv 21:12 *names* of·the twelve tribes of·the Sons of·IsraEl.

G2475 Ἰσρα•ηλίτης Israēlítēs *n/p.* (10x)

Roots:G2474

G2475 N/P-NSM Ἰσραηλίτης (2x)

Jn 1:47 "See! Truly an·Israelite in whom there·is no guile!"

Rm 11:1 For I·myself also am an·Israelite, from·among

G2475 N/P-NPM Ἰσραηλῖται (2x)

Rm 9:4 who are Israelites— of·whom *are* the adoption·as·

2Co 11:22 Hebrews? So·*am*·I. Are·they Israelites? So·*am*·I.

G2475 N/P-VPM Ἰσραηλῖται (5x)

Ac 2:22 "Men, Israelites, hear these words: Jesus of·

Ac 3:12 the people, "Men, Israelites, why do·yeu·marvel at

Ac 5:35 "Men, Israelites, take·heed to·yeurselves what

Ac 13:16 "Men, Israelites and the·ones reverently·fearing

Ac 21:28 ·yelling·out, "Men, Israelites, swiftly·help! This

EG2475 (1x)

Ac 7:24 he·forcefully·defended *his fellow Israelite* and made

G2476 ἵστημι hístēmi *v.* (155x)

στάω stáō [used in certain tenses]

Compare:G0450 G5087 G2749 See:G4739 G2525 G4714

G2476.1 V-FAI-3S στήσει (1x)

Mt 25:33 And in·fact, he·shall·set the sheep at his right·

G2476.1 V-FPI-2P σταθήσεσθε (1x)

Mk 13:9 gatherings, and yeu·shall·be·set before governors

G2476.1 V-PAI-3S ἵστησιν (1x)

Mt 4:5 into the Holy City and sets him on the topmost·ledge

G2476.1 V-AAI-3S ἔστησεν (5x)

Lk 4:9 him to JeruSalem, and he·set him on the topmost·

Lk 9:47 grabbing·hold of·a·little·child, he·set him near

Ac 22:30 ·then bringing Paul down, he·set *him* among them.

Mt 18:2 YeShua, summoning a·little·child, set him in *the*

Mk 9:36 And taking a·little·child, he·set him in *the* midst

G2476.1 V-2AAI-3P ἔστησαν (3x)

Ac 5:27 And bringing them, they·set *them* in the joint·

Ac 6:6 men·whom they·set in·the·sight of·the ambassadors,

Ac 6:13 and they·set·up false witnesses saying, "This man·

G2476.1 V-AAP-NPM στήσαντες (1x)

Jn 8:3 ·been·grabbed in adultery; and after·setting her in *the*

G2476.2 V-2AAI-3P ἔστησαν (1x)

Mt 26:15 over to·yeu." And they·settled with·him for·thirty

G2476.2 V-2AAP-NSF στᾶσα (1x)

Lk 7:38 and settling directly·at his feet right·behind *him*

G2476.2 V-API-1S ἐστάθην (1x)

Rv 13:1 And I·settled upon the sand of·the sea, and I·saw a·

G2476.2 V-APP-ASM σταθέντα (1x)

Ac 11:13 in his house, being·settled and declaring to·him,

G2476.2 V-APP-NSM σταθείς (6x)

Lk 18:11 "The Pharisee, after·being·settled, was·praying

Lk 18:40 And being·settled, Jesus commandingly·ordered

Lk 19:8 And Zacchaeus, after·being·settled, declared to the

Ac 2:14 But Peter, after·being·settled together with·the

Ac 17:22 So Paul, being·settled in *the* midst of·Mars'·Hill,

Ac 27:21 ·a·bite·of·food, Paul, after·being·settled in *the*

G2476.2 V-APP-NPM σταθέντες (2x)

Ac 5:20 "Traverse, and after·being·settled·*in*, speak in the

Ac 25:18 ·accusers, after·being·settled·in, were·bringing·up

G2476.2 V-RAP-APN ἑστῶτα (1x)

Lk 5:2 he·saw two sailboats having·settled directly·by the

G2476.3 V-FPI-3S σταθήσεται (2x)

Rm 14:4 or falls. And, he·shall·be·established, for God is

2Co 13:1 witnesses shall every utterance be·established.

G2476.3 V-PAI-1P ἱστῶμεν (1x)

Rm 3:31 happen! But·rather, we·establish Torah-Law *for*

G2476.3 V-AAI-3S ἔστησεν (1x)

Ac 17:31 On·account·that, he·established a·day in which he·

G2476.3 V-2AAI-3P ἔστησαν (1x)

Ac 1:23 And they·established two, Joseph being·called

G2476.3 V-AAN στῆσαι (3x)

Rm 10:3 and seeking to·establish their·own righteousness,

Rm 14:4 ·be·established, for God is able to·establish him.

Jud 1:24 ·stumblings, and to·establish *yeu* without·blemish

G2476.3 V-AAS-2S στήσῃς (1x)

Ac 7:60 "Lord, you·should·not establish this moral·failure

G2476.3 V-AAS-3S στήσῃ (1x)
Heb 10:9 the first in·order·that he·may·establish the second.
G2476.3 V-APN σταθῆναι (1x)
Lk 21:36 ·about to·happen, and to·be·established before the
G2476.3 V-APS-3S σταθῇ (1x)
Mt 18:16 witnesses every utterance may·be·established.
G2476.4 V-FPI-3S σταθήσεται (3x)
Lk 11:18 how shall his kingdom remain·established?
Mt 12:25 ·divided against itself shall·not remain·established.
Mt 12:26 ·then, how shall his kingdom remain·established?
G2476.4 V-APN σταθῆναι (4x)
Mk 3:24 that kingdom is·not able to·remain·established.
Mk 3:25 itself, that home is·not able to·remain·established.
Mk 3:26 he·is·not able to·remain·established, but·rather has
Rv 6:17 is·come, and who is·able to·remain·established?"
G2476.5 V-FDI-3P στήσονται (1x)
Rv 18:15 ·wealthy from her, shall·stand from a·distance on·
G2476.5 V-AAP-NPM στήσαντες (1x)
Ac 4:7 And standing them in the middle, they·inquired, "By
G2476.5 V-RAI-1S ἕστηκα (3x)
Ac 26:6 "And now I·stand being·judged over *the* expectation
Ac 26:22 personally·from God, I·stand even·unto this day,
Rv 3:20 'Behold, I·stand at the door and knock.
G2476.5 V-RAI-1P ἑστήκαμεν (1x)
Rm 5:2 into this grace in which we·stand, and we·boast in
G2476.5 V-RAI-2S ἕστηκας (2x)
Ac 7:33 feet, for the place in which you·stand is holy soil.
Rm 11:20 they·were·broken·off, and you stand in·the trust.
G2476.5 V-RAI-2P ἑστήκατε (5x)
Ac 1:11 why·do yeu·still·stand *there* looking·clearly·up
Mt 20:6 says to·them, 'Why·do yeu·stand here the whole
1Pe 5:12 this to·be *the* true grace of·God in which yeu·stand.
1Co 15:1 yeu·personally·received, and in which yeu·stand,
2Co 1:24 of·yeur joy— for by·the trust, yeu·stand.
G2476.5 V-RAI-3S ἕστηκεν (7x)
Jn 1:26 immerse in water, but one·stands *in·the* midst of·yeu
Jn 8:44 *the* beginning, and he·does·not stand in the truth,
Heb 10:11 every priest·that·offers·sacrifices stands each day
Jac 5:9 Behold, *the* judge stands before the doors.
1Co 7:37 *the·father* who stands immovably·steadfast in the
2Ti 2:19 the solid foundation of·God stands, having this
Rv 12:4 And the Dragon stands in·the·sight of·the woman,
G2476.5 V-RAI-3P ἑστήκασιν (3x)
Lk 8:20 mother and your brothers stand outside, wanting to·
Mt 12:47 mother and your brothers stand outside, seeking to·
Rv 8:2 I·saw the seven angels who stand in·the·sight of·God;
G2476.5 V-RAN ἑστάναι (3x)
Lk 13:25 door, and yeu·should·begin to·stand outside and
Ac 12:14 she·announced, "Peter is·standing before the gate
1Co 10:12 the·one presuming to·stand must·look·out lest
G2476.5 V-2RAP-ASN ἑστός (2x)
Mt 24:15 through DaniEl the prophet, standing in *the* holy
Mk 13:14 by DaniEl the prophet, standing where it·is·not
G2476.5 V-RAP-ASM ἑστῶτα (6x)
Jn 20:14 And she·observes Jesus standing *there*, yet she·had·
Ac 4:14 having·been·both·relieved·and·cured standing with·
Ac 7:55 God's glory, and Jesus standing at *the* right·hand of·
Ac 7:56 and the Son of·Clay·Man† standing at *the* right·hand
Rv 10:5 the angel which I·saw standing upon the sea and
Rv 19:17 And I·saw one angel standing in the sun; and he·
G2476.5 V-RAP-APM ἑστῶτας (6x)
Ac 5:23 security and the sentries standing outside before the
Mt 20:3 the third hour, he·saw others standing idle in the
Mt 20:6 hour, he·found others standing idle and says to·
Rv 7:1 these·things, I·saw four angels standing on the four
Rv 15:2 of·its name)— standing on the transparent, glassy
Rv 20:12 small and great, standing in·the·sight of·God, and
G2476.5 V-RAP-GSM ἑστῶτος (1x)
Rv 10:8 the hand of·*the*·angel, the·one standing upon the sea
G2476.5 V-RAP-GPM ἑστηκότων (5x)
Lk 9:27 truly, there·are some of·the·ones standing here, who
Mt 16:28 there·are some of·the·ones standing here who, no,
Mt 27:47 Now some of·the·ones standing there, after·hearing
Mk 9:1 that there·are some of·the·ones standing here, who,
Mk 11:5 And some of·the·ones standing there were·saying
G2476.5 V-RAP-NSN ἑστηκός (2x)
Rv 5:6 Elders, a·Lamb standing as having·been·slaughtered,
Rv 14:1 and behold, a·Lamb standing on the Mount Tsiyon
G2476.5 V-RAP-NSF ἑστῶσα (1x)
Jn 8:9 ·left·behind— and·also the wife standing in *the* midst.
G2476.5 V-RAP-NSM ἑστώς (10x)
Jn 3:29 ·the bridegroom, the·one standing and listening·for
Jn 6:22 crowd— the·one standing on·the·other·side of·the
Jn 18:18 And Peter was standing with them, also warming·
Lk 1:11 ·visible to·him an·angel of·Yahweh standing at *the*
Lk 5:1 of·God, he·himself was standing directly·by the lake
Lk 18:13 And the tax·collector, standing at·a·distance, was·
Ac 16:9 some man of·Macedonia standing and imploring
Ac 21:40 ·permitting him, Paul, while·standing on the stairs
Ac 24:21 one address that I·yelled·out standing among them,
Ac 25:10 Paul declared, "I·am standing at Caesar's Bema·
G2476.5 V-RAP-NPF ἑστῶσαι (1x)
Rv 11:4 Fine·Oil·Lampstands standing in·the·sight of·the
G2476.5 V-RAP-NPM ἑστηκότες (6x)
Jn 11:56 So·then, standing in the Sanctuary·Atrium, they·
Ac 5:25 in the prison·cell are standing in the Sanctuary·
Mt 6:5 *are*, because they·are·fond·of standing in the
Mk 3:31 come *along*, and standing outside, they·dispatched
Rv 7:9 and native·tongues, standing in·the·sight·of·the
Rv 18:10 standing from a·distance on·account·of the fear of·
G2476.6 V-RAP-ASM ἑστῶτα (1x)
Ac 22:25 Paul declared to the centurion standing·by, "Is·it·
G2476.6 V-RAP-NSM ἑστώς (2x)
Jn 12:29 ·then the crowd, the·one standing·by and hearing *it*
Jn 18:25 Simon Peter was standing·by and warming·himself.
G2476.6 V-RAP-NPM ἑστῶτες (1x)
Mt 26:73 ·while, the·ones standing·by declared to·Peter,
G2476.7 V-LAI-3S εἱστήκει (7x)
Jn 1:35 on·the next·day, John stood also *with* two from·
Jn 7:37 Sacred·Feast *of·Booths*, Jesus stood and yelled·out,
Jn 18:5 Judas, the·one handing him over, stood with them.
Jn 18:16 But Peter stood outside alongside the door.
Jn 20:11 But Mariam stood outside toward the chamber·
Lk 23:35 And the people stood *there* observing. And the
Mt 13:2 ·down *there*; and all the crowd stood on the shore.
G2476.7 V-LAI-3P εἱστήκεισαν (6x)
Jn 18:18 slaves and the assistants stood *there*, having·made
Jn 19:25 Now *these women* stood near the cross of·Jesus:
Lk 23:10 chief·priests and the scribes stood, legally·accusing
Lk 23:49 ·along with·him from Galilee, stood at·a·distance,
Ac 9:7 traveling·together with·him stood in·stunned·silence,
Mt 12:46 his mother and brothers stood outside, seeking to·
G2476.7 V-LAI-3P-ATT ἑστήκεσαν (1x)
Rv 7:11 And all the angels stood in·a·circle·around the
G2476.8 V-2AAI-3S ἔστη (11x)
Jn 20:19 Judeans, Jesus came and stood·still in the midst.
Jn 20:26 ·been·shut, Jesus came and stood·still in the midst
Jn 21:4 the·break·of·dawn, Jesus stood·still upon the shore;
Lk 6:8 And rising·up, he·stood·still.
Lk 6:17 walking·down with them, he·stood·still in a·level
Lk 8:44 garment, and at·once her flow of·blood stood·still.
Lk 24:36 these·things, Jesus himself stood·still in *the* midst
Ac 3:8 And upon·leaping·forth, he·stood·still; then he·was·
Ac 10:30 yet behold, a·man stood·still in·the·sight of·me in
Mt 2:9 ·of them, going·*on* until it·stood·still up·above where
Mt 27:11 Now YeShua stood·still before the governor.
G2476.8 V-2AAI-3P ἔστησαν (4x)
Lk 7:14 coffin, and the·ones bearing *him* stood·still. And he·
Lk 17:12 him ten leprous men who stood·still from·afar,
Rv 11:11 ·in upon them, and they·stood·still upon their feet,
Rv 18:17 ·many·as work the sea, stood·still from a·distance,
G2476.8 V-2AAM-2S στῆθι (3x)
Lk 6:8 hand, "Rouse·yourself and stand·still in the middle.
Ac 26:16 'But·yet rise·up and stand·still upon your feet, for
Jac 2:3 ·poor, "You·yourself must·stand·still over·there," or
G2476.8 V-2AAM-2P στῆτε (1x)
Eph 6:14 Stand·still accordingly, after·personally·girding
G2476.8 V-2AAN στῆναι (3x)
Ac 8:38 ·ordered the chariot to·stand·still. And they·both
Eph 6:11 yeu to·be·able to·stand·still specifically·against the
Eph 6:13 absolutely·all, *that yeu·may·be·able* to·stand·still.
G2476.8 V-2AAP-GSM στάντος (1x)
Ac 24:20 in me, with·me standing·still before the joint·
G2476.8 V-2AAP-NSM στάς (2x)
Mt 20:32 And after·standing·still, YeShua hollered·out·for
Mk 10:49 And after·standing·still, Jesus declared *to·them* to·
G2476.8 V-2AAS-2P στῆτε (1x)
Col 4:12 in·order·that yeu·may·stand·still, completely·
G2476.8 V-API-3S ἐστάθη (1x)
Rv 8:3 another angel came and stood·still at the Sacrifice·

G2477 ἱστορέω historéō *v.* (1x)
Roots:G1492
G2477.2 V-AAN ἱστορῆσαι (1x)
Gal 1:18 to JeruSalem to·see·and·personally·interview Peter,

G2478 ἰσχυρός ischyrós *adj.* (27x)
Roots:G2479 Compare:G0972 G1415 G2900
See:G2480 xLangAlso:H5794
G2478.1 A-NSM ἰσχυρός (4x)
Lk 11:21 the strong·man, having·been·fully·armed, should·
Lk 15:14 all *of·it*, there·occurred a·strong famine in that
Rv 18:8 ·burned with fire, because strong *is* Yahweh God,
Rv 18:21 And one strong angel took·up a·stone as a·great
G2478.1 A-NSF ἰσχυρά (1x)
Rv 18:10 Great City Babylon, the Strong City! Because in
G2478.1 A-NPM ἰσχυροί (3x)
Heb 11:34 were·enabled, did·become strong in battle, routed
1Co 4:10 *are* weak, but yeu *are* strong. Yeu *are* glorious,
1Jn 2:14 ·yeu, young·men, because yeu·are strong, and the
G2478.1 A-NPF ἰσχυραί (1x)
2Co 10:10 "His letters *are* weighty and strong, but his bodily
G2478.1 A-ASM ἰσχυρόν (5x)
Mt 12:29 unless first he·should·bind the strong·man? And
Mt 14:30 But looking·at the strong wind, he·was·afraid, and
Mk 3:27 unless he·should·bind the strong·man first, and
Rv 5:2 And I·saw a·strong angel officially·proclaiming with·
Rv 10:1 And I·saw another strong angel descending from·out
G2478.1 A-ASF ἰσχυράν (1x)
Heb 6:18 for·God to·lie, we·may·have a·strong consoling
G2478.1 A-APN ἰσχυρά (1x)
1Co 1:27 ·order·that he·may·put·to·shame the strong·things.
G2478.1 A-GSM ἰσχυροῦ (2x)
Mt 12:29 able to·enter into the strong·man's home and to·
Mk 3:27 to·thoroughly·plunder the strong·man's belongings,
G2478.1 A-GSF ἰσχυρᾶς (1x)
Heb 5:7 petitions and supplications with a·strong yell and
G2478.1 A-GPM ἰσχυρῶν (1x)
Rv 19:18 ·commanders, and flesh of·strong·men, and flesh
G2478.1 A-GPF ἰσχυρῶν (1x)
Rv 19:6 waters, and as a·voice of·strong thunderings, saying
G2478.2 A-NSM-C ἰσχυρότερος (4x)
Lk 3:16 yeu in·water, but the·one stronger·than me comes,
Lk 11:22 the·one stronger·than him should·conquer him
Mt 3:11 who·is·coming right·behind me is stronger·than me,
Mk 1:7 saying, "The·one stronger·than me comes right·
G2478.2 A-NSN-C ἰσχυρότερον (1x)
1Co 1:25 the weakness of·God is stronger·than the *strength*
G2478.2 A-NPM-C ἰσχυρότεροι (1x)
1Co 10:22 Lord to·jealousy? ¿! Are·we stronger·than he?

G2479 ἰσχύς ischýs *n.* (12x)
Compare:G0970 G1411 G1849 G2904 G4598-2
See:G2480 G2478 G2192 xLangAlso:H5797 H2428
G2479 N-NSF ἰσχύς (1x)
Rv 7:12 and the power, and the strength, *be* to·our God into
G2479 N-ASF ἰσχύν (1x)
Rv 5:12 and wealth and wisdom and strength and honor and
G2479 N-DSF ἰσχύϊ (2x)
2Pe 2:11 angels, being greater·in strength and power, do·not
Rv 18:2 And he·yelled·out in strength, a·great voice, saying,
G2479 N-GSF ἰσχύος (7x)

Lk 10:27 and from·out of·all your strength, and from·out
Mk 12:30 ·mind, and from·out of·all your strength.'' This
Mk 12:33 and from·out of·all the strength, and to·love one's
1Pe 4:11 as *one·attending* from·out of·strength which God
2Th 1:9 of·the Lord, 'and from the glory of·his strength,'
Eph 1:19 ·to the operation of·the strength of·his might
Eph 6:10 in *the* Lord and in the might of·his strength.
EG2479 (1x)
1Co 1:25 ·God is stronger·than the *strength* of·men·of·clay†.

G2480 ἰσχύω ischýō *v.* (30x)
Roots:G2479 Compare:G2729 G2594 G2901 G1410 See:G2478 G2001
G2480.ª V-AAI-3S ἴσχυσεν (1x)
Lk 8:43 ·healing, neither could be·cured·or·brought·relief,
G2480.1 V-FAI-3P ἰσχύσουσιν (1x)
Lk 13:24 shall·seek to·enter and shall·not have·strength.
G2480.1 V-PAI-1S ἰσχύω (2x)
Lk 16:3 estate·management. I·do·not have·strength to·dig;
Php 4:13 I·have·strength *to·do* all·things in the·one enabling
G2480.1 V-PAI-3S ἰσχύει (4x)
Gal 5:6 circumcision nor uncircumcision has·any strength,
Gal 6:15 circumcision nor uncircumcision has·any strength,
Mt 5:13 To not·even·one·purpose does·it·have·strength any·,
Jac 5:16 is·itself·operating *to* much *effect*. It·has·strength.
G2480.1 V-PAN ἰσχύειν (1x)
Mt 8:28 some not to·have·strength to·pass·by through that
G2480.1 V-PAP-GSM ἰσχύοντος (1x)
Lk 14:29 and not having·strength to·entirely·complete *it*, all
G2480.1 V-IAI-3S ἴσχυεν (1x)
Mk 5:4 not·even·one·man was·having·strength to·tame him.
G2480.1 V-IAI-3P ἴσχυον (2x)
Ac 6:10 And they·were·not having·strength to·withstand the
Ac 25:7 they·were·not having·strength to·exhibit *in·court*,
G2480.1 V-AAI-1P ἰσχύσαμεν (1x)
Ac 15:10 our fathers nor we·ourselves had·strength to·bear?
G2480.1 V-AAI-2S ἴσχυσας (1x)
Mk 14:37 Did·you·not have·strength to·keep·alert *for* one
G2480.1 V-AAI-2P ἰσχύσατε (1x)
Mt 26:40 did·yeu·all·not have·strength to·keep·alert with
G2480.1 V-AAI-3S ἴσχυσεν (2x)
Lk 6:48 that home, but did·not have·strength to·shake it, for
Lk 14:30 yet did·not have·strength to·entirely·complete *it*.'
G2480.1 V-AAI-3P ἴσχυσαν (5x)
Jn 21:6 and they·no longer had·strength to·draw it *back·in*
Lk 14:6 And they·did·not have·strength to·contradict him
Lk 20:26 And they·did·not have·strength to·grab·hold of·his
Mk 9:18 ·should·cast it out, yet they·did·not have·strength."
Rv 12:8 and they·did·not have·strength *to·overpower*; neither
EG2480.1 (1x)
Gal 6:15 ·rather *it·is* a·brand-new creation *that* has·strength.
G2480.2 V-IAI-3S ἴσχυεν (1x)
Ac 19:20 Lord was·growing and was·exercising·strength.
G2480.2 V-AAI-1P ἰσχύσαμεν (1x)
Ac 27:16 with·difficulty we·exercised·strength to·make the
G2480.2 V-AAI-3S ἴσχυσεν (1x)
Ac 19:16 spirit was in, exercised·*such*·strength against them
G2480.3 V-PAP-NPM ἰσχύοντες (2x)
Mt 9:12 to·them, "The·ones being·well have no need of·a·
Mk 2:17 says to·them, "The·ones being·well have no need
G2480.4 V-PAI-3S ἰσχύει (1x)
Heb 9:17 since not·at·any·time *is·it* in·force when the·one

G2481 ἴσως ísōs *adv.* (1x)
Roots:G2470 See:G2471
G2481 ADV ἴσως (1x)
Lk 20:13 beloved son. *It·is* likely *that* after·seeing this·one,

G2482 Ἰταλία Italía *n/l.* (4x)
See:G2483
G2482 N/L-ASF Ἰταλίαν (2x)
Ac 27:1 for us to·set·sail for Italy, they·were·handing both
Ac 27:6 ·ship of·AlexAndria sailing into Italy, the centurion
G2482 N/L-GSF Ἰταλίας (2x)
Ac 18:2 recently having·come from Italy with his wife
Heb 13:24 all the holy·ones. The·ones from Italy greet yeu.

G2483 Ἰταλικός Italikós *adj/g.* (1x)
Roots:G2482
G2483 A/G-GSF Ἰταλικῆς (1x)
Ac 10:1 a·battalion being·called the Italian *Battalion*,

G2484 Ἰτουραΐα Itouraía *adj/l.* (1x)
יְטוּר yᵉtûr [Hebrew]
Roots:H3195
G2484.2 A/L-GSF Ἰτουραίας (1x)
Lk 3:1 Philippus·II being·the·ruling·tetrarch of·Jetur and

G2485 ἰχθύδιον ichthýdiôn *n.* (2x)
Roots:G2486 G2444-3 Compare:G3795
G2485 N-APN ἰχθύδια (2x)
Mt 15:34 "Seven, and a·few small·fish."
Mk 8:7 And they·were·holding a·few small·fish. And upon·

G2486 ἰχθύς ichthýs *n.* (20x)
See:G2485 G3795
G2486.1 N-ASM ἰχθύν (3x)
Lk 11:11 shall·he·hand him a·stone? Or·if a·fish, ¿! instead
Mt 7:10 And if he·should·request a·fish, ¿! shall·hand him a·
Mt 17:27 and take·up the first fish ascending *on·the line*, and
G2486.1 N-GSM ἰχθύος (2x)
Lk 11:11 Or·if a·fish, ¿! instead of·a·fish, shall·he·hand him
Lk 24:42 ·handed him a·piece of·a·broiled fish and *a·piece*
G2486.2 N-NPM ἰχθύες (1x)
Lk 9:13 five loaves·of·bread and two fish, except·that after·
G2486.2 N-APM ἰχθύας (7x)
Lk 9:16 five loaves·of·bread and the two fish, looking·up to
Mt 14:17 here except five loaves·of·bread and two fish."
Mt 14:19 five loaves·of·bread and the two fish, looking·up to
Mt 15:36 ·of·bread and the fish *and* upon·giving·thanks, he·
Mk 6:38 "Five, and two fish."
Mk 6:41 five loaves·of·bread and the two fish, looking·up to
Mk 6:41 and he·distributed the two fish among·them·all.
G2486.2 N-GPM ἰχθύων (7x)
Jn 21:6 ·strength to·draw it *back·in* for the multitude of·fish.
Jn 21:8 ·boat, while·dragging the net of·fish (for they·were
Jn 21:11 ·*it being* exceedingly·full of·big fish (a·hundred
Lk 5:6 they·tightly·enclosed a·large multitude of·fish, and
Lk 5:9 ·him) over the catch of·the fish which they·caught.
Mk 6:43 ·baskets full of·*bread*·fragments and of·the fish.
1Co 15:39 flesh of·beasts, another of·fish, and another of·

G2487 ἴχνος íchnôs *n.* (3x)
Compare:G2240
G2487.2 N-DPN ἴχνεσιν (3x)
Rm 4:12 ·and·marching·orderly in·his foot·tracks, *that·is*, the
1Pe 2:21 yeu·should·follow·afterward in·his foot·tracks:
2Co 12:18 we·walked? *Is·he* not in·the same foot·tracks?

G2488 Ἰωά•θαμ Iōátham *n/p.* (2x)
יוֹתָם yôthạm [Hebrew]
Roots:H3147
G2488.3 N/P-PRI Ἰωάθαμ (2x)
Mt 1:9 Then UzzIah begot YoTham, and YoTham begot
Mt 1:9 UzzIah begot YoTham, and YoTham begot Achaz,

G2489 Ἰω•άννα Iōánna *n/p.* (2x)
Roots:G2491 See:G5529
G2489.2 N/P-NSF Ἰωάννα (1x)
Lk 24:10 ·was Mariam Magdalene, and Joanna, and Mariam
G2489.2 N/P-GSF Ἰωάννα (1x)
Lk 8:3 and Joanna, wife of·Chuza (personal·administrator

G2490 Ἰω•αννᾶς Iōannâs *n/p.* (1x)
יוֹחָנָן yôcнạnạn [Hebrew]
Roots:G2491
G2490.2 N/P-GSM Ἰωαννᾶ (1x)
Lk 3:27 *son* of·Johannes, *son* of·RhesaYah, *son* of·

G2491 Ἰω•άννης Iōánnēs *n/p.* (136x)
יוֹחָנָן yôcнạnạn [Hebrew]
Roots:H3110 See:G3138
G2491.2 N/P-NSM Ἰωάννης (40x)
Jn 1:6 His name *was* John.
Jn 1:15 John testifies concerning him and has·yelled·out,
Jn 1:26 John answered them, saying, "I·myself immerse in
Jn 1:28 across the Jordan *River*, where John was immersing.
Jn 1:29 On·the next·day, John looks·at Jesus, who·is·
Jn 1:32 And John testified, saying, "I·have·distinctly·viewed
Jn 1:35 Again, on·the next·day, John stood also *with* two
Jn 3:23 And John also was immersing in Ainon near to·
Jn 3:24 for John had·not·yet been·cast into the prison.
Jn 3:27 John answered and declared, "A·man·of·clay† is·not
Jn 4:1 Jesus makes and immerses more disciples than John,"
Jn 10:40 into the place where John was first immersing; and
Jn 10:41 him and were·saying, "John, in·fact, did not·even·
Jn 10:41 but all·things as·many·as John declared concerning
Lk 1:60 But·rather, he·shall·be·called John."
Lk 1:63 "His name is John." And they·all marveled.
Lk 3:16 John answered, saying to·absolutely·all *of·them*,
Lk 7:19 And John, summoning a·certain two of·his disciples,
Lk 7:20 men declared, "John the Immerser has·dispatched
Lk 7:33 "For John the Immerser has·come neither eating
Lk 9:7 by some that John has·been·awakened from·among
Lk 11:1 instruct us to·pray, just·as John also instructed his
Ac 1:5 Because in·fact, John immersed in·water, but yeu
Ac 10:37 the immersion which John officially·proclaimed,
Ac 11:16 how he·was·saying, 'John in·fact immersed in·
Ac 13:25 And as John was·completely·fulfilling his·own
Ac 19:4 "In·fact, John did·immerse *with* an·immersion of·
Mt 3:1 in those days, John the Immerser arrived·publicly,
Mt 3:4 And *this* same John was·having his apparel *made*
Mt 3:14 But John was·thoroughly·forbidding him, saying,
Mt 4:12 Now after·hearing that John was·handed·over *into*
Mt 11:2 Now John, after·hearing in the dungeon *of* the works
Mt 11:18 For John came neither eating nor drinking, and
Mt 14:2 to·his servant·boys, "This is John the Immerser; he·
Mt 14:4 For John was·saying to·him, "It·is·not proper for·
Mt 21:32 For John came to yeu by way of·righteousness, yet
Mk 1:4 John was·immersing in the wilderness and officially·
Mk 1:6 And John was having·dressed·himself·with camel's
Mk 6:14 he·was·saying, "John the Immersing·One was·
Mk 6:18 For John was·saying to·HerOd·AntiPas, "It·is·not
G2491.2 N/P-ASM Ἰωάννην (19x)
Jn 3:26 And they·came to John and declared to·him, "Rabbi,
Jn 5:33 have·dispatched specifically·for John, and he·has·
Lk 1:13 ·bear you a·son, and you·shall·call his name John.
Lk 3:2 — an·utterance of·God came to John the son of·
Lk 3:20 ·*these*·things— that he·permanently·shut John up in
Lk 9:9 declared, "I·myself beheaded John, but who is this,
Lk 9:19 answering, they·declared, "John the Immerser, but
Lk 20:6 ·are having·been·persuaded *for* John to·be a·prophet
Mt 3:13 the Jordan, directly·to John to·be·immersed by him.
Mt 14:3 ·AntiPas, after·taking·secure·hold·of John, bound
Mt 14:10 And after·sending·word, he·beheaded John in the
Mt 16:14 "In·fact, *some say* John the Immerser, and others
Mt 21:26 we·fear the crowd, for all hold John as a·prophet."
Mk 1:14 with John already·being·handed·over *to·prison*,
Mk 6:16 *of·him*, he·declared, "This is John, whom I·myself
Mk 6:17 after·dispatching, took·secure·hold·of John, and
Mk 6:20 for HerOd·AntiPas was·afraid·of John, having·seen
Mk 8:28 And they·answered, "John the Immerser, but some
Mk 11:32 for absolutely·all·men were·holding John, that
G2491.2 N/P-DSM Ἰωάννῃ (3x)
Lk 7:18 And the disciples of·John *the Immerser* reported·to
Lk 7:22 "Traversing, report to·John what·things yeu·saw
Mt 11:4 announce to·John those·things·which yeu·hear and
G2491.2 N/P-GSM Ἰωάννου (30x)
Jn 1:19 Now this is the testimony of·John, when the Judeans
Jn 1:40 him and already·hearing directly·from John.
Jn 3:25 ·and·discussion from·among John's disciples against
Jn 5:36 have the greater testimony *than·that* of·John, for the
Lk 3:15 in their hearts concerning John, if·perhaps he·
Lk 5:33 "Why·is·it·that the disciples of·John fast frequently,
Lk 7:24 And with·the messengers of·John going·off, *Jesus*
Lk 7:24 to·discourse to the crowds concerning John, "What
Lk 7:28 ·even·one prophet greater·than John the Immerser,
Lk 7:29 ·being·immersed·in the immersion of·John (even

Lk 16:16 and the prophets *were* until John. From then·on, the
Lk 20:4 The immersion of·John, was·it from·out·of·heaven,
Ac 1:22 beginning from the immersion of·John, unto the day
Ac 13:24 being·officially·proclaimed·in·advance by·John to·
Ac 18:25 ·acquainted·with merely the immersion of·John.
Ac 19:3 And they·declared, "Into John's immersion."
Mt 9:14 ·time, the disciples of·John came·alongside him,
Mt 11:7 to·say to·the crowds concerning John, "What·did
Mt 11:11 ·awakened one·greater·than John the Immerser.
Mt 11:12 And from the days of·John the Immerser until this·
Mt 11:13 prophets and the Torah-Law prophesied until John.
Mt 14:8 "Give me here the head of·John the Immerser on a·
Mt 17:13 he·declared to·them concerning John the Immerser.
Mt 21:25 The immersion of·John, from·what·source was·it?
Mk 1:9 of·Galilee and was·immersed by John in the Jordan.
Mk 2:18 Now the disciples of·John and the *disciples* of·the
Mk 2:18 "Why·is·it·that the disciples of·John and the
Mk 6:24 she·declared, "The head of·John the Immerser."
Mk 6:25 from·this·same·hour the head of·John the Immerser
Mk 11:30 The immersion of·John, was *it* from·out·of·heaven

EG2491.2 (1x)

Mt 3:7 are·coming to his immersion, *John* declared to·them,

G2491.3 N/P-NSM Ἰωάννης (14x)

Lk 9:49 And responding, John declared, "O·Captain, we·
Lk 9:54 *this*, his disciples, Jakob and John, declared, "Lord
Ac 1:13 (Peter, Jakob, John, and Andrew); (PhilIp and
Ac 3:1 Now Peter and John were·walking·up in·unison into
Ac 4:19 But answering, Peter and John declared to them,
Gal 2:9 Kephas·*(called·Peter)*, and John, the·ones seeming
Mt 10:2 Jakob (the·one of·Zebedee) and John his brother;
Mk 9:38 And John answered him, saying, "Mentor, we·saw
Mk 10:35 And Jakob and John, the Sons of·Zebedee,
Mk 13:3 Peter, Jakob, John and Andrew were·inquiring·of
Rv 1:4 John, To·the seven Called·Out·citizenries, to·the·
Rv 1:9 I, John, also yeur brother and partner·together in the
Rv 21:2 And I, John, saw the HOLY CITY, brand-new
Rv 22:8 And I, John, *am* the·one looking·upon these·things

G2491.3 N/P-ASM Ἰωάννην (15x)

Lk 5:10 *amazed were* Jakob and John, the·Sons of·Zebedee,
Lk 6:14 Andrew his brother, Jakob and John, and·PhilIp and
Lk 8:51 except Peter, Jakob, and John, and the father and
Lk 9:28 that·also personally·taking Peter, John, and Jakob,
Lk 22:8 And *Jesus* dispatched Peter and John, declaring,
Ac 3:3 after·seeing Peter and John intending to·enter into
Ac 3:11 who·was·healed securely·holding Peter and John, all
Ac 8:14 of·God, they·dispatched Peter and John to them,
Mt 4:21 Jakob (the·one of·Zebedee) and John his brother, in
Mt 17:1 ·takes Peter and Jakob and John his brother, and he·
Mk 1:19 of·Zebedee) and his brother John, and these·men
Mk 3:17 (the·one of·Zebedee) and John the brother of·Jakob
Mk 5:37 except Peter, Jakob, and John the brother of·Jakob.
Mk 9:2 ·takes Peter, Jakob, and John, and brings them up
Mk 14:33 him Peter, Jakob, and John, and he·began to·be·

G2491.3 N/P-DSM Ἰωάννῃ (2x)

Ac 3:4 ·intently upon him together with·John, declared,
Rv 1:1 through his angel, he·signified *it* to·his slave John,

G2491.3 N/P-GSM Ἰωάννου (4x)

Ac 4:13 the clarity·of·speech of·Peter and John, and grasping
Ac 12:2 Jakob, the brother of·John, with·a·dagger.
Mk 1:29 home of·Simon and Andrew, with Jakob and John.
Mk 10:41 ·be·greatly·displeased concerning Jakob and John.

EG2491.3 (2x)

Ac 8:25 Lord, *as Peter and John* returned·back to JeruSalem
Mt 20:20 him, with her sons *(Jakob and John), and she·was*

G2491.4 N/P-NSM Ἰωάννης (1x)

Ac 13:13 departing from them, John·*Mark* returned·back to

G2491.4 N/P-ASM Ἰωάννην (3x)

Ac 12:25 service (and·also personally·taking·along John,
Ac 13:5 they·were·having also John·*Mark as·their* assistant.
Ac 15:37 ·purposed to·personally·take·along John, the·one

G2491.4 N/P-GSM Ἰωάννου (1x)

Ac 12:12 of·Miri, the mother of·John (being·surnamed

G2491.5 N/P-ASM Ἰωάννην (1x)

Ac 4:6 ·priest and Caiaphas and YoChanan and AlexAnder,

G2492 Ἰώβ Iṓb *n/p.* (1x)

אִיּוֹב ʼıyôb [Hebrew]

Roots:H0347

G2492.2 N/P-PRI Ἰώβ (1x)

Jac 5:11 Yeu·heard of·the patient·endurance of·Job and saw

G2493 Ἰω•ήλ Iōḗl *n/p.* (1x)

יוֹאֵל yôʼel

Roots:H3100

G2493.2 N/P-PRI Ἰωήλ (1x)

Ac 2:16 having·been·declared through JoEl the prophet:

G2494 Ἰω•νάν Iōnán *n/p.* (1x)

Roots:G2491 G2495

G2494 N/P-PRI Ἰωνάν (1x)

Lk 3:30 *son* of·Yoseph, *son* of·Yonan, *son* of·ElYaQim,

G2495 Ἰωνᾶς Iōnâs *n/p.* (13x)

יוֹנָה yônạh [Hebrew]

Roots:H3124 See:G0920

G2495.2 N/P-NSM Ἰωνᾶς (2x)

Lk 11:30 For just·as Jonah was·a·sign to·the Ninevites, in·
Mt 12:40 For just·as Jonah was three days and three nights in

G2495.2 N/P-GSM Ἰωνᾶ (7x)

Lk 11:29 ·given to·it, except the sign of·Jonah the prophet.
Lk 11:32 ·repented at the official·proclamation of·Jonah; and
Lk 11:32 behold, one·of·larger·stature·than Jonah *is* here.
Mt 12:39 to·her, except the sign of·Jonah the prophet.
Mt 12:41 ·repented at the official·proclamation of·Jonah; and
Mt 12:41 behold, one·of·larger·stature·than Jonah *is* here.
Mt 16:4 ·given to·her, except the sign of·Jonah the prophet."

G2495.3 N/P-GSM Ἰωνᾶ (4x)

Jn 1:42 are Simon, the son of·Jonah. You·yourself shall·be·
Jn 21:15 "Simon, *son* of·Jonah, do·you·love me more·than
Jn 21:16 "Simon, *son* of·Jonah, do·you·love me?
Jn 21:17 "Simon, *son* of·Jonah, do·you·have·affection·for

G2496 Ἰω•ράμ Iōrám *n/p.* (2x)

Ἰηώ•ράμ Yēhōrám [Greek, Octuagint]

יוֹרָם yôrạm [Hebrew, informal]

יְהוֹרָם yᵉhôrạm [Hebrew, formal]

Roots:H3141 See:G2424-1

G2496.3 N/P-PRI Ἰωράμ (2x)

Mt 1:8 and JehoShaphat begot JehoRam†, and JehoRam†
Mt 1:8 begot JehoRam†, and JehoRam† begot UzzIah.

G2497 Ἰω•ρείμ Iōreím *n/p.* (1x)

Roots:G2496

G2497 N/P-PRI Ἰωρείμ (1x)

Lk 3:29 *son* of·EliEzer, *son* of·JoRim, *son* of·Matthat, *son*

G2498 Ἰω•σαφάτ Iōsaphát *n/p.* (2x)

Ἰηώ•σαφάτ Yēhōshaphát [Greek, Octuagint]

יְהוֹשָׁפָט yᵉhôshạphạṭ [Hebrew]

Roots:H3092

G2498.4 N/P-PRI Ἰωσαφάτ (2x)

Mt 1:8 Now Asa begot JehoShaphat, and JehoShaphat begot
Mt 1:8 JehoShaphat, and JehoShaphat begot JehoRam†, and

G2499 Ἰωσή Iōsḗ *n/p.* (3x)

Roots:G2500

G2499.1 N/P-GSM Ἰωσῆ (1x)

Mk 15:47 and Miryam (*mother* of·Jose), *being* somewhere·

G2499.2 N/P-GSM Ἰωσῆ (1x)

Lk 3:29 *son* of·Yose, *son* of·EliEzer, *son* of·JoRim, *son* of·

G2499.3 N/P-GSM Ἰωσῆ (1x)

Mk 15:40 (the mother of·little Jacob and of·Joses), and

G2500 Ἰωσῆς Iōsễs *n/p.* (4x)

Roots:G2501 Compare:G2499

G2500.2 N/P-NSM Ἰωσῆς (2x)

Ac 4:36 Now Yosef, the·one being·properly·called BarNabas
Mt 13:55 his brothers, *little*·Jacob, Joses, Simon and Jude,

G2500.2 N/P-GSM Ἰωσῆ (2x)

Mt 27:56 the mother of·*little*·Jacob and Joses, and the
Mk 6:3 and a·brother of·*little*·Jacob, Joses, Jude, and

G2501 Ἰωσήφ Iōsḗph *n/p.* (37x)

יוֹסֵף yôçẹph [Hebrew]

Roots:H3130

G2501.2 N/P-PRI Ἰωσήφ (8x)

Jn 4:5 to·the open·field that Jacob gave to·his son Joseph.
Ac 7:9 being·jealous, sold Joseph away into Egypt.
Ac 7:13 at the second·time, Joseph was·made·known to·his
Ac 7:13 to·his brothers, and Joseph's kindred became
Ac 7:14 *brothers*, Joseph summarily·called·for his father
Ac 7:18 rose·up, who had·not personally·known Joseph.
Heb 11:21 blessed each of·the Sons of·Joseph, and he·
Heb 11:22 By·trust, Joseph (as·he·was·completely·dying)

G2501.3 N/P-PRI Ἰωσήφ (1x)

Rv 7:8 From·among *the* tribe of·Joseph having·been·

EG2501.3 (1x)

Mt 2:22 HerOd·the·Great, *Joseph* was·afraid to·go·aside

G2501.4 N/P-PRI Ἰωσήφ (16x)

Jn 1:45 prophets: Jesus from Natsareth, the son of·Joseph."
Jn 6:42 Is this not Jesus, the son of·Joseph, whose father and
Lk 1:27 to·a·man whose name *was* Joseph, from·among *the*
Lk 2:4 And Joseph also walked·up from Galilee, out of·*the*·
Lk 2:16 diligently·found both Mariam and Joseph, and·also
Lk 2:33 And Joseph and his mother were·marveling at the·
Lk 2:43 ·behind in JeruSalem. And Joseph and his mother
Lk 3:23 thirty years·of·age, being a·son of·Joseph (as
Lk 4:22 "Is not this Joseph's son?
Mt 1:16 Now Jacob begot Joseph the husband of·Mariam,
Mt 1:18 Mariam already·being·espoused to·Joseph, prior·to
Mt 1:19 Now Joseph her husband, being a·righteous *man* and
Mt 1:20 a·vision·in·a·dream, saying, "Joseph, son of·David
Mt 1:24 Then Joseph, after·being·thoroughly·awakened from
Mt 2:13 appears to·Joseph according·to a·vision·in·a·dream,
Mt 2:19 ·to a·vision·in·a·dream) appears to·Joseph in Egypt,

EG2501.4 (1x)

Mk 15:46 *Jesus* down, *Joseph* tightly·enwrapped him in·the

G2501.5 N/P-PRI Ἰωσήφ (6x)

Jn 19:38 And after these·things, Joseph (the·one from
Lk 23:50 And behold, a·man, Joseph by·name, a·counselor
Mt 27:57 of Arimathaea, by·the·name·of Joseph, who also
Mt 27:59 after·taking the body, Joseph swathed it in·a·pure
Mk 15:43 Joseph came, the·one of Arimathaea, a·dignified
Mk 15:45 he·voluntarily·presented the body to·Joseph.

G2501.6 N/P-PRI Ἰωσήφ (1x)

Lk 3:24 ·Levi, *son* of·Malki, *son* of·Janna, *son* of·Joseph,

G2501.7 N/P-PRI Ἰωσήφ (1x)

Lk 3:26 *son* of·Shimei, *son* of·Joseph, *son* of·Jehudah,

G2501.8 N/P-PRI Ἰωσήφ (1x)

Lk 3:30 *son* of·Yehudah, *son* of·Yoseph, *son* of·Yonan,

G2501.9 N/P-PRI Ἰωσήφ (1x)

Ac 1:23 ·established two, Joseph being·called BarTsabas

G2502 Ἰω•σίας Iōsías *n/p.* (2x)

יֹאשִׁיָּה yôʼshıyạh [Hebrew]

Roots:H2977

G2502.2 N/P-NSM Ἰωσίας (1x)

Mt 1:11 Then JosIah begot YeKonYah and his brothers, upon

G2502.2 N/P-ASM Ἰωσίαν (1x)

Mt 1:10 MaNasseh begot Amon, and Amon begot JosIah.

G2503 ἰῶτα iỗta *n.* (1x)

G2503.1 N-LI ἰῶτα (1x)

Mt 5:18 should·pass·away, not one iota or one tiny·mark,

Kκ - Kappa

G2504 κα•γώ kagṓ *p:p.* (72x)
κα•μοί kamoî [dative case]
κα•μέ kamé [accusative case]
Roots:G2532 G1473

G2504.ª P:P-1NS-C καγώ (9x)
Jn 10:15 the Father knows me, so·even·I know the Father,
Mk 11:29 to·them, "I·shall·inquire·of yeu also one question;
1Th 3:5 ·of this, when·I could·quietly·bear·it no·longer, I·
1Co 7:40 my advice; and I·suppose also to·have God's Spirit
2Co 11:21 *this* in impulsiveness), I·also am·daringly·bold.
2Co 11:22 Are·they Hebrews? So·*am*·I. Are·they Israelites?
2Co 11:22 Are·they Israelites? So·*am*·I. Are·they *the*
2Co 11:22 Are·they *the* offspring† of·AbRaham? So·*am*·I.
2Co 12:20 I·do·not want, and·*that*·I should·be·found by·yeu

G2504.1 P:P-1NS-C καγώ (35x)
Jn 1:31 And·I had·not personally·known him, but·yet in·
Jn 1:33 And·I had·not personally·known him, but·yet the·
Jn 1:34 And·I have·clearly·seen, and have·testified, that this
Jn 5:17 Father works until this·moment, and·I·also work."
Jn 6:56 and drinking my blood, abides in me, and·I in him.
Jn 6:57 living Father dispatched me, and·I live through the
Jn 8:26 the·one sending me is true, and·I say to the world
Jn 10:27 My sheep listen·to my voice, and·I know them, and
Jn 10:28 And·I give to·them eternal life-above.
Jn 10:38 may·trust, that the Father *is* in me, and·I in him."
Jn 12:32 And·I, if I·should·be·elevated from·among the
Jn 14:20 *am* in my Father, and yeu *are* in me, and·I in yeu.
Jn 15:4 "Abide in me, and·I in yeu. Just·as the vine·sprout
Jn 15:5 The·one abiding in me and·I in him, the·same bears
Jn 17:21 Father, *are* in me, and·I in you— "in·order·that
Jn 17:26 you·loved me may·be in them, and·I in them."
Jn 20:15 ·me where you·laid him, and·I shall·take him away
Lk 2:48 Behold, your father and·I were·seeking you,
Lk 11:9 "And·I·myself say to·yeu, request, and it·shall·be·
Lk 16:9 "And·I say to·yeu: Make friends for·yeurselves
Lk 20:3 to them, "And·I shall·ask·of yeu one question, and
Lk 22:29 And·I bequeath to·yeu a·kingdom, just·as my
Ac 22:13 'Brother Saul, look·up!' And·I, in·the same hour,
Ac 22:19 "And·I declared, 'Lord, they·themselves are·fully·
Heb 8:9 continue in my covenant, and·I neglected them,'
Gal 6:14 world has·been·crucified to·me, and·I to·the world.
Mt 2:8 that upon·coming, I·also may·fall·prostrate to·him."
Mt 11:28 having·been·overloaded, and·I shall·refresh yeu.
Mt 26:15 ·do yeu·want to·give to·me? And·I shall·hand him
Rm 11:3 your sacrifice·altars, and·I alone am·all·that·is·left,
Jac 2:18 "You have trust, and·I have works." Show me your
Jac 2:18 as·a·result of·your works, and·I shall·show you my
Php 2:28 yeu·may·rejoice, and·*that*·I may·be less·grieved.
1Co 2:1 And·I, brothers, already·coming to yeu, came not
2Co 6:17 of·impurity,"› and·I shall·favorably·accept yeu,

G2504.2 P:P-1NS-C καγώ (20x)
Jn 15:9 ·as the Father loved me, so·also·I loved yeu. Abide
Jn 17:18 me into the world, I·also dispatch them into the
Ac 10:26 "Stand·up, *for* also·I myself am a·man·of·clay†.
Gal 4:12 be as I·myself *am*, because I·also *am* as yeu *are*.
Mt 10:32 before the men·of·clay†, I·also shall·affirm him
Mt 10:33 the men·of·clay†, him I·also shall·deny before my
Mt 16:18 And I·also say to·you that you·yourself are Peter·
Mt 21:24 declared to·them, "I·also shall·ask·of yeu one
Mt 21:24 *an·answer* to·me, I·also shall·declare to·yeu by
Rm 3:7 to his glory, why am I·also still judged as morally·
Php 2:19 to·yeu, that I·also may·be·well·in·*my*·soul, after·
1Co 7:8 for·them if they·should·remain even·as I·also *am*.
1Co 10:33 Just·as I·also willingly·adapt·for all *men* in·all
1Co 11:1 of·me, just·as I·also *am* of·Anointed-One.
2Co 11:18 boast according·to the flesh, I·also shall·boast.
Eph 1:15 On·account·of that, I·also, after·hearing·of the
Rv 2:6 the deeds of·the NicoLaitans, which I·also hate.
Rv 2:27 *by·its·maker*,"› as I·also have·received *authority*
Rv 3:10 ·endurance, I·also shall·purposefully·keep you
Rv 3:21 on my throne, even·as I·also overcame and did·sit·

G2504.3 P:P-1NS-C καγώ (3x)
Jn 20:21 *my* Father has·dispatched me, even·so·I send yeu."
Ac 26:29 *the* large, to·become such as even·I am, *though*
2Co 11:16 ·that, *for* a·little·while, even·I may·boast some.

G2504.4 P:P-1AS-C καμέ (2x)
Jn 7:28 "¿! So·do yeu·personally·know me, and do·yeu·
1Co 16:4 if it·should·be appropriate *for* me·also to·traverse,

G2504.4 P:P-1DS-C καμοί (3x)
Lk 1:3 it·seemed *good* to·me·also, having·closely·followed
Ac 8:19 saying, "Give me·also this authority, in·order·that
1Co 15:8 of·all, he·was·gazed·upon by·me·also, just·as·if

G2505 καθ•ά kathá *adv.* (1x)
Roots:G2596 G3739 Compare:G2531 See:G2509

G2505.1 ADV καθά (1x)
Mt 27:10 for the potter's field, just·as Yahweh appointed me

G2506 καθ•αίρεσις kathaírêsis *n.* (3x)
Roots:G2507

G2506.1 N-ASF καθαίρεσιν (3x)
2Co 10:4 in·God to *the* demolition of·strongholds—
2Co 10:8 (and not for yeur demolition), I·shall·not be·
2Co 13:10 Lord gave me to edification and not to demolition.

G2507 καθ•αιρέω kathairéō *v.* (9x)
Roots:G2596 G0138 Compare:G5465 G2524 G2647 G1474 See:G2737 xLangAlso:H5422

G2507.1 V-2AAN καθελεῖν (1x)
Mk 15:36 ·see whether EliJah comes to·lower him down."

G2507.1 V-2AAP-NSM καθελών (2x)
Lk 23:53 And after·lowering it down, he·swathed it in·a·
Mk 15:46 ·buying a·linen·cloth and lowering *Jesus* down,

G2507.1 V-2AAP-NPM καθελόντες (1x)
Ac 13:29 ·written concerning him, after·lowering *him* down

G2507.2 V-2AAI-3S καθεῖλεν (1x)
Lk 1:52 He·demoted powers from *their* thrones and elevated

G2507.3 V-FAI-1S καθελῶ (1x)
Lk 12:18 'This shall·I·do, I·shall·demolish my barns and

G2507.3 V-PAP-NPM καθαιροῦντες (1x)
2Co 10:5 demolishing elaborate·reasonings and every

G2507.3 V-PPN καθαιρεῖσθαι (1x)
Ac 19:27 her magnificence is·about to·be·demolished, whom

G2507.3 V-2AAP-NSM καθελών (1x)
Ac 13:19 And after·demolishing seven nations in *the* land of·

G2508 καθ•αίρω kathaírō *v.* (2x)
Roots:G2513 Compare:G2511 G0048 See:G2510-1 xLangEquiv:H2891

G2508.1 V-RPP-APM κεκαθαρμένους (1x)
Heb 10:2 once having·been·purified *so·as* to·have not·one·

G2508.3 V-PAI-3S καθαίρει (1x)
Jn 15:2 the *proper* fruit, he·trims·and·purifies it, in·order·

G2509 καθ•ά•περ kathápêr *adv.* (13x)
Roots:G2505 G4007

G2509 ADV καθάπερ (13x)
Heb 4:2 ·the·good·news, exactly·as they·also *had·been*, but·
Heb 5:4 ·called·forth by God, even exactly·as Aaron *was*.
Rm 4:6 exactly·as David also refers·to the supreme·
Rm 12:4 For exactly·as we·have many members in one body
1Th 2:11 Exactly·as yeu·have·seen (each one of·yeu), how
1Th 3:6 ·yearning to·see us, exactly·as we·ourselves also
1Th 3:12 all *men*, even exactly·as we·ourselves *do* toward
1Th 4:5 ·passion of·longing, even exactly·as the Gentiles,
1Co 12:12 For exactly·as the body is one and has many
2Co 1:14 that we·are yeur boasting, exactly·as yeu *are* also
2Co 3:13 And not exactly·as Moses *did*, who·was·placing a·
2Co 3:18 glory to glory, exactly·as from Yahweh's Spirit.
2Co 8:11 to·do *it*, that exactly·as *there·was* the eagerness to·

G2510 καθ•άπτω katháptō *v.* (1x)
Roots:G2596 G0681 See:G0680

G2510 V-AAI-3S καθῆψεν (1x)
Ac 28:3 out of·the warmth, fully·fastened·onto his hand.

G2511 καθ•αρίζω katharízō *v.* (30x)
Roots:G2513 Compare:G2508 G1571 G0048 See:G2512 G1245 G2514-1 xLangEquiv:H2891

G2511.1 V-FAI-3S-ATT καθαριεῖ (1x)
Heb 9:14 without·blemish to·God, purify yeur conscience

G2511.1 V-PAI-2P καθαρίζετε (2x)
Lk 11:39 "Now yeu Pharisees purify the outside of·the cup
Mt 23:25 ·acting·hypocrites! Because yeu·purify the outside

G2511.1 V-PAI-3S καθαρίζει (1x)
1Jn 1:7 Anointed, his Son, purifies us from all moral·failure

G2511.1 V-PAM-2P καθαρίζετε (1x)
Mt 10:8 Both·relieve·and·cure the·sick; purify lepers;

G2511.1 V-PPI-3S καθαρίζεται (1x)
Heb 9:22 ·to the Torah-Law, are·purified with blood. And

G2511.1 V-PPI-3P καθαρίζονται (2x)
Lk 7:22 lame·men walk, lepers are·purified, deaf·men hear
Mt 11:5 lame·men walk, lepers are·purified and deaf·men

G2511.1 V-PPN καθαρίζεσθαι (1x)
Heb 9:23 in the heavens) to·be·purified with·these *sacrifices*

G2511.1 V-AAI-3S ἐκαθάρισεν (2x)
Ac 10:15 ·time, "What God purified, you·yourself must·not
Ac 11:9 heaven, 'That·which God purified, you must·not

G2511.1 V-AAM-2S καθάρισον (1x)
Mt 23:26 "O·blind Pharisee, first purify the interior of·the

G2511.1 V-AAM-2P καθαρίσατε (1x)
Jac 4:8 and he·shall·draw·near to·yeu. Purify *yeur* hands,

G2511.1 V-AAN καθαρίσαι (3x)
Lk 5:12 if you·should·want, you·are·able to·purify me."
Mt 8:2 if you·should·want, you·are·able to·purify me."
Mk 1:40 "If you·should·want, you·are·able to·purify me."

G2511.1 V-AAP-NSM καθαρίσας (2x)
Ac 15:9 both us and them, purifying their hearts by·the trust.
Eph 5:26 ·and·make·*her*·holy, purifying her with·the

G2511.1 V-AAS-1P καθαρίσωμεν (1x)
2Co 7:1 dearly·beloved, we·should·purify ourselves from

G2511.1 V-AAS-3S καθαρίσῃ (2x)
Tit 2:14 all lawlessness,' and may·purify to·himself '*his*·
1Jn 1:9 us the moral·failures, and should·purify us from all

G2511.1 V-API-3S ἐκαθαρίσθη (3x)
Lk 4:27 yet not·even·one of·them was·purified, except
Mt 8:3 And immediately, his leprosy was·purified.
Mk 1:42 leprosy went·off from him, and he·was·purified.

G2511.1 V-API-3P ἐκαθαρίσθησαν (2x)
Lk 17:14 with them heading·on·out, *that* they·were·purified.
Lk 17:17 "Are·not·indeed the ten purified? But where *are*

G2511.1 V-APM-2S καθαρίσθητι (3x)
Lk 5:13 declaring, "I·want. Be·purified!" And immediately,
Mt 8:3 saying, "I·want·to. Be·purified." And immediately,
Mk 1:41 of·him and says to·him, "I·want·to. Be·purified."

G2511.2 V-PAP-NSN καθαρίζον (1x)
Mk 7:19 traverses·out into the outhouse, purging all the food

G2512 καθ•αρισμός katharismós *n.* (8x)
Roots:G2511 Compare:G0047 See:G2514-1 xLangEquiv:H2893

G2512.1 N-ASM καθαρισμόν (1x)
Heb 1:3 after·making purification of·our moral·failures

G2512.1 N-GSM καθαρισμοῦ (5x)
Jn 3:25 disciples against *the* Judeans concerning purification.
Lk 2:22 when the days of·her purification according·to the
Lk 5:14 and offer concerning your purification, just·as
Mk 1:44 your purification those·things·which Moses
2Pe 1:9 deathly·oblivious of·the purification from·his former

EG2512.1 (1x)
Mk 1:45 he·began to·officially·herald *his purification* often,

G2512.2 N-ASM καθαρισμόν (1x)
Jn 2:6 ·to the manner·of·purification of·the Judeans,

G2513 καθ•αρός katharós *adj.* (28x)
Roots:G2596 Compare:G0053 G4508 See:G2508 G2511 G0169 xLangEquiv:H2889 xLangAlso:H5355

G2513.2 A-NSM καθαρός (3x)
Jn 13:10 Moreover, he·is altogether pure. And yeu are pure,

Ac 18:6 yeur own·heads; I·myself *am* pure. From now·on, I·
Ac 20:26 day, that I·myself *am* pure from the blood of·all
G2513.2 A-NSF καθαρά (1x)
Jac 1:27 and Father— pure and uncontaminated religion is
G2513.2 A-NSN καθαρόν (4x)
Mt 23:26 in·order·that their exterior may·be pure also.
Tit 1:15 ·ones, not·even·one·thing *is* pure, but·rather even
Rv 21:18 And the CITY *was* pure gold, like pure glass.
Rv 21:21 And the broad·street of·the CITY *was* pure gold, as
G2513.2 A-NPM καθαροί (3x)
Jn 13:10 And yeu are pure, but·yet not·indeed all *of·yeu.*
Jn 13:11 "Yeu·are not·indeed all pure."
Mt 5:8 "Supremely·blessed *are* the pure in·the heart, because
G2513.2 A-NPN καθαρά (3x)
Lk 11:41 and behold, *suddenly* all·things are pure for·yeu?
Rm 14:20 In·fact, all·things *are* pure, but·yet *it·is* morally·
Tit 1:15 In·fact, to·the pure, all·things *are* pure.
G2513.2 A-ASM καθαρόν (1x)
Rv 22:1 And he·showed me a·pure river of·water of·
G2513.2 A-ASN καθαρόν (3x)
Rv 15:6 having·dressed·themselves in·pure and radiant
Rv 19:8 ·should·be·arrayed·with fine·linen, pure and radiant
Rv 19:14 ·themselves·with fine·linen, white and pure.
G2513.2 A-DSM καθαρῷ (1x)
Rv 21:18 And the CITY *was* pure gold, like pure glass.
G2513.2 A-DSF καθαρᾷ (3x)
Mt 27:59 the body, Joseph swathed it in·a·pure linen·cloth
1Ti 3:9 the Mystery of·the trust in a·pure conscience.
2Ti 1:3 from *my* forebears' *example* with a·pure conscience),
G2513.2 A-DSN καθαρῷ (1x)
Heb 10:22 the bodies having·been·bathed with·pure water.
G2513.2 A-DPM καθαροῖς (1x)
Tit 1:15 to·the pure, all·things *are* pure. But to·the·ones
G2513.2 A-GSF καθαρᾶς (3x)
1Pe 1:22 one·another from·out of·a·pure heart earnestly—
1Ti 1:5 of·the charge is love out of·a·pure heart, and of·a·
2Ti 2:22 the·ones calling·upon the Lord out of·a·pure heart.
G2513.3 A-NPM καθαροί (1x)
Jn 15:3 "Even·now yeu are trimmed·and·pure through the

G2514 καθ•αρότης katharótēs *n.* (1x)

Roots:G2513 Compare:G0047

G2514.2 N-ASF καθαρότητα (1x)
Heb 9:13 ·one·holy just·for the purification of·the flesh,

G2515 καθ•έδρα kathédra *n.* (3x)

Roots:G2596 G1476 Compare:G2362 G0968 G2435 See:G4410 xLangAlso:H4186

G2515 N-APF καθέδρας (2x)
Mt 21:12 moneychangers and the seats of·the·ones selling
Mk 11:15 moneychangers and the seats of·the·ones selling
G2515 N-GSF καθέδρας (1x)
Mt 23:2 and the Pharisees sat·down upon the seat of·Moses.

G2516 καθ•έζομαι kathézōmai *v.* (6x)

Roots:G2596 G1478-1 Compare:G2521 G2523 See:G1476

G2516.1 V-PNP-ASM καθεζόμενον (1x)
Lk 2:46 him in the Sanctuary·Courtyard, sitting·down in *the*
G2516.1 V-PNP-APM καθεζομένους (1x)
Jn 20:12 two angels in white sitting·down, one alongside the
G2516.1 V-PNP-NPM καθεζόμενοι (1x)
Ac 6:15 ·all the·ones who·were·sitting·down in the joint·
G2516.1 V-INI-1S ἐκαθεζόμην (1x)
Mt 26:55 staffs to·arrest me? I·was·sitting·down each day
G2516.1 V-INI-3S ἐκαθέζετο (2x)
Jn 4:6 ·the road·travel, was·sitting·down in·this·manner on
Jn 11:20 ·met him, but Mary was·sitting·down in the house.

G2517 καθ•εξῆς kathexēs *adv.* (5x)

Roots:G2596 G1836

G2517.2 ADV καθεξῆς (3x)
Lk 1:3 *a·thorough·account* in·consecutive·order, most·noble
Ac 11:4 explained·himself in·consecutive·order to·them,
Ac 18:23 and Phrygia in·consecutive·order, reaffirming all
G2517.3 ADV καθεξῆς (2x)
Lk 8:1 Now it·happened in the subsequent·order, that he·
Ac 3:24 and the·ones of·subsequent·order, as·many·as that·

G2518 καθ•εύδω katheúdō *v.* (23x)

Roots:G2596 G2107-2 Compare:G2837 G3573 G5258-1 G2530-3 See:G5258

G2518.2 V-PAP-NPM καθεύδοντες (1x)
1Th 5:7 For the·ones falling·asleep, sleep at·night, and the·
G2518.2 V-PAS-1P καθεύδωμεν (1x)
1Th 5:6 Accordingly, we·should·not fall·asleep, as even *do*
G2518.3 V-PAI-2S καθεύδεις (1x)
Mk 14:37 ·Peter, "Simon, do·you·sleep? Did·you·not have·
G2518.3 V-PAI-2P καθεύδετε (1x)
Lk 22:46 to·them, "Why·do yeu·sleep? Rising·up, be·in·
G2518.3 V-PAI-3S καθεύδει (3x)
Lk 8:52 She·did·not die, but·rather she·sleeps."
Mt 9:24 young·girl did·not die, but·rather she·sleeps." And
Mk 5:39 The little·child is·not dead, but·rather she·sleeps."
G2518.3 V-PAI-3P καθεύδουσιν (1x)
1Th 5:7 For the·ones falling·asleep, sleep at·night, and the·
G2518.3 V-PAM-2P καθεύδετε (2x)
Mt 26:45 says to·them, "Do·yeu·all·sleep *through* the·one
Mk 14:41 says to·them, "Do·yeu·all·sleep *through* the·one
G2518.3 V-PAN καθεύδειν (1x)
Mt 13:25 at the *time for* the men·of·clay† to·sleep, his enemy
G2518.3 V-PAP-APM καθεύδοντας (5x)
Mt 26:40 the disciples and finds them sleeping. And he·says
Mt 26:43 And coming, he·finds them sleeping again, for
Mk 13:36 ·coming suddenly he·should·find yeu sleeping.
Mk 14:37 he·comes and finds them sleeping. And he·says to·
Mk 14:40 ·returning·back, he·found them sleeping again for
G2518.3 V-PAP-NSM καθεύδων (2x)
Mk 4:38 was in the stern·of·the·boat, sleeping on the pillow.
Eph 5:14 he·says, "O·the·one sleeping, be·awakened and
G2518.3 V-PAS-1P καθεύδωμεν (1x)
1Th 5:10 ·keep·alert or we·should·sleep, we·should·live at·
G2518.3 V-PAS-3S καθεύδῃ (1x)
Mk 4:27 and should·sleep, and should·be·awakened night
G2518.3 V-IAI-3S ἐκάθευδεν (1x)
Mt 8:24 the breaking·waves, but he·himself was·sleeping.
G2518.3 V-IAI-3P ἐκάθευδον (1x)
Mt 25:5 lingering, all nodded·off and were·sleeping.
EG2518.3 (1x)
2Pe 2:3 and their total·destruction does·not nod·off *to·sleep.*

G2519 καθ•ηγητής kathēgētḗs *n.* (3x)

Roots:G2596 G2233 Compare:G1203 G1320 G4461 G4462 G5247 G5383 G0752 G2819-2 G1577-2 G1361 G5545-1 See:G2232 xLangEquiv:H7218-1

G2519.1 N-NSM καθηγητής (2x)
Mt 23:8 for one is yeur Preeminent·Leader, *that·is* the
Mt 23:10 for one is yeur Preeminent·Leader, *that·is* the
G2519.1 N-NPM καθηγηταί (1x)
Mt 23:10 ·even should·yeu·be·called preeminent·leaders, for

G2520 καθ•ήκω kathḗkō *v.* (2x)

Roots:G2596 G2240

G2520.2 V-PQP-APN καθήκοντα (1x)
Rm 1:28 mind, to·do the·things *which·are* not befitting;
G2520.2 V-PQP-NSN καθῆκον (1x)
Ac 22:22 the earth, for it·is·not befitting for·him to·live."

G2521 κάθ•ημαι káthēmai *v.* (89x)

Roots:G2596 G2247-2 Compare:G2516 G2523 G2650 See:G1476 G2515 xLangAlso:H3427

G2521.1 V-PNI-1S κάθημαι (1x)
Rv 18:7 she·says in her heart, 'I·sit·down a·queen, and I·am
G2521.1 V-PNI-2S-ATT κάθῃ (1x)
Ac 23:3 Even you·yourself sit·down judging me according·
G2521.1 V-PNI-3S κάθηται (2x)
Rv 17:9 mountains, wherever the woman sits·down on them.
Rv 17:15 ·saw, where the Prostitute sits·down, are peoples,
G2521.1 V-PNM-2S κάθου (7x)
Lk 20:42 declared to·my Lord, "Sit·down at my right·hand
Ac 2:34 declared to·my Lord, "Sit·down at my right·hand
Heb 1:13 at·any·time, "'Sit·down at my right·hand, until I·
Mt 22:44 declared to·my Lord, "Sit·down at my right·hand
Mk 12:36 declared to·my Lord, "Sit·down at my right·hand
Jac 2:3 "You·yourself must·sit·down here in·a·good·place,"
Jac 2:3 over·there," or "Sit·down here under my footstool,"
G2521.1 V-PNN καθῆσθαι (2x)
Mt 13:2 ·embark into the sailboat *and* to·sit·down *there*; and
Mk 4:1 embarking into the sailboat to·sit·down along the sea
G2521.1 V-PNP-ASF καθημένην (1x)
Rv 17:3 I·saw a·woman who·is·sitting·down upon a·scarlet
G2521.1 V-PNP-ASM καθήμενον (10x)
Lk 5:27 Levi by·name, sitting·down in the tax·booth.
Lk 8:35 demons had·come·out, sitting·down directly·at the
Lk 22:56 But after·seeing him sitting·down toward the
Mt 9:9 ·referred·to·as MattHew, who·is·sitting·down in the
Mt 26:64 'the Son of·Clay·Man† sitting·down at *the* right·
Mk 2:14 (the·one of·Alphaeus) sitting·down in the tax·
Mk 5:15 being·possessed·with·demons sitting·down and
Mk 14:62 ·upon the Son of·Clay·Man† sitting·down at *the*
Mk 16:5 ·tomb, they·saw a·young·man sitting·down on the
Rv 20:11 Throne, and the·one who·is·sitting·down on it,
G2521.1 V-PNP-APM καθημένους (5x)
Jn 2:14 *he·found* the exchangers·of·money sitting·down.
Lk 21:35 upon all the·ones who·are·sitting·down on *the* face
Mk 3:34 in·a·circle at·the·ones sitting·down around him, he·
Rv 4:4 twenty four Elders sitting·down, having·been·arrayed
Rv 9:17 the clear·vision, and the·ones sitting·down on them,
G2521.1 V-PNP-DSM καθημένῳ (8x)
Mt 23:22 of·God and by the·one who·is·sitting·down upon it
1Co 14:30 should·be·revealed to·another sitting·down, the
Rv 4:9 and thanks to·the·one who·is·sitting·down on the
Rv 5:13 saying, "To·the·one who·is·sitting·down upon the
Rv 6:4 ·given to·him, to·the·one who·is·sitting·down on it,
Rv 7:10 ·our God! To·the·one who·is·sitting·down upon the
Rv 14:15 a·loud voice to·the·one who·is·sitting·down on the
Rv 19:4 to·God, to·the·one who·is·sitting·down on the
G2521.1 V-PNP-DPN καθημένοις (1x)
Lk 7:32 ·children, the·ones sitting·down in a·marketplace
G2521.1 V-PNP-DPM καθημένοις (2x)
Lk 1:79 ·upon the·ones who·are·sitting·down in darkness
Mt 11:16 It·is like little·boys sitting·down in marketplaces
G2521.1 V-PNP-GSF καθημένης (1x)
Rv 17:1 Prostitute, the·one who·is·sitting·down upon the
G2521.1 V-PNP-GSM καθημένου (8x)
Mt 24:3 And with·him sitting·down upon the Mount of·
Mk 13:3 And with·him sitting·down upon the Mount of·
Rv 4:10 shall·fall in·the·sight of·the·one sitting·down on the
Rv 5:1 I·saw in the right·hand of·the·one sitting·down on the
Rv 5:7 of·the right·hand of·the·one sitting·down upon the
Rv 6:16 from *the* face of·the·one who·is·sitting·down on the
Rv 19:19 war against the·one who·is·sitting·down on the
Rv 19:21 ·sword of·the·one who·is·sitting·down upon the
G2521.1 V-PNP-GPM καθημένων (1x)
Rv 19:18 of·horses, and of·the·ones sitting·down on them,
G2521.1 V-PNP-NSM καθήμενος (16x)
Jn 12:15 King comes *to·you*, sitting·down upon a·donkey's
Lk 22:69 the Son of·Clay·Man† shall·be sitting·down at *the*
Ac 3:10 ·person, the·one sitting·down specifically·for the
Ac 8:28 Also, he·was returning·back and sitting·down in his
Ac 20:9 by·the·name·of EuTychus was·sitting·down in the
Col 3:1 Anointed-One is sitting·down at the·right·hand of·
Rv 4:2 the heaven, and upon the throne is·one·sitting·down.
Rv 4:3 And the·one sitting·down was in·clear·appearance
Rv 6:2 a·white horse and the·one who·is·sitting·down on it
Rv 6:5 a·black horse and the·one who·is·sitting·down on it
Rv 6:8 a·pale horse and the·one who·is·sitting·down upon it,
Rv 7:15 Temple. And the·one who·is·sitting·down on the
Rv 14:14 the thick·cloud *one* who·is·sitting·down like a·son
Rv 14:16 And the·one who·is·sitting·down on the thick·
Rv 19:11 a·white horse and the·one sitting·down upon it *was*
Rv 21:5 And the·one who·is·sitting·down upon the throne
G2521.1 V-PNP-NSM@ καθήμενος (1x)
Jn 9:8 Is this not the·one who·was·sitting·down and begging
G2521.1 V-PNP-NPF καθήμεναι (2x)
Lk 10:13 ·would·have repented, sitting·down in sackcloth

Mt 27:61 the other Miryam, sitting·down fully·before the
G2521.1 V-PNP-NPM καθήμενοι (6x)
Lk 5:17 and teachers·of·Torah-Law sitting·down, who were
Ac 2:2 ·filled all the house where they·were sitting·down.
Mt 20:30 behold, two blind·men are·sitting·down beside the
Mt 27:36 And sitting·down, they·were·keeping·guard·over
Mk 2:6 scribes were there, sitting·down yet pondering in
Rv 11:16 Elders, the·ones sitting·down in·the·sight·of·God
G2521.1 V-INI-3S ἐκάθητο (11x)
Jn 6:3 And there, he·was·sitting·down with his disciples.
Lk 18:35 a·certain blind·man sat·down directly·by the
Lk 22:55 and sitting·down·together, Peter sat·down in *the*
Ac 14:8 in·his feet who·was·sitting·down, inherently·being
Mt 13:1 from the home, was·sitting·down beside the sea.
Mt 15:29 walking·up upon the mountain, he·sat·down there.
Mt 26:58 and after·entering inside, he·sat·down with the
Mt 26:69 Now Peter was·sitting·down outside in the
Mt 28:2 the stone from the door and sat·down on·top of·it.
Mk 3:32 And a·crowd was·sitting·down around him, and
Mk 10:46 ·son of·Timaeus) was·sitting·down directly·by the
G2521.2 V-PNP-DPM καθημένοις (1x)
Mt 4:16 light. And to·the·ones who·are·fully·sitting in *the*
G2521.2 V-PNP-GSM καθημένου (1x)
Mt 27:19 But as·he·was·fully·seating himself upon the
G2521.2 V-PNP-NSM καθήμενος (1x)
Mt 4:16 people, the·ones who·are·fully·sitting in darkness,

Kκ

G2522 καθ•ημερινός kathēmêrinós *adj.* (1x)
Roots:G2596 G2250
G2522 A-DSF καθημερινῇ (1x)
Ac 6:1 were·intentionally·neglected in the daily service.

G2523 καθ•ίζω kathízō *v.* (48x)
Roots:G2516 Compare:G2521 See:G1940
xLangAlso:H3427
G2523.1 V-PAI-2P καθίζετε (1x)
1Co 6:4 ·matters, do·yeu·seat these *unrighteous·ones as·*
G2523.1 V-AAI-3S ἐκάθισεν (3x)
Heb 8:1 we·do·have such a·High·Priest who is·seated at *the*
Mk 16:19 ·up into the heaven and seated at *the* right·hand of·
Eph 1:20 ·among dead·men. And he·seated *him* at his·own
G2523.1 V-AAP-GSM καθίσαντος (1x)
Mt 5:1 upon the mountain. And after·seating himself, his
G2523.3 V-FAI-3S καθίσει (1x)
Mt 25:31 angels with him, then he·shall·sit upon his Throne
G2523.3 V-FDI-2P καθίσεσθε (1x)
Mt 19:28 of·Glory, yeu also shall·sit upon twelve thrones,
G2523.3 V-AAI-1S ἐκάθισα (1x)
Rv 3:21 even·as I·also overcame and did·sit·down with my
G2523.3 V-AAI-3S ἐκάθισεν (9x)
Jn 12:14 Jesus, finding a·young·donkey, sat·down on it,
Jn 19:13 Jesus outside, and he·sat·down on the Bema·
Lk 4:20 giving·*it*·back to·the assistant, he·sat·down, also
Lk 19:30 not·even·one man·of·clay† sat ever·at·any·time.
Heb 1:3 ·our moral·failures through himself, sat·down at *the*
Heb 10:12 of·moral·failures into perpetuity, sat·down at *the*
Heb 12:2 despising *it*, and sat·down at *the* right·hand of·the
Mk 11:7 they·threw their garments on·it, and he·sat upon it.
1Co 10:7 "The People sat·down to·eat and to·drink, and
G2523.3 V-AAI-3P ἐκάθισαν (3x)
Ac 13:14 gathering on·the day of·Sabbath, they·sat·down.
Mt 23:2 scribes and the Pharisees sat·down upon the seat of·
Rv 20:4 thrones, and they·sat upon them, and judgment
G2523.3 V-AAM-2P καθίσατε (2x)
Mt 26:36 to·the disciples, "Yeu·sit·down at·this·location,
Mk 14:32 says to·his disciples, "Yeu·sit·down here, until I·
G2523.3 V-AAN καθίσαι (6x)
Ac 2:30 he·would·raise·up the Anointed-One to·sit on his
Ac 8:31 that·he·would·climb·up to·sit·down together with·
Mt 20:23 I·myself shall·be·immersed·in, but to·sit at my
Mk 10:40 But to·sit at my right·hand and at my left is not
2Th 2:4 ' 'such·for him to·sit·down as God in the Temple
Rv 3:21 overcoming, I·shall·grant *for·him* to·sit with me on
G2523.3 V-AAP-NSM καθίσας (10x)
Jn 8:2 to him. And sitting·down, he·was·instructing them.
Lk 5:3 dry·ground. And sitting·down, he·was·instructing the
Lk 14:28 ·build a·tower, *does* not·indeed sit·down first *and*
Lk 14:31 king, *does* not·indeed sit·down first *and* takes·
Lk 16:6 accept your bill, and sitting·down quickly, write
Ac 12:21 in·royal clothing and sitting·down upon the Bema·
Ac 25:6 on·the next·day, after·sitting·down on the Bema·
Ac 25:17 on·the next·day), after·sitting·down on the Bema·
Mk 9:35 And after·sitting·down, he·hollered·out·for the
Mk 12:41 And after·sitting·down directly·opposite the
G2523.3 V-AAP-NPM καθίσαντες (2x)
Ac 16:13 to·be. And sitting·down, we·were·speaking to·the
Mt 13:48 *it* to the shore and sitting·down, they·collected the
G2523.3 V-AAS-1P καθίσωμεν (1x)
Mk 10:37 "Grant to·us that we·may·sit, one at your right·
G2523.3 V-AAS-3S καθίσῃ (1x)
Mt 19:28 the Son of·Clay·Man† should·sit upon his Throne
G2523.3 V-AAS-3P καθίσωσιν (1x)
Mt 20:21 that these two sons of·mine may·sit, one at your
G2523.3 V-ADS-2P καθίσησθε (1x)
Lk 22:30 in my kingdom, and may·sit on thrones judging
G2523.3 V-RAI-3S κεκάθικεν (1x)
Mk 11:2 not·even·one man·of·clay† has·sat. Loosening him,
G2523.4 V-AAI-3S ἐκάθισεν (2x)
Ac 2:3 were·made·visible to·them, and it·settled upon each
Ac 18:11 And he·settled *there* a·year and six lunar·months,
G2523.4 V-AAM-2P καθίσατε (1x)
Lk 24:49 yeu, but yeu·yeurselves must·settle in the City of·

G2524 καθ•ίημι kathíēmi *v.* (4x)
Roots:G2596 G2423-1 Compare:G2507 G5465
G2524 V-PPP-ASN καθιέμενον (1x)
Ac 10:11 at·the·four corners and being·sent·down to the
G2524 V-PPP-ASF καθιεμένην (1x)
Ac 11:5 a·great linen·sheet being·sent·down from·out of·the
G2524 V-AAI-3P καθῆκαν (2x)
Lk 5:19 ·up on the rooftop, they·sent him down through the
Ac 9:25 taking him by·night, sent·*him*·down *by* lowering

G2525 καθ•ίστημι kathístēmi *v.* (23x)
Roots:G2596 G2476 Compare:G2688-1 See:G2688
G2686-6
G2525.2 V-FAI-1S καταστήσω (2x)
Mt 25:21 over a·few·things, I·shall·fully·establish you over
Mt 25:23 over a·few·things, I·shall·fully·establish you over
G2525.2 V-FAI-1P καταστήσομεν (1x)
Ac 6:3 and wisdom, whom we·shall·fully·establish over this
G2525.2 V-FAI-3S καταστήσει (3x)
Lk 12:42 whom his lord shall·fully·establish over his
Lk 12:44 I·say to·yeu, that he·shall·fully·establish him over
Mt 24:47 I·say to·yeu, that he·shall·fully·establish him over
G2525.2 V-FPI-3P κατασταθήσονται (1x)
Rm 5:19 the many shall·be·fully·established *as* righteous.
G2525.2 V-PAI-3S καθίστησιν (2x)
Heb 7:28 the Torah-Law fully·establishes men·of·clay† *as*
2Pe 1:8 ·more·*and·more*, it·fully·establishes *yeu to·be*
G2525.2 V-PPI-3S καθίσταται (4x)
Heb 5:1 men·of·clay† is·fully·established on·behalf·of·men·
Heb 8:3 For every high·priest is·fully·established to·offer
Jac 3:6 ·manner, the tongue is·fully·established among our
Jac 4:4 of·the world is·fully·established·as an·enemy of·God
G2525.2 V-AAI-2S κατέστησας (1x)
Heb 2:7 ·glory and honor, and fully·established him over the
G2525.2 V-AAI-3S κατέστησεν (5x)
Lk 12:14 "Man·of·clay†, who fully·established me *as* estate·
Ac 7:10 king of·Egypt, and *Pharaoh* fully·established him,
Ac 7:27 declaring, "Who fully·established you *as* ruler and
Ac 7:35 declaring, "Who fully·established you *as* ruler and
Mt 24:45 slave whom his lord fully·established over his
G2525.2 V-AAS-2S καταστήσῃς (1x)
Tit 1:5 ·left·undone and should·fully·establish elders in·each
G2525.2 V-API-3P κατεστάθησαν (1x)
Rm 5:19 many are·fully·established *as* morally·disqualified,
EG2525.2 (1x)
Heb 7:28 after the Torah-Law), *fully·establishes the* Son *as*
G2525.4 V-PAP-NPM καθιστῶντες (1x)
Ac 17:15 And the·ones transporting Paul brought him as·far·

G2526 καθ•ό kathó *adv.* (4x)
Roots:G2596 G3739 See:G2526-3
G2526 ADV καθό (4x)
Rm 8:26 we·should·pray·for according·to·what is·necessary,
1Pe 4:13 rejoice, according·to·what *portion* yeu·share in·the
2Co 8:12 *it·is* well·acceptable according·to·what someone
2Co 8:12 may·have, not according·to·what he·does·not have

G2526-3 καθ•ο•έργον kathôérgôn *n.* (1x)
מְלָאכָה mĕlạ'kạh [corresponding Hebrew]
Roots:G2526 G2041 Compare:G2716-1 G2039
G3872
xLangEquiv:H4399
G2526-3.2 N-GPN καθοέργων (1x)
Heb 4:4 in the seventh day from all his prescribed·works."

G2527 καθ•όλου kathólôu *adv.* (1x)
Roots:G2596 G3650
G2527 ADV καθόλου (1x)
Ac 4:18 not to·enunciate nor·even to·instruct at·all in the

G2528 καθ•οπλίζω kathôplízō *v.* (1x)
Roots:G2596 G3695
G2528 V-RPP-NSM καθωπλισμένος (1x)
Lk 11:21 having·been·fully·armed, should·keep·watch·over

G2529 καθ•οράω kathôráō *v.* (1x)
Roots:G2596 G3708
G2529.3 V-PPI-3S καθορᾶται (1x)
Rm 1:20 invisible·things of·him are·quite·clearly·seen, both

G2530 καθ•ό•τι kathóti *adv.* (5x)
Roots:G2596 G3739 G5100
G2530.2 ADV καθότι (3x)
Lk 1:7 a·child *born* to·them, because·indeed EliSabeth was
Lk 19:9 ·come to·this house, because·indeed he·himself also
Ac 2:24 the pangs of·Death, because·indeed it·was not
G2530.3 ADV καθότι (2x)
Ac 2:45 them to·all, according·to any·particular need
Ac 4:35 ·out to·each·man, according·to any·particular need

G2531 καθ•ώς kathṓs *adv.* (182x)
Roots:G2596 G5613 Compare:G2505
G2531 ADV καθώς (182x)
Jn 1:23 the Way of·Yahweh,"ᐅ just·as Isaiah the prophet
Jn 3:14 "So just·as Moses elevated the serpent *upon a·sign·*
Jn 5:23 ·deeply·honor the Son, just·as they·deeply·honor the
Jn 5:30 not·even·one·thing of my·own·self. Just·as I·hear, I·
Jn 6:31 in the wilderness, just·as it·is having·been·written, '
Jn 6:57 "Just·as the living Father dispatched me, and·I live
Jn 6:58 of·the heaven. *It·is* not just·as *the time when* yeur
Jn 7:38 ·one trusting in me, just·as the Scripture declared, ᐅ
Jn 8:28 ·thing of my·own·self; but·rather just·as my Father
Jn 10:15 "Just·as the Father knows me, so·even·I know the
Jn 10:26 from·among my sheep, just·as I·declared to·yeu.
Jn 12:14 sat·down on it, just·as it·is having·been·written,
Jn 12:50 I·myself speak, *it·is* just·as the Father has·declared
Jn 13:15 ·example to·yeu in·order·that just·as I·myself did
Jn 13:33 Yeu·shall·seek me, and just·as I·declared to·the
Jn 13:34 that yeu·should·love one·another just·as I·loved yeu
Jn 14:27 peace I·give to·yeu. Not just·as the world gives *do*
Jn 14:31 the Father, even just·as the Father commanded me,
Jn 15:4 me, and·I in yeu. Just·as the vine·sprout is·not able
Jn 15:9 "Just·as the Father loved me, so·also·I loved yeu.
Jn 15:10 in my love, just·as I·myself have·observantly·kept
Jn 15:12 yeu·should·love one·another, just·as I·loved yeu.
Jn 17:2 Just·as *also* you·gave him authority over·all flesh, in·
Jn 17:11 ·that they·may·be one, just·as we·ourselves *are*.
Jn 17:14 not from·among the world, just·as I·myself am not
Jn 17:16 not from·among the world, just·as I·myself am not
Jn 17:18 "Just·as you·dispatched me into the world, I·also
Jn 17:21 ·order·that they·all may·be one, just·as you, Father,
Jn 17:22 ·that they·may·be one, just·as we·ourselves are one
Jn 17:23 and *that* you·loved them, just·as you·loved me.
Jn 19:40 with the aromatic·spices, just·as is *the* manner for·
Jn 20:21 "Peace *be* to·yeu. Just·as *my* Father has·dispatched
Lk 1:2 (just·as the·ones from *the* beginning handed·*them*·

Lk 1:55 into the coming·age, just·as he·spoke to our fathers.
Lk 1:70 just·as he·spoke through *the* mouth of·his holy
Lk 2:20 they·heard and saw, just·as it·was·spoken to them.
Lk 2:23 just·as it·has·been·written in Yahweh's Torah-Law,
Lk 5:14 purification, just·as Moses specifically·assigned, for
Lk 6:31 "And just·as yeu·want that the men·of·clay† should·
Lk 6:36 become compassionate, just·as yeur Father also is
Lk 11:1 instruct us to·pray, just·as John also instructed his
Lk 11:30 For just·as Jonah was a·sign to·the Ninevites, in·
Lk 17:26 "And just·as it·was in the days of·Noach, in·this·
Lk 19:32 ·dispatched found *it* just·as he·declared to·them.
Lk 22:13 ·off, they·found *it* just·as he·has·declared to·them.
Lk 22:29 ·I bequeath to·yeu a·kingdom, just·as my Father
Lk 24:24 and found *it* even in·this·manner just·as the women
Lk 24:39 flesh and bones, just·as yeu·observe me having.
Ac 2:4 ·in different bestowed·tongues, just·as the Spirit
Ac 2:22 him in *the* midst of·yeu, just·as yeu·yourselves also
Ac 7:17 "But just·as the time of·the promise was·drawing·
Ac 7:42 host of·the heaven, just·as it·has·been·written in a·
Ac 7:44 in the wilderness, *being* just·as the·one speaking to·
Ac 7:48 in temples made·by·hands, just·as the prophet says,
Ac 10:47 received the Holy Spirit just·as we·ourselves *did*
Ac 11:29 of·them just·as he·was·having·good·financial· *to·*
Ac 15:8 to·them the Holy Spirit, even just·as *he·gave* to·us;
Ac 15:14 *Peter* recounted·in·detail *that* just·as at·the·first,
Ac 15:15 do·mutually·agree, just·as it·has·been·written,
Ac 22:3 inherently·being a·zealot of·God, just·as yeu all are
Heb 3:7 Therefore, just·as the Holy Spirit says, "'Today if
Heb 4:3 complete·rest— just·as he·has·declared *concerning*
Heb 4:7 so·vast a·time), just·as it·has·been·declared,
Heb 5:3 And on·account·of this (just·as concerning the
Heb 5:6 Just·as he·says also in another *passage*, "'You *are*
Heb 8:5 just·as Moses had·been·divinely·instructed·by·
Heb 10:25 ·gathering of·ourselves, just·as *is* a·habit of·some
Heb 11:12 — *so·many* just·as the constellations·of·stars of·
Gal 2:7 had·been·entrusted *to·me*, just·as *the good·news* of·
Gal 3:6 *It·is of·trust* just·as with·AbRaham, *who* "'trusted
Gal 5:21 ·forewarn to·yeu, just·as also I·previously·declared
Mt 21:6 also doing just·as YeShua specifically·assigned to·
Mt 26:24 heads·on·out just·as it·has·been·written concerning
Mt 28:6 for he·is·awakened, just·as he·declared. Come·
Mk 4:33 to·them, just·as they·were·able to·hear *it*.
Mk 9:13 they·wanted, just·as it·has·been·written concerning
Mk 11:6 they·declared to·them just·as Jesus commanded,
Mk 14:16 and they·found *it* just·as he·declared to·them.
Mk 14:21 ·on·out, just·as it·has·been·written concerning
Mk 15:8 *for·him to·do* just·as he·was·doing regularly for·
Mk 16:7 ·shall·gaze·upon him, just·as he·declared to·yeu."
Rm 1:13 fruit among yeu also, just·as even·so among the
Rm 1:17 of·trust into trust. Just·as it·has·been·written, "
Rm 1:28 And just·as they·did·not examine·and·verify God
Rm 2:24 on·account·of yeu," just·as it·has·been·written.
Rm 3:4 man·of·clay† a·liar; just·as it·has·been·written,
Rm 3:8 But we·do·not *state* (just·as we·are·vilified, and just·
Rm 3:8 just·as we·are·vilified, and just·as some reply for·us
Rm 3:10 Just·as it·has·been·written: "There·is none
Rm 4:17 (just·as it·has·been·written, "'I·have·placed you *as*
Rm 8:36 Just·as it·has·been·written, "'For·your cause, we·
Rm 9:13 Just·as it·has·been·written, "'Jacob I·loved, but
Rm 9:29 And just·as IsaIah has·already·stated, "'Except
Rm 9:33 just·as it·has·been·written, "Behold, I·lay in
Rm 10:15 ·be·dispatched? Just·as it·has·been·written, "
Rm 11:8 just·as it·has·been·written, "GOD gave them a·
Rm 11:26 IsraEl shall·be·saved; just·as it·has·been·written,
Rm 15:3 himself, but·rather, just·as it·has·been·written,
Rm 15:7 yeu·must·each·receive one·another, just·as also the
Rm 15:9 on·behalf *of·his* mercy, just·as it·has·been·written,
Rm 15:21 But·rather just·as it·has·been·written, "'To·whom
Php 1:7 just·as it·is right for·me to·contemplate this on·
Php 2:12 beloved, just·as yeu·listened·and·obeyed always
Php 3:17 the·ones walking in·this·manner just·as yeu·hold us
1Pe 4:10 Just·as each·man received a·gracious·bestowment,
2Pe 1:14 ·tabernacle is abrupt, even just·as our Lord YeShua
2Pe 3:15 of·our Lord *as* Salvation— just·as also our beloved
1Th 1:5 ·of·assurance, just·as yeu·personally·know *that* we·
1Th 2:2 in Philippi, just·as yeu·personally·know, we·were·
1Th 2:4 But·rather just·as we·have·been·tested·and·proven
1Th 2:5 a·word of·flattery (just·as yeu·personally·know), nor
1Th 2:13 ·word of·men·of·clay†, but·rather just·as it·is truly
1Th 2:14 even just·as they·themselves *suffered* under the
1Th 3:4 ·about to·be·hard-pressed, even just·as it·happened,
1Th 4:1 Lord YeShua, just·as yeu·personally·received from
1Th 4:6 these·matters, just·as also we·previously·declared
1Th 4:11 ·with yeur own hands, just·as we·charged yeu,
1Th 4:13 yeu·should·not be·grieved, even just·as the rest,
1Th 5:11 and edify one the other, just·as also yeu·do.
2Th 1:3 concerning yeu, brothers, just·as it·is appropriate,
2Th 3:1 and may·be·glorified, even just·as *it·is* alongside
1Co 1:6 just·as the testimony of·the Anointed-One was·
1Co 1:31 in·order·that, just·as it·has·been·written, "The·
1Co 2:9 But·rather just·as it·has·been·written, "Eye did·not
1Co 4:17 in Anointed-One, just·as I·instruct everywhere
1Co 5:7 a·fresh·new lump·of·dough, just·as *indeed* yeu·are
1Co 8:2 ·thing, not·even·yet, just·as it·is·necessary *for·one*
1Co 10:6 ·after bad·things, just·as they·also longed·after
1Co 10:7 Yeu·must·not·even be idolaters, just·as *were* some
1Co 10:8 ·commit·sexual·immorality, just·as some of·them
1Co 10:9 ·try the Anointed-One, just·as some of·them also
1Co 10:10 ·must·not·even grumble, just·as some of·them
1Co 10:33 Just·as I·also willingly·adapt·for all *men* in·all
1Co 11:1 Be attentive·imitators of·me, just·as I·also *am* of·
1Co 11:2 the traditions, just·as I·handed·*them*·down to·yeu.
1Co 12:11 to·each·man individually just·as he·resolves.
1Co 12:18 each one of·them, in the Body just·as he·wanted.
1Co 13:12 I·shall·fully·know just·as also I·am·fully·known.
1Co 14:34 but·rather to·submit·themselves, just·as also the
1Co 15:38 God gives it a·body just·as he·determined, and to·
1Co 15:49 And just·as we·have·borne the derived·image of·
2Co 1:5 Because just·as the afflictions of·the Anointed-One
2Co 1:14 just·as also yeu·already·acknowledged us in part,
2Co 4:1 Service *of·the Spirit*, just·as we·are·shown·mercy,
2Co 6:16 a·temple of·the·living God, just·as God declared,
2Co 8:5 *this they·did*, not just·as we·expected, but·rather
2Co 8:6 Titus, in·order·that just·as he·began·previously,
2Co 8:15 Just·as it·has·been·written, "The·one did·not
2Co 9:3 on this part; that, just·as I·was·saying, yeu·may·be
2Co 9:7 each·man *sow* just·as he·is·preinclined in·*his*·heart,
2Co 9:9 Just·as it·has·been·written, "'*The·righteous·man*
2Co 10:7 for himself; because just·as he *is* of·Anointed-One
2Co 11:12 ·found *to·be lowly* even just·as we·ourselves *are*.
Eph 1:4 just·as he·selected us in him before *the* world's
Eph 3:3 to·me the Mystery (just·as I·previously·wrote *about*
Eph 4:4 and one Spirit— just·as also yeu·are·called·forth in
Eph 4:17 No·longer *are* yeu to·walk just·as the rest *of·the*
Eph 4:21 and are·instructed by him (just·as truth is in Jesus)
Eph 4:32 ·one·another, also just·as God graciously·forgave
Eph 5:2 and walk in love, just·as the Anointed-One also
Eph 5:3 among yeu, just·as is·befitting·for holy·ones,
Eph 5:25 ·love yeur·own wives, just·as the Anointed-One
Eph 5:29 and cherishingly·broods·over it— just·as even the
Col 1:6 ·*news* being·present among yeu, just·as *it·is* also in
Col 1:6 And it·is itself·bearing·fruit, just·as *it·does* also in
Col 1:7 just·as also yeu·learned *it* from EpAphras, our dear
Col 2:7 in the trust, just·as yeu·were·instructed, abounding
Col 3:13 a·fault specifically·against anyone, just·as also the
1Ti 1:3 Just·as I·implored you to·continue·on at Ephesus
1Jn 2:6 ·manner to·walk, just·as that·one already·walked.
1Jn 2:18 it·is *the* last hour. And just·as yeu·heard that the
1Jn 2:27 is not a·lie, even just·as it·already·instructed yeu),
1Jn 3:2 him, because we·shall·gaze·upon him just·as he·is.'
1Jn 3:3 in him cleanses himself, just·as that·one is morally·
1Jn 3:7 the righteousness is righteous, just·as that·one is
1Jn 3:12 not *doing* just·as Qain *did*, *who* was birthed·from·
1Jn 3:23 ·love one·another, just·as he·already·gave us *this*
1Jn 4:17 of·Tribunal·judgment, because just·as that·one is,
2Jn 1:4 in truth, just·as we·received a·commandment
2Jn 1:6 is the commandment, that just·as yeu·heard from *the*
3Jn 1:2 and to·be·healthy·and·sound, just·as your soul
3Jn 1:3 and testifying of·your truth, just·as you walk in truth

G2532 καί kaí *conj.* (9155x)
Compare:G1161 G5037 xLangAlso:HFC01
(abbreviated listing for G2532)

G2532.ª CONJ καί (2x)
(list for G2532.ª:CONJ excluded)
G2532.1 -- (1x)
(list for G2532.1:-- excluded)
G2532.1 CONJ καί (7741x)
(list for G2532.1:CONJ excluded)
EG2532.1 (10x)
(list for EG2532.1: excluded)
G2532.3 CONJ καί (753x)
(list for G2532.3:CONJ excluded)
EG2532.3 (3x)
(list for EG2532.3: excluded)
G2532.4 CONJ καί (217x)
(list for G2532.4:CONJ excluded)
G2532.5 CONJ καί (25x)
(list for G2532.5:CONJ excluded)
EG2532.5 (1x)
(list for EG2532.5: excluded)
G2532.6 CONJ καί (130x)
(list for G2532.6:CONJ excluded)
EG2532.6 (1x)
(list for EG2532.6: excluded)
G2532.7 CONJ καί (12x)
(list for G2532.7:CONJ excluded)
G2532.8 CONJ καί (29x)
(list for G2532.8:CONJ excluded)
EG2532.8 (4x)
(list for EG2532.8: excluded)
G2532.9 CONJ καί (5x)
(list for G2532.9:CONJ excluded)
EG2532.9 (1x)
(list for EG2532.9: excluded)
G2532.10 CONJ καί (91x)
(list for G2532.10:CONJ excluded)
EG2532.10 (10x)
(list for EG2532.10: excluded)
G2532.11 CONJ καί (45x)
(list for G2532.11:CONJ excluded)
G2532.12 CONJ καί (13x)
(list for G2532.12:CONJ excluded)
G2532.13 CONJ καί (9x)
(list for G2532.13:CONJ excluded)
G2532.14 CONJ καί (14x)
(list for G2532.14:CONJ excluded)
G2532.15 CONJ καί (21x)
(list for G2532.15:CONJ excluded)
G2532.16 CONJ καί (12x)
(list for G2532.16:CONJ excluded)
G2532.17 CONJ καί (1x)
(list for G2532.17:CONJ excluded)
G2532.18 CONJ καί (3x)
(list for G2532.18:CONJ excluded)
G2532.19 CONJ καί (1x)
(list for G2532.19:CONJ excluded)

G2533 Καϊάφας Kaïáphas *n/p.* (10x)
See:G0452

G2533.2 N/P-NSM Καϊάφας (2x)
Jn 11:49 one from·among them, *named* Caiaphas, being *the*
Jn 18:14 Now Caiaphas was the·one jointly·giving·counsel
G2533.2 N/P-ASM Καϊάφαν (3x)
Jn 18:24 ·been·bound, to Caiaphas the designated·high·priest
Ac 4:6 HannAs the high·priest and Caiaphas and YoChanan
Mt 26:57 led·*him*·away to Caiaphas the designated·high·priest
G2533.2 N/P-GSM Καϊάφα (4x)
Jn 18:13 for he·was *the* father-in-law of·Caiaphas, who was
Jn 18:28 they·led Jesus from Caiaphas to the Praetorian·hall

Lk 3:2 in·the·days of·HannAs and Caiaphas *the* high·priests
Mt 26:3 ·high·priest, the·one being·referred·to·as Caiaphas,
EG2533.2 (1x)
Jn 18:13 *Anointed-One having·been·bound to·Caiaphas, the*

G2534 καί•γε kaígê *conj.* (1x)
Roots:G2532 G1065
G2534.2 CONJ καί γέ (1x)
Lk 19:42 "If you·knew, even you, at·least in this your day,

G2535 Κάϊν Káïn *n/p.* (3x)
Ƙάϊν Qáïn [Greek, Octuagint]
קַיִן Qayin [Hebrew]
Roots:H7014
G2535.2 N/P-PRI Ƙάϊν (3x)
Heb 11:4 to·God a·much·better sacrifice than Qain, through
Jud 1:11 Because they·traversed in·the way of·Qain, and
1Jn 3:12 not *doing* just·as Qain *did, who* was birthed·from·

G2536 Καϊνάν Kaïnán *n/p.* (2x)
Ƙεϊνάν Qeïnán [Greek, Octuagint]
קֵינָן qeynan [Hebrew]
Roots:H7018 See:G2627
G2536.2 N/P-PRI Ƙεϊνάν (1x)
Lk 3:37 *son* of·Jared, *son* of·MahalalEl, *son* of·Qeinan,
G2536.3 N/P-PRI Ƙαϊνάν (1x)
Lk 3:36 *son* of·Qainan, *son* of·Arphaxad, *son* of·Shem, *son*

G2537 καινός kainós *adj.* (45x)
Compare:G3501 See:G2538 G0342 G1456
xLangEquiv:H2319 A2323
G2537.1 A-NSF καινή (6x)
Lk 22:20 "This cup *is* the brand-new covenant in my blood,
Ac 17:19 ·able to·know what this brand-new instruction *is*,
Gal 6:15 but·rather *it·is* a·brand-new creation *that has*·
Mk 1:27 "What is this? What *is* this brand-new instruction?
1Co 11:25 "This cup is the brand-new covenant in my blood.
2Co 5:17 in Anointed-One, *he·is* a·brand-new creation. The
G2537.1 A-NSN καινόν (2x)
Jn 19:41 ·garden, *there·was* a·brand-new chamber·tomb, in
Rv 2:17 the pebble, a·brand-new name having·been·written
G2537.1 A-NPN καινά (1x)
2Co 5:17 behold, all·things have·become brand-new.
G2537.1 A-ASM καινόν (3x)
Eph 2:15 in himself into one brand-new man·of·clay†, *thus*
Eph 4:24 ·yourselves·with the brand-new man·of·clay† (the·
Rv 21:1 And I·saw a·brand-new heaven and a·brand-new
G2537.1 A-ASF καινήν (11x)
Jn 13:34 "A·brand-new commandment I·give to·yeu, that
Heb 8:8 I·shall·completely·consummate a·brand-new with
Heb 8:13 In *that* he·says, "A·brand-new *covenant*," he·has·
2Pe 3:13 'a·Brand-New Heavens and a·Brand-New Earth,' in
1Jn 2:7 I·write no brand-new commandment to·yeu, but·
1Jn 2:8 On·the·other·hand, a·brand-new commandment I·
2Jn 1:5 ·though I·wrote a·brand-new commandment to·you,
Rv 5:9 And they·sing a·brand-new song, saying, "You·are
Rv 14:3 ·do·sing, as *singing* a·brand-new song in·the·sight
Rv 21:1 I·saw a·brand-new heaven and a·brand-new earth,
Rv 21:2 the HOLY CITY, brand-new JeruSalem, descending
G2537.1 A-ASN καινόν (6x)
Lk 5:36 but·if·so, then the brand-new *patch* makes·a·tear;
Ac 17:21 *attempting* to·say or to·hear something brand-new).
Mt 26:29 day whenever I·may·drink it brand-new with yeu
Mk 2:21 but·if·so, *then* the brand-new *patch, when·shrunk,*
Mk 14:25 that day whenever I·may·drink it brand-new in the
Rv 3:12 'And *I·shall·write upon him* my brand-new name.
G2537.1 A-APM καινούς (4x)
Lk 5:38 *is only* fit·to·be·cast into brand-new wineskins, and
Mt 9:17 they·cast fresh·new wine into brand-new wineskins,
Mk 2:22 *is only* fit·to·be·cast into brand-new wineskins."
2Pe 3:13 we·intently·await 'a·Brand-New Heavens and a·
G2537.1 A-APN καινά (2x)
Mt 13:52 treasure casts·forth *things* brand-new and old *to*·
Rv 21:5 "Behold, I·make all·things brand-new!" And he·
G2537.1 A-DSN καινῷ (1x)
Mt 27:60 laid it in his·own brand-new chamber·tomb, which
G2537.1 A-DPF καιναῖς (1x)
Mk 16:17 they·shall·speak in·brand-new bestowed·tongues;
G2537.1 A-GSF καινῆς (5x)
Heb 9:15 he·is *the* mediator of·a·brand-new covenant, so·
Mt 26:28 blood, the·one of·the brand-new covenant, the·one
Mk 14:24 blood, the·one of·the brand-new covenant, the·
2Co 3:6 ·qualified attendants of·a·brand-new covenant— not
Rv 3:12 of·my God, the brand-new JeruSalem, the·one
G2537.1 A-GSN καινοῦ (2x)
Lk 5:36 throws a·patch *from* a·brand-new garment upon an·
Lk 5:36 the·one from the brand-new *garment*, does·not
EG2537.1 (1x)
Heb 2:5 *that* he·subjugated the impending *brand-new* Land,

G2538 καινότης kainótēs *n.* (2x)
Roots:G2537 Compare:G3503 G3821
G2538 N-DSF καινότητι (2x)
Rm 6:4 also should·walk in brand-newness of·life-above.
Rm 7:6 such·for us to·be·slaves in brand-newness of·spirit,

G2539 καί•περ kaípêr *conj.* (6x)
Roots:G2532 G4007 Compare:G1499
G2539.1 CONJ καίπερ (1x)
Rv 17:8 the Scarlet·Beast that was, and is not, and·yet is.
G2539.2 CONJ καίπερ (5x)
Heb 5:8 Even·though being a·Son, he·learned the attentive·
Heb 7:5 even·though having·come·forth from·among the
Heb 12:17 no place for·repentance, even·though seeking it
Php 3:4 even·though I·myself *was once* also having
2Pe 1:12 these·things, even·though *yeu·are already*

G2540 καιρός kairós *n.* (88x)
Compare:G5550 G0165 G0874 See:G0170
G2540.1 N-NSM καιρός (17x)
Jn 7:6 Jesus says to·them, "My season is·not·yet here, but
Jn 7:6 is·not·yet here, but yeur season is always ready.
Jn 7:8 my season has·not·yet been·completely·fulfilled."
Lk 21:8 and, 'The season has·drawn·near.' Accordingly,
Mt 21:34 "And when the season of·the fruits drew·near, he·
Mt 26:18 The Mentor says, "My season is near·at·hand. I·do
Mk 1:15 "The season has·been·completely·fulfilled, and the
Mk 11:13 except leaves, for it·was not *the* season for·figs.
Mk 13:33 yeu·do·not personally·know when the season is.
1Pe 4:17 Because *it·is* the season *for* the judgment to·begin
1Co 7:29 *that* the season *is* having·been·drawn·tight·and·
2Co 6:2 Behold, now *is* the·well·acceptable season! Behold,
2Ti 4:3 For *the* season shall·be when they·shall·not bear·
2Ti 4:6 ·a·devotion, and the season of·my bodily·departure
Rv 1:3 ·been·written in it, for the season *is* near·at·hand.
Rv 11:18 WRATH came, and·also the season for·the dead
Rv 22:10 official·scroll, because the season is near·at·hand.
G2540.1 N-NPM καιροί (3x)
Lk 21:24 *the* seasons of·Gentiles should·be·completely·
Ac 3:19 to·be·rubbed·out, so·that seasons of·refreshing
2Ti 3:1 that in *the* last days perilous seasons shall·settle·in.
G2540.1 N-ASM καιρόν (17x)
Jn 5:4 For according·to a·certain·season, an·angel was·
Lk 1:20 which shall·be·completely·fulfilled in their season."
Lk 8:13 no root, who trust just·for a·season, and·then in a·
Lk 12:56 ·it that·yeu·do·not examine·and·verify this season?
Lk 19:44 you·did·not know the season of·your inspection."
Ac 12:1 But that very season, King HerOd·Agrippa violently·
Ac 19:23 And in that season, there·occurred no little
Heb 9:9 an·analogy for the season, then·currently·standing,
Heb 11:11 well·after·and·beyond *the* season of·maturity,
Rm 9:9 "'According·to this season I·shall·come, and there·
Rm 13:11 And having·seen the season, *know* that even·now,
1Pe 1:11 for which or what·kind·of season the Spirit of·
1Th 2:17 yeu just·for a·short season (in·personal·presence,
Eph 5:16 utterly·redeeming the season, because the days are
Col 4:5 *Called·Out·citizenry*, utterly·redeeming the season.
Rv 12:12 rage, having·seen that he·has *but* a·brief season."
Rv 12:14 place, where she·is·nourished there a·season, and
G2540.1 N-APM καιρούς (5x)
Ac 1:7 for·yeu to·know times or seasons which the Father
Ac 14:17 from·the·sky and fruit-bearing seasons, filling·up
Ac 17:26 ·determining prearranged seasons and the bounds
Gal 4:10 days, and lunar·months, and seasons, and years.
Rv 12:14 ·is·nourished there a·season, and seasons, and half
G2540.1 N-DSM καιρῷ (18x)
Lk 8:13 a·season, and·then in a·season of·proof·trial, they·
Lk 18:30 ·full many·times·over in this *present* season, and in
Lk 21:36 in every season that yeu·may·be·accounted·fully·
Ac 7:20 "Into which season Moses was·born, and he·was
Gal 6:9 the good; for in·due season we·shall·reap, not being·
Mt 12:1 In that season, YeShua traversed on·the various·
Mt 13:30 harvest, and in the season of·the harvest, I·shall·
Mt 14:1 In that season, HerOd·AntiPas the tetrarch heard of·
Mk 10:30 a·hundred·times·over now in this season, homes
Rm 3:26 of·his righteousness in the present season).
Rm 11:5 in the present season also, there·has·come·to·be a·
Rm 12:11 ·hot; in·the proper·season, by·being·subservient;
1Pe 1:5 a·Salvation ready to·be·revealed in *the* last season.
2Th 2:6 ·down in·order·for him to·be·revealed in his season.
2Co 6:2 I·favorably·heard you in·an·acceptable season, and
2Co 8:13 out of·equality, now in *this* season, *that* yeur
Eph 2:12 *remember* that in that season yeu·were apart·from
Eph 6:18 ·praying in Spirit in every season, and·also in this
G2540.1 N-DPM καιροῖς (5x)
Mt 21:41 who shall·render to·him the fruits in their seasons."
Tit 1:3 but in·due seasons made his Redemptive-word
1Ti 2:6 on·behalf of·all— the testimony in·due seasons,
1Ti 4:1 says that in later seasons some shall·withdraw·from
1Ti 6:15 who in·his·own seasons shall·show *he·is* the
G2540.1 N-GSM καιροῦ (6x)
Lk 4:13 the Slanderer withdrew from him only·for a·season.
Ac 13:11 ·at the sun— *but* only·for a·season." And at·once
Heb 9:10 ·*them* so·long·as·unto *the* season of·Rectification.
Rm 8:18 the afflictions of·the present season *are* not worthy
1Co 4:5 presently·judge anything before *the* season, until the
Rv 12:14 and seasons, and half a·season, away·from *the*
G2540.1 N-GPM καιρῶν (3x)
Mt 16:3 but are·not able *to·discern* the signs of·the seasons?
1Th 5:1 concerning the times and the seasons, brothers, yeu·
Eph 1:10 of·the complete·fulfillment of·the seasons): to·
G2540.2 N-ASM καιρόν (1x)
Rm 5:6 For yet, according·to due·season, Anointed-One
G2540.2 N-DSM καιρῷ (5x)
Lk 12:42 *them their* ration·of·food·staples in due·season?
Lk 20:10 "And in due·season, he·dispatched a·slave to the
Mt 24:45 to·give them the provision·of·food in due·season?
Mk 12:2 "And in·due·season, he·dispatched a·slave to the
1Pe 5:6 in·order·that he·may·elevate yeu in due·season—
G2540.2 N-GSM καιροῦ (1x)
Mt 8:29 ·you·come here to·torment us before due·season?"
G2540.3 N-ASM καιρόν (2x)
Ac 24:25 upon·partaking·of a·convenient·occasion, I·shall·
1Co 7:5 ·a·mutual·agreement specifically·for a·set·occasion,
G2540.3 N-DSM καιρῷ (2x)
Lk 13:1 On the same occasion, some·men were·present *who*·
Mt 11:25 ·*them*·into·judgment on that occasion, YeShua
EG2540.3 (1x)
Ac 19:15 And answering *on·one occasion*, the evil spirit
G2540.4 N-ASM καιρόν (2x)
Heb 11:15 they·would have·had opportunity to·return·back.
Gal 6:10 as we·have opportunity, we·should·work the

G2541 Καῖσαρ Kaîsar *n/p.* (31x)
Compare:G4575 See:G2542
G2541 N/P-ASM Καίσαρα (8x)
Jn 19:15 "We·have no king except Caesar."
Ac 25:8 nor·even against Caesar, did·I·morally·fail *in*
Ac 25:11 ·hand me over to·them. I·appeal·to Caesar."
Ac 25:12 answered, "You·have·appealed·to Caesar. To
Ac 25:12 ·appealed·to Caesar. To Caesar you·shall·traverse.
Ac 25:21 him to·be·kept until I·may·send him to Caesar."
Ac 26:32 ·fully·released, if·he·had·not appealed·to Caesar."
Ac 28:19 *this*, I·was·compelled to·appeal·to Caesar, though

Kκ

G2541 N/P-DSM Καίσαρι (9x)
Jn 19:12 making himself a·king speaks·against Caesar."
Lk 20:22 Is·it·proper for·us to·give tribute to·Caesar or not?
Lk 20:25 give·back the·things of·Caesar to·Caesar, and the·
Lk 23:2 forbidding *others* to·give tributes to·Caesar, saying
Ac 27:24 ·for you to·establish·proof to·Caesar, and behold,
Mt 22:17 ·it·proper to·give a·census·tribute to·Caesar or not?
Mt 22:21 render the·things of·Caesar to·Caesar, and the·
Mk 12:14 ·it·proper to·give a·census·tribute to·Caesar or not
Mk 12:17 "Give·back the·things of·Caesar to·Caesar, and
G2541 N/P-GSM Καίσαρος (13x)
Jn 19:12 this·man, you·are not Caesar's friend. Anyone
Lk 2:1 ·went·forth a·decree directly·from Caesar Augustus,
Lk 3:1 year of·the governing·term of·Tiberius Caesar—
Lk 20:24 And answering, they·declared, "Caesar's."
Lk 20:25 ·then, give·back the·things of·Caesar to·Caesar,
Ac 11:28 even happened in·the·days of·Claudius Caesar.
Ac 17:7 in·full·opposition to·the decrees of·Caesar, saying
Ac 25:10 "I·am standing at Caesar's Bema·judgment·seat,
Mt 22:21 They·say to·him, "Caesar's." Then he·says to·
Mt 22:21 "Well·then, render the·things of·Caesar to·Caesar,
Mk 12:16 And they·declared to·him, "Caesar's."
Mk 12:17 "Give·back the·things of·Caesar to·Caesar, and
Php 4:22 the·ones from·among Caesar's household.
EG2541 (1x)
Ac 18:2 Claudius *Caesar* having·thoroughly·arranged·for all

G2542 Καισάρεια Kaisárêia *n/l.* (17x)
Roots:G2541
G2542.2 N/L-ASF Καισάρειαν (7x)
Ac 9:30 brought him down to Caesarea and dispatched him
Ac 10:24 next·day, they·entered into Caesarea. And while·
Ac 12:19 ·down from Judea to Caesarea, *HerOd·Agrippa* was·
Ac 18:22 And after·coming·down to Caesarea, *then* walking·
Ac 23:33 after·entering into Caesarea and hand-delivering
Ac 25:6 *and·then* walking·down to Caesarea, on·the next·
Ac 25:13 and BerNiki arrived in Caesarea to·greet Festus.
G2542.2 N/L-DSF Καισαρείᾳ (2x)
Ac 10:1 there·was a·certain man in Caesarea, Cornelius by·
Ac 25:4 answered *for* Paul to·be·kept in Caesarea, and *that*
G2542.2 N/L-GSF Καισαρείας (6x)
Ac 11:11 having·been·dispatched from Caesarea to me.
Ac 21:16 of·the disciples from Caesarea also went·together
Ac 23:23 that they·should·traverse unto Caesarea from *the*
Ac 25:1 Festus walked·up from Caesarea to JeruSalem.
Mt 16:13 upon·coming into the district of·Caesarea Philippi,
Mk 8:27 disciples into the villages of·Caesarea Philippi. And
G2542.3 N/L-ASF Καισάρειαν (2x)
Ac 8:40 ·news in·all the cities, until he came to Caesarea.
Ac 21:8 Paul, going·forth, came to Caesarea. And entering

G2543 καί•τοι kaítôi *conj.* (1x)
Roots:G2532 G5104 Compare:G5106
G2543.3 CONJ καίτοι (1x)
Heb 4:3 complete·rest,'"' and·yet *he·declared this* with·the

G2544 καί•τοι•γε kaítôigê *conj.* (3x)
Roots:G2543 G1065
G2544.1 PRT τοι (1x)
Ac 14:17 And yet·indeed, he·did·not leave himself without·
G2544.2 CONJ καίτοιγε (2x)
Jn 4:2 (though·indeed Jesus himself was·not immersing, but·
Ac 17:27 and find·him, though·indeed inherently·being not

G2545 καίω kaíō *v.* (12x)
Compare:G4448 G2741 G5394 G1714 See:G2740 G2738 G1572 G2545 G0341-1 G2618 xLangAlso:H1197
G2545.1 V-FPS-1S καυθήσωμαι (1x)
1Co 13:3 my body in·order·that I·should·be·set·ablaze, and
G2545.1 V-PAI-3P καίουσιν (1x)
Mt 5:15 Neither do·they·set·ablaze a·lantern and place it
G2545.1 V-PPI-3S καίεται (1x)
Jn 15:6 and cast *them* into fire, and they·are·set·ablaze.
G2545.1 V-PPP-ASF καιομένην (1x)
Rv 19:20 Lake of·the Fire, the·one being·set·ablaze with the
G2545.1 V-PPP-DSF καιομένῃ (1x)
Rv 21:8 in the Lake, the·one being·set·ablaze with·fire and
G2545.1 V-PPP-NSN καιόμενον (1x)
Rv 8:8 a·great mountain being·set·ablaze with·fire was·cast
G2545.1 V-PPP-NSF καιομένη (1x)
Lk 24:32 not·indeed our heart being·set·ablaze within us, as
G2545.1 V-PPP-NSM καιόμενος (2x)
Jn 5:35 lantern, the·one being·set·ablaze and shining·forth,
Rv 8:10 from·out of·the heaven, being·set·ablaze as a·torch,
G2545.1 V-PPP-NPF καιόμεναι (2x)
Lk 12:35 ·girded·about and *yeur* lanterns being·set·ablaze.
Rv 4:5 lamps of·fire being·set·ablaze in·the·sight of·the
G2545.1 V-RPP-DSN κεκαυμένῳ (1x)
Heb 12:18 ·by·touch, nor having·been·set·ablaze with·fire,

G2546 κἀ•κεῖ kakêî *adv.* (11x)
Roots:G2532 G1563
G2546.1 ADV-C κἀκεῖ (9x)
Jn 11:54 ·to·as Ephraim. And he·was·lingering·awhile there
Ac 14:7 And they·were there, proclaiming·the·good·news.
Ac 22:10 Damascus, and·there it·shall·be·spoken to·you
Ac 25:20 to JeruSalem, and·there to·be·judged concerning
Ac 27:6 And·there, upon·finding a·sailing·ship of·
Mt 5:23 ·Altar, and·there you·should·recall·to·mind that
Mt 10:11 in it is worthy, and·there abide until yeu·should·
Mt 28:10 into Galilee, and·there they·shall·gaze·upon me."
Mk 1:35 into a·desolate place, and he·was·praying there.
G2546.2 ADV-C κἀκεῖ (2x)
Ac 17:13 by Paul, they·came there·also, stirring·up the
Mk 1:38 ·order·that I·may·officially·proclaim there·also. For

G2547 κἀ•κεῖ•θεν kakêîthên *adv.* (9x)
Roots:G2532 G1564
G2547.1 ADV-C κἀκεῖθεν (5x)
Ac 7:4 he·resided in Charan. And·from·there, after his
Ac 13:21 And·from·there, they·requested a·king, and God
Ac 14:26 And·from·there, they·sailed·off to Antioch, where
Ac 21:1 ·the next·day to Rhodes, and·from·there to Patara.
Ac 28:15 From·there, the brothers, upon·hearing the·things
G2547.2 ADV-C κἀκεῖθεν (1x)
Ac 27:12 counsel to·sail·away from·there·also, if·somehow
G2547.3 ADV-C κἀκεῖθεν (3x)
Ac 20:15 Sailing·off from·there, we·arrived the following
Ac 27:4 Sailing·on from·there, we·sailed·leeward·near·to
Mk 10:1 After·rising·up from·there, he·comes into the

G2548 κἀ•κεῖνος kakêînôs *p:d.* (23x)
Roots:G2532 G1565
G2548.1 P:D-NSM-C κἀκεῖνος (2x)
Lk 11:7 "And answering from·inside, that·man may·declare,
Lk 22:12 And·that·man shall·show yeu a·big upper·room
G2548.3 P:D-NPM-C κἀκεῖνοι (2x)
Mk 16:11 And·those *in·mourning*, hearing that he·lives and
Mk 16:13 And·those·men, going·off, announced *it* to·the rest
G2548.4 P:D-NPN-C κἀκεῖνα (2x)
Lk 11:42 these·things, and not·to·leave those·things *undone*.
Mt 23:23 these·things, and not·to·leave those·things *undone*.
G2548.6 P:D-APM-C κἀκείνους (1x)
Ac 18:19 ·arrived in Ephesus, and·these *two* he·left·behind
G2548.6 P:D-DPM-C κἀκείνοις (1x)
Mt 20:4 And·to·these he·declared, 'Yeu also head·on·out
G2548.7 P:D-NPN-C κἀκεῖνα (1x)
Mt 15:18 from·out of·the heart, and·these·things defile the
G2548.8 P:D-NSM-C κἀκεῖνος (2x)
Ac 5:37 right·behind him. He·also completely·perished.
2Ti 2:12 If we·are·denying *him*, he·also shall·be·denying us.
G2548.10 P:D-NPM-C κἀκεῖνοι (4x)
Jn 17:24 ·given to·me, I·want that they·also may·be with me
Ac 15:11 according·to that manner, they·also *are·saved*."
Heb 4:2 ·the·good·news, exactly·as they·also *had·been*, but·
1Co 10:6 ·things, just·as they·also longed·after *such·things*.
G2548.11 P:D-NSM-C κἀκεῖνος (1x)
Jn 19:35 is·true; this·one·also personally·knows that *what*
G2548.11 P:D-ASM-C κἀκεῖνον (1x)
Lk 20:11 another slave. And thrashing this·one·also, and
G2548.12 P:D-NPN-C κἀκεῖνα (1x)
Jn 10:16 It·is·mandatory·for me to·lead these·also, and they·
G2548.13 P:D-ASM-C κἀκεῖνον (1x)
Mk 12:4 after·casting·stones·at that·one·also, they·hit·*him*·
G2548.14 P:D-ASM-C κἀκεῖνον (1x)
Mk 12:5 ·dispatched another, and·this·one·also they·killed,
G2548.16 P:D-NSM-C κἀκεῖνος (2x)
Jn 6:57 the·one chewing me, he·likewise shall·live through
Jn 7:29 personally·from him. He·likewise dispatched me."
G2548.17 P:D-NSM-C κἀκεῖνος (1x)
Jn 14:12 that I·myself do, he·shall·do those·likewise. And

G2549 κακία kakía *n.* (11x)
Roots:G2556 Compare:G4507 G2550 xLangEquiv:H7451 xLangAlso:H5771 A5758
G2549.2 N-GSF κακίας (3x)
Ac 8:22 Now·then, repent of this depravity of·yours, and
Jac 1:21 and any·remaining·excess of·depravity, accept with
1Pe 2:16 liberty as a·cover-up for·the depravity, but·rather
G2549.3 N-ASF κακίαν (2x)
1Pe 2:1 Accordingly, with·yeu·laying·aside all malice, and
Col 3:8 wrath, rage, malice, revilement, *and* shameful·
G2549.3 N-DSF κακίᾳ (4x)
Rm 1:29 evil, greed, *and* malice; *being* exceedingly·full
Tit 3:3 pleasures, passing·through·life in malice and envy,
1Co 14:20 but·rather be·as·infants in·the malice. But in·the
Eph 4:31 be·expunged from yeu, together with·all malice.
G2549.3 N-GSF κακίας (1x)
1Co 5:8 leaven, nor·even with leaven of·malice or of·evil,
G2549.4 N-NSF κακία (1x)
Mt 6:34 Sufficient for·the day *is* its·own hardship.

G2550 κακο•ήθεια kakôḗthêia *n.* (1x)
Roots:G2556 G2239 Compare:G2549
G2550.2 N-GSF κακοηθείας (1x)
Rm 1:29 murder, strife, guile, *and* mischievousness; *being*

G2551 κακο•λογέω kakôlôgéō *v.* (4x)
Roots:G2556 G3056 Compare:G2127 xLangAlso:H7043
G2551.1 V-PAP-NSM κακολογῶν (2x)
Mt 15:4 ' and "the·one speaking·ill·of father or mother
Mk 7:10 '; and, "The·one speaking·ill·of father or mother
G2551.1 V-PAP-NPM κακολογοῦντες (1x)
Ac 19:9 and were·being·obstinate, speaking·ill·of The Way
G2551.1 V-AAN κακολογῆσαι (1x)
Mk 9:39 *that* also shall·be·able to·swiftly speak·ill·of me.

G2552 κακο•πάθεια kakôpáthêia *n.* (1x)
Roots:G2556 G3806
G2552 N-GSF κακοπαθείας (1x)
Jac 5:10 my brothers, the ill·hardship and the long-suffering

G2553 κακο•παθέω kakôpathéō *v.* (4x)
Roots:G2556 G3806 Compare:G5278 G2594 G3306 See:G2552 G4777
G2553.1 V-PAI-1S κακοπαθῶ (1x)
2Ti 2:9 in which I·suffer·hardship, as a·criminal, *even* as·far·
G2553.1 V-PAI-3S κακοπαθεῖ (1x)
Jac 5:13 *Is* any among yeu suffering·hardship? Let·him·pray.
G2553.2 V-AAM-2S κακοπάθησον (2x)
2Ti 2:3 ·then, you·yourself must·endure·hardship as a·good
2Ti 4:5 be·sober·minded in·all·things, endure·hardships, do

G2554 κακο•ποιέω kakôpôiéō *v.* (4x)
Roots:G2555 Compare:G2559
G2554.1 V-PAP-APM κακοποιοῦντας (1x)
1Pe 3:17 ·doing·good·things, than *for* doing·bad·things.
G2554.1 V-PAP-NSM κακοποιῶν (1x)
3Jn 1:11 of·God, but the·one doing·bad has·not clearly·seen
G2554.1 V-AAN κακοποιῆσαι (2x)
Lk 6:9 to·beneficially·do·good or to·do·bad, to·save a·soul
Mk 3:4 on·the various·Sabbaths, or to·do·bad? To·save a·

G2555 κακο•ποιός kakôpôiós *adj.* (5x)
Roots:G2556 G4160 See:G2554
G2555.2 A-NSM κακοποιός (2x)
Jn 18:30 "If this·man was·not a·criminal, we·would not
1Pe 4:15 *as* a·thief, or *as* a·criminal, or as one·interloping·
G2555.2 A-GPM κακοποιῶν (2x)

1Pe 2:12 they·speak·against yeu as criminals, as·a·result *of·*
1Pe 3:16 yeu as of·criminals, they·may·be·put·to·shame,
G2555.2 A-GPM@ κακοποιῶν (1x)
1Pe 2:14 in·fact, for retribution to·criminals and *for the*

G2556 κακός kakṓs *adj.* (53x)
Compare:G4190 G0092 G0096 G0955 G0983 G4469 G4550 G0824 G0113 See:G2560 G2549 G2570 G5501
xLangEquiv:H7451 xLangAlso:H7451-1
G2556.1 A-NSM κακός (1x)
Mt 24:48 "But if that bad slave should·declare in his heart,
G2556.1 A-NSN κακόν (3x)
Rm 7:21 *I·find* that the bad·thing *also* is·directly·laid·out
Jac 3:8 *It·is* unrestrainable, bad, *and* exceedingly·full of·
Rv 16:2 the earth, and it·became a·bad and evil pus·sore to
G2556.1 A-NPF κακαί (1x)
1Co 15:33 Do·not·be deceived. "Bad influences corrupt fine
G2556.1 A-ASN κακόν (7x)
Rm 7:19 *that* I·do, but·rather a·bad·thing which I·do·not
Rm 9:11 anything beneficially·good or bad, in·order·that the
Rm 12:21 by the bad, but·rather overcome the bad with the
Rm 13:4 But if you·should·do the bad·thing, be·afraid. For
Rm 16:19 ·good and *to·be* untainted in·regard·to the bad.
2Co 5:10 he·practiced— whether beneficially·good or bad.
3Jn 1:11 do·not attentively·imitate the bad, but·rather the
G2556.1 A-APM κακούς (3x)
Mt 21:41 He·shall·completely·destroy those bad·men badly,
Php 3:2 dogs; look·out·for the bad workmen; look·out·for
Rv 2:2 and that you·are·not able to·bear bad·men, and *that*
G2556.1 A-APN κακά (3x)
Lk 16:25 and likewise, Lazarus the bad·things. But now
Rm 3:8 "that we·should·do the bad·things in·order·that the
1Pe 3:12 *the* face of·Yahweh *is* against those·doing bad."
G2556.1 A-GSN κακοῦ (2x)
Heb 5:14 toward having discernment of·both good and bad.
Rm 12:21 Do·not be·overcome by the bad, but·rather
G2556.1 A-GPN κακῶν (3x)
Rm 1:30 braggers, *and* inventors of·bad·things; *being*
Rm 13:3 ·good works, but·rather for·the bad·ones. But do·
1Co 10:6 us not to·be men·longing·after bad·things, just·as
G2556.3 A-NSN κακόν (1x)
Rm 14:20 but·yet *it·is* morally·wrong for·the man·of·clay†
G2556.3 A-ASF κακήν (1x)
Col 3:5 impurity, burning·passion, wrong longing, and the
G2556.3 A-ASN κακόν (9x)
Ac 23:9 "We·find not·even·one wrong in this man·of·clay†,
Rm 2:9 of·a·man·of·clay† performing the wrong, of·Jew first
Rm 12:17 ·back to·not·even·one·man wrong for wrong,
Rm 13:4 upon the·one practicing the morally·wrong·thing.
Rm 13:10 Love works no wrong to·the neighbor.
1Pe 3:9 not rendering a·wrong for wrong, or a·defamation
1Th 5:15 *that* no one should·render wrong for wrong to·any
1Co 13:5 swiftly·provoked, *and* is·not reckoning the wrong.
2Co 13:7 God for·yeu not to·do not·even·one wrong; not in·
G2556.3 A-APN κακά (1x)
Ac 9:13 this man, what·many wrongs he·did to·your holy·
G2556.3 A-GSN κακοῦ (6x)
Jn 18:23 wrongly, testify concerning the wrong. But if *I*·
Rm 12:17 ·back to·not·even·one·man wrong for wrong,
1Pe 3:9 not rendering a·wrong for wrong, or a·defamation
1Pe 3:10 must·restrain his tongue from wrong and his lips
1Pe 3:11 "Veer·away from wrong and do *the* beneficially·
1Th 5:15 no one should·render wrong for wrong to·any *man*;
G2556.3 A-GPN κακῶν (2x)
Jac 1:13 for God is not·tempted with·moral·wrongs, and he·
1Ti 6:10 For one·root of·all the moral·wrongs is the
EG2556.3 (2x)
Ac 25:5 ·accuse this man, if there·is any *wrong* in him."
Jac 1:13 tempts not·even·one·man *with·moral·wrongs*.
G2556.4 A-NPM κακοί (1x)
Mk 7:21 ·clay†, the wicked deliberations do·proceed·forth:
G2556.4 A-NPN κακά (1x)
Tit 1:12 "Cretans *are* always liars, wicked wild·beasts, lazy

G2556.7 A-ASN κακόν (3x)
Lk 23:22 to them, "For what crime did this·one commit?
Mt 27:23 was·replying, "For what crime did·he·commit?
Mk 15:14 ·saying to·them, "For what crime did·he·commit?
G2556.8 A-ASN κακόν (2x)
Ac 16:28 ·should·inflict on·yourself not·one·bit·of harm, for
Ac 28:5 ·beast into the fire, *Paul* suffered no harm at·all.
G2556.8 A-APN κακά (1x)
2Ti 4:14 pointedly·did me much harm. May the Lord

G2557 κακο•ῦργος kakôûrgôs *adj.* (5x)
Roots:G2556 G2041
G2557.2 A-NSM κακοῦργος (1x)
2Ti 2:9 which I·suffer·hardship, as a·criminal, *even* as·far·
G2557.2 A-NPM κακοῦργοι (1x)
Lk 23:32 two others, *who·were* criminals, were·led together
G2557.2 A-APM κακούργους (1x)
Lk 23:33 ·crucified him, and·also the criminals, in·fact one
G2557.2 A-GPM κακούργων (1x)
Lk 23:39 of·the criminals who·were·hanging was·reviling
EG2557.2 (1x)
Lk 23:40 the other *criminal* was·reprimanding him, saying,

G2558 κακο•υχέω kakôuchéō *v.* (2x)
Roots:G2556 G2192 Compare:G2559 G3075 See:G4778 G2561
G2558 V-PPP-GPM κακουχουμένων (1x)
Heb 13:3 *with·them, and* the·ones being·maltreated, as
G2558 V-PPP-NPM κακουχούμενοι (1x)
Heb 11:37 ·destitute, being·hard-pressed, being·maltreated,

G2559 κακόω kakóō *v.* (6x)
Roots:G2556 Compare:G0984 G0091 G2554 See:G2561
G2559.1 V-FAI-3P κακώσουσιν (1x)
Ac 7:6 ·enslave them and shall·harm *them* four·hundred
G2559.1 V-FAP-NSM κακώσων (1x)
1Pe 3:13 And who *is* the·one *that* shall·harm yeu, if yeu·
G2559.1 V-AAN κακῶσαι (2x)
Ac 12:1 ·threw·forth his hands to·harm some of·the·ones
Ac 18:10 ·one·man shall·put·a·hand on·you to·harm you,
G2559.2 V-AAI-3P ἐκάκωσαν (1x)
Ac 14:2 roused·up and harmfully·affected the souls of·the
G2559.3 V-AAI-3S ἐκάκωσεν (1x)
Ac 7:19 ·against our kindred, badly·harmed our fathers, to·

G2560 κακῶς kakō̂s *adv.* (18x)
Roots:G2556 See:G5501
G2560.1 ADV κακῶς (4x)
Ac 23:5 You·shall·not declare *anything* badly of·a·ruler of·
Mt 15:22 my daughter *is* badly possessed·with·a·demon."
Mt 17:15 because he·is·lunatic and suffers badly, for he·has·
Mt 21:41 ·completely·destroy those bad·men badly, then he·
G2560.2 ADV κακῶς (10x)
Lk 5:31 ·of·healing, but·rather the·ones being badly·ill.
Lk 7:2 ·him, was·about to·completely·die, being badly·ill.
Mt 4:24 all the·ones being badly·ill, those·being·clenched
Mt 8:16 both·relieved·and·cured all the·ones being badly·ill,
Mt 9:12 ·of·healing, but·rather the·ones being badly·ill.
Mt 14:35 and brought to·him all the·ones being badly·ill,
Mk 1:32 to him all the·ones being badly·ill, and the·ones
Mk 1:34 many being badly·ill with·a·diversity·of illnesses,
Mk 2:17 but·rather the·ones being badly·ill. I·did·not come
Mk 6:55 on their mats the·ones being badly·ill, *to* wherever
EG2560.2 (1x)
Mt 9:20 a·woman *badly·ill*, discharging·a·flow·of·blood *for*
G2560.3 ADV κακῶς (2x)
Jn 18:23 him, "If I·spoke wrongly, testify concerning the
Jac 4:3 on·account·that yeu·request wrongly, in·order·that
EG2560.3 (1x)
2Co 10:10 in·fact, *the·one wrongly reckoning* replies, "His

G2561 κάκωσις kákōsis *n.* (1x)
Roots:G2559 Compare:G2558
G2561 N-ASF κάκωσιν (1x)
Ac 7:34 ·surely·seen the harmful·treatment of·my People

G2562 καλάμη kalámē *n.* (1x)
Roots:G2563 xLangAlso:H7179
G2562.2 N-ASF καλάμην (1x)
1Co 3:12 silver, precious stones, wood, hay, stubble—

G2563 κάλαμος kálamôs *n.* (12x)
See:G2562 xLangAlso:H7070 H5842 H7626
G2563.1 N-NSM κάλαμος (1x)
Rv 11:1 And he·gave to·me a·reed like a·rod, saying,
G2563.1 N-ASM κάλαμον (6x)
Lk 7:24 to·distinctly·view? A·reed being·shaken by a·wind?
Mt 11:7 to·distinctly·view? A·reed being·shaken by a·wind?
Mt 12:20 A·reed having·been·shattered he·did·not break·
Mt 27:29 *it* upon his head and·also a·reed in his right·hand,
Mt 27:30 at him, they·took the reed and were·beating at his
Rv 21:15 a·golden reed in·order·that he·should·measure the
G2563.1 N-DSM καλάμῳ (4x)
Mt 27:48 ·wine·vinegar and putting·it·on a·reed, was·giving
Mk 15:19 ·beating his head with·a·reed and were·spitting·on
Mk 15:36 ·wine·vinegar and putting·it·on a·reed, was·giving
Rv 21:16 the breadth. And with·the reed, he·measured the
G2563.2 N-GSM καλάμου (1x)
3Jn 1:13 want to·write to·you through ink and a·reed·pen.

G2564 καλέω kaléō *v.* (151x)
Compare:G2753 See:G2821 G1573-1 G3333 G4779 G0342-1 xLangAlso:H7121 A7123
G2564.1 V-FAI-1S καλέσω (1x)
Rm 9:25 also in Hosea, "I·shall·call *them* 'My People,'
G2564.1 V-FAI-2S καλέσεις (3x)
Lk 1:13 ·bear you a·son, and you·shall·call his name John.
Lk 1:31 ·and·birth a·son, and you·shall·call his name Jesus.
Mt 1:21 ·and·birth a·son, and you·shall·call his name
G2564.1 V-FAI-3P καλέσουσιν (1x)
Mt 1:23 ·and·birth a·son, and they·shall·call his name
G2564.1 V-FPI-2S κληθήσῃ (2x)
Jn 1:42 You·yourself shall·be·called Kephas *(a·piece·of·*
Lk 1:76 ·child, shall·be·called a·prophet of·the·Most·High,
G2564.1 V-FPI-3S κληθήσεται (9x)
Lk 1:32 "This·man shall·be great and shall·be·called *the* Son
Lk 1:35 *child*, being·born holy, shall·be·called God's Son.
Lk 1:60 "No·indeed! But·rather, he·shall·be·called John."
Lk 2:23 ·up a·primal·womb shall·be·called holy to·Yahweh
Mt 2:23 the prophets, "He·shall·be·called a·Natsarethan."
Mt 5:19 ·of·clay† in·this·manner, he·shall·be·called least in
Mt 5:19 ·instruct *them*, the·same shall·be·called great in the
Mt 21:13 "My house shall·be·called a·house of·prayer,"
Mk 11:17 "My house shall·be·called a·house of·prayer for·
G2564.1 V-FPI-3P κληθήσονται (2x)
Mt 5:9 they·themselves shall·be·called the·Sons of·God.
Rm 9:26 People,' there they·shall·be·called the·Sons of·
G2564.1 V-PAI-2P καλεῖτε (1x)
Lk 6:46 "And why·do yeu·call me, 'Lord, Lord,' and do·not
G2564.1 V-PAI-3S καλεῖ (3x)
Lk 20:44 So·then David calls him 'Lord'; how is·he also his
Mt 22:43 "So·then how·does David in Spirit call him 'Lord,
Mt 22:45 So·then, if David calls him 'Lord,' how is·he his
G2564.1 V-PAN καλεῖν (1x)
Heb 2:11 *the Initiator* is·not ashamed to·call them brothers,
G2564.1 V-PAP-NSF καλοῦσα (1x)
1Pe 3:6 listened·to·and·obeyed AbRaham, calling him lord.
G2564.1 V-PPI-3S καλεῖται (6x)
Lk 1:61 among your kinsfolk that is·called by·this name."
Lk 2:4 *the* city of·David (which is·called BethLechem), on·
Ac 28:1 then they·realized that the island was·called Melita.
Heb 3:13 day, even·for·as·along·as it·is·called "Today,"
Rv 11:8 *JeruSalem*, which spiritually is·called Sodom and
Rv 19:13 in·blood, and his name is·called The Word of·God
G2564.1 V-PPI-3P καλοῦνται (1x)
Lk 22:25 having·control·over them are·called 'benefactors.'
G2564.1 V-PPN καλεῖσθαι (3x)
Lk 1:62 *for* what he·might actually·want him to·be·called.
Mt 23:7 in the marketplaces, and to·be·called by the men·of·
1Co 15:9 who am not fit to·be·called an·ambassador, on·
G2564.1 V-PPP-ASN καλούμενον (3x)

Lk 19:29 the mount (the·one being·called *the Mount* of·
Lk 21:37 the mount, the·one being·called *the Mount* of·
Ac 27:16 ·near·to a·certain small·island being·called Clauda,
G2564.1 V-PPP-ASF καλουμένην (2x)
Lk 7:11 *that* he·was·traversing into a·city being·called Nain,
Ac 9:11 on the avenue, the·one being·called Straight, and
G2564.1 V-PPP-ASM καλούμενον (6x)
Lk 6:15 , and Simon, the·one being·called Zealot,
Lk 23:33 to the place, the·one being·called Skull, there they·
Ac 1:23 ·established two, Joseph being·called BarTsabas
Ac 15:37 ·take·along John, the·one being·called Mark.
Ac 27:8 we·came to some place being·called Good Harbors,
Rv 16:16 in·Hebrew being·called HarMeGiddon *(Mountain*
G2564.1 V-PPP-DSF καλουμένῃ (3x)
Lk 1:36 ·*pregnancy* for·her (the·woman being·called barren),
Ac 3:11 them in the colonnade being·called Solomon's,
Rv 1:9 the island, the·one being·called Patmos, on·account·
G2564.1 V-PPP-GSN καλουμένου (1x)
Ac 1:12 *the* mount, the·one being·called Olive·Orchard,
G2564.1 V-PPP-GSF καλουμένης (2x)
Lk 9:10 place *belonging·to* the·city being·called BethSaida.
Ac 10:1 from·among a·battalion being·called the Italian
G2564.1 V-PPP-GSM καλουμένου (1x)
Ac 7:58 ·at the feet of·a·young·man being·called Saul.
G2564.1 V-PPP-NSF καλουμένη (1x)
Lk 8:2 Mariam (the·one being·called Magdalene) from
G2564.1 V-PPP-NSF@ καλουμένη (1x)
Lk 10:39 And this·woman had a·sister called Mary, who,
G2564.1 V-PPP-NSM καλούμενος (5x)
Lk 19:2 ·*was* a·man being·called by·the·name·of Zacchaeus·
Ac 13:1 BarNabas, Simeon (the·one being·called Niger), and
Ac 27:14 *Crete*, the·one being·called EuroClydon *that·is*,
Rv 12:9 Serpent, the·one being·called Slanderer and the
Rv 19:11 ·down upon it *was* being·called Trustworthy and
G2564.1 V-IAI-3P ἐκάλουν (2x)
Lk 1:59 the little·child, and they·were·calling him ZacharIas
Ac 14:12 In·fact, both they·were·calling BarNabas, Zeus,
G2564.1 V-AAI-3S ἐκάλεσεν (3x)
Lk 14:16 man·of·clay† made a·great supper and called many.
Mt 1:25 her firstborn son. And he·called his name YeShua.
Mt 25:14 journeying·abroad, *who* called his·own slaves and
G2564.1 V-AAI-3P ἐκάλεσαν (1x)
Mt 10:25 as his lord. If they·called the master·of·the·house,
G2564.1 V-AAM-2S κάλεσον (1x)
Mt 20:8 to·his executive·manager, 'Call the workmen and
G2564.1 V-AAN καλέσαι (3x)
Lk 5:32 I·have·not come to·call righteous·men, but·rather
Mt 9:13 ' For I·did·not come to·call righteous·ones, but·
Mk 2:17 badly·ill. I·did·not come to·call righteous·men,
G2564.1 V-AAP-NSM καλέσας (1x)
Lk 19:13 And calling his ten slaves, he·gave ten more·silver·
G2564.1 V-AAS-2P καλέσητε (1x)
Mt 23:9 "And yeu·should·not call *anyone* yeur father upon
G2564.1 V-API-3S ἐκλήθη (3x)
Lk 2:21 the little·child, his name was·called Jesus, the *name*
Mt 27:8 Therefore that field is·called *AqelDama*, "Field of·
Jac 2:23 for righteousness." And he·was·called God's
G2564.1 V-APN κληθῆναι (3x)
Lk 15:19 and am no·longer worthy to·be·called your son;
Lk 15:21 and I·am no·longer worthy to·be·called your son.'
Ac 1:19 such·for this open·field to·be·called in·their own
G2564.1 V-APS-1P κληθῶμεν (1x)
1Jn 3:1 to·us, that we·should·be·called children of·God. On·
G2564.1 V-APS-2P κληθῆτε (2x)
Mt 23:8 "But yeu·yeurselves should·not be·called 'Rabbi,'
Mt 23:10 Nor·even should·yeu·be·called preeminent·leaders,
G2564.1 V-RPP-APM κεκλημένους (1x)
Mt 22:3 to·call·forth the·ones having·been·called to the
G2564.1 V-RPP-DPM κεκλημένοις (1x)
Mt 22:4 'Declare to·the·ones having·been·called, "Behold,
G2564.1 V-RPP-NPM κεκλημένοι (1x)
Mt 22:8 is ready, but the·ones having·been·called were not
EG2564.1 (5x)

Ac 13:9 Then Saul (the·one also *called* Paul), being·filled
Mt 10:3 of·Alphaeus) and *Judas called* Lebbaeus, the·one
Mt 10:25 more *shall·they·call* his·own family·members·in·
Mt 22:5 But neglecting *his call*, they·went·away, in·fact, one
Mk 2:14 *from·there*, he·saw Levi *called MattHew* (the·one
G2564.2 V-PAI-3S καλεῖ (1x)
1Co 10:27 if any·of·the non-trusting·ones call·for yeu, and
G2564.2 V-AAP-NSM καλέσας (2x)
Lk 7:39 *this*, the Pharisee, the·one calling·for him, declared
Mt 2:7 after·privately calling·for the Magian·astrologists,
G2564.2 V-AAP-NPM καλέσαντες (1x)
Ac 4:18 And calling·for them, they·charged them not to·
G2564.2 V-APP-GSM κληθέντος (1x)
Ac 24:2 And with·him being·called·for, Tertullus began to·
G2564.2 V-RAP-DSM κεκληκότι (1x)
Lk 14:12 ·was·saying also to·the·one having·called·for him,
G2564.2 V-RAP-NSM κεκληκώς (1x)
Lk 14:10 the·one having·called·for you should·come, he·
G2564.3 V-FPI-3S κληθήσεται (2x)
Heb 11:18 In YiTsaq, a·Seed shall·be·called·forth to·you,"
Rm 9:7 "In YiTsaq, a·Seed shall·be·called·forth to·you."
G2564.3 V-PAI-3S καλεῖ (1x)
Jn 10:3 his voice, and he·calls·forth his·own sheep each·by
G2564.3 V-PAM-2S καλεῖ (1x)
Lk 14:13 ·make a·reception, call·forth helplessly·poor·ones,
G2564.3 V-PAP-GSM καλοῦντος (4x)
Gal 5:8 *is* not from·out·of·the·one calling yeu forth.
Rm 4:17 ·to the dead·ones and calling·forth the·things not
Rm 9:11 but·rather as·a·result of·the·one calling·forth),
1Th 2:12 worthily of·God, the·one calling yeu forth into his
G2564.3 V-PAP-NSM καλῶν (1x)
1Th 5:24 Trustworthy *is* the·one calling yeu forth, who also
G2564.3 V-PPP-NSM καλούμενος (2x)
Heb 5:4 but·rather *it·is* the·one being·called·forth by God,
Heb 11:8 By·trust, AbRaham, being·called to·go·forth into
G2564.3 V-AAI-1S ἐκάλεσα (1x)
Mt 2:15 "From·out·of·Egypt I·called·forth my son."
G2564.3 V-AAI-3S ἐκάλεσεν (7x)
Mt 4:21 ·repairing their nets. And he·called them forth.
Mk 1:20 And immediately he·called them forth, and leaving
Rm 8:30 he·predetermined, these also he·called·forth; and
Rm 8:30 he·called·forth; and whom he·called·forth, these
Rm 9:24 even us, whom he·called·forth— not from·among
1Th 4:7 For God did·not call us forth toward impurity, but·
2Th 2:14 to which he·called yeu forth through our good·
G2564.3 V-AAM-2P καλέσατε (1x)
Mt 22:9 as·many·as yeu·might find, call·*them*·forth to the
G2564.3 V-AAN καλέσαι (1x)
Mt 22:3 his slaves to·call·forth the·ones having·been·called
G2564.3 V-AAP-ASM καλέσαντα (1x)
1Pe 1:15 according·to the·one already·calling yeu forth, *who·*
G2564.3 V-AAP-GSM καλέσαντος (4x)
Gal 1:6 ·are·transferring away·from the·one calling yeu forth
1Pe 2:9 ·excellencies of·the·one already·calling yeu forth out
2Pe 1:3 the recognition of·the·one already·calling us forth
2Ti 1:9 saving us and calling·*us*·forth with·a·holy calling,
G2564.3 V-AAP-NSM καλέσας (3x)
Lk 14:9 and the·one calling·forth *both* you and him, upon·
Gal 1:15 mother's womb and calling·*me*·forth through his
1Pe 5:10 of·all grace, the·one already·calling us forth into
G2564.3 V-API-2S ἐκλήθης (2x)
1Co 7:21 Are·you·called·forth *being* a·slave?
1Ti 6:12 to which also you·were·called·forth, and·also
G2564.3 V-API-2P ἐκλήθητε (7x)
Gal 5:13 brothers, yeu·yeurselves are·called·forth to liberty
1Pe 2:21 For toward this yeu·were·called·forth, because
1Pe 3:9 having·seen that yeu·were·called·forth to this in·
1Co 1:9 through whom yeu·are·called·forth into *the*
Eph 4:1 of·the calling by·which yeu·are·called·forth,
Eph 4:4 one Spirit— just·as also yeu·are·called·forth in one
Col 3:15 into which also yeu·were·called·forth in one Body
G2564.3 V-API-3S ἐκλήθη (5x)
Jn 2:2 And Jesus also was·called·forth to the wedding, and·

1Co 7:18 ·man *that* is·called·forth, having·been·circumcised,
1Co 7:18 Any·man *that* is·called·forth in uncircumcision,
1Co 7:20 in the calling in·which he·was·called·forth, in this
1Co 7:24 in that·*state*·which he·is·called·forth, brothers, in
G2564.3 V-APP-NSN κληθέν (1x)
Lk 2:21 Jesus, the *name* being·called·forth by the angel
G2564.3 V-APP-NSM κληθείς (2x)
1Co 7:22 For the·one being·called·forth in *the* Lord, *though*
1Co 7:22 likewise also the·one being·called·forth, *though*
G2564.3 V-APS-2S κληθῇς (2x)
Lk 14:8 "Whenever you·should·be·called·forth by any *man*
Lk 14:10 ·rather whenever you·should·be·called·forth, after·
G2564.3 V-RAI-3S κέκληκεν (2x)
1Co 7:15 in such·cases, but God has·called us forth in peace
1Co 7:17 ·as the Lord has·called·forth, in·this·manner let·
G2564.3 V-RPP-APM κεκλημένους (1x)
Lk 14:7 to the·ones having·been·called·forth, paying·close·
G2564.3 V-RPP-DPM κεκλημένοις (1x)
Lk 14:17 to·declare to·the·ones having·been·called·forth,
G2564.3 V-RPP-GPM κεκλημένων (1x)
Lk 14:24 men, the·ones having·been·called·forth, shall·taste
G2564.3 V-RPP-NSM κεκλημένος (1x)
Lk 14:8 ·than you may·be having·been·called·forth by him;
G2564.3 V-RPP-NPM κεκλημένοι (2x)
Heb 9:15 the·ones having·been·called·forth may·receive the
Rv 19:9 ·blessed *are* the·ones having·been·called·forth to the

G2565 καλλι•έλαιος kalliélaiôs *n.* (1x)
Roots:G2566 G1636
G2565 N-ASF καλλιέλαιον (1x)
Rm 11:24 ·grafted into a·cultivated·olive·tree, how·much

G2566 καλλίον kallíôn *adv.* (1x)
Roots:G2570
G2566 ADV-C κάλλιον (1x)
Ac 25:10 even as you·yourself realize better·than·most.

G2567 καλο•διδάσκαλος kalôdidáskalôs *adj.* (1x)
Roots:G2570 G1320 See:G2095
G2567 A-APF καλοδιδασκάλους (1x)
Tit 2:3 to·much wine, instructors·of·morally·good·things

G2569 καλο•ποιέω kalôpôiéō *v.* (1x)
Roots:G2570 G4160
G2569.2 V-PAP-NPM καλοποιοῦντες (1x)
2Th 3:13 yeu·should·not be·cowardly in·well·doing.

G2570 καλός kalós *adj.* (104x)
Compare:G0018 G2909 G4413 See:G5611 G2566 G2566-3 xLangAlso:H3303
G2570.1 A-NSM καλός (6x)
Jn 10:11 "I AM the good shepherd. The good shepherd lays·
Jn 10:11 good shepherd. The good shepherd lays·down his·
Jn 10:14 "I AM the good shepherd, and I·know my *sheep*,
1Ti 1:8 ·know that the Torah-Law *is* good, if someone
1Ti 4:6 ·the brothers, you·shall·be a·good attendant of·Jesus
2Ti 2:3 must·endure·hardship as a·good soldier of·Jesus
G2570.1 A-NSN καλόν (20x)
Lk 6:43 "For a·good tree is·not producing rotten fruit, neither
Lk 9:33 "O·Captain, it·is good for·us to·be here, and we·
Lk 14:34 "Salt *is* good, but if the salt should·become·bland,
Heb 13:9 For *it·is* good *for* the heart to·be·made·steadfast
Gal 4:18 But *it·is* good to·be·zealous always in *a* good *thing*,
Mt 13:38 field is the world, and the good seed, these are the
Mt 15:26 he·declared, "It·is not good to·take the children's
Mt 17:4 "Lord, it·is good for·us to·be here.
Mt 18:8 cast *it* from you. It·is good for·you to·enter into the
Mk 7:27 For it·is not good to·take the children's bread and
Mk 9:5 "Rabbi, it·is good for·us to·be here.
Mk 9:50 Salt *is* good, but if the salt should·become unsalty,
1Co 5:6 Yeur boasting *is* not good. Do·yeu·not personally·
1Co 7:1 yeu·wrote to·me, *it·is* good for·a·man·of·clay† not
1Co 7:8 to·the widows, it·is good for·them if they·should·
1Co 7:26 that *it·is* good for·a·man·of·clay† to·behave in·
1Co 9:15 to·me, for *it·is* good for·me to·die rather than that
1Ti 2:3 For this *is* good and fully·acceptable in·the·sight of·
1Ti 4:4 every creature of·God *is* good, and not·even·one *is*

1Ti 5:4 for that is good and fully·acceptable in·the·sight of·
G2570.1 A-NPF καλοί (1x)
1Pe 4:10 attending·to it as good estate·managers of·God's
G2570.1 A-NPN καλά (2x)
Tit 3:8 ·things are the good·things and profitable·things for·
1Ti 5:25 Likewise, also, the good works *of·some* are
G2570.1 A-ASM καλόν (11x)
Jn 2:10 man·of·clay† first places·out the good wine, and
Jn 2:10 ·yourself have·purposefully·kept the good wine until
Lk 3:9 every tree not producing good fruit is·chopped·down
Lk 6:43 fruit, neither *is* a·rotten tree producing good fruit.
Mt 3:10 tree not producing good fruit is·chopped·down and
Mt 7:19 tree not producing good fruit is·chopped·down and
Mt 12:33 the tree good, and its fruit good; or make the tree
1Ti 3:13 well do·acquire for·themselves good advancement,
1Ti 6:12 Be·striving·in the good striving of·the trust, grab·
1Ti 6:19 ·up·in·store for·themselves a·good foundation for
2Ti 4:7 I·have·strived·in the good striving; I·have·finished
G2570.1 A-ASF καλήν (10x)
Heb 13:18 ·confidence that we·have a·good conscience in
Mt 13:8 fell on the soil, the good·one, and were·giving fruit,
Mt 13:23 ·being·permeated·with·seed among the good soil,
Mk 4:8 And some fell into the good soil and was·giving fruit
Mk 4:20 ·being·permeated·with·seed among the good soil:
1Ti 1:18 ·may·strategically·war the good strategic·warfare,
1Ti 3:7 ·for him also to·have a·good testimony from the·ones
1Ti 6:12 and·also affirmed the good affirmation in·the·sight
1Ti 6:13 before Pontius Pilate the good affirmation)
2Ti 1:14 The good charge·fully·consigned·to·your·care, you·
G2570.1 A-ASN καλόν (12x)
Lk 6:38 and it·shall·be·given to·yeu; good measure, packed·
Heb 6:5 and after·tasting a·good utterance of·God, and·also
Gal 6:9 ·not be·cowardly *in* doing the good; for in·due
Mt 12:33 “Either make the tree good, and its fruit good; or
Mt 13:24 is·likened to·a·man·of·clay† sowing good seed in
Mt 13:27 ‘Sir, did·you·not·indeed sow good seed in your
Mt 13:37 “The·one sowing the good seed is the Son of·Clay·
Mt 26:10 to·the woman? For she·worked a·good deed to me.
Mk 14:6 ·troubles to·her? She·worked a·good work to me.
1Th 5:21 ·and·verify all·things; fully·hold·onto the good.
1Co 7:26 for·this to·inherently·be good on·account·of the
2Co 13:7 that yeu·yeurselves should·do the good, and *that*
G2570.1 A-APM καλούς (2x)
Mt 7:17 every beneficially·good tree produces good fruit, but
Mt 7:18 neither *is* a·rotten tree *able* to·produce good fruit.
G2570.1 A-APN καλά (3x)
Jn 10:32 answered them, “Many good works I·showed yeu
Mt 5:16 so·that they·may·see yeur good works and may·
Mt 13:48 ·down, they·collected the good into containers but
G2570.1 A-DSF καλῇ (1x)
Lk 8:15 “But the *seed* in the good soil, these are *the·ones*
G2570.1 A-DSN καλῷ (1x)
Gal 4:18 good to·be·zealous always in *a* good *thing*, and not
G2570.1 A-DPN καλοῖς (2x)
1Ti 5:10 being·attested·to by good works (if she·nurtured·
1Ti 6:18 ·good·work, to·be·wealthy in good deeds, to·be
G2570.1 A-GSF καλῆς (2x)
Jac 3:13 yeu? From·out of·the good behavior, let·him·show
1Ti 4:6 of·the trust and of·the good instruction, to·which
G2570.1 A-GSN καλοῦ (3x)
Jn 10:33 We·do·not stone you concerning a·good work, but·
Heb 5:14 toward having discernment of·both good and bad.
1Ti 3:1 ·assignment·of·oversight, he·longs·for a·good work.
G2570.1 A-GPN καλῶν (6x)
Heb 10:24 to a·keen·provoking of·love and good works,
1Pe 2:12 as criminals, as·a·result *of·yeur* good works (after·
Tit 2:7 ·forth *as* a·particular·pattern of·good works in the
Tit 2:14 People,' *one being* a·zealot of·good works.
Tit 3:8 ·have·a·considerable·care to·conduct good works.
Tit 3:14 *brothers* must·learn also to·conduct good works for
G2570.1 A/L-APM καλούς (1x)
Ac 27:8 to some place being·called Good Harbors, which
EG2570.1 (1x)
1Ti 5:25 are obvious·beforehand; and the *good works* being
G2570.2 A-APM καλούς (1x)
Mt 13:45 ·of·clay†, a·merchant seeking high·quality pearls,
G2570.3 A-ASN καλόν (1x)
Jac 2:7 they·themselves *that* revile the beautiful name, the·
G2570.3 A-DPM καλοῖς (1x)
Lk 21:5 that it·has·been·adorned with·beautiful stones and
G2570.5 A-NSM καλός (1x)
Rm 7:16 ·concur with·the Torah-Law that *it·is* morally·good.
G2570.5 A-NSN καλόν (1x)
Rm 14:21 *It·is* morally·good neither to·eat meat, nor·even to·
G2570.5 A-ASF καλήν (1x)
1Pe 2:12 the Gentiles, being morally·good in·order·that,
G2570.5 A-APN καλά (2x)
Rm 12:17 while·maintaining·oneself·in morally·good·things
2Co 8:21 ·maintaining·ourselves·in morally·good·things, not
G2570.5 A-DSF καλῇ (1x)
Lk 8:15 *the·ones* with a·morally·good and beneficially·good
G2570.6 A-ASM καλόν (1x)
Jac 4:17 having·seen *the* morally·good·thing to·do and not
G2570.6 A-ASN καλόν (2x)
Rm 7:18 *how* to·perform the morally·good·thing, I·do·not
Rm 7:21 for·myself to·do the morally·good·thing, *I·find* that
EG2570.6 (1x)
Rm 7:18 *the morally·good·thing* is·directly·laid·out before·
G2570.7 A-NSN καλόν (7x)
Mt 18:9 “It·is better for·you to·enter into the life-above with·
Mt 26:24 ·Man† is·handed·over! It·was better for·him if that
Mk 9:42 in me, it·is even·much better for·him if a·mill stone
Mk 9:43 chop it off. It·is better for·you to·enter into the
Mk 9:45 chop it off. It·is better for·you to·enter lame into
Mk 9:47 you, cast it out. It·is better for·you to·enter into the
Mk 14:21 ·Man† is·handed·over! It·was better for·him if

G2570-2 καλύβη kalýbē *n.* (3x)
Compare:G4633 G4634 G1409-1 G0106 See:G2570-1
xLangEquiv:H5521
G2570-2.3 N-GPF Καλυβῶν (1x)
Jn 7:2 Sacred·Feast, the *Sacred·Feast* of·Booths, was near·
EG2570-2.3 (2x)
Jn 7:14 halfway·through the Sacred·Feast *of·Booths*, Jesus
Jn 7:37 great *day* of·the Sacred·Feast *of·Booths*, Jesus stood

G2571 κάλυμα kályma *n.* (6x)
Roots:G2572 Compare:G2665 See:G0343 G2619
G2571.2 N-NSN κάλυμμα (3x)
2Co 3:14 even·unto the·present·day the same veil remains,
2Co 3:15 Moses is·read·aloud, a·veil is·laid·out upon their
2Co 3:16 *Anointed-One*, the veil is·entirely·removed.
G2571.2 N-ASN κάλυμμα (1x)
2Co 3:13 Moses *did*, who·was·placing a·veil over his face,
EG2571.2 (2x)
2Co 3:13 with·the *veil* being·fully·rendered·inoperative.
2Co 3:14 *the* certain *veil* which is·fully·rendered·inoperative

G2572 καλύπτω kalýptō *v.* (8x)
Compare:G2928 G4628-1 See:G1943 G2813 G2290 G2571 G4028
xLangEquiv:H3680
G2572.1 V-PAI-3S καλύπτει (1x)
Lk 8:16 after·igniting a·lantern, covers it with·a·vessel or
G2572.1 V-PPN καλύπτεσθαι (1x)
Mt 8:24 the sea, such·for the sailboat to·be·covered by the
G2572.1 V-AAM-2P καλύψατε (1x)
Lk 23:30 and to·the hills, “Cover us!”'
G2572.2 V-RPP-NSN κεκαλυμμένον (2x)
2Co 4:3 even·if our good·news is having·been·veiled, it·is
2Co 4:3 ·veiled, it·is having·been·veiled among the·ones
G2572.3 V-RPP-NSN κεκαλυμμένον (1x)
Mt 10:26 ·is not·even·one·thing having·been·concealed, that
G2572.4 V-FAI-3S καλύψει (2x)
Jac 5:20 and·also shall·cover·and·bury·over a·multitude
1Pe 4:8 love shall·cover·and·bury·over a·full·multitude of·

G2573 καλῶς kalŏs *adv.* (36x)
Roots:G2570 Compare:G2095
G2573.1 ADV καλῶς (26x)
Jn 4:17 Jesus says to·her, “You·declared well, ‘I·do·not
Jn 8:48 “*Do* we·ourselves not say well that you·yourself are
Jn 13:13 me Mentor and Lord, and yeu·say well, for I·am.
Jn 18:23 But if *I·spoke* well, why do·you·thrash me?
Lk 6:26 all the men·of·clay† should·declare well of·yeu! For
Lk 20:39 of·the scribes declared, “Mentor, well declared.”
Ac 10:33 to you, and you did well in·coming·directly *here*.
Ac 28:25 “The Holy Spirit spoke well through Isaiah the
Gal 5:7 Yeu·were·running well. Who cut·into·yeur·path
Mt 15:7 Isaiah did·prophesy well concerning yeu, saying,
Mk 7:6 to·them, “Isaiah prophesied well concerning yeu, the
Mk 7:37 “He·has·done all·things well. He·makes both the
Mk 12:28 ·seen that he·answered them well, inquired·of him,
Mk 16:18 on unhealthy·ones, and they·shall·be well.”
Jac 2:8 ·shall·love your neighbor as yourself,’” yeu·do well.
Jac 2:19 there·is one God. You·do well. The demons also
Php 4:14 Nevertheless yeu·did well sharing·together in·my
2Pe 1:19 word, to·which yeu·do well taking·heed as to·a·
1Co 7:37 to·keep·unmarried his virgin·daughter, does well.
1Co 7:38 the *father* giving·away·in·marriage does well, but
1Co 14:17 For in·fact, you give·thanks well, but·yet the
1Ti 3:4 one·conducting his·own house well, having his·
1Ti 3:12 their·children and their·own houses well.
1Ti 3:13 For the *men* already·attending well do·acquire for·
1Ti 5:17 having·conducted well must·be·considered· of·
3Jn 1:6 as·is·worthy of·God, *then* you·shall·do well.
G2573.2 ADV καλῶς (1x)
2Co 11:4 ·accept, yeu·were·bearing·with *him* beautifully.
G2573.3 ADV καλῶς (1x)
Heb 13:18 all·things, willing to·conduct·ourselves morally.
G2573.4 ADV καλῶς (1x)
Gal 4:17 yeu, *but* not for·moral·good, but·rather they·
G2573.5 ADV καλῶς (3x)
Lk 6:27 Love yeur enemies, do good to·the·ones hating yeu,
Mt 5:44 “Do good to·the·ones hating yeu, and pray on·behalf
Mt 12:12 ·such, it·is·proper to·do good on·the Sabbath·days
G2573.6 ADV καλῶς (1x)
Jac 2:3 “You·yourself must·sit·down here in·a·good·place,”
G2573.7 ADV καλῶς (3x)
Mk 7:9 to·them, “Clearly·full·well do·yeu·set·aside the
Mk 12:32 “Mentor, clearly·full·well did·you·declare in
Rm 11:20 Clearly·full·well, by·the lack·of·trust they·were·

G2574 κάμηλος kámēlŏs *n.* (6x)
גָּמָל gamal [Hebrew]
גמלא gamla [Armenian Syriac]
Roots:H1581 Compare:G3688 G2254-2 See:G2574-1
G2574 N-ASM κάμηλον (4x)
Lk 18:25 “For it·is easier *for* a·camel to·enter·in through a·
Mt 19:24 to·yeu, it·is easier *for* a·camel to·go through *the*
Mt 23:24 ·out the gnat, but swallowing·up the camel.
Mk 10:25 “It·is easier for·a·camel to·enter through the tiny·
G2574 N-GSM καμήλου (2x)
Mt 3:4 his apparel *made* from camel's hair and *was·girded·*
Mk 1:6 was having·dressed·himself·with camel's hair and

G2575 κάμινος káminŏs *n.* (4x)
Roots:G2545 See:G2574-2
xLangEquiv:H3564 xLangAlso:H3536 H4715 A0861
G2575 N-ASF κάμινον (2x)
Mt 13:42 they·shall·cast them into the furnace of·the fire,
Mt 13:50 they·shall·cast them into the furnace of·the fire,
G2575 N-DSF καμίνῳ (1x)
Rv 1:15 fine·brass (as having·been·refined in a·furnace), and
G2575 N-GSF καμίνου (1x)
Rv 9:2 of·the well, as smoke of·a·great furnace, and the sun

G2576 κα•μμύω kammýō *v.* (2x)
Roots:G2596 G3466-1 Compare:G3467 G2808 G0608
G2576 V-AAI-3P ἐκάμμυσαν (2x)
Ac 28:27 ears hardly heard, and they·fully·shut their eyes,

Mt 13:15 ears hardly heard, and they·fully·shut their eyes,

G2577 κάμνω kámnō *v.* (3x)
Compare:G2872 G1590 G0770
G2577.2 V-2AAS-2P κάμητε (1x)
Heb 12:3 lest yeu·should·become·fatigued, being·faint in·
G2577.2 V-RAI-2S κέκμηκας (1x)
Rv 2:3 ·account·of my name and have·not become·fatigued.
G2577.3 V-PAP-ASM κάμνοντα (1x)
Jac 5:15 shall·save the·one becoming·sickly·fatigued, and

G2578 κάμπτω kámptō *v.* (4x)
Compare:G2827 G5087
G2578.2 V-FAI-3S κάμψει (1x)
Rm 14:11 'every knee shall·bow to·me, and every tongue
G2578.2 V-PAI-1S κάμπτω (1x)
Eph 3:14 For·this gracious·cause, I·bow my knees to the
G2578.2 V-AAI-3P ἔκαμψαν (1x)
Rm 11:4 ·thousand men, who did·not bow a·knee to·Baal."
G2578.2 V-AAS-3S κάμψῃ (1x)
Php 2:10 of·Jesus, every knee should·bow (of·celestial·ones

G2579 κ•ἄν kán *cond.* (13x)
Roots:G2532 G1437 Compare:G3379 G0686
G2579.1 COND-C κἄν (3x)
Lk 13:9 And·if, in·fact, it·should·produce fruit, *good*! But·if·
Mk 16:18 ·up serpents; and·if they·should·drink something
Jac 5:15 ·awaken him; and·if he·may·be having·committed
G2579.2 COND-C κἄν (1x)
Mt 21:21 fig·tree, but·yet also·if yeu·should·declare to·this
G2579.3 COND-C κἄν (4x)
Ac 5:15 ·order·that with·Peter going·by, if·even his shadow
Heb 12:20 "If·even a·wild·beast should·lay·a·finger·on the
Mk 5:28 ·saying, "Because if·even I·should·lay·hold of·his
Mk 6:56 ·that they·may·lay·hold *of·him*, if·even *only* of·the
G2579.4 COND-C κἄν (4x)
Jn 8:14 to·them, "Though I·myself may·testify concerning
Jn 10:38 "But if I·do, though yeu·may·not trust me, trust the
Jn 11:25 trusting in me, though he·should·die, yet·shall·he·
Mt 26:35 to·him, "Though it·should·be·necessary·for me to·
G2579.5 COND-C κἄν (1x)
2Co 11:16 but if not, then·also accept me as impetuous in·

G2580 Κανᾶ Kanâ *n/l.* (4x)
Ꝁανᾶ Qanâ [Greek, Octuagint]
קָנָה qanah [Hebrew]
Roots:H7071 Compare:G2562-1
G2580.2 N/L-PRI Ꝁανᾶ (4x)
Jn 2:1 day, there·was·a·wedding in Qanah of·Galilee, and
Jn 2:11 of·miraculous·signs in Qanah of·Galilee and made
Jn 4:46 Jesus came again into Qanah of·Galilee, where he·
Jn 21:2 , and NathaniEl from Qanah in·Galilee, and the *sons*

G2581 Κανανίτης Kananítēs *n/g.* (2x)
קַנָּא qanna' [Hebrew]
Roots:H7067 Compare:G2207 G5478 See:G5477
G2581.2 N/G-NSM Κανανίτης (1x)
Mt 10:4 Simon the Zealot, and Judas IsCariot, the·one also
G2581.2 N/G-ASM Κανανίτην (1x)
Mk 3:18 *called Lebbaeus* Thaddaeus, and Simon the Zealot;

G2582 Κανδάκη Kandákē *n/p.* (1x)
G2582 N/P-GSF Κανδάκης (1x)
Ac 8:27 a·eunuch, a·potentate of·Candace, the queen of·

G2583 κανών kanṓn *n.* (6x)
Compare:G3358
EG2583 (1x)
1Ti 5:19 against an·elder, aside·from *this* standard:
G2583.3 N-ASM κανόνα (1x)
2Co 10:15 ·with yeu according·to our standard *of·service*, for
G2583.3 N-DSM κανόνι (3x)
Gal 6:16 ·and·march·orderly by·this standard, peace *be* upon
Php 3:16 ·orderly by·the same standard, to·contemplate the
2Co 10:16 to·boast by another·man's standard *of·service* for
G2583.3 N-GSM κανόνος (1x)
2Co 10:13 ·rather according·to the standard measure which

G2584 Καπερ•ναούμ Kapêrnaôúm *n/l.* (18x)
Roots:H3723 H5151
G2584.3 N/L-PRI Καπερναούμ (16x)
Jn 2:12 After this, he·walked·down to CaperNaum (he and
Jn 4:46 royal·official, whose son was·sick at CaperNaum.
Jn 6:17 across the sea toward CaperNaum. And even·now it·
Jn 6:24 sailboats and came to CaperNaum, seeking·for Jesus.
Jn 6:59 in a·gathering, while·instructing in CaperNaum.
Lk 4:23 ·things·as we·heard happening in CaperNaum, do
Lk 4:31 And he·came·down to CaperNaum, a·city of·Galilee
Lk 7:1 hearing of·the people, he·entered into CaperNaum.
Lk 10:15 "And you, CaperNaum, the·one being·elevated·up
Mt 4:13 he·resided in CaperNaum near·the·seashore, within
Mt 8:5 as·YeShua was·entering into CaperNaum, a·centurion
Mt 11:23 And you, CaperNaum, the·one being·elevated
Mt 17:24 And with·them coming to CaperNaum, the·ones
Mk 1:21 And they·traverse into CaperNaum. And
Mk 2:1 And again he·entered into CaperNaum after *some*
Mk 9:33 Then he·came to CaperNaum, and once·being in the
EG2584.3 (2x)
Lk 9:46 Then *in·CaperNaum*, a·discussion entered·in among
Mt 9:1 ·over and came into his·own city *of·CaperNaum*.

G2585 καπηλεύω kapēlêúō *v.* (1x)
Compare:G1389
G2585.3 V-PAP-NPM καπηλεύοντες (1x)
2Co 2:17 shortchanging·and·hustling the Redemptive-word

G2586 καπνός kapnós *n.* (13x)
See:G2585-2
xLangEquiv:H6227 xLangAlso:H6225
G2586 N-NSM καπνός (6x)
Rv 8:4 And the smoke of·the incense, *which·came* with·the
Rv 9:2 bottomless·pit, and there·ascended smoke out·of·the
Rv 9:2 out·of the well, as smoke of·a·great furnace, and the
Rv 9:17 mouths proceeds·forth fire and smoke and sulfur.
Rv 14:11 "And the smoke of·their torment ascends into ages
Rv 19:3 ·Yahweh,·HalleluYah! And her smoke ascends into
G2586 N-ASM καπνόν (2x)
Rv 18:9 ·should·look·upon the smoke of·her fiery·burning,
Rv 18:18 ·out, clearly·seeing the smoke of·her fiery·burning
G2586 N-GSM καπνοῦ (5x)
Ac 2:19 down·below: blood and fire and vapor of·smoke.
Rv 9:2 air were·darkened from·out·of the smoke of·the well.
Rv 9:3 And from·out·of the smoke there·came·forth locusts
Rv 9:18 fire, and as·a·result of·the smoke, and as·a·result
Rv 15:8 Temple was·overfilled with·smoke from·among the

G2587 Καππαδοκία Kappadôkía *n/l.* (2x)
xLangAlso:H3731
G2587 N/L-ASF Καππαδοκίαν (1x)
Ac 2:9 MesoPotamia and *in* Judea and Cappadocia, *in* Pontus
G2587 N/L-GSF Καππαδοκίας (1x)
1Pe 1:1 *throughout* Pontus, Galatia, Cappadocia, Asia, and

G2588 καρδία kardía *n.* (162x)
Compare:G3510
xLangEquiv:H3824 H3820 A3821
G2588.1 N-NSF καρδία (19x)
Jn 14:1 "Do·not be·troubled *in* yeur heart. Yeu·trust in God,
Jn 14:27 Do·not be·troubled in·yeur heart, nor·even be·timid
Jn 16:22 yeu again, and yeur heart shall·rejoice, and not·
Lk 12:34 yeur treasure is, there also yeur heart shall·be.
Lk 24:32 "Was·not·indeed our heart being·set·ablaze within
Ac 2:26 On·account·of that, my heart is·made·merry, and
Ac 4:32 of·the·ones trusting, the heart and the soul was one.
Ac 8:21 this matter, for your heart is not straight in·the·sight
Ac 28:27 For the heart of·this People became·thickly·
Heb 3:12 ·shall·be in any of·yeu an·evil heart of·distrust, in
Mt 6:21 yeur treasure is, there also yeur heart shall·be.
Mt 13:15 For the heart of·this People became·thickly·
Mt 15:8 with·their lips, but their heart is·distant, far·away
Mk 6:52 their heart was having·been·petrified·hard·as·stone.
Mk 7:6 with·*their*·lips, but their heart is·distant, far·away
Rm 1:21 their uncomprehending heart was·already·darkened.
2Co 6:11 to yeu; our heart has·been·broadened·wide·open.
1Jn 3:20 Because if our heart should·incriminate *us*, God is
1Jn 3:21 Beloved, if our heart should·not incriminate us,
G2588.1 N-NPF καρδίαι (2x)
Lk 21:34 ·at·any·time yeur hearts should·be·burdened with
Col 2:2 that their hearts may·be·comforted, being·knit·
G2588.1 N-ASF καρδίαν (16x)
Jn 12:40 their heart he·has·petrified·hard·as·stone in·order·
Jn 13:2 even·now having·cast into the heart of·Judas IsCariot
Jn 16:6 to·yeu, the grief has·completely·filled yeur heart.
Lk 4:18 ·heal the·ones *with* the heart having·been·shattered,
Ac 5:3 completely·filled your heart for·you to·lie to·the Holy
Ac 7:23 ·him, it·ascended upon his heart to·visit his brothers
Ac 13:22 *to·be* a·man according·to my·own heart, who shall·
Ac 16:14 ·opened·up her heart to·give·heed to·the·things
Ac 21:13 weeping and jointly·crushing my heart? For I·
Heb 13:9 good *for* the heart to·be·made·steadfast by·grace,
Mk 7:19 it·does·not traverse into his heart, but·rather into the
Mk 8:17 yeur heart still having·been·petrified·hard·as·stone?
Rm 2:5 hardness and *your* unrepentant heart, you·store·up
Jac 1:26 but·rather deluding his·own heart, this·man's
2Pe 2:14 having a·heart having·been·trained with·acts·of·
1Co 2:9 it·did·not ascend upon *the* heart of·a·man·of·clay†,
G2588.1 N-ASF@ καρδίαν (1x)
2Co 3:15 is·read·aloud, a·veil is·laid·out upon their hearts.
G2588.1 N-APF καρδίας (27x)
Lk 1:17 "to·turn fathers' hearts back·around toward *the*
Lk 16:15 but God knows yeur hearts; because the·thing
Lk 21:14 firmly·settle *it* in yeur hearts, not to·meditate·
Ac 14:17 seasons, filling·up our hearts with·nurturing and
Ac 15:9 both us and them, purifying their hearts by·the trust.
Heb 3:8 yeu·should·not harden yeur hearts, as in the Direct·
Heb 3:15 voice, yeu·should·not harden yeur hearts, as in the
Heb 4:7 his voice, yeu·should·not harden yeur hearts."
Heb 8:10 I·shall·inscribe them upon their hearts, and I·shall·
Heb 10:16 my Laws-of-Liberty upon their hearts, and upon
Heb 10:22 of·trust, the hearts having·been·sprinkled from
Gal 4:6 the Spirit of·his Son into yeur hearts, yelling·out,
Rm 8:27 the·one searching the hearts personally·knows what
Rm 16:18 they·thoroughly·delude the hearts of·the innocent
Jac 4:8 ·disqualified, and cleanse *yeur* hearts, *yeu who·are*
Jac 5:5 lived·luxuriously. Yeu·nourished yeur hearts, as in
Jac 5:8 Yeu·must·firmly·establish yeur hearts, because the
Php 4:7 shall·dutifully·keep yeur hearts and yeur mental·
1Th 2:4 ·rather God, the·one testing·and·proving our hearts.
1Th 3:13 ·order to·firmly·establish yeur hearts blameless in
2Th 2:17 may·he·comfort yeur hearts and firmly·establish
2Th 3:5 may the Lord fully·direct yeur hearts into the love
Eph 6:22 us, and *that* he·may·comfort yeur hearts.
Col 4:8 ·things concerning yeu and may·comfort yeur hearts,
1Jn 3:19 ·the truth and shall·reassure our hearts before him.
Rv 2:23 ·one searching kidneys and hearts. And I·shall·give
Rv 17:17 "For God gave in their hearts to·do his plan, and
G2588.1 N-DSF καρδίᾳ (37x)
Jn 12:40 with·the heart and may·be·turned·back·around, and
Lk 1:66 hearing *them* laid·*them*·up in their hearts, saying,
Lk 2:19 all these utterances, ruminating *on·them* in her heart.
Lk 2:51 ·guarding all these utterances in her heart.
Lk 8:15 a·morally·good and beneficially·good heart, who
Lk 12:45 if that slave should·declare in his heart, 'My lord
Lk 24:25 O stupid·ones, and slow in·the heart to·trust on all
Ac 2:37 *this*, they·were·fully·jabbed in·the heart, and they·
Ac 5:4 you·placed this action in your heart? You·did·not lie
Ac 7:51 and uncircumcised in·the heart and ears, yeu always
Ac 28:27 ears, and should·comprehend with·the heart, and
Heb 3:10 'Always, they·are·led·astray *in·their*·heart, and
Mt 5:8 *are* the pure in·the heart, because they·themselves
Mt 5:28 committed·adultery with·her even·now in his heart.
Mt 11:29 gentle and lowly in·the heart, and yeu·shall·find a·
Mt 12:40 three days and three nights in the heart of·the earth.
Mt 13:15 ears, and should·comprehend with·the heart, and
Mt 13:19 *seed* having·been·sown in his heart. This·person is
Mt 22:37 Yahweh your God with all your heart, and with all
Mt 24:48 that bad slave should·declare in his heart, 'My lord
Mk 11:23 and should·not be·hesitant in his heart, but·rather

Rm 9:2 grief is a·great and unceasing distress in·my heart.
Rm 10:6 "You·should·not declare in your heart, "Who
Rm 10:8 *even* in your mouth, and in your heart" (that is, the
Rm 10:9 and should·trust in your heart that God awakened
Rm 10:10 For with·*the*·heart, one·is·convinced unto
Jac 3:14 and contention in yeur hearts, do·not boast·over and
Php 1:7 on·account·of having yeu in my heart. Both in my
1Th 2:17 (in·personal·presence, not in·heart), diligently·
1Co 7:37 stands immovably·steadfast in the heart, not having
1Co 7:37 this·thing in his heart to·keep·unmarried his virgin·
2Co 5:12 ·boasting in a·surface·appearance and not in·heart.
2Co 8:16 same earnest·care into the heart of·Titus on·yeur
2Co 9:7 ·man *sow* just·as he·is·preinclined in·*his*·heart, not
Eph 5:19 and making·melody in yeur heart to·the Lord,
Col 3:16 singing with grace in yeur hearts to·the Lord.
Rv 18:7 because she·says in her heart, 'I·sit·down a·queen,

G2588.1 N-DPF καρδίαις (19x)

Lk 3:15 ·men were·pondering in their hearts concerning John
Lk 5:22 "Why·do yeu·ponder in yeur hearts?
Lk 24:38 And why·do debates ascend in yeur hearts?
Ac 7:39 and in·their hearts, they·turned·back·around to
Ac 7:54 ·things, they·were·thoroughly·irate to·the heart, and
Mt 9:4 ·do yeu·yeurselves cogitate evil·things in yeur hearts?
Mk 2:6 there, sitting·down yet pondering in their hearts,
Mk 2:8 "Why·do yeu·ponder these·things in yeur hearts?
Mk 4:15 the·one having·been·sown in their hearts.
Rm 2:15 of·the Torah-Law written in their hearts, with·their
Rm 5:5 has·been·poured·forth in our hearts through Holy
1Pe 3:15 Yahweh God holy in yeur hearts. And *be* ready
2Pe 1:19 should·rise·above·the·horizon in yeur hearts—
2Co 1:22 the earnest·deposit of·the Spirit in our hearts.
2Co 3:2 having·been·engraved in our hearts, being·known
2Co 4:6 did·radiate·brightly in our hearts, specifically·for *the*
2Co 7:3 that yeu·are in our hearts for *us* to·die·together and
Eph 3:17 Anointed-One to·reside in yeur hearts through the
Col 3:15 the peace of·God arbitrate in yeur hearts, into which

G2588.1 N-GSF καρδίας (35x)

Lk 1:51 ·men in·*the*·innermost·imagination of·their hearts.
Lk 6:45 beneficially·good treasure of·his heart, brings·forth
Lk 6:45 ·out of·the evil treasure of·his heart, brings·forth the
Lk 6:45 from·out of·the abundance of·the heart, his mouth
Lk 8:12 the Redemptive-word from their hearts, lest trusting,
Lk 9:47 seeing the discussion of·their heart, grabbing·hold
Lk 10:27 your God from·out of·all your heart, and from·out
Ac 2:46 in exuberant·celebration and simplicity of·heart,
Ac 8:22 the intention of·your heart shall·be·forgiven you.
Ac 8:37 "If you·trust from·out of·all the heart, it·is·proper."
Ac 11:23 with·determined·purpose of·heart to·continue·on
Heb 4:12 of·the·cogitations and intents of·the·heart.
Heb 10:22 ·alongside with a·true heart in full·assurance of·
Mt 12:34 from·out of·the abundance of·the heart the mouth
Mt 12:35 ·good treasure of·his heart casts·forth the
Mt 15:18 come·forth from·out of·the heart, and·these·things
Mt 15:19 For from·out of·the heart comes·forth evil
Mk 3:5 over the stony·hardness of·their hearts, he·says to·the
Mk 7:21 ·inside, from·out of·the heart of·the men·of·clay†,
Mk 12:30 your God from·out of·all your heart, and from·out
Mk 12:33 to·love him from·out of·all the heart, and from·out
Rm 2:29 and *with* a·circumcision *that·is* of·heart, in spirit,
Rm 6:17 from·out of·*the*·heart *to·that* particular·pattern of·
Rm 10:1 Brothers, in·fact my heart's good·purpose and
1Pe 1:22 one·another from·out of·a·pure heart earnestly—
1Pe 3:4 ·*to* the hidden man·of·clay† of·the heart, with the
1Co 14:25 the secrets of·his heart become apparent; and in·
2Co 2:4 and anguished·anxiety of·heart I·wrote to·yeu
2Co 3:3 of·stone, but·rather on fleshy tablets of·heart.
Eph 4:18 on·account·of the stony·hardness of·their heart,
Eph 6:5 and trembling, with fidelity of·yeur heart, as to·the
Col 3:22 but·rather with fidelity of·heart, reverently·fearing
1Ti 1:5 is love out of·a·pure heart, and of·a·beneficially·
2Ti 2:22 the·ones calling·upon the Lord out of·a·pure heart.
1Jn 3:20 *us*, God is greater·than our heart, and he·knows all·

G2588.1 N-GPF καρδιῶν (4x)

Lk 2:35 from·among many hearts should·be·revealed (and
Mt 18:35 his brother their trespasses from yeur hearts."
Rm 1:24 the longings of·their·own hearts, to·dishonor their·
1Co 4:5 shall·make·apparent the counsels of·the hearts. And

EG2588.1 (2x)

2Co 6:13 ·yeurselves, broaden·wide·open *yeur hearts* also.
2Co 7:2 Have·room·for us *in yeur hearts*; we·wronged no·

G2589 καρδιο•γνώστης kardiôgnṓstēs *n.* (2x)

Roots:G2588 G1097

G2589 N-NSM καρδιογνώστης (1x)

Ac 15:8 And God, the knower·of·the·heart, testified to·them

G2589 N-VSM καρδιογνῶστα (1x)

Ac 1:24 "You, O·Lord, knower·of·the·hearts of·all·men,

G2590 καρπός karpṓs *n.* (67x)

Roots:G0726 See:G2591 G2593 G2592
xLangEquiv:H6529 xLangAlso:H0003

G2590 N-NSM καρπός (8x)

Jn 15:16 should·bear fruit and yeur fruit should·remain, in·
Lk 1:42 and having·been·blessed *is* the fruit of·your womb.
Gal 5:22 But the fruit of·the Spirit is love, joy, peace,
Mt 21:19 to·it, "No·longer should fruit come·out·from you
Mk 4:29 "But whenever the fruit should·be·yielded·up,
Jac 3:18 And the fruit of·righteousness is·sown in peace by·
Php 1:22 *bodily* flesh, this *continues* a·fruit of·work for·me.
Eph 5:9 (for the fruit of·the Spirit *is* in all beneficial·

G2590 N-ASM καρπόν (35x)

Jn 4:36 ·of·service and gathers·together fruit into life-above
Jn 12:24 But if it·should·die, it·bears much fruit.
Jn 15:2 vine·sprout in me not bearing fruit, *the* same he·
Jn 15:2 bearing the *proper* fruit, he·trims·and·purifies it, in·
Jn 15:2 ·and·purifies it, in·order·that it·may·bear more fruit.
Jn 15:4 vine·sprout is·not able to·bear fruit of itself unless it·
Jn 15:5 him, the·same bears much fruit, because apart·from
Jn 15:8 is·glorified, that yeu·may·bear much fruit, and *that*
Jn 15:16 should·head·on·out and should·bear fruit and yeur
Lk 3:9 tree not producing good fruit is·chopped·down and is·
Lk 6:43 tree is not producing rotten fruit, neither *is* a·rotten
Lk 6:43 fruit, neither *is* a·rotten tree producing good fruit.
Lk 8:8 ·sprouted, it·produced fruit a·hundred·times·over."
Lk 13:6 vineyard, and he·came seeking fruit on it yet did·
Lk 13:7 three years, I·come seeking fruit on this fig·tree and
Lk 13:9 And·if, in·fact, it·should·produce fruit, *good*! But·
Heb 12:11 a·peaceful fruit of·righteousness for·the·ones
Heb 13:15 that·is, a·fruit of·lips giving·affirmation to·his
Mt 3:10 tree not producing good fruit is·chopped·down and
Mt 7:19 tree not producing good fruit is·chopped·down and
Mt 12:33 make the tree good, and its fruit good; or make the
Mt 12:33 the tree rotten, and its fruit rotten. For out of·the
Mt 13:8 the good·one, and were·giving fruit, in·fact some
Mt 13:26 the blade blossomed and produced fruit, then the
Mk 4:7 ·up and altogether·choked it, and it·gave no fruit.
Mk 4:8 the good soil and was·giving fruit, springing·up and
Mk 11:14 "May no·one any·longer eat fruit from·out of·you
Rm 1:13 , in·order·that I·may·have some fruit among yeu
Rm 6:21 Accordingly, what fruit were·yeu·having then in
Rm 6:22 to·God, yeu·have yeur fruit unto renewed·holiness,
Rm 15:28 ·sealing to·them this fruit, I·shall·go·aside through
Jac 5:7 ·the·soil waits·for the precious fruit of·the earth,
Jac 5:18 gave rain, and the earth blossomed·with its fruit.
Php 4:17 gift, but·rather I·anxiously·seek the fruit, the·one
Rv 22:2 *and* yielding·forth its fruit according·to each one's

G2590 N-APM καρπούς (11x)

Lk 3:8 "Now·then, produce fruits worthy of·the repentance,
Lk 12:17 no place·where I·shall·gather·together my fruits?'
Mt 3:8 Now·then, produce fruits worthy of·the repentance.
Mt 7:17 beneficially·good tree produces good fruit, but the
Mt 7:17 good fruit, but the rotten tree produces evil fruit.
Mt 7:18 tree is·not able to·produce evil fruit, neither *is* a·
Mt 7:18 neither *is* a·rotten tree *able* to·produce good fruit.
Mt 21:34 slaves to the tenant·farmers, to·receive its fruits.
Mt 21:41 who shall·render to·him the fruits in their seasons.
Mt 21:43 ·be·given to·a·nation producing the fruits of·it.
Rv 22:2 producing twelve *kinds·of* fruits, *and* yielding·forth

G2590 N-GSM καρποῦ (6x)

Lk 6:44 each tree is·known from·out of·its·own fruit. For not
Lk 20:10 they·should·give him of the fruit of·the vineyard.
Ac 2:30 with·an·oath *that* from·out of·*the*·fruit of·his loins,
Mt 12:33 For out of·the fruit, the tree is·known.
Mk 12:2 the tenant·farmers of the fruit of·the vineyard.
1Co 9:7 and does·not eat from·out of·its fruit? Or who

G2590 N-GPM καρπῶν (6x)

Mt 7:16 By their fruits, yeu·shall·recognize them.
Mt 7:20 by their fruits yeu·shall·recognize them.
Mt 21:34 "And when the season of·the fruits drew·near, he·
Jac 3:17 of·beneficially·good fruits, without·discrimination
Php 1:11 having·been·completely·filled of·*the*·fruits of·, of·
2Ti 2:6 man·that·works·the·soil to·partake first of·the fruits.

EG2590 (1x)

Mk 4:8 growing·more, and it·was·bearing *fruit*: one *seed*

G2591 Κάρπος Kárpôs *n/p.* (1x)

Roots:G2590

G2591.2 N/P-DSM Κάρπῳ (1x)

2Ti 4:13 that I·left·behind at Troas with Carpus, *as* you·are·

G2592 καρπο•φορέω karpôphôréō *v.* (8x)

Roots:G2593

G2592.1 V-PAI-3S καρποφορεῖ (2x)

Mt 13:23 *it*, who also·then bears·fruit and produces, in·fact,
Mk 4:28 For the earth automatically bears·fruit; first a·blade,

G2592.1 V-PAI-3P καρποφοροῦσιν (2x)

Lk 8:15 ·hold·onto *it* and bear·fruit with patient·endurance.
Mk 4:20 give·heed·and·accept *it*, and bear·fruit: one *seed*

G2592.1 V-PAP-NPM καρποφοροῦντες (1x)

Col 1:10 into all willing·compliance: bearing·fruit in every

G2592.1 V-PMP-NSN καρποφορούμενον (1x)

Col 1:6 And it·is itself·bearing·fruit, just·as *it·does* also in

G2592.1 V-AAN καρποφορῆσαι (1x)

Rm 7:5 in our members in·order to·bear·fruit for·Death.

G2592.1 V-AAS-1P καρποφορήσωμεν (1x)

Rm 7:4 ·men, in·order·that we·should·bear·fruit for·God.

G2593 καρπο•φόρος karpôphôrôs *adj.* (1x)

Roots:G2590 G5342 See:G2592

G2593.1 A-APM καρποφόρους (1x)

Ac 14:17 ·of·rain from·the·sky and fruit-bearing seasons,

G2594 καρτερέω kartêréō *v.* (1x)

Roots:G2904 Compare:G2901 G1414 G2480 G3306 G5278 G2553 See:G4342

G2594.2 V-AAI-3S ἐκαρτέρησεν (1x)

Heb 11:27 for he·mightily·endured as one·clearly·seeing

G2595 κάρφος kárphôs *n.* (6x)

G2595.2 N-ASN κάρφος (6x)

Lk 6:41 "And why do·you·look·at the speck·of·dust, the·one
Lk 6:42 *that* I·should·cast·out the speck·of·dust, the·one in
Lk 6:42 ·look·about to·cast·out the speck·of·dust, the·one in
Mt 7:3 And why do·you·look·at the speck·of·dust, the·one in
Mt 7:4 ·way *so* I·may·cast·out the speck·of·dust from your
Mt 7:5 ·about to·cast the speck·of·dust from·out of·your

G2596 κατά katá *prep.* (479x)

καθ- kath- [combining prefix]
κατ- kat- [alternate prefix]

Compare:G1519 G1538 See:G1722 G2736 G2633-1

G2596.1 PREP κατά (7x)

Lk 8:33 herd impulsively·dashed down the steep·overhang
Ac 8:26 "Rise·up and traverse down *on* the·south·side
Ac 8:36 And as they·traversed down the roadway, they·came
Mt 8:32 ·pigs impulsively·dashed down the steep·overhang
Mk 5:13 herd impulsively·dashed down the steep·overhang
Mk 14:3 ·flask, she·poured *the ointment* down his head.
2Co 8:2 ·their joy and their deep down poverty abounded to

G2596.2 PREP κατά (3x)

Heb 2:17 From·which, he·was·owing fully all·things to·the
Rm 11:21 For if God did·not spare the fully natural branches,
Phm 1:14 ·to a·compulsion, but·rather *be* fully voluntary.

G2596.3 PREP κατά (239x)

Jn 2:6 of·stone, according·to the manner·of·purification of·
Jn 5:4 For according·to a·certain·season, an·angel was·

Jn 7:24 Do·not unduly·judge according·to *mere*·appearance,
Jn 8:15 "Yeu·yeurselves judge according·to the flesh; I·
Jn 18:31 take him and judge him according·to yeur Oral-law.
Jn 19:7 have an·Oral-law, and according·to our Oral-law he·
Lk 1:9 *that* according·to the custom of·the Sanctuary·
Lk 1:38 May·it·happen to·me according·to your utterance."
Lk 2:22 days of·her purification according·to the Torah-Law
Lk 2:24 ·give a·sacrifice according·to the·thing having·been·
Lk 2:27 for·him according·to the prescribed·custom of·the
Lk 2:29 your slave in peace, according·to your utterance,
Lk 2:39 absolutely·all the·things according·to the Torah-Law
Lk 2:42 ·up with·them to JeruSalem according·to the custom
Lk 4:16 ·nurtured·and·reared. And according·to his custom,
Lk 22:22 ·Man† departs according·to the·thing having·been·
Lk 22:39 Then going·forth according·to his custom, *Jesus*
Lk 23:14 man·of·clay† according·to those·things·of·which
Lk 23:56 *over* the Sabbath according·to the commandment.
Ac 2:30 ·out of·*the*·fruit of·his loins, according·to the flesh,
Ac 3:17 that yeu·inflicted *the killing* according·to ignorance,
Ac 7:44 ·*him* to·make it, according·to the particular·pattern
Ac 13:22 of·Jesse, *to·be* a·man according·to my·own heart,
Ac 13:23 From this·man's Seed, according·to promise, God
Ac 15:11 Anointed to·be·saved; according·to that manner,
Ac 17:2 And according·to Paul's custom, he·entered·in
Ac 18:14 or an·evil, mischievous·deed according·to reason,
Ac 18:15 names, and *matters* according·to yeur Torah-Law,
Ac 19:20 In·this·manner, according·to might, the
Ac 22:3 having·been·educated·and·disciplined according·to
Ac 22:12 ·reverent man according·to the Torah-Law, being·
Ac 23:3 sit·down judging me according·to the Torah-Law,
Ac 23:31 the soldiers, according·to the *charge* having·
Ac 24:6 and determined to·judge according·to our Oral-law.
Ac 24:14 I·affirm to·you, that according·to The Way which
Ac 26:5 to·testify), that according·to the most·strict
Ac 27:25 turn·out according·to that·which has·been·spoken
Heb 2:4 of·Holy Spirit, according·to his·own determination.
Heb 5:6 to the coming·age according·to the assigned·order of·
Heb 5:10 a·High·Priest "'according·to the assigned·order of·
Heb 6:20 for the coming·age according·to the assigned·order
Heb 7:5 ·tithes·of the People according·to the Torah-Law,
Heb 7:11 to·be·raised·up according·to the assigned·order of·
Heb 7:11 not to·be·related according·to the assigned·order
Heb 7:15 fully·obvious, if, according·to the similarity of·
Heb 7:16 not according·to a·Torah-Law of·a·fleshly
Heb 7:16 but·rather according·to a·power of·an·
Heb 7:17 to the coming·age according·to the assigned·order
Heb 7:21 to the coming·age according·to the assigned·order
Heb 7:22 According·to so·vast *an·oath*, YeShua has·become
Heb 8:4 offering the presents according·to the Torah-Law,
Heb 8:5 ·make all·things according·to the particular·pattern,
Heb 8:9 Not according·to the covenant that I·made with·their
Heb 9:9 ·able to·make·completely·mature according·to *the*
Heb 9:22 And almost all·things, according·to the Torah-Law
Heb 9:27 And according·to as·much·as it·is·laid·away for·
Heb 10:8 ·things are·offered according·to the Torah-Law),
Heb 11:7 an·heir of·a·righteousness according·to trust.
Heb 11:13 These all died according·to trust, not receiving the
Heb 12:10 ·and·disciplining *us* according·to their supposing,
Gal 1:4 evil age currently·standing, according·to the will of·
Gal 1:11 by me is·not according·to a·man·of·clay†.
Gal 2:2 And I·walked·up according·to a·revelation, and set·
Gal 3:15 I·relate *this matter* according·to a·man·of·clay†,
Gal 3:29 Seed and *are* heirs according·to promise.
Gal 4:23 ·the maidservant has·been·born according·to flesh,
Gal 4:28 we·ourselves, brothers, according·to YiTsaq, are
Gal 4:29 ·one being·born according·to flesh was·persecuting
Gal 4:29 ·persecuting the·one *being·born* according·to Spirit,
Mt 1:20 appeared to·him according·to a·vision·in·a·dream,
Mt 2:12 after·being·divinely·instructed according·to a· not
Mt 2:13 appears to·Joseph according·to a·vision·in·a·dream,
Mt 2:16 two·years·of·age and below, according·to the time
Mt 2:19 of·Yahweh (according·to a·vision·in·a·dream)
Mt 2:22 So after·being·divinely·instructed according·to a·,

Mt 9:29 eyes, saying, "According·to yeur trust be·it to·yeu.
Mt 16:27 ·give·back to·each·man according·to his practice.'
Mt 23:3 do *it*, but do·not do according·to their works. For
Mt 25:15 one, to·each·man according·to his·own ability,
Mt 27:19 this·day according·to a·vision·in·a·dream on·
Mk 1:27 Because according·to authority he·orders even the
Mk 7:5 disciples not walk according·to the Oral·tradition of·
Rm 1:3 birthed·from·out of·David's Seed according·to flesh,
Rm 1:4 in power according·to a·spirit of·devoted·holiness,
Rm 2:2 the judgment of·God is according·to truth against
Rm 2:5 But according·to your hardness and *your* unrepentant
Rm 2:6 "'shall·render to·each·man according·to his deeds.'"
Rm 2:7 ·ones *working* according·to a·patient·endurance of·
Rm 2:16 of·the men·of·clay†. According·to my good·news,
Rm 3:5 *this line of·reasoning* according·to a·man·of·clay†).
Rm 4:1 our father to·have·found, according·to flesh?
Rm 4:4 ·of·service is·not reckoned according·to grace, but·
Rm 4:4 according·to grace, but·rather according·to the debt.
Rm 4:16 of·trust, in·order·that *it·may·be* according·to grace,
Rm 4:18 ·many nations according·to the·thing having·been·
Rm 5:6 For yet, according·to due·season, Anointed-One
Rm 7:22 in·the Torah-Law of·God according·to the inner
Rm 8:1 *for·the·ones* walking not according·to flesh, but·
Rm 8:1 according·to flesh, but·rather according·to Spirit.
Rm 8:4 the·ones walking not according·to flesh, but·rather
Rm 8:4 according·to flesh, but·rather according·to Spirit.
Rm 8:5 For the·ones being according·to flesh contemplate
Rm 8:5 flesh, but the·ones according·to Spirit *contemplate*
Rm 8:12 *but* not to·the flesh, to·live according·to the flesh.
Rm 8:13 For if yeu·live according·to flesh, yeu·are·about to·
Rm 8:27 over *the* holy·ones according·to *the will·of* God.
Rm 8:28 called·forth according·to *his* determined·purpose.
Rm 9:3 of·my brothers, my kinsmen according·to flesh,
Rm 9:5 and from·out of·whom, according·to the flesh, *is*
Rm 9:9 of·promise, "'According·to this season I·shall·come
Rm 9:11 ·purpose may·endure according·to God's Selection,
Rm 10:2 not according·to recognition·and·full·knowledge.
Rm 11:5 ·to·be a·remnant according·to a·Selection of·grace.
Rm 11:24 an·olive·tree·which·is·wild according·to nature,
Rm 11:24 how·much more shall·these, according·to nature,
Rm 11:28 In·fact, according·to the good·news, *they·are*
Rm 11:28 on·account·of yeu, but according·to the Selection,
Rm 12:6 gracious·bestowments according·to the grace
Rm 12:6 if prophecy, *then* according·to the proportion of·
Rm 15:5 one·another according·to Anointed-One Jesus,
Rm 16:25 ·firmly·establish yeu according·to my good·news
Rm 16:25 Anointed (according·to a·revealing of·*the*·Mystery
Rm 16:26 Scriptures, according·to a·full·appointment of·the
Jac 2:8 ·complete *the* Royal Law according·to the Scripture,
Jac 3:9 the·ones having·come·to·be according·to a·likeness
Jud 1:16 traversing according·to their·own longings. And
Jud 1:18 time, who·are·traversing according·to their·own
Php 1:20 according·to my eager·anticipation and expectation
Php 2:3 ·even·one·thing *be·done* according·to contention or
Php 3:5 from·among Hebrews; according·to Torah-Law, a·
Php 3:6 according·to zeal, persecuting the Called·Out·
Php 3:6 Called·Out·citizenry; according·to righteousness
Php 3:14 according·to *that* set·aim, I·pursue *it* toward the
Php 3:21 the body of·his glory, according·to the operation
Php 4:11 Not that I·say *this* according·to *a·particular* lacking
Php 4:19 ·fulfill yeur every need according·to his wealth in
1Pe 1:2 according·to *the* foreknowledge of·Father God, by a·
1Pe 1:3 YeShua Anointed, the·one according·to his large
1Pe 1:15 *conforming* according·to the·one already·calling
1Pe 1:17 presently·judging impartially according·to the work
1Pe 3:7 ·together *with·them* according·to knowledge, as
1Pe 4:6 in·fact according·to men·of·clay† in·*the*·flesh, but
1Pe 4:6 ·flesh, but may·live according·to God in·*the*·spirit.
1Pe 4:14 In·fact, according·to their·part, he·is·reviled; but
1Pe 4:14 he·is·reviled; but according·to yeur·part, he·is·
1Pe 4:19 even the·ones suffering according·to the will of·
2Pe 3:3 last days mockers, traversing according·to their own
2Pe 3:13 Nevertheless, according·to his pledge, we·intently·

2Pe 3:15 Paul wrote to·yeu (according·to the wisdom being·
2Th 1:12 and yeu in him, according·to the grace of·our God
2Th 2:9 whose arrival is according·to an·operation of·the
2Th 3:6 ·manner and not according·to the tradition which he·
Tit 1:1 of·truth (the·one according·to devout·reverence),
Tit 1:3 am·entrusted according·to a·full·appointment of·God
Tit 1:4 To·Titus, a·genuine child according·to a·shared trust.
Tit 1:9 Redemptive-word according·to the instruction in·
Tit 3:5 did), but·rather he·saved us according·to his mercy,
Tit 3:7 ·become heirs according·to an·Expectation of·eternal
1Co 1:26 not many *are* wise·men according·to flesh, not
1Co 2:1 yeu, came not according·to superiority of·discourse
1Co 3:3 fleshly, and walk according·to men·of·clay†?
1Co 3:8 his·own payment·of·service according·to his·own
1Co 3:10 According·to the grace of·God, the·one being·
1Co 7:6 *and* not according·to an·authoritative·assignment.
1Co 7:40 she·should·remain, according·to my advice; and I·
1Co 9:8 I·speak these·things according·to a·man·of·clay†?
1Co 10:18 Look·upon IsraEl according·to flesh. Are not·
1Co 15:3 of·our moral·failures according·to the Scriptures,
1Co 15:4 on·the third day according·to the Scriptures,
1Co 15:32 If according·to *the striving·of* men·of·clay†, I·
2Co 1:17 ·that I·purpose, do·I·purpose according·to flesh,
2Co 4:13 trust, according·to the·one having·been·written,
2Co 5:16 personally·know no·one·at·all according·to flesh.
2Co 5:16 we·have·known Anointed-One according·to flesh,
2Co 7:9 repentance, for yeu·were·grieved according·to God,
2Co 7:10 For the grief according·to God accomplishes
2Co 7:11 very·same·thing (to·grieve yeu according·to God),
2Co 8:3 that according·to *their* power, I·testify, even above·
2Co 8:8 ·not say *this* according·to fully·assigned·authority,
2Co 10:2 of·us as presently·walking according·to flesh.
2Co 10:3 we·do·not strategically·war according·to flesh.
2Co 10:7 ·look·at things according·to surface·appearance?
2Co 10:13 ·measure, but·rather according·to the standard
2Co 10:15 ·great along·with yeu according·to our standard
2Co 11:15 whose end shall·be according·to their works.
2Co 11:17 I·speak, I·do·not speak according·to *the* Lord,
2Co 11:18 Since many boast according·to the flesh, I·also
2Co 11:21 I·say *this* according·to *the implied·charge·of*
2Co 13:10 while·being·present, according·to the authority
Eph 1:5 Jesus Anointed, according·to the good·purpose of·
Eph 1:7 — the pardon of·trespasses according·to the wealth
Eph 1:9 Mystery of·his will (according·to his good·purpose
Eph 1:11 him, already·being·predetermined according·to *the*
Eph 1:11 ·one operating all things according·to the counsel
Eph 1:19 the·ones trusting, according·to the operation of·
Eph 2:2 ·times·past, yeu·walked according·to the present·age
Eph 2:2 present·age of·this world, according·to the prince of·
Eph 3:3 that according·to a·revelation, he·made·known to·
Eph 3:7 of·this *good·news* according·to the voluntary·present
Eph 3:7 ·one being·given to·me according·to the operation
Eph 3:11 according·to *the* determined·purpose of·the ages
Eph 3:16 in·order·that according·to the wealth of·his glory,
Eph 3:20 of·an·abundance, *to·do* according·to the power,
Eph 4:7 is·given to·each one of·us according·to the measure
Eph 4:16 ·joint, according·to an·effective·working of·each
Eph 4:22 ·off the old man·of·clay† according·to the previous
Eph 4:24 (the·one already·being·created according·to God in
Eph 6:5 ·obey the lords (*the·ones* according·to flesh) with
Eph 6:6 not according·to eyeservice as men-pleasers†, but·
Col 1:11 ·enabled with all power according·to the might of·
Col 1:25 an·attendant, according·to the estate·management
Col 1:29 I·labor·hard, striving according·to his operation,
Col 2:8 and an·empty delusion, according·to the tradition
Col 2:8 of·men·of·clay†, *that·is*, according·to the principles
Col 2:8 of·the world, and not according·to Anointed-One,
Col 2:22 with·usage)— *decrees* according·to 'the
Col 3:10 a·full·knowledge 'according·to *the* derived·image'
Col 3:20 ·to·and·obey the parents according·to all·things, for
Col 3:22 the·ones *who·are yeur* lords according·to flesh, not
Phm 1:14 should·not be as according·to a·compulsion, but·
1Ti 1:1 Anointed according·to a·full·appointment of·God

1Ti 1:11 according·to the glorious good·news of·the
1Ti 1:18 *my* child TimoThy, according·to the preceding
1Ti 5:21 doing not·even·one·thing according·to favoritism.
1Ti 6:3 with·the instruction according·to devout·reverence,
2Ti 1:1 through God's will, according·to *the* promise of·
2Ti 1:8 ·together in·the good·news according·to God's power
2Ti 1:9 with·a·holy calling, not according·to our works, but·
2Ti 1:9 but·rather according·to his·own determined·purpose
2Ti 2:8 from·among dead·men according·to my good·news,
2Ti 4:3 But·rather, according·to their·own longings, they·
2Ti 4:14 the Lord 'give·back to·him according·to his works,'
1Jn 5:14 if we·should·request anything according·to his will
2Jn 1:6 we·should·walk according·to his commandments.
Rv 2:23 ·give to·each·one of·yeu according·to yeur works.
Rv 18:6 and double to·her double according·to her works.
Rv 20:12 in the official·scrolls, according·to their works.
Rv 20:13 And each·one was·judged according·to their works
Rv 22:2 *and* yielding·forth its fruit according·to each one's

EG2596.3 (4x)

1Pe 3:3 adorning must·be, not *according·to* the outwardly,
1Pe 3:4 but·rather *according·to* the hidden man·of·clay† of·
2Pe 2:22 But it·has·befallen them *according·to* the true
Rv 21:17 cubits, *according·to* a·measure of·a·man·of·clay†,

G2596.4 PREP καθ´ (6x)

Ac 14:1 And accordingly *as in·Antiochia*, it·happened the
Heb 7:20 And accordingly, *he·was·made·priest*, *but* not
Rm 14:22 ·yourself have trust? *Then* accordingly, retain *the*
Tit 1:1 of·Jesus Anointed— accordingly *for·the* trust of·
1Co 14:27 in·a·bestowed·tongue, accordingly *let·it·be* two
Eph 5:33 also, yeu·yeurselves (accordingly each one in·that·

EG2596.4 (1x)

Eph 5:33 and *so·also* the wife *accordingly* (*as·the Bride*),

G2596.5 PREP κατά (66x)

Jn 18:29 ·accusation do·yeu·bring against this man·of·clay†?
Jn 19:11 having not·even·one·bit·of authority against me,
Lk 9:50 *him*, for whoever is not against us is on·behalf·of·us
Lk 11:23 ·one not being with me is against me, and the·one
Ac 4:26 ·gathered·together in·unison against Yahweh and
Ac 4:26 against Yahweh and against his Anointed-One."
Ac 6:13 cease speaking reviling utterances against this holy
Ac 14:2 the souls of·the Gentiles against the brothers.
Ac 16:22 And the crowd rose·up·together against them, and
Ac 19:16 in, exercised·*such*·strength against them such·for
Ac 21:28 instructing all·men everywhere against the People,
Ac 24:1 ·it·clear to·the governor *the·things* against Paul.
Ac 24:22 I·shall·thoroughly·ascertain the·things against yeu.
Ac 25:2 Judeans made·clear to·him *the·things* against Paul.
Ac 25:3 requesting an·influential·favor against *Paul*, that he·
Ac 25:7 bringing many burdensome complaints against Paul,
Ac 25:14 Festus set·forth the·things against Paul to·the king
Ac 25:15 ·clear *that* they·are·requesting justice against him.
Ac 25:27 also to·signify the legal·charge *laid* against him."
Ac 27:14 after, a·typhoon-like wind slammed against *Crete*,
Gal 3:21 *is* the Torah-Law against the promises of·God?
Gal 5:17 For the flesh longs against the Spirit, and the Spirit
Gal 5:17 the Spirit, and the Spirit against the flesh. And
Gal 5:23 *and* self-restraint— against such·things there·is no
Mt 5:11 ·declare all·manner·of evil utterance against yeu,
Mt 5:23 ·to·mind that your brother has anything against you,
Mt 10:35 I·came to·split "a·man·of·clay† against his father,
Mt 10:35 against his father, a·daughter against her mother,
Mt 10:35 and a·daughter-in-law against her mother-in-law;
Mt 12:14 upon·going·forth, took consultation against him,
Mt 12:25 being·divided against itself is·made·desolate, and
Mt 12:25 city or home being·divided against itself shall·not
Mt 12:30 ·one not being with me is against me, and the·one
Mt 12:32 whoever should·declare a·word against the Son of·
Mt 12:32 but whoever should·declare against the Holy Spirit,
Mt 20:11 *it*, they·were·grumbling against the master·of·the·
Mt 26:59 were·seeking false·testimony against YeShua, that
Mt 27:1 people took consultation against YeShua such·for
Mk 3:6 consultation with the HerOdians against him, on·
Mk 9:40 For whoever is not against yeu is on·behalf·of·yeu.
Mk 11:25 if yeu·have anything against anyone, forgive, in·
Mk 14:55 were·seeking testimony against Jesus in·order to·
Mk 14:56 For many were·falsely·testifying against him, and·
Mk 14:57 ·up, someone was·falsely·testifying against him,
Rm 8:31 ·*this* on·our behalf, who *is·able to·be* against us?
Rm 8:33 shall·call·to·account against God's Selected-Ones?
Rm 11:2 How he·confers with·God against IsraEl, saying,
Jac 3:14 do·not boast·over and utter·lies against the truth.
Jac 5:9 Do·not groan against one·another, brothers, lest yeu·
Jud 1:15 to·make Tribunal·judgment against all, and to·
Jud 1:15 *and* morally·disqualified·men spoke against him."
Php 1:12 the·things *which·happened* against me have·come
1Pe 2:11 longings, which strategically·war against the soul.
2Pe 2:11 power, do·not bring against themselves a·reviling
1Co 4:6 ·up over the *other*, *comparing* one against the other.
1Co 15:15 of·God, because we·testified against God that he·
2Co 10:5 is·lifting·itself·up against the absolute·knowledge
2Co 13:8 we·are·not able *to·do* anything against the truth,
Eph 6:21 may·personally·know the·things against me *and*
Col 2:14 after·rubbing·out the handwriting against us (the
Col 4:7 to·yeu all the·things *occurring* against me. *He·is* a·
1Ti 5:19 ·and·accept a·legal·accusation against an·elder,
Rv 2:4 'But·yet I·have *this* against you, that you·left your
Rv 2:14 'But·yet I·have a·few·things against you, because
Rv 2:20 'But·yet I·have a·few·things against you, because
Rv 12:7 and his angels waged·war against the Dragon; and

EG2596.5 (1x)

Ac 6:13 against this holy place and *against* the Torah-Law.

G2596.6 PREP καθ´ (42x)

Jn 21:25 Jesus did, which if each one should·be·written, I·
Lk 2:41 Now each year his parents traversed to JeruSalem
Lk 8:1 he·himself was·traveling·throughout each city and
Lk 8:4 were·traversing·onward toward him *from* each city,
Lk 9:6 ·forth, they·went·throughout each·of the villages,
Lk 9:23 himself and take·up his cross each day, and·then
Lk 11:3 'Give us each day our sustaining bread.
Lk 13:22 *Jesus* was·traversing·throughout each *of·the* cities
Lk 16:19 and fine·linen, splendidly being·merry each day.
Lk 19:47 And he·was instructing each day in the Sanctuary·
Lk 22:53 With·me being each day with yeu in the Sanctuary·
Ac 2:46 Each day, both while·diligently·continuing with·the·
Ac 2:46 Sanctuary·Atrium and breaking bread in·each house,
Ac 2:47 ·placing the·ones being·saved each day alongside
Ac 3:2 ·carried, whom they·were·laying each day alongside
Ac 5:15 to·bear·forth the sick in·each·of the broad·streets,
Ac 5:42 the Sanctuary·Atrium, and in·each house, they·did·
Ac 8:3 the Called·Out·citizenry. Traversing·into each *of* the
Ac 14:23 for·them elders for·each Called·Out·citizenry,
Ac 15:21 of·ancient generations, has in·each city the·ones
Ac 16:5 ·the trust and were·abounding in·number each day.
Ac 17:11 scrutinizing the Scriptures each day, *as·to* whether
Ac 17:17 and·also in the marketplace each and·every day
Ac 19:9 *the·things of·the kingdom of·God* each day in the
Ac 20:23 the Holy Spirit thoroughly·testifies in·each city,
Ac 21:19 *Paul* was·recounting·in·detail each and·every one
Ac 22:19 and thrashing in·each·of the gatherings, the·ones
Heb 3:13 But·rather exhort one·another each and·every day,
Heb 7:27 who does·not have a·necessity each day, just·as the
Heb 9:25 enters into the Holy·of·Holies each year with
Heb 10:1 same sacrifices (which they·offer each year into
Heb 10:3 ·again *is·made* of·moral·failures each year.
Heb 10:11 ·offers·sacrifices stands each day publicly·serving
Mt 19:3 ·clay† to·divorce his wife for·each and·every cause?
Mt 26:55 ·arrest me? I·was·sitting·down each day alongside
Mk 14:49 Each day I·was alongside yeu in the Sanctuary·
Rm 3:2 Much in·each and·every manner. For in·fact, first·of·
Rm 12:5 Body in Anointed-One, and each one the members
Tit 1:5 and should·fully·establish elders in·each city, as I·
1Co 14:31 For yeu·are·able, each one, all to·prophesy, in·
1Co 15:31 Each day I·die, as·sure·as *it·is* our boast, which I·
Rv 4:8 And *the* four living·beings, each one itself, was·

G2596.7 PREP καθ´ (10x)

Lk 10:31 "And by coincidence, a·certain priest·that·offers·
Lk 10:32 likewise a·Levite, happening by the place, coming
Ac 28:16 was·freely·permitted to·abide by himself together
Heb 6:13 ·having no·one·at·all greater by *which* to·swear,
Heb 6:13 greater by *which* to·swear, he·swore by himself,
Heb 6:16 men·of·clay† in·fact swear by the·one greater·than
Mt 26:63 ·oath,·I·solemnly·charge you by the·living God,
Jac 2:17 ·that it·should·have no works, is dead by itself.
1Co 12:8 but to·another a·word of·knowledge by the same
Eph 4:22 ·of·life (the·one being·corrupted by the delusional

G2596.8 PREP κατ´ (2x)

Jn 10:3 and he·calls·forth his·own sheep each·by name and
3Jn 1:14 Greet the friends each·by name.

G2596.9 PREP κατά (2x)

Ac 16:25 And at midnight Paul and Silas, while·praying,
2Ti 4:1 ·men and dead·men at his conspicuous·appearing

EG2596.9 (1x)

Col 2:6 Accordingly, *in the·same·manner* as yeu·personally·

G2596.10 PREP κατά (4x)

Ac 13:27 (the·ones being·read·aloud each and·every Sabbath
Ac 15:21 ·aloud in the gatherings each and·every Sabbath."
Ac 18:4 ·discussed in the gathering each and·every Sabbath,
1Co 16:2 Each first *day* of·the·week, let each·one of·yeu lay

G2596.11 PREP κατά (3x)

Lk 23:17 one·man to·them annually·at·this Sacred·Feast.
Mt 27:15 Now annually·at·this Sacred·Feast, the governor
Mk 15:6 Now annually·at·this Sacred·Feast, he·was·fully·

G2596.12 PREP κατά (58x)

Lk 2:31 which you·made·ready in front of·all the peoples;
Lk 4:14 and a·reputation went·forth concerning him in all the
Lk 6:23 in the heaven, for in the·same·manner, their fathers
Lk 6:26 well of·yeu! For in the·same·manner their fathers
Lk 8:39 he·went·away, officially·proclaiming in the whole
Lk 10:4 and yeu·should·greet not·even·one·man in the way.
Lk 15:14 ·*it*, there·occurred a·strong famine in that country,
Lk 17:30 "In the·same·manner shall·it·be in·that day *when*
Lk 23:5 "He·incites the people, instructing in all Judea,
Ac 3:13 handed·over, and yeu·denied him in front of·Pilate,
Ac 3:22 as myself; him yeu·shall·hear in all·things," "as·
Ac 9:31 in·fact, the Called·Out·citizenries in all of·Judea,
Ac 9:42 And it·became known in all Joppa, and many trusted
Ac 10:37 ·know the utterance occurring in all Judea,
Ac 11:1 and the brothers, the·ones being in Judea, heard that
Ac 13:1 among the Called·Out·citizenry being in Antioch,
Ac 15:23 to·*our*·brothers, the·ones in Antioch and Syria
Ac 15:36 we·should·visit our brothers in every city in
Ac 17:22 Athenians, I·observe how in all·things yeu *are*
Ac 19:23 And in that season, there·occurred no little
Ac 20:20 and have·instructed yeu publicly and in homes,
Ac 24:5 controversy among·all the Jews in The Land, and
Ac 24:12 ·crowd, neither in the gatherings, nor in the City.
Ac 24:14 the·things having·been·written in the Torah-Law
Ac 25:3 JeruSalem, while·they·make an·ambush in the way
Ac 26:11 ·honor·by·punishing them many·times in all the
Ac 26:13 day, O·king, I·saw in the way a·light from·heaven
Ac 27:27 ·about along the Adriatic·Sea, in *the* middle of·the
Heb 1:10 You, O·Lord, in *the* beginning laid·a·foundation·
Heb 3:3 glory than Moses, in as·much·as the·one planning·
Heb 3:8 in the Direct·Provocation, in the day of·the Proof·
Heb 4:15 but in all·points having·been·intently·tried in
Heb 4:15 having·been·intently·tried in similarity *to·us*, *yet*
Heb 9:5 is·not *the time for·us* to·say *anything* in particular.
Heb 9:9 the season, then·currently·standing, in which both
Heb 9:19 For with·every commandment in *the* Torah-Law
Gal 2:2 the Gentiles, but in private to·the·ones being·of·
Gal 2:11 to Antioch, I·withstood him in *his* face, because
Mt 14:13 in a·sailboat into a·desolate place in private. And
Mt 14:23 he·walked·up upon the mountain in private to·pray,
Mt 17:1 he·brings them up upon a·high mountain in private.
Mt 17:19 Then after·coming·alongside YeShua in private,
Mt 24:3 the disciples came·alongside him in private, saying
Mk 6:32 ·off to·a·desolate place in·the sailboat in private.
Mk 7:33 him aside from the crowd in private, *Jesus* cast his
Mk 9:2 them up upon a·high mountain in private, alone·by·

Mk 9:28 his disciples were·inquiring·of him in private,
Rm 1:15 In·this·manner, the *determined·purpose* in me *is*
Rm 14:15 *your* food, no·longer do·you·walk in love. Do·not
Rm 16:5 *greet* the Called·Out·citizenry *hosted* in their house.
2Th 2:3 thoroughly·delude yeu in not·even·one manner,
1Co 7:6 But I·say this in concession *concerning becoming*
1Co 14:40 must·be·done decently and in assigned·order.
1Co 16:19 ·the Called·Out·citizenry *hosted* in their house.
2Co 10:1 (*I*, who in personal·presence *am* in·fact lowly
Col 3:22 Yeu·must·listen·to·and·obey in all·things the·ones
Col 4:15 and the Called·Out·citizenry *hosted* in his house.
Phm 1:2 to·the Called·Out·citizenry *hosted* in your house.

G2596.13 PREP κατά (4x)
Lk 21:11 great earthquakes shall·be pervasive·in·all places,
Ac 8:1 were·dispersed pervasively·into·all the regions of·
Mt 24:7 and earthquakes shall·be pervasive·in·all places.
Mk 13:8 And earthquakes shall·be pervasive·in·all places,

G2596.14 PREP καθ´ (4x)
Ac 17:25 ·things, *himself being* pervasive·among all·things.
Ac 21:21 all the Jews *who·are* pervasive·among the Gentiles,
Ac 26:3 and issues *which·are* pervasive·among the·Judeans.
Eph 1:15 ·of the trust *which·is* pervasive·among yeu in the

G2596.15 PREP κατά (7x)
Lk 10:33 while·traveling, came adjacent·to *where* he *was*.
Ac 2:10 and *in* the parts of·Libya adjacent·to Cyrene, and
Ac 16:7 Coming adjacent·to Mysia, they·were·attempting to·
Ac 27:2 ·launched, intending to·sail adjacent·to the *coastal*
Ac 27:5 ·sailing·through the open·sea adjacent·to Cilicia and
Ac 27:7 and with·difficulty coming·to·be adjacent·to Cnidus,
Ac 27:7 ·sailed·leeward·near·to Crete, adjacent·to Salmone.

G2596.16 PREP κατά (2x)
Ac 16:7 they·were·attempting to·traverse toward Bithynia,
Ac 27:12 ·harbor of·Crete, looking·out toward *the* southwest

G2596.18 PREP κατ´ (2x)
Mt 20:17 ·took the twelve disciples aside privately by the
Mk 6:31 "Come·here yeu yeurselves aside privately into a·

G2596.19 PREP κατ´ (3x)
Ac 12:1 But that very season, King HerOd·Agrippa violently·
Ac 17:28 also certain of·yeur very·own poets have·declared,
Gal 3:1 truth, *before* whose very·own eyes YeShua Anointed

G2596.20 PREP καθ´ (6x)
Ac 25:23 regiment·commanders and the most prominent men
Gal 1:13 Judaism, that most exceedingly I·was·persecuting
Rm 7:13 may·become most exceedingly full·of·moral·failure
1Co 12:31 ·show to·yeu *the* most surpassingly·excellent way
2Co 1:8 in Asia, that most exceedingly, we·were·weighed·
2Co 4:17 for·us "a·most surpassingly·excellent unto

G2596.21 PREP κατά (1x)
Lk 1:18 "How shall·I·know this for·certain? For I·myself am

G2596.23 PREP κατά (1x)
1Co 11:4 having *his* head fully·covered, puts·to·shame his

G2597 κατα•βαίνω katabaínō *v.* (80x)
Roots:G2596 G0901-3 See:G2600

G2597.1 V-PAM-3S καταβαινέτω (1x)
Mt 24:17 must·not walk·down to·take·away anything out of·

G2597.1 V-PAP-GSM καταβαίνοντος (1x)
Jn 4:51 And with·him even·now walking·down, his slaves

G2597.1 V-PAP-GPM καταβαινόντων (2x)
Mt 17:9 And with·them walking·down off the mountain,
Mk 9:9 And with·them walking·down from the mountain,

G2597.1 V-IAI-3S κατέβαινεν (2x)
Lk 10:30 man·of·clay† was·walking·down from JeruSalem
Lk 10:31 priest·that·offers·sacrifices was·walking·down along

G2597.1 V-2AAI-3S κατέβη (6x)
Jn 2:12 After this, he·walked·down to CaperNaum (he and
Lk 2:51 And he·walked·down with them, and came to
Lk 18:14 "I·say to·yeu *that* this·man walked·down to his
Ac 7:15 So Jacob walked·down into Egypt, and he·
Ac 18:22 Called·Out·citizenry, he·walked·down to Antioch.
Ac 24:1 ·high·priest HananIah walked·down with the elders,

G2597.1 V-2AAI-3P κατέβησαν (4x)
Jn 6:16 occurred, his disciples walked·down to the sea,
Ac 8:38 to·stand·still. And they·both walked·down into the
Ac 14:25 in Perga, they·walked·down into Attalia.
Ac 16:8 And passing·by Mysia, they·walked·down to Troas.

G2597.1 V-2AAM-2S κατάβηθι (2x)
Jn 4:49 him, "Sir, walk·down prior·to my little·child dying.
Ac 10:20 after·rising·up, walk·down and traverse together

G2597.1 V-2AAM-3S καταβάτω (2x)
Lk 17:31 the home, must·not walk·down to·take them away;
Mk 13:15 on the rooftop must·not walk·down into the home,

G2597.1 V-2AAP-ASN καταβάν (1x)
Ac 23:10 squad·of·soldiers, upon·walking·down, to·seize

G2597.1 V-2AAP-DSM καταβάντι (1x)
Mt 8:1 And upon·walking·down from the mountain, large

G2597.1 V-2AAP-NSM καταβάς (4x)
Lk 6:17 And walking·down with them, he·stood·still in a·
Ac 10:21 Now after·walking·down to the men (the·ones
Ac 20:10 And walking·down, Paul fell·upon him, and after·
Ac 25:6 than ten days, *and·then* walking·down to Caesarea,

G2597.1 V-2AAP-NPM καταβάντες (2x)
Ac 8:15 who, after·walking·down, prayed concerning them,
Mk 3:22 the·ones already·walking·down from JeruSalem,

G2597.1 V-2AAS-3S καταβῇ (2x)
Jn 4:47 ·asking·of him that he·may·walk·down and may·heal
Ac 24:22 regiment·commander should·walk·down, I·shall·

G2597.1 V-RAP-NPM καταβεβηκότες (1x)
Ac 25:7 the Judeans having·walked·down from JeruSalem

G2597.2 V-FDI-3S καταβήσεται (2x)
Rm 10:7 or, "Who shall·descend into the bottomless·pit?
1Th 4:16 the Lord himself shall·descend from heaven with

G2597.2 V-PAI-3S καταβαίνει (1x)
Rv 16:21 ·of·a·talent·*(or·fifty·pounds)*) descends out of·the

G2597.2 V-PAN καταβαίνειν (1x)
Rv 13:13 that it·should·make fire to·descend from·out of·the

G2597.2 V-PAP-ASN καταβαῖνον (6x)
Jn 1:32 ·viewed the Spirit descending out of·heaven like a·
Jn 1:33 you·should·see the Spirit descending, and remaining
Ac 10:11 ·up, and a·certain vessel descending to him, as
Ac 11:5 a·clear·vision. A·certain vessel descending, as a·
Mt 3:16 he·saw the Spirit of·God descending like a·dove
Mk 1:10 and the Spirit like a·dove descending upon him.

G2597.2 V-PAP-ASF καταβαίνουσαν (3x)
Ac 8:26 the roadway, the·one descending from JeruSalem to
Rv 21:2 brand-new JeruSalem, descending from God out
Rv 21:10 the Holy JeruSalem, descending out of·the heaven

G2597.2 V-PAP-ASM καταβαίνοντα (3x)
Rv 10:1 another strong angel descending from·out of·the
Rv 18:1 ·things I·saw an·angel descending from·out of·the
Rv 20:1 And I·saw an·angel descending from·out of·the

G2597.2 V-PAP-APM καταβαίνοντας (1x)
Jn 1:51 angels of·God ascending and descending' upon the

G2597.2 V-PAP-NSN καταβαῖνον (1x)
Jac 1:17 endowment is from·above, descending from the

G2597.2 V-PAP-NSF καταβαίνουσα (1x)
Rv 3:12 JeruSalem, the·one descending out of·the heaven

G2597.2 V-PAP-NSM καταβαίνων (2x)
Jn 6:33 bread of·God is the·one descending from·out of·the
Jn 6:50 is the bread, the·one descending out of·the heaven,

G2597.2 V-IAI-3S κατέβαινεν (1x)
Jn 5:4 ·to·a·certain·season, an·angel was·descending on the

G2597.2 V-2AAI-1S κατέβην (1x)
Ac 7:34 groaning,' 'and I·descended to·snatch them out.

G2597.2 V-2AAI-3S κατέβη (6x)
Lk 8:23 And a·whirling of·wind descended upon the lake,
Mt 7:25 And the rain·storm descended, and the flood·waters
Mt 7:27 And the rain·storm descended, and the flood·waters
Eph 4:9 what is·it except that also he·descended first into
Rv 12:12 sea, because the Slanderer descended to yeu! *He·is*
Rv 20:9 And fire descended from God out of·the heaven and

G2597.2 V-2AAI-3P κατέβησαν (1x)
Ac 14:11 "The gods descended toward us being·in·the·

G2597.2 V-2AAM-2S κατάβηθι (1x)
Mt 27:40 If you·are a·son of·God, descend from the cross.

G2597.2 V-2AAM-2S-ATT κατάβα (1x)
Mk 15:30 save yourself, and descend from the cross!"

G2597.2 V-2AAM-3S καταβάτω (2x)
Mt 27:42 If he·is King of·IsraEl, let·him·descend now from
Mk 15:32 the King of·IsraEl, let·him·descend now from the

G2597.2 V-2AAN καταβῆναι (2x)
Lk 3:22 and the Holy Spirit descended in·a·bodily shape like
Lk 9:54 *that* we·should·declare fire to·descend from the

G2597.2 V-2AAP-NSM καταβάς (6x)
Jn 3:13 heaven, except the·one descending out of·the heaven
Jn 6:41 AM the bread, the·one descending out of·the heaven
Jn 6:51 living bread, the·one descending out of·the heaven.
Jn 6:58 is the bread, the·one descending out of·the heaven.
Mt 28:2 For Yahweh's angel, after·descending out of·heaven
Eph 4:10 The·one descending is himself also the·one

G2597.2 V-RAI-1S καταβέβηκα (2x)
Jn 6:38 because I·have·descended out of·the heaven, not in·
Jn 6:42 this·thing, 'I·have·descended out of·the heaven?

G2597.3 V-PAP-NPM καταβαίνοντες (1x)
Lk 22:44 like clots of·blood dropping·down upon the soil.

G2597.3 V-2AAI-3S κατέβη (1x)
Lk 19:6 And hastening, he·dropped·down; and rejoicing, he·

G2597.3 V-2AAM-2S κατάβηθι (1x)
Lk 19:5 "Zacchaeus, making·haste, drop·down. For today,

G2597.4 V-PAI-3S καταβαίνει (1x)
Jn 5:7 I·myself am·coming, another steps·down before me."

G2597.4 V-2AAP-NSM καταβάς (1x)
Mt 14:29 "Come." And after·stepping·down from the

G2598 κατα•βάλλω katabállō *v.* (3x)
Roots:G2596 G0906 Compare:G2311 G4815 G1080 See:G2602 G2845

G2598.1 V-PPP-NPM καταβαλλόμενοι (1x)
2Co 4:9 ·yet not being·forsaken; being·cast·down, but·yet

G2598.1 V-API-3S κατεβλήθη (1x)
Rv 12:10 legal·accuser of·our brothers is·cast·down, the·one

G2598.2 V-PMP-NPM καταβαλλόμενοι (1x)
Heb 6:1 ·of·maturity; not laying·down again *the* foundation

G2599 κατα•βαρέω katabaréō *v.* (1x)
Roots:G2596 G0916

G2599 V-AAI-1S κατεβάρησα (1x)
2Co 12:16 ·it·so, I·myself did·not impose·a·burden·on yeu.

G2600 κατά•βασις katábasis *n.* (1x)
Roots:G2597

G2600.2 N-DSF καταβάσει (1x)
Lk 19:37 even·now alongside the descent of·the Mount of·

G2601 κατα•βιβάζω katabibázō *v.* (2x)
Roots:G2596 G0973-1 See:G1688 G4246

G2601.1 V-FPI-2S καταβιβασθήσῃ (2x)
Lk 10:15 the heaven, you·shall·be·driven·down unto Hades.
Mt 11:23 unto the heaven, shall·be·driven·down unto Hades

G2602 κατα•βολή katabolḗ *n.* (11x)
Roots:G2598 Compare:G2310 G2845 G4815 See:G1080

G2602.4 N-ASF καταβολήν (1x)
Heb 11:11 a·miracle for an·ovulation of·a·single·seed *from*

G2602.5 N-GSF καταβολῆς (10x)
Jn 17:24 you·did·love me before *the* world's conception.
Lk 11:50 from *the* world's conception, may·be·sought·out
Heb 4:3 ·the works being·done from *the* world's conception.
Heb 9:26 many·times since *the* world's conception. But now
Mt 13:35 having·been·hidden from *the* world's conception."
Mt 25:34 ·made·ready for·yeu from *the* world's conception.
1Pe 1:20 ·been·foreknown before *the* world's conception, but
Eph 1:4 him before *the* world's conception for·us to·be holy
Rv 13:8 ·been·slaughtered from *the* world's conception.
Rv 17:8 life·above from *the* world's conception, looking·upon

G2603 κατα•βραβεύω katabrabeúō *v.* (1x)
Roots:G2596 G1018 Compare:G2729 G3884 G2940

G2603.4 V-PAM-3S καταβραβευέτω (1x)
Col 2:18 Let no·one manipulate·and·defraud yeu, *especially*

G2604 κατ•αγγελεύς katangêlêús *n.* (1x)
Roots:G2605

G2604 N-NSM καταγγελεύς (1x)
Ac 17:18 to·be an·ardent·proclaimer of·the strange·new

G2605 κατ•αγγέλλω katangéllō *v.* (20x)
Roots:G2596 G0032 See:G2604 G1804
G2605 V-PAI-1S καταγγέλλω (2x)
Ac 17:3 This Jesus (whom I·myself fully·proclaim to·yeu) is
Ac 17:23 ·knowing *him*, I·myself fully·proclaim this *God*
G2605 V-PAI-1P καταγγέλλομεν (1x)
Col 1:28 whom we·ourselves fully·proclaim, admonishing
G2605 V-PAI-2P καταγγέλλετε (1x)
1Co 11:26 ·drink this cup, yeu·fully·proclaim the Lord's
G2605 V-PAI-3P καταγγέλλουσιν (3x)
Ac 16:17 of·God Most·High, who fully·proclaim to·us *the*
Ac 16:21 and they·fully·proclaim customs which it·is·not
Php 1:16 In·fact, they·fully·proclaim Anointed-One out of·
G2605 V-PAN καταγγέλλειν (2x)
Ac 4:2 instructing the people and fully·proclaiming in Jesus
Ac 26:23 ·men *and* is·about to·fully·proclaim light to·the
G2605 V-PAP-DPM καταγγέλλουσιν (1x)
1Co 9:14 for·the·ones fully·proclaiming the good·news to·
G2605 V-PAP-NSM καταγγέλλων (1x)
1Co 2:1 or of·wisdom while·fully·proclaiming to·yeu the
G2605 V-PPI-3S καταγγέλλεται (3x)
Ac 13:38 of·moral·failures is·being·fully·proclaimed to·yeu.
Rm 1:8 that yeur trust is·being·fully·proclaimed in all the
Php 1:18 Anointed-One is·being·fully·proclaimed, and in
G2605 V-IAI-3P κατήγγελλον (1x)
Ac 13:5 they·were·fully·proclaiming the Redemptive-word
G2605 V-AAI-1P κατηγγείλαμεν (1x)
Ac 15:36 in which we·fully·proclaimed the Redemptive-word
G2605 V-2API-3S κατηγγέλη (1x)
Ac 17:13 of·God also was·fully·proclaimed in Berea by Paul
EG2605 (3x)
Ac 17:3 ·up from·among dead·men, and *fully·proclaiming*,
Php 1:17 But the *others fully·proclaim* out of·love, having·
2Co 10:14 yeu also, in *fully·proclaiming* the good·news of·

G2606 κατα•γελάω katagelā́ō *v.* (3x)
Roots:G2596 G1070
G2606 V-IAI-3P κατεγέλων (3x)
Lk 8:53 And they·were·laughing·down·at him, having·seen
Mt 9:24 she·sleeps." And they·were·laughing·down·at him.
Mk 5:40 And they·were·laughing·down at·him. But casting·

G2607 κατα•γινώσκω kataginṓskō *v.* (3x)
Roots:G2596 G1097
G2607.2 V-PAS-3S καταγινώσκῃ (2x)
1Jn 3:20 Because if our heart should·incriminate *us*, God is
1Jn 3:21 if our heart should·not incriminate us, *then* we·
G2607.2 V-RPP-NSM κατεγνωσμένος (1x)
Gal 2:11 *his* face, because he·was having·been·incriminated.

G2608 κατά•γνυμι katágnymi *v.* (4x)
Roots:G2596 G4486 Compare:G2806 G4937 See:G4366
G2608.2 V-AAI-3S κατεάξει (1x)
Mt 12:20 having·been·shattered he·did·not break·apart, and
G2608.2 V-AAI-3P κατέαξαν (2x)
Jn 19:32 soldiers came and in·fact broke·apart the legs of·the
Jn 19:33 ·now having·died, they·did·not break·apart his legs
G2608.2 V-2APS-3P κατεαγῶσιν (1x)
Jn 19:31 ·of Pilate that their legs should·be·broken·apart, and

G2609 κατ•άγω katágō *v.* (10x)
Roots:G2596 G0071 See:G0321
G2609.2 V-2AAI-1S κατήγαγον (1x)
Ac 23:28 ·were·calling him to·account, I·brought him down
G2609.2 V-2AAI-3P κατήγαγον (1x)
Ac 9:30 after·realizing *it*, the brothers brought him down to
G2609.2 V-2AAN καταγαγεῖν (1x)
Rm 10:6 heaven?" (that is, to·bring Anointed-One down),
G2609.2 V-2AAP-NSM καταγαγών (1x)
Ac 22:30 ·Sanhedrin to·come. And·then bringing Paul down
G2609.2 V-2AAS-2S καταγάγῃς (1x)
Ac 23:20 to·ask·of you that you·should·bring Paul down
G2609.2 V-2AAS-3S καταγάγῃ (1x)
Ac 23:15 ·commander that he·should·bring him down to yeu
G2609.3 V-2AAP-NPM καταγαγόντες (1x)
Lk 5:11 And mooring the sailboats upon the dry·ground,
G2609.3 V-2API-1S κατήχθημεν (2x)
Ac 21:3 we·were·sailing into Syria, and we·moored at Tyre,
Ac 27:3 with another *day of·sailing*, we·moored at Tsidon.
G2609.3 V-APP-NPM καταχθέντες (1x)
Ac 28:12 And after·being·moored at Syracuse, we·stayed·

G2610 κατ•αγωνίζομαι katagōnízômai *v.* (1x)
Roots:G2596 G0075 Compare:G0464 G5293
G2610.2 V-ADI-3P κατηγωνίσαντο (1x)
Heb 11:33 who through trust strenuously·subdued kingdoms,

G2611 κατα•δέω katadéō *v.* (1x)
Roots:G2596 G1210
G2611.2 V-AAI-3S κατέδησεν (1x)
Lk 10:34 coming·alongside *him*, he·bound·up his wounds,

G2612 κατά•δηλος katádēlôs *adj.* (1x)
Roots:G2596 G1212 See:G1552
G2612 A-NSN κατάδηλον (1x)
Heb 7:15 furthermore, it·is excessively fully·obvious, if,

G2613 κατα•δικάζω katadikázō *v.* (5x)
Roots:G2596 G1349 Compare:G2632
G2613.1 V-FPI-2S καταδικασθήσῃ (1x)
Mt 12:37 of·your words, you·shall·be·pronounced·guilty."
G2613.1 V-PAM-2P καταδικάζετε (1x)
Lk 6:37 ·not be·judged. Do·not pronounce·guilty, and no,
G2613.1 V-AAI-2P κατεδικάσατε (2x)
Mt 12:7 not have·pronounced·guilty the·ones without·guilt.
Jac 5:6 Yeu·pronounced·guilty *and* murdered the Righteous·
G2613.1 V-APS-2P καταδικασθῆτε (1x)
Lk 6:37 yeu·should·not be·pronounced·guilty. Fully·release

G2614 κατα•διώκω katadiṓkō *v.* (1x)
Roots:G2596 G1377
G2614.2 V-AAI-3P κατεδίωξαν (1x)
Mk 1:36 Simon and the·ones with him tracked him down.

G2615 κατα•δουλόω katadôulóō *v.* (2x)
Roots:G2596 G1402
G2615 V-PAI-3S καταδουλοῖ (1x)
2Co 11:20 yeu·bear·with·it, if anyone utterly·enslaves yeu,
G2615 V-AMS-3P καταδουλώσωνται (1x)
Gal 2:4 — in·order·that they·may·utterly·enslave us—

G2616 κατα•δυναστεύω katadynasteúō *v.* (2x)
Roots:G2596 G1413 Compare:G2634 G2961 xLangAlso:H6231 H7980
G2616.2 V-PAI-3P καταδυναστεύουσιν (1x)
Jac 2:6 ¿!·Is·it·not the wealthy·men *that* dominate yeu, and
G2616.2 V-PPP-APM καταδυναστευομένους (1x)
Ac 10:38 and healing all the·ones being·dominated by the

G2617 κατ•αισχύνω kataischýnō *v.* (13x)
Roots:G2596 G0153 Compare:G1788 See:G1870
G2617.1 V-FPI-3S καταισχυνθήσεται (2x)
Rm 9:33 any one trusting on him shall·not be·put·to·shame."
Rm 10:11 trusting on him shall·not be·put·to·shame."
G2617.1 V-PAI-2P καταισχύνετε (1x)
1Co 11:22 ·citizenry of·God, and put·to·shame the·ones not
G2617.1 V-PAI-3S καταισχύνει (3x)
Rm 5:5 And the Expectation does·not put·to·shame, because
1Co 11:4 *his* head fully·covered, puts·to·shame his head.
1Co 11:5 ·her head not·fully·veiled puts·to·shame her head,
G2617.1 V-PAS-3S καταισχύνῃ (2x)
1Co 1:27 world in·order·that he·may·put·to·shame the wise;
1Co 1:27 in·order·that he·may·put·to·shame the strong·
G2617.1 V-IPI-3P κατῃσχύνοντο (1x)
Lk 13:17 ·fully·set·opposed to·him were·put·to·shame. And
G2617.1 V-API-1S κατῃσχύνθην (1x)
2Co 7:14 concerning yeu, I·am·not put·to·shame; but·rather
G2617.1 V-APS-1P καταισχυνθῶμεν (1x)
2Co 9:4 ·say yeu *also*) should·be·put·to·shame in this firm·
G2617.1 V-APS-3S καταισχυνθῇ (1x)
1Pe 2:6 trusting on him, no, should·not be·put·to·shame."
G2617.1 V-APS-3P καταισχυνθῶσιν (1x)
1Pe 3:16 of·criminals, they·may·be·put·to·shame, the·ones

G2618 κατα•καίω katakaíō *v.* (12x)
Roots:G2596 G2545 Compare:G0355 G1714
G2618.2 V-FAI-3S κατακαύσει (2x)
Lk 3:17 but the chaff he·shall·completely·burn with·fire
Mt 3:12 the barn, but he·shall·completely·burn the chaff
G2618.2 V-FAI-3P κατακαύσουσιν (1x)
Rv 17:16 her flesh, and shall·completely·burn her with fire.
G2618.2 V-2FPI-3S κατακαήσεται (2x)
2Pe 3:10 *that·are* in it) shall·be·completely·burned·up.
1Co 3:15 work shall·be·completely·burned, he·shall·suffer·
G2618.2 V-FPI-3S κατακαυθήσεται (1x)
Rv 18:8 And she·shall·be·completely·burned with fire,
G2618.2 V-PPI-3S κατακαίεται (2x)
Heb 13:11 moral·failure, are·completely·burned outside the
Mt 13:40 are·collected and are·completely·burned in·fire, in·
G2618.2 V-IAI-3P κατέκαιον (1x)
Ac 19:19 scrolls, were·completely·burning *them* in·the·sight
G2618.2 V-AAN κατακαῦσαι (1x)
Mt 13:30 in bundles specifically to·completely·burn them,
G2618.2 V-2API-3S κατεκάη (2x)
Rv 8:7 third·part of·the trees was·completely·burned·up, and
Rv 8:7 ·up, and all green grass was·completely·burned·up.

G2619 κατα•καλύπτω katakalýptō *v.* (3x)
Roots:G2596 G2572 See:G0177
G2619.2 V-PPI-3S κατακαλύπτεται (1x)
1Co 11:6 For if a·woman is·not fully·veiled, also she·must·
G2619.2 V-PPM-3S κατακαλυπτέσθω (1x)
1Co 11:6 or to·be·shaved·bald, she·must·be·fully·veiled.
G2619.2 V-PPN κατακαλύπτεσθαι (1x)
1Co 11:7 a·man is·obligated not to·be·fully·veiling his head,

G2620 κατα•καυχάομαι katakaucháômai *v.* (4x)
Roots:G2596 G2744 Compare:G3528 G2358 G3166
G2620.1 V-PNI-2S κατακαυχᾶσαι (1x)
Rm 11:18 the branches. But if you·do·boast·over *them*, *it·is*
G2620.1 V-PNM-2S κατακαυχῶ (1x)
Rm 11:18 do·not boast·over the branches. But if you·do·
G2620.1 V-PNM-2P κατακαυχᾶσθε (1x)
Jac 3:14 yeur hearts, do·not boast·over and utter·lies against
G2620.2 V-PNI-3S κατακαυχᾶται (1x)
Jac 2:13 mercy boasts·triumphantly·over Tribunal·judgment.

G2621 κατά•κειμαι katákêimai *v.* (11x)
Roots:G2596 G2749
G2621.1 V-PNP-ASM κατακείμενον (1x)
Ac 9:33 Aeneas by·name, laying·down upon a·mat for
G2621.1 V-INI-3S κατέκειτο (2x)
Lk 5:25 of·them, taking·up what he·was·laying·down on,
Mk 2:4 mat on which the paralyzed·man was·laying·down.
G2621.2 V-PNN κατακεῖσθαι (1x)
Ac 28:8 *that* the father of·Poplius lay·ill, being·clenched
G2621.2 V-PNP-ASM κατακείμενον (1x)
Jn 5:6 Jesus, seeing this·man laying·ill and knowing that he·
G2621.2 V-INI-3S κατέκειτο (2x)
Jn 5:3 of·the·ones being·feeble were·laying·ill— blind, lame
Mk 1:30 mother-in-law was·laying·ill, burning·with·fever,
G2621.3 V-PNN κατακεῖσθαι (1x)
Mk 2:15 And it·happened, with him laying·back·to·eat in
G2621.3 V-PNP-ASM κατακείμενον (1x)
1Co 8:10 laying·back·and·eating in an·idol's·temple, shall
G2621.3 V-PNP-GSM κατακειμένου (1x)
Mk 14:3 as·he was·laying·back·and·eating, there·came a·
G2621.3 V-PNP-NPM κατακείμενοι (1x)
Lk 5:29 others that were laying·back·and·eating with them.

G2622 κατα•κλάω katakláō *v.* (2x)
Roots:G2596 G2806
G2622.2 V-AAI-3S κατέκλασεν (2x)
Lk 9:16 he·blessed them, and fully·broke *them*, and was·
Mk 6:41 ·blessed *it*. And he·fully·broke the loaves·of·bread

G2623 κατα•κλείω kataklêíō *v.* (2x)
Roots:G2596 G2808
G2623.2 V-AAI-1S κατέκλεισα (1x)
Ac 26:10 holy·ones I·myself permanently·shut·up in·prisons,
G2623.2 V-AAI-3S κατέκλεισεν (1x)

Κκ

Lk 3:20 all·*these*·things— that he·permanently·shut John up

G2624 κατα•κληρο•δοτέω kataklērôdôtéō *v.* (1x)
Roots:G2596 G2819 G1325

G2624.2 V-AAI-3S κατεκληροδότησεν (1x)
Ac 13:19 land of·Kenaan, he·fully·apportioned their land

G2625 κατα•κλίνω kataklínō *v.* (3x)
Roots:G2596 G2827

G2625.1 V-AAM-2P κατακλίνατε (1x)
Lk 9:14 "Make them fully·recline·back *by* fifty apiece *in*·

G2625.1 V-APS-2S κατακλιθῇς (1x)
Lk 14:8 ·banquet, you·should·not fully·recline·back in the

G2625.2 V-APN κατακλιθῆναι (1x)
Lk 24:30 with him fully·reclining·back·to·eat with them,

G2626 κατα•κλύζω kataklýzō *v.* (1x)
Roots:G2596 G2830 See:G2627 xLangAlso:H3999

G2626.2 V-APP-NSM κατακλυσθείς (1x)
2Pe 3:6 ·completely·destroyed, being·deluged with·water.

G2627 κατα•κλυσμός kataklysmós *n.* (4x)
Roots:G2626 Compare:G4215 G4132 xLangEquiv:H3999

G2627.2 N-NSM κατακλυσμός (2x)
Lk 17:27 the floating·ark, and·then the Deluge came and
Mt 24:39 they·did·not know … until the Deluge came, and

G2627.2 N-ASM κατακλυσμόν (1x)
2Pe 2:5 after·bringing a·Deluge upon a·world of·irreverent·

G2627.2 N-GSM κατακλυσμοῦ (1x)
Mt 24:38 the·ones that·were before the Deluge, *they·were*

G2628 κατ•α•κολουθέω katakôlôuthéō *v.* (2x)
Roots:G2596 G0190

G2628.2 V-AAP-NSF κατακολουθήσασα (1x)
Ac 16:17 *And* closely·following Paul and us, the·same·girl

G2628.2 V-AAP-NPF κατακολουθήσασαι (1x)
Lk 23:55 And closely·following, *the* women, also who were

G2629 κατα•κόπτω katakóptō *v.* (1x)
Roots:G2596 G2875

G2629.1 V-PAP-NSM κατακόπτων (1x)
Mk 5:5 yelling·out and fully·chopping·at himself with·stones

G2630 κατα•κρημνίζω katakrēmnízō *v.* (1x)
Roots:G2596 G2911

G2630.2 V-AAN κατακρημνίσαι (1x)
Lk 4:29 had·been·built, in·order to·throw him off·the·cliff.

G2631 κατά•κριμα katákrima *n.* (3x)
Roots:G2632 Compare:G1345

G2631 N-NSN κατάκριμα (1x)
Rm 8:1 not·even·one verdict·of·condemnation for·the·ones

G2631 N-ASN κατάκριμα (2x)
Rm 5:16 of·one *trespass* unto a·verdict·of·condemnation, but
Rm 5:18 men·of·clay† unto a·verdict·of·condemnation; even

G2632 κατα•κρίνω katakrínō *v.* (19x)
Roots:G2596 G2919 Compare:G2613

G2632 V-FAI-3S κατακρινεῖ (2x)
Lk 11:31 of·this generation, and she·shall·condemn them,
Mt 12:42 this generation, and shall·condemn it, because she·

G2632 V-FAI-3P κατακρινοῦσιν (4x)
Lk 11:32 with this generation, and they·shall·condemn it,
Mt 12:41 with this generation and shall·condemn it, because
Mt 20:18 and scribes, and they·shall·condemn him to·death
Mk 10:33 scribes. And they·shall·condemn him to·death and

G2632 V-FAP-NSM κατακρινῶν (1x)
Rm 8:34 Who·is the·one *that* shall·be·condemning? *It·is*

G2632 V-FPI-3S κατακριθήσεται (1x)
Mk 16:16 the·one not·already·trusting shall·be·condemned.

G2632 V-PAI-1S κατακρίνω (1x)
Jn 8:11 ·her, "Not·even·do I·myself condemn you. Traverse,

G2632 V-PAI-2S κατακρίνεις (1x)
Rm 2:1 you·judge the other, you·condemn yourself; for the·

G2632 V-AAI-3S κατέκρινεν (4x)
Jn 8:10 ·accusers? *Did* not·even·one·man condemn you?
Heb 11:7 house; through which he·condemned the world
Rm 8:3 moral·failure, condemned Moral·Failure in the flesh
2Pe 2:6 ·an·overturning·catastrophe, he·condemned *them*,

G2632 V-AAI-3P κατέκριναν (1x)
Mk 14:64 And they all condemned him to·be held·liable

G2632 V-API-3S κατεκρίθη (1x)
Mt 27:3 after·seeing that *YeShua* was·condemned, Judas, the·

G2632 V-APS-1P κατακριθῶμεν (1x)
1Co 11:32 we·should·not be·condemned together with·the

G2632 V-APS-2P κατακριθῆτε (1x)
Jac 5:9 brothers, lest yeu·should·be·condemned. Behold,

G2632 V-RPI-3S κατακέκριται (1x)
Rm 14:23 differently has·been·condemned if he·should·eat,

G2633 κατά•κρισις katákrisis *n.* (2x)
Roots:G2632

G2633 N-ASF κατάκρισιν (1x)
2Co 7:3 Not toward condemnation do·I·say *this*, for I·have·

G2633 N-GSF κατακρίσεως (1x)
2Co 3:9 For if the service of·the condemnation *had* glory, so·

G2634 κατα•κυριεύω katakyriêúō *v.* (4x)
Roots:G2596 G2961 Compare:G2616 xLangAlso:H7980

G2634.1 V-PAI-3P κατακυριεύουσιν (2x)
Mt 20:25 of·the Gentiles exercise·lordship·against them, and
Mk 10:42 ·over the Gentiles exercise·lordship·against them,

G2634.1 V-PAP-NPM κατακυριεύοντες (1x)
1Pe 5:3 as exercising·lordship·against the ones·assigned·by·

G2634.2 V-AAP-NSM κατακυριεύσας (1x)
Ac 19:16 leaping upon them and fully·dominating them, the

G2635 κατα•λαλέω katalaléō *v.* (5x)
Roots:G2637 Compare:G1225 G2723 xLangAlso:H3960

G2635 V-PAI-3S καταλαλεῖ (1x)
Jac 4:11 and judging his brother, he·speaks·against law and

G2635 V-PAI-3P καταλαλοῦσιν (1x)
1Pe 2:12 in·order·that, though they·speak·against yeu as

G2635 V-PAM-2P καταλαλεῖτε (1x)
Jac 4:11 Do·not speak·against one·another, brothers.

G2635 V-PAP-NSM καταλαλῶν (1x)
Jac 4:11 brothers. The·one speaking·against *his* brother and

G2635 V-PAS-3P καταλαλῶσιν (1x)
1Pe 3:16 ·order·that though they·should·speak·against yeu as

G2636 κατα•λαλία katalalía *n.* (2x)
Roots:G2637

G2636.2 N-NPF καταλαλιαί (1x)
2Co 12:20 ragings, contentions, backbitings, whisperings,

G2636.2 N-APF καταλαλιάς (1x)
1Pe 2:1 and hypocrisies, and envies, and all backbitings,

G2637 κατά•λαλος katálalôs *adj.* (1x)
Roots:G2596 G2980 Compare:G1228 See:G2636

G2637.2 A-APM καταλάλους (1x)
Rm 1:30 backbiters, detesters·of·God, abusively·insolent,

G2638 κατα•λαμβάνω katalambánō *v.* (15x)
Roots:G2596 G2983 Compare:G0726 G2729 G3528 G4084 G3539 G4920 See:G1949

G2638.1 V-PMI-1S καταλαμβάνομαι (1x)
Ac 10:34 "In truth, I·grasp that God is not one·who·is·

G2638.1 V-2AAI-3S κατέλαβεν (2x)
Jn 1:5 in the darkness, and the darkness did·not grasp it.
Rm 9:30 not pursuing righteousness, grasped righteousness,

G2638.1 V-2AAS-1S καταλάβω (1x)
Php 3:12 *it*, so·that also I·may·grasp onto that·for·which

G2638.1 V-2AAS-2P καταλάβητε (1x)
1Co 9:24 ·this·manner run, in·order·that yeu·may·grasp·*it*.

G2638.1 V-2AAS-3S καταλάβῃ (1x)
Mk 9:18 wherever *that spirit* should·grasp him, he·mangles

G2638.1 V-2AMN καταλαβέσθαι (1x)
Eph 3:18 yeu·may·have·full·strength to·grasp together with·

G2638.1 V-2AMP-NSM καταλαβόμενος (1x)
Ac 25:25 But I·myself, after·grasping him to·have·practiced

G2638.1 V-2AMP-NPM καταλαβόμενοι (1x)
Ac 4:13 and John, and grasping that they·were uneducated

G2638.1 V-API-1S κατελήφθην (1x)
Php 3:12 ·grasp onto that·for·which also I·am·grasped by the

G2638.1 V-RAN κατειληφέναι (1x)
Php 3:13 do·not reckon my·own·self to·have·grasped *it*. But

G2638.2 V-2AAS-3S καταλάβῃ (2x)
Jn 12:35 the light, lest darkness should·grab yeu. But the·
1Th 5:4 in·order·that the Day should·grab yeu as a·thief.

G2638.2 V-RPP-ASF κατειλημμένην (1x)
Jn 8:3 to him a·wife having·been·grabbed in adultery; and

G2638.3 V-API-3S κατειλήφθη (1x)
Jn 8:4 wife was·grabbed·suddenly *while* being·in·adultery,

G2639 κατα•λέγω katalégō *v.* (2x)
Roots:G2596 G3004 Compare:G0583

G2639.2 V-PPM-3S καταλεγέσθω (1x)
1Ti 5:9 Let a·solitary·widow be·registered *if she·is* not less·

EG2639.2 (1x)
1Ti 5:11 But decline *to·register* younger widows, for

G2640 κατά•λειμμα katáleimma *n.* (1x)
Roots:G2641 Compare:G3005 See:G2645 G5274-1 xLangAlso:H7611 H7605 H3499

G2640.3 N-NSN κατάλειμμα (1x)
Rm 9:27 sand of·the sea, the small·remnant shall·be·saved.

G2641 κατα•λείπω katalêípō *v.* (25x)
Roots:G2596 G3007 Compare:G5277 See:G1459

G2641.1 V-FAI-3S καταλείψει (3x)
Mt 19:5 cause a·man·of·clay† shall·leave·behind the father
Mk 10:7 cause a·man·of·clay† shall·leave·behind his father
Eph 5:31 ·this, a·man·of·clay† shall·leave·behind his father

G2641.1 V-PAI-3S καταλείπει (1x)
Lk 15:4 ·among them, does·not leave·behind the ninety-nine

G2641.1 V-PPP-GSF καταλειπομένης (1x)
Heb 4:1 with·a·promise being·left·behind *for·us* to·enter

G2641.1 V-2AAI-1S κατέλιπον (1x)
Tit 1:5 For·this, on·account·of·grace, I·left you behind in

G2641.1 V-2AAI-3S κατέλιπεν (2x)
Ac 18:19 and·these *two* he·left·behind at·that·location, but
Ac 24:27 ·favors with·the Judeans, left Paul behind having·

G2641.1 V-2AAI-3P κατέλιπον (1x)
Lk 20:31 the seven also; they·left·behind no children, and

G2641.1 V-2AAP-NSM καταλιπών (4x)
Lk 5:28 And leaving·behind absolutely·all, rising·up, he·
Mt 4:13 And upon·leaving Natsareth behind *and* coming *into*
Mt 16:4 And leaving them behind, he·went·off.
Mt 21:17 And leaving them behind, he·went·forth outside of·

G2641.1 V-2AAP-NPM καταλιπόντες (1x)
Ac 21:3 ·within·full·sight·of Cyprus and leaving it behind

G2641.1 V-2AAS-3S καταλίπῃ (1x)
Mk 12:19 should·die, and should·leave·behind a·wife, and

G2641.1 V-API-3S κατελείφθη (2x)
Jn 8:9 ·them; and Jesus alone was·left·behind— and·also the
Ac 2:31 that his soul 'was·not left·behind in Hades, neither

G2641.1 V-APN καταλειφθῆναι (1x)
1Th 3:1 ·longer, we·took·delight to·be·left·behind in Athens

G2641.1 V-RPP-NSM καταλελειμμένος (1x)
Ac 25:14 man having·been·left·behind *as* a·chained·prisoner

G2641.2 V-2AAI-3S κατέλιπεν (1x)
Lk 10:40 to·you that my sister abandoned me to·attend alone

G2641.2 V-AAP-APM καταλείψαντας (1x)
Ac 6:2 satisfactory to·us: abandoning the Redemptive-word

G2641.2 V-2AAP-NSM καταλιπών (1x)
Mk 14:52 But abandoning the linen·cloth, he·fled from them

G2641.3 V-2AAI-3S κατέλιπεν (1x)
Heb 11:27 By·trust, he·forsook Egypt (not fearing the rage

G2641.3 V-2AAP-NPM καταλιπόντες (1x)
2Pe 2:15 forsaking the straight way; they·are·led·astray,

G2641.4 V-2AAI-1S κατέλιπον (1x)
Rm 11:4 to·him? "'I·reserved to·myself seven·thousand

G2642 κατα•λιθάζω katalitházō *v.* (1x)
Roots:G2596 G3034

G2642 V-FAI-3S καταλιθάσει (1x)
Lk 20:6 all the people shall·fully·stone us to·death, for

G2643 κατ•αλλαγή katallagḗ *n.* (6x)
Roots:G2644 Compare:G0605 G2435

G2643.2 N-NSF καταλλαγή (1x)
Rm 11:15 ·away of·them *is* reconciliation for·*the*·world,

EG2643.2 (1x)
Rm 5:12 *a·reconciliation needed* on·account·of this: *that*

G2643.3 N-ASF καταλλαγήν (1x)
Rm 5:11 through whom now we·received the Reconciliation;
G2643.3 N-GSF καταλλαγῆς (2x)
2Co 5:18 giving to·us the Service of·the Reconciliation—
2Co 5:19 in us the Redemptive-word of·the Reconciliation.
EG2643.3 (1x)
2Co 6:3 Service *of·the Reconciliation* should·not be·blamed.

G2644 κατ•αλλάσσω katallássō *v.* (6x)
Roots:G2596 G0236 Compare:G1259 G2132 G2433 See:G0604 G2643
G2644.2 V-PAP-NSM καταλλάσσων (1x)
2Co 5:19 in Anointed-One presently·reconciling *the* world
G2644.2 V-AAP-GSM καταλλάξαντος (1x)
2Co 5:18 of·God, the·one already·reconciling us to·himself
G2644.2 V-2API-1P κατηλλάγημεν (1x)
Rm 5:10 ·being enemies, we·are·reconciled to·God through
G2644.2 V-2APM-2P καταλλάγητε (1x)
2Co 5:20 on·behalf of·Anointed-One, be·reconciled to·God!
G2644.2 V-2APM-3S καταλλαγήτω (1x)
1Co 7:11 or she·must·be·reconciled to·her husband. And a·
G2644.2 V-2APP-NPM καταλλαγέντες (1x)
Rm 5:10 more·so, after·being·reconciled, we·shall·be·saved

G2645 κατά•λοιπος katálôipôs *adj.* (1x)
Roots:G2596 G3062 See:G2640 xLangAlso:H7605 H3499
G2645.2 A-NPM κατάλοιποι (1x)
Ac 15:17 so·that the small·remnants of·the men·of·clay†

G2646 κατά•λυμα katályma *n.* (3x)
Roots:G2647 Compare:G3829 G5253 G3578 G0835 G3597 xLangAlso:H4411
G2646.2 N-NSN κατάλυμα (2x)
Lk 22:11 "Where is the local·travel·lodge, where I·may·eat
Mk 14:14 "Where is the local·travel·lodge where I·may·eat
G2646.2 N-DSN καταλύματι (1x)
Lk 2:7 there·was no place for·them at the local·travel·lodge.

G2647 κατα•λύω katalýō *v.* (17x)
Roots:G2596 G3089 Compare:G2673 G2507 See:G2646 xLangEquiv:H3885 xLangAlso:H4411
G2647.2 V-FAI-1S καταλύσω (1x)
Mk 14:58 'I·myself shall·demolish this Temple, the·one
G2647.2 V-FAI-3S καταλύσει (1x)
Ac 6:14 that this Jesus of·Natsareth shall·demolish this place
G2647.2 V-FPI-3S καταλυθήσεται (3x)
Lk 21:6 a·stone upon a·stone that shall·not be·demolished."
Ac 5:38 ·from·out of·men·of·clay†, it·shall·be·demolished.
Mt 24:2 upon a·stone that shall·not be·demolished, no."
G2647.2 V-PAM-2S κατάλυε (1x)
Rm 14:20 Do·not demolish the work of·God for·the·sake·of
G2647.2 V-PAP-NSM καταλύων (2x)
Mt 27:40 and saying, "The·one demolishing the Temple and
Mk 15:29 "Ah, the·one demolishing the Temple and
G2647.2 V-AAI-1S κατέλυσα (1x)
Gal 2:18 these·things which I·demolished, I·demonstrate
G2647.2 V-AAN καταλῦσαι (4x)
Ac 5:39 of·God, yeu·are·not able to·demolish it; *withdraw,*
Mt 5:17 ·not assume that I·came to·demolish the Torah-Law
Mt 5:17 prophets. I·did·not come to·demolish, but·rather to·
Mt 26:61 'I·am·able to·demolish the Temple of·God and
G2647.2 V-APS-3S καταλυθῇ (2x)
Mk 13:2 upon a·stone that should·not be·demolished, no."
2Co 5:1 of·the bodily·tent should·be·demolished, we·have
G2647.4 V-AAN καταλῦσαι (1x)
Lk 19:7 saying, "He·entered to·lodge with a·man *who·is*
G2647.4 V-AAS-3P καταλύσωσιν (1x)
Lk 9:12 and the countrysides, they·should·lodge and find

G2648 κατα•μανθάνω katamanthánō *v.* (1x)
Roots:G2596 G3129
G2648.2 V-2AAM-2P καταμάθετε (1x)
Mt 6:28 concerning apparel? Carefully·note the lilies of·the

G2649 κατα•μαρτυρέω katamartyréō *v.* (4x)
Roots:G2596 G3140
G2649 V-PAI-3P καταμαρτυροῦσιν (4x)
Mt 26:62 What *are* these·things they·testify·against you?
Mt 27:13 hear how·many·things they·testify·against you?
Mk 14:60 What·are these·things they·testify·against you?
Mk 15:4 See how·many·things they·testify·against you."

G2650 κατα•μένω kataménō *v.* (1x)
Roots:G2596 G3306 Compare:G2521 xLangAlso:H3427
G2650 V-PAP-NPM καταμένοντες (1x)
Ac 1:13 where they·were continuing·to·abide as·follows:

G2651 κατα•μόνας katamónas *adv.* (2x)
Roots:G2596 G3441 See:G5561
G2651.2 ADV καταμόνας (2x)
Lk 9:18 *usual time* to·be praying alone·by·himself, *that* the
Mk 4:10 And when he·was alone·by·himself, the·ones in·

G2652 κατ•ανά•θεμα katanáthêma *n.* (1x)
Roots:G2596 G0331 Compare:G2671
G2652.1 N-NSN κατανάθεμα (1x)
Rv 22:3 longer be any irrevocable·vow·to·destruction, but

G2653 κατ•ανα•θεματίζω katanathêmatízō *v.* (1x)
Roots:G2596 G0332 Compare:G2673 See:G2652
G2653.2 V-PAN καταναθεματίζειν (1x)
Mt 26:74 ·began to·take·an·irrevocable·vow·of·destruction

G2654 κατ•ανα•λίσκω katanalískō *v.* (1x)
Roots:G2596 G0355
G2654 V-PAP-NSN καταναλίσκον (1x)
Heb 12:29 for even our God *is* a·fully·consuming fire.

G2655 κατα•ναρκάω katanarkáō *v.* (3x)
Roots:G2596
G2655.3 V-FAI-1S καταναρκήσω (1x)
2Co 12:14 to yeu, and I·shall·not be·a·freeloader of·yeu. For
G2655.3 V-AAI-1S κατενάρκησα (2x)
2Co 11:9 I·was·not a·freeloader of·not·even·one·man. For
2Co 12:13 except that I myself was·not a·freeloader of·yeu?

G2656 κατα•νεύω katanêúō *v.* (1x)
Roots:G2596 G3506 Compare:G2678 See:G3573
G2656.2 V-AAI-3P κατένευσαν (1x)
Lk 5:7 And they·fully·beckoned to·the·ones participating, to·

G2657 κατα•νοέω katanôéō *v.* (14x)
Roots:G2596 G3539 Compare:G1689 G0816
G2657 V-PAI-2S κατανοεῖς (2x)
Lk 6:41 brother's eye, but do·not fully·observe the beam,
Mt 7:3 brother's eye, but do·not fully·observe the beam in
G2657 V-PAP-DSM κατανοοῦντι (1x)
Jac 1:23 ·resembled a·man fully·observing his natural face in
G2657 V-PAS-1P κατανοῶμεν (1x)
Heb 10:24 And we·should·fully·observe one·another to a·
G2657 V-IAI-1S κατενόουν (1x)
Ac 11:6 gazing·intently upon, I·was·fully·observing, and I·
G2657 V-IAI-3P κατενόουν (1x)
Ac 27:39 land, but they·were·fully·observing a·certain bay
G2657 V-AAI-3S κατενόησεν (2x)
Rm 4:19 in·the trust, he·did·not fully·observe his·own body,
Jac 1:24 For he·fully·observed himself and has·gone·away,
G2657 V-AAM-2P κατανοήσατε (3x)
Lk 12:24 "Fully·observe the ravens, because they·do·not
Lk 12:27 "Fully·observe how the lilies grow.
Heb 3:1 ·a·heavenly calling) fully·observe the Ambassador
G2657 V-AAN κατανοῆσαι (2x)
Ac 7:31 and with·him coming·alongside to·fully·observe *it,*
Ac 7:32 ·with·trembling, was·not daring to·fully·observe.
G2657 V-AAP-NSM κατανοήσας (1x)
Lk 20:23 But fully·observing their shrewd·cunning, he·

G2658 κατ•αντάω katantáō *v.* (13x)
Roots:G2596 G0470-2 Compare:G2064 G2185 G3854 G5348 See:G0528 G4876 G5221
G2658.2 V-AAI-1P κατηντήσαμεν (3x)
Ac 20:15 Sailing·off from·there, we·arrived the following
Ac 21:7 the voyage from Tyre, arrived at Ptolemais; and
Ac 28:13 ·roundabout from·there, we·arrived in Rhegium.
G2658.2 V-AAI-3S κατήντησεν (3x)
Ac 16:1 Then he·arrived in Derbe and Lystra.
Ac 18:19 Now he·arrived in Ephesus, and·these *two* he·left·
Ac 18:24 Now a·certain Jew arrived in Ephesus (Apollos
G2658.2 V-AAI-3P κατήντησαν (1x)
Ac 25:13 AgrIppa and BerNiki arrived in Caesarea to·greet
G2658.2 V-AAP-NPM καταντήσαντες (1x)
Ac 27:12 ·somehow they·might·be·able to·arrive at Phenice
G2658.3 V-AAI-3S κατήντησεν (1x)
1Co 14:36 from yeu? Or did·it·come·adjacent to yeu only?
G2658.4 V-AAI-3S κατήντησεν (1x)
1Co 10:11 for whom the ends of·the ages are·attained.
G2658.4 V-AAS-1S καταντήσω (1x)
Php 3:11 *in·order·that* if·somehow, I·may·attain to the
G2658.4 V-AAS-1P καταντήσωμεν (1x)
Eph 4:13 *for* so·long·as·until we·all should·attain unto the
G2658.5 V-AAN καταντῆσαι (1x)
Ac 26:7 day, expect *it* to·fully·come— concerning which

G2659 κατά•νυξις katányxis *n.* (1x)
Roots:G2660 See:G3506 G3571 xLangAlso:H8639
G2659.2 N-GSF κατανύξεως (1x)
Rm 11:8 gave them a·spirit of·a·stinging·numbness, eyes

G2660 κατα•νύσσω katanýssō *v.* (1x)
Roots:G2596 G3572
G2660.2 V-2API-3P κατενύγησαν (1x)
Ac 2:37 hearing *this,* they·were·fully·jabbed in·the heart,

G2661 κατ•αξιόω kataxiόō *v.* (4x)
Roots:G2596 G0515
G2661 V-API-3P κατηξιώθησαν (1x)
Ac 5:41 that they·were·accounted·fully·worthy to·be· on·
G2661 V-APN καταξιωθῆναι (1x)
2Th 1:5 yeu to·be·accounted·fully·worthy of·the kingdom
G2661 V-APP-NPM καταξιωθέντες (1x)
Lk 20:35 the·ones being·accounted·fully·worthy to·obtain
G2661 V-APS-2P καταξιωθῆτε (1x)
Lk 21:36 that yeu·may·be·accounted·fully·worthy to·utterly·

G2662 κατα•πατέω katapatéō *v.* (5x)
Roots:G2596 G3961 xLangAlso:H1758
G2662.1 V-PAN καταπατεῖν (1x)
Lk 12:1 such·that they·trampled·down one·another, *Jesus*
G2662.1 V-PPN καταπατεῖσθαι (1x)
Mt 5:13 to·be·cast out and to·be·trampled·down by the men·
G2662.1 V-AAP-NSM καταπατήσας (1x)
Heb 10:29 ·of·honor, the·one trampling·down the Son of·
G2662.1 V-AAS-3P καταπατήσωσιν (1x)
Mt 7:6 the pigs, lest they·should·trample them down among
G2662.1 V-API-3S κατεπατήθη (1x)
Lk 8:5 ·by the roadway, and it·was·trampled·down, and the

G2663 κατά•παυσις katápausis *n.* (9x)
Roots:G2664 Compare:G4520 G0372 xLangAlso:H4496
G2663.2 N-ASF κατάπαυσιν (8x)
Heb 3:11 'As·if they·shall·*ever*·enter into my complete·rest!'
Heb 3:18 'they·were·not to·enter into his complete·rest,' if·
Heb 4:1 ·enter into his complete·rest, we·should·be·alarmed,
Heb 4:3 trusting do·enter into the complete·rest— just·as he·
Heb 4:3 'as·if they·shall·*ever*·enter into my complete·rest,'"
Heb 4:5 As·if they·shall·*ever*·enter into my complete·rest."
Heb 4:10 already·entering into his complete·rest, he·himself
Heb 4:11 ·endeavor to·enter into that complete·rest, lest any·
G2663.2 N-GSF καταπαύσεως (1x)
Ac 7:49 Yahweh? Or what *is the* place of·my complete·rest?

G2664 κατα•παύω katapaúō *v.* (4x)
Roots:G2596 G3973 Compare:G0373 See:G2663 xLangAlso:H5117 H7673
G2664.1 V-AAI-3S κατέπαυσεν (1x)
Heb 4:10 he·himself also already·fully·ceased from his·own
G2664.3 V-AAI-3P κατέπαυσαν (1x)
Ac 14:18 these·things, they·fully·restrained the crowds not
G2664.4 V-AAI-3S κατέπαυσεν (1x)
Heb 4:4 ·manner, '"And God fully·rested in the seventh day
G2664.5 V-AAI-3S κατέπαυσεν (1x)
Heb 4:8 For if JoShua gave them complete·rest, he·would not

G2665 κατα•πέτασμα katapétasma *n.* (6x)
Roots:G2596 G4072 Compare:G2571 G1985-1
xLangEquiv:H6532 xLangAlso:H4539
G2665.1 N-NSN καταπέτασμα (3x)
Lk 23:45 was·darkened, and the curtain of·the Temple was·
Mt 27:51 And behold, the curtain of·the Temple is·torn in
Mk 15:38 And the curtain of·the Temple was·torn in two
G2665.1 N-ASN καταπέτασμα (1x)
Heb 9:3 And after the second curtain, *a·second* Tabernacle,
G2665.1 N-GSN καταπετάσματος (2x)
Heb 6:19 'and·also entering into the interior of·the curtain,'
Heb 10:20 he·inaugurated for·us through the curtain, that·is,

G2666 κατα•πίνω katapínō *v.* (7x)
Roots:G2596 G4095
xLangEquiv:H1104
G2666 V-PAP-NPM καταπίνοντες (1x)
Mt 23:24 ·out the gnat, but swallowing·up the camel.
G2666 V-2AAI-3S κατέπιεν (1x)
Rv 12:16 ·up her mouth, and swallowed·up the flood·water
G2666 V-API-3S κατεπόθη (1x)
1Co 15:54 ·written, "Death is·swallowed·up in victory."
G2666 V-API-3P κατεπόθησαν (1x)
Heb 11:29 (taking an·attempt) were·swallowed·up.
G2666 V-APS-3S καταποθῇ (2x)
2Co 2:7 such·a·man should·be·swallowed·up with·excessive
2Co 5:4 ·that the mortality may·be·swallowed·up by the
G2666.2 V-2AAS-3S καταπίῃ (1x)
1Pe 5:8 as a·roaring lion seeking whom he·may·swallow·up,

G2667 κατα•πίπτω katapíptō *v.* (2x)
Roots:G2596 G4098
G2667 V-PAN καταπίπτειν (1x)
Ac 28:6 ·with·fever or to·fall·down dead without·warning,
G2667 V-2AAP-GPM καταπεσόντων (1x)
Ac 26:14 "And with·all of·us already·falling·down upon the

G2668 κατα•πλέω katapléō *v.* (1x)
Roots:G2596 G4126
G2668 V-AAI-3P κατέπλευσαν (1x)
Lk 8:26 And they·sailed·down to the region of·the

G2669 κατα•πονέω katapônéō *v.* (2x)
Roots:G2596 G4188-1 Compare:G2872 G2577
See:G1278 G4190
G2669.2 V-PPP-ASM καταπονούμενον (1x)
2Pe 2:7 Lot being·worn·down·in·labored·anguish by the
G2669.2 V-PPP-DSM καταπονουμένῳ (1x)
Ac 7:24 for·the·one being·worn·down·in·labored·anguish,

G2670 κατα•ποντίζω katapôntízō *v.* (2x)
Roots:G2596 G4195 Compare:G1036
G2670 V-PPN καταποντίζεσθαι (1x)
Mt 14:30 and beginning to·be·plunged·down, he·yelled·out,
G2670 V-APS-3S καταποντισθῇ (1x)
Mt 18:6 neck, and *that* he·should·be·plunged·down in the

G2671 κατ•άρα katára *n.* (6x)
Roots:G2596 G0685 Compare:G2652 See:G2672
G2671.1 N-NSF κατάρα (1x)
Jac 3:10 same mouth come·forth blessing and cursing. My
G2671.2 N-NSF κατάρα (1x)
Gal 3:13 of·the Torah-Law, becoming a·curse on·our behalf
G2671.2 N-ASF κατάραν (1x)
Gal 3:10 of·Torah-Law, they·are under a·curse— for it·has·
G2671.2 N-GSF κατάρας (1x)
Gal 3:13 ·redeemed us out of·the curse of·the Torah-Law,
G2671.3 N-GSF κατάρας (2x)
Heb 6:8 and *is* close to·being·cursed, whose end *is* for
2Pe 2:14 *They·are* children of·*the*·curse,

G2672 κατ•αράομαι kataráômai *v.* (6x)
Roots:G2671 Compare:G2653 See:G1943-2 G0689-1
G2672 V-PNI-1P καταρώμεθα (1x)
Jac 3:9 And with it, we·curse the men·of·clay†, the·ones
G2672 V-PNM-2P καταρᾶσθε (1x)
Rm 12:14 the·ones persecuting yeu; bless and do·not curse.
G2672 V-PNP-APM καταρωμένους (2x)
Lk 6:28 bless the·ones cursing yeu, and pray on·behalf of·
Mt 5:44 yeur enemies, bless the·ones who·are·cursing yeu.
G2672 V-ADI-2S κατηράσω (1x)
Mk 11:21 which you·did·curse has·been·withered·away."
G2672 V-RPP-NPM κατηραμένοι (1x)
Mt 25:41 from me, the·ones having·been·cursed, into the

G2673 κατ•αργέω katargéō *v.* (27x)
Roots:G2596 G0691 Compare:G2647 G2758
G2673.2 V-FPI-3S καταργηθήσεται (2x)
1Co 13:8 knowledge, it·shall·be·fully·rendered·useless.
1Co 13:10 ·out of·a·portion shall·be·fully·rendered·useless.
G2673.2 V-PAI-1P καταργοῦμεν (1x)
Rm 3:31 So·then, do·we·fully·render·useless *the* Torah-Law
G2673.2 V-PAI-3S καταργεῖ (1x)
Lk 13:7 For·what·purpose·does·it also fully·render the soil
G2673.2 V-PPP-GPM καταργουμένων (1x)
1Co 2:6 present·age, the·ones being·fully·rendered·useless.
G2673.3 V-PPI-3S καταργεῖται (1x)
1Co 15:26 last enemy *that* is·fully·rendered·inert *is* Death.
G2673.3 V-AAP-NSM καταργήσας (1x)
Eph 2:15 after·fully·rendering·inert in his flesh the hostility
G2673.3 V-AAS-3S καταργήσῃ (1x)
1Co 1:28 in·order·that he·should·fully·render·inert the·
G2673.4 V-FAI-3S καταργήσει (2x)
2Th 2:8 mouth and shall·fully·render·inoperative with·the
1Co 6:13 but God shall·fully·render·inoperative even this
G2673.4 V-FPI-3P καταργηθήσονται (1x)
1Co 13:8 they·shall·be·fully·rendered·inoperative; if·also
G2673.4 V-PPI-3S καταργεῖται (1x)
2Co 3:14 certain *veil* which is·fully·rendered·inoperative in
G2673.4 V-PPP-GSN καταργουμένου (1x)
2Co 3:13 with·the *veil* being·fully·rendered·inoperative.
G2673.4 V-APS-3S καταργηθῇ (1x)
Rm 6:6 of·moral·failure may·be·fully·rendered·inoperative,
G2673.5 V-FAI-3S καταργήσει (1x)
Rm 3:3 ¿!·Shall their lack·of·trust fully·nullify the trust of·
G2673.5 V-PPP-ASF καταργουμένην (1x)
2Co 3:7 *Service of·Death* presently·being·fully·nullified)—
G2673.5 V-PPP-NSN καταργούμενον (1x)
2Co 3:11 *of·Death* is·being·fully·nullified on·account·of
G2673.5 V-AAN καταργῆσαι (1x)
Gal 3:17 such·for it to·fully·nullify the promise.
G2673.5 V-AAP-GSM καταργήσαντος (1x)
2Ti 1:10 *·is*, in·fact, *the·one* already·fully·nullifying Death,
G2673.5 V-API-1P κατηργήθημεν (1x)
Rm 7:6 But right·now, we·are·fully·nullified from the
G2673.5 V-API-2P κατηργήθητε (1x)
Gal 5:4 yeu·are·rendered·fully·nullified from the
G2673.5 V-RPI-3S κατήργηται (3x)
Gal 5:11 ·offense of·the cross has·been·fully·nullified.
Rm 4:14 ·void, and the promise has·been·fully·nullified.
Rm 7:2 should·die, she·has·been·fully·nullified from the
G2673.6 V-AAS-3S καταργήσῃ (2x)
Heb 2:14 he·may·fully·render·impotent the·one having the
1Co 15:24 whenever he·should·fully·render·impotent every
G2673.7 V-RAI-1S κατήργηκα (1x)
1Co 13:11 a·man, I·have·fully·put·to·rest the·things of·the

G2674 κατ•αριθμέω katarithméō *v.* (1x)
Roots:G2596 G0705 Compare:G4785
G2674 V-RPP-NSM κατηριθμημένος (1x)
Ac 1:17 he·was having·been·fully·numbered together with·

G2675 κατ•αρτίζω katartízō *v.* (13x)
Roots:G2596 G0739 Compare:G0600 G3340
G2675.1 V-AMI-2S κατηρτίσω (2x)
Heb 10:5 want, but you·completely·formed a·body for·me.
Mt 21:16 sucklings you·completely·formed strong·praise"?
G2675.1 V-RPN κατηρτίσθαι (1x)
Heb 11:3 ages to·have·been·completely·formed by·an· of·
G2675.1 V-RPP-APN κατηρτισμένα (1x)
Rm 9:22 of·wrath having·been·completely·formed for·total·
G2675.2 V-PAP-APM καταρτίζοντας (2x)
Mt 4:21 their father Zebedee, completely·repairing their nets
Mk 1:19 *were* in the sailboat completely·repairing the nets.
G2675.3 V-PAM-2P καταρτίζετε (1x)
Gal 6:1 spiritual) must·completely·reform such·a·man in a·
G2675.3 V-PPM-2P καταρτίζεσθε (1x)
2Co 13:11 be·glad. Be·completely·reformed, be·comforted
G2675.3 V-AAN καταρτίσαι (1x)
1Th 3:10 yeur face, and to·completely·reform the lackings
G2675.3 V-AAO-3S καταρτίσαι (2x)
Heb 13:21 may·he·completely·reform yeu unto every
1Pe 5:10 ·while, may he·himself completely·reform yeu,
G2675.3 V-RPP-NSM κατηρτισμένος (1x)
Lk 6:40 everyone having·been·completely·reformed shall·be
G2675.3 V-RPP-NPM κατηρτισμένοι (1x)
1Co 1:10 yeu·may·be having·been·completely·reformed into

G2676 κατ•άρτισις katártisis *n.* (1x)
Roots:G2675 Compare:G0342 G0605 G1357 G3824
G2676.1 N-ASF κατάρτισιν (1x)
2Co 13:9 we·well-wish, *even* yeur complete·reformation.

G2677 κατ•αρτισμός katartismós *n.* (1x)
Roots:G2675
G2677 N-ASM καταρτισμόν (1x)
Eph 4:12 toward the complete·development of·the holy·ones

G2678 κατα•σείω kataseíō *v.* (4x)
Roots:G2596 G4579 Compare:G3506 G2656
G2678.2 V-AAI-3S κατέσεισεν (1x)
Ac 21:40 on the stairs, motioned with·his hand to·the people
G2678.2 V-AAP-NSM κατασείσας (3x)
Ac 12:17 But motioning to·them with·his hand to·stay·silent,
Ac 13:16 Paul, standing·up and motioning with·his hand,
Ac 19:33 And AlexAnder, motioning with·his hand, was·

G2679 κατα•σκάπτω kataskáptō *v.* (2x)
Roots:G2596 G4626 Compare:G4485 G4938
G2679.2 V-AAI-3P κατέσκαψαν (1x)
Rm 11:3 completely·broke·down·and·foundationally·ruined
G2679.4 V-RPP-APN κατεσκαμμένα (1x)
Ac 15:16 of·it having·been·foundationally·ruined, and I·

G2680 κατα•σκευάζω kataskêuázō *v.* (11x)
Roots:G2596 G4632 Compare:G2090 G4294
See:G0180-2
G2680.1 V-FAI-3S κατασκευάσει (3x)
Lk 7:27 ·presence, who shall·fully·prepare your way before
Mt 11:10 ·presence, who shall·fully·prepare your way
Mk 1:2 personal·presence, who shall·fully·prepare your way
G2680.1 V-PPP-GSF κατασκευαζομένης (1x)
1Pe 3:20 with·a·floating·ark being·fully·prepared, in which
G2680.1 V-AAI-3S κατεσκεύασεν (1x)
Heb 11:7 ·apprehension, fully·prepared a·floating·ark for
G2680.1 V-RPP-ASM κατεσκευασμένον (1x)
Lk 1:17 a·People having·been·fully·prepared for·Yahweh."
G2680.1 V-RPP-GPM κατεσκευασμένων (1x)
Heb 9:6 with·these·things having·been·fully·prepared in·,
G2680.2 V-PPI-3S κατασκευάζεται (1x)
Heb 3:4 For every house is·planned·and·constructed by some
G2680.2 V-AAP-NSM κατασκευάσας (2x)
Heb 3:3 ·as the·one planning·and·constructing the house has
Heb 3:4 but the·one planning·and·constructing all·things *is*
G2680.2 V-API-3S κατεσκευάσθη (1x)
Heb 9:2 For a·Tabernacle was·planned·and·constructed; the

G2681 κατα•σκηνόω kataskēnóō *v.* (4x)
Roots:G2596 G4637 Compare:G3924-2 G4759-2
See:G2682
G2681.1 V-FAI-3S κατασκηνώσει (1x)
Ac 2:26 yet even my flesh shall·fully·encamp in expectation,
G2681.2 V-PAN κατασκηνοῦν (2x)
Mt 13:32 of·the sky to·come and to·nest on its branches.
Mk 4:32 birds of·the sky to·be·able to·nest under its shade.
G2681.2 V-AAI-3S κατεσκήνωσεν (1x)
Lk 13:19 and the birds of·the sky nested in its branches.

G2682 κατα•σκήνωσις kataskḗnōsis *n.* (2x)
Roots:G2681 See:G4633 G3925
G2682.2 N-APF κατασκηνώσεις (2x)
Lk 9:58 and the birds of·the sky *have* nests, but the Son of·
Mt 8:20 and the birds of·the sky *have* nests, but the Son of·

G2683 κατα•σκιάζω kataskiázō *v.* (1x)
Roots:G2596 G4639 See:G1982
G2683 V-PAP-NPN κατασκιάζοντα (1x)
Heb 9:5 of·glory fully·overshadowing the atonement·seat·

G2684 κατα•σκοπέω kataskôpéō *v.* (1x)
Roots:G2685
G2684.1 V-AAN κατασκοπῆσαι (1x)
Gal 2:4 came·in·with·ulterior·motives to·spy·out our liberty

G2685 κατά•σκοπος katáskôpôs *n.* (1x)
Roots:G2596 G4649 Compare:G1455
G2685 N-APM κατασκόπους (1x)
Heb 11:31 ·being·obstinate, accepting the spies with peace.

G2686 κατα•σοφίζομαι katasôphízômai *v.* (1x)
Roots:G2596 G4679
G2686.2 V-ADP-NSM κατασοφισάμενος (1x)
Ac 7:19 ·man, being·skillfully·shrewd·against our kindred,

G2687 κατα•στέλλω katastéllō *v.* (2x)
Roots:G2596 G4724
G2687.3 V-AAP-NSM καταστείλας (1x)
Ac 19:35 And after·fully·quieting·down the crowd, the
G2687.3 V-RPP-APM κατεσταλμένους (1x)
Ac 19:36 to·subsist having·been·fully·quieted·down and to·

G2688 κατ•άστημα katástēma *n.* (1x)
Roots:G2525 Compare:G0391 G1382
G2688.2 N-DSN καταστήματι (1x)
Tit 2:3 *they·be* in a·demeanor befitting·of·sacred·women, not

G2689 κατα•στολή katastôlḗ *n.* (1x)
Roots:G2687 Compare:G4749 G4158 G1742 G2440 G2441 xLangAlso:H4594
G2689.3 N-DSF καταστολῇ (1x)
1Ti 2:9 fully·modest·and·concealing·apparel with modesty·

G2690 κατα•στρέφω katastréphō *v.* (2x)
Roots:G2596 G4762
G2690 V-AAI-3S κατέστρεψεν (2x)
Mt 21:12 Sanctuary·Atrium, and he·overturned the tables
Mk 11:15 Sanctuary·Atrium, and he·overturned the tables

G2691 κατα•στρηνιάω katastrēniáō *v.* (1x)
Roots:G2596 G4763 Compare:G4684
G2691.2 V-AAS-3P καταστρηνιάσωσιν (1x)
1Ti 5:11 they·would·live·luxuriously·and·pleasurably·contrary·to

G2692 κατα•στροφή katastrôphḗ *n.* (2x)
Roots:G2690 Compare:G0646 G5289
G2692.2 N-DSF καταστροφῇ (2x)
2Pe 2:6 and Gomorrah with·an·overturning·catastrophe, he·
2Ti 2:14 toward an·overturning·catastrophic·ruin of·the·ones

G2693 κατα•στρώννυμι katastrṓnnymi *v.* (1x)
Roots:G2596 G4766 Compare:G3817 xLangAlso:H7819
G2693.3 V-API-3P κατεστρώθησαν (1x)
1Co 10:5 ·not take·delight, for they·were·struck·down in the

G2694 κατα•σύρω katasýrō *v.* (1x)
Roots:G2596 G4951
G2694 V-AAS-3S κατασύρῃ (1x)
Lk 12:58 from him, lest he·should·drag you down toward

G2695 κατα•σφάττω katasphátto *v.* (1x)
Roots:G2596 G4969 See:G4967
G2695 V-AAM-2P κατασφάξατε (1x)
Lk 19:27 *them* here, and fully·slaughter *them* before me.

G2696 κατα•σφραγίζω katasphragízō *v.* (1x)
Roots:G2596 G4972
G2696 V-RPP-ASN κατεσφραγισμένον (1x)
Rv 5:1 having·been·fully·sealed·up with·seven official·

G2697 κατ•άσχεσις katáschêsis *n.* (2x)
Roots:G2722 Compare:G2933 xLangEquiv:H0272 xLangAlso:H4181
G2697.2 N-ASF κατάσχεσιν (1x)
Ac 7:5 to·give it to·him for a·territorial·possession and to·his
G2697.2 N-DSF κατασχέσει (1x)
Ac 7:45 JoShua into the territorial·possession of·the Gentiles,

G2698 κατα•τίθημι katatíthēmi *v.* (3x)
Roots:G2596 G5087 Compare:G2343
G2698.1 V-AAI-3S κατέθηκεν (1x)
Mk 15:46 him in·the linen·cloth and fully·laid him in a·
G2698.2 V-2AMN καταθέσθαι (2x)
Ac 24:27 wanting to·store·up influential·favors with·the
Ac 25:9 wanting to·store·up influential·favor with·the

G2699 κατα•τομή katatômḗ *n.* (1x)
Roots:G2596 G5058-2 Compare:G0609 G4061
G2699.2 N-ASF κατατομήν (1x)
Php 3:2 bad workmen; look·out·for the mutilation·of·flesh!

G2700 κατα•τοξεύω katatôxêúō *v.* (1x)
Roots:G2596 G5115 Compare:G0190-2 xLangAlso:H3384
G2700 V-FPI-3S κατατοξευθήσεται (1x)
Heb 12:20 ·stones·at, or shall·be·shot·down with·a·javelin."

G2701 κατα•τρέχω katatréchō *v.* (1x)
Roots:G2596 G5143
G2701 V-2AAI-3S κατέδραμεν (1x)
Ac 21:32 who from·this·same·hour, ran·down to them,

G2702 κατα•φέρω kataphérō *v.* (3x)
Roots:G2596 G5342 Compare:G4784 See:G5586
G2702.2 V-PPP-NSM καταφερόμενος (1x)
Ac 20:9 becoming·weighed·down with·a·deep heavy·sleep.
G2702.2 V-APP-NSM κατενεχθείς (1x)
Ac 20:9 *and* after·being·weighed·down with heavy·sleep,
G2702.3 V-AAI-1S κατήνεγκα (1x)
Ac 26:10 ·executed, I·voted a·black·pebble *against·them.*

G2703 κατα•φεύγω kataphêúgō *v.* (2x)
Roots:G2596 G5343
G2703.1 V-2AAI-3P κατέφυγον (1x)
Ac 14:6 ·of *it, the ambassadors* fled·down to Lystra and
G2703.2 V-2AAP-NPM καταφυγόντες (1x)
Heb 6:18 the·ones fleeing·for·refuge) to·take·secure·hold of·

G2704 κατα•φθείρω kataphthéírō *v.* (2x)
Roots:G2596 G5351 Compare:G1311 See:G5356
G2704.2 V-2FPI-3P καταφθαρήσονται (1x)
2Pe 2:12 ·ignorant), they·shall·be·fully·corrupted in their
G2704.2 V-RPP-NPM κατεφθαρμένοι (1x)
2Ti 3:8 their mind having·been·fully·corrupted, disqualified

G2705 κατα•φιλέω kataphiléō *v.* (6x)
Roots:G2596 G5368
G2705 V-PAP-NSF καταφιλοῦσα (1x)
Lk 7:45 ·in, did·not let·up·on earnestly·kissing my feet.
G2705 V-IAI-3S κατεφίλει (1x)
Lk 7:38 of·her head, and she·was·earnestly·kissing his feet
G2705 V-IAI-3P κατεφίλουν (1x)
Ac 20:37 upon Paul's neck, they·were·earnestly·kissing him,
G2705 V-AAI-3S κατεφίλησεν (3x)
Lk 15:20 ·fell upon his neck and earnestly·kissed him.
Mt 26:49 "Be·well, Rabbi," and earnestly·kissed him.
Mk 14:45 "Rabbi, Rabbi," and he·earnestly·kissed him.

G2706 κατα•φρονέω kataphrônéō *v.* (9x)
Roots:G2596 G5426 Compare:G4065 See:G2707 xLangEquiv:H0959
G2706 V-FAI-3S καταφρονήσει (2x)
Lk 16:13 ·hold·tightly to·one and shall·despise the other.
Mt 6:24 ·shall·hold·tightly to·one and shall·despise the other
G2706 V-PAI-2S καταφρονεῖς (1x)
Rm 2:4 Or do·you·despise the wealth of·his kindness,
G2706 V-PAI-2P καταφρονεῖτε (1x)
1Co 11:22 in? Or do·yeu·despise the Called·Out·citizenry
G2706 V-PAM-3S καταφρονείτω (1x)
1Ti 4:12 Let no·man despise your youth, but·rather become
G2706 V-PAM-3P καταφρονείτωσαν (1x)
1Ti 6:2 masters that·trust·*in·Jesus,* do·not despise *them,*
G2706 V-PAP-APM καταφρονοῦντας (1x)
2Pe 2:10 longing, and·also despising sovereign·lordship.
G2706 V-AAP-NSM καταφρονήσας (1x)
Heb 12:2 patiently·endured a·cross of·shame, despising *it,*
G2706 V-AAS-2P καταφρονήσητε (1x)
Mt 18:10 ·see·to·it *that* yeu·should·not despise one of·these

G2707 κατα•φροντής kataphrôntḗs *n.* (1x)
Roots:G2706 Compare:G3060 G0989 xLangAlso:H0959
G2707 N-NPM καταφρονηταί (1x)
Ac 13:41 "Yeu·despisers, see, and intently·look, and be·

G2708 κατα•χέω katachéō *v.* (2x)
Roots:G2596 G5502-5 Compare:G1632 G4377-2 G4378 G4472 G0907
G2708 V-AAI-3S κατέχεεν (2x)
Mt 26:7 ·valuable ointment, and she·poured·*it*·down on his
Mk 14:3 upon·shattering the alabaster·flask, she·poured *the*

G2709 κατα•χθόνιος katachthóniôs *adj.* (1x)
Roots:G2596
G2709.2 A-GPM καταχθονίων (1x)
Php 2:10 and of·terrestrial·ones, and subterrestrial·ones),

G2710 κατα•χράομαι katachráômai *v.* (2x)
Roots:G2596 G5530
G2710 V-PNP-NPM καταχρώμενοι (1x)
1Co 7:31 ·ones using this world, as not abusing *it* … for the
G2710 V-ADN καταχρήσασθαι (1x)
1Co 9:18 without·charge, in·order not to·abuse my privilege

G2711 κατα•ψύχω katapsýchō *v.* (1x)
Roots:G2596 G5594
G2711 V-AAS-3S καταψύξῃ (1x)
Lk 16:24 ·his finger in·water and may·cool·down my tongue,

G2712 κατ•είδωλος katêídōlôs *adj.* (1x)
Roots:G2596 G1497
G2712 A-ASF κατείδωλον (1x)
Ac 17:16 upon·observing the city being utterly·idolatrous.

G2713 κατ•έν•αντι katénanti *adv.* (5x)
Roots:G2596 G1725 Compare:G0561
G2713.2 ADV κατέναντι (2x)
Mk 12:41 after·sitting·down directly·opposite the treasury·
Mk 13:3 of·Olives directly·opposite the Sanctuary·Estate,
G2713.3 ADV κατέναντι (3x)
Lk 19:30 Head·on·out into the village directly·before *yeu*; in
Mk 11:2 "Head·on·out into the village directly·before yeu,
Rm 4:17 *And being* directly·before God whom he·trusted

G2714 κατ•εν•ώπιον katênṓpiôn *prep.* (5x)
Roots:G2596 G1799
G2714 PREP κατενώπιον (5x)
Jud 1:24 without·blemish directly·in·the·sight of·his glory
2Co 2:17 ·out of·God *being* directly·in·the·sight of·God, we·
2Co 12:19 We·speak *being* directly·in·the·sight of·God in
Eph 1:4 and without·blemish directly·in·the·sight of·him—
Col 1:22 ·any·charge·of·wrong·doing directly·in·the·sight—

G2715 κατ•εξουσιάζω katêxôusiázō *v.* (2x)
Roots:G2596 G1850
G2715 V-PAI-3P κατεξουσιάζουσιν (2x)
Mt 20:25 *that·are* great exercise·authority·against them.
Mk 10:42 their great·ones exercise·authority·against them.

G2716 κατ•εργάζομαι katêrgázômai *v.* (26x)
Roots:G2596 G2038 Compare:G1090
G2716.2 V-PNI-1S κατεργάζομαι (3x)
Rm 7:15 For I·do·not know *why* I·perform that·which *I·do.*
Rm 7:17 *it·is* no·longer I·myself that·performs it, but·rather
Rm 7:20 *it·is* no·longer I·myself that·performs it, but·rather
G2716.2 V-PNN κατεργάζεσθαι (1x)
Rm 7:18 ·me, but *how* to·perform the morally·good·thing, I·
G2716.2 V-PNP-GSM κατεργαζομένου (1x)
Rm 2:9 every soul of·a·man·of·clay† performing the wrong,
G2716.2 V-PNP-NPM κατεργαζόμενοι (1x)
Rm 1:27 with males performing the dishonorable,·indecent·act
G2716.2 V-ADP-ASM κατεργασάμενον (1x)
1Co 5:3 the·one performing this·thing in·this·manner:
G2716.2 V-API-3S κατειργάσθη (1x)
2Co 12:12 of·an·ambassador were·performed among yeu
G2716.3 V-PNI-3S κατεργάζεται (7x)
Rm 4:15 For the Torah-Law accomplishes wrath (for where
Jac 1:3 ·testing of·yeur trust accomplishes patient·endurance.
Jac 1:20 wrath does·not accomplish God's righteousness.
2Co 4:17 momentary tribulation is·accomplishing for·us

2Co 7:10 according·to God accomplishes repentance unto
2Co 7:10 but the grief of·the world accomplishes death.
2Co 9:11 all fidelity, which is·accomplishing through us an·
G2716.3 V-PNM-2P κατεργάζεσθε (1x)
Php 2:12 and trembling, accomplish the *determined·purpose*
G2716.3 V-PNP-NSF κατεργαζομένη (1x)
Rm 7:13 *to·be* moral·failure, is·accomplishing death in·me
G2716.3 V-ADI-3S κατειργάσατο (3x)
Rm 7:8 through the commandment, accomplished in me all·
Rm 15:18 Anointed-One already·accomplished through me
2Co 7:11 *see* how·much diligence it·did·accomplish in·yeu,
G2716.3 V-ADN κατεργάσασθαι (1x)
1Pe 4:3 *was* sufficient for·us to·have·accomplished the will
G2716.3 V-ADP-NSM κατεργασάμενος (1x)
2Co 5:5 And the·one already·accomplishing for us this very·
G2716.3 V-ADP-NPM κατεργασάμενοι (1x)
Eph 6:13 evil day, and after·accomplishing absolutely·all,
G2716.4 V-PNI-3S κατεργάζεται (1x)
Rm 5:3 the tribulation fully·cultivates patient·endurance,
EG2716.4 (2x)
Rm 5:4 patient·endurance *fully·cultivates* proven·character,
Rm 5:4 and the proven·character *fully·cultivates* expectation.

G2718 κατ•έρχομαι katérchômai *v.* (13x)
Roots:G2596 G2064
G2718.1 V-PNP-NSF κατερχομένη (1x)
Jac 3:15 is not *that* which·is·coming·down from·above, but·
G2718.1 V-2AAI-1P κατήλθομεν (1x)
Ac 27:5 ·to Cilicia and PamPhylia, we·came·down to Myra,
G2718.1 V-2AAI-3S κατῆλθεν (2x)
Lk 4:31 And he·came·down to CaperNaum, a·city of·Galilee,
Ac 21:10 days, a·certain prophet came·down from Judea,
G2718.1 V-2AAI-3P κατῆλθον (2x)
Ac 11:27 those days, prophets came·down from JeruSalem
Ac 18:5 Silas and TimoThy came·down from Macedonia,
G2718.1 V-2AAN κατελθεῖν (1x)
Ac 9:32 it·happened *such·for* Peter to·come·down also to
G2718.1 V-2AAP-GPM κατελθόντων (1x)
Lk 9:37 on the next day, with·them coming·down from the
G2718.1 V-2AAP-NSM κατελθών (3x)
Ac 8:5 And Philippe, after·coming·down to a·city of·
Ac 12:19 *to·execution*. Then coming·down from Judea to
Ac 18:22 And after·coming·down to Caesarea, *then* walking·
G2718.1 V-2AAP-NPM κατελθόντες (1x)
Ac 15:1 And certain·men coming·down from Judea were·
G2718.2 V-2AAI-3P κατῆλθον (1x)
Ac 13:4 the Holy Spirit, these·men went·down to Seleucia.

G2719 κατ•εσθίω katêsthíō *v.* (15x)
Roots:G2596 G2068 Compare:G2068
xLangAlso:H0398
G2719 V-PAI-2P κατεσθίετε (2x)
Gal 5:15 But if yeu·bite and devour one·another, look·out
Mt 23:13 ·acting·hypocrites! Because yeu·devour the homes
G2719 V-PAI-3S κατεσθίει (2x)
2Co 11:20 utterly·enslaves yeu, if anyone devours *yeu*, if
Rv 11:5 from·out of·their mouth and devours their enemies.
G2719 V-PAI-3P κατεσθίουσιν (1x)
Lk 20:47 who devour the homes of·the widows, and pray
G2719 V-PAP-NPM κατεσθίοντες (1x)
Mk 12:40 The·ones devouring the homes of·the widows, and
G2719 V-2AAI-1S κατέφαγον (1x)
Rv 10:10 out of·the angel's hand and devoured it; and it·was
G2719 V-2AAI-3S κατέφαγεν (5x)
Jn 2:17 ·written, "'The zeal of·your house devours me."'
Lk 8:5 ·trampled·down, and the birds of·the sky devoured it.
Mt 13:4 roadway, and the birds came and devoured them.
Mk 4:4 and the birds of·the sky came and devoured it.
Rv 20:9 from God out of·the heaven and devoured them.
G2719 V-2AAM-2S κατάφαγε (1x)
Rv 10:9 ·says to·me, "Take and devour it; and it·shall·make
G2719 V-2AAP-NSM καταφαγών (1x)
Lk 15:30 came *home*, the·one devouring your livelihood
G2719 V-2AAS-3S καταφάγη (1x)
Rv 12:4 ·birth, in·order·that he·may·devour her child

G2720 κατ•ευθύνω katêuthýnō *v.* (3x)
Roots:G2596 G2116 Compare:G4929 G3594 G3329 G4291
G2720.2 V-AAN κατευθῦναι (1x)
Lk 1:79 and shadow of·death, to·fully·direct our feet into
G2720.2 V-AAO-3S κατευθύναι (2x)
1Th 3:11 our Lord YeShua Anointed, fully·direct our way to
2Th 3:5 And may the Lord fully·direct yeur hearts into the

G2721 κατ•εφ•ίστημι katêphístēmi *v.* (1x)
Roots:G2596 G2186
G2721.2 V-2AAI-3P κατεπέστησαν (1x)
Ac 18:12 Jews made·a·full·assault with·the·same· against·

G2722 κατ•έχω katéchō *v.* (19x)
Roots:G2596 G2192 See:G2697
G2722.1 V-PAP-NPM κατέχοντες (1x)
2Co 6:10 not·even·one·thing and·yet fully·having all·things.
G2722.2 V-PAI-2P κατέχετε (2x)
1Co 11:2 in·all·things, and fully·hold·onto the traditions,
1Co 15:2 if yeu·fully·hold·onto that·certain Redemptive-word
G2722.2 V-PAI-3P κατέχουσιν (1x)
Lk 8:15 ·hearing the Redemptive-word, fully·hold·onto *it* and
G2722.2 V-PAM-2P κατέχετε (1x)
1Th 5:21 ·and·verify all·things; fully·hold·onto the good.
G2722.2 V-PAN κατέχειν (1x)
Lk 14:9 ·begin with shame to·fully·hold·onto the very·last
G2722.2 V-PAP-NPM κατέχοντες (1x)
1Co 7:30 and the·ones buying, as not fully·holding·onto *it*;
G2722.2 V-PAS-1P κατέχωμεν (1x)
Heb 10:23 We·should·fully·hold·onto the affirmation of·the
G2722.2 V-IAI-3P κατεῖχον (1x)
Lk 4:42 ·came unto him and were·fully·holding·onto him,
G2722.2 V-IPI-1P κατειχόμεθα (1x)
Rm 7:6 ·dead *to·that* by that·which we·were·fully·held,
G2722.2 V-2AAS-1P κατάσχωμεν (3x)
Heb 3:6 provided·that we·should·fully·hold·onto the bold·
Heb 3:14 provided·that we·should·fully·hold·onto the
Mt 21:38 ·kill him and should·fully·hold·onto his inheritance
G2722.3 V-PAN κατέχειν (1x)
Phm 1:13 was·definitely·willing to·fully·retain alongside
G2722.4 V-PAP-ASN κατέχον (1x)
2Th 2:6 the·thing *that·is* holding·*him*·down in·order·for him
G2722.4 V-PAP-GPM κατεχόντων (1x)
Rm 1:18 of·men·of·clay† (the·ones holding·down the truth
G2722.4 V-PAP-NSM κατέχων (1x)
2Th 2:7 the·one holding·*him*·down at·this·moment *is·doing*
G2722.4 V-IPI-3S κατείχετο (1x)
Jn 5:4 from·whatever ailment by·which he·was·held·down.
G2722.5 V-IAI-3P κατεῖχον (1x)
Ac 27:40 ·wind, they·were·bearing·down toward the shore.

G2723 κατ•ηγορέω katēgôréō *v.* (23x)
Roots:G2725 Compare:G1458 G4316 See:G2724
G2723.2 V-FAI-1S κατηγορήσω (1x)
Jn 5:45 presume that I·myself shall·legally·accuse yeu to the
G2723.2 V-PAI-1P κατηγοροῦμεν (1x)
Ac 24:8 ·things of·which we·ourselves legally·accuse him."
G2723.2 V-PAI-2P κατηγορεῖτε (1x)
Lk 23:14 ·to those·things·of·which yeu·legally·accuse him.
G2723.2 V-PAI-3P κατηγοροῦσιν (2x)
Ac 24:13 concerning which now they·legally·accuse me.
Ac 25:11 ·these·things·which these·men legally·accuse me,
G2723.2 V-PAM-3P κατηγορείτωσαν (1x)
Ac 25:5 ·down·together *with·me*, legally·accuse this man, if
G2723.2 V-PAN κατηγορεῖν (4x)
Jn 8:6 they·may·have *something* to·legally·accuse him·of.
Lk 23:2 And they·began to·legally·accuse him, saying,
Ac 24:2 ·called·for, Tertullus began to·legally·accuse *Paul*,
Ac 24:19 to·be·here before you and to·legally·accuse *me*, if
G2723.2 V-PAP-GPM κατηγορούντων (1x)
Rm 2:15 and *with·their* reckonings legally·accusing or else
G2723.2 V-PAP-NSM κατηγορῶν (2x)
Jn 5:45 "There·is the·one legally·accusing yeu, Moses, in
Rv 12:10 ·down, the·one legally·accusing them in·the·sight
G2723.2 V-PAP-NPM κατηγοροῦντες (1x)
Lk 23:10 the scribes stood, legally·accusing him vigorously.
G2723.2 V-PPI-3S κατηγορεῖται (1x)
Ac 22:30 *as·to* why he·is·legally·accused personally·by the
G2723.2 V-PPN κατηγορεῖσθαι (1x)
Mt 27:12 But when he was·legally·accused by the chief·
G2723.2 V-PPP-NSM κατηγορούμενος (1x)
Ac 25:16 the·one being·legally·accused actually·holds the
G2723.2 V-IAI-3P κατηγόρουν (1x)
Mk 15:3 chief·priests were·legally·accusing him of·many·
G2723.2 V-AAN κατηγορῆσαι (1x)
Ac 28:19 anything *of·which* to·legally·accuse my nation.
G2723.2 V-AAS-3P κατηγορήσωσιν (3x)
Lk 11:54 mouth in·order·that they·may·legally·accuse him.
Mt 12:10 And in·order·that they·may·legally·accuse him,
Mk 3:2 ·days, in·order·that they·may·legally·accuse him.
EG2723.2 (1x)
Lk 23:15 ·yeurselves up to him *to·legally·accuse this·man*,

G2724 κατ•ηγορία katēgôría *n.* (4x)
Roots:G2725 Compare:G1462
G2724.2 N-ASF κατηγορίαν (3x)
Jn 18:29 "What legal·accusation do·yeu·bring against this
Lk 6:7 that they·might·find a·legal·accusation against·him.
1Ti 5:19 give·heed·and·accept a·legal·accusation against an·
G2724.2 N-DSF κατηγορίᾳ (1x)
Tit 1:6 not in legal·accusation of·an·unsaved·lifestyle or

G2725 κατ•ήγορος katḗgôrôs *n.* (7x)
Roots:G2596 G0058 See:G2723
G2725.2 N-NSM κατήγορος (1x)
Rv 12:10 because the legal·accuser of·our brothers is·cast·
G2725.2 N-NPM κατήγοροι (3x)
Jn 8:10 are those·men, your legal·accusers? *Did* not·even·
Ac 23:35 your legal·accusers also should·arrive·publicly."
Ac 25:18 whom, the legal·accusers, after·being·settled·in,
G2725.2 N-APM κατηγόρους (2x)
Ac 24:8 ·ordering his legal·accusers to·come to you,
Ac 25:16 actually·holds the legal·accusers face·to·face, and·
G2725.2 N-DPM κατηγόροις (1x)
Ac 23:30 you, charging his legal·accusers also to·say before

G2726 κατ•ήφεια katḗphêia *n.* (1x)
Roots:G2596 G5316 Compare:G1105
G2726.2 N-ASF κατήφειαν (1x)
Jac 4:9 ·distorted into mourning, and *yeur* joy into dejection.

G2727 κατ•ηχέω katēchéō *v.* (8x)
Roots:G2596 G2279 Compare:G1321
G2727.1 V-AAS-1S κατηχήσω (1x)
1Co 14:19 ·order·that *by·my·voice* I·may·inform others also,
G2727.1 V-API-2S κατηχήθης (1x)
Lk 1:4 concerning *the* sayings of·which you·were·informed.
G2727.1 V-API-3P κατηχήθησαν (1x)
Ac 21:21 Now they·are·informed concerning you, that you·
G2727.1 V-RPI-3P κατήχηνται (1x)
Ac 21:24 of·which·things they·have·been·informed you, it·
G2727.1 V-RPP-NSM κατηχημένος (1x)
Ac 18:25 This·man was having·been·informed·of The Way
G2727.2 V-PAP-DSM κατηχοῦντι (1x)
Gal 6:6 must·share with·the·one tutoring in all beneficially·
G2727.2 V-PPP-NSM κατηχούμενος (2x)
Gal 6:6 Now the·one being·tutored·in the Redemptive-word
Rm 2:18 the·things varying (being·tutored from·out of·the

G2728 κατ•ιόω katióō *v.* (1x)
Roots:G2596 G2447
G2728 V-RPI-3S κατίωται (1x)
Jac 5:3 gold and silver have·been·fully·rusted·down, and its

G2729 κατ•ισχύω katischýō *v.* (3x)
Roots:G2596 G2480 Compare:G2603 G3528
G2729.2 V-FAI-3P κατισχύσουσιν (1x)
Mt 16:18 and Hades' gates shall·not overpower it.
G2729.2 V-IAI-3P κατίσχυον (1x)
Lk 23:23 ·them and of·the chief·priests were·overpowering.
EG2729.2 (1x)
Rv 12:8 and they·did·not have·strength *to·overpower*; neither

G2730 κατ•οικέω katôikéō *v.* (47x)
Roots:G2596 G3611 Compare:G1927 G3484-1 See:G1460 G2733 G2732 G2729-1 G2733-3 xLangAlso:H3427
G2730.1 V-PAI-2S κατοικεῖς (1x)
Rv 2:13 your works, and where you·reside, *even* where the
G2730.1 V-PAI-2P κατοικεῖτε (1x)
Ac 7:4 ·settled him into this land in which yeu now reside.
G2730.1 V-PAI-3S κατοικεῖ (7x)
Lk 11:26 itself, and entering·in, they·reside there. And the
Ac 7:48 "But·yet the Most·High does·not reside in temples
Ac 17:24 Lord of·heaven and earth, resides not in temples
Mt 12:45 And *with* them·entering, he·resides there. And the
2Pe 3:13 Earth,' in which righteousness resides.
Col 2:9 all the complete·fullness of·Godhood resides bodily.
Rv 2:13 ·among yeu, where the Adversary-Accuser resides.
G2730.1 V-PAN κατοικεῖν (1x)
Ac 17:26 every nation of·men·of·clay† residing upon all the
G2730.1 V-PAP-APM κατοικοῦντας (7x)
Lk 13:4 ·and·beyond all men·of·clay† residing in JeruSalem?
Ac 9:22 the Jews, the·ones residing in Damascus, *by*
Rv 3:10 The Land, to·try the·ones residing upon the earth.
Rv 11:10 two prophets tormented the·ones residing on the
Rv 13:12 it·makes the earth and the·ones residing in her that
Rv 13:14 and it·deceives the·ones residing on the earth
Rv 14:6 good·news to·proclaim to·the·ones residing on the
G2730.1 V-PAP-DPM κατοικοῦσιν (3x)
Ac 11:29 service to the brothers, the·ones residing in Judea.
Rv 8:13 Woe, woe, woe to·the·ones residing on the earth—
Rv 13:14 Daemonic·Beast, saying to·the·ones residing on the
G2730.1 V-PAP-GPM κατοικούντων (2x)
Ac 22:12 being·attested·to by all the residing Jews,
Rv 6:10 avenge our blood on the·ones residing on the earth?
G2730.1 V-PAP-NSM κατοικῶν (1x)
Ac 1:20 desolate, and do·not let·there·be one residing in it,"
G2730.1 V-PAP-NPM κατοικοῦντες (5x)
Ac 2:5 And there·were Jews residing in JeruSalem, devout
Ac 13:27 For the·ones residing in JeruSalem, and their rulers,
Rv 11:10 And the·ones residing upon the earth shall·rejoice
Rv 13:8 And all the·ones residing upon the earth shall·fall·
Rv 17:8 total·destruction. And the·ones residing on the earth
G2730.1 V-AAI-3S κατῴκησεν (4x)
Ac 7:4 *the* land of·the·Kaldeans, he·resided in Charan. And·
Mt 2:23 And after·coming *there*, he·resided in a·city being·
Mt 4:13 *and* coming *into Galilee*, he·resided in CaperNaum
Jac 4:5 "The spirit that resides in us greatly·yearns *even*
G2730.1 V-AAN κατοικῆσαι (3x)
Ac 7:2 ·still in MesoPotamia, before he resided in Charan,
Eph 3:17 for·the Anointed-One to·reside in yeur hearts
Col 1:19 *of·God Most·High* takes·delight to·reside in him,
G2730.1 V-AAP-NSM κατοικήσας (1x)
Heb 11:9 *in* an·estranged·foreign *land*, residing in tents with
G2730.2 V-PAP-APM κατοικοῦντας (2x)
Ac 9:32 also to the holy·ones, the·ones residing·in Lod.
Ac 19:10 such·for all the·ones residing·in Asia to·hear the
G2730.2 V-PAP-DSM κατοικοῦντι (1x)
Mt 23:21 Temple, swears by it and by the·one residing·in it.
G2730.2 V-PAP-DPM κατοικοῦσιν (4x)
Ac 1:19 it·was known to·all the·ones residing·in JeruSalem,
Ac 4:16 *is* apparent to·all the·ones residing·in JeruSalem,
Ac 19:17 was known to·all the·ones residing·in Ephesus, to·
Rv 12:12 in them. Woe to·the·ones residing·in the earth and
G2730.2 V-PAP-NPM κατοικοῦντες (4x)
Ac 2:9 Elamites, and the·ones residing·in MesoPotamia and
Ac 2:14 and absolutely·all the·ones residing·in JeruSalem, be
Ac 9:35 And all the·ones residing·in Lod and Sharon saw
Rv 17:2 ·immorality. And the·ones residing·in the earth,

G2731 κατ•οίκησις katôíkēsis *n.* (1x)
Roots:G2730 See:G2733
G2731.1 N-ASF κατοίκησιν (1x)
Mk 5:3 who was·having his residence among the chamber·

G2732 κατ•οικητήριον katôikētēriôn *n.* (2x)
Roots:G2730 Compare:G2733
G2732 N-NSN κατοικητήριον (2x)
Eph 2:22 also are·built·together for a·residence of·God in
Rv 18:2 is·fallen, and is·become a·residence of·demons, and

G2733 κατ•οικία katôikía *n.* (1x)
Roots:G2730 Compare:G2732 G1886 See:G2731
G2733.1 N-GSF κατοικίας (1x)
Ac 17:26 seasons and the bounds of·their residency,

G2734 κατ•οπτρίζομαι katôptrízômai *v.* (1x)
Roots:G2596 G3700 Compare:G2072
G2734.2 V-PMP-NPM κατοπτριζόμενοι (1x)
2Co 3:18 (ourselves·seeing·and·reflecting the Lord's glory)

G2735 κατ•όρθωμα katórthōma *n.* (1x)
Roots:G2596 G3717 Compare:G1357
G2735.2 N-GPN κατορθωμάτων (1x)
Ac 24:2 ·of you, and with·upright·reforms occurring in·this

G2736 κάτω kátō *adv.* (11x)
κατωτέρω katōtérō [also]
Roots:G2596 See:G2737
G2736.1 ADV κάτω (2x)
Lk 4:9 ·are the Son of·God, cast yourself down from·here.
Ac 20:9 with heavy·sleep, he·fell down from the third·story
G2736.1 PREP κάτω (3x)
Jn 8:6 But after·stooping down, Jesus was·writing with·the
Jn 8:8 And again after·stooping down, he·was·writing into
Mt 4:6 of·God, cast yourself down. For it·has·been·written,
G2736.2 ADV κάτω (2x)
Mt 27:51 is·torn in two from top to bottom. And the earth is·
Mk 15:38 of·the Temple was·torn in two from top to bottom.
G2736.3 ADV κάτω (4x)
Jn 8:23 ·yeurselves are birthed·from down·below; I·myself
Ac 2:19 and signs on the earth down·below: blood and fire
Mt 2:16 from two·years·of·age and below, according·to the
Mk 14:66 Now with·Peter being down·below in the

G2737 κατώτερος katṓtêrôs *adj.* (1x)
Roots:G2736 Compare:G0086 See:G2507 G5465 xLangAlso:H8482
G2737.2 A-APN-C κατώτερα (1x)
Eph 4:9 first into the lowermost parts of·the earth?

G2738 καῦμα kaûma *n.* (2x)
Roots:G2545 See:G2739
G2738.2 N-NSN καῦμα (1x)
Rv 7:16 ·fall on them, nor·even any burning·radiation,
G2738.2 N-ASN καῦμα (1x)
Rv 16:9 ·by·the·sun with·great burning·radiation, and they·

G2739 καυματίζω kaumatízō *v.* (4x)
Roots:G2738
G2739.1 V-AAN καυματίσαι (1x)
Rv 16:8 and it·was·given to·him to·burn the men·of·clay†
G2739.2 V-API-3S ἐκαυματίσθη (2x)
Mt 13:6 ·above·the·horizon, it·was·burned·by·the·sun. And
Mk 4:6 ·the·horizon, it·was·burned·by·the·sun, and·then on·
G2739.2 V-API-3P ἐκαυματίσθησαν (1x)
Rv 16:9 the men·of·clay† were·burned·by·the·sun with·great

G2740 καῦσις kaûsis *n.* (1x)
Roots:G2545 Compare:G5395 See:G2741
G2740.2 N-ASF καῦσιν (1x)
Heb 6:8 whose end *is* for consumption·in·a·blazing·fire.

G2741 καυσόω kausóō *v.* (2x)
Roots:G2740 Compare:G4448 See:G2742
G2741.2 V-PPP-NPN καυσούμενα (2x)
2Pe 3:10 — being·consumed·in·a·blazing·fire; and·also *the*
2Pe 3:12 being·consumed·in·a·blazing·fire, are·liquefied.

G2742 καύσων kaúsōn *n.* (3x)
Roots:G2741
G2742 N-NSM καύσων (1x)
Lk 12:55 yeu·say, 'There·shall·be blazing·heat,' and it·
G2742 N-ASM καύσωνα (1x)
Mt 20:12 bearing the burden and the blazing·heat of·the day.
G2742 N-DSM καύσωνι (1x)
Jac 1:11 ·the·horizon together with·the blazing·heat, and 'it·

G2743 καυτηριάζω kautēriázō *v.* (1x)
Roots:G2545
G2743.2 V-RPP-GPM κεκαυτηριασμένων (1x)
1Ti 4:2 conscience having·been·seared *as·with a·hot·iron*,

G2744 καυχάομαι kaucháômai *v.* (40x)
Roots:G0849-3 G2172 Compare:G3166 G2620 See:G2745
G2744 V-FDI-1S καυχήσομαι (5x)
2Co 11:18 boast according·to the flesh, I·also shall·boast.
2Co 11:30 to·boast, I·shall·boast *about* the·things of·my
2Co 12:5 On·behalf of·such·a·man, I·shall·boast; but on·
2Co 12:5 ·behalf of·my·own·self, I·shall·not boast, except
2Co 12:9 rather, with·great·pleasure, I·shall·boast in my
G2744 V-FDI-1P καυχησόμεθα (1x)
2Co 10:13 But we·ourselves indeed·shall·not boast in the
G2744 V-PNI-1S καυχῶμαι (1x)
2Co 9:2 yeur eagerness, for·which I·boast over yeu to·*the*·
G2744 V-PNI-1P καυχώμεθα (2x)
Rm 5:2 which we·stand, and we·boast in expectation of·the
Rm 5:3 *so*, but·rather also we·boast in the tribulations,
G2744 V-PNI-2S καυχᾶσαι (3x)
Rm 2:17 the Torah-Law, and make·your·boast in God,
Rm 2:23 You who boast in Torah-Law, do·you·dishonor
1Co 4:7 also you·did·receive *it*, why do·you·boast, as *if* not
G2744 V-PNI-2P καυχᾶσθε (1x)
Jac 4:16 But now yeu·boast in yeur bragging.
G2744 V-PNI-3P καυχῶνται (2x)
2Co 11:12 ·order·that in what they·boast, they·may·be·found
2Co 11:18 Since many boast according·to the flesh, I·also
G2744 V-PNM-3S καυχάσθω (4x)
Jac 1:9 the brother of·the low·estate boast in his high·stature,
1Co 1:31 "The·one boasting, let·him·boast in Yahweh."
1Co 3:21 As·such, do·not·let·one boast in men·of·clay†, for
2Co 10:17 ·one who·is·boasting, let·him·boast in Yahweh."
G2744 V-PNN καυχᾶσθαι (4x)
Gal 6:14 But may·it·never happen for·me to·boast, except in
2Th 1:4 such·for we ourselves to·boast in yeu among the
2Co 11:30 If it·is·necessary to·boast, I·shall·boast *about* the·
2Co 12:1 it·is·not advantageous for·me to·boast, for I·shall·
G2744 V-PNP-APM καυχωμένους (1x)
2Co 5:12 the·ones who·are·boasting in a·surface·appearance
G2744 V-PNP-NSM καυχώμενος (3x)
1Co 1:31 ·written, "The·one boasting, let·him·boast in
2Co 10:17 But "the·one who·is·boasting, let·him·boast in
2Co 12:11 I·have·become impetuous in·boasting! Yeu
G2744 V-PNP-NPM καυχώμενοι (3x)
Rm 5:11 *so*, but·rather we·also are·boasting in God through
Php 3:3 to·God in·spirit, and boasting in Anointed-One
2Co 10:15 ·beyond·measure *that* we·are·boasting, *that·is*, in
G2744 V-ADN καυχήσασθαι (2x)
2Co 10:16 ·news, *and* not *for·us* to·boast by another·man's
2Co 12:6 For though I·should·want to·boast, I·shall·not be
G2744 V-ADS-1S καυχήσωμαι (2x)
2Co 10:8 even though I·should·boast somewhat excessively
2Co 11:16 ·that, *for* a·little·while, even·I may·boast some.
G2744 V-ADS-3S καυχήσηται (2x)
1Co 1:29 so·that all flesh may·not boast in·the·sight of·him.
Eph 2:9 ·out of·works, in·order·that not any may·boast.
G2744 V-ADS-3P καυχήσωνται (1x)
Gal 6:13 ·circumcised in·order·that they·may·boast in yeur
G2744 V-RNI-1S κεκαύχημαι (1x)
2Co 7:14 Because if I·have·boasted anything to·him
EG2744 (2x)
2Co 11:12 an·impromptu·occasion *to·boast of·themselves*,
2Co 12:6 But I·am·sparing *in·how I·boast*, lest any·man

G2745 καύχημα kaúchēma *n.* (11x)
Roots:G2744 See:G2746 xLangAlso:H8597
G2745.1 N-NSN καύχημα (1x)
1Co 9:16 ·proclaim·the·good·news, it·is not a·boast to·me,
G2745.1 N-ASN καύχημα (2x)
Rm 4:2 as·a·result of·works, he·has a·boast, but·yet not
Php 2:16 of·life·above— for *such* a·boast by·me in *the* day

G2745.2 N-NSN καύχημα (4x)
Php 1:26 that yeur boasting in me may·abound in Jesus
1Co 5:6 Yeur boasting *is* not good.
2Co 1:14 part, that we·are yeur boasting, exactly·as yeu *are*
2Co 9:3 brothers, lest our boasting on·yeur behalf should·
G2745.2 N-ASN καύχημα (3x)
Heb 3:6 bold·declaration and the boasting of·the Expectation
Gal 6:4 and then he·shall·have the boasting in himself alone
1Co 9:15 than that anyone should·make·void my boasting.
G2745.2 N-GSN καυχήματος (1x)
2Co 5:12 yeu an·impromptu·occasion for·boasting over us,

G2746 καύχησις kaúchēsis *n.* (13x)
Roots:G2744 See:G2745
G2746.1 N-NSF καύχησις (6x)
Rm 3:27 So·then, where *is* the boasting? It·is·excluded. On·
Jac 4:16 ·boast in yeur bragging. All such boasting is evil.
2Co 1:12 For this is our boasting, the testimony of·our
2Co 7:4 yeu, large *is* my boasting concerning yeu. I·have·
2Co 7:14 even in·this·manner our boasting (the·one *we·*
2Co 11:10 *such* that this boasting shall·not be·sealed·up in
G2746.1 N-GSF καυχήσεως (4x)
1Th 2:19 joy, or victor's·crown of·boasting? *Is·it* not·indeed
2Co 8:24 of·yeur love and of·our boasting over yeu, and *do·*
2Co 9:4 ·be·put·to·shame in this firm·assurance of·boasting.
2Co 11:17 impulsiveness, in this firm·assurance of·boasting.
EG2746.1 (1x)
2Co 11:1 ·while in·the impulsiveness *of·boasting*, but·yet
G2746.2 N-ASF καύχησιν (2x)
Rm 15:17 Accordingly, I·have a·boast in Jesus Anointed in·
1Co 15:31 I·die, as·sure·as *it·is* our boast, which I·have in

G2747 Κεγχρεαί Kênchrêaí *n/l.* (2x)
G2747.2 N/L-DPF Κεγχρεαῖς (2x)
Ac 18:18 already·having·shorn his head in Cenchrea, for he·
Rm 16:1 of·the Called·Out·citizenry, the·one in Cenchrea,

G2748 Κεδρών Kêdrṓn *n/l.* (1x)
Ḳεδρών Qêdrṓn [Greek, Octuagint]
קִדְרוֹן qidrôn [Hebrew]
Roots:H6939 Compare:G4075-1 G2952-8
xLangEquiv:H0730 xLangAlso:H0249
G2748.2 N/P-PRI Ḳέδρων (1x)
Jn 18:1 to·the·other·side of·the Brook Qidron, where there·

G2749 κεῖμαι kêîmai *v.* (29x)
Compare:G5087 G2476 See:G2837
G2749.1 V-PNI-1S κεῖμαι (1x)
Php 1:17 ·love, having·seen that I·am·laid·out for a·defense
G2749.1 V-PNI-1P κείμεθα (1x)
1Th 3:3 personally·know that we·are·laid·out to this.
G2749.1 V-PNI-3S κεῖται (7x)
Lk 2:34 "Behold, this *child* is·laid·out for a·downfall and a·
Lk 3:9 even·now also, the ax is·laid·out to the root of·the
Mt 3:10 even·now also, the ax is·laid·out to the root of·the
2Co 3:15 Moses is·read·aloud, a·veil is·laid·out upon their
1Ti 1:9 that Torah-Law is·not laid·out for·a·righteous·man,
1Jn 5:19 and the whole world is·laid·out in the Evil·One.
Rv 21:16 And the CITY lays·out foursquare, and its length is
G2749.1 V-PNP-ASN κείμενον (3x)
Jn 20:7 upon his head, *that* it·is·being·laid·out not with the
Lk 2:12 having·been·swaddled·*in·cloths*, laying·out in the
Lk 2:16 and·also the baby laying·out in the feeding·trough.
G2749.1 V-PNP-ASM κείμενον (1x)
1Co 3:11 foundation than the·one being·laid·out, which is
G2749.1 V-PNP-APN κείμενα (4x)
Jn 20:5 he·looked·at the strips·of·linen laying·out, however
Jn 20:6 And he·observes the strips·of·linen laying·out
Lk 12:19 beneficially·good·things being·laid·out for many
Lk 24:12 the strips·of·linen which·are·laying·out alone.
G2749.1 V-PNP-NSM κείμενος (2x)
Jn 11:41 where the·one having·died was laying·outstretched.
Lk 23:53 not·even·yet, not·even·one *man* being·laid·out.
G2749.1 V-PNP-NPF κείμεναι (1x)
Jn 2:6 And there·were laying·out there six ceremonial·water·
G2749.1 V-INI-3S ἔκειτο (2x)
Jn 20:12 the feet, where the body of·Jesus was·lain·out.
Mt 28:6 See the place where the Lord was·laid·out.
EG2749.1 (1x)
Jn 11:17 Jesus found him having *been·laid·to·rest* in the
G2749.2 V-PNP-ASF κειμένην (1x)
Jn 21:9 and a·small·broiled·fish being·set·out laying·upon *it*,
G2749.2 V-PNP-NSF κειμένη (1x)
Mt 5:14 A·city that·is·being·set·out high·upon a·mount is·
G2749.2 V-INI-3S ἔκειτο (2x)
Jn 19:29 ·then, there·was·set·out a·vessel exceedingly·full
Rv 4:2 and behold, a·throne was·set·out in the heaven, and
EG2749.2 (2x)
2Ti 2:20 of·earthenware, and some *are·set·out* in·fact unto
Rv 4:4 And all·around the throne *were·set·out* twenty four

G2750 κειρία kêiría *n.* (1x)
Compare:G1040 G3608 G4616
G2750.2 N-DPF κειρίαις (1x)
Jn 11:44 ·bound hand and foot with·swathes·of·linen, and his

G2751 κείρω kêírō *v.* (4x)
Compare:G3587
G2751 V-PAP-GSM κείροντος (1x)
Ac 8:32 in·the·direct·presence of·the·one shearing him, in·
G2751 V-AMM-3S κειράσθω (1x)
1Co 11:6 is·not fully·veiled, also she·must·be·shorn, but if
G2751 V-AMN κείρασθαι (1x)
1Co 11:6 for·a·woman to·be·shorn or to·be·shaved·bald,
G2751 V-AMP-NSM κειράμενος (1x)
Ac 18:18 ·him— *with·Paul* already·having·shorn his head in

G2752 κέλευμα kéleuma *n.* (1x)
Roots:G2753
G2752.2 N-DSN κελεύσματι (1x)
1Th 4:16 shall·descend from heaven with battle·cry, with a·

G2753 κελεύω kêlêúō *v.* (27x)
Roots:G3634-7 Compare:G1781 G1809 G2004
G4367 See:G2564
G2753.2 V-PAI-2S κελεύεις (1x)
Ac 23:3 Torah-Law, and you·commandingly·order *for* me
G2753.2 V-IAI-3P@ ἐκέλευον (1x)
Ac 16:22 garments, commandingly·ordered *for·Paul and*
G2753.2 V-AAI-1S ἐκέλευσα (2x)
Ac 25:17 ·judgment·seat, I·commandingly·ordered the man
Ac 25:21 I·commandingly·ordered him to·be·kept until I·
G2753.2 V-AAI-3S ἐκέλευσεν (17x)
Lk 18:40 Jesus commandingly·ordered him to·be·brought
Ac 5:34 ·all the people, commandingly·ordered to·make the
Ac 8:38 And he·commandingly·ordered the chariot to·stand·
Ac 12:19 he·commandingly·ordered *for·them* to·be·led·
Ac 21:33 ·him and commandingly·ordered *him* to·be·bound
Ac 21:34 he·commandingly·ordered him to·be·brought into
Ac 22:24 regiment·commander commandingly·ordered him
Ac 22:30 bonds and commandingly·ordered the chief·priests
Ac 23:10 — he·commandingly·ordered the squad·of·soldiers
Ac 23:35 And he·commandingly·ordered him to·be·
Ac 25:6 ·seat, *Festus* commandingly·ordered *for* Paul to·be·
Ac 27:43 and commandingly·ordered the·ones being·able
Mt 8:18 he·commandingly·ordered *to·make·ready* to·go·off
Mt 14:9 ·meal, he·commandingly·ordered *for·it* to·be·given
Mt 15:35 And he·commandingly·ordered the crowds to·sit·
Mt 18:25 to·repay, his lord commandingly·ordered *for* him
Mt 27:58 Then Pilate commandingly·ordered the body to·
G2753.2 V-AAM-2S κέλευσον (2x)
Mt 14:28 ·is·you yourself, commandingly·order me to·come
Mt 27:64 Now·then, commandingly·order *for* the grave to·
G2753.2 V-AAP-GSM κελεύσαντος (1x)
Ac 25:23 and with·Festus commandingly·ordering *that* Paul
G2753.2 V-AAP-NSM κελεύσας (2x)
Ac 24:8 commandingly·ordering his legal·accusers to·come
Mt 14:19 And after·commandingly·ordering the crowds to·
G2753.2 V-AAP-NPM κελεύσαντες (1x)
Ac 4:15 But commandingly·ordering them to·go·aside

G2754 κενο•δοξία kênôdôxía *n.* (1x)
Roots:G2755 Compare:G5450 G5243
G2754.2 N-ASF κενοδοξίαν (1x)
Php 2:3 according·to contention or self-conceit, but·rather

G2755 κενό•δοξος kênṓdôxôs *adj.* (1x)
Roots:G2756 G1391 Compare:G5187
G2755.2 A-NPM κενόδοξοι (1x)
Gal 5:26 ·not become self-conceited·men, challenging one·

G2756 κενός kênṓs *adj.* (18x)
Compare:G3152 G3762 See:G2758 G2761 G1246-2
G2756.1 A-NSM κενός (1x)
1Co 15:58 yeur wearisome·labor is not empty in *the* Lord.
G2756.1 A-NSF κενή (3x)
1Th 2:1 accessible·entrance to yeu has·not become empty.
1Co 15:10 upon me, was not empty. But·rather, I·labored·
1Co 15:14 *is* empty, and also yeur trust *is* empty.
G2756.1 A-NSN κενόν (1x)
1Co 15:14 our official·proclamation *is* empty, and also yeur
G2756.1 A-VSM κενέ (1x)
Jac 2:20 do·you·want to·know, O empty man·of·clay†, that
G2756.1 A-ASM κενόν (3x)
Lk 20:10 after·thrashing him, dispatched·*him*·forth empty.
Lk 20:11 ·treating *him*, they·dispatched·*him*·forth empty.
Mk 12:3 they·thrashed him and dispatched *him·back* empty.
G2756.1 A-APM κενούς (1x)
Lk 1:53 those·being·wealthy, he·dispatched·forth empty.
G2756.1 A-APN κενά (1x)
Ac 4:25 and *did* peoples meditate·upon empty·things?
G2756.1 A-DPM κενοῖς (1x)
Eph 5:6 Let not·one·man delude yeu with·empty words, for
G2756.1 A-GSF κενῆς (1x)
Col 2:8 the *use·of* philosophy and an·empty delusion,
G2756.2 A-ASM κενόν (1x)
Gal 2:2 lest·somehow I·should·run, or did·run, for naught.
G2756.2 A-ASN κενόν (3x)
Php 2:16 that I·did·not run for naught neither labored·hard
Php 2:16 ·not run for naught neither labored·hard for naught.
1Th 3:5 yeu and our wearisome·labor should·be for naught.
G2756.3 A-ASN κενόν (1x)
2Co 6:1 *with·him, it·is* not for nothing *that* we·implore also

G2757 κενο•φωνία kênôphōnía *n.* (2x)
Roots:G2756 G5456 Compare:G1261 G2214 G4804
G2757.2 N-APF κενοφωνίας (2x)
1Ti 6:20 ·away·from the profane, empty·discussions and *the*
2Ti 2:16 shun the profane *and* empty·discussions, for they·

G2758 κενόω kênṓō *v.* (5x)
Roots:G2756 Compare:G2673
G2758.1 V-AAI-3S ἐκένωσεν (1x)
Php 2:7 but·yet he·emptied himself, taking·hold·of *the*
G2758.1 V-APS-3S κενωθῇ (1x)
2Co 9:3 on·yeur behalf should·be·made·empty on this part;
G2758.2 V-AAS-3S κενώσῃ (1x)
1Co 9:15 than that anyone should·make·void my boasting.
G2758.2 V-APS-3S κενωθῇ (1x)
1Co 1:17 Anointed-One should·be·made·void *with·no·effect*.
G2758.2 V-RPI-3S κεκένωται (1x)
Rm 4:14 *are* heirs, the trust has·been·made·void, and the

G2759 κέντρον kéntrôn *n.* (5x)
Roots:G2758-1
G2759.2 N-NSN κέντρον (2x)
1Co 15:55 O·Death, where *is* your painful·sting? O·Hades,
1Co 15:56 But the painful·sting of·Death *is* Moral·Failure,
G2759.2 N-APN κέντρα (1x)
Rv 9:10 like scorpions, and there·were painful·stings in their
G2759.3 N-APN κέντρα (2x)
Ac 9:5 to·kick·the·heel·back directly·against cattle·prods."
Ac 26:14 to·kick·the·heel·back directly·against cattle·prods.'

G2760 κεντυρίων kêntyríōn *n.* (3x)
Compare:G1543
G2760.1 N-NSM κεντυρίων (1x)
Mk 15:39 And the Roman·centurion, the·one having·stood·
G2760.1 N-ASM κεντυρίωνα (1x)

Mk 15:44 summoning the Roman·centurion, he·inquired·of
G2760.1 N-GSM κεντυρίωνος (1x)
Mk 15:45 the Roman·centurion, he·voluntarily·presented the

G2761 κενῶς kênôs *adv.* (1x)
Roots:G2756
G2761 ADV κενῶς (1x)
Jac 4:5 ·presume that the Scripture says for·naught, "The

G2762 κεραία kêraía *n.* (2x)
Roots:G2768
G2762.3 N-NSF κεραία (1x)
Mt 5:18 not one iota or one tiny·mark, by·no·means, should·
G2762.3 N-ASF κεραίαν (1x)
Lk 16:17 ·pass·away, than one tiny·mark of·the Torah-Law

G2763 κεραμεύς kêramêús *n.* (3x)
Roots:G2766
G2763 N-NSM κεραμεύς (1x)
Rm 9:21 Or does·not the potter have authority *over* the clay,
G2763 N-GSM κεραμέως (2x)
Mt 27:7 *pieces·of·silver*, they·bought the potter's field as a·
Mt 27:10 same *pieces·of·silver* for the potter's field, just·as

G2764 κεραμικός kêramikôs *adj.* (1x)
Roots:G2766 Compare:G3749
G2764 A-NPN κεραμικά (1x)
Rv 2:27 of·iron, as the earthenware vessels are·shattered *by·*

G2765 κεράμιον kêrámiôn *n.* (2x)
Roots:G2766 Compare:G0030 G3582 G4632 G5201 G5473
G2765 N-ASN κεράμιον (2x)
Lk 22:10 ·of·clay† bearing a·pitcher of·water shall·meet·up
Mk 14:13 bearing a·pitcher of·water shall·approach·and·

G2766 κέραμος kéramôs *n.* (1x)
Roots:G2767 See:G2763 G2764 G2765
G2766.2 N-GPM κεράμων (1x)
Lk 5:19 him down through the tiles together with·the pallet

G2767 κεράννυμι kêránnymi *v.* (3x)
κεράω kêráō
[primary form, used in certain tenses]
Compare:G3396 See:G2768-1 G4786 G0185 G0194 xLangAlso:H4537
G2767.2 V-AAI-3S ἐκέρασεν (1x)
Rv 18:6 which she·blended·and·poured·out, blend·and·pour·
G2767.2 V-AAM-2P κεράσατε (1x)
Rv 18:6 ·and·poured·out, blend·and·pour·out to·her double.
G2767.2 V-RPP-GSM κεκερασμένου (1x)
Rv 14:10 the·one having·been·blended·and·poured undiluted

G2768 κέρας kéras *n.* (11x)
Compare:G4536 See:G2768-4 G4992-1 xLangEquiv:H7161 A7162
G2768 N-NPN κέρατα (2x)
Rv 17:12 "And the ten horns which you·saw are ten kings
Rv 17:16 And the ten horns which you·saw upon the Scarlet·
G2768 N-ASN κέρας (1x)
Lk 1:69 "And he·awakened a·horn of·Salvation for·us in the
G2768 N-APN κέρατα (6x)
Rv 5:6 ·been·slaughtered, having seven horns and seven
Rv 12:3 having seven heads and ten horns, and seven royal·
Rv 13:1 sea, having seven heads and ten horns, and upon its
Rv 13:11 it·was·having two horns like a·young·male·lamb,
Rv 17:3 of·revilement, having seven heads and ten horns.
Rv 17:7 the·one having the seven heads and the ten horns.
G2768 N-GPN κεράτων (2x)
Rv 9:13 one voice from·among the four horns of·the golden
Rv 13:1 ten horns, and upon its horns ten royal·turbans, and

G2768-4 κερατίνη kêratínē *n.* (1x)
Compare:G4536 G4992-1 See:G2768 xLangEquiv:H7782 xLangAlso:H8619 H2689
G2768-4.2 N-GSF κερατίνης (1x)
Heb 12:19 and to·a·reverberating shofar blast, and to·a·

G2769 κεράτιον kêrátiôn *n.* (1x)
Roots:G2768
G2769.2 N-GPN κερατίων (1x)
Lk 15:16 ·overfill his belly with the carob-pods that the pigs

G2770 κερδαίνω kêrdaínō *v.* (16x)
Roots:G2771 Compare:G4333 G3685
G2770 V-AAI-1S ἐκέρδησα (2x)
Mt 25:20 five talants·of·silver. See, I·gained another five
Mt 25:22 two talants·of·silver. See, I·gained another two
G2770 V-AAI-2S ἐκέρδησας (1x)
Mt 18:15 If he·should·listen·to you, you·gained your brother
G2770 V-AAI-3S ἐκέρδησεν (1x)
Mt 25:17 ·*received* the two, he also gained another two.
G2770 V-AAN κερδῆσαι (1x)
Ac 27:21 ·away from Crete nor·also to·gain this battering
G2770 V-AAP-NSM κερδήσας (1x)
Lk 9:25 a·man·of·clay† benefited, after·gaining the whole
G2770 V-AAS-1S κερδήσω (6x)
Php 3:8 ·to·dogs, in·order·that I·may·gain Anointed-One—
1Co 9:19 myself to·all, in·order·that I·may·gain *all* the more
1Co 9:20 I·became as a·Jew, in·order·that I·may·gain Jews;
1Co 9:20 as under Torah-Law, that I·may·gain the·ones *that*
1Co 9:21 , in·order·that I·may·gain *the·ones that are*
1Co 9:22 ·became as weak in·order·that I·may·gain the weak
G2770 V-AAS-1P κερδήσωμεν (1x)
Jac 4:13 and should·commercially·trade, and should·gain."
G2770 V-AAS-3S κερδήσῃ (2x)
Mt 16:26 being·benefited, if he·should·gain the whole world
Mk 8:36 a·man·of·clay†, if he·should·gain the whole world,
G2770 V-APS-3P κερδηθήσωνται (1x)
1Pe 3:1 Redemptive-word, they·may·be·gained through the

G2771 κέρδος kérdôs *n.* (3x)
Compare:G3786 G4200 G5622 G2039 See:G0146 G0147
G2771 N-NSN κέρδος (1x)
Php 1:21 For me to·live *is* Anointed-One, and to·die *is* gain.
G2771 N-NPN κέρδη (1x)
Php 3:7 But·yet, what·things that·were gains to·me, these·
G2771 N-GSN κέρδους (1x)
Tit 1:11 through·gracious·sounding·words for·shameful gain.

G2772 κέρμα kérma *n.* (1x)
Roots:G2751 Compare:G0694 G3546
G2772.3 N-NSN κέρμα (1x)
Jn 2:15 ·out the moneychangers' money and overturned the

G2773 κερματιστής kêrmatistḗs *n.* (1x)
Roots:G2772 Compare:G2855
G2773.2 N-APM κερματιστάς (1x)
Jn 2:14 *he·found* the exchangers·of·money sitting·down.

G2774 κεφάλαιον kêphálaiôn *n.* (2x)
Roots:G2776
G2774.2 N-NSN κεφάλαιον (1x)
Heb 8:1 being·said, *this·is the* summary: we·do·have such a·
G2774.3 N-GSN κεφαλαίου (1x)
Ac 22:28 "I·myself, with·a·large sum, procured this

G2775 κεφαλαιόω kêphalaiôō *v.* (1x)
Roots:G2776 Compare:G5135 See:G2774 G0346
G2775.2 V-AAI-3P ἐκεφαλαίωσαν (1x)
Mk 12:4 ·one·also, they·hit·*him*·in·the·head and dispatched

G2776 κεφαλή kêphalḗ *n.* (77x)
Compare:G3769 See:G2777 xLangEquiv:H7218 A7217 xLangAlso:H2180
EG2776 (1x)
Mk 15:17 victor's·crown, it·is·placed·around his *head*,
G2776.1 N-NSF κεφαλή (11x)
Mt 14:11 And his head was·brought on a·platter and was·
1Co 11:3 yeu to·personally·know that the head of·every man
1Co 11:3 the Anointed-One, and woman's head *is* the man,
1Co 11:3 head *is* the man, and Anointed-One's head *is* God.
1Co 12:21 of·you," nor again the head to·the feet, "I·have
Eph 4:15 in him who is the head, *namely* the Anointed-One,
Eph 5:23 because the husband is head of·the wife, even as
Eph 5:23 *is* head of·the entire·Called·Out·Citizenry. And he·
Col 1:18 And he·himself is the head of·the Body (the entire·
Col 2:10 *in him*, who is the head of·all principality and
Rv 1:14 His head and *his* hairs *are* white like wool (*as* white
G2776.1 N-NPF κεφαλαί (3x)
Rv 9:17 and sulfurous. And the heads of·the horses *were* as
Rv 9:17 heads of·the horses *were* as heads of·lions, and out
Rv 17:9 "The seven heads are seven mountains, wherever the
G2776.1 N-ASF κεφαλήν (30x)
Jn 13:9 feet merely, but·rather also my hands and my head."
Jn 19:30 And drooping his head, he·handed·over the spirit.
Lk 7:46 ·oil, you·did·not rub·oil·on my head, but she·herself
Lk 9:58 does·not have *a·place* where he·may·prop his head."
Lk 20:17 has·now·become the·distinct head corner *stone*"?
Ac 4:11 ·*is* the·one becoming the·distinct head corner *stone*.
Ac 18:6 "Yeur blood *be* upon yeur own·heads; I·myself *am*
Ac 18:18 ·*Paul* already·having·shorn his head in Cenchrea,
Ac 21:24 in·order·that they·may·shave their heads bald, and
Mt 6:17 when·fasting, rub·oil·on your head and wash your
Mt 8:20 does·not have anywhere he·may·prop his head."
Mt 14:8 "Give me here the head of·John the Immerser on a·
Mt 21:42 has·now·become the·distinct head corner *stone*.
Mt 26:7 ·down on his head as·he·was·reclining·at·the·meal.
Mt 27:29 they·put *it* upon his head and·also a·reed in his
Mt 27:30 they·took the reed and were·beating at his head.
Mk 6:24 And she·declared, "The head of·John the Immerser
Mk 6:25 ·give me from·this·same·hour the head of·John the
Mk 6:27 the king ordered for·his head to·be·brought. But·
Mk 6:28 and brought his head on a·platter, and he·gave it to·
Mk 12:10 has·now·become the·distinct head corner *stone*.
Mk 15:19 And they·were·beating his head with·a·reed and
Rm 12:20 you·shall·stack burning·coals of·fire on his head."
1Pe 2:7 ·one has·now·become the·distinct head corner *stone*
1Co 11:4 *his* head fully·covered, puts·to·shame his head.
1Co 11:5 head not·fully·veiled puts·to·shame her head, for
1Co 11:7 not to·be·fully·veiling his head, inherently·being
Eph 1:22 feet' and gave him *to·be* head over all *things* in·the
Col 2:19 and not securely·holding the Head, from·out of·
Rv 19:12 of·fire, and on his head *were* many royal·turbans,
G2776.1 N-APF κεφαλάς (13x)
Lk 21:28 ·up·straight and lift·up yeur heads, on·account·that
Mt 27:39 ·by were·reviling him, wagging their heads
Mk 15:29 ·reviling him, wagging their heads and saying,
Rv 4:4 they·had on their heads victor's·crowns made·of·gold.
Rv 9:7 battle; and on their heads *were something* as victor's·
Rv 9:19 *were* like serpents having heads, and they·do·bring·
Rv 12:3 fiery·red Dragon, having seven heads and ten horns,
Rv 12:3 ten horns, and seven royal·turbans upon his heads.
Rv 13:1 out of·the sea, having seven heads and ten horns,
Rv 13:1 ·turbans, and upon its heads a·name of·revilement.
Rv 17:3 of·revilement, having seven heads and ten horns.
Rv 17:7 the·one having the seven heads and the ten horns.
Rv 18:19 "And they·cast loose·dirt on their heads, and were·
G2776.1 N-DSF κεφαλῇ (4x)
Jn 19:2 of·thorns, they·put *it* on·his head and arrayed him
Jn 20:12 sitting·down, one alongside the head, and one
Mt 5:36 Neither should·you·swear by your head, because
1Co 11:5 with·her head not·fully·veiled puts·to·shame her
G2776.1 N-GSF κεφαλῆς (14x)
Jn 20:7 that was·upon his head, *that* it·is·being·laid·out not
Lk 7:38 *them* with·the hairs of·her head, and she·was·
Lk 7:44 and firmly·wiped *them* with·the hairs of·her head.
Lk 12:7 even the hairs of·yeur head all have·been·numbered.
Lk 21:18 And·yet a·hair from·among yeur head, no, it·
Ac 27:34 not·even·one hair shall·fall out·from yeur head."
Mt 10:30 But also the hairs of·yeur head are all having·been·
Mt 27:37 Then up·over his head, they·placed the cause of·his
Mk 14:3 ·flask, she·poured *the ointment* down his head.
1Co 11:4 or prophesying, having *his* head fully·covered,
1Co 11:10 authority on her head on·account·of the angels.
Rv 10:1 and a·rainbow *was* upon his head, and his face *was*
Rv 12:1 and upon her head a·victor's·crown of·twelve stars.
Rv 14:14 having on his head a·golden victor's·crown, and
G2776.1 N-GPF κεφαλῶν (1x)
Rv 13:3 one of·its heads as·though having·been·slaughtered

G2777 κεφαλίς kêphalís *n.* (1x)
Roots:G2776
G2777.2 N-DSF κεφαλίδι (1x)

Heb 10:7 *the* header of·an·official·scroll it·has·been·written

G2778 κῆνσος kē̃nsôs *n.* (4x)
Compare:G5056 G5411 See:G0582
G2778.2 N-ASM κῆνσον (3x)
Mt 17:25 earth take taxes or a·census·tribute? From their·
Mt 22:17 Is·it·proper to·give a·census·tribute to·Caesar or
Mk 12:14 Is·it·proper to·give a·census·tribute to·Caesar or
G2778.2 N-GSM κήνσου (1x)
Mt 22:19 for·me the currency of·the census·tribute." And

G2779 κῆπος kē̃pôs *n.* (5x)
Compare:G0290 G1638 G4808-1
xLangEquiv:H1588
G2779.1 N-ASM κῆπον (1x)
Lk 13:19 took *and* cast into his garden. And it·grew and
G2779.2 N-NSM κῆπος (2x)
Jn 18:1 Qidron, where there·was an·enclosed·garden, into
Jn 19:41 ·was·crucified, there·was an·enclosed·garden; and
G2779.2 N-DSM κήπῳ (2x)
Jn 18:26 I·myself see you in the enclosed·garden with him?
Jn 19:41 and in the enclosed·garden, *there·was* a·brand-new

G2780 κηπ•ουρός kēpôurốs *n.* (1x)
Roots:G2779 Compare:G1092 G0289
G2780 N-NSM κηπουρός (1x)
Jn 20:15 presuming that he·is the garden·keeper, says to·him

G2781 κηρίον kēríôn *n.* (1x)
Roots:G2444-3
G2781.2 N-GSN κηρίου (1x)
Lk 24:42 of·a·broiled fish and *a·piece* of·a·honey comb.

G2782 κήρυγμα kḗrygma *n.* (8x)
Roots:G2784 See:G2783
xLangEquiv:H7150
G2782.1 N-NSN κήρυγμα (3x)
1Co 2:4 my discourse and my official·proclamation *was* not
1Co 15:14 ·by·inference, our official·proclamation *is* empty,
2Ti 4:17 the official·proclamation may·be·fully·carried·forth
G2782.1 N-ASN κήρυγμα (3x)
Lk 11:32 they·repented at the official·proclamation of·Jonah;
Mt 12:41 ·repented at the official·proclamation of·Jonah; and
Rm 16:25 and the official·proclamation of·Jesus Anointed
G2782.1 N-DSN κηρύγματι (1x)
Tit 1:3 apparent by official·proclamation, with·which I·
G2782.1 N-GSN κηρύγματος (1x)
1Co 1:21 foolishness of·official·proclamation to·save the·

G2783 κῆρυξ kē̃ryx *n.* (3x)
Roots:G2784 See:G2782
G2783.2 N-NSM κήρυξ (2x)
1Ti 2:7 ·placed *as* an·official·proclaimer and an·ambassador
2Ti 1:11 I·myself was·placed *as* an·official·proclaimer, and
G2783.2 N-ASM κήρυκα (1x)
2Pe 2:5 *on-board,* an·official·proclaimer of·righteousness,

G2784 κηρύσσω kērýssō *v.* (61x)
Compare:G1229 G1256 G2605 See:G2783 G2782
xLangEquiv:A3745 xLangAlso:H7121
G2784.1 V-PAN κηρύσσειν (2x)
Mk 1:45 ·forth, he·began to·officially·herald *his purification*
Mk 5:20 he·went·off and began to·officially·herald in the
G2784.1 V-PAP-NSM κηρύσσων (1x)
Lk 8:1 officially·heralding and proclaiming·the·good·news
G2784.1 V-IAI-3P ἐκήρυσσον (1x)
Mk 7:36 more·abundantly they·were·officially·heralding *it.*
G2784.3 V-FAI-3P κηρύξουσιν (1x)
Rm 10:15 And how shall·they·officially·proclaim, unless
G2784.3 V-FPI-3S κηρυχθήσεται (2x)
Lk 12:3 private·chambers shall·be·officially·proclaimed the
Mt 24:14 of·the kingdom shall·be·officially·proclaimed in
G2784.3 V-PAI-1S κηρύσσω (2x)
Gal 2:2 good·news which I·officially·proclaim among the
Gal 5:11 brothers, if I·still officially·proclaim circumcision,
G2784.3 V-PAI-1P κηρύσσομεν (4x)
Rm 10:8 of·the trust which we·officially·proclaim):
1Co 1:23 so we·ourselves officially·proclaim Anointed-One
1Co 15:11 in·this·manner we·officially·proclaim, and in·
2Co 4:5 not ourselves *that* we·officially·proclaim, but·rather
G2784.3 V-PAI-3S κηρύσσει (2x)
Ac 19:13 yeu *by* Jesus whom Paul officially·proclaims."
2Co 11:4 who·is·coming does·officially·proclaim another
G2784.3 V-PAI-3P κηρύσσουσιν (1x)
Php 1:15 In·fact, some officially·proclaim the Anointed-One
G2784.3 V-PAM-2P κηρύσσετε (1x)
Mt 10:7 And while·traversing, officially·proclaim, saying,
G2784.3 V-PAN κηρύσσειν (4x)
Lk 9:2 ·dispatched them to·officially·proclaim the kingdom
Mt 4:17 ·on, YeShua began to·officially·proclaim and to·say
Mt 11:1 ·there to·instruct and to·officially·proclaim in their
Mk 3:14 that he·may·dispatch them to·officially·proclaim,
G2784.3 V-PAP-ASM κηρύσσοντα (1x)
Rv 5:2 ·strong angel officially·proclaiming with·a·loud voice
G2784.3 V-PAP-APM κηρύσσοντας (1x)
Ac 15:21 in·each city the·ones officially·proclaiming him,
G2784.3 V-PAP-GSM κηρύσσοντος (1x)
Rm 10:14 ·they·hear apart·from one·officially·proclaiming?
G2784.3 V-PAP-NSM κηρύσσων (12x)
Lk 3:3 officially·proclaiming an·immersion of·repentance
Lk 4:44 And he·was officially·proclaiming in the gatherings
Lk 8:39 And he·went·away, officially·proclaiming in the
Ac 20:25 whom I·went·throughout officially·proclaiming the
Ac 28:31 officially·proclaiming the kingdom of·God and
Mt 3:1 arrived·publicly, officially·proclaiming in the
Mt 4:23 and officially·proclaiming the good·news of·the
Mt 9:35 and officially·proclaiming the good·news of·the
Mk 1:4 and officially·proclaiming an·immersion of·
Mk 1:14 into Galilee officially·proclaiming the good·news
Mk 1:39 And he·was officially·proclaiming in their
Rm 2:21 The·one officially·proclaiming not to·steal, do·
G2784.3 V-PPI-3S κηρύσσεται (1x)
1Co 15:12 if Anointed-One is·officially·proclaimed that he·
G2784.3 V-IAI-3S ἐκήρυσσεν (3x)
Ac 8:5 was·officially·proclaiming the Anointed-One to·
Ac 9:20 he·was·officially·proclaiming the Anointed-One in
Mk 1:7 And he·was·officially·proclaiming, saying, "The·
G2784.3 V-IAI-3P ἐκήρυσσον (1x)
Mk 6:12 they·were·officially·proclaiming that men·should·
G2784.3 V-AAI-1P ἐκηρύξαμεν (2x)
1Th 2:9 any of·yeu), we·officially·proclaimed to yeu the
2Co 11:4 whom we·did·not already·officially·proclaim, or
G2784.3 V-AAI-3S ἐκήρυξεν (2x)
Ac 10:37 the immersion which John officially·proclaimed,
1Pe 3:19 to·the spirits in prison, he·officially·proclaimed
G2784.3 V-AAI-3P ἐκήρυξαν (1x)
Mk 16:20 those *disciples* officially·proclaimed *it* everywhere
G2784.3 V-AAM-2S κήρυξον (1x)
2Ti 4:2 Officially·proclaim the Redemptive-word! Stand·
G2784.3 V-AAM-2P κηρύξατε (2x)
Mt 10:27 in the ear, officially·proclaim upon the rooftops.
Mk 16:15 ·all the world, officially·proclaim the good·news
G2784.3 V-AAN κηρύξαι (3x)
Lk 4:18 to·officially·proclaim liberty to·subdued·captives
Lk 4:19 to·officially·proclaim an·acceptable Year of·
Ac 10:42 he·charged us to·officially·proclaim to·the people,
G2784.3 V-AAP-NSM κηρύξας (1x)
1Co 9:27 ·somehow, after·officially·proclaiming to·others,
G2784.3 V-AAS-1S κηρύξω (1x)
Mk 1:38 in·order·that I·may·officially·proclaim there·also.
G2784.3 V-API-3S ἐκηρύχθη (1x)
1Ti 3:16 by·angels, is·officially·proclaimed among Gentiles,
G2784.3 V-APN κηρυχθῆναι (2x)
Lk 24:47 of·moral·failures to·be·officially·proclaimed in his
Mk 13:10 the good·news first to·be·officially·proclaimed to
G2784.3 V-APP-GSN κηρυχθέντος (1x)
Col 1:23 (the·one already·being·officially·proclaimed to
G2784.3 V-APP-NSM κηρυχθείς (1x)
2Co 1:19 the·one being·officially·proclaimed among yeu
G2784.3 V-APS-3S κηρυχθῇ (2x)
Mt 26:13 good·news should·be·officially·proclaimed in the
Mk 14:9 good·news should·be·officially·proclaimed in the

G2785 κῆτος kē̃tôs *n.* (1x)
Roots:G5490 xLangAlso:H1709
G2785.2 N-GSN κήτους (1x)
Mt 12:40 nights in the belly of·the whale, in·this·manner the

G2786 Κηφᾶς Kēphâs *n/p.* (6x)
כֵּף keph [Hebrew]
Roots:H3710 Compare:G3037 See:G4074
xLangAlso:H6697 H5553
G2786.2 N/P-NSM Κηφᾶς (4x)
Jn 1:42 shall·be·called Kephas *(a·piece·of·hollow·rock),*"
Gal 2:9 to·me, Jacob, Kephas·*(called·Peter),* and John, the·
1Co 3:22 Paul, or Apollos, or Kephas·*(called·Peter),* or *the*
1Co 9:5 brothers of·the Lord, and *as* Kephas·*(called·Peter)*?
G2786.2 N/P-DSM Κηφᾷ (1x)
1Co 15:5 he·was·gazed·upon by·Kephas·*(called·Peter),* then
G2786.2 N/P-GSM Κηφᾶ (1x)
1Co 1:12 and "I *am* of·Kephas·*(called·Peter),*" and "I

G2787 κιβωτός kibōtốs *n.* (6x)
Κιβωτός Kibōtốs
xLangAlso:H0727 H8392
G2787.2 N-ASF κιβωτόν (3x)
Lk 17:27 Noach entered into the floating·ark, and·then the
Heb 11:7 fully·prepared a·floating·ark for *the* salvation of·
Mt 24:38 that day *that* Noach entered into the floating·ark,
G2787.2 N-GSF κιβωτοῦ (1x)
1Pe 3:20 ·Noach, with·a·floating·ark being·fully·prepared,
G2787.3 N-NSF Κιβωτός (1x)
Rv 11:19 heaven, and the Ark of·his covenant was·made·
G2787.3 N-ASF Κιβωτόν (1x)
Heb 9:4 a·golden censer and the Ark of·the covenant having·

G2788 κιθάρα kithára *n.* (4x)
Compare:G2796-1 G5568-1 G3476-1 See:G2789
xLangAlso:H3658 H5035
G2788.1 N-NSF κιθάρα (1x)
1Co 14:7 sound, whether flute or harp, if it·should·not give
G2788.1 N-APF κιθάρας (2x)
Rv 5:8 each·one *of·the·Elders* having harps and golden vials
Rv 15:2 on the transparent,·glassy sea, having harps of·God.
G2788.1 N-DPF κιθάραις (1x)
Rv 14:2 I·heard a·sound of·harpists harping with their harps.

G2789 κιθαρίζω kitharízō *v.* (2x)
Roots:G2788
G2789 V-PAP-GPM κιθαριζόντων (1x)
Rv 14:2 And I·heard a·sound of·harpists harping with their
G2789 V-PPP-NSN κιθαριζόμενον (1x)
1Co 14:7 *what tune* is·being·piped or is·being·harped?

G2790 κιθαρ•ῳδός kitharōdós *n.* (2x)
Roots:G2788 G5603
G2790 N-GPM κιθαρῳδῶν (2x)
Rv 14:2 And I·heard a·sound of·harpists harping with their
Rv 18:22 "And a·sound of·harpists, and musicians, and of·

G2791 Κιλικία Kilikía *n/l.* (8x)
G2791.2 N/L-ASF Κιλικίαν (3x)
Ac 15:23 in Antioch and Syria and Cilicia, the·ones from·
Ac 15:41 he·went·throughout Syria and Cilicia, reaffirming
Ac 27:5 the open·sea adjacent·to Cilicia and PamPhylia, we·
G2791.2 N/L-GSF Κιλικίας (5x)
Ac 6:9 Alexandrians, and the·ones from Cilicia and Asia,
Ac 21:39 a·Jew of·Tarsus, *a·city* of·Cilicia, a·citizen of·no
Ac 22:3 in Tarsus, *a·city* in·Cilicia, but having·been·reared
Ac 23:34 And ascertaining that *he·was* from Cilicia,
Gal 1:21 I·came into the vicinities of·Syria and Cilicia,

G2792 κινάμωμον kinámōmôn *n.* (1x)
Compare:G3030 G2368
xLangEquiv:H7076
G2792 N-ASN κινάμωμον (1x)
Rv 18:13 "and·also cinnamon, incense, ointments, and

G2793 κινδυνεύω kindynêúō *v.* (4x)
Roots:G2794
G2793.1 V-PAI-1P κινδυνεύομεν (1x)
Ac 19:40 For we·are·in·danger also to·be·called·to·account

G2793.1 V-PAI-3S κινδυνεύει (1x)
Ac 19:27 this our occupation is·in·danger of·coming into
G2793.1 V-IAI-3P ἐκινδύνευον (1x)
Lk 8:23 they·were·swamped *with·water* and were·in·danger.
G2793.2 V-PAI-1P κινδυνεύομεν (1x)
1Co 15:30 And why·do we·ourselves risk·danger every hour

G2794 κίνδυνος kíndynôs *n.* (9x)
See:G2793
G2794 N-NSM κίνδυνος (1x)
Rm 8:35 or famine, or nakedness, or danger, or dagger?
G2794 N-DPM κινδύνοις (8x)
2Co 11:26 many·times *I·was* in·dangers of·swollen·rivers,
2Co 11:26 in·dangers of·swollen·rivers, dangers of·robbers,
2Co 11:26 dangers of·robbers, dangers from·among *my·own*
2Co 11:26 *my·own* kindred, dangers from·among Gentiles,
2Co 11:26 dangers from·among Gentiles, dangers in a·city,
2Co 11:26 dangers in a·city, dangers in a·barren·wilderness,
2Co 11:26 dangers in a·barren·wilderness, dangers at sea,
2Co 11:26 at sea, *and in* dangers among false·brothers,

G2795 κινέω kinéō *v.* (8x)
Roots:G1510-1 Compare:G5015 See:G2796 G3334 G4787
G2795.1 V-FAI-1S κινήσω (1x)
Rv 2:5 to·you with·haste, and shall·stir your Lampstand out
G2795.1 V-PAP-ASM κινοῦντα (1x)
Ac 24:5 ·viral·pestilence, and stirring controversy among·all
G2795.1 V-PPI-1P κινούμεθα (1x)
Ac 17:28 in him, we·live and are·stirred and have·existence.
G2795.1 V-API-3S ἐκινήθη (1x)
Ac 21:30 And the whole City was·stirred, and the people
G2795.1 V-API-3P ἐκινήθησαν (1x)
Rv 6:14 every mountain and island was·stirred out of·their
G2795.2 V-PAP-NPM κινοῦντες (2x)
Mt 27:39 ·by were·reviling him, wagging their heads
Mk 15:29 ·by were·reviling him, wagging their heads and
G2795.4 V-AAN κινῆσαι (1x)
Mt 23:4 they·are·not willing *even* to·bother·with them.

G2796 κίνησις kínēsis *n.* (1x)
Roots:G2795
G2796 N-ASF κίνησιν (1x)
Jn 5:3 — *all·of·them* waiting·for the stirring of·the water.

G2797 Κίς Kís *n/p.* (1x)
Ḳίš Qísh [Greek, Octuagint]
קִישׁ qiysh [Hebrew]
Roots:H7027
G2797.2 N/P-PRI Ḳίς (1x)
Ac 13:21 gave to·them Saul son of·Qish, a·man from·among

G2798 κλάδος kládôs *n.* (11x)
Roots:G2806 Compare:G0902 G2814
G2798 N-NSM κλάδος (2x)
Mt 24:32 ·now, whenever its branch should·become tender
Mk 13:28 ·now, whenever its branch should·become tender
G2798 N-NPM κλάδοι (2x)
Rm 11:16 And if the root *is* holy, so *are* the branches.
Rm 11:19 "The branches were·broken·off in·order·that I·
G2798 N-APM κλάδους (2x)
Mt 21:8 and others were·chopping branches from the trees,
Mk 4:32 and it·produces great branches, such·for the birds
G2798 N-DPM κλάδοις (2x)
Lk 13:19 and the birds of·the sky nested in its branches."
Mt 13:32 of·the sky to·come and to·nest on its branches."
G2798 N-GPM κλάδων (3x)
Rm 11:17 And if some of·the branches were·broken·off, and
Rm 11:18 do·not boast·over the branches. But if you·do·
Rm 11:21 spare the fully natural branches, *take·heed* lest·

G2799 κλαίω klaíō *v.* (40x)
Compare:G1145 G2354 G2875 G3996 G0994
See:G2805
xLangEquiv:H1058
G2799 V-FAI-2P κλαύσετε (2x)
Jn 16:20 I·say to·yeu, that yeu shall·weep and shall·bewail,
Lk 6:25 Because yeu·shall·mourn and shall·weep.
G2799 V-FDI-3P κλαύσονται (1x)
Rv 18:9 ·in·voluptuous·luxury with her, shall·weep·for her,
G2799 V-PAI-2S κλαίεις (2x)
Jn 20:13 "Woman, why do·you·weep?" She·says to·them,
Jn 20:15 "Woman, why do·you·weep? Whom·do you·seek?
G2799 V-PAI-2P κλαίετε (1x)
Mk 5:39 "Why are·yeu·in·a·commotion and weeping? The
G2799 V-PAI-3P κλαίουσιν (1x)
Rv 18:11 And the merchants of·the earth do·weep and mourn
G2799 V-PAM-2S κλαῖε (2x)
Lk 7:13 over her and declared to·her, "Do·not weep."
Rv 5:5 Elders says to·me, "Do·not weep. Behold the Lion,
G2799 V-PAM-2P κλαίετε (3x)
Lk 8:52 but he·declared, "Do·not weep. She·did·not die,
Lk 23:28 "Daughters of·JeruSalem, do·not weep over me.
Lk 23:28 *Yet* moreover, weep over yeurselves and over yeur
G2799 V-PAN κλαίειν (1x)
Rm 12:15 those·rejoicing, and to·weep with those·weeping,
G2799 V-PAP-ASF κλαίουσαν (1x)
Jn 11:33 Now as·soon·as Jesus saw her weeping, and the
G2799 V-PAP-APM κλαίοντας (2x)
Jn 11:33 weeping, and the weeping Judeans coming·together
Mk 5:38 a·commotion, *people* weeping and clamoring
G2799 V-PAP-DPM κλαίουσιν (1x)
Mk 16:10 him, to·those·being in·mourning and weeping.
G2799 V-PAP-GPM κλαιόντων (1x)
Rm 12:15 those·rejoicing, and to·weep with those·weeping,
G2799 V-PAP-NSF κλαίουσα (3x)
Jn 20:11 outside toward the chamber·tomb weeping. Now·
Lk 7:38 his feet right·behind *him* while·weeping, she·began
Mt 2:18 distressing; *it·was* Rachel weeping *for* her children.
G2799 V-PAP-NSM κλαίων (1x)
Php 3:18 and now even *while* weeping, I·say *that they·are*
G2799 V-PAP-NPF κλαίουσαι (1x)
Ac 9:39 widows stood·by him, weeping and fully·exhibiting
G2799 V-PAP-NPM κλαίοντες (6x)
Lk 6:21 "Supremely·blessed *are* the·ones weeping now,
Ac 21:13 ·do yeu·continue weeping and jointly·crushing my
1Co 7:30 and the·ones weeping as not weeping; and the·ones
1Co 7:30 and the·ones weeping as not weeping; and the·ones
Rv 18:15 the fear of·her torment, weeping and mourning,
Rv 18:19 and were·yelling·out, weeping and mourning,
G2799 V-IAI-1S ἔκλαιον (1x)
Rv 5:4 And I·myself was·weeping much, because not·even·
G2799 V-IAI-3S ἔκλαιεν (2x)
Jn 20:11 as she·was·weeping, she·stooped·near·to·peer into
Mk 14:72 And reflecting·upon *it*, he·was·weeping.
G2799 V-IAI-3P ἔκλαιον (1x)
Lk 8:52 And all were·weeping and vividly·lamenting·over
G2799 V-AAI-2P ἐκλαύσατε (1x)
Lk 7:32 dance; we·bewailed for·yeu, and yeu·do·not weep.'
G2799 V-AAI-3S ἔκλαυσεν (3x)
Lk 19:41 ·drew·near, upon·seeing the City, he·wept over it,
Lk 22:62 And Peter, going·forth outside, wept bitterly.
Mt 26:75 And going·forth outside, he·wept bitterly.
G2799 V-AAM-2P κλαύσατε (2x)
Jac 4:9 Be·miserable, also mourn and weep. *Let* yeur
Jac 5:1 Come·on now, Wealthy·Men! Weep, howling over
G2799 V-AAS-3S κλαύσῃ (1x)
Jn 11:31 chamber·tomb in·order·that she·may·weep there."

G2800 κλάσις klásis *n.* (2x)
Roots:G2806 See:G2801
G2800 N-DSF κλάσει (2x)
Lk 24:35 he·was·known to·them in the breaking of·the bread
Ac 2:42 in·the fellowship, and in·the breaking of·the bread,

G2801 κλάσμα klásma *n.* (9x)
Roots:G2806 See:G2800
G2801 N-APN κλάσματα (1x)
Jn 6:12 the remaining·excess fragments, in·order·that not
G2801 N-GPN κλασμάτων (8x)
Jn 6:13 wicker·baskets with·fragments from·out of·the five
Lk 9:17 *was* twelve wicker·baskets of·*bread*·fragments.
Mt 14:20 the remaining·excess of·the fragments— twelve
Mt 15:37 full *of* the remaining·excess of·the fragments.
Mk 6:43 wicker·baskets full of·*bread*·fragments and of·the
Mk 8:8 And they·took·up an·abundance of·fragments, seven
Mk 8:19 wicker·baskets full of·fragments did·yeu·take·up?
Mk 8:20 completely·full of·fragments did·yeu·take·up?

G2802 Κλαύδη Klaúdē *n/l.* (1x)
G2802 N/L-ASF Κλαύδην (1x)
Ac 27:16 small·island being·called Clauda, with·difficulty

G2803 Κλαυδία Klaudía *n/p.* (1x)
Roots:G2804
G2803 N/P-NSF Κλαυδία (1x)
2Ti 4:21 and Pudens, and Linus, and Claudia, and all the

G2804 Κλαύδιος Klaúdiôs *n/p.* (3x)
Compare:G5086 G3505 See:G2541 G3079
G2804.1 N/P-ASM Κλαύδιον (1x)
Ac 18:2 on·account·of Claudius *Caesar* having·thoroughly·
G2804.1 N/P-GSM Κλαυδίου (1x)
Ac 11:28 even happened in·the·days of·Claudius Caesar.
G2804.2 N/P-NSM Κλαύδιος (1x)
Ac 23:26 "Claudius Lysias, to·the most·noble governor Felix

G2805 κλαυθμός klauthmós *n.* (9x)
Roots:G2799 Compare:G0995 G2355 See:G2805-1
G2805 N-NSM κλαυθμός (9x)
Lk 13:28 there *outside*, there·shall·be the weeping and the
Ac 20:37 And everyone was weeping a·long·while. And
Mt 2:18 Ramah— a·woeful·wailing and weeping and much
Mt 8:12 where there·shall·be the weeping and the gnashing
Mt 13:42 ·the fire, where there·shall·be the weeping and the
Mt 13:50 ·the fire, where there·shall·be the weeping and the
Mt 22:13 where there·shall·be the weeping and the
Mt 24:51 where there·shall·be the weeping and the
Mt 25:30 where there·shall·be the weeping and the

G2806 κλάω kláō *v.* (16x)
See:G2800 G2801
G2806.2 V-PAI-1P κλῶμεν (1x)
1Co 10:16 The bread which we·break, is·it not·indeed
G2806.2 V-PAP-NPM κλῶντες (1x)
Ac 2:46 in the Sanctuary·Atrium and breaking bread in·each
G2806.2 V-PPP-NSN κλώμενον (1x)
1Co 11:24 is my body, the·one being·broken over yeu. Do
G2806.2 V-AAI-1S ἔκλασα (1x)
Mk 8:19 When I·broke the five loaves·of·bread among the
G2806.2 V-AAI-3S ἔκλασεν (6x)
Lk 22:19 bread *and* giving·thanks, he·broke *it* and gave *it*
Mt 15:36 fish *and* upon·giving·thanks, he·broke *them* and
Mt 26:26 and blessing *it*, YeShua broke *it* and was·giving *it*
Mk 8:6 upon·giving·thanks, he·broke *the loaves·of·bread*,
Mk 14:22 *and* blessing *it*, Jesus broke *it* and gave *it* to·them
1Co 11:24 and after·giving·thanks, he·broke *it* and declared,
G2806.2 V-AAN κλάσαι (1x)
Ac 20:7 having·been·gathered·together to·break bread, Paul
G2806.2 V-AAP-NSM κλάσας (4x)
Lk 24:30 bread, he·blessed *it*, and after·breaking *it*, he·was·
Ac 20:11 Then after·walking·up and breaking bread, and
Ac 27:35 in·the·sight of·them·all, and after·breaking *it*, he·
Mt 14:19 he·blessed *it*. And after·breaking *bread*, he·gave
EG2806.2 (1x)
Mk 8:20 "And when *I·broke* the seven *loaves·of·bread*

G2807 κλείς klêís *n.* (6x)
Roots:G2808
G2807 N-NSF κλείς (1x)
Rv 9:1 And to·him was·given the key of·the well of·the
G2807 N-ASF κλεῖδα (3x)
Lk 11:52 yeu·took·away the key of·the absolute·knowledge.
Rv 3:7 "'The·one having the key of·David, the·one opening·
Rv 20:1 heaven, having the key of·the bottomless·pit and a·
G2807 N-APF κλεῖς (2x)
Mt 16:19 And I·shall·give to·you the keys of·the kingdom
Rv 1:18 ·Amen; and I·have the keys of·Hades and of·Death.

Kκ

G2808 κλείω klêíō *v.* (16x)
Compare:G2576 See:G4788 G0608
G2808 V-PAI-2P κλείετε (1x)
Mt 23:14 ·hypocrites! Because yeu·shut·up the kingdom of·
G2808 V-PAI-3S κλείει (2x)
Rv 3:7 the·one opening·up and not·even·one·man shuts, *who*
Rv 3:7 ·one·man shuts, *who* shuts and not·even·one·man
G2808 V-AAI-3S ἔκλεισεν (1x)
Rv 20:3 him into the bottomless·pit, and shut him up, and
G2808 V-AAN κλεῖσαι (2x)
Rv 3:8 ·up, and not·even·one·man is·able to·shut it, because
Rv 11:6 These have authority to·shut the sky, in·order·that
G2808 V-AAP-NSM κλείσας (1x)
Mt 6:6 your private·chamber, and after·shutting your door,
G2808 V-AAS-3S κλείσῃ (1x)
1Jn 3:17 need, and should·shut·up his inward·affections
G2808 V-API-3S ἐκλείσθη (2x)
Lk 4:25 when the heaven was·shut·up for·a·span·of three
Mt 25:10 And the door was·shut.
G2808 V-API-3P ἐκλείσθησαν (1x)
Ac 21:30 ·Courtyard, and immediately the doors were·shut.
G2808 V-APS-3P κλεισθῶσιν (1x)
Rv 21:25 And no, its gates may·not be·shut at·day's·end, for
G2808 V-RPI-3S κέκλεισται (1x)
Lk 11:7 Even·now, the door has·been·shut, and my little·
G2808 V-RPP-ASN κεκλεισμένον (1x)
Ac 5:23 we·found the dungeon having·been·shut with all
G2808 V-RPP-GPM κεκλεισμένων (2x)
Jn 20:19 and with·the doors having·been·shut where the
Jn 20:26 *and* with·the doors having·been·shut, Jesus came

G2809 κλέμμα klémma *n.* (1x)
Roots:G2813 See:G2812 G2829
G2809.2 N-GPN κλεμμάτων (1x)
Rv 9:21 sexual·immorality, nor from·out of·their thefts.

G2810 Κλεό•πας Klêópas *n/p.* (1x)
Roots:G2811 G3962
G2810.2 N/P-NSM Κλεόπας (1x)
Lk 24:18 the individual whose name *was* CleoPas declared to

G2811 κλέος klêós *n.* (1x)
Roots:G2564 Compare:G5345 G1391
G2811.2 N-NSN κλέος (1x)
1Pe 2:20 For what·kind·of merit *is·it*, if when yeu·are·being·

G2812 κλέπτης kléptēs *n.* (16x)
Roots:G2813 Compare:G3027 See:G2809
xLangEquiv:H1590
G2812.1 N-NSM κλέπτης (3x)
Jn 12:6 but·rather because he·was a·thief, and was·holding
Lk 12:33 heavens, where no thief draws·near, neither·does
1Pe 4:15 suffer as a·murderer, or *as* a·thief, or *as* a·criminal,
G2812.1 N-NPM κλέπται (3x)
Mt 6:19 obliterate, and where thieves break·in and steal.
Mt 6:20 obliterate, and where thieves do·not break·in nor·
1Co 6:10 nor thieves, nor covetous·men, nor drunkards, nor
G2812.2 N-NSM κλέπτης (2x)
Jn 10:1 ·up from·some·other·way, that·one is a·Thief and a·
Jn 10:10 "The Thief does·not come, except in·order·that he·
G2812.2 N-NPM κλέπται (1x)
Jn 10:8 ·which came before me are Thieves and robbers, but·
G2812.3 N-NSM κλέπτης (6x)
Lk 12:39 ·known in·which hour the thief would·come, he·
Mt 24:43 watch *of·the night* the thief comes, he·would·have
1Th 5:2 ·Yahweh, in·this·manner, comes as a·thief at night.
1Th 5:4 in·order·that the Day should·grab yeu as a·thief.
Rv 3:3 ·keep·alert, I·shall·come upon you as a·thief, and no,
Rv 16:15 "Behold, I·come as a·thief. Supremely·blessed *is*
G2812.4 N-NSM κλέπτης (1x)
2Pe 3:10 Day of·*the*·Lord shall·come as a·thief, in a·night in

G2813 κλέπτω kléptō *v.* (13x)
Compare:G3557 See:G2812 G2809
xLangEquiv:H1589
G2813 V-FAI-2S κλέψεις (2x)
Mt 19:18 commit·adultery," "You·shall·not steal,"
Rm 13:9 ·not murder. You·shall·not steal. You·shall·not
G2813 V-PAI-2S κλέπτεις (1x)
Rm 2:21 officially·proclaiming not to·steal, do·you·steal?
G2813 V-PAI-3P κλέπτουσιν (2x)
Mt 6:19 obliterate, and where thieves break·in and steal.
Mt 6:20 and where thieves do·not break·in nor·even steal.
G2813 V-PAM-3S κλεπτέτω (1x)
Eph 4:28 The·one stealing must·steal no·longer. But rather
G2813 V-PAN κλέπτειν (1x)
Rm 2:21 officially·proclaiming not to·steal, do·you·steal?
G2813 V-PAP-NSM κλέπτων (1x)
Eph 4:28 The·one stealing must·steal no·longer. But rather
G2813 V-AAI-3P ἔκλεψαν (1x)
Mt 28:13 ·declare, 'His disciples stole him, coming by·night
G2813 V-AAS-2S κλέψῃς (2x)
Lk 18:20 murder," "You·may·not steal," "You·may·not
Mk 10:19 murder," "You·may·not steal," "You·may·not
G2813 V-AAS-3S κλέψῃ (1x)
Jn 10:10 come, except in·order·that he·may·steal, and may·
G2813 V-AAS-3P κλέψωσιν (1x)
Mt 27:64 disciples, coming by·night, should·steal him, and

G2814 κλῆμα klē̃ma *n.* (5x)
Roots:G2806 Compare:G2798 See:G2814-1
G2814.2 N-NSN κλῆμα (2x)
Jn 15:4 ·I in yeu. Just·as the vine·sprout is·not able to·bear
Jn 15:6 as the *unfruitful* vine·sprout and is·already·withered,
G2814.2 N-NPN κλήματα (1x)
Jn 15:5 vine, yeu *are* the vine·sprouts. The·one abiding in
G2814.2 N-ASN κλῆμα (1x)
Jn 15:2 Every vine·sprout in me not bearing fruit, *the* same
EG2814.2 (1x)
Jn 15:2 same he·takes·away; and any *vine·sprout* bearing the

G2815 Κλήμης Klḗmēs *n/p.* (1x)
G2815.2 N/P-GSM Κλήμεντος (1x)
Php 4:3 ·me in the good·news, with Clement also, and *with*

G2816 κληρο•νομέω klērônômḗō *v.* (18x)
Roots:G2818 See:G2817 G2624-1 G4783-1
xLangEquiv:H5157
G2816.1 V-AAS-3S κληρονομήσῃ (1x)
Gal 4:30 maidservant, no, should·not be·heir with the son
G2816.2 V-FAI-3S κληρονομήσει (2x)
Mt 19:29 ·times·over and shall·inherit eternal life·above.
Rv 21:7 The·one overcoming shall·inherit all·things; and I·
G2816.2 V-FAI-3P κληρονομήσουσιν (4x)
Gal 5:21 such·things shall·not inherit God's kingdom.
Mt 5:5 because they·themselves shall·inherit the earth.
1Co 6:9 unrighteous·men shall·not inherit God's kingdom?
1Co 6:10 violently·or·exceedingly·greedy·men shall·inherit
G2816.2 V-PAI-3S κληρονομεῖ (1x)
1Co 15:50 does the corruption inherit the incorruptibility.
G2816.2 V-PAN κληρονομεῖν (1x)
Heb 1:14 on·account·of the·ones about to·inherit Salvation?
G2816.2 V-PAP-GPM κληρονομούντων (1x)
Heb 6:12 trust and long-suffering are·inheriting the promises
G2816.2 V-AAM-2P κληρονομήσατε (1x)
Mt 25:34 ·been·blessed of·my Father! Inherit the kingdom
G2816.2 V-AAN κληρονομῆσαι (2x)
Heb 12:17 long·afterward, wanting to·inherit the blessing,
1Co 15:50 and blood is·not able to·inherit God's kingdom;
G2816.2 V-AAS-1S κληρονομήσω (3x)
Lk 10:25 what should·I·do to·inherit eternal life·above?
Lk 18:18 what should·I·be·doing to·inherit eternal life·above
Mk 10:17 should·I·do that I·may·inherit eternal life·above?
G2816.2 V-AAS-2P κληρονομήσητε (1x)
1Pe 3:9 in·order·that yeu·should·inherit the·active·blessing.
G2816.2 V-RAI-3S κεκληρονόμηκεν (1x)
Heb 1:4 by·as·much·as he·has·inherited a·more·superb name

G2817 κληρο•νομία klērônomía *n.* (16x)
Roots:G2818 See:G2816
xLangEquiv:H5159
G2817.2 N-NSF κληρονομία (3x)
Lk 20:14 ·should·kill him, that the inheritance may·be ours.'
Gal 3:18 For if the inheritance *is* as·a·result of·Torah-Law,
Mk 12:7 ·should·kill him, and the inheritance shall·be ours.'
G2817.2 N-ASF κληρονομίαν (7x)
Lk 12:13 for·my brother to·divide the inheritance with me."
Ac 7:5 "But he·did·not give him an·inheritance in it, not·
Ac 20:32 and to·give yeu an·inheritance among all the·ones
Heb 11:8 to·receive for an·inheritance, listened·and·obeyed;
Mt 21:38 him and should·fully·hold·onto his inheritance.'
1Pe 1:4 shrivel-proof inheritance having·been·reserved in *the*
Eph 5:5 an·idolater— does·not have any·inheritance in the
G2817.2 N-GSF κληρονομίας (4x)
Heb 9:15 may·receive the promise of·the eternal inheritance.
Eph 1:14 ·deposit of·our inheritance for a·full·redemption
Eph 1:18 wealth of·the glory of·his inheritance in the holy·
Col 3:24 ·receive·in·full the rewarding of·the inheritance, for
EG2817.2 (2x)
Gal 3:18 ·bestowed *the inheritance* to·AbRaham through
Gal 3:19 for·whom *the inheritance* has·been·promised. *And*

G2818 κληρο•νόμος klērônómôs *n.* (15x)
Roots:G2819 G3551 See:G2816 G2817
G2818.2 N-NSM κληρονόμος (6x)
Lk 20:14 'This is the heir. Come·here! We·should·kill him,
Heb 11:7 became an·heir of·a·righteousness according·to
Gal 4:1 Now I·say *that* the heir, for·a·span·of time (as·long·
Gal 4:7 ·son; and if a·son, *then* also an·heir of·God through
Mt 21:38 'This is the heir. Come·here! We·should·kill him
Mk 12:7 'This is the heir! Come·here! We·should·kill him,
G2818.2 N-NPM κληρονόμοι (5x)
Gal 3:29 Seed and *are* heirs according·to promise.
Rm 4:14 ·ones birthed·from·out of·Torah-Law *are* heirs, the
Rm 8:17 *·are* children, then·also *we·are* heirs, heirs in·fact
Rm 8:17 then·also *we·are* heirs, heirs in·fact of·God and
Tit 3:7 we·should·become heirs according·to an·Expectation
G2818.2 N-ASM κληρονόμον (2x)
Heb 1:2 Son, whom he·placed *as* heir of·all·things, through
Rm 4:13 (the·one himself to·be *the* heir of·the world), but·
G2818.2 N-APM κληρονόμους (1x)
Jac 2:5 wealthy in trust and *to·be* heirs of·the kingdom which
G2818.2 N-DPM κληρονόμοις (1x)
Heb 6:17 to·fully·exhibit to·the heirs of·promise the

G2819 κλῆρος klē̃rôs *n.* (13x)
Roots:G2806 Compare:G3310 See:G2818 G2820
G1462-1 G3648
xLangEquiv:H1486 xLangAlso:H5159
G2819.1 N-NSM κλῆρος (1x)
Ac 1:26 ·gave·forth their lots, and the lot fell upon MatthIas.
G2819.1 N-ASM κλῆρον (5x)
Jn 19:24 among·themselves, and they·cast lots upon my
Lk 23:34 ·dividing·up his garments, they·cast lots.
Mt 27:35 casting lots in·order·that it·may·be·completely·
Mt 27:35 among·themselves, and they·cast lots over my
Mk 15:24 ·up his garments, while·casting lots upon them,
G2819.1 N-APM κλήρους (1x)
Ac 1:26 And they·gave·forth their lots, and the lot fell upon
G2819.2 N-ASM κλῆρον (2x)
Ac 1:17 ·clearly·obtained the allotted·portion of·this service.
Ac 1:25 to·take the allotted·portion of·this service and
G2819.3 N-GPM κλήρων (1x)
1Pe 5:3 ·lordship·against the ones·assigned·by·allotment,
G2819.4 N-ASM κλῆρον (1x)
Ac 26:18 ·failures and an·allotted·heritage among the·ones
G2819.4 N-GSM κλήρου (1x)
Col 1:12 the portion of·the allotted·heritage of·the holy·ones
G2819.5 N-NSM κλῆρος (1x)
Ac 8:21 ·is not a·portion nor·even a·small·chance for·you in

G2820 κληρόω klērôō *v.* (1x)
Roots:G2819 Compare:G2975 See:G4345
G2820.2 V-API-1P ἐκληρώθημεν (1x)
Eph 1:11 also we·are·assigned·an·allotted·heritage by him,

G2821 κλῆσις klē̃sis *n.* (12x)
Roots:G2564 See:G2822 G1577
xLangEquiv:H7150 xLangAlso:H4931
EG2821 (1x)

1Th 4:8 the·one presently·ignoring *this calling·forth, it·is*
G2821.1 N-NSF κλῆσις (1x)
Rm 11:29 gracious·bestowments and the calling of·God *are*
G2821.1 N-DSF κλήσει (2x)
1Co 7:20 ·man, in the calling in·which he·was·called·forth,
2Ti 1:9 us and calling·*us*·forth with·a·holy calling, not
G2821.1 N-GSF κλήσεως (5x)
Heb 3:1 *yeu* participants of·a·heavenly calling) fully·observe
Php 3:14 *it* toward the prize of·the upward calling of·God in
2Th 1:11 may·consider yeu deserving of·the calling, and *that*
Eph 4:1 of·the calling by·which yeu·are·called·forth,
Eph 4:4 ·called·forth in one expectation of·yeur calling—
G2821.2 N-ASF κλῆσιν (2x)
2Pe 1:10 ·endeavor to·make yeur calling·forth and Selection
1Co 1:26 For look·at yeur calling·forth, brothers: how·that
G2821.2 N-GSF κλήσεως (1x)
Eph 1:18 is the expectation of·his calling·forth, and what *is*

G2822 κλητός klētós *adj.* (11x)
Roots:G2564 See:G2821 G1577 G1577-3 G1945-1
xLangEquiv:H7148 H4744 xLangAlso:H4744-1
G2822.2 A-NSM κλητός (2x)
Rm 1:1 of·Jesus Anointed, called·forth *to·be* an·ambassador,
1Co 1:1 Paul, called·forth *to·be* an·ambassador of·Jesus
G2822.2 A-NPM κλητοί (3x)
Mt 20:16 the first last; for many are called·forth, but few *are*
Mt 22:14 "For many are called·forth, but few *are* Selected.
Rv 17:14 the·ones with him *are* called·forth, and Selected,
G2822.2 A-DPM κλητοῖς (4x)
Rm 1:7 Rome, beloved of·God, called·forth *as* holy·ones.
Rm 8:28 for·the·ones being called·forth according·to *his*
1Co 1:2 in Anointed-One Jesus, called·forth *to·be* holy·ones,
1Co 1:24 to·them, to·the·ones *who·are* called·forth, to·both
G2822.4 A-NPM κλητοί (1x)
Rm 1:6 are *the* called·forth·ones of·Jesus Anointed).
G2822.4 A-DPM κλητοῖς (1x)
Jud 1:1 in·YeShua Anointed, *to·yeu, the* called·forth·ones:

G2823 κλίβανος klíbanôs *n.* (2x)
Compare:G2289-1 xLangAlso:H8574
G2823.2 N-ASM κλίβανον (2x)
Lk 12:28 and tomorrow being·cast into an·oven, how·much
Mt 6:30 and tomorrow being·cast into an·oven, *¿!·shall·he*

G2824 κλίμα klíma *n.* (4x)
Roots:G2827
G2824.3 N-APN κλίματα (1x)
Gal 1:21 I·came into the vicinities of·Syria and Cilicia,
G2824.3 N-DPN κλίμασιν (2x)
Rm 15:23 a·place *to·publicly·work* in these vicinities, and
2Co 11:10 ·sealed·up in me within the vicinities of·Achaia.
EG2824.3 (1x)
2Co 13:2 if I·should·come into the *vicinity* again, I·shall·not

G2825 κλίνη klínē *n.* (12x)
Roots:G2827 Compare:G2845 G2895 See:G2826
xLangAlso:H4296 H6210
G2825.1 N-ASF κλίνην (2x)
Mk 4:21 measuring·basket or under the couch, *and* not in·
Rv 2:22 I·myself do·cast her upon a·couch *of·sickness*, and
G2825.1 N-GSF κλίνης (3x)
Lk 8:16 or places *it* beneath a·couch, but·rather he·puts *it* on
Lk 17:34 there·shall·be two *reclining* on one couch; the one
Mk 7:30 and her daughter having·been·cast upon the couch.
G2825.1 N-GPF κλινῶν (1x)
Mk 7:4 of·cups and pots and of·copper·vessels and couches.
EG2825.1 (2x)
Mt 8:6 ·boy has·been·cast paralyzed *on a·couch* at home,
Mt 8:14 having·been·cast *on a·couch* and burning·with·fever
G2825.2 N-ASF κλίνην (1x)
Mt 9:6 take·up your simple·couch and head·on·out to your
G2825.2 N-GSF κλίνης (2x)
Lk 5:18 a·man·of·clay† upon a·simple·couch who was
Mt 9:2 ·paralyzed·man having·been·cast on a·simple·couch.
G2825.2 N-GPF κλινῶν (1x)
Ac 5:15 and to·lay *them* on simple·couches and mats, in·

G2826 κλινίδιον klinídiôn *n.* (2x)
Roots:G2825 Compare:G2895 G2845
G2826 N-ASN κλινίδιον (1x)
Lk 5:24 be·awakened, and taking·up your pallet, traverse to
G2826 N-DSN κλινιδίῳ (1x)
Lk 5:19 the tiles together with·the pallet into the midst

G2827 κλίνω klínō *v.* (7x)
Compare:G2578 See:G0186 G0347 G2828
G2827.4 V-PAS-3S κλίνῃ (2x)
Lk 9:58 does·not have *a·place* where he·may·prop his head."
Mt 8:20 does·not have anywhere he·may·prop his head."
G2827.5 V-PAP-GPF κλινουσῶν (1x)
Lk 24:5 ·the *women* becoming alarmed and drooping the face
G2827.5 V-AAP-NSM κλίνας (1x)
Jn 19:30 And drooping his head, he·handed·over the spirit.
G2827.6 V-PAN κλίνειν (1x)
Lk 9:12 And the day began to·fade. Now the twelve,
G2827.6 V-RAI-3S κέκλικεν (1x)
Lk 24:29 evening, and the day has·faded." And he·entered·
G2827.7 V-AAI-3P ἔκλιναν (1x)
Heb 11:34 in battle, routed estranged·foreign garrisons.

G2828 κλισία klisía *n.* (1x)
Roots:G2827 See:G0186
G2828.3 N-APF κλισίας (1x)
Lk 9:14 ·recline·back *by* fifty apiece *in·each* reclined·group."

G2829 κλοπή klôpḗ *n.* (2x)
Roots:G2813 See:G2809
G2829 N-NPF κλοπαί (2x)
Mt 15:19 sexual·immoralities, thefts, false·testimonies, *and*
Mk 7:22 thefts, acts·of·coveting, evils, guile, debauchery,

G2830 κλύδων klýdōn *n.* (2x)
Compare:G2949 See:G2831
G2830.1 N-DSM κλύδωνι (1x)
Lk 8:24 ·reprimanded the wind and the surge of·water. And
G2830.2 N-DSM κλύδωνι (1x)
Jac 1:6 has·directly·resembled a·surging·wave of·a·sea

G2831 κλυδωνίζομαι klydōnízômai *v.* (1x)
Roots:G2830 Compare:G4494 G2949
G2831.2 V-PNP-NPM κλυδωνιζόμενοι (1x)
Eph 4:14 who·are·being·tossed·about·by·surging·waves

G2832 Κλωπᾶς Klōpâs *n/p.* (1x)
xLangEquiv:H0256
G2832.2 N/P-GSM Κλωπᾶ (1x)
Jn 19:25 sister (Miryam the *wife* of·Clopas), and Mariam

G2833 κνήθω knḗthō *v.* (1x)
G2833.2 V-PPP-NPM κνηθόμενοι (1x)
2Ti 4:3 ·up instructors for·themselves, those·tickling the ear;

G2834 Κνίδος Knídôs *n/l.* (1x)
G2834 N/L-ASF Κνίδον (1x)
Ac 27:7 ·difficulty coming·to·be adjacent·to Cnidus, *and*

G2835 κοδράντης kôdrántēs *n.* (2x)
See:G0787 G1220 G3016
G2835.1 N-NSM κοδράντης (1x)
Mk 12:42 ·poor widow cast·in two bits, which is a·quadran.
G2835.1 N-ASM κοδράντην (1x)
Mt 5:26 ·there until you·should·repay the very·last quadran.

G2836 κοιλία kôilía *n.* (23x)
Roots:G2836-1 Compare:G4751 G1064 G3388
See:G2835-1
xLangEquiv:H0990 xLangAlso:H7358 H3770
G2836.3 N-NSF κοιλία (3x)
Php 3:19 whose god *is* the belly, and *whose* glory *is* in their
1Co 6:13 *is* for·the belly, and the belly *is* for·the food, but
Rv 10:10 And when I·ate it, my belly was·made·bitter.
G2836.3 N-ASF κοιλίαν (4x)
Lk 15:16 And he·was·longing to·overfill his belly with the
Mt 15:17 passes·through into the belly and·then is·cast·out
Mk 7:19 but·rather into the belly, and·then traverses·out
Rv 10:9 it; and it·shall·make your belly bitter, but·yet it·
G2836.3 N-DSF κοιλίᾳ (3x)
Mt 12:40 days and three nights in the belly of·the whale, in·
Rm 16:18 Anointed, but·rather to·their·own belly. And
1Co 6:13 The food *is* for·the belly, and the belly *is* for·the
G2836.3 N-GSF κοιλίας (1x)
Jn 7:38 "from·out of·his belly shall·flow rivers of·living
G2836.4 N-NSF κοιλία (1x)
Lk 11:27 "Supremely·blessed *is* the womb bearing you, and
G2836.4 N-NPF κοιλίαι (1x)
Lk 23:29 *are* the barren, and *the* wombs that did·not bear,
G2836.4 N-ASF κοιλίαν (1x)
Jn 3:4 to·enter a·second·time into the womb of·his mother
G2836.4 N-DSF κοιλίᾳ (3x)
Lk 1:41 the babe skipped·about in her womb, and EliSabeth
Lk 1:44 ·about in my womb in an·exuberant·leaping·of·joy.
Lk 2:21 the angel prior·to him being·conceived in the womb.
G2836.4 N-GSF κοιλίας (6x)
Lk 1:15 Spirit, yet·even from·within his mother's womb.
Lk 1:42 and having·been·blessed *is* the fruit of·your womb.
Ac 3:2 ·out of·his mother's womb was·lifted·and·carried,
Ac 14:8 lame from·out of·his mother's womb, who never·at·
Gal 1:15 ·out of·my mother's womb and calling·*me*·forth
Mt 19:12 ·manner from·out *of·their* mother's womb. And

G2837 κοιμάω kôimáō *v.* (18x)
Roots:G2749 Compare:G2518 G5258 G3573
See:G1945-4
xLangEquiv:H7901
G2837.3 V-PPP-APM κοιμωμένους (1x)
Lk 22:45 he·found them being·laid·asleep due·to the grief,
G2837.3 V-PPP-GPM κοιμωμένων (1x)
Mt 28:13 him, coming by·night with·us being·laid·asleep.'
G2837.3 V-PPP-NSM κοιμώμενος (1x)
Ac 12:6 night Peter was being·laid·to·sleep between two
G2837.3 V-RPI-3S κεκοίμηται (1x)
Jn 11:12 if he·has·been·laid·asleep, he·shall·be·safe·and·
G2837.5 V-FPI-1P κοιμηθησόμεθα (1x)
1Co 15:51 In·fact, we·shall·not all be·laid·to·rest, but we·
G2837.5 V-PPI-3P κοιμῶνται (1x)
1Co 11:30 yeu, and a·significant·number are·laid·to·rest.
G2837.5 V-API-3S ἐκοιμήθη (2x)
Ac 7:60 And after·declaring this, he·was·laid·to·rest *in*
Ac 13:36 ·God in·his·own generation, was·laid·to·rest, and
G2837.5 V-API-3P ἐκοιμήθησαν (2x)
2Pe 3:4 since the fathers are·laid·to·rest, all·things remain·
1Co 15:6 unto this·moment, but some also are·laid·to·rest.
G2837.5 V-APP-APM κοιμηθέντας (2x)
1Th 4:14 ·him the·ones being·laid·to·rest through YeShua.
1Th 4:15 ·not precede the·ones already·being·laid·to·rest.
G2837.5 V-APP-NPM κοιμηθέντες (1x)
1Co 15:18 the·ones being·laid·to·rest in Anointed-One,
G2837.5 V-APS-3S κοιμηθῇ (1x)
1Co 7:39 husband should·be·laid·to·rest·*(that·is,·deceased)*,
G2837.5 V-RPI-3S κεκοίμηται (1x)
Jn 11:11 "Our friend Lazarus has·been·laid·to·rest. But·yet
G2837.5 V-RPP-GPM κεκοιμημένων (3x)
Mt 27:52 (the·ones having·been·laid·to·rest) are·awakened.
1Th 4:13 the·ones having·been·laid·to·rest, in·order·that
1Co 15:20 a·firstfruit of·the·ones having·been·laid·to·rest.

G2838 κοίμησις kôimēsis *n.* (1x)
Roots:G2837
G2838.1 N-GSF κοιμήσεως (1x)
Jn 11:13 the outstretched·resting of·the heavy·sleep.

G2839 κοινός kôinós *adj.* (13x)
Compare:G0952 G5337 G0462 G0169 G3393 G0234
See:G2840 G2844 G4862 G2840-1
EG2839 (1x)
1Co 10:13 yeu except *that·which is common to* mankind†.
G2839.1 A-NPN κοινά (1x)
Ac 4:32 absolutely·all·belongings *together in* common.
G2839.1 A-ASN κοινόν (1x)
Heb 10:29 he·was·made·holy) *to·be* a·common·thing, and
G2839.1 A-GSF κοινῆς (1x)
Jud 1:3 to·write to·yeu concerning the common Salvation, I·
G2839.2 A-ASF κοινήν (1x)
Tit 1:4 To·Titus, a·genuine child according·to a·shared trust.

Kκ

G2839.2 A-APN κοινά (1x)
Ac 2:44 they·were·having absolutely·all·belongings shared.
G2839.3 A-NSN κοινόν (2x)
Rm 14:14 that *there·is* nothing·at·all defiled through itself,
Rm 14:14 For·that·man, *it·is* defiled.
G2839.3 A-ASM κοινόν (1x)
Ac 10:28 ·to·not·even·one man·of·clay† *as* defiled or impure
G2839.3 A-ASN κοινόν (3x)
Ac 10:14 ·any·time have·I·eaten anything defiled or impure.
Ac 11:8 never·at·any·time did anything defiled or impure
Rm 14:14 reckoning something to·be defiled. For·that·man,
G2839.3 A-DPF κοιναῖς (1x)
Mk 7:2 of·his disciples eating bread with·defiled hands, that

G2840 κοινόω kôinóō *v.* (15x)
Roots:G2839 Compare:G5337 G3392
G2840.2 V-PAI-3S κοινοῖ (6x)
Mt 15:11 into the mouth *that* defiles the man·of·clay†, but·
Mt 15:11 *indeed*, this·thing defiles the man·of·clay†."
Mt 15:18 heart, and·these·things defile the man·of·clay†.
Mt 15:20 ·unwashed hands does·not defile the man·of·clay†.
Mk 7:20 man·of·clay†, that·thing defiles the man·of·clay†.
Mk 7:23 from·inside, and they·defile the man·of·clay†."
G2840.2 V-PAP-NSN κοινοῦν (1x)
Rv 21:27 ·not enter into it anyone defiling or committing an·
G2840.2 V-PAP-NPN κοινοῦντα (2x)
Mt 15:20 These are the·things defiling the man·of·clay†.
Mk 7:15 him, those are the·things defiling the man·of·clay†.
G2840.2 V-AAN κοινῶσαι (2x)
Mk 7:15 traversing into him is·able to·defile him, but·rather
Mk 7:18 into the man·of·clay† is·not able to·defile him,
G2840.2 V-RAI-3S κεκοίνωκεν (1x)
Ac 21:28 the Sanctuary·Courtyard and has·defiled this holy
G2840.2 V-RPP-APM κεκοινωμένους (1x)
Heb 9:13 the·ones having·been·defiled, makes·one·holy just·
G2840.3 V-PAM-2S κοίνου (2x)
Ac 10:15 purified, you·yourself must·not consider·defiled."
Ac 11:9 God purified, you must·not consider·defiled.'

G2841 κοινωνέω kôinōnéō *v.* (10x)
Roots:G2844 Compare:G3330 See:G2840-1
EG2841 (1x)
Mt 13:52 *things* brand-new and old *to·share with·others*."
G2841.1 V-PAI-2P κοινωνεῖτε (1x)
1Pe 4:13 ·to·what *portion* yeu·share in·the afflictions of·the
G2841.1 V-PAI-3S κοινωνεῖ (1x)
2Jn 1:11 "Be·well," shares in·his evil deeds.
G2841.1 V-PAM-2S κοινώνει (1x)
1Ti 5:22 quickly, nor·even share in·others' moral·failures.
G2841.1 V-PAM-3S κοινωνείτω (1x)
Gal 6:6 Redemptive-word must·share with·the·one tutoring in
G2841.1 V-PAP-NPM κοινωνοῦντες (1x)
Rm 12:13 holy·ones, by·sharing·with·others, by·pursuing
G2841.1 V-AAI-3S ἐκοινώνησεν (1x)
Php 4:15 ·even·one Called·Out·citizenry shared with·me in
EG2841.1 (1x)
Eph 5:4 but·yet rather *share* an·expression·of·thankfulness.
G2841.2 V-AAI-3P ἐκοινώνησαν (1x)
Rm 15:27 if the Gentiles have·a·common·fellowship in·their
G2841.2 V-RAI-3S κεκοινώνηκεν (1x)
Heb 2:14 little·children have·a·common·fellowship of·flesh

G2842 κοινωνία kôinōnía *n.* (20x)
Roots:G2844 Compare:G3352 G2140 See:G2840-1 xLangEquiv:H7803-2
G2842.3 N-NSF κοινωνία (8x)
Php 2:1 ·consolation of·love, if any fellowship of·Spirit, if
1Co 10:16 we·bless, is·it not·indeed fellowship of·the blood
1Co 10:16 we·break, is·it not·indeed fellowship of·the body
2Co 6:14 And what fellowship has·light alongside darkness
2Co 13:14 of·God, and the fellowship of·the Holy Spirit, *be*
Eph 3:9 for·all what *is* the fellowship of·the Mystery, the·
Phm 1:6 *praying* that the fellowship of·your trust may·
1Jn 1:3 with us, and our fellowship *is* also with the Father,
G2842.3 N-ASF κοινωνίαν (6x)
Php 3:10 resurrection, even the fellowship of·his afflictions,
1Co 1:9 yeu·are·called·forth into *the* fellowship of·his Son
2Co 8:4 and *take upon·us* the fellowship of·the service to the
1Jn 1:3 in·order·that yeu also may·have fellowship with us,
1Jn 1:6 we·should·declare that we·have fellowship with him,
1Jn 1:7 is in the light, we·have fellowship with one·another,
G2842.3 N-DSF κοινωνίᾳ (2x)
Ac 2:42 of·the ambassadors and in·the fellowship, and in·the
Php 1:5 for yeur fellowship in the good·news from *the* first
G2842.3 N-GSF κοινωνίας (1x)
Gal 2:9 BarNabas *the* right·hands of·fellowship, in·order·that
G2842.4 N-ASF κοινωνίαν (1x)
Rm 15:26 to·make a·certain common·welfare·fund for the
G2842.4 N-GSF κοινωνίας (2x)
Heb 13:16 the benevolence and common·welfare·fund, for
2Co 9:13 ·fidelity of·the common·welfare·fund for them and

G2843 κοινωνικός kôinōnikós *adj.* (1x)
Roots:G2844 Compare:G2130
G2843.1 A-APM κοινωνικούς (1x)
1Ti 6:18 deeds, to·be good·at·kind·giving *and* sociable,

G2844 κοινωνός kôinōnós *n.* (11x)
Roots:G2839 Compare:G4791 See:G2843 G2842 xLangEquiv:H7803-1
G2844.2 A-NPM κοινωνοί (6x)
Lk 5:10 ·Sons of·Zebedee, who were partners with·Simon.
Heb 10:33 while·yeu·were·becoming partners with·the·ones
Mt 23:30 fathers, we·would not be partners with·them in the
2Pe 1:4 these, yeu·may·become partners of·divine nature,
1Co 10:18 sacrifices, *also* partners of·the Sacrifice·Altar?
2Co 1:7 ·seen that just·as yeu·are partners of·the afflictions,
G2844.2 A-ASM κοινωνόν (1x)
Phm 1:17 if you·hold me *to·be* a·partner, purposely·receive
G2844.2 A-APM κοινωνούς (1x)
1Co 10:20 ·not want yeu to·become partners with·demons.
G2844.2 N-NSM κοινωνός (2x)
1Pe 5:1 of·the Anointed-One, and·also a·partner of·the glory
2Co 8:23 Titus, *he·is* my partner and coworker in·regard·to
EG2844.2 (1x)
2Co 1:7 ·this·manner *yeu·are* also *partners* of·the comforting

G2845 κοίτη kôítē *n.* (4x)
Roots:G2749 Compare:G2825 G2826 G2895 See:G2846 G2602 G1080 xLangAlso:H4904 A4903
G2845.1 N-NSF κοίτη (1x)
Heb 13:4 all *cultures*, and the bed *that·is* uncontaminated—
G2845.1 N-ASF κοίτην (1x)
Lk 11:7 are with me in the bed; I·am·not able to·rise·up and·
G2845.2 N-DPF κοίταις (1x)
Rm 13:13 not in·cohabitations and debaucheries, not in·
G2845.5 N-ASF κοίτην (1x)
Rm 9:10 also, having a·conception *of·twins* from·out of·one·

G2846 κοιτών kôitṓn *n.* (1x)
Roots:G2845
G2846 N-GSM κοιτῶνος (1x)
Ac 12:20 the·one over the king's bedroom, they·requested

G2847 κόκκινος kókkinôs *adj.* (6x)
Roots:G2848 Compare:G4209 G4450 G5402-1 xLangAlso:H8144 H8438
G2847.1 A-ASF κοκκίνην (1x)
Mt 27:28 him, they·placed a·scarlet military·cloak around
G2847.1 A-ASN κόκκινον (2x)
Rv 17:3 who·is·sitting·down upon a·scarlet demonic·beast,
Rv 18:16 and purple, and scarlet, and having·been·gilded
G2847.1 A-DSN κοκκίνῳ (1x)
Rv 17:4 ·one having·been·arrayed in·purple and scarlet, and
G2847.1 A-GSN κοκκίνου (2x)
Heb 9:19 ·male·goats, with water, scarlet wool, and hyssop,
Rv 18:12 and purple, silk, and scarlet, "and every citron

G2848 κόκκος kókkôs *n.* (7x)
xLangAlso:H8438
G2848 N-NSM κόκκος (1x)
Jn 12:24 I·say to·yeu, unless the kernel of·wheat, falling
G2848 N-ASM κόκκον (3x)
Lk 17:6 trust *that·grows* as a·kernel of·mustard·seed *does*,
Mt 17:20 trust *that·grows* as a·kernel of·mustard·seed *does*,
1Co 15:37 that·shall·be, but·rather a·bare kernel, whether it·
G2848 N-DSM κόκκῳ (3x)
Lk 13:19 "It·is like a·kernel of·mustard·seed, which a·man·
Mt 13:31 of·the heavens is like a·kernel of·mustard·seed
Mk 4:31 "*It·is* as a·kernel of·mustard·seed, which, whenever

G2849 κολάζω kôlázō *v.* (2x)
See:G2856 G2851
G2849.2 V-PPP-APM κολαζομένους (1x)
2Pe 2:9 ·day of·Tribunal·judgment to·be·sternly·punished—
G2849.2 V-AMS-3P κολάσωνται (1x)
Ac 4:21 of·how they·should·sternly·punish them on·account·

G2850 κολακεία kôlakeîa *n.* (1x)
G2850 N-GSF κολακείας (1x)
1Th 2:5 ·time did·we·come with a·word of·flattery (just·as

G2851 κόλασις kólasis *n.* (2x)
Roots:G2849 Compare:G5098
G2851 N-ASF κόλασιν (2x)
Mt 25:46 ·go·away into eternal tormenting·punishment, but
1Jn 4:18 because the fear has a·tormenting·punishment. But

G2852 κολαφίζω kôlaphízō *v.* (5x)
Roots:G2849 Compare:G4438 G5299
G2852 V-PAN κολαφίζειν (1x)
Mk 14:65 ·hood·over his face, even to·buffet him and to·say
G2852 V-PAS-3S κολαφίζῃ (1x)
2Co 12:7 ·*The*·Adversary in·order·that he·should·buffet me,
G2852 V-PPI-1P κολαφιζόμεθα (1x)
1Co 4:11 and go·naked, and are·buffeted, and are·unsettled·
G2852 V-PPP-NPM κολαφιζόμενοι (1x)
1Pe 2:20 if when yeu·are·being·buffeted for·morally·failing,
G2852 V-AAI-3P ἐκολάφισαν (1x)
Mt 26:67 they·spat in his face and buffeted him, and they·

G2853 κολλάω kôlláō *v.* (10x)
Compare:G4820 G4345 xLangAlso:H1692
G2853.2 V-PPN κολλᾶσθαι (3x)
Ac 5:13 ·one was·daring to·tightly·join·himself to·them, but·
Ac 9:26 was·intently·trying to·tightly·join·himself to·the
Ac 10:28 ·man that·is·a·Jew to·be·tightly·joined or to·come·
G2853.2 V-PPP-NSM κολλώμενος (2x)
1Co 6:16 that the·one being·tightly·joined to·the prostitute is
1Co 6:17 But the·one being·tightly·joined to·the Lord is one
G2853.2 V-PPP-NPM κολλώμενοι (1x)
Rm 12:9 evil, being·tightly·joined to·the beneficially·good
G2853.2 V-API-3S ἐκολλήθη (1x)
Lk 15:15 traversing, he·tightly·joined·himself to·one of·the
G2853.2 V-APM-2S κολλήθητι (1x)
Ac 8:29 "Go·alongside and be·tightly·joined to·this chariot.
G2853.2 V-APP-NPM κολληθέντες (1x)
Ac 17:34 But certain men, being·tightly·joined to·him,
G2853.3 V-APP-ASM κολληθέντα (1x)
Lk 10:11 of·yeur·own city, the·one being·stuck to·us, we·

G2854 κολλούριον kôllôúriôn *n.* (1x)
See:G2853
G2854.5 N-ASN κολλούριον (1x)
Rv 3:18 Also, smear eye·salve on your eyes, in·order·that

G2855 κολλυβιστής kôllybistḗs *n.* (3x)
Compare:G2773 G3027 See:G2854
G2855 N-GPM κολλυβιστῶν (3x)
Jn 2:15 and he·poured·out the moneychangers' money and
Mt 21:12 the tables of·the moneychangers and the seats of·
Mk 11:15 the tables of·the moneychangers and the seats of·

G2856 κολοβόω kôlôbóō *v.* (4x)
Roots:G2849
G2856.2 V-FPI-3P κολοβωθήσονται (1x)
Mt 24:22 the Selected-Ones, those Days shall·be·cut·short.
G2856.2 V-AAI-3S ἐκολόβωσεν (2x)
Mk 13:20 And except *that* Yahweh cut·short the Days, not
Mk 13:20 whom he·selected, he·cut·short the Days.
G2856.2 V-API-3P ἐκολοβώθησαν (1x)
Mt 24:22 And except those Days be·cut·short, not any flesh

G2857 Κολοσσαί Kôlôssaí *n/l.* (1x)
See:G2858
G2857.2 N/L-DPF Κολασσαῖς (1x)
Col 1:2 To·the·ones in Colossae, holy and trustworthy

G2859 κόλπος kólpôs *n.* (6x)
Compare:G3149 G4738 G4215
xLangEquiv:H2436 xLangAlso:H6747
G2859.1 N-ASM κόλπον (3x)
Jn 1:18 the·one being in the bosom of·the Father, that·one
Lk 6:38 *carrying·folds of·the garment around* yeur bosom.
Lk 16:22 ·away by the angels to AbRaham's bosom. But the
G2859.1 N-DSM κόλπῳ (1x)
Jn 13:23 Now reclining·at·the·meal at Jesus' bosom was one
G2859.1 N-DPM κόλποις (1x)
Lk 16:23 from a·distance, and Lazarus at his bosom.
G2859.2 N-ASM κόλπον (1x)
Ac 27:39 ·were·fully·observing a·certain bay having a·shore,

G2860 κολυμβάω kôlymbáō *v.* (1x)
See:G1579 G2861
G2860.3 V-PAN κολυμβᾶν (1x)
Ac 27:43 being·able to·swim, after·jumping·far·overboard

G2861 κολυμβήθρα kôlymbḗthra *n.* (5x)
Compare:G3041 See:G1579 G2860
G2861.2 N-NSF κολυμβήθρα (1x)
Jn 5:2 in JeruSalem, there·is a·pool having five colonnades;
G2861.2 N-ASF κολυμβήθραν (3x)
Jn 5:7 ·order·that he·should·cast me into the pool, but while
Jn 9:7 "Head·on·out, wash in the pool of·Siloam" (which
Jn 9:11 'Head·on·out to the pool of·Siloam and wash.
G2861.2 N-DSF κολυμβήθρᾳ (1x)
Jn 5:4 ·angel was·descending on the pool and was·troubling

Κκ

G2862 κολωνία kôlōnía *n.* (1x)
G2862 N-NSF κολωνία (1x)
Ac 16:12 province of·Macedonia, *and* a·colony; and we·

G2863 κομάω kômáō *v.* (2x)
Roots:G2864
G2863 V-PAS-3S κομᾷ (2x)
1Co 11:14 ·fact, that if a·man should·wear·long·hair, it·is a·
1Co 11:15 But if a·woman should·wear·long·hair, it·is a·

G2864 κόμη kómē *n.* (1x)
Compare:G2359 See:G2863 G2865
G2864 N-NSF κόμη (1x)
1Co 11:15 to·her, because the hair·of·the·head, instead of·a·

G2865 κομίζω kômízō *v.* (11x)
Compare:G5177 G2975 See:G1580 G4792 G2864 G2866
G2865.2 V-FDI-2P-ATT κομιεῖσθε (1x)
1Pe 5:4 yeu·shall·subsequently·obtain the undiminishable
G2865.2 V-FDI-3S-ATT κομιεῖται (2x)
Eph 6:8 this he·shall·subsequently·obtain personally·from
Col 3:25 doing·wrong shall·subsequently·obtain that·for· he·
G2865.2 V-FDP-NPM κομιούμενοι (1x)
2Pe 2:13 *And* they·shall·be·subsequently·obtaining a· for·
G2865.2 V-PMP-NPM κομιζόμενοι (1x)
1Pe 1:9 subsequently·obtaining the end of·yeur trust, *the*
G2865.2 V-AAP-NSF κομίσασα (1x)
Lk 7:37 after·subsequently·obtaining an·alabaster·flask of·
G2865.2 V-AMI-1S ἐκομισάμην (1x)
Mt 25:27 might be·subsequently·obtaining my·own together
G2865.2 V-AMI-3S ἐκομίσατο (1x)
Heb 11:19 (by analogy), he·subsequently·obtained him.
G2865.2 V-AMI-3P ἐκομίσαντο (1x)
Heb 11:39 the trust, did·not subsequently·obtain the promise
G2865.2 V-AMS-2P κομίσησθε (1x)
Heb 10:36 ·God, yeu·may·subsequently·obtain the promise.
G2865.2 V-AMS-3S κομίσηται (1x)
2Co 5:10 each·one may·subsequently·obtain the·things *done*

G2866 κομψότερον kômpsótêrôn *adv.* (1x)
Roots:G2865
G2866 ADV κομψότερον (1x)
Jn 4:52 the hour in which he·had gotten·better. And they·

G2867 κονιάω kôniáō *v.* (2x)
See:G2868
G2867 V-RPP-DPM κεκονιαμένοις (1x)
Mt 23:27 ·resemble graves having·been·whitewashed, which
G2867 V-RPP-VSM κεκονιαμένε (1x)
Ac 23:3 you, O·wall having·been·whitewashed! Even you·

G2868 κονι•ορτός kôniôrtós *n.* (5x)
Compare:G5522 G5515-2 See:G2867
xLangAlso:H0080
G2868 N-ASM κονιορτόν (5x)
Lk 9:5 city, jostle·off even the dust from yeur feet for a·
Lk 10:11 'Even the dust from·out of·yeur·own city, the·one
Ac 13:51 But shaking·off the dust of·their feet against them,
Ac 22:23 ·off the garments, and casting dust into the air,
Mt 10:14 home or that city, shake·off the dust of·yeur feet.

G2869 κοπάζω kôpázō *v.* (3x)
Roots:G2873 xLangAlso:H7918
G2869.2 V-AAI-3S ἐκόπασεν (3x)
Mt 14:32 embarking into the sailboat, the wind subsided.
Mk 4:39 And the wind subsided, and there·was a·great
Mk 6:51 sailboat, and the wind subsided. And they·were·

G2870 κοπετός kôpêtós *n.* (1x)
Roots:G2875 Compare:G3077 G3997
xLangAlso:H4553
G2870.2 N-ASM κοπετόν (1x)
Ac 8:2 and they·made great visceral·lamentation over him.

G2871 κοπή kôpḗ *n.* (1x)
Roots:G2875 See:G2873
xLangEquiv:H4347
G2871.2 N-GSF κοπῆς (1x)
Heb 7:1 returning·back from the carnage of·the kings, and

G2872 κοπιάω kôpiáō *v.* (23x)
Roots:G2873 Compare:G2577 G4903
G2872.1 V-RAP-NSM κεκοπιακώς (1x)
Jn 4:6 ·then Jesus, having·become·weary as·a·result of·the
G2872.2 V-PAI-1S κοπιῶ (1x)
Col 1:29 for which·thing also I·labor·hard, striving
G2872.2 V-PAI-1P κοπιῶμεν (2x)
1Co 4:12 and we·labor·hard, working with·our·own hands.
1Ti 4:10 For to this also we·labor·hard and are·reproached,
G2872.2 V-PAI-3S κοπιᾷ (2x)
Lk 12:27 grow. They·do·not labor·hard, they·do·not·even
Mt 6:28 how they·grow; they·do·not labor·hard, neither do·
G2872.2 V-PAM-3S κοπιάτω (1x)
Eph 4:28 no·longer. But rather let·him·labor·hard, working
G2872.2 V-PAP-ASM κοπιῶντα (1x)
2Ti 2:6 the hard·laboring man·that·works·the·soil to·partake
G2872.2 V-PAP-APF κοπιώσας (1x)
Rm 16:12 and Tryphosa, the·ones laboring·hard in *the* Lord.
G2872.2 V-PAP-APM κοπιῶντας (2x)
Ac 20:35 that in·this·manner, laboring·hard, it·is·mandatory
1Th 5:12 ·know the·ones laboring·hard among yeu, and are·
G2872.2 V-PAP-DSM κοπιῶντι (1x)
1Co 16:16 ·everyone, the·one coworking and laboring·hard.
G2872.2 V-PAP-NPM κοπιῶντες (2x)
Mt 11:28 to me, all the·ones laboring·hard and having·been·
1Ti 5:17 honor, especially the·ones laboring·hard in word
G2872.2 V-AAI-1S ἐκοπίασα (2x)
Php 2:16 ·not run for naught neither labored·hard for naught.
1Co 15:10 But·rather, I·labored·hard, more·abundantly
G2872.2 V-AAI-3S ἐκοπίασεν (2x)
Rm 16:6 who, in·many·ways, labored·hard among us.
Rm 16:12 Persis, who repeatedly labored·hard in *the* Lord.
G2872.2 V-AAP-NPM κοπιάσαντες (1x)
Lk 5:5 ·him, "O·Captain, after·laboring·hard all through the
G2872.2 V-RAI-1S κεκοπίακα (1x)
Gal 4:11 ·for yeu, lest·somehow I·have·labored·hard for yeu
G2872.2 V-RAI-2S κεκοπίακας (1x)
Rv 2:3 and you·have·labored·hard on·account·of my name
G2872.2 V-RAI-2P κεκοπιάκατε (1x)
Jn 4:38 which yeu·yeurselves have·not labored·hard. Others
G2872.2 V-RAI-3P κεκοπιάκασιν (1x)
Jn 4:38 ·not labored·hard. Others have·labored·hard, and

G2873 κόπος kópôs *n.* (19x)
Roots:G2875 Compare:G2872 G3449 G2041 G4192
xLangAlso:H5999 H3018
G2873.2 N-DSM κόπῳ (2x)
2Th 3:8 but·rather were·working in weariness and travail
2Co 11:27 *subsisting* in weariness and travail, in
G2873.3 N-NSM κόπος (2x)
1Th 3:5 ·trying yeu and our wearisome·labor should·be for
1Co 15:58 having·seen that yeur wearisome·labor is not
G2873.3 N-ASM κόπον (4x)
Jn 4:38 and yeu have·entered into their wearisome·labors."
1Th 2:9 brothers, our wearisome·labor and the travail, for
1Co 3:8 ·of·service according·to his·own wearisome·labor.
Rv 2:2 your works, and your wearisome·labor, and your
G2873.3 N-DPM κόποις (3x)
2Co 6:5 in chaos, in wearisome·labors, in sleeplessness, in
2Co 10:15 *that·is*, in other·men's wearisome·labors, but
2Co 11:23 … in wearisome·labors more·abundantly, in
G2873.3 N-GSM κόπου (2x)
Heb 6:10 yeur work and *yeur* wearisome·labor of·love,
1Th 1:3 of·the trust, and the wearisome·labor of·the love,
G2873.3 N-GPM κόπων (1x)
Rv 14:13 ·may·rest from·out of·their wearisome·labors, and
G2873.4 N-ASM κόπον (1x)
Lk 18:5 personally·presenting *her* wearisome·troubles to·me,
G2873.4 N-APM κόπους (4x)
Lk 11:7 personally·present *your* wearisome·troubles to·me.
Gal 6:17 ·man personally·present wearisome·troubles to·me,
Mt 26:10 yeu·personally·present wearisome·troubles to·the
Mk 14:6 yeu·personally·present wearisome·troubles to·her?

G2874 κοπρία kôpría *n.* (2x)
See:G2875 xLangAlso:H0830
G2874 N-ASF κοπρίαν (2x)
Lk 13:8 I·should·dig around it and should·cast manure *on·it.*
Lk 14:35 for soil, nor·even for manure, *but·rather* men·cast

G2875 κόπτω kóptō *v.* (8x)
Compare:G5058-2 G3076 G2354 See:G2870 G2859 G1249-2 xLangAlso:H5594 H2404
G2875.1 V-IAI-3P ἔκοπτον (2x)
Mt 21:8 roadway, and others were·chopping branches from
Mk 11:8 roadway, and others were·chopping limbs out of·
G2875.3 V-FDI-3P κόψονται (3x)
Mt 24:30 all the tribes of·the earth shall·vividly·lament,' and
Rv 1:7 the tribes of·the earth shall·vividly·lament over him.'
Rv 18:9 ·weep·for her, and shall·vividly·lament over her,
G2875.3 V-IMI-3P ἐκόπτοντο (2x)
Lk 8:52 all were·weeping and vividly·lamenting·over her,
Lk 23:27 also were·vividly·lamenting and were·bewailing·
G2875.3 V-AMI-2P ἐκόψασθε (1x)
Mt 11:17 for·yeu, and yeu·did·not vividly·lament.'

G2876 κόραξ kórax *n.* (1x)
Roots:G2880
xLangEquiv:H6158
G2876 N-APM κόρακας (1x)
Lk 12:24 "Fully·observe the ravens, because they·do·not

G2877 κοράσιον kôrásiôn *n.* (8x)
Compare:G5008
G2877 N-NSN κοράσιον (5x)
Mt 9:24 "Depart! For the young·girl did·not die, but·rather
Mt 9:25 of·her hand, and the young·girl was·awakened.
Mk 5:41 *from·Aramaic*, is "Young·girl, I·say to·you, be·
Mk 5:42 And immediately, the young·girl rose·up and was·
Mk 6:28 to·the young·girl, and the young·girl gave it to·her
G2877 N-DSN κορασίῳ (3x)
Mt 14:11 a·platter and was·given to·the young·girl, and she·
Mk 6:22 the king declared to·the young·girl, "Request·of
Mk 6:28 and he·gave it to·the young·girl, and the young·

G2878 κορβᾶν kôrbân *n/t.* (2x)
κορβανᾶς kôrbanâs
Ⱪορβᾶν Qôrbân [Greek, Octuagint]
קָרְבָּן qọr·ḇạn [Hebrew]
Roots:H7133 Compare:G1435
G2878.1 HEB Ⱪορβᾶν (1x)
Mk 7:11 is *now* Qorban, a·voluntary·offering·of·sacrifice,'"
G2878.3 N-ASM κορβανᾶν (1x)
Mt 27:6 to·cast them into the Temple·Treasury, since it·is

G2879 Κορέ Kôrê *n/p.* (1x)
קֹרַח Qọrạch [Hebrew]
Roots:H7141
G2879.2 N/P-PRI Κορέ (1x)
Jud 1:11 ·perished in·the hostile·grumbling of·Korah.

G2880 κορέννυμι kôrénnymi *v.* (2x)
Compare:G1705 G5526 G0714 G0700 G2100
See:G2876
G2880.2 V-APP-NPM κορεσθέντες (1x)
Ac 27:38 And after·being·stuffed·full·to·excess with·, they·
G2880.3 V-RPP-NPM κεκορεσμένοι (1x)
1Co 4:8 ·are having·been·stuffed·full·to·nauseating·excess.

G2881 Κορίνθιος Kôrínthiôs *adj/g.* (2x)
Roots:G2882
G2881 A/G-VPM Κορίνθιοι (1x)
2Co 6:11 O·*yeu*·Corinthians, we·have·opened·up our mouth
G2881 A/G-GPM Κορινθίων (1x)
Ac 18:8 and many of·the Corinthians hearing *Paul* were·

G2882 Κόρινθος Kórinthôs *n/l.* (6x)
See:G2881
G2882 N/L-ASF Κόρινθον (2x)
Ac 18:1 ·things, Paul came to Corinth, being·deported out
2Co 1:23 that to·spare yeu, I·did·not·yet come to Corinth.
G2882 N/L-DSF Κορίνθῳ (4x)
Ac 19:1 with Apollos being in Corinth, it·happened *that* Paul
1Co 1:2 the·one being in Corinth— ones·having·been·
2Co 1:1 of·God, the·one being at Corinth, together with·all
2Ti 4:20 Erastus remained at Corinth, but Trophimus, being·

G2883 Κορνήλιος Kôrnēliôs *n/p.* (10x)
G2883 N/P-NSM Κορνήλιος (5x)
Ac 10:1 man in Caesarea, Cornelius by·name, a·centurion
Ac 10:22 And they·declared, "Cornelius, a·centurion, a·
Ac 10:24 ·awaiting them, Cornelius was calling·together his
Ac 10:25 happened to·enter, Cornelius met·up with·him.
Ac 10:30 And Cornelius replied, "Four days ago I·was
G2883 N/P-VSM Κορνήλιε (2x)
Ac 10:3 toward him and declaring to·him, "Cornelius."
Ac 10:31 and he·disclosed, 'Cornelius, your prayer is·heard,
G2883 N/P-DSM Κορνηλίῳ (1x)
Ac 10:7 angel (the·one speaking to·Cornelius) went·away,
G2883 N/P-GSM Κορνηλίου (2x)
Ac 10:17 (the·ones having·been·dispatched from Cornelius),
Ac 10:21 having·been·dispatched to him from Cornelius),

G2884 κόρος kôrôs *n.* (1x)
כֹּר ḳôr [Hebrew]
Roots:H3734 Compare:G1115-1 G0943
G2884.1 N-APM κόρους (1x)
Lk 16:7 he·declared, 'A·hundred kor·measures of·wheat.'

G2885 κοσμέω kôsmêō *v.* (10x)
Roots:G2889 Compare:G5021
G2885.1 V-RPP-ASM κεκοσμημένον (2x)
Lk 11:25 ·been·swept and having·been·put·in·proper·order.
Mt 12:44 ·been·swept and having·been·put·in·proper·order.
G2885.2 V-PAN κοσμεῖν (1x)
1Ti 2:9 also, *I·resolve·for* the women to·adorn themselves in
G2885.2 V-PAS-3P κοσμῶσιν (1x)
Tit 2:10 in·order·that they·may·adorn *themselves·with* the
G2885.2 V-IAI-3P ἐκόσμουν (1x)
1Pe 3:5 the holy wives also were·adorning themselves, the·
G2885.2 V-RPI-3S κεκόσμηται (1x)
Lk 21:5 that it·has·been·adorned with·beautiful stones and
G2885.2 V-RPP-ASF κεκοσμημένην (1x)
Rv 21:2 as a·bride having·been·adorned for·her husband.
G2885.2 V-RPP-NPM κεκοσμημένοι (1x)
Rv 21:19 *were* having·been·adorned·with all·manner·of
G2885.3 V-PAI-2P κοσμεῖτε (1x)
Mt 23:29 of·the prophets and decorate the chamber·tombs
G2885.4 V-AAI-3P ἐκόσμησαν (1x)
Mt 25:7 virgins are·awakened, and they·trimmed their lamps

G2886 κοσμικός kôsmikôs *adj.* (2x)
Roots:G2889
G2886.1 A-ASN κοσμικόν (1x)
Heb 9:1 ·ministry *to·God*, and·also the worldly holy·place.
G2886.1 A-APF κοσμικάς (1x)
Tit 2:12 the irreverence and the worldly longings, we·should·

G2887 κόσμιος kősmiôs *adj.* (2x)
Roots:G2889
G2887 A-ASM κόσμιον (1x)
1Ti 3:2 sober-minded, self-controlled, orderly, hospitable,
G2887 A-DSF κοσμίῳ (1x)
1Ti 2:9 in orderly, fully·modest·and·concealing·apparel with

G2888 κοσμο•κράτωρ kôsmôkrátōr *n.* (1x)
Roots:G2889 G2902
G2888.2 N-APM κοσμοκράτορας (1x)
Eph 6:12 ·against the mighty·world·powers of·the darkness

G2889 κόσμος kősmôs *n.* (187x)
Roots:G2865 Compare:G3625 G1093 See:G2885
G2886
xLangEquiv:H8398
G2889.2 N-NSM κόσμος (1x)
1Pe 3:3 whose adorning must·be, not *according·to* the
G2889.3 N-NSM κόσμος (31x)
Jn 1:10 in the world, and the world came·to·be through him,
Jn 1:10 ·to·be through him, yet the world did·not know him.
Jn 3:17 but·rather in·order·that the world through him may·
Jn 7:7 The world is·not able to·hate yeu, but it·hates me,
Jn 12:19 ·thing? See, the world went·off right·behind him.
Jn 14:17 of·Truth, whom the world is·not able to·receive,
Jn 14:19 "Yet a·little·while, and the world observes me no
Jn 14:27 Not just·as the world gives *do* I·myself give to·yeu.
Jn 14:31 But·rather, in·order·that the world may·know that
Jn 15:18 "If the world hates yeu, yeu·know that it·has·hated
Jn 15:19 the world, the world would affectionately·favor its·
Jn 15:19 On·account·of this, the world hates yeu.
Jn 16:20 and shall·bewail, but the world shall·rejoice, and
Jn 17:14 Redemptive-word, and the world hated them because
Jn 17:21 "in·order·that the world may·trust that you·yourself
Jn 17:23 "and in·order·that the world may·know that you·
Jn 17:25 "O·Righteous Father, the world did·not know you,
Heb 11:38 (of·whom the world was not worthy), being·
Gal 6:14 through whom *the* world has·been·crucified to·me,
Mt 13:38 Now the field is the world, and the good seed,
Rm 3:19 and all the world may·become liable·under·justice
Jac 3:6 *is* a·fire; *it·is* the world of·unrighteousness. In·this·
2Pe 3:6 the world at·that·time was·completely·destroyed,
1Co 1:21 the wisdom of·God) the world through the wisdom
1Co 3:22 Kephas·*(called·Peter)*, or *the* world, or life-above,
1Co 6:2 the world? And if the world is·judged by yeu, are·
1Jn 2:17 And the world passes·away, and its longing, but
1Jn 3:1 On·account·of that, the world does·not know us,
1Jn 3:13 ·not marvel, my brothers, if the world hates yeu.
1Jn 4:5 from·among the world, and the world hears them.
1Jn 5:19 of·God, and the whole world is·laid·out in the Evil·
G2889.3 N-ASM κόσμον (45x)
Jn 1:9 every child·of·clay† coming into the world.
Jn 3:16 ·manner, God loved the world, such·that he·gave his
Jn 3:17 into the world in·order·that he·may·presently·judge
Jn 3:17 ·that he·may·presently·judge the world, but·rather
Jn 3:19 the Light has·come into the world, and the men·of·
Jn 6:14 the Prophet, the·one who·is·coming into the world."
Jn 8:26 and·I say to the world these·things which I·heard
Jn 9:39 did·come into this world in·order·that the·ones not
Jn 10:36 ·holy and dispatched into the world, *of·him* yeu·
Jn 11:27 of·God, the·one who·is·coming into the world."
Jn 12:46 have·come into the world, in·order·that anyone,
Jn 12:47 ·that I·may·presently·judge the world, but·rather in·
Jn 12:47 but·rather in·order·that I·may·save the world.
Jn 16:8 ·one shall·convict the world concerning moral·failure
Jn 16:21 the joy that a·child·of·clay† is·born into the world.
Jn 16:28 and have·come into the world. Again, I·leave the
Jn 16:28 Again, I·leave the world, and traverse to the Father.
Jn 16:33 ·courage; I·myself have·overcome the world."
Jn 17:5 I·was·having with you before the world existed.
Jn 17:18 you·dispatched me into the world, I·also dispatch
Jn 17:18 into the world, I·also dispatch them into the world.
Jn 18:37 to this I·have·come into the world, in·order·that I·
Jn 21:25 ·imagine not·even the world itself to·have·room·for
Lk 9:25 the whole world but already·completely·losing
Ac 17:24 God, the·one making the world and all the·things
Heb 10:5 he·who·is·entering into the world says,
Heb 11:7 which he·condemned the world and became an·
Mt 16:26 if he·should·gain the whole world, and should·
Mk 8:36 if he·should·gain the whole world, yet should·
Mk 14:9 ·be·officially·proclaimed in the whole world, also
Mk 16:15 into absolutely·all the world, officially·proclaim
Rm 3:6 Otherwise how·does God judge the world?
Rm 5:12 Moral·Failure entered into the world and Death
1Co 6:2 that the holy·ones shall·judge the world? And if the
2Co 5:19 presently·reconciling *the* world to·himself, while·
1Ti 1:15 into the world to·save morally·disqualified·ones,
1Ti 6:7 we·carried not·even·one·thing into the world, *and it·*
1Jn 2:15 Do·not love the world, nor·even the·things in the
1Jn 2:15 If any·man should·love the world, the love of·the
1Jn 4:1 many false·prophets have·gone·out into the world.
1Jn 4:9 Son into the world, in·order·that we·may·live
1Jn 5:4 ·born from·out·of·God overcomes the world. And
1Jn 5:4 the victory (the·one overcoming the world): our trust.
1Jn 5:5 Who is the·one overcoming the world, if·not the·one
2Jn 1:7 many impostors entered into the world, the·ones not
G2889.3 N-DSM κόσμῳ (37x)
Jn 1:10 *This Light* was in the world, and the world came·to·
Jn 6:33 of·the heaven, and giving life-above to·the world."
Jn 7:4 these·things, make yourself apparent to·the world."
Jn 9:5 Inasmuch·as I·should·be in the world, I·am a·light of·
Jn 12:25 his soul in this world shall·vigilantly·keep it unto
Jn 13:1 his·own, the·ones in the world, he·loved them to *the*
Jn 14:22 yourself to·us, and not·indeed to·the world?"
Jn 16:33 ·have peace. In the world, yeu·have tribulation,
Jn 17:11 And I·am no longer in the world, but these·men are
Jn 17:11 but these·men are in the world, and I·myself do·
Jn 17:12 ·was with them in the world, I·myself was·guarding
Jn 17:13 these·things I·speak in the world, in·order·that they·
Jn 18:20 with·freeness·of·speech to·the world. I·myself
Gal 6:14 world has·been·crucified to·me, and·I to·the world.
Mt 18:7 "Woe to·the world due·to its scandalous·traps, for
Mt 26:13 ·be·officially·proclaimed in the whole world, also
Rm 1:8 yeur trust is·being·fully·proclaimed in all the world.
Rm 5:13 moral·failure was in *the* world, but moral·failure
Php 2:15 yeu·are·apparent as brilliant·lights in *the* world
1Pe 5:9 in·yeur brotherhood *while·still* in *this* world.
2Pe 1:4 ·from the corruption *caused* by worldly longing.
2Pe 2:5 ·bringing a·Deluge upon a·world of·irreverent·men;
1Co 4:9 ·become a·public·spectacle to·the world, to·angels,
1Co 7:31 and the·ones using this world, as not abusing *it* …
1Co 8:4 an·idol *is* nothing·at·all in *the* world, and that *there*·
1Co 11:32 ·not be·condemned together with·the world.
1Co 14:10 kinds of·voices in *the* world, and not·even·one of·
2Co 1:12 ·ourselves in the world and more·abundantly
Eph 2:12 ·of·Resurrection, and without·God in the world.
Col 1:6 yeu, just·as *it·is* also in all the world. And it·is itself·
Col 2:20 living in *the* world, are·yeu·subject·to·decrees
1Ti 3:16 is·trusted *upon* in *the* world, is·taken·up into glory.
1Jn 2:15 world, nor·even the·things in the world. If any·man
1Jn 2:16 Because all *that·is* in the world, the longing of·the
1Jn 4:3 that it·is·come, and now is in the world, even·now.
1Jn 4:4 greater is the·one in yeu, than the·one in the world.
1Jn 4:17 that·one is, so·also are we·ourselves in this world.

G2889.3 N-GSM κόσμου (73x)
Jn 1:29 the·one taking·away the moral·failure of·the world!
Jn 4:42 is truly the Savior of·the world, the Anointed-One.
Jn 6:51 shall·give on·behalf of·the life† of·the world."
Jn 8:12 "I AM the light of·the world. The·one following me,
Jn 8:23 Yeu·yeurselves are from·among this world; I·myself
Jn 8:23 this world; I·myself am not from·among this world.
Jn 9:5 I·should·be in the world, I·am a·light of·the world."
Jn 11:9 stumble, because he·looks·at the light of·this world.
Jn 12:31 ·is now a·Tribunal·judgment of·this world. The
Jn 12:31 The prince of·this world shall now be·cast·out
Jn 13:1 that he·should·walk·on from·among this world to the
Jn 14:30 for the prince of·this world comes, and he·does·
Jn 15:19 "If yeu·were from·among the world, the world
Jn 15:19 but yeu·are not from·among the world, but·rather I·
Jn 15:19 selected yeu from·among the world. On·account·of
Jn 16:11 because the prince of·this world has·been·judged.
Jn 17:6 ·given to·me from·among the world. They·were
Jn 17:9 *It·is* not concerning the world *that* I·ask, but·rather
Jn 17:14 they·are not from·among the world, just·as I·myself
Jn 17:14 just·as I·myself am not from·among the world.
Jn 17:15 them up out·from·among the world, but·rather that
Jn 17:16 "They·are not from·among the world, just·as I·
Jn 17:16 just·as I·myself am not from·among the world.
Jn 17:24 you·did·love me before *the* world's conception.
Jn 18:36 "My kingdom is not from·among this world. If my
Jn 18:36 kingdom was from·among this world, my assistants
Lk 11:50 being·poured·out from *the* world's conception,
Lk 12:30 these·things, the nations of·the world seek·after.
Heb 4:3 ·the works being·done from *the* world's conception.
Heb 9:26 ·suffer many·times since *the* world's conception.
Gal 4:3 ·been·enslaved under the principles of·the world.
Mt 4:8 him all the kingdoms of·the world and their glory,
Mt 5:14 are the light of·the world. A·city that·is·being·set·
Mt 13:35 having·been·hidden from *the* world's conception."
Mt 24:21 has·not been since *the* world's beginning until the
Mt 25:34 ·made·ready for·yeu from *the* world's conception.
Rm 1:20 For from *the* world's creation, the invisible·things
Rm 4:13 himself to·be *the* heir of·the world), but·rather *is*
Rm 11:12 if their trespass *became* wealth for·*the*·world, and
Rm 11:15 of·them *is* reconciliation for·*the*·world, what *shall*
Jac 1:27 ·keep oneself unstained from the world.
Jac 2:5 the helplessly·poor of·this world *to·be* wealthy in
Jac 4:4 that the friendship of·the world is hostility with·God?
Jac 4:4 ·friend of·the world is·fully·established·as an·enemy
1Pe 1:20 ·been·foreknown before *the* world's conception, but
2Pe 2:5 and *if* he·did·not spare *the* ancient world, but·rather
2Pe 2:20 of·the world by a·recognition·and·acknowledgment
1Co 1:20 not·indeed make·foolish the wisdom of·this world?
1Co 1:27 of·the world in·order·that he·may·put·to·shame the
1Co 1:27 of·the world in·order·that he·may·put·to·shame the
1Co 1:28 the bastardly·things of·the world and the·things
1Co 2:12 *it·was* not the spirit of·the world *that* we·ourselves
1Co 3:19 For the wisdom of·this world is foolishness with
1Co 4:13 as scum of·the world, an·offscouring of·all·things
1Co 5:10 with·the sexually·immoral·people of·this world, or
1Co 5:10 yeu·are·obligated to·go·forth out of·the world.
1Co 7:31 for the schematic·layout of·this world passes·away.
1Co 7:33 is·anxious·about the·things of·the world, how he·
1Co 7:34 is·anxious·about the·things of·the world, how she·
2Co 7:10 but the grief of·the world accomplishes death.
Eph 1:4 us in him before *the* world's conception for·us to·be
Eph 2:2 ·to the present·age of·this world, according·to the
Col 2:8 ·*is*, according·to the principles of·the world, and not
Col 2:20 from the principles of·the world, why, as·though
1Jn 2:2 concerning *the moral·failures·of* the whole world.
1Jn 2:16 Father, but·rather is birthed·from·out of·the world.
1Jn 3:17 whoever should·have the world's livelihood, and
1Jn 4:5 ·themselves are from·out of·the world, on·account·of
1Jn 4:5 ·of that they·speak from·among the world, and the
1Jn 4:14 has·dispatched the Son *to·be* Savior of·the world.
Rv 11:15 "The kingdoms of·the world are·become *the*
Rv 13:8 ·been·slaughtered from *the* world's conception.
Rv 17:8 ·scroll of·the life-above from *the* world's conception,

G2890 Κούαρτος Kôúartôs *n/p.* (1x)
G2890.2 N/P-NSM Κούαρτος (1x)
Rm 16:23 greets yeu, *as* also *does* Quartus, the brother.

G2891 κοῦμι kôûmi *aram.* (1x)
ϗοῦμι qôûmi [Greek, Octuagint]
קוּם qûm̱ [Aramaic]
Roots:A6966
G2891 ARAM ϗοῦμι (1x)
Mk 5:41 ·the hand, he·says to·her, "Talitha qumi," which,

G2892 κουστωδία kôustōdía *n.* (3x)
Compare:G4688
G2892 N-ASF κουστωδίαν (1x)
Mt 27:65 to·them, "Yeu·have a·sentinel·guard. Head·on·out
G2892 N-GSF κουστωδίας (2x)
Mt 27:66 with the sentinel·guard *and·by* officially·sealing
Mt 28:11 behold, some of·the sentinel·guard, after·coming

G2893 κουφίζω kôuphízō *v.* (2x)
G2893 V-IAI-3P ἐκούφιζον (1x)
Ac 27:38 they·were·lightening the sailing·ship, *by* casting·
EG2893 (1x)
Ac 27:18 ·storm, the next·day they·did *lighten the ship by*

G2894 κόφινος kóphinôs *n.* (6x)
Compare:G4553 G4711
G2894 N-NPM κόφινοι (1x)
Lk 9:17 *was* twelve wicker·baskets of·*bread*·fragments.
G2894 N-APM κοφίνους (5x)
Jn 6:13 twelve wicker·baskets with·fragments from·out of·
Mt 14:20 of·the fragments— twelve wicker·baskets full.
Mt 16:9 *men*, and how·many wicker·baskets yeu·took·up?
Mk 6:43 ·up twelve wicker·baskets full of·*bread*·fragments
Mk 8:19 *men*, how·many wicker·baskets full of·fragments

G2895 κράββατος krábbatôs *n.* (13x)
Compare:G2825 G2826 G2845
G2895 N-ASM κράββατον (9x)
Jn 5:8 "Be·awakened, take·up your mat and walk."
Jn 5:9 And he·took·up his mat and was·walking, and on the
Jn 5:10 It·is·not proper for·you to·take·up *your* mat."
Jn 5:11 ·man declared to·me, 'Take·up your mat and walk.'"
Jn 5:12 declaring to·you, 'Take·up your mat and walk'?
Mk 2:4 ·digging·through, they·lowered the mat on which
Mk 2:9 'Be·awakened, and take·up your mat and walk'?
Mk 2:11 ·awakened, and take·up your mat, and head·on·out
Mk 2:12 and after·taking·up the mat, he·went·forth in·front
G2895 N-DSM κραββάτῳ (1x)
Ac 9:33 by·name, laying·down upon a·mat for eight years,
G2895 N-DPM κραββάτοις (1x)
Mk 6:55 ·began to·carry·about on their mats the·ones being
G2895 N-GPM κραββάτων (1x)
Ac 5:15 ·lay *them* on simple·couches and mats, in·order·that
EG2895 (1x)
Ac 9:34 Rise·up and toss·aside your *mat*." And immediately

G2896 κράζω krázō *v.* (59x)
Compare:G0310 G0994 G2019 G5455 See:G0349 G2906 xLangAlso:H2199 H7768
G2896.1 V-2FDI-3P κεκράξονται (1x)
Lk 19:40 these should·keep·silent, the stones shall·yell·out."
G2896.1 V-PAI-1P κράζομεν (1x)
Rm 8:15 of·adoption·as·sons, by which we·yell·out, "Abba,
G2896.1 V-PAI-3S κράζει (5x)
Lk 9:39 him, and suddenly he·yells·out; and it·convulses
Mt 15:23 "Dismiss her, because she·yells·out after us."
Rm 9:27 But IsaIah yells·out concerning IsraEl, '" Although
Jac 5:4 having·been·robbed by yeu, it·yells·out. And the
Rv 12:2 she·yelled·out experiencing·birthing·pain and
G2896.1 V-PAN κράζειν (1x)
Mk 10:47 of·Natsareth, he·began to·yell·out and to·say,
G2896.1 V-PAP-ASN κρᾶζον (2x)
Ac 21:36 of·the people were·following, yelling·out, "Take
Gal 4:6 of·his Son into yeur hearts, yelling·out, "Abba,
G2896.1 V-PAP-APM κράζοντας (1x)
Mt 21:15 that he·did and·also the boys yelling·out in the
G2896.1 V-PAP-GPM κραζόντων (1x)
Ac 19:34 ·a·span·of about two hours— yelling·out, "Great
G2896.1 V-PAP-NSM κράζων (2x)
Mk 5:5 and in the tombs, yelling·out and fully·chopping·at
Rv 14:15 out of·the Temple, yelling·out in a·loud voice to·
G2896.1 V-PAP-NPN κράζοντα (1x)
Lk 4:41 were·coming·out of many, yelling·out and saying,
G2896.1 V-PAP-NPM κράζοντες (4x)
Ac 14:14 garments, rushed·in among the crowd, yelling·out
Ac 21:28 while·yelling·out, "Men, Israelites, swiftly·help!
Mt 9:27 blind·men followed him, yelling·out and saying,
Rv 7:10 and yelling·out with·a·loud voice, saying, "The
G2896.1 V-IAI-3S ἔκραζεν (4x)
Lk 18:39 But he·himself was·yelling·out so·much *the* more
Ac 16:17 Paul and us, the·same·girl was·yelling·out, saying,
Mk 3:11 ·down·before him and was·yelling·out, saying,
Mk 10:48 ·keep·silent, but he·was·yelling·out so·much the
G2896.1 V-IAI-3P ἔκραζον (11x)
Jn 12:13 to meet him, and were·yelling·out, "Hosanna!
Jn 19:12 him, but the Judeans were·yelling·out, saying, "If
Ac 19:28 full of·rage, and they·were·yelling·out, saying,
Ac 19:32 ·course, some were·yelling·out a·certain·thing,
Mt 20:31 ·silent, but they·were·yelling·out more·loudly,
Mt 21:9 and the·ones following, were·yelling·out, saying,
Mt 27:23 But the *crowds* were·yelling·out more·abundantly,
Mk 11:9 and the·ones following were·yelling·out, saying,
Rv 6:10 And they·were·yelling·out with·a·loud voice, saying
Rv 18:18 and they·were·yelling·out, clearly·seeing the
Rv 18:19 on their heads, and were·yelling·out, weeping and
G2896.1 V-AAI-1S ἔκραξα (1x)
Ac 24:21 this one address that I·yelled·out standing among
G2896.1 V-AAI-3S ἔκραξεν (11x)
Jn 7:28 Accordingly, Jesus yelled·out in the Sanctuary·
Jn 7:37 *of·Booths*, Jesus stood and yelled·out, saying, "If
Jn 12:44 And Jesus yelled·out and declared, "The·one
Ac 7:60 bowing the knees, he·yelled·out with·a·loud voice,
Ac 23:6 and the other Pharisees, he·yelled·out in the joint·
Mt 14:30 to·be·plunged·down, he·yelled·out, saying, "Lord
Rv 7:2 ·the·living God, and he·yelled·out with·a·loud voice
Rv 10:3 and he·yelled·out with·a·loud voice, just·as *when* a·
Rv 10:3 a·lion roars. And when he·yelled·out, the Seven
Rv 18:2 And he·yelled·out in strength, a·great voice, saying,
Rv 19:17 in the sun; and he·yelled·out with·a·loud voice,
G2896.1 V-AAI-3P ἔκραξαν (5x)
Mt 8:29 And behold, they·yelled·out, saying, "What·does·
Mt 14:26 ·is a·phantom!" and they·yelled·out from the fear.
Mt 20:30 that YeShua passes·by, they·yelled·out, saying,
Mk 15:13 And they·yelled·out again, "Crucify him!"
Mk 15:14 And they·yelled·out the more·abundantly,
G2896.1 V-AAP-NSN κράξαν (2x)
Mk 1:26 ·convulsing him and yelling·out with·a·loud voice,
Mk 9:26 And after·yelling·out and convulsing him
G2896.1 V-AAP-NSM κράξας (4x)
Mt 27:50 But YeShua, after·yelling·out again with·a·loud
Mk 5:7 And yelling·out with·a·loud voice, he·declared,
Mk 9:24 the father of·the little·child, yelling·out with tears,
Mk 15:39 ·manner, upon·yelling·out, he·breathed·his·last,
G2896.1 V-AAP-NPM κράξαντες (1x)
Ac 7:57 Then yelling·out with·a·loud voice, they·stopped·up
G2896.1 V-2RAI-3S κέκραγεν (1x)
Jn 1:15 testifies concerning him and has·yelled·out, saying,

G2897 κραιπάλη kraipálē *n.* (1x)
Roots:G0138 Compare:G3178 G0810 See:G0726
G2897.2 N-DSF κραιπάλῃ (1x)
Lk 21:34 ·burdened with the·aftermath·of·indulgence, and

G2898 κρανίον kraníôn *n.* (4x)
Roots:G2768 G2444-3 xLangEquiv:H1538 xLangAlso:G1115
G2898 N-ASN κρανίον (1x)
Lk 23:33 to the place, the·one being·called Skull, there they·
G2898 N-GSN κρανίου (3x)
Jn 19:17 being·referred·to·as *the* Place of·a·Skull, which is·

Mt 27:33 that is being·referred·to·as, *the* Place of·a·Skull,
Mk 15:22 ·interpreted *from·Hebrew*, is *the* Place of·a·Skull.

G2899 κράσπεδον kráspêdôn *n.* (5x)
Compare:G5440 xLangAlso:H6734

G2899.3 N-APN κράσπεδα (1x)
Mt 23:5 tefillin and enlarge the fringes of·their garments.

G2899.3 N-GSN κρασπέδου (4x)
Lk 8:44 ·behind, she·laid·hold of·the fringe of·his garment,
Mt 9:20 ·behind, she·laid·hold of·the fringe of·his garment,
Mt 14:36 ·may merely lay·hold of·the fringe of·his garment,
Mk 6:56 *of·him*, if·even *only* of·the fringe of·his garment.

G2900 κραταιός krataiós *adj.* (1x)
Roots:G2904 Compare:G2478 G1415 G0972 See:G2903 G2901-2 G2900-1 xLangEquiv:H1368

G2900.1 A-ASF κραταιάν (1x)
1Pe 5:6 be·humbled under the mighty hand of·God, in·

G2901 κραταιόω krataiṓō *v.* (4x)
Roots:G2900 Compare:G2594 G2480 xLangAlso:H2388

G2901.1 V-APN κραταιωθῆναι (1x)
Eph 3:16 ·grant yeu to·be·made·mighty with·power through

G2901.2 V-PPM-2P κραταιοῦσθε (1x)
1Co 16:13 " Be·manly! Become·mighty!"

G2901.2 V-IPI-3S ἐκραταιοῦτο (2x)
Lk 1:80 was·growing, and was·becoming·mighty in·spirit,
Lk 2:40 was·growing and was·becoming·mighty in·spirit,

G2902 κρατέω kratéō *v.* (47x)
Roots:G2904 Compare:G1840 G2480 G4599 G5293 See:G2888 G1467-1

G2902.2 V-FAI-3S κρατήσει (1x)
Mt 12:11 shall·not·indeed take·secure·hold·of it and pull·it·

G2902.2 V-PAS-1P κρατῶμεν (1x)
Heb 4:14 Son of·God, we·should·take·secure·hold of·the

G2902.2 V-AAI-1P ἐκρατήσαμεν (1x)
Ac 24:6 whom also we·took·secure·hold·of and determined

G2902.2 V-AAI-2P ἐκρατήσατε (2x)
Mt 26:55 ·Atrium, and yeu·did·not take·secure·hold·of me.
Mk 14:49 and yeu·did·not take·secure·hold·of me. "But·

G2902.2 V-AAI-3S ἐκράτησεν (2x)
Mt 9:25 upon·entering, he·took·secure·hold of·her hand,
Mk 6:17 after·dispatching, took·secure·hold·of John, and

G2902.2 V-AAN κρατῆσαι (3x)
Heb 6:18 ·for·refuge) to·take·secure·hold of·the Expectation
Mk 3:21 hearing *of·it*, went·out to·take·secure·hold·of him,
Mk 12:12 they·were·seeking to·take·secure·hold·of him, yet

G2902.2 V-AAP-NSM κρατήσας (4x)
Lk 8:54 outside and taking·secure·hold of·her by·the hand,
Mt 14:3 HerOd·AntiPas, after·taking·secure·hold·of John,
Mk 1:31 her, after·taking·secure·hold·of her hand, and
Mk 5:41 And after·taking·secure·hold of·the little·child by·

G2902.2 V-AAP-NPM κρατήσαντες (2x)
Mt 22:6 And the rest, taking·secure·hold of·his slaves,
Mk 14:1 were·seeking how, after·taking·secure·hold *of·him*,

G2902.2 V-AAS-3P κρατήσωσιν (1x)
Mt 26:4 in·order·that they·may·take·secure·hold·of YeShua

G2902.2 V-RAN κεκρατηκέναι (1x)
Ac 27:13 *and* supposing to·have·taken·secure·hold of·the

G2902.3 V-PAI-2S κρατεῖς (1x)
Rv 2:13 *is*, and you·securely·hold my name and did·not

G2902.3 V-PAI-2P κρατεῖτε (1x)
Mk 7:8 of·God, yeu·securely·hold·to the Oral·tradition of·

G2902.3 V-PAI-3P κρατοῦσιν (1x)
Mk 14:51 nakedness, and the young·men securely·held him.

G2902.3 V-PAM-2S κράτει (1x)
Rv 3:11 I·come swiftly. Securely·hold that·which you·have,

G2902.3 V-PAM-2P κρατεῖτε (1x)
2Th 2:15 stand·fast and securely·hold·to the traditions

G2902.3 V-PAN κρατεῖν (1x)
Mk 7:4 they·personally·received to·securely·hold, *such·as*

G2902.3 V-PAP-APM κρατοῦντας (3x)
Rv 2:14 ·have there ones·securely·holding·to the instruction
Rv 2:15 also have ones·securely·holding·to the instruction
Rv 7:1 corners of·the earth, securely·holding the four winds

G2902.3 V-PAP-GSM κρατοῦντος (1x)
Ac 3:11 ·man who·was·healed securely·holding Peter and

G2902.3 V-PAP-NSM κρατῶν (2x)
Col 2:19 and not securely·holding the Head, from·out·of·
Rv 2:1 'These·things says the·one securely·holding the seven

G2902.3 V-PAP-NPM κρατοῦντες (1x)
Mk 7:3 ·do·not eat, securely·holding·to the Oral·tradition

G2902.3 V-PAS-2P κρατῆτε (1x)
Jn 20:23 *moral·failures* yeu·should·securely·hold, they·have·

G2902.3 V-PPN κρατεῖσθαι (1x)
Ac 2:24 not possible *for·Jesus* to·be·securely·held by him.

G2902.3 V-IPI-3P ἐκρατοῦντο (1x)
Lk 24:16 But their eyes were·securely·held, *such·for them*

G2902.3 V-AAI-3S ἐκράτησεν (1x)
Rv 20:2 And he·securely·held the Dragon, the original

G2902.3 V-AAI-3P ἐκράτησαν (4x)
Mt 26:50 their hands on YeShua and securely·held him.
Mt 28:9 And coming·alongside, they·securely·held his feet
Mk 9:10 And they·securely·held the saying toward
Mk 14:46 ·threw their hands on him and securely·held him.

G2902.3 V-AAM-2P κρατήσατε (3x)
Mt 26:48 I·should·kiss, that·is him. Securely·hold him."
Mk 14:44 it·is him. Securely·hold him and lead·*him*·away
Rv 2:25 ·have, securely·hold even·until I·should·come.

G2902.3 V-AAN κρατῆσαι (1x)
Mt 21:46 Yet while·seeking to·securely·hold him, they·

G2902.3 V-AAP-NSM κρατήσας (2x)
Mt 18:28 denarii, and securely·holding him, he·was·
Mk 9:27 But after·securely·holding him by·the hand, Jesus

G2902.3 V-AAP-NPM κρατήσαντες (1x)
Mt 26:57 the·ones securely·holding YeShua led·*him*·away to

G2902.3 V-RPI-3P κεκράτηνται (1x)
Jn 20:23 ·securely·hold, they·have·been·securely·held."

G2903 κράτιστος krátistôs *adj.* (4x)
Roots:G2904 Compare:G3841 See:G2900 G2909 xLangAlso:H0117

G2903.2 A-VSM κράτιστε (3x)
Lk 1:3 in·consecutive·order, most·noble TheoPhilus,
Ac 24:3 everywhere and in·every·way, most·noble Felix.
Ac 26:25 "I·am·not raving·mad, most·noble Festus, but·

G2903.2 A-DSM κρατίστῳ (1x)
Ac 23:26 Claudius Lysias, to·the most·noble governor Felix,

G2904 κράτος krátôs *n.* (12x)
Compare:G0970 G1411 G1413 G1849 G2479 See:G2594 G2900 G2902 G2903 G2908 G2909 G3841 G4031 xLangEquiv:H1397

G2904.1 N-NSN κράτος (6x)
Jud 1:25 *be* glory and majesty, might and authority, both
1Pe 4:11 is the glory and the might into the ages of·ages.
1Pe 5:11 *be* the glory and the might into the ages of·ages.
1Ti 6:16 , to·whom *be* honor and might eternal. So·be·it,·
Rv 1:6 ·him *be* the glory and the might into the ages of·ages.
Rv 5:13 honor and the glory and the might, into the ages of·

G2904.1 N-ASN κράτος (3x)
Ac 19:20 In·this·manner, according·to might, the
Heb 2:14 ·impotent the·one having the might of·Death, that·
Col 1:11 all power according·to the might of·his glory into

G2904.1 N-DSN κράτει (1x)
Eph 6:10 in *the* Lord and in the might of·his strength.

G2904.1 N-GSN κράτους (1x)
Eph 1:19 ·to the operation of·the strength of·his might

G2904.2 N-ASN κράτος (1x)
Lk 1:51 "He·did a·mighty·thing with his arm; he·thoroughly·

G2905 κραυγάζω kraugázō *v.* (7x)
Roots:G2906 Compare:G0994 G0310

G2905 V-FAI-3S κραυγάσει (1x)
Mt 12:19 ·in·strife, neither shall·he·yell·out, nor·even·shall

G2905 V-PAP-GPM κραυγαζόντων (1x)
Ac 22:23 And with·them yelling·out, and flinging·off the

G2905 V-AAI-3S ἐκραύγασεν (2x)
Jn 11:43 these·things, he·yelled·out with·a·loud voice,
Mt 15:22 *who*, upon·coming·forth yelled·out to·him,

G2905 V-AAI-3P ἐκραύγασαν (3x)
Jn 18:40 So·then they·all yelled·out again, saying, "Not this·
Jn 19:6 and the assistants saw him, they·yelled·out, saying,
Jn 19:15 But they·yelled·out, "Take·*him*·away, take·*him*·

G2906 κραυγή kraugḗ *n.* (6x)
Roots:G2896 Compare:G0213-2 See:G2905

G2906.1 N-NSF κραυγή (1x)
Mt 25:6 "And at·the·middle of·night, a·yell has·occurred,

G2906.1 N-DSF κραυγῇ (1x)
Rv 14:18 he·hollered·out with·a·loud yell to·the·one having

G2906.1 N-GSF κραυγῆς (1x)
Heb 5:7 and supplications with·a·strong yell and tears toward

G2906.2 N-NSF κραυγή (3x)
Ac 23:9 And there·occurred a·great *amount·of* yelling. And
Eph 4:31 rage, and wrath, and yelling, and revilement, be·
Rv 21:4 neither mourning, nor yelling, nor·also continual·

G2907 κρέας kréas *n.* (2x)

G2907 N-APN κρέα (2x)
Rm 14:21 *It·is* morally·good neither to·eat meat, nor·even to·
1Co 8:13 *then* no, I·should·not eat meat unto the coming·age,

G2908 κρεῖσσον krêîssôn *adj.* (3x)
Roots:G2909 See:G2900

G2908.2 A-NSN κρεῖσσον (2x)
Php 1:23 *which·is even* so·much more significantly·better.
1Co 7:9 ·marry. For it·is significantly·better to·marry than

G2908.2 A-ASN κρεῖσσον (1x)
1Co 7:38 giving·away·in·marriage does significantly·better.

G2909 κρείττων krêíttōn *adj.* (17x)
Roots:G2904 Compare:G2570 See:G2908 G2900 G2903

G2909.1 A-GSM κρείττονος (1x)
Heb 7:7 contradiction, the lesser is·blessed by the mightier.

G2909.2 A-NSM κρείττων (1x)
Heb 1:4 ·made so·much significantly·better·than the angels,

G2909.2 A-NSN κρεῖττον (2x)
1Pe 3:17 For *it·is* significantly·better, if the will of·God is·
2Pe 2:21 For it·was significantly·better for·them not to·have·

G2909.2 A-ASF κρείττονα (1x)
Heb 10:34 *the* heavens a·significantly·better and an·enduring

G2909.2 A-ASN κρεῖττον (2x)
Heb 11:40 ·at something significantly·better concerning us:
1Co 11:17 not for the significantly·better, but·rather for the

G2909.2 A-APN κρείττονα (3x)
Heb 6:9 yeu *of·*the significantly·better·things and *of·the*
Heb 12:24 speaking significantly·better·things— contrary·to
1Co 12:31 the significantly·better gracious·bestowments.

G2909.2 A-DPF κρείττοσιν (2x)
Heb 8:6 has·been·enacted upon significantly·better promises.
Heb 9:23 themselves with·significantly·better sacrifices than

G2909.2 A-GSF κρείττονος (5x)
Heb 7:19 superseding·introduction of·a·significantly·better
Heb 7:22 a·surety of·a·significantly·better covenant.
Heb 8:6 also *the* mediator of·a·significantly·better covenant,
Heb 11:16 ·stretch·themselves·toward a·significantly·better,
Heb 11:35 ·order·that they·may·obtain a·significantly·better.

G2910 κρεμάννυμι krêmánnymi *v.* (7x)
Compare:G4029 See:G2911 G1582 xLangAlso:H8518

G2910 V-PMP-ASN κρεμάμενον (1x)
Ac 28:4 saw the venomous·beast hanging out·from his hand,

G2910 V-PMP-NSM κρεμάμενος (1x)
Gal 3:13 ·accursed *is* any one being·hung on an·arbor·tree."

G2910 V-PPI-3P κρέμανται (1x)
Mt 22:40 On these two commandments is·hung all the

G2910 V-AAP-NPM κρεμάσαντες (2x)
Ac 5:30 ·yeurselves abusively·manhandled, hanging *him* on
Ac 10:39 whom they·executed *by* hanging on an·arbor·tree.

G2910 V-APP-GPM κρεμασθέντων (1x)
Lk 23:39 ·the criminals who·were·hanging was·reviling him,

G2910 V-APS-3S κρεμασθῇ (1x)
Mt 18:6 a·donkey-sized millstone should·be·hung upon his

G2911 κρημνός krēmnős *n.* (3x)
Roots:G2910 See:G2911-2
G2911.2 N-GSM κρημνοῦ (3x)
Lk 8:33 ·dashed down the steep·overhang into the lake and
Mt 8:32 ·dashed down the steep·overhang into the sea and
Mk 5:13 ·dashed down the steep·overhang into the sea.

G2912 Κρής Krḗs *n/g.* (2x)
Roots:G2914
G2912 N/G-NPM Κρῆτες (2x)
Ac 2:11 Cretans and Arabians— we·hear them speaking in·
Tit 1:12 of·their own, declared, "Cretans *are* always liars,

G2913 Κρήσκης Krḗskēs *n/p.* (1x)
G2913.2 N/P-NSM Κρήσκης (1x)
2Ti 4:10 he·departed to ThessaloNica, Crescens to Galatia,

G2914 Κρήτη Krḗtē *n/l.* (7x)
G2914 N/L-ASF Κρήτην (2x)
Ac 27:7 we·sailed·leeward·near·to Crete, adjacent·to
Ac 27:13 they·were·sailing·near Crete, very·close·to *shore*.
G2914 N/L-DSF Κρήτῃ (1x)
Tit 1:5 I·left you behind in Crete, that you·should·fully·set·
G2914 N/L-GSF Κρήτης (2x)
Ac 27:12 *there, which·is* a·harbor of·Crete, looking·out
Ac 27:21 not to·be·sailing·away from Crete nor·also to·gain
EG2914 (2x)
Ac 27:8 which was near *the* city *of* Lasea *(in·Crete)*.
Ac 27:14 wind slammed against *Crete*, the·one being·called

Κκ

G2915 κριθή krithḗ *n.* (1x)
Compare:G4447-1 G4621 See:G2916 xLangEquiv:H8184
G2915 N-GSF κριθῆς (1x)
Rv 6:6 and three dry·measures of·barley for·a·denarius; and

G2916 κρίθινος kríthinôs *adj.* (2x)
Roots:G2915
G2916 A-APM κριθίνους (1x)
Jn 6:9 here, who has five barley loaves·of·bread, and two
G2916 A-GPM κριθίνων (1x)
Jn 6:13 from·out of·the five barley loaves·of·bread, which

G2917 κρίμα kríma *n.* (30x)
Roots:G2919 Compare:G2920 See:G4792-3 xLangAlso:H4941
G2917.2 N-NSN κρίμα (5x)
Rm 2:2 But we·have·seen that the judgment of·God is
Rm 3:8 Of·such·men, the judgment is just.
Rm 5:16 For in·fact, the judgment *was* as·a·result of·one
2Pe 2:3 *·teachers* for·whom judgment from·long·ago is·not
Rv 20:4 ·sat upon them, and judgment was·given to·them—
G2917.2 N-NPN κρίματα (1x)
Rm 11:33 How inexplorable *are* his judgments, and his ways
G2917.2 N-ASN κρίμα (15x)
Jn 9:39 Jesus declared, "For judgment, I·myself did·come
Lk 20:47 "These shall·receive more·abundant judgment."
Lk 24:20 rulers handed him over to a·judgment of·death, and
Gal 5:10 troubling yeu shall·bear the judgment, whoever he·
Mt 23:13 that, yeu·shall·receive more·abundant judgment.
Mk 12:40 "These shall·receive more·abundant judgment."
Rm 2:3 ·yourself shall·utterly·escape the judgment of·God?
Rm 13:2 ·to *it* shall·receive judgment for·themselves.
Jac 3:1 having·seen that we·shall·receive greater judgment.
Jud 1:4 ·about of·antiquity to this judgment, irreverent·men
1Pe 4:17 *it·is* the season *for* the judgment to·begin with the
1Co 11:29 eats and drinks judgment to·himself, not
1Co 11:34 yeu·should·come·together into judgment. And as·
1Ti 5:12 being·held·in judgment, because they·set·aside the
Rv 17:1 I·shall·show to·you the judgment of·the Great
G2917.2 N-APN κρίματα (1x)
1Co 6:7 yeu, because yeu·hold judgment among them.
G2917.2 N-DSN κρίματι (1x)
Lk 23:40 God, *seeing* how you·are in the same judgment?
G2917.2 N-GSN κρίματος (2x)
Ac 24:25 and the impending judgment *that* shall·be, Felix,
Heb 6:2 ·resurrection of·the·dead, and of·eternal judgment.
EG2917.2 (2x)
Mk 13:11 they·should·bring *yeu for·judgment*, while·handing
Rm 5:18 as through one trespass, *judgment came* upon all
G2917.3 N-ASN κρίμα (1x)
Rv 18:20 God decided yeur just·claim as·a·result of·her
G2917.4 N-DSN κρίματι (1x)
Mt 7:2 by whatever standard·of·judgment yeu·unduly·judge,
G2917.5 N-ASN κρίμα (1x)
1Ti 3:6 ·fall to an·accusational·judgment of·the Slanderer.

G2918 κρίνον krínôn *n.* (2x)
Compare:G4677 G2924-3 xLangEquiv:H7799
G2918 N-APN κρίνα (2x)
Lk 12:27 "Fully·observe how the lilies grow. They·do·not
Mt 6:28 apparel? Carefully·note the lilies of·the field, how

G2919 κρίνω krínō *v.* (112x)
Compare:G3354 G4793 G4822 G4588-3 G1340-1 See:G2917 G2920 G2632 xLangAlso:H8199
G2919.1 V-FAI-1S κρινῶ (1x)
Lk 19:22 'From·out of·your·own mouth shall·I·judge you,
G2919.1 V-FAI-1P κρινοῦμεν (1x)
1Co 6:3 ·not personally·know that we·shall·judge angels?
G2919.1 V-FAI-3S κρινεῖ (2x)
Jn 12:48 which I·spoke. The·same shall·judge him at the last
Rm 2:27 ·out of·natural uncircumcision *indeed* judge you,
G2919.1 V-FAI-3P κρινοῦσιν (1x)
1Co 6:2 ·know that the holy·ones shall·judge the world?
G2919.1 V-FPI-2P κριθήσεσθε (1x)
Mt 7:2 yeu·unduly·judge, yeu·shall·be·judged. And by
G2919.1 V-FPI-3P κριθήσονται (1x)
Rm 2:12 Torah-Law shall·be·judged through Torah-Law.
G2919.1 V-PAI-1S κρινῶ (4x)
Jn 5:30 Just·as I·hear, I·judge. And my verdict is righteous,
Jn 8:15 I·myself do·not presently·judge not·even·one·man.
Jn 12:47 ·not trust, I·myself do·not presently·judge him, for
Ac 15:19 Therefore, I·myself judge *for·us* not to·further·
G2919.1 V-PAI-2S κρίνεις (3x)
Rm 2:1 For in that·which you·judge the other, you·condemn
Jac 4:11 But if you·judge law, you·are not a·doer of·law,
Rv 6:10 the Truthful·One, do·you·not judge and avenge our
G2919.1 V-PAI-2P κρίνετε (4x)
Jn 8:15 "Yeu·yeurselves judge according·to the flesh; I·
Lk 12:57 Now, why·do yeu·not judge what·is·right even by
Ac 13:46 ·shove it away and presently·judge yeurselves not
1Co 5:12 not·indeed presently·judge the·ones inside?
G2919.1 V-PAI-3S κρινεῖ (10x)
Jn 5:22 not·even·does the Father judge, not·even·one·man,
Jn 7:51 "¿!·Does our Oral-law judge the man·of·clay†,
Heb 13:4 God presently·judges sexually·immoral·people and
Rm 2:16 at a·Day when God judges the secrets of·the men·
Rm 3:6 Otherwise how·does God judge the world?
Rm 14:5 In·fact, someone judges one·day *to·be* above·and·
Rm 14:5 day, yet someone *else* judges every day *to·be alike*.
Jac 4:11 brother, he·speaks·against law and judges law. But
1Co 5:13 the·ones outside, God presently·judges. So·then:
Rv 19:11 and in righteousness he·judges and wages·war.
G2919.1 V-PAM-2P κρίνετε (1x)
1Co 4:5 yeu·must·not presently·judge anything before *the*
G2919.1 V-PAM-3S κρινέτω (2x)
Rm 14:3 the·one not eating must·not judge the·one eating,
Col 2:16 do·not·let anyone judge yeu *concerning matters* in
G2919.1 V-PAN κρίνειν (5x)
Jn 8:26 many·things to·speak and to·judge concerning yeu.
Ac 17:31 a·day in which he·intends 'to·judge The Land by
Ac 24:6 ·hold·of and determined to·judge according·to our
1Co 5:12 ·with·me, to also presently·judge the·ones outside
2Ti 4:1 Anointed (the·one about to·judge living·men and
G2919.1 V-PAP-ASM κρίνοντα (2x)
Jn 12:48 utterances, has *this* one presently·judging him: the
1Pe 1:17 the·one presently·judging impartially according·to
G2919.1 V-PAP-DSM κρίνοντι (1x)
1Pe 2:23 ·handing *his cause* over to·the·one judging justly;
G2919.1 V-PAP-NSM κρίνων (6x)
Jn 8:50 glory; there·is One presently·seeking and judging.
Ac 23:3 you·yourself sit·down judging me according·to the
Rm 2:1 Therefore, *for* anyone presently·judging— you·are
Rm 2:1 yourself; for the·one judging, you·practice the same·
Jac 4:11 speaking·against *his* brother and judging his brother,
Rv 18:8 strong *is* Yahweh God, the·one judging her.
G2919.1 V-PAP-NPM κρίνοντες (2x)
Lk 22:30 and may·sit on thrones judging the twelve tribes
Mt 19:28 ·sit upon twelve thrones, judging the twelve tribes
G2919.1 V-PAS-1S κρινῶ (2x)
Jn 8:16 And yet if I·myself should·judge, my verdict is true,
Jn 12:47 come in·order·that I·may·presently·judge the world,
G2919.1 V-PAS-3S κρίνῃ (1x)
Jn 3:17 in·order·that he·may·presently·judge the world, but·
G2919.1 V-PPI-1S κρίνομαι (1x)
Rm 3:7 why am I·also still judged as morally·disqualified?
G2919.1 V-PPI-3S κρίνεται (3x)
Jn 3:18 The·one trusting in him is·not presently·judged, but
Ac 26:8 Why is·it·judged *to·be* incredible with yeu, that God
1Co 6:2 world? And if the world is·judged by yeu, are·yeu
G2919.1 V-PPN κρίνεσθαι (5x)
Ac 25:9 there to·be·judged concerning these·things before
Ac 25:10 it·is·mandatory·for me to·be·judged. I·wronged
Ac 25:20 and·there to·be·judged concerning these·matters.
Rm 3:4 and may·overcome when you are·being·judged.'"
Jac 2:12 so do: as ones·about to·be·judged through *the* Law
G2919.1 V-PPP-NSM κρινόμενος (1x)
Ac 26:6 "And now I·stand being·judged over *the* expectation
G2919.1 V-PPP-NPM κρινόμενοι (1x)
1Co 11:32 But presently·being·judged, we·are·correctively·
G2919.1 V-IPI-1P ἐκρινόμεθα (1x)
1Co 11:31 ourselves *properly*, we·would not be·judged.
G2919.1 V-AAI-2S ἔκρινας (2x)
Lk 7:43 And he·declared to·him, "You·judged uprightly."
Rv 16:5 divinely·holy, because you·judged these·things.
G2919.1 V-AAI-3S ἔκρινεν (1x)
Rv 19:2 his verdicts; because he·judged the Great Prostitute,
G2919.1 V-AAM-2P κρίνατε (6x)
Jn 7:24 ·to *mere*·appearance, but·rather judge the righteous
Jn 18:31 ·yeurselves take him and judge him according·to
Ac 4:19 ·God to·listen·to yeu rather than to·God, yeu·judge.
Rm 14:13 but·rather yeu·must·judge this all·the·more:
1Co 10:15 ·men; yeu·yeurselves judge what I·disclose:
1Co 11:13 Judge·already among yeurselves in·unison, is·it
G2919.1 V-AAN κρῖναι (1x)
1Pe 4:5 to·the·one having readiness to·judge *the·ones* living
G2919.1 V-AAP-APM κρίναντας (1x)
2Co 5:14 us, after·already·*conclusively*·judging this·thing:
G2919.1 V-AAP-NPM κρίναντες (2x)
Ac 13:27 , they·completely·fulfilled *them* in·judging *him*.
Ac 21:25 ·by·letter, judging for·them to·observantly·keep
G2919.1 V-API-3P ἐκρίθησαν (2x)
Rv 20:12 And the dead·ones are·judged out of·the·things
Rv 20:13 them. And each·one was·judged according·to their
G2919.1 V-APN κριθῆναι (1x)
Rv 11:18 the season for·the dead to·be·judged, and·also *for*·
G2919.1 V-APS-2P κριθῆτε (2x)
Lk 6:37 ·judge, and no, yeu·should·not be·judged. Do·not
Mt 7:1 unduly·judge in·order·that yeu·should·not be·judged.
G2919.1 V-APS-3P κριθῶσιν (2x)
1Pe 4:6 in·order·that they·may·be·judged in·fact according·
2Th 2:12 in·order·that they·all may·be·judged, the·ones not
G2919.1 V-RAI-1S κέκρικα (1x)
1Co 5:3 being·present, I·have·judged the·one performing
G2919.1 V-RAI-2P κεκρίκατε (1x)
Ac 16:15 saying, "If yeu·have·judged me to·be trustworthy
G2919.1 V-RAI-3S κέκρικεν (1x)
1Co 7:37 his·own will, and has·judged this·thing in his heart
G2919.1 V-RPI-3S κέκριται (2x)
Jn 3:18 but the·one not trusting has·been·judged even·now,
Jn 16:11 because the prince of·this world has·been·judged.
G2919.2 V-AAI-1S ἔκρινα (3x)
Ac 25:25 to the Revered·Emperor, I·decided to·send him *on*,
1Co 2:2 For I·decided not to·personally·know anything

2Co 2:1 But I·decided this for·my·own·self, not again to·
G2919.2 V-AAI-3S ἔκρινεν (2x)
Ac 20:16 for Paul decided to·sail·directly·by Ephesus, so·
Rv 18:20 prophets, because God decided yeur just·claim as·
G2919.2 V-AAP-GSM κρίναντος (1x)
Ac 3:13 ·Pilate, with·that·one deciding to·fully·release *him*.
G2919.2 V-API-3S ἐκρίθη (1x)
Ac 27:1 And as·soon·as it·was·decided for us to·set·sail for
G2919.2 V-RAI-1S κέκρικα (1x)
Tit 3:12 me to NicoPolis, for I·have·decided to·winter there.
G2919.2 V-RPP-APN κεκριμένα (1x)
Ac 16:4 ·keep, the·ones having·been·decided by the
G2919.3 V-PAP-NSM κρίνων (1x)
Rm 14:22 the·one not calling himself into·judgment by what
G2919.3 V-PPI-1S κρίνομαι (2x)
Ac 23:6 ·dead·men, *that* I·myself am·called·into·judgment."
Ac 24:21 ·men, I·myself am·called·into·judgment by yeu
G2919.4 V-PPI-3S κρίνεται (1x)
1Co 6:6 brother goes·to·court·to·be·judged against a·brother,
G2919.4 V-PPN κρίνεσθαι (1x)
1Co 6:1 the other, go·to·court·to·be·judged before the
G2919.4 V-APN κριθῆναι (1x)
Mt 5:40 for·you to·go·to·court·to·be·judged and to·take your
G2919.5 V-PAI-2S κρίνεις (2x)
Rm 14:10 why·do you·yourself unduly·judge your brother?
Jac 4:12 Who are you·yourself that unduly·judges the other?
G2919.5 V-PAI-2P κρίνετε (1x)
Mt 7:2 standard·of·judgment yeu·unduly·judge, yeu·shall·
G2919.5 V-PAM-2P κρίνετε (3x)
Jn 7:24 "Do·not unduly·judge according·to *mere*·appearance
Lk 6:37 "Also, do·not unduly·judge, and no, yeu·should·not
Mt 7:1 "Do·not unduly·judge in·order·that yeu·should·not
G2919.5 V-PAP-NSM κρίνων (2x)
Rm 2:3 ·clay† (the·one unduly·judging the·ones practicing
Rm 14:4 the·one unduly·judging another·man's household·
G2919.5 V-PAS-1P κρίνωμεν (1x)
Rm 14:13 no·longer should·we·unduly·judge one·another,
G2919.5 V-PPI-3S κρίνεται (1x)
1Co 10:29 ·reason·is my liberty unduly·judged by another

G2920 κρίσις krísis *n.* (48x)

Roots:G2919 Compare:G2917 G1349 See:G4793-1
xLangAlso:H4941

G2920.1 N-NSF κρίσις (4x)
Jn 3:19 "And this is the verdict, that the Light has·come into
Jn 5:30 ·hear, I·judge. And my verdict is righteous, because
Jn 8:16 if I·myself should·judge, my verdict is true, because
Ac 8:33 In his humiliation, his verdict was·taken·away. And
G2920.1 N-NPF κρίσεις (2x)
Rv 16:7 Almighty, true and righteous *are* your verdicts."
Rv 19:2 and righteous *are* his verdicts; because he·judged
G2920.1 N-ASF κρίσιν (3x)
Jn 7:24 ·appearance, but·rather judge the righteous verdict."
Jud 1:9 , did·not dare to·bring·up a·verdict of·revilement,
2Pe 2:11 a·reviling verdict personally·before Yahweh.
G2920.1 N-GSF κρίσεως (1x)
2Th 1:5 *This·is* an·indication of·the righteous verdict of·God,
G2920.2 N-DSF κρίσει (1x)
Mt 5:21 should·murder shall·be held·liable to·the tribunal.
G2920.4 N-NSF κρίσις (1x)
Jac 2:13 For the tribunal·justice without·forgiving·favor *is*
G2920.4 N-ASF κρίσιν (4x)
Lk 11:42 and neglect the tribunal·justice and the love of·
Mt 12:18 he·shall·announce tribunal·justice to·the Gentiles.
Mt 12:20 he·should·cast·forth tribunal·justice into victory.
Mt 23:23 of·the Torah-Law: the tribunal·justice, and the
G2920.5 N-DSF κρίσει (1x)
Mt 5:22 ·be held·liable to·the Tribunal *of·the Hell·Canyon*.
G2920.5 N-GSF κρίσεως (1x)
Mt 23:33 ·yeu·escape from the Tribunal of·the Hell·Canyon?
G2920.6 N-NSF κρίσις (2x)
Jn 12:31 "There·is now a·Tribunal·judgment of·this world.
Rv 18:10 in one hour your Tribunal·judgment came.'
G2920.6 N-ASF κρίσιν (7x)
Jn 5:22 he·has·given all the Tribunal·judgment to·the Son,
Jn 5:24 he·does·not come into Tribunal·judgment, but·rather
Jn 5:27 authority also to·make Tribunal·judgment, because
Jud 1:6 ·murky·shroud for Tribunal·judgment of·a·great day.
Jud 1:15 to·make Tribunal·judgment against all, and to·
2Pe 2:4 having·been·reserved for a·Tribunal·judgment;
1Ti 5:24 preceding *them* to Tribunal·judgment; and also
G2920.6 N-GSF κρίσεως (9x)
Jn 16:8 righteousness, and concerning Tribunal·judgment.
Jn 16:11 and concerning Tribunal·judgment, because the
Heb 10:27 apprehension of·Tribunal·judgment and a·fiery
Mt 12:36 it in *the* Day of·Final·Tribunal·judgment.
Mk 3:29 he·is held·liable of·eternal Tribunal·judgment."
Jac 2:13 mercy boasts·triumphantly·over Tribunal·judgment.
2Pe 2:9 a·day of·Tribunal·judgment to·be·sternly·punished
1Jn 4:17 ·speech in the day of·Tribunal·judgment, because
Rv 14:7 the hour of·his Tribunal·judgment did·come! And
G2920.7 N-DSF κρίσει (5x)
Lk 10:14 ·Tyre and Tsidon at the Final·Tribunal than for·yeu.
Lk 11:31 shall·be·awakened in the Final·Tribunal with the
Lk 11:32 shall·rise·up in the Final·Tribunal with this
Mt 12:41 shall·rise·up in the Final·Tribunal with this
Mt 12:42 shall·be·awakened in the Final·Tribunal with this
G2920.8 N-NSF κρίσις (1x)
Heb 9:27 ·then *to·have* a·Final·Tribunal·judgment after that
G2920.8 N-GSF κρίσεως (6x)
Jn 5:29 into a·resurrection of·Final·Tribunal·judgment.
Mt 10:15 in *the* Day of·Final·Tribunal·judgment, than for·
Mt 11:22 in *the* Day of·Final·Tribunal·judgment than for·yeu.
Mt 11:24 in *the* Day of·Final·Tribunal·judgment than for·you
Mk 6:11 in *the* Day of·Final·Tribunal·judgment than for·that
2Pe 3:7 for a·Day of·Final·Tribunal·judgment and total·

G2921 Κρίσπος Kríspŏs *n/p.* (2x)

G2921.2 N/P-NSM Κρίσπος (1x)
Ac 18:8 And Crispus, the director·of·the·gathering, trusted
G2921.2 N/P-ASM Κρίσπον (1x)
1Co 1:14 not·even·one of·yeu, except Crispus and Gaius,

G2922 κριτήριον kritḗriŏn *n.* (3x)

Roots:G2923

G2922.2 N-APN κριτήρια (2x)
Jac 2:6 yeu, and *the* same *that* draw yeu into arbitrations?
1Co 6:4 if yeu·should·have arbitrations of·secular·matters,
G2922.2 N-GPN κριτηρίων (1x)
1Co 6:2 yeu, are·yeu unworthy of·the·smallest arbitrations?

G2923 κριτής kritḗs *n.* (18x)

Roots:G2919 Compare:G1348 G0758 G4588-1
See:G2922
xLangEquiv:H8199 xLangAlso:H1781

G2923 N-NSM κριτής (9x)
Lk 12:58 the judge, and the judge should·hand you over to·
Lk 18:2 a·certain city there·was a·certain judge— *one* who·
Lk 18:6 "Hear what the unjust judge says.
Ac 10:42 ·determined by God *to·be* Judge of·living·men and
Ac 18:15 ·definitely·not willing to·be judge of·these·things."
Mt 5:25 to·the judge, and the judge should·hand you over
Jac 4:11 law, you·are not a·doer of·law, but·rather a·judge.
Jac 5:9 Behold, *the* judge stands before the doors.
2Ti 4:8 the Lord, the righteous judge, shall·yield·forth to·me
G2923 N-NPM κριταί (3x)
Lk 11:19 On·account·of that, they shall·be yeur judges.
Mt 12:27 On·account·of that, they shall·be yeur judges.
Jac 2:4 and are·become judges with·evil deliberations?
G2923 N-ASM κριτήν (2x)
Lk 12:58 he·should·drag you down toward the judge, and the
Ac 24:10 many years of·you being a·judge to·this nation,
G2923 N-APM κριτάς (1x)
Ac 13:20 fifty years, he·gave *to·them* judges, until SamuEl
G2923 N-DSM κριτῇ (2x)
Heb 12:23 heavens, and to·God, Judge of·all, and to·spirits
Mt 5:25 should·hand you over to·the judge, and the judge
EG2923 (1x)
1Co 6:4 ·yeu·seat these *unrighteous·ones as·judges*, the·ones

G2924 κριτικός kritikŏs *adj.* (1x)

Roots:G2923 Compare:G0144 G1252 G1253

G2924.4 A-NSM κριτικός (1x)
Heb 4:12 and *he·is* a·discerner of·the·cogitations and

G2925 κρούω krŏúō *v.* (9x)

G2925 V-PAI-1S κρούω (1x)
Rv 3:20 ·stand at the door and knock. If anyone should·hear
G2925 V-PAM-2P κρούετε (2x)
Lk 11:9 and yeu·shall·find; knock, and it·shall·be·opened·
Mt 7:7 and yeu·shall·find; knock, and it·shall·be·opened·
G2925 V-PAN κρούειν (1x)
Lk 13:25 ·begin to·stand outside and to·knock at·the door,
G2925 V-PAP-DSM κρούοντι (2x)
Lk 11:10 and to·the·one knocking, it·shall·be·opened·up.
Mt 7:8 finds; and to·the·one knocking it·shall·be·opened·up.
G2925 V-PAP-NSM κρούων (1x)
Ac 12:16 But Peter was·persisting·in knocking. And
G2925 V-AAP-GSM κρούσαντος (2x)
Lk 12:36 *with·him* coming and knocking, they·may·open·up
Ac 12:13 And as·Peter *was* knocking *at* the door of·the gate,

G2927 κρυπτός kryptŏs *adj.* (20x)

Roots:G2928 Compare:G3466 See:G2931 G2926
xLangAlso:H8587 A7328 H7328-1

G2927.1 A-NSM κρυπτός (1x)
1Pe 3:4 ·rather *according·to* the hidden man·of·clay† of·the
G2927.1 A-NSN κρυπτόν (4x)
Lk 8:17 "For there·is not *anything* hidden, that shall·not
Lk 12:2 shall·not be·revealed, nor hidden that shall·not be·
Mt 10:26 shall·not be·revealed, and hidden, that shall·not
Mk 4:22 For there·is not anything hidden, which should·not
G2927.1 A-APN κρυπτά (2x)
1Co 4:5 shall·illuminate the hidden·things of·the darkness
2Co 4:2 we·have·renounced the hidden·things of·shame,
G2927.2 A-NPN κρυπτά (1x)
1Co 14:25 And in·this·manner, the secrets of·his heart
G2927.2 A-APN κρυπτά (1x)
Rm 2:16 when God judges the secrets of·the men·of·clay†.
G2927.2 A-DSN κρυπτῷ (3x)
Jn 7:4 *that* does anything in secret when he·himself seeks to·
Jn 7:10 the Sacred·Feast, not openly, but·rather as in secret.
Jn 18:20 And I·spoke nothing·at·all in secret.
G2927.3 A-ASN κρυπτόν (1x)
Lk 11:33 a·lantern, places *it* in hiding, nor·even under the
G2927.4 A-DSN κρυπτῷ (7x)
Mt 6:4 so·that your merciful·act may·be in private. And your
Mt 6:4 Father, the·one looking·on in private, shall himself
Mt 6:6 to·your Father, the·one in private. And your Father,
Mt 6:6 the·one looking·on in private, shall·give·back to·
Mt 6:18 to·your Father, the·one in private. And your Father,
Mt 6:18 the·one looking·on in private, shall·give·back to·
Rm 2:29 the·one *vigilantly·keeping* in private, *he·is* a·Jew,

G2928 κρύπτω krýptō *v.* (16x)

Compare:G2572 G2990 G4628-1 See:G2927 G2931
xLangAlso:H6845

G2928.1 V-AAI-1S ἔκρυψα (1x)
Mt 25:25 ·afraid, upon·going·off, I·hid your talant·of·silver
G2928.1 V-AAI-3S ἔκρυψεν (1x)
Mt 13:44 a·man·of·clay†, after·finding *it*, hides *it*. And
G2928.1 V-AAI-3P ἔκρυψαν (1x)
Rv 6:15 and every free·man, hid themselves in the caves
G2928.1 V-AAM-2P κρύψατε (1x)
Rv 6:16 "Fall on us, and hide us from *the* face of·the·one
G2928.1 V-2API-3S ἐκρύβη (4x)
Jn 8:59 him, but Jesus hid·himself and went·forth from·out
Jn 12:36 and after·going·off, he·was·hidden from them.
Lk 19:42 peace! But now they·are·already·hidden from your
Heb 11:23 (being·born) was·hid three·lunar·months by his
G2928.1 V-2APN κρυβῆναι (2x)
Mt 5:14 ·set·out high·upon a·mount is·not able to·be·hidden.
1Ti 5:25 being otherwise, are·not able to·be·hidden, *likewise*
G2928.1 V-RPI-3S κέκρυπται (1x)
Col 3:3 and yeur life·above has·been·hidden together with·the

G2928.1 V-RPP-APN κεκρυμμένα (1x)
Mt 13:35 ·belch·forth *things* having·been·hidden from *the*
G2928.1 V-RPP-DSM κεκρυμμένῳ (1x)
Mt 13:44 is like treasure having·been·hidden in a·field,
G2928.1 V-RPP-GSM κεκρυμμένου (1x)
Rv 2:17 ·give to·him to·eat from the hidden manna, and I·
G2928.1 V-RPP-NSN κεκρυμμένον (1x)
Lk 18:34 this utterance was having·been·hidden from them,
G2928.2 V-RPP-NSM κεκρυμμένος (1x)
Jn 19:38 but having·been·under·cover on·account·of the fear

G2929 κρυσταλλίζω krystallízō *v.* (1x)
Roots:G2930
G2929.2 V-PAP-DSM κρυσταλλίζοντι (1x)
Rv 21:11 stone, even·as a·jasper stone, resembling·crystal),

G2930 κρύσταλλος krýstallôs *n.* (2x)
See:G2929
xLangEquiv:H7140
G2930.2 N-ASM κρύσταλλον (1x)
Rv 22:1 of·life-above, radiant as crystal, proceeding·forth out
G2930.2 N-DSM κρυστάλλῳ (1x)
Rv 4:6 *there·is* a·transparent,·glassy sea, like crystal. And in

G2931 κρυφῆ kryphē̂ *adv.* (1x)
Roots:G2928 Compare:G2977 See:G2927 G2930-2 G2931-1
G2931 ADV κρυφῇ (1x)
Eph 5:12 ·things which·are·occurring among them secretly.

G2932 κτάομαι ktáômai *v.* (7x)
Compare:G5608 G0059 G4046 See:G2933 G2935
G2932.1 V-PNI-1S-C κτῶμαι (1x)
Lk 18:12 I·tithe all·things, *on* as·many·things·as I·procure.'
G2932.1 V-PNN κτᾶσθαι (1x)
Ac 8:20 ·present of·God may·be·procured through valuables.
G2932.1 V-ADI-1S ἐκτησάμην (1x)
Ac 22:28 with·a·large sum, procured this citizenship." And
G2932.1 V-ADI-3S ἐκτήσατο (1x)
Ac 1:18 in·fact, this·man procured an·open·field out of·the
G2932.1 V-ADM-2P κτήσασθε (1x)
Lk 21:19 In yeur patient·endurance, yeu·procure yeur souls.
G2932.1 V-ADS-2P κτήσησθε (1x)
Mt 10:9 Yeu·should·not procure gold, nor·even silver, nor·
G2932.2 V-PNN κτᾶσθαι (1x)
1Th 4:4 of·yeu to·personally·know·how to·possess his·own

G2933 κτῆμα ktē̂ma *n.* (4x)
Roots:G2932 Compare:G2697 See:G2935
G2933.2 N-ASN κτῆμα (1x)
Ac 5:1 together with·Sapphira his wife, sold a·possession,
G2933.2 N-APN κτήματα (3x)
Ac 2:45 And they·were·selling·off the possessions and the
Mt 19:22 ·grieved, for he·was holding many possessions.
Mk 10:22 ·grieved, for he·was holding many possessions.

G2934 κτῆνος ktē̂nôs *n.* (4x)
Roots:G2932 Compare:G2342 G2353 See:G2934-1 xLangEquiv:H4735 xLangAlso:H0929
G2934.3 N-APN κτήνη (1x)
Rv 18:13 and wheat, "and livestock, sheep, horses, and
G2934.4 N-ASN κτῆνος (1x)
Lk 10:34 mounting him upon his·own beast, he·brought him
G2934.4 N-APN κτήνη (1x)
Ac 23:24 *be certain* to·provide beasts *for·them* in·order·that
G2934.4 N-GPN κτηνῶν (1x)
1Co 15:39 of·men·of·clay†, another flesh of·beasts, another

G2935 κτήτωρ ktḗtōr *n.* (1x)
Roots:G2932 Compare:G2962 See:G2933
G2935 N-NPM κτήτορες (1x)
Ac 4:34 were·subsisting *being* possessors of·open·fields or

G2936 κτίζω ktízō *v.* (14x)
Compare:G2932 G4160 See:G2937 G2938 G2939
G2936 V-AAI-2S ἔκτισας (1x)
Rv 4:11 the power, because you·yourself created all things,
G2936 V-AAI-3S ἔκτισεν (3x)
Mk 13:19 beginning of·creation which God created unto the
1Ti 4:3 ·from foods— which God created for partaking with
Rv 10:6 the ages of·ages ('who created the heaven, and the·
G2936 V-AAP-ASM κτίσαντα (1x)
Rm 1:25 to·the creation instead·of the·one creating *it* (*the·*
G2936 V-AAP-DSM κτίσαντι (1x)
Eph 3:9 ·ages in God, the·one creating all things through
G2936 V-AAP-GSM κτίσαντος (1x)
Col 3:10 ·to *the* derived·image' of·the·one creating him—
G2936 V-AAS-3S κτίσῃ (1x)
Eph 2:15 decrees), in·order·that he·should·create the two in
G2936 V-API-3S ἐκτίσθη (2x)
1Co 11:9 For also man is·not created on·account·of the
Col 1:16 Because in him, all·things are·created: the·ones in
G2936 V-API-3P ἐκτίσθησαν (1x)
Rv 4:11 and through your will, they·exist and are·created."
G2936 V-APP-ASM κτισθέντα (1x)
Eph 4:24 (the·one already·being·created according·to God in
G2936 V-APP-NPM κτισθέντες (1x)
Eph 2:10 of·him, already·being·created in Anointed-One
G2936 V-RPI-3S ἔκτισται (1x)
Col 1:16 All·things have·been·created through him and for

G2937 κτίσις ktísis *n.* (20x)
Roots:G2936 See:G2938 G2939
G2937.1 N-NSF κτίσις (5x)
Gal 6:15 ·rather *it·is* a·brand-new creation *that has·strength.*
Rm 8:20 For the creation was·made·subject to·the futility,
Rm 8:21 that the creation itself also shall·be·set·free from
Rm 8:22 ·know that the entire creation groans·together and
2Co 5:17 in Anointed-One, *he·is* a·brand-new creation. The
G2937.1 N-DSF κτίσει (2x)
Mk 16:15 ·proclaim the good·news to·all the creation.
Rm 1:25 ·ministered to·the creation instead·of the·one
G2937.1 N-GSF κτίσεως (8x)
Heb 9:11 made·by·human·hand, that·is, not of·this creation.
Mk 10:6 But from creation's beginning, God " made them
Mk 13:19 from *the* beginning of·creation which God created
Rm 1:20 For from *the* world's creation, the invisible·things
Rm 8:19 eager·anticipation of·the creation fully·awaits the
2Pe 3:4 ·this·manner *as they·were* from creation's beginning.
Col 1:15 of·the invisible God, *the* firstborn of·all creation.
Rv 3:14 true witness, the beginning of·the creation of·God:
EG2937.1 (1x)
Rm 8:23 And not merely *the creation*, but·rather we·
G2937.3 N-NSF κτίσις (1x)
Heb 4:13 ·is not a·creature *that·is* not·completely·apparent
G2937.3 N-DSF κτίσει (1x)
Col 1:23 ·officially·proclaimed to every creature under the
G2937.4 N-NSF κτίσις (1x)
Rm 8:39 nor any other created·thing shall·be·able to·separate
G2937.5 N-DSF κτίσει (1x)
1Pe 2:13 to·every created·governance of·mankind† on·

G2938 κτίσμα ktísma *n.* (5x)
Roots:G2936 See:G2937 G2939
G2938.2 N-NSN κτίσμα (1x)
1Ti 4:4 Because every creature of·God *is* good, and not·
G2938.2 N-ASN κτίσμα (1x)
Rv 5:13 And every creature which is in the heaven, and on
G2938.2 N-GPN κτισμάτων (2x)
Jac 1:18 for us to·be a·certain firstfruit of·his creatures.
Rv 8:9 and the third·part of·the creatures (the·ones in the sea
EG2938.2 (1x)
Lk 12:24 nor·even do·they·reap. For·such *creatures*, there·is

G2939 κτίστης ktístēs *n.* (1x)
Roots:G2936 Compare:G1217 G5079 See:G2937 G2938
G2939 N-DSM κτίστῃ (1x)
1Pe 4:19 beneficial·well·doing, as to·a·trustworthy Creator.

G2940 κυβεία kybêía *n.* (1x)
Compare:G3180 G3834 G2603 G3884
G2940.4 N-DSF κυβείᾳ (1x)
Eph 4:14 by the artful·manipulation of·men·of·clay†, *and*

G2941 κυβέρνησις kybérnēsis *n.* (1x)
See:G2942
G2941.2 N-APF κυβερνήσεις (1x)
1Co 12:28 ·healing, supportive·helps, sound·guidance, *and*

G2942 κυβερνήτης kybêrnḗtēs *n.* (2x)
Compare:G4408-1 See:G2941
G2942.2 N-NSM κυβερνήτης (1x)
Rv 18:17 "And every *ship's* pilot, and all aboard the
G2942.2 N-DSM κυβερνήτῃ (1x)
Ac 27:11 centurion was·convinced by·the pilot and by·the

G2943 κυκλό•θεν kyklṓthên *adv.* (4x)
Roots:G2943-1 Compare:G2945 G2944 See:G2945
G2943 ADV κυκλόθεν (4x)
Rv 4:3 stone, and *there·was* a·rainbow all·around the throne,
Rv 4:4 And all·around the throne *were·set·out* twenty four
Rv 4:8 apiece overflowing of·eyes, all·around and inwardly.
Rv 5:11 *the* voice of·many angels all·around the throne and

G2944 κυκλόω kyklṓō *v.* (5x)
Roots:G2943-1 Compare:G2947 See:G2633-3 G2945 G2943
G2944.2 V-PPP-ASF κυκλουμένην (1x)
Lk 21:20 ·see JeruSalem being·surrounded by army·camps,
G2944.2 V-AAI-3P ἐκύκλωσαν (2x)
Jn 10:24 So·then the Judeans surrounded him and were·
Rv 20:9 of·the earth, and they·surrounded the garrison of·
G2944.2 V-AAP-GPM κυκλωσάντων (1x)
Ac 14:20 But, with·the disciples surrounding him, after·
G2944.2 V-APP-NPN κυκλωθέντα (1x)
Heb 11:30 fell·down, being·surrounded for·a·span·of seven

G2945 κύκλῳ kýklō *n.* (7x)
Roots:G2943-1 Compare:G4029 See:G2945-1 G4033-1 G2943 xLangAlso:H5439
G2945.1 N-DSM κύκλῳ (1x)
Mk 3:34 looking·around in·a·circle at·the·ones sitting·down
G2945.2 N-DSM κύκλῳ (2x)
Rv 4:6 of·the throne, and in·a·circle·around the throne, *are*
Rv 7:11 all the angels stood in·a·circle·around the throne and
G2945.3 N-DSM κύκλῳ (1x)
Rm 15:19 and around·in·a·circuit to·as·far·as Illyricum).
G2945.4 N-DSM κύκλῳ (3x)
Lk 9:12 ·order·that going·off into the encircling villages and
Mk 6:6 he·was·heading·around·to the encircling villages,
Mk 6:36 after·going·off into the encircling countrysides and

G2946 κύλισμα kýlisma *n.* (1x)
Roots:G2947
G2946 N-ASN κύλισμα (1x)
2Pe 2:22 *keeps·on* bathing·herself in a·wallowing of·muck."

G2947 κυλιόω kyliṓō *v.* (1x)
Roots:G2949 Compare:G2944 G1507 See:G2946
G2947 V-IEI-3S ἐκυλίετο (1x)
Mk 9:20 upon the soil, he·was·rolling·about foaming.

G2948 κυλλός kyllṓs *adj.* (4x)
κυλλόν kyllṓn [neuter]
Roots:G2949 Compare:G0376 G5560 See:G2947
G2948.3 A-ASM κυλλόν (1x)
Mk 9:43 to·enter into the life-above crippled, than having the
G2948.3 A-ASN κυλλόν (1x)
Mt 18:8 the life-above lame or crippled, rather·than having
G2948.3 A-APM κυλλούς (2x)
Mt 15:30 lame, blind, mute, crippled, and many others, and
Mt 15:31 ·ones speaking, crippled·ones healthy·and·sound,

G2949 κῦμα kŷma *n.* (5x)
Compare:G2830 xLangAlso:H1530
G2949.2 N-NPN κύματα (2x)
Mk 4:37 ·wind, and the breaking·waves were·breaking into
Jud 1:13 wild breaking·waves of·the·sea presently·foaming·
G2949.2 N-GPN κυμάτων (3x)
Ac 27:41 was·broken by the force of·the breaking·waves.
Mt 8:24 sailboat to·be·covered by the breaking·waves, but
Mt 14:24 being·tormented under the breaking·waves, for

G2950 κύμβαλον kýmbalôn *n.* (1x)
Roots:G2949 See:G2949-3
xLangEquiv:H4700 xLangAlso:H6767
G2950 N-NSN κύμβαλον (1x)
1Co 13:1 a·reverberating bronze·gong or a·clanging cymbal.

G2951 κύμινον kýminôn *n.* (1x)
xLangEquiv:H3646
G2951 N-ASN κύμινον (1x)
Mt 23:23 mint and the dill and the cumin, but yeu·left the

G2952 κυνάριον kynáriôn *n.* (4x)
Roots:G2965
G2952 N-NPN κυνάρια (2x)
Mt 15:27 For even the puppies eat from the little·crumbs,
Mk 7:28 For even the puppies beneath the table eat from the
G2952 N-DPN κυναρίοις (2x)
Mt 15:26 the children's bread and to·cast *it* to·the puppies."
Mk 7:27 the children's bread and to·cast *it* to·the puppies."

G2953 Κύπριος Kýpriôs *n/g.* (3x)
Roots:G2954
G2953.2 N/G-NSM Κύπριος (1x)
Ac 4:36 ·Consoling), *was* a·Levite *and* of·Cyprus by·birth,
G2953.2 N/G-NPM Κύπριοι (1x)
Ac 11:20 from·among them were men of·Cyprus and Cyrene
G2953.2 N/G-DSM Κυπρίῳ (1x)
Ac 21:16 *them* a·certain·man, Mnason of·Cyprus, an·early

G2954 Κύπρος Kýprôs *n/l.* (5x)
See:G2953
G2954 N/L-ASF Κύπρον (4x)
Ac 13:4 Also from·there, they·sailed·off to Cyprus.
Ac 15:39 ·taking *John*·Mark, to·sail·away to Cyprus.
Ac 21:3 Now after·coming·within·full·sight·of Cyprus and
Ac 27:4 we·sailed·leeward·near·to Cyprus, on·account·of
G2954 N/L-GSF Κύπρου (1x)
Ac 11:19 ·throughout as·far·as·to Phoenicia, Cyprus, and

G2955 κύπτω kýptō *v.* (3x)
Roots:G2949
G2955 V-AAP-NSM κύψας (3x)
Jn 8:6 ·accuse him·of. But after·stooping down, Jesus was·
Jn 8:8 And again after·stooping down, he·was·writing into
Mk 1:7 I·am not fit, *even* after·stooping·down, to·loose the

G2956 Κυρηναῖος Kyrēnaîos *n/g.* (6x)
Roots:G2957
G2956.1 N/G-ASM Κυρηναῖον (2x)
Mt 27:32 they·found a·man·of·clay†, a·Cyrenian, Simon
Mk 15:21 who·was·passing·by, Simon, a·Cyrenian, coming
G2956.1 N/G-GSM Κυρηναίου (1x)
Lk 23:26 countryside, Simon, a·Cyrenian, they·placed the
G2956.1 N/G-GPM Κυρηναίων (1x)
Ac 6:9 of·Freedmen, with Cyrenians and Alexandrians, and
G2956.2 N/G-NSM Κυρηναῖος (1x)
Ac 13:1 Niger), and Lucius of·Cyrene, Manaen also (*who·*
G2956.2 N/G-NPM Κυρηναῖοι (1x)
Ac 11:20 them were men of·Cyprus and Cyrene, who, after·

G2957 Κυρήνη Kyrḗnē *n/l.* (1x)
See:G2956
G2957 N/L-ASF Κυρήνην (1x)
Ac 2:10 the parts of·Libya adjacent·to Cyrene, and the·ones

G2958 Κυρήνιος Kyrḗniôs *n/p.* (1x)
G2958 N/P-GSM Κυρηνίου (1x)
Lk 2:2 first occurred with·Cyrenius being·governor of·Syria)

G2959 Κυρία Kyría *n/p.* (2x)
Roots:G2962 xLangAlso:H1404 H1172
G2959.1 N/P-VSF Κυρία (1x)
2Jn 1:5 And now I·ask·of you, my·Lady, not as·though I·
G2959.1 N/P-DSF Κυρίᾳ (1x)
2Jn 1:1 The Elder. To·a·Selected lady and her children—

G2960 κυριακός kyriakốs *adj.* (2x)
Roots:G2962 See:G2453
G2960.2 A-ASN κυριακόν (1x)
1Co 11:20 in·unison, it·is not to·eat *the* Lord's supper.
G2960.2 A-DSF κυριακῇ (1x)
Rv 1:10 ·to·be in *the* Spirit on the Lord's day and heard right·

G2961 κυριεύω kyriêúō *v.* (7x)
Roots:G2962 See:G2634
G2961.1 V-FAI-3S κυριεύσει (1x)
Rm 6:14 For moral·failure shall·not lord·over yeu, for yeu·
G2961.1 V-PAI-1P κυριεύομεν (1x)
2Co 1:24 Not because we·lord·over yeur trust, but·rather are
G2961.1 V-PAI-3S κυριεύει (2x)
Rm 6:9 no·longer dies. Death no·longer lords·over him.
Rm 7:1 that the Torah-Law lords·over the man·of·clay† for·
G2961.1 V-PAI-3P κυριεύουσιν (1x)
Lk 22:25 "The kings of·the Gentiles lord·over them; and the·
G2961.1 V-PAP-GPM κυριευόντων (1x)
1Ti 6:15 of·the·ones reigning, and Lord of·the·ones lording,
G2961.2 V-AAS-3S κυριεύσῃ (1x)
Rm 14:9 in·order·that he·may·exercise·lordship·over both

G2962 κύριος kýriôs *n.* (597x)
Κύριος Kýrhiôs [Representation of יְהֹוָה]
אֲדֹנָי 'ădònay [Hebrew]
Roots:G2963-1 Compare:G0935 G1203 G3617
See:G2962-1 G2964 G2959 G2960 G2955-1
xLangEquiv:H0136 xLangAlso:H3068
G2962.1 N-NSM κύριος (124x)
Jn 4:1 Accordingly, as·soon·as the Lord knew that the
Jn 13:13 ·yeurselves hail me Mentor and Lord, and yeu·say
Jn 13:14 I·myself washed yeur feet *being* Lord and Mentor,
Jn 15:15 does·not personally·know what his lord does; but I·
Jn 20:28 and declared to·him, "My Lord and my God.
Jn 21:7 says to·Peter, "It·is the Lord." Now·then, after·
Jn 21:7 after·hearing that it·was the Lord, Simon Peter
Jn 21:12 you·yourself?" having·seen that it·was the Lord.
Lk 2:11 ·and·birthed who is *the* Anointed-One, *the* Lord.
Lk 6:5 "The Son of·Clay·Man† is Lord also of·the Sabbath.
Lk 7:13 And seeing her, the Lord empathized over her and
Lk 7:31 And the Lord declared, "So·then to·what shall·I·
Lk 10:1 these·things, the Lord expressly·indicated seventy
Lk 11:39 And the Lord declared to·him, "Now yeu Pharisees
Lk 12:37 those slaves, whom the lord, upon·coming, shall·
Lk 12:42 And the Lord declared, "Who then is the
Lk 12:42 ·manager, whom his lord shall·fully·establish over
Lk 12:43 that slave, whom his lord, upon·coming, shall·find
Lk 12:45 in his heart, 'My lord is·delayed in·coming *back*,'
Lk 12:46 the lord of·that slave shall·come in a·day when he·
Lk 13:15 So·then the Lord answered him and declared, "O·
Lk 14:23 And the lord declared to the slave, 'Go·out into the
Lk 16:3 should·I·do? Because my lord removes from me the
Lk 16:8 "And the lord applauded the unjust estate·manager,
Lk 17:6 And the Lord declared, "If yeu·were·having trust
Lk 18:6 Then the Lord declared, "Hear what the unjust
Lk 19:31 ·declare to·him, 'Because the Lord has need of·it.
Lk 19:34 And they·declared, "The Lord has need of·it.
Lk 22:31 Then the Lord declared, "Simon, Simon, behold,
Lk 22:61 turning·around, the Lord looked·clearly·at Peter.
Lk 24:34 saying, "The Lord really is·awakened and was·
Ac 1:21 *the* time in which the Lord Jesus came·in and went·
Ac 2:47 People. And the Lord was·placing the·ones being·
Ac 9:5 Lord?" And the Lord declared, "It·is·I Myself,
Ac 9:6 you·want me to·do?" And the Lord *said* to him,
Ac 9:10 Ananias by·name. And the Lord declared to him in
Ac 9:11 And the Lord *said* to him, "Rising·up, traverse on
Ac 9:15 But the Lord declared to him, "Traverse! Because
Ac 9:17 "Brother Saul, the Lord, Jesus, the·one being·made·
Ac 10:36 through Jesus Anointed— This·one is Lord of·all.
Ac 12:17 ·an·account to·them how the Lord brought him out
Ac 13:47 it·has·been·commanded to·us *by* the Lord, "I·
Ac 16:10 concluding that the Lord has·summoned us to·
Ac 16:14 God, of·whom the Lord thoroughly·opened·up her
Ac 17:24 the·same·one inherently·being Lord of·heaven and
Ac 18:9 And the Lord declared to·Paul through a·clear·
Ac 22:10 ·I·do, Lord?" And the Lord declared to me,
Ac 23:11 following night, the Lord, upon·standing·over him
Heb 7:14 our Lord has·risen·above·the·horizon from·among
Gal 4:1 ·one·thing from·a·slave, *though* being lord of·all,
Mt 10:25 and the slave as his lord. If they·called the master·
Mt 12:8 the Son of·Clay·Man† is Lord even of·the Sabbath.
Mt 18:25 to·repay, his lord commandingly·ordered *for* him
Mt 18:27 So empathizing, the lord of·that slave fully·
Mt 18:32 Then after·summoning him, his lord says to·him,
Mt 18:34 And being·angry, his lord handed him over to·the
Mt 21:3 yeu·shall·declare, 'The Lord has need of·them,'
Mt 24:42 personally·know in·which hour yeur Lord comes.
Mt 24:45 prudent slave whom his lord fully·established over
Mt 24:46 that slave, whom his lord, upon·coming, shall·find
Mt 24:48 in his heart, 'My lord is·delayed in·coming *back*,'
Mt 24:50 the lord of·that slave shall·come on a·day when he·
Mt 25:19 after a·long time, the lord of·those slaves comes
Mt 25:21 His lord replied to·him, 'Well·done, O·
Mt 25:23 His lord replied to·him, 'Well·done, O·
Mt 25:26 "And answering, his lord declared to·him, 'O·evil
Mt 28:6 See the place where the Lord was·laid·out.
Mk 2:28 the Son of·Clay·Man† is Lord also of·the Sabbath.
Mk 11:3 ·do this?' Yeu·declare 'The Lord has need of·him.
Mk 13:35 ·not personally·know when the lord of·the home
Mk 16:19 Now·then in·fact, after the Lord spoke to·them,
Rm 10:12 this same *Lord Jesus is* Lord of·all, being·wealthy
Jac 1:12 of·life-above, which the Lord promised to·the·ones
Jac 4:15 to·say, "If the Lord should·will, then we·should·
Jac 5:15 ·sickly·fatigued, and the Lord shall·awaken him;
Php 2:11 ·affirm that Jesus Anointed *is* Lord, to *the* glory of·
Php 4:5 to·all men·of·clay†. The Lord *is* near·at·hand.
2Pe 1:14 even just·as our Lord YeShua Anointed made·
2Pe 3:9 The Lord is·not tardy *concerning* the promise, as
1Th 3:11 Father himself, and our Lord YeShua Anointed,
1Th 3:12 And may the Lord make yeu to·increase·more and
1Th 4:6 on·account·that the Lord *is* avenger concerning all
1Th 4:16 Because the Lord himself shall·descend from
2Th 2:8 ·revealed, whom the Lord shall·consume with·the
2Th 2:16 Now our Lord YeShua Anointed himself, and God,
2Th 3:3 But trustworthy is the Lord, who shall·firmly·
2Th 3:5 And may the Lord fully·direct yeur hearts into the
2Th 3:16 Now may the Lord of·Peace himself grant yeu
2Th 3:16 *matter* at every turn. The Lord *be* with yeu all.
1Co 3:5 yeu·trusted, even as the Lord gave to·each·man?
1Co 4:4 But the·one scrutinizing me is *the* Lord.
1Co 4:5 *the* season, until the Lord should·come, who also
1Co 4:19 yeu promptly, if the Lord should·determine, and I·
1Co 6:13 but·rather for·the Lord, and the Lord for·the body.
1Co 7:10 *yet* not I·myself, but·rather the Lord, a·wife *is* not
1Co 7:12 rest I·myself say, not the Lord— if any brother has
1Co 7:17 each·one according·as the Lord has·called·forth,
1Co 8:6 *exist* for him) and one Lord, Jesus Anointed
1Co 9:14 the Lord thoroughly·assigned for·the·ones fully·
1Co 11:23 ·down to·yeu, that the Lord Jesus, on·the night in
1Co 12:5 there·are varieties of·services, but the same Lord.
1Co 15:47 man·of·clay† *is* the Lord from·out of·heaven.
1Co 16:7 alongside yeu, if the Lord should·freely·permit.
2Co 3:17 Now the Lord is the Spirit, and where the Spirit of·
2Co 10:8 our authority, which the Lord gave us for
2Co 10:18 ·approved, but·rather whom the Lord commends.
2Co 13:10 ·to the authority which the Lord gave me to
Eph 4:5 one Lord, one trust, one immersion,
Eph 5:29 — just·as even the Lord *does for* the entire·Called·
Eph 6:9 having·seen that yeur same Lord also is in *the*
1Ti 6:15 of·the·ones reigning, and Lord of·the·ones lording,
2Ti 1:16 May the Lord give mercy to·*the*·house of·
2Ti 1:18 May the Lord grant to·him to·find mercy
2Ti 2:7 For may the Lord give to·you comprehension in all·
2Ti 3:11 I·underwent, but the Lord snatched me from·out
2Ti 4:8 of·righteousness, which the Lord, the righteous
2Ti 4:14 me much harm. May the Lord 'give·back to·him
2Ti 4:17 But the Lord stood·by me and enabled me, in·order·
2Ti 4:18 And the Lord shall·snatch me away·from every evil
2Ti 4:22 The Lord Jesus Anointed *be* with your spirit.
Rv 1:8 beginning and end," says the Lord, "the·one being,
Rv 11:8 and Egypt, where also our Lord was·crucified.

Rv 17:14 ·conquer them, because he·is Lord of·lords, and
Rv 19:16 KING OF·KINGS, AND LORD OF·LORDS.
G2962.1 N-NPM κύριοι (4x)
Ac 16:19 And with·her lords seeing that the expectation of·
1Co 8:5 earth (just·as there·are many gods, and many lords),
Eph 6:9 And the lords: They·must·do the same·things toward
Col 4:1 *Now* the lords: Yeu·must·personally·furnish to·the
G2962.1 N-VSM κύριε (108x)
Jn 6:34 So·then they·declared to him, "Lord, always give us
Jn 6:68 Peter answered him, "Lord, to whom shall·we·go?
Jn 8:11 She·declared, "Not·even·one, Lord." And Jesus
Jn 9:36 "Who is·he, Lord, in·order·that I·may·trust in him?
Jn 9:38 And he·replied, "Lord, I·trust." And he·fell·prostrate
Jn 11:3 to him, saying, "Lord, see, he·whom you·are·fond·
Jn 11:12 his disciples declared, "Lord, if he·has·been·laid·
Jn 11:21 Martha declared to Jesus, "Lord, if you·were here,
Jn 11:27 to·him, "Yes, Lord. I·myself have·trusted that
Jn 11:32 at his feet, saying to·him, "Lord, if you·were here,
Jn 11:34 him?" They·said to·him, "Lord, come and see.
Jn 11:39 says to·him, "O·Lord, even·now he·smells·bad,
Jn 13:6 that·one says to·him, "Lord, do·you·yourself wash
Jn 13:9 Simon Peter says to·him, "Lord, not my feet merely,
Jn 13:25 upon Jesus' chest, says to·him, "Lord, who is·it?
Jn 13:36 says to·him, "Lord, where·do you·head·on·out?
Jn 13:37 Peter says to·him, "Lord, why am·I·not able to·
Jn 14:5 says to·him, "Lord, we·do·not personally·know to·
Jn 14:8 Philip says to·him, "Lord, show us the Father, and
Jn 14:22 says to·him, "Lord, how has·it·happened that you·
Jn 21:15 to·him, "Yes, Lord; you·yourself personally·know
Jn 21:16 to·him, "Yes, Lord; you·yourself personally·know
Jn 21:17 to·him, "Lord, you·yourself personally·know all·
Jn 21:20 at the supper and declared, "Lord, who is the·one
Jn 21:21 Peter says to·Jesus, "Lord, and what *about* this·
Lk 5:8 because I·am a·man full·of·moral·failure, Lord."
Lk 5:12 ·petitioned him, saying, "Lord, if you·should·want,
Lk 6:46 "And why·do yeu·call me, 'Lord, Lord,' and do·not
Lk 6:46 why·do yeu·call me, 'Lord, Lord,' and do·not do
Lk 7:6 to him, saying to·him, "Lord, do·not be·harassed.
Lk 9:54 and John, declared, "Lord, do·you·want *that* we·
Lk 9:57 declared to him, "Lord, I·shall·follow you wherever
Lk 9:59 But the·man declared, "Lord, freely·permit me to·
Lk 9:61 another also declared, "Lord, I·shall·follow you, but
Lk 10:17 with joy, saying, "Lord, even the demons are·
Lk 10:21 ·affirm to·you, O·Father, Lord of·the heaven and
Lk 10:40 *him*, she·declared, "Lord, does·it·not matter to·
Lk 11:1 disciples declared to him, "Lord, instruct us to·pray,
Lk 12:41 But Peter declared to·him, "Lord, do·you·say this
Lk 13:8 answering, he·says to·him, 'Lord, leave it this year
Lk 13:23 someone declared to him, "Lord, *is·it so* that the·
Lk 13:25 at·the door, saying, 'Lord, Lord, open·up to·us,'
Lk 13:25 door, saying, 'Lord, Lord, open·up to·us,' and
Lk 14:22 the slave declared, 'Lord, it·has·happened as you·
Lk 17:37 they·say to·him, "Where, Lord?" And he·declared
Lk 18:41 And he·declared, "Lord, that I·may·receive·my·
Lk 19:8 to the Lord, "Behold, Lord, the half of·my holdings
Lk 19:16 came·close, saying, 'Lord, your mina actively·
Lk 19:18 second came, saying, 'Lord, your mina produced
Lk 19:20 another came, saying, 'Lord, behold, *here·is* your
Lk 19:25 they·declared to·him, 'Lord, he·*already*·has ten
Lk 22:33 And *Simon* declared to·him, "Lord, I·am ready to·
Lk 22:38 And they·declared, "Lord, behold, here *are* two
Lk 22:49 they·declared to·him, "Lord, shall·we·smite with
Lk 23:42 And he·was·saying to·Jesus, "Lord, recall me to·
Ac 1:6 ·inquiring·of him, saying, "Lord, do·you at this time
Ac 1:24 "You, O·Lord, knower·of·the·hearts of·all·men,
Ac 7:59 *Lord*, even while·saying, "Lord Jesus, accept my
Ac 7:60 with·a·loud voice, "Lord, you·should·not·establish
Ac 9:5 "Who are·you, Lord?" And the Lord declared, "It·is·
Ac 9:6 ·amazed, he·declared, "Lord, what·do you·want me
Ac 9:10 "Behold, I·myself Lord."
Ac 9:13 But Ananias answered, "Lord, I·have·heard of
Ac 10:4 "What is·it, Lord?" And he·declared to·him, "Your
Ac 10:14 "Not·any·such·thing, Lord, because never·at·
Ac 11:8 'Not·any·such·thing, Lord, because never·at·any·
Ac 22:8 'Who are·you, Lord?' And he·declared to me, 'It·
Ac 22:10 'What should·I·do, Lord?' And the Lord declared
Ac 22:19 "And·I declared, 'Lord, they·themselves are·fully·
Ac 26:15 'Who are·you, Lord?' And he·declared, 'It·is·I
Heb 1:10 And, "'You, O·Lord, in *the* beginning laid·a·
Mt 7:21 "Not everyone saying to·me, 'Lord, Lord,' shall·
Mt 7:21 saying to·me, 'Lord, Lord,' shall·enter into the
Mt 7:22 to·me at that Day, 'Lord, Lord, ¿!·Did·we·not
Mt 7:22 Day, 'Lord, Lord, ¿!·Did·we·not prophesy in·your
Mt 8:2 ·prostrate to·him, saying, "Lord, if you·should·want,
Mt 8:6 and saying, "Lord, my servant·boy has·been·cast
Mt 8:8 the centurion was·replying, "Lord, I·am not fit in·
Mt 8:21 disciples declared to·him, "Lord, freely·permit me
Mt 8:25 awakened him, saying, "Lord, save us! We·
Mt 9:28 ·able to·do this?" They·say to·him, "Yes, Lord."
Mt 11:25 ·affirm to·you, O·Father, Lord of·the heaven and
Mt 13:51 all these·things?" They·say to·him, "Yes, Lord."
Mt 14:28 him, Peter declared, "Lord, if it·is·you yourself,
Mt 14:30 ·down, he·yelled·out, saying, "Lord, save me.
Mt 15:22 "Show·mercy on·me, O·Lord, O·Son of·David;
Mt 15:25 ·prostrate to·him, saying, "Lord, swiftly·help me.
Mt 15:27 "Yes *it·is*, Lord. For even the puppies eat from the
Mt 16:22 "*God* be·favorable to·you, Lord. No, this shall·not
Mt 17:4 Peter declared to·YeShua, "Lord, it·is good for·us
Mt 17:15 "Lord, show·mercy on·my son, because he·is·
Mt 18:21 him, declared, "Lord, how·many·times shall my
Mt 18:26 to·him, saying, 'Lord, be·patient toward me, and
Mt 20:30 "Show·mercy on·us, O·Lord, Son of·David.
Mt 20:31 "Show·mercy on·us, O·Lord, Son of·David.
Mt 20:33 They·say to·him, "Lord, that our eyes may·be·
Mt 25:11 came also, saying, 'Lord, Lord, open·up to·us.
Mt 25:11 came also, saying, 'Lord, Lord, open·up to·us.
Mt 25:20 ·of·silver, saying, 'Lord, you·handed·over to·me
Mt 25:22 ·silver, declared, 'Lord, you·handed·over to·me
Mt 25:24 talant·of·silver, declared, 'Lord, I·knew you that
Mt 25:37 ·answer him, saying, 'Lord, when did·we·see you
Mt 25:44 ·answer him, saying, 'Lord, when did·we·see you
Mt 26:22 of·them began to·say to·him, "Lord, is·it·I myself?
Mk 7:28 "Yes *it·is*, Lord. For even the puppies beneath the
Mk 9:24 with tears, was·saying, "Lord, I·trust! Swiftly·help
Rv 4:11 "You·are worthy, O·Lord, to·receive the glory and
Rv 22:20 Yes, come, Lord Jesus.
G2962.1 N-ASM κύριον (52x)
Jn 11:2 the·one rubbing·oil·on the Lord with·ointment, and
Jn 20:2 to·them, "They·took·away the Lord from·out·of·the
Jn 20:13 "Because they·took·away my Lord, and I·have·not
Jn 20:18 disciples that she·has·clearly·seen the Lord, and
Jn 20:20 the disciples were·glad after·seeing the Lord.
Jn 20:25 to·him, "We·have·clearly·seen the Lord." But he·
Lk 12:36 ·awaiting their·own lord when he·shall·break·camp
Lk 19:8 after·being·settled, declared to·the Lord, "Behold,
Lk 20:44 So·then David calls him 'Lord'; how is·he also his
Ac 2:36 whom yeu crucified, both Lord and Anointed-One."
Ac 8:24 "Yeu·yeurselves petition to the Lord on·my behalf,
Ac 9:27 to·them how *Saul* saw the Lord along the roadway,
Ac 9:35 him, *and* they·turned·back·around toward the Lord.
Ac 9:42 known in all Joppa, and many trusted on the Lord.
Ac 11:17 ·*are* already·trusting on the Lord Jesus Anointed),
Ac 11:20 proclaiming·the·good·news of·the Lord Jesus.
Ac 15:17 of·the men·of·clay† may·seek·out the Lord, even
Ac 16:31 "Trust on the Lord Jesus Anointed, and you·shall·
Ac 17:27 *for·them* to·seek the Lord, if perhaps they·might·
Ac 20:21 a·trust (the·one toward our Lord Jesus Anointed).
Ac 21:20 *these·things*, they·were·glorifying the Lord. And·
Heb 12:14 not·even·one·man shall·gaze·upon the Lord.
Heb 13:20 ·up from·among dead·men our Lord YeShua (the
Mt 10:24 the instructor, nor·even a·slave above his lord.
Mt 22:43 how·does David in Spirit call him 'Lord,' saying,
Mt 22:45 So·then, if David calls him 'Lord,' how is·he his
Mk 12:37 himself refers·to him *as* 'Lord,' so from·what·
Rm 4:24 ·awakening Jesus our Lord from·among dead·men,
Rm 10:9 with your mouth, "Jesus *is* Lord," and should·trust
Rm 13:14 dress·yeurselves·with the Lord Jesus Anointed,
Jud 1:4 only Master, God and our Lord YeShua Anointed.
Php 3:20 ·fully·await *the* Savior, *the* Lord Jesus Anointed,
1Pe 2:13 ·governance of·mankind† on·account·of the Lord,
1Pe 3:6 listened·to·and·obeyed AbRaham, calling him lord.
1Th 2:15 the *Judeans* killing the Lord YeShua and their·own
1Th 5:27 On·oath,·I·charge yeu by·the Lord for·the letter to·
1Co 2:8 *it*, they·would·have not crucified the Lord of·glory.
1Co 6:14 *who* even awakened the Lord *from·death*, also
1Co 9:1 clearly·seen Jesus Anointed our Lord? Are yeu·
1Co 10:22 Or do·we·provoke the Lord to·jealousy?
1Co 12:3 ·man is·able to·declare, "Jesus *is* Lord," except by
1Co 16:22 ·not have·affection·for the Lord Jesus Anointed,
2Co 4:5 but·rather Anointed-One Jesus *the* Lord, and we·
2Co 4:14 the·one awakening the Lord Jesus shall·awaken us
2Co 5:8 the body and to·be·at·home alongside the Lord.
2Co 11:17 I·do·not speak according·to *the* Lord, but·rather
2Co 12:8 I·implored the Lord three·times in·order·that it·
Eph 6:24 all the·ones loving our Lord Jesus Anointed with
Col 2:6 the Anointed-One, Jesus the Lord, *so* walk·yeu in
Col 4:1 having·seen that yeu also have a·Lord in *the* heavens
Phm 1:5 trust which you·have toward the Lord Jesus and for
2Ti 2:22 with the·ones calling·upon the Lord out of·a·pure
G2962.1 N-DSM κυρίῳ (95x)
Lk 14:21 that slave announced these·things to·his lord. Then
Lk 16:5 'How·much·do you·owe to·my lord?'
Lk 17:5 Then the ambassadors declared to·the Lord, "Add
Lk 20:42 "Yahweh declared to·my Lord, "Sit·down at my
Ac 2:34 "Yahweh declared to·my Lord, "Sit·down at my
Ac 5:14 but *of·the·ones* trusting in·the Lord, even·more
Ac 11:23 ·purpose of·heart to·continue·on with·the Lord,
Ac 11:24 an·ample crowd was·placed·alongside the Lord.
Ac 13:2 as·they were·publicly·serving for·the Lord, and·also
Ac 14:3 boldly·speaking·with·clarity in the Lord (the·one
Ac 14:23 they·placed·the·direct·care·of them to·the Lord, in
Ac 16:15 me to·be trustworthy to·the Lord, *then come·along*,
Ac 18:8 ·the·gathering, trusted on·the Lord together with·all
Ac 20:19 being·a·slave to·the Lord with all humility·of·mind
Ac 25:26 absolutely·certain to·write *to·my* Lord *Nero*.
Gal 5:10 for yeu in *the* Lord, that yeu·shall·contemplate not·
Mt 18:31 and coming to·their lord, they·clearly·related all
Mt 22:44 "Yahweh declared to·my Lord, "Sit·down at my
Mk 12:36 "Yahweh declared to·my Lord, "Sit·down at my
Rm 6:11 but alive to·God in Jesus Anointed our Lord.
Rm 6:23 *is* eternal life-above in Jesus Anointed our Lord.
Rm 8:39 the love of·God in Anointed-One, Jesus our Lord.
Rm 14:4 ·servant? To·his·own lord he·stands·fast or falls.
Rm 14:6 day, earnestly·regards *it* unto·*the*·Lord; and the·
Rm 14:6 day, unto·*the*·Lord he·does·not earnestly·regard *it*.
Rm 14:6 The·one eating, eats unto·*the*·Lord, for to·God he·
Rm 14:6 the·one not eating, unto·*the*·Lord he·does·not eat,
Rm 14:8 we·should·live, we·live to·the Lord; or·also
Rm 14:8 we·should·die, we·die to·the Lord. Accordingly,
Rm 14:14 and have·been·convinced by *the* Lord Jesus, that
Rm 16:2 yeu·may·welcome her in *the* Lord, as·is·worthy of·
Rm 16:8 Greet my well-beloved Amplias in *the* Lord.
Rm 16:11 of·Narcissus, the·ones being in *the* Lord.
Rm 16:12 the·ones laboring·hard in *the* Lord. Greet the
Rm 16:12 Persis, who repeatedly labored·hard in *the* Lord.
Rm 16:13 the One-Selected in *the* Lord, and his mother and
Rm 16:18 ·these are·not slaves to·our Lord Jesus Anointed,
Rm 16:22 the·one writing the letter, greet yeu in *the* Lord.
Php 1:14 of·the brothers in *the* Lord, having·confidence by·
Php 2:19 But I·do·expect, in *the* Lord Jesus, to·send
Php 2:24 But I·have·confidence in *the* Lord that also I·
Php 2:29 So·then, welcome him in *the* Lord with all joy, and
Php 3:1 my brothers: Rejoice in *the* Lord! In·fact, *it·is* not
Php 4:1 in·this·manner stand·fast in *the* Lord, *my* dearly·
Php 4:2 SynTyche to·contemplate the same·thing in *the* Lord.
Php 4:4 Rejoice in *the* Lord always, *and* again I·shall·declare
Php 4:10 Now I·rejoiced in *the* Lord greatly, that even·now
2Pe 3:8 "one day *is* with *the* Lord as a·thousand years, and
1Th 1:1 ·*is* in Father God and *in* Lord YeShua Anointed.

1Th 3:8 now we·live, if you should·stand·fast in *the* Lord.
1Th 4:1 yeu and exhort *yeu* by *the* Lord YeShua, just·as yeu·
1Th 4:17 we·shall·be always together with·*the*·Lord.
1Th 5:12 are·conducting yeu in *the* Lord, and admonishing
2Th 1:1 in God our Father and *the* Lord YeShua Anointed.
2Th 3:4 And we·have·confidence in *the* Lord concerning yeu
1Co 4:17 and trustworthy in *the* Lord, who shall·cause yeu
1Co 6:13 sexual·immorality, but·rather for·the Lord, and the
1Co 6:17 But the·one being·tightly·joined to·the Lord is one
1Co 7:22 For the·one being·called·forth in *the* Lord, *though*
1Co 7:32 of·the Lord, how he·shall·accommodate the Lord.
1Co 7:35 ·attending·well to·the Lord without·distraction.
1Co 7:39 she·wants, merely *that he·be* in *the* Lord.
1Co 9:1 Lord? Are yeu·yeurselves not my work in *the* Lord?
1Co 9:2 are the official·seal of·my commission in *the* Lord.
1Co 11:11 neither *is* woman apart·from man, in *the* Lord.
1Co 15:31 which I·have in Anointed-One Jesus our Lord.
1Co 15:58 yeur wearisome·labor is not empty in *the* Lord.
1Co 16:19 greet yeu much in *the* Lord, together with·the
2Co 2:12 ·door having·been·opened·up to·me by *the* Lord),
2Co 8:5 first they·gave their·own·selves to·the Lord and *then*
Eph 1:15 *·is* pervasive·among yeu in the Lord Jesus and *of*
Eph 2:21 ·together, grows into a·holy temple in *the* Lord,
Eph 3:11 he·made in Anointed-One, Jesus our Lord—
Eph 4:1 the chained·prisoner in *the* Lord, implore yeu to·
Eph 4:17 this and attest *to·it* in *the* Lord: No·longer *are* yeu
Eph 5:8 but now *yeu·are* light in *the* Lord. Walk as children
Eph 5:10 ·and·verifying what is most·satisfying to·the Lord.
Eph 5:19 and making·melody in yeur heart to·the Lord,
Eph 5:22 ·yeurselves to·yeur·own husbands, as to·the Lord,
Eph 6:1 Listen·to·and·obey yeur parents in *the* Lord, for this
Eph 6:7 ·intent, being·slaves to·the Lord and not to·men·of·
Eph 6:10 brothers, be·enabled in *the* Lord and in the might
Eph 6:21 brother and trustworthy attendant in *the* Lord
Col 3:16 singing with grace in yeur hearts to·the Lord.
Col 3:18 ·yeur·own husbands, as is·appropriate in *the* Lord.
Col 3:20 all·things, for this is most·satisfying to·the Lord.
Col 3:23 *it* out of·a·soul's·desire as to·the Lord and not to·
Col 3:24 for yeu·are·slaves to·the Lord Anointed-One.
Col 4:7 attendant, and a·fellow·slave in the Lord,
Col 4:17 which you·personally·received in *the* Lord, that
Phm 1:16 more to·you, both in *the* flesh and in *the* Lord?
Phm 1:20 derive·profit·from you in *the* Lord; refresh my
Phm 1:20 Lord; refresh my inward·affections in *the* Lord.
1Ti 1:12 gratitude to·Anointed-One Jesus our Lord, the·one
Rv 14:13 the·ones dying in *the* Lord from·this·moment·on.'

G2962.1 N-DPM κυρίοις (5x)

Lk 16:13 ·servant is·able to·be·a·slave to·two lords, for
Ac 16:16 ·personally·furnishing her lords with·much income
Mt 6:24 No·one·at·all is·able to·be·a·slave to·two lords. For
Eph 6:5 the slaves: Listen·to·and·obey the lords (*the·ones*
Col 3:22 the·ones *who·are yeur* lords according·to flesh, not

G2962.1 N-GSM κυρίου (183x)

Jn 6:23 they·ate the bread, with·the Lord giving·thanks.
Jn 13:16 a·slave is not greater·than his lord; neither *is* an·
Jn 15:20 'A·slave is not greater·than his lord.' If they·
Lk 1:43 that the mother of·my Lord should·come to me?
Lk 1:76 *the* personal·presence of·*the*·Lord to·make·ready his
Lk 10:2 Accordingly, petition the Lord of·the harvest, that
Lk 12:47 that slave, the·one knowing his lord's will and not
Lk 16:5 summoning each one of·his lord's needy·debtors, he·
Lk 22:61 quietly·recalled the word of·the Lord, how he·
Lk 24:3 they·did·not find the body of·the Lord Jesus.
Ac 4:33 the testimonies of·the resurrection of·the Lord Jesus,
Ac 8:16 ·been·immersed in the name of·the Lord Jesus).
Ac 8:25 speaking the Redemptive-word of·the Lord, *as Peter*
Ac 9:1 the disciples of·the Lord, after·coming·alongside the
Ac 9:29 was·speaking in the name of·the Lord Jesus, and
Ac 9:31 in·the reverent·fear·and·awe of·the Lord and in·the
Ac 10:48 in the name of·the Lord. Then they·asked him to·
Ac 11:16 I·recalled·to·mind the utterance of·*the*·Lord, how
Ac 13:11 And now behold, the Lord's hand *is* against you,
Ac 13:12 being·astounded at the instruction of·the Lord.
Ac 13:48 ·glorifying the Redemptive-word of·the Lord. And
Ac 13:49 of·the Lord was·thoroughly·carried throughout the
Ac 15:11 ·trust through the grace of·*the*·Lord Jesus Anointed
Ac 15:26 on·behalf·of·the name of·our Lord Jesus Anointed.
Ac 15:35 ·news of·the Redemptive-word of·the Lord, with
Ac 15:36 ·proclaimed the Redemptive-word of·the Lord, *and*
Ac 16:32 to·him the Redemptive-word of·the Lord, and to·all
Ac 18:25 accurately the·things concerning the Lord *Jesus*,
Ac 19:5 ·were·immersed into the name of·the Lord Jesus.
Ac 19:10 to·hear the Redemptive-word of·the Lord Jesus, both
Ac 19:13 to·name the name of·the Lord Jesus over the·ones
Ac 19:17 and the name of·the Lord Jesus was·magnified.
Ac 19:20 the Redemptive-word of·the Lord was·growing and
Ac 20:24 which I·received personally·from the Lord Jesus,
Ac 20:35 to·remember the words of·the Lord Jesus that he·
Ac 21:13 on·behalf·of·the name of·the Lord Jesus."
Ac 21:14 "The will of·the Lord be·done."
Ac 22:16 ·failures, calling·upon the name of·the Lord.'
Ac 28:31 the·things concerning the Lord Jesus Anointed—
Heb 2:3 being·spoken through the Lord, it·was·confirmed to
Gal 1:3 Father God, and *from* our Lord YeShua Anointed,
Gal 1:19 ambassadors, except Jacob, the Lord's brother.
Gal 6:14 except in the cross of·our Lord YeShua Anointed,
Gal 6:17 bear in my body the marks of·the Lord YeShua.
Gal 6:18 the grace of·our Lord YeShua Anointed *be* with
Mt 9:38 So·then, petition the Lord of·the harvest, that he·
Mt 25:18 dug in the earth and hid·away his lord's money.
Mt 25:21 Enter into the joy of·your lord.'
Mt 25:23 Enter into the joy of·your lord.'
Mk 16:20 with·the Lord working·together *alongside* and
Rm 1:4 of·the·dead; *specifically*, Jesus Anointed our Lord,
Rm 1:7 from God our Father and *the* Lord Jesus Anointed.
Rm 5:1 peace toward God through our Lord Jesus Anointed,
Rm 5:11 ·boasting in God through our Lord Jesus Anointed,
Rm 5:21 eternal life-above through Jesus Anointed our Lord.
Rm 7:25 to·God through Jesus Anointed our Lord. So
Rm 10:13 would call·upon the name of·*the*·Lord shall·be·
Rm 14:8 or·also whether we·should·die, we·are the Lord's.
Rm 15:6 the God and Father of·our Lord Jesus Anointed.
Rm 15:30 brothers, on·account·of our Lord Jesus Anointed,
Rm 16:20 The grace of·our Lord Jesus Anointed *be* with yeu.
Rm 16:24 The grace of·our Lord Jesus Anointed *be* with yeu
Jac 1:1 a·slave of·God and of·*the*·Lord YeShua Anointed.
Jac 1:7 he·shall·receive anything personally·from the Lord.
Jac 2:1 do·not hold the trust of·our Lord YeShua Anointed
Jac 4:10 Be·humbled in·the·sight of·the Lord, and he·shall·
Jac 5:7 until the returning·Presence of·the Lord. Behold, the
Jac 5:8 the returning·Presence of·the Lord has·drawn·near.
Jac 5:14 ·oil·on him with·olive·oil in the name of·the Lord.
Jud 1:17 by the ambassadors of·our Lord YeShua Anointed,
Jud 1:21 ·awaiting the mercy of·our Lord YeShua Anointed
Php 1:2 from God our Father and *from* Lord Jesus Anointed.
Php 3:8 of·Anointed-One, Jesus my Lord— on·account·of
Php 4:23 The grace of·our Lord Jesus Anointed *be* with yeu
1Pe 1:3 the God and Father of·our Lord YeShua Anointed,
2Pe 1:2 *the* full·knowledge of·God and of·YeShua our Lord.
2Pe 1:8 ·and·acknowledgment of·our Lord YeShua Anointed
2Pe 1:11 the eternal kingdom of·our Lord and Savior YeShua
2Pe 1:16 and initial·arrival of·our Lord YeShua Anointed.
2Pe 2:20 ·and·acknowledgment of·the Lord and Savior
2Pe 3:2 *·stated* by·our ambassadors of·the Lord and Savior—
2Pe 3:10 But the Day of·*the*·Lord shall·come as a·thief, in a·
2Pe 3:15 the long-suffering of·our Lord *as* Salvation— just·
2Pe 3:18 grace and in·*the*·knowledge of·our Lord and Savior
1Th 1:1 God our Father, and *the* Lord YeShua Anointed.
1Th 1:3 of·the Expectation, of·our Lord YeShua Anointed),
1Th 1:6 ·imitators of·us and of·the Lord, after·accepting the
1Th 1:8 Redemptive-word of·the Lord has·been·echoed·forth.
1Th 2:19 yeu, *being* before our Lord YeShua Anointed at his
1Th 3:13 returning·Presence of·our Lord YeShua Anointed
1Th 4:2 what charges we·gave yeu through the Lord YeShua.
1Th 4:15 For this we·say to·yeu by *the* Lord's word, that we·
1Th 4:15 surviving to the returning·Presence of·the Lord), no
1Th 4:17 thick·clouds to approach·and·meet the Lord in *the*
1Th 5:9 of·Salvation through our Lord YeShua Anointed,
1Th 5:23 returning·Presence of·our Lord YeShua Anointed.
1Th 5:28 The grace of·our Lord YeShua Anointed *be* with
2Th 1:2 from God our Father and *the* Lord YeShua Anointed.
2Th 1:7 us at the revealing of·the Lord YeShua from heaven
2Th 1:8 the good·news of·our Lord YeShua Anointed,
2Th 1:9 from *the* personal·presence of·the Lord, 'and from
2Th 1:12 that the name of·our Lord YeShua Anointed may·
2Th 1:12 of·our God and of·*the*·Lord YeShua Anointed.
2Th 2:1 returning·Presence of·our Lord YeShua Anointed,
2Th 2:13 yeu (O·brothers having·been·loved by *the* Lord),
2Th 2:14 of·the·glory of·our Lord YeShua Anointed.
2Th 3:1 of·the Lord may·run·unhindered and may·be·
2Th 3:6 brothers, in our Lord's name, YeShua Anointed, to·
2Th 3:12 and exhort through our Lord YeShua Anointed, in·
2Th 3:18 The grace of·our Lord YeShua Anointed *be* with
Tit 1:4 from Father God and *the* Lord Jesus Anointed our
1Co 1:2 ·calling·upon the name of·our Lord Jesus Anointed
1Co 1:3 from God our Father, and Lord Jesus Anointed.
1Co 1:7 ·awaiting the revealing of·our Lord Jesus Anointed,
1Co 1:8 ·to·account in the Day of·our Lord Jesus Anointed.
1Co 1:9 *the* fellowship of·his Son Jesus Anointed our Lord.
1Co 1:10 through the name of·our Lord Jesus Anointed, in·
1Co 5:4 "In the name of·our Lord Jesus Anointed, with·yeu
1Co 5:4 together with·the power of·our Lord Jesus Anointed,
1Co 5:5 spirit may·be·saved in the Day of·the Lord Jesus."
1Co 6:11 ·as·righteous in the name of·the Lord Jesus, and by
1Co 7:22 *being* a·slave, he·is *the* Lord's freedman, likewise
1Co 7:25 have an·authoritative·assignment of·*the*·Lord. But
1Co 7:25 ·shown·mercy from *the* Lord to·be trustworthy.
1Co 7:32 ·man is·anxious·about the·things of·the Lord, how
1Co 7:34 the·things of·the Lord in·order·that she·may·be
1Co 9:5 and *as* the brothers of·the Lord, and *as* Kephas·
1Co 10:21 Yeu·are·not able to·drink *the* Lord's cup and·also
1Co 10:21 to·participate·and·belong to·*the*·Lord's table and·
1Co 11:23 personally·received from the Lord that·which also
1Co 11:26 yeu·fully·proclaim the Lord's death even·until
1Co 11:27 the cup of·the Lord in·an·unworthy·manner,
1Co 11:27 ·be held·liable of·the body and blood of·the Lord.
1Co 11:29 to·himself, not discerning the Lord's body.
1Co 11:32 ·disciplined by *the* Lord, in·order·that we·should·
1Co 14:37 I·write to·yeu are commandments of·the Lord.
1Co 15:57 us the victory through our Lord Jesus Anointed.
1Co 15:58 in the work of·the Lord, having·seen that yeur
1Co 16:10 for he·works the work of·*the*·Lord, as also I·
1Co 16:23 The grace of·the Lord Jesus Anointed *be* with yeu
2Co 1:2 from God our Father and *from* Lord Jesus Anointed.
2Co 1:3 the God and Father of·our Lord Jesus Anointed, the
2Co 1:14 ·as yeu *are* also ours in the Day of·the Lord Jesus.
2Co 3:18 (ourselves·seeing·and·reflecting the Lord's glory)
2Co 4:10 body the mortal·deadness of·the Lord Jesus, that
2Co 5:6 we·are·presently·absent·abroad from the Lord—
2Co 5:11 having·seen the fear of·the Lord, we·persuade
2Co 8:9 For yeu·know the grace of·our Lord Jesus Anointed,
2Co 8:19 us to the glory of·the same Lord, and·also *showing*
2Co 8:21 'merely in·the·sight of·*the*·Lord, but·rather also in·
2Co 11:31 The God and Father of·our Lord Jesus Anointed,
2Co 12:1 I·shall·come to visions and revelations of·*the*·Lord.
2Co 13:14 The grace of·the Lord Jesus Anointed, and the
Eph 1:2 from God our Father and *our* Lord Jesus Anointed.
Eph 1:3 the God and Father of·our Lord Jesus Anointed, the·
Eph 1:17 in·order·that the God of·our Lord Jesus Anointed,
Eph 3:14 my knees to the Father of·our Lord Jesus Anointed,
Eph 5:17 ones·comprehending what the will of·the Lord *is*.
Eph 5:20 and Father in *the* name of·our Lord Jesus Anointed,
Eph 6:4 ·and·discipline and admonition of·the·Lord.
Eph 6:8 ·obtain personally·from the Lord, whether *he·be*
Eph 6:23 trust from Father God and *the* Lord Jesus Anointed.
Col 1:2 from God our Father and *the* Lord Jesus Anointed.
Col 1:3 to·the God and Father of·our Lord Jesus Anointed,
Col 1:10 yeu to·walk worthily of·the Lord into all willing·
Col 3:17 deed, *do* all in *the* Lord Jesus' name, giving·thanks

Col 3:24 that from *the* Lord yeu·shall·receive·in·full the
Phm 1:3 from God our Father and *the* Lord Jesus Anointed.
Phm 1:25 The grace of·our Lord Jesus Anointed *be* with yeur
1Ti 1:1 of·God our Savior, and Lord Jesus Anointed, our
1Ti 1:2 from God our Father and Jesus Anointed our Lord.
1Ti 1:14 of·our Lord increased·evermore·above·and·beyond
1Ti 5:21 in·the·sight of·God, and of·Lord Jesus Anointed,
1Ti 6:3 (the·ones of·our Lord Jesus Anointed) and with·the
1Ti 6:14 conspicuous·appearing of·our Lord Jesus Anointed
2Ti 1:2 from Father God and Anointed-One Jesus our Lord.
2Ti 1:8 be·ashamed·of the testimony of·our Lord, nor·even
2Ti 2:14 of·the Lord not to·quarrel·over·the·trifling·nuances·
2Ti 2:24 ·is·mandatory·for a·slave of·*the*·Lord not to·quarrel
2Ti 4:1 in·the·sight of·God and the Lord Jesus Anointed
2Jn 1:3 God, and personally·from *the* Lord Jesus Anointed,
Rv 11:15 are·become *the kingdoms* of·our Lord and of·his
Rv 22:21 The grace of·our Lord Jesus Anointed *be* with yeu

G2962.1 N-GPM κυρίων (2x)
Rv 17:14 them, because he·is Lord of·lords, and King of·
Rv 19:16 KING OF·KINGS, AND LORD OF·LORDS.

EG2962.1 (5x)
Ac 2:25 For David says this in·regard·to *his·Lord,* " I·was·
Ac 7:59 ·at Stephen while·he·is·calling·upon *the Lord*, even
Rm 10:12 Greek— for this same *Lord Jesus is* Lord of·all,
Jac 2:1 ·our Lord YeShua Anointed (*the Lord* of·Glory) with
1Co 1:2 Lord Jesus Anointed— both their *Lord* and ours.

G2962.2 N-VSM κύριε (11x)
Jn 4:11 The woman says to·him, "Sir, you·have not·even a·
Jn 4:15 The woman says to him, "Sir, give me this water, in·
Jn 4:19 The woman says to·him, "Sir, I·observe that you·
Jn 4:49 ·official says to him, "Sir, walk·down prior·to my
Jn 5:7 feeble·man answered him, "Sir, I·have no man·of·
Jn 12:21 ·asking·of him, saying, "Sir, we·want to·see Jesus.
Jn 20:15 ·keeper, says to·him, "Sir, if you·yourself bore
Mt 13:27 declared to·him, 'Sir, did·you·not·indeed sow
Mt 21:30 'I·myself *will*, sir,' yet he·did·not go·off.
Mt 27:63 saying, "Sir, we·are·mindful·of that thing the
Rv 7:14 And I·have·declared to·him, "Sir, you·yourself

G2962.2 N-VPM κύριοι (1x)
Ac 16:30 outside, he·replied, "Sirs, what is·necessary·for

G2962.5 N-NSM κύριος (5x)
Lk 20:13 "Then the owner of·the vineyard declared, 'What
Lk 20:15 "So·then what shall the owner of·the vineyard do
Mt 20:8 ·early·evening occurring, the owner of·the vineyard
Mt 21:40 "So·then, whenever the owner of·the vineyard
Mk 12:9 "So·then, what·shall the owner of·the vineyard do?

G2962.5 N-NPM κύριοι (1x)
Lk 19:33 were·loosing the colt, its owners declared to them,

G2962.5 N-GPM κυρίων (1x)
Mt 15:27 the·ones falling from the table of·their owners."

G2962-1 Κύῥιος Kýrhiôs *n/p.* (165x)

יְהֹוָה yĕhvạh [The Hebrew Name]
Ἰηώυά Yēhōvá [a Greek transliteration]
Ἰηώ Yēhō [a Greek prefix]

Roots:H3068 Compare:G2962 G2316 G2424 xLangEquiv:H3068 xLangAlso:H0430 H0410 A0426 H0433

G2962-1.2 N-NSM Κύῥιος (1x)
Rm 14:11 '*As·surely·as* I·myself live,' says Yahweh,

G2962-1.2 N-VSM Κύῥιε (2x)
Ac 4:29 And at·the present, O·Yahweh, take·notice·of their
Rm 11:3 "'Yahweh, they·killed your prophets and

G2962-1.2 N-ASM Κύῥιον (16x)
Lk 1:16 Sons of·IsraEl back·around to Yahweh their God.
Lk 1:46 "My soul does·magnify Yahweh,
Lk 4:8 ·shall·fall·prostrate *directly·before* Yahweh your God,
Lk 4:12 "You·shall·not thoroughly·try Yahweh your God.
Lk 10:27 ""You·shall·love Yahweh your God from·out of·
Lk 20:37 burning·bush, *just* as·soon·as he·says Yahweh,
Ac 2:25 " I·was·clearly·keeping Yahweh in·the·sight of·me
Ac 11:21 turned·back·around to Yahweh trusting *in·Jesus*.
Heb 8:11 his brother, saying, "Know Yahweh," because all
Mt 4:7 "You·shall·not thoroughly·try Yahweh your God."
Mt 4:10 ·fall·prostrate *directly·before* Yahweh your God,
Mt 22:37 ""You·shall·love Yahweh your God with all your
Mk 12:30 And you·shall·love Yahweh your God from·out
Rm 15:11 And again, "'Splendidly·praise Yahweh, all the
1Pe 3:15 But make Yahweh God holy in yeur hearts.
2Co 3:16 ·back·around to Yahweh *through Anointed-One*,

G2962-1.2 N-DSM Κυῥίῳ (6x)
Gal 3:6 *who* "'trusted in·Yahweh, and it·was·reckoned to·
Rm 4:3 "'And AbRaham trusted in·Yahweh, and it·was·
Jac 2:23 "'And AbRaham trusted in·Yahweh, and it·was·
2Pe 2:11 a·reviling verdict personally·before Yahweh.
1Co 1:31 "The·one boasting, let·him·boast in Yahweh."
2Co 10:17 ·one who·is·boasting, let·him·boast in Yahweh.

G2962-1.2 N-GSM Κυῥίου (10x)
Jn 6:45 "And they·shall·be all instructed of·Yahweh."
Lk 1:45 having·been·spoken to·her directly·from Yahweh."
Lk 4:4 alone, but·rather upon every utterance of·Yahweh.'"
Ac 4:26 ·together in·unison against Yahweh and against his
Mt 1:22 the·thing being·uttered by Yahweh through the
Mt 2:15 the·thing being·uttered by Yahweh through the
Mt 4:4 ·is·proceeding·forth through *the* mouth of·Yahweh.'"
Mt 21:42 This came·to·be directly·from Yahweh, and it·is
Mk 12:11 This came·to·be directly·from Yahweh, and it·is
2Ti 1:18 ·him to·find mercy personally·from Yahweh in that

G2962-1.2 N/P-NSM Κύῥιος (53x)
Lk 1:25 "In·this·manner has Yahweh done for·me, in *the*
Lk 1:28 ·having·been·graciously·favored. Yahweh *is* with
Lk 1:32 Son of·the·Most·High, and Yahweh God shall·give
Lk 1:58 kinsfolk heard that Yahweh was·making·great his
Lk 1:68 "Blessed *be* Yahweh, God of·IsraEl, because he·
Lk 2:15 having·occurred, which Yahweh made·known to·us
Lk 20:42 ·scroll of·Psalms, "Yahweh declared to·my Lord,
Ac 2:34 he·himself says, "Yahweh declared to·my Lord,
Ac 2:39 at·a·distance, as·many·as Yahweh our God would
Ac 3:22 to the fathers, "Yahweh yeur God shall·raise·up a·
Ac 7:33 "And Yahweh declared to·him, "Loosen the shoes
Ac 7:37 Sons of·IsraEl, "Yahweh yeur God shall·raise·up
Ac 7:49 shall·yeu·build for·me, says Yahweh? Or what *is*
Ac 12:11 ·personally·know truly that Yahweh dispatched his
Ac 15:17 upon them, says Yahweh, the·one doing all these·
Heb 7:21 to him, "'Yahweh swore and shall·not have·regret,
Heb 8:2 ·the true Tabernacle, which Yahweh set·up and not
Heb 8:8 *the* days come,' says Yahweh, 'and I·shall·
Heb 8:9 covenant, and·I neglected them,' says Yahweh.
Heb 8:10 after those days,' says Yahweh, 'giving my
Heb 10:16 them after those days, says Yahweh, giving my
Heb 10:30 shall·recompense," says Yahweh. And again,
Heb 10:30 And again, "'Yahweh shall·sheriff his People.
Heb 12:6 For whom Yahweh loves, he·correctively·
Heb 13:6 while·exercising·courage, "'Yahweh *is* for·me a·
Mt 22:44 "Yahweh declared to·my Lord, "Sit·down at my
Mt 27:10 the potter's field, just·as Yahweh appointed me."
Mk 5:19 to·them what·many·things Yahweh did for·you, and
Mk 12:29 "Listen, O·IsraEl: Yahweh our God, Yahweh is
Mk 12:29 O·IsraEl: Yahweh our God, Yahweh is one.
Mk 12:36 the Holy Spirit, "Yahweh declared to·my Lord,
Mk 13:20 And except *that* Yahweh cut·short the Days, not
Rm 4:8 Supremely·blessed *is* a·man to·whom Yahweh, no,
Rm 9:28 because Yahweh shall·make a·concise·working·of
Rm 9:29 "'Except Yahweh of·Hosts left·behind offspring†
Rm 12:19 ·me; I·myself shall·recompense,'" says Yahweh.
Jac 5:11 of·Yahweh, that Yahweh is very·empathetic and
Jud 1:5 ·seen this: that Yahweh, after·*first*·saving a·People
Jud 1:9 "'May Yahweh reprimand you.'"
Jud 1:14 "Behold, Yahweh came with a·myriad·tens·of·
1Pe 2:3 if·ever "yeu·tasted that Yahweh *is* kind."
2Pe 2:9 *then·indeed* Yahweh— does·personally·know·how
1Co 3:20 And again, "Yahweh knows the deliberations of·
1Co 14:21 they·shall·not·even listen·to me," says Yahweh.
2Co 6:17 and be·distinctly·detached,"" says Yahweh, "
2Co 6:18 sons and daughters,"" says Yahweh Almighty.
2Ti 2:19 official·seal, "' Yahweh already·knows the·ones
Rv 4:8 holy, holy *is* Yahweh, *El Shaddai* God Almighty,
Rv 18:8 with fire, because strong *is* Yahweh God, the·one
Rv 19:6 ·Yahweh,·HalleluYah! Because Yahweh, God
Rv 21:22 see a·Temple in it, for Yahweh, *El Shaddai* God
Rv 22:5 of·sun light, because Yahweh God illuminates them
Rv 22:6 and true." And Yahweh, God of·the holy prophets,

G2962-1.2 N/P-VSM Κύῥιε (7x)
Jn 12:38 which he·declared, "'O·Yahweh, who trusted *that*·
Rm 10:16 IsaIah says, "'O·Yahweh, who trusted *that·which*
Rv 11:17 "We·give·thanks to·you, O·Yahweh, God
Rv 15:3 *are* your works, O·Yahweh, God Almighty.
Rv 15:4 should·not reverently·fear you, O·Yahweh, and
Rv 16:5 "You·are righteous, O·Yahweh, the·one being, and
Rv 16:7 ·Altar saying, "Yes, O·Yahweh, God Almighty,

G2962-1.2 N/P-DSM Κυῥίῳ (6x)
Lk 1:17 a·People having·been·fully·prepared for·Yahweh."
Lk 2:22 him up to JeruSalem to·present *him* to·Yahweh—
Lk 2:23 a·primal·womb shall·be·called holy to·Yahweh"—
Lk 2:38 responded·likewise·in·affirmation to·Yahweh and
Mt 5:33 ·falsely, but shall·render to·Yahweh your oaths."
Rv 19:1 the honor, and the power *are* to·Yahweh our God!

G2962-1.2 N/P-GSM Κυῥίου (60x)
Jn 1:23 "Make·straight the Way of·Yahweh,"" just·as IsaIah
Jn 12:13 *is* the·one who·is·coming in Yahweh's name," the
Jn 12:38 And to·whom is·revealed the arm of·Yahweh?"
Lk 1:6 in all the commandments and regulations of·Yahweh.
Lk 1:9 ·incense after·entering into the Temple of·Yahweh.
Lk 1:11 ·visible to·him an·angel of·Yahweh standing at *the*
Lk 1:15 For he·shall·be great in·the·sight of·Yahweh. And,
Lk 1:38 the female·slave of·Yahweh! May·it·happen to·me
Lk 1:66 little·child be?" And Yahweh's hand was with him.
Lk 2:9 And behold, Yahweh's angel stood·over them, and
Lk 2:9 and Yahweh's glory radiated·brightly·all·around
Lk 2:23 just·as it·has·been·written in Yahweh's Torah-Law,
Lk 2:24 having·been·declared in Yahweh's Torah-Law, "'a·
Lk 2:26 death before he·should·see Yahweh's Anointed-One.
Lk 2:39 ·to the Torah-Law of·Yahweh, they·returned·back
Lk 3:4 'Make·ready the Way of·Yahweh; yeu·must·make his
Lk 4:18 "'Yahweh's Spirit *is* upon me for·the·cause·of
Lk 4:19 ·proclaim an·acceptable Year of·Yahweh."
Lk 5:17 And the power of·Yahweh was *present* to·heal them.
Lk 13:35 the·one who·is·coming in *the* name of·Yahweh.'"
Lk 19:38 who·is·coming in *the* name of·Yahweh!' Peace in
Ac 2:20 the great and conspicuous Day of·Yahweh coming.
Ac 2:21 ·call·upon the name of·Yahweh shall·be·saved."
Ac 3:19 ·come from *the* personal·presence of·Yahweh,
Ac 5:9 are·mutually·agreed·together to·try Yahweh's Spirit?
Ac 5:19 But an·angel of·Yahweh, *coming* through the night,
Ac 7:30 an·angel of·Yahweh was·made·visible to·him in
Ac 7:31 *it*, *the* voice of·Yahweh came·to·be alongside him,
Ac 8:26 And the·angel of·Yahweh spoke to Philippe, saying,
Ac 8:39 ·up out of·the water, Yahweh's Spirit snatched
Ac 11:21 And *the* hand of·Yahweh was with them, and a·
Ac 12:7 And behold, an·angel of·Yahweh stood·over *him*,
Ac 12:23 And at·once, an·angel of·Yahweh smote him,
Ac 13:10 cease perverting the straight ways of·Yahweh?
Ac 18:25 having·been·informed·of The Way of·Yahweh.
Heb 12:5 do·not have·little·respect of·Yahweh's corrective·,
Mt 1:20 behold, an·angel of·Yahweh appeared to·him
Mt 1:24 as the angel of·Yahweh specifically·assigned him,
Mt 2:13 behold, an·angel of·Yahweh appears to·Joseph
Mt 2:19 behold, an·angel of·Yahweh (according·to a·
Mt 3:3 'Make·ready the Way of·Yahweh; yeu·must·make his
Mt 21:9 who·is·coming in *the* name of·Yahweh!" Hosanna
Mt 23:39 the·one who·is·coming in *the* name of·Yahweh.'"
Mt 28:2 a·great earthquake. For Yahweh's angel, after·
Mk 1:3 'Make·ready the Way of·Yahweh; yeu·must·make
Mk 11:9 *is* the·one who·is·coming in *the* name of·Yahweh."
Mk 11:10 that·is·coming in *the* name of·Yahweh. Hosanna
Rm 11:34 "' For who knew Yahweh's mind?
Jac 5:4 have·entered 'into the ears of·Yahweh of·Hosts.'
Jac 5:10 of·the prophets who spoke in·the name of·Yahweh.
Jac 5:11 and saw the end·result of·Yahweh, that Yahweh is

1Pe 1:25 but the utterance of·Yahweh endures to the coming·
1Pe 3:12 Because the eyes of·Yahweh *are* upon righteous·
1Pe 3:12 but *the* face of·Yahweh *is* against those·doing bad.
1Th 5:2 accurately that the Day of·Yahweh, in·this·manner,
1Co 2:16 For "'who knew Yahweh's mind that he·shall·
1Co 10:26 "'the Land *is* Yahweh's, and its complete·fullness
1Co 10:28 "'the Land *is* Yahweh's, and its complete·fullness
2Co 3:17 Spirit, and where the Spirit of·Yahweh *is*, there *is*
2Co 3:18 glory to glory, exactly·as from Yahweh's Spirit.

EG2962-1.2 (4x)
Lk 1:17 shall·go·onward in·the·sight of *Yahweh* in *the* spirit
Heb 2:12 saying *to·Yahweh*, "'I·shall·announce your name
Rm 9:28 For *Yahweh is* entirely·completing *the* matter and
Rm 15:9 you among Gentiles, *O·Yahweh*, and shall·make·

G2963 κυριότης kyriótēs *n.* (4x)
Roots:G2962 Compare:G0932 G2232 G1481

G2963.1 N-ASF κυριότητα (1x)
Jud 1:8 flesh, ignore sovereign·lordship, and revile glorious·

G2963.1 N-GSF κυριότητος (1x)
2Pe 2:10 and·also despising sovereign·lordship. *They·are*

G2963.2 N-NPF κυριότητες (1x)
Col 1:16 whether thrones, or dominions, or principalities,

G2963.2 N-GSF κυριότητος (1x)
Eph 1:21 and authority, power and dominion, and every

G2964 κυρόω kyróō *v.* (2x)
Roots:G2963-1 Compare:G4300 See:G2962

G2964.1 V-RPP-ASF κεκυρωμένην (1x)
Gal 3:15 of·a·man·of·clay† *once* having·been·ratified, *that*

G2964.2 V-AAN κυρῶσαι (1x)
2Co 2:8 Therefore I·implore yeu to·ratify *yeur* love for him.

G2965 κύων kýōn *n.* (5x)
See:G2952
xLangEquiv:H3611

G2965 N-NSM κύων (1x)
2Pe 2:22 true proverb, "'A·dog *keeps·on* returning to his·

G2965 N-NPM κύνες (2x)
Lk 16:21 Moreover, even the dogs were·coming·*along and*
Rv 22:15 But outside *are* the dogs, and the·ones utilizing·

G2965 N-APM κύνας (1x)
Php 3:2 Look·out·for the dogs; look·out·for the bad

G2965 N-DPM κυσίν (1x)
Mt 7:6 the·thing *which·is* holy to·the dogs, nor·even should·

G2966 κῶλον kṓlôn *n.* (1x)
Roots:G2849 Compare:G4430

G2966.2 N-NPN κῶλα (1x)
Heb 3:17 the·ones morally·failing, whose slain·bodies fell in

G2967 κωλύω kōlýō *v.* (23x)
Roots:G2849 Compare:G1465 G2008

G2967.1 V-PAI-3S κωλύει (1x)
Ac 8:36 *here·is* water. What prevents me to·be·immersed?

G2967.1 V-PPN κωλύεσθαι (1x)
Heb 7:23 *they·were* being·prevented to·personally·continue

G2967.1 V-AAN κωλῦσαι (1x)
Ac 11:17 , then who *am* I? Was·I able to·prevent God?

G2967.1 V-AAS-2S κωλύσῃς (1x)
Lk 6:29 outer·garment, you·should·not prevent *him from*

G2967.1 V-API-1S ἐκωλύθην (1x)
Rm 1:13 to yeu (but was·prevented even·until here·and·now)

G2967.2 V-PAI-3S κωλύει (1x)
3Jn 1:10 brothers, and he·forbids the·ones being·resolved *to·*

G2967.2 V-PAM-2P κωλύετε (6x)
Lk 9:50 declared to him, "Do·not forbid *him*, for whoever is
Lk 18:16 to·come to me, and do·not forbid them, for of·such
Mt 19:14 little·children, and do·not forbid them to·come to
Mk 9:39 But Jesus declared, "Do·not forbid him, for there·is
Mk 10:14 ·come to me, and do·not forbid them, for of·such
1Co 14:39 do·not forbid to·speak with·bestowed·tongues.

G2967.2 V-PAN κωλύειν (1x)
Ac 24:23 *him·at* ease, and to·forbid not·one of·his own·

G2967.2 V-PAP-ASM κωλύοντα (1x)
Lk 23:2 the nation, and forbidding *others* to·give tributes to·

G2967.2 V-PAP-GPM κωλυόντων (2x)
1Th 2:16 by·forbidding us to·speak to·the Gentiles in·order·
1Ti 4:3 forbidding to·marry— *and commanding* to·abstain·

G2967.2 V-AAI-1P ἐκωλύσαμεν (2x)
Lk 9:49 in your name; and we·forbade him, because he·
Mk 9:38 does·not follow us, and we·forbade him, because

G2967.2 V-AAI-2P ἐκωλύσατε (1x)
Lk 11:52 and yeu·forbade the·ones who·were·entering."

G2967.2 V-AAI-3S ἐκώλυσεν (2x)
Ac 27:43 to·thoroughly·save Paul, forbade them of·the
2Pe 2:16 of·a·man·of·clay† forbade the irrational·conduct

G2967.2 V-AAN κωλῦσαι (1x)
Ac 10:47 "Is any·man able to·forbid water *such·for* these not

G2967.2 V-APP-NPM κωλυθέντες (1x)
Ac 16:6 of·Galatia, they·were·being·forbidden by the Holy

G2968 κώμη kṓmē *n.* (28x)
Roots:G2749 Compare:G4172 See:G2969
xLangEquiv:H3723

G2968 N-ASF κώμην (13x)
Jn 11:30 had·not·yet come into the village, but·rather was in
Lk 8:1 ·throughout each city and village, officially·heralding
Lk 9:52 they·entered into a·village of·the·Samaritans, as·
Lk 9:56 And they·traversed to another village.
Lk 10:38 that he·himself entered into a·certain village, and a·
Lk 17:12 into a·certain village, there·approached·and·met
Lk 19:30 "Head·on·out into the village directly·before *yeu*;
Lk 24:13 on that·same day to a·village with·the name
Lk 24:28 And they·drew·near to the village, where they·
Mt 10:11 whatever city or village yeu·should·enter, verify·
Mt 21:2 ·should·traverse into the village fully·in·front of·yeu
Mk 8:26 ·should·not·even enter into the village, nor·even
Mk 11:2 "Head·on·out into the village directly·before yeu,

G2968 N-APF κώμας (10x)
Lk 9:6 each·of·the villages, proclaiming·the·good·news, and
Lk 9:12 ·that going·off into the encircling villages and the
Lk 13:22 each *of·the* cities and villages, instructing and
Ac 8:25 ·the·good·news in·many villages of·the Samaritans.
Mt 9:35 around the cities and the villages, instructing in their
Mt 14:15 after·going·off into the villages, they·may·buy
Mk 6:6 ·around·to the encircling villages, while·instructing.
Mk 6:36 countrysides and villages, they·should·buy bread
Mk 6:56 he·was·traversing, whether into villages, or cities,
Mk 8:27 his disciples into the villages of·Caesarea Philippi.

G2968 N-DSF κώμῃ (1x)
Mk 8:26 should·you·declare *this* to·anyone in the village."

G2968 N-GSF κώμης (4x)
Jn 7:42 ·David, and from the village of·BethLechem, where
Jn 11:1 BethAny, from·among the village of·Mary and her
Lk 5:17 ·come from·out of·every village of·Galilee and
Mk 8:23 he·led him outside of·the village. And after·spitting

G2969 κωμό•πολις kōmópôlis *n.* (1x)
Roots:G2968 G4172 Compare:G4172 See:G2968

G2969 N-APF κωμοπόλεις (1x)
Mk 1:38 ·head·out into the neighboring towns, in·order·that

G2970 κῶμος kṓmôs *n.* (3x)
Roots:G2749 Compare:G1792

G2970 N-NPM κῶμοι (1x)
Gal 5:21 murders, intoxications, revelries, and things like

G2970 N-DPM κώμοις (2x)
Rm 13:13 as in daylight, not in·revelries and intoxications,
1Pe 4:3 excesses·of·wine, revelries, drinking·parties, and

G2971 κών•ωψ kṓnōps *n.* (1x)
Roots:G2759 G3700

G2971.2 N-ASM κώνωπα (1x)
Mt 23:24 the·ones thoroughly·filtering·out the gnat, but

G2972 Κῶς Kṓs *n/l.* (1x)

G2972 N/L-ASF Κῶν (1x)
Ac 21:1 them, we·went sailing·straight to Cos, and on·the

G2973 Κωσάμ Kōsám *n/p.* (1x)
Ḳωσάμ Qōsám [Greek, Octuagint]
קֶסֶם qeçem [Hebrew]
Roots:H7081 Compare:G4436

G2973.2 N/P-PRI Ḳωσάμ (1x)
Lk 3:28 *son* of·Addi, *son* of·Qosam, *son* of·ElModam, *son*

G2974 κωφός kōphós *adj.* (14x)
Roots:G2875 Compare:G0216 G1769 G4623 G4602
xLangEquiv:H2795

G2974.2 A-NSN κωφόν (1x)
Mk 9:25 "Spirit, the·one mute and deaf, I·myself order you,

G2974.2 A-NPM κωφοί (2x)
Lk 7:22 walk, lepers are·purified, deaf·men hear, dead·men
Mt 11:5 lepers are·purified and deaf·men hear, dead·men

G2974.2 A-ASM κωφόν (1x)
Mk 7:32 to·him a·deaf·man *with* a·speech·impediment, and

G2974.2 A-APM κωφούς (1x)
Mk 7:37 He·makes both the deaf to·hear and the mute to·

G2974.3 A-NSM κωφός (4x)
Lk 1:22 to·them, yet was·thoroughly·remaining mute.
Lk 11:14 ·the demon going·out, the mute·man spoke. And
Mt 9:33 with·the demon being·cast·out, the mute spoke, and
Mt 12:22 *being* blind and mute, and he·both·relieved·and·

G2974.3 A-NSN κωφόν (1x)
Lk 11:14 ·out a·demon, and it was mute. And it·happened,

G2974.3 A-ASM κωφόν (2x)
Mt 9:32 ·of·clay†, a·mute being·possessed·with·a·demon.
Mt 12:22 such·for the blind and mute·man both to·speak and

G2974.3 A-APM κωφούς (2x)
Mt 15:30 *those that·were* lame, blind, mute, crippled, and
Mt 15:31 to·marvel, while·looking·at muted·ones speaking,

Αα Ββ Γγ Δδ Εε Ζζ Ηη Θθ Ιι Κκ Λλ Μμ Νν Ξξ Οο Ππ Ρρ Σσ Ττ Υυ Φφ Χχ Ψψ Ωω

Λλ - Lambda

G2975 λαγχάνω lanchánō *v.* (4x)
Compare:G2013 G5177 G2865 G2820
G2975.1 V-2AAS-1P λάχωμεν (1x)
Jn 19:24 but·rather we·should·determine·by·lot concerning it
G2975.2 V-2AAI-3S ἔλαχεν (1x)
Ac 1:17 with·us, and he·clearly·obtained the allotted·portion
G2975.2 V-2AAP-DPM λαχοῦσιν (1x)
2Pe 1:1 To·the·ones already·clearly·obtaining an·equally·
G2975.3 V-2AAI-3S ἔλαχεν (1x)
Lk 1:9 ·priesthood, he·clearly·obtained·the·lot, the·one·to·
G2976 Λάζαρος Lázarôs *n/p.* (15x)
Roots:H0499
G2976 N/P-NSM Λάζαρος (8x)
Jn 11:1 ·man was sick, *named* Lazarus, from BethAny,
Jn 11:2 feet with·her hair, whose brother Lazarus was·sick).
Jn 11:11 "Our friend Lazarus has·been·laid·to·rest. But·yet
Jn 11:14 to·them with·clarity·of·speech, "Lazarus is·dead.
Jn 12:1 Jesus came to BethAny where Lazarus was, the·one
Jn 12:2 was·attending *to·them*, but Lazarus was one of·the·
Lk 16:20 ·beggar by·the·name·of Lazarus who had·been·cast
Lk 16:25 ·things, and likewise, Lazarus the bad·things. But
G2976 N/P-VSM Λάζαρε (1x)
Jn 11:43 ·out with·a·loud voice, "Lazarus, come·over·here,
G2976 N/P-ASM Λάζαρον (6x)
Jn 11:5 Jesus loved Martha, also her sister, and Lazarus.
Jn 12:9 but·rather in·order·that they·may·see Lazarus also,
Jn 12:10 ·counsel in·order·that they·may·kill Lazarus also,
Jn 12:17 when he·hollered·out·for Lazarus from·among the
Lk 16:23 from·a·distance, and Lazarus at his bosom.
Lk 16:24 on·me, and send Lazarus in·order·that he·may·dip
G2977 λάθρα láthra *adv.* (4x)
Roots:G2990 Compare:G2931 G2398 See:G2977-2
G2977 ADV λάθρα (4x)
Jn 11:28 ·out·for Mary her sister, privately declaring, "The
Ac 16:37 And now do·they·cast us out privately? For no *way*
Mt 1:19 ·and·scorn, resolved to·dismiss her privately.
Mt 2:7 Then HerOd·the·Great, after·privately calling·for the
G2978 λαῖλαψ laîlaps *n.* (3x)
Compare:G4578 G5494
G2978.1 N-GSF λαίλαπος (1x)
2Pe 2:17 ·clouds being·driven by a·whirlwind, for·whom the
G2978.2 N-NSF λαῖλαψ (2x)
Lk 8:23 he·fell·asleep. And a·whirling of·wind descended
Mk 4:37 And there·happens a·great whirling of·wind, and
G2979 λακτίζω laktízō *v.* (2x)
G2979.1 V-PAN λακτίζειν (2x)
Ac 9:5 for·you to·kick·the·heel·back directly·against cattle·
Ac 26:14 hard for·you to·kick·the·heel·back directly·against
G2980 λαλέω laléō *v.* (302x)
Compare:G3004 G2036 G5346 G4483 See:G2981 xLangEquiv:H1696
G2980 V-FAI-1S λαλήσω (3x)
Jn 14:30 "Not any·longer shall·I·speak much with yeu, for
Jn 16:25 when no longer shall·I·speak to·yeu in proverbs,
1Co 14:21 and in other lips I·shall·speak to·this People; and
G2980 V-FAI-1P λαλήσομεν (1x)
3Jn 1:14 you straight·away, and we·shall·speak mouth to
G2980 V-FAI-2P λαλήσετε (1x)
Mt 10:19 ·be·given to·yeu in that hour what yeu·shall·speak.
G2980 V-FAI-3S λαλήσει (6x)
Jn 9:21 ask him. He·himself shall·speak concerning himself.
Jn 16:13 "For he·shall·not speak from himself, but·rather as·
Jn 16:13 he·should·hear, *that* shall·he·speak, and he·shall·
Ac 10:6 ·by *the* sea. This·man shall·speak to·you what is·
Ac 10:32 who coming·directly, shall·speak to·you. This·
Ac 11:14 who shall·speak to you utterances by which you·
G2980 V-FAI-3P λαλήσουσιν (1x)
Mk 16:17 they·shall·speak in·brand-new bestowed·tongues;
G2980 V-FPI-3S λαληθήσεται (4x)
Ac 9:6 into the city, and it·shall·be·spoken to·you what is·
Ac 22:10 and·there it·shall·be·spoken to·you concerning
Mt 26:13 she·herself did shall·be·spoken·of for a·memorial
Mk 14:9 she·herself did shall·be·spoken·of for a·memorial
G2980 V-FPP-GPN λαληθησομένων (1x)
Heb 3:5 of·the·things which·were·to·be·spoken·later),
G2980 V-PAI-1S λαλῶ (17x)
Jn 6:63 The utterances that I·myself speak to·yeu, *they* are
Jn 7:17 ·God, or *whether* I·myself speak from my·own·self.
Jn 8:25 "Even the·same·which I·spoke to·yeu from·the
Jn 8:28 ·as my Father instructed me, I·speak these·things.
Jn 8:38 "I·myself speak that·which I·have·clearly·seen from·
Jn 12:50 "Accordingly, whatever I·myself speak, *it·is* just·as
Jn 12:50 has·declared to·me; in·this·manner I·speak."
Jn 14:10 "The utterances that I·myself speak to·yeu, I·do·not
Jn 14:10 speak to·yeu, I·do·not speak from my·own·self, but
Jn 17:13 to you, and these·things I·speak in the world, in·
Ac 26:26 to whom also I·speak, being·boldly·confident, for
Mt 13:13 "On·account·of that, I·speak to·them in parables,
Rm 7:1 (for I·speak to·the·ones·knowing Torah-Law), that
1Co 9:8 ¿! Do I·speak these·things according·to a·man·of·
2Co 11:17 That·which I·speak, I·do·not speak according·to
2Co 11:17 ·which I·speak, I·do·not speak according·to *the*
2Co 11:23 Being·beyond·reason, I·speak— I·myself *am*
G2980 V-PAI-1P λαλοῦμεν (10x)
Jn 3:11 I·say to·you, we·speak that which we·personally·
Heb 2:5 *brand-new* Land, concerning which we·speak.
Heb 6:9 ·Salvation, even though we·speak in·this·manner.
1Th 2:4 with·the good·news, in·this·manner we·speak, not
1Co 2:6 But we·do·speak wisdom among the·ones *being*
1Co 2:7 But·rather we·speak God's wisdom in a·Mystery,
1Co 2:13 Which·things also we·speak, not with instructive
2Co 2:17 *being* directly·in·the·sight·of·God, we·speak in *the*
2Co 4:13 ' we·ourselves also trust and therefore speak,
2Co 12:19 to·yeu? We·speak *being* directly·in·the·sight·of·
G2980 V-PAI-2S λαλεῖς (4x)
Jn 4:27 ·do you·seek?" or, "Why·do you·speak with her?
Jn 16:29 "See, now you·speak with·clarity·of·speech, and
Jn 19:10 ·then Pilate says·to·him, "Do·you·not speak to·me?
Mt 13:10 to·him, "Why·do you·speak to·them in parables?
G2980 V-PAI-3S λαλεῖ (16x)
Jn 3:31 ·out·of·the·earth, and speaks from·out·of·the·earth.
Jn 3:34 For he·whom God dispatched speaks the utterances
Jn 7:26 But see, he·speaks with·clarity·of·speech, and they·
Jn 8:44 ·should·speak a·lie, he·speaks from·out·of·his·own
Jn 16:18 We·do·not personally·know what *it·is* he·speaks."
Lk 5:21 "Who is this who speaks revilements·of·God?
Lk 6:45 of·the·abundance·of·the·heart, his mouth speaks.
Mt 12:34 of·the·abundance·of·the·heart the mouth speaks.
Mk 2:7 ·manner, does this·man speak revilements·of·God?
Rm 3:19 the Torah-Law says, it·speaks to·the·ones with the
Jud 1:16 And their mouth speaks outrageous·things, while·
1Pe 4:11 If any·man speaks *to·others*, *let·him·be* as *one*·
1Co 14:2 in·a·bestowed·tongue speaks not to·men·of·clay†,
1Co 14:2 but in·*the*·Spirit, he·does·speak mysteries.
1Co 14:3 the·one prophesying speaks to·men·of·clay† *for*
1Co 14:27 ·if any·man does·speak in·a·bestowed·tongue,
G2980 V-PAI-3P λαλοῦσιν (2x)
1Co 12:30 of·healing. Not all speak in·bestowed·tongues.
1Jn 4:5 on·account·of that they·speak from·among the
G2980 V-PAM-2S λαλεῖ (3x)
Ac 18:9 Do·not be·afraid, but·rather speak, and you·should·
Tit 2:1 But you·yourself speak that·which is·suitable·for the
Tit 2:15 Speak these·things, and exhort and reprove with all
G2980 V-PAM-2P λαλεῖτε (4x)
Ac 5:20 and after·being·settled·*in*, speak in the Sanctuary·
Mk 13:11 to·yeu in that hour, that speak, for it·is not yeu·
Jac 2:12 In·this·manner yeu·must·speak and so do: as ones·
Eph 4:25 the lying, "Each·man must·speak truth with his
G2980 V-PAM-3S λαλείτω (1x)
1Co 14:28 And·thus, he·must·speak to·himself and to·God.
G2980 V-PAM-3P λαλείτωσαν (1x)
1Co 14:29 Now *let* prophets speak two or three, and *let* the
G2980 V-PAN λαλεῖν (20x)
Jn 8:26 I·have many·things to·speak and to·judge concerning
Lk 4:41 he·was·not giving·leave·for them to·speak, because
Lk 7:15 dead·man sat·up and began to·speak. And he·gave
Ac 2:4 they·began to·speak·in different bestowed·tongues,
Ac 4:17 ·threaten them to·speak no·longer to·not·even·one
Ac 4:20 are·not able not to·speak the·things·which we·saw
Ac 4:29 slaves *the ability* to·speak your Redemptive-word
Ac 5:40 *them*, they·charged *them* not to·speak in the name
Ac 11:15 And as I began to·speak, the Holy Spirit fell upon
Mt 12:22 and mute·man both to·speak and to·look·about.
Mt 12:34 are·yeu·able to·speak beneficially·good·things?
Mk 1:34 he·was·not allowing the demons to·speak, because
Mk 7:37 both the deaf to·hear and the mute to·speak."
Rm 15:18 I·shall·not venture to·speak of·any·of·such·things
Php 1:14 ·more daringly·bold to·speak the Redemptive-word
1Th 1:8 such·for us not to·have need to·speak anything.
1Co 14:5 I·want yeu all to·speak with·bestowed·tongues, but
1Co 14:34 ·freely·permitted for·them to·speak, but·rather to·
1Co 14:35 for·women to·speak in a·convened·Called·Out·
1Co 14:39 do·not forbid to·speak with·bestowed·tongues.
G2980 V-PAP-ASF λαλοῦσαν (1x)
Ac 26:14 the earth, I·heard a·voice speaking to me, and
G2980 V-PAP-ASM λαλοῦντα (1x)
Heb 12:25 Yeu·should·not shun the·one speaking. For if
G2980 V-PAP-APM λαλοῦντας (1x)
Mt 15:31 ·looking·at muted·ones speaking, crippled·ones
G2980 V-PAP-DSM λαλοῦντι (2x)
Heb 12:24 blood speaking significantly·better·things—
1Co 14:11 I·shall·be a·barbarian to·the·one speaking, also
G2980 V-PAP-GSF λαλούσης (1x)
Rv 4:1 which I·heard *was* as a·trumpet speaking with me,
G2980 V-PAP-GSM λαλοῦντος (17x)
Jn 1:37 two disciples heard him speaking, and they·followed
Jn 8:30 With·him speaking these·things, many trusted in him
Lk 8:49 While·he was·yet speaking, there·comes someone
Lk 22:47 And while·he was·yet speaking, behold a·crowd.
Lk 22:60 And at·once, with·him still speaking, the rooster
Ac 6:11 "We·have·heard him speaking reviling utterances
Ac 7:38 the angel, the·one speaking with·him on Mount
Ac 10:44 As·Peter was·yet speaking these utterances, the
Ac 14:9 The·same·man was·hearing Paul speaking, who
Ac 22:9 *distinctly*·hear the voice of·the·one speaking to·me.
Mt 9:18 With·him speaking these·things to·them, behold, a·
Mt 12:46 And with·him still speaking to·the crowds, behold,
Mt 17:5 While·he was·yet speaking, behold, a·thick·cloud
Mt 26:47 And with·him still speaking, behold, Judas, one of·
Mk 5:35 As·he was·still speaking, one·came from *the house*·
Mk 14:43 And immediately, while·yet speaking of·him,
2Co 13:3 ·seek a·proof of·the Anointed-One speaking in me,
G2980 V-PAP-GPM λαλούντων (5x)
Lk 24:36 And with·them speaking these·things, Jesus
Ac 2:6 ·hearing them speaking in·his·own·distinct dialect.
Ac 2:11 — we·hear them speaking in·our native·tongues the
Ac 4:1 And as·they were·speaking to the people, the priests·
Ac 10:46 ·hearing them speaking in·bestowed·tongues and
G2980 V-PAP-NSN λαλοῦν (2x)
Mt 10:20 the Spirit of·yeur Father *is* the·one speaking in yeu.
Rv 13:5 ·was·given to·it a·mouth speaking great·things and
G2980 V-PAP-NSF λαλοῦσα (1x)
Rv 10:8 from·out·of·the heaven *was* speaking with me again,
G2980 V-PAP-NSM λαλῶν (17x)
Jn 4:26 *Yes*, the·one speaking to·you."
Jn 7:18 The·man speaking from himself seeks his·own glory,
Jn 9:37 him, and it·is the·same·one speaking with you."
Lk 5:4 Now as·soon·as he·ceased speaking, he·declared to
Ac 6:13 ·of·clay† does·not cease speaking reviling utterances
Ac 7:44 ·as the·one speaking to·Moses thoroughly·assigned
Ac 10:7 ·as the angel (the·one speaking to·Cornelius) went·
2Pe 3:16 also in all his letters, speaking in them concerning
1Co 12:3 to·yeu, that not·even·one·man speaking by God's
1Co 14:2 For the·one speaking in·a·bestowed·tongue speaks
1Co 14:4 The·one speaking in·a·bestowed·tongue does·edify
1Co 14:5 than the·one speaking with·bestowed·tongues,

1Co 14:6 ·come to yeu speaking with·bestowed·tongues,
1Co 14:11 speaking, also the·one speaking with me *shall·be*
1Co 14:13 the·one speaking in·a·bestowed·tongue must·pray
1Co 14:18 I·give·thanks to·my God, speaking more·than all
Rv 21:15 And the·one speaking with me was·holding a·

G2980 V-PAP-NPF λαλοῦσαι (1x)
1Ti 5:13 also and meddlers, speaking things·which are·not

G2980 V-PAP-NPM λαλοῦντες (7x)
Ac 2:7 "Behold, are not all these ones speaking Galileans?
Ac 11:19 and Antioch, speaking the Redemptive-word to·
Ac 20:30 men shall·rise·up, speaking perverse·things, to·
Mt 10:20 ·yeurselves are not the·ones speaking, but·rather
Mk 13:11 for it·is not yeu·yeurselves speaking, but·rather the
1Co 14:9 being·spoken? For yeu·shall·be speaking into *thin*
Eph 5:19 speaking to·yeurselves in·psalms and hymns and

G2980 V-PAS-1S λαλῶ (1x)
1Co 13:1 If·ever I·should·speak with·the bestowed·tongues

G2980 V-PAS-3S λαλῇ (1x)
Jn 8:44 in him. Whenever he·should·speak a·lie, he·speaks

G2980 V-PAS-3P λαλῶσιν (1x)
1Co 14:23 and all should·speak with·bestowed·tongues,

G2980 V-PMI-3S λαλεῖται (1x)
Heb 11:4 *although* already·dying, he·himself still speaks.

G2980 V-PPN λαλεῖσθαι (1x)
Heb 2:3 an·initial *announcement* being·spoken through the

G2980 V-PPP-ASM λαλούμενον (1x)
Mk 5:36 upon·hearing the word being·spoken, Jesus says to·

G2980 V-PPP-DPN λαλουμένοις (2x)
Lk 2:33 at the·things being·spoken concerning him.
Ac 16:14 to·give·heed to·the·things being·spoken by Paul.

G2980 V-PPP-NSN λαλούμενον (1x)
1Co 14:9 shall·it·be·known, the·thing being·spoken? For

G2980 V-PPP-NSF λαλουμένη (1x)
Ac 17:19 instruction *is, which·is* being·spoken by you?

G2980 V-IAI-1S ἐλάλουν (1x)
1Co 13:11 I·was an·infant, I·was·speaking as an·infant, I·

G2980 V-IAI-1P ἐλαλοῦμεν (1x)
Ac 16:13 sitting·down, we·were·speaking to·the women

G2980 V-IAI-3S ἐλάλει (18x)
Jn 4:27 they·marveled that he·was·speaking with a·woman.
Jn 7:13 not·even·one was·speaking with·freeness·of·speech
Jn 10:6 ·*of*·things it·was that he·was·speaking to·them *about*
Lk 1:64 tongue *loosed*, and he·was·speaking, blessing God.
Lk 2:38 to·Yahweh and was·speaking concerning him to·all
Lk 9:11 them, he·was·speaking to·them concerning the
Lk 24:32 within us, as he·was·speaking with·us along the
Ac 6:10 wisdom and the Spirit by·which he·was·speaking.
Ac 9:29 ·speaking·with·clarity, *Saul* was·speaking in the
Ac 18:25 in·the spirit, he·was·speaking and was·instructing
Heb 4:8 ·rest, he·would not have·spoken after·these·things
Mt 13:34 ·from·a·parable, he·was·not speaking to·them,
Mk 2:2 the door. And he·was·speaking the Redemptive-word
Mk 4:33 parables, he·was·speaking the Redemptive-word to·
Mk 4:34 And he·was·not speaking to·them apart·from a·
Mk 7:35 tongue was·loosed, and he·was·speaking correctly.
Mk 8:32 And he·was·speaking the saying with·clarity·of·
Rv 13:11 ·male·lamb, and it·was·speaking as a·dragon.

G2980 V-IAI-3P ἐλάλουν (4x)
Ac 4:31 Spirit, and they·were·speaking the Redemptive-word
Ac 11:20 after·entering into Antioch, were·speaking to the
Ac 19:6 and they·were·speaking with·bestowed·tongues and
Ac 26:31 they·were·speaking among one·another, saying,

G2980 V-AAI-1S ἐλάλησα (9x)
Jn 12:48 him: the Redemptive-word which I·spoke. The·same
Jn 12:49 I·myself did·not speak from·out·of·my·own·self.
Jn 15:22 "Except *for·that* I·came and I·spoke to·them, they·
Jn 18:20 "I·myself spoke with·freeness·of·speech to·the
Jn 18:20 come·together. And I·spoke nothing·at·all in secret
Jn 18:21 ·of·the·ones having·heard what I·spoke to·them.
Jn 18:23 Jesus answered him, "If I·spoke wrongly, testify
Lk 24:44 "These *are* the words which I·spoke to·you, while·
2Co 4:13 "'I·trusted, therefore I·spoke,'" we·ourselves also

G2980 V-AAI-1P ἐλαλήσαμεν (1x)
2Co 7:14 ·shame; but·rather as we·spoke all·things to·yeu in

G2980 V-AAI-2P ἐλαλήσατε (1x)
Lk 12:3 in the light; and that·which yeu·spoke to the ear in

G2980 V-AAI-3S ἐλάλησεν (32x)
Jn 7:46 in·this·manner *has* a·man·of·clay† spoken as *does*
Jn 8:12 In·due·course, Jesus spoke again to·them, saying, "I
Jn 8:20 These utterances Jesus spoke at the treasury·room,
Jn 12:36 These·things Jesus spoke, and after·going·off, he·
Jn 12:41 when he·saw his glory and spoke concerning him.
Jn 17:1 Jesus spoke these·things and lifted·up his eyes to the
Lk 1:55 into the coming·age, just·as he·spoke to our fathers.
Lk 1:70 just·as he·spoke through *the* mouth of·his holy
Lk 2:50 comprehend the utterance which he·spoke to·them.
Lk 11:14 demon going·out, the mute·man spoke. And the
Lk 24:6 Recall·to·mind how he·spoke to·yeu while·still
Ac 2:31 foreseeing *this*, he·spoke concerning the
Ac 3:21 ·all·things, of·which God spoke through *the* mouth
Ac 7:6 And God spoke in·this·manner, that his "offspring†
Ac 8:26 And the·angel of·Yahweh spoke to Philippe, saying,
Ac 9:27 the roadway, and that he·spoke to·him, and how he·
Ac 23:9 if a·spirit or an·angel spoke to·him, we·should·not
Ac 28:21 arriving·publicly announced or spoken any evil
Ac 28:25 "The Holy Spirit spoke well through Isaiah the
Heb 1:2 spoke to·us in these last days by *his* Son, whom he·
Heb 7:14 tribe Moses spoke not·even·one·thing concerning
Mt 9:33 ·the demon being·cast·out, the mute spoke, and the
Mt 13:3 And he·spoke many·things to·them in parables,
Mt 13:33 Another parable he·spoke to·them: "The kingdom
Mt 13:34 YeShua spoke all these·things to·the crowds in
Mt 14:27 But immediately YeShua spoke to·them, saying,
Mt 23:1 Then YeShua spoke to·the crowds and to·his
Mt 28:18 And coming·alongside, YeShua spoke to·them,
Mk 6:50 And immediately he·spoke with them, and he·says
Rv 1:12 ·about to·look·at the voice that spoke with me. And
Rv 17:1 the seven vials, and he·spoke with me, saying to·me
Rv 21:9 last punishing·blows), and he·spoke with me,

G2980 V-AAI-3P ἐλάλησαν (11x)
Lk 24:25 in·the heart to·trust on all that the prophets spoke.
Ac 3:24 of·subsequent·order, as·many·as that·spoke, also
Ac 16:32 And they·spoke to·him the Redemptive-word of·the
Ac 26:22 and Moses spoke of·as·being·about·to·happen:
Heb 13:7 ·are·governing among·yeu, who spoke to·yeu the
Jac 5:10 of·the prophets who spoke in·the name of·Yahweh.
Jud 1:15 *and* morally·disqualified·men spoke against him."
2Pe 1:21 Spirit, men·of·clay† (the holy·ones in·God) spoke.
Rv 10:3 ·out, the Seven Thunders spoke their·own voices.
Rv 10:4 when the Seven Thunders spoke their·own voices, I·
Rv 10:4 those·things·which the Seven Thunders spoke, and

G2980 V-AAN λαλῆσαι (22x)
Lk 1:19 ·sight of·God; and I·am·dispatched to·speak to you,
Lk 1:20 ·silent, and not being·able to·speak, even·until *the*
Lk 1:22 ·coming·forth, he·was·not able to·speak to·them.
Lk 11:37 Now as *Jesus* was·speaking, a·certain Pharisee
Ac 14:1 Jews, and in·this·manner to·speak, such·for a·large
Ac 16:6 by·the Holy Spirit to·speak the Redemptive-word in
Ac 21:39 you, freely·permit me to·speak to the people.
Ac 23:18 ·man to you, having something to·speak to·you."
Mt 12:46 brothers stood outside, seeking to·speak with·him.
Mt 12:47 stand outside, seeking to·speak with·you."
Mk 16:19 after the Lord spoke to·them, he·was·taken·up
Jac 1:19 ·be swift to·hear, slow to·speak, *and* slow to wrath.
1Pe 3:10 tongue from wrong and his lips not to·speak guile."
1Th 2:2 ·were·boldly·confident in·our God to·speak to yeu
1Th 2:16 by·forbidding us to·speak to·the Gentiles in·order·
1Co 3:1 brothers, am·not able to·speak to·yeu as to·
1Co 14:19 ·Out·assembly, I·determine to·speak five words
2Co 12:4 is·not being·proper for·a·man·of·clay† to·speak.
Eph 6:20 ·with·clarity as it·is·mandatory·for me to·speak.
Col 4:3 Redemptive-word (*that·is*, to·speak the Mystery of·
Col 4:4 it apparent, as it·is·mandatory·for me to·speak.
2Jn 1:12 to·come to yeu, and to·speak mouth to mouth, in·

G2980 V-AAP-GSM λαλήσαντος (1x)
Ac 23:7 And with·him speaking that, there·occurred a·

G2980 V-AAP-NSM λαλήσας (2x)
Heb 1:1 After·speaking in·many·portions and with·many·
Heb 5:5 a·high·priest, but·rather the·one speaking to him,

G2980 V-AAP-NPM λαλήσαντες (2x)
Ac 8:25 ·testifying and speaking the Redemptive-word of·the
Ac 14:25 And speaking the Redemptive-word in Perga, they·

G2980 V-AAS-1S λαλήσω (2x)
Jn 12:49 what I·should·declare and what I·should·speak.
1Co 14:6 ·I·benefit yeu, unless I·should·speak to·yeu either

G2980 V-AAS-2P λαλήσητε (2x)
Mt 10:19 ·anxious·about how or what yeu·should·speak, for
Mk 13:11 ·beforehand what yeu·should·speak, nor·even

G2980 V-AAS-3S λαλήσῃ (3x)
Ac 3:22 '«as·many·things·as he·would speak to yeu.»'
Mk 9:6 ·not personally·known what he·should·speak, for
Rv 13:15 ·image of·the Daemonic·Beast should·speak, and

G2980 V-AAS-3P λαλήσωσιν (1x)
Mt 12:36 which if the men·of·clay† should·speak *it*, they·

G2980 V-API-3S ἐλαλήθη (2x)
Lk 2:20 they·heard and saw, just·as it·was·spoken to them.
Heb 11:18 to whom it·was·spoken, "In YiTsaq, a·Seed

G2980 V-APN λαληθῆναι (2x)
Ac 13:42 for·these utterances to·be·spoken to·them at the
Ac 13:46 Redemptive-word of·God first to·be·spoken to·yeu,

G2980 V-APP-GSN λαληθέντος (1x)
Lk 2:17 utterance, the·one being·spoken to·them concerning

G2980 V-APP-GSF λαληθείσης (1x)
Heb 9:19 in *the* Torah-Law already·being·spoken by Moses

G2980 V-APP-GPN λαληθέντων (1x)
Lk 2:18 the·things·that were·being·spoken to them by the

G2980 V-APP-NSM λαληθείς (1x)
Heb 2:2 For if the word being·spoken through angels was

G2980 V-RAI-1S λελάληκα (9x)
Jn 8:40 me, a·man·of·clay† that has·spoken to·yeu the truth,
Jn 14:25 "These·things have·I·spoken to·yeu, while·abiding
Jn 15:3 the Redemptive-word which I·have·spoken to·yeu.
Jn 15:11 "These·things have·I·spoken to·yeu in·order·that
Jn 16:1 "These·things I·have·spoken to·yeu, in·order·that
Jn 16:4 "But·rather these·things have·I·spoken to·yeu, that
Jn 16:6 But·rather because I·have·spoken these·things to·yeu
Jn 16:25 "These·things I·have·spoken to·yeu in proverbs.
Jn 16:33 "I·have·spoken these·things to·yeu, in·order·that in

G2980 V-RAI-3S λελάληκεν (2x)
Jn 9:29 personally·know that God has·spoken to·Moses. But
Jn 12:29 were·saying, "An·angel has·spoken to·him."

G2980 V-RPI-3S λελάληται (1x)
Ac 27:25 according·to that·which has·been·spoken to·me.

G2980 V-RPP-DPN λελαλημένοις (1x)
Lk 1:45 of·the·things having·been·spoken to·her directly·

EG2980 (7x)
Jn 18:23 the wrong. But if *I·spoke* well, why do·you·thrash
Ac 10:15 And a·voice *spoke* to him again for a·second·time,
Ac 15:27 also *to·yeu* the same·things through *spoken* word.
Heb 12:19 *for* a·word not to·be·further *spoken* to·them.
1Pe 4:11 *let·him·be* as *one·speaking* eloquent·words of·God
2Th 2:15 ·were·instructed, whether through *spoken* word or
1Co 7:35 upon·yeu, but·rather *I·speak* pertaining·to *what is*

G2981 λαλιά laliá *n.* (4x)
Roots:G2980 xLangAlso:H4057

G2981 N-NSF λαλιά (2x)
Mt 26:73 them, for even your speech makes you plain.
Mk 14:70 you·are a·Galilean; even your speech is·alike."

G2981 N-ASF λαλιάν (2x)
Jn 4:42 ·longer do·we·trust on·account·of your speech, for
Jn 8:43 "Why do·yeu·not know my speech? *It·is* because

G2982 λαμά lamá *heb.* (2x)
λαμμᾶ lammâ
מָה mạh [Hebrew]
Roots:H4100

G2982 HEB λαμμᾶ (2x)
Mt 27:46 voice, saying, "Eli, Eli, lama shebaq-thani?
Mk 15:34 voice, saying, "Eloi, Eloi, lama shebaq-thani?

Αα Ββ Γγ Δδ Εε Ζζ Ηη Θθ Ιι Κκ Λλ Μμ Νν Ξξ Οο Ππ Ρρ Σσ Ττ Υυ Φφ Χχ Ψψ Ωω

G2983 λαμβάνω lambánō *v.* (265x)
Compare:G1209 G0138 G0680 G2902 See:G5274 G4033-2
xLangEquiv:H3947

G2983.1 V-PAI-3S λαμβάνει (5x)
Jn 21:13 Then Jesus comes and takes the bread and gives *it*
Lk 9:39 And behold, a·spirit takes him, and suddenly he·
Heb 5:4 And not unto·himself *does* anyone take the honor,
Mt 10:38 And whoever does·not take his cross and follow
2Co 11:20 devours *yeu*, if anyone takes *from·yeu*, if anyone
G2983.1 V-PAI-3P λαμβάνουσιν (1x)
Mt 17:25 the kings of·the earth take taxes or a·census·tribute
G2983.1 V-PAM-3S λαμβανέτω (1x)
Rv 22:17 And the·one willing, let·him·take the water of·
G2983.1 V-PAP-NSM λαμβάνων (1x)
2Ti 1:5 while·taking recollection of·the trust without·
G2983.1 V-PAP-NPM λαμβάνοντες (1x)
3Jn 1:7 name, they·went·forth, taking not·one·thing from
G2983.1 V-PPP-NSM λαμβανόμενος (1x)
Heb 5:1 high·priest being·taken from·among men·of·clay†
G2983.1 V-2AAI-1S ἔλαβον (2x)
Mt 27:9 saying, "And they·took the thirty pieces·of·silver,
Rv 10:10 Then I·took the tiny·official·scroll out of·the
G2983.1 V-2AAI-1P ἐλάβομεν (2x)
Lk 5:5 all through the night, we·took nothing·at·all. But at
Mt 16:7 "*It·is* because we·did·not take bread."
G2983.1 V-2AAI-2P ἐλάβετε (1x)
Mt 16:8 ·deliberate among yeurselves that yeu·took no bread
G2983.1 V-2AAI-3S ἔλαβεν (13x)
Jn 6:11 Then Jesus took the loaves·of·bread, and after·
Jn 19:1 Then accordingly, Pilate took Jesus and flogged *him*.
Jn 19:27 that hour, the disciple took her into his·own *home*.
Lk 6:4 into the house of·God and took and ate the Intended·
Lk 20:30 And the second took the *same* wife, and this·man
Lk 20:31 And the third took her, and in·like·manner, the
Ac 24:27 two·years, Porcius Festus took succession *after*
Ac 28:15 upon·seeing *them*, Paul took courage, giving·
Mt 8:17 saying, "He·himself took our sicknesses, and he·
Mk 12:20 brothers, and the first·one took a·wife, and·then
Mk 12:21 And the second took her, and he·died, and neither
1Co 11:23 he·was·handed·over, took *unleavened* bread,
Rv 5:8 And when he·took the official·scroll, the four living·
G2983.1 V-2AAI-3P ἔλαβον (10x)
Jn 12:13 they·took the boughs of·palm·trees, and went·forth
Jn 19:23 Jesus, the soldiers took his outer·garments and
Jn 19:40 So·then they·took the body of·Jesus and bound it
Mt 12:14 upon·going·forth, took consultation against him,
Mt 22:15 the Pharisees took consultation on·specifically·how
Mt 25:3 their·own lamps, did·not take oil among their·own·
Mt 25:4 But the prudent took oil in their containers with their
Mt 27:1 the elders of·the people took consultation against
Mt 27:30 And after·spitting at him, they·took the reed and
Mk 12:22 And the seven took her, and they·did·not leave
G2983.1 V-2AAM-2S λάβε (2x)
Rv 10:8 saying, "Head·on·out! Take the tiny·official·scroll,
Rv 10:9 And he·says to·me, "Take and devour it; and it·
G2983.1 V-2AAM-2P λάβετε (7x)
Jn 18:31 to·them, "Yeu·yeurselves take him and judge him
Jn 19:6 says to·them, "Yeu·yeurselves take him and crucify
Lk 22:17 he·declared, "Take this, and thoroughly·distribute
Mt 26:26 ·the disciples, and he·declared, "Take, eat! This is
Mk 14:22 *it* to·them, and he·declared, "Take, eat! This is
Jac 5:10 Take *for* an·explicit·example, my brothers, the ill·
1Co 11:24 he·broke *it* and declared, "Take, eat! This is my
G2983.1 V-2AAN λαβεῖν (10x)
Jn 10:18 it down, and I·have authority to·take it again. This
Ac 1:25 to·take the allotted·portion of·this service and
Ac 15:14 God visited Gentiles to·take from·among *them* a·
Mt 5:40 ·to·court·to·be·judged and to·take your inner·tunic,
Mt 15:26 "It·is not good to·take the children's bread and to·
Mt 16:5 *of·the sea*, his disciples had·forgotten to·take bread.
Mk 7:27 For it·is not good to·take the children's bread and
Mk 8:14 Now *the disciples* forgot to·take bread, and except
Rv 5:9 "You·are worthy to·take the official·scroll and to·
Rv 6:4 who·is·sitting·down on it, to·take the peace from the
G2983.1 V-2AAO-3S λάβοι (1x)
Ac 1:20 and "May·another take his assignment·of·oversight.
G2983.1 V-2AAP-NSF λαβοῦσα (4x)
Jn 12:3 ·then, taking a·Roman·pound of·extremely·valuable
Mt 13:33 is like leaven, which upon·taking *it*, a·woman
Rm 7:8 Moral·Failure, taking impromptu·occasion through
Rm 7:11 Moral·Failure, taking impromptu·occasion through
G2983.1 V-2AAP-NSF@ λαβοῦσα (1x)
Lk 13:21 leaven, which a·woman took *and* incorporated into
G2983.1 V-2AAP-NSM λαβών (23x)
Jn 13:4 the garments. And taking a·towel, he·tightly·girded
Lk 9:16 And after·taking the five loaves·of·bread and the
Lk 20:29 And the first·one, after·taking a·wife, died
Lk 22:19 And after·taking *unleavened* bread and *and* giving·
Lk 24:30 ·back·to·eat with them, after·taking the bread, he·
Lk 24:43 And taking *it*, he·ate in·the·sight of·them.
Ac 16:3 ·forth together with·him. And taking *TimoThy*, he·
Ac 27:35 And after·declaring these·things and taking bread,
Heb 9:19 to·all the People, after·taking the blood of·calves
Mt 13:31 ·mustard·seed (which after·taking, a·man·of·clay†
Mt 14:19 the grass, and upon·taking the five loaves·of·bread
Mt 15:36 And after·taking the seven loaves·of·bread and the
Mt 26:26 as·they were·eating, after·taking the *unleavened*
Mt 26:27 And after·taking the cup and giving·thanks, he·
Mt 27:24 *that* a·commotion is·being·made, taking water, he·
Mt 27:48 them, after·running and taking a·sponge and
Mt 27:59 And after·taking the body, Joseph swathed it in·a·
Mk 6:41 And after·taking the five loaves·of·bread and the
Mk 8:6 the soil. And after·taking the seven loaves·of·bread
Mk 9:36 And taking a·little·child, he·set him in *the* midst of·
Mk 14:22 as·they were·eating, after·taking *the unleavened*
Mk 14:23 And after·taking the cup *and* giving·thanks, he·
2Co 11:8 other Called·Out·citizenries, taking wages *of·them*,
G2983.1 V-2AAP-NSM@ λαβών (1x)
Lk 13:19 ·seed, which a·man·of·clay† took *and* cast into his
G2983.1 V-2AAP-NPF λαβοῦσαι (2x)
Mt 25:1 to·ten virgins, who, taking their lamps, went·forth
Mt 25:3 ·who *were* foolish, upon·taking their·own lamps,
G2983.1 V-2AAP-NPM λαβόντες (9x)
Ac 2:23 ·God) *was* given·over, being·taken through lawless
Ac 9:25 Then the disciples, taking him by·night, sent·*him*·
Ac 17:9 And after·taking the security·bail personally·from
Ac 17:15 ·going·back, taking *with·them* a·commandment to
Heb 11:29 of·which the Egyptians (taking an·attempt) were·
Mt 27:6 And the chief·priests, taking the pieces·of·silver,
Mt 27:7 And after·taking consultation, from·out of·the·same
Mt 28:12 with the elders and taking consultation, they·gave
Mt 28:15 So taking the money, they·did as they·were·
G2983.1 V-2AAS-1S λάβω (1x)
Jn 10:17 lay·down my soul in·order·that I·may·take it again.
G2983.1 V-2AAS-3S λάβῃ (4x)
Jn 6:7 that each·one of·them may·take some small·piece."
Lk 20:28 childless, that his brother should·take his wife and
Mk 12:19 children, that his brother should·take his wife and
Rv 3:11 not·even·one·man should·take your victor's·crown.
G2983.1 V-RAI-2S εἴληφας (1x)
Rv 11:17 ·is·coming, because you·have·taken your great
G2983.1 V-RAI-3S εἴληφεν (3x)
1Co 10:13 A·proof·trial has·not taken yeu except *that·which*
Rv 5:7 And he·came and has·taken the official·scroll out of·
Rv 8:5 And the angel has·taken the censer·for·frankincense,
EG2983.1 (1x)
1Co 11:25 In·like·manner also, *he·took* the cup after eating·
G2983.2 V-FDI-1P λημψόμεθα (1x)
Jac 3:1 having·seen that we·shall·receive greater judgment.
G2983.2 V-FDI-2P λήψεσθε (7x)
Jn 5:43 ·come in his·own name, that·man yeu·shall·receive.
Jn 16:24 "Request, and yeu·shall·receive, in·order·that yeur
Ac 1:8 But·rather yeu·shall·receive power, with·the Holy
Ac 2:38 and yeu·shall·receive the voluntary·present of·the
Mt 20:7 and whatever may·be right, *that* yeu·shall·receive.'
Mt 21:22 in the prayer while·trusting, yeu·shall·receive."
Mt 23:13 that, yeu·shall·receive more·abundant judgment.
G2983.2 V-FDI-3S λήψεται (9x)
Jn 16:14 ·me, he·shall·receive and shall·announce·in·detail
Jn 16:15 *of·Truth* shall·receive and shall·announce·in·detail
Mt 10:41 name shall·receive a·prophet's payment·of·service;
Mt 10:41 name shall·receive a·righteous·man's payment·of·
Mt 19:29 my name, shall·receive a·hundred·times·over and
Jac 1:7 that he·shall·receive anything personally·from the
Jac 1:12 ·approved, he·shall·receive the victor's·crown of·
1Co 3:8 each·man shall·receive his·own payment·of·service
1Co 3:14 *foundation*, he·shall·receive a·payment·of·service.
G2983.2 V-FDI-3P λήψονται (4x)
Lk 20:47 "These shall·receive more·abundant judgment."
Mt 20:10 *forward*, assumed that they·shall·receive more, yet
Mk 12:40 "These shall·receive more·abundant judgment."
Rm 13:2 ·to *it* shall·receive judgment for·themselves.
G2983.2 V-PAI-1S λαμβάνω (2x)
Jn 5:34 But I·myself receive the testimony not from a·man·
Jn 5:41 "I·do·not receive glory personally·from men·of·
G2983.2 V-PAI-1P λαμβάνομεν (2x)
1Jn 3:22 we·may·request, we·receive personally·from him,
1Jn 5:9 Though we·receive the testimony of·men·of·clay†,
G2983.2 V-PAI-2S λαμβάνεις (1x)
Lk 20:21 and do·not receive *the* personal·appearance *of·any*
G2983.2 V-PAI-2P λαμβάνετε (5x)
Jn 3:11 ·clearly·seen, and yeu·do·not receive our testimony.
Jn 5:43 Father's name, and yeu·do·not receive me. If another
Mk 11:24 ·yeu·are·praying, trust that yeu·do·receive *them*,
Jac 4:3 and do·not receive on·account·that yeu·request
2Co 11:4 ·proclaim, or *if* yeu·receive another spirit, which
G2983.2 V-PAI-3S λαμβάνει (11x)
Jn 3:32 and·yet not·even·one·man receives his testimony.
Jn 4:36 And the·one reaping receives payment·of·service and
Jn 7:23 If a·man-child·of·clay† receives circumcision on a·
Jn 13:20 receiving anyone I·may·send, receives me; and the·
Jn 13:20 and the·one receiving me receives the·one sending
Lk 11:10 everyone, the·one requesting receives, and the·one
Gal 2:6 ·me. God does·not receive *the* personal·appearance
Mt 7:8 For any one requesting receives; and the·one seeking
1Co 9:24 in·fact all run, but *that only* one receives the prize?
Rv 14:9 and its derived·image, and receives *its* etching in
Rv 14:11 night, nor·does anyone receiving the etching of·its
G2983.2 V-PAI-3P λαμβάνουσιν (3x)
Heb 7:8 *are* tithes *that* dying men·of·clay† receive, but there
Mk 4:16 the Redemptive-word, immediately receive it with
Rv 17:12 a·kingdom, but·yet they·do·receive authority as
G2983.2 V-PAM-2P λαμβάνετε (1x)
2Jn 1:10 this instruction, yeu·must·not receive him into a·
G2983.2 V-PAN λαμβάνειν (4x)
Jn 3:27 ·of·clay† is·not able to·receive not·even·one·thing,
Jn 7:39 the·ones trusting in him were·about to·receive, for
Ac 20:35 more supremely·blessed to·give than to·receive.'"
Heb 11:8 which he·was·about to·receive for an·inheritance,
G2983.2 V-PAP-NSM λαμβάνων (6x)
Jn 12:48 ·ignoring me and not receiving my utterances, has
Jn 13:20 I·say to·yeu, the·one receiving anyone I·may·send
Jn 13:20 me; and the·one receiving me receives the·one
Heb 7:9 even Levi, the·one receiving tithes, has·tithed
Mt 13:20 and straight·away *is* receiving it with joy.
Rv 2:17 ·one·man did·know except the·one receiving *it*.'"
G2983.2 V-PAP-NPM λαμβάνοντες (4x)
Jn 5:44 able to·trust, receiving glory personally·from one·
Heb 7:5 the Sons of·Levi receiving the Sanctuary·priesthood,
Mt 17:24 CaperNaum, the·ones receiving the two·drachma
Rm 5:17 more *that* the·ones receiving the superabundance
G2983.2 V-PAS-3S λαμβάνῃ (1x)
Ac 8:19 I·should·lay *my* hands, he·may·receive Holy Spirit.
G2983.2 V-PPP-NSN λαμβανόμενον (1x)
1Ti 4:4 ·*be* discarded *when* being·received with thanksgiving
G2983.2 V-IAI-3P ἐλάμβανον (1x)
Ac 8:17 on them, and they·were·receiving Holy Spirit.
G2983.2 V-2AAI-1S ἔλαβον (3x)

Jn 10:18 This commandment I·received personally·from my
Ac 20:24 the service, which I·received personally·from the
2Co 11:24 Five·times by *the* Jews I·received forty *stripes*
G2983.2 V-2AAI-1P ἐλάβομεν (5x)
Jn 1:16 ·fullness, we·ourselves all received even grace in·
Rm 1:5 through whom we·received grace and commission
Rm 5:11 through whom now we·received the Reconciliation;
1Co 2:12 of·the world *that* we·ourselves received, but·rather
2Jn 1:4 just·as we·received a·commandment personally·from
G2983.2 V-2AAI-2S ἔλαβες (2x)
1Co 4:7 what·do you·have that you·did·not receive? And if
1Co 4:7 receive? And if also you·did·receive *it*, why do·
G2983.2 V-2AAI-2P ἐλάβετε (9x)
Ac 7:53 *yeu* who received the Torah-Law as an·institution
Ac 19:2 to them, "Did·yeu·receive Holy Spirit after·trusting
Gal 3:2 to·learn from yeu, did·yeu·receive the Spirit as·a·
Mt 10:8 ·out demons. Yeu·received freely·without·charge;
Rm 8:15 For yeu·did·not receive a·spirit of·slavery again to
Rm 8:15 but·rather yeu·received a·Spirit of·adoption·as·sons
2Co 11:4 spirit, which yeu·did·not already·receive, or
Col 4:10 concerning whom yeu·received commandments; if
1Jn 2:27 which yeu·yourselves already·received from him
G2983.2 V-2AAI-3S ἔλαβεν (6x)
Jn 19:30 Accordingly, when Jesus received the wine·vinegar
Heb 2:2 and inattentive·disregard received a·just reward·for·
Heb 11:11 also, Sarah herself received a·miracle for an·
Mk 15:23 ·mingled·with·myrrh, but he·did·not receive *it*.
Rm 4:11 And he·received *the* sign of·circumcision, an·
1Pe 4:10 Just·as each·man received a·gracious·bestowment,
G2983.2 V-2AAI-3P ἔλαβον (9x)
Jn 1:12 But as·many·as did·receive him, to·them he·gave
Jn 17:8 to·me, and they·themselves received *them*; and they·
Ac 10:47 not to·be·immersed, *these* who received the Holy
Heb 11:35 Women received their dead from·out of·a·
Heb 11:36 And others received a·trial of·*cruel*·mockings and
Mt 20:9 about the eleventh hour received a·denarius apiece.
Mt 20:10 more, yet they also received *the* same, a·denarius
Rv 17:12 ten kings who did·not·yet receive a·kingdom, but·
Rv 20:4 derived·image, and did·not receive the etching upon
G2983.2 V-2AAM-2P λάβετε (1x)
Jn 20:22 Then he·says to·them, "Receive Holy Spirit!
G2983.2 V-2AAN λαβεῖν (11x)
Jn 6:21 Then they·were·willing to·receive him into the
Jn 14:17 the world is·not able to·receive, because it·does·not
Lk 19:12 a·distant country to·receive for·himself a·kingdom
Ac 3:3 was·asking to·receive a·merciful·act·of·charity.
Ac 3:5 anticipating to·receive something personally·from
Ac 10:43 in him *is* to·receive pardon of·moral·failures
Ac 26:18 God, for·them to·receive pardon of·moral·failures
Heb 10:26 ·failing voluntarily after receiving the recognition
Mt 21:34 slaves to the tenant·farmers, to·receive its fruits.
Rv 4:11 "You·are worthy, O·Lord, to·receive the glory and
Rv 5:12 ·one having·been·slaughtered) to·receive the power
G2983.2 V-2AAO-3S λάβοι (1x)
Ac 25:16 and·also may·receive a·place to·defend·himself
G2983.2 V-2AAP-ASM λαβόντα (1x)
Lk 19:15 with him coming·back after·receiving the kingdom,
G2983.2 V-2AAP-APM λαβόντας (1x)
Rv 19:20 which he·deceived the·ones receiving the etching
G2983.2 V-2AAP-NSF λαβοῦσα (1x)
Heb 2:3 which after·receiving an·initial *announcement*
G2983.2 V-2AAP-NSM λαβών (12x)
Jn 3:33 The·one receiving his testimony did·stamp·his·own·
Jn 13:30 Accordingly, after·receiving the morsel, that·one
Jn 18:3 So·then, after·receiving the battalion and·also
Ac 2:33 right·hand of·God and·also receiving the Promise
Ac 9:19 And after·receiving nourishment, he·was·
Ac 26:10 ·up in·prisons, receiving authority personally·from
Mt 25:16 "And traversing, the·one receiving the five talents·
Mt 25:18 But going·off, the·one receiving the one *talant·of·*
Mt 25:20 "And coming·alongside, the·one receiving the five
Mt 25:22 coming·alongside also, the·one receiving the two
2Pe 1:17 For he·received personally·from Father God honor

1Co 4:7 ·receive *it*, why do·you·boast, as *if* not receiving *it*?
G2983.2 V-2AAP-NPM λαβόντες (2x)
Heb 11:13 according·to trust, not receiving the promises,
Mt 20:11 "And after·receiving *it*, they·were·grumbling
G2983.2 V-2AAS-1P λάβωμεν (2x)
Heb 4:16 of·Grace, in·order·that we·may·receive mercy and
Gal 3:14 — in·order·that we·may·receive the promise of·the
G2983.2 V-2AAS-2P λάβητε (1x)
Rv 18:4 in·order·that yeu·may·not receive from·out of·her
G2983.2 V-2AAS-3S λάβῃ (4x)
Mk 10:30 who·should·not receive a·hundred·times·over now
Mk 12:2 in·order·that he·may·receive directly·from the
Jac 5:7 it, until he·should·receive early·autumn and latter·
1Co 14:5 the convened·Called·Out·assembly may·receive.
G2983.2 V-2AAS-3P λάβωσιν (3x)
Ac 8:15 concerning them, that they·may·receive Holy Spirit.
Heb 9:15 having·been·called·forth may·receive the promise
1Co 9:25 *do·this* in·order·that they·may·receive a·corruptible
G2983.2 V-RAI-1S εἴληφα (1x)
Rv 2:27 ' as I·also have·received *authority* personally·from
G2983.2 V-RAI-2S εἴληφας (1x)
Rv 3:3 by·what·means you·have·received and heard, so·then
G2983.2 V-RAP-NSM εἰληφώς (2x)
Ac 16:24 who, upon·having·received such a·charge, cast
Mt 25:24 ·alongside, the·one having·received the one talant·
EG2983.2 (1x)
Mt 25:17 And likewise, the·one *having·received* the two, he
G2983.3 V-2AAI-1S ἔλαβον (2x)
Php 3:12 Not that even·now I·took·hold·of *it*, or even·now
2Co 12:16 shrewdly·cunning, I·took·hold·of yeu with·guile.
G2983.3 V-2AAI-3S ἔλαβεν (3x)
Jn 13:12 he·washed their feet and took·hold·of his garments,
Lk 5:26 And astonishment took·hold·of absolutely·all, and
Lk 7:16 a·reverent·fear·and·awe took·hold·of absolutely·all
G2983.3 V-2AAP-NSM λαβών (2x)
Mt 17:27 *(worth four drachmas)*. Taking·hold·of that, give
Php 2:7 himself, taking·hold·of *the* fundamental·nature of·
G2983.3 V-2AAP-NPM λαβόντες (5x)
Mt 21:35 the tenant·farmers, after·taking·hold of·his slaves,
Mt 21:39 And after·taking·hold·of him, they·cast·*him*·forth
Mt 26:52 the·ones taking·hold·of a·dagger shall·completely·
Mk 12:3 "But after·taking·hold·of *him*, they·thrashed him
Mk 12:8 And after·taking·hold·of him, they·killed *him* and
G2983.4 V-2AAI-2P ἐλάβετε (2x)
Mt 16:9 *men*, and how·many wicker·baskets yeu·took·up?
Mt 16:10 *men*, and how·many woven·baskets yeu·took·up?
G2983.5 V-2AAP-NSM λαβών (1x)
2Pe 1:9 already·becoming deathly·oblivious of·the

G2984 Λάμεχ Lámĕch *n/p.* (1x)
לֶמֶךְ lemek [Hebrew]
Roots:H3929
G2984 N/P-PRI Λάμεχ (1x)
Lk 3:36 *son* of·Shem, *son* of·Noach, *son* of·Lemek,

G2985 λαμπάς lampás *n.* (9x)
Roots:G2989 Compare:G3088 G5322 See:G2986 G2987 G2988 G2987-1
G2985.1 N-NPF λαμπάδες (3x)
Ac 20:8 And there·was a·significant·number·of lamps in the
Mt 25:8 of·yeur oil, because our lamps are·extinguished.'
Rv 4:5 and *there·are* seven lamps of·fire being·set·ablaze
G2985.1 N-APF λαμπάδας (3x)
Mt 25:1 who, taking their lamps, went·forth to approach·
Mt 25:3 foolish, upon·taking their·own lamps, did·not take
Mt 25:7 are·awakened, and they·trimmed their lamps.
G2985.1 N-GPF λαμπάδων (1x)
Mt 25:4 prudent took oil in their containers with their lamps.
G2985.2 N-NSF λαμπάς (1x)
Rv 8:10 ·the heaven, being·set·ablaze as a·torch, and it·fell
G2985.2 N-GPF λαμπάδων (1x)
Jn 18:3 there with searchlights and torches and weapons.

G2986 λαμπρός lamprós *adj.* (9x)
Roots:G2989 Compare:G3045 G3167 G5459 G2298 See:G2985 G2987 G2988 xLangAlso:H1966
G2986.1 A-NSM λαμπρός (1x)
Rv 22:16 the star, the·one radiant and brilliantly·dawning."
G2986.1 A-ASM λαμπρόν (1x)
Rv 22:1 ·pure river of·water of·life-above, radiant as crystal,
G2986.1 A-ASN λαμπρόν (2x)
Rv 15:6 ·dressed·themselves in·pure and radiant flax·linen,
Rv 19:8 ·be·arrayed·with fine·linen, pure and radiant." (for
G2986.1 A-DSF λαμπρᾷ (1x)
Ac 10:30 stood·still in·the·sight of·me in radiant clothing,
G2986.3 A-NPN λαμπρά (1x)
Rv 18:14 ·things and the splendid·things went·away from
G2986.3 A-ASF λαμπράν (2x)
Lk 23:11 *him* and arraying him in·splendid clothing, he·sent
Jac 2:3 the·one prominently·wearing the splendid clothing,
G2986.3 A-DSF λαμπρᾷ (1x)
Jac 2:2 *with* a·prominent·gold·ring, in splendid clothing, and

G2987 λαμπρότης lamprótēs *n.* (1x)
Roots:G2986 Compare:G0796 G5458 See:G2985 G2988 G2987-1
G2987 N-ASF λαμπρότητα (1x)
Ac 26:13 ·light from·heaven beyond the brilliance of·the sun

G2988 λαμπρῶς lamprỗs *adv.* (1x)
Roots:G2986 Compare:G0134 See:G2985 G2986 G2987
G2988.2 ADV λαμπρῶς (1x)
Lk 16:19 ·cloak and fine·linen, splendidly being·merry each

G2989 λάμπω lámpō *v.* (7x)
Compare:G0826 G1823 G2014 G5316 G5461 See:G2985 G2986 G2987 G2988 G1584 xLangAlso:H5050 H5051
G2989 V-PAI-3S λάμπει (2x)
Lk 17:24 *part* under heaven, radiates·brightly to the *other·*
Mt 5:15 lampstand, and it·radiates·brightly for·all the·ones
G2989 V-AAI-3S ἔλαμψεν (3x)
Ac 12:7 *him*, and a·light radiated·brightly in the jailhouse.
Mt 17:2 And his face radiated·brightly as the sun, and his
2Co 4:6 out of·darkness, who did·radiate·brightly in our
G2989 V-AAM-3S λαμψάτω (1x)
Mt 5:16 *let* yeur light radiate·brightly before the men·of·
G2989 V-AAN λάμψαι (1x)
2Co 4:6 *for* light to·radiate·brightly out of·darkness, who

G2990 λανθάνω lanthánō *v.* (6x)
Compare:G2928 See:G0227 G3024 G1950
G2990.ª V-PAN λανθάνειν (1x)
Ac 26:26 not·even·one·thing, to·be·hidden from·him; for
G2990.ª V-2AAI-3S ἔλαθεν (1x)
Lk 8:47 seeing that she·was·not hidden, came trembling;
G2990.1 V-2AAN λαθεῖν (1x)
Mk 7:24 ·man to·know *it*, but he·was·not able to·lay·hidden.
G2990.2 V-PAI-3S λανθάνει (1x)
2Pe 3:5 For this is·oblivious·to them (willingly) that by·the
G2990.2 V-PAM-3S λανθανέτω (1x)
2Pe 3:8 this one·thing, do·not be·oblivious, O·yeu beloved,
G2990.2 V-2AAI-3P@ ἔλαθον (1x)
Heb 13:2 this some are·hosting angels, being·oblivious *of·it*.

G2991 λα•ξευτός laxĕutós *adj.* (1x)
Roots:G2991-2 Compare:G2998-1
G2991.3 A-DSN λαξευτῷ (1x)
Lk 23:53 *that·was* chiseled·out·within·a·mass·of·stone,

G2992 λαός laós *n.* (150x)
Compare:G1218 G1577 xLangEquiv:H5971 A5972 xLangAlso:H3816
G2992.1 N-NSM λαός (15x)
Jn 8:2 ·Atrium, and all the people were·coming to him.
Lk 1:21 And the people were intently·awaiting Zacharias,
Lk 7:29 *this*, all the people already·being·immersed·in the
Lk 18:43 And all the people seeing *it*, gave strong·praise to·
Lk 19:48 ·all the people were·very·attentive to·hear him,
Lk 20:6 ·clay†,' all the people shall·fully·stone us to·death,
Lk 21:38 And all the people were·rising·early·and·going to

Lk 23:35 And the people stood *there* observing.
Ac 3:9 And all the people saw him walking·along and
Ac 3:11 and John, all the people ran·together toward them in
Ac 5:13 to·them, but·yet the people were·magnifying them;
Ac 18:10 ·account·that I·have for·myself many people in this
Mt 4:16 the people, the·ones who·are·fully·sitting in
Mt 27:25 And responding, all the people declared, "His
1Pe 2:10 ·ones *who* in·times·past *were* not a·people, but *are*

G2992.1 N-NPM λαοί (3x)
Ac 4:25 and *did* peoples meditate·upon empty·things?
Rm 15:11 And applaud him, all the peoples!'"
Rv 17:15 the Prostitute sits·down, are peoples, and crowds,

G2992.1 N-ASM λαόν (23x)
Lk 3:18 he·was·proclaiming·good·news to·the people.
Lk 3:21 when absolutely·all the people were·immersed,
Lk 9:13 we·ourselves should·buy food for all these people."
Lk 20:1 with·him instructing the people in the Sanctuary·
Lk 20:9 to·relay this parable to·the people, "A·certain man·
Lk 20:19 ·against them, yet they·feared the people.
Lk 22:2 they·may·eliminate him, for they·feared the people.
Lk 23:5 saying, "He·incites the people, instructing in all
Lk 23:13 the chief·priests, the rulers, and the people, Pilate
Lk 23:14 to·me as one·turning·away the people, and behold,
Ac 3:12 *this*, Peter answered to·the people, "Men, Israelites,
Ac 4:1 as·they were·speaking to·the people, the priests·that·
Ac 4:2 ·of them instructing the people and fully·proclaiming
Ac 4:17 any·further among the people— with·threatening,
Ac 4:21 ·punish them on·account·of the people, because all
Ac 5:25 in the Sanctuary·Atrium and instructing the people."
Ac 5:26 for they·feared the people, lest they·should·be·
Ac 5:37 a·significant·number·of people right·behind him.
Ac 6:12 And they·jointly·stirred·up the people, the elders,
Ac 13:15 of·exhortation specifically·for the people, say·on."
Ac 21:39 you, freely·permit me to·speak to·the people."
Mk 11:32 *·stopped, for* they·were·afraid·of the people, for
Rv 14:6 nation, and tribe, and native·tongue, and people,

G2992.1 N-DSM λαῷ (15x)
Lk 2:10 to·yeu of·great joy, which shall·be to·all the people.
Lk 21:23 ·need upon the land and WRATH on this people.
Ac 5:12 and wonders occurred among the people— (and
Ac 5:20 speak in the Sanctuary·Atrium to·the people all the
Ac 5:34 among·all the people, commandingly·ordered to·
Ac 6:8 wonders and miraculous·signs among the people.
Ac 10:2 many merciful·acts for·the people and continually
Ac 10:41 not to·all the people, but·rather to·witnesses
Ac 10:42 us to·officially·proclaim to·the people, and to·
Ac 12:4 to·bring him out to·the people after the Passover.
Ac 21:40 motioned with·his hand to·the people. And with·a·
Mt 4:23 every illness and every disease among the people.
Mt 9:35 every illness and every disease among the people.
Mt 26:5 lest a·commotion should·occur among the people."
Mt 27:64 him, and should·declare to·the people, 'He·is·

G2992.1 N-DPM λαοῖς (2x)
Ac 4:27 together with·Gentiles and with·peoples of·IsraEl,
Rv 10:11 to·prophesy again over many peoples, and nations,

G2992.1 N-GSM λαοῦ (21x)
Lk 1:10 And the entire multitude of·the people were praying
Lk 3:15 And the people were·intently·awaiting, and all·men
Lk 6:17 and a·large multitude of·people from all *over* Judea
Lk 7:1 in the hearing of·the people, he·entered into
Lk 8:47 in·the·sight of·all the people, on·account·of what
Lk 19:47 of·the people were·seeking to·completely·destroy
Lk 20:26 in·the·direct·presence of·the people. And
Lk 20:45 And in·the·hearing of·all the people, he·declared
Lk 22:66 ·of elders of·the people were·gathered·together
Lk 23:27 him a·large multitude of·the people, and·also of·
Lk 24:19 and word directly·before God and all the people.
Ac 12:11 all the anticipated·evil of·the people of·Judea."
Ac 21:30 was·stirred, and the people came running·together.
Ac 21:36 For the multitude of·the people were·following,
Mt 2:4 and *the* scribes of·the people, he·was·inquiring
Mt 21:23 and the elders of·the people came·alongside him,
Mt 26:3 the elders of·the people were·gathered·together in
Mt 26:47 from the chief·priests and elders of·the people.
Mt 27:1 and the elders of·the people took consultation
Mk 14:2 lest there·shall·be a·commotion of·the people."
Rv 5:9 tribe, and native·tongue, and people, and nation;

G2992.1 N-GPM λαῶν (3x)
Lk 2:31 which you·made·ready in front of·all the peoples;
Rv 7:9 nations, and tribes, and peoples, and native·tongues,
Rv 11:9 And from·among the peoples and tribes and native·

EG2992.1 (7x)
Ac 5:15 such·for *the people* to·bear·forth the sick in·each·of
Mk 1:5 to him, and·also the *people* of·JeruSalem, and all
Mk 5:38 and observes a·commotion, *people* weeping and
Mk 6:41 ·that they·should·place·*them*·before *the people*, and
Rm 11:32 ·confined all the *peoples* to an·obstinate·attitude,
Rm 11:32 ·order·that he·may·show·mercy to·all the *peoples*.
2Ti 3:5 So·then, turn·yourself·away·and·avoid these *people*!

G2992.2 N-NSM λαός (10x)
Ac 7:17 God swore to·AbRaham, the People grew and were·
Heb 7:11 under it the People had·the·Torah-Law·enacted),
Mt 15:8 " This People draws·near to·me with·their mouth
Mk 7:6 " This People deeply·honors me with·*their*·lips, but
Rm 9:26 'Yeu *are* not my People,' there they·shall·be·called
1Pe 2:9 a·holy nation, a·People for an·acquired·possession
1Pe 2:10 a·people, but *are* now God's People, the·ones not
1Co 10:7 ·been·written, "The People sat·down to·eat and
2Co 6:16 they·themselves shall·be my·own distinct People.
Rv 18:4 from·among her, my People, in·order·that yeu·may·

G2992.2 N-NPM λαοί (1x)
Rv 21:3 and they·themselves shall·be his Peoples, and God,

G2992.2 N-ASM λαόν (21x)
Lk 1:17 to·make·ready a·People having·been·fully·prepared
Lk 7:16 "God visited his People."
Ac 2:47 having grace alongside all the People. And the Lord
Ac 13:17 fathers, and elevated the People in the Sojourning
Ac 13:31 to JeruSalem, who are his witnesses to the People.
Ac 15:14 Gentiles to·take from·among *them* a·People for his
Ac 28:26 "Traverse toward this People, and declare,
Heb 7:5 to·receive·tithes·of the People according·to the
Heb 8:10 they·themselves shall·be my·own distinct People.
Heb 9:19 both the official·scroll itself and all the People,
Heb 10:30 And again, "'Yahweh shall·sheriff his People.'"
Heb 13:12 he·may·make·holy the People through his·own
Mt 1:21 for he·himself shall·save his People from their
Mt 2:6 ·leading, one·who shall·shepherd my People IsraEl.
Rm 9:25 "I·shall·call *them* 'My People,' *who·were* not my
Rm 9:25 People,' *who·were* not my People, and *call·her*
Rm 10:21 my hands toward a·People being·obstinate and
Rm 11:1 ¿!·Did God shove·away his People? May·it·never
Rm 11:2 did·not shove·away his People which he·foreknew.
Jud 1:5 Yahweh, after·*first*·saving a·People out of·Egypt's
Tit 2:14 to·himself '*his·own* extraordinary People,' *one being*

G2992.2 N-DSM λαῷ (12x)
Lk 1:68 he·visited and made a·ransoming for·his People!
Lk 1:77 knowledge of·Salvation to·his People unto a·pardon
Ac 4:10 to·yeu all, and to·all the People of·IsraEl, that by
Ac 13:24 ·in·advance by·John to·all the People of·IsraEl,
Ac 19:4 saying to·the People that they·should·trust in the·
Ac 26:23 to·fully·proclaim light to·the People and to·the
Ac 28:17 ·even·one·thing antagonistic to·the People or to·the
Heb 4:9 ·remaining a·Sabbath·Rest for·the People of·God.
Heb 9:19 by Moses to·all the People, after·taking the blood
Heb 11:25 ·maltreated·together with·the People of·God than
2Pe 2:1 ·to·be false·prophets also among the People, even as
1Co 14:21 other lips I·shall·speak to·this People; and in·this·

G2992.2 N-GSM λαοῦ (17x)
Jn 11:50 ·of·clay† should·die on·behalf·of·the People, and
Jn 18:14 ·be·completely·destroyed on·behalf·of·the People.
Lk 2:32 of·Gentiles and *for the* glory of·your People IsraEl."
Ac 3:23 ' "shall·be·exterminated from·among the People."
Ac 4:8 to them, "Rulers of·the People, and elders of·IsraEl,
Ac 7:34 the harmful·treatment of·my People *who·are* in
Ac 13:17 The God of·this People IsraEl selected our fathers,
Ac 21:28 all·men everywhere against the People, the
Ac 23:5 declare *anything* badly of·a·ruler of·your People.'"
Ac 26:17 you out from·among the People, and *from·among*
Ac 28:27 the heart of·this People became·thickly·calloused,
Heb 2:17 ·atonement·for the moral·failures of·the People.
Heb 5:3 (just·as concerning the People, in·this·manner also
Heb 7:27 ·afterward *on·behalf* of·the·ones of·the People, for
Heb 9:7 and *on·behalf* of·the ignorant·errors of·the People,
Mt 13:15 the heart of·this People became·thickly·calloused,
Rm 15:10 " Be·merry, O·Gentiles, with his People."

G2993 Λαο•δίκεια Laôdíkêia *n/l.* (5x)
Roots:G2992 G1349

G2993.2 N/L-ASF Λαοδίκειαν (1x)
Rv 1:11 to Sardis, and to PhilAdelphia, and to LaoDicea."

G2993.2 N/L-DSF Λαοδικείᾳ (3x)
Col 2:1 and *for* the·ones in LaoDicea, and *for* as·many·as
Col 4:13 yeu, and the·ones in LaoDicea, and the·ones in
Col 4:15 Greet the brothers in LaoDicea, and *greet* Nymphas

G2993.2 N/L-GSF Λαοδικείας (1x)
Col 4:16 should·read·aloud the *letter* from·out of·LaoDicea.

G2994 Λαο•δικεύς Laôdikêús *n/g.* (2x)
Roots:G2993

G2994 N/G-GPM Λαοδικέων (2x)
Col 4:16 convened·Called·Out·assembly of·LaoDiceans, and
Rv 3:14 ·the Called·Out·citizenry of·the·LaoDiceans write,

G2995 λάρυγξ lárynx *n.* (1x)
Compare:G5333-2
xLangEquiv:H1627

G2995 N-NSM λάρυγξ (1x)
Rm 3:13 "'Their throat *is* a·grave having·been·opened·up;

G2996 Λασαία Lasaía *n/l.* (1x)

G2996 N/L-NSF Λασαία (1x)
Ac 27:8 which was near *the* city *of* Lasea *(in·Crete)*.

G2997 λάσχω láschō *v.* (1x)

G2997 V-AAI-3S ἐλάκησεν (1x)
Ac 1:18 ·downhill headfirst, he·burst·open in·the·middle,

G2998 λα•τομέω latômêō *v.* (2x)
Roots:G2998-1 Compare:G2991-2 G2875 G4249 G5058-2 G0594-1 See:G2991 G2998-2 xLangAlso:H2672 H3738

G2998 V-AAI-3S ἐλατόμησεν (1x)
Mt 27:60 chamber·tomb, which he·hewed·out in the solid·

G2998 V-RPP-NSN λελατομημένον (1x)
Mk 15:46 which was having·been·hewed out of·solid·rock,

G2999 λατρεία latrêía *n.* (5x)
Roots:G3000 Compare:G3009 See:G2999-1 G2999-2 xLangEquiv:A6402 xLangAlso:H5656

G2999 N-NSF λατρεία (1x)
Rm 9:4 ·of·the·Torah-Law, and the ritual·ministry *to·God*,

G2999 N-ASF λατρείαν (2x)
Jn 16:2 yeu might·presume to·offer a·ritual·ministry to·God.
Rm 12:1 to·God, *which·is* yeur reasonable ritual·ministry.

G2999 N-APF λατρείας (1x)
Heb 9:6 Tabernacle, further·finishing the ritual·ministries.

G2999 N-GSF λατρείας (1x)
Heb 9:1 was·having regulations of·ritual·ministry *to·God*,

G3000 λατρεύω latrêúō *v.* (21x)
Compare:G3008 G1247 See:G2999
xLangEquiv:A6399 xLangAlso:H6398 H5647

G3000 V-FAI-2S λατρεύσεις (2x)
Lk 4:8 and "to·him only shall·you·ritually·minister.'"
Mt 4:10 and "to·him only shall·you·ritually·minister.'"

G3000 V-FAI-3P λατρεύσουσιν (2x)
Ac 7:7 ·shall·come·forth and shall·ritually·minister to·me in
Rv 22:3 in it; and his slaves shall·ritually·minister to·him.

G3000 V-PAI-1S λατρεύω (4x)
Ac 24:14 ·sect, in·this·manner I·ritually·minister to·God my
Ac 27:23 ·him·whose I·am and to·whom I·ritually·minister,
Rm 1:9 my witness, to·whom I·ritually·minister in my spirit
2Ti 1:3 to·God (to·whom I·ritually·minister from *my*

G3000 V-PAI-3P λατρεύουσιν (2x)
Heb 8:5 who ritually·minister unto·an·explicit·pattern and
Rv 7:15 ·the throne of·God and ritually·minister to·him day

G3000 V-PAN λατρεύειν (3x)
Lk 1:74 enemies) to·ritually·minister to·him without·fear
Ac 7:42 handed them over to·ritually·minister to·the host of·
Heb 9:14 ·order·for *yeu* to·ritually·minister to·the·living God
G3000 V-PAP-ASM λατρεύοντα (1x)
Heb 9:9 ·to *the* conscience of·the·one ritually·ministering;
G3000 V-PAP-APM λατρεύοντας (1x)
Heb 10:2 ·offered through the·ones ritually·ministering, once
G3000 V-PAP-NSN λατρεῦον (1x)
Ac 26:7 earnestness, while·ritually·ministering *to·God* night
G3000 V-PAP-NSF λατρεύουσα (1x)
Lk 2:37 ·Estate, ritually·ministering *to·God* with·fastings
G3000 V-PAP-NPM λατρεύοντες (2x)
Heb 13:10 the·ones who·are·ritually·ministering in·the
Php 3:3 the·ones ritually·ministering to·God in·spirit, and
G3000 V-PAS-1P λατρεύωμεν (1x)
Heb 12:28 which we·may·ritually·minister to·God quite·
G3000 V-AAI-3P ἐλάτρευσαν (1x)
Rm 1:25 reverenced and ritually·ministered to·the creation

G3001 λάχανον láchanôn *n.* (4x)
Compare:G1008 G5451 xLangAlso:H3419
G3001.1 N-ASN λάχανον (1x)
Lk 11:42 and the rue and all·manner·of garden·plants, and
G3001.1 N-APN λάχανα (1x)
Rm 14:2 but the·one being·weak, eats garden·plants.
G3001.1 N-GPN λαχάνων (2x)
Mt 13:32 it·is bigger·than the garden·plants and becomes a·
Mk 4:32 becomes greater·than all the garden·plants, and it·

G3002 Λεββαῖος Lĕbbaîôs *n/p.* (2x)
See:G2280
G3002.2 N/P-NSM Λεββαῖος (1x)
Mt 10:3 and *Judas called* Lebbaeus, the·one being·
EG3002.2 (1x)
Mk 3:18 , and *Judas called Lebbaeus* Thaddaeus, and

G3003 λεγεών lĕgĕṓn *n.* (4x)
Compare:G4686
G3003.1 N-NSM λεγεών (2x)
Lk 8:30 name?" And he·declared, "Legion," because many
Mk 5:9 "My name *is* Legion, because we·are many.
G3003.1 N-ASM λεγεῶνα (1x)
Mk 5:15 the·one *who·was* having·held the legion. And they·
G3003.1 N-APM λεγεῶνας (1x)
Mt 26:53 ·present to·me more than twelve legions of·angels?

G3004 λέγω lĕgō *v.* (1370x)
Compare:G2036 G5346 G4483 G2980 See:G3056 G4816 xLangAlso:H0559 H1696 H5002
G3004.1 V-PAI-1S λέγω (206x)
Jn 1:51 "Certainly, most·certainly, I·say to·yeu, from this·
Jn 3:3 "Certainly, most·certainly, I·say to·you, unless
Jn 3:5 "Certainly, most·certainly, I·say to·you, unless
Jn 3:11 "Certainly, most·certainly, I·say to·you, we·speak
Jn 4:35 the harvest'? Behold, I·say to·yeu, lift·up yeur eyes
Jn 5:19 "Certainly, most·certainly, I·say to·yeu, the Son is·
Jn 5:24 "Certainly, most·certainly, I·say to·yeu, the·one
Jn 5:25 "Certainly, most·certainly, I·say to·yeu, an·hour is·
Jn 5:34 a·man·of·clay†, but·rather I·say these·things that
Jn 6:26 "Certainly, most·certainly, I·say to·yeu, yeu·seek
Jn 6:32 "Certainly, most·certainly, I·say to·yeu, Moses has·
Jn 6:47 "Certainly, most·certainly, I·say to·yeu, the·one
Jn 6:53 "Certainly, most·certainly, I·say to·yeu, unless yeu·
Jn 8:26 me is true, and·I say to the world these·things which
Jn 8:34 "Certainly, most·certainly, I·say to·yeu that any one
Jn 8:45 "And because I·myself say the truth, yeu·do·not trust
Jn 8:46 moral·failure? And if·what I·say *is the* truth, why·do
Jn 8:51 "Certainly, most·certainly, I·say to·yeu, if anyone
Jn 8:58 "Certainly, most·certainly, I·say to·yeu, prior·to
Jn 10:1 "Certainly, most·certainly, I·say to·yeu, the·one not
Jn 10:7 "Certainly, most·certainly, I·say to·yeu, I AM the
Jn 12:24 "Certainly, most·certainly, I·say to·yeu, unless the
Jn 13:16 "Certainly, most·certainly, I·say to·yeu, a·slave is
Jn 13:18 "I·do·not say *this* concerning yeu all.
Jn 13:20 "Certainly, most·certainly, I·say to·yeu, the·one
Jn 13:21 "Certainly, most·certainly, I·say to·yeu that one
Jn 13:33 to·come,' so·also do·I·say to·yeu at·this·moment.
Jn 13:38 Certainly, most·certainly, I·say to·you, a·rooster,
Jn 14:12 "Certainly, most·certainly, I·say to·yeu, the·one
Jn 16:7 "But·yet I·myself say to·yeu the truth; it·is·more·
Jn 16:20 "Certainly, most·certainly, I·say to·yeu, that yeu
Jn 16:23 "Certainly, most·certainly, I·say to·yeu, as·many·
Jn 16:26 in my name, and I·do·not say to·yeu that I·myself
Jn 21:18 "Certainly, most·certainly, I·say to·you, when
Lk 3:8 *for·our* father.' For I·say to·yeu that God is·able
Lk 4:24 Then he·declared, "Certainly I·say to·yeu, that not·
Lk 4:25 "But I·say to·yeu in truth, many widows were in
Lk 5:24 ·the·one having·been·paralyzed), "I·say to·you, be·
Lk 6:27 "But·rather I·say to·yeu, to·the·ones hearing: "Love
Lk 6:46 Lord, Lord,' and do·not do the·things·which I·say?
Lk 7:8 soldiers under my·own·self, and I·say to·this·man,
Lk 7:9 ·the crowd following him, "I·say to·yeu, not·even in
Lk 7:14 ·declared, "Young·man, I·say to·you, be·awakened
Lk 7:26 A·prophet? Yes, I·say to·yeu, and much·more
Lk 7:28 "For I·say to·yeu, among those·born of·women
Lk 7:47 "As·such, on·account·of·grace I·say to·you, her
Lk 9:27 "But I·say to·yeu truly, there·are some of·the·ones
Lk 10:12 "But I·say to·yeu, that it·shall·be more·tolerable at
Lk 10:24 For I·say to·yeu, that many prophets and kings
Lk 11:8 "I·say to·yeu, even·though already·rising·up, he·
Lk 11:9 "And·I·myself say to·yeu, request, and it·shall·be·
Lk 11:51 *of·God.* Yes, I·say to·yeu, it·shall·be·sought·out
Lk 12:4 "And I·say to·yeu, my friends, do·not be·afraid of
Lk 12:5 the Hell·Canyon. Yes, I·say to·yeu, fear this·one.
Lk 12:8 "Also I·say to·yeu, anyone who·should·affirm me
Lk 12:22 "On·account·of that, I·say to·yeu, do·not be·
Lk 12:27 they·do·not·even spin, and·yet I·say to·yeu, not·
Lk 12:37 shall·find keeping·alert. Certainly I·say to·yeu,
Lk 12:44 Truly I·say to·yeu, that he·shall·fully·establish him
Lk 12:51 ·give peace on the·earth? I·say to·yeu, no·indeed,
Lk 12:59 I·say to·you, no, you·should·not come·forth from·
Lk 13:3 "I·say to·yeu, no·indeed, but·yet, unless yeu·should·
Lk 13:5 "I·say to·yeu, no·indeed, but·yet, unless yeu·should·
Lk 13:24 gate, because many, I·say to·yeu, shall·seek to·
Lk 13:27 But he·shall·declare, 'I·say to·yeu, I·do·not
Lk 13:35 And certainly I·say to·yeu, no, yeu·should·not see
Lk 14:24 'For I·say to·yeu, that not·even·one of·those men,
Lk 15:7 "I·say to·yeu, that in·this·manner, there·shall·be
Lk 15:10 "In·this·manner, I·say to·yeu, *that such* joy occurs
Lk 16:9 "And·I say to·yeu: Make friends for·yeurselves
Lk 17:34 "I·say to·yeu, in·that night there·shall·be two
Lk 18:8 I·say to·yeu that he·shall·make retribution for·them
Lk 18:14 "I·say to·yeu *that* this·man walked·down to his
Lk 18:17 Certainly I·say to·yeu, whoever, if he·should·not
Lk 18:29 And he·declared to·them, "Certainly I·say to·yeu,
Lk 19:26 "(For I·say to·yeu, that to·any one having, *more*
Lk 19:40 he·declared to·them, "I·say to·yeu that if these
Lk 20:8 "Neither *do* I·myself say to·yeu by what·kind·of
Lk 21:3 And he·declared, "Truly I·say to·yeu, that this
Lk 21:32 "Certainly I·say to·yeu, this generation·of·
Lk 22:16 For I·say to·yeu that no, I·should·not eat any·
Lk 22:18 For I·say to·yeu: No, I·should·not·ever drink of·the
Lk 22:34 And he·declared, "I·say to·you, Peter, a·rooster,
Lk 22:37 "For I·say to·yeu, that still it·is·mandatory·for this
Lk 23:43 declared to·him, "Certainly I·say to·you, today,
Ac 5:38 now *these are* the·things I·say to·yeu: Withdraw
Gal 1:9 ·have·already·stated, so at·this·moment I·say again,
Gal 3:17 And this I·say, Torah-Law (the·one having·
Gal 4:1 Now I·say *that* the heir, for·a·span·of time (as·long·
Gal 5:2 See, I Paul say to·yeu, that if yeu·should·be·
Gal 5:16 So I·say, walk in·Spirit, and no, yeu·would·not
Mt 3:9 *for·our* father.' For I·say to·yeu that God is·able
Mt 5:18 "For certainly I·say to·yeu, until the heaven and the
Mt 5:20 "For I·say to·yeu, that unless yeur righteousness
Mt 5:22 But I·myself say to·yeu that any one being·angry
Mt 5:26 Certainly I·say to·you, no, you·should·not come·
Mt 5:28 But I·myself say to·yeu that everyone looking·upon
Mt 5:32 But I·myself say to·yeu, that whoever should·
Mt 5:34 "But I·myself say to·yeu not to·swear at·all: neither
Mt 5:39 But I·myself say to·yeu, not to·stand·opposed·to the
Mt 5:44 But I·myself say to·yeu, love yeur enemies, bless
Mt 6:2 by the men·of·clay†. Certainly I·say to·yeu, they·
Mt 6:5 to·the men·of·clay†. Certainly I·say to·yeu, they·
Mt 6:16 *to·be* fasting. Certainly I·say to·yeu that they·
Mt 6:25 "On·account·of that, I·say to·yeu, do·not be·
Mt 6:29 And·yet I·say to·yeu, not·even Solomon, in all his
Mt 8:9 soldiers under my·own·self, and I·say to·this *man*,
Mt 8:10 ·ones following, "Certainly I·say to·yeu, not·even
Mt 8:11 And I·say to·yeu that many shall·come from east
Mt 10:15 Certainly I·say to·yeu, it·shall·be more·tolerable
Mt 10:23 into the other, for certainly I·say to·yeu, no, yeu·
Mt 10:27 "What I·say to·yeu in the darkness, declare in the
Mt 10:42 in a·disciple's name, certainly I·say to·yeu, no, he·
Mt 11:9 A·prophet? Yes, I·say to·yeu, and much·more·
Mt 11:11 "Certainly I·say to·yeu, among those·born of·
Mt 11:22 Moreover I·say to·yeu, it·shall·be more·tolerable
Mt 11:24 So·even·more, I·say to·yeu that it·shall·be more·
Mt 12:6 "But I·say to·yeu that one·greater·than the
Mt 12:31 "On·account·of that, I·say to·yeu, all·manner·of
Mt 12:36 "But I·say to·yeu, that for·every idle utterance,
Mt 13:17 For certainly I·say to·yeu, that many prophets and
Mt 16:18 And I·also say to·you that you·yourself are Peter·
Mt 16:28 "Certainly I·say to·yeu, there·are some of·the·ones
Mt 17:12 "But I·say to·yeu, that EliJah came even·now, and
Mt 17:20 ·of yeur lack·of·trust. For certainly I·say to·yeu, if
Mt 18:3 and declared, "Certainly I·say to·yeu, unless yeu·
Mt 18:10 one of·these little·ones, for I·say to·yeu that
Mt 18:13 he·should·happen to·find it, certainly I·say to·yeu,
Mt 18:18 "Certainly I·say to·yeu, as·many·things·as yeu·
Mt 18:19 "Again I·say to·yeu, that if two of·yeu should·
Mt 18:22 says to·him, "I·do·not say to·you, up·to seven·
Mt 19:9 And I·say to·yeu, that whoever should·divorce his
Mt 19:23 to·his disciples, "Certainly I·say to·yeu that *it·is*
Mt 19:24 "And again I·say to·yeu, it·is easier *for* a·camel to·
Mt 19:28 declared to·them, "Certainly I·say to·yeu, that yeu,
Mt 21:21 declared to·them, "Certainly I·say to·yeu, if yeu·
Mt 21:27 "Neither do I·myself say to·yeu by what·kind·of
Mt 21:31 says to·them, "Certainly I·say to·yeu that the tax·
Mt 21:43 "On·account·of that, I·say to·yeu, the kingdom of·
Mt 23:36 "Certainly I·say to·yeu, all these·things shall·come
Mt 23:39 For I·say to·yeu, no, yeu·should·not see me from
Mt 24:2 look·for all these·things. Certainly I·say to·yeu, no,
Mt 24:34 "Certainly I·say to·yeu, *that* this generation·of·
Mt 24:47 Certainly I·say to·yeu, that he·shall·fully·establish
Mt 25:12 he·declared, 'Certainly I·say to·yeu, I·do·not
Mt 25:40 shall·declare to·them, 'Certainly I·say to·yeu, in
Mt 25:45 saying, 'Certainly I·say to·yeu, in as·much·as
Mt 26:13 "Certainly I·say to·yeu, wherever this good·news
Mt 26:21 he·declared, "Certainly I·say to·yeu, that one
Mt 26:29 "But I·say to·yeu, no, I·should·not drink from this·
Mt 26:34 replied to·him, "Certainly I·say to·you, that in this
Mt 26:64 ·yourself declared *it*. Moreover I·say to·yeu, from
Mk 2:11 "I·say to·you, be·awakened, and take·up your mat,
Mk 3:28 "Certainly I·say to·yeu, that all the moral·failings
Mk 5:41 is "Young·girl, I·say to·you, be·awakened!"
Mk 6:11 a·testimony against·them. Certainly I·say to·yeu,
Mk 8:12 seek·for a·sign? Certainly I·say to·yeu, 'As·if a·
Mk 9:1 he·was·saying to·them, "Certainly I·say to·yeu, that
Mk 9:13 "But·yet I·say to·yeu that indeed EliJah has·come,
Mk 9:41 yeu·are of·Anointed-One, certainly I·say to·yeu, no
Mk 10:15 Certainly I·say to·yeu, whoever, if he·should·not
Mk 10:29 Jesus declared, "Certainly I·say to·yeu, there·is
Mk 11:23 For certainly I·say to·yeu that whoever should·
Mk 11:24 On·account·of that, I·say to·yeu, all·things, as·
Mk 12:43 he·says to·them, "Certainly I·say to·yeu, that this
Mk 13:30 "Certainly I·say to·yeu, that this generation·of·
Mk 13:37 "And what I·say to·yeu, I·say to·all.
Mk 13:37 "And what I·say to·yeu, I·say to·all. Keep·alert!"
Mk 14:9 Certainly I·say to·yeu, wherever this good·news
Mk 14:18 Jesus declared, "Certainly I·say to·yeu, that one
Mk 14:25 "Certainly I·say to·yeu, no, I·should·not drink

Mk 14:30 says to·him, "Certainly I·say to·you, that this·day,
Rm 3:5 the wrath?" (I·say *this line of·reasoning* according·
Rm 6:19 I·say *this* after·the·manner·of·men† on·account·of
Rm 9:1 I·say *the* truth in Anointed-One, I·do·not lie, with·
Rm 10:18 But·yet I·say, ¿!·Did they·not hear?
Rm 10:19 But·yet I·say, ¿!·Did IsraEl not know?
Rm 11:1 Accordingly, I·say, ¿!·Did God shove·away his
Rm 11:11 Accordingly, I·say, ¿!·Did they·slip·up in·order·
Rm 11:13 For I·say *this* to·yeu, the Gentiles, in as·much·as
Rm 12:3 grace being·given to·me, I·say to·every·man being
Rm 15:8 Now I·say *it·was·necessary·for* Jesus Anointed to·
Php 3:18 now even *while* weeping, I·say *that they·are* the
Php 4:11 Not that I·say *this* according·to *a·particular* lacking
1Co 1:12 Now I·say this, that each·one of·yeu says, "In·fact,
1Co 6:5 I·say *this* to yeur·own embarrassment.
1Co 7:6 But I·say this in concession *concerning becoming*
1Co 7:8 But I·say to·the unmarried and to·the widows, it·is
1Co 7:12 But to·the rest I·myself say, not the Lord— if any
1Co 7:35 And I·say this specifically·for yeur own advantage;
1Co 10:15 I·say *this* as to·prudent·men; yeu·yourselves
1Co 10:29 "Conscience," I·say, not·indeed your·own, but·
1Co 15:34 some are ignorant of·God. I·say *this* to yeur·own
2Co 6:13 for the same due·reciprocation (I·say *this* as to·*my*·
2Co 7:3 Not toward condemnation do·I·say *this*, for I·have·
2Co 8:8 I·do·not say *this* according·to fully·assigned·
2Co 11:16 Again I·say, not anyone should·suppose me to·be
2Co 11:21 I·say *this* according·to *the implied·charge·of*
2Co 11:21 someone may·be·daringly·bold, (I·say *this* in
Eph 4:17 Accordingly, I·say this and attest *to·it* in *the* Lord:
Eph 5:32 mystery, but I·myself do·say *this* in·regard·to
Col 2:4 And this I·say, lest any·man should·defraud yeu with
Phm 1:21 ·shall·do also above·and·beyond that·which I·say.
2Ti 2:7 Understand what I·say. For may the Lord give to·you
1Jn 5:16 concerning that·thing do·I·say that he·should·ask.
Rv 2:24 'But to·yeu I·say, and to·the rest in Thyatira (as·

G3004.1 V-PAI-1P λέγομεν (4x)

Jn 8:48 "*Do* we·ourselves not say well that you·yourself are
Ac 21:23 "So·then do this·thing which we·say to·you. With·
Rm 4:9 upon the Uncircumcision also? For we·say that 'the
1Th 4:15 For this we·say to·yeu by *the* Lord's word, that we·

G3004.1 V-PAI-2S λέγεις (19x)

Jn 1:22 sending us, what·do you·say concerning yourself?
Jn 8:5 Accordingly, what·do you·yourself say?"
Jn 8:33 have·we·been·enslaved. How·do you·yourself say,
Jn 8:52 and the prophets; and you·yourself say, 'If someone
Jn 9:17 again, "What·do you·yourself say concerning him,
Jn 12:34 and how·do you·yourself say, 'It·is·mandatory·
Jn 14:9 Father; so·then how·do you·yourself say, 'Show us
Jn 16:29 ·clarity·of·speech, and say not·even·one proverb.
Jn 18:34 "From yourself, do·you say this·thing, or did·
Jn 18:37 answered, "You·yourself say *it·rightly* because I
Lk 8:45 and press·against *you*, and you·say, 'Who·is the·
Lk 12:41 to·him, "Lord, do·you·say this parable to us, or
Lk 20:21 we·personally·know that you·say and instruct
Lk 23:3 him, he·replied, "You·yourself say *it·rightly*."
Mt 27:11 was·replying to·him, "You·yourself say *it·rightly*."
Mk 5:31 the crowd pressing·in·around you and say, 'Who
Mk 15:2 he·declared to·him, "You·yourself say *it·rightly*."
1Co 14:16 ·now he·does·not personally·know what you·say?
Rv 3:17 because you·say, "I·am wealthy.

G3004.1 V-PAI-2S@ λέγεις (3x)

Lk 22:60 I·do·not personally·know what you·are·saying."
Mt 26:70 "I·do·not personally·know what you·are·saying."
Mk 14:68 ·acquainted·with what you·yourself are·saying."

G3004.1 V-PAI-2P λέγετε (20x)

Jn 4:20 on this mountain; and yeu say, that in JeruSalem is
Jn 4:35 "¿!·Do·not yeu·yourselves say, 'There·are yet four·
Jn 8:54 me; of·whom yeu·yourselves say that he·is yeur God
Jn 9:19 "Is this yeur son, who yeu say was·born blind?
Jn 9:41 not have moral·failure. But now yeu·say, 'We·look·
Jn 10:36 world, *of·him* yeu·yourselves say 'You·revile·God,
Jn 13:13 me Mentor and Lord, and yeu·say well, for I·am.
Lk 7:33 nor drinking wine, and yeu·say, 'He·has a·demon.
Lk 7:34 eating and drinking, and yeu·say, 'Behold a·man·
Lk 9:20 "And who·do yeu·yeurselves say me to·be?
Lk 11:18 remain·established? "Yeu·say that I cast·out
Lk 12:54 *the* west, immediately yeu·say, 'There·comes a·
Lk 12:55 *yeu·should·see the* south·wind blowing, yeu·say,
Lk 22:70 to them, "Yeu·yeurselves say *it·rightly* because I
Mt 15:5 But yeu·yeurselves say, 'Whoever should·declare
Mt 16:2 "With·early·evening occurring, yeu·say, '*It·shall*·
Mt 16:15 "But yeu·yeurselves, who·do yeu·say me to·be?
Mt 23:30 and say, 'If we·were in the days of·our fathers,
Mk 7:11 But yeu·yeurselves say, 'If a·man·of·clay† should·
Mk 8:29 "But who·do yeu·yeurselves say me to·be?

G3004.1 V-PAI-3S λέγει (331x)

Jn 1:21 are you·yourself, EliJah?" And he·says, "I·am not.
Jn 1:29 who·is·coming toward him, and he·says, "See the
Jn 1:36 ·clearly·upon Jesus walking·along, he·says, "See
Jn 1:38 distinctly·viewing them following, says to·them,
Jn 1:39 He·says to·them, "Come and see.
Jn 1:41 finds his·own brother Simon and says to·him, "We·
Jn 1:43 and he·finds PhilIp and says to·him, "Follow me.
Jn 1:45 PhilIp finds NathaniEl and says to·him, "We·have·
Jn 1:46 ·out of·Natsareth?" PhilIp says to·him, "Come and
Jn 1:47 coming toward him and says concerning him, "See!
Jn 1:48 NathaniEl says to·him, "From·what·source do·you·
Jn 1:49 NathaniEl answered and says to·him, "Rabbi, you·
Jn 1:51 Then he·says to·him, "Certainly, most·certainly, I·
Jn 2:3 And lacking wine, the mother of·Jesus says to him,
Jn 2:4 Jesus says to·her, "Woman, what·does·this·have to·
Jn 2:5 His mother says to·the attendants, "Whatever he·
Jn 2:7 Jesus says to·them, "Overfill the ceremonial·water·
Jn 2:8 And he·says to·them, "Draw·*it*·out now and bring *it*
Jn 2:10 and says to·him, "Every man·of·clay† first places·
Jn 3:4 NicoDemus says to him, "How·is a·man·of·clay† able
Jn 4:7 ·Samaria to·draw·out water. Jesus says to·her, "Give
Jn 4:9 Accordingly, the Samaritan woman says to·him,
Jn 4:11 The woman says to·him, "Sir, you·have not·even a·
Jn 4:15 The woman says to him, "Sir, give me this water,
Jn 4:16 Jesus says to·her, "Head·on·out, holler·out·for your
Jn 4:17 Jesus says to·her, "You·declared well, 'I·do·not
Jn 4:19 The woman says to·him, "Sir, I·observe that you·
Jn 4:21 Jesus says to·her, "Woman, trust me, because an·
Jn 4:25 The woman says to·him, "I·personally·know that
Jn 4:26 Jesus says to·her, "It·is·I Myself.
Jn 4:28 ·off into the city, and she·says to·the men·of·clay†,
Jn 4:34 Jesus says to·them, "My food is that I·may·do the
Jn 4:49 The royal·official says to him, "Sir, walk·down
Jn 4:50 Jesus says to·him, "Depart, your son lives.
Jn 5:6 *sickness* even·now a·long time, says to·him, "Do·
Jn 5:8 Jesus says to·him, "Be·awakened, take·up your mat
Jn 6:5 crowd is·come toward him, Jesus says to PhilIp,
Jn 6:8 Andrew, Simon Peter's brother, says to·him,
Jn 6:12 But as they·are·filled·up, he·says to·his disciples,
Jn 6:20 But he·says to·them, "It·is·I Myself.
Jn 6:42 ·know? So·then how·is·it *that* he·says this·thing, 'I·
Jn 7:6 So·then Jesus says to·them, "My season is·not·yet
Jn 7:50 *and* being one from·among them) says to them,
Jn 8:22 ·that he·shall·kill himself? Because he·says, 'Where
Jn 8:39 Jesus says to·them, "If yeu·were AbRaham's
Jn 9:12 is this·man?" He·says, "I·do·not personally·know.
Jn 11:7 Then after that he·says to·the disciples, "We·should·
Jn 11:11 he·declared, and after that he·says to·them, "Our
Jn 11:13 *disciples* presumed that he·says *this* concerning the
Jn 11:23 Jesus says to·her, "Your brother shall·rise·up.
Jn 11:24 Martha says to·him, "I·personally·know that he·
Jn 11:27 She·says to·him, "Yes, Lord.
Jn 11:39 Jesus says, "Take·away the stone.
Jn 11:39 the sister of·the·one having·died, says to·him, "O·
Jn 11:40 Jesus says to·her, "Did·I·not declare to·you, that, if
Jn 11:44 ·about with·a·sweat·towel. Jesus says to·them,
Jn 12:4 Simon's *son*, the·one about to·hand him over) says,
Jn 13:6 to Simon Peter, and that·one says to·him, "Lord,
Jn 13:8 Peter says to·him, "No, you·should·not wash my
Jn 13:9 Simon Peter says to·him, "Lord, not my feet merely,
Jn 13:10 Jesus says to·him, "The·one having·been·bathed
Jn 13:25 falling·back upon Jesus' chest, says to·him, "Lord
Jn 13:27 So·then Jesus says to·him, "What you·do, do more·
Jn 13:29 the money·bag, that Jesus says to·him, "Buy *those*·
Jn 13:31 When he·went·forth, Jesus says, "Now the Son of·
Jn 13:36 Simon Peter says to·him, "Lord, where·do you·
Jn 13:37 Peter says to·him, "Lord, why am·I·not able to·
Jn 14:5 Thomas says to·him, "Lord, we·do·not personally·
Jn 14:6 Jesus says to·him, "I AM the way, and the truth
Jn 14:8 PhilIp says to·him, "Lord, show us the Father, and
Jn 14:9 Jesus says to·him, "Am·I so·vast a·time with yeu,
Jn 14:22 Judas *Thaddaeus*, not IsCariot, says to·him, "Lord
Jn 16:17 "What is this that he·says to·us, 'A·little·while, and
Jn 16:18 "What is this·thing that he·says, 'A·little·while?
Jn 18:5 Jesus says to·them, "I AM.
Jn 18:17 servant·girl (the doorkeeper) says to·Peter, "Are
Jn 18:17 of·this man·of·clay†?" That·man says, "I·am not.
Jn 18:26 earlobe Peter chopped·off, says, "¿!·Did·not I·
Jn 18:38 Pilate says to·him, "What is truth?
Jn 18:38 to the Judeans, and he·says to·them, "I·myself find
Jn 19:4 Pilate went·forth outside again and says to·them,
Jn 19:5 the purple garment. And *Pilate* says to·them, "See,
Jn 19:6 Pilate says to·them, "Yeu·yeurselves take him and
Jn 19:9 again into the Praetorian·hall and says to·Jesus,
Jn 19:10 So·then Pilate says to·him, "Do·you·not speak to·
Jn 19:14 *the* sixth hour, and he·says to·the Judeans, "See
Jn 19:15 Pilate says to·them, "Shall·I·crucify yeur King?
Jn 19:26 ·nearby whom he·loved, he·says to·his mother,
Jn 19:27 Then he·says to·the disciple, "Behold your mother!
Jn 19:28 Scripture may·be·fully·completed, says, "I·thirst!
Jn 19:35 ·also personally·knows that *what* he·says *is* true, in·
Jn 19:37 And again another Scripture says, "They·shall·
Jn 20:2 whom Jesus was·fond·of, and she·says to·them,
Jn 20:13 why do·you·weep?" She·says to·them, "Because
Jn 20:15 Jesus says to·her, "Woman, why do·you·weep?
Jn 20:15 that he·is the garden·keeper, says to·him, "Sir, if
Jn 20:16 Jesus says to·her, "Mariam.
Jn 20:16 being·turned·back·around, says to·him *in·Aramaic*,
Jn 20:17 Jesus says to·her, "Do·not lay·hold·of·me, for I·
Jn 20:19 ·still in the midst. And he·says to·them, "Peace *be*
Jn 20:22 this, he·puffed·on *them*. Then he·says to·them,
Jn 20:27 Then he·says to·Thomas, "Bring your finger here,
Jn 20:29 Jesus says to·him, "Thomas, because you·have·
Jn 21:3 Simon Peter says to·them, "I·head·on·out to·fish.
Jn 21:5 So Jesus says to·them, "Little·children, ¿! do·yeu·
Jn 21:7 that disciple whom Jesus loved says to·Peter, "It·is
Jn 21:10 Jesus says to·them, "Bring of the small·fry which
Jn 21:12 Jesus says to·them, "Come·here! Dine!" And not·
Jn 21:15 when they·had·dined, Jesus says to·Simon Peter,
Jn 21:15 more·than these·things?" He·says to·him, "Yes,
Jn 21:15 that I·have·affection·for you." He·says to·him,
Jn 21:16 He·says to·him again a·second·time, "Simon, *son*
Jn 21:16 ·Jonah, do·you·love me?" He·says to·him, "Yes,
Jn 21:16 that I·have·affection·for you." He·says to·him,
Jn 21:17 He·says to·him the third·time, "Simon, *son* of·
Jn 21:17 Jesus says to·him, "Feed my sheep.
Jn 21:19 And after·declaring this, he·says to·him, "Follow
Jn 21:21 Upon·seeing this·man, Peter says to·Jesus, "Lord,
Jn 21:22 Jesus says to·him, "If I·should·want him to·remain
Lk 3:11 And answering, he·says to·them, "The·one having
Lk 5:39 wants fresh·new *wine*, for he·says, 'The old is finer
Lk 9:33 ·for EliJah," not personally·knowing what he·says.
Lk 11:24 and not finding *any*, it·says, 'I·shall·return·back
Lk 11:45 ·one of·the experts·in·Torah-Law says to·him,
Lk 13:8 "And answering, he·says to·him, 'Lord, leave it
Lk 16:7 ·measures of·wheat.' And he·says to·him, '*Here*,
Lk 16:29 AbRaham says to·him, 'They·have Moses and the
Lk 18:6 "Hear what the unjust judge says.
Lk 19:22 "And he·says to·him, 'From·out of·your·own
Lk 20:42 And David himself says in a·scroll of·Psalms,
Lk 22:11 of·the home, 'The Mentor says to·you, "Where is
Lk 24:36 in *the* midst of·them, and says to·them, "Peace *be*
Ac 2:17 in the last days, says God, *that* I·shall·pour·forth

Ac 2:25 For David says this in·regard·to *his·Lord*, " I·was·
Ac 2:34 into the heavens, but he·himself says, "Yahweh
Ac 7:48 in temples made·by·hands, just·as the prophet says,
Ac 7:49 ·of house shall·yeu·build for·me, says Yahweh?
Ac 8:34 you, concerning whom·does the prophet say this?
Ac 12:8 And he·did so. Then he·says to·him, "Cast your·
Ac 13:35 Therefore he·says also in another *Psalm*, "You·
Ac 15:17 has·been·surnamed upon them, says Yahweh, the·
Ac 21:11 feet, he·declared, "Thus says the Holy Spirit, 'in·
Ac 21:37 the barracks, he·says to·the regiment·commander,
Heb 1:6 ·bring the Firstborn into The Land, he·says, " And
Heb 1:7 And, in·fact, he·says unto the angels, "*This·is*
Heb 3:7 Therefore, just·as the Holy Spirit says, "Today if
Heb 5:6 Just·as he·says also in another *passage*, "You *are*
Heb 8:8 For finding·fault with·them, he·says, "'Behold,
Heb 8:8 *the* days come,' says Yahweh, 'and I·shall·
Heb 8:9 covenant, and·I neglected them,' says Yahweh.
Heb 8:10 of·IsraEl after those days,' says Yahweh, 'giving
Heb 10:5 he·who·is·entering into the world says,
Heb 10:16 them after those days, says Yahweh, giving my
Heb 10:30 I·myself shall·recompense,'" says Yahweh. And
Gal 3:16 and·to·his Seed. He·does·not say, "And to·the
Gal 4:30 But·yet what·does the Scripture say? "Cast·out the
Mt 4:6 and he·says to·him, "If you·are *the* Son of·God, cast
Mt 4:9 and he·says to·him, "All these·things I·shall·give to·
Mt 4:10 Then YeShua says to·him, "Head·on·out,
Mt 4:19 And he·says to·them, "Come·here, *fall·in* right·
Mt 8:4 Then YeShua says to·him, "Clearly·see·to·it *that*
Mt 8:7 And YeShua says to·him, "After·going *to·him*, I·
Mt 8:20 And YeShua says to·him, "The foxes have burrows,
Mt 8:26 And he·says to·them, "Why are·yeu timid, O·yeu·
Mt 9:6 moral·failures," (then he·says to·the paralyzed·man)
Mt 9:9 in the tax·booth. And he·says to·him, "Follow me.
Mt 9:24 says to·them, "Depart! For the young·girl did·not
Mt 9:28 came·alongside him. And YeShua says to·them,
Mt 9:37 Then he·says to·his disciples, "In·fact, the harvest
Mt 12:13 Then he·says to·the man·of·clay†, "Stretch·out
Mt 12:44 Then it·says, 'I·shall·return into my house from·
Mt 13:51 YeShua says to·them, "Did·yeu·comprehend all
Mt 14:31 grabbed·hold of·him, and says to·him, "O·you·
Mt 15:34 And YeShua says to·them, "How·many loaves·of·
Mt 16:15 He·says to·them, "But yeu·yeurselves, who·do
Mt 17:25 He·says, "Yes.
Mt 17:26 Peter says to·him, "From the others.
Mt 18:22 YeShua says to·him, "I·do·not say to·you, up·to
Mt 18:32 after·summoning him, his lord says to·him, 'Evil
Mt 19:8 He·says to·them, "*It·was* pertaining·to yeur
Mt 19:18 He·says to·him, "Which·ones?
Mt 19:20 The young·man says to·him, "All these·things I·
Mt 20:6 he·found others standing idle and says to·them,
Mt 20:7 no·one·at·all hired us.' He·says to·them, 'Also
Mt 20:8 of·the vineyard says to·his executive·manager,
Mt 20:21 "What·do you·want?" She·says to·him, "Declare
Mt 20:23 And he·says to·them, "In·fact, yeu·shall·drink of·
Mt 21:13 and he·says to·them, "It·has·been·written, "My
Mt 21:16 are·saying?" And YeShua says to·them, "Yes!
Mt 21:19 it, except merely leaves, and he·says to·it, "No·
Mt 21:31 YeShua says to·them, "Certainly I·say to·yeu
Mt 21:42 YeShua says to·them, "Did·yeu·not·even·at·any·
Mt 21:45 *it·was* concerning them *that* he·says *these·things*.
Mt 22:8 "Then he·says to·his slaves, 'In·fact the wedding is
Mt 22:12 And he·says to·him, 'O·associate, how did·you·
Mt 22:20 And he·says to·them, "Whose derived·image and
Mt 22:21 Then he·says to·them, "Well·then, render the·
Mt 22:43 He·says to·them, "So·then how·does David in
Mt 26:18 declare to·him, 'The Mentor says, "My season is
Mt 26:25 is·it·I myself?" He·says to·him, "You·yourself
Mt 26:31 Then YeShua says to·them, "All yeu shall·be·
Mt 26:35 Peter says to·him, "Though it·should·be·
Mt 26:36 ·to·as GethSemane, and he·says to·the disciples,
Mt 26:38 Then he·says to·them, "My soul is exceedingly·
Mt 26:40 finds them sleeping. And he·says to·Peter, "So,
Mt 26:45 Then he·comes to·his disciples and says to·them,
Mt 26:52 Then YeShua says to·him, "Return·back your
Mt 26:64 YeShua says to·him, "You·yourself declared *it*.
Mt 26:71 *servant·girl* saw him and says to·the·ones there,
Mt 27:13 Then Pilate says to·him, "Do·you·not hear how·
Mt 27:22 Pilate says to·them, "So·then what shall·I·do with·
Mt 28:10 Then YeShua says to·them, "Do·not be·afraid!
Mk 1:38 And he·says to·them, "We·should·head·out into
Mk 1:41 his hand, he·laid·hold of·him and says to·him, "I·
Mk 1:44 and he·says to·him, "Clearly·see·to·it *that* you·
Mk 2:5 after·seeing their trust, says to·the paralyzed·man,
Mk 2:10 ·failures—" *then* he·says to·the paralyzed·man,
Mk 2:14 in the tax·booth, and he·says to·him, "Follow me.
Mk 2:17 And after·hearing *that*, Jesus says to·them, "The·
Mk 3:3 And *Jesus* says to·the man·of·clay†, the·one having
Mk 3:4 And he·says to·them, "Is·it·proper to·beneficially·
Mk 3:5 of·their hearts, he·says to·the man·of·clay†,
Mk 3:34 at·the·ones sitting·down around him, he·says, "See
Mk 4:13 And he·says to·them, "Do·yeu·not personally·
Mk 4:35 with·early·evening occurring, he·says to·them,
Mk 5:19 did·not allow him, but·rather says to·him, "Head·
Mk 5:36 ·spoken, Jesus says to·the director·of·the·gathering
Mk 5:39 And after·entering, he·says to·them, "Why are·
Mk 5:41 of·the little·child by·the hand, he·says to·her,
Mk 6:38 But he·says to·them, "How·many loaves·of·bread
Mk 6:50 he·spoke with them, and he·says to·them, "Be·of·
Mk 7:18 Then he·says to·them, "So, are yeu·yeurselves also
Mk 7:28 And she·answered and says to·him, "Yes *it·is*, Lord
Mk 7:34 to the heaven, he·sighed·heavily and says to·him,
Mk 8:1 after·summoning his disciples, Jesus says to·them,
Mk 8:12 after·sighing·deeply in·his spirit, he·says, "Why·
Mk 8:17 And upon·knowing *it*, Jesus says to·them, "Why·
Mk 8:29 And he·himself says to·them, "But who·do yeu·
Mk 8:29 to·be?" And answering, Peter says to·him, "You·
Mk 9:5 Now responding *to·this*, Peter says to·Jesus, "Rabbi,
Mk 9:19 But answering him, he·says, "O distrusting
Mk 9:35 he·hollered·out·for the twelve and says to·them,
Mk 10:11 And he·says to·them, "Whoever should·divorce
Mk 10:23 after·looking·around, Jesus says to·his disciples,
Mk 10:24 Jesus, answering again, says to·them, "Children,
Mk 10:27 after·looking·clearly·upon them, Jesus says,
Mk 10:42 Jesus, upon·summoning them, says to·them,
Mk 10:51 And responding, Jesus says to·him, "What·do
Mk 11:2 and says to·them, "Head·on·out into the village
Mk 11:21 ·to·mind·and·considering *it*, Peter says to·him,
Mk 11:22 And answering, Jesus says to·them, "Have God's
Mk 11:23 that the·things·which he·says are·coming·to·be; it·
Mk 11:33 And Jesus answering says to·them, "Neither do
Mk 12:16 And they·brought *it*. And he·says to·them,
Mk 12:43 And summoning his disciples, he·says to·them,
Mk 13:1 ·Atrium, one of·his disciples says to·him, "Mentor
Mk 14:13 two of·his disciples and says to·them, "Head·on·
Mk 14:14 ·of·the·house, 'The Mentor says, "Where is the
Mk 14:27 Then Jesus says to·them, "All yeu·shall·be·
Mk 14:30 And Jesus says to·him, "Certainly I·say to·you,
Mk 14:32 *is* GethSemane. And *Jesus* says to·his disciples,
Mk 14:34 Then he·says to·them, "My soul is exceedingly·
Mk 14:37 and finds them sleeping. And he·says to·Peter,
Mk 14:41 ·comes the third·time, and *sternly* says to·them,
Mk 14:45 immediately going·toward him, he·says, "Rabbi,
Mk 14:61 was·inquiring·of him, and he·says to·him, "Are
Mk 14:63 after·tearing·apart his·own tunics, says, "What
Mk 14:67 after·looking·clearly·at him, she·says, "You
Mk 16:6 And he·says to·them, "Do·not be·utterly·amazed.
Rm 3:19 that as·much·as the Torah-Law says, it·speaks to·
Rm 4:3 For what·does the Scripture say? "'And AbRaham
Rm 9:15 For he·says to·Moses, " I·shall·show·gracious·
Rm 9:17 For the Scripture says to·Pharaoh, "For this same·
Rm 9:25 As he·says also in Hosea, "I·shall·call *them* 'My
Rm 10:6 birthed·from·out·of·trust, says *it* in·this·manner,
Rm 10:8 But·yet what·does it·say? "The utterance is near
Rm 10:11 For the Scripture says, " Everyone trusting on
Rm 10:16 the good·news. For IsaIah says, "'O·Yahweh,
Rm 10:19 IsraEl not know? First Moses says, "'I·myself
Rm 10:20 But IsaIah is·quite·daringly·bold and says, " I·
Rm 10:21 But to IsraEl he·says, " The whole day·long I·
Rm 11:2 personally·know what the Scripture says by EliJah?
Rm 11:4 But·rather what says the response·of·Yahweh to·
Rm 11:9 And David says, "Let their table be·made into a·
Rm 12:19 ·me; I·myself shall·recompense,'" says Yahweh.
Rm 14:11 '*As·surely·as* I·myself live,' says Yahweh,"
Rm 15:10 And again he·says, " Be·merry, O·Gentiles, with
Rm 15:12 And again, IsaIah says, " There·shall·be the root
Jac 4:5 do·yeu·presume that the Scripture says for·naught, '
Jac 4:6 he·gives greater grace. Therefore he·says, " God
1Co 1:12 I·say this, that each·one of·yeu says, "In·fact, I·
1Co 9:8 does·not·indeed the Torah-Law say these·things also
1Co 9:10 Or does·he·say *this* altogether on·account·of us?
1Co 12:3 ·one·man speaking by God's Spirit says, "Jesus *is*
1Co 14:21 they·shall·not·even listen·to·me," says Yahweh.
1Co 14:34 ·themselves, just·as also the Oral-law says.
2Co 6:2 for he·says, "'I·favorably·heard you in·an·
2Co 6:17 and be·distinctly·detached,"" says Yahweh, "
2Co 6:18 sons and daughters,"" says Yahweh Almighty.
Eph 4:8 Therefore he·says, "After·ascending on·high, by·
Eph 5:14 Therefore he·says, "O·the·one sleeping, be·
1Ti 4:1 Now the Spirit expressly says that in later seasons
1Ti 5:18 For the Scripture says, "'You·shall·not muzzle an·
Rv 1:8 beginning and end," says the Lord, "the·one being,
Rv 2:1 write, 'These·things says the·one securely·holding
Rv 2:7 what the Spirit says to·the Called·Out·citizenries. To·
Rv 2:8 in·Smyrna write, 'These·things says the First and the
Rv 2:11 what the Spirit says to·the Called·Out·citizenries.
Rv 2:12 write, 'These·things says the·one having the sharp,
Rv 2:17 what the Spirit says to·the Called·Out·citizenries.
Rv 2:18 Thyatira write, 'These·things says the Son of·God,
Rv 2:29 what the Spirit says to·the Called·Out·citizenries.'"
Rv 3:1 Sardis write, 'These·things says the·one having the
Rv 3:6 what the Spirit says to·the Called·Out·citizenries.'"
Rv 3:7 PhilAdelphia write, 'These·things says the Holy·One,
Rv 3:13 what the Spirit says to·the Called·Out·citizenries.'"
Rv 3:14 write, 'These·things says the Sure·One, the·Amen,
Rv 3:22 what the Spirit says to·the Called·Out·citizenries.'"
Rv 5:5 And one from·among the Elders says to·me, "Do·not
Rv 10:9 the tiny·official·scroll." And he·says to·me, "Take
Rv 10:11 And he·says to·me, "It·is·mandatory·for you to·
Rv 14:13 "Yes," says the Spirit, "in·order·that they·may·
Rv 17:15 And he·says to·me, "The *Many* Waters which
Rv 18:7 and mourning, because she·says in her heart, 'I·sit·
Rv 19:9 Then *the angel* says to·me, "Write, 'Supremely·
Rv 19:9 " And he·says to·me, "These are the true sayings
Rv 19:10 feet to·fall·prostrate to·him. And he·says to·me,
Rv 21:5 all·things brand-new!" And he·says to·me, "Write,
Rv 22:9 Then he·says to·me, "Clearly·see·to·it *that* you·do·
Rv 22:10 And he·says to·me, "You·should·not seal·up the
Rv 22:20 The·one testifying these·things says, "Yes, I·come

G3004.1 V-PAI-3P λέγουσιν (54x)

Jn 7:26 ·of·speech, and they·say nothing·at·all to·him.
Jn 8:4 they·say to·him, "Mentor, this wife was·grabbed·
Jn 9:17 They·say to·the blind·man again, "What·do you·
Jn 11:8 The disciples say to·him, "Rabbi, the Judeans now
Jn 11:34 "Where have·yeu·laid him?" They·said to·him,
Jn 16:29 His disciples say to·him, "See, now you·speak
Jn 20:13 And those *angels* say to·her, "Woman, why do·
Jn 21:3 "I·head·on·out to·fish." They·say to·him, "We·
Lk 9:18 "Who·do the crowds say me to·be?
Lk 17:37 And answering, they·say to·him, "Where, Lord?
Lk 20:41 to them, "How·do they·say *it·is·mandatory·for* the
Lk 24:23 ·seen a·vision of·angels who say *that* he·himself *is*
Ac 23:8 For in·fact, *the* Sadducees say *that* there·is not a·
Ac 24:14 according·to The Way which they·say *is* a·sect, in·
Mt 9:28 that I·am·able to·do this?" They·say to·him, "Yes,
Mt 11:18 eating nor drinking, and they·say, 'He·has a·
Mt 11:19 came eating and drinking, and they·say, 'Behold,
Mt 13:51 all these·things?" They·say to·him, "Yes, Lord.
Mt 14:17 And they·say to·him, "We·do·not have *anything*
Mt 15:33 And his disciples say to·him, "From·what·source

Mt 16:13 "Who·do the men·of·clay† say me to·be— *me*, the
Mt 17:10 why·do the scribes say that it·is·mandatory·for
Mt 19:7 *Then* they·say to·him, "So·then why·did Moses
Mt 19:10 His disciples say to·him, "If the legal·charge of·
Mt 20:7 They·say to·him, 'Because no·one·at·all hired us.
Mt 20:22 to·be·immersed·in *it*?" They·say to·him, "We·
Mt 20:33 They·say to·him, "Lord, that our eyes may·be·
Mt 21:16 "Do·you·hear what these *boys* are·saying?" And
Mt 21:31 will of·the father?" They·say to·him, "The first·
Mt 21:41 They·say to·him, "He·shall·completely·destroy
Mt 22:21 They·say to·him, "Caesar's.
Mt 22:42 Whose son is·he?" They·say to·him, "*The Son*
Mt 23:3 do according·to their works. For they·say *it*, and·yet
Mt 27:22 ·to·as Anointed-One?" They·all say to·him, "Let·
Mk 1:37 And upon·finding him, they·say to·him, "All *men*
Mk 2:18 And they·come and say to·him, "Why·is·it·that the
Mk 4:38 And they·thoroughly·awaken him and say to·him,
Mk 6:35 disciples, after·coming·alongside him, say, "The
Mk 6:37 *something* to·eat." And they·say to·him, "Upon·
Mk 6:38 And already·knowing, they·say, "Five, and two
Mk 8:19 of·fragments did·yeu·take·up?" They·say to·him,
Mk 8:27 "Who·do the men·of·clay† say me to·be?
Mk 9:11 "Why·do the scribes say that it·is·mandatory·for
Mk 11:28 and they·say to·him, "By what·kind·of authority
Mk 11:33 And answering, they·say to·Jesus, "We·do·not
Mk 12:14 And upon·coming, they·say to·him, "Mentor,
Mk 12:18 come to him, who say *that there·is* not to·be a·
Mk 12:35 "How·do the scribes say that the Anointed-One is
Mk 14:12 the Passover, his disciples say to·him, "Going·
1Co 15:12 how·do some among yeu say that there·is no
1Ti 1:7 not understanding— neither what they·say, nor
Rv 2:24 of·the Adversary-Accuser," as they·say), I·shall·cast
Rv 6:16 Then they·say to·the mountains and to·the solid·
Rv 22:17 And the Spirit and the Bride say, "Come!" And

G3004.1 V-PAM-2S λέγε (1x)

Ac 22:27 declared to·him, "Say *it* to·me whether you·

G3004.1 V-PAM-2P λέγετε (7x)

Lk 10:5 home yeu·should·enter, first say, 'Peace to·this
Lk 10:9 ·and·cure the sick in it, and say to·them, 'The
Lk 11:2 "Whenever yeu·should·pray, say, 'Our Father, the·
Lk 17:10 ·thoroughly·assigned to·yeu, yeu also must·say,
Ac 13:15 of·exhortation specifically·for the people, say·on."
Gal 4:21 Say to·me, the·ones wanting to·be under
2Jn 1:10 into a·home, and yeu·must·not say to·him, "Be·

G3004.1 V-PAM-3S λεγέτω (1x)

Jac 1:13 No·one being·tempted must·ever·say, "I·am·

G3004.1 V-PAN λέγειν (30x)

Jn 16:12 "I·have yet many·things to·say to·yeu, but·yet yeu·
Lk 3:8 and yeu·should·not begin to·say within yeurselves,
Lk 4:21 And he·began to·say to them, "Today, this Scripture
Lk 6:42 Or how are·you·able to·say to your brother,
Lk 7:49 ·at·the·meal began to·say within themselves, "Who
Lk 11:27 it·happened, as he was·saying these·things, *that* a·
Lk 11:29 crowds being·amassed·together, he·began to·say,
Lk 12:1 one·another, *Jesus* began to·say to his disciples,
Lk 13:26 "Then yeu·shall·begin to·say, 'We·ate and drank
Lk 23:30 Then shall·they·begin "to·say to·the mountains,
Ac 17:21 other than *attempting* to·say or to·hear something
Ac 23:30 charging his legal·accusers also to·say before you
Heb 8:13 In *that* he·says, "A·brand-new *covenant*," he·has·
Heb 9:5 is not *the time for·us* to·say *anything* in particular.
Heb 13:6 Such·for us to·say, while·exercising·courage,
Mt 3:9 And yeu·should·not presume to·say within yeurselves
Mt 4:17 YeShua began to·officially·proclaim and to·say,
Mt 11:7 were·departing, YeShua began to·say to·the crowds
Mt 13:54 them to·be·astounded, and to·say, "From·what·
Mt 26:22 grieved, each·one of·them began to·say to·him,
Mk 9:26 as one·dead— such·for many to·say that he·died.
Mk 10:28 Then Peter began to·say to·him, "Behold, we·
Mk 10:47 he·began to·yell·out and to·say, "O·Jesus, the
Mk 13:5 And Jesus answering them began to·say, "Look·out
Mk 14:19 ·began to·be·grieved and to·say to·him one·by·one
Mk 14:65 even to·buffet him and to·say to·him, "Prophesy
Mk 14:69 again, began to·say to·the·ones standing·nearby,
Rm 3:8 and just·as some reply for·us to·say), "that we·
Jac 4:15 Instead, yeu *ought* to·say, "If the Lord should·will,
Tit 2:8 not·even·one mediocre thing to·say concerning yeu

G3004.1 V-PAP-ASF λέγουσαν (10x)

Lk 3:22 and a·voice occurred from·out of·heaven, saying,
Ac 9:4 the earth, he·heard a·voice saying to·him, "Saul,
Ac 26:14 to me, and saying in·the Hebrew language, 'Saul,
Rv 6:6 in *the* midst of·the four living·beings saying, "A·dry·
Rv 6:7 *the* voice of·the fourth living·being saying, "Come
Rv 9:14 saying to·the sixth angel who was·holding the
Rv 10:4 a·voice from·out of·the heaven saying to·me, "Seal·
Rv 11:12 voice from·out of·the heaven saying to·them,
Rv 12:10 And I·heard a·loud voice saying in the heaven,
Rv 18:4 voice from·out of·the heaven, saying: "Come·out

G3004.1 V-PAP-ASM λέγοντα (5x)

Lk 23:2 to·give tributes to·Caesar, saying himself to·be *the*
Ac 7:59 ·calling·upon *the Lord*, even while·saying, "Lord
Ac 22:18 and saw him saying to·me, 'Make·haste and go·
Rv 4:8 have a·rest·break day and night, saying, "Holy, holy,
Rv 14:7 saying with a·loud voice, "Fear God and give glory

G3004.1 V-PAP-APM λέγοντας (8x)

Lk 24:34 saying, "The Lord really is·awakened and was·
Ac 6:11 Then they·secretly·induced men to·say, "We·have·
Ac 6:13 and they·set·up false witnesses saying, "This man·
Mt 21:15 ·out in the Sanctuary·Atrium, saying, "Hosanna
Mk 1:27 ·question·and·discuss among themselves, saying,
Mk 2:12 all to·be·astonished and to·glorify God, saying,
Rv 5:13 the·ones in them, I·heard saying, "To·the·one who·
Rv 19:6 and as a·voice of·strong thunderings, saying,

G3004.1 V-PAP-DPM λέγουσιν (2x)

Lk 7:32 and hollering·out to·one·another, and saying, 'We·
Mt 11:17 and saying, 'We·played·flute for·yeu, and yeu·

G3004.1 V-PAP-GSN λέγοντος (14x)

Lk 3:4 a·scroll of·the·words of·Isaiah the prophet, saying, "
Mt 1:22 ·uttered by Yahweh through the prophet, saying,
Mt 2:15 Yahweh through the prophet, saying, "From·out
Mt 2:17 being·uttered by Jeremiah the prophet, saying,
Mt 4:14 being·uttered through Isaiah the prophet, saying,
Mt 8:17 through Isaiah the prophet, saying, "He·himself
Mt 12:17 being·uttered through Isaiah the prophet, saying,
Mt 13:35 being·uttered through the prophet, saying, "I·
Mt 21:4 the·thing being·uttered through the prophet, saying,
Mt 22:31 of·the·thing being·uttered to·yeu by God, saying,
Mt 27:9 through Jeremiah the prophet, saying, "And they·
Rv 6:1 ·beings (as a·voice of·a·thunder) saying, "Come and
Rv 6:3 I·heard the second living·being saying, "Come and
Rv 6:5 I·heard the third living·being saying, "Come and

G3004.1 V-PAP-GSF λεγούσης (6x)

Ac 11:7 And I·heard a·voice saying to·me, 'Peter, after·
Ac 22:7 to the hard·ground and heard a·voice saying to·me,
Rv 1:11 saying, "I AM the Alpha and the Omega,
Rv 14:13 a·voice from·out of·the heaven saying to·me,
Rv 16:1 voice from·out of·the Temple saying to·the seven
Rv 21:3 voice from·out of·the heaven saying, "Behold, the

G3004.1 V-PAP-GSM λέγοντος (11x)

Lk 9:34 But with·him saying these·things, there·came a·
Lk 11:53 And with·him saying these·things to them, the
Lk 13:17 And with·him saying these·things, all the·ones
Ac 6:14 For we·have·heard him saying that this Jesus of·
Heb 7:21 a·swearing·of·oath through the·one saying to him,
Mt 3:3 *of* by Isaiah the prophet, saying, "A·voice of·one·
Mk 14:58 "We·ourselves heard him saying, 'I·myself shall·
Rv 8:13 flying in mid-heaven, saying with·a·loud voice,
Rv 16:5 I·heard the angel of·the waters saying, "You·are
Rv 16:7 another from·among the Sacrifice·Altar saying,
Rv 19:1 crowd in the heaven, saying, "Splendidly·praise·

G3004.1 V-PAP-GPM λεγόντων (5x)

Lk 2:13 of·*the*·heavenly host praising God and saying,
Lk 8:20 it·is·announced to·him, *with·several* saying, "Your
Lk 21:5 And with·some saying concerning the Sanctuary·
Rv 2:9 the revilement of·the·ones saying themselves to·be
Rv 3:9 Adversary-Accuser (the·ones saying themselves to·be

G3004.1 V-PAP-NSN λέγον (2x)

Ac 20:23 thoroughly·testifies in·each city, saying that bonds
Ac 28:26 saying, "Traverse toward this People, and declare,

G3004.1 V-PAP-NSF λέγουσα (24x)

Jn 11:32 she·fell·down at his feet, saying to·him, "Lord, if
Jn 19:24 may·be·completely·fulfilled, the·one saying,
Lk 1:24 ·hiding herself *for* five lunar·months, saying,
Lk 9:35 a·voice from·out of·the thick·cloud, saying, "This
Lk 15:9 friends and the close·neighbors saying, 'Rejoice·
Lk 18:3 and she·was·coming to him, saying, 'Avenge me
Ac 16:15 her household, she·implored *us*, saying, "If yeu·
Ac 16:17 us, the·same·girl was·yelling·out, saying, "These
Mt 3:17 a·voice from·out of·the heavens, saying, "This is
Mt 13:14 the prophecy of·Isaiah, the·one saying, "Hearing
Mt 15:22 upon·coming·forth yelled·out to·him, saying,
Mt 15:25 she·was·falling·prostrate to·him, saying, "Lord,
Mt 17:5 ·voice from·out of·the thick·cloud, saying, "This
Mt 21:10 all the City was·shaken, saying, "Who is this?
Mt 26:69 servant·girl came·alongside him, saying, "You·
Mt 27:19 dispatched to him, saying, "Have·nothing·to·do
Mk 6:25 to the king, she·requested *it*, saying, "I·want that
Mk 9:7 a·voice came out of·the thick·cloud, saying, "This
Mk 15:28 was·completely·fulfilled, the·one saying, "And
Jac 2:23 Scripture is·completely·fulfilled, the·one saying,
Rv 4:1 a·trumpet speaking with me, saying, "Walk·up here,
Rv 10:8 speaking with me again, and saying, "Head·on·out!
Rv 16:17 from the throne, saying, "It·has·happened!"
Rv 19:5 came·forth out of·the throne, saying, "Splendidly·

G3004.1 V-PAP-NSM λέγων (187x)

Jn 1:15 concerning him and has·yelled·out, saying, "This
Jn 1:26 John answered them, saying, "I·myself immerse in
Jn 1:32 And John testified, saying, "I·have·distinctly·
Jn 4:10 of·God, and who is the·one saying to·you, 'Give me
Jn 7:28 Sanctuary·Atrium, instructing and saying, "¿!·So·
Jn 7:37 Jesus stood and yelled·out, saying, "If any·man
Jn 8:12 Jesus spoke again to·them, saying, "I AM the light
Jn 12:23 And Jesus answered them, saying, "The hour has·
Lk 1:63 requesting a·writing·tablet, he·wrote, saying, "His
Lk 1:67 was·filled with·Holy Spirit and prophesied, saying,
Lk 3:16 John answered, saying to·absolutely·all *of·them*,
Lk 4:4 Jesus answered to him, saying, "It·has·been·written,
Lk 4:34 saying, "Let·*us*·be! What·does·this·have to·do·
Lk 4:35 And Jesus reprimanded him, saying, "Be·muzzled!
Lk 5:8 Peter fell·down·at Jesus' knees, saying, "Go·forth
Lk 5:12 on *his* face, he·petitioned him, saying, "Lord, if
Lk 7:6 centurion sent friends to him, saying to·him, "Lord,
Lk 7:19 sent *them* to Jesus, saying, "Are you·yourself the·
Lk 7:20 has·dispatched us to you, saying, 'Are you·yourself
Lk 7:39 him, declared within himself, saying, "If this·man
Lk 8:8 a·hundred·times·over." While·saying these·things,
Lk 8:30 And Jesus inquired·of him, saying, "What is your
Lk 8:38 together with·him, but Jesus dismissed him, saying,
Lk 8:49 ·*of* the director·of·the·gathering, saying to·him,
Lk 8:50 *it*, answered him, saying, "Do·not be·afraid.
Lk 8:54 of·her by·the hand, hollered·out, saying, "Girl, be·
Lk 9:18 And he·inquired·of them, saying, "Who·do the
Lk 9:38 a·man of the crowd shouted·out, saying, "Mentor,
Lk 10:25 ·up, and thoroughly·trying him, he·said, "Mentor,
Lk 11:45 "Mentor, *when* saying these·things, you·abusively·
Lk 12:16 And he·declared a·parable to them, saying, "The
Lk 12:17 And he·pondered within himself, saying, 'What
Lk 14:3 the experts·in·Torah-Law and Pharisees, saying,
Lk 14:7 ·were·selecting the foremost·places, saying to them,
Lk 15:3 And he·declared this parable to them, saying,
Lk 15:6 friends and the close·neighbors, saying to·them,
Lk 17:4 should·turn·back·around to you, saying, 'I·repent,'
Lk 18:2 saying, "In a·certain city there·was a·certain judge
Lk 18:13 but·rather was·beating at his chest, saying, 'God,
Lk 18:18 ruler inquired·of him, saying, "Beneficially·good
Lk 18:38 And he·cried·out, saying, "Jesus, O·Son of·David,
Lk 18:41 saying, "What·do you·want *that* I·should·do for·
Lk 19:16 "Then the first came·close, saying, 'Lord, your
Lk 19:18 And the second came, saying, 'Lord, your mina

Lk 19:20 "And another came, saying, 'Lord, behold, *here*·is
Lk 19:42 saying, "If you·knew, even you, at·least
Lk 19:46 saying to·them, "It·has·been·written, "My house
Lk 22:19 he·broke *it* and gave *it* to·them, saying, "This is
Lk 22:20 also the cup after eating·supper, saying, "This cup
Lk 22:42 saying, "Father, if you·are·definitely·willing to·
Lk 22:57 But he·denied him, saying, "Woman, I·do·not
Lk 22:59 someone else was·strongly·asserting, saying, "In
Lk 23:3 And Pilate inquired·of him, saying, "Are you·
Lk 23:39 who·were·hanging was·reviling him, saying, "If
Lk 23:40 *criminal* was·reprimanding him, saying, "Are·not·
Lk 23:47 ·*was* happening, glorified God, saying, "Really,
Lk 24:7 saying, 'It·is·mandatory·for the Son of·Clay·Man†
Ac 2:40 ·thoroughly·testifying and was·exhorting, saying,
Ac 3:25 bequeathed unto our fathers, saying to AbRaham, "
Ac 5:25 ·close, someone reported to·them, saying, "Behold
Ac 5:28 saying, "¿!·Did·we·not charge a·charge to·yeu not
Ac 5:36 Theudas rose·up, saying himself to·be someone
Ac 8:9 the Gentiles of·Samaria, saying himself to·be
Ac 8:19 saying, "Give me·also this authority, in·order·that
Ac 8:26 of·Yahweh spoke to Philippe, saying, "Rise·up and
Ac 10:26 But Peter roused him, saying, "Stand·up, *for* also·
Ac 11:4 ·himself in·consecutive·order to·them, saying,
Ac 12:7 on·the side, he·awakened him, saying, "Rise·up in
Ac 15:13 *half-brother of·Jesus)* answered, saying, "Men,
Ac 16:9 standing and imploring him, saying, "Crossing into
Ac 16:28 hollered·out with·a·loud voice, saying, "You·
Ac 19:4 an·immersion of·repentance, saying to·the People
Ac 19:26 crowd *by* persuading *them*, saying that the *gods*
Ac 21:21 pervasive·among the Gentiles, saying for·them not
Ac 21:40 ·addressed *them* in·the Hebrew language, saying,
Ac 22:26 ·announced to·the regiment·commander, saying,
Ac 24:2 Tertullus began to·legally·accuse *Paul*, saying,
Ac 25:14 ·things against Paul to·the king, saying, "There·is
Ac 26:22 and great, saying not·even·one·thing aside·from
Ac 27:10 saying to·them, "Men, I·observe that the
Ac 27:24 saying *to·me*, 'Do·not be·afraid, Paul.
Ac 27:33 ·all·of·them to·partake of·nourishment, saying,
Heb 2:6 someone thoroughly·testified, saying, "What is
Heb 2:12 saying *to·Yahweh*, "I·shall·announce your name
Heb 4:7 "Today," saying *it* by David (after so·vast a·time),
Heb 6:14 saying, "Most assuredly, blessing I·shall·indeed·
Heb 8:11 and each·man his brother, saying, "Know
Heb 9:20 saying, "This *is* the blood of·the covenant which
Heb 10:8 *After* saying above, that "Sacrifice and offering
Heb 12:26 But now he·has·promised, saying, "Yet once·
Mt 1:20 to·him according·to a·vision·in·a·dream, saying,
Mt 2:13 ·Joseph according·to a·vision·in·a·dream, saying,
Mt 2:20 saying, "After·being·awakened, personally·take the
Mt 3:2 and saying, "Yeu·must·repent, for the kingdom of·
Mt 3:14 John was·thoroughly·forbidding him, saying, "I·
Mt 5:2 ·up his mouth, he·was·instructing them, saying,
Mt 7:21 "Not everyone saying to·me, 'Lord, Lord,' shall·
Mt 8:2 ·*him*, was·falling·prostrate to·him, saying, "Lord, if
Mt 8:3 ·out his hand, laid·hold of·him saying, "I·want·to.
Mt 8:6 and saying, "Lord, my servant·boy has·been·cast
Mt 9:18 *to·YeShua*, was·falling·prostrate to·him, saying,
Mt 9:29 he·laid·hold of·their eyes, saying, "According·to
Mt 9:30 YeShua sternly·warned them, saying, "Clearly·see·
Mt 10:5 after·charging them, saying, "Yeu·should·not go·
Mt 13:3 many·things to·them in parables, saying, "Behold,
Mt 13:24 parable he·put·forth·directly to·them, saying,
Mt 13:31 parable he·put·forth·directly to·them, saying,
Mt 14:27 YeShua spoke to·them, saying, "Be·of·good·
Mt 14:30 to·be·plunged·down, he·yelled·out, saying,
Mt 15:4 For God commanded, saying, "Deeply·honor your
Mt 15:7 IsaIah did·prophesy well concerning yeu, saying,
Mt 16:13 was·asking·of his disciples, saying, "Who·do the
Mt 16:22 *aside*, began to·reprimand him, saying, "*God* be·
Mt 17:9 YeShua commanded them, saying, "Yeu·should·
Mt 17:14 ·alongside him, kneeling·down to·him and saying,
Mt 17:25 YeShua preempted him, saying, "What·do you
Mt 18:26 slave was·falling·prostrate to·him, saying, 'Lord,
Mt 18:28 him, he·was·strangling *him*, saying, 'Repay me
Mt 18:29 his fellow·slave was·imploring him, saying, 'Be·
Mt 21:2 saying to·them, "Yeu·should·traverse into the
Mt 21:37 son to them, saying, 'They·shall·be·respectful·of
Mt 22:1 YeShua declared to·them again by parables, saying,
Mt 22:4 he·dispatched other slaves, saying, 'Declare to·
Mt 22:35 inquired·of *him*, trying him and saying,
Mt 22:42 saying, "What·do yeu suppose concerning the
Mt 22:43 'Lord,' saying,
Mt 23:2 saying, "The scribes and the Pharisees sat·down
Mt 25:20 another five talants·of·silver, saying, 'Lord, you·
Mt 25:45 Then he·shall·answer them, saying, 'Certainly I·
Mt 26:27 ·thanks, he·gave *it* to·them, saying, "Drink out
Mt 26:39 on his face, praying and saying, "O·my Father, if
Mt 26:42 ·time, after·going·off, he·prayed, saying, "O·My
Mt 26:48 him over gave them a·sign, saying, "Whomever I·
Mt 26:65 ·high·priest tore·apart his garments, saying, "He·
Mt 26:70 *it* before *them* all, saying, "I·do·not personally·
Mt 27:4 saying, "I·morally·failed in·handing·over blood
Mt 27:11 the governor inquired·of him, saying, "Are you·
Mt 27:24 hands fully·in·front·of·the crowd, saying, "I·am
Mt 27:46 YeShua shouted·out with·a·loud voice, saying,
Mt 28:9 YeShua approached·and·met them, saying, "Be·of·
Mt 28:18 YeShua spoke to·them, saying, "All authority is·
Mk 1:7 And he·was·officially·proclaiming, saying, "The·
Mk 1:15 and saying, "The season has·been·completely·
Mk 1:24 saying, "Let·*us*·be! What·does·this·have to·do·
Mk 1:25 And Jesus reprimanded him, saying, "Be·muzzled!
Mk 1:40 even kneeling·down to·him and saying to·him, "If
Mk 3:33 And he·answered them, saying, "Who is my
Mk 5:9 name?" And he·answered, saying, "My name *is*
Mk 5:23 and was·imploring him repeatedly, saying, "My
Mk 8:15 And he·thoroughly·charged them, saying,
Mk 8:26 him to his house, saying, "You·should·not·even
Mk 8:27 he·was·inquiring·of his disciples, saying to·them,
Mk 8:33 he·reprimanded Peter, saying, "Get·yourself·back
Mk 9:25 he·reprimanded the impure spirit, saying to·him,
Mk 9:38 And John answered him, saying, "Mentor, we·saw
Mk 11:17 And he·was·instructing, saying to·them, "Has·it·
Mk 12:6 him also last to·them, saying, 'They·shall·be·
Mk 12:26 ·bush) God declared to·him, saying, "I·myself
Mk 14:44 had·given them a·prearranged·signal, saying,
Mk 14:60 midst, inquired·of Jesus, saying, "Do·you·not
Mk 14:68 But he·denied *it*, saying, "I·do·not personally·
Mk 15:4 Pilate inquired·of him again, saying, "Do·you·not
Mk 15:9 So Pilate answered them, saying, "Do·yeu·want
Mk 15:34 Jesus cried·out with·a·loud voice, saying, "Eloi
Mk 15:36 *it* to·him to·drink, saying, "Let·us·leave *him*·
Rm 2:22 The·one saying not to·commit·adultery, do·you·
Rm 11:2 How he·confers with·God against IsraEl, saying,
Jud 1:14 Adam, prophesied·of·these, saying, "Behold,
1Co 11:25 the cup after eating·supper, saying, "This cup is
1Jn 2:4 The·one saying, "I·have·known him," yet not
1Jn 2:6 The·one saying he·abides in him is·obligated himself
1Jn 2:9 The·one saying *himself* to·be in the light, and hating
2Jn 1:11 For the·one saying to·him, "Be·well," shares in·his
Rv 1:17 his right hand upon me, saying to·me, "Do·not be·
Rv 7:3 saying, "Yeu·may·not bring·harm·to the earth,
Rv 7:13 from·among the Elders answered, saying to·me,
Rv 10:9 I·went·aside to the angel, saying to·him, "Give to·
Rv 11:1 to·me a·reed like a·rod, saying, "Rouse·yourself
Rv 13:14 of·the Daemonic·Beast, saying to·the·ones residing
Rv 14:8 there·followed another angel, saying, "Babylon is·
Rv 14:9 angel followed them, saying with a·loud voice, "If
Rv 14:18 having the sharp sickle, saying, "Thrust·in your
Rv 17:1 and he·spoke with me, saying to·me, "Come·over·
Rv 18:2 in strength, a·great voice, saying, "Babylon the
Rv 18:21 cast *it* into the sea, saying, "In·this·manner with·
Rv 19:17 he·yelled·out with·a·loud voice, saying to·all the
Rv 21:9 and he·spoke with me, saying, "Come·over·here!

G3004.1 V-PAP-NPN λέγοντα (2x)

Lk 4:41 of many, yelling·out and saying, "You·yourself are
Mk 3:11 ·down·before him and was·yelling·out, saying,

G3004.1 V-PAP-NPF λέγουσαι (5x)

Jn 11:3 his sisters dispatched to him, saying, "Lord, see,
Lk 24:23 his body, they·came, saying also *that* they·had·
Mt 25:9 But the prudent answered, saying, '*Not·so*, lest
Mt 25:11 rest *of·the* virgins came also, saying, 'Lord, Lord,
Rv 11:15 great voices in the heaven, saying, "The kingdoms

G3004.1 V-PAP-NPM λέγοντες (154x)

Jn 4:31 the disciples were·imploring·of him, saying, "Rabbi
Jn 4:51 him, and announced *to·him*, saying, "Your boy
Jn 6:52 were·quarreling among one·another, saying, "How·
Jn 7:15 the Judeans were·marveling, saying, "How·does
Jn 9:2 And his disciples asked·of him, saying, "Rabbi, who
Jn 9:19 And they·asked·of them, saying, "Is this yeur son,
Jn 10:33 The Judeans answered him, saying, "We·do·not
Jn 11:31 went·out, they·followed her, saying, "She·heads·
Jn 12:21 of·Galilee, and were·asking·of him, saying, "Sir,
Jn 18:40 So·then they·all yelled·out again, saying, "Not
Jn 19:6 saw him, they·yelled·out, saying, "Crucify *him*,
Jn 19:12 but the Judeans were·yelling·out, saying, "If you·
Lk 1:66 laid·*them*·up in their hearts, saying, "What then
Lk 3:10 the crowds were·inquiring·of him, saying, "So·then
Lk 3:14 ·officers also were·inquiring·of him, saying, "And
Lk 4:36 ·speaking·together among one·another, saying,
Lk 5:21 and the Pharisees began to·ponder, saying, "Who is
Lk 5:26 and were·filled with·reverent·fear·and·awe, saying,
Lk 5:30 were·grumbling toward his disciples, saying, "Why
Lk 7:4 they·were·imploring him earnestly, saying, "He·is
Lk 7:16 and they·were·glorifying God, saying, "A·great
Lk 8:9 his disciples were·inquiring·of him, saying, "What
Lk 8:24 they·thoroughly·awakened him, saying, "Captain,
Lk 8:25 ·afraid, they·marveled, saying among one·another,
Lk 10:17 the seventy returned·back with joy, saying, "Lord,
Lk 13:25 outside and to·knock at·the door, saying, 'Lord,
Lk 13:31 ·came·alongside certain Pharisees, saying to·him,
Lk 14:30 saying, 'This man·of·clay† began to·build yet did·
Lk 15:2 and the scribes were·murmuring, saying, "This·
Lk 17:13 ·themselves lifted·*up their* voices, saying, "Jesus,
Lk 19:7 *this*, absolutely·all were·murmuring, saying, "He·
Lk 19:14 a·delegation right·behind him, saying, 'We·do·not
Lk 19:38 saying, "Having·been·blessed *is* the King who·
Lk 20:2 and declared to him, saying, "Declare to·us, by
Lk 20:5 ·reckoned·together alongside themselves, saying,
Lk 20:14 deliberated among themselves, saying, 'This is the
Lk 20:21 And they·inquired·of him, saying, "Mentor, we·
Lk 20:28 saying, "Mentor, Moses wrote to·us, if any·man's
Lk 21:7 And they·inquired·of him, saying, "So·then Mentor
Lk 21:8 for many shall·come in my name, saying, 'I AM,'
Lk 22:64 and were·inquiring·of him, saying, "Prophesy,
Lk 22:66 into their·own joint·council·of·Sanhedrin, saying,
Lk 23:2 And they·began to·legally·accuse him, saying,
Lk 23:5 But they·were·strongly·insisting, saying, "He·
Lk 23:18 altogether·at·once, they·screamed·out, saying,
Lk 23:21 But they·were·exclaiming, saying, "Crucify *him*,
Lk 23:35 with·them were·sneering·at *him*, saying, "He·
Lk 23:37 and saying, "If you·yourself are the king of·the
Lk 24:29 But they·personally·compelled him, saying,
Ac 1:6 they·were·inquiring·of him, saying, "Lord, do·you
Ac 2:7 and were·marveling, saying among one·another,
Ac 2:12 and were·thoroughly·perplexed, saying one to
Ac 4:16 saying, "What shall·we·do to·these men·of·clay†?
Ac 5:23 saying, "In·fact, we·found the dungeon having·
Ac 8:10 *the* least unto *the* greatest, saying, "This·man is the
Ac 11:3 saying, "You·entered·in alongside men being
Ac 11:18 and they·were·glorifying God, saying, "So also
Ac 13:15 ·the·gathering dispatched to them, saying, "Men,
Ac 14:11 their voices, saying in·the·language·of·Lycaonia,
Ac 14:15 and saying, "Men, why·do yeu·do these·things?
Ac 14:18 And with·difficulty while·saying these·things,
Ac 15:5 of·the Pharisees having·trusted, saying, "It·is·
Ac 15:24 (dislodging·and·disturbing yeur souls, saying, '*It*·
Ac 16:35 dispatched the enforcement·officers, saying,
Ac 17:7 to·the decrees of·Caesar, saying *that* there·is
Ac 17:19 to Mars'·Hill·*(also·called·AreoPagus)*, saying,

Ac 18:13 saying, "This·man persistently·persuades men·of·
Ac 19:13 the evil spirits, saying, "On·oath,·we·charge yeu
Ac 19:28 ·rage, and they·were·yelling·out, saying, "Great
Ac 22:22 they·lifted·up their voices, saying, "Away·with
Ac 23:9 ·up, they·were·thoroughly·fighting, saying, "We·
Ac 23:12 over·to·destruction, saying neither to·eat nor to·
Ac 26:31 they·were·speaking among one·another, saying,
Heb 11:14 For the·ones saying such·things make·it·clear that
Mt 2:2 saying, "Where is the·one being·reproduced·and·
Mt 6:31 So·then, yeu·should·not be·anxious, saying, 'what
Mt 8:25 his disciples awakened him, saying, "Lord, save
Mt 8:27 the men·of·clay† marveled, saying, "What·manner·
Mt 8:29 behold, they·yelled·out, saying, "What·does·this·
Mt 8:31 the demons were·imploring him, saying, "If you·
Mt 9:14 of·John came·alongside him, saying, "Why·do we·
Mt 9:27 followed him, yelling·out and saying, "O·Son of·
Mt 9:33 and the crowds marveled, saying, "Never·at·any·
Mt 10:7 And while·traversing, officially·proclaim, saying,
Mt 12:10 him, they·inquired·of him, saying, "Is·it·proper
Mt 12:38 scribes and Pharisees answered, saying, "Mentor,
Mt 13:36 disciples came·alongside him, saying, "Explain
Mt 14:15 his disciples came·alongside him, saying, "The
Mt 14:26 sea, the disciples were·troubled, saying, "It·is a·
Mt 14:33 *alongside*, fell·prostrate to·him, saying, "Truly
Mt 15:1 from JeruSalem come·alongside YeShua saying,
Mt 15:23 ·alongside were·imploring·of him, saying,
Mt 16:7 they·were·deliberating among themselves, saying,
Mt 17:10 his disciples inquired·of him, saying, "So·then
Mt 18:1 disciples came·alongside YeShua, saying, "Who
Mt 19:3 ·alongside him, trying him and saying to·him, "Is·
Mt 19:25 were tremendously astounded, saying, "Who then
Mt 20:12 saying, 'These last·ones did one hour, and you·
Mt 20:30 that YeShua passes·by, they·yelled·out, saying,
Mt 20:31 but they·were·yelling·out more·loudly, saying—
Mt 21:9 and the·ones following, were·yelling·out, saying,
Mt 21:20 *this*, the disciples marveled, saying, "How·is the
Mt 21:23 of·the people came·alongside him, saying, "By
Mt 21:25 ·deliberating closely·among themselves, saying,
Mt 22:16 to·him along·with the HerOdians, saying, "Mentor
Mt 22:23 came·alongside him, the·ones saying *there·is* not
Mt 22:24 saying, "Mentor, Moses declared, if a·certain·man
Mt 23:16 *yeu* blind guides, the·ones saying, 'Whoever
Mt 24:3 came·alongside him in private, saying, "Declare to·
Mt 24:5 many shall·come in my name, saying, 'I AM the
Mt 25:37 the righteous shall·answer him, saying, 'Lord,
Mt 25:44 "Then they also shall·answer him, saying, 'Lord,
Mt 26:8 his disciples are·greatly·displeased, saying, "To
Mt 26:17 disciples came·alongside YeShua, saying to·him,
Mt 26:68 saying, "Prophesy to·us, O·Anointed-One, who is
Mt 27:23 were·yelling·out more·abundantly, saying, "Let·
Mt 27:29 him, they·were·mocking him, saying, "*Ah*! Be·
Mt 27:40 and saying, "The·one demolishing the Temple and
Mt 27:54 they·feared tremendously, saying, "Truly this
Mt 27:63 saying, "Sir, we·are·mindful·of that thing the
Mt 28:13 saying, "Yeu·must·declare, 'His disciples stole
Mk 5:12 all the demons implored him, saying, "Send us
Mk 5:35 *the house·of* the director·of·the·gathering, saying,
Mk 6:2 hearing *him* were·astounded, saying, "From·what·
Mk 7:37 ·astounded above·and·beyond·excess, saying,
Mk 8:16 ·were·deliberating among one·another, saying, "*It*·
Mk 9:11 And they·were·inquiring·of him, saying, "Why·do
Mk 10:26 beyond·excess, saying among themselves, "Then
Mk 10:35 approach·close to·him, saying, "Mentor, we·
Mk 10:49 ·hollered·out·for the blind·man, saying to·him,
Mk 11:9 and the·ones following were·yelling·out, saying,
Mk 11:31 they·were·reckoning among themselves, saying,
Mk 12:18 a·resurrection, and they·inquired·of him, saying,
Mk 13:6 For many shall·come in my name, saying, 'I AM
Mk 14:4 ·displeased alongside themselves, and saying,
Mk 14:57 was·falsely·testifying against him, saying,
Mk 15:29 him, wagging their heads and saying, "Ah, the·
Jac 4:13 Come·on now, the·ones saying, "Today or
2Pe 3:4 and saying, "Where is the promise of·his returning·
2Ti 2:18 the truth, saying the resurrection even·now to·
Rv 4:10 victor's·crowns in·the·sight of·the throne, saying,
Rv 5:9 And they·sing a·brand-new song, saying, "You·are
Rv 5:12 saying with·a·loud voice, "Worthy is the Lamb
Rv 6:10 they·were·yelling·out with·a·loud voice, saying,
Rv 7:10 and yelling·out with·a·loud voice, saying, "The
Rv 7:12 saying, "So·be·it,·Amen! The blessing, and the
Rv 11:17 saying, "We·give·thanks to·you, O·Yahweh, God
Rv 13:4 *directly·before* the Daemonic·Beast, saying, "Who *is*
Rv 15:3 and the song of·the Lamb, saying, "Great and
Rv 18:10 ·account·of the fear of·her torment, saying, 'Woe,
Rv 18:16 and saying, 'Woe, woe, the Great City,
Rv 18:18 the smoke of·her fiery·burning, saying, 'What *city*
Rv 18:19 ·out, weeping and mourning, saying, 'Woe, woe,
Rv 19:4 who·is·sitting·down on the throne, saying, "So·be·

G3004.1 V-PAS-1S λέγω (2x)

Heb 11:32 And what more should·I·say? For the time shall·
Phm 1:19 ·pay *it*, not that I·should·say to·you that even you·

G3004.1 V-PAS-1P λέγωμεν (1x)

2Co 9:4 we·ourselves (not that we·should·say yeu *also*)

G3004.1 V-PAS-2P λέγητε (1x)

1Co 1:10 in·order·that yeu all should·say the same·thing,

G3004.1 V-PAS-3S λέγῃ (3x)

Jn 2:5 "Whatever he·might say to·yeu, do *it*.
Jac 2:14 brothers, though someone should·say he·has trust
1Co 3:4 For whenever someone should·say, "In·fact, I·

G3004.1 V-PAS-3P λέγωσιν (1x)

1Th 5:3 For whenever they·should·say, "Peace and security,

G3004.1 V-PPI-3S λέγεται (3x)

Jn 1:38 ·being·translated *from Hebrew*, is·to·say Mentor),
Jn 20:16 (which is·to·say, "O·my·*great*·Mentor").
Heb 7:13 these·things are·said, has·participated·with·and·

G3004.1 V-PPN λέγεσθαι (2x)

Lk 9:7 ·perplexed, on·account·of *that* it·was·said by some
Heb 3:15 Explicitly it·is·said, "'Today, if yeu·should·hear

G3004.1 V-PPP-APN λεγόμενα (1x)

Lk 18:34 neither were·they·knowing the·things being·said.

G3004.1 V-PPP-DPN λεγομένοις (5x)

Ac 8:6 were·giving·heed to·the·things being·said by Philippe
Ac 13:45 were·contradicting the·things being·said by Paul,
Ac 27:11 rather than by·the·things being·said by Paul.
Ac 28:24 they·were·persuaded by·the·things being·said, but
Heb 8:1 Now concerning the·things being·said, *this·is the*

G3004.1 V-IAI-1S ἔλεγον (2x)

Php 3:18 ·about, of·whom I·was·saying to·yeu many·times,
2Co 9:3 part; that, just·as I·was·saying, yeu·may·be having·

G3004.1 V-IAI-2P ἐλέγετε (1x)

Lk 17:6 ·seed *does*, yeu·might say to·this mulberry-fig·tree,

G3004.1 V-IAI-3S ἔλεγεν (64x)

Jn 2:21 But he·was·saying this concerning the temple of·his
Jn 2:22 recalled·to·mind that he·was·saying this to·them.
Jn 5:18 Sabbath— moreover he·was·saying also *that* God
Jn 6:6 And he·was·saying this, trying him, for he·himself
Jn 6:65 And he·was·saying, "On·account·of that, I·have·
Jn 8:27 ·not know that he·was·saying to·them *concerning* the
Jn 8:31 So·then, Jesus was·saying to *those* Judeans, the·ones
Jn 9:9 *But* that·man was·saying, "It·is·I myself.
Jn 12:29 standing·by and hearing *it*, was·saying, "*It·was*
Jn 12:33 And he·was·saying this, signifying what·kind·of
Lk 3:7 Accordingly, he·was·saying to·the crowds
Lk 5:36 And he·was also saying a·parable to them, "Not·
Lk 6:5 And he·was·saying to·them, "The Son of·Clay·Man†
Lk 6:20 eyes to his disciples, he·was·saying, "Supremely·
Lk 9:23 Then *Jesus* was·saying to *them* all, "If any·man
Lk 10:2 Now·then, he·was·saying to them, "In·fact, the
Lk 12:54 And he·was·saying also to·the crowds, "Whenever
Lk 13:14 ·cured on·the Sabbath, was·saying to·the crowd,
Lk 13:18 But he·was·saying, "To·what is the kingdom of·
Lk 14:7 And he·was·saying a·parable to·the·ones having·
Lk 14:12 Then he·was·saying also to·the·one having·called·
Lk 16:1 And he·was·saying also toward his disciples,
Lk 16:5 ·his lord's needy·debtors, he·was·saying to·the first,
Lk 18:1 Then also he·was·saying a·parable to·them, *how*
Lk 21:10 Then he·was·saying to·them, "Nation shall·be·
Lk 23:34 Then Jesus was·saying, "Father, forgive them, for
Lk 23:42 And he·was·saying to·Jesus, "Lord, recall me to·
Ac 4:32 And not·even one was·saying *for* any of·his
Ac 11:16 utterance of·*the*·Lord, how he·was·saying, 'John
Ac 13:25 ·fulfilling his·own running·race, he·was·saying,
Ac 28:17 ·them coming·together, he·was·saying to them,
Mt 9:21 for she·was·saying within herself, "If merely I·
Mt 14:4 For John was·saying to·him, "It·is·not proper for·
Mk 2:25 And he·himself was·saying to·them, "Did·yeu·not·
Mk 2:27 And *Jesus* was·saying to·them, "The Sabbath
Mk 3:23 after·summoning them, he·was·saying to·them in
Mk 4:2 and in his instruction, he·was·saying to·them,
Mk 4:9 And he·was·saying to·them, "The·one having ears
Mk 4:11 And he·was·saying to·them, "It·has·been·given to·
Mk 4:21 And he·was·saying to·them, "¿! Is·it·ever·the·
Mk 4:24 And he·was·saying to·them, "Look·out·for how
Mk 4:26 And he·was·saying, "In·this·manner is the
Mk 4:30 And he·was·saying, "To·what should·we·liken the
Mk 5:8 (For *Jesus* was·saying to·him, "Impure spirit, come·
Mk 5:28 For she·was·saying, "Because if·even I·should·lay·
Mk 5:30 ·himself·about in the crowd, was·saying, "Who
Mk 6:4 But Jesus was·saying to·them, "A·prophet is not
Mk 6:10 And he·was·saying to·them, "In·whatever·place
Mk 6:14 was openly·well·known. And he·was·saying,
Mk 6:18 For John was·saying to·HerOd·AntiPas, "It·is·not
Mk 7:9 And he·was·saying to·them, "Clearly·full·well do·
Mk 7:14 all the crowd, he·was·saying to·them, "Listen·to
Mk 7:20 And he·was·saying, "The·thing proceeding·forth
Mk 8:21 And he·was·saying to·them, "How do·yeu·not
Mk 8:24 And looking·up, he·was·saying, "I·look·upon the
Mk 9:1 And he·was·saying to·them, "Certainly I·say to·yeu,
Mk 9:24 ·child, yelling·out with tears, was·saying, "Lord,
Mk 9:31 his disciples, and he·was·saying to·them, "The
Mk 12:35 in the Sanctuary·Atrium, Jesus was·saying,
Mk 12:38 And he·was·saying to·them in his instruction,
Mk 14:31 But he·was·saying out *all the* more vehemently,
Mk 14:36 And he·was·saying, "Abba, Father, all·things *are*
Mk 15:14 But Pilate was·saying to·them, "For what crime
Rm 7:7 longing, except·that the Torah-Law was·saying,

G3004.1 V-IAI-3P ἔλεγον (69x)

Jn 4:33 So·then the disciples were·saying among one·another
Jn 4:42 Also they·were·saying to·the woman, "No·longer
Jn 5:10 Judeans were·saying to·the·one having·been·both·
Jn 6:14 a·miraculous·sign, the men·of·clay† were·saying,
Jn 6:42 And they·were·saying, "Is this not Jesus, the son of·
Jn 7:11 him at the Sacred·Feast and were·saying, "Where is
Jn 7:12 In·fact, they·were·saying, "He·is a·beneficially·
Jn 7:12 ·good·man," but others were·saying, "No, but·
Jn 7:25 from·among the·men of·JeruSalem were·saying, "Is
Jn 7:31 crowd trusted in him and were·saying, "Whenever
Jn 7:40 many from·among the crowd were·saying, "Truly
Jn 7:41 Others were·saying, "This is the Anointed-One.
Jn 7:41 But others were·saying, "For ¿! is·it from·out of·
Jn 8:6 But they·were·saying this, trying him in·order·that
Jn 8:19 So·then they·were·saying to·him, "Where is your
Jn 8:22 So·then the Judeans were·saying, "Is·it·that he·
Jn 8:25 So·then they·were·saying to·him, "Who are you·
Jn 9:8 previously that he·was blind) were·saying, "Is this
Jn 9:9 Some were·saying, "This is·he.
Jn 9:10 Accordingly, they·were·saying to·him, "How·are
Jn 9:16 some from·among the Pharisees were·saying, "This
Jn 9:16 the Sabbath." Others were·saying, "How·is a·man·
Jn 10:20 And many from·among them were·saying, "He·has
Jn 10:21 Others were·saying, "These·things are not the
Jn 10:24 Judeans surrounded him and were·saying to·him,
Jn 10:41 And many came to him and were·saying, "John, in·
Jn 11:36 So·then the Judeans were·saying, "See how fond·
Jn 11:47 a·joint·council·of·Sanhedrin and were·saying,
Jn 11:56 ·seeking Jesus and were·saying among one·another,
Jn 12:29 has·occurred." Others were·saying, "An·angel
Jn 16:18 So·then they·were·saying, "What is this·thing that
Jn 19:3 and they·were·saying, "*Ah*! Be·well, O·King of·the

λλ

Jn 19:21 chief·priests of·the Judeans were·saying to·Pilate,
Jn 20:25 So the other disciples were·saying to·him, "We·
Lk 4:22 of·his mouth. And·also they·were·saying, "Is not
Lk 22:65 And they·were·saying many other reviling *things*
Lk 24:10 with·them, who were·saying these·things to the
Ac 2:13 And while·jeering, others were·saying, "These·
Ac 9:21 hearing *him* were·astonished and were·saying, "Is
Ac 12:15 to·be in·this·manner. But they·were·saying, "It·is
Ac 17:18 him. And some were·saying, "What·is·it *that* this
Ac 21:4 days; these·same·men were·saying to·Paul through
Ac 28:4 his hand, they·were·saying among one·another,
Ac 28:6 ·changing·their·minds, they·were·saying him to·be
Mt 9:34 But the Pharisees were·saying, "He·casts·out the
Mt 12:23 all the crowds were·astonished and were·saying,
Mt 21:11 And the crowds were·saying, "This is YeShua the
Mt 26:5 But they·were·saying, "Not on the feast·day, lest a·
Mt 27:41 ·priests with the scribes and elders were·saying,
Mt 27:47 there, after·hearing *that*, were·saying, "This·man
Mt 27:49 But the rest were·saying, "Leave *him·alone*, we·
Mk 2:16 ·disqualified·men, were·saying to·his disciples,
Mk 2:24 And the Pharisees were·saying to·him, "See, why·
Mk 3:21 to·take·secure·hold·of him, for they·were·saying,
Mk 3:22 ·walking·down from JeruSalem, were·saying "He·
Mk 3:30 Because they·were·saying, "He·has an·impure
Mk 4:41 ·and·awe, and they·were·saying to one·another,
Mk 5:31 And his disciples were·saying to·him, "You·look·
Mk 6:15 Others were·saying, "It·is EliJah.
Mk 6:15 And others were·saying, "It·is a·prophet, or as
Mk 11:5 of·the·ones standing there were·saying to·them,
Mk 14:2 But they·were·saying, "Not on the feast *day*, lest
Mk 14:31 And also, all were·saying likewise.
Mk 14:70 ·ones standing·nearby were·saying again to·Peter,
Mk 15:31 while·mocking, were·saying among one·another
Mk 15:35 after·hearing *that*, were·saying, "Behold, he·
Mk 16:3 And they·were·saying among themselves, "Who
Jud 1:18 how·that they·were·saying to·yeu that there·shall·
Rv 5:14 And the four living·beings were·saying, "So·be·it,·

EG3004.1 (26x)

Jn 4:1 that the Pharisees *had* heard *it said* that "Jesus makes
Jn 9:9 But others *were·saying*, "He·is like him.
Jn 12:28 a·voice from·out of·the heaven, *saying*, "Both I·
Lk 9:19 John the Immerser, but others *say* EliJah, and others
Lk 9:19 *say* EliJah, and others *say* that some prophet of·the
Lk 20:27 the·ones being·contradictory *by·saying that* there·is
Lk 22:34 ·utterly·deny three·times, *saying that* you·do·not
Ac 7:32 *saying*, "I·myself *am* the God of·your fathers, the
Ac 9:6 me to·do?" And the Lord *said* to him, "Rise·up and
Ac 9:11 And the Lord *said* to him, "Rising·up, traverse on
Ac 9:20 Anointed-One in the gatherings, *saying*, "This is
Ac 10:13 And there·came a·voice to him, *saying*, "Peter,
Ac 15:1 from Judea were·instructing the brothers, *saying*,
Ac 17:18 strange·new demigods." *They·said this* because
Gal 3:8 ·the·good·news·in·advance to·AbRaham, *saying*,
Mt 16:14 "In·fact, *some say* John the Immerser, and others
Mt 16:14 John the Immerser, and others *say* EliJah, but *yet*
Mt 16:14 *say* EliJah, but *yet* others *say* JeremIah, or one of·
Mt 23:18 "And·also *yeu·say*, 'Whoever should·swear by the
Mt 26:74 ·vow·of·destruction and to·swear, *saying*, "I·do·
Mt 27:44 And *saying* the same·thing also, the robbers (the·
Mt 27:46 lama shebaq-thani?" That·is *to·say*, "My God,
Mk 1:11 a·voice from·out of·the heavens, *saying*, "You·
Mk 8:28 "John the Immerser, but some *say*, EliJah, and
Mk 10:33 *saying*, "Behold, we·walk·up to JeruSalem, and
Rm 4:7 *saying*, '" Supremely·blessed *are·they* whose

G3004.3 V-PAI-1S λέγω (1x)

Jn 15:15 "No·longer do·I·refer·to yeu *as* slaves, because the

G3004.3 V-PAI-2S λέγεις (3x)

Lk 18:19 "Why·do you·refer·to me *as* beneficially·good?
Mt 19:17 "Why·do you·refer·to me *as* beneficially·good?
Mk 10:18 "Why·do you·refer·to me *as* beneficially·good?

G3004.3 V-PAI-2P λέγετε (2x)

Mk 14:71 ·know this man·of·clay† to·whom yeu·refer."
Mk 15:12 ·do *to·the·one* whom yeu·refer·to·as King of·the

G3004.3 V-PAI-3S λέγει (5x)

Jn 13:22 being·at·a·loss concerning who he·is·referring·to.
Jn 13:24 ·be, concerning the·man·to·whom he·is·referring.
Lk 20:37 burning·bush, *just* as·soon·as he·says Yahweh,
Mk 12:37 So·then David himself refers·to him *as* 'Lord,' so
Rm 4:6 ·as David also refers·to the supreme·blessedness of·

G3004.3 V-PAN λέγειν (2x)

Ac 10:28 to·me to·refer·to not·even·one man·of·clay† *as*
Eph 5:12 even to·refer·to the·things which·are·occurring

G3004.3 V-PAP-ASF λέγουσαν (1x)

Rv 2:20 woman JeZebel, the·one referring·to herself *as* a·

G3004.3 V-PPI-3S λέγεται (5x)

Jn 19:17 Place of·a·Skull, which is·referred·to in·Hebrew *as*
Ac 9:36 is·referred·to·as Dorcas·*(meaning·Gazelle)*. She·
Heb 9:2 ·Show bread, which is·referred·to·as *the* Holy·Place
Mt 13:55 mother referred·to·as Mariam·*(meaning·bitterly·*?
Rv 8:11 the name of·the star is·referred·to·as Wormwood,

G3004.3 V-PPN λέγεσθαι (1x)

Heb 11:24 renounced being·referred·to·as son of·Pharaoh's

G3004.3 V-PPP-ASN λεγόμενον (2x)

Mt 26:36 to an·open·field being·referred·to·as GethSemane,
2Th 2:4 ·himself over all *that·is* being·referred·to·as God or

G3004.3 V-PPP-ASF λεγομένην (4x)

Jn 4:5 to a·city of·Samaria being·referred·to·as Sychar *(or·*
Jn 11:54 *and* into a·city being·referred·to·as Ephraim. And
Ac 3:2 the·one being·referred·to·as Stately·and·Elegant, to·
Mt 2:23 in a·city being·referred·to·as Natsareth *(meaning·a·*

G3004.3 V-PPP-ASM λεγόμενον (8x)

Jn 19:13 in a·place being·referred·to·as Stone·Pavement, but
Jn 19:17 ·forth unto the *place* being·referred·to·as *the* Place
Mt 4:18 Simon (the·one being·referred·to·as Peter) and
Mt 9:9 ·man·of·clay†, *Levi* being·referred·to·as MattHew,
Mt 27:16 being·referred·to·as BarAbbas·*(meaning·son·of·*.
Mt 27:17 the·one being·referred·to·as Anointed-One?
Mt 27:22 the·one being·referred·to·as Anointed-One?
Mt 27:33 coming to a·place being·referred·to·as GolGotha,

G3004.3 V-PPP-GSF λεγομένης (2x)

Ac 6:9 gathering, the·one being·referred·to·as *the Gathering*
Eph 2:11 by the·one being·referred·to·as *the* Circumcision,

G3004.3 V-PPP-GSM λεγομένου (1x)

Mt 26:3 ·high·priest, the·one being·referred·to·as Caiaphas,

G3004.3 V-PPP-NSF λεγομένη (2x)

Lk 22:1 ·near, the·one being·referred·to·as Passover.
Heb 9:3 Tabernacle, the·one being·referred·to·as *the* Holy

G3004.3 V-PPP-NSM λεγόμενος (12x)

Jn 4:25 the·one being·referred·to·as Anointed-One.
Jn 9:11 "A·man·of·clay† being·referred·to·as Jesus, he·
Jn 11:16 ·then Thomas (the·one being·referred·to·as Twin)
Jn 20:24 the twelve, the·one being·referred·to·as Twin) was
Jn 21:2 and Thomas (the·one being·referred·to·as Twin),
Lk 22:47 a·crowd. And the·one being·referred·to·as Judas,
Mt 1:16 the·one being·referred·to·as Anointed-One.
Mt 10:2 first, Simon (the·one being·referred·to·as Peter) and
Mt 26:14 twelve, the·one being·referred·to·as Judas IsCariot
Mt 27:33 GolGotha, that is being·referred·to·as, *the* Place
Mk 15:7 there·was the·one being·referred·to·as BarAbbas,
Col 4:11 and JeShua (the·one being·referred·to·as Justus).

G3004.3 V-PPP-NPM λεγόμενοι (2x)

1Co 8:5 even if·perhaps they·are being·referred·to·as gods,
Eph 2:11 the·ones being·referred·to·as *the* Uncircumcision

G3004.3 V-IAI-3S ἔλεγεν (1x)

Jn 6:71 Now he·was·referring·to Judas IsCariot, *the son* of·

EG3004.3 (1x)

Mk 15:22 him to *the* place *being·referred·to·as* GolGotha,

G3004.4 V-PAI-1S λέγω (5x)

Jn 13:19 From this·moment·on, I·relate *it* to·yeu before it·
Gal 3:15 Brothers, I·relate *this matter* according·to a·man·
Mk 11:33 "Neither do I·myself relate to·yeu by what·kind·of
1Co 15:51 Behold, I·relay to·yeu a·mystery. In·fact, we·
1Ti 2:7 and an·ambassador— (I·relate *the* truth in

G3004.4 V-PAI-3S λέγει (1x)

Jn 12:22 PhilIp comes and relays *this* to·Andrew, and again

G3004.4 V-PAI-3P λέγουσιν (2x)

Jn 12:22 and again Andrew and PhilIp relay *it* to·Jesus.
Mk 1:30 ·fever, and immediately they·related *this* to·him

G3004.4 V-PAN λέγειν (5x)

Lk 20:9 Then he·began to·relay this parable to the people,
Ac 17:18 ·peddler actually·supposes to·relate *to·others*?
Heb 5:11 yet the·explanation·is·difficult to·relay *to·yeu* since
Mk 10:32 again the twelve, he·began to·relate to·them the
Mk 12:1 And he·began to·relate to·them in parables.

G3004.4 V-PAP-NSM λέγων (1x)

Ac 1:3 forty days, and·also relating the·things concerning

G3004.4 V-PAS-3P λέγωσιν (1x)

Mk 8:30 that not·even·to·one·man should·they·relate *this*

G3004.4 V-PPN λέγεσθαι (1x)

Heb 7:11 and not to·be·related according·to the assigned·

G3004.4 V-IAI-1S ἔλεγον (2x)

Ac 25:20 ·question, was·relating·as·to whether he·might·be·
2Th 2:5 yet alongside yeu, I·was·relating these·things to·yeu

G3004.4 V-IAI-3S ἔλεγεν (1x)

Lk 13:6 And he·was·relaying this parable, "A·certain·man

G3004.4 V-IAI-3P ἔλεγον (1x)

Lk 9:31 ·made·visible in glory, were·relating his exodus

G3004.6 V-PAN λέγειν (3x)

Lk 7:24 going·off, *Jesus* began to·discourse to the crowds
Ac 24:10 ·the governor beckoning for·him to·discourse, Paul
Ac 26:1 ·permitted for·you to·discourse on·your·own behalf.

G3005 λεῖμμα lêîmma *n.* (1x)

Roots:G3007 Compare:G3062 See:G2640 G2645
xLangAlso:H3499 H7611

G3005.2 N-NSN λεῖμμα (1x)

Rm 11:5 there·has·come·to·be a·remnant according·to a·

G3006 λεῖος lêîôs *adj.* (1x)

Compare:G5138
xLangEquiv:H2512

G3006 A-APF λείας (1x)

Lk 3:5 roadways *shall·be made* into smooth *roadways*;

G3007 λείπω lêípō *v.* (6x)

Compare:G5302 See:G3005 G1587 G1952 G1257

G3007.4 V-PAI-3S λείπει (1x)

Lk 18:22 for·yourself, one·thing remains·left·undone. Sell

G3007.4 V-PAP-APN λείποντα (1x)

Tit 1:5 the·things remaining·left·undone and should·fully·

G3007.4 V-PAS-3S λείπῃ (1x)

Tit 3:13 not·even·one·thing may·remain·left·undone for·.

G3007.5 V-PPI-3S λείπεται (1x)

Jac 1:5 So, if any of·yeu is·deficient of·wisdom, let·him·

G3007.5 V-PPP-NPM λειπόμενοι (2x)

Jac 1:4 and entirely·whole, being·deficient in not·one·thing.
Jac 2:15 naked and should·be being·deficient of·the daily

G3008 λειτ•ουργέω lêitôurgḗō *v.* (4x)

Roots:G3011 Compare:G3000 G1247 See:G3009
G3008-1 G3008-2 xLangAlso:H5647 A8120

G3008.1 V-PAP-GPM λειτουργούντων (1x)

Ac 13:2 And as·they were·publicly·serving for·the Lord,

G3008.1 V-PAP-NSM λειτουργῶν (1x)

Heb 10:11 stands each day publicly·serving and offering

EG3008.1 (1x)

Rm 15:23 no·longer having a·place *to·publicly·work* in these

G3008.2 V-AAN λειτουργῆσαι (1x)

Rm 15:27 also to·publicly·work·charity to·them in the

G3009 λειτ•ουργία lêitôurgía *n.* (6x)

Roots:G3008 Compare:G1248 G3000 See:G3010
G3008-1
xLangEquiv:H8053-1 xLangAlso:H5656

G3009.1 N-DSF λειτουργίᾳ (1x)

Php 2:17 upon the sacrifice and public·service of·yeur trust,

G3009.1 N-GSF λειτουργίας (4x)

Lk 1:23 ·as the days of·his public·service were·fulfilled, *that*
Heb 8:6 a·more·superb public·service, by·as·much·as he·is
Heb 9:21 blood, and all the vessels of·the public·service.
Php 2:30 ·utterly·supply yeur lack of·public·service, the·one

G3009.2 N-GSF λειτουργίας (1x)

2Co 9:12 Because the service of·this public·charity, not

G3010 λειτ•ουργικός lêitôurgikôs *adj.* (1x)
Roots:G3011 Compare:G1248 See:G3008 G3009 xLangAlso:H5656
G3010.1 A-NPN λειτουργικά (1x)
Heb 1:14 Are·they not·indeed all publicly·serving spirits,

G3011 λειτ•ουργός lêitôurgôs *n.* (4x)
Roots:G2992 G2041 Compare:G1249 G2819-2 G2999-2 See:G3008-1 xLangEquiv:H7763-1 xLangAlso:H8053-1
G3011.2 N-NSM λειτουργός (1x)
Heb 8:2 a·public·servant of·the holy·things and of·the true
G3011.2 N-NPM λειτουργοί (1x)
Rm 13:6 ·are God's public·servants, diligently·continuing in
G3011.2 N-ASM λειτουργόν (2x)
Rm 15:16 for me to·be a·public·servant of·Jesus Anointed
Php 2:25 yeur ambassador and public·servant *concerning* my

G3012 λέντιον lêntiôn *n.* (2x)
Compare:G4676
G3012.2 N-ASN λέντιον (1x)
Jn 13:4 the garments. And taking a·towel, he·tightly·girded
G3012.2 N-DSN λεντίῳ (1x)
Jn 13:5 ·firmly·wipe *them* with·the towel with·which he·was

G3013 λεπίς lêpís *n.* (1x)
Roots:G3016-3 See:G3014 G3015 xLangAlso:H7193
G3013.2 N-NPF λεπίδες (1x)
Ac 9:18 immediately, *something* like scales fell·off from his

G3014 λέπρα lêpra *n.* (4x)
Roots:G3016-3 See:G3013 G3015 xLangAlso:H6883
G3014.2 N-NSF λέπρα (3x)
Lk 5:13 And immediately, the leprosy went·off from him.
Mt 8:3 And immediately, his leprosy was·purified.
Mk 1:42 *this*, immediately, the leprosy went·off from him,
G3014.2 N-GSF λέπρας (1x)
Lk 5:12 behold, a·man full of·leprosy; and after·seeing

G3015 λεπρός lêprôs *adj.* (9x)
Roots:G3016-3 See:G3014 G3013
G3015.2 A-NPM λεπροί (1x)
Lk 17:12 ·approached·and·met him ten leprous men who
G3015.3 A-NSM λεπρός (2x)
Mt 8:2 And behold, a·leper, after·coming *toward·him*, was·
Mk 1:40 And a·leper came to him, imploring him, even
G3015.3 A-NPM λεπροί (3x)
Lk 4:27 "And many lepers were in IsraEl in·the·days of·
Lk 7:22 lame·men walk, lepers are·purified, deaf·men hear
Mt 11:5 and lame·men walk, lepers are·purified and deaf·
G3015.3 A-APM λεπρούς (1x)
Mt 10:8 ·relieve·and·cure the·sick; purify lepers; awaken
G3015.3 A-GSM λεπροῦ (2x)
Mt 26:6 ·to·be in BethAny, in Simon the leper's home,
Mk 14:3 in the home of·Simon the leper, as·he was·laying·

G3016 λεπτόν lêptôn *n.* (3x)
Roots:G3013 See:G2835 G0787 G1220
G3016.2 N-ASN λεπτόν (1x)
Lk 12:59 even until you·should·give·back the very·last bit."
G3016.2 N-APN λεπτά (2x)
Lk 21:2 a·certain needy widow casting two bits *in* there.
Mk 12:42 helplessly·poor widow cast·in two bits, which is

G3017 Λευΐ Lêuí *n/p.* (5x)
לֵוִי lêviy [Hebrew]
Roots:H3878 Compare:G3018
G3017.2 N/P-PRI Λευΐ (2x)
Heb 7:5 the·ones from·among the Sons of·Levi receiving the
Heb 7:9 to·make a·declaration, even Levi, the·one receiving
G3017.3 N/P-PRI Λευΐ (1x)
Rv 7:7 *the* tribe of·Levi having·been·officially·sealed,
G3017.4 N/P-PRI Λευΐ (1x)
Lk 3:24 *son* of·Matthat, *son* of·Levi, *son* of·Malki, *son* of·
G3017.5 N/P-PRI Λευΐ (1x)
Lk 3:29 *son* of·JoRim, *son* of·Matthat, *son* of·Levi,

G3018 Λευΐς Lêuís *n/p.* (4x)
לֵוִי lêviy
Roots:G3017 See:G3156
G3018.2 N/P-NSM Λευΐς (1x)
Lk 5:29 And Levi made a·great reception for·him in his·own
G3018.2 N/P-ASM Λευΐν (2x)
Lk 5:27 distinctly·viewed a·tax·collector, Levi by·name,
Mk 2:14 ·on *from·there*, he·saw Levi *called MattHew* (the·
EG3018.2 (1x)
Mt 9:9 ·man·of·clay†, *Levi* being·referred·to·as MattHew,

G3019 Λευΐτης Lêuítēs *n/g.* (3x)
Roots:G3017 xLangEquiv:H3881
G3019 N/G-NSM Λευΐτης (2x)
Lk 10:32 "And likewise a·Levite, happening by the place,
Ac 4:36 Son of·Consoling), *was* a·Levite *and* of·Cyprus by·
G3019 N/G-APM Λευΐτας (1x)
Jn 1:19 ·offer·sacrifices and Levites from·out of·JeruSalem

G3020 Λευϊτικός Lêuïtikôs *adj/g.* (1x)
Roots:G3019
G3020 A/G-GSF Λευϊτικῆς (1x)
Heb 7:11 was through the Levitical sacred·priesthood, (for

G3021 λευκαίνω lêukaínō *v.* (2x)
Roots:G3022
G3021 V-AAI-3P ἐλεύκαναν (1x)
Rv 7:14 their long·robes, and they·whitened their long·robes
G3021 V-AAN λευκᾶναι (1x)
Mk 9:3 a·cloth-fuller on the earth is·not *even* able to·whiten.

G3022 λευκός lêukôs *adj.* (25x)
See:G3021 G1258-1 xLangEquiv:H3836
G3022 A-NSM λευκός (3x)
Lk 9:29 and his attire *was* white *and* radiantly·shimmering.
Rv 6:2 I·saw, and behold, a·white horse and the·one who·
Rv 19:11 ·been·opened·up, and behold a·white horse and
G3022 A-NSF λευκή (1x)
Rv 14:14 I·saw, and behold, a·white thick·cloud, and upon
G3022 A-NSN λευκόν (2x)
Mt 28:3 was as lightning, and his apparel white as snow.
Rv 1:14 hairs *are* white like wool (*as* white as snow), and his
G3022 A-NPF λευκαί (3x)
Jn 4:35 ·open·fields, because they·are white even·now unto
Rv 1:14 His head and *his* hairs *are* white like wool (*as* white
Rv 6:11 And white long·robes were·given to·each·one·of·
G3022 A-NPN λευκά (2x)
Mt 17:2 the sun, and his garments became white as the light.
Mk 9:3 became glistening, exceedingly white as snow, such·
G3022 A-ASM λευκόν (1x)
Rv 20:11 And I·saw a·Great White Throne, and the·one
G3022 A-ASF λευκήν (3x)
Mt 5:36 you·are·not able to·make one hair white or black.
Mk 16:5 ·side, having·been·arrayed·with a·white long·robe,
Rv 2:17 manna, and I·shall·give him a·white pebble, also on
G3022 A-ASN λευκόν (1x)
Rv 19:14 ·themselves·with fine·linen, white and pure.
G3022 A-APF λευκάς (2x)
Rv 7:9 having·been·arrayed·with white long·robes and
Rv 7:13 having·been·arrayed·with the white long·robes?
G3022 A-APN λευκά (1x)
Rv 3:18 ·that you·may·be·wealthy, and·also white garments,
G3022 A-DSF λευκῇ (1x)
Ac 1:10 two men had·stood·nearby them in white clothing,
G3022 A-DPM λευκοῖς (1x)
Rv 19:14 the heaven were·following him upon white horses,
G3022 A-DPN λευκοῖς (4x)
Jn 20:12 she·observes two angels in white sitting·down, one
Rv 3:4 and they·shall·walk·along with me in white, because
Rv 3:5 the·same shall·be·arrayed in white garments, and no
Rv 4:4 ·down, having·been·arrayed in white garments, and

G3023 λέων lêōn *n.* (9x)
Compare:G3001-1 G3463-3 xLangEquiv:A0744 H0738
G3023.1 N-NSM λέων (1x)
Rv 10:3 with·a·loud voice, just·as *when* a·lion roars. And
G3023.1 N-DSM λέοντι (1x)
Rv 4:7 the first living·being *is* like a·lion, and the second
G3023.1 N-GSM λέοντος (1x)
Rv 13:2 and its mouth as a·mouth of·a·lion. And the Dragon
G3023.1 N-GPM λεόντων (3x)
Heb 11:33 promises, stopped·up *the* mouths of·lions,
Rv 9:8 hair of·women, and their teeth were as *teeth* of·lions.
Rv 9:17 of·the horses *were* as heads of·lions, and out of·their
G3023.2 N-NSM λέων (1x)
1Pe 5:8 strolls·about as a·roaring lion seeking whom he·
G3023.2 N-GSM λέοντος (1x)
2Ti 4:17 And·thus I·was·snatched out of·a·lion's mouth.
G3023.3 N-NSM λέων (1x)
Rv 5:5 "Do·not weep. Behold the Lion, the·one being from·

G3024 λήθη lḗthē *n.* (1x)
Roots:G2990 Compare:G1953 See:G2983
G3024.3 N-ASF λήθην (1x)
2Pe 1:9 already·becoming deathly·oblivious of·the

G3025 ληνός lēnôs *n.* (5x)
See:G5276
G3025.3 N-NSF ληνός (1x)
Rv 14:20 And the winepress was·trampled outside the City,
G3025.3 N-ASF ληνόν (3x)
Mt 21:33 around it, and he·dug a·winepress in it and·also
Rv 14:19 cast *it* into the great winepress of·the Rage of·God.
Rv 19:15 and he·himself tramples the winepress of·the wine
G3025.3 N-GSF ληνοῦ (1x)
Rv 14:20 blood came·forth out of·the winepress, even·up·to

G3026 λῆρος lêrôs *n.* (1x)
G3026.1 N-NSM λῆρος (1x)
Lk 24:11 appeared in·the·sight of·them as idle·chatter, and

G3027 λῃστής lēistḗs *n.* (15x)
Compare:G2812 G2855 G3986-2 xLangAlso:H6530 H1416 H7703
G3027.1 N-NSM λῃστής (2x)
Jn 10:1 ·some·other·way, that·one is a·Thief and a·robber.
Jn 18:40 And BarAbbas was a·robber.
G3027.1 N-NPM λῃσταί (3x)
Jn 10:8 before me are Thieves and robbers, but·yet the sheep
Mt 27:38 *there·were* two robbers being·crucified together
Mt 27:44 the same·thing also, the robbers (the·ones being·
G3027.1 N-ASM λῃστήν (3x)
Lk 22:52 ·yeu·come·out, as against an·armed·robber, with
Mt 26:55 ·come·out as against an·armed·robber with daggers
Mk 14:48 ·yeu·come·forth, as against an·armed·robber, with
G3027.1 N-APM λῃστάς (2x)
Lk 10:36 a·neighbor to·the·one falling among the robbers?"
Mk 15:27 with·him, they·crucify two robbers: one at his·
G3027.1 N-DPM λῃσταῖς (1x)
Lk 10:30 and surrounded, he·fell·among robbers, who also,
G3027.1 N-GPM λῃστῶν (4x)
Lk 19:46 " but yeu·yeurselves made it "a·den of·robbers.'"
Mt 21:13 " but yeu·yeurselves made it "a·den of·robbers.'"
Mk 11:17 But yeu·yeurselves made it "a·den of·robbers'".
2Co 11:26 of·swollen·rivers, dangers of·robbers, dangers

G3028 λῆψις lêpsis *n.* (1x)
Roots:G2983 See:G3336
G3028.1 N-GSF λήψεως (1x)
Php 4:15 in *the* matter of·giving and of·receiving, except yeu

G3029 λίαν lían *adv.* (14x)
Compare:G4970 G4971 xLangAlso:H3966
G3029.1 ADV λίαν (3x)
Mt 4:8 personally·takes him up to a·very high mountain and
2Co 11:5 ·fallen·short of·the very highest of·ambassadors.
2Co 12:11 ·I·fall·short of·the very highest of·ambassadors,
G3029.2 ADV λίαν (2x)
2Jn 1:4 I·rejoiced very·much that I·have·found from·among

λλ

3Jn 1:3 For I·rejoiced very·much, with·*the*·brothers coming
G3029.3 ADV λίαν (7x)
Lk 23:8 ·seeing Jesus, HerOd·AntiPas was·exceedingly glad,
Mt 2:16 Magian·astrologists, was·enraged exceedingly. And
Mt 8:28 from·out·of·the chamber·tombs, exceedingly fierce,
Mt 27:14 such·for the governor to·marvel exceedingly.
Mk 6:51 And they·were·exceedingly astonished among
Mk 9:3 garments became glistening, exceedingly white as
2Ti 4:15 for exceedingly he·has·stood·opposed·to our
G3029.4 ADV λίαν (2x)
Mk 1:35 after·already·rising·up very·early while·still·night,
Mk 16:2 And very·early, at·the·watch·of·dawn of·the first

G3030 λίβανος líbanôs *n.* (2x)
לְבוֹנָה lĕbônạh [Hebrew]
Roots:H3828 Compare:G2368 G2792 See:G3031
G3030.2 N-ASM λίβανον (2x)
Mt 2:11 ·him presents: *being* gold, frankincense, and myrrh.
Rv 18:13 incense, ointments, and frankincense, "and wine

G3031 λιβανωτός libanōtós *adj.* (2x)
Roots:G3030 Compare:G2369
G3031.2 A-ASM λιβανωτόν (2x)
Rv 8:3 ·Altar, having a·golden censer·for·frankincense; and
Rv 8:5 the angel has·taken the censer·for·frankincense, and

G3032 Λιβερτῖνος Libertînôs *n/g.* (1x)
Compare:G0558
G3032 N/G-GPM Λιβερτίνων (1x)
Ac 6:9 being·referred·to·as *the Gathering* of·Freedmen, with

G3033 Λιβύη Libýē *n/l.* (1x)
Roots:G3047
G3033 N/L-GSF Λιβύης (1x)
Ac 2:10 Egypt and *in* the parts of·Libya adjacent·to Cyrene,

G3034 λιθάζω litházō *v.* (8x)
Roots:G3037 See:G3036
G3034 V-PAI-1P λιθάζομεν (1x)
Jn 10:33 saying, "We·do·not stone you concerning a·good
G3034 V-PAI-2P λιθάζετε (1x)
Jn 10:32 ·account·of which of·those works do·yeu·stone me?
G3034 V-AAN λιθάσαι (1x)
Jn 11:8 the Judeans now were·seeking to·stone you, and do·
G3034 V-AAP-NPM λιθάσαντες (1x)
Ac 14:19 after·persuading the crowds and stoning Paul, they·
G3034 V-AAS-3P λιθάσωσιν (1x)
Jn 10:31 stones again in·order·that they·should·stone him.
G3034 V-API-1S ἐλιθάσθην (1x)
2Co 11:25 ·beaten·with·rods three·times, I·was·stoned once,
G3034 V-API-3P ἐλιθάσθησαν (1x)
Heb 11:37 They·were·stoned *to·death*, they·were·sawed·in·
G3034 V-APS-3P λιθασθῶσιν (1x)
Ac 5:26 they·feared the people, lest they·should·be·stoned.

G3035 λίθινος líthinôs *adj.* (3x)
Roots:G3037
xLangEquiv:H0068 A0069
G3035 A-NPF λίθιναι (1x)
Jn 2:6 six ceremonial·water·basins of·stone, according·to the
G3035 A-APN λίθινα (1x)
Rv 9:20 silver, bronze, stone, and wood, which neither are·
G3035 A-DPF λιθίναις (1x)
2Co 3:3 God, not on tablets of·stone, but·rather on fleshy

G3036 λιθο•βολέω lithôbôléō *v.* (9x)
Roots:G3037 G0906 See:G3034 G2642-1
G3036 V-FPI-3S λιθοβοληθήσεται (1x)
Heb 12:20 ·on the mountain, it·shall·be·cast·stones·at, or
G3036 V-PAP-NSF λιθοβολοῦσα (2x)
Lk 13:34 and casting·stones·at the·ones having·been·
Mt 23:37 and casting·stones·at the·ones having·been·
G3036 V-PPN λιθοβολεῖσθαι (1x)
Jn 8:5 commanded for·us to·cast·stones·at such·women.
G3036 V-IAI-3P ἐλιθοβόλουν (2x)
Ac 7:58 of·the City, they·were·casting·stones·at *him*, and
Ac 7:59 And they·were·casting·stones·at Stephen while·he·
G3036 V-AAN λιθοβολῆσαι (1x)
Ac 14:5 *the ambassadors* and to·cast·stones·at them,
G3036 V-AAP-NPM λιθοβολήσαντες (1x)
Mk 12:4 to them, and after·casting·stones·at that·one·also,
G3036 V-API-3P ἐλιθοβόλησαν (1x)
Mt 21:35 they·killed, and *one* whom they·cast·stones·at.

G3037 λίθος líthôs *n.* (66x)
Compare:G4074 G2786 G5586 G2995-1 G3139
See:G3035 G3034 G3036
xLangEquiv:H0068 A0069 xLangAlso:H0070
G3037 N-NSM λίθος (8x)
Jn 11:38 Now it·was a·cave, and a·stone was·resting upon it
Lk 21:6 in which there·shall·not·be·left a·stone upon a·stone
Ac 4:11 is "the stone being·disdainfully·rejected by yeu,
Mt 24:2 there·should·not·be·left here a·stone upon a·stone
Mk 9:42 better for·him if a·mill stone be·set around his neck,
Mk 13:2 No, there·should·not·be·left a·stone upon a·stone
Mk 16:4 they·observed that the stone had·been·rolled·away,
1Pe 2:8 and "a·stone of·stumbling and a·solid·rock of·
G3037 N-NPM λίθοι (4x)
Lk 19:40 these should·keep·silent, the stones shall·yell·out."
Mt 4:3 ·God, declare that these stones should·become bread.
Mk 13:1 see what·manner·of stones and what·manner·of
1Pe 2:5 And yeu·yeurselves, as living stones, are·built·up,
G3037 N-ASM λίθον (26x)
Jn 8:7 ·moral·failure, let·him·cast the first stone at her."
Jn 11:39 Jesus says, "Take·away the stone." Martha, the
Jn 11:41 So·then they·took·away the stone *from the place*
Jn 20:1 ·at the stone having·been·taken·away from·among
Lk 4:11 you·should·stub your foot directly·against a·stone."
Lk 11:11 bread, ¿! shall·he·hand him a·stone? Or·if a·fish,
Lk 19:44 and they·shall·not leave in you stone upon stone,
Lk 20:17 ·been·written, "*The* stone which the builders
Lk 20:18 falling upon that stone shall·be·dashed·to·pieces;
Lk 24:2 they·found the stone having·been·rolled·away from
Mt 4:6 you·should·stub your foot directly·against a·stone.'"
Mt 7:9 son should·request bread, ¿! shall·hand him a·stone?
Mt 21:42 in the Scriptures, "A·stone which the builders
Mt 21:44 ·one falling on this stone shall·be·dashed·to·pieces,
Mt 24:2 be·left here a·stone upon a·stone that shall·not be·
Mt 27:60 and after·rolling a·great stone to·the door of·the
Mt 27:66 sentinel·guard *and·by* officially·sealing the stone.
Mt 28:2 coming·alongside, rolled·away the stone from the
Mk 12:10 this Scripture? "A·stone which the builders
Mk 15:46 of·solid·rock, and he·rolled a·stone over the door
Mk 16:3 "Who shall·roll·away for·us the stone at the door
Rm 9:33 I·lay in Tsiyon a·stone of·stumbling and a·solid·
1Pe 2:4 yeu·are·coming·alongside, the·living stone, in·fact,
1Pe 2:6 I·lay in Tsiyon a·chief·corner stone, Selected, *being*
1Pe 2:7 to·those·being·obstinate, "A·stone, which the·ones
Rv 18:21 And one strong angel took·up a·stone as a·great
G3037 N-APM λίθους (3x)
Jn 8:59 ·then they·took·up stones in·order·that they·may·cast
Jn 10:31 lifted·up·and·carried stones again in·order·that
1Co 3:12 *with* gold, silver, precious stones, wood, hay,
G3037 N-DSM λίθῳ (12x)
Lk 4:3 of·God, declare to·this stone that it·should·become
Lk 19:44 ·shall·not leave in you stone upon stone, because
Lk 21:6 ·shall·not be·left a·stone upon a·stone that shall·not
Ac 17:29 like gold or silver or stone etched by·*the*·art and
Mk 13:2 ·not be·left a·stone upon a·stone that should·not be·
Rm 9:32 For they·stumbled at·the stumbling stone,
Rv 4:3 like a·jasper and a·sardius stone, and *there·was* a·
Rv 17:4 ·gilded with·gold and precious stones and pearls,
Rv 18:16 ·gilded with gold, and precious stones, and pearls!
Rv 21:11 her brilliance *was* like a·precious stone, even·as a·
Rv 21:11 stone, even·as a·jasper stone, resembling·crystal),
Rv 21:19 ·been·adorned·with all·manner·of precious stones.
G3037 N-DPM λίθοις (3x)
Lk 21:5 ·adorned·with·beautiful stones and vow·offerings,
Mk 5:5 ·out and fully·chopping·at himself with·stones.
2Co 3:7 ·engraved in writing on stones, came·into·being in
G3037 N-GSM λίθου (2x)
Lk 22:41 drew·away from them about a·stone's cast, and
Rv 18:12 "cargo of·gold, silver, precious stones, and pearls,
G3037 N-GPM λίθων (2x)
Lk 3:8 is·able from·out·of·these stones to·awaken children
Mt 3:9 is·able from·out·of·these stones to·awaken children
EG3037 (6x)
Lk 20:17 has·now·become the·distinct head corner *stone*'"?
Ac 4:11 the·one becoming the·distinct head corner *stone*."
Mt 21:42 the·distinct head corner *stone*. This came·to·be
Mk 12:10 has·now·become the·distinct head corner *stone*.
1Pe 2:7 has·now·become the·distinct head corner *stone*,'"
Eph 2:20 Anointed himself being *the* chief·corner *stone*,

G3038 λιθό•στρωτος lithóstrōtôs *adj.* (1x)
Roots:G3037 G4766 See:G1042
G3038.2 A-ASN λιθόστρωτον (1x)
Jn 19:13 in a·place being·referred·to·as Stone·Pavement, but

G3039 λικμάω likmáō *v.* (2x)
Compare:G0229
G3039.2 V-FAI-3S λικμήσει (2x)
Lk 20:18 it·should·fall, it·shall·grind him to·powder."
Mt 21:44 it·should·fall, it·shall·grind him to·powder."

G3040 λιμήν limḗn *n.* (3x)
Compare:G2568 See:G3041 xLangAlso:H4231
G3040.1 N-ASM λιμένα (1x)
Ac 27:12 to·winter *there, which·is* a·harbor of·Crete,
G3040.1 N-GSM λιμένος (1x)
Ac 27:12 And with·the harbor inherently·being unsuitable,
G3040.2 A/L-APM Λιμένας (1x)
Ac 27:8 some place being·called Good Harbors, which was

G3041 λίμνη límnē *n.* (10x)
Roots:G3040 Compare:G2861 G4215 See:G2288
G1067
G3041.1 N-ASF λίμνην (3x)
Lk 5:1 was standing directly·by the lake of·Gennesaret.
Lk 8:23 of·wind descended upon the lake, and they·were·
Lk 8:33 ·overhang into the lake and was·utterly·drowned.
G3041.1 N-GSF λίμνης (1x)
Lk 8:22 ·go·through to the other·side of·the lake." And they·
G3041.2 N-ASF λίμνην (1x)
Lk 5:2 having·settled directly·by the lake's·edge; then after·
G3041.3 N/L-ASF λίμνην (4x)
Rv 19:20 still·living, into the Lake of·the Fire, the·one
Rv 20:10 them, was·cast into the Lake of·the Fire and sulfur
Rv 20:14 and Hades were·cast into the Lake of·the Fire. This
Rv 20:15 life-above, he·was·cast into the Lake of·the Fire.
G3041.3 N/L-DSF λίμνῃ (1x)
Rv 21:8 their portion *is* in the Lake, the·one being·set·ablaze

G3042 λιμός limós *n.* (12x)
Roots:G3007 Compare:G3061
xLangEquiv:H7458
G3042.2 N-DSM λιμῷ (3x)
Lk 15:17 I·myself am·completely·perishing with·hunger!
2Co 11:27 in sleeplessness many·times, in hunger and thirst,
Rv 6:8 with a·straight·sword, and with hunger, and with
G3042.3 N-NSM λιμός (5x)
Lk 4:25 six lunar·months, as great famine occurred over all
Lk 15:14 all *of·it*, there·occurred a·strong famine in that
Ac 7:11 "Now there·came a·famine over all the land of·
Rm 8:35 calamity, or persecution, or famine, or nakedness,
Rv 18:8 and mourning, and famine. And she·shall·be·
G3042.3 N-NPM λιμοί (3x)
Lk 21:11 ·in·all places, also famines and viral·pestilences,
Mt 24:7 kingdom against kingdom. And famines, and viral·
Mk 13:8 places, and there·shall·be famines and agitations.
G3042.3 N-ASM λιμόν (1x)
Ac 11:28 *that* there·was·about to·be a·great famine over all

G3043 λίνον línôn *n.* (2x)
Compare:G1040
xLangEquiv:H6594 H6593 xLangAlso:H8336
G3043.1 N-ASN λίνον (1x)
Mt 12:20 he·did·not break·apart, and flax, being·smoldering
G3043.2 N-ASN λίνον (1x)
Rv 15:6 ·themselves in·pure and radiant flax·linen, and

G3044 Λῖνος Lînôs *n/p.* (1x)
Roots:G3043
G3044 N/P-NSM Λῖνος (1x)
2Ti 4:21 you, and Pudens, and Linus, and Claudia, and all
G3045 λιπαρός liparós *adj.* (1x)
Compare:G2986 G4684-1 G4684 G5172 G4764
G3045.2 A-NPN λιπαρά (1x)
Rv 18:14 and all the sumptuous·things and the splendid·
G3046 λίτρα lítra *n.* (2x)
Compare:G1220 G5007
G3046 N-ASF λίτραν (1x)
Jn 12:3 ·then, taking a·Roman·pound of·extremely·valuable
G3046 N-APF λίτρας (1x)
Jn 19:39 about *a·weight* of·a·hundred Roman·pounds.
G3047 λίψ líps *n.* (1x)
Compare:G3558 G4689 See:G5566
G3047.2 N-ASM λίβα (1x)
Ac 27:12 looking·out toward *the* southwest and northwest.
G3048 λογία lôgía *n.* (2x)
Roots:G3056 Compare:G2842 See:G4816
G3048.2 N-NPF λογῖαι (1x)
1Co 16:2 ·be no contributions whenever I·should·come.
G3048.2 N-GSF λογίας (1x)
1Co 16:1 Now concerning the contribution, the·one for the
G3049 λογίζομαι lôgízômai *v.* (45x)
Roots:G3056 Compare:G5426 See:G3053
G3049.1 V-PNM-2P λογίζεσθε (1x)
Php 4:8 any high·praise, take·a·reckoning·of these·things.
G3049.2 V-FPI-3S λογισθήσεται (1x)
Rm 2:26 shall·it·not·indeed be·reckoned for circumcision?
G3049.2 V-PNI-1S λογίζομαι (5x)
Rm 8:18 For I·reckon that the afflictions of·the present
Php 3:13 do·not reckon my·own·self to·have·grasped *it*.
1Pe 5:12 (the trustworthy brother as·how I·reckon *it*), I·
2Co 10:2 with·which I·reckon to·be·daringly·bold against
2Co 11:5 For I·reckon not·one·bit to·have·fallen·short of·the
G3049.2 V-PNI-1P λογιζόμεθα (1x)
Rm 3:28 Accordingly, we·reckon *that* a·man·of·clay† *is* to·
G3049.2 V-PNI-2S λογίζῃ (1x)
Rm 2:3 And do·you·reckon this, O man·of·clay† (the·one
G3049.2 V-PNI-3S λογίζεται (5x)
Rm 4:4 ·of·service is·not reckoned according·to grace, but·
Rm 4:5 as·righteous, his trust is·reckoned for righteousness
Rm 4:6 to·whom God reckons righteousness apart·from
Rm 9:8 children of·the promise are·reckoned for offspring†.
1Co 13:5 swiftly·provoked, *and* is·not reckoning the wrong.
G3049.2 V-PNM-2P λογίζεσθε (1x)
Rm 6:11 yeu·yeurselves must·reckon also yeurselves to·be
G3049.2 V-PNM-3S λογιζέσθω (3x)
1Co 4:1 Let a·man·of·clay† reckon us in·this·manner: as
2Co 10:7 to·be of·Anointed-One, let·him·reckon this again
2Co 10:11 Let such·a·man reckon this, "Such·as we·are in·
G3049.2 V-PNP-APM λογιζομένους (1x)
2Co 10:2 ·bold against some— the·ones reckoning of·us as
G3049.2 V-PNP-DSM λογιζομένῳ (1x)
Rm 14:14 except to·the·one reckoning something to·be
G3049.2 V-PNP-NSM λογιζόμενος (1x)
2Co 5:19 while·not presently·reckoning their trespasses to·
G3049.2 V-PPN λογίζεσθαι (1x)
Rm 4:24 us, to·whom it·is·about to·be·reckoned— the·ones
G3049.2 V-INI-1S ἐλογιζόμην (1x)
1Co 13:11 as an·infant, I·was·reckoning as an·infant. But
G3049.2 V-INI-3P ἐλογίζοντο (1x)
Mk 11:31 And they·were·reckoning among themselves,
G3049.2 V-ADN λογίσασθαι (1x)
2Co 3:5 we·are sufficient by ourselves to·reckon anything as
G3049.2 V-ADP-NSM λογισάμενος (1x)
Heb 11:19 reckoning that God *was* able to·awaken *him* even
G3049.2 V-ADS-3S λογίσηται (2x)
Rm 4:8 Yahweh, no, should·not reckon moral·failure."
2Co 12:6 *I·boast*, lest any·man should·reckon to me above
G3049.2 V-AOO-3S λογισθείη (1x)
2Ti 4:16 *men* forsook me; may·it·not be·reckoned to·them.
G3049.2 V-API-1P ἐλογίσθημεν (1x)
Rm 8:36 all the day·long; we·are·reckoned as sheep for·
G3049.2 V-API-3S ἐλογίσθη (9x)
Lk 22:37 " And he·was·reckoned among *the* lawless·ones,"
Gal 3:6 trusted in·Yahweh, and it·was·reckoned to·him for
Mk 15:28 saying, "And he·was·reckoned with lawless·ones.
Rm 4:3 trusted in·Yahweh, and it·was·reckoned to·him for
Rm 4:9 we·say that 'the trust was·reckoned to·AbRaham for
Rm 4:10 So·then how was·it·reckoned? *With·him* being in
Rm 4:22 And therefore "it·was·reckoned to·him for
Rm 4:23 ·of him merely, that it·was·reckoned to·him,
Jac 2:23 trusted in·Yahweh, and it·was·reckoned to·him for
G3049.2 V-APN λογισθῆναι (2x)
Ac 19:27 goddess Artemis to·be·reckoned as nothing·at·all.
Rm 4:11 ·for righteousness to·be·reckoned to·them also,
EG3049.2 (4x)
Rm 2:3 *the* same·things)— *do·you·reckon* that you·yourself
Rm 4:11 trust— the *righteousness reckoned while·still* in the
2Co 10:10 in·fact, *the·one wrongly reckoning* replies, "His
2Co 12:16 yeu. But·yet *yeu·reckon that*, inherently·being
G3050 λογικός lôgikós *adj.* (2x)
Roots:G3056
G3050 A-ASF λογικήν (1x)
Rm 12:1 to·God, *which·is* yeur reasonable ritual·ministry.
G3050.3 A-ASN λογικόν (1x)
1Pe 2:2 babies, eagerly·crave the rational milk *of·the*
G3051 λόγιον lógiôn *n.* (4x)
Roots:G3052 Compare:G5538 G4487 See:G5537
xLangAlso:H2833
G3051 N-APN λόγια (3x)
Ac 7:38 who accepted living eloquent·words to·give to·us—
Rm 3:2 they·are·entrusted·with the eloquent·words of·God.
1Pe 4:11 *let·him·be* as *one·speaking* eloquent·words of·God;
G3051 N-GPN λογίων (1x)
Heb 5:12 ·principles of·the eloquent·words of·God. And
G3052 λόγιος lógiôs *adj.* (1x)
Roots:G3056 See:G3051
G3052 A-NSM λόγιος (1x)
Ac 18:24 by·birth), an·eloquent man being powerful in the
G3053 λογισμός lôgismós *n.* (2x)
Roots:G3049 G2469-1
G3053.1 N-GPM λογισμῶν (1x)
Rm 2:15 and *with·their* reckonings legally·accusing or else
G3053.4 N-APM λογισμούς (1x)
2Co 10:5 demolishing elaborate·reasonings and every
G3054 λογο•μαχέω lôgômachéō *v.* (1x)
Roots:G3056 G3164 See:G3055
G3054.2 V-PAN λογομαχεῖν (1x)
2Ti 2:14 not to·quarrel·over·the·trifling·nuances·of·words
G3055 λογο•μαχία lôgômachía *n.* (1x)
Roots:G3056 G3164 See:G3054
G3055.2 N-APF λογομαχίας (1x)
1Ti 6:4 and quarrels·over·the·trifling·nuances·of·words,
G3056 λόγος lógôs *n.* (349x)
Roots:G3004 Compare:G4487 G4229 G0982
See:G3048 G3049
xLangEquiv:H1697
G3056.1 N-NSM λόγος (13x)
Jn 15:25 in·order·that the word may·be·completely·fulfilled,
Lk 4:32 his instruction, because his word was with authority
Lk 4:36 saying, "What a·word *is* this! Because with
Lk 5:15 But the word went·throughout even·more
Ac 13:15 within yeu a·word of·exhortation specifically·for
Heb 2:2 For if the word being·spoken through angels was
Heb 7:28 weakness, but the word of·the swearing·of·oath
Mt 5:37 "But yeur word must·be, 'Yes' *for* 'yes' *and*
Rm 9:9 For this *is* the word of·promise, "According·to this
1Co 12:8 is·given through the Spirit a·word of·wisdom, but
1Co 12:8 ·wisdom, but to·another a·word of·knowledge by
2Ti 2:17 And their word, as gangrene, shall·have a·
1Jn 2:7 old commandment is the word which yeu·heard from
G3056.1 N-NPM λόγοι (7x)
Lk 21:33 earth shall·pass·away, but my words, no, may·not
Lk 24:44 "These *are* the words which I·spoke to yeu, while·
Ac 15:15 And to·this, the words of·the prophets do·
Mt 24:35 earth shall·pass·away, but my words, no, should·
Mk 13:31 earth shall·pass·away, but my words, no, should·
Rv 21:5 "Write, because these words are true and
Rv 22:6 ·declared to·me, "These words *are* trustworthy and
G3056.1 N-ASM λόγον (17x)
Jn 4:41 And many more trusted on·account·of his·own word.
Jn 8:55 I·have·seen him, and I·observantly·keep his word.
Jn 15:20 ·kept my word, they·shall·observantly·keep yeurs
Lk 12:10 "And all who shall·declare a·word against the Son
Ac 20:24 But·yet not·even·one word causes *me concern*,
Heb 12:19 *·for them to·request for* a·word not to·be·further
Mt 8:8 my roof, but·rather merely declare a·word, and my
Mt 12:32 And whoever should·declare a·word against the
Mt 15:23 But he·did·not answer her a·word. And his
Mt 22:46 ·man was·able to·answer him a·word, nor·even·did
Mt 26:44 ·prayed for a·third·time, declaring the same words.
Mk 5:36 immediately upon·hearing the word being·spoken,
Mk 14:39 ·going·off, he·prayed, declaring the same words.
2Pe 1:19 we·have more·firmly the prophetic word, to·which
1Th 2:13 yeu·did·accept *it* not *as* a·word of·men·of·clay†,
1Co 14:9 yeu·should·give a·clearly·discernible word, how
Rv 12:11 Lamb, and through the word of·their testimony;
G3056.1 N-APM λόγους (11x)
Ac 2:22 Israelites, hear these words: Jesus of·Natsareth, a·
Ac 5:5 And upon·hearing these words, AnanIas fell·down
Ac 5:24 heard these words, they·were·thoroughly·perplexed
Mt 10:14 ·not·even hear yeur words, while·going·forth·from
1Co 14:19 I·determine to·speak five words through my
1Co 14:19 ·than ten·thousand words in a·bestowed·tongue.
Rv 1:3 and the·ones hearing the words of·the prophecy and
Rv 22:7 ·one observantly·keeping the words of·the prophecy
Rv 22:9 observantly·keeping the words of·this official·scroll.
Rv 22:10 "You·should·not seal·up the words of·the prophecy
Rv 22:18 to·everyone hearing the words of·the prophecy of·
G3056.1 N-DSM λόγῳ (23x)
Jn 2:22 the Scripture and the word which Jesus declared.
Jn 4:50 the man·of·clay† trusted the word that Jesus declared
Lk 7:7 to you, but·rather declare with·a·word, and my
Lk 24:19 powerful in deed and word directly·before God and
Ac 20:2 and exhorting them often in·word, he·came into
Ac 20:38 especially over the words which he·had·declared,
Mt 8:16 the spirits with·a·word and both·relieved·and·cured
Mk 12:13 in·order·that they·should·entrap him in·*his*·words.
Rm 15:18 ·obedience among·Gentiles, by·word and deed,
Jac 3:2 If any·man does·not slip·up in word, the·same *is* a·
1Th 1:5 come·to·be among yeu in word merely, but·rather
1Th 2:5 at·any·time did·we·come with a·word of·flattery
1Th 4:15 ·say to·yeu by *the* Lord's word, that we·ourselves,
2Th 2:17 yeu in every beneficially·good word and work.
2Th 3:14 ·not listen·to·and·obey our word through this·letter
1Co 1:5 by him, in every word and in·all knowledge—
1Co 4:20 kingdom of·God *is* not in word, but·rather in power
2Co 8:7 in·trust, and in·word, and in·knowledge, and in·all
2Co 10:11 this, "Such·as we·are in·word through *our* letters
Col 3:17 what soever yeu·should·do in word or in deed, *do*
1Ti 4:12 ·example of·the ones·that·trust, in word, in conduct
1Ti 5:17 the·ones laboring·hard in word and instruction.
1Jn 3:18 ·children, we·should·not love in·word, nor·even in·
G3056.1 N-DPM λόγοις (12x)
Lk 1:20 because you·did·not trust my words, which shall·be·
Lk 4:22 they·were·marveling at the gracious words, the·ones
Lk 23:9 ·of him with a·significant·number·of words. But
Ac 2:40 ·many other words, he·was·thoroughly·testifying
Ac 7:22 and he·was powerful in words and in deeds.
Ac 15:24 yeu with·words (dislodging·and·disturbing yeur
Mk 10:24 the disciples were·amazed at his words. But Jesus,
1Th 4:18 As·such, comfort one·another with these words.
1Co 2:4 not with persuasive words of·mankind's† wisdom,
1Co 2:13 not with instructive words of·mankind's† wisdom,

Eph 5:6 not·one·man delude yeu with·empty words, for on·
3Jn 1:10 he·does, gossiping·against us with·evil words. And
G3056.1 N-GSM λόγου (9x)
Lk 20:20 ·that they·may·grab·hold of·his words, in·order·to·
Lk 22:61 And Peter quietly·recalled the word of·the Lord,
Ac 15:27 also *to·yeu* the same·things through *spoken* word.
Ac 18:15 since it·is an·issue concerning a·word and names,
Ac 22:22 ·were·listening·to him even·until this word, and
Heb 13:22 brothers, bear·with the word of·exhortation, for
1Pe 3:1 through the behavior of·the wives without a·word
2Th 2:2 through spirit, nor through word, nor through letter
2Th 2:15 whether through *spoken* word or through our letter
G3056.1 N-GPM λόγων (5x)
Lk 3:4 ·been·written in a·scroll of·the·words of·IsaIah the
Ac 20:35 and to·remember the words of·the Lord Jesus that
Mt 12:37 of·your words, you·shall·be·regarded·as·righteous,
Mt 12:37 of·your words, you·shall·be·pronounced·guilty."
Rv 22:19 *anything* from the words of·*the*·scroll of·this
EG3056.1 (1x)
Mt 22:22 And upon·hearing *these words*, they·marveled, and
G3056.2 N-NSM λόγος (16x)
Jn 4:37 For in this *case*, the saying is true, 'One is the·one
Jn 6:60 "This is a·hard saying; who is·able to·hear it?
Jn 7:36 What *manner·of* saying is this that he·declared,
Jn 12:38 in·order·that the saying of·IsaIah the prophet may·
Jn 18:9 in·order·that the saying may·be·completely·fulfilled,
Jn 18:32 that the saying of·Jesus may·be·completely·fulfilled
Jn 21:23 So·then this saying went·forth among the brothers,
Lk 7:17 And this saying concerning him went·forth among
Ac 6:5 And the saying was·satisfactory in·the·sight of·the
Mt 28:15 And this saying is·widely·promoted closely·among
Tit 3:8 Trustworthy *is* the saying. And concerning these·
1Co 15:54 then shall·occur the saying, the·one having·
1Ti 1:15 The saying *is* trustworthy and deserving of·all full·
1Ti 3:1 Trustworthy *is* the saying: "If any·man longingly·
1Ti 4:9 Trustworthy *is* the saying and worthy of·all full·
2Ti 2:11 Trustworthy *is* the saying: "For if we·died·together
G3056.2 N-NPM λόγοι (2x)
Lk 24:17 to them, "What sayings *are* these that yeu·toss·
Rv 19:9 "These are the true sayings of·God."
G3056.2 N-ASM λόγον (10x)
Jn 4:39 in him on·account·of the saying of·the woman,
Jn 7:40 So·then after·hearing the saying, many from·among
Jn 19:8 when Pilate heard this saying, he·was all·the·more
Jn 19:13 Accordingly, after·hearing this saying, Pilate
Mt 15:12 *this* saying, are·tripped·up·and·fallen·away?
Mt 19:11 "Not all·men have·room·for this saying, but·rather
Mt 19:22 But after·hearing the saying, the young·man went·
Mk 7:29 to·her, "On·account·of this saying, head·on·out.
Mk 8:32 he·was·speaking the saying with·clarity·of·speech.
Mk 9:10 they·securely·held the saying toward themselves,
G3056.2 N-APM λόγους (10x)
Jn 10:19 among the Judeans on·account·of these sayings.
Jn 14:24 ·loving me does·not observantly·keep my sayings.
Lk 9:28 eight days after these sayings, that·also personally·
Lk 9:44 Yeu·yeurselves must·let these sayings be·placed into
Ac 16:36 the prison·warden announced this saying to Paul,
Mt 7:24 anyone that hears these sayings of·mine and does
Mt 7:26 "And everyone hearing these sayings of·mine, and
Mt 7:28 when YeShua entirely·completed these sayings, the
Mt 19:1 when YeShua finished these sayings, he·moved·on
Mt 26:1 YeShua finished all these sayings, he·declared to·his
G3056.2 N-DSM λόγῳ (5x)
Lk 1:29 she·was·thoroughly·troubled over his saying, and
Ac 7:29 Then Moses fled at this saying, and was a·sojourner
Gal 5:14 Torah-Law is·completely·fulfilled in one saying, in
Mk 10:22 And after·glowering at the saying, he·went·away
Rm 13:9 it·is·summed·up in this saying, explicitly, "'You·
G3056.2 N-DPM λόγοις (2x)
Rm 3:4 ·may·be·regarded·as·righteous in your sayings, and
2Pe 2:3 ·commercially·exploit yeu with·fabricated sayings,
G3056.2 N-GSM λόγου (1x)
Jn 15:20 "Remember the saying that I·myself declared to·

G3056.2 N-GPM λόγων (2x)
Lk 1:4 concerning *the* sayings of·which you·were·informed.
Lk 6:47 me, both hearing my sayings and doing them, I·
G3056.4 N-NSM λόγος (2x)
1Co 2:4 And my discourse and my official·proclamation *was*
2Co 10:10 and his discourse *is* having·been·utterly·disdained
G3056.4 N-ASM λόγον (1x)
1Co 4:19 the discourse of·the·ones having·been·puffed·up,
G3056.4 N-DSM λόγῳ (2x)
Mt 22:15 ·how they·should·ensnare him in *his* discourse.
2Co 11:6 though *I·am* untrained in·the·discourse, yet *it·is* not
G3056.4 N-GSM λόγου (3x)
Ac 14:12 the·one who·was·officially·leading the discourse.
Ac 15:32 the brothers through much discourse *in·kind*, and
1Co 2:1 according·to superiority of·discourse or of·wisdom
EG3056.5 (1x)
Eph 4:29 beneficially·good *conversation*, particularly·for the
G3056.6 N-NSM λόγος (2x)
Eph 4:29 ·let any rotten conversation proceed·forth from·out
Col 4:6 Yeur conversation always *is to·be* with grace having·
G3056.6 N-ASM λόγον (1x)
Ac 20:7 the conversation so·long·as·unto midnight.
EG3056.6 (9x)
Ac 11:2 were·discriminating *the matter* alongside him,
Ac 17:32 "We·shall·hear you again concerning this *matter*."
Ac 18:15 a·word and names, and *matters* according·to yeur
Ac 20:7 bread, Paul was·discussing *matters* with·them,
Ac 20:9 With·Paul discussing *matters* over a·longer·*period*,
Ac 24:25 *Paul* discussing *matters* concerning righteousness,
Mk 9:14 mutually·questioning·and·discussing *a·matter* with·
Mk 10:10 inquired·of him again concerning the same *matter*.
Rm 14:23 *the matter* differently has·been·condemned if he·
G3056.7 N-NSM λόγος (1x)
Heb 5:11 Concerning which, the matter *means* much to·us,
G3056.7 N-ASM λόγον (5x)
Ac 19:38 ·him have a·matter specifically·against any·man,
Mk 1:45 often, and to·widely·promote the matter, such·for
Rm 9:28 entirely·completing *the* matter and cutting·*it*·short
Rm 9:28 ·make a·concise·working·of *the* matter upon the
Php 4:15 shared with·me in *the* matter of·giving and of·
G3056.7 N-DSM λόγῳ (1x)
Ac 8:21 ·even a·small·chance for·you in this matter, for your
G3056.7 N-GSM λόγου (1x)
Ac 15:6 gathered·together to·see concerning this matter.
EG3056.7 (5x)
Mt 27:24 after·seeing that *reasoning with·them* benefits
Rm 3:5 *this line of·reasoning* according·to a·man·of·clay†).
Rm 3:7 *But the reasoning states*, "For if by my lie, the truth
1Co 12:15 ¿! from this *reasoning*, is·it not from·among
1Co 12:16 ¿! from this *reasoning*, is·it not from·among
G3056.8 N-NSM λόγος (1x)
1Co 1:18 For the reasoning (the·one of·the cross) is
G3056.8 N-ASM λόγον (1x)
Tit 2:8 healthy·and·sound reasoning *that·is* faultless in·order·
G3056.8 N-GSM λόγου (1x)
1Co 1:17 ·news, not with wisdom of·reasoning, lest the
EG3056.8 (1x)
Php 3:4 other·man presumes *a·reason* to·have·confidence in
G3056.9 N-ASM λόγον (2x)
Ac 18:14 an·evil, mischievous·deed according·to reason, O
1Pe 3:15 ·man requesting·of yeu a·reason concerning the
G3056.9 N-DSM λόγῳ (1x)
Ac 10:29 I·inquire, for·what reason did·yeu·send·for me?
G3056.9 N-GSM λόγου (1x)
Mt 5:32 his wife, personally·aside·from a·reason of·sexual·,
G3056.10 N-ASM λόγον (1x)
Col 2:23 ·very·things are in·fact a·rationalization of·wisdom,
G3056.11 N-NSM λόγος (1x)
Ac 11:22 Now the account concerning them was·heard
G3056.11 N-ASM λόγον (10x)
Lk 16:2 Give·forth an·account of·your estate·management,
Ac 1:1 In·fact, the first account I·made, O TheoPhilus, *was*
Ac 19:40 ·be·able to·render an·account of·this riotous·mob."

Heb 13:17 as ones·that·shall·be·giving·forth an·account—
Mt 12:36 *it*, they·shall·give·back an·account concerning it in
Mt 18:23 who wanted to·tally·up an·accounting among his
Mt 25:19 comes and tally·ups an·accounting with them.
Rm 14:12 ·one of·us shall·give account concerning himself
Php 4:17 fruit, the·one increasing·more into yeur account.
1Pe 4:5 ·who shall·give·forth an·account to·the·one having
G3056.12 N-NSM λόγος (1x)
Heb 4:13 to·his eyes, to whom our reckoning *is·due*.
EG3056.12 (1x)
Lk 10:30 And taking·up *the question*, Jesus declared, "A·
G3056.13 N-ASM λόγον (3x)
Lk 20:3 "And·I shall·ask·of yeu one question, and yeu·must·
Mt 21:24 "I·also shall·ask·of yeu one question, which if yeu·
Mk 11:29 "I·shall·inquire·of yeu also one question; so·then
G3056.14 N-NSM λόγος (6x)
Jn 1:1 At *the* beginning was the Word, and the Word was
Jn 1:1 was the Word, and the Word was alongside God,
Jn 1:1 Word was alongside God, and the Word was God.
Jn 1:14 And the Word became flesh and encamped among us
1Jn 5:7 heaven: the Father, the Word, and the Holy Spirit.
Rv 19:13 ·blood, and his name is·called The Word of·God.
G3056.14 N-ASM λόγον (1x)
Ac 10:36 The Word which *God* dispatched to·the Sons of·
G3056.14 N-DSM λόγῳ (2x)
2Pe 3:5 (willingly) that by·the Word of·God, there·were
2Pe 3:7 But now, by·the·same Word, the heavens and the
G3056.14 N-GSM λόγου (2x)
Lk 1:2 ·becoming eyewitnesses and assistants of·the Word),
1Jn 1:1 ·by·touch, concerning the Word of·the life-above;
G3056.15 N-NSM λόγος (2x)
Jn 10:35 pertaining·to whom the Holy-word of·God came,
Rm 9:6 not as·though the Holy-word of·God has·fallen·short.
G3056.15 N-ASM λόγον (1x)
Mk 7:13 invalidating the Holy-word of·God by·yeur Oral·
EG3056.15 (1x)
1Pe 2:2 the rational milk *of·the Redemptive-word*, *which·is*
G3056.16 N-NSM λόγος (23x)
Jn 8:37 because my Redemptive-word does·not have·room in
Jn 12:48 ·judging him: the Redemptive-word which I·spoke.
Jn 14:24 "But the Redemptive-word which yeu·hear is not
Jn 17:17 holy in your truth. Your Redemptive-word is truth.
Lk 8:11 scattering·of·seed is the Redemptive-word of·God.
Ac 6:7 And the Redemptive-word of·God was·growing·*in*·
Ac 12:24 But the Redemptive-word of·God was·growing and
Ac 13:26 God, to·yeu the Redemptive-word of·this Salvation
Ac 13:49 And the Redemptive-word of·the Lord was·
Ac 17:13 knew that the Redemptive-word of·God also was·
Ac 19:20 ·to might, the Redemptive-word of·the Lord was·
Heb 4:2 *·been*, but·yet the Redemptive-word *through* hearing
Mk 4:15 roadway, where the Redemptive-word is·sown: and
1Th 1:8 For from yeu, the Redemptive-word of·the Lord has·
2Th 3:1 us in·order·that the Redemptive-word of·the Lord
Tit 2:5 ·order·that the Redemptive-word of·God should·not·be
1Co 14:36 Or did the Redemptive word of·God come·forth
2Co 1:18 because our Redemptive-word toward yeu did·not
Eph 6:19 *·penetrating* Redemptive-word may·be·given to·me,
Col 3:16 Let the Redemptive-word of·Anointed-One indwell
2Ti 2:9 bonds, but·yet the Redemptive-word of·God has·not
1Jn 1:10 him a·liar, and his Redemptive-word is not in us.
1Jn 2:14 strong, and the Redemptive-word of·God abides in
G3056.16 N-ASM λόγον (81x)
Jn 5:24 the·one hearing my Redemptive-word and trusting the·
Jn 5:38 And yeu·do·not have his Redemptive-word abiding in
Jn 8:43 yeu·are·not able to·hear my Redemptive-word.
Jn 8:51 should·observantly·keep my Redemptive-word, no,
Jn 8:52 should·observantly·keep my Redemptive-word, no,
Jn 14:23 ·shall·observantly·keep my Redemptive-word. And
Jn 15:3 through the Redemptive-word which I·have·spoken to·
Jn 17:6 they·have·observantly·kept your Redemptive-word.
Jn 17:14 ·myself have·given them your Redemptive-word, and
Lk 5:1 ·upon him to·hear the Redemptive-word of·God, he·
Lk 8:12 and he·takes·away the Redemptive-word from their

Lk 8:13 who with joy accept the Redemptive-word; yet these
Lk 8:15 after·hearing the Redemptive-word, fully·hold·onto *it*
Lk 8:21 the·ones hearing the Redemptive-word of·God and
Lk 10:39 feet, also was·listening·to his Redemptive-word.
Lk 11:28 the·ones hearing the Redemptive-word of·God and
Ac 2:41 ·fully·accepting his Redemptive-word with·pleasure,
Ac 4:4 of·the·ones hearing the Redemptive-word trusted, and
Ac 4:29 *the ability* to·speak your Redemptive-word with all
Ac 4:31 ·were·speaking the Redemptive-word of·God with
Ac 6:2 abandoning the Redemptive-word of·God to·attend
Ac 8:4 *the regions* proclaiming the Redemptive-word.
Ac 8:14 Samaria had·accepted the Redemptive-word of·God,
Ac 8:25 and speaking the Redemptive-word of·the Lord, *as*
Ac 10:44 fell upon all the·ones hearing the Redemptive-word.
Ac 11:1 Gentiles also accepted the Redemptive-word of·God.
Ac 11:19 speaking the Redemptive-word to·no·one except
Ac 13:5 ·fully·proclaiming the Redemptive-word of·God in
Ac 13:7 Saul, sought to·hear the Redemptive-word of·God.
Ac 13:44 ·together to·hear the Redemptive-word of·God.
Ac 13:46 necessary for·the Redemptive-word of·God first to·
Ac 13:48 were·glorifying the Redemptive-word of·the Lord.
Ac 14:25 And speaking the Redemptive-word in Perga, they·
Ac 15:7 to·hear the Redemptive-word of·the good·news
Ac 15:35 ·the·good·news of·the Redemptive-word of·the Lord
Ac 15:36 ·fully·proclaimed the Redemptive-word of·the Lord,
Ac 16:6 Holy Spirit to·speak the Redemptive-word in Asia.
Ac 16:32 they·spoke to·him the Redemptive-word of·the Lord
Ac 17:11 ·*Jews*·who accepted the Redemptive-word with all
Ac 18:11 instructing the Redemptive-word of·God among
Ac 19:10 ·in Asia to·hear the Redemptive-word of·the Lord
Heb 6:1 the initiating Redemptive-word of·the Anointed-One,
Heb 13:7 who spoke to·yeu the Redemptive-word of·God,
Gal 6:6 ·in the Redemptive-word must·share with·the·one
Mt 13:19 hearing the Redemptive-word of·the kingdom yet
Mt 13:20 hearing the Redemptive-word and straight·away *is*
Mt 13:21 on·account·of the Redemptive-word, straight·away
Mt 13:22 is the·one hearing the Redemptive-word, and·yet the
Mt 13:22 ·wealth altogether·choke the Redemptive-word, and
Mt 13:23 hearing the Redemptive-word and comprehending *it*,
Mk 2:2 And he·was·speaking the Redemptive-word to·them.
Mk 4:14 "The·one sowing sows the Redemptive-word.
Mk 4:15 and he·takes·away the Redemptive-word, the·one
Mk 4:16 they·should·hear the Redemptive-word, immediately
Mk 4:17 on·account·of the Redemptive-word, immediately
Mk 4:18 these *are* the·ones hearing the Redemptive-word,
Mk 4:19 — they·altogether·choke the Redemptive-word, and
Mk 4:20 hear the Redemptive-word, give·heed·and·accept *it*,
Mk 4:33 he·was·speaking the Redemptive-word to·them,
Mk 16:20 and confirming the Redemptive-word through the
Jac 1:21 ·mildness the implanted Redemptive-word, the·one
Php 1:14 ·bold to·speak the Redemptive-word without·fear.
Php 2:16 ·forward *the* Redemptive-word of·life-above— for
1Th 1:6 after·accepting the Redemptive-word, along·with
1Th 2:13 God's Redemptive-word of·hearing directly·from us,
1Th 2:13 it·is truly, God's Redemptive-word, which operates
Tit 1:3 in·due seasons made his Redemptive-word apparent by
2Co 2:17 ·and·hustling the Redemptive-word of·God. But·
2Co 4:2 handling the Redemptive-word of·God with·guile,
2Co 5:19 in us the Redemptive-word of·the Reconciliation.
Eph 1:13 after·hearing the Redemptive-word of·the truth, the
Col 1:25 to·completely·fulfill the Redemptive-word of·God,
2Ti 2:15 rightly·dissecting the Redemptive-word of·truth.
2Ti 4:2 ·proclaim the Redemptive-word! Stand·forward when·
1Jn 2:5 should·observantly·keep his Redemptive-word, in him
Rv 1:2 who testified·to the Redemptive-word of·God, and *to*
Rv 1:9 Patmos, on·account·of the Redemptive-word of·God,
Rv 3:8 and observantly·kept my Redemptive-word, and did·
Rv 3:10 ·kept the Redemptive-word of·my patient·endurance,
Rv 6:9 on·account·of the Redemptive-word of·God, and on·
Rv 20:4 and on·account·of the Redemptive-word of·God, and

G3056.16 N-APM λόγους (2x)
Lk 9:26 be·ashamed·of me and my Redemptive-words, the
Mk 8:38 ·ashamed·of me and of·my Redemptive-words in this

G3056.16 N-DSM λόγῳ (9x)
Jn 8:31 yeu should·continue in my Redemptive-word, yeu·are
Ac 14:3 ·one testifying to·the Redemptive-word of·his grace
Ac 20:32 to·God, and to·the Redemptive-word of·his grace,
Jac 1:18 he·bred us by·the·Redemptive-word of·truth, for us
1Pe 2:8 ·stumble at·the Redemptive-word, being·obstinate. To
1Pe 3:1 to·the Redemptive-word, they·may·be·gained through
1Co 15:2 that·certain Redemptive-word I·proclaimed to·yeu,
2Co 6:7 by *the* Redemptive-word of·truth, by God's power,
Col 1:5 ·heard·before in the Redemptive-word of·the truth of·

G3056.16 N-DPM λόγοις (3x)
1Ti 4:6 ·and·trained·by the Redemptive-words of·the trust and
1Ti 6:3 having·healthy·and·sound Redemptive-words (the·
2Ti 4:15 he·has·stood·opposed·to our Redemptive-words.

G3056.16 N-GSM λόγου (9x)
Jn 17:20 ·be·trusting in me through their Redemptive-word—
Ac 6:4 prayer and in·the service of·the Redemptive-word."
Heb 5:13 *is* inexperienced with·*the*·Redemptive-word of·—
Jac 1:22 Now become doers of·*the*·Redemptive-word, and not
Jac 1:23 if any is a·hearer of·*the*·Redemptive-word, and not a·
1Pe 1:23 ·*of·seed* through *the* Redemptive-word of·God,
Tit 1:9 ·to the trustworthy Redemptive-word according·to the
Col 4:3 ·up to·us a·door for·the Redemptive-word (*that·is*, to·
1Ti 4:5 God's Redemptive-word and an·earnest·request.

G3056.16 N-GPM λόγων (1x)
2Ti 1:13 of·healthy·and·sound Redemptive-words, which you·

G3056.17 N-NSM λόγος (1x)
Heb 4:12 For the Word† of·God *is* living and active, and *he*·

G3057 λόγχη lônchē *n.* (1x)
Compare:G0160-1 G0956 G1002 G2759
xLangAlso:H7013 H7014

G3057.1 N-DSF λόγχῃ (1x)
Jn 19:34 soldiers jabbed his side with·the·tip·of·a·lance, and

G3058 λοιδορέω lôidôréō *v.* (4x)
Roots:G3060 Compare:G3679 G0987 G1796 G2706
G4065 See:G3059 G1589-3

G3058 V-PAI-2S λοιδορεῖς (1x)
Ac 23:4 declared, "Do·you·defame God's high·priest?

G3058 V-PPP-NSM λοιδορούμενος (1x)
1Pe 2:23 who, being·defamed, was·not defaming·in·reply;

G3058 V-PPP-NPM λοιδορούμενοι (1x)
1Co 4:12 with·our·own hands. Being·defamed, we·bless.

G3058 V-AAI-3P ἐλοιδόρησαν (1x)
Jn 9:28 So·then they·defamed him and declared, "You·

G3059 λοιδορία lôidôría *n.* (3x)
Roots:G3060 Compare:G1426 See:G3058

G3059 N-ASF λοιδορίαν (1x)
1Pe 3:9 a·wrong for wrong, or a·defamation for defamation,

G3059 N-GSF λοιδορίας (2x)
1Pe 3:9 wrong, or a·defamation for defamation, but on·the·
1Ti 5:14 impromptu·occasion for·defamation by·the·one

G3060 λοίδορος lôídôrôs *adj.* (2x)
Compare:G0989 G2707 See:G3058 G3059

G3060.1 A-NPM λοίδοροι (1x)
1Co 6:10 nor drunkards, nor defamatory·men, nor violently·

G3060.2 A-NSM λοίδορος (1x)
1Co 5:11 or an·idolater, or a·defamer, or a·drunkard, or *is*

G3061 λοιμός lôimós *n.* (3x)
Compare:G3042 G2288 xLangAlso:H1698

G3061.1 N-NPM λοιμοί (2x)
Lk 21:11 also famines and viral·pestilences, and there·
Mt 24:7 And famines, and viral·pestilences, and earthquakes

G3061.1 N-ASM λοιμόν (1x)
Ac 24:5 after·finding this man *to·be* a·viral·pestilence, and

G3062 λοιποί lôipôí *adj.* (41x)
Roots:G3007 Compare:G3005 See:G3063 G3064
G2645 xLangAlso:H3499

G3062.1 A-APN λοιπά (2x)
Mk 4:19 and the·things concerning the remaining longings
Rv 3:2 firmly·establish the·things remaining that are·about

G3062.1 A-GPM λοιπῶν (1x)
Rv 8:13 the earth— from·out·of the remaining voices of·the

G3062.2 A-NPM λοιποί (15x)
Lk 18:11 I·am not just·as the rest of·the men·of·clay† *are*:
Ac 28:9 with·this happening, the rest also, the·ones having
Gal 2:13 And the rest *of·the* Jews also were·hypocritical·
Mt 22:6 And the rest, taking·secure·hold of·his slaves,
Mt 27:49 But the rest were·saying, "Leave *him·alone*, we·
Rm 11:7 ·obtain *it*, and the rest were·petrified·hard·as·stone,
1Th 4:13 ·not be·grieved, even just·as the rest, the·ones not
1Th 5:6 as even *do* the rest, but·rather we·should·keep·alert
1Co 9:5 even·as also *do* the rest *of·the* ambassadors, and *as*
Eph 2:3 ·were by·nature children of·wrath, even as the rest.
1Ti 5:20 morally·failing in·order·that the rest also may·have
Rv 9:20 And the rest of·the men·of·clay† who were·not
Rv 11:13 And the rest became alarmed and gave glory to·the
Rv 19:21 And the rest were·killed with the straight·sword of·
Rv 20:5 First Resurrection. But the rest of·the dead did·not

G3062.2 A-NPF λοιπαί (2x)
Lk 24:10 of·*little*·Jacob, and the rest *that·were* together
Mt 25:11 "But eventually, the rest *of·the* virgins came also,

G3062.2 A-NPN λοιπά (1x)
Eph 4:17 *are* yeu to·walk just·as the rest *of·the* Gentiles also

G3062.2 A-APM λοιπούς (3x)
Lk 18:9 they·are righteous, and utterly·disdaining the rest.
Ac 2:37 to Peter and to·the rest of·the·ambassadors, "Men,
Ac 27:44 And the rest *got there*, in·fact, some·men on planks

G3062.2 A-APF λοιπάς (2x)
2Pe 3:16 as *they·do* also the rest of·Scriptures, to their own
2Co 12:13 beyond the rest *of·the* Called·Out·citizenries,

G3062.2 A-APN λοιπά (1x)
1Co 11:34 I·may·come, I·shall·thoroughly·arrange the rest.

G3062.2 A-DPM λοιποῖς (7x)
Lk 8:10 kingdom of·God, but to·the rest, *it·is* in parables, in·
Lk 24:9 all these·things to·the eleven and to·all the rest.
Mk 16:13 announced *it* to·the rest *in·mourning*, but·neither·
Php 1:13 to·all in the Praetorian·court, and to·all the rest.
1Co 7:12 But to·the rest I·myself say, not the Lord— if any
2Co 13:2 ·already·morally·failed and to·all the rest— that if
Rv 2:24 to·yeu I·say, and to·the rest in Thyatira (as·many·

G3062.2 A-DPN λοιποῖς (1x)
Rm 1:13 also, just·as even·so among the rest *of·the* Gentiles.

G3062.2 A-GPM λοιπῶν (4x)
Ac 5:13 Now, of·the rest, not·even·one was·daring to·
Ac 17:9 personally·from Jason and the rest, they·dismissed
Php 4:3 also, and *with* the rest of·my coworkers, the names
1Co 15:37 it·may·happen·to·be of·wheat or some of·the rest;

G3062.2 A-GPN λοιπῶν (2x)
Lk 12:26 ·is·least, why are·yeu·anxious concerning the rest?
Rv 12:17 ·off to·make war with the rest of·her offspring†,

G3063 λοιπόν lôipón *adj.* (14x)
Roots:G3062 Compare:G1534 G2089

G3063.2 A-NSN λοιπόν (6x)
Php 3:1 One·thing remaining, my brothers: Rejoice in *the*
Php 4:8 One·thing remaining, brothers: As·many·things·as
1Th 4:1 Now·then, one·thing remaining, brothers: We·ask·
2Th 3:1 One·thing remaining, brothers: Pray concerning us
1Co 7:29 *with* the *time which* is remaining … even the·ones
Eph 6:10 *Now* one·thing remaining: My brothers, be·enabled

G3063.2 A-ASN λοιπόν (5x)
Ac 27:20 laying·upon *us*, all remaining expectation for·us
Heb 10:13 *Now* one·thing *is still* remaining: waiting·for *the*
Mt 26:45 ·all·sleep *through* the·one remaining *moment* and
Mk 14:41 ·all·sleep *through* the·one remaining *moment* and
1Co 4:2 Now *with* such·a·thing remaining, it·is·sought in the

G3063.3 A-ASN λοιπόν (2x)
1Co 1:16 also the household of·Stephanas. Finally, I·do·not
2Co 13:11 Finally, brothers, be·glad.

G3063.4 A-ASN λοιπόν (1x)
2Ti 4:8 Henceforth, there·is·laid·away for·me the victor's·

G3064 λοιποῦ lôipôû *adj.* (1x)
Roots:G3062

G3064.2 A-GSN λοιποῦ (1x)
Gal 6:17 From·henceforth, let no·man personally·present

G3065 Λουκᾶς Lôukâs *n/p.* (3x)
G3065.2 N/P-NSM Λουκᾶς (3x)
Col 4:14 Luke, the beloved practitioner·of·healing, and
Phm 1:24 AristArchus, Demas, Luke, *these* my coworkers.
2Ti 4:11 Only Luke is with me.

G3066 Λούκιος Lôúkiôs *n/p.* (2x)
G3066.2 N/P-NSM Λούκιος (2x)
Ac 13:1 ·called Niger), and Lucius of·Cyrene, Manaen also
Rm 16:21 my coworker, and·also Lucius, Jason, and

G3067 λουτρόν lôutrôn *n.* (2x)
Roots:G3068
G3067.1 N-GSN λουτροῦ (1x)
Tit 3:5 ·to his mercy, through a·bath of·regeneration and a·
G3067.2 N-DSN λουτρῷ (1x)
Eph 5:26 purifying her with·the bathing of·the water by an·

G3068 λούω lôúō *v.* (6x)
Compare:G3538 G4150 G0907 G0048 See:G0628
xLangEquiv:H7364
G3068 V-AAI-3S ἔλουσεν (1x)
Ac 16:33 hour of·the night, he·bathed off *their* punishing·
G3068 V-AAP-DSM λούσαντι (1x)
Rv 1:5 the·one loving us and already·bathing us *clean* from
G3068 V-AAP-NPM λούσαντες (1x)
Ac 9:37 ·sick, she died. And after·bathing her, they·laid *her*
G3068 V-AMP-NSF λουσαμένη (1x)
2Pe 2:22 and "a·sow *keeps·on* bathing·herself in a·wallowing
G3068 V-RPP-NSM λελουμένος (1x)
Jn 13:10 to·him, "The·one having·been·bathed has no need
G3068 V-RPP-NPM λελουμένοι (1x)
Heb 10:22 the bodies having·been·bathed with·pure water.

G3069 Λύδδα Lýdda *n/l.* (3x)
לֹד lód
Roots:H3850
G3069.2 N/L-ASF Λύδδαν (2x)
Ac 9:32 also to the holy·ones, the·ones residing·in Lod.
Ac 9:35 And all the·ones residing·in Lod and Sharon saw
G3069.2 N/L-GSF Λύδδης (1x)
Ac 9:38 Now being *as* Lod *was* near to·Joppa, *and* after·

G3070 Λυδία Lydía *n/p.* (2x)
Compare:G4554 xLangAlso:H5614
G3070 N/P-NSF Λυδία (1x)
Ac 16:14 by·the·name·of Lydia from *the*·city of·Thyatira, a·
G3070 N/P-ASF Λυδίαν (1x)
Ac 16:40 they·entered into *the house·of* Lydia. And seeing

G3071 Λυκαονία Lykaônía *n/l.* (1x)
Roots:G3074 See:G3072
G3071 N/L-GSF Λυκαονίας (1x)
Ac 14:6 Lystra and Derbe, the cities of·Lycaonia, and to·the

G3072 Λυκαονιστί Lykaônistí *adv/g.* (1x)
Roots:G3071
G3072 ADV Λυκαονιστί (1x)
Ac 14:11 their voices, saying in·the·language·of·Lycaonia,

G3073 Λυκία Lykía *n/l.* (1x)
Roots:G3074
G3073 N/L-GSF Λυκίας (1x)
Ac 27:5 we·came·down to Myra, *a·city* of·Lycia.

G3074 λύκος lýkôs *n.* (6x)
See:G3022
xLangEquiv:H2061
G3074 N-NSM λύκος (1x)
Jn 10:12 and flees; and the wolf snatches them and scatters
G3074 N-NPM λύκοι (2x)
Ac 20:29 burdensome wolves shall·enter·in among yeu,
Mt 7:15 but inwardly, they·are violently·greedy wolves.
G3074 N-ASM λύκον (1x)
Jn 10:12 sheep, he·observes the wolf coming and leaves the
G3074 N-GPM λύκων (2x)
Lk 10:3 as adolescent·male·lambs in *the* midst of·wolves.
Mt 10:16 yeu as sheep in *the* midst of·wolves. Accordingly,

G3075 λυμαίνομαι lymaínômai *v.* (1x)
Compare:G4199 See:G3089
G3075.1 V-INI-3S ἐλυμαίνετο (1x)
Ac 8:3 Saul was·brutally·ravaging the Called·Out·citizenry.

G3076 λυπέω lypéō *v.* (27x)
Roots:G3077 Compare:G2875 G3996 G3600
See:G4036 G4818
xLangEquiv:H3013
G3076.1 V-PAI-1S-C λυπῶ (1x)
2Co 2:2 For if I·myself grieve yeu, then who would·be the·
G3076.1 V-PAM-2P λυπεῖτε (1x)
Eph 4:30 And do·not grieve the Holy Spirit of·God, by
G3076.1 V-AAI-1S ἐλύπησα (1x)
2Co 7:8 Because even·though I·grieved yeu with the letter, I·
G3076.1 V-AAI-3S ἐλύπησεν (1x)
2Co 7:8 *it* that the·same letter did·grieve yeu, even·though *it*·
G3076.1 V-API-2P ἐλυπήθητε (1x)
2Co 7:9 but·rather that yeu·were·grieved to repentance, for
G3076.1 V-APN λυπηθῆναι (1x)
2Co 7:11 this very·same·thing (to·grieve yeu according·to
G3076.1 V-RAI-3S λελύπηκεν (2x)
2Co 2:5 But if any·man has·caused·grief, *it·is* not me *that*
2Co 2:5 *it·is* not me *that* he·has·grieved (other·than in part)
EG3076.1 (1x)
Jn 11:33 in·the spirit; yet he·troubled himself *to·grieve*,
G3076.2 V-FPI-2P λυπηθήσεσθε (1x)
Jn 16:20 shall·rejoice, and yeu shall·be·grieved, but·yet yeur
G3076.2 V-PPI-3S λυπεῖται (1x)
Rm 14:15 But if your brother is·grieved through *your* food,
G3076.2 V-PPN λυπεῖσθαι (2x)
Mt 26:37 he·began to·be·grieved and to·be·intensely·
Mk 14:19 And they·began to·be·grieved and to·say to·him
G3076.2 V-PPP-NSM λυπούμενος (3x)
Mt 19:22 the young·man went·away being·grieved, for he·
Mk 10:22 at the saying, he·went·away being·grieved, for he·
2Co 2:2 except the·one being·grieved as·a·result of·me?
G3076.2 V-PPP-NPM λυπούμενοι (2x)
Mt 26:22 And being tremendously grieved, each·one of·them
2Co 6:10 as being·grieved yet always rejoicing, as
G3076.2 V-PPS-2P λυπῆσθε (1x)
1Th 4:13 in·order·that yeu·should·not be·grieved, even
G3076.2 V-API-2P ἐλυπήθητε (2x)
2Co 7:9 I·do·rejoice, not that yeu·were·grieved, but·rather
2Co 7:9 repentance, for yeu·were·grieved according·to God,
G3076.2 V-API-3S ἐλυπήθη (2x)
Jn 21:17 Peter was·grieved because he·declared to·him
Mt 14:9 And the king was·grieved, but on·account·of the
G3076.2 V-API-3P ἐλυπήθησαν (2x)
Mt 17:23 And they·were tremendously grieved.
Mt 18:31 ·were·happening, were tremendously grieved, and
G3076.2 V-APP-NPM λυπηθέντες (1x)
1Pe 1:6 *although* being·grieved a·little·bit at·this·moment
G3076.2 V-APS-2P λυπηθῆτε (1x)
2Co 2:4 tears, not that yeu·should·be·grieved, but·rather that

G3077 λύπη lýpē *n.* (16x)
Compare:G2870 G3997 G3601 G4192 See:G3076
G0253 G4036 G3077-1 xLangAlso:H3015
G3077.1 N-NSF λύπη (5x)
Jn 16:6 ·things to·yeu, the grief has·completely·filled yeur
Jn 16:20 ·grieved, but·yet yeur grief shall·become a·distinct
Rm 9:2 that my grief is a·great and unceasing distress in·my
2Co 7:10 For the grief according·to God accomplishes
2Co 7:10 Salvation without·regret, but the grief of·the world
G3077.1 N-ASF λύπην (4x)
Jn 16:21 ·and·give·birth, she·has grief because her hour is·
Jn 16:22 yeu·yeurselves in·fact now have grief. But I·shall·
Php 2:27 on·me also, lest I·should·have grief upon grief.
2Co 2:3 *to·yeu*, I·should·have grief from them·by·whom it·
G3077.1 N-APF λύπας (1x)
1Pe 2:19 conscience *toward* God undergoes grief, suffering
G3077.1 N-DSF λύπῃ (2x)
Php 2:27 on·me also, lest I·should·have grief upon grief.
2Co 2:7 ·man should·be·swallowed·up with·excessive grief.
G3077.1 N-GSF λύπης (2x)
Lk 22:45 he·found them being·laid·asleep due·to the grief,
2Co 9:7 in·*his*·heart, not out of·grief nor out of·compulsion,
G3077.2 N-GSF λύπης (1x)
Heb 12:11 to·be joyous, but·rather grievous. But eventually,
G3077.3 N-DSF λύπῃ (1x)
2Co 2:1 ·self, not again to·come to yeu in grievousness.

G3078 Λυσ•ανίας Lysanías *n/p.* (1x)
Roots:G3080
G3078.2 N/P-GSM Λυσανίου (1x)
Lk 3:1 and with·Lysanias being·the·ruling·tetrarch of·

G3079 Λυσίας Lysías *n/p.* (4x)
See:G2804
G3079 N/P-NSM Λυσίας (3x)
Ac 23:26 "Claudius Lysias, to·the most·noble governor Felix
Ac 24:7 But Lysias the regiment·commander, after·coming·
Ac 24:22 "Whenever Lysias the regiment·commander
EG3079 (1x)
Ac 21:37 And *Lysias* the *regiment·commander* replied,

G3080 λύσις lýsis *n.* (1x)
Roots:G3089 Compare:G0647
G3080.2 N-ASF λύσιν (1x)
1Co 7:27 to·a·woman? Do·not seek a·break·up. Have·you·

G3081 λυσι•τελεῖ lysitêlêî *v.* (1x)
Roots:G3080 G5056 Compare:G3786 G4050
See:G0255
G3081.2 V-PAI-3S λυσιτελεῖ (1x)
Lk 17:2 It·is·a·better·end for·him that a·donkey-sized

G3082 Λύστρα Lýstra *n/l.* (6x)
G3082 N/L-ASF Λύστραν (3x)
Ac 14:6 *it, the ambassadors* fled·down to Lystra and Derbe,
Ac 14:21 ·number, they·returned·back to Lystra, and *to*
Ac 16:1 Then he·arrived in Derbe and Lystra. And behold, a·
G3082 N/L-DPN Λύστροις (3x)
Ac 14:8 And at Lystra, *there·was* a·certain man disabled in·
Ac 16:2 ·attested·to by the brothers in Lystra and Iconium.
2Ti 3:11 at Iconium, *and* at Lystra; what persecutions I·

G3083 λύτρον lýtrôn *n.* (2x)
Roots:G3089 Compare:G0058-1 See:G3084
xLangEquiv:H6306 xLangAlso:H6299 H1353
G3083.2 N-ASN λύτρον (2x)
Mt 20:28 and to·give his soul *to·be* a·ransom for many."
Mk 10:45 and to·give his soul *to·be* a·ransom for many."

G3084 λυτρόω lytrôō *v.* (3x)
Roots:G3083 Compare:G1805 G0059 See:G3085
G3086 G0628-2 G1589-5
xLangEquiv:H6299
G3084 V-PMN λυτροῦσθαι (1x)
Lk 24:21 he·himself is the·one intending to·ransom IsraEl.
G3084 V-AMS-3S λυτρώσηται (1x)
Tit 2:14 behalf in·order·that he·may·ransom us from all
G3084 V-API-2P ἐλυτρώθητε (1x)
1Pe 1:18 or gold *that* yeu·were·ransomed from·out of·yeur

G3085 λύτρωσις lýtrōsis *n.* (3x)
Roots:G3084 Compare:G0058-1 See:G3086
xLangEquiv:H6304
G3085 N-ASF λύτρωσιν (3x)
Lk 1:68 he·visited and made a·ransoming for·his People!
Lk 2:38 to·all the·ones awaiting a·ransoming in JeruSalem.
Heb 9:12 finding·in·himself an·eternal ransoming *for·us*.

G3086 λυτρωτής lytrōtḗs *n.* (1x)
Roots:G3084 Compare:G0059 See:G3085 G1805
G3086.1 N-ASM λυτρωτήν (1x)
Ac 7:35 dispatched *to·be* a·ruler and a·ransomer by *the* hand

G3087 λυχνία lychnía *n.* (12x)
Roots:G3088 xLangAlso:H4501 A5043
G3087.1 N-ASF λυχνίαν (3x)
Lk 11:33 *places it* on the lampstand, in·order·that the·ones
Mt 5:15 ·basket, but·rather on the lampstand, and it·radiates·
Mk 4:21 not in·order·that it·should·be·put on the lampstand?
G3087.1 N-GSF λυχνίας (1x)
Lk 8:16 but·rather he·puts *it* on a·lampstand, in·order·that

G3087.2 N-NSF λυχνία (1x)
Heb 9:2 in which also *was* the Menorah·Lampstand, and the
G3087.6 N-NPF λυχνίαι (1x)
Rv 11:4 ·trees and the two Fine·Oil·Lampstands standing in·
G3087.7 N-NPF λυχνίαι (1x)
Rv 1:20 and the seven Lampstands which you·saw are *the*
G3087.7 N-ASF λυχνίαν (1x)
Rv 2:5 ·haste, and shall·stir your Lampstand out of·its place,
G3087.7 N-APF λυχνίας (2x)
Rv 1:12 turning·about, I·saw seven Golden Lampstands,
Rv 1:20 and the seven Golden Lampstands: the seven stars
G3087.7 N-GPF λυχνιῶν (2x)
Rv 1:13 in *the* midst of·the seven Lampstands, *one* like a·son
Rv 2:1 ·about in *the* midst of·the seven Golden Lampstands:

G3088 λύχνος lýchnôs *n.* (14x)
Roots:G3022 Compare:G2985 G5322 See:G3087 xLangAlso:H5216
G3088.1 N-NSM λύχνος (6x)
Jn 5:35 That·man was the lantern, the·one being·set·ablaze
Lk 11:34 "The lantern of·the body is the eye.
Lk 11:36 radiant·shimmer of·a·lantern may·illuminate you."
Mt 6:22 "The lantern of·the body is the eye.
Mk 4:21 ·Is·it·ever·the·case·that the lantern is·brought *forth*
Rv 21:23 of·God illuminated it, and the Lamb *is* its lantern.
G3088.1 N-NPM λύχνοι (1x)
Lk 12:35 ·girded·about and *yeur* lanterns being·set·ablaze.
G3088.1 N-ASF λύχνον (4x)
Lk 8:16 "Not·even·one·man, after·igniting a·lantern, covers
Lk 11:33 Not·even·one·man, after·igniting a·lantern, places
Lk 15:8 one drachma, does·not·indeed ignite a·lantern, and
Mt 5:15 Neither do·they·set·ablaze a·lantern and place it
G3088.1 N-DSM λύχνῳ (1x)
2Pe 1:19 ·do well taking·heed as to·a·lantern shining·forth in
G3088.1 N-GSM λύχνου (2x)
Rv 18:23 and a·light of·a·lantern, no should·not·ever shine·
Rv 22:5 they·do·not have need of·a·lantern, nor·even of·

G3089 λύω lýō *v.* (43x)
Compare:G4486 G2352 G0630 G0622 G4977 See:G0360 G0630 G1262 G1956 G2647 G3083 G3886
G3089.1 V-FPI-3S λυθήσεται (1x)
Rv 20:7 Adversary-Accuser shall·be·loosened from·out of·his
G3089.1 V-PAI-2P λύετε (2x)
Lk 19:31 any·man should·ask·of yeu, 'Why do·yeu·loose *it*?
Lk 19:33 declared to·them, "Why·do yeu·loose the colt?
G3089.1 V-PAI-3S λύει (1x)
Lk 13:15 each·one of·yeu on·the Sabbath loosen his ox or
G3089.1 V-PAI-3P λύουσιν (1x)
Mk 11:4 door at the fork·in·the·road, and they·loose him.
G3089.1 V-PAP-GPM λυόντων (1x)
Lk 19:33 And as·they were·loosing the colt, its owners
G3089.1 V-PAP-NPM λύοντες (1x)
Mk 11:5 "What·are yeu·doing, loosening the colt?
G3089.1 V-AAI-3S ἔλυσεν (1x)
Ac 22:30 personally·by the Judeans, he·loosed him from the
G3089.1 V-AAM-2S λῦσον (2x)
Ac 7:33 declared to·him, "Loosen the shoes from·your feet,
Rv 9:14 was·holding the trumpet, "Loosen the four angels,
G3089.1 V-AAM-2P λύσατε (1x)
Jn 11:44 Jesus says to·them, "Loose him, and allow·him to·
G3089.1 V-AAN λῦσαι (5x)
Lk 3:16 ·whose shoes I·am not fit to·loose. He·himself shall·
Ac 13:25 the shoes of·whose feet I·am not worthy to·loose.'
Mk 1:7 *even* after·stooping·down, to·loose the strap of·his
Rv 5:2 ·up the official·scroll and to·loosen its official·seals?
Rv 5:5 to·open·up the official·scroll and to·loosen its seven
G3089.1 V-AAP-NSM λύσας (1x)
Ac 2:24 whom God raised·up, loosing the pangs of·Death,
G3089.1 V-AAP-NPM λύσαντες (3x)
Lk 19:30 ·one man·of·clay† sat ever·at·any·time. Loosing it,
Mt 21:2 and a·colt with her. Loosening *them*, bring *them*
Mk 11:2 not·even·one man·of·clay† has·sat. Loosening him,
G3089.1 V-AAS-1S λύσω (1x)
Jn 1:27 am not *even* worthy that I·may·loosen his shoe strap.
G3089.1 V-AAS-2S λύσῃς (1x)
Mt 16:19 and whatever you·should·loose on the earth shall·
G3089.1 V-AAS-2P λύσητε (1x)
Mt 18:18 and as·many·things·as yeu·should·loose on the
G3089.1 V-AAS-3S λύσῃ (1x)
Ac 24:26 to·him by Paul, that he·may·loose him. Therefore,
G3089.1 V-API-3S ἐλύθη (1x)
Mk 7:35 the impediment of·his tongue was·loosed, and he·
G3089.1 V-API-3P ἐλύθησαν (1x)
Rv 9:15 And the four angels were·loosened, the·ones having·
G3089.1 V-APN λυθῆναι (2x)
Lk 13:16 was·it·not binding·for *her* to·be·loosed from this
Rv 20:3 it·is·mandatory·for him to·be·loosed a·short time.
G3089.1 V-APP-GSF λυθείσης (1x)
Ac 13:43 And with·the gathering being·let·loose, many of·
G3089.1 V-RPP-NSN λελυμένον (1x)
Mt 16:19 on the earth shall·be having·been·loosed in the
G3089.1 V-RPP-NPN λελυμένα (1x)
Mt 18:18 on the earth shall·be having·been·loosed in the
G3089.2 V-IAI-3S ἔλυεν (1x)
Jn 5:18 because not merely was·he·breaking the Sabbath—
G3089.2 V-IPI-3S ἐλύετο (1x)
Ac 27:41 unshakable, but the stern was·broken by the force
G3089.2 V-AAP-NSM λύσας (1x)
Eph 2:14 one, and already·breaking·down the middle·wall
G3089.2 V-AAS-3S λύσῃ (1x)
Mt 5:19 Accordingly, whoever should·break one of·these
G3089.2 V-APN λυθῆναι (1x)
Jn 10:35 came, and the Scripture is·not able to·be·broken …
G3089.2 V-APS-3S λυθῇ (1x)
Jn 7:23 of·Moses should·not be·broken, are·yeu·irritated
G3089.2 V-RPI-2S λέλυσαι (1x)
1Co 7:27 ·up. Have·you·been·broken·up from a·woman?
G3089.3 V-AAM-2P λύσατε (1x)
Jn 2:19 and declared to·them, "Tear·down this temple, and
G3089.3 V-AAS-3S λύσῃ (1x)
1Jn 3:8 ·made·apparent: that he·should·tear·down the works
G3089.4 V-FPI-3P λυθήσονται (2x)
2Pe 3:10 and *the* elements shall·be·dissolved— being·
2Pe 3:12 heavens, being·set·on·fire, shall·be·dissolved, and
G3089.4 V-PPP-GPN λυομένων (1x)
2Pe 3:11 with·all these·things being·dissolved, *determine*

G3090 Λωΐς Lōḯs *n/p.* (1x)
See:G5095 G2131
G3090 N/P-DSM Λωΐδι (1x)
2Ti 1:5 first in your grandmother Lois and your mother

G3091 Λώτ Lṓt *n/p.* (4x)
לוֹט lôṭ [Hebrew]
Roots:H3876
G3091.2 N/P-PRI Λώτ (4x)
Lk 17:28 also as it·was in the days of·Lot: they·were·eating,
Lk 17:29 but on·that day *when* Lot went·forth from Sodom,
Lk 17:32 "Remember Lot's wife.
2Pe 2:7 righteous Lot being·worn·down·in·labored·anguish

Μμ - Mu

G3092 Ματθάθ Maáth *n/p.* (1x)
G3092 N/P-PRI Ματθάθ (1x)
Lk 3:26 *son* of·Maath, *son* of·Mattathias, *son* of·Shimei, *son*

G3093 Μαγδαλά Magdalá *n/l.* (1x)
מִגְדָּל mɪgdal [Hebrew]
Roots:H4026 Compare:G1148 G4444 See:G3094
G3093.2 N/L-PRI Μαγδαλά (1x)
Mt 15:39 into the borders of·Magdala·*(that·is,·the·Tower)*.

G3094 Μαγδαληνή Magdalēnḗ *n/p.* (12x)
Roots:G3093
G3094.2 N/P-NSF Μαγδαληνή (11x)
Jn 19:25 the *wife* of·Clopas), and Mariam Magdalene.
Jn 20:1 ·being still dark), Mariam Magdalene comes to the
Jn 20:18 Mariam Magdalene came announcing to·the
Lk 8:2 Mariam (the·one being·called Magdalene) from
Lk 24:10 It·was Mariam Magdalene, and Joanna, and
Mt 27:56 Among whom was Mariam Magdalene, and
Mt 27:61 And there was Mariam Magdalene, and the other
Mt 28:1 first *dawn* of·the·week, Mariam Magdalene and the
Mk 15:40 even among whom was Mariam Magdalene, and
Mk 15:47 And Mariam Magdalene and Miryam (*mother* of·
Mk 16:1 already·elapsing, Mariam Magdalene and Mariam
G3094.2 N/P-DSF Μαγδαληνῇ (1x)
Mk 16:9 *Jesus* did·appear first to·Mariam Magdalene, from

G3095 μαγεία magêía *n.* (1x)
Roots:G3096 Compare:G4021
G3095.2 N-DPF μαγείαις (1x)
Ac 8:11 *for* the longest time with·the dark·occult·powers.

G3096 μαγεύω magêúō *v.* (1x)
Roots:G3097 See:G3095
G3096 V-PAP-NSM μαγεύων (1x)
Ac 8:9 city practicing·dark·occult·powers and astonishing

G3097 μάγος mágôs *n.* (6x)
See:G3096 G3095 xLangAlso:H7248
G3097.1 N-NPM μάγοι (1x)
Mt 2:1 ·the·Great, behold, Magian·astrologists from *the* east
G3097.1 N-APM μάγους (1x)
Mt 2:7 ·for the Magian·astrologists, precisely·ascertained
G3097.1 N-GPM μάγων (2x)
Mt 2:16 ·mocked by the Magian·astrologists, was·enraged
Mt 2:16 personally·from the Magian·astrologists.
G3097.2 N-NSM μάγος (1x)
Ac 13:8 But Elymas, the occultist (for so his name is·
G3097.2 N-ASM μάγον (1x)
Ac 13:6 ·found a·certain Jewish occultist, a·false·prophet,

G3098 Μαγώγ Magṓg *n/p.* (1x)
מָגוֹג magôg [Hebrew]
Roots:H4031 See:G1136
G3098.1 N/P-PRI Μαγώγ (1x)
Rv 20:8 of·the earth, Gog and Magog, to·gather them

G3099 Μαδιάν Madián *n/l.* (1x)
מִדְיָן mɪdyan [Hebrew]
Roots:H4080 xLangAlso:H6989
G3099.2 N/L-PRI Μαδιάμ (1x)
Ac 7:29 was a·sojourner in *the* land of·Midian, where he·

G3100 μαθητεύω mathētêúō *v.* (4x)
Roots:G3101 Compare:G1321
G3100.1 V-AAI-3S ἐμαθήτευσεν (1x)
Mt 27:57 who also himself became·a·disciple of·YeShua.
G3100.1 V-APP-NSM μαθητευθείς (1x)
Mt 13:52 that, every scribe already·being·discipled into the
G3100.2 V-AAM-2P μαθητεύσατε (1x)
Mt 28:19 "Accordingly, while·traversing, disciple all the
G3100.2 V-AAP-NPM μαθητεύσαντες (1x)
Ac 14:21 to·that city and discipling a·significant·number,

G3101 μαθητής mathētḗs *n.* (280x)
Roots:G3129 Compare:G1320 See:G3102 G4827
xLangEquiv:H8527

G3101.2 N-NSM μαθητής (20x)

Jn 9:28 "You·yourself are that·man's disciple, but we·
Jn 18:15 Jesus, and *so was* another disciple. But that disciple
Jn 18:15 disciple. But that disciple was known to·the
Jn 18:16 In·due·course, the other disciple, who was known
Jn 19:27 from that hour, the disciple took her into his·own
Jn 19:38 from Arimathaea) being a·disciple of·Jesus but
Jn 20:3 Peter and the other disciple went·forth, and they·
Jn 20:4 yet the other disciple more·swiftly outran Peter and
Jn 20:8 Then accordingly, the other disciple entered also,
Jn 21:7 In·due·course, that disciple whom Jesus loved says
Jn 21:23 among the brothers, "This disciple does·not die."
Jn 21:24 This is the disciple, the·one testifying concerning
Lk 6:40 "A·disciple is not above his instructor, but everyone
Lk 14:26 his·own soul also, he·is·not able to·be my disciple.
Lk 14:27 right·behind me, is·not able to·be my disciple.
Lk 14:33 all his holdings, he·is·not able to·be my disciple.
Ac 9:10 And there·was a·certain disciple at Damascus,
Ac 9:26 all afraid of·him, not trusting that he·was a·disciple.
Ac 16:1 And behold, a·certain disciple was there, TimoThy
Mt 10:24 "A·disciple is not above the instructor, nor·even a·

G3101.2 N-NPM μαθηταί (111x)

Jn 1:37 And the two disciples heard him speaking, and they·
Jn 2:2 ·called·forth to the wedding, and·also his disciples.
Jn 2:11 And his disciples trusted in him.
Jn 2:12 his brothers, and his disciples), and they·remained
Jn 2:17 And his disciples recalled·to·mind that it·was
Jn 2:22 dead·men, his disciples recalled·to·mind that he·
Jn 3:22 these·things, Jesus and his disciples came into the
Jn 4:2 himself was·not immersing, but·rather his disciples),
Jn 4:8 (for his disciples had·gone·off to the city in·order·that
Jn 4:27 And his disciples came upon this, and they·marveled
Jn 4:31 the meanwhile, the disciples were·imploring·of him,
Jn 4:33 So·then the disciples were·saying among one·another
Jn 6:11 and the disciples to·the·ones reclining·for·the·meal,
Jn 6:16 ·evening occurred, his disciples walked·down to the
Jn 6:22 that one into which his disciples embarked, and that
Jn 6:22 ·boat, but·rather *that* his disciples went·off alone—
Jn 6:24 was not there, nor his disciples, they also embarked
Jn 6:61 in himself that his disciples are·grumbling about this,
Jn 7:3 into Judea, that your disciples also may·observe the
Jn 8:31 in my Redemptive-word, yeu·are truly my disciples;
Jn 9:2 And his disciples asked·of him, saying, "Rabbi, who
Jn 9:27 yeu·yeurselves also want to·become his disciples?"
Jn 9:28 disciple, but we·ourselves are Moses' disciples.
Jn 11:8 The disciples say to·him, "Rabbi, the Judeans now
Jn 11:12 Accordingly, his disciples declared, "Lord, if he·
Jn 12:16 But his disciples did·not know these·things at·the
Jn 13:22 Accordingly, the disciples were·looking to one·
Jn 13:35 everyone shall·know that yeu·are disciples to·me, if
Jn 15:8 and *that* yeu·shall·become my·personal disciples.
Jn 16:29 His disciples say to·him, "See, now you·speak
Jn 18:1 which he·himself entered *along* with his disciples.
Jn 20:10 So·then, the disciples went·off again to their·own
Jn 20:19 the disciples were having·been·gathered·together
Jn 20:20 Accordingly, the disciples were·glad after·seeing
Jn 20:25 So the other disciples were·saying to·him, "We·
Jn 20:26 eight days, again his disciples were inside, and
Jn 21:4 shore; however, the disciples had·not seen that it·
Jn 21:8 And the other disciples came in·the small·boat,
Lk 5:33 "Why·is·it·that the disciples of·John fast frequently
Lk 6:1 the grain·fields, and his disciples were·plucking the
Lk 7:11 of·his disciples were·traversing·together with·him,
Lk 7:18 And the disciples of·John *the Immerser* reported·to
Lk 8:9 And his disciples were·inquiring·of him, saying,
Lk 8:22 into a·sailboat with his disciples, and he·declared to
Lk 9:18 ·himself, *that* the disciples were·together with·him.
Lk 9:54 And after·seeing *this*, his disciples, Jakob and John,
Lk 18:15 ·may·lay·hold of·them, but the disciples seeing *it*,
Lk 22:39 of·Olives. And his disciples also followed him.
Ac 9:25 Then the disciples, taking him by·night, sent·*him*·
Ac 9:38 was in this *city*, the disciples dispatched two men to
Ac 13:52 And the disciples were·completely·filled with·joy
Ac 19:30 the public·assembly, the disciples were·not letting
Mt 5:1 ·seating himself, his disciples came·alongside him.
Mt 8:23 into the sailboat, his disciples followed him.
Mt 8:25 And coming·alongside, his disciples awakened him,
Mt 9:14 At·that·time, the disciples of·John came·alongside
Mt 9:14 Pharisees fast often, but your disciples do·not fast?
Mt 9:19 YeShua followed him, and *so·did* his disciples.
Mt 12:1 and *when* his disciples were·hungry, they·also
Mt 12:2 "Behold, your disciples do that·which it·is·not
Mt 13:10 coming·alongside, the disciples declared to·him,
Mt 13:36 And his disciples came·alongside him, saying,
Mt 14:12 And his disciples, after·coming·alongside, took·
Mt 14:15 occurring, his disciples came·alongside him,
Mt 14:19 ·the disciples, and the disciples *gave bread* to·the
Mt 14:26 upon the sea, the disciples were·troubled, saying,
Mt 15:2 "Why·do your disciples walk·contrary·to the Oral·
Mt 15:12 Then his disciples, after·coming·alongside,
Mt 15:23 his disciples coming·alongside were·imploring·of
Mt 15:33 And his disciples say to·him, "From·what·source
Mt 15:36 ·his disciples, and the disciples *gave* to·the crowd.
Mt 16:5 *of·the sea*, his disciples had·forgotten to·take bread.
Mt 17:6 And upon·hearing *it*, the disciples fell on their faces
Mt 17:10 And his disciples inquired·of him, saying, "So·
Mt 17:13 Then the disciples comprehended that he·declared
Mt 17:19 YeShua in private, the disciples declared, "Why·
Mt 18:1 same hour, the disciples came·alongside YeShua,
Mt 19:10 His disciples say to·him, "If the legal·charge of·
Mt 19:13 and pray. And the disciples reprimanded them.
Mt 19:25 upon·hearing *this*, his disciples were tremendously
Mt 21:6 And traversing, the disciples, also doing just·as
Mt 21:20 And seeing *this*, the disciples marveled, saying,
Mt 24:1 yet his disciples came·alongside to·fully·exhibit
Mt 24:3 Mount of·Olives, the disciples came·alongside him
Mt 26:8 ·seeing *this*, his disciples are·greatly·displeased,
Mt 26:17 ·Bread, the disciples came·alongside YeShua,
Mt 26:19 And the disciples did as YeShua appointed them,
Mt 26:35 And·also, all the disciples declared likewise.
Mt 26:56 Then leaving him, all the disciples fled.
Mt 27:64 the third day, lest his disciples, coming by·night,
Mt 28:13 "Yeu·must·declare, 'His disciples stole him,
Mt 28:16 Now the eleven disciples traversed into Galilee to
Mk 2:18 Now the disciples of·John and the *disciples* of·the
Mk 2:18 ·him, "Why·is·it·that the disciples of·John and the
Mk 2:18 of·the Pharisees fast, but your disciples do·not fast?
Mk 2:23 and his disciples began to·make a·pathway,
Mk 5:31 And his disciples were·saying to·him, "You·look·
Mk 6:1 his·own fatherland, and his disciples followed him.
Mk 6:29 And with·his disciples hearing *of·it*, they·came and
Mk 6:35 a·late hour, his disciples, after·coming·alongside
Mk 7:5 him, "Why·do your disciples not walk according·to
Mk 7:17 the crowd, his disciples were·inquiring·of him
Mk 8:4 And his disciples answered him, "From·what·source
Mk 8:27 Jesus went·out with his disciples into the villages
Mk 9:28 into a·house, his disciples were·inquiring·of him in
Mk 10:10 in the home, his disciples inquired·of him again
Mk 10:13 and the disciples were·reprimanding the·ones
Mk 10:24 And the disciples were·amazed at his words.
Mk 11:14 And his disciples were·listening.
Mk 14:12 ·sacrificing the Passover, his disciples say to·him,
Mk 14:16 And his disciples went·forth and came into the

G3101.2 N-ASM μαθητήν (3x)

Jn 19:26 his mother and the disciple standing·nearby whom
Jn 20:2 and to the other disciple whom Jesus was·fond·of,
Jn 21:20 ·about, Peter looks·at the disciple following *them*

G3101.2 N-APM μαθητάς (41x)

Jn 4:1 Jesus makes and immerses more disciples than John,"
Lk 5:30 ·them were·grumbling toward his disciples, saying,
Lk 6:13 ·was day, he·hailed his disciples *to·himself* and was·
Lk 6:20 lifting·up his eyes to his disciples, he·was·saying,
Lk 9:1 And calling·together his twelve disciples, he·gave
Lk 9:14 And he·declared to his disciples, "Make them fully·
Lk 9:43 ·things which Jesus did, he·declared to his disciples,
Lk 10:22 turning·around toward the disciples, he·declared,
Lk 10:23 ·himself *to·be* alongside his disciples, he·declared
Lk 11:1 to·pray, just·as John also instructed his disciples."
Lk 12:1 *Jesus* began to·say to his disciples, "First·of·all,
Lk 12:22 Then he·declared to his disciples, "On·account·of
Lk 16:1 And he·was·saying also toward his disciples,
Lk 17:1 And *Jesus* declared to the disciples, "It·is not·
Lk 17:22 Then he·declared to the disciples, "Days shall·
Lk 22:45 prayer *and* coming to the disciples, he·found them
Ac 9:1 ·menace and murder against the disciples of·the Lord,
Ac 11:26 in Antioch *that* "The disciples *are* 'Christians,'
Ac 18:23 in·consecutive·order, reaffirming all the disciples.
Ac 19:1 And finding some disciples,
Ac 19:9 he·distinctly·detached the disciples *from·them*,
Ac 20:1 Paul, after·summoning the disciples and embracing
Ac 20:30 to·draw·away the disciples right·behind them.
Ac 21:4 after·diligently·finding the disciples, we·stayed·over
Mt 10:1 And summoning his twelve disciples, he·gave to·
Mt 12:49 ·forth his hand over his disciples, he·declared,
Mt 14:22 YeShua compelled his disciples to·embark into
Mt 15:32 And after·summoning his disciples, YeShua
Mt 16:13 Philippi, was·asking·of his disciples, saying,
Mt 20:17 personally·took the twelve disciples aside privately
Mt 21:1 of·Olives), then YeShua dispatched two disciples,
Mt 22:16 they·dispatched their disciples to·him along·with
Mt 26:40 And he·comes to the disciples and finds them
Mt 26:45 Then he·comes to his disciples and says to·them,
Mk 6:45 he·compelled his disciples to·embark into the
Mk 8:1 ·eat), after·summoning his disciples, Jesus says to·
Mk 8:27 way, he·was·inquiring·of his disciples, saying to·
Mk 8:33 ·about and seeing his disciples, he·reprimanded
Mk 9:14 upon·coming to the *other* disciples, he·saw a·large
Mk 9:31 For he·was·instructing his disciples, and he·was·
Mk 12:43 And summoning his disciples, he·says to·them,

G3101.2 N-DSM μαθητῇ (3x)

Jn 19:27 Then he·says to·the disciple, "Behold your mother!
Ac 21:16 Mnason of·Cyprus, an·early disciple, with·whom
Mt 10:25 sufficient for·the disciple that he·should·become as

G3101.2 N-DPM μαθηταῖς (43x)

Jn 6:11 he·thoroughly·doled·*it*·out to·the disciples, and the
Jn 6:12 they·are·filled·up, he·says to·his disciples, "Gather·
Jn 6:22 did·not enter·together with·his disciples into the
Jn 11:7 after that he·says to·the disciples, "We·should·head·
Jn 18:1 together with·his disciples to·the·other·side of·the
Jn 20:18 to·the disciples that she·has·clearly·seen the Lord,
Jn 21:1 himself apparent again to·the disciples at the Sea of·
Jn 21:14 ·apparent to·his disciples, after·being·awakened
Lk 9:16 was·giving *them* to·the disciples to·place·before the
Lk 19:39 "Mentor, reprimand your disciples."
Lk 20:45 of·all the people, he·declared to·his disciples,
Ac 9:26 ·trying to·tightly·join·himself to·the disciples, but
Ac 14:28 ·were·lingering there together with·the disciples.
Ac 18:27 encouraging the disciples *there* to·fully·accept
Mt 9:10 ·together·at·the·meal with·YeShua and his disciples.
Mt 9:11 the Pharisees declared to·his disciples, "Why·does
Mt 9:37 Then he·says to·his disciples, "In·fact, the harvest
Mt 11:1 *these·things* to·his twelve disciples, he·walked·on
Mt 14:19 he·gave the loaves·of·bread to·the disciples, and
Mt 15:36 ·broke *them* and gave *them* to·his disciples, and the
Mt 16:20 his disciples in·order·that they·should·declare to·
Mt 16:21 to·show to·his disciples that it·is·mandatory·for
Mt 16:24 Then YeShua declared to·his disciples, "If any·
Mt 17:16 And I·brought him to·your disciples, and they·
Mt 19:23 And YeShua declared to·his disciples, "Certainly
Mt 23:1 YeShua spoke to·the crowds and to·his disciples,
Mt 26:1 all these sayings, he·declared to·his disciples,
Mt 26:26 and was·giving *it* to·the disciples, and he·declared,
Mt 26:36 and he·says to·the disciples, "Yeu·sit·down at·
Mt 28:7 declare to·his disciples that he·was·awakened from
Mt 28:8 ·great joy, they·ran to·announce *it* to·his disciples.
Mt 28:9 they·were·traversing to·announce *it* to·his disciples,

Mk 2:15 ·at·the·meal with·Jesus and his disciples. For there·
Mk 2:16 ·disqualified·men, were·saying to·his disciples,
Mk 3:9 And he·declared to·his disciples that a·small·boat
Mk 4:34 he·was·explaining all·things to·his disciples.
Mk 6:41 to·his disciples in·order·that they·should·place·
Mk 8:6 to·his disciples in·order·that they·may·place·*them*·
Mk 8:34 the crowd *to·him* along·with his disciples, *Jesus*
Mk 9:18 I·declared to·your disciples that they·should·cast it
Mk 10:23 ·around, Jesus says to·his disciples, "How
Mk 14:32 And *Jesus* says to·his disciples, "Yeu·sit·down
Mk 16:7 head·on·out! Declare to·his disciples and to·Peter
G3101.2 N-GSM μαθητοῦ (1x)
Mt 10:42 of·cold *water* to·drink merely in a·disciple's name,
G3101.2 N-GPM μαθητῶν (47x)
Jn 1:35 John stood also *with* two from·among his disciples.
Jn 3:25 ·discussion from·among John's disciples against *the*
Jn 6:3 And there, he·was·sitting·down with his disciples.
Jn 6:8 One from·among his disciples, Andrew, Simon Peter's
Jn 6:60 many from·among his disciples, upon·hearing *this*,
Jn 6:66 of·this, many of·his disciples went·off to the·things
Jn 11:54 he·was·lingering·awhile there with his disciples.
Jn 12:4 So·then one from·among his disciples (Judas
Jn 13:5 then he·began to·wash the disciples' feet and to·
Jn 13:23 bosom was one of·his disciples whom Jesus loved.
Jn 16:17 *some* from·among his disciples declared among
Jn 18:2 Jesus did·gather there together with his disciples.
Jn 18:17 also from·among the disciples of·this man·of·clay†?
Jn 18:19 asked Jesus concerning his disciples and concerning
Jn 18:25 you·yourself not also from·among his disciples?"
Jn 20:30 other signs in·the·sight of·his disciples, which are
Jn 21:2 ·Zebedee, and two others from·among his disciples.
Jn 21:12 of·the disciples was·daring to·verify·by·inquiring·
Lk 6:17 and·also the crowd of·his disciples, and a·large
Lk 7:19 summoning a·certain two of·his disciples, sent *them*
Lk 9:40 your disciples in·order·that they·should·cast him out
Lk 11:1 he·ceased, a·certain·one of·his disciples declared to
Lk 19:29 of·Olives), he·dispatched two of·his disciples,
Lk 19:37 ·all the multitude of·the disciples began rejoicing,
Lk 22:11 where I·may·eat the Passover with my disciples?"'
Ac 1:15 in *the* midst of·the disciples (and it·was a·crowd
Ac 6:1 And in these days of·the disciples multiplying, there·
Ac 6:2 ·summoning the multitude of·the disciples, declared,
Ac 6:7 and the number of·the disciples were·multiplied in
Ac 9:19 Now Saul was among the disciples at Damascus *for*
Ac 11:29 So some of·the disciples, each of·them just·as he·
Ac 14:20 But, with·the disciples surrounding him, after·
Ac 14:22 reaffirming the souls of·the disciples, exhorting
Ac 15:10 ·yoke upon the neck of·the disciples, which neither
Ac 20:7 with·the disciples having·been·gathered·together to·
Ac 21:16 And *some* of·the disciples from Caesarea also
Mt 8:21 And another of·his disciples declared to·him, "Lord
Mt 11:2 *and* sending·word by·two of·his disciples,
Mt 26:18 the Passover alongside you with my disciples.""'
Mk 3:7 And Jesus departed with his disciples to the sea.
Mk 7:2 And after·seeing some of·his disciples eating bread
Mk 8:10 into the sailboat with his disciples, he·came into the
Mk 10:46 from Jericho with his disciples and a·significant
Mk 11:1 Mount of·Olives, he·dispatches two of·his disciples
Mk 13:1 Sanctuary·Atrium, one of·his disciples says to·him,
Mk 14:13 And he·dispatches two of·his disciples and says
Mk 14:14 where I·may·eat the Passover with my disciples?"'
EG3101.2 (11x)
Jn 11:13 his death, but those *disciples* presumed that he·says
Lk 19:36 traversing, *other disciples* were·spreading·out their
Ac 9:2 that if·ever he·should·find any *disciples* of·The Way,
Ac 16:2 This *disciple* was·attested·to by the brothers in
Ac 21:5 we·were·traversing, with·all *the disciples* seeing us
Ac 21:6 sailing·ship, and those *disciples* returned·back to
Mk 2:18 disciples of·John and the *disciples* of·the Pharisees
Mk 2:18 disciples of·John and the *disciples* of·the Pharisees
Mk 8:7 *them*, he·declared *to·his disciples* to·place them also
Mk 8:14 Now *the disciples* forgot to·take bread, and except
Mk 16:20 ·forth, those *disciples* officially·proclaimed *it*

G3102 μαθήτρια mathḗtria *n.* (1x)
Roots:G3101
G3102.2 N-NSF μαθήτρια (1x)
Ac 9:36 a·certain female·disciple by·the·name·of Tabitha,

G3103 Μαθου•σάλα Mathôusála *n/p.* (1x)
מְתוּשֶׁלַח mᵉthûshẹlạcн [Hebrew]
Μεθου•σέλαχ Mêthôushélach
[Greek, Octuagint]
Roots:H4968 Compare:G0130 See:G4527 G2627
G3103.2 N/P-PRI Μεθουσέλαχ (1x)
Lk 3:37 *son* of·MethuShelach, *son* of·Enoch, *son* of·Jared,

G3104 Μαϊνάν Maïnán *n/p.* (1x)
G3104 N/P-PRI Μαϊνάν (1x)
Lk 3:31 *son* of·Melea, *son* of·Mainan, *son* of·Mattatha, *son*

G3105 μαίνομαι maínômai *v.* (5x)
See:G3130 G3132 G3131-2 xLangAlso:H7696
G3105.2 V-PNI-1S μαίνομαι (1x)
Ac 26:25 But he·replied, "I·am·not raving·mad, most·noble
G3105.2 V-PNI-2S μαίνῃ (2x)
Ac 12:15 they·declared to·her, "You·are·raving·mad!" But
Ac 26:24 voice, "Paul, you·are·raving·mad! The many
G3105.2 V-PNI-2P μαίνεσθε (1x)
1Co 14:23 shall·they·not declare that yeu·are·raving·mad?
G3105.2 V-PNI-3S μαίνεται (1x)
Jn 10:20 "He·has a·demon and is·raving·mad; why·do yeu·

G3106 μακαρίζω makarízō *v.* (2x)
Roots:G3107 See:G3108 xLangAlso:H0833
G3106.1 V-FAI-3P-ATT μακαριοῦσιν (1x)
Lk 1:48 generations shall·pronounce me supremely·blessed.
G3106.1 V-PAI-1P μακαρίζομεν (1x)
Jac 5:11 we·pronounce·them·supremely·blessed, the·ones

G3107 μακάριος makáriôs *adj.* (50x)
Compare:G2128 See:G3108 G3106
xLangAlso:H0835
G3107.1 A-NSM μακάριος (16x)
Lk 7:23 And supremely·blessed is·he who should·not be·
Lk 12:43 Supremely·blessed *is* that slave, whom his lord,
Lk 14:14 you·shall·be supremely·blessed because they·do·
Lk 14:15 declared to·him, "Supremely·blessed *is·he* that
Mt 11:6 And he·is supremely·blessed, whoever *he·is*, if he·
Mt 16:17 declared to·him, "Supremely·blessed are·you,
Mt 24:46 Supremely·blessed *is* that slave, whom his lord,
Rm 4:8 Supremely·blessed *is* a·man to·whom Yahweh, no,
Rm 14:22 in·the·sight of·God. Supremely·blessed *is* the·one
Jac 1:12 Supremely·blessed *is* a·man that patiently·endures
Jac 1:25 ·work, this·man shall·be supremely·blessed in his
1Ti 6:15 shall·show *he·is* the supremely·blessed and only
Rv 1:3 Supremely·blessed *are both* the·one reading·aloud
Rv 16:15 I·come as a·thief. Supremely·blessed *is* the·one
Rv 20:6 Supremely·blessed and holy *is* the·one having part
Rv 22:7 I·come swiftly! Supremely·blessed *is* the·one
G3107.1 A-NSF μακαρία (2x)
Lk 1:45 "And supremely·blessed *is* the·one trusting that
Lk 11:27 declared to·him, "Supremely·blessed *is* the womb
G3107.1 A-NSF-C μακαριωτέρα (1x)
1Co 7:40 But she·is supremely·blessed if in·this·manner she·
G3107.1 A-NSN μακάριον (1x)
Ac 20:35 'It·is more supremely·blessed to·give than to·
G3107.1 A-NPM μακάριοι (26x)
Jn 13:17 ·know these·things, supremely·blessed are·yeu if
Jn 20:29 you·have·trusted. Supremely·blessed *are* the·ones
Lk 6:20 he·was·saying, "Supremely·blessed *are* the
Lk 6:21 "Supremely·blessed *are* the·ones hungering now,
Lk 6:21 ·be·stuffed·full. "Supremely·blessed *are* the·ones
Lk 6:22 "Supremely·blessed are·yeu, whenever the men·of·
Lk 10:23 privately, "Supremely·blessed *are* the eyes
Lk 11:28 ·a·matter·of·fact, supremely·blessed *are* the·ones
Lk 12:37 "Supremely·blessed *are* those slaves, whom the
Lk 12:38 *them* in·this·manner, supremely·blessed are those
Mt 5:3 "Supremely·blessed *are* the helplessly·poor in·the
Mt 5:4 "Supremely·blessed *are* the·ones mourning, because
Mt 5:5 "Supremely·blessed *are* the calmly·mild·ones,
Mt 5:6 "Supremely·blessed *are* the·ones hungering and
Mt 5:7 "Supremely·blessed *are* the merciful, because they·
Mt 5:8 "Supremely·blessed *are* the pure in·the heart, because
Mt 5:9 "Supremely·blessed *are* the peacemakers, because
Mt 5:10 "Supremely·blessed *are* the·ones having·been·
Mt 5:11 "Supremely·blessed are·yeu whenever *men* should·
Mt 13:16 "But supremely·blessed *are* yeur eyes, because
Rm 4:7 *saying*, '" Supremely·blessed *are·they* whose
1Pe 3:14 ·of righteousness, *yeu·are* supremely·blessed. And
1Pe 4:14 *yeu·are* supremely·blessed, because the Spirit of·
Rv 14:13 "Write, 'Supremely·blessed *are* the dead·ones,
Rv 19:9 "Write, 'Supremely·blessed *are* the·ones having·
Rv 22:14 Supremely·blessed *are* the·ones doing his
G3107.1 A-NPF μακάριαι (1x)
Lk 23:29 they·shall·declare, 'Supremely·blessed *are* the
G3107.1 A-ASM μακάριον (1x)
Ac 26:2 ·considered myself supremely·blessed, King
G3107.1 A-ASF μακαρίαν (1x)
Tit 2:13 while·awaiting the supremely·blessed Expectation
G3107.1 A-GSM μακαρίου (1x)
1Ti 1:11 glorious good·news of·the supremely·blessed God,

G3108 μακαρισμός makarismós *n.* (3x)
Roots:G3106
G3108 N-NSM μακαρισμός (2x)
Gal 4:15 what was the supreme·blessedness yeu *spoke·of*?
Rm 4:9 So·then, *is* this supreme·blessedness upon the
G3108 N-ASM μακαρισμόν (1x)
Rm 4:6 ·to the supreme·blessedness of·the man·of·clay† to·

G3109 Μακεδονία Makêdônía *n/l.* (23x)
Roots:G3110
G3109 N/L-NSF Μακεδονία (1x)
Rm 15:26 For Macedonia and Achaia delighted to·make a·
G3109 N/L-ASF Μακεδονίαν (11x)
Ac 16:9 saying, "Crossing into Macedonia, swiftly·help us.
Ac 16:10 we·sought to·go·forth into Macedonia, concluding
Ac 19:21 *that* after·going·throughout Macedonia and Achaia,
Ac 19:22 ·ones attending to·him into Macedonia, TimoThy
Ac 20:1 *them*, went·forth to·traverse into Macedonia.
1Co 16:5 whenever I·should·go·throughout Macedonia, for
1Co 16:5 Macedonia, for I·am·to·go·throughout Macedonia.
2Co 1:16 to·go through yeu into Macedonia, and to·come
2Co 2:13 ·leave·of them, I·went·forth into Macedonia.
2Co 7:5 For even with·us coming into Macedonia, our flesh
1Ti 1:3 (*even* while·I·was·traversing into Macedonia), *do·so*
G3109 N/L-DSF Μακεδονίᾳ (3x)
1Th 1:7 to·all the·ones trusting in Macedonia and Achaia.
1Th 1:8 Not merely in Macedonia and Achaia, but·rather
1Th 4:10 the brothers, the·ones in all Macedonia. But we·
G3109 N/L-GSF Μακεδονίας (7x)
Ac 16:12 a·foremost city of·the province of·Macedonia, *and*
Ac 18:5 and TimoThy came·down from Macedonia, Paul
Ac 20:3 he·made a·plan to·return·back through Macedonia.
Php 4:15 when I·went·forth from Macedonia, not·even·one
2Co 1:16 and to·come again from Macedonia to yeu, and by
2Co 8:1 unto the Called·Out·citizenries of·Macedonia,
2Co 11:9 from Macedonia utterly·fulfilled·in·particular; and
EG3109 (1x)
Ac 19:1 the uppermost districts *of·Macedonia*, came to

G3110 Μακεδών Makêdṓn *n/g.* (5x)
Roots:G3372 See:G3109
G3110.2 N/G-NPM Μακεδόνες (1x)
2Co 9:4 ·perhaps if *any* Macedonians should·come together
G3110.2 N/G-DPM Μακεδόσιν (1x)
2Co 9:2 for·which I·boast over yeu to·the·Macedonians, that
G3110.2 N/G-GSM Μακεδόνος (1x)
Ac 27:2 with·AristArchus (a·Macedonian of·ThessaloNica)
G3110.3 N/G-NSM Μακεδών (1x)
Ac 16:9 there·was some man of·Macedonia standing and
G3110.3 N/G-APM Μακεδόνας (1x)
Ac 19:29 Gaius and AristArchus, men·of·Macedonia, Paul's

G3111 μάκελλον mákêllôn *n.* (1x)

G3111 N-DSN μακέλλῳ (1x)

1Co 10:25 Every thing being·sold in a·meat·market, eat *it*,

G3112 μακράν makrán *adv.* (10x)

Roots:G3117 Compare:G4207 See:G3598

G3112 ADV μακράν (10x)

Jn 21:8 (for they·were not at·a·distance from the dry·ground,
Lk 7:6 with·him not being·off at·a·distance from the home,
Lk 15:20 But with·him still being·off at·a·distance, his father
Ac 2:39 and for·all the·ones at·a·distance, as·many·as
Ac 17:27 inherently·being not at·a·distance from each one
Ac 22:21 you forth unto *the* Gentiles at·a·distance.'"
Mt 8:30 Now there·was at·a·distance from them a·herd of·
Mk 12:34 "You·are not at·a·distance from the kingdom of·
Eph 2:13 yeu·yourselves, once being at·a·distance, are·made
Eph 2:17 'peace to·yeu, the·ones at·a·distance, and to·the·

G3113 μακρό•θεν makrṓthên *adv.* (14x)

Roots:G3117

G3113 ADV μακρόθεν (14x)

Lk 16:23 he·clearly·sees AbRaham from a·distance, and
Lk 18:13 the tax·collector, standing at·a·distance, was·not
Lk 22:54 Now Peter was·following at·a·distance.
Lk 23:49 from Galilee, stood at·a·distance, clearly·seeing
Mt 26:58 Peter was·following him from a·distance up·to the
Mt 27:55 women were there observing from a·distance, who
Mk 5:6 But upon·seeing Jesus from a·distance, he·ran and
Mk 8:3 way, for some of·them have·come *from* a·distance."
Mk 11:13 ·seeing a·fig·tree in·the·distance having leaves,
Mk 14:54 Peter followed him from a·distance, as·far·as to
Mk 15:40 ·were also women observing from a·distance, even
Rv 18:10 standing from a·distance on·account·of the fear of·
Rv 18:15 her, shall·stand from a·distance on·account·of the
Rv 18:17 ·many·as work the sea, stood·still from a·distance,

G3114 μακρο•θυμέω makrôthyméō *v.* (10x)

Roots:G3115-1 See:G3115 G3116

G3114.1 V-PAI-3S μακροθυμεῖ (2x)

2Pe 3:9 tardiness, but·rather is·long-suffering toward us, not
1Co 13:4 The Love is·long-suffering *and* is·beneficially·kind

G3114.1 V-PAP-NSM μακροθυμῶν (1x)

Jac 5:7 of·the earth, suffering·with·long·patience over it,

G3114.3 V-PAM-2P μακροθυμεῖτε (1x)

1Th 5:14 support the weak, be·patient toward all *men*.

G3114.3 V-PAP-NSM μακροθυμῶν (1x)

Lk 18:7 night to him, yet while·being·patient toward them?

G3114.3 V-AAM-2S μακροθύμησον (2x)

Mt 18:26 saying, 'Lord, be·patient toward me, and I·shall·
Mt 18:29 ·imploring him, saying, 'Be·patient with me, and

G3114.3 V-AAM-2P μακροθυμήσατε (2x)

Jac 5:7 Accordingly, be·patient brothers, until the returning·
Jac 5:8 also must·be·patient. Yeu·must·firmly·establish yeur

G3114.3 V-AAP-NSM μακροθυμήσας (1x)

Heb 6:15 ·this·manner, after·patiently·waiting, he·obtained

G3115 μακρο•θυμία makrôthymía *n.* (14x)

Roots:G3115-1 Compare:G0463 G4343 G5281 G4710 See:G3116 G3114

G3115.1 N-NSF μακροθυμία (2x)

Gal 5:22 joy, peace, long-suffering, kindness, beneficial·
1Pe 3:20 ·time, the long-suffering of·God was·waiting·for

G3115.1 N-ASF μακροθυμίαν (4x)

2Pe 3:15 resolutely·consider the long-suffering of·our Lord
Col 1:11 ·endurance and long-suffering with joyfulness—
Col 3:12 humility·of·mind, gentleness, long-suffering,
1Ti 1:16 the entirety *of·his* long-suffering, specifically·for a·

G3115.1 N-DSF μακροθυμίᾳ (4x)

Rm 9:22 bore with much long-suffering *the* vessels of·
2Co 6:6 by knowledge, by long-suffering, by kindness, by
2Ti 3:10 ·purpose, *my* trust, *my* long-suffering, *my* love, *my*
2Ti 4:2 *and* exhort with all long-suffering and instruction!

G3115.1 N-GSF μακροθυμίας (4x)

Heb 6:12 through trust and long-suffering are·inheriting the
Rm 2:4 forbearance, and long-suffering, not·knowing that
Jac 5:10 ill·hardship and the long-suffering of·the prophets
Eph 4:2 and gentleness, with long-suffering, bearing·with

G3116 μακρο•θυμώς makrôthymṓs *adv.* (1x)

Roots:G3115-1 See:G3114 G3115

G3116.2 ADV μακροθύμως (1x)

Ac 26:3 Therefore, I·petition you to·hear me patiently.

G3117 μακρός makrṓs *adj.* (5x)

Roots:G3372 Compare:G0568 G4206 See:G3112

G3117.2 A-ASF μακράν (2x)

Lk 15:13 ·all, journeyed·abroad into a·distant country, and
Lk 19:12 traversed into a·distant country to·receive for·

G3117.3 A-APN μακρά (3x)

Lk 20:47 and pray lengthy *prayers* for·an·outward·showing
Mt 23:13 and for·a·pretense are·praying lengthy *prayers*.
Mk 12:40 and for·a·pretense praying lengthy *prayers*.

G3118 μακρο•χρόνιος makrôchrṓniôs *adj.* (1x)

Roots:G3117 G5550

G3118 A-NSM μακροχρόνιος (1x)

Eph 6:3 with·you, and you·shall·be a·long·time on the earth.

G3119 μαλακία malakía *n.* (3x)

Roots:G3120 Compare:G3554 G0769 See:G3119-1 xLangAlso:H4251

G3119.2 N-ASF μαλακίαν (3x)

Mt 4:23 every illness and every disease among the people.
Mt 9:35 every illness and every disease among the people.
Mt 10:1 ·relieve·and·cure every illness and every disease.

G3120 μαλακός malakṓs *adj.* (4x)

Compare:G0527 See:G3119

G3120.1 A-APN μαλακά (1x)

Mt 11:8 the·ones prominently·wearing the soft *garments* are

G3120.1 A-DPN μαλακοῖς (2x)

Lk 7:25 ·of·clay† having·been·enrobed in soft garments?
Mt 11:8 ·of·clay† having·been·enrobed in soft garments?

G3120.2 A-NPM μαλακοί (1x)

1Co 6:9 nor adulterers, nor effeminate·men, nor men·who·

G3121 Μαλελε•ήλ Malêlêél *n/p.* (1x)

מַהֲלַלְאֵל mahălal'el [Hebrew]

Roots:H4111 See:G2627

G3121.2 N/P-PRI Μαλελεήλ (1x)

Lk 3:37 *son* of·Jared, *son* of·MahalalEl, *son* of·Qeinan,

G3122 μάλιστα málista *adv.* (13x)

Roots:G3118-3 See:G3123

G3122.2 ADV μάλιστα (12x)

Ac 20:38 being·distressed especially over the words which
Ac 25:26 forth before yeu, and especially before you, O·
Ac 26:3 especially with·you being an·expert in·all customs
Gal 6:10 ·good toward all, but especially toward the family·
Php 4:22 ·ones greet yeu, especially the·ones from·among
2Pe 2:10 but especially the·ones *falling·in* right·behind flesh,
Tit 1:10 ·delude·the·mind, especially the·ones from·among
Phm 1:16 a·slave, a·brother beloved, especially to·me, but
1Ti 4:10 of·all men·of·clay†, especially of·those·that·trust.
1Ti 5:8 ·for his·own, and especially for·the family·members
1Ti 5:17 of·double honor, especially the·ones laboring·hard
2Ti 4:13 the official·scrolls, *but* especially the parchments.

EG3122.2 (1x)

2Co 1:11 *especially* with·yeu also assisting·together by·the

G3123 μᾶλλον mâllôn *adv.* (84x)

Roots:G3118-3 Compare:G0235 G2228 See:G3122

G3123.1 ADV μᾶλλον (47x)

Jn 5:18 the Judeans were·seeking *all* the·more to·kill him,
Jn 19:8 Pilate heard this saying, he·was all·the·more afraid,
Lk 5:15 word went·throughout even·more concerning him,
Lk 11:13 gifts to·yeur children, how·much more the Father,
Lk 12:24 "By·how·much more *do* yeu·yourselves surpass·
Lk 12:28 into an·oven, how·much more *shall·he·enrobe* yeu,
Lk 18:39 he·himself was·yelling·out so·much *the* more—
Ac 5:14 Lord, even·more were·being·placed·alongside *the*
Ac 9:22 But Saul was·enabled *all* the·more, and was·
Ac 20:35 declared, 'It·is more supremely·blessed to·give
Ac 22:2 Hebrew language, they·personally·held more still).
Heb 9:14 how·much more shall the blood of·the
Heb 10:25 *one·another*, and so·much the·more, as·much·as
Heb 12:25 so·much more·so we·ourselves *shall·not·escape*,
Gal 4:27 the desolate·woman has·many more children than
Mt 6:26 ·not yeu·yourselves *of* more surpassing·value *than*
Mt 6:30 an·oven, ¿! *shall·he* not much more *enrobe* yeu, O·
Mt 7:11 to·yeur children, how·much more shall yeur Father,
Mt 10:25 how·much more *shall·they·call* his·own family·
Mt 18:13 ·say to·yeu, he·rejoices more over that·same *sheep*
Mk 10:48 but he·was·yelling·out so·much the more— "O·
Mk 14:31 But he·was·saying out *all the* more vehemently,
Rm 5:9 his blood, so·much more·so we·shall·be·saved from
Rm 5:10 ·his Son, so·much more·so, after·being·reconciled,
Rm 5:15 the many died, so·much more did·abound the grace
Rm 5:17 *then* so·much *the* more *that* the·ones receiving the
Rm 11:12 how·much more their complete·fullness?
Rm 11:24 ·olive·tree, how·much more shall·these,
Rm 14:13 ·rather yeu·must·judge this all·the·more: *purpose*
Php 1:9 that yeur love may·abound yet more and more in
Php 1:9 more and more in recognition·and·full·knowledge
Php 1:23 *which·is even* so·much more significantly·better.
Php 2:12 but·rather now so·much more in my absence),
Php 3:4 to·have·confidence in flesh, I·myself *have* more:
2Pe 1:10 brothers, all·the·more quickly·endeavor to·make
1Th 4:1 ·God in·order·that yeu·may·abound more·and·more.
1Th 4:10 ·implore yeu, brothers, to·abound more·and·more,
1Co 9:12 *should* not we·ourselves *participate* more? But·yet
1Co 12:22 But·rather, so·much more *those* members of·the
1Co 14:18 to·my God, speaking more·than all of·yeu with·
2Co 3:8 indeed, how·much more shall the Service of·the
2Co 3:11 on·account·of glory, so·much more *surpassing is*
2Co 5:8 *preferring* all·the·more to·be·absent·abroad from·
2Co 7:7 on·behalf·of me, such·for me to·rejoice more.
2Co 7:13 and more·exceedingly *all* the·more, we·rejoiced
Phm 1:16 to·me, but how·much more to·you, both in *the*
1Ti 6:2 they·are brothers; but·rather more, be·slaves *to·them*

G3123.2 ADV μᾶλλον (28x)

Jn 3:19 men·of·clay† loved the darkness rather than the light,
Lk 10:20 are·subject to·yeu, but rather rejoice because yeur
Ac 4:19 ·the·sight of·God to·listen·to yeu rather than to·God,
Ac 5:29 ·comply with·God rather than with·men·of·clay†.
Ac 27:11 and by·the shipowner, rather than by·the·things
Heb 11:25 choosing rather to·be·maltreated·together with·
Gal 4:9 after·knowing God, or rather being·known by God,
Mt 10:6 but traverse rather to the sheep, the·ones having·
Mt 10:28 the soul. But rather be·afraid·of the·one being·able
Mt 25:9 and yeu. But traverse rather toward the·ones selling
Mt 27:24 nothing·at·all, but·yet rather *that* a·commotion is·
Mk 5:26 but·yet *with·her* coming rather to the more·harm.
Mk 15:11 crowd that rather he·should·fully·release BarAbbas
Rm 8:34 the·one dying, but rather also, being·awakened,
Php 1:12 me have·come rather for a·continual·advancement
1Co 5:2 ·been·puffed·up, and did·not·indeed rather mourn,
1Co 6:7 judgment among them. Rather, why not·indeed *let*
1Co 6:7 not·indeed *let* yeurselves·be·wronged? Rather, why
1Co 7:21 if·also you·are·able to·become free, use *it* rather.
1Co 9:15 for *it·is* good for·me to·die rather than that anyone
2Co 2:7 yeu *ought* rather to·graciously·forgive *him*, and to·
2Co 12:9 Accordingly rather, with·great·pleasure, I·shall·
Eph 4:28 ·steal no·longer. But rather let·him·labor·hard,
Eph 5:4 but·yet rather *share* an·expression·of·thankfulness.
Eph 5:11 works of·the darkness, but rather yet refute *them*.
Phm 1:9 rather on·account·of the love, I·implore *you*, *I* Paul,
1Ti 1:4 contrarily·present speculations rather than God's
2Ti 3:4 fond·of·sensual·pleasures rather than *being* fond·of·

EG3123.2 (1x)

1Ti 4:7 myths, and train yourself *rather* to devout·reverence.

G3123.3 ADV μᾶλλον (2x)

Mk 7:36 even·much more·abundantly they·were·officially·
Mk 9:42 trusting in me, it·is even·much better for·him if a·

G3123.4 ADV μᾶλλον (6x)

Jn 12:43 men·of·clay† more·especially indeed·than·even the
Heb 12:9 not much more·especially be·in·subjection to·the
Heb 12:13 but more·especially *so·that* it·may·be·healed.

1Co 14:1 but more·especially that yeu·may·prophesy.
1Co 14:5 *I·want* more·especially that yeu·should·prophesy,
2Co 3:9 *had* glory, so·much more·especially *does* the

G3124 Μάλχος Málchôs *n/p.* (1x)
מֶלֶךְ mëlëḵ [Hebrew]
Roots:H4429
G3124.2 N/P-NSM Μάλχος (1x)
Jn 18:10 And the slave's name was Malchus.

G3125 μάμμη mámmē *n.* (1x)
G3125 N-DSF μάμμῃ (1x)
2Ti 1:5 indwelt first in your grandmother Lois and your

G3126 μαμμωνᾶς mammōnâs *aram.* (5x)
Compare:G4149
G3126.2 ARAM μαμωνᾶ (2x)
Lk 16:9 from·out of·the material·wealth of·the unrighteous·
Lk 16:11 with the unrighteous material·wealth, who shall·
EG3126.2 (1x)
Lk 16:12 with another·man's *material·wealth*, who shall·give
G3126.3 ARAM μαμωνᾶ (2x)
Lk 16:13 able to·be·a·slave to·God and to·Material·Wealth."
Mt 6:24 able to·be·a·slave to·God and to·Material·Wealth.

G3127 Μαναήν Manaḗn *n/p.* (1x)
G3127 N/P-PRI Μαναήν (1x)
Ac 13:1 , and Lucius of·Cyrene, Manaen also (*who·was*

G3128 Μανασσῆς Manassễs *n/p.* (3x)
מְנַשֶּׁה mᵉnaš̱ẖeh [Hebrew]
Roots:H4519
G3128.3 N/P-GSM Μανασσῆ (1x)
Rv 7:6 *the* tribe of·MaNasseh having·been·officially·sealed,
G3128.5 N/P-NSM Μανασσῆς (1x)
Mt 1:10 begot MaNasseh, and MaNasseh begot Amon, and
G3128.5 N/P-ASM Μανασσῆ (1x)
Mt 1:10 Now Hezekiah begot MaNasseh, and MaNasseh

G3129 μανθάνω manthánō *v.* (25x)
μαθέω mathéō
[alternate form, used in certain tenses]
Compare:G1321 See:G3100 G4827
xLangAlso:H3925
G3129 V-PAI-3P μανθάνουσιν (1x)
1Ti 5:13 And also at·the·same·time, they·learn *to·be* idle,
G3129 V-PAM-3S μανθανέτω (1x)
1Ti 2:11 A·woman must·learn in stillness with all subjection.
G3129 V-PAM-3P μανθανέτωσαν (2x)
Tit 3:14 And our *brothers* must·learn also to·conduct good
1Ti 5:4 or grandchildren, they·must·learn first at·their·own
G3129 V-PAP-APN μανθάνοντα (1x)
2Ti 3:7 always learning, and·yet never·even being·able to·
G3129 V-PAS-3P μανθάνωσιν (1x)
1Co 14:31 to·prophesy, in·order·that all may·learn, and all
G3129 V-2AAI-1S ἔμαθον (1x)
Php 4:11 *a·particular* lacking; for I·myself learned, *that* in
G3129 V-2AAI-2S ἔμαθες (2x)
2Ti 3:14 in the·things·which you·already·learned and are·
2Ti 3:14 ·personally·known from whom you·learned *them*,
G3129 V-2AAI-2P ἐμάθετε (4x)
Rm 16:17 the instruction which yeu learned, and veer·away
Php 4:9 These·things, which also yeu·learned, and
Eph 4:20 *that* yeu·yeurselves learned Anointed-One,
Col 1:7 just·as also yeu·learned *it* from EpAphras, our dear
G3129 V-2AAI-3S ἔμαθεν (1x)
Heb 5:8 being a·Son, he·learned the attentive·obedience
G3129 V-2AAM-2P μάθετε (4x)
Mt 9:13 But upon·departing, learn what it·means, "I·want
Mt 11:29 my yoke upon yeu, and learn from me, because I·
Mt 24:32 Now from the fig·tree, yeu·must·learn the parable:
Mk 13:28 from the fig·tree, yeu·must·learn the parable:
G3129 V-2AAN μαθεῖν (3x)
Gal 3:2 This merely I·want to·learn from yeu, did·yeu·
1Co 14:35 And if they·want to·learn anything, they·must·
Rv 14:3 and not·even·one·man was·able to·learn the song
G3129 V-2AAP-NSM μαθών (2x)
Jn 6:45 every·man hearing and learning personally·from the
Ac 23:27 I·snatched him out, upon·learning that he·was a·
G3129 V-2AAS-2P μάθητε (1x)
1Co 4:6 ·account·of yeu, in·order·that yeu·may·learn in us
G3129 V-RAP-NSM μεμαθηκώς (1x)
Jn 7:15 ·know *the Sacred·*Writings, not having·learned?"

G3130 μανία manía *n.* (1x)
Roots:G3105 See:G3132
G3130 N-ASF μανίαν (1x)
Ac 26:24 studies do·twist you about into raving·madness."

G3131 μάννα mánna *heb.* (5x)
מָן maṉ [Hebrew]
Roots:H4478
G3131.2 HEB μάννα (5x)
Jn 6:31 Our fathers ate the manna in the wilderness, just·as
Jn 6:49 Yeur fathers ate the manna in the wilderness, and
Jn 6:58 *when* yeur fathers ate the manna and died. The·one
Heb 9:4 *was* a·golden urn having the manna, and Aaron's
Rv 2:17 ·him to·eat from the hidden manna, and I·shall·give

G3132 μαντεύομαι mantéúômai *v.* (1x)
Roots:G3105 Compare:G4395 G5537 G4436 G2813-1 See:G3130 G3131-1 G3131-2 xLangAlso:H7080
G3132.2 V-PNP-NSF μαντευομένη (1x)
Ac 16:16 lords with·much income by·maniacal·soothsaying.

G3133 μαραίνω maraínō *v.* (1x)
Compare:G4570 G3583 See:G0263
G3133.2 V-FPI-3S μαρανθήσεται (1x)
Jac 1:11 the wealthy·man shall·be·shriveled·up along his

G3134 μαρὰν ἀθά maràn athá *aram.* (2x)
μαρὰνα θά maràna thá [as a response]
G3134.2 ARAM μαράν (1x)
1Co 16:22 Anathema MaranAtha *(devoted·to·destruction at·*
EG3134.2 (1x)
1Co 16:22 *(devoted·to·destruction at·the·Lord's·coming)*.

G3135 μαργαρίτης margarítēs *n.* (9x)
xLangEquiv:H4772-1 xLangAlso:H6443
G3135 N-NPM μαργαρῖται (1x)
Rv 21:21 the twelve gates *were* twelve pearls; again, each
G3135 N-ASM μαργαρίτην (1x)
Mt 13:46 one extremely·valuable pearl, after·going·off, has·
G3135 N-APM μαργαρίτας (2x)
Mt 7:6 nor·even should·yeu·cast yeur pearls before the pigs
Mt 13:45 ·of·clay†, a·merchant seeking high·quality pearls,
G3135 N-DPM μαργαρίταις (3x)
1Ti 2:9 or gold, or pearls, or extremely·expensive attire,
Rv 17:4 ·gold and precious stones and pearls, *and* having a·
Rv 18:16 ·gilded with gold, and precious stones, and pearls!
G3135 N-GSM μαργαρίτου (2x)
Rv 18:12 precious stones, and pearls, "and of·fine·linen,
Rv 21:21 of·the gates was *made* out of·one pearl. And the

G3136 Μάρθα Mártha *n/p.* (13x)
G3136.2 N/P-NSF Μάρθα (8x)
Jn 11:20 Accordingly, Martha, as·soon·as she·heard that
Jn 11:21 Then Martha declared to Jesus, "Lord, if you·were
Jn 11:24 Martha says to·him, "I·personally·know that he·
Jn 11:30 was in the place where Martha went·and·met him.
Jn 11:39 ·away the stone." Martha, the sister of·the·one
Jn 12:2 for·him there, and Martha was·attending *to·them*,
Lk 10:38 by·the·name·of Martha hospitably·received him
Lk 10:40 But Martha was·distracted concerning much
G3136.2 N/P-VSF Μάρθα (2x)
Lk 10:41 Jesus declared to·her, "Martha, Martha, you·are·
Lk 10:41 to·her, "Martha, Martha, you·are·anxious and are·
G3136.2 N/P-ASF Μάρθαν (2x)
Jn 11:5 And Jesus loved Martha, also her sister, and Lazarus.
Jn 11:19 the *women* in·company·with Martha and Mary, in·
G3136.2 N/P-GSF Μάρθας (1x)
Jn 11:1 ·among the village of·Mary and her sister Martha.

G3137 Μαριάμ Mariám *n/p.* (56x)
Μαρία María [informal]
מִרְיָם mıryam̱ [Hebrew formal]
Roots:H4813
EG3137.2 (2x)
Jn 19:25 near the cross of·Jesus: *Mariam* his mother, his
Lk 3:23 *as·well·as being a·grandson of·Mariam's father*, Eli,
G3137.4 N/P-NSF Μαρία (5x)
Lk 24:10 and Joanna, and Mariam *the mother* of·*little*·Jacob,
Mt 27:56 Mariam Magdalene, and Mariam the mother of·
Mt 28:1 Magdalene and the other Mariam came to·observe
Mk 15:40 was Mariam Magdalene, and Mariam (the mother
Mk 16:1 Mariam Magdalene and Mariam (the *mother* of·
G3137.4 N/P-DSF Μαρίᾳ (1x)
Ac 1:14 together with·women and Mariam the mother of·
G3137.4 N/P-GSF Μαρίας (5x)
Lk 1:41 ·as Elisabeth heard the greeting of·Mariam, *that* the
Mt 1:16 begot Joseph the husband of·Mariam, from·out of·
Mt 1:18 mother Mariam already·being·espoused to·Joseph,
Mt 2:11 they·found the little·child with Mariam his mother.
Mk 6:3 the carpenter, the son of·Mariam, and a·brother of·
G3137.4 N/P-PRI Μαριάμ (13x)
Lk 1:27 And the virgin's name *was* Mariam.
Lk 1:30 "Do·not be·afraid, Mariam, for you·found grace
Lk 1:34 Then Mariam declared to the angel, "How shall this
Lk 1:38 And Mariam declared, "Behold, the female·slave
Lk 1:39 And Mariam, rising·up in these days, traversed into
Lk 1:46 And Mariam declared, "My soul does·magnify
Lk 1:56 And Mariam abided together with·her about three
Lk 2:5 ·be·enrolled·in·the·census together with·Mariam, his
Lk 2:16 ·haste and diligently·found both Mariam and Joseph,
Lk 2:19 But Mariam was·closely·guarding all these
Lk 2:34 them, and he·declared to Mariam his mother,
Mt 1:20 ·not be·afraid to·personally·take Mariam *for* your
Mt 13:55 referred·to·as Mariam·*(meaning·bitterly·rebellious)*
G3137.5 N/P-NSF Μαρία (12x)
Jn 19:25 the *wife* of·Clopas), and Mariam Magdalene.
Jn 20:1 ·being still dark), Mariam Magdalene comes to the
Jn 20:11 But Mariam stood outside toward the chamber·
Jn 20:18 Mariam Magdalene came announcing to·the
Lk 8:2 spirits and sicknesses: Mariam (the·one being·called
Lk 24:10 It·was Mariam Magdalene, and Joanna, and
Mt 27:56 Among whom was Mariam Magdalene, and
Mt 27:61 And there was Mariam Magdalene, and the other
Mt 28:1 first *dawn* of·the·week, Mariam Magdalene and the
Mk 15:40 even among whom was Mariam Magdalene, and
Mk 15:47 And Mariam Magdalene and Miryam (*mother* of·
Mk 16:1 Sabbath already·elapsing, Mariam Magdalene and
G3137.5 N/P-VSF Μαρία (1x)
Jn 20:16 Jesus says to·her, "Mariam." That·woman, being·
G3137.5 N/P-DSF Μαρίᾳ (1x)
Mk 16:9 *Jesus* did·appear first to·Mariam Magdalene, from
G3137.6 N/P-NSF Μαρία (3x)
Jn 19:25 his mother's sister (Miryam the *wife* of·Clopas),
Mt 27:61 and the other Miryam, sitting·down fully·before
Mk 15:47 And Mariam Magdalene and Miryam (*mother* of·
G3137.7 N/P-GSF Μαρίας (1x)
Ac 12:12 he·came to the home of·Miri, the mother of·John
G3137.8 N/P-NSF Μαρία (6x)
Jn 11:2 (It·was *that* Mary, the·one rubbing·oil·on the Lord
Jn 11:20 went·and·met him, but Mary was·sitting·down in
Jn 11:32 So as·soon·as Mary came where Jesus was, upon·
Jn 12:3 of·authentic spikenard, Mary rubbed·oil·on the feet
Lk 10:39 And this·woman had a·sister called Mary, who,
Lk 10:42 is needed, and Mary selected the beneficially·good
G3137.8 N/P-ASF Μαρίαν (4x)
Jn 11:19 in·company·with Martha and Mary, in·order·that
Jn 11:28 she·went·off and hollered·out for Mary her sister,
Jn 11:31 her, seeing that Mary rose·up quickly and went·out
Jn 11:45 coming alongside Mary and distinctly·viewing the·
G3137.8 N/P-GSF Μαρίας (1x)
Jn 11:1 from·among the village of·Mary and her sister

G3137.9 N/P-PRI Μαριάμ (1x)
Rm 16:6 Greet Maria, who, in·many·ways, labored·hard

G3138 Μάρκος Márkôs *n/p.* (8x)
See:G2491 G0921

G3138.2 N/P-NSM Μάρκος (3x)
1Pe 5:13 ·*yeu*, greets yeu, and *so·does* *John*·Mark, my son.
Col 4:10 ·war, greets yeu, also *John*·Mark (the cousin of·
Phm 1:24 *John*·Mark, AristArchus, Demas, Luke, *these* my

G3138.2 N/P-ASM Μάρκον (4x)
Ac 12:25 ·along John, the·one being·surnamed Mark).
Ac 15:37 ·take·along John, the·one being·called Mark.
Ac 15:39 personally·taking *John*·Mark, to·sail·away to
2Ti 4:11 is with me. Taking·up *John*·Mark, bring·him with

G3138.2 N/P-GSM Μάρκου (1x)
Ac 12:12 mother of·John (being·surnamed Mark), where a·

G3139 μάρμαρος mármarôs *n.* (1x)
Compare:G3037

G3139 N-GSM μαρμάρου (1x)
Rv 18:12 "and of·bronze, iron, and marble,

G3140 μαρτυρέω martyrḗō *v.* (79x)
Roots:G3144 Compare:G3143 See:G3141 G3142

G3140.1 V-PMP-NPM μαρτυρούμενοι (1x)
1Th 2:11 personally·encouraging yeu and being·a·witness,

G3140.1 V-PPP-NSM μαρτυρούμενος (2x)
Ac 26:22 even·unto this day, being·a·witness to·both small
Heb 7:8 ·*stature who·is still* being·a·witness because he·lives

G3140.2 V-FAI-3S μαρτυρήσει (1x)
Jn 15:26 the Father, that·one shall·testify concerning me.

G3140.2 V-PAI-1S μαρτυρῶ (5x)
Jn 7:7 it·hates me, because I·myself testify concerning it,
Gal 4:15 ·blessedness yeu *spoke·of*? For I·testify to·yeu that,
Rm 10:2 For I·testify for·them that they·have a·zeal of·God,
2Co 8:3 according·to *their* power, I·testify, even above·and·
Col 4:13 For I·testify for·him, that he·has much zeal over

G3140.2 V-PAI-1P μαρτυροῦμεν (4x)
Jn 3:11 ·know and testify what we·have·clearly·seen, and
1Jn 1:2 we·have·clearly·seen *it*, and testify, and announce
1Jn 4:14 have·distinctly·viewed and testify that the Father
3Jn 1:12 And also, we·ourselves testify, and *all·of* yeu·

G3140.2 V-PAI-2S μαρτυρεῖς (1x)
Jn 8:13 declared to·him, "You testify concerning yourself;

G3140.2 V-PAI-2P μαρτυρεῖτε (4x)
Jn 3:28 Yeu·yeurselves testify to·me that I·declared, 'I·
Jn 15:27 "And yeu also do·testify, because yeu·are with me
Lk 11:48 "Then·by·inference, yeu·testify and gladly·consent
Mt 23:31 "As·such, yeu·testify against·yeurselves that yeu·

G3140.2 V-PAI-3S μαρτυρεῖ (9x)
Jn 1:15 John testifies concerning him and has·yelled·out,
Jn 3:32 and heard, that·thing he·testifies; and·yet not·even·
Jn 5:32 that the testimony which he·testifies concerning me
Jn 5:36 works which I·myself do; it·testifies concerning me,
Jn 8:18 (the·one sending me), he·testifies concerning me."
Jn 10:25 Father's name, these·things testify concerning me.
Ac 22:5 ·high·priest *HananIah* is also a·witness for·me, and
Heb 7:17 For he·testifies, "You *are* a·priest·that·offers·a·
Heb 10:15 *of·this*, the Holy Spirit also testifies to·us, with it

G3140.2 V-PAI-3P μαρτυροῦσιν (1x)
Ac 10:43 ·this·one, all the prophets do·testify— *that* anyone

G3140.2 V-PAN μαρτυρεῖν (1x)
Ac 26:5 from·the·start (if they·should·determine to·testify),

G3140.2 V-PAP-DSM μαρτυροῦντι (1x)
Ac 14:3 the Lord (the·one testifying to·the Redemptive-word

G3140.2 V-PAP-GSF μαρτυρούσης (1x)
Jn 4:39 the saying of·the woman, testifying, "He·declared

G3140.2 V-PAP-GSM μαρτυροῦντος (1x)
Heb 11:4 ·be righteous, with·God testifying concerning his

G3140.2 V-PAP-GPM μαρτυρούντων (1x)
3Jn 1:3 with·*the*·brothers coming and testifying of·your truth

G3140.2 V-PAP-NSN μαρτυροῦν (1x)
1Jn 5:6 And the Spirit is the·one testifying, because the Spirit

G3140.2 V-PAP-NSM μαρτυρῶν (4x)
Jn 5:32 There·is another, the·one testifying concerning me,
Jn 8:18 I·myself am one testifying concerning my·own·self,
Jn 21:24 disciple, the·one testifying concerning these·things
Rv 22:20 The·one testifying these·things says, "Yes, I·come

G3140.2 V-PAP-NPF μαρτυροῦσαι (1x)
Jn 5:39 Yet those are the·ones testifying concerning me.

G3140.2 V-PAP-NPM μαρτυροῦντες (2x)
1Jn 5:7 there·are three, the·ones testifying in the heaven: the
1Jn 5:8 And there·are three, the·ones testifying on the earth:

G3140.2 V-PAS-1S μαρτυρῶ (2x)
Jn 5:31 "If I·myself should·testify concerning my·own·self,
Jn 8:14 I·myself may·testify concerning my·own·self, my

G3140.2 V-IAI-3S ἐμαρτύρει (1x)
Jn 12:17 the crowd *from BethAny* was·testifying, the·one

G3140.2 V-IAI-3P ἐμαρτύρουν (1x)
Lk 4:22 And they all were·testifying for·him, and they·were·

G3140.2 V-AAI-1P ἐμαρτυρήσαμεν (1x)
1Co 15:15 of·God, because we·testified against God that he·

G3140.2 V-AAI-3S ἐμαρτύρησεν (5x)
Jn 1:32 And John testified, saying, "I·have·distinctly·viewed
Jn 4:44 for Jesus himself already·testified that, "A·prophet
Jn 13:21 in·the spirit, and he·testified and declared,
Ac 15:8 the knower·of·the·heart, testified to·them, giving
Rv 1:2 who testified·to the Redemptive-word of·God, and *to*

G3140.2 V-AAI-3P ἐμαρτύρησαν (1x)
3Jn 1:6 who already·testified of·your love in·the·sight of·a·

G3140.2 V-AAM-2S μαρτύρησον (1x)
Jn 18:23 "If I·spoke wrongly, testify concerning the wrong.

G3140.2 V-AAN μαρτυρῆσαι (2x)
Ac 23:11 ·manner it·is·mandatory·for you to·testify also to
Rv 22:16 Jesus, sent my angel to·testify to·yeu these·things

G3140.2 V-AAP-GSM μαρτυρήσαντος (1x)
1Ti 6:13 Jesus (the·one testifying before Pontius Pilate the

G3140.2 V-AAP-NSM μαρτυρήσας (1x)
Ac 13:22 as king, for·whom also testifying, he·declared,

G3140.2 V-AAS-1S μαρτυρήσω (1x)
Jn 18:37 the world, in·order·that I·may·testify to·the truth.

G3140.2 V-AAS-3S μαρτυρήσῃ (3x)
Jn 1:7 in·order·that he·may·testify concerning the Light, in·
Jn 1:8 in·order·that he·may·testify concerning the Light.
Jn 2:25 no need that anyone should·testify concerning the

G3140.2 V-RAI-1S μεμαρτύρηκα (1x)
Jn 1:34 And·I have·clearly·seen, and have·testified, that this

G3140.2 V-RAI-2S μεμαρτύρηκας (1x)
Jn 3:26 Jordan, to·whom you·yourself have·testified, see,

G3140.2 V-RAI-3S μεμαρτύρηκεν (5x)
Jn 5:33 ·for John, and he·has·testified to·the truth.
Jn 5:37 the·one sending me, has·testified concerning me.
Jn 19:35 the·one having·clearly·seen *it* has·testified, and his
1Jn 5:9 of·God which he·has·testified concerning his Son.
1Jn 5:10 the testimony that God has·testified concerning his

G3140.2 V-RPI-3S μεμαρτύρηται (1x)
Heb 11:5 it·has·been·testified *of·him* to·have·fully·satisfied

G3140.3 V-PPP-APM μαρτυρουμένους (1x)
Ac 6:3 ·among yeurselves seven men being·attested·to, full

G3140.3 V-PPP-NSF μαρτυρουμένη (2x)
Rm 3:21 has·been·made·apparent, being·attested·to by the
1Ti 5:10 being·attested·to by good works (if she·nurtured·

G3140.3 V-PPP-NSM μαρτυρούμενος (2x)
Ac 10:22 ·fearing God and being·attested·to by the whole
Ac 22:12 ·to the Torah-Law, being·attested·to by all the

G3140.3 V-IPI-3S ἐμαρτυρεῖτο (1x)
Ac 16:2 This *disciple* was·attested·to by the brothers in

G3140.3 V-API-3S ἐμαρτυρήθη (1x)
Heb 11:4 through which he·was·attested to·be righteous,

G3140.3 V-API-3P ἐμαρτυρήθησαν (1x)
Heb 11:2 For in this, the elders·of·old are·attested·to.

G3140.3 V-APP-NPM μαρτυρηθέντες (1x)
Heb 11:39 all these, already·being·attested·to through the

G3140.3 V-RPI-3S μεμαρτύρηται (1x)
3Jn 1:12 Demetrius has·been·attested·to by all·men, and by

G3141 μαρτυρία martyría *n.* (37x)
Roots:G3144 See:G3142

G3141 N-NSF μαρτυρία (15x)
Jn 1:19 Now this is the testimony of·John, when the Judeans
Jn 5:31 concerning my·own·self, my testimony is not
Jn 5:32 ·know that the testimony which he·testifies
Jn 8:13 concerning yourself; your testimony is not legally·
Jn 8:14 concerning my·own·self, my testimony is true,
Jn 8:17 Torah-Law that the testimony of·two men·of·clay† is
Jn 19:35 *it* has·testified, and his testimony is true; this·one·
Jn 21:24 and we·personally·know that his testimony is true.
Mk 14:59 ·manner was their testimony equal·in·substance.
Tit 1:13 This testimony is true. On·account·of which cause,
1Jn 5:9 testimony of·men·of·clay†, the testimony of·God is
1Jn 5:9 because this is the testimony of·God which he·has·
1Jn 5:11 And this is the testimony, that God gave to·us
3Jn 1:12 ·*of* yeu·personally·know that our testimony is true.
Rv 19:10 ·prostrate to·God, for the testimony of·Jesus is the

G3141 N-NPF μαρτυρίαι (1x)
Mk 14:56 him, and·yet the testimonies were not equal·in·

G3141 N-ASF μαρτυρίαν (19x)
Jn 1:7 The·same came for a·testimony, in·order·that he·may·
Jn 3:11 ·clearly·seen, and yeu·do·not receive our testimony.
Jn 3:32 and·yet not·even·one·man receives his testimony.
Jn 3:33 receiving his testimony did·stamp·his·own·seal that
Jn 5:34 But I·myself receive the testimony not from a·man·
Jn 5:36 I·myself have the greater testimony *than·that* of·John
Ac 22:18 ·heed·and·accept your testimony concerning me.'
Mk 14:55 ·Sanhedrin were·seeking testimony against Jesus
1Ti 3:7 ·for him also to·have a·good testimony from the·ones
1Jn 5:9 Though we·receive the testimony of·men·of·clay†,
1Jn 5:10 in the Son of·God has the testimony in himself; the·
1Jn 5:10 he·has·not trusted in the testimony that God has·
Rv 1:2 of·God, and *to* the testimony of·Jesus Anointed, and
Rv 1:9 and on·account·of the testimony of·Jesus Anointed.
Rv 6:9 on·account·of the testimony which they·were·holding
Rv 11:7 whenever they·should·finish their testimony, the
Rv 12:17 ·God and having the testimony of·Jesus Anointed.
Rv 19:10 and of·your brothers having the testimony of·Jesus.
Rv 20:4 ·beheaded on·account·of the testimony of·Jesus and

G3141 N-GSF μαρτυρίας (2x)
Lk 22:71 need do·we·have of·any·further testimony? For
Rv 12:11 through the word of·their testimony; and they·did·

G3142 μαρτύριον martýriôn *n.* (20x)
Roots:G3144 See:G3141
xLangEquiv:H5715 xLangAlso:H1697

G3142.1 N-NSN μαρτύριον (3x)
2Th 1:10 — because our testimony among yeu was·trusted.
1Co 1:6 just·as the testimony of·the Anointed-One was·
2Co 1:12 is our boasting, the testimony of·our conscience—

G3142.1 N-ASN μαρτύριον (15x)
Lk 5:14 specifically·assigned, for a·testimony to·them."
Lk 9:5 the dust from yeur feet for a·testimony against them."
Lk 21:13 And it·shall·result to·yeu for a·testimony.
Ac 4:33 were·giving·forth the testimonies of·the resurrection
Heb 3:5 (for a·testimony of·the·things which·were·to·be·
Mt 8:4 specifically·assigned, for a·testimony to·them."
Mt 10:18 because·of me, for a·testimony to·them and to·the
Mt 24:14 in all The Land for a·testimony to·all the nations,
Mk 1:44 specifically·assigned, for a·testimony to·them."
Mk 6:11 ·dirt beneath yeur feet for a·testimony against·them.
Mk 13:9 and kings for·my cause, for a·testimony to·them.
Jac 5:3 and its rust shall·be testimony against yeu and shall·
1Co 2:1 ·fully·proclaiming to·yeu the testimony of·God.
1Ti 2:6 on·behalf of·all— the testimony in·due seasons,
2Ti 1:8 ·should·not be·ashamed·of the testimony of·our Lord

G3142.1 N-GSN μαρτυρίου (2x)
Ac 7:44 "The Tabernacle of·Testimony was with our fathers
Rv 15:5 Temple of·the Tabernacle of·the Testimony in the

G3143 μαρτύρομαι martýrômai *v.* (3x)
Roots:G3144 Compare:G3140

G3143.2 V-PNI-1S μαρτύρομαι (3x)
Ac 20:26 Therefore I·attest to·yeu in the present day, that I·
Gal 5:3 And I·attest again to·every man·of·clay† being·
Eph 4:17 Accordingly, I·say this and attest *to·it* in *the* Lord:

G3144 μάρτυς mártys *n.* (34x)
See:G3141 G3142 G3143 xLangAlso:H5707
G3144.1 N-NSM μάρτυς (7x)
Ac 22:15 Because you·shall·be his witness to all men·of·
Rm 1:9 For God is my witness, to·whom I·ritually·minister
Php 1:8 For God is my witness, how I·greatly·yearn·after
1Pe 5:1 the fellow-elder, and a·witness of·the afflictions of·
1Th 2:5 nor with a·pretext for·covetousness (God *is* witness),
Rv 1:5 Anointed, *who·is* the trustworthy witness, *and* the
Rv 3:14 the trustworthy and true witness, the beginning of·
G3144.1 N-NPM μάρτυρες (9x)
Lk 24:48 "And yeu·yeurselves are witnesses of·these·things.
Ac 1:8 ·upon yeu, and yeu·shall·be witnesses to·me both in
Ac 2:32 this Jesus, of·which we·ourselves all are witnesses.
Ac 3:15 dead·men, to·which we·ourselves are witnesses.
Ac 5:32 we·ourselves are his witnesses of·these utterances;
Ac 7:58 ·at *him*, and the witnesses laid·aside their garments
Ac 10:39 we·ourselves are witnesses of·all·the·things which
Ac 13:31 to JeruSalem, who are his witnesses to the People.
1Th 2:10 Yeu *are* witnesses, and God *also*, how in·a·
G3144.1 N-ASM μάρτυρα (3x)
Ac 1:22 ·men *for* one to·become a·witness together with·us
Ac 26:16 you *to·be* an·assistant and a·witness, both of·the·
2Co 1:23 I·myself do·call·upon God *for* a·witness upon my
G3144.1 N-APM μάρτυρας (1x)
Ac 6:13 and they·set·up false witnesses saying, "This man·
G3144.1 N-DPM μάρτυσιν (3x)
Ac 10:41 but·rather to·witnesses having·been·elected· by
Heb 10:28 ·from compassion upon two or three witnesses.
Rv 11:3 I·shall·give *unto* my two witnesses, and they·shall·
G3144.1 N-GPM μαρτύρων (8x)
Heb 12:1 a·cloud of·witnesses that·is·encircling·about us—
Mt 18:16 mouth of·two or three witnesses every utterance
Mt 26:65 What further need have·we of·witnesses? See, now
Mk 14:63 "What need do·we·have of·any·further witnesses?
2Co 13:1 At *the* mouth of·two or three witnesses shall every
1Ti 5:19 "except at *the mouth* of·two or three witnesses."
1Ti 6:12 good affirmation in·the·sight of·many witnesses.
2Ti 2:2 me through many witnesses, place·the·direct·care·of
G3144.2 N-NSM μάρτυς (1x)
Rv 2:13 AntiPas *was* my trustworthy martyr, who was·killed
G3144.2 N-GSM μάρτυρος (1x)
Ac 22:20 the blood of·your martyr Stephen was·poured·out,
G3144.2 N-GPM μαρτύρων (1x)
Rv 17:6 from·out of·the blood of·the martyrs of·Jesus. And

G3145 μασσάομαι massáômai *v.* (1x)
Roots:G3145-1 Compare:G5176 See:G3155
G3145 V-INI-3P ἐμασσῶντο (1x)
Rv 16:10 ·into·darkness. And they·gnawed their tongues as·

G3146 μαστιγόω mastigóō *v.* (7x)
Roots:G3148 Compare:G1194 G3147 G5417 See:G3147
G3146.1 V-FAI-2P μαστιγώσετε (1x)
Mt 23:34 and *some* from·among them yeu·shall·flog in yeur
G3146.1 V-FAI-3P μαστιγώσουσιν (2x)
Mt 10:17 ·councils·of·Sanhedrin, and they·shall·flog yeu in
Mk 10:34 And they·shall·mock him, and shall·flog him, and
G3146.1 V-AAI-3S ἐμαστίγωσεν (1x)
Jn 19:1 Then accordingly, Pilate took Jesus and flogged *him*.
G3146.1 V-AAN μαστιγῶσαι (1x)
Mt 20:19 for *them* to·mock, and to·flog, and to·crucify *him*.
G3146.1 V-AAP-NPM μαστιγώσαντες (1x)
Lk 18:33 And after·flogging *him*, they·shall·kill him.
G3146.2 V-PAI-3S μαστιγοῖ (1x)
Heb 12:6 ·correctively·disciplines, and he·whips every son

G3147 μαστίζω mastízō *v.* (1x)
Roots:G3148 Compare:G1194 G3146 See:G3146
G3147 V-PAN μαστίζειν (1x)
Ac 22:25 ·it·proper for·yeu to·scourge a·man·of·clay† *who·is*

G3148 μάστιξ mástix *n.* (6x)
Roots:G3145 Compare:G4127 G5416 See:G3146 G3147
G3148.2 N-APF μάστιγας (1x)
Mk 3:10 ·*them* as were·having scourges to·press·toward him
G3148.2 N-GSF μάστιγος (2x)
Mk 5:29 body that she·has·been·healed from the scourge.
Mk 5:34 be healthy·and·sound away·from your scourge."
G3148.2 N-GPF μαστίγων (1x)
Lk 7:21 ·and·cured many from illnesses, scourges, and evil
G3148.3 N-DPF μάστιξιν (1x)
Ac 22:24 to·be·interrogated by·scourgings in·order·that he·
G3148.3 N-GPF μαστίγων (1x)
Heb 11:36 a·trial of·*cruel*·mockings and scourgings, and

G3149 μαστός mastós *n.* (3x)
Roots:G3145 Compare:G4738 G2859 xLangAlso:H7699
G3149 N-NPM μαστοί (2x)
Lk 11:27 bearing you, and *the* breasts which nursed *you*.
Lk 23:29 did·not bear, and *the* breasts which did·not nurse.
G3149 N-DPM μαστοῖς (1x)
Rv 1:13 ·with a·golden band directly·against the breasts.

G3150 ματαιο•λογία mataiôlogía *n.* (1x)
Roots:G3151
G3150 N-ASF ματαιολογίαν (1x)
1Ti 1:6 ·turned·aside to idle·talk, already·missing·the·mark,

G3151 ματαιο•λόγος mataiôlógôs *adj.* (1x)
Roots:G3152 G3004 Compare:G4691 G5397 See:G3150
G3151 A-NPM ματαιολόγοι (1x)
Tit 1:10 and idle·talkers and those·that·delude·the·mind,

G3152 μάταιος mátaiôs *adj.* (6x)
Roots:G3155 Compare:G2756 See:G3153 G3154 xLangAlso:H7723 H1892
G3152 A-NSM μάταιος (1x)
Jac 1:26 deluding his·own heart, this·man's religion *is* futile.
G3152 A-NSF ματαία (1x)
1Co 15:17 been·awakened, yeur trust *is* futile— yeu·are still
G3152 A-NPM μάταιοι (2x)
Tit 3:9 for they·are unprofitable and futile·things.
1Co 3:20 the deliberations of·the wise, that they·are futile."
G3152 A-GSF ματαίας (1x)
1Pe 1:18 ·out of·yeur futile manner·of·life handed·down·by·
G3152 A-GPM ματαίων (1x)
Ac 14:15 ·yeu to·turn·back·around from these futilities to the

G3153 ματαιότης mataiótēs *n.* (3x)
Roots:G3152
G3153.1 N-DSF ματαιότητι (2x)
Rm 8:20 the creation was·made·subject to·the futility, not
Eph 4:17 ·*the* Gentiles also walk, in a·futility of·their mind,
G3153.1 N-GSF ματαιότητος (1x)
2Pe 2:18 ·are·enunciating outrageous·things of·futility, *it·is*

G3154 ματαιόω mataióō *v.* (1x)
Roots:G3152
G3154.2 V-API-3P ἐματαιώθησαν (1x)
Rm 1:21 but·rather they·already·became·futile in their

G3155 μάτην mátēn *adv.* (2x)
Roots:G3145 See:G3152 G3153 G3154 xLangAlso:H7723
G3155.2 ADV μάτην (2x)
Mt 15:9 But futilely do·they·reverence me, teaching *the*
Mk 7:7 And futilely do·they·reverence me, teaching *the*

G3156 Ματθα•ῖος Matthaîos *n/p.* (8x)
מַתִּתְיָה matִthyah
Roots:G3161 See:G3018 xLangEquiv:H4993
G3156.2 N/P-NSM Ματθαῖος (2x)
Ac 1:13 Thomas); (BarTholomew and MattHew); (Jakob
Mt 10:3 Thomas and MattHew the tax·collector *(the·one of·*
G3156.2 N/P-ASM Ματθαῖον (3x)
Lk 6:15 MattHew *of·Alphaeus* and Thomas, Jakob (the·one
Mt 9:9 being·referred·to·as MattHew, who·is·sitting·down in
Mk 3:18 and BarTholomew, and MattHew *of·Alphaeus*, and
EG3156.2 (3x)
Mt 9:10 while·he is·reclining·at·a·meal in *MattHew's* home,
Mk 2:14 ·*there*, he·saw Levi *called MattHew* (the·one of·
Mk 2:15 him laying·back·to·eat in *MattHew's* home, *that*

G3157 Ματθάν Matthán *n/p.* (2x)
מַתָּן matan [Hebrew]
Roots:H4977
G3157 N/P-PRI Ματθάν (2x)
Mt 1:15 EleAzar, and EleAzar begot Matthan, and Matthan
Mt 1:15 EleAzar begot Matthan, and Matthan begot Jacob.

G3158 Ματθάτ Matthát *n/p.* (2x)
Roots:G3161 See:G3156 G3159
G3158.2 N/P-PRI Ματθάτ (1x)
Lk 3:29 *son* of·JoRim, *son* of·Matthat, *son* of·Levi,
G3158.3 N/P-PRI Ματθάτ (1x)
Lk 3:24 *son* of·Matthat, *son* of·Levi, *son* of·Malki, *son* of·

G3159 Ματθ•ίας Matthías *n/p.* (2x)
Roots:G3161 See:G3156
G3159.2 N/P-ASM Ματθίαν (2x)
Ac 1:23 (who was·surnamed Justus) and MatthIas.
Ac 1:26 and the lot fell upon MatthIas. And he·was·fully·

G3160 Ματταθ•ά Mattathá *n/p.* (1x)
Roots:G3161 Compare:G3190 xLangEquiv:H4992
G3160 N/P-PRI Ματταθά (1x)
Lk 3:31 *son* of·Mainan, *son* of·Mattatha, *son* of·Nathan,

G3161 Ματταθ•ίας Mattathías *n/p.* (2x)
מַתִּתְיָהוּ matithyahû [Hebrew]
Roots:H4993 See:G3156 G3159 G3158
G3161.2 N/P-GSM Ματταθίου (1x)
Lk 3:25 *son* of·MattathIas, *son* of·Amots, *son* of·Nachum,
G3161.3 N/P-GSM Ματταθίου (1x)
Lk 3:26 *son* of·Maath, *son* of·MattathIas, *son* of·Shimei, *son*

G3162 μάχαιρα máchaira *n.* (29x)
Roots:G3163 Compare:G4501 G3584-1 G5113-3 xLangEquiv:H2719
G3162.1 N-NSF μάχαιρα (2x)
Rm 8:35 or famine, or nakedness, or danger, or dagger?
Rv 6:4 And there·was·given to·him a·great dagger.
G3162.1 N-NPF μάχαιραι (1x)
Lk 22:38 behold, here *are* two daggers." And he·declared
G3162.1 N-ASF μάχαιραν (11x)
Jn 18:10 Now·then, having a·dagger, Simon Peter drew it
Jn 18:11 to·Peter, "Cast your dagger into the sheath! The
Lk 22:36 And the·one not having a·dagger, let·him·sell his
Ac 16:27 ·opened·up, drawing his·dagger, he·was·about to·
Heb 4:12 above·and·beyond any double-edged dagger,
Mt 10:34 I·did·not come to·cast peace, but·rather a·dagger.
Mt 26:51 his hand, drew·out his dagger. And smiting the
Mt 26:52 to·him, "Return·back your dagger into its place,
Mt 26:52 taking·hold·of a·dagger shall·completely·perish by
Mk 14:47 standing·nearby, upon·drawing the dagger, struck
Eph 6:17 of·custodial·Salvation and the dagger of·the Spirit,
G3162.1 N-DSF μαχαίρᾳ (5x)
Lk 22:49 "Lord, shall·we·smite with *the* dagger?"
Ac 12:2 Jakob, the brother of·John, with·a·dagger.
Mt 26:52 ·of a·dagger shall·completely·perish by a·dagger.
Rv 13:10 If any·man kills with a·dagger, it·is·mandatory·for
Rv 13:10 it·is·mandatory·for him to·be·killed with a·dagger.
G3162.1 N-GSF μαχαίρας (4x)
Lk 21:24 And they·shall·fall by·the·edge of·a·dagger, and
Heb 11:34 escaped *the* edge of·*the*·dagger, from weakness
Heb 11:37 ·died by murder with·a·dagger. They·went·about
Rv 13:14 which has the gash by·the dagger, and·yet lived.
G3162.1 N-GPF μαχαιρῶν (5x)
Lk 22:52 against an·armed·robber, with daggers and staffs?
Mt 26:47 him *was* a·large crowd with daggers and staffs,
Mt 26:55 as against an·armed·robber with daggers and staffs
Mk 14:43 with him a·large crowd with daggers and staffs,
Mk 14:48 against an·armed·robber, with daggers and staffs
G3162.3 N-ASF μάχαιραν (1x)
Rm 13:4 without·reason *that* he·bears the sword, for he·is

G3163 μάχη máchē *n.* (4x)
Roots:G3164 Compare:G0073 G2054 G5379 G4171 See:G3162 xLangAlso:H4079
G3163.2 N-NPF μάχαι (2x)
Jac 4:1 From·what·source *are* wars and quarrels among yeu
2Co 7:5 on every·side. Outwardly *are* quarrels, inwardly *are*
G3163.2 N-APF μάχας (2x)
Tit 3:9 genealogies, strifes, and quarrels of·Torah-Law, for
2Ti 2:23 having·seen that they·give·birth *to* quarrels.

G3164 μάχομαι máchômai *v.* (4x)
Compare:G0075 G0483 G2051 G4170 See:G3163 G3162 G1264
G3164.1 V-PNI-2P μάχεσθε (1x)
Jac 4:2 yeu·are·not able to·obtain. Yeu·fight and wage·war,
G3164.1 V-PNP-DPM μαχομένοις (1x)
Ac 7:26 ·himself·visible to·them as·they·were·fighting, and
G3164.2 V-PNN μάχεσθαι (1x)
2Ti 2:24 ·for a·slave of·*the*·Lord not to·quarrel, but·rather
G3164.2 V-INI-3P ἐμάχοντο (1x)
Jn 6:52 the Judeans were·quarreling among one·another,

G3165 μέ mé *p:p.* (307x)
See:G1691
(abbreviated listing for G3165)
G3165.1 P:P-1AS μέ (293x)
(list for G3165.1:P:P-1AS excluded)
EG3165.1 (5x)
(list for EG3165.1: excluded)
G3165.2 P:P-1AS μέ (3x)
(list for G3165.2:P:P-1AS excluded)
G3165.3 P:P-1AS μέ (6x)
(list for G3165.3:P:P-1AS excluded)

G3166 μεγαλ•αυχέω mêgalauchéō *v.* (1x)
Roots:G3173 G0849-3 Compare:G2744 G2620 See:G0837
G3166 V-PAI-3S μεγαλαυχεῖ (1x)
Jac 3:5 is a·small member, yet it·boasts·greatly. Behold, a·

G3167 μεγαλεῖος mêgalêîôs *adj.* (2x)
Roots:G3173 Compare:G2986 See:G3168 G3170 G3170-1
G3167.1 A-APN μεγαλεῖα (2x)
Lk 1:49 the powerful·one did magnificent·things for·me, and
Ac 2:11 ·our native·tongues the magnificent·things of·God."

G3168 μεγαλειότης mêgalêiótēs *n.* (3x)
Roots:G3167 Compare:G3172 G3170-1
G3168 N-ASF μεγαλειότητα (1x)
Ac 19:27 also her magnificence is·about to·be·demolished,
G3168 N-DSF μεγαλειότητι (1x)
Lk 9:43 they·all were·astounded at the magnificence of·God.
G3168 N-GSF μεγαλειότητος (1x)
2Pe 1:16 yeu·were·being beholders of·that magnificence.

G3169 μεγαλο•πρεπής mêgalôprêpḗs *adj.* (1x)
Roots:G3173 G4241
G3169.2 A-GSF μεγαλοπρεποῦς (1x)
2Pe 1:17 ·carried·forth to·him by the magnificent glory,

G3170 μεγαλύνω mêgalýnō *v.* (8x)
Roots:G3173 See:G3167 G3170-1
G3170.1 V-IAI-3S ἐμεγάλυνεν (1x)
Lk 1:58 heard that Yahweh was·making·great his mercy with
G3170.1 V-APN μεγαλυνθῆναι (1x)
2Co 10:15 ·grown·further) to·be·made·great along·with yeu
G3170.2 V-PAI-3P μεγαλύνουσιν (1x)
Mt 23:5 their tefillin and enlarge the fringes of·their
G3170.3 V-FPI-3S μεγαλυνθήσεται (1x)
Php 1:20 also), Anointed-One shall·be·magnified in my
G3170.3 V-PAI-3S μεγαλύνει (1x)
Lk 1:46 Mariam declared, "My soul does·magnify Yahweh,
G3170.3 V-PAP-GPM μεγαλυνόντων (1x)
Ac 10:46 in·bestowed·tongues and magnifying God. Then
G3170.3 V-IAI-3S ἐμεγάλυνεν (1x)
Ac 5:13 to·them, but·yet the people were·magnifying them;
G3170.3 V-IPI-3S ἐμεγαλύνετο (1x)
Ac 19:17 and the name of·the Lord Jesus was·magnified.

G3171 μεγάλως mêgálōs *adv.* (1x)
Roots:G3173
G3171 ADV μεγάλως (1x)
Php 4:10 Now I·rejoiced in *the* Lord greatly, that even·now

G3172 μεγαλωσύνη mêgalōsýnē *n.* (3x)
Roots:G3173 Compare:G3168 See:G3174
G3172.2 N-NSF μεγαλωσύνη (1x)
Jud 1:25 Savior, *be* glory and majesty, might and authority,
G3172.3 N-GSF μεγαλωσύνης (2x)
Heb 1:3 at *the* right·hand of·the Divine·Majesty on high,
Heb 8:1 ·hand of·the throne of·the Divine·Majesty in the

G3173 μέγας mégas *adj.* (194x)
μεγάλη mêgálē [feminine]
μεγάλοι mêgálôi [plural]
μεγάλ- mêgál- [other forms]
Compare:G4183 See:G3176 G3170 G3187 xLangEquiv:H1419
G3173.1 A-NSM μέγας (24x)
Lk 1:15 For he·shall·be great in·the·sight of·Yahweh. And,
Lk 1:32 "This·man shall·be great and shall·be·called *the* Son
Lk 4:25 and six lunar·months, as great famine occurred over
Lk 7:16 God, saying, "A·great prophet has·been·awakened
Lk 9:48 least among yeu all, the·same shall·be great."
Ac 5:5 *and* expired. And great reverent·fear came upon all
Ac 5:11 And great reverent·fear came upon all the Called·
Ac 8:1 that·very day, there·was a·great persecution against
Ac 16:26 And without·warning there·was a·great earthquake,
Mt 5:19 *them*, the·same shall·be·called great in the kingdom
Mt 8:24 And behold, a·great tempest occurred in the sea,
Mt 20:26 whoever should·want to·become great among yeu,
Mt 28:2 And behold, there·occurred a·great earthquake. For
Mk 10:43 whoever should·want to·become great among yeu,
Mk 16:4 ·been·rolled·away, for it·was tremendously great.
1Ti 6:6 with self-sufficiency is a·great means·of·gain.
Rv 6:12 and behold, there·was a·great earthquake; and the
Rv 8:10 sounded, and there·fell a·great star from·out of·the
Rv 11:11 upon their feet, and great fear fell upon the·ones
Rv 11:13 in that hour there·happened a·great earthquake, and
Rv 12:3 in the heaven; and behold a·great fiery·red Dragon,
Rv 12:9 And the great Dragon was·cast·out, the original
Rv 16:18 and lightnings. And there·was a·great earthquake,
Rv 16:18 the earth, so·vast an·earthquake, *and* so great!
G3173.1 A-NSF μεγάλη (35x)
Jn 19:31 (for that Sabbath was the great day), the Judeans
Lk 21:23 Days! For there·shall·be great dire·need upon the
Ac 4:33 of·the Lord Jesus, and great grace was upon them
Ac 7:11 of·Egypt and Kenaan, and a·great tribulation, and
Ac 8:8 And there·was great joy in that city.
Ac 8:10 "This·man is the great power of·God."
Ac 19:28 ·out, saying, "Great *is* Artemis of·the·Ephesians.
Ac 19:34 two hours— yelling·out, "Great *is* Artemis of·the
Ac 23:9 And there·occurred a·great *amount·of* yelling. And
Mt 7:27 that home, and it·fell; and great was its downfall.
Mt 8:26 the winds and the sea, and there·was a·great calm.
Mt 15:28 "O woman, great *is* your trust! It·is·done for·you
Mt 22:36 which·one *is the* great commandment in the
Mt 24:21 "For then there·shall·be a·Great Tribulation, such·
Mk 4:37 And there·happens a·great whirling·of·wind, and
Mk 4:39 the wind subsided, and there·was a·great calm.
Mk 5:11 on·the·side·of the mountains, a·great herd of·pigs
Rm 9:2 that my grief is a·great and unceasing distress in·my
1Co 16:9 For a·great and active door has·opened·up to·me,
Rv 6:4 And there·was·given to·him a·great dagger.
Rv 6:17 because the GREAT DAY of·his WRATH is·come,
Rv 11:19 thunderings, and an·earthquake, and great hail.
Rv 14:8 is·fallen, is·fallen, the Great City, because she·has·
Rv 16:17 air, and there·came·forth a·great voice from the
Rv 16:19 And the Great City became three parts, and the
Rv 16:19 the Great was·recalled·to·mind in·the·sight·of·God
Rv 16:21 And great hail (*each hailstone* about *the* weight·
Rv 16:21 its punishing·blow was tremendously great.
Rv 17:5 MYSTERY, BABYLON THE GREAT, THE
Rv 17:18 woman whom you·saw is the Great City, the·one
Rv 18:2 saying, "Babylon the Great is·fallen, is·fallen, and
Rv 18:10 'Woe, woe, the Great City Babylon, the Strong
Rv 18:16 'Woe, woe, the Great City, the·one having·been·
Rv 18:19 'Woe, woe, the Great City, in which all the·ones
Rv 18:21 ·manner with·violence, the Great City Babylon
G3173.1 A-NSN μέγα (7x)
Lk 6:49 And the wreckage of·that home became great."
1Co 9:11 spiritual·things, *is·it* a·great·thing if we·ourselves
2Co 11:15 Accordingly, *it·is* no great·thing if his attendants
Eph 5:32 This is a·great mystery, but I·myself do·say *this* in·
1Ti 3:16 And admittedly, great is the Mystery of·the Way·
Rv 8:8 and *something* as a·great mountain being·set·ablaze
Rv 12:1 And a·great sign was·made·visible in the heaven: a·
G3173.1 A-NPM μεγάλοι (4x)
Lk 21:11 And great earthquakes shall·be pervasive·in·all
Mt 20:25 ·ones *that·are* great exercise·authority against them
Mk 10:42 their great·ones exercise·authority against them.
Rv 19:5 ·fearing him, both the small and the great!"
G3173.1 A-NPF μεγάλαι (1x)
Rv 11:15 sounded, and there·became great voices in the
G3173.1 A-NPN μεγάλα (2x)
Lk 21:11 ·shall·be frightening·things and great signs from
Rv 15:3 ·the Lamb, saying, "Great and marvelous *are* your
G3173.1 A-ASM μέγαν (12x)
Lk 2:9 And they·were·frightened *with* great fear.
Ac 8:2 and they·made great visceral·lamentation over him.
Ac 8:9 of·Samaria, saying himself to·be someone great;
Ac 11:28 *that* there·was·about to·be a·great famine over all
Heb 4:14 So·then having a·great High·Priest, having·gone·
Heb 13:20 our Lord YeShua (the great shepherd of·the sheep
Mt 27:60 solid·rock, and after·rolling a·great stone to·the
Mk 4:41 ·frightened *with* a·great reverent·fear·and·awe, and
Rv 12:12 to yeu! *He·is* having great rage, having·seen that
Rv 16:12 poured·out his vial upon the great river EuPhrates,
Rv 18:21 angel took·up a·stone as a·great millstone, and cast
Rv 20:11 And I·saw a·Great White Throne, and the·one
G3173.1 A-ASF μεγάλην (19x)
Lk 2:10 behold, I·proclaim·good·news to·yeu of·great joy,
Lk 5:29 And Levi made a·great reception for·him in his·own
Ac 2:20 blood, prior·to the great and conspicuous Day of·
Ac 10:11 him, as *being* a·great linen·sheet having·been·tied
Ac 11:5 descending, as a·great linen·sheet being·sent·down
Ac 15:3 *to God*. And they·were·causing great joy for·all the
Heb 10:35 ·declaration, which has great reward·for·service.
Mt 2:10 they·rejoiced *with* tremendously great joy.
Rv 1:10 day and heard right·behind me a·great voice, as of·
Rv 2:22 committing·adultery with her into great tribulation,
Rv 11:12 And they·heard a·great voice from·out of·the
Rv 11:17 because you·have·taken your great power and
Rv 13:2 it his power, and his throne, and great authority.
Rv 14:19 and cast *it* into the great winepress of·the Rage of·
Rv 18:1 from·out of·the heaven, having great authority; and
Rv 19:1 after these·things, I·heard a·great voice of·a·large
Rv 19:2 because he·judged the Great Prostitute, who was·
Rv 20:1 the key of·the bottomless·pit and a·great chain in his
Rv 21:10 and showed me the Great CITY, the Holy
G3173.1 A-ASN μέγα (9x)
Lk 13:19 And it·grew and became a·great tree, and the birds
Lk 14:16 "A·certain man·of·clay† made a·great supper and
Lk 16:26 and yeu there·has·been·firmly·set a·great chasm,
Mt 4:16 ·sitting in darkness, they·did·see a·great light. And
Rv 15:1 sign in the heaven, great and marvelous, seven
Rv 16:9 ·clay† were·burned·by·the·sun with·great burning·,
Rv 17:6 And seeing her, I·marveled with·great marvel.
Rv 21:10 me away in spirit to a·great and high mountain, and
Rv 21:12 also having a·wall great and high, having twelve
G3173.1 A-APM μεγάλους (3x)
Mk 4:32 the garden·plants, and it·produces great branches,
Rv 13:16 all, the small and the great, also the wealthy and
Rv 20:12 dead·ones, small and great, standing in·the·sight
G3173.1 A-APF μεγάλας (2x)
Ac 8:13 ·observing both signs and great miracles occurring.

Mk 13:2 to·him, "Do·you·look·upon these great structures?
G3173.1 A-APN μεγάλα (4x)
Ac 6:8 full of·trust and power, was·doing great wonders and
Mt 24:24 false·prophets, and they·shall·give great signs and
Rv 13:5 to·it a·mouth speaking great·things and revilements.
Rv 13:13 And it·does great signs, so that it·should·make fire
G3173.1 A-DSM μεγάλῳ (3x)
Lk 8:37 them, because they·were·clenched with·great fear.
Ac 26:22 being·a·witness to·both small and great, saying
Rv 9:14 having·been·bound in the great river EuPhrates
G3173.1 A-DSF μεγάλῃ (6x)
Jn 7:37 the last day, on·the great *day* of·the Sacred·Feast *of·*
Ac 4:33 And with·great power, the ambassadors were·
Mk 5:42 And they·were·astonished with·great astonishment.
2Ti 2:20 But in a·great home there·are not merely vessels
Rv 18:2 And he·yelled·out in strength, a·great voice, saying,
Rv 18:18 'What *city is* like the Great City!'
G3173.1 A-DPM μεγάλοις (1x)
Rv 11:18 name, the small and the great, and·also *for·you* to·
G3173.1 A-GSM μεγάλου (5x)
Jn 6:18 was·thoroughly·roused *due·to* a·great wind blowing.
Tit 2:13 ·appearing of·the glory of·our great God and Savior,
Rv 6:13 ·green·figs while·being·shaken by a·great wind.
Rv 12:14 two wings of·the great eagle were·given that she·
Rv 19:17 ·gathered·together for the supper of·the great God,
G3173.1 A-GSF μεγάλης (14x)
Lk 24:52 him, returned·back to JeruSalem with great joy.
Ac 19:27 *for* the sanctuary of·the great goddess Artemis to·
Ac 19:35 temple·custodian of·the great goddess Artemis, and
Mt 24:31 his angels with a·great sound of·a·trumpet, and
Mt 28:8 with reverent·fear·and·awe and with·great joy,
Jud 1:6 ·murky·shroud for Tribunal·judgment of·a·great day.
Rv 7:14 ·ones coming out of·The GREAT TRIBULATION,
Rv 9:2 out of·the well, as smoke of·a·great furnace, and the
Rv 11:8 *shall·lay* in the broad·street of·the great City *that·is*
Rv 14:2 waters, and as a·voice of·a·great thunder. And I·
Rv 16:1 And I·heard a·great voice from·out of·the Temple
Rv 16:14 to the battle of·that great day of·God Almighty.
Rv 17:1 to·you the judgment of·the Great Prostitute, the·one
Rv 21:3 And I·heard a·great voice from·out of·the heaven
G3173.1 A-GPM μεγάλων (1x)
Rv 19:18 ·men, *both* free and slave, both small and great."
G3173.2 A-NSF μεγάλη (1x)
Mt 22:38 This is *the* foremost and greatest commandment.
G3173.2 A-GSM μεγάλου (2x)
Ac 8:10 from *the* least unto *the* greatest, saying, "This·man
Heb 8:11 from *the* least of·them unto *the* greatest of·them.
G3173.3 A-ASN μέγα (2x)
Lk 22:12 yeu a·big upper·room having·been·spread·out *for·*
Mk 14:15 yeu a·big upper·room having·been·spread·out *for·*
G3173.3 A-GPM μεγάλων (1x)
Jn 21:11 *with·it being* exceedingly·full of·big fish (a·
G3173.4 A-ASF μεγάλην (2x)
Mk 15:37 after·sending·away *his spirit with* a·loud voice,
Rv 12:10 And I·heard a·loud voice saying in the heaven,
G3173.4 A-DSF μεγάλῃ (29x)
Jn 11:43 these·things, he·yelled·out with·a·loud voice,
Lk 1:42 And she·exclaimed with·a·loud voice, and declared,
Lk 4:33 demon, and he·screamed·out with·a·loud voice,
Lk 8:28 ·before him, and with·a·loud voice he·declared,
Lk 19:37 praising God with·a·loud voice concerning all *the*
Lk 23:46 And hollering·out with·a·loud voice, Jesus
Ac 7:57 Then yelling·out with·a·loud voice, they·stopped·up
Ac 7:60 the knees, he·yelled·out with·a·loud voice, "Lord,
Ac 8:7 impure spirits, crying·out with·a·loud voice, were·
Ac 14:10 *Paul* declared with·a·loud voice, "Stand upright
Ac 16:28 But Paul hollered·out with·a·loud voice, saying,
Ac 26:24 Festus replied *to* these·things with·a·loud voice,
Mt 27:46 ninth hour YeShua shouted·out with·a·loud voice,
Mt 27:50 YeShua, after·yelling·out again with·a·loud voice,
Mk 1:26 ·convulsing him and yelling·out with·a·loud voice,
Mk 5:7 And yelling·out with·a·loud voice, he·declared,
Mk 15:34 hour, Jesus cried·out with·a·loud voice, saying,
Rv 5:2 angel officially·proclaiming with·a·loud voice,
Rv 5:12 saying with·a·loud voice, "Worthy is the Lamb
Rv 6:10 And they·were·yelling·out with·a·loud voice, saying
Rv 7:2 God, and he·yelled·out with·a·loud voice to·the four
Rv 7:10 and yelling·out with·a·loud voice, saying, "The
Rv 8:13 flying in mid-heaven, saying with·a·loud voice,
Rv 10:3 and he·yelled·out with·a·loud voice, just·as *when* a·
Rv 14:7 saying with a·loud voice, "Fear God and give glory
Rv 14:9 angel followed them, saying with a·loud voice, "If
Rv 14:15 ·the Temple, yelling·out in a·loud voice to·the·one
Rv 14:18 and he·hollered·out with·a·loud yell to·the·one
Rv 19:17 sun; and he·yelled·out with·a·loud voice, saying
G3173.4 A-DPF μεγάλαις (1x)
Lk 23:23 And they·were·insisting with·loud voices,
G3173.4 A-GSF μεγάλης (1x)
Lk 17:15 ·healed, returned·back with a·loud voice glorifying
G3173.5 A-ASM μέγαν (1x)
Heb 10:21 and *having* a·high priest over the house of·God—
G3173.5 A-DSM μεγάλῳ (1x)
Lk 4:38 was being·clenched with·a·high fever, and they·
G3173.6 A-NSM μέγας (1x)
Heb 11:24 Moses (after·becoming full·grown) renounced

G3174 μέγεθος mégêthôs *n.* (1x)
Roots:G3173 Compare:G3168 See:G3172 xLangEquiv:H1433
G3174.1 N-NSN μέγεθος (1x)
Eph 1:19 and what *is* the surpassing greatness of·his power

G3175 μεγιστᾶνες mêgistânês *n.* (3x)
Roots:G3176
G3175 N-NPM μεγιστᾶνες (2x)
Rv 6:15 of·the earth, and the greatest·men, and the wealthy·
Rv 18:23 your merchants were the greatest·men of·the earth,
G3175 N-DPM μεγιστᾶσιν (1x)
Mk 6:21 ·supper on·his birthday for·his greatest·men and the

G3176 μέγιστος mégistôs *adj.* (1x)
Roots:G3173 See:G3187
G3176 A-NPN-S μέγιστα (1x)
2Pe 1:4 he·has·endowed to·us the most·greatest and precious

G3177 μεθ•ερμηνεύω mêthêrmēnêúō *v.* (7x)
Roots:G3326 G2059 Compare:G1329
G3177.1 V-PPP-NSN μεθερμηνευόμενον (6x)
Jn 1:41 which, when·being·interpreted *from·Hebrew*, is
Ac 4:36 (which, when·being·interpreted *from·Aramaic*, is
Mt 1:23 ⁻ which, when·being·interpreted *from·Hebrew*, is
Mk 5:41 which, when·being·interpreted *from·Aramaic*, is
Mk 15:22 which, when·being·interpreted *from·Hebrew*, is
Mk 15:34 ' Which, when·being·interpreted *from·Aramaic*,
G3177.2 V-PPI-3S μεθερμηνεύεται (1x)
Ac 13:8 (for so his name is·interpreted *from·Arabic*), stood·

G3178 μέθη méthē *n.* (3x)
Compare:G2897 See:G3184 G3182-1 G3183
G3178.2 N-NPF μέθαι (1x)
Gal 5:21 envyings, murders, intoxications, revelries, and
G3178.2 N-DSF μέθῃ (1x)
Lk 21:34 ·of·indulgence, and with·intoxication, and with·
G3178.2 N-DPF μέθαις (1x)
Rm 13:13 daylight, not in·revelries and intoxications, not in·

G3179 μεθ•ίστημι mêthístēmi *v.* (5x)
μεθ•ιστάνω mêthistánō [1 Corinthians 13:2]
Roots:G3326 G2476 Compare:G3346 G0851
G3179.2 V-PAN μεθιστάνειν (1x)
1Co 13:2 all the trust, as·such to·relocate mountains, and
G3179.2 V-AAI-3S μετέστησεν (1x)
Col 1:13 of·the authority of·darkness and relocated *us* into
G3179.4 V-AAP-NSM μεταστήσας (1x)
Ac 13:22 And after·relieving him from·duty, he·awakened
G3179.4 V-APS-1S μετασταθῶ (1x)
Lk 16:4 whenever I·should·be·relieved·from·duty of·the
G3179.7 V-AAI-3S μετέστησεν (1x)
Ac 19:26 Asia, this Paul has·won·over an·ample crowd *by*

G3180 μεθ•οδεία mêthôdêía *n.* (2x)
Roots:G3326 G3593 Compare:G2940 G3884 G3834
G3180.2 N-ASF μεθοδείαν (1x)
Eph 4:14 shrewd·cunning pertaining·to the trickery of·deceit.
G3180.2 N-APF μεθοδείας (1x)
Eph 6:11 specifically·against the trickeries of·the Slanderer,

G3181 μεθ•όριος mêthốriôs *n.* (1x)
Roots:G3326 G3725
G3181.2 N-APN μεθόρια (1x)
Mk 7:24 he·went·off into the common·borders of·Tyre and

G3182 μεθύσκω mêthýskō *v.* (3x)
Roots:G3184 See:G3182-1 G3183 xLangAlso:H7937
G3182.3 V-PPN μεθύσκεσθαι (1x)
Lk 12:45 ·girls, and to·eat and to·drink and to·be·drunk,
G3182.3 V-PPN-2P μεθύσκεσθε (1x)
Eph 5:18 And not to·be·drunk with·wine, in which is *the*
G3182.3 V-PPP-NPM μεθυσκόμενοι (1x)
1Th 5:7 at·night, and the·ones being·drunk, get·drunk at·

G3183 μέθυσος méthysôs *n.* (2x)
Roots:G3184 Compare:G3630 G3943 G3632 See:G3182 G3182-1 xLangEquiv:H7910
G3183.2 N-NSM μέθυσος (1x)
1Co 5:11 or a·defamer, or a·drunkard, or *is* violently·or·
G3183.2 N-NPM μέθυσοι (1x)
1Co 6:10 covetous·men, nor drunkards, nor defamatory·men

G3184 μεθύω mêthýō *v.* (7x)
Roots:G3178 Compare:G3631-1 G3943 G3942-1 G3632-3 See:G3182 G3183 G3182-1 xLangAlso:H7937
G3184.2 V-PAI-3S μεθύει (1x)
1Co 11:21 ·fact, one goes·hungry, and another gets·drunk.
G3184.2 V-PAI-3P μεθύουσιν (1x)
1Th 5:7 and the·ones being·drunk, get·drunk at·night.
G3184.2 V-PAP-ASF μεθύουσαν (1x)
Rv 17:6 And I·saw the woman getting·drunk from·out of·the
G3184.2 V-PAP-GPM μεθυόντων (1x)
Mt 24:49 to·eat and to·drink with the·ones getting·drunk,
G3184.2 V-API-3P ἐμεθύσθησαν (1x)
Rv 17:2 ·in the earth, they·are·made·drunk from·out of·the
G3184.3 V-PAI-3P μεθύουσιν (1x)
Ac 2:15 For these·men are·not drunk as yeu assume, for it·is
G3184.3 V-APS-3P μεθυσθῶσιν (1x)
Jn 2:10 wine, and whenever they·should·be·drunk, then the

G3185 μεῖζον meîzôn *adv.* (1x)
Roots:G3187
G3185.2 ADV μεῖζον (1x)
Mt 20:31 but they·were·yelling·out more·loudly, saying—

G3186 μειζότερος mêizốtêrôs *adj.* (1x)
Roots:G3187
G3186.1 A-ASF-C μειζοτέραν (1x)
3Jn 1:4 I·have no joy even·greater·than these·things, that I·

G3187 μείζων meízōn *adj.* (45x)
Roots:G3173 Compare:G1640 G4119 See:G3176 G3185 G3186
G3187.1 A-NSM-C μείζων (26x)
Jn 4:12 ¿! Are you·yourself greater·than our father Jacob,
Jn 8:53 ¿! Are you·yourself greater·than our father AbRaham
Jn 10:29 has·given *them* to·me, is greater·than all; and not·
Jn 13:16 to·yeu, a·slave is not greater·than his lord; neither
Jn 13:16 *is* an·ambassador greater·than the·one sending him.
Jn 14:28 the Father,' because my Father is greater·than me.
Jn 15:20 'A·slave is not greater·than his lord.' If they·
Lk 7:28 there·is not·even·one prophet greater·than John the
Lk 7:28 least·one in the kingdom of·God is greater·than he."
Lk 9:46 among them *as·to* which of·them would·be greater.
Lk 22:24 *concerning* which of·them is·reputed to·be greater.
Lk 22:26 "But·rather the·one greater among yeu, let·him·be
Lk 22:27 For who *is* greater, the·one reclining·at·the·meal,
Mt 11:11 ·has·not been·awakened one·greater·than John the
Mt 11:11 in the kingdom of·the heavens is greater·than he.
Mt 12:6 ·yeu that one·greater·than the Sanctuary·Courtyard
Mt 18:1 "Who then is greater in the kingdom of·the heavens?

Mt 18:4 this·one is the·one *who·is* greater in the kingdom
Mt 23:11 "But the·one *who·is* greater among·yeu shall·be
Mt 23:17 For which is greater, the gold, or the Temple, the·
Mk 4:32 it·springs·up and becomes greater·than all the
Mk 9:34 among one·another who *would·be* greater.
Rm 9:12 to·her, "'The greater shall·be·a·slave to·the lesser.
1Co 14:5 that yeu·should·prophesy, for greater *is* the·one
1Jn 3:20 ·incriminate *us*, God is greater·than our heart, and
1Jn 4:4 have·overcome them, because greater is the·one in
G3187.1 A-NSF-C μείζων (3x)
Mk 12:31 ·is no other commandment greater·than these."
1Co 13:13 *and* Love; but *the* greater of·these *is* the Love.
1Jn 5:9 the testimony of·God is greater, because this is the
G3187.1 A-NSN-C μεῖζον (1x)
Mt 23:19 For which *is* greater, the present or the Sacrifice·
G3187.1 A-NPM-C μείζονες (1x)
2Pe 2:11 whereas angels, being greater·in strength and
G3187.1 A-ASM-C μείζονα (1x)
Heb 11:26 of·the Anointed-One *to·be* greater wealth *than* the
G3187.1 A-ASF-C μείζονα (4x)
Jn 5:36 But I·myself have the greater testimony *than·that* of·
Jn 15:13 "A·love greater·than this, has not·even·one·man,
Jn 19:11 me over to·you has a·greater moral·failure."
Jac 4:6 But he·gives greater grace. Therefore he·says, '" God
G3187.1 A-ASN-C μεῖζον (1x)
Jac 3:1 having·seen that we·shall·receive greater judgment.
G3187.1 A-APN-C μείζονα (3x)
Jn 1:50 You·shall·gaze·upon greater·things·than these."
Jn 5:20 and he·shall·show him works greater·than these, that
Jn 14:12 ·do those·likewise. And greater *works* than·these
G3187.1 A-GSM-C μείζονος (2x)
Heb 6:13 since he·was·having no·one·at·all greater by *which*
Heb 6:16 in·fact swear by the·one greater·than *themselves,*
G3187.1 A-GSF-C μείζονος (1x)
Heb 9:11 ·directly through the greater and more·complete
G3187.2 A-NSN-C μεῖζον (1x)
Mt 13:32 ·be·grown, it·is bigger·than the garden·plants and
G3187.2 A-APF-C μείζονας (1x)
Lk 12:18 my barns and shall·build bigger·ones; and there I·

G3188 μέλαν mélan *adj.* (3x)
Roots:G3189
G3188 A-DSN μέλανι (1x)
2Co 3:3 us, having·been·engraved not with·ink, but·rather
G3188 A-GSN μέλανος (2x)
2Jn 1:12 *so* through a·sheet·of·paper and ink, but·rather I·
3Jn 1:13 want to·write to·you through ink and a·reed·pen.

G3189 μέλας mélas *adj.* (3x)
See:G3188 G3435
G3189 A-NSM μέλας (2x)
Rv 6:5 I·saw, and behold, a·black horse and the·one who·
Rv 6:12 the sun became *as* black as sackcloth made·of·hair,
G3189 A-ASF μέλαιναν (1x)
Mt 5:36 you·are·not able to·make one hair white or black.

G3190 Μελεᾶς Mêlêâs *n/p.* (1x)
Compare:G3160
G3190 N/P-PRI Μελεᾶ (1x)
Lk 3:31 *son* of·Melea, *son* of·Mainan, *son* of·Mattatha, *son*

G3191 μελετάω mêlêtáō *v.* (3x)
Roots:G3199 Compare:G5426 G0096-1 See:G3191-1 G4304
G3191.2 V-PAM-2S μελέτα (1x)
1Ti 4:15 Meditate·upon these·things; be in these·things in·
G3191.2 V-AAI-3P ἐμελέτησαν (1x)
Ac 4:25 and *did* peoples meditate·upon empty·things?
G3191.3 V-PAM-2P μελετᾶτε (1x)
Mk 13:11 ·should·speak, nor·even premeditate, but·rather

G3192 μέλι méli *n.* (4x)
See:G3193
xLangEquiv:H1706
G3192 N-NSN μέλι (3x)
Mt 3:4 and his nourishment was locusts and wild honey.
Rv 10:9 but·yet it·shall·be in your mouth sweet as honey."
Rv 10:10 ·was in my mouth sweet as honey. And when I·ate
G3192 N-ASN μέλι (1x)
Mk 1:6 his loins, and *was* eating locusts and wild honey.

G3193 μελίσσιος mêlíssiôs *adj.* (1x)
Roots:G3192
G3193 A-GSN μελισσίου (1x)
Lk 24:42 of·a·broiled fish and *a·piece* of a·honey comb.

G3194 Μελίτη Mêlítē *n/l.* (1x)
G3194 N/L-NSF Μελίτη (1x)
Ac 28:1 then they·realized that the island was·called Melita.

G3195 μέλλω méllō *v.* (111x)
Roots:G3199 Compare:G1764
G3195.1 V-PAI-1S μέλλω (1x)
Rv 3:16 cold nor fervently·hot, I·intend to·vomit you out of·
G3195.1 V-PAI-2S μέλλεις (2x)
Jn 14:22 ·it·happened that you·intend to·manifest yourself
Ac 22:16 And now, what·is·it *that* you·are·about *to·do*?
G3195.1 V-PAI-2P μέλλετε (1x)
Ac 5:35 what yeu·intend to·accomplish concerning these
G3195.1 V-PAI-3S μέλλει (5x)
Jn 7:35 "Where·does this·man intend to·traverse that we·
Jn 7:35 ·not find him? ¿!·Does he·intend to·traverse into the
Ac 17:31 he·established a·day in which he·intends ·to·judge
Mt 2:13 to·you, for HerOd·the·Great intends to·seek the little·
Rv 12:5 a·male who imminently·intends to·shepherd all the
G3195.1 V-PAP-ASN μέλλον (1x)
Lk 13:9 you·shall·chop it down for the·thing intended.'"
G3195.1 V-PAP-ASM μέλλοντα (1x)
Ac 13:34 dead·men, no·longer intending to·return·back to
G3195.1 V-PAP-APM μέλλοντας (2x)
Ac 3:3 after·seeing Peter and John intending to·enter into the
Ac 23:15 as intending to·thoroughly·ascertain *something*
G3195.1 V-PAP-GSM μέλλοντος (1x)
Ac 18:14 And while·Paul was·intending to·open·up his
G3195.1 V-PAP-GPM μελλόντων (2x)
Ac 27:30 ·a·pretense as·though intending to·extend anchors
2Pe 2:6 ·out an·explicit·example for·those·intending to·be·;
G3195.1 V-PAP-NSM μέλλων (4x)
Lk 22:23 it·might·be intending to·accomplish this·thing.
Lk 24:21 he·himself is the·one intending to·ransom IsraEl.
Ac 20:7 *matters* with·them, intending to·go·onward on·the
Ac 20:13 ·assigned, intending himself to·go·on·foot.
G3195.1 V-PAP-NPM μέλλοντες (4x)
Ac 20:13 to Assos, *while* from·there intending to·take Paul
Ac 22:29 immediately, the·ones intending to·interrogate him
Ac 23:20 as·though intending to·inquire more·precisely
Ac 27:2 we·launched, intending to·sail adjacent·to the
G3195.1 V-PAS-3S μέλλῃ (1x)
Rv 10:7 seventh angel, whenever he·should·intend to·sound,
G3195.1 V-IAI-3S ἔμελλεν (1x)
Ac 12:6 when HerOd·Agrippa was·intending to·bring him
EG3195.1 (1x)
2Co 10:9 ·not seem as if *I·intended* to·utterly·frighten yeu
G3195.2 V-PAI-1P μέλλομεν (1x)
1Th 3:4 to·yeu that we·are·about to·be·hard-pressed, even
G3195.2 V-PAI-3S μέλλει (4x)
Lk 9:44 Son of·Clay·Man† is·about to·be·handed·over into
Mt 17:22 Son of·Clay·Man† is·about to·be·handed·over into
Rm 4:24 ·of us, to·whom it·is·about to·be·reckoned— the·
Rv 1:19 are, and the·things·which are·about to·be after
G3195.2 V-PAN μέλλειν (4x)
Ac 11:28 the Spirit *that* there·was·about to·be a·great famine
Ac 19:27 also her magnificence is·about to·be·demolished,
Ac 23:30 the man, *which·was* about to·be *carried·out* by the
Ac 28:6 ·anticipating him about to·be·swollen·with·fever or
G3195.2 V-PAP-ASM μέλλοντα (1x)
Ac 23:27 the Judeans and·also *was* about to·be·eliminated by
G3195.2 V-PAP-GSF μελλούσης (1x)
1Pe 5:1 and·also a·partner of·the glory about to·be·revealed.
G3195.2 V-PAP-NSM μέλλων (1x)
Ac 21:37 And as Paul was·about to·be·brought into the
G3195.2 V-PAP-NPM μέλλοντες (2x)
Jac 2:12 and so do: as ones·about to·be·judged through *the*
Rv 6:11 ·fulfilled, the·ones about to·be·killed also as they·
G3195.2 V-PAS-3S μέλλῃ (1x)
Mk 13:4 all these·things are·about to·be·entirely·completed?
G3195.2 V-IAI-3P ἔμελλον (1x)
Ac 21:27 seven days were·about to·be·entirely·completed,
G3195.3 V-PAI-1S μέλλω (1x)
Mt 20:22 to·drink the cup that I·myself am·about to·drink?
G3195.3 V-PAI-2S μέλλεις (1x)
Ac 22:26 saying, "Clearly·see what you·are·about to·do, for
G3195.3 V-PAI-2P μέλλετε (1x)
Rm 8:13 if yeu·live according·to flesh, yeu·are·about to·die.
G3195.3 V-PAI-3S μέλλει (7x)
Lk 19:11 of·God is·about to·be·made·totally·apparent at·
Ac 23:3 to him, "God is·about to·pummel you, O·wall
Ac 26:23 dead·men *and* is·about to·fully·proclaim light to·
Mt 16:27 "For the Son of·Clay·Man† is·about to·come in the
Rv 2:10 Behold, the Slanderer is·about to·cast *some* from·
Rv 3:2 ·establish the·things remaining that are·about to·die,
Rv 17:8 is not. And it·is·about to·ascend from·out of·the
G3195.3 V-PAN μέλλειν (1x)
Ac 25:4 and *that* he·himself was·about to·depart *for·there*
G3195.3 V-PAP-APM μέλλοντας (1x)
Heb 1:14 on·account·of the·ones about to·inherit Salvation?
G3195.3 V-PAP-DSM μέλλοντι (1x)
Ac 20:3 against·him by the Jews as·he·was·about to·sail into
G3195.3 V-PAP-GSN μέλλοντος (1x)
Heb 10:27 a·fiery indignation, *which·is* about ·to·devour
G3195.3 V-PAP-GSF μελλούσης (1x)
Rv 12:4 of·the woman, the·one about to·produce·birth, in·
G3195.3 V-PAP-GSM μέλλοντος (1x)
2Ti 4:1 Jesus Anointed (the·one about to·judge living·men
G3195.3 V-PAP-GPN μελλόντων (1x)
Ac 26:22 and Moses spoke of·as·being·about to·happen:
G3195.3 V-PAP-GPM μελλόντων (2x)
1Ti 1:16 a·primary·example for·the·ones about to·trust on
Rv 8:13 of·the three angels, the·ones about to·sound!"
G3195.3 V-PAP-NSM μέλλων (4x)
Jn 12:4 Simon's *son*, the·one about to·hand him over) says,
Ac 26:2 *for* I·am·about to·make·my·defense this·day before
Heb 8:5 ·divinely·instructed·by·Yahweh when·he·was·about
Mt 11:14 *it*, he·himself is EliJah, the·one about to·come.
G3195.3 V-IAI-1S ἔμελλον (1x)
Rv 10:4 spoke their·own voices, I·was·about to·write. And
G3195.3 V-IAI-3S ἔμελλεν (4x)
Jn 6:6 had·personally·known what he·was·about to·do.
Lk 9:31 exodus which he·was·about to·completely·fulfill in
Lk 10:1 city and place where he·himself was·about to·come.
Ac 16:27 his·dagger, he·was·about to·eliminate himself,
G3195.3 V-IAI-3S-ATT ἤμελλεν (3x)
Jn 6:71 for *it·was* this·man *that* was·about to·hand him over
Lk 19:4 him, because *Jesus* was·about to·go through that
Heb 11:8 into the place which he·was·about to·receive for
G3195.3 V-IAI-3P ἔμελλον (1x)
Jn 7:39 the·ones trusting in him were·about to·receive, for
G3195.4 V-PAI-3P μέλλουσιν (1x)
Jn 6:15 So Jesus, knowing that they·are·about to·come and
G3195.4 V-PAP-ASF μέλλουσαν (1x)
Heb 13:14 but·rather we·seek·for the·one about·to·come.
G3195.4 V-PAP-DSM μέλλοντι (2x)
Mt 12:32 in this present·age, nor in the·one about·to·come.
Eph 1:21 ·age, but·rather also in the·one about·to·come.
G3195.4 V-PAP-GSF μελλούσης (2x)
1Ti 4:8 for·the present *age*, and for·the *age* about·to·come."
Rv 3:10 of·the proof·trial, the·one about to·come upon all
G3195.4 V-PAP-GSM μέλλοντος (1x)
Heb 6:5 *the* miraculous·powers of·*the*·age about·to·come,
G3195.4 V-PAP-GPN μελλόντων (1x)
Heb 11:20 Jacob and Esau concerning things·to·come.
G3195.4 V-PAP-NPN μέλλοντα (2x)
Rm 8:38 ·currently·standing, nor things·about·to·come,
1Co 3:22 ·currently·standing, or things·about·to·come— all
G3195.5 V-PAI-2S μέλλεις (1x)
Rv 2:10 not·one·bit·of which·things you·are·about to·suffer.

G3195.5 V-PAI-3S μέλλει (1x)
Mt 17:12 the Son of·Clay·Man† is·about to·suffer under
G3195.5 V-IAI-3S-ATT ἤμελλεν (4x)
Jn 4:47 and may·heal his son, for he·was·about to·die.
Jn 12:33 signifying what·kind·of death he·was·about to·die.
Jn 18:32 signifying what·kind·of death he·was·about to·die.
Lk 7:2 dearly·valued by·him, was·about to·completely·die,
G3195.6 V-PAP-APN μέλλοντα (1x)
Lk 21:36 all these·things, the·ones being·about to·happen,
G3195.6 V-PAS-3S μέλλῃ (1x)
Lk 21:7 whenever these·things should·be·about to·happen?
G3195.6 V-IAI-3S ἔμελλεν (2x)
Jn 11:51 he·prophesied that Jesus was·about to·die on·behalf
Ac 27:33 And even·until daylight was·about to·occur, Paul
G3195.7 V-FAI-2P μελλήσετε (1x)
Mt 24:6 And yeu·shall·happen to·hear·of wars and rumors
G3195.8 V-PAN μέλλειν (2x)
Ac 24:15 *that though it·is* still·impending, there·shall·be a·
Ac 27:10 I·observe that the impending voyage shall·be with
G3195.8 V-PAP-ASN μέλλον (1x)
1Ti 6:19 a·good foundation for the impending *age*, in·order·
G3195.8 V-PAP-ASF μέλλουσαν (3x)
Heb 2:5 *that* he·subjugated the impending *brand-new* Land,
Gal 3:23 in·order·for the impending trust to·be·revealed.
Rm 8:18 alongside the impending glory to·be·revealed in us.
G3195.8 V-PAP-APN μέλλοντα (1x)
Mk 10:32 to·them the impending·things·about to·befall him,
G3195.8 V-PAP-GSN μέλλοντος (1x)
Ac 24:25 self-restraint, and the impending judgment *that*
G3195.8 V-PAP-GSF μελλούσης (2x)
Lk 3:7 ·indication to·yeu to·flee from the impending wrath?
Mt 3:7 ·indication to·yeu to·flee from the impending wrath?
G3195.8 V-PAP-GSM μέλλοντος (1x)
Rm 5:14 violation, who is a·figure of·the·one impending.
G3195.8 V-PAP-GPN μελλόντων (3x)
Heb 9:11 ·Priest of·the impending beneficially·good·things,
Heb 10:1 of·the impending beneficially·good *activities* (not
Col 2:17 ·things are a·shadow of·the·things impending, but
G3195.9 V-PAI-3P μέλλουσιν (1x)
Ac 20:38 that no·longer would·they·*be·able* to·observe his

G3196 μέλος mélôs *n.* (35x)

G3196 N-NSN μέλος (5x)
Jac 3:5 the tongue is a·small member, yet it·boasts·greatly.
1Co 12:14 the Body is not one member, but·rather many.
1Co 12:19 And if they·were all one member, where·is the
1Co 12:26 And if one member suffers, all the members
1Co 12:26 *with·it*; or·if one member is·glorified, all the
G3196 N-NPN μέλη (12x)
Rm 12:4 in one body, but all the members have not the same
Rm 12:5 and each one the members of·one·another.
1Co 6:15 that yeur bodies are members of·Anointed-One?
1Co 12:12 members, and all the members of·the one body
1Co 12:20 But now in·fact *they·are* many members, but one
1Co 12:22 so·much more *those* members of·the Body, the·
1Co 12:25 ·rather *that* the members should·be·anxious the
1Co 12:26 suffers, all the members suffer·together *with·it*;
1Co 12:26 is·glorified, all the members rejoice·together.
1Co 12:27 Body and members from·among a·portion *of·it*,
Eph 4:25 ' because we·are members of·one·another.
Eph 5:30 because we·are members of·his Body, from·out·of·
G3196 N-APN μέλη (10x)
Rm 6:13 ·not·even present yeur members *as* instruments of·
Rm 6:13 dead·men, and yeur members *as* instruments of·
Rm 6:19 For just·as yeu·presented yeur members *as* slaves
Rm 6:19 now yeu·must·present yeur members *as* slaves to·
Rm 12:4 For exactly·as we·have many members in one body
1Co 6:15 after·taking·up the members of·Anointed-One,
1Co 6:15 should·I·make *them* members of·a·prostitute?
1Co 12:12 body is one and has many members, and all the
1Co 12:18 ·now, God himself·placed the members, each one
Col 3:5 Accordingly, deaden yeur members *to* the·things
G3196 N-DPN μέλεσιν (5x)
Rm 7:5 did·operate in our members in·order to·bear·fruit
Rm 7:23 Law in my members, strategically·warring·against
Rm 7:23 of·Moral·Failure, the·one being in my members.
Jac 3:6 is·fully·established among our members, the·one
Jac 4:1 which·are·strategically·warring in yeur members?
G3196 N-GPN μελῶν (2x)
Mt 5:29 that one of·your members should·completely·perish,
Mt 5:30 that one of·your members should·completely·perish,
EG3196 (1x)
1Co 12:23 And those *members* of·the body, which·we·

G3197 Μελχί Mêlchí *n/p.* (2x)

מַלְכִּי mạl·ḳıy [Hebrew]
Roots:H4428 xLangAlso:H4439 H4441 H4443
G3197.2 N/P-PRI Μελχί (2x)
Lk 3:24 ·Matthat, *son* of·Levi, *son* of·Malki, *son* of·Janna,
Lk 3:28 *son* of·Malki, *son* of·Addi, *son* of·Qosam, *son* of·

G3198 Μελχι•σεδέκ Mêlchisêdék *n/p.* (9x)

Μελχι•σεδέϗ Mêlchisêdéq
[Greek, Octuagint]
מַלְכִּי־צֶדֶק mạl·ḳıy-tsẹdeq [Hebrew]
Roots:H4442
G3198.2 N/P-PRI Μελχισεδέκ (9x)
Heb 5:6 ·order of·MalkiTsedeq·*(King·of·Righteousness)*,"
Heb 5:10 according·to the assigned·order of·MalkiTsedeq."
Heb 6:20 according·to the assigned·order of·MalkiTsedeq.
Heb 7:1 For this MalkiTsedeq (King of·Salem, Priest of·
Heb 7:10 of·*his*·father when MalkiTsedeq met·up with·him.
Heb 7:11 ·to the assigned·order of·MalkiTsedeq and not to·
Heb 7:15 ·to the similarity of·MalkiTsedeq, another priest·
Heb 7:17 according·to the assigned·order of·MalkiTsedeq."
Heb 7:21 according·to the assigned·order of·MalkiTsedeq"")

G3199 μέλω mélō *v.* (10x)

See:G3191 G3195
G3199.2 V-PAM-3S μελέτω (1x)
1Co 7:21 ·forth *being* a·slave? Let·it·matter not to·you, but·
G3199.2 V-PQI-3S μέλει (7x)
Jn 10:13 ·worker, and it·does·not matter to·him concerning
Lk 10:40 "Lord, does·it·not matter to·you that my sister
Mt 22:16 in truth, and it·does·not matter to·you concerning
Mk 4:38 "Mentor, does·it·not matter to·you that we·
Mk 12:14 and *that* it·does·not matter to·you concerning
1Pe 5:7 upon him, because it·matters to·him concerning yeu
1Co 9:9 ' ¿!·Do the oxen matter to·God?
G3199.2 V-IAI-3S ἔμελεν (2x)
Jn 12:6 this, not because it·was·mattering to·him concerning
Ac 18:17 ·even·one of·these·things was·mattering to·Gallio.

G3200 μεμβράνα mêmbrána *n.* (1x)

Compare:G5489 G1992
G3200 N-APF μεμβράνας (1x)
2Ti 4:13 the official·scrolls, *but* especially the parchments.

G3201 μέμφομαι mémphômai *v.* (3x)

Compare:G3469 See:G3437 G3470
G3201.2 V-PNI-3S μέμφεται (1x)
Rm 9:19 to·me, "Why still does·he·find·fault? For who has·
G3201.2 V-PNP-NSM μεμφόμενος (1x)
Heb 8:8 For finding·fault with·them, he·says, "'Behold,
G3201.2 V-ADI-3P ἐμέμψαντο (1x)
Mk 7:2 that is, with·unwashed *hands*, they·found·fault.

G3202 μεμψί•μοιρος mêmpsímôirôs *adj.* (1x)

Roots:G3201 Compare:G1113 See:G3313
G3202.2 A-NPM μεμψίμοιροι (1x)
Jud 1:16 grumblers, malcontented·faultfinders, traversing

G3303 μέν mén *prt.* (196x)

Compare:G3375 See:G1161
G3303 PRT μέν (193x)
Jn 7:12 crowds concerning him. In·fact, they·were·saying,
Jn 10:41 "John, in·fact, did not·even·one miraculous·sign,
Jn 11:6 he·heard that he·was·sick, in·fact he·remained two
Jn 16:9 moral·failure, in·fact because they·did·not trust in
Jn 16:22 "And accordingly, yeu·yeurselves in·fact now have
Jn 19:24 lots upon my attire." In·fact, in·due·course, the
Jn 19:32 the *Roman* soldiers came and in·fact broke·apart the
Jn 20:30 Now·then in·fact, Jesus also did many other signs
Lk 3:16 to·absolutely·all *of·them*, "In·fact, I·myself immerse
Lk 3:18 Accordingly in·fact, also exhorting many other·
Lk 8:5 sowed, *there·was* that·which in·fact fell directly·by
Lk 10:2 he·was·saying to them, "In·fact, the harvest *is* large,
Lk 10:6 And, in·fact, if a·son of·peace should·be there,
Lk 11:48 because they·themselves in·fact killed them, and
Lk 13:9 And·if, in·fact, it·should·produce fruit, *good*! But·
Lk 22:22 And in·fact, the Son of·Clay·Man† departs
Lk 23:33 and·also the criminals, in·fact one at *the* right·
Lk 23:41 And we·ourselves in·fact justly, for we·receive·in·
Lk 23:56 and ointments, and in·fact, they·kept·still *over* the
Ac 1:1 In·fact, the first account I·made, O TheoPhilus,
Ac 1:5 Because in·fact, John immersed in·water, but yeu
Ac 1:6 Accordingly in·fact, after·coming·together, they·
Ac 1:18 (Accordingly in·fact, this·man procured an·open·
Ac 2:41 Accordingly in·fact, after·fully·accepting his
Ac 3:21 Whom in·fact it·is·mandatory·for heaven to·accept
Ac 3:22 "For Moses in·fact declared to the fathers,
Ac 4:16 ·clay†? For that in·fact a·notable miraculous·sign
Ac 5:23 saying, "In·fact, we·found the dungeon having·
Ac 5:41 the *ambassadors*, in·fact, were·departing from in·
Ac 8:4 Accordingly in·fact, the·ones being·dispersed went·
Ac 8:25 In·due·course, in·fact, after·thoroughly·testifying
Ac 9:7 ·him stood in·stunned·silence, in·fact hearing the
Ac 9:31 Accordingly in·fact, the Called·Out·citizenries in
Ac 11:16 he·was·saying, 'John in·fact immersed in·water,
Ac 11:19 Accordingly in·fact, the·ones being·dispersed by
Ac 12:5 Accordingly in·fact, Peter was·kept in the prison·
Ac 13:4 Accordingly in·fact, after·being·sent·forth by the
Ac 13:36 "For in·fact David, after·tending to·the counsel of·
Ac 14:3 Accordingly in·fact, they lingered a·sufficient time,
Ac 14:4 ·the city was·torn·in·two. And in·fact, the·one *part*
Ac 14:12 In·fact, both they·were·calling BarNabas, Zeus, and
Ac 15:3 Accordingly in·fact, being·sent·onward·on·their·
Ac 15:30 Accordingly in·fact, after·being·dismissed, they·
Ac 16:5 Accordingly in·fact, the Called·Out·citizenries
Ac 17:12 Accordingly in·fact, many from·among them
Ac 17:17 Accordingly in·fact, he·was·having·discussions in
Ac 17:30 "Accordingly in·fact, after·previously·overlooking
Ac 17:32 And in·fact, after·hearing of·a·resurrection of·
Ac 18:14 to·the Jews, "Accordingly in·fact, if it·were some
Ac 19:4 Then Paul declared, "In·fact, John did·immerse
Ac 19:32 In·fact, in·due·course, some were·yelling·out a·
Ac 19:38 "Accordingly in·fact, if Demetrius and the
Ac 21:39 But Paul declared, "In·fact, I·myself am a·man·of·
Ac 22:3 "I·myself am in·fact a·man *who·is* a·Jew, having·
Ac 22:9 being together with·me, in·fact, did·distinctly·view
Ac 23:8 For in·fact, *the* Sadducees say *that* there·is not a·
Ac 23:18 So·then in·fact, the *centurion*, personally·taking
Ac 23:22 So·then in·fact, the regiment·commander
Ac 23:31 So·then in·fact, the soldiers, according·to the
Ac 25:4 Now·then in·fact, Festus answered *for* Paul to·be·
Ac 25:11 For if in·fact, I·am·a·harmful·offender, or have·
Ac 26:4 "Accordingly in·fact, all the Judeans have·
Ac 26:9 "Accordingly in·fact, I·myself (within·myself)
Ac 27:21 "O Men, in·fact it·was·necessary *for·yeu* to·
Ac 27:41 they·ran the boat aground; and in·fact, the bow,
Ac 27:44 the rest *got there*, in·fact, some·men on planks,
Ac 28:5 Now·then, in·fact, after·jostling·off the venomous·
Ac 28:22 ·things you·contemplate, for in·fact, as·concerning
Ac 28:24 And in·fact, they·were·persuaded by·the·things
Heb 1:7 And, in·fact, he·says unto the angels, "'*This·is* the·
Heb 3:5 And in·fact, Moses *was* trustworthy in all his house
Heb 6:16 For men·of·clay† in·fact swear by·the·one greater·
Heb 7:2 all·things. First, in·fact, being·translated *from*·
Heb 7:5 And in·fact, the·ones from·among the Sons of·Levi
Heb 7:8 And here *and·now*, in·fact, *are* tithes *that* dying
Heb 7:11 Accordingly in·fact, if perfection was·through the
Heb 7:18 For there·is, in·fact, a·cancellation of·a·preceding
Heb 7:21 (For in·fact, the priests·that·offer·sacrifices were
Heb 7:23 And, in·fact, many·in·number are the·ones

Mμ

Heb 8:4 For if, in·fact, he·were on earth, he·would not·even
Heb 9:1 Accordingly in·fact, the first Tabernacle also was·
Heb 9:6 the priests·that·offer·sacrifices, in·fact, continually
Heb 9:23 a·necessity *for* the·things (in·fact, *the* explicit·
Heb 10:11 And in·fact, every priest·that·offers·sacrifices stands
Heb 10:33 in·fact, while·yeu·were·being·made·a·public·
Heb 11:15 And in·fact, if they·were·reminiscing of·that
Heb 12:9 Furthermore, in·fact, we·had fathers of·our flesh,
Heb 12:10 For in·fact, they, just·for few days, were·
Heb 12:11 And in·fact, all education·and·discipline,
Gal 4:8 Moreover in·fact, when not having·seen God, yeu·
Gal 4:23 But·rather in·fact, the·one birthed·from·out of·the
Gal 4:24 the two covenants. One in·fact *is* from Mount Sinai
Mt 3:11 In·fact, I·myself immerse yeu in water for
Mt 9:37 he·says to·his disciples, "In·fact, the harvest *is* large
Mt 10:13 And if, in·fact the home should·be worthy, *let* yeur
Mt 13:4 he·himself *went·forth* to·sow, in·fact, some *seeds*
Mt 13:8 ·one, and were·giving fruit, in·fact some *seed* a·
Mt 13:23 ·then bears·fruit and produces, in·fact, some *seed*
Mt 13:32 which in·fact is smaller·than all the variety·of·
Mt 16:3 ·acting·hypocrites, in·fact yeu·know to·discern the
Mt 16:14 And they·declared, "In·fact, *some say* John the
Mt 17:11 declared to·them, "In·fact EliJah does·come first
Mt 20:23 he·says to·them, "In·fact, yeu·shall·drink of·my
Mt 21:35 *handled·them·dishonorably*. In·fact, *there·was*
Mt 22:5 *his call*, they·went·away, in·fact, one to his·own
Mt 22:8 he·says to·his slaves, 'In·fact the wedding is ready,
Mt 23:27 ·whitewashed, which in·fact outwardly appear
Mt 23:28 "In·this·manner, in·fact, yeu also outwardly
Mt 25:15 And in·fact, to·one he·gave five talants·of·silver,
Mt 25:33 And in·fact, he·shall·set the sheep at his right·hand
Mt 26:24 "In·fact, the Son of·Clay·Man† heads·on·out just·
Mt 26:41 ·may·not enter into a·proof·trial. In·fact, the spirit
Mk 1:8 In·fact, I·myself immersed yeu in water, but he·
Mk 4:4 he *began* to·sow, that, in·fact, *seed* fell directly·by
Mk 9:12 to·them, "EliJah, in·fact, after·coming first, does·
Mk 10:39 And Jesus declared to·them, "In·fact, the cup that
Mk 12:5 and·then many others (in·fact, thrashing some and
Mk 14:21 "In·fact, the Son of·Clay·Man† heads·on·out, just·
Mk 14:38 ·may·not enter into a·proof·trial. In·fact, the spirit
Mk 16:19 Now·then in·fact, after the Lord spoke to·them,
Rm 1:8 First in·fact, I·give·thanks to·my God through Jesus
Rm 2:7 In·fact, to·the·ones *working* according·to a·patient·
Rm 2:8 of·being·contentious, and in·fact, being·obstinate to·
Rm 2:25 For in·fact, circumcision benefits if you·should·
Rm 3:2 in·each and·every manner. For in·fact, first·of·all,
Rm 5:16 one already·morally·failing. For in·fact, the
Rm 6:11 ·reckon also yeurselves to·be in·fact dead to·the
Rm 7:12 As·such, in·fact, the Torah-Law *is* holy, and the
Rm 7:25 So accordingly in·fact, with·the mind, I myself am·
Rm 8:10 if Anointed-One *is* in yeu, in·fact, the body *is* dead
Rm 8:17 *we·are* heirs, heirs in·fact of·God and co-heirs
Rm 9:21 ·the same lump·of·clay to·make, in·fact, one vessel
Rm 10:1 Brothers, in·fact my heart's good·purpose and
Rm 11:13 ·as I·myself am in·fact an·ambassador of·Gentiles,
Rm 11:22 a·severe·cutting-off from·God! In·fact, upon the·
Rm 11:28 In·fact, according·to the good·news, *they·are*
Rm 14:2 In·fact, one trusts that·he·may·eat all·things, but
Rm 14:5 In·fact, someone judges one·day *to·be* above·and·
Rm 14:20 ·God for·the·sake·of food. In·fact, all·things *are*
Rm 16:19 But·yet I·want yeu, in·fact, to·be wise in·regard·
Jac 3:17 *that·is* from·above is first, in·fact, morally·clean,
Jud 1:8 these *irreverent* dreamers, in·fact, contaminate flesh,
Jud 1:10 But in·fact, these·men revile what·many·things
Jud 1:22 And in·fact, show·mercy to·some while·using·
Php 1:15 In·fact, some officially·proclaim the Anointed-One
Php 1:16 In·fact, they·fully·proclaim Anointed-One out of·
Php 1:28 ·fully·set·opposed— which in·fact is an·indicator
Php 2:23 Accordingly in·fact, I·expect to·send this·man
Php 3:1 Rejoice in *the* Lord! In·fact, *it·is* not tiresome for·
Php 3:13 to·have·grasped *it*. But in·fact, *there·is* one·thing
1Pe 1:20 In·fact, *a·sacrificial·lamb*, with·him·having·been·
1Pe 2:4 ·living stone, in·fact, having·been·rejected·as·unfit
1Pe 2:14 as being·sent through him, in·fact, for retribution
1Pe 3:18 to·God, in·fact having·been·put·to·death in·flesh,
1Pe 4:6 they·may·be·judged in·fact according·to men·of·
1Pe 4:14 rests upon yeu. In·fact, according·to their·part, he·
1Th 2:18 we·wanted to·come to yeu, in·fact I Paul, also
Tit 1:15 In·fact, to·the pure, all·things *are* pure.
1Co 1:12 each·one of·yeu says, "In·fact, I·myself am of·
1Co 1:18 cross) is foolishness, in·fact, to·the·ones who·are·
1Co 1:23 *which·is* in·fact a·scandalous·offense to·Jews and
1Co 2:15 the spiritual·one scrutinizes, in·fact, all·things, but
1Co 3:4 someone should·say, "In·fact, I·myself am of·Paul,
1Co 5:3 For I, in·fact, even·though being·absent in·the body
1Co 6:4 Accordingly in·fact, if yeu·should·have arbitrations
1Co 6:7 Accordingly in·fact, even·now there·is altogether a·
1Co 7:7 gracious·bestowment from·out of·God, in·fact, one
1Co 9:24 the·ones running in a·stadium·race in·fact all run,
1Co 9:25 in·all·things. Accordingly in·fact, those *runners*
1Co 11:7 For in·fact a·man is·obligated not to·be·fully·
1Co 11:14 the nature itself instruct yeu, in·fact, that if a·man
1Co 11:18 For in·fact first·of·all, as·yeu are·coming·together
1Co 11:21 prior·to *others*; and in·fact, one goes·hungry, and
1Co 12:8 For in·fact to·one is·given through the Spirit a·
1Co 12:20 But now in·fact *they·are* many members, but one
1Co 12:28 even, in·fact, some·of·whom *which* God laid·out
1Co 14:17 For in·fact, you give·thanks well, but·yet the
1Co 15:39 same flesh, but·rather in·fact *there·is* one *kind·of*
1Co 15:40 terrestrial bodies, but·yet in·fact the glory of·the
1Co 15:51 I·relay to·yeu a·mystery. In·fact, we·shall·not all
2Co 2:16 In·fact, to·some *we·are* an·aroma of·death unto
2Co 4:12 As·such in·fact, the death operates in us, but the
2Co 8:17 Because in·fact, he·accepted the exhortation; but
2Co 9:1 For, in·fact, concerning the service to the holy·ones,
2Co 10:1 who in personal·presence *am* in·fact lowly among
2Co 10:10 Because in·fact, *the·one wrongly reckoning*
2Co 11:4 For in·fact, if the·one who·is·coming does·
2Co 12:12 In·fact, the signs of·an·ambassador were·
Eph 4:11 And he·himself, in·fact, *is the·one who* gave·forth
Col 2:23 ·very·things are in·fact a·rationalization of·wisdom,
2Ti 1:10 Anointed, *who·is*, in·fact, *the·one* already·fully·
2Ti 2:20 and some *are·set·out* in·fact unto honor, and some
2Ti 4:4 and in·fact, they·shall·turn the inner·sense·of·hearing

EG3303 (3x)

Heb 10:33 and *in·fact*, while·yeu·were·becoming partners
Rm 9:30 ·then, what shall·we·state? *In·fact*, that Gentiles,
1Co 14:18 *In·fact*, I·give·thanks to·my God, speaking more·

G3304 μεν•οῦν•γε mĕnôungĕ *prt.* (4x)
Roots:G3303 G3767 G1065

G3304.1 PRT μενοῦνγε (4x)

Lk 11:28 declared, "As·a·matter·of·fact, supremely·blessed
Rm 9:20 As·a·matter·of·fact, O man·of·clay†, who are you·
Rm 10:18 ¿!·Did they·not hear? As·a·matter·of·fact,
Php 3:8 Moreover, as·a·matter·of·fact, also— I·resolutely·

G3305 μέν•τοι mĕntôi *conj.* (7x)
Roots:G3303 G5104

G3305.1 CONJ μέντοι (1x)

Jn 12:42 Yet·at·the·same·time, consequently·in·fact, many

G3305.2 CONJ μέντοι (6x)

Jn 4:27 with a·woman. However, not·even·one·man
Jn 7:13 However, not·even·one was·speaking with·freeness·
Jn 20:5 the strips·of·linen laying·out, however, he·did·not
Jn 21:4 stood·still upon the shore; however, the disciples
Jac 2:8 If however, yeu·complete *the* Royal Law according·
2Ti 2:19 However·in·fact, the solid foundation of·God

G3306 μένω mĕnō *v.* (121x)
Compare:G5278 G2594 G2553 See:G3438

G3306.1 V-FAI-2P μενεῖτε (1x)

1Jn 2:24 ·remain in yeu, you also shall·remain in the Son,

G3306.1 V-FAI-3S μενεῖ (1x)

1Co 3:14 any·man's work shall·remain which he·built·upon

G3306.1 V-PAI-3S μενεῖ (6x)

Jn 3:36 but·rather the wrath of·God does·remain upon him.
Jn 9:41 Accordingly, yeur moral·failure remains.
2Co 3:14 the·present·day the same veil remains, not being·
2Co 9:9 ·poor·in·need; his righteousness remains into the
2Ti 2:13 we·do·not·trust, that·one still·remains trustworthy;
1Jn 3:9 moral·failure, because his Seed remains in him. And

G3306.1 V-PAI-3P μένουσιν (1x)

1Co 15:6 whom the majority remain unto this·moment, but

G3306.1 V-PAM-2P μένετε (1x)

Lk 10:7 And remain in the same home, eating and drinking

G3306.1 V-PAM-3S μενέτω (2x)

1Co 7:11 if she·is·separated, she·must·remain unmarried, or
1Co 7:20 he·was·called·forth, in this he·must·remain.

G3306.1 V-PAN μένειν (2x)

Jn 21:22 "If I·should·want him to·remain until I·come, what·
Jn 21:23 "If I·should·want him to·remain until I·come, what·

G3306.1 V-PAP-ASN μένον (1x)

Jn 1:33 the Spirit descending, and remaining upon him, the·

G3306.1 V-PAP-NSN μένον (2x)

Ac 5:4 While·remaining, was·it·not·indeed remaining your·
2Co 3:11 *is* the·one *of·the Spirit* remaining in glory.

G3306.1 V-PAS-3S μένῃ (1x)

Jn 15:16 fruit and yeur fruit should·remain, in·order·that

G3306.1 V-IAI-3S ἔμενεν (1x)

Ac 5:4 ·remaining, was·it·not·indeed remaining your·own?

G3306.1 V-AAI-3S ἔμεινεν (4x)

Jn 7:9 these·things to·them, he·remained in Galilee.
Jn 11:6 that he·was·sick, in·fact he·remained two days still
Ac 27:41 bow, after·getting·stuck, remained unshakable,
2Ti 4:20 Erastus remained at Corinth, but Trophimus, being·

G3306.1 V-AAI-3P ἔμειναν (2x)

Jn 2:12 his disciples), and they·remained there not many
Mt 11:23 it·would·have remained as·long·as·unto the

G3306.1 V-AAM-2P μείνατε (2x)

Mt 26:38 ·grieved unto death. Yeu·remain here and keep·
Mk 14:34 ·grieved unto death. Yeu·remain here and keep·

G3306.1 V-AAN μεῖναι (1x)

Rv 17:10 it·is·mandatory·for him to·remain a·little·while.

G3306.1 V-AAS-3S μείνῃ (6x)

Jn 15:6 "If someone should·not remain in me, he·is·already·
Jn 15:11 to·yeu in·order·that my joy may·remain in yeu, and
Jn 19:31 in·order·that the bodies should·not remain upon the
Heb 12:27 ·that the·things not being·shaken may·remain.
1Co 7:40 if in·this·manner she·should·remain, according·to
1Jn 2:24 ·heard from *the* beginning should·remain in yeu,

G3306.1 V-AAS-3P μείνωσιν (2x)

Ac 27:31 "Unless these should·remain with the sailing·ship,
1Co 7:8 good for·them if they·should·remain even·as I·also

G3306.2 V-FAI-1S μενῶ (1x)

Php 1:25 ·seen that I·shall·abide and shall·continue·together

G3306.2 V-FAI-2P μενεῖτε (2x)

Jn 15:10 ·keep my commandments, yeu·shall·abide in my
1Jn 2:27 it·already·instructed yeu), yeu·shall·abide in him.

G3306.2 V-PAI-1S μενῶ (1x)

Jn 15:10 my Father's commandments and abide in his love.

G3306.2 V-PAI-1P μένομεν (1x)

1Jn 4:13 By this we·know that we·abide in him, and he·

G3306.2 V-PAI-2S μένεις (1x)

Jn 1:38 is·to·say Mentor), "where·do you·abide?"

G3306.2 V-PAI-3S μενεῖ (17x)

Jn 1:39 They·came and saw where he·abides, and they·
Jn 6:56 flesh, and drinking my blood, abides in me, and·I in
Jn 12:24 into the soil, should·die, it abides alone. But if it·
Jn 12:34 ·the Torah-Law that the Anointed-One abides to the
Jn 14:17 ·know him, because he·abides personally·with yeu,
Heb 7:3 of·God, he·abides a·priest·that·offers·a·sacrifice into
1Jn 2:10 The·one loving his brother abides in the light, and
1Jn 2:14 and the Redemptive-word of·God abides in yeu, and
1Jn 2:17 doing the will of·God abides into the coming·age.
1Jn 2:27 already·received from him presently·abides in yeu,
1Jn 3:14 not presently·loving the brother abides in Death.
1Jn 3:17 how·does the love of·God presently·abide in him?
1Jn 3:24 his commandments presently·abides in *God*, and
1Jn 3:24 And by this we·know that he·presently·abides in us,
1Jn 4:12 If we·should·love one·another, God abides in us,

1Jn 4:15 is the Son of·God, God abides in him, and he·
1Jn 4:16 and the·one abiding in the Love abides in God, and
G3306.2 V-PAM-2P μένετε (3x)
Lk 9:4 yeu·should·enter into, there abide, and from·there
Mk 6:10 into a·home, there abide until yeu·should·go·forth
1Jn 2:28 And now, dear·children, abide in him, in·order·
G3306.2 V-PAM-3S μενέτω (1x)
1Jn 2:24 Accordingly, let·it·abide in yeu, that·which yeu
G3306.2 V-PAN μένειν (2x)
Ac 28:16 but Paul was·freely·permitted to·abide by himself
1Jn 2:6 The·one saying he·abides in him is·obligated himself
G3306.2 V-PAP-ASF μένουσαν (2x)
1Jn 3:15 does·not have eternal life-above abiding in him.
2Jn 1:2 on·account·of the truth abiding in us and *which* shall·
G3306.2 V-PAP-ASM μένοντα (1x)
Jn 5:38 yeu·do·not have his Redemptive-word abiding in yeu,
G3306.2 V-PAP-GSM μένοντος (1x)
1Pe 1:23 *which·is* living and abiding to the coming·age—
G3306.2 V-PAP-NSM μένων (7x)
Jn 14:10 my·own·self, but the Father abiding in me, he·
Jn 14:25 have·I·spoken to·yeu, while·abiding with yeu.
Jn 15:5 *are* the vine·sprouts. The·one abiding in me and·I in
1Jn 3:6 Any one abiding in him does·not morally·fail.
1Jn 4:16 God is love; and the·one abiding in the Love abides
2Jn 1:9 the·one walking·contrary·to and not abiding in the
2Jn 1:9 ·not have God. The·one abiding in the instruction
G3306.2 V-PAS-3S μένῃ (1x)
Jn 14:16 that he·may·abide with yeu into the coming·age,
G3306.2 V-IAI-3S ἔμενεν (2x)
Lk 8:27 a·garment, and was·not abiding in *any* home, but·
Ac 18:3 being of·the same·trade, he·was·abiding with them
G3306.2 V-AAI-1P ἐμείναμεν (2x)
Ac 21:7 after·greeting the brothers, we·abided with them
Ac 21:8 being from·among the seven), we·abided with him.
G3306.2 V-AAI-3S ἔμεινεν (5x)
Jn 1:32 out of·heaven like a·dove, and he·abided upon him.
Jn 4:40 to·abide with them, and he·abided there two days.
Jn 10:40 John was first immersing; and there he·abided.
Lk 1:56 And Mariam abided together with·her about three
Ac 28:30 And Paul abided a·whole two·years in his·own
G3306.2 V-AAI-3P ἔμειναν (1x)
Jn 1:39 saw where he·abides, and they·abided with him that
G3306.2 V-AAM-2S μεῖνον (1x)
Lk 24:29 ·compelled him, saying, "Abide with us, because
G3306.2 V-AAM-2P μείνατε (4x)
Jn 15:4 "Abide in me, and·I in yeu.
Jn 15:9 loved me, so·also·I loved yeu. Abide in my love.
Ac 16:15 entering into my house, yeu·must·abide *there*."
Mt 10:11 it is worthy, and·there abide until yeu·should·go·
G3306.2 V-AAN μεῖναι (5x)
Jn 4:40 him, they·were·asking him to·abide with them, and
Lk 19:5 today, it·is·necessary·for me to·abide in your house.
Lk 24:29 And he·entered·in to·abide together with·them.
Ac 9:43 *such·for* him to·abide a·significant·number·of days
Ac 18:20 But with·them asking *him* to·abide a·longer time
G3306.2 V-AAP-NPM μείναντες (1x)
Ac 20:15 to Samos. And after·abiding in Trogyllium, the
G3306.2 V-AAS-2P μείνητε (2x)
Jn 15:4 not·even *can* yeu unless yeu·should·abide in me.
Jn 15:7 "If yeu·should·abide in me and my utterances
G3306.2 V-AAS-3S μείνῃ (3x)
Jn 12:46 trusting in me, should·not abide in the darkness.
Jn 15:4 ·bear fruit of itself unless it·should·abide in the vine,
Jn 15:7 in me and my utterances should·abide in yeu, yeu·
G3306.3 V-PAI-3P μένουσιν (1x)
Ac 20:23 city, saying that bonds and tribulations await me.
G3306.3 V-IAI-3P ἔμενον (1x)
Ac 20:5 ·on·beforehand, these·men were·awaiting us at
G3306.4 V-PAI-3S μενεῖ (3x)
Jn 8:35 And the slave does·not continue·*to·remain* in the
Jn 8:35 *but* the Son continues·*to·remain* into the coming·age.
1Co 13:13 right·now, these three·things continue: Trust,
G3306.4 V-PAM-2S μένε (1x)
2Ti 3:14 But you·yourself must·continue in the·things·which
G3306.4 V-PAM-3S μενέτω (2x)
Heb 13:1 The brotherly·affection must·continue.
1Co 7:24 brothers, in that·*state* he·must·continue with God.
G3306.4 V-PAN μένειν (1x)
Heb 7:24 But *this·man*, on·account·of him continuing to the
G3306.4 V-PAP-ASF μένουσαν (1x)
Heb 13:14 For here we·have no continuing city, but·rather
G3306.4 V-AAS-2P μείνητε (1x)
Jn 8:31 "If yeu should·continue in my Redemptive-word,
G3306.4 V-AAS-3P μείνωσιν (1x)
1Ti 2:15 provided·that *such women* should·continue in trust
G3306.4 V-LAI-3P μεμενήκεισαν (1x)
1Jn 2:19 ·among us, they·would have·continued with us.
EG3306.4 (1x)
Ac 8:11 ·of *that he·continued* to·have·astonished them *for*
G3306.5 V-PAI-3S μενεῖ (1x)
1Pe 1:25 the utterance of·Yahweh endures to the coming·age.
G3306.5 V-PAP-ASF μένουσαν (2x)
Jn 6:27 but·rather for·the full·meal enduring into eternal
Heb 10:34 ·significantly·better and an·enduring subsistence.
G3306.5 V-PAS-3S μένῃ (1x)
Rm 9:11 determined·purpose may·endure according·to God's

G3307 μερίζω mĕrízō *v.* (14x)
Roots:G3313 Compare:G0873 G5563 G1252
See:G3311 G3312 xLangAlso:H6385
G3307.2 V-AAI-3S ἐμέρισεν (2x)
Rm 12:3 seeing·as God imparted to·each·man a·measure
1Co 7:17 ·*know that* as God imparted to·each·man, each·one
G3307.3 V-AAI-3S ἐμέρισεν (3x)
Heb 7:2 to·whom also AbRaham distributed a·tenth *part*
Mk 6:41 *the people*, and he·distributed the two fish among·
2Co 10:13 standard measure which God distributed to·us, a·
G3307.4 V-AMN μερίσασθαι (1x)
Lk 12:13 declare for·my brother to·divide the inheritance
G3307.4 V-API-3S ἐμερίσθη (1x)
Mt 12:26 Adversary-Accuser, he·is·divided against himself.
G3307.4 V-APP-NSF μερισθεῖσα (2x)
Mt 12:25 "Every kingdom being·divided against itself is·
Mt 12:25 and every city or home being·divided against itself
G3307.4 V-APS-3S μερισθῇ (2x)
Mk 3:24 And if a·kingdom should·be·divided against itself,
Mk 3:25 And if a·home should·be·divided against itself, that
G3307.4 V-RPI-3S μεμέρισται (2x)
Mk 3:26 ·up against himself and has·been·divided, he·is·not
1Co 1:13 The Anointed-One, has·he·been·divided? ¿! Was
G3307.5 V-RPI-3S@ μεμέρισται (1x)
1Co 7:34 There·is·a·distinct·difference *also between* the

G3308 μέριμνα mĕrimna *n.* (6x)
Roots:G3307 Compare:G5431 G4928 See:G3309
G3308 N-NSF μέριμνα (2x)
Mt 13:22 and·yet the anxiety of·this present·age and the
2Co 11:28 daily turmoil: the anxiety of·all the Called·Out·
G3308 N-NPF μέριμναι (1x)
Mk 4:19 yet the anxieties of·this present·age— and the
G3308 N-ASF μέριμναν (1x)
1Pe 5:7 flinging all yeur anxiety upon him, because it·
G3308 N-DPF μερίμναις (1x)
Lk 21:34 and with·anxieties of·things·that·pertain·to·this·,
G3308 N-GPF μεριμνῶν (1x)
Lk 8:14 are·altogether·choked by anxieties and wealth and

G3309 μεριμνάω mĕrimnáō *v.* (19x)
Roots:G3308 Compare:G3349 See:G1959
G3309 V-FAI-3S μεριμνήσει (2x)
Mt 6:34 tomorrow shall·be·anxious·about the·things of·itself
Php 2:20 who genuinely shall·be·anxious·about the·things
G3309 V-PAI-2S μεριμνᾷς (1x)
Lk 10:41 Martha, you·are·anxious and are·disturbed about
G3309 V-PAI-2P μεριμνᾶτε (1x)
Lk 12:26 ·is·least, why are·yeu·anxious concerning the rest?
G3309 V-PAI-3S μεριμνᾷ (4x)
1Co 7:32 unmarried·man is·anxious·about the·things of·the
1Co 7:33 ·one marrying is·anxious·about the·things of·the
1Co 7:34 unmarried·woman is·anxious·about the·things of·
1Co 7:34 ·one marrying is·anxious·about the·things of·the
G3309 V-PAM-2P μεριμνᾶτε (5x)
Lk 12:11 the authorities, do·not be·anxious·about how or
Lk 12:22 I·say to·yeu, do·not be·anxious·about yeur soul,
Mt 6:25 I·say to·yeu, do·not be·anxious·about yeur soul,
Mt 6:28 "And why are·yeu·anxious concerning apparel?
Php 4:6 Be·anxious·about not·even·one·thing, but·rather in
G3309 V-PAP-NSM μεριμνῶν (2x)
Lk 12:25 from·among yeu by·being·anxious is·able to·add
Mt 6:27 from·among yeu by·being·anxious is·able to·add
G3309 V-PAS-3P μεριμνῶσιν (1x)
1Co 12:25 *that* the members should·be·anxious the same
G3309 V-AAS-2P μεριμνήσητε (3x)
Mt 6:31 "So·then, yeu·should·not be·anxious, saying, 'what
Mt 6:34 yeu·should·not be·anxious for tomorrow, for
Mt 10:19 yeu over, yeu·should·not be·anxious·about how or

G3310 μερίς mĕrís *n.* (5x)
Roots:G3313 See:G3311 xLangAlso:H2506
G3310.1 N-NSF μερίς (2x)
Ac 8:21 There·is not a·portion nor·even a·small·chance for·
2Co 6:15 ·*Ruin)*? Or what portion has·one·that·trusts with a·
G3310.1 N-ASF μερίδα (2x)
Lk 10:42 Mary selected the beneficially·good portion, which
Col 1:12 us for the portion of·the allotted·heritage of·the
G3310.2 N-GSF μερίδος (1x)
Ac 16:12 is a·foremost city of·the province of·Macedonia,

G3311 μερισμός mĕrismŏs *n.* (2x)
Roots:G3307 See:G3310
G3311.1 N-DPM μερισμοῖς (1x)
Heb 2:4 ·of miracles and with·distributions of·Holy Spirit,
G3311.2 N-GSM μερισμοῦ (1x)
Heb 4:12 ·penetrating even·unto a·dividing of·soul and spirit

G3312 μεριστής mĕristḗs *n.* (1x)
Roots:G3307 See:G1348
G3312.2 N-ASM μεριστήν (1x)
Lk 12:14 me *as* estate·executor or distributor over yeu?

G3313 μέρος mĕrŏs *n.* (46x)
See:G0266 G3310 xLangAlso:H2506
G3313.ª N-ASN μέρος (1x)
Heb 9:5 is not *the time for·us* to·say *anything* in particular.
G3313.1 N-NSN μέρος (1x)
Rv 21:8 the·ones *who·are* false, their portion *is* in the Lake,
G3313.1 N-ASN μέρος (7x)
Jn 13:8 ·not wash you, you·do·not have a·portion with me."
Lk 12:46 and shall·lay his portion with the·ones distrusting.
Lk 15:12 me the portion of·substance being·stashed·away
Ac 5:2 And bringing a·certain portion, he·laid *it* directly·at
Mt 24:51 him in·two and shall·lay his portion with the stage·
1Co 14:27 at·the most three·men, and a·portion apiece, and
Rv 22:19 God shall·remove his portion from *the* scroll of·
G3313.1 N-APN μέρη (1x)
Jn 21:6 the net to the right·hand portions of·the sailboat, and
G3313.1 N-DSN μέρει (1x)
1Pe 4:16 ·ashamed, but let·him·glorify God in this portion.
G3313.1 N-GSN μέρους (5x)
1Co 12:27 Body and members from·among a·portion *of·it*,
1Co 13:9 For we·know from·out of·a·portion *of·the whole*,
1Co 13:9 *whole*, and we·prophesy from·out of·a·portion.
1Co 13:10 from·out of·a·portion shall·be·fully·rendered·.
1Co 13:12 ·this·moment, I·know from·out of·a·portion, but
EG3313.1 (2x)
Rm 11:16 Now if the *portion of·dough offered as·a* firstfruit
1Pe 4:13 rejoice, according·to·what *portion* yeu·share in·the
G3313.2 N-NSN μέρος (2x)
Jn 19:23 and made four parts, a·part for·each soldier, and·
Ac 23:6 already·knowing that the one part were Sadducees
G3313.2 N-ASN μέρος (2x)
Lk 11:36 ·of·light, not having any part opaquely·dark, *the*
Rv 20:6 ·blessed and holy *is* the·one having part in the First
G3313.2 N-APN μέρη (6x)
Jn 19:23 outer·garments and made four parts, a·part for·each

Ac 2:10 Egypt and *in* the parts of·Libya adjacent·to Cyrene,
Ac 20:2 after·going·throughout those parts and exhorting
Mk 8:10 disciples, he·came into the parts of·Dalmanutha.
Eph 4:9 first into the lowermost parts of·the earth?
Rv 16:19 the Great City became three parts, and the cities of·

G3313.2 N-DSN μέρει (1x)
2Co 9:3 behalf should·be·made·empty on this part; that, just·

G3313.2 N-GSN μέρους (6x)
Ac 23:9 *that·were* of·the Pharisees' part, upon·rising·up,
Rm 11:25 has·happened to·IsraEl *only* in part, *and* only·until
Rm 15:15 I·wrote to·yeu in part as once·again·reminding
2Co 1:14 also yeu·already·acknowledged us in part, that we·
2Co 2:5 *that* he·has·grieved (other·than in part), in·order·that
Eph 4:16 an·effective·working of·each individual part in *its*

G3313.3 N-ASN μέρος (1x)
1Co 11:18 to·subsist among yeu; and I·partly trust some *of·it*

G3313.3 N-GSN μέρους (1x)
Rm 15:24 if first I·should·be partly replenished by yeu.

G3313.4 N-DSN μέρει (1x)
Col 2:16 in drinking, or in participating of·a·Sacred·Feast or

G3313.5 N-ASN μέρος (1x)
Lk 24:42 And they·handed him a·piece of·a·broiled fish and

EG3313.5 (1x)
Lk 24:42 a·piece of·a·broiled fish and *a·piece* of·a·honey

G3313.6 N-APN μέρη (4x)
Ac 19:1 ·throughout the uppermost districts *of·Macedonia*,
Mt 2:22 ·a·dream, he·departed into the districts of·Galilee.
Mt 15:21 YeShua departed into the district of·Tyre and
Mt 16:13 upon·coming into the district of·Caesarea Philippi

G3313.7 N-ASN μέρος (1x)
Ac 19:27 merely this our occupation is·in·danger of·coming

G3313.9 N-DSN μέρει (1x)
2Co 3:10 ·not·even been·glorified in this particular·aspect:

G3314 μεσ•ημβρία mêsēmbría *n.* (8x)
Roots:G3319 G2250 Compare:G3558

G3314.1 N-ASF μεσημβρίαν (1x)
Ac 22:6 ·near to·Damascus around midday, it·happened

EG3314.1 (6x)
Jn 4:6 on the well. It·was *midday* about *the* sixth hour, *and*
Jn 19:14 of·the Passover, and *it·was midday* about *the* sixth
Lk 23:44 Now it·was *midday* about *the* sixth hour, and
Ac 10:9 upon the rooftop to·pray *at·midday* about *the* sixth
Mt 27:45 Now from *midday*, *the* sixth hour, there·was
Mk 15:33 And *at·midday*, with·*the*·sixth hour occurring,

G3314.2 N-ASF μεσημβρίαν (1x)
Ac 8:26 ·up and traverse down *on* the·south·side toward the

G3315 μεσιτεύω mêsitêúō *v.* (1x)
Roots:G3316

G3315.2 V-AAI-3S ἐμεσίτευσεν (1x)
Heb 6:17 ·nature of·his counsel, ratified *it* by·an·oath

G3316 μεσίτης mêsítēs *n.* (7x)
Roots:G3319
xLangEquiv:H4965-1

G3316.1 N-NSM μεσίτης (4x)
Heb 8:6 also *the* mediator of·a·significantly·better covenant,
Heb 9:15 this, he·is *the* mediator of·a·brand-new covenant,
Gal 3:20 Now the mediator is not *a·mediator* of·one *party*,
1Ti 2:5 God, and *there·is* one mediator *between* God and

G3316.1 N-DSM μεσίτῃ (1x)
Heb 12:24 to·YeShua, mediator of·a·fresh·new covenant,

G3316.1 N-GSM μεσίτου (1x)
Gal 3:19 ·assigned through angels in *the* hand of·a·mediator.

EG3316.1 (1x)
Gal 3:20 Now the mediator is not *a·mediator* of·one *party*,

G3317 μεσο•νύκτιον mêsônýktiōn *n.* (4x)
Roots:G3319 G3571 Compare:G4404 G0219
See:G5610

G3317.1 N-ASN μεσονύκτιον (1x)
Ac 16:25 And at midnight Paul and Silas, while·praying,

G3317.1 N-GSN μεσονυκτίου (3x)
Lk 11:5 and shall·traverse to him at·midnight, and should·
Ac 20:7 the conversation so·long·as·unto midnight.
Mk 13:35 *whether* at·early·evening, or at·midnight, or at·

G3318 Μεσο•ποταμία Mêsôpôtamía *n/l.* (2x)
Roots:G3319 G4215
xLangEquiv:H0763 xLangAlso:H6307

G3318.2 N/L-ASF Μεσοποταμίαν (1x)
Ac 2:9 and the·ones residing·in MesoPotamia and *in* Judea

G3318.2 N/L-DSF Μεσοποταμίᾳ (1x)
Ac 7:2 AbRaham while·he·was·still in MesoPotamia, before

G3319 μέσος mếsôs *adj.* (60x)
Roots:G3326 See:G3322 G0303-1

G3319.1 A-NSM μέσος (1x)
Ac 1:18 headfirst, he·burst·open in·the·middle, and all his

G3319.1 A-ASN μέσον (6x)
Jn 19:18 him, *one* on·each·side and Jesus in·*the*·middle.
Lk 6:8 "Rouse·yourself and stand·still in the middle." And
Lk 23:45 curtain of·the Temple was·torn *down the* middle.
Ac 27:27 the Adriatic·Sea, in *the* middle of·the night the
Mt 14:24 the sailboat was even·now in·*the*·middle of·the sea,
1Co 6:5 ·be·able to·discern up *the* middle for·his brothers?

G3319.1 A-DSN μέσῳ (1x)
Ac 4:7 And standing them in the middle, they·inquired, "By

G3319.1 A-GSF μέσης (1x)
Mt 25:6 "And at·the·middle of·night, a·yell has·occurred,

G3319.1 A-GSN μέσου (1x)
2Th 2:7 *is·doing so* until he·should·come out of·*the*·middle.

G3319.2 A-NSM μέσος (1x)
Jn 1:26 in water, but one·stands *in·the* midst of·yeu, whom

G3319.2 A-ASN μέσον (8x)
Jn 20:19 Jesus came and stood·still in the midst. And he·says
Jn 20:26 Jesus came and stood·still in the midst *of·them.* And
Lk 4:35 flinging him in the midst, came·forth from him,
Lk 5:19 together with·the pallet into the midst before Jesus.
Mt 13:25 darnel·weeds up *in·the* midst of·the wheat, and he·
Mk 3:3 "Rouse·yourself *forth* into the midst *of·us.*"
Mk 7:31 Sea of·Galilee, through *the* midst of·the borders of·
Mk 14:60 after·standing·up in the midst, inquired·of Jesus,

G3319.2 A-DSN μέσῳ (31x)
Jn 8:3 in adultery; and after·setting her in *the* midst,
Jn 8:9 ·left·behind— and·also the wife standing in *the* midst.
Lk 2:46 sitting·down in *the* midst of·the instructors, both
Lk 8:7 And other *seed* fell in *the* midst of·the thorns; and the
Lk 10:3 as adolescent·male·lambs in *the* midst of·wolves.
Lk 21:21 ·ones in *the* midst of·it must·depart·beyond·reach;
Lk 22:27 But I·myself am in *the* midst of·yeu as the·one
Lk 22:55 igniting a·fire in *the* midst of·the courtyard and
Lk 22:55 ·together, Peter sat·down in *the* midst of·them.
Lk 24:36 Jesus himself stood·still in *the* midst of·them, and
Ac 1:15 in these days, in *the* midst of·the disciples (and it·
Ac 2:22 did through him in *the* midst of·yeu, just·as yeu·
Ac 17:22 being·settled in *the* midst of·Mars'·Hill, replied,
Ac 27:21 after·being·settled in *the* midst of·them, declared,
Heb 2:12 to·my brothers. In *the* midst of·*the*·gathering, I·
Mt 10:16 yeu as sheep in *the* midst of·wolves. Accordingly,
Mt 14:6 of·HerOdias danced in their midst and satisfied
Mt 18:2 a·little·child, set him in *the* midst of·them
Mt 18:20 in my name, there am·I in *the* midst of·them."
Mk 6:47 the sailboat was in *the* midst of·the sea, and he *was*
Mk 9:36 ·child, he·set him in *the* midst of·them, then taking
Php 2:15 irreproachable, in the·midst of·a·warped and
1Th 2:7 we·were pleasantly·engageable in *the* midst of·yeu,
Rv 1:13 and in *the* midst of·the seven Lampstands, *one* like
Rv 2:1 the·one strolling·about in *the* midst of·the seven
Rv 2:7 which is in *the* midst of·the paradise of·God.
Rv 4:6 And in *the* midst of·the throne, and in·a·circle·around
Rv 5:6 and behold, in *the* midst of·the throne and of·the
Rv 5:6 living·beings, and in *the* midst of·the Elders, a·Lamb
Rv 6:6 I·heard a·voice in *the* midst of·the four living·beings
Rv 22:2 In *the* midst of·its broad·street, and on·both sides of·

G3319.2 A-GSN μέσου (9x)
Jn 8:59 Sanctuary·Atrium going through *the* midst of·them,
Lk 4:30 after·going through *the* midst of·them, departed.
Lk 17:11 he·himself went through *the* midst of·Samaria and
Ac 17:33 Paul went·forth from·among *the* midst of·them.
Ac 23:10 to·seize him from·among *the* midst of·them, and
Mt 13:49 ·ones from·out of·*the*·midst of·the righteous·ones,
1Co 5:2 ·be·entirely·expelled from·among *the* midst of·yeu.
2Co 6:17 ·must·come·out from·among *the* midst of·them and
Col 2:14 it away out of·the midst *of·us*, already·firmly·

G3319.3 A-GSF μέσης (1x)
Ac 26:13 at·mid day, O·king, I·saw in the way a·light from·

G3320 μεσό•τοιχον mêsốtôichôn *n.* (1x)
Roots:G3319 G5109 Compare:G5418

G3320 N-ASN μεσότοιχον (1x)
Eph 2:14 ·down the middle·wall of·hedging *between us*,

G3321 μεσ•ουράνημα mêsôuránēma *n.* (3x)
Roots:G3319 G3772

G3321 N-DSN μεσουρανήματι (3x)
Rv 8:13 an angel flying in mid-heaven, saying with·a·loud
Rv 14:6 angel who·is·flying in *the* mid-heaven, having *the*
Rv 19:17 to·the·ones flying in mid-heaven, "Come·here!

G3322 μεσόω mêsốō *v.* (1x)
Roots:G3319

G3322.2 V-PAP-GSF μεσούσης (1x)
Jn 7:14 But even·now halfway·through the Sacred·Feast *of·*

G3323 Μεσσίας Mêssías *n/p.* (2x)
מָשִׁיחַ mąšhiyąch [Hebrew]
Χριστός Christós [Greek translation]
Roots:H4899 Compare:G5547

G3323.2 N/P-NSM Μεσσίας (1x)
Jn 4:25 "I·personally·know that Messiah is·coming, the·one

G3323.2 N/P-ASM Μεσσίαν (1x)
Jn 1:41 says to·him, "We·have·found the Messiah," which,

G3324 μεστός mêstós *adj.* (8x)
Compare:G4134

G3324 A-NSF μεστή (2x)
Jac 3:8 bad, *and* exceedingly·full of·deadly venom.
Jac 3:17 readily·compliant, exceedingly·full of·mercy and

G3324 A-NSN μεστόν (1x)
Jn 19:29 ·set·out a·vessel exceedingly·full of·wine·vinegar.

G3324 A-NPM μεστοί (2x)
Mt 23:28 yeu·are exceedingly·full of·stage·acting·hypocrisy
Rm 15:14 also are exceedingly·full of·beneficial·goodness,

G3324 A-ASN μεστόν (1x)
Jn 21:11 ·ground, *with·it being* exceedingly·full of·big fish

G3324 A-APM μεστούς (2x)
Rm 1:29 malice; *being* exceedingly·full of·envy, murder,
2Pe 2:14 eyes exceedingly·full of·alluring·adultery and not·

G3325 μεστόω mêstốō *v.* (1x)
Roots:G3324 Compare:G4130

G3325.1 V-RPP-NPM μεμεστωμένοι (1x)
Ac 2:13 These·men·are having·been·excessively·filled with·.

G3326 μετά mêtá *prep.* (474x)
Compare:G1722 G4862 See:G0575 G1537 G1519
G3319 G4314
(abbreviated listing for G3326)

G3326.1 PREP μετά (355x)
(list for G3326.1:PREP excluded)

G3326.2 PREP μεθ΄ (14x)
(list for G3326.2:PREP excluded)

G3326.3 PREP μετά (98x)
(list for G3326.3:PREP excluded)

EG3326.3 (1x)
(list for EG3326.3: excluded)

G3326.4 PREP μετά (6x)
(list for G3326.4:PREP excluded)

G3327 μετα•βαίνω mêtabaínō *v.* (12x)
Roots:G3326 G0901-3

G3327 V-FDI-3S μεταβήσεται (1x)
Mt 17:20 to·there,' and it·shall·walk·on. And nothing·at·all

G3327 V-PAM-2P μεταβαίνετε (1x)
Lk 10:7 payment·of·service. Do·not walk·on out·from home

G3327 V-2AAI-3S μετέβη (1x)
Mt 11:1 disciples, he·walked·on from·there to·instruct and

G3327 V-2AAM-2S μετάβηθι (2x)
Jn 7:3 declared to·him, "Walk·on from·here and head·on·out

Mt 17:20 to·this mountain, 'Walk·on from·here to·there,'
G3327 V-2AAP-NSM μεταβάς (3x)
Ac 18:7 And walking·on from·there, he·came into a·home
Mt 12:9 And walking·on from·there, he·went into their
Mt 15:29 And walking·on from·there, YeShua came near·to
G3327 V-2AAS-3S μεταβῇ (2x)
Jn 13:1 has·come, that he·should·walk·on from·among this
Mt 8:34 ·implored *him* that he·should·walk·on from their
G3327 V-RAI-1P μεταβεβήκαμεν (1x)
1Jn 3:14 that we·ourselves have·walked·on out·from Death
G3327 V-RAI-3S μεταβέβηκεν (1x)
Jn 5:24 ·judgment, but·rather has·walked·on out·from the

G3328 μετα•βάλλω mêtabállō *v.* (1x)
Roots:G3326 G0906
G3328.2 V-PMP-NPM μεταβαλλόμενοι (1x)
Ac 28:6 presently·changing·their·minds, they·were·saying

G3329 μετ•άγω mêtágō *v.* (2x)
Roots:G3326 G0071 Compare:G2116 G3594 G2720 G3608-1
G3329.3 V-PAI-1P μετάγομεν (1x)
Jac 3:3 them to·our *will*, and we·steer their whole body.
G3329.3 V-PPI-3S μετάγεται (1x)
Jac 3:4 winds, *and·yet* they·are·steered by a·very·small

G3330 μετα•δίδωμι mêtadídōmi *v.* (6x)
Roots:G3326 G1325 Compare:G2841 See:G2130 G5543
G3330.2 V-PAN μεταδιδόναι (1x)
Eph 4:28 *amply·enough* to·kindly·give to·the·one having
G3330.2 V-PAP-NSM μεταδιδούς (1x)
Rm 12:8 exhortation; the·one kindly·giving, *kindly·giving*
G3330.2 V-2AAM-3S μεταδότω (1x)
Lk 3:11 having two tunics must·kindly·give to·the·one not
G3330.2 V-2AAN μεταδοῦναι (1x)
1Th 2:8 ·for yeu, we·were·delighted to·kindly·give to·yeu,
G3330.2 V-2AAS-1S μεταδῶ (1x)
Rm 1:11 to·see yeu that I·may·kindly·give to·yeu some
EG3330.2 (1x)
Rm 12:8 the·one kindly·giving, *kindly·giving* with fidelity;

G3331 μετά•θεσις mêtáthêsis *n.* (3x)
Roots:G3346
G3331.1 N-NSF μετάθεσις (1x)
Heb 7:12 there·occurs out·of·necessity also a·transfer of·law.
G3331.1 N-GSF μεταθέσεως (1x)
Heb 11:5 ⁼ for before his transfer, it·has·been·testified *of·*
G3331.3 N-ASF μετάθεσιν (1x)
Heb 12:27 the transfer·and·removal of·the·things being·

G3332 μετ•αίρω mêtaírō *v.* (2x)
Roots:G3326 G0142
G3332.2 V-AAI-3S μετῆρεν (2x)
Mt 13:53 finished these parables, he·moved·on from·there.
Mt 19:1 finished these sayings, he·moved·on from Galilee

G3333 μετα•καλέω mêtakalêō *v.* (4x)
Roots:G3326 G2564 Compare:G4341
G3333 V-FMI-1S μετακαλέσομαι (1x)
Ac 24:25 ·occasion, I·shall·summarily·call·for you."
G3333 V-AMI-3S μετεκαλέσατο (2x)
Ac 7:14 'Joseph summarily·called·for his father Jacob and
Ac 20:17 to Ephesus, he·summarily·called·for the elders of·
G3333 V-AMM-2S μετακάλεσαι (1x)
Ac 10:32 send to Joppa and summarily·call·for Simon, who

G3334 μετα•κινέω mêtakinêō *v.* (1x)
Roots:G3326 G2795 Compare:G4531 See:G0277 G4787
G3334.1 V-PPP-NPM μετακινούμενοι (1x)
Col 1:23 ·settled, and *are* not being·stirred·away from the

G3335 μετα•λαμβάνω mêtalambánō *v.* (8x)
Roots:G3326 G2983 See:G3336
G3335 V-PAI-3S μεταλαμβάνει (1x)
Heb 6:7 also it·is·cultivated, it·partakes of·blessings from
G3335 V-PAN μεταλαμβάνειν (1x)
2Ti 2:6 man·that·works·the·soil to·partake first of·the fruits.
G3335 V-IAI-3P μετελάμβανον (1x)
Ac 2:46 ·each house, they·were·partaking of·nourishment in
G3335 V-2AAN μεταλαβεῖν (2x)
Ac 27:33 absolutely·all·of·them to·partake of·nourishment,
Heb 12:10 in·order·for *us* to·partake of·his holiness.
G3335 V-2AAP-NSM μεταλαβών (1x)
Ac 24:25 And upon·partaking·of a·convenient·occasion, I·
EG3335 (2x)
Rm 14:20 for·the man·of·clay† *to·partake*, for·the·one *being*
Rm 15:1 ·ourselves, the·ones *being* able *to·partake*, ought

G3336 μετά•ληψις mêtálēpsis *n.* (1x)
Roots:G3335 See:G3028
G3336 N-ASF μετάληψιν (1x)
1Ti 4:3 which God created for partaking with thanksgiving

G3337 μετ•αλλάσσω mêtallássō *v.* (2x)
Roots:G3326 G0236
G3337 V-AAI-3P μετήλλαξαν (2x)
Rm 1:25 who exchanged the truth of·God with the lie, and
Rm 1:26 for even their females exchanged the natural sexual·

G3338 μετα•μέλλομαι mêtaméllômai *v.* (6x)
Roots:G3326 G3199 Compare:G3340 See:G0278
G3338.1 V-PNI-1S μεταμέλομαι (1x)
2Co 7:8 with the letter, I·am·not regretting *it*, even·though I·
G3338.1 V-INI-1S μετεμελόμην (1x)
2Co 7:8 regretting *it*, even·though I·was·regretting *it*, for I·
G3338.1 V-AOP-NSM μεταμεληθείς (1x)
Mt 21:29 But eventually having·regret, he·went·off.
G3338.2 V-FOI-3S μεταμεληθήσεται (1x)
Heb 7:21 ""Yahweh swore and shall·not have·regret, 'You
G3338.2 V-AOI-2P μετεμελήθητε (1x)
Mt 21:32 *this*, did·not eventually have·regret, *so·as* to·trust
G3338.2 V-AOP-NSM μεταμεληθείς (1x)
Mt 27:3 him over, upon·having·regret, returned·back the

G3339 μετα•μορφόω mêtamôrphôō *v.* (4x)
מֶטָמֹרְפֵּז mẹṭamórphẹz
[Hebrew, New Testament]
Roots:G3326 G3445 Compare:G0236 G3345 G4833 xLangEquiv:H4301-1
G3339 V-PPI-1P μεταμορφούμεθα (1x)
2Co 3:18 glory)— are·being·metamorphosed into·the same
G3339 V-PPM-2P μεταμορφοῦσθε (1x)
Rm 12:2 but·rather be·metamorphosed by·the renewing of·
G3339 V-API-3S μετεμορφώθη (2x)
Mt 17:2 And he·was·metamorphosed before them. And his
Mk 9:2 And he·was·metamorphosed before them.

G3340 μετα•νοέω mêtanôēō *v.* (34x)
Roots:G3326 G3539 Compare:G3338 G2675 See:G3341
G3340.2 V-FAI-3P μετανοήσουσιν (1x)
Lk 16:30 to them from dead·men, they·shall·repent.'
G3340.2 V-PAI-1S μετανοῶ (1x)
Lk 17:4 to you, saying, 'I·repent,' you·shall·forgive him.
G3340.2 V-PAM-2P μετανοεῖτε (3x)
Mt 3:2 and saying, "Yeu·must·repent, for the kingdom of·
Mt 4:17 to·officially·proclaim and to·say, "Repent, for the
Mk 1:15 of·God has·drawn·near. Yeu·must·repent and trust
G3340.2 V-PAN μετανοεῖν (2x)
Ac 17:30 charges all the men·of·clay† everywhere to·repent.
Ac 26:20 *for·them* to·repent and to·turn·back·around
G3340.2 V-PAP-DSM μετανοοῦντι (2x)
Lk 15:7 one morally·disqualified·man repenting, rather·than
Lk 15:10 over one morally·disqualified·man repenting."
G3340.2 V-PAS-2P μετανοῆτε (2x)
Lk 13:3 but·yet, unless yeu·should·repent, yeu·shall all
Lk 13:5 but·yet, unless yeu·should·repent, yeu·shall all
G3340.2 V-AAI-3S μετενόησεν (1x)
Rv 2:21 her sexual·immorality, yet she·did·not repent.
G3340.2 V-AAI-3P μετενόησαν (9x)
Lk 10:13 long·ago they·would·have repented, sitting·down
Lk 11:32 ·shall·condemn it, because they·repented at the
Mt 11:20 miracles happened, because they·did·not repent.
Mt 11:21 long·ago they·would·have repented in sackcloth
Mt 12:41 and shall·condemn it, because they·repented at the
Rv 9:20 ·blows did·not·even repent out·from·among the
Rv 9:21 and neither did·they·repent out·from·among their
Rv 16:9 ·blows. And they·did·not repent *as* to·give him
Rv 16:11 and they·did·not repent out·from·among their
G3340.2 V-AAM-2S μετανόησον (5x)
Ac 8:22 Now·then, repent of this depravity of·yours, and
Rv 2:5 from·what·source you·have·fallen, and repent, and
Rv 2:16 'Repent! But·if·not, I·come to·you swiftly, and I·
Rv 3:3 so·then observantly·keep *it* and repent. Accordingly,
Rv 3:19 Accordingly, be·zealous and repent.
G3340.2 V-AAM-2P μετανοήσατε (2x)
Ac 2:38 Peter replied to them, "Repent, and each·one of·yeu
Ac 3:19 Accordingly, yeu·must·repent and turn·back·around
G3340.2 V-AAP-GPM μετανοησάντων (1x)
2Co 12:21 ·morally·failed and not repenting concerning the
G3340.2 V-AAS-2S μετανοήσῃς (1x)
Rv 2:5 out of·its place, unless you·should·repent.
G3340.2 V-AAS-3S μετανοήσῃ (2x)
Lk 17:3 reprimand him; and if he·should·repent, forgive him
Rv 2:21 in·order·that she·should·repent out·from·among her
G3340.2 V-AAS-3P μετανοήσωσιν (2x)
Mk 6:12 ·officially·proclaiming that men·should·repent.
Rv 2:22 if they·should·not repent out·from·among their

G3341 μετά•νοια mêtánôia *n.* (24x)
Roots:G3340 Compare:G3338 G3338-1 G3337-2 See:G0278
G3341.2 N-ASF μετάνοιαν (14x)
Lk 5:32 but·rather morally·disqualified·men to repentance."
Lk 24:47 And for·repentance and pardon of·moral·failures
Ac 5:31 ·own right·hand, to·grant repentance to·IsraEl and
Ac 11:18 God granted the repentance unto life-above."
Ac 20:21 Jews and Greeks, a·repentance (the·one toward
Heb 6:6 ·and·renew·them again to repentance, *that·is*,
Mt 3:11 immerse yeu in water for repentance, but the·one
Mt 9:13 but·rather morally·disqualified·ones to repentance."
Mk 2:17 but·rather morally·disqualified·men to repentance."
Rm 2:4 that the kindness of·God leads you to repentance?
2Pe 3:9 but·rather for·all to·have·room for repentance.
2Co 7:9 but·rather that yeu·were·grieved to repentance, for
2Co 7:10 ·to God accomplishes repentance unto Salvation
2Ti 2:25 God should·give to·them repentance for *the*
G3341.2 N-GSF μετανοίας (10x)
Lk 3:3 an·immersion of·repentance unto a·pardon of·moral·
Lk 3:8 produce fruits worthy of·the repentance, and yeu·
Lk 15:7 righteous·men who have no need of·repentance.
Ac 13:24 an·immersion of·repentance being·officially· by·
Ac 19:4 ·immerse *with* an·immersion of·repentance, saying
Ac 26:20 God, practicing works worthy of·the repentance.
Heb 6:1 *the* foundation— of·repentance from dead works,
Heb 12:17 he·found no place for·repentance, even·though
Mt 3:8 Now·then, produce fruits worthy of·the repentance.
Mk 1:4 an·immersion of·repentance unto a·pardon of·moral·

G3342 μετα•ξύ mêtaxý *adv.* (13x)
Roots:G3326 G4862 Compare:G0303-1
G3342.1 ADV μεταξύ (7x)
Lk 11:51 completely·perishing between the Sacrifice·Altar
Lk 16:26 And on·top·of all these·things, between us and yeu
Ac 12:6 Peter was being·laid·to·sleep between two soldiers,
Ac 15:9 ·did·not·even make·one·distinction between both us
Mt 18:15 head·on·out and reprove him between you and him
Mt 23:35 whom yeu·murdered between the Temple and the
Rm 2:15 else exonerating·themselves between one·another,
EG3342.1 (4x)
Ac 23:7 there·occurred a·controversy *between* the Pharisees
1Co 7:34 ·is·a·distinct·difference *also between* the wife and
Eph 2:14 ·down the middle·wall of·hedging *between us*,
1Ti 2:5 and *there·is* one mediator *between* God and men·of·
G3342.2 ADV μεταξύ (1x)
Jn 4:31 But in the meanwhile, the disciples were·imploring·
G3342.3 ADV μεταξύ (1x)
Ac 13:42 to·be·spoken to·them at the next Sabbath.

G3343 μετα•πέμπω mêtapémpō *v.* (8x)
Roots:G3326 G3992
G3343.2 V-PNP-NSM μεταπεμπόμενος (1x)
Ac 24:26 he·was·sending·for him more·frequently and was·
G3343.2 V-ADI-2P μετεπέμψασθε (1x)
Ac 10:29 I·inquire, for·what reason did·yeu·send·for me?
G3343.2 V-ADI-3S μετεπέμψατο (1x)
Ac 24:24 (herself·being a·Judean), Felix sent·for Paul, and
G3343.2 V-ADM-2S μετάπεμψαι (2x)
Ac 10:5 now send men to Joppa and send·for Simon, who is·
Ac 11:13 men to Joppa and send·for Simon being·surnamed
G3343.2 V-ADN μεταπέμψασθαι (1x)
Ac 10:22 ·instructed by a·holy angel to·send·for you into his
G3343.2 V-ADS-3S μεταπέμψηται (1x)
Ac 25:3 *Paul*, that he·may·send·for him *to·walk·up* to
G3343.2 V-APP-NSM μεταπεμφθείς (1x)
Ac 10:29 Therefore, after·being·sent·for, I·came *to·yeu*

G3344 μετα•στρέφω mêtastréphō *v.* (3x)
Roots:G3326 G4762 xLangAlso:H2015
G3344.2 V-2FPI-3S μεταστραφήσεται (1x)
Ac 2:20 The sun shall·be·distorted into darkness and the
G3344.2 V-AAN μεταστρέψαι (1x)
Gal 1:7 troubling yeu and willing to·distort the good·news
G3344.2 V-2APM-3S μεταστραφήτω (1x)
Jac 4:9 *Let* yeur laughter be·distorted into mourning, and

G3345 μετα•σχηματίζω mêtaschēmatízō *v.* (5x)
Roots:G3326 G4976 Compare:G0236 G3339 G3346 G1744
G3345.1 V-FAI-3S μετασχηματίσει (1x)
Php 3:21 who shall·transform the body of·our humble·estate
G3345.3 V-PMI-3S μετασχηματίζεται (1x)
2Co 11:14 himself is·disguised as an·angel of·light.
G3345.3 V-PMP-NPM μετασχηματιζόμενοι (1x)
2Co 11:13 ·of·guile, disguising·themselves as ambassadors
G3345.3 V-PPI-3P μετασχηματίζονται (1x)
2Co 11:15 if his attendants also are·disguised as attendants
G3345.4 V-AAI-1S μετεσχημάτισα (1x)
1Co 4:6 brothers, I·portrayed·as·an·example as·to myself

G3346 μετα•τίθημι mêtatíthēmi *v.* (6x)
Roots:G3326 G5087 Compare:G3179 G0236 See:G0276
G3346.2 V-PAP-NPM μετατιθέντες (1x)
Jud 1:4 this judgment, irreverent·men transferring the grace
G3346.2 V-PEI-2P μετατίθεσθε (1x)
Gal 1:6 so quickly yeu·are·transferring away·from the·one
G3346.2 V-PPP-GSF μετατιθεμένης (1x)
Heb 7:12 sacred·priesthood being·transferred, there·occurs
G3346.2 V-AAI-3S μετέθηκεν (1x)
Heb 11:5 ·not found, on·account·that God transferred him;
G3346.2 V-API-3S μετετέθη (1x)
Heb 11:5 By·trust, Enoch was·transferred *such·for* him not
G3346.2 V-API-3P μετετέθησαν (1x)
Ac 7:16 And they·were·transferred into Shekem and laid in

G3347 μετ•έπ•ειτα mêtépêita *adv.* (1x)
Roots:G3326 G1899 Compare:G1534 G1899
G3347.2 ADV μετέπειτα (1x)
Heb 12:17 ·known that even long·afterward, wanting to·

G3348 μετ•έχω mêtéchō *v.* (9x)
Roots:G3326 G2192 Compare:G3335
G3348.1 V-PAI-3P μετέχουσιν (1x)
1Co 9:12 If others participate in·*this*·privilege among·yeu,
EG3348.1 (1x)
1Co 9:12 ·yeu, *should* not we·ourselves *participate* more?
G3348.2 V-PAI-1S μετέχω (1x)
1Co 10:30 ·gratitude, I·myself participate·neighborly, why
G3348.3 V-PAI-1P μετέχομεν (1x)
1Co 10:17 *of·us* participate·and·belong *by·eating* from·out
G3348.3 V-PAN μετέχειν (1x)
1Co 10:21 able to·participate·and·belong to·*the*·Lord's table
G3348.3 V-2AAI-3S μετέσχεν (1x)
Heb 2:14 likewise·personally participated·and·belonged·to
G3348.3 V-RAI-3S μετέσχηκεν (1x)
Heb 7:13 has·participated·with·and·belongs·to another tribe
G3348.4 V-PAN μετέχειν (1x)
1Co 9:10 ·grain in expectation to·participate·by·eating of·his
G3348.4 V-PAP-NSM μετέχων (1x)
Heb 5:13 for anyone *still* participating·by·drinking milk *is*

G3349 μετε•ωρίζω mêtêōrízō *v.* (1x)
Roots:G3326 G0142 G0109 Compare:G3309
G3349.3 V-PPM-2P μετεωρίζεσθε (1x)
Lk 12:29 and do·not be·in·suspense *concerning these·things*

G3350 μετ•οικεσία mêtôikêsía *n.* (4x)
Roots:G3326 G3624 See:G3351
G3350.2 N-ASF μετοικεσίαν (1x)
Mt 1:12 Now after the Babylonian exile, YeKonYah begot
G3350.2 N-GSF μετοικεσίας (3x)
Mt 1:11 his brothers, upon *the time* of·the Babylonian exile.
Mt 1:17 from David until the Babylonian exile *are* fourteen
Mt 1:17 And from the Babylonian exile until the

G3351 μετ•οικίζω mêtôikízō *v.* (2x)
Roots:G3326 G3624 See:G3350
G3351.1 V-AAI-3S μετῴκισεν (1x)
Ac 7:4 father died, *God* transferred·and·settled him into this
G3351.3 V-FAI-1S-ATT μετοικιῶ (1x)
Ac 7:43 ·prostrate to·them. And I·shall·exile yeu far·beyond

G3352 μετ•οχή mêtôchḗ *n.* (1x)
Roots:G3348 Compare:G2842
G3352 N-NSF μετοχή (1x)
2Co 6:14 for what participation has·righteousness with

G3353 μέτ•οχος mḗtôchôs *adj.* (6x)
Roots:G3348 Compare:G4791 G4805 G2083 xLangAlso:H2270
G3353.1 A-DPM μετόχοις (1x)
Lk 5:7 ·fully·beckoned to·the·ones participating, to·the·ones
G3353.2 A-NPM μέτοχοι (2x)
Heb 3:1 brothers (*yeu* participants of·a·heavenly calling)
Heb 12:8 (of·which all have·become participants), then·by·
G3353.2 A-APM μετόχους (1x)
Heb 6:4 ·present, and becoming participants of·Holy Spirit,
G3353.3 A-NPM μέτοχοι (1x)
Heb 3:14 For we·have·become partaking·companions of·,
G3353.3 A-APM μετόχους (1x)
Heb 1:9 ·joy above·and·beyond your companions."

G3354 μετρέω mêtrḗō *v.* (10x)
Roots:G3358 Compare:G2919 G4793 See:G1267-1
G3354.1 V-PAI-2P μετρεῖτε (2x)
Lk 6:38 that yeu·measure, it·shall·be·additionally·measured·
Mk 4:24 whatever standard·of·measurement yeu·measure,
G3354.1 V-AAI-3S ἐμέτρησεν (2x)
Rv 21:16 And with·the reed, he·measured the CITY at
Rv 21:17 And he·measured its wall, a·hundred *and* forty four
G3354.1 V-AAM-2S μέτρησον (1x)
Rv 11:1 "Rouse·yourself and measure the Temple of·God,
G3354.1 V-AAS-2S μετρήσης (1x)
Rv 11:2 outside, and you·should·not measure it, because it·
G3354.1 V-AAS-3S μετρήσῃ (1x)
Rv 21:15 reed in·order·that he·should·measure the CITY,
G3354.2 V-FPI-3S μετρηθήσεται (1x)
Mk 4:24 *comprehension* shall·be·measured·out to·yeu. And
G3354.3 V-PAI-2P μετρεῖτε (1x)
Mt 7:2 standard·of·measurement yeu·unduly·measure, it·
G3354.3 V-PAP-NPM μετροῦντες (1x)
2Co 10:12 But·rather those unduly·measuring themselves by

G3355 μετρητής mêtrētḗs *n.* (1x)
Roots:G3354
G3355.2 N-APM μετρητάς (1x)
Jn 2:6 ·room·for two or three ten·gallon·measures apiece.

G3356 μετριο•παθέω mêtriôpathḗō *v.* (1x)
Roots:G3357 G3806
G3356 V-PAN μετριοπαθεῖν (1x)
Heb 5:2 *also* being·able to·be·moderate with·the·ones being·

G3357 μετρίως mêtríōs *adv.* (1x)
Roots:G3358 Compare:G5234 See:G0280
G3357.2 ADV μετρίως (1x)
Ac 20:12 ·alive, and they·were·comforted beyond·measure.

G3358 μέτρον mḗtrôn *n.* (13x)
Compare:G2583 See:G3354 xLangAlso:H4060 H5429
G3358.1 N-ASN μέτρον (7x)
Lk 6:38 ·shall·be·given to·yeu; good measure, packed·down
Mt 23:32 completely·fulfill even the measure of·yeur fathers.
Rm 12:3 ·as God imparted to·each·man a·measure of·trust.
2Co 10:13 according·to the standard measure which God
Eph 4:7 according·to the measure of·the voluntary·present
Eph 4:13 a·complete man, into a·measure of·maturity of·the
Rv 21:17 cubits, *according·to* a·measure of·a·man·of·clay†,
G3358.1 N-DSN μέτρῳ (1x)
Eph 4:16 individual part in *its* measure. He·himself·produces
G3358.1 N-GSN μέτρου (2x)
Jn 3:34 God does·not give the Spirit as·a·result of·measure.
2Co 10:13 to·us, a·measure *of·service* actually·reaching also
G3358.3 N-DSN μέτρῳ (3x)
Lk 6:38 same standard·of·measurement that yeu·measure, it·
Mt 7:2 by whatever standard·of·measurement yeu·unduly·,
Mk 4:24 whatever standard·of·measurement yeu·measure,

G3359 μέτ•ωπον mḗtōpôn *n.* (8x)
Roots:G3326
xLangEquiv:H4696
G3359.2 N-ASN μέτωπον (2x)
Rv 17:5 And upon her forehead *was* a·name having·been·
Rv 20:4 receive the etching upon their foreheads, *nor* even in
G3359.2 N-GSN μετώπου (1x)
Rv 14:9 and receives *its* etching in his forehead, or in his
G3359.2 N-GPN μετώπων (5x)
Rv 7:3 ·seal the slaves of·our God in their foreheads."
Rv 9:4 ·not have the official·seal of·God in their foreheads.
Rv 13:16 on their right hand or upon their foreheads.
Rv 14:1 of·his Father having·been·written in their foreheads.
Rv 22:4 his face, and his name *shall·be* in their foreheads.

G3360 μέχρι mḗchri *adv.* (17x)
μεχρίς mêchrís
Roots:G3372 Compare:G0891 G2193
G3360.1 ADV μέχρι (3x)
Heb 3:6 Expectation *being* steadfast as·long·as·unto *the* end.
Heb 3:14 ·assurance, *being* steadfast as·long·as·unto *the* end
Mt 11:23 it·would·have remained as·long·as·unto the present
G3360.2 ADV μέχρις (4x)
Heb 12:4 Yet·not as·far·as·unto *sweating* blood did·yeu·
Rm 15:19 and around·in·a·circuit to·as·far·as Illyricum).
Php 2:8 becoming attentively·obedient as·far·as·unto death,
2Ti 2:9 as·a·criminal, *even* as·far·as·unto bonds, but·yet
G3360.3 ADV μέχρι (3x)
Mk 13:30 should·not pass·away, so·long·as·until all these·
Eph 4:13 *for* so·long·as·until we·all should·attain unto the
1Ti 6:14 *for* so·long·as·until the conspicuous·appearing of·
G3360.4 ADV μέχρι (3x)
Ac 20:7 the conversation so·long·as·unto midnight.
Heb 9:10 imposed *on·them* so·long·as·unto *the* season of·
Mt 13:30 to·be·grown·together so·long·as·unto the harvest,
G3360.5 ADV μέχρι (4x)
Ac 10:30 ago I·was fasting so·far·as·unto this·same hour;
Mt 28:15 ·among Judeans so·far·as·unto the present·day.
Rm 5:14 already·reigned from Adam so·far·as·unto Moses,
Php 2:30 he·was·drawn·near so·far·as·unto death, ignoring·

G3361 μή mḗ *prt.* (865x)
Compare:G3756 See:G3362 G3363 G3364 G3372 G3373 G3375 G3378 G3385
(abbreviated listing for G3361)
G3361.1 NEG μή (75x)
(list for G3361.1:NEG excluded)
G3361.1 NEG-ADJ μή (26x)
(list for G3361.1:NEG-ADJ excluded)
G3361.1 NEG-ADV μή (10x)
(list for G3361.1:NEG-ADV excluded)
G3361.1 NEG-CONJ μή (6x)
(list for G3361.1:NEG-CONJ excluded)
G3361.1 NEG-N μή (20x)

(list for G3361.1:NEG-N excluded)
G3361.1 NEG-PREP μή (14x)
(list for G3361.1:NEG-PREP excluded)
G3361.1 NEG-V μή (595x)
(list for G3361.1:NEG-V excluded)
G3361.1 NEG-VC μή (30x)
(list for G3361.1:NEG-VC excluded)
G3361.2 NEG μή (2x)
(list for G3361.2:NEG excluded)
G3361.2 NEG-N μή (7x)
(list for G3361.2:NEG-N excluded)
G3361.2 NEG-V μή (2x)
(list for G3361.2:NEG-V excluded)
G3361.3 NEG-CONJ μή (13x)
(list for G3361.3:NEG-CONJ excluded)
G3361.5 NEG-RHET μή (46x)
(list for G3361.5:NEG-RHET excluded)
EG3361.5 (1x)
(list for EG3361.5: excluded)
G3361.7 NEG-V μή (1x)
(list for G3361.7:NEG-V excluded)
G3361.8 NEG μή (1x)
(list for G3361.8:NEG excluded)
G3361.8 NEG-V μή (14x)
(list for G3361.8:NEG-V excluded)
G3361.9 NEG-V μή (1x)
(list for G3361.9:NEG-V excluded)
G3361.10 NEG-VC μή (1x)
(list for G3361.10:NEG-VC excluded)

G3362 ἐ•άν μή êán mḗ *cond.* (38x)
Roots:G3361 G1437
G3362.2 NEG-COND ἐάν μή (36x)
Jn 3:2 ·signs that you·yourself do unless God should·be with
Jn 3:3 I·say to·you, unless someone should·be·born from·
Jn 3:5 I·say to·you, unless someone should·be·born from·
Jn 3:27 ·one·thing, unless it·may·be having·been·given to·
Jn 4:48 to him, “Unless yeu·*all*·should·see signs and
Jn 6:44 is·able to·come to me, unless the Father (the·one
Jn 6:53 I·say to·yeu, unless yeu·should·eat the flesh of·the
Jn 6:65 ·come to me, unless it·should·be having·been·given
Jn 7:51 man·of·clay†, unless it·should·hear directly·from
Jn 8:24 yeur moral·failures. For unless yeu·should·trust that
Jn 12:24 ·certainly, I·say to·yeu, unless the kernel of·wheat,
Jn 15:4 to·bear fruit of itself unless it·should·abide in the
Jn 15:4 not·even *can* yeu unless yeu·should·abide in me.
Jn 20:25 he·declared to·them, “Unless I·may·see the imprint
Lk 13:3 no·indeed, but·yet, unless yeu·should·repent, yeu·
Lk 13:5 no·indeed, but·yet, unless yeu·should·repent, yeu·
Ac 8:31 ·able *to·know them*, unless some·man should·guide
Ac 15:1 *saying*, “Unless yeu·should·be·circumcised in·the
Ac 27:31 to·the soldiers, “Unless these should·remain with
Mt 5:20 I·say to·yeu, that unless yeur righteousness should·
Mt 12:29 his belongings, unless first he·should·bind the
Mt 18:3 I·say to·yeu, unless yeu·should·be·turned·back and
Mt 18:35 do to·yeu, unless each·one·of yeu·should·forgive
Mt 26:42 able to·pass·away from me unless I·should·drink it,
Mk 3:27 into his home, unless he·should·bind the strong·
Mk 7:3 all the Judeans, unless they·should·wash their hands
Mk 7:4 a·marketplace, unless they·should·immerse *their*
Rm 10:15 ·proclaim, unless they·should·be·dispatched?
2Th 2:3 *·not come·to·stand*, unless there·should·come the
1Co 9:16 is·to·me, unless I·should·proclaim·the·good·news!
1Co 14:6 shall·I·benefit yeu, unless I·should·speak to·yeu
1Co 14:9 *For* unless yeu·should·give a·clearly·discernible
1Co 15:36 you sow is·not giving·life, unless it·should·die.
2Ti 2:5 ·not victoriously·crowned unless he·should·contend
Rv 2:5 out of·its place, unless you·should·repent.
Rv 3:3 repent. Accordingly, unless you·should·keep·alert,
G3362.3 NEG-COND ἐάν μή (2x)
Jn 5:19 by himself, but·only what he·should·look·upon the
Gal 2:16 of·works of·Torah-Law, but·only through a·trust

G3363 ἵνα μή hína mḗ *prep.* (33x)
Roots:G3361 G2443
G3363.2 NEG-CONJ ἵνα μή (33x)
Jn 3:20 toward the light, lest his deeds should·be·refuted.
Jn 5:14 morally·fail no·longer, lest something worse
Jn 12:35 yeu·have the light, lest darkness should·grab yeu.
Jn 18:28 Praetorian·hall, lest they·should·be·contaminated,
Lk 8:12 from their hearts, lest trusting, they·should·be·saved
Lk 16:28 ·testify to·them, lest they·themselves also should·
Lk 18:5 ·shall·avenge her, lest she·should·greatly·pester me
Ac 5:26 they·feared the people, lest they·should·be·stoned.
Heb 3:13 “Today,” lest any from·among yeu should·be·
Heb 4:11 into that complete·rest, lest any·man should·fall
Heb 11:28 of·the blood, lest the·one savagely·terminating
Heb 12:3 against himself, lest yeu·should·become·fatigued,
Heb 12:13 tracks for·yeur feet, lest the lame *limb* should·
Mt 26:5 on the feast·day, lest a·commotion should·occur
Mk 3:9 ·of the crowd, lest they·should·press·in·against him.
Rm 11:25 of·this mystery, lest yeu·should·be·full·of·notions
Rm 15:20 is·already·named, lest I·should·build upon
Jac 5:9 ·another, brothers, lest yeu·should·be·condemned.
Jac 5:12 “No, No,” lest yeu·should·fall into hypocrisy.
Php 2:27 but·rather on·me also, lest I·should·have grief
2Pe 3:17 Lest after·being·led·away·together with·the error
1Co 1:15 lest any should·declare that I·immersed in my·own
1Co 1:17 not with wisdom of·reasoning, lest the cross of·the
1Co 8:13 ·age, lest I·should·cause·the·moral·failure·of my
1Co 9:12 we·quietly·bear all·things, lest we·should·give any
1Co 11:34 ·eat at home, lest yeu·should·come·together into
1Co 16:2 ·up as he·may·prosper, lest there·should·be no
2Co 2:3 I·wrote this same·thing to·yeu, lest coming *to·yeu*,
2Co 9:3 So I·sent the brothers, lest our boasting on·yeur
Col 2:4 And this I·say, lest any·man should·defraud yeu
Col 3:21 ·irritate yeur children, lest they·should·be·dejected.
1Ti 3:6 lest being·inflated·with·self-conceit he·should·fall
Rv 16:15 his garments, lest he·should·walk·along naked,

G3365 μηδ•αμῶς mēdamō̂s *adv.* (2x)
Roots:G3361 Compare:G3761
G3365.2 ADV μηδαμῶς (2x)
Ac 10:14 But Peter declared, “Not·any·such·thing, Lord,
Ac 11:8 But I·declared, ‘Not·any·such·thing, Lord, because

G3366 μη•δέ mēdḗ *conj.* (57x)
Roots:G3361 G1161 Compare:G3761 G3756 G3383
G3366.2 CONJ-NEG μηδέ (10x)
Mt 6:25 what yeu·should·drink, nor·even for·yeur body,
Mt 10:9 Yeu·should·not procure gold, nor·even silver, nor·
Mt 10:9 nor·even silver, nor·even copper·coinage in yeur
Mk 2:2 no·longer to·have·room, not·even alongside the door
Mk 6:11 should·not accept yeu, or·should·not·even hear yeu
Mk 8:26 house, saying, “You·should·not·even enter into the
Rm 6:13 And·yeu·must·not·even present yeur members *as*
1Co 10:7 Yeu·must·not·even be idolaters, just·as *were* some
1Co 10:10 We·must·not·even grumble, just·as some of·them
Eph 5:3 impurity or greed, must·not·even be·named among
G3366.3 CONJ-NEG μηδέ (46x)
Jn 4:15 ·that I·may·not thirst, nor·even should·come here to·
Jn 14:27 ·not be·troubled in·yeur heart, nor·even be·timid.
Lk 3:14 ·man, nor·even should·yeu·extort·by·false·charges,
Lk 10:4 a·pouch, nor a·knapsack, nor·even shoes, and yeu·
Lk 12:22 what yeu·should·eat, nor·even for·yeur body,
Lk 12:47 not making·ready, nor·even doing pertaining·to his
Lk 14:12 holler·out·for your friends, nor·even your brothers,
Lk 14:12 nor·even your brothers, nor·even your kinsmen,
Lk 14:12 your kinsmen, nor·even wealthy close·neighbors,
Lk 16:26 to yeu should·not be·able; nor·even may the·ones
Lk 17:23 ·off *after·them*, nor·even should·yeu·pursue *them*.
Ac 4:18 them not to·enunciate nor·even to·instruct at·all in
Ac 21:21 the children, nor·even to·walk after·the customs.
Ac 23:8 ·is not a·resurrection, *also* not·even an·angel nor a·
Heb 12:5 corrective·discipline, nor·even be·faint *when*
Mt 7:6 *·is* holy to·the dogs, nor·even should·yeu·cast yeur
Mt 10:10 a·knapsack for *yeur* journey, nor·even two tunics,
Mt 10:10 nor·even two tunics, nor·even shoes, nor·even a·
Mt 10:10 tunics, nor·even shoes, nor·even a·staff, for the
Mt 10:14 should·not accept yeu or·should·not·even hear yeur
Mt 22:29 having·seen the Scriptures, nor·even the power of·
Mt 23:10 Nor·even should·yeu·be·called preeminent·leaders,
Mt 24:20 ·not happen in·winter, nor·even on a·Sabbath.
Mk 8:26 into the village, nor·even should·you·declare *this*
Mk 12:24 having·seen the Scriptures, nor·even the power
Mk 13:11 what yeu·should·speak, nor·even premeditate,
Mk 13:15 walk·down into the home, nor·even enter *it*, to·
Rm 9:11 not·yet being·born nor·even practicing anything
Rm 14:21 ·good neither to·eat meat, nor·even to·drink wine,
Rm 14:21 nor·even to·drink wine, nor·even *anything* by
1Pe 3:14 of·their fear, nor·even should·yeu·be·troubled.”
1Pe 5:2 but·rather voluntarily; nor·even for·shameful·gain,
1Pe 5:3 nor·even as exercising·lordship·against the ones·
2Th 3:10 does·not want to·work, nor·even *then* must·he·eat.
1Co 5:8 not with old leaven, nor·even with leaven of·malice
1Co 10:8 Nor·even should·we·commit·sexual·immorality,
1Co 10:9 Nor·even should·we·thoroughly·try the
2Co 4:2 walking in shrewd·cunning nor·even handling the
Col 2:21 ·should·not lay·hold·of, nor·even should·you·taste,
Col 2:21 ·you·taste, nor·even should·you·lay·a·finger·on *it*,
1Ti 1:4 nor·even to·give·heed to·myths and to·endless
1Ti 5:22 on·not·one·man quickly, nor·even share in·others
1Ti 6:17 to·be·arrogant nor·even to·have·placed·their· upon
2Ti 1:8 testimony of·our Lord, nor·even of·me his chained·
1Jn 2:15 Do·not love the world, nor·even the·things in the
1Jn 3:18 we·should·not love in·word, nor·even in·tongue,
G3366.4 CONJ-NEG μηδέ (1x)
1Co 5:11 no,·not·even to·eat·together with·such·a·man.

G3367 μηδ•είς mēdêís *adj.* (91x)
μηδ•εμία mēdêmía [irregular feminine]
μηδ•έν mēdén [neuter]
Roots:G3361 G1520 Compare:G3762
G3367.1 A-NSM μηδείς (11x)
Gal 6:17 let no·man personally·present wearisome·troubles
Mt 9:30 “Clearly·see·to·it *that* no·one knows *I·did this*.
Mk 5:43 them repeatedly that no·one should·know this, and
Mk 11:14 declared to·it, “May no·one any·longer eat fruit
Jac 1:13 No·one being·tempted must·ever·say, “I·am·
Tit 2:15 ·assigned·authority. Let not·one·man disparage you
1Co 3:21 As·such, do·not·let·one boast in men·of·clay†, for
1Co 10:24 Let no·man seek his·own, but·rather each·man the
Eph 5:6 Let not·one·man delude you with·empty words, for
Col 2:18 Let no·one manipulate·and·defraud yeu, *especially*
1Ti 4:12 Let no·man despise your youth, but·rather become
G3367.1 A-ASM μηδένα (4x)
Ac 9:7 the sound·of·the·voice, but observing no·one.
Ac 24:23 ease, and to·forbid not·one of·his own·company
1Th 3:3 *for* no·one to·be·woefully·shaken by these
Tit 3:2 to·revile no·man, to·be not·quarrelsome, *but* fair,
G3367.1 A-DSM μηδενί (7x)
Ac 11:19 the Redemptive-word to·no·one except to·Jews
Ac 23:22 *for·him* to·divulge “to·no·one that you·made these·
Mt 8:4 ·it *that* you·should·declare *this* to·no·one. But·rather
Mt 16:20 ·that they·should·declare to·no·one that he·himself
Mt 17:9 Yeu·should·declare the clear·vision to·no·man, until
Rm 13:8 Owe not·one·man not·even·one·thing, except to·
1Ti 5:22 Lay·forth hands on·not·one·man quickly, nor·even
G3367.2 A-ASN μηδέν (3x)
Ac 27:33 ·of·food, each·taking·to·yeurselves not·one·thing.
1Ti 6:4 while·being·fully·acquainted·with not·one·thing,
3Jn 1:7 they·went·forth, taking not·one·thing from the
G3367.2 A-DSN μηδενί (1x)
Jac 1:4 and entirely·whole, being·deficient in not·one·thing.
G3367.2 A-GSN μηδενός (1x)
1Th 4:12 and *that* yeu·may·have need of·not·one·thing.
G3367.3 A-ASF μηδεμίαν (2x)
Heb 10:2 to·have not·one·bit further a·moral·consciousness
2Co 6:3 *yeu* while·giving not·one·bit·of an·instance·of· in
G3367.3 A-ASN μηδέν (8x)

Lk 3:13 to them, "Exact not·one·bit more·than the·thing
Lk 4:35 came·forth from him, injuring him not·one·bit.
Ac 15:28 to·us, to·put on·yeu not·one·bit·of a·larger burden
Ac 16:28 ·should·inflict on·yourself not·one·bit·of harm, for
Mk 5:26 belongings with not·one·bit *of·it* being·beneficial,
2Th 3:11 ·manner, who·are·working not·one·bit, but·rather
2Co 11:5 For I·reckon not·one·bit to·have·fallen·short of·the
Rv 2:10 'Fear not·one·bit·of which·things you·are·about to·

G3367.4 A-NSN μηδέν (2x)
Ac 8:24 that not·even·one of·these·things·which yeu·have·
Gal 6:3 ·be something, being not·even·one·thing, he·deludes

G3367.4 A-ASM μηδένα (3x)
Jn 8:10 and distinctly·viewing not·even·one besides the wife,
Ac 10:28 to·me to·refer·to not·even·one man·of·clay† *as*
2Th 2:3 thoroughly·delude yeu in not·even·one manner,

G3367.4 A-ASF μηδεμίαν (5x)
Ac 13:28 And after·finding not·even·one cause of·death *in·*
Ac 25:17 here (making not·even·one postponement on·the
Ac 28:18 ·of there not subsisting even·one cause for·death
1Pe 3:6 ·good and not being·afraid *of* not·even·one terror.
1Ti 5:14 to·give not·even·one impromptu·occasion for·

G3367.4 A-ASN μηδέν (23x)
Lk 6:35 and lend, fully·expecting not·even·one·thing—
Lk 9:3 to them, "Take·up not·even·one·thing for the journey
Ac 4:21 finding not·even·one·thing of·how they·should·
Ac 10:20 hesitating *for* not·even·one·thing, on·account·that
Ac 11:12 hesitating *for* not·even·one·thing. Moreover,
Ac 19:36 and to·accomplish not·even·one·thing rashly.
Ac 21:25 to·observantly·keep not·even·one such·thing,
Ac 23:29 but having not·even·one allegation worthy of·
Ac 25:25 to·have·practiced not·even·one·thing worthy of·
Ac 28:6 and observing not·even·one·thing out·of·place
Mk 1:44 you·should·declare not·even·one·thing to·not·even·
Mk 6:8 that they·should·take·up not·even·one·thing for *their*
Rm 13:8 Owe not·one·man not·even·one·thing, except to·
Jac 1:6 trust, hesitating *for* not·even·one·thing. For the·one
Php 2:3 *Let* not·even·one·thing *be·done* according·to
Php 4:6 Be·anxious·about not·even·one·thing, but·rather in
Tit 2:8 ·embarrassed, having not·even·one mediocre thing
Tit 3:13 in·order·that not·even·one·thing may·remain·left·
1Co 10:25 scrutinizing not·even·one·thing on·account·of the
1Co 10:27 scrutinizing not·even·one·thing on·account·of the
2Co 6:10 as having not·even·one·thing and·yet fully·having
2Co 13:7 to God for·yeu not to·do not·even·one wrong; not
1Ti 5:21 doing not·even·one·thing according·to favoritism.

G3367.4 A-DSN μηδενί (4x)
Php 1:28 not being·scared (in not·even·one·thing) by the·
1Co 1:7 in not·even·one gracious·bestowment while·fully·
2Co 6:3 ·of·stumbling in not·even·one·thing, in·order·that
2Co 7:9 in not·even·one·thing, yeu·should·have·suffered·

G3367.4 A-GSN μηδενός (2x)
Ac 19:40 with·there·inherently·being not·even·one cause
Ac 23:14 ·to·destruction to·taste not·even·one·thing until

G3367.5 A-NSM μηδείς (3x)
1Co 3:18 Let not·even·one·man thoroughly·delude himself.
1Jn 3:7 Dear·children, let not·even·one·man deceive yeu.
Rv 3:11 in·order·that not·even·one·man should·take your

G3367.5 A-ASM μηδένα (2x)
Lk 3:14 "·violently·shake·and·intimidate not·even·one·man,
Lk 10:4 and yeu·should·greet not·even·one·man in the way.

G3367.5 A-DSM μηδενί (9x)
Lk 5:14 charged him to·declare *it* not·even·to·one·man,
Lk 8:56 to·declare to·not·even·one·man the·thing having·
Lk 9:21 *them* to·declare not·even·to·one·man this·thing,
Ac 4:17 to·speak no·longer to·not·even·one man·of·clay† in
Mk 1:44 not·even·one·thing to·not·even·one·man. But·rather
Mk 7:36 they·should·declare *it* to·not·even·one·man. But·as·
Mk 8:30 that not·even·to·one·man should·they·relate *this*
Mk 9:9 they·should·give·an·account not·even·to·one·man
Rm 12:17 *is* giving·back to·not·even·one·man wrong for

G3367.6 A-NSN μηδέν (1x)
Mt 27:19 saying, "Have·nothing·to·do with that righteous·

G3368 μη•δέ•πο•τε mēdépôtê *adv.* (1x)
Roots:G3366 G4218

G3368 ADV μηδέποτε (1x)
2Ti 3:7 learning, and·yet never·even being·able to·come to

G3369 μη•δέ•πω mēdépō *adv.* (1x)
Roots:G3366 G4452

G3369 ADV μηδέπω (1x)
Heb 11:7 the·things not·even·yet being·looked·upon, being·

G3370 Μῆδος Mē̂dôs *n/g.* (1x)
xLangAlso:H4074

G3370 N/G-NPM Μῆδοι (1x)
Ac 2:9 Parthians and Medes and Elamites, and the·ones

G3371 μηκ•έτι mēkéti *adv.* (21x)
Roots:G3361 G2089

G3371.1 ADV μηκέτι (19x)
Jn 5:14 healthy·and·sound; morally·fail no·longer, lest
Jn 8:11 Traverse, and morally·fail no·longer!"
Ac 4:17 to·speak no·longer to·not·even·one man·of·clay† in
Ac 13:34 dead·men, no·longer intending to·return·back to
Mt 21:19 and he·says to·it, "No·longer should fruit come
Mk 1:45 matter, such·for *Jesus* no·longer to·be·able to·enter
Mk 2:2 ·together, such·for *them* no·longer to·have·room,
Mk 9:25 out·of·him, and you·may·enter no·longer into him.
Rm 6:6 may·be·fully·rendered·inoperative, no·longer *for* us
Rm 14:13 no·longer should·we·unduly·judge one·another,
Rm 15:23 But right·now, no·longer having a·place *to·*
1Pe 4:2 in·order no·longer to·live·naturally the remainder·of
1Th 3:1 ·we·could·quietly·bear *it* no·longer, we·took·delight
1Th 3:5 when·I could·quietly·bear·it no·longer, I·sent·word
2Co 5:15 the·ones living should·no·longer live to·themselves
Eph 4:14 in·order·that we·may no·longer be infants, who·
Eph 4:17 *to·it* in *the* Lord: No·longer *are* you to·walk just·as
Eph 4:28 The·one stealing must·steal no·longer. But rather
1Ti 5:23 No·longer drink·water·only, but·rather use a·little

G3371.2 ADV μηκέτι (2x)
Ac 25:24 *that* it·is·not necessary·for him to·live any·longer.
Mk 11:14 to·it, "May no·one any·longer eat fruit from·out

G3372 μῆκος mē̂kôs *n.* (3x)
Compare:G3173 See:G3117 G3110
xLangEquiv:H0753

G3372 N-NSN μῆκος (3x)
Eph 3:18 what *is* the breadth, and length, and depth, and
Rv 21:16 lays·out foursquare, and its length is as·vast and
Rv 21:16 thousand stadia. The length and the breadth and

G3373 μηκύνω mēkýnō *v.* (1x)
Roots:G3372 Compare:G0837

G3373.3 V-PPS-3S μηκύνηται (1x)
Mk 4:27 and should·be·grown·to·length, he·himself does·not

G3374 μηλωτή mēlōtḗ *n.* (1x)

G3374 N-DPF μηλωταῖς (1x)
Heb 11:37 ·a·dagger. They·went·about in sheepskins *and* in

G3375 μήν mḗn *prt.* (1x)
Roots:G3303 G2229 Compare:G3303

G3375 PRT μήν (1x)
Heb 6:14 "'Most assuredly, blessing I·shall·indeed·bless

G3376 μήν mḗn *n.* (18x)
Compare:G3561 G4582 See:G2250
xLangEquiv:H2320

G3376.1 N-ASM μῆνα (1x)
Rv 9:15 the hour, day, lunar·month, and year, in·order·that

G3376.1 N-APM μῆνας (14x)
Lk 1:24 ·entirely·hiding herself *for* five lunar·months, saying
Lk 1:56 about three lunar·months and·then returned·back to
Lk 4:25 ·a·span·of three years and six lunar·months, as great
Ac 7:20 ·nurtured in his father's house three lunar·months.
Ac 18:11 *there* a·year and six lunar·months, instructing the
Ac 19:8 ·clarity for·a·span·of three lunar·months, discussing
Ac 20:3 continuing *there* also *for* three lunar·months. *But*
Ac 28:11 the island *for* three lunar·months, we·sailed·away
Gal 4:10 ·meticulously·keep days, and lunar·months, and
Jac 5:17 on the earth *for* three years and six lunar·months.
Rv 9:5 they·should·be·tormented five lunar·months. And
Rv 9:10 ·bring·harm·to the men·of·clay† five lunar·months.
Rv 11:2 ·shall·trample the Holy City forty two lunar·months.
Rv 13:5 ·given to·it to·do *this for* forty two lunar·months.

G3376.1 N-DSM μηνί (1x)
Lk 1:26 And in the sixth lunar·month, the angel GabriEl was·

G3376.1 PRT μήν (1x)
Lk 1:36 this is *the* sixth lunar·month *of·pregnancy* for·her

G3376.2 N-ASM μῆνα (1x)
Rv 22:2 its fruit according·to each one's month. And the

G3376-2 μῆνις mē̂nis *n.* (2x)
Compare:G2373-2 G2372 G3709 See:G3455-1
xLangEquiv:H0639-1 xLangAlso:H0342 H5156

G3376-2.2 N-DSF μῆνει (2x)
Heb 3:11 Even·as I·swore in my flared·anger, 'As·if they·
Heb 4:3 "'As I·swore in my flared·anger, 'as·if they·shall·

G3377 μηνύω mēnýō *v.* (4x)
Roots:G3145 G3415 Compare:G5346 G1718 G1583

G3377.1 V-AAI-3S ἐμήνυσεν (1x)
Lk 20:37 even Moses brought·it·to·attention at the burning·

G3377.1 V-AAP-ASM μηνύσαντα (1x)
1Co 10:28 ·of that·one bringing·it·to·*yeur*·attention, and the

G3377.1 V-AAS-3S μηνύσῃ (1x)
Jn 11:57 he·is, he·should·bring·it·to·*their*·attention, so·that

G3377.1 V-APP-GSF μηνυθείσης (1x)
Ac 23:30 ·a·plot being·brought·to·my attention against the

G3379 μή•πο•τε mḗpôtê *adv.* (26x)
μή πο•τέ mḗ pôté
ἵνα μή•πο•τε hína mḗpôtê
Roots:G3361 G4218 G2443 Compare:G3363 G3381
G3387 xLangAlso:H6435

G3379.1 ADV μήποτε (1x)
Heb 9:17 men·are·dead, since not·at·any·time *is·it* in·force

G3379.2 ADV μήποτε (6x)
Lk 4:11 *their* palms, lest·at·any·time you·should·stub your
Lk 21:34 ·heed to·yeurselves, lest·at·any·time yeur hearts
Heb 2:1 lest·at·any·time we·should·drift·away *from·it.*
Mt 4:6 *their* palms, lest·at·any·time you·should·stub your
Mt 5:25 way with him, lest·at·any·time the legal·adversary
Mk 4:12 lest·at·any·time they·should·turn·back·around,

G3379.3 ADV μήποτε (13x)
Lk 12:58 ·been·released from him, lest he·should·drag you
Lk 14:8 ·place, lest a·more·honorable·man·than you may·be
Lk 14:12 nor·even wealthy close·neighbors, lest they also
Ac 28:27 ·fully·shut their eyes, lest they·should·see with·the
Heb 3:12 Look·out, brothers, lest there·shall·be in any of·
Heb 4:1 ·rest, we·should·be·alarmed, lest any from·among
Mt 7:6 before the pigs, lest they·should·trample them down
Mt 13:15 ·fully·shut their eyes, lest they·should·see with·the
Mt 13:29 'No, lest while·collecting the darnel·weeds, yeu·
Mt 15:32 them without·eating, lest they·should·be·faint on
Mt 25:9 '*Not·so*, lest there·should·not be·sufficient *oil* for·
Mt 27:64 until the third day, lest his disciples, coming by·
Mk 14:2 the feast *day*, lest there·shall·be a·commotion of·

EG3379.3 (1x)
Lk 21:34 ·pertain·to·this·natural·life, and·also *lest* that day

G3379.4 ADV μήποτε (2x)
Lk 14:29 Lest·perhaps, with·him laying *the* foundation, and
Ac 5:39 *withdraw*, lest·perhaps yeu·should·be·found *to·be*

G3379.5 ADV μήποτε (2x)
Lk 3:15 concerning John, if·perhaps he·himself might·be the
2Ti 2:25 ·in·opposition— if·perhaps God should·give to·

G3379.6 ADV μήποτε (1x)
Jn 7:26 they·say nothing·at·all to·him. Perhaps the rulers

G3380 μή•πω mḗpō *adv.* (2x)
Roots:G3361 G4452

G3380 ADV μήπω (2x)
Heb 9:8 *was* not·yet to·have·been·made·apparent with·the
Rm 9:11 (for *with·the twins* not·yet being·born nor·even

G3381 μή•πως mḗpōs *conj.* (12x)
μή πώς mḗ pṓs
Roots:G3361 G4458

G3381.1 CONJ μήπως (9x)

Ac 27:29 And fearing lest·somehow they·should·fall into
Gal 2:2 being·of·reputation, lest·somehow I·should·run, or
Gal 4:11 ·for yeu, lest·somehow I·have·labored·hard for yeu
1Th 3:5 ·know yeur trust, lest·somehow the Tempting·One
1Co 8:9 But look·out! Lest·somehow this privilege of·yeurs
1Co 9:27 lest·somehow, after·officially·proclaiming to·
2Co 11:3 But I·fear, lest·somehow, as the Serpent
2Co 12:20 For I·fear, lest·somehow after·coming, I·should·
2Co 12:20 yeu·do·not want. Lest·somehow *there·be* strifes,

G3381.2 CONJ μήπως (3x)

Rm 11:21 *take·heed* lest·perhaps he·should·not·even spare
2Co 2:7 lest·perhaps such·a·man should·be·swallowed·up
2Co 9:4 Lest·perhaps if *any* Macedonians should·come

G3382 μηρός mērós *n.* (1x)

xLangEquiv:H3409 A3410

G3382 N-ASM μηρόν (1x)

Rv 19:16 garment and on his thigh the name having·been·

G3383 μή•τε mḗtê *conj.* (37x)

Roots:G3361 G5037

G3383.2 CONJ μήτε (16x)

Lk 7:33 John the Immerser has·come neither eating bread
Lk 9:3 not·even·one·thing for the journey, neither staffs, nor
Lk 9:3 staffs, nor knapsack, neither bread, neither money;
Lk 9:3 knapsack, neither bread, neither money; neither to·
Lk 9:3 bread, neither money; neither to·have two tunics
Ac 23:12 over·to·destruction, saying neither to·eat nor to·
Ac 23:21 themselves over·to·destruction, neither to·eat nor
Ac 27:20 And with·neither sun nor constellations·of·stars
Heb 7:3 without·lineage, having neither beginning of·days,
Mt 5:34 to·yeu not to·swear at·all: neither by the heaven,
Mt 5:36 Neither should·you·swear by your head, because
Mt 11:18 For John came neither eating nor drinking, and
Jac 5:12 brothers, do·not swear, neither by·the heaven, nor
2Th 2:2 ·disturbed *by·any delusion* (neither through spirit,
1Ti 1:7 not understanding— neither what they·say, nor
Rv 7:3 Yeu·may·not bring·harm·to the earth, neither the sea,

G3383.3 CONJ μήτε (19x)

Lk 7:33 has·come neither eating bread nor drinking wine,
Lk 9:3 journey, neither staffs, nor knapsack, neither bread,
Ac 23:8 *also* not·even an·angel nor a·spirit, but *the*
Ac 23:12 saying neither to·eat nor to·drink until they·
Ac 23:21 ·to·destruction, neither to·eat nor to·drink until
Ac 27:20 ·neither sun nor constellations·of·stars appearing
Heb 7:3 having neither beginning of·days, nor end of·life†,
Mt 5:35 nor by the earth, because it·is his foot stool,
Mt 5:35 it·is his foot stool, nor toward JeruSalem, because
Mt 11:18 For John came neither eating nor drinking, and
Jac 5:12 swear, neither by·the heaven, nor by·the earth, nor
Jac 5:12 heaven, nor by·the earth, nor by·any other oath.
2Th 2:2 in the mind, nor to·be·woefully·disturbed *by·any*
2Th 2:2 (neither through spirit, nor through word, nor
2Th 2:2 nor through word, nor through letter as·though
1Ti 1:7 what they·say, nor concerning certain·things·which
Rv 7:1 should·not blow on the earth, nor on the sea, nor on
Rv 7:1 blow on the earth, nor on the sea, nor on any tree.
Rv 7:3 ·to the earth, neither the sea, nor the trees, even·until

G3383.4 CONJ μήτε (1x)

Eph 4:27 nor·even give place to·the Slanderer.

G3383.5 CONJ μήτε (1x)

Mk 3:20 ·for them not to·be·able so·much·as to·eat bread.

G3384 μήτηρ mḗtēr *n.* (88x)

Compare:G3994 See:G3388 G3159-1
xLangEquiv:H0517

G3384 N-NSF μήτηρ (33x)

Jn 2:1 Qanah of·Galilee, and the mother of·Jesus was there.
Jn 2:3 And lacking wine, the mother of·Jesus says to him,
Jn 2:5 His mother says to·the attendants, "Whatever he·
Jn 2:12 to CaperNaum (he and his mother, and his brothers,
Jn 19:25 the cross of·Jesus: *Mariam* his mother, his mother's
Jn 19:27 to·the disciple, "Behold your mother!" And from
Lk 1:43 to·me, that the mother of·my Lord should·come to
Lk 1:60 And answering, his mother declared, "No·indeed!
Lk 2:33 And Joseph and his mother were marveling at the·
Lk 2:43 And Joseph and his mother did·not know *of·it.*
Lk 2:48 were·astounded. And his mother declared to him,
Lk 2:51 ·them. And his mother was·thoroughly·guarding all
Lk 8:19 And *his* mother and his brothers came·directly
Lk 8:20 *·several* saying, "Your mother and your brothers
Lk 8:21 ·declared to them, "My mother and my brothers are
Lk 12:53 and son against father; mother against daughter,
Gal 4:26 up·above is free, which is *the* mother of·us all.
Mt 12:46 crowds, behold, his mother and brothers stood
Mt 12:47 "Behold, your mother and your brothers stand
Mt 12:48 "Who is my mother? And who are my brothers?
Mt 12:49 he·declared, "Behold my mother and my brothers!
Mt 12:50 *the* same is my brother, and sister, and mother."
Mt 13:55 his mother referred·to·as Mariam *(meaning·*
Mt 20:20 Then the mother of·the·Sons of·Zebedee came·
Mt 27:56 and Mariam the mother of·*little*·Jacob and Joses,
Mt 27:56 and Joses, and the mother of·the·Sons of·Zebedee.
Mk 3:31 his brothers and his mother come *along*, and
Mk 3:32 "Behold, your mother and your brothers seek·for
Mk 3:33 "Who is my mother, or my brothers?
Mk 3:34 "See, my mother and my brothers!
Mk 3:35 this·one is my brother, and my sister, and mother."
Mk 15:40 and Mariam (the mother of·little Jacob and of·
Rv 17:5 GREAT, THE MOTHER OF·THE PROSTITUTES

G3384 N-ASF μητέρα (26x)

Jn 6:42 father and mother we·ourselves personally·know?
Jn 19:26 Jesus seeing his mother and the disciple standing·
Lk 2:34 and he·declared to Mariam his mother, "Behold,
Lk 8:51 and John, and the father and the mother of·the girl.
Lk 14:26 considerately·hate his father, and mother, and wife
Lk 18:20 ' "Deeply·honor your father and your mother.' "
Mt 2:13 ·take the little·child and his mother, and flee into
Mt 2:14 the little·child and his mother by·night and departed
Mt 2:20 ·take the little·child and his mother, and traverse
Mt 2:21 ·took the little·child and his mother and came into
Mt 10:37 affectionately·favoring father or mother over me is
Mt 15:4 "Deeply·honor your father and mother,' and
Mt 15:4 ·ill·of father or mother must·completely·die *the*
Mt 15:6 deeply·honor his father or his mother.' And·thus,
Mt 19:5 father and the mother and shall·be·tightly·bonded
Mt 19:19 "'Deeply·honor your father and mother,'" and
Mt 19:29 or sisters or father or mother or wife or children or
Mk 5:40 the little·child's father and mother and the·ones with
Mk 7:10 Deeply·honor your father and your mother'; and,
Mk 7:10 ·ill·of father or mother must·completely·die *the*
Mk 10:7 shall·leave·behind his father and mother, and shall·
Mk 10:19 rob,' "Deeply·honor your father and mother.' "
Mk 10:29 or sisters or father or mother or wife or children or
Rm 16:13 in *the* Lord, and his mother and mine.
Eph 5:31 shall·leave·behind his father and mother, and shall·
Eph 6:2 "'Deeply·honor your father and mother'" (which is

G3384 N-APF μητέρας (2x)

Mk 10:30 brothers and sisters and mothers and children and
1Ti 5:2 older·women as mothers, younger·women as sisters,

G3384 N-DSF μητρί (12x)

Jn 19:26 whom he·loved, he·says to·his mother, "Woman,
Lk 7:12 ·died, an·only son of·his mother, and she·herself
Lk 7:15 And he·gave him to·his mother.
Lk 12:53 and daughter against mother; mother-in-law
Ac 1:14 with·women and Mariam the mother of·Jesus, and·
Mt 14:11 ·the young·girl, and she·brought *it* to·her mother.
Mt 15:5 ·declare to·his father or to·his mother, "Although
Mk 6:24 *of·the room*, she·declared to·her mother, "What
Mk 6:28 ·girl, and the young·girl gave it to·her mother.
Mk 7:11 ·declare to·his father or to·his mother, "Although
Mk 7:12 do·not·even·one·thing for·his father or his mother,
2Ti 1:5 your grandmother Lois and your mother EuNiki, and

G3384 N-GSF μητρός (12x)

Jn 3:4 ·time into the womb of·his mother and to·be·born?
Jn 19:25 *Mariam* his mother, his mother's sister (Miryam
Lk 1:15 Spirit, yet·even from·within his mother's womb.
Ac 3:2 from·out of·his mother's womb was·lifted·and·carried
Ac 12:12 to the home of·Miri, the mother of·John (being·
Ac 14:8 ·being lame from·out·of·his mother's womb, who
Gal 1:15 ·detaching me from·out of·my mother's womb and
Mt 1:18 For with·his mother Mariam already·being·espoused
Mt 2:11 the little·child with Mariam his mother. And falling·
Mt 10:35 his father, a·daughter against her mother, and a·
Mt 14:8 And after·being·urged·on by her mother, she·replied
Mt 19:12 in·this·manner from·out *of·their* mother's womb.

EG3384 (3x)

Lk 24:10 Joanna, and Mariam *the mother* of·*little*·Jacob, and
Mk 15:47 Magdalene and Miryam (*mother* of·Jose), *being*
Mk 16:1 and Mariam (the *mother* of·*little*·Jacob) and Salome

G3385 μή•τι mḗti *prt.* (13x)

Roots:G3361 G5100

G3385.ª PRT-I μήτι (8x)

Jn 4:29 to·me all the·many·things I·did! Could this be the
Jn 8:22 Judeans were·saying, "Is·it·that he·shall·kill himself
Lk 6:39 a·parable to·them: "Is·it possible·for *the* blind to·
Ac 10:47 "Is any·man able to·forbid water *such·for* these not
Mt 12:23 ·astonished and were·saying, "Could this be the
Mk 14:19 and to·say to·him one·by·one, "Is·it I·myself?
Mk 14:19 "Is·it I·myself?" And another, "Is·it I·myself?
1Co 6:3 angels? How·much·more still of·secular·matters?

G3385.2 PRT-I μήτι (5x)

Jn 7:31 the Anointed-One should·come, ¿! shall·he·do more
Jn 18:35 Pilate answered, "¿! Am·I myself a·Jew?
Mt 7:16 them. "¿!·Do men·collect a·cluster·of·grapes from
Mk 4:21 to·them, "¿!·Is·it·ever·the·case·that the lantern is·
Jac 3:11 ¿!·Does the wellspring gush·forth at the same

G3387 μή•τις mḗtis *prt.* (1x)
μή τὶς mḗ tìs

Roots:G3361 G5100

G3387 PRT μήτις (1x)

Ac 27:42 lest·any might·thoroughly·escape by·swimming·

G3388 μήτρα mḗtra *n.* (2x)

Roots:G3384 Compare:G1064 G2836
xLangEquiv:H7358 xLangAlso:H0990 H7356

G3388.2 N-ASF μήτραν (1x)

Lk 2:23 thoroughly·opening·up a·primal·womb shall·be·

G3388.2 N-GSF μήτρας (1x)

Rm 4:19 ·of·age, nor the deadness of·Sarah's primal·womb.

G3389 μητρ•αλῴας mētralṓias *n.* (1x)

Roots:G3384 G0257 Compare:G3390-1 G3970-1
See:G3964

G3389.2 N-DPM μητραλῴαις (1x)

1Ti 1:9 for·thrashers·of·fathers and thrashers·of·mothers,

G3391 μία mía *n.* (79x)

Roots:G1520 Compare:G1520 See:G1775

G3391.1 N-NSF μία (15x)

Jn 10:16 and *together* it·shall·become one flock *and* one
Lk 17:35 grinding in·unison; one shall·be·personally·taken,
Ac 4:32 the heart and the soul was one. And not·even one
Ac 19:34 he·was a·Jew, there·came one voice from·out·of·
Gal 4:24 are the two covenants. One in·fact *is* from Mount
Mt 5:18 ·away, not one iota or one tiny·mark, by·no·means,
Mt 19:6 no·longer two, but·rather one flesh. Accordingly,
Mt 24:41 at the mill-house; one is·personally·taken, and one
Mt 24:41 one is·personally·taken, and one is·left.
Mt 26:69 the courtyard, and one servant·girl came·alongside
Mk 10:8 ·such, they·are no·longer two, but·rather one flesh.
Mk 14:66 courtyard, *along* comes one of·the servant·girls
2Pe 3:8 O·yeu beloved, that "one day *is* with *the* Lord as
2Pe 3:8 a·thousand years, and a·thousand years as one day."
Eph 4:5 one Lord, one trust, one immersion,

G3391.1 N-ASF μίαν (32x)

Lk 9:33 and we·should·make three tabernacles; one·for you,
Lk 9:33 tabernacles; one·for you, one·for Moses, and one·
Lk 9:33 ·for you, one·for Moses, and one·for EliJah," not
Lk 15:8 *·silver*, if she·should·completely·lose one drachma,
Lk 16:17 the earth to·pass·away, than one tiny·mark of·the
Lk 17:22 ·come when yeu·shall·long to·see one of·the days
Ac 12:10 And going·forth, they·went·onward one alleyway,
Ac 21:7 the brothers, we·abided with them one day.

Ac 28:13 Rhegium. And after one day, with·*the*·south·wind
Heb 10:12 he·himself, after·offering one sacrifice on·behalf
Mt 5:19 whoever should·break one of·these least
Mt 5:36 because you·are·not able to·make one hair white or
Mt 17:4 ·make three tabernacles here: one for·you, and one
Mt 17:4 here: one for·you, and one for·Moses, and one for·
Mt 17:4 for·you, and one for·Moses, and one for·EliJah."
Mt 19:5 ·his wife, and the two shall·be distinctly one flesh'"?
Mt 20:12 'These last·ones did one hour, and you·made them
Mt 21:19 And seeing one fig·tree by the roadway, he·came
Mt 26:40 have·strength to·keep·alert with me *for* one hour?
Mk 9:5 we·should·make three tabernacles: one for·you, and
Mk 9:5 one for·you, and one for·Moses, and one for·EliJah
Mk 9:5 for·you, and one for·Moses, and one for·EliJah."
Mk 10:8 and the two shall·be distinctly one flesh.'' As·such,
Mk 14:37 ·you·not have·strength to·keep·alert *for* one hour?
1Co 6:16 two,'' he·replies, '"shall·be distinctly one flesh."'
2Co 11:24 by *the* Jews I·received forty *stripes* minus one.
Eph 5:31 wife, and the two shall·be distinctly one flesh.'"
Rv 9:13 sounded, and I·heard one voice from·among the
Rv 13:3 And I·saw one of·its heads as·though having·been·
Rv 17:12 ·do·receive authority as kings *for* one hour with the
Rv 17:13 "These have *just* one plan, and they·thoroughly·
Rv 17:17 his plan, and to·do *just* one plan, also to·give their
G3391.1 N-DSF μιᾷ (12x)
Lk 5:12 And it·happened with him being in one of·the cities,
Lk 8:22 Now it·happened on one of·the days that he·himself
Lk 13:10 Now he·was instructing in one of·the gatherings on
Lk 20:1 And it·happened, *that* on one of·those days, with·
Heb 10:14 For by·one offering, he·has·made·fully·complete
Php 1:27 in one spirit, with·one soul struggling·together for·
1Co 10:8 and twenty·three thousand fell in one day.
Eph 4:4 also yeu·are·called·forth in one expectation of·yeur
Rv 18:8 her punishing·blows shall·come in one day: death,
Rv 18:10 City! Because in one hour your Tribunal·judgment
Rv 18:17 Because in·one hour such·vast wealth is·desolated.
Rv 18:19 of·her valuableness! Because in·one hour, she·is·
G3391.1 N-GSF μιᾶς (8x)
Lk 14:18 "And with one *intent*, they·all began to·excuse·
Lk 17:34 night there·shall·be two *reclining* on one couch; the
Lk 22:59 And with·an·interval·of about one hour, someone
Ac 24:21 other·than concerning this one address that I·
Heb 12:16 as Esau, who for one full·meal gave·away his
Tit 1:6 ·any·charge·of·wrong·doing, a·husband of·one wife,
1Ti 3:2 ·all·blame·and·suspicion, a·husband of·one wife,
1Ti 3:12 Stewards must·be husbands of·one wife, conducting
G3391.2 N-NSF μία (1x)
Rv 9:12 The first woe went·away; behold, there·come two
G3391.2 N-ASF μίαν (4x)
Mt 28:1 ·it·growing·light toward the first *dawn* of·the·week,
Tit 3:10 that·is·divisively·selective after a·first and second
1Co 16:2 Each first *day* of·the·week, let each·one of·yeu lay
Rv 6:1 when the Lamb opened·up *the* first from·among the
G3391.2 N-DSF μιᾷ (4x)
Jn 20:1 Now, on·the first *day* of·the week at·the·watch·of·
Jn 20:19 on·that *same* day, the first *day* of·the week, and
Lk 24:1 Now on·the first *day* of·the week, with·*the*·sunrise
Ac 20:7 And on·the first *day* of·the week, with·the disciples
G3391.2 N-GSF μιᾶς (1x)
Mk 16:2 at·the·watch·of·dawn of·the first *day* of·*the*·week,
G3391.3 N-NSF μία (1x)
Mk 12:42 upon·coming, a·certain helplessly·poor widow
G3391.3 N-DSF μιᾷ (1x)
Lk 5:17 And it·happened on a·certain day, even while he·

G3392 μιαίνω miaínō *v.* (5x)
Compare:G2840 See:G3393 G0283 G1591-2 G3392-1
xLangEquiv:H2930
G3392 V-PAI-3P μιαίνουσιν (1x)
Jud 1:8 *irreverent* dreamers, in·fact, contaminate flesh,
G3392 V-APS-3P μιανθῶσιν (2x)
Jn 18:28 ·hall, lest they·should·be·contaminated, but·rather
Heb 12:15 and through this, many should·be·contaminated;
G3392 V-RPI-3S μεμίανται (1x)
Tit 1:15 their mind and conscience has·been·contaminated.
G3392 V-RPP-DPM μεμιασμένοις (1x)
Tit 1:15 to·the·ones having·been·contaminated and *to·the*

G3393 μίασμα míasma *n.* (1x)
Roots:G3392 Compare:G0234 G2839 G0167 G4507
See:G3394 G0283
G3393.2 N-APN μιάσματα (1x)
2Pe 2:20 ·escaping·from the contaminations of·the world by

G3394 μιασμός miasmốs *n.* (1x)
Roots:G3392 See:G3393
G3394.1 N-GSM μιασμοῦ (1x)
2Pe 2:10 who·are·traversing in a·contaminating longing,

G3395 μίγμα mígma *n.* (1x)
Roots:G3396 See:G3398-2
G3395.1 N-ASN μίγμα (1x)
Jn 19:39 to Jesus by·night, bringing a·mixture of·myrrh and

G3396 μίγνυμι mígnymi *v.* (4x)
Compare:G2767 See:G3395 G3398-2 G1961-1
G4830-3 G2650-3 G4783-2
G3396 V-AAI-3S ἔμιξεν (1x)
Lk 13:1 whose blood Pilate mixed with their sacrifices.
G3396 V-RPP-ASN μεμιγμένον (1x)
Mt 27:34 wine·vinegar to·drink having·been·mixed with gall
G3396 V-RPP-ASF μεμιγμένην (1x)
Rv 15:2 ·glassy sea having·been·mixed with·fire, and·also
G3396 V-RPP-NPN μεμιγμένα (1x)
Rv 8:7 hail and fire having·been·mixed with·blood, and

G3397 μικρόν mikrốn *adj.* (16x)
Roots:G3398 Compare:G3641
G3397.2 A-ASM μικρόν (1x)
Mt 26:39 And going·onward a·little·bit, he·fell on his face,
G3397.2 A-ASN μικρόν (1x)
Mk 14:35 And going·onward a·little·bit, he·fell on the soil
G3397.3 A-ASM μικρόν (1x)
Mk 14:70 *it* again. And a·little·while after, the·ones
G3397.3 A-ASN μικρόν (13x)
Jn 13:33 "Dear·children, yet a·little·while I·am with yeu.
Jn 14:19 "Yet a·little·while, and the world observes me no
Jn 16:16 "A·little·while, and yeu·do·not observe me, and
Jn 16:16 and again, a·little·while, and yeu·shall·gaze·upon
Jn 16:17 that he·says to·us, 'A·little·while, and yeu·do·not
Jn 16:17 and again, a·little·while, and yeu·shall·gaze·upon
Jn 16:18 this·thing that he·says, 'A·little·while?' We·do·not
Jn 16:19 which I·declared, 'A·little·while, and yeu·do·not
Jn 16:19 and again, a·little·while, and yeu·shall·gaze·upon
Heb 10:37 For yet, as·long·as a·little·while, the·one who·is·
Mt 26:73 And coming·alongside after a·little·while, the·ones
2Co 11:1 ·bear·with me a·little·while in·the impulsiveness
2Co 11:16 impetuous in·order·that, *for* a·little·while, even·I

G3398 μικρός mikrốs *adj.* (30x)
μικρότερος mikrốterŏs [comparative]
Compare:G1646
G3398.1 A-NSM μικρός (1x)
Lk 19:3 ·to for the crowd, because he·was small of·stature.
G3398.1 A-NSN μικρόν (1x)
Jac 3:5 in·this·manner, the tongue is a·small member, yet·it·
G3398.1 A-NSN-C μικρότερον (1x)
Mt 13:32 which in·fact is smaller·than all the variety·of·
G3398.1 A-NPM μικροί (1x)
Rv 19:5 ·reverently·fearing him, both the small and the great
G3398.1 A-APM μικρούς (2x)
Rv 13:16 And it·makes all, the small and the great, also the
Rv 20:12 And I·saw the dead·ones, small and great,
G3398.1 A-DSM μικρῷ (1x)
Ac 26:22 this day, being·a·witness to·both small and great,
G3398.1 A-DPM μικροῖς (1x)
Rv 11:18 ·fearing your name, the small and the great, and·
G3398.1 A-GPM μικρῶν (1x)
Rv 19:18 ·men, *both* free and slave, both small and great."
G3398.2 A-NSF μικρά (2x)
Gal 5:9 A·little leaven leavens the whole lump·of·dough.
1Co 5:6 ·yeu·not personally·know that a·little leaven leavens
G3398.2 A-NSN μικρόν (1x)
Lk 12:32 "Do·not be·afraid, Little Flock, because yeur
G3398.2 A-ASF μικράν (1x)
Rv 3:8 ·able to·shut it, because you·have a·little power, and
G3398.2 A-GSM μικροῦ (1x)
Mk 15:40 Mariam (the mother of·little Jacob and of·Joses),
G3398.2 A-GPM μικρῶν (6x)
Lk 17:2 ·cause·the·moral·failure·of one of·these little·ones.
Mt 10:42 ·give to·one of·these little·ones a·cup of·cold
Mt 18:6 ·moral·failure·of one of·these little·ones, the·ones
Mt 18:10 yeu·should·not despise one of·these little·ones, for
Mt 18:14 one of·these little·ones should·completely·perish.
Mk 9:42 ·the·moral·failure·of one of·the little·ones, the·ones
G3398.3 A-NSM-C μικρότερος (4x)
Lk 7:28 the Immerser, but the least·one in the kingdom of·
Lk 9:48 me, for the·one inherently·being least among yeu all
Mt 11:11 But the·one *who·is* least in the kingdom of·the
Mk 4:31 in the earth, *is* least of·all the variety·of·seeds that·
G3398.3 A-GSM μικροῦ (2x)
Ac 8:10 were·giving·heed, from *the* least unto *the* greatest,
Heb 8:11 ·know me, from *the* least of·them unto *the* greatest
G3398.4 A-ASM μικρόν (4x)
Jn 7:33 declared to·them, "Yet a·short time am·I with yeu,
Jn 12:35 declared to·them, "Yet a·short time is the light with
Rv 6:11 ·them that they·should·rest yet *for* a·short time, until
Rv 20:3 it·is·mandatory·for him to·be·loosed a·short time.

G3399 Μίλητος Mílētŏs *n/l.* (3x)
G3399 N/L-ASF Μίλητον (1x)
Ac 20:15 the following *day* we·came to Miletus,
G3399 N/L-DSF Μιλήτῳ (1x)
2Ti 4:20 Trophimus, being·sick, I·left·behind at Miletus.
G3399 N/L-GSF Μιλήτου (1x)
Ac 20:17 And from Miletus, after·sending·word to Ephesus,

G3400 μίλιον míliŏn *n.* (1x)
G3400 N-ASN μίλιον (1x)
Mt 5:41 ·upon you *to·head·out·for* one mile, head·on·out

G3401 μιμέομαι mimếŏmai *v.* (4x)
See:G3402
G3401.2 V-PNM-2S μιμοῦ (1x)
3Jn 1:11 Beloved·man, do·not attentively·imitate the bad,
G3401.2 V-PNM-2P μιμεῖσθε (1x)
Heb 13:7 trust yeu·are·to·attentively·imitate, observing·
G3401.2 V-PNN μιμεῖσθαι (2x)
2Th 3:7 ·seen how it·is·necessary to·attentively·imitate us,
2Th 3:9 a·model·example for·yeu to·attentively·imitate us.

G3402 μιμητής mimētḗs *n.* (7x)
Roots:G3401
G3402.2 N-NPM μιμηταί (7x)
Heb 6:12 ·slothful, but attentive·imitators of·the·ones *who*
1Pe 3:13 if yeu·should·become attentive·imitators of·the
1Th 1:6 ·yeurselves did·become attentive·imitators of·us and
1Th 2:14 did·become attentive·imitators of·the Called·Out·
1Co 4:16 I·implore yeu, become attentive·imitators of·me.
1Co 11:1 Be attentive·imitators of·me, just·as I·also *am* of·
Eph 5:1 Accordingly, become attentive·imitators of·God, as

G3403 μιμνήσκω mimnḗskō *v.* (3x)
Roots:G3415
EG3403.1 (1x)
Gal 2:10 Merely *they·reminded us* that we·should·remember
G3403.2 V-PNM-2P μιμνῄσκεσθε (1x)
Heb 13:3 Keep·in·mind the chained·prisoners, as having·
G3403.3 V-PNI-2S μιμνῄσκη (1x)
Heb 2:6 mortal·man†, that you·are·actively·mindful of·him?

G3404 μισέω misếō *v.* (43x)
Roots:G3411-1 Compare:G4768-2 G0655 G0948
G2190 G4768 See:G3404-1
xLangEquiv:H8130 A8131
G3404.1 V-FAI-2S μισήσεις (1x)
Mt 5:43 ·shall·love your neighbor and shall·hate your enemy
G3404.1 V-FAI-3S μισήσει (2x)
Lk 16:13 to·two lords, for either he·shall·hate the one and

Mt 6:24 to·two lords. For either he·shall·hate the one and
G3404.1 V-FAI-3P μισήσουσιν (2x)
Mt 24:10 one·another over, and shall·hate one·another.
Rv 17:16 the Scarlet·Beast, these shall·hate the Prostitute,
G3404.1 V-PAI-1S μισῶ (3x)
Rm 7:15 ·want *to·do*, but·rather I·do that·thing which I·hate.
Rv 2:6 the deeds of·the NicoLaitans, which I·also hate.
Rv 2:15 instruction of·the NicoLaitans, which·thing I·hate.
G3404.1 V-PAI-2S μισεῖς (1x)
Rv 2:6 But·yet you·have this, that you·hate the deeds of·the
G3404.1 V-PAI-3S μισεῖ (6x)
Jn 3:20 any one practicing mediocrity hates the light, and
Jn 7:7 able to·hate yeu, but it·hates me, because I·myself
Jn 15:18 "If the world hates yeu, yeu·know that it·has·hated
Jn 15:19 On·account·of this, the world hates yeu.
Jn 15:23 "The·one hating me, hates my Father also.
1Jn 3:13 ·not marvel, my brothers, if the world hates yeu.
G3404.1 V-PAN μισεῖν (1x)
Jn 7:7 The world is·not able to·hate yeu, but it·hates me,
G3404.1 V-PAP-APM μισοῦντας (1x)
Mt 5:44 "Do good to·the·ones hating yeu, and pray on·behalf
G3404.1 V-PAP-DPM μισοῦσιν (1x)
Lk 6:27 Love yeur enemies, do good to·the·ones hating yeu,
G3404.1 V-PAP-GPM μισούντων (1x)
Lk 1:71 and from·among *the* hand of·all the·ones hating us;
G3404.1 V-PAP-NSM μισῶν (4x)
Jn 15:23 "The·one hating me, hates my Father also.
1Jn 2:9 *himself* to·be in the light, and hating his brother, is in
1Jn 2:11 But the·one hating his brother is in the darkness,
1Jn 3:15 Any one presently·hating his brother is a·
G3404.1 V-PAP-NPM μισοῦντες (2x)
Jud 1:23 *them* from·out of·the fire, hating even the tunic
Tit 3:3 malice and envy, detestable·men hating one·another.
G3404.1 V-PAS-3S μισῇ (1x)
1Jn 4:20 "I·love God," and he·should·hate his brother, he·is
G3404.1 V-PPP-NPM μισούμενοι (4x)
Lk 21:17 And yeu·shall·be being·hated by all on·account·of
Mt 10:22 And yeu·shall·be being·hated by all *men* on·
Mt 24:9 ·kill yeu, and yeu·shall·be being·hated by all the
Mk 13:13 And yeu·shall·be being·hated by all *men* on·
G3404.1 V-IAI-3P ἐμίσουν (1x)
Lk 19:14 "But his citizens were·hating him, and they·
G3404.1 V-AAI-1S ἐμίσησα (1x)
Rm 9:13 ·been·written, "Jacob I·loved, but Esau I·hated."
G3404.1 V-AAI-2S ἐμίσησας (1x)
Heb 1:9 You·loved righteousness and hated lawlessness.
G3404.1 V-AAI-3S ἐμίσησεν (2x)
Jn 17:14 and the world hated them because they·are not
Eph 5:29 For not·even·one·man ever hated his·own flesh,
G3404.1 V-AAI-3P ἐμίσησαν (1x)
Jn 15:25 "They·personally·hated me freely·without·cause.
G3404.1 V-AAS-3P μισήσωσιν (1x)
Lk 6:22 whenever the men·of·clay† should·hate yeu, and
G3404.1 V-RAI-3S μεμίσηκεν (1x)
Jn 15:18 yeu, yeu·know that it·has·hated me first·before *it*·
G3404.1 V-RAI-3P μεμισήκασιν (1x)
Jn 15:24 also they·have·clearly·seen and have·hated both me
EG3404.1 (1x)
Jn 15:18 ·know that it·has·hated me first·before *it·hated* yeu.
G3404.2 V-RPP-GSN μεμισημένου (1x)
Rv 18:2 ·cell of·every impure and intensely·hated fowl.
G3404.3 V-PAI-3S μισεῖ (1x)
Lk 14:26 to me and does·not considerately·hate his father,
G3404.3 V-PAP-NSM μισῶν (1x)
Jn 12:25 it; and the·one considerately·hating his soul in this

G3405 μισθ•απο•δοσία misthapôdôsía *n.* (3x)
Roots:G3406 Compare:G0469 G0489
G3405.1 N-ASF μισθαποδοσίαν (2x)
Heb 10:35 ·declaration, which has great reward·for·service.
Heb 11:26 he·was·intently·looking to the reward·for·service.
G3405.2 N-ASF μισθαποδοσίαν (1x)
Heb 2:2 ·disregard received a·just reward·for·disservice,

G3406 μισθ•απο•δότης misthapôdótēs *n.* (1x)
Roots:G3408 G0591 See:G3405
G3406.3 N-NSM μισθαποδότης (1x)
Heb 11:6 *that* he·comes·to·be an·appropriate·rewarder to·

G3407 μίσθιος místhiôs *adj.* (2x)
Roots:G3408 Compare:G3411 xLangAlso:H7916
G3407.2 A-NPM μίσθιοι (1x)
Lk 15:17 father's hired·men have·an·abundance of·bread,
G3407.2 A-GPM μισθίων (1x)
Lk 15:19 your son; make me as one of·your hired·men."'

G3408 μισθός misthós *n.* (29x)
Compare:G0489 G3405 See:G3409 G3406 G3407 xLangEquiv:H7939 xLangAlso:H4909
G3408.1 N-NSM μισθός (7x)
Lk 6:23 for, behold, yeur payment·of·service *is* large in the
Lk 6:35 — "and yeur payment·of·service shall·be large, and
Mt 5:12 ·for·joy, because yeur payment·of·service *is* large
Rm 4:4 working, the payment·of·service is·not reckoned
Jac 5:4 Behold, the payment·of·service for·the workmen
1Co 9:18 Now·then, the payment·of·service: What is *the*
Rv 22:12 swiftly, and my payment·of·service *is* with me, to·
G3408.1 N-ASM μισθόν (18x)
Jn 4:36 receives payment·of·service and gathers·together
Mt 5:46 loving yeu, what payment·of·service do·yeu·have?
Mt 6:1 ·not have a·payment·of·service personally·from yeur
Mt 6:2 ·yeu, they·completely·have their payment·of·service.
Mt 6:5 ·yeu, they·completely·have their payment·of·service.
Mt 6:16 that they·completely·have their payment·of·service.
Mt 10:41 shall·receive a·prophet's payment·of·service; and
Mt 10:41 ·receive a·righteous·man's payment·of·service.
Mt 10:42 ·not completely·lose his payment·of·service."
Mt 20:8 render to·them the payment·of·service, beginning
Mk 9:41 ·not completely·lose his payment·of·service.
2Pe 2:13 ·be·subsequently·obtaining a·payment·of·service,
2Pe 2:15 loved a·payment·of·service for·unrighteousness.
1Co 3:8 his·own payment·of·service according·to his·own
1Co 3:14 *foundation*, he·shall·receive a·payment·of·service.
1Co 9:17 voluntarily, I·have a·payment·of·service, but *even*
2Jn 1:8 that·we·may·fully·receive a·full payment·of·service.
Rv 11:18 ·*you* to·give the payment·of·service to·your slaves
G3408.1 N-GSM μισθοῦ (4x)
Lk 10:7 is worthy of·his payment·of·service. Do·not walk·on
Ac 1:18 ·field out of·the payment·of·service for·the injustice
Jud 1:11 the error of·BalaAm for·a·payment·of·service, and
1Ti 5:18 workman *is* deserving of·his payment·of·service.

G3409 μισθόω misthôō *v.* (5x)
Roots:G3408 Compare:G5099 See:G3410 G3411 xLangEquiv:H7936
G3409 V-AMI-3S ἐμισθώσατο (1x)
Mt 20:7 to·him, 'Because no·one·at·all hired us.' He·says
G3409 V-AMN μισθώσασθαι (1x)
Mt 20:1 ·out at·the·same·time as·dawn to·hire workmen into
EG3409 (3x)
Mt 20:2 ·agreeing with the workmen *to·hire them* for a·
Mt 20:9 upon·coming *forward*, the·ones *hired* about the
Mt 20:10 But the first·ones *hired*, upon·coming *forward*,

G3410 μίσθωμα místhōma *n.* (1x)
Roots:G3409 See:G3411
G3410 N-DSN μισθώματι (1x)
Ac 28:30 a·whole two·years in his·own hired·house. And he·

G3411 μισθωτός misthōtós *n.* (4x)
Roots:G3409 Compare:G3407 See:G3410
G3411 N-NSM μισθωτός (3x)
Jn 10:12 "But the hired·worker, not even being a·shepherd
Jn 10:13 And the hired·worker flees, because he·is a·hired·
Jn 10:13 flees, because he·is a·hired·worker, and it·does·not
G3411 N-GPM μισθωτῶν (1x)
Mk 1:20 in the sailboat with the hired·workers, they·went·off

G3412 Μιτυλήνη Mitylḗnē *n/l.* (1x)
G3412.2 N/L-ASF Μιτυλήνην (1x)
Ac 20:14 after·taking him aboard, we·came to Mitylene.

G3413 Μι•χα•ήλ Michaḗl *n/p.* (2x)
מִיכָאֵל mıykạ'el [Hebrew]
Roots:H4317 Compare:G1043
G3413.2 N/P-PRI Μιχαήλ (2x)
Jud 1:9 Now MiChaEl the chief·angel, when verbally·
Rv 12:7 war in the heaven. MiChaEl and his angels waged·

G3414 μνᾶ mnâ *n.* (9x)
μνᾶς mnâs [comparative]
See:G1406 G1220 xLangEquiv:H4488 xLangAlso:H8255
G3414.3 N-NSF μνᾶ (3x)
Lk 19:16 'Lord, your mina actively·earned ten more·minas.
Lk 19:18 'Lord, your mina produced five more·minas.
Lk 19:20 behold, *here·is* your mina which I·was·holding
G3414.3 N-ASF-C μνᾶν (1x)
Lk 19:24 standing·nearby, 'Take·away the mina from him,
G3414.4 N-APF-C μνᾶς (5x)
Lk 19:13 slaves, he·gave ten more·silver·minas to·them and
Lk 19:16 Lord, your mina actively·earned ten more·minas.'
Lk 19:18 'Lord, your mina produced five more·minas.'
Lk 19:24 and give *it* to·the·one having the ten more·minas.'
Lk 19:25 'Lord, he·*already*·has ten more·minas!'

G3415 μνάομαι mnáômai *v.* (21x)
Roots:G3416-1 See:G3403 G3421
G3415.1 V-API-1S ἐμνήσθην (1x)
Ac 11:16 "Then I·recalled·to·mind the utterance of·*the*·Lord,
G3415.1 V-API-3S ἐμνήσθη (2x)
Mt 26:75 And Peter was·*suddenly*·mindful of·the utterance
Rv 16:19 the Great was·recalled·to·mind in·the·sight of·God
G3415.1 V-API-3P ἐμνήσθησαν (5x)
Jn 2:17 And his disciples recalled·to·mind that it·was
Jn 2:22 his disciples recalled·to·mind that he·was·saying
Jn 12:16 then they·recalled·to·mind that these·things were
Lk 24:8 And they·recalled·to·mind his utterances.
Ac 10:31 merciful·acts were·recalled·to·mind in·the·sight
G3415.1 V-APM-2S μνήσθητι (2x)
Lk 16:25 declared, 'Child, recall·to·mind that you, in your
Lk 23:42 to·Jesus, "Lord, recall me to·mind whenever you·
G3415.1 V-APM-2P μνήσθητε (2x)
Lk 24:6 ·rather is·awakened. Recall·to·mind how he·spoke
Jud 1:17 But yeu, beloved, recall·to·mind the utterances,
G3415.1 V-APS-1S μνησθῶ (2x)
Heb 8:12 no, I·should·not recall·to·mind any·longer.'
Heb 10:17 no, I·should·not recall·to·mind any·longer."
G3415.1 V-APS-2S μνησθῇς (1x)
Mt 5:23 and·there you·should·recall·to·mind that your
G3415.3 V-API-1P ἐμνήσθημεν (1x)
Mt 27:63 saying, "Sir, we·are·mindful·of that thing the
G3415.3 V-APN μνησθῆναι (3x)
Lk 1:54 his servant·boy IsraEl, being·mindful of·*his*·mercy
Lk 1:72 our fathers, and to·be·mindful of·his holy covenant;
2Pe 3:2 To·be·mindful of·the utterances having·been·
G3415.3 V-RPI-2P μέμνησθε (1x)
1Co 11:2 that yeu·have·been·mindful of·me in·all·things,
G3415.3 V-RPP-NSM μεμνημένος (1x)
2Ti 1:4 (having·been·mindful of·your tears)— while·greatly·

G3416 Μνάσων Mnásōn *n/p.* (1x)
G3416 N/P-DSM Μνάσωνι (1x)
Ac 21:16 with *them* a·certain·man, Mnason of·Cyprus, an·

G3417 μνεία mnêía *n.* (7x)
Roots:G3415 G3403 Compare:G0364 G3419 G3420
G3417.1 N-ASF μνείαν (4x)
Rm 1:9 of·his Son, how unceasingly I·make mention of·yeu
1Th 1:2 all of·yeu, making mention of·yeu in our prayers,
Eph 1:16 on·behalf of·yeu, making mention of·yeu in my
Phm 1:4 to·my God, making mention of·you always in my
G3417.1 N-DSF μνείᾳ (1x)
Php 1:3 I·give·thanks to·my God upon every mention of·yeu,
G3417.2 N-ASF μνείαν (1x)
2Ti 1:3 without·ceasing I·have a·reminder concerning you in
G3417.4 N-ASF μνείαν (1x)
1Th 3:6 a·beneficially·good remembrance of·us always,

G3418 μνῆμα mnē̂ma *n.* (7x)
Roots:G3415 Compare:G3422 See:G3419 xLangAlso:H6913

G3418.2 N-NSN μνῆμα (1x)
Ac 2:29 ·dead and buried, and his tomb is with us even·unto

G3418.2 N-ASN μνῆμα (1x)
Lk 24:1 they·came to the tomb, bringing aromatic·spices

G3418.2 N-APN μνήματα (1x)
Rv 11:9 shall·not allow their corpses to·be·placed in tombs.

G3418.2 N-DSN μνήματι (2x)
Lk 23:53 in a·tomb *that·was* chiseled·out·within·a·mass·of·
Ac 7:16 Shekem and laid in the tomb that AbRaham's *son*

G3418.2 N-DPN μνήμασιν (2x)
Lk 8:27 ·not abiding in *any* home, but·rather in the tombs.
Mk 5:5 on the mountains and in the tombs, yelling·out and

G3419 μνημεῖον mnēmêîôn *n.* (42x)
Roots:G3420 Compare:G3422 G5028 See:G3418 G3417 xLangAlso:H6913

G3419.2 N-NSN μνημεῖον (2x)
Jn 19:41 ·garden, *there·was* a·brand-new chamber·tomb, in
Jn 19:42 ·day, because the chamber·tomb was near·at·hand.

G3419.2 N-NPN μνημεῖα (2x)
Lk 11:44 Because yeu·are as the chamber·tombs, the
Mt 27:52 and the chamber·tombs are·opened·up, and many

G3419.2 N-ASN μνημεῖον (16x)
Jn 11:31 to the chamber·tomb in·order·that she·may·weep
Jn 11:38 himself, comes to the chamber·tomb. Now it·was
Jn 20:1 Magdalene comes to the chamber·tomb and looks·at
Jn 20:3 went·forth, and they·came to the chamber·tomb.
Jn 20:4 outran Peter and came first to the chamber·tomb.
Jn 20:6 him, and he·entered into the chamber·tomb. And he·
Jn 20:8 ·one coming first to the chamber·tomb. And he·saw
Jn 20:11 stood outside toward the chamber·tomb weeping.
Jn 20:11 she·stooped·near·to·peer into the chamber·tomb,
Lk 23:55 did·distinctly·view the chamber·tomb and how his
Lk 24:12 Peter ran to the chamber·tomb, and stooping·near·
Lk 24:22 after·coming at·early·sunrise to the chamber·tomb;
Lk 24:24 with·us went·off to the chamber·tomb, and found *it*
Ac 13:29 the arbor·tree, they·laid *him* in a·chamber·tomb.
Mk 16:2 they·went to the chamber·tomb with·the sun
Mk 16:5 upon·entering into the chamber·tomb, they·saw a·

G3419.2 N-APN μνημεῖα (3x)
Lk 11:47 yeu·build the chamber·tombs of·the prophets, and
Lk 11:48 and yeu·yeurselves build their chamber·tombs.
Mt 23:29 and decorate the chamber·tombs of·the righteous,

G3419.2 N-DSN μνημείῳ (4x)
Jn 11:17 *been·laid·to·rest* in the chamber·tomb four days
Mt 27:60 it in his·own brand-new chamber·tomb, which he·
Mk 6:29 ·away his corpse and laid it in the chamber·tomb.
Mk 15:46 and fully·laid him in a·chamber·tomb which was

G3419.2 N-DPN μνημείοις (2x)
Jn 5:28 all the·ones in the chamber·tombs shall·hear his
Mk 5:3 his residence among the chamber·tombs. And not·

G3419.2 N-GSN μνημείου (10x)
Jn 12:17 from·among the chamber·tomb and awakened him
Jn 20:1 ·been·taken·away from·among the chamber·tomb.
Jn 20:2 the Lord from·out·of the chamber·tomb, and we·
Lk 24:2 having·been·rolled·away from the chamber·tomb.
Lk 24:9 ·back from the chamber·tomb, they·announced all
Mt 27:60 to·the door of·the chamber·tomb, he·went·off.
Mt 28:8 coming·forth swiftly from the chamber·tomb, with
Mk 15:46 ·rolled a·stone over the door of·the chamber·tomb.
Mk 16:3 for·us the stone at the door of·the chamber·tomb?"
Mk 16:8 they·fled from the chamber·tomb; and they·

G3419.2 N-GPN μνημείων (3x)
Mt 8:28 ·forth from·out·of the chamber·tombs, exceedingly
Mt 27:53 ·forth from·among the chamber·tombs after his
Mk 5:2 him out·of·the chamber·tombs a·man·of·clay† with

G3420 μνήμη mnḗmē *n.* (1x)
Roots:G3403 Compare:G3419

G3420 N-ASF μνήμην (1x)
2Pe 1:15 *the ability* to·make recollection of·these·things.

G3421 μνημονεύω mnēmônêúō *v.* (24x)
Roots:G3420 xLangAlso:H2142

G3421.2 V-PAI-2P μνημονεύετε (4x)
Mt 16:9 ·not·yet understand, nor·even remember the five
Mk 8:18 do·yeu·not hear?' "And do·yeu·not remember?
1Th 2:9 For yeu·remember, brothers, our wearisome·labor
2Th 2:5 Do·yeu·not remember, that while·being yet

G3421.2 V-PAI-3S μνημονεύει (1x)
Jn 16:21 ·birth the little·child, she·remembers the tribulation

G3421.2 V-PAM-2S μνημόνευε (3x)
2Ti 2:8 Remember *that* Jesus Anointed, birthed·from·out·of·
Rv 2:5 remember from·what·source you·have·fallen, and
Rv 3:3 remember by·what·means you·have·received and

G3421.2 V-PAM-2P μνημονεύετε (5x)
Jn 15:20 "Remember the saying that I·myself declared to·
Lk 17:32 "Remember Lot's wife.
Heb 13:7 Remember the·ones who·are·governing among·yeu
Eph 2:11 Therefore remember, that yeu *were* at·one·time the
Col 4:18 by·my·own hand, Paul: Remember my bonds. The

G3421.2 V-PAN μνημονεύειν (1x)
Ac 20:35 of·the weak, and to·remember the words of·the

G3421.2 V-PAP-NPM μνημονεύοντες (2x)
Ac 20:31 keep·alert, remembering that for·three·years, I·
1Th 1:3 unceasingly remembering yeu before our God and

G3421.2 V-PAS-1P μνημονεύωμεν (1x)
Gal 2:10 *us* that we·should·remember the helplessly·poor,

G3421.2 V-PAS-2P μνημονεύητε (1x)
Jn 16:4 hour should·come, yeu·may·remember that I·myself

G3421.2 V-AAI-3S ἐμνημόνευσεν (2x)
Heb 11:22 ·completely·dying) remembered concerning the
Rv 18:5 heaven," and God remembered her wrong·doings.

EG3421.2 (3x)
Jn 18:24 (*Remember that* HannAs dispatched him, having·
1Th 4:1 from us, *remember* how it·is·mandatory·for you to·
Eph 2:12 *And remember* that in that season yeu·were apart·

G3421.3 V-IAI-3P ἐμνημόνευον (1x)
Heb 11:15 ·fact, if they·were·reminiscing of·that *fatherland*

G3422 μνημόσυνον mnēmósynôn *n.* (3x)
Roots:G3421 Compare:G3418 See:G3419 xLangAlso:H2146

G3422.2 N-ASN μνημόσυνον (3x)
Ac 10:4 ·acts ascended for a·memorial in·the·sight·of·God.
Mt 26:13 did shall·be·spoken·of for a·memorial of·her."
Mk 14:9 did shall·be·spoken·of for a·memorial of·her."

G3423 μνηστεύω mnēstêúō *v.* (3x)
Roots:G3415 Compare:G0718

G3423.2 V-APP-GSF μνηστευθείσης (1x)
Mt 1:18 mother Mariam already·being·espoused to·Joseph,

G3423.2 V-RPP-ASF μεμνηστευμένην (1x)
Lk 1:27 a·veiled·virgin having·been·espoused to·a·man

G3423.2 V-RPP-DSF μεμνηστευμένῃ (1x)
Lk 2:5 together with·Mariam, his espoused wife, being

G3424 μογι•λάλος môgilálôs *adj.* (1x)
Roots:G3425 G2980 Compare:G0216 G1769 xLangAlso:H0483

G3424.2 A-ASM μογιλάλον (1x)
Mk 7:32 to·him a·deaf·man *with* a·speech·impediment, and

G3425 μόγις mógis *adv.* (1x)
See:G3433

G3425.2 ADV μόγις (1x)
Lk 9:39 along·with foam, and hardly does·it·depart from

G3426 μόδιος módiôs *n.* (3x)

G3426.1 N-ASM μόδιον (3x)
Lk 11:33 nor·even under the measuring·basket, but·rather
Mt 5:15 place it under the measuring·basket, but·rather on
Mk 4:21 it·should·be·placed under the measuring·basket or

G3427 μοί môí *p:p.* (242x)
Compare:G3450 See:G1698 G1519-1
(abbreviated listing for G3427)

G3427.ª P:P-1DS μοί (1x)
(list for G3427.ª:P:P-1DS excluded)

G3427.1 P:P-1DS μοί (225x)
(list for G3427.1:P:P-1DS excluded)

EG3427.1 (2x)
(list for EG3427.1: excluded)

G3427.2 P:P-1DS μοί (8x)
(list for G3427.2:P:P-1DS excluded)

G3427.3 P:P-1DS-HEB μοί (1x)
(list for G3427.3:P:P-1DS-HEB excluded)

G3427.4 P:P-1DS μοί (4x)
(list for G3427.4:P:P-1DS excluded)

G3427.5 P:P-1DS μοί (1x)
(list for G3427.5:P:P-1DS excluded)

G3428 μοιχαλίς môichalís *n.* (7x)
Roots:G3432 See:G3430

G3428.1 N-NSF μοιχαλίς (3x)
Mt 12:39 generation (*who·is* also an·adulteress) seeks·for a·
Mt 16:4 generation (*who·is* also an·adulteress) seeks·for a·
Rm 7:3 she·shall·bear·the·public·title·of an·adulteress. But

G3428.1 N-VPF μοιχαλίδες (1x)
Jac 4:4 Yeu·adulterers and adulteresses, do·yeu·not

G3428.1 N-ASF μοιχαλίδα (1x)
Rm 7:3 not to·be an·adulteress by·becoming *yoked·together*

G3428.1 N-DSF μοιχαλίδι (1x)
Mk 8:38 (*known·as* the adulteress and morally·disqualified),

G3428.2 N-GSF μοιχαλίδος (1x)
2Pe 2:14 exceedingly·full of·alluring·adultery and not·fully·

G3429 μοιχάω môicháō *v.* (6x)
Roots:G3432

G3429 V-PNI-3S μοιχᾶται (5x)
Mt 5:32 ·marry her·having·been·divorced commits·adultery.
Mt 19:9 should·marry another, does·commit·adultery. And
Mt 19:9 ·divorced, upon·marrying, does·commit·adultery."
Mk 10:11 ·marry another commits·adultery against her.
Mk 10:12 ·be·married to·another, she·commits·adultery."

G3429 V-PNN μοιχᾶσθαι (1x)
Mt 5:32 ·immorality, causes her to·commit·adultery, and

G3430 μοιχεία môichêía *n.* (4x)
Roots:G3431 Compare:G4202 See:G3428 xLangEquiv:H5004 H5005

G3430 N-NSF μοιχεία (1x)
Gal 5:19 which are *these*: adultery, sexual·immorality,

G3430 N-NPF μοιχεῖαι (2x)
Mt 15:19 murders, adulteries, sexual·immoralities, thefts,
Mk 7:21 do·proceed·forth: adulteries, sexual·immoralities,

G3430 N-DSF μοιχείᾳ (1x)
Jn 8:3 to him a·wife having·been·grabbed in adultery; and

G3431 μοιχεύω môichêúō *v.* (14x)
Roots:G3432 Compare:G4203 See:G3430 xLangEquiv:H5003

G3431 V-FAI-2S μοιχεύσεις (4x)
Mt 5:27 ancient·ones, "You·shall·not commit·adultery."
Mt 19:18 murder," "You·shall·not commit·adultery,"
Rm 13:9 "You·shall·not commit·adultery. You·shall·not
Jac 2:11 ' Now if you·shall·not commit·adultery, but you·

G3431 V-PAI-2S μοιχεύεις (1x)
Rm 2:22 ·adultery, do·you·commit·adultery? The·one

G3431 V-PAI-3S μοιχεύει (2x)
Lk 16:18 wife and marrying another commits·adultery, and
Lk 16:18 ·divorced from *her* husband commits·adultery.

G3431 V-PAN μοιχεύειν (1x)
Rm 2:22 not to·commit·adultery, do·you·commit·adultery?

G3431 V-PAP-APM μοιχεύοντας (1x)
Rv 2:22 and the·ones committing·adultery with her into

G3431 V-PPP-NSF μοιχευομένη (1x)
Jn 8:4 *while* being·in·adultery, in·the·actual·crime·itself.

G3431 V-AAI-3S ἐμοίχευσεν (1x)
Mt 5:28 ·for her, committed·adultery with·her even·now in

G3431 V-AAS-2S μοιχεύσῃς (3x)
Lk 18:20 "You·may·not commit·adultery," "You·may·
Mk 10:19 "You·may·not commit·adultery," "You·may·
Jac 2:11 declaring, "You·may·not commit·adultery," also

G3432 μοιχός môichós *n.* (4x)
See:G3430 G3428 G3431

G3432.1 N-NPM μοιχοί (2x)

Lk 18:11 ·greedy·men, unrighteous·men, adulterers, or
1Co 6:9 nor idolaters, nor adulterers, nor effeminate·men,
G3432.1 N-VPM μοιχοί (1x)
Jac 4:4 Yeu·adulterers and adulteresses, do·yeu·not
G3432.1 N-APM μοιχούς (1x)
Heb 13:4 ·judges sexually·immoral·people and adulterers.

G3433 μόλις mốlis *adv.* (6x)
Roots:G3425
G3433.1 ADV μόλις (4x)
Ac 14:18 And with·difficulty while·saying these·things,
Ac 27:7 days, and with·difficulty coming·to·be adjacent·to
Ac 27:8 And sailing·near it with·difficulty, we·came to some
Ac 27:16 with·difficulty we·exercised·strength to·make the
G3433.2 ADV μόλις (2x)
Rm 5:7 For scarcely over a·righteous·man shall anyone die,
1Pe 4:18 " If the righteous·man scarcely is·saved, where

G3434 Μολόχ Môlôch *n/p.* (1x)
מֹלֶךְ mólęḵ [Hebrew]
Roots:H4432 Compare:G0935
G3434.2 N/P-PRI Μολόχ (1x)
Ac 7:43 Also, yeu·took·up the tabernacle of·Molek, and the

G3435 μολύνω môlýnō *v.* (3x)
Roots:G3189 Compare:G2840 G3392 G3470 G4695 See:G3436 xLangAlso:H2936
G3435.2 V-PPI-3S μολύνεται (1x)
1Co 8:7 and their conscience (being weak) is·tarnished.
G3435.2 V-AAI-3P ἐμόλυναν (1x)
Rv 3:4 even in Sardis which did·not tarnish their garments;
G3435.2 V-API-3P ἐμολύνθησαν (1x)
Rv 14:4 These are·they who are·not tarnished with women,

G3436 μολυσμός môlysmốs *n.* (1x)
Roots:G3435 Compare:G2839 G3394 xLangAlso:H2613
G3436.1 N-GSM μολυσμοῦ (1x)
2Co 7:1 ·purify ourselves from all tarnishing of·flesh and

G3437 μομφή mômphḗ *n.* (1x)
Roots:G3201
G3437.2 N-ASF μομφήν (1x)
Col 3:13 should·hold a·fault specifically·against anyone,

G3438 μονή mônḗ *adj.* (2x)
Roots:G3306
G3438.2 A-NPF μοναί (1x)
Jn 14:2 "In my Father's home are many abodes, but·if·not, I·
G3438.2 N-ASF μονήν (1x)
Jn 14:23 ·come to him, and shall·make our·abode with him.

G3439 μονο•γενής mônôgênḗs *adj.* (9x)
Roots:G3441 G1084
G3439.2 A-NSM μονογενής (1x)
Jn 1:18 ·seen God ever·at·any·time. The only·begotten Son,
G3439.2 A-ASM μονογενῆ (3x)
Jn 3:16 world, such·that he·gave his only·begotten Son, in·
Heb 11:17 promises was·offering·up his only·begotten *son*,
1Jn 4:9 because God has·dispatched his only·begotten Son
G3439.2 A-GSM μονογενοῦς (2x)
Jn 1:14 (*the* glory as of·the·only·begotten directly·from *the*
Jn 3:18 trusted in the name of·the only·begotten Son of·God.
G3439.3 A-NSM μονογενής (1x)
Lk 9:38 ·look upon my son, because he·is my only·child.
G3439.3 A-NSF μονογενής (1x)
Lk 8:42 because there·was to·him an·only·child, a·daughter
G3439.4 A-NSM μονογενής (1x)
Lk 7:12 ·procession·for one·having·died, an·only son of·his

G3440 μόνον mốnôn *adv.* (67x)
Roots:G3441 Compare:G0574
G3440 ADV μόνον (66x)
Jn 5:18 to·kill him, because not merely was·he·breaking the
Jn 11:52 not on·behalf·of the nation merely, but·rather in·
Jn 12:9 ·did·not come on·account·of Jesus merely, but·rather
Jn 13:9 "Lord, not my feet merely, but·rather also my hands
Jn 17:20 But not concerning these·men merely do·I·ask, but·
Lk 8:50 "Do·not be·afraid. Merely trust, and she·shall·be·
Ac 8:16 they·were·subsisting merely having·been·immersed
Ac 11:19 Redemptive-word to·no·one except to·Jews merely.
Ac 18:25 being·fully·acquainted·with merely the immersion
Ac 19:26 and observe that not merely at·Ephesus, but·yet
Ac 19:27 So *that* not merely this our occupation is·in·danger
Ac 21:13 am in·a·state·of·readiness not merely to·be·bound,
Ac 26:29 well-wish to·God, *that* not merely you, but·rather
Ac 27:10 much damage·and·loss, not merely of·the cargo
Heb 9:10 *which·stood* merely in ceremonial·foods and drinks
Heb 12:26 once·more I·myself do·shake not merely the earth
Gal 1:23 But they·were hearing merely, "The·one
Gal 2:10 Merely *they·reminded us* that we·should·remember
Gal 3:2 This merely I·want to·learn from yeu, did·yeu·
Gal 4:18 good *thing*, and not merely with me being·present
Gal 5:13 are·called·forth to liberty; merely *do* not *use* the
Gal 6:12 to·be·circumcised merely in·order·that they·should·
Mt 5:47 if yeu·should·greet yeur brothers merely, what·do
Mt 8:8 under my roof, but·rather merely declare a·word, and
Mt 9:21 herself, "If merely I·should·lay·hold of·his garment
Mt 10:42 a·cup of·cold *water* to·drink merely in a·disciple's
Mt 14:36 him in·order·that they·may merely lay·hold of·the
Mt 21:19 ·even·one·thing on it, except merely leaves, and
Mt 21:21 ·not be·hesitant, not merely shall·yeu·do the·thing
Mk 5:36 "Do·not be·afraid, merely trust."
Mk 6:8 "… except a·staff merely. No knapsack, no bread,
Rm 1:32 are worthy of·death), not merely do *the* same, but·
Rm 3:29 Or *is·he* the God of·Jews merely? *Is·he* not·indeed
Rm 4:12 *·are* not from·among *the* Circumcision merely, but·
Rm 4:16 ·from·out of·the Torah-Law merely, but·rather also
Rm 4:23 it·was·not written on·account·of him merely, that
Rm 5:3 And not merely *so*, but·rather also we·boast in the
Rm 5:11 And not merely *so*, but·rather we·also are·boasting
Rm 8:23 And not merely *the creation*, but·rather we·
Rm 9:10 And not merely *this*. Moreover with·Rebeqah also,
Rm 9:24 ·forth— not from·among Jews merely, but·yet also
Rm 13:5 to·submit·oneself, not merely on·account·of the
Jac 1:22 of·*the*·Redemptive-word, and not merely hearers,
Jac 2:24 ·as·righteous, and not as·a·result of·trust merely.
Php 1:27 Merely live·as·a·good·citizen (as·is·worthy of·the
Php 1:29 on·behalf·of·Anointed-One, not merely to·trust in
Php 2:12 (not as in my presence merely, but·rather now so·
Php 2:27 on·him, and not on·him merely, but·rather on·me
1Pe 2:18 ·fear, not merely to·the beneficially·good·ones and
1Th 1:5 ·to·be among yeu in word merely, but·rather also in
1Th 1:8 has·been·echoed·forth. Not merely in Macedonia
1Th 2:8 not the good·news of·God merely, but·rather also
2Th 2:7 even·now. *It·is just* merely *that* the·one holding·
1Co 7:39 to·whomever she·wants, merely *that he·be* in *the*
1Co 15:19 we·are merely having·placed·our·expectation in
2Co 7:7 and not by his arrival merely, but·rather also by the
2Co 8:10 since last·year began·previously not merely to·do,
2Co 8:19 And not merely *that*— but·rather also after·him·
2Co 8:21 ·good·things, not 'merely in·the·sight of·*the*·Lord,
2Co 9:12 not merely is·it utterly·fulfilling·in·particular the
Eph 1:21 name being·named, not merely in this present·age,
1Ti 5:13 the homes, and not merely idle, but·rather
2Ti 2:20 home there·are not merely vessels made·of·gold
2Ti 4:8 And not to·me merely, but·rather also to·all the·ones
1Jn 2:2 and not concerning ours merely, but·rather also
1Jn 5:6 *and* not by the water merely, but·rather by the water
EG3440 (1x)
Lk 17:10 because we·have·done *merely* that·which we·were·

G3441 μόνος mốnôs *adj.* (50x)
Roots:G3306 See:G3443 G3440
G3441.3 A-NSM μόνος (12x)
Jn 6:15 he·departed again to·a·mountain alone *by* himself.
Jn 8:9 last·of·them; and Jesus alone was·left·behind— and·
Jn 8:16 true, because I·am not alone, but·rather *it·is* I·myself
Jn 12:24 should·die, it abides alone. But if it·should·die, it·
Jn 16:32 And·yet I·am not alone, because the Father is with
Lk 5:21 ·able to·forgive moral·failures, except God alone?"
Lk 9:36 voice occurring, Jesus was·found alone. And they·
Heb 9:7 year, the high·priest *went* alone, *but* not apart·from
Mt 14:23 with·early·evening occurring, he·was there alone.
Mk 6:47 of·the sea, and he *was* alone upon the dry·ground.
Rm 11:3 your sacrifice·altars, and·I alone am·all·that·is·left,
Rv 15:4 your name? Because *you* alone *are* divinely·holy,
G3441.3 A-NPM μόνοι (2x)
Jn 6:22 *that* his disciples went·off alone— *they·sought·for*
1Th 3:1 we·took·delight to·be·left·behind in Athens alone,
G3441.3 A-ASM μόνον (4x)
Jn 8:29 The Father did·not leave me alone, because I·myself
Jn 16:32 *cares*, and should·leave me alone. And·yet I·am
Gal 6:4 he·shall·have the boasting in himself alone, and not
Mk 9:8 not·even·one·man, other·than Jesus alone with them
G3441.3 A-ASF μόνην (1x)
Lk 10:40 my sister abandoned me to·attend alone? So·then
G3441.3 A-APM μόνους (1x)
Lk 6:4 it·is·not proper to·eat except alone *for* the priests·that·
G3441.3 A-APN μόνα (1x)
Lk 24:12 ·of·linen which·are·laying·out alone. And·then he·
G3441.3 A-DSM μόνῳ (2x)
Lk 4:4 shall·live not upon bread alone, but·rather upon every
Mt 4:4 shall·live not upon bread alone, but·rather upon every
G3441.3 A-GSM μόνου (1x)
Mt 18:15 between you and him alone. If he·should·listen·to
G3441.4 A-APM μόνους (1x)
Mk 9:2 ·high mountain in private, alone·by·themselves. And
G3441.5 A-NSM μόνος (8x)
Lk 24:18 to him, "*Are* you only sojourning in JeruSalem,
Mt 24:36 the angels of·the heavens, except my Father only.
Rm 16:4 ·my soul, for·whom not only I·myself give·thanks,
1Co 9:6 Or *are* only BarNabas and I·myself *excluded*? ¿!·
1Ti 6:15 *he·is* the supremely·blessed and only Power, the
1Ti 6:16 the only·one having immortality, dwelling *in*
2Ti 4:11 Only Luke is with me.
2Jn 1:1 in truth, and not I·myself only, but·rather also all
G3441.5 A-NPM μόνοι (2x)
Php 4:15 matter of·giving and of·receiving, except yeu only.
Col 4:11 being·referred·to·as Justus). Only these coworkers
G3441.5 A-ASM μόνον (2x)
Jn 17:3 that they·may·know you, the only true God, and
Jud 1:4 into debauchery and denying the only Master, God
G3441.5 A-APM μόνους (2x)
1Co 14:36 from yeu? Or did·it·come·adjacent to yeu only?
Rv 9:4 any tree), but·yet only the men·of·clay† who do·not
G3441.5 A-DSM μόνῳ (5x)
Lk 4:8 and "to·him only shall·you·ritually·minister.'"
Mt 4:10 and "to·him only shall·you·ritually·minister.'"
Rm 16:27 to·the·only wise God, to·him *be* the glory through
Jud 1:25 to·the·only wise God our Savior, *be* glory and
1Ti 1:17 incorruptible, invisible, to·the·only wise God, *be*
G3441.5 A-DPM μόνοις (1x)
Mt 12:4 him, except only for·the priests·that·offer·sacrifices?
G3441.5 A-GSM μόνου (1x)
Jn 5:44 the glory, the·one personally·from the only God?
G3441.5 ADV μόνον (1x)
Mt 17:8 they·saw not·even·one·man, except YeShua only.
EG3441.5 (3x)
Jn 12:29 was·saying, "*It·was only* thunder *that* has·occurred.
Mk 2:7 to·forgive moral·failures, except one *only*: God?
Mk 13:32 heaven, neither the Son, except the Father *only*.

G3442 μον•όφθαλμος mônốphthalmôs *adj.* (2x)
Roots:G3441 G3788
G3442 A-ASM μονόφθαλμον (2x)
Mt 18:9 to·enter into the life·above with·one·eye, rather·than
Mk 9:47 into the kingdom of·God with·one·eye, than having

G3443 μονόω mônốō *v.* (1x)
Roots:G3441 Compare:G5503
G3443 V-RPP-NSF μεμονωμένη (1x)
1Ti 5:5 and having·been·left·all·alone, has·placed·her·

G3444 μορφή môrphḗ *n.* (4x)
Roots:G3313 Compare:G1491 G4976 G5326 See:G3445 G3446 G4832
G3444.1 N-DSF μορφῇ (1x)
Mk 16:12 from·among them in another form while·walking,
G3444.2 N-ASF μορφήν (1x)

Php 2:7 taking·hold·of *the* fundamental·nature of·a·slave,
G3444.2 N-DSF μορφῇ (1x)
Php 2:6 who, subsisting in *the* fundamental·nature of·God,
EG3444.2 (1x)
Heb 2:16 ·hold— not *of·the fundamental·nature* of·angels

G3445 μορφόω môrphŏō *v.* (1x)
Roots:G3444 Compare:G2675 G4111 See:G3339 G4833
G3445 V-APS-3S μορφωθῇ (1x)
Gal 4:19 Anointed-One should·be·fundamentally·formed in

G3446 μόρφωσις mŏrphōsis *n.* (2x)
Roots:G3445
G3446.1 N-ASF μόρφωσιν (2x)
Rm 2:20 having the formula of·the absolute·knowledge and
2Ti 3:5 having a·formula of·devout·reverence, but having·

G3447 μοσχο•ποιέω môschôpôiĕō *v.* (1x)
Roots:G3448 G4160
G3447 V-AAI-3P ἐμοσχοποίησαν (1x)
Ac 7:41 And they·made·a·calf in those days and brought·

G3448 μόσχος mŏschôs *adj.* (6x)
xLangEquiv:H5695 xLangAlso:H7794
G3448 A-ASM μόσχον (3x)
Lk 15:23 And bringing the fattened calf, sacrifice *it*.
Lk 15:27 father sacrificed the fattened calf, because he·fully·
Lk 15:30 you·sacrificed for·him the fattened calf.'
G3448 N-DSM μόσχῳ (1x)
Rv 4:7 the second living·being *is* like a·calf, and the third
G3448 N-GPM μόσχων (2x)
Heb 9:12 through blood of·adult·male·goats and calves, but
Heb 9:19 ·taking the blood of·calves and of·adult·male·goats

G3449 μόχθος mŏchthôs *n.* (3x)
Roots:G3425 Compare:G2873 G5605 xLangAlso:H5999
G3449.1 N-ASM μόχθον (1x)
1Th 2:9 our wearisome·labor and the travail, for working
G3449.1 N-DSM μόχθῳ (2x)
2Th 3:8 were·working in weariness and travail night and day
2Co 11:27 *subsisting* in weariness and travail, in

G3450 μοῦ môû *p:p.* (588x)
Compare:G3427 See:G1700
(abbreviated listing for G3450)
G3450.1 P:P-1GS μοῦ (61x)
(list for G3450.1:P:P-1GS excluded)
G3450.2 P:P-1GS μοῦ (520x)
(list for G3450.2:P:P-1GS excluded)
EG3450.2 (1x)
(list for EG3450.2: excluded)
G3450.3 P:P-1GS μοῦ (6x)
(list for G3450.3:P:P-1GS excluded)

G3451 μουσικός môusikŏs *adj.* (1x)
G3451.2 A-GPM μουσικῶν (1x)
Rv 18:22 a·sound of·harpists, and musicians, and of·flute·

G3452 μυελός myêlŏs *n.* (1x)
G3452 N-GPM μυελῶν (1x)
Heb 4:12 and even of·the·joints and marrow, and *he·is* a·

G3453 μυέω myĕō *v.* (1x)
Roots:G3466-1 Compare:G1321 See:G3466
G3453.2 V-RPI-1S μεμύημαι (1x)
Php 4:12 I·have·been·shown·how also to·be·stuffed·full

G3454 μῦθος mŷthôs *n.* (5x)
Roots:G3466 See:G3453
G3454 N-APM μύθους (2x)
1Ti 4:7 shun the profane and age-old, senile myths, and train
2Ti 4:4 the truth and shall·be·turned·aside to the myths.
G3454 N-DPM μύθοις (3x)
2Pe 1:16 following·out myths having·been·skillfully·devised
Tit 1:14 giving·heed to·Jewish myths and commandments
1Ti 1:4 nor·even to·give·heed to·myths and to·endless

G3455 μυκάομαι mykâômai *v.* (1x)
G3455.3 V-PNI-3S μυκᾶται (1x)
Rv 10:3 voice, just·as *when* a·lion roars. And when he·

G3456 μυκτηρίζω myktērízō *v.* (1x)
Roots:G3455 Compare:G1702
G3456.2 V-PPI-3S μυκτηρίζεται (1x)
Gal 6:7 ·not be·deceived; God is·not ridiculed, for whatever

G3457 μυλικός mylikŏs *adj.* (1x)
Roots:G3458
G3457 A-NSM μυλικός (1x)
Mk 9:42 it·is even·much better for·him if a·mill stone be·set

G3458 μύλος mýlôs *n.* (4x)
Roots:G3433 See:G3457 G3459 xLangAlso:H7347
G3458.2 N-NSM μύλος (2x)
Lk 17:2 for·him that a·donkey-sized millstone be·set around
Mt 18:6 that a·donkey-sized millstone should·be·hung upon
G3458.2 N-ASM μύλον (1x)
Rv 18:21 angel took·up a·stone as a·great millstone, and cast
G3458.2 N-GSM μύλου (1x)
Rv 18:22 in you. And a·sound of·a·millstone, no, should·not

G3459 μύλων mýlōn *n.* (1x)
Roots:G3458
G3459 N-DSM μύλωνι (1x)
Mt 24:41 *women shall·be* grinding at the mill-house; one is·

G3460 Μύρα Mýra *n/l.* (1x)
G3460 N/L-APN Μύρα (1x)
Ac 27:5 PamPhylia, we·came·down to Myra, *a·city* of·Lycia

G3461 μυριάς myriás *n.* (7x)
Roots:G3463
xLangEquiv:H7233
G3461.1 N-NPM μυριάδες (1x)
Rv 9:16 *was* twice ten·thousand times·ten·thousand *(which·is*
G3461.1 N-APM μυριάδας (1x)
Ac 19:19 five times·ten·thousand pieces·of·silver *(which·is*
G3461.1 N-GPM μυριάδων (1x)
Rv 9:16 ten·thousand times·ten·thousand *(which·is two·*
G3461.2 N-DPM μυριάσιν (2x)
Heb 12:22 and to·a·myriad·tens·of·thousands of·angels,
Jud 1:14 with a·myriad·tens·of·thousands of·his holy·ones,
G3461.3 N-NPM μυριάδες (1x)
Ac 21:20 how·many tens·of·thousands of·Judeans there·are
G3461.3 N-GPM μυριάδων (1x)
Lk 12:1 ·gathered of·the tens·of·thousands, such·that they·

G3462 μυρίζω myrízō *v.* (1x)
Roots:G3464 Compare:G0218 G1472 G5548
G3462 V-AAN μυρίσαι (1x)
Mk 14:8 She·came·beforehand to·apply·ointment·to my

G3463 μύριοι mýriôi *adj.* (3x)
See:G3461
G3463.1 A-APM μυρίους (2x)
1Co 4:15 yeu·may·have ten·thousand strict·elementary· in
1Co 14:19 others also, rather·than ten·thousand words in a·
G3463.1 A-GPM μυρίων (1x)
Mt 18:24 ·man delinquent of·ten·thousand talants·of·silver.

G3464 μύρον mýrôn *n.* (15x)
Compare:G4666 See:G3462 xLangAlso:H4753
G3464 N-NSN μύρον (2x)
Jn 12:5 "This ointment, why was·it·not sold·off for·three·
Mt 26:9 For this ointment was·able to·be·sold·off for·much,
G3464 N-ASN μύρον (2x)
Mt 26:12 For she·herself, casting this ointment on my body,
Rv 18:13 cinnamon, incense, ointments, and frankincense,
G3464 N-APN μύρα (1x)
Lk 23:56 ·made·ready aromatic·spices and ointments, and
G3464 N-DSN μύρῳ (3x)
Jn 11:2 the·one rubbing·oil·on the Lord with·ointment, and
Lk 7:38 ·kissing his feet and was·rubbing·on the ointment.
Lk 7:46 but she·herself rubbed·oil·on my feet with·ointment.
G3464 N-GSN μύρου (6x)
Jn 12:3 ·pound of·extremely·valuable ointment of·authentic
Jn 12:3 ·filled from·out of·the aroma of·the ointment.
Lk 7:37 ·obtaining an·alabaster·flask of·ointment
Mt 26:7 an·alabaster·flask of·deeply·valuable ointment, and
Mk 14:3 ·flask of·extremely·expensive ointment of·authentic
Mk 14:4 "Why·has this total·ruin of·the ointment occurred?
EG3464 (1x)
Mk 14:3 ·flask, she·poured *the ointment* down his head.

G3465 Μυσία Mysía *n/l.* (2x)
G3465 N/L-ASF Μυσίαν (2x)
Ac 16:7 Coming adjacent·to Mysia, they·were·attempting to·
Ac 16:8 And passing·by Mysia, they·walked·down to Troas.

G3466 μυ•στήριον mystḗriôn *n.* (29x)
Roots:G3466-1 Compare:G2927 See:G3453 G3454 xLangEquiv:A7328 H7328-1 xLangAlso:H8587
G3466.2 N-APN μυστήρια (1x)
1Co 14:2 but in·*the*·Spirit, he·does·speak mysteries.
G3466.3 N-NSN μυστήριον (2x)
Eph 5:32 This is a·great mystery, but I·myself do·say *this* in·
Rv 1:20 *"Now this·is* the mystery of·the seven stars which
G3466.3 N-ASN μυστήριον (3x)
Mk 4:11 ·given to·yeu to·know the mystery of·the kingdom
Rm 11:25 brothers, to·be·ignorant of·this mystery, lest yeu·
1Co 15:51 Behold, I·relay to·yeu a·mystery. In·fact, we·
G3466.3 N-APN μυστήρια (3x)
Lk 8:10 ·been·given to·know the mysteries of·the kingdom
Mt 13:11 to·yeu to·know the mysteries of·the kingdom of·
1Co 13:2 and should·have·seen all the mysteries and all the
G3466.3 N-GPN μυστηρίων (1x)
1Co 4:1 and estate·managers of·God's mysteries.
G3466.4 N-NSN μυστήριον (2x)
1Ti 3:16 is the Mystery of·the Way·of·Devout·Reverence.
Rv 10:7 even the Mystery of·God should·be·finished, as he·
G3466.4 N-ASN μυστήριον (6x)
Eph 1:9 already·making·known to·us the Mystery of·his will
Eph 3:3 he·made·known to·me the Mystery (just·as I·
Eph 6:19 *·me* to·make·known the Mystery of·the good·news,
Col 1:26 the Mystery, the·one having·been·hidden·away
Col 4:3 (*that·is*, to·speak the Mystery of·the Anointed-One
1Ti 3:9 *but* holding the Mystery of·the trust in a·pure
G3466.4 N-DSN μυστηρίῳ (2x)
1Co 2:7 we·speak God's wisdom in a·Mystery, the·one
Eph 3:4 comprehension in the Mystery of·the Anointed-One)
G3466.4 N-GSN μυστηρίου (4x)
Rm 16:25 ·to a·revealing of·*the*·Mystery having·been· from·
Eph 3:9 *is* the fellowship of·the Mystery, the·one having·
Col 1:27 the wealth of·the glory of·this Mystery among the
Col 2:2 into a·full·knowledge of·the Mystery of·God and
EG3466.4 (2x)
Rm 16:26 with *the Mystery* already·being·made·known to
Eph 3:5 *This·is the Mystery* (which in other generations·of·
G3466.5 N-NSN μυστήριον (1x)
2Th 2:7 For the mystery of·the Lawlessness operates even·
G3466.6 N-NSN μυστήριον (1x)
Rv 17:5 having·been·written, MYSTERY, BABYLON THE
G3466.6 N-ASN μυστήριον (1x)
Rv 17:7 shall·declare to·you the MYSTERY of·the woman,

G3467 μυ•ωπάζω myōpázō *v.* (1x)
Roots:G3466-1 G3700 Compare:G2576 See:G4694
G3467.4 V-PAP-NSM μυωπάζων (1x)
2Pe 1:9 being·dangerously·nearsighted, already·becoming

G3468 μώλ•ωψ mōlōps *n.* (1x)
See:G3433 G3700
G3468.3 N-DSM μώλωπι (1x)
1Pe 2:24 thrashed·and·swollen·body yeu·are·already·healed.'

G3469 μωμάομαι mōmáômai *v.* (2x)
Roots:G3470
G3469 V-ADS-3S μωμήσηται (1x)
2Co 8:20 this·thing: *that* not anyone should·blame us in this
G3469 V-APS-3S μωμηθῇ (1x)
2Co 6:3 Service *of·the Reconciliation* should·not be·blamed.

G3470 μῶμος mōmôs *n.* (1x)
Roots:G3201 See:G3469 xLangAlso:H3971
G3470.2 N-NPM μῶμοι (1x)
2Pe 2:13 *·are* stains and blemishes, luxuriously·indulging in

G3471 μωραίνω mōraínō *v.* (4x)
Roots:G3474
G3471.2 V-APS-3S μωρανθῇ (2x)

Lk 14:34 good, but if the salt should·become·bland, in what·
Mt 5:13 but if the salt should·become·bland, in what·manner
G3471.3 V-AAI-3S ἐμώρανεν (1x)
1Co 1:20 Did God not·indeed make·foolish the wisdom of·
G3471.4 V-API-3P ἐμωράνθησαν (1x)
Rm 1:22 to·be wise, they·already·became·foolish,

G3472 μωρία mōría *n.* (5x)
Roots:G3474
G3472 N-NSF μωρία (3x)
1Co 1:18 the·one of·the cross) is foolishness, in·fact, to·the·
1Co 2:14 Spirit of·God, for they·are foolishness to·him. And
1Co 3:19 the wisdom of·this world is foolishness with God.
G3472 N-ASF μωρίαν (1x)
1Co 1:23 ·offense to·Jews and foolishness to·Greeks.
G3472 N-GSF μωρίας (1x)
1Co 1:21 the foolishness of·official·proclamation to·save

G3473 μωρο•λογία mōrôlôgía *n.* (1x)
Roots:G3474 G3004 Compare:G0148
G3473 N-NSF μωρολογία (1x)
Eph 5:4 *nor* even an·obscenity, or foolish·conversation, or

G3474 μωρός mōrós *adj.* (13x)
Roots:G3466-1 Compare:G0781 G0878 See:G3471 G3472
xLangEquiv:H3684
G3474.2 A-NPF μωραί (3x)
Mt 25:2 them were prudent, and the *other* five *were* foolish.
Mt 25:3 Those·who *were* foolish, upon·taking their·own
Mt 25:8 And the foolish declared to·the prudent, 'Give to·us
G3474.2 A-APF μωράς (2x)
Tit 3:9 But shun foolish speculations, genealogies, strifes,
2Ti 2:23 shun the foolish and uneducated·and·undisciplined
G3474.2 A-APN μωρά (1x)
1Co 1:27 ·rather God selected the foolish·things of·the world
G3474.2 A-DSM μωρῷ (1x)
Mt 7:26 doing them, shall·be·likened to·a·foolish man, who
G3474.3 A-NSM μωρός (1x)
1Co 3:18 present·age, let·him·become a·fool, in·order·that
G3474.3 A-NPM μωροί (1x)
1Co 4:10 ·ourselves *are* fools on·account·of Anointed-One,
G3474.3 A-VSM μωρέ (1x)
Mt 5:22 whoever should·declare, 'You·fool,' shall·be held·
G3474.3 A-VPM μωροί (2x)
Mt 23:17 O·fools and blind·men! For which is greater, the
Mt 23:19 O·fools and blind·men! For which *is* greater, the
G3474.4 A-NSN μωρόν (1x)
1Co 1:25 because the foolishness of·God is wiser·than the

G3475 Μωσῆς Mōsễs *n/p.* (81x)
Μωσεύς Mōsêús
Μωϋσῆς Mōÿsễs
מֹשֶׁה móshęh [Hebrew]
Μωσε Mōshê [Greek, Octuagint]
Roots:H4872 See:G0002
xLangEquiv:A4873
G3475.2 N/P-NSM Μωσῆς (43x)
Jn 1:45 ·him, "We·have·found whom Moses wrote *about* in
Jn 3:14 "So just·as Moses elevated the serpent *upon a·sign*·
Jn 5:45 ·is the·one legally·accusing yeu, Moses, in whom
Jn 6:32 ·certainly, I·say to·yeu, Moses has·not given yeu
Jn 7:19 "¿!·Has·not Moses given yeu the Torah-Law?
Jn 7:22 "On·account·of that Moses has·given to·yeu the
Jn 8:5 in the Torah-Law, Moses commanded for·us to·cast·
Lk 5:14 purification, just·as Moses specifically·assigned, for
Lk 9:30 ·together with·him, who were Moses and EliJah—
Lk 20:28 saying, "Mentor, Moses wrote to·us, if any·man's
Lk 20:37 ·awakened, even Moses brought·it·to·attention at
Ac 3:22 "For Moses in·fact declared to the fathers,
Ac 6:14 the customs which Moses handed·down to·us."
Ac 7:20 "Into which season Moses was·born, and he·was
Ac 7:22 And Moses was·educated·and·disciplined in·all *the*
Ac 7:29 Then Moses fled at this saying, and was a·sojourner
Ac 7:31 Now upon·seeing *it*, Moses marveled at·the clear·
Ac 7:32 God of·Jacob." But Moses, being terrified·with·
Ac 7:37 "This Moses is the·one declaring to·the Sons of·
Ac 7:40 *As* for this Moses who brought us out of·*the*·land of·
Ac 15:21 For Moses, from·out of·ancient generations, has in·
Ac 26:22 the prophets and Moses spoke of·as·being·about
Heb 3:2 producing him, as also Moses *was trustworthy* in all
Heb 3:5 And in·fact, Moses *was* trustworthy in all his house
Heb 7:14 ·to which tribe Moses spoke not·even·one·thing
Heb 8:5 just·as Moses had·been·divinely·instructed·by·
Heb 11:23 By·trust, Moses (being·born) was·hid three·
Heb 11:24 By·trust, Moses (after·becoming full·grown)
Heb 12:21 was frightful, *such·that* Moses declared, "I·am
Mt 8:4 offer the present that Moses specifically·assigned, for
Mt 17:3 And behold, Moses and EliJah were·made·visible
Mt 19:7 ·him, "So·then why·did Moses command *us* to·give
Mt 19:8 hardness·of·heart *that* Moses freely·permitted yeu
Mt 22:24 saying, "Mentor, Moses declared, if a·certain·man
Mk 1:44 those·things·which Moses specifically·assigned, for
Mk 7:10 For Moses declared, "Deeply·honor your father
Mk 10:3 to·them, "What did·Moses command yeu?
Mk 10:4 And they·declared, "Moses freely·permitted *us* to·
Mk 12:19 "Mentor, Moses wrote for·us that if any·man's
Rm 10:5 For Moses describes the righteousness, the·one
Rm 10:19 ¿!·Did IsraEl not know? First Moses says, "I·
2Co 3:13 And not exactly·as Moses *did*, who·was·placing a·
2Co 3:15 the·present·day, whenever Moses is·read·aloud, a·
G3475.2 N/P-ASM Μωσῆν (5x)
Lk 16:29 says to·him, 'They·have Moses and the prophets.
Ac 6:11 reviling utterances against Moses and *against* God.
Ac 7:35 "This Moses whom they·renounced, declaring,
Heb 3:3 ·been·counted·worthy of·more glory than Moses, in
1Co 10:2 and all were·immersed into Moses in the cloud and
G3475.2 N/P-DSM Μωϋσεῖ (9x)
Jn 5:46 For if yeu·were·trusting in·Moses, yeu·would be·
Jn 9:29 personally·know that God has·spoken to·Moses. But
Lk 9:33 one·for you, one·for Moses, and one·for EliJah,"
Ac 7:44 ·one speaking to·Moses thoroughly·assigned *for·him*
Mt 17:4 one for·you, and one for·Moses, and one for·EliJah.
Mk 9:4 them, EliJah together with·Moses, and they·were
Mk 9:5 one for·you, and one for·Moses, and one for·EliJah
Rm 9:15 For he·says to·Moses, " I·shall·show·gracious·
2Ti 3:8 Jambres stood·opposed·to Moses, in·this·manner
G3475.2 N/P-GSM Μωσέως (23x)
Jn 1:17 the Torah-Law was·given through Moses, the grace
Jn 7:22 (not that it·is from·out of·Moses, but·rather from·out
Jn 7:23 ·that the Torah-Law of·Moses should·not be·broken,
Jn 9:28 disciple, but we·ourselves are Moses' disciples.
Lk 2:22 ·to the Torah-Law of·Moses were·fulfilled, they·
Lk 16:31 'If they·do·not hear Moses and the prophets,
Lk 24:27 And beginning from Moses and all the prophets,
Lk 24:44 concerning me in the Torah-Law of·Moses, *the*
Ac 13:39 ·regarded·as·innocent by the Torah-Law of·Moses.
Ac 15:1 ·circumcised in·the manner of·Moses, yeu·are·not
Ac 15:5 *them* to·observantly·keep the Torah-Law of·Moses."
Ac 21:21 you·instruct a·defection away·from Moses *to* all
Ac 28:23 Jesus, both from the Torah-Law of·Moses and the
Heb 3:16 after·coming·forth out of·Egypt through Moses.
Heb 9:19 already·being·spoken by Moses to·all the People,
Heb 10:28 Anyone setting·aside Moses' Torah-Law died
Mt 23:2 and the Pharisees sat·down upon the seat of·Moses.
Mk 12:26 ·yeu·not read·aloud in the scroll of·Moses, how
Rm 5:14 ·reigned from Adam so·far·as·unto Moses, even
Jud 1:9 he·was·discussing about *the* body of·Moses), did·not
1Co 9:9 it·has·been·written in the Torah-Law of·Moses,
2Co 3:7 ·intently into the face of·Moses on·account·of the
Rv 15:3 And they·sing the song of·Moses, a·slave of·God,
EG3475.2 (1x)
Ac 7:38 "This *Moses* is the·one already·coming among the

Nν - Nu

G3476 Ναασσών Naassṓn *n/p.* (3x)
נַחְשׁוֹן nachshôn [Hebrew]
Roots:H5177
G3476.2 N/P-PRI Ναασσών (3x)
Lk 3:32 *son* of·BoAz, *son* of·Salmon, *son* of·Nachshon,
Mt 1:4 and AmmiNadab begot Nachshon, and Nachshon
Mt 1:4 begot Nachshon, and Nachshon begot Salmon.

G3477 Ναγγαί Nangaí *n/p.* (1x)
xLangAlso:H5052
G3477 N/P-PRI Ναγγαί (1x)
Lk 3:25 *son* of·Nachum, *son* of·Esli, *son* of·Naggai,

G3478 Ναζαρέτ Nazarét *n/l.* (12x)
Ναζαρέθ Nazaréth [Hellenized]
נְצֶרֶת natsęręth [Hebrew]
Νατσαρέθ Natsaréth [proper transliteration]
נָצְרַת natsrath [later Hebrew]
Roots:H5341-3 See:G3479 G3480 xLangAlso:H5342
G3478.2 N/L-PRI Νατσαρέθ (9x)
Jn 1:45 ·also the prophets: Jesus from Natsareth, the son of·
Lk 1:26 God to a·city of·Galilee whose name *is* Natsareth,
Lk 2:51 with them, and came to Natsareth, and was being·
Lk 4:16 Now he·came to Natsareth, where he·was having·
Ac 10:38 anointed Jesus *who·was* from Natsareth with·Holy
Mt 2:23 being·referred·to·as Natsareth *(meaning·a·Hidden·,*
Mt 4:13 And upon·leaving Natsareth behind *and* coming *into*
Mt 21:11 the prophet, the·one from Natsareth of·Galilee."
Mk 1:9 days *that* Jesus came from Natsareth of·Galilee and
G3478.3 N/L-PRI Νατσαρέθ (3x)
Jn 1:46 beneficially·good to·be from·out of·Natsareth?"
Lk 2:4 from Galilee, out of·*the*·city of·Natsareth, into Judea,
Lk 2:39 city of·Natsareth *(which·means: A·Hidden·Branch).*

G3479 Ναζαρηνός Nazarēnós *n/g.* (4x)
נְצֵרִין natsęriyn [Aramaic root]
Νατσαρηνός Natsarēnós
[proper transliteration]
Roots:A5341-2 Compare:G5546 See:G3480 G3478
xLangEquiv:H5341-4 xLangAlso:H5139 H5341-3
G3479.1 N/G-VSM Νατσαρηνέ (2x)
Lk 4:34 and you, O·YeShua of·Natsareth? Did·you·come to·
Mk 1:24 you, O·YeShua of·Natsareth? Did·you·come to·
G3479.1 N/G-GSM Νατσαρηνοῦ (1x)
Mk 14:67 "You also were with Jesus of·Natsareth."
G3479.2 N/G-ASM Νατσαρηνόν (1x)
Mk 16:6 Yeu·seek Jesus the Natsarethan, the·one having·

G3480 Ναζωραῖος Nazōraîos *n/g.* (15x)
נְצֶרְתִי natsęręthiy [Hebrew root]
Νατσωραῖος Natsōraîos
[proper transliteration]
Roots:G3478 Compare:G5546 See:G3479
xLangEquiv:H5341-4 A5341-2 xLangAlso:H5139 H4899-1
G3480.2 N/G-NSM Νατσωραῖος (1x)
Mt 2:23 the prophets, "He·shall·be·called a·Natsarethan."
G3480.3 N/G-NSM Νατσωραῖος (5x)
Jn 19:19 was, "JESUS OF·NATSARETH THE KING OF·
Lk 18:37 to·him that Jesus of·Natsareth was·passing·by.
Ac 6:14 that this Jesus of·Natsareth shall·demolish this place
Ac 22:8 'It·is·I Myself, Jesus of·Natsareth, whom you·
Mk 10:47 ·hearing that it·was Jesus of·Natsareth, he·began
G3480.3 N/G-ASM Νατσωραῖον (3x)
Jn 18:5 They·answered him, "Jesus of·Natsareth." Jesus
Jn 18:7 ·seek?" And they·declared, "Jesus of·Natsareth."
Ac 2:22 hear these words: Jesus of·Natsareth, a·man
G3480.3 N/G-GSM Νατσωραίου (5x)
Lk 24:19 "Concerning Jesus of·Natsareth, who became a·
Ac 3:6 name of·Jesus Anointed of·Natsareth, be·awakened
Ac 4:10 the name of·Jesus Anointed of·Natsareth, whom yeu
Ac 26:9 ·things contrary to the name of·Jesus of·Natsareth.

Mt 26:71 "This·one also was with YeShua of·Natsareth."
G3480.4 N/G-GPM Νατσωραίων (1x)
Ac 24:5 *being* a·champion of·the sect of·the Natsarethans,

G3481 Ναθάν Nathán *n/p.* (1x)
נָתָן nathan [Hebrew]
Roots:H5416
G3481.2 N/P-PRI Ναθάν (1x)
Lk 3:31 *son* of·Mattatha, *son* of·Nathan, *son* of·David,

G3482 Ναθανα•ήλ Nathanaél *n/p.* (6x)
נְתַנְאֵל nethan'el [Hebrew]
Roots:H5417
G3482.2 N/P-PRI Ναθαναήλ (6x)
Jn 1:45 Philip finds NathaniEl and says to·him, "We·have·
Jn 1:46 And NathaniEl declared to·him, "Is·it·possible *for*
Jn 1:47 Jesus saw NathaniEl coming toward him and says
Jn 1:48 NathaniEl says to·him, "From·what·source do·you·
Jn 1:49 NathaniEl answered and says to·him, "Rabbi, you·
Jn 21:2 ·to·as Twin), and NathaniEl from Qanah in·Galilee,

G3483 ναί naí *prt.* (37x)
G3483 PRT ναί (34x)
Jn 11:27 She·says to·him, "Yes, Lord. I·myself have·trusted
Jn 21:15 He·says to·him, "Yes, Lord; you·yourself
Jn 21:16 me?" He·says to·him, "Yes, Lord; you·yourself
Lk 7:26 ·gone·forth to·see? A·prophet? Yes, I·say to·yeu,
Lk 10:21 and you·revealed them to·infants. Yes, Father,
Lk 11:51 ·Altar and the house *of·God*. Yes, I·say to·yeu, it·
Lk 12:5 *a·person* into the Hell·Canyon. Yes, I·say to·yeu,
Ac 5:8 ·so·much?" And she·declared, "Yes, for·so·much."
Ac 22:27 And he·replied, "Yes."
Mt 5:37 "But yeur word must·be, 'Yes' *for* 'yes' *and* 'No'
Mt 5:37 'Yes' *for* 'yes' *and* 'No' *for* 'no.
Mt 9:28 ·able to·do this?" They·say to·him, "Yes, Lord."
Mt 11:9 yeu·go·forth to·see? A·prophet? Yes, I·say to·yeu,
Mt 11:26 Yes, Father, because in·this·manner it·became a·
Mt 13:51 all these·things?" They·say to·him, "Yes, Lord."
Mt 15:27 And she·declared, "Yes *it·is*, Lord.
Mt 17:25 He·says, "Yes." And when he·entered into the
Mt 21:16 to·them, "Yes! Have·yeu·not·even·at·any·time
Mk 7:28 she·answered and says to·him, "Yes *it·is*, Lord.
Rm 3:29 not·indeed also of·Gentiles? Yes, of·Gentiles also,
Jac 5:12 But yeur "Yes," let·it·be "Yes," and *yeur* "No
Jac 5:12 "Yes," let·it·be "Yes," and *yeur* "No, No," lest
2Co 1:17 with me there·should·be the "Yes, yes" and·then
2Co 1:17 me there·should·be the "Yes, yes" and·then the
2Co 1:18 toward yeu did·not become "Yes" and·then "No.
2Co 1:19 and me), did·not become "Yes" and·then "No,"
2Co 1:19 "No," but·rather in him has·become "Yes."
2Co 1:20 promises, in him *is* the "Yes," and in him *is* the
Phm 1:20 Yes, brother, may I·myself derive·profit·from you
Rv 1:7 shall·vividly·lament over him.' Yes, So·be·it,·Amen.
Rv 14:13 " "Yes," says the Spirit, "in·order·that they·may·
Rv 16:7 the Sacrifice·Altar saying, "Yes, O·Yahweh, God
Rv 22:20 testifying these·things says, "Yes, I·come swiftly.
Rv 22:20 So·be·it,·Amen. Yes, come, Lord Jesus.
EG3483 (3x)
Jn 4:26 "It·is·I Myself. *Yes*, the·one speaking to·you.
Eph 1:8 *Yes, the wealth of·his grace* which he·abounded to
Eph 1:12 for a·high·praise of·his glory, *yes us*, the·ones

G3484 Ναΐν Naín *n/l.* (1x)
xLangAlso:H4999
G3484.2 N/L-PRI Ναΐν (1x)
Lk 7:11 he·was·traversing into a·city being·called Nain, and

G3485 ναός naós *n.* (47x)
Roots:G3484-1 Compare:G2411 G4638 G0039
See:G3511
xLangEquiv:H1964 A1965
G3485.2 N-APM ναούς (1x)
Ac 19:24 a·silversmith making silver temples of·Artemis,
G3485.2 N-DPM ναοῖς (2x)
Ac 7:48 ·High does·not reside in temples made·by·hands,
Ac 17:24 and earth, resides not in temples made·by·hands,
G3485.3 N-NSM ναός (2x)
Jn 2:20 "*In* forty six years, this Temple was·built, and you,
Mt 23:17 the gold, or the Temple, the·one making the gold
G3485.3 N-ASM ναόν (7x)
Lk 1:9 ·incense after·entering into the Temple of·Yahweh.
Mt 26:61 'I·am·able to·demolish the Temple of·God and to·
Mt 27:40 "The·one demolishing the Temple and building *it*
Mk 14:58 'I·myself shall·demolish this Temple, the·one
Mk 15:29 the·one demolishing the Temple and building *it*
2Th 2:4 ·for him to·sit·down as God in the Temple of·God,'
Rv 11:1 "Rouse·yourself and measure the Temple of·God,
G3485.3 N-DSM ναῷ (5x)
Lk 1:21 him *that he·would·presume* to·linger in the Temple.
Lk 1:22 he·has·clearly·seen a·vision in the Temple. And he·
Mt 23:16 should·swear "by the Temple," it·is nothing·at·all,
Mt 23:21 And the·one swearing by the Temple, swears by it
Mt 27:5 the pieces·of·silver at the Temple, he·departed. And
G3485.3 N-GSM ναοῦ (6x)
Lk 23:45 and the curtain of·the Temple was·torn *down the*
Mt 23:16 "by the gold of·the Temple," he·is·obligated!'
Mt 23:35 whom yeu·murdered between the Temple and the
Mt 27:51 behold, the curtain of·the Temple is·torn in two
Mk 15:38 And the curtain of·the Temple was·torn in two
Rv 11:2 inwardly *toward* the Temple, you·must·cast·forth
G3485.4 N-NSM ναός (4x)
1Co 3:16 personally·know that yeu·are a·temple of·God, and
1Co 3:17 God shall·corrupt. For the temple of·God is holy,
1Co 6:19 ·know that yeur body is a·temple of·the Holy Spirit
2Co 6:16 For yeu·yeurselves are a·temple of·the·living God,
G3485.4 N-ASM ναόν (3x)
Jn 2:19 "Tear·down this temple, and in three days I·shall·
1Co 3:17 If anyone corrupts the temple of·God, this·one God
Eph 2:21 ·together, grows into a·holy temple in *the* Lord,
G3485.4 N-DSM-HEB ναῷ (1x)
2Co 6:16 what mutual·compact has·a·temple of·God with
G3485.4 N-GSM ναοῦ (1x)
Jn 2:21 he·was·saying this concerning the temple of·his body
EG3485.4 (1x)
1Co 3:17 of·God is holy, which *temple* yeu·yeurselves are.
G3485.5 N-NSM ναός (3x)
Rv 11:19 And the Temple of·God was·opened·up in the
Rv 15:5 and behold, the Temple of·the Tabernacle of·the
Rv 15:8 And the Temple was·overfilled with·smoke from·
G3485.5 N-ASM ναόν (2x)
Rv 15:8 were·able to·enter into the Temple, even·until the
Rv 21:22 And I·did·not see a·Temple in it, for Yahweh, *El*
G3485.5 N-DSM ναῷ (2x)
Rv 7:15 day and night in his Temple. And the·one who·is·
Rv 11:19 ·his covenant was·made·visible in his Temple. And
G3485.5 N-GSM ναοῦ (5x)
Rv 14:15 angel came·forth out of·the Temple, yelling·out in
Rv 14:17 angel came·forth out of·the Temple, the·one in the
Rv 15:6 angels came·forth from·out of·the Temple, having
Rv 16:1 a·great voice from·out of·the Temple saying to·the
Rv 16:17 ·forth a·great voice from the Temple of·the heaven,
G3485.6 N-NSM ναός (1x)
Rv 21:22 God Almighty, and the Lamb are its Temple.
G3485.6 N-DSM ναῷ (1x)
Rv 3:12 I·shall·make a·pillar in the Temple of·my God, and

G3486 Ναούμ Naôúm *n/p.* (1x)
נַחוּם nachûm [Hebrew]
Roots:H5151
G3486.2 N/P-PRI Ναούμ (1x)
Lk 3:25 *son* of·Amots, *son* of·Nachum, *son* of·Esli, *son* of·

G3487 νάρδος nárdôs *n.* (2x)
xLangEquiv:H5373
G3487.2 N-GSF νάρδου (2x)
Jn 12:3 ·valuable ointment of·authentic spikenard, Mary
Mk 14:3 ·expensive ointment of·authentic spikenard. And

G3488 Νάρκισσος Nárkissôs *n/p.* (1x)
G3488.2 N/P-GSM Ναρκίσσου (1x)
Rm 16:11 from·among the *household* of·Narcissus, the·ones

G3489 ναυ•αγέω nauagéō *v.* (2x)
Roots:G3491 G0071
G3489.2 V-AAI-1S ἐναυάγησα (1x)
2Co 11:25 ·stoned once, I·was·shipwrecked three·times, *and*
G3489.2 V-AAI-3P ἐναυάγησαν (1x)
1Ti 1:19 some, after·shoving·*it*·away, are·shipwrecked,

G3490 ναύ•κληρος naúklērôs *n.* (1x)
Roots:G3491 G2819 Compare:G4143 See:G3492 G3489
G3490.2 N-DSM ναυκλήρῳ (1x)
Ac 27:11 by·the pilot and by·the shipowner, rather than by·

G3491 ναῦς naûs *n.* (1x)
Roots:G3493-1 Compare:G4143 See:G3490 G3492 G3489 G3517 xLangAlso:H0590
G3491 N-ASF ναῦν (1x)
Ac 27:41 *a·broad sand·bar*, they·ran the boat aground; and

G3492 ναύτης naútēs *n.* (3x)
Roots:G3491 Compare:G5257 See:G3490
G3492.2 N-NPM ναῦται (2x)
Ac 27:27 of·the night the sailors were·surmising for·them to·
Rv 18:17 the company of·ships, and sailors, and as·many·as
G3492.2 N-GPM ναυτῶν (1x)
Ac 27:30 But with·the sailors seeking to·flee out·from the

G3493 Ναχώρ Nachốr *n/p.* (1x)
נָחוֹר nachôr [Hebrew]
Roots:H5152
G3493.2 N/P-PRI Ναχώρ (1x)
Lk 3:34 *son* of·AbRaham, *son* of·Terach, *son* of·Nachor,

G3494 νεανίας nêanías *n.* (5x)
Roots:G3501 See:G3495 G3494-1
G3494.2 N-NSM νεανίας (1x)
Ac 20:9 And a·certain young·man by·the·name·of EuTychus
G3494.2 N-ASM νεανίαν (3x)
Ac 23:17 ·replying, "Lead this young·man to the regiment·
Ac 23:18 asked *me* to·bring this young·man to you, having
Ac 23:22 ·commander dismissed the young·man, charging
G3494.2 N-GSM νεανίου (1x)
Ac 7:58 ·at the feet of·a·young·man being·called Saul.

G3495 νεανίσκος nêanískôs *n.* (10x)
Roots:G3501 See:G3494
G3495 N-NSM νεανίσκος (3x)
Mt 19:20 The young·man says to·him, "All these·things I·
Mt 19:22 saying, the young·man went·away being·grieved,
Mk 14:51 (But·also a certain young·man was·following him
G3495 N-NPM νεανίσκοι (3x)
Ac 2:17 and yeur young·men shall·gaze·upon clear·visions,
Ac 5:10 and expired. And the young·men entering, found
Mk 14:51 nakedness, and the young·men securely·held him.
G3495 N-VSM νεανίσκε (1x)
Lk 7:14 And he·declared, "Young·man, I·say to·you, be·
G3495 N-VPM νεανίσκοι (2x)
1Jn 2:13 I·write to·yeu, young·men, because yeu·have·
1Jn 2:14 I·already·wrote to·yeu, young·men, because yeu·
G3495 N-ASM νεανίσκον (1x)
Mk 16:5 ·tomb, they·saw a·young·man sitting·down on the

G3496 Νεά•πολις Nêápôlis *n/l.* (1x)
Roots:G3501 G4172
G3496.2 N/L-ASF Νεάπολιν (1x)
Ac 16:11 ·of·Thrace, also the following *day* to NeaPolis,

G3497 Νεεμάν Nêêmán *n/p.* (1x)
נַעֲמָן na'ăman [Hebrew]
Roots:H5283
G3497.2 N/P-PRI Νεεμάν (1x)
Lk 4:27 of·them was·purified, except Naaman the Syrian."

G3498 νεκρός nêkrós *adj.* (133x)
Roots:G3500-1 Compare:G2253 See:G3499 G3500
xLangAlso:H4191
G3498 A-NSM νεκρός (9x)
Lk 7:15 And the dead·man sat·up and began to·speak.
Lk 15:24 this son of·mine was dead and came·alive·again;
Lk 15:32 this your brother was dead and came·alive·again;

Ac 20:9 down from the third·story and was·taken·up dead.
Mk 9:26 and he·became as one·dead— such·for many to·
Rv 1:17 him, I·fell toward his feet as dead. And he·laid his
Rv 1:18 *I·AM* the·one living, and was dead; and behold, I·
Rv 2:8 First and the Last, who became dead and·yet lived:
Rv 3:1 you·have the name that you·live, yet you·are dead.

G3498 A-NSF νεκρά (4x)
Rm 7:8 For apart·from Torah-Law, moral·failure *was* dead.
Jac 2:17 ·that it·should·have no works, is dead by itself.
Jac 2:20 trust, completely·apart·from the works, is dead?
Jac 2:26 also, the trust apart·from the works is dead.

G3498 A-NSN νεκρόν (2x)
Rm 8:10 in·fact, the body *is* dead through moral·failure.
Jac 2:26 body apart·from spirit is dead, in·this·manner also,

G3498 A-NPM νεκροί (14x)
Jn 5:25 now is, when the dead·ones shall·hear the voice of·
Lk 7:22 deaf·men hear, dead·men are·awakened, *and the*
Lk 20:37 Now, *concerning* that the dead are·awakened, even
Mt 11:5 and deaf·men hear, dead·men are·awakened and *the*
Mt 28:4 keeping·guard are·shaken and became as·if dead.
1Th 4:16 trumpet, and the dead·ones in Anointed-One shall·
1Co 15:15 by·inference, dead·men are·not awakened.
1Co 15:16 For if dead·men are·not awakened, not·even
1Co 15:29 of·the dead, if dead·men are·not awakened at·all?
1Co 15:32 advantage to·me, if dead·men are·not awakened?
1Co 15:35 shall·declare, "How·are the dead·men awakened?
1Co 15:52 it·shall·sound, and the dead shall·be·awakened
Rv 14:13 'Supremely·blessed *are* the dead·ones, the·ones
Rv 20:12 And the dead·ones are·judged out·of·the·things

G3498 A-ASM νεκρόν (1x)
Ac 28:6 ·with·fever or to·fall·down dead without·warning,

G3498 A-ASF νεκράν (1x)
Ac 5:10 ·men entering, found her dead, and carrying·*her*·out

G3498 A-APM νεκρούς (19x)
Jn 5:21 the Father awakens the dead and gives·life·to *them*;
Lk 9:60 ·him, "Leave the dead·ones to·bury their·own dead,
Lk 9:60 the dead·ones to·bury their·own dead, but you·
Ac 26:8 incredible with yeu, that God awakens dead·men?
Heb 11:35 received their dead from·out of·a·resurrection.
Mt 8:22 me, and allow the dead·ones to·bury their·own dead
Mt 8:22 and allow the dead·ones to·bury their·own dead."
Mt 10:8 purify lepers; awaken dead·ones; cast·out demons.
Rm 4:17 ·one giving·life·to the dead·ones and calling·forth
Rm 6:11 yeurselves to·be in·fact dead to·the Moral·Failure,
1Pe 4:5 readiness to·judge *the·ones* living and *the* dead·ones.
2Co 1:9 but·rather upon God (the·one awakening the dead).
Eph 2:1 yeu·yeurselves were·once dead in·the trespasses and
Eph 2:5 even *with* us being dead in·the trespasses, he·made·
Col 2:13 And *although* yeu *were* dead, being in·the
2Ti 4:1 ·one about to·judge living·men and dead·men at his
Rv 20:12 And I·saw the dead·ones, small and great, standing
Rv 20:13 And the Sea gave·forth the dead·ones in her, and
Rv 20:13 Death and Hades gave·forth the dead·ones in them.

G3498 A-DPM νεκροῖς (2x)
Heb 9:17 ·and·covenant *is* of·force after men·are·dead, since
1Pe 4:6 ·the·good·news·already·proclaimed also to·the·dead:

G3498 A-GSM νεκροῦ (1x)
Rv 16:3 and it·became as blood of·a·dead·man. And every

G3498 A-GPM νεκρῶν (77x)
Jn 2:22 when he·was·awakened from·among dead·men, his
Jn 12:1 ·died, whom he·awakened from·among dead·men.
Jn 12:9 also, whom he·awakened from·among dead·men.
Jn 12:17 ·tomb and awakened him from·among dead·men.
Jn 20:9 ·for him to·rise·up from·among dead·men.
Jn 21:14 after·being·awakened from·among dead·men.
Lk 9:7 that John has·been·awakened from·among dead·men,
Lk 16:30 ·traverse to them from dead·men, they·shall·repent.
Lk 16:31 someone should·rise·up from·among dead·men.'"
Lk 20:35 the resurrection from·out of·the dead, neither marry
Lk 20:38 So he·is not a·God of·dead·men, but·rather of·
Lk 24:5 "Why among the dead do·yeu·seek the·one living?
Lk 24:46 and to·rise·up from·among dead·men on·the third
Ac 3:15 God awakened from·among dead·men, to·which
Ac 4:2 the resurrection, the·one from·among dead·men.
Ac 4:10 whom God awakened from·among dead·men, by
Ac 10:41 with·him after he rose·up from·among dead·men.
Ac 10:42 by God *to·be* Judge of·living·men and dead·men.
Ac 13:30 But God awakened him from·among dead·men—
Ac 13:34 he·raised him up from·among dead·men, no·longer
Ac 17:3 to·suffer and to·rise·up from·among dead·men, and
Ac 17:31 after·raising him up from·among dead·men."
Ac 17:32 of·a·resurrection of·dead·men, they·were·jeering.
Ac 23:6 even *the* resurrection of·dead·men, *that* I·myself
Ac 24:15 there·shall·be a·resurrection of·dead·men, both
Ac 24:21 Concerning *the* resurrection of·dead·men, I·myself
Ac 26:23 ·a·resurrection from·among dead·men *and* is·about
Heb 6:2 of·hands, and of·the·resurrection of·the·dead, and
Heb 11:19 *him* even from·among dead·men, from·which also
Heb 13:20 ·one bringing·up from·among dead·men our Lord
Gal 1:1 the·one awakening him from·among dead·men),
Mt 14:2 he himself is·already·awakened from the dead, and
Mt 17:9 ·Clay·Man† should·rise·up from·among dead·men."
Mt 22:31 the resurrection of·the dead, did·yeu·not read·
Mt 22:32 is not the God of·dead·men, but·rather of·living·
Mt 23:27 but inwardly they·overflow of·dead *men's* bones
Mt 27:64 'He·is·awakened from the dead,' and the last error
Mt 28:7 that he·was·awakened from the dead, and behold,
Mk 6:14 ·One was·awakened from·among dead·men, and
Mk 6:16 is·already·awakened from·among dead·men."
Mk 9:9 of·Clay·Man† should·rise·up from·among dead·men.
Mk 9:10 it·should·mean to·rise·up from·among the dead.
Mk 12:25 ·rise·up from·among dead·men, they·neither
Mk 12:26 "Now concerning the dead, that they·are·
Mk 12:27 He·is not the God of·dead·men, but·rather a·God
Rm 1:4 from·out of·a·resurrection of·the·dead; *specifically*,
Rm 4:24 ·awakening Jesus our Lord from·among dead·men,
Rm 6:4 ·awakened from·among dead·men through the glory
Rm 6:9 ·awakened from·among dead·men, Anointed-One
Rm 6:13 as those·that·are·alive from·among dead·men, and
Rm 7:4 ·awakened from·among dead·men, in·order·that we·
Rm 8:11 awakening Jesus from·among dead·men dwells in
Rm 8:11 the Anointed-One from·among dead·men shall also
Rm 10:7 to·bring Anointed-One up from·among dead·men).
Rm 10:9 him from·among dead·men, you·shall·be·saved.
Rm 11:15 *be*, except life-above from·among dead·men?
Rm 14:9 ·may·exercise·lordship·over both *the* dead and *the*
Php 3:11 ·attain to the exceptional·resurrection of·the dead.
1Pe 1:3 of·YeShua Anointed from·among dead·men—
1Pe 1:21 awakening him from·among dead·men and giving
1Th 1:10 he·awakened from·among dead·men, YeShua, the·
1Co 15:12 ·been·awakened from·among dead·men, how·do
1Co 15:12 yeu say that there·is no resurrection of·dead·men?
1Co 15:13 if there·is no resurrection of·dead·men, not·even
1Co 15:20 has·been·awakened from·among dead·men. He·
1Co 15:21 a·man·of·clay† *came* resurrection of·dead·men.
1Co 15:29 the·ones being·immersed on·behalf of·the dead, if
1Co 15:29 then are·they·immersed on·behalf of·the dead?
1Co 15:42 also *is* the resurrection of·the dead. It·is·sown in
Eph 1:20 after·awakening him from·among dead·men. And
Eph 5:14 and rise·up from·out of·the dead, and the
Col 1:18 *the* firstborn from·out of·the dead, in·order·that in
Col 2:12 ·one already·awakening him from·out of·the dead.
2Ti 2:8 ·awakened from·among dead·men according·to my
Rv 1:5 *and* the firstborn from·out of·the dead, and the chief·
Rv 11:18 and·also the season for·the dead to·be·judged,
Rv 20:5 But the rest of·the dead did·not come·alive·again

G3498 A-GPN νεκρῶν (2x)
Heb 6:1 foundation— of·repentance from dead works, and
Heb 9:14 yeur conscience from dead works in·order·for *yeu*

EG3498 (1x)
2Co 5:15 behalf and already·being·awakened *from the dead*.

G3499 νεκρόω nêkrŏō *v.* (3x)
Roots:G3498 Compare:G2348 See:G3500

G3499.1 V-AAM-2P νεκρώσατε (1x)
Col 3:5 Accordingly, deaden yeur members *to* the·things

G3499.1 V-RPP-ASN νενεκρωμένον (1x)
Rm 4:19 body, even·now having·been·deadened, subsisting

G3499.1 V-RPP-GSM νενεκρωμένου (1x)
Heb 11:12 were·born from·him·having·been·deadened *of*—

G3500 νέκρωσις nékrōsis *n.* (2x)
Roots:G3499 Compare:G2288 G1044

G3500.2 N-ASF νέκρωσιν (2x)
Rm 4:19 ·of·age, nor the deadness of·Sarah's primal·womb.
2Co 4:10 in the body the mortal·deadness of·the Lord Jesus,

G3501 νέος nêŏs *adj.* (24x)
νεώτερος nêṓtêrŏs [comparative]
Compare:G2537 See:G3503 G0365
xLangAlso:H6810 H6996 H5288

G3501.2 A-APF νέας (1x)
Tit 2:4 ·train the young·women to·be·affectionate·to·their·

G3501.3 A-NSM-C νεώτερος (4x)
Jn 21:18 to·you, when you·were younger, you·were·girding
Lk 15:12 And the younger of·them declared to·the father,
Lk 15:13 days after, the younger son, gathering·together
Lk 22:26 among yeu, let·him·be as the younger, and the·one

G3501.3 A-NPM-C νεώτεροι (2x)
Ac 5:6 And the younger·men, rising·up, tightly·wrapped him
1Pe 5:5 Likewise, *yeu* younger·men, be·submitted *to·yeur*

G3501.3 A-APM-C νεωτέρους (2x)
Tit 2:6 exhort the younger·men to·be·self-controlled.
1Ti 5:1 *him* as a·father, *likewise* younger·men as brothers,

G3501.3 A-APF-C νεωτέρας (3x)
1Ti 5:2 older·women as mothers, younger·women as sisters,
1Ti 5:11 But decline *to·register* younger widows, for
1Ti 5:14 ·of·grace, I·resolve *for* younger *widows* to·marry,

G3501.4 A-NSM νέος (2x)
Lk 5:37 But·if·so, the fresh·new wine shall·burst the
Mk 2:22 But·if·so, the fresh·new wine bursts the wineskins,

G3501.4 A-NSN νέον (1x)
1Co 5:7 ·order·that yeu·may·be a·fresh·new lump·of·dough,

G3501.4 A-ASM νέον (8x)
Lk 5:37 "And not·even·one·man casts fresh·new wine into
Lk 5:38 "But·rather fresh·new wine *is only* fit·to·be·cast into
Lk 5:39 old *wine* immediately wants fresh·new *wine*, for he·
Mt 9:17 Neither do·men·cast fresh·new wine into old
Mt 9:17 ·destroyed. But·rather they·cast fresh·new wine into
Mk 2:22 And not·even·one·man casts fresh·new wine into
Mk 2:22 "But·rather fresh·new wine *is only* fit·to·be·cast
Col 3:10 ·yeurselves·with the fresh·new *man·of·clay†*, the·

G3501.4 A-GSF νέας (1x)
Heb 12:24 to·YeShua, mediator of·a·fresh·new covenant,

G3502 νεοσσός nêŏssŏ́s *n.* (1x)
Roots:G3501

G3502 N-APM νεοσσούς (1x)
Lk 2:24 of·turtledoves or two of·the·Offspring of·a·dove."'

G3503 νεότης nêŏ́tēs *n.* (5x)
Roots:G3501 Compare:G2538
xLangEquiv:H5271

G3503.2 N-GSF νεότητος (5x)
Lk 18:21 ·things I·vigilantly·kept from·among my youth."
Ac 26:4 my way·of·life from·among *my* youth (the·one
Mt 19:20 ·things I·vigilantly·kept from·out of·my youth, yet
Mk 10:20 ·things I·vigilantly·kept from·out of·my youth."
1Ti 4:12 Let no·man despise your youth, but·rather become

G3504 νεό•φυτος nêŏ́phytŏs *adj.* (1x)
Roots:G3501 G5453 Compare:G5040 G0313

G3504.3 A-ASM νεόφυτον (1x)
1Ti 3:6 *and* not one·newly·come·to·the·trust, lest being·

G3505 Νέρων Nérōn *n/p.* (1x)
See:G2804 G5086

EG3505 (1x)
Ac 25:26 absolutely·certain to·write *to·my* Lord *Nero*.

G3506 νεύω nêúō *v.* (2x)
Compare:G4591 G2678 G3573 See:G1962 G2656 G3573

G3506.2 V-PAI-3S νεύει (1x)
Jn 13:24 So·then, Simon Peter beckoned to·him to·inquire

G3506.2 V-AAP-GSM νεύσαντος (1x)

Ac 24:10 with·the governor beckoning for·him to·discourse,

G3507 νεφέλη nêphélē *n.* (24x)
Roots:G3509
xLangEquiv:H5645 xLangAlso:H6051 H0108
G3507.2 N-NSF νεφέλη (5x)
Lk 9:34 saying these·things, there·came a·thick·cloud, and
Ac 1:9 he·was·lifted·up, and a·thick·cloud received him up
Mt 17:5 behold, a·thick·cloud full·of·light overshadowed
Mk 9:7 Then there·was a·thick·cloud overshadowing them,
Rv 14:14 and behold, a·white thick·cloud, and upon the
G3507.2 N-NPF νεφέλαι (2x)
Jud 1:12 thick·clouds without·water being·carried·about by
2Pe 2:17 without·water, thick·clouds being·driven by a·
G3507.2 N-ASF νεφέλην (5x)
Lk 9:34 they·were·afraid to·enter into the thick·cloud.
Lk 12:54 ·see the thick·cloud rising·above·the·horizon from
Rv 10:1 having·been·arrayed·with a·thick·cloud; and a·
Rv 14:14 and upon the thick·cloud *one* who·is·sitting·down
Rv 14:16 who·is·sitting·down on the thick·cloud cast·in his
G3507.2 N-DSF νεφέλῃ (2x)
Lk 21:27 Son of·Clay·Man† coming in a·thick·cloud' with
Rv 11:12 to the heaven in the thick·cloud, and their enemies
G3507.2 N-DPF νεφέλαις (2x)
Mk 13:26 of·Clay·Man† coming in thick·clouds' with much
1Th 4:17 ·them in *the* thick·clouds to approach·and·meet the
G3507.2 N-GSF νεφέλης (4x)
Lk 9:35 there·came a·voice from·out of·the thick·cloud,
Mt 17:5 a·voice from·out of·the thick·cloud, saying,
Mk 9:7 and a·voice came out of·the thick·cloud, saying,
Rv 14:15 ·the·one who·is·sitting·down on the thick·cloud,
G3507.2 N-GPF νεφελῶν (4x)
Mt 24:30 coming upon the thick·clouds of·the heaven' with
Mt 26:64 and 'coming upon the thick·clouds of·the heaven."
Mk 14:62 'coming with the thick·clouds of·the heaven.'"
Rv 1:7 Behold, 'he·comes with the thick·clouds,' and '

G3508 Νεφθαλείμ Nêphthaleím *n/g.* (3x)
נַפְתָּלִי naph·ṭaliy [Hebrew]
Roots:H5321
G3508.3 N/G-PRI Νεφθαλείμ (1x)
Rv 7:6 *the* tribe of·Naphtali having·been·officially·sealed,
G3508.4 N/G-PRI Νεφθαλείμ (2x)
Mt 4:13 within *the* borders of·Zebulun and Naphtali,
Mt 4:15 "O·Land of·Zebulun and land of·Naphtali, *by the*

G3509 νέφος nêphôs *n.* (3x)
Compare:G1105 G2217 See:G3507
xLangEquiv:H6051 xLangAlso:H5645 H7834
G3509.1 N-ASN νέφος (2x)
Heb 12:1 so·vast a·cloud of·witnesses that·is·encircling·
1Co 10:1 all our fathers were under the cloud, and all went
G3509.1 N-DSF νέφη (1x)
1Co 10:2 were·immersed into Moses in the cloud and in the

G3510 νεφρός nêphrôs *n.* (1x)
Compare:G1271 G2259-2 See:G2588
xLangEquiv:H3629
G3510.2 N-APM νεφρούς (1x)
Rv 2:23 that I AM the·one searching kidneys and hearts.

G3511 νεω•κόρος nêōkôrôs *adj.* (1x)
Roots:G3485
G3511.1 A-ASF νεωκόρον (1x)
Ac 19:35 Ephesians is·being temple·custodian of·the great

G3512 νεωτερικός nêōtêrikôs *adj.* (1x)
Roots:G3501
G3512 A-APF νεωτερικάς (1x)
2Ti 2:22 So flee the youthful longings, but pursue

G3513 νή nê *prt.* (1x)
Roots:G3483
G3513 PRT νή (1x)
1Co 15:31 Each day I·die, as·sure·as *it·is* our boast, which I·

G3514 νήθω nêthō *v.* (2x)
G3514 V-PAI-3S νήθει (2x)
Lk 12:27 ·do·not labor·hard, they·do·not·even spin, and·yet
Mt 6:28 they·do·not labor·hard, neither do·they·spin.

G3515 νη•πιάζω nēpiázō *v.* (1x)
Roots:G3516
G3515.1 V-PAM-2P νηπιάζετε (1x)
1Co 14:20 but·rather be·as·infants in·the malice. But in·the

G3516 νή•πιος nḗpiôs *adj.* (14x)
Roots:G2031 Compare:G1025 See:G3516-1
G3516.2 A-NSM νήπιος (6x)
Heb 5:13 of·righteousness— for he·is *still* an·infant.
Gal 4:1 for·a·span·of time (as·long·as he·is an·infant), varies
1Co 13:11 When I·was an·infant, I·was·speaking as an·
1Co 13:11 I·was·speaking as an·infant, I·was·contemplating
1Co 13:11 ·was·contemplating as an·infant, I·was·reckoning
1Co 13:11 as an·infant, I·was·reckoning as an·infant. But
G3516.2 A-NPM νήπιοι (2x)
Gal 4:3 we·ourselves, when we·were infants, were having·
Eph 4:14 be infants, who·are·being·tossed·about·by·surging·
G3516.2 A-DPM νηπίοις (3x)
Lk 10:21 ·men, and you·revealed them to·infants. Yes,
Mt 11:25 intelligent·men, and you·revealed them to·infants.
1Co 3:1 as to·fleshly·ones, as to·infants in Anointed-One.
G3516.2 A-GSM νηπίου (1x)
1Co 13:11 I·have·fully·put·to·rest the·things of·the infant.
G3516.2 A-GPM νηπίων (2x)
Mt 21:16 " From·out *of·the* mouth of·infants and sucklings
Rm 2:20 of·impetuous·men, an·instructor of·infants, having

G3517 Νηρεύς Nērêús *n/p.* (1x)
Roots:G3491
G3517 N/P-ASM Νηρέα (1x)
Rm 16:15 PhiloLogus, and Julia, Nereus, and his sister, and

G3518 Νηρί Nērí *n/p.* (1x)
נֵרִיָּה nēriyah [Hebrew]
Roots:H5374
G3518.2 N/P-PRI Νηρί (1x)
Lk 3:27 of·ZorubBabel, *son* of·ShealtiEl, *son* of·NeriYah,

G3519 νησίον nēsíôn *n.* (1x)
Roots:G3520 G2444-3
G3519 N-ASN νησίον (1x)
Ac 27:16 ·near·to a·certain small·island being·called Clauda,

G3520 νῆσος nē̂sôs *n.* (9x)
Roots:G3491 See:G3519
xLangEquiv:H0339
G3520 N-NSF νῆσος (3x)
Ac 28:1 then they·realized that the island was·called Melita.
Rv 6:14 and every mountain and island was·stirred out of·
Rv 16:20 And every island fled·away, and mountains were·
G3520 N-ASF νῆσον (2x)
Ac 13:6 And going·throughout the island, even·as·far·as
Ac 27:26 ·for us to·be·cast·away upon some island."
G3520 N-DSF νήσῳ (3x)
Ac 28:9 sicknesses on the island, were·coming·alongside,
Ac 28:11 after having·wintered on the island *for* three lunar·
Rv 1:9 came·to·be in the island, the·one being·called
G3520 N-GSF νήσου (1x)
Ac 28:7 *belonging* to·the foremost·man of·the island, *a·man*

G3521 νη•στεία nēstêía *n.* (8x)
Roots:G3522 Compare:G0776
G3521.1 N-DSF νηστείᾳ (3x)
Mt 17:21 kind does·not depart except by prayer and fasting."
Mk 9:29 able to·come·forth, except by prayer and fasting."
1Co 7:5 ·off·and·give·yeurselves to·the fasting and to·the
G3521.1 N-DPF νηστείαις (3x)
Lk 2:37 ·ministering *to·God* with·fastings and petitions night
2Co 6:5 in wearisome·labors, in sleeplessness, in fastings,
2Co 11:27 hunger and thirst, in fastings many·times, in cold
G3521.1 N-GPF νηστειῶν (1x)
Ac 14:23 with fasting, they·placed·the·direct·care·of them
G3521.2 N-ASF νηστείαν (1x)
Ac 27:9 on·account·of the fast·*Day·of·Atonement* also even·

G3522 νη•στεύω nēstêúō *v.* (21x)
Roots:G3523 See:G3521
G3522 V-FAI-3P νηστεύσουσιν (3x)
Lk 5:35 ·be·lifted·away from them, they·shall·fast in those
Mt 9:15 ·be·lifted·away from them, and then they·shall·fast.
Mk 2:20 from them, and then they·shall·fast in those days.
G3522 V-PAI-1S νηστεύω (1x)
Lk 18:12 I·fast twice in·the week, I·tithe all·things, *on* as·
G3522 V-PAI-1P νηστεύομεν (1x)
Mt 9:14 ·do we·ourselves and the Pharisees fast often, but
G3522 V-PAI-3P νηστεύουσιν (4x)
Lk 5:33 "Why·is·it·that the disciples of·John fast frequently,
Mt 9:14 Pharisees fast often, but your disciples do·not fast?"
Mk 2:18 and the *disciples* of·the Pharisees fast, but your
Mk 2:18 ·the Pharisees fast, but your disciples do·not fast?"
G3522 V-PAN νηστεύειν (3x)
Lk 5:34 to·make the Sons of·the bride-chamber to·fast, while
Mk 2:19 the Sons of·the bride-chamber able to·fast, while
Mk 2:19 among themselves, they·are·not able to·fast.
G3522 V-PAP-GPM νηστευόντων (1x)
Ac 13:2 ·serving for·the Lord, and·also fasting, the Holy
G3522 V-PAP-NSM νηστεύων (3x)
Ac 10:30 days ago I·was fasting so·far·as·unto this·same
Mt 6:17 "But you, when·fasting, rub·oil·on your head and
Mt 6:18 to·the men·of·clay† *to·be* fasting, but·rather to·your
G3522 V-PAP-NPM νηστεύοντες (2x)
Mt 6:16 to·the men·of·clay† *to·be* fasting. Certainly I·say to·
Mk 2:18 *disciples* of·the Pharisees were fasting. And they·
G3522 V-PAS-2P νηστεύητε (1x)
Mt 6:16 "But whenever yeu·should·fast, do·not become
G3522 V-AAP-NSM νηστεύσας (1x)
Mt 4:2 And after·fasting forty days and forty nights,
G3522 V-AAP-NPM νηστεύσαντες (1x)
Ac 13:3 Then after·fasting and praying, and after·laying·

G3523 νῆ•στις nē̂stis *adj.* (2x)
Roots:G2068
G3523.1 A-APM νήστεις (2x)
Mt 15:32 I·do·not want to·dismiss them without·eating, lest
Mk 8:3 if I·should·dismiss them without·eating to·their·own

G3524 νηφάλεος nēphálêôs *adj.* (3x)
νηφάλιος nēpháliôs
Roots:G3525
G3524.2 A-ASM νηφάλεον (1x)
1Ti 3:2 ·husband of·one wife, sober-minded, self-controlled,
G3524.2 A-APM νηφαλίους (2x)
Tit 2:2 to·be sober-minded, morally·worthy·of·reverent·
1Ti 3:11 not slanderers, *being* sober-minded *and* trustworthy

G3525 νήφω nḗphō *v.* (6x)
Compare:G3562 G5430 G5431 See:G3524 G0366 G1594
G3525.1 V-PAP-NPM νήφοντες (1x)
1Pe 1:13 ·mind, being·sober, place·yeur·expectation
G3525.1 V-PAS-1P νήφωμεν (1x)
1Th 5:8 of·day, should·be·sober, dressing·ourselves·with
G3525.1 V-AAM-2P νήψατε (1x)
1Pe 5:8 Be·sober, keep·alert! Because yeur legal·adversary,
G3525.2 V-PAM-2S νῆφε (1x)
2Ti 4:5 But you·yourself be·sober·minded in all·things,
G3525.2 V-PAS-1P νήφωμεν (1x)
1Th 5:6 we·should·keep·alert and should·be·sober·minded.
G3525.3 V-AAM-2P νήψατε (1x)
1Pe 4:7 be·self-controlled, and be·sensible to the prayers.

G3526 Νίγερ Nígêr *n/p.* (1x)
G3526.2 N/P-PRI Νίγερ (1x)
Ac 13:1 Simeon (the·one being·called Niger), and Lucius

G3527 Νικάνωρ Nikánōr *n/p.* (1x)
Roots:G3528 Compare:G4736 See:G1675
G3527.2 N/P-ASM Νικάνορα (1x)
Ac 6:5 and·also Philippe, ProChorus, Nicanor, Timon,

G3528 νικάω nikáō *v.* (28x)
Roots:G3529 Compare:G2729 G2274 G2620 G0234-1 See:G5245
G3528.1 V-FAI-3S νικήσει (2x)
Rv 11:7 war with them, and shall·conquer them, and shall·
Rv 17:14 Lamb, and the Lamb shall·conquer them, because

G3528.1 V-PAP-NSM νικῶν (1x)
Rv 6:2 ·given to·him, and he·came·forth conquering, so that
G3528.1 V-AAN νικῆσαι (1x)
Rv 13:7 war with the holy·ones, and to·conquer them.' And
G3528.1 V-AAS-3S νικήσῃ (2x)
Lk 11:22 ·than him should·conquer him after·coming·upon
Rv 6:2 ·came·forth conquering, so that he·should·conquer.
G3528.2 V-PAI-3S νικᾷ (1x)
1Jn 5:4 ·been·born from·out of·God overcomes the world.
G3528.2 V-PAM-2S νικᾷ (1x)
Rm 12:21 by the bad, but·rather overcome the bad with the
G3528.2 V-PAP-APM νικῶντας (1x)
Rv 15:2 and·also the·ones overcoming (out·from·among
G3528.2 V-PAP-DSM νικῶντι (2x)
Rv 2:7 ·Out·citizenries. To·the·one overcoming, I·shall·give
Rv 2:17 ·citizenries. To·the·one overcoming, I·shall·give to·
G3528.2 V-PAP-NSM νικῶν (7x)
1Jn 5:5 Who is the·one overcoming the world, if·not the·one
Rv 2:11 to·the Called·Out·citizenries. The·one overcoming,
Rv 2:26 'And the·one overcoming and the·one fully·keeping
Rv 3:5 'The·one overcoming, the·same shall·be·arrayed in
Rv 3:12 'Him, the·one overcoming, I·shall·make a·pillar in
Rv 3:21 'To·him, the·one overcoming, I·shall·grant *for·him*
Rv 21:7 The·one overcoming shall·inherit all·things; and I·
G3528.2 V-PPM-2S νικῶ (1x)
Rm 12:21 Do·not be·overcome by the bad, but·rather
G3528.2 V-AAI-1S ἐνίκησα (1x)
Rv 3:21 throne, even·as I·also overcame and did·sit·down
G3528.2 V-AAI-3P ἐνίκησαν (1x)
Rv 12:11 And they·themselves overcame him through the
G3528.2 V-AAP-NSF νικήσασα (1x)
1Jn 5:4 this is the victory (the·one overcoming the world):
G3528.2 V-AAS-2S νικήσῃς (1x)
Rm 3:4 in your sayings, and may·overcome when you are·
G3528.2 V-RAI-1S νενίκηκα (1x)
Jn 16:33 ·good·courage; I·myself have·overcome the world.
G3528.2 V-RAI-2P νενικήκατε (3x)
1Jn 2:13 ·yeu, young·men, because yeu·have·overcome the
1Jn 2:14 in yeu, and yeu·have·overcome the Evil·One.
1Jn 4:4 dear·children, and have·overcome them, because
G3528.3 V-AAI-3S ἐνίκησεν (1x)
Rv 5:5 Root of·David)! He·victoriously·prevailed *such* to·

G3529 νίκη níkē *n.* (1x)
See:G3534 G3528
G3529.2 N-NSF νίκη (1x)
1Jn 5:4 And this is the victory (the·one overcoming the

G3530 Νικό•δημος Nikódēmôs *n/p.* (5x)
Roots:G3534 G1218
G3530.2 N/P-NSM Νικόδημος (5x)
Jn 3:1 from·among the Pharisees, NicoDemus *was* his name,
Jn 3:4 NicoDemus says to him, "How·is a·man·of·clay†
Jn 3:9 NicoDemus answered and declared to·him, "How·are
Jn 7:50 NicoDemus (the·one coming alongside *Jesus* by·
Jn 19:39 And NicoDemus came also, the·one coming at·the

G3531 Νικο•λαΐτης Nikôlaḯtēs *n/g.* (2x)
Roots:G3534 G2992 Compare:G2819-2 G1361 G5545-1 See:G3532
G3531.2 N/G-GPM Νικολαϊτῶν (2x)
Rv 2:6 that you·hate the deeds of·the NicoLaitans, which I·
Rv 2:15 ·to the instruction of·the NicoLaitans, which·thing I·

G3532 Νικό•λαος Nikólaôs *n/p.* (1x)
Roots:G3534 G2992 Compare:G4736 See:G3531 G1675
G3532.2 N/P-ASM Νικόλαον (1x)
Ac 6:5 ParMenas, and NicoLaos, a·convert·to·Judaism of·

G3533 Νικό•πολις Nikópôlis *n/l.* (1x)
Roots:G3534 G4172
G3533.2 N/L-ASF Νικόπολιν (1x)
Tit 3:12 to·come to me to NicoPolis, for I·have·decided to·

G3534 νῖκος nîkôs *n.* (4x)
Roots:G3529 Compare:G2275 See:G5380
G3534.2 N-NSN νῖκος (1x)
1Co 15:55 painful·sting? O·Hades, where *is* your victory?
G3534.2 N-ASN νῖκος (3x)
Mt 12:20 he·should·cast·forth tribunal·justice into victory.
1Co 15:54 ·written, "'Death is·swallowed·up in victory.'"
1Co 15:57 the·one giving us the victory through our Lord

G3535 Νινευΐ Ninêuḯ *n/l.* (1x)
נִינְוֵה niyn^e^veh [Hebrew]
Roots:H5210 See:G3536
G3535.2 N/L-PRI Νινευΐ (1x)
Lk 11:32 "Men of·Nineveh shall·rise·up in the Final·Tribunal

G3536 Νινευΐτης Ninêuḯtēs *n/g.* (2x)
Roots:G3535
G3536.1 N/G-NPM Νινευῖται (1x)
Mt 12:41 "Men of·Nineveh shall·rise·up in the Final·Tribunal
G3536.2 N/G-DPM Νινευΐταις (1x)
Lk 11:30 Jonah was a·sign to·the Ninevites, in·this·manner

G3537 νιπτήρ niptḗr *n.* (1x)
Roots:G3538
G3537 N-ASM νιπτῆρα (1x)
Jn 13:5 he·casts water into the wash·basin; then he·began

G3538 νίπτω níptō *v.* (17x)
Compare:G3068 G4150 G0637 See:G3537 G0633
G3538 V-PAI-2S νίπτεις (1x)
Jn 13:6 "Lord, do·you·yourself wash my feet?
G3538 V-PAN νίπτειν (2x)
Jn 13:5 the wash·basin; then he·began to·wash the disciples
Jn 13:14 ·yeurselves are·obligated to·wash one·another's feet
G3538 V-PMI-3P νίπτονται (1x)
Mt 15:2 elders? For they·do·not wash their hands whenever
G3538 V-AAI-1S ἔνιψα (1x)
Jn 13:14 Accordingly, if I·myself washed yeur feet *being*
G3538 V-AAI-3S ἔνιψεν (2x)
Jn 13:12 Now·then, when he·washed their feet and took·
1Ti 5:10 ·received·strangers, if she·washed *the* holy·ones
G3538 V-AAS-1S νίψω (1x)
Jn 13:8 him, "If I·should·not wash you, you·do·not have a·
G3538 V-AAS-2S νίψῃς (1x)
Jn 13:8 "No, you·should·not wash my feet *even* to the
G3538 V-AMI-1S ἐνιψάμην (1x)
Jn 9:15 clay upon my eyes, and I·washed, and I·look·about.
G3538 V-AMI-3S ἐνίψατο (1x)
Jn 9:7 Accordingly, he·went·away and washed, and he·came
G3538 V-AMM-2S νίψαι (3x)
Jn 9:7 to·him, "Head·on·out, wash in the pool of·Siloam"
Jn 9:11 to the pool of·Siloam and wash.' And after·going·off
Mt 6:17 ·fasting, rub·oil·on your head and wash your face,
G3538 V-AMN νίψασθαι (1x)
Jn 13:10 ·bathed has no need other·than to·wash the feet.
G3538 V-AMP-NSM νιψάμενος (1x)
Jn 9:11 And after·going·off and washing, I·received·sight."
G3538 V-AMS-3P νίψωνται (1x)
Mk 7:3 all the Judeans, unless they·should·wash their hands

G3539 νοιέω nôiḗō *v.* (14x)
Roots:G3563 Compare:G0143 G4920 G1252 G0191 See:G3540
G3539.2 V-PAI-1P νοοῦμεν (1x)
Heb 11:3 By·trust, we·understand the ages to·have·been·
G3539.2 V-PAI-2P νοεῖτε (5x)
Mt 15:17 Do·yeu·not·yet understand that any thing
Mt 16:9 "Do·yeu·not·yet understand, nor·even remember the
Mt 16:11 ·it that yeu·do·not understand that·I·declared *this*
Mk 7:18 ·comprehension? Do·yeu·not understand that any
Mk 8:17 have bread? Do·yeu·not·yet understand, nor·even
G3539.2 V-PAM-2S νόει (1x)
2Ti 2:7 Understand what I·say. For may the Lord give to·you
G3539.2 V-PAM-3S νοείτω (2x)
Mt 24:15 place," (the·one reading, he·must·understand),
Mk 13:14 mandatory" (the·one reading must·understand),
G3539.2 V-PAP-NPM νοοῦντες (1x)
1Ti 1:7 teachers·of·Torah-Law, not understanding— neither
G3539.2 V-PPP-NPN νοούμενα (1x)
Rm 1:20 and divinity, being·understood by·the things·made
G3539.2 V-AAN νοῆσαι (1x)
Eph 3:4 yeu·are·able to·understand my comprehension in
G3539.2 V-AAS-3P νοήσωσιν (1x)
Jn 12:40 with·the eyes nor should·understand with·the heart
G3539.3 V-PAI-1P νοοῦμεν (1x)
Eph 3:20 those·things·which we·request or have·in·mind—

G3540 νόημα nốēma *n.* (6x)
Roots:G3539 Compare:G1270 G1761 G1771 G1963 See:G0050 G2657
G3540.1 N-APN νοήματα (1x)
2Co 4:4 the mental·perceptions of·the non-trusting·ones,
G3540.3 N-NPN νοήματα (2x)
2Co 3:14 their mental·dispositions were·petrified·hard·as·.
2Co 11:3 yeur mental·disposition should·be·corrupted from
G3540.3 N-APN νοήματα (1x)
Php 4:7 hearts and yeur mental·dispositions in Anointed-One
G3540.4 N-APN νοήματα (1x)
2Co 2:11 for we·are·not ignorant of·his mental·schemes.
G3540.5 N-ASN νόημα (1x)
2Co 10:5 ·of·war *of* every mental·scheming unto the

G3541 νόθος nốthôs *adj.* (1x)
See:G3576
G3541 A-NPM νόθοι (1x)
Heb 12:8 then·by·inference, yeu·are bastards and not sons.

G3542 νομή nômḗ *n.* (2x)
See:G3551
xLangEquiv:H4829 H4830
G3542.1 N-ASF νομήν (1x)
Jn 10:9 ·in and shall·go·forth, and he·shall·find pasture.
G3542.3 N-ASF νομήν (1x)
2Ti 2:17 shall·have a·susceptible·body·as·pasture, of·whom

G3543 νομίζω nômízō *v.* (15x)
Roots:G3551 Compare:G5274
G3543.2 V-PAI-1S νομίζω (1x)
1Co 7:26 Accordingly, I·deem for·this to·inherently·be
G3543.2 V-PAI-3S νομίζει (1x)
1Co 7:36 *father* deems to·have·improper·etiquette toward his
G3543.2 V-IPI-3S ἐνομίζετο (1x)
Lk 3:23 a·son of·Joseph (as deemed·by·law), *as·well·as*
G3543.3 V-IPI-3S ἐνομίζετο (1x)
Ac 16:13 a·river, where prayer was·accustomed to·be. And
G3543.5 V-PAN νομίζειν (1x)
Ac 17:29 of·God, we·ought not to·assume *for* the divine to·
G3543.5 V-PAP-GPM νομιζόντων (1x)
1Ti 6:5 truth— assuming the Way·of·Devout·Reverence
G3543.5 V-PAP-NSM νομίζων (1x)
Ac 16:27 ·eliminate himself, assuming the chained·prisoners
G3543.5 V-IAI-3S ἐνόμιζεν (1x)
Ac 7:25 So he·was·assuming *for* his brothers to·comprehend
G3543.5 V-IAI-3P ἐνόμιζον (1x)
Ac 21:29 in the City, whom they·were·assuming that Paul
G3543.5 V-AAI-2S ἐνόμισας (1x)
Ac 8:20 to total·destruction, because you·assumed *that* the
G3543.5 V-AAI-3P ἐνόμισαν (1x)
Mt 20:10 ·coming *forward*, assumed that they·shall·receive
G3543.5 V-AAP-NPM νομίσαντες (2x)
Lk 2:44 But assuming him to·be in the caravan, they·went a·
Ac 14:19 *him* outside of·the city assuming him to·have·died.
G3543.5 V-AAS-2P νομίσητε (2x)
Mt 5:17 "Yeu·should·not assume that I·came to·demolish the
Mt 10:34 "Yeu·should·not assume that I·came to·cast peace

G3544 νομικός nômikṓs *adj.* (9x)
Roots:G3551 See:G3544-1
G3544.2 A-APF νομικάς (1x)
Tit 3:9 strifes, and quarrels of·Torah-Law, for they·are
G3544.3 A-ASM νομικόν (1x)
Tit 3:13 Diligently send Zenas the lawyer and Apollos
G3544.4 A-NSM νομικός (2x)
Lk 10:25 behold, a·certain expert·in·Torah-Law stood·up,
Mt 22:35 *who·was* an·expert·in·Torah-Law, inquired·of *him*
G3544.4 A-NPM νομικοί (1x)
Lk 7:30 Pharisees and the experts·in·Torah-Law refused the
G3544.4 A-APM νομικούς (1x)

Lk 14:3 declared to the experts·in·Torah-Law and Pharisees,
G3544.4 A-DPM νομικοῖς (2x)
Lk 11:46 to·yeu also, the experts·in·Torah-Law! Because
Lk 11:52 "Woe to·yeu, the experts·in·Torah-Law! Because
G3544.4 A-GPM νομικῶν (1x)
Lk 11:45 ·one of·the experts·in·Torah-Law says to·him,

G3545 νομίμως nômímōs *adv.* (2x)
Roots:G3551
G3545.1 ADV νομίμως (2x)
1Ti 1:8 *is* good, if someone should·use it legitimately
2Ti 2:5 ·crowned unless he·should·contend legitimately.

G3546 νόμισμα nómisma *n.* (1x)
Roots:G3543 Compare:G0694 G2772
G3546 N-ASN νόμισμα (1x)
Mt 22:19 ·exhibit for·me the currency of·the census·tribute."

G3547 νομο•διδάσκαλος nômôdidáskalôs *n.* (3x)
Roots:G3551 G1320
G3547 N-NSM νομοδιδάσκαλος (1x)
Ac 5:34 ·name·of GamaliEl, a·teacher·of·Torah-Law, *being*
G3547 N-NPM νομοδιδάσκαλοι (2x)
Lk 5:17 Pharisees and teachers·of·Torah-Law sitting·down,
1Ti 1:7 wanting to·be teachers·of·Torah-Law, not

G3548 νομο•θεσία nômôthêsía *n.* (1x)
Roots:G3550 See:G3549
G3548.2 N-NSF νομοθεσία (1x)
Rm 9:4 covenants, and the enacting·of·the·Torah-Law, and

G3549 νομο•θετέω nômôthêtéō *v.* (2x)
Roots:G3550 Compare:G1303 xLangAlso:H2710 H3772
G3549.2 V-RPI-3S νενομοθέτηται (1x)
Heb 8:6 which has·been·enacted upon significantly·better
G3549.4 V-LPI-3S νενομοθέτητο (1x)
Heb 7:11 under it the People had·the·Torah-Law·enacted),

G3550 νομο•θέτης nômôthétēs *n.* (1x)
Roots:G3551 G5087 See:G3549 G3548
G3550.2 N-NSM νομοθέτης (1x)
Jac 4:12 There·is the one lawmaker, the·one being·able to·

G3551 νόμος nómôs *n.* (200x)
תּוֹרָה ṭôrạh [Hebrew]
Compare:G3862 G1206-2 See:G3544 G3544-1 G0458 G0460 xLangEquiv:H8451
G3551.2 N-NSM νόμος (4x)
Gal 3:21 For if the law being·able to·give·life-above was·
Gal 5:23 self-restraint— against such·things there·is no law.
Rm 2:14 not having Torah-Law are a·law to·themselves,
Rm 4:15 (for where there·is no law, *there·is* not·even a·
G3551.2 N-ASM νόμον (3x)
Rm 7:21 By·inference, I·find the law in·the *circumstance*
Jac 4:11 he·speaks·against law and judges law. But if you·
Jac 4:11 But if you·judge law, you·are not a·doer of·law,
G3551.2 N-GSM νόμου (5x)
Heb 7:12 there·occurs out of·necessity also a·transfer of·law.
Rm 3:27 On·account·of what·kind·of law? The·one of·
Rm 5:13 ·failure is·not imputed *with·there* being no law.
Jac 4:11 his brother, he·speaks·against law and judges law.
Jac 4:11 law, you·are not a·doer of·law, but·rather a·judge.
G3551.3 N-NSM Νόμος (27x)
Jn 1:17 Because the Torah-Law was·given through Moses,
Jn 7:23 in·order·that the Torah-Law of·Moses should·not be·
Lk 16:16 "The Torah-Law and the prophets *were* until John.
Heb 7:19 For the Torah-Law made not·even·one·thing
Heb 7:28 For the Torah-Law fully·establishes men·of·clay†
Heb 10:1 For the Torah-Law, having a·shadow of·the
Gal 3:12 And the Torah-Law is not as·a·result of·trust, but·
Gal 3:17 And this I·say, Torah-Law (the·one having·
Gal 3:19 *for* what *purpose is* the Torah-Law? On·account·of·
Gal 3:21 So·then, *is* the Torah-Law against the promises of·
Gal 3:24 As·such, the Torah-Law has·become our strict·
Gal 5:14 For all the Torah-Law is·completely·fulfilled in one
Mt 7:12 to·them, for this is the Torah-Law and the prophets.
Mt 11:13 the prophets and the Torah-Law prophesied until
Mt 22:40 commandments is·hung all the Torah-Law and the
Rm 3:19 ·know that as·much·as the Torah-Law says, it·
Rm 4:15 For the Torah-Law accomplishes wrath (for where
Rm 5:20 Torah-Law came·in·with·an·ulterior·motive in·
Rm 7:1 , that the Torah-Law lords·over the man·of·clay†
Rm 7:7 shall·we·state? *Is* the Torah-Law moral·failure?
Rm 7:7 longing, except·that the Torah-Law was·saying,
Rm 7:12 As·such, in·fact, the Torah-Law *is* holy, and the
Rm 7:14 we·personally·know that the Torah-Law is spiritual,
1Co 9:8 Or does·not·indeed the Torah-Law say these·things
1Co 15:56 and the power of·Moral·Failure *is* the Torah-Law.
1Ti 1:8 we·personally·know that the Torah-Law *is* good, if
1Ti 1:9 this: that Torah-Law is·not laid·out for·a·righteous·
G3551.3 N-ASM Νόμον (48x)
Jn 7:19 Moses given yeu the Torah-Law? And·yet not·even·
Jn 7:19 from·among yeu does the Torah-Law. Why·do yeu·
Lk 2:22 according·to the Torah-Law of·Moses were·fulfilled
Lk 2:39 the·things according·to the Torah-Law of·Yahweh,
Ac 7:53 *yeu* who received the Torah-Law as·an·institution
Ac 15:5 *them* to·observantly·keep the Torah-Law of·Moses."
Ac 15:24 and to·observantly·keep the Torah-Law,' to·whom
Ac 18:13 to·reverence God contrary·to the Torah-Law."
Ac 21:24 ·march·orderly, vigilantly·keeping the Torah-Law.
Ac 22:12 man according·to the Torah-Law, being·attested·to
Ac 23:3 judging me according·to the Torah-Law, and you·
Ac 24:14 having·been·written in the Torah-Law and the
Ac 25:8 "Neither against the Torah-Law of·the Jews, nor
Heb 7:5 ·of the People according·to the Torah-Law, that·is,
Heb 7:16 not according·to a·Torah-Law of·a·fleshly
Heb 7:28 (the·one after the Torah-Law), *fully·establishes the*
Heb 8:4 offering the presents according·to the Torah-Law,
Heb 9:19 in *the* Torah-Law already·being·spoken by Moses
Heb 9:22 ·things, according·to the Torah-Law, are·purified
Heb 10:8 ·things are·offered according·to the Torah-Law),
Heb 10:28 Moses' Torah-Law died completely·apart·from
Gal 3:23 under Torah-Law, having·been·jointly·confined in·
Gal 4:4 ·out of·a·woman, coming·to·be under Torah-Law,
Gal 4:5 ·kinsman·redeem the·ones under Torah-Law, that
Gal 4:21 ·ones wanting to·be under Torah-Law, do·yeu·not
Gal 4:21 under Torah-Law, do·yeu·not hear the Torah-Law?
Gal 5:3 he·is under·an·obligation to·do all the Torah-Law.
Gal 5:18 ·are·led by·Spirit, yeu·are not under Torah-Law.
Gal 6:13 ·circumcised, vigilantly·keep Torah-Law, but·yet
Mt 5:17 that I·came to·demolish the Torah-Law or the
Rm 2:14 the·ones not having Torah-Law, should·do by·
Rm 2:14 these *Gentiles* not having Torah-Law are a·law to·
Rm 2:25 benefits if you·should·practice Torah-Law. But if
Rm 2:27 And *if* completing the Torah-Law, *shall·not* the·one
Rm 3:31 ·we·fully·render·useless *the* Torah-Law through the
Rm 3:31 But·rather, we·establish Torah-Law *for what it·is*.
Rm 6:14 for yeu·are not under Torah-Law, but·rather under
Rm 6:15 because we·are not under Torah-Law, but·rather
Rm 7:1 (for I·speak to·the·ones·knowing Torah-Law), that
Rm 9:31 But IsraEl, pursuing a·Torah-Law of·righteousness,
Rm 9:31 already·attain to *the* Torah-Law of·righteousness.
Rm 13:8 the other has·completely·fulfilled *the* Torah-Law.
Jac 2:10 shall·observantly·keep the whole Torah-Law, but
Php 3:5 Hebrews; according·to Torah-Law, a·Pharisee;
1Co 9:20 to·the·ones *that* are·under Torah-Law, as under
1Co 9:20 Torah-Law, as under Torah-Law, that I·may·gain
1Co 9:20 I·may·gain the·ones *that* are·under *the* Torah-Law;
Eph 2:15 (*namely* the Torah-Law of·the commandments
G3551.3 N-DSM Νόμῳ (28x)
Jn 1:45 Moses wrote *about* in the Torah-Law, and·also the
Jn 8:5 Now in the Torah-Law, Moses commanded for·us to·
Jn 8:17 also, it·has·been·written in yeur Torah-Law that the
Jn 10:34 Is·it not having·been·written in yeur Torah-Law,
Jn 15:25 the·one having·been·written in their Torah-Law,
Lk 2:23 just·as it·has·been·written in Yahweh's Torah-Law,
Lk 2:24 having·been·declared in Yahweh's Torah-Law, "'a·
Lk 10:26 What has·been·written in the Torah-Law? How·do
Lk 24:44 concerning me in the Torah-Law of·Moses, *the*
Ac 13:39 ·regarded·as·innocent by the Torah-Law of·Moses.
Gal 2:19 am·dead to·Torah-Law in·order·that I·may·live
Gal 3:11 that by Torah-Law not·even·one is·regarded·as·
Gal 5:4 by Torah-Law, yeu·are·rendered·fully·nullified from
Mt 12:5 did·yeu·not read·aloud in the Torah-Law, that on·
Mt 22:36 *is the* great commandment in the Torah-Law?"
Rm 2:12 ·fail with Torah-Law shall·be·judged through
Rm 2:17 and you·rely·upon the Torah-Law, and make·
Rm 2:20 ·knowledge and of·the truth within the Torah-Law.
Rm 2:23 You who boast in Torah-Law, do·you·dishonor
Rm 3:19 to·the·ones with the Torah-Law, in·order·that every
Rm 7:2 has·been·bound by·Torah-Law to·the living husband
Rm 7:4 also were·put·to·death to·the Torah-Law through the
Rm 7:16 ·not want, I·concur with·the Torah-Law that *it·is*
Rm 7:22 ·pleasure in·the Torah-Law of·God according·to the
Php 3:6 righteousness (the·one in *the* Torah-Law), becoming
1Co 7:39 has·been·bound by·Torah-Law over a·lifetime as·
1Co 9:9 For it·has·been·written in the Torah-Law of·Moses,
1Co 14:21 In the Torah-Law it·has·been·written, "In other·
G3551.3 N-GSM Νόμου (58x)
Jn 12:34 heard from·out of·the Torah-Law that the
Lk 2:27 ·to the prescribed·custom of·the Torah-Law,
Lk 16:17 than one tiny·mark of·the Torah-Law to·fall.
Ac 6:13 against this holy place and *against* the Torah-Law.
Ac 13:15 after the reading·aloud of·the Torah-Law and the
Ac 18:15 ·to yeur Torah-Law, yeu·shall·review·the·matter
Ac 21:20 they·inherently·are all zealots of·the Torah-Law.
Ac 21:28 against the People, the Torah-Law, and this place.
Ac 28:23 Jesus, both from the Torah-Law of·Moses and the
Gal 2:16 as·a·result of·works of·Torah-Law, but·only
Gal 2:16 ·a·result of·works of·Torah-Law— on·account·that
Gal 2:16 ·as·righteous as·a·result of·works of·Torah-Law.
Gal 2:19 For I·myself through Torah-Law, am·dead to·
Gal 2:21 *is* through Torah-Law, then·by·inference,
Gal 3:2 the Spirit as·a·result of·works of·Torah-Law, or as·a·
Gal 3:5 yeu, *is·it* as·a·result of·works of·Torah-Law, or as·a·
Gal 3:10 birthed·from·out of·works of·Torah-Law, they·are
Gal 3:10 in the official·scroll of·the Torah-Law to·do them."
Gal 3:13 us out of·the curse of·the Torah-Law, becoming a·
Gal 3:18 the inheritance *is* as·a·result of·Torah-Law, *it·is* no·
Gal 3:21 really would be as·a·result of·Torah-Law.
Mt 5:18 should·pass·away from the Torah-Law until all
Mt 23:23 ·left the weightier *matters* of·the Torah-Law: the
Rm 2:12 Torah-Law shall·be·judged through Torah-Law.
Rm 2:13 not the hearers of·the Torah-Law *that·are* righteous
Rm 2:13 of·the Torah-Law shall·be·regarded·as·righteous.
Rm 2:14 the·things *contained* in·the Torah-Law, these
Rm 2:15 ·indicate the work of·the Torah-Law written in their
Rm 2:18 varying (being·tutored from·out of·the Torah-Law).
Rm 2:23 God through the violation of·the Torah-Law?
Rm 2:25 if you·should·be a·transgressor of·Torah-Law, your
Rm 2:26 ·keep the righteous·acts of·the Torah-Law, his
Rm 2:27 circumcision *being* a·transgressor of·Torah-Law?
Rm 3:20 ·that, as·a·result *of·the* deeds of·Torah-Law, '
Rm 3:20 ' for through Torah-Law *is the* recognition of·
Rm 3:21 apart·from Torah-Law has·been·made·apparent,
Rm 3:21 being·attested·to by the Torah-Law and the
Rm 3:28 by·a·trust apart·from works of·Torah-Law.
Rm 4:13 promise *is* not through Torah-Law to·AbRaham or
Rm 4:14 if the·ones birthed·from·out of·Torah-Law *are* heirs,
Rm 4:16 *who·is* birthed·from·out of·the Torah-Law merely,
Rm 5:13 For even·until *the* Torah-Law, moral·failure was in
Rm 7:2 from the *particular* Torah-Law of·the husband.
Rm 7:3 she·is freed from the Torah-Law *such·for* herself not
Rm 7:5 the·ones through the Torah-Law, did·operate in our
Rm 7:6 ·are·fully·nullified from the Torah-Law, being·dead
Rm 7:7 Moral·Failure, except through Torah-Law, for also
Rm 7:8 longing. For apart·from Torah-Law, moral·failure
Rm 7:9 I·myself was·living apart·from Torah-Law once, but
Rm 8:3 the·thing *which·is* impossible of·the Torah-Law, in
Rm 8:4 from the Torah-Law may·be·completely·fulfilled in
Rm 9:32 ·though *it·were* as·a·result of·works of·Torah-Law.
Rm 10:4 *is the* end of·Torah-Law for righteousness to·
Rm 10:5 the·one from·out of·the Torah-Law, "'The man·

Rm 13:10 love *is* Torah-Law's complete·fulfillment.
Jac 2:9 being·convicted by the Torah-Law as transgressors.
Jac 2:11 you·have·become a·transgressor of·Torah-Law.
Php 3:9 righteousness (the·one from·out of·Torah-Law), but·
EG3551.3 (3x)
Gal 3:19 violations, *Torah-Law* was·placed·alongside *the*
Gal 3:19 *And the Torah-Law was* being·thoroughly·assigned
Rm 2:28 *of·vigilantly·keeping Torah-Law* that·is a·Jew,
G3551.4 N-ASM νόμον (1x)
Rm 7:23 but I·look·at another Law in my members,
G3551.4 N-DSM νόμῳ (2x)
Rm 7:23 ·a·war·prisoner *of* me to·the Law of·Moral·Failure,
Rm 7:25 but with·the flesh, *a·slave* to·Moral·Failure's Law.
G3551.4 N-GSM νόμου (1x)
Rm 8:2 me free from the Law of·Moral·Failure and Death.
G3551.5 N-ASM νόμον (1x)
Jac 2:8 yeu·complete *the* Royal Law according·to the
G3551.5 N-DSM νόμῳ (2x)
Rm 7:23 ·warring·against the Royal-Law of·my mind and
Rm 7:25 I myself am·a·slave to·God's Royal-Law, but with·
G3551.6 N-NSM νόμος (2x)
Jn 7:51 "¿!·Does our Oral-law judge the man·of·clay†,
1Co 14:34 ·themselves, just·as also the Oral-law says.
G3551.6 N-ASM νόμον (5x)
Jn 7:49 the·one not knowing the Oral-law, they·are utterly·
Jn 18:31 him and judge him according·to yeur Oral-law."
Jn 19:7 "We·ourselves have an·Oral-law, and according·to
Jn 19:7 and according·to our Oral-law he·is·due to·die,
Ac 24:6 and determined to·judge according·to our Oral-law.
G3551.6 N-GSM νόμου (2x)
Ac 22:3 *the* precise·manner of·*the*·Oral-law of·this esteemed·
Ac 23:29 ·account concerning issues of·their Oral-law, but
G3551.7 N-NSM νόμος (1x)
Rm 8:2 For the Law-of-Liberty of·the Spirit of·the life-above
G3551.7 N-ASM νόμον (2x)
Gal 6:2 utterly·fulfill the Law-of-Liberty of·the Anointed-One
Jac 1:25 ·near·to·peer into the complete Law of·Liberty, and
G3551.7 N-APM νόμους (2x)
Heb 8:10 'giving my Laws-of-Liberty into their innermost·
Heb 10:16 Yahweh, giving my Laws-of-Liberty upon their
G3551.7 N-DSM νόμῳ (1x)
Rm 8:7 for it·is·not subject to·the Law-of-Liberty of·God, for
G3551.7 N-GSM νόμου (1x)
Jac 2:12 ·about to·be·judged through *the* Law of·Liberty.
G3551.8 N-GSM νόμου (1x)
Rm 3:27 ·indeed, but·rather on·account·of a·Law of·Trust.

G3552 νοσέω nôséō *v.* (1x)
Roots:G3554 See:G3553
G3552.3 V-PAP-NSM νοσῶν (1x)
1Ti 6:4 but·yet sickly·harping·on about disputable·questions

G3553 νόσημα nṓsēma *n.* (1x)
Roots:G3552
G3553 N-DSN νοσήματι (1x)
Jn 5:4 from·whatever ailment by·which he·was·held·down.

G3554 νόσος nṓsôs *n.* (12x)
Compare:G0769 G3119 G0771 See:G3553
G3554.1 N-ASF νόσον (3x)
Mt 4:23 both·relieving·and·curing every illness and every
Mt 9:35 both·relieving·and·curing every illness and every
Mt 10:1 and to·both·relieve·and·cure every illness and every
G3554.1 N-APF νόσους (4x)
Lk 9:1 the demons, and to·both·relieve·and·cure illnesses.
Ac 19:12 and *for* the illnesses to·be·removed from them,
Mt 8:17 sicknesses, and he·lifted·and·carried the illnesses.
Mk 3:15 authority to·both·relieve·and·cure the illnesses, and
G3554.1 N-DPF νόσοις (3x)
Lk 4:40 to him, with·a·diversity·of illnesses *being·present*;
Mt 4:24 ·clenched by·a·diversity·of illnesses and torments,
Mk 1:34 being badly·ill with·a·diversity·of illnesses, and he·
G3554.1 N-GPF νόσων (2x)
Lk 6:17 came to·hear him and to·be·healed of·their illnesses,
Lk 7:21 ·relieved·and·cured many from illnesses, scourges,

G3555 νοσσιά nôssiá *n.* (1x)
Roots:G3502 See:G3556
G3555 N-ASF νοσσιάν (1x)
Lk 13:34 as a·hen *gathers* her brood under *her* wings, and

G3556 νοσσίον nôssíôn *n.* (1x)
Roots:G3502 G2444-3 See:G3555
G3556 N-APN νοσσία (1x)
Mt 23:37 as a·hen completely·gathers her chicks under her

G3557 νοσφίζομαι nôsphízômai *v.* (3x)
Compare:G2813
G3557.2 V-PMP-APM νοσφιζομένους (1x)
Tit 2:10 *and* not pilfering, but·rather indicating all
G3557.2 V-AMI-3S ἐνοσφίσατο (1x)
Ac 5:2 and he·pilfered *part* of the price, with·his wife also
G3557.2 V-AMN νοσφίσασθαι (1x)
Ac 5:3 ·lie to·the Holy Spirit, and to·pilfer *part* of the price

G3558 νότος nṓtôs *n.* (7x)
Compare:G3047 G3314 See:G1005 G0395 G1424
xLangEquiv:H1864 xLangAlso:H5045
G3558.1 N-ASM νότον (1x)
Lk 12:55 whenever *yeu·should·see the* south·wind blowing,
G3558.1 N-GSM νότου (2x)
Ac 27:13 And with·the·south·wind blowing·softly, *and*
Ac 28:13 after one day, with·*the*·south·wind springing·up,
G3558.2 N-GSM νότου (4x)
Lk 11:31 "*The* queen of·the·south shall·be·awakened in the
Lk 13:29 and from north and south, and shall·recline·at·the·
Mt 12:42 *The* queen *of·the* south shall·be·awakened in the
Rv 21:13 *are* three gates; on *the* south *are* three gates; *and*

G3559 νου•θεσία nôuthêsía *n.* (3x)
Roots:G3560
G3559.2 N-ASF νουθεσίαν (2x)
Tit 3:10 ·selective after a·first and second admonition,
1Co 10:11 ·are·written specifically·for our admonition, for
G3559.2 N-DSF νουθεσίᾳ (1x)
Eph 6:4 ·and·discipline and admonition of·the·Lord.

G3560 νου•θετέω nôuthêtéō *v.* (8x)
Roots:G3563 G5087 Compare:G3867 G0363
See:G3559
G3560.2 V-PAI-1S νουθετῶ (1x)
1Co 4:14 ·rather, as my beloved children, I·admonish *yeu.*
G3560.2 V-PAM-2P νουθετεῖτε (2x)
1Th 5:14 yeu, brothers, admonish the disorderly·ones,
2Th 3:15 as an·enemy, but·rather admonish *him* as a·brother
G3560.2 V-PAN νουθετεῖν (1x)
Rm 15:14 who·are·being·able also to·admonish one·another.
G3560.2 V-PAP-APM νουθετοῦντας (1x)
1Th 5:12 ·conducting yeu in *the* Lord, and admonishing yeu,
G3560.2 V-PAP-NSM νουθετῶν (1x)
Ac 20:31 ·three·years, I·did·not cease admonishing each one
G3560.2 V-PAP-NPM νουθετοῦντες (2x)
Col 1:28 fully·proclaim, admonishing every man·of·clay†
Col 3:16 instructing and admonishing yeurselves in·psalms

G3561 νου•μηνία nôumēnía *n.* (1x)
Roots:G3501 G3376 See:G2250 xLangAlso:H2320
G3561 N-GSF νουμηνίας (1x)
Col 2:16 of·a·Sacred·Feast or of·a·new·moon or of·Sabbaths

G3562 νουν•εχῶς nôunêchōs *adv.* (1x)
Roots:G3563 G2192 Compare:G5430 G3525
G3562.2 ADV νουνεχῶς (1x)
Mk 12:34 that the·same·man answered sensibly, declared to·

G3563 νοῦς nôûs *n.* (24x)
Roots:G1097 Compare:G5590 G1271 See:G3539
G3540
G3563.1 N-NSM νοῦς (2x)
Tit 1:15 but·rather even their mind and conscience has·
Rv 17:9 "Here *is* the mind·*(or·understanding)*, the·one
G3563.1 N-ASM νοῦν (6x)
Rm 1:28 them over to·a·disqualified mind, to·do the·things
Rm 11:34 '" For who knew Yahweh's mind? Or who became
1Co 2:16 Yahweh's mind that he·shall·conclusively·weigh·a·
1Co 2:16 ' But we·ourselves have Anointed-One's mind.
1Ti 6:5 men·of·clay†, *their* minds also having·been·robbed
2Ti 3:8 ·clay† *with* their mind having·been·fully·corrupted,
G3563.1 N-DSM νοΐ (3x)
Rm 7:25 So accordingly in·fact, with·the mind, I myself am·
Rm 14:5 Let each·man be·fully·assured in his·own mind.
1Co 1:10 ·completely·reformed into the same mind and in
G3563.1 N-GSM νοός (6x)
Rm 7:23 Royal-Law of·my mind and making·a·war·prisoner
Rm 12:2 by·the renewing of·yeur mind, in·order·for yeu to·
2Th 2:2 yeu not quickly to·be·shaken in the mind, nor to·be·
Eph 4:17 ·*the* Gentiles also walk, in a·futility of·their mind,
Eph 4:23 *yeu* to·be·rejuvenated in·the spirit of·yeur mind—
Col 2:18 being·puffed·up for·no·reason by his mind of·flesh,
G3563.2 N-NSM νοῦς (1x)
1Co 14:14 spirit prays, but my understanding is unfruitful.
G3563.2 N-ASM νοῦν (3x)
Lk 24:45 ·opened·up their understanding to·comprehend the
Php 4:7 ·and·over all understanding, shall·dutifully·keep
Rv 13:18 ·one having the understanding, let·him·calculate
G3563.2 N-DSM νοΐ (2x)
1Co 14:15 and I·shall·pray with·the understanding also. I·
1Co 14:15 I·shall·make·song with·the understanding also.
G3563.2 N-GSM νοός (1x)
1Co 14:19 words through my understanding, in·order·that

G3564 Νυμφᾶς Nymphâs *n/p.* (1x)
Roots:G3565 G1435
G3564.2 N/P-ASM Νύμφαν (1x)
Col 4:15 LaoDicea, and *greet* Nymphas and the Called·Out·

G3565 νύμφη nýmphē *n.* (9x)
See:G3566 G3567
xLangEquiv:H3618
G3565.1 N-NSF νύμφη (1x)
Rv 22:17 And the Spirit and the Bride say, "Come!" And
G3565.1 N-ASF νύμφην (3x)
Jn 3:29 "The·one having the bride is a·bridegroom. But the
Rv 21:2 ·made·ready as a·bride having·been·adorned for·her
Rv 21:9 I·shall·show you the Bride, the Lamb's wife.
G3565.1 N-GSF νύμφης (1x)
Rv 18:23 you; and a·voice of·bridegroom and of·bride, no,
EG3565.1 (1x)
Eph 5:33 the wife *accordingly* (*as·the Bride*), in·order·that
G3565.2 N-NSF νύμφη (1x)
Lk 12:53 daughter-in-law, and daughter-in-law against her
G3565.2 N-ASF νύμφην (2x)
Lk 12:53 mother-in-law against her daughter-in-law, and
Mt 10:35 her mother, and a·daughter-in-law against her

G3566 νυμφίος nymphíôs *n.* (16x)
Roots:G3565 Compare:G1059-2 G3995 See:G3567
xLangEquiv:H2860
G3566 N-NSM νυμφίος (9x)
Jn 3:29 "The·one having the bride is a·bridegroom. But the
Lk 5:34 to·fast, while the bridegroom is with them?
Lk 5:35 the bridegroom should·be·lifted·away from them,
Mt 9:15 to·mourn, as·long·as the bridegroom is with them?
Mt 9:15 the bridegroom should·be·lifted·away from them,
Mt 25:6 'Behold, the bridegroom comes! Go·forth to
Mt 25:10 going·off to·buy *oil*, the bridegroom came, and
Mk 2:19 able to·fast, while the bridegroom is with them?
Mk 2:20 the bridegroom should·be·lifted·away from them,
G3566 N-ASM νυμφίον (2x)
Jn 2:9 ·of·the·banquet hollered·out·for the bridegroom
Mk 2:19 as they·do·have the bridegroom among themselves,
G3566 N-GSM νυμφίου (5x)
Jn 3:29 But the friend of·the bridegroom, the·one standing
Jn 3:29 with·joy on·account·of the bridegroom's voice.
Mt 25:1 went·forth to·approach·and·meet the bridegroom.
Mt 25:5 Now with·the bridegroom lingering, all nodded·off
Rv 18:23 in you; and a·voice of·bridegroom and of·bride, no

G3567 νυμφών nymphṓn *n.* (3x)
Roots:G3565 See:G3566
G3567 N-GSM νυμφῶνος (3x)
Lk 5:34 to·make the Sons of·the bride-chamber to·fast, while
Mt 9:15 ¿!·Are the Sons of·the bride-chamber able to·mourn,

Mk 2:19 "¿! Are the Sons of the bride-chamber able to fast,

G3568 νῦν nŷn *adv.* (141x)
See:G3569 G3570

G3568.1 ADV νῦν (126x)
Jn 2:8 he says to them, "Draw *it* out now and bring *it* to the
Jn 4:18 had five husbands, and now, he whom you have is
Jn 4:23 "But yet an hour comes, and now is, when the true
Jn 5:25 an hour is coming, and now is, when the dead ones
Jn 8:40 But now yeu seek to kill me, a man of clay† that
Jn 8:52 declared to him, "Now we have known that you
Jn 9:21 But now by what means he looks about, we do not
Jn 9:41 would not have moral failure. But now yeu say,
Jn 11:8 "Rabbi, the Judeans now were seeking to stone you,
Jn 11:22 But yet I personally know, even now, that as
Jn 12:27 "Now my soul has been troubled, and what should
Jn 12:31 "There is now a Tribunal judgment of this world.
Jn 12:31 prince of this world shall now be cast out outside.
Jn 13:31 forth, Jesus says, "Now the Son of Clay Man† is
Jn 13:36 you are not able to follow me now, but you shall
Jn 14:29 "And now I have declared *it* to yeu prior to *it*
Jn 15:22 having moral failure, but now they do not have a
Jn 15:24 moral failure. But now also they have clearly seen
Jn 16:5 "But now I head on out toward the one sending me,
Jn 16:22 accordingly, yeu yourselves in fact now have grief.
Jn 16:29 him, "See, now you speak with clarity of speech,
Jn 16:30 Now we have seen that you have seen all things,
Jn 16:32 an hour comes, and now has come that yeu should
Jn 17:5 "And now, you, O Father, glorify me (*along* with
Jn 17:7 "Now they have known that all things, as much as
Jn 17:13 "And now I come to you, and these things I speak
Jn 18:36 over to the Judeans. So now my kingdom is not
Lk 1:48 ' for behold, from now on all the generations shall
Lk 2:29 "Master, now dismiss your slave in peace,
Lk 5:10 "Do not be afraid. From now on, you shall be
Lk 6:21 blessed *are* the ones hungering now, because yeu
Lk 6:21 blessed *are* the ones weeping now, because yeu
Lk 6:25 to yeu, the ones laughing now! Because yeu shall
Lk 11:39 declared to him, "Now yeu Pharisees purify the
Lk 12:52 "For from now on there shall be five in one house
Lk 16:25 the bad things. But now this one is comforted, and
Lk 19:42 your peace! But now they are already hidden from
Lk 22:36 he declared to them, "But yet now, the one having
Lk 22:69 From now on, the Son of Clay Man† shall be
Ac 2:33 forth this, which yeu now look upon and hear.
Ac 3:17 "And now, brothers, I have seen that yeu inflicted
Ac 5:38 "And now *these are* the things I say to yeu:
Ac 7:4 settled him into this land in which yeu now reside.
Ac 7:34 ' 'And now, come over here, I shall dispatch you
Ac 7:52 coming of the Righteous One, now of whom, yeu
Ac 10:5 And now send men to Joppa and send for Simon,
Ac 10:33 well in coming directly *here*. Now accordingly,
Ac 12:11 Peter declared, "Now I personally know truly that
Ac 13:11 And now behold, the Lord's hand *is* against you,
Ac 15:10 "Now, accordingly, why do yeu try God, to put a
Ac 16:36 yeu should be fully released. Now accordingly,
Ac 16:37 cast *us* into prison. And now do they cast us out
Ac 17:30 the times of ignorance, God now charges all the
Ac 18:6 I myself *am* pure. From now on, I shall traverse to
Ac 20:22 "And now behold, having been bound in the spirit,
Ac 20:25 "And now behold, I myself personally know that
Ac 22:1 fathers, hear my defense *which I make* now to yeu."
Ac 22:16 And now, what is it *that* you are about *to do*?
Ac 23:15 Now accordingly, yeu yourselves together with the
Ac 23:21 should eliminate him. And now they are ready,
Ac 24:13 concerning which now they legally accuse me.
Ac 24:25 answered, "Holding it for now, depart. And
Ac 26:6 "And now I stand being judged over *the* expectation
Ac 26:17 the Gentiles— 'to whom now I dispatch you,
Heb 2:8 to him. But now we do not yet clearly see all
Heb 9:5 forgiveness), concerning which, now is not *the*
Heb 9:24 into the heaven itself, now to be manifested in the
Heb 9:26 *the* world's conception. But now only once, at *the*
Heb 12:26 at that time. But now he has promised, saying,
Gal 1:23 us in times past now proclaims the good news, the
Gal 2:20 lives in me. And that which now I live in flesh, I
Gal 3:3 Spirit, are yeu finishing further now in *the* flesh?
Gal 4:9 But now, after knowing God, or rather being known
Gal 4:29 according to Spirit, even in this manner *it is* now.
Mt 26:65 of witnesses? See, now yeu heard his revilement
Mt 27:42 is King of IsraEl, let him descend now from the
Mt 27:43 in God. Let him rescue him now, if he wants him,
Mk 10:30 not receive a hundred times over now in this
Mk 15:32 the King of IsraEl, let him descend now from the
Rm 5:9 So then, now being regarded as righteous by his
Rm 5:11 Anointed, through whom now we received the
Rm 6:19 in this manner now yeu must present yeur
Rm 6:21 in those things of which now yeu are ashamed?
Rm 8:1 *there is* now not even one verdict of condemnation
Rm 11:30 to God, but now yeu are shown mercy by the
Rm 11:31 also, these now are obstinate in order that by
Rm 13:11 out of heavy sleep, for now our Salvation *is*
Rm 16:26 but now with him already being made apparent—
Jac 4:13 Come on now, the ones saying, "Today or
Jac 4:16 But now yeu boast in yeur bragging.
Jac 5:1 Come on now, Wealthy Men! Weep, howling over
Jud 1:25 might and authority, both now and into all the
Php 1:20 of speech (as always, *so* now also), Anointed-One
Php 1:30 such as yeu saw in me, and now hear *to be* in me.
Php 2:12 presence merely, but rather now so much more in
Php 3:18 to yeu many times, and now even *while* weeping,
1Pe 1:12 things which are now reported in detail to yeu
1Pe 2:10 *were* not a people, but *are* now God's People, the
1Pe 2:10 but now being shown compassionate mercy.
1Pe 2:25 being led astray, but yet are now returned to the
1Pe 3:21 corresponding pattern, which even now saves us, *is*
2Pe 3:7 But now, by the same Word, the heavens and the
2Pe 3:18 To him *be* glory both now and to *the* day of *the*
1Th 3:8 Because now we live, if yeu should stand fast in *the*
2Th 2:6 And now yeu personally know the thing *that is*
1Co 3:2 Moreover neither yet now are yeu able,
1Co 7:14 yeur children are impure, but now they are holy.
1Co 12:20 But now in fact *they are* many members, but one
1Co 16:12 of *his* will that he should come now, but he
2Co 5:16 As such, from now on, we ourselves personally
2Co 5:16 according to flesh, yet now we know *him* no
2Co 6:2 ' Behold, now *is* the well acceptable season!
2Co 6:2 the well acceptable season! Behold, now *is the* day
2Co 8:13 But rather out of equality, now in *this* season, *that*
2Co 13:2 time even while being absent now, I do write to
Eph 2:2 of the air, of the spirit now operating in the Sons of
Eph 3:5 the Sons of clay†, as it is now revealed to his holy
Eph 3:10 may be made known now to the principalities and
Eph 5:8 yeu were once darkness, but now *yeu are* light in
Col 1:24 Now, I rejoice in my afflictions on yeur behalf, and
2Ti 1:10 but now being made apparent through the
1Jn 2:18 is coming, even now many have become
1Jn 2:28 And now, dear children, abide in him, in order that
1Jn 3:2 Beloved, now we are children of God, and it is not
1Jn 4:3 yeu have heard that it is come, and now is in the
2Jn 1:5 And now I ask of you, my Lady, not as though I

G3568.2 ADV νῦν (1x)
2Co 7:9 *But* right now I do rejoice, not that yeu were

G3568.3 ADV νῦν (13x)
Ac 4:29 And at the present, O Yahweh, take notice of their
Gal 4:25 and corresponds to JeruSalem at the present, and is
Mt 24:21 *the* world's beginning until the present, neither, no,
Mk 13:19 which God created unto the present, and no, it
Rm 3:26 of his righteousness in the present season).
Rm 8:18 that the afflictions of the present season *are* not
Rm 8:22 experiences birthing pain even up to the present.
Rm 11:5 in this manner, in the present season also, there
Php 1:5 good news from *the* first day even unto the present,
Tit 2:12 and with devout reverence in the present age,
1Ti 4:8 having promise of life above for the present *age*, and
1Ti 6:17 the wealthy ones in the present age not to be
2Ti 4:10 Demas forsook me, loving the present age, and he

G3568.4 ADV νῦν (1x)
Jn 21:10 Bring of the small fry which yeu caught just now."

G3569 τα•νῦν tanŷn *adv.* (3x)
τὰ νῦν tà nŷn
Roots:G3588 G3568 See:G3570

G3569.2 ADV-C τανῦν (2x)
Ac 20:32 "And at the present, brothers, I place the direct
Ac 27:22 And at the present, I urgently recommend for yeu

EG3569.2 (1x)
2Th 2:2 Anointed-One is currently standing *at the present*.

G3570 νυνί nyní *adv.* (22x)
Roots:G3568 See:G3569

G3570.1 ADV νυνί (2x)
Col 1:21 by the evil works, so now he utterly reconciled
Phm 1:9 as an old man and now also a chained prisoner of

EG3570.1 (1x)
Rm 3:24 *are* now being regarded as righteous as a free

G3570.2 ADV νυνί (9x)
Rm 7:6 But right now, we are fully nullified from the
Rm 7:17 So right now, *it is* no longer I myself that performs
Rm 15:23 But right now, no longer having a place *to*
Rm 15:25 But right now, I traverse to JeruSalem, attending
1Co 13:13 And right now, these three things continue: Trust,
1Co 14:6 So right now, brothers, if I should come to yeu
2Co 8:11 So right now also, yeu must further finish to do *it*,
Eph 2:13 But right now in Anointed-One Jesus, yeu
Col 3:8 But right now yeu yourselves also must put off all

G3570.3 ADV νυνί (4x)
Heb 11:16 But even now, they longingly stretch themselves
Rm 6:22 But even now, after being set free from Moral
1Co 12:18 But even now, God himself placed the members,
2Co 8:22 in many things, but even now much more diligent,

G3570.4 ADV νυνί (1x)
Phm 1:11 not useful to you, but just now *is* easily useful to

G3570.5 ADV νυνί (5x)
Heb 8:6 But now in fact, he has obtained a more superb
Rm 3:21 But now in fact, God's righteousness apart from
1Co 5:11 But now in fact, I wrote to yeu not to associate
1Co 15:20 But, now in fact, Anointed-One has been
Col 1:26 but now in fact is made apparent to his holy ones

G3571 νύξ nýx *n.* (68x)
Compare:G3317
xLangEquiv:H3915 A3916

G3571 N-NSF νύξ (7x)
Jn 9:4 for as long as it is day. Night is coming, when not
Jn 13:30 And it was night.
Ac 27:27 Now as soon as the fourteenth night was come,
Rm 13:12 The night continually advanced, and the day has
Rv 8:12 forth for the third part of it, and the night likewise.
Rv 21:25 be shut at day's end, for night shall not be there.
Rv 22:5 And there shall not be night there. Also, they do not

G3571 N-ASF νύκτα (5x)
Lk 2:37 *to God* with fastings and petitions night and day.
Ac 20:31 cease admonishing each one, night and day with
Ac 26:7 while ritually ministering *to God* night and day,
Mk 4:27 sleep, and should be awakened night and day, but
2Th 3:8 in weariness and travail night and day specifically

G3571 N-APF νύκτας (4x)
Lk 21:37 Atrium, but *during* the nights, upon going forth,
Mt 4:2 forty days and forty nights, eventually he hungered.
Mt 12:40 was three days and three nights in the belly of the
Mt 12:40 shall be three days and three nights in the heart of

G3571 N-DSF νυκτί (15x)
Jn 11:10 man should walk along in the night, he stumbles,
Jn 21:3 And on that night, they caught nothing at all.
Lk 12:20 one! This night, they are demanding back your
Lk 17:34 "I say to yeu, in that night there shall be two
Ac 12:6 him forth, on that night Peter was being laid to
Ac 18:9 to Paul through a clear vision at night, "Do not be
Ac 23:11 And on the following night, the Lord, upon
Ac 27:23 For there stood by me this night an angel of God,
Mt 26:31 by me and shall fall away on this night. For it has

Mt 26:34 I·say to·you, that in this night, prior·to a·rooster
Mk 14:27 me and·shall·fall·away on this night, because it·
Mk 14:30 that this·day, *even* in this night, prior·to a·rooster
2Pe 3:10 ·Lord shall·come as a·thief, in a·night in which the
1Th 5:2 ·Yahweh, in·this·manner, comes as a·thief at night.
1Co 11:23 the Lord Jesus, on·the night in which he·was·

G3571 N-GSF νυκτός (34x)
Jn 3:2 The·same came to Jesus by·night and declared to·him,
Jn 7:50 ·one coming alongside *Jesus* by·night *and* being one
Jn 19:39 at·the first to Jesus by·night, bringing a·mixture of·
Lk 2:8 ·field and vigilantly·keeping the night watches over
Lk 5:5 after·laboring·hard all through the night, we·took
Lk 18:7 the·ones crying·out day and night to him, yet
Ac 5:19 ·Yahweh, *coming* through the night, opened·up the
Ac 9:24 gates both day and night so·that they·may·eliminate
Ac 9:25 disciples, taking him by·night, sent·*him*·down *by*
Ac 16:9 was·made·visible to·Paul through the night: there·
Ac 16:33 in the same hour of·the night, he·bathed off *their*
Ac 17:10 Paul and Silas through the night to Berea— who,
Ac 23:23 unto Caesarea from *the* third hour of·the night.
Ac 23:31 they·brought *him* through the night to AntiPatris.
Ac 27:27 ·Sea, in *the* middle of·the night the sailors were·
Mt 2:14 little·child and his mother by·night and departed into
Mt 14:25 in·*the*·fourth watch of·the night, YeShua went·off
Mt 25:6 "And at·the·middle of·night, a·yell has·occurred,
Mt 27:64 his disciples, coming by·night, should·steal him,
Mt 28:13 him, coming by·night with·us being·laid·asleep.'
Mk 5:5 And constantly, night and day, he·was on the
Mk 6:48 *the* fourth watch of·the night, he·comes toward
1Th 2:9 the travail, for working night and day (specifically
1Th 3:10 Night and day, *we·are* abundantly petitioning *him*
1Th 5:5 of·Day. We·are not of·night nor·even of·darkness.
1Th 5:7 the·ones falling·asleep, sleep at·night, and the·ones
1Th 5:7 and the·ones being·drunk, get·drunk at·night.
1Ti 5:5 ·on in·the petitions and in·the prayers night and day.
2Ti 1:3 concerning you in my petitions night and day
Rv 4:8 they·do·not have a·rest·break day and night, saying,
Rv 7:15 ritually·minister to·him day and night in his Temple.
Rv 12:10 them in·the·sight of·our God day and night.
Rv 14:11 do·not have a·rest·break day or night, nor·does
Rv 20:10 and they·shall·be·tormented day and night into the

EG3571 (3x)
Mt 24:43 ·known in·which watch *of·the night* the thief comes
Mt 26:45 the·one remaining *moment* and rest·yeurselves?
Mk 14:41 the·one remaining *moment* and rest·yeurselves?

G3572 νύσσω nýssō *v.* (1x)
Compare:G1574 See:G2660

G3572.2 V-AAI-3S ἔνυξεν (1x)
Jn 19:34 But·rather one of·the soldiers jabbed his side with·

G3573 νυστάζω nystázō *v.* (2x)
Roots:G3506 Compare:G3572-1 G2518 G2107-2 G5258-1 See:G1963-1 G2656 xLangAlso:H5123

G3573.2 V-PAI-3S νυστάζει (1x)
2Pe 2:3 and their total·destruction does·not nod·off *to·sleep*.

G3573.2 V-AAI-3P ἐνύσταξαν (1x)
Mt 25:5 lingering, all nodded·off and were·sleeping.

G3574 νυχθ•ήμερον nychthḗmêrôn *n.* (1x)
Roots:G3571 G2250

G3574 N-ASN νυχθήμερον (1x)
2Co 11:25 I·have·continued·on *for* a·night·and·a·day in the

G3575 Νῶε Nôê *n/p.* (8x)
נֹחַ nọach [Hebrew]
Roots:H5146 See:G2627

G3575.2 N/P-PRI Νῶε (8x)
Lk 3:36 *son* of·Shem, *son* of·Noach, *son* of·Lemek,
Lk 17:26 it·was in the days of·Noach, in·this·manner shall·
Lk 17:27 even·until that day *when* Noach entered into the
Heb 11:7 ·trust, Noach, after·being·divinely·instructed·by·
Mt 24:37 just·as *were* the days of·Noach, in·this·manner also
Mt 24:38 even·until that day *that* Noach entered into the
1Pe 3:20 *this·moment* in *the* days of·Noach, with·a·floating·
2Pe 2:5 world, but·rather vigilantly·kept Noach, *the* eighth

G3576 νωθρός nōthrós *adj.* (2x)
Roots:G3541 Compare:G1021 G3636

G3576.1 A-NPM νωθροί (2x)
Heb 5:11 since yeu·have·become bastardly·slothful with·the
Heb 6:12 ·that yeu·should·not become bastardly·slothful, but

G3577 νῶτος nō̂tôs *n.* (1x)
Compare:G4383

G3577 N-ASM νῶτον (1x)
Rm 11:10 and let their back continually *be* altogether·bent·

Ξξ - Xi

G3578 ξενία xênía *n.* (2x)
Roots:G3581 Compare:G1958 G2646 See:G3580

G3578.2 N-ASF ξενίαν (2x)
Ac 28:23 him in the guest·accommodations, to·whom he·
Phm 1:22 ·ready for·me also guest·accommodations, for I·

G3579 ξενίζω xênízō *v.* (14x)
Roots:G3581 Compare:G0324 G0526

G3579.1 V-AAI-3S ἐξένισεν (2x)
Ac 10:23 inviting them in, *Peter* hosted *them*. And on·the
Ac 28:7 who was·warmly·welcoming us. He·hosted *us for*

G3579.1 V-AAP-NPM ξενίσαντες (1x)
Heb 13:2 for through this some are·hosting angels, being·

EG3579.1 (4x)
Rm 16:5 Also *greet* the Called·Out·citizenry *hosted* in their
1Co 16:19 with·the Called·Out·citizenry *hosted* in their
Col 4:15 Nymphas and the Called·Out·citizenry *hosted* in his
Phm 1:2 and to·the Called·Out·citizenry *hosted* in your

G3579.2 V-PPI-3S ξενίζεται (3x)
Ac 10:6 This·man is·a·guest *staying* with a·certain·man,
Ac 10:18 the·one being·surnamed Peter, is·a·guest here.
Ac 10:32 shall·speak to·you. This·man is·a·guest in *the*

G3579.2 V-APS-1P ξενισθῶμεν (1x)
Ac 21:16 ·early disciple, with·whom we·should·be·guests.

G3579.3 V-PAP-APN ξενίζοντα (1x)
Ac 17:20 For you·carry certain strange·things to our ears.

G3579.4 V-PPI-3P ξενίζονται (1x)
1Pe 4:4 in which they·think·it·is·strange of·yeu not *to·be*

G3579.5 V-PPM-2P ξενίζεσθε (1x)
1Pe 4:12 Beloved, do·not be·strangely·surprised at the fiery·

G3580 ξενο•δοχέω xênôdôchéō *v.* (1x)
Roots:G3581 G1209 Compare:G5264 G5381 See:G3578

G3580.3 V-AAI-3S ἐξενοδόχησεν (1x)
1Ti 5:10 ·children, if she·hospitably·received·strangers, if

G3581 ξένος xénôs *adj.* (15x)
Compare:G0241 G0245 G0915 G3927 See:G3579 G3578

G3581.2 A-NPM ξένοι (4x)
Ac 17:21 and the foreigners temporarily·residing·there were·
Heb 11:13 that they·were foreigners and foreign·residents on
Eph 2:12 of·IsraEl, and foreigners from·the covenants of·the
Eph 2:19 yeu·are no·longer foreigners and sojourners, but·

G3581.2 A-DPM ξένοις (1x)
Mt 27:7 the potter's field as a·burial·place for·the foreigners.

G3581.3 A-NSM ξένος (2x)
Mt 25:35 ·gave me drink. I·was a·stranger, and yeu·gathered
Mt 25:43 I·was a·stranger, and yeu·did·not gather me in,

G3581.3 A-ASM ξένον (2x)
Mt 25:38 When did·we·see you a·stranger, and gathered·
Mt 25:44 or thirsting, or *being* a·stranger, or naked, or sick,

G3581.3 A-APM ξένους (1x)
3Jn 1:5 ·may·work for the brothers and for the strangers—

G3581.5 A-NSM ξένος (1x)
Rm 16:23 Gaius, my local·host (and *local·host* of·the whole

EG3581.5 (1x)
Rm 16:23 my local·host (and *local·host* of·the whole Called·

G3581.6 A-DPF ξέναις (1x)
Heb 13:9 ·about by·diverse and strange·new instructions. For

G3581.6 A-GPN ξένων (1x)
Ac 17:18 an·ardent·proclaimer of·the strange·new demigods.

G3581.7 A-GSN ξένου (1x)
1Pe 4:12 , as·though *it·is* a·strange·new·thing befalling yeu.

G3582 ξέστης xéstēs *n.* (2x)
Compare:G0030 G2765 G4632 G4713 G5473 See:G3586 G3587

G3582.3 N-GPM ξεστῶν (2x)
Mk 7:4 ·washings of·cups and pots and of·copper·vessels
Mk 7:8 *such·as the* ceremonial·washings of·pots and cups,

G3583 ξηραίνω xēraínō *v.* (16x)
Roots:G3584 See:G0369-2
xLangEquiv:H3001 xLangAlso:H2717
G3583.1 V-API-3S ἐξηράνθη (3x)
Mk 5:29 the well of·her blood was·dried·up, and she·knew
Rv 14:15 because the harvest of·the earth is·dried·up."
Rv 16:12 and its water was·dried·up, in·order·that the way
G3583.2 V-AAI-3S ἐξήρανεν (1x)
Jac 1:11 ·the blazing·heat, and it·withered the grass, and its
G3583.2 V-API-3S ἐξηράνθη (2x)
Jn 15:6 *unfruitful* vine·sprout and is·already·withered, and
1Pe 1:24 "The grass is·withered, and its flower already·
G3583.2 V-RPP-ASF ἐξηραμμένην (3x)
Mk 3:1 ·was a·man·of·clay† there having the withered hand.
Mk 3:3 man·of·clay†, the·one having the withered hand,
Mk 11:20 the fig·tree having·been·withered from·out of·*the*·
G3583.3 V-PPI-3S ξηραίνεται (1x)
Mk 9:18 grates his teeth and withers·away. And I·declared
G3583.3 V-API-3S ἐξηράνθη (5x)
Lk 8:6 ·being·sprouted, it·withered·away on·account·of *the*
Mt 13:6 ·of it not having root, it·is·already·withered·away.
Mt 21:19 And at·once the fig·tree is·withered·away.
Mt 21:20 "How·is the fig·tree withered·away *all* at·once?
Mk 4:6 on·account·of it·not having root, it·withered·away.
G3583.3 V-RPI-3S ἐξήρανται (1x)
Mk 11:21 which you·did·curse has·been·withered·away."

G3584 ξηρός xērôs *adj.* (7x)
Roots:G3582 See:G3583
xLangEquiv:H2724 xLangAlso:H3004
G3584.1 A-DSN ξηρῷ (1x)
Lk 23:31 ·sap, what should·be·done to the parched·one?"
G3584.2 N-ASF ξηράν (1x)
Mt 23:15 ·about the sea and the parched·ground to·make one
G3584.2 N-GSF ξηρᾶς (1x)
Heb 11:29 Red Sea as through parched·ground, of·which the
G3584.3 A-NSF ξηρά (1x)
Lk 6:6 man·of·clay† there and his right hand was withered.
G3584.3 A-GPM ξηρῶν (1x)
Jn 5:3 ·ill— blind, lame, withered— *all·of·them* waiting·for
G3584.3 N-ASF ξηράν (2x)
Lk 6:8 man·of·clay†, the·one having the withered hand,
Mt 12:10 a·man·of·clay† having the hand withered. And in·

G3585 ξύλινος xýlinôs *adj.* (2x)
Roots:G3586
G3585 A-NPN ξύλινα (1x)
2Ti 2:20 ·silver, but·rather also of·wood and of·earthenware
G3585 A-APN ξύλινα (1x)
Rv 9:20 bronze, stone, and wood, which neither are·able to·

G3586 ξύλον xýlôn *n.* (19x)
Roots:G3582 Compare:G1186 G5208 G4464 G0902-1 G4716 See:G3585-1 G3586-3 xLangAlso:H6086 A0636
G3586.1 N-ASN ξύλον (1x)
Rv 18:12 "and every citron wood, "and every *type·of* ivory
G3586.1 N-APN ξύλα (1x)
1Co 3:12 silver, precious stones, wood, hay, stubble—
G3586.1 N-GSN ξύλου (1x)
Rv 18:12 vessel *made* out of·*the*·most·precious wood, "and
G3586.3 N-GPN ξύλων (5x)
Lk 22:52 against an·armed·robber, with daggers and staffs?
Mt 26:47 a·large crowd with daggers and staffs, from the
Mt 26:55 ·armed·robber with daggers and staffs to·arrest me
Mk 14:43 crowd with daggers and staffs, directly·from the
Mk 14:48 ·robber, with daggers and staffs to·arrest me?
G3586.4 N-ASN ξύλον (1x)
Ac 16:24 prison·cell and secured their feet in the stocks.
G3586.5 N-NSN ξύλον (1x)
Rv 22:2 river, *was the* arbor·tree of·Life-above, producing
G3586.5 N-ASN ξύλον (2x)
1Pe 2:24 ·own body upon the arbor·tree, in·order·that we·
Rv 22:14 *to·reach* upon the arbor·tree of·Life-above and may·
G3586.5 N-DSN ξύλῳ (1x)
Lk 23:31 ·things to the arbor·tree *which·is* green·with·sap,
G3586.5 N-GSN ξύλου (6x)
Ac 5:30 ·manhandled, hanging *him* on an·arbor·tree.
Ac 10:39 whom they·executed *by* hanging on an·arbor·tree.
Ac 13:29 *him* down from the arbor·tree, they·laid *him* in a·
Gal 3:13 ·accursed *is* any one being·hung on an·arbor·tree.
Rv 2:7 to·him to·eat from·out of·the arbor·tree of·Life-above,
Rv 22:2 And the leaves of·the arbor·tree *were* for *the*

G3587 ξυράω xyráō *v.* (3x)
Roots:G3582 Compare:G2751 See:G3587-1 G3586
xLangAlso:H1548
G3587 V-PPN ξυρᾶσθαι (1x)
1Co 11:6 or to·be·shaved·bald, she·must·be·fully·veiled.
G3587 V-ADS-3P ξυρήσωνται (1x)
Ac 21:24 for them in·order·that they·may·shave their heads
G3587 V-RPP-DSF ἐξυρημένῃ (1x)
1Co 11:5 the same as·the *woman* having·been·shaved·bald.

Oo - Omicron

G3588 ὁ hô *t.* (12326x)
ἡ hē [feminine]
τό tô [neuter (each with various inflections)]
xLangEquiv:HFA00 xLangAlso:HFP50
(abbreviated listing for G3588)
G3588.ª T-NSM ὁ (1x)
(list for G3588.ª:T-NSM excluded)
G3588.ª T-DSF τῇ (1x)
(list for G3588.ª:T-DSF excluded)
G3588.ª T-GSM τοῦ (1x)
(list for G3588.ª:T-GSM excluded)
G3588.1 -- (2x)
(list for G3588.1:-- excluded)
G3588.1 T-NSM ὁ (1063x)
(list for G3588.1:T-NSM excluded)
G3588.1 T-NSF ἡ (575x)
(list for G3588.1:T-NSF excluded)
G3588.1 T-NSN τό (349x)
(list for G3588.1:T-NSN excluded)
G3588.1 T-NPM οἱ (565x)
(list for G3588.1:T-NPM excluded)
G3588.1 T-NPF αἱ (85x)
(list for G3588.1:T-NPF excluded)
G3588.1 T-NPN τά (136x)
(list for G3588.1:T-NPN excluded)
G3588.1 T-ASM τόν (788x)
(list for G3588.1:T-ASM excluded)
G3588.1 T-ASF τήν (928x)
(list for G3588.1:T-ASF excluded)
G3588.1 T-ASN τό (638x)
(list for G3588.1:T-ASN excluded)
G3588.1 T-APM τούς (380x)
(list for G3588.1:T-APM excluded)
G3588.1 T-APF τάς (178x)
(list for G3588.1:T-APF excluded)
G3588.1 T-APN τά (273x)
(list for G3588.1:T-APN excluded)
G3588.1 T-DSM τῷ (341x)
(list for G3588.1:T-DSM excluded)
G3588.1 T-DSF τῇ (549x)
(list for G3588.1:T-DSF excluded)
G3588.1 T-DSN τῷ (225x)
(list for G3588.1:T-DSN excluded)
G3588.1 T-DPM τοῖς (227x)
(list for G3588.1:T-DPM excluded)
G3588.1 T-DPF ταῖς (94x)
(list for G3588.1:T-DPF excluded)
G3588.1 T-DPN τοῖς (97x)
(list for G3588.1:T-DPN excluded)
G3588.1 T-GSM τοῦ (727x)
(list for G3588.1:T-GSM excluded)
G3588.1 T-GSF τῆς (758x)
(list for G3588.1:T-GSF excluded)
G3588.1 T-GSN τοῦ (342x)
(list for G3588.1:T-GSN excluded)
G3588.1 T-GPM τῶν (531x)
(list for G3588.1:T-GPM excluded)
G3588.1 T-GPF τῶν (67x)
(list for G3588.1:T-GPF excluded)
G3588.1 T-GPN τῶν (149x)
(list for G3588.1:T-GPN excluded)
G3588.1 T-APF τάς (1x)
(list for G3588.1:T-APF excluded)
G3588.1 T-GSM τοῦ (1x)
(list for G3588.1:T-GSM excluded)
EG3588.1 (11x)
(list for EG3588.1: excluded)
G3588.2 T-DSF τῇ (1x)
(list for G3588.2:T-DSF excluded)
G3588.3 T-NSM ὁ (596x)

(list for G3588.3:T-NSM excluded)
G3588.3 T-NSF ἡ (44x)
(list for G3588.3:T-NSF excluded)
G3588.3 T-NSN τό (31x)
(list for G3588.3:T-NSN excluded)
G3588.3 T-NPM οἱ (272x)
(list for G3588.3:T-NPM excluded)
G3588.3 T-NPF αἱ (7x)
(list for G3588.3:T-NPF excluded)
G3588.3 T-NPN τά (11x)
(list for G3588.3:T-NPN excluded)
G3588.3 T-ASM τόν (101x)
(list for G3588.3:T-ASM excluded)
G3588.3 T-ASF τήν (37x)
(list for G3588.3:T-ASF excluded)
G3588.3 T-ASN τό (29x)
(list for G3588.3:T-ASN excluded)
G3588.3 T-APM τούς (151x)
(list for G3588.3:T-APM excluded)
G3588.3 T-APF τάς (6x)
(list for G3588.3:T-APF excluded)
G3588.3 T-APN τά (9x)
(list for G3588.3:T-APN excluded)
G3588.3 T-DSM τῷ (93x)
(list for G3588.3:T-DSM excluded)
G3588.3 T-DSM@ τῷ (1x)
(list for G3588.3:T-DSM@ excluded)
G3588.3 T-DSF τῇ (14x)
(list for G3588.3:T-DSF excluded)
G3588.3 T-DSN τῷ (3x)
(list for G3588.3:T-DSN excluded)
G3588.3 T-DPM τοῖς (136x)
(list for G3588.3:T-DPM excluded)
G3588.3 T-DPF ταῖς (13x)
(list for G3588.3:T-DPF excluded)
G3588.3 T-DPN τοῖς (6x)
(list for G3588.3:T-DPN excluded)
G3588.3 T-GSM τοῦ (89x)
(list for G3588.3:T-GSM excluded)
G3588.3 T-GSF τῆς (25x)
(list for G3588.3:T-GSF excluded)
G3588.3 T-GSN τοῦ (10x)
(list for G3588.3:T-GSN excluded)
Oo
G3588.3 T-GPM τῶν (116x)
(list for G3588.3:T-GPM excluded)
G3588.3 T-GPF τῶν (3x)
(list for G3588.3:T-GPF excluded)
G3588.3 T-GPN τῶν (6x)
(list for G3588.3:T-GPN excluded)
EG3588.3 (19x)
(list for EG3588.3: excluded)
***EG3588.3* T-GPM** (1x)
(list for EG3588.3:T-GPM excluded)
G3588.4 T-NSN τό (36x)
(list for G3588.4:T-NSN excluded)
G3588.4 T-NPF αἱ (1x)
(list for G3588.4:T-NPF excluded)
G3588.4 T-NPN τά (21x)
(list for G3588.4:T-NPN excluded)
G3588.4 T-ASN τό (30x)
(list for G3588.4:T-ASN excluded)
G3588.4 T-APN τά (130x)
(list for G3588.4:T-APN excluded)
G3588.4 T-DSM τῷ (1x)
(list for G3588.4:T-DSM excluded)
G3588.4 T-DSN τῷ (2x)
(list for G3588.4:T-DSN excluded)
G3588.4 T-DPN τοῖς (16x)
(list for G3588.4:T-DPN excluded)
G3588.4 T-GSN τοῦ (1x)
(list for G3588.4:T-GSN excluded)
G3588.4 T-GPM τῶν (2x)
(list for G3588.4:T-GPM excluded)
G3588.4 T-GPN τῶν (12x)
(list for G3588.4:T-GPN excluded)
EG3588.4 (6x)
(list for EG3588.4: excluded)
G3588.6 T-ASN τό (10x)
(list for G3588.6:T-ASN excluded)
G3588.6 T-ASN@ τό (1x)
(list for G3588.6:T-ASN@ excluded)
G3588.6 T-DSM τῷ (1x)
(list for G3588.6:T-DSM excluded)
G3588.6 T-GSM τοῦ (2x)
(list for G3588.6:T-GSM excluded)
EG3588.6 (2x)
(list for EG3588.6: excluded)
G3588.7 T-NSM ὁ (1x)
(list for G3588.7:T-NSM excluded)
G3588.7 T-NPM οἱ (2x)
(list for G3588.7:T-NPM excluded)
G3588.7 T-APM τούς (2x)
(list for G3588.7:T-APM excluded)
G3588.7 T-GSM τοῦ (1x)
(list for G3588.7:T-GSM excluded)
G3588.8 T-NSM ὁ (2x)
(list for G3588.8:T-NSM excluded)
G3588.8 T-NSF ἡ (2x)
(list for G3588.8:T-NSF excluded)
G3588.8 T-NPM οἱ (1x)
(list for G3588.8:T-NPM excluded)
G3588.8 T-NPF αἱ (4x)
(list for G3588.8:T-NPF excluded)
G3588.8 T-ASM τόν (5x)
(list for G3588.8:T-ASM excluded)
G3588.8 T-ASF τήν (22x)
(list for G3588.8:T-ASF excluded)
G3588.8 T-ASN τό (5x)
(list for G3588.8:T-ASN excluded)
G3588.8 T-APM τούς (5x)
(list for G3588.8:T-APM excluded)
G3588.8 T-APF τάς (23x)
(list for G3588.8:T-APF excluded)
G3588.8 T-APN τά (3x)
(list for G3588.8:T-APN excluded)
G3588.8 T-DSM τῷ (8x)
(list for G3588.8:T-DSM excluded)
G3588.8 T-DSF τῇ (7x)
(list for G3588.8:T-DSF excluded)
G3588.8 T-DSN τῷ (5x)
(list for G3588.8:T-DSN excluded)
G3588.8 T-DPM τοῖς (4x)
(list for G3588.8:T-DPM excluded)
G3588.8 T-DPF ταῖς (3x)
(list for G3588.8:T-DPF excluded)
G3588.8 T-DPN τοῖς (5x)
(list for G3588.8:T-DPN excluded)
G3588.8 T-GSM τοῦ (3x)
(list for G3588.8:T-GSM excluded)
G3588.8 T-GSF τῆς (7x)
(list for G3588.8:T-GSF excluded)
G3588.8 T-GPM τῶν (1x)
(list for G3588.8:T-GPM excluded)
G3588.8 T-GPF τῶν (1x)
(list for G3588.8:T-GPF excluded)
G3588.8 T-GPN τῶν (1x)
(list for G3588.8:T-GPN excluded)
EG3588.8 (13x)
(list for EG3588.8: excluded)
G3588.9 T-APM τούς (2x)
(list for G3588.9:T-APM excluded)
G3588.11 T-APN τά (1x)
(list for G3588.11:T-APN excluded)

G3589 ὀγδοή•κοντα ôgdôḗkônta *n.* (2x)
Roots:G3590
xLangEquiv:H8084
G3589.1 N-NUI ὀγδοήκοντα (1x)
Lk 16:7 '*Here*, accept your bill, and write eighty.'
G3589.2 N-GPN ὀγδοηκοντατεσσάρων (1x)
Lk 2:37 she *was* a·widow for·about eighty·four years, who

G3590 ὄγδοος ógdôôs *adj.* (5x)
Roots:G3638 See:G3589 xLangAlso:H8066
G3590 A-NSM ὄγδοος (2x)
Rv 17:11 is not, even it·itself is an·eighth *king* and is from·
Rv 21:20 the seventh, chrysolite; the eighth, beryl; the ninth
G3590 A-ASM ὄγδοον (1x)
2Pe 2:5 vigilantly·kept Noach, *the* eighth *soul on-board*,
G3590 A-DSF ὀγδόῃ (2x)
Lk 1:59 And it·occurred on the eighth day, *that* they·came
Ac 7:8 YiTsaq and circumcised him on·the eighth day; and

G3591 ὄγκος ónkôs *n.* (1x)
Roots:G0044-1 See:G0043 G5246
G3591.2 N-ASM ὄγκον (1x)
Heb 12:1 ·us·already·laying·aside every hindrance and the

G3592 ὅ•δε hóde̊ *p:d.* (12x)
ἥ•δε hḗdê [feminine]
τό•δε tódê [neuter]
Roots:G3588 G1161 Compare:G3778 G3779 See:G5602
G3592.ª P:D-ASF τήνδε (1x)
Jac 4:13 or tomorrow we·should·traverse into that city, and
G3592.1 P:D-NSM ὅδε (1x)
Lk 16:25 the bad·things. But now this·one is·comforted, and
G3592.1 P:D-DSF τῇδε (1x)
Lk 10:39 And this·woman had a·sister called Mary, who,
G3592.2 P:D-APN τάδε (8x)
Ac 15:23 writing *this letter of* these·things through their·own
Rv 2:1 of·Ephesus write, 'These·things says the·one
Rv 2:8 in·Smyrna write, 'These·things says the First and the
Rv 2:12 Pergamos write, 'These·things says the·one having
Rv 2:18 in Thyatira write, 'These·things says the Son of·
Rv 3:1 in Sardis write, 'These·things says the·one having
Rv 3:7 PhilAdelphia write, 'These·things says the Holy·One,
Rv 3:14 write, 'These·things says the Sure·One, the·Amen,
G3592.3 P:D-APN τάδε (1x)
Ac 21:11 and feet, he·declared, "Thus says the Holy Spirit,

G3593 ὁδεύω hôdêúō *v.* (1x)
Roots:G3598 See:G1353
G3593 V-PAP-NSM ὁδεύων (1x)
Lk 10:33 "But some Samaritan, while·traveling, came

G3594 ὁδ•ηγέω hôdēgéō *v.* (5x)
Roots:G3595 Compare:G4291 G0071 G1643 G2720 G3329 See:G2526-1 xLangAlso:H5148
G3594.1 V-FAI-3S ὁδηγήσει (2x)
Jn 16:13 of·Truth, should·come, he·shall·guide yeu into all
Rv 7:17 shall·shepherd them and shall·guide them to living
G3594.1 V-PAN ὁδηγεῖν (1x)
Lk 6:39 "Is·it possible·for *the* blind to·guide *the* blind?
G3594.1 V-PAS-3S ὁδηγῇ (1x)
Mt 15:14 And if a·blind·man should·guide a·blind·man, both
G3594.1 V-AAS-3S ὁδηγήσῃ (1x)
Ac 8:31 *to·know them*, unless some·man should·guide me?

G3595 ὁδ•ηγός hôdēgós *n.* (5x)
Roots:G3598 G2233
G3595.1 N-NPM ὁδηγοί (1x)
Mt 15:14 them. They·are blind guides of·blind·men. And if
G3595.1 N-VPM ὁδηγοί (2x)
Mt 23:16 "Woe to·yeu, *yeu* blind guides, the·ones saying,
Mt 23:24 O·blind guides, the·ones thoroughly·filtering·out
G3595.1 N-ASM ὁδηγόν (1x)
Rm 2:19 within·yourself to·be a·guide of·blind·men, a·light
G3595.1 N-GSM ὁδηγοῦ (1x)
Ac 1:16 (the·one becoming a·guide to·the·ones arresting

G3596 ὁδοι•πορέω hôdôipôréō *v.* (1x)
Roots:G3598 G4198 See:G3597 G3597-1
G3596.1 V-PAP-GPM ὁδοιπορούντων (1x)
Ac 10:9 *household·servants* traveling·along·the·road and

G3597 ὁδοι•πορία hôdôipôría *n.* (2x)
Roots:G3596 See:G3597-1 G4197
G3597.1 N-DPF ὁδοιπορίαις (1x)
2Co 11:26 In·road·travels, many·times *I·was* in·dangers of·
G3597.1 N-GSF ὁδοιπορίας (1x)
Jn 4:6 ·weary as·a·result of·the road·travel, was·sitting·down

G3598 ὁδός hôdôs *n.* (108x)
Compare:G5147 G5163 G4505 G4646 G2161-1 G1240-1 See:G3593 G1353-1 xLangEquiv:H1870
G3598.1 N-NSF ὁδός (5x)
Jn 14:6 "I AM the way, and the truth, and the life-above.
Mt 7:13 gate, and spacious *is* the way, the·one leading·off to
Mt 7:14 gate, and the way having·been·pressed·down, the·
2Pe 2:2 ·account·of whom, the way of·truth shall·be·reviled.
Rv 16:12 was·dried·up, in·order·that the way of·the kings
G3598.1 N-NPF ὁδοί (2x)
Rm 11:33 *are* his judgments, and his ways untraceable!
Rv 15:3 Righteous and true *are* your ways, the King of·the
G3598.1 N-ASF ὁδόν (19x)
Jn 14:4 head·on·out, and yeu·personally·know the way."
Jn 14:5 ·then how are·we·able to·personally·know the way?"
Lk 1:79 to·fully·direct our feet into *the* way of·peace."
Lk 7:27 who shall·fully·prepare your way before you.
Lk 10:4 and yeu·should·greet not·even·one·man in the way.
Ac 8:39 any·longer, for he·traversed on·his way rejoicing.
Ac 16:17 who fully·proclaim to·us *the* way of·Salvation."
Ac 25:3 ·they·make an·ambush in the way to·eliminate him.
Ac 26:13 I·saw in the way a·light from·heaven beyond the
Heb 9:8 this·thing: *that* the way of·the Holy·of·Holies *was*
Heb 10:20 ·carved and living way which he·inaugurated for·
Mt 11:10 who shall·fully·prepare your way before you.
Mk 1:2 who shall·fully·prepare your way before you.
Mk 11:8 and they·were·spreading *them* out in the roadway.
Rm 3:17 And a·way of·peace, they·did·not know.
2Pe 2:15 forsaking the straight way; they·are·led·astray,
2Pe 2:21 not to·have·recognized the way of·righteousness,
1Th 3:11 YeShua Anointed, fully·direct our way to yeu.
1Co 12:31 to·yeu *the* most surpassingly·excellent way.
G3598.1 N-APF ὁδούς (6x)
Lk 1:76 ·presence of·*the*·Lord to·make·ready his ways;
Lk 3:5 and the rough,·jagged roadways *shall·be made* into
Ac 2:28 You·made·known to·me *the* ways of·life-above†;
Ac 13:10 ·not cease perverting the straight ways of·Yahweh?
Heb 3:10 and they·themselves did·not know my ways.'
1Co 4:17 to·recall·to·mind·and·consider my ways, the·ones
G3598.1 N-DSF ὁδῷ (14x)
Lk 10:31 ·sacrifices was·walking·down along that way. And
Lk 12:58 give effort on the way to·have·been·released from
Lk 24:32 as he·was·speaking with·us along the way, and as
Lk 24:35 the·things *that occurred* along the way, and how
Mt 5:25 such·time *as* you·are on the way with him, lest·at·
Mt 15:32 ·eating, lest they·should·be·faint on the way."
Mt 21:32 For John came to yeu by way of·righteousness, yet
Mk 8:3 houses, they·shall·be·faint on the way, for some of·
Mk 8:27 And along the way, he·was·inquiring·of his
Mk 9:33 yeu·deliberated among yeurselves along the way?"
Mk 9:34 for along the way they·discussed among one·
Jac 2:25 the messengers and casting·*them*·forth another way?
Jud 1:11 Because they·traversed in·the way of·Qain, and
2Pe 2:15 ·led·astray, following·out the way of·BalaAm *the*
G3598.1 N-DPF ὁδοῖς (3x)
Ac 14:16 ·for all the nations to·traverse in·their·own ways.
Rm 3:16 Shattered·ruin and misery *are* in their ways.
Jac 1:8 ·in·his·soul *is* completely·unstable in all his ways.
G3598.1 N-GSF ὁδοῦ (3x)
Mt 2:12 into their·own country through another way.
Mt 8:28 not to·have·strength to·pass·by through that way.
Jac 5:20 from·out of·*the*·error of·his way shall·save a·soul
EG3598.1 (5x)
Lk 5:18 and they·were·seeking *a·way* to·carry him in and
Lk 19:4 because *Jesus* was·about to·go through that *way*.
Ac 16:37 out privately? For no *way*, but·rather coming *here*
Rm 14:13 a·stumbling·block or a·trap in·a·brother's *way*.
1Ti 4:8 "For the *way·of* bodily training is profitable just·for
G3598.2 N-ASF ὁδόν (1x)
Mk 2:23 his disciples began to·make a·pathway, plucking the
G3598.3 N-ASF ὁδόν (15x)
Lk 8:5 in·fact fell directly·by the roadway, and it·was·
Lk 8:12 "And the·ones directly·by the roadway are the·ones
Lk 18:35 ·man sat·down directly·by the roadway begging.
Ac 8:26 down *on* the·south·side toward the roadway, the·one
Ac 8:36 as they·traversed down the roadway, they·came to
Mt 4:15 land of·Naphtali, *by the* roadway of·sea, beyond the
Mt 10:5 "Yeu·should·not go·off to a·roadway of·Gentiles,
Mt 13:4 some *seeds* fell directly·by the roadway, and the
Mt 13:19 ·permeated·with·seed directly·by the roadway.
Mt 20:30 blind·men are·sitting·down beside the roadway.
Mk 4:4 ·fact, *seed* fell directly·by the roadway, and the birds
Mk 4:15 the *individuals* directly·by the roadway, where the
Mk 10:17 ·traversing·forth into *the* same roadway, one·man,
Mk 10:46 was·sitting·down directly·by the roadway begging.
Mk 11:8 ·out their garments in the roadway, and others were·
G3598.3 N-APF ὁδούς (2x)
Lk 14:23 'Go·out into the roadways and hedges, and compel
Mt 22:10 going·forth into the roadways, gathered·together
G3598.3 N-DSF ὁδῷ (9x)
Lk 9:57 while·traversing along the roadway, *that* a·certain·
Lk 19:36 ·out their garments beneath *him* in the roadway.
Ac 9:17 to·you along the roadway in·which you·were·going,
Ac 9:27 saw the Lord along the roadway, and that he·spoke
Mt 20:17 aside privately by the roadway, and he·declared to·
Mt 21:8 ·out their·own garments in the roadway, and others
Mt 21:8 and they·were·spreading *them* out in the roadway.
Mk 10:32 And they·were on the roadway, walking·up toward
Mk 10:52 ·sight and was·following Jesus along the roadway.
G3598.3 N-GSF ὁδοῦ (1x)
Mt 21:19 seeing one fig·tree by the roadway, he·came to it
G3598.3 N-GPF ὁδῶν (1x)
Mt 22:9 to the exit·areas of·the roadways, and as·many·as
EG3598.3 (1x)
Lk 3:5 roadways *shall·be made* into smooth *roadways*;
G3598.4 N-ASF ὁδόν (5x)
Lk 2:44 caravan, they·went a·day's journey, then they·were·
Lk 9:3 "Take·up not·even·one·thing for the journey, neither
Ac 1:12 which is near JeruSalem, being a·Sabbath's journey.
Mt 10:10 nor a·knapsack for *yeur* journey, nor·even two
Mk 6:8 ·take·up not·even·one·thing for *their* journey, *saying*,
G3598.4 N-GSF ὁδοῦ (1x)
Lk 11:6 came·directly to me out·from a·journey, and I·do·
G3598.6 N-ASF ὁδόν (8x)
Jn 1:23 "Make·straight the Way of·Yahweh,'" just·as IsaIah
Lk 3:4 'Make·ready the Way of·Yahweh; yeu·must·make
Ac 18:25 having·been·informed·of The Way of·Yahweh.
Ac 19:9 speaking·ill·of The Way in·the·sight of·the
Ac 22:4 "*It·is·I* who persecuted this Way even·unto *their*
Ac 24:14 ·you, that according·to The Way which they·say *is*
Mt 3:3 'Make·ready the Way of·Yahweh; yeu·must·make
Mk 1:3 'Make·ready the Way of·Yahweh; yeu·must·make
G3598.6 N-GSF ὁδοῦ (3x)
Ac 9:2 he·should·find any *disciples* of·The Way, whether
Ac 19:23 there·occurred no little disturbance about The Way.
Ac 24:22 more·precisely concerning The Way, he·deferred
G3598.7 N-ASF ὁδόν (4x)
Lk 20:21 but·rather *that* you·instruct the Way of·God in truth
Ac 18:26 explained to·him the Way of·God more·precisely.
Mt 22:16 and *that* you·instruct the Way of·God in truth, and
Mk 12:14 ·clay†, but·rather instruct the Way of·God in truth

G3599 ὀδούς ôdôús *n.* (13x)
Roots:G2068 Compare:G1661 xLangEquiv:H8127 A8128 xLangAlso:H7161
G3599.1 N-ASM ὀδόντα (1x)
Mt 5:38 "An·eye for an·eye, and a·tooth for a·tooth."
G3599.1 N-GSM ὀδόντος (1x)
Mt 5:38 "An·eye for an·eye, and a·tooth for a·tooth."
G3599.2 N-NPM ὀδόντες (1x)
Rv 9:8 hair of·women, and their teeth were as *teeth* of·lions.
G3599.2 N-APM ὀδόντας (2x)
Ac 7:54 heart, and they·were·gnashing *their* teeth at him.
Mk 9:18 ·at·the·mouth and grates his teeth and withers·away
G3599.2 N-GPM ὀδόντων (7x)
Lk 13:28 weeping and the gnashing of·teeth, whenever yeu·
Mt 8:12 ·shall·be the weeping and the gnashing of·the teeth."
Mt 13:42 ·shall·be the weeping and the gnashing of·teeth.
Mt 13:50 ·shall·be the weeping and the gnashing of·teeth."
Mt 22:13 ·be the weeping and the gnashing of·the teeth.'
Mt 24:51 ·be the weeping and the gnashing of·the teeth.
Mt 25:30 ·be the weeping and the gnashing of·the teeth.
EG3599.2 (1x)
Rv 9:8 hair of·women, and their teeth were as *teeth* of·lions.

G3600 ὀδυνάω ôdynáō *v.* (4x)
Roots:G3601 Compare:G0085 G4727 G3076
G3600 V-PPI-1S ὀδυνῶμαι (1x)
Lk 16:24 my tongue, because I·am·distressed in this blaze.
G3600 V-PPI-2S-IRR ὀδυνᾶσαι (1x)
Lk 16:25 now this·one is·comforted, and you are·distressed.
G3600 V-PPP-NPM ὀδυνώμενοι (2x)
Lk 2:48 father and·I were·seeking you, being·distressed."
Ac 20:38 being·distressed especially over the words which

G3601 ὀδύνη ôdýnē *n.* (2x)
Roots:G1416 Compare:G2870 G3077 G3997 G0318 G4192 G0217-3 See:G3602 xLangAlso:H4470
G3601 N-NSF ὀδύνη (1x)
Rm 9:2 grief is a·great and unceasing distress in·my heart.
G3601 N-DPF ὀδύναις (1x)
1Ti 6:10 ·entirely·impaled themselves on·many distresses.

G3602 ὀδυρμός ôdyrmôs *n.* (2x)
Roots:G1416 Compare:G3997 G3077-1 See:G3601
G3602 N-NSM ὀδυρμός (1x)
Mt 2:18 and weeping and much distressing; *it·was* Rachel
G3602 N-ASM ὀδυρμόν (1x)
2Co 7:7 yeur great·yearning, yeur distressing, yeur fervency

G3604 Ὀζ•ίας Ôzías *n/p.* (2x)
עֻזִּיָּה 'ụziyạh [Hebrew]
Roots:H5818
G3604.2 N/P-NSM Ὀζίας (1x)
Mt 1:9 Then UzzIah begot YoTham, and YoTham begot
G3604.2 N/P-ASM Ὀζίαν (1x)
Mt 1:8 begot JehoRam†, and JehoRam† begot UzzIah.

G3605 ὄζω ôzō *v.* (1x)
Compare:G2174-2 See:G3744
G3605.2 V-PAI-3S ὄζει (1x)
Jn 11:39 "O·Lord, even·now he·smells·bad, for it·is *the*

G3606 ὅ•θεν hóthên *adv.* (15x)
Roots:G3739
G3606.1 ADV ὅθεν (7x)
Lk 11:24 ·return·back to·my house from·which I·came·out.'
Heb 2:17 From·which, he·was·owing fully all·things to·the
Heb 3:1 From·which·cause, O·holy brothers (*yeu*
Heb 7:25 from·which·place he·is·able also to·save·them to
Heb 11:19 even from·among dead·men, from·which also
Mt 12:44 ·return into my house from·which I·came·out;' and
Mt 14:7 From·which, with an·oath, he·affirmed to·give her
G3606.2 ADV ὅθεν (1x)
Ac 28:13 Sailing·roundabout from·there, we·arrived in
G3606.3 ADV ὅθεν (3x)
Ac 14:26 where they·were having·been·directly·handed to·
Mt 25:24 and gathering·together from·where you·did·not
Mt 25:26 and gather·together from·where I·did·not winnow·
G3606.4 ADV ὅθεν (4x)
Ac 26:19 "By·which *cause*, O·King AgrIppa, I·did·not
Heb 8:3 both presents and sacrifices, by·which *pattern*, *it·is*
Heb 9:18 by·which *necessity*, not·even the first *covenant*
1Jn 2:18 ·of·the·Anointed-One, by·which we·know that it·is

G3607 ὀθόνη ôthónē *n.* (2x)
See:G3608
G3607.1 N-ASF ὀθόνην (2x)
Ac 10:11 a·great linen·sheet having·been·tied at·the·four
Ac 11:5 as a·great linen·sheet being·sent·down from·out of·
G3608 ὀθόνιον ôthóniôn *n.* (5x)
Roots:G3607 Compare:G2750
G3608 N-APN ὀθόνια (3x)
Jn 20:5 ·peer·in, he·looked·at the strips·of·linen laying·out,
Jn 20:6 And he·observes the strips·of·linen laying·out
Lk 24:12 the strips·of·linen which·are·laying·out alone.
G3608 N-DPN ὀθονίοις (1x)
Jn 19:40 of·Jesus and bound it in·strips·of·linen with the
G3608 N-GPN ὀθονίων (1x)
Jn 20:7 ·being·laid·out not with the strips·of·linen, but·rather
G3609 οἰκεῖος ôikêîôs *adj.* (3x)
Roots:G3624 Compare:G3615
G3609.2 A-NPM οἰκεῖοι (1x)
Eph 2:19 ·the holy·ones and *are* family·members of·God,
G3609.2 A-APM οἰκείους (1x)
Gal 6:10 especially toward the family·members of·the trust.
G3609.2 A-GPM οἰκείων (1x)
1Ti 5:8 especially for·the family·members, he·has·denied the
G3610 οἰκέτης ôikḗtēs *n.* (5x)
Roots:G3611 Compare:G2321-1
G3610.1 N-NSM οἰκέτης (1x)
Lk 16:13 "Not·even·one household·servant is·able to·be·a·
G3610.1 N-NPM οἰκέται (1x)
1Pe 2:18 the household·servants: be·submitting·yourselves
G3610.1 N-ASM οἰκέτην (1x)
Rm 14:4 another·man's household·servant? To·his·own lord
G3610.1 N-GPM οἰκετῶν (1x)
Ac 10:7 of·his household·servants and a·devoutly·reverent
EG3610.1 (1x)
Ac 10:9 with·those *household·servants* traveling·along·the·
G3611 οἰκέω ôikḗō *v.* (9x)
Roots:G3624 Compare:G2730 See:G1774 G3625 xLangAlso:H3427
G3611.1 V-PAI-3S οἰκεῖ (4x)
Rm 7:18 ·is, in my flesh) dwells no beneficially·good·thing;
Rm 8:9 in Spirit, if·perhaps God's Spirit dwells in yeu. But
Rm 8:11 Jesus from·among dead·men dwells in yeu, *then*
1Co 3:16 of·God, and *that* the Spirit of·God dwells in yeu?
G3611.1 V-PAN οἰκεῖν (2x)
1Co 7:12 she·herself gives·glad·consent to·dwell with him,
1Co 7:13 *if* he·himself gives·glad·consent to·dwell with her,
G3611.1 V-PAP-NSF οἰκοῦσα (2x)
Rm 7:17 that·performs it, but·rather the·one dwelling in me,
Rm 7:20 that·performs it, but·rather the·one dwelling in me,
G3611.1 V-PAP-NSM οἰκῶν (1x)
1Ti 6:16 having immortality, dwelling *in* unapproachable
G3612 οἴκημα ôíkēma *n.* (1x)
Roots:G3611 See:G3613
G3612.2 N-DSN οἰκήματι (1x)
Ac 12:7 and a·light radiated·brightly in the jailhouse. And
G3613 οἰκητήριον ôikētḗriôn *n.* (2x)
Roots:G3611 See:G3612
G3613.1 N-ASN οἰκητήριον (1x)
2Co 5:2 to·fully·dress·ourselves·with our housing, the·one
G3613.2 N-ASN οἰκητήριον (1x)
Jud 1:6 ·behind their·own dwelling·place, he·has·reserved
G3614 οἰκία ôikía *n.* (99x)
Roots:G3624 Compare:G1430 G0833 G1886 G0933 G3485 See:G3612-1 xLangAlso:H1004 A1005
G3614.1 N-NSF οἰκία (8x)
Jn 12:3 hair, and the home was·completely·filled from·out
Ac 10:6 Simon a·tanner, whose home is directly·by *the* sea
Ac 18:7 ·is·reverencing God, whose home was adjoining the
Mt 10:13 And if, in·fact the home should·be worthy, *let* yeur
Mt 12:25 and every city or home being·divided against itself
Mk 3:25 And if a·home should·be·divided against itself, that
Mk 3:25 against itself, that home is·not able to·remain·
2Co 5:1 that if our earthly home of·the bodily·tent should·
G3614.1 N-ASF οἰκίαν (39x)
Lk 4:38 he·entered into Simon's home. And Simon's
Lk 6:48 He·is like a·man·of·clay† building a·home, who also
Lk 6:49 ·of·clay† building a·home apart·from a·foundation
Lk 7:36 entering into the Pharisee's home, *Jesus* reclined·at·
Lk 7:44 "I·entered into your home, you·gave·me no water
Lk 8:51 And entering into the home, he·did·not allow not·
Lk 9:4 "And whatever home yeu·should·enter into, there
Lk 10:5 "And into whatever home yeu·should·enter, first say
Lk 10:7 Do·not walk·on out·from home to home.
Lk 15:8 a·lantern, and sweep the home, and seek carefully
Lk 18:29 ·yeu, there·is not·even·one·man that left home, or
Lk 22:10 follow him into the home where he·traverses·in.
Ac 9:17 ·off and entered into the home. And after·laying his
Ac 10:17 ·inquiry for·Simon's home, they·stood·over at the
Ac 11:11 ·standing·over *the gate* at the home where I·was,
Ac 12:12 ·aware, he·came to the home of·Miri, the mother
Ac 18:7 he·came into a·home of·someone by·the·name·of
Mt 2:11 And coming into the home, they·found the little·
Mt 7:24 man who built his home upon the solid·rock.
Mt 7:26 to·a·foolish man, who built his home upon the sand.
Mt 8:14 And YeShua, upon·coming into Peter's home, saw
Mt 9:23 upon·coming into the ruler's home and seeing the
Mt 9:28 And after·coming into the home, the blind·men
Mt 10:12 And while·entering into the home, greet it.
Mt 12:29 the strong·man's home and to·thoroughly·plunder
Mt 12:29 And then he·shall·thoroughly·plunder his home.
Mt 13:36 crowds, YeShua went *back* into the home. And his
Mt 17:25 when he·entered into the home, YeShua preempted
Mt 24:43 and would not·have let his home to·be·broken·into.
Mk 1:29 they·went into the home of·Simon and Andrew,
Mk 3:27 not·even·one already·entering into his home, unless
Mk 3:27 and then he·shall·thoroughly·plunder his home.
Mk 6:10 ·place yeu·should·enter into a·home, there abide
Mk 7:24 And upon·entering into the home, he·was·wanting
Mk 10:29 there·is not·even·one that left home or brothers or
Mk 13:15 must·not walk·down into the home, nor·even enter
Mk 13:34 ·abroad, upon·leaving his home and giving
2Co 5:1 a·structure, a·home not·made·by·human·hand,
2Jn 1:10 yeu·must·not receive him into a·home, and yeu·
G3614.1 N-APF οἰκίας (8x)
Lk 20:47 who devour the homes of·the widows, and pray
Mt 19:29 And everyone who left homes or brothers or sisters
Mt 23:13 Because yeu·devour the homes of·the widows and
Mk 10:30 now in this season, homes and brothers and sisters
Mk 12:40 The·ones devouring the homes of·the widows, and
1Co 11:22 ¿! For do·yeu·not have homes to·eat and to·drink
1Ti 5:13 *to·be* idle, going·roundabout the homes, and not
2Ti 3:6 ·ones impersonating·their·way into the homes, and
G3614.1 N-DSF οἰκίᾳ (27x)
Jn 8:35 does·not continue·*to·remain* in the home into the
Jn 11:31 with her in the home and personally·consoling her,
Jn 14:2 "In my Father's home are many abodes, but·if·not, I·
Lk 5:29 reception for·him in his·own home, and there·was a·
Lk 6:48 the stream burst·directly·against that home, but did·
Lk 7:37 in the Pharisee's home, after·subsequently·obtaining
Lk 8:27 and was·not abiding in *any* home, but·rather in the
Lk 10:7 And remain in the same home, eating and drinking
Lk 15:25 ·going·*along*, he·drew·near to·the home *and* heard
Lk 17:31 his belongings in the home, must·not walk·down
Ac 9:11 and seek in Judas' home for a·man·of·Tarsus, Saul
Ac 10:32 This·man is·a·guest in *the* home of·Simon, a·
Ac 16:32 of·the Lord, and to·all the·ones in his home.
Ac 17:5 And assaulting the home of·Jason, they·were·
Mt 5:15 and it·radiates·brightly for·all the·ones in the home.
Mt 7:25 and they·fell·directly·against that home; yet it·did·
Mt 7:27 blew, and they·surged·against that home, and it·fell;
Mt 8:6 ·cast paralyzed *on a·couch* at home, dreadfully being·
Mt 9:10 ·he is·reclining·at·a·meal in *MattHew's* home, *that*
Mt 13:57 in his·own fatherland and in his·own home."
Mt 26:6 ·to·be in BethAny, in Simon the leper's home,
Mk 2:15 laying·back·to·eat in *MattHew's* home, *that* many
Mk 6:4 and among his kinsmen, and in his·own home."
Mk 9:33 and once·being in the home, he·was·inquiring·of
Mk 10:10 And in the home, his disciples inquired·of him
Mk 14:3 being in BethAny in the home of·Simon the leper,
2Ti 2:20 But in a·great home there·are not merely vessels
G3614.1 N-GSF οἰκίας (9x)
Lk 6:49 And the wreckage of·that home became great."
Lk 7:6 being·off at·a·distance from the home, the centurion
Lk 10:7 Do·not walk·on out·from home to home.
Lk 22:11 yeu·shall·declare to·the master of·the home, 'The
Mt 10:14 words, while·going·forth·from the home or that
Mt 13:1 after·going·forth from the home, was·sitting·down
Mt 24:17 walk·down to·take·away anything out of·his home.
Mk 13:15 enter *it*, to·take·away anything out of·his home.
Mk 13:35 ·know when the lord of·the home comes, *whether*
G3614.1 N-GPF οἰκιῶν (1x)
Ac 4:34 possessors of·open·fields or homes, upon·selling
EG3614.1 (4x)
Jn 19:27 that hour, the disciple took her into his·own *home*.
Jn 20:10 the disciples went·off again to their·own *homes*.
Lk 15:27 'Your brother comes *home*! And your father
Lk 15:30 this son of·yours came *home*, the·one devouring
G3614.3 N-NSF οἰκία (1x)
Jn 4:53 And he·himself trusted, and his whole household.
G3614.3 N-ASF οἰκίαν (1x)
1Co 16:15 yeu·personally·know the household of·Stephanas,
G3614.3 N-GSF οἰκίας (1x)
Php 4:22 the·ones from·among Caesar's household.
G3615 οἰκιακός ôikiakós *n.* (2x)
Roots:G3614 Compare:G3609
G3615.1 N-NPM οἰκιακοί (1x)
Mt 10:36 *shall·be* his·own family·members·in·his·home."
G3615.1 N-APM οἰκιακούς (1x)
Mt 10:25 *·they·call* his·own family·members·in·his·home?
G3616 οἰκο•δεσ•ποτέω ôikôdêspôtêō *v.* (1x)
Roots:G3617
G3616.4 V-PAN οἰκοδεσποτεῖν (1x)
1Ti 5:14 ·children, to·attend·to·the·operations·of·the·home,
G3617 οἰκο•δεσ•πότης ôikôdêspótēs *n.* (12x)
Roots:G3624 G1203 See:G3616
G3617.1 N-NSM οἰκοδεσπότης (5x)
Lk 12:39 the master·of·the·house had·personally·known in·
Lk 13:25 ·once the master·of·the·house should·be·roused,
Lk 14:21 ·angry, the master·of·the·house declared to·his
Mt 21:33 ·certain man·of·clay†, a·master·of·the·house, who
Mt 24:43 the master·of·the·house had·personally·known in·
G3617.1 N-ASM οἰκοδεσπότην (1x)
Mt 10:25 If they·called the master·of·the·house, BaalZebul,·
G3617.1 N-DSM οἰκοδεσπότῃ (3x)
Mt 13:52 is like a·man·of·clay†, a·master·of·the·house, who
Mt 20:1 is like a·man·of·clay†, a·master·of·the·house, who
Mk 14:14 ·enter, yeu·declare to·the master·of·the·house,
G3617.1 N-GSM οἰκοδεσπότου (2x)
Mt 13:27 slaves of·the master·of·the·house declared to·him,
Mt 20:11 ·were·grumbling against the master·of·the·house,
G3617.2 N-DSM οἰκοδεσπότῃ (1x)
Lk 22:11 And yeu·shall·declare to·the master of·the home,
G3618 οἰκο•δομέω ôikôdômĕō *v.* (39x)
Roots:G3624 G1185-1 See:G3619 xLangAlso:H1129 A1124
G3618.1 V-FAI-1S οἰκοδομήσω (3x)
Lk 12:18 ·demolish my barns and shall·build bigger·ones;
Mt 16:18 I·shall·build my entire·Called·Out·Citizenry,
Mk 14:58 three days I·shall·build another not·made·by·hand.
G3618.1 V-FAI-2P οἰκοδομήσετε (1x)
Ac 7:49 stool. What·kind·of house shall·yeu·build for·me,
G3618.1 V-PAI-1S οἰκοδομῶ (1x)
Gal 2:18 "For if I·build again these·things which I·
G3618.1 V-PAI-2P οἰκοδομεῖτε (3x)
Lk 11:47 to·yeu! Because yeu·build the chamber·tombs of·
Lk 11:48 and yeu·yeurselves build their chamber·tombs.
Mt 23:29 ·acting·hypocrites! Because yeu·build the graves

G3618.1 V-PAN οἰκοδομεῖν (1x)
Lk 14:30 'This man·of·clay† began to·build yet did·not
G3618.1 V-PAP-DSM οἰκοδομοῦντι (1x)
Lk 6:48 "He·is like a·man·of·clay† building a·home, who
G3618.1 V-PAP-GPM οἰκοδομούντων (1x)
Ac 4:11 ·rejected by yeu, the·ones building; *this·is* the·one
G3618.1 V-PAP-NSM οἰκοδομῶν (2x)
Mt 27:40 demolishing the Temple and building *it* in three
Mk 15:29 demolishing the Temple and building *it* in three
G3618.1 V-PAP-NPM οἰκοδομοῦντες (4x)
Lk 20:17 *The* stone which the builders rejected·as·unfit, the·
Mt 21:42 "A·stone which the builders rejected·as·unfit, the·
Mk 12:10 "A·stone which the builders rejected·as·unfit, the·
1Pe 2:7 A·stone, which the·ones building rejected·as·unfit,
G3618.1 V-PAS-1S οἰκοδομῶ (1x)
Rm 15:20 ·named, lest I·should·build upon another·man's
G3618.1 V-PPI-2P οἰκοδομεῖσθε (1x)
1Pe 2:5 as living stones, are·built·up, *being* a·spiritual
G3618.1 V-IAI-3P ᾠκοδόμουν (1x)
Lk 17:28 ·selling, they·were·planting, they·were·building;
G3618.1 V-AAI-3S ᾠκοδόμησεν (6x)
Lk 7:5 nation, and he·himself built the gathering·place for·
Ac 7:47 "And *it·was* Solomon *who* built a·house for·him.
Mt 7:24 him to·a·prudent man who built his home upon the
Mt 7:26 ·likened to·a·foolish man, who built his home upon
Mt 21:33 he·dug a·winepress in it and·also built a·tower,"
Mk 12:1 and dug a·vat·for·a·winepress, and built a·tower,"
G3618.1 V-AAN οἰκοδομῆσαι (2x)
Lk 14:28 from·among yeu, wanting to·build a·tower, *does*
Mt 26:61 the Temple of·God and to·build it after three days.
G3618.1 V-AAP-DSM οἰκοδομήσαντι (1x)
Lk 6:49 is like a·man·of·clay† building a·home apart·from
G3618.1 V-API-3S ᾠκοδομήθη (1x)
Jn 2:20 *In* forty six years, this Temple was·built, and you, in
G3618.1 V-LPI-3S ᾠκοδόμητο (1x)
Lk 4:29 on which their city had·been·built, in·order·to·throw
G3618.2 V-PAI-3S οἰκοδομεῖ (4x)
1Co 8:1 The knowledge puffs·up, but the Love edifies.
1Co 10:23 are·proper for·me, but·yet not all·things edify.
1Co 14:4 speaking in·a·bestowed·tongue does·edify himself,
1Co 14:4 ·one prophesying edifies a·convened·Called·Out·.
G3618.2 V-PAM-2P οἰκοδομεῖτε (1x)
1Th 5:11 ·comfort one·another, and edify one the other,
G3618.2 V-PPI-3S οἰκοδομεῖται (1x)
1Co 14:17 give·thanks well, but·yet the other is·not edified.
G3618.2 V-PPP-NPF οἰκοδομούμεναι (1x)
Ac 9:31 and Samaria were·having peace, being·edified. And
G3618.3 V-FPI-3S οἰκοδομηθήσεται (1x)
1Co 8:10 of·him who·is weak be·reinforced to·eat those·

G3619 οἰκο•δομή ôikôdômḗ *n.* (18x)
Roots:G3624 G1185-1 Compare:G1739 See:G3618
G3619.2 N-NSF οἰκοδομή (2x)
1Co 3:9 yeu·are God's cultivated·soil, God's structure.
Eph 2:21 the entire structure, being·fitly·framed·together,
G3619.2 N-NPF οἰκοδομαί (1x)
Mk 13:1 ·of stones and what·manner·of structures *these are*!
G3619.2 N-ASF οἰκοδομήν (1x)
2Co 5:1 (from·out·of·God) a·structure, a·home not·made·
G3619.2 N-APF οἰκοδομάς (2x)
Mt 24:1 for·him the structures of·the Sanctuary·Estate.
Mk 13:2 "Do·you·look·upon these great structures? No,
G3619.3 N-ASF οἰκοδομήν (10x)
Rm 15:2 ·*conscience* for·his good·benefit unto edification.
1Co 14:3 speaks to·men·of·clay† *for* edification, and
1Co 14:5 ·Called·Out·assembly may·receive edification.
1Co 14:12 toward the edification of·the Called·Out·citizenry.
1Co 14:26 All·things must·occur specifically·for edification.
2Co 10:8 which the Lord gave us for edification (and not for
2Co 13:10 which the Lord gave me to edification and not to
Eph 4:12 a·work of·service, unto an·edification of·the Body
Eph 4:16 ·growth of·the Body for its·own edification in love.
Eph 4:29 particularly·for the needed edification, in·order·that
G3619.3 N-GSF οἰκοδομῆς (2x)
Rm 14:19 of·peace and the·things edifying to one·another.
2Co 12:19 dearly·beloved, on·behalf of·yeur edification.

G3621 οἰκο•νομέω ôikônômêō *v.* (1x)
Roots:G3623 See:G3622
G3621 V-PAN οἰκονομεῖν (1x)
Lk 16:2 ·shall·not be·able to·manage·the·estate any·longer.'

G3622 οἰκο•νομία ôikônômía *n.* (8x)
Roots:G3623 See:G3621
G3622.2 N-ASF οἰκονομίαν (6x)
Lk 16:3 removes from me the estate·management. I·do·not
1Co 9:17 involuntarily, an·estate·management *of·the grace*
Eph 1:10 for an·estate·management of·the complete·
Eph 3:2 ·heard of·the estate·management of·the grace of·
Col 1:25 according·to the estate·management of·God, the·
1Ti 1:4 rather than God's estate·management, the·one in trust
G3622.2 N-GSF οἰκονομίας (2x)
Lk 16:2 ·forth an·account of·your estate·management, for
Lk 16:4 ·duty of·the estate·management, they·may·accept

G3623 οἰκο•νόμος ôikônómôs *n.* (11x)
Roots:G3624 G3551 Compare:G2012 G1249 G5009-1 See:G3621 G3622
xLangEquiv:H5532-1 xLangAlso:H5532
G3623.2 N-NSM οἰκονόμος (3x)
Lk 12:42 the trustworthy and prudent estate·manager, whom
Lk 16:3 "And the estate·manager declared within himself,
Rm 16:23 Erastus, the estate·manager of·the city, greets yeu
G3623.2 N-NPM οἰκονόμοι (1x)
1Pe 4:10 ·to it as good estate·managers of·God's manifold
G3623.2 N-ASM οἰκονόμον (3x)
Lk 16:1 ·of·clay† who was·retaining an·estate·manager, and
Lk 16:8 lord applauded the unjust estate·manager, because
Tit 1:7 ·of·wrong·doing as an·estate·manager of·God), not
G3623.2 N-APM οἰκονόμους (2x)
Gal 4:2 ·guardians and estate·managers even·up·to the day·
1Co 4:1 and estate·managers of·God's mysteries.
G3623.2 N-DPM οἰκονόμοις (1x)
1Co 4:2 it·is·sought in the estate·managers that each·man
EG3623.2 (1x)
Lk 16:1 and this *estate·manager* was·slandered to·him as·

G3624 οἶκος ôîkôs *n.* (121x)
Compare:G1430 G0833 G2732 G2733 G1886 G0933 G3485 See:G3614 G3612-1
xLangEquiv:H1004 A1005
G3624.1 N-NSM οἶκος (15x)
Lk 11:17 ·desolate, and a·house *thoroughly·divided* against
Lk 13:35 "Behold, yeur house is·left to·yeu desolate.
Lk 14:23 *them* to·come·in, that my house may·be·overfilled.
Lk 19:46 ·been·written, "My house is a·house of·prayer,"
Lk 19:46 ·written, "My house is a·house of·prayer," but
Ac 2:36 "Now·then, all *the* house of·IsraEl must·know
Ac 7:42 of·the prophets, "O·house of·IsraEl, ¿! did·yeu·
Heb 3:4 For every house is·planned·and·constructed by some
Heb 3:6 his·own house, of·whose house are we·ourselves—
Mt 21:13 "My house shall·be·called a·house of·prayer,"
Mt 21:13 "My house shall·be·called a·house of·prayer,"
Mt 23:38 "Behold, yeur house is·left to·yeu desolate!
Mk 11:17 "My house shall·be·called a·house of·prayer
Mk 11:17 "My house shall·be·called a·house of·prayer for·
1Pe 2:5 stones, are·built·up, *being* a·spiritual house, a·holy
G3624.1 N-ASM οἶκον (58x)
Jn 2:16 ·not make my Father's house a·house of·commerce."
Jn 2:16 ·not make my Father's house a·house of·commerce."
Jn 7:53 And each·man traversed to his·own house.
Lk 1:23 were·fulfilled, *that* he·went·off to his·own house.
Lk 1:33 And he·shall·reign over the house of·Jacob into the
Lk 1:40 and she·entered into the house of·ZacharIas and
Lk 1:56 ·months and·then returned·back to·her·own house.
Lk 5:24 and taking·up your pallet, traverse to your house."
Lk 5:25 on, he·went·off to his·own house, glorifying God.
Lk 6:4 how he·entered into the house of·God and took and
Lk 7:10 And upon·returning·back to the house, the·ones
Lk 8:39 ·back to·your·own house and give·an·account·of
Lk 8:41 he·was·imploring him to·enter into his house,
Lk 9:61 me to·orderly·take·leave·of the·ones at my house."
Lk 10:38 ·of Martha hospitably·received him into her house.
Lk 11:17 a·house *thoroughly·divided* against a·house falls.
Lk 11:24 ·return·back to my house from·which I·came·out.'
Lk 12:39 not have·allowed his house to·be·broken·into.
Lk 14:1 with him going into a·house of·a·certain·man of·the
Lk 15:6 And coming to the house, he·calls·together the
Lk 16:27 that you·may·send him to my father's house,
Lk 18:14 to his house having·been·regarded·as·righteous
Lk 22:54 him into the house of·the [designated]·high·priest.
Ac 2:2 it·completely·filled all the house where they·were
Ac 2:46 breaking bread in·each house, they·were·partaking
Ac 5:42 Sanctuary·Atrium, and in·each house, they·did·not
Ac 7:10 him, governing over Egypt and all his house.
Ac 7:47 "And *it·was* Solomon *who* built a·house for·him.
Ac 7:49 stool. What·kind·of house shall·yeu·build for·me,
Ac 10:22 angel to·send·for you into his house, and to·hear
Ac 11:12 with·me, and we·entered into the man's house.
Ac 16:15 *and* entering into my house, yeu·must·abide *there*
Ac 16:34 them up into his house, he·placed·forth a·meal·
Ac 21:8 And entering into the house of·Philippe (the
Heb 3:6 as a·son over his·own house, of·whose house are
Heb 8:8 a·brand-new covenant with the house of·IsraEl and
Heb 8:8 the house of·IsraEl and with the house of·Judah.
Heb 10:21 and *having* a·high priest over the house of·God—
Mt 9:6 your simple·couch and head·on·out to your house."
Mt 9:7 And upon·being·awakened, he·went·off to his house.
Mt 12:4 How he·entered into the house of·God and ate the
Mt 12:44 ·shall·return into my house from·which I·came·out
Mk 2:1 *some* days, and it·was·heard that he·was in a·house.
Mk 2:11 take·up your mat, and head·on·out to your house."
Mk 2:26 How he·entered into the house of·God in·the·days
Mk 3:19 Then they·went into a·house.
Mk 5:19 "Head·on·out to your house, to your *kinsfolk*, and
Mk 5:38 ·comes to the house of·the director·of·the·gathering
Mk 7:17 And when he·entered into a·house away·from the
Mk 7:30 And after·going·off to her house, she·found the
Mk 8:3 ·eating to their·own houses, they·shall·be·faint on
Mk 8:26 And he·dispatched him to his house, saying, "You·
Mk 9:28 And after·entering into a·house, his disciples were·
Rm 16:5 Called·Out·citizenry *hosted* in their house. Greet
1Co 16:19 ·the Called·Out·citizenry *hosted* in their house.
Col 4:15 and the Called·Out·citizenry *hosted* in his house.
Phm 1:2 to·the Called·Out·citizenry *hosted* in your house.
1Ti 5:4 at·their·own house to·show·devout·reverence and to·
G3624.1 N-APM οἴκους (3x)
Lk 16:4 they·may·accept me into their houses.'
Ac 8:3 Traversing·into each *of* the houses *and* dragging·off
Tit 1:11 Such·men overturn whole houses, instructing things·
G3624.1 N-DSM οἴκῳ (16x)
Jn 11:20 ·met him, but Mary was·sitting·down in the house.
Lk 1:69 of·Salvation for·us in the house of·his servant·boy
Lk 10:5 yeu·should·enter, first say, 'Peace to·this house.'
Lk 12:52 five in one house having·been·thoroughly·divided,
Lk 19:5 it·is·necessary·for me to·abide in your house."
Lk 19:9 Salvation did·come to·this house, because·indeed
Ac 7:20 ·nurtured in his father's house three lunar·months.
Ac 10:2 ·fearing God together with·all his house, both doing
Ac 10:30 ninth hour while·praying in my house, yet behold,
Ac 11:13 he·saw the angel in his house, being·settled and
Ac 18:8 on·the Lord together with·all his house; and many
Heb 3:2 as also Moses *was trustworthy* in all his house.
Heb 3:5 trustworthy in all his house as a·domestic·attendant
Heb 8:10 that I·shall·enact with·the house of·IsraEl after
1Ti 3:15 ·oneself among God's house, the·same·which is a·
2Ti 1:16 the Lord give mercy *to·the*·house of·OnesiPhorus,
G3624.1 N-DPM οἴκοις (1x)
Mt 11:8 the soft *garments* are in the houses of·the kings.
G3624.1 N-GSM οἴκου (12x)
Jn 2:17 ·written, "The zeal of·your house devours me."
Lk 1:27 *was* Joseph, from·among *the* house of·David. And
Lk 2:4 him being from·among *the* house and paternal·lineage
Lk 11:51 the Sacrifice·Altar and the house *of·God*. Yes, I·say

Ac 19:16 to·utterly·flee from·out·of·that house naked and
Heb 3:3 ·one planning·and·constructing the house has more
Heb 11:7 ·ark for *the* salvation of·his house; through which
Mt 10:6 having·completely·perished of·*the*·house of·IsraEl.
Mt 15:24 having·completely·perished of·*the*·house of·IsraEl.
1Pe 4:17 the judgment to·begin with the house of·God. And
1Ti 3:4 one·conducting his·own house well, having his·
1Ti 3:5 has·not seen·how to·conduct his·own house, how
G3624.1 N-GPM οἴκων (1x)
1Ti 3:12 their·children and their·own houses well.
EG3624.1 (6x)
Lk 8:49 ·from *the house·of* the director·of·the·gathering,
Ac 16:40 prison, they·entered into *the house·of* Lydia. And
Heb 3:3 the house has more honor *than the house* itself.
Heb 8:13 the first *covenant with·the house of·IsraEl*. Now
Mk 5:35 from *the house·of* the director·of·the·gathering,
1Co 1:11 brothers, by the·ones *of·the house* of·Chloe, that
G3624.2 N-NSM οἶκος (3x)
Ac 11:14 you·shall·be·saved, you and all your household.'
Ac 16:15 ·immersed, and·also her household, she·implored
Ac 16:31 and you·shall·be·saved, you and your household."
G3624.2 N-ASM οἶκον (2x)
1Co 1:16 (And I·immersed also the household of·Stephanas.
2Ti 4:19 and Aquila, and the household of·OnesiPhorus.
EG3624.2 (1x)
Ac 16:33 ·was·immersed at·once, he and all his *household*.
G3624.3 N-APM οἴκους (1x)
Ac 20:20 and have·instructed yeu publicly and in homes,
G3624.3 N-DSM οἴκῳ (2x)
1Co 11:34 is·hungry, let·him·eat at home, lest yeu·should·
1Co 14:35 ·must·inquire·of their·own menfolk at home. For

G3625 οἰκουμένη ôikôumĕnē *n.* (15x)
Roots:G3611 Compare:G1093 G2889 xLangEquiv:H0776 A0772 A0778 xLangAlso:H0127 H8398
G3625.1 N-NSF οἰκουμένη (1x)
Ac 19:27 whom all Asia and The Land reverences."
G3625.1 N-ASF οἰκουμένην (8x)
Lk 2:1 *that* all The Land was·to·be·enrolled·in·a·census.
Ac 11:28 to·be a·great famine over all The Land, which even
Ac 17:6 "The·ones upsetting The Land, these·men are·
Ac 17:31 he·intends 'to·judge The Land by righteousness' by
Ac 24:5 among·all the Jews in The Land, and *being* a·
Heb 1:6 ·should·bring the Firstborn into The Land, he·says,
Heb 2:5 *that* he·subjugated the impending *brand-new* Land,
Rv 12:9 the·one deceiving all The Land; he·was·cast·out into
G3625.1 N-DSF οἰκουμένῃ (2x)
Lk 21:26 the·things which·are·coming·upon The Land, for
Mt 24:14 in all The Land for a·testimony to·all the nations,
G3625.1 N-GSF οἰκουμένης (4x)
Lk 4:5 all the kingdoms of·The Land in a·moment of·time.
Rm 10:18 their utterances to the utmost·parts of·The Land."'
Rv 3:10 about to·come upon all The Land, to·try the·ones
Rv 16:14 of·the earth and of·all The Land, to·gather them

G3626 οἰκ•ουρός ôikôurŏs *adj.* (1x)
Roots:G3624
G3626 A-APF οἰκουρούς (1x)
Tit 2:5 *·and·*morally·clean, housekeepers, beneficially·good,

G3627 οἰκτείρω ôiktêírō *v.* (2x)
οἰκτερέω ôiktêrĕō
[prolonged, in certain tenses]
Roots:G3629-1 Compare:G1653 G2433 See:G3628 G3629 xLangAlso:H7355
G3627.1 V-FAI-1S οἰκτειρήσω (1x)
Rm 9:15 and I·shall·compassionately·show·pity on·whom I·
G3627.1 V-PAS-1S οἰκτείρω (1x)
Rm 9:15 on·whom I·would compassionately·show·pity."'

G3628 οἰκτιρμός ôiktirmŏs *n.* (5x)
Roots:G3627 See:G3629 xLangEquiv:H7356 A7359
G3628.2 N-NPM οἰκτιρμοί (1x)
Php 2:1 of·Spirit, if any inward·affections and compassions,
G3628.2 N-GPM οἰκτιρμῶν (2x)
Heb 10:28 died completely·apart·from compassion upon two
Col 3:12 , dress·yeurselves·with compassionate inward·,
G3628.3 N-GPM οἰκτιρμῶν (2x)
Rm 12:1 brothers, through the tender·compassions of·God,
2Co 1:3 the Father of·the tender·compassions and God of·

G3629 οἰκτίρμων ôiktírmōn *adj.* (3x)
Roots:G3627 See:G3628
G3629 A-NSM οἰκτίρμων (2x)
Lk 6:36 just·as yeur Father also is compassionate.
Jac 5:11 that Yahweh is very·empathetic and compassionate.
G3629 A-NPM οἰκτίρμονες (1x)
Lk 6:36 "Accordingly, become compassionate, just·as yeur

G3630 οἰνο•πότης ôinŏpŏtēs *n.* (2x)
Roots:G3631 G4095 Compare:G3943 G3183 G5314 See:G3632 G3631-1 xLangAlso:H5433 H2151
G3630 N-NSM οἰνοπότης (2x)
Lk 7:34 a·glutton and an·excessive·wine-drinker, a·friend
Mt 11:19 a·glutton and an·excessive·wine-drinker, a·friend

G3631 οἶνος ôinŏs *n.* (36x)
Compare:G1098 G3690 See:G3632-2 G0749-5 G0749-4
xLangEquiv:H3196
G3631 N-NSM οἶνος (4x)
Lk 5:37 But·if·so, the fresh·new wine shall·burst the
Mt 9:17 wineskins are·burst, and the wine pours·out, and the
Mk 2:22 But·if·so, the fresh·new wine bursts the wineskins,
Mk 2:22 the wineskins, and the wine pours·out, and the
G3631 N-ASM οἶνον (18x)
Jn 2:3 of·Jesus says to him, "They·do·not have wine."
Jn 2:9 tasted the water having·been·made wine, yet had·not
Jn 2:10 ·clay† first places·out the good wine, and whenever
Jn 2:10 ·purposefully·kept the good wine until this·moment."
Jn 4:46 where he·made the water *into* wine. And there·was
Lk 1:15 no, he·should·not drink wine nor intoxicating·drink,
Lk 5:37 not·even·one·man casts fresh·new wine into old
Lk 5:38 "But·rather fresh·new wine *is only* fit·to·be·cast into
Lk 7:33 neither eating bread nor drinking wine, and yeu·say,
Lk 10:34 wounds, pouring·in oil and wine. And mounting
Mt 9:17 Neither do·men·cast fresh·new wine into old
Mt 9:17 But·rather they·cast fresh·new wine into brand-new
Mk 2:22 not·even·one·man casts fresh·new wine into old
Mk 2:22 "But·rather fresh·new wine *is only* fit·to·be·cast
Mk 15:23 him wine to·drink having·been·mingled·with·
Rm 14:21 meat, nor·even to·drink wine, nor·even *anything*
Rv 6:6 you·should·not bring·harm·to the oil and the wine."
Rv 18:13 and frankincense, "and wine, oil, fine·flour, and
G3631 N-DSM οἴνῳ (4x)
Tit 2:3 to·much wine, instructors·of·morally·good·things
Eph 5:18 And not to·be·drunk with·wine, in which is *the*
1Ti 3:8 not giving·heed to·much wine, not of·shameful·
1Ti 5:23 but·rather use a·little wine on·account·of your
G3631 N-GSM οἴνου (7x)
Jn 2:3 And lacking wine, the mother of·Jesus says to him,
Rv 14:8 nations drink from·out·of·the wine of·the rage of·her
Rv 14:10 same shall·drink from·out·of·the wine of·the Rage
Rv 16:19 ·give to·her the cup of·the wine of·the Rage of·his
Rv 17:2 from·out·of·the wine of·her sexual·immorality."
Rv 18:3 nations have·drunk from·out·of·the wine of·the rage
Rv 19:15 tramples the winepress of·the wine of·the Rage and
EG3631 (3x)
Lk 5:39 ·even·one·man drinking old *wine* immediately wants
Lk 5:39 *wine* immediately wants fresh·new *wine*, for he·says
Lk 5:39 'The old is finer *wine*.'"

G3632 οἰνο•φλυγία ôinŏphlygía *n.* (1x)
Roots:G3631 G5397 Compare:G3943 See:G3631-1 G3630
G3632.2 N-DPF οἰνοφλυγίαις (1x)
1Pe 4:3 debaucheries, longings, excesses·of·wine, revelries,

G3633 οἴομαι ôíŏmai *v.* (3x)
οἶμαι ôîmai [shorter]
Roots:G3634
G3633.2 V-PNI-1S-C οἶμαι (1x)
Jn 21:25 each one should·be·written, I·imagine not·even the
G3633.2 V-PNM-3S οἰέσθω (1x)
Jac 1:7 man·of·clay† must·not imagine that he·shall·receive
G3633.2 V-PNP-NPM οἰόμενοι (1x)
Php 1:16 ·cleanness·of·motive, imagining *also* to·bring·on

G3634 οἷος hôîŏs *p:k.* (17x)
Compare:G5108 G3697 See:G3745 G3588 G3739
EG3634 (1x)
1Co 15:47 ·of·clay† *was* from·out·of·soil, *as* dusty·clay.
G3634.1 P:K-NSM οἷος (1x)
Rv 16:18 ·was a·great earthquake, such·as did·not happen
G3634.1 P:K-NPM οἷοι (2x)
1Th 1:5 *that* we·behaved·ourselves as·such among yeu, on·
2Co 10:11 reckon this, "Such·as we·are in·word through *our*
G3634.1 P:K-ASM οἷον (2x)
Php 1:30 the same strenuous·struggle such·as yeu·saw in me,
2Co 12:20 should·be·found by·yeu such·as yeu·do·not want.
G3634.1 P:K-APN οἵους (1x)
2Co 12:20 ·coming, I·should·find yeu such·as I·do·not want
G3634.1 P:R-NSF οἵα (1x)
Mt 24:21 a·Great Tribulation, such·as has·not been since
G3634.1 P:R-NPN οἷα (1x)
Mk 9:3 white as snow, such·as a·cloth-fuller on the earth is·
EG3634.1 (1x)
Mk 7:4 to·securely·hold, *such·as the* ceremonial·washings
G3634.2 P:K-NSM οἷος (2x)
1Co 15:48 As *was* the dusty·clay·man, such also *are* the
1Co 15:48 the dusty·clay·men; and as *is* the heavenly·man,
G3634.2 P:R-NSF οἵα (1x)
Mk 13:19 ·be a·Tribulation, such as has·not happened from
G3634.3 P:R-NPN οἷα (1x)
2Ti 3:11 *my* afflictions— such·as·what happened to·me at
G3634.4 P:K-APN οἵους (1x)
2Ti 3:11 *and* at Lystra; what persecutions I·underwent, but
G3634.5 P:K-GSN οἵου (1x)
Lk 9:55 ·not personally·know of·what·manner of·spirit yeu
G3634.6 P:K-NSN οἷον (1x)
Rm 9:6 But *it·is* not as·though the Holy-word of·God has·

G3635 ὀκνέω ŏknĕō *v.* (1x)
Compare:G1019 G1252 G5549 See:G3636
G3635.4 V-AAN ὀκνῆσαι (1x)
Ac 9:38 *him* not to·amble·along in·going·through to them.

G3636 ὀκνηρός ŏknērŏs *adj.* (3x)
Roots:G3635 Compare:G3576 xLangAlso:H6102
G3636.2 A-NPM ὀκνηροί (1x)
Rm 12:11 in·the diligence, *by* not *being* slothful; in·the spirit
G3636.2 A-VSM ὀκνηρέ (1x)
Mt 25:26 'O·evil and slothful slave! You·had·personally·
G3636.3 A-NSN ὀκνηρόν (1x)
Php 3:1 In·fact, *it·is* not tiresome for·me to·write the same·

G3637 ὀκτα•ήμερος ŏktaēmêrŏs *adj.* (1x)
Roots:G3638 G2250
G3637 A-NSM ὀκταήμερος (1x)
Php 3:5 ·circumcision *at* eight·days·of·age from·among *the*

G3638 ὀκτώ ŏktō *n.* (5x)
See:G3590 xLangAlso:H8083
G3638 N-NUI ὀκτώ (5x)
Jn 20:26 And after eight days, again his disciples were inside
Lk 2:21 And when eight days were·fulfilled to·circumcise
Lk 9:28 And it·happened about eight days after these sayings
Ac 9:33 laying·down upon a·mat for eight years, *and* who
1Pe 3:20 which a·few (that·is eight souls) were·thoroughly·

G3639 ὄλεθρος ŏlêthrŏs *n.* (4x)
Compare:G0684 G4938 See:G3644 G3645
G3639.2 N-NSM ὄλεθρος (1x)
1Th 5:3 an·unexpected savage·termination assaults them,
G3639.2 N-ASM ὄλεθρον (3x)
2Th 1:9 justice with·an·eternal savage·termination from *the*
1Co 5:5 for a·savage·termination of·the flesh, in·order·that
1Ti 6:9 down in a·savage·termination and total·destruction.

G3640 ὀλιγό•πιστος ŏligŏpistŏs *adj.* (5x)
Roots:G3641 G4102
G3640.2 A-VSM ὀλιγόπιστε (1x)

Mt 14:31 and says to·him, "O·you·of·little·trust, why·did
G3640.2 A-VPM ὀλιγόπιστοι (4x)
Lk 12:28 more *shall·he·enrobe* yeu, O·yeu·of·little·trust?
Mt 6:30 not much more *enrobe* yeu, O·yeu·of·little·trust?
Mt 8:26 "Why are·yeu timid, O·yeu·of·little·trust?" Then
Mt 16:8 declared to·them, "O·yeu·of·little·trust, why·do

G3641 ὀλίγος ôlígôs *adj.* (43x)
Compare:G3397 G3398 xLangAlso:H4592
G3641.2 A-ASM ὀλίγον (1x)
Rv 12:12 rage, having·seen that he·has *but* a·brief season."
G3641.3 A-ASM ὀλίγον (2x)
Jac 4:14 one·appearing just·for a·brief·moment and then
1Ti 4:8 training is profitable just·for a·brief·moment, "but
G3641.3 A-DSN ὀλίγῳ (1x)
Ac 26:28 "In *such* a·brief·moment, do·you·persuade me to·
G3641.4 A-DSM ὀλίγῳ (1x)
Eph 3:3 Mystery (just·as I·previously·wrote *about* briefly,
G3641.5 A-GPN ὀλίγων (1x)
1Pe 5:12 I·reckon *it*), I·wrote briefly to·yeu— exhorting
G3641.6 A-NPM ὀλίγοι (7x)
Lk 10:2 but the workmen *are* few. Accordingly, petition the
Lk 13:23 *is·it so* that the·ones being·saved *are* few?" And
Ac 17:12 trusted, and·also not a·few of·the dignified Greek
Mt 7:14 ·off to the life-above, and few are the·ones finding it
Mt 9:37 the harvest *is* large, but the workmen *are* few.
Mt 20:16 for many are called·forth, but few *are* Selected."
Mt 22:14 "For many are called·forth, but few *are* Selected."
G3641.6 A-NPF ὀλίγαι (2x)
Ac 17:4 ·reverent Greek·men and not a·few of·the foremost
1Pe 3:20 being·fully·prepared, in which a·few (that·is eight
G3641.6 A-APF ὀλίγας (2x)
Lk 12:48 shall·be·thrashed with·few *punishing·blows*. "So
Heb 12:10 they, just·for few days, were·educating·and·
G3641.6 A-APN ὀλίγα (7x)
Mt 15:34 "Seven, and a·few small·fish."
Mt 25:21 over a·few·things, I·shall·fully·establish you over
Mt 25:23 over a·few·things, I·shall·fully·establish you over
Mk 8:7 And they·were·holding a·few small·fish. And upon·
Rv 2:14 'But·yet I·have a·few·things against you, because
Rv 2:20 'But·yet I·have a·few·things against you, because
Rv 3:4 'You·have a·few names even in Sardis which did·not
G3641.6 A-DPM ὀλίγοις (1x)
Mk 6:5 laying his hands upon·a·few unhealthy·ones *whom*
G3641.7 A-NSM ὀλίγος (2x)
Ac 12:18 occurring, there·was no little disturbance among
Ac 19:23 season, there·occurred no little disturbance about
G3641.7 A-NSN ὀλίγον (1x)
Jac 3:5 yet it·boasts·greatly. Behold, a·little fire kindles
G3641.7 A-ASM ὀλίγον (1x)
Ac 14:28 And *it·was* no little time *that* they·were·lingering
G3641.7 A-ASF ὀλίγην (1x)
Ac 19:24 personally·furnished no little income for·the
G3641.7 A-ASN ὀλίγον (2x)
Lk 7:47 "But to·whom little is·forgiven, *the same* loves little.
Lk 7:47 to·whom little is·forgiven, *the same* loves little."
G3641.7 A-DSM ὀλίγῳ (1x)
1Ti 5:23 ·only, but·rather use a·little wine on·account·of
G3641.7 A-DSN ὀλίγῳ (1x)
Ac 26:29 this·day, both among *the* little and among *the* large
G3641.7 A-GSM ὀλίγου (1x)
Ac 27:20 days, and with·no little wintry·storm laying·upon
G3641.7 A-GSF ὀλίγης (1x)
Ac 15:2 with·it·becoming of·no little controversy to·Paul
G3641.8 A-ASM ὀλίγον (1x)
1Pe 5:10 YeShua— after·our·suffering a·little·while, may
G3641.8 ADV ὀλίγον (2x)
Mk 6:31 a·desolate place, and rest a·little·while!" For there·
Rv 17:10 it·is·mandatory·for him to·remain a·little·while.
G3641.9 A-ASM ὀλίγον (1x)
1Pe 1:6 *although* being·grieved a·little·bit at·this·moment
G3641.10 A-ASM ὀλίγον (1x)
Lk 5:3 *Jesus* asked·of him to·head·off a·little·way from the
G3641.10 ADV ὀλίγον (1x)
Mk 1:19 And walking·forward a·little·way from·there, he·
G3641.11 A-ASN ὀλίγον (1x)
2Co 8:15 much, and the·one did·not decrease·to the less.

G3642 ὀλιγό•ψυχος ôligópsychôs *adj.* (1x)
Roots:G3641 G5590
G3642.2 A-APM ὀλιγοψύχους (1x)
1Th 5:14 personally·encourage the fainthearted, support the

G3643 ὀλιγ•ωρέω ôligōréō *v.* (1x)
Roots:G3641
G3643.2 V-PAM-2S ὀλιγώρει (1x)
Heb 12:5 do·not have·little·respect of·Yahweh's corrective·

G3644 ὀλοθρευτής ôlôthrêutḗs *n.* (1x)
Roots:G3645
G3644.1 N-GSM ὀλοθρευτοῦ (1x)
1Co 10:10 ·completely·destroyed by the savage·terminator.

G3645 ὀλοθρεύω ôlôthrêúō *v.* (1x)
Roots:G3639 See:G3644
G3645.2 V-PAP-NSM ὀλοθρεύων (1x)
Heb 11:28 lest the·one savagely·terminating the firstborn

G3646 ὁλο•καύτωμα hôlôkaútōma *n.* (3x)
Roots:G3650 G2545 Compare:G2593-2 See:G3645-1 G3646-1 xLangAlso:H1890 A5928 H5930
G3646.1 N-APN ὁλοκαυτώματα (2x)
Heb 10:6 In·burnt·offerings, even concerning moral·failure,
Heb 10:8 "Sacrifice and offering and burnt·offerings, even
G3646.1 N-GPN ὁλοκαυτωμάτων (1x)
Mk 12:33 is more·than all the burnt·offerings and the

G3647 ὁλο•κληρία hôlôklēría *n.* (1x)
Roots:G3648 Compare:G3651
G3647.4 N-ASF ὁλοκληρίαν (1x)
Ac 3:16 ·man this perfect·soundness fully·in·front of·yeu all.

G3648 ὁλό•κληρος hôlóklērôs *adj.* (2x)
Roots:G3650 G2819 Compare:G3651 See:G3647
G3648.2 A-NPM ὁλόκληροι (1x)
Jac 1:4 ·may·be complete and entirely·whole, being·deficient
G3648.3 A-NSN ὁλόκληρον (1x)
1Th 5:23 ·perfect. And may every·single·part of·yeur spirit,

G3649 ὀλολύζω ôlôlýzō *v.* (1x)
Compare:G0214 G2360 G5207-2 See:G3648-1 xLangEquiv:H3213 xLangAlso:H3214
G3649 V-PAP-NPM ὀλολύζοντες (1x)
Jac 5:1 Wealthy·Men! Weep, howling over yeur miseries,

G3650 ὅλος hôlôs *adj.* (114x)
Compare:G3956 See:G3654
G3650.1 A-NSM ὅλος (1x)
1Jn 5:19 ·out of·God, and the whole world is·laid·out in the
G3650.1 A-NSF ὅλη (5x)
Jn 4:53 And he·himself trusted, and his whole household.
Ac 19:29 And the whole city was·filled with·mass·confusion
Ac 21:30 And the whole City was·stirred, and the people
Mk 1:33 And the whole city was having·been·completely·
1Co 14:23 if the whole Called·Out·citizenry should·come·
G3650.1 A-NSN ὅλον (11x)
Jn 11:50 not *that* the whole nation should·completely·perish.
Lk 11:34 should·be clear·and·focused, your whole body is
Lk 11:36 "Now·then, if your whole body *is* full·of·light, not
Lk 11:36 part opaquely·dark, *the* whole shall·be full·of·light
Mt 5:29 and not *that* your whole body should·be·cast into
Mt 5:30 and not *that* your whole body should·be·cast into
Mt 6:22 ·be clear·and·focused, your whole body shall·be
Mt 6:23 should·be evil, your whole body shall·be opaquely·
Mk 15:1 scribes and the whole joint·council·of·Sanhedrin,
1Co 12:17 If the whole body *is* an·eye, where·is the sense·
1Co 12:17 ·of·hearing placed? If *the* whole *body is* hearing,
G3650.1 A-ASM ὅλον (7x)
Jn 7:23 I·made a·whole man·of·clay† healthy·and·sound on
Lk 9:25 ·clay† benefited, after·gaining the whole world but
Ac 11:26 them to·be·gathered·together a·whole year among
Mt 16:26 ·benefited, if he·should·gain the whole world, and
Mk 8:36 ·of·clay†, if he·should·gain the whole world, yet
Mk 14:9 should·be·officially·proclaimed in the whole world,
Jac 2:10 shall·observantly·keep the whole Torah-Law, but
G3650.1 A-ASF ὅλην (7x)
Lk 8:39 ·proclaiming in the whole city what·many·things
Ac 28:30 And Paul abided a·whole two·years in his·own
Mt 20:6 'Why·do yeu·stand here the whole day idle?
Mt 27:27 ·hall, gathered·together the whole battalion against
Mk 6:55 *and* running·around that whole surrounding·region,
Mk 15:16 And they·call·together the whole battalion.
Rm 10:21 he·says, " The whole day·long I·spread·out my
G3650.1 A-ASN ὅλον (5x)
Gal 5:9 A·little leaven leavens the whole lump·of·dough.
Jac 3:2 ·mature man, able also to·bridle the whole body.
Jac 3:3 them to·our *will*, and we·steer their whole body.
Jac 3:6 our members, the·one staining the whole body, and
1Co 5:6 a·little leaven leavens the whole lump·of·dough?
G3650.1 A-APM ὅλους (1x)
Tit 1:11 Such·men overturn whole houses, instructing things·
G3650.1 A-DSM ὅλῳ (1x)
Mt 26:13 ·be·officially·proclaimed in the whole world, also
G3650.1 A-DSF ὅλῃ (2x)
Lk 1:65 among the whole mountainous·region of·Judea,
Rv 13:3 And it·was·marveled among the whole earth, *which*
G3650.1 A-GSM ὅλου (1x)
1Jn 2:2 concerning *the moral·failures·of* the whole world.
G3650.1 A-GSF ὅλης (2x)
Ac 13:49 ·thoroughly·carried throughout the whole region.
Rm 16:23 (and *local·host* of·the whole Called·Out·citizenry),
G3650.1 A-GSN ὅλου (1x)
Ac 10:22 and being·attested·to by the whole nation of·the
EG3650.1 (2x)
Rm 11:16 firstfruit *is* holy, the *whole* lump·of·dough *is* also
1Co 13:9 we·know from·out of·a·portion *of·the whole*, and
G3650.2 A-NSM ὅλος (1x)
Mt 22:40 two commandments is·hung all the Torah-Law and
G3650.2 A-NSF ὅλη (2x)
Ac 19:27 is·about to·be·demolished, whom all Asia and The
Ac 21:31 that all JeruSalem has·been·stirred·up·into·an·
G3650.2 A-NSN ὅλον (5x)
Mt 1:22 And all this has·happened, in·order·that it·may·be·
Mt 21:4 But all this has·happened in·order·that it·may·be·
Mt 26:56 "But all this has·happened in·order·that the
Mt 26:59 the elders and all the joint·council·of·Sanhedrin
Mk 14:55 chief·priests and all the joint·council·of·Sanhedrin
G3650.2 A-ASM ὅλον (6x)
Lk 8:43 who after·specifically·consuming all *her* livelihood
Ac 2:2 wind, and it·completely·filled all the house where
Ac 2:47 and having grace alongside all the People. And the
Ac 7:10 him, governing over Egypt and all his house.
Gal 5:3 he·is under·an·obligation to·do all the Torah-Law.
Mk 12:44 as·many·as she·was·holding, all her livelihood."
G3650.2 A-ASF ὅλην (13x)
Lk 23:44 and there·was a·darkness over all the land until *the*
Ac 5:11 reverent·fear came upon all the Called·Out·citizenry
Ac 7:11 Now there·came a·famine over all the land of·Egypt
Ac 11:28 ·was·about to·be a·great famine over all The Land,
Mt 4:23 And YeShua was·heading·out all around Galilee,
Mt 4:24 And his fame went·off into all Syria. And they·
Mt 9:26 of·this *awakening* went·forth into all that land.
Mt 14:35 place dispatched into all that surrounding·region
Mk 1:28 his fame went·forth unto all the region·surrounding
Mk 1:39 in their gatherings among all Galilee and casting·
Mk 15:33 darkness came·to·be over all the land until *the*
Rm 8:36 ·your cause, we·are·put·to·death all the day·long;
Rv 12:9 Adversary-Accuser, the·one deceiving all The Land;
G3650.2 A-ASN ὅλον (3x)
Lk 13:21 seah·measures of·flour, until all was·leavened."
Ac 22:30 ·priests and all their joint·council·of·Sanhedrin to·
Mt 13:33 seah·measures of·flour, until all was·leavened."
G3650.2 A-DSM ὅλῳ (4x)
Ac 18:8 trusted on·the Lord together with·all his house; and
Heb 3:2 as also Moses *was trustworthy* in all his house.
Heb 3:5 in·fact, Moses *was* trustworthy in all his house as
Rm 1:8 yeur trust is·being·fully·proclaimed in all the world.
G3650.2 A-DSF ὅλῃ (9x)

Lk 7:17 concerning him went·forth among all Judea and
Ac 15:22 elders, together with·all the Called·Out·citizenry,
Mt 9:31 ·forth, they·widely·promoted it in all that land.
Mt 22:37 ·shall·love Yahweh your God with all your heart,
Mt 22:37 all your heart, and with all your soul, and with all
Mt 22:37 all your soul, and with all your innermost·mind."
Mt 24:14 shall·be·officially·proclaimed in all The Land for
1Th 4:10 all the brothers, the·ones in all Macedonia. But
2Co 1:1 with·all the holy·ones, the·ones being in all Achaia:
G3650.2 A-DSN ὅλῳ (1x)
Php 1:13 *the* Anointed-One to·become apparent to·all in the
G3650.2 A-GSM ὅλου (1x)
Jn 19:23 *continuously* from·the·start throughout all *of·it*.
G3650.2 A-GSF ὅλης (21x)
Lk 4:14 ·forth concerning him in all the surrounding·region.
Lk 5:5 "O·Captain, after·laboring·hard all through the night,
Lk 10:27 ·love Yahweh your God from·out of·all your heart,
Lk 10:27 ·all your heart, and from·out of·all your soul, and
Lk 10:27 your soul, and from·out of·all your strength, and
Lk 10:27 strength, and from·out of·all your innermost·mind,
Lk 23:5 the people, instructing in all Judea, beginning from
Ac 8:37 "If you·trust from·out of·all the heart, it·is·proper.
Ac 9:31 the Called·Out·citizenries in all of·Judea, Galilee
Ac 9:42 And it·became known in all Joppa, and many trusted
Ac 10:37 the utterance occurring in all Judea, beginning
Mk 12:30 Yahweh your God from·out of·all your heart, and
Mk 12:30 ·all your heart, and from·out of·all your soul, and
Mk 12:30 soul, and from·out of·all your innermost·mind,
Mk 12:30 innermost·mind, and from·out of·all your strength
Mk 12:33 And to·love him from·out of·all the heart, and
Mk 12:33 the heart, and from·out of·all the comprehension,
Mk 12:33 the comprehension, and from·out of·all the soul,
Mk 12:33 ·all the soul, and from·out of·all the strength, and
Rv 3:10 the·one about to·come upon all The Land, to·try
Rv 16:14 to the kings of·the earth and of·all The Land, to·
G3650.3 A-NSM ὅλος (2x)
Jn 9:34 "You·yourself were·born altogether in moral·failures
Jn 13:10 Moreover, he·is altogether pure. And yeu are pure,

G3651 ὁλο•τελής hôlôtêlḗs *adj.* (1x)
Roots:G3650 G5056 Compare:G3648 G3647
G3651 A-APM ὁλοτελεῖς (1x)
1Th 5:23 make yeu·yeurselves holy, absolutely·perfect. And

Oo

G3652 Ὀλυμπᾶς Ôlympâs *n/p.* (1x)
G3652 N/P-ASM Ὀλυμπᾶν (1x)
Rm 16:15 and his sister, and Olympas, and all the holy·

G3653 ὄλυνθος ólynthôs *n.* (1x)
Compare:G4810
G3653 N-APM ὀλύνθους (1x)
Rv 6:13 casts its unripe·green·figs while·being·shaken by a·

G3654 ὅλως hólōs *adv.* (5x)
Roots:G3650
G3654.1 ADV ὅλως (1x)
1Co 6:7 even·now there·is altogether a·deterioration among
G3654.2 ADV ὅλως (1x)
1Co 5:1 It·is·heard all·over *that there·is* sexual·immorality
G3654.3 ADV ὅλως (2x)
Mt 5:34 I·myself say to·yeu not to·swear at·all: neither by
1Co 15:29 if dead·men are·not awakened at·all? Why then
EG3654.3 (1x)
Gal 1:7 is not *actually* another *good·news* at·all. However,

G3655 ὄμβρος ómbrôs *n.* (1x)
Compare:G1027 G1028 G5205
G3655 N-NSM ὄμβρος (1x)
Lk 12:54 yeu·say, 'There·comes a·thunderstorm,' and in·

G3656 ὁμ•ιλέω hômilḗō *v.* (4x)
Roots:G3658
G3656.2 V-PAN ὁμιλεῖν (1x)
Lk 24:15 And it·happened, with them conversing, then
G3656.2 V-IAI-3S ὡμίλει (1x)
Ac 24:26 him more·frequently and was·conversing with·him.
G3656.2 V-IAI-3P ὡμίλουν (1x)
Lk 24:14 they·themselves were·conversing alongside one·
G3656.2 V-AAP-NSM ὁμιλήσας (1x)
Ac 20:11 ·a·bite·to·eat and conversing over a·long·while in·

G3657 ὁμ•ιλία hômilía *n.* (1x)
Roots:G3658 Compare:G3656
G3657.3 N-NPF ὁμιλίαι (1x)
1Co 15:33 ·be deceived. "Bad influences corrupt fine moral·

G3658 ὅμ•ιλος hómilôs *n.* (1x)
Roots:G3674 G0138 Compare:G3793 See:G3656
G3658.2 N-NSM ὅμιλος (1x)
Rv 18:17 and all aboard the company of·ships, and sailors,

G3659 ὄμμα ómma *n.* (1x)
Roots:G3700 Compare:G3788 G5168
G3659.2 N-APN ὄμματα (1x)
Mk 8:23 And after·spitting into his eyes *and* laying his hands

G3660 ὀμνύω ômnýō *v.* (27x)
ὀμόω ômóō
[another prolonged form, used in certain tenses]
xLangAlso:H7650
G3660 V-PAI-3S ὀμνύει (3x)
Mt 23:20 swearing by the Sacrifice·Altar, swears by it and
Mt 23:21 ·one swearing by the Temple, swears by it and by
Mt 23:22 swearing by the heaven, swears by the throne of·
G3660 V-PAI-3P ὀμνύουσιν (1x)
Heb 6:16 For men·of·clay† in·fact swear by the·one greater·
G3660 V-PAM-2P ὀμνύετε (1x)
Jac 5:12 my brothers, do·not swear, neither by·the heaven,
G3660 V-PAN ὀμνύειν (2x)
Mt 26:74 ·vow·of·destruction and to·swear, *saying*, "I·do·
Mk 14:71 ·bind·*himself*·over·to·destruction and to·swear,
G3660 V-AAI-1S ὤμοσα (2x)
Heb 3:11 Even·as I·swore in my flared·anger, 'As·if they·
Heb 4:3 *obstinate·ones*, "'As I·swore in my flared·anger,
G3660 V-AAI-3S ὤμοσεν (8x)
Lk 1:73 an·oath which he·swore to our father AbRaham,
Ac 2:30 and having·seen that God swore to·him with·an·oath
Ac 7:17 was·drawing·near which God swore to·AbRaham,
Heb 3:18 And to·whom did·he·swear *that* 'they·were·not
Heb 6:13 greater by *which* to·swear, he·swore by himself,
Heb 7:21 to him, "'Yahweh swore and shall·not have·regret,
Mk 6:23 And he·swore to·her, "Whatever you·should·
Rv 10:6 and he·swore by the·one living into the ages of·ages
G3660 V-AAN ὀμόσαι (2x)
Heb 6:13 no·one·at·all greater by *which* to·swear, he·swore
Mt 5:34 "But I·myself say to·yeu not to·swear at·all: neither
G3660 V-AAP-NSM ὀμόσας (3x)
Mt 23:20 "So·then, the·one swearing by the Sacrifice·Altar,
Mt 23:21 And the·one swearing by the Temple, swears by it
Mt 23:22 And the·one swearing by the heaven, swears by the
G3660 V-AAS-2S ὀμόσῃς (1x)
Mt 5:36 Neither should·you·swear by your head, because
G3660 V-AAS-3S ὀμόσῃ (4x)
Mt 23:16 saying, 'Whoever should·swear "by the Temple,"
Mt 23:16 nothing·at·all, but whoever should·swear "by the
Mt 23:18 'Whoever should·swear by the Sacrifice·Altar, it·
Mt 23:18 ·at·all, but whoever should·swear by the present,

G3661 ὁμο•θυμαδόν hômôthymadón *adv.* (12x)
Roots:G3674 G2372
G3661.2 ADV ὁμοθυμαδόν (12x)
Ac 1:14 diligently·continuing with·the·same·determination
Ac 2:1 absolutely·all with·the·same·determination in·unison.
Ac 2:46 ·diligently·continuing with·the·same·determination
Ac 4:24 toward God with·the·same·determination, and
Ac 5:12 ·were absolutely·all with·the·same·determination in
Ac 7:57 ·dashed upon him with·the·same·determination.
Ac 8:6 *together* with·the·same·determination, were·giving·
Ac 12:20 but with·the·same·determination, they·were·
Ac 15:25 to·us, being with·the·same·determination, to·send
Ac 18:12 made·a·full·assault with·the·same·determination.
Ac 19:29 ·impulsively·dashed with·the·same·determination
Rm 15:6 in·order·that with·the·same·determination *and* with

G3662 ὁμοιάζω hômôiázō *v.* (1x)
Roots:G3664 Compare:G3945
G3662 V-PAI-3S ὁμοιάζει (1x)
Mk 14:70 you·are a·Galilean; even your speech is·alike."

G3663 ὁμοιο•παθής hômôiôpathḗs *adj.* (2x)
Roots:G3664 G3806
G3663 A-NSM ὁμοιοπαθής (1x)
Jac 5:17 EliJah was a·man·of·clay† of·like·passions with·us,
G3663 A-NPM ὁμοιοπαθεῖς (1x)
Ac 14:15 also are men·of·clay† of·like·passions with·yeu,

G3664 ὅμοιος hómôiôs *adj.* (47x)
Roots:G3674 Compare:G2470 See:G3662
G3664.1 A-NSM ὅμοιος (12x)
Jn 8:55 him,' I·shall·be a·liar like yeurselves. But·rather I·
Jn 9:9 others *were·saying*, "He·is like him." *But* that·man
Lk 6:47 doing them, I·shall·indicate to·yeu what he·is like.
Lk 6:48 "He·is like a·man·of·clay† building a·home, who
Lk 6:49 not doing, is like a·man·of·clay† building a·home
Mt 13:52 kingdom of·the heavens is like a·man·of·clay†, a·
Rv 4:3 ·down was in·clear·appearance like a·jasper and a·
Rv 4:3 the throne, in·clear·appearance like an·emerald.
Rv 11:1 And he·gave to·me a·reed like a·rod, saying,
Rv 13:4 ·Beast, saying, "Who *is* like the Daemonic·Beast?
Rv 14:14 *one* who·is·sitting·down like a·son of·clay·man†,
Rv 21:11 ·God (even her brilliance *was* like a·precious stone,
G3664.1 A-NSF ὁμοία (14x)
Lk 13:18 "To·what is the kingdom of·God like? And to·what
Lk 13:19 "It·is like a·kernel of·mustard·seed, which a·man·
Lk 13:21 It·is like leaven, which a·woman took *and*
Mt 13:31 of·the heavens is like a·kernel of·mustard·seed
Mt 13:33 "The kingdom of·the heavens is like leaven, which
Mt 13:44 of·the heavens is like treasure having·been·hidden
Mt 13:45 kingdom of·the heavens is like a·man·of·clay†, a·
Mt 13:47 of·the heavens is like a·dragnet after·being·cast
Mt 20:1 kingdom of·the heavens is like a·man·of·clay†, a·
Mt 22:39 "And *the* second *is* like it, "You·shall·love your
Mk 12:31 And *the* second *is* like it, "You·shall·love your
Rv 4:6 throne *there·is* a·transparent,·glassy sea, like crystal.
Rv 18:18 'What *city is* like the Great City!'
Rv 21:18 And the CITY *was* pure gold, like pure glass.
G3664.1 A-NSN ὅμοιον (4x)
Rv 4:7 And the first living·being *is* like a·lion, and the
Rv 4:7 and the second living·being *is* like a·calf, and the
Rv 4:7 and the fourth living·being *is* like a·flying eagle.
Rv 13:2 Daemonic·Beast which I·saw was like a·leopard, and
G3664.1 A-NPM ὅμοιοι (7x)
Lk 7:31 of·this generation? And to·what are·they like?
Lk 7:32 "They·are like little·children, the·ones sitting·down
Lk 12:36 *must·be* like men·of·clay† who·are·awaiting their·
1Jn 3:2 ·be·made·apparent, 'we·shall·be like him, because
Rv 1:15 and his feet like fine·brass (as having·been·refined
Rv 2:18 eyes as a·blaze of·fire and his feet like fine·brass:
Rv 9:7 *were something* as victor's·crowns like gold, and their
G3664.1 A-NPF ὅμοιαι (1x)
Rv 9:19 *tails*, for their tails *were* like serpents having heads,
G3664.1 A-NPN ὅμοια (3x)
Gal 5:21 revelries, and things like these … of·which I·
Mt 11:16 this generation? It·is like little·boys sitting·down
Rv 9:7 ·the locusts *were* like horses having·been·made·ready
G3664.1 A-ASM ὅμοιον (3x)
Ac 17:29 to·assume *for* the divine to·be like gold or silver or
Jud 1:7 As *in* like manner to·these *angels*, Sodom and
Rv 1:13 seven Lampstands, *one* like a·son of·clay·man†,
G3664.1 A-APF ὁμοίας (1x)
Rv 9:10 And they·have tails like scorpions, and there·were
G3664.1 A-APN ὅμοια (2x)
Rv 13:11 it·was·having two horns like a·young·male·lamb,
Rv 16:13 And I·saw three impure spirits like frogs *come* out

G3665 ὁμοιότης hômôiótēs *n.* (2x)
Roots:G3664 See:G3667 G3669
G3665 N-ASF ὁμοιότητα (2x)
Heb 4:15 having·been·intently·tried in similarity *to·us*, *yet*

Heb 7:15 if, according·to the similarity of·MalkiTsedeq,

G3666 ὁμοιόω hômôiốō *v.* (15x)
Roots:G3664 Compare:G1503 G3846 G4833 xLangAlso:H1819

G3666.1 V-FAI-1S ὁμοιώσω (5x)
Lk 7:31 "So·then to·what shall·I·liken the men·of·clay† of·
Lk 13:18 of·God like? And to·what shall·I·liken it?
Lk 13:20 he·declared, "To·what shall·I·liken the kingdom
Mt 7:24 and does them, I·shall·liken him to·a·prudent man
Mt 11:16 "But to·what shall·I·liken this generation?

G3666.1 V-FPI-3S ὁμοιωθήσεται (2x)
Mt 7:26 not doing them, shall·be·likened to·a·foolish man,
Mt 25:1 of·the heavens shall·be·likened to·ten virgins, who,

G3666.1 V-AAS-1P ὁμοιώσωμεν (1x)
Mk 4:30 ·saying, "To·what should·we·liken the kingdom of·

G3666.1 V-API-1P ὡμοιώθημεν (1x)
Rm 9:29 as Sodom, and would be·likened as Gomorrah."

G3666.1 V-API-3S ὡμοιώθη (3x)
Mt 13:24 of·the heavens is·likened to·a·man·of·clay† sowing
Mt 18:23 of·the heavens is·likened to·a·man·of·clay†, a·king
Mt 22:2 of·the heavens is·likened to·a·certain·man·of·clay†,

G3666.2 V-APP-NPM ὁμοιωθέντες (1x)
Ac 14:11 toward us being·in·the·likeness of·men·of·clay†."

G3666.2 V-APS-2P ὁμοιωθῆτε (1x)
Mt 6:8 "Accordingly, yeu·should·not be·like them, for yeur

G3666.3 V-APN ὁμοιωθῆναι (1x)
Heb 2:17 all·things to·the brothers to·become·like *them*, that

G3667 ὁμοίωμα hômôíōma *n.* (7x)
Roots:G3666 Compare:G1504 See:G3665 G3669 xLangAlso:H8403 H8544

G3667.1 N-NPN ὁμοιώματα (1x)
Rv 9:7 And the semblances of·the locusts *were* like horses

G3667.2 N-DSN ὁμοιώματι (5x)
Rm 1:23 ·a·resemblance of·a·derived·image of·corruptible
Rm 5:14 ·failing after the resemblance of·Adam's violation,
Rm 6:5 ·fused·together in·the resemblance of·his death,
Rm 8:3 ·own Son in *the* resemblance of·morally·failing flesh
Php 2:7 becoming in *the* resemblance of·men·of·clay†.

EG3667.2 (1x)
Rm 6:5 ·shall·be also *in·the resemblance* of·his resurrection

G3668 ὁμοίως hômôíōs *adv.* (30x)
Roots:G3664

G3668 ADV ὁμοίως (30x)
Jn 5:19 should·do, these·things also the Son does likewise.
Jn 6:11 reclining·for·the·meal, and likewise from·out of·the
Jn 21:13 *it* to·them, and the small·broiled·fish likewise.
Lk 3:11 *any*, and the·one having food must·do likewise."
Lk 5:10 And likewise also *amazed were* Jakob and John, the·
Lk 5:33 and make petitions, and likewise the·ones of·the
Lk 6:31 ·do to·yeu, also yeu·yeurselves do likewise to·them.
Lk 10:32 "And likewise a·Levite, happening by the place,
Lk 10:37 "Traverse, and you·yourself do likewise."
Lk 13:5 ·repent, yeu·shall all likewise completely·perish."
Lk 16:25 beneficially·good·things, and likewise, Lazarus the
Lk 17:28 "Likewise, *it·shall·be* also as it·was in·the days of·
Lk 17:31 to·take them away; and likewise, the·one in·the
Lk 22:36 let·him·take·it·up, and likewise a·knapsack. And
Heb 9:21 Moreover likewise, he·sprinkled the Tabernacle
Mt 22:26 Likewise the second also, and the third, even·unto
Mt 26:35 And·also, all the disciples declared likewise.
Mt 27:41 Likewise while·mocking *him* also, the chief·priests
Mk 4:16 "And these are·they likewise, the·ones being·
Mk 15:31 Likewise also, the chief·priests, while·mocking,
Rm 1:27 And likewise also the males, leaving the natural
Jac 2:25 And likewise also Rachav the prostitute, was·she·
Jud 1:8 Likewise also these *irreverent* dreamers, in·fact,
1Pe 3:1 *Now* likewise the wives: be·submitting·yeurselves
1Pe 3:7 *Now* likewise the husbands: *be* dwelling·together
1Pe 5:5 Likewise, *yeu* younger·men, be·submitted *to·yeur*
1Co 7:3 kind·marital·duty being·due, and likewise also the
1Co 7:4 but·rather the husband. And likewise also, the
1Co 7:22 *the* Lord's freedman, likewise also the·one being·
Rv 8:12 ·forth for·the third·part of·it, and the night likewise.

G3669 ὁμοίωσις hômôíōsis *n.* (1x)
Roots:G3666 Compare:G4610-1 G1504 G3855-2 See:G3665 G3667 xLangAlso:H6754 A6755 H8403 H1823

G3669 N-ASF ὁμοίωσιν (1x)
Jac 3:9 having·come·to·be according·to a·likeness of·God.

G3670 ὁμο•λογέω hômôlôgéō *v.* (23x)
Roots:G3674 G3056 Compare:G5335 G1861 See:G1843 G3672

G3670.1 V-FAI-1S ὁμολογήσω (2x)
Mt 7:23 And then I·shall·affirm to·them, 'Not·even·at·any·
Mt 10:32 the men·of·clay†, I·also shall·affirm him by·name

G3670.1 V-FAI-3S ὁμολογήσει (2x)
Lk 12:8 Son of·Clay·Man† also shall·affirm him by·name
Mt 10:32 "Now·then, anyone who shall·affirm me by·name

G3670.1 V-PAI-1S ὁμολογῶ (1x)
Ac 24:14 "But this I·affirm to·you, that according·to The

G3670.1 V-PAI-3S ὁμολογεῖ (2x)
1Jn 4:2 every spirit which affirms Jesus Anointed having·
1Jn 4:3 And every spirit that does·not affirm Jesus, the

G3670.1 V-PAI-3P ὁμολογοῦσιν (2x)
Ac 23:8 nor a·spirit, but *the* Pharisees affirm both·things.
Tit 1:16 They·affirm to·have·seen God, but in·the works

G3670.1 V-PAP-GPM ὁμολογούντων (1x)
Heb 13:15 ·is, a·fruit of·lips giving·affirmation to·his name.

G3670.1 V-PAP-NPM ὁμολογοῦντες (1x)
2Jn 1:7 the world, the·ones not affirming Jesus Anointed as·

G3670.1 V-PPI-3S ὁμολογεῖται (1x)
Rm 10:10 and with·*the*·mouth affirmation·is·made unto

G3670.1 V-IAI-3P ὡμολόγουν (1x)
Jn 12:42 ·of the Pharisees they·were·not affirming *him*, in·

G3670.1 V-AAI-2S ὡμολόγησας (1x)
1Ti 6:12 you·were·called·forth, and·also affirmed the good

G3670.1 V-AAI-3S ὡμολόγησεν (3x)
Jn 1:20 And he·affirmed and did·not deny, but he·affirmed,
Jn 1:20 and did·not deny, but he·affirmed, "I·myself am not
Mt 14:7 with an·oath, he·affirmed to·give her whatever

G3670.1 V-AAP-NPM ὁμολογήσαντες (1x)
Heb 11:13 embracing *them*, and affirming that they·were

G3670.1 V-AAS-2S ὁμολογήσῃς (1x)
Rm 10:9 If you·should·affirm with your mouth, "Jesus *is*

G3670.1 V-AAS-3S ὁμολογήσῃ (3x)
Jn 9:22 even·now that if any·man should·affirm *Jesus to·be*
Lk 12:8 ·yeu, anyone who should·affirm me by·name before
1Jn 4:15 Whoever should·affirm that Jesus is the Son of·God

G3670.3 V-PAS-1P ὁμολογῶμεν (1x)
1Jn 1:9 If we·should·confess our moral·failures, he·is

G3671 ὁμο•λογία hômôlôgía *n.* (6x)
Roots:G3674 G3056 Compare:G5335 G1861 See:G3670

G3671 N-ASF ὁμολογίαν (3x)
Heb 10:23 ·hold·onto the affirmation of·the Expectation
1Ti 6:12 affirmed the good affirmation in·the·sight of·many
1Ti 6:13 before Pontius Pilate the good affirmation)

G3671 N-GSF ὁμολογίας (3x)
Heb 3:1 and High·Priest of·our affirmation, Anointed-One
Heb 4:14 we·should·take·secure·hold of·the affirmation.
2Co 9:13 God over the affirmation of·yeur subjection to·the

G3672 ὁμο•λογουμένως hômôlôgôuménōs *adv.* (1x)
Roots:G3670

G3672 ADV ὁμολογουμένως (1x)
1Ti 3:16 And admittedly, great is the Mystery of·the Way·

G3673 ὁμό•τεχνος hômótêchnôs *adj.* (1x)
Roots:G3674 G5078

G3673 A-ASM ὁμότεχνον (1x)
Ac 18:3 ·account·of being of·the same·trade, he·was·abiding

G3674 ὁμοῦ hômôû *adv.* (3x)
Compare:G0260 See:G3676

G3674.1 ADV ὁμοῦ (1x)
Jn 21:2 *Now* at·the·same·place, there·was Simon Peter, and

G3674.2 ADV ὁμοῦ (2x)
Jn 4:36 and the·one reaping may·rejoice at·the·same·time.
Jn 20:4 But the two·men were·running at·the·same·time, yet

G3675 ὁμό•φρων hômóphrōn *adj.* (1x)
Roots:G5424 G3674 Compare:G2473

G3675 A-NPM ὁμόφρονες (1x)
1Pe 3:8 *be* of·the·same·mind, sympathetic·toward·one·

G3676 ὅμως hốmōs *conj.* (3x)
Roots:G3674

G3676.2 CONJ ὅμως (1x)
Jn 12:42 Yet·at·the·same·time, consequently·in·fact, many

G3676.3 CONJ ὅμως (1x)
1Co 14:7 And·in·the·same·manner the soulless,·inanimate·

G3676.4 CONJ ὅμως (1x)
Gal 3:15 ·of·clay†, that·in·the·same·manner, a·covenant of·

G3677 ὄναρ ónar *n.* (6x)
Compare:G1798 G3701 xLangAlso:H2472

G3677 N-OI ὄναρ (6x)
Mt 1:20 to·him according·to a·vision·in·a·dream, saying,
Mt 2:12 according·to a·vision·in·a·dream not to·return·back
Mt 2:13 to·Joseph according·to a·vision·in·a·dream, saying,
Mt 2:19 ·Yahweh (according·to a·vision·in·a·dream) appears
Mt 2:22 according·to a·vision·in·a·dream, he·departed into
Mt 27:19 according·to a·vision·in·a·dream on·account·of

G3678 ὀνάριον ônáriôn *n.* (1x)
Roots:G3688

G3678 N-ASN ὀνάριον (1x)
Jn 12:14 And Jesus, finding a·young·donkey, sat·down on it

G3679 ὀνειδίζω ônêidízō *v.* (10x)
Roots:G3681 Compare:G3058 See:G3680 xLangAlso:H2616

G3679 V-PAN ὀνειδίζειν (1x)
Mt 11:20 Then he·began to·reproach the cities in which the

G3679 V-PAP-GSM ὀνειδίζοντος (1x)
Jac 1:5 ·simplicity·and·fidelity and without reproaching, and

G3679 V-PAP-GPM ὀνειδιζόντων (1x)
Rm 15:3 "The reproaches of·the·ones reproaching you fell

G3679 V-PPI-1P ὀνειδιζόμεθα (1x)
1Ti 4:10 this also we·labor·hard and are·reproached, because

G3679 V-PPI-2P ὀνειδίζεσθε (1x)
1Pe 4:14 If yeu·are·reproached for *the* name of·

G3679 V-IAI-3P ὠνείδιζον (2x)
Mt 27:44 ·together with·him) were·reproaching him.
Mk 15:32 ·together with·him were·reproaching him.

G3679 V-AAI-3S ὠνείδισεν (1x)
Mk 16:14 ·at·a·meal, and he·reproached *them* for·their lack·

G3679 V-AAS-3P ὀνειδίσωσιν (2x)
Lk 6:22 yeu *from·their·company*, and should·reproach *yeu*,
Mt 5:11 are·yeu whenever *men* should·reproach yeu and

G3680 ὀνειδισμός ônêidismós *n.* (5x)
Roots:G3679 Compare:G2008-1 G1650 G1649 G1426 G3059 xLangEquiv:H2781 xLangAlso:H2617

G3680 N-NPM ὀνειδισμοί (1x)
Rm 15:3 "The reproaches of·the·ones reproaching you fell

G3680 N-ASM ὀνειδισμόν (3x)
Heb 11:26 ·considering the reproach of·the Anointed-One *to·*
Heb 13:13 the arrayed·encampment, bearing his reproach.
1Ti 3:7 ·order·that he·should·not fall into reproach and *into*

G3680 N-DPM ὀνειδισμοῖς (1x)
Heb 10:33 ·spectacle both by·reproaches and tribulations,

G3681 ὄνειδος ônêidôs *n.* (1x)
See:G3679 G3680 G3686 xLangEquiv:H2781 xLangAlso:H2617

G3681 N-ASN ὄνειδος (1x)
Lk 1:25 to·remove my lowly·reproach among men·of·clay†

G3682 Ὀνήσιμος Ônḗsimôs *n/p.* (2x)
Roots:G3685

G3682.2 N/P-ASM Ὀνήσιμον (1x)
Phm 1:10 I·implore you concerning my child Onesimus,

G3682.2 N/P-DSM Ὀνησίμῳ (1x)
Col 4:9 together with·Onesimus, the trustworthy and

Αα Ββ Γγ Δδ Εε Ζζ Ηη Θθ Ιι Κκ Λλ Μμ Νν Ξξ Οο Ππ Ρρ Σσ Ττ Υυ Φφ Χχ Ψψ Ωω

G3683 Ὀνησί•φορος Ônēsíphôrôs *n/p.* (2x)
Roots:G3685 G5411
G3683.2 N/P-GSM Ὀνησιφόρου (2x)
2Ti 1:16 give mercy to·*the*·house of·OnesiPhorus, because
2Ti 4:19 and Aquila, and the household of·OnesiPhorus.
G3684 ὀνικός ônikős *adj.* (2x)
Roots:G3688
G3684.2 A-NSM ὀνικός (2x)
Lk 17:2 ·end for·him that a·donkey-sized millstone be·set
Mt 18:6 ·him that a·donkey-sized millstone should·be·hung
G3685 ὀνίνημι ônínēmi *v.* (1x)
See:G3682
G3685.2 V-2ADO-1S ὀναίμην (1x)
Phm 1:20 brother, may I·myself derive·profit·from you in
G3686 ὄνομα ônôma *n.* (231x)
Compare:G1097 G3685 See:G3687 G2176
xLangEquiv:H8034 A8036
G3686.1 N-NSN ὄνομα (38x)
Jn 1:6 personally·from God. His name *was* John.
Jn 3:1 Pharisees, NicoDemus *was* his name, a·ruler of·the
Jn 18:10 And the slave's name was Malchus.
Lk 1:5 the daughters of·Aaron, and her name *was* EliSabeth.
Lk 1:26 God to a·city of·Galilee whose name *is* Natsareth,
Lk 1:27 ·been·espoused to·a·man whose name *was* Joseph,
Lk 1:27 And the virgin's name *was* Mariam.
Lk 1:49 magnificent·things for·me, and holy *is* his name.
Lk 1:63 he·wrote, saying, "His name is John." And they·
Lk 2:21 the little·child, his name was·called Jesus, the *name*
Lk 2:25 ·of·clay† in JeruSalem, whose name *was* Simeon,
Lk 8:30 "What is your name?" And he·declared, "Legion,"
Lk 8:41 behold, there·came a·man whose name *was* Jairus,
Lk 11:2 in the heavens, your name, let·it·be·made·holy!
Lk 24:13 day to a·village with·the name Emmaus, being·a·
Lk 24:18 the individual whose name *was* CleoPas declared
Ac 3:16 and personally·know. *Jesus'* name and the trust
Ac 4:12 For there·is not·even another name under the heaven
Ac 13:6 a·false·prophet, whose name *was* BarJoshua,
Ac 13:8 (for so his name is·interpreted *from·Arabic*), stood·
Mt 6:9 ·one in the heavens, your name, let·it·be·made·holy!
Mk 5:9 "What *is* your name?" And he·answered, saying,
Mk 5:9 he·answered, saying, "My name *is* Legion, because
Mk 6:14 heard *of·him*, for his name was openly·well·known.
Mk 14:32 to an·open·field of·which the name *is* GethSemane
Rm 2:24 For "the name of·God is·reviled among the
Rm 9:17 and that my name may·be·thoroughly·announced in
2Th 1:12 that the name of·our Lord YeShua Anointed may·
1Ti 6:1 of·all honor, in·order·that the name of·God and the
Rv 2:17 a·brand-new name having·been·written which not·
Rv 6:8 who·is·sitting·down upon it, his name *is* Death, and
Rv 8:11 and the name of·the star is·referred·to·as
Rv 9:11 of·the bottomless·pit. *The* name for·him in·Hebrew
Rv 9:11 he·has *this* name, Apollyon·*(Total·Destroyer)*.
Rv 13:1 ·turbans, and upon its heads a·name of·revilement.
Rv 17:5 upon her forehead *was* a·name having·been·written,
Rv 19:13 ·dipped in·blood, and his name is·called The Word
Rv 22:4 his face, and his name *shall·be* in their foreheads.
G3686.1 N-NPN ὀνόματα (5x)
Lk 10:20 rejoice because yeur names are·already·written in
Mt 10:2 And the names of·the twelve ambassadors are these:
Php 4:3 rest of·my coworkers, the names of·whom *are* in
Rv 13:8 ·prostrate to·it, whose names have·not been·written
Rv 17:8 shall·marvel, whose names have·not been·written in
G3686.1 N-ASN ὄνομα (67x)
Jn 1:12 of·God, to·the·ones trusting upon his name,
Jn 2:23 many trusted in his name, observing his miraculous·
Jn 3:18 he·has·not trusted in the name of·the only·begotten
Jn 10:3 he·calls·forth his·own sheep each·by name and leads
Jn 12:28 Father, glorify your name." Accordingly, there·
Jn 15:21 ·they·do to·yeu on·account·of my name, because
Jn 17:6 "I·made your name apparent to·the men·of·clay†
Jn 17:26 And I·made·known to·them your name, and shall·
Lk 1:13 ·bear you a·son, and you·shall·call his name John.
Lk 1:31 ·and·birth a·son, and you·shall·call his name Jesus.
Lk 6:22 *yeu*, and should·cast·out yeur name as evil,
Lk 21:17 ·be being·hated by all on·account·of my name.
Ac 2:21 who himself·should·call·upon the name of·Yahweh
Ac 8:16 having·been·immersed in the name of·the Lord
Ac 9:14 ·bind all the·ones who·are·calling·upon your name."
Ac 9:15 ·Selection to·bear my name in·the·sight of·Gentiles
Ac 9:21 JeruSalem who·are·calling·upon this name, and·also
Ac 15:17 upon whom my name has·been·surnamed upon
Ac 19:5 *this*, they·were·immersed into the name of·the Lord
Ac 19:13 ·it·upon·themselves to·name the name of·the Lord
Ac 19:17 them all, and the name of·the Lord Jesus was·
Ac 22:16 moral·failures, calling·upon the name of·the Lord.
Ac 26:9 ·things contrary to·the name of·Jesus of·Natsareth.
Heb 1:4 a·more·superb name above·and·beyond theirs.
Heb 2:12 "'I·shall·announce your name to·my brothers. In
Heb 6:10 yeu·have·indicated for his name, already·attending
Mt 1:21 ·call his name YeShua·*(meaning·Yahweh·Saves)*,
Mt 1:23 a·son, and they·shall·call his name ImmanuEl,"
Mt 1:25 And he·called his name YeShua.
Mt 10:22 by all *men* on·account·of my name. But the·one
Mt 10:41 in a·prophet's name shall·receive a·prophet's
Mt 10:41 a·righteous·man's name shall·receive a·righteous·
Mt 10:42 to·drink merely in a·disciple's name, certainly I·say
Mt 18:20 having·been·gathered·together in my name, there
Mt 24:9 ·hated by all the nations on·account·of my name.
Mt 28:19 immersing them in the name of·the Father, and
Mk 3:16 on·Simon, he·laid a·name "Peter·*(a·piece·of·rock)*
Mk 13:13 ·hated by all *men* on·account·of my name. "But
Rm 10:13 "'all who would call·upon the name of·*the*·Lord
Jac 2:7 *that* revile the beautiful name, the·one being·
Php 2:9 and graciously·bestowed on·him a·name, the·one
Php 2:9 on·him a·name, the·one above every name,
1Co 1:2 place who·are·calling·upon the name of·our Lord
1Co 1:13 Or were·yeu·immersed in the name of·Paul?
1Co 1:15 should·declare that I·immersed in my·own name.
2Ti 2:19 the·one naming the name of·Anointed-One, must·
1Jn 2:12 have·been·forgiven yeu on·account·of his name.
1Jn 5:13 to·the·ones trusting in the name of·the Son of·God
1Jn 5:13 in·order·that yeu·may·trust in the name of·the Son
3Jn 1:14 Greet the friends each·by name.
Rv 2:3 ·labored·hard on·account·of my name and have·not
Rv 2:13 and you·securely·hold my name and did·not deny
Rv 3:1 your works, that you·have the name that you·live, yet
Rv 3:5 no, I·shall·not rub·out his name out of·the scroll of·
Rv 3:5 I·shall·explicitly·affirm his name in·the·sight of·my
Rv 3:8 my Redemptive-word, and did·not deny my name.
Rv 3:12 'And I·shall·write upon him the name of·my God,
Rv 3:12 of·my God, and the name of·the CITY of·my God,
Rv 3:12 'And *I·shall·write upon him* my brand-new name.
Rv 11:18 ·ones who·are·reverently·fearing your name, the
Rv 13:6 toward God, to·revile his name, and his Tabernacle,
Rv 13:17 the etching, or the name of·the Daemonic·Beast, or
Rv 14:1 thousand, having the name of·his Father having·
Rv 15:4 and should·glorify your name? Because *you* alone
Rv 16:9 and they·reviled the name of·God— the·one
Rv 19:12 ·turbans, having a·name having·been·written that
Rv 19:16 on his thigh the name having·been·written, KING
G3686.1 N-APN ὀνόματα (5x)
Mk 3:17 of·Jakob, also on·them he·laid a·name: BoanErges,
Rv 3:4 'You·have a·few names even in Sardis which did·not
Rv 11:13 ·killed seven thousand names of·men·of·clay†.
Rv 21:12 the gates, and names having·been·inscribed, which
Rv 21:14 on them *are the* names of·the twelve ambassadors
G3686.1 N-DSN ὀνόματι (64x)
Jn 5:43 have·come in my Father's name, and yeu·do·not
Jn 5:43 another should·come in his·own name, that·man yeu·
Jn 10:25 ·myself do in my Father's name, these·things testify
Jn 12:13 *is* the·one who·is·coming in Yahweh's name," the
Jn 14:13 yeu·should·request in my name, that·thing shall·I·
Jn 14:14 yeu·should·request something in my name, I·myself
Jn 14:26 the Father shall·send in my name, that·one shall·
Jn 15:16 ·request·of the Father in my name, he·may·give *it*
Jn 16:23 request·of the Father in my name, he·shall·give *it*
Jn 16:24 ·did·not request not·even·one·thing in my name.
Jn 16:26 day, yeu·shall·request in my name, and I·do·not
Jn 17:11 guard by your·own name these whom you·have·
Jn 17:12 I·myself was·guarding them in your name. "I·
Jn 20:31 that trusting, yeu·may·have life-above in his name.
Lk 1:59 ·calling him ZacharIas, after the name of·his father.
Lk 1:61 among your kinsfolk that is·called by·this name."
Lk 9:48 ·accept this little·child in my name accepts me. And
Lk 9:49 ·out the demons in your name; and we·forbade him,
Lk 10:17 even the demons are·subject to·us in your name."
Lk 13:35 *is* the·one who·is·coming in *the* name of·Yahweh."
Lk 19:38 the King who·is·coming in *the* name of·Yahweh!'
Lk 21:8 for many shall·come in my name, saying, 'I AM,'
Lk 24:47 to·be·officially·proclaimed in his name to all the
Ac 2:38 be·immersed in the name of·Jesus Anointed for
Ac 3:6 to·you. In the name of·Jesus Anointed of·Natsareth,
Ac 4:7 power, or by what·kind·of name, did yeu·yeurselves
Ac 4:10 that by the name of·Jesus Anointed of·Natsareth,
Ac 4:17 ·longer to·not·even·one man·of·clay† in this name."
Ac 4:18 nor·even to·instruct at·all in the name of·Jesus.
Ac 5:28 to·yeu not to·instruct in this name? And behold,
Ac 5:40 *them* not to·speak in the name of·Jesus, and they·
Ac 9:27 ·with·clarity at Damascus in the name of·Jesus.
Ac 9:29 *Saul* was·speaking in the name of·the Lord Jesus,
Ac 10:48 for·them to·be·immersed in the name of·the Lord.
Ac 15:14 to·take from·among *them* a·People for his name.
Ac 16:18 "I·charge you in the name of·Jesus Anointed to·
Heb 13:15 ·is, a·fruit of·lips giving·affirmation to·his name.
Mt 7:22 ¿!·Did·we·not prophesy in·your name, and in·your
Mt 7:22 in·your name, and in·your name cast·out demons,
Mt 7:22 ·out demons, and in·your name do many miracles?
Mt 12:21 "And in his name, Gentiles shall·place·their·
Mt 18:5 ·accept one such little·child in my name accepts me.
Mt 21:9 *is* the·one who·is·coming in *the* name of·Yahweh!"
Mt 23:39 *is* the·one who·is·coming in *the* name of·Yahweh."
Mt 24:5 For many shall·come in my name, saying, 'I AM
Mk 9:37 little·children such·as·these in my name accepts me,
Mk 9:38 casting·out demons in·your name, one·who does·
Mk 9:39 shall·do a·miracle in my name *that* also shall·be·
Mk 9:41 ·cup of·water to·drink in my name, because yeu·are
Mk 11:9 *is* the·one who·is·coming in *the* name of·Yahweh."
Mk 11:10 the·one that·is·coming in *the* name of·Yahweh.
Mk 13:6 For many shall·come in my name, saying, 'I AM
Mk 16:17 "in my name shall·they·cast·out demons; they·
Rm 15:9 *O·Yahweh*, and shall·make·song to·your name.'"
Jac 5:10 of·the prophets who spoke in·the name of·Yahweh.
Jac 5:14 ·oil·on him with·olive·oil in the name of·the Lord.
Php 2:10 that at the name of·Jesus, every knee should·bow
1Pe 4:14 yeu·are·reproached for *the* name of·Anointed-One,
2Th 3:6 brothers, in our Lord's name, YeShua Anointed, to·
1Co 5:4 "In the name of·our Lord Jesus Anointed, with·yeu
1Co 6:11 ·are·regarded·as·righteous in the name of·the Lord
Eph 5:20 ·*our* God and Father in *the* name of·our Lord Jesus
Col 3:17 *do* all in *the* Lord Jesus' name, giving·thanks to·the
1Jn 3:23 that we·should·already·trust on·the name of·his Son
G3686.1 N-GSN ὀνόματος (17x)
Lk 21:12 kings and governors for·the·cause·of my name.
Ac 3:16 And at the trust of·his name, *this·trust* stabilized
Ac 4:30 wonders to·be·done through the name of·your holy
Ac 5:41 to·be·dishonorably·treated on·behalf of·his name.
Ac 8:12 kingdom of·God and the name of·Jesus Anointed,
Ac 9:16 ·for him to·suffer on·behalf of·my name."
Ac 10:43 pardon of·moral·failures through his name."
Ac 15:26 their souls on·behalf of·the name of·our Lord Jesus
Ac 21:13 at JeruSalem on·behalf of·the name of·the Lord
Mt 19:29 ·of·land, for·the·cause·of my name, shall·receive
Rm 1:5 of·trust among all the Gentiles concerning his name,
1Co 1:10 yeu, brothers, through the name of·our Lord Jesus
Eph 1:21 and dominion, and every name being·named, not
3Jn 1:7 For on·behalf of·the name, they·went·forth, taking
Rv 13:17 of·the Daemonic·Beast, or the number of·his name.
Rv 14:11 ·does anyone receiving the etching of·its name."

Oo

Rv 15:2 *and* out·from·among the number of·its name)—
G3686.1 N-GPN ὀνομάτων (3x)
Ac 1:15 (and it·was a·crowd of·names in·unison *of* about a·
Ac 18:15 it·is an·issue concerning a·word and names, and
Rv 17:3 ·beast, overflowing of·names of·revilement, having
EG3686.1 (2x)
Lk 2:21 was·called Jesus, the *name* being·called·forth by the
Ac 4:10 dead·men, by this *name* does this·man stand·nearby
G3686.2 N-DSN ὀνόματι (14x)
Lk 5:27 ·viewed a·tax·collector, Levi by·name, sitting·down
Lk 23:50 a·man, Joseph by·name, a·counselor inherently·
Ac 5:1 But a·certain man, AnanIas by·name, together with·
Ac 9:10 disciple at Damascus, AnanIas by·name. And the
Ac 9:11 home for a·man·of·Tarsus, Saul by·name. For,
Ac 9:33 man·of·clay†, Aeneas by·name, laying·down upon
Ac 10:1 in Caesarea, Cornelius by·name, a·centurion from·
Ac 12:13 a·servant·girl (Rhoda by·name) came·alongside
Ac 16:1 was there, TimoThy by·name, a·son of·a·certain
Ac 18:24 in Ephesus (Apollos by·name, of·AlexAndria by·
Ac 21:10 prophet came·down from Judea, Agabus by·name.
Ac 27:1 Julius by·name, from·*the*·Revered·Emperor's
Mt 27:32 a·Cyrenian, Simon by·name, *and* they·pressed·
Mk 5:22 of·the directors·of·the·gathering, Jairus by·name.
G3686.3 N-DSN ὀνόματι (16x)
Lk 1:5 priest·that·offers·sacrifices by·the·name·of ZacharIas,
Lk 10:38 woman by·the·name·of Martha hospitably·received
Lk 16:20 helpless·beggar by·the·name·of Lazarus who had·
Lk 19:2 being·called by·the·name·of Zacchaeus·*(meaning*·,
Ac 5:34 a·certain·man, a·Pharisee by·the·name·of GamaliEl,
Ac 8:9 a·certain man by·the·name·of Simon was·previously
Ac 9:12 ·vision a·man by·the·name·of AnanIas entering·in
Ac 9:36 a·certain female·disciple by·the·name·of Tabitha,
Ac 11:28 one from·among them by·the·name·of Agabus,
Ac 16:14 a·woman by·the·name·of Lydia from·*the*·city of·
Ac 17:34 ·Hill, and a·woman by·the·name·of Damaris, and
Ac 18:2 and he·found a·certain Jew by·the·name·of Aquila
Ac 18:7 into a·home of·someone by·the·name·of Justus,
Ac 19:24 For someone by·the·name·of Demetrius, a·
Ac 20:9 young·man by·the·name·of EuTychus was·sitting·
Ac 28:7 of·the island, *a·man* by·the·name·of Poplius who

G3687 ὀνομάζω ônômázō *v.* (14x)
Roots:G3686 See:G2028
G3687.1 V-PAN ὀνομάζειν (1x)
Ac 19:13 took·it·upon·themselves to·name the name of·the
G3687.1 V-PAP-NSM ὀνομάζων (1x)
2Ti 2:19 "Everyone, the·one naming the name of·
G3687.1 V-PPI-3S ὀνομάζεται (2x)
1Co 5:1 ·immorality which is·not·even named among the
Eph 3:15 ·lineage in *the* heavens and upon earth is·named:
G3687.1 V-PPM-3S ὀνομαζέσθω (1x)
Eph 5:3 or greed, must·not·even be·named among yeu, just·
G3687.1 V-PPP-GSN ὀνομαζομένου (1x)
Eph 1:21 and every name being·named, not merely in this
G3687.1 V-PPP-NSM ὀνομαζόμενος (1x)
1Co 5:11 any·man being·named a·brother should·actually·be
G3687.1 V-AAI-3S ὠνόμασεν (2x)
Lk 6:13 twelve of them whom also he·named ambassadors.
Lk 6:14 Simon (whom also he·named Peter), and Andrew his
G3687.1 V-API-3S ὠνομάσθη (1x)
Rm 15:20 not where Anointed-One is·already·named, lest I·
EG3687.1 (4x)
Jn 11:1 Now a·certain·man was sick, *named* Lazarus, from
Jn 11:49 one from·among them, *named* Caiaphas, being *the*
Ac 24:1 and *with* a·certain orator *named* Tertullus, who
Ac 25:19 and concerning some·man *named* Jesus, having·

G3688 ὄνος ônôs *n.* (6x)
Compare:G5268 G2574 G2254-2 See:G3678 G3684 xLangEquiv:H2543
G3688 N-NSM ὄνος (1x)
Lk 14:5 "Which of·yeu shall·have a·donkey or an·ox fallen
G3688 N-ASM ὄνον (1x)
Lk 13:15 his ox or *his* donkey from the feeding·trough, even
G3688 N-ASF ὄνον (3x)
Mt 21:2 yeu·shall·find a·donkey having·been·tied·up, and a·
Mt 21:5 and having·mounted upon a·donkey even *upon* a·
Mt 21:7 brought the donkey and the colt, and they·put their
G3688 N-GSF ὄνου (1x)
Jn 12:15 comes *to·you*, sitting·down upon a·donkey's colt.

G3689 ὄντως ôntōs *adv.* (10x)
Roots:G5607
G3689 ADV ὄντως (10x)
Jn 8:36 should·set yeu free, yeu·shall really be free·men.
Lk 23:47 God, saying, "Really, this man·of·clay† was a·
Lk 24:34 "The Lord really is·awakened and was·gazed·upon
Gal 3:21 ·already·given, the righteousness really would be
Mk 11:32 were·holding John, that he·was really a·prophet.)
2Pe 2:18 the·ones really already·escaping·from the·ones
1Co 14:25 ·God, announcing that God is really among yeu.
1Ti 5:3 Honor widows *that·are* really solitary·widows.
1Ti 5:5 Now the·one *that·is* really a·solitary·widow, and
1Ti 5:16 ·relief to·the·ones *that·are* really solitary·widows.

G3690 ὄξος ôxôs *n.* (7x)
Roots:G3691 Compare:G1098 G3631 xLangAlso:H2558
G3690 N-ASN ὄξος (3x)
Jn 19:30 when Jesus received the wine·vinegar, he·declared,
Lk 23:36 ·alongside *him* and offering wine·vinegar to·him
Mt 27:34 him wine·vinegar to·drink having·been·mixed with
G3690 N-GSN ὄξους (4x)
Jn 19:29 ·set·out a·vessel exceedingly·full of·wine·vinegar.
Jn 19:29 a·sponge with·wine·vinegar and putting·it·on
Mt 27:48 and filling *it* with·wine·vinegar and putting·it·on a·
Mk 15:36 a·sponge of·wine·vinegar and putting·it·on a·reed,

G3691 ὀξύς ôxýs *adj.* (8x)
See:G0188
G3691.1 A-NSF ὀξεῖα (2x)
Rv 1:16 of·his mouth, a·sharp double-edged straight·sword
Rv 19:15 of·his mouth proceeds·forth a·sharp straight·sword,
G3691.1 A-ASF ὀξεῖαν (1x)
Rv 2:12 ·things says the·one having the sharp, double-edged
G3691.1 A-ASN ὀξύ (4x)
Rv 14:14 victor's·crown, and in his hand a·sharp sickle.
Rv 14:17 in the heaven, he also *was* having a·sharp sickle.
Rv 14:18 yell to·the·one having the sharp sickle, saying,
Rv 14:18 "Thrust·in your sharp sickle and collect·for·
G3691.2 A-NPM ὀξεῖς (1x)
Rm 3:15 "Their feet *are* swift to·pour·out blood.

G3692 ὀπή ôpḗ *n.* (2x)
Roots:G3700 Compare:G4693 G4978-1 G5169 G5174-1 xLangAlso:H2356 H5366 H2288
G3692.1 N-GSF ὀπῆς (1x)
Jac 3:11 gush·forth at the same narrow·opening *with·both* the
G3692.2 N-DPF ὀπαῖς (1x)
Heb 11:38 and *in* caves and in·the caverns of·the earth.

G3693 ὄπισ•θεν ópisthên *adv.* (7x)
Roots:G3700 See:G3694
G3693.2 ADV ὄπισθεν (3x)
Lk 8:44 Coming·alongside *him* from·behind, she·laid·hold
Mt 9:20 ·alongside *YeShua* from·behind, she·laid·hold of·the
Mk 5:27 already·coming in the crowd from·behind *him*, she·
G3693.3 ADV ὄπισθεν (2x)
Lk 23:26 the cross on·him, *for·him* to·carry *it* behind Jesus.
Rv 4:6 ·beings overflowing of·eyes forward and behind.
G3693.4 ADV ὄπισθεν (1x)
Rv 5:1 ·inside and on·the·back, having·been·fully·sealed·up
G3693.5 ADV ὄπισθεν (1x)
Mt 15:23 "Dismiss her, because she·yells·out after us."

G3694 ὀπίσω ôpísō *adv.* (36x)
Roots:G3700 See:G3693
G3694.2 ADV ὀπίσω (1x)
Jn 18:6 they·went·off backwards and fell down·on·the·
G3694.3 ADV ὀπίσω (25x)
Jn 1:15 ·one who·is·coming right·behind me has·come·to·be
Jn 1:27 he (the·one who·is·coming right·behind me who has·
Jn 1:30 I·myself declared, 'Right·behind me comes a·man
Jn 12:19 ·thing? See, the world went·off right·behind him."
Lk 7:38 directly·at his feet right·behind *him* while·weeping,
Lk 9:23 If any·man wants to·come right·behind me, he·must·
Lk 14:27 bear his cross and come right·behind me, is·not
Lk 19:14 and they·dispatched a·delegation right·behind him,
Lk 21:8 yeu·should·not traverse right·behind them.
Ac 5:37 a·significant·number·of people right·behind him.
Ac 20:30 to·draw·away the disciples right·behind them.
Mt 3:11 but the·one who·is·coming right·behind me is
Mt 4:19 "Come·here, *fall·in* right·behind me, and I·shall·
Mt 10:38 take his cross and follow right·behind me, he·is not
Mt 16:24 "If any·man wants to·come right·behind me, he·
Mk 1:7 "The·one stronger·than me comes right·behind me,
Mk 1:17 "Come·here, *fall·in* right·behind me! And I·shall·
Mk 1:20 the hired·workers, they·went·off right·behind him.
Mk 8:34 "Whoever wants to·come right·behind me, let·him·
Jud 1:7 even going·off to·the·back·*end* of·different flesh,
2Pe 2:10 but especially the·ones *falling·in* right·behind flesh,
1Ti 5:15 *falling·in* right·behind the Adversary-Accuser.
Rv 1:10 Lord's day and heard right·behind me a·great voice,
Rv 12:15 water as a·flood·water right·behind the woman,
Rv 13:3 *which·fell·in line* right·behind the Daemonic·Beast.
G3694.4 ADV ὀπίσω (7x)
Jn 6:66 disciples went·off to·the·things left·behind, and no·
Jn 20:14 ·turned·around toward the·things left·behind. And
Lk 9:62 *then* looking to·the·things left·behind, is well-suited
Lk 17:31 the field must·not return to·the·things left·behind.
Mt 24:18 return *to·the·things* left·behind to·take·away his
Mk 13:16 ·not return to·the·things left·behind to·take·up his
Php 3:13 the·things left·behind and stretching·myself·toward
G3694.5 ADV ὀπίσω (3x)
Lk 4:8 declared to·him, "Get·yourself·back behind me,
Mt 16:23 ·declared to·Peter, "Get·yourself·back behind me,
Mk 8:33 Peter, saying, "Get·yourself·back behind me,

G3695 ὁπλίζω hôplízō *v.* (1x)
Roots:G3696
G3695 V-AMM-2P ὁπλίσασθε (1x)
1Pe 4:1 yeu·yourselves must·arm·yourselves with·the same

G3696 ὅπλον hôplôn *n.* (6x)
See:G3695
G3696.1 N-APN ὅπλα (2x)
Rm 6:13 *as* instruments of·unrighteousness to·Moral·Failure,
Rm 6:13 members *as* instruments of·righteousness to·God.
G3696.2 N-NPN ὅπλα (1x)
2Co 10:4 For the weapons of·our strategic·warfare *are* not
G3696.2 N-GPN ὅπλων (1x)
Jn 18:3 there with searchlights and torches and weapons.
G3696.4 N-APN ὅπλα (1x)
Rm 13:12 ·ourselves·with the weapons·and·armor of·light.
G3696.4 N-GPN ὅπλων (1x)
2Co 6:7 the weapons·and·armor of·righteousness on·the

G3697 ὁ•ποῖος hôpôîôs *adj.* (5x)
Roots:G3739 G4169 Compare:G3634 See:G5108
G3697.ª A-NSN ὁποῖος (3x)
Ac 26:29 *the* large, to·become such as even·I am, *though*
Jac 1:24 immediately, he·forgot what·sort·of·man he·was.
1Co 3:13 ·and·prove each·man's work for·what·type it·is.
G3697.ª A-NPM ὁποῖοι (1x)
Gal 2:6 *important*— whatever·manner·of·men they once
G3697.ª A-ASF ὁποίαν (1x)
1Th 1:9 us, what·manner of·accessible·entrance we·have to

G3698 ὁ•πό•τε hôpốtê *adv.* (1x)
Roots:G3739 G4218
G3698.2 ADV ὁπότε (1x)
Lk 6:3 that David did that·one·time·when he·was·hungry,

G3699 ὅ•που hôpôu *adv.* (82x)
Roots:G3739 G4225
G3699.1 ADV ὅπου (1x)
Mk 6:10 to·them, "In·whatever·place yeu·should·enter into
G3699.2 ADV ὅπου (14x)
Jn 21:18 were·strolling·about wherever you·were·wanting.
Lk 9:57 I·shall·follow you wherever you·should·go·away."

Lk 17:37 And he·declared to·them, "Wherever the body *is*,
Mt 8:19 I·shall·follow you wherever you·should·go·away."
Mt 24:28 "For wherever the corpse should·be, there the
Mt 26:13 "Certainly I·say to·yeu, wherever this good·news
Mk 6:55 being badly·ill, *to* wherever they·were·hearing,
Mk 6:56 And wherever he·was·traversing, whether into
Mk 9:18 and wherever *that spirit* should·grasp him, he·
Mk 14:9 Certainly I·say to·yeu, wherever this good·news
Mk 14:14 And wherever he·should·enter, yeu·declare to·the
Jac 3:4 by a·very·small rudder, wherever the sudden·
Rv 14:4 following the Lamb wherever he·may·head·on·out.
Rv 17:9 are seven mountains, wherever the woman sits·

G3699.3 ADV ὅπου (66x)

Jn 1:28 across the Jordan *River*, where John was immersing.
Jn 3:8 The breeze blows where it·wants, and you hear the
Jn 4:20 is the place where it·is·mandatory to·fall·prostrate."
Jn 4:46 into Qanah of·Galilee, where he·made the water *into*
Jn 6:23 Tiberias near to·the place where they·ate the bread,
Jn 6:62 of·Clay·Man† ascending to·where he·was previously
Jn 7:34 and shall·not find *me*, and where I AM, *there* yeu·
Jn 7:36 and shall·not find *me*? And where I AM, *there* yeu·
Jn 7:42 the village of·BethLechem, where David was *from*?
Jn 8:21 in yeur moral·failures. Where I·myself head·on·out,
Jn 8:22 Because he·says, 'Where I·myself head·on·out,
Jn 10:40 the Jordan into the place where John was first
Jn 11:30 was in the place where Martha went·and·met him.
Jn 11:32 So as·soon·as Mary came where Jesus was, upon·
Jn 12:1 Jesus came to BethAny where Lazarus was, the·one
Jn 12:26 to·me, let·him·follow me; and where I AM, there
Jn 13:33 to·the Judeans, 'Where I·myself head·on·out, yeu
Jn 13:36 answered him, "Where I·head·on·out, you·are·not
Jn 14:3 ·receive yeu to myself in·order·that where I AM,
Jn 14:4 And yeu·personally·know to·where *it·is that* I·myself
Jn 17:24 that they·also may·be with me where I AM, in·
Jn 18:1 Brook Qidron, where there·was an·enclosed·garden,
Jn 18:20 and in the Sanctuary·Atrium where the Judeans
Jn 19:18 where they·crucified him, and·also two others with
Jn 19:20 title because the place where Jesus was·crucified
Jn 19:41 Now in the place where he·was·crucified, there·was
Jn 20:12 and one alongside the feet, where the body of·Jesus
Jn 20:19 with·the doors having·been·shut where the disciples
Jn 21:18 you, and shall·carry *you* where you·do·not want."
Lk 12:33 treasure in the heavens, where no thief draws·near,
Lk 12:34 "For where yeur treasure is, there also yeur heart
Lk 22:11 is the local·travel·lodge, where I·may·eat the
Ac 17:1 ·came to ThessaloNica where the gathering·place of·
Heb 6:20 where a·forerunner entered on·behalf of·us—
Heb 9:16 For where *there·is* a·last·will·and·covenant, *it·is* a·
Heb 10:18 And, where *there·is* pardon of·these·things,
Mt 6:19 treasures upon the earth, where moth and corrosion
Mt 6:19 corrosion obliterate, and where thieves break·in and
Mt 6:20 treasures in heaven, where neither moth nor
Mt 6:20 nor corrosion obliterate, and where thieves do·not
Mt 6:21 For where yeur treasure is, there also yeur heart
Mt 13:5 fell upon the rocky·places, where it·was·not having
Mt 25:24 man·of·clay†, reaping where you·did·not sow and
Mt 25:26 ·personally·known that I·reap where I·did·not sow
Mt 26:57 the designated·high·priest, where the scribes and
Mt 28:6 See the place where the Lord was·laid·out.
Mk 2:4 crowd, they·pulled·apart the roof where he·was, and
Mk 4:5 fell upon the rocky·ground, where it·was·not having
Mk 4:15 ·by the roadway, where the Redemptive·word is·
Mk 5:40 him, and he·traverses·in where the little·child was
Mk 9:44 where "their worm does·not completely·die, and
Mk 9:46 where "their worm does·not completely·die, and
Mk 9:48 where "their worm completely·does·not die, and
Mk 13:14 the prophet, standing where it·is·not mandatory"
Mk 14:14 is the local·travel·lodge where I·may·eat the
Mk 16:6 See the place where they·laid him!
Rm 15:20 *but* not where Anointed-One is·already·named,
Jac 3:16 For where jealousy and contention *is*, there *is*
1Co 3:3 yeu·are yet fleshly. For where *there·is* among yeu
Col 3:11 where there·is·not therein Greek and Jew,

Rv 2:13 and where you·reside, *even* where the throne of·the
Rv 2:13 closely·among yeu, where the Adversary-Accuser
Rv 11:8 is·called Sodom and Egypt, where also our Lord
Rv 12:6 into the wilderness, where she·has a·place having·
Rv 12:14 into her place, where she·is·nourished there a·
Rv 20:10 ·the Fire and sulfur, where the Daemonic·Beast and

G3699.4 ADV ὅπου (1x)

2Pe 2:11 whereas angels, being greater·in strength and power

G3700 ὀπτάνομαι ôptánômai *v.* (26x)

ὄπτομαι óptômai
[primary middle voice, used in certain tenses]

Compare:G3708 G0991 G1492 G1718 G2014 G2300 G2334 G4648 G5316 See:G3799-1 G3799 G3708

G3700.1 V-FPI-1S ὀφθήσομαι (1x)

Ac 26:16 of·the·things·in·which I·shall·be·made·visible to·,

G3700.1 V-FPI-3S ὀφθήσεται (1x)

Heb 9:28 , he·shall·be·made·visible to·the·ones who·are·

G3700.1 V-API-1S ὤφθην (1x)

Ac 26:16 your feet, for I·was·made·visible to·you for this·

G3700.1 V-API-3S ὤφθη (9x)

Lk 1:11 And there·was·made·visible to·him an·angel of·
Lk 22:43 And there·was·made·visible to·him an·angel from
Ac 7:2 "The God of·Glory was·made·visible to·our father
Ac 7:26 day, he·made·himself·visible to·them as·they·were·
Ac 7:30 an·angel of·Yahweh was·made·visible to·him in
Ac 16:9 a·clear·vision was·made·visible to·Paul through the
Rv 11:19 the Ark of·his covenant was·made·visible in his
Rv 12:1 And a·great sign was·made·visible in the heaven: a·
Rv 12:3 And another sign was·made·visible in the heaven;

G3700.1 V-API-3P ὤφθησαν (2x)

Ac 2:3 tongues as of·fire were·made·visible to·them, and it·
Mt 17:3 Moses and EliJah were·made·visible to·them,

G3700.1 V-APP-GSM ὀφθέντος (1x)

Ac 7:35 of·*the*·angel, the·one being·made·visible to·him in

G3700.1 V-APP-NSM ὀφθείς (1x)

Ac 9:17 Jesus, the·one being·made·visible to·you along the

G3700.1 V-APP-NPM ὀφθέντες (1x)

Lk 9:31 who, upon·being·made·visible in glory, were·

G3700.2 V-PNP-NSM ὀπτανόμενος (1x)

Ac 1:3 ·proofs, while·being·gazed·upon by·them throughout

G3700.2 V-API-3S ὤφθη (8x)

Lk 24:34 really is·awakened and was·gazed·upon by·Simon.
Ac 13:31 *Jesus* who was·gazed·upon over many·more days
Mk 9:4 And they·gazed·upon them, EliJah together with·
1Co 15:5 that he·was·gazed·upon by·Kephas·*(called·Peter)*,
1Co 15:6 he·was·gazed·upon by·upwards·of five·hundred
1Co 15:7 After·that, he·was·gazed·upon by·Jacob, *and* then
1Co 15:8 And last of·all, he·was·gazed·upon by·me·also,
1Ti 3:16 ·as·righteous in Spirit, is·gazed·upon by·angels, is·

G3701 ὀπτασία ôptasía *n.* (4x)

Compare:G3677 G3705 G1798 G1611 See:G3700 xLangAlso:H4758

G3701.1 N-ASF ὀπτασίαν (2x)

Lk 1:22 they·realized that he·has·clearly·seen a·vision in the
Lk 24:23 *that* they·had·clearly·seen a·vision of·angels who

G3701.1 N-APF ὀπτασίας (1x)

2Co 12:1 for I·shall·come to visions and revelations of·*the*·

G3701.1 N-DSF ὀπτασίᾳ (1x)

Ac 26:19 I·did·not become obstinate to·the heavenly vision.

G3702 ὀπτός ôptós *adj.* (1x)

See:G3701-1 xLangAlso:H6748

G3702 A-GSM ὀπτοῦ (1x)

Lk 24:42 And they·handed him a·piece of·a·broiled fish and

G3703 ὀπ•ώρα ôpôra *n.* (1x)

Roots:G3796 G5610

G3703.2 N-NSF ὀπώρα (1x)

Rv 18:14 "And the juicy·ripe·fruit of·the longing of·your

G3704 ὅ•πως hópōs *adv.* (57x)

Roots:G3739 G4459

EG3704. [a] (1x)

Mt 13:28 ·want *us* to·go·off *so·that* we·may·collect them?

G3704.1 ADV ὅπως (5x)

Lk 11:37 him in·such·a·manner·so·that he·should·dine next·
Ac 9:12 on·him in·such·a·manner·so·that he·may·receive·."
Ac 9:17 me in·such·a·manner·so·that you·may·receive·your·
Mt 6:16 faces in·such·a·manner·so·that they·may·be· to·the
Mt 8:17 in·such·a·manner·so·that *the prophecy* may·be·

G3704.2 ADV ὅπως (16x)

Jn 11:57 ·to·*their*·attention, so·that they·may·apprehend him
Lk 16:26 ·firmly·set a·great chasm, so·that the·ones wanting
Lk 16:28 *send him* so·that he·may·thoroughly·testify to·them
Ac 3:19 to·be·rubbed·out, so·that seasons of·refreshing
Ac 9:24 both day and night so·that they·may·eliminate him.
Ac 15:17 so·that the small·remnants of·the men·of·clay†
Ac 20:16 ·directly·by Ephesus, so·that it·should·not happen
Heb 9:15 covenant, so·that with·death already·occurring for
Mt 5:16 before the men·of·clay†, so·that they·may·see yeur
Mt 5:45 so·that yeu·may·become the·Sons of·yeur Father,
Mt 6:4 so·that your merciful·act may·be in private.
Mt 6:5 broad·streets to·pray so·that they·may·be·apparent
Mt 6:18 so·that you·may·not be·appearing to·the men·of·
Mk 5:23 your hands on·her, so·that she·may·be·saved and
Rm 3:4 " So·that you·may·be·regarded·as·righteous in
1Co 1:29 so·that all flesh may·not boast in·the·sight of·him.

G3704.3 ADV ὅπως (31x)

Lk 2:35 that *the* deliberations from·among many hearts
Lk 7:3 asking him to·come that he·may·thoroughly·save his
Lk 10:2 of·the harvest, that he·should·cast·forth workmen
Ac 8:15 concerning them, that they·may·receive Holy Spirit.
Ac 8:24 ·my behalf, that not·even·one of·these·things·which
Ac 9:2 ·to the gatherings, that if·ever he·should·find any
Ac 23:15 ·the regiment·commander that he·should·bring him
Ac 23:20 to·ask·of you that you·should·bring Paul down
Ac 23:23 ·spearmen, that they·should·traverse unto
Ac 24:26 ·be·given to·him by Paul, that he·may·loose him.
Ac 25:3 against *Paul*, that he·may·send·for him *to·walk·up*
Ac 25:26 you, O·King AgrIppa, that, after·the investigation
Heb 2:9 with·glory and honor, that by·the·grace of·God he·
Gal 1:4 ·behalf of·our moral·failures, that he·may·snatch us
Mt 2:8 announce *it* to·me, that upon·coming, I·also may·
Mt 2:23 *·Branch)*, that it·may·be·completely·fulfilled, the·
Mt 6:2 and in the avenues, that they·may·be·glorified by the
Mt 8:34 they·implored *him* that he·should·walk·on from
Mt 9:38 of·the harvest, that he·should·cast·forth workmen
Mt 12:17 that it·may·be·completely·fulfilled, the·thing
Mt 13:35 that it·may·be·completely·fulfilled, the·thing
Mt 23:35 that upon yeu may·come all *the* righteous blood
Mt 26:59 ·testimony against YeShua, that they·may·put him
Rm 9:17 I·fully·awakened you, that I·may·indicate my
Rm 9:17 by you, and that my name may·be·thoroughly·
Jac 5:16 on·behalf of·one·another, that yeu·may·be·healed.
1Pe 2:9 ·possession— that yeu·should·proclaim·forth the
2Th 1:12 that the name of·our Lord YeShua Anointed may·
2Co 8:11 ·further·finish to·do *it*, that exactly·as *there·was*
2Co 8:14 for yeur lacking, that there·may·be equality.
Phm 1:6 *praying* that the fellowship of·your trust may·

G3704.4 ADV ὅπως (4x)

Lk 24:20 And·also specifically·how the chief·priests and our
Mt 12:14 on·specifically·how they·may·completely·destroy
Mt 22:15 consultation on·specifically·how they·should· him
Mk 3:6 on·specifically·how they·should·completely· him.

G3705 ὅραμα hórama *n.* (12x)

Roots:G3708 Compare:G3701 See:G3706 G3707

G3705.2 N-NSN ὅραμα (2x)

Ac 10:17 might·be *meant·by* the clear·vision which he·saw,
Ac 16:9 And a·clear·vision was·made·visible to·Paul

G3705.2 N-ASN ὅραμα (5x)

Ac 7:31 Moses marveled at·the clear·vision, and with·him
Ac 11:5 and in a·trance I·saw a·clear·vision. A·certain vessel
Ac 12:9 but he·was·supposing to·look·upon a·clear·vision.
Ac 16:10 as·soon·as he·saw the clear·vision, immediately
Mt 17:9 "Yeu·should·declare the clear·vision to·no·man,

G3705.2 N-DSN ὁράματι (3x)

Ac 9:10 Lord declared to him in a·clear·vision, "O·AnanIas.

Oo

Ac 9:12 and he·saw in a·clear·vision a·man by·the·name·of
Ac 10:3 He·saw openly in a·clear·vision, about *the* ninth
G3705.2 N-GSN ὁράματος (2x)
Ac 10:19 ·Peter was·cogitating about the clear·vision, the
Ac 18:9 Lord declared to·Paul through a·clear·vision at night

G3706 ὅρασις hốrasis *n.* (4x)
Roots:G3708 See:G3705 G3707
G3706.2 N-APF ὁράσεις (1x)
Ac 2:17 yeur young·men shall·gaze·upon clear·visions, and
G3706.2 N-DSF ὁράσει (1x)
Rv 9:17 I·saw the horses in the clear·vision, and the·ones
G3706.3 N-DSF ὁράσει (2x)
Rv 4:3 sitting·down was in·clear·appearance like a·jasper
Rv 4:3 the throne, in·clear·appearance like an·emerald.

G3707 ὁρατός hôratốs *adj.* (1x)
Roots:G3708 See:G3706
G3707.2 A-NPN ὁρατά (1x)
Col 1:16 the earth, the·ones clearly·visible and the·ones

G3708 ὁράω hôráō *v.* (59x)
Compare:G1492 G1896 G2300 G2334 G3700
See:G3705 G3706 G3707 G4308
G3708.2 V-PAI-1S ὁρῶ (1x)
Ac 8:23 For I·clearly·see you being in a·gall of·bitterness
G3708.2 V-PAI-1P ὁρῶμεν (1x)
Heb 2:8 But now we·do·not·yet clearly·see all things having·
G3708.2 V-PAI-3S ὁρᾷ (1x)
Lk 16:23 in torments, he·clearly·sees AbRaham from a·
G3708.2 V-PAM-2S ὁρᾶ (1x)
Ac 22:26 saying, "Clearly·see what you·are·about to·do,
G3708.2 V-PAM-2P ὁρᾶτε (1x)
Jac 2:24 Now·then yeu·clearly·see that as·a·result of·works,
G3708.2 V-PAP-NSM ὁρῶν (1x)
Heb 11:27 ·endured as one·clearly·seeing the Invisible-One.
G3708.2 V-PAP-NPF ὁρῶσαι (1x)
Lk 23:49 stood at·a·distance, clearly·seeing these·things.
G3708.2 V-PAP-NPM ὁρῶντες (2x)
1Pe 1:8 — in whom, not clearly·seeing at·this·moment but
Rv 18:18 they·were·yelling·out, clearly·seeing the smoke
G3708.2 V-IAI-3P-ATT ἑώρων (1x)
Jn 6:2 because they·were·clearly·seeing his miraculous·signs
G3708.2 V-RAI-1S-ATT ἑώρακα (3x)
Jn 1:34 And·I have·clearly·seen, and have·testified, that this
Jn 8:38 speak that·which I·have·clearly·seen from·beside my
1Co 9:1 Have·I·not·indeed clearly·seen Jesus Anointed our
G3708.2 V-RAI-1P-ATT ἑωράκαμεν (5x)
Jn 3:11 ·know and testify what we·have·clearly·seen, and
Jn 20:25 ·saying to·him, "We·have·clearly·seen the Lord."
1Jn 1:1 ·heard, which we·have·clearly·seen with·our eyes,
1Jn 1:2 is·made·apparent, and we·have·clearly·seen *it*, and
1Jn 1:3 That·which we·have·clearly·seen and have·heard,
G3708.2 V-RAI-2S-ATT ἑώρακας (4x)
Jn 8:57 years·of·age, and have·you·clearly·seen AbRaham?
Jn 9:37 to·him, "Even you·have·clearly·seen him, and it·is
Jn 20:29 "Thomas, because you·have·clearly·seen me, you·
Ac 22:15 ·of·clay† of·what you·have·clearly·seen and heard.
G3708.2 V-RAI-2P-ATT ἑωράκατε (4x)
Jn 5:37 ever·at·any·time, nor have·clearly·seen his shape.
Jn 6:36 to·yeu, also yeu·have·clearly·seen me and do·not
Jn 8:38 that·which yeu·have·clearly·seen from·beside yeur
Jn 14:7 ·on, yeu·do·know him, and have·clearly·seen him."
G3708.2 V-RAI-3S-ATT ἑώρακεν (12x)
Jn 1:18 Not·even·one·man has·clearly·seen God ever·at·any·
Jn 3:32 And what he·has·clearly·seen and heard, that·thing
Jn 6:46 Not that any·man has·clearly·seen the Father, except
Jn 6:46 ·from God; this·one has·clearly·seen the Father.
Jn 14:9 having·clearly·seen me has·clearly·seen the Father;
Jn 20:18 to·the disciples that she·has·clearly·seen the Lord,
Lk 1:22 they·realized that he·has·clearly·seen a·vision in the
Col 2:18 ·which he·has·not clearly·seen, being·puffed·up
1Jn 3:6 Any one morally·failing has·not clearly·seen him,
1Jn 4:20 his brother whom he·has·clearly·seen, in·what·way
1Jn 4:20 ·able to·love God whom he·has·not clearly·seen?
3Jn 1:11 but the·one doing·bad has·not clearly·seen God.
G3708.2 V-RAI-3P-ATT ἑωράκασιν (3x)
Jn 15:24 But now also they·have·clearly·seen and have·hated
Lk 9:36 ·one of·those·things·which they·have·clearly·seen.
Col 2:1 and *for* as·many·as have·not clearly·seen my face in
G3708.2 V-RAN-ATT ἑωρακέναι (1x)
Lk 24:23 also *that* they·had·clearly·seen a·vision of·angels
G3708.2 V-RAP-NSM-ATT ἑωρακώς (2x)
Jn 14:9 The·one having·clearly·seen me has·clearly·seen
Jn 19:35 Now the·one having·clearly·seen *it* has·testified,
G3708.2 V-RAP-NPM-ATT ἑωρακότες (1x)
Jn 4:45 accepted him, having·clearly·seen all·the·things that
G3708.2 V-LAI-3S-ATT ἑωράκει (1x)
Ac 7:44 ·to the particular·pattern which he·had·clearly·seen.
G3708.3 V-PAM-2S ὅρα (5x)
Heb 8:5 Tabernacle: "For clearly·see·to·it," he·replies,
Mt 8:4 to·him, "Clearly·see·to·it *that* you·should·declare
Mk 1:44 to·him, "Clearly·see·to·it *that* you·should·declare
Rv 19:10 he·says to·me, "Clearly·see·to·it *that* you·do·not
Rv 22:9 he·says to·me, "Clearly·see·to·it *that* you·do·not
G3708.3 V-PAM-2P ὁρᾶτε (7x)
Lk 12:15 to them, "Yeu·clearly·see·to·it, and be·vigilant
Mt 9:30 them, saying, "Clearly·see·to·it *that* no·one knows
Mt 16:6 declared to·them, "Clearly·see·to·it also *that* yeu·
Mt 18:10 "Clearly·see·to·it *that* yeu·should·not despise one
Mt 24:6 rumors of·wars. Clearly·see·to·it *that* yeu·are·not
Mk 8:15 saying, "Clearly·see·to·it *that* yeu·look·out for the
1Th 5:15 Clearly·see·to·it *that* no one should·render wrong
G3708.4 V-PAI-1S ὁρῶ (1x)
Mk 8:24 the men·of·clay† as how I·clearly·envision trees,

G3709 ὀργή ôrgḗ *n.* (36x)
Roots:G3713 Compare:G2372 G3950 G3376-2
G1557 G2347 See:G3710 G3711
xLangEquiv:H5678
G3709.3 N-NSF ὀργή (2x)
Jac 1:20 For man's wrath does·not accomplish God's
Eph 4:31 bitterness, and rage, and wrath, and yelling, and
G3709.3 N-ASF ὀργήν (2x)
Jac 1:19 swift to·hear, slow to·speak, *and* slow to wrath.
Col 3:8 must·put·off all·these things: wrath, rage, malice,
G3709.3 N-GSF ὀργῆς (2x)
Mk 3:5 ·at them with wrath, while·being·jointly·grieved over
1Ti 2:8 hands, completely·apart·from wrath and debate.
G3709.4 N-NSF ὀργή (5x)
Jn 3:36 life·above, but·rather the wrath of·God does·remain
Rm 1:18 For God's wrath is·revealed from heaven against all
1Th 2:16 So, the wrath already·anticipated upon them *is* for
Eph 5:6 on·account·of these·things the wrath of·God comes
Col 3:6 on·account·of which·things the wrath of·God comes
G3709.4 N-ASF ὀργήν (5x)
Rm 3:5 unrighteous, the·one bringing·on the wrath?" (I·say
Rm 4:15 For the Torah-Law accomplishes wrath (for where
Rm 9:22 willing to·indicate his wrath and to·make·known
Rm 13:4 of·God, an·avenger *to·execute* wrath upon the·one
Rm 13:5 not merely on·account·of the wrath, but·rather also
G3709.4 N-DSF ὀργῇ (1x)
Rm 12:19 ·rather yeu·must·give place to·the wrath *of·God*,
G3709.4 N-GSF ὀργῆς (4x)
Lk 3:7 ·indication to·yeu to·flee from the impending wrath?
Mt 3:7 ·indication to·yeu to·flee from the impending wrath?
Rm 9:22 vessels of·wrath having·been·completely·formed
Eph 2:3 And we·were by·nature children of·wrath, even as
EG3709.4 (1x)
Rm 1:19 *the wrath is·revealed* on·account·that, the·thing
G3709.5 N-NSF ὀργή (1x)
Rm 2:8 unrighteousness, *he·shall·render* Rage and Wrath,
G3709.5 N-ASF ὀργήν (2x)
Rm 2:5 heart, you·store·up Wrath for·yourself in a·Day of·
1Th 5:9 God did·not place us for Wrath, but·rather for
G3709.5 N-GSF ὀργῆς (1x)
1Th 1:10 who·is·snatching us away·from the coming Wrath.
EG3709.5 (1x)
Rv 16:6 blood to·drink, for they·are deserving *of·Wrath*."
G3709.6 N-GSF ὀργῆς (2x)
Rm 2:5 for·yourself in a·Day of·Wrath and of·*the*·revelation
Rm 5:9 ·so we·shall·be·saved from the Wrath through him.
G3709.7 N-NSF ὀργή (2x)
Lk 21:23 ·need upon the land and WRATH on this people.
Rv 11:18 are·angered, and your WRATH came, and·also the
G3709.7 N-GSF ὀργῆς (2x)
Rv 6:16 throne, and from the WRATH OF·THE LAMB,
Rv 6:17 the GREAT DAY of·his WRATH is·come, and who
G3709.8 N-GSF ὀργῆς (3x)
Rv 14:10 into the cup of·his Wrath; and he·shall·be·
Rv 16:19 ·her the cup of·the wine of·the Rage of·his Wrath.
Rv 19:15 wine of·the Rage and the Wrath of·God Almighty.

G3710 ὀργίζω ôrgízō *v.* (8x)
Roots:G3709 Compare:G4768 See:G3949 G3711
G3710.2 V-PPM-2P ὀργίζεσθε (1x)
Eph 4:26 "'Be·angry, but do·not morally·fail!'" Do·not·let
G3710.2 V-PPP-NSM ὀργιζόμενος (1x)
Mt 5:22 to·yeu that any one being·angry with·his brother for·
G3710.2 V-API-3S ὠργίσθη (3x)
Lk 15:28 "Then he·was·angry and was·not willing to·enter.
Mt 22:7 upon·hearing *this*, the king was·angry, and sending
Rv 12:17 And the Dragon was·angry toward the woman, and
G3710.2 V-API-3P ὠργίσθησαν (1x)
Rv 11:18 And the nations are·angered, and your WRATH
G3710.2 V-APP-NSM ὀργισθείς (2x)
Lk 14:21 to·his lord. Then being·angry, the master·of·the·
Mt 18:34 And being·angry, his lord handed him over to·the

G3711 ὀργίλος ôrgílôs *adj.* (1x)
Roots:G3709 Compare:G2373-1 See:G3710
G3711 A-ASM ὀργίλον (1x)
Tit 1:7 not self-pleasing, not easily·angered, not continually·

G3712 ὀργυιά ôrguiá *n.* (2x)
Roots:G3713
G3712 N-APF ὀργυιάς (2x)
Ac 27:28 they·found *it to·be* twenty fathoms; and after·
Ac 27:28 ·line again, they·found *it to·be* fifteen fathoms.

G3713 ὀρέγομαι ôrégômai *v.* (3x)
Compare:G3735
G3713.2 V-PMI-3S ὀρέγεται (1x)
1Ti 3:1 "If any·man longingly·stretches·himself·toward an·,
G3713.2 V-PMI-3P ὀρέγονται (1x)
Heb 11:16 they·longingly·stretch·themselves·toward a·
G3713.2 V-PMP-NPM ὀρεγόμενοι (1x)
1Ti 6:10 some are·longingly·stretching·themselves·toward.

G3714 ὀρεινός ôrêinốs *adj.* (2x)
Roots:G3735 Compare:G5561 G1015
G3714.2 A-ASF ὀρεινήν (1x)
Lk 1:39 traversed into the mountainous·region with haste,
G3714.2 A-DSF ὀρεινῇ (1x)
Lk 1:65 among the whole mountainous·region of·Judea,

G3715 ὄρεξις ốrêxis *n.* (1x)
Roots:G3713 Compare:G1939
G3715 N-DSF ὀρέξει (1x)
Rm 1:27 are·inflamed in their lust toward one·another;

G3716 ὀρθο•ποδέω ôrthôpôdéō *v.* (1x)
Roots:G3717 G4228
G3716.2 V-PAI-3P ὀρθοποδοῦσιν (1x)
Gal 2:14 I·saw that they·did·not walk·uprightly toward the

G3717 ὀρθός ôrthốs *adj.* (2x)
Roots:G3735 See:G3723
G3717.1 A-NSM ὀρθός (1x)
Ac 14:10 with·a·loud voice, "Stand upright on your feet.
G3717.3 A-APF ὀρθάς (1x)
Heb 12:13 and make level tracks for·yeur feet, lest the lame

G3718 ὀρθο•τομέω ôrthôtôméō *v.* (1x)
Roots:G3717 G5058-2 Compare:G0873 G1266
G1371 See:G5114
G3718.2 V-PAP-ASM ὀρθοτομοῦντα (1x)
2Ti 2:15 workman rightly·dissecting the Redemptive-word of·

G3719 ὀρθρίζω ôrthrízō *v.* (1x)
Roots:G3722 See:G3721
G3719.2 V-IAI-3S ὤρθριζεν (1x)

Lk 21:38 all the people were·rising·early·and·going to him

G3720 ὀρθρινός ôrthrinôs *adj.* (1x)
Roots:G3722 Compare:G4407 G5459 G0395 G0827 See:G3721

G3720.3 A-NSM ὀρθρινός (1x)
Rv 22:16 the star, the·one radiant and brilliantly·dawning."

G3721 ὄρθριος órthriôs *adj.* (1x)
Roots:G3722 Compare:G4404 G4405 G4407 G3798 See:G3719 G3720

G3721.2 A-NPF ὄρθριαι (1x)
Lk 24:22 astonished us, after·coming at·early·sunrise to the

G3722 ὄρθρος órthrôs *n.* (3x)
Compare:G4404 G4405 G4407 G0827 G2246 See:G3720 G3735 G0142

G3722.1 N-ASM ὄρθρον (1x)
Ac 5:21 ·Atrium at the sunrise and were·instructing. Now the

G3722.1 N-GSM ὄρθρου (2x)
Jn 8:2 And with·*the*·sunrise, he·came·directly again into the
Lk 24:1 ·the week, with·*the*·sunrise deep *below·the·horizon*,

G3723 ὀρθῶς ôrthôs *adv.* (4x)
Roots:G3717

G3723.1 ADV ὀρθῶς (3x)
Lk 7:43 And he·declared to·him, "You·judged uprightly."
Lk 10:28 to·him, "You·answered uprightly. Do this, and
Lk 20:21 that you·say and instruct uprightly, and do·not

G3723.2 ADV ὀρθῶς (1x)
Mk 7:35 tongue was·loosed, and he·was·speaking correctly.

G3724 ὁρίζω hôrízō *v.* (8x)
Roots:G3725 Compare:G2309 G4316 See:G0873 G4309

G3724.2 V-PAI-3S ὁρίζει (1x)
Heb 4:7 again he·specifically·determined a·certain day,

G3724.2 V-AAI-3S ὥρισεν (1x)
Ac 17:31 whom he·specifically·determined, after·holding·

G3724.2 V-AAI-3P ὥρισαν (1x)
Ac 11:29 *to·do so*, specifically·determined to·send service to

G3724.2 V-AAP-NSM ὁρίσας (1x)
Ac 17:26 specifically·determining prearranged seasons and

G3724.2 V-APP-GSM ὁρισθέντος (1x)
Rm 1:4 the·one being·specifically·determined *to·be the* Son

G3724.2 V-RPP-ASN ὡρισμένον (1x)
Lk 22:22 ·to the·thing having·been·specifically·determined.

G3724.2 V-RPP-NSM ὡρισμένος (1x)
Ac 10:42 the·one having·been·specifically·determined by

G3724.3 V-RPP-DSF ὡρισμένῃ (1x)
Ac 2:23 ·man (by·the specifically·determined counsel and

G3725 ὅριον hóriôn *n.* (11x)
See:G3724 G3734 xLangAlso:H1366

G3725.2 N-APN ὅρια (3x)
Mt 15:39 into the borders of·Magdala·*(that·is,·the·Tower)*.
Mt 19:1 and came into the borders of·Judea beyond the
Mk 10:1 he·comes into the borders of·Judea through the

G3725.2 N-DPN ὁρίοις (2x)
Mt 2:16 within all of·its *outermost* borders, from two·years·
Mt 4:13 ·the·seashore, within *the* borders of·Zebulun and

G3725.2 N-GPN ὁρίων (6x)
Ac 13:50 and BarNabas and cast them out from their borders.
Mt 8:34 *him* that he·should·walk·on from their borders.
Mt 15:22 a·Kenaanite woman from those borders, *who*,
Mk 5:17 to·implore *Jesus* to·go·away from their borders.
Mk 7:31 going·forth from·among the borders of·Tyre and
Mk 7:31 through *the* midst of·the borders of·DecaPolis.

G3726 ὁρκίζω hôrkízō *v.* (3x)
Roots:G3727 Compare:G1844

G3726.3 V-PAI-1S ὁρκίζω (2x)
Mk 5:7 of·God Most·High? On·oath,·I·charge you by·God,
1Th 5:27 On·oath,·I·charge yeu by·the Lord for·the letter to·

G3726.3 V-PAI-1P ὁρκίζομεν (1x)
Ac 19:13 spirits, saying, "On·oath,·we·charge yeu *by* Jesus

G3727 ὅρκος hórkôs *n.* (11x)
See:G3725 G3728

G3727.3 N-NSM ὅρκος (1x)
Heb 6:16 ·than *themselves*, and the oath for confirmation *is*

G3727.3 N-ASM ὅρκον (2x)
Lk 1:73 an·oath which he·swore to our father AbRaham,
Jac 5:12 nor by·the earth, nor by·any other oath. But yeur

G3727.3 N-APM ὅρκους (3x)
Mt 5:33 ·falsely, but shall·render to·Yahweh your oaths.'"
Mt 14:9 but on·account·of the oath and the·ones reclining·
Mk 6:26 *yet* on·account·of the oath and the·ones reclining·

G3727.3 N-DSM ὅρκῳ (2x)
Ac 2:30 that God swore to·him with·an·oath *that* from·out
Heb 6:17 ·nature of·his counsel, ratified *it* by·an·oath

G3727.3 N-GSM ὅρκου (2x)
Mt 14:7 From·which, with an·oath, he·affirmed to·give her
Mt 26:72 And again he·denied *it* with an·oath, "I·do·not

EG3727.3 (1x)
Heb 7:22 According·to so·vast *an·oath*, YeShua has·become

G3728 ὁρκ•ωμοσία hôrkōmôsía *n.* (4x)
Roots:G3727 G3660

G3728 N-GSF ὁρκωμοσίας (4x)
Heb 7:20 ·*priest, but* not apart·from a·swearing·of·oath.
Heb 7:21 ·become *priests* apart·from a·swearing·of·oath, but
Heb 7:21 this·one with a·swearing·of·oath through the·one
Heb 7:28 but the word of·the swearing·of·oath (the·one after

G3729 ὁρμάω hôrmáō *v.* (5x)
Roots:G3730 See:G0874

G3729.2 V-AAI-3S ὥρμησεν (3x)
Lk 8:33 and the herd impulsively·dashed down the steep·
Mt 8:32 the entire herd of·pigs impulsively·dashed down the
Mk 5:13 and the herd impulsively·dashed down the steep·

G3729.2 V-AAI-3P ὥρμησαν (2x)
Ac 7:57 ·up their ears and impulsively·dashed upon him
Ac 19:29 they·impulsively·dashed with·the·same· into the

G3730 ὁρμή hôrmḗ *n.* (2x)
Compare:G3709 See:G3729 G3731

G3730.2 N-NSF ὁρμή (1x)
Ac 14:5 as·soon·as there·became a·violent·attempt (both

G3730.3 N-NSF ὁρμή (1x)
Jac 3:4 wherever the sudden·impulse of·the·one piloting

G3731 ὅρμημα hórmēma *n.* (1x)
Roots:G3730

G3731.1 N-DSN ὁρμήματι (1x)
Rv 18:21 saying, "In·this·manner with·violence, the Great

G3732 ὄρνεον órnêôn *n.* (3x)
Roots:G3733 Compare:G4071

G3732 N-NPN ὄρνεα (1x)
Rv 19:21 and all the fowls were·stuffed·full from·among

G3732 N-DPN ὀρνέοις (1x)
Rv 19:17 voice, saying to·all the fowls, to·the·ones flying in

G3732 N-GSN ὀρνέου (1x)
Rv 18:2 ·cell of·every impure and intensely·hated fowl.

G3733 ὄρνις órnis *n.* (2x)
Roots:G3735 Compare:G0220 xLangAlso:H8650-1

G3733.2 N-NSM ὄρνις (2x)
Lk 13:34 your children, as a·hen *gathers* her brood under
Mt 23:37 your children as a·hen completely·gathers her

G3734 ὁρο•θεσία hôrôthêsía *n.* (1x)
Roots:G3725 G5087

G3734.2 N-APF ὁροθεσίας (1x)
Ac 17:26 seasons and the bounds of·their residency,

G3735 ὄρος órôs *n.* (67x)
Compare:G1015 G3733 See:G0142 G3714 xLangEquiv:H2022

G3735.1 N-NSN ὄρος (3x)
Lk 3:5 ·be·completely·filled, and every mountain and hill
Rv 6:14 being·rolled·up; and every mountain and island
Rv 8:8 as a·great mountain being·set·ablaze with·fire was·

G3735.1 N-NPN ὄρη (2x)
Rv 16:20 island fled·away, and mountains were·not found.
Rv 17:9 "The seven heads are seven mountains, wherever the

G3735.1 N-ASN ὄρος (15x)
Jn 6:3 Then Jesus went·up upon the mountain. And there, he·
Jn 6:15 he·departed again to a·mountain alone *by* himself.
Lk 4:5 him up upon a·high mountain, showed to·him all the
Lk 6:12 days *that* he·went·forth to the mountain to·pray, and
Lk 9:28 Jakob, he·walked·up upon the mountain to·pray.
Mt 4:8 him up to a·very high mountain and shows him all the
Mt 5:1 he·walked·up upon the mountain. And after·seating
Mt 14:23 he·walked·up upon the mountain in private to·
Mt 15:29 Then walking·up upon the mountain, he·sat·down
Mt 17:1 he·brings them up upon a·high mountain in private.
Mt 28:16 into Galilee to the mountain where YeShua
Mk 3:13 Then *Jesus* walks·up upon the mountain, and he·
Mk 6:46 ·of them, he·went·off to the mountain to·pray.
Mk 9:2 and brings them up upon a·high mountain in private,
Rv 21:10 spirit to a·great and high mountain, and showed me

G3735.1 N-APN ὄρη (6x)
Lk 21:21 in Judea must·flee into the mountains; and the·ones
Mt 18:12 leaving the ninety-nine on the mountains, *and* seek
Mt 24:16 "then the·ones in Judea must·flee to the mountains.
Mk 5:11 there, on·the·side·of the mountains, a·great herd
Mk 13:14 the·ones in Judea must·flee into the mountains.
1Co 13:2 trust, as·such to·relocate mountains, and should·

G3735.1 N-DSN ὄρει (8x)
Jn 4:20 Our fathers fell·prostrate on this mountain; and yeu
Jn 4:21 ·coming when, neither on this mountain, nor·even in
Lk 8:32 of·pigs being·fed on the mountain, and they·were·
Heb 12:18 come·alongside a·mountain being·verified·by·,
Mt 17:20 *does*, yeu·shall·declare to·this mountain, 'Walk·
Mt 21:21 ·yet also·if yeu·should·declare to·this mountain,
Mk 11:23 whoever should·declare to·this mountain, 'Be·
2Pe 1:18 ·being together with·him on the holy mountain.

G3735.1 N-DPN ὄρεσιν (4x)
Lk 23:30 shall·they·begin "to·say to·the mountains, "Fall
Heb 11:38 in barren·wildernesses, and *in* mountains, and *in*
Mk 5:5 and day, he·was on the mountains and in the tombs,
Rv 6:16 Then they·say to·the mountains and to·the solid·

G3735.1 N-GSN ὄρους (5x)
Lk 9:37 with·them coming·down from the mountain, a·large
Heb 12:20 ·finger·on the mountain, it·shall·be·cast·stones·at,
Mt 8:1 upon·walking·down from the mountain, large crowds
Mt 17:9 with·them walking·down off the mountain, YeShua
Mk 9:9 ·down from the mountain, he·thoroughly·charged

G3735.1 N-GPN ὀρέων (1x)
Rv 6:15 caves and among the solid·rocks of·the mountains.

G3735.2 N-NSN ὄρος (1x)
Gal 4:25 For *this* Hagar is Mount Sinai in Arabia, and

G3735.2 N-ASN ὄρος (10x)
Jn 8:1 But Jesus traversed to the Mount of·Olives.
Lk 19:29 and BethAny alongside the mount (the·one being·
Lk 21:37 ·sleeping·out·in·the·open upon the mount, the·one
Lk 22:39 *Jesus* traversed to the Mount of·Olives. And his
Mt 21:1 to BethPhage (toward the Mount of·Olives), then
Mt 26:30 ·a·psalm, they·went·out to the Mount of·Olives.
Mk 11:1 and BethAny, alongside the Mount of·Olives, he·
Mk 13:3 ·down upon the Mount of·Olives directly·opposite
Mk 14:26 ·a·psalm, they·went·out to the Mount of·Olives.
Rv 14:1 a·Lamb standing on the Mount Tsiyon, and with

G3735.2 N-DSN ὄρει (3x)
Ac 7:38 the·one speaking with·him on Mount Sinai, and
Heb 8:5 the·one being·shown to·you on the mount."
Heb 12:22 yeu·have·come·alongside Mount Tsiyon and the·

G3735.2 N-GSN ὄρους (7x)
Lk 4:29 him unto the brow of·the mount on which their city
Lk 19:37 ·now alongside the descent of·the Mount of·Olives,
Ac 1:12 to JeruSalem from *the* mount, the·one being·called
Ac 7:30 ·visible to·him in the wilderness of·Mount Sinai, in
Gal 4:24 One in·fact *is* from Mount Sinai, bearing·children
Mt 5:14 that·is·being·set·out high·upon a·mount is·not able
Mt 24:3 with·him sitting·down upon the Mount of·Olives,

EG3735.2 (2x)
Lk 19:29 mount (the·one being·called *the Mount* of·Olives),
Lk 21:37 mount, the·one being·called *the Mount* of·Olives.

G3736 ὀρύσσω ôryssō *v.* (3x)
xLangAlso:H3738 H5365 H2864

G3736 V-AAI-3S ὤρυξεν (3x)
Mt 21:33 a·hedge around it, and he·dug a·winepress in it

Mt 25:18 receiving the one *talant·of·silver* dug in the earth
Mk 12:1 around *it*, and dug a·vat·for·a·winepress, and built

G3737 ὀρφανός ôrphanós *adj.* (2x)
xLangEquiv:H3490

G3737.3 A-APM ὀρφανούς (2x)
Jn 14:18 I·shall·not leave yeu orphans. I·do·come alongside
Jac 1:27 is this: to·visit *the* orphans and widows in their

G3738 ὀρχέομαι ôrchéômai *v.* (4x)
Compare:G5525
xLangEquiv:H4246 xLangAlso:H4234

G3738 V-ADI-2P ὠρχήσασθε (2x)
Lk 7:32 for·yeu, and yeu·did·not dance; we·bewailed for·
Mt 11:17 for·yeu, and yeu·did·not dance; we·bewailed for·

G3738 V-ADI-3S ὠρχήσατο (1x)
Mt 14:6 the daughter of·HerOdias danced in their midst and

G3738 V-ADP-GSF ὀρχησαμένης (1x)
Mk 6:22 HerOdias entering·in and dancing and satisfying

G3739 ὅς hós *p:r.* (1360x)
ἥ hḗ [feminine]
ὅ hó [neuter]
Roots:G3588 Compare:G3754 G0243 G2087
See:G3757 G3753

G3739.ª P:R-ASM ὅν (1x)
Ac 23:29 I·found him being·called·to·account concerning

G3739.ª P:R-DSF ᾗ (1x)
Lk 24:13 that·same day to a·village with·the name Emmaus,

G3739.1 P:R-NSM ὅς (191x)
Jn 1:27 ·coming right·behind me who has·come·to·be ahead
Jn 1:30 ·behind me comes a·man who has·come·to·be ahead
Jn 3:26 to·him, "Rabbi, he·who was with you beyond the
Jn 4:12 greater·than our father Jacob, who gave us the well?
Jn 4:14 But whoever should·drink from·out·of the water that
Jn 4:29 Come·here! See a·man·of·clay† who declared to·me
Jn 10:29 "My Father, who has·given *them* to·me, is greater·
Jn 18:13 he·was *the* father-in-law of·Caiaphas, who was *the*
Jn 18:16 ·course, the other disciple, who was known to·the
Jn 21:20 *the·one* whom Jesus loved, who also sat·back upon
Lk 2:11 a·Savior is·reproduced·and·birthed who is *the*
Lk 5:18 a·simple·couch who was having·been·paralyzed,
Lk 5:21 "Who is this who speaks revilements·of·God?
Lk 6:16 and Judas IsCariot, who also was a·betrayer.
Lk 6:48 like a·man·of·clay† building a·home, who also dug
Lk 7:2 a·certain centurion's slave, who was dearly·valued
Lk 7:23 And supremely·blessed is·he who should·not be·
Lk 7:27 personal·presence, who shall·fully·prepare your
Lk 8:18 ·with·comprehension, for whoever should·have
Lk 8:18 shall·be·given; and whoever should·not have, from
Lk 8:27 from·out·of the city, who was·having demons for a·
Lk 9:24 For whoever should·want to·save his soul's·desire
Lk 9:24 ·lose it, but whoever should·completely·lose his
Lk 9:26 "For whoever would be·ashamed·of me and my
Lk 9:48 and declared to·them, "Whoever should·accept this
Lk 9:48 name accepts me. And whoever should·accept me
Lk 9:50 "Do·not forbid *him*, for whoever is not against us is
Lk 12:8 "Also I·say to·yeu, anyone who should·affirm me
Lk 12:10 "And all who shall·declare a·word against the Son
Lk 16:1 man·of·clay† who was·retaining an·estate·manager,
Lk 16:20 ·the·name·of Lazarus who had·been·cast alongside
Lk 17:7 or shepherding, who shall·declare immediately *to*·
Lk 17:31 "In that day, whoever shall·be upon the rooftop,
Lk 17:33 "Whoever should·seek to·save his soul's·desire
Lk 17:33 ·lose it; and whoever should·completely·lose his
Lk 18:17 Certainly I·say to·yeu, whoever, if he·should·not
Lk 18:30 no, who should·not receive·in·full many·times·
Lk 23:51 a·city of·the Judeans, who also himself awaited the
Lk 24:19 Jesus of·Natsareth, who became a·man, a·prophet
Ac 1:23 being·called BarTsabas (who was·surnamed Justus)
Ac 2:21 ·be, *that* anyone who himself·should·call·upon the
Ac 3:3 who, after·seeing Peter and John intending to·enter
Ac 5:36 about four·hundred), who *himself* was·eliminated.
Ac 7:18 king rose·up, who had·not personally·known
Ac 7:38 and with·our fathers. *It·is·he* who accepted living
Ac 7:40 *As* for this Moses who brought us out of·*the*·land of·
Ac 7:46 who found grace in·the·sight of·God and requested
Ac 8:27 the queen of·the·Ethiopians, who was over all her
Ac 8:27 all her treasury *and* who had·come to JeruSalem to·
Ac 9:33 eight years, *and* who was having·been·paralyzed.
Ac 10:5 Joppa and send·for Simon, who is·surnamed Peter.
Ac 10:32 summarily·call·for Simon, who is·surnamed Peter,
Ac 10:32 who is·surnamed Peter, who coming·directly,
Ac 10:38 the·same who went·throughout doing·good·deeds
Ac 11:14 who shall·speak to you utterances by which you·
Ac 11:23 who, after·coming·directly and seeing the grace of·
Ac 13:7 who was co-opting the proconsul, Sergius Paulus,
Ac 13:22 according·to my·own heart, who shall·do all my
Ac 13:31 *Jesus* who was·gazed·upon over many·more days
Ac 14:8 mother's womb, who never·at·any·time had·walked
Ac 14:9 Paul speaking, who after·gazing·intently at·him and
Ac 14:15 to the living God, 'who made the heaven, and the
Ac 14:16 Who, in the generations having·long·past, gave·
Ac 16:24 who, upon·having·received such a·charge, cast
Ac 18:27 ·fully·accept *Apollos*, who upon·arriving·publicly,
Ac 21:32 who from·this·same·hour, ran·down to them,
Ac 22:4 "*It·is·I* who persecuted this Way even·unto *their*
Ac 28:7 ·name·of Poplius who was·warmly·welcoming us.
Heb 1:3 by·the utterance of·his power) who, after·making
Heb 5:7 *a·high·priest*, who in the days of·his flesh, *was*
Heb 7:16 (who has·come·to·be *a·priest·that·offers·a·sacrifice*,
Heb 7:27 who does·not have a·necessity each day, just·as the
Heb 8:1 we·do·have such a·High·Priest who is·seated at *the*
Heb 9:14 the blood of·the Anointed-One, who through *the*
Heb 12:2 ·Finisher of·the Trust— who, because of·the joy
Heb 12:16 or profane·person as Esau, who for one full·meal
Mt 5:19 Accordingly, whoever should·break one of·these
Mt 5:19 of·the heavens; but whoever should·do and should·
Mt 5:21 murder," and "whoever should·murder shall·be
Mt 5:22 "Now whoever should·declare to·his brother,
Mt 5:22 ·council·of·Sanhedrin. But whoever should·declare,
Mt 5:31 "It·was·uttered, 'Whoever should·divorce his wife
Mt 5:32 ·myself say to·yeu, that whoever should·divorce his
Mt 5:32 her to·commit·adultery, and whoever should·marry
Mt 10:14 And whoever should·not accept yeu or·should·not·
Mt 10:38 And whoever does·not take his cross and follow
Mt 10:42 And whoever should·give to·one of·these little·
Mt 11:6 And he·is supremely·blessed, whoever *he·is*, if he·
Mt 11:10 personal·presence, who shall·fully·prepare your
Mt 12:32 And whoever should·declare a·word against the
Mt 12:32 ·be·forgiven him, but whoever should·declare
Mt 13:23 and comprehending *it*, who also·then bears·fruit
Mt 13:46 who upon·finding one extremely·valuable pearl,
Mt 15:5 yeu·yeurselves say, 'Whoever should·declare to·his
Mt 16:25 For whoever should·want to·save his soul's·desire
Mt 16:25 ·lose it, and whoever should·completely·lose his
Mt 18:5 And whoever should·accept one such little·child in
Mt 18:6 "But whoever would entice·or·cause·the·moral·
Mt 18:23 to·a·man·of·clay†, a·king, who wanted to·tally·up
Mt 18:28 found one of·his fellow·slaves who was·owing him
Mt 19:9 And I·say to·yeu, that whoever should·divorce his
Mt 19:29 And everyone who left homes or brothers or sisters
Mt 20:26 among yeu, but·rather whoever should·want to·
Mt 20:27 and whoever should·want to·be foremost among
Mt 23:16 the·ones saying, 'Whoever should·swear "by the
Mt 23:16 it·is nothing·at·all, but whoever should·swear
Mt 23:18 "And·also *yeu·say*, 'Whoever should·swear by the
Mt 23:18 it·is nothing·at·all, but whoever should·swear by
Mt 27:57 by·the·name·of Joseph, who also himself
Mk 1:2 personal·presence, who shall·fully·prepare your way
Mk 3:19 and Judas IsCariot, who also handed him over.
Mk 3:29 But whoever should·revile against the Holy Spirit
Mk 3:35 For whoever should·do the will of·God, this·one is
Mk 4:25 "For whoever should·maturely·utilize·what·he·has,
Mk 4:25 and whoever does·not maturely·utilize·what·he·has,
Mk 5:3 who was·having his residence among the chamber·
Mk 8:35 For whoever should·want to·save his soul's·desire
Mk 8:35 ·lose it, but whoever should·completely·lose his
Mk 8:38 "For whoever would be·ashamed·of me and of·my
Mk 9:37 "Whoever should·accept one of·the little·children
Mk 9:37 name accepts me, and whoever should·accept me,
Mk 9:38 demons in·your name, one·who does·not follow us,
Mk 9:39 for there·is not·even·one who shall·do a·miracle in
Mk 9:40 For whoever is not against yeu is on·behalf of·yeu.
Mk 9:41 For whoever should·give yeu a·cup of·water to·
Mk 9:42 "But whoever would entice·or·cause·the·moral·
Mk 10:11 he·says to·them, "Whoever should·divorce his
Mk 10:15 Certainly I·say to·yeu, whoever, if he·should·not
Mk 10:43 among yeu, but·rather whoever should·want to·
Mk 10:44 And whoever of·yeu should·want to·become
Mk 11:23 certainly I·say to·yeu that whoever should·declare
Mk 15:43 a·dignified counselor who also himself was
Rm 1:25 the·one creating *it* (*the·one* who is blessed into the
Rm 2:6 who·himself "'shall·render to·each·man according·
Rm 2:23 You who boast in Torah-Law, do·you·dishonor
Rm 3:30 since·indeed *it·is* one God who, *from·among both*,
Rm 4:16 birthed·from·out·of·AbRaham's trust, who is father
Rm 4:25 who was·handed·over on·account·of our trespasses,
Rm 5:14 resemblance of·Adam's violation, who is a·figure
Rm 8:34 rather also, being·awakened, who is even at *the*
Rm 8:34 right·hand of·God, who also makes·intercession
Rm 10:13 For "'all who would call·upon the name of·*the*·
Rm 16:5 my well-beloved Epaenetus, who is a·firstfruit of·
Jac 4:4 Accordingly, whoever would be·definitely·willing
Php 2:6 who, subsisting in *the* fundamental·nature of·God,
Php 3:21 who shall·transform the body of·our humble·estate
1Pe 2:22 "Who did·not commit moral·failure, neither was
1Pe 2:23 who, being·defamed, was·not defaming·in·reply;
1Pe 2:24 who himself carried·up our moral·failures in his·
1Pe 3:22 who, traversing into heaven, is at *the* right·hand of·
2Pe 2:15 *the son* of·Beor who loved a·payment·of·service
1Th 5:24 *is* the·one calling yeu forth, who also shall·do *it*.
2Th 3:3 is the Lord, who shall·firmly·establish yeu and
Tit 2:14 who gave himself on·our behalf in·order·that 'he·
1Co 1:8 who also shall·confirm yeu unto *the* end, *being* not·
1Co 1:30 in Anointed-One Jesus, who is·made to·us wisdom
1Co 4:5 the Lord should·come, who also shall·illuminate the
1Co 4:17 I·sent to·yeu TimoThy, who is my beloved child,
1Co 4:17 in *the* Lord, who shall·cause yeu to·recall·to·
1Co 7:37 *the·father* who stands immovably·steadfast in the
1Co 10:13 But God *is* trustworthy, who shall·not let yeu to·
1Co 11:27 As·such, whoever should·eat this bread or
1Co 15:9 the least of·the ambassadors, who am not fit to·be·
2Co 1:10 *It·is* he·who already·snatched us from·out·of·so·
2Co 3:6 who also made us sufficiently·qualified attendants
2Co 4:4 good·news of·the Anointed-One— who is 'God's
2Co 4:6 out of·darkness, who did·radiate·brightly in our
2Co 10:1 of·Anointed-One (*I*, who in personal·presence *am*
2Co 13:3 speaking in me, who is·not weak toward yeu, but·
Eph 1:14 who is the earnest·deposit of·our inheritance for
Eph 4:15 ·grow·up *in* all things in him who is the head,
Col 1:7 our dear fellow·slave, who is a·trustworthy
Col 1:13 *It·is* he·who has·already·snatched us from·out·of·
Col 1:15 *It·is the Son* who is *the* derived·image of·the
Col 1:18 ; *it·is Anointed·One himself* who is *the* beginning,
Col 2:10 having·been·completely·fulfilled *in him*, who is the
Col 4:9 and beloved brother, who is from·among yeu.
1Ti 2:4 who wants all men·of·clay† to·be·saved and to·come
1Ti 4:10 upon the·living God, who is *the* Savior of·all men·
1Jn 2:5 But whoever should·observantly·keep his
1Jn 3:17 But whoever should·have the world's livelihood,
1Jn 4:6 God hears us. Whoever is not birthed·from·out·of·
1Jn 4:15 Whoever should·affirm that Jesus is the Son of·God
Rv 1:2 who testified·to the Redemptive-word of·God, and *to*
Rv 2:8 First and the Last, who became dead and·yet lived:
Rv 2:13 trustworthy martyr, who was·killed closely·among
Rv 2:14 instruction of·BalaAm, who was·instructing with
Rv 9:14 saying to·the sixth angel who was·holding the
Rv 10:6 into the ages of·ages ('who created the heaven, and
Rv 12:5 a·son, a·male who imminently·intends to·shepherd
Rv 20:2 Dragon, the original Serpent, who is Slanderer and

G3739.1 P:R-NSF ἥ (3x)

Lk 2:37 for·about eighty·four years, who did·not withdraw
Lk 10:39 had a·sister called Mary, who, sitting·down·near at
Ac 9:36 ·name·of Tabitha, who (by·thorough·translation

G3739.1 P:R-NSN ὅ (2x)

Jn 6:9 There·is a little·boy here, who has five barley loaves·
Jn 15:26 of·Truth, who proceeds·forth personally·from the

G3739.1 P:R-NPM οἵ (25x)

Jn 1:13 who are·born, not from·out of·blood, nor from·out
Lk 5:10 the·Sons of·Zebedee, who were partners with·
Lk 5:17 ·Torah-Law sitting·down, who were having·come
Lk 6:17 ·coast of·Tyre and Tsidon, who came to·hear him
Lk 8:13 they·should·hear, *are those* who with joy accept the
Lk 8:13 yet these have no root, who trust just·for a·season,
Lk 9:27 some of·the·ones standing here, who no, shall·not
Lk 9:31 who, upon·being·made·visible in glory, were·
Lk 10:30 and surrounded,·he·fell·among robbers, who also,
Lk 13:30 "And behold, there·are last who shall·be first, and
Lk 13:30 shall·be first, and there·are first who shall·be last."
Lk 17:12 him ten leprous men who stood·still from·afar,
Lk 20:47 who devour the homes of·the widows, and pray
Lk 24:23 ·had·clearly·seen a·vision of·angels who say *that*
Ac 1:11 who also declared, "Yeu·men of·Galilee, why·do
Heb 11:33 who through trust strenuously·subdued kingdoms,
Mk 4:16 among the rocky·places: ones·who, whenever they·
Rm 16:7 among the ambassadors, who also have·come·to·be
Jac 5:10 the long-suffering of·the prophets who spoke in·the
1Pe 2:8 ' *It·is* they·who presently·stumble at·the
1Pe 4:5 they·who shall·give·forth an·account to·the·one
3Jn 1:6 who already·testified of·your love in·the·sight of·a·
Rv 8:2 I·saw the seven angels who stand in·the·sight of·God;
Rv 9:20 the rest of·the men·of·clay† who were·not killed by
Rv 14:4 These are·they who are·not tarnished with women,

G3739.1 P:R-NPF αἵ (4x)

Lk 8:2 women who were having·been·both·relieved·and·
Lk 23:27 ·also of·women, who also were·vividly·lamenting
Lk 24:10 together with·them, who were·saying these·things
Mk 15:41 (women·who also, when he·was in Galilee, were·

G3739.1 P:R-NPN ἅ (1x)

Rv 1:4 also from the seven Spirits who are in·the·sight of·his

G3739.1 P:R-ASM ὅν (113x)

Jn 1:15 saying, "This was·he of·whom I·declared, 'The·one
Jn 1:26 *in·the* midst of·yeu, whom yeu·yeurselves do·not
Jn 1:33 declared to·me, 'Upon whom you·should·see the
Jn 1:45 to·him, "We·have·found whom Moses wrote *about*
Jn 3:34 For he·whom God dispatched speaks the utterances
Jn 4:18 husbands, and now, he·whom you·have is not your
Jn 5:38 in yeu, because the·same·one whom he·dispatched,
Jn 5:45 Moses, in whom yeu·yeurselves have·placed·yeur·
Jn 6:29 yeu·should·trust in that·one whom he·dispatched."
Jn 7:25 "Is this not he·whom they·seek to·kill?
Jn 7:28 me is true, whom yeu·yeurselves do·not personally·
Jn 8:54 the·one glorifying me; of·whom yeu·yeurselves say
Jn 9:19 "Is this yeur son, who yeu say was·born blind?
Jn 10:36 "*yet* whom the Father made·holy and dispatched
Jn 11:3 "Lord, see, he·whom you·are·fond·of is·sick."
Jn 12:1 ·one having·died, whom he·awakened from·among
Jn 12:9 ·see Lazarus also, whom he·awakened from·among
Jn 13:23 bosom was one of·his disciples whom Jesus loved.
Jn 15:26 should·come, whom I·myself shall·send to·yeu
Jn 17:3 God, and Jesus Anointed, whom you·dispatched.
Jn 19:26 and the disciple standing·nearby whom he·loved,
Jn 19:37 "'They·shall·gaze·upon him·whom they·pierced.'"
Jn 20:2 and to the other disciple whom Jesus was·fond·of,
Jn 21:7 In·due·course, that disciple whom Jesus loved says
Jn 21:20 disciple following *them* (*the·one* whom Jesus loved,
Lk 6:14 Simon (whom also he·named Peter), and Andrew his
Lk 12:42 and prudent estate·manager, whom his lord shall·
Lk 12:43 Supremely·blessed *is* that slave, whom his lord,
Lk 20:18 ·to·pieces; but upon whomever it·should·fall, it·
Lk 23:25 ·of insurrection and murder, whom they·requested.
Ac 2:24 whom God raised·up, loosing the pangs of·Death,
Ac 2:36 made this same Jesus, whom yeu crucified, both
Ac 3:2 was·lifted·and·carried, whom they·were·laying each
Ac 3:13 ·boy, Jesus, whom yeu·yeurselves handed·over,
Ac 3:15 the Initiator of·the life-above, whom God awakened
Ac 3:16 *this·trust* stabilized this·man whom yeu·observe and
Ac 3:21 Whom in·fact it·is·mandatory·for heaven to·accept
Ac 4:10 ·Jesus Anointed of·Natsareth, whom yeu crucified,
Ac 4:10 whom yeu crucified, whom God awakened from·
Ac 4:22 forty years·of·age, on whom this miraculous·sign
Ac 4:27 your holy servant·boy Jesus whom you·anointed,
Ac 5:30 Jesus, whom yeu·yeurselves abusively·manhandled,
Ac 7:35 "This Moses whom they·renounced, declaring,
Ac 9:5 "It·is·I Myself, Jesus, whom you·yourself persecute.
Ac 10:21 "Behold, it·is·I myself whom yeu·seek. What *is*
Ac 10:39 and in JeruSalem— whom they·executed *by*
Ac 13:37 But he·whom God awakened did·not see decay.
Ac 14:23 ·of them to·the Lord, in whom they·had·trusted.
Ac 17:3 "This Jesus (whom I·myself fully·proclaim to·yeu)
Ac 17:23 *the·one to·*whom yeu·show·devout·reverence
Ac 19:13 yeu *by* Jesus whom Paul officially·proclaims."
Ac 21:29 in the City, whom they·were·assuming that Paul
Ac 22:8 Jesus of·Natsareth, whom you·yourself persecute.'
Ac 24:6 ·Courtyard, whom also we·took·secure·hold·of and
Ac 25:19 Jesus, having·died, whom Paul was·professing to·
Ac 26:15 ·is·I Myself, Jesus, whom you·yourself persecute.
Ac 26:26 concerning these·things, to whom also I·speak,
Ac 28:4 a·murderer, whom, after·being·thoroughly·saved
Ac 28:8 Paul entered·in alongside him, and after·praying *and*
Heb 1:2 last days by *his* Son, whom he·placed *as* heir of·all·
Heb 2:10 *Father God* (on·account·of whom all·things *exist*
Heb 4:13 to·his eyes, to whom our reckoning *is·due*.
Heb 7:13 *priest*, concerning whom these·things are·said,
Heb 11:18 to whom it·was·spoken, "'In YiTsaq, a·Seed
Heb 12:6 For whom Yahweh loves, he·correctively·
Heb 12:6 he·whips every son whom he·personally·accepts.'"
Heb 12:7 sons, for what son is·he whom a·father does·not
Mt 7:9 ·of·clay† is·there from·among yeu, who if his son
Mt 12:18 Behold my servant·boy, whom I·decidedly·chose,
Mt 12:18 my beloved, in whom my soul takes·delight.
Mt 21:35 In·fact, *there·was one* whom they·thrashed, and
Mt 21:35 they·thrashed, and *one* whom they·killed, and *one*
Mt 21:35 they·killed, and *one* whom they·cast·stones·at.
Mt 21:44 ·dashed·to·pieces, but on whomever it·should·fall,
Mt 23:35 of·BerekYah, whom yeu·murdered between the
Mt 24:45 trustworthy and prudent slave whom his lord fully·
Mt 24:46 Supremely·blessed *is* that slave, whom his lord,
Mt 26:48 a·sign, saying, "Whomever I·should·kiss, that·is
Mt 27:9 ·one having·been·appraised, who was·appraised by
Mt 27:15 a chained·prisoner, whomever they·were·wanting.
Mk 6:16 This is John, whom I·myself beheaded. He·himself
Mk 14:44 ·signal, saying, "Whomever I·should·kiss, it·is
Mk 14:71 ·know this man·of·clay† to·whom yeu·refer."
Mk 15:12 I·should·do *to·the·one* whom yeu·refer·to·as King
Rm 3:25 whom God personally·determined *to·be* an·atoning·
Rm 9:15 '" I·shall·show·gracious·mercy on·whom I·would
Rm 9:15 and I·shall·compassionately·show·pity on·whom I·
Rm 9:18 Accordingly, on·whom he·determines, he·shows·
Rm 9:18 he·shows·mercy, and on·whom he·determines,
Rm 10:14 ·they·call·upon *him* in whom they·did·not trust?
Php 3:8 on·account·of whom I·suffered·the·damage·and·loss
1Pe 1:8 whom not having·seen, yeu·love— in whom, not
1Pe 1:8 yeu·love— in whom, not clearly·seeing at·this·
1Pe 2:4 *It·is·he* to whom yeu·are·coming·alongside, the·
2Pe 1:17 my beloved Son, in whom I·myself take·delight."
1Th 1:10 of·the heavens, whom he·awakened from·among
2Th 2:8 the Lawless·One shall·be·revealed, whom the Lord
1Co 8:11 ·perish, on·account·of whom Anointed-One died?
1Co 15:15 the Anointed-One, whom he·did·not awaken, if·
2Co 1:10 in whom we·have·placed·our·expectation that
2Co 8:22 brother, whom we·tested·and·proved many·times
2Co 10:18 is verifiably·approved, but·rather whom the Lord
2Co 11:4 whom we·did·not already·officially·proclaim, or
Eph 6:22 whom I·sent to yeu for this very·purpose, that yeu·
Col 1:28 whom we·ourselves fully·proclaim, admonishing
Col 4:8 whom I·sent to yeu for this same purpose, in·order·
Phm 1:10 my child Onesimus, whom I·begot in my bonds.
Phm 1:12 whom I·sent·back *to·you*. So you·yourself
Phm 1:13 whom I·myself was·definitely·willing to·fully·
2Ti 4:15 of·whom also you·yourself must·be·vigilant, for
1Jn 4:20 not loving his brother whom he·has·clearly·seen,
1Jn 4:20 ·he·able to·love God whom he·has·not clearly·seen
3Jn 1:1 ·the well-beloved Gaius, whom I·myself do·love in

G3739.1 P:R-ASF ἥν (4x)

Lk 13:16 of·AbRaham, whom the Adversary-Accuser bound,
Ac 19:27 is·about to·be·demolished, whom all Asia and The
1Ti 6:15 who in·his·own seasons shall·show *he·is* the
Rv 17:18 "And the woman whom you·saw is the Great City,

G3739.1 P:R-ASN ὅ (6x)

Jn 4:22 *directly·before* whom yeu·do·not personally·know.
Jn 4:22 *directly·before* whom we·ourselves fall·prostrate,
Jn 14:17 the Spirit of·Truth, whom the world is·not able to·
Jn 14:26 *who·is* the Holy Spirit, whom the Father shall·send
Jn 17:2 eternal life-above to all whom you·have·given to·him.
Ac 5:32 ·also *is* the Holy Spirit, whom God gave to·the·ones

G3739.1 P:R-APM οὕς (36x)

Jn 5:21 ·manner the Son gives·life-above·to whom he·wants.
Jn 10:35 them gods pertaining·to whom the Holy-word of·
Jn 13:18 yeu all. I·myself personally·know whom I·selected,
Jn 17:6 to·the·men·of·clay† whom you·have·given to·me
Jn 17:11 your·own name these whom you·have·given to·me,
Jn 17:24 "Father, those·whom you·have·given to·me, I·want
Jn 18:9 "From·among them whom you·have·given to·me, I·
Lk 6:13 was·selecting twelve of them whom also he·named
Lk 12:37 ·blessed *are* those slaves, whom the lord, upon·
Lk 13:4 "Or those eighteen, upon whom the tower in Siloam
Ac 1:2 Holy Spirit to·the ambassadors whom he·selected;
Ac 5:25 "Behold, the men whom yeu·placed in the prison·
Ac 6:3 and wisdom, whom we·shall·fully·establish over this
Ac 6:6 men·whom they·set in·the·sight of·the ambassadors,
Ac 15:17 all the Gentiles, upon whom my name has·been·
Ac 17:7 whom Jason has·hospitably·received, and all these·
Ac 24:19 of·whom it·is·necessary *for·them* to·be·here before
Ac 25:16 To whom I·answered, 'It·is not *the* manner of·the·
Ac 26:17 the Gentiles— 'to whom now I·dispatch you,
Heb 6:7 for·those on·account·of whom also it·is·cultivated,
Gal 4:19 for·whom I·experience·birthing·pain again even·
Mk 3:13 and he·summons those·whom he was·wanting,
Mk 13:20 ·account·of the Selected-Ones whom he·selected,
Rm 8:29 Because whom he·did·foreknow, also he·did·
Rm 8:30 Now these·whom he·predetermined, these also he·
Rm 8:30 also he·called·forth; and whom he·called·forth,
Rm 8:30 ·as·righteous; and whom he·regarded·as·righteous,
Rm 9:24 even us, whom he·called·forth— not from·among
Php 3:18 many stroll·about, of·whom I·was·saying to·yeu
2Pe 2:2 *ways* to·total·destruction, on·account·of whom, the
Tit 1:11 of·whom it·is·mandatory·to·silence·mouths. Such·
1Co 10:11 ·for our admonition, for whom the ends of·the
1Co 16:3 whomever yeu·should·verifiably·approve through
1Ti 1:20 and AlexAnder, whom I·handed·over to·the
2Jn 1:1 and her children— whom I·myself do·love in truth,
3Jn 1:6 — whom *if* sending·onward·on·their·journey, as·is·

G3739.1 P:R-DSM ᾧ (58x)

Jn 1:47 Truly an·Israelite in whom there·is no guile!"
Jn 3:26 the Jordan, to·whom you·yourself have·testified, see
Jn 13:26 "It·is that·man to·whom I·shall·hand the morsel,
Lk 1:27 having·been·espoused to·a·man whose name *was*
Lk 2:25 ·was·a·man·of·clay† in JeruSalem, whose name *was*
Lk 4:6 to·me, and I·do·give it to·whomever I·should·want.
Lk 7:4 worthy for·whom this shall·be·personally·furnished,
Lk 7:43 that *it·is the·one* to·whom he·graciously·forgave the
Lk 7:47 "But to·whom little is·forgiven, *the same* loves little.
Lk 8:41 behold, there·came a·man whose name *was* Jairus,
Lk 10:22 the Son, and *he* to·whomever the Son should·
Lk 12:48 "So to·anyone to·whom much is·given, personally·
Lk 12:48 and to·whom *others* place·the·direct·care·of much
Lk 24:18 And answering, the individual whose name *was*
Ac 5:36 himself to·be someone (to·whom a·number of·men
Ac 7:7 And the nation to·whom they·should·be·enslaved, I·

Ac 7:39 *the·one* to·whom our fathers did·not want to·become
Ac 8:19 authority, in·order·that on·whomever I·should·lay
Ac 10:6 ·man, Simon a·tanner, whose home is directly·by
Ac 13:6 Jewish occultist, a·false·prophet, whose name *was*
Ac 13:22 to·them David as king, for·whom also testifying,
Ac 17:31 ' by *that* man whom he·specifically·determined,
Ac 19:16 them, the man·of·clay†, whom the evil spirit was
Ac 21:16 ·early disciple, with·whom we·should·be·guests.
Ac 27:23 ·him·whose I·am and to·whom I·ritually·minister,
Heb 7:2 to·whom also AbRaham distributed a·tenth *part*
Heb 7:4 what·stature this·man *was*, to·whom even the
Heb 13:21 YeShua Anointed— to·whom *be* the glory to the
Gal 1:5 to·whom *be* the glory to the ages of·ages.
Gal 3:19 the Seed should·come for·whom *the inheritance*
Mt 3:17 "This is my beloved Son, in whom I·take·delight."
Mt 11:27 except the Son, and to·whomever the Son should·
Mt 17:5 my beloved Son, in whom I·take·delight. Listen·to
Mk 1:11 are my beloved Son, in whom I·take·delight."
Rm 1:9 is my witness, to·whom I·ritually·minister in my
Rm 4:6 of·the man·of·clay† to·whom God reckons
Rm 4:8 Supremely·blessed *is* a·man to·whom Yahweh, no,
Rm 16:27 to·*the*·only wise God, to·him *be* the glory through
Jac 1:17 Father of·lights— with whom there·is·not therein
1Pe 4:11 through YeShua Anointed, to·whom is the glory
1Pe 5:9 whom yeu·must·stand·up·against, solid in·the trust,
2Pe 1:9 For in·whom these *qualities* are·not present, he·is
1Co 7:39 she·is free to·be·married to·whomever she·wants,
2Co 2:10 For·whom yeu·graciously·forgive anything, I·
2Co 2:10 anything (for·whom I·have·graciously·forgiven *it*),
Eph 1:7 in whom we·have the ransom·in·full through his
Eph 1:11 In whom also we·are·assigned·an·allotted·heritage
Eph 1:13 in whom yeu also *already·placed·yeur·expectation*,
Eph 1:13 of·yeur Salvation— in whom also, after·trusting,
Eph 2:21 in whom the entire structure, being·fitly·framed·
Eph 2:22 in whom yeu also are·built·together for a·residence
Eph 3:12 in whom we·have the freeness·of·speech and the
Col 1:14 in whom we·have the ransom·in·full through his
Col 2:11 in whom also yeu·are·already·circumcised with·a·
1Ti 6:16 men·of·clay† to·see), to·whom *be* honor and might
2Ti 1:3 gratitude to·God (to·whom I·ritually·minister from
2Ti 1:12 ashamed, for I·have·seen in·whom I·have·trusted,
2Ti 4:18 into his heavenly kingdom, to·whom *be* glory into

G3739.1 P:R-DSF ᾗ (1x)

Lk 1:26 by God to a·city of·Galilee whose name *is* Natsareth

G3739.1 P:R-DSN ᾧ (4x)

Rm 6:16 that yeu·are slaves to·whom yeu·present yeurselves
Rm 6:16 *Yeu·are slaves* to·whom yeu·listen·and·obey,
Eph 4:30 by whom yeu·are·already·officially·sealed to *the*
Col 2:3 in whom are hidden·away all the treasures of·

G3739.1 P:R-DPM οἷς (23x)

Lk 19:15 to·be·hailed to·him (*each·one* to·whom he·gave the
Ac 1:3 to·whom also he·established·proof·of himself being·
Ac 15:24 to·whom we·did·not thoroughly·charge *such*·
Ac 17:34 to·him, trusted, among whom also *was* Dionysius,
Ac 20:25 all, among whom I·went·throughout officially·
Ac 28:23 to·whom he·was·explaining·himself, while·
Gal 2:5 to·them, not·even just·for an·hour, did·we·yield to·
Gal 3:1 by·the truth, *before* whose very·own eyes YeShua
Mt 19:11 but·rather those·to·whom it·has·been·given.
Mt 20:23 *to·them* for·whom it·has·been·made·ready by my
Mk 10:40 ·*given to·them* for·whom it·has·been·made·ready."
Rm 4:24 ·account·of us, to·whom it·is·about·to·be·reckoned
Rm 15:21 ·written, "To·whom it·is·not·reported·in·detail
Rm 16:4 on·behalf·of my soul, for·whom not only I·myself
Jud 1:13 stars— for·whom have·been·reserved the deep·
Php 2:15 generation, among whom yeu·are·apparent as
2Pe 2:3 *false·teachers* for·whom judgment from·long·ago
2Pe 2:17 by a·whirlwind, for·whom the deep·murky·shroud
2Co 4:4 in whom the god of·this present·age blinded the
Eph 2:3 Among whom also we all had·our·manner·of·life in·
Col 1:27 to·whom God determined to·make·known what *is*
Col 3:7 among whom yeu·yeurselves also once walked,
Rv 7:2 to·the four angels, to·whom it was·given to·bring·

G3739.1 P:R-DPF αἷς (2x)

Mt 27:56 Among whom was Mariam Magdalene, and
Mk 15:40 from·a·distance, even among whom was Mariam

G3739.1 P:R-DPN οἷς (1x)

Rm 1:6 among whom also yeu·yeurselves are *the* called·

G3739.1 P:R-GSM οὗ (53x)

Jn 1:27 has·come·to·be ahead of·me) of·whom I·myself am
Jn 1:30 This is·he concerning whom I·myself declared,
Jn 4:46 ·was·a·certain royal·official, whose son was·sick at
Jn 6:42 the son of·Joseph, whose father and mother we·
Jn 18:26 being a·kinsman of·him·whose earlobe Peter
Lk 3:16 ·than me comes, the strap of·whose shoes I·am not
Lk 3:17 whose winnowing·fork *is* in his hand, and he·shall·
Lk 7:27 This is *he*, concerning whom it·has·been·written,
Lk 8:35 found the man·of·clay† from whom the demons had·
Lk 8:38 Now the man from whom the demons had·come·out
Lk 9:9 is this, concerning whom I·myself hear such·things?
Lk 17:1 to·come, but woe *to·him* through whom they·come!
Lk 22:22 man·of·clay† through whom he·is·handed·over!"
Ac 7:52 of·the Righteous·One, now of·whom, yeu have·
Ac 13:25 after me, the shoes of·whose feet I·am not worthy
Ac 18:7 Justus, who·is·reverencing God, whose home was
Ac 21:11 at JeruSalem shall·bind the man who owns this belt
Ac 24:8 to you, personally·from whom you·shall·be·able,
Ac 25:15 concerning whom, with·me being at JeruSalem, the
Ac 25:18 Concerning whom, the legal·accusers, after·being·
Ac 25:24 observe this·man, about whom all the multitude
Ac 25:26 concerning whom I·do·not have something
Ac 27:23 night an·angel of·God, of·him·whose I·am and to·
Heb 1:2 heir of·all·things, through whom also he·made the
Heb 2:10 all·things *exist* and through whom all·things *exist*),
Heb 3:6 a·son over his·own house, of·whose house are we·
Heb 12:26 whose *own* voice shook the earth at·that·time.
Heb 13:23 ·fully·released, with whom I·shall·gaze·upon yeu
Gal 6:14 Lord YeShua Anointed, through whom *the* world
Mt 3:11 me is stronger·than me, whose shoes I·am not fit to·
Mt 3:12 whose winnowing·fork *is* in his hand, and he·shall·
Mt 11:10 this is·he, concerning whom it·has·been·written,
Mt 18:7 man·of·clay† through whom the scandalous·trap
Mt 26:24 woe to·that man·of·clay† through whom the Son
Mk 1:7 me comes right·behind me, of·whom I·am not fit,
Mk 14:21 woe to·that man·of·clay† through whom the Son
Rm 1:5 through whom we·received grace and commission
Rm 2:29 *and* not in·letter— whose high·praise *is* not from·
Rm 4:17 *And being* directly·before God whom he·trusted
Rm 5:2 through whom also we·have the embraceable·access
Rm 5:11 Jesus Anointed, through whom now we·received
Rm 10:14 shall·they·trust *him* of·whom they·did·not hear?
Rm 14:15 food, on·behalf·of·whom Anointed-One died.
1Pe 2:24 'by·whose thrashed·and·swollen·body yeu·are·
2Th 2:9 *O·the Lawless·One*, whose arrival is according·to
1Co 1:9 through whom yeu·are·called·forth into *the*
1Co 8:6 the Father (from·out of·whom *are* all·things and
1Co 8:6 Jesus Anointed (through whom *are* all·things and
2Co 8:18 with him the brother, whose high·praise *is* in the
Eph 3:15 from·out of·whom *the* entire paternal·lineage in *the*
Eph 4:16 from·out of·whom all the Body is·being·fitly·
Col 4:10 concerning whom yeu·received commandments; if
Rv 20:11 ·is·sitting·down on it, from whose face the earth

G3739.1 P:R-GSF ἧς (10x)

Jn 11:2 feet with·her hair, whose brother Lazarus was·sick).
Lk 8:2 ·called Magdalene) from whom had·gone·forth seven
Ac 16:14 who·is·reverencing God, of·whom the Lord
Heb 6:8 and *is* close to·being·cursed, whose end *is* for
Heb 11:10 the foundations whose architectural·designer and
Mt 1:16 of·Mariam, from·out of·whom was·born YeShua,
Mk 7:25 about him, a·woman whose young·daughter was·
Mk 16:9 Magdalene, from whom he·had·cast·out seven
1Pe 3:6 *It·is* of·her·whom yeu·did·become children, while·
Rv 17:2 with whom the kings of·the earth committed·sexual·

G3739.1 P:R-GSN οὗ (3x)

Tit 3:6 whom he·poured·forth on us abundantly through
1Jn 3:24 as·a·result of·the Spirit whom he·already·gave to·us

Rv 13:12 the first Daemonic·Beast, whose own deadly gash

G3739.1 P:R-GPM ὧν (28x)

Jn 17:9 concerning those·whom you·have·given to·me,
Lk 6:34 personally·from whom yeu·expect to·receive·in·full,
Lk 13:1 concerning the Galileans, whose blood Pilate mixed
Ac 22:5 the council·of·elders, personally·from whom I also
Heb 3:17 the·ones morally·failing, whose slain·bodies fell in
Heb 11:38 (of·whom the world was not worthy), being·
Heb 13:7 of·God, whose trust yeu·are·to·attentively·imitate,
Rm 3:14 "Whose mouth overflows of·evil·prayer and of·
Rm 4:7 *are·they* whose violations·of·law are·forgiven and
Rm 4:7 and whose moral·failures are·fully·covered·over·
Rm 9:4 are Israelites— of·whom *are* the adoption·as·sons,
Rm 9:5 of·whom *are* the fathers, and from·out of·whom,
Rm 9:5 the fathers, and from·out of·whom, according·to the
Php 3:19 whose end *is* total·destruction, whose god *is* the
Php 3:19 whose end *is* total·destruction, whose god *is* the
Php 4:3 of·my coworkers, the names of·whom *are* in *the*
1Co 3:5 other than attendants through whom yeu·trusted,
1Co 15:6 ·occasion·only, from·among whom the majority
2Co 2:3 grief from them·by·whom it·was·necessary·for me
2Co 11:15 attendants of·righteousness, whose end shall·be
2Co 12:17 through any of·them whom I·have·dispatched to
1Ti 1:15 morally·disqualified·ones, of·whom I·myself am
1Ti 1:20 of·whom are Hymenaeus and AlexAnder, whom I·
2Ti 1:15 Asia are·turned·away·from me, of·whom *also* are
2Ti 2:17 ·body·as·pasture, of·whom is Hymenaeus and
Rv 13:8 shall·fall·prostrate to·it, whose names have·not
Rv 17:8 the earth shall·marvel, whose names have·not been·
Rv 20:8 into battle, the number of·whom *is* as the sand of·

G3739.1 P:R-GPF ὧν (1x)

1Pe 3:3 whose adorning must·be, not *according·to* the

G3739.1 P:R-GPN ὧν (2x)

Ac 7:45 ·possession of·the Gentiles, whom God thrust·out
Heb 13:11 bodies of·these animals, whose blood is·carried

G3739.2 ADV οὗ (1x)

Heb 13:10 from·among which the·ones who·are·ritually·

G3739.2 N-NSF ἥ (1x)

Heb 9:2 the first, in which also *was* the Menorah·

G3739.2 P:R-NSM ὅς (8x)

Jn 19:17 Place of·a·Skull, which is·referred·to in·Hebrew *as*
Gal 3:16 And to·your single·seed, which is Anointed-One.
Mk 4:31 as a·kernel of·mustard·seed, which, whenever it·
1Th 2:13 God's Redemptive·word, which operates also in
1Co 3:11 than the·one being·laid·out, which is Jesus the
Eph 5:5 ·person, or greedy·man— which is an·idolater—
Col 1:27 among the Gentiles, which is Anointed-One in yeu
Rv 13:4 *directly·before* the Dragon which gave authority to·

G3739.2 P:R-NSF ἥ (1x)

Mt 25:13 nor·even the hour in which the Son of·Clay·Man†

G3739.2 P:R-NSN ὅ (46x)

Jn 1:9 the true Light which illuminates every child·of·clay†
Jn 1:38 "Rabbi" (which, when·being·translated *from*
Jn 1:41 the Messiah," which, when·being·interpreted *from*·
Jn 1:42 ·*hollow·rock*)," which is·translated *from·Hebrew*
Jn 9:7 pool of·Siloam" (which *from·Hebrew* is·translated *as*
Jn 20:16 "Rabboni!" (which is·to·say, "O·my·*great*·
Lk 5:3 into one of·the sailboats, which was Simon's, *Jesus*
Lk 6:2 "Why·do yeu·do that·which it·is·not proper to·do on
Lk 8:5 as he·himself sowed, *there·was* that·which in·fact fell
Ac 1:12 the·one being·called Olive·Orchard, which is near
Ac 4:36 by the ambassadors (which, when·being·interpreted
Heb 7:2 "King of·Salem," which is, King of·Peace.
Gal 1:7 which is not *actually* another *good·news at·all*.
Mt 1:23 name ImmanuEl, which, when·being·interpreted
Mt 13:32 which in·fact is smaller·than all the variety·of·
Mk 3:17 ·them he·laid a·name: BoanErges, which is, "Sons
Mk 4:22 hidden, which should·not be·made·apparent,
Mk 5:41 qumi," which, when·being·interpreted *from*·
Mk 7:34 "Ephphatha," which is, "Be·thoroughly·opened·
Mk 12:42 ·poor widow cast·in two bits, which is a·quadran.
Mk 15:16 inside the courtyard, which is *the* Praetorian·hall.
Mk 15:22 ·*to·as* GolGotha, which, when·being·interpreted

Mk 15:34 shebaq-thani?" Which, when·being·interpreted
Mk 15:46 in a·chamber·tomb which was having·been·hewed
Php 2:5 *for* this·thing among yeurselves, which *was* also in
1Pe 3:4 ·undisturbable spirit, which is extremely·precious
1Pe 3:21 *The* corresponding·pattern, which even now saves
2Th 3:17 of·Paul by·my·own hand, which is a·signature in
1Co 15:36 Impetuous·one, that·which you sow is·not
1Co 15:37 And that·which you·sow, you·sow not the body
Eph 3:5 *This·is the Mystery* (which in other generations·of·
Eph 6:17 dagger of·the Spirit, which is an·utterance of·God.
Col 1:24 on·behalf of·his Body, which is the entire·Called·
Col 2:14 us (the decrees which were sternly·opposed to·us),
1Ti 2:10 ·good works (which is·befitting·for women who·
1Ti 4:14 in you, which was·given to·you through prophecy,
2Ti 1:6 the gracious·bestowment of·God, which is in you
1Jn 2:27 anointing which yeu·yeurselves already·received
1Jn 4:2 of·God: every spirit which affirms Jesus Anointed
1Jn 4:3 ·of·the·Anointed-One, of·which yeu·have·heard that
Rv 2:7 ·out of·the arbor·tree of·Life-above, which is in *the*
Rv 5:13 And every creature which is in the heaven, and on
Rv 13:14 ·image for·the Daemonic·Beast, which has the gash
Rv 20:12 another official·scroll was·opened·up, which is *the*
Rv 21:8 ·set·ablaze with·fire and sulfur, which is *the* Second
Rv 21:17 *·to* a·measure of·a·man·of·clay†, which is *that* of·

G3739.2 P:R-NPM οἵ (3x)

Lk 23:29 did·not bear, and *the* breasts which did·not nurse.'
Ac 7:40 "Make for·us gods which shall·traverse·before us.
Rv 5:6 seven horns and seven eyes which are the seven

G3739.2 P:R-NPF αἵ (2x)

Rv 4:5 in·the·sight of·the throne, which are the seven Spirits
Rv 5:8 golden vials overflowing with·incense, which are the

G3739.2 P:R-NPN ἅ (9x)

Jn 10:16 And I·have other sheep which are not from·among
Jn 20:30 in·the·sight of·his disciples, which are not having·
Mk 11:23 that the·things·which he says are·coming·to·be; it·
2Pe 3:16 *that·are* hard·to·understand— which *the* unlearned
Col 2:17 which·things are a·shadow of·the·things impending
Col 2:22 which all are *subject* to perishing with·usage)—
Rv 13:14 *means·of* the miraculous·signs which it was·given
Rv 21:12 and names having·been·inscribed, which are *the*
Rv 22:6 slaves the·things·*of*·which it·is·mandatory to·be·

G3739.2 P:R-ASM ὅν (38x)

Jn 12:38 may·be·completely·fulfilled, which he·declared,
Jn 12:48 him: the Redemptive-word which I·spoke. The·same
Jn 14:24 "But the Redemptive-word which yeu·hear is not
Jn 15:3 the Redemptive-word which I·have·spoken to·yeu.
Jn 18:1 an·enclosed·garden, into which he·himself entered
Jn 18:9 may·be·completely·fulfilled, which *Jesus* declared,
Jn 18:32 may·be·completely·fulfilled which he·declared,
Lk 1:73 an·oath which he·swore to our father AbRaham,
Lk 13:19 of·mustard·seed, which a·man·of·clay† took *and*
Lk 19:30 ·been·tied, on which not·even·one man·of·clay†
Lk 20:17 "*The* stone which the builders rejected·as·unfit,
Ac 1:24 ·all·men, expressly·indicate which one from·among
Ac 7:44 ·to the particular·pattern which he·had·clearly·seen.
Ac 10:36 The Word which *God* dispatched to·the Sons of·
Ac 15:10 the neck of·the disciples, which neither our fathers
Ac 27:25 according·to that·which has·been·spoken to·me.
Ac 27:39 bay having a·shore, into which they·purposed, if
Heb 9:9 then·currently·standing, in which both presents
Heb 11:8 ·forth into the place which he·was·about to·receive
Mt 2:9 And behold, the star which they·saw in the east was·
Mt 2:16 time which he·precisely·ascertained personally·from
Mt 13:31 like a·kernel of·mustard·seed (which after·taking,
Mt 13:44 ·been·hidden in a·field, which a·man·of·clay†,
Mt 21:24 yeu one question, which if yeu·should·declare *an*·
Mt 21:42 "A·stone which the builders rejected·as·unfit,
Mk 11:2 ·been·tied, on which not·even·one man·of·clay†
Mk 12:10 "A·stone which the builders rejected·as·unfit,
Rm 6:17 ·pattern of·instruction which is·handed·down *to·yeu*
Rm 11:2 did·not shove·away his People which he·foreknew.
Jac 1:12 the victor's·crown of·life-above, which the Lord
1Pe 2:7 "A·stone, which the·ones building rejected·as·unfit

1Co 10:16 Anointed-One? The bread which we·break, is·it
1Ti 6:16 *in* unapproachable light which no·one·at·all sees
2Ti 4:8 the victor's·crown of·righteousness, which the Lord,
1Jn 2:7 commandment is the word which yeu·heard from *the*
Rv 7:9 a·large crowd which not·even·one·man was·able to·
Rv 10:5 And the angel which I·saw standing upon the sea
Rv 12:16 swallowed·up the flood·water which the Dragon

G3739.2 P:R-ASF ἥν (73x)

Jn 5:32 that the testimony which he·testifies concerning me
Jn 6:21 upon the dry·ground for which they·were·heading.
Jn 6:27 into eternal life-above, which the Son of·Clay·Man†
Jn 6:51 is my flesh, which I·myself shall·give on·behalf of·
Jn 8:40 to·yeu the truth, which I·heard personally·from God.
Jn 17:22 "And the glory which you·have·given to·me I·
Jn 17:24 they·may·observe my glory, which you·gave to·me
Jn 17:26 "in·order·that the love with·which you·loved me
Lk 9:31 his exodus which he·was·about to·completely·fulfill
Lk 13:21 It·is like leaven, which a·woman took *and*
Lk 15:9 I·found the drachma which I·completely·lost.'
Lk 19:20 *here·is* your mina which I·was·holding *for·you*,
Ac 1:4 Promise of·the Father, which yeu·heard from·me.
Ac 1:16 to·be·completely·fulfilled, which the Holy Spirit
Ac 7:3 and come·over·here into a·land which I·shall·show
Ac 7:4 ·settled him into this land in which yeu now reside.
Ac 7:45 Which also our fathers, after·receiving·it·in·turn,
Ac 8:32 of·the Scripture which he·was·reading·aloud was
Ac 10:21 the motivation on·account·of which yeu·are·here?
Ac 11:6 Which gazing·intently upon, I·was·fully·observing,
Ac 20:24 and the service, which I·received personally·from
Ac 20:28 of·God, which he·himself·acquired through his·
Ac 23:28 ·charge on·account·of which they·were·calling him
Ac 24:14 that according·to The Way which they·say *is* a·sect
Ac 24:15 ·expectation in God, which these·men themselves
Ac 26:7 to which *promise* our twelve·tribes, in earnestness,
Ac 27:17 Which after·taking·*it*·up, they·used emergency·
Heb 2:11 ·out of·one *Father*. On·account·of which cause,
Heb 6:19 Which *Expectation* we·have as an·anchor of·the
Heb 7:14 ·among Judah, in·regard·to which tribe Moses
Heb 8:2 of·the true Tabernacle, which Yahweh set·up and
Heb 10:20 and living way which he·inaugurated for·us
Gal 1:23 the trust which once he·was·fiercely·ransacking."
Gal 2:4 ·motives to·spy·out our liberty which we·have in
Mt 13:33 heavens is like leaven, which upon·taking *it*, a·
Mt 13:48 which when it·was·completely·filled, after·hauling
Mt 15:13 ·declared, "Every plant which my heavenly Father
Mk 11:21 fig·tree which you·did·curse has·been·withered·
Rm 1:27 the due·payback which is·mandatory·for their error.
Rm 16:17 traps contrary·to the instruction which yeu learned
1Pe 3:20 ·ark being·fully·prepared, in which a·few (that·is
1Pe 5:12 this to·be *the* true grace of·God in which yeu·stand.
2Pe 3:12 Day of·God— through which *the* heavens, being·
2Th 3:6 ·to the tradition which he·personally·received from
Tit 1:2 Expectation of·eternal life-above, which God (the·
Tit 1:13 is true. On·account·of which cause, reprove them
1Co 2:7 ·been·hidden·away, which God predetermined
1Co 2:8 which not·even·one of·the rulers of·this present·age
1Co 15:31 ·as *it·is* our boast, which I·have in Anointed-One
2Co 2:4 ·may·know the love which I·have more·abundantly
2Co 9:2 ·know yeur eagerness, for·which I·boast over yeu
2Co 13:10 according·to the authority which the Lord gave
Eph 1:9 his good·purpose which he·personally·determined
Eph 1:20 which he·operated in the Anointed-One, after·
Eph 2:4 on·account·of his large love with·which he·loved us,
Eph 3:11 determined·purpose of·the ages which he·made in
Col 1:5 in the heavens— which yeu·already·heard·before in
Col 3:15 yeur hearts, into which also yeu·were·called·forth
Col 4:17 ·for the service which you·personally·received in
Phm 1:5 of·your love and trust which you·have toward the
1Ti 1:19 ·good conscience. Which concerning the trust,
1Ti 6:12 life-above, to which also you·were·called·forth,
1Ti 6:21 which some, who·are·making·a·profession *of·trust*,
2Ti 1:6 On·account·of which cause I·remind·and·admonish
2Ti 1:12 On·account·of which cause also I·suffer these·

1Jn 1:5 then is the announcement which we·have·heard from
1Jn 2:7 an·old commandment which yeu·were·having from
1Jn 5:9 testimony of·God which he·has·testified concerning
2Jn 1:5 to·you, but·rather that·which we·were·having from
Rv 1:1 Revelation of·Jesus Anointed, which God gave to·
Rv 4:1 the heaven and the first voice which I·heard *was* as a·
Rv 6:9 ·account·of the testimony which they·were·holding.
Rv 10:8 And the voice which I·heard from·out·of·the heaven

G3739.2 P:R-ASN ὅ (87x)

Jn 3:11 ·you, we·speak that which we·personally·know and
Jn 4:38 yeu to·reap *that·for* which yeu·yeurselves have·not
Jn 6:22 except that one into which his disciples embarked,
Jn 6:39 completely·lose any *sheep* which he·has·given me
Jn 8:38 speak that·which I·have·clearly·seen from·beside my
Jn 8:38 yeu do that·which yeu·have·clearly·seen from·beside
Jn 17:4 ·completed the work, which *likewise* you·have·given
Jn 18:11 the sheath! The cup which the Father has·given me,
Lk 2:15 ·one having·occurred, which Yahweh made·known
Lk 2:31 which you·made·ready in front of·all the peoples;
Lk 2:50 comprehend the utterance which he·spoke to·them.
Lk 8:18 ·taken·away even that·which he·presumes to·have."
Lk 11:6 I·do·not have that·which I·shall·place·before him.'
Lk 12:3 in the light; and that·which yeu·spoke to the ear in
Lk 17:10 ·done *merely* that·which we·were·obligated to·do.'
Ac 2:33 he·poured·forth this, which yeu now look·upon
Ac 3:6 with·me, but that·thing which I·do·have, I·give to·
Ac 10:17 might·be *meant·by* the clear·vision which he·saw,
Ac 10:37 the immersion which John officially·proclaimed,
Ac 11:30 Which also they·did, dispatching *it* to the elders
Ac 13:2 Saul for the work to·which I·have·summoned them.
Ac 14:26 for the work which they·completely·fulfilled.
Ac 21:23 "So·then do this·thing which we·say to·you. With·
Ac 26:10 Which·thing also I·did in JeruSalem, and many of·
Heb 9:7 not apart·from blood, which he·offered on·behalf
Gal 1:8 contrary·to that·which we·already·proclaimed to·yeu
Gal 1:9 ·yeu contrary·to that·which yeu·personally·received,
Gal 2:2 the good·news which I·officially·proclaim among
Gal 2:10 this very·thing which I·diligently·endeavored to·do.
Gal 2:20 lives in me. And that·which now I·live in flesh, I·
Mt 12:2 your disciples do that·which it·is·not proper to·do
Mt 12:36 for·every idle utterance, which if the men·of·clay†
Mt 13:12 ·has, even that·which he·has shall·be·taken·away
Mt 25:29 ·has, even that·which he·has shall·be·taken·away
Mt 27:60 brand-new chamber·tomb, which he·hewed·out in
Mk 2:24 ·do on the Sabbath·days that·which is·not proper?
Mk 4:25 ·has, even that·which he·has shall·be·taken·away
Rm 1:2 (which he·promised·beforehand through his prophets
Rm 6:10 For in·that·which he·died, he·died to·the Moral·
Rm 6:10 ·one·occasion·only, but in·that·which he·lives, he·
Rm 7:15 For I·do·not know *why* I·perform that·which *I·do*.
Rm 7:15 For I·do·not practice that·thing which I·want *to·do*,
Rm 7:15 ·want *to·do*, but·rather I·do that·thing which I·hate.
Rm 7:16 But if I·do that which I·do·not want, I·concur with·
Rm 7:19 not *the* beneficially·good·thing which I·want *to·do*,
Rm 7:19 I·do, but·rather a·bad·thing which I·do·not want,
Rm 7:20 Now if that·which I·myself do·not want, *if* that·
Rm 10:8 utterance of·the trust which we·officially·proclaim)
Rm 11:7 did·not obtain that which it·still·anxiously·seeks,
1Pe 2:8 being·obstinate. To which *end·result*, they·are also
2Th 1:11 For which also we·pray always concerning yeu,
2Th 2:14 to which he·called yeu forth through our good·
Tit 1:3 ·proclamation, with·which I·myself am·entrusted
1Co 3:14 ·man's work shall·remain which he·built·upon *the*
1Co 4:6 *of·men* above that·which has·been·written, in·order·
1Co 10:16 The cup of·blessing which we·bless, is·it not·
1Co 11:23 from the Lord that·which also I·handed·down to·
1Co 15:1 to·yeu the good·news which I·proclaimed to·yeu,
1Co 15:1 to·yeu, which also yeu·personally·received, and in
1Co 15:3 first-of-all, that·which also I·personally·received,
2Co 3:14 certain *veil* which is·fully·rendered·inoperative in
2Co 11:4 another spirit, which yeu·did·not already·receive,
2Co 11:4 good·news, which yeu·did·not already·accept,
2Co 11:17 That·which I·speak, I·do·not speak according·to

2Co 12:6 ·reckon to me above that·which he·looks·upon me
2Co 12:13 For what is·it in·which yeu·were·inferior beyond
Eph 3:4 pertaining·to which, upon·reading·*it*·aloud, yeu·are·
Col 1:29 for which·thing also I·labor·hard, striving
Col 3:25 shall·subsequently·obtain that·for·which he·did·,
Col 4:3 on·account·of which also I·have·been·bound),
Phm 1:21 ·shall·do also above·and·beyond that·which I·say.
1Ti 1:11 ·blessed God, with·which I·myself was·entrusted.
1Ti 2:7 for which I·myself was·placed *as* an·official·
2Ti 1:11 for which I·myself was·placed *as* an·official·
1Jn 1:1 That·which was from *the* beginning, which we·
1Jn 1:1 from *the* beginning, which we·have·heard, which
1Jn 1:1 ·have·heard, which we·have·clearly·seen with·our
1Jn 1:1 ·seen with·our eyes, which we·distinctly·viewed,
1Jn 1:3 That·which we·have·clearly·seen and have·heard,
1Jn 2:8 commandment I·do·write to·yeu, which is true in
1Jn 2:24 let·it·abide in yeu, that·which yeu already·heard
1Jn 2:24 beginning. If that·which yeu·already·heard from
Rv 2:15 instruction of·the NicoLaitans, which·thing I·hate.
Rv 2:17 having·been·written which not·even·one·man did·
Rv 2:25 Nevertheless, that·which yeu·presently·have,
Rv 3:11 I·come swiftly. Securely·hold that·which you·have,
Rv 13:2 And the Daemonic·Beast which I·saw was like a·

G3739.2 P:R-APM οὕς (8x)
Lk 6:4 Intended·Show bread, which it·is·not proper to·eat
Lk 11:27 bearing you, and *the* breasts which nursed *you*."
Lk 24:44 "These *are* the words which I·spoke to yeu, while·
Ac 1:7 to·know times or seasons which the Father placed in
Ac 7:43 Remphan, the figures which yeu·made *in·order* to·
Ac 28:15 and *the* Three Taverns, which upon·seeing *them*,
Mt 12:4 Intended·Show bread, which was not being·proper
Mk 2:26 the Intended·Show bread, which it·is·not proper to·

G3739.2 P:R-APF ἅς (3x)
Heb 10:1 with·the same sacrifices (which they·offer each
2Th 2:15 ·hold·to the traditions which yeu·were·instructed,
Rv 1:20 and the seven Lampstands which you·saw are *the*

G3739.2 P:R-APN ἅ (54x)
Jn 2:23 observing his miraculous·signs which he·was·doing.
Jn 5:36 of·John, for the works which the Father gave me
Jn 5:36 , *they·are* the same works which I·myself do; it·
Jn 6:2 his miraculous·signs which he·was·doing upon the·
Jn 6:13 ·of·bread, which remained·in·excess by·the·ones
Jn 8:26 the world these·things which I·heard personally·from
Jn 11:45 and distinctly·viewing the·things·which Jesus did,
Jn 14:26 yeu *concerning* all·things which I·declared to·yeu.
Jn 15:24 them the works which not·even·one other·man has·
Jn 17:8 to·them the utterances which you·have·given to·me,
Lk 6:46 Lord, Lord,' and do·not do the·things·which I·say?
Lk 10:24 wanted to·see the·things·which yeu look·upon, and
Lk 10:24 *them*, and to·hear the·things·which yeu·hear, and
Lk 21:6 "*As·for* these·things which yeu·observe, days shall·
Lk 24:1 bringing aromatic·spices which they·made·ready,
Ac 4:20 ·not able not to·speak the·things·which we·saw and
Ac 6:14 ·change the customs which Moses handed·down to·
Ac 8:6 ·upon the miraculous·signs which he·was·doing.
Ac 11:9 from·out of·the heaven, 'That·which God purified,
Ac 16:21 they·fully·proclaim customs which it·is·not proper
Ac 25:7 against Paul, which they·were·not having·strength
Heb 2:13 I·myself and the little·children which God gave to·
Gal 1:20 (Now the·things·which I·write to·yeu— Behold, in·
Gal 2:18 if I·build again these·things which I·demolished, I·
Gal 5:17 yeu·may·not do these·things which yeu·might want
Gal 5:21 and things like these … of·which I·forewarn to·yeu,
Mt 13:17 longed to·see *the·things* which yeu·look·upon, and
Mt 13:17 *them*, and to·hear *the·things* which yeu·hear, and
Mk 7:4 other·things which they·personally·received to·
Rm 9:23 of·mercy, which he·made·ready·in·advance for
Php 4:9 These·things, which also yeu·learned, and
1Pe 1:12 ·attending·to·us the·same·things which are now
1Pe 1:12 from heaven— which·things angels long to·stoop·
2Th 3:4 yeu·do and shall·do the·things·which we·charge yeu
Tit 1:11 houses, instructing things·which are·not mandatory,
Tit 2:1 But you·yourself speak that·which is·suitable·for the
1Co 2:9 ·a·man·of·clay†, the·things·which God made·ready
1Co 2:13 Which·things also we·speak, not with instructive
2Co 12:4 utterances, which is·not being·proper for·a·man·
Col 3:6 on·account·of which·things the wrath of·God comes
1Ti 4:3 to·abstain·from foods— which God created for
2Ti 2:2 And the·things·which you·heard personally·from me
3Jn 1:10 I·shall·quietly·recollect his deeds which he·does,
Rv 1:19 "Write the·things·which you·saw, and the·things·
Rv 1:19 ·things·which you·saw, and the·things·which are,
Rv 1:19 ·which are, and the·things·which are·about to·be
Rv 2:6 the deeds of·the NicoLaitans, which I·also hate.
Rv 2:10 not·one·bit·of which·things you·are·about to·suffer.
Rv 3:4 ·few names even in Sardis which did·not tarnish their
Rv 4:1 ·show you things·which it·is·mandatory to·happen
Rv 9:20 and wood, which neither are·able to·look·about,
Rv 17:12 "And the ten horns which you·saw are ten kings
Rv 17:15 "The *Many* Waters which you·saw, where the
Rv 17:16 And the ten horns which you·saw upon the Scarlet·

G3739.2 P:R-DSM ᾧ (14x)
Jn 2:22 the Scripture and the word which Jesus declared.
Ac 1:21 during all *the* time in which the Lord Jesus came·in
Ac 4:31 in which they·were having·been·gathered·together;
Ac 7:20 "Into which season Moses was·born, and he·was
Ac 7:33 feet, for the place in which you·stand is holy soil.
Ac 17:23 I·found a·pedestal on which had·been·inscribed,
Ac 20:38 especially over the words which he·had·declared,
Ac 27:8 being·called Good Harbors, which was near *the* city
Heb 6:17 By which *confirmation*, God, being·resolved more·
Mk 2:4 they·lowered the mat on which the paralyzed·man
Rm 7:6 being·dead *to·that* by that·which we·were·fully·held,
2Pe 1:19 the prophetic word, to·which yeu·do well taking·
Eph 5:18 with·wine, in which is *the* unsaved·lifestyle, but·
Eph 6:16 trust (with which yeu·shall·be·able to·extinguish

G3739.2 P:R-DSF ᾗ (28x)
Jn 4:52 ·from them the hour in which he·had gotten·better.
Jn 4:53 *it·was* at that hour, in which Jesus declared to·him,
Jn 5:28 because an·hour is·coming in which all the·ones in
Jn 17:5 yourself) with·the glory which I·was·having with
Lk 5:9 ·him) over the catch of·the fish which they·caught.
Lk 6:49 on the earth, which the stream burst·directly·against
Lk 11:22 his whole·armor in which he·had·confided and
Lk 19:30 directly·before *yeu*; in which traversing·in, yeu·
Lk 21:15 a·mouth and wisdom, which all the·ones who·are·
Lk 22:7 ·Bread, in which it·was·mandatory·for the Passover
Ac 2:8 our own·distinct dialect into which we·were·born?
Ac 9:17 to·you along the roadway in·which you·were·going,
Ac 17:31 ·that, he·established a·day in which he·intends·
Heb 9:4 on·all·sides with·gold, in which *was* a·golden urn
Gal 5:1 ·fast in·the liberty with·which Anointed-One set us
Mt 24:44 comes at·an·hour which yeu·do·not presume.
Mk 7:13 by·yeur Oral·tradition, which yeu·handed·down.
Rm 5:2 trust into this grace in which we·stand, and we·boast
2Pe 3:10 in a·night in which the heavens shall·pass·away
1Th 3:9 over all the joy with·which we·rejoice on·account·of
1Co 7:20 in the calling in·which he·was·called·forth, in this
1Co 11:23 on·the night in which he·was·handed·over, took
2Co 7:7 by the consoling with·which he·was·comforted in
2Co 10:2 confidence with·which I·reckon to·be·daringly·
2Co 12:21 and debauchery which they·practiced.
Eph 1:6 grace— in which he·graciously·favored us in the·
1Ti 4:6 instruction, to·which you·have·closely·followed.
Rv 18:19 the Great City, in which all the·ones having ships

G3739.2 P:R-DSN ᾧ (23x)
Jn 5:4 from·whatever ailment by·which he·was·held·down.
Jn 13:5 towel with·which he·was having·been·tightly·girded.
Jn 19:41 a·brand-new chamber·tomb, in which, not·even·yet
Ac 4:12 the men·of·clay† by which it·is·necessary·for us to·
Ac 6:10 wisdom and the Spirit by·which he·was·speaking.
Ac 10:12 in which all the four-footed·animals of·the earth
Ac 13:41 in yeur days, a·work which, no, yeu·may·not·ever
Ac 20:28 entire little·flock, among which the Holy Spirit
Heb 10:29 of·the covenant (by which he·was·made·holy) *to·*
Mt 26:50 ·associate, *attend* to *that* for·which you·are·here!"
Rm 2:1 man·of·clay†! For in that·which you·judge the other
Rm 8:15 a·Spirit of·adoption·as·sons, by which we·yell·out,
Rm 14:21 wine, nor·even *anything* by which your brother
Php 3:12 I·may·grasp onto that·for·which also I·am·grasped
Php 4:10 in which also yeu·were·earnestly·concerned, but
1Pe 3:19 in which, also traversing·to·the spirits in prison, he·
1Pe 4:4 in which they·think·it·is·strange of·yeu not *to·be*
2Pe 2:19 — for that·by·which someone has·been·defeated,
1Co 7:24 Each·man, in that·*state*·which he·is·called·forth,
1Co 15:1 yeu·personally·received, and in which yeu·stand,
Col 2:12 in which also yeu·are·already·awakened·together
2Ti 2:9 in which I·suffer·hardship, as a·criminal, *even* as·far·
Rv 18:6 In the cup which she·blended·and·poured·out,

G3739.2 P:R-DPM οἷς (3x)
2Pe 2:12 ·reviling in matters·of·which they·are·ignorant),
2Pe 3:13 Earth,' in which righteousness resides.
2Pe 3:16 concerning these·things, in which are some·things

G3739.2 P:R-DPF αἷς (9x)
Lk 13:14 There·are six days in which it·is·necessary to·work
Lk 21:6 days shall·come in which there·shall·not be·left a·
Lk 23:29 Days are·coming in which they·shall·declare,
Ac 15:36 in every city in which we·fully·proclaimed the
Heb 10:32 previous days in which, after·being·enlightened,
Mt 11:20 to·reproach the cities in which the large·majority
2Pe 3:1 I·write to·yeu, in which I·thoroughly·awaken yeur
Eph 2:2 in which·things in·times·past, yeu·walked
Rv 2:13 my trust, even in the days in which AntiPas *was* my

G3739.2 P:R-DPN οἷς (10x)
Lk 1:78 mercy, in which, a·light·rising·over·the·horizon
Lk 9:43 with·all marveling over all·things which Jesus did,
Ac 2:22 and wonders and signs, which God did through him
Ac 11:14 to you utterances by which you·shall·be·saved, you
Ac 24:18 in which·things they·found me *so·doing*, having·
Heb 6:18 matters·of·consequence in which *it·was* impossible
Gal 4:9 ·poor principles— to·which yeu·want to·be·slaves,
Eph 2:10 ·good works, which God made·ready·in·advance
2Ti 3:14 in the·things·which you·already·learned and are·
Rv 19:20 in·the·sight of·it, with which he·deceived the·ones

G3739.2 P:R-GSM οὗ (6x)
Jn 10:12 not even being a·shepherd over·that·which are not
Ac 2:32 raised·up this Jesus, of·which we·ourselves all are
Heb 5:11 Concerning which, the matter *means* much to·us,
Heb 12:14 apart·from which not·even·one·man shall·gaze·
2Co 10:13 ·to the standard measure which God distributed
Col 2:19 ·holding the Head, from·out of·which all the Body

G3739.2 P:R-GSF ἧς (26x)
Ac 1:25 from·among which Judas walked·contrary·to, *in·*
Ac 3:25 of·the unilateral·covenant which God bequeathed
Ac 7:17 of·the promise was·drawing·near which God swore
Ac 26:7 *it* to·fully·come— concerning which expectation,
Heb 2:5 *brand-new* Land, concerning which we·speak.
Heb 6:10 ·labor of·love, which yeu·have·indicated for his
Heb 7:13 from which not·even·one·man has·given·attention
Heb 7:19 *does*, through which we·draw·near to·God.
Heb 9:20 the blood of·the covenant which God commanded
Heb 11:4 than Qain, through which he·was·attested to·be
Heb 11:7 of·his house; through which he·condemned the
Heb 11:15 of·that *fatherland* from which they·came·out,
Heb 11:29 through parched·ground, of·which the Egyptians
Heb 12:8 corrective·discipline (of·which all have·become
Heb 12:19 ·a·voice of·utterances, of·which the·ones hearing
Heb 12:28 through which we·may·ritually·minister to·God
Mk 13:19 from *the* beginning of·creation which God created
Jac 2:5 heirs of·the kingdom which he·promised to·the·ones
1Pe 4:11 ·*attending* from·out of·strength which God supplies
2Th 1:5 of·God, on·behalf of·which also yeu·suffer—
2Co 1:4 the comfort with·which we·ourselves are·comforted
2Co 10:8 concerning our authority, which the Lord gave us
Eph 1:8 *the wealth of·his grace* which he·abounded to us in
Eph 4:1 of·the calling by·which yeu·are·called·forth,
Col 1:25 of·which I·myself am·made an·attendant,
1Ti 6:10 which some are·longingly·stretching·themselves·

G3739.2 P:R-GSN οὗ (13x)

Jn 7:39 this concerning the Spirit, which the·ones trusting in
Lk 4:18 *is* upon me for·the·cause·of which he·anointed me,
Lk 4:29 the brow of·the mount on which their city had·been·
Ac 3:15 from·among dead·men, to·which we·ourselves are
Ac 19:40 ·one cause about which we·shall·be·able to·render
Mk 14:32 they·come to an·open·field of·which the name *is*
Mk 14:72 ·considered the utterance which Jesus declared to·
1Co 6:19 Spirit *who·is* in yeu, which yeu·have from God,
1Co 10:30 ·reviled over that·for·which I·myself give·thanks?
1Co 15:2 through which also yeu·are·saved, if yeu·fully·
Eph 6:20 on·behalf of·which I·am·an·elder·spokesman in a·
Col 1:23 Expectation of·the good·news which yeu·heard
Col 1:23 creature under the heaven), of·which I, Paul, am·

G3739.2 P:R-GPM ὧν (3x)

Lk 1:4 concerning *the* sayings of·which you·were·informed.
2Ti 1:13 which you·heard personally·from me, in trust and
Rv 1:20 the mystery of·the seven stars which you·saw in my

G3739.2 P:R-GPF ὧν (3x)

Ac 9:36 works and merciful·acts which she·was·doing.
1Ti 1:6 from·which, some are·already·turned·aside to idle·
1Ti 6:4 ·of·words, from·out of·which becomes envy, strife,

G3739.2 P:R-GPN ὧν (24x)

Jn 7:31 more miraculous·signs than these which this·man did
Jn 21:10 "Bring of the small·fry which yeu·caught just·now.
Lk 3:19 all *the* evils which HerOd·AntiPas committed,
Ac 3:21 ·a·reconstitution of·all·things, of·which God spoke
Ac 8:24 that not·even·one of·these·things·which yeu·have·
Ac 10:39 are witnesses of·all·the·things which he·did both in
Ac 13:39 from everything from·which yeu·were·not able·to
Ac 15:29 From·among which·things *if* yeu·thoroughly·keep·
Ac 21:24 ·that, of·which·things they·have·been·informed
Ac 22:10 all·things which have·been·assigned for·you to·do.
Ac 24:8 these·things of·which we·ourselves legally·accuse
Ac 24:13 ·things concerning which now they·legally·accuse
Ac 25:11 at·all to·these·things·which these·men legally·
Ac 26:2 all·the·things for·which I·am·called·to·account by
Ac 26:16 a·witness, both of·the·things·which you·saw and
Ac 26:16 and of·the·things·in·which I·shall·be·made·visible
Heb 5:8 ·obedience from the·things·which he·suffered.
Heb 9:5 ·of·favorable·forgiveness), concerning which, now
Jud 1:15 their irreverent deeds which they·irreverently·did,
Jud 1:15 concerning all the harsh·things which irreverent *and*
2Pe 3:6 through which the world at·that·time was·
Tit 3:5 (of·the·ones in righteousness which we·ourselves did)
1Co 7:1 concerning the·things·of·which yeu·wrote to·me, *it*·
2Co 1:6 of·the same afflictions which we·ourselves also

G3739.3 P:R-NSN ὅ (4x)

Lk 19:26 not having, even what he·has shall·be·taken·away
Mt 20:4 ·out into the vineyard, and whatever may·be right I·
Mk 5:33 personally·knowing what has·happened in her,
1Co 15:10 But by·the·grace of·God I·am what I·am, and his

G3739.3 P:R-ASF ἥν (7x)

Lk 8:47 the people, on·account·of what cause she·laid·hold
Lk 9:4 "And whatever home yeu·should·enter into, there
Lk 10:5 "And into whatever home yeu·should·enter, first say
Lk 10:8 "So into whatever city yeu·should·enter, and they·
Lk 10:10 "But into whatever city yeu·should·enter, and they·
Ac 22:24 on·account·of what cause they·were·exclaiming in·
Mt 10:11 "And into whatever city or village yeu·should·

G3739.3 P:R-ASN ὅ (51x)

Jn 3:11 ·know and testify what we·have·clearly·seen, and
Jn 3:32 And what he·has·clearly·seen and heard, that·thing
Jn 13:7 and declared to·him, "What I·myself do, you·
Jn 13:27 Jesus says to·him, "What you·do, do more·swiftly.
Jn 15:7 yeu·shall·request whatever yeu·should·determine,
Jn 15:16 in·order·that whatever yeu·should·request·of the
Jn 19:22 Pilate answered, "What I·have·written, I·have·
Lk 9:33 ·for EliJah," not personally·knowing what he·says.
Lk 19:21 ·of·clay†. You·take·up what you·did·not lay·down
Lk 19:21 ·did·not lay·down, and reap what you·did·not sow.
Lk 19:22 man·of·clay†, taking·up what I·did·not lay·down,
Lk 19:22 ·not lay·down, and reaping what I·did·not sow.
Lk 22:60 I·do·not personally·know what you·are·saying."
Ac 14:11 And the crowds, after·seeing what Paul did, they·
Gal 6:7 God is·not ridiculed, for whatever a·man·of·clay†
Mt 10:27 "What I·say to·yeu in the darkness, declare in the
Mt 10:27 declare in the light; and what yeu·hear in the ear,
Mt 14:7 he·affirmed to·give her whatever she·may·request.
Mt 15:5 ·benefited as·a·result of·me, whatever *it·should·be*,
Mt 16:19 of·the heavens, and whatever you·should·bind on
Mt 16:19 in the heavens, and whatever you·should·loose on
Mt 18:28 *him*, saying, 'Repay me what you·owe *me*.
Mt 19:6 one flesh. Accordingly, what God yoked·together,
Mt 20:7 ·out into the vineyard, and whatever may·be right,
Mt 20:15 proper for·me to·do whatever I·should·want with
Mt 26:13 whole world, also what she·herself did shall·be·
Mk 6:22 ·girl, "Request·of me whatever you·should·want,
Mk 6:23 to·her, "Whatever you·should·request of·me, I·
Mk 7:11 ·benefited as·a·result of·me, whatever *it·should·be*,
Mk 10:9 Accordingly, what God yoked·together, a·man·of·
Mk 10:35 you·should·do for·us whatever we·should·request.
Mk 11:23 ·be; it·shall·be to·him whatever he·may·declare.
Mk 13:11 premeditate, but·rather whatever should·be·given
Mk 14:8 She·herself made·do with·what she·had. She·came·
Mk 14:9 the whole world, also what she·herself did shall·be·
Rm 4:21 ·being·fully·assured that, what *God* has·promised,
Rm 8:24 an·expectation, for what man expectantly·awaits
Rm 8:25 if we·expectantly·await for·what we·do·not look·
Rm 12:3 more·than what is·necessary to·contemplate
Php 3:16 Nevertheless, for what we·already·attained, let·us·
1Co 7:36 so happens, let·him·do what he·will, he·does·not
1Co 10:13 let yeu to·be·tried above what yeu·are·able, but·
1Co 10:15 ·men; yeu·yeurselves judge what I·disclose:
2Co 11:12 But what I·presently·do, and *what* I·shall·do, *is*
Eph 6:8 having·seen that whatever beneficially·good·thing
Col 3:17 And anything what soever yeu·should·do in word
Col 3:23 And anything what soever *that* yeu·should·do, be·
1Jn 3:22 And whatever·thing we·may·request, we·receive
1Jn 5:15 that he·hears us, whatever·thing we·might request,
3Jn 1:5 ·man, trustworthily do·you·do whatever *good·deed*
Rv 1:11 and, "What you·look·upon, write in an·official·

G3739.3 P:R-APN ἅ (17x)

Jn 5:19 ·upon the Father doing, for whatever that *the Father*
Jn 11:46 and declared to·them what·things Jesus did.
Jn 12:50 "Accordingly, whatever I·myself speak, *it·is* just·as
Jn 18:21 these·men personally·know what I·myself declared.
Lk 7:22 Traversing, report to·John what·things yeu·saw and
Lk 12:12 yeu in the same hour what is·necessary to·declare."
Ac 8:30 ·so, *that* you·know what·things you·read·aloud?
Ac 10:15 again for·a·second·time, "What God purified, you·
Ac 28:22 personally·from you what·things you·contemplate,
Mk 9:9 ·even·to·one·man *concerning* what·things they·saw,
Mk 13:37 "And what I·say to·yeu, I·say to·all.
2Co 1:13 ·yeu, other than what yeu·currently·read·aloud or
2Co 5:10 the body, pertaining·to what he·practiced—
1Ti 1:7 not understanding— neither what they·say, nor
2Ti 2:7 Understand what I·say. For may the Lord give to·you
1Jn 5:15 requests, whatever·things *that* we·have·requested
Rv 1:1 to·show to·his slaves what is·mandatory to·happen

G3739.3 P:R-DSN ᾧ (8x)

Lk 5:25 of·them, taking·up what he·was·laying·down on,
Mt 7:2 by whatever standard·of·judgment yeu·unduly·judge,
Mt 7:2 by whatever standard·of·measurement yeu·unduly·
Mk 4:24 By whatever standard·of·measurement yeu·measure
Rm 14:22 into·judgment by what he·verifiably·approves.
Rm 16:2 ·stand·by her in whatever matter·of·consequence
2Co 11:12 *of·themselves*, in·order·that in what they·boast,
2Co 11:21 But in whatever *manner* someone may·be·

G3739.3 P:R-DPM οἷς (1x)

Php 4:11 I·myself learned, *that* in whatever·state I·am, to·be

G3739.3 P:R-GPN ὧν (3x)

Lk 23:41 appropriate·*punishment* for·what we·practiced.
Ac 22:15 men·of·clay† of·what you·have·clearly·seen and
Mt 6:8 for yeur Father has·seen what·things *are* needed

G3739.4 P:R-NPM οἵ (1x)

Ac 28:10 these also honored us with·many honors.

G3739.4 P:R-GSM οὗ (1x)

Jn 13:24 ·be, concerning the·man·to·whom he·is·referring.

G3739.4 P:R-GPM ὧν (1x)

2Th 2:10 ·perishing, because these did·not accept the love

G3739.5 P:R-NSM ὅς (2x)

Ac 16:2 This *disciple* was·attested·to by the brothers in
Ac 24:6 this·same·man also was·attempting to·profane the

G3739.5 P:R-APM οὕς (1x)

Ac 19:25 After·mustering·together these·men, and·also the

G3739.5 P:R-APN ἅ (1x)

1Co 14:37 ·him·acknowledge that these·things I·write to·yeu

G3739.5 P:R-DSM ᾧ (1x)

Ac 8:10 to·this they·all were·giving·heed, from *the* least unto

G3739.5 P:R-DSN ᾧ (2x)

Rm 5:12 into all men·of·clay† upon this·very *point*: *that* all
1Pe 1:6 In this yeu·leap·for·joy, *although* being·grieved a·

G3739.5 P:R-DPM οἷς (1x)

1Pe 1:12 *And* it·was·revealed to·these·men that *it·was* not

G3739.5 P:R-GSF ἧς (1x)

1Pe 1:10 Concerning this Salvation, the prophets sought·*it*·

G3739.5 P:R-GSN οὗ (1x)

Eph 3:7 ·was·made a·steward of·this *good·news* according·to

G3739.5 P:R-GPF ὧν (1x)

2Pe 1:4 Through these he·has·endowed to·us the most·

G3739.6 P:R-NSM ὅς (20x)

Jn 8:40 to·kill me, a·man·of·clay† that has·spoken to·yeu
Jn 9:24 they·hollered·out·for the man·of·clay† that was blind
Lk 1:61 ·even·one among your kinsfolk that is·called by·this
Lk 7:49 "Who is this that also forgives moral·failures?
Lk 14:15 "Supremely·blessed *is·he* that shall·eat bread in
Lk 14:33 ·among yeu that does·not orderly·take·leave·of all
Lk 18:29 to·yeu, there·is not·even·one·man that left home,
Lk 21:6 a·stone upon a·stone that shall·not be·demolished."
Ac 19:35 for what man·of·clay† is·there that does·not know
Gal 3:10 Utterly·accursed *is* everyone that does·not continue
Mt 12:11 shall·there·be from·among yeu that shall·have one
Mt 24:2 a·stone upon a·stone that shall·not be·demolished,
Mt 27:33 ·to·as GolGotha, that is being·referred·to·as, *the*
Mk 10:29 to·yeu, there·is not·even·one that left home or
Mk 13:2 a·stone upon a·stone that should·not be·demolished,
Rm 8:32 He·that did·not spare his·own Son, but·rather
Jac 1:12 ·blessed *is* a·man that patiently·endures a·proof·trial
Jac 4:12 Who are you·yourself that unduly·judges the other?
1Co 2:16 mind that he·shall·conclusively·weigh·a·matter·for
1Co 6:5 yeu? Not·even one that shall·be·able to·discern up

G3739.6 P:R-NSN ὅ (16x)

Jn 1:3 not·even one·thing came·to·be that has·come·to·be.
Jn 20:7 and the sweat·towel that was upon his head, *that* it·
Lk 8:17 not *anything* hidden, that shall·not become apparent
Lk 8:17 *anything* hidden·away, that shall·not be·known and
Lk 12:2 having·been·altogether·concealed that shall·not be·
Lk 12:2 be·revealed, nor hidden that shall·not be·known.
Mt 10:26 having·been·concealed, that shall·not be·revealed,
Mt 10:26 be·revealed, and hidden, that shall·not be·known.
Mk 4:4 as he *began* to·sow, that, in·fact, *seed* fell directly·
Mk 7:11 whatever *it·should·be*, that·thing is *now* Qorban,
Mk 7:15 ·outside of·the man·of·clay†, that traversing into
Mk 15:42 since it·was preparation·day (that is, *a·day*
Rm 14:23 Now anything that *is* not from·out of·trust is
Jac 4:5 for·naught, "The spirit that resides in us greatly·
1Jn 4:3 And every spirit that does·not affirm Jesus, the
Rv 17:11 And the Scarlet·Beast that was and is not, even it·

G3739.6 P:R-NPM οἵ (3x)

Jn 6:64 there·are some from·among yeu that do·not trust."
Lk 5:29 and others that were laying·back·and·eating with
Rm 15:21 ·gaze·upon *him*, and those·that have·not heard

G3739.6 P:R-NPF αἵ (1x)

Lk 23:29 the barren, and *the* wombs that did·not bear, and

G3739.6 P:R-NPN ἅ (1x)

Lk 12:20 shall·be those·things·which you·made·ready?

G3739.6 P:R-ASM ὅν (5x)

Jn 6:51 and also the bread that I·myself shall·give is my
Jn 7:36 What *manner·of* saying is this that he·declared,

Lk 21:4 in·absolutely·all the livelihood that she·was·holding.
Ac 15:11 Anointed to·be·saved; according·to that manner,
2Ti 4:13 The cape that I·left·behind at Troas with Carpus, *as*

G3739.6 P:R-ASF ἥν (9x)
Jn 4:32 have a·full·meal to·eat that yeu·yeurselves do·not
Heb 8:9 Not according·to the covenant that I·made with·their
Heb 8:10 *is* the unilateral·covenant that I·shall·enact with·the
Heb 10:16 the unilateral·covenant that I·shall·bequeath unto
1Jn 2:25 is the promise that he·himself did·already·promise
1Jn 3:11 Because this is the message that yeu·heard from *the*
1Jn 4:16 ·known and have·trusted the Love that God has in
1Jn 5:10 ·not trusted in the testimony that God has·testified
1Jn 5:14 this is the freeness·of·speech that we·have toward

G3739.6 P:R-ASN ὅ (22x)
Jn 4:5 near·by to·the open·field that Jacob gave to·his son
Jn 4:14 ·age, but·rather the water that I·shall·give him, it·
Jn 6:14 So·then, seeing that Jesus did a·miraculous·sign, the
Jn 6:37 "All that the Father gives me shall·come toward me;
Jn 14:13 And anything that yeu·should·request in my name,
Jn 16:17 "What is this that he·says to·us, 'A·little·while, and
Jn 16:18 "What is this·thing that he·says, 'A·little·while?
Lk 6:3 Did·yeu·not·even read·aloud this·thing that David did
Ac 7:16 and laid in the tomb that AbRaham's *son Jacob*
Ac 23:19 "What is·it that you·have to·announce to·me?
Heb 8:3 this·man to·have something also that he·may·offer.
Mt 8:4 and offer the present that Moses specifically·assigned
Mt 20:22 ·yeu·able to·drink the cup that I·myself am·about
Mt 20:22 And the immersion that I·myself am·immersed·in
Mt 20:23 the immersion that I·myself shall·be·immersed·in,
Mk 10:38 ·yeu·able to·drink the cup that I·myself drink·of?
Mk 10:38 be·immersed·in the immersion that I·myself *am*
Mk 10:39 "In·fact, the cup that I·myself drink, yeu·shall·
Mk 10:39 and in·the immersion that I·myself am·immersed,
1Co 4:7 And what·do you·have that you·did·not receive?
Rv 17:8 *The* Scarlet·Beast that you·saw, it·was and is not.
Rv 19:12 a·name having·been·written that not·even·one·man

G3739.6 P:R-APM οὕς (2x)
Jn 17:12 "I·vigilantly·kept those·that you·have·given to·me,
Lk 24:17 sayings *are* these that yeu·toss·back·and·forth to

G3739.6 P:R-APN ἅ (22x)
Jn 3:2 to·do these miraculous·signs that you·yourself do
Jn 4:45 him, having·clearly·seen all·the·things that he·did in
Jn 5:20 Son and shows him all·things that he·himself does,
Jn 6:63 ·even·one·thing. The utterances that I·myself speak
Jn 7:3 disciples also may·observe the works that you do.
Jn 10:6 ·*sort·of*·things it·was that he·was·speaking to·them
Jn 10:25 "The works that I·myself do in my Father's name,
Jn 14:10 me? "The utterances that I·myself speak to·yeu, I·
Jn 14:12 in me, the works that I·myself do, he·shall·do
Jn 15:15 because all·things that I·heard personally·from my
Lk 10:23 eyes looking·upon the·things·that yeu·look·upon.
Ac 3:18 But those·things·which God fully·announced·
Mt 11:4 announce to·John those·things·which yeu·hear and
Mt 21:15 ·seeing the marvelous·things that he·did and·also
Mk 1:44 purification those·things·which Moses specifically·
1Co 10:20 *No,* but·rather *I·reply* that those·things *which* the
1Co 12:23 And those *members* of·the body, which·we·
2Co 1:17 levity? Or the·things·that I·purpose, do·I·purpose
Col 2:18 one·intruding·into those·things·which he·has·not
2Jn 1:8 completely·lose those·things·for·which we·worked,
Rv 3:2 ·establish the·things remaining that are·about to·die,
Rv 10:4 to·me, "Seal·up those·things·which the Seven

G3739.6 P:R-DSM ᾧ (1x)
Jn 4:50 man·of·clay† trusted the word that Jesus declared to·

G3739.6 P:R-DSF ᾗ (4x)
Lk 12:40 Son of·Clay·Man† comes in·that hour you·do·not
Lk 17:29 but on·that day *when* Lot went·forth from Sodom,
Lk 17:30 "In·the·same·manner shall·it·be in·that day *when*
Mt 24:50 *him*, and at an·hour that he·does·not know,

G3739.6 P:R-DSN ᾧ (4x)
Lk 6:38 same standard·of·measurement that yeu·measure, it·
Heb 2:18 For in that he·has·suffered, he·himself being·tried,
Heb 10:10 By that will, we·are the·ones having·been·made·
Rm 8:3 ·the Torah-Law, in that it·was·being·weak through

G3739.6 P:R-DPF αἷς (1x)
2Th 1:4 and tribulations that yeu·hold·up·*under*.

G3739.6 P:R-DPN οἷς (3x)
Lk 2:20 praising God over all·the·things that they·heard and
Lk 24:25 in·the heart to·trust on all that the prophets spoke.
Rm 6:21 then in those·things·of·which now yeu·are·ashamed

G3739.6 P:R-GSM οὗ (1x)
Jn 15:20 "Remember the saying that I·myself declared to·

G3739.6 P:R-GSF ἧς (9x)
Lk 1:20 even·until *the* day that these·things should·occur,
Lk 7:45 ·kiss, but she·herself since that *moment* I·entered·in,
Lk 17:27 ·given·away·in·marriage, even·until that day *when*
Ac 1:22 of·John, unto the day that he·was·taken·up from us,
Ac 20:18 are·fully·acquainted, from that first day since I·
Ac 24:21 this one address that I·yelled·out standing among
Mt 24:38 giving·away·in·marriage, even·until that day *that*
Col 1:6 ·as *it·does* also in yeu since that day yeu·heard *it* and
Col 1:9 we·ourselves also (since that day *when* we·heard *of*·

G3739.6 P:R-GSN οὗ (2x)
Jn 4:14 ·drink from·out of·the water that I·myself shall·give
Mt 18:19 any matter·of·consequence that they·may·request,

G3739.6 P:R-GPF ὧν (1x)
Lk 19:37 voice concerning all *the* miracles that they·saw,

G3739.6 P:R-GPN ὧν (9x)
Jn 13:29 to·him, "Buy *those·things* that we·have need·of for
Lk 9:36 days not·even·one of·those·things·which they·have·.
Lk 15:16 belly with the carob-pods that the pigs were·eating,
Lk 23:14 according·to those·things·of·which yeu·legally·
Ac 1:1 *was* concerning all that Jesus began both to·do and
Ac 21:19 each and·every one of·those·things·which God did
Ac 26:22 ·one·thing aside·from those·things·which both the
Rm 15:18 of·any of·such·things except·what Anointed-One
Eph 3:20 operating in us, those·things·which we·request or

EG3739.6 (2x)
Mt 23:34 and scribes, and *some* from·among them yeu·
Mt 23:34 ·kill and shall·crucify, and *some* from·among them

G3739.7 P:R-NSM ὅς (2x)
Rm 14:5 In·fact, someone judges one·day *to·be* above·and·
Rm 14:5 *another* day, yet someone *else* judges every day *to*·

G3739.7 P:R-NSN ὅ (3x)
Mt 13:23 and produces, in·fact, some *seed* a·hundredfold,
Mt 13:23 some *seed* a·hundredfold, some *seed* sixtyfold, and
Mt 13:23 some *seed* sixtyfold, and some *seed* thirtyfold."

G3739.7 P:R-NPN ἅ (3x)
Mt 13:4 ·*forth* to·sow, in·fact, some *seeds* fell directly·by
2Ti 2:20 and of·earthenware, and some *are·set·out* in·fact
2Ti 2:20 ·*out* in·fact unto honor, and some unto dishonor.

G3739.7 P:R-ASN ὅ (3x)
Mt 13:8 were·giving fruit, in·fact some *seed* a·hundredfold,
Mt 13:8 some *seed* a·hundredfold, some *seed* sixtyfold, and
Mt 13:8 some *seed* sixtyfold, and some *seed* thirtyfold.

G3739.7 P:R-APM οὕς (4x)
Ac 27:44 rest *got there*, in·fact, some·men on planks, and
Ac 27:44 ·men on planks, and some·men on some·of·the
Jud 1:22 show·mercy to·some while·using·discernment.
1Co 12:28 even, in·fact, some·of·whom *which* God laid·out

G3739.7 P:R-DPM οἷς (2x)
2Co 2:16 In·fact, to·some *we·are* an·aroma of·death unto
2Co 2:16 unto death, and to·some an·aroma of·life-above

G3739.8 P:R-ASN ὅ (1x)
1Co 4:2 Now *with* such·a·thing remaining, it·is·sought in the

G3739.8 P:R-APN ἅ (1x)
Rv 5:13 and beneath the earth, and such·as are upon the sea,

G3739.8 P:R-DPM οἷς (1x)
Lk 12:24 sow nor·even do·they·reap. For·such *creatures*,

G3739.8 P:R-DPN οἷς (2x)
Ac 26:12 "And among such *activities*, while·traversing to
Heb 13:9 ·not beneficial·to the·ones walking in such·things.

G3739.8 P:R-GSN οὗ (1x)
Lk 7:47 "As·such, on·account·of·grace I·say to·you, her

G3739.8 P:R-GPM ὧν (1x)
Rm 3:8 ·things may·come." Of·such·men, the judgment is

G3739.8 P:R-GPN ὧν (1x)
Ac 25:18 not·even·one accusation of·such·things *as* I·myself

G3739.9 P:R-NSM ὅς (3x)
Rm 14:2 In·fact, one trusts that·he·may·eat all·things, but
1Co 7:7 from·out of·God, in·fact, one in·this·manner, and
1Co 11:21 ·to *others*; and in·fact, one goes·hungry, and

G3739.9 P:R-ASM ὅν (1x)
Lk 23:33 and·also the criminals, in·fact one at *the* right·hand

G3739.9 P:R-ASN ὅ (1x)
Rm 9:21 lump·of·clay to·make, in·fact, one vessel to honor

G3739.9 P:R-DSM ᾧ (2x)
Mt 25:15 And in·fact, to·one he·gave five talants·of·silver,
1Co 12:8 For in·fact to·one is·given through the Spirit a·

G3739.10 P:R-NSM ὅς (2x)
1Co 7:7 one in·this·manner, and another in·that·manner.
1Co 11:21 ·fact, one goes·hungry, and another gets·drunk.

G3739.10 P:R-ASN ὅ (1x)
Rm 9:21 ·fact, one vessel to honor and another to dishonor?

G3739.10 P:R-DSM ᾧ (2x)
Mt 25:15 five talants·of·silver, and to·another two, and to·
Mt 25:15 to·another two, and to·another one, to·each·man

G3739.11 P:R-ASM ὅν (1x)
Lk 23:33 ·fact one at *the* right·hand, and the·other at *the* left.

G3739.11 P:R-APM οὕς (1x)
Jud 1:23 And others save with a·fear while·snatching *them*

G3739.12 P:R-DPM οἷς (1x)
Lk 12:1 In the·meanwhile, with·the crowd being·completely·

G3739.13 P:R-DSF ᾗ (3x)
Lk 12:46 shall·come in a·day when he·does·not anticipate
Lk 12:46 *him*, and at an·hour when he·does·not know, and
Mt 24:50 shall·come on a·day when he·does·not anticipate

G3739.13 P:R-DPF αἷς (1x)
Lk 1:25 for·me, in *the* days when he·took·notice·of *me*, to·

G3739.13 P:R-GSF ἧς (1x)
Ac 1:2 even·until *the* day when he·was·taken·up, after·

G3739.14 ADV οὗ (1x)
Rm 9:26 *that* in the place where it·was·uttered to·them,

G3739.14 P:R-DSM ᾧ (1x)
Jn 11:6 two days still in *the same* place where he·was.

G3739.14 P:R-DSF ᾗ (1x)
Ac 11:11 at the home where I·was, having·been·dispatched

G3740 ὁσάκις hôsákis *adv.* (3x)
Roots:G3739 See:G0302

G3740 ADV ὁσάκις (3x)
1Co 11:25 Do this, as·often·as yeu·would·drink *it*, as my
1Co 11:26 For as·often·as yeu·should·eat this bread, and
Rv 11:6 ·any punishing·blow, as·often·as they·should·want.

G3741 ὅσιος hôsiôs *adj.* (8x)
Compare:G1342 G2413 G0040 G2126 See:G3742 G3743
xLangEquiv:H2623

G3741.2 A-NSM ὅσιος (3x)
Heb 7:26 ·befitting·for us, *who·is* divinely·holy, innocent,
Rv 15:4 Because *you* alone *are* divinely·holy, because
Rv 16:5 that·was, and the·one divinely·holy, because you·

G3741.2 A-ASM ὅσιον (1x)
Tit 1:8 righteous, divinely·holy, self-restrained,

G3741.2 A-APM ὁσίους (1x)
1Ti 2:8 ·pray in every place, lifting·up divinely·holy hands,

G3741.3 A-APN ὅσια (1x)
Ac 13:34 to·yeu the trustworthy, Divine·Promises of·David.

G3741.4 A-ASM ὅσιον (2x)
Ac 2:27 shall·you·give your Divine·Holy·One to·see decay.
Ac 13:35 ·shall·not give your Divine·Holy·One to·see decay.

G3742 ὁσιότης hôsiótēs *n.* (2x)
Roots:G3741 Compare:G0041 G0038 G0042 See:G3743 G3742-1

G3742 N-DSF ὁσιότητι (2x)
Lk 1:75 in divine·holiness and righteousness in·the·sight·of·
Eph 4:24 in righteousness and in·divine·holiness of·the truth)

G3743 ὁσίως hôsíōs *adv.* (1x)
Roots:G3741 See:G3742

G3743.1 ADV ὁσίως (1x)

1Th 2:10 how in·a·divinely·holy·manner and righteously

G3744 ὀσμή ôsmḗ *n.* (6x)
Roots:G3605 Compare:G3750-2 G2174-2 See:G2175 xLangEquiv:H7381 A7382

G3744.1 N-NSF ὀσμή (2x)
2Co 2:16 In·fact, to·some *we·are* an·aroma of·death unto
2Co 2:16 death, and to·some an·aroma of·life-above unto

G3744.1 N-ASF ὀσμήν (3x)
Php 4:18 personally·from yeu, a·soothing aroma, a·sacrifice
2Co 2:14 and making·apparent the aroma of·his knowledge
Eph 5:2 and a·sacrifice to·God for a·soothing aroma.

G3744.1 N-GSF ὀσμῆς (1x)
Jn 12:3 ·filled from·out of·the aroma of·the ointment.

G3745 ὅσ•ος hốsôs *p:k.* (113x)
Roots:G3739

G3745.1 P:K-NPM ὅσοι (29x)
Jn 1:12 But as·many·as did·receive him, to·them he·gave
Lk 4:40 with·the sun sinking·down, as·many·as were sick,
Lk 9:5 And *for* as·many·as should·not accept yeu, while·
Ac 3:24 ·ones of·subsequent·order, as·many·as that·spoke,
Ac 4:6 and AlexAnder, and as·many·as were from·among
Ac 4:34 in·a·bind, for as·many·as were·subsisting *being*
Ac 5:36 And all (as·many·as were·persuaded by·him) were·
Ac 5:37 And all (as·many·as were·convinced by·him) were·
Ac 10:45 ·astonished, as·many·as came·together with·Peter,
Ac 13:48 ·trusted (as·many·as were having·been·assigned to
Heb 2:15 he·may·release them, as·many·as·who (through
Gal 3:10 For as·many·as are birthed·from·out of·works of·
Gal 3:27 For as·many·of·yeu·as are·immersed into *the*
Gal 6:12 As·much·as they·want to·project·a·good·
Gal 6:16 And as·many·as shall·conform·and·march·orderly
Mt 14:36 of·his garment, and as·many·as did·lay·hold *of·it*
Mk 3:10 ·and·cured many, such·for as·many *of·them* as
Mk 6:11 And *for* as·many·as should·not accept yeu, or·
Mk 6:56 of·his garment. And as·many·as were·laying·hold
Rm 2:12 For as·many·as did·morally·fail without·
Rm 2:12 ·Torah-Law. And as·many·as did·morally·fail with
Rm 6:3 ·yeu·not·know, that as·many·as are·immersed into
Rm 8:14 For as·many·as are·led by·God's Spirit, these are
Php 3:15 as·many·as *would·become* completely·mature,
Col 2:1 LaoDicea, and *for* as·many·as have·not clearly·seen
1Ti 6:1 Let as·many slaves as are under a·yoke resolutely·
Rv 2:24 to·the rest in Thyatira (as·many·as do·not have this
Rv 13:15 ·speak, and should·make as·many·as would not
Rv 18:17 ·ships, and sailors, and as·many·as work the sea,

G3745.1 P:K-NPF ὅσαι (1x)
2Co 1:20 For as·many·as *are* God's promises, in him *is* the

G3745.1 P:K-NPN ὅσα (7x)
Rm 15:4 For as·many·things·as were·previously·written,
Php 4:8 remaining, brothers: As·many·things·as are true,
Php 4:8 as·many·things·as *are* morally·worthy·of·reverent·
Php 4:8 ·reverent·respect, as·many·things·as *are* righteous,
Php 4:8 *are* righteous, as·many·things·as *are* morally·clean,
Php 4:8 ·clean, as·many·things·as *are* of·kind·sentiment, as·
Php 4:8 ·sentiment, as·many·things·as *are* of·fine·reputation

G3745.1 P:K-APM ὅσους (4x)
Ac 2:39 the·ones at·a·distance, as·many·as Yahweh our God
Mt 22:9 of·the roadways, and as·many·as yeu·might find,
Mt 22:10 gathered·together all, as·many·as they·found,
Rv 3:19 'As·many·as I·may·have·affection·for, I·myself

G3745.1 P:K-APF ὅσας (1x)
Mk 3:28 revilements, as·many·things·as they·would revile.

G3745.1 P:K-APN ὅσα (17x)
Jn 10:41 ·sign, but all·things as·many·as John declared
Jn 16:13 but·rather as·many·things·as he·should·hear, *that*
Jn 16:15 "All·things, as·many·things·as the Father has, are
Jn 16:23 to·yeu, as·many·things·as yeu·would request·of·the
Lk 4:23 yourself. As·many·things·as we·heard happening in
Lk 12:3 Because as·many·things·as yeu·declared in the
Lk 18:12 I·tithe all·things, *on* as·many·things·as I·procure.'
Lk 18:22 Sell all·things, as·many·things·as you·have, and
Ac 3:22 all·things," as·many·things·as he·would speak to
Ac 4:28 to·do as·many·things·as your hand and your counsel
Mt 18:18 I·say to·yeu, as·many·things·as yeu·should·bind
Mt 18:18 heaven, and as·many·things·as yeu·should·loose
Mk 9:13 and they·did to·him as·many·things·as they·wanted,
Mk 11:24 all·things, as·many·things·as yeu·would request
Mk 12:44 cast·in all·things, as·many·as she·was·holding, all
Jud 1:10 *in* as·many·things·as they·are·fully·acquainted·with
Rv 1:2 of·Jesus Anointed, and *to* as·many·things·as he·saw.

G3745.2 P:K-NPN ὅσα (1x)
Jn 21:25 ·are also many other·things, as·much·as Jesus did,

G3745.2 P:K-ASN ὅσον (7x)
Jn 6:11 small·broiled·fish as·much·as they·were·wanting.
Heb 3:3 in as·much·as the·one planning·and·constructing
Heb 9:27 according·to as·much·as it·is·laid·away for·the
Mt 25:40 I·say to·yeu, in as·much·as yeu·did *it* to·one of·the
Mt 25:45 I·say to·yeu, in as·much·as yeu·did·not do *it* to·
Mk 7:36 But as·much·as he·himself thoroughly·charged
Rm 11:13 the Gentiles, in as·much·as I·myself am in·fact

G3745.2 P:K-APN ὅσα (14x)
Jn 11:22 even now, that as·much·as you·should·request·of
Jn 15:14 if yeu·should·do as·much·as I·myself command
Jn 17:7 that all·things, as·much·as you·have·given to·me,
Mt 7:12 all·things, as·much·as yeu·should·want that the
Mt 13:44 ·heads·on·out and sells all (as·much·as he·has) and
Mt 13:46 has·sold·off all (as·much·as he·was·holding) and
Mt 17:12 but·yet they·did to him as·much·as they·wanted.
Mt 18:25 children and all·things as·much·as he·was·holding,
Mt 21:22 And all·things, as·much·as yeu·may·request in the
Mt 23:3 whatever as·much·as they·should·declare to·yeu
Mt 28:20 ·keep all·things as·much·as I·commanded yeu.
Mk 10:21 lack, head·on·out, sell as·much·as you·have, and
Rm 3:19 ·personally·know that as·much·as the Torah-Law
Rv 18:7 As·much·as she·glorified herself and lived·in·

G3745.2 P:K-DSN ὅσῳ (3x)
Heb 1:4 by·as·much·as he·has·inherited a·more·superb
Heb 8:6 ·superb public·service, by·as·much·as he·is also *the*
Heb 10:25 ·much the·more, as·much·as yeu·look·upon the

G3745.2 P:K-GPM ὅσων (1x)
Lk 11:8 ·awakened shall·give him as·much·as he·has·need.

G3745.3 P:K-NSN ὅσον (1x)
Rv 21:16 its length is as·vast and as·long·as the breadth. And

G3745.3 P:K-ASM ὅσον (5x)
Gal 4:1 heir, for·a·span·of time (as·long·as he·is an·infant),
Mk 2:19 is with them? *For* as·long a·time as they·do·have
Rm 7:1 for·a·span·of time, *that·is, for* as·long·as he·lives?
2Pe 1:13 ·resolutely·consider·it right, for as·long·as I·am in
1Co 7:39 ·Torah-Law over a·lifetime as·long·as her husband

G3745.3 P:K-ASN ὅσον (2x)
Heb 10:37 "For yet, as·long·as a·little·while, the·one who·
Mt 9:15 able to·mourn, as·long·as the bridegroom is with

G3745.4 P:K-APN ὅσα (16x)
Lk 8:39 and give·an·account·of what·many·things God did
Lk 8:39 in the whole city what·many·things Jesus did·for·
Lk 9:10 ·an·account to *Jesus* what·many·things they·did.
Ac 4:23 ·company and reported what·many·things *that* the
Ac 9:13 concerning this man, what·many wrongs he·did to·
Ac 9:16 to·him what·many·things it·is·mandatory·for him
Ac 9:39 and fully·exhibiting what·many inner·tunics and
Ac 14:27 they·reported·in·detail what·many·things *that* God
Ac 15:4 they·reported·in·detail what·many·things *that* God
Ac 15:12 recounting·in·detail what·many miraculous·signs
Mk 3:8 — after·hearing what·many·things he·was·doing, a·
Mk 5:19 ·in·detail to·them what·many·things Yahweh did
Mk 5:20 ·herald in the DecaPolis what·many·things Jesus did
Mk 6:30 to·him all·things, even what·many·things they·did,
Mk 6:30 they·did, and what·many·things they·instructed.
Jud 1:10 revile what·many·things they·do·not personally·

G3745.5 P:K-APN ὅσα (2x)
Jn 4:29 who declared to·me all the·many·things I·did! Could
Jn 4:39 "He·declared to·me all the·many·things I·did."

G3745.6 P:K-NPM ὅσοι (1x)
Jn 10:8 All the·many·which came before me are Thieves and

G3745.7 P:K-APN ὅσα (1x)
2Ti 1:18 Day; and in·how·many·things he·attended *to·me* at

G3746 ὅσ•περ hốspêr *p:r.* (1x)
Roots:G3739 G4007

G3746 P:R-ASM-P ὅνπερ (1x)
Mk 15:6 ·prisoner, whom·specifically they·requested.

G3747 ὀστέον ôstéôn *n.* (5x)
ὀστοῦν ôstôûn [contracted]
xLangEquiv:H6106 xLangAlso:H1634

G3747 N-NSN-C ὀστοῦν (1x)
Jn 19:36 ·be·completely·fulfilled, "A·bone of·him shall·not

G3747 N-APN ὀστέα (1x)
Lk 24:39 does·not have flesh and bones, just·as yeu·observe

G3747 N-GPN ὀστέων (3x)
Heb 11:22 and he·gave·a·command concerning his bones.
Mt 23:27 they·overflow of·dead *men's* bones and of·all
Eph 5:30 from·out of·his flesh, and from·out of·his bones.

G3748 ὅσ•τις hốstis *p:r.* (146x)
ἥ•τις hḗtis [feminine]
ὅ•τι hốti [neuter]
Roots:G3739 G5100 Compare:G3754
(abbreviated listing for G3748)

G3748.ª P:R-ASN ὅ τί (1x)
(list for G3748.ª:P:R-ASN excluded)

G3748.2 P:R-NPM οἵτινες (2x)
(list for G3748.2:P:R-NPM excluded)

G3748.3 P:R-NPM οἵτινες (1x)
(list for G3748.3:P:R-NPM excluded)

G3748.4 P:R-NSM ὅστις (10x)
(list for G3748.4:P:R-NSM excluded)

G3748.4 P:R-NSF ἥτις (9x)
(list for G3748.4:P:R-NSF excluded)

G3748.4 P:R-NPM οἵτινες (46x)
(list for G3748.4:P:R-NPM excluded)

G3748.4 P:R-NPF αἵτινες (6x)
(list for G3748.4:P:R-NPF excluded)

G3748.5 P:R-NSM ὅστις (11x)
(list for G3748.5:P:R-NSM excluded)

G3748.5 P:R-NPM οἵτινες (1x)
(list for G3748.5:P:R-NPM excluded)

G3748.7 P:R-NSF ἥτις (3x)
(list for G3748.7:P:R-NSF excluded)

G3748.7 P:R-NPM οἵτινες (1x)
(list for G3748.7:P:R-NPM excluded)

G3748.7 P:R-ASN ὅ τί (1x)
(list for G3748.7:P:R-ASN excluded)

G3748.8 P:R-NPM οἵτινες (1x)
(list for G3748.8:P:R-NPM excluded)

G3748.9 P:R-NSM ὅστις (1x)
(list for G3748.9:P:R-NSM excluded)

G3748.9 P:R-NPM οἵτινες (3x)
(list for G3748.9:P:R-NPM excluded)

G3748.10 P:R-NPM οἵτινες (1x)
(list for G3748.10:P:R-NPM excluded)

G3748.11 P:R-NPF αἵτινες (1x)
(list for G3748.11:P:R-NPF excluded)

G3748.11 P:R-NPN ἅτινα (1x)
(list for G3748.11:P:R-NPN excluded)

G3748.12 P:R-NSM ὅστις (1x)
(list for G3748.12:P:R-NSM excluded)

G3748.12 P:R-NSF ἥτις (25x)
(list for G3748.12:P:R-NSF excluded)

G3748.12 P:R-NPM οἵτινες (3x)
(list for G3748.12:P:R-NPM excluded)

G3748.12 P:R-NPF αἵτινες (4x)
(list for G3748.12:P:R-NPF excluded)

G3748.12 P:R-NPN ἅτινα (3x)
(list for G3748.12:P:R-NPN excluded)

G3748.13 P:R-NPN ἅτινα (1x)
(list for G3748.13:P:R-NPN excluded)

G3748.15 P:R-NPN ἅτινα (1x)
(list for G3748.15:P:R-NPN excluded)

G3748.16 P:R-ASN ὅ τί (2x)
(list for G3748.16:P:R-ASN excluded)

G3748.18 P:R-NSM ὅστις (2x)
(list for G3748.18:P:R-NSM excluded)
G3748.19 P:R-NSM ὅστις (1x)
(list for G3748.19:P:R-NSM excluded)
G3748.19 P:R-NSF ἥτις (2x)
(list for G3748.19:P:R-NSF excluded)
G3748.19 P:R-NSN ὅ τί (1x)
(list for G3748.19:P:R-NSN excluded)

G3749 ὀστράκινος ôstrákinôs *adj.* (3x)
Compare:G2764
G3749.1 A-NPN ὀστράκινα (1x)
2Ti 2:20 but·rather also of·wood and of·earthenware, and
G3749.1 A-DPN ὀστρακίνοις (1x)
2Co 4:7 But we·have this treasure in earthenware vessels, in·
EG3749.1 (1x)
1Th 4:4 ·how to·possess his·own *earthenware* vessel in

G3750 ὄσφρησις ósphrēsis *n.* (1x)
Roots:G3605 See:G3750-1 G3750-2
G3750.1 N-NSF ὄσφρησις (1x)
1Co 12:17 *is* hearing, where·is the sense·of·smell placed?

G3751 ὀσφῦς ôsphŷs *n.* (8x)
xLangEquiv:H4975
G3751.1 N-NPF ὀσφύες (1x)
Lk 12:35 "Yeur loins must·be having·been·girded·about and
G3751.1 N-ASF ὀσφύν (3x)
Mt 3:4 ·*girded·with* a·leather belt around his loins, and his
Mk 1:6 hair and with·a·leather belt around his loins, and *was*
Eph 6:14 after·personally·girding yeur·own loins with truth
G3751.1 N-APF ὀσφύας (1x)
1Pe 1:13 girding·up the loins of·yeur innermost·mind, being·
G3751.1 N-DSF ὀσφύϊ (1x)
Heb 7:10 for he·was yet in the loins of·*his*·father when
G3751.1 N-GSF ὀσφύος (2x)
Ac 2:30 *that* from·out of·*the*·fruit of·his loins, according·to
Heb 7:5 ·come·forth from·among the loins of·AbRaham.

G3752 ὅτ•αν hótan *conj.* (122x)
Roots:G3753 G0302
G3752.1 CONJ ὅταν (119x)
Jn 2:10 the good wine, and whenever they·should·be·drunk,
Jn 4:25 ·as Anointed-One. Whenever that·one should·come,
Jn 5:7 I·have no man·of·clay†, whenever the water should·
Jn 7:27 ·source he·is. Now whenever the Anointed-One
Jn 7:31 were·saying, "Whenever the Anointed-One should·
Jn 8:28 declared to·them, "Whenever yeu·should·elevate the
Jn 8:44 ·is not truth in him. Whenever he·should·speak a·lie,
Jn 10:4 "And whenever he·should·cast·forth his·own sheep,
Jn 13:19 ·happens in·order·that, whenever it·should·happen,
Jn 14:29 in·order·that, whenever it·should·happen, yeu·
Jn 15:26 "But whenever the Companion/Intercessor should·
Jn 16:4 have·I·spoken to·yeu, that whenever the hour
Jn 16:13 "But whenever that·one, the Spirit of·Truth, should·
Jn 16:21 "Whenever the woman should·reproduce·and·give·
Jn 16:21 her hour is·come, but whenever she·may·birth the
Jn 21:18 But whenever you·should·grow·agedly·old, you·
Lk 5:35 and then, whenever the bridegroom should·be·
Lk 6:22 ·blessed are·yeu, whenever the men·of·clay†
Lk 6:22 and whenever they·should·distinctly·separate yeu
Lk 6:26 "Woe to·yeu, whenever all the men·of·clay†
Lk 8:13 upon the solid·rock, whenever they·should·hear,
Lk 9:26 ·ashamed·of that·man whenever he·should·come in
Lk 11:2 he·declared to·them, "Whenever yeu·should·pray,
Lk 11:21 "Whenever the strong·man, having·been·fully·
Lk 11:24 "Whenever the impure spirit should·go·forth from
Lk 11:34 also full·of·light; but whenever *your eye* should·be
Lk 11:36 ·be full·of·light, as whenever the radiant·shimmer
Lk 12:11 "And whenever they·should·bring yeu before the
Lk 12:54 ·the crowds, "Whenever yeu·should·see the thick·
Lk 12:55 And whenever *yeu·should·see the* south·wind
Lk 13:28 ·teeth, whenever yeu·should·gaze·upon AbRaham,
Lk 14:8 "Whenever you·should·be·called·forth by any *man*
Lk 14:10 "But·rather whenever you·should·be·called·forth,
Lk 14:10 in·order·that whenever the·one having·called·for
Lk 14:12 him, "Whenever you·should·make a·luncheon or
Lk 14:13 "But·rather whenever you·should·make a·reception
Lk 16:4 whenever I·should·be·relieved·from·duty of·the
Lk 16:9 in·order·that, whenever yeu·may·cease·living,
Lk 17:10 In·this·manner, whenever yeu·should·do all the·
Lk 21:7 *that shall·be* whenever these·things should·be·about
Lk 21:9 "But whenever yeu·should·hear·of wars and chaos,
Lk 21:20 "And whenever yeu·should·see JeruSalem being·
Lk 21:30 Whenever they·should·bud, even·now while·
Lk 21:31 ·manner, whenever yeu·should·see these·things
Lk 23:42 recall me to·mind whenever you·should·come into
Ac 23:35 ·thoroughly·hear you whenever your legal·accusers
Ac 24:22 them, declaring, "Whenever Lysias the regiment·
Heb 1:6 And again, whenever he·should·bring the Firstborn
Mt 5:11 ·blessed are·yeu whenever *men* should·reproach yeu
Mt 6:2 Accordingly, whenever you·should·do a·merciful·act
Mt 6:5 "And whenever you·should·pray, you·shall·not be
Mt 6:6 "But you, whenever you·should·pray, enter into your
Mt 6:16 "But whenever yeu·should·fast, do·not become
Mt 9:15 But days shall·come, whenever the bridegroom
Mt 10:19 But whenever they·should·hand yeu over, yeu·
Mt 10:23 But whenever they·should·persecute yeu in this
Mt 12:43 "Now whenever the impure spirit should·come·out
Mt 13:32 ·of·seeds. But whenever it·should·be·grown, it·is
Mt 15:2 wash their hands whenever they·should·eat bread."
Mt 19:28 in The Regeneration whenever the Son of·Clay·
Mt 21:40 "So·then, whenever the owner of·the vineyard
Mt 23:15 ·to·Judaism, and whenever he·should·become·one,
Mt 24:15 "Accordingly, whenever yeu·should·see " the
Mt 24:32 "Even·now, whenever its branch should·become
Mt 24:33 ·then yeu·yeurselves, whenever yeu·should·see all
Mt 25:31 "But whenever the Son of·Clay·Man† should·come
Mt 26:29 until that day whenever I·may·drink it brand-new
Mk 2:20 But days shall·come, whenever the bridegroom
Mk 3:11 impure spirits, whenever one·was·observing him,
Mk 4:15 is·sown: and whenever they·should·hear, the
Mk 4:16 ·places: ones·who, whenever they·should·hear the
Mk 4:29 "But whenever the fruit should·be·yielded·up,
Mk 4:31 ·seed, which, whenever it·should·be·sown in the
Mk 4:32 But whenever it·should·be·sown, it·springs·up and
Mk 8:38 ·be·ashamed·of him, whenever he·should·come in
Mk 9:9 what·things they·saw, except whenever the Son of·
Mk 11:25 "And whenever yeu·should·stand·fast while·yeu·
Mk 12:23 in the resurrection, whenever they·should·rise·up,
Mk 12:25 "For whenever they·should·rise·up from·among
Mk 13:4 what *shall·be* the sign whenever all these·things
Mk 13:7 And whenever yeu·should·hear·of wars and rumors
Mk 13:11 "But whenever they·should·bring *yeu for·judgment*
Mk 13:14 "But whenever yeu·should·see " the Abomination
Mk 13:28 "Even·now, whenever its branch should·become
Mk 13:29 whenever yeu·should·see these·things happening,
Mk 14:7 yeurselves. And whenever yeu·should·want, yeu·
Mk 14:25 until that day whenever I·may·drink it brand-new
Rm 11:27 ·them," ·whenever I·should·remove their moral·
Jac 1:2 all joy whenever yeu·should·entirely·fall·into diverse
1Th 5:3 For whenever they·should·say, "Peace and security,
2Th 1:10 whenever he·should·come to·be·glorified in his
Tit 3:12 Whenever I·shall·send Artemas to you, or Tychicus,
1Co 3:4 For whenever someone should·say, "In·fact, I·
1Co 13:10 But whenever the complete should·come, then
1Co 14:26 brothers? Whenever yeu·should·come·together,
1Co 15:24 ·that, the end, whenever he·should·hand·over the
1Co 15:24 whenever he·should·fully·render·impotent every
1Co 15:28 And whenever all·things should·be·made·subject
1Co 15:54 So whenever this corruptible *being* should·dress·
1Co 16:2 ·be no contributions whenever I·should·come.
1Co 16:3 And whenever I·should·arrive·publicly, whomever
1Co 16:5 yeu, whenever I·should·go·throughout Macedonia,
1Co 16:12 but he·shall·come whenever he·should·have·.
2Co 10:6 ·disregard, whenever yeur attentive·obedience
2Co 12:10 of·Anointed-One, for whenever I·may·be·weak,
2Co 13:9 ·are·glad, whenever we·ourselves should·be·weak,
Col 3:4 Whenever the Anointed-One, *who·is* our life·above,
Col 4:16 And whenever the letter should·be·read·aloud
1Ti 5:11 for whenever they·would·live·luxuriously·and· the
1Jn 2:28 in·order·that whenever he·should·be·made·apparent
1Jn 5:2 the children of·God, whenever we·love God and
Rv 4:9 And whenever the living·beings shall·give glory and
Rv 9:5 ·scorpion, whenever he·should·strike a·man·of·clay†
Rv 10:7 seventh angel, whenever he·should·intend to·sound,
Rv 11:7 And whenever they·should·finish their testimony,
Rv 12:4 her child whenever she·should·produce·birth.
Rv 17:10 did·not·yet come; and whenever he·should·come,
Rv 18:9 over her, whenever they·should·look·upon the
Rv 20:7 And whenever the thousand years should·be·
G3752.2 CONJ ὅταν (3x)
Jn 9:5 Inasmuch·as I·should·be in the world, I·am a·light of·
Rm 2:14 (For inasmuch·as Gentiles, the·ones not having
1Co 15:27 feet." But inasmuch·as *God* should·declare that

G3753 ὅ•τε hôtê *adv.* (105x)
Roots:G3739 G5037 Compare:G2259 See:G3757
G3753.2 ADV ὅτε (105x)
Jn 1:19 the testimony of·John, when the Judeans dispatched
Jn 2:22 Accordingly, when he·was·awakened from·among
Jn 4:21 me, because an·hour is·coming when, neither on this
Jn 4:23 and now is, when the true ones·that·fall·prostrate
Jn 4:45 So·then, when he·came into Galilee, the Galileans
Jn 5:25 and now is, when the dead·ones shall·hear the
Jn 6:24 So·then, when the crowd saw that Jesus was not
Jn 9:4 Night is·coming, when not·even·one·man is·able to·
Jn 9:14 And it·was a·Sabbath when Jesus made the clay and
Jn 12:16 at·the first, but·rather when Jesus was·glorified,
Jn 12:17 being with him when he·hollered·out·for Lazarus
Jn 12:41 IsaIah declared these·things when he·saw his glory
Jn 13:12 Now·then, when he·washed their feet and took·
Jn 13:31 When he·went·forth, Jesus says, "Now the Son of·
Jn 16:25 But·yet an·hour comes, when no longer shall·I·
Jn 17:12 "When I·was with them in the world, I·myself was·
Jn 19:6 Accordingly, when the chief·priests and the
Jn 19:8 Now·then, when Pilate heard this saying, he·was all·
Jn 19:23 Now·then, when they·crucified Jesus, the soldiers
Jn 19:30 Accordingly, when Jesus received the wine·vinegar
Jn 20:24 ·to·as Twin) was not with them when Jesus came.
Jn 21:15 Accordingly, when they·had·dined, Jesus says to·
Jn 21:18 ·certainly, I·say to·you, when you·were younger,
Lk 2:21 And when eight days were·fulfilled to·circumcise
Lk 2:22 Now when the days of·her purification according·to
Lk 2:42 And when he·was twelve years·of·age, after·
Lk 4:25 in the days of·EliJah, when the heaven was·shut·up
Lk 6:13 And when it·was day, he·hailed his disciples *to*·
Lk 13:35 *the time* should·come when yeu·should·declare, "
Lk 15:30 But when this son of·yours came *home*, the·one
Lk 17:22 "Days shall·come when yeu·shall·long to·see one
Lk 22:14 And when the hour came, *Jesus* sat·back·to·eat,
Lk 22:35 to·them, "When I·dispatched yeu without·any
Lk 23:33 And when they·went·off to the place, the·one
Ac 1:13 And when they·entered, they·walked·up into the
Ac 8:12 But when they·trusted Philippe as·he·was·
Ac 8:39 And when they·walked·up out of·the water,
Ac 11:2 Now when Peter walked·up to JeruSalem, the·ones
Ac 12:6 And when HerOd·Agrippa was·intending to·bring
Ac 21:5 And when it·happened *for* us to·properly·finish·out
Ac 21:35 And when he·came to the stairs, *the need* befell
Ac 22:20 And when the blood of·your martyr Stephen was·
Ac 27:39 And when it·was day, they·were·not recognizing
Ac 28:16 And when we·came to Rome, the centurion
Heb 7:10 in the loins of·*his*·father when MalkiTsedeq met·up
Heb 9:17 ·any·time *is·it* in·force when the·one bequeathing
Gal 1:15 But when God took·delight (the·one specially·
Gal 2:11 But when Peter came to Antioch, I·withstood him
Gal 2:12 with the Gentiles. But when they·came, he·was·
Gal 2:14 But·rather, when I·saw that they·did·not walk·
Gal 4:3 ·this·manner, we·ourselves, when we·were infants,
Gal 4:4 But when the complete·fullness of·time was·come,
Mt 7:28 it·happened *that* when YeShua entirely·completed
Mt 9:25 But when the crowd was·cast·out, upon·entering,

Αα Ββ Γγ Δδ Εε Ζζ Ηη Θθ Ιι Κκ Λλ Μμ Νν Ξξ Οο Ππ Ρρ Σσ Ττ Υυ Φφ Χχ Ψψ Ωω

Mt 11:1 And it·happened *that* when YeShua finished
Mt 12:3 what David did, when he·himself was·hungry, and
Mt 13:26 And when the blade blossomed and produced fruit,
Mt 13:48 which when it·was·completely·filled, after·hauling
Mt 13:53 And it·happened *that* when YeShua finished these
Mt 17:25 And when he·entered into the home, YeShua
Mt 19:1 And it·happened *that* when YeShua finished these
Mt 21:1 And when they·drew·near to JeruSalem and came to
Mt 21:34 "And when the season of·the fruits drew·near, he·
Mt 26:1 And it·happened *that* when YeShua finished all
Mt 27:31 And when they·had·mocked him, they·stripped the
Mk 1:32 And with·early·evening occurring, when the sun
Mk 2:25 read·aloud what David did, when he·had need and
Mk 4:10 And when he·was alone·by·himself, the·ones in·
Mk 6:21 ·happy·occasion, when HerOd·AntiPas was·making
Mk 7:17 And when he·entered into a·house away·from the
Mk 8:19 When I·broke the five loaves·of·bread among the
Mk 8:20 "And when *I·broke* the seven *loaves·of·bread*
Mk 11:1 And when they·drew·near to JeruSalem, to
Mk 11:19 And when early·evening occurred, he·was·
Mk 14:12 ·Bread, when they·were·sacrificing the Passover,
Mk 15:20 And when they·mocked him, they·stripped the
Mk 15:41 (women·who also, when he·was in Galilee, were·
Rm 2:16 at a·Day when God judges the secrets of·the men·
Rm 6:20 For when yeu·were slaves of·Moral·Failure, yeu·
Rm 7:5 For when we·were in the flesh, the intense·cravings
Rm 13:11 now our Salvation *is* nearer than when we·trusted.
Jud 1:9 the chief·angel, when verbally·contending with·the
Php 4:15 good·news *among·yeu*, when I·went·forth from
1Pe 3:20 ·being·obstinate in·times·past, when at·one·time,
1Th 3:4 For even when we·were alongside yeu, we·were·
2Th 3:10 For even when we·were alongside yeu, this we·
Tit 3:4 But when the kindness of·God our Savior and *his*
1Co 13:11 When I·was an·infant, I·was·speaking as an·
1Co 13:11 as an·infant. But when I·have·become a·man, I·
Col 3:7 also once walked, when yeu·were·living with them.
2Ti 4:3 *the* season shall·be when they·shall·not bear·with the
Rv 1:17 And when I·saw him, I·fell toward his feet as dead.
Rv 5:8 And when he·took the official·scroll, the four living·
Rv 6:1 And I·saw when the Lamb opened·up *the* first from·
Rv 6:3 And when he·opened·up the second official·seal, I·
Rv 6:5 And when *the Lamb* opened·up the third official·seal,
Rv 6:7 And when he·opened·up the fourth official·seal, I·
Rv 6:9 And when *the Lamb* opened·up the fifth official·seal,
Rv 6:12 And I·saw when he·opened·up the sixth official·seal
Rv 8:1 And when *the Lamb* opened·up the seventh official·
Rv 10:3 ·as *when* a·lion roars. And when he·yelled·out, the
Rv 10:4 And when the Seven Thunders spoke their·own
Rv 10:10 mouth sweet as honey. And when I·ate it, my belly
Rv 12:13 And when the Dragon saw that he·was·cast to the
Rv 22:8 and hearing *them*. And when I·heard and looked, I·

G3754 ὅ•τι hóti *conj.* (1115x)
Roots:G3748 Compare:G2443 G3704
(abbreviated listing for G3754)
G3754.ª CONJ ὅτι (3x)
(list for G3754.ª:CONJ excluded)
G3754.1 CONJ ὅτι (634x)
(list for G3754.1:CONJ excluded)
EG3754.1 (5x)
(list for EG3754.1: excluded)
G3754.2 CONJ ὅτι (19x)
(list for G3754.2:CONJ excluded)
EG3754.2 (1x)
(list for EG3754.2: excluded)
G3754.3 CONJ ὅτι (451x)
(list for G3754.3:CONJ excluded)
G3754.4 CONJ ὅτι (1x)
(list for G3754.4:CONJ excluded)
G3754.5 CONJ ὅτι (1x)
(list for G3754.5:CONJ excluded)

G3755 ὅ•του hótôu *p:r.* (6x)
Roots:G3748
G3755 P:R-GSN-ATT ὅτου (6x)
Jn 9:18 ·his·sight, until such·time *that* they·hollered·out·for
Lk 13:8 year also, until such·time *that* I·should·dig around it
Lk 15:8 seek carefully until such·time *that* she·should·find *it*
Lk 22:16 of·it until such·time *that* it·should·be·completely·
Lk 22:18 of·the vine, until such·time the kingdom of·God
Mt 5:25 swiftly, for·as·long·as such·time *as* you·are on the

G3756 οὐ ôu *prt.* (1643x)
οὐκ ôuk [before a vowel]
οὐχ ôuch [before an aspirate]
Compare:G3361 See:G3364 G3372
(abbreviated listing for G3756)
G3756.1 NEG οὐ (12x)
(list for G3756.1:NEG excluded)
G3756.1 NEG-ADJ οὐ (9x)
(list for G3756.1:NEG-ADJ excluded)
G3756.1 NEG-ADV οὐ (8x)
(list for G3756.1:NEG-ADV excluded)
G3756.1 NEG-EMPH οὐ (94x)
(list for G3756.1:NEG-EMPH excluded)
G3756.1 NEG-N οὐ (16x)
(list for G3756.1:NEG-N excluded)
G3756.1 NEG-V οὐκ (48x)
(list for G3756.1:NEG-V excluded)
EG3756.1 (1x)
(list for EG3756.1: excluded)
G3756.2 NEG οὐκ (30x)
(list for G3756.2:NEG excluded)
G3756.2 NEG-ADJ οὐ (40x)
(list for G3756.2:NEG-ADJ excluded)
G3756.2 NEG-ADV οὐχ (72x)
(list for G3756.2:NEG-ADV excluded)
G3756.2 NEG-CONJ οὐχ (3x)
(list for G3756.2:NEG-CONJ excluded)
G3756.2 NEG-N οὐκ (83x)
(list for G3756.2:NEG-N excluded)
G3756.2 NEG-PREP οὐ (75x)
(list for G3756.2:NEG-PREP excluded)
G3756.2 NEG-RHET οὐκ (11x)
(list for G3756.2:NEG-RHET excluded)
G3756.2 NEG-V οὐκ (1099x)
(list for G3756.2:NEG-V excluded)
G3756.2 NEG-VC οὐχ (20x)
(list for G3756.2:NEG-VC excluded)
G3756.3 NEG-V οὐκ (5x)
(list for G3756.3:NEG-V excluded)
G3756.4 NEG-ADJ οὐκ (1x)
(list for G3756.4:NEG-ADJ excluded)
G3756.4 NEG-ADV οὐχ (1x)
(list for G3756.4:NEG-ADV excluded)
G3756.4 NEG-PREP οὐ (1x)
(list for G3756.4:NEG-PREP excluded)
G3756.4 NEG-V οὐ (6x)
(list for G3756.4:NEG-V excluded)
G3756.5 NEG-ADJ οὐχ (2x)
(list for G3756.5:NEG-ADJ excluded)
G3756.6 NEG-RHET οὐ (5x)
(list for G3756.6:NEG-RHET excluded)
G3756.7 NEG-V οὐ (1x)
(list for G3756.7:NEG-V excluded)

G3757 οὗ hôû *adv.* (29x)
Roots:G3739
G3757.ª ADV οὗ (3x)
Ac 21:26 ·ceremonial·cleansing *would·be*, at which *time* the
Php 3:20 in *the* heavens, out·from which also we·fully·await
1Co 16:6 onward·on·my·journey wherever I·may·traverse.
G3757.2 ADV οὗ (24x)
Jn 11:41 stone *from the place* where the·one having·died was
Lk 4:16 where he·was having·been·nurtured·and·reared.
Lk 4:17 he·found the place where it·was having·been·written
Lk 10:1 every city and place where he·himself was·about to·
Lk 22:10 follow him into the home where he·traverses·in.
Lk 24:28 to the village, where they·were·traversing, and he·
Ac 1:13 ·chamber, where they·were continuing·to·abide as·
Ac 2:2 ·filled all the house where they·were sitting·down.
Ac 7:29 in *the* land of·Midian, where he·begot two sons.
Ac 12:12 Mark), where a·significant·number were having·
Ac 16:13 city beside a·river, where prayer was·accustomed
Ac 20:6 in·only five days, where we·lingered seven days.
Ac 20:8 where they·were having·been·gathered·together.
Ac 25:10 ·judgment·seat, where it·is·mandatory·for me to·
Ac 28:14 where finding brothers, we·were·exhorted to·stay·
Mt 2:9 ·*on* until it·stood·still up·above where the little·child
Mt 18:20 "For where two or three are having·been·gathered·
Mt 26:36 "Yeu·sit·down at·this·location, where going·aside,
Mt 28:16 Galilee to the mountain where YeShua assigned
Rm 4:15 accomplishes wrath (for where there·is no law,
Rm 5:20 ·more. But where Moral·Failure increased·more,
2Co 3:17 is the Spirit, and where the Spirit of·Yahweh *is*,
Col 3:1 seek the·things up·above, where Anointed-One is
Rv 17:15 which you·saw, where the Prostitute sits·down,
G3757.2 P:R-GSN οὗ (1x)
Lk 23:53 ·out·within·a·mass·of·stone, where there·was not,
G3757.4 ADV οὗ (1x)
Heb 3:9 when yeur fathers tried me, tested·and·proved me,

G3758 οὐά ôuá *inj.* (5x)
G3758 INJ οὐά (1x)
Mk 15:29 heads and saying, "Ah, the·one demolishing the
EG3758 (4x)
Jn 8:10 besides the wife, declared to·her, "*Ah*, the wife.
Jn 19:3 and they·were·saying, "*Ah*! Be·well, O·King of·the
Mt 27:29 they·were·mocking him, saying, "*Ah*! Be·well,
Mk 15:18 and they·began to·greet him, "*Ah*! Be·well, O·

G3759 οὐαί ôuaí *inj.* (47x)
xLangAlso:H1958 H1945
G3759 INJ οὐαί (43x)
Lk 6:24 "Moreover, woe to·yeu, the wealthy! Because yeu·
Lk 6:25 "Woe to·yeu, the·ones having·been·filled·up!
Lk 6:25 Because yeu·shall·hunger. Woe to·yeu, the·ones
Lk 6:26 "Woe to·yeu, whenever all the men·of·clay† should·
Lk 10:13 "Woe to·you, Chorazin! Woe to·you, BethSaida!
Lk 10:13 "Woe to·you, Chorazin! Woe to·you, BethSaida!
Lk 11:42 "But·rather, woe to·yeu, Pharisees! Because yeu·
Lk 11:43 "Woe to·yeu, Pharisees! Because yeu·love the first·
Lk 11:44 "Woe to·yeu, scribes and Pharisees, O·stage·
Lk 11:46 And *Jesus* declared, "Woe to·yeu also, the experts·
Lk 11:47 "Woe to·yeu! Because yeu·build the chamber·
Lk 11:52 "Woe to·yeu, the experts·in·Torah-Law! Because
Lk 17:1 ·traps not to·come, but woe *to·him* through whom
Lk 21:23 "But woe to·the·ones being in pregnancy and to·
Lk 22:22 ·determined. Moreover, woe to·that man·of·clay†
Mt 11:21 "Woe to·you, Chorazin! Woe to·you, BethSaida!
Mt 11:21 "Woe to·you, Chorazin! Woe to·you, BethSaida!
Mt 18:7 "Woe to·the world due·to its scandalous·traps, for
Mt 18:7 to·come! Nevertheless, woe to·that man·of·clay†
Mt 23:13 "But woe to·yeu, Scribes and Pharisees, O·stage·
Mt 23:14 "Woe to·yeu, Scribes and Pharisees, O·stage·
Mt 23:15 "Woe to·yeu, Scribes and Pharisees, O·stage·
Mt 23:16 "Woe to·yeu, *yeu* blind guides, the·ones saying,
Mt 23:23 "Woe to·yeu, Scribes and Pharisees, O·stage·
Mt 23:25 "Woe to·yeu, Scribes and Pharisees, O·stage·
Mt 23:27 "Woe to·yeu, Scribes and Pharisees, O·stage·
Mt 23:29 "Woe to·yeu, Scribes and Pharisees, O·stage·
Mt 24:19 "And woe to·the·ones being in pregnancy and to·
Mt 26:24 concerning him, but woe to·that man·of·clay†
Mk 13:17 "And woe to·the·ones being in pregnancy and to·
Mk 14:21 concerning him, but woe to·that man·of·clay†
Jud 1:11 Woe to·them! Because they·traversed in·the way
1Co 9:16 for necessity is·laid·upon me; and woe is to·me,
Rv 8:13 saying with·a·loud voice, "Woe, woe, woe to·the·
Rv 8:13 ·a·loud voice, "Woe, woe, woe to·the·ones residing
Rv 8:13 "Woe, woe, woe to·the·ones residing on the earth

Rv 12:12 encamping in them. Woe to·the·ones residing·in
Rv 18:10 of·her torment, saying, 'Woe, woe, the Great City
Rv 18:10 saying, 'Woe, woe, the Great City Babylon, the
Rv 18:16 and saying, 'Woe, woe, the Great City, the·one
Rv 18:16 and saying, 'Woe, woe, the Great City, the·one
Rv 18:19 and mourning, saying, 'Woe, woe, the Great City,
Rv 18:19 saying, 'Woe, woe, the Great City, in which all

G3759 N-OI οὐαί (4x)

Rv 9:12 The first woe went·away; behold, there·come two
Rv 9:12 behold, there·come two woes still after these·things.
Rv 11:14 The second woe went·away; behold, the third woe
Rv 11:14 went·away; behold, the third woe comes swiftly.

G3760 οὐ•δα•μῶς ôudamỗs *adv.* (1x)

Roots:G3762

G3760 ADV οὐδαμῶς (1x)

Mt 2:6 *the* land of·Judah, are by·no·means least among the

G3761 οὐ•δέ ôudé *adv.* (137x)

Roots:G3756 G1161 Compare:G3366

G3761.ª ADV οὐδ´ (7x)

Lk 20:8 Jesus declared to·them, "Neither *do* I·myself say to·
Heb 9:25 Not in·order·that he·should·offer himself many·
Mt 9:17 Neither do·men·cast fresh·new wine into old
Mt 21:27 ·himself replied to·them, "Neither do I·myself say
Mk 11:33 says to·them, "Neither do I·myself relate to·yeu
Rm 9:7 Neither because they·are offspring† of·AbRaham,
2Th 3:8 Neither as·a·free·present did·we·eat personally·from

G3761.1 ADV οὐδέ (1x)

Heb 9:12 *He·came·directly*, however·not through blood of·

G3761.2 ADV οὐδέ (42x)

Jn 1:3 and apart·from him not·even one·thing came·to·be
Jn 5:22 For not·even·does the Father judge, not·even·one·
Jn 8:11 declared to·her, "Not·even·do I·myself condemn
Jn 15:4 in the vine, in·this·manner, not·even *can* yeu unless
Jn 21:25 should·be·written, I·imagine not·even the world
Lk 6:3 declared, "Did·yeu·not·even read·aloud this·thing
Lk 7:9 "I·say to·yeu, not·even in IsraEl did·I·find so·vast a·
Lk 12:27 They·do·not labor·hard, they·do·not·even spin,
Lk 12:27 and·yet I·say to·yeu, not·even Solomon in all his
Lk 18:13 was·not willing to·lift·up not·even his eyes to the
Lk 23:40 saying, "Are·not·even you·yourself afraid·of God
Ac 4:32 soul was one. And not·even one was·saying *for* any
Ac 7:5 him an·inheritance in it, not·even a·foot step, and·yet
Ac 19:2 "But·yet, we·did·not·even hear whether there·is a·
Heb 8:4 he·would not·even be a·priest·that·offers·a·sacrifice,
Heb 9:18 by·which *necessity*, not·even the first *covenant*
Gal 2:3 But·yet not·even Titus (the·one together with·me
Gal 2:5 to·them, not·even just·for an·hour, did·we·yield to·
Mt 6:29 And·yet I·say to·yeu, not·even Solomon, in all his
Mt 8:10 "Certainly I·say to·yeu, not·even in IsraEl did·I·find
Mt 24:36 ·one·at·all personally·knows, not·even the angels
Mt 25:45 ·these *my brothers*, yeu·did·not·even do *it* to·me.
Mt 27:14 he·did·not answer to him not·even one utterance,
Mk 6:31 and they·were·not·even having·opportunity to·eat.
Mk 12:10 "Did·yeu·not·even read·aloud this Scripture?
Mk 13:32 ·one·at·all personally·knows, not·even the angels,
Mk 14:59 Yet not·even in·this·manner was their testimony
Rm 3:10 "There·is none righteous," "not·even one."
Rm 4:15 there·is no law, *there·is* not·even a·violation).
Rm 11:21 *·heed* lest·perhaps he·should·not·even spare you.
1Co 4:3 Moreover, I·scrutinize not·even my·own·self.
1Co 5:1 sexual·immorality which is·not·even named among
1Co 6:5 a·wise·man among yeu? Not·even one that shall·be·
1Co 11:14 Or does·not·even the nature itself instruct yeu, in·
1Co 14:21 in·this·manner, they·shall·not·even listen·to me,"
1Co 15:13 not·even Anointed-One has·been·awakened.
1Co 15:16 not·even Anointed-One has·been·awakened.
2Co 3:10 ·been·glorified, has·not·even been·glorified in this
1Ti 6:7 *and it·is* plain that we·are·not·even able to·carry
1Ti 6:16 no·one·at·all sees (*which* it·is·not·even possible *for*
1Jn 2:23 one who·is·denying the Son does·not·even have the
Rv 9:4 vegetation of·the earth (not·even any green·thing nor·

G3761.3 ADV οὐδέ (31x)

Jn 11:50 nor·even ponder that it·is·more·advantageous for·us
Jn 14:17 it·does·not observe him, nor·even knows him. But
Lk 11:33 *it* in hiding, nor·even under the measuring·basket,
Lk 12:24 because they·do·not sow nor·even do·they·reap.
Lk 12:24 there·is not a·dispensary nor·even a·barn, yet God
Lk 17:21 nor·even shall·they·declare, 'Behold, here *it·is*!' or
Lk 21:15 be·able to·declare·against nor·even to·withstand.
Ac 8:21 ·is not a·portion nor·even a·small·chance for·you in
Ac 9:9 not looking·about, and neither ate nor·even drank.
Ac 17:25 nor·even is·waited·upon by *the* hands of·men·of·
Heb 13:5 I·may·not·ever give·up·on you, nor·even no, I·
Gal 3:28 There·is·not therein Jew nor·even Greek, there·is·
Gal 3:28 there·is·not therein slave nor·even free, there·is·
Mt 6:20 and where thieves do·not break·in nor·even steal.
Mt 6:26 neither do·they·reap, nor·even do·they·gather into
Mt 10:24 above the instructor, nor·even a·slave above his
Mt 11:27 the Father; nor·even·does anyone fully·know the
Mt 12:19 shall·he·yell·out, nor·even·shall any·man hear his
Mt 16:9 Do·yeu·not·yet understand, nor·even remember the
Mt 16:10 Nor·even the seven loaves·of·bread of·the four·
Mt 22:46 to·answer him a·word, nor·even·did anyone dare
Mt 25:13 ·do·not personally·know the day nor·even the hour
Mk 8:17 Do·yeu·not·yet understand, nor·even comprehend?
Rm 9:16 on·the·one wanting *it*, nor·even on·the·one running
1Th 5:5 We·are not of·night nor·even of·darkness.
1Ti 2:12 nor·even *for·her* to·take·a·stance·of·authority·over
Rv 5:3 ·one·man in the heaven, nor·even upon the earth,
Rv 5:3 nor·even upon the earth, nor·even beneath the earth,
Rv 7:16 neither shall·they·thirst any·longer, nor·even, no,
Rv 7:16 should·fall on them, nor·even any burning·radiation
Rv 9:4 earth (not·even any green·thing nor·even any tree),

G3761.4 ADV οὐδέ (2x)

Gal 6:13 For neither·even·do they·themselves, being·
Mk 16:13 *in·mourning*, but·neither·even·did those *mourners*

G3761.4 ADV-NEG οὐδέ (1x)

Mt 6:15 their trespasses, neither·even·shall yeur Father

G3761.5 ADV οὐδέ (42x)

Jn 7:5 For neither were his brothers trusting in him.
Jn 8:42 out·from God. For neither have·I·come of my·own·
Jn 13:16 not greater·than his lord; neither *is* an·ambassador
Lk 6:43 is·not producing rotten fruit, neither *is* a·rotten tree
Lk 7:7 Therefore neither did·I·consider my·own·self
Lk 8:17 become apparent; neither *anything* hidden·away,
Lk 12:33 draws·near, neither·does moth thoroughly·ruin.
Lk 16:31 and the prophets, neither shall·they·be·persuaded,
Lk 23:15 "Moreover, neither·did HerOd·AntiPas, for I·sent
Ac 2:27 soul in Hades, neither shall·you·give your Divine·
Ac 2:31 ·not left·behind in Hades, neither did·his flesh see
Ac 4:34 For neither was anyone subsisting among them in·a·
Ac 16:21 proper for·us to·personally·accept, neither to·do,
Ac 20:24 causes *me concern*, neither do·I·hold my soul *as*
Heb 10:8 ·did·not want, neither did·you·take·delight *in·them*
Gal 1:1 from men·of·clay†, neither through a·man·of·clay†,
Gal 1:12 For I·myself neither personally·received it from a·
Gal 1:17 neither did·I·go·up to JeruSalem toward the·ones
Mt 5:15 Neither do·they·set·ablaze a·lantern and place it
Mt 6:26 because they·do·not sow, neither do·they·reap, nor·
Mt 6:28 they·do·not labor·hard, neither do·they·spin.
Mt 7:18 able to·produce evil fruit, neither *is* a·rotten tree
Mt 12:4 ·proper for·him to·eat, neither for·the·ones with
Mt 12:19 ·not engage·in·strife, neither shall·he·yell·out,
Mt 13:13 they·do·not hear, neither do·they·comprehend.
Mt 23:14 do·not enter·in, neither do·yeu·allow the·ones
Mt 24:21 beginning until the present, neither, no, it·should·
Mk 4:22 be·made·apparent, neither·did *anything* become
Mk 11:26 yeu·yeurselves do·not forgive, neither yeur Father
Mk 12:21 her, and he·died, and neither *did* he·himself leave
Mk 13:32 the·ones in heaven, neither the Son, except the
Mk 14:68 *him*, neither am·I·fully·acquainted·with what you·
Rm 2:28 *Torah-Law* that·is a·Jew, neither the·one with an·
Rm 8:7 Law-of-Liberty of·God, for neither is·it·able *to·be*).
Php 2:16 I·did·not run for naught neither labored·hard for
1Pe 2:22 did·not commit moral·failure, neither was guile
1Co 11:16 *any·other* such custom, neither *do* the Called·
1Co 15:50 able to·inherit God's kingdom; neither does the
1Jn 3:6 has·not clearly·seen him, neither has·known him.
Rv 5:3 to·open·up the official·scroll, neither to·look·upon it.
Rv 7:16 any·longer, neither shall·they·thirst any·longer, nor·
Rv 21:23 no need of·the sun, neither of·the moon, in·order·

G3761.6 ADV οὐδέ (11x)

Jn 1:13 not from·out of·blood, nor from·out of·*the*·will of·
Jn 1:13 ·out of·*the*·will of·flesh, nor from·out of·*the*·will of·
Jn 6:24 that Jesus was not there, nor his disciples, they also
Jn 16:3 ·yeu, because they·did·not know the Father, nor me.
Lk 6:44 ·men·collect figs, nor from·out of·a·bramble·bush
Ac 24:18 neither with crowd, nor with a·commotion. "But
Gal 4:14 in my flesh, nor did·yeu·spit·*me*·out, but·rather
2Pe 1:8 *yeu to·be* neither idle nor unfruitful in the
1Th 2:3 birthed·from·out of·deceit, nor from·out of·impurity,
1Co 2:6 wisdom of·this present·age, nor of·the rulers of·this
2Co 7:12 ·of the·one doing·wrong, nor because·of the·one

G3762 οὐ•δε•ίς ôudêís *adj.* (236x)

οὐ•δε•μία ôudêmía [feminine]
οὐ•δ•έν ôudén [neuter]

Roots:G3761 G1520 Compare:G3367

G3762.1 A-NSM οὐδείς (31x)

Jn 7:13 not·even·one was·speaking with·freeness·of·speech
Jn 7:19 Torah-Law? And·yet not·even·one from·among yeu
Jn 8:11 She·declared, "Not·even·one, Lord." And Jesus
Jn 10:29 greater·than all; and not·even·one is·able to·snatch
Jn 14:6 truth, and the life·above. Not·even·one comes to the
Jn 15:24 the works which not·even·one other·man has·done,
Jn 16:5 ·one sending me, and not·even·one from·among yeu
Jn 17:12 ·given to·me, and not·even·one from·among them
Jn 19:41 which, not·even·yet, not·even·one *man* was·laid.
Jn 21:12 Dine!" And not·even·one of·the disciples was·
Lk 1:61 to her, "There·is not·even·one among your kinsfolk
Lk 4:24 "Certainly I·say to·yeu, that not·even·one prophet is
Lk 4:27 the prophet, yet not·even·one of·them was·purified,
Lk 7:28 ·women there·is not·even·one prophet greater·than
Lk 14:24 'For I·say to·yeu, that not·even·one of·those men,
Lk 16:13 "Not·even·one household·servant is·able to·be·a·
Lk 19:30 ·tied, on which not·even·one man·of·clay† sat
Lk 23:53 not·even·yet, not·even·one *man* being·laid·out.
Ac 5:13 not·even·one was·daring to·tightly·join·himself to·
Gal 3:11 Torah-Law not·even·one is·regarded·as·righteous
Mk 3:27 belongings, not·even·one already·entering into his
Mk 9:39 him, for there·is not·even·one who shall·do a·
Mk 10:29 I·say to·yeu, there·is not·even·one that left home
Mk 11:2 ·tied, on which not·even·one man·of·clay† has·sat.
Mk 12:34 And not·even·one was·daring any·longer to·
Rm 14:7 For not·even·one of·us lives to·himself, and not·
Rm 14:7 lives to·himself, and not·even·one dies to·himself.
Jac 3:8 But not·even·one among·clay·men† is·able to·tame
1Co 2:8 which not·even·one of·the rulers of·this present·age
1Co 2:11 in·this·manner not·even·one *being* personally·
1Co 8:4 *the* world, and that *there·is* not·even·one other God,

G3762.1 A-NSF οὐδεμία (3x)

Ac 27:22 "For there·shall·be not·even·one loss of·soul from·
Jac 3:12 In·this·manner, not·even·one wellspring *is·able*
Php 4:15 not·even·one Called·Out·citizenry shared with·me

G3762.1 A-NSN οὐδέν (3x)

Ac 18:17 And not·even·one of·these·things was·mattering
Rm 8:1 now not·even·one verdict·of·condemnation for·the·
1Co 14:10 *the* world, and not·even·one of·them *is* without·

G3762.1 A-ASM οὐδένα (2x)

Jn 18:9 to·me, I·did·not completely·lose not·even·one."
1Co 1:14 to·God that I·immersed not·even·one of·yeu,

G3762.1 A-ASF οὐδεμίαν (6x)

Jn 16:29 ·clarity·of·speech, and say not·even·one proverb.
Jn 18:38 "I·myself find in him not·even·one fault.
Jn 19:4 ·that yeu·may·know that I·find not·even·one fault in
Lk 4:26 yet to not·even·one of·them was EliJah sent, except
Ac 25:18 were·bringing·up not·even·one accusation of·such·
Mk 6:5 he·was·not able to·do there not·even·one miracle,

G3762.1 A-ASN οὐδέν (9x)
Jn 10:41 in·fact, did not·even·one miraculous·sign, but all·
Lk 9:36 days not·even·one of·those·things·which they·have·
Lk 18:34 comprehended not·even·one of·these·things; also,
Lk 23:4 the crowds, "I·find not·even·one fault in this man·
Lk 23:14 in·the·sight of·yeu, found not·even·one fault in
Lk 23:22 commit? I·found not·even·one cause for·death in
Ac 15:9 and he·did·not·even make·one·distinction between
Ac 23:9 saying, "We·find not·even·one wrong in this man·
Ac 25:10 ·judged. I·wronged not·even·one *of* the·Judeans,
G3762.1 A-DSM οὐδενί (2x)
Ac 4:12 the Salvation is not in not·even·one other. For there·
Ac 8:16 he·was having·fallen upon not·even·one of·them,
G3762.1 A-DSN οὐδενί (1x)
1Co 9:15 But I·myself used not·even·one of·these·things,
G3762.1 A-GSM οὐδενός (2x)
Ac 27:34 yeur salvation, for not·even·one hair shall·fall out·
Mt 22:16 ·not matter to·you concerning not·even·one *man*,
G3762.1 A-GSN οὐδενός (1x)
Ac 20:24 But·yet not·even·one word causes *me concern*,
G3762.2 A-NSN οὐδέν (7x)
Lk 12:2 there·is not·even·one·thing having·been·altogether·
Lk 23:15 and behold, not·even·one·thing worthy of·death
Gal 2:6 it·thoroughly·means not·even·one·thing to·me. God
Mt 10:26 there·is not·even·one·thing having·been·concealed,
Mk 7:15 There·is not·even·one·thing from·outside of·the
Tit 1:15 *to·the* non-trusting·ones, not·even·one·thing *is* pure,
1Ti 4:4 of·God *is* good, and not·even·one *is to·be* discarded
G3762.2 A-ASN οὐδέν (45x)
Jn 3:27 is·not able to·receive not·even·one·thing, unless it·
Jn 5:19 Son is·not able to·do not·even·one·thing by himself,
Jn 5:30 am·not able to·do not·even·one·thing of my·own·self
Jn 6:63 The flesh does·not benefit not·even·one·thing. The
Jn 8:28 and *that* I·do not·even·one·thing of my·own·self;
Jn 9:33 he·would·not be·able to·do not·even·one·thing."
Jn 11:49 do·not personally·know not·even·one·thing,
Jn 12:19 how yeu·do·not benefit not·even·one·thing? See,
Jn 14:30 and he·does·not have not·even·one·thing in me.
Jn 15:5 me, yeu·are·not able to·do not·even·one·thing.
Jn 16:23 day yeu·shall·not ask·of me not·even·one·thing.
Jn 16:24 yeu·did·not request not·even·one·thing in my
Lk 4:2 days, he·did·not eat not·even·one·thing. And upon·
Lk 10:19 power of·the enemy; and not·even·one·thing, no,
Lk 20:40 ·they·daring to·inquire·of him not·even·one·thing.
Lk 23:9 But *Jesus* answered him not·even·one·thing.
Lk 23:41 "But this·man practiced not·even·one·thing amiss."
Ac 4:14 they·were·having not·even·one·thing to·declare· *it*.
Ac 17:21 ·their·leisure·time for not·even·one·thing, other
Ac 20:20 how I·kept·back not·even·one·thing of·the·things
Ac 26:22 saying not·even·one·thing aside·from those·things·
Ac 26:26 of·these·things, not·even·one·thing, to·be·hidden
Ac 26:31 practices not·even·one·thing worthy of·death or of·
Ac 28:17 having·committed not·even·one·thing antagonistic
Heb 2:8 to·him all things, not·even·one·thing did *God* leave
Heb 7:14 spoke not·even·one·thing concerning a·sacred·
Heb 7:19 made not·even·one·thing completely·mature, but
Gal 2:6 — not·even·one·thing did·they·further·impart to·me.
Gal 4:1 an·infant), varies not·even·one·thing from·a·slave,
Mt 5:13 To not·even·one·purpose does·it·have·strength any·
Mt 21:19 he·came to it and found not·even·one·thing on it,
Mt 27:12 and the elders, he·answered not·even·one·thing.
Mk 7:12 to·no·longer do not·even·one·thing for·his father or
Mk 14:60 Do·you·not answer not·even·one·thing? What·are
Mk 14:61 ·keeping·silent and answered not·even·one·thing.
Mk 15:4 "Do·you·not answer not·even·one·thing? See
Mk 15:5 ·no·longer answering not·even·one·thing, such·for
Mk 16:8 ·one·man did·they·declare not·even·one·thing, for
1Co 4:4 For I·am·conscious·of not·even·one·thing against·,
1Co 8:2 he·has·known not·even·one·thing, not·even·yet,
1Co 13:3 ·not have love, it·benefits not·even·one·thing.
2Co 12:11 for *in* not·even·one·thing did·I·fall·short of·the
Phm 1:14 to·do not·even·one·thing apart·from your input,
1Ti 6:7 For we·carried not·even·one·thing into the world,
2Ti 2:14 ·nuances·of·words for not·even·one·thing useful,
G3762.2 A-DSN οὐδενί (2x)
Mk 9:29 to·them, "By not·even·one·thing is this kind able
Php 1:20 that in not·even·one·thing shall·I·be·ashamed,
G3762.2 A-GSN οὐδενός (2x)
Lk 22:35 And they·declared, "Not·even·one·thing."
Rv 3:17 ·wealthy and have need of·not·even·one·thing," yet
EG3762.2 (1x)
Mk 15:3 ·many·things, *but he·answered not·even·one·thing*.
G3762.3 A-ASF οὐδεμίαν (1x)
Jn 19:11 ·not having not·even·one·bit·of authority against
G3762.3 A-ASN οὐδέν (2x)
Gal 5:2 Anointed-One shall·benefit yeu not·even·one·bit.
Gal 5:10 yeu·shall·contemplate not·even·one·bit otherwise,
G3762.4 A-NSM οὐδείς (55x)
Jn 1:18 Not·even·one·man has·clearly·seen God ever·at·any·
Jn 3:2 an·instructor, for not·even·one·man is·able to·do
Jn 3:13 "And not·even·one·man has·ascended into the
Jn 3:32 he·testifies; and·yet not·even·one·man receives his
Jn 4:27 a·woman. However, not·even·one·man declared,
Jn 6:44 Not·even·one·man is·able to·come to me, unless the
Jn 6:65 to·yeu that not·even·one·man is·able to·come to me,
Jn 7:4 For *there·is* not·even·one·man *that* does anything in
Jn 7:27 ·come, not·even·one·man knows from·what·source
Jn 7:30 to·apprehend him, but not·even·one·man threw his
Jn 7:44 him, but·yet not·even·one·man threw hands on him.
Jn 8:10 legal·accusers? *Did* not·even·one·man condemn you
Jn 8:20 ·Atrium. And not·even·one·man apprehended him,
Jn 9:4 is·coming, when not·even·one·man is·able to·work.
Jn 10:18 "Not·even·one·man takes it away from me, but·
Jn 13:28 Now not·even·one·man who·was·reclining·at·the·
Jn 15:13 ·love greater·than this, has not·even·one·man, that
Jn 16:22 ·rejoice, and not·even·one·man takes·away yeur
Lk 5:36 to them, "Not·even·one·man throws a·patch *from* a·
Lk 5:37 "And not·even·one·man casts fresh·new wine into
Lk 5:39 Also, not·even·one·man drinking old *wine*
Lk 8:16 "Not·even·one·man, after·igniting a·lantern, covers
Lk 9:62 unto him, "Not·even·one·man, upon·throwing his
Lk 10:22 my Father. And not·even·one·man knows who the
Lk 11:33 "Not·even·one·man, after·igniting a·lantern, places
Lk 15:16 ·eating, yet not·even·one·man was·giving him
Lk 18:29 to·yeu, there·is not·even·one·man that left home,
Ac 18:10 and not·even·one·man shall·put·a·hand on·you
Heb 7:13 which not·even·one·man has·given·attention at·the
Heb 12:14 which not·even·one·man shall·gaze·upon the
Gal 3:15 ·ratified, *that* not·even·one·man sets·it·aside or
Mt 9:16 "Now not·even·one·man throws a·patch of·
Mt 22:46 And not·even·one·man was·able to·answer him a·
Mk 2:21 "Also, not·even·one·man sews a·patch of·
Mk 2:22 And not·even·one·man casts fresh·new wine into
Mk 5:3 ·tombs. And not·even·one·man was·able to·bind
Mk 5:4 And not·even·one·man was·having·strength to·tame
1Co 3:11 For not·even·one·man is·able to·lay another
1Co 12:3 to·yeu, that not·even·one·man speaking by God's
1Co 12:3 And not·even·one·man is·able to·declare,
1Co 14:2 For not·even·one·man listens·with·comprehension,
Eph 5:29 For not·even·one·man ever hated his·own flesh,
2Ti 2:4 Not·even·one·man who·is·strategically·going·to·war
2Ti 4:16 not·even·one·man appeared·publicly·together
1Jn 4:12 Not·even·one·man has·distinctly·viewed God ever·
Rv 2:17 ·written which not·even·one·man did·know except
Rv 3:7 the·one opening·up and not·even·one·man shuts,
Rv 3:7 shuts, *who* shuts and not·even·one·man opens·up"':
Rv 3:8 ·opened·up, and not·even·one·man is·able to·shut it,
Rv 5:3 And not·even·one·man in the heaven, nor·even upon
Rv 5:4 much, because not·even·one·man was·found worthy
Rv 7:9 crowd which not·even·one·man was·able to·number,
Rv 14:3 Elders; and not·even·one·man was·able to·learn the
Rv 18:11 over her, because not·even·one·man buys their
Rv 19:12 ·written that not·even·one·man personally·knows,
G3762.4 A-ASM οὐδένα (10x)
Jn 5:22 the Father judge, not·even·one·man, but·rather he·
Jn 8:15 I·myself do·not presently·judge not·even·one·man.
Jn 18:31 "It·is·not proper for·us to·kill not·even·one·man,"
Lk 8:51 he·did·not allow not·even·one·person to·enter·in,
Mt 17:8 ·up their eyes, they·saw not·even·one·man, except
Mk 5:37 allow not·even·one·man to·follow·along with·him,
Mk 7:24 he·was·wanting not·even·one·man to·know *it*, but
Mk 9:8 they·saw no·longer not·even·one·man, other·than
Jac 1:13 tempts not·even·one·man *with·moral·wrongs*.
Php 2:20 For I·have not·even·one·man of·such·kindred·soul,
G3762.4 A-DSM οὐδενί (2x)
Lk 9:36 and they·announced to·not·even·one·man in those
Mk 16:8 And to·not·even·one·man did·they·declare not·
G3762.4 A-GSM οὐδενός (5x)
Lk 8:43 be·cured·or·brought·relief, by not·even·one·man.
Ac 20:33 "I·longed·for not·even·one·man's silver or gold or
Mk 12:14 matter to·you concerning not·even·one·man, for
1Co 2:15 but he·himself is·scrutinized by not·even·one·man.
2Co 11:9 I·was·not a·freeloader of·not·even·one·man. For
G3762.5 A-NSM οὐδείς (1x)
Rv 15:8 of·his power. And none·at·all were·able to·enter
G3762.5 A-NSF οὐδεμία (1x)
1Jn 1:5 light, and in him there·is not darkness, none·at·all.
G3762.5 A-NSN οὐδέν (1x)
Ac 25:11 But if there·is no *validity* at·all to·these·things·
G3762.5 A-ASF οὐδεμίαν (1x)
2Co 7:5 Macedonia, our flesh has·had no relaxation at·all,
G3762.5 A-ASN οὐδέν (1x)
Ac 28:5 ·beast into the fire, *Paul* suffered no harm at·all.
G3762.6 A-NSN οὐδέν (11x)
Jn 8:54 my·own·self, my glory is nothing·at·all. It·is my
Ac 21:24 concerning you, it·is nothing·at·all. But·rather *that*
Mt 17:20 And nothing·at·all shall·be·impossible for·yeu.
Mt 23:16 "by the Temple," it·is nothing·at·all, but whoever
Mt 23:18 by the Sacrifice·Altar, it·is nothing·at·all, but
Rm 14:14 Jesus, that *there·is* nothing·at·all defiled through
1Co 7:19 The circumcision is nothing·at·all, and the
1Co 7:19 and the uncircumcision is nothing·at·all, but·rather
1Co 8:4 ·personally·know that an·idol *is* nothing·at·all in *the*
1Co 13:2 and should·not have love, I·am nothing·at·all.
2Co 12:11 of·ambassadors, even·though I·am nothing·at·all.
G3762.6 A-ASN οὐδέν (9x)
Jn 7:26 ·of·speech, and they·say nothing·at·all to·him.
Jn 18:20 come·together. And I·spoke nothing·at·all in secret
Jn 21:3 And on that night, they·caught nothing·at·all.
Lk 5:5 through the night, we·took nothing·at·all. But at your
Ac 5:36 ·dissolved, and they·became nothing·at·all.
Ac 19:27 goddess Artemis to·be·reckoned as nothing·at·all.
Mt 26:62 to·him, "Do·you·answer nothing·at·all? What *are*
Mt 27:24 *reasoning with·them* benefits nothing·at·all, but·yet
Mk 11:13 to it, he·found nothing·at·all except leaves, for it·
G3762.7 A-NSM οὐδείς (10x)
Lk 18:19 ·good? No·one·at·all *is* beneficially·good, except
Ac 25:11 me, no·one·at·all is·able to·gratuitously·hand me
Mt 6:24 "No·one·at·all is·able to·be·a·slave to·two lords.
Mt 11:27 my Father, and no·one·at·all fully·knows the Son,
Mt 19:17 *There·is* no·one·at·all beneficially·good except
Mt 20:7 They·say to·him, 'Because no·one·at·all hired us.'
Mt 24:36 that day and hour no·one·at·all personally·knows,
Mk 10:18 *There·is* no·one·at·all beneficially·good except
Mk 13:32 that day and hour no·one·at·all personally·knows,
1Ti 6:16 *in* unapproachable light which no·one·at·all sees
G3762.7 A-ASM οὐδένα (6x)
Ac 5:23 But opening·up, we·found no·one·at·all inside."
Ac 9:8 ·opened·up, he·was·looking·upon no·one·at·all. And
2Co 5:16 personally·know no·one·at·all according·to flesh.
2Co 7:2 *hearts*; we·wronged no·one·at·all, we·corrupted no·
2Co 7:2 no·one·at·all, we·corrupted no·one·at·all, *and* we·
2Co 7:2 no·one·at·all, *and* we·swindled no·one·at·all.
G3762.7 A-DSM οὐδενί (1x)
Jn 8:33 offspring†, and to·no·one·at·all, ever·at·any·time,
G3762.7 A-GSM οὐδενός (1x)
Heb 6:13 since he·was·having no·one·at·all greater by
G3762.8 A-ASN οὐδέν (1x)
Gal 4:12 as yeu *are*. Not·at·all did·yeu·bring·harm·to me.

G3763 οὐ•δέ•πο•τε ôudépôtê *adv.* (16x)
Roots:G3761 G4218
G3763.1 ADV οὐδέποτε (6x)
Heb 10:11 which not·even·at·any·time is·able to·entirely·
Mt 7:23 to·them, 'Not·even·at·any·time did·I·know yeu! '
Mt 21:16 "Yes! Have·yeu·not·even·at·any·time read·aloud,
Mt 21:42 "Did·yeu·not·even·at·any·time read·aloud in the
Mt 26:33 I·myself not·even·at·any·time shall·be·tripped·up·.
Mk 2:25 "Did·yeu·not·even·at·any·time read·aloud what
G3763.2 ADV οὐδέποτε (10x)
Jn 7:46 answered, "Never·at·any·time in·this·manner *has* a·
Lk 15:29 to·you, and never·at·any·time did·I·neglect your
Lk 15:29 and never·at·any·time did·you·give me a·young·
Ac 10:14 because never·at·any·time have·I·eaten anything
Ac 11:8 Lord, because never·at·any·time did anything
Ac 14:8 womb, who never·at·any·time had·walked.
Heb 10:1 activities), never·at·any·time is·it·able with·the
Mt 9:33 "Never·at·any·time did·it·appear in·this·manner in
Mk 2:12 saying, "Never·at·any·time did·we·see *it* in·this·
1Co 13:8 The Love never·at·any·time falls·short. But if·also

G3764 οὐ•δέ•πω ôudépō *adv.* (5x)
Roots:G3761 G4452
G3764 ADV οὐδέπω (5x)
Jn 7:39 not·yet *given*, because Jesus was·not·yet glorified).
Jn 19:41 ·tomb, in which, not·even·yet, not·even·one *man*
Jn 20:9 For not·even·yet had·they·seen the Scripture *which*·
Lk 23:53 where there·was not, not·even·yet, not·even·one
1Co 8:2 ·known not·even·one·thing, not·even·yet, just·as it·

G3765 οὐκ•έτι ôukéti *adv.* (39x)
οὐκ ἔτι ôuk éti
Roots:G3756 G2089
G3765.1 NEG-ADV οὐκέτι (1x)
2Co 1:23 that to·spare yeu, I·did·not·yet come to Corinth.
G3765.2 NEG-ADV οὐκέτι (32x)
Jn 4:42 woman, "No·longer do·we·trust on·account·of your
Jn 6:66 and no·longer were·they·walking·along with him.
Jn 15:15 "No·longer do·I·refer·to yeu *as* slaves, because the
Lk 15:19 and am no·longer worthy to·be·called your son;
Lk 15:21 of·you, and I·am no·longer worthy to·be·called
Lk 20:40 And no·longer were·they daring to·inquire·of him
Ac 20:25 of·God, shall·gaze·upon my face no·longer.
Ac 20:38 that no·longer would·they·*be·able* to·observe his
Heb 10:18 ·things, *there·is* no·longer an·offering concerning
Heb 10:26 no·longer is·there·still·remaining a·sacrifice
Gal 2:20 and I·live. No·longer I·myself, but Anointed-One
Gal 3:18 ·Torah-Law, *it·is* no·longer as·a·result·of·promise.
Gal 3:25 we·are no·longer under a·strict·elementary·school·
Gal 4:7 As·such, you·are no·longer a·slave, but·rather a·son
Mt 19:6 As·such, they·are no·longer two, but·rather one
Mk 7:12 yeu·allow him to·no·longer do not·even·one·thing
Mk 9:8 ·all·around, they·saw no·longer not·even·one·man,
Mk 10:8 ' As·such, they·are no·longer two, but·rather one
Mk 15:5 Jesus was·no·longer answering not·even·one·thing,
Rm 6:9 ·among dead·men, Anointed-One no·longer dies.
Rm 6:9 no·longer dies. Death no·longer lords·over him.
Rm 7:17 right·now, *it·is* no·longer I·myself that·performs it,
Rm 7:20 ·thing I·do, *it·is* no·longer I·myself that·performs it
Rm 11:6 *it·is* by·grace, *it·is* no·longer as·a·result·of·works,
Rm 11:6 otherwise the grace becomes no·longer grace. But
Rm 11:6 of·works, *then* it·is no·longer grace, otherwise the
Rm 11:6 grace, otherwise the work is no·longer work.
Rm 14:15 through *your* food, no·longer do·you·walk in love
2Co 5:16 yet now we·know *him* no·longer *in·this·manner*.
Eph 2:19 consequently, yeu·are no·longer foreigners and
Phm 1:16 no·longer as·a·slave, but·rather above a·slave, a·
Rv 18:14 went·away from you, and no·longer, no, you·
G3765.3 NEG-ADV οὐκέτι (6x)
Lk 22:16 no, I·should·not eat any·longer from·out·of·it until
Ac 8:39 eunuch did·not see him any·longer, for he·traversed
Mt 22:46 ·even·did anyone dare any·longer to·inquire·of him
Mk 12:34 ·even·one was·daring any·longer to·inquire·of him
Mk 14:25 no, I·should·not drink any·longer from·out·of·the
Rv 18:11 not·even·one·man buys their cargo any·longer—

G3766 οὐκ•οῦν ôukôûn *adv.* (1x)
Roots:G3756 G3767
G3766.2 ADV οὐκοῦν (1x)
Jn 18:37 declared to·him, "So·then·indeed, you·yourself are

G3767 οὖν ôûn *conj.* (525x)
Compare:G1352 G2596 G5106 See:G3766
G3767.2 CONJ οὖν (245x)
Jn 1:22 Accordingly, they·declared to·him, "Who are·you?
Jn 2:18 Accordingly, the Judeans answered and declared to·
Jn 2:22 Accordingly, when he·was·awakened from·among
Jn 3:29 ·of the bridegroom's voice. Accordingly, this (my
Jn 4:1 Accordingly, as·soon·as the Lord knew that the
Jn 4:9 Accordingly, the Samaritan woman says to·him,
Jn 4:30 Accordingly, they·went·forth out·of·the city and
Jn 4:53 Accordingly, the father knew that *it·was* at that hour,
Jn 5:10 Accordingly, the Judeans were·saying to·the·one
Jn 5:18 Accordingly, on·account·of that, the Judeans were·
Jn 6:10 grass in the place. Accordingly, the men sat·back·to·
Jn 6:13 Accordingly, they·gathered·together and overfilled
Jn 6:30 Accordingly, they·declared to·him, "So·then what
Jn 6:32 Accordingly, Jesus declared to·them, "Certainly,
Jn 6:41 Accordingly, the Judeans were·grumbling
Jn 6:45 of·Yahweh." Accordingly, every·man hearing and
Jn 6:53 Accordingly, Jesus declared to·them, "Certainly,
Jn 6:60 Accordingly, many from·among his disciples, upon·
Jn 6:68 Accordingly, Simon Peter answered him, "Lord, to
Jn 7:3 Accordingly, his brothers declared to him, "Walk·on
Jn 7:28 Accordingly, Jesus yelled·out in the Sanctuary·
Jn 7:35 Accordingly, the Judeans declared among themselves
Jn 7:43 Accordingly, there·was a·severing·schism among the
Jn 8:5 to·cast·stones·at such·women. Accordingly, what·do
Jn 8:13 Accordingly, the Pharisees declared to·him, "You
Jn 8:24 Accordingly, I·declared to·yeu that yeu·shall·die in
Jn 8:28 Then accordingly, Jesus declared to·them,
Jn 8:38 from·beside my Father, and accordingly, yeu do
Jn 8:42 Accordingly, Jesus declared to·them, "If God was
Jn 8:52 Accordingly, the Judeans declared to·him, "Now
Jn 8:57 Accordingly, the Judeans declared to him, "You·are
Jn 9:7 ·Been·Dispatched). Accordingly, he·went·away and
Jn 9:10 Accordingly, they·were·saying to·him, "How·are
Jn 9:18 Accordingly, the Judeans did·not trust concerning
Jn 9:25 Accordingly, that·man answered and declared,
Jn 9:41 'We·look·about.' Accordingly, yeur moral·failure
Jn 10:19 Accordingly, there·was a·severing·schism again
Jn 10:31 Accordingly, the Judeans lifted·up·and·carried
Jn 10:39 Accordingly, they·were·seeking again to·apprehend
Jn 11:12 Accordingly, his disciples declared, "Lord, if he·
Jn 11:14 Then accordingly, Jesus declared to·them with·
Jn 11:20 Accordingly, Martha, as·soon·as she·heard that
Jn 11:38 Accordingly, Jesus, again being·exasperated in
Jn 11:47 Accordingly, the chief·priests and the Pharisees
Jn 11:54 Accordingly, Jesus was·no longer strolling·about
Jn 12:2 Accordingly, they·made a·supper for·him there, and
Jn 12:7 Accordingly, Jesus declared, "Leave her *alone*.
Jn 12:28 your name." Accordingly, there·came a·voice
Jn 12:35 Accordingly, Jesus declared to·them, "Yet a·short
Jn 12:50 eternal life-above. "Accordingly, whatever I·myself
Jn 13:14 Accordingly, if I·myself washed yeur feet *being*
Jn 13:22 Accordingly, the disciples were·looking to one·
Jn 13:30 Accordingly, after·receiving the morsel, that·one
Jn 16:17 Accordingly, *some* from·among his disciples
Jn 16:22 "And accordingly, yeu·yourselves in·fact now have
Jn 18:4 Accordingly, Jesus, having·seen all the·things that·
Jn 18:8 to·yeu that I AM. Accordingly, if yeu·seek me,
Jn 18:27 Accordingly, Peter denied *it* again, and immediately
Jn 18:29 Accordingly, Pilate went·out to them and declared,
Jn 18:31 yeur Oral-law." Accordingly, the Judeans declared
Jn 18:37 Accordingly, Pilate declared to·him, "So·then·
Jn 19:1 Then accordingly, Pilate took Jesus and flogged *him*.
Jn 19:6 Accordingly, when the chief·priests and the
Jn 19:13 Accordingly, after·hearing this saying, Pilate
Jn 19:16 Then accordingly, he·handed him over to·them that
Jn 19:21 Accordingly, the chief·priests of·the Judeans were·
Jn 19:24 Accordingly, they·declared among one·another,
Jn 19:26 Accordingly, Jesus seeing his mother and the
Jn 19:30 Accordingly, when Jesus received the wine·vinegar,
Jn 19:32 Accordingly, the *Roman* soldiers came and in·fact
Jn 20:3 Accordingly, Peter and the other disciple went·forth,
Jn 20:8 Then accordingly, the other disciple entered also,
Jn 20:20 his hands and his side. Accordingly, the disciples
Jn 21:6 and yeu·shall·find." Accordingly, they·cast *the net*
Jn 21:15 Accordingly, when they·had·dined, Jesus says to·
Lk 3:7 Accordingly, he·was·saying to·the crowds traversing·
Lk 3:9 to the root of·the trees. Accordingly, every tree not
Lk 3:18 Accordingly in·fact, also exhorting many other·
Lk 4:7 Accordingly, if you should·fall·prostrate in·the·sight
Lk 6:36 "Accordingly, become compassionate, just·as yeur
Lk 8:18 "Accordingly, look·out·for how *well* yeu·listen·
Lk 10:2 but the workmen *are* few. Accordingly, petition the
Lk 10:37 with him." Accordingly, Jesus declared to·him,
Lk 11:34 body is the eye. Accordingly, whenever your eye
Lk 12:7 all have·been·numbered. "Accordingly, do·not be·
Lk 12:40 "Accordingly, yeu·yourselves become ready also,
Lk 13:14 it·is·necessary to·work. Accordingly, coming on
Lk 14:33 "Accordingly in·this·manner, anyone from·among
Lk 19:12 Accordingly, he·declared, "A·man·of·clay†, a·
Lk 21:8 has·drawn·near.' Accordingly, yeu·should·not
Lk 21:14 "Accordingly, firmly·settle *it* in yeur hearts, not to·
Lk 21:36 "Accordingly, stay·alert, petitioning in every
Lk 23:16 "Accordingly, after·correctively·disciplining him,
Ac 1:6 Accordingly in·fact, after·coming·together, they·
Ac 1:18 (Accordingly in·fact, this·man procured an·open·
Ac 1:21 "Accordingly, it·is·mandatory of·the men going·
Ac 2:30 Accordingly, inherently·being a·prophet and having·
Ac 2:41 Accordingly in·fact, after·fully·accepting his
Ac 3:19 "Accordingly, yeu·must·repent and turn·back·
Ac 5:41 Accordingly, the *ambassadors*, in·fact, were·
Ac 8:4 Accordingly in·fact, the·ones being·dispersed went·
Ac 9:31 Accordingly in·fact, the Called·Out·citizenries in
Ac 10:29 ·expressing·opposition. Accordingly, I·inquire,
Ac 10:33 ·directly *here*. Now accordingly, we·ourselves *are*
Ac 11:19 Accordingly in·fact, the·ones being·dispersed by
Ac 12:5 Accordingly in·fact, Peter was·kept in the prison·
Ac 13:4 Accordingly in·fact, after·being·sent·forth by the
Ac 13:40 Accordingly, look·out, lest it·should·come upon
Ac 14:3 Accordingly in·fact, they·lingered a·sufficient time,
Ac 15:3 Accordingly in·fact, being·sent·onward·on·their·
Ac 15:10 "Now, accordingly, why·do yeu·try God, to·put a·
Ac 15:27 "Accordingly, we·have·dispatched Judas and Silas,
Ac 15:30 Accordingly in·fact, after·being·dismissed, they·
Ac 16:5 Accordingly in·fact, the Called·Out·citizenries
Ac 16:11 Accordingly, sailing from Troas, we·sailed·straight
Ac 16:36 ·be·fully·released. Now accordingly, going·forth,
Ac 17:12 Accordingly in·fact, many from·among them
Ac 17:17 Accordingly in·fact, he·was·having·discussions in
Ac 17:20 to our ears. Accordingly, we·resolve to·know what
Ac 17:29 Accordingly, inherently·being kindred of·God, we·
Ac 17:30 "Accordingly in·fact, after·previously·overlooking
Ac 18:14 to the Jews, "Accordingly in·fact, if it·were some
Ac 19:38 "Accordingly in·fact, if Demetrius and the
Ac 23:15 Now accordingly, yeu·yourselves together with·the
Ac 25:17 "Accordingly, with·them coming·together here
Ac 26:4 "Accordingly in·fact, all the Judeans have·
Ac 26:9 "Accordingly in·fact, I·myself (within·myself)
Ac 28:20 Accordingly, on·account·of this cause, I·
Heb 2:14 Accordingly, since the little·children have·a·
Heb 4:1 Accordingly, with·a·promise being·left·behind *for*·
Heb 4:11 Accordingly, we·should·quickly·endeavor to·enter
Heb 4:16 Accordingly, we·should·be·coming·alongside with
Heb 7:11 Accordingly in·fact, if perfection was through the
Heb 9:1 Accordingly in·fact, the first Tabernacle also was·
Heb 9:23 Accordingly, *it·was* a·necessity *for* the·things (in·
Heb 10:19 Accordingly brothers, by the blood of·YeShua,
Heb 10:35 Accordingly, yeu·should·not cast·away yeur bold·

Heb 13:15 Accordingly, on·account·of him, we·should·
Gal 5:1 Accordingly, stand·fast in·the liberty with·which
Gal 6:10 Accordingly, as we·have opportunity, we·should·
Mt 3:10 to the root of·the trees. Accordingly, every tree not
Mt 5:19 Accordingly, whoever should·break one of·these
Mt 6:2 "Accordingly, whenever you·should·do a·merciful·
Mt 6:8 "Accordingly, yeu·should·not be·like them, for yeur
Mt 6:22 of·the body is the eye. Accordingly, if your eye
Mt 6:34 "Accordingly, yeu·should·not be·anxious for
Mt 7:12 "Accordingly, all·things, as·much·as yeu·should·
Mt 7:24 "Accordingly, anyone that hears these sayings of·
Mt 10:16 *the* midst of·wolves. Accordingly, become prudent
Mt 10:26 Accordingly, do·not fear them.
Mt 10:31 Accordingly, do·not be·afraid; yeu·yeurselves
Mt 13:40 "Accordingly, just·as the darnel·weeds are·
Mt 18:4 Accordingly, whoever should·humble himself as
Mt 19:6 two, but·rather one flesh. Accordingly, what God
Mt 23:3 Accordingly, everything, whatever as·much·as they·
Mt 24:15 "Accordingly, whenever yeu·should·see " the
Mt 24:26 "Accordingly, if they·should·declare to·yeu,
Mt 24:42 "Accordingly, keep·alert, because yeu·do·not
Mt 25:13 "Accordingly, keep·alert, because yeu·do·not
Mt 25:27 Accordingly, it·was·mandatory·for you to·cast my
Mt 28:19 "Accordingly, while·traversing, disciple all the
Mk 10:9 Accordingly, what God yoked·together, a·man·of·
Mk 12:27 but·rather a·God of·living·men. Accordingly, yeu
Mk 13:35 Accordingly, keep·alert— for yeu·do·not
Rm 2:26 Accordingly, if the·one uncircumcised should·
Rm 3:28 Accordingly, we·reckon *that* a·man·of·clay† *is* to·
Rm 4:1 Accordingly, what shall·we·state *for* AbRaham our
Rm 5:1 Accordingly, already·being·regarded·as·righteous
Rm 6:4 Accordingly, we·are·already·buried·together with·
Rm 6:12 Accordingly, *each·one·of* you·must·not·let Moral·
Rm 6:21 Accordingly, what fruit were·yeu·having then in
Rm 7:3 Accordingly, if she·should·come to·another man
Rm 7:25 our Lord. So accordingly in·fact, with·the mind, I
Rm 8:12 So accordingly brothers, we·are under·an·
Rm 9:14 Accordingly, what shall·we·state?
Rm 9:18 Accordingly, on·whom he·determines, he·shows·
Rm 11:1 Accordingly, I·say, ¿!·Did God shove·away his
Rm 11:5 Accordingly in·this·manner, in the present season
Rm 11:11 Accordingly, I·say, ¿!·Did they·slip·up in·order·
Rm 11:19 Accordingly, you·shall·declare, "The branches
Rm 11:22 Accordingly, see *both* a·benevolent·kindness and
Rm 12:1 Accordingly, I·implore yeu, brothers, through the
Rm 12:20 Accordingly, "'If your enemy should·hunger,
Rm 13:7 Accordingly, render the dues to·all·ones *in·superior*
Rm 13:10 no wrong to·the neighbor. Accordingly, love *is*
Rm 13:12 ·drawn·near. Accordingly, we·should·put·away
Rm 14:8 we·die to·the Lord. Accordingly, both whether we·
Rm 14:13 Accordingly, no·longer should·we·unduly·judge
Rm 14:16 Accordingly, do·not·let yeur good·benefit be·
Rm 14:19 Accordingly, we·should·pursue the·things of·
Rm 15:17 Accordingly, I·have a·boast in Jesus Anointed in·
Rm 15:28 Accordingly, after·further·finishing this
Rm 16:19 to all *men*. Accordingly, I·rejoice over yeu.
Jac 4:4 is hostility with·God? Accordingly, whoever would
Jac 4:7 Accordingly, submit·yeurselves to·God.
Jac 5:7 Accordingly, be·patient brothers, until the returning·
Php 2:1 Accordingly, if *there·is* any exhortation in
Php 2:23 Accordingly in·fact, I·expect to·send this·man
Php 2:28 Accordingly, I·sent him more·diligently, in·order·
Php 3:15 Accordingly, as·many·as *would·become*
1Pe 2:1 Accordingly, with·yeu·laying·aside all malice, and
1Pe 2:13 Accordingly, submit·yeurselves to·every created·
1Pe 4:1 Accordingly, with·Anointed-One already·suffering
1Pe 4:7 has·drawn·near. Accordingly, be·self-controlled,
1Pe 5:6 Accordingly, be·humbled under the mighty hand of·
2Pe 3:11 Accordingly, with·all these·things being·dissolved,
2Pe 3:17 Accordingly, O·yeu beloved, while·foreknowing
1Th 5:6 Accordingly, we·should·not fall·asleep, as even *do*
2Th 2:15 So accordingly, brothers, stand·fast and securely·
1Co 4:16 Accordingly, I·implore yeu, become attentive·
1Co 5:7 Accordingly, purge·out the old leaven in·order·that
1Co 6:4 Accordingly in·fact, if yeu·should·have arbitrations
1Co 6:7 Accordingly in·fact, even·now there·is altogether a·
1Co 7:26 Accordingly, I·deem for·this to·inherently·be good
1Co 9:25 ·self-restraint in·all·things. Accordingly in·fact,
1Co 14:26 Accordingly, how is·it *to·be*, brothers?
1Co 15:11 Accordingly, whether *it·was* I·myself or those
1Co 16:11 Accordingly, not anyone should·utterly·disdain
1Co 16:18 spirit and yeurs. Accordingly, acknowledge the·
2Co 7:1 Accordingly, having these promises, dearly·beloved,
2Co 8:24 Accordingly, indicate for them the indicator of·
2Co 9:5 Accordingly, I·resolutely·considered *it* necessary to·
2Co 11:15 Accordingly, *it·is* no great·thing if his attendants
2Co 12:9 in weakness." Accordingly rather, with·great·
Eph 4:17 Accordingly, I·say this and attest *to·it* in *the* Lord:
Eph 5:1 Accordingly, become attentive·imitators of·God, as
Eph 5:7 Accordingly, do·not become co-participants with·
Eph 5:15 Accordingly, look·out *then for* precisely how yeu·
Eph 6:14 Stand·still accordingly, after·personally·girding
Col 2:6 Accordingly, *in·the·same·manner* as yeu·personally·
Col 2:16 Accordingly, do·not·let anyone judge yeu
Col 3:5 Accordingly, deaden yeur members *to* the·things
Col 3:12 Accordingly, as Selected-Ones of·God (holy and
1Ti 2:8 Accordingly, I·resolve *for* the men to·pray in every
1Ti 5:14 Accordingly, on·account·of·grace, I·resolve *for*
2Ti 1:8 Accordingly, you·should·not be·ashamed·of the
2Ti 2:1 Accordingly, you, my child, be·enabled in the grace,
2Ti 2:21 Accordingly, if anyone should·entirely·purify
2Ti 4:1 Accordingly, I·myself thoroughly·urge *you* in·the·
1Jn 2:24 Accordingly, let·it·abide in yeu, that·which yeu
3Jn 1:8 Accordingly, we·ourselves ought to·fully·receive·
Rv 2:5 Accordingly, remember from·what·source you·have·
Rv 3:3 'Accordingly, remember by·what·means you·have·
Rv 3:3 *it* and repent. Accordingly, unless you·should·keep·
Rv 3:19 correctively·discipline. Accordingly, be·zealous

G3767.3 CONJ οὖν (20x)

Jn 3:25 In·due·course, there·occurred a·question·and·
Jn 4:5 In·due·course, he·comes to a·city of·Samaria being·
Jn 4:46 In·due·course, Jesus came again into Qanah of·
Jn 6:19 In·due·course, having·rowed about twenty·five or
Jn 8:12 In·due·course, Jesus spoke again to·them, saying, "I
Jn 8:21 In·due·course, Jesus declared again to·them, "I·
Jn 11:3 In·due·course, his sisters dispatched to him, saying,
Jn 12:1 In·due·course, six days before the Passover, Jesus
Jn 18:16 outside alongside the door. In·due·course, the other
Jn 18:19 In·due·course, the designated·high·priest asked Jesus
Jn 18:28 In·due·course, they·led Jesus from Caiaphas to the
Jn 19:20 In·due·course, many of·the Judeans read·aloud this
Jn 19:24 ' In·fact, in·due·course, the soldiers did these·
Jn 19:31 In·due·course, since it·was preparation·day, in·
Jn 20:19 In·due·course, with·it·being *almost* early·evening
Jn 21:7 In·due·course, that disciple whom Jesus loved says
Ac 8:25 In·due·course, in·fact, after·thoroughly·testifying
Ac 19:32 In·fact, in·due·course, some were·yelling·out a·
Ac 28:9 In·due·course, with·this happening, the rest also,
Mk 3:31 In·due·course, his brothers and his mother come

G3767.4 CONJ οὖν (181x)

Jn 1:21 And they·asked·of him, "So·then, who are you·
Jn 1:25 and declared to·him, "So·then why·do you·immerse,
Jn 2:20 So·then the Judeans declared, "*In* forty six years,
Jn 4:6 well was there. So·then Jesus, having·become·weary
Jn 4:11 well is deep. So·then from·what·source do·you·have
Jn 4:28 So·then, the woman left her water·jar and went·off
Jn 4:33 So·then the disciples were·saying among one·another
Jn 4:40 So·then *just* as·soon·as the Samaritans came toward
Jn 4:45 So·then, when he·came into Galilee, the Galileans
Jn 4:52 So·then he·inquired personally·from them the hour
Jn 5:4 and was·troubling the water. So·then, the first·one
Jn 5:12 So·then they·asked·of him, "Who is the man·of·
Jn 5:19 So·then Jesus answered and declared to·them,
Jn 6:5 So·then, after·lifting·up the eyes and surveying that a·
Jn 6:14 So·then, seeing that Jesus did a·miraculous·sign, the
Jn 6:21 Then they·were·willing to·receive him into the
Jn 6:24 So·then, when the crowd saw that Jesus was not
Jn 6:28 So·then they·declared to·him, "What·do we·do in·
Jn 6:30 ·declared to·him, "So·then what miraculous·sign *do*
Jn 6:34 So·then they·declared to·him, "Lord, always give us
Jn 6:42 ·ourselves personally·know? So·then how·is·it *that*
Jn 6:52 So·then the Judeans were·quarreling among one·
Jn 6:62 So·then, *what* if yeu·should·observe the Son of·Clay·
Jn 6:67 So·then Jesus declared to·the twelve, "And *do* yeu·
Jn 7:6 So·then Jesus says to·them, "My season is·not·yet
Jn 7:25 So·then, some from·among the·men of·JeruSalem
Jn 7:30 So·then they·were·seeking to·apprehend him, but
Jn 7:33 So·then Jesus declared to·them, "Yet a·short time
Jn 7:40 So·then after·hearing the saying, many from·among
Jn 7:45 So·then the assistants came to the chief·priests and
Jn 7:47 Then the Pharisees answered them, "¿!·Have even
Jn 8:19 So·then they·were·saying to·him, "Where is your
Jn 8:22 So·then the Judeans were·saying, "Is·it·that he·
Jn 8:25 So·then they·were·saying to·him, "Who are you·
Jn 8:31 So·then, Jesus was·saying to *those* Judeans, the·ones
Jn 8:36 So·then, if the Son should·set yeu free, yeu·shall
Jn 8:41 of·yeur father." So·then they·declared to·him,
Jn 8:48 So·then the Judeans answered and declared to·him,
Jn 8:59 So·then they·took·up stones in·order·that they·may·
Jn 9:8 So·then the close·neighbors (and the·ones observing
Jn 9:12 So·then they·declared to·him, "Where is this·man?
Jn 9:16 So·then some from·among the Pharisees were·saying
Jn 9:19 say was·born blind? So·then at·this·moment, how
Jn 9:24 So·then for a·second·time they·hollered·out·for the
Jn 9:28 So·then they·defamed him and declared, "You·
Jn 10:7 So·then Jesus declared to·them again, "Certainly,
Jn 10:24 So·then the Judeans surrounded him and were·
Jn 11:16 So·then Thomas (the·one being·referred·to·as
Jn 11:21 Then Martha declared to Jesus, "Lord, if you·were
Jn 11:31 So·then the Judeans, the·ones being·with her in the
Jn 11:36 So·then the Judeans were·saying, "See how fond·
Jn 11:41 So·then they·took·away the stone *from the place*
Jn 11:45 So·then many from·among the Judeans, the·ones
Jn 11:53 So·then, from that day *forth*, they·took·counsel·
Jn 11:56 So·then, standing in the Sanctuary·Atrium, they·
Jn 12:4 So·then one from·among his disciples (Judas
Jn 12:19 So·then the Pharisees declared among themselves,
Jn 12:29 So·then the crowd, the·one standing·by and hearing
Jn 13:6 So·then he·comes to Simon Peter, and that·one says
Jn 13:24 So·then, Simon Peter beckoned to·him to·inquire
Jn 13:27 entered into that·man. So·then Jesus says to·him,
Jn 16:18 So·then they·were·saying, "What is this·thing that
Jn 18:3 So·then, after·receiving the battalion and·also
Jn 18:7 So·then he·inquired·of them again, "Whom·do yeu·
Jn 18:11 So·then Jesus declared to·Peter, "Cast your dagger
Jn 18:12 And·then the battalion, the regiment·commander,
Jn 18:17 So·then the servant·girl (the doorkeeper) says to·
Jn 18:25 warming·himself. So·then they·declared to·him,
Jn 18:31 So·then Pilate declared to·them, "Yeu·yeurselves
Jn 18:33 So·then Pilate entered into the Praetorian·hall again
Jn 18:39 at the Passover. So·then, do·yeu·resolve *that* I·
Jn 18:40 So·then they·all yelled·out again, saying, "Not this·
Jn 19:10 So·then Pilate says to·him, "Do·you·not speak to·
Jn 19:40 So·then they·took the body of·Jesus and bound it
Jn 20:2 So·then she·runs and comes to Simon Peter and to
Jn 20:6 So·then, Simon Peter comes following him, and he·
Jn 20:10 So·then, the disciples went·off again to·their·own
Jn 21:9 So·then, as they·disembarked upon the dry·ground,
Jn 21:13 Then Jesus comes and takes the bread and gives *it*
Jn 21:23 So·then this saying went·forth among the brothers,
Lk 3:10 ·of him, saying, "So·then what shall·we·do?
Lk 6:9 So·then Jesus declared to them, "I·shall·inquire·of
Lk 7:31 Lord declared, "So·then to·what shall·I·liken the
Lk 7:42 ·forgave them·both. So·then declare *to·me*, which
Lk 10:36 "So·then, which of·these three·men seems to·you
Lk 10:40 me to·attend alone? So·then declare to·her that
Lk 11:13 "So·then, if yeu, inherently·being evil, personally·
Lk 11:35 So·then, keep·a·watch *that* the light, the·one in you
Lk 12:26 "So·then, if yeu·are·not·even able *to·do* that·thing·

Lk 13:15 So·then the Lord answered him and declared, "O·
Lk 16:11 So·then, if yeu·did·not become trustworthy with
Lk 16:27 "Then he·declared, 'So·then I·implore·of you,
Lk 20:5 he·shall·declare, 'So·then why did·yeu·not trust
Lk 20:15 they·killed *him*. "So·then what shall the owner
Lk 20:17 them, he·declared, "So·then, what is this having·
Lk 20:33 "So·then, in the resurrection, whose wife of·them
Lk 20:44 So·then David calls him 'Lord'; how is·he also his
Lk 21:7 ·of him, saying, "So·then Mentor, when shall
Lk 22:36 Then he·declared to·them, "But·yet now, the·one
Lk 22:70 So they·all replied, "So·then, you·yourself are the
Lk 23:22 him. "So·then after·correctively·disciplining him,
Ac 2:33 So·then, after·being·elevated to·the right·hand of·
Ac 10:23 So·then inviting them in, *Peter* hosted *them*.
Ac 10:33 So·then, from·this·same·hour I·sent to you, and
Ac 15:39 So·then a·sharp·disagreement occurred, such·for
Ac 19:3 to them, "So·then into what were·yeu·immersed?
Ac 20:28 "So·then take·heed to·yeurselves, and to·the entire
Ac 21:23 "So·then do this·thing which we·say to·you.
Ac 22:29 So·then immediately, the·ones intending to·
Ac 23:18 So·then in·fact, the *centurion*, personally·taking
Ac 23:22 So·then in·fact, the regiment·commander
Ac 23:31 So·then in·fact, the soldiers, according·to the
Ac 25:23 So·then on·the next·day, with·AgrÎppa and BerNiki
Ac 26:22 So·then after·obtaining assistance personally·from
Heb 4:14 So·then having a·great High·Priest, having·gone·
Gal 3:19 So·then, *for* what *purpose is* the Torah-Law?
Gal 3:21 So·then, *is* the Torah-Law against the promises of·
Gal 4:15 So·then, what was the supreme·blessedness yeu
Mt 5:23 "So·then, if you·should·bring your present to the
Mt 5:48 "So·then, yeu·yeurselves shall·be complete *in·this·*
Mt 6:9 "So·then, yeu·yeurselves pray in·this·manner: 'Our
Mt 6:23 whole body shall·be opaquely·dark. So·then, if the
Mt 6:31 "So·then, yeu·should·not be·anxious, saying, 'what
Mt 7:11 So·then, if yeu·yeurselves, being evil, personally·
Mt 9:38 So·then, petition the Lord of·the harvest, that he·
Mt 12:12 So·then, by·how·much·does a·man·of·clay†
Mt 12:26 he·is·divided against himself. So·then, how shall
Mt 13:27 seed in your field? So·then, from·what·source are
Mt 13:56 alongside us? So·then from·what·source *does* this·
Mt 17:10 ·of him, saying, "So·then why·do the scribes say
Mt 18:26 So·then falling·down, the slave was·falling·
Mt 18:29 So·then falling·down at his feet, his fellow·slave
Mt 19:7 *Then* they·say to·him, "So·then why·did Moses
Mt 21:25 he·shall·declare to·us, 'So·then why did·yeu·not
Mt 21:40 "So·then, whenever the owner of·the vineyard
Mt 22:17 So·then declare to·us, what·do you suppose?
Mt 22:28 "So·then, in the resurrection whose wife shall·she·
Mt 22:43 He·says to·them, "So·then how·does David in
Mt 22:45 So·then, if David calls him 'Lord,' how is·he
Mt 23:20 "So·then, the·one swearing by the Sacrifice·Altar,
Mt 25:28 So·then, take·away the talant·of·silver from him
Mt 26:54 But·then how·should the Scriptures be·completely·
Mt 27:17 So·then, with·them having·been·gathered·together,
Mt 27:22 Pilate says to·them, "So·then what shall·I·do with·
Mk 11:31 he·shall·declare, 'So·then why did·yeu·not trust
Mk 12:6 "So·then, yet having one son, his well-beloved, he·
Mk 12:9 "So·then, what·shall the owner of·the vineyard do?
Mk 12:23 "So·then in the resurrection, whenever they·
Mk 12:37 So·then David himself refers·to him *as* 'Lord,' so
Mk 15:12 again to·them, "So·then, what·do yeu·want *that* I·
Rm 2:21 So·then, the·one instructing someone·else, do·you·
Rm 3:1 So·then what *is* the Jew's superior·benefit?
Rm 3:9 So·then what, are·we *Jews* any·better·off?
Rm 3:27 So·then, where *is* the boasting?
Rm 3:31 So·then, do·we·fully·render·useless *the* Torah-Law
Rm 4:9 So·then, *is* this supreme·blessedness upon the
Rm 4:10 So·then how was·it·reckoned?
Rm 5:9 So·then, now being·regarded·as·righteous by his
Rm 6:1 So·then, what shall·we·state?
Rm 6:15 So·then, what?
Rm 7:7 So·then, what shall·we·state?
Rm 7:13 So·then, the beneficially·good, has·it·become death
Rm 8:31 So·then, what shall·we·state toward these·things?
Rm 9:16 So·then, consequently, *it·depends* not on·the·one
Rm 9:19 So·then, you·shall·declare to·me, "Why still does·
Rm 9:30 So·then, what shall·we·state?
Rm 10:14 So·then, how shall·they·call·upon *him* in whom
Rm 11:7 So·then, what *happened*?
Rm 14:12 So·then, consequently, each·one of·us shall·give
Php 2:29 So·then, welcome him in *the* Lord with all joy, and
1Pe 2:7 So·then the honor *is* to·yeu, to·the·ones presently·
1Co 3:5 So·then, who is Paul, and who *is* Apollos, other
1Co 8:4 So·then, concerning the feeding·upon the·things
1Co 10:19 So·then, what do·I·reply?
1Co 10:31 So·then whether yeu·eat, or drink, or anything
1Co 14:15 So·then, which is·it?
2Co 3:12 So·then, having such an·expectation, we·use
2Co 5:6 So·then, *we·are* exercising·courage always even
2Co 5:11 So·then, having·seen the fear of·the Lord, we·
Col 3:1 So·then, if yeu·are·already·awakened·together with·
Phm 1:17 So·then, if you·hold me *to·be* a·partner, purposely·

G3767.5 CONJ οὖν (12x)

Jn 6:15 So Jesus, knowing that they·are·about to·come and
Jn 6:43 So Jesus answered and declared to·them, "Do·not
Jn 11:32 So as·soon·as Mary came where Jesus was, upon·
Jn 19:5 So Jesus came·forth outside bearing the thorny
Jn 19:38 Pilate freely·permitted *him*. So he·came and took·
Jn 19:42 So they·laid Jesus there on·account·of the Judeans
Jn 20:25 So the other disciples were·saying to·him, "We·
Jn 21:5 So Jesus says to·them, "Little·children, ¿! do·yeu·
Lk 15:28 and was·not willing to·enter. So coming·out, his
Mt 1:17 So all the generations·of·offspring from AbRaham
Mt 13:28 declared to·him, 'So do·you·want *us* to·go·off *so·*
Rm 5:18 So consequently, as through one trespass, *judgment*

G3767.6 CONJ οὖν (66x)

Jn 4:48 Now·then Jesus declared to him, "Unless yeu·*all·*
Jn 7:11 Now·then, the Judeans were·seeking him at the
Jn 9:15 Now·then, the Pharisees again also were·asking·of
Jn 11:6 Now·then, as·soon·as he·heard that he·was·sick, in·
Jn 11:17 Now·then, after·going *to·him*, Jesus found him
Jn 11:33 Now as·soon·as Jesus saw her weeping, and the
Jn 12:3 Now·then, taking a·Roman·pound of·extremely·
Jn 12:9 Now·then, a·large crowd from·among the Judeans
Jn 12:17 Now·then, the crowd *from BethAny* was·testifying,
Jn 12:21 Now·then, the·same *Greeks* came·alongside PhilÎp,
Jn 13:12 Now·then, when he·washed their feet and took·
Jn 16:19 Now·then, Jesus knew that they·were·wanting to·
Jn 18:6 Now·then, as·soon·as he·declared to·them, "I AM,"
Jn 18:10 Now·then, having a·dagger, Simon Peter drew it
Jn 19:4 Now·then, Pilate went·forth outside again and says
Jn 19:8 Now·then, when Pilate heard this saying, he·was all·
Jn 19:23 Now·then, when they·crucified Jesus, the soldiers
Jn 19:29 Now·then, there·was·set·out a·vessel exceedingly·
Jn 20:11 the chamber·tomb weeping. Now·then, as she·was·
Jn 20:21 Now·then, Jesus declared to·them again, "Peace *be*
Jn 20:30 Now·then in·fact, Jesus also did many other signs
Jn 21:7 "It·is the Lord." Now·then, after·hearing that it·was
Lk 3:8 "Now·then, produce fruits worthy of·the repentance,
Lk 10:2 Now·then, he·was·saying to·them, "In·fact, the
Lk 11:36 "Now·then, if your whole body *is* full·of·light, not
Lk 20:29 "Now·then, there·were seven brothers.
Lk 23:20 Now·then, wanting to·fully·release Jesus, Pilate
Ac 2:36 "Now·then, all *the* house of·IsraEl must·know
Ac 6:3 Now·then, brothers, inspect from·among yeurselves
Ac 8:22 Now·then, repent of this depravity of·yours, and
Ac 10:32 Now·then, send to Joppa and summarily·call·for
Ac 11:17 Now·then, since God gave to·them the equally·
Ac 13:38 "Now·then, men, brothers, be·it known to·yeu that
Ac 15:2 Now·then, with·it·becoming of·no little controversy
Ac 17:23 'TO·AN·UNKNOWN GOD.' Now·then, *the·one*
Ac 19:36 Now·then, with·these·things being·indisputable, it·
Ac 21:22 Now·then, why is *this*?
Ac 23:21 Now·then, you·yourself should·not be·persuaded
Ac 25:1 Now·then, three days after walking·over into·the
Ac 25:4 Now·then in·fact, Festus answered *for* Paul to·be·
Ac 25:5 "Now·then," he·replies, "the·ones among yeu *who·*
Ac 28:5 Now·then, in·fact, after·jostling·off the venomous·
Ac 28:28 "Now·then, be·it known to·yeu that the custodial·
Heb 4:6 Now·then, since it·is·still·remaining *for* some to·
Gal 3:5 Now·then, the·one fully·supplying the Spirit to·yeu
Mt 3:8 Now·then, produce fruits worthy of·the repentance.
Mt 10:32 "Now·then, anyone who shall·affirm me by·name
Mt 13:18 "Now·then, yeu·yeurselves hear the parable of·
Mt 22:9 Now·then, yeu·traverse to the exit·areas of·the
Mt 27:64 Now·then, commandingly·order *for* the grave to·
Mk 16:19 Now·then in·fact, after the Lord spoke to·them,
Jac 4:17 Now·then, *anyone* having·seen *the* morally·good·
1Th 4:1 Now·then, one·thing remaining, brothers: We·ask·of
1Co 6:15 of·Anointed-One? Now·then, after·taking·up the
1Co 9:18 Now·then, the payment·of·service: What is *the*
1Co 11:20 Now·then, as·yeu are·coming·together in·unison,
1Co 14:11 Now·then, if I·should·not personally·know the
1Co 14:23 Now·then, if the whole Called·Out·citizenry
2Co 1:17 Now·then, in·purposefully·planning that, ¿!·did
2Co 5:20 Now·then, we·are·elder·spokesmen on·behalf of·
Eph 2:19 Now·then, consequently, yeu·are no·longer
Eph 4:1 Now·then, I·myself, the chained·prisoner in *the*
Col 2:20 Now·then, if yeu·did·die together with·
1Ti 2:1 Now·then, I·exhort first of·all *for* petitions, prayers,
1Ti 3:2 Now·then, it·is·mandatory·for the overseer to·be
2Ti 2:3 Now·then, you·yourself must·endure·hardship as a·

G3767.7 CONJ οὖν (1x)

Mt 22:21 he·says to·them, "Well·then, render the·things of·

G3768 οὔ•πω ôúpō *adv.* (23x)

Roots:G3756 G4452

G3768 NEG-ADV οὔπω (23x)

Jn 2:4 to·do·with·me and you? My hour has·not·yet come."
Jn 3:24 for John had·not·yet been·cast into the prison.
Jn 7:6 says to·them, "My season is·not·yet here, but yeur
Jn 7:8 this Sacred·Feast. I·myself do·not·yet walk·up to this
Jn 7:8 my season has·not·yet been·completely·fulfilled."
Jn 7:30 his hand on him, because his hour had·not·yet come.
Jn 7:39 for Holy Spirit was not·yet *given*, because Jesus
Jn 8:20 him, because his hour had·not·yet come.
Jn 8:57 to him, "You·are not·yet fifty years·of·age, and
Jn 11:30 Now Jesus had·not·yet come into the village, but·
Jn 20:17 lay·hold of·me, for I·have·not·yet ascended to my
Ac 8:16 (For as·of·yet, he·was having·fallen upon not·even·
Heb 2:8 to·him. But now we·do·not·yet clearly·see all
Heb 12:4 Yet·not as·far·as·unto *sweating* blood did·yeu·
Mt 15:17 Do·yeu·not·yet understand that any thing
Mt 16:9 "Do·yeu·not·yet understand, nor·even remember the
Mt 24:6 *these·things* to·happen, but·still the end is not·yet.
Mk 8:17 ·do·not have bread? Do·yeu·not·yet understand,
Mk 13:7 *such·things* to·happen, but·rather the end *is* not·yet.
1Co 3:2 and not food, for yeu·were·not·yet able *to·bear it*.
1Jn 3:2 of·God, and it·is·not·yet made·apparent what we·
Rv 17:10 is, *and* the other did·not·yet come; and whenever
Rv 17:12 are ten kings who did·not·yet receive a·kingdom,

G3769 οὐρά ôurá *n.* (5x)

Compare:G2771-1 G2776
xLangEquiv:H2180 xLangAlso:H7218

G3769 N-NSF οὐρά (1x)

Rv 12:4 And his tail dragged the third·part of·the stars of·the

G3769 N-NPF οὐραί (1x)

Rv 9:19 *their tails*, for their tails *were* like serpents having

G3769 N-APF οὐράς (1x)

Rv 9:10 And they·have tails like scorpions, and there·were

G3769 N-DPF οὐραῖς (1x)

Rv 9:10 and there·were painful·stings in their tails, and their

EG3769 (1x)

Rv 9:19 in their mouth *and in their tails*, for their tails *were*

G3770 οὐράνιος ôuránîôs *adj.* (6x)

Roots:G3772

G3770.2 A-NSM οὐράνιος (4x)

Mt 6:14 their trespasses, your heavenly Father also shall·
Mt 6:26 into barns, yet your heavenly Father nourishes them
Mt 6:32 seek·after) for your heavenly Father has·seen that

Mt 15:13 "Every plant which my heavenly Father did·not
G3770.2 A-DSF οὐρανίῳ (1x)
Ac 26:19 I·did·not become obstinate to·the heavenly vision.
G3770.2 A-GSF οὐρανίου (1x)
Lk 2:13 ·to·be a·multitude of·the·heavenly host praising God

G3771 οὐρανό•θεν ôuranóthên *adv.* (2x)
Roots:G3772
G3771.1 ADV οὐρανόθεν (1x)
Ac 14:17 us seasons·of·rain from·the·sky and fruit-bearing
G3771.2 ADV οὐρανόθεν (1x)
Ac 26:13 I·saw in the way a·light from·heaven beyond the

G3772 οὐρανός ôuranós *n.* (285x)
Compare:G0109 G3321 See:G3735 G0142
xLangEquiv:H8064 A8065 xLangAlso:H7549
G3772.1 N-NSM οὐρανός (9x)
Lk 4:25 ·EliJah, when the heaven was·shut·up for·a·span·of
Lk 21:33 "The heaven and the earth shall·pass·away, but my
Ac 7:49 "The heaven *is* my throne, and the earth *is* my foot
Mt 5:18 certainly I·say to·yeu, until the heaven and the earth
Mt 24:35 "The heaven and the earth shall·pass·away, but my
Mk 13:31 "The heaven and the earth shall·pass·away, but my
Rv 6:14 And heaven was·utterly·separated as an·official·
Rv 20:11 face the earth and the heaven fled·away. And there·
Rv 21:1 earth, for the first heaven and the first earth passed·
G3772.1 N-NPM οὐρανοί (7x)
Heb 1:10 the earth; and the heavens are works of·your hands
Mt 3:16 And behold, the heavens were·opened·up to·him,
2Pe 3:5 Word of·God, there·were heavens from·antiquity,
2Pe 3:7 by·the·same Word, the heavens and the earth are
2Pe 3:10 the heavens shall·pass·away with·a·whirring·noise ·
2Pe 3:12 — through which *the* heavens, being·set·on·fire,
Rv 12:12 be·merry, the heavens and the·ones encamping in
G3772.1 N-VSM οὐρανέ (1x)
Rv 18:20 "Be·merry over her, O·Heaven, and the holy
G3772.1 N-ASM οὐρανόν (42x)
Jn 1:51 ·shall·gaze·upon the heaven having·been·opened·up,
Jn 3:13 ·even·one·man has·ascended into the heaven, except
Jn 17:1 and lifted·up his eyes to the heaven, and he·declared,
Lk 2:15 went·away from them into the heaven, also *that* the
Lk 3:21 ·immersed and praying, the heaven was·opened·up,
Lk 9:16 two fish, looking·up to the heaven, he·blessed them,
Lk 15:18 I·morally·failed against the heaven, and in·the·
Lk 15:21 I·morally·failed against the heaven and in·the·sight
Lk 16:17 But it·is easier·for the heaven and the earth to·pass·
Lk 17:24 ·out of·the·one *part* under heaven, radiates·brightly
Lk 17:24 to the *other·part* under heaven, in·this·manner also
Lk 18:13 his eyes to the heaven, but·rather was·beating at his
Lk 24:51 from them and was·carried·up into the heaven.
Ac 1:10 ·intently toward the heaven with·him departing,
Ac 1:11 *there* looking·clearly·up into the heaven? This·same
Ac 1:11 from yeu into the heaven, shall·come in·this·manner
Ac 1:11 ·distinctly·viewed him traversing into the heaven."
Ac 2:5 devout men from every nation under the heaven.
Ac 3:21 ·fact it·is·mandatory·for heaven to·accept even·until
Ac 4:12 name under the heaven having·been·given among
Ac 4:24 God, 'the·one making the heaven, and the earth,
Ac 7:55 after·gazing·intently into the heaven, he·saw God's
Ac 10:11 he·observed the heaven having·been·opened·up,
Ac 10:16 and the vessel was·taken·up again into the heaven.
Ac 11:10 ·all *of·it* was·drawn·up again into the heaven.
Ac 14:15 God, 'who made the heaven, and the earth, and the
Heb 9:24 true, but·rather into the heaven itself, now to·be·
Heb 12:26 not merely the earth, but·rather also the heaven.⇨
Mt 14:19 two fish, looking·up to the heaven, he·blessed *it*.
Mk 6:41 two fish, looking·up to the heaven, he·blessed *it*.
Mk 7:34 upon·looking·up to the heaven, he·sighed·heavily
Mk 16:19 he·was·taken·up into the heaven and seated at *the*
Rm 10:6 "Who shall·ascend into heaven?" (that is, to·
Jac 5:12 do·not swear, neither by·the heaven, nor by·the
1Pe 3:22 who, traversing into heaven, is at *the* right·hand of·
Col 1:23 to every creature under the heaven), of·which I,
Rv 10:5 sea and upon the earth lifted his hand to the heaven,
Rv 10:6 ·ages ('who created the heaven, and the·things in it,
Rv 11:12 And they·ascended to the heaven in the thick·cloud
Rv 14:7 to·the·one 'having·made the heaven, and the earth,
Rv 19:11 And I·saw the heaven having·been·opened·up, and
Rv 21:1 And I·saw a·brand-new heaven and a·brand-new
G3772.1 N-APM οὐρανούς (5x)
Ac 2:34 did·not ascend into the heavens, but he·himself says,
Ac 7:56 I·observe the heavens having·been·opened·up, and
Heb 4:14 ·Priest, having·gone·through the heavens, YeShua
Mk 1:10 the water, he·saw the heavens being·split·open, and
2Pe 3:13 ·await 'a·Brand-New Heavens and a·Brand-New
G3772.1 N-DSM οὐρανῷ (39x)
Jn 3:13 the Son of·Clay·Man†, the·one being in the heaven.
Lk 6:23 payment·of·service *is* large in the heaven, for in the·
Lk 11:2 Your will be·done, as in heaven, so·also on the
Lk 15:7 ·shall·be *such* joy in the heaven over one morally·
Lk 18:22 and you·shall·have treasure in heaven. And come·
Lk 19:38 ' Peace in heaven and glory in *the* highest!"
Ac 2:19 I·shall·give wonders in the heaven up·above and
Mt 5:34 at·all: neither by the heaven, because it·is God's
Mt 6:10 Your will be·done— as in heaven, so·also on the
Mt 6:20 store·up for·yeurselves treasures in heaven, where
Mt 18:18 shall·be having·been·bound in the heaven, and as·
Mt 18:18 earth shall·be having·been·loosed in the heaven.
Mt 19:21 and you·shall·have treasure in heaven. And come·
Mt 22:30 but·rather they·are as God's angels in heaven.
Mt 23:22 And the·one swearing by the heaven, swears by the
Mt 24:30 of·Clay·Man† shall·be·apparent in the heaven. And
Mt 28:18 authority is·given to·me in heaven and upon earth.
Mk 10:21 and you·shall·have treasure in heaven. And come·
Mk 13:32 the angels, the·ones in heaven, neither the Son,
1Co 8:5 ·referred·to·as gods, whether in heaven or upon the
1Jn 5:7 three, the·ones testifying in the heaven: the Father,
Rv 4:1 a·door having·been·opened·up in the heaven and the
Rv 4:2 a·throne was·set·out in the heaven, and upon the
Rv 5:3 And not·even·one·man in the heaven, nor·even upon
Rv 5:13 every creature which is in the heaven, and on the
Rv 8:1 there·was silence in the heaven *for* about half·an·hour
Rv 11:15 there·became great voices in the heaven, saying,
Rv 11:19 of·God was·opened·up in the heaven, and the Ark
Rv 12:1 sign was·made·visible in the heaven: a·woman
Rv 12:3 sign was·made·visible in the heaven; and behold a·
Rv 12:7 And there·was war in the heaven. MiChaEl and his
Rv 12:8 was their place found any·longer in the heaven.
Rv 12:10 ·loud voice saying in the heaven, "At·this·moment
Rv 13:6 Tabernacle, and the·ones encamping in the heaven.
Rv 14:17 of·the Temple, the·one in the heaven, he also *was*
Rv 15:1 And I·saw another sign in the heaven, great and
Rv 15:5 of·the Testimony in the heaven is·opened·up.
Rv 19:1 a·great voice of·a·large crowd in the heaven, saying,
Rv 19:14 the armies in the heaven were·following him upon
G3772.1 N-DPM οὐρανοῖς (40x)
Lk 10:20 yeur names are·already·written in the heavens."
Lk 11:2 'Our Father, the·one in the heavens, your name, let·
Lk 12:33 an·inexhaustible treasure in the heavens, where no
Heb 8:1 of·the throne of·the Divine·Majesty in the heavens,
Heb 9:23 of·the·things in the heavens) to·be·purified with·
Heb 10:34 to·have in *the* heavens a·significantly·better and
Heb 12:23 having·been·enrolled in *the* heavens, and to·God,
Mt 5:12 ·service *is* large in the heavens. For in·this·manner
Mt 5:16 may·glorify yeur Father, the·one in the heavens.
Mt 5:45 Father, the·one in *the* heavens, because he·raises his
Mt 5:48 ·as yeur Father, the·one in the heavens, is complete.
Mt 6:1 personally·from yeur Father, the·one in the heavens.
Mt 6:9 Our Father, the·one in the heavens, your name, let·it·
Mt 7:11 the·one in the heavens, give beneficially·good·
Mt 7:21 doing the will of·my Father, the·one in *the* heavens.
Mt 10:32 by·name before my Father, the·one in *the* heavens.
Mt 10:33 ·deny before my Father, the·one in *the* heavens.
Mt 12:50 of·my Father, the·one in *the* heavens, *the* same is
Mt 16:17 but·rather my Father, the·one in the heavens.
Mt 16:19 shall·be having·been·bound in the heavens, and
Mt 16:19 earth shall·be having·been·loosed in the heavens."
Mt 18:10 their angels in *the* heavens look·upon the face of·
Mt 18:10 the face of·my Father, the·one in *the* heavens.
Mt 18:14 of·yeur Father, the·one in *the* heavens, it·is not a·
Mt 18:19 personally·by my Father, the·one in *the* heavens.
Mt 23:9 for one is yeur Father, the·one in the heavens.
Mk 11:25 also (the·one in the heavens) may·forgive yeu yeur
Mk 11:26 Father (the·one in the heavens) shall·forgive yeur
Mk 12:25 but·rather are as angels, the·ones in the heavens.
Mk 13:25 powers, the·ones in the heavens, shall·be·shaken.
Php 3:20 ·citizenship inherently·is in *the* heavens, out·from
1Pe 1:4 having·been·reserved in *the* heavens for us—
2Co 5:1 not·made·by·human·hand, eternal in the heavens.
Eph 1:10 both the·things in the heavens and the·things on
Eph 3:15 *the* entire paternal·lineage in *the* heavens and upon
Eph 6:9 same Lord also is in *the* heavens, and there·is not
Col 1:5 ·one being·laid·away for·yeu in the heavens— which
Col 1:16 are·created: the·ones in the heavens, and the·ones
Col 1:20 ·things upon the earth or the·things in the heavens.
Col 4:1 ·seen that yeu also have a·Lord in *the* heavens.
G3772.1 N-GSM οὐρανοῦ (82x)
Jn 1:32 the Spirit descending out of·heaven like a·dove, and
Jn 3:13 except the·one descending out of·the heaven, the Son
Jn 3:27 having·been·given to·him from·out of·the heaven.
Jn 3:31 who·is·coming from·out of·the heaven is up·above
Jn 6:31 He·gave them bread from·out of·the heaven to·eat.⇨"
Jn 6:32 yeu the bread from·out of·the heaven, but·rather my
Jn 6:32 gives yeu the true bread from·out of·the heaven,
Jn 6:33 is the·one descending from·out of·the heaven, and
Jn 6:38 because I·have·descended out of·the heaven, not in·
Jn 6:41 the bread, the·one descending out of·the heaven."
Jn 6:42 'I·have·descended out of·the heaven?'"
Jn 6:50 the·one descending out of·the heaven, in·order·that
Jn 6:51 bread, the·one descending out of·the heaven. "If
Jn 6:58 the·one descending out of·the heaven. *It·is* not just·
Jn 12:28 there·came a·voice from·out of·the heaven, *saying*,
Lk 3:22 and a·voice occurred from·out of·heaven, saying,
Lk 9:54 fire to·descend from the heaven and to·consume
Lk 10:15 ·up unto the heaven, you·shall·be·driven·down
Lk 10:18 falling as lightning from·out of·heaven.
Lk 10:21 ·you, O·Father, Lord of·the heaven and the earth,
Lk 11:13 the Father, the·one out of·heaven, shall·give Holy
Lk 11:16 personally·from him a·sign from·out of·heaven.
Lk 17:29 and sulfur from heaven and completely·destroyed
Lk 20:4 of·John, was·it from·out of·heaven, or from·out of·
Lk 20:5 we·should·declare, 'From·out of·heaven,' he·shall·
Lk 21:11 ·be frightening·things and great signs from heaven.
Lk 22:43 to·him an·angel from heaven, strengthening him.
Ac 2:2 a·reverberating·sound from·out of·the heaven, just·as
Ac 7:42 to·ritually·minister to·the host of·the heaven, just·as
Ac 9:3 a·light from the heaven flashed·all·around him.
Ac 11:5 ·sent·down from·out of·the heaven by·four corners,
Ac 11:9 for a·second·time from·out of·the heaven, 'That·
Ac 17:24 ·one inherently·being Lord of·heaven and earth,
Ac 22:6 suddenly from·out of·the heaven *for* a·significant
Gal 1:8 from·out of·heaven should·proclaim·a·good·news
Mt 11:23 ·elevated unto the heaven, shall·be·driven·down
Mt 11:25 ·you, O·Father, Lord of·the heaven and the earth,
Mt 16:1 ·exhibit for·them a·sign from·out of·the heaven.
Mt 21:25 ·source was·it? From·out of·heaven or from·out
Mt 21:25 "If we·should·declare, 'From·out of·heaven,' he·
Mt 24:29 the stars shall·fall from the heaven, and the powers
Mt 24:30 upon the thick·clouds of·the heaven' with power
Mt 26:64 and 'coming upon the thick·clouds of·the heaven.'"
Mt 28:2 ·descending out of·heaven *and* coming·alongside,
Mk 8:11 ·from him a·sign from the heaven, trying him.
Mk 11:30 of·John, was *it* from·out of·heaven, or from·out
Mk 11:31 "If we·should·declare, 'From·out of·heaven,' he·
Mk 13:25 and the stars of·the heaven shall·be falling·away,
Mk 13:27 of·earth as·far·as·to *the* uttermost·part of·heaven.
Mk 14:62 'coming with the thick·clouds of·the heaven.'"
Rm 1:18 For God's wrath is·revealed from heaven against all
1Pe 1:12 Spirit already·being·dispatched from heaven—
2Pe 1:18 ·carried·forth from·out of·heaven, while·being
1Th 4:16 himself shall·descend from heaven with battle·cry,

2Th 1:7 of·the Lord YeShua from heaven with *the* angels of·
1Co 15:47 man·of·clay† *is* the Lord from·out of·heaven.
2Co 5:2 ·with our housing, the·one from·out of·heaven,
2Co 12:2 ·a·man being·snatched·up unto *the* third heaven.
Rv 3:12 the·one descending out of·the heaven from my God
Rv 6:13 and the stars of·the heaven fell to the earth, as *when*
Rv 8:10 a·great star from·out of·the heaven, being·set·ablaze
Rv 9:1 a·star having·fallen from·out of·the heaven to the
Rv 10:1 from·out of·the heaven, having·been·arrayed·with a·
Rv 10:4 I·heard a·voice from·out of·the heaven saying to·me
Rv 10:8 which I·heard from·out of·the heaven *was* speaking
Rv 11:12 ·great voice from·out of·the heaven saying to·them
Rv 11:13 alarmed and gave glory to·the God of·the heaven.
Rv 12:4 third·part of·the stars of·the heaven and cast them to
Rv 13:13 fire to·descend from·out of·the heaven to the earth
Rv 14:2 I·heard a·voice from·out of·the heaven, as a·voice
Rv 14:13 a·voice from·out of·the heaven saying to·me,
Rv 16:11 ·reviled the God of·the heaven as·a·result of·their
Rv 16:17 voice from the Temple of·the heaven, from the
Rv 16:21 descends out of·the heaven upon the men·of·
Rv 18:1 an·angel descending from·out of·the heaven, having
Rv 18:4 ·heard another voice from·out of·the heaven, saying:
Rv 18:5 moral·failures followed even·up·to the heaven, and
Rv 20:1 an·angel descending from·out of·the heaven, having
Rv 20:9 from God out of·the heaven and devoured them.
Rv 21:2 God out of·the heaven, having·been·made·ready as
Rv 21:3 a·great voice from·out of·the heaven saying,
Rv 21:10 descending out of·the heaven from God,

G3772.1 N-GPM οὐρανῶν (42x)
Lk 21:26 for the powers of·the heavens shall·be·shaken.
Heb 7:26 ·men, and becoming higher·than the heavens;
Heb 12:25 *imparting·divine·instruction* from *the* heavens,
Mt 3:2 for the kingdom of·the heavens has·drawn·near."
Mt 3:17 behold, a·voice from·out of·the heavens, saying,
Mt 4:17 for the kingdom of·the heavens has·drawn·near."
Mt 5:3 spirit, because theirs is the kingdom of·the heavens.
Mt 5:10 because theirs is the kingdom of·the heavens.
Mt 5:19 least in the kingdom of·the heavens; but whoever
Mt 5:19 shall·be·called great in the kingdom of·the heavens.
Mt 5:20 ·not·ever enter into the kingdom of·the heavens.
Mt 7:21 into the kingdom of·the heavens, but·rather the·one
Mt 8:11 YiTsaq, and Jacob in the kingdom of·the heavens.
Mt 10:7 'The kingdom of·the heavens has·drawn·near.'
Mt 11:11 in the kingdom of·the heavens is greater·than he.
Mt 11:12 the kingdom of·the heavens is·seized·by·force,
Mt 13:11 mysteries of·the kingdom of·the heavens, but to·
Mt 13:24 of·the heavens is·likened to·a·man·of·clay† sowing
Mt 13:31 "The kingdom of·the heavens is like a·kernel of·
Mt 13:33 "The kingdom of·the heavens is like leaven, which
Mt 13:44 Again, the kingdom of·the heavens is like treasure
Mt 13:45 the kingdom of·the heavens is like a·man·of·clay†
Mt 13:47 the kingdom of·the heavens is like a·dragnet
Mt 13:52 into the kingdom of·the heavens is like a·man·of·
Mt 16:19 keys of·the kingdom of·the heavens, and whatever
Mt 18:1 Who then is greater in the kingdom of·the heavens?"
Mt 18:3 ·should·not enter into the kingdom of·the heavens.
Mt 18:4 ·one *who·is* greater in the kingdom of·the heavens.
Mt 18:23 of·the heavens is·likened to·a·man·of·clay†, a·king
Mt 19:12 ·account·of the kingdom of·the heavens. The·one
Mt 19:14 to·me, for of·such is the kingdom of·the heavens."
Mt 19:23 ·man shall·enter into the kingdom of·the heavens.
Mt 20:1 "For the kingdom of·the heavens is like a·man·of·
Mt 22:2 of·the heavens is·likened to·a·certain·man·of·clay†,
Mt 23:14 the kingdom of·the heavens before men·of·clay†!
Mt 24:29 and the powers of·the heavens shall·be·shaken.
Mt 24:31 from *the* uttermost·parts of·*the*·heavens unto *the*
Mt 24:36 not·even the angels of·the heavens, except my
Mt 25:1 the kingdom of·the heavens shall·be·likened to·ten
Mk 1:11 there·came a·voice from·out of·the heavens, *saying*,
1Th 1:10 ·await his Son from·out of·the heavens, whom he·
Eph 4:10 ascending high·above all the heavens, that he·may·

EG3772.1 (1x)
Mt 25:14 For *the kingdom of·the heavens is* just·as a·man·of·

G3772.2 N-NSM οὐρανός (3x)
Mt 16:2 '*It·shall·be* fine·weather, for the sky is·fiery·red.'
Mt 16:3 today, for the sky is·fiery·red *and* glowering.
Jac 5:18 And he·prayed again, and the sky gave rain, and the

G3772.2 N-ASM οὐρανόν (1x)
Rv 11:6 have authority to·shut the sky, in·order·that it·

G3772.2 N-GSM οὐρανοῦ (13x)
Lk 8:5 ·trampled·down, and the birds of·the sky devoured it.
Lk 9:58 burrows, and the birds of·the sky *have* nests, but the
Lk 12:56 ·examine·and·verify the face of·the sky and of·the
Lk 13:19 tree, and the birds of·the sky nested in its branches
Ac 10:12 and the creeping·things, and the birds of·the sky.
Ac 11:6 and the creeping·things, and the birds of·the sky.
Heb 11:12 constellations·of·stars of·the sky in·the multitude
Mt 6:26 ·clearly at the birds of·the sky, because they·do·not
Mt 8:20 burrows, and the birds of·the sky *have* nests, but the
Mt 13:32 such·for the birds of·the sky to·come and to·nest
Mt 16:3 yeu·know to·discern the face of·the sky, but are·not
Mk 4:4 and the birds of·the sky came and devoured it.
Mk 4:32 such·for the birds of·the sky to·be·able to·nest

G3773 Οὐρβανός Ôurbanós *n/p.* (1x)

G3773.2 N/P-ASM Οὐρβανόν (1x)
Rm 16:9 Greet Urbanus, our coworker in Anointed-One, and

G3774 Οὐρ•ίας Ôurías *n/p.* (1x)

אוּרִיָּה 'ûrıyạh [Hebrew]
Roots:H0223

G3774.2 N/P-GSM Οὐρίου (1x)
Mt 1:6 birthed·from·out of·the·one *having·been* UrIah's *wife*).

G3775 οὖς ôûs *n.* (37x)

Compare:G0189 See:G5621
xLangEquiv:H0241

G3775 N-NSN οὖς (2x)
1Co 2:9 "Eye did·not see, and ear did·not hear, and it·did·
1Co 12:16 And if the ear should·declare, "Because I·am not

G3775 N-NPN ὦτα (2x)
Mt 13:16 they·look·upon, and yeur ears, because they·hear.
1Pe 3:12 upon righteous·men, and his ears *are·open* to their

G3775 N-ASN οὖς (11x)
Lk 12:3 and that·which yeu·spoke to the ear in the private·
Lk 22:50 designated·high·priest and removed his right ear.
Mt 10:27 what yeu·hear in the ear, officially·proclaim upon
Rv 2:7 'The·one having an·ear, let·him·hear what the Spirit
Rv 2:11 'The·one having an·ear, let·him·hear what the Spirit
Rv 2:17 'The·one having an·ear, let·him·hear what the Spirit
Rv 2:29 'The·one having an·ear, let·him·hear what the Spirit
Rv 3:6 'The·one having an·ear, let·him·hear what the Spirit
Rv 3:13 'The·one having an·ear, let·him·hear what the Spirit
Rv 3:22 'The·one having an·ear, let·him·hear what the Spirit
Rv 13:9 If any·man has an·ear, let·him·hear.

G3775 N-APN ὦτα (16x)
Lk 1:44 sound of·your greeting occurred in my ears, the babe
Lk 8:8 ·out, "The·one having ears to·hear, let·him·hear.
Lk 9:44 ·let these sayings be·placed into yeur ears— "for
Lk 14:35 "The·one having ears to·hear, let·him·hear.
Ac 7:57 they·stopped·up their ears and impulsively·dashed
Ac 11:22 ·heard among the ears of·the Called·Out·citizenry,
Mt 11:15 "The·one having ears to·hear, let·him·hear.
Mt 13:9 The·one having ears to·hear, let·him·hear.
Mt 13:43 "The·one having ears to·hear, let·him·hear.
Mk 4:9 to·them, "The·one having ears to·hear, let·him·hear.
Mk 4:23 "If any·man has ears to·hear, let·him·hear.
Mk 7:16 If any·man has ears to·hear, let·him·hear.
Mk 7:33 cast his fingers into his ears, and after·spitting, he·
Mk 8:18 do·yeu·not look? And having ears, do·yeu·not hear
Rm 11:8 not to·look·upon, and ears *for·them* not to·hear
Jac 5:4 have·entered 'into the ears of·Yahweh of·Hosts.'

G3775 N-DPN ὠσίν (6x)
Lk 4:21 has·been·completely·fulfilled in yeur ears."
Ac 7:51 and uncircumcised in·the heart and ears, yeu always
Ac 28:27 ·thickly·calloused, and their ears hardly heard, and
Ac 28:27 eyes, and should·hear with·the ears, and should·
Mt 13:15 ·thickly·calloused, and their ears hardly heard, and
Mt 13:15 eyes, and should·hear with·the ears, and should·

G3776 οὐσία ôusía *n.* (2x)

Roots:G5607 Compare:G5223

G3776 N-ASF οὐσίαν (1x)
Lk 15:13 his substance while·living in·an·unsaved·lifestyle.

G3776 N-GSF οὐσίας (1x)
Lk 15:12 the portion of·substance being·stashed·away *for·me*

G3777 οὔ•τε óútê *conj.* (95x)

Roots:G3756 G5037

G3777.a CONJ οὔτε (1x)
Rv 21:4 nor yelling, nor·also continual·anguish. It·shall·

G3777.2 CONJ οὔτε (34x)
Jn 4:21 an·hour is·coming when, neither on this mountain,
Jn 8:19 answered, "Neither do·yeu·personally·know me, nor
Jn 9:3 Jesus answered, "Neither this·man morally·failed, nor
Lk 14:35 It·is neither well-suited for soil, nor·even for
Lk 20:35 from·out of·the dead, neither marry nor are·given·
Lk 20:36 For neither are·they·able to·die any·longer, for
Ac 15:10 neck of·the disciples, which neither our fathers nor
Ac 19:37 *who·are* neither despoilers·of·temple·sanctuaries,
Ac 24:12 or making a·turmoil of·a·crowd, neither in the
Ac 24:13 Neither are·they·able to·establish·proof *against* me
Ac 25:8 *declaring*, "Neither against the Torah-Law of·the
Ac 28:21 Judea concerning you, neither *have* any of·the
Gal 5:6 For in YeShua Anointed, neither circumcision nor
Gal 6:15 in Anointed-One YeShua, neither circumcision nor
Mt 6:20 in heaven, where neither moth nor corrosion
Mt 12:32 it·shall·not be·forgiven him, neither in this present·
Mt 22:30 in the resurrection, neither do·they·marry nor are·
Mk 12:25 from·among dead·men, they·neither marry nor
Rm 8:38 For I·have·been·convinced that neither death, nor
1Th 2:6 glory from·among men·of·clay†, neither from yeu
1Co 3:2 *to·bear it*. Moreover neither yet now are·yeu·able,
1Co 3:7 As·such, neither is the·one planting anything, nor
1Co 6:9 *No*, neither sexually·immoral·men, nor idolaters,
1Co 8:8 commend us to·God. For neither if we·should·eat,
1Co 11:11 Nevertheless, neither *is* man apart·from woman,
1Co 11:11 man apart·from woman, neither *is* woman apart·
3Jn 1:10 ·satisfied with these·things, neither does he·himself
Rv 3:15 works, that you·are neither cold nor fervently·hot.
Rv 3:16 you·are lukewarm, and neither cold nor fervently·
Rv 5:4 ·read·aloud the official·scroll, neither to·look·upon it
Rv 9:20 punishing·blows did·not·even repent out·from·
Rv 9:20 and wood, which neither are·able to·look·about,
Rv 12:8 ·not have·strength *to·overpower*; neither was their
Rv 21:4 shall·not be any·longer, neither mourning, nor

EG3777.2 (1x)
Rv 20:4 the etching upon their foreheads, ***nor*** even in their

G3777.3 CONJ οὔτε (47x)
Jn 1:25 are not the Anointed-One, nor EliJah, nor the
Jn 1:25 not the Anointed-One, nor EliJah, nor the Prophet?
Jn 5:37 his voice ever·at·any·time, nor have·clearly·seen his
Jn 8:19 Neither do·yeu·personally·know me, nor my Father.
Jn 9:3 "Neither this·man morally·failed, nor his parents, but·
Lk 20:35 neither marry nor are·given·away·in·marriage.
Ac 15:10 neither our fathers nor we·ourselves had·strength
Ac 24:12 And they·did·not·even find me in the Sanctuary·
Ac 24:12 ·crowd, neither in the gatherings, nor in the City.
Ac 25:8 Torah-Law of·the Jews, nor against the Sanctuary·
Gal 1:12 it from a·man·of·clay†, nor was·I·instructed, but·
Gal 5:6 neither circumcision nor uncircumcision has·any
Gal 6:15 neither circumcision nor uncircumcision has·any
Mt 6:20 where neither moth nor corrosion obliterate, and
Mt 12:32 in this present·age, nor in the·one about·to·come.
Mt 22:30 neither do·they·marry nor are·they·given·away·in·,
Mk 12:25 they·neither marry nor are·given·in·marriage,
Rm 8:38 ·been·convinced that neither death, nor life†, nor
Rm 8:38 death, nor life†, nor angels, nor principalities, nor
Rm 8:38 nor life†, nor angels, nor principalities, nor powers
Rm 8:38 angels, nor principalities, nor powers, nor things·
Rm 8:38 nor powers, nor things·currently·standing, nor
Rm 8:38 ·currently·standing, nor things·about·to·come,

Rm 8:39 nor height, nor depth, nor any other created·thing
Rm 8:39 nor height, nor depth, nor any other created·thing
Rm 8:39 nor height, nor depth, nor any other created·thing
1Th 2:3 of·deceit, nor from·out of·impurity, nor in guile.
1Th 2:5 (just·as yeu·personally·know), nor with a·pretext
1Th 2:6 nor seeking glory from·among men·of·clay†, neither
1Th 2:6 men·of·clay†, neither from yeu nor from others,
1Co 3:7 is the·one planting anything, nor the·one watering,
1Co 6:9 neither sexually·immoral·men, nor idolaters, nor
1Co 6:9 ·immoral·men, nor idolaters, nor adulterers, nor
1Co 6:9 idolaters, nor adulterers, nor effeminate·men, nor
1Co 6:9 effeminate·men, nor men·who·have·sex·with·men,
1Co 6:10 nor thieves, nor covetous·men, nor drunkards, nor
1Co 6:10 nor thieves, nor covetous·men, nor drunkards, nor
1Co 6:10 nor thieves, nor covetous·men, nor drunkards, nor
Rv 3:15 that you·are neither cold nor fervently·hot. Oh·that
Rv 3:16 and neither cold nor fervently·hot, I·intend to·
Rv 9:20 neither are·able to·look·about, nor to·hear, nor to·
Rv 9:20 are·able to·look·about, nor to·hear, nor to·walk;
Rv 9:21 ·from·among their murders, nor from·out of·their
Rv 9:21 ·of·poisonous·drugs, nor from·out of·their sexual·
Rv 9:21 of·their sexual·immorality, nor from·out of·their
Rv 20:4 to·the Daemonic·Beast nor his derived·image, and
Rv 21:4 any·longer, neither mourning, nor yelling, nor·also

G3777.4 CONJ οὔτε (5x)

Jn 4:21 neither on this mountain, nor·even in JeruSalem,
Lk 14:35 neither well-suited for soil, nor·even for manure,
Ac 19:37 ·temple·sanctuaries, nor·even those·reviling yeur
Ac 25:8 the Sanctuary·Courtyard, nor·even against Caesar,
1Co 8:8 ·eat, do·we·excel, nor·even if we·should·not eat,

G3777.5 CONJ οὔτε (7x)

Jn 4:11 "Sir, you·have not·even a·bucket·for·drawing·water,
Jn 5:37 concerning me. Not·even yeu·have·heard his voice
Lk 12:26 "So·then, if yeu·are·not·even able *to·do* that·thing·
Ac 4:12 other. For there·is not·even another name under the
Ac 28:21 "We·ourselves do·not·even anticipate·receiving
Mk 5:3 ·man was·able to·bind him, not·even with·chains,
1Th 2:5 For not·even at·any·time did·we·come with a·word

G3778 ο•ὗτος hôûtôs *p:d.* (343x)

ο•ὗτοι hôûtôi [nominative masculine plural]
α•ὕτη haútē [nominative feminine singular]
α•ὗται haûtai [nominative feminine plural]

Roots:G3588 G0846 Compare:G3592 See:G3779 G5023 G5025 G5026 G5124 G5125 G5126 G5127 G5128 G5129 G5130

Oo

G3778.2 P:D-NSM οὗτος (166x)

Jn 1:15 ·out, saying, "This was·he of·whom I·declared,
Jn 1:30 This is·he concerning whom I·myself declared,
Jn 1:34 ·seen, and have·testified, that this is the Son of·God
Jn 1:41 This·man *Andrew* first finds his·own brother Simon
Jn 2:20 "*In* forty six years, this Temple was·built, and you,
Jn 4:29 to·me all the·many·things I·did! Could this be the
Jn 4:42 and we·personally·know that this is truly the Savior
Jn 4:47 This·man, after·hearing that Jesus comes from·out
Jn 6:14 men·of·clay† were·saying, "This is truly the Prophet
Jn 6:42 And they·were·saying, "Is this not Jesus, the son of·
Jn 6:42 So·then how·is·it *that* he·says this·thing, 'I·have·
Jn 6:46 personally·from God; this·one has·clearly·seen the
Jn 6:50 This is the bread, the·one descending out of·the
Jn 6:52 saying, "How·is this·man able to·give us the flesh
Jn 6:58 "This is the bread, the·one descending out of·the
Jn 6:60 upon·hearing *this*, declared, "This is a·hard saying;
Jn 6:71 *son* of·Simon, for *it·was* this·man *that* was·about to·
Jn 7:15 saying, "How·does this·man personally·know *the*
Jn 7:25 were·saying, "Is this not he·whom they·seek to·kill?
Jn 7:26 Perhaps the rulers truly do·know that this truly is the
Jn 7:31 miraculous·signs than these which this·man did?
Jn 7:35 "Where·does this·man intend to·traverse that we·
Jn 7:36 What *manner·of* saying is this that he·declared,
Jn 7:40 the crowd were·saying, "Truly this is the Prophet.
Jn 7:41 Others were·saying, "This is the Anointed-One.
Jn 7:46 a·man·of·clay† spoken as *does* this man·of·clay†."
Jn 7:49 But·rather this crowd, the·one not knowing the
Jn 9:2 "Rabbi, who morally·failed, this·man or his parents,
Jn 9:3 Jesus answered, "Neither this·man morally·failed, nor
Jn 9:8 were·saying, "Is this not the·one who·was·sitting·
Jn 9:9 Some were·saying, "This is·he." But others *were·*
Jn 9:16 the Pharisees were·saying, "This man·of·clay† is not
Jn 9:19 ·asked·of them, saying, "Is this yeur son, who yeu
Jn 9:20 declared, "We·personally·know that this is our son,
Jn 9:24 ·ourselves personally·know that this man·of·clay† is
Jn 9:33 Except this·man was personally·from God, he·
Jn 11:37 declared, "Was·not this·man, the·one opening·up
Jn 11:37 to·make *it·be* also that this·man should·not die?
Jn 11:47 "What·do we·do, because this man·of·clay† does
Jn 12:34 to·be·elevated'? "Who is this Son of·Clay·Man†?
Jn 18:30 declared to·him, "If this·man was not a·criminal,
Jn 21:21 "Lord, and what *about* this·man?"
Jn 21:23 So·then this saying went·forth among the brothers,
Jn 21:24 This is the disciple, the·one testifying concerning
Lk 1:29 ·pondering what·manner·of greeting this might·be.
Lk 1:32 "This·man shall·be great and shall·be·called *the* Son
Lk 1:36 ·son in her old·age, and this is *the* sixth lunar·month
Lk 2:34 "Behold, this *child* is·laid·out for a·downfall and
Lk 4:22 ·also they·were·saying, "Is not this Joseph's son?
Lk 4:36 "What a·word *is* this! Because with authority and
Lk 5:21 saying, "Who is this who speaks revilements of·God
Lk 7:17 And this saying concerning him went·forth among
Lk 7:27 This is *he*, concerning whom it·has·been·written,
Lk 7:39 saying, "If this·man were a·prophet, he·would·be
Lk 7:49 themselves, "Who is this that also forgives moral·
Lk 8:25 "What *manner·of man* is this? Because he·orders
Lk 9:9 John, but who is this, concerning whom I·myself
Lk 9:35 ·the thick·cloud, saying, "This is my beloved Son.
Lk 14:30 saying, 'This man·of·clay† began to·build yet did·
Lk 15:2 "This·man welcomes morally·disqualified·men and
Lk 15:24 Because this son of·mine was dead and came·alive·
Lk 15:30 But when this son of·yours came *home*, the·one
Lk 15:32 and to·be·glad, because this your brother was dead
Lk 16:1 ·manager, and this *estate·manager* was·slandered
Lk 17:18 glory to·God, *none* except this resident·alien."
Lk 18:11 ·men, adulterers, or even as this tax·collector.
Lk 18:14 "I·say to·yeu *that* this·man walked·down to his
Lk 19:2 was a·chief·tax·collector, and this·man was wealthy
Lk 20:14 among themselves, saying, 'This is the heir.
Lk 20:28 ·having a·wife, and this·man should·die childless,
Lk 20:30 took the *same* wife, and this·man died childless.
Lk 22:56 servant·girl declared, "This·man was also together
Lk 22:59 "In truth, this·man also was with him, for he·is
Lk 23:22 "For what crime did this·one commit?
Lk 23:35 others, let·him·save himself— if this·man is the
Lk 23:38 and Hebrew: "THIS IS THE KING OF·THE
Lk 23:41 "But this·man practiced not·even·one·thing amiss.
Lk 23:47 "Really, this man·of·clay† was a·righteous·man.
Lk 23:52 This·man, after·coming·alongside Pilate, requested
Ac 1:18 in·fact, this·man procured an·open·field out of·the
Ac 4:9 what·means this·man has·been·made·safe·and·well—
Ac 4:10 this *name* does this·man stand·nearby in·the·sight
Ac 4:11 This is "the stone being·disdainfully·rejected by
Ac 6:13 false witnesses saying, "This man·of·clay† does·not
Ac 6:14 this Jesus of·Natsareth shall·demolish this place and
Ac 7:19 This·man, being·skillfully·shrewd·against our
Ac 7:36 This·man brought them out, after·doing wonders
Ac 7:37 "This Moses is the·one declaring to·the Sons of·
Ac 7:38 "This *Moses* is the·one already·coming among the
Ac 7:40 ·traverse·before us. *As* for this Moses who brought
Ac 8:10 *the* greatest, saying, "This·man is the great power
Ac 9:15 "Traverse! Because this·man is my vessel of·
Ac 9:20 in the gatherings, *saying*, "This is the Son of·God!"
Ac 9:21 were·saying, "Is this not the·one already·fiercely·
Ac 9:22 Damascus, *by* conclusively·proving that this is the
Ac 10:6 This·man is·a·guest *staying* with a·certain·man,
Ac 10:6 is directly·by *the* sea. This·man shall·speak to·you
Ac 10:32 shall·speak to·you. This·man is·a·guest in *the*
Ac 10:36 through Jesus Anointed— This·one is Lord of·all.
Ac 13:7 *who·was* an·intelligent man. This·man, summoning
Ac 17:3 ·men, and *fully·proclaiming*, "This Jesus (whom I·
Ac 17:18 ·is·it *that* this two-bit·peddler actually·supposes to·
Ac 18:13 "This·man persistently·persuades men·of·clay†
Ac 18:25 This·man was having·been·informed·of The Way
Ac 18:26 And this·man began to·boldly·speak·with·clarity in
Ac 19:26 almost throughout·all Asia, this Paul has·won·over
Ac 21:28 Israelites, swiftly·help! This is the man·of·clay†
Ac 22:26 you·are·about to·do, for this man·of·clay† is a·
Ac 26:31 saying, "This man·of·clay† practices not·even·
Ac 26:32 replied to·Festus, "This man·of·clay† was·able to·
Ac 28:4 among one·another, "This man·of·clay† is entirely
Heb 3:3 For this·man has·been·counted·worthy of·more
Heb 7:1 For this MalkiTsedeq (King of·Salem, Priest of·God
Heb 7:4 Now observe what·stature this·man *was*, to·whom
Mt 3:3 For this is·he, the·one being·uttered *of* by IsaIah the
Mt 3:17 of·the heavens, saying, "This is my beloved Son,
Mt 7:12 in·this·manner to·them, for this is the Torah-Law
Mt 8:27 "What·manner·of *clay·being* is this that even the
Mt 9:3 declared within themselves, "This·man reviles·God."
Mt 10:22 ·enduring to *the* end, this·one shall·be·saved.
Mt 11:10 For this is·he, concerning whom it·has·been·
Mt 12:23 and were·saying, "Could this be the Son of·David?
Mt 12:24 Pharisees declared, "This·man does·not cast·out
Mt 13:19 in his heart. This·person is the·one already·being·
Mt 13:20 among the rocky·places, this·person is the·one
Mt 13:22 among the thorns, this·person is the·one hearing
Mt 13:23 the good soil, this·person is the·one hearing the
Mt 13:55 ¿!·Is this not the carpenter's son?
Mt 14:2 and declared to·his servant·boys, "This is John the
Mt 15:8 " This People draws·near to·me with·their mouth
Mt 17:5 ·cloud, saying, "This is my beloved Son, in whom
Mt 18:4 himself as this little·child, this·one is the·one *who·is*
Mt 21:10 all the City was·shaken, saying, "Who is this?"
Mt 21:11 And the crowds were·saying, "This is YeShua the
Mt 21:38 declared among themselves, 'This is the heir.
Mt 26:61 declared, "This·man was·disclosing, 'I·am·able
Mt 26:71 says to·the·ones there, "This·one also was with
Mt 27:37 *was* having·been·written, "THIS IS YESHUA,
Mt 27:47 were·saying, "This·man hollers·out·for EliJah."
Mt 27:54 tremendously, saying, "Truly this was God's Son.
Mt 27:58 This·man, upon·coming·alongside Pilate, requested
Mt 28:15 ·instructed. And this saying is·widely·promoted
Mk 2:7 ·manner, does this·man speak revilements of·God?
Mk 3:35 should·do the will of·God, this·one is my brother,
Mk 4:41 "Who then is this, that even the wind and the sea
Mk 6:3 Is this not the carpenter, the son of·Mariam, and a·
Mk 6:16 after·hearing *of·him*, he·declared, "This is John,
Mk 7:6 it·has·been·written, " This People deeply·honors me
Mk 9:7 ·the thick·cloud, saying, "This is my beloved Son.
Mk 12:7 declared among themselves, 'This is the heir!
Mk 14:69 standing·nearby, "This·man is from·among them.
Mk 15:39 he·declared, "Truly this man·of·clay† was a·son
Rm 4:9 So·then, *is* this supreme·blessedness upon the
Rm 8:9 ·not have Anointed-One's Spirit, this·one is not his.
Rm 9:9 For this *is* the word of·promise, "According·to this
Jac 1:23 not a·doer, this·one has·directly·resembled a·man
Jac 1:25 and personally·continuing *in·it*, this·man being not
Jac 1:25 of·the·work, this·man shall·be supremely·blessed
1Pe 2:7 rejected·as·unfit, this·one has·now·become the·
2Pe 1:17 the magnificent glory, "This is my beloved Son, in
1Jn 2:22 not the Anointed-One? This·one is the adversary·
1Jn 5:6 This is the·one coming through water and blood,
1Jn 5:20 in his Son Jesus Anointed. This is the true God and
2Jn 1:7 Anointed as·coming in flesh. This is the impostor
2Jn 1:9 the instruction of·Anointed-One, this·one has both
Rv 20:14 into the Lake of·the Fire. This is the Second Death

G3778.2 P:D-NSF αὕτη (62x)

Jn 1:19 Now this is the testimony of·John, when the Judeans
Jn 3:19 "And this is the verdict, that the Light has·come into
Jn 3:29 the bridegroom's voice. Accordingly, this (my joy)
Jn 8:4 ·him, "Mentor, this wife was·grabbed·suddenly *while*
Jn 11:4 hearing *that*, declared, "This sickness is not toward
Jn 12:30 and declared, "This voice has·happened not on·

Jn 15:12 "This is my commandment, that yeu·should·love
Jn 17:3 "And this is the eternal life-above, that they·may·
Lk 2:2 (*And* this enrollment first occurred with·Cyrenius
Lk 4:21 "Today, this Scripture has·been·completely·fulfilled
Lk 8:9 "What might·be *meant·by* this parable?
Lk 8:11 "Now the parable is this: The scattering·of·seed is
Lk 11:29 he·began to·say, "This is an·evil generation.
Lk 21:3 I·say to·yeu, that this helplessly·poor widow cast *in*
Lk 21:32 I·say to·yeu, this generation·of·offspring, no,
Lk 22:53 "But·yet this is yeur hour, and the jurisdiction of·
Ac 5:38 and let them be, because if this counsel or this work
Ac 8:26 from JeruSalem to Gaza." (This is a·wilderness).
Ac 8:32 Scripture which he·was·reading·aloud was this,
Ac 17:19 ·we·able to·know what this brand-new instruction
Ac 21:11 shall·bind the man who owns this belt, and they·
Heb 8:10 "·Because this *is* the unilateral·covenant that I·
Heb 10:16 "·This *is* the unilateral·covenant that I·shall·
Mt 9:26 And the disclosure of·this *awakening* went·forth
Mt 13:54 ·source *does* this·man *have* this wisdom and·also
Mt 21:42 head corner *stone*. This came·to·be directly·from
Mt 22:20 "Whose derived·image and inscription *is* this?"
Mt 22:38 This is *the* foremost and greatest commandment.
Mt 24:34 I·say to·yeu, *that* this generation·of·offspring, no,
Mt 26:8 "To what·purpose *is* this total·ruin?
Mk 1:27 "What is this? What *is* this brand-new instruction?
Mk 8:12 he·says, "Why·does this generation seek·for a·sign
Mk 12:11 This came·to·be directly·from Yahweh, and it·is
Mk 12:16 "Whose *is* this derived·image and inscription?
Mk 12:30 your strength." This commandment *is* foremost.
Mk 12:43 I·say to·yeu, that this helplessly·poor widow has·
Mk 13:30 I·say to·yeu, that this generation·of·offspring, no,
Mk 14:4 saying, "Why·has this total·ruin of·the ointment
Rm 7:10 is·found in·me for life-above, this *resulted* in death.
Rm 11:27 And this *is* personally my unilateral·covenant to·
Jac 1:27 pure and uncontaminated religion is this: to·visit *the*
Jac 3:15 This wisdom is not *that* which·is·coming·down
Tit 1:13 This testimony is true.
1Co 8:9 But look·out! Lest·somehow this privilege of·yeurs
1Co 9:3 My defense to·the·ones scrutinizing me is this:
2Co 1:12 For this is our boasting, the testimony of·our
2Co 2:6 Sufficient to·such·a·man *is* this public·penalty, the·
2Co 11:10 me, *such* that this boasting shall·not be·sealed·up
Eph 3:8 ·the·least of·all holy·ones, this grace was·given: to·
1Jn 1:5 This then is the announcement which we·have·heard
1Jn 2:25 And this is the promise that he·himself did·already·
1Jn 3:11 Because this is the message that yeu·heard from *the*
1Jn 3:23 And this is his commandment, that we·should·
1Jn 5:3 For this is the love of·God, that we·should·
1Jn 5:4 overcomes the world. And this is the victory (the·
1Jn 5:9 of·God is greater, because this is the testimony of·
1Jn 5:11 And this is the testimony, that God gave to·us
1Jn 5:11 to·us eternal life-above, and this life-above is in his
1Jn 5:14 And this is the freeness·of·speech that we·have
2Jn 1:6 And this is the Love, that we·should·walk according·
2Jn 1:6 ·walk according·to his commandments. This is the
Rv 20:5 This *is* the First Resurrection.

G3778.2 P:D-NPM οὗτοι (1x)

Rm 9:6 not all the·ones from·among IsraEl, *are* this IsraEl.

EG3778.2 (4x)

Jn 1:9 *This* was the true Light which illuminates every child·
Jn 1:10 *This Light* was in the world, and the world came·to·
Heb 2:3 so·vast a·Salvation? *This Salvation*, which after·
Mt 13:54 ·man *have* this wisdom and·also *do these* miracles?

G3778.3 P:D-NPM οὗτοι (76x)

Jn 6:5 shall·we·buy bread in·order·that these may·eat?
Jn 17:11 longer in the world, but these·men are in the world,
Jn 17:25 but I·myself knew you, and these knew that you
Jn 18:21 to·them. See, these·men personally·know what I·
Lk 8:13 accept the Redemptive-word; yet these have no root,
Lk 8:14 falling among the thorns, these are the·ones hearing,
Lk 8:15 in the good soil, these are *the·ones* with a·morally·
Lk 8:21 mother and my brothers are these, the·ones hearing
Lk 13:2 "Do·yeu·suppose that these Galileans became
Lk 13:4 do·yeu·presume that these·men were delinquent
Lk 19:40 "I·say to·yeu that if these should·keep·silent, the
Lk 20:47 ·showing. "These shall·receive more·abundant
Lk 21:4 For absolutely·all these·men cast from·out·of·their
Lk 24:17 sayings *are* these that yeu·toss·back·and·forth to
Lk 24:44 And he·declared to·them, "These *are* the words
Ac 1:14 These all were diligently·continuing with·the·same·
Ac 2:7 "Behold, are not all these ones speaking Galileans?
Ac 2:15 For these·men are·not drunk as yeu assume, for it·is
Ac 11:12 not·even·one·thing. Moreover, these six brothers
Ac 13:4 the Holy Spirit, these·men went·down to Seleucia.
Ac 16:17 ·out, saying, "These men·of·clay† are slaves of·
Ac 16:20 they·declared, "These men·of·clay†, inherently·
Ac 17:6 upsetting The Land, these·men are·presently here
Ac 17:7 ·received, and all these·men practice *things* in·full·
Ac 17:11 Now these *Berean Jews* were more·noble·than the·
Ac 20:5 going·on·beforehand, these·men were·awaiting us
Ac 24:15 in God, which these·men themselves also await,
Ac 25:11 to·these·things·which these·men legally·accuse me
Ac 27:31 ·the soldiers, "Unless these should·remain with the
Heb 11:13 These all died according·to trust, not receiving the
Heb 11:39 And all these, already·being·attested·to through
Gal 6:12 ·appearance in the·flesh, these·men compel yeu to·
Mt 4:3 ·son of·God, declare that these stones should·become
Mt 13:38 and the good seed, these are the Sons of·the
Mt 20:12 saying, 'These last·ones did one hour, and you·
Mt 20:21 to·him, "Declare that these two sons of·mine may·
Mt 21:16 to·him, "Do·you·hear what these *boys* are·saying?
Mt 25:46 "And these shall·go·away into eternal tormenting·
Mt 26:62 What *are* these·things they·testify·against you?
Mk 4:15 "Now these are the *individuals* directly·by the
Mk 4:16 "And these are·they likewise, the·ones being·
Mk 4:18 "And these are the·ones who·are being·permeated·
Mk 4:18 among the thorns: these *are* the·ones hearing the
Mk 4:20 "But these are the·ones already·being·permeated·
Mk 12:40 *prayers*. "These shall·receive more·abundant
Mk 14:60 What·are these·things they·testify·against you?
Rm 2:14 *contained* in·the Torah-Law, these *Gentiles* not
Rm 8:14 are·led by·God's Spirit, these are the·Sons of·God.
Rm 11:24 ·tree, how·much more shall·these, according·to
Rm 11:31 in·this·manner also, these now are·obstinate in·
Jud 1:8 Likewise also these *irreverent* dreamers, in·fact,
Jud 1:10 But in·fact, these·men revile what·many·things
Jud 1:12 These are dangerous·sea·reefs at yeur love·feasts,
Jud 1:16 These are grumblers, malcontented·faultfinders,
Jud 1:19 These are the·ones dividing·apart·along·sectarian·
2Pe 2:12 But these *false·teachers* (as natural, irrational
2Pe 2:17 These are wellsprings without·water, thick·clouds
1Co 16:17 lacking on·yeur *part*, these·men utterly·supplied.
Col 4:11 ·to·as Justus). Only these coworkers for the
1Ti 3:10 And also these·men must·be·tested·and·proven first
2Ti 3:8 Moses, in·this·manner these also stand·opposed·to
1Jn 5:7 Word, and the Holy Spirit. And these three are one.
Rv 7:13 "Who are these, the·ones having·been·arrayed·with
Rv 7:14 And he·declared to·me, "These are the·ones coming
Rv 11:4 These are the two olive·trees and the two Fine·Oil·
Rv 11:6 These have authority to·shut the sky, in·order·that
Rv 11:10 presents to·one·another because these two prophets
Rv 14:4 These are·they who are·not tarnished with women,
Rv 14:4 for they·are virgins. These are the·ones following
Rv 14:4 ·head·on·out. These were·kinsman·redeemed from
Rv 17:13 "These have *just* one plan, and they·thoroughly·
Rv 17:14 These shall·wage·war with the Lamb, and the
Rv 17:16 ·saw upon the Scarlet·Beast, these shall·hate the
Rv 19:9 " And he·says to·me, "These are the true sayings
Rv 21:5 "Write, because these words are true and
Rv 22:6 he·declared to·me, "These words *are* trustworthy

G3778.3 P:D-NPF αὗται (3x)

Lk 21:22 "Because these are Days of·Vengeance, of·the·One
Ac 20:34 Now yeu·yeurselves know that these hands tended
Gal 4:24 ·things are being·an·allegory, for these are the two

EG3778.3 (1x)

2Pe 2:19 *These false·teachers* who·are·promising liberty to·

G3778.4 P:D-NSM οὗτος (26x)

Jn 1:2 The·same was at *the* beginning alongside God.
Jn 1:7 The·same came for a·testimony, in·order·that he·may·
Jn 1:33 remaining upon him, the·same is the·one immersing
Jn 3:2 The·same came to Jesus by·night and declared to·him,
Jn 3:26 have·testified, see, the·same·man immerses, and all
Jn 7:18 glory of·the·one sending him, the·same·man is true,
Jn 15:5 in me and·I in him, the·same bears much fruit,
Lk 2:25 name *was* Simeon, and the·same man·of·clay† *was*
Lk 9:24 soul's·desire for·my cause, the·same shall·save it.
Lk 9:48 least among yeu all, the·same shall·be great."
Lk 20:17 rejected·as·unfit, the·same has·now·become the·
Lk 23:51 The·same was not having·voted·together with·the
Ac 1:11 ·clearly·up into the heaven? This·same Jesus, the·
Ac 3:10 that he·himself was the·same·person, the·one
Ac 14:9 The·same·man was·hearing Paul speaking, who
Ac 17:24 ·things in it, the·same·one inherently·being Lord
Mt 5:19 should·instruct *them*, the·same shall·be·called great
Mt 21:42 rejected·as·unfit, the·same has·now·become the·
Mt 24:13 ·enduring to *the* end, the·same shall·be·saved.
Mt 26:23 with me in the dish, the·same shall·hand me over.
Mk 8:35 *for·that* of·the good·news, the·same shall·save it.
Mk 12:10 rejected·as·unfit, the·same has·now·become the·
Mk 13:13 ·enduring to *the* end, the·same shall·be·saved.
Jac 3:2 slip·up in word, the·same *is* a·completely·mature
1Co 8:3 loves God, the·same has·been·absolutely·known by
Rv 3:5 'The·one overcoming, the·same shall·be·arrayed in

G3778.4 P:D-NSF αὕτη (1x)

Ac 16:17 Paul and us, the·same·girl was·yelling·out, saying,

G3778.4 P:D-NPM οὗτοι (3x)

Jn 12:21 Now·then, the·same *Greeks* came·alongside Philip,
Ac 24:20 Or·else these same·men *here*, let·them·declare if
Gal 3:7 birthed·from·out·of·trust, the·same are the·Sons of·

G3779 ο•ὕτω hôútō *adv.* (214x)

ο•ὕτως hôútōs [before a vowel]

Roots:G3778 Compare:G3592 xLangAlso:H3651

G3779.1 ADV οὕτως (200x)

Jn 3:8 "*So·also*, in·this·manner, is any one having·been·born
Jn 3:14 the wilderness, in·this·manner, it·is·mandatory·for
Jn 3:16 For in·this·manner, God loved the world, such·that
Jn 4:6 road·travel, was·sitting·down in·this·manner on the
Jn 5:21 and gives·life·to *them*; even in·this·manner the Son
Jn 5:26 life-above in himself, in·this·manner, he·gave also
Jn 7:46 "Never·at·any·time in·this·manner *has* a·man·of·
Jn 8:59 of·them, and in·this·manner, he·was·passing·on
Jn 11:48 If we·should·leave him alone in·this·manner, all
Jn 12:50 Father has·declared to·me; in·this·manner I·speak.
Jn 15:4 ·abide in the vine, in·this·manner, not·even *can* yeu
Jn 18:22 "Do·you·answer the high·priest in·this·manner?"
Jn 21:1 and he·made *himself* apparent in·this·manner.
Lk 1:25 "In·this·manner has Yahweh done for·me, in *the*
Lk 2:48 "Child, why·did you·do us in·this·manner? Behold,
Lk 9:15 And they·did *so* in·this·manner, and absolutely·all
Lk 10:21 Yes, Father, because in·this·manner, it·became a·
Lk 11:30 a·sign to·the Ninevites, in·this·manner also the
Lk 12:21 "In·this·manner *is* the·one storing·up·treasure for·
Lk 12:28 "So if God in·this·manner enrobes the grass, today
Lk 12:38 ·find *them* in·this·manner, supremely·blessed are
Lk 12:43 upon·coming, shall·find doing in·this·manner.
Lk 12:54 a·thunderstorm,' and in·this·manner it·happens.
Lk 14:33 "Accordingly in·this·manner, anyone from·among
Lk 15:7 "I·say to·yeu, that in·this·manner, there·shall·be
Lk 15:10 "In·this·manner, I·say to·yeu, *that such* joy occurs
Lk 17:10 In·this·manner, whenever yeu·should·do all the·
Lk 17:24 *·part* under heaven, in·this·manner also shall·be
Lk 17:26 the days of·Noach, in·this·manner shall·it·be also
Lk 19:31 *it*?' In·this·manner yeu·shall·declare to·him,
Lk 21:31 "In·this·manner, whenever yeu·should·see these·
Lk 22:26 But yeu *shall* not *be* in·this·manner. "But·rather
Lk 24:24 and found *it* even in·this·manner just·as the women
Lk 24:46 to·them, "In·this·manner it·has·been·written, so·
Lk 24:46 so·also in·this·manner it·was·mandatory·for the

Ac 1:11 into the heaven, shall·come in·this·manner as yeu·
Ac 3:18 to·suffer in·this·manner, he·completely·fulfilled.
Ac 7:6 And God spoke in·this·manner, that his "offspring†
Ac 7:8 of·circumcision. And in·this·manner, *AbRaham*
Ac 8:32 shearing him, in·this·manner he·did·not open·up his
Ac 12:15 ·strongly·asserting *for·it* to·be in·this·manner. But
Ac 13:34 ·back to decay, in·this·manner he·has·declared,
Ac 13:47 For in·this·manner it·has·been·commanded to·us
Ac 14:1 of·the Jews, and in·this·manner to·speak, such·for
Ac 17:11 these·things might·actually·be in·this·manner.
Ac 17:33 And in·this·manner, Paul went·forth from·among
Ac 19:20 In·this·manner, according·to might, the
Ac 20:11 over a·long·while in·this·manner even·unto *the*
Ac 20:13 for in·this·manner he·was having·been·thoroughly·
Ac 20:35 *in* all·things, that in·this·manner, laboring·hard, it·
Ac 21:11 the Holy Spirit, 'in·this·manner the Judeans at
Ac 22:24 they·were·exclaiming in·this·manner against him.
Ac 23:11 JeruSalem, in·this·manner it·is·mandatory·for you
Ac 24:9 professing these·things to·hold *true* in·this·manner.
Ac 24:14 *is* a·sect, in·this·manner I·ritually·minister to·God
Ac 27:17 the sail, they·were·carried·along in·this·manner.
Ac 27:25 I·trust God, that in·this·manner, it·shall turn·out
Ac 27:44 sailing·ship. And in·this·manner it·happened *that*
Ac 28:14 seven days. And in·this·manner we·went toward
Heb 4:4 concerning the seventh *day* in·this·manner, "And
Heb 5:3 the People, in·this·manner also concerning himself)
Heb 5:5 In·this·manner also, Anointed-One did·not glorify
Heb 6:9 ·Salvation, even though we·speak in·this·manner.
Heb 6:15 And in·this·manner, after·patiently·waiting, he·
Heb 9:6 having·been·fully·prepared in·this·manner, the
Heb 9:28 in·this·manner, the Anointed-One, after·being·
Heb 10:33 partners with·the·ones being·used in·this·manner.
Heb 12:21 And in·this·manner the·thing being·made·
Gal 3:3 In·this·manner, are·yeu stupid?
Gal 4:3 Even in·this·manner, we·ourselves, when we·were
Gal 4:29 according·to Spirit, even in·this·manner *it·is* now.
Gal 6:2 of·one·another, and in·this·manner utterly·fulfill the
Mt 1:18 birth of·YeShua Anointed was in·this·manner. For
Mt 2:5 For in·this·manner it·has·been·written through the
Mt 3:15 at·this·moment, for in·this·manner it·is befitting·for
Mt 5:12 the heavens. For in·this·manner they·persecuted the
Mt 5:16 In·this·manner, *let* yeur light radiate·brightly before
Mt 5:19 the men·of·clay† in·this·manner, he·shall·be·called
Mt 5:47 ·indeed even the tax·collectors *greet* in·this·manner?
Mt 6:9 "So·then, yeu·yeurselves pray in·this·manner: 'Our
Mt 6:30 And if God in·this·manner enrobes the grass of·the
Mt 7:12 yeu·yeurselves do even in·this·manner to·them, for
Mt 7:17 In·this·manner, every beneficially·good tree
Mt 9:33 ·at·any·time did·it·appear in·this·manner in IsraEl."
Mt 11:26 because in·this·manner it·became a·delightful·
Mt 12:40 of·the whale, in·this·manner the Son of·Clay·
Mt 12:45 first·ones. "In·this·manner shall·it·be also to·this
Mt 13:40 ·burned in·fire, in·this·manner shall·it·be at the
Mt 13:49 In·this·manner shall·it·be at the entire·completion
Mt 17:12 as·much·as they·wanted. "In·this·manner also, the
Mt 18:14 "In·this·manner, before *the face* of·yeur Father,
Mt 18:35 "In·this·manner also, shall my heavenly Father do
Mt 19:8 *the* beginning it·has·not happened in·this·manner.
Mt 19:10 of·the man·of·clay† is in·this·manner with his wife
Mt 19:12 ·who were·born in·this·manner from·out *of·their*
Mt 20:16 "In·this·manner, the last shall·be first, and the first
Mt 20:26 "But it·shall·not be in·this·manner among yeu, but·
Mt 23:28 "In·this·manner, in·fact, yeu also outwardly appear
Mt 24:27 as·far·as·to *the* west, in·this·manner also shall·be
Mt 24:33 "In·this·manner, so·then yeu·yeurselves, whenever
Mt 24:37 the days of·Noach, in·this·manner also shall·be
Mt 24:39 ·all·of·them. "In·this·manner also shall·be the
Mt 24:46 upon·coming, shall·find *him* doing in·this·manner.
Mt 26:54 it·is·mandatory·for *it* to·happen in·this·manner?"
Mk 2:7 "Why in·this·manner, does this·man speak
Mk 2:8 *these·things* in·this·manner within themselves, he·
Mk 2:12 "Never·at·any·time did·we·see *it* in·this·manner."
Mk 4:26 And he·was·saying, "In·this·manner is the
Mk 4:40 "Why are·yeu timid in·this·manner? How·is·it *that*
Mk 10:43 But it·shall·not be in·this·manner among yeu, but·
Mk 13:29 "In·this·manner, so·then yeu·yeurselves, whenever
Mk 14:59 Yet not·even in·this·manner was their testimony
Mk 15:39 after·seeing that in·this·manner, upon·yelling·out
Rm 1:15 In·this·manner, the *determined·purpose* in me *is*
Rm 4:18 ·been·declared, "'In·this·manner shall·be your
Rm 5:12 ·Failure, also in·this·manner Death went·through
Rm 5:15 ·bestowment *is* also in·this·manner (but·yet not as
Rm 5:18 ·of·condemnation; even in·this·manner, through
Rm 5:19 ·disqualified, also in·this·manner through the
Rm 5:21 in Death, even in·this·manner Grace may·reign
Rm 6:4 of·the Father, in·this·manner we·ourselves also
Rm 6:11 In·this·manner, yeu·yeurselves must·reckon also
Rm 6:19 Lawlessness, in·this·manner now yeu·must·present
Rm 9:20 "Why did·you·make me in·this·manner?"
Rm 10:6 of·trust, says *it* in·this·manner, "You·should·not
Rm 11:5 Accordingly in·this·manner, in the present season
Rm 11:26 And in·this·manner all IsraEl shall·be·saved; just·
Rm 11:31 in·this·manner also, these now are·obstinate in·
Rm 12:5 in·this·manner, we (the many) are one Body in
Rm 15:20 And in·this·manner, *I·am* aspiring to·proclaim·
Jac 1:11 completely·perishes. In·this·manner also, the
Jac 2:12 In·this·manner yeu·must·speak and so do: as ones·
Jac 2:17 Even in·this·manner, the trust, provided·that it·
Jac 2:26 ·from spirit is dead, in·this·manner also, the trust
Jac 3:5 Even in·this·manner, the tongue is a·small member,
Jac 3:6 world of·unrighteousness. In·this·manner, the tongue
Jac 3:10 kindly·needed·for these·things to·be in·this·manner.
Jac 3:12 Or a·vine, figs? In·this·manner, not·even·one
Php 3:17 the·ones walking in·this·manner just·as yeu·hold us
Php 4:1 joy and victor's·crown) in·this·manner stand·fast in
1Pe 2:15 Because in·this·manner, it·is the will of·God, *by*
1Pe 3:5 For in·this·manner in·times·past, the holy wives also
2Pe 1:11 For in·this·manner, the accessible·entrance shall·
2Pe 3:4 ·things remain·constant in·this·manner *as they·were*
1Th 2:4 with·the good·news, in·this·manner we·speak, not
1Th 2:8 In·this·manner, ourselves·yearning·for yeu, we·
1Th 4:14 died and rose·up, in·this·manner also God shall·
1Th 4:17 in *the* air. And in·this·manner, we·shall·be always
1Th 5:2 that the Day of·Yahweh, in·this·manner, comes as
2Th 3:17 a·signature in every letter. I·write in·this·manner.
1Co 2:11 in him? Even in·this·manner not·even·one *being*
1Co 3:15 he·himself shall·be·saved, but in·this·manner, as
1Co 4:1 Let a·man·of·clay† reckon us in·this·manner: as
1Co 5:3 the·one performing this·thing in·this·manner:
1Co 6:5 yeur·own embarrassment. In·this·manner, is·there
1Co 7:7 of·God, in·fact, one in·this·manner, and another in·
1Co 7:17 has·called·forth, in·this·manner let·him·walk. And
1Co 7:17 And in·this·manner I·thoroughly·assign among
1Co 7:26 good for·a·man·of·clay† to·behave in·this·manner:
1Co 7:40 ·blessed if in·this·manner she·should·remain,
1Co 8:12 But by·morally·failing in·this·manner toward the
1Co 9:14 Even in·this·manner, the Lord thoroughly·assigned
1Co 9:15 ·order·that it·should·be·done in·this·manner to me,
1Co 9:24 receives the prize? In·this·manner run, in·order·
1Co 9:26 Now·then, in·this·manner I·myself do·run, *but* not
1Co 9:26 not as uncertainly; in·this·manner I·do·box, *but*
1Co 11:12 *is* from·out of·the man, in·this·manner the man *is*
1Co 11:28 himself, and in·this·manner let·him·eat from·out
1Co 12:12 many) are one body, in·this·manner also *is* the
1Co 14:9 In·this·manner, so·also *are* yeu, through the
1Co 14:12 *It·is* even in·this·manner *with* yeu·yeurselves.
1Co 14:21 People; and in·this·manner, they·shall·not·even
1Co 14:25 And in·this·manner, the secrets of·his heart
1Co 14:25 apparent; and in·this·manner falling·down on *his*
1Co 15:11 in·this·manner we·officially·proclaim, and in·
1Co 15:11 ·proclaim, and in·this·manner yeu·trusted.
1Co 15:22 within Adam die, even in·this·manner, all within
1Co 15:42 In·this·manner also *is* the resurrection of·the dead
1Co 15:45 And in·this·manner it·has·been·written, "The
1Co 16:1 even yeu·yeurselves must·do in·this·manner:
2Co 1:5 abound in us, in·this·manner our comforting also
2Co 1:7 of·the afflictions, in·this·manner *yeu·are* also
2Co 7:14 to·yeu in truth, even in·this·manner our boasting
2Co 8:6 even in·this·manner he·should·further·finish among
2Co 8:11 to·be·willing, in·this·manner *that there·may·be the*
2Co 9:5 *for* the·same to·be ready in·this·manner: as a·
2Co 10:7 even in·this·manner *are* we·ourselves of·
2Co 11:3 ·cunning, in·this·manner yeur mental·disposition
Eph 4:20 But *it·was* not in·this·manner *that* yeu·yeurselves
Eph 5:24 to·the Anointed-One, in·this·manner also the
Eph 5:28 In·this·manner, the husbands are·obligated to·love
Col 3:13 graciously·forgave yeu, in·this·manner yeu also *do*
2Ti 3:8 stood·opposed·to Moses, in·this·manner these also
1Jn 2:6 him is·obligated himself also in·this·manner to·walk,
1Jn 4:11 Beloved, if in·this·manner, God loved us, we·
Rv 2:15 In·this·manner, you·yourself also have ones·
Rv 3:16 'In·this·manner *then*, because you·are lukewarm,
Rv 9:17 And in·this·manner I·saw the horses in the clear·
Rv 11:5 it·is·mandatory·for him to·be·killed in·this·manner.
Rv 18:21 saying, "In·this·manner with·violence, the Great

EG3779.1 (1x)

Mt 5:48 yeu·yeurselves shall·be complete *in·this·manner*,

G3779.2 ADV οὕτως (3x)

Jn 14:31 me, I·do *it just* in·that·manner. "Be·awake, we·
1Co 7:7 one in·this·manner, and another in·that·manner.
Eph 5:33 (accordingly each one in·that·manner) must·love

G3779.3 ADV οὕτως (10x)

Lk 6:10 And he·did so, and his hand was·restored as·
Ac 7:1 "Are these·things so?"
Ac 12:8 And he·did so. Then he·says to·him, "Cast your·
Ac 13:8 the occultist (for so his name is·interpreted *from*·
Gal 1:6 I·marvel that so quickly yeu·are·transferring away·
Mt 26:40 And he·says to·Peter, "So, did·yeu·all·not have·
Mk 7:18 Then he·says to·them, "So, are yeu·yeurselves also
Jac 2:12 In·this·manner yeu·must·speak and so do: as ones·
1Co 7:36 ·be past·her·prime and financial·need so happens,
Rv 16:18 the earth, so·vast an·earthquake, *and* so great!

G3780 οὐχί ôuchí *prt.* (59x)

Roots:G3756

G3780 NEG οὐχί (10x)

Jn 13:10 And yeu are pure, but·yet not·indeed all *of·yeu*."
Jn 13:11 that, he·declared, "Yeu·are not·indeed all pure."
Lk 1:60 his mother declared, "No·indeed! But·rather, he·
Lk 12:51 on the earth? I·say to·yeu, no·indeed, but·rather
Lk 13:3 "I·say to·yeu, no·indeed, but·yet, unless yeu·
Lk 13:5 "I·say to·yeu, no·indeed, but·yet, unless yeu·
Lk 16:30 And he·declared, 'No·indeed, father AbRaham!
Rm 3:27 law? The·one of·works? No·indeed, but·rather on·
1Co 10:29 I·say, not·indeed your·own, but·rather of·the
2Co 10:13 But we·ourselves indeed·shall·not boast in the

G3780 PRT-I οὐχί (46x)

Jn 7:42 Has·not·indeed the Scripture declared, that the
Jn 11:9 answered, "Are·there not·indeed twelve hours of·the
Jn 14:22 yourself to·us, and not·indeed to·the world?
Lk 6:39 to·guide *the* blind? Shall·they·not·indeed both fall
Lk 12:6 "Are·not·indeed five little·sparrows sold for·two
Lk 14:28 to·build a·tower, *does* not·indeed sit·down first
Lk 14:31 another king, *does* not·indeed sit·down first *and*
Lk 15:8 ·lose one drachma, does·not·indeed ignite a·lantern,
Lk 17:8 But·rather shall·he·not·indeed declare to·him,
Lk 17:17 Jesus declared, "Are·not·indeed the ten purified?
Lk 22:27 *Is·it* not·indeed the·one reclining·at·the·meal?
Lk 24:26 Is·it·not·indeed mandatory·for the Anointed-One
Lk 24:32 one·another, "Was not·indeed our heart being·set·
Ac 5:4 ·remaining, was·it·not·indeed remaining your·own?
Ac 7:50 Did·not·indeed my hand make all these·things?
Heb 1:14 Are·they not·indeed all publicly·serving spirits,
Heb 3:17 years? *Was·it* not·indeed the·ones morally·failing,
Mt 5:46 ·of·service do·yeu·have? Do·not·indeed even the
Mt 5:47 *·is* superior *to·others*? Do not·indeed even the tax·
Mt 6:25 yeu·should·dress·yeurselves. Is not·indeed the soul
Mt 10:29 Are·not·indeed two little·sparrows sold for·an·
Mt 12:11 ·Sabbaths, shall·not·indeed take·secure·hold·of it
Mt 13:27 to·him, 'Sir, did·you·not·indeed sow good seed in

Mt 13:55 not the carpenter's son? Is·not·indeed his mother
Mt 13:56 his sisters, are·they not all indeed alongside us?
Mt 18:12 should·be·led·astray, does·he·not·indeed traverse,
Mt 20:13 Did·you·not·indeed mutually·agree with·me for·
Rm 2:26 uncircumcision, shall·it·not·indeed be·reckoned for
Rm 3:29 of·Jews merely? *Is·he* not·indeed also of·Gentiles?
Rm 8:32 of·us all, how shall·he·not·indeed, together with·
1Th 2:19 ·crown of·boasting? *Is·it* not·indeed even yeu,
1Co 1:20 present·age? Did God not·indeed make·foolish the
1Co 3:3 and dissensions, are·yeu not·indeed fleshly, and
1Co 3:4 "I *am* of·Apollos," are·yeu not·indeed fleshly?
1Co 5:2 ·been·puffed·up, and did·not·indeed rather mourn,
1Co 5:12 yeu·yeurselves not·indeed presently·judge the·ones
1Co 6:1 the unrighteous·ones, and not·indeed before the
1Co 6:7 Rather, why not·indeed *let* yeurselves·be·wronged?
1Co 6:7 Rather, why not·indeed *let* yeurselves·be·robbed?
1Co 8:10 an·idol's·temple, shall not·indeed the conscience
1Co 9:1 ·I not free? Have·I·not·indeed clearly·seen Jesus
1Co 9:8 a·man·of·clay†? Or does·not·indeed the Torah-Law
1Co 10:16 which we·bless, is·it not·indeed fellowship of·the
1Co 10:16 we·break, is·it not·indeed fellowship of·the body
1Co 10:18 ·to flesh. Are not·indeed the·ones eating of·the
2Co 3:8 indeed, how·much more shall the Service of·the

EG3780 (2x)
Ac 5:4 ·sold·off, inherently·was·it *not·indeed* in your·own
Rm 2:27 the Torah-Law, *shall·not* the·one birthed·from·out

EG3780.- (1x)
Rm 2:27 ·out of·natural uncircumcision *indeed* judge you,

G3781 ὀφειλέτης ôphêilḗtēs *n.* (9x)
Roots:G3784 Compare:G5533 See:G3783 G3782

G3781.1 N-DPM ὀφειλέταις (1x)
Mt 6:12 ·debts, also as we·ourselves forgive our debtors.

EG3781.1 (2x)
Lk 12:58 ·officer should·cast you into *debtors'* prison.
Mt 5:25 assistant, and you·shall·be·cast into *debtors'* prison.

G3781.2 N-NSM ὀφειλέτης (2x)
Gal 5:3 ·circumcised, that he·is under·an·obligation to·do all
Rm 1:14 I·am under·an·obligation both to·Greeks and to·

G3781.2 N-NPM ὀφειλέται (2x)
Rm 8:12 brothers, we·are under·an·obligation, *but* not to·the
Rm 15:27 and they·are under·an·obligation for·them. For if

G3781.3 N-NSM ὀφειλέτης (1x)
Mt 18:24 to·him, one·man delinquent of·ten·thousand

G3781.3 N-NPM ὀφειλέται (1x)
Lk 13:4 these·men were delinquent above·and·beyond all

G3782 ὀφειλή ôphêilḗ *n.* (2x)
Roots:G3784 See:G3783 G3781

G3782.1 N-ASF ὀφειλήν (1x)
Mt 18:32 I·forgave you all that indebtedness, since you·

G3782.2 N-APF ὀφειλάς (1x)
Rm 13:7 render the dues to·all·ones *in·superior authority*:

G3783 ὀφείλημα ôphêílēma *n.* (2x)
Roots:G3784 See:G3781 G3782

G3783.1 N-ASN ὀφείλημα (1x)
Rm 4:4 according·to grace, but·rather according·to the debt.

G3783.2 N-APN ὀφειλήματα (1x)
Mt 6:12 And forgive us our moral·debts, also as we·

G3784 ὀφείλω ôphêílō *v.* (42x)
ὀφειλέω ôphêiléō
[prolonged form, in certain tenses]
Roots:G3786 Compare:G5535 G0315 See:G3781 G3782 G3783 G3785

G3784.ª V-PAI-3S ὀφείλει (1x)
1Co 7:36 ·be past·her·prime and financial·need so happens,

G3784.1 V-PAI-2S ὀφείλεις (3x)
Lk 16:5 to·the first, 'How·much·do you·owe to·my lord?
Lk 16:7 'And you, how·much·do you·owe?' And he·
Mt 18:28 'Repay me what you·owe *me*.'

G3784.1 V-PAI-3S ὀφείλει (1x)
Phm 1:18 if he·wronged you, or owes *you* anything, impute

G3784.1 V-PAM-2P ὀφείλετε (1x)
Rm 13:8 Owe not·one·man not·even·one·thing, except to·

G3784.1 V-PPP-ASN ὀφειλόμενον (2x)
Mt 18:30 until he·should·repay the *amount* being·owed.
Mt 18:34 he·should·repay all the *amount* being·owed him.

G3784.1 V-IAI-3S ὤφειλεν (3x)
Lk 7:41 ·debtors; the one was·owing five·hundred denarii
Heb 2:17 From·which, he·was·owing fully all·things to·the
Mt 18:28 of·his fellow·slaves who was·owing him a·hundred

G3784.2 V-PAI-1P ὀφείλομεν (4x)
2Th 1:3 We·are·indebted to·give·thanks to·God always
2Th 2:13 we·ourselves are·indebted to·give·thanks always
1Jn 3:16 and we·ourselves are·indebted to·lay·down *our·own*
1Jn 4:11 we·ourselves also are·indebted to·love one·another.

G3784.2 V-PAP-DSM ὀφείλοντι (1x)
Lk 11:4 for we also forgive everyone being·indebted to·us.

G3784.3 V-PAI-2P ὀφείλετε (2x)
Jn 13:14 yeu·yeurselves are·obligated to·wash one·another's
1Co 5:10 by·inference, yeu·are·obligated to·go·forth out

G3784.3 V-PAI-3S ὀφείλει (7x)
Heb 5:3 himself), he·is·obligated to·offer *sacrifices* on·
Mt 23:16 "by the gold of·the Temple," he·is·obligated!'
Mt 23:18 by the present, the·one upon it, he·is·obligated.'
1Co 11:7 in·fact a·man is·obligated not to·be·fully·veiling
1Co 11:10 that, the woman is·obligated to·have authority
2Co 12:14 the children are·not obligated to·store·up for·the
1Jn 2:6 saying he·abides in him is·obligated himself also in·

G3784.3 V-PAI-3P ὀφείλουσιν (2x)
Rm 15:27 they·are·obligated also to·publicly·work·charity
Eph 5:28 the husbands are·obligated to·love their·own

G3784.3 V-IAI-1P ὠφείλομεν (1x)
Lk 17:10 ·done *merely* that·which we·were·obligated to·do.'

G3784.4 V-PAI-1P ὀφείλομεν (3x)
Ac 17:29 ·being kindred of·God, we·ought not to·assume
Rm 15:1 the·ones *being* able *to·partake*, ought to·bear *with*
3Jn 1:8 we·ourselves ought to·fully·receive·and·host such·

G3784.4 V-PAI-3S ὀφείλει (1x)
1Co 9:10 because the·one plowing ought to·plow in

EG3784.4 (2x)
Jac 4:15 Instead, you *ought* to·say, "If the Lord should·will,
2Co 2:7 ·contrary, yeu *ought* rather to·graciously·forgive

G3784.6 V-PAI-3S ὀφείλει (1x)
Jn 19:7 and according·to our Oral-law he·is·due to·die,

G3784.6 V-PAP-NPM ὀφείλοντες (1x)
Heb 5:12 For even after the time being·due *for·yeu* to·be

G3784.6 V-PPP-ASF ὀφειλομένην (1x)
1Co 7:3 to·the wife the kind·marital·duty being·due, and

G3784.6 V-IAI-1S ὤφειλον (1x)
2Co 12:11 me, for I·myself was·due to·be·commended by

EG3784.7 (4x)
Rm 13:7 *authority*: the tribute to·the·one *due* the tribute, the
Rm 13:7 *due* the tribute, the tax to·the·one *due* the tax, the
Rm 13:7 the reverent·fear to·the·one *due* the reverent·fear,
Rm 13:7 reverent·fear, the honor to·the·one *due* the honor.

G3785 ὄφελον ôphêlôn *inj.* (4x)
Roots:G3784

G3785.2 INJ ὄφελον (4x)
Gal 5:12 Oh·that even they·were·chopped·off, the·ones
1Co 4:8 us. And oh·that it·were·actually·so *that* yeu·did·
2Co 11:1 Oh·that yeu·would·bear·with me a·little·while in·
Rv 3:15 cold nor fervently·hot. Oh·that you·would·be cold

G3786 ὄφελος ôphêlôs *n.* (3x)
Roots:G3784-1 Compare:G2771 G4200 G5622 See:G3784 G5624

G3786.2 N-NSN ὄφελος (3x)
Jac 2:14 What *is* the advantage, my brothers, though
Jac 2:16 ·needs of·the body— what *is* the advantage?
1Co 15:32 at Ephesus, what *is* the advantage to·me, if dead·

G3787 ὀφθαλμο•δουλεία ôphthalmôdôulêía *n.* (2x)
Roots:G3788 G1397

G3787 N-ASF ὀφθαλμοδουλείαν (1x)
Eph 6:6 not according·to eyeservice as men-pleasers†, but·

G3787 N-DPF ὀφθαλμοδουλείαις (1x)
Col 3:22 ·to flesh, not with eyeservice as men-pleasers†,

G3788 ὀφθαλμός ôphthalmṓs *n.* (103x)
Roots:G3700 Compare:G3659 G5168 xLangAlso:H5869

G3788.1 N-NSM ὀφθαλμός (15x)
Lk 11:34 "The lantern of·the body is the eye. Accordingly,
Lk 11:34 whenever your eye should·be clear·and·focused,
Mt 5:29 "So if your right eye entraps you, pluck it out and
Mt 6:22 "The lantern of·the body is the eye. Accordingly, if
Mt 6:22 if your eye should·be clear·and·focused, your
Mt 6:23 But if your eye should·be evil, your whole body
Mt 18:9 And if your eye entraps you, pluck it out and cast *it*
Mt 20:15 my things? Is your eye evil, because I·myself am
Mk 7:22 evils, guile, debauchery, an·evil eye, revilement,
Mk 9:47 "And if your eye should·entrap you, cast it out.
1Co 2:9 just·as it·has·been·written, "Eye did·not see, and
1Co 12:16 "Because I·am not an·eye, I·am not from·among
1Co 12:17 If the whole body *is* an·eye, where·is the sense·
1Co 12:21 And *the* eye is·not able to·declare to·the hand, "I·
Rv 1:7 ' and 'every eye shall·gaze·upon him, and·also they·

G3788.1 N-NPM ὀφθαλμοί (16x)
Jn 9:10 ·saying to·him, "How·are your eyes opened·up?
Lk 2:30 because my eyes saw your custodial·Salvation,
Lk 4:20 ·sat·down, also with·the eyes of·all·them that·were
Lk 10:23 ·blessed *are* the eyes looking·upon the·things·that
Lk 24:16 But their eyes were·securely·held, *such·for them*
Lk 24:31 And their eyes were·thoroughly·opened·up, and
Mt 9:30 And their eyes were·opened·up; and YeShua sternly·
Mt 13:16 "But supremely·blessed *are* yeur eyes, because
Mt 20:33 "Lord, that our eyes may·be·opened·up."
Mt 20:34 and immediately their eyes received·sight, and
Mt 26:43 for their eyes were having·been·weighed·down.
Mk 14:40 for their eyes were having·been·weighed·down,
Rm 11:10 " Let their eyes be·darkened, *such·for them* not
1Pe 3:12 Because the eyes of·Yahweh *are* upon righteous·
Rv 1:14 white as snow), and his eyes *are* as a·blaze of·fire,
Rv 19:12 His eyes *were* as a·blaze of·fire, and on his head

G3788.1 N-ASM ὀφθαλμόν (1x)
Mt 5:38 ·heard that it·was·uttered, "An·eye for an·eye, and

G3788.1 N-APM ὀφθαλμούς (37x)
Jn 4:35 ·say to·yeu, lift·up yeur eyes and distinctly·view the
Jn 6:5 So·then, after·lifting·up the eyes and surveying that a·
Jn 9:6 he·smeared the clay over the eyes of·the blind·man,
Jn 9:11 clay and smeared·*it*·over my eyes, and he·declared
Jn 9:14 when Jesus made the clay and opened·up his eyes.
Jn 9:15 "He·put clay upon my eyes, and I·washed, and I·
Jn 9:17 him, because he·opened·up your eyes." And he·
Jn 9:21 or who opened·up his eyes, we·ourselves do·not
Jn 9:26 ·did he·do to·you? How·did he·open·up your eyes?"
Jn 9:30 ·what·source he·is, and·yet he·opened·up my eyes.
Jn 9:32 ·man opened·up eyes of·one·having·been·born blind.
Jn 10:21 ¿!·Is a·demon able to·open·up blind eyes?"
Jn 11:37 this·man, the·one opening·up the eyes of·the blind,
Jn 11:41 And Jesus lifted the eyes upward and declared,
Jn 12:40 "He·has·blinded their eyes, and their heart he·has·
Jn 17:1 these·things and lifted·up his eyes to the heaven, and
Lk 6:20 And lifting·up his eyes to his disciples, he·was·
Lk 16:23 Hades, after·lifting·up his eyes while·subsisting in
Lk 18:13 willing to·lift·up not·even his eyes to the heaven,
Ac 9:40 And she·opened·up her eyes; and upon·seeing
Ac 26:18 to·open·up their eyes, *and* to·turn·*them*·back·
Ac 28:27 and they·fully·shut their eyes, lest they·should·
Gal 3:1 *before* whose very·own eyes YeShua Anointed was·
Gal 4:15 possible, digging·out yeur own·eyes, yeu·would
Mt 13:15 and they·fully·shut their eyes, lest they·should·
Mt 17:8 And lifting·up their eyes, they·saw not·even·one·
Mt 18:9 rather·than having two eyes *and* to·be·cast into the
Mk 8:18 'Having eyes, do·yeu·not look?
Mk 8:25 again laid his hands upon his eyes and made him to·
Mk 9:47 ·one·eye, than having two eyes *and* to·be·cast into
Rm 11:8 a·spirit of·a·stinging·numbness, eyes *for·them* not
2Pe 2:14 having eyes exceedingly·full of·alluring·adultery
Eph 1:18 the eyes of·yeur innermost·understanding having·
1Jn 2:11 ·is·heading, because the darkness blinded his eyes.

Rv 2:18 of·God, the·one having his eyes as a·blaze of·fire
Rv 3:18 smear eye·salve on your eyes, in·order·that you·
Rv 5:6 having seven horns and seven eyes which are the
G3788.1 N-DSM ὀφθαλμῷ (8x)
Lk 6:41 the·one in your brother's eye, but do·not fully·
Lk 6:41 fully·observe the beam, the·one in your·own eye?
Lk 6:42 the speck·of·dust, the·one in your eye,' *while* you·
Lk 6:42 not looking·at the beam in your own·eye? "O·stage·
Lk 6:42 ·out the speck·of·dust, the·one in your brother's eye.
Mt 7:3 ·dust, the·one in your brother's eye, but do·not fully·
Mt 7:3 but do·not fully·observe the beam in your·own eye?
Mt 7:4 And behold, the beam *is* in your·own eye?
G3788.1 N-DPM ὀφθαλμοῖς (7x)
Jn 12:40 ·should·not see with·the eyes nor should·understand
Ac 28:27 lest they·should·see with·the eyes, and should·
Heb 4:13 and having·been·vulnerably·exposed to·his eyes, to
Mt 13:15 lest they·should·see with·the eyes, and should·
Mt 21:42 ·from Yahweh, and it·is marvelous in our eyes"?
Mk 12:11 ·from Yahweh, and it·is marvelous in our eyes.'"
1Jn 1:1 which we·have·clearly·seen with·our eyes, which
G3788.1 N-GSM ὀφθαλμοῦ (6x)
Lk 6:42 cast·out the beam from your·own eye, and then you·
Mt 5:38 it·was·uttered, "An·eye for an·eye, and a·tooth for
Mt 7:4 I·may·cast·out the speck·of·dust from your eye!' And
Mt 7:5 cast the beam from·out of·your·own eye, and then
Mt 7:5 the speck·of·dust from·out of·your brother's eye.
1Co 15:52 in an·instant, in a·twinkling of·an·eye, at the last
G3788.1 N-GPM ὀφθαλμῶν (11x)
Lk 19:42 But now they·are·already·hidden from your eyes.
Ac 9:8 but with·his *dazed* eyes having·been·opened·up, he·
Ac 9:18 scales fell·off from his eyes. And he·received·sight
Mt 9:29 Then he·laid·hold of·their eyes, saying,
Mt 20:34 YeShua laid·hold of·their eyes, and immediately
Rm 3:18 "There·is no fear of·God fully·before their eyes."
1Jn 2:16 flesh, and the longing of·the eyes, and the bragging
Rv 4:6 four living·beings overflowing of·eyes forward and
Rv 4:8 six wings apiece overflowing of·eyes, all·around and
Rv 7:17 God shall·rub·away every tear from their eyes."
Rv 21:4 God shall·rub·away every tear from their eyes.' And
EG3788.1 (1x)
Lk 11:34 ·of·light; but whenever *your* *eye* should·be evil,
G3788.2 N-GPM ὀφθαλμῶν (1x)
Ac 1:9 a·thick·cloud received him up from their eyesight.

Oo

G3789 ὄφις ôphis *n.* (14x)
Roots:G3700 Compare:G1404 G4567 G4566 G1228 xLangEquiv:H5175
G3789.1 N-NPM ὄφεις (1x)
Mt 10:16 become prudent as the serpents and untainted as
G3789.1 N-VPM ὄφεις (1x)
Mt 23:33 O·serpents, O·offspring of·vipers, in·what·way
G3789.1 N-ASM ὄφιν (3x)
Jn 3:14 just·as Moses elevated the serpent *upon a·sign·pole*
Lk 11:11 ¿! instead of·a·fish, shall·he·hand him a·serpent?
Mt 7:10 ·should·request a·fish, ¿! shall·hand him a·serpent?
G3789.1 N-APM ὄφεις (1x)
Mk 16:18 "they·shall·take·up serpents; and·if they·should·
G3789.1 N-DPM ὄφεσιν (1x)
Rv 9:19 for their tails *were* like serpents having heads, and
G3789.1 N-GPM ὄφεων (2x)
Lk 10:19 the·one to·trample upon serpents and scorpions,
1Co 10:9 they·were·completely·destroyed by the serpents.
G3789.3 N-NSM ὄφις (3x)
2Co 11:3 lest·somehow, as the Serpent thoroughly·deluded
Rv 12:9 Dragon was·cast·out, the original Serpent, the·one
Rv 12:15 And the Serpent cast out of·his mouth water as a·
G3789.3 N-ASM ὄφιν (1x)
Rv 20:2 the Dragon, the original Serpent, who is Slanderer
G3789.3 N-GSM ὄφεως (1x)
Rv 12:14 half a·season, away·from *the* face of·the Serpent.

G3790 ὀφρῦς ôphrŷs *n.* (1x)
Roots:G3700 Compare:G4750
G3790.1 N-GSF ὀφρύος (1x)
Lk 4:29 and drove him unto the brow of·the mount on which

G3791 ὀχλέω ôchléō *v.* (2x)
Roots:G3793 See:G1776
G3791.2 V-PPP-APM ὀχλουμένους (1x)
Ac 5:16 *the* sick and *those* being·harassed by impure spirits.
G3791.2 V-PPP-NPM ὀχλούμενοι (1x)
Lk 6:18 also the·ones being·harassed by impure spirits.

G3792 ὀχλο•ποιέω ôchlôpôiéō *v.* (1x)
Roots:G3793 G4160
G3792.2 V-AAP-NPM ὀχλοποιήσαντες (1x)
Ac 17:5 and raising·a·mob, were·making·a·commotion·in

G3793 ὄχλος óchlôs *n.* (179x)
Roots:G2192 Compare:G3658 See:G3791
G3793.1 N-NSM ὄχλος (46x)
Jn 6:2 And a·large crowd was·following him, because they·
Jn 6:5 and surveying that a·large crowd is·come toward him,
Jn 6:22 On·the next·day, the crowd— the·one standing on·
Jn 6:24 So·then, when the crowd saw that Jesus was not
Jn 7:20 The crowd answered and declared, "You·have a·
Jn 7:49 But·rather this crowd, the·one not knowing the
Jn 12:9 Now·then, a·large crowd from·among the Judeans
Jn 12:12 On·the next·day, a·large crowd (the·one coming to
Jn 12:17 Now·then, the crowd *from BethAny* was·testifying,
Jn 12:18 On·account·of that, the crowd *from JeruSalem* also
Jn 12:29 So·then the crowd, the·one standing·by and hearing
Jn 12:34 The crowd answered him, "We·ourselves heard
Lk 5:29 and there·was a·large crowd of·tax·collectors and
Lk 6:17 in a·level place, and·also the crowd of·his disciples,
Lk 6:19 And the entire crowd was·seeking to·lay·hold of·
Lk 7:11 ·together with·him, and·also a·large crowd.
Lk 7:12 a·widow. And a·significant crowd of·the city *was*
Lk 8:40 Jesus returned·back, the crowd fully·accepted him,
Lk 9:37 from the mountain, a·large crowd met·up with·him.
Lk 13:17 And all the crowd was·rejoicing over all the
Lk 22:47 was·yet speaking, behold a·crowd. And the·one
Ac 1:15 disciples (and it·was a·crowd of·names in·unison *of*
Ac 6:7 also a·large crowd of·the priests·that·offer·sacrifices
Ac 11:24 And an·ample crowd was·placed·alongside the
Ac 16:22 And the crowd rose·up·together against them, and
Mt 9:25 But when the crowd was·cast·out, upon·entering,
Mt 13:2 ·down *there*; and all the crowd stood on the shore.
Mt 20:29 ·forth from Jericho, a·large crowd followed him.
Mt 20:31 And the crowd reprimanded them that they·should·
Mt 21:8 And the very·large crowd spread·out their·own
Mt 26:47 and with him *was* a·large crowd with daggers and
Mk 2:13 sea, and all the crowd was·coming alongside him,
Mk 3:20 And a·crowd was·coming·together again, such·for
Mk 3:32 And a·crowd was·sitting·down around him, and
Mk 4:1 the sea. And a·large crowd was·gathered·together to
Mk 4:1 the sea, and all the crowd was alongside the sea
Mk 5:21 *sea*, a·large crowd is·already·gathered·together to
Mk 5:24 with him, and a·large crowd was·following him,
Mk 9:15 And immediately all the crowd, after·seeing him,
Mk 9:25 that the crowd came·running·together·toward *them*,
Mk 11:18 him, because all the crowd was·astounded at his
Mk 12:37 And the large crowd was·hearing him with·
Mk 12:41 was·observing how the crowd cast copper·coinage
Mk 14:43 and with him a·large crowd with daggers and
Mk 15:8 And the crowd, upon·shouting·out, began to·request
Rv 7:9 and behold, a·large crowd which not·even·one·man
G3793.1 N-NPM ὄχλοι (29x)
Lk 3:10 And the crowds were·inquiring·of him, saying, "So·
Lk 4:42 a·desolate place. And the crowds were·seeking him,
Lk 5:15 him, and large crowds came·together to·hear *him*,
Lk 8:42 ·out, the crowds were·altogether·constricting him.
Lk 8:45 "Captain, the crowds confine you and press·against
Lk 9:11 And the crowds, after·knowing *it*, followed him.
Lk 9:18 them, saying, "Who·do the crowds say me to·be?
Lk 11:14 the mute·man spoke. And the crowds marveled.
Lk 14:25 large crowds were·traversing·together with·him,
Lk 23:48 And all the crowds convening·publicly upon that
Ac 8:6 And the crowds, *being together* with·the·same·
Ac 14:11 And the crowds, after·seeing what Paul did, they·
Mt 4:25 And large crowds followed him from Galilee and
Mt 7:28 these sayings, the crowds were·astounded at his
Mt 8:1 from the mountain, large crowds followed him.
Mt 9:8 But the crowds seeing *it*, marveled, and they·glorified
Mt 9:33 the mute spoke, and the crowds marveled, saying,
Mt 12:15 And large crowds followed him, and he·both·
Mt 12:23 And all the crowds were·astonished and were·
Mt 13:2 And large crowds were·gathered·together to him,
Mt 14:13 after·hearing *of·this*, the crowds followed him on·
Mt 15:30 And large crowds came·alongside him, having
Mt 19:2 And large crowds followed him, and he·both·
Mt 21:9 And the crowds, the·ones preceding and the·ones
Mt 21:11 And the crowds were·saying, "This is YeShua the
Mt 22:33 hearing *this*, the crowds were·astounded at his
Mk 6:33 Yet the crowds saw them heading·on·out, and many
Mk 10:1 and again, crowds were·traversing·together toward
Rv 17:15 sits·down, are peoples, and crowds, and nations,
G3793.1 N-ASM ὄχλον (32x)
Jn 7:12 "No, but·rather he·deceives the crowd."
Jn 11:42 but·yet on·account·of the crowd, the·one having·
Lk 5:1 it·happened, with the crowd pressing·upon him to·
Lk 5:19 him in on·account·of the crowd, walking·up on the
Lk 8:19 ·not able to·encounter him on·account·of the crowd.
Lk 9:12 to·him, "Dismiss the crowd, in·order·that going·off
Ac 11:26 ·citizenry and to·instruct an·ample crowd. Also *it*·
Ac 14:14 garments, rushed·in among the crowd, yelling·out
Ac 17:8 And they·troubled the crowd and the rulers·of·the·
Ac 19:26 Paul has·won·over an·ample crowd *by* persuading
Ac 19:35 And after·fully·quieting·down the crowd, the
Ac 21:27 they·were·stirring·up all the crowd into·an·uproar,
Mt 9:23 flute·players and the crowd being·in·a·commotion,
Mt 14:5 ·kill him, he·feared the crowd, because they·were·
Mt 14:14 YeShua saw a·large crowd, and he·empathized
Mt 15:10 And upon·summoning the crowd, he·declared to·
Mt 15:32 "I·empathize over the crowd, because even·now
Mt 15:33 such·as to·stuff·full so·vast a·crowd?"
Mt 17:14 ·them coming to·the crowd, a·certain·man·of·clay†
Mt 21:26 of·men·of·clay†,' we·fear the crowd, for all hold
Mk 2:4 to·him on·account·of the crowd, they·pulled·apart
Mk 3:9 ·attend to·him on·account·of the crowd, lest they·
Mk 4:36 after·sending·away the crowd, they·personally·took
Mk 5:31 "You·look·at the crowd pressing·in·around you
Mk 6:34 after·coming·ashore, saw a·large crowd, and he·
Mk 6:45 until he·himself should·dismiss the crowd.
Mk 7:14 And upon·summoning all the crowd, he·was·saying
Mk 8:2 "I·empathize over the crowd, because even·now
Mk 8:34 And after·summoning the crowd *to·him* along·with
Mk 9:14 *other* disciples, he·saw a·large crowd about them,
Mk 12:12 him, yet they·feared the crowd, for they·knew that
Mk 15:11 the chief·priests incited the crowd that rather he·
G3793.1 N-APM ὄχλους (19x)
Lk 5:3 he·was·instructing the crowds from·out of·the
Lk 7:24 began to·discourse to·the crowds concerning John,
Lk 23:4 to the chief·priests and *to* the crowds, "I·find not·
Ac 13:45 But after·seeing the crowds, the Jews were·filled
Ac 14:18 they·fully·restrained the crowds not to·sacrifice
Ac 14:19 and after·persuading the crowds and stoning Paul,
Ac 17:13 they·came there·also, stirring·up the crowds.
Mt 5:1 And seeing the crowds, he·walked·up upon the
Mt 8:18 And YeShua, seeing large crowds about him, he·
Mt 9:36 But after·seeing the crowds, he·empathized
Mt 13:36 Then after·sending·away the crowds, YeShua went
Mt 14:15 passed·away. Dismiss the crowds, in·order·that
Mt 14:19 ·commandingly·ordering the crowds to·recline on
Mt 14:22 the other·side, until he·should·dismiss the crowds.
Mt 14:23 And after·dismissing the crowds, he·walked·up
Mt 15:31 such·for the crowds to·marvel, while·looking·at
Mt 15:39 And after·dismissing the crowds, he·embarked into
Mt 21:46 ·hold him, they·feared the crowds, since·now *the*
Mt 27:20 persuaded the crowds that they·should·request
G3793.1 N-DSM ὄχλῳ (12x)
Jn 7:43 ·schism among the crowd on·account·of him.
Lk 7:9 ·around, he·declared to·the crowd following him, "I·

Lk 9:16 *them* to·the disciples to·place·before the crowd.
Lk 13:14 ·the Sabbath, was·saying to·the crowd, "There·are
Ac 21:34 *and some* another·thing among the crowd. And not
Mt 15:36 ·his disciples, and the disciples *gave* to·the crowd.
Mt 27:15 to·fully·release to·the crowd a chained·prisoner,
Mk 5:27 *and* already·coming in the crowd from·behind *him*,
Mk 5:30 ·turning·himself·about in the crowd, was·saying,
Mk 8:6 And he·charged the crowd to·sit·back upon the soil.
Mk 8:6 ·*them*·forth, and they·placed *them* before the crowd.
Mk 15:15 being·resolved to·make the crowd content, fully·
G3793.1 N-DPM ὄχλοις (11x)
Jn 7:12 much grumbling among the crowds concerning him.
Lk 3:7 to·the crowds traversing·forth to·be·immersed by him
Lk 12:54 And he·was·saying also to·the crowds, "Whenever
Ac 14:13 ·was·wanting to·sacrifice together with·the crowds.
Mt 11:7 YeShua began to·say to·the crowds concerning John
Mt 12:46 And with·him still speaking to·the crowds, behold,
Mt 13:34 spoke all these·things to·the crowds in parables.
Mt 14:19 and the disciples *gave bread* to·the crowds.
Mt 15:35 ·ordered the crowds to·sit·back upon the soil.
Mt 23:1 Then YeShua spoke to·the crowds and to·his
Mt 26:55 hour, YeShua declared to·the crowds, "Did·yeu·
G3793.1 N-GSM ὄχλου (25x)
Jn 5:13 Jesus carefully·slipped·away, with·a·crowd being in
Jn 7:31 And many from·among the crowd trusted in him and
Jn 7:32 Pharisees heard the crowd grumbling these·things
Jn 7:40 saying, many from·among the crowd were·saying,
Lk 8:4 And with·a·large crowd being·assembled·together,
Lk 9:38 behold, a·man of the crowd shouted·out, saying,
Lk 11:27 a·certain woman from·among the crowd, lifting·up
Lk 12:1 with·the crowd being·completely·gathered of·the
Lk 12:13 someone from·among the crowd declared to·him,
Lk 18:36 And hearing a·crowd traversing·through, he·
Lk 19:3 and was·not able·to for the crowd, because he·was
Lk 19:39 of·the Pharisees from among·the crowd declared to
Lk 22:6 to·hand him over to·them without·any of·the crowd.
Ac 19:33 AlexAnder forward out of·the crowd, with·the Jews
Ac 21:35 the soldiers on·account·of the force of·the crowd.
Ac 24:12 anyone, or making a·turmoil of·a·crowd, neither in
Ac 24:18 Sanctuary·Courtyard, neither with crowd, nor with
Mt 27:24 ·his·own hands fully·in·front of·the crowd, saying,
Mk 7:17 into a·house away·from the crowd, his disciples
Mk 7:33 after·taking him aside from the crowd in private,
Mk 8:1 In those days (with·*the*·crowd being immense and
Mk 9:17 ·man, answering from·among the crowd, declared,
Mk 10:46 his disciples and a·significant crowd, BarTimaeus
Rv 19:1 I·heard a·great voice of·a·large crowd in the heaven,
Rv 19:6 And I·heard as a·voice of·a·large crowd, and as a·
G3793.1 N-GPM ὄχλων (1x)
Lk 11:29 And with·the crowds being·amassed·together, he·
EG3793.1 (4x)
Mt 21:46 crowds, since·now *the crowds* were·holding him
Mt 27:23 But the *crowds* were·yelling·out more·abundantly,
Mk 8:7 *to·his disciples* to·place them also before *the crowd*.
Rv 7:9 was·able to·number, *a·crowd* from·among all nations

G3794 ὀχύρωμα ôchýrōma *n.* (1x)
Roots:G2192 Compare:G4443-1 xLangAlso:H4686
G3794.1 N-GPN ὀχυρωμάτων (1x)
2Co 10:4 in·God to *the* demolition of·strongholds—

G3795 ὀψάριον ôpsáriôn *n.* (5x)
Roots:G3702 G2444-3 Compare:G2485
G3795.2 N-ASN ὀψάριον (2x)
Jn 21:9 and a·small·broiled·fish being·set·out laying·upon
Jn 21:13 *it* to·them, and the small·broiled·fish likewise.
G3795.2 N-APN ὀψάρια (1x)
Jn 6:9 loaves·of·bread, and two small·broiled·fish, but·yet
G3795.2 N-GPN ὀψαρίων (1x)
Jn 6:11 ·out of·the small·broiled·fish as·much·as they·were·
G3795.3 N-GPN ὀψαρίων (1x)
Jn 21:10 "Bring of the small·fry which yeu·caught just·now.

G3796 ὀψέ ôpsé *adv.* (3x)
Roots:G3700 Compare:G2073 G3317 See:G3798 G3694
G3796.2 ADV ὀψέ (1x)
Mt 28:1 And after·the·close of·the·joint·Sabbaths, with·it·
G3796.3 ADV ὀψέ (2x)
Mk 11:19 And when early·evening occurred, he·was·
Mk 13:35 ·the home comes, *whether* at·early·evening, or at·

G3797 ὄψιμος ôpsimôs *adj.* (1x)
Roots:G3796 Compare:G4406 xLangEquiv:H4456
G3797.2 A-ASM ὄψιμον (1x)
Jac 5:7 ·should·receive early·autumn and latter·spring rain.

G3798 ὄψιος ôpsiôs *adj.* (15x)
Roots:G3796 Compare:G2073 G3721
G3798.1 A-GSF ὀψίας (1x)
Mk 11:11 even·now with·the hour being late, he·went·out to
G3798.2 A-NSF ὀψία (1x)
Jn 6:16 Now as early·evening occurred, his disciples walked·
G3798.2 A-GSF ὀψίας (13x)
Jn 20:19 with·it·being *almost* early·evening on·that *same*
Mt 8:16 And with·early·evening occurring, they·brought to·
Mt 14:15 And with·early·evening occurring, his disciples
Mt 14:23 private to·pray, and with·early·evening occurring,
Mt 16:2 ·declared to·them, "With·early·evening occurring,
Mt 20:8 "So with·early·evening occurring, the owner of·the
Mt 26:20 And with·early·evening occurring, he·was·
Mt 27:57 And with·early·evening occurring, there·came a·
Mk 1:32 And with·early·evening occurring, when the sun
Mk 4:35 in the same day, with·early·evening occurring, he·
Mk 6:47 And with·early·evening occurring, the sailboat was
Mk 14:17 And with·early·evening occurring, he·comes with
Mk 15:42 And even·now, with·early·evening occurring,

G3799 ὄψις ôpsis *n.* (3x)
Roots:G3700 Compare:G4383 G2397 G1491 See:G3799-1
G3799.3 N-NSF ὄψις (1x)
Rv 1:16 is·proceeding·forth,' and his appearance *is* as the
G3799.3 N-ASF ὄψιν (1x)
Jn 7:24 ·judge according·to *mere*·appearance, but·rather
G3799.4 N-NSF ὄψις (1x)
Jn 11:44 his facial·appearance had·been·bound·about with·a·

G3799-1 ὄψομαι ôpsômai *v.* (32x)
Roots:G3700 Compare:G3708 See:G3799
G3799-1.2 V-FDI-1S ὄψομαι (2x)
Jn 16:22 now have grief. But I·shall·gaze·upon yeu again,
Heb 13:23 ·released, with whom I·shall·gaze·upon yeu, if
G3799-1.2 V-FDI-1P ὀψόμεθα (1x)
1Jn 3:2 like him, because we·shall·gaze·upon him just·as
G3799-1.2 V-FDI-2S-ATT ὄψει (2x)
Jn 1:50 You·shall·gaze·upon greater·things·than these."
Jn 11:40 if you·should·trust, you·shall·gaze·upon the glory
G3799-1.2 V-FDI-2P ὄψεσθε (10x)
Jn 1:51 this·moment·on, yeu·shall·gaze·upon the heaven
Jn 16:16 again, a·little·while, and yeu·shall·gaze·upon me,
Jn 16:17 again, a·little·while, and yeu·shall·gaze·upon me,'
Jn 16:19 again, a·little·while, and yeu·shall·gaze·upon me'?
Lk 17:22 Son of·Clay·Man†, and yeu·shall·not gaze·upon *it*.
Ac 20:25 the kingdom of·God, shall·gaze·upon my face no·
Mt 26:64 from this·moment·on, yeu·shall·gaze·upon 'the
Mt 28:7 yeu into Galilee. There yeu·shall·gaze·upon him.
Mk 14:62 "I AM, and yeu·shall·gaze·upon the Son of·Clay·
Mk 16:7 into Galilee. There yeu·shall·gaze·upon him, just·
G3799-1.2 V-FDI-3S ὄψεται (4x)
Jn 3:36 ·obstinate to·the Son shall·not gaze·upon life-above,
Lk 3:6 and all flesh shall·gaze·upon the custodial·Salvation
Heb 12:14 not·even·one·man shall·gaze·upon the Lord.
Rv 1:7 ' and 'every eye shall·gaze·upon him, and·also they·
G3799-1.2 V-FDI-3P ὄψονται (9x)
Jn 19:37 says, "'They·shall·gaze·upon him·whom they·
Lk 21:27 "And then they·shall·gaze·upon 'the Son of·Clay·
Ac 2:17 and yeur young·men shall·gaze·upon clear·visions,
Mt 5:8 heart, because they·themselves shall·gaze·upon God.
Mt 24:30 shall·vividly·lament,' and they·shall·gaze·upon '
Mt 28:10 into Galilee, and·there they·shall·gaze·upon me."
Mk 13:26 And at·that·time, they·shall·gaze·upon 'the Son
Rm 15:21 ·detail concerning him, they·shall·gaze·upon *him*,
Rv 22:4 And they·shall·gaze·upon his face, and his name
G3799-1.2 V-ADS-2P ὄψησθε (1x)
Lk 13:28 ·teeth, whenever yeu·should·gaze·upon AbRaham,
G3799-1.3 V-FDI-2S-ATT ὄψει (1x)
Mt 27:4 to us? You·yourself shall·review·the·matter *and be*
G3799-1.3 V-FDI-2P ὄψεσθε (2x)
Ac 18:15 yeu·shall·review·the·matter yeurselves, for I·
Mt 27:24 Yeu·yeurselves shall·review·the·matter *and be*

G3800 ὀψώνιον ôpsōniôn *n.* (4x)
Roots:G3795 Compare:G4620
G3800.2 N-NPN ὀψώνια (1x)
Rm 6:23 For the wages of·Moral·Failure *is* death, but the
G3800.2 N-ASN ὀψώνιον (1x)
2Co 11:8 other Called·Out·citizenries, taking wages *of·them*,
G3800.2 N-DPN ὀψωνίοις (2x)
Lk 3:14 ·false·charges, and be·satisfied with·yeur wages."
1Co 9:7 ·goes·to·war at·any·time with·his·own wages? Who

Ππ - Pi

G3802 παγιδεύω pagidêúō *v.* (1x)
Roots:G3803 Compare:G4624
G3802 V-AAS-3P παγιδεύσωσιν (1x)
Mt 22:15 on·specifically·how they·should·ensnare him in *his*

G3803 παγίς pagís *n.* (5x)
Roots:G4078 Compare:G4625 G1029 See:G3802 xLangAlso:H4170
G3803.1 N-NSF παγίς (1x)
Lk 21:35 "For as a·snare it·shall·come upon all the·ones
G3803.1 N-ASF παγίδα (3x)
Rm 11:9 "Let their table be·made into a·snare, and into a·
1Ti 3:7 fall into reproach and *into* a·snare of·the Slanderer.
1Ti 6:9 ·wealthy fall into a·proof·trial and a·snare, and *into*
G3803.1 N-GSF παγίδος (1x)
2Ti 2:26 of·the Slanderer's snare, having·been·captured·alive

G3804 πάθημα páthēma *n.* (17x)
Roots:G3806 Compare:G2347
G3804.1 N-NPN παθήματα (2x)
Rm 8:18 For I·reckon that the afflictions of·the present
2Co 1:5 Because just·as the afflictions of·the Anointed-One
G3804.1 N-ASN πάθημα (1x)
Heb 2:9 *the* angels on·account·of the affliction of·Death, *but*·
G3804.1 N-APN παθήματα (1x)
1Pe 1:11 ·testifying·beforehand the afflictions *to·come* upon
G3804.1 N-DPN παθήμασιν (3x)
1Pe 4:13 yeu·share in·the afflictions of·the Anointed-One, so
Col 1:24 Now, I·rejoice in my afflictions on·yeur behalf,
2Ti 3:11 *my* persecutions, *and my* afflictions— such·as·what
G3804.1 N-GPN παθημάτων (7x)
Heb 2:10 Salvation completely·mature through afflictions.
Heb 10:32 ·endured a·large struggle of·afflictions—
Php 3:10 of·his afflictions, becoming·fundamentally·like·
1Pe 5:1 and a·witness of·the afflictions of·the Anointed-One,
1Pe 5:9 *that* the same afflictions *are* to·be·further·finished
2Co 1:6 of·the same afflictions which we·ourselves also
2Co 1:7 yeu·are partners of·the afflictions, in·this·manner
EG3804.1 (1x)
Rm 9:17 same·purpose *for affliction* I·fully·awakened you,
G3804.3 N-NPN παθήματα (1x)
Rm 7:5 the flesh, the intense·cravings of·the moral·failures,
G3804.3 N-DPN παθήμασιν (1x)
Gal 5:24 the flesh together with·the intense·cravings and the

Ππ

G3805 παθητός pathētós *adj.* (1x)
Roots:G3806 See:G3804
G3805.2 A-NSM παθητός (1x)
Ac 26:23 Anointed-One *is·to·be* subjected·to·suffering, that

G3806 πάθος páthôs *n.* (3x)
Roots:G3958 Compare:G3804 G2372 See:G3805
G3806.3 N-ASN πάθος (1x)
Col 3:5 ·immorality, impurity, burning·passion, wrong
G3806.3 N-APN πάθη (1x)
Rm 1:26 them over to dishonorable burning·passions, for
G3806.3 N-DSN πάθει (1x)
1Th 4:5 not in *the* burning·passion of·longing, even exactly·

G3807 παιδ•αγωγός paidagōgós *n.* (3x)
Roots:G3816 G0071
G3807.3 N-NSM παιδαγωγός (1x)
Gal 3:24 our strict·elementary·school·teacher *to·bring·us* to
G3807.3 N-ASM παιδαγωγόν (1x)
Gal 3:25 no·longer under a·strict·elementary·school·teacher.
G3807.3 N-APM παιδαγωγούς (1x)
1Co 4:15 ten·thousand strict·elementary·school·teachers in

G3808 παιδάριον paidáriôn *n.* (2x)
Roots:G3816 See:G3813 G3814
G3808 N-NSN παιδάριον (1x)
Jn 6:9 "There·is a little·boy here, who has five barley loaves·
G3808 N-DPN παιδαρίοις (1x)
Mt 11:16 generation? It·is like little·boys sitting·down in

G3809 παιδεία paidêía *n.* (6x)
Roots:G3811 See:G3810 xLangAlso:H4148 H7626
G3809.1 N-NSF παιδεία (1x)
Heb 12:11 all education·and·discipline, particularly·for the
G3809.1 N-ASF παιδείαν (1x)
2Ti 3:16 ·straight, *and* for education·and·discipline (the·one
G3809.1 N-DSF παιδείᾳ (1x)
Eph 6:4 them in *the* education·and·discipline and admonition
G3809.2 N-ASF παιδείαν (1x)
Heb 12:7 If yeu·patiently·endure corrective·discipline, God
G3809.2 N-GSF παιδείας (2x)
Heb 12:5 of·Yahweh's corrective·discipline, nor·even be·
Heb 12:8 completely·apart·from corrective·discipline (of·

G3810 παιδευτής paidêutḗs *n.* (2x)
Roots:G3811 See:G3809
G3810 N-ASF παιδευτήν (1x)
Rm 2:20 an·educator·and·disciplinarian of·impetuous·men,
G3810 N-APM παιδευτάς (1x)
Heb 12:9 of·our flesh, educators·and·disciplinarians, and

G3811 παιδεύω paidêúō *v.* (13x)
Roots:G3816 See:G3809 G3810 xLangAlso:H3256
G3811.1 V-PAP-ASM παιδεύοντα (1x)
2Ti 2:25 educating·and·disciplining with gentleness the·ones
G3811.1 V-PAP-NSF παιδεύουσα (1x)
Tit 2:12 presently·educating·and·disciplining us in·order·that
G3811.1 V-IAI-3P ἐπαίδευον (1x)
Heb 12:10 were·educating·and·disciplining *us* according·to
G3811.1 V-API-3S ἐπαιδεύθη (1x)
Ac 7:22 And Moses was·educated·and·disciplined in·all *the*
G3811.1 V-RPP-NSM πεπαιδευμένος (1x)
Ac 22:3 *and* having·been·educated·and·disciplined *the*
G3811.2 V-PAI-1S παιδεύω (1x)
Rv 3:19 ·for, I·myself reprove and correctively·discipline.
G3811.2 V-PAI-3S παιδεύει (2x)
Heb 12:6 Yahweh loves, he·correctively·disciplines, and he·
Heb 12:7 whom a·father does·not correctively·discipline?
G3811.2 V-PPI-1P παιδευόμεθα (1x)
1Co 11:32 ·judged, we·are·correctively·disciplined by *the*
G3811.2 V-PPP-NPM παιδευόμενοι (1x)
2Co 6:9 we·live, as being·correctively·disciplined and not
G3811.2 V-AAP-NSM παιδεύσας (2x)
Lk 23:16 "Accordingly, after·correctively·disciplining him,
Lk 23:22 "So·then after·correctively·disciplining him, I·
G3811.2 V-APS-3P παιδευθῶσιν (1x)
1Ti 1:20 in·order·that they·may·be·correctively·disciplined

G3812 παιδιό•θεν paidióthên *adv.* (1x)
Roots:G3813
G3812 ADV παιδιόθεν (1x)
Mk 9:21 ·him?" And he·declared, "From·young·childhood.

G3813 παιδίον paidíôn *n.* (53x)
Roots:G3816 G2444-3 Compare:G5043 G5040 G4168 See:G3808 xLangAlso:H2945
G3813.1 N-NSN παιδίον (9x)
Lk 1:66 "What then shall this little·child be?
Lk 1:80 And the little·child was·growing, and was·
Lk 2:40 And the little·child was·growing and was·becoming·
Lk 18:17 accept the kingdom of·God as a·little·child, no,
Mt 2:9 until it·stood·still up·above where the little·child was.
Mt 18:4 should·humble himself as this little·child, this·one is
Mk 5:39 and weeping? The little·child is·not dead, but·
Mk 5:40 ·in where the little·child was reclining·as·a·corpse.
Mk 10:15 kingdom of·God as·though *he·is* a·little·child, no,
G3813.1 N-NPN παιδία (5x)
Lk 11:7 has·been·shut, and my little·children are with me in
Heb 2:13 I·myself and the little·children which God gave
Heb 2:14 the little·children have·a·common·fellowship of·
Mt 19:13 Then little·children were·brought to·him in·order·
1Co 14:20 be not little·children in·the contemplations, but·
G3813.1 N-VSN παιδίον (1x)
Lk 1:76 "And you, little·child, shall·be·called a·prophet of·
G3813.1 N-VPN παιδία (3x)
Jn 21:5 Jesus says to·them, "Little·children, ¿! do·yeu·have
1Jn 2:13 I·presently·write to·yeu, little·children, because
1Jn 2:18 Little·children, it·is *the* last hour.
G3813.1 N-ASN παιδίον (16x)
Jn 4:49 "Sir, walk·down prior·to my little·child dying."
Jn 16:21 she·may·birth the little·child, she·remembers the
Lk 1:59 *that* they·came to·circumcise the little·child, and
Lk 2:21 days were·fulfilled to·circumcise the little·child, his
Lk 2:27 the parents brought in the little·child Jesus, to·do
Lk 9:48 "Whoever should·accept this little·child in my name
Heb 11:23 ·that they·saw *he·was* a·handsome little·child; and
Mt 2:11 home, they·found the little·child with Mariam his
Mt 2:13 ·awakened, personally·take the little·child and his
Mt 2:13 to·seek the little·child to·completely·destroy him."
Mt 2:14 he·personally·took the little·child and his mother
Mt 2:20 ·awakened, personally·take the little·child and his
Mt 2:21 he·personally·took the little·child and his mother
Mt 18:2 And YeShua, summoning a·little·child, set him in
Mt 18:5 should·accept one such little·child in my name
Mk 9:36 And taking a·little·child, he·set him in *the* midst of·
G3813.1 N-APN παιδία (5x)
Lk 18:16 declared, "Allow the little·children to·come to·me,
Mt 18:3 ·back and should·become as the little·children, no,
Mt 19:14 declared, "Allow the little·children, and do·not
Mk 10:13 And they·were·bringing little·children to·him, that
Mk 10:14 to·them, "Allow the little·children to·come to·me,
G3813.1 N-DPN παιδίοις (1x)
Lk 7:32 "They·are like little·children, the·ones sitting·down
G3813.1 N-GSN παιδίου (7x)
Lk 2:17 being·spoken to·them concerning this little·child.
Lk 9:47 of·their heart, grabbing·hold of·a·little·child, he·set
Mt 2:8 ·inquiring precisely concerning the little·child; and
Mt 2:20 for the·ones seeking the little·child's soul have·died.
Mk 5:40 he·personally·takes the little·child's father and
Mk 5:41 ·taking·secure·hold of·the little·child by·the hand,
Mk 9:24 the father of·the little·child, yelling·out with tears,
G3813.1 N-GPN παιδίων (4x)
Mt 14:21 men, apart·from women and little·children.
Mt 15:38 men, apart·from women and little·children.
Mk 7:28 table eat from the young·children's little·crumbs."
Mk 9:37 ·accept one of·the little·children such·as·these in
EG3813.1 (2x)
Mk 9:20 And they·brought *the little·child* to him, and upon·
Mk 9:20 the spirit convulsed *the little·child*. And falling upon

G3814 παιδίσκη paidískē *n.* (14x)
Roots:G3816 Compare:G0010-4 See:G3808 xLangAlso:H5291 H8198
G3814.2 N-NSF παιδίσκη (5x)
Jn 18:17 So·then the servant·girl (the doorkeeper) says to·
Lk 22:56 ·intently at·him, a·certain servant·girl declared,
Ac 12:13 door of·the gate, a·servant·girl (Rhoda by·name)
Mt 26:69 and one servant·girl came·alongside him, saying,
Mk 14:69 And the servant·girl, after·seeing him again, began
G3814.2 N-ASF παιδίσκην (1x)
Ac 16:16 to prayer, *that* a·certain servant·girl having a·spirit
G3814.2 N-APF παιδίσκας (1x)
Lk 12:45 the servant·boys and the servant·girls, and to·eat
G3814.2 N-GPF παιδισκῶν (1x)
Mk 14:66 of·the servant·girls of·the designated·high·priest.
EG3814.2 (1x)
Mt 26:71 to the gate·*area*, another *servant·girl* saw him and
G3814.3 N-ASF παιδίσκην (1x)
Gal 4:30 say? "Cast·out the maidservant and her son, for
G3814.3 N-GSF παιδίσκης (4x)
Gal 4:22 sons, one birthed·from·out the maidservant, and one
Gal 4:23 ·out of·the maidservant has·been·born according·to
Gal 4:30 son, for the son of·the maidservant, no, should·not
Gal 4:31 we·are not children of·a·maidservant, but·rather

G3815 παίζω paízō *v.* (1x)
Roots:G3816 Compare:G1070 See:G1702 xLangAlso:H6711
G3815.3 V-PAN παίζειν (1x)
1Co 10:7 and to·drink, and they·rose·up to·sexually·play."

G3816 παῖς paîs *n.* (25x)
Roots:G3817 Compare:G5043 See:G3813 G3814 G3815 xLangAlso:H5288 H5650

G3816.1 N-NSM παῖς (3x)
Jn 4:51 and announced *to·him*, saying, "Your boy lives."
Lk 2:43 their returning·back, the boy Jesus remained·behind
Mt 17:18 And the boy was·both·relieved·and·cured from

G3816.1 N-ASM παῖδα (2x)
Lk 9:42 impure spirit and healed the boy, and he·gave him
Ac 20:12 And they·brought the boy *home* being·alive, and

G3816.1 N-APM παῖδας (2x)
Mt 2:16 *soldiers*, he·eliminated all the boys, the·ones in
Mt 21:15 that he·did and·also the boys yelling·out in the

EG3816.1 (1x)
Mt 21:16 "Do·you·hear what these *boys* are·saying?

G3816.2 N-NSF παῖς (1x)
Lk 8:54 ·the hand, hollered·out, saying, "Girl, be·awake."

G3816.2 N-GSF παιδός (1x)
Lk 8:51 and John, and the father and the mother of·the girl.

G3816.3 N-NSM παῖς (5x)
Lk 7:7 with·a·word, and my servant·boy shall·be·healed.
Mt 8:6 "Lord, my servant·boy has·been·cast paralyzed *on a·*
Mt 8:8 declare a·word, and my servant·boy shall·be·healed.
Mt 8:13 And his servant·boy was·healed in the *very* same
Mt 12:18 "Behold my servant·boy, whom I·decidedly·chose

G3816.3 N-ASM παῖδα (3x)
Ac 3:13 fathers,' he·glorified his·own servant·boy, Jesus,
Ac 3:26 God, after·raising·up his·own servant·boy Jesus,
Ac 4:27 ·together against your holy servant·boy Jesus whom

G3816.3 N-APM παῖδας (1x)
Lk 12:45 and should·begin to·beat the servant·boys and the

G3816.3 N-DPM παισίν (1x)
Mt 14:2 and declared to·his servant·boys, "This is John the

G3816.3 N-GSM παιδός (4x)
Lk 1:54 "He·helped·and·supported his servant·boy IsraEl,
Lk 1:69 for·us in the house of·his servant·boy David,
Ac 4:25 ·one, through *the* mouth of·your servant·boy David,
Ac 4:30 through the name of·your holy servant·boy, Jesus."

G3816.3 N-GPM παίδων (1x)
Lk 15:26 summoning one of·his servant·boys, he·inquired

G3817 παίω paíō *v.* (5x)
Compare:G5180 G3960 G4141 G4474 G2693

G3817.1 V-AAI-3S ἔπαισεν (2x)
Jn 18:10 Simon Peter drew it and struck the slave of·the
Mk 14:47 upon·drawing the dagger, struck the slave of·the

G3817.1 V-AAP-NSM παίσας (2x)
Lk 22:64 "Prophesy, who is the·one striking you?
Mt 26:68 O·Anointed-One, who is the·one striking you?

G3817.1 V-AAS-3S παίσῃ (1x)
Rv 9:5 whenever he·should·strike a·man·of·clay†.

G3819 πάλαι pálai *adv.* (6x)
Roots:G3825 Compare:G4218 G4386 G4413 See:G1597 G3820

G3819.1 ADV πάλαι (3x)
Lk 10:13 in yeu, long·ago they·would·have repented,
Heb 1:1 and with·many·methods long·ago to·the fathers by
Mt 11:21 and Tsidon, long·ago they·would·have repented in

G3819.2 ADV πάλαι (1x)
Mk 15:44 ·of him whether he·died long·before·now.

G3819.3 ADV πάλαι (1x)
Jud 1:4 having·been·previously·written·about of·antiquity to

G3819.4 ADV πάλαι (1x)
2Pe 1:9 of·the purification from·his former moral·failures.

G3820 παλαιός palaiós *adj.* (19x)
Roots:G3819 See:G3821 G3822 xLangAlso:A6268 H5769 H3453

G3820.1 A-NSM παλαιός (2x)
Lk 5:39 fresh·new *wine*, for he·says, 'The old is finer *wine*.
Rm 6:6 our old man·of·clay† is·already·crucified·together

G3820.1 A-NSF παλαιά (1x)
1Jn 2:7 from *the* beginning. The old commandment is the

G3820.1 A-ASM παλαιόν (3x)
Lk 5:39 not·even·one·man drinking old *wine* immediately
Eph 4:22 yeu to·put·off the old man·of·clay† according·to
Col 3:9 ·already·stripped·off the old man·of·clay† together

G3820.1 A-ASF παλαιάν (2x)
1Co 5:7 Accordingly, purge·out the old leaven in·order·that
1Jn 2:7 to·yeu, but·rather an·old commandment which yeu·

G3820.1 A-ASN παλαιόν (1x)
Lk 5:36 *from* a·brand-new garment upon an·old garment;

G3820.1 A-APM παλαιούς (3x)
Lk 5:37 casts fresh·new wine into old wineskins. But·if·so,
Mt 9:17 do·men·cast fresh·new wine into old wineskins.
Mk 2:22 casts fresh·new wine into old wineskins. But·if·so,

G3820.1 A-APN παλαιά (1x)
Mt 13:52 *things* brand-new and old *to·share with·others*."

G3820.1 A-DSF παλαιᾷ (1x)
1Co 5:8 ·observe·the·sacred·feast, not with old leaven, nor·

G3820.1 A-DSN παλαιῷ (3x)
Lk 5:36 *garment*, does·not mutually·agree with·the old·one.
Mt 9:16 a·patch of·unprocessed cloth onto an·old garment,
Mk 2:21 a·patch of·unprocessed cloth on an·old garment,

G3820.1 A-GSF παλαιᾶς (1x)
2Co 3:14 upon the reading·aloud of·the old covenant; *it·is*

G3820.1 A-GSN παλαιοῦ (1x)
Mk 2:21 takes·away its complete·fullness from·the old, and

G3821 παλαιότης palaiótēs *n.* (1x)
Roots:G3820 Compare:G2538

G3821.1 N-DSF παλαιότητι (1x)
Rm 7:6 of·spirit, and not in·oldness of·*the*·letter.

G3822 παλαιόω palaióō *v.* (4x)
Roots:G3820

G3822.2 V-FPI-3P παλαιωθήσονται (1x)
Heb 1:11 they·all shall·become·old·and·worn·out as *does* a·

G3822.2 V-PPP-APN παλαιούμενα (1x)
Lk 12:33 pouches not becoming·old·and·worn·out, *but ones·*

G3822.3 V-RAI-3S πεπαλαίωκεν (1x)
Heb 8:13 *covenant*," he·has·made·obsolete the first

G3822.4 V-PPP-NSN παλαιούμενον (1x)
Heb 8:13 Now the·thing presently·being·made·obsolete and

G3822-5 παλάμη palámē *n.* (2x)
Compare:G5495 xLangEquiv:H3709

G3822-5.1 N-GPF παλάμῃ (2x)
Lk 4:11 ·shall·lift you upon *their* palms, lest·at·any·time
Mt 4:6 They·shall·lift you upon *their* palms, lest·at·any·time

G3823 πάλη pálē *n.* (1x)
Roots:G3825-2 Compare:G0119 See:G3825

G3823 N-NSF πάλη (1x)
Eph 6:12 it·is not for·our wrestling specifically·against blood

G3824 παλιγ•γενεσία palingênêsía *n.* (2x)
Roots:G3825 G1078 Compare:G0342 G0365 G0605 G1357 G2676

G3824.2 N-GSF παλιγγενεσίας (1x)
Tit 3:5 through a·bath of·regeneration and a·renewing of·

G3824.3 N-DSF παλιγγενεσίᾳ (1x)
Mt 19:28 me, in The Regeneration whenever the Son of·

G3825 πάλιν pálin *adv.* (142x)
Roots:G3825-2 Compare:G0509 See:G1597 G3823

G3825.1 ADV πάλιν (141x)
Jn 1:35 Again, on·the next·day, John stood also *with* two
Jn 4:3 he·left Judea and went·off again into Galilee.
Jn 4:13 drinking from·out of·this water shall·thirst again.
Jn 4:46 In·due·course, Jesus came again into Qanah of·
Jn 4:54 This *is* again *the* second miraculous·sign *that* Jesus
Jn 6:15 him king, he·departed again to·a·mountain alone *by*
Jn 8:2 And with·*the*·sunrise, he·came·directly again into the
Jn 8:8 And again after·stooping down, he·was·writing into
Jn 8:12 In·due·course, Jesus spoke again to·them, saying, "I
Jn 8:21 In·due·course, Jesus declared again to·them, "I·
Jn 9:15 Now·then, the Pharisees again also were·asking·of
Jn 9:17 They·say to·the blind·man again, "What·do you·
Jn 9:26 Then they·declared to·him again, "What·did he·do
Jn 9:27 Why·do yeu·want to·hear *it* again? "¿!·Do yeu·
Jn 10:7 So·then Jesus declared to·them again, "Certainly,
Jn 10:17 lay·down my soul in·order·that I·may·take it again.
Jn 10:18 it down, and I·have authority to·take it again. This
Jn 10:19 there·was a·severing·schism again among the
Jn 10:31 stones again in·order·that they·should·stone him.
Jn 10:39 they·were·seeking again to·apprehend him. But
Jn 10:40 And he·went·away again beyond the Jordan into the
Jn 11:7 "We·should·head·out into Judea again."
Jn 11:8 to·stone you, and do·you·head·on·out there again?"
Jn 11:38 Accordingly, Jesus, again being·exasperated in
Jn 12:22 *this* to·Andrew, and again Andrew and Philip relay
Jn 12:28 "Both I·glorified *it*, and I·shall·glorify *it* again."
Jn 12:39 ·not able to·trust, because *as* IsaIah declared again,
Jn 13:12 his garments, after·sitting·back again, he·declared
Jn 14:3 for·yeu, I·come again and shall·personally·receive
Jn 16:16 yeu·do·not observe me, and again, a·little·while,
Jn 16:17 yeu·do·not observe me, and again, a·little·while,
Jn 16:19 yeu·do·not observe me, and again, a·little·while,
Jn 16:22 But I·shall·gaze·upon yeu again, and yeur heart
Jn 16:28 have·come into the world. Again, I·leave the world
Jn 18:7 So·then he·inquired·of them again, "Whom·do yeu·
Jn 18:27 Peter denied *it* again, and immediately a·rooster
Jn 18:33 into the Praetorian·hall again and hollered·out·for
Jn 18:38 And after·declaring this, he·went·out again to the
Jn 18:40 So·then they·all yelled·out again, saying, "Not this·
Jn 19:4 Pilate went·forth outside again and says to·them,
Jn 19:9 and he·entered again into the Praetorian·hall and says
Jn 19:37 And again another Scripture says, "They·shall·
Jn 20:10 the disciples went·off again to·their·own *homes*.
Jn 20:21 Now·then, Jesus declared to·them again, "Peace
Jn 20:26 And after eight days, again his disciples were
Jn 21:1 Jesus made himself apparent again to·the disciples at
Jn 21:16 He·says to·him again a·second·time, "Simon, *son*
Lk 13:20 And again he·declared, "To·what shall·I·liken the
Lk 23:20 to·fully·release Jesus, Pilate addressed *them* again.
Ac 10:15 And a·voice *spoke* to him again for a·second·time,
Ac 10:16 and the vessel was·taken·up again into the heaven
Ac 11:10 and absolutely·all *of·it* was·drawn·up again into the
Ac 17:32 "We·shall·hear you again concerning this *matter*.
Ac 18:21 in JeruSalem, but I·shall·return·back again to yeu,
Ac 27:28 and dropping·the·measuring·line again, they·found
Heb 1:5 have·begotten you"? And again, "I·myself shall·
Heb 1:6 And again, whenever he·should·bring the Firstborn
Heb 2:13 And again, " I·myself shall·be having·confidence
Heb 2:13 ·confidence on him." And again, "Behold, I·
Heb 4:5 And in this *passage* again, "As·if they·shall·*ever*·
Heb 4:7 again he·specifically·determined a·certain day,
Heb 5:12 to·instruct yeu again *about* certain·things·which
Heb 6:1 ·of maturity; not laying·down again *the* foundation
Heb 6:6 to·reinstate·and·renew·them again to repentance,
Heb 10:30 ' says Yahweh. And again, "Yahweh shall·
Gal 1:9 ·stated, so at·this·moment I·say again, if any·man
Gal 1:17 into Arabia, and again returned·back to Damascus.
Gal 2:1 fourteen years, I·walked·up again to JeruSalem with
Gal 2:18 "For if I·build again these·things which I·
Gal 4:9 God, how·is·it *that* yeu·return again to the weak and
Gal 4:9 to·be·slaves, *once* again starting·over·from·the·top?
Gal 4:19 ·whom I·experience·birthing·pain again even·until
Gal 5:1 us free, and do·not again be·held·in by·a·yoke of·
Gal 5:3 And I·attest again to·every man·of·clay† being·
Mt 4:7 was·replying to·him, "Again, it·has·been·written,
Mt 4:8 Again, the Slanderer personally·takes him up to a·
Mt 5:33 "Again, yeu·heard that it·was·uttered to·the ancient·
Mt 13:44 "Again, the kingdom of·the heavens is like treasure
Mt 13:45 "Again, the kingdom of·the heavens is like a·man·
Mt 13:47 "Again, the kingdom of·the heavens is like a·
Mt 18:19 "Again I·say to·yeu, that if two of·yeu should·
Mt 19:24 "And again I·say to·yeu, it·is easier *for* a·camel to·
Mt 20:5 Again, going·forth about *the* sixth and ninth hour,
Mt 21:36 Again, he·dispatched other slaves more·than at·the
Mt 22:1 YeShua declared to·them again by parables, saying,
Mt 22:4 "Again, he·dispatched other slaves, saying,
Mt 26:42 Again for a·second·time, after·going·off, he·
Mt 26:43 coming, he·finds them sleeping again, for their

Mt 26:44 And leaving them, going·off again, he·prayed for
Mt 26:72 And again he·denied *it* with an·oath, "I·do·not
Mt 27:50 YeShua, after·yelling·out again with·a·loud voice,
Mk 2:1 And again he·entered into CaperNaum after *some*
Mk 2:13 And he·went·forth again beside the sea, and all the
Mk 3:1 And he·entered again into the gathering, and there·
Mk 3:20 And a·crowd was·coming·together again, such·for
Mk 4:1 Then he·began again to·instruct directly·by the sea.
Mk 5:21 And with·Jesus crossing·over again in the sailboat
Mk 7:31 And again, going·forth from·among the borders of·
Mk 8:13 embarking into the sailboat again, he·went·off to
Mk 8:25 After·that, *Jesus* again laid his hands upon his eyes
Mk 10:1 of·the Jordan, and again, crowds were·traversing·
Mk 10:1 toward him, and again, as he·had·been·accustomed
Mk 10:10 his disciples inquired·of him again concerning the
Mk 10:24 But Jesus, answering again, says to·them,
Mk 10:32 And personally·taking again the twelve, he·began
Mk 11:27 And they·come again to JeruSalem. And with·him
Mk 12:4 And again he·dispatched another slave to them, and
Mk 12:5 And again he·dispatched another, and·this·one·also
Mk 14:39 And again, after·going·off, he·prayed, declaring
Mk 14:40 ·back, he·found them sleeping again for their eyes
Mk 14:61 ·even·one·thing. Again the designated·high·priest
Mk 14:69 servant·girl, after·seeing him again, began to·say
Mk 14:70 And he·was·denying *it* again. And a·little·while
Mk 14:70 ·ones standing·nearby were·saying again to·Peter,
Mk 15:4 And Pilate inquired·of him again, saying, "Do·you·
Mk 15:12 And responding, Pilate declared again to·them,
Mk 15:13 And they·yelled·out again, "Crucify him!"
Rm 8:15 yeu·did·not receive a·spirit of·slavery again to fear,
Rm 11:23 ·grafted·in, for God is able to·engraft them again.
Rm 15:10 And again he·says, "" Be·merry, O·Gentiles, with
Rm 15:11 And again, ""Splendidly·praise Yahweh, all the
Rm 15:12 And again, IsaIah says, "" There·shall·be the root
Jac 5:18 And he·prayed again, and the sky gave rain, and the
Php 1:26 in Jesus Anointed through my arrival to yeu again.
Php 2:28 in·order·that seeing him again, yeu·may·rejoice,
Php 4:4 in *the* Lord always, *and* again I·shall·declare,
2Pe 2:20 *they* once·again are·being·entangled in·these·things
1Co 3:20 And again, "Yahweh knows the deliberations of·
1Co 7:5 should·come·together in·unison again, in·order·that
1Co 12:21 no need of·you," nor again the head to·the feet,
2Co 1:16 Macedonia, and to·come again from Macedonia to
2Co 2:1 this for·my·own·self, not again to·come to yeu in
2Co 3:1 Do·we·begin again to·commend ourselves?
2Co 5:12 For not again do·we·commend ourselves to·yeu,
2Co 10:7 let·him·reckon this again for himself; because
2Co 11:16 Again I·say, not anyone should·suppose me to·be
2Co 12:19 Again, do·yeu·suppose that we·make·our·defense
2Co 12:21 *And* lest, after·coming again, my God may·
2Co 13:2 if I·should·come into the *vicinity* again, I·shall·not
Rv 10:8 heaven *was* speaking with me again, and saying,
Rv 10:11 ·mandatory·for you to·prophesy again over many

G3825.4 ADV πάλιν (1x)

1Jn 2:8 On·the·other·hand, a·brand-new commandment I·

G3826 παμ•πληθεί pamplēthêí *adv.* (1x)

Roots:G3956 G4128

G3826.2 ADV παμπληθεί (1x)

Lk 23:18 And altogether·at·once, they·screamed·out, saying,

G3827 πάμ•πολυς pámpolys *adj.* (1x)

Roots:G3956 G4183 Compare:G5246

G3827 A-GSM παμπόλλου (1x)

Mk 8:1 days (with·*the*·crowd being immense and not having

G3828 Παμ•φυλία Pamphylía *n/l.* (5x)

Roots:G3956 G5443 See:G5561

G3828.2 N/L-ASF Παμφυλίαν (3x)

Ac 2:10 also *in* Phrygia and PamPhylia, *in* Egypt and *in* the
Ac 14:24 ·throughout Pisidia, they·came to PamPhylia.
Ac 27:5 adjacent·to Cilicia and PamPhylia, we·came·down

G3828.2 N/L-GSF Παμφυλίας (2x)

Ac 13:13 *him*) came to Perga in·PamPhylia. And departing
Ac 15:38 withdrawing from them from PamPhylia and not

G3829 παν•δοχεῖον pandôchêîon *n.* (1x)

Roots:G3956 G1209 Compare:G2646 See:G3830

G3829.2 N-ASN πανδοχεῖον (1x)

Lk 10:34 he·brought him to an·inn and took·care of·him.

G3830 παν•δοχεύς pandôchêús *n.* (1x)

Roots:G3956 G1209 See:G3829

G3830 N-DSM πανδοχεῖ (1x)

Lk 10:35 he·gave *them* to·the innkeeper, and declared to·

G3831 παν•ήγυρις panḗgyris *n.* (1x)

Roots:G3956 G0058 Compare:G0421-1 G1859 G1840-5 xLangAlso:H6116 H4150

G3831.2 N-DSF πανηγύρει (1x)

Heb 12:23 to·a·national,·festive·assembly, and to·a·Called·

G3832 παν•οικί panôikí *adv.* (1x)

Roots:G3956 G3624

G3832 ADV πανοικί (1x)

Ac 16:34 with·the·whole·household having·trusted in·God.

G3833 παν•οπλία panôplía *n.* (3x)

Roots:G3956 G3696

G3833 N-ASF πανοπλίαν (3x)

Lk 11:22 he·takes·away his whole·armor in which he·had·
Eph 6:11 Dress·yeurselves·with the whole·armor of·God,
Eph 6:13 that, take·up the whole·armor of·God in·order·that

G3834 παν•ουργία panôurgía *n.* (5x)

Roots:G3835 Compare:G2940 G3180 xLangAlso:H6195

G3834.2 N-ASF πανουργίαν (1x)

Lk 20:23 fully·observing their shrewd·cunning, he·declared

G3834.2 N-DSF πανουργίᾳ (4x)

1Co 3:19 entrapping the wise in their·own shrewd·cunning.""
2Co 4:2 not walking in shrewd·cunning nor·even handling
2Co 11:3 Eve by his shrewd·cunning, in·this·manner yeur
Eph 4:14 *and* by *the* shrewd·cunning pertaining·to the

G3835 παν•οῦργος panôûrgôs *n.* (1x)

Roots:G3956 G2041 See:G3834

G3835.3 N-NSM πανοῦργος (1x)

2Co 12:16 inherently·being shrewdly·cunning, I·took·hold·

G3836 παν•ταχό•θεν pantachṓthên *adv.* (1x)

Roots:G3837

G3836 ADV πανταχόθεν (1x)

Mk 1:45 places, and they·came to him from·everywhere.

G3837 παν•ταχοῦ pantachôû *adv.* (7x)

Roots:G3956

G3837 ADV πανταχοῦ (7x)

Lk 9:6 ·news, and both·relieving·and·curing everywhere.
Ac 17:30 charges all the men·of·clay† everywhere to·repent.
Ac 21:28 ·clay† instructing all·men everywhere against the
Ac 24:3 ·of thanksgiving both everywhere and in·every·way,
Ac 28:22 known to·us that everywhere it·is·spoken·against."
Mk 16:20 officially·proclaimed *it* everywhere, with·the Lord
1Co 4:17 just·as I·instruct everywhere among every Called·

G3838 παν•τελής pantêlḗs *adj.* (2x)

Roots:G3956 G5056

G3838.2 A-ASN παντελές (1x)

Lk 13:11 ·able to·pull·herself·up·straight to the full·height.

G3838.4 A-ASN παντελές (1x)

Heb 7:25 also to·save·them to the uttermost (the·ones who·

G3839 πάντη pántē *adv.* (1x)

Roots:G3956

G3839 ADV πάντη (1x)

Ac 24:3 both everywhere and in·every·way, most·noble

G3840 πάντο•θεν pántôthên *adv.* (2x)

Roots:G3956

G3840.2 ADV πάντοθεν (1x)

Heb 9:4 having·been·overlaid on·all·sides with·gold, in

G3840.3 ADV πάντοθεν (1x)

Lk 19:43 you, and shall·confine you on·every·side,

G3841 παντο•κράτωρ pantôkrátōr *n.* (10x)

Roots:G3956 G2904 Compare:G4522-2 xLangEquiv:H7706

G3841 N-NSM παντοκράτωρ (8x)

2Co 6:18 sons and daughters,"" says Yahweh Almighty.
Rv 1:8 ·was, and the·one who·is·coming, the Almighty."
Rv 4:8 *is* Yahweh, *El Shaddai* God Almighty, the·one who·
Rv 11:17 to·you, O·Yahweh, God Almighty, the·one being,
Rv 15:3 works, O·Yahweh, God Almighty. Righteous and
Rv 16:7 Yes, O·Yahweh, God Almighty, true and righteous
Rv 19:6 Because Yahweh, God Almighty, reigns.
Rv 21:22 for Yahweh, *El Shaddai* God Almighty, and the

G3841 N-GSM παντοκράτορος (2x)

Rv 16:14 to the battle of·that great day of·God Almighty.
Rv 19:15 wine of·the Rage and the Wrath of·God Almighty.

G3842 πάντ•ο•τε pántôtê *adv.* (42x)

Roots:G3956 G3753 Compare:G0104 G1539

G3842.1 ADV πάντοτε (40x)

Jn 6:34 ·declared to him, "Lord, always give us this bread.
Jn 7:6 is·not·yet here, but yeur season is always ready.
Jn 8:29 alone, because I·myself always do the·things *that*·
Jn 11:42 ·personally·known that you·hear me always, but·yet
Jn 12:8 For yeu always have the helplessly·poor among
Jn 12:8 But me, yeu·have not always."
Jn 18:20 to·the world. I·myself always instructed in the
Jn 18:20 ·Atrium where the Judeans always come·together.
Lk 15:31 'Child, you·yourself are always with me, and all
Lk 18:1 *·purpose* it·is·to·be·mandatory always to·pray and
Heb 7:25 through him), always living to make·intercession
Gal 4:18 But *it·is* good to·be·zealous always in *a* good *thing*,
Mt 26:11 For yeu always have the helplessly·poor among
Mt 26:11 yeurselves, but me, yeu·do·not always have.
Mk 14:7 For yeu always have the helplessly·poor among
Mk 14:7 But me, yeu·have not always.
Rm 1:10 always in my prayers.
Php 1:4 always in every petition of·mine on·behalf of·yeu all
Php 1:20 with all clarity·of·speech (as always, *so* now also),
Php 2:12 just·as yeu·listened·and·obeyed always (not as in
Php 4:4 Rejoice in *the* Lord always, *and* again I·shall·declare
1Th 1:2 We·give·thanks to·God always concerning all of·
1Th 3:6 ·good remembrance of·us always, greatly·yearning
1Th 4:17 we·shall·be always together with·*the*·Lord.
1Th 5:15 wrong to·any *man*; but·rather always pursue the
1Th 5:16 Rejoice always.
2Th 1:3 to·give·thanks to·God always concerning yeu,
2Th 1:11 For which also we·pray always concerning yeu,
2Th 2:13 ·indebted to·give·thanks always to·God concerning
1Co 1:4 I·give·thanks to·my God always concerning yeu for
1Co 15:58 unstirrable·from *the Trust*, always abounding in
2Co 2:14 *be* to·God— the·one always causing us to·triumph
2Co 4:10 always carrying·about in the body the mortal·
2Co 5:6 exercising·courage always even while·personally·
Eph 5:20 giving·thanks always on·behalf of·all·things *to·our*
Col 1:3 Jesus Anointed, praying always concerning yeu,
Col 4:6 Yeur conversation always *is to·be* with grace having·
Col 4:12 greets yeu, always striving on·yeur behalf in the
Phm 1:4 God, making mention of·you always in my prayers,
2Ti 3:7 always learning, and·yet never·even being·able to·

G3842.2 ADV πάντοτε (2x)

1Th 2:16 *these same Judeans* at·all·times to·utterly·fulfill *the*
2Co 9:8 in all *things* at·all·times, yeu·may·abound to every

G3843 πάντως pántōs *adv.* (9x)

Roots:G3956

G3843.1 ADV πάντως (2x)

1Co 5:10 not altogether with·the sexually·immoral·people
1Co 9:10 Or does·he·say *this* altogether on·account·of·us?

G3843.2 ADV πάντως (4x)

Lk 4:23 to them, "Entirely, yeu·shall·declare to·me this
Ac 21:22 ·binding·for a·multitude entirely to·come·together,
Ac 28:4 "This man·of·clay† is entirely a·murderer, whom,
1Co 16:12 yeu with the brothers, yet entirely, it·was not *the*

G3843.3 ADV πάντως (2x)

Ac 18:21 "It·is·mandatory·for me by·all·means to·make the
1Co 9:22 things in·order·that by·all·means I·may·save some.

G3843.4 ADV πάντως (1x)

Rm 3:9 No, by·no·means, for we·already·legally·charged

G3844 παρά pará *prep.* (201x)
παρ- par- [alternate prefix]
Compare:G4314 G3326

EG3844 (1x)
Jn 13:3 has·given all·things to·him, *directly* into his hands,

G3844.1 PREP παρά (6x)
Jn 19:25 Now *these women* stood near the cross of·Jesus:
Lk 9:47 ·hold of·a·little·child, he·set him near himself
Ac 7:16 purchased for·a·price of·silver·pieces near the Sons
Mt 4:18 And while·walking near the Sea of·Galilee, YeShua
Mt 15:29 ·on from·there, YeShua came near·to the Sea of·
Mk 3:21 And the·ones near *of·kin·to* him, hearing *of·it*, went·

G3844.2 PREP παρ´ (1x)
Lk 11:37 ·such·a·manner·so·that he·should·dine next·to him.

G3844.3 PREP παρά (6x)
Ac 16:13 we·went·forth outside of·the city beside a·river,
Heb 11:12 as the innumerable sand beside the shoreline of·
Mt 13:1 from the home, was·sitting·down beside the sea.
Mt 20:30 two blind·men are·sitting·down beside the roadway
Mk 1:16 And walking beside the Sea of·Galilee, he·saw
Mk 2:13 And he·went·forth again beside the sea, and all the

G3844.4 PREP παρά (15x)
Jn 1:14 as of·the·only·begotten directly·from *the* Father), full
Jn 1:40 him and already·hearing directly·from John.
Jn 7:51 unless it·should·hear directly·from him beforehand,
Lk 1:37 because any utterance directly·from God shall·not
Lk 1:45 having·been·spoken to·her directly·from Yahweh."
Lk 2:1 ·went·forth a·decree directly·from Caesar Augustus,
Lk 6:19 because power came·forth directly·from him and
Lk 8:49 there·comes someone directly·from *the house·of*
Mt 2:4 people, he·was·inquiring directly·from them where
Mt 21:42 *stone*. This came·to·be directly·from Yahweh, and
Mk 12:2 he·may·receive directly·from the tenant·farmers of
Mk 12:11 This came·to·be directly·from Yahweh, and it·is
Mk 14:43 daggers and staffs, directly·from the chief·priests
Jac 1:27 Directly·from *our* God and Father— pure and
1Th 2:13 God's Redemptive-word of·hearing directly·from us,

G3844.5 PREP παρ´ (61x)
Jn 1:6 ·clay† having·been·dispatched personally·from God.
Jn 4:9 request *some* to·drink personally·from me, being a·
Jn 4:52 So·then he·inquired personally·from them the hour
Jn 5:41 I·do·not receive glory personally·from men·of·clay†,
Jn 5:44 ·trust, receiving glory personally·from one·another,
Jn 5:44 the glory, the·one personally·from the only God?
Jn 6:45 hearing and learning personally·from the Father
Jn 6:46 except the·one being personally·from God; this·one
Jn 7:29 him, because I·am personally·from him. He·likewise
Jn 8:26 these·things which I·heard personally·from him."
Jn 8:40 truth, which I·heard personally·from God. AbRaham
Jn 9:16 "This man·of·clay† is not personally·from God,
Jn 9:33 Except this·man was personally·from God, he·
Jn 10:18 I·received personally·from my Father."
Jn 15:15 all·things that I·heard personally·from my Father I·
Jn 15:26 shall·send to·yeu personally·from the Father, the
Jn 15:26 who proceeds·forth personally·from the Father,
Jn 16:27 that I·myself came·forth personally·from God.
Jn 16:28 "I·came·forth personally·from the Father, and have·
Jn 17:7 ·as you·have·given to·me, are personally·from you,
Jn 17:8 ·knew truly that I·came·forth personally·from you,
Lk 6:34 ·lend *to·them* personally·from whom yeu·expect to·
Lk 11:16 *him*, were·seeking personally·from him a·sign
Lk 12:48 ·whom much is·given, personally·from him much
Ac 2:33 of·the Holy Spirit personally·from the Father, he·
Ac 3:2 the merciful·act·of·charity personally·from the·ones
Ac 3:5 to·receive something personally·from them.
Ac 9:2 he·requested personally·from him letters for
Ac 9:14 he·has authority personally·from the chief·priests
Ac 10:22 and to·hear utterances personally·from you."
Ac 17:9 ·taking the security·bail personally·from Jason and
Ac 20:24 service, which I·received personally·from the Lord
Ac 22:5 all the council·of·elders, personally·from whom I
Ac 24:8 to you, personally·from whom you·shall·be·able,
Ac 26:10 authority personally·from the chief·priests. And
Ac 26:12 and an·executive·charge personally·from the chief·
Ac 26:22 after·obtaining assistance personally·from God, I·
Ac 28:22 to·hear personally·from you what·things you·
Mt 2:7 precisely·ascertained personally·from them the time
Mt 2:16 which he·precisely·ascertained personally·from the
Mt 6:1 a·payment·of·service personally·from yeur Father,
Mt 20:20 and requesting something personally·from him.
Mk 8:11 with·him, seeking personally·from him a·sign from
Jac 1:5 of·wisdom, let·him·request personally·from God,
Jac 1:7 he·shall·receive anything personally·from the Lord.
Php 4:18 accepting personally·from EpAphroditus the·things
Php 4:18 the·things *which·were·sent* personally·from yeu, a·
2Pe 1:17 For he·received personally·from Father God honor
2Th 3:8 ·present did·we·eat personally·from anyone's bread,
1Co 16:2 each·one of·yeu lay *aside* personally·from himself,
Eph 6:8 he·shall·subsequently·obtain personally·from the
2Ti 1:13 which you·heard personally·from me, in trust and
2Ti 1:18 to·him to·find mercy personally·from Yahweh in
2Ti 2:2 ·things·which you·heard personally·from me through
1Jn 3:22 we·may·request, we·receive personally·from him,
1Jn 5:15 *that* we·have·requested personally·from him.
2Jn 1:3 mercy, *and* peace, personally·from Father God, and
2Jn 1:3 Father God, and personally·from *the* Lord Jesus
2Jn 1:4 a·commandment personally·from the Father.
Rv 2:27 have·received *authority* personally·from my Father.
Rv 3:18 ·counsel to·you to·buy personally·from me gold

G3844.6 PREP παρ´ (1x)
Mk 5:26 and expending all her personal belongings with not·

G3844.7 PREP παρά (2x)
Jn 8:38 ·which I·have·clearly·seen from·beside my Father,
Jn 8:38 yeu·have·clearly·seen from·beside yeur father."

G3844.8 PREP παρά (7x)
Jn 5:34 receive the testimony not from a·man·of·clay†, but·
Gal 1:12 neither personally·received it from a·man·of·clay†,
1Th 4:1 YeShua, just·as yeu·personally·received from us,
2Th 3:6 the tradition which he·personally·received from us.
1Co 12:15 ·among the body," ¿! from this *reasoning*, is·it
1Co 12:16 ·among the body," ¿! from this *reasoning*, is·it
2Ti 3:14 having·personally·known from whom you·learned

G3844.9 PREP παρά (1x)
Lk 10:39 Mary, who, sitting·down·near at Jesus' feet, also

G3844.10 PREP παρά (10x)
Lk 7:38 and settling directly·at his feet right·behind *him*
Lk 8:35 had·come·out, sitting·down directly·at the feet of·
Lk 8:41 And falling directly·at the feet of·Jesus, he·was·
Lk 17:16 and he·fell·down on *his* face directly·at his feet,
Ac 4:35 and they·were·laying *them*·down directly·at the
Ac 4:37 the value and laid *it* directly·at the ambassadors' feet
Ac 5:2 portion, he·laid *it* directly·at the ambassadors' feet.
Ac 5:10 And she·fell·down at·once directly·at his feet and
Ac 7:58 laid·aside their garments directly·at the feet of·a·
Mt 15:30 they·quickly·deposited them directly·at the feet of·

G3844.11 PREP παρά (1x)
Ac 22:3 having·been·reared in this city personally·at the feet

G3844.12 PREP παρά (6x)
Lk 1:30 for you·found grace personally·before God.
Lk 2:52 and graciousness personally·before God and men·
Gal 3:11 is·regarded·as·righteous personally·before God,
Rm 2:13 *that·are* righteous personally·before God, but·rather
1Pe 2:20 ·good, this *is* graciousness personally·before God.
2Pe 2:11 a·reviling verdict personally·before Yahweh.

G3844.13 PREP παρά (33x)
Jn 1:39 where he·abides, and they·abided with him that day,
Jn 4:40 him, they·were·asking him to·abide with them, and
Jn 14:23 ·come to him, and shall·make our·abode with him.
Jn 14:25 have·I·spoken to·yeu, while·abiding with yeu.
Jn 17:5 glorify me (*along* with yourself) with·the glory
Jn 17:5 with·the glory which I·was·having with you before
Lk 18:27 ·things *which·are* impossible with men·of·clay† are
Lk 18:27 with men·of·clay† are possible with God."
Lk 19:7 "He·entered to·lodge with a·man *who·is* morally·
Ac 9:43 ·number·of days in Joppa with a·certain Simon, a·
Ac 10:6 This·man is·a·guest *staying* with a·certain·man,
Ac 18:3 of·the same·trade, he·was·abiding with them and
Ac 18:20 *him* to·abide a·longer time with them, he·did·not
Ac 21:7 ·greeting the brothers, we·abided with them one day
Ac 21:8 being from·among the seven), we·abided with him.
Ac 21:16 along·with us, bringing with *them* a·certain·man,
Ac 26:8 Why is·it·judged *to·be* incredible with yeu, that God
Mt 19:26 declared to·them, "With men·of·clay† this is
Mt 19:26 this is impossible, but with God all·things are
Mt 22:25 "Now there·were with us seven brothers, and the
Mk 10:27 Jesus says, "With men·of·clay† *it·is* impossible,
Mk 10:27 *it·is* impossible, but·yet not with God, for with
Mk 10:27 not with God, for with God all·things are possible.
Rm 2:11 For there·is no partiality with God.
Rm 9:14 ·we·state? ¿!·Is·there unrighteousness with God?
Jac 1:17 from the Father of·lights— with whom there·is·not
2Pe 3:8 that "one day *is* with *the* Lord as a·thousand years,
2Th 1:6 since *it·is* a·righteous·thing with God to·recompense
1Co 3:19 wisdom of·this world is foolishness with God. For
1Co 7:24 brothers, in that·*state* he·must·continue with God.
2Co 1:17 according·to flesh, that with me there·should·be
Eph 6:9 in *the* heavens, and there·is not partiality with him.
2Ti 4:13 cape that I·left·behind at Troas with Carpus, *as* you·

G3844.14 PREP παρ´ (1x)
Jn 14:17 him, because he·abides personally·with yeu, and

G3844.15 PREP παρ´ (3x)
Mt 21:25 they·were·deliberating closely·among themselves,
Mt 28:15 is·widely·promoted closely·among Judeans so·far·
Rv 2:13 martyr, who was·killed closely·among yeu, where

G3844.16 PREP παρά (14x)
Lk 5:1 he·himself was standing directly·by the lake of·
Lk 5:2 sailboats having·settled directly·by the lake's·edge;
Lk 8:5 *·was* that·which in·fact fell directly·by the roadway,
Lk 8:12 "And the·ones directly·by the roadway are the·ones
Lk 18:35 blind·man sat·down directly·by the roadway
Ac 10:6 a·tanner, whose home is directly·by *the* sea. This·
Ac 10:32 *the* home of·Simon, a·tanner, directly·by *the* sea.'
Mt 13:4 in·fact, some *seeds* fell directly·by the roadway,
Mt 13:19 already·being·permeated·with·seed directly·by the
Mk 4:1 Then he·began again to·instruct directly·by the sea.
Mk 4:4 that, in·fact, *seed* fell directly·by the roadway, and
Mk 4:15 these are the *individuals* directly·by the roadway,
Mk 5:21 ·together to him, and he·was directly·by the sea.
Mk 10:46 was·sitting·down directly·by the roadway

G3844.17 PREP παρά (4x)
Lk 10:7 drinking the·things *provided* personally·by them, for
Ac 22:30 he·is·legally·accused personally·by the Judeans,
Mt 18:19 it·shall·happen for·them personally·by my Father,
1Pe 2:4 by men·of·clay†, but Selected personally·by God,

G3844.18 PREP παρ´ (2x)
Lk 3:13 the·thing directly having·been·thoroughly·assigned
Col 4:16 the letter should·be·read·aloud directly·to yeu,

G3844.19 PREP παρ´ (1x)
Rm 11:27 And this *is* personally my unilateral·covenant to·

G3844.20 PREP παρ´ (2x)
Rm 11:25 ·be full·of·notions personally·about yeurselves:
Rm 12:16 full·of·notions personally·about yeurselves.

G3844.21 PREP παρά (6x)
Heb 2:7 you·made him lesser than *the* supreme·angels; you·
Heb 2:9 ·degree having·been·made·lesser than *the* angels on·
Heb 3:3 has·been·counted·worthy of·more glory than Moses,
Heb 9:23 with·significantly·better sacrifices than these.
Heb 11:4 offered to·God a·much·better sacrifice than Qain,
1Co 3:11 ·lay another foundation than the·one being·laid·out

G3844.22 PREP παρ´ (1x)
Rm 12:3 not to·overly·esteem·himself more·than what is·

G3844.23 PREP παρά (5x)
Lk 13:2 morally·disqualified above·and·beyond all the
Lk 13:4 were delinquent above·and·beyond all men·of·clay†
Heb 1:4 a·more·superb name above·and·beyond theirs.
Heb 1:9 *·the* oil of·exuberant·joy above·and·beyond your
Rm 14:5 one·day *to·be* above·and·beyond *another* day, yet

G3844.24 PREP παρά (1x)

Heb 11:11 ·and·gave·birth well·after·and·beyond *the* season
G3844.25 PREP παρά (1x)
2Co 11:24 by *the* Jews I·received forty *stripes* minus one.
G3844.26 PREP παρά (8x)
Ac 18:13 ·clay† to·reverence God contrary·to the Torah-Law
Heb 12:24 ·better·things— contrary·to *that·of* Abel.
Gal 1:8 to·yeu contrary·to that·which we·already·proclaimed
Gal 1:9 ·news to·yeu contrary·to that·which yeu·personally·
Rm 1:26 sexual·intercourse for the·one contrary·to nature.
Rm 4:18 *AbRaham*, contrary·to expectation, trusted on an·
Rm 11:24 according·to nature, and·yet contrary·to nature,
Rm 16:17 and the traps contrary·to the instruction which yeu
G3844.27 PREP παρά (1x)
Rm 1:25 to·the creation instead·of the·one creating *it* (*the*·

G3845 παρα•βαίνω parabaínō *v.* (4x)
Roots:G3844 G0901-3 See:G3848
G3845.1 V-PAI-2P παραβαίνετε (1x)
Mt 15:3 yeu·yeurselves walk·contrary·to the commandment
G3845.1 V-PAI-3P παραβαίνουσιν (1x)
Mt 15:2 your disciples walk·contrary·to the Oral·tradition of·
G3845.1 V-PAP-NSM παραβαίνων (1x)
2Jn 1:9 Anyone, the·one walking·contrary·to and not
G3845.1 V-2AAI-3S παρέβη (1x)
Ac 1:25 ·among which Judas walked·contrary·to, *in·order*

G3846 παρα•βάλλω parabállō *v.* (2x)
Roots:G3844 G0906 Compare:G1448 G2020 G3666
G3846.2 V-2AAS-1P παραβάλωμεν (1x)
Mk 4:30 what·kind·of analogy should·we·cast·directly·at it?
G3846.3 V-2AAI-1P παρεβάλομεν (1x)
Ac 20:15 *day of·sailing*, we·drew·alongside to Samos. And

G3847 παρά•βασις parábasis *n.* (7x)
Roots:G3845
G3847 N-NSF παράβασις (2x)
Heb 2:2 and every violation and inattentive·disregard
Rm 4:15 there·is no law, *there·is* not·even a·violation).
G3847 N-DSF παραβάσει (1x)
1Ti 2:14 being·deluded, has·come·to·be in violation.
G3847 N-GSF παραβάσεως (2x)
Rm 2:23 God through the violation of·the Torah-Law?
Rm 5:14 after the resemblance of·Adam's violation, who is
G3847 N-GPF παραβάσεων (2x)
Heb 9:15 a·full·ransom (from·the violations *that·were* under
Gal 3:19 ·of·grace, *because* of·the violations, *Torah-Law*

G3848 παρα•βάτης parabátēs *n.* (5x)
Roots:G3845 Compare:G3892
G3848 N-NSM παραβάτης (2x)
Rm 2:25 But if you·should·be a·transgressor of·Torah-Law,
Jac 2:11 you·have·become a·transgressor of·Torah-Law.
G3848 N-NPM παραβάται (1x)
Jac 2:9 being·convicted by the Torah-Law as transgressors.
G3848 N-ASM παραβάτην (2x)
Gal 2:18 I·demonstrate my·own·self *to·be* a·transgressor.
Rm 2:27 circumcision *being* a·transgressor of·Torah-Law?

G3849 παρα•βιάζομαι parabiázômai *v.* (2x)
Roots:G3844 G0971 Compare:G2600-1
G3849.2 V-ADI-3S παρεβιάσατο (1x)
Ac 16:15 ·abide *there*." And she·personally·compelled us.
G3849.2 V-ADI-3P παρεβιάσαντο (1x)
Lk 24:29 But they·personally·compelled him, saying,

G3850 παρα•βολή parabôlḗ *n.* (50x)
Roots:G3846 Compare:G3942 See:G0238 xLangAlso:H4912
G3850.1 N-NSF παραβολή (2x)
Lk 8:9 "What might·be *meant·by* this parable?"
Lk 8:11 "Now the parable is this: The scattering·of·seed is
G3850.1 N-ASF παραβολήν (25x)
Lk 5:36 And he·was also saying a·parable to them, "Not·
Lk 6:39 And he·declared a·parable to·them: "Is·it possible·
Lk 12:16 And he·declared a·parable to them, saying, "The
Lk 12:41 "Lord, do·you·say this parable to us, or even to all
Lk 13:6 And he·was·relaying this parable, "A·certain·man
Lk 14:7 And he·was·saying a·parable to the·ones having·
Lk 15:3 And he·declared this parable to them, saying,
Lk 18:1 Then also he·was·saying a·parable to·them, *how*
Lk 18:9 And he·declared also this parable to certain ones
Lk 19:11 *it*, *Jesus* declared a·parable, on·account·of him
Lk 20:9 Then he·began to·relay this parable to the people,
Lk 20:19 he·declared this parable specifically·against them,
Lk 21:29 And he·declared to·them a·parable: "See the fig·
Mt 13:18 ·then, yeu·yeurselves hear the parable of·the·one
Mt 13:24 Another parable he·put·forth·directly to·them,
Mt 13:31 Another parable he·put·forth·directly to·them,
Mt 13:33 Another parable he·spoke to·them: "The kingdom
Mt 13:36 "Explain to·us the parable of·the darnel·weeds of·
Mt 15:15 declared to·him, "Explain this parable to·us."
Mt 21:33 "Hear another parable. "There·was a·certain man·
Mt 24:32 the fig·tree, yeu·must·learn the parable: "Even·
Mk 4:10 with·the twelve) asked him *about* the parable.
Mk 4:13 "Do·yeu·not personally·know this parable? How·
Mk 12:12 he·declared the parable specifically·against them.
Mk 13:28 the fig·tree, yeu·must·learn the parable: "Even·
G3850.1 N-APF παραβολάς (3x)
Mt 13:53 when YeShua finished these parables, he·moved·on
Mt 21:45 And after·hearing his parables, the chief·priests
Mk 4:13 How·else then shall·yeu·know all the parables?
G3850.1 N-DPF παραβολαῖς (12x)
Lk 8:10 but to·the rest, *it·is* in parables, in·order·that "
Mt 13:3 he·spoke many·things to·them in parables, saying,
Mt 13:10 "Why·do you·speak to·them in parables?"
Mt 13:13 that, I·speak to·them in parables, because looking,
Mt 13:34 these·things to·the crowds in parables. And apart·
Mt 13:35 ·open·up my mouth in parables; I·shall·belch·forth
Mt 22:1 YeShua declared to·them again by parables, saying,
Mk 3:23 he·was·saying to·them in parables, "How·is·it
Mk 4:2 ·was·instructing them many·things by parables, and
Mk 4:11 outside, all·*these*·things are·done in the parables,
Mk 4:33 And with·many such parables, he·was·speaking the
Mk 12:1 And he·began to·relate to·them in parables. "A·
G3850.1 N-GSF παραβολῆς (4x)
Lk 8:4 city, *Jesus* declared *the·following* through a·parable:
Mt 13:34 in parables. And apart·from a·parable, he·was·not
Mk 4:34 he·was·not speaking to·them apart·from a·parable.
Mk 7:17 were·inquiring·of him concerning the parable.
G3850.2 N-NSF παραβολή (1x)
Heb 9:9 The·same·which *was* an·analogy for the season,
G3850.2 N-DSF παραβολῇ (2x)
Heb 11:19 from·which also (by analogy), he·subsequently·
Mk 4:30 what·kind·of analogy should·we·cast·directly·at it?
G3850.3 N-ASF παραβολήν (1x)
Lk 4:23 "Entirely, yeu·shall·declare to·me this adage, 'O·

G3851 παρα•βουλεύομαι parabôulêúômai *v.* (1x)
Roots:G3844 G1011
G3851.2 V-ADP-NSM παραβουλευσάμενος (1x)
Php 2:30 death, ignoring·the·personal·warning·of the soul,

G3852 παρ•αγγελία parangêlía *n.* (6x)
Roots:G3853
G3852 N-ASF παραγγελίαν (2x)
Ac 16:24 who, upon·having·received such a·charge, cast
1Ti 1:18 I·place·the·direct·care·of this charge to·you, *my*
G3852 N-APF παραγγελίας (1x)
1Th 4:2 For yeu·personally·know what charges we·gave yeu
G3852 N-DSF παραγγελίᾳ (1x)
Ac 5:28 "¿!·Did·we·not charge a·charge to·yeu not to·
G3852 N-GSF παραγγελίας (1x)
1Ti 1:5 Now the·end·purpose of·the charge is love out·of·a·
EG3852 (1x)
Ac 23:31 ·to the *charge* having·been·thoroughly·assigned to·

G3853 παρ•αγγέλλω parangéllō *v.* (31x)
Roots:G3844 G0032
G3853.2 V-PAI-1S παραγγέλλω (3x)
Ac 16:18 declared to·the spirit, "I·charge you in the name
1Co 7:10 And to·the·ones having·married I·charge, *yet* not I·
1Ti 6:13 I·charge you in·the·sight·of God (the·one giving·
G3853.2 V-PAI-1P παραγγέλλομεν (3x)
2Th 3:4 ·do and shall·do the·things·which we·charge yeu.
2Th 3:6 Now we·charge yeu, brothers, in our Lord's name,
2Th 3:12 Now the·ones such·as·these, we·charge and exhort
G3853.2 V-PAI-3S παραγγέλλει (1x)
Ac 17:30 of·ignorance, God now charges all the men·of·
G3853.2 V-PAM-2S παράγγελλε (3x)
1Ti 4:11 You·must·charge and instruct these·things.
1Ti 5:7 And charge *them with* these·things, in·order·that
1Ti 6:17 Charge the wealthy·ones in the present age not to·
G3853.2 V-PAN παραγγέλλειν (1x)
Ac 15:5 them and to·charge *them* to·observantly·keep the
G3853.2 V-PAP-NSM παραγγέλλων (1x)
1Co 11:17 Now in·this charging, I·do·not applaud *yeu*,
G3853.2 V-IAI-1P παρηγγέλλομεν (1x)
2Th 3:10 alongside yeu, this we·were·charging yeu, that if
G3853.2 V-IAI-3S παρήγγελλεν (1x)
Lk 8:29 (For he·was·charging the impure spirit to·come·
G3853.2 V-AAI-1P παρηγγείλαμεν (2x)
Ac 5:28 saying, "¿!·Did·we·not charge a·charge to·yeu not
1Th 4:11 ·with yeur own hands, just·as we·charged yeu,
G3853.2 V-AAI-3S παρήγγειλεν (7x)
Lk 5:14 And he·himself charged him to·declare *it* not·even·
Lk 8:56 were·astonished, but he·charged them to·declare to·
Lk 9:21 ·forbidding them, he·charged *them* to·declare not·
Ac 1:4 being·huddled·close·together, *Jesus* charged them,
Ac 10:42 And he·charged us to·officially·proclaim to·the
Mk 6:8 And he·charged them that they·should·take·up not·
Mk 8:6 And he·charged the crowd to·sit·back upon the soil.
G3853.2 V-AAI-3P παρήγγειλαν (2x)
Ac 4:18 And calling·for them, they·charged them not to·
Ac 5:40 *and* thrashing *them*, they·charged *them* not to·speak
G3853.2 V-AAP-NSM παραγγείλας (3x)
Ac 23:22 the young·man, charging *for·him* to·divulge "to·
Ac 23:30 ·this·same·hour to you, charging his legal·accusers
Mt 10:5 twelve YeShua dispatched, after·charging them,
G3853.2 V-AAP-NPM παραγγείλαντες (1x)
Ac 16:23 *them* into prison, charging the prison·warden to·
G3853.2 V-AAS-2S παραγγείλῃς (1x)
1Ti 1:3 , *do·so* in·order·that you·may·charge some not to·
EG3853.2 (1x)
1Ti 6:18 *Charge them* to·do·beneficially·good·work, to·be·

G3854 παρα•γίνομαι paragínômai *v.* (38x)
Roots:G3844 G1096 Compare:G1448 G2064 G2240 G2658 G3918 See:G4836
G3854.1 V-2ADI-3S παρεγένετο (1x)
Lk 19:16 "Then the first came·close, saying, 'Lord, your
G3854.1 V-2ADI-3P παρεγένοντο (1x)
Ac 20:18 And as·soon·as they·came·close to him, he·
G3854.1 V-2ADP-ASM παραγενόμενον (1x)
Ac 9:39 with·them. After·coming·directly *to·Joppa*, they·
G3854.1 V-2ADP-NSM παραγενόμενος (2x)
Lk 14:21 "So coming·close, that slave announced these·
Ac 5:25 Then coming·close, someone reported to·them,
G3854.1 V-2ADP-NPM παραγενόμενοι (2x)
Lk 7:4 And coming·close to Jesus, they·were·imploring him
Lk 7:20 And coming·close to him, the men declared, "John
G3854.2 V-PNI-3S παραγίνεται (1x)
Mt 3:13 At·that·time, YeShua comes·directly from Galilee
G3854.2 V-2ADI-1S παρεγενόμην (1x)
Lk 12:51 Do·yeu·suppose that I·came·directly to·give peace
G3854.2 V-2ADI-3S παρεγένετο (2x)
Jn 8:2 And with·*the*·sunrise, he·came·directly again into the
Lk 11:6 since·just·now a·friend of·mine came·directly to me
G3854.2 V-2ADI-3P παρεγένοντο (3x)
Lk 8:19 mother and his brothers came·directly toward him,
Ac 13:14 from Perga, came·directly to Antiochia of·Pisidia.
Ac 21:18 alongside Jacob; and all the elders came·directly.
G3854.2 V-2ADP-APM παραγενομένους (1x)
Lk 22:52 and *the* elders coming·directly toward him,
G3854.2 V-2ADP-NSM παραγενόμενος (5x)
Ac 9:26 Now after·coming·directly to JeruSalem, Saul was·
Ac 10:32 ·surnamed Peter, who coming·directly, shall·speak
Ac 10:33 and you did well in·coming·directly *here*. Now

Ππ

Ac 11:23 who, after·coming·directly and seeing the grace
Ac 23:16 ·Paul's sister, coming·directly after·hearing of·the
G3854.2 V-2ADP-NSM@ παραγενόμενος (1x)
Heb 9:11 ·good·things, came·directly through the greater
G3854.2 V-2ADP-NPM παραγενόμενοι (2x)
Ac 5:22 But the assistants, coming·directly *to·the dungeon*,
Ac 17:10 Berea— who, after·coming·directly *there*, went·
EG3854.2 (1x)
Heb 9:12 *He·came·directly*, however·not through blood of·
G3854.3 V-PNI-3S παραγίνεται (1x)
Mk 14:43 speaking of·him, Judas comes·openly, being one
G3854.3 V-IDI-3P παρεγίνοντο (1x)
Jn 3:23 there. And they·came·openly and were·immersed,
G3854.3 V-2ADI-1S παρεγενόμην (1x)
Ac 24:17 ·more years, I·came·openly doing merciful·acts
G3854.3 V-2ADP-NPM παραγενόμενοι (1x)
Ac 14:27 And after·coming·openly and gathering·together
G3854.4 V-PNI-3S@ παραγίνεται (1x)
Mt 3:1 the Immerser arrived·publicly, officially·proclaiming
G3854.4 V-2ADI-3P παρεγένοντο (1x)
Mt 2:1 from *the* east arrived·publicly in JeruSalem,
G3854.4 V-2ADP-GSM παραγενομένου (1x)
Ac 25:7 And with·him arriving·publicly, the Judeans having·
G3854.4 V-2ADP-NSM παραγενόμενος (4x)
Ac 5:21 ·him, after·arriving·publicly, they·called·together
Ac 18:27 who upon·arriving·publicly, joined·in·and·helped
Ac 24:24 days, after·arriving·publicly together with·his wife
Ac 28:21 any of·the brothers arriving·publicly announced or
G3854.4 V-2ADP-NPM παραγενόμενοι (1x)
Ac 15:4 And arriving·publicly in JeruSalem, they·were·fully·
G3854.4 V-2ADS-1S παραγένωμαι (1x)
1Co 16:3 And whenever I·should·arrive·publicly, whomever
G3854.4 V-2ADS-3P παραγένωνται (1x)
Ac 23:35 your legal·accusers also should·arrive·publicly."

G3855 παρ•άγω parágō *v.* (10x)
Roots:G3844 G0071
G3855.2 V-PAI-3S παράγει (1x)
Mt 20:30 ·hearing that YeShua passes·by, they·yelled·out,
G3855.2 V-PAP-ASM παράγοντα (1x)
Mk 15:21 ·upon a·certain·man who·was·passing·by, Simon,
G3855.3 V-PAP-DSM παράγοντι (1x)
Mt 9:27 And with·YeShua passing·on from·there, two blind·
G3855.3 V-PAP-NSM παράγων (3x)
Jn 9:1 And while·passing·on *through*, he·saw a·man·of·clay†
Mt 9:9 And while·passing·on from·there, YeShua saw a·
Mk 2:14 Then passing·on *from·there*, he·saw Levi *called*
G3855.3 V-IAI-3S παρῆγεν (1x)
Jn 8:59 and in·this·manner, he·was·passing·on *through*.
G3855.4 V-PAI-3S παράγει (1x)
1Co 7:31 for the schematic·layout of·this world passes·away.
G3855.4 V-PMI-3S παράγεται (2x)
1Jn 2:8 yeu, because the darkness is·passing·away, and the
1Jn 2:17 And the world passes·away, and its longing, but

G3856 παρα•δειγματίζω paradeîgmatízō *v.* (2x)
Roots:G3844 G1165
G3856.2 V-PAP-APM παραδειγματίζοντας (1x)
Heb 6:6 and exposing·*him*·to·public·ridicule·and·scorn.
G3856.2 V-AAN παραδειγματίσαι (1x)
Mt 1:19 her to·be·exposed·to·public·ridicule·and·scorn,

G3857 παράδεισος parádêisôs *n.* (3x)
xLangEquiv:H6508 xLangAlso:H1588
G3857.3 N-DSM παραδείσῳ (1x)
Lk 23:43 today, you·shall·be with me in the paradise."
G3857.4 N-ASM παράδεισον (1x)
2Co 12:4 how he·was·snatched·up into Paradise, and heard
G3857.5 N-GSM παραδείσου (1x)
Rv 2:7 which is in *the* midst of·the paradise of·God.'"

G3858 παρα•δέχομαι paradéchômai *v.* (5x)
Roots:G3844 G1209 Compare:G3880
G3858.2 V-PNI-3S παραδέχεται (1x)
Heb 12:6 he·whips every son whom he·personally·accepts."
G3858.2 V-PNN παραδέχεσθαι (1x)
Ac 16:21 it·is·not proper for·us to·personally·accept, neither
G3858.3 V-FNI-3P παραδέξονται (1x)
Ac 22:18 they·shall·not give·heed·and·accept your testimony
G3858.3 V-PNI-3P παραδέχονται (1x)
Mk 4:20 hear the Redemptive-word, give·heed·and·accept *it*,
G3858.3 V-PNM-2S παραδέχου (1x)
1Ti 5:19 Do·not give·heed·and·accept a·legal·accusation

G3859 παρα•δια•τριβή paradiatribḗ *n.* (1x)
Roots:G3844 G1304 Compare:G0485 G3859
G3859.2 N-NPF παραδιατριβαί (1x)
1Ti 6:5 *and* idle·disputations of·thoroughly·corrupted men·

G3860 παρα•δίδωμι paradídōmi *v.* (124x)
Roots:G3844 G1325 Compare:G0325 G0591 G1929
G3860.2 V-IAI-3P παρεδίδουν (1x)
Ac 16:4 the cities, they·were·handing·down to·them the
G3860.2 V-AAI-1S παρέδωκα (3x)
1Co 11:2 the traditions, just·as I·handed·*them*·down to·yeu.
1Co 11:23 the Lord that·which also I·handed·down to·yeu,
1Co 15:3 For I·handed·down to·yeu, first-of-all, that·which
G3860.2 V-AAI-2P παρεδώκατε (1x)
Mk 7:13 ·yeur Oral·tradition, which yeu·handed·down. And
G3860.2 V-AAI-3S παρέδωκεν (1x)
Ac 6:14 the customs which Moses handed·down to·us."
G3860.2 V-2AAI-3P παρέδοσαν (1x)
Lk 1:2 beginning handed·*them*·down to·us after·becoming
G3860.2 V-API-2P παρεδόθητε (1x)
Rm 6:17 of·instruction which is·handed·down *to·yeu*.
G3860.2 V-APP-DSF παραδοθείσῃ (1x)
Jud 1:3 trust already·being·handed·down only·once to·the
G3860.2 V-APP-GSF παραδοθείσης (1x)
2Pe 2:21 holy commandment being·handed·down to·them.
G3860.3 V-APP-NSM παραδοθείς (1x)
Ac 15:40 went·forth after·being·directly·handed to·the grace
G3860.3 V-RPP-NPM παραδεδομένοι (1x)
Ac 14:26 they·were having·been·directly·handed to·the
G3860.4 V-FAI-1S παραδώσω (1x)
Mt 26:15 to·give to·me? And·I shall·hand him over to·yeu.
G3860.4 V-FAI-3S παραδώσει (6x)
Jn 13:21 ·yeu that one from·among yeu shall·hand me over."
Mt 10:21 "And brother shall·hand·over brother to death, and
Mt 26:21 that one from·among yeu shall·hand me over."
Mt 26:23 with me in the dish, the·same shall·hand me over.
Mk 13:12 "Now brother shall·hand·over brother to death,
Mk 14:18 the·one eating with·me, shall·hand me over."
G3860.4 V-FAI-3P παραδώσουσιν (7x)
Ac 21:11 owns this belt, and they·shall·hand *him* over into
Mt 10:17 the men·of·clay†, for they·shall·hand yeu over to
Mt 20:19 and shall·hand him over to·the Gentiles for *them*
Mt 24:9 "Then they·shall·hand yeu over for tribulation and
Mt 24:10 ·and·fall·away, and shall·hand one·another over,
Mk 10:33 ·condemn him to·death and shall·hand him over
Mk 13:9 ·out·for yeurselves, for they·shall·hand yeu over to
G3860.4 V-FAP-NSM παραδώσων (1x)
Jn 6:64 and who was the·one to·be·handing him over.
G3860.4 V-FPI-2P παραδοθήσεσθε (1x)
Lk 21:16 "But yeu·shall·be·handed·over both by parents,
G3860.4 V-FPI-3S παραδοθήσεται (3x)
Lk 18:32 For he·shall·be·handed·over to·the Gentiles, and
Mt 20:18 of·Clay·Man† shall·be·handed·over to·the chief·
Mk 10:33 of·Clay·Man† shall·be·handed·over to·the chief·
G3860.4 V-PAI-2S παραδίδως (1x)
Lk 22:48 "Judas, do·you·hand·over the Son of·Clay·Man†
G3860.4 V-PAN παραδιδόναι (2x)
Jn 6:71 for *it·was* this·man *that* was·about to·hand him over,
Jn 12:4 Simon's *son*, the·one about to·hand him over) says,
G3860.4 V-PAP-ASM παραδιδόντα (1x)
Jn 13:11 he·had·personally·known the·one handing him over
G3860.4 V-PAP-GSM παραδιδόντος (1x)
Lk 22:21 behold, the hand of·the·one handing me over *is*
G3860.4 V-PAP-NSM παραδιδούς (11x)
Jn 18:2 And Judas, the·one handing him over, also had·
Jn 18:5 And even Judas, the·one handing him over, stood
Jn 19:11 On·account·of that, the·one handing me over to·
Jn 21:20 "Lord, who is the·one handing you over?
Ac 22:4 captively·binding and handing·over into prisons
Mt 26:25 And answering, Judas (the·one handing him over)
Mt 26:46 Behold, the·one handing me over has·drawn·near.
Mt 26:48 But the·one handing him over gave them a·sign,
Mt 27:3 was·condemned, Judas, the·one handing him over,
Mk 14:42 Behold, the·one handing me over has·drawn·near.
Mk 14:44 And the·one handing him over had·given them a·
G3860.4 V-PAP-NPM παραδιδόντες (2x)
Lk 21:12 yeu and shall·persecute *yeu*, handing *yeu* over to
Mk 13:11 ·bring *yeu for·judgment*, while·handing yeu over,
G3860.4 V-PAS-3P παραδιδῶσιν (1x)
Mt 10:19 But whenever they·should·hand yeu over, yeu·
G3860.4 V-PPI-1P παραδιδόμεθα (1x)
2Co 4:11 the·ones living, are·handed·over to death on·
G3860.4 V-PPI-3S παραδίδοται (7x)
Lk 22:22 man·of·clay† through whom he·is·handed·over!"
Mt 26:2 Son of·Clay·Man† is·handed·over to·be·crucified."
Mt 26:24 the Son of·Clay·Man† is·handed·over! It·was
Mt 26:45 and the Son of·Clay·Man† is·handed·over into *the*
Mk 9:31 "The Son of·Clay·Man† is·handed·over into *the*
Mk 14:21 the Son of·Clay·Man† is·handed·over! It·was
Mk 14:41 the Son of·Clay·Man† is·handed·over into the
G3860.4 V-PPN παραδίδοσθαι (2x)
Lk 9:44 of·Clay·Man† is·about to·be·handed·over into *the*
Mt 17:22 of·Clay·Man† is·about to·be·handed·over into *the*
G3860.4 V-IAI-3S παρεδίδου (2x)
Ac 8:3 and women, he·was·handing·*them*·over to prison.
1Pe 2:23 he·was·not threatening, but was·handing *his cause*
G3860.4 V-IAI-3P παρεδίδουν (1x)
Ac 27:1 us to·set·sail for Italy, they·were·handing both Paul
G3860.4 V-IPI-3S παρεδίδοτο (1x)
1Co 11:23 on·the night in which he·was·handed·over, took
G3860.4 V-AAI-1S παρέδωκα (1x)
1Ti 1:20 whom I·handed·over to·the Adversary-Accuser in·
G3860.4 V-AAI-1P παρεδώκαμεν (1x)
Jn 18:30 a·criminal, we·would not have·handed him over to·
G3860.4 V-AAI-2S παρέδωκας (2x)
Mt 25:20 'Lord, you·handed·over to·me five talants·of·
Mt 25:22 'Lord, you·handed·over to·me two talants·of·
G3860.4 V-AAI-2P παρεδώκατε (1x)
Ac 3:13 Jesus, whom yeu·yeurselves handed·over, and yeu·
G3860.4 V-AAI-3S παρέδωκεν (17x)
Jn 19:16 Then accordingly, he·handed him over to·them
Jn 19:30 And drooping his head, he·handed·over the spirit.
Lk 23:25 whom they·requested. But he·handed Jesus over
Ac 7:42 Then God turned·around and handed them over to·
Ac 28:16 the centurion handed·over the chained·prisoners
Mt 18:34 And being·angry, his lord handed him over to·the
Mt 25:14 called his·own slaves and handed·over his holdings
Mt 27:26 he·handed·*him*·over in·order·that he·may·be·
Mk 3:19 and Judas IsCariot, who also handed him over.
Mk 15:15 he·handed·*him*·over in·order·that he·should·be·
Rm 1:24 Therefore God also handed them over to impurity
Rm 1:26 On·account·of that, God handed them over to
Rm 1:28 ·and·full·knowledge, God handed them over to a·
Rm 8:32 his·own Son, but·rather handed him over on·behalf
2Pe 2:4 *deepest dungeon of·Hades*), he·handed *them* over
Eph 5:2 also loved us and handed himself over on·our behalf,
Eph 5:25 ·Called·Out·Citizenry and handed himself over on·
G3860.4 V-AAI-3P παρέδωκαν (6x)
Jn 18:35 nation and the chief·priests handed you over to·me.
Lk 24:20 the chief·priests and our rulers handed him over to
Mt 27:2 him, they·led·*him*·away and handed him over to·
Mt 27:18 that on·account·of envy they·handed him over.
Mk 15:1 ·carried·*him*·away and handed·*him*·over to·Pilate.
Eph 4:19 having·become·apathetic, handed themselves over
G3860.4 V-2AAN παραδοῦναι (3x)
Lk 20:20 of·his words, in·order to·hand him over to·the
Lk 22:6 ·was·seeking a·good·opportunity to·hand him over
1Co 5:5 *yeu·are* to·hand·over such·a·man to·the
G3860.4 V-2AAP-GSM παραδόντος (1x)

Gal 2:20 loving me, and already·handing himself over on·
G3860.4 V-2AAP-NSM παραδούς (3x)
Ac 12:4 placed *him* in prison, handing *him* over to·four
Mt 10:4 and Judas IsCariot, the·one also handing him over.
Mt 27:4 "I·morally·failed in·handing·over blood *that·is*
G3860.4 V-2AAS-1S παραδῶ (1x)
1Co 13:3 holdings, and though I·should·hand·over my body
G3860.4 V-2AAS-3S παραδῶ (9x)
Jn 13:2 *son* of·Simon, that he·should·hand him over,
Lk 12:58 judge, and the judge should·hand you over to·the
Lk 22:4 the wardens, how he·may·hand him over to·them.
Mt 5:25 ·any·time the legal·adversary should·hand you over
Mt 5:25 judge, and the judge should·hand you over to·the
Mt 26:16 ·opportunity in·order·that he·may·hand him over.
Mk 14:10 ·priests, in·order·that he·should·hand him over to·
Mk 14:11 how he·should·conveniently hand him over.
1Co 15:24 end, whenever he·should·hand·over the kingdom
G3860.4 V-API-1S παρεδόθην (1x)
Ac 28:17 ·fathers, was·handed·over *as* a·chained·prisoner
G3860.4 V-API-3S παρεδόθη (4x)
Lk 10:22 "All·things are·handed·over to·me by my Father.
Mt 4:12 after·hearing that John was·handed·over *into prison*,
Mt 11:27 "All·things are·handed·over to·me by my Father,
Rm 4:25 who was·handed·over on·account·of our trespasses,
G3860.4 V-APN παραδοθῆναι (2x)
Lk 24:7 the Son of·Clay·Man† to·be·handed·over into *the*
Mk 1:14 with John already·being·handed·over *to·prison*,
G3860.4 V-APS-1S παραδοθῶ (1x)
Jn 18:36 ·that I·should·not be·handed·over to·the Judeans.
G3860.4 V-RAP-DPM παραδεδωκόσιν (1x)
Ac 15:26 men·of·clay† having·handed·over their souls on
G3860.4 V-RPI-3S παραδέδοται (1x)
Lk 4:6 their glory, because it·has·been·handed·over to·me,
G3860.4 V-LAI-3P παραδεδώκεισαν (1x)
Mk 15:10 that the chief·priests had·handed him over through
EG3860.4 (3x)
Ac 8:20 with·you, be *handed·over* to total·destruction,
Mt 10:21 to death, and father *shall·hand·over* child, and
Mk 13:12 to death, and father *shall·hand·over* child; and
G3860.5 V-2AAS-3S παραδῷ (1x)
Mk 4:29 the fruit should·be·yielded·up, immediately he·

G3861 παρά•δοξος parádôxôs *adj.* (1x)
Roots:G3844 G1391
G3861.2 A-APN παράδοξα (1x)
Lk 5:26 "We·saw things·way·beyond·believable today."

Ππ

G3862 παρά•δοσις parádôsis *n.* (13x)
Roots:G3860 Compare:G3551 xLangAlso:H6905-1
G3862.1 N-ASF παράδοσιν (2x)
2Th 3:6 ·to the tradition which he·personally·received from
Col 2:8 delusion, according·to the tradition of·men·of·clay†,
G3862.1 N-APF παραδόσεις (2x)
2Th 2:15 ·hold·to the traditions which yeu·were·instructed,
1Co 11:2 and fully·hold·onto the traditions, just·as I·
G3862.3 N-ASF παράδοσιν (7x)
Mt 15:2 walk·contrary·to the Oral·tradition of·the elders?
Mt 15:3 commandment of·God through yeur Oral·tradition?
Mt 15:6 commandment of·God through yeur Oral·tradition.
Mk 7:3 securely·holding·to the Oral·tradition of·the elders.
Mk 7:5 not walk according·to the Oral·tradition of·the elders
Mk 7:8 ·securely·hold·to the Oral·tradition of·men·of·clay†,
Mk 7:9 yeu·may·observantly·keep yeur·own Oral·tradition.
G3862.3 N-DSF παραδόσει (1x)
Mk 7:13 the Holy-word of·God by·yeur Oral·tradition, which
G3862.3 N-GPF παραδόσεων (1x)
Gal 1:14 a·zealot of·my forefathers' Oral·traditions.

G3863 παρα•ζηλόω parazēlôō *v.* (4x)
Roots:G3844 G2206
G3863.2 V-FAI-1S παραζηλώσω (1x)
Rm 10:19 "I·myself shall·provoke yeu to·jealousy with
G3863.2 V-PAI-1P παραζηλοῦμεν (1x)
1Co 10:22 Or do·we·provoke the Lord to·jealousy?
G3863.2 V-AAN παραζηλῶσαι (1x)
Rm 11:11 to·the Gentiles, to·provoke them to·jealousy.
G3863.2 V-AAS-1S παραζηλώσω (1x)
Rm 11:14 somehow I·may·provoke·to·jealousy *them who·*

G3864 παρα•θαλάσσιος parathalássiôs *adj.* (1x)
Roots:G3844 G2281
G3864 A-ASF παραθαλασσίαν (1x)
Mt 4:13 he·resided in CaperNaum near·the·seashore, within

G3865 παρα•θεωρέω paratheōréō *v.* (1x)
Roots:G3844 G2334 Compare:G0272 G3928 G1950
G3865.3 V-IPI-3P παρεθεωροῦντο (1x)
Ac 6:1 their widows were·intentionally·neglected in the daily

G3866 παρα•θήκη parathḗkē *n.* (1x)
Roots:G3908 Compare:G0728 See:G3872
G3866.2 N-ASF παραθήκην (1x)
2Ti 1:12 able to·vigilantly·keep my trust·deposit toward that

G3867 παρ•αινέω parainéō *v.* (3x)
Roots:G3844 G0134 Compare:G3560 G0363 G3870
G3867.2 V-PAI-1S παραινῶ (1x)
Ac 27:22 I·urgently·recommend·for yeu to·cheer·up. "For
G3867.3 V-IAI-3S παρῄνει (1x)
Ac 27:9 ·by, Paul was·making·an·urgent·recommendation,
EG3867.3 (1x)
Ac 27:21 with·my *urgent·recommendation*, *such·for·us* not

G3868 παρ•αιτέομαι paraitéômai *v.* (11x)
Roots:G3844 G0154 Compare:G0665 G0654 G0114 G4026
G3868.2 V-PNM-2S παραιτοῦ (3x)
Tit 3:10 Shun a·man·of·clay† that·is·divisively·selective
1Ti 4:7 So shun the profane and age-old,·senile myths, and
2Ti 2:23 But shun the foolish and uneducated·and·
G3868.2 V-ADI-3P παρῃτήσαντο (1x)
Heb 12:19 of·which the·ones hearing shunned *it*, *such·for*
G3868.2 V-ADP-NPM παραιτησάμενοι (1x)
Heb 12:25 *the·ones* already·shunning the·one imparting·
G3868.2 V-ADS-2P παραιτήσησθε (1x)
Heb 12:25 Look·out! Yeu·should·not shun the·one speaking
G3868.3 V-PNI-1S παραιτοῦμαι (1x)
Ac 25:11 worthy of·death, I·do·not decline to·die. But if
G3868.3 V-PNM-2S παραιτοῦ (1x)
1Ti 5:11 But decline *to·register* younger widows, for
G3868.4 V-PNN παραιτεῖσθαι (1x)
Lk 14:18 *intent*, they·all began to·excuse·themselves. The
G3868.4 V-RPP-ASM παρῃτημένον (2x)
Lk 14:18 I·ask *that* you have me excused.'
Lk 14:19 I·ask *that* you have me excused.'

G3869 παρα•καθ•ίζω parakathízō *v.* (1x)
Roots:G3844 G2523
G3869 V-AAP-NSF παρακαθίσασα (1x)
Lk 10:39 called Mary, who, sitting·down·near at Jesus' feet,

G3870 παρα•καλέω parakaléō *v.* (109x)
Roots:G3844 G2564 Compare:G2065 See:G3874
G3870.1 V-AAI-1S παρεκάλεσα (1x)
Ac 28:20 ·account·of this cause, I·personally·called·for yeu,
G3870.2 V-PAI-1P παρακαλοῦμεν (1x)
1Co 4:13 Being·reviled, we·entreat. We·have·now·become
G3870.2 V-IAI-3S παρεκάλει (1x)
Lk 15:28 So coming·out, his father was·entreating him.
G3870.3 V-PAI-1S παρακαλῶ (18x)
Ac 24:4 hindrance upon you, I·implore you in·your·own
Ac 27:34 Therefore I·implore yeu to·each·take *some*
Heb 13:19 But I·implore *yeu* all·the·more to·do this, in·
Heb 13:22 And I·implore yeu, brothers, bear·with the word
Rm 12:1 Accordingly, I·implore yeu, brothers, through the
Rm 15:30 Now I·implore yeu, brothers, on·account·of our
Rm 16:17 Now I·implore yeu, brothers, to·keep·a·watch·of
Php 4:2 I·implore EuOdia and I·implore SynTyche to·
Php 4:2 EuOdia and I·implore SynTyche to·contemplate the
1Pe 2:11 Dearly·beloved, I·implore *yeu* as sojourners and
1Co 1:10 Now I·implore yeu, brothers, through the name of·
1Co 4:16 Accordingly, I·implore yeu, become attentive·
1Co 16:15 I·implore yeu, brothers, (yeu·personally·know
2Co 2:8 Therefore I·implore yeu to·ratify *yeur* love for him.
2Co 10:1 Now I, Paul, I·myself do·implore yeu through the
Eph 4:1 ·prisoner in *the* Lord, implore yeu to·walk worthily
Phm 1:9 rather on·account·of the love, I·implore *you*, *I* Paul
Phm 1:10 I·implore you concerning my child Onesimus,
G3870.3 V-PAI-1P παρακαλοῦμεν (2x)
1Th 4:10 in all Macedonia. But we·implore yeu, brothers,
2Co 6:1 *it·is* not for nothing *that* we·implore also *for* yeu to·
G3870.3 V-PAI-3P παρακαλοῦσιν (2x)
Mk 7:32 ·impediment, and they·implore him in·order·that
Mk 8:22 a·blind·man to·him and implore him in·order·that
G3870.3 V-PAN παρακαλεῖν (1x)
Mk 5:17 And they·began to·implore *Jesus* to·go·away from
G3870.3 V-PAP-GSM παρακαλοῦντος (1x)
2Co 5:20 of·Anointed-One, as God imploring *yeu* through
G3870.3 V-PAP-NSM παρακαλῶν (3x)
Ac 16:9 man of·Macedonia standing and imploring him,
Mt 8:5 a·centurion came·alongside him, imploring him
Mk 1:40 a·leper came to him, imploring him, even kneeling·
G3870.3 V-PAP-NPM παρακαλοῦντες (1x)
Ac 9:38 two men to him, imploring *him* not to·amble·along
G3870.3 V-IAI-1P παρεκαλοῦμεν (1x)
Ac 21:12 residing·in·that·place, were·imploring him not to·
G3870.3 V-IAI-3S παρεκάλει (7x)
Lk 8:31 And they·were·imploring him, in·order·that he·
Lk 8:41 ·at the feet of·Jesus, he·was·imploring him to·enter
Ac 27:33 Paul was·imploring absolutely·all·of·them to·
Mt 18:29 feet, his fellow·slave was·imploring him, saying,
Mk 5:10 And he·was·imploring him much that he·should·not
Mk 5:18 having·been·possessed·with·demons was·imploring
Mk 5:23 and was·imploring him repeatedly, saying, "My
G3870.3 V-IAI-3P παρεκάλουν (8x)
Lk 7:4 ·close to Jesus, they·were·imploring him earnestly,
Lk 8:32 the mountain, and they·were·imploring him that he·
Ac 13:42 the Gentiles were·imploring for·these utterances
Ac 19:31 sending·word to him, they·were·imploring *him* not
Ac 25:2 ·*things* against Paul. And they·were·imploring him,
Mt 8:31 And the demons were·imploring him, saying, "If
Mt 14:36 and they·were·imploring him in·order·that they·
Mk 6:56 marketplaces and were·imploring him in·order·that
G3870.3 V-AAI-1S παρεκάλεσα (2x)
2Co 12:8 Over this·matter, I·implored the Lord three·times
1Ti 1:3 Just·as I·implored you to·continue·on at Ephesus
G3870.3 V-AAI-2S παρεκάλεσας (1x)
Mt 18:32 all that indebtedness, since you·implored *of* me.
G3870.3 V-AAI-3S παρεκάλεσεν (2x)
Ac 8:31 And he·implored Philippe that·he·would·climb·up
Ac 16:15 and·also her household, she·implored *us*, saying,
G3870.3 V-AAI-3P παρεκάλεσαν (3x)
Ac 16:39 And coming, they·implored them, and after·
Mt 8:34 And after·seeing him, they·implored *him* that he·
Mk 5:12 And all the demons implored him, saying, "Send us
G3870.3 V-AAN παρακαλέσαι (1x)
Mt 26:53 I·am·not able at·this·moment to·implore my Father
EG3870.3 (1x)
2Co 6:3 *We·implore yeu* while·giving not·one·bit·of an·
G3870.4 V-PAI-1S παρακαλῶ (2x)
1Pe 5:1 the·ones among yeu, I·exhort *as* the fellow-elder,
1Ti 2:1 Now·then, I·exhort first of·all *for* petitions, prayers,
G3870.4 V-PAI-1P παρακαλοῦμεν (3x)
1Th 4:1 brothers: We·ask·of yeu and exhort *yeu* by *the* Lord
1Th 5:14 Now we·exhort yeu, brothers, admonish the
2Th 3:12 such·as·these, we·charge and exhort through our
G3870.4 V-PAM-2S παρακάλει (4x)
Tit 2:6 Likewise, exhort the younger·men to·be·
Tit 2:15 Speak these·things, and exhort and reprove with all
1Ti 5:1 chastise an·older·man, but·rather exhort *him* as a·
1Ti 6:2 These·things instruct and exhort.
G3870.4 V-PAM-2P παρακαλεῖτε (1x)
Heb 3:13 But·rather exhort one·another each and·every day,
G3870.4 V-PAN παρακαλεῖν (1x)
Tit 1:9 in·order·that he·may·be able also to·exhort by the
G3870.4 V-PAP-NSM παρακαλῶν (4x)
Lk 3:18 in·fact, also exhorting many other·things, he·was·

Rm 12:8 or the·one exhorting, on the exhortation; the·one
Jud 1:3 to·yeu, exhorting *yeu* to·strenuously·struggle·for the
1Pe 5:12 briefly to·yeu— exhorting and further·testifying

G3870.4 V-PAP-NPM παρακαλοῦντες (3x)
Ac 14:22 souls of·the disciples, exhorting *them* to·continue
Heb 10:25 ·habit of·some, but·rather exhorting *one·another*,
1Th 2:11 his children, exhorting and personally·encouraging

G3870.4 V-IAI-3S παρεκάλει (2x)
Ac 2:40 ·thoroughly·testifying and was·exhorting, saying,
Ac 11:23 And he·was·exhorting them·all with·determined·

G3870.4 V-AAI-1S παρεκάλεσα (2x)
1Co 16:12 Apollos, I repeatedly entreated him in·order·that
2Co 12:18 I·exhorted Titus, and I·dispatched·*him*·together·

G3870.4 V-AAI-3P παρεκάλεσαν (1x)
Ac 15:32 prophets also themselves, exhorted the brothers

G3870.4 V-AAM-2S παρακάλεσον (1x)
2Ti 4:2 reprimand, *and* exhort with all long-suffering and

G3870.4 V-AAN παρακαλέσαι (2x)
2Co 8:6 such·for us to·exhort Titus, in·order·that just·as he·
2Co 9:5 ·considered *it* necessary to·exhort the brothers, that

G3870.4 V-AAP-NSM παρακαλέσας (1x)
Ac 20:2 ·throughout those parts and exhorting them often in·

G3870.4 V-API-1P παρεκλήθημεν (1x)
Ac 28:14 brothers, we·were·exhorted to·stay·over with them

G3870.5 V-FPI-3P παρακληθήσονται (1x)
Mt 5:4 because they·themselves shall·be·comforted.

G3870.5 V-PAM-2P παρακαλεῖτε (2x)
1Th 4:18 As·such, comfort one·another with these words.
1Th 5:11 Therefore yeu·must·comfort one·another, and

G3870.5 V-PAN παρακαλεῖν (1x)
2Co 1:4 in·order·for us to·be·able to·comfort the·ones in

G3870.5 V-PAP-NSM παρακαλῶν (2x)
2Co 1:4 the·one comforting us in all our tribulation, in·order·
2Co 7:6 But·yet God, the·one comforting the·ones *that·are*

G3870.5 V-PPI-1P παρακαλούμεθα (2x)
2Co 1:4 with·which we·ourselves are·comforted by God.
2Co 1:6 and Salvation, or·whether we·are·comforted, *it·is*

G3870.5 V-PPI-3S παρακαλεῖται (1x)
Lk 16:25 But now this·one is·comforted, and you are·

G3870.5 V-PPM-2P παρακαλεῖσθε (1x)
2Co 13:11 ·reformed, be·comforted, contemplate the same·

G3870.5 V-PPS-3P παρακαλῶνται (1x)
1Co 14:31 ·that all may·learn, and all may·be·comforted.

G3870.5 V-AAI-3S παρεκάλεσεν (1x)
2Co 7:6 the·ones *that·are* feeling·low, comforted us by the

G3870.5 V-AAI-3P παρεκάλεσαν (1x)
Ac 16:40 And seeing the brothers, they·comforted them and

G3870.5 V-AAN παρακαλέσαι (2x)
1Th 3:2 ·firmly·establish yeu and to·comfort yeu concerning
2Co 2:7 to·graciously·forgive *him*, and to·comfort *him*, lest·

G3870.5 V-AAO-3S παρακαλέσαι (1x)
2Th 2:17 may·he·comfort yeur hearts and firmly·establish

G3870.5 V-AAS-3S παρακαλέσῃ (2x)
Eph 6:22 us, and *that* he·may·comfort yeur hearts.
Col 4:8 ·things concerning yeu and may·comfort yeur hearts,

G3870.5 V-API-1P παρεκλήθημεν (1x)
1Th 3:7 and dire·need, we·are·comforted over yeu through

G3870.5 V-API-3S παρεκλήθη (1x)
2Co 7:7 the consoling with·which he·was·comforted in yeu,

G3870.5 V-API-3P παρεκλήθησαν (1x)
Ac 20:12 ·alive, and they·were·comforted beyond·measure.

G3870.5 V-APN παρακληθῆναι (1x)
Mt 2:18 And she·was·not willing to·be·comforted, because

G3870.5 V-APS-3P παρακληθῶσιν (1x)
Col 2:2 their hearts may·be·comforted, being·knit·together in

G3870.5 V-RPI-1P παρακεκλήμεθα (1x)
2Co 7:13 ·account·of that, we·have·been·comforted in yeur

G3871 παρα•καλύπτω parakalýptō *v.* (1x)
Roots:G3844 G2572

G3871.2 V-RPP-NSN παρακεκαλυμμένον (1x)
Lk 9:45 and it·was having·been·tightly·veiled from them,

G3872 παρα•κατα•θήκη parakatathḗkē *n.* (2x)
Roots:G3844 G2698 Compare:G3866 G2526-3 xLangAlso:H4399

G3872.3 N-ASF παρακαταθήκην (2x)
1Ti 6:20 ·keep the charge·fully·consigned·to·your·care,
2Ti 1:14 The good charge·fully·consigned·to·your·care, you·

G3873 παρά•κειμαι parákeîmai *v.* (2x)
Roots:G3844 G2749

G3873.1 V-PNI-3S παράκειται (2x)
Rm 7:18 *morally·good·thing* is·directly·laid·out before·me,
Rm 7:21 the bad·thing *also* is·directly·laid·out before·me.

G3874 παρά•κλησις paráklēsis *n.* (29x)
Roots:G3870 Compare:G3888 See:G3875

G3874.1 N-GSF παρακλήσεως (1x)
2Co 8:4 ·petitioning us with much entreaty for·us to·accept

G3874.2 N-NSF παράκλησις (2x)
Php 2:1 if *there·is* any exhortation in Anointed-One, if any
1Th 2:3 For our exhortation *was* not birthed·from·out of·

G3874.2 N-ASF παράκλησιν (2x)
1Co 14:3 *for* edification, and exhortation, and personal·
2Co 8:17 Because in·fact, he·accepted the exhortation; but

G3874.2 N-DSF παρακλήσει (4x)
Ac 9:31 Lord and in·the exhortation·and·comfort of·the Holy
Ac 15:31 ·*it*·aloud, they·rejoiced over the exhortation.
Rm 12:8 or the·one exhorting, on the exhortation; the·one
1Ti 4:13 reading·aloud *of·Scripture*, to·the exhortation, *and*

G3874.2 N-GSF παρακλήσεως (3x)
Ac 13:15 yeu a·word of·exhortation specifically·for the
Heb 12:5 of·the exhortation which thoroughly·relates to·yeu
Heb 13:22 bear·with the word of·exhortation, for through

G3874.3 N-ASF παράκλησιν (1x)
Phm 1:7 we·have much gratitude and comfort in your love,

G3874.3 N-DSF παρακλήσει (2x)
2Co 7:4 with·the comfort, I·am·abounding·above·and·
2Co 7:13 we·have·been·comforted in yeur comfort; and

G3874.3 N-GSF παρακλήσεως (4x)
Rm 15:4 patient·endurance and the comfort of·the Scriptures
Rm 15:5 patient·endurance and of·the comfort grant to·yeu
2Co 1:3 of·the tender·compassions and God of·all comfort,
2Co 1:4 through the comfort with·which we·ourselves are·

G3874.4 N-NSF παράκλησις (1x)
2Co 1:5 in us, in·this·manner our comforting also abounds

G3874.4 N-GSF παρακλήσεως (3x)
2Co 1:6 *it·is* on·behalf·of·yeur comforting and Salvation,
2Co 1:6 *it·is* on·behalf·of·yeur comforting and Salvation
2Co 1:7 ·manner *yeu·are* also *partners* of·the comforting.

G3874.5 N-ASF παράκλησιν (3x)
Lk 2:25 and devout, awaiting the·consoling of·IsraEl. And
Heb 6:18 to·lie, we·may·have a·strong consoling (*we·being*
2Th 2:16 *us* eternal consoling and a·beneficially·good

G3874.5 N-DSF παρακλήσει (1x)
2Co 7:7 also by the consoling with·which he·was·comforted

G3874.5 N-GSF παρακλήσεως (1x)
Ac 4:36 *from·Aramaic*, is Son of·Consoling), *was* a·Levite

G3874.6 N-ASF παράκλησιν (1x)
Lk 6:24 Because yeu·completely·have yeur consolation.

G3875 παρά•κλητος paráklētos *n.* (5x)
Roots:G3844 G2822 See:G3874

G3875.4 N-NSM παράκλητος (3x)
Jn 14:26 "But the Companion/Intercessor, *who·is* the Holy
Jn 15:26 whenever the Companion/Intercessor should·come,
Jn 16:7 go·away, the Companion/Intercessor shall·not come

G3875.4 N-ASM παράκλητον (2x)
Jn 14:16 he·shall·give yeu another Companion/Intercessor,
1Jn 2:1 ·fail, we·have a·Companion/Intercessor alongside

G3876 παρ•ακοή parakoḗ *n.* (3x)
Roots:G3878 Compare:G5218 G0506

G3876.2 N-NSF παρακοή (1x)
Heb 2:2 violation and inattentive·disregard received a·just

G3876.2 N-ASF παρακοήν (1x)
2Co 10:6 to·avenge all inattentive·disregard, whenever yeur

G3876.2 N-GSF παρακοῆς (1x)
Rm 5:19 the inattentive·disregard of·one man·of·clay†, the

G3877 παρ•α•κολουθέω parakolouthéō *v.* (4x)
Roots:G3844 G0190 Compare:G4748 G4964

G3877.1 V-FAI-3S παρακολουθήσει (1x)
Mk 16:17 these signs shall·closely·follow the·ones already·

G3877.1 V-RAI-2S παρηκολούθηκας (2x)
1Ti 4:6 instruction, to·which you·have·closely·followed.
2Ti 3:10 you·yourself have·closely·followed my instruction,

G3877.1 V-RAP-DSM παρηκολουθηκότι (1x)
Lk 1:3 ·also, having·closely·followed all·things accurately

G3878 παρ•ακούω parakoúō *v.* (2x)
Roots:G3844 G0191 Compare:G0506

G3878.2 V-AAS-3S παρακούσῃ (2x)
Mt 18:17 And if he·should·disregard them, declare *it* to·the
Mt 18:17 also he·should·disregard the convened·Called·Out·

G3879 παρα•κύπτω parakýptō *v.* (5x)
Roots:G3844 G2955

G3879 V-AAI-3S παρέκυψεν (1x)
Jn 20:11 she·was·weeping, she·stooped·near·to·peer into the

G3879 V-AAN παρακύψαι (1x)
1Pe 1:12 ·things angels long to·stoop·near·and·peer into.

G3879 V-AAP-NSM παρακύψας (3x)
Jn 20:5 And stooping·near·to·peer·in, he·looked·at the
Lk 24:12 and stooping·near·to·peer·in, he·looked·upon the
Jac 1:25 But the·one stooping·near·to·peer into the complete

G3880 παρα•λαμβάνω paralambánō *v.* (51x)
Roots:G3844 G2983 Compare:G3858 G4355

G3880.2 -- (1x)
Lk 17:36 in the field; one shall·be·personally·taken, and the

G3880.2 V-FPI-3S παραληφθήσεται (2x)
Lk 17:34 couch; the one shall·be·personally·taken, and the
Lk 17:35 in·unison; one shall·be·personally·taken, and the

G3880.2 V-PAI-3S παραλαμβάνει (8x)
Lk 11:26 it·traverses and personally·takes *to·itself* seven
Mt 4:5 Then the Slanderer personally·takes him up into the
Mt 4:8 Again, the Slanderer personally·takes him up to a·
Mt 12:45 he·traverses and personally·takes with himself
Mt 17:1 six days, YeShua personally·takes Peter and Jakob
Mk 5:40 ·all·of·them, he·personally·takes the little·child's
Mk 9:2 after six days, Jesus personally·takes Peter, Jakob,
Mk 14:33 Then he·personally·takes with him Peter, Jakob,

G3880.2 V-PAI-3P παραλαμβάνουσιν (1x)
Mk 4:36 the crowd, they·personally·took him as·soon·as he·

G3880.2 V-PPI-3S παραλαμβάνεται (2x)
Mt 24:40 the field; the one is·personally·taken, and the *other*
Mt 24:41 at the mill-house; one is·personally·taken, and one

G3880.2 V-2AAI-3S παρέλαβεν (4x)
Mt 1:24 ·assigned him, and he·personally·took *her for* his
Mt 2:14 ·being·awakened, he·personally·took the little·child
Mt 2:21 ·being·awakened, he·personally·took the little·child
Mt 20:17 JeruSalem, YeShua personally·took the twelve

G3880.2 V-2AAI-3P παρέλαβον (1x)
Jn 19:16 ·be·crucified. And they·personally·took Jesus and

G3880.2 V-2AAM-2S παράλαβε (3x)
Mt 2:13 ·being·awakened, personally·take the little·child
Mt 2:20 ·being·awakened, personally·take the little·child
Mt 18:16 ·not hear *you, then* personally·take with you one

G3880.2 V-2AAN παραλαβεῖν (1x)
Mt 1:20 ·should·not be·afraid to·personally·take Mariam *for*

G3880.2 V-2AAP-ASM παραλαβόντα (1x)
Ac 15:39 and *for* BarNabas, personally·taking *John*·Mark,

G3880.2 V-2AAP-NSM παραλαβών (10x)
Lk 9:10 they·did. And personally·taking them, he·quietly·
Lk 9:28 these sayings, that·also personally·taking Peter,
Lk 18:31 Now personally·taking the twelve, he·declared to
Ac 16:33 And personally·taking them in the same hour of·
Ac 21:24 after·personally·taking these·men, be·
Ac 21:26 Then Paul, after·personally·taking the men on·the
Ac 21:32 ran·down to them, personally·taking soldiers and
Ac 23:18 the *centurion*, personally·taking him, brought
Mt 26:37 Then personally·taking *with·him* Peter and the two
Mk 10:32 they·were·afraid. And personally·taking again the

G3880.2 V-2AAP-NPM παραλαβόντες (1x)
Mt 27:27 ·the governor, after·personally·taking YeShua into
G3880.3 V-FDI-1S παραλήψομαι (1x)
Jn 14:3 I·come again and shall·personally·receive yeu to
G3880.3 V-PAP-NPM παραλαμβάνοντες (1x)
Heb 12:28 personally·receiving an·unshakable kingdom,
G3880.3 V-2AAI-1S παρέλαβον (3x)
Gal 1:12 For I·myself neither personally·received it from a·
1Co 11:23 For I·myself personally·received from the Lord
1Co 15:3 that·which also I·personally·received, that
G3880.3 V-2AAI-2S παρέλαβες (1x)
Col 4:17 the service which you·personally·received in *the*
G3880.3 V-2AAI-2P παρελάβετε (5x)
Gal 1:9 ·to that·which yeu·personally·received, let·him·be
Php 4:9 also yeu·learned, and personally·received, and
1Th 4:1 YeShua, just·as yeu·personally·received from us,
1Co 15:1 to·yeu, which also yeu·personally·received, and in
Col 2:6 as yeu·personally·received the Anointed-One, Jesus
G3880.3 V-2AAI-3S παρέλαβεν (1x)
2Th 3:6 the tradition which he·personally·received from us.
G3880.3 V-2AAI-3P παρέλαβον (2x)
Jn 1:11 ·own, and his·own did·not personally·receive him.
Mk 7:4 which they·personally·received to·securely·hold,
G3880.3 V-2AAP-NPM παραλαβόντες (1x)
1Th 2:13 because after·personally·receiving God's
EG3880.3 (1x)
Gal 1:12 but·rather *I·personally·received it* through a·

G3881 παρα•λέγομαι paralégômai *v.* (2x)
Roots:G3844 G3004
G3881.2 V-PNP-NPM παραλεγόμενοι (1x)
Ac 27:8 And sailing·near it with·difficulty, we·came to some
G3881.2 V-INI-3P παρελέγοντο (1x)
Ac 27:13 ·taking·up·anchor, they·were·sailing·near Crete,

G3882 παρ•άλιος paráliôs *adj.* (1x)
Roots:G3844 G0251
G3882 A-GSF παραλίου (1x)
Lk 6:17 and JeruSalem, and from·the sea·coast of·Tyre and

G3883 παρ•αλλαγή parallagḗ *n.* (1x)
Roots:G3844 G0236
G3883.2 N-NSF παραλλαγή (1x)
Jac 1:17 with whom there·is·not therein an·alteration, nor *the*

G3884 παρα•λογίζομαι paralôgízômai *v.* (2x)
Roots:G3844 G3049 Compare:G2603 G3180
G3884.2 V-PNP-NPM παραλογιζόμενοι (1x)
Jac 1:22 not merely hearers, defrauding yeur·own·selves.
G3884.2 V-PNS-3S παραλογίζηται (1x)
Col 2:4 this I·say, lest any·man should·defraud yeu with

G3885 παρα•λυτικός paralytikós *adj.* (10x)
Roots:G3886
G3885.1 A-NSM παραλυτικός (2x)
Mt 8:6 my servant·boy has·been·cast paralyzed *on a·couch*
Mk 2:4 mat on which the paralyzed·man was·laying·down.
G3885.1 A-ASM παραλυτικόν (2x)
Mt 9:2 to·him a·paralyzed·man having·been·cast on a·
Mk 2:3 to him, bringing a·paralyzed·man being·carried by
G3885.1 A-APM παραλυτικούς (1x)
Mt 4:24 and those·being·lunatic, and those·paralyzed. And
G3885.1 A-DSM παραλυτικῷ (5x)
Mt 9:2 trust, YeShua declared to·the paralyzed·man, "Child,
Mt 9:6 (then he·says to·the paralyzed·man), "Upon·being·
Mk 2:5 their trust, says to·the paralyzed·man, "Child, your
Mk 2:9 is easier to·declare to·the paralyzed·man, 'The
Mk 2:10 ·failures—" *then* he·says to·the paralyzed·man,

G3886 παρα•λύω paralýō *v.* (5x)
Roots:G3844 G3089
G3886.1 V-RPP-DSM παραλελυμένῳ (1x)
Lk 5:24 (he·declared to·the·one having·been·paralyzed),
G3886.1 V-RPP-NSM παραλελυμένος (2x)
Lk 5:18 a·simple·couch who was having·been·paralyzed,
Ac 9:33 eight years, *and* who was having·been·paralyzed.
G3886.1 V-RPP-NPM παραλελυμένοι (1x)
Ac 8:7 many *of·the·ones* having·been·paralyzed and lame
G3886.2 V-RPP-APN παραλελυμένα (1x)
Heb 12:12 ·upright the limp hands and the paralyzed knees,

G3887 παρα•μένω paraménō *v.* (3x)
Roots:G3844 G3306
G3887.2 V-FAI-1S παραμενῶ (1x)
1Co 16:6 And it·may·be·that I·shall·abide·nearby or even
G3887.3 V-PAN παραμένειν (1x)
Heb 7:23 being·prevented to·personally·continue on· death.
G3887.3 V-AAP-NSM παραμείνας (1x)
Jac 1:25 Law of·Liberty, and personally·continuing *in·it*,

G3888 παρα•μυθέομαι paramythéômai *v.* (4x)
Roots:G3844 G3454 Compare:G2292 G3874 G4389
G3888.3 V-PNM-2P παραμυθεῖσθε (1x)
1Th 5:14 ·ones, personally·encourage the fainthearted,
G3888.3 V-PNP-NPM παραμυθούμενοι (2x)
Jn 11:31 in the home and personally·consoling her, seeing
1Th 2:11 exhorting and personally·encouraging yeu and
G3888.3 V-ADS-3P παραμυθήσωνται (1x)
Jn 11:19 in·order·that they·should·personally·console them

G3889 παρα•μυθία paramythía *n.* (1x)
Roots:G3888 See:G3890
G3889 N-ASF παραμυθίαν (1x)
1Co 14:3 and exhortation, and personal·consolation.

G3890 παρα•μύθιον paramýthiôn *n.* (1x)
Roots:G3889
G3890 N-NSN παραμύθιον (1x)
Php 2:1 Anointed-One, if any personal·consolation of·love,

G3891 παρα•νομέω paranôméō *v.* (1x)
Roots:G3844 G3551 Compare:G3845 See:G3892 G3848
G3891.2 V-PAP-NSM παρανομῶν (1x)
Ac 23:3 *for* me to·be·pummeled contrary·to·Torah-Law?"

G3892 παρα•νομία paranômía *n.* (2x)
Roots:G3844 G3551 Compare:G3848 G0458 See:G3891 G3845 G3892-1
G3892.2 N-GSF παρανομίας (1x)
2Pe 2:16 a·reproof of·his·own transgression: a·voiceless
EG3892.2 (1x)
Jac 2:10 he·has·become held·liable of·all *transgressions*.

G3893 παρα•πικραίνω parapikraínō *v.* (1x)
Roots:G3844 G4087 See:G3894 xLangAlso:H7378
G3893.2 V-AAI-3P παρεπίκραναν (1x)
Heb 3:16 after·hearing, some did·directly·provoke, but·yet

G3894 παρα•πικρασμός parapikrasmós *n.* (2x)
Roots:G3893 xLangEquiv:H4808 xLangAlso:H4809
G3894.2 N-DSM παραπικρασμῷ (2x)
Heb 3:8 yeur hearts, as in the Direct·Provocation, in the
Heb 3:15 harden yeur hearts, as in the Direct·Provocation."

G3895 παρα•πίπτω parapíptō *v.* (1x)
Roots:G3844 G4098 See:G3900
G3895.2 V-2AAP-APM παραπεσόντας (1x)
Heb 6:6 and·then *once* personally·falling·away … *it·is*

G3896 παρα•πλέω parapléō *v.* (1x)
Roots:G3844 G4126
G3896 V-AAN παραπλεῦσαι (1x)
Ac 20:16 for Paul decided to·sail·directly·by Ephesus, so·

G3897 παρα•πλήσιον paraplḗsiôn *adv.* (1x)
Roots:G3844 G4139
G3897.2 ADV παραπλήσιον (1x)
Php 2:27 For even he·was·sick almost to·death, but·yet God

G3898 παρα•πλησίως paraplēsíōs *adv.* (1x)
Roots:G3844 G4139 See:G3897
G3898.3 ADV παραπλησίως (1x)
Heb 2:14 he·himself likewise·personally participated·and·

G3899 παρα•πορεύομαι parapôrêúômai *v.* (5x)
Roots:G3844 G4198
G3899.2 V-PNN παραπορεύεσθαι (1x)
Mk 2:23 *for* him to·be·traversing·directly through the grain·
G3899.2 V-PNP-NPM παραπορευόμενοι (3x)
Mt 27:39 the·ones traversing·directly·by were·reviling him,
Mk 11:20 at·dawn, as·they·were·traversing·directly·by *it*,
Mk 15:29 the·ones traversing·directly·by were·reviling him,
G3899.2 V-INI-3P παρεπορεύοντο (1x)
Mk 9:30 they·were·traversing·directly through Galilee, and

G3900 παρά•πτωμα paráptōma *n.* (24x)
Roots:G3895 Compare:G0266 G0458 G3892 See:G4417 xLangAlso:H6588
G3900.3 N-NSN παράπτωμα (3x)
Rm 5:15 in·this·manner (but·yet not as the trespass). For if
Rm 5:20 in·order·that the trespass may·increase·more. But
Rm 11:12 Now if their trespass *became* wealth for·*the*·world,
G3900.3 N-APN παραπτώματα (10x)
Mt 6:14 ·forgive the men·of·clay† their trespasses, yeur
Mt 6:15 the men·of·clay† their trespasses, neither·even·shall
Mt 6:15 ·even·shall yeur Father forgive yeur trespasses.
Mt 18:35 ·forgive his brother their trespasses from yeur
Mk 11:25 in the heavens) may·forgive yeu yeur trespasses.
Mk 11:26 in the heavens) shall·forgive yeur trespasses."
Rm 4:25 was·handed·over on·account·of our trespasses, and
Jac 5:16 Explicitly·confess *yeur* trespasses to·one·another,
2Co 5:19 ·not presently·reckoning their trespasses to·them,
Col 2:13 him, graciously·forgiving us all the trespasses—
G3900.3 N-DSN παραπτώματι (4x)
Gal 6:1 ·of·clay† should·be·overtaken in some trespass, yeu
Rm 5:15 For if by·the trespass of·the one, the many died, so·
Rm 5:17 For if by·the one trespass, Death reigned through
Rm 11:11 But·rather, through·their trespass, the Salvation
G3900.3 N-DPN παραπτώμασιν (3x)
Eph 2:1 were·once dead in·the trespasses and in·the moral·
Eph 2:5 dead in·the trespasses, he·made·*us*·alive·together in·
Col 2:13 being in the trespasses and the uncircumcision of·
G3900.3 N-GSN παραπτώματος (1x)
Rm 5:18 as through one trespass, *judgment came* upon all
G3900.3 N-GPN παραπτωμάτων (2x)
Rm 5:16 of·many trespasses unto a·verdict·of·righteousness.
Eph 1:7 blood— the pardon of·trespasses according·to the
EG3900.3 (1x)
Rm 5:16 of·one *trespass* unto a·verdict·of·condemnation, but

G3901 παρα•ρρυέω pararrhyéō *v.* (1x)
Roots:G3844 G4482
G3901.3 V-2AAS-1P παραρρυῶμεν (1x)
Heb 2:1 lest·at·any·time we·should·drift·away *from·it*.

G3902 παρά•σημος parásēmôs *n.* (1x)
Roots:G3844 G4591
G3902.2 N-DSN παρασήμῳ (1x)
Ac 28:11 with·a·figurehead of·the·twin·sons·of·Zeus

G3903 παρα•σκευάζω paraskêuázō *v.* (4x)
Roots:G3844 G4632 Compare:G2090 G2680 See:G0532
G3903.1 V-PAP-GPM παρασκευαζόντων (1x)
Ac 10:10 but with·the·others making·preparation, a·trance
G3903.1 V-RPI-3S παρεσκεύασται (1x)
2Co 9:2 Achaia has·been·making·preparation since last·year;
G3903.2 V-RPP-NPM παρεσκευασμένοι (1x)
2Co 9:3 yeu·may·be having·been·personally·prepared.
G3903.3 V-FDI-3S παρασκευάσεται (1x)
1Co 14:8 sound, who shall·prepare·himself for battle?

G3904 παρα•σκευή paraskêuḗ *n.* (6x)
Roots:G3903
G3904.2 N-NSF παρασκευή (4x)
Jn 19:14 Now it·was preparation·day of·the Passover, and *it*·
Jn 19:31 ·course, since it·was preparation·day, in·order·that
Lk 23:54 And *that* day was preparation·day, and a·Sabbath
Mk 15:42 occurring, since it·was preparation·day (that is, *a*·
G3904.2 N-ASF παρασκευήν (2x)
Jn 19:42 on·account·of the Judeans' preparation·day, because
Mt 27:62 which is after the preparation·day, the chief·priests

G3905 παρα•τείνω paratêínō *v.* (1x)
Roots:G3844 G5037-1
G3905.2 V-IAI-3S παρέτεινεν (1x)
Ac 20:7 next·day; and he·was·prolonging the conversation

G3906 παρα•τηρέω paratēréō *v.* (6x)
Roots:G3844 G5083 See:G3907
G3906.1 V-PMI-2P παρατηρεῖσθε (1x)
Gal 4:10 Yeu·meticulously·keep days, and lunar·months,
G3906.2 V-PMP-NPM παρατηρούμενοι (1x)
Lk 14:1 they·themselves were meticulously·watching him.
G3906.2 V-IAI-3P παρετήρουν (3x)
Lk 6:7 and the Pharisees were·meticulously·watching him,
Ac 9:24 And they·were·meticulously·watching the gates
Mk 3:2 And they·were·meticulously·watching him, *as·to*
G3906.2 V-AAP-NPM παρατηρήσαντες (1x)
Lk 20:20 And meticulously·watching *him*, they·dispatched

G3907 παρα•τήρησις paratērēsis *n.* (1x)
Roots:G3906
G3907 N-GSF παρατηρήσεως (1x)
Lk 17:20 ·God does·not come with meticulous·observation,

G3908 παρα•τίθημι paratíthēmi *v.* (19x)
Roots:G3844 G5087 Compare:G0728 G0394 See:G3866
G3908.2 V-FAI-1S παραθήσω (1x)
Lk 11:6 I·do·not have that·which I·shall·place·before him.'
G3908.2 V-PPP-ASN παρατιθέμενον (1x)
1Co 10:27 to·traverse, eat anything being·placed·before yeu,
G3908.2 V-PPP-APN παρατιθέμενα (1x)
Lk 10:8 yeu, eat *such·things as are* being·placed·before yeu.
G3908.2 V-AAI-3S παρέθηκεν (1x)
Ac 16:34 up into his house, he·placed·forth a·meal·table and
G3908.2 V-AAI-3P παρέθηκαν (1x)
Mk 8:6 ·may·place *them*·forth, and they·placed *them* before
G3908.2 V-2AAN παραθεῖναι (1x)
Mk 8:7 *them*, he·declared *to·his disciples* to·place them also
G3908.2 V-2AAS-3P παραθῶσιν (2x)
Mk 6:41 in·order·that they·should·place·*them*·before *the*
Mk 8:6 in·order·that they·may·place·*them*·forth, and they·
G3908.2 V-APN παρατιθέναι (1x)
Lk 9:16 *them* to·the disciples to·place·before the crowd.
G3908.3 V-PMP-NSM παρατιθέμενος (1x)
Ac 17:3 and putting·forth·directly that it·was·mandatory·for
G3908.3 V-AAI-3S παρέθηκεν (2x)
Mt 13:24 Another parable he·put·forth·directly to·them,
Mt 13:31 Another parable he·put·forth·directly to·them,
G3908.4 V-FDI-1S παραθήσομαι (1x)
Lk 23:46 hands I·shall·place·the·direct·care·of my spirit.'"
G3908.4 V-PMI-1S παρατίθεμαι (2x)
Ac 20:32 brothers, I·place·the·direct·care·of yeu to·God,
1Ti 1:18 I·place·the·direct·care·of this charge to·you, *my*
G3908.4 V-PPM-3P παρατιθέσθωσαν (1x)
1Pe 4:19 will of·God must·place·the·direct·care·of their·own
G3908.4 V-2AMI-2S παράθου (1x)
2Ti 2:2 place·the·direct·care·of these·things to·trustworthy
G3908.4 V-2AMI-3P παρέθεντο (2x)
Lk 12:48 and to·whom *others* place·the·direct·care·of much,
Ac 14:23 fasting, they·placed·the·direct·care·of them to·the

G3909 παρα•τυγχάνω paratynchánō *v.* (1x)
Roots:G3844 G5177
G3909 V-PAP-APM παρατυγχάνοντας (1x)
Ac 17:17 and·every day alongside the·ones chancing·nearby.

G3910 παρ•αυτίκα parautíka *adv.* (1x)
Roots:G3844 G0846
G3910 ADV παραυτίκα (1x)
2Co 4:17 momentary tribulation is·accomplishing for·us

G3911 παρα•φέρω paraphérō *v.* (2x)
Roots:G3844 G5342
G3911.5 V-2AAM-2S παρένεγκε (1x)
Mk 14:36 *are* possible to·you. Personally·carry this cup
G3911.5 V-2AAN παρενεγκεῖν (1x)
Lk 22:42 you·are·definitely·willing to·personally·carry this

G3912 παρα•φρονέω paraphrônéō *v.* (1x)
Roots:G3844 G5426
G3912 V-PAP-NSM παραφρονῶν (1x)
2Co 11:23 of·Anointed-One? Being·beyond·reason, I·speak

G3913 παρα•φρονία paraphrônía *n.* (1x)
Roots:G3912
G3913.1 N-ASF παραφρονίαν (1x)
2Pe 2:16 ·clay† forbade the irrational·conduct of·the prophet.

G3914 παρα•χειμάζω parachêimázō *v.* (4x)
Roots:G3844 G5492
G3914 V-FAI-1S παραχειμάσω (1x)
1Co 16:6 ·abide·nearby or even shall·winter alongside yeu,
G3914 V-AAN παραχειμάσαι (2x)
Ac 27:12 ·might·be·able to·arrive at Phenice to·winter *there*,
Tit 3:12 me to NicoPolis, for I·have·decided to·winter there.
G3914 V-RAP-DSM παρακεχειμακότι (1x)
Ac 28:11 And after having·wintered on the island *for* three

G3915 παρα•χειμασία parachêimasía *n.* (1x)
Roots:G3914
G3915 N-ASF παραχειμασίαν (1x)
Ac 27:12 ·being unsuitable, particularly·for wintering·in, the

G3916 παρα•χρῆμα parachrēma *adv.* (19x)
Roots:G3844 G5536 Compare:G2112
G3916.2 ADV παραχρῆμα (19x)
Lk 1:64 And his mouth was·opened·up at·once, and his
Lk 4:39 it·left her. And at·once rising·up, she·was·attending
Lk 5:25 And at·once, rising·up in·the·sight of·them, taking·
Lk 8:44 fringe of·his garment, and at·once her flow of·blood
Lk 8:47 ·laid·hold of·him, and how at·once, she·was·healed.
Lk 8:55 spirit returned, and she·stood·up at·once, and he·
Lk 13:13 on·her, and at·once she·is·straightened·upright,
Lk 18:43 And at·once, he·received·his·sight and was·
Lk 19:11 ·God is·about to·be·made·totally·apparent at·once.
Lk 22:60 what you·are·saying." And at·once, with·him still
Ac 3:7 hand, he·pulled·him·up. And at·once, his feet and
Ac 5:10 And she·fell·down at·once directly·at his feet and
Ac 9:18 eyes. And he·received·sight at·once. And rising·up,
Ac 12:23 And at·once, an·angel of·Yahweh smote him,
Ac 13:11 ·for·a·season." And at·once there·fell upon him
Ac 16:26 of·the dungeon to·be·shaken. And at·once, all the
Ac 16:33 ·blows; and he·was·immersed at·once, he and all
Mt 21:19 coming·age." And at·once the fig·tree is·withered·
Mt 21:20 "How·is the fig·tree withered·away *all* at·once?"

G3917 πάρδαλις párdalis *n.* (1x)
xLangAlso:H5246 A5245
G3917 N-DSF παρδάλει (1x)
Rv 13:2 ·Beast which I·saw was like a·leopard, and its feet

G3918 πάρ•ειμι párêimi *v.* (23x)
Roots:G3844 G1510 See:G3952 G4840
G3918.1 V-PXI-3S πάρεστιν (1x)
Jn 11:28 "The Mentor is·near, and he·hollers·out·for you.
G3918.2 V-PXP-DPN παροῦσιν (1x)
Heb 13:5 being·satisfied with·the·things being·at·hand, for
G3918.3 V-PXI-1P πάρεσμεν (1x)
Ac 10:33 all in·the·sight of·God. We·are·present to·hear all
G3918.3 V-PXI-3S πάρεστιν (1x)
2Pe 1:9 in·whom these *qualities* are·not present, he·is blind,
G3918.3 V-PXI-3P πάρεισιν (1x)
Ac 17:6 The Land, these·men are·presently here also,
G3918.3 V-PXN παρεῖναι (2x)
Gal 4:18 not merely with me being·present alongside yeu.
Gal 4:20 I·was·wanting to·be·present alongside yeu at·this·
G3918.3 V-PXP-ASN παρόν (1x)
Heb 12:11 ·discipline, particularly·for the present, does·not
G3918.3 V-PXP-DSF παρούσῃ (1x)
2Pe 1:12 having·been·firmly·established in·the present truth.
G3918.3 V-PXP-GSN παρόντος (1x)
Col 1:6 with·the *good·news* being·present among yeu, just·as
G3918.3 V-PXP-NSM παρών (6x)
1Co 5:3 ·absent in·the body but being·present in·the spirit,
1Co 5:3 even·now, as·though being·present, I·have·judged
2Co 10:2 to·be·bold when·I·am·present with·the confidence
2Co 11:9 And while·being·present alongside yeu and
2Co 13:2 ·forewarn as·though being·present the second·time
2Co 13:10 *yeu* with·abrupt·sharpness while·being·present,
G3918.3 V-PXP-NPM παρόντες (1x)
2Co 10:11 *shall·we·be* also in·deed while·being·present."
G3918.3 V-IXI-3P παρῆσαν (2x)
Lk 13:1 some·men were·present *who·were* reporting to·him
Ac 12:20 ·determination, they·were·present alongside him.
G3918.4 V-PXI-2S πάρει (1x)
Mt 26:50 *attend* to *that* for·which you·are·here!" Then
G3918.4 V-PXI-2P πάρεστε (1x)
Ac 10:21 the motivation on·account·of which yeu·are·here?"
G3918.4 V-PXI-3S πάρεστιν (1x)
Jn 7:6 "My season is·not·yet here, but yeur season is always
G3918.4 V-PXN παρεῖναι (1x)
Ac 24:19 it·is·necessary *for·them* to·be·here before you and

G3919 παρ•εισ•άγω parêiságō *v.* (1x)
Roots:G3844 G1521
G3919.2 V-FAI-3P παρεισάξουσιν (1x)
2Pe 2:1 who shall·privately·introduce factions·and· of·total·

G3920 παρ•είσ•ακτος parêísaktôs *adj.* (1x)
Roots:G3919
G3920 A-APM παρεισάκτους (1x)
Gal 2:4 *still*, on·account·of the infiltrating, false·brothers

G3921 παρ•εισ•δύνω parêisdýnō *v.* (1x)
Roots:G3844 G1519 G1416
G3921.2 V-AAI-3P παρεισέδυσαν (1x)
Jud 1:4 men·of·clay† crept·into·place·unawares, the·ones

G3922 παρ•εισ•έρχομαι parêisérchômai *v.* (2x)
Roots:G3844 G1525
G3922.2 V-2AAI-3S παρεισῆλθεν (1x)
Rm 5:20 Torah-Law came·in·with·an·ulterior·motive in· the
G3922.2 V-2AAI-3P παρεισῆλθον (1x)
Gal 2:4 who came·in·with·ulterior·motives to·spy·out our

G3923 παρ•εισ•φέρω parêisphérō *v.* (1x)
Roots:G3844 G1533 Compare:G2023 G3618
G3923.3 V-AAP-NPM παρεισενέγκαντες (1x)
2Pe 1:5 Now also *besides* this, applying all diligence, yeu·

G3924 παρ•εκτός parêktós *adv.* (3x)
Roots:G3844 G1622
G3924.2 ADV παρεκτός (1x)
2Co 11:28 the·things *that·are* externally·pressing, *there·is*
G3924.4 ADV παρεκτός (2x)
Ac 26:29 ·I am, *though* personally·aside·from these bonds."
Mt 5:32 his wife, personally·aside·from a·reason of·sexual·

G3925 παρ•εμ•βολή parêmbôlḗ *n.* (10x)
Roots:G3844 G1685 Compare:G4753 G4760 See:G2682 xLangAlso:H4264
G3925.2 N-GSF παρεμβολῆς (2x)
Heb 13:11 ·burned outside the arrayed·encampment.
Heb 13:13 to him outside the arrayed·encampment, bearing
G3925.3 N-ASF παρεμβολήν (1x)
Rv 20:9 and they·surrounded the garrison of·the holy·ones
G3925.3 N-APF παρεμβολάς (1x)
Heb 11:34 in battle, routed estranged·foreign garrisons.
G3925.4 N-ASF παρεμβολήν (6x)
Ac 21:34 ·ordered him to·be·brought into the barracks.
Ac 21:37 was·about to·be·brought into the barracks, he·says
Ac 22:24 him to·be·brought into the barracks, declaring for·
Ac 23:10 midst of·them, and to·bring *him* into the barracks.
Ac 23:16 and entering into the barracks, he·reported *it* to·
Ac 23:32 returned·back to the barracks *in·JeruSalem*, after·

G3926 παρ•εν•οχλέω parênôchléō *v.* (1x)
Roots:G3844 G1776
G3926 V-PAN παρενοχλεῖν (1x)
Ac 15:19 judge *for·us* not to·further·harass the·ones from the

G3927 παρ•επί•δημος parêpídēmôs *adj.* (3x)
Roots:G3844 G1927 Compare:G3941 G3581 G0241 See:G0590
G3927 A-NPM παρεπίδημοι (1x)
Heb 11:13 they·were foreigners and foreign·residents on the
G3927 A-APM παρεπιδήμους (1x)
1Pe 2:11 sojourners and foreign·residents to·abstain·from the
G3927 A-DPM παρεπιδήμοις (1x)
1Pe 1:1 To·Selected foreign·residents of·*the*·Diaspora

G3928 παρ•έρχομαι parérchômai *v.* (31x)
Roots:G3844 G2064 Compare:G0272 G3865 G1950 See:G0492

G3928.1 V-2AAP-NSM παρελθών (3x)
Lk 12:37 ·at·the·table, and coming·near, he·shall·attend to·
Lk 17:7 of·the field, 'After·coming·aside, sit·back·and·eat'?
Ac 24:7 regiment·commander, after·coming·near with much
G3928.3 V-PNI-3S παρέρχεται (1x)
Lk 18:37 to·him that Jesus of·Natsareth was·passing·by.
G3928.3 V-2AAN παρελθεῖν (2x)
Mt 8:28 some not to·have·strength to·pass·by through that
Mk 6:48 upon the sea, and was·wanting to·pass·by them.
G3928.3 V-2AAP-NPM παρελθόντες (1x)
Ac 16:8 And passing·by Mysia, they·walked·down to Troas.
G3928.3 V-2RAN παρεληλυθέναι (1x)
Ac 27:9 also even·now to·have·passed·by, Paul was·
G3928.3 V-2RAP-NSM παρεληλυθώς (1x)
1Pe 4:3 of·*our*·natural·life already·having·passed·by *was*
G3928.4 V-FDI-3S παρελεύσεται (1x)
Jac 1:10 because as a·flower of·grass, he·shall·pass·away.
G3928.4 V-FDI-3P παρελεύσονται (4x)
Lk 21:33 "The heaven and the earth shall·pass·away, but my
Mt 24:35 "The heaven and the earth shall·pass·away, but my
Mk 13:31 "The heaven and the earth shall·pass·away, but my
2Pe 3:10 the heavens shall·pass·away with·a·whirring·noise ·
G3928.4 V-2AAI-3S παρῆλθεν (3x)
Mt 14:15 the hour even·now *has* passed·away. Dismiss the
2Co 5:17 creation. The ancient·things passed·away; behold,
Rv 21:1 heaven and the first earth passed·away; and the Sea,
G3928.4 V-2AAM-3S παρελθέτω (1x)
Mt 26:39 if it·is possible, let this cup pass·away from me.
G3928.4 V-2AAN παρελθεῖν (2x)
Lk 16:17 the heaven and the earth to·pass·away, than one
Mt 26:42 if this cup is·not able to·pass·away from me unless
G3928.4 V-2AAS-3S παρέλθῃ (6x)
Lk 21:32 ·of·offspring, no, should·not pass·away, until all
Mt 5:18 heaven and the earth should·pass·away, not one iota
Mt 5:18 ·mark, by·no·means, should·pass·away from the
Mt 24:34 ·of·offspring, no, should·not pass·away, until all
Mk 13:30 no, should·not pass·away, so·long·as·until all
Mk 14:35 possible, the hour may·pass·away from him.
G3928.4 V-2AAS-3P παρέλθωσιν (3x)
Lk 21:33 ·away, but my words, no, may·not pass·away.
Mt 24:35 but my words, no, should·not·ever pass·away.
Mk 13:31 but my words, no, should·not·ever pass·away.
G3928.5 V-PNI-2P παρέρχεσθε (1x)
Lk 11:42 ·of garden·plants, and neglect the tribunal·justice
G3928.5 V-2AAI-1S παρῆλθον (1x)
Lk 15:29 to·you, and never·at·any·time did·I·neglect your

G3929 πάρ•εσις párêsis *n.* (1x)
Roots:G3935

G3929 N-ASF πάρεσιν (1x)
Rm 3:25 the reprieve·from·punishment of·the moral·failings

G3930 παρ•έχω paréchō *v.* (17x)
Roots:G3844 G2192

EG3930 (1x)
Lk 18:4 "But after these *persistent appeals*, he·declared
G3930.2 V-PAM-2S πάρεχε (1x)
Lk 6:29 you on the cheek, hold·forth the other *cheek* also,
G3930.2 V-PMP-NSM παρεχόμενος (1x)
Tit 2:7 *continue* holding·yourself·forth *as* a·particular·
G3930.2 V-2AAP-NSM παρασχών (1x)
Ac 17:31 ·determined, after·holding·forth trust to·all *men*·
G3930.3 V-2AAI-3P παρέσχον (1x)
Ac 22:2 Hebrew language, they·personally·held more still).
G3930.4 V-PAI-2P παρέχετε (2x)
Mt 26:10 "Why·do yeu·personally·present wearisome· to·the
Mk 14:6 Why·do yeu·personally·present wearisome·troubles
G3930.4 V-PAM-2S πάρεχε (1x)
Lk 11:7 'Do·not personally·present *your* wearisome·troubles
G3930.4 V-PAM-3S παρεχέτω (1x)
Gal 6:17 no·man personally·present wearisome·troubles to·
G3930.4 V-PAN παρέχειν (1x)
Lk 18:5 ·of this widow personally·presenting *her* wearisome·
G3930.5 V-IAI-3P παρεῖχον (1x)
Ac 28:2 the barbarians were·personally·exhibiting to·us an·
G3930.6 V-FAI-3S παρέξει (1x)
Lk 7:4 worthy for·whom this shall·be·personally·furnished,
G3930.6 V-PAP-DSM παρέχοντι (1x)
1Ti 6:17 (the·one personally·furnishing to·us abundantly all·
G3930.6 V-PMM-2P παρέχεσθε (1x)
Col 4:1 the lords: Yeu·must·personally·furnish to·the slaves
G3930.6 V-IAI-3S παρεῖχεν (1x)
Ac 16:16 ·met us, who was·personally·furnishing her lords
G3930.6 V-IMI-3S παρείχετο (1x)
Ac 19:24 temples of·Artemis, personally·furnished no little
G3930.7 V-PAI-3P παρέχουσιν (1x)
1Ti 1:4 which contrarily·present speculations rather than

G3931 παρ•ηγορία parēgôría *n.* (1x)
Roots:G3844 G0058

G3931.2 N-NSF παρηγορία (1x)
Col 4:11 who did·become a·personal·comfort to·me.

G3932 παρθενία parthenía *n.* (1x)
Roots:G3933 See:G3931-1 xLangAlso:H1331

G3932 N-GSF παρθενίας (1x)
Lk 2:36 with a·husband seven years from her virginity,

G3933 παρθένος parthénôs *n.* (15x)
Compare:G0022 G3494-1 See:G3932 xLangAlso:H5959

G3933.1 N-NSF παρθένος (2x)
1Co 7:28 ·fail; and if the virgin should·marry, she·did·not
1Co 7:34 the wife and the virgin. The unmarried·woman is·
G3933.1 N-NPF παρθένοι (3x)
Mt 25:7 Then all those virgins are·awakened, and they·
Mt 25:11 eventually, the rest *of·the* virgins came also, saying
Rv 14:4 with women, for they·are virgins. These are the·
G3933.1 N-ASF παρθένον (1x)
2Co 11:2 *yeu as* a·morally·clean virgin to·the Anointed-One.
G3933.1 N-DPF παρθένοις (1x)
Mt 25:1 of·the heavens shall·be·likened to·ten virgins, who,
G3933.1 N-GSF παρθένου (1x)
Lk 1:27 house of·David. And the virgin's name *was* Mariam.
G3933.1 N-GPF παρθένων (1x)
1Co 7:25 And concerning the virgins, I·do·not have an·
EG3933.1 (1x)
Mt 25:2 And five *virgins* from·among them were prudent,
G3933.2 N-NPF παρθένοι (1x)
Ac 21:9 had daughters, four virgin·daughters prophesying.
G3933.2 N-ASF παρθένον (2x)
1Co 7:36 ·improper·etiquette toward his virgin·daughter, if
1Co 7:37 heart to·keep·unmarried his virgin·daughter, does
G3933.3 N-NSF παρθένος (1x)
Mt 1:23 "Behold, the veiled·virgin shall·be in pregnancy
G3933.3 N-ASF παρθένον (1x)
Lk 1:27 toward a·veiled·virgin having·been·espoused to·a·

G3934 Πάρθος Párthôs *n/g.* (1x)

G3934 N/G-NPM Πάρθοι (1x)
Ac 2:9 Parthians and Medes and Elamites, and the·ones

G3935 παρ•ίημι paríēmi *v.* (1x)
Roots:G3844 G2423-1

G3935.2 V-RPP-APF παρειμένας (1x)
Heb 12:12 Therefore raise·upright the limp hands and the

G3936 παρ•ίστημι parístēmi *v.* (42x)
παρ•ιστάνω paristánō [prolonged]
Roots:G3844 G2476 Compare:G4921 G1433

G3936.1 V-RAI-3S παρέστηκεν (1x)
Ac 4:10 *name* does this·man stand·nearby in·the·sight of·yeu
G3936.1 V-RAP-ASM-C παρεστῶτα (1x)
Jn 19:26 and the disciple standing·nearby whom he·loved,
G3936.1 V-RAP-DPM παρεστῶσιν (3x)
Lk 19:24 "And he·declared to·the·ones standing·nearby,
Ac 23:2 for·the·ones standing·nearby him to·pummel his
Mk 14:69 again, began·to·say to·the·ones standing·nearby,
G3936.1 V-RAP-GPM παρεστηκότων (2x)
Mk 14:47 one of·the·ones standing·nearby, upon·drawing
Mk 15:35 some of·the·ones standing·nearby, after·hearing
G3936.1 V-RAP-NSM παρεστηκώς (3x)
Jn 18:22 one of·the assistants standing·nearby gave a·slap
Lk 1:19 GabriEl, the·one standing·near in·the·sight of·God;
Mk 15:39 the·one having·stood·nearby out in·front of·him,
G3936.1 V-RAP-NPM-C παρεστῶτες (2x)
Ac 23:4 Now the·ones standing·nearby declared, "Do·you·
Mk 14:70 after, the·ones standing·nearby were·saying again
G3936.1 V-LAI-3P παρειστήκεισαν (1x)
Ac 1:10 behold, two men had·stood·nearby them in white
G3936.2 V-2AAI-3S παρέστη (2x)
Ac 27:23 For there·stood·by me this night an·angel of·God,
2Ti 4:17 But the Lord stood·by me and enabled me, in·order·
G3936.2 V-AAI-3P παρέστησαν (2x)
Ac 4:26 The kings of·the earth stood·by *ready*, and the rulers
Ac 9:39 and all the widows stood·by him, weeping and
G3936.2 V-2AAS-2P παραστῆτε (1x)
Rm 16:2 of·the holy·ones, and *that* yeu·may·stand·by her in
EG3936.2 (1x)
1Pe 3:15 *be* ready always to *present* *a·gracious* defense to·
G3936.3 V-FDI-1P παραστησόμεθα (1x)
Rm 14:10 ·shall all stand·directly·at the Bema·judgment·seat
G3936.4 V-FAI-3S παραστήσει (2x)
Mt 26:53 my Father, and he·shall·present to·me more than
2Co 4:14 through Jesus, and shall·present *us* together with·
G3936.4 V-PAI-2P παριστάνετε (1x)
Rm 6:16 yeu·are slaves to·whom yeu·present yeurselves *as*
G3936.4 V-PAM-2P παριστάνετε (1x)
Rm 6:13 And·yeu·must·not·even present yeur members *as*
G3936.4 V-AAI-2P παρεστήσατε (1x)
Rm 6:19 For just·as yeu·presented yeur members *as* slaves
G3936.4 V-AAI-3S παρέστησεν (1x)
Ac 9:41 holy·ones and the widows, he·presented her alive.
G3936.4 V-AAI-3P παρέστησαν (1x)
Ac 23:33 to·the governor, also presented Paul before·him.
G3936.4 V-AAM-2P παραστήσατε (2x)
Rm 6:13 but·rather yeu·must·present yeurselves to·God, as
Rm 6:19 ·this·manner now yeu·must·present yeur members
G3936.4 V-AAN παραστῆσαι (6x)
Lk 2:22 him up to JeruSalem to·present *him* to·Yahweh—
Ac 23:24 Also *be certain* to·provide beasts *for·them* in·order·
Rm 12:1 tender·compassions of·God, to·present yeur bodies
2Co 11:2 yeu to·one husband, to·present *yeu as* a·morally·
Col 1:22 flesh through the death, to·present yeu holy and
2Ti 2:15 Quickly·endeavor to·present yourself verifiably·
G3936.4 V-AAS-1P παραστήσωμεν (1x)
Col 1:28 in·order·that we·may·present every man·of·clay†
G3936.4 V-AAS-3S παραστήσῃ (1x)
Eph 5:27 that he·may·present her to·himself glorious, the
G3936.4 V-RAI-3S παρέστηκεν (1x)
Mk 4:29 sickle, because the harvest has·presented *itself*."
G3936.5 V-AAI-3S παρέστησεν (1x)
Ac 1:3 also he·established·proof·of himself being·alive after
G3936.5 V-2AAN παραστῆναι (1x)
Ac 27:24 ·is·mandatory·for you to·establish·proof to·Caesar,
G3936.5 V-AAN παραστῆσαι (1x)
Ac 24:13 Neither are·they·able to·establish·proof *against* me
G3936.6 V-PAI-3S παρίστησιν (1x)
1Co 8:8 But food does·not commend us to·God. For neither

G3937 Παρ•μενᾶς Parmenâs *n/p.* (1x)
Roots:G3844 G3306 Compare:G4736 See:G1675

G3937.2 N/P-ASM Παρμενᾶν (1x)
Ac 6:5 Nicanor, Timon, ParMenas, and NicoLaos, a·

G3938 πάρ•οδος párôdôs *n.* (1x)
Roots:G3844 G3598 Compare:G1353-1 G0824-2

G3938.3 N-DSF παρόδῳ (1x)
1Co 16:7 to·see yeu at·this·moment in route, but *instead*, I·

G3939 παρ•οικέω parôikéō *v.* (2x)
Roots:G3844 G3611 Compare:G1927 G0589 G2730 See:G3940 G3941 xLangEquiv:H1481

G3939.2 V-PAI-2S παροικεῖς (1x)
Lk 24:18 "*Are* you only sojourning in JeruSalem, and did·not

G3939.2 V-AAI-3S παρῴκησεν (1x)
Heb 11:9 By·trust, he·sojourned in the land of·promise as *in*

G3940 παρ•οικία parôikía *n.* (2x)
Roots:G3941 See:G3939
xLangEquiv:H4033

G3940.2 N-GSF παροικίας (1x)
1Pe 1:17 *during* the time of·yeur sojourning *here* in reverent·

G3940.3 N-DSF παροικίᾳ (1x)
Ac 13:17 elevated the People in the Sojourning in *the* land

G3941 πάρ•οικος párôikôs *adj.* (4x)
Roots:G3844 G3624 Compare:G3927 G0241
See:G3939 G3940
xLangEquiv:H1616

G3941.2 A-NSM πάροικος (1x)
Ac 7:29 at this saying, and was a·sojourner in *the* land of·

G3941.2 A-NSN πάροικον (1x)
Ac 7:6 shall·be a·sojourner in an·estranged·foreign land, and

G3941.2 A-NPM πάροικοι (1x)
Eph 2:19 ·are no·longer foreigners and sojourners, but·rather

G3941.2 A-APM παροίκους (1x)
1Pe 2:11 I·implore *yeu* as sojourners and foreign·residents

G3942 παρ•οιμία parôimía *n.* (5x)
Roots:G3844 G3633 Compare:G3850 See:G0238

G3942.2 N-ASF παροιμίαν (2x)
Jn 10:6 Jesus declared this proverb to·them, but those
Jn 16:29 ·clarity·of·speech, and say not·even·one proverb.

G3942.2 N-DPF παροιμίαις (2x)
Jn 16:25 ·things I·have·spoken to·yeu in proverbs. But·yet
Jn 16:25 longer shall·I·speak to·yeu in proverbs, but·rather I·

G3942.2 N-GSF παροιμίας (1x)
2Pe 2:22 ·has·befallen them *according·to* the true proverb,

G3943 πάρ•οινος párôinôs *adj.* (2x)
Roots:G3844 G3631 Compare:G3632 G3183 G3630

G3943.2 A-ASM πάροινον (2x)
Tit 1:7 not easily·angered, not continually·near·wine, not a·
1Ti 3:3 not continually·near·wine, not a·violent·man, not of·

G3944 παρ•οίχομαι parôíchômai *v.* (1x)
Roots:G3844 G3634-2 Compare:G0599-5

G3944.2 V-RNP-DPF παρῳχημέναις (1x)
Ac 14:16 in the generations having·long·past, gave·leave·for

G3945 παρ•ομοιάζω parômôiázō *v.* (1x)
Roots:G3946 Compare:G3662

G3945.2 V-PAI-2P παρομοιάζετε (1x)
Mt 23:27 Because yeu·resemble graves having·been·

G3946 παρ•όμοιος parómôiôs *adj.* (2x)
Roots:G3844 G3664 See:G3945

G3946.2 A-APN παρόμοια (2x)
Mk 7:8 and many other such similar·things do·yeu·do."
Mk 7:13 And many such similar·things do·yeu·do."

G3947 παρ•οξύνω parôxýnō *v.* (2x)
Roots:G3844 G3691 Compare:G1690 See:G3948

G3947.2 V-IPI-3S παρωξύνετο (1x)
Ac 17:16 his spirit was·keenly·provoked within himself,

G3947.3 V-PPI-3S παροξύνεται (1x)
1Co 13:5 seek its·own, is·not swiftly·provoked, *and* is·not

G3948 παρ•οξυσμός parôxysmós *n.* (2x)
Roots:G3947 Compare:G2373-2

G3948.1 N-ASM παροξυσμόν (1x)
Heb 10:24 one·another to a·keen·provoking of·love and

G3948.2 N-NSM παροξυσμός (1x)
Ac 15:39 So·then a·sharp·disagreement occurred, such·for

G3949 παρ•οργίζω parôrgízō *v.* (2x)
Roots:G3844 G3710 Compare:G2042 G4360
See:G3950 xLangAlso:H3707

G3949.1 V-FAI-1S παροργιῶ (1x)
Rm 10:19 a·nation, *and* I·shall·personally·anger yeu with a·

G3949.1 V-PAM-2P παροργίζετε (1x)
Eph 6:4 And fathers: Do·not personally·anger yeur children,

G3950 παρ•οργισμός parôrgismós *n.* (1x)
Roots:G3949 Compare:G5176-2 G2372 G3709
See:G3949-1 xLangAlso:H3708

G3950 N-DSM παροργισμῷ (1x)
Eph 4:26 ·not·let the sun go·down upon yeur personal·anger,

G3951 παρ•οτρύνω parôtrýnō *v.* (1x)
Roots:G3844

G3951.2 V-AAI-3P παρώτρυναν (1x)
Ac 13:50 But the Jews personally·stirred·up the women

G3952 παρ•ουσία parôusía *n.* (24x)
Roots:G3918 Compare:G4383

G3952.1 N-NSF παρουσία (1x)
2Co 10:10 and strong, but his bodily presence *is* weak, and

G3952.1 N-DSF παρουσίᾳ (1x)
Php 2:12 (not as in my presence merely, but·rather now so·

G3952.2 N-NSF παρουσία (1x)
2Th 2:9 *O·the Lawless·One*, whose arrival is according·to

G3952.2 N-DSF παρουσίᾳ (3x)
1Co 16:17 I·rejoice upon the arrival of·Stephanas and
2Co 7:6 feeling·low, comforted us by the arrival of·Titus,
2Co 7:7 and not by his arrival merely, but·rather also by the

G3952.2 N-GSF παρουσίας (1x)
Php 1:26 in Jesus Anointed through my arrival to yeu again.

G3952.3 N-ASF παρουσίαν (1x)
2Pe 1:16 to·yeu the power and initial·arrival of·our Lord

G3952.4 N-ASF παρουσίαν (1x)
2Pe 3:12 and hastening the imminent·arrival of·the Day of·

G3952.5 N-NSF παρουσία (4x)
Mt 24:27 also shall·be the returning·Presence of·the Son of·
Mt 24:37 also shall·be the returning·Presence of·the Son of·
Mt 24:39 also shall·be the returning·Presence of·the Son of·
Jac 5:8 hearts, because the returning·Presence of·the Lord

G3952.5 N-ASF παρουσίαν (1x)
1Th 4:15 surviving to the returning·Presence of·the Lord), no

G3952.5 N-DSF παρουσίᾳ (5x)
1Th 2:19 Lord YeShua Anointed at his returning·Presence?
1Th 3:13 our Father, at the returning·Presence of·our Lord
1Th 5:23 unto the returning·Presence of·our Lord YeShua
1Co 15:23 of·Anointed-One, at his returning·Presence—
1Jn 2:28 be·ashamed before him at his returning·Presence.

G3952.5 N-GSF παρουσίας (5x)
Mt 24:3 *shall·be* the sign of·your returning·Presence, and of·
Jac 5:7 brothers, until the returning·Presence of·the Lord.
2Pe 3:4 is the promise of·his returning·Presence? For since
2Th 2:1 on·behalf of·the returning·Presence of·our Lord
2Th 2:8 conspicuous·appearing of·his returning·Presence.

G3953 παρ•οψίς parôpsís *n.* (2x)
Roots:G3844 G3795 Compare:G4094 G5165

G3953.2 N-GSF παροψίδος (2x)
Mt 23:25 of·the cup and of·the serving·bowl, but from·inside
Mt 23:26 of·the cup and of·the serving·bowl, in·order·that

G3954 πα•ρρησία parrhēsía *n.* (31x)
Roots:G3956 G4483 Compare:G2294 G4006
See:G3955

G3954.2 N-NSF παρρησία (2x)
2Co 7:4 Large *is* my freeness·of·speech toward yeu, large *is*
1Jn 5:14 And this is the freeness·of·speech that we·have

G3954.2 N-ASF παρρησίαν (5x)
Heb 10:19 of·YeShua, having freeness·of·speech upon the
Eph 3:12 in whom we·have the freeness·of·speech and the
Phm 1:8 ·having much freeness·of·speech in Anointed-One
1Jn 3:21 us, *then* we·have freeness·of·speech toward God.
1Jn 4:17 ·order·that we·may·have freeness·of·speech in the

G3954.2 N-DSF παρρησίᾳ (4x)
Jn 7:4 he·himself seeks to·be in freeness·of·speech *publicly*.
Jn 7:13 was·speaking with·freeness·of·speech concerning
Jn 11:54 strolling·about with·freeness·of·speech among the
Jn 18:20 ·myself spoke with·freeness·of·speech to·the world.

G3954.2 N-GSF παρρησίας (1x)
Heb 4:16 ·alongside with freeness·of·speech to·the Throne

G3954.3 N-ASF παρρησίαν (2x)
Ac 4:13 Now observing the clarity·of·speech of·Peter and
1Jn 2:28 ·apparent, we·may·have clarity·of·speech, and

G3954.3 N-DSF παρρησίᾳ (8x)
Jn 7:26 But see, he·speaks with·clarity·of·speech, and they·
Jn 10:24 declare *it* to·us with·clarity·of·speech."
Jn 11:14 Jesus declared to·them with·clarity·of·speech,
Jn 16:25 ·detail to·yeu with·clarity·of·speech concerning the
Jn 16:29 See, now you·speak with·clarity·of·speech, and say
Mk 8:32 he·was·speaking the saying with·clarity·of·speech.
Php 1:20 but·rather with all clarity·of·speech (as always,
Eph 6:19 ·up of·my mouth with clarity·of·speech, *for·me* to·

G3954.3 N-GSF παρρησίας (4x)
Ac 2:29 ·declare to yeu with clarity·of·speech concerning the
Ac 4:29 your Redemptive-word with all clarity·of·speech,
Ac 4:31 the Redemptive-word of·God with clarity·of·speech.
Ac 28:31 — with all clarity·of·speech, without·hindrance.

G3954.4 N-ASF παρρησίαν (1x)
1Ti 3:13 ·also much boldness·of·speech·with·clarity in *the*

G3954.4 N-DSF παρρησίᾳ (1x)
2Co 3:12 we·use much boldness·of·speech·with·clarity.

G3954.5 N-ASF παρρησίαν (2x)
Heb 3:6 ·should·fully·hold·onto the bold·declaration and the
Heb 10:35 ·not cast·away yeur bold·declaration, which has

G3954.5 N-DSF παρρησίᾳ (1x)
Col 2:15 *of·them* with a·bold·declaration *(his Resurrection)*,

G3955 πα•ρρησιάζομαι parrhēsiázômai *v.* (9x)
Roots:G3954 Compare:G0662 G2292 G5111

G3955.2 V-PNN παρρησιάζεσθαι (1x)
Ac 18:26 this·man began to·boldly·speak·with·clarity in the

G3955.2 V-PNP-NSM παρρησιαζόμενος (1x)
Ac 9:29 And boldly·speaking·with·clarity, *Saul* was·

G3955.2 V-PNP-NPM παρρησιαζόμενοι (1x)
Ac 14:3 ·sufficient time, boldly·speaking·with·clarity in the

G3955.2 V-INI-3S ἐπαρρησιάζετο (1x)
Ac 19:8 he·was·boldly·speaking·with·clarity for·a·span·of

G3955.2 V-ADI-3S ἐπαρρησιάσατο (1x)
Ac 9:27 and how he·boldly·spoke·with·clarity at Damascus

G3955.2 V-ADP-NPM παρρησιασάμενοι (1x)
Ac 13:46 But after·boldly·speaking·with·clarity, Paul and

G3955.2 V-ADS-1S παρρησιάσωμαι (1x)
Eph 6:20 that in it, I·may·boldly·speak·with·clarity as it·is·

G3955.3 V-PNP-NSM παρρησιαζόμενος (1x)
Ac 26:26 whom also I·speak, being·boldly·confident, for I·

G3955.3 V-ADI-1P ἐπαρρησιασάμεθα (1x)
1Th 2:2 ·personally·know, we·were·boldly·confident in our

G3956 πᾶς pâs *adj.* (1246x)
πᾶν pân [including all forms of declension]
πᾶμ- pâm- [soft prefix]
Compare:G3650 G5100 See:G3843 G0537
xLangEquiv:H3605 A3606

G3956.1 A-NSM πᾶς (24x)
Jn 8:2 into the Sanctuary·Atrium, and all the people were·
Lk 7:29 And upon·hearing *this*, all the people already·being·
Lk 12:10 "And all who shall·declare a·word against the Son
Lk 13:17 to·him were·put·to·shame. And all the crowd was·
Lk 18:43 him, glorifying God. And all the people seeing *it*,
Lk 20:6 'From·out of·men·of·clay†,' all the people shall·
Lk 21:38 And all the people were·rising·early·and·going to
Ac 2:36 "Now·then, all *the* house of·IsraEl must·know
Ac 3:9 And all the people saw him walking·along and
Ac 3:11 ·holding Peter and John, all the people ran·together
Ac 11:14 you·shall·be·saved, you and all your household.'
Ac 13:39 by him, everyone trusting is·regarded·as·innocent
Gal 5:14 For all the Torah-Law is·completely·fulfilled in one
Mt 13:2 *and* to·sit·down *there*; and all the crowd stood on
Mt 27:25 And responding, all the people declared, "His
Mk 2:13 again beside the sea, and all the crowd was·coming
Mk 4:1 along the sea, and all the crowd was alongside the
Mk 9:15 And immediately all the crowd, after·seeing him,
Mk 11:18 for they·were·afraid·of him, because all the crowd
Rm 3:19 mouth may·be·stopped·up, and all the world may·
Rm 10:13 For "all who would call·upon the name of·*the*·
Rm 11:26 And in·this·manner all IsraEl shall·be·saved; just·
Rv 8:7 trees was·completely·burned·up, and all green grass
Rv 18:17 every *ship's* pilot, and all aboard the company of·

G3956.1 A-NSF πᾶσα (18x)
Lk 3:6 and all flesh shall·gaze·upon the custodial·Salvation

Ac 13:44 coming Sabbath, almost all the city *of·Antiochia*
Ac 27:20 ·storm laying·upon *us*, all remaining expectation
Heb 12:11 And in·fact, all education·and·discipline,
Gal 2:16 of·Torah-Law— on·account·that all flesh shall·not
Mt 2:3 HerOd·the·Great was·troubled, and all JeruSalem with
Mt 3:5 was·traversing·out to him, and all Judea, and all the
Mt 3:5 and all Judea, and all the region·surrounding the
Mt 21:10 entering into JeruSalem, all the City was·shaken,
Mt 28:18 to·them, saying, "All authority is·given to·me in
Mk 1:5 And all the region of·Judea was·traversing·out to
Jac 4:16 yeu·boast in yeur bragging. All such boasting is
1Pe 1:24 on·account·that "' All flesh *is* as grass, and every
1Co 1:29 so·that all flesh may·not boast in·the·sight of·him.
1Co 15:39 All flesh *is* not the same flesh, but·rather in·fact
Eph 4:31 Let all bitterness, and rage, and wrath, and yelling,
2Ti 3:16 All Scripture *is* breathed·into·and·inspired·by·God,
1Jn 5:17 All unrighteousness is moral·failure, and there·is

G3956.1 A-NSN πᾶν (9x)

Ac 15:12 And all the multitude stayed·silent and were·
Ac 22:5 also a·witness for·me, and all the council·of·elders,
Ac 25:24 this·man, about whom all the multitude of·the
Mt 23:35 that upon yeu may·come all *the* righteous blood
Eph 4:16 from·out of·whom all the Body is·being·fitly·
Col 1:19 because all the complete·fullness *of·God Most·High*
Col 2:9 because in *Anointed-One* all the complete·fullness
Col 2:19 the Head, from·out of·which all the Body grows·up
1Jn 2:16 Because all *that·is* in the world, the longing of·the

G3956.1 A-NPM πάντες (172x)

Jn 1:7 Light, in·order·that through him all *men* may·trust.
Jn 1:16 complete·fullness, we·ourselves all received even
Jn 3:26 the·same·man immerses, and all *men* come to him.
Jn 5:23 in·order·that all *men* should·deeply·honor the Son,
Jn 5:28 an·hour is·coming in which all the·ones in the
Jn 6:45 "And they·shall·be all instructed of·Yahweh."
Jn 7:21 "I·did one work, and yeu all marvel.
Jn 10:8 All the·many·which came before me are Thieves and
Jn 11:48 him alone in·this·manner, all *men* shall·trust in him
Jn 13:10 And yeu are pure, but·yet not·indeed all *of·yeu*."
Jn 13:11 that, he·declared, "Yeu·are not·indeed all pure."
Jn 17:21 "in·order·that they·all may·be one, just·as you,
Jn 18:40 So·then they·all yelled·out again, saying, "Not this·
Lk 1:63 "His name is John." And they·all marveled.
Lk 1:66 and all the·ones hearing *them* laid·*them*·up in their
Lk 2:3 And all traversed to·be·enrolled, each·one into his·
Lk 2:18 And all the·ones hearing *it* marveled concerning the·
Lk 2:47 And all the·ones hearing him were·astonished at his
Lk 4:22 And they all were·testifying for·him, and they·were·
Lk 4:28 And hearing these·things, everyone in the gathering
Lk 6:26 Woe to·yeu, whenever all the men·of·clay† should·
Lk 8:40 him, for they·were all intently·awaiting him.
Lk 8:52 And all were·weeping and vividly·lamenting·over
Lk 9:17 And they·all ate and were·stuffed·full.
Lk 9:43 And they·all were·astounded at the magnificence of·
Lk 13:3 ·repent, yeu·shall all likewise completely·perish.
Lk 13:5 ·repent, yeu·shall all likewise completely·perish."
Lk 13:17 these·things, all the·ones being·fully·set·opposed
Lk 13:27 are·yeu? Withdraw from me, all *yeu* workmen of·
Lk 14:18 one *intent*, they·all began to·excuse·themselves.
Lk 14:29 to·entirely·complete *it*, all the·ones observing *it*
Lk 15:1 And all the tax·collectors and the morally·
Lk 20:38 but·rather of·living·men, for all live to·him."
Lk 21:15 which all the·ones who·are·fully·set·opposed to·
Lk 22:70 So they·all replied, "So·then, you·yourself are the
Lk 23:48 And all the crowds convening·publicly upon that
Lk 23:49 Now all his acquaintances, and the women
Ac 1:14 These all were diligently·continuing with·the·same·
Ac 2:7 And they·all were·astonished and were·marveling,
Ac 2:7 "Behold, are not all these ones speaking Galileans?
Ac 2:12 And all were·astonished and were·thoroughly·
Ac 2:32 this Jesus, of·which we·ourselves all are witnesses.
Ac 2:44 And all the·ones trusting were in·unison, and they·
Ac 3:24 And even all the prophets from SamuEl and the·ones
Ac 4:21 ·of the people, because all *men* were·glorifying God
Ac 5:17 rising·up, and all the·ones together with·him
Ac 5:36 *himself* was·eliminated. And all (as·many·as were·
Ac 5:37 He·also completely·perished. And all (as·many·as
Ac 8:1 ·one in JeruSalem; and all besides the ambassadors
Ac 8:10 to·this they·all were·giving·heed, from *the* least unto
Ac 9:21 But all the·ones hearing *him* were·astonished and
Ac 9:26 to·the disciples, but they·were all afraid of·him, not
Ac 9:35 And all the·ones residing·in Lod and Sharon saw
Ac 10:33 we·ourselves *are* all in·the·sight of·God. We·are·
Ac 10:43 "To·this·one, all the prophets do·testify— *that*
Ac 16:33 ·was·immersed at·once, he and all his *household*.
Ac 17:7 has·hospitably·received, and all these·men practice
Ac 17:21 (Now all Athenians and the foreigners temporarily·
Ac 18:17 the director·of·the·gathering, all the Greeks
Ac 19:7 And there·were about twelve men *in* all.
Ac 20:25 I·myself personally·know that yeu all, among
Ac 21:18 alongside Jacob; and all the elders came·directly.
Ac 21:20 ·trusted? And they·inherently·are all zealots of·the
Ac 21:24 heads bald, and *so·that* all may·know how·that, of·
Ac 22:3 ·being a·zealot of·God, just·as yeu all are this·day.
Ac 25:24 "King AgrIppa, and all the men being·present·
Ac 26:4 "Accordingly in·fact, all the Judeans have·
Ac 27:36 they·themselves were all of·a·cheerful·outlook,
Heb 1:6 "' And fall·prostrate to·him, all angels of·God!"'
Heb 1:11 and they·all shall·become·old·and·worn·out as
Heb 1:14 Are·they not·indeed all publicly·serving spirits,
Heb 2:11 being·made·holy *are* all birthed·from·out of·one
Heb 3:16 ·directly·provoke, but·yet not all the·ones *did·so*
Heb 8:11 Yahweh," because all shall·personally·know me,
Heb 11:13 These all died according·to trust, not receiving the
Heb 11:39 And all these, already·being·attested·to through
Heb 12:8 ·discipline (of·which all have·become participants)
Gal 1:2 and all the brothers together with·me.
Gal 3:26 For yeu·are all the·Sons of·God through the trust in
Gal 3:28 and female, for yeu are all one in Anointed-One
Mt 11:13 For all the prophets and the Torah-Law prophesied
Mt 11:28 "Come·here to me, all the·ones laboring·hard and
Mt 12:23 And all the crowds were·astonished and were·
Mt 14:20 And they·all ate and were·stuffed·full.
Mt 15:37 And all ate and were·stuffed·full.
Mt 19:11 to·them, "Not all·men have·room·for this saying,
Mt 21:26 we·fear the crowd, for all hold John as·a·prophet.
Mt 22:28 shall·she·be of·the seven? For they·all held her."
Mt 23:8 *that·is* the Anointed-One, and yeu all are brothers.
Mt 25:31 ·come in his glory, and all the holy angels with
Mt 26:27 "Drink out of·it, all *of·yeu*,
Mt 26:31 says to·them, "All yeu shall·be·tripped·up by me
Mt 26:33 ·him, "Even if all·men shall·be·tripped·up by you
Mt 26:35 And·also, all the disciples declared likewise.
Mt 26:52 its place, for all the·ones taking·hold·of a·dagger
Mt 26:56 Then leaving him, all the disciples fled.
Mt 27:1 ·the·break·of·dawn occurring, all the chief·priests
Mt 27:22 ·to·as Anointed-One?" They·all say to·him, "Let·
Mk 1:5 *people* of·JeruSalem, and all were·immersed by him
Mk 1:27 And they·were all amazed, such·for *them* to·
Mk 1:37 him, they·say to·him, "All *men* seek·for you.
Mk 5:12 And all the demons implored him, saying, "Send us
Mk 5:20 ·things Jesus did for·him, and all were·marveling.
Mk 6:42 And they·all ate and were·stuffed·full.
Mk 6:50 For they·all saw him and were·troubled.
Mk 7:3 For the Pharisees and all the Judeans, unless they·
Mk 12:44 For they all cast·in from·out·of·their abundance,
Mk 14:23 he·gave *it* to·them. And they·all drank out·of·it.
Mk 14:27 says to·them, "All yeu·shall·be·tripped·up by me
Mk 14:29 "Even if all shall·be·tripped·up·and·fall·away,
Mk 14:31 And also, all were·saying likewise.
Mk 14:53 the designated·high·priest, and all the chief·priests
Mk 14:64 to·yeu?" And they all condemned him to·be·held·
Rm 3:12 They all veered·away. At·the·same·time, they·are·
Rm 3:23 For all morally·failed and are·destitute of·the glory
Rm 5:12 ·clay† upon this·very *point*: *that* all morally·failed.
Rm 9:6 has·fallen·short. For not all the·ones from·among
Rm 9:7 offspring† of·AbRaham, *are* they·all *his* children.
Rm 10:16 But·yet not all listened·to·and·obeyed the good·
Rm 14:10 For we·shall all stand·directly·at the Bema·
Rm 15:11 And applaud him, all the peoples!"'
Php 2:21 For all the·men seek their·own, not the·things·of
Php 4:22 All the holy·ones greet yeu, especially the·ones
1Pe 3:8 Now finally all *of·yeu*: *be* of·the·same·mind,
1Pe 5:5 *to·yeur* elders. And all *of·yeu*, being·submitted to·
1Th 5:5 Yeu·yeurselves are all the·Sons of·Light and the·
2Th 2:12 in·order·that they·all may·be·judged, the·ones not
Tit 3:15 All *that·are* with me greet you.
1Co 1:10 Anointed, in·order·that yeu all should·say the
1Co 8:1 We·personally·know that we·all have knowledge.
1Co 9:24 ·ones running in a·stadium·race in·fact all run, but
1Co 10:1 want yeu to·be·ignorant that all our fathers were
1Co 10:1 were under the cloud, and all went through the sea,
1Co 10:2 and all were·immersed into Moses in the cloud and
1Co 10:3 And all ate the same spiritual food,
1Co 10:4 and all drank the same spiritual drink, for they·
1Co 10:17 one Body. For all *of·us* participate·and·belong *by*·
1Co 12:13 by one Spirit we·ourselves were all immersed into
1Co 12:13 slave or free; and all are·given·drink into one
1Co 12:29 Not all *are* ambassadors. Not all *are* prophets.
1Co 12:29 all *are* ambassadors. Not all *are* prophets. Not all
1Co 12:29 Not all *are* prophets. Not all *are* instructors. Not
1Co 12:29 *are* instructors. Not all *are operating·in* miracles.
1Co 12:30 Not all have gracious·bestowments of·healing.
1Co 12:30 of·healing. Not all speak in·bestowed·tongues.
1Co 12:30 ·bestowed·tongues. Not all thoroughly·translate.
1Co 14:23 and all should·speak with·bestowed·tongues,
1Co 14:24 But if all should·prophesy, and someone should·
1Co 14:31 ·are·able, each one, all to·prophesy, in·order·that
1Co 14:31 all to·prophesy, in·order·that all may·learn, and
1Co 14:31 ·that all may·learn, and all may·be·comforted.
1Co 15:22 For just·as all within Adam die, even in·this·
1Co 15:22 Adam die, even in·this·manner, all within the
1Co 15:51 In·fact, we·shall·not all be·laid·to·rest, but we·
1Co 15:51 all be·laid·to·rest, but we·shall all be·changed,
1Co 16:20 All the brothers greet yeu.
2Co 3:18 And we·ourselves all— with·a·face having·been·
2Co 5:14 died on·behalf of·all, then·by·inference, all died.
2Co 13:13 All the holy·ones greet yeu.
Eph 2:3 also we all had·our·manner·of·life in·times·past in
Eph 4:13 *for* so·long·as·until we·all should·attain unto the
Col 2:3 in whom are hidden·away all the treasures of·
2Ti 1:15 This you·personally·know, that all the·ones in Asia
2Ti 3:12 And also, all the·ones determining to·live with·
2Ti 4:16 ·together with·me, but·rather all *men* forsook me;
2Ti 4:21 and Linus, and Claudia, and all the brothers.
1Jn 2:19 ·apparent that they·were not all from·among us.
2Jn 1:1 only, but·rather also all the·ones having·known the
Rv 7:11 And all the angels stood in·a·circle·around the
Rv 13:8 And all the·ones residing upon the earth shall·fall·
Rv 18:19 Great City, in which all the·ones having ships in
Rv 19:5 "Splendidly·praise our God, all·yeu his slaves, and

G3956.1 A-NPF πᾶσαι (15x)

Lk 1:48 ' for behold, from now·on all the generations shall·
Lk 12:7 even the hairs of·yeur head all have·been·numbered.
Ac 3:25 "And in·your Seed all the paternal·lineages of·the
Ac 9:39 the upper·chamber, and all the widows stood·by
Ac 16:26 And at·once, all the doors were·opened·up, and
Ac 27:37 Now in the sailing·ship, all *told*, we·were two·
Mt 1:17 So all the generations·of·offspring from AbRaham
Mt 10:30 hairs of·yeur head are all having·been·numbered.
Mt 13:56 his sisters, are·they not all indeed alongside us?
Mt 24:30 And at·that·time, 'all the tribes of·the earth shall·
Mt 25:5 with·the bridegroom lingering, all nodded·off and
Mt 25:7 Then all those virgins are·awakened, and they·
Rm 16:4 but·rather also all the Called·Out·citizenries of·the
Rv 1:7 him;' 'and all the tribes of·the earth shall·vividly·
Rv 2:23 with death; and all the Called·Out·citizenries shall·

G3956.1 A-NPN πάντα (45x)

Jn 17:10 "So·then, all my·things are yours, and your·things
Lk 1:65 dwelling·around them. And all these utterances

Lk 4:7 ·fall·prostrate in·the·sight of·me, all shall·be yours."
Lk 12:30 For all these·things, the nations of·the world seek·
Lk 12:31 of·God, and all these·things shall·be·added to·yeu.
Lk 15:31 always with me, and all the·things *that·are* mine,
Lk 18:31 JeruSalem, and all the·things having·been·written
Ac 1:18 he·burst·open in·the·middle, and all his intestines
Ac 10:12 in which all the four-footed·animals of·the earth
Ac 15:17 may·seek·out the Lord, even all the Gentiles, upon
Ac 15:18 "Known to·God are all his works from the·
Gal 3:8 *saying*, "'In you, all the nations shall·be·blessed.
Mt 5:18 ·away from the Torah-Law until all should·happen.
Mt 6:33 righteousness, and all these·things shall·be·added
Mt 13:56 ·what·source *does* this·man *do* all these·things?
Mt 23:36 "Certainly I·say to·yeu, all these·things shall·come
Mt 24:8 But all these *are the* beginning of·birth·pangs.
Mt 24:34 pass·away, until all these·things should·happen.
Mt 25:32 And all the nations shall·be·gathered·together
Mk 3:28 I·say to·yeu, that all the moral·failings shall·be·
Mk 7:23 All these evil·things proceed·forth from·inside, and
Mk 13:30 so·long·as·until all these·things should·happen.
Rm 11:36 him, and to him, *are* all things. To·him *be* glory
Rm 12:4 in one body, but all the members have not the same
Rm 15:11 "'Splendidly·praise Yahweh, all the Gentiles!
1Co 3:22 or things·about·to·come— all *of·it* is yeurs,
1Co 9:22 ·every one, I·have·become all things in·order·that
1Co 10:11 Now all these impressive·examples were·
1Co 11:12 through the woman, but all things *are* from·out
1Co 12:12 has many members, and all the members of·the
1Co 12:19 And if they·were all one member, where·is the
1Co 12:26 if one member suffers, all the members suffer·
1Co 12:26 one member is·glorified, all the members rejoice·
1Co 15:28 in·him, in·order·that God may·be all in all.
1Co 16:14 In love, all of·yeu, BE!
2Co 4:15 For all things *are* on·account·of yeu in·order·that,
2Co 5:18 And all things *are* from·out of·God, the·one
Col 2:22 which all are *subject* to perishing with·usage)—
Col 3:11 *or* free, but·rather Anointed-One *is* all, and in all.
2Ti 4:17 may·be·fully·carried·forth and *that* all the Gentiles
Rv 15:4 divinely·holy, because "all the nations shall·come
Rv 18:3 Because all the nations have·drunk from·out of·the
Rv 18:14 ·away from you, and all the sumptuous·things and
Rv 18:23 ·and·supplying·of·poisonous·drugs, all the nations
Rv 19:21 of·his mouth; and all the fowls were·stuffed·full

G3956.1 A-ASM πάντα (9x)

Lk 9:13 we·ourselves should·buy food for all these people."
Ac 20:18 ·what·manner I·have·been with yeu at·all time,
Ac 21:27 ·Courtyard, they·were·stirring·up all the crowd
Heb 9:19 both the official·scroll itself and all the People,
Mk 7:14 And upon·summoning all the crowd, he·was·saying
Php 4:7 extending·itself·above·and·over all understanding,
1Pe 2:1 with·yeu·laying·aside all malice, and all guile, and
2Th 2:4 ·exalting·himself over all *that·is* being·referred·to·as
Col 2:2 in love, and into all wealth of·the full·assurance of·

G3956.1 A-ASF πᾶσαν (37x)

Jn 5:22 but·rather he·has·given all the Tribunal·judgment
Jn 16:13 should·come, he·shall·guide yeu into all the truth.
Lk 2:1 ·from Caesar Augustus, *that* all The Land was·to·be·
Lk 3:3 And he·went into all the region·surrounding the
Lk 4:25 ·months, as great famine occurred over all the land,
Lk 10:19 and scorpions, and upon all the power of·the
Ac 2:17 I·shall·pour·forth from my Spirit upon all flesh, and
Ac 5:21 ·of·Sanhedrin and all the council·of·aged·men of·
Ac 7:14 ·called·for his father Jacob and all his kinsfolk, in
Ac 20:27 *as* not to·report·in·detail to·yeu all the counsel of·
Ac 26:20 and·then in·JeruSalem and unto all the region of·
Mt 3:15 ·for us to·completely·fulfill all righteousness." Then
Mt 18:32 'Evil slave! I·forgave you all that indebtedness,
Mt 27:45 there·was darkness over all the land until the·
Mk 5:33 ·down·before him and declared to·him all the truth.
Rm 1:18 is·revealed from heaven against all irreverence and
Rm 10:18 clear·articulation went·forth into all the earth, and
Jac 1:2 My brothers, resolutely·consider·it all joy whenever
Jac 1:21 Therefore, putting·away all filthiness and any·
Jud 1:3 Beloved, while·making all diligence to·write to·yeu
1Pe 2:1 Accordingly, with·yeu·laying·aside all malice, and
1Pe 5:7 flinging all yeur anxiety upon him, because it·
2Pe 1:5 *besides* this, applying all diligence, yeu·must·fully·
Tit 2:10 but·rather indicating all beneficially·good trust, in·
Tit 3:2 *but* fair, indicating all gentleness to all men·of·clay†
1Co 13:2 all the mysteries and all the absolute·knowledge,
1Co 13:2 ·knowledge, and if·ever I·should·have all the trust,
1Co 15:24 ·impotent every principality and all authority and
2Co 9:8 And God *is* able *to·cause* all grace to·abound toward
2Co 9:8 yeu, in·order·that having all self-sufficiency in all
2Co 9:11 being·enriched in everything to all fidelity, which
2Co 10:6 in readiness to·avenge all inattentive·disregard,
Col 1:10 worthily of·the Lord into all willing·compliance:
Col 1:11 the might of·his glory into all patient·endurance and
Rv 5:6 of·God having·been·dispatched into all the earth.
Rv 13:7 ' And authority was·given to·it over all tribes, and
Rv 13:12 And it·exercises all the authority of·the first

G3956.1 A-ASN πᾶν (6x)

Jn 6:37 "All that the Father gives me shall·come toward me;
Jn 17:2 ·give eternal life-above to all whom you·have·given
Ac 17:26 nation of·men·of·clay† residing upon all the face
Mt 18:34 until he·should·repay all the *amount* being·owed
Eph 3:19 ·be·completely·filled to all the complete·fullness
2Ti 3:17 ·equipped toward all beneficially·good works.

G3956.1 A-APM πάντας (82x)

Jn 2:24 ·them, on·account·of him knowing all *men·of·clay†*,
Jn 12:32 the earth, I·shall·draw all *men* toward myself.
Lk 1:65 ·and·awe happened on all the·ones dwelling·around
Lk 5:9 enveloped him (and all the·ones together with·him)
Lk 6:10 And looking·around·upon them all, he·declared to·
Lk 6:19 came·forth directly·from him and healed *them* all.
Lk 9:23 Then *Jesus* was·saying to *them* all, "If any·man
Lk 12:41 do·you·say this parable to us, or even to all?"
Lk 13:2 ·disqualified above·and·beyond all the Galileans,
Lk 13:4 above·and·beyond all men·of·clay† residing in
Lk 13:28 YiTsaq, and Jacob, and all the prophets in the
Lk 21:35 ·come upon all the·ones who·are·sitting·down on
Ac 4:33 ·the Lord Jesus, and great grace was·upon them all.
Ac 5:5 great reverent·fear came upon all the·ones hearing
Ac 5:11 Called·Out·citizenry, and upon all the·ones hearing
Ac 9:14 ·priests to·bind all the·ones who·are·calling·upon
Ac 10:38 ·deeds and healing all the·ones being·dominated by
Ac 10:44 the Holy Spirit fell upon all the·ones hearing the
Ac 11:23 he·was·exhorting them·all with·determined· of·
Ac 18:2 *Caesar* having·thoroughly·arranged·for all the Jews
Ac 18:23 in·consecutive·order, reaffirming all the disciples.
Ac 19:10 two years, such·for all the·ones residing·in Asia
Ac 19:17 reverent·fear·and·awe fell upon them all, and the
Ac 21:21 a·defection away·from Moses *to* all the Jews *who·*
Ac 21:28 ·of·clay† instructing all·men everywhere against
Ac 22:15 ·shall·be his witness to all men·of·clay† of·what
Ac 26:29 merely you, but·rather also all the·ones hearing me
Ac 27:24 God has·graciously·given you all the·ones sailing
Ac 27:44 *that* they·all made·it·thoroughly·safe upon the dry·
Ac 28:30 he·was·fully·accepting all the·ones traversing·in
Heb 13:24 Greet all the·ones who·are·governing among·yeu,
Heb 13:24 ·are·governing among·yeu, and all the holy·ones.
Gal 6:10 ·should·work the beneficially·good toward all, but
Mt 2:4 And after·gathering·together all the chief·priests and
Mt 2:16 dispatching *soldiers*, he·eliminated all the boys, the·
Mt 4:24 And they·brought to·him all the·ones being·badly·ill
Mt 8:16 and both·relieved·and·cured all the·ones being
Mt 12:15 him, and he·both·relieved·and·cured them all.
Mt 14:35 ·region and brought to·him all the·ones being
Mt 21:12 ·Estate of·God and cast·out all the·ones selling and
Mt 22:10 the roadways, gathered·together all, as·many·as
Mt 26:1 *that* when YeShua finished all these sayings, he·
Mk 1:32 they·were·bringing to him all the·ones being
Mk 2:12 ·front of·them·all, such·for all to·be·astonished and
Rm 3:9 both Jews and Greeks, all to·be under moral·failure.
Rm 3:22 trust of·Jesus Anointed *is* for all and *is* upon all the·
Rm 3:22 *is* for all and *is* upon all the·ones trusting, for there·
Rm 5:12 Death went·through into all men·of·clay† upon
Rm 5:18 *judgment came* upon all men·of·clay† unto a·
Rm 5:18 *of·righteousness came* upon all men·of·clay† unto
Rm 10:12 ·wealthy to all the·ones who·are·calling·upon him.
Rm 11:32 For God jointly·confined all the *peoples* to an·
Rm 11:32 ·order·that he·may·show·mercy to·all the *peoples*.
Rm 16:15 and Olympas, and all the holy·ones together
Rm 16:19 ·obedience is·already·broadcast to all *men*.
Jud 1:15 and to·thoroughly·convict all the irreverent·ones
Jud 1:25 both now and into all the ages. So·be·it,·Amen.
Php 1:7 ·the good·news, yeu all are·being partners·together
Php 1:8 I·greatly·yearn·after yeu all in inward·affections of·
Php 2:26 since·now he·was greatly·yearning·for yeu all, and
1Pe 2:17 Honor all·men. Love the brotherhood.
2Pe 3:9 ·be·destroyed, but·rather for·all to·have·room for
1Th 3:12 love toward one·another and toward all *men*, even
1Th 4:10 For even yeu·do this toward all the brothers, the·
1Th 5:14 support the weak, be·patient toward all *men*.
1Th 5:15 ·good, both for one·another, and to all *men*.
1Th 5:26 Greet all the brothers with a·holy kiss.
Tit 3:2 *but* fair, indicating all gentleness to all men·of·clay†.
1Co 7:7 For I·want all men·of·clay† to·be also as myself.
1Co 14:5 I·want yeu all to·speak with·bestowed·tongues, but
1Co 15:25 even·until he·should·place all the enemies under
2Co 2:3 to·rejoice, having·confidence in yeu all that my joy
2Co 2:5 , in·order·that I·may·not be·a·burden·upon yeu all.
2Co 5:10 For it·is·mandatory·for every one of·us to·be·
2Co 9:13 ·fund for them and for all *the helplessly·poor*.
Eph 1:15 the Lord Jesus and *of* the love for all the holy·ones,
Eph 3:9 and to·illuminate for·all what *is* the fellowship of·
Col 1:4 Jesus and *of·yeur* love, the·one for all the holy·ones
Phm 1:5 toward the Lord Jesus and for all the holy·ones,
1Ti 2:4 who wants all men·of·clay† to·be·saved and to·come
2Ti 2:24 but·rather to·be pleasantly·engageable to all *men*,
Rv 13:16 And it·makes all, the small and the great, also the

G3956.1 A-APF πάσας (10x)

Lk 1:75 righteousness in·the·sight of·him, all the days of·
Lk 4:5 mountain, showed to·him all the kingdoms of·The
Ac 8:40 he·proclaimed·the·good·news in·all the cities, until
Ac 26:11 ·punishing them many·times in all the gatherings,
Mt 4:8 high mountain and shows him all the kingdoms of·the
Mt 9:35 And YeShua was·heading·out all around the cities
Mt 28:20 I·myself am with yeu *for* all the days, even·unto
Mk 4:13 How·else then shall·yeu·know all the parables?
1Pe 2:1 and hypocrisies, and envies, and all backbitings,
Eph 3:21 Anointed-One Jesus, unto all the generations of·

G3956.1 A-APN πάντα (81x)

Jn 4:39 "He·declared to·me all the·many·things I·did."
Jn 15:21 "But·yet all these·things shall·they·do to·yeu on·
Jn 18:4 Jesus, having·seen all the·things that·were·coming
Lk 2:19 Mariam was·closely·guarding all these utterances,
Lk 2:51 mother was·thoroughly·guarding all these utterances
Lk 7:1 And since *Jesus* fully·finished all his utterances in the
Lk 9:1 them power and authority over all the demons, and to·
Lk 9:7 the tetrarch heard all the·things which·are·happening
Lk 12:18 and there I·shall·gather·together all my produce
Lk 15:14 And with·him spending all *of·it*, there·occurred a·
Lk 16:14 fond·of·money, also were·hearing all these·things,
Lk 17:10 yeu·should·do all the·things already·being·
Lk 18:21 he·declared, "All these·things I·vigilantly·kept
Lk 18:28 "Behold, we·ourselves left all and followed you.
Lk 21:22 to·completely·fulfill all the·things having·been·
Lk 21:24 ·shall·be·made·prisoners·of·war into all the nations
Lk 21:29 "See the fig·tree, and all the trees.
Lk 21:32 no, should·not pass·away, until all should·happen.
Lk 21:36 ·fully·worthy to·utterly·escape all these·things, the·
Lk 24:9 ·tomb, they·announced all these·things to·the
Lk 24:47 ·proclaimed in his name to all the nations,
Ac 4:24 the earth, and the sea, and all the·things in them.
Ac 5:20 Sanctuary·Atrium to·the people all the utterances of·
Ac 7:50 Did·not·indeed my hand make all these·things?
Ac 10:33 to·hear all the·things having·been·specifically·
Ac 13:22 ·to my·own heart, who shall·do all my will."

Ac 14:15 the earth, and the sea, and all the·things in them.
Ac 14:16 having·long·past, gave·leave·for all the nations to·
Ac 15:17 says Yahweh, the·one doing all these·things."
Ac 17:24 the·one making the world and all the·things in it,
Heb 2:8 ' For in making·subordinate to·him all things, not·
Heb 2:8 clearly·see all things having·been·made·subordinate
Heb 9:21 also with·the blood, and all the vessels of·the
Mt 4:9 he·says to·him, "All these·things I·shall·give to·you,
Mt 6:32 (For all these·things the Gentiles seek·after) for yeur
Mt 8:33 the city, they·announced all the·things *occurring*,
Mt 13:34 YeShua spoke all these·things to·the crowds in
Mt 13:41 ·shall·collect from·out of·his kingdom all the traps,
Mt 13:44 he·heads·on·out and sells all (as·much·as he·has)
Mt 13:46 after·going·off, has·sold·off all (as·much·as he·
Mt 13:51 to·them, "Did·yeu·comprehend all these·things?
Mt 18:31 lord, they·clearly·related all the·things that·were·
Mt 19:20 says to·him, "All these·things I·vigilantly·kept
Mt 19:27 "Behold, we·ourselves left all and followed you.
Mt 23:5 But all their works *that* they·do *are* specifically·for
Mt 24:2 ·them, "Do·not look·for all these·things. Certainly
Mt 24:6 for it·is·mandatory·for all *these·things* to·happen,
Mt 24:33 whenever yeu·should·see all these·things, yeu·
Mt 28:19 while·traversing, disciple all the nations,
Mk 5:26 ·of·healing and expending all her personal
Mk 7:19 ·out into the outhouse, purging all the food?
Mk 10:20 "Mentor, all these·things I·vigilantly·kept from·
Mk 10:28 "Behold, we·ourselves left all and followed you.
Mk 13:4 ·*be* the sign whenever all these·things are·about to·
Mk 13:10 first to·be·officially·proclaimed to all the nations.
Rm 8:32 with·him, also graciously·bestow to·us all things?
Rm 16:26 already·being·made·known to all the Gentiles—
Php 3:21 to·be·able even to·subject all things to·himself.
Php 4:18 But I·completely·have all and do·abound; I·have·
1Co 10:31 or anything *that* yeu·do, do all to God's glory.
1Co 10:33 Just·as I·also willingly·adapt·for all *men* in·all
1Co 12:6 but it·is the same God, the·one operating all in all.
1Co 12:11 But all these·things operate by·the one and the
1Co 13:2 prophecy, and should·have·seen all the mysteries
1Co 13:3 ·for *the helpless·beggars using* all my holdings,
Eph 1:10 : to·reconsolidate·under·one·head all things in
Eph 1:11 of·the·one operating all things according·to the
Eph 1:22 And 'he·subjugated all *things* under his feet' and
Eph 1:22 him *to·be* head over all *things* in·the entire·Called·
Eph 1:23 of·the·one who·is·completely·filling all in all.
Eph 3:9 in God, the·one creating all things through Jesus
Eph 4:15 in love, we·should·grow·up *in* all things in him
Eph 6:16 which yeu·shall·be·able to·extinguish all the fiery
Col 2:13 him, graciously·forgiving us all the trespasses—
Col 3:17 in word or in deed, *do* all in *the* Lord Jesus' name,
Col 4:7 shall·make·known to·yeu all the·things *occurring*
1Ti 6:13 ·the·sight of·God (the·one giving·life·to all things)
Rv 4:11 power, because you·yourself created all things, and
Rv 5:13 are upon the sea, and all the·ones in them, I·heard
Rv 12:5 who imminently·intends to·shepherd all the nations
Rv 14:8 City, because she·has·made all nations drink from·

G3956.1 A-DSM παντί (10x)

Lk 2:10 to·yeu of·great joy, which shall·be to·all the people.
Ac 1:21 men going·together with·us during all *the* time in
Ac 4:10 ·it known to·yeu all, and to·all the People of·IsraEl,
Ac 5:34 *being* highly·valued among·all the people,
Ac 10:2 ·reverently·fearing God together with·all his house,
Ac 10:41 not to·all the people, but·rather to·witnesses
Ac 13:24 ·proclaimed·in·advance by·John to·all the People
Heb 9:19 already·being·spoken by Moses to·all the People,
1Pe 2:18 ·yeurselves to·the masters with all reverent·fear,
Col 1:6 among yeu, just·as *it·is* also in all the world. And it·

G3956.1 A-DSF πάσῃ (35x)

Lk 7:17 all Judea and among all the surrounding·region.
Lk 12:27 not·even Solomon in all his glory was·arrayed as
Ac 1:8 both in JeruSalem, and in all Judea, and in·Samaria,
Ac 5:23 the dungeon having·been·shut with all security and
Ac 7:22 was·educated·and·disciplined in·all *the* wisdom of·
Ac 23:1 have·been·living·as·a·good·citizen in·all conscience
Mt 6:29 not·even Solomon, in all his glory, was·arrayed as
Mk 16:15 ·proclaim the good·news to·all the creation.
Rm 1:29 having·been·completely·filled with·all, sexual·
Rm 9:17 name may·be·thoroughly·announced in all the earth
Php 1:9 ·and·full·knowledge and with·all keen·perception,
Php 1:20 ·be·ashamed, but·rather with all clarity·of·speech
1Pe 1:15 ·yeurselves must·become holy in all *yeur* behavior,
1Th 3:7 that, brothers, in all our tribulation and dire·need,
1Th 3:9 to·God concerning yeu, over all the joy with·which
2Th 2:9 of·the Adversary-Accuser with all power and signs
2Th 2:10 and with all the delusion of·unrighteousness in the·
1Co 1:5 by him, in every word and in·all knowledge—
2Co 1:4 the·one comforting us in all our tribulation, in·order·
2Co 7:4 ·above·and·beyond with·the joy in all our tribulation
2Co 8:7 and in·knowledge, and in·all diligence, and (as·a·
2Co 12:12 ·performed among yeu with all patient·endurance,
Eph 1:8 he·abounded to us in all wisdom and thoughtful·
Eph 4:31 be·expunged from yeu, together with·all malice.
Eph 5:9 fruit of·the Spirit *is* in all beneficial·goodness and
Eph 6:18 presently·staying·alert with all perseverance—
Col 1:9 ·and·full·knowledge of·his will in all wisdom and
Col 1:11 being·enabled with all power according·to the
Col 1:28 instructing every man·of·clay† in all wisdom, in·
Col 3:16 among yeu abundantly in all wisdom, instructing
1Ti 2:2 ·quiet natural·life in all devout·reverence and in·
1Ti 2:11 A·woman must·learn in stillness with all subjection.
1Ti 5:2 ·women as sisters, with all moral·cleanliness.
2Ti 4:2 *and* exhort with all long-suffering and instruction!
Rv 11:6 and to·smite the earth with·any punishing·blow, as·

G3956.1 A-DSN παντί (4x)

Rm 4:16 the promise to·be steadfast to·all the offspring†, not
2Co 7:11 *what* vindication! In all *things* yeu·demonstrated
2Co 9:8 having all self-sufficiency in all *things* at·all·times,
2Co 11:9 utterly·fulfilled·in·particular; and in all *things*, I·

G3956.1 A-DPM πᾶσιν (46x)

Lk 2:38 ·speaking concerning him to·all the·ones awaiting a·
Lk 9:48 inherently·being least among yeu all, the·same shall·
Lk 24:9 all these·things to·the eleven and to·all the rest.
Ac 1:19 And it·was known to·all the·ones residing·in
Ac 2:39 for·yeur children, and for·all the·ones at·a·distance,
Ac 2:45 ·thoroughly·distributing them to·all, according·to
Ac 4:10 be·it known to·yeu all, and to·all the People of·
Ac 4:16 through them *is* apparent to·all the·ones residing·in
Ac 15:3 And they·were·causing great joy for·all the brothers.
Ac 16:32 of·the Lord, and to·all the·ones in his home.
Ac 17:30 ·ignorance, God now charges all the men·of·clay†
Ac 17:31 ·holding·forth trust to·all *men·of·clay†* after·raising
Ac 19:17 And this was known to·all the·ones residing·in
Ac 20:32 among all the·ones having·been·made·holy.
Ac 20:36 the knees, he·prayed together with·them all.
Ac 24:5 and stirring controversy among·all the Jews in The
Heb 5:9 Salvation to·all the·ones listening·to·and·obeying
Mt 5:15 and it·radiates·brightly for·all the·ones in the home
Mk 6:41 and he·distributed the two fish among·them·all.
Mk 13:37 "And what I·say to·yeu, I·say to·all. Keep·alert!"
Rm 1:7 To·all the·ones being in Rome, beloved of·God,
Rm 13:7 render the dues to·all·ones *in·superior authority*:
Jac 1:5 the·one giving to·all with·simplicity·and·fidelity and
Php 1:1 slaves of·Jesus Anointed. To·all the holy·ones in
Php 1:13 to·all in the Praetorian·court, and to·all the rest.
Php 1:25 and shall·continue·together with·yeu all for yeur
Php 2:17 ·rejoice and·also do·rejoice·together with·yeu all.
Php 4:5 Yeur fairness, let·it·be·known to·all men·of·clay†.
1Pe 5:14 Peace to·yeu, to·all the·ones in Anointed-One
1Th 1:7 to·become model·examples to·all the·ones trusting
1Th 2:15 ·God, even *being* antagonists to·all men·of·clay†
1Th 5:27 Lord for·the letter to·be·read·aloud to·all the holy
2Th 1:4 patient·endurance and trust in all yeur persecutions
2Th 1:10 and to·be·marveled at by·all the·ones trusting in
Tit 2:11 ·Salvation, became·apparent to·all men·of·clay†—
1Co 1:2 *to·be* holy·ones, together with·all *those* in every
1Co 9:19 I·make·a·slave·of myself to·all, in·order·that I·
1Co 15:7 ·upon by·Jacob, *and* then by·all the ambassadors.
2Co 1:1 being at Corinth, together with·all the holy·ones,
2Co 13:2 having·already·morally·failed and to·all the rest—
Eph 3:18 ·strength to·grasp together with·all the holy·ones
Eph 4:6 the·one over all and throughout all and in yeu all.
1Ti 4:15 continual·advancement may·be apparent among all.
2Ti 3:9 their irrational·resentment shall·be obvious to·all, as
2Ti 4:8 merely, but·rather also to·all the·ones having·loved
Rv 21:8 and idolaters, and all the·ones *who·are* false, their

G3956.1 A-DPF πάσαις (6x)

Lk 1:6 traversing blamelessly in all the commandments and
Lk 24:27 he·was·expounding to·them in all the Scriptures
Jac 1:8 ·in·his·soul *is* completely·unstable in all his ways.
2Pe 3:16 Even·as *he·does* also in all his letters, speaking in
1Co 7:17 ·assign among all the Called·Out·citizenries.
1Co 14:33 as in all the convened·Called·Out·assemblies of·

G3956.1 A-DPN πᾶσιν (25x)

Lk 12:44 he·shall·fully·establish him over all his holdings.
Lk 13:17 the crowd was·rejoicing over all the glorious·things
Lk 14:33 that does·not orderly·take·leave·of all his holdings,
Lk 16:26 And on·top·of all these·things, between us and yeu
Lk 24:21 Moreover together with·all these·things, today
Lk 24:25 slow in·the heart to·trust on all that the prophets
Ac 17:25 giving life† and breath to·all·things, *himself being*
Heb 13:4 Highly·valued *is* the wedding in all *cultures*, and
Gal 3:10 ·not continue in all the·things having·been·written
Gal 6:6 with·the·one tutoring in all beneficially·good·things.
Mt 2:16 ·ones in BethLechem and within all of·its *outermost*
Mt 23:20 ·Altar, swears by it and by all the·things upon it.
Mt 24:14 all The Land for a·testimony to·all the nations, and
Mt 24:47 he·shall·fully·establish him over all his holdings.
Mk 11:17 ·be·called a·house of·prayer for·all the nations"?
Rm 1:5 ·attentive·obedience of·trust among all the Gentiles
Rm 8:37 in all these·things we·gain·a·decisive·victory
Tit 2:9 masters *and* to·be most·satisfying in all *things*, not
1Co 10:33 I·also willingly·adapt·for all *men* in·all *things*, not
1Co 12:6 but it·is the same God, the·one operating all in all.
1Co 15:28 in·him, in·order·that God may·be all in all.
Eph 1:23 of·the·one who·is·completely·filling all in all.
Col 3:11 *or* free, but·rather Anointed-One *is* all, and in all.
Col 3:14 And over all these·things, *dress·yeurselves·with* the
Rv 19:17 ·out with·a·loud voice, saying to·all the fowls, to·

G3956.1 A-GSM παντός (7x)

Lk 8:47 she·announced to·him, in·the·sight of·all the people
Lk 20:45 And in·the·hearing of·all the people, he·declared
Lk 24:19 and word directly·before God and all the people.
Ac 13:10 "O *you·are* full of·all guile and all mischief, O·Son
Heb 2:9 ·grace of·God he·should·taste death on·behalf of·all.
Heb 2:15 fear of·death) were all *their* lifetime held·in
2Co 7:1 ·should·purify ourselves from all tarnishing of·flesh

G3956.1 A-GSF πάσης (33x)

Jn 17:2 *also* you·gave him authority over·all flesh, in·order·
Lk 6:17 a·large multitude of·people from all *over* Judea and
Lk 21:35 who·are·sitting·down on *the* face of·all the earth.
Ac 4:29 your Redemptive-word with all clarity·of·speech,
Ac 8:27 ·the·Ethiopians, who was over all her treasury *and*
Ac 12:11 ·Agrippa's hand and *from* all the anticipated·evil of·
Ac 13:10 *you·are* full of·all guile and all mischief, O·Son of·
Ac 13:10 ·Son of·Slanderer! O·Enemy of·all Righteousness,
Ac 17:11 accepted the Redemptive-word with all eagerness,
Ac 19:26 at·Ephesus, but·yet almost throughout·all Asia,
Ac 20:19 ·a·slave to·the Lord with all humility·of·mind, and
Ac 28:31 Lord Jesus Anointed— with all clarity·of·speech,
Mt 23:27 ·overflow of·dead *men's* bones and of·all impurity.
Rm 15:13 Expectation completely·fill yeu with·all joy and
Rm 15:14 having·been·completely·filled with·all knowledge,
Php 2:29 welcome him in *the* Lord with all joy, and hold
1Pe 5:10 But the God of·all grace, the·one already·calling us
Tit 2:14 ·that 'he·may·ransom us from all lawlessness,' and
Tit 2:15 exhort and reprove with all fully·assigned·authority.
2Co 1:3 of·the tender·compassions and God of·all comfort,
Eph 1:21 high·above all principality and authority, power
Eph 4:2 with all humility·of·mind and gentleness, with
Eph 4:19 into an·occupation of·all impurity with greediness

Eph 6:18 Through all prayer and petition, be·presently·
Col 1:15 of·the invisible God, *the* firstborn of·all creation.
Col 2:10 who is the head of·all principality and authority—
1Ti 1:15 *is* trustworthy and deserving of·all full·acceptance:
1Ti 3:4 with all impeccable·integrity·worthy·of·reverent·
1Ti 4:9 *is* the saying and worthy of·all full·acceptance.
1Ti 6:1 ·consider their·own masters worthy of·all honor, in·
1Jn 1:7 his Son, purifies us from all moral·failure.
1Jn 1:9 and should·purify us from all unrighteousness.
Rv 7:4 ·been·officially·sealed from·among all *the* tribes of·

G3956.1 A-GSN παντός (1x)

Rv 7:9 to·number, *a·crowd* from·among all nations, and

G3956.1 A-GPM πάντων (96x)

Jn 10:29 *them* to·me, is greater·than all; and not·even·one
Jn 13:18 say *this* concerning yeu all. I·myself personally·
Lk 1:71 and from·among *the* hand of·all the·ones hating us;
Lk 2:31 which you·made·ready in front of·all the peoples;
Lk 3:15 ·intently·awaiting, and all·men were·pondering in
Lk 4:15 in their gatherings, being·glorified by all.
Lk 4:20 also with·the eyes of·all·them that·were in the
Lk 8:45 laying·hold of·me?" But with·everyone denying *it*,
Lk 9:43 of·God. But with·all marveling over all·things
Lk 11:50 in·order·that the blood of·all the prophets, the
Lk 21:3 helplessly·poor widow cast *in* more·than them·all.
Lk 21:17 yeu·shall·be being·hated by all on·account·of my
Lk 24:27 beginning from Moses and all the prophets, he·
Ac 1:24 knower·of·the·hearts of·all·men, expressly·indicate
Ac 3:16 ·man this perfect·soundness fully·in·front of·yeu all.
Ac 3:18 ·beforehand through *the* mouth of·all his prophets,
Ac 3:21 spoke through *the* mouth of·all his holy prophets
Ac 10:36 through Jesus Anointed— This·one is Lord of·all.
Ac 19:19 ·completely·burning *them* in·the·sight of·all *men*.
Ac 19:34 there·came one voice from·out of·all *present*, for·
Ac 20:26 that I·myself *am* pure from the blood of·all *men*.
Ac 21:5 ·forth, we·were·traversing, with·all *the disciples*
Ac 22:12 Torah-Law, being·attested·to by all the residing
Ac 26:3 with·you being an·expert in·all customs and issues
Ac 26:14 "And with·all of·us already·falling·down upon the
Ac 27:35 ·gave·thanks to·God in·the·sight of·them·all, and
Heb 12:14 Pursue peace with all *men*, also the renewed·
Heb 12:23 and to·God, Judge of·all, and to·spirits of·
Heb 13:25 The grace *be* with yeu all. So·be·it,·Amen.
Gal 2:14 good·news, I·declared to·Peter before *them* all, "If
Gal 4:1 ·one·thing from·a·slave, *though* being lord of·all,
Gal 4:26 up·above is free, which is *the* mother of·us all.
Mt 10:22 yeu·shall·be being·hated by all *men* on·account·of
Mt 22:27 And last of·all, the wife died also.
Mt 26:70 But he·denied *it* before *them* all, saying, "I·do·not
Mk 2:12 mat, he·went·forth in·front of·them·all, such·for all
Mk 9:35 *the same* shall·be last of·all and attendant of·all.
Mk 9:35 *the same* shall·be last of·all and attendant of·all."
Mk 10:44 ·want to·become foremost, shall·be slave of·all.
Mk 12:43 widow has·cast·in more·than all the·ones casting
Mk 13:13 yeu·shall·be being·hated by all *men* on·account·of
Rm 1:8 through Jesus Anointed on·behalf of·all of·yeu, that
Rm 4:11 in·order·for him to·be father of·all the·ones trusting
Rm 4:16 ·out of·AbRaham's trust, who is father of·us all
Rm 8:32 him over on·behalf of·us all, how shall·he·not·
Rm 10:12 same *Lord Jesus is* Lord of·all, being·wealthy to
Rm 12:17 ·good·things in·the·sight of·all men·of·clay†,'
Rm 12:18 part, behaving·peacefully with all men·of·clay†.
Rm 15:33 the God of·Peace *be* with yeu all. So·be·it,·Amen.
Rm 16:24 Jesus Anointed *be* with yeu all. So·be·it,·Amen.
Jac 2:10 he·has·become held·liable of·all *transgressions*.
Jud 1:15 to·make Tribunal·judgment against all, and to·
Php 1:4 of·mine on·behalf of·yeu all while·making the
Php 1:7 for·me to·contemplate this on·behalf of·all of·yeu,
Php 4:23 Jesus Anointed *be* with yeu all. So·be·it,·Amen.
1Th 1:2 ·give·thanks to·God always concerning all of·yeu,
1Th 3:13 ·our Lord YeShua Anointed with all his holy·ones.
1Th 4:6 Lord *is* avenger concerning all these·matters, just·as
2Th 1:3 the love of·each one of·yeu all, toward one·another,
2Th 3:2 evil men·of·clay†, for not all·men *have* the trust.
2Th 3:16 The Lord *be* with yeu all.
2Th 3:18 YeShua Anointed *be* with yeu all. So·be·it,·Amen.
Tit 3:15 The grace *be* with yeu all. So·be·it,·Amen.
1Co 9:19 *though* being free from·among all *men·of·clay†*, I·
1Co 14:18 more·than all of·yeu with·bestowed·tongues.
1Co 14:24 ·man, he·is·convicted by all, he·is·scrutinized by
1Co 14:24 he·is·convicted by all, he·is·scrutinized by all.
1Co 15:8 And last of·all, he·was·gazed·upon by·me·also,
1Co 15:10 ·hard, more·abundantly than·them all; but not I·
1Co 15:19 we·are of·all men·of·clay† most·pitied.
1Co 16:24 My love *be* with yeu all in Anointed-One Jesus.
2Co 2:3 in yeu all that my joy is *preferred* by·all of·yeu.
2Co 3:2 ·known and being·read·aloud by all men·of·clay†,
2Co 5:14 that if one died on·behalf of·all, then·by·inference,
2Co 5:15 he·died on·behalf of·all in·order·that the·ones
2Co 7:13 because his spirit has·been·refreshed by yeu all.
2Co 7:15 the attentive·obedience of·yeu all, how with
2Co 13:14 ·the Holy Spirit, *be* with yeu all. So·be·it,·Amen.
Eph 3:8 the·one *who·is* less·than·the·least of·all holy·ones,
Eph 4:6 one God and Father of·all: the·one over all and
Eph 4:6 Father of·all: the·one over all and throughout all
Eph 4:6 the·one over all and throughout all and in yeu all.
Eph 4:10 also the·one ascending high·above all the heavens,
Eph 6:18 — even with·petition concerning all the holy·ones
Eph 6:24 The Grace *be* with all the·ones loving our Lord
1Ti 2:1 ·of·thankfulness to·be·made over all men·of·clay†,
1Ti 2:2 on·behalf of·kings and all the·ones being in superior·
1Ti 2:6 *as* a·substitutionary·ransom on·behalf of·all— the
1Ti 4:10 who is *the* Savior of·all men·of·clay†, especially
1Ti 5:20 In·the·sight of·all, you·must·reprove the·ones
2Ti 3:11 but the Lord snatched me from·out of·all *of·them*.
3Jn 1:12 Demetrius has·been·attested·to by all·men, and by
Rv 8:3 he·should·give *it* with·the prayers of·all the holy·ones
Rv 18:24 ·ones, and of·all the·ones having·been·slaughtered
Rv 19:18 ·down on them, and flesh of·all·men, *both* free and
Rv 22:21 Jesus Anointed *be* with yeu all. So·be·it,·Amen.

G3956.1 A-GPF πασῶν (7x)

Lk 19:37 God with·a·loud voice concerning all *the* miracles
Ac 7:10 snatched him out from·among all his tribulations,
Mk 6:33 Then they·ran·together on·foot from all the cities
Mk 12:28 "Which commandment is foremost of·all?"
Mk 12:29 him, "*The* foremost of·all the commandments *is*,
2Co 8:18 ·news throughout all the Called·Out·citizenries.
2Co 11:28 the anxiety of·all the Called·Out·citizenries.

G3956.1 A-GPN πάντων (23x)

Jn 3:31 who·is·coming from·above is up·above all. The·one
Jn 3:31 ·is·coming from·out of·the heaven is up·above all.
Lk 3:19 Philippus) and concerning all *the* evils which
Lk 7:18 reported·to him concerning all these·things.
Lk 7:35 Wisdom is·regarded·as·righteous by all her children.
Lk 20:32 So last of·all, the wife died also.
Lk 24:14 concerning all these·things having·befallen *in·*
Ac 1:1 *was* concerning all that Jesus began both to·do and
Ac 9:32 And while·going throughout all *the regions*, it·
Ac 24:8 to·recognize concerning all these·things of·which
Heb 4:4 in the seventh day from all his prescribed·works."
Mt 13:32 in·fact is smaller·than all the variety·of·seeds. But
Mt 24:9 and yeu·shall·be being·hated by all the nations on·
Mk 4:31 the earth, *is* least of·all the variety·of·seeds that·are
Mk 4:32 ·up and becomes greater·than all the garden·plants,
Mk 12:22 they·did·not leave offspring†. Last of·all, the wife
Mk 12:33 himself, is more·than all the burnt·offerings and
Rm 9:5 the·one being God over all, blessed into the ages.
Jud 1:15 ·ones among·them concerning all their irreverent
Jud 1:15 ·did, and concerning all the harsh·things which
2Pe 3:11 Accordingly, with·all these·things being·dissolved,
1Ti 2:1 Now·then, I·exhort first of·all *for* petitions, prayers,
1Ti 6:10 For one·root of·all the moral·wrongs is the

EG3956.1 (1x)

Ac 7:14 Jacob and all his kinsfolk, in *all*, seventy five souls.

G3956.2 A-NPN πάντα (39x)

Jn 1:3 All·things came·to·be through him, and apart·from
Jn 10:41 miraculous·sign, but all·things as·many·as John
Jn 16:15 "All·things, as·many·things·as the Father has, are
Jn 17:7 "Now they·have·known that all·things, as·much·as
Lk 10:22 he·declared, "All·things are·handed·over to·me by
Lk 11:41 and behold, *suddenly* all·things are pure for·yeu?
Lk 14:17 'Come, because all·things are·even·now ready.
Heb 2:10 *God* (on·account·of whom all·things *exist* and
Heb 2:10 all·things *exist* and through whom all·things *exist*),
Heb 4:13 in·the·sight·of·him, but all·things *are* naked and
Heb 9:22 And almost all·things, according·to the Torah-Law,
Mt 11:27 "All·things are·handed·over to·me by my Father,
Mt 19:26 impossible, but with God all·things are possible."
Mt 22:4 *are* having·been·sacrificed, and all·things *are* ready
Mk 4:11 ·ones *that·are* outside, all·*these*·things are·done in
Mk 9:23 "If you·are·able to·trust, all·things *are* possible to·
Mk 10:27 with God, for with God all·things are possible."
Mk 14:36 "Abba, Father, all·things *are* possible to·you.
Rm 14:20 In·fact, all·things *are* pure, but·yet *it·is* morally·
2Pe 3:4 ·to·rest, all·things remain·constant in·this·manner
Tit 1:15 In·fact, to·the pure, all·things *are* pure. But to·the·
1Co 3:21 boast in men·of·clay†, for all·things are yeurs.
1Co 6:12 All·things are·proper for·me, but·yet not all·things
1Co 6:12 for·me, but·yet not all·things are·advantageous.
1Co 6:12 are·advantageous. All·things are·proper for·me,
1Co 8:6 (from·out of·whom *are* all·things and we·ourselves
1Co 8:6 (through whom *are* all·things and we·ourselves
1Co 10:23 All·things are·proper for·me, but·yet not all·
1Co 10:23 for·me, but·yet not all·things are·advantageous.
1Co 10:23 are·advantageous. All·things are·proper for·me,
1Co 10:23 are·proper for·me, but·yet not all·things edify.
1Co 14:26 All·things must·occur specifically·for edification
1Co 14:40 *Even·so*, all·things must·be·done decently and in
1Co 15:27 ·declare that "all·things have·been·subjugated,"
2Co 5:17 ·away; behold, all·things have·become brand-new
2Co 12:19 but *we·do* all·things, dearly·beloved, on·behalf
Col 1:16 Because in him, all·things are·created: the·ones in
Col 1:16 authorities. All·things have·been·created through
Col 1:17 all·things, and by him all·things have·consisted.

G3956.2 A-APN πάντα (78x)

Jn 3:35 loves the Son and has·given all·things into his hand.
Jn 4:25 ·come, he·shall·announce·in·detail to·us all·things."
Jn 4:29 ·clay† who declared to·me all the·many·things I·did!
Jn 4:45 him, having·clearly·seen all·the·things that he·did in
Jn 5:20 Son and shows him all·things that he·himself does,
Jn 13:3 that the Father has·given all·things to·him, *directly*
Jn 14:26 ·one shall·instruct yeu *concerning* all·things, and
Jn 14:26 ·remind yeu *concerning* all·things which I·declared
Jn 15:15 yeu *to·be* friends, because all·things that I·heard
Jn 16:30 we·have·seen that you·have·seen all·things, and
Jn 21:17 ·yourself personally·know all·things; you·yourself
Lk 18:12 in·the week, I·tithe all·things, *on* as·many·things·
Lk 18:22 ·left·undone. Sell all·things, as·many·things·as
Lk 24:44 "It·is·mandatory·for all·things to·be·completely·,
Ac 3:22 as myself; him yeu·shall·hear in all·things,'' "as·
Ac 17:22 I·observe how in all·things yeu *are* more·filled·
Ac 17:25 ·things, *himself being* pervasive·among all·things.
Ac 20:35 I·exemplified·to·yeu *in* all·things, that in·this·
Heb 1:3 also *the·one* upholding all·things by·the utterance
Heb 2:8 You·subjugated all·things beneath his feet.
Heb 2:17 he·was·owing fully all·things to·the brothers to·
Heb 3:4 the·one planning·and·constructing all·things *is* God.
Heb 8:5 "*that* you·should·make all·things according·to the
Gal 3:22 jointly·confined all·things under moral·failure in·
Mt 7:12 "Accordingly, all·things, as·much·as yeu·should·
Mt 17:11 does·come first and shall·reconstitute all·things.
Mt 18:25 children and all·things as·much·as he·was·holding,
Mt 21:22 And all·things, as·much·as yeu·may·request in the
Mt 28:20 them to·observantly·keep all·things as·much·as I·
Mk 4:34 he·was·explaining all·things to·his disciples.
Mk 6:30 Jesus and reported·to·him all·things, even what·
Mk 7:37 saying, "He·has·done all·things well. He·makes
Mk 9:12 after·coming first, does·reconstitute all·things.
Mk 11:11 after·looking·around·upon all·things, even·now
Mk 11:24 I·say·to·yeu, all·things, as·many·things·as yeu·

Mk 12:44 of·her destitution cast·in all·things, as·many·as
Mk 13:23 Behold, I·have·already·stated all·things to·yeu.
Rm 8:28 ·the·ones loving God, all·things work·together to
Rm 14:2 one trusts that·he·may·eat all·things, but the·one
Php 2:14 Do all·things completely·apart·from grumblings
Php 3:8 — I·resolutely·consider all·things to·be a·total·loss
Php 3:8 I·suffered·the·damage·and·loss of·all·things, and
Php 4:13 I·have·strength *to·do* all·things in the·one enabling
2Pe 1:3 ·his divine power, all·things pertaining·to life·above
1Th 5:21 Examine·and·verify all·things; fully·hold·onto the
Tit 2:7 Concerning all·things, *continue* holding·yourself·
1Co 2:10 Spirit, for the Spirit searches all·things, even, the
1Co 2:15 ·one scrutinizes, in·fact, all·things, but he·himself
1Co 9:12 but·rather we·quietly·bear all·things, lest we·
1Co 9:25 exercises·self-restraint in·all·things. Accordingly
1Co 11:2 yeu·have·been·mindful of·me in·all·things, and
1Co 13:7 It·quietly·bears all·things, trusts all·things,
1Co 13:7 all·things, trusts all·things, expectantly·awaits all·
1Co 13:7 expectantly·awaits all·things, patiently·endures
1Co 13:7 ·awaits all·things, patiently·endures all·things.
1Co 15:27 For *God* "" subjugated all·things under his feet.""
1Co 15:27 already·subjugating all·things to *Anointed-One*.
1Co 15:28 whenever all·things should·be·made·subject to·
1Co 15:28 ·subject to·the·one subjecting all·things in·him,
2Co 2:9 whether yeu·are attentively·obedient in all·things.
2Co 6:10 not·even·one·thing and·yet fully·having all·things.
2Co 7:14 but·rather as we·spoke all·things to·yeu in truth,
Eph 3:20 ·is·being·able, above·and·beyond all·things, to·do
Eph 4:10 heavens, that he·may·completely·fill all·things).
Eph 5:13 But all·things being·refuted are·made·apparent by
Eph 6:21 shall·make·known to·yeu all·things. *He·is* the
Col 1:20 ·utterly·reconcile through him all·things to himself,
Col 3:8 yeu·yourselves also must·put·off all·these things:
Col 3:20 ·to·and·obey the parents according·to all·things, for
Col 3:22 ·listen·to·and·obey in all·things the·ones *who·are*
Col 4:9 They·shall·make·known to·yeu all·things, the·ones
1Ti 4:8 is profitable specifically·for all·things, having
1Ti 6:17 to·us abundantly all·things for full·enjoyment).
2Ti 2:10 that, I·patiently·endure all·things on·account·of the
1Jn 2:20 the Holy·One, and yeu·personally·know all·things.
1Jn 3:20 is greater·than our heart, and he·knows all·things.
Rv 21:5 "Behold, I·make all·things brand-new!" And he·
Rv 21:7 The·one overcoming shall·inherit all·things; and I·

G3956.2 A-DPM πᾶσιν (1x)

Php 4:12 In any and in every *circumstance*, I·have·been·

G3956.2 A-DPN πᾶσιν (14x)

Ππ

Lk 1:3 having·closely·followed all·things accurately from·
Lk 2:20 and praising God over all·the·things that they·heard
Lk 3:20 he·added even this upon all·*these*·things— that he·
Lk 9:43 But with·all marveling over all·things which Jesus
Ac 24:14 trusting in·all the·things having·been·written in
Heb 13:18 we·have a·good conscience in all·things, willing
1Pe 4:11 in·order·that God, in all·things, may·be·glorified
Tit 2:10 ·*with* the instruction of·God our Savior in all·things.
2Co 11:6 ·being·made·apparent unto yeu in all·things.
Eph 6:16 Over all·*these*·things, after·taking·up the tall·shield
Col 1:18 in·order·that in all·things he·himself may·come
1Ti 3:11 *being* sober-minded *and* trustworthy in all·things.
2Ti 2:7 the Lord give to·you comprehension in all·things.
2Ti 4:5 be·sober·minded in all·things, endure·hardships, do

G3956.2 A-GPM πάντων (2x)

1Pe 4:8 And above all, *continue* having earnest love among
Col 1:17 And he·himself is before all·things, and by him all·

G3956.2 A-GPN πάντων (12x)

Ac 3:21 ·until *the* times of·a·reconstitution of·all·things, of·
Ac 10:39 are witnesses of·all·the·things which he·did both in
Ac 22:10 concerning all·things which have·been·assigned
Ac 26:2 concerning all·the·things for·which I·am·called·to·
Heb 1:2 whom he·placed *as* heir of·all·things, through whom
Heb 7:2 distributed a·tenth *part* from all·things. First, in·fact,
Jac 5:12 But above all·things, my brothers, do·not swear,
1Pe 4:7 But the end of·all·things has·drawn·near.
1Co 4:13 an·offscouring of·all·things unto this·moment.

Eph 5:20 ·thanks always on·behalf of·all·things *to·our* God
1Jn 2:27 presently·instructs yeu concerning all·things (and
3Jn 1:2 I·well-wish *to·God* concerning all·things, *such·as*

G3956.3 A-NSF πᾶσα (1x)

Mt 12:31 that, I·say to·yeu, all·manner·of moral·failure and

G3956.3 A-ASF πᾶσαν (1x)

Rm 7:8 accomplished in me all·manner·of longing. For

G3956.3 A-ASN πᾶν (2x)

Lk 11:42 and the rue and all·manner·of garden·plants, and
Mt 5:11 ·lying, should·declare all·manner·of evil utterance

G3956.3 A-DSM παντί (1x)

Rv 21:19 having·been·adorned·with all·manner·of precious

G3956.3 A-GSF πάσης (1x)

Ac 24:3 ·accept *this* with all·manner·of thanksgiving both

G3956.4 A-APN πάντα (1x)

Heb 4:15 but in all·points having·been·intently·tried in

G3956.5 A-NSM πᾶς (19x)

Jn 2:10 says to·him, "Every man·of·clay† first places·out
Jn 6:45 ⁼ Accordingly, every·man hearing and learning
Heb 3:4 For every house is·planned·and·constructed by some
Heb 5:1 For every high·priest being·taken from·among men·
Heb 8:3 For every high·priest is·fully·established to·offer
Heb 10:11 in·fact, every priest·that·offers·sacrifices stands
Mt 13:52 ·of that, every scribe already·being·discipled into
Rm 3:4 God be true, but every man·of·clay† a·liar; just·as
Jac 1:19 my beloved brothers, every man·of·clay† must·be
1Co 11:4 Every man praying or prophesying, having *his*
Eph 5:5 this·thing, that every sexually·immoral·person, or
1Jn 2:23 Every one who·is·denying the Son does·not·even
1Jn 3:10 the children of·the Slanderer. Every one not doing
1Jn 5:1 Every one trusting that Jesus is the Anointed-One
1Jn 5:1 ·born from·out of·God; and every one loving *God*,
Rv 1:7 thick·clouds,' and 'every eye shall·gaze·upon him,
Rv 6:15 and the powerful·men, and every slave, and every
Rv 6:15 ·men, and every slave, and every free·man, hid
Rv 18:17 "And every *ship's* pilot, and all aboard the

G3956.5 A-NSF πᾶσα (18x)

Lk 3:5 Every canyon shall·be·completely·filled, and every
Lk 11:17 ·them, "Every kingdom being·thoroughly·divided
Ac 3:23 "And it·shall·be *that* every soul who would not
Heb 2:2 was steadfast, and every violation and inattentive·
Mt 12:25 declared to·them, "Every kingdom being·divided
Mt 12:25 itself is·made·desolate, and every city or home
Mt 15:13 answering, he·declared, "Every plant which my
Mk 9:49 ·salted with·fire, and every sacrifice shall·be·salted
Rm 13:1 Let·every soul submit·itself to·the·superior
Rm 14:11 to·me, and every tongue shall·explicitly·affirm
Jac 1:17 Every beneficially·good act·of·giving and every
Jac 3:7 For every species of·wild·beasts, also of·birds, and
Php 2:11 and every tongue should·explicitly·affirm that
1Pe 1:24 *is* as grass, and every man·of·clay's† glory *is* as *the*
2Pe 1:20 this first, that every prophecy of·Scripture does·not
1Co 11:5 But every woman who·is·praying or prophesying
Rv 16:3 as blood of·a·dead·man. And every living soul in
Rv 16:20 And every island fled·away, and mountains were·

G3956.5 A-NSN πᾶν (20x)

Lk 2:23 "'Every male thoroughly·opening·up a·primal·
Lk 3:5 shall·be·completely·filled, and every mountain and
Lk 3:9 of·the trees. Accordingly, every tree not producing
Mt 3:10 of·the trees. Accordingly, every tree not producing
Mt 7:17 In·this·manner, every beneficially·good tree
Mt 7:19 Every tree not producing good fruit is·chopped·
Mt 12:36 "But I·say to·yeu, that for·every idle utterance,
Mt 18:16 three witnesses every utterance may·be·established
Rm 3:19 in·order·that every mouth may·be·stopped·up, and
Rm 14:11 Yahweh,⁼ "'every knee shall·bow to·me, and
Jac 1:17 ·good act·of·giving and every complete endowment
Jac 3:16 *is*, there *is* instability and every mediocre activity.
Php 2:10 at the name of·Jesus, every knee should·bow (of·
1Co 6:18 Flee the sexual·immorality. Every moral·failing,
2Co 13:1 three witnesses shall every utterance be·established
1Ti 4:4 Because every creature of·God *is* good, and not·
1Jn 4:2 ·know the Spirit of·God: every spirit which affirms

1Jn 4:3 And every spirit that does·not affirm Jesus, the
1Jn 5:4 Because every one having·been·born from·out of·
Rv 6:14 ·scroll being·rolled·up; and every mountain and

G3956.5 A-ASM πάντα (8x)

Jn 1:9 Light which illuminates every child·of·clay† coming
Lk 4:37 him was·proceeding·forth into every place in·the
Heb 12:1 with·us·already·laying·aside every hindrance and
Heb 12:6 ·disciplines, and he·whips every son whom he·
Php 4:21 Greet every holy·one in Anointed-One Jesus.
Col 1:28 ·proclaim, admonishing every man·of·clay† and
Col 1:28 man·of·clay† and instructing every man·of·clay† in
Col 1:28 ·that we·may·present every man·of·clay† complete

G3956.5 A-ASF πᾶσαν (16x)

Lk 10:1 his personal·presence, into every city and place
Ac 5:42 And every day in the Sanctuary·Atrium, and in·each
Ac 15:36 we·should·visit our brothers in every city in which
Mt 4:23 and·also both·relieving·and·curing every illness and
Mt 4:23 ·and·curing every illness and every disease among
Mt 9:35 and both·relieving·and·curing every illness and
Mt 9:35 ·and·curing every illness and every disease among
Mt 10:1 ·out and to·both·relieve·and·cure every illness and
Mt 10:1 ·relieve·and·cure every illness and every disease.
Rm 2:9 and calamity, upon every soul of·a·man·of·clay†
Rm 14:5 day, yet someone *else* judges every day *to·be alike*.
Php 4:19 ·completely·fulfill yeur every need according·to his
2Th 1:11 he·may·completely·fulfill every good·purpose of·
1Co 15:24 he·should·fully·render·impotent every and all
1Co 15:30 why·do we·ourselves risk·danger every hour?
2Co 4:2 ourselves to every man·of·clay's† conscience in·the·

G3956.5 A-ASN πᾶν (17x)

Jn 15:2 Every vine·sprout in me not bearing fruit, *the* same
Ac 17:26 ·one blood he·made every nation of·men·of·clay†
Php 2:9 on·him a·name, the·one above every name,
Tit 1:16 particularly·for every beneficially·good work.
Tit 3:1 ready particularly·for every beneficially·good work,
1Co 10:25 Every thing being·sold in a·meat·market, eat *it*,
2Co 9:8 yeu·may·abound to every beneficially·good work.
2Co 10:5 elaborate·reasonings and every elevated·thing *that*
2Co 10:5 ·prisoners·of·war *of* every mental·scheming unto
2Ti 2:21 ·been·made·ready for every beneficially·good work
Rv 5:13 And every creature which is in the heaven, and on
Rv 7:17 'And God shall·rub·away every tear from their eyes.
Rv 14:6 residing on the earth, and to·every nation, and tribe,
Rv 18:12 and scarlet, "and every citron wood, "and every
Rv 18:12 every citron wood, "and every *type·of* ivory vessel,
Rv 18:12 ·*of* ivory vessel, and every *type·of* vessel *made* out
Rv 21:4 'And God shall·rub·away every tear from their eyes.

G3956.5 A-DSM παντί (17x)

Lk 6:30 But give to·every one requesting·of you, and of the·
Lk 21:36 stay·alert, petitioning in every season that yeu·
Gal 5:3 again to·every man·of·clay† being·circumcised, that
Rm 2:10 and peace, to·every·man, the·one who·is·working
Rm 12:3 ·given to·me, I·say to·every·man being among yeu,
Php 1:18 *Just that* moreover, in·every manner, whether in·
Php 4:12 I·have·seen·how to·abound. In any and in every
1Pe 3:15 *a·gracious* defense to·every·man requesting·of yeu
1Th 1:8 and Achaia, but·rather also in every place yeur trust
2Th 2:17 ·establish yeu in every beneficially·good word and
2Th 3:16 Peace throughout every *matter* at every turn. The
1Co 1:2 with·all *those* in every place who·are·calling·upon
1Co 1:5 yeu·are·enriched by him, in every word and in·all
2Co 2:14 aroma of·his knowledge in every place through us.
Eph 4:14 being·carried·about by·every wind of·instruction,
Eph 6:18 be·presently·praying in Spirit in every season, and·
1Ti 2:8 ·resolve *for* the men to·pray in every place, lifting·up

G3956.5 A-DSF πάσῃ (8x)

Ac 2:43 And reverent·fear·and·awe came upon·every soul,
Php 1:3 I·give·thanks to·my God upon every mention of·yeu,
Php 1:4 always in every petition of·mine on·behalf of·yeu all
1Pe 2:13 submit·yeurselves to·every created·governance of·
2Th 3:17 which is a·signature in every letter. I·write in·this·
1Co 4:17 everywhere among every Called·Out·citizenry.
Eph 1:3 already·blessing us with every spiritual blessing by

Col 1:23 ·being·officially·proclaimed to every creature under
G3956.5 A-DSN παντί (8x)
Lk 4:4 alone, but·rather upon every utterance of·Yahweh.'"
Ac 10:35 but·rather in every nation, the·one who·is·
Heb 13:21 ·reform yeu unto every beneficially·good work
Mt 4:4 ·rather upon every utterance that·is·proceeding·forth
Col 1:10 bearing·fruit in every beneficially·good work and
Col 4:12 ·been·completely·fulfilled in every will of·God.
1Ti 5:10 if she·diligently·followed·through in·every work).
1Jn 4:1 Beloved, do·not trust every spirit, but·rather test·
G3956.5 A-DPM πᾶσιν (2x)
1Co 8:7 ·knowledge *of·this is* not in every·man. And some,
1Co 9:22 ·that I·may·gain the weak. To·every one, I·have·
G3956.5 A-GSM παντός (3x)
2Th 3:6 ·withdraw yeurselves from every brother walking in·
2Th 3:16 grant yeu Peace throughout every *matter* at every
1Co 11:3 to·personally·know that the head of·every man is
G3956.5 A-GSF πάσης (5x)
Lk 5:17 having·come from·out of·every village of·Galilee
Heb 6:16 *is* to·them an·utter·end of·every conflict.
Heb 9:19 For with·every commandment in *the* Torah-Law
Eph 4:16 through every amply·supplying connection·joint,
Rv 5:9 by your blood— from·out of·every tribe, and native·
G3956.5 A-GSN παντός (8x)
Ac 2:5 JeruSalem, devout men from every nation under the
Mt 13:47 ·together from·among every kind *of·creature*,
1Th 5:22 Abstain from every aspect of·evil.
Eph 1:21 and dominion, and every name being·named, not
Phm 1:6 recognition of·every beneficially·good·thing among
2Ti 4:18 Lord shall·snatch me away·from every evil work.
Rv 18:2 of·demons, and a·prison of·every impure spirit, and
Rv 18:2 impure spirit, and a·prison·cell of·every impure and
EG3956.5 (1x)
Ac 27:21 Now with *every soul* subsisting a·long·while
G3956.6 A-ASM πάντα (1x)
Rm 3:2 Much in·each and·every manner. For in·fact, first·of·
G3956.6 A-ASF πᾶσαν (2x)
Ac 17:17 in the marketplace each and·every day alongside
Mt 19:3 ·clay† to·divorce his wife for·each and·every cause?
G3956.6 A-ASN πᾶν (3x)
Ac 13:27 the·ones being·read·aloud each and·every Sabbath)
Ac 15:21 ·aloud in the gatherings each and·every Sabbath."
Ac 18:4 in the gathering each and·every Sabbath, and was·
G3956.7 A-NSM πᾶς (16x)
Jn 18:37 to·the truth. Everyone being birthed·from·out of·the
Lk 6:40 but everyone having·been·completely·reformed
Lk 11:10 "For everyone, the·one requesting receives, and
Lk 14:11 Because for·everyone, the·one elevating himself
Lk 16:16 and everyone forcefully·presses·himself toward it.
Lk 18:14 "Because *this·goes* for·everyone: "The·one
Gal 3:10 "Utterly·accursed *is* everyone that does·not
Mt 5:28 say to·yeu that everyone looking·upon a·woman
Mt 7:21 "Not everyone saying to·me, 'Lord, Lord,' shall·
Mt 7:26 "And everyone hearing these sayings of·mine, and
Mt 19:29 And everyone who left homes or brothers or sisters
Mk 9:49 "For everyone shall·be·salted with·fire, and every
Rm 10:11 Scripture says, '" Everyone trusting on him shall·
1Co 9:25 And everyone striving·for·a·prize exercises·
2Ti 2:19 ' And, "Everyone, the·one naming the name of·
Rv 22:15 and the idolaters, and everyone being·fond·of and
G3956.7 A-NPM πάντες (4x)
Jn 13:35 By this, everyone shall·know that yeu·are disciples
Lk 4:40 as·many·as were sick, everyone brought them to
Mk 7:14 "Listen·to me, everyone, and comprehend!
Mk 14:50 Then leaving him, everyone fled.
G3956.7 A-APM πάντας (6x)
Jn 2:15 ·small·cords, he·cast·out everyone from·among the
Lk 4:36 And amazement came·to·be upon everyone, and
Lk 8:54 he·himself, after·casting·out everyone outside and
Ac 9:40 But Peter, after·casting everyone forth outside,
Ac 28:2 kindling a·fire, they·each·received everyone of·us,
Mk 6:39 And he·ordered them to·make everyone recline,
G3956.7 A-DSM παντί (6x)
Lk 11:4 for we also forgive everyone being·indebted to·us.
Mt 25:29 "(For to·everyone maturely·utilizing·what·he·has,
Rm 1:16 God's power to Salvation to·everyone trusting, both
Rm 10:4 ·Torah-Law for righteousness to·everyone trusting.
1Co 16:16 ·the·ones such·as·these, and to·everyone, the·one
Rv 22:18 For I·jointly·testify to·everyone hearing the words
G3956.7 A-GPM πάντων (2x)
Ac 16:26 ·opened·up, and everyone's bonds were·slackened.
Ac 20:37 And everyone was weeping a·long·while.
G3956.8 A-NPN πάντα (1x)
Jn 19:28 ·seen that even·now everything has·been·finished,
G3956.8 A-APN πάντα (3x)
Mt 18:26 me, and I·shall·give·back to·you everything.'
Mt 18:29 with me, and I·shall·repay you everything.'
Mt 23:3 Accordingly, everything, whatever as·much·as
G3956.8 A-DSN παντί (9x)
Php 4:6 not·even·one·thing, but·rather in everything (in·the
1Th 5:18 In everything give·thanks, for this *is* the·will of·
1Co 1:5 that in everything yeu·are·enriched by him, in every
2Co 6:4 But·rather in everything, *we·are* presently·
2Co 7:16 I·rejoice that in everything, I·am·more·encouraged
2Co 8:7 just·as yeu·abound in everything, in·trust, and in·
2Co 9:11 being·enriched in everything to all fidelity, which
2Co 11:6 moreover in everything, *we·are* already·being·
Eph 5:24 also the wives to·their·own husbands in everything.
G3956.8 A-GPN πάντων (1x)
Ac 13:39 from everything from·which yeu·were·not able·to
G3956.9 A-DSM παντί (1x)
2Co 4:8 Being·hard-pressed on every·side, but·yet not being·
G3956.9 A-DSN παντί (1x)
2Co 7:5 *we·are* being·hard-pressed on every·side. Outwardly
EG3956.9 (1x)
2Th 2:2 nor to·be·woefully·disturbed *by·any delusion*
G3956.10 A-NSM πᾶς (1x)
Lk 6:19 And the entire crowd was·seeking to·lay·hold of·
G3956.10 A-NSF πᾶσα (5x)
Mt 8:32 And behold, the entire herd of·pigs impulsively·
Mt 8:34 And behold, the entire city came·out to meet·up
Rm 8:22 ·know that the entire creation groans·together and
Eph 2:21 in whom the entire structure, being·fitly·framed·
Eph 3:15 from·out of·whom *the* entire paternal·lineage in *the*
G3956.10 A-NSN πᾶν (1x)
Lk 1:10 And the entire multitude of·the people were praying
G3956.10 A-ASM πάντα (1x)
Lk 4:13 And after·entirely·completing *the* entire proof·trial,
G3956.10 A-DSN παντί (1x)
Ac 20:28 to·yeurselves, and to·the entire little·flock, among
G3956.10 A-GSN παντός (1x)
Ac 6:5 was·satisfactory in·the·sight of·the entire multitude.
EG3956.10 (1x)
Jac 4:17 Now·then, *anyone* having·seen *the* morally·good·
G3956.11 A-ASF πᾶσαν (1x)
1Ti 1:16 may·indicate the entirety *of·his* long-suffering,
G3956.12 A-NSM πᾶς (22x)
Jn 3:8 in·this·manner, is any one having·been·born from·
Jn 3:15 in·order·that any one trusting in him should·not
Jn 3:16 only·begotten Son, in·order·that any one trusting in
Jn 3:20 For any one practicing mediocrity hates the light,
Jn 8:34 ·certainly, I·say to·yeu that any one committing the
Lk 6:47 "Any one who·is·coming toward me, both hearing
Gal 3:13 "Utterly·accursed *is* any one being·hung on an·
Mt 5:22 I·myself say to·yeu that any one being·angry with·
Mt 7:8 For any one requesting receives; and the·one seeking
Rm 9:33 ·rock of·scandalous·offense, and any one trusting
Eph 4:29 Do·not·let any rotten conversation proceed·forth
1Jn 2:29 ·is righteous, *then* yeu·know that any one doing the
1Jn 3:3 And any one having this Expectation in him cleanses
1Jn 3:4 Any one committing the moral·failure also commits
1Jn 3:6 Any one abiding in him does·not morally·fail.
1Jn 3:6 him does·not morally·fail. Any one morally·failing
1Jn 3:9 Any one having·been·born from·out of·God does·not
1Jn 3:15 Any one presently·hating his brother is a·
1Jn 3:15 yeu·personally·know that any man-killer† does·not
1Jn 4:7 ·from·out of·God; and any one presently·loving has·
1Jn 5:18 We·personally·know that any one having·been·born
Rv 18:22 any·longer in you. And any craftsman of·any trade
G3956.12 A-NSF πᾶσα (4x)
Mt 24:22 Days be·cut·short, not any flesh would be·saved
Mk 13:20 cut·short the Days, not any flesh would be·saved;
Rm 3:20 ·not be·regarded·as·righteous any flesh in·the·sight
Eph 5:3 But sexual·immorality, and·also any impurity or
G3956.12 A-NSN πᾶν (7x)
Lk 1:37 because any utterance directly·from God shall·not
Mt 15:17 ·yeu·not·yet understand that any thing traversing
Mk 7:18 Do·yeu·not understand that any thing traversing
Eph 5:13 by the light, for any thing being·made·apparent is
1Jn 2:21 yeu·do·personally·know it, and that any lie is not
Rv 7:16 ·fall on them, nor·even any burning·radiation,
Rv 22:3 ·no longer be any irrevocable·vow·to·destruction,
G3956.12 A-ASF πᾶσαν (1x)
Heb 4:12 above·and·beyond any double-edged dagger,
G3956.12 A-ASN πᾶν (4x)
Jn 15:2 same he·takes·away; and any *vine·sprout* bearing the
Rv 7:1 on the earth, nor on the sea, nor on any tree.
Rv 9:4 of·the earth (not·even any green·thing nor·even any
Rv 9:4 (not·even any green·thing nor·even any tree), but·yet
G3956.12 A-DSM παντί (1x)
Lk 19:26 "(For I·say to·yeu, that to·any one having, *more*
G3956.12 A-DSF πάσῃ (1x)
2Co 1:4 us to·be·able to·comfort the·ones in any tribulation,
G3956.12 A-GSF πάσης (2x)
Heb 7:7 And apart·from any contradiction, the lesser is·
Rv 18:22 And any craftsman of·any trade, no, should·not be·
G3956.12 A-GSN παντός (2x)
Mt 18:10 to·yeu that throughout any *matter·of·consequence*,
Mt 18:19 earth concerning any matter·of·consequence that
G3956.13 A-NSM πᾶς (17x)
Jn 4:13 declared to·her, "Anyone drinking from·out of·this
Jn 6:40 ·the·one sending me, that anyone, the·one observing
Jn 11:26 And anyone, the·one living and trusting in me, no,
Jn 12:46 the world, in·order·that anyone, the·one trusting in
Jn 16:2 an·hour is·come that anyone killing yeu might·
Jn 19:12 not Caesar's friend. Anyone making himself a·king
Lk 12:8 "Also I·say to·yeu, anyone who·should·affirm me
Lk 14:33 in·this·manner, anyone from·among yeu that does·
Lk 16:18 "Anyone divorcing his wife and marrying another
Lk 16:18 commits·adultery, and anyone marrying the·one
Lk 20:18 "Anyone falling upon that stone shall·be·dashed·
Ac 2:21 And it·shall·be, *that* anyone who himself·should·
Heb 5:13 for anyone *still* participating·by·drinking milk *is*
Mt 7:24 "Accordingly, anyone that hears these sayings of·
Mt 10:32 "Now·then, anyone who·shall·affirm me by·name
Rm 2:1 Therefore, *for* anyone presently·judging— you·are
2Jn 1:9 Anyone, the·one walking·contrary·to and not abiding
G3956.13 A-NSN πᾶν (1x)
Rv 21:27 there·should·not enter into it anyone defiling or
G3956.13 A-ASM πάντα (1x)
Ac 10:43 prophets do·testify— *that* anyone trusting in him
G3956.13 A-ASN πᾶν (1x)
Jn 6:39 that I·should·not completely·lose any *sheep* which
G3956.13 A-DSM παντί (1x)
Lk 12:48 "So to·anyone to·whom much is·given, personally·
G3956.13 A-GSM παντός (1x)
Mt 13:19 "*Concerning* anyone hearing the Redemptive-word
G3956.14 A-NSN πᾶν (1x)
Rm 14:23 from·out·of·trust. Now anything that *is* not from·
G3956.14 A-ASN πᾶν (5x)
Ac 10:14 never·at·any·time have·I·eaten anything defiled or
Ac 11:8 because never·at·any·time did anything defiled or
1Co 10:27 to·traverse, eat anything being·placed·before yeu,
Col 3:17 And anything what soever yeu·should·do in word
Col 3:23 And anything what soever *that* yeu·should·do, be·

G3957 πάσχα páscha *aram.* (30x)

פֶּסַח ṗeçacн

Compare:G1945-5 See:G0106 G5333-3 xLangEquiv:H6453

G3957.2 ARAM πάσχα (28x)

Jn 2:13 Now the Judeans' Passover was near·at·hand, and
Jn 2:23 in JeruSalem at the Passover among the Sacred·Feast,
Jn 6:4 And the Passover, the Sacred·Feast of·the Judeans,
Jn 11:55 Now the Judeans' Passover was near·at·hand. And
Jn 11:55 to JeruSalem before the Passover, in·order·that
Jn 12:1 ·course, six days before the Passover, Jesus came to
Jn 13:1 And before the Sacred·Feast of·the Passover, Jesus,
Jn 18:28 but·rather that they·may·eat the Passover.
Jn 18:39 ·release to·yeu one·man at the Passover. So·then,
Jn 19:14 Now it·was preparation·day of·the Passover, and *it*
Lk 2:41 for·the *Judeans'* Sacred·Feast of·the Passover.
Lk 22:1 ·near, the·one being·referred·to·as Passover.
Lk 22:7 it·was·mandatory·for the Passover to·be·sacrificed.
Lk 22:8 make·ready for·us the Passover, that we·may·eat *it*.
Lk 22:11 where I·may·eat the Passover with my disciples?
Lk 22:13 And they·made·ready the Passover.
Lk 22:15 I·longed to·eat this Passover with yeu before my
Ac 12:4 to·bring him out to·the people after the Passover.
Heb 11:28 By·trust, he·has·done the Passover and the
Mt 26:2 that after two days the Passover occurs, and·then
Mt 26:17 ·should·make·ready for·you to·eat the Passover?"
Mt 26:18 near·at·hand. I·do the Passover alongside you with
Mt 26:19 them, and they·made·ready the Passover.
Mk 14:1 *the Judeans' Sacred·Feast·of* the Passover and the
Mk 14:12 when they·were·sacrificing the Passover, his
Mk 14:12 ·ready in·order·that you·may·eat the Passover?"
Mk 14:14 ·lodge where I·may·eat the Passover with my
Mk 14:16 And they·made·ready the Passover.

EG3957.2 (1x)

Jn 4:45 JeruSalem at the Sacred·Feast *of*·Passover, for they·

G3957.3 ARAM πάσχα (1x)

1Co 5:7 our Passover·lamb, is·already·sacrificed on·our

G3958 πάσχω páschō *v.* (44x)

πάθω páthō [in certain tenses]

πένθω pénthō [in certain tenses]

Compare:G2553 G2210 G0984 G3949 See:G3806

G3958.2 V-PAI-1S πάσχω (1x)

2Ti 1:12 ·account·of which cause also I·suffer these·things.

G3958.2 V-PAI-1P πάσχομεν (1x)

2Co 1:6 same afflictions which we·ourselves also suffer).

Ππ

G3958.2 V-PAI-2P πάσχετε (1x)

2Th 1:5 of·God, on·behalf of·which also yeu·suffer—

G3958.2 V-PAI-3S πάσχει (2x)

Mt 17:15 son, because he·is·lunatic and suffers badly, for
1Co 12:26 And if one member suffers, all the members

G3958.2 V-PAM-3S πασχέτω (1x)

1Pe 4:15 For do·not·let any of·yeu suffer as a·murderer, or

G3958.2 V-PAN πάσχειν (3x)

Mt 17:12 Son of·Clay·Man† is·about to·suffer under them."
Php 1:29 in him, but·rather also to·suffer on·behalf of·him,
1Pe 3:17 to·suffer *for* beneficially·doing·good·things, than

G3958.2 V-PAO-2P πάσχοιτε (1x)

1Pe 3:14 even·though yeu·may·actually·suffer on·account·of

G3958.2 V-PAP-NSM πάσχων (2x)

1Pe 2:19 *toward* God undergoes grief, suffering unjustly.
1Pe 2:23 defaming·in·reply; when·suffering, he·was·not

G3958.2 V-PAP-NPM πάσχοντες (2x)

1Pe 2:20 when suffering for·beneficially·doing·good, this *is*
1Pe 4:19 As·such, even the·ones suffering according·to the

G3958.2 V-2AAI-1S ἔπαθον (1x)

Mt 27:19 righteous·man, for I·suffered many·things this·day

G3958.2 V-2AAI-2P ἐπάθετε (2x)

Gal 3:4 Did·yeu·suffer so·many·things for·no·reason— if·
1Th 2:14 the·same·manner yeu also suffered under yeur·own

G3958.2 V-2AAI-3S ἔπαθεν (5x)

Ac 28:5 ·beast into the fire, *Paul* suffered no harm at·all.
Heb 5:8 ·obedience from the·things·which he·suffered.
Heb 13:12 through his·own blood, suffered outside the gate.
1Pe 2:21 because Anointed-One also suffered on·our behalf
1Pe 3:18 Anointed-One also suffered only·once concerning

G3958.2 V-2AAN παθεῖν (12x)

Lk 9:22 ·for the Son of·Clay·Man† to·suffer many·things,
Lk 17:25 it·is·mandatory·for him to·suffer many·things and
Lk 22:15 to·eat this Passover with yeu before my suffering.
Lk 24:26 ·for the Anointed-One to·suffer these·things, and
Lk 24:46 ·mandatory·for the Anointed-One to·suffer and to·
Ac 1:3 ·of himself being·alive after his suffering by many
Ac 3:18 *for* the Anointed-One to·suffer in·this·manner, he·
Ac 9:16 it·is·mandatory·for him to·suffer on·behalf of·my
Ac 17:3 ·for the Anointed-One to·suffer and to·rise·up from·
Heb 9:26 ·for him to·already·suffer many·times since *the*
Mt 16:21 to JeruSalem, and to·suffer many·things from the
Mk 8:31 the Son of·Clay·Man† to·suffer many·things and to·

G3958.2 V-2AAP-APM παθόντας (1x)

1Pe 5:10 YeShua— after·our·suffering a·little·while, may

G3958.2 V-2AAP-GSM παθόντος (1x)

1Pe 4:1 with·Anointed-One already·suffering on·behalf of·us

G3958.2 V-2AAP-NSF παθοῦσα (1x)

Mk 5:26 and·also already·suffering many·things under many

G3958.2 V-2AAP-NSM παθών (1x)

1Pe 4:1 Because the·one already·suffering in flesh has·been·

G3958.2 V-2AAS-3S πάθῃ (1x)

Mk 9:12 ·Clay·Man†, that he·should·suffer many·things and

G3958.2 V-2RAI-3S πέπονθεν (1x)

Heb 2:18 For in that he·has·suffered, he·himself being·tried,

G3958.2 V-2RAI-3P πεπόνθασιν (1x)

Lk 13:2 Galileans, because they·have·suffered such·things?

EG3958.2 (2x)

1Pe 4:16 But if *any·man suffers* as "a·Christian," a·Little·
1Th 2:14 even just·as they·themselves *suffered* under the

G3958.4 V-PAN πάσχειν (1x)

Rv 2:10 ·bit·of which·things you·are·about to·suffer. Behold

G3959 Πάταρα Pátara *n/l.* (1x)

G3959 N/L-APN Πάταρα (1x)

Ac 21:1 ·the next·day to Rhodes, and·from·there to Patara.

G3960 πατάσσω patássō *v.* (10x)

Roots:G3817 Compare:G5180 xLangAlso:H5221 H5217

G3960 V-FAI-1S πατάξω (2x)

Mt 26:31 it·has·been·written, "I·shall·smite the shepherd,
Mk 14:27 it·has·been·written, "I·shall·smite the shepherd,

G3960 V-FAI-1P πατάξομεν (1x)

Lk 22:49 "Lord, shall·we·smite with *the* dagger?

G3960 V-AAI-3S ἐπάταξεν (2x)

Lk 22:50 a·certain one from·among them smote the slave of·
Ac 12:23 at·once, an·angel of·Yahweh smote him, because

G3960 V-AAN πατάξαι (1x)

Rv 11:6 them into blood, and to·smite the earth with·any

G3960 V-AAP-NSM πατάξας (3x)

Ac 7:24 ·down·in·labored·anguish, smiting the Egyptian.
Ac 12:7 in the jailhouse. And tapping Peter on·the side, he·
Mt 26:51 drew·out his dagger. And smiting the slave of·the

G3960 V-AAS-3S πατάσσῃ (1x)

Rv 19:15 ' in·order·that with it he·should·smite the nations;

G3961 πατέω patéō *v.* (5x)

Roots:G3817

G3961 V-FAI-3P πατήσουσιν (1x)

Rv 11:2 to·the Gentiles. And they·shall·trample the Holy

G3961 V-PAI-3S πατεῖ (1x)

Rv 19:15 of·iron, and he·himself tramples the winepress of·

G3961 V-PAN πατεῖν (1x)

Lk 10:19 the authority, the·one to·trample upon serpents and

G3961 V-PPP-NSM πατουμένη (1x)

Lk 21:24 And JeruSalem shall·be being·trampled by Gentiles

G3961 V-API-3S ἐπατήθη (1x)

Rv 14:20 And the winepress was·trampled outside the City,

G3962 πατήρ patḗr *n.* (428x)

Compare:G1118 G3966 See:G3967 G3971 xLangEquiv:H0001 A0002 xLangAlso:G0005

G3962.1 N-NSM πατήρ (17x)

Jn 4:53 Accordingly, the father knew that *it·was* at that hour,
Jn 8:39 "AbRaham is our father." Jesus says to·them, "If
Jn 8:56 "Yeur father AbRaham leaped·for·joy that he·should·
Lk 1:67 And his father ZacharIas was·filled with·Holy Spirit
Lk 2:48 Behold, your father and·I were·seeking you,
Lk 12:53 Father shall·be·thoroughly·divided against son, and
Lk 15:20 still being·off at·a·distance, his father saw him,
Lk 15:22 "But the father declared to his slaves, 'Bring·out
Lk 15:27 *home*! And your father sacrificed the fattened calf,
Lk 15:28 So coming·out, his father was·entreating him.
Heb 12:7 ·he whom a·father does·not correctively·discipline
Mt 10:21 brother to death, and father *shall·hand·over* child,
Mk 9:24 And immediately the father of·the little·child,
Mk 13:12 brother to death, and father *shall·hand·over* child;
Rm 4:16 ·out of·AbRaham's trust, who is father of·us all
Jac 2:21 AbRaham our father, was·it·not as·a·result of·works
1Th 2:11 one of·yeu), how as a·father *does·for* his children,

G3962.1 N-NPM πατέρες (20x)

Jn 4:20 Our fathers fell·prostrate on this mountain; and yeu
Jn 6:31 Our fathers ate the manna in the wilderness, just·as
Jn 6:49 Yeur fathers ate the manna in the wilderness, and
Jn 6:58 just·as *the time when* yeur fathers ate the manna and
Lk 6:23 in the·same·manner, their fathers were·doing *this*
Lk 6:26 in the·same·manner their fathers were·doing to·the
Lk 11:47 of·the prophets, and yeur fathers killed them.
Ac 7:11 a·great tribulation, and our fathers were·not finding
Ac 7:15 Egypt, and he·completely·died, he and our fathers.
Ac 7:39 *the·one* to·whom our fathers did·not want to·become
Ac 7:45 Which also our fathers, after·receiving·it·in·turn,
Ac 7:51 the Holy Spirit. As yeur fathers *are*, so·also *are* yeu
Ac 7:52 of·the prophets did yeur fathers not persecute?
Ac 15:10 which neither our fathers nor we·ourselves had·
Heb 3:9 when yeur fathers tried me, tested·and·proved me,
Rm 9:5 of·whom *are* the fathers, and from·out of·whom,
2Pe 3:4 For since the fathers are·laid·to·rest, all·things
1Co 10:1 to·be·ignorant that all our fathers were under the
Eph 6:4 And fathers: Do·not personally·anger yeur children,
Col 3:21 *Now* the fathers: Yeu·must·not contentiously·

G3962.1 N-VSM πάτερ (6x)

Lk 15:12 ·them declared to·the father, 'Father, give me the
Lk 15:18 and shall·declare to·him, "Father, I·morally·failed
Lk 15:21 declared to·him, 'Father, I·morally·failed against
Lk 16:24 he·himself declared, 'Father AbRaham, show·
Lk 16:27 'So·then I·implore·of you, father, that you·may·
Lk 16:30 ·declared, 'No·indeed, father AbRaham! But·yet if

G3962.1 N-VPM πατέρες (4x)

Ac 7:2 "Men, brothers and fathers, listen: "The God of·
Ac 22:1 "Men, brothers and fathers, hear my defense *which*
1Jn 2:13 I·write to·yeu, fathers, because yeu·have·known
1Jn 2:14 I·already·wrote to·yeu, fathers, because yeu·have·

G3962.1 N-ASM πατέρα (42x)

Jn 6:42 the son of·Joseph, whose father and mother we·
Lk 1:73 an·oath which he·swore to our father AbRaham,
Lk 3:8 'We·have AbRaham *for·our* father.' For I·say to·yeu
Lk 8:51 and John, and the father and the mother of·the girl.
Lk 9:59 freely·permit me to·go·off first to·bury my father."
Lk 11:11 "Now which father among·yeu, *if* the son shall·
Lk 14:26 me and does·not considerately·hate his father, and
Lk 15:18 I·shall·traverse toward my father and shall·declare
Lk 15:20 rising·up, he·came toward his father. But with·him
Lk 18:20 ' "Deeply·honor your father and your mother.
Ac 7:4 And·from·there, after his father died, *God*
Ac 7:14 Joseph summarily·called·for his father Jacob and all
Ac 16:3 ·all had·seen that his father inherently·was a·Greek.
Ac 28:8 And it·happened *that* the father of·Poplius lay·ill,
Mt 3:9 'We·have AbRaham *for·our* father.' For I·say to·yeu
Mt 4:22 the sailboat and their father, they·followed him.
Mt 8:21 ·permit me first to·go·off and to·bury my father."
Mt 10:37 The·one affectionately·favoring father or mother

Mt 15:4 saying, "Deeply·honor your father and mother,"
Mt 15:4 and "the·one speaking·ill·of father or mother must·
Mt 15:6 no, he·should·not deeply·honor his father or his
Mt 19:5 a·man·of·clay† shall·leave·behind the father and the
Mt 19:19 "'Deeply·honor your father and mother,'" and
Mt 19:29 or brothers or sisters or father or mother or wife or
Mt 23:9 And yeu·should·not call *anyone* yeur father upon the
Mk 1:20 them forth, and leaving their father Zebedee in the
Mk 5:40 ·personally·takes the little·child's father and mother
Mk 7:10 "Deeply·honor your father and your mother"; and
Mk 7:10 "The·one speaking·ill·of father or mother must·
Mk 9:21 And *Jesus* inquired·of his father, "About how·long
Mk 10:7 ·of·clay† shall·leave·behind his father and mother,
Mk 10:19 rob," "Deeply·honor your father and mother.'"
Mk 10:29 or brothers or sisters or father or mother or wife or
Mk 15:21 from *the* countryside (the father of·AlexAnder and
Rm 4:1 ·we·state *for* AbRaham our father to·have·found,
Rm 4:11 in·order·for him to·be father of·all the·ones trusting
Rm 4:12 ·*for him to·be* a·father of·circumcision to·the·ones
Rm 4:17 "'I·have·placed you *as* a·father of·many nations'").
Rm 4:18 ·for himself to·become the father of·many nations
Eph 5:31 ·of·clay† shall·leave·behind his father and mother,
Eph 6:2 "'Deeply·honor your father and mother'" (which is
1Ti 5:1 but·rather exhort *him* as a·father, *likewise* younger·

G3962.1 N-APM πατέρας (12x)

Lk 1:55 into the coming·age, just·as he·spoke to our fathers."
Ac 3:22 For Moses in·fact declared to the fathers, "Yahweh
Ac 3:25 which God bequeathed unto our fathers, saying to
Ac 7:12 in Egypt, Jacob dispatched·forth our fathers first.
Ac 7:19 kindred, badly·harmed our fathers, to·make *them*
Ac 13:17 People IsraEl selected our fathers, and elevated the
Ac 13:32 ·news, the promise occurring toward the fathers,
Ac 13:36 and was·laid alongside his fathers and saw decay.
Ac 26:6 of·the promise being·made by God to the fathers,
Ac 28:25 well through IsaIah the prophet to our fathers,
Heb 12:9 Furthermore, in·fact, we·had fathers of·our flesh,
1Co 4:15 but·yet *yeu·have* not many fathers, for in

G3962.1 N-DSM πατρί (10x)

Lk 1:62 And they·were·making·gestures to·his father, *for*
Lk 9:42 healed the boy, and he·gave him back to·his father.
Lk 12:53 against son, and son against father; mother against
Lk 15:12 the younger of·them declared to·the father, 'Father
Lk 15:29 answering *him*, he·declared to·his father, 'Behold,
Ac 7:2 ·visible to·our father AbRaham while·he·was·still in
Mt 15:5 'Whoever should·declare to·his father or to·his
Mk 7:11 a·man·of·clay† should·declare to·his father or to·his
Mk 7:12 ·longer do not·even·one·thing for·his father or his
Php 2:22 together with·a·father, he·has·been·subservient to·

G3962.1 N-DPM πατράσιν (3x)

Ac 7:44 of·Testimony was with our fathers in the wilderness
Heb 1:1 with·many·methods long·ago to·the fathers by the
Heb 8:9 covenant that I·made with·their fathers in *the* day

G3962.1 N-GSM πατρός (18x)

Jn 4:12 Are you·yourself greater·than our father Jacob, who
Jn 8:53 Are you·yourself greater·than our father AbRaham,
Lk 1:32 shall·give to·him the Throne of·his father David.
Lk 1:59 ·calling him ZacharIas, after the name of·his father.
Lk 15:17 of·my father's hired·men have·an·abundance of·
Lk 16:27 that you·may·send him to my father's house,
Ac 7:20 *and* he·was·nurtured in his father's house three
Ac 16:1 (one·that·trusts), but his·father *was* a·Greek.
Heb 7:10 yet in the loins of·*his*·father when MalkiTsedeq
Gal 4:2 ·managers even·up·to the day·set·forth by·the father.
Mt 2:22 in Judea in·the·stead of·his father HerOd·the·Great,
Mt 4:21 the sailboat with their father Zebedee, completely·
Mt 10:35 "a·man·of·clay† against his father, a·daughter
Mt 21:31 which one·did the will of·the father?" They·say
Mk 11:10 *is the* kingdom of·our father David, the·one that·
Rm 4:12 in the uncircumcised trust of·our father AbRaham.
Rm 9:10 *of·twins* from·out of·one·man, our father YiTsaq—
1Co 5:1 such·for someone to·have the father's wife.

G3962.1 N-GPM πατέρων (12x)

Lk 1:17 "to·turn fathers' hearts back·around toward *the*
Lk 1:72 *promised* mercy with our fathers, and to·be·mindful
Lk 11:48 ·consent to·the deeds of·yeur fathers, because they·
Ac 3:13 of·Jacob, the God of·our fathers,' he·glorified his·
Ac 5:30 The God of·our fathers awakened Jesus, whom yeu·
Ac 7:32 "I·myself *am* the God of·your fathers, the God of·
Ac 7:38 on Mount Sinai, and with·our fathers. *It·is·he* who
Ac 7:45 thrust·out from *the* face of·our fathers. *It·was with*
Ac 22:14 'The God of·our fathers handpicked you to·know
Mt 23:30 If we·were in the days of·our fathers, we·would not
Mt 23:32 completely·fulfill even the measure of·yeur fathers.
Rm 15:8 ·order to·confirm the promises *made* to·the fathers,

EG3962.1 (10x)

Jn 5:19 for whatever that *the Father* should·do, these·things
Lk 3:23 *as·well·as being a·grandson of·Mariam's father*, Eli,
Ac 7:16 near the Sons of·Chamor *the father* of·Shekem.
Ac 7:45 *It·was with our fathers* until the days of·David,
Heb 2:10 For it·was·befitting·for *Father God* (on·account·of
Heb 2:11 all birthed·from·out of·one *Father*. On·account·of
1Co 7:36 if any *father* deems to·have·improper·etiquette
1Co 7:37 Nevertheless, *the·father* who stands immovably·
1Co 7:38 even the *father* giving·away·in·marriage does
1Co 7:38 well, but the *father* not giving·away·in·marriage

G3962.2 N-NSM πατήρ (93x)

Jn 3:35 The Father loves the Son and has·given all·things
Jn 4:23 for even the Father seeks the·ones such·as·these
Jn 5:17 them, "My Father works until this·moment, and·I·
Jn 5:20 For the Father is·a·friend·to the Son and shows him
Jn 5:21 "For just·as the Father awakens the dead and gives·
Jn 5:22 For not·even·does the Father judge, not·even·one·
Jn 5:26 For just·as the Father has life-above in himself, in·
Jn 5:36 for the works which the Father gave me (in·order·
Jn 5:36 concerning me, that the Father has·dispatched me.
Jn 5:37 "And Father himself, the·one sending me, has·
Jn 6:27 to·yeu, for God the Father officially·sealed this·one.
Jn 6:32 of·the heaven, but·rather my Father gives yeu the
Jn 6:37 "All that the Father gives me shall·come toward me;
Jn 6:44 ·come to me, unless the Father (the·one sending me
Jn 6:57 "Just·as the living Father dispatched me, and·I live
Jn 8:16 but·rather *it·is* I·myself and Father, the·one sending
Jn 8:18 concerning my·own·self, and Father (the·one
Jn 8:19 "Where is your Father?" Jesus answered, "Neither
Jn 8:28 ·self; but·rather just·as my Father instructed me, I·
Jn 8:29 me is with me. The Father did·not leave me alone,
Jn 8:42 "If God was yeur Father, yeu·would love me, for I·
Jn 8:54 glory is nothing·at·all. It·is my Father *that·is* the·one
Jn 10:15 "Just·as the Father knows me, so·even·I know the
Jn 10:17 "On·account·of that, the Father loves me, because
Jn 10:29 "My Father, who has·given *them* to·me, is greater·
Jn 10:30 I·myself and the Father are one."
Jn 10:36 "*yet* whom the Father made·holy and dispatched
Jn 10:38 and may·trust, that the Father *is* in me, and·I in
Jn 12:26 ·attend to·me, the Father shall·deeply·honor him.
Jn 12:49 ·out of·my·own·self. But·rather Father (the·one
Jn 12:50 speak, *it·is* just·as the Father has·declared to·me;
Jn 13:3 (having·seen that the Father has·given all·things to·
Jn 14:10 I·myself *am* in the Father, and the Father is in me?
Jn 14:10 from my·own·self, but the Father abiding in me,
Jn 14:11 I·myself *am* in the Father, and the Father *is* in me.
Jn 14:13 shall·I·do, that the Father may·be·glorified in the
Jn 14:23 Redemptive-word. And my Father shall·love him,
Jn 14:26 the Holy Spirit, whom the Father shall·send in my
Jn 14:28 the Father,' because my Father is greater·than me.
Jn 14:31 Father, even just·as the Father commanded me, I·
Jn 15:1 "I AM the true vine, and my Father is the farmer.
Jn 15:8 "In·this my Father is·glorified, that yeu·may·bear
Jn 15:9 "Just·as the Father loved me, so·also·I loved yeu.
Jn 16:15 "All·things, as·many·things·as the Father has, are
Jn 16:27 For the Father himself is·a·friend·to yeu, because
Jn 16:32 ·yet I·am not alone, because the Father is with me.
Jn 18:11 The cup which the Father has·given me, no, ¿!·
Jn 20:21 *be* to·yeu. Just·as *my* Father has·dispatched me,
Lk 6:36 become compassionate, just·as yeur Father also is
Lk 10:21 to·infants. Yes, Father, because in·this·manner, it·
Lk 10:22 the Son is, except the Father, and who the Father is
Lk 10:22 the Father, and who the Father is, except the Son,
Lk 11:13 children, how·much more the Father, the·one out
Lk 12:30 "And yeur Father personally·knows that yeu·have·
Lk 12:32 Flock, because yeur Father takes·delight to·give
Lk 22:29 a·kingdom, just·as my Father bequeathed to·me,
Ac 1:7 times or seasons which the Father placed in his·own
Gal 4:6 Son into yeur hearts, yelling·out, "Abba, Father!"
Mt 5:48 *in·this·manner*, just·as yeur Father, the·one in the
Mt 6:4 in private. And your Father, the·one looking·on in
Mt 6:6 in private. And your Father, the·one looking·on in
Mt 6:8 ·like them, for yeur Father has·seen what·things *are*
Mt 6:14 trespasses, yeur heavenly Father also shall·forgive
Mt 6:15 neither·even·shall yeur Father forgive yeur
Mt 6:18 in private. And your Father, the·one looking·on in
Mt 6:26 barns, yet yeur heavenly Father nourishes them.
Mt 6:32 for yeur heavenly Father has·seen that yeu·have·
Mt 7:11 how·much more shall yeur Father, the·one in the
Mt 11:26 Yes, Father, because in·this·manner it·became a·
Mt 11:27 the Son, except the Father; nor·even·does anyone
Mt 15:13 plant which my heavenly Father did·not plant
Mt 16:17 *this* to·you, but·rather my Father, the·one in the
Mt 18:35 also, shall my heavenly Father do to·yeu, unless
Mt 23:9 earth, for one is yeur Father, the·one in the heavens.
Mt 24:36 the angels of·the heavens, except my Father only.
Mk 11:25 forgive, in·order·that yeur Father also (the·one
Mk 11:26 do·not forgive, neither yeur Father (the·one in the
Mk 13:32 heaven, neither the Son, except the Father *only*.
Mk 14:36 ·saying, "Abba, Father, all·things *are* possible to·
Rm 8:15 ·as·sons, by which we·yell·out, "Abba, Father!"
1Pe 1:3 Blessed *be* the God and Father of·our Lord YeShua
1Th 3:11 Now may our God and Father himself, and our
2Th 2:16 and God, even our Father, the·one loving us, and
1Co 8:6 ·*is but* one God, the Father (from·out of·whom *are*
2Co 1:3 Blessed *be* the God and Father of·our Lord Jesus
2Co 1:3 Anointed, the Father of·the tender·compassions and
2Co 11:31 The God and Father of·our Lord Jesus Anointed,
Eph 1:3 Blessed *be* the God and Father of·our Lord Jesus
Eph 1:17 Jesus Anointed, the Father of·Glory, may·give to·
Eph 4:6 one God and Father of·all: the·one over all and
1Jn 3:1 what·manner·of love the Father has·given to·us,
1Jn 4:14 and testify that the Father has·dispatched the Son *to*·
1Jn 5:7 testifying in the heaven: the Father, the Word, and

G3962.2 N-VSM πάτερ (18x)

Jn 11:41 and declared, "Father, I·give·thanks to·you that
Jn 12:27 and what should·I·declare? 'Father, save me out
Jn 12:28 Father, glorify your name.
Jn 17:1 and he·declared, "Father, the hour has·come.
Jn 17:5 "And now, you, O·Father, glorify me (*along* with
Jn 17:11 "Holy Father, guard by your·own name these whom
Jn 17:21 ·all may·be one, just·as you, Father, *are* in me,
Jn 17:24 "Father, those·whom you·have·given to·me, I·want
Jn 17:25 "O·Righteous Father, the world did·not know you,
Lk 10:21 "I·explicitly·affirm to·you, O·Father, Lord of·the
Lk 11:2 ·pray, say, 'Our Father, the·one in the heavens,
Lk 22:42 saying, "Father, if you·are·definitely·willing to·
Lk 23:34 Then Jesus was·saying, "Father, forgive them, for
Lk 23:46 ·a·loud voice, Jesus declared, "Father, "into your
Mt 6:9 pray in·this·manner: 'Our Father, the·one in the
Mt 11:25 "I·explicitly·affirm to·you, O·Father, Lord of·the
Mt 26:39 praying and saying, "O·my Father, if it·is possible,
Mt 26:42 he·prayed, saying, "O·My Father, if this cup is·

G3962.2 N-ASM πατέρα (53x)

Jn 5:18 also *that* God *was* his·own Father, making himself
Jn 5:19 but·only what he·should·look·upon the Father doing,
Jn 5:23 just·as they·deeply·honor the Father. The·one not
Jn 5:23 does·not deeply·honor the Father, the·one sending
Jn 5:45 that I·myself shall·legally·accuse yeu to the Father.
Jn 6:46 that any·man has·clearly·seen the Father, except the·
Jn 6:46 ·from God; this·one has·clearly·seen the Father.
Jn 6:57 and·I live through the Father, so the·one chewing
Jn 8:19 me, nor my Father. If yeu·had·personally·known me
Jn 8:19 also yeu·would have·personally·known my Father."

Jn 8:27 that he·was·saying to·them *concerning* the Father.
Jn 8:41 out of·sexual·immorality. We·have one Father, God!
Jn 8:49 but·rather I·deeply·honor my Father, and yeu
Jn 10:15 me, so·even·I know the Father, and I·lay·down my
Jn 13:1 this world to the Father, already·loving his·own, the·
Jn 14:6 Not·even·one comes to the Father, except through
Jn 14:7 me, yeu·would·have known my Father also, and
Jn 14:8 "Lord, show us the Father, and it·suffices for·us.
Jn 14:9 ·clearly·seen me has·clearly·seen the Father; so·then
Jn 14:9 'Show us the Father'?
Jn 14:12 ·he·do, because I·myself traverse to my Father.
Jn 14:16 "And I·myself shall·ask·of the Father, and he·shall·
Jn 14:28 'I·traverse to the Father,' because my Father is
Jn 14:31 world may·know that I·love the Father, even just·as
Jn 15:16 whatever yeu·should·request·of the Father in my
Jn 15:23 "The·one hating me, hates my Father also.
Jn 15:24 ·seen and have·hated both me and my Father.
Jn 16:3 ·yeu, because they·did·not know the Father, nor me.
Jn 16:10 because I·head·on·out toward my Father, and yeu·
Jn 16:16 because I·myself head·on·out toward the Father."
Jn 16:17 'I·myself head·on·out toward the Father'?
Jn 16:23 ·things·as yeu·would request·of the Father in my
Jn 16:26 that I·myself shall·ask·of the Father concerning yeu
Jn 16:28 I·leave the world, and traverse to the Father."
Jn 20:17 for I·have·not·yet ascended to my Father. But you·
Jn 20:17 'I·ascend to my Father *who·is* also yeur Father, and
Jn 20:17 to my Father *who·is* also yeur Father, and *to* my
Heb 1:5 "'I·myself shall·be his·own distinct Father, and he·
Mt 5:16 good works and may·glorify yeur Father, the·one in
Mt 11:27 ·even·does anyone fully·know the Father, except
Mt 26:53 able at·this·moment to·implore my Father, and he·
Rm 15:6 yeu·may·glorify the God and Father of·our Lord
Jac 3:9 With it, we·bless *our* God and Father. And with it,
1Pe 1:17 And if yeu·presently·call·upon Father, the·one
2Co 6:18 and "I·shall·be yeur·own distinct Father, and yeu·
Eph 2:18 the embraceable·access to the Father by one Spirit.
Eph 3:14 I·bow my knees to the Father of·our Lord Jesus
1Jn 1:2 which was alongside the Father, and is·made·
1Jn 2:1 a·Companion/Intercessor alongside the Father, Jesus
1Jn 2:13 ·children, because yeu·have·known the Father.
1Jn 2:22 the·one who·is·denying the Father and the Son.
1Jn 2:23 Son does·not·even have the Father. [(but·he·that·
2Jn 1:9 this·one has both the Father and the Son.

G3962.2 N-DSM πατρί (22x)

Jn 4:21 in JeruSalem, shall·yeu·fall·prostrate to·the Father.
Jn 4:23 ·prostrate shall·fall·prostrate to·the Father in spirit
Jn 8:38 I·have·clearly·seen from·beside my Father, and
Jn 14:10 trust that I·myself *am* in the Father, and the Father
Jn 14:11 me that I·myself *am* in the Father, and the Father *is*
Jn 14:20 ·know that I·myself *am* in my Father, and yeu *are*
Heb 12:9 ·especially be·in·subjection to·the Father of·spirits,
Mt 6:1 ·of·service personally·from yeur Father, the·one in
Mt 6:6 your door, pray to·your Father, the·one in private.
Mt 6:18 *to·be* fasting, but·rather to·your Father, the·one in
Jac 1:27 Directly·from *our* God and Father— pure and
Jud 1:1 To·the·ones in Father God, having·been·made·holy
Php 4:20 Now to·our God and Father *be* glory into the ages
1Th 1:1 of·the·ThessaloNicans *which·is* in Father God and *in*
2Th 1:1 of·the·ThessaloNicans in God our Father and *the*
1Co 15:24 to·the·one *who·is* God and Father, whenever he·
Eph 5:20 of·all·things *to·our* God and Father in *the* name of·
Col 1:3 We·give·thanks to·the God and Father of·our Lord
Col 1:12 while·giving·thanks to·the Father: the·one already·
Col 3:17 giving·thanks to·the God and Father through him.
1Jn 2:24 yeu also shall·remain in the Son, and in the Father.
Rv 1:6 ·offer·a·sacrifice to·his God and Father. To·him *be*

G3962.2 N-GSM πατρός (80x)

Jn 1:14 as of·the·only·begotten directly·from *the* Father), full
Jn 1:18 in the bosom of·the Father, that·one recounted·*him*·
Jn 2:16 Do·not make my Father's house a·house of·
Jn 5:30 my·own will, but·rather the Father's will, the·one
Jn 5:43 "I·myself have·come in my Father's name, and yeu·
Jn 6:39 "And this is the Father's will, the·one sending me,
Jn 6:45 and learning personally·from the Father comes to me
Jn 6:65 ·been·given to·him birthed·from·out of·my Father."
Jn 10:18 I·received personally·from my Father."
Jn 10:25 that I·myself do in my Father's name, these·things
Jn 10:29 ·able to·snatch *them* from·out of·my Father's hand.
Jn 10:32 I·showed yeu from·out of·my Father; on·account·of
Jn 10:37 I·do·not do the works of·my Father, do·not trust me
Jn 14:2 "In my Father's home are many abodes, but·if·not, I·
Jn 14:21 me shall·be·loved by my Father, and I·myself shall·
Jn 14:24 mine, but·rather *that* of·the·Father, the·one sending
Jn 15:10 ·observantly·kept my Father's commandments and
Jn 15:15 personally·from my Father I·made·known to·yeu.
Jn 15:26 shall·send to·yeu personally·from the Father, the
Jn 15:26 proceeds·forth personally·from the Father, that·one
Jn 16:25 to·yeu with·clarity·of·speech concerning the Father.
Jn 16:28 "I·came·forth personally·from the Father, and have·
Lk 2:49 ·for me to·be among the·things of·my Father?"
Lk 9:26 ·own glory, and *that* of·the Father, and of·the holy
Lk 10:22 are·handed·over to·me by my Father. And not·
Lk 24:49 dispatch the Promise of·my Father upon yeu, but
Ac 1:4 ·wait·around for·the Promise of·the Father, which
Ac 2:33 Spirit personally·from the Father, he·poured·forth
Gal 1:1 through YeShua Anointed and Father God, the·one
Gal 1:3 *be* to·yeu and peace from Father God, and *from* our
Gal 1:4 according·to the will of·our God and Father,
Mt 5:45 yeu·may·become the·Sons of·yeur Father, the·one
Mt 7:21 the·one doing the will of·my Father, the·one in *the*
Mt 10:20 but·rather the Spirit of·yeur Father *is* the·one
Mt 10:29 the soil without yeur Father *personally·knowing.*
Mt 10:32 ·affirm him by·name before my Father, the·one in
Mt 10:33 him I·also shall·deny before my Father, the·one in
Mt 11:27 are·handed·over to·me by my Father, and no·one·
Mt 12:50 should·do the will of·my Father, the·one in *the*
Mt 13:43 the sun in the kingdom of·their Father. "The·one
Mt 16:27 to·come in the glory of·his Father with his angels,
Mt 18:10 look·upon the face of·my Father, the·one in *the*
Mt 18:14 before *the face* of·yeur Father, the·one in *the*
Mt 18:19 ·happen for·them personally·by my Father, the·one
Mt 20:23 for·whom it·has·been·made·ready by my Father."
Mt 25:34 the·ones having·been·blessed of·my Father! Inherit
Mt 26:29 brand-new with yeu in the kingdom of·my Father."
Mt 28:19 them in the name of·the Father, and of·the Son, and
Mk 8:38 ·come in the glory of·his Father with the holy
Rm 1:7 and peace from God our Father and *the* Lord Jesus
Rm 6:4 through the glory of·the Father, in·this·manner we·
Jac 1:17 descending from the Father of·lights— with whom
Php 1:2 peace, from God our Father and *from* Lord Jesus
Php 2:11 Jesus Anointed *is* Lord, to *the* glory of·Father God.
1Pe 1:2 according·to *the* foreknowledge of·Father God, by a·
2Pe 1:17 For he·received personally·from Father God honor
1Th 1:1 ·yeu, and peace, from God our Father, and *the* Lord
1Th 1:3 yeu before our God and Father (*yeur* work of·the
1Th 3:13 before God, even our Father, at the returning·
2Th 1:2 peace, from God our Father and *the* Lord YeShua
Tit 1:4 mercy, *and* peace, from Father God and *the* Lord
1Co 1:3 and peace, from God our Father, and Lord Jesus
2Co 1:2 peace, from God our Father and *from* Lord Jesus
Eph 1:2 and peace, from God our Father and *our* Lord Jesus
Eph 6:23 and love with trust from Father God and *the* Lord
Col 1:2 and peace, from God our Father and *the* Lord Jesus
Col 2:2 of·the Mystery of·God and Father, and of·the
Phm 1:3 and peace, from God our Father and *the* Lord Jesus
1Ti 1:2 *and* peace from God our Father and Jesus Anointed
2Ti 1:2 *and* peace, from Father God and Anointed-One
1Jn 1:3 our fellowship *is* also with the Father, and with his
1Jn 2:15 the world, the love of·the Father is not in him.
1Jn 2:16 is not birthed·from·out of·the Father, but·rather is
2Jn 1:3 mercy, *and* peace, personally·from Father God, and
2Jn 1:3 Jesus Anointed, the Son of·the Father, in truth and
2Jn 1:4 a·commandment personally·from the Father.
Rv 2:27 have·received *authority* personally·from my Father.
Rv 3:5 his name in·the·sight of·my Father, and in·the·sight
Rv 3:21 and did·sit·down with my Father on his throne.
Rv 14:1 the name of·his Father having·been·written in their

G3962.3 N-NSM πατήρ (1x)

Jn 8:44 *disposition*, because he·is a·liar and the father of·it.

G3962.3 N-DSM πατρί (1x)

Jn 8:38 yeu·have·clearly·seen from·beside yeur father."

G3962.3 N-GSM πατρός (3x)

Jn 8:41 Yeu·yeurselves do the deeds of·yeur father." So·then
Jn 8:44 are birthed·from·out *of·yeur* father the Slanderer, and
Jn 8:44 to·do the longings of·yeur father. That·one was a·

G3962.4 N-GPM πατέρων (1x)

Heb 11:23 was·hid three·lunar·months by his parents, on·

G3962.5 N-APM πατέρας (1x)

Rm 11:28 *they·are* beloved on·account·of the patriarchs.

G3962.5 N-GPM πατέρων (1x)

Jn 7:22 of·Moses, but·rather from·out of·the patriarchs), and

G3963 Πάτμος Pátmôs *n/l.* (1x)

G3963 N/L-DSF Πάτμῳ (1x)

Rv 1:9 island, the·one being·called Patmos, on·account·of

G3964 πατρ•αλῴας patralṓias *n.* (1x)

Roots:G3962 G0257 Compare:G3970-1 G3390-1 See:G3389

G3964.2 N-DPM πατραλῴαις (1x)

1Ti 1:9 and for·profane·ones, for·thrashers·of·fathers and

G3965 πατριά patriá *n.* (4x)

Roots:G3962 Compare:G1078 G3609 G5207 See:G5336-3 G3967 G3971 xLangAlso:H4940

G3965.1 N-NSF πατριά (1x)

Eph 3:15 from·out of·whom *the* entire paternal·lineage in *the*

G3965.1 N-NPF πατριαί (1x)

Ac 3:25 in·your Seed all the paternal·lineages of·the earth

G3965.1 N-GSF πατριᾶς (1x)

Lk 2:4 from·among *the* house and paternal·lineage of·David,

EG3965.1 (1x)

Mt 1:1 A·record of·*the·paternal* origin (*via·adoption*) of·

G3966 πατρι•άρχης patriárchēs *n.* (4x)

Roots:G3965 G0757

G3966 N-NSM πατριάρχης (1x)

Heb 7:4 to·whom even the patriarch AbRaham gave a·tenth

G3966 N-NPM πατριάρχαι (1x)

Ac 7:9 "And the patriarchs, being·jealous, sold Joseph away

G3966 N-APM πατριάρχας (1x)

Ac 7:8 *begot* Jacob; and Jacob *begot* the twelve patriarchs.

G3966 N-GSM πατριάρχου (1x)

Ac 2:29 clarity·of·speech concerning the patriarch David,

G3967 πατρικός patrikṓs *adj.* (1x)

Roots:G3962 Compare:G4269 See:G3971

G3967.2 A-GPM πατρικῶν (1x)

Gal 1:14 a·zealot of·my forefathers' Oral·traditions.

G3968 πατρίς patrís *n.* (10x)

Roots:G3962

G3968.1 N-ASF πατρίδα (3x)

Heb 11:14 ·things make·it·clear that they·seek a·fatherland.
Mt 13:54 coming into his·own fatherland, he·was·instructing
Mk 6:1 from·there and came into his·own fatherland, and his

G3968.1 N-DSF πατρίδι (5x)

Jn 4:44 "A·prophet has no honor in his·own fatherland."
Lk 4:23 CaperNaum, do also here in your·own fatherland.'"
Lk 4:24 ·one prophet is acceptable in his·own fatherland.
Mt 13:57 except in his·own fatherland and in his·own home
Mk 6:4 ·honor, except in his·own fatherland, and among his

EG3968.1 (2x)

Heb 11:15 ·were·reminiscing of·that *fatherland* from which
Heb 11:16 ·toward a·significantly·better *fatherland*, that·is,

G3969 Πατρο•βᾶς Patrôbâs *n/p.* (1x)

Roots:G3962 G0979

G3969.2 N/P-ASM Πατρόβαν (1x)

Rm 16:14 Phlegon, Hermas, PatroBas, Hermes, and the

G3970 πατρο•παρά•δοτος patrôparádôtôs *adj.* (1x)

Roots:G3962 G3860

G3970 A-GSF πατροπαραδότου (1x)

1Pe 1:18 futile manner·of·life handed·down·by·your·fathers,

Ππ

G3971 πατρῷος patrōôs *adj.* (3x)
Roots:G3962 Compare:G4269 See:G3967
G3971.3 A-DSM πατρῴῳ (1x)
Ac 24:14 ·minister to·God my esteemed·Father, trusting in·all
G3971.3 A-DPN πατρῴοις (1x)
Ac 28:17 customs of·our esteemed·fathers, was·handed·over
G3971.3 A-GSM πατρῴου (1x)
Ac 22:3 ·Oral-law of·this esteemed·father, inherently·being a·

G3972 Παῦλος Paûlôs *n/p.* (176x)
Roots:G3973 Compare:G4074 See:G4549
G3972.3 N/P-NSM Παῦλος (80x)
Ac 13:9 Saul (the·one also *called* Paul), being·filled with·
Ac 13:16 Then Paul, standing·up and motioning with·his
Ac 13:46 ·boldly·speaking·with·clarity, Paul and BarNabas
Ac 14:11 crowds, after·seeing what Paul did, they·lifted·up
Ac 14:14 ambassadors, BarNabas and Paul, after·hearing *of*·
Ac 15:35 So Paul and BarNabas were·lingering in Antioch,
Ac 15:36 Now after some days, Paul declared to BarNabas,
Ac 15:38 But Paul was·not considering·it·appropriate to·
Ac 15:40 And Paul, picking Silas, went·forth after·being·
Ac 16:3 Paul wanted this·man to·go·forth together with·him.
Ac 16:18 But being·thoroughly·stressed·out, Paul, even
Ac 16:25 And at midnight Paul and Silas, while·praying,
Ac 16:28 But Paul hollered·out with·a·loud voice, saying,
Ac 16:37 But Paul replied to them, "After publicly thrashing
Ac 17:22 So Paul, being·settled in *the* midst of·Mars'·Hill,
Ac 17:33 And in·this·manner, Paul went·forth from·among
Ac 18:1 And after these·things, Paul came to Corinth, being·
Ac 18:5 ·down from Macedonia, Paul was·clenched in·the
Ac 18:18 And Paul, still continuing·on *there* a·sufficient
Ac 19:4 Then Paul declared, "In·fact, John did·immerse
Ac 19:13 yeu *by* Jesus whom Paul officially·proclaims."
Ac 19:21 ·things were·completely·fulfilled, Paul placed *it* in
Ac 19:26 ·all Asia, this Paul has·won·over an·ample crowd
Ac 20:1 the commotion ceased, Paul, after·summoning the
Ac 20:7 to·break bread, Paul was·discussing *matters* with·
Ac 20:10 And walking·down, Paul fell·upon him, and after·
Ac 20:16 for Paul decided to·sail·directly·by Ephesus, so·
Ac 21:13 But Paul answered, "Why·do yeu·continue
Ac 21:18 on·the following *day*, Paul had·entered together
Ac 21:26 Then Paul, after·personally·taking the men on·the
Ac 21:29 whom they·were·assuming that Paul brought into
Ac 21:37 And as Paul was·about to·be·brought into the
Ac 21:39 But Paul declared, "In·fact, I·myself am a·man·of·
Ac 21:40 after·freely·permitting him, Paul, while·standing
Ac 22:25 him with·the straps, Paul declared to the centurion
Ac 22:28 procured this citizenship." And Paul replied, "But
Ac 23:1 And Paul, after·gazing·intently at·the joint·council·
Ac 23:3 Then Paul declared to him, "God is·about to·
Ac 23:5 And Paul replied, "I·had·not seen, brothers, that he·
Ac 23:6 Then Paul, already·knowing that the one part were
Ac 23:10 lest Paul should·be·thoroughly·drawn·apart by
Ac 23:17 one of·the centurions, Paul was·replying, "Lead
Ac 23:18 "After·summoning me, Paul, the chained·prisoner,
Ac 24:10 beckoning for·him to·discourse, Paul answered,
Ac 25:10 Then Paul declared, "I·am standing at Caesar's
Ac 25:19 ·died, whom Paul was·professing to·be·alive.
Ac 25:23 ·ordering *that* Paul be·brought·forth,
Ac 26:1 ·own behalf." Then Paul, after·stretching·forth his
Ac 26:29 And Paul declared, "I·would well-wish to·God,
Ac 27:9 ·by, Paul was·making·an·urgent·recommendation,
Ac 27:21 without·a·bite·of·food, Paul, after·being·settled in
Ac 27:31 Paul declared to·the centurion and to·the soldiers,
Ac 27:33 ·occur, Paul was·imploring absolutely·all·of·them
Ac 28:8 ·fevers and dysentery. Paul entered·in alongside
Ac 28:15 which upon·seeing *them*, Paul took courage,
Ac 28:30 And Paul abided a·whole two·years in his·own
Gal 1:1 Paul, an·ambassador— (not from men·of·clay†,
Gal 5:2 See, I Paul say to·yeu, that if yeu·should·be·
Rm 1:1 Paul, a·slave of·Jesus Anointed, called·forth *to·be*
Php 1:1 Paul and TimoThy, slaves of·Jesus Anointed.
2Pe 3:15 just·as also our beloved brother Paul wrote to·yeu
1Th 1:1 Paul, Silvanus, and TimoThy.
1Th 2:18 to·come to yeu, in·fact I Paul, also once and again,
2Th 1:1 Paul, Silvanus, and TimoThy.
Tit 1:1 Paul, a·slave of·God and an·ambassador of·Jesus
1Co 1:1 Paul, called·forth *to·be* an·ambassador of·Jesus
1Co 1:13 ·he·been·divided? ¿!·Was Paul crucified on·yeur
1Co 3:5 So·then, who is Paul, and who *is* Apollos, other
1Co 3:22 Whether Paul, or Apollos, or Kephas·*(called·Peter)*
2Co 1:1 Paul, an·ambassador of·Jesus Anointed through
2Co 10:1 Now I, Paul, I·myself do·implore yeu through the
Eph 1:1 Paul, an·ambassador of·Jesus Anointed through
Eph 3:1 ·this, on·account·of·grace, I, Paul, *am* the chained·
Col 1:1 Paul, an·ambassador of·Jesus Anointed through
Col 1:23 heaven), of·which I, Paul, am·made an·attendant.
Phm 1:1 Paul, a·chained·prisoner of·Jesus Anointed, and
Phm 1:9 I·implore *you*, *I* Paul, being such as an·old·man
Phm 1:19 I, Paul, wrote *this* by·my·own hand; I·myself
1Ti 1:1 Paul, an·ambassador of·Jesus Anointed according·to
2Ti 1:1 Paul, an·ambassador of·Jesus Anointed through
G3972.3 N/P-VSM Παῦλε (3x)
Ac 23:11 declared, "Be·of·good·courage, Paul. For as you·
Ac 26:24 with·a·loud voice, "Paul, you·are·raving·mad! The
Ac 27:24 'Do·not be·afraid, Paul. It·is·mandatory·for you
G3972.3 N/P-ASM Παῦλον (33x)
Ac 13:13 sailing·away from Paphos, Paul (*and* the·ones in·
Ac 13:50 ·roused·up persecution against Paul and BarNabas
Ac 14:12 BarNabas, Zeus, and Paul, Hermes, since·now he·
Ac 14:19 the crowds and stoning Paul, they·were·dragging
Ac 15:2 them, they·arranged *for* Paul and BarNabas, and
Ac 16:19 went·out *from·her*, after·grabbing Paul and Silas,
Ac 16:36 the prison·warden announced this saying to Paul,
Ac 17:10 the brothers sent·forth both Paul and Silas through
Ac 17:14 the brothers dispatched·forth Paul to·traverse as
Ac 17:15 And the·ones transporting Paul brought him as·far·
Ac 19:1 it·happened *that* Paul, after·going·throughout the
Ac 19:15 I·know, and Paul I·am·fully·acquainted·with, but
Ac 20:13 *while* from·there intending to·take Paul aboard, for
Ac 21:8 ·day, the·ones in·company·with Paul, going·forth,
Ac 21:32 and the soldiers, they·ceased beating Paul.
Ac 22:30 to·come. And·then bringing Paul down, he·set *him*
Ac 23:12 to·eat nor to·drink until they·should·kill Paul.
Ac 23:14 ·taste not·even·one·thing until we·should·kill Paul.
Ac 23:20 ·of you that you·should·bring Paul down tomorrow
Ac 23:24 ·*them* in·order·that after·mounting Paul upon *one*,
Ac 23:31 ·assigned·to·them, taking·up Paul, they·brought
Ac 23:33 to·the governor, also presented Paul before·him.
Ac 24:23 ·arranged·for the centurion to·keep Paul, and·also
Ac 24:24 a·Judean), Felix sent·for Paul, and he·heard him
Ac 24:27 ·the Judeans, left Paul behind having·been·bound.
Ac 25:4 Festus answered *for* Paul to·be·kept in Caesarea,
Ac 25:6 commandingly·ordered *for* Paul to·be·brought.
Ac 25:14 Festus set·forth the·things against Paul to·the king,
Ac 26:1 Then AgrIppa replied to Paul, "It·is·freely·
Ac 26:28 But AgrIppa replied to Paul, "In *such* a·brief·
Ac 27:1 Italy, they·were·handing both Paul and certain other
Ac 27:43 being·resolved to·thoroughly·save Paul, forbade
Ac 28:17 it·happened *that* Paul called·together the·ones
G3972.3 N/P-DSM Παύλῳ (16x)
Ac 13:43 converts·to·Judaism followed Paul and BarNabas,
Ac 15:2 of·no little controversy to·Paul and BarNabas and
Ac 15:22 to Antioch together with·Paul and BarNabas;
Ac 15:25 yeu together with·our beloved BarNabas and Paul,
Ac 16:9 a·clear·vision was·made·visible to·Paul through the
Ac 16:17 *And* closely·following Paul and us, the·same·girl
Ac 16:29 ·trembling, he·fell·down·before Paul and Silas.
Ac 17:2 And according·to Paul's custom, he·entered·in
Ac 17:4 ·convinced and joined·alongside with·Paul and Silas
Ac 18:9 the Lord declared to·Paul through a·clear·vision at
Ac 18:12 ·assault with·the·same·determination against·Paul.
Ac 21:4 these·same·men were·saying to·Paul through the
Ac 23:16 entering into the barracks, he·reported *it* to·Paul.
Ac 25:9 with·the Judeans, answering Paul, he·declared,
Ac 27:3 at Tsidon. And·also treating Paul humanely, Julius
Ac 28:16 ·battalion, but Paul was·freely·permitted to·abide
G3972.3 N/P-GSM Παύλου (30x)
Ac 13:45 the·things being·said by Paul, contradicting and
Ac 14:9 The·same·man was·hearing Paul speaking, who
Ac 15:12 BarNabas and Paul recounting·in·detail what·many
Ac 16:14 to·give·heed to·the·things being·spoken by Paul.
Ac 17:13 was·fully·proclaimed in Berea by Paul, they·came
Ac 17:16 Now while·Paul was·waiting·for them at Athens,
Ac 18:14 And while·Paul was·intending to·open·up his
Ac 19:6 And with·Paul laying his hands on·them, the Holy
Ac 19:11 through the hands of·Paul, was·doing miracles
Ac 19:29 men·of·Macedonia, Paul's traveling·companions,
Ac 19:30 And while·Paul was·resolving to·enter into the
Ac 20:9 ·a·deep heavy·sleep. With·Paul discussing *matters*
Ac 20:37 And affectionately·falling upon Paul's neck, they·
Ac 21:11 ·coming to us and taking·up Paul's belt, and·also
Ac 21:30 And grabbing·hold of·Paul, they·were·drawing
Ac 23:16 And the son of·Paul's sister, coming·directly after·
Ac 24:1 ·it·clear to·the governor *the·things* against Paul.
Ac 24:26 valuables shall·be·given to·him by Paul, that he·
Ac 25:2 made·clear to·him *the·things* against Paul. And they·
Ac 25:7 many burdensome complaints against Paul, which
Ac 25:21 "But with·Paul appealing to·be·reserved for the
Ac 27:11 rather than by·the·things being·said by Paul.
Ac 28:3 And as·Paul *was* bundling·together a·multitude of·
Ac 28:25 ·dismissed·themselves, with·Paul declaring one
2Th 3:17 The salutation of·Paul by·my·own hand, which is
1Co 1:12 "In·fact, I·myself am of·Paul," and "I *am* of·
1Co 1:13 Or were·yeu·immersed in the name of·Paul?
1Co 3:4 "In·fact, I·myself am of·Paul," and someone·else,
1Co 16:21 The salutation of·Paul by·my·own hand.
Col 4:18 salutation by·my·own hand, Paul: Remember my
EG3972.3 (13x)
Ac 14:10 *Paul* declared with·a·loud voice, "Stand upright
Ac 16:22 commandingly·ordered *for·Paul and Silas* to·be·
Ac 18:2 out of·Rome). *And Paul* came·alongside them.
Ac 18:8 many of·the Corinthians hearing *Paul* were·trusting,
Ac 18:18 with·him— *with·Paul* already·having·shorn his
Ac 20:11 even·unto *the* first·light·of·day, *Paul* went·forth.
Ac 21:19 ·greeting them, *Paul* was·recounting·in·detail each
Ac 22:27 And coming·alongside *Paul*, the regiment·
Ac 24:2 ·for, Tertullus began to·legally·accuse *Paul*, saying,
Ac 24:25 But with *Paul* discussing *matters* concerning
Ac 25:3 requesting an·influential·favor against *Paul*, that he·
Ac 26:24 And with *Paul* still·making·his·defense, Festus
Ac 28:5 venomous·beast into the fire, *Paul* suffered no harm
G3972.4 N/P-DSM Παύλῳ (1x)
Ac 13:7 the proconsul, Sergius Paulus, *who·was* an·

G3973 παύω paúō *v.* (15x)
Compare:G1587 G4932 See:G0373 G2664 G3972
G3973.2 V-FDI-2S παύσῃ (1x)
Ac 13:10 Righteousness, shall·you·not cease perverting the
G3973.2 V-FDI-3P παύσονται (1x)
1Co 13:8 if·also bestowed·tongues, they·shall·cease; if·also
G3973.2 V-PMI-1S παύομαι (1x)
Eph 1:16 I·do·not cease giving·thanks on·behalf of·yeu,
G3973.2 V-PMI-1P παυόμεθα (1x)
Col 1:9 we·heard *of·it*) do·not cease praying on·yeur behalf
G3973.2 V-PMI-3S παύεται (1x)
Ac 6:13 "This man·of·clay† does·not cease speaking reviling
G3973.2 V-IMI-3P ἐπαύοντο (1x)
Ac 5:42 in·each house, they·did·not cease instructing and
G3973.2 V-AMI-1S ἐπαυσάμην (1x)
Ac 20:31 for·three·years, I·did·not cease admonishing each
G3973.2 V-AMI-3S ἐπαύσατο (2x)
Lk 5:4 Now as·soon·as he·ceased speaking, he·declared to
Lk 11:1 place, *that* as·soon·as he·ceased, a·certain·one of·
G3973.2 V-AMI-3P ἐπαύσαντο (3x)
Lk 8:24 the surge of·water. And they·ceased, and there·was
Ac 21:32 and the soldiers, they·ceased beating Paul.
Heb 10:2 ¿!·would·they not have·ceased being·offered
G3973.2 V-AMN παύσασθαι (1x)
Ac 20:1 Now after the commotion ceased, Paul, after·

Αα Ββ Γγ Δδ Εε Ζζ Ηη Θθ Ιι Κκ Λλ Μμ Νν Ξξ Οο Ππ Ρρ Σσ Ττ Υυ Φφ Χχ Ψψ Ωω

G3973.3 V-AAM-3S παυσάτω (1x)
1Pe 3:10 beneficially·good days must·restrain his tongue
G3973.3 V-RPI-3S πέπαυται (1x)
1Pe 4:1 in flesh has·been·restrained from·moral·failure,

G3974 Πάφος Páphôs *n/l.* (2x)
G3974 N/L-GSF Πάφου (2x)
Ac 13:6 the island, even·as·far·as Paphos, they·found a·
Ac 13:13 And sailing·away from Paphos, Paul (*and* the·ones

G3975 παχύνω pachýnō *v.* (2x)
Roots:G4078
G3975.4 V-API-3S ἐπαχύνθη (2x)
Ac 28:27 heart of·this People became·thickly·calloused, and
Mt 13:15 heart of·this People became·thickly·calloused, and

G3976 πέδη pédē *n.* (3x)
Roots:G4228 Compare:G0254 G1199 G5498-2 xLangAlso:H5178
G3976 N-APF πέδας (1x)
Mk 5:4 him, and the shackles to·have·been·shattered. And
G3976 N-DPF πέδαις (2x)
Lk 8:29 ·chains, even being·vigilantly·kept in·shackles. And
Mk 5:4 ·times to·have·been·bound with·shackles and chains,

G3977 πεδινός pêdinós *adj.* (1x)
Roots:G4228 Compare:G2117
G3977 A-GSM πεδινοῦ (1x)
Lk 6:17 with them, he·stood·still in a·level place, and·also

G3978 πεζεύω pêzêúō *v.* (1x)
Roots:G4228 See:G3979
G3978 V-PAN πεζεύειν (1x)
Ac 20:13 ·assigned, intending himself to·go·on·foot.

G3979 πεζῇ pêzēi *adv.* (3x)
Roots:G4228 See:G3978
G3979 ADV πεζῇ (2x)
Mt 14:13 the crowds followed him on·foot from the cities.
Mk 6:33 him. Then they·ran·together on·foot from all the
EG3979 (1x)
Ac 28:14 in·this·manner we·went toward Rome *on·foot*.

G3980 πειθ•αρχέω pêitharchêō *v.* (4x)
Roots:G3982 G0757 Compare:G0700 G5226 G5255 G5293
G3980.2 V-PAN πειθαρχεῖν (2x)
Ac 5:29 "It·is·mandatory to·readily·comply with·God rather
Tit 3:1 and authorities, to·readily·comply, to·be ready
G3980.2 V-PAP-DPM πειθαρχοῦσιν (1x)
Ac 5:32 God gave to·the·ones readily·complying with·him."
G3980.2 V-AAP-APM πειθαρχήσαντας (1x)
Ac 27:21 *for·yeu* to·readily·comply with·my *urgent·*

G3981 πειθός pêithós *adj.* (1x)
Roots:G3982 See:G3988
G3981 A-DPM πειθοῖς (1x)
1Co 2:4 *was* not with persuasive words of·mankind's†

G3982 πείθω pêíthō *v.* (56x)
Compare:G4100 G4104 G1679 See:G3981 G2138 G4006 xLangAlso:H0983
G3982.1 V-FAI-1P πείσομεν (1x)
Mt 28:14 by the governor, we·ourselves shall·persuade him,
G3982.1 V-FPI-3P πεισθήσονται (1x)
Lk 16:31 prophets, neither shall·they·be·persuaded, though
G3982.1 V-PAI-1P πείθομεν (1x)
2Co 5:11 the fear of·the Lord, we·persuade men·of·clay†.
G3982.1 V-PAI-2S πείθεις (1x)
Ac 26:28 a·brief·moment, do·you·persuade me to·become
G3982.1 V-PAP-NSM πείθων (2x)
Ac 19:8 discussing (and persuading) the·things concerning
Ac 28:23 of·God, and·also persuading them concerning
G3982.1 V-PMM-2P πείθεσθε (1x)
Heb 13:17 Be·persuaded by·the·ones who·are·governing
G3982.1 V-PMP-DPM πειθομένοις (1x)
Rm 2:8 and are·being·persuaded by·the unrighteousness, *he·*
G3982.1 V-PPI-1S πείθομαι (1x)
Ac 26:26 being·boldly·confident, for I·am·persuaded *for* not
G3982.1 V-PPN πείθεσθαι (3x)
Gal 3:1 ·an·evil·eye·on yeu to·not be·persuaded by·the truth,
Gal 5:7 ·path *such·for* yeu to·not be·persuaded by·the truth?
Jac 3:3 horses' mouths specifically to·persuade them to·our
G3982.1 V-PPP-GSM πειθομένου (1x)
Ac 21:14 And with·him not being·persuaded, we·kept·still,
G3982.1 V-IAI-3S ἔπειθεν (1x)
Ac 18:4 and·every Sabbath, and was·persuading Jews and
G3982.1 V-IAI-3P ἔπειθον (1x)
Ac 13:43 with·them, were·persuading them to·continue·on
G3982.1 V-IPI-3P ἐπείθοντο (2x)
Ac 5:36 And all (as·many·as were·persuaded by·him) were·
Ac 28:24 they·were·persuaded by·the·things being·said, but
G3982.1 V-AAI-3P ἔπεισαν (1x)
Mt 27:20 chief·priests and the elders persuaded the crowds
G3982.1 V-AAP-NSM πείσας (1x)
Ac 19:26 has·won·over an·ample crowd *by* persuading *them*,
G3982.1 V-AAP-NPM πείσαντες (2x)
Ac 12:20 alongside him. And persuading Blastus, the·one
Ac 14:19 and Iconium, and after·persuading the crowds and
G3982.1 V-API-3P ἐπείσθησαν (1x)
Ac 5:40 And they·were·persuaded by·him. And after·
G3982.1 V-APP-NPM πεισθέντες (1x)
Heb 11:13 them from·afar, and being·persuaded·of *them*,
G3982.1 V-APS-2S πεισθῇς (1x)
Ac 23:21 you·yourself should·not be·persuaded by·them,
G3982.1 V-RPI-1S πέπεισμαι (1x)
Rm 15:14 I myself also have·been·persuaded concerning yeu
G3982.1 V-RPI-1P πεπείσμεθα (1x)
Heb 6:9 beloved, we·have·been·persuaded concerning yeu
G3982.1 V-RPP-NSM πεπεισμένος (1x)
Lk 20:6 ·death, for they·are having·been·persuaded *for* John
G3982.2 V-IPI-3S ἐπείθετο (1x)
Ac 27:11 But the centurion was·convinced by·the pilot and
G3982.2 V-IPI-3P ἐπείθοντο (1x)
Ac 5:37 And all (as·many·as were·convinced by·him) were·
G3982.2 V-API-3P ἐπείσθησαν (1x)
Ac 17:4 ·among them were·convinced and joined·alongside
G3982.2 V-RPI-1S πέπεισμαι (4x)
Rm 8:38 For I·have·been·convinced that neither death, nor
Rm 14:14 ·know, and have·been·convinced by *the* Lord
2Ti 1:5 mother EuNiki, and I·have·been·convinced that *is* in
2Ti 1:12 ·have·trusted, and I·have·been·convinced that he·is
G3982.3 V-2RAI-1S πέποιθα (2x)
Gal 5:10 I·myself do·have·confidence for yeu in *the* Lord,
Php 2:24 But I·have·confidence in *the* Lord that also I·
G3982.3 V-2RAI-1P πεποίθαμεν (2x)
Heb 13:18 us, for we·have·confidence that we·have a·good
2Th 3:4 And we·have·confidence in *the* Lord concerning yeu
G3982.3 V-2RAI-2S πέποιθας (1x)
Rm 2:19 And you·have·confidence within·yourself to·be a·
G3982.3 V-2RAI-3S πέποιθεν (2x)
Mt 27:43 "He·has·confidence in God. Let·him·rescue him
2Co 10:7 If any·man has·confidence in·himself to·be of·
G3982.3 V-2RAN πεποιθέναι (1x)
Php 3:4 ·man presumes *a·reason* to·have·confidence in flesh,
G3982.3 V-2RAP-APM πεποιθότας (3x)
Lk 18:9 to certain ones having·confidence in themselves that
Mk 10:24 it·is for·the·ones having·confidence in the
Php 1:14 in *the* Lord, having·confidence by·my bonds, *are*
G3982.3 V-2RAP-NSM πεποιθώς (5x)
Heb 2:13 " I·myself shall·be having·confidence on him."
Php 1:6 having·confidence of·this very·thing— that the·one
Php 1:25 And having·this confidence, I·have·seen that I·
2Co 2:3 ·for me to·rejoice, having·confidence in yeu all that
Phm 1:21 Having·confidence in·your attentive·obedience, I·
G3982.3 V-2RAP-NPM πεποιθότες (1x)
Php 3:3 Jesus, and not having·confidence in flesh,
G3982.3 V-2LAI-3S ἐπεποίθει (1x)
Lk 11:22 in which he·had·confided and thoroughly·doles·out
G3982.4 V-PAI-1S πείθω (1x)
Gal 1:10 at·this·moment, do·I·comply·with men·of·clay†, or
EG3982.4 (1x)
Gal 1:10 ·I·comply·with men·of·clay†, or *comply·with* God?
G3982.6 V-2RAP-NPM πεποιθότες (1x)
2Co 1:9 ·that we·may·not be having·reliance upon ourselves,
G3982.8 V-FAI-1P πείσομεν (1x)
1Jn 3:19 ·from·out of·the truth and shall·reassure our hearts

G3983 πεινάω pêináō *v.* (23x)
See:G3993 G4361 xLangAlso:H7456
G3983.1 V-FAI-2P πεινάσετε (1x)
Lk 6:25 ·been·filled·up! Because yeu·shall·hunger. Woe to·
G3983.1 V-FAI-3P πεινάσουσιν (1x)
Rv 7:16 They·shall·not hunger any·longer, neither shall·
G3983.1 V-PAI-1P πεινῶμεν (1x)
1Co 4:11 the very·present hour, also we·hunger, and should·
G3983.1 V-PAP-ASM πεινῶντα (2x)
Mt 25:37 when did·we·see you hungering, and nourished
Mt 25:44 Lord, when did·we·see you hungering, or thirsting
G3983.1 V-PAP-NPM πεινῶντες (2x)
Lk 6:21 "Supremely·blessed *are* the·ones hungering now,
Mt 5:6 ·blessed *are* the·ones hungering and thirsting·for the
G3983.1 V-PAS-3S πεινᾷ (1x)
Rm 12:20 enemy should·hunger, provide·some·food·for him
G3983.1 V-AAI-3S ἐπείνασεν (2x)
Lk 4:2 being·entirely·completed, eventually he·hungered.
Mt 4:2 forty days and forty nights, eventually he·hungered.
G3983.1 V-AAS-3S πεινάσῃ (1x)
Jn 6:35 me, no, he·should·not hunger, and the·one trusting
G3983.2 V-PAI-3S πεινᾷ (1x)
1Co 11:21 and in·fact, one goes·hungry, and another gets·
G3983.3 V-PAI-3S πεινᾷ (1x)
1Co 11:34 And if any·man is·hungry, let·him·eat at home,
G3983.3 V-PAN πεινᾶν (1x)
Php 4:12 ·how also to·be·stuffed·full and to·be·hungry, even
G3983.3 V-PAP-APM πεινῶντας (1x)
Lk 1:53 He·filled·up those·being·hungry with·beneficially·,
G3983.3 V-AAI-1S ἐπείνασα (2x)
Mt 25:35 For I·was·hungry, and yeu·gave me to·eat.
Mt 25:42 For I·was·hungry, and yeu·did·not give me
G3983.3 V-AAI-3S ἐπείνασεν (5x)
Lk 6:3 David did that·one·time·when he·was·hungry, him
Mt 12:3 did, when he·himself was·hungry, and the·ones
Mt 21:18 the City with·the·break·of·dawn, he·was·hungry.
Mk 2:25 did, when he·had need and was·hungry, he and the·
Mk 11:12 coming·forth from BethAny, he·was·hungry.
G3983.3 V-AAI-3P ἐπείνασαν (1x)
Mt 12:1 and *when* his disciples were·hungry, they·also began

G3984 πεῖρα pêîra *n.* (2x)
Roots:G4008 Compare:G3986 See:G3987
G3984.1 N-ASF πεῖραν (1x)
Heb 11:36 And others received a·trial of·*cruel*·mockings and
G3984.2 N-ASF πεῖραν (1x)
Heb 11:29 Egyptians (taking an·attempt) were·swallowed·up

G3985 πειράζω pêirázō *v.* (39x)
Roots:G3984 Compare:G1381 G1598 See:G3986 G3987 xLangEquiv:H5254
G3985.1 V-PAI-2P πειράζετε (4x)
Lk 20:23 he·declared to them, "Why·do yeu·try me?
Ac 15:10 "Now, accordingly, why·do yeu·try God, to·put a·
Mt 22:18 declared, "Why·do yeu·try me, O·stage·acting·
Mk 12:15 he·declared to·them, "Why·do yeu·try me?
G3985.1 V-PAM-2P πειράζετε (1x)
2Co 13:5 Try yeurselves, whether yeu·are in the trust.
G3985.1 V-PAP-NSM πειράζων (2x)
Jn 6:6 And he·was·saying this, trying him, for he·himself
Mt 22:35 inquired·of *him*, trying him and saying,
G3985.1 V-PAP-NPM πειράζοντες (5x)
Jn 8:6 But they·were·saying this, trying him in·order·that
Lk 11:16 And others, trying *him*, were·seeking personally·
Mt 19:3 also came·alongside him, trying him and saying to·
Mk 8:11 ·from him a·sign from the heaven, trying him.
Mk 10:2 And upon·coming·alongside to·try him, the
G3985.1 V-PPP-DPM πειραζομένοις (1x)
Heb 2:18 he·is·able to·swiftly·help the·ones being·tried.
G3985.1 V-PPP-NSM πειραζόμενος (3x)
Lk 4:2 being·tried *for* forty days by the Slanderer.

Heb 11:17 AbRaham, when·being·tried, had·offered·up
Mk 1:13 in the wilderness forty days, being·tried by the
G3985.1 V-IAI-3S ἐπείρασεν (1x)
1Th 3:5 lest·somehow the Tempting·One was·trying yeu and
G3985.1 V-AAI-3P ἐπείρασαν (2x)
Heb 3:9 when yeur fathers tried me, tested·and·proved me,
1Co 10:9 just·as some of·them also tried *him*, and they·
G3985.1 V-AAN πειράσαι (2x)
Ac 5:9 are·mutually·agreed·together to·try Yahweh's Spirit?
Rv 3:10 upon all The Land, to·try the·ones residing upon the
G3985.1 V-AMI-2S ἐπειράσω (1x)
Rv 2:2 bad·men, and *that* you·tried the·ones professing to·
G3985.1 V-APN πειρασθῆναι (2x)
Mt 4:1 wilderness by the Spirit to·be·tried by the Slanderer.
1Co 10:13 who shall·not let yeu to·be·tried above what yeu·
G3985.1 V-APP-NSM πειρασθείς (1x)
Heb 2:18 he·has·suffered, he·himself being·tried, he·is·able
G3985.1 V-APS-2S πειρασθῇς (1x)
Gal 6:1 ·of yourself, lest you·yourself also should·be·tried.
G3985.1 V-APS-2P πειρασθῆτε (1x)
Rv 2:10 yeu into prison in·order·that yeu·may·be·tried, and
G3985.2 V-IAI-3S ἐπείρασεν (1x)
Ac 24:6 this·same·man also was·attempting to·profane the
G3985.2 V-IAI-3P ἐπείραζον (1x)
Ac 16:7 ·to Mysia, they·were·attempting to·traverse toward
EG3985.2 (1x)
Ac 17:21 ·even·one·thing, other than *attempting* to·say or
G3985.3 V-PAI-3S πειράζει (1x)
Jac 1:13 he·himself tempts not·even·one·man *with·moral·*
G3985.3 V-PAP-NSM πειράζων (2x)
Mt 4:3 coming·alongside him, the Tempting·One declared,
1Th 3:5 lest·somehow the Tempting·One was·trying yeu
G3985.3 V-PAP-NPM@ πειράζοντες (1x)
Mt 16:1 And upon·coming·alongside to·tempt *YeShua*, the
G3985.3 V-PAS-3S πειράζῃ (1x)
1Co 7:5 Adversary-Accuser may·not tempt yeu on·account·of
G3985.3 V-PPI-1S πειράζομαι (1x)
Jac 1:13 ·tempted must·ever·say, "I·am·tempted by God,"
G3985.3 V-PPI-3S πειράζεται (1x)
Jac 1:14 But each·man is·tempted, being·drawn·forth by his·
G3985.3 V-PPP-NSM πειραζόμενος (1x)
Jac 1:13 No·one being·tempted must·ever·say, "I·am·
G3985.3 V-API-3P ἐπειράσθησαν (1x)
Heb 11:37 ·sawed·in·half, they·were·tempted, they·died by

G3986 πειρασμός pêirasmós *n.* (21x)
Roots:G3985 Compare:G4451 G2347 G1382
xLangEquiv:H4531
G3986.1 N-NSM πειρασμός (1x)
1Co 10:13 A·proof·trial has·not taken yeu except *that·which*
G3986.1 N-ASM πειρασμόν (11x)
Lk 4:13 after·entirely·completing *the* entire proof·trial, the
Lk 11:4 may·you·not carry us into a·proof·trial, but·rather
Lk 22:40 *in·order·for yeu* not to·enter into a·proof·trial."
Lk 22:46 ·order·that yeu·should·not enter into a·proof·trial."
Gal 4:14 yeu·did·not utterly·disdain my proof·trial, the·one
Mt 6:13 may·you·not carry us into a·proof·trial, but·rather
Mt 26:41 ·that yeu·may·not enter into a·proof·trial. In·fact,
Mk 14:38 ·that yeu·may·not enter into a·proof·trial. In·fact,
Jac 1:12 a·man that patiently·endures a·proof·trial, because
1Pe 4:12 (occurring specifically·for a·proof·trial among·yeu)
1Ti 6:9 to·become·wealthy fall into a·proof·trial and a·snare,
G3986.1 N-DSM πειρασμῷ (1x)
1Co 10:13 but·rather together with·the proof·trial, also
G3986.1 N-DPM πειρασμοῖς (3x)
Lk 22:28 ·remained·constantly with me in my proof·trials.
Jac 1:2 yeu·should·entirely·fall·into diverse proof·trials,
1Pe 1:6 it·is·being·necessary) in diverse proof·trials—
G3986.1 N-GSM πειρασμοῦ (4x)
Lk 8:13 and·then in a·season of·proof·trial, they·withdraw.
Heb 3:8 in the day of·the Proof·Trial in the wilderness,
2Pe 2:9 devoutly·reverent·men out of·proof·trials, and to·
Rv 3:10 you from·out of·the hour of·the proof·trial, the·one
G3986.1 N-GPM πειρασμῶν (1x)

Ac 20:19 with·many tears, and with·proof·trials, the·ones

G3987 πειράω pêiráō *v.* (3x)
Roots:G3984 Compare:G1598 See:G3985 G3986
xLangAlso:H5254
G3987.2 V-INI-3S ἐπειρᾶτο (1x)
Ac 9:26 Saul was·intently·trying to·tightly·join·himself to·
G3987.2 V-INI-3P ἐπειρῶντο (1x)
Ac 26:21 were·intently·trying to·abusively·manhandle *me*.
G3987.2 V-RPP-ASM πεπειραμένον (1x)
Heb 4:15 in all·points having·been·intently·tried in similarity

G3988 πεισμονή pêismonḗ *n.* (1x)
Roots:G3982 See:G3981
G3988.1 N-NSF πεισμονή (1x)
Gal 5:8 The persuading *is* not from·out of·the·one calling

G3989 πέλαγος pélagôs *n.* (2x)
Compare:G2281 G0899 G1037
G3989.1 N-ASN πέλαγος (1x)
Ac 27:5 after·sailing·through the open·sea adjacent·to Cilicia
G3989.2 N-DSN πελάγει (1x)
Mt 18:6 ·be·plunged·down in the open·depth of·the sea.

G3990 πελεκίζω pêlêkízō *v.* (1x)
Roots:G4141
G3990 V-RPP-GPM πεπελεκισμένων (1x)
Rv 20:4 of·the·ones having·been·beheaded on·account·of the

G3991 πέμπτος pémptôs *adj.* (4x)
Roots:G4002
xLangEquiv:H2549
G3991 A-NSM πέμπτος (3x)
Rv 9:1 And the fifth angel sounded, and I·saw a·star having·
Rv 16:10 And the fifth angel poured·out his vial upon the
Rv 21:20 the fifth, sardonyx; the sixth, sardius; the
G3991 A-ASF πέμπτην (1x)
Rv 6:9 *the Lamb* opened·up the fifth official·seal, I·saw

G3992 πέμπω pémpō *v.* (82x)
Compare:G2423-1 G1856 See:G4724
G3992.1 V-FAI-1S πέμψω (5x)
Jn 15:26 whom I·myself shall·send to·yeu personally·from
Jn 16:7 yeu; but if I·should·depart, I·shall·send him to yeu.
Lk 20:13 'What should·I·do? I·shall·send my beloved son.
Tit 3:12 Whenever I·shall·send Artemas to you, or Tychicus,
1Co 16:3 *yeur* letters, these I·shall·send to·carry yeur
G3992.1 V-FAI-3S πέμψει (2x)
Jn 14:26 Spirit, whom the Father shall·send in my name,
2Th 2:11 ·account·of this, God shall·send them an·effective
G3992.1 V-FAI-3P πέμψουσιν (1x)
Rv 11:10 and they·shall·send presents to·one·another
G3992.1 V-PAI-1S πέμπω (1x)
Jn 20:21 *my* Father has·dispatched me, even·so·I send yeu."
G3992.1 V-PAN πέμπειν (1x)
Ac 25:25 to the Revered·Emperor, I·decided to·send him *on*,
G3992.1 V-PAP-ASM πέμποντα (1x)
Ac 25:27 to·me unreasonable to·send a·chained·prisoner,
G3992.1 V-PPP-DPM πεμπομένοις (1x)
1Pe 2:14 or to·governors, as being·sent through him, in·fact,
G3992.1 V-AAI-1S ἔπεμψα (8x)
Ac 10:33 So·then, from·this·same·hour I·sent to you, and
Ac 23:30 by the Judeans, I·sent *him* from·this·same·hour to
Php 2:28 Accordingly, I·sent him more·diligently, in·order·
1Co 4:17 On·account·of that, I·sent to·yeu TimoThy, who is
2Co 9:3 So I·sent the brothers, lest our boasting on·yeur
Eph 6:22 whom I·sent to yeu for this very·purpose, that yeu·
Col 4:8 whom I·sent to yeu for this same purpose, in·order·
Rv 22:16 "I, Jesus, sent my angel to·testify to·yeu these·
G3992.1 V-AAI-1P ἐπέμψαμεν (1x)
1Th 3:2 and we·sent TimoThy, our brother, and attendant of·
G3992.1 V-AAI-2P ἐπέμψατε (1x)
Php 4:16 Because even in ThessaloNica yeu·sent also once
G3992.1 V-AAI-3S ἔπεμψεν (3x)
Lk 7:6 from the home, the centurion sent friends to him,
Lk 7:19 a·certain two of·his disciples, sent *them* to Jesus,
Lk 15:15 country, and *the citizen* sent him into his fields to·
G3992.1 V-AAM-2S πέμψον (5x)

Lk 16:24 show·mercy on·me, and send Lazarus in·order·that
Ac 10:5 And now send men to Joppa and send·for Simon,
Ac 10:32 Now·then, send to Joppa and summarily·call·for
Mk 5:12 implored him, saying, "Send us into the pigs, in·
Rv 1:11 in an·official·scroll, and send *it* to·the Called·Out·
G3992.1 V-AAN πέμψαι (8x)
Lk 20:11 And he·further·proceeded to·send another slave.
Lk 20:12 And he·further·proceeded to·send a·third. But also
Ac 11:29 *to·do so*, specifically·determined to·send service to
Ac 15:22 Called·Out·citizenry, to·send men being·selected
Ac 15:25 ·the·same·determination, to·send selected men to
Php 2:19 *the* Lord Jesus, to·send TimoThy promptly to·yeu,
Php 2:23 I·expect to·send this·man from·this·same·hour as·
Php 2:25 I·resolutely·considered *it* necessary to·send to yeu
G3992.1 V-AAP-ASM πέμψαντα (7x)
Jn 5:23 ·not deeply·honor the Father, the·one sending him.
Jn 7:33 and·then I·head·on·out toward the·one sending me.
Jn 12:44 ·not trust in me, but·rather in the·one sending me.
Jn 12:45 the·one observing me observes the·one sending me.
Jn 13:20 the·one receiving me receives the·one sending me."
Jn 15:21 they·do·not personally·know the·one sending me.
Jn 16:5 now I·head·on·out toward the·one sending me, and
G3992.1 V-AAP-DSM πέμψαντι (1x)
Jn 5:24 Redemptive-word and trusting the·one sending me has
G3992.1 V-AAP-DPM πέμψασιν (1x)
Jn 1:22 ·that we·may·give an·answer to·the·ones sending us,
G3992.1 V-AAP-GSM πέμψαντος (10x)
Jn 4:34 is that I·may·do the will of·the·one sending me, and
Jn 5:30 but·rather the Father's will, the·one sending me.
Jn 6:38 ·own will, but·rather the will of·the·one sending me.
Jn 6:39 the Father's will, the·one sending me, that I·should·
Jn 6:40 this is the will of·the·one sending me, that anyone,
Jn 7:16 is not mine, but·rather *from* the·one sending me.
Jn 7:18 seeking the glory of·the·one sending him, the·same·
Jn 9:4 to·be·working the works of·the·one sending me, for·
Jn 13:16 *is* an·ambassador greater·than the·one sending him.
Jn 14:24 but·rather *that of·the·*Father, the·one sending me.
G3992.1 V-AAP-NSM πέμψας (12x)
Jn 1:33 him, but·yet the·one sending me to·immerse in
Jn 5:37 Father himself, the·one sending me, has·testified
Jn 6:44 unless the Father (the·one sending me) should·draw
Jn 7:28 my·own·self, but·rather the·one sending me is true,
Jn 8:16 ·rather *it·is* I·myself and Father, the·one sending me.
Jn 8:18 ·self, and Father (the·one sending me), he·testifies
Jn 8:26 concerning yeu. But·yet the·one sending me is true,
Jn 8:29 And the·one sending me is with me.
Jn 12:49 But·rather Father (the·one sending me), he·himself
Mt 2:8 And sending them to BethLechem, he·declared,
Mt 22:7 the king was·angry, and sending his troops, he·
Rm 8:3 the flesh, God, after·sending his·own Son in *the*
G3992.1 V-AAS-1S πέμψω (2x)
Jn 13:20 the·one receiving anyone I·may·send, receives me;
Ac 25:21 him to·be·kept until I·may·send him to Caesar.
G3992.1 V-AAS-2S πέμψῃς (1x)
Lk 16:27 you, father, that you·may·send him to my father's
G3992.1 V-API-3S ἐπέμφθη (1x)
Lk 4:26 to not·even·one of·them was EliJah sent, except into
G3992.1 V-APP-NPM πεμφθέντες (1x)
Lk 7:10 to the house, the·ones being·sent found the sick
EG3992.1 (1x)
Lk 16:28 for I·have five brothers; *send him* so·that he·may·
G3992.3 V-AAI-1S ἔπεμψα (1x)
1Th 3:5 ·bear·it no·longer, I·sent·word in·order·to·know
G3992.3 V-AAP-NSM πέμψας (3x)
Ac 20:17 And from Miletus, after·sending·word to Ephesus,
Mt 11:2 ·the Anointed-One *and* sending·word by·two of·his
Mt 14:10 And after·sending·word, he·beheaded John in the
G3992.3 V-AAP-NPM πέμψαντες (1x)
Ac 19:31 being friends with·him, sending·word to him,
G3992.4 V-AAM-2S πέμψον (2x)
Rv 14:15 on the thick·cloud, "Thrust·in your sickle and reap
Rv 14:18 sickle, saying, "Thrust·in your sharp sickle and

G3993 πένης pénēs *n.* (1x)
Compare:G4434 See:G3998 G4188-1
G3993.3 N-DPM πένησιν (1x)
2Co 9:9 dispersed; he·gave to·the working·poor·in·need; his

G3994 πενθερά pênthêrá *n.* (6x)
Roots:G3995 Compare:G3384
xLangEquiv:H2545 xLangAlso:H0517
G3994 N-NSF πενθερά (3x)
Lk 4:38 And Simon's mother-in-law was being·clenched
Lk 12:53 against mother; mother-in-law against her
Mk 1:30 But Simon's mother-in-law was·laying·ill, burning·
G3994 N-ASF πενθεράν (2x)
Lk 12:53 and daughter-in-law against her mother-in-law."
Mt 8:14 saw *Peter's* mother-in-law having·been·cast *on a·*
G3994 N-GSF πενθερᾶς (1x)
Mt 10:35 and a·daughter-in-law against her mother-in-law;

G3995 πενθερός pênthêrós *n.* (1x)
Compare:G1059-2 G3566 See:G3994
xLangAlso:H2524 H2859
G3995 N-NSM πενθερός (1x)
Jn 18:13 for he·was *the* father-in-law of·Caiaphas, who was

G3996 πενθέω pênthéō *v.* (13x)
Roots:G3997 Compare:G3602 G2875 G3076 G2799 G1145 See:G3996-1 G2664-2
xLangEquiv:H0056
G3996 V-FAI-1S πενθήσω (1x)
2Co 12:21 among yeu, and I·shall·mourn many of·the·ones
G3996 V-FAI-2P πενθήσετε (1x)
Lk 6:25 now! Because yeu·shall·mourn and shall·weep.
G3996 V-PAI-3P πενθοῦσιν (1x)
Rv 18:11 of·the earth do·weep and mourn over her, because
G3996 V-PAN πενθεῖν (1x)
Mt 9:15 Sons of·the bride-chamber able to·mourn, as·long·as
G3996 V-PAP-DPM πενθοῦσιν (1x)
Mk 16:10 him, to·those·being in·mourning and weeping.
G3996 V-PAP-NPM πενθοῦντες (3x)
Mt 5:4 "Supremely·blessed *are* the·ones mourning, because
Rv 18:15 the fear of·her torment, weeping and mourning,
Rv 18:19 were·yelling·out, weeping and mourning, saying,
G3996 V-AAI-2P ἐπενθήσατε (1x)
1Co 5:2 and did·not·indeed rather mourn, in·order·that the·
G3996 V-AAM-2P πενθήσατε (1x)
Jac 4:9 Be·miserable, also mourn and weep. *Let* yeur
EG3996 (3x)
Mk 16:11 And·those *in·mourning*, hearing that he·lives and
Mk 16:13 *it* to·the rest *in·mourning*, but·neither·even·did
Mk 16:13 but·neither·even·did those *mourners* trust.

G3997 πένθος pénthôs *n.* (5x)
Roots:G3958 Compare:G3602 G2870 G3803-2 G3077 See:G3996
xLangEquiv:H0060
G3997 N-NSN πένθος (5x)
Jac 4:9 yeur laughter be·distorted into mourning, and *yeur*
Rv 18:7 ·a·vast·quantity·of torment and mourning, because
Rv 18:7 not a·widow, and no, I·should·not see mourning.'
Rv 18:8 in one day: death, and mourning, and famine.
Rv 21:4 ·not be any·longer, neither mourning, nor yelling,

G3998 πενιχρός pênichrós *adj.* (1x)
Roots:G3993 Compare:G4434
xLangEquiv:H0034
G3998 A-ASF πενιχράν (1x)
Lk 21:2 And he·saw also a·certain needy widow casting two

G3999 πεντά•κις pêntákis *adv.* (1x)
Roots:G4002
G3999 ADV πεντάκις (1x)
2Co 11:24 Five·times by *the* Jews I·received forty *stripes*

G4000 πεντακισ•χίλιοι pêntakischílîôi *n.* (6x)
Roots:G3999 G5507
G4000 N-NPM πεντακισχίλιοι (4x)
Jn 6:10 ·to·eat; the number *was* about five·thousand *men.*
Lk 9:14 For there·were about five·thousand men. And he·
Mt 14:21 And the·ones eating were about five·thousand men,
Mk 6:44 ·the loaves·of·bread were about five·thousand men.
G4000 N-APM πεντακισχιλίους (1x)
Mk 8:19 five loaves·of·bread among the five·thousand *men,*
G4000 N-GPM πεντακισχιλίων (1x)
Mt 16:9 the five loaves·of·bread of·the five·thousand *men,*

G4001 πεντα•κόσιοι pêntakósîôi *n.* (2x)
Roots:G4002 G1540
G4001 N-APN πεντακόσια (1x)
Lk 7:41 the one was·owing five·hundred denarii *(about one*
G4001 N-DPM πεντακοσίοις (1x)
1Co 15:6 by·upwards·of five·hundred brothers upon·one·

G4002 πέντε pêntê *n.* (37x)
See:G3991
xLangEquiv:H2568 xLangAlso:H2549
G4002 N-NUI πέντε (37x)
Jn 4:18 For you·have·had five husbands, and now, he·whom
Jn 5:2 there·is a·pool having five colonnades; in·Hebrew, *it·*
Jn 6:9 a little·boy here, who has five barley loaves·of·bread,
Jn 6:13 from·out of·the five barley loaves·of·bread, which
Lk 1:24 was·entirely·hiding herself *for* five lunar·months,
Lk 9:13 there·are not more than five loaves·of·bread and two
Lk 9:16 And after·taking the five loaves·of·bread and the
Lk 12:6 "Are·not·indeed five little·sparrows sold for·two
Lk 12:52 "For from now·on there·shall·be five in one house
Lk 14:19 declared, 'I·bought five yoked·teams of·oxen, and
Lk 16:28 for I·have five brothers; *send him* so·that he·may·
Lk 19:18 'Lord, your mina produced five more·minas.'
Lk 19:19 'Be you also over five cities.'
Ac 4:4 and the number of·the men was about five thousand.
Ac 7:14 and all his kinsfolk, in *all*, seventy five souls.'
Ac 19:19 *it to·be* five times·ten·thousand pieces·of·silver
Ac 20:6 ·came to them in Troas in·only five days, where we·
Ac 24:1 And after five days, the designated·high·priest
Mt 14:17 have *anything* here except five loaves·of·bread and
Mt 14:19 and upon·taking the five loaves·of·bread and the
Mt 16:9 nor·even remember the five loaves·of·bread of·the
Mt 25:2 And five *virgins* from·among them were prudent,
Mt 25:2 them were prudent, and the *other* five *were* foolish.
Mt 25:15 And in·fact, to·one he·gave five talants·of·silver,
Mt 25:16 the·one receiving the five talants·of·silver worked
Mt 25:16 same, and produced another five talants·of·silver.
Mt 25:20 the·one receiving the five talants·of·silver brought
Mt 25:20 ·of·silver brought another five talants·of·silver,
Mt 25:20 you·handed·over to·me five talants·of·silver. See,
Mt 25:20 See, I·gained another five talants·of·silver upon
Mk 6:38 already·knowing, they·say, "Five, and two fish.
Mk 6:41 And after·taking the five loaves·of·bread and the
Mk 8:19 When I·broke the five loaves·of·bread among the
1Co 14:19 I·determine to·speak five words through my
Rv 9:5 that they·should·be·tormented five lunar·months.
Rv 9:10 ·bring·harm·to the men·of·clay† five lunar·months.
Rv 17:10 And they·are seven kings. The five fell, and the

G4003 πεντε•και•δέκατος pêntêkaidékatôs *adj.* (1x)
Roots:G4002 G2532 G1182
G4003 A-DSN πεντεκαιδεκάτῳ (1x)
Lk 3:1 Now in *the* fifteenth year of·the governing·term of·

G4004 πεντή•κοντα pêntḗkônta *n.* (8x)
Roots:G4002 See:G4005
G4004.1 N-NUI πεντήκοντα (6x)
Jn 8:57 him, "You·are not·yet fifty years·of·age, and have·
Lk 7:41 *wages*), and the other fifty *denarii (about a·month*
Lk 9:14 Make them fully·recline·back *by* fifty apiece *in·each*
Lk 16:6 your bill, and sitting·down quickly, write fifty.'
Ac 13:20 *which·took* about four·hundred and fifty years, he·
Mk 6:40 ·eat in·rows, rows by a·hundred, and by fifty *deep.*
EG4004.1 (1x)
Ac 19:19 pieces·of·silver *(which·is fifty thousand drachmas).*
G4004.2 N-GPM πεντηκοντατριῶν (1x)
Jn 21:11 ·full·of·big fish (a·hundred *and* fifty·three); and·yet

G4005 πεντη•κοστή pêntēkôstḗ *n.* (3x)
Roots:G4004 Compare:G1439-1 See:G2250
xLangAlso:H7620
G4005.2 N/T-GSF πεντηκοστῆς (3x)
Ac 2:1 with the day of·Pentecost to·be·completely·fulfilled,
Ac 20:16 ·him, to·be in JeruSalem *on* the day of·Pentecost.
1Co 16:8 I·shall·stay·over in Ephesus until the Pentecost.

G4006 πεποίθησις pêpôíthēsis *n.* (6x)
Roots:G3982 Compare:G2294
G4006 N-ASF πεποίθησιν (2x)
Php 3:4 I·myself *was once* also having confidence in flesh. If
2Co 3:4 And such confidence we·have through the
G4006 N-DSF πεποιθήσει (4x)
2Co 1:15 And in·this confidence, I·was·definitely·willing to·
2Co 8:22 more·diligent, with·much confidence, the·one *he·*
2Co 10:2 ·present with·the confidence with·which I·reckon
Eph 3:12 embraceable·access with confidence through trust

G4008 πέραν péran *adv.* (23x)
See:G1276 G1599-1
G4008.1 ADV πέραν (2x)
Jn 1:28 ·things happened in BethAbara across the Jordan
Jn 6:17 the sailboat, they·were·going across the sea toward
G4008.2 ADV πέραν (15x)
Jn 6:1 Jesus went·off *to·the* other·side of·the Sea of·Galilee,
Jn 6:22 — the·one standing on·the·other·side of·the sea,
Jn 6:25 Now after·finding him on·the·other·side of·the sea,
Jn 18:1 with·his disciples to·the·other·side of·the Brook
Lk 8:22 "We·should·go·through to the other·side of·the lake.
Mt 8:18 *to·make·ready* to·go·off to the other·side *of·the Sea*
Mt 8:28 with·him coming to the other·side into the region of·
Mt 14:22 and to·go·on·ahead·of him to the other·side, until
Mt 16:5 And after·coming to the other·side *of·the sea*, his
Mk 4:35 "We·should·go·through to the other·side *of·the Sea*
Mk 5:1 And they·came·over to the other·side of·the sea, into
Mk 5:21 in the sailboat to the other·side *of·the sea*, a·large
Mk 6:45 and to·go·on·ahead to the other·side *of·the sea*
Mk 8:13 again, he·went·off to the other·side *of·the sea.*
Mk 10:1 of·Judea through the other·side of·the Jordan, and
G4008.3 ADV πέραν (6x)
Jn 3:26 he·who was with you beyond the Jordan, to·whom
Jn 10:40 And he·went·away again beyond the Jordan into the
Mt 4:15 *by the* roadway of·sea, beyond the Jordan, O·
Mt 4:25 JeruSalem and Judea, and *from* beyond the Jordan.
Mt 19:1 came into the borders of·Judea beyond the Jordan.
Mk 3:8 ·then from Edom, and *from* beyond the Jordan, and

G4009 πέρας péras *n.* (4x)
See:G4008 G4070
G4009.2 N-APN πέρατα (1x)
Rm 10:18 their utterances to the utmost·parts of·The Land."
G4009.2 N-GPN περάτων (2x)
Lk 11:31 she·came from·out of·the utmost·parts of·the earth
Mt 12:42 she·came from·out of·the utmost·parts of·the earth
G4009.3 N-NSN πέρας (1x)
Heb 6:16 *is* to·them an·utter·end of·every conflict.

G4010 Πέργαμος Pérgamôs *n/l.* (2x)
Roots:G4444
G4010.2 N/L-ASF Πέργαμον (1x)
Rv 1:11 and to Smyrna, and to Pergamos, and to Thyatira,
G4010.2 N/L-DSF Περγάμῳ (1x)
Rv 2:12 angel of·the Called·Out·citizenry in Pergamos write,

G4011 Πέργη Pérgē *n/l.* (3x)
Roots:G4444 See:G4010
G4011.2 N/L-ASF Πέργην (1x)
Ac 13:13 ·with *him*) came to Perga in·PamPhylia. And
G4011.2 N/L-DSF Πέργῃ (1x)
Ac 14:25 the Redemptive·word in Perga, they·walked·down
G4011.2 N/L-GSF Πέργης (1x)
Ac 13:14 after·going·throughout from Perga, came·directly

G4012 περί pêrí *prep.* (353x)
Roots:G4008 See:G4038
G4012.1 PREP περί (11x)
Lk 13:8 also, until such·time *that* I·should·dig around it and
Lk 17:2 that a·donkey-sized millstone be·set around his neck
Lk 22:49 And the·ones around him, upon·seeing the·thing
Ac 22:6 and drawing·near to·Damascus around midday, it·
Mt 3:4 and *was·girded·with* a·leather belt around his loins,

Mk 1:6 camel's hair and with·a·leather belt around his loins,
Mk 3:8 the Jordan, and *from* around Tyre and Tsidon—
Mk 3:32 And a·crowd was·sitting·down around him, and
Mk 3:34 in·a·circle at·the·ones sitting·down around him, he·
Mk 9:42 for·him if a·mill stone be·set around his neck, and
Jud 1:7 Sodom and Gomorrah and the cities around them, *in*

G4012.2 PREP περί (26x)

Jn 6:61 that his disciples are·grumbling about this, declared
Lk 7:3 And after·hearing about Jesus, he·dispatched elders
Lk 10:41 ·are·anxious and are·disturbed about many·things.
Lk 23:8 on·account·of hearing many·things about him; and
Lk 24:4 with them thoroughly·perplexing about this, behold
Ac 5:24 they·were·thoroughly·perplexed about them as·to
Ac 10:9 the rooftop to·pray *at·midday* about *the* sixth hour.
Ac 10:19 while·Peter was·cogitating about the clear·vision,
Ac 19:23 there·occurred no little disturbance about The Way.
Ac 19:40 not·even·one cause about which we·shall·be·able
Ac 22:6 *for* a·significant light to·flash·all·around about me.
Ac 25:24 with·us, observe this·man, about whom all the
Ac 28:7 Now in about the same place, there·were *some* open·
Ac 28:15 brothers, upon·hearing the·things about us, came·
Mt 8:18 seeing large crowds about him, he·commandingly·
Mt 20:3 "And going·forth *midmorning* about the third hour,
Mt 20:5 Again, going·forth about *the* sixth and ninth hour,
Mt 20:6 "Now going·forth about the eleventh hour, he·
Mt 20:9 *forward*, the·ones *hired* about the eleventh hour
Mt 27:46 And about the ninth hour YeShua shouted·out
Mk 5:27 After·hearing about Jesus *and* already·coming in
Mk 6:48 was contrary to·them. And about *the* fourth watch
Mk 7:25 For after·hearing about him, a·woman whose
Mk 9:14 disciples, he·saw a·large crowd about them, and
Jud 1:9 ·the Slanderer (he·was·discussing about *the* body of·
1Ti 6:4 sickly·harping·on about disputable·questions and

EG4012.2 (2x)

Jn 21:21 "Lord, and what *about* this·man?
2Co 11:30 to·boast, I·shall·boast *about* the·things of·my

G4012.3 PREP περί (289x)

Jn 1:7 in·order·that he·may·testify concerning the Light, in·
Jn 1:8 in·order·that he·may·testify concerning the Light.
Jn 1:15 John testifies concerning him and has·yelled·out,
Jn 1:22 sending us, what·do you·say concerning yourself?
Jn 1:30 This is·he concerning whom I·myself declared,
Jn 1:47 coming toward him and says concerning him, "See!
Jn 2:21 But he·was·saying this concerning the temple of·his
Jn 2:25 anyone should·testify concerning the man·of·clay†,
Jn 3:25 disciples against *the* Judeans concerning purification.
Jn 5:31 "If I·myself should·testify concerning my·own·self,
Jn 5:32 ·is another, the·one testifying concerning me, and I·
Jn 5:32 the testimony which he·testifies concerning me is
Jn 5:36 which I·myself do; it·testifies concerning me, that
Jn 5:37 sending me, has·testified concerning me. Not·even
Jn 5:39 Yet those are the·ones testifying concerning me.
Jn 5:46 ·trusting in·me, for that·man wrote concerning me.
Jn 6:41 the Judeans were·grumbling concerning him,
Jn 7:7 me, because I·myself testify concerning it, that its
Jn 7:12 much grumbling among the crowds concerning him.
Jn 7:13 ·speaking with·freeness·of·speech concerning him,
Jn 7:17 his will, he·shall·know concerning the instruction,
Jn 7:32 the crowd grumbling these·things concerning him,
Jn 7:39 (But he·declared this concerning the Spirit, which
Jn 8:13 to·him, "You testify concerning yourself; your
Jn 8:14 I·myself may·testify concerning my·own·self, my
Jn 8:18 I·myself am one testifying concerning my·own·self,
Jn 8:18 (the·one sending me), he·testifies concerning me."
Jn 8:26 many·things to·speak and to·judge concerning yeu.
Jn 8:46 ·among yeu convicts me concerning moral·failure?
Jn 9:17 "What·do you·yourself say concerning him, because
Jn 9:18 the Judeans did·not trust concerning him that he·was
Jn 9:21 him. He·himself shall·speak concerning himself."
Jn 10:13 and it·does·not matter to·him concerning the sheep.
Jn 10:25 Father's name, these·things testify concerning me.
Jn 10:33 "We·do·not stone you concerning a·good work,
Jn 10:33 work, but·rather concerning a·revilement·of·God.
Jn 10:41 as·many·as John declared concerning this·man were
Jn 11:13 And Jesus had·declared *this* concerning his death,
Jn 11:13 that he·says *this* concerning the outstretched·resting
Jn 11:19 ·personally·console them concerning their brother.
Jn 12:6 ·mattering to·him concerning the helplessly·poor,
Jn 12:41 when he·saw his glory and spoke concerning him.
Jn 13:18 "I·do·not say *this* concerning yeu all. I·myself
Jn 13:22 being·at·a·loss concerning who he·is·referring·to.
Jn 13:24 ·be, concerning the·man·to·whom he·is·referring.
Jn 15:22 ·not have a·pretense concerning their moral·failure.
Jn 15:26 the Father, that·one shall·testify concerning me.
Jn 16:8 shall·convict the world concerning moral·failure, and
Jn 16:8 moral·failure, and concerning righteousness, and
Jn 16:8 righteousness, and concerning Tribunal·judgment.
Jn 16:9 Concerning moral·failure, in·fact because they·did·
Jn 16:10 and concerning righteousness, because I·head·on·
Jn 16:11 and concerning Tribunal·judgment, because the
Jn 16:19 among one·another concerning this·thing which I·
Jn 16:25 to·yeu with·clarity·of·speech concerning the Father.
Jn 16:26 I·myself shall·ask·of the Father concerning yeu.
Jn 17:9 "I·myself ask concerning them. *It·is* not concerning
Jn 17:9 concerning them. *It·is* not concerning the world *that*
Jn 17:9 but·rather concerning those·whom you·have·given
Jn 17:20 "But not concerning these·men merely do·I·ask,
Jn 17:20 also concerning the·ones who·shall·be·trusting in
Jn 18:19 ·high·priest asked Jesus concerning his disciples
Jn 18:19 his disciples and concerning his instruction.
Jn 18:23 "If I·spoke wrongly, testify concerning the wrong.
Jn 18:34 or did·others declare·it to·you concerning me?
Jn 19:24 ·rather we·should·determine·by·lot concerning it,
Jn 21:24 the·one testifying concerning these·things and
Lk 1:1 a·thorough·account concerning the activities having·
Lk 1:4 ·may·fully·know the security concerning *the* sayings
Lk 2:17 they·thoroughly·made·it·known·to·all concerning
Lk 2:17 being·spoken to·them concerning this little·child.
Lk 2:18 *it* marveled concerning the·things·that were·being·
Lk 2:27 Jesus, to·do concerning for·him according·to the
Lk 2:33 at the·things being·spoken concerning him.
Lk 2:38 to·Yahweh and was·speaking concerning him to·all
Lk 3:15 were·pondering in their hearts concerning John, if·
Lk 3:19 being·reproved by him concerning HerOdias (the
Lk 3:19 ·his brother PhilIppus) and concerning all *the* evils
Lk 4:10 "He·shall·command his angels concerning you, to·
Lk 4:14 and a·reputation went·forth concerning him in all
Lk 4:37 an·echoing·rumor concerning him was·proceeding·
Lk 4:38 ·high fever, and they·asked·of him concerning her.
Lk 5:14 ·sacrifices, and offer concerning your purification,
Lk 5:15 word went·throughout even·more concerning him,
Lk 7:17 And this saying concerning him went·forth among
Lk 7:18 reported·to him concerning all these·things.
Lk 7:24 began to·discourse to the crowds concerning John,
Lk 7:27 This is *he*, concerning whom it·has·been·written,
Lk 9:9 but who is this, concerning whom I·myself hear
Lk 9:11 he·was·speaking to·them concerning the kingdom
Lk 9:45 ·were·afraid to·ask him concerning this utterance.
Lk 10:40 Martha was·distracted concerning much attendance
Lk 11:53 him to·speak·off-hand concerning more·things,
Lk 12:26 ·is·least, why are·yeu·anxious concerning the rest?
Lk 13:1 *who·were* reporting to·him concerning the Galileans,
Lk 16:2 'What *is* this I·hear concerning you?
Lk 19:37 praising God with·a·loud voice concerning all *the*
Lk 21:5 ·some saying concerning the Sanctuary·Courtyard,
Lk 22:32 "But I·myself petitioned concerning you, *Simon*,
Lk 22:37 ' for even the·things concerning me have an·end.
Lk 24:14 alongside one·another concerning all these·things
Lk 24:19 ·declared to·him, "Concerning Jesus of·Natsareth,
Lk 24:27 in all the Scriptures the·things concerning himself.
Lk 24:44 the·things having·been·written concerning me in
Ac 1:1 O TheoPhilus, *was* concerning all that Jesus began
Ac 1:3 and·also relating the·things concerning the kingdom
Ac 1:16 ·declared through David's mouth concerning Judas
Ac 2:29 yeu with clarity·of·speech concerning the patriarch
Ac 2:31 *this*, he·spoke concerning the resurrection of·the
Ac 7:52 fully·announcing·beforehand concerning the coming
Ac 8:12 ·proclaiming the·things concerning the kingdom of·
Ac 8:15 after·walking·down, prayed concerning them, that
Ac 8:34 "I·petition you, concerning whom·does the prophet
Ac 8:34 ·does the prophet say this? Concerning himself, or
Ac 8:34 Concerning himself, or concerning someone else?
Ac 9:13 I·have·heard of many·things concerning this man,
Ac 11:22 Now the account concerning them was·heard
Ac 13:29 ·all the·things having·been·written concerning him,
Ac 15:2 to the ambassadors and elders concerning this issue.
Ac 15:6 gathered·together to·see concerning this matter.
Ac 17:32 "We·shall·hear you again concerning this *matter*."
Ac 18:15 But since it·is an·issue concerning a·word and
Ac 18:25 accurately the·things concerning the Lord *Jesus*,
Ac 19:8 and persuading) the·things concerning the kingdom
Ac 19:25 ·men, and·also the workmen concerning the *trades*
Ac 19:39 But if yeu·seek anything concerning other·matters,
Ac 19:40 to·be·called·to·account concerning today's uproar,
Ac 21:21 Now they·are·informed concerning you, that you·
Ac 21:24 ·things they·have·been·informed concerning you,
Ac 21:25 "Now concerning the Gentiles having·trusted, we·
Ac 22:10 ·be·spoken to·you concerning all·things which
Ac 22:18 ·heed·and·accept your testimony concerning me.'
Ac 23:6 a·son of·a·Pharisee; *it·is* concerning *the* Expectation
Ac 23:11 For as you·thoroughly·testified concerning me to
Ac 23:15 *something* more·precisely concerning him; and we·
Ac 23:20 more·precisely *about* something concerning him.
Ac 23:29 being·called·to·account concerning issues of·their
Ac 24:8 him, to·recognize concerning all these·things of·
Ac 24:10 ·composure I·give·an·account concerning myself,
Ac 24:13 *against* me of·the·things concerning which now
Ac 24:21 other·than concerning this one address that I·
Ac 24:21 them, 'Concerning *the* resurrection of·dead·men,
Ac 24:22 having·seen more·precisely concerning The Way,
Ac 24:24 ·for Paul, and he·heard him concerning the trust in
Ac 24:25 *Paul* discussing *matters* concerning righteousness,
Ac 25:9 there to·be·judged concerning these·things before
Ac 25:15 concerning whom, with·me being at JeruSalem, the
Ac 25:16 a·place to·defend·himself concerning the allegation
Ac 25:18 Concerning whom, the legal·accusers, after·being·
Ac 25:19 him concerning their·own superstitious·religion,
Ac 25:19 ·religion, and concerning some·man *named* Jesus,
Ac 25:20 being·at·a·loss concerning this disputable·question,
Ac 25:20 and·there to·be·judged concerning these·matters.
Ac 25:26 concerning whom I·do·not have something
Ac 26:2 ·day before you concerning all·the·things for·which
Ac 26:7 *it* to·fully·come— concerning which expectation,
Ac 26:26 king is·fully·acquainted concerning these·things, to
Ac 28:21 ·receiving letters from Judea concerning you,
Ac 28:21 announced or spoken any evil concerning you.
Ac 28:22 ·contemplate, for in·fact, as·concerning this sect,
Ac 28:23 and·also persuading them concerning Jesus, both
Ac 28:31 and instructing the·things concerning the Lord
Heb 2:5 *brand-new* Land, concerning which we·speak.
Heb 4:4 somewhere he·has·declared concerning the seventh
Heb 4:8 ·spoken after these·things concerning another day.
Heb 5:3 on·account·of this (just·as concerning the People,
Heb 5:3 People, in·this·manner also concerning himself),
Heb 5:11 Concerning which, the matter *means* much to·us,
Heb 6:9 we·have·been·persuaded concerning yeu *of* the
Heb 7:14 not·even·one·thing concerning a·sacred·priesthood
Heb 9:5 ·seat·of·favorable·forgiveness), concerning which,
Heb 10:6 In·burnt·offerings, even concerning moral·failure,
Heb 10:7 ·scroll it·has·been·written concerning me— to·do
Heb 10:8 burnt·offerings, even concerning moral·failure,
Heb 10:18 no·longer an·offering concerning moral·failure.
Heb 10:26 ·remaining a·sacrifice concerning moral·failures,
Heb 11:7 ·being·divinely·instructed·by·Yahweh concerning
Heb 11:20 Jacob and Esau concerning things·to·come.
Heb 11:22 ·dying) remembered concerning the exodus of·
Heb 11:22 and he·gave·a·command concerning his bones.
Heb 11:32 ·for me in·giving·an·account concerning Gideon,
Heb 11:40 ·at something significantly·better concerning us:

Heb 13:11 through the high·priest concerning moral·failure,
Heb 13:18 Pray concerning us, for we·have·confidence that
Mt 2:8 ·*it*·by·inquiring precisely concerning the little·child;
Mt 4:6 "He·shall·command his angels concerning you," and
Mt 6:28 "And why are·yeu·anxious concerning apparel?
Mt 9:36 the crowds, he·empathized concerning them,
Mt 11:7 began to·say to·the crowds concerning John,
Mt 11:10 this is·he, concerning whom it·has·been·written, '
Mt 12:36 *it*, they·shall·give·back an·account concerning it in
Mt 15:7 Isaiah did·prophesy well concerning yeu, saying,
Mt 16:11 that·I·declared *this* to·yeu not concerning bread,
Mt 17:13 that he·declared to·them concerning John the
Mt 18:19 on the earth concerning any matter·of·consequence
Mt 20:24 the ten were·greatly·displeased concerning the two
Mt 21:45 Pharisees knew that *it·was* concerning them *that*
Mt 22:16 ·not matter to·you concerning not·even·one *man*,
Mt 22:31 "Now concerning the resurrection of·the dead, did·
Mt 22:42 ·do yeu suppose concerning the Anointed-One?
Mt 24:36 "But concerning that day and hour no·one·at·all
Mt 26:24 ·on·out just·as it·has·been·written concerning him,
Mt 26:28 the·one being·poured·out concerning many for
Mk 1:30 they·related *this* to·him concerning her.
Mk 1:44 ·sacrifices, and offer concerning your purification
Mk 4:19 ·wealth— and the·things concerning the remaining
Mk 5:16 ·possessed·with·demons, and concerning the pigs.
Mk 7:6 "Isaiah prophesied well concerning yeu, the stage·
Mk 7:17 were·inquiring·of him concerning the parable.
Mk 8:30 ·to·one·man should·they·relate *this* concerning him.
Mk 10:10 inquired·of him again concerning the same *matter*.
Mk 10:41 to·be·greatly·displeased concerning Jakob and
Mk 12:14 ·not matter to·you concerning not·even·one·man,
Mk 12:26 "Now concerning the dead, that they·are·
Mk 13:32 "But concerning that day and hour no·one·at·all
Mk 14:21 ·out, just·as it·has·been·written concerning him,
Mk 14:24 the·one being·poured·out concerning many.
Rm 1:3 concerning his Son: the·one coming·to·be birthed·
Rm 8:3 ·morally·failing flesh and concerning moral·failure,
Rm 14:12 ·us shall·give account concerning himself to·God.
Rm 15:14 myself also have·been·persuaded concerning yeu,
Rm 15:21 ·whom it·is·not reported·in·detail concerning him,
Jud 1:3 all diligence to·write to·yeu concerning the common
Jud 1:15 the irreverent·ones among·them concerning all their
Jud 1:15 which they·irreverently·did, and concerning all the
Php 1:27 ·absent, I·may·hear the·things concerning yeu—
Php 2:19 ·*my*·soul, after·knowing the·things concerning yeu.
Php 2:20 shall·be·anxious·about the·things concerning yeu.
Php 2:23 ·as I·should·fully·see the·things concerning me.
1Pe 1:10 Concerning this Salvation, the prophets sought·*it*·
1Pe 1:10 *for·it* after·prophesying to yeu concerning the grace
1Pe 3:15 ·of yeu a·reason concerning the Expectation in yeu
1Pe 3:18 also suffered only·once concerning moral·failures,
1Pe 5:7 him, because it·matters to·him concerning yeu.
2Pe 1:12 ·remind yeu always concerning these·things, even·
2Pe 3:16 speaking in them concerning these·things, in
1Th 1:2 ·give·thanks to·God always concerning all of·yeu,
1Th 1:9 For they·themselves report concerning us, what·
1Th 3:2 yeu and to·comfort yeu concerning yeur trust,
1Th 3:9 are·we·able to·recompense to·God concerning yeu,
1Th 4:6 the Lord *is* avenger concerning all these·matters,
1Th 4:9 But concerning the brotherly·affection, yeu·have no
1Th 4:13 concerning the·ones having·been·laid·to·rest, in·
1Th 5:1 Now concerning the times and the seasons, brothers,
1Th 5:25 Brothers, pray concerning us.
2Th 1:3 to·give·thanks to·God always concerning yeu,
2Th 1:11 For which also we·pray always concerning yeu,
2Th 2:13 to·give·thanks always to·God concerning yeu (O·
2Th 3:1 brothers: Pray concerning us in·order·that the
Tit 2:7 Concerning all·things, *continue* holding·yourself·
Tit 2:8 ·even·one mediocre thing to·say concerning yeu *all*.
Tit 3:8 *is* the saying. And concerning these·things, I·resolve
1Co 1:4 I·give·thanks to·my God always concerning yeu for
1Co 1:11 For it·was·made·plain to·me concerning yeu, my
1Co 7:1 Now concerning the·things·of·which yeu·wrote to·
1Co 7:25 And concerning the virgins, I·do·not have an·
1Co 7:37 but has authority concerning his·own will, and
1Co 8:1 Now concerning the·things sacrificed·to·idols: We·
1Co 8:4 So·then, concerning the feeding·upon the·things
1Co 12:1 Now concerning the spiritual *bestowments*,
1Co 16:1 Now concerning the contribution, the·one for the
1Co 16:12 Now concerning *our* brother Apollos, I repeatedly
2Co 9:1 For, in·fact, concerning the service to the holy·ones
2Co 10:8 somewhat excessively concerning our authority,
Eph 6:18 — even with·petition concerning all the holy·ones
Eph 6:22 that yeu·may·know the·things concerning us, and
Col 1:3 Jesus Anointed, praying always concerning yeu,
Col 2:1 ·a·huge strenuous·struggle I·have concerning yeu,
Col 4:3 at·the·same·time praying also concerning us, that
Col 4:8 ·that he·may·know the·things concerning yeu and
Col 4:10 of·BarNabas, concerning whom yeu·received
Phm 1:10 I·implore you concerning my child Onesimus,
1Ti 1:7 ·say, nor concerning certain·things·which they·so·
1Ti 1:19 ·good conscience. Which concerning the trust,
1Ti 6:21 *of·trust*, missed·the·mark concerning the trust.
2Ti 1:3 without·ceasing I·have a·reminder concerning you in
2Ti 2:18 who missed·the·mark concerning the truth, saying
2Ti 3:8 ·fully·corrupted, disqualified concerning the trust.
1Jn 1:1 our hands verified·by·touch, concerning the Word
1Jn 2:2 is *the* atonement concerning our moral·failures, and
1Jn 2:2 our moral·failures, and not concerning ours merely,
1Jn 2:2 but·rather also concerning *the moral·failures·of* the
1Jn 2:26 ·wrote to·yeu concerning the·ones who·are·leading
1Jn 2:27 presently·instructs yeu concerning all·things (and
1Jn 4:10 *to·be the* atonement concerning our moral·failures.
1Jn 5:9 of·God which he·has·testified concerning his Son.
1Jn 5:10 testimony that God has·testified concerning his Son.
1Jn 5:16 unto death; not concerning that·thing do·I·say that
3Jn 1:2 ·man, I·well-wish *to·God* concerning all·things,

EG4012.3 (20x)
Jn 8:27 that he·was·saying to·them *concerning* the Father.
Jn 12:49 a·commandment *concerning* what I·should·declare
Jn 14:26 that·one shall·instruct yeu *concerning* all·things,
Jn 14:26 ·quietly·remind yeu *concerning* all·things which I·
Lk 12:29 and do·not be·in·suspense *concerning these·things*.
Lk 18:31 ·written through the prophets *concerning* the Son
Lk 20:37 "Now, *concerning* that the dead are·awakened,
Lk 22:24 among them, *concerning* which of·them is·reputed
Heb 4:3 ·as he·has·declared *concerning the obstinate·ones*,
Heb 8:12 and *concerning* their moral·failures and their
Heb 11:1 ·awaited, a·conviction *concerning* actions not
Mt 13:19 "*Concerning* anyone hearing the Redemptive-word
Mk 3:28 Sons of·clay†, and·also *concerning* revilements, as·
Rm 12:3 is·necessary to·contemplate *concerning himself*,
Php 1:10 ·and·verify yeu (*concerning* the·things varying
Php 2:25 and public·servant *concerning* my needs),
2Pe 3:9 The Lord is·not tardy *concerning* the promise, as
1Co 7:6 this in concession *concerning becoming married*,
Col 2:16 do·not·let anyone judge yeu *concerning matters* in
2Ti 2:14 Quietly·remind *them concerning* these·things—

G4012.4 PREP περί (4x)
Jn 11:19 alongside the *women* in·company·with Martha and
Ac 13:13 Paul (*and* the·ones in·company·with *him*) came to
Ac 21:8 on·the·next·day, the·ones in·company·with Paul,
Mk 4:10 alone·by·himself, the·ones in·company·with him

G4012.5 PREP περί (1x)
Rv 15:6 ·girded·about·with golden bands around *their* chests

G4013 περι•άγω pêriágō *v.* (6x)
Roots:G4012 G0071 Compare:G3332 See:G5217

G4013.1 V-PAN περιάγειν (1x)
1Co 9:5 ¿!·Do we·not have privilege to·lead·about a·wife

G4013.2 V-IAI-3S περιῆγεν (3x)
Mt 4:23 And YeShua was·heading·out all around Galilee,
Mt 9:35 And YeShua was·heading·out all around the cities
Mk 6:6 ·trust. And he·was·heading·around·to the encircling

G4013.3 V-PAI-2P περιάγετε (1x)
Mt 23:15 Because yeu·head·round·about the sea and the

G4013.4 V-PAP-NSM περιάγων (1x)
Ac 13:11 then darkness; and moving·about, he·was·seeking

G4014 περι•αιρέω pêriairéō *v.* (4x)
Roots:G4012 G0138 Compare:G0343 G0851 G0579 G1601 G1807

G4014.2 V-PPI-3S περιαιρεῖται (1x)
2Co 3:16 *Anointed-One*, the veil is·entirely·removed.

G4014.2 V-IPI-3S περιῃρεῖτο (1x)
Ac 27:20 for·us to·be·saved was·entirely·removed.

G4014.2 V-2AAN περιελεῖν (1x)
Heb 10:11 ·time is·able to·entirely·remove moral·failures.

G4014.2 V-2AAP-NPM περιελόντες (1x)
Ac 27:40 And entirely·removing the anchors, they·were·

G4015 περι•αστράπτω pêriastráptō *v.* (2x)
Roots:G4012 G0797

G4015 V-AAI-3S περιήστραψεν (1x)
Ac 9:3 a·light from the heaven flashed·all·around him.

G4015 V-AAN περιαστράψαι (1x)
Ac 22:6 *for* a·significant light to·flash·all·around about me.

G4016 περι•βάλλω pêribállō *v.* (24x)
Roots:G4012 G0906 Compare:G1746 xLangAlso:H5844

G4016.1 V-FAI-3P περιβαλοῦσιν (1x)
Lk 19:43 and your enemies shall·cast a·palisade around you

G4016.1 V-2AMM-2S περιβαλοῦ (1x)
Ac 12:8 he·says to·him, "Cast your·garment around you and

G4016.2 V-FMI-3S περιβαλεῖται (1x)
Rv 3:5 ·one overcoming, the·same shall·be·arrayed in white

G4016.2 V-2AAI-1P περιεβάλομεν (1x)
Mt 25:38 ·*you*·in? Or naked, and arrayed *you with·clothing*?

G4016.2 V-2AAI-2P περιεβάλετε (2x)
Mt 25:36 naked, and yeu·arrayed me *with·clothing*. I·was·
Mt 25:43 in, naked, and yeu·did·not array me *with·clothing*,

G4016.2 V-2AAI-3P περιέβαλον (1x)
Jn 19:2 they·put *it* on·his head and arrayed him *with* a·purple

G4016.2 V-2AAP-NSM περιβαλών (1x)
Lk 23:11 , after·mocking *him* and arraying him in·splendid

G4016.2 V-2AMI-3S περιεβάλετο (2x)
Lk 12:27 in all his glory was·arrayed as one of·these.
Mt 6:29 in all his glory, was·arrayed as one of·these.

G4016.2 V-2AMS-1P περιβαλώμεθα (1x)
Mt 6:31 '*with* what *clothing* should·we·be·arrayed?'

G4016.2 V-2AMS-2S περιβάλῃ (1x)
Rv 3:18 garments, in·order·that you·may·be·arrayed, and

G4016.2 V-2AMS-3S περιβάληται (1x)
Rv 19:8 ·granted that she·should·be·arrayed·with fine·linen,

G4016.2 V-RPP-ASM περιβεβλημένον (2x)
Mk 16:5 ·side, having·been·arrayed·with a·white long·robe,
Rv 10:1 heaven, having·been·arrayed·with a·thick·cloud;

G4016.2 V-RPP-APM περιβεβλημένους (1x)
Rv 4:4 Elders sitting·down, having·been·arrayed in white

G4016.2 V-RPP-NSF περιβεβλημένη (3x)
Rv 12:1 a·woman having·been·arrayed·with the sun, and
Rv 17:4 *is* the·one having·been·arrayed in·purple and scarlet,
Rv 18:16 City, the·one having·been·arrayed·with fine·linen,

G4016.2 V-RPP-NSM περιβεβλημένος (2x)
Mk 14:51 *with* a·linen·cloth having·been·arrayed over *his*
Rv 19:13 and having·been·arrayed·with a·garment having·

G4016.2 V-RPP-NPM περιβεβλημένοι (3x)
Rv 7:9 Lamb, having·been·arrayed·with white long·robes
Rv 7:13 these, the·ones having·been·arrayed·with the white
Rv 11:3 *and* sixty days, having·been·arrayed·with sackcloth.

G4017 περι•βλέπω pêriblépō *v.* (7x)
Roots:G4012 G0991

G4017.1 V-AMP-NSM περιβλεψάμενος (5x)
Lk 6:10 And looking·around·upon them all, he·declared to·
Mk 3:5 And looking·around·at them with wrath, while·
Mk 3:34 And looking·around in·a·circle at·the·ones sitting·
Mk 10:23 And after·looking·around, Jesus says to·his
Mk 11:11 And after·looking·around·upon all·things, even·

G4017.2 V-IMI-3S περιεβλέπετο (1x)
Mk 5:32 And he·was·looking·all·around to·see the·one

G4017.2 V-AMP-NPM περιβλεψάμενοι (1x)
Mk 9:8 And suddenly, after·looking·all·around, they·saw

G4018 περι•βόλαιον pêribólaiôn *n.* (2x)
Roots:G4016 Compare:G1742 xLangAlso:H3830
G4018.2 N-NSN περιβόλαιον (1x)
Heb 1:12 And as a·mantle, you·shall·roll them up, and they·
G4018.2 N-GSN περιβολαίου (1x)
1Co 11:15 ·of·the·head, instead of·a·mantle, has·been·given

G4019 περι•δέω pêridéō *v.* (1x)
Roots:G4012 G1210
G4019 V-LPI-3S περιεδέδετο (1x)
Jn 11:44 facial·appearance had·been·bound·about with·a·.

G4020 περι•εργάζομαι pêriêrgázômai *v.* (1x)
Roots:G4012 G2038 Compare:G3095 G0244
See:G4021
G4020.3 V-PNP-APM περιεργαζομένους (1x)
2Th 3:11 ·one·bit, but·rather who·are·meddling·busybodies.

G4021 περί•εργος pêriêrgôs *adj.* (2x)
Roots:G4012 G2041 Compare:G3095 G0244
See:G4020
G4021.2 A-NPM περίεργοι (1x)
1Ti 5:13 but·rather gossipers also and meddlers, speaking
G4021.3 A-APN περίεργα (1x)
Ac 19:19 the meddling·in·dark·arts, after·bringing·together

G4022 περι•έρχομαι pêriérchômai *v.* (4x)
Roots:G4012 G2064 Compare:G4108
G4022.1 V-2AAI-3P περιῆλθον (1x)
Heb 11:37 with·a·dagger. They·went·about in sheepskins
G4022.2 V-PNP-NPF περιερχόμεναι (1x)
1Ti 5:13 they·learn *to·be* idle, going·roundabout the homes,
G4022.3 V-2AAP-NPM περιελθόντες (1x)
Ac 28:13 Sailing·roundabout from·there, we·arrived in
G4022.4 V-PNP-GPM περιερχομένων (1x)
Ac 19:13 Then certain of·the itinerant Jews, *being* exorcists,

G4023 περι•έχω pêriéchō *v.* (5x)
Roots:G4012 G2192
EG4023 (1x)
Rm 2:14 by·nature the·things *contained* in·the Torah-Law,
G4023.2 V-PAI-3S περιέχει (1x)
1Pe 2:6 Therefore also it·is·contained in·the Scripture,
G4023.2 V-PAP-ASF περιέχουσαν (1x)
Ac 23:25 he·wrote a·letter containing this particular·pattern:
EG4023.2 (1x)
Eph 2:15 of·the commandments *contained* in decrees), in·
G4023.3 V-2AAI-3S περιέσχεν (1x)
Lk 5:9 For amazement enveloped him (and all the·ones

G4024 περι•ζώννυμι pêrizōnnymi *v.* (8x)
Roots:G4012 G2224
G4024.1 V-RPP-ASM περιεζωσμένον (1x)
Rv 1:13 and having·been·girded·about·with a·golden band
G4024.1 V-RPP-NPF περιεζωσμέναι (1x)
Lk 12:35 loins must·be having·been·girded·about and *yeur*
G4024.1 V-RPP-NPM περιεζωσμένοι (1x)
Rv 15:6 and having·been·girded·about·with golden bands
EG4024.1 (1x)
Mt 3:4 from camel's hair and *was·girded·with* a·leather belt
G4024.2 V-FMI-3S περιζώσεται (1x)
Lk 12:37 I·say to·yeu, that he·shall·gird·himself·about, and
G4024.2 V-AMM-2S περίζωσαι (1x)
Ac 12:8 him, "Gird·yourself·about and shod·yourself·with
G4024.2 V-AMP-NSM περιζωσάμενος (1x)
Lk 17:8 ·for·supper, and after·girding·yourself·about, attend
G4024.3 V-AMP-NPM περιζωσάμενοι (1x)
Eph 6:14 after·personally·girding yeur·own loins with truth

G4025 περί•θεσις pêríthêsis *n.* (1x)
Roots:G4060
G4025 N-GSF περιθέσεως (1x)
1Pe 3:3 ·braiding·of·hair and a·draping of·golden·articles, or

G4026 περι•ΐστημι pêriḯstēmi *v.* (4x)
Roots:G4012 G2476 Compare:G0665 G3868
G4026.1 V-2AAI-3P περιέστησαν (1x)
Ac 25:7 ·walked·down from JeruSalem stood·around, also
G4026.2 V-RAP-ASM-C περιεστῶτα (1x)
Jn 11:42 the crowd, the·one having·stood·by, I·declared *it*
G4026.3 V-PMM-2S περιΐστασο (2x)
Tit 3:9 But shun foolish speculations, genealogies, strifes,
2Ti 2:16 But shun the profane *and* empty·discussions, for

G4027 περι•κάθ•αρμα pêrikátharma *n.* (1x)
Roots:G4012 G2508
G4027.2 N-NPN περικαθάρματα (1x)
1Co 4:13 We·have·now·become as scum of·the world, an·

G4028 περι•καλύπτω pêrikalýptō *v.* (3x)
Roots:G4012 G2572
G4028.2 V-RPP-ASF περικεκαλυμμένην (1x)
Heb 9:4 covenant having·been·overlaid on·all·sides with·
G4028.3 V-PAN περικαλύπτειν (1x)
Mk 14:65 ·on him, and upon·putting·a·hood·over his face,
G4028.3 V-AAP-NPM περικαλύψαντες (1x)
Lk 22:64 And putting·a·hood·over him, they·were·

G4029 περί•κειμαι pêríkêimai *v.* (5x)
Roots:G4012 G2749 Compare:G2139 G2910 G2945
G4029.2 V-PNI-3S περίκειται (2x)
Lk 17:2 ·him that a·donkey-sized millstone be·set around his
Heb 5:2 since he·himself also is·beset·with weakness.
G4029.3 V-PNI-3S περίκειται (1x)
Mk 9:42 better for·him if a·mill stone be·set around his neck,
G4029.4 V-PNP-ASN περικείμενον (1x)
Heb 12:1 a·cloud of·witnesses that·is·encircling·about us—
G4029.5 V-PNI-1S περίκειμαι (1x)
Ac 28:20 of·IsraEl *that* I·am·entirely·bound·with this chain."

G4030 περι•κεφαλαία pêrikêphalaía *n.* (2x)
Roots:G4012 G2776
xLangEquiv:H3553 xLangAlso:H6959
G4030.2 N-ASF περικεφαλαίαν (2x)
1Th 5:8 and *with·the* Expectation of·Salvation for·a·helmet.
Eph 6:17 also accept the helmet of·custodial·Salvation and

G4031 περι•κρατής pêrikratḗs *adj.* (1x)
Roots:G4012 G2904
G4031.2 A-NPM περικρατεῖς (1x)
Ac 27:16 ·strength to·make the skiff mighty·secure.

G4032 περι•κρύπτω pêrikrýptō *v.* (1x)
Roots:G4012 G2928
G4032.2 V-IAI-3S περιέκρυβεν (1x)
Lk 1:24 conceived and was·entirely·hiding herself *for* five

G4033 περι•κυκλόω pêrikyklóō *v.* (1x)
Roots:G4012 G2944
G4033.2 V-FAI-3P περικυκλώσουσιν (1x)
Lk 19:43 around you, and shall·completely·surround you,

G4034 περι•λάμπω pêrilámpō *v.* (2x)
Roots:G4012 G2989 xLangAlso:H5050 H5051
G4034 V-AAI-3S περιέλαμψεν (1x)
Lk 2:9 Yahweh's glory radiated·brightly·all·around them.
G4034 V-AAP-ASN περιλάμψαν (1x)
Ac 26:13 of·the sun radiating·brightly·all·around me and

G4035 περι•λείπω pêrilêípō *v.* (2x)
Roots:G4012 G3007
G4035.2 V-POP-NPM περιλειπόμενοι (2x)
1Th 4:15 the·ones living (the·ones surviving to the returning·
1Th 4:17 the·ones *still* surviving) shall·be·snatched·up at·

G4036 περί•λυπος pêrílypôs *adj.* (5x)
Roots:G4012 G3077 See:G4818
G4036 A-NSM περίλυπος (2x)
Lk 18:23 these·things, he·became exceedingly·grieved, for
Mk 6:26 And the king became exceedingly·grieved, *yet* on·
G4036 A-NSF περίλυπος (2x)
Mt 26:38 "My soul is exceedingly·grieved unto death. Yeu·
Mk 14:34 "My soul is exceedingly·grieved unto death. Yeu·
G4036 A-ASM περίλυπον (1x)
Lk 18:24 him becoming exceedingly·grieved, declared,

G4037 περι•μένω pêriménō *v.* (1x)
Roots:G4012 G3306 Compare:G4328 G1679
See:G0362
G4037 V-PAN περιμένειν (1x)
Ac 1:4 but·rather to·patiently·wait·around for·the Promise

G4038 πέριξ périx *adv.* (1x)
Roots:G4012
G4038.1 ADV πέριξ (1x)
Ac 5:16 a·multitude *out* of·the cities all·around JeruSalem,

G4039 περι•οικέω pêriôikéō *v.* (1x)
Roots:G4012 G3611
G4039 V-PAP-APM περιοικοῦντας (1x)
Lk 1:65 happened on all the·ones dwelling·around them.

G4040 περί•οικος pêríôikôs *adj.* (1x)
Roots:G4012 G3624 Compare:G1069 G4139 G2192
G4040.2 A-NPM περίοικοι (1x)
Lk 1:58 And her·surrounding·neighbors and her kinsfolk

G4041 περι•ούσιος pêriôúsiôs *adj.* (1x)
Roots:G4012 G1510 xLangAlso:H5459
G4041.2 A-ASM περιούσιον (1x)
Tit 2:14 ·purify to·himself *'his·own* extraordinary People,'

G4042 περι•οχή pêriôché *n.* (1x)
Roots:G4023
G4042.2 N-NSF περιοχή (1x)
Ac 8:32 Now the passage of·the Scripture which he·was·

G4043 περι•πατέω pêripatéō *v.* (96x)
Roots:G4012 G3961 Compare:G0901-3 G4198
See:G1704 xLangAlso:H1980 H1869
G4043.1 V-FAI-3S περιπατήσει (1x)
Jn 8:12 me, no he·shall·not stroll·about in the darkness, but·
G4043.1 V-PAI-3S περιπατεῖ (2x)
1Pe 5:8 ·adversary, Slanderer, strolls·about as a·roaring lion
1Jn 2:11 is in the darkness, and strolls·about in the darkness,
G4043.1 V-PAI-3P περιπατοῦσιν (1x)
Php 3:18 (For many stroll·about, of·whom I·was·saying to·
G4043.1 V-PAN περιπατεῖν (2x)
Lk 20:46 the·ones delighting to·stroll·about in long·robes,
Mk 12:38 the·ones wanting to·stroll·about in long·robes,
G4043.1 V-PAP-APM περιπατοῦντας (1x)
Mk 8:24 how I·clearly·envision trees, *but* strolling·about."
G4043.1 V-PAP-NSM περιπατῶν (1x)
Rv 2:1 in his right·hand, the·one strolling·about in *the* midst
G4043.1 V-PAP-NPM περιπατοῦντες (1x)
2Co 10:3 For while·strolling·about in *bodily* flesh, we·do·not
G4043.1 V-PAS-1P περιπατῶμεν (1x)
1Jn 1:6 with him, yet should·stroll·about in the darkness,
G4043.1 V-IAI-2S περιεπάτεις (1x)
Jn 21:18 and were·strolling·about wherever you·were·
G4043.1 V-IAI-3S περιεπάτει (1x)
Jn 11:54 ·no longer strolling·about with·freeness·of·speech
G4043.2 V-FAI-3P περιπατήσουσιν (2x)
Rv 3:4 their garments; and they·shall·walk·along with me in
Rv 21:24 of·the·ones being·saved, shall·walk in its light,
G4043.2 V-PAI-3P περιπατοῦσιν (2x)
Lk 7:22 the·blind receive·their·sight, lame·men walk, lepers
Mt 11:5 ·men receive·their·sight and lame·men walk, lepers
G4043.2 V-PAM-2S περιπατεῖ (7x)
Jn 5:8 "Be·awakened, take·up your mat and walk."
Jn 5:11 'Take·up your mat and walk.'"
Jn 5:12 'Take·up your mat and walk'?
Lk 5:23 you,' or to·declare, 'Be·awakened and walk'?
Ac 3:6 Anointed of·Natsareth, be·awakened and walk!"
Mt 9:5 you?' or to·declare, 'Be·awakened and walk?'
Mk 2:9 'Be·awakened, and take·up your mat and walk'?
G4043.2 V-PAN περιπατεῖν (3x)
Jn 7:1 in Galilee, for he·was·not willing to·walk in Judea,
Ac 3:12 or devout·reverence we·have·made him to·walk?
Rv 9:20 are·able to·look·about, nor to·hear, nor to·walk;'
G4043.2 V-PAP-ASM περιπατοῦντα (4x)
Jn 6:19 stadia, they·observe Jesus walking·along on the sea
Ac 3:9 saw him walking·along and splendidly·praising God.
Mt 14:26 And after·seeing him walking upon the sea, the
Mk 6:49 But after·seeing him walking upon the sea, they·
G4043.2 V-PAP-APM περιπατοῦντας (1x)
Mt 15:31 ·ones healthy·and·sound, lame·ones walking, and
G4043.2 V-PAP-DSM περιπατοῦντι (1x)
Jn 1:36 ·looking·clearly·upon Jesus walking·along, he·says,

G4043.2 V-PAP-DPM περιπατοῦσιν (1x)
Mk 16:12 form while·walking, as·they·were·traversing into
G4043.2 V-PAP-GSM περιπατοῦντος (1x)
Mk 11:27 to JeruSalem. And with·him walking along the
G4043.2 V-PAP-NSM περιπατῶν (5x)
Ac 3:8 the Sanctuary·Courtyard, walking·along and leaping
Mt 4:18 And while·walking near the Sea of·Galilee, YeShua
Mt 14:25 went·off toward them, walking upon the sea.
Mk 1:16 And walking beside the Sea of·Galilee, he·saw
Mk 6:48 he·comes toward them, walking upon the sea, and
G4043.2 V-PAP-NPM περιπατοῦντες (2x)
Lk 11:44 and the men·of·clay† walking over *them* have·not
Lk 24:17 ·and·forth to one·another while·walking·along, and
G4043.2 V-PAS-3S περιπατῇ (3x)
Jn 11:9 ·the daylight? If any·man should·walk·along in the
Jn 11:10 But if any·man should·walk·along in the night, he·
Rv 16:15 his garments, lest he·should·walk·along naked,
G4043.2 V-IAI-3S περιεπάτει (6x)
Jn 5:9 And he·took·up his mat and was·walking, and on the
Jn 7:1 And after these·things, Jesus was·walking in Galilee,
Jn 10:23 And Jesus was·walking in the Sanctuary·Atrium at
Ac 3:8 he·stood·still; then he·was·walking; then he·entered
Ac 14:10 And he·was·leaping and walking.
Mk 5:42 the young·girl rose·up and was·walking, for she·
G4043.2 V-IAI-3P περιεπάτουν (1x)
Jn 6:66 and no·longer were·they·walking·along with him.
G4043.2 V-AAI-3S περιεπάτησεν (1x)
Mt 14:29 from the sailboat, Peter walked upon the water to·
G4043.2 V-LAI-3S περιπεπατήκει (1x)
Ac 14:8 womb, who never·at·any·time had·walked.
G4043.3 V-PAI-1P περιπατοῦμεν (1x)
2Co 5:7 for we·presently·walk through trust, not through
G4043.3 V-PAI-2S περιπατεῖς (2x)
Rm 14:15 *your* food, no·longer do·you·walk in love. Do·not
3Jn 1:3 testifying of·your truth, just·as you walk in truth.
G4043.3 V-PAI-2P περιπατεῖτε (2x)
1Co 3:3 fleshly, and walk according·to men·of·clay†?
Eph 5:15 look·out *then for* precisely how yeu·walk, not as
G4043.3 V-PAI-3S περιπατεῖ (1x)
Eph 4:17 the rest *of the* Gentiles also walk, in a·futility of·
G4043.3 V-PAI-3P περιπατοῦσιν (1x)
Mk 7:5 "Why·do your disciples not walk according·to the
G4043.3 V-PAM-2P περιπατεῖτε (6x)
Jn 12:35 light with yeu. Walk for·as·long·as yeu·have the
Gal 5:16 So I·say, walk in·Spirit, and no, yeu·would·not
Eph 5:2 and walk in love, just·as the Anointed-One also
Eph 5:8 *yeu are* light in *the* Lord. Walk as children of·light
Col 2:6 Anointed-One, Jesus the Lord, *so* walk·yeu in him,
Col 4:5 Walk in wisdom toward the·ones outside *the Called·*
G4043.3 V-PAM-3S περιπατείτω (1x)
1Co 7:17 has·called·forth, in·this·manner let·him·walk. And
G4043.3 V-PAN περιπατεῖν (4x)
Ac 21:21 the children, nor·even to·walk after·the customs.
1Th 4:1 ·for yeu to·walk and to·agreeably·comply with·God
Eph 4:17 No·longer *are* yeu to·walk just·as the rest *of the*
1Jn 2:6 himself also in·this·manner to·walk, just·as that·one
G4043.3 V-PAP-ASM περιπατοῦντα (1x)
3Jn 1:4 ·things, that I·hear·of my children walking in truth.
G4043.3 V-PAP-APM περιπατοῦντας (4x)
Php 3:17 ·a·watch·of the·ones walking in·this·manner just·as
2Th 3:11 we·hear *that there are* some walking among yeu
2Co 10:2 of·us as presently·walking according·to flesh.
2Jn 1:4 from·among your children *those* walking in truth,
G4043.3 V-PAP-DPM περιπατοῦσιν (2x)
Rm 8:1 Jesus, *for the ones* walking not according·to flesh,
Rm 8:4 in us, the·ones walking not according·to flesh, but·
G4043.3 V-PAP-GSM περιπατοῦντος (1x)
2Th 3:6 every brother walking in·a·disorderly·manner and
G4043.3 V-PAP-NSM περιπατῶν (1x)
Jn 12:35 ·grab yeu. But the·one walking in the darkness
G4043.3 V-PAP-NPM περιπατοῦντες (1x)
2Co 4:2 ·things of·shame, not walking in shrewd·cunning
G4043.3 V-PAS-1P περιπατῶμεν (2x)
1Jn 1:7 But if we·should·walk in the light as he·himself is in
2Jn 1:6 is the Love, that we·should·walk according·to his
G4043.3 V-PAS-2P περιπατῆτε (2x)
1Th 4:12 in·order·that yeu·may·walk decently toward the·
2Jn 1:6 yeu·heard from *the* beginning, yeu·should·walk in it.
G4043.3 V-AAI-1P περιεπατήσαμεν (1x)
2Co 12:18 not in·the same spirit *that* we·walked? *Is he* not
G4043.3 V-AAI-2P περιεπατήσατε (2x)
Eph 2:2 ·things in·times·past, yeu·walked according·to the
Col 3:7 whom yeu·yeurselves also once walked, when yeu·
G4043.3 V-AAI-3S περιεπάτησεν (1x)
1Jn 2:6 ·manner to·walk, just·as that·one already·walked.
G4043.3 V-AAN περιπατῆσαι (3x)
1Th 2:12 for yeu to·walk worthily of·God, the·one calling
Eph 4:1 Lord, implore yeu to·walk worthily of·the calling
Col 1:10 *such for* yeu to·walk worthily of·the Lord into all
G4043.3 V-AAP-NPM περιπατήσαντες (1x)
Heb 13:9 ·not beneficial·to the·ones walking in such·things.
G4043.3 V-AAS-1P περιπατήσωμεν (3x)
Rm 6:4 we·ourselves also should·walk in brand-newness of·
Rm 13:13 We·should·walk decently, as in daylight, not in·
Eph 2:10 ·in·advance in·order·that we·should·walk in them.

G4044 περι•πείρω pêripêírō *v.* (1x)
Roots:G4012 G4008 Compare:G1338 G1574
G4044.2 V-AAI-3P περιέπειραν (1x)
1Ti 6:10 and they·entirely·impaled themselves on·many

G4045 περι•πίπτω pêripíptō *v.* (3x)
Roots:G4012 G4098
G4045.2 V-2AAI-3S περιέπεσεν (1x)
Lk 10:30 to Jericho, and surrounded,·he·fell·among robbers,
G4045.2 V-2AAP-NPM περιπεσόντες (1x)
Ac 27:41 And upon·falling·surrounded into a·place where·
G4045.3 V-2AAS-2P περιπέσητε (1x)
Jac 1:2 whenever yeu·should·entirely·fall·into diverse proof·

G4046 περι•ποιέομαι pêripôiéômai *v.* (2x)
Roots:G4012 G4160 Compare:G0059 G2932 G5608 G5177 See:G4047
G4046.2 V-PMI-3P περιποιοῦνται (1x)
1Ti 3:13 ·attending well do·acquire for·themselves good
G4046.2 V-AMI-3S περιεποιήσατο (1x)
Ac 20:28 ·God, which he·himself·acquired through his·own

G4047 περι•ποίησις pêripôíēsis *n.* (5x)
Roots:G4046 xLangAlso:H5459
G4047.1 N-ASF περιποίησιν (2x)
1Th 5:9 but·rather for acquisition of·Salvation through our
2Th 2:14 good·news, for the·acquisition of·the·glory of·our
G4047.2 N-ASF περιποίησιν (1x)
1Pe 2:9 nation, a·People for an·acquired·possession— that
G4047.2 N-GSF περιποιήσεως (1x)
Eph 1:14 a·full·redemption of·the acquired·possession, for a·
G4047.3 N-ASF περιποίησιν (1x)
Heb 10:39 but·rather of·a·trust to a·preservation of·*the*·soul.

G4048 περι•ρρήγνυμι pêrirrhḗgnymi *v.* (1x)
Roots:G4012 G4486
G4048.2 V-AAP-NPM περιρρήξαντες (1x)
Ac 16:22 after·completely·tearing·away their garments,

G4049 περι•σπάω pêrispáō *v.* (1x)
Roots:G4012 G4685 Compare:G5182 See:G4048-4 G0563
G4049.2 V-IPI-3S περιεσπᾶτο (1x)
Lk 10:40 But Martha was·distracted concerning much

G4050 περισσεία pêrissêía *n.* (4x)
Roots:G4052 Compare:G0100 G3062 G3063 See:G4051 G5248 xLangAlso:H3504
G4050.2 N-NSF περισσεία (1x)
2Co 8:2 ·test of·tribulation, the superabundance of·their joy
G4050.2 N-ASF περισσείαν (1x)
Rm 5:17 the·ones receiving the superabundance of·grace and
G4050.4 N-ASF περισσείαν (1x)
Jac 1:21 all filthiness and any·remaining·excess of·depravity,
G4050.5 N-ASF περισσείαν (1x)
2Co 10:15 ·to our standard *of service*, for a·great·advantage

G4051 περίσσευμα pêrísseuma *n.* (5x)
Roots:G4052 Compare:G0100 See:G4050
G4051.1 N-NSN περίσσευμα (2x)
2Co 8:13 season, *that* yeur abundance *may be a supply* for
2Co 8:14 in·order·that their abundance also may·be *a supply*
G4051.1 N-APN περισσεύματα (1x)
Mk 8:8 ·full. And they·took·up an·abundance of·fragments,
G4051.1 N-GSN περισσεύματος (2x)
Lk 6:45 "For from·out of·the abundance of·the heart, his
Mt 12:34 For from·out of·the abundance of·the heart the

G4052 περισσεύω pêrissêúō *v.* (39x)
Roots:G4053 Compare:G4121 G5242 See:G5248 xLangAlso:H3498
G4052.1 V-PAI-1S περισσεύω (1x)
Php 4:18 all and do·abound; I·have·been·completely·filled,
G4052.1 V-PAI-2P περισσεύετε (1x)
2Co 8:7 Moreover, just·as yeu·abound in everything, in·
G4052.1 V-PAI-3S περισσεύει (2x)
2Co 1:5 ·as the afflictions of·the Anointed-One abound in us,
2Co 1:5 our comforting also abounds through Anointed-One.
G4052.1 V-PAN περισσεύειν (4x)
Rm 15:13 ·one to·trust, for yeu to·abound in the Expectation
Php 4:12 to·be·humbled, and I·have·seen·how to·abound. In
Php 4:12 to·be·hungry, even to·abound and to·be·lacking.
1Th 4:10 ·implore yeu, brothers, to·abound more·and·more,
G4052.1 V-PAP-NPM περισσεύοντες (2x)
1Co 15:58 ·from *the Trust*, always abounding in the work
Col 2:7 trust, just·as yeu·were·instructed, abounding in it in
G4052.1 V-PAS-2P περισσεύητε (3x)
1Th 4:1 ·God in·order·that yeu·may·abound more·and·more.
2Co 8:7 in·the love, *see* that yeu·should·abound in this grace
2Co 9:8 in all *things* at·all·times, yeu·may·abound to every
G4052.1 V-PAS-3S περισσεύῃ (2x)
Php 1:9 this I·pray, that yeur love may·abound yet more and
Php 1:26 yeur boasting in me may·abound in Jesus Anointed
G4052.1 V-IAI-3P ἐπερίσσευον (1x)
Ac 16:5 in·the trust and were·abounding in·number each day
G4052.1 V-AAI-3S ἐπερίσσευσεν (4x)
Rm 3:7 my lie, the truth of·God abounded to his glory, why
Rm 5:15 died, so·much more did·abound the grace of·God
2Co 8:2 and their deep down poverty abounded to the wealth
Eph 1:8 *the wealth of his grace* which he·abounded to us in
G4052.1 V-AAN περισσεῦσαι (1x)
2Co 9:8 *is* able *to cause* all grace to·abound toward yeu, in·
G4052.1 V-AAO-3S περισσεύσαι (1x)
1Th 3:12 make yeu to·increase·more and abound in·the love
G4052.1 V-AAS-3S περισσεύσῃ (2x)
Mt 5:20 yeur righteousness should·abound more·than *that*
2Co 4:15 expression·of·thankfulness should·abound to the
G4052.2 V-FPI-3S περισσευθήσεται (2x)
Mt 13:12 ·be·given, and he·shall·have·an·abundance. But
Mt 25:29 ·be·given, and he·shall·have·an·abundance. But
G4052.2 V-PAI-3P περισσεύουσιν (1x)
Lk 15:17 father's hired·men have·an·abundance of·bread,
G4052.3 V-PAN περισσεύειν (1x)
Lk 12:15 because not in the abundance from·out of·one's
G4052.3 V-PAP-GSN περισσεύοντος (2x)
Lk 21:4 these·men cast from·out of·their abundance into the
Mk 12:44 all cast·in from·out of·their abundance, but she·
G4052.4 V-PAI-1P περισσεύομεν (1x)
1Co 8:8 neither if we·should·eat, do·we·excel, nor·even if
G4052.4 V-PAI-3S περισσεύει (1x)
2Co 3:9 *does* the service of·the righteousness excel in glory.
G4052.4 V-PAP-NSF περισσεύουσα (1x)
2Co 9:12 holy·ones, but·rather *it is* excelling also through
G4052.4 V-PAS-2P περισσεύητε (1x)
1Co 14:12 yeu·must·seek that yeu·may·excel toward the
G4052.5 V-PAP-ASN περισσεῦον (2x)
Mt 14:20 ·took·up the remaining·excess of·the fragments—
Mt 15:37 full *of* the remaining·excess of·the fragments.
G4052.5 V-AAI-3S ἐπερίσσευσεν (1x)
Jn 6:13 which remained·in·excess by·the·ones having·been·
G4052.5 V-AAP-APN περισσεύσαντα (1x)

Jn 6:12 “Gather·together the remaining·excess fragments,

G4052.5 V-AAP-NSN περισσεῦσαν (1x)

Lk 9:17 And the remaining·excess taken·up by·them *was*

G4053 περισσός pêrissós *adj.* (9x)

Roots:G4012 Compare:G4056 G5247 See:G4051 G1537
xLangEquiv:H7227

G4053.2 A-GSN περισσοῦ (1x)

Eph 3:20 above·and·beyond from·out of·an·abundance, *to·do*

G4053.3 ADV περισσόν (1x)

Jn 10:10 life-above, and that·they·may·have *it* abundantly.

G4053.4 A-NSN περισσόν (1x)

Rm 3:1 So·then what *is* the Jew's superior·benefit? Or what

G4053.4 A-ASN περισσόν (1x)

Mt 5:47 merely, what·do yeu·do *that·is* superior *to·others*?

G4053.4 A-GSM περισσοῦ (1x)

Mt 5:35 because it·is *the* City of·the superior King.

G4053.5 A-NSN περισσόν (1x)

2Co 9:1 the holy·ones, it·is superfluous for·me to·write to·

G4053.6 A-NSN περισσόν (1x)

Mt 5:37 And the·thing in·excess of·these·things is birthed·

G4053.6 A-GSN περισσοῦ (1x)

Mk 6:51 astonished among themselves beyond excess, and

G4053.7 A-GSN περισσοῦ (1x)

Mk 14:31 ·saying out *all the* more vehemently, “Even·if it·

G4054 περισσότερον pêrissótêrôn *adj.* (4x)

Roots:G4055

G4054.1 A-NSN-C περισσότερον (1x)

Heb 6:17 being·resolved more·abundantly to·fully·exhibit

G4054.1 A-ASM-C περισσότερον (1x)

1Co 15:10 I·labored·hard, more·abundantly than·them all;

G4054.1 A-ASN-C περισσότερον (1x)

Mk 7:36 even·much more·abundantly they·were·officially· *it*

G4054.2 A-NSN-C περισσότερον (1x)

Heb 7:15 And furthermore, it·is excessively fully·obvious, if

G4055 περισσότερος pêrissótêrôs *adj.* (12x)

Roots:G4053 See:G4056 G4054

G4055.1 A-ASF-C περισσοτέραν (3x)

1Co 12:23 we·place·around *them* more·abundant honor; and

1Co 12:23 our indecent·parts have more·abundant decorum.

1Co 12:24 the Body, giving more·abundant honor to·the·one

G4055.1 A-ASN-C περισσότερον (3x)

Lk 20:47 “These shall·receive more·abundant judgment.”

Mt 23:13 that, yeu·shall·receive more·abundant judgment.

Mk 12:40 “These shall·receive more·abundant judgment.”

G4055.2 A-NSN-C περισσότερον (1x)

Mt 11:9 Yes, I·say to·yeu, and much·more·than a·prophet.

G4055.2 A-ASM-C περισσότερον (1x)

Lk 7:26 Yes, I·say to·yeu, and much·more than·a·prophet.

G4055.2 A-ASN-C περισσότερον (2x)

Lk 12:4 these·things not having anything much·more to·do.

Lk 12:48 ·of much, from·him they·shall·request much·more.

G4055.3 A-DSF-C περισσοτέρᾳ (1x)

2Co 2:7 ·man should·be·swallowed·up with·excessive grief.

G4055.4 A-ASN-C περισσότερον (1x)

2Co 10:8 ·boast somewhat excessively concerning our

G4056 περισσοτέρως pêrissôtérōs *adv.* (13x)

Roots:G4055

G4056.1 ADV περισσοτέρως (9x)

Heb 2:1 ·for us more·abundantly to·give·heed to·the·things

Mk 15:14 And they·yelled·out the more·abundantly,

1Th 2:17 diligently·endeavored the·more·abundantly to·see

2Co 1:12 in the world and more·abundantly toward yeu.

2Co 2:4 the love which I·have more·abundantly for yeu.

2Co 7:15 inward·affections are more·abundant toward yeu,

2Co 11:23 … in wearisome·labors more·abundantly, in

2Co 11:23 in imprisonments more·abundantly, *and* in

2Co 12:15 even·though the·more·abundantly *I·am* loving

G4056.2 ADV περισσοτέρως (2x)

Heb 13:19 But I·implore *yeu* all·the·more to·do this, in·

Php 1:14 bonds, *are* all·the·more daringly·bold to·speak the

G4056.3 ADV περισσοτέρως (2x)

Gal 1:14 inherently·being more·exceedingly a·zealot of·my

2Co 7:13 yeur comfort; and more·exceedingly *all* the·more,

G4057 περισσῶς pêrissôs *adv.* (5x)

Roots:G4053 Compare:G4056 See:G5249

G4057.1 ADV ἐκπερισσοῦ (3x)

Mt 27:23 *crowds* were·yelling·out more·abundantly, saying,

1Th 3:10 and day, *we·are* abundantly petitioning *him* above·

1Th 5:13 to·resolutely·consider them abundantly with love

G4057.2 ADV περισσῶς (2x)

Ac 26:11 ·against them beyond·excess, I·was·persecuting

Mk 10:26 And they·were·astounded beyond·excess, saying

G4058 περιστερά pêristêrá *n.* (10x)

Compare:G5167
xLangEquiv:H3123

G4058.2 N-NPF περιστεραί (1x)

Mt 10:16 prudent as the serpents and untainted as the doves.

G4058.2 N-ASF περιστεράν (4x)

Jn 1:32 Spirit descending out of·heaven like a·dove, and he·

Lk 3:22 descended in·a·bodily shape like a·dove upon him,

Mt 3:16 Spirit of·God descending like a·dove and coming

Mk 1:10 and the Spirit like a·dove descending upon him.

G4058.2 N-APF περιστεράς (4x)

Jn 2:14 oxen, sheep, and doves; and·also *he·found* the

Jn 2:16 he·declared to·the·ones selling the doves, “Take·

Mt 21:12 and the seats of·the·ones selling the doves,

Mk 11:15 and the seats of·the·ones selling the doves,

G4058.2 N-GPF περιστερῶν (1x)

Lk 2:24 of·turtledoves or two of·the·Offspring of·a·dove.”

G4059 περι•τέμνω pêritémnō *v.* (18x)

Roots:G4012 G5114 Compare:G1986 See:G4061
xLangEquiv:H4135 xLangAlso:H5243

G4059.2 V-PAI-2P περιτέμνετε (1x)

Jn 7:22 on a·Sabbath, yeu·circumcise a·man-child·of·clay†.

G4059.2 V-PAN περιτέμνειν (2x)

Ac 15:5 “It·is·mandatory to·circumcise them and to·charge

Ac 21:21 saying for·them not to·circumcise the children,

G4059.2 V-PPM-3S περιτεμνέσθω (1x)

1Co 7:18 ·forth in uncircumcision, must·not be·circumcised.

G4059.2 V-PPN περιτέμνεσθαι (3x)

Ac 15:24 saying, ‘*It·is·necessary* to·be·circumcised and to·

Gal 6:12 compel yeu to·be·circumcised merely in·order·that

Gal 6:13 yeu to·be·circumcised in·order·that they·may·boast

G4059.2 V-PPP-DSM περιτεμνομένῳ (1x)

Gal 5:3 again to·every man·of·clay† being·circumcised, that

G4059.2 V-PPP-NPM περιτεμνόμενοι (1x)

Gal 6:13 ·themselves, being·circumcised, vigilantly·keep

G4059.2 V-PPS-2P περιτέμνησθε (2x)

Ac 15:1 “Unless yeu·should·be·circumcised in·the manner

Gal 5:2 that if yeu·should·be·circumcised, Anointed-One

G4059.2 V-2AAI-3S περιέτεμεν (2x)

Ac 7:8 *AbRaham* begot YiTsaq and circumcised him on·the

Ac 16:3 taking *TimoThy*, he·circumcised him on·account·of

G4059.2 V-2AAN περιτεμεῖν (2x)

Lk 1:59 day, *that* they·came to·circumcise the little·child,

Lk 2:21 days were·fulfilled to·circumcise the little·child, his

G4059.2 V-API-2P περιετμήθητε (1x)

Col 2:11 also yeu·are·already·circumcised with·a· not·made·

G4059.2 V-APN περιτμηθῆναι (1x)

Gal 2:3 being a·Greek) was·compelled to·be·circumcised.

G4059.2 V-RPP-NSM περιτετμημένος (1x)

1Co 7:18 is·called·forth, having·been·circumcised, must·not

G4060 περι•τίθημι pêritíthêmi *v.* (8x)

Roots:G4012 G5087 Compare:G1746

G4060.1 V-PAI-1P περιτίθεμεν (1x)

1Co 12:23 upon·these we·place·around *them* more·abundant

G4060.1 V-PAI-3S περιτιθέασιν (1x)

Mk 15:17 victor's·crown, it·is·placed·around his *head*,

G4060.1 V-AAI-3S περιέθηκεν (2x)

Mt 21:33 “planted a·vineyard and placed a·hedge around it,

Mk 12:1 “planted a·vineyard, and placed a·hedge around *it*,

G4060.1 V-AAI-3P περιέθηκαν (1x)

Mt 27:28 ·stripping him, they·placed a·scarlet military·cloak

G4060.2 V-2AAP-NSM περιθείς (2x)

Mt 27:48 *it* with·wine·vinegar and putting·it·on a·reed, was·

Mk 15:36 a·sponge of·wine·vinegar and putting·it·on a·reed,

G4060.2 V-2AAP-NPM περιθέντες (1x)

Jn 19:29 with·wine·vinegar and putting·it·on hyssop,

G4061 περι•τομή pêritômḗ *n.* (36x)

מוּלָה mûlaḥ [Hebrew]

Roots:G4059 Compare:G0203 G2699
xLangEquiv:H4139

G4061.1 N-NSF περιτομή (2x)

Rm 2:28 ·appearance, *that·is*, with a·circumcision in·flesh.

Rm 2:29 ·*is* a·Jew, and *with* a·circumcision *that·is* of·heart,

G4061.1 N-ASF περιτομήν (2x)

Jn 7:23 ·of·clay† receives circumcision on a·Sabbath in·

Gal 5:11 if I·still officially·proclaim circumcision, why·am

G4061.1 N-DSF περιτομῇ (3x)

Php 3:5 with·a·circumcision *at* eight·days·of·age from·

Col 2:11 yeu·are·already·circumcised with·a·circumcision,

Col 2:11 ·the flesh by the circumcision of·the Anointed-One

G4061.2 N-ASF περιτομήν (1x)

Jn 7:22 Moses has·given to·yeu the circumcision (not that it·

G4061.2 N-GSF περιτομῆς (3x)

Ac 7:8 And he·gave to·him a·covenant of·circumcision. And

Rm 3:1 ·benefit? Or what *is* the profit of·the circumcision?

Rm 4:11 ·received *the* sign of·circumcision, an·official·seal

G4061.3 N-NSF περιτομή (6x)

Gal 5:6 Anointed, neither circumcision nor uncircumcision

Gal 6:15 YeShua, neither circumcision nor uncircumcision

Rm 2:25 For in·fact, circumcision benefits if you·should·

Rm 2:25 your circumcision has·become uncircumcision.

1Co 7:19 The circumcision is nothing·at·all, and the

Col 3:11 Greek and Jew, circumcision and uncircumcision,

G4061.3 N-ASF περιτομήν (1x)

Rm 2:26 shall·it·not·indeed be·reckoned for circumcision?

G4061.3 N-DSF περιτομῇ (2x)

Rm 4:10 ·it·reckoned? *With·him* being in circumcision, or in

Rm 4:10 uncircumcision? Not in circumcision, but·rather in

G4061.3 N-GSF περιτομῆς (2x)

Rm 2:27 through letter and circumcision *being* a·transgressor

Rm 4:12 *to·be* a·father of·circumcision to·the·ones *who·are*

G4061.4 N-NSF περιτομή (1x)

Php 3:3 For we·ourselves are the Circumcision, the·ones

G4061.4 N-ASF περιτομήν (3x)

Gal 2:9 Gentiles, and they·themselves to the Circumcision.

Rm 3:30 as·righteous: *the* Circumcision as·a·result of·trust

Rm 4:9 supreme·blessedness upon the Circumcision *only*, or

G4061.4 N-GSF περιτομῆς (10x)

Ac 10:45 from·among *the* Circumcision trusting *in·Jesus*

Ac 11:2 ·among *the* Circumcision were·discriminating *the*

Gal 2:7 of·the Circumcision *had·been·entrusted* to·Peter

Gal 2:8 ·Peter unto a·commission of·the Circumcision, also

Gal 2:12 fearing the·ones from·among *the* Circumcision.

Rm 4:12 *who·are* not from·among *the* Circumcision merely,

Rm 15:8 an·attendant of·*the*·Circumcision on·behalf of·

Tit 1:10 especially the·ones from·among *the* Circumcision,

Eph 2:11 being·referred·to·as *the* Circumcision, *which·is*

Col 4:11 the·ones being from·among *the* Circumcision, who

G4062 περι•τρέπω pêritrépō *v.* (1x)

Roots:G4012 G5157 Compare:G4962 G4045-1 G3344

G4062.2 V-PAI-3S περιτρέπει (1x)

Ac 26:24 The many studies do·twist you about into raving·

G4063 περι•τρέχω pêritréchō *v.* (1x)

Roots:G4012 G5143

G4063 V-2AAP-NPM περιδραμόντες (1x)

Mk 6:55 *and* running·around that whole surrounding·region,

G4064 περι•φέρω pêriphérō *v.* (5x)

Roots:G4012 G5342

G4064 V-PAN περιφέρειν (1x)

Mk 6:55 ·region, they·began to·carry·about on their mats

G4064 V-PAP-NPM περιφέροντες (1x)

2Co 4:10 always carrying·about in the body the mortal·

G4064 V-PPM-2P περιφέρεσθε (1x)

Heb 13:9 Do·not·be carried·about by·diverse and strange·

Αα Ββ Γγ Δδ Εε Ζζ Ηη Θθ Ιι Κκ Λλ Μμ Νν Ξξ Οο Ππ Ρρ Σσ Ττ Υυ Φφ Χχ Ψψ Ωω

G4064 V-PPP-NPF περιφερόμεναι (1x)
Jud 1:12 ·clouds without·water being·carried·about by winds
G4064 V-PPP-NPM περιφερόμενοι (1x)
Eph 4:14 ·waves and being·carried·about by·every wind of·

G4065 περι•φρονέω pêriphrônêō *v.* (1x)
Roots:G4012 G5426 Compare:G1848 G2706 G3058
G4065.3 V-PAM-3S περιφρονείτω (1x)
Tit 2:15 ·authority. Let not·one·man disparage you.

G4066 περί•χωρος pêríchōrôs *adj.* (10x)
Roots:G4012 G5561 See:G1093
G4066.2 A-NSM περίχωρος (1x)
Mt 3:5 and all the region·surrounding the Jordan *River*,
G4066.2 A-ASF περίχωρον (2x)
Lk 3:3 he·went into all the region·surrounding the Jordan
Mk 1:28 went·forth unto all the region·surrounding Galilee.
G4066.2 A-GSF περιχώρου (1x)
Lk 8:37 multitude of·the region·surrounding the Gadarenes
G4066.3 A-ASF περίχωρον (3x)
Ac 14:6 cities of·Lycaonia, and to·the surrounding·region.
Mt 14:35 into all that surrounding·region and brought to·him
Mk 6:55 ·around that whole surrounding·region, they·began
G4066.3 A-DSF περιχώρῳ (1x)
Lk 7:17 all Judea and among all the surrounding·region.
G4066.3 A-GSF περιχώρου (2x)
Lk 4:14 ·forth concerning him in all the surrounding·region.
Lk 4:37 ·forth into every place in·the surrounding·region.

G4067 περί•ψωμα pêrípsōma *n.* (1x)
Roots:G4012
G4067.2 N-NSN περίψημα (1x)
1Co 4:13 of·the world, an·offscouring of·all·things unto

G4068 περπερεύομαι pêrpêrêúômai *v.* (1x)
Roots:G4008
G4068 V-PNI-3S περπερεύεται (1x)
1Co 13:4 The Love does·not brag. It·is·not puffed·up,

G4069 Περσίς Pêrsís *n/p.* (1x)
G4069.2 N/P-ASF Περσίδα (1x)
Rm 16:12 Greet the well-beloved Persis, who repeatedly

G4070 πέρυσι pérysi *adv.* (2x)
Roots:G4009
G4070.2 ADV πέρυσι (2x)
2Co 8:10 for·yeu, who since last·year began·previously not
2Co 9:2 has·been·making·preparation since last·year; and

G4071 πετεινόν pêtêinón *n.* (14x)
Roots:G4072 Compare:G3732
G4071.2 N-NPN πετεινά (7x)
Lk 8:5 and it·was·trampled·down, and the birds of·the sky
Lk 9:58 have burrows, and the birds of·the sky *have* nests,
Lk 13:19 a·great tree, and the birds of·the sky nested in its
Ac 10:12 and the creeping·things, and the birds of·the sky.
Mt 8:20 have burrows, and the birds of·the sky *have* nests,
Mt 13:4 the roadway, and the birds came and devoured them
Mk 4:4 ·by the roadway, and the birds of·the sky came and
G4071.2 N-APN πετεινά (4x)
Ac 11:6 and the creeping·things, and the birds of·the sky.
Mt 6:26 "Look·clearly at the birds of·the sky, because they·
Mt 13:32 a·tree, such·for the birds of·the sky to·come and
Mk 4:32 branches, such·for the birds of·the sky to·be·able
G4071.2 N-GPN πετεινῶν (3x)
Lk 12:24 *do* yeu·yeurselves surpass·the·value of·the birds?
Rm 1:23 of·corruptible Clay·Man†, and·also of·birds, and
Jac 3:7 of·wild·beasts, also of·birds, and of·creeping·things,

G4072 πέτομαι pétômai *v.* (5x)
πετάομαι pêtáômai [prolongation]
πτάομαι ptáômai [contracted]
G4072 V-PNP-ASM πετώμενον (1x)
Rv 14:6 And I·saw another angel who·is·flying in *the*
G4072 V-PNP-DSM πετωμένῳ (1x)
Rv 4:7 and the fourth living·being *is* like a·flying eagle.
G4072 V-PNP-DPN πετωμένοις (1x)
Rv 19:17 to·all the fowls, to·the·ones flying in mid-heaven,
G4072 V-PNP-GSM πετωμένου (1x)
Rv 8:13 And I·saw and heard an angel flying in mid-heaven,
G4072 V-PNS-3S πέτηται (1x)
Rv 12:14 great eagle were·given that she·may·fly into the

G4073 πέτρα pétra *n.* (17x)
Roots:G4073-3 Compare:G1023-1 G3023-1
See:G4074
xLangEquiv:H6697
G4073.1 N-NSF πέτρα (1x)
1Pe 2:8 of·stumbling and a·solid·rock of·scandalous·offense.
G4073.1 N-NPF πέτραι (1x)
Mt 27:51 earth is·shaken, and the solid·rocks are·split·open,
G4073.1 N-ASF πέτραν (6x)
Lk 6:48 and laid a·foundation on the solid·rock. And with·a·
Lk 6:48 it, for it·had·been·founded upon the solid·rock.
Lk 8:6 other *seed* fell upon the solid·rock, and once·being·
Mt 7:24 man who built his home upon the solid·rock.
Mt 7:25 fall, for it·had·been·founded upon the solid·rock.
Rm 9:33 ·stumbling and a·solid·rock of·scandalous·offense,
G4073.1 N-APF πέτρας (1x)
Rv 6:15 caves and among the solid·rocks of·the mountains.
G4073.1 N-DSF πέτρᾳ (1x)
Mt 27:60 which he·hewed·out in the solid·rock, and after·
G4073.1 N-DPF πέτραις (1x)
Rv 6:16 ·say to·the mountains and to·the solid·rocks, "Fall
G4073.1 N-GSF πέτρας (2x)
Lk 8:13 "And the·ones upon the solid·rock, whenever they·
Mk 15:46 was having·been·hewed out of·solid·rock, and he·
EG4073.1 (1x)
Lk 8:6 ·away on·account·of *the solid·rock* not holding
G4073.2 N-NSF πέτρα (1x)
1Co 10:4 *them*, and the Solid·Rock was the Anointed-One.
G4073.2 N-DSF πέτρᾳ (1x)
Mt 16:18 "But upon this Solid·Rock I·shall·build my
G4073.2 N-GSF πέτρας (1x)
1Co 10:4 from·out of·that·spiritual Solid·Rock following

G4074 Πέτρος Pétrôs *n/p.* (168x)
Roots:G4073-3 Compare:G3037 G2786 G5586
See:G4613 G4073
xLangEquiv:H3710 xLangAlso:H5553 H6697
G4074.2 N/P-NSM Πέτρος (104x)
Jn 1:42 ·*rock*)," which is·translated *from·Hebrew as* Peter.
Jn 6:68 Accordingly, Simon Peter answered him, "Lord, to
Jn 13:8 Peter says to·him, "No, you·should·not wash my
Jn 13:9 Simon Peter says to·him, "Lord, not my feet merely,
Jn 13:24 So·then, Simon Peter beckoned to·him to·inquire
Jn 13:36 Simon Peter says to·him, "Lord, where·do you·
Jn 13:37 Peter says to·him, "Lord, why am·I·not able to·
Jn 18:10 having a·dagger, Simon Peter drew it and struck
Jn 18:15 And Simon Peter was·following Jesus, and *so was*
Jn 18:16 But Peter stood outside alongside the door.
Jn 18:18 ·warming·themselves. And Peter was standing with
Jn 18:25 Now Simon Peter was standing·by and warming·
Jn 18:26 a·kinsman of·him·whose earlobe Peter chopped·off,
Jn 18:27 Accordingly, Peter denied *it* again, and
Jn 20:3 Accordingly, Peter and the other disciple went·forth,
Jn 20:6 So·then, Simon Peter comes following him, and he·
Jn 21:2 *Now* at·the·same·place, there·was Simon Peter, and
Jn 21:3 Simon Peter says to·them, "I·head·on·out to·fish.
Jn 21:7 the Lord, Simon Peter tightly·girded *his* fishing·coat
Jn 21:11 Simon Peter walked·up and drew the net upon the
Jn 21:17 ·for me?" Peter was·grieved because he·declared
Jn 21:20 So after·turning·himself·about, Peter looks·at the
Jn 21:21 Upon·seeing this·man, Peter says to·Jesus, "Lord,
Lk 5:8 after·seeing *it*, Simon Peter fell·down·at Jesus' knees,
Lk 8:45 with·everyone denying *it*, Peter and the·ones with
Lk 9:20 me to·be?" And answering, Peter declared, "The
Lk 9:32 Now Peter and the·ones together with·him were
Lk 9:33 ·departing from him, *that* Peter declared to Jesus,
Lk 12:41 But Peter declared to·him, "Lord, do·you·say this
Lk 18:28 Then Peter declared, "Behold, we·ourselves left all
Lk 22:54 ·priest. Now Peter was·following at·a·distance.
Lk 22:55 and sitting·down·together, Peter sat·down in *the*
Lk 22:58 from·among them." And Peter declared, "Man·
Lk 22:60 And Peter declared, "Man·of·clay†, I·do·not
Lk 22:61 ·clearly·at Peter. And Peter quietly·recalled the
Lk 22:62 And Peter, going·forth outside, wept bitterly.
Lk 24:12 But rising·up, Peter ran to the chamber·tomb, and
Ac 1:13 ·were continuing·to·abide as·follows: (Peter, Jakob,
Ac 1:15 a·hundred *and* twenty), Peter, after·standing·up,
Ac 2:14 But Peter, after·being·settled together with·the
Ac 2:38 And Peter replied to them, "Repent, and each·one
Ac 3:1 Now Peter and John were·walking·up in·unison into
Ac 3:4 And Peter, gazing·intently upon him together with·
Ac 3:6 Then Peter declared, "Silver and gold, it·does·not
Ac 3:12 And seeing *this*, Peter answered to the people,
Ac 4:8 Then Peter, being·filled with·Holy Spirit, declared to
Ac 4:19 But answering, Peter and John declared to them,
Ac 5:3 But Peter declared, "AnanIas, why *has* the
Ac 5:8 And Peter answered to·her, "Declare to·me whether
Ac 5:9 So Peter declared to her, "How *is·it* that yeu are·
Ac 5:29 But answering, Peter and the ambassadors declared,
Ac 8:20 But Peter declared to him, "May your silver,
Ac 9:34 And Peter declared to·him, "Aeneas, Jesus the
Ac 9:38 to·Joppa, *and* after·hearing that Peter was in this
Ac 9:39 And rising·up, Peter went·together with·them.
Ac 9:40 But Peter, after·casting everyone forth outside,
Ac 10:5 Joppa and send·for Simon, who is·surnamed Peter.
Ac 10:9 drawing·near to·the city, Peter walked·up upon the
Ac 10:14 But Peter declared, "Not·any·such·thing, Lord,
Ac 10:17 But as Peter was·thoroughly·perplexed in himself
Ac 10:18 Simon, the·one being·surnamed Peter, is·a·guest
Ac 10:21 to him from Cornelius), Peter declared, "Behold,
Ac 10:23 And on·the next·day, Peter went·forth together
Ac 10:26 But Peter roused him, saying, "Stand·up, *for* also·I
Ac 10:32 ·for Simon, who is·surnamed Peter, who coming·
Ac 10:34 Then Peter, opening·up his mouth, declared, "In
Ac 10:46 and magnifying God. Then Peter responded,
Ac 11:2 Now when Peter walked·up to JeruSalem, the·ones
Ac 11:4 Peter explained·himself in·consecutive·order to·
Ac 12:5 Accordingly in·fact, Peter was·kept in the prison·
Ac 12:6 forth, on·that night Peter was being·laid·to·sleep
Ac 12:11 And after·coming to himself, Peter declared,
Ac 12:16 But Peter was·persisting·in knocking. And
Ac 12:18 the soldiers as·to what was·become of·Peter.
Ac 15:7 occurring, after·rising·up, Peter declared to them,
Gal 2:7 of·the Circumcision *had·been·entrusted* to·Peter
Gal 2:11 But when Peter came to Antioch, I·withstood him
Mt 10:2 first, Simon (the·one being·referred·to·as Peter) and
Mt 14:28 And answering him, Peter declared, "Lord, if it·
Mt 14:29 ·down from the sailboat, Peter walked upon the
Mt 15:15 Now responding, Peter declared to·him, "Explain
Mt 16:16 And answering, Simon Peter declared, "You·
Mt 16:18 ·you that you·yourself are Peter·*(a·piece·of·rock)*.
Mt 16:22 And Peter, purposely·taking him *aside*, began to·
Mt 17:4 Now responding *to·this*, Peter declared to·YeShua,
Mt 17:26 Peter says to·him, "From the others.
Mt 18:21 Then Peter, coming·alongside him, declared,
Mt 19:27 Then responding, Peter declared to·him, "Behold,
Mt 26:33 And answering, Peter declared to·him, "Even if
Mt 26:35 Peter says to·him, "Though it·should·be·
Mt 26:58 But Peter was·following him from a·distance up·to
Mt 26:69 Now Peter was·sitting·down outside in the
Mt 26:75 And Peter was·*suddenly*·mindful of·the utterance
Mk 8:29 to·be?" And answering, Peter says to·him, "You·
Mk 8:32 ·taking him *aside*, Peter began to·reprimand him.
Mk 9:5 Now responding *to·this*, Peter says to·Jesus, "Rabbi,
Mk 10:28 Then Peter began to·say to·him, "Behold, we·
Mk 11:21 ·to·mind·and·considering *it*, Peter says to·him,
Mk 13:3 directly·opposite the Sanctuary·Estate, Peter, Jakob
Mk 14:29 But Peter replied to·him, "Even if all shall·be·
Mk 14:54 But Peter followed him from a·distance, as·far·as
Mk 14:72 And Peter recalled·to·mind·and·considered the
1Pe 1:1 Peter, an·ambassador of·YeShua Anointed.
2Pe 1:1 Shimon Peter, a·slave and an·ambassador of·
G4074.2 N/P-VSM Πέτρε (3x)
Lk 22:34 "I·say to·you, Peter, a·rooster, no, it·shall·not

Ac 10:13 to him, *saying*, "Peter, after·standing·up, make·
Ac 11:7 a·voice saying to·me, 'Peter, after·standing·up,
G4074.2 N/P-ASM Πέτρον (26x)
Jn 13:6 So·then he·comes to Simon Peter, and that·one says
Jn 18:16 *him* to·the doorkeeper, and she·brought·in Peter.
Jn 20:2 she·runs and comes to Simon Peter and to the other
Lk 6:14 Simon (whom also he·named Peter), and Andrew his
Lk 8:51 not·even·one·person to·enter·in, except Peter, Jakob
Lk 9:28 sayings, that·also personally·taking Peter, John, and
Lk 22:8 And *Jesus* dispatched Peter and John, declaring,
Ac 2:37 heart, and they·declared to Peter and to·the rest of·
Ac 3:3 who, after·seeing Peter and John intending to·enter
Ac 3:11 who·was·healed securely·holding Peter and John, all
Ac 8:14 of·God, they·dispatched Peter and John to them,
Ac 9:32 it·happened *such·for* Peter to·come·down also to
Ac 9:40 ·up her eyes; and upon·seeing Peter, she·sat·up.
Ac 10:25 And as·soon·as Peter happened to·enter, Cornelius
Ac 11:13 Joppa and send·for Simon being·surnamed Peter,
Ac 12:3 Judeans, he·further·proceeded to·arrest Peter also.
Ac 12:14 ·in, she·announced, "Peter is·standing before the
Gal 1:18 to·see·and·personally·interview Peter, and I·stayed·
Mt 4:18 Simon (the·one being·referred·to·as Peter) and
Mt 17:1 days, YeShua personally·takes Peter and Jakob and
Mt 26:37 Then personally·taking *with·him* Peter and the two
Mk 3:16 ·Simon, he·laid a·name "Peter·*(a·piece·of·rock)*";
Mk 5:37 to·follow·along with·him, except Peter, Jakob, and
Mk 9:2 six days, Jesus personally·takes Peter, Jakob, and
Mk 14:33 Then he·personally·takes with·him Peter, Jakob,
Mk 14:67 And seeing Peter warming·himself, after·looking·
G4074.2 N/P-DSM Πέτρῳ (16x)
Jn 18:11 So·then Jesus declared to·Peter, "Cast your dagger
Jn 18:17 (the doorkeeper) says to·Peter, "Are you·yourself
Jn 21:7 disciple whom Jesus loved says to·Peter, "It·is the
Jn 21:15 they·had·dined, Jesus says to·Simon Peter, "Simon
Lk 22:61 the Lord looked·clearly·at Peter. And Peter
Ac 10:45 as·many·as came·together with·Peter, because
Gal 2:8 (for the·one operating in·Peter unto a·commission
Gal 2:14 of·the good·news, I·declared to·Peter before *them*
Mt 16:23 But turning·around, he·declared to·Peter, "Get·
Mt 17:24 ·drachma *tax* came·alongside Peter and declared,
Mt 26:40 finds them sleeping. And he·says to·Peter, "So,
Mt 26:73 the·ones standing·by declared to·Peter, "Truly
Mk 8:33 seeing his disciples, he·reprimanded Peter, saying,
Mk 14:37 them sleeping. And he·says to·Peter, "Simon, do·
Mk 14:70 standing·nearby were·saying again to·Peter,
Mk 16:7 ·his disciples and to·Peter that he·goes·on·ahead·of
G4074.2 N/P-GSM Πέτρου (13x)
Jn 1:40 Andrew, Simon Peter's brother, was one from·
Jn 1:44 from·among the city of·Andrew and Peter.
Jn 6:8 his disciples, Andrew, Simon Peter's brother, says to·
Jn 20:4 the other disciple more·swiftly outran Peter and came
Ac 4:13 observing the clarity·of·speech of·Peter and John,
Ac 5:15 and mats, in·order·that with·Peter going·by, if·even
Ac 10:19 But while·Peter was·cogitating about the clear·
Ac 10:44 As·Peter was·yet speaking these utterances, the
Ac 12:7 in the jailhouse. And tapping Peter on·the side, he·
Ac 12:13 And as·Peter *was* knocking *at* the door of·the gate,
Ac 12:14 And after·recognizing Peter's voice, she·did·not
Mt 8:14 And YeShua, upon·coming into Peter's home, saw
Mk 14:66 Now with·Peter being·down·below in the
EG4074.2 (6x)
Jn 21:19 by·what·kind·of death *Peter* shall·glorify God. And
Ac 8:25 of·the Lord, *as Peter and John* returned·back to
Ac 10:23 So·then inviting them in, *Peter* hosted *them*. And
Ac 12:4 and after·apprehending *Peter*, *HerOd·Agrippa* placed
Ac 15:14 Shimon *Peter* recounted·in·detail *that* just·as at·
Mt 8:14 home, saw *Peter's* mother-in-law having·been·cast

G4075 πετρ•ώδης pêtrṓdēs *adj.* (4x)
Roots:G4073-3 G1491 See:G4073 G4074
G4075.2 A-ASN πετρῶδες (1x)
Mk 4:5 *seed* fell upon the rocky·ground, where it·was·not
G4075.3 A-APN πετρώδη (3x)
Mt 13:5 *seeds* fell upon the rocky·places, where it·was·not
Mt 13:20 ·with·seed among the rocky·places, this·person is
Mk 4:16 ·with·seed among the rocky·places: ones·who,

G4076 πήγανον pḗganôn *n.* (1x)
Roots:G4078
G4076 N-ASN πήγανον (1x)
Lk 11:42 the mint and the rue and all·manner·of garden·

G4077 πηγή pēgḗ *n.* (12x)
Roots:G4078
xLangEquiv:H4599 xLangAlso:H4002
G4077.1 N-NSF πηγή (3x)
Jn 4:14 it·shall·be in him a·wellspring of·water springing·up
Jac 3:11 ¿!·Does the wellspring gush·forth at the same
Jac 3:12 not·even·one wellspring *is·able* to·produce *both*
G4077.1 N-NPF πηγαί (1x)
2Pe 2:17 These are wellsprings without·water, thick·clouds
G4077.1 N-APF πηγάς (4x)
Rv 7:17 shall·guide them to living wellsprings of·waters.
Rv 8:10 of·the rivers, and upon the wellsprings of·waters;
Rv 14:7 and the earth, and sea,' and wellsprings of·waters!"
Rv 16:4 the rivers and into the wellsprings of·waters, and
G4077.1 N-GSF πηγῆς (1x)
Rv 21:6 thirsting from·out of·the wellspring of·the water of·
G4077.2 N-NSF πηγή (2x)
Jn 4:6 Now Jacob's well was there. So·then Jesus, having·
Mk 5:29 And immediately, the well of·her blood was·dried·
G4077.2 N-DSF πηγῇ (1x)
Jn 4:6 was·sitting·down in·this·manner on the well. It·was

G4078 πήγνυμι pḗgnymi *v.* (1x)
Compare:G4338 G1574 G1335-2 See:G4362 G3975
G4078.2 V-AAI-3S ἔπηξεν (1x)
Heb 8:2 Tabernacle, which Yahweh set·up and not a·man·

G4079 πηδάλιον pēdáliôn *n.* (2x)
Roots:G4228 See:G3976
G4079.2 N-GSN πηδαλίου (1x)
Jac 3:4 they·are·steered by a·very·small rudder, wherever the
G4079.2 N-GPN πηδαλίων (1x)
Ac 27:40 at·the·same·time slackening the rudder cables, and

G4080 πηλίκος pēlíkôs *adj.* (2x)
Roots:G4225 Compare:G2245 G4119
G4080.2 A-NSM πηλίκος (1x)
Heb 7:4 Now observe what·stature this·man *was*, to·whom
G4080.3 A-DPN πηλίκοις (1x)
Gal 6:11 Yeu·see with·what·sizable letters I·write to·yeu by·

G4081 πηλός pēlôs *n.* (6x)
Compare:G1004 See:G4080-1 xLangAlso:H2563
H2916
G4081 N-ASM πηλόν (5x)
Jn 9:6 down·on·the·open·ground and made clay out of·the
Jn 9:6 saliva, and he·smeared the clay over the eyes of·the
Jn 9:11 ·to·as Jesus, he·made clay and smeared·*it*·over my
Jn 9:14 when Jesus made the clay and opened·up his eyes.
Jn 9:15 So he·declared to·them, "He·put clay upon my eyes,
G4081 N-GSM πηλοῦ (1x)
Rm 9:21 potter have authority *over* the clay, from·out of·the

G4082 πήρα pḗra *n.* (6x)
Compare:G0905 G1101 G2223
G4082.2 N-ASF πήραν (5x)
Lk 9:3 journey, neither staffs, nor knapsack, neither bread,
Lk 10:4 lift·and·carry a·pouch, nor a·knapsack, nor·even
Lk 22:36 let·him·take·it·up, and likewise a·knapsack. And
Mt 10:10 nor a·knapsack for *yeur* journey, nor·even two
Mk 6:8 "… except a·staff merely. No knapsack, no bread,
G4082.2 N-GSF πήρας (1x)
Lk 22:35 yeu without·any pouch, knapsack, or shoes, ¿!·Did

G4083 πῆχυς pêchys *n.* (4x)
xLangAlso:H0520 A0521
G4083.2 N-GPM πηχῶν (2x)
Jn 21:8 ·ground, but·rather about two·hundred cubits away).
Rv 21:17 a·hundred *and* forty four cubits, *according·to* a·
G4083.4 N-ASM πῆχυν (2x)
Lk 12:25 by·being·anxious is·able to·add one half·step to his
Mt 6:27 by·being·anxious is·able to·add one half·step to his

G4084 πιάζω piázō *v.* (12x)
Roots:G0971 Compare:G4815 G4085 G0234-1
See:G4085
G4084.2 V-AAP-NSM πιάσας (1x)
Ac 3:7 And after·gripping him by·the right hand, he·pulled·
G4084.3 V-AAI-3S ἐπίασεν (1x)
Jn 8:20 And not·even·one·man apprehended him, because
G4084.3 V-AAN πιάσαι (4x)
Jn 7:30 So·then they·were·seeking to·apprehend him, but
Jn 7:44 from·among them were·wanting to·apprehend him,
Jn 10:39 they·were·seeking again to·apprehend him. But
2Co 11:32 under·continual·guard, wanting to·apprehend me.
G4084.3 V-AAP-NSM πιάσας (1x)
Ac 12:4 and after·apprehending *Peter*, *HerOd·Agrippa* placed
G4084.3 V-AAS-3P πιάσωσιν (2x)
Jn 7:32 assistants in·order·that they·should·apprehend him.
Jn 11:57 ·*their*·attention, so·that they·may·apprehend him.
G4084.3 V-API-3S ἐπιάσθη (1x)
Rv 19:20 And the Daemonic·Beast was·apprehended, and
G4084.5 V-AAI-2P ἐπιάσατε (1x)
Jn 21:10 Bring of·the small·fry which yeu·caught just·now."
G4084.5 V-AAI-3P ἐπίασαν (1x)
Jn 21:3 And on that night, they·caught nothing·at·all.

G4085 πιέζω piézō *v.* (1x)
Roots:G4084 Compare:G2346
G4085 V-RPP-ASN@ πεπιεσμένον (1x)
Lk 6:38 ·given to·yeu; good measure, packed·down, shaken

G4086 πιθανο•λογία pithanôlôgía *n.* (1x)
Roots:G3982 G3056
G4086 N-DSF πιθανολογίᾳ (1x)
Col 2:4 should·defraud yeu with persuasive·conversation.

G4087 πικραίνω pikraínō *v.* (4x)
Roots:G4089 See:G4088 xLangAlso:H4843
G4087 V-FAI-3S πικρανεῖ (1x)
Rv 10:9 and it·shall·make your belly bitter, but·yet it·shall·
G4087 V-PPM-2P πικραίνεσθε (1x)
Col 3:19 the wives, and do·not become·bitter toward them.
G4087 V-API-3S ἐπικράνθη (1x)
Rv 10:10 And when I·ate it, my belly was·made·bitter.
G4087 V-API-3P ἐπικράνθησαν (1x)
Rv 8:11 of·the waters, because they·were·made·bitter.

G4088 πικρία pikría *n.* (4x)
Roots:G4089 See:G4087 G4087-1 xLangAlso:H4751
G4088.1 N-NSF πικρία (1x)
Eph 4:31 Let all bitterness, and rage, and wrath, and yelling,
G4088.1 N-GSF πικρίας (3x)
Ac 8:23 you being in a·gall of·bitterness and a·joint·bond of·
Heb 12:15 lest any root of·bitterness sprouting upward
Rm 3:14 mouth overflows of·evil·prayer and of·bitterness.

G4089 πικρός pikrṓs *adj.* (2x)
Roots:G4078 See:G4087 G4088-1
xLangEquiv:H4751
G4089.1 A-ASM πικρόν (1x)
Jac 3:14 But if yeu·have bitter jealousy and contention in
G4089.1 A-ASN πικρόν (1x)
Jac 3:11 ·opening *with·both* the fresh *water* and the bitter?

G4090 πικρῶς pikrôs *adv.* (2x)
Roots:G4089 See:G4088
G4090.1 ADV πικρῶς (2x)
Lk 22:62 And Peter, going·forth outside, wept bitterly.
Mt 26:75 And going·forth outside, he·wept bitterly.

G4091 Πιλᾶτος Pilâtôs *n/p.* (56x)
G4091.2 N/P-NSM Πιλᾶτος (39x)
Jn 18:29 Accordingly, Pilate went·out to them and declared,
Jn 18:31 So·then Pilate declared to·them, "Yeu·yeurselves
Jn 18:33 So·then Pilate entered into the Praetorian·hall again
Jn 18:35 Pilate answered, "¿! Am·I myself a·Jew?
Jn 18:37 Accordingly, Pilate declared to·him, "So·then·
Jn 18:38 Pilate says to·him, "What is truth?
Jn 19:1 Then accordingly, Pilate took Jesus and flogged *him*.
Jn 19:4 Now·then, Pilate went·forth outside again and says
Jn 19:6 *him*, crucify *him*!" Pilate says to·them, "Yeu·

Jn 19:8 Now·then, when Pilate heard this saying, he·was all·
Jn 19:10 So·then Pilate says to·him, "Do·you·not speak to·
Jn 19:12 ·a·result of·this, Pilate was·seeking to·fully·release
Jn 19:13 after·hearing this saying, Pilate brought Jesus
Jn 19:15 crucify him!" Pilate says to·them, "Shall·I·
Jn 19:19 And Pilate also wrote a·title and placed *it* on the
Jn 19:22 Pilate answered, "What I·have·written, I·have·
Jn 19:38 the body of·Jesus, and Pilate freely·permitted *him*.
Lk 13:1 the Galileans, whose blood Pilate mixed with their
Lk 23:3 And Pilate inquired·of him, saying, "Are you·
Lk 23:4 Then Pilate declared to the chief·priests and *to* the
Lk 23:6 But Pilate, after·hearing "Galilee," inquired whether
Lk 23:12 same day, both Pilate and HerOd·AntiPas became
Lk 23:13 the chief·priests, the rulers, and the people, Pilate
Lk 23:20 to·fully·release Jesus, Pilate addressed *them* again.
Lk 23:24 And Pilate rendered·judgment *for* their request to·
Ac 4:27 both HerOd·AntiPas and Pontius Pilate, together
Mt 27:13 Then Pilate says to·him, "Do·you·not hear how·
Mt 27:17 ·been·gathered·together, Pilate declared to·them,
Mt 27:22 Pilate says to·them, "So·then what shall·I·do with·
Mt 27:24 And Pilate, after·seeing that *reasoning with·them*
Mt 27:58 of·YeShua. Then Pilate commandingly·ordered the
Mt 27:65 So Pilate replied to·them, "Yeu·have a·sentinel·
Mk 15:2 And Pilate inquired·of him, "Are you·yourself the
Mk 15:4 And Pilate inquired·of him again, saying, "Do·you·
Mk 15:9 So Pilate answered them, saying, "Do·yeu·want
Mk 15:12 And responding, Pilate declared again to·them,
Mk 15:14 But Pilate was·saying to·them, "For what crime
Mk 15:15 So Pilate, being·resolved to·make the crowd
Mk 15:44 And Pilate marveled if, even·now, he·has·died.

G4091.2 N/P-ASM Πιλάτον (7x)
Jn 19:31 , the Judeans asked·of Pilate that their legs should·
Jn 19:38 Judeans, asked·of Pilate that he·may·take·away the
Lk 23:1 ·all the multitude of·them led him to Pilate.
Ac 13:28 they·requested·of Pilate for·him to·be·executed.
Mt 27:62 and the Pharisees gathered·together to Pilate,
Mk 15:5 not·even·one·thing, such·for Pilate to·marvel.
Mk 15:43 ·daringly·bold, he·went·in to Pilate and requested

G4091.2 N/P-DSM Πιλάτῳ (6x)
Jn 19:21 chief·priests of·the Judeans were·saying to·Pilate,
Lk 23:11 in·splendid clothing, he·sent him back to·Pilate.
Lk 23:52 ·man, after·coming·alongside Pilate, requested the
Mt 27:2 and handed him over to·Pontius Pilate the governor.
Mt 27:58 ·man, upon·coming·alongside Pilate, requested the
Mk 15:1 ·carried·*him*·away and handed·*him*·over to·Pilate.

G4091.2 N/P-GSM Πιλάτου (3x)
Lk 3:1 — (with·Pontius Pilate being·governor of·Judea, and
Ac 3:13 and yeu·denied him in front of·Pilate, with·that·one
1Ti 6:13 (the·one testifying before Pontius Pilate the good

EG4091.2 (1x)
Jn 19:5 and the purple garment. And *Pilate* says to·them,

G4092 πίμπρημι pímprēmi *v.* (1x)
πρέω prĕō [an alternate in certain tenses]

G4092.3 V-PPN πίμπρασθαι (1x)
Ac 28:6 him about to·be·swollen·with·fever or to·fall·down

G4093 πινακίδιον pinakídiôn *n.* (1x)
Roots:G4094 G2444-3

G4093.2 N-ASN πινακίδιον (1x)
Lk 1:63 And requesting a·writing·tablet, he·wrote, saying,

G4094 πίναξ pínax *n.* (5x)
Roots:G4109 Compare:G3953 G5165

G4094 N-DSF πίνακι (4x)
Mt 14:8 me here the head of·John the Immerser on a·platter."
Mt 14:11 his head was·brought on a·platter and was·given
Mk 6:25 ·hour the head of·John the Immerser on a·platter."
Mk 6:28 and brought his head on a·platter, and he·gave it to·

G4094 N-GSM πίνακος (1x)
Lk 11:39 outside of·the cup and the platter, but yeur inward·

G4095 πίνω pínō *v.* (75x)
πίω píō [an alternate in certain tenses]
πόω pôō [another form for certain tenses]
Compare:G2994-1 G5202 See:G4222 G2666

G4095 V-FDI-2S πίεσαι (1x)
Lk 17:8 ·things, you·yourself shall·eat and shall·drink'?

G4095 V-FDI-2P πίεσθε (2x)
Mt 20:23 to·them, "In·fact, yeu·shall·drink of·my cup and
Mk 10:39 that I·myself drink, yeu·shall·drink; and in·the

G4095 V-FDI-3S πίεται (1x)
Rv 14:10 *the* same shall·drink from·out of·the wine of·the

G4095 V-PAI-1S πίνω (2x)
Mk 10:38 the cup that I·myself drink·of? And be·immersed·
Mk 10:39 the cup that I·myself drink, yeu·shall·drink; and

G4095 V-PAI-2P πίνετε (2x)
Lk 5:30 "Why do·yeu·eat and drink with tax·collectors and
1Co 10:31 So·then whether yeu·eat, or drink, or anything

G4095 V-PAI-3S πίνει (2x)
Mk 2:16 "How·is·it that he·eats and drinks with the tax·
1Co 11:29 ·manner, eats and drinks judgment to·himself,

G4095 V-PAI-3P πίνουσιν (1x)
Lk 5:33 the·ones of·the Pharisees, but yours eat and drink?"

G4095 V-PAM-3S πινέτω (2x)
Jn 7:37 ·man should·thirst, let·him·come to me and drink.
1Co 11:28 from·out of·the bread and drink from·out of·the

G4095 V-PAN πίνειν (5x)
Lk 12:45 ·girls, and to·eat and to·drink and to·be·drunk,
Mt 20:22 the cup that I·myself am·about to·drink? And the
Mt 24:49 fellow·slaves and to·eat and to·drink with the·ones
1Co 10:21 Yeu·are·not able to·drink *the* Lord's cup and·also
1Co 11:22 For do·yeu·not have homes to·eat and to·drink in?

G4095 V-PAP-NSM πίνων (8x)
Jn 4:13 to·her, "Anyone drinking from·out of·this water
Jn 6:54 ·one chewing my flesh, and drinking my blood, has
Jn 6:56 chewing my flesh, and drinking my blood, abides in
Lk 7:33 ·come neither eating bread nor drinking wine, and
Lk 7:34 of·Clay·Man† has·come eating and drinking, and
Mt 11:18 came neither eating nor drinking, and they·say,
Mt 11:19 of·Clay·Man† came eating and drinking, and they·
1Co 11:29 ·one eating and drinking in·an·unworthy·manner,

G4095 V-PAP-NPM πίνοντες (2x)
Lk 10:7 same home, eating and drinking the·things *provided*
Mt 24:38 ·*were* chewing *a·full·meal* and drinking, marrying

G4095 V-PAS-1S πίνω (2x)
Mt 26:29 until that day whenever I·may·drink it brand-new
Mk 14:25 until that day whenever I·may·drink it brand-new

G4095 V-PAS-2P πίνητε (3x)
Lk 22:30 in·order·that yeu·may·eat and may·drink at my
1Co 11:25 Do this, as·often·as yeu·would·drink *it*, as my
1Co 11:26 ·should·eat this bread, and should·drink this cup,

G4095 V-PAS-3S πίνῃ (1x)
1Co 11:27 should·eat this bread or should·drink the cup of·

G4095 V-IAI-3P ἔπινον (3x)
Lk 17:27 they·were·drinking, they·were·marrying·wives,
Lk 17:28 ·eating, they·were·drinking, they·were·buying,
1Co 10:4 for they·were·drinking from·out of·that·spiritual

G4095 V-2AAI-1P ἐπίομεν (1x)
Lk 13:26 to·say, 'We·ate and drank in·the·sight of·you, and

G4095 V-2AAI-3S ἔπιεν (2x)
Jn 4:12 us the well? Even he·himself drank out of·it, and his
Ac 9:9 not looking·about, and neither ate nor·even drank.

G4095 V-2AAI-3P ἔπιον (2x)
Mk 14:23 he·gave *it* to·them. And they·all drank out of·it.
1Co 10:4 and all drank the same spiritual drink, for they·

G4095 V-2AAM-2S πίε (1x)
Lk 12:19 Rest, eat, drink, *and* be·merry.

G4095 V-2AAM-2P πίετε (1x)
Mt 26:27 *it* to·them, saying, "Drink out of·it, all *of·yeu*,

G4095 V-2AAN πιεῖν (14x)
Jn 4:7 "Give me *some* to·drink,"
Jn 4:9 a·Jew, request *some* to·drink personally·from me,
Jn 4:10 'Give me *some* to·drink,' you would·have·requested·
Ac 23:12 saying neither to·eat nor to·drink until they·should·
Ac 23:21 neither to·eat nor to·drink until they·should·
Mt 20:22 yeu·are·requesting. Are·yeu·able to·drink the cup
Mt 27:34 him wine·vinegar to·drink having·been·mixed with
Mt 27:34 and after·tasting *it*, he·was·not willing to·drink *it*.
Mk 10:38 yeu·are·requesting. Are·yeu·able to·drink the cup
Mk 15:23 wine to·drink having·been·mingled·with·myrrh,
Rm 14:21 to·eat meat, nor·even to·drink wine, nor·even
1Co 9:4 ¿!·Do we·not have privilege to·eat and to·drink?
1Co 10:7 People sat·down to·eat and to·drink, and they·rose·
Rv 16:6 and you·gave them blood to·drink, for they·are

G4095 V-2AAP-NSF πιοῦσα (1x)
Heb 6:7 For the soil, after·drinking the rain which·is·coming

G4095 V-2AAP-NSM πιών (1x)
Lk 5:39 Also, not·even·one·man drinking old *wine*

G4095 V-2AAS-1S πίω (6x)
Jn 18:11 has·given me, no, ¿!·should·I·not·indeed drink it?
Lk 17:8 to·me until I·should·eat and should·drink; and·then
Lk 22:18 No, I·should·not·ever drink of·the produce of·the
Mt 26:29 no, I·should·not drink from this·moment·on from·
Mt 26:42 able to·pass·away from me unless I·should·drink it,
Mk 14:25 no, I·should·not drink any·longer from·out of·the

G4095 V-2AAS-1P πίωμεν (2x)
Mt 6:31 should·we·eat?' or, 'What should·we·drink?' or,
1Co 15:32 "'We·should·eat and should·drink, for tomorrow

G4095 V-2AAS-2P πίητε (3x)
Jn 6:53 ·the Son of·Clay·Man†, and should·drink his blood,
Lk 12:29 yeu·should·eat, or what yeu·should·drink, and do·
Mt 6:25 ·should·eat, even what yeu·should·drink, nor·even

G4095 V-2AAS-3S πίῃ (2x)
Jn 4:14 But whoever should·drink from·out of·the water that
Lk 1:15 no, he·should·not drink wine nor intoxicating·

G4095 V-2AAS-3P πίωσιν (1x)
Mk 16:18 and·if they·should·drink something deadly, no,

G4095 V-RAI-3S πέπωκεν (1x)
Rv 18:3 Because all the nations have·drunk from·out of·the

G4096 πιότης piótēs *n.* (1x)
Roots:G4104-2 Compare:G3045-1 See:G4095
xLangAlso:H4924

G4096.1 N-GSF πιότητος (1x)
Rm 11:17 of·the root and the plumpness of·the olive·tree,

G4097 πιπράσκω pipráskō *v.* (9x)
πράω práō
[base of the reduplicated and prolonged form, occurs as an alternate in certain tenses]
Roots:G4008 Compare:G4453 G1710
xLangAlso:H4376

G4097.1 V-PPP-GPM πιπρασκομένων (1x)
Ac 4:34 ·bringing the values of·the·things being·sold·off,

G4097.1 V-IAI-3P ἐπίπρασκον (1x)
Ac 2:45 And they·were·selling·off the possessions and the

G4097.1 V-API-3S ἐπράθη (1x)
Jn 12:5 why was·it·not sold·off for·three·hundred denarii

G4097.1 V-APN πραθῆναι (3x)
Mt 18:25 ·ordered *for* him to·be·sold·off, even his wife and
Mt 26:9 For this ointment was·able to·be·sold·off for·much,
Mk 14:5 ·thing was·able to·be·sold·off for·upwards·of three·

G4097.1 V-APP-NSN πραθέν (1x)
Ac 5:4 your·own? And being·sold·off, inherently·was·it *not*·

G4097.1 V-RAI-3S πέπρακεν (1x)
Mt 13:46 pearl, after·going·off, has·sold·off all (as·much·

G4097.1 V-RPP-NSM πεπραμένος (1x)
Rm 7:14 fleshly, having·been·sold·off under Moral·Failure.

G4098 πίπτω píptō *v.* (90x)
πέτω pétō
[basis for the reduplicated and contracted form; occurs as an alternate in certain tenses]
Compare:G2667 G4417 See:G4072
xLangEquiv:H5307 A5308

G4098.1 V-FDI-3S πεσεῖται (2x)
Ac 27:34 for not·even·one hair shall·fall out·from yeur

Mt 10:29 not one from·among them shall·fall upon the soil
G4098.1 V-FNI-3P πεσοῦνται (5x)
Lk 6:39 *the* blind? Shall·they·not·indeed both fall into a·pit?
Lk 21:24 And they·shall·fall by·the·edge of·a·dagger, and
Mt 15:14 should·guide a·blind·man, both shall·fall into a·pit
Mt 24:29 brightness, and the stars shall·fall from the heaven,
Rv 4:10 twenty four Elders shall·fall in·the·sight of·the·one
G4098.1 V-PAI-3S πίπτει (3x)
Lk 11:17 a·house *thoroughly·divided* against a·house falls.
Mk 5:22 And upon·seeing him, he·falls toward his feet
Rm 14:4 To·his·own lord he·stands·fast or falls. And, he·
G4098.1 V-PAI-3S@ πίπτει (1x)
Mt 17:15 badly, for he·has·already·fallen many·times into
G4098.1 V-PAP-GPN πιπτόντων (2x)
Lk 16:21 with the little·crumbs, the·ones falling from the
Mt 15:27 the little·crumbs, the·ones falling from the table
G4098.1 V-2AAI-1S ἔπεσον (3x)
Ac 22:7 And I·fell to the hard·ground and heard a·voice
Rv 1:17 And when I·saw him, I·fell toward his feet as dead.
Rv 19:10 And I·fell before his feet to·fall·prostrate to·him.
G4098.1 V-2AAI-3S ἔπεσεν (29x)
Lk 6:49 burst·directly·against, and immediately it·fell. And
Lk 8:5 *there·was* that·which in·fact fell directly·by the
Lk 8:6 "And other *seed* fell upon the solid·rock, and once·
Lk 8:7 "And other *seed* fell in *the* midst of·the thorns; and
Lk 8:8 "And other *seed* fell on the beneficially·good soil, and
Lk 13:4 upon whom the tower in Siloam fell and killed them,
Ac 1:26 their lots, and the lot fell upon Matthias. And he·
Ac 20:9 ·down with heavy·sleep, he·fell down from the
Heb 3:17 morally·failing, whose slain·bodies fell in the
Mt 7:25 home; yet it·did·not fall, for it·had·been·founded
Mt 7:27 they·surged·against that home, and it·fell; and great
Mt 13:4 in·fact, some *seeds* fell directly·by the roadway,
Mt 13:5 But other *seeds* fell upon the rocky·places, where it·
Mt 13:7 And others fell among the thorns, and the thorns
Mt 13:8 But others fell on the soil, the good·one, and were·
Mt 26:39 And going·onward a·little·bit, he·fell on his face,
Mk 4:4 that, in·fact, *seed* fell directly·by the roadway, and
Mk 4:5 But other *seed* fell upon the rocky·ground, where it·
Mk 4:7 And some fell into the thorns, and the thorns sprung·
Mk 4:8 And some fell into the good soil and was·giving fruit
Mk 14:35 And going·onward a·little·bit, he·fell on the soil
Rv 8:10 angel sounded, and there·fell a·great star from·out
Rv 8:10 ·set·ablaze as a·torch, and it·fell upon the third·part
Rv 11:11 feet, and great fear fell upon the·ones observing
Rv 11:13 and the tenth·part of·the City fell. And in the
Rv 14:8 saying, "Babylon is·fallen, is·fallen, the Great
Rv 14:8 "Babylon is·fallen, is·fallen, the Great City,
Rv 18:2 "Babylon the Great is·fallen, is·fallen, and is·
Rv 18:2 Babylon the Great is·fallen, is·fallen, and is·become
G4098.1 V-2AAI-3P ἔπεσαν (8x)
Jn 18:6 ·off backwards and fell down·on·the·open·ground.
Mt 17:6 upon·hearing *it*, the disciples fell on their faces and
1Co 10:8 and twenty·three thousand fell in one day.
Rv 6:13 and the stars of·the heaven fell to the earth, as *when*
Rv 7:11 the four living·beings, and they·fell on their faces
Rv 11:16 of·God on their thrones, fell upon their faces, and
Rv 16:19 and the cities of·the nations fell. And Babylon the
Rv 17:10 they·are seven kings. The five fell, and the one is,
G4098.1 V-2AAM-2P πέσετε (2x)
Lk 23:30 "to·say to·the mountains, "Fall on us!" and to·the
Rv 6:16 mountains and to·the solid·rocks, "Fall on us, and
G4098.1 V-2AAN πεσεῖν (1x)
Lk 16:17 than one tiny·mark of·the Torah-Law to·fall.
G4098.1 V-2AAP-ASM πεσόντα (1x)
Lk 10:18 the Adversary-Accuser falling as lightning from·out
G4098.1 V-2AAP-APM πεσόντας (1x)
Rm 11:22 In·fact, upon the·ones falling, a·severe·cutting-off
G4098.1 V-2AAP-NSN πεσόν (1x)
Lk 8:14 "And the *seed* falling among the thorns, these are
G4098.1 V-2AAP-NSM πεσών (8x)
Jn 12:24 unless the kernel of·wheat, falling into the soil,
Lk 5:12 and after·seeing Jesus *and* falling on *his* face, he·
Lk 8:41 of·the gathering. And falling directly·at the feet of·
Lk 20:18 "Anyone falling upon that stone shall·be·dashed·
Ac 9:4 And falling upon the earth, he·heard a·voice saying
Ac 10:25 Cornelius met·up with·him. *And* falling at his feet,
Mt 21:44 "And the·one falling on this stone shall·be·dashed·
Mk 9:20 convulsed *the little·child*. And falling upon the soil,
G4098.1 V-2AAS-2P πέσητε (1x)
Jac 5:12 "No, No," lest yeu·should·fall into hypocrisy.
G4098.1 V-2AAS-3S πέσῃ (5x)
Lk 20:18 but upon whomever it·should·fall, it·shall·grind
Heb 4:11 that complete·rest, lest any·man should·fall by the
Mt 21:44 but on whomever it·should·fall, it·shall·grind him
1Co 10:12 to·stand must·look·out lest he·should·fall.
Rv 7:16 no, *that* the sunray should·fall on them, nor·even
G4098.1 V-2AAS-3P πέσωσιν (1x)
Rm 11:11 ·up in·order·that they·should·fall? May·it·never
G4098.1 V-RAP-ASM πεπτωκότα (1x)
Rv 9:1 and I·saw a·star having·fallen from·out of·the
G4098.2 V-2AAI-1S ἔπεσα (1x)
Rv 22:8 and looked, I·fell·down to·fall·prostrate before the
G4098.2 V-2AAI-3S ἔπεσεν (4x)
Jn 11:32 was, upon·seeing him, she·fell·down at his feet,
Lk 17:16 and he·fell·down on *his* face directly·at his feet,
Ac 5:10 And she·fell·down at·once directly·at his feet and
Heb 11:30 the walls of·Jericho fell·down, being·surrounded
G4098.2 V-2AAI-3P ἔπεσαν (3x)
Rv 5:8 the twenty·four Elders fell·down in·the·sight of·the
Rv 5:14 the twenty·four Elders fell·down and fell·prostrate
Rv 19:4 the four living·beings fell·down and fell·prostrate
G4098.2 V-2AAP-NSM πεσών (4x)
Mt 4:9 ·you, if upon·falling·down, you·should·fall·prostrate
Mt 18:26 So·then falling·down, the slave was·falling·
Mt 18:29 So·then falling·down at his feet, his fellow·slave
1Co 14:25 apparent; and in·this·manner falling·down on *his*
G4098.2 V-2AAP-NSM@ πεσών (1x)
Ac 5:5 these words, Ananias fell·down *and* expired. And
G4098.2 V-2AAP-NPM πεσόντες (1x)
Mt 2:11 his mother. And falling·down, they·fell·prostrate
G4098.2 V-RAP-ASF πεπτωκυῖαν (1x)
Ac 15:16 of·David, the·one having·fallen·down. And I·

G4099 Πισιδία Pisidía *n/l.* (2x)

G4099 N/L-ASF Πισιδίαν (1x)
Ac 14:24 And going·throughout Pisidia, they·came to
G4099 N/L-GSF Πισιδίας (1x)
Ac 13:14 Perga, came·directly to Antiochia of·Pisidia. And

G4100 πιστεύω pistêúō *v.* (250x)

Roots:G4102 Compare:G1380 See:G4104 G2667-1
xLangEquiv:H0539 A0540
G4100.1 V-FAI-1P πιστεύσομεν (1x)
Mt 27:42 now from the cross, and we·shall·trust on·him.
G4100.1 V-FAI-2P πιστεύσετε (2x)
Jn 3:12 ·do·not trust, how shall·yeu·trust if I·should·declare
Jn 5:47 *Sacred*·Writings, how shall·yeu·trust my utterances?
G4100.1 V-FAI-3P πιστεύσουσιν (2x)
Jn 11:48 alone in·this·manner, all *men* shall·trust in him,
Rm 10:14 ·not trust? And how shall·they·trust *him* of·whom
G4100.1 V-FAP-GPM πιστευσόντων (1x)
Jn 17:20 concerning the·ones who·shall·be·trusting in me
G4100.1 V-PAI-1S πιστεύω (5x)
Jn 9:38 And he·replied, "Lord, I·trust." And he·fell·
Ac 8:37 he·declared, "I·trust Jesus Anointed to·be the Son
Ac 27:25 men, cheer·up! For I·trust God, that in·this·
Mk 9:24 was·saying, "Lord, I·trust! Swiftly·help my lack·
1Co 11:18 ·subsist among yeu; and I·partly trust some *of·it*.
G4100.1 V-PAI-1P πιστεύομεν (6x)
Jn 4:42 "No·longer do·we·trust on·account·of your speech,
Jn 16:30 "By this, we·trust that you·came·forth from God.
Ac 15:11 But·rather we·trust through the grace of·*the*·Lord
Rm 6:8 ·died together with·Anointed-One, we·trust also that
1Th 4:14 For if we·trust that YeShua died and rose·up, in·
2Co 4:13 ' we·ourselves also trust and therefore speak,
G4100.1 V-PAI-2S πιστεύεις (8x)
Jn 1:50 the fig·tree,' do·you·trust? You·shall·gaze·upon
Jn 9:35 to·him, "You·yourself, do·you·trust in the Son of·
Jn 11:26 should·not die to·the coming·age. Do·you·trust this?
Jn 14:10 Do·you·not trust that I·myself *am* in the Father, and
Ac 8:37 Philippe declared, "If you·trust from·out of·all the
Ac 26:27 King Agrippa, do·you·trust the prophets?
Ac 26:27 the prophets? I·personally·know that you·trust."
Jac 2:19 You·yourself trust that there·is one God.
G4100.1 V-PAI-2P πιστεύετε (9x)
Jn 3:12 earthly·things, and yeu·do·not trust, how shall·yeu·
Jn 5:38 he·dispatched, him yeu·yourselves do·not trust.
Jn 5:47 But if yeu·do·not trust those *Sacred*·Writings, how
Jn 6:36 also yeu·have·clearly·seen me and do·not trust.
Jn 8:45 because I·myself say the truth, yeu·do·not trust me.
Jn 8:46 *is the* truth, why·do yeu·yourselves not trust me?
Jn 10:25 "I·declared *it* to·yeu, and yeu·do·not trust. "The
Jn 10:26 But·yet yeu·yourselves do·not trust, for yeu·are not
Jn 16:31 "*So* at·this·moment, do·yeu·trust?
G4100.1 V-PAI-3S πιστεύει (3x)
Jn 12:44 ·one trusting in me, does·not trust in me, but·rather
Rm 14:2 In·fact, one trusts that·he·may·eat all·things, but
1Co 13:7 It·quietly·bears all·things, trusts all·things,
G4100.1 V-PAI-3P πιστεύουσιν (4x)
Jn 6:64 ·are some from·among yeu that do·not trust." For
Jn 16:9 ·failure, in·fact because they·did·not trust in me;
Lk 8:13 have no root, who trust just·for a·season, and·then
Jac 2:19 The demons also trust *that*, and they·shudder.
G4100.1 V-PAM-2S πίστευε (2x)
Lk 8:50 "Do·not be·afraid. Merely trust, and she·shall·be·
Mk 5:36 "Do·not be·afraid, merely trust."
G4100.1 V-PAM-2P πιστεύετε (10x)
Jn 10:37 ·do·not do the works of·my Father, do·not trust me.
Jn 12:36 For·as·long·as yeu·have the light, trust in the light,
Jn 14:1 be·troubled *in* yeur heart. Yeu·trust in God, trust
Jn 14:1 Yeu·trust in God, trust also in me.
Jn 14:11 Trust me that I·myself *am* in the Father, and the
Jn 14:11 *is* in me. But·if·not, trust me on·account·of the
Mt 9:28 says to·them, "Do·yeu·trust that I·am·able to·do
Mk 1:15 has·drawn·near. Yeu·must·repent and trust in the
Mk 11:24 as·yeu·are·praying, trust that yeu·do·receive *them*
1Jn 4:1 Beloved, do·not trust every spirit, but·rather test·
G4100.1 V-PAN πιστεύειν (5x)
Jn 12:39 ·of that, they·were·not able to·trust, because *as*
Lk 24:25 ·ones, and slow in·the heart to·trust on all that the
Rm 15:13 ·all joy and peace in the·one to·trust, for yeu to·
Php 1:29 of·Anointed-One, not merely to·trust in him, but·
1Ti 1:16 ·example for·the·ones about to·trust on him to
G4100.1 V-PAP-ASM πιστεύοντα (1x)
Ac 10:43 do·testify— *that* anyone trusting in him *is* to·
G4100.1 V-PAP-APM πιστεύοντας (5x)
Ac 22:19 in·each·of the gatherings, the·ones trusting on you.
Rm 3:22 all and *is* upon all the·ones trusting, for there·is no
1Pe 1:21 (the·ones through him trusting in God, the·one
1Co 1:21 of·official·proclamation to·save the·ones trusting.
Eph 1:19 toward us, the·ones trusting, according·to the
G4100.1 V-PAP-DSM πιστεύοντι (4x)
Mk 9:23 to·trust, all·things *are* possible to·the·one trusting."
Rm 1:16 power to Salvation to·everyone trusting, both to·
Rm 4:5 ·one not working, but trusting on the·one regarding
Rm 10:4 ·Torah-Law for righteousness to·everyone trusting.
G4100.1 V-PAP-DPM πιστεύουσιν (11x)
Jn 1:12 children of·God, to·the·ones trusting upon his name
Gal 3:22 the promise may·be·given to·the·ones trusting.
Rm 4:24 to·be·reckoned— the·ones trusting on the·one
1Pe 2:7 honor *is* to·yeu, to·the·ones presently·trusting. But
1Th 1:7 ·examples to·all the·ones trusting in Macedonia and
1Th 2:10 ·behaved·ourselves among·yeu, the·ones trusting.
1Th 2:13 which operates also in yeu, the·ones trusting.
2Th 1:10 to·be·marveled at by·all the·ones trusting in that
1Co 14:22 a·sign, not to·the·ones trusting, but·rather to·the
1Co 14:22 ·ones, but·rather for·the·ones trusting.
1Jn 5:13 I·wrote to·yeu, to·the·ones trusting in the name of·
G4100.1 V-PAP-GPM πιστευόντων (3x)

Mt 18:6 one of·these little·ones, the·ones trusting in me, it·
Mk 9:42 one of·the little·ones, the·ones trusting in me, it·is
Rm 4:11 to·be father of·all the·ones trusting *God* through *the*
G4100.1 V-PAP-NSM πιστεύων (24x)
Jn 3:15 in·order·that any one trusting in him should·not
Jn 3:16 in·order·that any one trusting in him should·not
Jn 3:18 The·one trusting in him is·not presently·judged, but
Jn 3:18 but the·one not trusting has·been·judged even·now,
Jn 3:36 "The·one trusting in the Son has eternal life-above,
Jn 5:24 my Redemptive-word and trusting the·one sending me
Jn 6:35 he·should·not hunger, and the·one trusting in me, no
Jn 6:40 observing the Son, and trusting in him, may·have
Jn 6:47 I·say to·yeu, the·one trusting in me has eternal
Jn 7:38 The·one trusting in me, just·as the Scripture declared
Jn 11:25 and the life-above. The·one trusting in me, though
Jn 11:26 And anyone, the·one living and trusting in me, no,
Jn 12:44 and declared, "The·one trusting in me, does·not
Jn 12:46 in·order·that anyone, the·one trusting in me,
Jn 14:12 ·certainly, I·say to·yeu, the·one trusting in me, the
Ac 13:39 everyone trusting is·regarded·as·innocent from
Ac 24:14 ·God my esteemed·Father, trusting in·all the·things
Rm 9:33 ·offense, and any one trusting on him shall·not be·
Rm 10:11 says, '" Everyone trusting on him shall·not be·
1Pe 2:6 *being* dearly·precious; and the·one trusting on him,
1Jn 5:1 Every one trusting that Jesus is the Anointed-One
1Jn 5:5 the world, if·not the·one trusting that Jesus is the
1Jn 5:10 The·one trusting in the Son of·God has the
1Jn 5:10 in himself; the·one not trusting God has·made *God*
G4100.1 V-PAP-NPM πιστεύοντες (8x)
Jn 6:64 who they·are, the·ones not trusting, and who was
Jn 7:39 the Spirit, which the·ones trusting in him were·about
Jn 20:31 of·God; and that trusting, yeu·may·have life-above
Ac 2:44 And all the·ones trusting were in·unison, and they·
Ac 5:14 but *of·the·ones* trusting in·the Lord, even·more
Ac 9:26 all afraid of·him, not trusting that he·was a·disciple.
Mt 21:22 in the prayer while·trusting, yeu·shall·receive."
1Pe 1:8 not clearly·seeing at·this·moment but trusting *him*,
G4100.1 V-PAS-2P πιστεύητε (2x)
Jn 10:38 "But if I·do, though yeu·may·not trust me, trust the
1Jn 5:13 *is* eternal, and in·order·that yeu·may·trust in the
G4100.1 V-IAI-2P ἐπιστεύετε (2x)
Jn 5:46 For if yeu·were·trusting in·Moses, yeu·would be·
Jn 5:46 ·trusting in·Moses, yeu·would be·trusting in·me, for
G4100.1 V-IAI-3P ἐπίστευον (4x)
Jn 7:5 For neither were his brothers trusting in him.
Jn 12:11 were·heading·on·out and were·trusting in Jesus.
Jn 12:37 ·signs before them, they·were·not trusting in him,
Ac 18:8 of·the Corinthians hearing *Paul* were·trusting, and
G4100.1 V-AAI-1S ἐπίστευσα (1x)
2Co 4:13 having·been·written, "'I·trusted, therefore I·spoke
G4100.1 V-AAI-1P ἐπιστεύσαμεν (2x)
Gal 2:16 we·ourselves also trusted in Anointed-One
Rm 13:11 now our Salvation *is* nearer than when we·trusted.
G4100.1 V-AAI-2S ἐπίστευσας (2x)
Lk 1:20 should·occur, because you·did·not trust my words,
Mt 8:13 "Head·on·out; and as you·trusted, *so* be·it·done to·
G4100.1 V-AAI-2P ἐπιστεύσατε (7x)
Lk 20:5 'So·then why did·yeu·not trust him?
Mt 21:25 'So·then why did·yeu·not trust him?
Mt 21:32 way of·righteousness, yet yeu·did·not trust him.
Mk 11:31 'So·then why did·yeu·not trust him?
1Co 3:5 than attendants through whom yeu·trusted, even as
1Co 15:2 except excluding·that yeu·trusted for·no·reason *in·*
1Co 15:11 ·proclaim, and in·this·manner yeu·trusted.
G4100.1 V-AAI-3S ἐπίστευσεν (14x)
Jn 4:50 And the man·of·clay† trusted the word that Jesus
Jn 4:53 And he·himself trusted, and his whole household.
Jn 7:48 the rulers or from·among the Pharisees trust in him?
Jn 12:38 "'O·Yahweh, who trusted *that·which* we·ourselves
Jn 20:8 And he·saw and trusted.
Ac 8:13 And Simon himself also trusted. And after·being·
Ac 13:12 ·happened, the proconsul trusted, being·astounded
Ac 18:8 the director·of·the·gathering, trusted on·the Lord
Gal 3:6 ·as with·AbRaham, *who* "trusted in·Yahweh, and
Rm 4:3 say? "'And AbRaham trusted in·Yahweh, and it·
Rm 4:17 *being* directly·before God whom he·trusted (*who·is*
Rm 4:18 contrary·to expectation, trusted on an·Expectation
Rm 10:16 O·Yahweh, who trusted *that·which* we·ourselves
Jac 2:23 "'And AbRaham trusted in·Yahweh, and it·was·
G4100.1 V-AAI-3P ἐπίστευσαν (22x)
Jn 2:11 And his disciples trusted in him.
Jn 2:22 this to·them. And they·trusted the Scripture and the
Jn 2:23 among the Sacred·Feast, many trusted in his name,
Jn 4:39 Samaritans from·among that city trusted in him on·
Jn 4:41 And many more trusted on·account·of his·own word.
Jn 7:31 And many from·among the crowd trusted in him and
Jn 8:30 ·him speaking these·things, many trusted in him.
Jn 9:18 the Judeans did·not trust concerning him that he·
Jn 10:42 And many trusted in him there.
Jn 11:45 the·things·which Jesus did, trusted in him.
Jn 12:42 from·among the chief·rulers also trusted in him.
Jn 17:8 personally·from you, and they·trusted that you did·
Ac 4:4 of·the·ones hearing the Redemptive-word trusted, and
Ac 8:12 when they·trusted Philippe as·he·was·proclaiming
Ac 9:42 known in all Joppa, and many trusted on the Lord.
Ac 13:48 of·the Lord. And they·trusted (as·many·as were
Ac 17:12 ·fact, many from·among them trusted, and·also not
Ac 17:34 men, being·tightly·joined to·him, trusted, among
Mt 21:32 tax·collectors and the prostitutes did·trust him, but
Mk 16:13 but·neither·even·did those *mourners* trust.
Mk 16:14 they·did·not trust the·ones distinctly·viewing him
Rm 10:14 ·upon *him* in whom they·did·not trust? And how
G4100.1 V-AAM-2S πίστευσον (2x)
Jn 4:21 says to·her, "Woman, trust me, because an·hour is·
Ac 16:31 And they·declared, "Trust on the Lord Jesus
G4100.1 V-AAM-2P πιστεύσατε (1x)
Jn 10:38 yeu·may·not trust me, trust the works in·order·that
G4100.1 V-AAN πιστεῦσαι (7x)
Jn 5:44 How·are yeu·yeurselves able to·trust, receiving glory
Ac 14:1 multitude both of·Jews and·also of·Greeks to·trust.
Ac 15:7 of·the good·news through my mouth, and to·trust.
Heb 11:6 who·is·coming·alongside God to·trust that he·is,
Mt 21:32 did·not eventually have·regret, *so·as* to·trust him.
Mk 9:23 to·him, "If you·are·able to·trust, all·things *are*
2Th 2:11 *from·truth* in·order·for them to·trust the lie,
G4100.1 V-AAP-APM πιστεύσαντας (1x)
Jud 1:5 ·*that* he·completely·destroyed the·ones not trusting.
G4100.1 V-AAP-DPM πιστεύσασιν (2x)
Ac 11:17 also *he·gave* to·us *who·are* already·trusting on the
Mk 16:17 shall·closely·follow the·ones already·trusting: "in
G4100.1 V-AAP-GPM πιστευσάντων (1x)
Ac 4:32 And of·the multitude of·the·ones trusting, the heart
G4100.1 V-AAP-NSF πιστεύσασα (1x)
Lk 1:45 ·blessed *is* the·one trusting that there·shall·be a·
G4100.1 V-AAP-NSM πιστεύσας (2x)
Ac 11:21 turned·back·around to Yahweh trusting *in·Jesus*.
Mk 16:16 "The·one already·trusting and already·being·
G4100.1 V-AAP-NPM πιστεύσαντες (6x)
Jn 20:29 ·blessed *are* the·ones not seeing, and·yet trusting."
Lk 8:12 their hearts, lest trusting, they·should·be·saved.
Ac 19:2 "Did·yeu·receive Holy Spirit after·trusting?" And
Heb 4:3 For the·ones trusting do·enter into the complete·rest
2Th 2:12 ·all may·be·judged, the·ones not trusting the truth,
Eph 1:13 after·trusting, yeu·are·already·officially·sealed
G4100.1 V-AAS-1S πιστεύσω (2x)
Jn 9:36 "Who is·he, Lord, in·order·that I·may·trust in him?
Jn 20:25 ·cast my hand into his side, no, I·may·not trust."
G4100.1 V-AAS-1P πιστεύσωμεν (3x)
Jn 6:30 in·order·that we·may·see and should·trust in·you?
Mk 15:32 the cross in·order·that we·may·see and may·trust."
1Jn 3:23 that we·should·already·trust on·the name of·his
G4100.1 V-AAS-2S πιστεύσῃς (2x)
Jn 11:40 that, if you·should·trust, you·shall·gaze·upon the
Rm 10:9 *is* Lord," and should·trust in your heart that God
G4100.1 V-AAS-2P πιστεύσητε (14x)
Jn 4:48 ·see signs and wonders, no, yeu·may·not trust."
Jn 6:29 is the work of·God, that yeu·should·trust in that·one
Jn 8:24 moral·failures. For unless yeu·should·trust that I
Jn 10:38 in·order·that yeu·may·know, and may·trust, that
Jn 11:15 not there, in·order·that yeu·may·trust; but·yet we·
Jn 13:19 whenever it·should·happen, yeu·may·trust that I
Jn 14:29 ·that, whenever it·should·happen, yeu·may·trust.
Jn 19:35 *what* he·says *is* true, in·order·that yeu may·trust.
Jn 20:31 ·been·written in·order·that yeu·may·trust that Jesus
Lk 22:67 ·should·declare *it* to·yeu, no, yeu·should·not trust.
Ac 13:41 no, yeu·may·not·ever trust, though someone
Mt 24:23 'There *he·is*!' yeu·should·not trust *it*.
Mt 24:26 in the private·chambers,' yeu·should·not trust *it*.
Mk 13:21 'Behold, there *he·is*!' yeu·should·not trust *it*.
G4100.1 V-AAS-3S πιστεύσῃ (3x)
Jn 12:47 my utterances and should·not trust, I·myself do·not
Jn 17:21 "in·order·that the world may·trust that you·yourself
Mk 11:23 but·rather should·trust that the·things·which he·
G4100.1 V-AAS-3P πιστεύσωσιν (3x)
Jn 1:7 Light, in·order·that through him all *men* may·trust.
Jn 11:42 I·declared *it* in·order·that they·may·trust that you
Ac 19:4 to·the People that they·should·trust in the·one who·
G4100.1 V-API-3S ἐπιστεύθη (2x)
2Th 1:10 — because our testimony among yeu was·trusted.
1Ti 3:16 ·proclaimed among Gentiles, is·trusted *upon* in *the*
G4100.1 V-RAI-1S πεπίστευκα (2x)
Jn 11:27 Lord. I·myself have·trusted that you·yourself are
2Ti 1:12 for I·have·seen in·whom I·have·trusted, and I·
G4100.1 V-RAI-1P πεπιστεύκαμεν (2x)
Jn 6:69 And we·ourselves have·trusted and have·known that
1Jn 4:16 ·ourselves have·known and have·trusted the Love
G4100.1 V-RAI-2S πεπίστευκας (1x)
Jn 20:29 ·seen me, you·have·trusted. Supremely·blessed *are*
G4100.1 V-RAI-2P πεπιστεύκατε (1x)
Jn 16:27 ·a·friend·to me, and have·trusted that I·myself
G4100.1 V-RAI-3S πεπίστευκεν (2x)
Jn 3:18 even·now, because he·has·not trusted in the name
1Jn 5:10 a·liar, because he·has·not trusted in the testimony
G4100.1 V-RAP-APM πεπιστευκότας (1x)
Jn 8:31 to *those* Judeans, the·ones having·trusted in·him,
G4100.1 V-RAP-DPM πεπιστευκόσιν (1x)
Ac 18:27 *them* much, the·ones having·trusted through the
G4100.1 V-RAP-GPM πεπιστευκότων (3x)
Ac 19:18 many of·the·ones having·trusted were·*now*·coming
Ac 21:20 ·Judeans there·are, the·ones having·trusted? And
Ac 21:25 the Gentiles having·trusted, we·ourselves
G4100.1 V-RAP-NSM πεπιστευκώς (1x)
Ac 16:34 with·the·whole·household having·trusted in·God.
G4100.1 V-RAP-NPM πεπιστευκότες (2x)
Ac 15:5 of·the Pharisees having·trusted, saying, "It·is·
Tit 3:8 ·that the·ones having·trusted in·God may·have·a·
G4100.1 V-LAI-3P πεπιστεύκεισαν (1x)
Ac 14:23 ·of them to·the Lord, in whom they·had·trusted.
EG4100.1 (1x)
Heb 11:6 that he·is, and *to·trust that* he·comes·to·be an·
G4100.2 V-PPI-3S πιστεύεται (1x)
Rm 10:10 ·*the*·heart, one·is·convinced unto righteousness,
G4100.3 V-FAI-3S πιστεύσει (1x)
Lk 16:11 material·wealth, who shall·entrust to·yeu the true
G4100.3 V-IAI-3S ἐπίστευεν (1x)
Jn 2:24 But Jesus himself was·not entrusting himself to·them
G4100.3 V-API-1S ἐπιστεύθην (2x)
Tit 1:3 ·which I·myself am·entrusted according·to a·full·
1Ti 1:11 ·blessed God, with·which I·myself was·entrusted.
G4100.3 V-API-3P ἐπιστεύθησαν (1x)
Rm 3:2 ·of·all, they·are·entrusted·with the eloquent·words
G4100.3 V-APN πιστευθῆναι (1x)
1Th 2:4 ·proven by God to·be·entrusted with·the good·news,
G4100.3 V-RPI-1S πεπίστευμαι (1x)
1Co 9:17 *of·the grace of·God* has *still* been·entrusted *to·me*.
G4100.3 V-RPI-1S@ πεπίστευμαι (1x)
Gal 2:7 of·the Uncircumcision had·been·entrusted *to·me*,
EG4100.3 (1x)
Gal 2:7 of·the Circumcision *had·been·entrusted* to·Peter

G4101 πιστικός pistikós *adj.* (2x)
Roots:G4102 Compare:G0228 G1103

G4101.2 A-GSF πιστικῆς (2x)
Jn 12:3 ·extremely·valuable ointment of·authentic spikenard,
Mk 14:3 ·expensive ointment of·authentic spikenard. And

G4102 πίστις pístis *n.* (252x)
Roots:G3982 See:G4100 G4103 G0513-1
xLangAlso:H0539

G4102.1 N-NSF πίστις (36x)
Lk 7:50 to the woman, “Your trust has·saved you; traverse
Lk 8:25 “Where is yeur trust?” And being·afraid, they·
Lk 8:48 be·of·good·courage. Your trust has·made you
Lk 17:19 depart. Your trust has·made you safe·and·well.
Lk 18:42 “Receive·your·sight. Your trust has·saved you.”
Lk 22:32 *Simon*, in·order·that your trust should·not cease,
Ac 3:16 *Jesus'* name and the trust (the·one through him)
Heb 11:1 Now trust is a·firm·assurance of·things·being·
Gal 5:6 but·rather trust which·is·itself·operating through
Gal 5:22 kindness, beneficial·goodness, trust,
Mt 9:22 be·of·good·courage; your trust has·made you safe·
Mt 15:28 O woman, great *is* your trust! It·is·done for·you as
Mk 5:34 “Daughter, your trust has·made you safe·and·well.
Mk 10:52 “Head·on·out, your trust has·made you safe·and·
Rm 1:8 of·yeu, that yeur trust is·being·fully·proclaimed in
Rm 4:5 the irreverent as·righteous, his trust is·reckoned for
Rm 4:9 we·say that 'the trust was·reckoned to·AbRaham for
Rm 4:14 *are* heirs, the trust has·been·made·void, and the
Rm 10:17 Consequently, the trust *comes* as·a·result of·
Jac 2:14 have works? *¿!* Is the trust not able to·save him?
Jac 2:17 Even in·this·manner, the trust, provided·that it·
Jac 2:20 man·of·clay†, that the trust, completely·apart·from
Jac 2:22 ·at how the trust was·working·together with·his
Jac 2:22 of·the works, the trust is·made·completely·mature.
Jac 2:26 in·this·manner also, the trust apart·from the works
1Th 1:8 in every place yeur trust toward God has·gone·forth,
2Th 1:3 because yeur trust grows·exceedingly, and the love
2Th 3:2 evil men·of·clay†, for not all·men *have* the trust.
1Co 2:5 in·order·that yeur trust should·not be in *the* wisdom
1Co 12:9 and to·someone·else, trust by the same Spirit, but
1Co 13:13 these three·things continue: Trust, Expectation,
1Co 15:14 *is* empty, and also yeur trust *is* empty.
1Co 15:17 has·not been·awakened, yeur trust *is* futile—
Eph 4:5 one Lord, one trust, one immersion,
1Jn 5:4 victory (the·one overcoming the world): our trust.
Rv 13:10 the patient·endurance and the trust of·the holy·ones

G4102.1 N-ASF πίστιν (55x)
Lk 5:20 And seeing their trust, he·declared to·him, “Man·of·
Lk 7:9 to·yeu, not·even in IsraEl did·I·find so·vast a·trust.”
Lk 17:5 declared to·the Lord, “Add trust to·us.”
Lk 17:6 “If yeu·were·having trust *that·grows* as a·kernel of·
Lk 18:8 ·*back*, shall·he·find then *such* a·trust on the earth?
Ac 14:9 at·him and seeing that he·has trust to·be·saved,
Ac 17:31 after·holding·forth trust to·all *men·of·clay†* after·
Ac 20:21 toward God), and a·trust (the·one toward our
Heb 11:7 an·heir of·a·righteousness according·to trust.
Heb 11:13 These all died according·to trust, not receiving the
Heb 13:7 of·God, whose trust yeu·are·to·attentively·imitate,
Gal 1:23 proclaims·the·good·news, the trust which once he·
Gal 3:23 But before the trust *was* to·come, we·were·
Gal 3:23 in·order·for the impending trust to·be·revealed.
Mt 8:10 to·yeu, not·even in IsraEl did·I·find so·vast a·trust.
Mt 9:2 And upon·seeing their trust, YeShua declared to·the
Mt 9:29 saying, “According·to yeur trust be·it to·yeu.”
Mt 17:20 to·yeu, if yeu·should·have trust *that·grows* as a·
Mt 21:21 to·yeu, if yeu·should·have trust and should·not be·
Mt 23:23 and the mercy, and the trust. “It·is·mandatory to·
Mk 2:5 And Jesus, after·seeing their trust, says to·the
Mk 4:40 ·manner? How·is·it *that* yeu·do·not have trust?”
Mk 11:22 “Have God's *type·of* trust.
Rm 1:17 birthed·from·out of·trust into trust. Just·as it·has·
Rm 3:3 their lack·of·trust fully·nullify the trust of·God?
Rm 14:22 Do·you·yourself have trust? *Then* accordingly,
Jac 2:1 brothers, do·not hold the trust of·our Lord YeShua
Jac 2:14 someone should·say he·has trust but should·not
Jac 2:18 shall·declare, “You have trust, and·I have works.
Jac 2:18 Show me your trust as·a·result of·your works,
Jac 2:18 and·I shall·show you my trust as·a·result of·my
1Pe 1:21 — such·for yeur trust and expectation to·be in
2Pe 1:1 ·obtaining an·equally·valuable trust with·us in *the*
1Th 3:5 ·word in·order to·know yeur trust, lest·somehow the
1Th 3:6 ·proclaiming·good·news to·us of·yeur trust and love
Tit 1:1 — accordingly *for·the* trust of·God's Selected-Ones
Tit 1:4 a·genuine child according·to a·shared trust. Grace,
Tit 2:10 indicating all beneficially·good trust, in·order·that
1Co 13:2 and if·ever I·should·have all the trust, as·such to·
Eph 1:15 after·hearing·of the trust *which·is* pervasive·among
Col 1:4 after·hearing *both* of·yeur trust in Anointed-One
Phm 1:5 hearing of·your love and trust which you·have
1Ti 1:19 holding trust and a·beneficially·good conscience.
1Ti 1:19 Which concerning the trust, some, after·shoving·*it*·
1Ti 5:8 ·the family·members, he·has·denied the trust and is
1Ti 5:12 ·in judgment, because they·set·aside the first trust.
1Ti 6:11 righteousness, devout·reverence, trust, love,
1Ti 6:21 ·*trust*, missed·the·mark concerning the trust. Grace
2Ti 2:18 ·occurred, and they·overturn the trust of·some.
2Ti 2:22 but pursue righteousness, trust, love, peace, with
2Ti 3:8 ·fully·corrupted, disqualified concerning the trust.
2Ti 4:7 ·finished the race·course; I·have·fully·kept the trust.
Rv 2:13 my name and did·not deny my trust, even in the
Rv 2:19 and the service, and the trust, even your patient·
Rv 14:12 the commandments of·God and the trust of·Jesus.

G4102.1 N-DSF πίστει (58x)
Ac 3:16 And at the trust of·his name, *this·trust* stabilized
Ac 6:7 ·sacrifices were·listening·to·and·obeying the trust.
Ac 14:22 exhorting *them* to·continue in·the trust, and how·
Ac 15:9 both us and them, purifying their hearts by·the trust.
Ac 16:5 were·made·solid in·the trust and were·abounding in·
Ac 26:18 the·ones having·been·made·holy by·a·trust, the
Heb 4:2 ·together with·the Trust within·the·ones hearing *it*.
Heb 11:3 By·trust, we·understand the ages to·have·been·
Heb 11:4 By·trust, Abel offered to·God a·much·better
Heb 11:5 By·trust, Enoch was·transferred *such·for* him not
Heb 11:7 By·trust, Noach, after·being·divinely·instructed·
Heb 11:8 By·trust, AbRaham, being·called to·go·forth into
Heb 11:9 By·trust, he·sojourned in the land of·promise as *in*
Heb 11:11 By·trust also, Sarah herself received a·miracle for
Heb 11:17 By·trust, AbRaham, when·being·tried, had·
Heb 11:20 By·trust, YiTsaq blessed Jacob and Esau
Heb 11:21 By·trust, Jacob (when·he·was·dying) blessed
Heb 11:22 By·trust, Joseph (as·he·was·completely·dying)
Heb 11:23 By·trust, Moses (being·born) was·hid three·
Heb 11:24 By·trust, Moses (after·becoming full·grown)
Heb 11:27 By·trust, he·forsook Egypt (not fearing the rage
Heb 11:28 By·trust, he·has·done the Passover and the
Heb 11:29 By·trust, they·crossed the Red Sea as through
Heb 11:30 By·trust, the walls of·Jericho fell·down, being·
Heb 11:31 By·trust, Rachav the prostitute did·not
Gal 2:20 in flesh, I·live in the trust of·the Son of·God, the·
Rm 3:28 *is* to·be·regarded·as·righteous by·a·trust apart·from
Rm 4:19 And not being·weak in·the trust, he·did·not fully·
Rm 4:20 but·rather was·enabled by·the trust, already·giving
Rm 5:2 we·have the embraceable·access by·the trust into this
Rm 11:20 and you stand in·the trust. Do·not·be arrogant,
Rm 14:1 ·receive the·one being·weak in·the trust, *though* not
Jac 1:6 But let·him·request in trust, hesitating *for* not·even·
Jac 2:5 of·this world *to·be* wealthy in trust and *to·be* heirs of·
Jud 1:3 ·for the trust already·being·handed·down only·once
Jud 1:20 building·up yeurselves in·yeur holy trust, *yeu* who·
Php 1:27 struggling·together for·the trust of·the good·news,
Php 3:9 from·out of·God *based* upon the trust)—
1Pe 5:9 ·stand·up·against, solid in·the trust, having·seen
2Pe 1:5 along·with yeur trust: Courageous·Moral·Excellence
2Th 2:13 in renewed·holiness of·Spirit and in·trust of·truth,
Tit 1:13 ·that they·may·be·healthy·and·sound in the trust,
Tit 2:2 self-controlled, healthy·and·sound in·the trust, in·the
Tit 3:15 ·ones having·affection·for us in the trust. The grace
1Co 16:13 Stand·fast in the trust! “" Be·manly! Become·
2Co 1:24 of·yeur joy— for by·the trust, yeu·stand.
2Co 8:7 ·as yeu·abound in everything, in·trust, and in·word,
2Co 13:5 whether yeu·are in the trust. Examine·and·verify
Col 1:23 yeu·persist in·the trust, having·been·founded and
Col 2:7 and being·made·steadfast in the trust, just·as yeu·
1Ti 1:2 To·TimoThy, a·genuine child in trust. Grace, mercy,
1Ti 1:4 than God's estate·management, the·one in trust.
1Ti 2:7 lie)— an·instructor of·Gentiles in trust and truth.
1Ti 2:15 *such women* should·continue in trust and love and
1Ti 3:13 boldness·of·speech·with·clarity in *the* trust, the·one
1Ti 4:12 in love, in spirit, in trust, *and* in moral·cleanliness.
2Ti 1:13 you·heard personally·from me, in trust and love,
2Ti 3:10 upbringing, *my* determined·purpose, *my* trust, *my*

G4102.1 N-GSF πίστεως (95x)
Ac 6:5 Stephen, a·man full of·trust and of·Holy Spirit, and·
Ac 6:8 Now Stephen, full of·trust and power, was·doing
Ac 11:24 and full of·Holy Spirit and trust. And an·ample
Ac 13:8 ·thoroughly·turn the proconsul away·from the trust.
Ac 14:27 that he·opened·up *the* door of·trust to·the Gentiles.
Ac 24:24 he·heard him concerning the trust in Anointed-One
Heb 6:1 from dead works, and of·trust toward God,
Heb 6:12 of·the·ones *who* through trust and long-suffering
Heb 10:22 a·true heart in full·assurance of·trust, the hearts
Heb 10:38 the righteous·man shall·live as·a·result of·trust,
Heb 10:39 but·rather of·a·trust to·a·preservation of·*the*·soul
Heb 11:6 But apart·from trust, *it·is* impossible to·fully·
Heb 11:33 who through trust strenuously·subdued kingdoms,
Heb 11:39 ·being·attested·to through the trust, did·not
Heb 12:2 Initiator and Complete·Finisher of·the Trust— who
Gal 2:16 but·only through a·trust of·YeShua Anointed, we·
Gal 2:16 ·righteous as·a·result of·trust of·Anointed-One and
Gal 3:2 of·Torah-Law, or as·a·result of·a·hearing of·trust?
Gal 3:5 of·Torah-Law, or as·a·result of·a·hearing of·trust?
Gal 3:7 that the·ones birthed·from·out of·trust, the·same are
Gal 3:8 birthed·from·out of·trust, announced·the·good·news·
Gal 3:9 ·ones birthed·from·out of·trust are·blessed together
Gal 3:11 “the righteous·one shall·live as·a·result of·trust.”
Gal 3:12 the Torah-Law is·not as·a·result of·trust, but·rather,
Gal 3:14 ·receive the promise of·the Spirit through the trust.
Gal 3:22 ·order·that, as·a·result of·trust in·YeShua Anointed
Gal 3:24 ·may·be·regarded·as·righteous as·a·result of·trust.
Gal 3:25 But with·the Trust coming, we·are no·longer under
Gal 3:26 the·Sons of·God through the trust in Anointed-One
Gal 5:5 an·expectation of·righteousness as·a·result of·trust.
Gal 6:10 especially toward the family·members of·the trust.
Rm 1:5 for an·attentive·obedience of·trust among all the
Rm 1:12 among yeu through the mutual trust, both of·yeu
Rm 1:17 is·revealed, birthed·from·out of·trust into trust.
Rm 1:17 the righteous·man shall·live as·a·result of·trust.”
Rm 3:22 God's righteousness through trust of·Jesus Anointed
Rm 3:25 ·for favorable·forgiveness through the trust in his
Rm 3:26 the·one birthed·from·out of·a·trust of·Jesus
Rm 3:27 ·indeed, but·rather on·account·of a·Law of·Trust.
Rm 3:30 *the* Circumcision as·a·result of·trust and *the*
Rm 3:30 of·trust and *the* Uncircumcision through the trust.
Rm 3:31 *the* Torah-Law through the trust? May·it·never
Rm 4:11 an·official·seal of·the righteousness of·the trust—
Rm 4:12 in the uncircumcised trust of·our father AbRaham.
Rm 4:13 , but·rather *is* through a·righteousness of·trust.
Rm 4:16 *righteousness is* as·a·result of·trust, in·order·that
Rm 4:16 *who·is* birthed·from·out of·AbRaham's trust, who is
Rm 5:1 ·regarded·as·righteous as·a·result of·trust, we·have
Rm 9:30 the righteousness birthed·from·out of·trust.
Rm 9:32 *they·pursued it* not as·a·result of·trust, but·rather
Rm 10:6 the·one birthed·from·out of·trust, says *it* in·this·
Rm 10:8 utterance of·the trust which we·officially·proclaim)
Rm 12:3 ·as God imparted to·each·man a·measure of·trust.
Rm 12:6 *then* according·to the proportion of·the trust;
Rm 14:23 because *it·is* not from·out of·trust. Now anything
Rm 14:23 that *is* not from·out of·trust is moral·failure.
Rm 16:26 Gentiles— for an·attentive·obedience of·trust),
Jac 1:3 ·testing of·yeur trust accomplishes patient·endurance.

Jac 2:24 ·as·righteous, and not as·a·result of·trust merely.
Jac 5:15 ·well-being *along* with·the trust shall·save the·one
Php 1:25 yeur continual·advancement and joy of·the trust,
Php 2:17 and public·service of·yeur trust, I·do·rejoice and·
Php 3:9 but·rather the·one through a·trust of·Anointed-One
1Pe 1:5 by God's power through trust for a·Salvation ready
1Pe 1:7 in·order·that the proof·testing of·yeur trust (*being*
1Pe 1:9 subsequently·obtaining the end of·yeur trust, *the*
1Th 1:3 Father (*yeur* work of·the trust, and the wearisome·
1Th 3:2 yeu and to·comfort yeu concerning yeur trust,
1Th 3:7 we·are·comforted over yeu through yeur trust.
1Th 3:10 to·completely·reform the lackings of·yeur trust.
1Th 5:8 ·with *the* full·chest·armor of·trust and love, and
2Th 1:4 on·behalf of·yeur patient·endurance and trust in all
2Th 1:11 ·beneficial·goodness and work of·trust in power,
2Co 1:24 Not because we·lord·over yeur trust, but·rather are
2Co 4:13 the same spirit of·the trust, according·to·the·one
2Co 5:7 for we·presently·walk through trust, not through
2Co 10:15 ·expectation (with·yeur trust being·grown·further)
Eph 2:8 ·are having·been·saved through the trust. And this
Eph 3:12 ·access with confidence through trust of·him.
Eph 3:17 in yeur hearts through the trust, having·been·rooted
Eph 4:13 ·attain unto the oneness of·the trust, and of·the
Eph 6:16 after·taking·up the tall·shield of·the trust (with
Eph 6:23 brothers, and love with trust from Father God and
Col 2:5 and the stability of·yeur trust in Anointed-One.
Col 2:12 *with·him* through the trust of·the effective·work of·
Phm 1:6 that the fellowship of·your trust may·become active
1Ti 1:5 conscience, and of·a·trust without·hypocrisy—
1Ti 1:14 ·evermore·above·and·beyond with trust and love,
1Ti 3:9 holding the Mystery of·the trust in a·pure conscience
1Ti 4:1 some shall·withdraw·from the trust, giving·heed to·
1Ti 4:6 ·by the Redemptive-words of·the trust and of·the good
1Ti 6:10 They·are·utterly·led·astray from the trust, and they·
1Ti 6:12 ·in the good striving of·the trust, grab·hold of·the
2Ti 1:5 ·taking recollection of·the trust without·hypocrisy in
2Ti 3:15 you wise to Salvation through a·trust, the·one in

EG4102.1 (8x)
Ac 3:16 the trust of·his name, *this·trust* stabilized this·man
Ac 26:18 having·been·made·holy by·a·trust, the *trust* in me.
Heb 11:4 and through the·same *trust*, *although* already·
Gal 3:6 *It·is of·trust* just·as with·AbRaham, *who* "trusted
Rm 3:24 *yet those trusting in Jesus are now* being·regarded·
1Co 9:5 ·lead·about a·wife (a·sister *in·the Trust*) even·as also
1Co 15:58 unstirrable·from *the Trust*, always abounding in
1Ti 6:21 who·are·making·a·profession *of·trust*, missed·the·

G4103 πιστός pistós *adj.* (68x)
Roots:G3982 See:G4102

G4103.1 A-NSM πιστός (32x)
Lk 12:42 "Who then is the trustworthy and prudent estate·
Lk 16:10 "The·one *being* trustworthy with very·little is also
Lk 16:10 with very·little is also trustworthy with much. And
Lk 19:17 Because you·became trustworthy in very·little, be
Heb 2:17 ·merciful and trustworthy High·Priest in·the·things
Heb 3:5 And in·fact, Moses *was* trustworthy in all his house
Heb 10:23 without·slouching (for trustworthy *is* the·one
Mt 24:45 "Who then is the trustworthy and prudent slave
Mt 25:21 slave! You·were trustworthy over a·few·things, I·
Mt 25:23 slave! You·were trustworthy over a·few·things, I·
1Th 5:24 Trustworthy *is* the·one calling yeu forth, who also
2Th 3:3 But trustworthy is the Lord, who shall·firmly·
Tit 3:8 Trustworthy *is* the saying.
1Co 1:9 God *is* trustworthy, through whom yeu·are·called·
1Co 4:2 that each·man should·be·found trustworthy.
1Co 7:25 ·shown·mercy from *the* Lord to·be trustworthy.
1Co 10:13 But God *is* trustworthy, who shall·not let yeu to·
2Co 1:18 But God *is* trustworthy, because our
Eph 6:21 the beloved brother and trustworthy attendant in *the*
Col 1:7 fellow·slave, who is a·trustworthy attendant on·yeur
Col 4:7 *He·is* a·beloved brother, a·trustworthy attendant, and
1Ti 1:15 The saying *is* trustworthy and deserving of·all full·
1Ti 3:1 Trustworthy *is* the saying: "If any·man longingly·
1Ti 4:9 Trustworthy *is* the saying and worthy of·all full·
2Ti 2:11 Trustworthy *is* the saying: "For if we·died·together
2Ti 2:13 ·trust, that·one still·remains trustworthy; he·is·not
1Jn 1:9 our moral·failures, he·is trustworthy and righteous
Rv 1:5 Jesus Anointed, *who·is* the trustworthy witness, *and*
Rv 2:10 ten days. Become trustworthy even·unto death, and
Rv 2:13 in which AntiPas *was* my trustworthy martyr, who
Rv 3:14 the Sure·One,·the·Amen, the trustworthy and true
Rv 19:11 upon it *was* being·called Trustworthy and True,

G4103.1 A-NPF πιστοί (5x)
Lk 16:11 ·then, if yeu·did·not become trustworthy with the
Lk 16:12 ·did·not become trustworthy with another·man's
Rv 17:14 *are* called·forth, and Selected, and trustworthy."
Rv 21:5 because these words are true and trustworthy."
Rv 22:6 "These words *are* trustworthy and true." And

G4103.1 A-VSM πιστέ (2x)
Mt 25:21 ·done, O·beneficially·good and trustworthy slave!
Mt 25:23 ·done, O·beneficially·good and trustworthy slave!

G4103.1 A-ASM πιστόν (3x)
Heb 3:2 being trustworthy to·the·one producing him, as also
Heb 11:11 ·resolutely·considered *him* trustworthy, the·one
1Ti 1:12 ·resolutely·considered me trustworthy, placing·me

G4103.1 A-ASF πιστήν (1x)
Ac 16:15 yeu·have·judged me to·be trustworthy to·the Lord,

G4103.1 A-ASN πιστόν (1x)
1Co 4:17 is my beloved child, and trustworthy in *the* Lord,

G4103.1 A-APF πιστάς (1x)
1Ti 3:11 *being* sober-minded *and* trustworthy in all·things.

G4103.1 A-APN πιστά (2x)
Ac 13:34 ·shall·give to·yeu the trustworthy, Divine·Promises
Tit 1:6 of·one wife, having trustworthy children not in legal·

G4103.1 A-DSM πιστῷ (2x)
1Pe 4:19 beneficial·well·doing, as to·a·trustworthy Creator.
Col 4:9 with·Onesimus, the trustworthy and beloved

G4103.1 A-DPM πιστοῖς (2x)
Col 1:2 ·ones in Colossae, holy and trustworthy brothers in
2Ti 2:2 ·of these·things to·trustworthy men·of·clay† who

G4103.1 A-GSM πιστοῦ (2x)
1Pe 5:12 Through Silvanus (the trustworthy brother as·how
Tit 1:9 ·to the trustworthy Redemptive-word according·to the

EG4103.1 (1x)
Heb 3:2 him, as also Moses *was trustworthy* in all his house.

G4103.2 A-NSM πιστός (1x)
Jn 20:27 And do·not be distrusting, but·rather trusting."

G4103.2 A-NPF πιστοί (1x)
Ac 10:45 *the* Circumcision trusting *in·Jesus* were·astonished,

G4103.2 A-DSM πιστῷ (1x)
Gal 3:9 are·blessed together with·the trusting of·AbRaham.

G4103.2 A-DPM πιστοῖς (1x)
1Ti 4:3 for·the·ones trusting and having·fully·known the

G4103.3 A-NSM πιστός (1x)
1Ti 5:16 If anyone (a·man·that·trusts or a·woman·that·trusts)

G4103.3 A-NSF πιστή (1x)
1Ti 5:16 (a·man·that·trusts or a·woman·that·trusts) has

G4103.3 A-NPF πιστοί (1x)
1Ti 6:2 *to·them*, because they·are ones·that·trust and *are*

G4103.3 A-APM πιστούς (1x)
1Ti 6:2 the·ones having masters that·trust·*in·Jesus*, do·not

G4103.3 A-DSM-HEB πιστῷ (1x)
2Co 6:15 portion has·one·that·trusts with a·non-trusting·one

G4103.3 A-DPM πιστοῖς (1x)
Eph 1:1 in Ephesus, and to·those·that·trust in Anointed-One

G4103.3 A-GSF πιστῆς (1x)
Ac 16:1 of·a·certain Jewish woman (one·that·trusts), but his·

G4103.3 A-GPM πιστῶν (2x)
1Ti 4:10 of·all men·of·clay†, especially of·those·that·trust.
1Ti 4:12 become a·model·example of·the ones·that·trust, in

G4103.4 A-ASN πιστόν (1x)
3Jn 1:5 Beloved·man, trustworthily do·you·do whatever

G4104 πιστόω pistóō *v.* (1x)
Roots:G4103 See:G4100

G4104 V-API-2S ἐπιστώθης (1x)
2Ti 3:14 and are·assured·of, having·personally·known from

G4105 πλανάω planáō *v.* (39x)
Roots:G4106 Compare:G0538 G5574 See:G0635

G4105.2 V-PPP-NPM πλανώμενοι (1x)
Heb 11:38 worthy), being·wanderers in barren·wildernesses

G4105.3 V-PAP-GPM πλανώντων (1x)
1Jn 2:26 concerning the·ones who·are·leading yeu astray.

G4105.3 V-PPI-2P πλανᾶσθε (2x)
Mk 12:24 on·account·of this·thing *that* yeu·are·led·astray, *in*
Mk 12:27 Accordingly, yeu are·largely led·astray."

G4105.3 V-PPI-3P πλανῶνται (1x)
Heb 3:10 'Always, they·are·led·astray in·*their*·heart, and

G4105.3 V-PPM-2P πλανᾶσθε (1x)
Mt 22:29 to·them, "Yeu·are·led·astray, not having·seen the

G4105.3 V-PPN πλανᾶσθαι (1x)
Rv 2:20 ·prophetess, to·instruct and to·lead·astray my slaves

G4105.3 V-PPP-ASN πλανώμενον (1x)
Mt 18:12 the mountains, *and* seek the·one being·led·astray?

G4105.3 V-PPP-DPM πλανωμένοις (1x)
Heb 5:2 ·the·ones being·ignorant and being·led·astray, since

G4105.3 V-PPP-NPN πλανώμενα (1x)
1Pe 2:25 For yeu·were as sheep being·led·astray, but·yet are

G4105.3 V-API-3P ἐπλανήθησαν (2x)
2Pe 2:15 the straight way; they·are·led·astray, following·out
Rv 18:23 ·poisonous·drugs, all the nations were·led·astray.

G4105.3 V-APS-3S πλανηθῇ (2x)
Mt 18:12 them should·be·led·astray, does·he·not·indeed
Jac 5:19 if anyone among yeu should·be·led·astray from the

G4105.3 V-RPP-DPN πεπλανημένοις (1x)
Mt 18:13 ninety-nine, the·ones not having·been·led·astray.

G4105.4 V-FAI-3P πλανήσουσιν (3x)
Mt 24:5 'I AM the Anointed-One,' and shall·deceive many.
Mt 24:11 shall·be·awakened and shall·deceive many.
Mk 13:6 'I AM *the Anointed-One*,' and shall·deceive many.

G4105.4 V-PAI-1P πλανῶμεν (1x)
1Jn 1:8 we·do·not have moral·failure, we·deceive ourselves,

G4105.4 V-PAI-3S πλανᾷ (2x)
Jn 7:12 "No, but·rather he·deceives the crowd."
Rv 13:14 and it·deceives the·ones residing on the earth

G4105.4 V-PAM-3S πλανάτω (1x)
1Jn 3:7 Dear·children, let not·even·one·man deceive yeu.

G4105.4 V-PAP-NSM πλανῶν (2x)
Rv 12:9 the Adversary-Accuser, the·one deceiving all The
Rv 20:10 the Slanderer, the·one deceiving them, was·cast

G4105.4 V-PAP-NPM πλανῶντες (1x)
2Ti 3:13 more·wicked·thing, deceiving and being·deceived.

G4105.4 V-PPM-2P πλανᾶσθε (4x)
Gal 6:7 Do·not be·deceived; God is·not ridiculed, for
Jac 1:16 Do·not be·deceived, my beloved brothers.
1Co 6:9 inherit God's kingdom? Do·not be·deceived! *No*,
1Co 15:33 Do·not·be deceived. "Bad influences corrupt fine

G4105.4 V-PPP-NPM πλανώμενοι (2x)
Tit 3:3 stupid, obstinate, being·deceived, being·slaves to·
2Ti 3:13 more·wicked·thing, deceiving and being·deceived.

G4105.4 V-AAI-3S ἐπλάνησεν (1x)
Rv 19:20 of·it, with which he·deceived the·ones receiving

G4105.4 V-AAN πλανῆσαι (2x)
Mt 24:24 ·as, if possible, to·deceive even the Selected-Ones
Rv 20:8 and shall·go·forth to·deceive the nations, the·ones in

G4105.4 V-AAS-3S πλανήσῃ (3x)
Mt 24:4 "Look·out *that* not anyone should·deceive yeu.
Mk 13:5 "Look·out lest anyone should·deceive yeu.
Rv 20:3 him, in·order·that he·should·not deceive the nations

G4105.4 V-APS-2P πλανηθῆτε (1x)
Lk 21:8 "Look·out, *that* yeu·may·not be·deceived, for many

G4105.4 V-RPI-2P πεπλάνησθε (1x)
Jn 7:47 "¿!·Have even yeu·yeurselves been·deceived?

G4106 πλάνη plánē *n.* (10x)
Roots:G4108 Compare:G0539

G4106.2 N-GSF πλάνης (1x)
2Th 2:11 them an·effective deviation *from·truth* in·order·for

G4106.3 N-NSF πλάνη (1x)
Mt 27:64 and the last error shall·be worse·than the first.

G4106.3 N-DSF πλάνῃ (3x)
Jud 1:11 ·out the error of·BalaAm for·a·payment·of·service,
2Pe 2:18 ·from the·ones conducting·themselves in error.
2Pe 3:17 ·together with·the error of·the unscrupulous·men,
G4106.3 N-GSF πλάνης (3x)
Rm 1:27 the due·payback which is·mandatory·for their error.
Jac 5:20 ·disqualified·man from·out of·*the*·error of·his way
1Jn 4:6 we·know the spirit of·truth and the spirit of·error.
G4106.4 N-GSF πλάνης (2x)
1Th 2:3 exhortation *was* not birthed·from·out of·deceit, nor
Eph 4:14 shrewd·cunning pertaining·to the trickery of·deceit.

G4107 πλανήτης planḗtēs *n.* (1x)
Roots:G4108 Compare:G4009-2
G4107.2 N-NPM πλανῆται (1x)
Jud 1:13 ·upon their·own shame, erratic·wandering stars—

G4108 πλάνος plánôs *adj.* (5x)
See:G2965
G4108.4 A-NSM πλάνος (2x)
Mt 27:63 ·of that thing the impostor declared *while·he·was*
2Jn 1:7 This is the impostor and the adversary·of·the·
G4108.4 A-NPM πλάνοι (2x)
2Co 6:8 and good·reputation, as impostors and·yet true,
2Jn 1:7 Because many impostors entered into the world, the·
G4108.4 A-DPM πλάνοις (1x)
1Ti 4:1 the trust, giving·heed to·impostrous spirits and to·

G4109 πλάξ pláx *n.* (3x)
Roots:G4111
xLangEquiv:H3871
G4109 N-NPF πλάκες (1x)
Heb 9:4 ·one blossoming), and the tablets of·the covenant.
G4109 N-DPF πλαξίν (2x)
2Co 3:3 ·living God, not on tablets of·stone, but·rather on
2Co 3:3 of·stone, but·rather on fleshy tablets of·heart.

G4110 πλάσμα plásma *n.* (1x)
Roots:G4111 See:G4112 G4109
G4110 N-NSN πλάσμα (1x)
Rm 9:20 God? ¿!·Shall the·thing molded state to·the·one

G4111 πλάσσω plássō *v.* (2x)
See:G4110 G4109
G4111 V-AAP-DSM πλάσαντι (1x)
Rm 9:20 ·thing molded state to·the·one already·molding *it*,
G4111 V-API-3S ἐπλάσθη (1x)
1Ti 2:13 For Adam was·molded first, then Eve.

G4112 πλαστός plastós *adj.* (1x)
Roots:G4111 See:G4110
G4112.3 A-DPM πλαστοῖς (1x)
2Pe 2:3 ·commercially·exploit yeu with·fabricated sayings,

G4113 πλατεῖα platêîa *n.* (9x)
Roots:G4116 Compare:G4505 G1353-1 See:G4115
xLangEquiv:H7339 xLangAlso:H2351
G4113.2 N-NSF πλατεῖα (1x)
Rv 21:21 And the broad·street of·the CITY *was* pure gold, as
G4113.2 N-APF πλατείας (3x)
Lk 10:10 ·out into the same broad·streets, yeu·must·declare,
Lk 14:21 Go·out quickly into the broad·streets and alleyways
Ac 5:15 the sick in·each·of the broad·streets, and to·lay *them*
G4113.2 N-DPF πλατείαις (2x)
Lk 13:26 of·you, and you·instructed in our broad·streets.'
Mt 12:19 ·shall any·man hear his voice in the broad·streets.
G4113.2 N-GSF πλατείας (2x)
Rv 11:8 corpses *shall·lay* in the broad·street of·the great City
Rv 22:2 In *the* midst of·its broad·street, and on·both sides of·
G4113.2 N-GPF πλατειῶν (1x)
Mt 6:5 and in the corners of·the broad·streets to·pray so·that

G4114 πλάτος plátôs *n.* (4x)
Roots:G4116 Compare:G2148-1
xLangEquiv:H7341
G4114 N-NSN πλάτος (3x)
Eph 3:18 ·all the holy·ones what *is* the breadth, and length,
Rv 21:16 is·as·vast and as·long·as the breadth. And with·the
Rv 21:16 The length and the breadth and its height are equal
G4114 N-ASN πλάτος (1x)
Rv 20:9 And they·walked·up on the breadth of·the earth, and

G4115 πλατύνω platýnō *v.* (3x)
Roots:G4116 See:G4113
xLangEquiv:H7337
G4115.1 V-PAI-3P πλατύνουσιν (1x)
Mt 23:5 by·the men·of·clay†. "They·broaden their tefillin
G4115.2 V-APM-2P πλατύνθητε (1x)
2Co 6:13 : Yeu·yeurselves, broaden·wide·open *yeur hearts*
G4115.2 V-RPI-3S πεπλάτυνται (1x)
2Co 6:11 to yeu; our heart has·been·broadened·wide·open.

G4116 πλατύς platýs *adj.* (2x)
Roots:G4111 Compare:G5561 G2149 See:G4113
G4114 G4115 xLangAlso:H7342
G4116.2 A-NSF πλατεῖα (1x)
Mt 7:13 obstructed·and·narrow gate, because broad *is* the
EG4116.2 (1x)
Ac 27:41 where·two·seas·met *producing a·broad sand·bar*,

G4117 πλέγμα plégma *n.* (1x)
Roots:G4120 Compare:G1708
G4117.2 N-DPN πλέγμασιν (1x)
1Ti 2:9 Not with braids·of·hair, or gold, or pearls, or

G4118 πλεῖστος plêîstôs *adj.* (3x)
Roots:G4183
G4118.1 A-NSM πλεῖστος (1x)
Mt 21:8 And the very·large crowd spread·out their·own
G4118.2 A-ASN πλεῖστον (1x)
1Co 14:27 *let·it·be* two or at·the most three·men, and a·
G4118.3 A-NPF πλεῖσται (1x)
Mt 11:20 cities in which the large·majority of·his miracles

G4119 πλείων plêíōn *adj.* (61x)
πλεῖον plêîōn [neuter]
πλέον plêôn
Roots:G4183 Compare:G4080 See:G4133
G4119.ª A-NPM-C πλείονες (1x)
Heb 7:23 And, in·fact, many·in·number are the·ones
G4119.1 A-NPM-C πλείους (1x)
Jn 4:41 And many more trusted on·account·of his·own word.
G4119.1 A-ASM-C πλείονα (1x)
Jn 15:2 ·and·purifies it, in·order·that it·may·bear more fruit.
G4119.1 A-ASN-C πλεῖον (3x)
Lk 7:42 declare *to·me*, which of·them shall·love him more?"
Lk 7:43 *the·one* to·whom he·graciously·forgave the more."
2Ti 2:16 ·continually·advance toward more irreverence.
G4119.1 A-APM-C πλείονας (1x)
1Co 9:19 I·may·gain *all* the more *brothers in·Anointed-One*.
G4119.1 A-APN-C πλείονα (1x)
Mt 20:10 assumed that they·shall·receive more, yet they
G4119.1 A-GPN-C πλειόνων (1x)
Lk 11:53 him to·speak·off-hand concerning more·things,
EG4119.1 (4x)
Mt 13:12 ·utilizes·what·he·has, to·him *more* shall·be·given,
Mt 25:29 ·utilizing·what·he·has, *more* shall·be·given, and
Mk 2:3 Then *more* come to him, bringing a·paralyzed·man
Mk 4:25 ·utilize·what·he·has, to·him *more* shall·be·given,
G4119.2 A-ASF-C πλείονα (1x)
Heb 11:4 Abel offered to·God a·much·better sacrifice than
G4119.3 A-NPM-C πλείονες (1x)
Ac 28:23 a·day for·him, many·more were·coming alongside
G4119.3 A-APM-C πλείονας (3x)
Ac 27:20 ·of·stars appearing over many·more days, and
Php 1:14 And many·more of·the brothers in *the* Lord,
2Co 9:2 and from·out of·yeur zeal, it·stirred·up many·more.
G4119.3 A-APF-C πλείους (3x)
Ac 13:31 was·gazed·upon over many·more days by·the·ones
Ac 21:10 And with·us still·staying·over *for* many·more days,
Ac 25:14 as they·were·lingering there *for* many·more days,
G4119.3 A-DPM-C πλείοσιν (1x)
Ac 2:40 And with·many other words, he·was·thoroughly·
G4119.3 A-GPN-C πλειόνων (2x)
Ac 24:17 "And after many·more years, I·came·openly doing
2Co 4:15 grace through the many·more *occasions*, the
G4119.4 A-NPM-C πλείους (3x)
Ac 19:32 And the majority had·not personally·known for·
Ac 27:12 ·for wintering·in, the majority placed counsel to·
1Co 15:6 from·among whom the majority remain unto this·
G4119.4 A-DPM-C πλείοσιν (1x)
1Co 10:5 But·yet with the majority of·them, God did·not
G4119.4 A-GPM-C πλειόνων (1x)
2Co 2:6 public·penalty, the·one *inflicted* by the majority.
G4119.5 A-NSN-C πλεῖον (4x)
Lk 9:13 "Among·us there·are not more than five loaves·of·
Lk 12:23 "The soul is more·than the physical·nourishment,
Mt 6:25 ·indeed the soul more·than the physical·nourishment
Mk 12:33 as himself, is more·than all the burnt·offerings
G4119.5 A-NPM-C πλείους (2x)
Ac 23:13 And there·were more·than forty·men having·made
Ac 23:21 who·lay·in·wait·for him *are* more·than forty men,
G4119.5 A-NPF-C πλείους (1x)
Ac 24:11 to·know that there·are not more than twelve days
G4119.5 A-ASF-C πλείονα (1x)
Heb 3:3 ·and·constructing the house has more honor *than the*
G4119.5 A-ASN-C πλεῖον (5x)
Jn 21:15 of·Jonah, do·you·love me more·than these·things?
Lk 3:13 "Exact not·one·bit more·than the·thing directly
Lk 21:3 helplessly·poor widow cast *in* more·than them·all.
Mt 5:20 righteousness should·abound more·than *that* of·the
Mk 12:43 ·poor widow has·cast·in more·than all the·ones
G4119.5 A-APM-C πλείονας (2x)
Jn 4:1 "Jesus makes and immerses more disciples than John,
Mt 21:36 he·dispatched other slaves more·than at·the first,
G4119.5 A-APF-C πλείους (2x)
Ac 25:6 after·lingering·awhile among them *for* more than ten
Mt 26:53 and he·shall·present to·me more than twelve
G4119.5 A-APN-C πλείονα (2x)
Jn 7:31 ·come, ¿! shall·he·do more miraculous·signs than
Rv 2:19 even the last·ones *are* more·than the first·ones.
G4119.5 A-GSF-C πλείονος (1x)
Heb 3:3 ·man has·been·counted·worthy of·more glory than
G4119.5 A-GPN-C πλειόνων (1x)
Ac 4:22 the man·of·clay† was more·than forty years·of·age,
EG4119.5 (1x)
Mt 6:25 ·nourishment, and the body *more·than* the apparel?
G4119.7 A-ASN-C πλέον (1x)
Ac 15:28 ·put on·yeu not·one·bit·of a·larger burden besides
G4119.8 A-NSN-C πλεῖον (4x)
Lk 11:31 and behold, one·of·larger·stature·than Solomon *is*
Lk 11:32 and behold, one·of·larger·stature·than Jonah *is*
Mt 12:41 and behold, one·of·larger·stature·than Jonah *is*
Mt 12:42 behold, one·of·a·larger·stature·than Solomon *is*
G4119.9 A-ASM-C πλείονα (1x)
Ac 18:20 ·them asking *him* to·abide a·longer time with them,
G4119.9 A-ASN-C πλεῖον (1x)
Ac 20:9 ·Paul discussing *matters* over a·longer·*period*, *and*
G4119.10 A-ASN-C πλεῖον (3x)
Ac 4:17 ·that it·may·not disseminate any·further among the
Ac 24:4 ·that I·should·not·be any·further hindrance upon
2Ti 3:9 they·shall·not continually·advance any·further, for

G4120 πλέκω plékō *v.* (3x)
Compare:G1707 See:G1708 G4117
G4120 V-AAP-NPM πλέξαντες (3x)
Jn 19:2 And the soldiers, after·braiding a·victor's·crown out
Mt 27:29 And after·braiding a·victor's·crown out·of·thorns,
Mk 15:17 ·cloak. And after·braiding a·thorny victor's·crown

G4121 πλεονάζω plêônázō *v.* (9x)
Roots:G4119 Compare:G0837 G4052
G4121.2 V-PAI-3S πλεονάζει (1x)
2Th 1:3 one of·yeu all, toward one·another, increases·more,
G4121.2 V-PAP-ASM πλεονάζοντα (1x)
Php 4:17 ·seek the fruit, the·one increasing·more into yeur
G4121.2 V-PAP-NPN πλεονάζοντα (1x)
2Pe 1:8 and increasing·more·*and·more*, it·fully·establishes
G4121.2 V-AAI-3S ἐπλεόνασεν (1x)
Rm 5:20 But where Moral·Failure increased·more, Grace
G4121.2 V-AAO-3S πλεονάσαι (1x)

1Th 3:12 the Lord make yeu to·increase·more and abound
G4121.2 V-AAS-3S πλεονάσῃ (2x)
Rm 5:20 in·order·that the trespass may·increase·more. But
Rm 6:1 ·Failure in·order·that Grace may·increase·more?
G4121.3 V-AAP-NSF πλεονάσασα (1x)
2Co 4:15 in·order·that, *by* the ever·increasing grace through
G4121.4 V-AAI-3S ἐπλεόνασεν (1x)
2Co 8:15 "The·one did·not increase·to the much, and the·

G4122 πλεον•εκτέω plêônêktéō *v.* (5x)
Roots:G4123 Compare:G4851 G2770 G1710 See:G4124
G4122.3 V-PAN πλεονεκτεῖν (1x)
1Th 4:6 *for·yeu* not to·overstep and to·swindle his brother in
G4122.3 V-AAI-1S ἐπλεονέκτησα (1x)
2Co 12:17 ¿!·Did I·swindle yeu through any of·them whom
G4122.3 V-AAI-1P ἐπλεονεκτήσαμεν (1x)
2Co 7:2 no·one·at·all, *and* we·swindled no·one·at·all.
G4122.3 V-AAI-3S ἐπλεονέκτησεν (1x)
2Co 12:18 brother. ¿!·Did Titus swindle anything from·yeu?
G4122.3 V-APS-1P πλεονεκτηθῶμεν (1x)
2Co 2:11 in·order·that we·should·not be·swindled by the

G4123 πλεον•έκτης plêônéktēs *n.* (4x)
Roots:G4119 G2192 See:G4122 G4124
G4123.2 N-NSM πλεονέκτης (1x)
Eph 5:5 or impure·person, or greedy·man— which is an·
G4123.4 N-NSM πλεονέκτης (1x)
1Co 5:11 ·be a·sexually·immoral·man, or covetous, or an·
G4123.4 N-NPM πλεονέκται (1x)
1Co 6:10 nor thieves, nor covetous·men, nor drunkards, nor
G4123.4 N-DPM πλεονέκταις (1x)
1Co 5:10 ·this world, or with·the covetous, or ones·who·are·

G4124 πλεον•εξία plêônêxía *n.* (10x)
Roots:G4123 Compare:G0724 See:G4122
G4124.2 N-NSF πλεονεξία (1x)
Eph 5:3 and·also any impurity or greed, must·not·even be·
G4124.2 N-DSF πλεονεξίᾳ (2x)
Rm 1:29 sexual·immorality, evil, greed, *and* malice; *being*
2Pe 2:3 And in greed, they·shall·commercially·exploit yeu
G4124.2 N-GSF πλεονεξίας (1x)
Lk 12:15 ·it, and be·vigilant due·to the greed, because not in
G4124.3 N-DSF πλεονεξίᾳ (1x)
Eph 4:19 into an·occupation of·all impurity with greediness.
G4124.4 N-ASF πλεονεξίαν (1x)
Col 3:5 wrong longing, and the covetousness— which is
G4124.4 N-GSF πλεονεξίας (1x)
1Th 2:5 , nor with a·pretext for·covetousness (God *is*
G4124.5 N-NPF πλεονεξίαι (1x)
Mk 7:22 thefts, acts·of·coveting, evils, guile, debauchery,
G4124.5 N-ASF πλεονεξίαν (1x)
2Co 9:5 not as·though·some act·of·coveting *was·occurring*.
G4124.5 N-DPF πλεονεξίαις (1x)
2Pe 2:14 a·heart having·been·trained with·acts·of·coveting.

G4125 πλευρά plêurá *n.* (5x)
xLangEquiv:H6763 A5967
G4125.2 N-ASF πλευράν (5x)
Jn 19:34 ·the soldiers jabbed his side with·the·tip·of·a·lance,
Jn 20:20 to·them his hands and his side. Accordingly, the
Jn 20:25 and may·cast my hand into his side, no, I·may·not
Jn 20:27 and cast *it* into my side. And do·not be distrusting,
Ac 12:7 And tapping Peter on·the side, he·awakened him,

G4126 πλέω plḗō *v.* (7x)
πλεύω plêúō
[an alternate form in certain tenses]
Roots:G4150 Compare:G3493-1 G4130 See:G0636 G4143 G4142 xLangAlso:H1980
G4126 V-PAN πλεῖν (1x)
Ac 27:2 we·launched, intending to·sail adjacent·to the
G4126 V-PAP-ASN πλέον (1x)
Ac 27:6 a·sailing·ship of·AlexAndria sailing into Italy, the
G4126 V-PAP-APM πλέοντας (1x)
Ac 27:24 ·graciously·given you all the·ones sailing with you.
G4126 V-PAP-GPM πλεόντων (1x)
Lk 8:23 But while·they were·sailing, he·fell·asleep. And a·
G4126 V-IAI-1P ἐπλέομεν (1x)
Ac 21:3 behind on·the·left·side, we·were·sailing into Syria,
EG4126 (2x)
Ac 20:15 and with·another *day of·sailing*, we·drew·alongside
Ac 27:3 And with another *day of·sailing*, we·moored at

G4127 πληγή plēgḗ *n.* (23x)
Roots:G4141 Compare:G1668 G3148 G5134 xLangEquiv:H5061 xLangAlso:H4046 H5063
G4127.2 N-NSF πληγή (1x)
Rv 16:21 hail, because its punishing·blow was tremendously
G4127.2 N-NPF πληγαί (2x)
Rv 15:8 even·until the seven punishing·blows of·the seven
Rv 18:8 ·account·of that, her punishing·blows shall·come in
G4127.2 N-APF πληγάς (6x)
Lk 10:30 ·stripping him and placing punishing·blows *on·him*,
Ac 16:23 after·placing many punishing·blows upon·them,
Rv 15:1 having the last seven punishing·blows, because in
Rv 15:6 seven punishing·blows, having·dressed·themselves
Rv 16:9 having authority over these punishing·blows. And
Rv 22:18 him the punishing·blows having·been·written in
G4127.2 N-DSF πληγῇ (1x)
Rv 11:6 the earth with·any punishing·blow, as·often·as they·
G4127.2 N-DPF πληγαῖς (3x)
2Co 6:5 in punishing·blows, in imprisonments, in chaos, in
2Co 11:23 in punishing·blows beyond·measure, in
Rv 9:20 killed by these punishing·blows did·not·even repent
G4127.2 N-GSF πληγῆς (1x)
Rv 16:21 God as·a·result of·the punishing·blow of·the hail,
G4127.2 N-GPF πληγῶν (4x)
Lk 12:48 things·deserving of·punishing·blows, shall·be·
Ac 16:33 he·bathed off *their* punishing·blows; and he·was·
Rv 18:4 ·may·not receive from·out·of·her punishing·blows,
Rv 21:9 overflowing of·the seven last punishing·blows), and
EG4127.2 (2x)
Lk 12:47 shall·be·thrashed with·many *punishing·blows*.
Lk 12:48 shall·be·thrashed with·few *punishing·blows*. "So
G4127.3 N-NSF πληγή (2x)
Rv 13:3 and its deadly gash was·both·relieved·and·cured.
Rv 13:12 own deadly gash was·both·relieved·and·cured.
G4127.3 N-ASF πληγήν (1x)
Rv 13:14 Daemonic·Beast, which has the gash by·the dagger,

G4128 πλῆθος plễthôs *n.* (32x)
Roots:G4130
G4128.2 N-NSN πλῆθος (19x)
Jn 5:3 a·large multitude of·the·ones being·feeble were·
Lk 1:10 And the entire multitude of·the people were praying
Lk 2:13 there·came·to·be a·multitude of·*the*·heavenly host
Lk 6:17 disciples, and a·large multitude of·people from all
Lk 8:37 ·all the multitude of·the region·surrounding the
Lk 19:37 absolutely·all the multitude of·the disciples began
Lk 23:1 rising·up, absolutely·all the multitude of·them led
Lk 23:27 ·was·following him a·large multitude of·the people
Ac 2:6 was·happening, the multitude came·together and
Ac 5:16 There·came·together also a·multitude *out* of·the
Ac 14:4 But the multitude of·the city was·torn·in·two.
Ac 15:12 And all the multitude stayed·silent and were·
Ac 17:4 both a·large multitude of·the·ones who·are·being·
Ac 21:22 It·is·binding·for a·multitude entirely to·come·
Ac 21:36 For the multitude of·the people were·following,
Ac 23:7 the Sadducees, and the multitude was·torn·in·two.
Ac 25:24 ·man, about whom all the multitude of·the Judeans
Mk 3:7 And a·large multitude from Galilee followed him,
Mk 3:8 ·things he·was·doing, a·large multitude came to him
G4128.2 N-NPN πλήθη (1x)
Ac 5:14 *the Called·Out·citizenry*, multitudes both of·men
G4128.2 N-ASN πλῆθος (6x)
Lk 5:6 this, they·tightly·enclosed a·large multitude of·fish,
Ac 6:2 after·summoning the multitude of·the disciples,
Ac 14:1 to·speak, such·for a·large multitude both of·Jews
Ac 15:30 ·together the multitude, they·hand-delivered the
Ac 28:3 bundling·together a·multitude of·kindling·sticks and
Jac 5:20 ·cover·and·bury·over a·multitude of·moral·failures.
G4128.2 N-DSN πλήθει (1x)
Heb 11:12 ·of·stars of·the sky in·the multitude *of·them*, and
G4128.2 N-GSN πλήθους (4x)
Jn 21:6 ·strength to·draw it *back·in* for the multitude of·fish.
Ac 4:32 And of·the multitude of·the·ones trusting, the heart
Ac 6:5 ·satisfactory in·the·sight of·the entire multitude. And
Ac 19:9 Way in·the·sight of·the multitude, after·withdrawing
G4128.3 N-ASN πλῆθος (1x)
1Pe 4:8 shall·cover·and·bury·over a·full·multitude of·moral·

G4129 πληθύνω plēthýnō *v.* (12x)
Roots:G4128
G4129 V-FAI-1S πληθυνῶ (1x)
Heb 6:14 you, and multiplying I·shall·indeed·multiply you.
G4129 V-PAP-GPM πληθυνόντων (1x)
Ac 6:1 days of·the disciples multiplying, there·happened a·
G4129 V-PAP-NSM πληθύνων (1x)
Heb 6:14 you, and multiplying I·shall·indeed·multiply you.
G4129 V-IPI-3S ἐπληθύνετο (2x)
Ac 6:7 number of·the disciples were·multiplied in JeruSalem
Ac 12:24 of·God was·growing and was·multiplied.
G4129 V-IPI-3P ἐπληθύνοντο (1x)
Ac 9:31 ·comfort of·the Holy Spirit, they·were·multiplying.
G4129 V-AAO-3S πληθύναι (1x)
2Co 9:10 ·he·supply and multiply yeur scattering·of·seed,
G4129 V-API-3S ἐπληθύνθη (1x)
Ac 7:17 the People grew and were·multiplied in Egypt,
G4129 V-APN πληθυνθῆναι (1x)
Mt 24:12 And on·account·of the·thing to·be·multiplied, the
G4129 V-APO-3S πληθυνθείη (3x)
Jud 1:2 mercy, and peace, and love be·multiplied to·yeu.
1Pe 1:2 May grace and peace be·multiplied to·yeu.
2Pe 1:2 May grace and peace be·multiplied to·yeu in *the*

G4130 πλήθω plḗthō *v.* (24x)
πλέω pléō
[a primary, but alternate form used only for certain tenses]
Compare:G3325 G0700 G2100 See:G4140 xLangEquiv:H4390 A4391
G4130.1 V-FPI-3S πλησθήσεται (1x)
Lk 1:15 ·drink, and he·shall·be·filled with·Holy Spirit, yet·
G4130.1 V-AAI-3P ἔπλησαν (1x)
Lk 5:7 And they·came and filled both the sailboats, such·for
G4130.1 V-AAP-NSM πλήσας (1x)
Mt 27:48 taking a·sponge and filling *it* with·wine·vinegar
G4130.1 V-AAP-NPM πλήσαντες (1x)
Jn 19:29 *soldiers*, after·filling a·sponge with·wine·vinegar
G4130.1 V-API-3S ἐπλήσθη (4x)
Lk 1:41 womb, and ElisaBeth was·filled with·Holy Spirit.
Lk 1:67 And his father ZacharIas was·filled with·Holy Spirit
Ac 19:29 the whole city was·filled with·mass·confusion.
Mt 22:10 wedding was·filled with·those·reclining·at·the·.
G4130.1 V-API-3P ἐπλήσθησαν (7x)
Lk 5:26 God and were·filled with·reverent·fear·and·awe,
Lk 6:11 But they·themselves were·filled with·irrational· and
Ac 2:4 And absolutely·all were·filled with·Holy Spirit, and
Ac 3:10 and they·were·filled with·amazement and
Ac 4:31 and absolutely·all were·filled with·Holy Spirit, and
Ac 5:17 of·the Sadducees), they·were·filled with·jealousy,
Ac 13:45 the crowds, the Jews were·filled with·jealousy and
G4130.1 V-API-3P@ ἐπλήσθησαν (1x)
Lk 4:28 everyone in the gathering was·filled with·rage.
G4130.1 V-APP-NSM πλησθείς (2x)
Ac 4:8 Then Peter, being·filled with·Holy Spirit, declared to
Ac 13:9 also *called* Paul), being·filled with·Holy Spirit and
G4130.1 V-APS-2S πλησθῇς (1x)
Ac 9:17 ·your·sight and may·be·filled with·Holy Spirit."
G4130.3 V-API-3S ἐπλήσθη (1x)
Lk 1:57 time was·fulfilled for·her to·reproduce·and·give·
G4130.3 V-API-3P ἐπλήσθησαν (4x)
Lk 1:23 the days of·his public·service were·fulfilled, *that* he·
Lk 2:6 for·her to·reproduce·and·give·birth were·fulfilled.
Lk 2:21 when eight days were·fulfilled to·circumcise the
Lk 2:22 Torah-Law of·Moses were·fulfilled, they·brought

G4131 πλήκτης plḗktēs *n.* (2x)
Roots:G4141 See:G1605
G4131.2 N-ASM πλήκτην (2x)
Tit 1:7 not continually·near·wine, not a·violent·man, not of·
1Ti 3:3 not continually·near·wine, not a·violent·man, not of·

G4132 πλήμμυρα plḗmmyra *n.* (1x)
Roots:G4130 Compare:G2627 G4215 G5493
G4132.2 N-GSF πλημμύρας (1x)
Lk 6:48 the solid·rock. And with·a·flash·flood happening,

G4133 πλήν plḗn *adv.* (32x)
Roots:G4119 Compare:G0235 G1508
G4133.1 ADV πλήν (13x)
Lk 6:24 "Moreover, woe to·yeu, the wealthy! Because yeu·
Lk 10:11 we·do·wipe·*it*·off against·yeu. Moreover, know
Lk 10:14 So·moreover, it·shall·be more·tolerable for·Tyre
Lk 10:20 "Moreover, do·not rejoice in this, that the spirits
Lk 11:41 Moreover, yeu·give a·merciful·act·of·charity, one·
Lk 12:31 "Moreover, seek the kingdom of·God, and all
Lk 19:27 'Moreover, those my enemies, the·ones not
Lk 22:21 "*And* moreover, behold, the hand of·the·one
Lk 22:22 ·been·specifically·determined. Moreover, woe to·
Lk 23:28 do·not weep over me. *Yet* moreover, weep over
Mt 11:22 Moreover I·say to·yeu, it·shall·be more·tolerable
Mt 26:64 "You·yourself declared *it*. Moreover I·say to·yeu,
Php 1:18 *it·matter? Just that* moreover, in·every manner,
G4133.2 ADV πλήν (9x)
Lk 13:33 "Nevertheless, it·is·necessary·for me to·traverse
Lk 18:8 in haste. "Nevertheless, the Son of·Clay·Man†,
Lk 22:42 this cup from me … nevertheless not my will, but·
Mt 18:7 *for* scandalous·traps to·come! Nevertheless, woe to·
Mt 26:39 pass·away from me. Nevertheless not as I·myself
Php 3:16 Nevertheless, for what we·already·attained, let·us·
Php 4:14 Nevertheless yeu·did well sharing·together in·my
1Co 11:11 Nevertheless, neither *is* man apart·from woman,
Rv 2:25 Nevertheless, that·which yeu·presently·have,
G4133.3 ADV πλήν (3x)
Lk 6:35 "So·even·more, love yeur enemies, and beneficially·
Mt 11:24 So·even·more, I·say to·yeu that it·shall·be more·
Eph 5:33 So·even·more also, yeu·yeurselves (accordingly
G4133.4 ADV πλήν (4x)
Jn 8:10 and distinctly·viewing not·even·one besides the wife,
Ac 8:1 in JeruSalem; and all besides the ambassadors were·
Ac 15:28 a·larger burden besides these·things of·necessity:
Mk 12:32 one God, and there·is not another besides him."
EG4133.4 (1x)
2Pe 1:5 Now also *besides* this, applying all diligence, yeu·
G4133.5 ADV πλήν (2x)
Ac 20:23 other·than that the Holy Spirit thoroughly·testifies
Ac 27:22 of·soul from·among yeu, other·than *that* of·the

G4134 πλήρης plḗrēs *adj.* (19x)
Roots:G4130 Compare:G3324 See:G0187
xLangAlso:H4392
G4134.1 A-NSM πλήρης (6x)
Lk 4:1 And Jesus, full of·Holy Spirit, returned·back from
Lk 5:12 behold, a·man full of·leprosy; and after·seeing
Ac 6:8 Now Stephen, full of·trust and power, was·doing
Ac 7:55 But *Stephen*, inherently·being full of·Holy Spirit,
Ac 11:24 a·beneficially·good man and full of·Holy Spirit
Ac 13:10 declared, "O *you·are* full of·all guile and all
G4134.1 A-NSF πλήρης (2x)
Jn 1:14 directly·from *the* Father), full of·grace and truth.
Ac 9:36 She·herself was full of·beneficially·good works
G4134.1 A-NPM πλήρεις (1x)
Ac 19:28 *these·things*, they·were·becoming full of·rage, and
G4134.1 A-ASM πλήρη (2x)
Ac 6:5 they·selected Stephen, a·man full of·trust and of·
2Jn 1:8 that·we·may·fully·receive a·full payment·of·service.
G4134.1 A-APM πλήρεις (4x)
Ac 6:3 seven men being·attested·to, full of·Holy Spirit and
Mt 14:20 of·the fragments— twelve wicker·baskets full.
Mk 6:43 twelve wicker·baskets full of·*bread*·fragments and
Mk 8:19 wicker·baskets full of·fragments did·yeu·take·up?
G4134.1 A-APF πλήρεις (1x)
Mt 15:37 And they·took·up seven woven·baskets full *of* the
EG4134.1 (2x)
Ac 2:28 you·shall·completely·fill me *full* of·euphoria with
Mk 8:8 ·abundance of·fragments, seven woven·baskets *full*.
G4134.2 A-ASM πλήρη (1x)
Mk 4:28 a·head·of·grain, after·that, fully·ripe grain in the

G4135 πληρο•φορέω plērôphôréō *v.* (5x)
Roots:G4134 G5409 See:G4136
G4135.1 V-AAM-2S πληροφόρησον (1x)
2Ti 4:5 ·news·of·redemption, fully·carry·out your service.
G4135.1 V-APS-3S πληροφορηθῇ (1x)
2Ti 4:17 the official·proclamation may·be·fully·carried·forth
G4135.2 V-PPM-3S πληροφορείσθω (1x)
Rm 14:5 *alike*. Let each·man be·fully·assured in his·own
G4135.2 V-APP-NSM πληροφορηθείς (1x)
Rm 4:21 and already·being·fully·assured that, what *God* has·
G4135.3 V-RPP-GPN πεπληροφορημένων (1x)
Lk 1:1 the activities having·been·fully·evidenced among us

G4136 πληρο•φορία plērôphôría *n.* (4x)
Roots:G4135 Compare:G4006 G5287
G4136 N-ASF πληροφορίαν (1x)
Heb 6:11 toward the full·assurance of·the Expectation, even·
G4136 N-DSF πληροφορίᾳ (2x)
Heb 10:22 with a·true heart in full·assurance of·trust, the
1Th 1:5 Spirit and with much fullness·of·assurance, just·as
G4136 N-GSF πληροφορίας (1x)
Col 2:2 all wealth of·the full·assurance of·comprehension,

G4137 πληρόω plērôō *v.* (90x)
Roots:G4134 Compare:G5055 G0535 See:G4138
G4138-1 G4845
G4137.1 V-FAI-2S πληρώσεις (1x)
Ac 2:28 of·life-above†; you·shall·completely·fill me *full* of·
G4137.1 V-FPI-3S πληρωθήσεται (1x)
Lk 3:5 Every canyon shall·be·completely·filled, and every
G4137.1 V-PMP-GSM-T πληρουμένου (1x)
Eph 1:23 ·fullness of·the·one who·is·completely·filling all in
G4137.1 V-PPM-2P πληροῦσθε (1x)
Eph 5:18 ·lifestyle, but·rather be·completely·filled in Spirit
G4137.1 V-PPP-NSN πληρούμενον (1x)
Lk 2:40 in·spirit, being·completely·filled with·wisdom. And
G4137.1 V-IPI-3P ἐπληροῦντο (1x)
Ac 13:52 the disciples were·completely·filled with·joy and
G4137.1 V-AAI-3S ἐπλήρωσεν (2x)
Ac 2:2 forceful wind, and it·completely·filled all the house
Ac 5:3 the Adversary-Accuser completely·filled your heart
G4137.1 V-AAO-3S πληρώσαι (1x)
Rm 15:13 of·the Expectation completely·fill yeu with·all joy
G4137.1 V-AAS-3S πληρώσῃ (1x)
Eph 4:10 heavens, that he·may·completely·fill all·things).
G4137.1 V-API-3S ἐπληρώθη (2x)
Jn 12:3 and the home was·completely·filled from·out of·the
Mt 13:48 which when it·was·completely·filled, after·hauling
G4137.1 V-APS-1S πληρωθῶ (1x)
2Ti 1:4 in·order·that I·may·be·completely·filled with·joy—
G4137.1 V-APS-2P πληρωθῆτε (2x)
Eph 3:19 in·order·that yeu·may·be·completely·filled to all
Col 1:9 yeu·may·be·completely·filled with·the recognition·
G4137.1 V-APS-3S πληρωθῇ (1x)
Jn 15:11 in yeu, and *that* yeur joy may·be·completely·filled.
G4137.1 V-RAI-2P πεπληρώκατε (1x)
Ac 5:28 yeu·have·completely·filled JeruSalem with·yeur
G4137.1 V-RAI-3S πεπλήρωκεν (1x)
Jn 16:6 to·yeu, the grief has·completely·filled yeur heart.
G4137.1 V-RPI-1S πεπλήρωμαι (2x)
Php 4:18 ·abound; I·have·been·completely·filled, accepting
2Co 7:4 yeu. I·have·been·completely·filled with·the comfort
G4137.1 V-RPP-APM πεπληρωμένους (1x)
Rm 1:29 having·been·completely·filled with·all
G4137.1 V-RPP-NSF πεπληρωμένη (2x)
Jn 16:24 yeur joy may·be having·been·completely·filled.
1Jn 1:4 our joy should·be having·been·completely·filled.
G4137.1 V-RPP-NPM πεπληρωμένοι (2x)
Rm 15:14 ·goodness, having·been·completely·filled with·all
Php 1:11 having·been·completely·filled of·*the*·fruits of·
G4137.2 V-FAI-3S πληρώσει (1x)
Php 4:19 And my God shall·completely·fulfill yeur every
G4137.2 V-FDI-3P πληρώσονται (1x)
Rv 6:11 their brothers shall·be·completely·fulfilled, the·ones
G4137.2 V-FPI-3P πληρωθήσονται (1x)
Lk 1:20 words, which shall·be·completely·fulfilled in their
G4137.2 V-PAN πληροῦν (1x)
Lk 9:31 he·was·about to·completely·fulfill in JeruSalem.
G4137.2 V-PAS-2S πληροῖς (1x)
Col 4:17 in *the* Lord, that you·may·completely·fulfill it!"
G4137.2 V-PPI-3S πληροῦται (1x)
Gal 5:14 For all the Torah-Law is·completely·fulfilled in one
G4137.2 V-IAI-3S ἐπλήρου (1x)
Ac 13:25 as John was·completely·fulfilling his·own running·
G4137.2 V-IPI-3S ἐπληροῦτο (1x)
Ac 7:23 as forty·years time was·completely·fulfilled in·him,
G4137.2 V-IPI-3P ἐπληροῦντο (1x)
Ac 9:23 ·number·of days were·completely·fulfilled, the Jews
G4137.2 V-AAI-3S ἐπλήρωσεν (1x)
Ac 3:18 to·suffer in·this·manner, he·completely·fulfilled.
G4137.2 V-AAI-3P ἐπλήρωσαν (2x)
Ac 13:27 , they·completely·fulfilled *them* in·judging *him*.
Ac 14:26 for the work which they·completely·fulfilled.
G4137.2 V-AAM-2P πληρώσατε (2x)
Mt 23:32 Yeu·yeurselves completely·fulfill even the
Php 2:2 completely·fulfill my joy, that yeu·should·
G4137.2 V-AAN πληρῶσαι (3x)
Mt 3:15 ·for us to·completely·fulfill all righteousness." Then
Mt 5:17 come to·demolish, but·rather to·completely·fulfill.
Col 1:25 for yeu, to·completely·fulfill the Redemptive-word
G4137.2 V-AAP-NPM πληρώσαντες (1x)
Ac 12:25 JeruSalem after·completely·fulfilling the service
G4137.2 V-AAS-3S πληρώσῃ (1x)
2Th 1:11 *that* he·may·completely·fulfill every good·purpose
G4137.2 V-API-3S ἐπληρώθη (5x)
Ac 19:21 And as these·things were·completely·fulfilled, Paul
Mt 2:17 Then was·completely·fulfilled, the·thing being·
Mt 27:9 Then was·completely·fulfilled the·thing being·
Mk 15:28 the Scripture was·completely·fulfilled, the·one
Jac 2:23 And the Scripture is·completely·fulfilled, the·one
G4137.2 V-APN πληρωθῆναι (3x)
Lk 21:22 of·the·One to·completely·fulfill all the·things
Lk 24:44 ·for all·things to·be·completely·fulfilled, the·things
Ac 1:16 ·for this·Scripture to·be·completely·fulfilled, which
G4137.2 V-APP-GSF πληρωθείσης (1x)
Ac 24:27 But having·completely·fulfilled two·years, Porcius
G4137.2 V-APP-GPN πληρωθέντων (1x)
Ac 7:30 with·forty years being·completely·fulfilled, an·angel
G4137.2 V-APS-3S πληρωθῇ (20x)
Jn 12:38 the prophet may·be·completely·fulfilled, which he·
Jn 13:18 ·that the Scripture may·be·completely·fulfilled,
Jn 15:25 ·that the word may·be·completely·fulfilled, the·one
Jn 17:12 ·that the Scripture may·be·completely·fulfilled.
Jn 18:9 ·that the saying may·be·completely·fulfilled, which
Jn 18:32 of·Jesus may·be·completely·fulfilled which he·
Jn 19:24 the Scripture may·be·completely·fulfilled, the·one
Jn 19:36 that the Scripture should·be·completely·fulfilled,
Lk 22:16 ·time *that* it·should·be·completely·fulfilled in the
Mt 1:22 in·order·that it·may·be·completely·fulfilled, the·
Mt 2:15 in·order·that it·may·be·completely·fulfilled, the·
Mt 2:23 that it·may·be·completely·fulfilled, the·thing
Mt 4:14 in·order·that it·may·be·completely·fulfilled, the·
Mt 8:17 *the prophecy* may·be·completely·fulfilled, the·one
Mt 12:17 that it·may·be·completely·fulfilled, the·thing
Mt 13:35 that it·may·be·completely·fulfilled, the·thing
Mt 21:4 in·order·that it·may·be·completely·fulfilled, the·
Mt 27:35 in·order·that it·may·be·completely·fulfilled, the·
Rm 8:4 ·the Torah-Law may·be·completely·fulfilled in us,
2Co 10:6 attentive·obedience should·be·completely·fulfilled.
G4137.2 V-APS-3P πληρωθῶσιν (4x)
Lk 21:24 seasons of·Gentiles should·be·completely·fulfilled.

Mt 26:54 the Scriptures be·completely·fulfilled that *state* it·
Mt 26:56 of·the prophets may·be·completely·fulfilled." Then
Mk 14:49 the Scriptures may·be·completely·fulfilled ..."
G4137.2 V-RAI-3S πεπλήρωκεν (1x)
Rm 13:8 the other has·completely·fulfilled *the* Torah-Law.
G4137.2 V-RAN πεπληρωκέναι (1x)
Rm 15:19 me to·have·completely·fulfilled the good·news of·
G4137.2 V-RPI-3S πεπλήρωται (4x)
Jn 3:29 this (my joy) has·been·completely·fulfilled.
Jn 7:8 my season has·not·yet been·completely·fulfilled."
Lk 4:21 this Scripture has·been·completely·fulfilled in yeur
Mk 1:15 "The season has·been·completely·fulfilled, and the
G4137.2 V-RPP-ASF πεπληρωμένην (1x)
Jn 17:13 joy having·been·completely·fulfilled in themselves.
G4137.2 V-RPP-APN πεπληρωμένα (1x)
Rv 3:2 works having·been·completely·fulfilled in·the·sight
G4137.2 V-RPP-NSF πεπληρωμένη (1x)
2Jn 1:12 our joy may·be having·been·completely·fulfilled.
G4137.2 V-RPP-NPM πεπληρωμένοι (2x)
Col 2:10 in him, having·been·completely·fulfilled *in him*,
Col 4:12 and having·been·completely·fulfilled in every will
G4137.5 V-AAI-3S ἐπλήρωσεν (1x)
Lk 7:1 And since *Jesus* fully·finished all his utterances in the

G4138 πλήρωμα plḗrōma *n.* (18x)
Roots:G4137 See:G4138-1
G4138.1 N-NSN πλήρωμα (10x)
Gal 4:4 But when the complete·fullness of·time was·come,
Mt 9:16 it·takes·away its complete·fullness from the
Mk 2:21 takes·away its complete·fullness from·the old, and
Rm 11:12 how·much more their complete·fullness?
Rm 11:25 only·until the complete·fullness of·the Gentiles
1Co 10:26 Land *is* Yahweh's, and its complete·fullness."
1Co 10:28 Land *is* Yahweh's, and its complete·fullness."
Eph 1:23 his Body, the complete·fullness of·the·one who·is·
Col 1:19 because all the complete·fullness *of·God Most·High*
Col 2:9 all the complete·fullness of·Godhood resides bodily.
G4138.1 N-ASN πλήρωμα (1x)
Eph 3:19 ·filled to all the complete·fullness of·God.
G4138.1 N-DSN πληρώματι (1x)
Rm 15:29 ·come in complete·fullness of·blessing of·the
G4138.1 N-GSN πληρώματος (2x)
Jn 1:16 And from·out of·his complete·fullness, we·ourselves
Eph 4:13 of·the complete·fullness of·the Anointed-One—
EG4138.1 (1x)
1Th 2:16 ·fulfill *the complete·fullness·of* their moral·failures.
G4138.2 N-APN πληρώματα (1x)
Mk 8:20 woven·baskets completely·full of·fragments did·
G4138.4 N-NSN πλήρωμα (1x)
Rm 13:10 love *is* Torah-Law's complete·fulfillment.
G4138.4 N-GSN πληρώματος (1x)
Eph 1:10 of·the complete·fulfillment of·the seasons): to·

G4139 πλησίον plēsíôn *adv.* (17x)
Compare:G1069 G4040
xLangEquiv:H7453 xLangAlso:H7468
G4139.1 ADV πλησίον (1x)
Jn 4:5 ·as Sychar *(or·intoxicating)*, near·by to·the open·field
G4139.2 ADV πλησίον (16x)
Lk 10:27 ·mind,'' and "your neighbor as yourself.'"
Lk 10:29 "And who is my neighbor?"
Lk 10:36 ·you to·have·become a·neighbor to·the·one falling
Ac 7:27 the·one morally·wronging the neighbor shoved him
Heb 8:11 *anymore* instruct each·man his neighbor, and each·
Gal 5:14 ·one, "'You·shall·love your neighbor as yourself.'"
Mt 5:43 "You·shall·love your neighbor and shall·hate your
Mt 19:19 and "'You·shall·love your neighbor as yourself.'"
Mt 22:39 it, "You·shall·love your neighbor as yourself.'
Mk 12:31 it, "You·shall·love your neighbor as yourself.'
Mk 12:33 strength, and to·love one's neighbor as himself, is
Rm 13:9 "'You·shall·love your neighbor as yourself.'"
Rm 13:10 works no wrong to·the neighbor. Accordingly,
Rm 15:2 ·adapt to·his neighbor's *weak·conscience* for his
Jac 2:8 "'You·shall·love your neighbor as yourself,'" yeu·
Eph 4:25 ·man must·speak truth with his neighbor,'" because

G4140 πλησμονή plēsmônḗ *n.* (1x)
Roots:G4130
G4140.2 N-ASF πλησμονήν (1x)
Col 2:23 specifically·against an·indulgence of·the flesh.

G4141 πλήσσω plḗssō *v.* (1x)
Roots:G4111 Compare:G1194 G3817 G3960 G5180 See:G1605 G4131
G4141.1 V-2API-3S ἐπλήγη (1x)
Rv 8:12 and the third·part of·the sun was·pounded, and the

G4142 πλοιάριον plôiáriôn *n.* (6x)
Roots:G4143 Compare:G3491 G4627
G4142 N-NSN πλοιάριον (2x)
Jn 6:22 that there·had·been no other small·boat there except
Mk 3:9 that a·small·boat should·diligently·attend to·him on·
G4142 N-NPN πλοιάρια (2x)
Jn 6:23 Now other small·boats came out·from Tiberias near
Mk 4:36 the sailboat. And other small·boats were also with
G4142 N-ASN πλοιάριον (1x)
Jn 6:22 with·his disciples into the small·boat, but·rather *that*
G4142 N-DSN πλοιαρίῳ (1x)
Jn 21:8 disciples came in·the small·boat, while·dragging the

G4143 πλοῖον plôîôn *n.* (69x)
Roots:G4126 Compare:G3491 G4627 See:G4142 xLangAlso:H0591
G4143.1 N-NSN πλοῖον (4x)
Jn 6:21 And immediately, the sailboat came·to·be upon the
Mt 8:24 the sea, such·for the sailboat to·be·covered by the
Mt 14:24 But the sailboat was even·now in·*the*·middle of·the
Mk 6:47 with·early·evening occurring, the sailboat was in
G4143.1 N-ASN πλοῖον (19x)
Jn 6:17 after·embarking into the sailboat, they·were·going
Jn 6:21 to·receive him into the sailboat. And immediately,
Jn 21:3 and walked·up into the sailboat straight·away. And
Lk 8:22 that he·himself embarked into a·sailboat with his
Lk 8:37 ·him embarking into the sailboat, he·returned·back.
Mt 4:22 immediately, leaving the sailboat and their father,
Mt 8:23 And embarking into the sailboat, his disciples
Mt 9:1 after·embarking into the sailboat, he·crossed·over and
Mt 13:2 ·for him to·embark into the sailboat *and* to·sit·down
Mt 14:22 to·embark into the sailboat and to·go·on·ahead·of
Mt 14:32 with·him embarking into the sailboat, the wind
Mt 15:39 he·embarked into the sailboat and came into the
Mk 4:1 he *was* embarking into the sailboat to·sit·down along
Mk 4:37 ·waves were·breaking into the sailboat, such·for it
Mk 5:18 *Jesus* was·embarking into the sailboat, the·one
Mk 6:45 to·embark into the sailboat and to·go·on·ahead to
Mk 6:51 he·walked·up toward them into the sailboat, and the
Mk 8:10 after·embarking into the sailboat with his disciples
Mk 8:13 *and* embarking into the sailboat again, he·went·off
G4143.1 N-APN πλοῖα (5x)
Jn 6:24 they also embarked into the sailboats and came to
Lk 5:2 Now he·saw two sailboats having·settled directly·by
Lk 5:7 they·came and filled both the sailboats, such·for them
Lk 5:11 And mooring the sailboats upon the dry·ground,
Rv 18:19 City, in which all the·ones having ships in the sea
G4143.1 N-DSN πλοίῳ (10x)
Lk 5:7 ·ones in the other sailboat *that·was* already·coming
Mt 4:21 his brother, in the sailboat with their father Zebedee
Mt 14:13 departed from·there in a·sailboat into a·desolate
Mt 14:33 And the·ones in the sailboat, after·coming
Mk 1:19 ·men *were* in the sailboat completely·repairing the
Mk 1:20 their father Zebedee in the sailboat with the hired·
Mk 4:36 him as·soon·as he·was in the sailboat. And other
Mk 5:21 crossing·over again in the sailboat to the other·side
Mk 6:32 ·off to·a·desolate place in·the sailboat in private.
Mk 8:14 ·not having *any* in the sailboat among themselves.
G4143.1 N-GSN πλοίου (6x)
Jn 6:19 sea and coming near to·the sailboat. And they·were·
Jn 21:6 the right·hand portions of·the sailboat, and yeu·shall·
Lk 5:3 ·was·instructing the crowds from·out of·the sailboat.
Mt 14:29 And after·stepping·down from the sailboat, Peter
Mk 5:2 ·him coming·forth out of·the sailboat, immediately
Mk 6:54 ·them coming·forth out of·the sailboat, immediately
G4143.1 N-GPN πλοίων (2x)
Lk 5:3 But embarking into one of·the sailboats, which was
Rv 8:9 the third·part of·the ships were·thoroughly·ruined.
G4143.2 N-NSN πλοῖον (1x)
Ac 21:3 at Tyre, for the sailing·ship was unloading its cargo
G4143.2 N-NPN πλοῖα (1x)
Jac 3:4 Behold also the sailing·ships, being so·vast, and *are*
G4143.2 N-ASN πλοῖον (8x)
Ac 20:13 going·onward to the sailing·ship, sailed to Assos,
Ac 20:38 And they·were·seeing him off to the sailing·ship.
Ac 21:2 And after·finding a·sailing·ship sailing·over to
Ac 21:6 we·embarked into the sailing·ship, and those
Ac 27:6 ·there, upon·finding a·sailing·ship of·AlexAndria
Ac 27:17 ·cables, undergirding the sailing·ship. And, fearing
Ac 27:38 they·were·lightening the sailing·ship, *by* casting·
Ac 27:39 if it·were·possible, to·propel the sailing·ship.
G4143.2 N-DSN πλοίῳ (4x)
Ac 27:2 And after·embarking·upon a·sailing·ship of·, we·
Ac 27:31 these should·remain with the sailing·ship, yeu are·
Ac 27:37 Now in the sailing·ship, all *told*, we·were two·
Ac 28:11 we·sailed·away in a·sailing·ship of·AlexAndria
G4143.2 N-GSN πλοίου (6x)
Ac 27:10 of·the cargo and of·the sailing·ship, but·yet also
Ac 27:15 with·the sailing·ship being·snatched·up·together
Ac 27:19 we·flung the sailing·ship's tackle *overboard*.
Ac 27:22 ·among yeu, other·than *that* of·the sailing·ship.
Ac 27:30 seeking to·flee out·from the sailing·ship, and with·
Ac 27:44 of·the *broken·pieces* from the sailing·ship. And in·
G4143.3 N-GPN πλοίων (1x)
Rv 18:17 and all aboard the company of·ships, and sailors,
EG4143.3 (2x)
Ac 27:18 *lighten the ship by* throwing·the·cargo·overboard.
Rv 18:17 "And every *ship's* pilot, and all aboard the

G4144 πλόος plôôs *n.* (3x)
Roots:G4126
G4144 N-ASM πλοῦν (2x)
Ac 21:7 ·thoroughly·accomplishing the voyage from Tyre,
Ac 27:10 I·observe that the impending voyage shall·be with
G4144 N-GSM πλοός (1x)
Ac 27:9 ·elapsing, and with·the voyage being even·now

G4145 πλούσιος plôúsiôs *adj.* (28x)
Roots:G4149
G4145.1 A-NSM πλούσιος (13x)
Lk 16:1 "There·was·a·certain wealthy man·of·clay† who
Lk 16:19 "There·was·a·certain wealthy man·of·clay†, and
Lk 16:22 bosom. But the wealthy·man died also and was·
Lk 18:23 ·grieved, for he·was tremendously wealthy.
Lk 19:2 a·chief·tax·collector, and this·man was wealthy.
Mt 19:23 ·difficult *that* a·wealthy·man shall·enter into the
Mt 27:57 occurring, there·came a·wealthy man·of·clay† of
Jac 1:10 but the wealthy in his·own humiliation, because as
Jac 1:11 also, the wealthy·man shall·be·shriveled·up along
2Co 8:9 Anointed, how·that being wealthy, on·account·of
Eph 2:4 But God, being wealthy in mercy, on·account·of his
Rv 2:9 the poverty (but you·are wealthy). And *I·personally*·
Rv 3:17 you·say, "I·am wealthy. I·have·become·wealthy
G4145.1 A-NPM πλούσιοι (4x)
Mk 12:41 many that·were·wealthy were·casting·in much.
Jac 2:6 ¿!·Is·it·not the wealthy·men *that* dominate yeu, and
Jac 5:1 Come·on now, Wealthy·Men! Weep, howling over
Rv 6:15 and the greatest·men, and the wealthy·men, and the
G4145.1 A-ASM πλούσιον (3x)
Lk 18:25 of·a·needle, than *for* a·wealthy·man to·enter into
Mt 19:24 of·a·needle than *for* a·wealthy·man to·enter into
Mk 10:25 ·the needle, than for·a·wealthy·man to·enter into
G4145.1 A-APM πλουσίους (4x)
Lk 14:12 your kinsmen, nor·even wealthy close·neighbors,
Lk 21:1 looking·up, he·saw the wealthy·men casting their
Jac 2:5 helplessly·poor of·this world *to·be* wealthy in trust
Rv 13:16 the great, also the wealthy and the helplessly·poor,
G4145.1 A-DPM πλουσίοις (2x)
Lk 6:24 woe to·yeu, the wealthy! Because yeu·completely·

1Ti 6:17 Charge the wealthy·ones in the present age not to·
G4145.1 A-GSM πλουσίου (2x)
Lk 12:16 of·a·certain wealthy man·of·clay† brought·forth·
Lk 16:21 the·ones falling from the wealthy·man's table.

G4146 πλουσίως plôusíōs *adv.* (4x)
Roots:G4145
G4146 ADV πλουσίως (4x)
2Pe 1:11 shall·be·fully·supplied abundantly to·yeu into the
Tit 3:6 he·poured·forth on us abundantly through Jesus
Col 3:16 indwell among yeu abundantly in all wisdom,
1Ti 6:17 ·furnishing to·us abundantly all·things for full·

G4147 πλουτέω plôutéō *v.* (12x)
Roots:G4148
G4147.1 V-PAN πλουτεῖν (1x)
1Ti 6:9 the·ones being·resolved to·become·wealthy fall into
G4147.1 V-PAP-NSM πλουτῶν (1x)
Lk 12:21 ·up·treasure for·himself, becoming·wealthy, yet
G4147.1 V-AAI-2P ἐπλουτήσατε (1x)
1Co 4:8 Even·now yeu·became·wealthy! Yeu·reigned *as·*
G4147.1 V-AAI-3P ἐπλούτησαν (2x)
Rv 18:3 merchants of·the earth became·wealthy out of·the
Rv 18:19 ships in the sea became·wealthy as·a·result of·her
G4147.1 V-AAP-NPM πλουτήσαντες (1x)
Rv 18:15 ·things, the·ones becoming·wealthy from her,
G4147.1 V-AAS-2P πλουτήσητε (1x)
2Co 8:9 ·yeurselves by·this poverty may·become·wealthy.
G4147.1 V-RAI-1S πεπλούτηκα (1x)
Rv 3:17 "I·am wealthy. I·have·become·wealthy and have
G4147.2 V-PAN πλουτεῖν (1x)
1Ti 6:18 ·do·beneficially·good·work, to·be·wealthy in good
G4147.2 V-PAP-APM πλουτοῦντας (1x)
Lk 1:53 and those·being·wealthy, he·dispatched·forth
G4147.2 V-PAP-NSM πλουτῶν (1x)
Rm 10:12 *Jesus is* Lord of·all, being·wealthy to all the·ones
G4147.2 V-AAS-2S πλουτήσῃς (1x)
Rv 3:18 fire, in·order·that you·may·be·wealthy, and·also

G4148 πλουτίζω plôutízō *v.* (3x)
Roots:G4149 See:G4147
G4148.1 V-PAP-NPM πλουτίζοντες (1x)
2Co 6:10 as helplessly·poor yet making·wealthy many, as
G4148.2 V-PPP-NPM πλουτιζόμενοι (1x)
2Co 9:11 being·enriched in everything to all fidelity, which
G4148.2 V-API-2P ἐπλουτίσθητε (1x)
1Co 1:5 that in everything yeu·are·enriched by him, in every

G4149 πλοῦτος plôûtôs *n.* (25x)
Roots:G4130 Compare:G3126 See:G4145 G4148 xLangAlso:H6239 H2428
G4149.1 N-NSM πλοῦτος (4x)
Jac 5:2 Yeur wealth has·rotted, and yeur garments have·
Eph 1:18 ·forth, and what *is* the wealth of·the glory of·his
Col 1:27 to·make·known what *is* the wealth of·the glory of·
Rv 18:17 Because in·one hour such·vast wealth is·desolated.
G4149.1 N-NSN πλοῦτος (2x)
Rm 11:12 if their trespass *became* wealth for·*the*·world, and
Rm 11:12 and their deterioration, wealth for·*the*·Gentiles;
G4149.1 N-ASM πλοῦτον (10x)
Heb 11:26 of·the Anointed-One *to·be* greater wealth *than* the
Rm 9:23 ·that he·may·make·known the wealth of·his glory
Php 4:19 yeur every need according·to his wealth in glory in
2Co 8:2 poverty abounded to the wealth of·their fidelity—
Eph 1:7 of·trespasses according·to the wealth of·his grace.
Eph 2:7 upcoming ages the surpassing wealth of·his grace,
Eph 3:8 Gentiles the untraceable wealth of·the Anointed-One
Eph 3:16 in·order·that according·to the wealth of·his glory,
Col 2:2 in love, and into all wealth of·the full·assurance of·
Rv 5:12 to·receive the power and wealth and wisdom and
G4149.1 N-GSM πλούτου (6x)
Lk 8:14 ·choked by anxieties and wealth and pleasures of·the
Mt 13:22 delusional·nature of·wealth altogether·choke the
Mk 4:19 — and the delusional·nature of·wealth— and the·
Rm 2:4 Or do·you·despise the wealth of·his kindness,
Rm 11:33 O *the* depth of·wealth, both of·*the*·wisdom and
1Ti 6:17 upon *the* uncertainty of·wealth, but·rather in the
EG4149.1 (3x)
Lk 16:11 ·wealth, who shall·entrust to·yeu the true *wealth*?
Lk 16:12 who shall·give to·yeu *wealth of* yeur·own?
Eph 1:8 *Yes, the wealth of·his grace* which he·abounded to

G4150 πλύνω plýnō *v.* (1x)
Compare:G3068 G3538 See:G0637 xLangAlso:H3526
G4150.2 V-AAI-3P ἔπλυναν (1x)
Rv 7:14 and they·laundered their long·robes, and they·

G4151 πνεῦμα pnêûma *n.* (394x)
Roots:G4154 Compare:G5590 G0417 G4157 G0444 G5326 G0378-3 See:G4152 xLangEquiv:H7307 A7308 xLangAlso:H7496 H5397
G4151.1 N-NSN πνεῦμα (1x)
Jn 3:8 The breeze blows where it·wants, and you·hear the
G4151.2 N-ASN πνεῦμα (1x)
Rv 13:15 ·given to·it to·give breath to·the derived·image of·
G4151.2 N-DSN πνεύματι (1x)
2Th 2:8 the Lord shall·consume with·the breath of·his
G4151.3 N-NSN πνεῦμα (8x)
Jn 3:6 ·one having·been·born from·out of·the Spirit is spirit.
Jn 6:63 I·myself speak to·yeu, *they* are spirit, and *they* are
Lk 24:39 me and see, because a·spirit does·not have flesh
Jac 4:5 says for·naught, "The spirit that resides in us
1Co 6:17 ·one being·tightly·joined to·the Lord is one spirit.
1Jn 4:2 the Spirit of·God: every spirit which affirms Jesus
1Jn 4:3 And every spirit that does·not affirm Jesus, the
Rv 19:10 the testimony of·Jesus is the spirit of·prophecy."
G4151.3 N-NPN πνεύματα (2x)
Rv 4:5 of·the throne, which are the seven Spirits of·God.
Rv 5:6 are the seven Spirits of·God having·been·dispatched
G4151.3 N-ASN πνεῦμα (11x)
Lk 24:37 alarmed, they·were·supposing to·observe a·spirit.
Rm 8:15 For yeu·did·not receive a·spirit of·slavery again to
Rm 11:8 "GOD gave them a·spirit of·a·stinging·numbness,
1Co 2:12 Now, *it·was* not the spirit of·the world *that* we·
1Co 15:45 *came·into·being* as a·spirit, giving·life·above.
2Co 4:13 Having the same spirit of·the trust, according·to
2Co 11:4 or *if* yeu·receive another spirit, which yeu·did·not
Eph 1:17 of·Glory, may·give to·yeu a·spirit of·wisdom and
2Ti 1:7 God did·not give us a·spirit of·timidity, but·rather
1Jn 4:6 ·a·result of·this, we·know the spirit of·truth and the
1Jn 4:6 we·know the spirit of·truth and the spirit of·error.
G4151.3 N-APN πνεύματα (2x)
1Jn 4:1 but·rather test·and·prove the spirits whether they·are
Rv 3:1 ·things says the·one having the Spirits of·God and the
G4151.3 N-DSN πνεύματι (22x)
Jn 4:23 shall·fall·prostrate to·the Father in spirit and in·truth,
Jn 4:24 ·*before* him to·fall·prostrate in spirit and in·truth."
Lk 1:17 ·sight of *Yahweh* in *the* spirit and power of·EliJah,
Lk 1:80 ·growing, and was·becoming·mighty in·spirit, and
Lk 2:40 was·becoming·mighty in·spirit, being·completely·
Ac 18:5 ·clenched in·the spirit *and* was·thoroughly·testifying
Ac 18:25 being·fervently·hot in·the spirit, he·was·speaking
Gal 6:1 ·reform such·a·man in a·spirit of·gentleness,
Mt 5:3 *are* the helplessly·poor in·the spirit, because theirs is
Rm 2:29 a·circumcision *that·is* of·heart, in spirit, *and* not in·
Rm 12:11 slothful; in·the spirit, by·being·fervently·hot; in·
Php 1:27 — that yeu·stand·fast in one spirit, with·one soul
Php 3:3 the·ones ritually·ministering to·God in·spirit, and
1Pe 4:6 ·flesh, but may·live according·to God in·*the*·spirit.
1Co 4:21 a·rod or with love, also in·a·spirit of·gentleness?
1Co 5:3 ·the body but being·present in·the spirit, even·now,
2Co 12:18 *Is·he* not in·the same spirit *that* we·walked?
Col 2:5 I·am together with·yeu in·the spirit, rejoicing and
1Ti 4:12 in conduct, in love, in spirit, in trust, *and* in moral·
1Jn 4:1 do·not trust every spirit, but·rather test·and·prove
Rv 17:3 And he·carried me away in spirit into a·wilderness.
Rv 21:10 And he·carried me away in spirit to a·great and
G4151.3 N-GSN πνεύματος (4x)
Lk 9:55 personally·know of·what·manner of·spirit yeu are.
Rm 7:6 us to·be·slaves in brand-newness of·spirit, and not
Jac 2:26 For just·as the body apart·from spirit is dead, in·
2Th 2:2 *by·any delusion* (neither through spirit, nor through
G4151.3 N-GPN πνευμάτων (4x)
Heb 12:9 be·in·subjection to·the Father of·spirits, and shall·
1Co 12:10 to·another discerning of·spirits, but to·someone·
1Co 14:12 Since yeu·are zealots of·spiritual *bestowments*,
Rv 1:4 , also from the seven Spirits who are in·the·sight of·
EG4151.3 (2x)
Mk 15:37 Jesus, after·sending·away *his spirit with* a·loud
1Jn 4:3 is the *spirit* of·the Adversary·of·the·Anointed-One,
G4151.4 N-NSN πνεῦμα (10x)
Lk 1:47 and my spirit leaped·for·joy in God my Savior.
Lk 8:55 And her spirit returned, and she·stood·up at·once,
Ac 17:16 at Athens, his spirit was·keenly·provoked within
Mt 26:41 In·fact, the spirit *is* eager, but the flesh *is* weak.
Mk 14:38 In·fact, the spirit *is* eager, but the flesh *is* weak.
1Th 5:23 And may every·single·part of·yeur spirit, soul, and
1Co 2:11 man·of·clay†, except the spirit of·the man·of·clay†
1Co 5:5 flesh, in·order·that the spirit may·be·saved in the
1Co 14:14 ·pray in·a·bestowed·tongue, my spirit prays, but
2Co 7:13 of·Titus, because his spirit has·been·refreshed by
G4151.4 N-NPN πνεύματα (1x)
1Co 14:32 And *the* spirits of·prophets are·subject to·prophets
G4151.4 N-ASN πνεῦμα (6x)
Jn 19:30 And drooping his head, he·handed·over the spirit.
Lk 23:46 hands I·shall·place·the·direct·care·of my spirit.'"
Ac 7:59 "Lord Jesus, accept my spirit."
Mt 27:50 ·out again with·a·loud voice, sent·away his spirit.
Rm 1:4 in power according·to a·spirit of·devoted·holiness,
1Co 16:18 For they·refreshed my spirit and yeurs.
G4151.4 N-DSN πνεύματι (15x)
Jn 11:33 with·her, he·was·exasperated in·the spirit; yet he·
Jn 13:21 Jesus was·troubled in·the spirit, and he·testified
Ac 19:21 placed *it* in his spirit, *that* after·going·throughout
Ac 20:22 behold, having·been·bound in·the spirit, I·myself
Mk 2:8 immediately in·his spirit that they·are·pondering
Mk 8:12 And after·sighing·deeply in·his spirit, he·says,
Rm 1:9 to·whom I·ritually·minister in my spirit in the good·
Rm 8:16 himself jointly·testifies with·our spirit that we·are
1Co 6:20 in yeur body and in yeur spirit, which are God's.
1Co 7:34 ·be holy, both in·body and in·spirit. But the·one
1Co 14:15 is·it? I·shall·pray with·the spirit, and I·shall·pray
1Co 14:15 I·shall·make·song with·the spirit, and I·shall·
1Co 14:16 when you·should·bless with·the spirit, how·shall
2Co 2:13 I·did·not have an·ease in·my spirit, *for* me not to·
Eph 4:23 *yeu* to·be·rejuvenated in·the spirit of·yeur mind—
G4151.4 N-DPN πνεύμασιν (2x)
Heb 12:23 ·all, and to·spirits of·righteous·men having·been·
1Pe 3:19 which, also traversing to·the spirits in prison, he·
G4151.4 N-GSN πνεύματος (7x)
Heb 4:12 even·unto a·dividing of·soul and spirit, and even
Gal 6:18 Anointed *be* with yeur spirit. So·be·it,·Amen.
1Pe 3:4 of·the calmly·mild and quietly·undisturbable spirit,
1Co 5:4 ·gathered·together, also with·my spirit, together
2Co 7:1 all tarnishing of·flesh and spirit, further·finishing
Phm 1:25 Anointed *be* with yeur spirit. So·be·it,·Amen.
2Ti 4:22 Jesus Anointed *be* with your spirit. Grace *be* with
G4151.5 N-NSN πνεῦμα (1x)
Ac 23:9 this man·of·clay†, but if a·spirit or an·angel spoke
G4151.5 N-NPN πνεύματα (1x)
Heb 1:14 all publicly·serving spirits, being·dispatched into
G4151.5 N-ASN πνεῦμα (1x)
Ac 23:8 *also* not·even an·angel nor a·spirit, but *the*
G4151.5 N-APN πνεύματα (1x)
Heb 1:7 the·one making his angels spirits and his attendants
G4151.6 N-NSN πνεῦμα (9x)
Lk 9:39 And behold, a·spirit takes him, and suddenly he·
Lk 11:24 "Whenever the impure spirit should·go·forth from
Ac 19:15 *on·one occasion*, the evil spirit declared, "Jesus I·
Ac 19:16 the man·of·clay†, whom the evil spirit was in,
Mt 12:43 whenever the impure spirit should·come·out from
Mk 1:26 And the impure spirit, after·convulsing him and
Mk 5:8 was·saying to·him, "Impure spirit, come·forth out

Mk 9:20 *Jesus*, immediately the spirit convulsed *the little·*
Mk 9:25 spirit, saying to·him, "Spirit, the·one mute and

G4151.6 N-NPN πνεύματα (4x)
Lk 10:20 in this, that the spirits are·subject to·yeu, but rather
Mk 3:11 And the impure spirits, whenever one·was·
Mk 5:13 after·coming·out, the impure spirits entered into
Rv 16:14 For they·are spirits of·demons, doing miraculous·

G4151.6 N-ASN πνεῦμα (6x)
Lk 4:33 a·man·of·clay† having a·spirit of·an·impure demon,
Lk 13:11 ·was a·woman having a·spirit of·sickness even
Ac 16:16 having a·spirit of·Pythonic·divination approached·
Mk 3:30 they·were·saying, "He·has an·impure spirit."
Mk 7:25 was·having an·impure spirit, upon·coming, she·fell·
Mk 9:17 I·brought to you my son, having a·mute spirit,

G4151.6 N-APN πνεύματα (7x)
Lk 11:26 *to·itself* seven other spirits more·evil·than itself,
Ac 8:7 For impure spirits, crying·out with·a·loud voice,
Ac 19:12 and·also *for* the evil spirits to·go·forth from them.
Ac 19:13 over the·ones having the evil spirits, saying, "On·
Mt 8:16 and he·cast·out the spirits with·a·word and both·
Mt 12:45 himself seven other spirits more·evil·than himself.
Rv 16:13 And I·saw three impure spirits like frogs *come* out

G4151.6 N-DSN πνεύματι (6x)
Lk 8:29 ·was·charging the impure spirit to·come·forth from
Lk 9:42 Jesus reprimanded the impure spirit and healed the
Ac 16:18 turning·about, declared to·the spirit, "I·charge
Mk 1:23 there·was a·man·of·clay† with an·impure spirit, and
Mk 5:2 ·tombs a·man·of·clay† with an·impure spirit,
Mk 9:25 he·reprimanded the impure spirit, saying to·him,

G4151.6 N-DPN πνεύμασιν (3x)
Lk 4:36 power he·orders the impure spirits, and they·come·
Mk 1:27 he·orders even the impure spirits, and they·listen·
1Ti 4:1 giving·heed to·impostrous spirits and to·instructions

G4151.6 N-GSN πνεύματος (2x)
Eph 2:2 authority of·the air, of·the spirit now operating in
Rv 18:2 and a·prison of·every impure spirit, and a·prison·

G4151.6 N-GPN πνευμάτων (6x)
Lk 6:18 also the·ones being·harassed by impure spirits. And
Lk 7:21 scourges, and evil spirits; and to·many *that·were*
Lk 8:2 ·relieved·and·cured from evil spirits and sicknesses:
Ac 5:16 and *those* being·harassed by impure spirits. *And* the·
Mt 10:1 to·them authority *over* impure spirits, such·for them
Mk 6:7 he·was·giving them authority *over* the impure spirits.

EG4151.6 (2x)
Mk 9:18 and wherever *that spirit* should·grasp him, he·
Mk 9:26 him repeatedly, *the spirit* came·forth, and he·

Ππ

G4151.7 N-NSN πνεῦμα (58x)
Jn 6:63 The Spirit is the·one giving·life-above.
Jn 14:26 *who·is* the Holy Spirit, whom the Father shall·send
Jn 15:26 ·from the Father, the Spirit of·Truth, who
Jn 16:13 But whenever that·one, the Spirit of·Truth, should·
Lk 3:22 and the Holy Spirit descended in·a·bodily shape like
Lk 4:18 "'Yahweh's Spirit *is* upon me for·the·cause·of
Lk 12:12 "For the Holy Spirit shall·instruct yeu in the same
Ac 1:16 which the Holy Spirit previously·declared through
Ac 2:4 bestowed·tongues, just·as the Spirit was·giving them
Ac 8:29 And the Spirit declared to·Philippe, "Go·alongside
Ac 8:39 out of·the water, Yahweh's Spirit snatched Philippe
Ac 10:19 about the clear·vision, the Spirit declared to·him,
Ac 10:44 these utterances, the Holy Spirit fell upon all the·
Ac 11:12 And the Spirit declared to·me to·go·together with·
Ac 11:15 I began to·speak, the Holy Spirit fell upon them,
Ac 13:2 and·also fasting, the Holy Spirit declared, "Now·
Ac 16:7 toward Bithynia, but the Spirit did·not let them.
Ac 19:6 his hands on·them, the Holy Spirit came upon them,
Ac 20:23 that the Holy Spirit thoroughly·testifies in·each
Ac 20:28 among which the Holy Spirit has·placed yeu *to·be*
Ac 21:11 "Thus says the Holy Spirit, 'in·this·manner the
Ac 28:25 "The Holy Spirit spoke well through Isaiah the
Heb 3:7 Therefore, just·as the Holy Spirit says, "'Today if
Heb 10:15 And *of·this*, the Holy Spirit also testifies to·us,
Gal 5:17 against the Spirit, and the Spirit against the flesh.
Mt 10:20 speaking, but·rather the Spirit of·yeur Father *is*
Mk 1:12 And straight·away the Spirit casts him forth into the
Mk 13:11 ·yeurselves speaking, but·rather the Holy Spirit.
Rm 8:9 in Spirit, if·perhaps God's Spirit dwells in yeu.
Rm 8:10 Now the Spirit *is* life-above through righteousness,
Rm 8:11 and if the Spirit of·the·one awakening Jesus from·
Rm 8:16 The Spirit himself jointly·testifies with·our spirit
Rm 8:26 the Spirit also is·helpful·and·works·together·
Rm 8:26 ·necessary, but·rather the Spirit himself intercedes
1Pe 1:11 what·kind·of season the Spirit of·Anointed-One in
1Pe 4:14 supremely·blessed, because the Spirit of·glory and
1Co 2:10 his Spirit, for the Spirit searches all·things, even,
1Co 2:11 the·things of·God, except the Spirit of·God.
1Co 3:16 of·God, and *that* the Spirit of·God dwells in yeu?
1Co 12:4 of·gracious·bestowments, but the same Spirit.
1Co 12:11 one and the very·same Spirit, dispensing to·each·
2Co 3:6 for the letter kills, but the Spirit gives·life-above.
2Co 3:17 Now the Lord is the Spirit, and where the Spirit of·
2Co 3:17 the Spirit, and where the Spirit of·Yahweh *is*, there
1Ti 4:1 Now the Spirit expressly says that in later seasons
1Jn 5:6 And the Spirit is the·one testifying, because the Spirit
1Jn 5:6 is the·one testifying, because the Spirit is the truth.
1Jn 5:7 the Word, and the Holy Spirit. And these three are
1Jn 5:8 testifying on the earth: the Spirit, and the water, and
Rv 2:7 let·him·hear what the Spirit says to·the Called·Out·
Rv 2:11 let·him·hear what the Spirit says to·the Called·Out·
Rv 2:17 let·him·hear what the Spirit says to·the Called·Out·
Rv 2:29 let·him·hear what the Spirit says to·the Called·Out·
Rv 3:6 let·him·hear what the Spirit says to·the Called·Out·
Rv 3:13 let·him·hear what the Spirit says to·the Called·Out·
Rv 3:22 let·him·hear what the Spirit says to·the Called·Out·
Rv 14:13 "Yes," says the Spirit, "in·order·that they·may·
Rv 22:17 And the Spirit and the Bride say, "Come!" And

G4151.7 N-ASN πνεῦμα (30x)
Jn 1:32 "I·have·distinctly·viewed the Spirit descending out
Jn 1:33 whom you·should·see the Spirit descending, and
Jn 3:34 God does·not give the Spirit as·a·result of·measure.
Jn 14:17 the Spirit of·Truth, whom the world is·not able to·
Lk 12:10 reviling against the Holy Spirit, it·shall·not be·
Ac 5:3 heart for·you to·lie to·the Holy Spirit, and to·pilfer
Ac 5:9 ·agreed·together to·try Yahweh's Spirit? Behold, the
Ac 5:32 and so·also *is* the Holy Spirit, whom God gave to·
Ac 8:18 ·viewing that the Holy Spirit is·given through the
Ac 10:47 who received the Holy Spirit just·as we·ourselves
Ac 15:8 giving to·them the Holy Spirit, even just·as *he·gave*
Heb 10:29 and abusively·insulting the Spirit of·Grace?
Gal 3:2 yeu, did·yeu·receive the Spirit as·a·result of·works
Gal 3:5 ·then, the·one fully·supplying the Spirit to·yeu and
Gal 4:6 sons, God dispatched·forth the Spirit of·his Son into
Gal 6:8 but the·one sowing into the Spirit, shall·reap eternal
Mt 3:16 ·him, and he·saw the Spirit of·God descending like
Mt 12:18 takes·delight. I·shall·place my Spirit upon him,
Mk 1:10 being·split·open, and the Spirit like a·dove
Mk 3:29 should·revile against the Holy Spirit does·not have
Rm 8:11 mortal bodies through his Spirit indwelling within
Jud 1:19 ·or·partisan·lines, soulish, not having *the* Spirit.
1Th 4:8 the·one also already·giving to us his Holy Spirit.
1Th 5:19 Do·not quench the Spirit.
1Co 2:12 received, but·rather the Spirit, the·one from·out
1Co 7:40 advice; and I·suppose also to·have God's Spirit.
1Co 12:8 ·another a·word of·knowledge by the same Spirit,
1Co 12:13 or free; and all are·given·drink into one Spirit.
Eph 4:30 And do·not grieve the Holy Spirit of·God, by
1Jn 4:2 By this yeu·presently·know the Spirit of·God: every

G4151.7 N-DSN πνεύματι (23x)
Lk 2:27 And he·came by the Spirit into the Sanctuary·
Lk 4:1 Jordan and was·led by the Spirit into the wilderness,
Lk 10:21 Jesus leaped·for·joy in·the Spirit and declared,
Ac 6:10 wisdom and the Spirit by·which he·was·speaking.
Ac 7:51 always do·violently·oppose the Holy Spirit. As yeur
Ac 11:16 ·water, but yeu shall·be·immersed in Holy Spirit.'
Ac 15:28 For it·seemed·good to·the Holy Spirit, and to·us,
Mt 12:28 ·out the demons by God's Spirit, then·by·inference,
Mk 12:36 For David himself declared by the Holy Spirit,
Rm 8:13 But if *by·the·*Spirit yeu·put·to·death the practices
Rm 8:14 For as·many·as are·led by·God's Spirit, these are
Jud 1:20 holy trust, *yeu* who·are·praying by Holy Spirit,
1Pe 1:12 with Holy Spirit already·being·dispatched from
1Pe 3:18 in·flesh, but being·given·life-above in·the Spirit,
1Co 6:11 of·the Lord Jesus, and by the Spirit of·our God.
1Co 12:3 not·even·one·man speaking by God's Spirit says,
1Co 12:9 ·else, trust by the same Spirit, but to·another,
1Co 12:9 ·bestowments of·healing by the same Spirit,
1Co 12:13 For even by one Spirit we·ourselves were all
2Co 3:3 ·ink, but·rather *with·the·*Spirit of·the·living God,
Eph 1:13 ·sealed with·the Holy Spirit of·the promise,
Col 1:8 ·one also making·plain to·us yeur love in *the* Spirit.
Rv 1:10 I·came·to·be in *the* Spirit on the Lord's day and

G4151.7 N-GSN πνεύματος (52x)
Jn 3:6 ·one having·been·born from·out of·the Spirit is spirit.
Jn 3:8 is any one having·been·born from·out of·the Spirit."
Jn 7:39 But he·declared this concerning the Spirit, which the·
Lk 2:26 to·him by the Holy Spirit *that he·was* not to·see
Lk 4:14 returned·back in the power of·the Spirit to Galilee,
Ac 1:8 power, with·the Holy Spirit coming·upon yeu, and
Ac 2:17 *that* I·shall·pour·forth from my Spirit upon all flesh
Ac 2:18 I·shall·pour·forth from my Spirit, and they·shall·
Ac 2:33 the Promise of·the Holy Spirit personally·from the
Ac 2:38 ·receive the voluntary·present of·the Holy Spirit.
Ac 9:31 ·comfort of·the Holy Spirit, they·were·multiplying.
Ac 10:45 ·present of·the Holy Spirit has·been·poured·forth,
Ac 11:28 signified through the Spirit *that* there·was·about
Ac 13:4 after·being·sent·forth by the Holy Spirit, these·men
Ac 16:6 ·being·forbidden by the Holy Spirit to·speak the
Ac 21:4 ·saying to·Paul through the Spirit not to·walk·up to
Heb 9:8 with·the Holy Spirit making·plain this·thing: *that*
Heb 9:14 who through *the* eternal Spirit offered himself
Gal 3:14 ·may·receive the promise of·the Spirit through the
Gal 5:17 For the flesh longs against the Spirit, and the Spirit
Gal 5:22 But the fruit of·the Spirit is love, joy, peace,
Gal 6:8 shall·reap eternal life-above from·out of·the Spirit.
Mt 4:1 ·up into the wilderness by the Spirit to·be·tried by the
Mt 12:31 revilement of·the *Holy* Spirit shall·not be·forgiven
Mt 12:32 should·declare against the Holy Spirit, it·shall·not
Mt 28:19 Father, and of·the Son, and of·the Holy Spirit,
Rm 8:2 For the Law-of-Liberty of·the Spirit of·the life-above
Rm 8:5 ·to Spirit *contemplate* the·things of·the Spirit.
Rm 8:6 but the disposition of·the Spirit *is* life-above and
Rm 8:23 having the firstfruit of·the Spirit, even we·ourselves
Rm 8:27 ·knows what the disposition of·the Spirit *is*, how
Rm 15:19 with *the* power of·God's Spirit, such·for me to·
Rm 15:30 ·of the love of·the Spirit, to·strive·together with·
Php 1:19 an·ample·supply of·the Spirit of·Jesus Anointed
1Pe 1:2 of·Father God, by a·renewed·holiness of·Spirit— to
1Pe 1:22 truth through *the* Spirit unto a·brotherly·affection
2Pe 1:21 ·carried·along by *the* Holy Spirit, men·of·clay†
1Co 2:10 revealed *them* to·us through his Spirit, for the Spirit
1Co 2:14 does·not accept the·things of·the Spirit of·God, for
1Co 6:19 body is a·temple of·the Holy Spirit *who·is* in yeu,
1Co 12:7 manifestation of·the Spirit is·given to·each·man
1Co 12:8 ·one is·given through the Spirit a·word of·wisdom,
2Co 1:22 the earnest·deposit of·the Spirit in our hearts.
2Co 3:18 glory to glory, exactly·as from Yahweh's Spirit.
2Co 5:5 also giving to·us the earnest·deposit of·the Spirit.
2Co 13:14 and the fellowship of·the Holy Spirit, *be* with yeu
Eph 3:16 ·made·mighty with·power through his Spirit in the
Eph 4:3 to·fully·keep the oneness of·the Spirit in the joint·
Eph 5:9 (for the fruit of·the Spirit *is* in all beneficial·
Eph 6:17 ·Salvation and the dagger of·the Spirit, which is an·
1Jn 3:24 us, as·a·result of·the Spirit whom he·already·gave
1Jn 4:13 because he·has·given to·us from·out of·his Spirit.

G4151.7 N/P-GSN πνεύματος (1x)
2Co 3:8 more shall the Service of·the Spirit be in glory?

EG4151.7 (4x)
Jn 16:15 from·out of·me, *the Spirit of·Truth* shall·receive
2Co 3:10 ·of the surpassing glory *of·the Service of·the Spirit*.
2Co 3:11 *surpassing is* the·one *of·the Spirit* remaining in

2Co 4:1 having this Service *of·the* Spirit, just·as we·are·
G4151.8 N-NSN πνεῦμα (7x)
Jn 4:24 God *is* Spirit, and it·is·mandatory·for the·ones
Jn 7:39 ·about to·receive, for Holy Spirit was not·yet *given*,
Lk 1:35 declared to·her, "Holy Spirit shall·come upon you,
Lk 2:25 ·consoling of·IsraEl. And Holy Spirit was upon him.
Ac 19:2 ·did·not·even hear whether there·is a·Holy Spirit."
Eph 4:4 ·*is* one Body, and one Spirit— just·as also yeu·are·
Rv 11:11 a·half days, *the* Spirit of·life-above from·out of·
G4151.8 N-ASN πνεῦμα (12x)
Jn 20:22 Then he·says to·them, "Receive Holy Spirit!
Lk 11:13 shall·give Holy Spirit to·the·ones requesting·of
Ac 8:15 concerning them, that they·may·receive Holy Spirit.
Ac 8:17 on them, and they·were·receiving Holy Spirit.
Ac 8:19 ·should·lay *my* hands, he·may·receive Holy Spirit."
Ac 19:2 "Did·yeu·receive Holy Spirit after·trusting?
Gal 4:29 the·one *being·born* according·to Spirit, even in·this·
Rm 8:1 according·to flesh, but·rather according·to Spirit.
Rm 8:4 according·to flesh, but·rather according·to Spirit.
Rm 8:5 the·ones according·to Spirit *contemplate* the·things
Rm 8:9 ·man does·not have Anointed-One's Spirit, this·one
Rm 8:15 ·rather yeu·received a·Spirit of·adoption·as·sons,
G4151.8 N-DSN πνεύματι (28x)
Jn 1:33 him, the·same is the·one immersing in Holy Spirit.'
Lk 3:16 shall·immerse yeu in Holy Spirit and in·fire,
Ac 1:5 but yeu shall·be·immersed in Holy Spirit after not *too*
Ac 10:38 from Natsareth with·Holy Spirit and with·power,
Gal 3:3 After·beginning in·*the*·Spirit, are·yeu·finishing·
Gal 5:5 For we·ourselves, by·*the*·Spirit, fully·await an·
Gal 5:16 So I·say, walk in·Spirit, and no, yeu·would·not
Gal 5:18 But if yeu·are·led by·Spirit, yeu·are·not under
Gal 5:25 If we·live in·Spirit, we·should·conform·and·march·
Gal 5:25 ·should·conform·and·march·orderly also in·Spirit.
Mt 3:11 shall·immerse yeu in Holy Spirit and in·fire,
Mt 22:43 "So·then how·does David in Spirit call him 'Lord,
Mk 1:8 but he·himself shall·immerse yeu in Holy Spirit."
Rm 8:9 in flesh, but·rather in Spirit, if·perhaps God's Spirit
Rm 9:1 conscience jointly·testifying with·me in Holy Spirit,
Rm 14:17 righteousness, peace, and joy in Holy Spirit.
Rm 15:16 having·been·made·holy by Holy Spirit.
1Th 1:5 in power and in Holy Spirit and with much fullness·
1Co 12:3 "Jesus *is* Lord," except by Holy Spirit.
1Co 14:2 ·comprehension, but in·*the*·Spirit, he·does·speak
2Co 6:6 by kindness, by Holy Spirit, by love without·
Eph 2:18 the embraceable·access to the Father by one Spirit.
Eph 2:22 are·built·together for a·residence of·God in Spirit.
Eph 3:5 to·his holy ambassadors and prophets by *the* Spirit):
Eph 5:18 but·rather be·completely·filled in Spirit—
Eph 6:18 petition, be·presently·praying in Spirit in every
1Ti 3:16 is·regarded·as·righteous in Spirit, is·gazed·upon
Rv 4:2 And immediately I·came·to·be in Spirit, and behold,
G4151.8 N-GSN πνεύματος (30x)
Jn 3:5 ·be·born from·out of·water and of·Spirit, he·is·not
Lk 1:15 and he·shall·be·filled with·Holy Spirit, yet·even
Lk 1:41 womb, and EliSabeth was·filled with·Holy Spirit.
Lk 1:67 was·filled with·Holy Spirit and prophesied, saying,
Lk 4:1 And Jesus, full of·Holy Spirit, returned·back from
Ac 1:2 ·commands through Holy Spirit to·the ambassadors
Ac 2:4 And absolutely·all were·filled with·Holy Spirit, and
Ac 4:8 Then Peter, being·filled with·Holy Spirit, declared to
Ac 4:31 and absolutely·all were·filled with·Holy Spirit, and
Ac 6:3 being·attested·to, full of·Holy Spirit and wisdom,
Ac 6:5 full of·trust and of·Holy Spirit, and·also Philippe,
Ac 7:55 ·being full of·Holy Spirit, after·gazing·intently into
Ac 9:17 ·your·sight and may·be·filled with·Holy Spirit."
Ac 11:24 ·good man and full of·Holy Spirit and trust. And
Ac 13:9 , being·filled with·Holy Spirit and gazing·intently
Ac 13:52 ·completely·filled with·joy and with·Holy Spirit.
Heb 2:4 and with·distributions of·Holy Spirit, according·to
Heb 6:4 ·present, and becoming participants of·Holy Spirit,
Mt 1:18 in a·pregnancy birthed·from·out of·Holy Spirit.
Mt 1:20 ·conceived in her is birthed·from·out of·Holy Spirit.
Rm 5:5 in our hearts through Holy Spirit, the·one already·
Rm 15:13 in the Expectation by *the* power of·Holy Spirit.
Php 2:1 of·love, if any fellowship of·Spirit, if any inward·
1Th 1:6 ·with much tribulation *and* with joy of·Holy Spirit,
2Th 2:13 Salvation in renewed·holiness of·Spirit and in·trust
Tit 3:5 a·bath of·regeneration and a·renewing of·Holy Spirit,
1Co 2:4 but·rather in demonstration of·Spirit and of·power,
1Co 2:13 ·rather with instructions of·Holy Spirit, comparing
2Co 3:6 not of·letter, but·rather of·Spirit, for the letter kills,
2Ti 1:14 ·must·vigilantly·keep through Holy Spirit, the·one
EG4151.8 (1x)
Eph 6:18 and·also in this same *Spirit*, presently·staying·alert

G4152 πνευματικός pnêumatikós *adj.* (26x)
Roots:G4151 Compare:G5591 G5446
G4152.1 A-NSM πνευματικός (4x)
Rm 7:14 ·know that the Torah-Law is spiritual, but I·myself
1Pe 2:5 stones, are·built·up, *being* a·spiritual house, a·holy
1Co 2:15 And the spiritual·one scrutinizes, in·fact, all·things,
1Co 14:37 to·be a·prophet or spiritual, let·him·acknowledge
G4152.1 A-NSN πνευματικόν (4x)
1Co 15:44 a·soulish body; it·is·awakened a·spiritual body.
1Co 15:44 ·is a·soulish body, and there·is a·spiritual body.
1Co 15:46 Moreover, the spiritual *was* not first, but·rather
1Co 15:46 ·rather the soulish, then·afterward the spiritual.
G4152.1 A-NPM πνευματικοί (1x)
Gal 6:1 (the·ones *who·are* spiritual) must·completely·reform
G4152.1 A-ASN πνευματικόν (3x)
Rm 1:11 gracious·bestowment *which·is* spiritual, in·order·for
1Co 10:3 And all ate the same spiritual food,
1Co 10:4 and all drank the same spiritual drink, for they·
G4152.1 A-APF πνευματικάς (1x)
1Pe 2:5 to·carry·up spiritual sacrifices well·acceptable to·
G4152.1 A-APN πνευματικά (4x)
1Co 2:13 comparing spiritual·things with·spiritual·things.
1Co 9:11 we·ourselves sowed to·yeu the spiritual·things, *is·it*
1Co 14:1 and zealously·desire the spiritual *bestowments*,
Eph 6:12 specifically·against the spiritual·things of·evil in
G4152.1 A-DSF πνευματικῇ (2x)
Eph 1:3 already·blessing us with every spiritual blessing by
Col 1:9 ·his will in all wisdom and spiritual comprehension,
G4152.1 A-DPM πνευματικοῖς (1x)
1Co 3:1 able to·speak to·yeu as to·spiritual·ones, but·rather
G4152.1 A-DPF πνευματικαῖς (2x)
Eph 5:19 in·psalms and hymns and spiritual songs, singing
Col 3:16 in·psalms and hymns and spiritual songs, singing
G4152.1 A-DPN πνευματικοῖς (2x)
Rm 15:27 in·their spiritual·things, they·are·obligated also to·
1Co 2:13 comparing spiritual·things with·spiritual·things.
G4152.1 A-GSF πνευματικῆς (1x)
1Co 10:4 from·out of·that·spiritual Solid·Rock following
G4152.1 A-GPN πνευματικῶν (1x)
1Co 12:1 Now concerning the spiritual *bestowments*,

G4153 πνευματικῶς pnêumatikōs *adv.* (3x)
Roots:G4152
G4153.1 ADV πνευματικῶς (2x)
1Co 2:14 to·know *it*, because it·is·investigated spiritually.
Rv 11:8 *that·is JeruSalem*, which spiritually is·called Sodom
EG4153.1 (1x)
Jn 9:39 ·ones not *spiritually* looking·about may·look·about,

G4154 πνέω pnéō *v.* (7x)
Compare:G0416 G5594 G5445-5 See:G4157
G4154.2 V-PAI-3S πνεῖ (1x)
Jn 3:8 The breeze blows where it·wants, and you·hear the
G4154.2 V-PAP-ASM πνέοντα (1x)
Lk 12:55 *yeu·should·see the* south·wind blowing, yeu·say,
G4154.2 V-PAP-GSM πνέοντος (1x)
Jn 6:18 was·thoroughly·roused *due·to* a·great wind blowing.
G4154.2 V-PAS-3S πνέῃ (1x)
Rv 7:1 in·order·that wind should·not blow on the earth, nor
G4154.2 V-AAI-3P ἔπνευσαν (2x)
Mt 7:25 and the winds blew, and they·fell·directly·against
Mt 7:27 came, and the winds blew, and they·surged·against
G4154.3 V-PAP-DSF πνεούσῃ (1x)
Ac 27:40 to·the blowing·wind, they·were·bearing·down

G4155 πνίγω pnígō *v.* (2x)
Roots:G4154 See:G4156 G0638 G4846
G4155.2 V-IAI-3S ἔπνιγεν (1x)
Mt 18:28 and securely·holding him, he·was·strangling *him*,
G4155.3 V-IPI-3P ἐπνίγοντο (1x)
Mk 5:13 ·thousand *of·them*, and they·were·drowned in the

G4156 πνικτός pniktós *adj.* (3x)
Roots:G4155
G4156.2 A-ASN πνικτόν (1x)
Ac 21:25 *from* blood, *from* a·strangled·animal, and *from*
G4156.2 A-GSN πνικτοῦ (2x)
Ac 15:20 and *from* the strangled·animal, and *from* the blood
Ac 15:29 and from·blood, and from·a·strangled·animal, and

G4157 πνοή pnôḗ *n.* (2x)
Roots:G4154 Compare:G0417 G4151 G5590
See:G0378-3 xLangAlso:H5397
G4157.2 N-GSF πνοῆς (1x)
Ac 2:2 heaven, just·as of·a·rushing forceful wind, and it·
G4157.3 N-ASF πνοήν (1x)
Ac 17:25 with·himself giving life† and breath to·all·things,

G4158 ποδ•ήρης pôdḗrēs *adj.* (1x)
Roots:G4228 Compare:G4749 G2689 G2440 G1361-4 See:G2066 xLangAlso:H4598 H0906 H4254
G4158.2 A-ASM ποδήρη (1x)
Rv 1:13 having·dressed·himself·with a·foot·length·robe, and

G4159 πό•θεν póthên *adv.* (28x)
Roots:G4213
G4159.1 ADV-I πόθεν (28x)
Jn 1:48 says to·him, "From·what·source do·you·know me?
Jn 2:9 wine, yet had·not seen from·what·source it·was (but
Jn 3:8 ·yet you·have·not seen from·what·source it·comes or
Jn 4:11 is deep. So·then from·what·source do·you·have the
Jn 6:5 to Philip, "From·what·source shall·we·buy bread in·
Jn 7:27 ·know this·man, *and* from·what·source he·is. Now
Jn 7:27 not·even·one·man knows from·what·source he·is."
Jn 7:28 do·yeu·personally·know from·what·source I·am?
Jn 8:14 I·personally·know from·what·source I·came and
Jn 8:14 But yeu have·not seen from·what·source I·come and
Jn 9:29 we·do·not personally·know from·what·source he·is.
Jn 9:30 do·not personally·know from·what·source he·is, and·
Jn 19:9 says to·Jesus, "From·what·source are you·yourself?
Lk 1:43 And from·what·source *is* this *granted* to·me, that the
Lk 13:25 personally·know yeu. From·what·source are·yeu?
Lk 13:27 personally·know yeu. From·what·source are·yeu?
Lk 20:7 *as* to·not personally·know from·what·source *it·was*.
Mt 13:27 field? So·then, from·what·source are the darnel·
Mt 13:54 and to·say, "From·what·source *does* this·man *have*
Mt 13:56 us? So·then from·what·source *does* this·man *do* all
Mt 15:33 "From·what·source *should·we·find* for·ourselves
Mt 21:25 The immersion of·John, from·what·source was·it?
Mk 6:2 saying, "From·what·source *does* this·man *do* these·
Mk 8:4 him, "From·what·source shall·someone be·able to·
Mk 12:37 'Lord,' so from·what·source is his Son?
Jac 4:1 From·what·source *are* wars and quarrels among yeu
Rv 2:5 remember from·what·source you·have·fallen, and
Rv 7:13 long·robes? And from·what·source did·they·come?

G4160 ποιέω pôiéō *v.* (611x)
Compare:G4238 G2038 G2716 G2936 See:G4161 xLangEquiv:H6213
G4160.1 V-FAI-1S ποιήσω (6x)
Jn 14:13 in my name, that·thing shall·I·do, that the Father
Jn 14:14 something in my name, I·myself shall·do *it*.
Lk 12:18 declared, 'This shall·I·do, I·shall·demolish my
Lk 16:4 I·know what I·shall·do, in·order·that, whenever I·
Mt 27:22 "So·then what shall·I·do with·YeShua, the·one
2Co 11:12 I·presently·do, and *what* I·shall·do, *is* in·order·
G4160.1 V-FAI-1P ποιήσομεν (6x)
Lk 3:10 ·of him, saying, "So·then what shall·we·do?"
Lk 3:12 "Mentor, what shall·we·do?"
Lk 3:14 "And what·shall we·ourselves do?" And he·declared
Ac 2:37 "Men, brothers, what shall·we·do?"
Ac 4:16 saying, "What shall·we·do to·these men·of·clay†?

Heb 6:3 And this we·shall·do, if·ever God should·freely·
G4160.1 V-FAI-2S ποιήσεις (2x)
Phm 1:21 ·seen that you·shall·do also above·and·beyond
3Jn 1:6 as·is·worthy of·God, *then* you·shall·do well.
G4160.1 V-FAI-2P ποιήσετε (2x)
Mt 21:21 be·hesitant, not merely shall·yeu·do the·thing *that*
2Th 3:4 also yeu·do and shall·do the·things·which we·charge
G4160.1 V-FAI-3S ποιήσει (11x)
Jn 7:31 should·come, ¿! shall·he·do more miraculous·signs
Jn 14:12 that I·myself do, he·shall·do those·likewise. And
Jn 14:12 And greater *works* than·these shall·he·do, because
Lk 20:15 what shall the owner of·the vineyard do to·them?
Ac 13:22 ·to my·own heart, who shall·do all my will.
Heb 13:6 be·afraid of·what a·man·of·clay† shall·do to·me."
Mt 18:35 shall my heavenly Father do to·yeu, unless each·
Mt 21:40 ·come, what shall·he·do to·those tenant·farmers?
Mk 9:39 for there·is not·even·one who shall·do a·miracle in
Mk 12:9 the owner of·the vineyard do? He·shall·come and
1Th 5:24 *is* the·one calling yeu forth, who also shall·do *it*.
G4160.1 V-FAI-3P ποιήσουσιν (3x)
Jn 15:21 all these·things shall·they·do to·yeu on·account·of
Jn 16:3 And these·things shall·they·do to·yeu, because they·
1Co 15:29 Otherwise what shall·they·do, the·ones being·
G4160.1 V-FAP-NSM ποιήσων (1x)
Ac 24:17 years, I·came·openly doing merciful·acts for my
G4160.1 V-PAI-1S ποιῶ (21x)
Jn 5:36 *are* the same works which I·myself do; it·testifies
Jn 8:28 I AM, and *that* I·do not·even·one·thing of my·own·
Jn 8:29 because I·myself always do the·things *that·are*
Jn 10:25 "The works that I·myself do in my Father's name,
Jn 10:37 "If I·do·not do the works of·my Father, do·not trust
Jn 10:38 "But if I·do, though yeu·may·not trust me, trust the
Jn 13:7 to·him, "What I·myself do, you·yourself do·not
Jn 14:12 me, the works that I·myself do, he·shall·do those·
Jn 14:31 Father commanded me, I·do *it just* in·that·manner.
Lk 20:8 to·yeu by what·kind·of authority I·do these·things."
Mt 21:24 to·yeu by what·kind·of authority I·do these·things.
Mt 21:27 to·yeu by what·kind·of authority I·do these·things.
Mt 26:18 season is near·at·hand. I·do the Passover alongside
Mk 11:29 to·yeu by what·kind·of authority I·do these·things.
Mk 11:33 to·yeu by what·kind·of authority I·do these·things.
Rm 7:15 I·want *to·do*, but·rather I·do that·thing which I·hate
Rm 7:16 But if I·do that which I·do·not want, I·concur with·
Rm 7:19 I·want *to·do*, *that* I·do, but·rather a·bad·thing
Rm 7:20 do·not want, *if* that·thing I·do, *it·is* no·longer I·
1Co 9:23 And this I·do on·account·of the good·news, in·
2Co 11:12 But what I·presently·do, and *what* I·shall·do, *is*
G4160.1 V-PAI-1P ποιοῦμεν (4x)
Jn 6:28 to him, "What·do we·do in·order·that we·may·work
Jn 11:47 and were·saying, "What·do we·do, because this
1Jn 1:6 in the darkness, we·do·lie, and do·not do the truth.
1Jn 3:22 ·keep his commandments and do the·things *that·are*
G4160.1 V-PAI-2S ποιεῖς (11x)
Jn 2:18 do·you·show to·us, *seeing* that you·do these·things?
Jn 3:2 miraculous·signs that you·yourself do unless God
Jn 6:30 miraculous·sign *do* you·yourself do, in·order·that
Jn 7:3 disciples also may·observe the works that you do.
Jn 7:4 in freeness·of·speech *publicly*. If you·do these·things,
Jn 13:27 Jesus says to·him, "What you·do, do more·swiftly.
Lk 20:2 by what·kind·of authority do·you·do these·things?
Mt 21:23 By what·kind·of authority do·you·do these·things?
Mk 11:28 By what·kind·of authority do·you·do these·things?
Jac 2:19 that there·is one God. You·do well. The demons
3Jn 1:5 ·man, trustworthily do·you·do whatever *good·deed*
G4160.1 V-PAI-2P ποιεῖτε (16x)
Jn 8:38 yeu do that·which yeu·have·clearly·seen from·
Jn 8:41 "Yeu·yeurselves do the deeds of·yeur father.
Lk 6:2 to·them, "Why·do yeu·do that·which it·is·not proper
Lk 6:46 Lord, Lord,' and do·not do the·things·which I·say?
Ac 14:15 "Men, why·do yeu·do these·things?
Mt 5:47 brothers merely, what·do yeu·do *that·is* superior *to·*
Mk 7:8 and many other such similar·things do·yeu·do."
Mk 7:13 And many such similar·things do·yeu·do."
Mk 11:3 ·man should·declare to·yeu, 'Why·do yeu·do this?
Mk 11:5 to·them, "What·are yeu·doing, loosening the colt?
Jac 2:8 ·shall·love your neighbor as yourself,'" yeu·do well.
2Pe 1:19 prophetic word, to·which yeu·do well taking·heed
1Th 4:10 For even yeu·do this toward all the brothers, the·
1Th 5:11 and edify one the other, just·as also yeu·do.
2Th 3:4 yeu, that also yeu·do and shall·do the·things·which
1Co 10:31 or drink, or anything *that* yeu·do, do all to God's
G4160.1 V-PAI-3S ποιεῖ (17x)
Jn 5:19 should·do, these·things also the Son does likewise.
Jn 5:20 him all·things that he·himself does, and he·shall·
Jn 7:4 For *there·is* not·even·one·man *that* does anything in
Jn 7:19 not·even·one from·among yeu does the Torah-Law.
Jn 7:51 and should·know what *it·is that* he·does?"
Jn 11:47 this man·of·clay† does many miraculous·signs?
Jn 14:10 Father abiding in me, he·himself does the works.
Jn 15:15 personally·know what his lord does; but I·have·
Lk 7:8 'Do this,' and he·does *it*."
Mt 6:3 your left·hand know what your right·hand is·doing,
Mt 7:24 these sayings of·mine and does them, I·shall·liken
Mt 8:9 'Do this,' and he·does *it*."
1Co 7:37 to·keep·unmarried his virgin·daughter, does well.
1Co 7:38 even the *father* giving·away·in·marriage does well,
1Co 7:38 giving·away·in·marriage does significantly·better.
3Jn 1:10 his deeds which he·does, gossiping·against us with·
Rv 13:13 And it·does great signs, so that it·should·make fire
G4160.1 V-PAI-3P ποιοῦσιν (11x)
Lk 6:33 For even the morally·disqualified·ones do the same.
Lk 23:31 "Because if they·do these·things to the arbor·tree
Lk 23:34 for they·do·not personally·know what they·do."
Mt 5:46 Do·not·indeed even the tax·collectors do the same?
Mt 5:47 *that·is* superior *to·others*? Do not·indeed even the
Mt 6:2 you, just·as the stage·acting·hypocrites do in the
Mt 12:2 "Behold, your disciples do that·which it·is·not
Mt 23:3 For they·say *it*, and·yet they·do·not do *it*.
Mt 23:5 all their works *that* they·do *are* specifically·for them
Mk 2:24 "See, why·do they·do on the Sabbath·days that·
Rm 1:32 of·death), not merely do *the* same, but·rather also
G4160.1 V-PAM-2S ποιεῖ (3x)
Lk 10:28 "You·answered uprightly. Do this, and you·shall·
Lk 10:37 "Traverse, and you·yourself do likewise."
Rm 13:3 ·of the authority? Do the beneficially·good·thing,
G4160.1 V-PAM-2P ποιεῖτε (13x)
Lk 6:27 "Love yeur enemies, do good to·the·ones hating yeu
Lk 6:31 ·do to·yeu, also yeu·yeurselves do likewise to·them.
Lk 22:19 the·one being·given on·yeur behalf. Do this as my
Mt 5:44 who·are·cursing yeu. "Do good to·the·ones hating
Mt 7:12 ·do to·yeu, yeu·yeurselves do even in·this·manner
Mt 23:3 yeu·must·observantly·keep *that·thing* and do *it*, but
Mt 23:3 and do *it*, but do·not do according·to their works.
Jac 2:12 In·this·manner yeu·must·speak and so do: as ones·
Php 2:14 Do all·things completely·apart·from grumblings
1Co 10:31 or anything *that* yeu·do, do all to God's glory.
1Co 11:24 the·one being·broken over yeu. Do this as my
1Co 11:25 covenant in my blood. Do this, as·often·as yeu·
Eph 6:9 And the lords: They·must·do the same·things
G4160.1 V-PAM-3S ποιείτω (2x)
Lk 3:11 *any*, and the·one having food must·do likewise."
1Co 7:36 financial·need so happens, let·him·do what he·will
G4160.1 V-PAN ποιεῖν (22x)
Jn 3:2 ·even·one·man is·able to·do these miraculous·signs
Jn 5:19 the Son is·not able to·do not·even·one·thing by
Jn 5:30 "I·myself am·not able to·do not·even·one·thing of
Jn 6:6 had·personally·known what he·was·about to·do.
Jn 7:17 If any·man should·want to·do his will, he·shall·know
Jn 8:44 Slanderer, and yeu·want to·do the longings of·yeur
Jn 9:16 ·of·moral·failure, able to·do such miraculous·signs?
Jn 9:33 he·would·not be·able to·do not·even·one·thing."
Jn 15:5 me, yeu·are·not able to·do not·even·one·thing.
Lk 6:2 ·do yeu·do that·which it·is·not proper to·do on the
Ac 1:1 all that Jesus began both to·do and to·instruct,
Ac 9:6 ·be·spoken to·you what is·mandatory·for you to·do."
Ac 10:6 shall·speak to·you what is·necessary·for you to·do."
Ac 16:21 for·us to·personally·accept, neither to·do, being
Ac 16:30 ·for me to·do in·order·that I·may·be·saved?
Ac 22:26 "Clearly·see what you·are·about to·do, for this
Mt 6:1 "Take·heed not to·do yeur merciful·act before the
Mt 12:2 do that·which it·is·not proper to·do on a·Sabbath."
Mt 12:12 As·such, it·is·proper to·do good on·the Sabbath·
Rm 1:28 to a·disqualified mind, to·do the·things *which·are*
Rm 7:21 wanting for·myself to·do the morally·good·thing, *I·*
Jac 4:17 having·seen *the* morally·good·thing to·do and not
G4160.1 V-PAP-ASM ποιοῦντα (3x)
Jn 5:19 ·only what he·should·look·upon the Father doing, for
Lk 12:43 upon·coming, shall·find doing in·this·manner.
Mt 24:46 upon·coming, shall·find *him* doing in·this·manner.
G4160.1 V-PAP-APM ποιοῦντας (1x)
1Pe 3:12 *the* face of·Yahweh *is* against those·doing bad."
G4160.1 V-PAP-DSM ποιοῦντι (1x)
Jac 4:17 morally·good·thing to·do and not doing *it*, to·him it·
G4160.1 V-PAP-GSM ποιοῦντος (1x)
Mt 6:3 "But as·you are·doing a·merciful·act, do·not·let your
G4160.1 V-PAP-NSM ποιῶν (15x)
Jn 3:21 But the·one doing the truth comes to the light, in·
Lk 6:47 hearing my sayings and doing them, I·shall·indicate
Ac 10:2 his house, both doing many merciful·acts for·the
Ac 15:17 says Yahweh, the·one doing all these·things."
Mt 7:21 heavens, but·rather the·one doing the will of·my
Mt 7:26 of·mine, and not doing them, shall·be·likened to·a·
Rm 2:3 such·things, and·yet doing *the* same·things)— *do·*
Rm 3:12 ·useless; there·is none doing benevolent·kindness;
Rm 12:20 give him drink; for *by* doing this, you·shall·stack
1Ti 4:16 persist in·them, for in·doing this you·shall·save
1Ti 5:21 prejudice, doing not·even·one·thing according·to
1Jn 2:17 and its longing, but the·one doing the will of·God
1Jn 2:29 yeu·know that any one doing the righteousness has·
1Jn 3:7 deceive yeu. The·one doing the righteousness is
1Jn 3:10 Every one not doing righteousness is not birthed·
G4160.1 V-PAP-NPN ποιοῦντα (1x)
Rv 16:14 ·are spirits of·demons, doing miraculous·signs, to·
G4160.1 V-PAP-NPM ποιοῦντες (7x)
Lk 8:21 hearing the Redemptive-word of·God and doing it."
Ac 19:14 there·were certain·men *who·were* doing this·thing:
Gal 6:9 And we·should·not be·cowardly *in* doing the good;
2Pe 1:10 and Selection firm. For in·doing these·things, no,
Eph 2:3 of·our flesh, doing the determinations·of·the·will
Eph 6:6 slaves of·the Anointed-One, doing the will of·God
Rv 22:14 ·blessed *are* the·ones doing his commandments, in·
G4160.1 V-PAS-1S ποιῶ (2x)
Jn 4:34 "My food is that I·may·do the will of·the·one
Jn 6:38 heaven, not in·order·that I·may·do my·own will,
G4160.1 V-PAS-2S ποιῇς (3x)
Mt 6:2 whenever you·should·do a·merciful·act, you·
Mk 11:28 in·order·that you·should·do these·things?
Rm 13:4 ·good·thing. But if you·should·do the bad·thing,
G4160.1 V-PAS-2P ποιῆτε (7x)
Jn 13:15 ·myself did for·yeu, also yeu·yeurselves should·do.
Jn 13:17 supremely·blessed are·yeu if yeu·should·do them.
Jn 15:14 my friends, if yeu·should·do as·much·as I·myself
Gal 5:17 in·order·that yeu·may·not do these·things which
2Co 13:7 but·rather that yeu·yeurselves should·do the good,
Col 3:17 anything what soever yeu·should·do in word or in
Col 3:23 what soever *that* yeu·should·do, be·working *it* out
G4160.1 V-PAS-3S ποιῇ (3x)
Jn 5:19 whatever that *the Father* should·do, these·things also
Jn 9:31 may·be reverent·of·God, and should·do his will,
Rm 2:14 having Torah-Law, should·do by·nature the·things
G4160.1 V-PAS-3P ποιῶσιν (3x)
Lk 6:31 ·as yeu·want that the men·of·clay† should·do to·yeu,
Heb 13:17 an·account— in·order·that they·may·do this with
Mt 7:12 ·want that the men·of·clay† should·do to·yeu, yeu·
G4160.1 V-IAI-2P ἐποιεῖτε (1x)
Jn 8:39 AbRaham's children, yeu·would do the works of·
G4160.1 V-IAI-3S ἐποίει (10x)
Jn 2:23 observing his miraculous·signs which he·was·doing.
Jn 5:16 to·kill him, because he·was·doing these·things on a·

Jn 6:2 miraculous·signs which he·was·doing upon the·ones
Ac 6:8 full of·trust and power, was·doing great wonders and
Ac 8:6 ·upon the miraculous·signs which he·was·doing.
Ac 9:36 works and merciful·acts which she·was·doing.
Ac 16:18 And this she·did over many days.
Ac 19:11 the hands of·Paul, was·doing miracles (*and* not
Mk 3:8 ·hearing what·many·things he·was·doing, a·large
Mk 15:8 ·*him to·do* just·as he·was·doing regularly for·them.
G4160.1 V-IAI-3P ἐποίουν (2x)
Lk 6:23 ·same·manner, their fathers were·doing *this* to·the
Lk 6:26 their fathers were·doing to·the false·prophets.
G4160.1 V-IMI-3P ἐποιοῦντο (1x)
Ac 27:18 ·by·the·storm, the next·day they·did *lighten the*
G4160.1 V-AAI-1S ἐποίησα (7x)
Jn 4:29 declared to·me all the·many·things I·did! Could this
Jn 4:39 "He·declared to·me all the·many·things I·did."
Jn 7:21 and declared to·them, "I·did one work, and yeu all
Jn 13:15 to·yeu in·order·that just·as I·myself did for·yeu,
Jn 15:24 "If I·did·not do among them the works which not·
Ac 26:10 Which·thing also I·did in JeruSalem, and many of·
1Ti 1:13 I·was·shown·mercy, because I·did *it* ignorantly in
G4160.1 V-AAI-1P ἐποιήσαμεν (2x)
Mt 7:22 ·out demons, and in·your name do many miracles?
Tit 3:5 in righteousness which we·ourselves did), but·rather
G4160.1 V-AAI-2S ἐποίησας (3x)
Jn 18:35 ·priests handed you over to·me. What·did you·do?"
Lk 2:48 "Child, why·did you·do us in·this·manner?
Ac 10:33 to you, and you did well in·coming·directly *here*.
G4160.1 V-AAI-2P ἐποιήσατε (6x)
Ac 4:7 or by what·kind·of name, did yeu·yeurselves do this?
Mt 25:40 I·say to·yeu, in as·much·as yeu·did *it* to·one of·the
Mt 25:40 ·the least of·these my brothers, yeu·did *it* to·me.'
Mt 25:45 ·yeu, in as·much·as yeu·did·not do *it* to·one of·the
Mt 25:45 ·these *my brothers*, yeu·did·not·even do *it* to·me.'
Php 4:14 Nevertheless yeu·did well sharing·together in·my
G4160.1 V-AAI-3S ἐποίησεν (46x)
Jn 2:11 Jesus did this initiating of·miraculous·signs in Qanah
Jn 4:45 ·clearly·seen all·the·things that he·did in JeruSalem
Jn 4:54 second miraculous·sign *that* Jesus did, coming from·
Jn 6:14 So·then, seeing that Jesus did a·miraculous·sign, the
Jn 7:31 miraculous·signs than these which this·man did?"
Jn 8:40 personally·from God. AbRaham did·not do this.
Jn 9:26 ·declared to·him again, "What·did he·do to·you?
Jn 10:41 "John, in·fact, did not·even·one miraculous·sign,
Jn 11:45 ·viewing the·things·which Jesus did, trusted in him.
Jn 11:46 and declared to·them what·things Jesus did.
Jn 20:30 Now·then in·fact, Jesus also did many other signs
Jn 21:25 many other·things, as·much·as Jesus did, which if
Lk 1:49 the powerful·one did magnificent·things for·me, and
Lk 1:51 "He·did a·mighty·thing with his arm; he·thoroughly·
Lk 6:3 that David did that·one·time when he·was·hungry,
Lk 6:10 "Stretch·forth your hand." And he·did so, and his
Lk 8:39 ·an·account·of what·many·things God did for·you."
Lk 8:39 the whole city what·many·things Jesus did for·him.
Lk 9:43 over all·things which Jesus did, he·declared to his
Lk 9:54 heaven and to·consume them, even as EliJah did?"
Lk 16:8 unjust estate·manager, because he·did prudently.
Lk 17:9 because he·did the·things already·being·thoroughly·
Ac 2:22 and signs, which God did through him in *the* midst
Ac 9:13 man, what·many wrongs he·did to·your holy·ones
Ac 10:39 are witnesses of·all·the·things which he·did both in
Ac 12:8 ·with your sandals." And he·did so. Then he·says
Ac 14:11 after·seeing what Paul did, they·lifted·up their
Ac 14:27 ·detail what·many·things *that* God did with them,
Ac 15:4 ·in·detail what·many·things *that* God did with them.
Ac 15:12 ·signs and wonders God did through them among
Ac 21:19 one of·those·things·which God did among the
Heb 7:27 People, for he·did this upon·one·occasion·only,
Mt 1:24 ·awakened from the heavy·sleep, did as the angel
Mt 12:3 "Did·yeu·not read·aloud what David did, when he·
Mt 13:28 to·them, 'A·hostile man·of·clay† did this.' Then
Mt 13:58 And he·did·not do many miracles there on·
Mt 20:5 about *the* sixth and ninth hour, he·did likewise.
Mt 21:15 the marvelous·things that he·did and·also the boys
Mt 21:31 Out of·the two, which one·did the will of·the
Mt 26:12 ointment on my body, did *it* specifically·for my
Mt 26:13 also what she·herself did shall·be·spoken·of for a·
Mk 2:25 ·even·at·any·time read·aloud what David did, when
Mk 5:19 to·them what·many·things Yahweh did for·you, and
Mk 5:20 the DecaPolis what·many·things Jesus did for·him,
Mk 14:8 She·herself made·do with·what she·had. She·came·
Mk 14:9 also what she·herself did shall·be·spoken·of for a·
G4160.1 V-AAI-3P ἐποίησαν (12x)
Jn 12:16 him, and *that* they·did these·things to·him.
Jn 19:24 ·fact, in·due·course, the soldiers did these·things.
Lk 9:10 ·an·account to *Jesus* what·many·things they·did.
Lk 9:15 And they·did *so* in·this·manner, and absolutely·all
Ac 11:30 Which also they·did, dispatching *it* to the elders
Mt 17:12 recognize him, but·yet they·did to·him as·much·as
Mt 20:12 saying, 'These last·ones did one hour, and you·
Mt 21:36 at·the first, and they·did to·them in·like·manner.
Mt 26:19 And the disciples did as YeShua appointed them,
Mt 28:15 taking the money, they·did as they·were·instructed
Mk 6:30 all·things, even what·many·things they·did, and
Mk 9:13 has·come, and they·did to·him as·many·things·as
G4160.1 V-AAM-2S ποίησον (7x)
Jn 13:27 "What you·do, do more·swiftly."
Lk 4:23 we·heard happening in CaperNaum, do also here in
Lk 7:8 he·comes; and to·my slave, 'Do this,' and he·does *it*.
Ac 21:23 "So·then do this·thing which we·say to·you.
Mt 8:9 he·comes; and to·my slave, 'Do this,' and he·does *it*.
2Ti 4:5 in all·things, endure·hardships, do *the* work of·a·
Rv 2:5 you·have·fallen, and repent, and do the first works;
G4160.1 V-AAM-2P ποιήσατε (2x)
Jn 2:5 "Whatever he·might say to·yeu, do *it*."
1Co 16:1 even yeu·yeurselves must·do in·this·manner:
G4160.1 V-AAM-3S ποιησάτω (1x)
1Pe 3:11 from wrong and do *the* beneficially·good·thing;
G4160.1 V-AAN ποιῆσαι (30x)
Lk 2:27 in the little·child Jesus, to·do concerning for·him
Lk 11:42 love of·God. It·is·mandatory to·do these·things,
Lk 12:4 these·things not having anything much·more to·do.
Lk 17:10 ·done *merely* that·which we·were·obligated to·do.'
Ac 4:28 to·do as·many·things·as your hand and your counsel
Ac 9:6 "Lord, what·do you·want me to·do?" And the Lord
Ac 22:10 ·things which have·been·assigned for·you to·do.'
Heb 10:7 ·been·written concerning me— to·do your will,
Heb 10:9 I·come, *I·am* the·one to·do your will, O·God."
Heb 13:19 But I·implore *yeu* all·the·more to·do this, in·
Heb 13:21 beneficially·good work in·order to·do his will,
Gal 2:10 this very·thing which I·diligently·endeavored to·do.
Gal 3:10 in the official·scroll of·the Torah-Law to·do them."
Gal 5:3 that he·is under·an·obligation to·do all the
Mt 9:28 "Do·yeu·trust that I·am·able to·do this?
Mt 20:15 ·it·not proper for·me to·do whatever I·should·want
Mt 23:23 "It·is·mandatory to·do these·things, and not to·
Mk 6:5 And he·was·not able to·do there not·even·one
Mk 7:12 him to·no·longer do not·even·one·thing for·his
Mk 10:36 "What·do yeu·want me to·do for·yeu?
Rm 4:21 what *God* has·promised, *God* was able also to·do.
2Co 8:10 ·year began·previously not merely to·do, but·rather
2Co 8:11 So right·now also, yeu·must·further·finish to·do *it*,
2Co 13:7 to God for·yeu not to·do not·even·one wrong; not
Eph 3:20 all·things, to·do above·and·beyond from·out of·
Phm 1:14 I·determined to·do not·even·one·thing apart·from
Rv 13:5 And authority was·given to·it to·do *this for* forty
Rv 13:14 ·signs which it was·given to·do in·the·sight of·the
Rv 17:17 For God gave in their hearts to·do his plan, and to·
Rv 17:17 hearts to·do his plan, and to·do *just* one plan, also
G4160.1 V-AAO-3P-A ποιήσειαν (1x)
Lk 6:11 alongside one·another what they·might do to·Jesus.
G4160.1 V-AAP-ASF ποιήσασαν (1x)
Mk 5:32 ·looking·all·around to·see the·one doing this·thing.
G4160.1 V-AAP-DSM ποιήσαντι (1x)
Jac 2:13 ·forgiving·favor *is* for·the·one not doing mercy, but
G4160.1 V-AAP-NSM ποιήσας (9x)
Lk 6:49 But the·one hearing and not doing, is like a·man·of·
Lk 10:25 "Mentor, what should·I·do to·inherit eternal
Lk 12:47 not making·ready, nor·even doing pertaining·to his
Lk 12:48 but doing things·deserving of·punishing·blows,
Lk 18:18 Mentor, what should·I·be·doing to·inherit eternal
Ac 7:36 brought them out, after·doing wonders and signs in
Gal 3:12 "'The man·of·clay† doing them shall·live by them
Rm 10:5 "'The man·of·clay† doing them shall·live by them
Rv 19:20 ·Prophet, the·one doing the miraculous·signs in·
G4160.1 V-AAP-NPM ποιήσαντες (4x)
Jn 5:29 ·forth; the·ones already·doing the beneficially·good,
Lk 5:6 And after·doing this, they·tightly·enclosed a·large
Heb 10:36 ·endurance in·order·that, after·doing the will of·
Mt 21:6 traversing, the disciples, also doing just·as YeShua
G4160.1 V-AAS-1S ποιήσω (11x)
Jn 17:4 you·have·given to·me in·order·that I·should·do *it*.
Lk 12:17 saying, 'What should·I·do, because I·have no
Lk 16:3 within himself, 'What should·I·do? Because my
Lk 18:41 "What·do you·want *that* I·should·do for·you?
Lk 20:13 declared, 'What should·I·do? I·shall·send my
Ac 22:10 And I·declared, 'What should·I·do, Lord?
Mt 19:16 beneficially·good·thing should·I·do in·order·that I·
Mt 20:32 "What·do yeu·want *that* I·should·do for·yeu?
Mk 10:17 ·good Mentor, what should·I·do that I·may·inherit
Mk 10:51 "What·do you·want *that* I·should·do for·you?
Mk 15:12 ·do yeu·want *that* I·should·do *to·the·one* whom
G4160.1 V-AAS-1P ποιήσωμεν (2x)
Rm 3:8 , "that we·should·do the bad·things in·order·that
Jac 4:15 then we·should·live, and should·do this or that.
G4160.1 V-AAS-2S ποιήσῃς (1x)
Mk 10:35 we·want that you·should·do for·us whatever we·
G4160.1 V-AAS-2P ποιήσητε (1x)
Lk 17:10 ·manner, whenever yeu·should·do all the·things
G4160.1 V-AAS-3S ποιήσῃ (4x)
Mt 5:19 but whoever should·do and should·instruct *them*,
Mt 12:50 For whoever should·do the will of·my Father, the·
Mk 3:35 For whoever should·do the will of·God, this·one is
Eph 6:8 beneficially·good·thing each·man should·do, this
G4160.1 V-AAS-3P ποιήσωσιν (1x)
Lk 19:48 yet they·were·not finding how they·may·do *it*, for
G4160.1 V-RAI-1S πεποίηκα (1x)
Jn 13:12 ·them, "Yeu·must·know what I·have·done for·yeu.
G4160.1 V-RAI-1P πεποιήκαμεν (1x)
Lk 17:10 slaves, because we·have·done *merely* that·which
G4160.1 V-RAI-3S πεποίηκεν (4x)
Jn 15:24 not·even·one other·man has·done, they·would·not
Lk 1:25 "In·this·manner has Yahweh done for·me, in *the*
Heb 11:28 By·trust, he·has·done the Passover and the
Mk 7:37 ·excess, saying, "He·has·done all·things well. He·
G4160.1 V-RAN πεποιηκέναι (1x)
Jn 12:18 they·heard him to·have·done this miraculous·sign.
G4160.1 V-RAP-GSM πεποιηκότος (1x)
Jn 12:37 with·him having·done so·many miraculous·signs
G4160.1 V-RAP-NSM πεποιηκώς (1x)
Ac 21:33 he·might·be, and what *it·was* he·was·having·done.
EG4160.1 (26x)
Lk 12:26 ·are·not·even able *to·do* that·thing·which·is·least,
Ac 11:29 ·as he·was·having·good·financial·means *to·do so*,
Ac 22:16 what·is·it *that* you·are·about *to·do*? Upon·rising·up
Ac 25:5 among yeu *who·are* able *to·do so*, after·walking·
Gal 5:17 ·not do these·things which yeu·might want *to·do*.
Mt 21:21 shall·yeu·do the·thing *that is·done* to·the fig·tree,
Mk 6:20 him, he·was·continuing *to·do* many·things, yet
Mk 9:22 him, but·yet if you·are·able *to·do* something,
Mk 15:8 began to·request *for·him to·do* just·as he·was·doing
Rm 7:15 I·do·not know *why* I·perform that·which *I·do*. For I·
Rm 7:15 practice that·thing which I·want *to·do*, but·rather I·
Rm 7:18 ·thing; for to·want *to·do the morally·good·thing* is·
Rm 7:19 *the* beneficially·good·thing which I·want *to·do*, *that*
Rm 12:8 *and* the·one showing·mercy, *doing so* with
Php 4:13 I·have·strength *to·do* all·things in·the·one enabling
2Th 2:7 holding·*him*·down at·this·moment *is·doing so* until
2Co 8:21 *We·do this* while·maintaining·ourselves·in

Αα Ββ Γγ Δδ Εε Ζζ Ηη Θθ Ιι Κκ Λλ Μμ Νν Ξξ Οο Ππ Ρρ Σσ Ττ Υυ Φφ Χχ Ψψ Ωω

2Co 11:21 ·ourselves were·*too*·weak to·do *these same·things*
2Co 13:8 For we·are·not able to·do anything against the truth
Eph 3:20 from·out of·an·abundance, to·do according·to the
Col 3:17 ·do in word or in deed, do all in *the* Lord Jesus
Phm 1:8 to·order you to·do the appropriate·thing,
1Jn 3:12 not doing just·as Qain *did, who* was birthed·from·
1Jn 3:12 not *doing* just·as Qain did, *who* was birthed·from·
2Jn 1:12 *all,* I·am·definitely·not willing to·do *so* through a·
3Jn 1:10 and he·forbids the·ones being·resolved to·do *so* and
G4160.2 V-PAI-3S ποιεῖ (1x)
1Jn 3:4 ·failure also commits the violation·of·the·Royal-Law
G4160.2 V-PAP-APM ποιοῦντας (1x)
Mt 13:41 and·also the·ones committing the Lawlessness,
G4160.2 V-PAP-NSN ποιοῦν (1x)
Rv 21:27 it anyone defiling or committing an·abomination or
G4160.2 V-PAP-NSM ποιῶν (4x)
Jn 8:34 to·yeu that any one committing the moral·failure is
1Jn 3:4 Any one committing the moral·failure also commits
1Jn 3:8 The·one committing the moral·failure is birthed·from·
Rv 22:15 and everyone being·fond·of and committing a·lie.
G4160.2 V-AAI-1S ἐποίησα (1x)
2Co 11:7 Or did·I·commit a·moral·failure in·humbling my·
G4160.2 V-AAI-3S ἐποίησεν (5x)
Lk 3:19 all *the* evils which HerOd·AntiPas committed,
Lk 23:22 what crime did this·one commit? I·found not·even·
Mt 27:23 "For what crime did·he·commit?" But the *crowds*
Mk 15:14 "For what crime did·he·commit?" And they·
1Pe 2:22 "Who did·not commit moral·failure, neither was
G4160.2 V-AAP-NSM ποιήσας (1x)
1Co 5:2 mourn, in·order·that the·one committing this deed
G4160.2 V-AAP-NSM@ ποιήσας (1x)
Ac 28:17 I·myself, having·committed not·even·one·thing
G4160.2 V-AAS-3S ποιήσῃ (1x)
1Co 6:18 provided·that a·man·of·clay† should·commit *it,* is
G4160.2 V-RAP-NSM πεποιηκώς (1x)
Jac 5:15 and·if he·may·be having·committed moral·failures,
G4160.2 V-LAI-3P πεποιήκεισαν (1x)
Mk 15:7 who had·committed murder in the insurrection.
G4160.3 V-FAI-1S ποιήσω (3x)
Mt 4:19 right·behind me, and I·shall·make yeu fishers of·
Rv 3:9 , behold, I·shall·make them that they·should·come
Rv 3:12 the·one overcoming, I·shall·make a·pillar in the
G4160.3 V-FAI-1P ποιήσομεν (2x)
Jn 14:23 ·come to him, and shall·make our·abode with him.
Mt 28:14 shall·persuade him, and shall·make yeu *secure*
G4160.3 V-FAI-3S ποιήσει (5x)
Lk 18:7 And, ¿! shall·not God make retribution for·his·own
Lk 18:8 I·say to·yeu that he·shall·make retribution for·them
Rm 9:28 Yahweh shall·make a·concise·working·of *the*
1Co 10:13 with·the proof·trial, also shall·make the exit·out,
Rv 11:7 from·out of·the bottomless·pit) shall·make war with
G4160.3 V-FAI-3P ποιήσουσιν (2x)
Jn 16:2 "They·shall·make yeu cut·off·from·the·gatherings.
Rv 17:16 the Prostitute, and they·shall·make her desolate
G4160.3 V-PAI-1S ποιῶ (1x)
Rv 21:5 declared, "Behold, I·make all·things brand-new!"
G4160.3 V-PAI-1P ποιοῦμεν (1x)
1Jn 1:10 we·have·not morally·failed, we·make him a·liar,
G4160.3 V-PAI-2S ποιεῖς (2x)
Jn 8:53 are·dead. Whom·do you·yourself make yourself *out*
Jn 10:33 you, being a·man·of·clay†, make yourself God."
G4160.3 V-PAI-2P ποιεῖτε (1x)
Mt 23:15 ·become·one, yeu·make him twice·as·much a·son
G4160.3 V-PAI-3S ποιεῖ (5x)
Jn 4:1 *it said* that "Jesus makes and immerses more disciples
Mt 26:73 them, for even your speech makes you plain."
Mk 7:37 "He·has·done all·things well. He·makes both the
Rv 13:12 ·Beast in·the·sight of·it, and it·makes the earth and
Rv 13:16 And it·makes all, the small and the great, also the
G4160.3 V-PAM-2P ποιεῖτε (4x)
Jn 2:16 these·things from·here. Do·not make my Father's
Lk 3:4 the Way of·Yahweh; yeu·must·make his highways
Mt 3:3 the Way of·Yahweh; yeu·must·make his highways
Mk 1:3 the Way of·Yahweh; yeu·must·make his highways
G4160.3 V-PAN ποιεῖν (3x)
Jn 5:27 ·gave him authority also to·make Tribunal·judgment,
Ac 7:19 our fathers, to·make *them* put·out·and·expose their
Mk 2:23 and his disciples began to·make a·pathway,
G4160.3 V-PAP-ASM ποιοῦντα (1x)
Ac 24:12 alongside anyone, or making a·turmoil of·a·crowd
G4160.3 V-PAP-DPM ποιοῦσιν (1x)
Jac 3:18 is·sown in peace by·the·ones making peace.
G4160.3 V-PAP-NSM ποιῶν (5x)
Jn 5:18 *was* his·own Father, making himself equal with·God
Jn 19:12 not Caesar's friend. Anyone making himself a·king
Ac 19:24 ·of Demetrius, a·silversmith making silver temples
Heb 1:7 "*This·is* the·one making his angels spirits and his
Eph 2:15 one brand-new man·of·clay†, *thus* making peace,
G4160.3 V-PAP-NPM ποιοῦντες (1x)
Ac 25:3 ·*up* to JeruSalem, while·they·make an·ambush in
G4160.3 V-PAS-2S ποιῇς (2x)
Lk 14:12 "Whenever you·should·make a·luncheon or a·
Lk 14:13 But·rather whenever you·should·make a·reception,
G4160.3 V-PAS-3S ποιῇ (1x)
Rv 13:13 signs, so that it·should·make fire to·descend from·
G4160.3 V-PMI-1S ποιοῦμαι (1x)
Rm 1:9 of·his Son, how unceasingly I·make mention of·yeu
G4160.3 V-PMI-3P ποιοῦνται (1x)
Lk 5:33 of·John fast frequently, and make petitions, and
G4160.3 V-PMM-2P ποιεῖσθε (1x)
Rm 13:14 Anointed, and do·not make provision for longings
G4160.3 V-PMN ποιεῖσθαι (2x)
2Pe 1:10 ·more quickly·endeavor to·make yeur calling·forth
2Pe 1:15 *the ability* to·make recollection of·these·things.
G4160.3 V-PMP-NSM ποιούμενος (5x)
Lk 13:22 instructing and making a·circuitous·route toward
Jud 1:3 Beloved, while·making all diligence to·write to·yeu
Php 1:4 ·mine on·behalf of·yeu all while·making the petition
Eph 1:16 ·thanks on·behalf of·yeu, making mention of·yeu
Phm 1:4 I·give·thanks to·my God, making mention of·you
G4160.3 V-PMP-NPM ποιούμενοι (1x)
1Th 1:2 concerning all of·yeu, making mention of·yeu in
G4160.3 V-PPN ποιεῖσθαι (1x)
1Ti 2:1 *and* expressions·of·thankfulness to·be·made over all
G4160.3 V-IAI-3S ἐποίει (2x)
Ac 9:39 Dorcas was·making while·she·was·still with them.
Mk 6:21 when HerOd·AntiPas was·making a·supper on·his
G4160.3 V-IAI-3P ἐποίουν (1x)
Mk 3:6 immediately were·making consultation with the
G4160.3 V-AAI-1S ἐποίησα (2x)
Jn 7:23 with·me because I·made a·whole man·of·clay†
Heb 8:9 ·to the covenant that I·made with·their fathers in *the*
G4160.3 V-AAI-2S ἐποίησας (3x)
Mt 20:12 did one hour, and you·made them equal to·us, the·
Rm 9:20 *it,* "Why did·you·make me in·this·manner?
Rv 5:10 and, you·made us *to·be* to·our God kings and
G4160.3 V-AAI-2P ἐποιήσατε (4x)
Lk 19:46 of·prayer," but yeu·yeurselves made it "a·den
Ac 7:43 the figures which yeu·made *in·order* to·fall·prostrate
Mt 21:13 of·prayer," but yeu·yeurselves made it "a·den
Mk 11:17 nations"? But yeu·yeurselves made it "a·den of·
G4160.3 V-AAI-3S ἐποίησεν (23x)
Jn 4:46 into Qanah of·Galilee, where he·made the water *into*
Jn 9:6 he·spat down·on·the·open·ground and made clay out
Jn 9:11 ·clay† being·referred·to·as Jesus, he·made clay and
Jn 9:14 And it·was a·Sabbath when Jesus made the clay and
Jn 19:7 he·is·due to·die, because he·made himself *out to·be*
Lk 1:68 because he·visited and made a·ransoming for·his
Lk 5:29 And Levi made a·great reception for·him in his·own
Lk 11:40 the·one making the outside also make the inside?
Lk 14:16 "A·certain man·of·clay† made a·great supper and
Ac 2:36 must·know securely that God made this same Jesus,
Ac 7:24 *his fellow Israelite* and made vengeance for·the·one
Ac 7:50 Did·not·indeed my hand make all these·things?
Ac 14:15 to the living God, 'who made the heaven, and the
Ac 17:26 from·out of·one blood he·made every nation of·
Heb 1:2 of·all·things, through whom also he·made the ages.
Mt 19:4 from *the* beginning "made them male and female,"
Mt 22:2 a·king, who made a·wedding·banquet for·his son
Mk 3:14 And he·made twelve *ambassadors*, that they·
Mk 8:25 hands upon his eyes and made him to·receive·sight,
Mk 10:6 creation's beginning, God " made them male and
2Co 5:21 moral·failure made *himself* a·reparation·for·moral·
Eph 3:11 of·the ages which he·made in Anointed-One, Jesus
Rv 1:6 And he·made us kings and priests·that·offer·a·sacrifice
G4160.3 V-AAI-3P ἐποίησαν (2x)
Jn 12:2 Accordingly, they·made a·supper for·him there, and
Jn 19:23 took his outer·garments and made four parts, a·part
G4160.3 V-AAM-2S ποίησον (2x)
Lk 15:19 worthy to·be·called your son; make me as one of·
Ac 7:40 declaring to·Aaron, "Make for·us gods which
G4160.3 V-AAM-2P ποιήσατε (6x)
Jn 6:10 Jesus declared, "Make the men·of·clay† to·sit·back·
Lk 12:33 ·act·of·charity. *Thus* make for·yeurselves pouches
Lk 16:9 ·I say to·yeu: Make friends for·yeurselves from·out
Heb 12:13 and make level tracks for·yeur feet, lest the lame
Mt 12:33 "Either make the tree good, and its fruit good; or
Mt 12:33 and its fruit good; or make the tree rotten, and its
G4160.3 V-AAN ποιῆσαι (15x)
Jn 11:37 eyes of·the blind, able to·make *it·be* also that this·
Lk 5:34 to them, "¿! Are yeu·able to·make the Sons of·the
Ac 5:34 commandingly·ordered to·make the ambassadors
Ac 7:44 to·Moses thoroughly·assigned *for·him* to·make it,
Ac 18:21 ·for me by·all·means to·make the Sacred·Feast,
Mt 5:36 because you·are·not able to·make one hair white or
Mt 23:15 the parched·ground to·make one convert·to·Judaism
Mk 14:7 yeu·should·want, yeu·are·able to·do well by·them.
Mk 15:15 So Pilate, being·resolved to·make the crowd
Rm 9:21 from·out of·the same lump·of·clay to·make, in·fact,
Jud 1:15 to·make Tribunal·judgment against all, and to·
Rv 12:17 the woman, and he·went·off to·make war with the
Rv 13:7 And it·was·given to·it 'to·make war with the holy·
Rv 13:14 on the earth, to·make a·derived·image for·the
Rv 19:19 having·been·gathered·together to·make war against
G4160.3 V-AAP-DSM ποιήσαντι (1x)
Rv 14:7 fall·prostrate to·the·one 'having·made the heaven,
G4160.3 V-AAP-NSM ποιήσας (8x)
Jn 2:15 And making a·lash out of·small·cords, he·cast·out
Jn 5:11 them, "The·one making me healthy·and·sound, that·
Jn 5:15 it·was Jesus, the·one making him healthy·and·sound
Lk 11:40 ·ones! ¿! Did·not the·one making the outside also
Ac 4:24 you *are* God, 'the·one making the heaven, and the
Ac 17:24 God, the·one making the world and all the·things
Mt 19:4 ·yeu·not read·aloud that the·one making *them* from
Eph 2:14 is our peace, the·one already·making the both one,
G4160.3 V-AAP-NPM ποιήσαντες (2x)
Ac 23:12 some of·the Judeans, making a·secret·mob, vowed·
Mk 15:1 the chief·priests, after·making consultation with
G4160.3 V-AAS-1S ποιήσω (1x)
1Co 6:15 of·Anointed-One, should·I·make *them* members
G4160.3 V-AAS-1P ποιήσωμεν (3x)
Lk 9:33 to·be here, and we·should·make three tabernacles;
Mt 17:4 If you·want, we·should·make three tabernacles here
Mk 9:5 to·be here. And we·should·make three tabernacles:
G4160.3 V-AAS-2S ποιήσῃς (1x)
Heb 8:5 "*that* you·should·make all·things according·to the
G4160.3 V-AAS-3S ποιήσῃ (1x)
Rv 13:15 should·speak, and should·make as·many·as would
G4160.3 V-AAS-3P ποιήσωσιν (3x)
Jn 6:15 seize him in·order·that they·should·make him king,
Mt 12:16 ·that they·should·not make him openly·known,
Mk 3:12 ·that they·should·not make him openly·known.
G4160.3 V-AMI-1S ἐποιησάμην (1x)
Ac 1:1 In·fact, the first account I·made, O TheoPhilus, *was*
G4160.3 V-AMI-3P ἐποιήσαντο (1x)
Ac 8:2 Stephen, and they·made great visceral·lamentation
G4160.3 V-AMN ποιήσασθαι (1x)
Rm 15:26 delighted to·make a·certain common·welfare·fund
G4160.3 V-AMP-NSM ποιησάμενος (2x)

Ac 25:17 ·together here (making not·even·one postponement
Heb 1:3 ·his power) who, after·making purification of·our
G4160.3 V-RAI-3S πεποίηκεν (1x)
1Jn 5:10 the·one not trusting God has·made *God* himself a·
G4160.3 V-RAP-DPM πεποιηκόσιν (1x)
Ac 3:12 or devout·reverence we·have·made him to·walk?
G4160.3 V-RAP-NPM πεποιηκότες (2x)
Jn 18:18 stood *there*, having·made a·fire·of·coals because it·
Ac 23:13 forty·men having·made this sworn·conspiracy.
G4160.3 V-RPP-GPM πεποιημένων (1x)
Heb 12:27 as *of·things* having·been·made, in·order·that the·
EG4160.3 (4x)
Ac 24:17 merciful·acts for my nation, and *making* offerings;
Heb 10:3 a·reminder·again *is·made* of·moral·failures each
Mt 3:4 John was·having his apparel *made* from camel's hair
2Co 7:14 our boasting (the·one *we·made* before Titus) has·
G4160.4 V-PAI-3S ποιεῖ (5x)
Mt 7:17 every beneficially·good tree produces good fruit,
Mt 7:17 good fruit, but the rotten tree produces evil fruit.
Mt 13:23 *it*, who also·then bears·fruit and produces, in·fact,
Mk 4:32 the garden·plants, and it·produces great branches,
1Jn 3:9 from·out of·God does·not commit moral·failure,
G4160.4 V-PAN ποιεῖν (2x)
Mt 7:18 ·good tree is·not able to·produce evil fruit, neither *is*
Mt 7:18 neither *is* a·rotten tree *able* to·produce good fruit.
G4160.4 V-PAP-APM ποιοῦντας (1x)
Rm 16:17 ·a·watch·of the·ones producing the dissensions
G4160.4 V-PAP-DSN ποιοῦντι (1x)
Mt 21:43 and shall·be·given to·a·nation producing the fruits
G4160.4 V-PAP-NSN ποιοῦν (6x)
Lk 3:9 every tree not producing good fruit is·chopped·down
Lk 6:43 "For a·good tree is·not producing rotten fruit, neither
Lk 6:43 fruit, neither *is* a·rotten tree producing good fruit.
Mt 3:10 every tree not producing good fruit is·chopped·
Mt 7:19 Every tree not producing good fruit is·chopped·
Rv 22:2 arbor·tree of·Life·above, producing twelve *kinds·of*
G4160.4 V-PAP-NSM ποιῶν (1x)
Heb 13:21 in·order to·do his will, producing in yeu the·thing
G4160.4 V-PMI-3S ποιεῖται (1x)
Eph 4:16 He·himself·produces the maturing·growth of·the
G4160.4 V-AAI-3S ἐποίησεν (4x)
Lk 8:8 ·sprouted, it·produced fruit a·hundred·times·over."
Lk 19:18 'Lord, your mina produced five more·minas.
Mt 13:26 when the blade blossomed and produced fruit, then
Mt 25:16 *the* same, and produced another five talants·of·
G4160.4 V-AAM-2P ποιήσατε (2x)
Lk 3:8 "Now·then, produce fruits worthy of·the repentance,
Mt 3:8 Now·then, produce fruits worthy of·the repentance.
G4160.4 V-AAN ποιῆσαι (2x)
Jac 3:12 ·Is a·fig·tree able, my brothers, to·produce olives?
Jac 3:12 not·even·one wellspring *is·able* to·produce *both* salt
G4160.4 V-AAP-DSM ποιήσαντι (1x)
Heb 3:2 being trustworthy to·the·one producing him, as also
G4160.4 V-AAS-3S ποιήσῃ (1x)
Lk 13:9 And·if, in·fact, it·should·produce fruit, *good*! But·
EG4160.4 (1x)
Ac 27:41 where·two·seas·met *producing a·broad sand·bar*,
G4160.5 V-FAI-1S ποιήσω (1x)
Mk 1:17 right·behind me! And I·shall·cause yeu to·become
G4160.5 V-PAI-3S ποιεῖ (1x)
Mt 5:32 ·sexual·immorality, causes her to·commit·adultery,
G4160.5 V-PMI-1S ποιοῦμαι (1x)
Ac 20:24 But·yet not·even·one word causes *me concern*,
G4160.5 V-IAI-3P ἐποίουν (1x)
Ac 15:3 *to God*. And they·were·causing great joy for·all the
G4160.5 V-AAM-2P ποιήσατε (1x)
Col 4:16 directly·to yeu, cause that it·should·be·read·aloud
G4160.5 V-AAS-3S ποιήσῃ (1x)
Rv 12:15 woman, in·order·that he·may·cause this *woman to·*
EG4160.5 (2x)
Mt 8:28 exceedingly fierce, such·that *it·caused* some not to·
2Co 9:8 And God *is* able *to·cause* all grace to·abound toward
G4160.6 V-PAI-2P ποιεῖτε (1x)
Ac 21:13 answered, "Why·do yeu·continue weeping and
G4160.6 V-IAI-3S ἐποίει (1x)
Mk 6:20 ·hearing him, he·was·continuing *to·do* many·things
G4160.6 V-AAN ποιῆσαι (1x)
Lk 1:72 to·continue *the promised* mercy with our fathers,
G4160.6 V-AAP-NSM ποιήσας (3x)
Lk 10:37 he·declared, "The·one continuing the act·of·mercy
Ac 18:23 And after·continuing *there for* some time, he·went·
Ac 20:3 continuing *there* also *for* three lunar·months.
G4160.6 V-AAP-NPM ποιήσαντες (1x)
Ac 15:33 And after·continuing *there* a·time, they·were·
G4160.6 V-AAS-1P ποιήσωμεν (1x)
Jac 4:13 into that city, and should·continue there *for* one
G4160.6 V-RAI-1S πεποίηκα (1x)
2Co 11:25 *and* I·have·continued·on *for* a·night·and·a·day
EG4160.6 (2x)
Mt 24:22 any flesh would be·saved *to·continue living*; but
1Pe 4:8 And above all, *continue* having earnest love among
G4160.7 V-PAI-3S ποιεῖ (1x)
Rv 13:12 And it·exercises all the authority of·the first

G4161 ποίημα pôíēma *n.* (2x)

Roots:G4160 Compare:G2041 See:G4162 G4163
xLangEquiv:H4639
G4161.2 N-DPN ποιήμασιν (1x)
Rm 1:20 divinity, being·understood by·the things·made—
G4161.3 N-NSN ποίημα (1x)
Eph 2:10 For we·are a·product of·him, already·being·created

G4162 ποίησις pôíēsis *n.* (1x)

Roots:G4160 See:G4161 G4163
G4162 N-DSF ποιήσει (1x)
Jac 1:25 this·man shall·be supremely·blessed in his doing.

G4163 ποιητής pôiētḗs *n.* (6x)

Roots:G4160 See:G4161 G4162
G4163.1 N-NSM ποιητής (3x)
Jac 1:23 of·*the*·Redemptive·word, and not a·doer, this·one
Jac 1:25 a·forgetful hearer, but·rather a·doer of·the·work,
Jac 4:11 ·judge law, you·are not a·doer of·law, but·rather a·
G4163.1 N-NPM ποιηταί (2x)
Rm 2:13 but·rather, the *faultless* doers of·the Torah-Law
Jac 1:22 Now become doers of·*the*·Redemptive·word, and not
G4163.3 N-GPM ποιητῶν (1x)
Ac 17:28 also certain of·yeur very·own poets have·declared,

G4164 ποικίλος pôikílôs *adj.* (10x)

Compare:G1313 See:G4182 xLangAlso:H1261
G4164.1 A-DPM ποικίλοις (2x)
Jac 1:2 yeu·should·entirely·fall·into diverse proof·trials,
1Pe 1:6 it·is being·necessary) in diverse proof·trials—
G4164.1 A-DPF ποικίλαις (2x)
Heb 13:9 ·not·be carried·about by·diverse and strange·new
Tit 3:3 being·deceived, being·slaves to·diverse longings and
G4164.2 A-DPF ποικίλαις (5x)
Lk 4:40 to him, with·a·diversity·of illnesses *being·present*;
Heb 2:4 and wonders, and with·a·diversity·of miracles and
Mt 4:24 those·being·clenched by·a·diversity·of illnesses and
Mk 1:34 many being badly·ill with·a·diversity·of illnesses,
2Ti 3:6 being·led·away with·a·diversity·of longings,
G4164.3 A-GSF ποικίλης (1x)
1Pe 4:10 it as good estate·managers of·God's manifold grace.

G4165 ποιμαίνω pôimaínō *v.* (11x)

Roots:G4166 Compare:G1006 xLangAlso:H7462
G4165.1 V-FAI-3S ποιμανεῖ (4x)
Mt 2:6 ·leading, one·who shall·shepherd my People IsraEl.
Rv 2:27 " And he·shall·shepherd them with a·rod of·iron, as
Rv 7:17 amidst the·throne, shall·shepherd them and shall·
Rv 19:15 nations; and he·himself shall·shepherd them with
G4165.1 V-PAI-3S ποιμαίνει (1x)
1Co 9:7 of·its fruit? Or who shepherds a·flock, and does·not
G4165.1 V-PAM-2S ποίμαινε (1x)
Jn 21:16 He·says to·him, "Shepherd my sheep."
G4165.1 V-PAN ποιμαίνειν (2x)
Ac 20:28 overseers, to·shepherd the Called·Out·citizenry of·
Rv 12:5 a·male who imminently·intends to·shepherd all the
G4165.1 V-PAP-ASM ποιμαίνοντα (1x)
Lk 17:7 having a·slave plowing or shepherding, who shall·
G4165.1 V-AAM-2P ποιμάνατε (1x)
1Pe 5:2 Shepherd the little·flock of·God among yeu,
G4165.4 V-PAP-NPM ποιμαίνοντες (1x)
Jud 1:12 shepherding·and·feeding themselves without·fear.

G4166 ποιμήν pôimḗn *n.* (18x)

Compare:G4461 G2519 G2819-2 See:G0750 G4165
G4168 G4167
xLangEquiv:H7321-1 xLangAlso:H7473
G4166 N-NSM ποιμήν (7x)
Jn 10:2 ·in through the door is shepherd of·the sheep.
Jn 10:11 "I AM the good shepherd. The good shepherd lays·
Jn 10:11 shepherd. The good shepherd lays·down his·own
Jn 10:12 not even being a·shepherd over·that·which are not
Jn 10:14 "I AM the good shepherd, and I·know my *sheep*,
Jn 10:16 it·shall·become one flock *and* one shepherd.
Mt 25:32 just·as the shepherd distinctly·separates the sheep
G4166 N-NPM ποιμένες (3x)
Lk 2:8 And there·were shepherds in the same region,
Lk 2:15 *that* the men·of·clay†, the shepherds, declared to
Lk 2:20 And the shepherds returned, glorifying and praising
G4166 N-ASM ποιμένα (6x)
Heb 13:20 Lord YeShua (the great shepherd of·the sheep by
Mt 9:36 ·been·flung·about, as sheep not having a·shepherd.
Mt 26:31 "I·shall·smite the shepherd, and the sheep of·the
Mk 6:34 "as sheep not having a·shepherd,'" and he·began
Mk 14:27 "I·shall·smite the shepherd, and the sheep shall·
1Pe 2:25 now returned to the Shepherd and Overseer of·yeur
G4166 N-APM ποιμένας (1x)
Eph 4:11 ·of·redemption, and the shepherds and instructors
G4166 N-GPM ποιμένων (1x)
Lk 2:18 ·that were·being·spoken to them by the shepherds.

G4167 ποίμνη pôímnē *n.* (5x)

צֹנֶא tsōne‘ [Hebrew]

Roots:G4165 Compare:G0750 See:G4168
xLangEquiv:H6629 H6792 xLangAlso:H5739
G4167 N-NSF ποίμνη (1x)
Jn 10:16 and *together* it·shall·become one flock *and* one
G4167 N-ASF ποίμνην (2x)
Lk 2:8 vigilantly·keeping the night watches over their flock.
1Co 9:7 fruit? Or who shepherds a·flock, and does·not eat
G4167 N-GSF ποίμνης (2x)
Mt 26:31 sheep of·the flock shall·be·thoroughly·scattered."
1Co 9:7 and does·not eat from·out of·the milk of·the flock?

G4168 ποίμνιον pôímniôn *n.* (5x)

צֹאנָן tsōnean [Hebrew diminutive]

Roots:G4167 G2444-3 Compare:G5040 G3813
G0034 G1577 See:G4166
xLangEquiv:H6792 xLangAlso:H5739
G4168.1 N-ASN ποίμνιον (1x)
1Pe 5:2 Shepherd the little·flock of·God among yeu,
G4168.1 N-DSN ποιμνίῳ (1x)
Ac 20:28 and to·the entire little·flock, among which the
G4168.1 N-GSN ποιμνίου (2x)
Ac 20:29 among yeu, who·are·not sparing the little·flock.
1Pe 5:3 but·rather being model·examples to·the little·flock.
G4168.1 N/G-NSN ποίμνιον (1x)
Lk 12:32 "Do·not be·afraid, Little Flock, because yeur

G4169 π•οῖος pôîôs *p:i.* (34x)

Roots:G4226 G3634 Compare:G4217
G4169.2 P:I-NSF ποία (4x)
Lk 6:32 the·ones loving yeu, what·kind·of grace is·it to·yeu
Lk 6:33 ·doing·good to·yeu, what·kind·of grace is·it to·yeu?
Lk 6:34 ·expect to·receive·in·full, what·kind·of grace is·it
Jac 4:14 tomorrow! For what·kind·of *essence is* yeur life†?
G4169.2 P:I-NSN ποῖον (1x)
1Pe 2:20 For what·kind·of merit *is·it*, if when yeu·are·being·
G4169.2 P:I-ASM ποῖον (2x)
Ac 7:49 my foot stool. What·kind·of house shall·yeu·build
1Pe 1:11 ·searching for which or what·kind·of season the
G4169.2 P:I-DSM ποίῳ (3x)

Jn 12:33 this, signifying what·kind·of death he·was·about
Jn 18:32 signifying what·kind·of death he·was·about to·die.
Jn 21:19 ·declared, signifying by·what·kind·of death *Peter*
G4169.2 P:I-DSF ποίᾳ (10x)
Lk 20:2 Declare to·us, by what·kind·of authority do·you·do
Lk 20:8 I·myself say to·yeu by what·kind·of authority I·do
Ac 4:7 they·inquired, "By what·kind·of power, or by what·
Mt 21:23 "By what·kind·of authority do·you·do these·
Mt 21:24 shall·declare to·yeu by what·kind·of authority I·do
Mt 21:27 I·myself say to·yeu by what·kind·of authority I·do
Mk 4:30 Or what·kind·of analogy should·we·cast·directly·at
Mk 11:28 to·him, "By what·kind·of authority do·you·do
Mk 11:29 ·declare to·yeu by what·kind·of authority I·do
Mk 11:33 relate to·yeu by what·kind·of authority I·do these·
G4169.2 P:I-DSN ποίῳ (2x)
Ac 4:7 what·kind·of power, or by what·kind·of name, did
1Co 15:35 And in·what·kind·of body do·they·come?
G4169.2 P:I-GSM ποίου (1x)
Rm 3:27 It·is·excluded. On·account·of what·kind·of law?
G4169.2 P:I-GSF ποίας (1x)
Lk 5:19 finding through what·kind·of *means* they·may·carry
G4169.3 P:I-NSF ποία (2x)
Mt 22:36 "Mentor, which·one *is the* great commandment in
Mk 12:28 well, inquired·of him, "Which commandment is
G4169.3 P:I-ASF ποίαν (1x)
Rv 3:3 no, you·should·not know which hour I·shall·come
G4169.3 P:I-ASN ποῖον (1x)
Jn 10:32 of·my Father; on·account·of which of·those works
G4169.3 P:I-APF ποίας (1x)
Mt 19:18 He·says to·him, "Which·ones?" And YeShua
G4169.3 P:I-DSF ποίᾳ (3x)
Lk 12:39 ·house had·personally·known in·which hour the
Mt 24:42 yeu·do·not personally·know in·which hour yeur
Mt 24:43 had·personally·known in·which watch *of·the night*
G4169.3 P:I-GSF ποίας (1x)
Ac 23:34 the governor inquired from·which province he·was
G4169.4 P:I-NSF ποῖα (1x)
Lk 24:19 And he·declared to·them, "Like·what?" And they·

G4170 πολεμέω pôlêmĕō *v.* (7x)
Roots:G4171 Compare:G4754 G3164 See:G1606-2
xLangAlso:H3898
G4170 V-FAI-1S πολεμήσω (1x)
Rv 2:16 to·you swiftly, and I·shall·wage·war against them
G4170 V-FAI-3P πολεμήσουσιν (1x)
Rv 17:14 These shall·wage·war with the Lamb, and the
G4170 V-PAI-2P πολεμεῖτε (1x)
Jac 4:2 Yeu·fight and wage·war, but yeu·do·not have, on·
G4170 V-PAI-3S πολεμεῖ (1x)
Rv 19:11 and in righteousness he·judges and wages·war.
G4170 V-AAI-3S ἐπολέμησεν (1x)
Rv 12:7 and the Dragon (and his angels) waged·war,
G4170 V-AAI-3P ἐπολέμησαν (1x)
Rv 12:7 MiChaEl and his angels waged·war against the
G4170 V-AAN πολεμῆσαι (1x)
Rv 13:4 Daemonic·Beast? Who is·able to·wage·war against it

G4171 πόλεμος pôlĕmŏs *n.* (18x)
Compare:G3163 G1611-2 See:G4170 G1606-2
G4171.1 N-NSM πόλεμος (1x)
Rv 12:7 And there·was war in the heaven.
G4171.1 N-NPM πόλεμοι (1x)
Jac 4:1 From·what·source *are* wars and quarrels among yeu
G4171.1 N-ASM πόλεμον (5x)
Lk 14:31 who·is·traversing to·engage·in war against another
Rv 11:7 of·the bottomless·pit) shall·make war with them,
Rv 12:17 woman, and he·went·off to·make war with the rest
Rv 13:7 it·was·given to·it ·to·make war with the holy·ones,
Rv 19:19 ·gathered·together to·make war against the·one
G4171.1 N-APM πολέμους (3x)
Lk 21:9 "But whenever yeu·should·hear·of wars and chaos,
Mt 24:6 And yeu·shall·happen to·hear·of wars and rumors
Mk 13:7 And whenever yeu·should·hear·of wars and rumors
G4171.1 N-GPM πολέμων (2x)
Mt 24:6 ·hear·of wars and rumors of·wars. Clearly·see·to·it
Mk 13:7 ·should·hear·of wars and rumors of·wars, do·not
G4171.2 N-ASM πόλεμον (5x)
1Co 14:8 sound, who shall·prepare·himself for battle?
Rv 9:7 like horses having·been·made·ready for battle; and on
Rv 9:9 ·sound of·chariots, of·many horses running to battle.
Rv 16:14 ·gather them together to the battle of·that great day
Rv 20:8 to·gather them together into battle, the number of·
G4171.2 N-DSM πολέμῳ (1x)
Heb 11:34 did·become strong in battle, routed estranged·

G4172 πόλις pôlis *n.* (171x)
Roots:G4183 Compare:G3390 G2968 G2969
See:G4171 G2414 G0897
xLangEquiv:H5892
EG4172 (1x)
Lk 4:26 sent, except into *the city* Tsarephath of·Tsidon, to a·
G4172.2 N-NSF πόλις (9x)
Lk 4:29 mount on which their city had·been·built, in·order
Ac 13:44 almost all the city *of·Antiochia* did·gather·together
Ac 16:12 which is a·foremost city of·the province of·
Ac 19:29 And the whole city was·filled with·mass·confusion
Ac 27:8 which was near *the city of* Lasea *(in·Crete)*.
Mt 5:14 of·the world. A·city that·is·being·set·out high·upon
Mt 8:34 And behold, the entire city came·out to meet·up
Mt 12:25 is·made·desolate, and every city or home being·
Mk 1:33 whole city was having·been·completely·gathered
G4172.2 N-NPF πόλεις (3x)
Jud 1:7 Sodom and Gomorrah and the cities around them, *in*
2Pe 2:6 and *if* after·incinerating *the* cities of·Sodom and
Rv 16:19 three parts, and the cities of·the nations fell.
G4172.2 N-ASF πόλιν (42x)
Jn 4:5 he·comes to a·city of·Samaria being·referred·to·as
Jn 4:8 had·gone·off to the city in·order·that they·may·buy
Jn 4:28 water·jar and went·off into the city, and she·says to·
Jn 11:54 *and* into a·city being·referred·to·as Ephraim. And
Lk 1:26 was·dispatched by God to a·city of·Galilee whose
Lk 1:39 mountainous·region with haste, into a·city of·Judah,
Lk 2:3 traversed to·be·enrolled, each·one into his·own city.
Lk 2:4 into Judea, to *the* city of·David (which is·called
Lk 2:39 Galilee to their·own city of·Natsareth *(which·means:*
Lk 4:31 he·came·down to CaperNaum, a·city of·Galilee, and
Lk 7:11 *that* he·was·traversing into a·city being·called Nain,
Lk 8:1 was·traveling·throughout each city and village,
Lk 8:4 ·onward toward him *from* each city, *Jesus* declared
Lk 8:34 going·off, they·announced *it* in the city and in the
Lk 8:39 in the whole city what·many·things Jesus did for·
Lk 10:1 personal·presence, into every city and place where
Lk 10:8 "So into whatever city yeu·should·enter, and they·
Lk 10:10 "But into whatever city yeu·should·enter, and they·
Ac 8:5 PhilIppe, after·coming·down to a·city of·Samaria,
Ac 9:6 Rise·up and enter into the city, and it·shall·be·spoken
Ac 14:20 after·rising·up, he·entered into the city, and on·the
Ac 14:21 ·the·good·news to·that city and discipling a·
Ac 15:21 has in·each city the·ones officially·proclaiming
Ac 15:36 ·visit our brothers in every city in which we·fully·
Ac 16:20 ·being Jews, do·exceedingly·trouble our city,
Ac 17:5 ·a·mob, were·making·a·commotion·in the city. And
Ac 17:16 upon·observing the city being utterly·idolatrous.
Ac 19:35 that does·not know *that* the·city of·the Ephesians
Ac 20:23 Holy Spirit thoroughly·testifies in·each city, saying
Heb 13:14 here we·have no continuing city, but·rather we·
Mt 2:23 he·resided in a·city being·referred·to·as Natsareth
Mt 8:33 and going·off into the city, they·announced all the·
Mt 9:1 ·over and came into his·own city *of·CaperNaum*.
Mt 10:5 ·should·not enter into *any* city of·the·Samaritans,
Mt 10:11 And into whatever city or village yeu·should·enter,
Mt 22:7 ·destroyed those murderers and torched their city.
Mt 23:34 gatherings and shall·persecute from city to city,
Mk 1:45 to·be·able to·enter openly into a·city, but·rather was
Mk 5:14 fled and gave·a·detailed·report in the city and in the
Jac 4:13 or tomorrow we·should·traverse into that city, and
Tit 1:5 and should·fully·establish elders in·each city, as I·
2Co 11:32 the city of·the·Damascenes under·continual·guard
G4172.2 N-APF πόλεις (9x)
Lk 13:22 ·throughout each *of·the* cities and villages,
Ac 8:40 he·proclaimed·the·good·news in·all the cities, until
Ac 14:6 Lystra and Derbe, the cities of·Lycaonia, and to·the
Ac 16:4 ·throughout the cities, they·were·handing·down to·
Ac 26:11 *them* even as·far·as to the foreign cities.
Mt 9:35 was·heading·out all around the cities and the
Mt 10:23 no, yeu·may·not finish the cities of·IsraEl, until
Mt 11:20 Then he·began to·reproach the cities in which the
Mk 6:56 whether into villages, or cities, or countrysides,
G4172.2 N-DSF πόλει (16x)
Lk 2:11 to·yeu this·day, in *the* city of·David, a·Savior is·
Lk 7:37 a·woman in the city who was full·of·moral·failure,
Lk 10:12 at that Day for·Sodom, than for·that city.
Lk 18:2 "In a·certain city there·was a·certain judge— *one*
Lk 18:3 there·was a·widow in that city, and she·was·coming
Ac 8:8 And there·was great joy in that city.
Ac 8:9 in the *same* city practicing·dark·occult·powers and
Ac 10:9 ·along·the·road and drawing·near to·the city, Peter
Ac 11:5 "I·myself was in *the* city *of* Joppa praying, and in a·
Ac 16:12 and we·were in that city lingering·awhile·for some
Ac 18:10 ·that I·have for·myself many people in this city."
Ac 22:3 but having·been·reared in this city personally·at the
Mt 10:15 Day of·Final·Tribunal·judgment, than for·that city.
Mt 10:23 they·should·persecute yeu in this city, flee into the
Mk 6:11 Day of·Final·Tribunal·judgment than for·that city."
2Co 11:26 ·among Gentiles, dangers in a·city, dangers in a·
G4172.2 N-DPF πόλεσιν (2x)
Lk 4:43 kingdom of·God to·the other cities also, because I·
Mt 11:1 to·instruct and to·officially·proclaim in their cities.
G4172.2 N-GSF πόλεως (26x)
Jn 1:44 BethSaida, from·among the city of·Andrew and
Jn 4:30 they·went·forth out of·the city and were·coming
Jn 4:39 of·the Samaritans from·among that city trusted in
Lk 2:4 ·up from Galilee, out of·*the*·city of·Natsareth, into
Lk 4:29 they·cast him forth outside of·the city and drove him
Lk 7:12 Now as he·drew·near to·the gate of·the city, behold,
Lk 7:12 And a·significant crowd of·the city *was* together
Lk 8:27 a·certain man from·out of·the city, who was·having
Lk 9:5 while·yeu·are·going·forth from that city, jostle·off
Lk 9:10 place *belonging·to* the·city being·called BethSaida.
Lk 10:11 the dust from·out of·yeur·own city, the·one being·
Lk 14:21 broad·streets and alleyways of·the city, and bring·
Lk 23:51 *he·was* of Arimathaea, a·city of·the Judeans, who
Ac 13:50 and·also the foremost·men of·the city *of·Antiochia*,
Ac 14:4 But the multitude of·the city was·torn·in·two. And
Ac 14:13 the·one being·before their city, after·bringing bulls
Ac 14:19 ·dragging *him* outside of·the city assuming him to·
Ac 16:13 we·went·forth outside of·the city beside a·river,
Ac 16:14 by·the·name·of Lydia from·*the*·city of·Thyatira, a·
Ac 16:39 they·were·asking *of·them* to·go·out of·the city.
Ac 21:5 until *we·were* outside of·the city. And bowing the
Ac 21:39 a·citizen of·no obscure city. And I·petition you,
Ac 25:23 most prominent men of·the city, and with·Festus
Mt 10:14 ·forth·from the home or that city, shake·off the
Mt 23:34 gatherings and shall·persecute from city to city,
Rm 16:23 Erastus, the estate·manager of·the city, greets yeu
G4172.2 N-GPF πόλεων (6x)
Lk 5:12 with him being in one of·the cities, behold, a·man
Lk 19:17 in very·little, be having authority over ten cities.'
Lk 19:19 'Be you also over five cities.'
Ac 5:16 also a·multitude *out* of·the cities all·around
Mt 14:13 the crowds followed him on·foot from the cities.
Mk 6:33 ·together on·foot from all the cities and went there
EG4172.2 (5x)
Ac 9:38 that Peter was in this *city*, the disciples dispatched
Ac 21:39 *who·is* a·Jew of·Tarsus, *a·city* of·Cilicia, a·citizen
Ac 22:3 having·been·born in Tarsus, *a·city* in·Cilicia, but
Ac 27:5 we·came·down to Myra, *a·city* of·Lycia.
Rv 18:18 fiery·burning, saying, 'What *city is* like the Great
G4172.4 N-NSF πόλις (3x)
Ac 21:30 And the whole City was·stirred, and the people
Mt 5:35 because it·is *the* City of·the superior King.
Mt 21:10 into JeruSalem, all the City was·shaken, saying,

G4172.4 N-ASF πόλιν (13x)
Lk 19:41 he·drew·near, upon·seeing the City, he·wept over
Lk 22:10 with·yeu entering into the City, a·man·of·clay†
Ac 12:10 the·one leading to the City, which automatically
Ac 24:12 ·crowd, neither in the gatherings, nor in the City.
Mt 4:5 ·takes him up into the Holy City and sets him on the
Mt 21:18 heading·back into the City with·the·break·of·dawn,
Mt 26:18 "Head·on·out into the City to·a·particular·man and
Mt 27:53 ·entered into the Holy City and were·manifested
Mt 28:11 after·coming into the City, announced to·the
Mk 14:13 "Head·on·out into the City, and a·man·of·clay†
Mk 14:16 went·forth and came into the City, and they·found
Rv 11:2 And they·shall·trample the Holy City forty two
Rv 20:9 of·the holy·ones and the City having·been·loved.
G4172.4 N-DSF πόλει (3x)
Lk 23:19 occurring in the City and·also for·murder).
Lk 24:49 must·settle in the City of·JeruSalem until yeu·
Ac 21:29 together with·him in the City, whom they·were·
G4172.4 N-GSF πόλεως (6x)
Jn 19:20 was·crucified was near to·the City. And it·was
Ac 7:58 ·out outside of·the City, they·were·casting·stones·at
Mt 21:17 he·went·forth outside of·the City into BethAny,
Mk 11:19 he·was·traversing·forth outside of·the City.
Rv 11:8 the broad·street of·the great City *that·is JeruSalem*,
Rv 11:13 and the·tenth·part of·the City fell. And in the
EG4172.4 (1x)
Mt 27:32 as·they·were·coming·out *of·the City*, they·found a·
G4172.5 N-NSF πόλις (8x)
Rv 14:8 is·fallen, the Great City, because she·has·made all
Rv 16:19 And the Great City became three parts, and the
Rv 17:18 whom you·saw is the Great City, the·one having a·
Rv 18:10 'Woe, woe, the Great City Babylon, the Strong
Rv 18:10 City Babylon, the Strong City! Because in one
Rv 18:16 woe, the Great City, the·one having·been·arrayed·
Rv 18:19 'Woe, woe, the Great City, in which all the·ones
Rv 18:21 the Great City Babylon shall·be·cast·down, and
G4172.5 N-DSF πόλει (1x)
Rv 18:18 'What *city is* like the Great City!'
G4172.5 N-GSF πόλεως (1x)
Rv 14:20 the winepress was·trampled outside the City, and
G4172.6 N-NSF πόλις (3x)
Rv 21:16 And the CITY lays·out foursquare, and its length is
Rv 21:18 was *of* jasper. And the CITY *was* pure gold, like
Rv 21:23 And the CITY has no need of·the sun, neither of·
G4172.6 N-ASF πόλιν (7x)
Heb 11:10 for he·was·waiting·for the CITY having the
Heb 11:16 their God, for he·made·ready a·CITY for them.
Rv 21:2 John, saw the HOLY CITY, brand-new JeruSalem,
Rv 21:10 and showed me the Great CITY, the Holy
Rv 21:15 in·order·that he·should·measure the CITY, and its
Rv 21:16 reed, he·measured the CITY at twelve thousand
Rv 22:14 and may·enter by·the gates into the CITY.
G4172.6 N-DSF πόλει (1x)
Heb 12:22 Tsiyon and the·living God's CITY, to·a·heavenly
G4172.6 N-GSF πόλεως (5x)
Rv 3:12 God, and the name of·the CITY of·my God, the
Rv 21:14 And the wall of·the CITY *is* having twelve
Rv 21:19 wall of·the CITY *were* having·been·adorned·with
Rv 21:21 And the broad·street of·the CITY *was* pure gold, as
Rv 22:19 and from·out of·the HOLY CITY, and *from* the·

G4173 πολιτ•άρχης pôlitárchēs *n.* (2x)
Roots:G4172 G0757
G4173 N-APM πολιτάρχας (2x)
Ac 17:6 certain brothers to·the rulers·of·the·city, crying·out,
Ac 17:8 crowd and the rulers·of·the·city *that·were* hearing

G4174 πολιτεία pôlitêía *n.* (2x)
Roots:G4177 Compare:G4175 G1577 xLangEquiv:H0249-2 xLangAlso:H0249-1
G4174.1 N-ASF πολιτείαν (1x)
Ac 22:28 with·a·large sum, procured this citizenship." And
G4174.1 N-GSF πολιτείας (1x)
Eph 2:12 ·utterly·alienated from·the citizenship of·IsraEl,

G4175 πολίτευμα pôlítêuma *n.* (1x)
Roots:G4176 Compare:G4174 G4847 G1577 G2840-1 xLangAlso:H3816
G4175.2 N-NSN πολίτευμα (1x)
Php 3:20 For our communal·citizenship inherently·is in *the*

G4176 πολιτεύομαι pôlitêúômai *v.* (2x)
Roots:G4177
G4176 V-PNM-2P πολιτεύεσθε (1x)
Php 1:27 Merely live·as·a·good·citizen (as·is·worthy of·the
G4176 V-RPI-1S πεπολίτευμαι (1x)
Ac 23:1 I·myself have·been·living·as·a·good·citizen in·all

G4177 πολίτης pôlítēs *n.* (5x)
Roots:G4172 Compare:G1577 See:G4174 G4175 G4176 G4847 xLangAlso:H0249 H0249-1 H0249-2
G4177 N-NSM πολίτης (1x)
Ac 21:39 *a·city* of·Cilicia, a·citizen of·no obscure city.
G4177 N-NPM πολῖται (1x)
Lk 19:14 "But his citizens were·hating him, and they·
G4177 N-GPM πολιτῶν (1x)
Lk 15:15 ·himself to·one of·the citizens of·that country, and
EG4177 (2x)
Lk 15:15 of·that country, and *the citizen* sent him into his
Ac 22:28 I·myself, also, *am* having·been·born *a·citizen*."

G4178 πολλά•κις pôllákis *adv.* (18x)
Roots:G4183
G4178 ADV πολλάκις (18x)
Jn 18:2 the place, because many·times Jesus did·gather there
Ac 26:11 ·honor·by·punishing them many·times in all the
Heb 6:7 which·is·coming upon it many·times and producing
Heb 9:25 ·that he·should·offer himself many·times, just·as
Heb 9:26 ·for him to·already·suffer many·times since *the*
Heb 10:11 ·serving and offering many·times the same
Mt 17:15 for he·has·already·fallen many·times into the fire
Mt 17:15 ·times into the fire and many·times into the water.
Mk 5:4 him many·times to·have·been·bound with·shackles
Mk 9:22 And many·times it·cast him even into fire and into
Rm 1:13 that many·times I·personally·determined to·come
Php 3:18 of·whom I·was·saying to·yeu many·times, and
2Co 8:22 we·tested·and·proved many·times being diligent in
2Co 11:23 *and* in *facing various* deaths many·times!
2Co 11:26 In·road·travels, many·times *I·was* in·dangers of·
2Co 11:27 travail, in sleeplessness many·times, in hunger
2Co 11:27 and thirst, in fastings many·times, in cold and
2Ti 1:16 ·OnesiPhorus, because many·times he·refreshed me

G4179 πολλα•πλασίων pôllaplasíōn *adj.* (1x)
Roots:G4183 G4111 G4120 Compare:G1542
G4179.2 A-APN πολλαπλασίονα (1x)
Lk 18:30 should·not receive·in·full many·times·over in this

G4180 πολυ•λογία pôlylôgía *n.* (1x)
Roots:G4183 G3056
G4180 N-DSF πολυλογίᾳ (1x)
Mt 6:7 that they·shall·be·heard by·their long·discourse.

G4181 πολυ•μερῶς pôlymerôs *adv.* (1x)
Roots:G4183 G3313 Compare:G4187
G4181 ADV πολυμερῶς (1x)
Heb 1:1 After·speaking in·many·portions and with·many·

G4182 πολυ•ποίκιλος pôlypôíkilôs *adj.* (1x)
Roots:G4183 G4164 Compare:G1313
G4182.2 A-NSM πολυποίκιλος (1x)
Eph 3:10 ·that the extensively·manifold wisdom of·God

G4183 πολύς pôlýs *adj.* (366x)
πολλός pôllôs
[alternate, with its various forms]
Compare:G3173 See:G4118 G4119 G4214
G4183.1 A-NSM πολύς (4x)
Jn 6:10 Now there·was much grass in the place.
Jn 7:12 And there·was much grumbling among the crowds
Heb 5:11 which, the matter *means* much to·us, yet the·
Mt 2:18 a·woeful·wailing and weeping and much distressing;
G4183.1 A-NSN πολύ (3x)
Lk 12:48 ·given, personally·from him much shall·be·sought,
Rm 3:2 Much in·each·and·every manner.
1Pe 1:7 of·yeur trust (*being* much more·precious·than gold
G4183.1 A-NPN πολλά (2x)
Jn 3:23 near to·Salim because there·was much water there.
Rv 8:3 and there·was·given to·him much incense, in·order·
G4183.1 A-ASM πολύν (4x)
Jn 12:24 But if it·should·die, it·bears much fruit.
Jn 15:5 ·I in him, the·same bears much fruit, because apart·
Jn 15:8 is·glorified, that yeu·may·bear much fruit, and *that*
Col 4:13 I·testify for·him, that he·has much zeal over yeu,
G4183.1 A-ASF πολλήν (7x)
Lk 10:40 was·distracted concerning much attendance *to·them*
Ac 16:16 lords with·much income by·maniacal·soothsaying.
Mt 13:5 ·places, where it·was·not having much earth, and
Mk 4:5 ·ground, where it·was·not having much soil, and
Phm 1:7 For we·have much gratitude and comfort in your
Phm 1:8 while·having much freeness·of·speech in
1Ti 3:13 and·also much boldness·of·speech·with·clarity in
G4183.1 A-ASN πολύ (7x)
Lk 7:47 have·been·forgiven, because she·loved much. "But
Lk 12:48 "So to·anyone to·whom much is·given, personally·
Lk 12:48 *others* place·the·direct·care·of much, from·him
Ac 18:27 joined·in·and·helped *them* much, the·ones
Jac 5:16 ·a·righteous·man is·itself·operating *to* much *effect*.
2Co 8:15 The·one did·not increase·to the much, and the·one
2Co 8:22 in many·things, but even·now much more·diligent,
G4183.1 A-APN πολλά (6x)
Jn 14:30 "Not any·longer shall·I·speak much with yeu, for
Mk 5:10 And he·was·imploring him much that he·should·not
Mk 12:41 many that·were·wealthy were·casting·in much.
1Co 16:19 and Little·Prisca greet yeu much in *the* Lord,
2Ti 4:14 coppersmith, pointedly·did me much harm. May
Rv 5:4 And I·myself was·weeping much, because not·even·
G4183.1 A-DSM πολλῷ (4x)
1Th 2:2 to yeu the good·news of·God with much striving.
Tit 2:3 slanderers, not having·been·enslaved to·much wine,
1Co 2:3 and in reverent·fear, and in much trembling.
1Ti 3:8 ambiguous·of·word, not giving·heed to·much wine,
G4183.1 A-DSF πολλῇ (7x)
Rm 9:22 power, bore with much long-suffering *the* vessels
1Th 1:5 in Holy Spirit and with much fullness·of·assurance,
1Th 1:6 Redemptive-word, along·with much tribulation *and*
1Th 2:17 ·abundantly to·see yeur face with much longing.
2Co 3:12 we·use much boldness·of·speech·with·clarity.
2Co 6:4 as attendants of·God: in much patient·endurance, in
2Co 8:22 ·now much more·diligent, with·much confidence,
G4183.1 A-DSN πολλῷ (3x)
Lk 16:10 ·little is also trustworthy with much. And the·one
Lk 16:10 with very·little is also unrighteous with much.
Heb 12:9 ·we not much more·especially be·in·subjection to·
G4183.1 A-GSF πολλῆς (10x)
Lk 21:27 in a·thick·cloud' with power and much glory.
Ac 15:7 And with·much mutual·questioning·and·discussion
Ac 24:2 "While·obtaining much peace on·account·of you,
Ac 24:7 ·commander, after·coming near with much force,
Ac 25:23 and BerNiki coming with much pomp and entering
Ac 27:10 ·be with a·battering and much damage·and·loss,
Mt 24:30 ·clouds of·the heaven' with power and much glory.
Mk 13:26 in thick·clouds' with much power and glory.
2Co 2:4 For out of·much tribulation and anguished·anxiety
2Co 8:4 they·were·petitioning us with much entreaty for·us
G4183.1 A-GSN πολλοῦ (1x)
Mt 26:9 this ointment was·able to·be·sold·off for·much, and
G4183.1 A-GPF πολλῶν (1x)
Ac 14:22 the kingdom of·God through many tribulations."
G4183.2 A-NSM πολύς (1x)
Ac 18:10 on·account·that I·have for·myself many people in
G4183.2 A-NPM πολλοί (76x)
Jn 2:23 among the Sacred·Feast, many trusted in his name,
Jn 4:39 And many of·the Samaritans from·among that city
Jn 6:60 Accordingly, many from·among his disciples, upon·
Jn 6:66 As·a·result of·this, many of·his disciples went·off to
Jn 7:31 And many from·among the crowd trusted in him and
Jn 7:40 after·hearing the saying, many from·among the

Jn 8:30 With·him speaking these·things, many trusted in
Jn 10:20 And many from·among them were·saying, "He·has
Jn 10:41 And many came to him and were·saying, "John, in·
Jn 10:42 And many trusted in him there.
Jn 11:19 And many from·among the Judeans had·come
Jn 11:45 So·then many from·among the Judeans, the·ones
Jn 11:55 was near·at·hand. And many walked·up out of·the
Jn 12:11 because on·account·of him, many of·the Judeans
Jn 12:42 ·time, consequently·in·fact, many from·among the
Jn 19:20 In·due·course, many of·the Judeans read·aloud this
Lk 1:1 Since·indeed many took·it·upon·themselves to·fully·
Lk 1:14 exuberant·leaping·of·joy, and many shall·rejoice at
Lk 4:27 "And many lepers were in IsraEl in·the·days of·
Lk 10:24 For I·say to·yeu, that many prophets and kings
Lk 13:24 obstructed·and·narrow gate, because many, I·say
Lk 21:8 yeu·may·not be·deceived, for many shall·come in
Ac 4:4 But many of·the·ones hearing the Redemptive-word
Ac 8:7 *them*, and many *of·the·ones* having·been·paralyzed
Ac 9:42 known in all Joppa, and many trusted on the Lord.
Ac 13:43 ·the gathering being·let·loose, many of·the Jews
Ac 17:12 Accordingly in·fact, many from·among them
Ac 18:8 ·all his house; and many of·the Corinthians hearing
Ac 19:18 Also, many of·the·ones having·trusted were·*now*·
Heb 12:15 and through this, many should·be·contaminated;
Mt 7:13 to the total·destruction, and many are the·ones who·
Mt 7:22 Many shall·declare to·me at that Day, 'Lord, Lord,
Mt 8:11 And I·say to·yeu that many shall·come from east
Mt 9:10 *that* behold, even many tax·collectors and morally·
Mt 13:17 I·say to·yeu, that many prophets and righteous·
Mt 19:30 "But many *who·are* first shall·be last, and *the* last
Mt 20:16 and the first last; for many are called·forth, but
Mt 22:14 "For many are called·forth, but few *are* Selected.
Mt 24:5 For many shall·come in my name, saying, 'I AM
Mt 24:10 And then many shall·be·tripped·up·and·fall·away,
Mt 24:11 And many false·prophets shall·be·awakened and
Mk 2:2 And immediately, many were·gathered·together,
Mk 2:15 in *MattHew's* home, *that* many tax·collectors and
Mk 2:15 disciples. For there·were many, and they·followed
Mk 5:9 "My name *is* Legion, because we·are many."
Mk 6:2 in the gathering, and many hearing *him* were·
Mk 6:31 For there·were many coming and heading·on·out,
Mk 6:33 them heading·on·out, and many recognized him.
Mk 10:31 "But many *who·are* first shall·be last, and the last
Mk 10:48 And many were·reprimanding him that he·should·
Mk 11:8 And many spread·out their garments in the roadway
Mk 12:41 And many that·were·wealthy were·casting·in
Mk 13:6 For many shall·come in my name, saying, 'I AM
Mk 14:56 For many were·falsely·testifying against him, and·
Rm 5:15 trespass of·the one, the many died, so·much more
Rm 5:19 man·of·clay†, the many are·fully·established *as*
Rm 5:19 of·the one, the many shall·be·fully·established *as*
Rm 12:5 in·this·manner, we (the many) are one Body in
Jac 3:1 My brothers, not many *of·yeu should* become
Php 3:18 (For many stroll·about, of·whom I·was·saying to·
2Pe 2:2 And many shall·follow·out their *ways* to·total·
Tit 1:10 For there·are many insubordinate and idle·talkers
1Co 1:26 ·forth, brothers: how·that not many *are* wise·men
1Co 1:26 ·men according·to flesh, not many *are* powerful,
1Co 1:26 not many *are* powerful, not many *are* noblemen.
1Co 8:5 the earth (just·as there·are many gods, and many
1Co 8:5 earth (just·as there·are many gods, and many lords),
1Co 10:17 Because *though being* the many, we·are one bread
1Co 11:30 On·account·of that, many *are* weak and
1Co 16:9 *there·are* many who·are·being·fully·set·opposed.
2Co 2:17 ·are not as the many, shortchanging·and·hustling
2Co 11:18 Since many boast according·to the flesh, I·also
1Jn 2:18 even now many have·become adversaries·of·the·
1Jn 4:1 of·God, because many false·prophets have·gone·out
2Jn 1:7 Because many impostors entered into the world, the·
Rv 8:11 wormwood; and many men·of·clay† died as·a·
G4183.2 A-NPF πολλαί (6x)
Jn 14:2 "In my Father's home are many abodes, but·if·not, I·
Lk 4:25 I·say to·yeu in truth, many widows were in IsraEl in
Lk 7:47 to·you, her many moral·failures have·been·forgiven
Lk 8:3 and Susanna, and many others, who were·attending
Mt 27:55 Now many women were there observing from a·
Mk 15:41 to·him); and·also many other·women, the·ones
G4183.2 A-NPN πολλά (11x)
Jn 21:25 And there·are also many other·things, as·much·as
Lk 8:30 "Legion," because many demons entered into him.
Ac 2:43 came upon·every soul, and many wonders and signs
Ac 5:12 hands of·the ambassadors, many signs and wonders
Ac 26:24 you·are·raving·mad! The many studies do·twist
Gal 4:27 the desolate·woman has·many more children than
Mt 27:52 are·opened·up, and many bodies of·holy·ones
Mk 7:4 eat. And there·are many other·things which they·
1Co 12:12 of·the one body (being many) are one body, in·
1Co 12:14 the Body is not one member, but·rather many.
1Co 12:20 But now in·fact *they·are* many members, but one
G4183.2 A-APM πολλούς (22x)
Lk 1:16 "And he·shall·turn many of·the Sons of·IsraEl back·
Lk 7:21 he·both·relieved·and·cured many from illnesses,
Lk 14:16 man·of·clay† made a·great supper and called many.
Ac 10:27 ·entered·in and found many having·come·together.
Ac 26:10 in JeruSalem, and many of·the holy·ones I·myself
Heb 2:10 all·things *exist*), in·bringing many sons to glory,
Gal 1:14 in Judaism above many my·own·age among my
Mt 3:7 But upon·seeing *that* many of·the Pharisees and
Mt 8:16 to·him many being·possessed·with·demons, and he·
Mt 15:30 blind, mute, crippled, and many others, and they·
Mt 24:5 'I AM the Anointed-One,' and shall·deceive many.
Mt 24:11 shall·be·awakened and shall·deceive many.
Mk 1:34 he·both·relieved·and·cured many being·badly·ill
Mk 3:10 For he·both·relieved·and·cured many, such·for as·
Mk 6:13 they·were·rubbing·oil·on many that·were·unhealthy
Mk 9:26 as one·dead— such·for many to·say that he·died.
Mk 12:5 ·this·one·also they·killed, and·then many others
Mk 13:6 'I AM *the Anointed-One*,' and shall·deceive many.
Rm 5:15 one man·of·clay†, Jesus Anointed, to the many.
1Co 4:15 but·yet *yeu·have* not many fathers, for in
2Co 6:10 as helplessly·poor yet making·wealthy many, as
2Co 12:21 I·shall·mourn many of·the·ones having·already·
G4183.2 A-APF πολλάς (11x)
Jn 2:12 disciples), and they·remained there not many days.
Lk 12:47 shall·be·thrashed with·many *punishing·blows*.
Lk 15:13 "And not many days after, the younger son,
Ac 1:5 ·be·immersed in Holy Spirit after not *too* many days."
Ac 8:25 proclaim·the·good·news in·many villages of·the
Ac 10:2 his house, both doing many merciful·acts for·the
Ac 16:18 And this she·did over many days. But being·
Ac 16:23 after·placing many punishing·blows upon·them,
Mt 7:22 ·out demons, and in·your name do many miracles?
Mt 13:58 And he·did·not do many miracles there on·
1Ti 6:9 ·trial and a·snare, and *into* many stupid and injurious
G4183.2 A-APN πολλά (38x)
Jn 8:26 I·have many·things to·speak and to·judge concerning
Jn 10:32 Jesus answered them, "Many good works I·showed
Jn 11:47 this man·of·clay† does many miraculous·signs?
Jn 16:12 "I·have yet many·things to·say to·yeu, but·yet yeu·
Jn 20:30 in·fact, Jesus also did many other signs in·the·sight
Lk 3:18 in·fact, also exhorting many other·things, he·was·
Lk 9:22 the Son of·Clay·Man† to·suffer many·things, and to·
Lk 10:41 ·are·anxious and are·disturbed about many·things.
Lk 12:19 you·have many beneficially·good·things being·
Lk 12:19 ·good·things being·laid·out for many years. Rest,
Lk 17:25 to·suffer many·things and to·be·rejected·as·unfit
Lk 22:65 And they·were·saying many other reviling *things*
Lk 23:8 ·while on·account·of hearing many·things about him
Ac 25:7 also bringing many burdensome complaints against
Ac 26:9 to·be·necessary to·practice many·things contrary to
Mt 13:3 And he·spoke many·things to·them in parables,
Mt 16:21 to JeruSalem, and to·suffer many·things from the
Mt 19:22 ·grieved, for he·was holding many possessions.
Mt 27:19 for I·suffered many·things this·day according·to
Mk 1:34 ·of illnesses, and he·cast·out many demons. And
Mk 4:2 he·was·instructing them many·things by parables,
Mk 5:26 and·also already·suffering many·things under many
Mk 6:13 And they·were·casting·out many demons, and with·
Mk 6:20 him, he·was·continuing *to·do* many·things, yet
Mk 6:34 ' and he·began to·instruct them *in* many·things.
Mk 7:8 of·pots and cups, and many other such similar·things
Mk 7:13 yeu·handed·down. And many such similar·things
Mk 8:31 to·suffer many·things and to·be·rejected·as·unfit by
Mk 9:12 that he·should·suffer many·things and should·be·
Mk 10:22 ·grieved, for he·was holding many possessions.
Mk 15:3 were·legally·accusing him of·many·things, *but he*·
Rm 12:4 For exactly·as we·have many members in one body
Rm 16:6 Maria, who, in·many·ways, labored·hard among
Jac 3:2 For in·many·things, absolutely·all *of·us* slip·up.
1Co 12:12 the body is one and has many members, and all
2Jn 1:12 Having many·things to·write to·yeu *all*, I·am·
3Jn 1:13 I·was·having many·things to·write, but·yet I·do·not
Rv 19:12 and on his head *were* many royal·turbans, having
G4183.2 A-DSM πολλῷ (1x)
Jn 4:41 And many more trusted on·account·of his·own word.
G4183.2 A-DPM πολλοῖς (5x)
Lk 7:21 and evil spirits; and to·many *that·were* blind, he·
Lk 8:29 ·of·clay†, for many times it·had·altogether·seized
Mt 27:53 into the Holy City and were·manifested to·many.
Rm 8:29 ·for his *Son* to·be firstborn among many brothers.
Rv 10:11 ·for you to·prophesy again over many peoples, and
G4183.2 A-DPF πολλαῖς (4x)
Lk 2:36 herself having·well-advanced in many days, *being*
Ac 28:10 these also honored us with·many honors. And
Mk 4:33 And with·many such parables, he·was·speaking the
1Ti 6:10 ·entirely·impaled themselves on·many distresses.
G4183.2 A-DPN πολλοῖς (2x)
Ac 1:3 after his suffering by many positive·proofs, while·
2Co 8:22 many·times being diligent in many·things, but
G4183.2 A-GSM πολλοῦ (1x)
Ac 15:32 the brothers through much discourse *in·kind*, and
G4183.2 A-GPM πολλῶν (20x)
Lk 2:34 for a·downfall and a·raising·again of·many in IsraEl,
Lk 4:41 demons also were·coming·out of many, yelling·out
Ac 8:7 voice, were·coming·out of·many of·the·ones having
Ac 9:13 "Lord, I·have·heard of many·things concerning this
Ac 15:35 of·the Lord, with many others also.
Heb 9:28 'to·carry·up moral·failures for the many,' for a·
Mt 8:30 ·distance from them a·herd of·many pigs being·fed.
Mt 20:28 and to·give his soul *to·be* a·ransom for many."
Mt 24:12 the love of·the many shall·be·chilled.
Mt 26:28 ·one being·poured·out concerning many for pardon
Mt 26:60 And with·many false·witnesses coming·alongside
Mk 5:26 ·things under many practitioners·of·healing and
Mk 10:45 and to·give his soul *to·be* a·ransom for many."
Mk 14:24 the·one being·poured·out concerning many.
Rm 16:2 she·herself did·become a·patroness of·many, and
1Co 10:33 of·the many in·order·that they·may·be·saved.
1Ti 6:12 good affirmation in·the·sight of·many witnesses.
2Ti 2:2 ·heard personally·from me through many witnesses,
Rv 5:11 and I·heard *the* voice of·many angels all·around the
Rv 9:9 as the·sound of·chariots, of·many horses running to
G4183.2 A-GPF πολλῶν (2x)
Lk 2:35 that *the* deliberations from·among many hearts
2Co 9:12 through many expressions·of·thankfulness to·God.
G4183.2 A-GPN πολλῶν (18x)
Lk 12:7 Yeu·surpass·the·value of·many little·sparrows.
Ac 20:19 all humility·of·mind, and with·many tears, and
Ac 24:10 ·fully·acquainted from·among many years of·you
Gal 3:16 ·the seeds," as upon many *offspring†*, but·rather as
Mt 10:31 surpass·the·value of·many little·sparrows.
Mt 25:21 I·shall·fully·establish you over many·things. Enter
Mt 25:23 I·shall·fully·establish you over many·things. Enter
Rm 4:17 "'I·have·placed you *as* a·father of·many nations'").
Rm 4:18 to·become the father of·many nations according·to
Rm 5:16 ·bestowment *is* as·a·result of·many trespasses unto
Rm 15:23 a·great·yearning for these·many years to·come to
2Co 1:11 on·our behalf, birthed·from·out of·many persons,
2Co 1:11 *may·be·bestowed* upon us through many *persons*,

Ππ

2Co 2:4 of·heart I·wrote to·yeu through many tears, not that
Rv 1:15 , and his voice as *the* sound of·many waters,
Rv 14:2 of·the heaven, as a·voice of·many waters, and as a·
Rv 17:1 the·one who·is·sitting·down upon the Many Waters,
Rv 19:6 ·large crowd, and as a·voice of·many waters, and as
EG4183.2 (1x)
Rv 17:15 he·says to·me, "The *Many* Waters which you·saw
G4183.3 A-NSM πολύς (22x)
Jn 6:2 And a·large crowd was·following him, because they·
Jn 6:5 eyes and surveying that a·large crowd is·come toward
Jn 12:9 Now·then, a·large crowd from·among the Judeans
Jn 12:12 On·the next·day, a·large crowd (the·one coming to
Lk 5:29 home, and there·was a·large crowd of·tax·collectors
Lk 6:23 yeur payment·of·service *is* large in the heaven, for
Lk 6:35 and yeur payment·of·service shall·be large, and yeu·
Lk 7:11 ·together with·him, and·also a·large crowd.
Lk 9:37 from the mountain, a·large crowd met·up with·him.
Lk 10:2 "In·fact, the harvest *is* large, but the workmen *are*
Ac 6:7 in JeruSalem tremendously; also a·large crowd of·the
Ac 11:21 with them, and a·large number turned·back·around
Mt 5:12 because yeur payment·of·service *is* large in the
Mt 9:37 "In·fact, the harvest *is* large, but the workmen *are*
Mt 20:29 ·forth from Jericho, a·large crowd followed him.
Mt 26:47 and with him *was* a·large crowd with daggers and
Mk 4:1 the sea. And a·large crowd was·gathered·together to
Mk 5:21 *sea*, a·large crowd is·already·gathered·together to
Mk 5:24 with him, and a·large crowd was·following him,
Mk 12:37 And the large crowd was·hearing him with·
Mk 14:43 twelve, and with him a·large crowd with daggers
Rv 7:9 and behold, a·large crowd which not·even·one·man
G4183.3 A-NSF πολλή (2x)
2Co 7:4 Large *is* my freeness·of·speech toward yeu, large *is*
2Co 7:4 freeness·of·speech toward yeu, large *is* my boasting
G4183.3 A-NSN πολύ (6x)
Jn 5:3 these *colonnades*, a·large multitude of·the·ones
Lk 6:17 of·his disciples, and a·large multitude of·people
Lk 23:27 there·was·following him a·large multitude of·the
Ac 17:4 and Silas, both a·large multitude of·the·ones who·
Mk 3:7 the sea. And a·large multitude from Galilee followed
Mk 3:8 ·many·things he·was·doing, a·large multitude came
G4183.3 A-NPM πολλοί (8x)
Lk 5:15 concerning him, and large crowds came·together to·
Lk 14:25 Now large crowds were·traversing·together with·
Mt 4:25 And large crowds followed him from Galilee and
Mt 8:1 from the mountain, large crowds followed him.
Mt 12:15 from·there. And large crowds followed him, and
Mt 13:2 And large crowds were·gathered·together to him,
Mt 15:30 And large crowds came·alongside him, having
Mt 19:2 And large crowds followed him, and he·both·
G4183.3 A-ASM πολύν (3x)
Mt 14:14 upon·going·forth, YeShua saw a·large crowd, and
Mk 6:34 after·coming·ashore, saw a·large crowd, and he·
Mk 9:14 *other* disciples, he·saw a·large crowd about them,
G4183.3 A-ASF πολλήν (3x)
Ac 28:29 having a·large questioning·and·discussion among
Heb 10:32 yeu·patiently·endured a·large struggle of·
Eph 2:4 mercy, on·account·of his large love with·which he·
G4183.3 A-ASN πολύ (3x)
Lk 5:6 this, they·tightly·enclosed a·large multitude of·fish,
Ac 14:1 ·manner to·speak, such·for a·large multitude both
1Pe 1:3 the·one according·to his large mercy begetting us
G4183.3 A-APM πολλούς (1x)
Mt 8:18 And YeShua, seeing large crowds about him, he·
G4183.3 A-DSF πολλῇ (1x)
2Co 8:2 that in a·large proof·test of·tribulation, the
G4183.3 A-DSN πολλῷ (1x)
Ac 26:29 *the* little and among *the* large, to·become such as
G4183.3 A-GSM πολλοῦ (3x)
Lk 8:4 And with·a·large crowd being·assembled·together,
Rv 19:1 I·heard a·great voice of·a·large crowd in the
Rv 19:6 And I·heard as a·voice of·a·large crowd, and as a·
G4183.3 A-GSF πολλῆς (2x)
Ac 21:40 to·the people. And with·a·large silence occurring,
Ac 23:10 So·now with·a·large controversy occurring, the
G4183.3 A-GSN πολλοῦ (1x)
Ac 22:28 answered, "I·myself, with·a·large sum, procured
G4183.4 A-ASN πολύ (1x)
Mk 12:27 Accordingly, yeu are·largely led·astray."
G4183.6 A-APN πολλά (3x)
Mt 9:14 we·ourselves and the Pharisees fast often, but your
Mk 1:45 to·officially·herald *his purification* often, and to·
Rm 15:22 ·of·which also, I·was·hindered often *from* coming
G4183.6 A-DSM πολλῷ (1x)
Ac 20:2 parts and exhorting them often in·word, he·came
G4183.7 A-ASM πολύν (2x)
Jn 5:6 he·had·been *in·the sickness* even·now a·long time,
Mt 25:19 "Now after a·long time, the lord of·those slaves
G4183.7 A-ASN πολύ (2x)
Ac 27:14 But not long after, a·typhoon-like wind slammed
Ac 28:6 ·them anticipating over a·long·while and observing
G4183.7 A-GSF πολλῆς (1x)
Ac 27:21 subsisting a·long·while without·a·bite·of·food,
G4183.8 A-NSF πολλή (1x)
Mk 6:35 place is desolate, and even·now *it·is* a·late hour.
G4183.8 A-GSF πολλῆς (1x)
Mk 6:35 And even·now with·it·becoming a·late hour, his
G4183.9 A-NPN πολλά (1x)
Mk 9:26 after·yelling·out and convulsing him repeatedly, *the*
G4183.9 A-APN πολλά (6x)
Mk 3:12 And repeatedly, he·was·stringently·forbidding them
Mk 5:23 and was·imploring him repeatedly, saying, "My
Mk 5:38 *people* weeping and clamoring repeatedly.
Mk 5:43 he·thoroughly·charged them repeatedly that no·one
Rm 16:12 Persis, who repeatedly labored·hard in *the* Lord.
1Co 16:12 brother Apollos, I repeatedly entreated him in·
G4183.10 A-DSM πολλῷ (6x)
Rm 5:9 by his blood, so·much more·so we·shall·be·saved
Rm 5:10 death of·his Son, so·much more·so, after·being·
Rm 5:15 one, the many died, so·much more did·abound the
Rm 5:17 through the one·man, *then* so·much *the* more *that*
2Co 3:9 *had* glory, so·much more·especially *does* the
2Co 3:11 on·account·of glory, so·much more *surpassing is*
G4183.10 A-DSN πολλῷ (7x)
Lk 18:39 But he·himself was·yelling·out so·much *the* more
Heb 12:25 on the earth, so·much more·so we·ourselves
Mt 6:30 into an·oven, ¿!·*shall·he* not much more *enrobe* yeu
Mk 10:48 ·silent, but he·was·yelling·out so·much the more
Php 1:23 *which·is even* so·much more significantly·better.
Php 2:12 merely, but·rather now so·much more in my
1Co 12:22 But·rather, so·much more *those* members of·the

G4184 πολύ•σπλαγχνος pôlýsplanchnôs *adj.* (1x)
Roots:G4183 G4698
G4184 A-NSM πολύσπλαγχνος (1x)
Jac 5:11 that Yahweh is very·empathetic and compassionate

G4185 πολυ•τελής pôlytélês *adj.* (3x)
Roots:G4183 G5056 Compare:G1784 G5093
G4185.1 A-DSM πολυτελεῖ (1x)
1Ti 2:9 or gold, or pearls, or extremely·expensive attire,
G4185.1 A-GSF πολυτελοῦς (1x)
Mk 14:3 an·alabaster·flask of·extremely·expensive ointment
G4185.2 A-NSN πολυτελές (1x)
1Pe 3:4 which is extremely·precious in·the·sight of·God.

G4186 πολύ•τιμος pôlýtimôs *adj.* (2x)
Roots:G4183 G5092 Compare:G0927
G4186 A-ASM πολύτιμον (1x)
Mt 13:46 who upon·finding one extremely·valuable pearl,
G4186 A-GSF πολυτίμου (1x)
Jn 12:3 a·Roman·pound of·extremely·valuable ointment of·

G4187 πολυ•τρόπως pôlytrópōs *adv.* (1x)
Roots:G4183 G5158 Compare:G4181
G4187 ADV πολυτρόπως (1x)
Heb 1:1 ·portions and with·many·methods long·ago to·the

G4188 πόμα pôma *n.* (2x)
Roots:G4095 Compare:G4213 xLangAlso:H8249
G4188 N-ASN πόμα (1x)
1Co 10:4 all drank the same spiritual drink, for they·were·
G4188 N-DPN πόμασιν (1x)
Heb 9:10 merely in ceremonial·foods and drinks, and in·

G4189 πονηρία pônēría *n.* (7x)
Roots:G4190 Compare:G2556 G4549-1 See:G4188-2
G4189.1 N-NPF πονηρίαι (1x)
Mk 7:22 thefts, acts·of·coveting, evils, guile, debauchery,
G4189.1 N-ASF πονηρίαν (1x)
Mt 22:18 But YeShua, knowing their evil, declared, "Why·
G4189.1 N-DSF πονηρίᾳ (1x)
Rm 1:29 unrighteousness, sexual·immorality, evil, greed,
G4189.1 N-GSF πονηρίας (3x)
Lk 11:39 yeur inward·part overflows with·extortion and evil.
1Co 5:8 with leaven of·malice or of·evil, but·rather with
Eph 6:12 ·against the spiritual·things of·evil in the heavenly·
G4189.1 N-GPF πονηριῶν (1x)
Ac 3:26 to·turn·away each·one *of·yeu* from yeur evils."

G4190 πονηρός pônērós *adj.* (76x)
Roots:G4192 Compare:G2556 G4550 See:G4189
G4191 G4188-2 G1278 G2669
xLangEquiv:H7451-1 xLangAlso:H7451
G4190.1 A-NSM πονηρός (6x)
Lk 6:45 beneficially·good. And the evil man·of·clay†, from·
Lk 11:34 but whenever *your eye* should·be evil, your body *is*
Mt 6:23 But if your eye should·be evil, your whole body
Mt 12:35 ·good·things, and the evil man·of·clay† from·out
Mt 20:15 my things? Is your eye evil, because I·myself am
Mk 7:22 evils, guile, debauchery, an·evil eye, revilement,
G4190.1 A-NSF πονηρά (5x)
Lk 11:29 "This is an·evil generation. It·seeks·for a·sign,
Heb 3:12 ·shall·be in any of·yeu an·evil heart of·distrust, in
Mt 12:39 he·declared to·them, "An·evil generation (*who·is*
Mt 16:4 An·evil generation (*who·is* also an·adulteress)
Jac 4:16 All such boasting is evil.
G4190.1 A-NSN πονηρόν (4x)
Ac 18:14 some wrong·doing or an·evil, mischievous·deed
Ac 19:15 *on·one occasion*, the evil spirit declared, "Jesus I·
Ac 19:16 the man·of·clay†, whom the evil spirit was in,
Rv 16:2 and it·became a·bad and evil pus·sore to the men·
G4190.1 A-NPM πονηροί (5x)
Lk 11:13 if yeu, inherently·being evil, personally·know·how
Mt 7:11 if yeu·yeurselves, being evil, personally·know·how
Mt 12:34 O·offspring of·vipers, being evil, in·what·way are·
Mt 15:19 ·out of·the heart comes·forth evil deliberations,
2Ti 3:13 But evil men·of·clay† and adept·smooth·talkers
G4190.1 A-NPF πονηραί (2x)
Eph 5:16 ·redeeming the season, because the days are evil.
1Ti 6:4 becomes envy, strife, revilements, evil suspicions,
G4190.1 A-NPN πονηρά (4x)
Jn 3:19 rather than the light, for their deeds were evil.
Jn 7:7 I·myself testify concerning it, that its works are evil.
Mk 7:23 All these evil·things proceed·forth from·inside, and
1Jn 3:12 Because his·own works were evil, and the·ones
G4190.1 A-VSM πονηρέ (3x)
Lk 19:22 mouth shall·I·judge you, O·evil slave. You·had·
Mt 18:32 his lord says to·him, 'Evil slave! I·forgave you all
Mt 25:26 lord declared to·him, 'O·evil and slothful slave!
G4190.1 A-ASN πονηρόν (5x)
Lk 6:22 should·cast·out yeur name as evil, because·of the
Lk 6:45 evil treasure of·his heart, brings·forth the evil. "For
Ac 28:21 announced or spoken any evil concerning you.
Mt 5:11 should·declare all·manner·of evil utterance against
Rm 12:9 utterly·detesting the evil, being·tightly·joined to·
G4190.1 A-APM πονηρούς (4x)
Ac 17:5 ·taking·to·themselves certain evil men of·the riffraff
Mt 7:17 good fruit, but the rotten tree produces evil fruit.
Mt 7:18 ·good tree is·not able to·produce evil fruit, neither *is*
Mt 22:10 they·found, both *the* evil and *the* beneficially·good
G4190.1 A-APN πονηρά (4x)
Ac 19:12 them, and·also *for* the evil spirits to·go·forth from
Ac 19:13 Jesus over the·ones having the evil spirits, saying,
Mt 9:4 ·do yeu·yeurselves cogitate evil·things in yeur hearts?
Mt 12:35 from·out of·his evil treasure casts·forth evil·things.

G4190.1 A-DSF πονηρᾷ (2x)
Mt 12:45 ·this·manner shall·it·be also to·this evil generation.
Eph 6:13 ·may·be·able to·withstand *them* in the evil day, and
G4190.1 A-DPM πονηροῖς (1x)
3Jn 1:10 he·does, gossiping·against us with·evil words. And
G4190.1 A-DPN πονηροῖς (2x)
Col 1:21 enemies in·*your*·innermost·mind by the evil works,
2Jn 1:11 "Be·well," shares in·his evil deeds.
G4190.1 A-GSM πονηροῦ (4x)
Jn 17:15 ·should·guard them beyond·reach of·the Evil·One.
Lk 6:45 man·of·clay†, from·out of·the evil treasure of·his
Gal 1:4 us out from·among the evil age currently·standing,
Mt 12:35 ·of·clay† from·out of·his evil treasure casts·forth
G4190.1 A-GSF πονηρᾶς (1x)
Heb 10:22 having·been·sprinkled from an·evil conscience,
G4190.1 A-GSN πονηροῦ (2x)
1Th 5:22 Abstain from every aspect of·evil.
2Ti 4:18 shall·snatch me away·from every evil work. And
G4190.1 A-GPM πονηρῶν (2x)
Jac 2:4 and are·become judges with·evil deliberations?
2Th 3:2 away·from the absurd and evil men·of·clay†, for not
G4190.1 A-GPN πονηρῶν (3x)
Lk 3:19 and concerning all *the* evils which HerOd·AntiPas
Lk 7:21 illnesses, scourges, and evil spirits; and to·many
Lk 8:2 ·been·both·relieved·and·cured from evil spirits and
G4190.2 A-ASM πονηρόν (1x)
1Co 5:13 ·expel the evil·person from·among yeurselves in·
G4190.2 A-DSM πονηρῷ (1x)
Mt 5:39 not to·stand·opposed·to the evil·person, but·rather
G4190.3 A-NSM πονηρός (2x)
Mt 13:19 yet not comprehending *it*, the Evil·One comes and
1Jn 5:18 himself, and the Evil·One does·not lay·hold of·him
G4190.3 A-ASM πονηρόν (2x)
1Jn 2:13 ·men, because yeu·have·overcome the Evil·One. I·
1Jn 2:14 in yeu, and yeu·have·overcome the Evil·One.
G4190.3 A-DSM πονηρῷ (1x)
1Jn 5:19 and the whole world is·laid·out in the Evil·One.
G4190.3 A-GSM πονηροῦ (7x)
Lk 11:4 but·rather snatch us away·from the Evil·One.'"
Mt 5:37 of·these·things is birthed·from·out of·the Evil·One.
Mt 6:13 snatch us away from the Evil·One, because yours is
Mt 13:38 But the darnel·weeds are the Sons of·the Evil·One.
2Th 3:3 yeu and shall·vigilantly·keep *yeu* from the Evil·One.
Eph 6:16 to·extinguish all the fiery arrows of·the Evil·One),
1Jn 3:12 birthed·from·out of·the Evil·One and slaughtered his
G4190.4 A-APM πονηρούς (3x)
Lk 6:35 he·himself is kind to the ungrateful and evil·ones.
Mt 5:45 ·horizon over evil·ones and beneficially·good·ones,
Mt 13:49 ·separate the evil·ones from·out of·*the*·midst of·the

G4191 πονηρότερος pônērṓtêrôs *adj.* (2x)
Roots:G4190
G4191 A-APN-C πονηρότερα (2x)
Lk 11:26 *to·itself* seven other spirits more·evil·than itself,
Mt 12:45 himself seven other spirits more·evil·than himself.

G4192 πόνος pốnôs *n.* (3x)
Roots:G3993 Compare:G5605 G3449 G2873 G3077 G3601 See:G1278 G2669 G4190 xLangAlso:H5999
G4192.2 N-NSM πόνος (1x)
Rv 21:4 nor yelling, nor·also continual·anguish. It·shall·not
G4192.2 N-GSM πόνου (1x)
Rv 16:10 their tongues as·a·result of·the continual·anguish,
G4192.2 N-GPM πόνων (1x)
Rv 16:11 ·a·result of·their continual·anguish and as·a·result

G4193 Ποντικός Pôntikṓs *adj/g.* (1x)
Roots:G4195
G4193.2 A/G-ASM Ποντικόν (1x)
Ac 18:2 Jew by·the·name·of Aquila (of·Pontus by·birth,

G4194 Πόντιος Pốntiôs *n/p.* (4x)
G4194.2 N/P-NSM Πόντιος (1x)
Ac 4:27 *they·being* both HerOd·AntiPas and Pontius Pilate,
G4194.2 N/P-DSM Ποντίῳ (1x)
Mt 27:2 and handed him over to·Pontius Pilate the governor.
G4194.2 N/P-GSM Ποντίου (2x)
Lk 3:1 Caesar— (with·Pontius Pilate being·governor of·
1Ti 6:13 (the·one testifying before Pontius Pilate the good

G4195 Πόντος Pốntôs *n/l.* (2x)
See:G4193
G4195.2 N/L-ASM Πόντον (1x)
Ac 2:9 and *in* Judea and Cappadocia, *in* Pontus and Asia,
G4195.2 N/L-GSM Πόντου (1x)
1Pe 1:1 of·*the*·Diaspora *throughout* Pontus, Galatia,

G4196 Πόπλιος Pốpliôs *n/p.* (2x)
G4196.2 N/P-DSM Ποπλίῳ (1x)
Ac 28:7 *a·man* by·the·name·of Poplius who was·warmly·
G4196.2 N/P-GSM Ποπλίου (1x)
Ac 28:8 it·happened *that* the father of·Poplius lay·ill, being·

G4197 πορεία pôrêía *n.* (2x)
Roots:G4198 Compare:G4330 See:G3597 xLangAlso:H1979
G4197.2 N-ASF πορείαν (1x)
Lk 13:22 and making a·circuitous·route toward JeruSalem.
G4197.3 N-DPF πορείαις (1x)
Jac 1:11 ·shriveled·up along his proceedings·throughout·life.

G4198 πορεύομαι pôrêúômai *v.* (154x)
Roots:G3984 Compare:G4043 G0402 G0672 G5563 See:G1607 G4197 G4365 xLangEquiv:H3212
G4198.1 V-FDI-1S πορεύσομαι (2x)
Lk 15:18 Rising·up, I·shall·traverse toward my father and
Ac 18:6 From now·on, I·shall·traverse to the Gentiles.
G4198.1 V-FDI-2S πορεύσῃ (1x)
Ac 25:12 ·to Caesar. To Caesar you·shall·traverse."
G4198.1 V-FDI-3S πορεύσεται (1x)
Lk 11:5 yeu shall·have a·friend, and shall·traverse to him at·
G4198.1 V-FDI-3P πορεύσονται (1x)
1Co 16:4 to·traverse, they·shall·traverse together with·me.
G4198.1 V-PNI-1S πορεύομαι (8x)
Jn 11:11 ·been·laid·to·rest. But·yet I·traverse, in·order·that
Jn 14:2 *that* to·yeu. I·traverse to·make·ready a·place for·yeu
Jn 14:12 shall·he·do, because I·myself traverse to my Father
Jn 14:28 rejoice that I·declared, 'I·traverse to the Father,'
Jn 16:28 I·leave the world, and traverse to the Father.
Lk 14:19 yoked·teams of·oxen, and I·traverse to·test them
Ac 20:22 in·the spirit, I·myself traverse to JeruSalem, not
Rm 15:25 But right·now, I·traverse to JeruSalem, attending
G4198.1 V-PNI-3S πορεύεται (6x)
Jn 10:4 ·cast·forth his·own sheep, he·traverses before them,
Lk 7:8 'Traverse,' and he·traverses; and to·another, 'Come,
Lk 11:26 "Then it·traverses and personally·takes *to·itself*
Lk 15:4 in the wilderness, and·then traverse after the·one
Mt 8:9 'Traverse,' and he·traverses; and to·another, 'Come
Mt 12:45 Then he·traverses and personally·takes with
G4198.1 V-PNM-2S πορεύου (11x)
Jn 8:11 I·myself condemn you. Traverse, and morally·fail
Jn 20:17 to my Father. But you·traverse to my brothers and
Lk 5:24 and taking·up your pallet, traverse to your house.
Lk 7:50 "Your trust has·saved you; traverse in peace."
Lk 10:37 Jesus declared to·him, "Traverse, and you·yourself
Ac 8:26 "Rise·up and traverse down *on* the·south·side
Ac 9:15 declared to him, "Traverse! Because this·man is my
Ac 10:20 ·up, walk·down and traverse together with·them,
Ac 22:10 to me, 'Upon·rising·up, traverse into Damascus,
Ac 22:21 he·declared to me, 'Traverse, because I·myself
Mt 2:20 and his mother, and traverse into *the* land of·IsraEl,
G4198.1 V-PNM-2P πορεύεσθε (5x)
Ac 5:20 "Traverse, and after·being·settled·*in*, speak in the
Ac 16:36 Now accordingly, going·forth, traverse in peace."
Mt 10:6 but traverse rather to the sheep, the·ones having·
Mt 22:9 Now·then, yeu·traverse to the exit·areas of·the
Mt 25:9 for·us and yeu. But traverse rather toward the·ones
G4198.1 V-PNN πορεύεσθαι (17x)
Jn 7:35 ·does this·man intend to·traverse that we·ourselves
Jn 7:35 him? ¿!·Does he·intend to·traverse into the Diaspora
Lk 9:51 ·himself firmly·set his face to·traverse to JeruSalem,
Lk 10:38 it·happened, with them traversing, that he·himself
Lk 13:33 it·is·necessary·for me to·traverse today, and
Lk 17:11 And with him traversing to JeruSalem, it·happened
Lk 22:33 "Lord, I·am ready to·traverse with you, even unto
Lk 24:28 made·as·though he·would·traverse further.
Ac 9:3 And in the *regular·course·of* traversing, it·occurred
Ac 14:16 ·for all the nations to·traverse in·their·own ways.
Ac 16:7 they·were·attempting to·traverse toward Bithynia,
Ac 17:14 dispatched·forth Paul to·traverse as toward the sea,
Ac 19:21 and Achaia, *for·him* to·traverse to JeruSalem,
Ac 23:32 ·for the horsemen to·traverse *onward* together
Ac 25:20 he·might·be·definitely·willing to·traverse to
1Co 10:27 ·for yeu, and yeu·want to·traverse, eat anything
1Co 16:4 *for* me·also to·traverse, they·shall·traverse together
G4198.1 V-PNP-ASM πορευόμενον (1x)
Ac 1:11 as yeu·distinctly·viewed him traversing into the
G4198.1 V-PNP-APM πορευομένους (2x)
Ac 26:13 me and the·ones traversing together with·me.
2Pe 2:10 flesh, who·are·traversing in a·contaminating
G4198.1 V-PNP-DSM πορευομένῳ (1x)
Ac 22:6 "And with·me traversing and drawing·near to·
G4198.1 V-PNP-DPM πορευομένοις (1x)
Mk 16:12 while·walking, as·they·were·traversing into *the*
G4198.1 V-PNP-GSM πορευομένου (1x)
Lk 19:36 And with·him traversing, *other disciples* were·
G4198.1 V-PNP-GPF πορευομένων (1x)
Mt 28:11 Now as·they were·traversing, behold, some of·the
G4198.1 V-PNP-GPM πορευομένων (2x)
Lk 9:57 it·happened to·them, while·traversing along the
Ac 16:16 *later*, it·happened with·us traversing to prayer,
G4198.1 V-PNP-NSN πορευόμενον (1x)
Lk 9:53 his face was *as* one·who·is·traversing to JeruSalem.
G4198.1 V-PNP-NSM πορευόμενος (3x)
Lk 14:31 "Or what king, who·is·traversing to·engage·in war
Ac 26:12 such *activities*, while·traversing to Damascus with
1Ti 1:3 (*even* while·I·was·traversing into Macedonia), *do·so*
G4198.1 V-PNP-NPF πορευόμεναι (1x)
Ac 9:31 And while·traversing in·the reverent·fear·and·awe
G4198.1 V-PNP-NPM πορευόμενοι (7x)
Lk 1:6 in·the·sight of·God, traversing blamelessly in all the
Lk 8:14 hearing, yet while·traversing, are·altogether·choked
Lk 24:13 from·among them were traversing on that·same
Mt 10:7 And while·traversing, officially·proclaim, saying,
Jud 1:16 ·faultfinders, traversing according·to their·own
Jud 1:18 time, who·are·traversing according·to their·own
2Pe 3:3 last days mockers, traversing according·to their own
G4198.1 V-PNS-1S πορεύωμαι (2x)
Rm 15:24 just as·soon·as I·should·traverse for Spain, I·shall·
1Co 16:6 onward·on·my·journey wherever I·may·traverse.
G4198.1 V-INI-1S ἐπορευόμην (1x)
Ac 22:5 letters to the brothers and traversed into Damascus,
G4198.1 V-INI-1P ἐπορευόμεθα (1x)
Ac 21:5 upon·going·forth, we·were·traversing, with·all *the*
G4198.1 V-INI-3S ἐπορεύετο (4x)
Lk 7:6 And Jesus was·traversing together with·them. And
Lk 7:11 on the next·day *that* he·was·traversing into a·city
Lk 19:28 ·declaring these·things, *Jesus* traversed·on ahead,
Ac 8:39 see him any·longer, for he·traversed on·his way
G4198.1 V-INI-3P ἐπορεύοντο (5x)
Lk 2:3 And all traversed to·be·enrolled, each·one into his·
Lk 2:41 each year his parents traversed to JeruSalem for·the
Lk 24:28 to the village, where they·were·traversing, and he·
Ac 8:36 And as they·traversed down the roadway, they·came
Mt 28:9 And as they·were·traversing to·announce *it* to·his
G4198.1 V-ADS-1P πορευσώμεθα (1x)
Jac 4:13 "Today or tomorrow we·should·traverse into that
G4198.1 V-AOI-3S ἐπορεύθη (10x)
Jn 7:53 And each·man traversed to·his·own house.
Jn 8:1 But Jesus traversed to the Mount of·Olives.
Lk 1:39 in these days, traversed into the mountainous·region
Lk 4:42 occurring, going·forth, he·traversed into a·desolate
Lk 19:12 a·certain nobleman, traversed into a·distant
Lk 22:39 ·to his custom, *Jesus* traversed to the Mount of·
Ac 8:27 And rising·up, he·traversed, and behold, *there·was*

Ac 12:17 And going·forth, he·traversed into another place.
Mt 12:1 season, YeShua traversed on·the various·Sabbaths
Mt 19:15 his hands on·them, he·traversed·on from·there.

G4198.1 V-AOI-3P ἐπορεύθησαν (4x)
Lk 9:56 And they·traversed to another village.
Mt 2:9 And after·listening·to the king, they·traversed. And
Mt 28:16 Now the eleven disciples traversed into Galilee to
Jud 1:11 Woe to·them! Because they·traversed in·the way

G4198.1 V-AOM-2S πορεύθητι (4x)
Lk 7:8 and I·say to·this·man, 'Traverse,' and he·traverses;
Ac 9:11 to him, "Rising·up, traverse on the avenue, the·one
Ac 28:26 saying, "Traverse toward this People, and declare,
Mt 8:9 and I·say to·this *man*, 'Traverse,' and he·traverses;

G4198.1 V-AON πορευθῆναι (2x)
Ac 1:25 ·contrary·to, *in·order* to·traverse into his·own place.
Ac 20:1 *them*, went·forth to·traverse into Macedonia.

G4198.1 V-AOP-ASM πορευθέντα (1x)
Ac 27:3 Julius freely·permitted *him* to·traverse to his·friends

G4198.1 V-AOP-NSF πορευθεῖσα (1x)
Mk 16:10 That·one, after·traversing, announced *it* to·the·

G4198.1 V-AOP-NSM πορευθείς (7x)
Lk 14:10 ·be·called·forth, after·traversing, sit·back·to·eat in
Lk 15:15 And traversing, he·tightly·joined·himself to·one of·
Mt 17:27 ·should·not trip them up, after·traversing to the sea
Mt 25:16 "And traversing, the·one receiving the five talants·
Mt 26:14 ·to·as Judas IsCariot, upon·traversing to the chief·
1Pe 3:19 in which, also traversing to·the spirits in prison,
1Pe 3:22 who, traversing into heaven, is at *the* right·hand of·

G4198.1 V-AOP-NSM@ πορευθείς (1x)
Mt 18:12 ·led·astray, does·he·not·indeed traverse, leaving

G4198.1 V-AOP-NPF πορευθεῖσαι (1x)
Mt 28:7 Then traversing swiftly, declare to·his disciples that

G4198.1 V-AOP-NPM πορευθέντες (12x)
Lk 7:22 declared to·them, "Traversing, report to·John what·
Lk 9:13 two fish, except·that after·traversing, we·ourselves
Lk 9:52 personal·presence. And traversing, they·entered into
Lk 13:32 he·declared to·them, "Traversing, yeu·declare to·
Lk 22:8 John, declaring, "Traversing, make·ready for·us the
Mt 2:8 he·declared, "Upon·traversing, verify·*it*·by·inquiring
Mt 11:4 declared to·them, "Traversing, announce to·John
Mt 21:6 And traversing, the disciples, also doing just·as
Mt 22:15 Then traversing, the Pharisees took consultation
Mt 27:66 And traversing, they·secured the grave with the
Mt 28:19 "Accordingly, while·traversing, disciple all the
Mk 16:15 ·declared to·them, "Traversing into absolutely·all

G4198.1 V-AOS-1S πορευθῶ (1x)
Jn 14:3 And if I·should·traverse and should·make·ready a·

G4198.1 V-AOS-2P πορευθῆτε (2x)
Lk 21:8 yeu·should·not traverse right·behind them.
Mt 21:2 to·them, "Yeu·should·traverse into the village fully·

G4198.1 V-AOS-3S πορευθῇ (1x)
Lk 16:30 But·yet if someone should·traverse to them from

G4198.1 V-AOS-3P πορευθῶσιν (1x)
Ac 23:23 that they·should·traverse unto Caesarea from *the*

G4198.1 V-RNP-APM πεπορευμένους (1x)
1Pe 4:3 of·the Gentiles— having·traversed in debaucheries,

G4198.2 V-PNI-3S πορεύεται (1x)
Lk 22:22 Son of·Clay·Man† departs according·to·the·thing

G4198.2 V-PNM-2S πορεύου (5x)
Jn 4:50 Jesus says to·him, "Depart, your son lives.
Lk 8:48 trust has·made you safe·and·well; depart in peace."
Lk 13:31 "Go·out, and depart from·here, because HerOd·
Lk 17:19 to·him, "Rising·up, depart. Your trust has·made
Ac 24:25 Holding it for·now, depart. And upon·partaking·of

G4198.2 V-PNM-2P πορεύεσθε (1x)
Mt 25:41 ·ones at *the* left·hand, 'Depart from me, the·ones

G4198.2 V-PNN πορεύεσθαι (1x)
Lk 4:42 ·onto him, *such·for·him* not to·depart from them.

G4198.2 V-PNP-GSM πορευομένου (1x)
Ac 1:10 toward the heaven with·him departing, behold, two

G4198.2 V-PNP-GPM πορευομένων (1x)
Mt 11:7 And as·these·men were·departing, YeShua began to·

G4198.2 V-INI-3S ἐπορεύετο (3x)
Jn 4:50 word that Jesus declared to·him, and he·departed.
Lk 4:30 after·going through *the* midst of·them, departed.
Mt 24:1 And going·forth, YeShua was·departing from the

G4198.2 V-INI-3P ἐπορεύοντο (1x)
Ac 5:41 *ambassadors*, in·fact, were·departing from in·front

G4198.2 V-AOI-3S ἐπορεύθη (1x)
2Ti 4:10 the present age, and he·departed to ThessaloNica,

G4198.2 V-AOP-NPM πορευθέντες (2x)
Lk 17:14 to·them, "After·departing, yeu·must·fully·exhibit
Mt 9:13 But upon·departing, learn what it·means, "I·want

G4198.2 V-AOS-1S πορευθῶ (1x)
Jn 16:7 to yeu; but if I·should·depart, I·shall·send him to

G4199 πορθέω pôrthéō *v.* (3x)
Compare:G3075

G4199 V-IAI-1S ἐπόρθουν (1x)
Gal 1:13 ·citizenry of·God and was·fiercely·ransacking it.

G4199 V-IAI-3S ἐπόρθει (1x)
Gal 1:23 the trust which once he·was·fiercely·ransacking."

G4199 V-AAP-NSM πορθήσας (1x)
Ac 9:21 not the·one already·fiercely·ransacking the·ones in

G4200 πορισμός pôrismós *n.* (2x)
Compare:G2771 G3786

G4200.3 N-NSM πορισμός (1x)
1Ti 6:6 with self-sufficiency is a·great means·of·gain.

G4200.3 N-ASM πορισμόν (1x)
1Ti 6:5 ·of·Devout·Reverence *itself* to·be a·means·of·gain.

G4201 Πόρκιος Pórkiôs *n/p.* (1x)

G4201.2 N/P-ASM Πόρκιον (1x)
Ac 24:27 ·fulfilled two·years, Porcius Festus took

G4202 πορνεία pôrnêía *n.* (26x)
Roots:G4203 Compare:G3430 See:G4204-1 xLangEquiv:H8457 xLangAlso:H2184

G4202.3 N-NSF πορνεία (4x)
Gal 5:19 are *these*: adultery, sexual·immorality, impurity,
1Co 5:1 all·over *that there·is* sexual·immorality among yeu,
1Co 5:1 yeu, and such sexual·immorality which is·not·even
Eph 5:3 But sexual·immorality, and·also any impurity or

G4202.3 N-NPF πορνεῖαι (2x)
Mt 15:19 murders, adulteries, sexual·immoralities, thefts,
Mk 7:21 ·forth: adulteries, sexual·immoralities, murders,

G4202.3 N-ASF πορνείαν (3x)
Ac 21:25 a·strangled·animal, and *from* sexual·immorality."
1Co 6:18 Flee the sexual·immorality. Every moral·failing,
Col 3:5 ·things upon the earth: sexual·immorality, impurity,

G4202.3 N-APF πορνείας (1x)
1Co 7:2 But on·account·of the sexual·immoralities, each

G4202.3 N-DSF πορνείᾳ (5x)
Mt 19:9 wife, except over sexual·immorality, and should·
Rm 1:29 with·all unrighteousness, sexual·immorality, evil,
1Co 6:13 body *is* not for·the sexual·immorality, but·rather
2Co 12:21 impurity and sexual·immorality and debauchery
Rv 19:2 the earth with her sexual·immorality, and he·

G4202.3 N-GSF πορνείας (11x)
Jn 8:41 ·not been·born out of·sexual·immorality. We·have
Ac 15:20 idols, and *from* the sexual·immorality, and *from*
Ac 15:29 and from·sexual·immorality. From·among which·
Mt 5:32 ·aside·from a·reason of·sexual·immorality, causes
1Th 4:3 for·yeu to·abstain from the sexual·immorality,
Rv 2:21 ·repent out·from·among her sexual·immorality, yet
Rv 9:21 nor from·out of·their sexual·immorality, nor from·
Rv 14:8 of·the wine of·the rage of·her sexual·immorality."
Rv 17:2 from·out of·the wine of·her sexual·immorality."
Rv 17:4 and impurity of·her sexual·immorality.
Rv 18:3 wine of·the rage of·her sexual·immorality, and the

G4203 πορνεύω pôrnêúō *v.* (8x)
Roots:G4204 Compare:G0766 G2037-1 G3431 See:G1608 xLangAlso:H2181

G4203.4 V-PAP-NSM πορνεύων (1x)
1Co 6:18 the·one committing·sexual·immorality morally·

G4203.4 V-PAS-1P πορνεύωμεν (1x)
1Co 10:8 Nor·even should·we·commit·sexual·immorality,

G4203.4 V-AAI-3P ἐπόρνευσαν (3x)
1Co 10:8 some of·them committed·sexual·immorality, and
Rv 17:2 of·the earth committed·sexual·immorality. And the·
Rv 18:3 of·the earth committed·sexual·immorality with her,

G4203.4 V-AAN πορνεῦσαι (2x)
Rv 2:14 ·to·idols, and to·commit·sexual·immorality.
Rv 2:20 my slaves to·commit·sexual·immorality and to·eat

G4203.4 V-AAP-NPM πορνεύσαντες (1x)
Rv 18:9 the·ones committing·sexual·immorality and living·

G4204 πόρνη pórnē *n.* (12x)
Roots:G4205 Compare:G3511-2 See:G4202 G4204-1 xLangAlso:H2181

G4204.1 N-NSF πόρνη (3x)
Heb 11:31 the prostitute did·not completely·perish·together
Jac 2:25 likewise also Rachav the prostitute, was·she·not
Rv 17:15 which you·saw, where the Prostitute sits·down, are

G4204.1 N-NPF πόρναι (2x)
Mt 21:31 the tax·collectors and the prostitutes precede yeu
Mt 21:32 the tax·collectors and the prostitutes did·trust him,

G4204.1 N-ASF πόρνην (2x)
Rv 17:16 these shall·hate the Prostitute, and they·shall·
Rv 19:2 because he·judged the Great Prostitute, who was·

G4204.1 N-DSF πόρνῃ (1x)
1Co 6:16 the·one being·tightly·joined·to·the prostitute is one

G4204.1 N-GSF πόρνης (2x)
1Co 6:15 ·make *them* members of·a·prostitute? May·it·never
Rv 17:1 the judgment of·the Great Prostitute, the·one who·

G4204.1 N-GPF πορνῶν (2x)
Lk 15:30 your livelihood with prostitutes, you·sacrificed for·
Rv 17:5 MOTHER OF·THE PROSTITUTES AND OF·THE

G4205 πόρνος pórnôs *n.* (10x)
Compare:G4097 G2064-3 G2504-2 See:G4204 G4203 G4202

G4205.3 N-NSM πόρνος (3x)
Heb 12:16 *there·be* any sexually·immoral or profane·person
1Co 5:11 should·actually·be a·sexually·immoral·man, or
Eph 5:5 this·thing, that every sexually·immoral·person, or

G4205.3 N-NPM πόρνοι (2x)
1Co 6:9 *No*, neither sexually·immoral·men, nor idolaters,
Rv 22:15 ·drugs, and the sexually·immoral·persons, and the

G4205.3 N-APM πόρνους (1x)
Heb 13:4 God presently·judges sexually·immoral·people and

G4205.3 N-DPM πόρνοις (4x)
1Co 5:9 not to·associate·with sexually·immoral·people,
1Co 5:10 with·the sexually·immoral·people of·this world, or
1Ti 1:10 for·sexually·immoral·men, for·men·who·have·sex·
Rv 21:8 and murderers, and sexually·immoral·persons, and

G4206 πόρρω pórrhō *adv.* (3x)
Roots:G4253 Compare:G3117 G0568 See:G4207 G1451

G4206.3 ADV πόρρω (3x)
Lk 14:32 with·the·other being yet far·away, dispatching a·
Mt 15:8 lips, but their heart is·distant, far·away from me.
Mk 7:6 ·lips, but their heart is·distant, far·away from me.

G4207 πόρρω•θεν pórrhōthên *adv.* (2x)
Roots:G4206 Compare:G3112

G4207.1 ADV πόρρωθεν (2x)
Lk 17:12 him ten leprous men who stood·still from·afar,
Heb 11:13 but·rather seeing them from·afar, and being·

G4208 πορρωτέρω pôrrhōtérō *adv.* (1x)
Roots:G4206

G4208 ADV-C πορρωτέρω (1x)
Lk 24:28 made·as·though he·would·traverse further.

G4209 πορφύρα pôrphýra *n.* (5x)
Compare:G2847 G5191 xLangEquiv:H0713 A0711 xLangAlso:H8504

G4209.2 N-DSF πορφύρα (1x)
Rv 17:4 *is* the·one having·been·arrayed in·purple and scarlet,

G4209.2 N-GSF πορφύρας (1x)
Rv 18:12 "and of·fine·linen, and purple, silk, and scarlet,

G4209.3 N-ASF πορφύραν (3x)
Lk 16:19 and he·was·wearing a·purple·cloak and fine·linen,
Mk 15:17 And they·dress him with·a·purple·cloak. And
Mk 15:20 him, they·stripped the purple·cloak from·him, and

G4210 πορφυροῦς pôrphyrôûs *adj.* (3x)
Roots:G4209
G4210 A-ASN πορφυροῦν (3x)
Jn 19:2 on·his head and arrayed him *with* a·purple garment,
Jn 19:5 thorny victor's·crown and the purple garment. And
Rv 18:16 ·been·arrayed·with fine·linen, and purple, and

G4211 πορφυρό•πωλις pôrphyrốpōlis *n.* (1x)
Roots:G4209 G4453
G4211.1 N-NSF πορφυρόπωλις (1x)
Ac 16:14 of·Thyatira, a·seller·of·purple·cloth, *a·woman*

G4212 ποσά•κις pôsákis *adv.* (3x)
Roots:G4214
G4212 ADV ποσάκις (3x)
Lk 13:34 How·many·times I·wanted to·completely·gather
Mt 18:21 "Lord, how·many·times shall my brother
Mt 23:37 How·many·times I·wanted to·completely·gather

G4213 πόσις pốsis *n.* (3x)
Roots:G4095 Compare:G4188 See:G1035
G4213.1 N-NSF πόσις (1x)
Rm 14:17 ·God is not *about* feeding and drinking, but·rather
G4213.1 N-DSF πόσει (1x)
Col 2:16 in feeding, or in drinking, or in participating of·a·
G4213.2 N-NSF πόσις (1x)
Jn 6:55 is a·full·meal, and my blood truly is a·full·drink.

G4214 πόσ•ος pốsôs *p:q.* (27x)
Roots:G3739 Compare:G4183
G4214.1 P:Q-ASF πόσην (1x)
2Co 7:11 God), *see* how·much diligence it·did·accomplish
G4214.1 P:Q-ASN πόσον (2x)
Lk 16:5 to·the first, 'How·much·do you·owe to·my lord?
Lk 16:7 'And you, how·much·do you·owe?
G4214.1 P:Q-DSN πόσῳ (11x)
Lk 11:13 gifts to·yeur children, how·much more the Father,
Lk 12:24 them. "By·how·much more *do* yeu·yeurselves
Lk 12:28 into an·oven, how·much more *shall·he·enrobe* yeu,
Heb 9:14 how·much more shall the blood of·the
Heb 10:29 By·how·much, do·yeu·suppose, shall·he·be·
Mt 7:11 gifts to·yeur children, how·much more shall yeur
Mt 10:25 ·Master-Of-Dung, how·much more *shall·they·call*
Mt 12:12 by·how·much·does a·man·of·clay† surpass·the·
Rm 11:12 wealth for·*the*·Gentiles; how·much more their
Rm 11:24 ·cultivated·olive·tree, how·much more shall·these
Phm 1:16 especially to·me, but how·much more to·you,
G4214.2 P:Q-NPM πόσοι (1x)
Lk 15:17 he·declared, 'How·many of·my father's hired·
G4214.2 P:Q-NPF πόσαι (1x)
Ac 21:20 brother, how·many tens·of·thousands of·Judeans
G4214.2 P:Q-APM πόσους (5x)
Mt 15:34 to·them, "How·many loaves·of·bread do·yeu·have
Mt 16:9 *men*, and how·many wicker·baskets yeu·took·up?
Mk 6:38 to·them, "How·many loaves·of·bread do·yeu·have
Mk 8:5 ·of them, "How·many loaves·of·bread do·yeu·have?
Mk 8:19 five·thousand *men*, how·many wicker·baskets full
G4214.2 P:Q-APF πόσας (1x)
Mt 16:10 *men*, and how·many woven·baskets yeu·took·up?
G4214.2 P:Q-APN πόσα (2x)
Mt 27:13 ·not hear how·many·things they·testify·against you
Mk 15:4 See how·many·things they·testify·against you."
G4214.2 P:Q-GPN πόσων (1x)
Mk 8:20 *men*, how·many woven·baskets completely·full of·
G4214.3 P:Q-NSM πόσος (1x)
Mk 9:21 his father, "About how·long a·time has·it·been *that*
G4214.5 P:Q-NSN πόσον (1x)
Mt 6:23 in you, is darkness, how·dense *is* the darkness!

G4215 ποταμός pôtamốs *n.* (19x)
Roots:G4095 Compare:G5493 G4224 G2627 G4132 G3041 See:G4214-1 G4216 xLangAlso:H5104 H2975 A5103
G4215.1 N-NSM ποταμός (2x)
Lk 6:48 happening, the stream burst·directly·against that
Lk 6:49 earth, which the stream burst·directly·against, and
G4215.2 N-NPM ποταμοί (1x)
Jn 7:38 from·out·of·his belly shall·flow rivers of·living water
G4215.2 N-ASM ποταμόν (3x)
Ac 16:13 outside of·the city beside a·river, where prayer
Rv 16:12 ·out his vial upon the great river EuPhrates, and its
Rv 22:1 he·showed me a·pure river of·water of·life-above,
G4215.2 N-APM ποταμούς (1x)
Rv 16:4 angel poured·out his vial into the rivers and into the
G4215.2 N-DSM ποταμῷ (2x)
Mk 1:5 him in the Jordan River, explicitly·confessing their
Rv 9:14 great river EuPhrates *(that·is,·Good·Rushing·River)*."
G4215.2 N-GSM ποταμοῦ (1x)
Rv 22:2 and on·both sides of·the river, *was the* arbor·tree
G4215.2 N-GPM ποταμῶν (1x)
Rv 8:10 it·fell upon the third·part of·the rivers, and upon the
EG4215.2 (3x)
Jn 1:28 in BethAbara across the Jordan *River*, where John
Lk 3:3 ·surrounding the Jordan *River*, officially·proclaiming
Mt 3:5 and all the region·surrounding the Jordan *River*,
G4215.3 N-GPM ποταμῶν (1x)
2Co 11:26 ·times *I·was* in·dangers of·swollen·rivers, dangers
G4215.4 N-NPM ποταμοί (2x)
Mt 7:25 ·storm descended, and the flood·waters came, and
Mt 7:27 ·storm descended, and the flood·waters came, and
G4215.4 N-ASM ποταμόν (2x)
Rv 12:15 of·his mouth water as a·flood·water right·behind
Rv 12:16 and swallowed·up the flood·water which the

G4216 ποταμο•φόρητος pôtamôphốrētôs *adj.* (1x)
Roots:G4215 G5409
G4216.2 A-ASF ποταμοφόρητον (1x)
Rv 12:15 this *woman to·be* carried·away·by·the·flood·water.

G4217 ποτα•πός pôtapốs *adj.* (7x)
Roots:G4219 G4226 Compare:G3634 See:G4169
G4217 A-NSM ποταπός (2x)
Lk 1:29 and was·pondering what·manner·of greeting this
Mt 8:27 saying, "What·manner·of *clay·being* is this that
G4217 A-NSF ποταπή (1x)
Lk 7:39 he·would·be knowing who and what·manner *is* the
G4217 A-NPM ποταποί (1x)
Mk 13:1 "Mentor, see what·manner·of stones and what·
G4217 A-NPF ποταπαί (1x)
Mk 13:1 ·of stones and what·manner·of structures *these are*!
G4217 A-ASF ποταπήν (1x)
1Jn 3:1 See, what·manner·of love the Father has·given to·us
G4217 A-APM ποταπούς (1x)
2Pe 3:11 *determine* what·manner is·necessary·for yeu to·

G4218 πο•τέ pôtê *prt.* (32x)
Roots:G4225 G5037 Compare:G0530 G3819 G4386 G4413 G3753 See:G4219 G3698
G4218.2 PRT ποτέ (4x)
Heb 1:5 to·which of·the angels did·he·declare at·any·time,
Heb 1:13 which of·the angels has·he·declared at·any·time,
1Th 2:5 For not·even at·any·time did·we·come with a·word
1Co 9:7 strategically·goes·to·war at·any·time with·his·own
G4218.3 PRT ποτέ (1x)
Eph 2:11 that yeu *were* at·one·time the nations among flesh
G4218.4 PRT ποτέ (10x)
Lk 22:32 trust should·not cease, and once you return, you·
Gal 1:23 the trust which once he·was·fiercely·ransacking."
Gal 2:6 — whatever·manner·of·men they once were, it·
Rm 7:9 I·myself was·living apart·from Torah-Law once, but
Rm 11:30 yeu·yeurselves also once were·obstinate to·God,
Tit 3:3 For we·ourselves also were once stupid, obstinate,
Eph 2:13 Jesus, yeu·yeurselves, once being at·a·distance,
Eph 5:8 For yeu·were once darkness, but now *yeu·are* light
Col 1:21 And yeu·yeurselves, once existing *as·those* having·
Col 3:7 among whom yeu·yeurselves also once walked,
EG4218.4 (1x)
Php 3:4 even·though I·myself *was* once also having
G4218.5 PRT ποτέ (8x)
Gal 1:23 us in·times·past now proclaims·the·good·news, the
1Pe 2:10 *Yeu·are* the·ones *who* in·times·past *were* not a·
1Pe 3:5 For in·this·manner in·times·past, the holy wives also
1Pe 3:20 to·those·being·obstinate in·times·past, when at·
2Pe 1:21 ·of·clay† *was* prophecy carried·forth in·times·past.
Eph 2:2 in which·things in·times·past, yeu·walked
Eph 2:3 we all had·our·manner·of·life in·times·past in the
Phm 1:11 The·one *who* in·times·past *was* not·useful to·you,
G4218.6 PRT ποτέ (1x)
Jn 9:13 ·man to the Pharisees, the·one formerly *being* blind.
EG4218.6 (2x)
Mk 5:15 the·one *formerly* being·possessed·with·demons
Rm 6:17 *be* gratitude, that *formerly* yeu·were *the* slaves of·
G4218.7 PRT ποτέ (1x)
Gal 1:13 For yeu·heard of·my former manner·of·life in
G4218.8 PRT ποτέ (2x)
Rm 1:10 if·somehow even·now at·last *that* I·shall·prosper
Php 4:10 that even·now at·last yeur·earnest·concern over
G4218.9 PRT ποτέ (2x)
2Pe 1:10 these·things, no, yeu·should·not ever slip·up.
Eph 5:29 For not·even·one·man ever hated his·own flesh,

G4219 πό•τε pốtê *prt.* (19x)
Roots:G4226 G5037 Compare:G3753 See:G2193 G4218
G4219.1 PRT-I πότε (12x)
Jn 6:25 ·declared to·him, "Rabbi, when did·you·come here?
Lk 12:36 ·own lord when he·shall·break·camp from·among
Lk 17:20 by the Pharisees *as·to* when the kingdom of·God
Lk 21:7 "So·then Mentor, when shall these·things be?
Mt 24:3 "Declare to·us, when shall these·things be?
Mt 25:37 saying, 'Lord, when did·we·see you hungering,
Mt 25:38 When did·we·see you a·stranger, and gathered·
Mt 25:39 When did·we·see you sick, or in prison, and came
Mt 25:44 saying, 'Lord, when did·we·see you hungering,
Mk 13:4 "Declare to·us, when·shall these·things be?
Mk 13:33 for yeu·do·not personally·know when the season
Mk 13:35 — for yeu·do·not personally·know when the lord
G4219.2 PRT-I πότε (7x)
Jn 10:24 to·him, "How·long are·you·keeping our soul in·
Lk 9:41 perverse generation, how·long shall·I·be alongside
Mt 17:17 perverse generation, how·long shall·I·be with yeu?
Mt 17:17 ·I·be with yeu? How·long shall·I·put·up·with yeu?
Mk 9:19 generation, how·long shall·I·be alongside yeu?
Mk 9:19 alongside yeu? How·long shall·I·put·up·with yeu?
Rv 6:10 ·a·loud voice, saying, "How·long, Master, the Holy

G4220 πότερον pốtêrôn *adv.* (1x)
Roots:G4226
G4220.2 ADV-I πότερον (1x)
Jn 7:17 concerning the instruction, whether it·is from·out·of·

G4221 ποτήριον pôtḗriôn *n.* (33x)
Roots:G4095 Compare:G2866-1
G4221.1 N-NSN ποτήριον (6x)
Lk 22:20 Likewise also the cup after eating·supper, saying,
Lk 22:20 saying, "This cup *is* the brand-new covenant in
Mt 26:42 "O·My Father, if this cup is·not able to·pass·away
1Co 10:16 The cup of·blessing which we·bless, is·it not·
1Co 11:25 ·manner also, *he·took* the cup after eating·supper,
1Co 11:25 saying, "This cup is the brand-new covenant in
G4221.1 N-ASN ποτήριον (19x)
Jn 18:11 into the sheath! The cup which the Father has·
Lk 22:17 And after·accepting *the* cup *and* giving·thanks, he·
Lk 22:42 ·willing to·personally·carry this cup from me …
Mt 10:42 to·one of·these little·ones a·cup of·cold *water* to·
Mt 20:22 Are·yeu·able to·drink the cup that I·myself am·
Mt 20:23 yeu·shall·drink of·my cup and be·immersed·in
Mt 26:27 And after·taking the cup and giving·thanks, he·
Mt 26:39 if it·is possible, let this cup pass·away from me.
Mk 9:41 whoever should·give yeu a·cup of·water to·drink in
Mk 10:38 Are·yeu·able to·drink the cup that I·myself drink·
Mk 10:39 "In·fact, the cup that I·myself drink, yeu·shall·
Mk 14:23 And after·taking the cup *and* giving·thanks, he·
Mk 14:36 to·you. Personally·carry this cup away·from me.
1Co 10:21 ·not able to·drink *the* Lord's cup and·also *the* cup
1Co 10:21 Lord's cup and·also *the* cup of·demons. Yeu·are·
1Co 11:26 and should·drink this cup, yeu·fully·proclaim
1Co 11:27 bread or should·drink the cup of·the Lord in·an·
Rv 16:19 of·God, to·give to·her the cup of·the wine of·the

Ππ

Rv 17:4 and pearls, *and* having a·golden cup in her hand
G4221.1 N-DSN ποτηρίῳ (2x)
Rv 14:10 ·and·poured undiluted into the cup of·his Wrath;
Rv 18:6 In the cup which she·blended·and·poured·out,
G4221.1 N-GSN ποτηρίου (4x)
Lk 11:39 purify the outside of·the cup and the platter, but
Mt 23:25 yeu·purify the outside of·the cup and of·the
Mt 23:26 purify the interior of·the cup and of·the serving·
1Co 11:28 ·out·of·the bread and drink from·out·of·the cup.
G4221.1 N-GPN ποτηρίων (2x)
Mk 7:4 *such·as the* ceremonial·washings of·cups and pots
Mk 7:8 *the* ceremonial·washings of·pots and cups, and many

G4222 ποτίζω pôtízō *v.* (15x)
Roots:G4095
G4222.1 V-PAM-2S πότιζε (1x)
Rm 12:20 if he·should·thirst, give him drink; for *by* doing
G4222.1 V-IAI-3S ἐπότιζεν (2x)
Mt 27:48 putting·it·on a·reed, was·giving *it* to·him to·drink.
Mk 15:36 ·on a·reed, was·giving *it* to·him to·drink, saying,
G4222.1 V-AAI-1P ἐποτίσαμεν (1x)
Mt 25:37 nourished *you*? Or thirsting, and gave·*you*·drink?
G4222.1 V-AAI-2P ἐποτίσατε (2x)
Mt 25:35 ·thirsty, and yeu·gave me drink. I·was a·stranger,
Mt 25:42 I·was·thirsty, and yeu·did·not give·drink to·me.
G4222.1 V-AAS-3S ποτίσῃ (2x)
Mt 10:42 little·ones a·cup of·cold *water* to·drink merely in a·
Mk 9:41 should·give yeu a·cup of·water to·drink in my name
G4222.1 V-API-1P ἐποτίσθημεν (1x)
1Co 12:13 or free; and all are·given·drink into one Spirit.
G4222.2 V-PAI-3S ποτίζει (1x)
Lk 13:15 feeding·trough, even leading·*him*·off to·watering?
G4222.2 V-PAP-NSM ποτίζων (2x)
1Co 3:7 anything, nor the·one watering, but·rather God, the·
1Co 3:8 But the·one planting and the·one watering are one,
G4222.2 V-AAI-3S ἐπότισεν (1x)
1Co 3:6 I·myself planted, Apollos watered, but·yet God
G4222.2 V-RAI-3S πεπότικεν (1x)
Rv 14:8 she·has·made all nations drink from·out·of·the wine
G4222.3 V-AAI-1S ἐπότισα (1x)
1Co 3:2 I·fed yeu milk and not food, for yeu·were·not·yet

G4223 Ποτίολοι Pôtíôlôi *n/l.* (1x)
G4223.2 N/L-APM Ποτιόλους (1x)
Ac 28:13 ·up, we·came on·the·second·day to Puteoli,

G4224 πότος pôtôs *n.* (1x)
Roots:G4095 Compare:G0712 G1062 G1403
xLangAlso:H4960
G4224 N-DPM πότοις (1x)
1Pe 4:3 excesses·of·wine, revelries, drinking·parties, and

G4225 πού pôú *prt.* (6x)
Compare:G4214 See:G4226
G4225.ª PRT πού (2x)
Jn 1:39 They·came and saw where he·abides, and they·
1Jn 2:11 and does·not personally·know where he·is·heading,
G4225.1 PRT πού (2x)
Heb 2:6 But somewhere, someone thoroughly·testified,
Heb 4:4 For somewhere he·has·declared concerning the
G4225.2 PRT πού (1x)
Rm 4:19 subsisting somewhere·near a·hundred·years·of·age,
G4225.3 PRT πού (1x)
Mk 15:47 ·Jose), *being* somewhere·nearby, were·observing

G4226 ποῦ pôû *prt.* (44x)
See:G4225
G4226.2 PRT-I ποῦ (41x)
Jn 1:38 *Hebrew*, is·to·say Mentor), "where·do you·abide?
Jn 3:8 from·what·source it·comes or where it·heads·on·out.
Jn 7:11 Sacred·Feast and were·saying, "Where is that·man?
Jn 7:35 among themselves, "Where·does this·man intend to·
Jn 8:10 "*Ah*, the wife. Where are those·men, your legal·
Jn 8:14 from·what·source I·came and where I·head·on·out.
Jn 8:14 from·what·source I·come and where I·head·on·out.
Jn 8:19 they·were·saying to·him, "Where is your Father?
Jn 9:12 So·then they·declared to·him, "Where is this·man?
Jn 11:34 and he·declared, "Where have·yeu·laid him?
Jn 11:57 that if any·man should·know where he·is, he·
Jn 12:35 does·not personally·know where he·is·heading.
Jn 13:36 says to·him, "Lord, where·do you·head·on·out?
Jn 14:5 Lord, we·do·not personally·know to·where *it·is that*
Jn 16:5 yeu asks·of me, 'Where·do you·head·on·out?
Jn 20:2 ·tomb, and we·have·not seen where they·laid him."
Jn 20:13 Lord, and I·have·not seen where they·laid him."
Jn 20:15 him away, declare to·me where you·laid him, and·I
Lk 8:25 And he·declared to·them, "Where is yeur trust?
Lk 9:58 ·Man† does·not have *a·place* where he·may·prop his
Lk 12:17 I·have no place·where I·shall·gather·together my
Lk 17:17 the ten purified? But where *are* the *other* nine?
Lk 17:37 And answering, they·say to·him, "Where, Lord?
Lk 22:9 they·declared to·him, "Where do·you·want *that* we·
Lk 22:11 says to·you, "Where is the local·travel·lodge,
Heb 11:8 being·fully·acquainted·with where he·was·going.
Mt 2:2 saying, "Where is the·one being·reproduced·and·
Mt 2:4 directly·from them where the Anointed-One is·born.
Mt 8:20 ·Man† does·not have anywhere he·may·prop his
Mt 26:17 "Where do·you·want that·we·should·make·ready
Mk 14:12 ·him, "Going·aside, where do·you·want *that* we·
Mk 14:14 The Mentor says, "Where is the local·travel·lodge
Rm 3:27 So·then, where *is* the boasting?
1Pe 4:18 ·man scarcely is·saved, where shall·appear the
2Pe 3:4 and saying, "Where is the promise of·his returning·
1Co 1:20 Where *is the* wise?
1Co 1:20 Where *is the* wise? Where *is the* scribe?
1Co 1:20 Where *is the* scribe? Where *is the* disputer of·this
1Co 15:55 "O·Death, where *is* your painful·sting?
1Co 15:55 painful·sting? O·Hades, where *is* your victory?
Rv 2:13 ·know your works, and where you·reside, *even*
G4226.3 PRT-I ποῦ (3x)
1Co 12:17 body *is* an·eye, where·is the sense·of·hearing
1Co 12:17 *body is* hearing, where·is the sense·of·smell
1Co 12:19 ·were all one member, where·is the Body placed?

G4227 Πούδης Pôúdēs *n/p.* (1x)
G4227.2 N/P-NSM Πούδης (1x)
2Ti 4:21 EuBulus greets you, and Pudens, and Linus, and

G4228 πούς pôús *n.* (96x)
Compare:G0939 See:G4158
G4228 N-NSM πούς (3x)
Mt 18:8 "So if your hand or your foot entraps you, chop it
Mk 9:45 And if your foot should·entrap you, chop it off.
1Co 12:15 If the foot should·declare, "Because I·am not a·
G4228 N-NPM πόδες (7x)
Ac 5:9 Spirit? Behold, the feet of·the·ones burying your
Rm 3:15 "Their feet *are* swift to·pour·out blood.
Rm 10:15 the feet of·the·ones who·are·proclaiming·good·
Rv 1:15 and his feet like fine·brass (as having·been·refined
Rv 2:18 eyes as a·blaze of·fire and his feet like fine·brass:
Rv 10:1 face *was* as the sun, and his feet as pillars of·fire.
Rv 13:2 was like a·leopard, and its feet *were* as *the feet* of·a·
G4228 N-ASM πόδα (3x)
Lk 4:11 you·should·stub your foot directly·against a·stone."
Mt 4:6 you·should·stub your foot directly·against a·stone.'"
Rv 10:2 And he·placed his right foot upon the sea, and the
G4228 N-APM πόδας (55x)
Jn 11:2 ·ointment, and firmly·wiping his feet with·her hair,
Jn 11:32 him, she·fell·down at his feet, saying to·him,
Jn 11:44 ·been·bound hand and foot with·swathes·of·linen,
Jn 12:3 Mary rubbed·oil·on the feet of·Jesus and firmly·
Jn 12:3 feet of·Jesus and firmly·wiped his feet with·her hair,
Jn 13:5 ·began to·wash the disciples' feet and to·firmly·wipe
Jn 13:6 "Lord, do·you·yourself wash my feet?"
Jn 13:8 No, you·should·not wash my feet *even* to the coming·
Jn 13:9 "Lord, not my feet merely, but·rather also my hands
Jn 13:10 no need other·than to·wash the feet. Moreover, he·
Jn 13:12 when he·washed their feet and took·hold·of his
Jn 13:14 if I·myself washed yeur feet *being* Lord and
Jn 13:14 are·obligated to·wash one·another's feet.
Lk 1:79 of·death, to·fully·direct our feet into *the* way of·
Lk 7:38 and settling directly·at his feet right·behind *him*
Lk 7:38 she·began to·shower his feet with·tears and was·
Lk 7:38 ·was·earnestly·kissing his feet and was·rubbing·on
Lk 7:44 you·gave·me no water for my feet, but she·herself
Lk 7:44 but she·herself showered my feet with·the tears and
Lk 7:45 ·in, did·not let·up·on earnestly·kissing my feet.
Lk 7:46 but she·herself rubbed·oil·on my feet with·ointment.
Lk 8:35 sitting·down directly·at the feet of·Jesus, having·
Lk 8:41 And falling directly·at the feet of·Jesus, he·was·
Lk 10:39 who, sitting·down·near at Jesus' feet, also was·
Lk 15:22 give *him* a·ring for his hand and shoes for his feet.
Lk 17:16 *his* face directly·at his feet, giving·thanks to·him.
Lk 24:39 See my hands and my feet, that I AM myself.
Lk 24:40 he·fully·exhibited for·them his hands and his feet.
Ac 4:35 ·*them*·down directly·at the ambassadors' feet, and it·
Ac 4:37 value and laid *it* directly·at the ambassadors' feet.
Ac 5:2 portion, he·laid *it* directly·at the ambassadors' feet.
Ac 5:10 ·fell·down at·once directly·at his feet and expired.
Ac 7:58 directly·at the feet of·a·young·man being·called
Ac 10:25 *And* falling at his feet, he·fell·prostrate *to·him*.
Ac 14:10 "Stand upright on your feet." And he·was·leaping
Ac 16:24 prison·cell and secured their feet in the stocks.
Ac 21:11 ·also binding his·own hands and feet, he·declared,
Ac 22:3 in this city personally·at the feet of·GamaliEl, *and*
Ac 26:16 ·up and stand·still upon your feet, for I·was·made·
Mt 15:30 ·deposited them directly·at the feet of·YeShua.
Mt 18:8 having two hands or two feet *and* to·be·cast into the
Mt 18:29 So·then falling·down at his feet, his fellow·slave
Mt 22:13 'After·binding him hand and foot, take him away
Mt 28:9 they·securely·held his feet and fell·prostrate to·him
Mk 5:22 And upon·seeing him, he·falls toward his feet
Mk 7:25 spirit, upon·coming, she·fell·down toward his feet.
Mk 9:45 life-above, than having two feet *and* to·be·cast into
Rm 16:20 the Adversary-Accuser under yeur feet in haste.
1Co 15:25 ·should·place all the enemies under his·own feet.
1Co 15:27 *God* " subjugated all·things under his feet." But
Eph 1:22 'he·subjugated all *things* under his feet' and gave
Eph 6:15 and shodding·yeur·own feet in a·state·of·readiness
1Ti 5:10 if she·washed *the* holy·ones' feet, if she·gave·relief
Rv 1:17 when I·saw him, I·fell toward his feet as dead. And
Rv 11:11 and they·stood·still upon their feet, and great fear
G4228 N-DPM ποσίν (5x)
Jn 20:12 head, and one alongside the feet, where the body
Ac 14:8 man disabled in·his feet who·was·sitting·down,
Heb 12:13 and make level tracks for·yeur feet, lest the lame
Mt 7:6 them down among their feet, then turning·around,
1Co 12:21 nor again the head to·the feet, "I·have no need
G4228 N-GSM ποδός (1x)
Ac 7:5 an·inheritance in it, not·even a·foot step, and·yet he·
G4228 N-GPM ποδῶν (19x)
Lk 9:5 even the dust from yeur feet for a·testimony against
Lk 20:43 I·should·lay·out your enemies *as* your foot stool."'
Ac 2:35 I·should·lay·out your enemies *as* your foot stool."'
Ac 7:33 'Loosen the shoes from·your feet, for the place in
Ac 7:49 and the earth *is* my foot stool. What·kind·of house
Ac 13:25 me, the shoes of·whose feet I·am not worthy to·
Ac 13:51 But shaking·off the dust of·their feet against them,
Heb 1:13 I·should·lay·out your enemies *as* your foot stool"?
Heb 2:8 You·subjugated all·things beneath his feet." For in
Heb 10:13 his enemies should·be·laid·out *as* his foot stool.
Mt 5:35 by the earth, because it·is his foot stool, nor toward
Mt 10:14 home or that city, shake·off the dust of·yeur feet.
Mt 22:44 I·should·lay·out your enemies *as* your foot stool"?
Mk 6:11 ·off the loose·dirt beneath yeur feet for a·testimony
Mk 12:36 I·should·lay·out your enemies *as* your foot stool."
Rv 3:9 and should·fall·prostrate in·the·sight of·your feet, and
Rv 12:1 and the moon beneath her feet, and upon her head
Rv 19:10 And I·fell before his feet to·fall·prostrate to·him.
Rv 22:8 ·down to·fall·prostrate before the feet of·the angel,
EG4228 (3x)
Heb 12:13 lest the lame *limb* should·be·turned·aside, but
Rv 10:2 foot upon the sea, and the left *foot* on the earth,
Rv 13:2 and its feet *were* as *the feet* of·a·bear, and its mouth

G4229 πρᾶγμα prâgma *n.* (16x)
Roots:G4238 Compare:G0982 G3056 See:G4231 G4230
G4229.1 N-ASN πρᾶγμα (1x)
Ac 5:4 How *is·it* that you·placed this action in your heart?
G4229.1 N-GPN πραγμάτων (1x)
Heb 11:1 *concerning* actions not being·looked·upon.
G4229.2 N-NSN πρᾶγμα (1x)
Jac 3:16 *is*, there *is* instability and every mediocre activity.
G4229.2 N-GPN πραγμάτων (2x)
Lk 1:1 the activities having·been·fully·evidenced among us
Heb 10:1 same *as* a·direct·representation of·the activities),
EG4229.2 (2x)
Ac 26:12 "And among such *activities*, while·traversing to
Heb 10:1 of·the impending beneficially·good *activities* (not
G4229.3 N-ASN πρᾶγμα (1x)
1Co 6:1 having a·matter·of·consequence specifically·against
G4229.3 N-DSN πράγματι (3x)
Rm 16:2 matter·of·consequence she·may·have·need of·yeu,
1Th 4:6 his brother in the matter·of·consequence, on·
2Co 7:11 to·be morally·clean in the matter·of·consequence.
G4229.3 N-GSN πράγματος (1x)
Mt 18:19 earth concerning any matter·of·consequence that
G4229.3 N-GPN πραγμάτων (1x)
Heb 6:18 two unalterable matters·of·consequence in which
EG4229.3 (1x)
Mt 18:10 that throughout any *matter·of·consequence*, their
EG4229.4 (2x)
Rm 15:28 this *consequential·matter of·gracious·benevolence*,
2Co 8:8 *in·the consequential·matter of·gracious·benevolence*,

G4230 πραγματεία pragmatêía *n.* (1x)
Roots:G4231
G4230.2 N-DPF πραγματείαις (1x)
2Ti 2:4 with·the business·pursuits of·the natural·life, in·

G4231 πραγματεύομαι pragmatêúômai *v.* (1x)
Roots:G4229 See:G4230
G4231.1 V-ADM-2P πραγματεύσασθε (1x)
Lk 19:13 to them, 'Keep·yourselves·busy until I·come·*back*.

G4232 πραιτώριον praitốriôn *n.* (8x)
G4232.1 N-NSN πραιτώριον (1x)
Mk 15:16 which is *the* Praetorian·hall. And they·call·
G4232.1 N-ASN πραιτώριον (5x)
Jn 18:28 from Caiaphas to the Praetorian·hall, and it·was
Jn 18:28 did·not enter into the Praetorian·hall, lest they·
Jn 18:33 Pilate entered into the Praetorian·hall again and
Jn 19:9 he·entered again into the Praetorian·hall and says to·
Mt 27:27 YeShua into the Praetorian·hall, gathered·together
G4232.1 N-DSN πραιτωρίῳ (1x)
Ac 23:35 ·vigilantly·kept in HerOd·Agrippa's Praetorian·hall.
G4232.2 N-DSN πραιτωρίῳ (1x)
Php 1:13 apparent to·all in the Praetorian·court, and to·all

G4233 πράκτωρ práktōr *n.* (2x)
Roots:G4238
G4233.2 N-NSM πράκτωρ (1x)
Lk 12:58 and the debt·collection·officer should·cast you
G4233.2 N-DSM πράκτορι (1x)
Lk 12:58 ·hand you over to·the debt·collection·officer, and

G4234 πρᾶξις prâxis *n.* (7x)
Roots:G4238 Compare:G1838 xLangAlso:H4611
G4234.1 N-ASF πρᾶξιν (2x)
Mt 16:27 ·give·back to·each·man according·to his practice.'
Rm 12:4 but all the members have not the same practice,
G4234.1 N-APF πράξεις (2x)
Ac 19:18 ·confessing and reporting their practices in·detail.
Rm 8:13 ·Spirit yeu·put·to·death the practices of·the body,
G4234.1 N-DSF πράξει (1x)
Lk 23:51 with·the counsel and with·their practice; *he·was* of
G4234.1 N-DPF πράξεσιν (1x)
Col 3:9 ·off the old man·of·clay† together with·his practices
EG4234.1 (1x)
1Co 9:18 ·of·service: What is *the voluntary* practice for·me?

G4235 πρᾶος prâôs *adj.* (1x)
Roots:G4239 Compare:G5011 See:G4236
G4235 N-NSM πρᾶος (1x)
Mt 11:29 from me, because I·am gentle and lowly in·the

G4236 πραότης praốtēs *n.* (9x)
Roots:G4235 Compare:G4240 G5011
G4236.1 N-NSF πραότης (1x)
Gal 5:23 gentleness, *and* self-restraint— against such·things
G4236.1 N-ASF πραότητα (3x)
Tit 3:2 *but* fair, indicating all gentleness to all men·of·clay†.
Col 3:12 humility·of·mind, gentleness, long-suffering,
1Ti 6:11 trust, love, patient·endurance, *and* gentleness.
G4236.1 N-DSF πραότητι (1x)
2Ti 2:25 with gentleness the·ones who·are·thoroughly·
G4236.1 N-GSF πραότητος (4x)
Gal 6:1 ·a·man in a·spirit of·gentleness, keeping·a·watch·of
1Co 4:21 a·rod or with love, also in·a·spirit of·gentleness?
2Co 10:1 do·implore yeu through the gentleness and fairness
Eph 4:2 with all humility·of·mind and gentleness, with

G4237 πρασιά prasiá *n.* (2x)
G4237.2 N-NPF πρασιαί (2x)
Mk 6:40 And they·sat·back·to·eat in·rows, rows by a·
Mk 6:40 they·sat·back·to·eat in·rows, rows by a·hundred,

G4238 πράσσω prássō *v.* (39x)
Compare:G4160 See:G4234 xLangAlso:H6466
G4238.1 V-FAI-2P πράξετε (1x)
Ac 15:29 ·guarding yeurselves, yeu·shall·practice well.
G4238.1 V-PAI-1S πράσσω (3x)
Rm 7:15 For I·do·not practice that·thing which I·want *to·do*,
Rm 7:19 which I·do·not want, that·thing *is what* I·practice.
1Co 9:17 For if I·practice this·thing voluntarily, I·have a·
G4238.1 V-PAI-2S πράσσεις (1x)
Rm 2:1 for the·one judging, you·practice the same·things.
G4238.1 V-PAI-2P πράσσετε (1x)
Php 4:9 and saw in me, practice— and the God of·peace
G4238.1 V-PAI-3S πράσσει (1x)
Ac 26:31 man·of·clay† practices not·even·one·thing worthy
G4238.1 V-PAI-3P πράττουσιν (1x)
Ac 17:7 and all these·men practice *things* in·full·opposition
G4238.1 V-PAP-APM πράσσοντας (3x)
Ac 26:20 ·around toward God, practicing works worthy of·
Rm 2:2 ·to truth against the·ones practicing such·things.
Rm 2:3 ·one unduly·judging the·ones practicing such·things,
G4238.1 V-PAP-DSM πράσσοντι (1x)
Rm 13:4 upon the·one practicing the morally·wrong·thing.
G4238.1 V-PAP-DPM πράσσουσιν (1x)
Rm 1:32 also give·glad·consent to·the·ones practicing *them*.
G4238.1 V-PAP-NSM πράσσων (1x)
Jn 3:20 For any one practicing mediocrity hates the light,
G4238.1 V-PAP-NPM πράσσοντες (2x)
Gal 5:21 that the·ones practicing such·things shall·not
Rm 1:32 of·God (that the·ones practicing such·things are
G4238.1 V-PAS-2S πράσσῃς (1x)
Rm 2:25 benefits if you·should·practice Torah-Law. But if
G4238.1 V-AAI-1P ἐπράξαμεν (1x)
Lk 23:41 appropriate·*punishment* for·what we·practiced.
G4238.1 V-AAI-3S ἔπραξεν (2x)
Lk 23:41 "But this·man practiced not·even·one·thing amiss."
2Co 5:10 the body, pertaining·to what he·practiced—
G4238.1 V-AAI-3P ἔπραξαν (1x)
2Co 12:21 and debauchery which they·practiced.
G4238.1 V-AAN πρᾶξαι (1x)
Ac 26:9 *it* to·be·necessary to·practice many·things contrary
G4238.1 V-AAP-GPM πραξάντων (2x)
Ac 19:19 of·the·ones practicing the meddling·in·dark·arts,
Rm 9:11 nor·even practicing anything beneficially·good or
G4238.1 V-AAP-NPM πράξαντες (1x)
Jn 5:29 and the·ones already·practicing the mediocrity,
G4238.1 V-RAI-1S πέπραχα (1x)
Ac 25:11 ·offender, or have·practiced anything worthy of·
G4238.1 V-RAN πεπραχέναι (1x)
Ac 25:25 him to·have·practiced not·even·one·thing worthy
G4238.1 V-RPP-NSN πεπραγμένον (2x)
Lk 23:15 worthy of·death is having·been·practiced by·him.
Ac 26:26 ·thing was not having·been·practiced in a·corner.
G4238.2 V-PAN πράσσειν (4x)
Lk 22:23 it·might·be intending to·accomplish this·thing.
Ac 5:35 what yeu·intend to·accomplish concerning these
Ac 19:36 and to·accomplish not·even·one·thing rashly.
1Th 4:11 to·keep·still, and to·accomplish yeur·own *tasks*,
G4238.3 V-AAI-1S ἔπραξα (1x)
Lk 19:23 I·myself might·have reclaimed my·own together
G4238.4 V-PAI-2P πράσσετε (1x)
Lk 3:13 to them, "Exact not·one·bit more·than the·thing
G4238.5 V-AAI-2P ἐπράξατε (1x)
Ac 3:17 brothers, I·have·seen that yeu·inflicted *the killing*
G4238.5 V-AAS-2S πράξῃς (1x)
Ac 16:28 "You·should·inflict on·yourself not·one·bit·of
EG4238.5 (1x)
2Co 2:6 this public·penalty, the·one *inflicted* by the majority
G4238.6 V-PAI-1S πράσσω (1x)
Eph 6:21 against me *and* how I·fare, Tychicus shall·make·

G4239 πραΰς praÿs *adj.* (3x)
Compare:G4235 G2261 G5011 See:G4240 G4236
G4239.1 A-NSM πραΰς (1x)
Mt 21:5 comes to·you, calmly·mild and having·mounted
G4239.1 A-NPM πραεῖς (1x)
Mt 5:5 "Supremely·blessed *are* the calmly·mild·ones,
G4239.1 A-GSN πραέος (1x)
1Pe 3:4 of·the calmly·mild and quietly·undisturbable spirit,

G4240 πραΰτης praÿtēs *n.* (3x)
Roots:G4239 Compare:G4236 See:G4235
G4240.1 N-DSF πραΰτητι (2x)
Jac 1:21 accept with a·calm·mildness the implanted
Jac 3:13 ·show his works with a·calm·mildness of·wisdom.
G4240.1 N-GSF πραΰτητος (1x)
1Pe 3:15 with a·calm·mildness and a·reverent·fear·and·awe,

G4241 πρέπω prêpō *v.* (7x)
Compare:G0433 G1832
G4241.2 V-PQI-3S πρέπει (1x)
Tit 2:1 that·which is·suitable·for the healthy·and·sound
G4241.3 V-PQI-3S πρέπει (2x)
Eph 5:3 among yeu, just·as is·befitting·for holy·ones,
1Ti 2:10 (which is·befitting·for women who·are·making·a·
G4241.3 V-PQP-NSN πρέπον (2x)
Mt 3:15 ·manner it·is befitting·for us to·completely·fulfill all
1Co 11:13 in·unison, is·it befitting·for a·woman to·pray to·
G4241.3 V-IAI-3S ἔπρεπεν (2x)
Heb 2:10 For it·was·befitting·for *Father God* (on·account·of
Heb 7:26 For such a·High·Priest was·befitting·for us, *who·is*

G4242 πρεσβεία prêsbêía *n.* (2x)
Roots:G4243 Compare:G4244
G4242.3 N-ASF πρεσβείαν (2x)
Lk 14:32 yet far·away, dispatching a·delegation, he·asks·of
Lk 19:14 and they·dispatched a·delegation right·behind him

G4243 πρεσβεύω prêsbêúō *v.* (2x)
Roots:G4244-1 See:G4244 G4246
G4243.2 V-PAI-1S πρεσβεύω (1x)
Eph 6:20 of·which I·am·an·elder·spokesman in a·chain, that
G4243.2 V-PAI-1P πρεσβεύομεν (1x)
2Co 5:20 Now·then, we·are·elder·spokesmen on·behalf·of·

G4244 πρεσβυτέριον prêsbytériôn *n.* (3x)
Roots:G4245 Compare:G1087 G4892 See:G4850 G4242 xLangAlso:H2205
G4244.1 N-NSN πρεσβυτέριον (2x)
Lk 22:66 it·became day, the council·of·elders of·the people
Ac 22:5 ·me, and all the council·of·elders, personally·from
G4244.1 N-GSN πρεσβυτερίου (1x)
1Ti 4:14 *the* laying·on of·the hands of·the council·of·elders.

G4245 πρεσβύτερος prêsbýtêrôs *adj.* (68x)
Roots:G4244-1 Compare:G1088 G1087 G1985 G2819-2 See:G4243 G4244 G4242-1 xLangEquiv:H2205 xLangAlso:H7869
G4245.1 A-NSM πρεσβύτερος (1x)

Lk 15:25 "Now his older son was in a·field, and as he·was·
G4245.2 A-NPM πρεσβύτεροι (1x)
Ac 2:17 ·visions, and yeur older·men shall·dream dreams.
G4245.2 A-DSM πρεσβυτέρῳ (1x)
1Ti 5:1 You·should·not chastise an·older·man, but·rather
G4245.2 A-GPM πρεσβυτέρων (1x)
Jn 8:9 beginning from the older·men unto the last·of·them;
G4245.3 A-APF πρεσβυτέρας (1x)
1Ti 5:2 older·women as mothers, younger·women as sisters,
G4245.4 A-NPM πρεσβύτεροι (10x)
Ac 4:23 *that* the chief·priests and the elders declared to them.
Ac 25:15 the chief·priests and the elders of·the Judeans
Mt 21:23 the chief·priests and the elders of·the people came·
Mt 26:3 scribes, and the elders of·the people were·gathered·
Mt 26:57 the scribes and the elders were·gathered·together.
Mt 26:59 Now the chief·priests and the elders and all the
Mt 27:1 all the chief·priests and the elders of·the people took
Mt 27:20 But the chief·priests and the elders persuaded the
Mk 11:27 the scribes, and the elders come alongside him,
Mk 14:53 all the chief·priests and the elders and the scribes
G4245.4 A-VPM πρεσβύτεροι (1x)
Ac 4:8 "Rulers of·the People, and elders of·IsraEl,
G4245.4 A-APM πρεσβυτέρους (4x)
Lk 7:3 about Jesus, he·dispatched elders of·the Judeans to
Lk 22:52 ·Estate, and *the* elders coming·directly toward him
Ac 4:5 the next·day, *that* their rulers and elders and scribes
Ac 6:12 ·stirred·up the people, the elders, and the scribes.
G4245.4 A-DPM πρεσβυτέροις (3x)
Lk 20:1 the scribes stood·over *him* together with·the elders,
Ac 23:14 the chief·priests and the elders, declared, "With·
Mt 27:3 pieces·of·silver to·the chief·priests and the elders,
G4245.4 A-GPM πρεσβυτέρων (13x)
Lk 9:22 to·be·rejected·as·unfit by the elders and chief·priests
Ac 24:1 HananIah walked·down with the elders, and *with* a·
Mt 15:2 ·contrary·to the Oral·tradition of·the elders? For
Mt 16:21 many·things from the elders and chief·priests and
Mt 26:47 from the chief·priests and elders of·the people.
Mt 27:12 the chief·priests and the elders, he·answered not·
Mt 27:41 ·priests with the scribes and elders were·saying,
Mt 28:12 ·being·gathered·together with the elders and taking
Mk 7:3 securely·holding·to the Oral·tradition of·the elders.
Mk 7:5 ·to the Oral·tradition of·the elders, but·rather eat the
Mk 8:31 and to·be·rejected·as·unfit by the elders, chief·
Mk 14:43 the chief·priests and the scribes and the elders.
Mk 15:1 ·making consultation with the elders and scribes
G4245.5 A-NPM πρεσβύτεροι (5x)
Rv 4:10 the twenty four Elders shall·fall in·the·sight of·the·
Rv 5:8 and the twenty·four Elders fell·down in·the·sight of·
Rv 5:14 And the twenty·four Elders fell·down and fell·
Rv 11:16 And the twenty four Elders, the·ones sitting·down
Rv 19:4 And the twenty four Elders and the four living·
G4245.5 A-APM πρεσβυτέρους (1x)
Rv 4:4 the twenty four Elders sitting·down, having·been·
G4245.5 A-GPM πρεσβυτέρων (6x)
Rv 5:5 And one from·among the Elders says to·me, "Do·not
Rv 5:6 and in *the* midst of·the Elders, a·Lamb standing as
Rv 5:11 and the living·beings and the Elders, and thousands
Rv 7:11 ·circle·around the throne and the Elders and the four
Rv 7:13 Then one from·among the Elders answered, saying
Rv 14:3 living·beings, and of·the Elders; and not·even·one·
EG4245.5 (1x)
Rv 5:8 of·the Lamb, each·one *of·the·Elders* having harps
G4245.6 A-NSM πρεσβύτερος (2x)
2Jn 1:1 The Elder. To·a·Selected lady and her children—
3Jn 1:1 The Elder. To·the well-beloved Gaius, whom I·
G4245.6 A-NPM πρεσβύτεροι (4x)
Ac 15:6 ambassadors and the elders gathered·together to·see
Ac 15:23 *From* the ambassadors, the elders, and the brothers
Ac 21:18 alongside Jacob; and all the elders came·directly.
1Ti 5:17 The elders having·conducted well must·be·
G4245.6 A-APM πρεσβυτέρους (7x)
Ac 11:30 dispatching *it* to·the elders through *the* hands of·
Ac 14:23 for·them elders for·each Called·Out·citizenry,
Ac 15:2 to the ambassadors and elders concerning this issue.
Ac 20:17 ·called·for the elders of·the Called·Out·citizenry.
Jac 5:14 ·him·summon the elders of·the Called·Out·citizenry
1Pe 5:1 Elders, the·ones among yeu, I·exhort *as* the
Tit 1:5 ·undone and should·fully·establish elders in·each city
G4245.6 A-DPM πρεσβυτέροις (2x)
Ac 15:22 to·the ambassadors and the elders, together with·all
1Pe 5:5 *yeu* younger·men, be·submitted *to·yeur* elders. And
G4245.6 A-GSM πρεσβυτέρου (1x)
1Ti 5:19 a·legal·accusation against an·elder, aside·from *this*
G4245.6 A-GPM πρεσβυτέρων (2x)
Ac 15:4 the ambassadors and the elders, and they·reported·
Ac 16:4 by the ambassadors and the elders, the·ones in
G4245.7 A-NPM πρεσβύτεροι (1x)
Heb 11:2 For in this, the elders·of·old are·attested·to.

G4246 πρεσβύτης prêsbýtēs *n.* (3x)
Compare:G1088 G4247 G1123-1 See:G4245 G4243 xLangAlso:H2205
G4246.1 N-NSM πρεσβύτης (2x)
Lk 1:18 for·certain? For I·myself am an·old·man, and my
Phm 1:9 *I* Paul, being such as an·old·man and now also a·
G4246.1 N-APM πρεσβύτας (1x)
Tit 2:2 *for* old·men to·be sober-minded, morally·worthy·of·

G4247 πρεσβῦτις prêsbŷtis *n.* (1x)
Roots:G4246 Compare:G1088 G1123-1
G4247 N-APF πρεσβύτιδας (1x)
Tit 2:3 *for* old·women likewise, *that they·be* in a·demeanor

G4248 πρηνής prēnḗs *adj.* (1x)
Roots:G4253
G4248.2 A-NSM πρηνής (1x)
Ac 1:18 and falling·downhill headfirst, he·burst·open in·

G4249 πρίζω prízō *v.* (1x)
Compare:G1371 G3192-1 See:G1282
G4249 V-API-3P ἐπρίσθησαν (1x)
Heb 11:37 they·were·sawed·in·half, they·were·tempted,

G4250 πρίν prín *adv.* (14x)
Roots:G4253
G4250.1 ADV πρίν (10x)
Jn 4:49 "Sir, walk·down prior·to my little·child dying.
Jn 8:58 I·say to·yeu, prior·to AbRaham coming·to·be, I
Jn 14:29 now I·have·declared *it* to·yeu prior·to *it* happening,
Lk 22:61 he·declared to·him, "Prior·to a·rooster crowing,
Ac 2:20 and the moon into blood, prior·to the great and
Mt 1:18 already·being·espoused to·Joseph, prior·to them
Mt 26:34 that in this night, prior·to a·rooster crowing, you·
Mt 26:75 had·declared to·him, "Prior·to a·rooster crowing,
Mk 14:30 *even* in this night, prior·to a·rooster crowing twice
Mk 14:72 declared to·him, "Prior·to a·rooster crowing twice
G4250.2 ADV πρίν (4x)
Lk 2:26 *that he·was* not to·see death before he·should·see
Lk 22:34 ·not crow this·day before you·shall·utterly·deny
Ac 7:2 while·he·was·still in MesoPotamia, before he resided
Ac 25:16 man·of·clay† to total·destruction, before the·one

G4251 Πρίσκα Príska *n/p.* (1x)
Compare:G0207 See:G4252
G4251.2 N/P-ASF Πρίσκαν (1x)
2Ti 4:19 Greet Prisca and Aquila, and the household of·

G4252 Πρίσκιλλα Prískilla *n/p.* (5x)
Roots:G4251 See:G0207
G4252.1 N/P-NSF Πρίσκιλλα (3x)
Ac 18:18 into Syria, and Little·Prisca and Aquila *were*
Ac 18:26 him, Aquila and Little·Prisca purposely·took him
1Co 16:19 yeu. Aquila and Little·Prisca greet yeu much in
G4252.1 N/P-ASF Πρίσκιλλαν (2x)
Ac 18:2 Italy with his wife Little·Prisca *(that·is, Priscilla)*,
Rm 16:3 Greet Little·Prisca and Aquila, my coworkers in

G4253 πρό prố *prep.* (49x)
See:G4250
G4253.1 PREP πρό (42x)
Jn 1:48 declared to·him, "Before Philip hollered·out·for you
Jn 5:7 I·myself am·coming, another steps·down before me."
Jn 10:8 All the·many·which came before me are Thieves and
Jn 11:55 out of·the region to JeruSalem before the Passover,
Jn 12:1 In·due·course, six days before the Passover, Jesus
Jn 13:1 And before the Sacred·Feast of·the Passover, Jesus,
Jn 13:19 I·relate *it* to·yeu before it·happens in·order·that,
Jn 17:5 glory which I·was·having with you before the world
Jn 17:24 to·me because you·did·love me before *the* world's
Lk 1:76 for you·shall·traverse before *the* personal·presence
Lk 7:27 my messenger before your personal·presence, who
Lk 9:52 ·dispatched messengers before his personal·presence
Lk 10:1 them up by·twos before his personal·presence, into
Lk 11:38 ·not first immerse *his hands* before the luncheon.
Lk 21:12 "But before absolutely·all these·things, they·shall·
Lk 22:15 to·eat this Passover with yeu before my suffering.
Ac 5:23 and the sentries standing outside before the doors.
Ac 5:36 For before these days, Theudas rose·up, saying
Ac 12:6 ·guarding the prison·cell, *standing* before the door.
Ac 12:14 she·announced, "Peter is·standing before the gate!
Ac 14:13 that·offers·sacrifices, the·one being before their city,
Ac 21:38 the Egyptian, *the·one* before these days already·
Ac 23:15 him; and we·ourselves, before he shall·draw·near,
Heb 11:5 transferred him;" for before his transfer, it·has·
Gal 1:17 toward the·ones *who·were* ambassadors before me,
Gal 3:23 But before the trust *was* to·come, we·were·
Mt 5:12 they·persecuted the prophets, the·ones before yeu.
Mt 6:8 what·things *are* needed before yeu·yeurselves have
Mt 8:29 ·you·come here to·torment us before due·season?
Mt 11:10 my messenger before your personal·presence, who
Mt 24:38 in the days, the·ones that·were before the Deluge,
Mk 1:2 my messenger before your personal·presence, who
Rm 16:7 also have·come·to·be in Anointed-One before me.
Jac 5:9 Behold, *the* judge stands before the doors.
1Pe 1:20 with·him·having·been·foreknown before *the*
Tit 1:2 ·one without·falsehood) promised before time eternal
1Co 2:7 ·away, which God predetermined before the ages to
1Co 4:5 ·not presently·judge anything before *the* season,
Eph 1:4 he·selected us in him before *the* world's conception
Col 1:17 And he·himself is before all·things, and by him all·
2Ti 1:9 in *the* Anointed-One, Jesus— before time eternal—
2Ti 4:21 Quickly·endeavor to·come before winter. EuBulus
G4253.2 PREP πρό (3x)
Lk 2:21 ·forth by the angel prior·to him being·conceived in
Ac 13:24 People of·IsraEl, prior·to *the* personal·appearance
Gal 2:12 For prior·to certain·men coming from Jacob, he·
EG4253.2 (1x)
1Co 5:9 I·wrote to·yeu in the *prior* letter not to·associate·
G4253.3 PREP πρό (1x)
2Co 12:2 in Anointed-One fourteen years ago (whether in
G4253.4 PREP πρό (2x)
Jac 5:12 But above all·things, my brothers, do·not swear,
1Pe 4:8 And above all, *continue* having earnest love among

G4254 προ•άγω prôágō *v.* (18x)
Roots:G4253 G0071 Compare:G5348 G5217 G4393
G4254.2 V-PAI-3P προάγουσιν (1x)
Mt 21:31 tax·collectors and the prostitutes precede yeu into
G4254.2 V-PAP-APF προαγούσας (1x)
1Ti 1:18 according·to the preceding prophecies over you,
G4254.2 V-PAP-GSF προαγούσης (1x)
Heb 7:18 a·cancellation of·a·preceding commandment on·
G4254.2 V-PAP-NPF πρoάγουσαι (1x)
1Ti 5:24 ·clay† are obvious·beforehand, preceding *them* to
G4254.2 V-PAP-NPM προάγοντες (2x)
Mt 21:9 And the crowds, the·ones preceding and the·ones
Mk 11:9 And the·ones preceding and the·ones following
G4254.3 V-FAI-1S προάξω (2x)
Mt 26:32 to·be·awakened, I·shall·go·on·ahead·of yeu into
Mk 14:28 to·be·awakened, I·shall·go·on·ahead·of yeu into
G4254.3 V-PAI-3S προάγει (2x)
Mt 28:7 and behold, he·goes·on·ahead·of yeu into Galilee.
Mk 16:7 and to·Peter that he·goes·on·ahead·of yeu into
G4254.3 V-PAN προάγειν (2x)
Mt 14:22 into the sailboat and to·go·on·ahead·of him to the
Mk 6:45 into the sailboat and to·go·on·ahead to the other·
G4254.3 V-PAP-NSM προάγων (1x)

Mk 10:32 and Jesus was going·on·ahead·of them, and they·

G4254.3 V-PAP-NPM προάγοντες (1x)

Lk 18:39 the·ones going·on·ahead were·reprimanding him,

G4254.3 V-IAI-3S προῆγεν (1x)

Mt 2:9 they·saw in the east was·going·on·ahead·of them,

G4254.4 V-PAN προάγειν (1x)

Ac 12:6 HerOd·AgrIppa was·intending to·bring him forth, on·

G4254.4 V-2AAI-1S προήγαγον (1x)

Ac 25:26 "Therefore I·brought him forth before yeu, and

G4254.4 V-2AAP-NSM προαγαγών (1x)

Ac 16:30 And bringing them outside, he·replied, "Sirs, what

G4255 προ•αιρέομαι prôairéômai *v.* (1x)
Roots:G4253 G0138

G4255.2 V-PNI-3S προαιρεῖται (1x)

2Co 9:7 each·man *sow* just·as he·is·preinclined in·*his*·heart,

G4256 προ•αιτιάομαι prôaitiáômai *v.* (1x)
Roots:G4253 G0156

G4256 V-ADI-1P προητιασάμεθα (1x)

Rm 3:9 ·means, for we·already·legally·charged both Jews

G4257 προ•ακούω prôakôúō *v.* (1x)
Roots:G4253 G0191

G4257 V-AAI-2P προηκούσατε (1x)

Col 1:5 heavens— which yeu·already·heard·before in the

G4258 προ•α•μαρτάνω prôamartánō *v.* (2x)
Roots:G4253 G0264

G4258 V-RAP-DPM προημαρτηκόσιν (1x)

2Co 13:2 to·the·ones having·already·morally·failed and to·

G4258 V-RAP-GPM προημαρτηκότων (1x)

2Co 12:21 of·the·ones having·already·morally·failed and not

G4259 προ•αύλιον prôaúliôn *n.* (1x)
Roots:G4253 G0833 See:G1886

G4259.2 N-ASN προαύλιον (1x)

Mk 14:68 outside into the entryway·of·the·courtyard, and a·

G4260 προ•βαίνω prôbaínō *v.* (5x)
Roots:G4253 G0901-3

G4260.1 V-2AAP-NSM προβάς (2x)

Mt 4:21 And walking·forward from·there, he·saw two other

Mk 1:19 And walking·forward a·little·way from·there, he·

G4260.2 V-RAP-NSF προβεβηκυῖα (2x)

Lk 1:18 and my wife *is* having·well-advanced in her days.

Lk 2:36 of·Asher, herself having·well-advanced in many

G4260.2 V-RAP-NPM προβεβηκότες (1x)

Lk 1:7 and both were having·well-advanced in their days.

G4261 προ•βάλλω prôbállō *v.* (2x)
Roots:G4253 G0906 Compare:G4264 G0985 G1631 G5453

G4261 V-AAP-GPM προβαλόντων (1x)

Ac 19:33 of·the crowd, with·the Jews pushing him forward.

G4261.2 V-2AAS-3P προβάλωσιν (1x)

Lk 21:30 Whenever they·should·bud, even·now while·

G4262 προ•βατικός prôbatikós *adj.* (1x)
Roots:G4263

G4262.2 A-DSF προβατικῇ (1x)

Jn 5:2 Now at the Sheep·Gate in JeruSalem, there·is a·pool

G4263 πρό•βατον próbatôn *n.* (46x)
Roots:G4260 Compare:G0721 G0704

G4263.2 N-NSN πρόβατον (1x)

Ac 8:32 this, " He·was·driven as a·sheep to *the* butchering;

G4263.2 N-NPN πρόβατα (12x)

Jn 10:3 doorkeeper opens·up, and the sheep hear his voice,

Jn 10:4 before them, and the sheep follow him, because

Jn 10:8 and robbers, but·yet the sheep did·not hear them.

Jn 10:12 ·which are not *even* his·own sheep, he·observes the

Jn 10:27 "My sheep listen·to my voice, and·I know them,

Mt 10:16 I·myself dispatch yeu as sheep in *the* midst of·

Mt 18:12 any man·of·clay† *has* a·hundred sheep, and one

Mt 26:31 the shepherd, and the sheep of·the flock shall·be·

Mk 6:34 they·were "as sheep not having a·shepherd," and

Mk 14:27 and the sheep shall·be·thoroughly·scattered."

Rm 8:36 ·long; we·are·reckoned as sheep for·butchering."

1Pe 2:25 For yeu·were as sheep being·led·astray, but·yet are

G4263.2 N-ASN πρόβατον (2x)

Lk 15:6 because I·found my sheep, the·one having·become·

Mt 12:11 from·among yeu that shall·have one sheep, that if

G4263.2 N-APN πρόβατα (16x)

Jn 2:14 he·found the·ones selling oxen, sheep, and doves;

Jn 2:15 the Sanctuary·Atrium, also the sheep and the oxen;

Jn 10:3 and he·calls·forth his·own sheep each·by name and

Jn 10:4 he·should·cast·forth his·own sheep, he·traverses

Jn 10:12 the wolf coming and leaves the sheep and flees; and

Jn 10:12 and the wolf snatches them and scatters the sheep.

Jn 10:16 And I·have other sheep which are not from·among

Jn 21:16 He·says to·him, "Shepherd my sheep."

Jn 21:17 Jesus says to·him, "Feed my sheep.

Lk 15:4 yeu, having a·hundred sheep, that after·completely·

Mt 9:36 and having·been·flung·about, as sheep not having

Mt 10:6 but traverse rather to the sheep, the·ones having·

Mt 15:24 dispatched except to the sheep, the·ones having·

Mt 25:32 shepherd distinctly·separates the sheep from the

Mt 25:33 in·fact, he·shall·set the sheep at his right·hand, but

Rv 18:13 "and livestock, sheep, horses, and carriages, "and

G4263.2 N-GSN προβάτου (1x)

Mt 12:12 ·of·clay† surpass·the·value of·a·sheep? As·such, it·

G4263.2 N-GPN προβάτων (9x)

Jn 10:1 into the yard·pen of·the sheep, but·rather walking·up

Jn 10:2 ·in through the door is shepherd of·the sheep.

Jn 10:7 ·certainly, I·say to·yeu, I AM the door of·the sheep.

Jn 10:11 lays·down his·own soul on·behalf of·the sheep.

Jn 10:13 and it·does·not matter to·him concerning the sheep.

Jn 10:15 and I·lay·down my soul on·behalf of·the sheep.

Jn 10:26 for yeu·are not from·among my sheep, just·as I·

Heb 13:20 (the great shepherd of·the sheep by an·eternal

Mt 7:15 who do·come to yeu in sheep's apparel, but inwardly

EG4263.2 (5x)

Jn 6:39 that I·should·not completely·lose any *sheep* which

Jn 6:39 from·among it *(that·is, the sheep pen)*, but·rather

Jn 10:14 shepherd, and I·know my *sheep*, and am·known by

Mt 12:11 sheep, that if this *sheep* should·fall into a·pit on·

Mt 18:13 he·rejoices more over that·same *sheep* than over

G4264 προ•βιβάζω prôbibázō *v.* (2x)
Roots:G4253 G0973-1 Compare:G4261 G1688 See:G2601

G4264.1 V-AAI-3P προεβίβασαν (1x)

Ac 19:33 But they·pressed AlexAnder forward out of·the

G4264.2 V-APP-NSF προβιβασθεῖσα (1x)

Mt 14:8 And after·being·urged·on by her mother, she·replied

G4265 προ•βλέπω prôblépō *v.* (1x)
Roots:G4253 G0991

G4265 V-AMP-GSM προβλεψαμένου (1x)

Heb 11:40 with·God previously·looking·at something

G4266 προ•γίνομαι prôgínômai *v.* (1x)
Roots:G4253 G1096 See:G4269

G4266 V-RAP-GPN προγεγονότων (1x)

Rm 3:25 of·the moral·failings having·already·occurred)—

G4267 προ•γινώσκω prôginṓskō *v.* (5x)
Roots:G4253 G1097

G4267 V-PAP-NPM προγινώσκοντες (2x)

Ac 26:5 Foreknowing me from·the·start (if they·should·

2Pe 3:17 O·yeu beloved, while·foreknowing *these·things*,

G4267 V-AAI-3S προέγνω (2x)

Rm 8:29 Because whom he·did·foreknow, also he·did·

Rm 11:2 ·not shove·away his People which he·foreknew. Or

G4267 V-RPP-GSM προεγνωσμένου (1x)

1Pe 1:20 with·him·having·been·foreknown before *the*

G4268 πρό•γνωσις prógnōsis *n.* (2x)
Roots:G4267

G4268 N-ASF πρόγνωσιν (1x)

1Pe 1:2 according·to *the* foreknowledge of·Father God, by a·

G4268 N-DSF προγνώσει (1x)

Ac 2:23 ·determined counsel and foreknowledge of·God)

G4269 πρό•γονος prógônôs *n.* (2x)
Roots:G4266 Compare:G3967 G3971

G4269.1 N-DPM προγόνοις (1x)

1Ti 5:4 to·give·back compensations to·their·forebears, for

G4269.1 N-GPM προγόνων (1x)

2Ti 1:3 I·ritually·minister from *my* forebears' *example* with

G4270 προ•γράφω prôgráphō *v.* (5x)
Roots:G4253 G1125

G4270.1 V-AAI-1S προέγραψα (1x)

Eph 3:3 the Mystery (just·as I·previously·wrote *about* briefly

G4270.1 V-2API-3S προεγράφη (3x)

Gal 3:1 YeShua Anointed was·previously·written among yeu

Rm 15:4 as·many·things·as were·previously·written, they·

Rm 15:4 ·written, they·were·previously·written for our

G4270.1 V-RPP-NPM προγεγραμμένοι (1x)

Jud 1:4 the·ones having·been·previously·written·about of· to

G4271 πρό•δηλος pródēlôs *adj.* (3x)
Roots:G4253 G1212

G4271.2 A-NSN πρόδηλον (1x)

Heb 7:14 For *it·is* obvious·beforehand that our Lord has·

G4271.2 A-NPF πρόδηλοι (1x)

1Ti 5:24 men·of·clay† are obvious·beforehand, preceding

G4271.2 A-NPN πρόδηλα (1x)

1Ti 5:25 good works *of·some* are obvious·beforehand; and

G4272 προ•δίδωμι prôdídōmi *v.* (1x)
Roots:G4253 G1325

G4272.2 V-AAI-3S προέδωκεν (1x)

Rm 11:35 "Or who first·gave to·him that it·shall·be·

G4273 προ•δότης prôdótēs *n.* (3x)
Roots:G4272

G4273.1 N-NSM προδότης (1x)

Lk 6:16 and Judas IsCariot, who also was a·betrayer.

G4273.1 N-NPM προδόται (2x)

Ac 7:52 ·whom, yeu have·become betrayers and murderers,

2Ti 3:4 betrayers, rash, having·been·inflated·with·

G4274 πρό•δρομος pródrômôs *adj.* (1x)
Roots:G4390

G4274.2 A-NSM πρόδρομος (1x)

Heb 6:20 where a·forerunner entered on·behalf of·us—

G4275 προ•είδω prôéídō *v.* (2x)
Roots:G4253 G1492

G4275.1 V-2AAP-NSF προϊδοῦσα (1x)

Gal 3:8 And the Scripture, foreseeing that God regards·as·

G4275.1 V-2AAP-NSM προϊδών (1x)

Ac 2:31 foreseeing *this*, he·spoke concerning the resurrection

G4276 προ•ελπίζω prôêlpízō *v.* (2x)
Roots:G4253 G1679 See:G0560

G4276.2 V-RAP-APM προηλπικότας (1x)

Eph 1:12 the·ones already·having·placed·our·expectation in

EG4276.2 (1x)

Eph 1:13 also *already·placed·yeur·expectation*, after·hearing

G4277 προ•έπω prôépō *v.* (3x)
Roots:G4253 G2036 Compare:G4280 G4302

G4277 V-2AAI-1S προεῖπον (1x)

Gal 5:21 to·yeu, just·as also I·previously·declared, that the·

G4277 V-AAI-1P προείπαμεν (1x)

1Th 4:6 just·as also we·previously·declared to·yeu and

G4277 V-2AAI-3S προεῖπεν (1x)

Ac 1:16 the Holy Spirit previously·declared through David's

G4278 προ•εν•άρχομαι prôênárchômai *v.* (2x)
Roots:G4253 G1728

G4278 V-ADI-2P προενήρξασθε (1x)

2Co 8:10 who since last·year began·previously not merely

G4278 V-ADI-3S προενήρξατο (1x)

2Co 8:6 in·order·that just·as he·began·previously, even in·

G4279 προ•επ•αγγέλλομαι prôêpangéllômai *v.* (1x)
Roots:G4253 G1861

G4279 V-ADI-3S προεπηγγείλατο (1x)

Rm 1:2 (which he·promised·beforehand through his prophets

G4280 προ•ερέω prôêréō *v.* (10x)
Roots:G4253 G2046 Compare:G4277 G4302

G4280 V-RAI-1S προείρηκα (4x)

Mt 24:25 Behold, I·have·already·stated *this* to·yeu.

Mk 13:23 Behold, I·have·already·stated all·things to·yeu.

2Co 7:3 do·I·say *this*, for I·have·already·stated that yeu·are
2Co 13:2 I·have·already·stated— and I·do·presently·
G4280 V-RAI-1P προειρήκαμεν (1x)
Gal 1:9 As we·have·already·stated, so at·this·moment I·say
G4280 V-RAI-3S προείρηκεν (1x)
Rm 9:29 And just·as IsaIah has·already·stated, "Except
G4280 V-RAN προειρηκέναι (1x)
Heb 10:15 testifies to·us, with it having·been·already·stated,
G4280 V-RPP-GPN προειρημένων (1x)
Jud 1:17 the·ones having·been·already·stated by the
G4280 V-RPP-GPM προειρημένων (1x)
2Pe 3:2 of·the utterances having·been·already·stated by the
EG4280 (1x)
2Pe 3:2 commandment *having·been·already·stated* by·our

G4281 προ•έρχομαι prôérchômai *v.* (9x)
Roots:G4253 G2064 Compare:G1826
G4281.1 V-INI-3S προήρχετο (1x)
Lk 22:47 one of·the twelve, went·before them, and he·
G4281.1 V-2AAI-3P προῆλθον (1x)
Mk 6:33 the cities and went there before them, and together,·
G4281.2 V-2AAP-NPM προελθόντες (1x)
Ac 20:5 going·on·beforehand, these·men were·awaiting us at
G4281.2 V-2AAS-3P προέλθωσιν (1x)
2Co 9:5 the brothers, that they·should·go·beforehand to yeu,
G4281.3 V-FDI-3S προελεύσεται (1x)
Lk 1:17 And he·himself shall·go·onward in·the·sight of
G4281.3 V-2AAI-3P προῆλθον (1x)
Ac 12:10 And going·forth, they·went·onward one alleyway,
G4281.3 V-2AAP-NSM προελθών (2x)
Mt 26:39 And going·onward a·little·bit, he·fell on his face,
Mk 14:35 And going·onward a·little·bit, he·fell on the soil
G4281.3 V-2AAP-NPM προελθόντες (1x)
Ac 20:13 Now we·ourselves, going·onward to the sailing·

G4282 προ•ετοιμάζω prôêtôimázō *v.* (2x)
Roots:G4253 G2090
G4282 V-AAI-3S προητοίμασεν (2x)
Rm 9:23 ·mercy, which he·made·ready·in·advance for glory
Eph 2:10 God made·ready·in·advance in·order·that we·

G4283 προ•ευ•αγγελίζομαι prôêuangêlízômai *v.* (1x)
Roots:G4253 G2097
G4283 V-ADI-3S προευηγγελίσατο (1x)
Gal 3:8 announced·the·good·news·in·advance to·AbRaham,

G4284 προ•έχομαι prôéchômai *v.* (1x)
Roots:G4253 G2192
G4284.3 V-PNI-1P προεχόμεθα (1x)
Rm 3:9 So·then what, are·we *Jews* any·better·off? No, by·

G4285 προ•ηγέομαι prôēgêômai *v.* (1x)
Roots:G4253 G2233
G4285.2 V-PNP-NPM προηγούμενοι (1x)
Rm 12:10 ·the honor, by·showing·deference·to one·another;

G4286 πρό•θεσις prôthêsis *n.* (16x)
Roots:G4388 Compare:G1012
G4286.3 N-NSF πρόθεσις (1x)
Rm 9:11 the determined·purpose may·endure according·to
G4286.3 N-ASF πρόθεσιν (4x)
Rm 8:28 called·forth according·to *his* determined·purpose.
Eph 1:11 ·to *the* determined·purpose of·the·one operating all
Eph 3:11 according·to *the* determined·purpose of·the ages
2Ti 1:9 according·to his·own determined·purpose and grace,
G4286.3 N-DSF προθέσει (2x)
Ac 11:23 them·all with·determined·purpose of·heart to·
2Ti 3:10 *my* upbringing, *my* determined·purpose, *my* trust,
G4286.3 N-GSF προθέσεως (1x)
Ac 27:13 of·the determined·purpose, after·taking·up·anchor,
EG4286.3 (4x)
Rm 1:15 In·this·manner, the *determined·purpose* in me *is*
Rm 14:9 For to this *determined·purpose* Anointed-One also
Php 2:12 the *determined·purpose* of·yeur·own Salvation!
1Jn 3:8 For this *determined·purpose* the Son of·God was·
G4286.4 N-NSF πρόθεσις (1x)
Heb 9:2 the Table, and the Intended·Show bread, which·is·
G4286.4 N-GSF προθέσεως (3x)
Lk 6:4 and took and ate the Intended·Show bread, which·it·
Mt 12:4 the house of·God and ate the Intended·Show bread,
Mk 2:26 high·priest and ate the Intended·Show bread, which

G4287 προ•θέσμιος prôthésmiôs *n.* (1x)
προ•θεσμία prôthêsmía [feminine]
Roots:G4253 G5087 See:G2250
G4287.2 N-GSF προθεσμίας (1x)
Gal 4:2 ·managers even·up·to the day·set·forth by·the father.

G4288 προ•θυμία prôthymía *n.* (6x)
Roots:G4289 Compare:G2432 G4710 See:G4290
G4288.2 N-NSF προθυμία (2x)
2Co 8:11 exactly·as *there·was* the eagerness to·be·willing,
2Co 8:12 For if the eagerness is·set·forth, *it·is* well·
G4288.2 N-ASF προθυμίαν (2x)
2Co 8:19 same Lord, and·also *showing* yeur eagerness)—
2Co 9:2 For I·personally·know yeur eagerness, for·which I·
G4288.2 N-GSF προθυμίας (1x)
Ac 17:11 Redemptive-word with all eagerness, scrutinizing
EG4288.2 (1x)
2Co 8:11 *that there·may·be the eagerness* to·further·finish *it*

G4289 πρό•θυμος prôthymôs *adj.* (4x)
Roots:G4253 G2372 Compare:G2432 G4705 See:G4288 G4290
G4289.2 A-NSN πρόθυμον (3x)
Mt 26:41 In·fact, the spirit *is* eager, but the flesh *is* weak.
Mk 14:38 In·fact, the spirit *is* eager, but the flesh *is* weak.
Rm 1:15 in me *is* eager also to·proclaim·the·good·news to·
EG4289.2 (1x)
2Co 8:10 to·do, but·rather also *were·eager* to·be·willing.

G4290 προ•θύμως prôthýmōs *adv.* (1x)
Roots:G4289 Compare:G2432 See:G4288
G4290 ADV προθύμως (1x)
1Pe 5:2 ·gain, but·rather with·a·cheerful·eagerness;

G4291 προ•ΐστημι prôístēmi *v.* (9x)
Roots:G4253 G2476 Compare:G2720 G3594 G4929 G0390 See:G4367-1 G4368
G4291.2 V-PMN προΐστασθαι (2x)
Tit 3:8 may·have·a·considerable·care to·conduct good works
Tit 3:14 our *brothers* must·learn also to·conduct good works
G4291.2 V-PMP-ASM προϊστάμενον (1x)
1Ti 3:4 one·conducting his·own house well, having his·
G4291.2 V-PMP-APM προϊσταμένους (1x)
1Th 5:12 ·hard among yeu, and are·conducting yeu in *the*
G4291.2 V-PMP-NSM προϊστάμενος (1x)
Rm 12:8 *or* the·one conducting *a·group·or·group·effort*,
G4291.2 V-PMP-NPM προϊστάμενοι (1x)
1Ti 3:12 of·one wife, conducting their·children and their·
G4291.2 V-2AAN προστῆναι (1x)
1Ti 3:5 any·man has·not seen·how to·conduct his·own house
G4291.2 V-RAP-NPM προεστῶτες (1x)
1Ti 5:17 elders having·conducted well must·be·considered·
EG4291.2 (1x)
Rm 12:8 *a·group·or·group·effort*, *conducting* with diligence;

G4292 προ•καλέομαι prôkalêômai *v.* (1x)
Roots:G4253 G2564 Compare:G3947 G3893
G4292.2 V-PMP-NPM προκαλούμενοι (1x)
Gal 5:26 self-conceited·men, challenging one·another,

G4293 προ•κατ•αγγέλλω prôkatangéllō *v.* (4x)
Roots:G4253 G2605
G4293 V-AAI-3S προκατήγγειλεν (1x)
Ac 3:18 God fully·announced·beforehand through *the* mouth
G4293 V-AAI-3P προκατήγγειλαν (1x)
Ac 3:24 ·spoke, also fully·announced·beforehand these days
G4293 V-AAP-APM προκαταγγείλαντας (1x)
Ac 7:52 the·ones fully·announcing·beforehand concerning
G4293 V-RPP-ASF προκατηγγελμένην (1x)
2Co 9:5 the·one having·been·fully·announced·beforehand,

G4294 προ•κατ•αρτίζω prôkatartízō *v.* (1x)
Roots:G4253 G2675 Compare:G2680
G4294.2 V-AAS-3P προκαταρτίσωσιν (1x)
2Co 9:5 yeu, and should·completely·rectify yeur beneficial·

G4295 πρό•κειμαι prókêimai *v.* (5x)
Roots:G4253 G2749
G4295.1 V-PNP-ASM προκείμενον (1x)
Heb 12:1 the strenuous·race being·laid·out·before us—
G4295.1 V-PNP-GSF προκειμένης (2x)
Heb 6:18 ·hold of·the Expectation being·laid·out·before *us*.
Heb 12:2 who, because of·the joy being·laid·out·before him,
G4295.3 V-PNI-3S πρόκειται (1x)
2Co 8:12 For if the eagerness is·set·forth, *it·is* well·
G4295.3 V-PNI-3P πρόκεινται (1x)
Jud 1:7 flesh, are·presently·set·forth·as a·public·example,

G4296 προ•κηρύσσω prôkēryssō *v.* (2x)
Roots:G4253 G2784
G4296.2 V-AAP-GSM προκηρύξαντος (1x)
Ac 13:24 ·repentance being·officially·proclaimed·in·advance
G4296.2 V-RPP-ASM προκεκηρυγμένον (1x)
Ac 3:20 ·one having·been·officially·proclaimed·in·advance.

G4297 προ•κοπή prôkôpé *n.* (3x)
Roots:G4298
G4297.2 N-NSF προκοπή (1x)
1Ti 4:15 ·that your continual·advancement may·be apparent
G4297.2 N-ASF προκοπήν (2x)
Php 1:12 for a·continual·advancement of·the good·news,
Php 1:25 ·yeu all for yeur continual·advancement and joy of·

G4298 προ•κόπτω prôkóptō *v.* (6x)
Roots:G4253 G2875
G4298.2 V-FAI-3P προκόψουσιν (3x)
2Ti 2:16 for they·shall·continually·advance toward more
2Ti 3:9 they·shall·not continually·advance any·further, for
2Ti 3:13 adept·smooth·talkers shall·continually·advance the
G4298.2 V-IAI-1S προέκοπτον (1x)
Gal 1:14 And I·was·continually·advancing in Judaism above
G4298.2 V-IAI-3S προέκοπτεν (1x)
Lk 2:52 And Jesus was·continually·advancing in·wisdom,
G4298.2 V-AAI-3S προέκοψεν (1x)
Rm 13:12 The night continually·advanced, and the day has·

G4299 πρό•κριμα prókrima *n.* (1x)
Roots:G4253 G2919 Compare:G4346
G4299.2 N-GSN προκρίματος (1x)
1Ti 5:21 *instructions* completely·apart·from prejudice, doing

G4300 προ•κυρόω prôkyrôō *v.* (1x)
Roots:G4253 G2964
G4300 V-RPP-ASF προκεκυρωμένην (1x)
Gal 3:17 ·covenant having·been·previously·ratified by God

G4301 προ•λαμβάνω prôlambánō *v.* (3x)
Roots:G4253 G2983
G4301.ª V-PAI-3S προλαμβάνει (1x)
1Co 11:21 in eating, each·one takes his·own supper prior·to
G4301.ª V-2AAI-3S προέλαβεν (1x)
Mk 14:8 She·came·beforehand to·apply·ointment·to my
G4301.ª V-APS-3S προληφθῇ (1x)
Gal 6:1 though a·man·of·clay† should·be·overtaken in some

G4302 προ•λέγω prôlégō *v.* (3x)
Roots:G4253 G3004 Compare:G4277 G4280
G4302.2 V-PAI-1S προλέγω (2x)
Gal 5:21 like these … of·which I·forewarn to·yeu, just·as
2Co 13:2 — and I·do·presently·forewarn as·though being·
G4302.2 V-IAI-1P προελέγομεν (1x)
1Th 3:4 yeu, we·were·saying·beforehand to·yeu that we·

G4303 προ•μαρτύρομαι prômartýrômai *v.* (1x)
Roots:G4253 G3143
G4303.2 V-PNP-NSN προμαρτυρόμενον (1x)
1Pe 1:11 ·plain, when·testifying·beforehand the afflictions

G4304 προ•μελετάω prômêlêtáō *v.* (1x)
Roots:G4253 G3191
G4304 V-PAN προμελετᾶν (1x)
Lk 21:14 hearts, not to·meditate·beforehand *what* to·plead.

G4305 προ•μεριμνάω prômêrimnáō *v.* (1x)
Roots:G4253 G3309
G4305 V-PAM-2P προμεριμνᾶτε (1x)
Mk 13:11 do·not be·anxious·beforehand what yeu·should·

G4306 προ•νοέω prŏnŏĕō *v.* (4x)
Roots:G4253 G3539 Compare:G3936 G3930 See:G4307
G4306.2 V-PAI-3S προνοεῖ (1x)
1Ti 5:8 if anyone does·not maintain·provision·for his·own,
G4306.3 V-PMP-NPM προνοούμενοι (2x)
Rm 12:17 while·maintaining·oneself·in morally·good·things
2Co 8:21 *this* while·maintaining·ourselves·in morally·good·,
EG4306.3 (1x)
1Pe 2:12 *Maintain* yeur behavior among the Gentiles, being

G4307 πρό•νοια prŏnŏia *n.* (2x)
Roots:G4306
G4307.1 N-GSF προνοίας (1x)
Ac 24:2 in·this nation on·account·of your providence,
G4307.2 N-ASF πρόνοιαν (1x)
Rm 13:14 and do·not make provision for longings of·the

G4308 προ•οράω prŏŏráō *v.* (2x)
Roots:G4253 G3708 Compare:G1896
G4308.2 V-RAP-NPM προεωρακότες (1x)
Ac 21:29 (For they·were previously·having·clearly·seen the
G4308.3 V-IMI-1S προωρώμην (1x)
Ac 2:25 *Lord,* " I·was·clearly·keeping Yahweh in·the·sight

G4309 προ•ορίζω prŏŏrízō *v.* (6x)
Roots:G4253 G3724
G4309.2 V-AAI-3S προώρισεν (4x)
Ac 4:28 hand and your counsel predetermined to·happen.
Rm 8:29 also he·did·predetermine *to·become* fundamentally·
Rm 8:30 Now these·whom he·predetermined, these also he·
1Co 2:7 ·hidden·away, which God predetermined before the
G4309.2 V-AAP-NSM προορίσας (1x)
Eph 1:5 already·predetermining us for adoption·as·sons into
G4309.2 V-APP-NPM προορισθέντες (1x)
Eph 1:11 him, already·being·predetermined according·to *the*

G4310 προ•πάσχω prŏpáschō *v.* (1x)
Roots:G4253 G3958
G4310 V-2AAP-NPM προπαθόντες (1x)
1Th 2:2 But·rather even after·previously·suffering, and

G4311 προ•πέμπω prŏpĕmpō *v.* (9x)
Roots:G4253 G3992 Compare:G4317 G4902
G4311.1 V-AAM-2S πρόπεμψον (1x)
Tit 3:13 Diligently send Zenas the lawyer and Apollos
G4311.1 V-AAM-2P προπέμψατε (1x)
1Co 16:11 him, but send him onward·on·his·journey in
G4311.1 V-AAP-NSM προπέμψας (1x)
3Jn 1:6 *if* sending·onward·on·their·journey, as·is·worthy of·
G4311.1 V-AAS-2P προπέμψητε (1x)
1Co 16:6 ·that yeu may·send me onward·on·my·journey
G4311.1 V-APN προπεμφθῆναι (2x)
Rm 15:24 ·through, and to·be·sent·onward by yeu *from*
2Co 1:16 to yeu, and by yeu to·be·sent·onward into Judea.
G4311.1 V-APP-NPM προπεμφθέντες (1x)
Ac 15:3 in·fact, being·sent·onward·on·their·journey by the
G4311.2 V-PAP-GPM προπεμπόντων (1x)
Ac 21:5 ·traversing, with·all *the disciples* seeing us off
G4311.2 V-IAI-3P προέπεμπον (1x)
Ac 20:38 his face. And they·were·seeing him off to the

G4312 προ•πετής prŏpĕtḗs *adj.* (2x)
Roots:G4253 G4098
G4312.2 A-NPM προπετεῖς (1x)
2Ti 3:4 betrayers, rash, having·been·inflated·with·
G4312.3 A-ASN προπετές (1x)
Ac 19:36 and to·accomplish not·even·one·thing rashly.

G4313 προ•πορεύομαι prŏpŏrĕúŏmai *v.* (2x)
Roots:G4253 G4198 Compare:G4365
G4313.1 V-FDI-2S προπορεύσῃ (1x)
Lk 1:76 of·the·Most·High, for you·shall·traverse before *the*
G4313.1 V-FDI-3P προπορεύσονται (1x)
Ac 7:40 Make for·us gods which shall·traverse·before us. *As*

G4314 πρός prŏs *prep.* (716x)
Roots:G4253 Compare:G3844 G1909 xLangAlso:H0413 H0854
G4314.ª PREP πρός (4x)
Mt 13:30 in bundles specifically to·completely·burn them,
Mk 5:11 Now there·was there, on·the·side·of the mountains,
Jac 3:3 in the horses' mouths specifically to·persuade them
1Th 2:9 night and day (specifically not to·be·a·burden·upon
G4314.1 PREP πρός (88x)
Jn 1:29 looks·at Jesus, who·is·coming toward him, and he·
Jn 1:47 Jesus saw NathaniEl coming toward him and says
Jn 3:20 the light, and does·not come toward the light, lest
Jn 4:30 ·forth out of·the city and were·coming toward him.
Jn 4:40 as·soon·as the Samaritans came toward him, they·
Jn 4:47 into Galilee, he·went·off toward him and was·
Jn 6:5 that a·large crowd is·come toward him, Jesus says to
Jn 6:37 the Father gives me shall·come toward me; and the·
Jn 6:37 me; and the·one who·is·coming toward me, no, I·
Jn 7:33 yeu, and·then I·head·on·out toward the·one sending
Jn 11:4 "This sickness is not toward death, but·rather on·
Jn 12:32 the earth, I·shall·draw all *men* toward myself."
Jn 16:5 "But now I·head·on·out toward the·one sending me,
Jn 16:10 because I·head·on·out toward my Father, and yeu·
Jn 16:16 because I·myself head·on·out toward the Father."
Jn 16:17 and 'I·myself head·on·out toward the Father'?
Jn 20:11 Mariam stood outside toward the chamber·tomb
Lk 1:27 toward a·veiled·virgin having·been·espoused to·a·
Lk 1:28 And entering *this·realm* toward her, the angel
Lk 5:30 among·them were·grumbling toward his disciples,
Lk 6:47 "Any one who·is·coming toward me, both hearing
Lk 7:44 And turning·around toward the woman, he·replied
Lk 8:4 *others that* were·traversing·onward toward him *from*
Lk 8:19 and his brothers came·directly toward him, yet were·
Lk 10:22 And turning·around toward the disciples, he·
Lk 12:58 lest he·should·drag you down toward the judge,
Lk 14:5 And answering toward them, he·declared, "Which
Lk 15:18 Rising·up, I·shall·traverse toward my father and
Lk 15:20 "And rising·up, he·came toward his father. But
Lk 16:1 And he·was·saying also toward his disciples,
Lk 18:11 ·settled, was·praying these·things toward himself,
Lk 22:56 after·seeing him sitting·down toward the firelight
Lk 24:29 with us, because it·is toward evening, and the day
Ac 3:11 John, all the people ran·together toward them in the
Ac 4:24 their·voice toward God with·the·same·determination
Ac 10:3 an·angel of·God entering *this·realm* toward him and
Ac 13:32 ·news, the promise occurring toward the fathers,
Ac 14:11 gods descended toward us being·in·the·likeness of·
Ac 24:16 a·conscience void·of·offense toward God and
Ac 28:26 saying, "Traverse toward this People, and declare,
Ac 28:30 ·accepting all the·ones traversing·in toward him,
Heb 4:13 ·vulnerably·exposed to·his eyes, to whom our
Heb 5:7 a·strong yell and tears toward the·one being·able to·
Heb 5:14 ·trained through habit toward having discernment
Heb 6:11 the same diligence toward the full·assurance of·the
Gal 1:17 did·I·go·up to JeruSalem toward the·ones *who·were*
Gal 2:14 that they·did·not walk·uprightly toward the truth
Gal 6:10 we·should·work the beneficially·good toward all,
Gal 6:10 all, but especially toward the family·members of·
Mt 14:25 of·the night, YeShua went·off toward them, '
Mt 21:1 and came to BethPhage (toward the Mount of·Olives
Mt 25:9 But traverse rather toward the·ones selling *oil* and
Mk 5:22 And upon·seeing him, he·falls toward his feet
Mk 6:33 before them, and together,·they·came toward him.
Mk 6:45 to the other·side *of·the sea* toward BethSaida, until
Mk 6:48 of·the night, he·comes toward them, walking upon
Mk 6:51 And he·walked·up toward them into the sailboat,
Mk 7:25 spirit, upon·coming, she·fell·down toward his feet.
Mk 9:10 they·securely·held the saying toward themselves,
Mk 10:1 crowds were·traversing·together toward him, and
Mk 10:50 ·garment *and* rising·up, he·came toward Jesus.
Rm 4:2 of·works, he·has a·boast, but·yet not toward God.
Rm 5:1 of·trust, we·have peace toward God through our
Rm 8:31 So·then, what shall·we·state toward these·things?
Rm 10:21 ·out my hands toward a·People being·obstinate
Rm 15:32 in·order·that I·may·come toward yeu with joy
Php 2:30 yeur lack of·public·service, the·one toward me.
1Th 1:8 in every place yeur trust toward God has·gone·forth,
1Th 4:12 yeu·may·walk decently toward the·ones outside *the*
1Th 5:14 support the weak, be·patient toward all *men.*
1Co 4:21 ·do yeu·want? Should·I·come toward yeu with a·
1Co 12:2 even·as yeu·were·led toward the voiceless idols.
1Co 14:12 ·seek that yeu·may·excel toward the edification
2Co 1:12 in the world and more·abundantly toward yeu.
2Co 1:18 because our Redemptive-word toward yeu did·not
2Co 3:4 we·have through the Anointed-One toward God.
2Co 7:3 Not toward condemnation do·I·say *this,* for I·have·
2Co 7:4 Large *is* my freeness·of·speech toward yeu, large *is*
Eph 4:12 toward the complete·development of·the holy·ones
Eph 6:9 lords: They·must·do the same·things toward them,
Col 3:19 the wives, and do·not become·bitter toward them.
Col 4:5 Walk in wisdom toward the·ones outside *the Called·*
Phm 1:5 and trust which you·have toward the Lord Jesus and
2Ti 3:17 having·been·properly·equipped toward all
1Jn 3:21 us, *then* we·have freeness·of·speech toward God.
1Jn 5:14 is the freeness·of·speech that we·have toward him,
Rv 1:17 And when I·saw him, I·fell toward his feet as dead.
Rv 13:6 ·up its mouth in revilement toward God, to·revile his
EG4314.1 (2x)
Ac 24:16 ·offense toward God and *toward* the men·of·clay†.
1Pe 2:19 on·account·of conscience *toward* God undergoes
G4314.2 PREP πρός (422x)
Jn 1:42 And he·brought him to Jesus. And Jesus, looking·
Jn 2:3 wine, the mother of·Jesus says to him, "They·do·not
Jn 3:2 The·same came to Jesus by·night and declared to·him,
Jn 3:4 NicoDemus says to him, "How·is·a·man·of·clay† able
Jn 3:21 the·one doing the truth comes to the light, in·order·
Jn 3:26 And they·came to John and declared to·him, "Rabbi,
Jn 3:26 the·same·man immerses, and all *men* come to him."
Jn 4:15 The woman says to him, "Sir, give me this water, in·
Jn 4:48 Now·then Jesus declared to him, "Unless yeu·*all·*
Jn 4:49 The royal·official says to him, "Sir, walk·down
Jn 5:40 "And yeu·do·not want to·come to me, in·order·that
Jn 5:45 that I·myself shall·legally·accuse yeu to the Father.
Jn 6:5 toward him, Jesus says to PhilIp, "From·what·source
Jn 6:17 ·had·become dark, and Jesus had·not come to them.
Jn 6:28 So·then they·declared to him, "What·do we·do in·
Jn 6:34 So·then they·declared to him, "Lord, always give us
Jn 6:35 of·life-above. The·one who·is·coming to me, no, he·
Jn 6:44 Not·even·one·man is·able to·come to me, unless the
Jn 6:45 learning personally·from the Father comes to me.
Jn 6:65 that not·even·one·man is·able to·come to me, unless
Jn 6:68 Peter answered him, "Lord, to whom shall·we·go?
Jn 7:3 Accordingly, his brothers declared to him, "Walk·on
Jn 7:37 "If any·man should·thirst, let·him·come to me and
Jn 7:45 So·then the assistants came to the chief·priests and
Jn 7:50 *and* being one from·among them) says to them,
Jn 8:2 and all the people were·coming to him. And sitting·
Jn 8:3 and the Pharisees brought to him a·wife having·been·
Jn 8:7 after·pulling·himself·up·straight, he·declared to them,
Jn 8:31 So·then, Jesus was·saying to *those* Judeans, the·ones
Jn 8:57 Accordingly, the Judeans declared to him, "You·are
Jn 9:13 They·brought *the* same·man to the Pharisees, the·one
Jn 10:41 And many came to him and were·saying, "John, in·
Jn 11:3 In·due·course, his sisters dispatched to him, saying,
Jn 11:15 yeu·may·trust; but·yet we·should·head·out to him.
Jn 11:21 Then Martha declared to Jesus, "Lord, if you·were
Jn 11:29 heard *it,* she·is·roused swiftly and goes to him.
Jn 11:46 some from·among them went·off to the Pharisees
Jn 13:1 ·should·walk·on from·among this world to the Father
Jn 13:3 ·forth from God and was·heading·on·out to God),
Jn 13:6 So·then he·comes to Simon Peter, and that·one says
Jn 14:3 shall·personally·receive yeu to myself in·order·that
Jn 14:6 the life-above. Not·even·one comes to the Father,
Jn 14:12 ·he·do, because I·myself traverse to my Father.
Jn 14:23 shall·love him, and we·shall·come to him, and
Jn 14:28 'I·head·on·out, and I·come *back* to yeu.' If yeu·
Jn 14:28 rejoice that I·declared, 'I·traverse to the Father,'
Jn 16:7 the Companion/Intercessor shall·not come to yeu;
Jn 16:7 yeu; but if I·should·depart, I·shall·send him to yeu.
Jn 16:28 I·leave the world, and traverse to the Father."

Jn 17:11 in the world, and I·myself do·come to you. “Holy
Jn 17:13 “And now I·come to you, and these·things I·speak
Jn 18:13 Then they·led him away first to HannAs *the proper*
Jn 18:24 him, having·been·bound, to Caiaphas the
Jn 18:29 Accordingly, Pilate went·out to them and declared,
Jn 18:38 ·declaring this, he·went·out again to the Judeans,
Jn 19:39 also, the·one coming at·the first to Jesus by·night,
Jn 20:2 So·then she·runs and comes to Simon Peter and to
Jn 20:2 comes to Simon Peter and to the other disciple whom
Jn 20:10 the disciples went·off again to their·own *homes*.
Jn 20:17 of·me, for I·have·not·yet ascended to my Father.
Jn 20:17 to my Father. But you·traverse to my brothers and
Jn 20:17 declare to·them, ‘I·ascend to my Father *who·is* also
Jn 21:22 him to·remain until I·come, what·is·that to you?
Jn 21:23 him to·remain until I·come, what·is·that to you?
Lk 1:13 But the angel declared to him, “Do·not be·afraid,
Lk 1:18 Then ZacharIas declared to the angel, “How shall·I·
Lk 1:19 of·God; and I·am·dispatched to·speak to you, and
Lk 1:34 Then Mariam declared to the angel, “How shall this
Lk 1:43 that the mother of·my Lord should·come to me?
Lk 1:55 into the coming·age, just·as he·spoke to our fathers.”
Lk 1:61 And they·declared to her, “There·is not·even·one
Lk 1:73 an·oath which he·swore to our father AbRaham,
Lk 1:80 until *the* day of·his official·showing to IsraEl.
Lk 2:15 the shepherds, declared to one·another, “Now·
Lk 2:18 the·things·that were·being·spoken to them by the
Lk 2:20 they·heard and saw, just·as it·was·spoken to them.
Lk 2:34 blessed them, and he·declared to Mariam his mother
Lk 2:48 And his mother declared to him, “Child, why·did
Lk 2:49 And he·declared to them, “How *is·it* that yeu·were·
Lk 3:9 ·now also, the ax is·laid·out to the root of·the trees.
Lk 3:12 came to·be·immersed, and they·declared to him,
Lk 3:13 And he·declared to them, “Exact not·one·bit more·
Lk 3:14 do?” And he·declared to them, “Yeu·should·
Lk 4:4 And Jesus answered to him, saying, “It·has·been·
Lk 4:21 And he·began to·say to them, “Today, this Scripture
Lk 4:23 And he·declared to them, “Entirely, yeu·shall·
Lk 4:26 yet to not·even·one of·them was EliJah sent, except
Lk 4:26 *the city* Tsarephath of·Tsidon, to a·woman *who was*
Lk 4:40 everyone brought them to him, with·a·diversity·of
Lk 4:43 And he·declared to them, “It·is·mandatory·for me
Lk 5:4 ·soon·as he·ceased speaking, he·declared to Simon,
Lk 5:10 And Jesus declared to Simon, “Do·not be·afraid.
Lk 5:22 deliberations, answering, declared to them, “Why·
Lk 5:31 And answering, Jesus declared to them, “The·ones
Lk 5:33 Now they·declared to him, “Why·is·it·that the
Lk 5:34 And he·declared to them, “¿! Are yeu·able to·make
Lk 5:36 And he·was also saying·a·parable to them, “Not·
Lk 6:3 And responding to them, Jesus declared, “Did·yeu·
Lk 6:9 So·then Jesus declared to them, “I·shall·inquire·of
Lk 7:3 he·dispatched elders of·the Judeans to him, asking
Lk 7:4 And coming·close to Jesus, they·were·imploring him
Lk 7:6 the centurion sent friends to him, saying to·him,
Lk 7:7 did·I·consider my·own·self deserving to·come to you,
Lk 7:19 two of·his disciples, sent *them* to Jesus, saying,
Lk 7:20 And coming·close to him, the men declared, “John
Lk 7:20 John the Immerser has·dispatched us to you, saying,
Lk 7:24 *Jesus* began to·discourse to the crowds concerning
Lk 7:40 And answering, Jesus declared to him, “Simon, I·
Lk 7:50 And he·declared to the woman, “Your trust has·
Lk 8:21 And answering, he·declared to them, “My mother
Lk 8:22 his disciples, and he·declared to them, “We·should·
Lk 8:35 what·was·happening. And they·came to Jesus and
Lk 9:3 And he·declared to them, “Take·up not·even·one·
Lk 9:13 But he·declared to them, “Yeu·yeurselves give
Lk 9:14 And he·declared to his disciples, “Make them fully·
Lk 9:23 Then *Jesus* was·saying to *them* all, “If any·man
Lk 9:33 from him, *that* Peter declared to Jesus, “O·Captain,
Lk 9:43 ·things which Jesus did, he·declared to his disciples,
Lk 9:50 And Jesus declared to him, “Do·not forbid *him*, for
Lk 9:57 roadway, *that* a·certain·man declared to him, “Lord
Lk 9:59 And he·declared to another, “Follow me.
Lk 10:2 Now·then, he·was·saying to them, “In·fact, the
Lk 10:26 He·declared to him, “What has·been·written in the
Lk 10:29 to·regard himself as·righteous, declared to Jesus,
Lk 11:1 a·certain·one of·his disciples declared to him,
Lk 11:5 And he·declared to them, “Which from·among yeu
Lk 11:5 a·friend, and shall·traverse to him at·midnight, and
Lk 11:6 ·now a·friend of·mine came·directly to me out·from
Lk 11:39 And the Lord declared to him, “Now yeu Pharisees
Lk 11:53 And with·him saying these·things to them, the
Lk 12:1 one·another, *Jesus* began to·say to his disciples,
Lk 12:3 the light; and that·which yeu·spoke to the ear in the
Lk 12:15 Then he·declared to them, “Yeu·clearly·see·to·it,
Lk 12:16 And he·declared a·parable to them, saying, “The
Lk 12:22 Then he·declared to his disciples, “On·account·of
Lk 12:41 “Lord, do·you·say this parable to us, or even to all
Lk 12:41 Lord, do·you·say this parable to us, or even to all?
Lk 13:7 “So he·declared to the vinedresser, ‘Behold, *for*
Lk 13:23 Then someone declared to him, “Lord, *is·it so* that
Lk 13:34 ·stones·at the·ones having·been·dispatched to you!
Lk 14:3 Jesus declared to the experts·in·Torah-Law and
Lk 14:7 a·parable to the·ones having·been·called·forth,
Lk 14:7 ·were·selecting the foremost·places, saying to them,
Lk 14:23 And the lord declared to the slave, ‘Go·out into the
Lk 14:25 ·him, and turning·around, he·declared to them,
Lk 14:26 “If any·man comes to me and does·not
Lk 15:3 And he·declared this parable to them, saying,
Lk 15:22 “But the father declared to his slaves, ‘Bring·out
Lk 16:26 ·ones wanting to·cross from·here to yeu should·not
Lk 16:26 ·even may the·ones from·there cross·over to us.’
Lk 16:30 But·yet if someone should·traverse to them from
Lk 17:1 And *Jesus* declared to the disciples, “It·is not·
Lk 17:22 Then he·declared to the disciples, “Days shall·
Lk 18:3 in that city, and she·was·coming to him, saying,
Lk 18:7 the·ones crying·out day and night to him, yet while·
Lk 18:9 he·declared also this parable to certain ones having·
Lk 18:16 “Allow the little·children to·come to me, and do·
Lk 18:31 personally·taking the twelve, he·declared to them,
Lk 18:40 commandingly·ordered him to·be·brought to him,
Lk 19:5 ·up, he·saw him, and declared to him, “Zacchaeus,
Lk 19:8 after·being·settled, declared to the Lord, “Behold,
Lk 19:9 And Jesus declared to him, “Today, Salvation did·
Lk 19:13 more·silver·minas to·them and declared to them,
Lk 19:33 the colt, its owners declared to them, “Why·do
Lk 19:35 And they·brought it to Jesus, and flinging their·
Lk 19:39 Pharisees from among·the crowd declared to him,
Lk 20:2 and declared to him, saying, “Declare to·us, by
Lk 20:3 And answering, he·declared to them, “And·I shall·
Lk 20:9 Then he·began to·relay this parable to the people,
Lk 20:10 he·dispatched a·slave to the tenant·farmers in·
Lk 20:23 their shrewd·cunning, he·declared to them, “Why·
Lk 20:41 But he·declared to them, “How·do they·say *it·is·*
Lk 21:38 the people were·rising·early·and·going to him in
Lk 22:15 And he·declared to them, “With·longing, I·longed
Lk 22:45 from the prayer *and* coming to the disciples, he·
Lk 22:52 Then Jesus declared to the chief·priests, *the*
Lk 22:70 Son of·God?” And he·declared to them, “Yeu·
Lk 23:4 Then Pilate declared to the chief·priests and *to* the
Lk 23:7 he·sent him up to HerOd·AntiPas, himself being also
Lk 23:14 declared to them, “Yeu·brought this man·of·clay†
Lk 23:15 I·sent yeu·yeurselves up to him *to·legally·accuse*
Lk 23:22 And *for* the third·time, he·declared to them, “For
Lk 23:28 But turning·around toward them, Jesus declared,
Lk 24:5 toward the earth, *the men* declared to them, “Why
Lk 24:10 who were·saying these·things to the ambassadors.
Lk 24:12 he·went·off, marveling to himself at·the·thing
Lk 24:17 And he·declared to them, “What sayings *are* these
Lk 24:17 that yeu·toss·back·and·forth to one·another while·
Lk 24:18 whose name *was* CleoPas declared to him, “*Are*
Lk 24:25 Then he·himself declared to them, “O stupid·ones,
Lk 24:32 And they·declared to one·another, “Was not·
Lk 24:44 *are* the words which I·spoke to yeu, while·still
Ac 1:7 And he·declared to them, “It·is not·for·yeu to·know
Ac 2:12 were·thoroughly·perplexed, saying one to another,
Ac 2:29 brothers, it·is·being·proper to·declare to yeu with
Ac 2:37 in·the heart, and they·declared to Peter and to·the
Ac 2:38 And Peter replied to them, “Repent, and each·one
Ac 3:12 And seeing *this*, Peter answered to the people,
Ac 3:22 “For Moses in·fact declared to the fathers,
Ac 3:22 ’ ⇐as·many·things·as he·would speak to yeu.⇒
Ac 3:25 bequeathed unto our fathers, saying to AbRaham, ⇐
Ac 4:1 And as·they were·speaking to the people, the priests·
Ac 4:8 being·filled with·Holy Spirit, declared to them,
Ac 4:19 Peter and John declared to them, “Whether it·is
Ac 4:23 ·released, they·went to their·own·company and
Ac 4:23 *that* the chief·priests and the elders declared to them.
Ac 5:9 So Peter declared to her, “How *is·it* that yeu are·
Ac 5:35 And *then* he·declared to *the joint·council*, “Men,
Ac 7:3 and declared to him, ‘Go·forth from·among your
Ac 8:14 of·God, they·dispatched Peter and John to them,
Ac 8:20 But Peter declared to him, “May your silver,
Ac 8:24 “Yeu·yeurselves petition to the Lord on·my behalf,
Ac 8:26 And the·angel of·Yahweh spoke to PhilIppe, saying,
Ac 9:6 me to·do?” And the Lord *said* to him, “Rise·up and
Ac 9:10 And the Lord declared to him in a·clear·vision, “O·
Ac 9:11 And the Lord *said* to him, “Rising·up, traverse on
Ac 9:15 But the Lord declared to him, “Traverse! Because
Ac 9:27 grabbing him, brought *him* to the ambassadors and
Ac 9:32 *such·for* Peter to·come·down also to the holy·ones,
Ac 9:38 the disciples dispatched two men to him, imploring
Ac 9:40 he·prayed. And turning·back·around to the body,
Ac 10:13 And there·came a·voice to him, *saying*, “Peter,
Ac 10:15 And a·voice *spoke* to him again for a·second·time,
Ac 10:21 Now after·walking·down to the men (the·ones
Ac 10:21 men (the·ones having·been·dispatched to him from
Ac 10:28 And he·replied to them, “Yeu·yeurselves are·
Ac 10:33 So·then, from·this·same·hour I·sent to you, and
Ac 11:11 having·been·dispatched from Caesarea to me.
Ac 11:14 who shall·speak to you utterances by which you·
Ac 11:20 Antioch, were·speaking to the Hellenistic·Jews,
Ac 11:30 also they·did, dispatching *it* to the elders through
Ac 12:5 prayer over him was being·made to God by the
Ac 12:8 And the angel declared to him, “Gird·yourself·
Ac 12:15 And they·declared to her, “You·are·raving·mad!”
Ac 12:21 ·AgrIppa was·delivering·a·public·address to them.
Ac 13:15 the directors·of·the·gathering dispatched to them,
Ac 13:31 to JeruSalem, who are his witnesses to the People.
Ac 15:2 to·walk·up to JeruSalem to the ambassadors and
Ac 15:7 after·rising·up, Peter declared to them, “Men,
Ac 15:25 to·send selected men to yeu together with·our
Ac 15:33 from the brothers *to·return* to the ambassadors
Ac 15:36 some days, Paul declared to BarNabas, “Now·then
Ac 16:36 the prison·warden announced this saying to Paul,
Ac 16:37 But Paul replied to them, “After publicly thrashing
Ac 17:15 taking *with·them* a·commandment to Silas and
Ac 17:15 and TimoThy, that they·should·come to him as
Ac 18:6 shaking·out his garments, he·declared to them,
Ac 18:14 ·open·up his mouth, Gallio declared to the Jews,
Ac 18:21 but I·shall·return·back again to yeu, God willing.
Ac 19:2 he·declared to them, “Did·yeu·receive Holy Spirit
Ac 19:2 after·trusting?” And they·declared to him, “But·
Ac 19:3 And he·declared to them, “So·then into what were·
Ac 19:31 friends with·him, sending·word to him, they·were·
Ac 20:6 Unleavened·Bread, and we·came to them in Troas
Ac 20:18 And as·soon·as they·came·close to him, he·
Ac 21:11 And after·coming to us and taking·up Paul's belt,
Ac 21:37 “Is·it·proper for·me to·declare something to you?
Ac 21:39 you, freely·permit me to·speak to the people.”
Ac 22:1 fathers, hear my defense *which I·make* now to yeu.”
Ac 22:5 whom I also accepted letters to the brothers and
Ac 22:8 Lord?’ And he·declared to me, ‘It·is·I Myself,
Ac 22:10 And the Lord declared to me, ‘Upon·rising·up,
Ac 22:13 after·coming to me and standing·over *me*, he·
Ac 22:15 you·shall·be his witness to all men·of·clay† of·
Ac 22:21 “And he·declared to me, ‘Traverse, because I·
Ac 22:25 straps, Paul declared to the centurion standing·by,
Ac 23:3 Then Paul declared to him, “God is·about to·
Ac 23:15 that he·should·bring him down to yeu tomorrow, as

Ac 23:17 "Lead this young·man to the regiment·commander,
Ac 23:18 him, brought *him* to the regiment·commander and
Ac 23:18 asked *me* to·bring this young·man to you, having
Ac 23:22 to·no·one that you·made these·things clear to me."
Ac 23:24 they·should·bring·*him*·thoroughly·safe to Felix the
Ac 23:30 I·sent *him* from·this·same·hour to you, charging
Ac 25:16 To whom I·answered, 'It·is not *the* manner of·the·
Ac 25:21 him to·be·kept until I·may·send him to Caesar."
Ac 25:22 Then Agrippa replied to Festus, "I·resolve also to·
Ac 26:1 Then Agrippa replied to Paul, "It·is·freely·
Ac 26:6 of·the promise being·made by God to the fathers,
Ac 26:9 to·practice many·things contrary to the name of·
Ac 26:14 earth, I·heard a·voice speaking to me, and saying
Ac 26:26 ·acquainted concerning these·things, to whom also
Ac 26:28 But Agrippa replied to Paul, "In *such* a·brief·
Ac 27:3 ·permitted *him* to·traverse to his·friends to·obtain
Ac 28:17 ·them coming·together, he·was·saying to them,
Ac 28:21 And they·declared to him, "We·ourselves do·not·
Ac 28:25 well through Isaiah the prophet to our fathers,
Heb 1:13 But to which of·the angels has·he·declared at·any·
Heb 5:5 a·high·priest, but·rather the·one speaking to him,
Heb 7:21 a·swearing·of·oath through the·one saying to him,
Heb 11:18 to whom it·was·spoken, "In YiTsaq, a·Seed
Heb 13:13 Now·then, we·should·go·forth to him outside the
Mt 2:12 ·in·a·dream not to·return·back to HerOd·the·Great,
Mt 3:5 Then JeruSalem was·traversing·out to him, and all
Mt 3:10 ·now also, the ax is·laid·out to the root of·the trees.
Mt 3:13 to the Jordan, directly·to John to·be·immersed by
Mt 3:14 by you, and do·you·yourself come to me?
Mt 3:15 And answering, YeShua declared to him, "Allow
Mt 7:15 the false·prophets, who do·come to yeu in sheep's
Mt 10:6 but traverse rather to the sheep, the·ones having·
Mt 10:13 ·not be worthy, *let* yeur peace be·returned to yeu.
Mt 11:28 "Come·here to me, all the·ones laboring·hard and
Mt 13:2 And large crowds were·gathered·together to him,
Mt 14:28 commandingly·order me to·come to you upon the
Mt 14:29 Peter walked upon the water to·go to YeShua.
Mt 17:14 And with·them coming to the crowd, a·certain·
Mt 19:14 and do·not forbid them to·come to me, for of·such
Mt 21:32 For John came to yeu by way of·righteousness, yet
Mt 21:34 he·dispatched his slaves to the tenant·farmers, to·
Mt 21:37 eventually, he·dispatched his son to them, saying,
Mt 23:34 behold, I·myself dispatch to yeu prophets and
Mt 23:37 ·stones·at the·ones having·been·dispatched to you!
Mt 25:36 I·was in prison, and yeu·came to me.'
Mt 25:39 ·we·see you sick, or in prison, and came to you?
Mt 26:14 Judas IsCariot, upon·traversing to the chief·priests,
Mt 26:18 "Head·on·out into the City to a·particular·man and
Mt 26:40 And he·comes to the disciples and finds them
Mt 26:45 Then he·comes to his disciples and says to·them,
Mt 26:57 ·holding YeShua led·*him*·away to Caiaphas the
Mt 27:4 And they·declared, "What·is·that to us?
Mt 27:14 And he·did·not answer to him not·even one
Mt 27:19 ·judgment·seat, his wife dispatched to him, saying,
Mt 27:62 and the Pharisees gathered·together to Pilate,
Mk 1:5 the region of·Judea was·traversing·out to him, and·
Mk 1:32 sun sank·down, they·were·bringing to him all the·
Mk 1:40 And a·leper came to him, imploring him, even
Mk 1:45 places, and they·came to him from·everywhere.
Mk 2:3 Then *more* come to him, bringing a·paralyzed·man
Mk 3:7 And Jesus departed with his disciples to the sea. And
Mk 3:8 he·was·doing, a·large multitude came to him.
Mk 3:13 ·whom he was·wanting, and they·went·off to him.
Mk 3:31 they·dispatched to him while·hollering·out·for
Mk 4:1 And a·large crowd was·gathered·together to him,
Mk 4:41 ·and·awe, and they·were·saying to one·another,
Mk 5:15 And they·come to Jesus and observe the·one
Mk 5:19 "Head·on·out to your house, to your *kinsfolk*, and
Mk 6:25 upon·entering·in immediately with haste to the king
Mk 7:31 of·Tyre and Tsidon, he·came to the Sea of·Galilee,
Mk 9:14 And upon·coming to the *other* disciples, he·saw a·
Mk 9:17 "Mentor, I·brought to you my son, having a·mute
Mk 9:19 ·long shall·I·put·up·with yeu? Bring him to me."
Mk 9:20 And they·brought *the little·child* to him, and upon·
Mk 10:7 mother, and shall·be·tightly·bonded to his wife,
Mk 10:14 "Allow the little·children to·come to me, and do·
Mk 11:7 And they·brought the colt to Jesus, and they·threw
Mk 12:2 ·season, he·dispatched a·slave to the tenant·farmers
Mk 12:4 And again he·dispatched another slave to them, and
Mk 12:6 he·dispatched him also last to them, saying,
Mk 12:13 And they·dispatched to him some of·the Pharisees
Mk 12:18 Then *the* Sadducees come to him, who say *that*
Mk 13:22 shall·give signs and wonders to utterly·lead·astray,
Mk 14:10 one of·the twelve, went·off to the chief·priests,
Mk 14:53 they·led Jesus away to the designated·high·priest,
Mk 15:43 Being·daringly·bold, he·went·in to Pilate and
Rm 1:10 I·shall·prosper by the will of·God to·come to yeu.
Rm 1:13 ·times I·personally·determined to·come to yeu (but
Rm 10:1 heart's good·purpose and petition to God on·behalf
Rm 10:21 But to IsraEl he·says, " The whole day·long I·
Rm 15:22 also, I·was·hindered often *from* coming to yeu.
Rm 15:23 ·yearning for these·many years to·come to yeu,
Rm 15:24 ·traverse for Spain, I·shall·come to yeu, for I·
Rm 15:29 I·have·seen that, in·coming to yeu, I·shall·come
Rm 15:30 with·me in the prayers to God on·my behalf,
Php 1:26 in Jesus Anointed through my arrival to yeu again.
Php 2:25 *it* necessary to·send to yeu EpAphroditus, my
Php 4:6 of·yeurs, make·*them*·be·known directly·to God.
1Pe 2:4 *It·is·he* to whom yeu·are·coming·alongside, the·
1Pe 3:15 And *be* ready always to *present a·gracious* defense
2Pe 3:16 the rest of·Scriptures, to their own total·destruction
1Th 1:9 what·manner of·accessible·entrance we·have to yeu,
1Th 1:9 and how yeu·turned·back·around to God from the
1Th 2:1 that our accessible·entrance to yeu has·not become
1Th 2:2 ·confident in our God to·speak to yeu the good·news
1Th 2:18 Therefore we·wanted to·come to yeu, in·fact I Paul
1Th 3:6 with·TimoThy coming from yeu to us, *he·brings*
1Th 3:11 YeShua Anointed, fully·direct our way to yeu.
Tit 3:2 *but* fair, indicating all gentleness to all men·of·clay†.
Tit 3:12 Whenever I·shall·send Artemas to you, or Tychicus,
Tit 3:12 or Tychicus, quickly·endeavor to·come to me to
1Co 2:1 And·I, brothers, already·coming to yeu, came not
1Co 4:18 ·up, as·though *it·is* not me who·is·coming to yeu.
1Co 4:19 But I·shall·come to yeu promptly, if the Lord
1Co 6:5 I·say *this* to yeur·own embarrassment. In·this·
1Co 13:12 ·view, but then face to face. At·this·moment, I·
1Co 14:6 brothers, if I·should·come to yeu speaking with·
1Co 15:34 of·God. I·say *this* to yeur·own embarrassment.
1Co 16:5 Now I·shall·come to yeu, whenever I·should·go·
1Co 16:11 in peace in·order·that he·may·come to me, for I·
1Co 16:12 him in·order·that he·should·come to yeu with the
2Co 1:15 I·was·definitely·willing to·come to yeu previously
2Co 1:16 and to·come again from Macedonia to yeu, and by
2Co 2:1 ·own·self, not again to·come to yeu in grievousness
2Co 3:1 some *do*, of·letters of·recommendation to yeu, or *of*·
2Co 3:16 one·should·turn·back·around to Yahweh *through*
2Co 4:2 commending ourselves to every man·of·clay's†
2Co 6:11 we·have·opened·up our mouth to yeu; our heart
2Co 7:12 — for·it to·become·apparent to yeu in·the·sight of·
2Co 8:17 ·diligent, of·his·own·choice, he·went·forth to yeu.
2Co 8:19 (the·one being·attended·to by us to the glory of·the
2Co 10:4 but·rather powerful in·God to *the* demolition of·
2Co 12:14 at·the·ready *for* a·third·time to·come to yeu, and
2Co 12:17 any of·them whom I·have·dispatched to yeu?
2Co 13:1 This *is the* third·time I·am·coming to yeu. "At *the*
2Co 13:7 Now I·well-wish to God for·yeu not to·do not·
Eph 2:18 *of·us* have the embraceable·access to the Father by
Eph 3:14 ·cause, I·bow my knees to the Father of·our Lord
Eph 5:31 mother, and shall·be·tightly·bonded to his wife,
Eph 6:22 whom I·sent to yeu for this very·purpose, that yeu·
Col 4:8 whom I·sent to yeu for this same purpose, in·order·
Col 4:10 commandments; if he·should·come to yeu, accept
1Ti 3:14 to·you, expecting to·come to you more·promptly.
1Ti 4:7 myths, and train yourself *rather* to devout·reverence.
2Ti 2:24 but·rather to·be pleasantly·engageable to all *men*,
2Ti 4:9 Quickly·endeavor to·come to me promptly,
2Jn 1:10 If any·man comes to yeu *all*, and does·not bring this
2Jn 1:12 and ink, but·rather I·expect to·come to yeu, and to·
2Jn 1:12 to yeu, and to·speak mouth to mouth, in·order·that
3Jn 1:14 ·away, and we·shall·speak mouth to mouth. Peace
Rv 10:9 And I·went·aside to the angel, saying to·him, "Give
Rv 12:5 ·iron; and her child was·snatched·up to God, and *to*
Rv 12:12 sea, because the Slanderer descended to yeu! *He·is*
Rv 21:9 And there·came to me one of·the seven angels (of·

G4314.3 PREP πρός (14x)

Jn 4:35 because they·are white even·now unto harvest.
Lk 9:62 And Jesus declared unto him, "Not·even·one·man,
Lk 18:1 ·them, *how* unto *this·purpose* it·is·to·be·mandatory
Ac 3:25 ·covenant which God bequeathed unto our fathers,
Heb 1:7 And, in·fact, he·says unto the angels, "*This·is*
Heb 1:8 But unto the Son *he·says*, "Your throne, O·God,
Heb 10:16 ·covenant that I·shall·bequeath unto them after
Rm 15:2 *·conscience* for his good·benefit unto edification.
Jac 4:5 that resides in us greatly·yearns *even* unto envy"?
2Co 1:20 "So·be·it,·Amen" for·God unto glory through us.
1Jn 5:16 ·failing a·moral·failure *which·is* not unto death, he·
1Jn 5:16 (*that·is*, to·the·ones morally·failing not unto death).
1Jn 5:16 unto death). There·is moral·failure unto death; not
1Jn 5:17 ·failure, and there·is moral·failure not unto death.

G4314.4 PREP πρός (74x)

Jn 1:1 the Word, and the Word was alongside God, and the
Jn 1:2 The·same was at *the* beginning alongside God.
Jn 7:50 NicoDemus (the·one coming alongside *Jesus* by·
Jn 11:19 ·among the Judeans had·come alongside the *women*
Jn 11:45 the Judeans, the·ones coming alongside Mary and
Jn 14:18 ·not leave yeu orphans. I·do·come alongside yeu.
Jn 18:16 But Peter stood outside alongside the door. In·due·
Jn 20:12 in white sitting·down, one alongside the head, and
Jn 20:12 the head, and one alongside the feet, where the
Lk 6:11 and were·conferring alongside one·another what
Lk 9:41 how·long shall·I·be alongside yeu and shall·put·
Lk 10:23 Then turning·himself *to·be* alongside his disciples,
Lk 16:20 ·of Lazarus who had·been·cast alongside his gate,
Lk 19:29 to BethPhage and BethAny alongside the mount
Lk 19:37 drawing·near, even·now alongside the descent of·
Lk 20:5 And they·reckoned·together alongside themselves,
Lk 24:14 were·conversing alongside one·another concerning
Ac 2:47 God, and having grace alongside all the People.
Ac 3:2 whom they·were·laying each day alongside the door
Ac 5:10 carrying·*her*·out, buried *her* alongside her husband.
Ac 7:31 *it, the* voice of·Yahweh came·to·be alongside him,
Ac 9:29 ·was·mutually·questioning·and·discussing alongside
Ac 11:2 were·discriminating *the matter* alongside him,
Ac 11:3 saying, "You·entered·in alongside men being
Ac 12:20 ·determination, they·were·present alongside him.
Ac 13:36 was·laid·to·rest, and was·laid alongside his fathers
Ac 15:2 ·and·discussion *occurring* alongside them, they·
Ac 17:2 Paul's custom, he·entered·in alongside them, and
Ac 17:17 and·every day alongside the·ones chancing·nearby.
Ac 21:18 ·entered together with·us *to·come* alongside Jacob;
Ac 24:12 ·Courtyard discussing *anything* alongside anyone,
Ac 28:8 and dysentery. Paul entered·in alongside him, and
Ac 28:23 ·him, many·more were·coming alongside him in
Heb 9:20 covenant which God commanded alongside yeu."
Gal 1:18 Peter, and I·stayed·over alongside him fifteen days.
Gal 2:5 good·news should·remain·constantly alongside yeu.
Gal 4:18 not merely with me being·present alongside yeu.
Gal 4:20 to·be·present alongside yeu at·this·moment and to·
Mt 13:56 his sisters, are·they not all indeed alongside us?
Mt 26:18 I·do the Passover alongside you with my disciples.
Mt 26:55 ·sitting·down each day alongside yeu instructing in
Mk 1:33 was having·been·completely·gathered alongside the
Mk 2:2 no·longer to·have·room, not·even alongside the door
Mk 2:13 and all the crowd was·coming alongside him, and
Mk 4:1 and all the crowd was alongside the sea upon the
Mk 6:3 Simon? And are not his sisters here alongside us?
Mk 6:30 gathered·themselves·together alongside Jesus and
Mk 7:1 of·the scribes gathered·together alongside him, after·
Mk 9:16 ·do yeu·mutually·question·and·discuss alongside?

Mk 9:19 generation, how·long shall·I·be alongside yeu?
Mk 11:1 BethPhage and BethAny, alongside the Mount of·
Mk 11:4 the colt outside having·been·tied alongside the door
Mk 11:27 the scribes, and the elders come alongside him,
Mk 14:4 being·greatly·displeased alongside themselves, and
Mk 14:49 Each day I·was alongside yeu in the Sanctuary·
Mk 14:54 and warming·himself alongside the firelight.
Rm 8:18 not worthy *to·be·compared* alongside the impending
1Th 3:4 For even when we·were alongside yeu, we·were·
2Th 2:5 that while·being yet alongside yeu, I·was·relating
2Th 3:1 may·be·glorified, even just·as *it·is* alongside yeu,
2Th 3:10 For even when we·were alongside yeu, this we·
1Co 2:3 And I·myself came·to·be alongside yeu in weakness
1Co 16:6 ·abide·nearby or even shall·winter alongside yeu,
1Co 16:7 I·expect to·stay·over some time alongside yeu, if
1Co 16:10 he·may·come·to·be alongside yeu without·fear,
2Co 5:8 the body and to·be·at·home alongside the Lord.
2Co 6:14 And what fellowship has·light alongside darkness?
2Co 6:15 has·Anointed-One alongside BeliaI·*(the·Worthless·*
2Co 11:9 And while·being·present alongside yeu and
Phm 1:13 ·definitely·willing to·fully·retain alongside myself,
1Jn 1:2 eternal life-above, which was alongside the Father,
1Jn 2:1 ·have a·Companion/Intercessor alongside the Father,
Rv 3:20 ·up the door, I·shall·enter·in alongside him, and
Rv 22:18 ·place *anything additional* alongside these·things,
EG4314.4 (2x)
Mt 14:33 the sailboat, after·coming *alongside*, fell·prostrate
Mk 16:20 Lord working·together *alongside* and confirming
G4314.5 PREP πρός (26x)
Jn 4:33 ·then the disciples were·saying among one·another,
Jn 6:52 the Judeans were·quarreling among one·another,
Jn 7:35 the Judeans declared among themselves, "Where·
Jn 12:19 So·then the Pharisees declared among themselves,
Jn 16:17 ·among his disciples declared among one·another,
Jn 19:24 Accordingly, they·declared among one·another,
Lk 4:36 they·were·speaking·together among one·another,
Lk 8:25 they·marveled, saying among one·another, "What
Lk 20:14 the tenant·farmers deliberated among themselves,
Lk 22:23 began to·question·and·discuss among themselves,
Lk 23:12 ·previously being in hostility among themselves.
Ac 2:7 and were·marveling, saying among one·another,
Ac 4:15 they·rigorously·conferred among one·another,
Ac 26:31 they·were·speaking among one·another, saying,
Ac 28:4 his hand, they·were·saying among one·another,
Ac 28:25 And being discordant among one·another, they·
Mk 1:27 ·for *them* to·mutually·question·and·discuss among,
Mk 8:16 And they·were·deliberating among one·another,
Mk 9:33 ·was·it *that* yeu·deliberated among yeurselves along
Mk 9:34 the way they·discussed among one·another who
Mk 10:26 beyond·excess, saying among themselves, "Then
Mk 11:31 And they·were·reckoning among themselves,
Mk 12:7 those tenant·farmers declared among themselves,
Mk 15:31 ·mocking, were·saying among one·another with
Mk 16:3 And they·were·saying among themselves, "Who
2Co 12:21 my God may·humble me among yeu, and I·
G4314.6 PREP πρός (17x)
Jn 10:35 "If he·declared them gods pertaining·to whom the
Lk 12:47 ·ready, nor·even doing pertaining·to his will, shall·
Lk 14:6 to·contradict him pertaining·to these·things.
Lk 19:42 this your day, the·things pertaining·to your peace!
Ac 9:2 him letters for Damascus pertaining·to the gatherings,
Ac 28:10 they·supplied *us* the·things pertaining·to the need.
Heb 2:17 High·Priest in·the·things pertaining·to God, in·
Heb 5:1 of·men·of·clay† in·the·things pertaining·to God, in·
Mt 19:8 "*It·was* pertaining·to yeur hardness·of·heart *that*
Mk 10:5 to·them, "Pertaining·to yeur hardness·of·heart, he·
Rm 15:17 in Jesus Anointed in·the·things pertaining·to God.
2Pe 1:3 divine power, all·things pertaining·to life-above and
1Co 7:35 upon·yeu, but·rather *I·speak* pertaining·to *what is*
2Co 3:13 his face, *which·is* pertaining·to the Sons of·IsraEl
2Co 5:10 through the body, pertaining·to what he·practiced
Eph 3:4 pertaining·to which, upon·reading·*it*·aloud, yeu·are·
Eph 4:14 by *the* shrewd·cunning pertaining·to the trickery

G4314.7 PREP πρός (5x)
Lk 4:11 you·should·stub your foot directly·against a·stone."
Ac 9:5 to·kick·the·heel·back directly·against cattle·prods."
Ac 26:14 to·kick·the·heel·back directly·against cattle·prods.'
Mt 4:6 you·should·stub your foot directly·against a·stone.'"
Rv 1:13 ·with a·golden band directly·against the breasts.
G4314.8 PREP πρός (17x)
Lk 20:19 he·declared this parable specifically·against them,
Ac 6:1 Hellenistic·Jews specifically·against the Hebrews,
Ac 19:38 ·him have a·matter specifically·against any·man,
Ac 23:30 you the·things *they·have* specifically·against him.
Ac 24:19 ·actually·have anything specifically·against me.
Ac 25:19 certain issues specifically·against him concerning
Heb 12:4 strenuously·struggling specifically·against the
Mk 12:12 he·declared the parable specifically·against them.
1Co 6:1 a·matter·of·consequence specifically·against the
Eph 6:11 to·stand·still specifically·against the trickeries of·
Eph 6:12 not for·our wrestling specifically·against blood and
Eph 6:12 but·rather: specifically·against the principalities,
Eph 6:12 principalities, specifically·against the authorities,
Eph 6:12 specifically·against the mighty·world·powers of·
Eph 6:12 ·age, *and* specifically·against the spiritual·things
Col 2:23 any value specifically·against an·indulgence of·the
Col 3:13 should·hold a·fault specifically·against anyone,
G4314.9 PREP πρός (23x)
Jn 5:33 ·yeurselves have·dispatched specifically·for John,
Lk 14:28 ·has the *means* specifically·for *its* full·development
Lk 14:32 he·asks·of the *conditions* specifically·for peace.
Ac 3:10 sitting·down specifically·for the merciful·act·of·
Ac 13:15 a·word of·exhortation specifically·for the people,
Ac 27:34 for this is·inherently specific·for yeur salvation,
Mt 5:28 looking·upon a·woman specifically to·long·for her,
Mt 23:5 ·do *are* specifically·for them to·be·distinctly·viewed
Mt 26:12 did *it* specifically·for my preparation·of·burial.
Rm 3:26 ·a·trust of·Jesus (specifically·as an·indicator·of·his
1Pe 4:12 (occurring specifically·for a·proof·trial among·yeu)
2Th 3:8 travail night and day specifically·for *us* not to·be·a·
1Co 7:5 ·result of·a·mutual·agreement specifically·for a·set·,
1Co 7:35 And I·say this specifically·for yeur own advantage;
1Co 10:11 they·are·written specifically·for our admonition,
1Co 12:7 is·given to·each·man specifically·for the advantage
1Co 14:26 All·things must·occur specifically·for edification.
2Co 2:16 And who *is* sufficient specifically·for these·things?
2Co 4:6 in our hearts, specifically·for *the* illumination of·the
2Co 5:12 ·have *an·answer* specifically·for the·ones who·are·
2Co 11:8 taking wages *of·them*, specifically·for yeur service.
1Ti 1:16 specifically·for a·primary·example for·the·ones
1Ti 4:8 ·Reverence is profitable specifically·for all·things,
G4314.10 PREP πρός (9x)
Jn 13:28 ·at·the·meal knew particularly why he·declared this
Ac 27:12 ·being unsuitable, particularly·for wintering·in, the
Heb 12:11 ·and·discipline, particularly·for the present, does·
Mt 6:1 ·of·clay†, particularly for·it to·be·distinctly·viewed
Tit 1:16 disqualified particularly·for every beneficially·good
Tit 3:1 to·be ready particularly·for every beneficially·good
Eph 4:29 ·good *conversation*, particularly·for the needed
Eph 6:11 ·armor of·God, particularly·for yeu to·be·able to·
2Ti 3:16 and *is* profitable particularly·for instruction, for
G4314.11 PREP πρός (10x)
Jn 5:35 and yeu wanted just·for a·short·while to·leap·for·joy
Lk 8:13 no root, who trust just·for a·season, and·then in a·
Heb 9:13 ·defiled, makes·one·holy just·for the purification
Heb 12:10 For in·fact, they, just·for few days, were·
Gal 2:5 to·them, not·even just·for an·hour, did·we·yield to·
Jac 4:14 a·vapor, one·appearing just·for a·brief·moment and
1Th 2:17 ·removed from yeu just·for a·short season (in·
2Co 7:8 yeu, even·though *it·was* just·for a·short·while.
Phm 1:15 he·departed just·for a·short·while in·order·that
1Ti 4:8 bodily training is profitable just·for a·brief·moment,
G4314.15 PREP πρός (3x)
2Ti 3:16 profitable particularly·for instruction, for reproof,
2Ti 3:16 instruction, for reproof, for setting·straight, *and* for
2Ti 3:16 setting·straight, *and* for education·and·discipline

G4315 προ•σάββατον prôsábbatôn *n.* (1x)
Roots:G4253 G4521 Compare:G3904
G4315 N-NSN προσάββατον (1x)
Mk 15:42 preparation·day (that is, *a·day* before·a·Sabbath),
G4316 προσ•αγορεύω prôsagôrěúō *v.* (1x)
Roots:G4314 G0058 Compare:G2723 G1951
G4316.2 V-APP-NSM προσαγορευθείς (1x)
Heb 5:10 being·specifically·designated by God a·High·Priest
G4317 προσ•άγω prôságō *v.* (4x)
Roots:G4314 G0071 Compare:G4311
G4317.2 V-2AAM-2S προσάγαγε (1x)
Lk 9:41 yeu and shall·put·up·with yeu? Escort your son here
G4317.2 V-2AAP-NPM προσαγαγόντες (1x)
Ac 16:20 And escorting them to·the court·officers, they·
G4317.2 V-2AAS-3S προσαγάγῃ (1x)
1Pe 3:18 ·ones, in·order·that he·may·escort us to·God, in·
G4317.3 V-PAN προσάγειν (1x)
Ac 27:27 for·them to·be·heading·toward some country.
G4318 προσ•αγωγή prôsagōgḗ *n.* (3x)
Roots:G4317 Compare:G1529 See:G0072
G4318.3 N-ASF προσαγωγήν (3x)
Rm 5:2 also we·have the embraceable·access by·the trust
Eph 2:18 the both *of·us* have the embraceable·access to the
Eph 3:12 and the embraceable·access with confidence
G4319 προσ•αιτέω prôsaitéō *v.* (3x)
Roots:G4314 G0154
G4319.1 V-PAP-NSM προσαιτῶν (3x)
Jn 9:8 this not the·one who·was·sitting·down and begging?"
Lk 18:35 ·man sat·down directly·by the roadway begging.
Mk 10:46 was·sitting·down directly·by the roadway begging.
G4320 προσ•ανα•βαίνω prôsanabaínō *v.* (1x)
Roots:G4314 G0305
G4320.1 V-2AAM-2S προσανάβηθι (1x)
Lk 14:10 to·you, 'Friend, walk·further·up higher.' Then
G4321 προσ•ανα•λίσκω prôsanalískō *v.* (1x)
Roots:G4314 G0355 Compare:G4325
G4321.2 V-AAP-NSF προσαναλώσασα (1x)
Lk 8:43 years, who after·specifically·consuming all *her*
G4322 προσ•ανα•πληρόω prôsanaplēróō *v.* (2x)
Roots:G4314 G0378
G4322 V-PAP-NSF προσαναπληροῦσα (1x)
2Co 9:12 is·it utterly·fulfilling·in·particular the lackings of·
G4322 V-AAI-3P προσανεπλήρωσαν (1x)
2Co 11:9 from Macedonia utterly·fulfilled·in·particular; and
G4323 προσ•ανα•τίθημι prôsanatíthēmi *v.* (2x)
Roots:G4314 G0394
G4323.2 V-2AMI-3P προσανέθεντο (1x)
Gal 2:6 — not·even·one·thing did·they·further·impart to·me.
G4323.3 V-2AMI-1S προσανεθέμην (1x)
Gal 1:16 I·did·not immediately confer with·flesh and blood,
G4324 προσ•απειλέω prôsapěiléō *v.* (1x)
Roots:G4314 G0546
G4324.3 V-AMP-NPM προσαπειλησάμενοι (1x)
Ac 4:21 So after·further·threatening·them, they·dismissed
G4325 προσ•δαπανάω prôsdapanáō *v.* (1x)
Roots:G4314 G1159 Compare:G4321 See:G1550
G4325.2 V-AAS-2S προσδαπανήσῃς (1x)
Lk 10:35 And whatever you·might spend·further, when I
G4326 προσ•δέομαι prôsdéômai *v.* (1x)
Roots:G4314 G1189
G4326.1 V-PNP-NSM προσδεόμενος (1x)
Ac 17:25 ·of·clay†, *as·though* being·in·a·bind·for anything,
G4327 προσ•δέχομαι prôsdéchômai *v.* (14x)
Roots:G4314 G1209 Compare:G1551 G0324
G4327.2 V-PNI-3S προσδέχεται (1x)
Lk 15:2 "This·man welcomes morally·disqualified·men and
G4327.2 V-PNM-2P προσδέχεσθε (1x)
Php 2:29 So·then, welcome him in *the* Lord with all joy, and
G4327.2 V-ADI-2P προσεδέξασθε (1x)
Heb 10:34 with·my bonds, and yeu·welcomed with joy the
G4327.2 V-ADP-NPM προσδεξάμενοι (1x)

Heb 11:35 ·beaten·to·death, not welcoming the blood·bribe
G4327.2 V-ADS-2P προσδέξησθε (1x)
Rm 16:2 in·order·that yeu·may·welcome her in *the* Lord, as·
G4327.3 V-PNI-3P προσδέχονται (1x)
Ac 24:15 God, which these·men themselves also await, *that*
G4327.3 V-PNP-DPM προσδεχομένοις (2x)
Lk 2:38 him to·all the·ones awaiting a·ransoming in
Lk 12:36 like men·of·clay† who·are·awaiting their·own lord
G4327.3 V-PNP-NSM προσδεχόμενος (2x)
Lk 2:25 and devout, awaiting the·consoling of·IsraEl. And
Mk 15:43 who also himself was awaiting the kingdom of·
G4327.3 V-PNP-NPM προσδεχόμενοι (3x)
Ac 23:21 now they·are ready, awaiting the promise from
Jud 1:21 God's love, *yeu* who·are·awaiting the mercy of·our
Tit 2:13 while·awaiting the supremely·blessed Expectation
G4327.3 V-INI-3S προσεδέχετο (1x)
Lk 23:51 who also himself awaited the kingdom of·God.

G4328 προσ•δοκάω prôsdôkáō *v.* (16x)
Roots:G4314 G1209 Compare:G5348 G4037 G1679
G4328.1 V-PAI-1P προσδοκῶμεν (1x)
Mt 11:3 ·one who·is·coming, or do·we·anticipate another?
G4328.1 V-PAI-3S προσδοκᾷ (2x)
Lk 12:46 in a·day when he·does·not anticipate *him*, and at
Mt 24:50 on a·day when he·does·not anticipate *him*, and at
G4328.1 V-PAP-APM προσδοκῶντας (1x)
2Pe 3:12 while·anticipating and hastening the imminent·
G4328.1 V-PAP-GPM προσδοκώντων (1x)
Ac 28:6 but with·them anticipating over a·long·while and
G4328.1 V-PAP-NSM προσδοκῶν (1x)
Ac 3:5 ·attention to·them, anticipating to·receive something
G4328.1 V-PAP-NPM προσδοκῶντες (1x)
Ac 27:33 ·day is·the·fourteenth day of·anticipating, *and·still*
G4328.1 V-IAI-3P προσεδόκων (1x)
Ac 28:6 But they·were·anticipating him about to·be·swollen·
G4328.2 V-PAI-1P προσδοκῶμεν (1x)
2Pe 3:13 according·to his pledge, we·intently·await ᶠa·
G4328.2 V-PAP-GSM προσδοκῶντος (1x)
Lk 3:15 And the people were·intently·awaiting, and all·men
G4328.2 V-PAP-NSM προσδοκῶν (2x)
Lk 1:21 And the people were intently·awaiting ZacharIas,
Ac 10:24 into Caesarea. And while·intently·awaiting them,
G4328.2 V-PAP-NPM προσδοκῶντες (2x)
Lk 8:40 him, for they·were all intently·awaiting him.
2Pe 3:14 *yeu* beloved, while·intently·awaiting these·things,
G4328.2 V-PAS-1P προσδοκῶμεν (2x)
Lk 7:19 ·is·coming? Or should·we·intently·await another?
Lk 7:20 ·is·coming? Or should·we·intently·await another?

Ππ

G4329 προσ•δοκία prôsdôkía *n.* (2x)
Roots:G4328
G4329.1 N-GSF προσδοκίας (1x)
Lk 21:26 and for·apprehension·of the·things which·are·
G4329.2 N-GSF προσδοκίας (1x)
Ac 12:11 and *from* all the anticipated·evil of·the people of·

G4330 προσ•εάω prôsêáō *v.* (1x)
Roots:G4314 G1439
G4330 V-PAP-GSM προσεῶντος (1x)
Ac 27:7 us progress·forward, we·sailed·leeward·near·to

G4331 προσ•εγγίζω prôsêngízō *v.* (1x)
Roots:G4314 G1448
G4331 V-AAN προσεγγίσαι (1x)
Mk 2:4 being·able to·further·draw·near to·him on·account·of

G4332 προσ•εδρεύω prôsêdrêúō *v.* (1x)
Roots:G4314 G1476 Compare:G1247 See:G2145
G4332 V-PAP-NPM προσεδρεύοντες (1x)
1Co 9:13 the·ones sitting·alongside·and·attending to·the

G4333 προσ•εργάζομαι prôsêrgázômai *v.* (1x)
Roots:G4314 G2038 Compare:G2770 G3685
G4333.4 V-ADI-3S προσειργάσατο (1x)
Lk 19:16 'Lord, your mina actively·earned ten more·minas.

G4334 προσ•έρχομαι prôsérchômai *v.* (86x)
Roots:G4314 G2064
G4334.1 V-2AAP-NSM προσελθών (2x)
Mt 26:49 And immediately, going·toward YeShua, he·
Mk 14:45 upon·coming *and* immediately going·toward him,
G4334.2 V-2AAM-2S πρόσελθε (1x)
Ac 8:29 to·Philippe, "Go·alongside and be·tightly·joined to·
G4334.2 V-2AAP-NPM προσελθόντες (1x)
Mt 26:50 you·are·here!" Then going·alongside, they·threw
G4334.3 V-PNI-3S προσέρχεται (1x)
1Ti 6:3 does·not come·alongside having·healthy·and·sound
G4334.3 V-PNI-3P προσέρχονται (2x)
Mt 9:14 the disciples of·John came·alongside him, saying,
Mt 15:1 from JeruSalem come·alongside YeShua saying,
G4334.3 V-PNN προσέρχεσθαι (2x)
Ac 10:28 or to·come·alongside one·of·a·different·ethnic·,
Ac 24:23 ·company to·tend *to·him* or to·come·alongside him.
G4334.3 V-PNP-ASM προσερχόμενον (1x)
Heb 11:6 ·for the·one who·is·coming·alongside God to·trust
G4334.3 V-PNP-APM προσερχομένους (2x)
Heb 7:25 (the·ones who·are·coming·alongside God through
Heb 10:1 ·completely·mature the·ones coming·alongside *it*.
G4334.3 V-PNP-GSM προσερχομένου (2x)
Lk 9:42 And with·him yet coming·alongside, the demon
Ac 7:31 and with·him coming·alongside to·fully·observe *it*,
G4334.3 V-PNP-NPM προσερχόμενοι (2x)
Lk 23:36 were·mocking him, coming·alongside *him* and
1Pe 2:4 ·*is·he* to whom yeu·are·coming·alongside, the·living
G4334.3 V-PNS-1P προσερχώμεθα (2x)
Heb 4:16 we·should·be·coming·alongside with freeness·of·
Heb 10:22 we·should·come·alongside with a·true heart in
G4334.3 V-INI-3P προσήρχοντο (1x)
Ac 28:9 on the island, were·coming·alongside, and they·
G4334.3 V-2AAI-3S προσῆλθεν (7x)
Ac 12:13 by·name) came·alongside to·listen·attentively.
Ac 18:2 *And Paul* came·alongside them.
Mt 8:5 into CaperNaum, a·centurion came·alongside him,
Mt 17:14 a·certain·man·of·clay† came·alongside him,
Mt 20:20 of·the·Sons of·Zebedee came·alongside him, with
Mt 26:7 there·came·alongside him a·woman having an·
Mt 26:69 and one servant·girl came·alongside him, saying,
G4334.3 V-AAI-3P προσῆλθον (17x)
Jn 12:21 Now·then, the·same *Greeks* came·alongside Philip,
Lk 13:31 same day, there·came·alongside certain Pharisees,
Mt 4:11 behold, angels came·alongside and were·attending
Mt 5:1 ·seating himself, his disciples came·alongside him.
Mt 9:28 the home, the blind·men came·alongside him. And
Mt 13:36 And his disciples came·alongside him, saying,
Mt 14:15 occurring, his disciples came·alongside him,
Mt 15:30 And large crowds came·alongside him, having
Mt 17:24 the two·drachma *tax* came·alongside Peter and
Mt 18:1 hour, the disciples came·alongside YeShua, saying,
Mt 19:3 The Pharisees also came·alongside him, trying him
Mt 21:14 blind·men and lame·men came·alongside him in
Mt 21:23 and the elders of·the people came·alongside him,
Mt 22:23 *some* Sadducees came·alongside him, the·ones
Mt 24:1 his disciples came·alongside to·fully·exhibit for·him
Mt 24:3 of·Olives, the disciples came·alongside him in
Mt 26:17 ·Bread, the disciples came·alongside YeShua,
G4334.3 V-2AAP-GPM προσελθόντων (1x)
Mt 26:60 with·many false·witnesses coming·alongside, *still*
G4334.3 V-2AAP-NSF προσελθοῦσα (2x)
Lk 8:44 Coming·alongside *him* from·behind, she·laid·hold
Mt 9:20 years. After·coming·alongside *YeShua* from·behind,
G4334.3 V-2AAP-NSM προσελθών (21x)
Lk 7:14 And coming·alongside, he·laid·hold of·the coffin,
Lk 10:34 And coming·alongside *him*, he·bound·up his
Lk 23:52 This·man, after·coming·alongside Pilate,
Ac 9:1 after·coming·alongside the designated·high·priest
Ac 22:26 hearing *that*, coming·alongside, he·announced to·
Ac 22:27 And coming·alongside *Paul*, the regiment·
Mt 4:3 And coming·alongside him, the Tempting·One
Mt 8:19 And one scribe coming·alongside, declared to·him,
Mt 17:7 Then coming·alongside, YeShua laid·hold of·them
Mt 18:21 Then Peter, coming·alongside him, declared,
Mt 19:16 And behold, one coming·alongside him declared,
Mt 21:28 two children, and coming·alongside the first, he·
Mt 21:30 "And coming·alongside the second, he·declared
Mt 25:20 "And coming·alongside, the·one receiving the five
Mt 25:22 "And coming·alongside also, the·one receiving the
Mt 25:24 "But also coming·alongside, the·one having·
Mt 27:58 This·man, upon·coming·alongside Pilate,
Mt 28:2 out of·heaven *and* coming·alongside, rolled·away
Mt 28:18 And coming·alongside, YeShua spoke to·them,
Mk 1:31 And coming·alongside, he·awakened her, after·
Mk 12:28 of·the scribes, coming·alongside *and* having·seen
G4334.3 V-2AAP-NPF προσελθοῦσαι (1x)
Mt 28:9 ·cheer." And coming·alongside, they·securely·held
G4334.3 V-2AAP-NPM προσελθόντες (16x)
Lk 8:24 And coming·alongside *him*, they·thoroughly·
Lk 9:12 Now the twelve, coming·alongside, declared to·him
Lk 20:27 Then coming·alongside *him*, certain of·the·
Ac 23:14 ·men, after·coming·alongside the chief·priests and
Mt 8:25 And coming·alongside, his disciples awakened him,
Mt 13:10 And coming·alongside, the disciples declared to·
Mt 13:27 So after·coming·alongside, the slaves of·the
Mt 14:12 his disciples, after·coming·alongside, took·away
Mt 15:12 his disciples, after·coming·alongside, declared to·
Mt 15:23 disciples coming·alongside were·imploring·of him,
Mt 16:1 And upon·coming·alongside to·tempt *YeShua*, the
Mt 17:19 Then after·coming·alongside YeShua in private,
Mt 26:60 eventually, two false·witnesses coming·alongside,
Mt 26:73 And coming·alongside after a·little·while, the·ones
Mk 6:35 his disciples, after·coming·alongside him, say,
Mk 10:2 And upon·coming·alongside to·try him, the
G4334.3 V-2RAI-2P προσεληλύθατε (2x)
Heb 12:18 yeu·have·not come·alongside a·mountain being·
Heb 12:22 But·rather yeu·have·come·alongside Mount

G4335 προσ•ευχή prôsêuché *n.* (40x)
Roots:G4336 Compare:G1162 G0685 See:G2171
G4335.1 N-NSF προσευχή (3x)
Ac 10:31 'Cornelius, your prayer is·heard, and your
Ac 12:5 in the prison·cell. But earnest prayer over him was
Ac 16:13 beside a·river, where prayer was·accustomed to·be
G4335.1 N-NPF προσευχαί (2x)
Ac 10:4 to·him, "Your prayers and your merciful·acts
Rv 5:8 with·incense, which are the prayers of·the holy·ones.
G4335.1 N-ASF προσευχήν (1x)
Ac 16:16 it·happened with·us traversing to prayer, *that* a·
G4335.1 N-APF προσευχάς (3x)
1Pe 3:7 in·order·for yeur prayers not to·be·chopped·down.
1Pe 4:7 be·self-controlled, and be·sensible to the prayers.
1Ti 2:1 first of·all *for* petitions, prayers, intercessions, *and*
G4335.1 N-DSF προσευχῇ (11x)
Lk 6:12 ·through·the·night *continuing* in the prayer of·God.
Ac 1:14 with·the·same·determination in·the prayer and the
Ac 6:4 shall·diligently·continue in·the prayer and in·the
Mt 17:21 kind does·not depart except by prayer and fasting."
Mt 21:22 ·as yeu·may·request in the prayer while·trusting,
Mk 9:29 able to·come·forth, except by prayer and fasting."
Rm 12:12 ·enduring; in·the prayer, by·diligently·continuing;
Jac 5:17 with·us, and he·prayed in·prayer *for* it·not to·
Php 4:6 in everything (in·the prayer and in·the petition with
1Co 7:5 ·give·yeurselves to·the fasting and to·the prayer, and
Col 4:2 Diligently·continue in·the prayer, keeping·alert in it
G4335.1 N-DPF προσευχαῖς (6x)
Ac 2:42 and in·the breaking of·the bread, and in·the prayers.
Rm 15:30 to·strive·together with·me in the prayers to God
Col 4:12 on·yeur behalf in the prayers, in·order·that yeu·
1Ti 5:5 ·on in·the petitions and in·the prayers night and day.
Rv 8:3 ·that he·should·give *it* with·the prayers of·all the
Rv 8:4 *which·came* with·the prayers of·the holy·ones,
G4335.1 N-GSF προσευχῆς (6x)
Lk 19:46 "My house is a·house of·prayer," but yeu·
Lk 22:45 And after·rising·up from the prayer *and* coming to
Ac 3:1 ·Courtyard at the *afternoon* hour of·prayer, *being* the
Mt 21:13 My house shall·be·called a·house of·prayer,'' but
Mk 11:17 My house shall·be·called a·house of·prayer for·all
Eph 6:18 Through all prayer and petition, be·presently·

G4335.1 N-GPF προσευχῶν (5x)
Rm 1:10 always in my prayers. Petitioning, if·somehow
1Th 1:2 all of·yeu, making mention of·yeu in our prayers,
Eph 1:16 of·yeu, making mention of·yeu in my prayers—
Phm 1:4 God, making mention of·you always in my prayers,
Phm 1:22 yeur prayers I·shall·be·graciously·given to·yeu.
EG4335.1 (3x)
Lk 20:47 and pray lengthy *prayers* for·an·outward·showing.
Mt 23:13 and for·a·pretense are·praying lengthy *prayers*.
Mk 12:40 and for·a·pretense praying lengthy *prayers*.

G4336 προσ•εύχομαι **prôsêúchômai** *v.* (88x)
Roots:G4314 G2172 Compare:G2172 G1793 G4727 xLangEquiv:H6279 xLangAlso:H8605 H6419
G4336.1 V-FDI-1S προσεύξομαι (2x)
1Co 14:15 So·then, which is·it? I·shall·pray with·the spirit,
1Co 14:15 spirit, and I·shall·pray with·the understanding
G4336.1 V-PNI-1S προσεύχομαι (1x)
Php 1:9 And this I·pray, that yeur love may·abound yet more
G4336.1 V-PNI-1P προσευχόμεθα (1x)
2Th 1:11 For which also we·pray always concerning yeu,
G4336.1 V-PNI-3S προσεύχεται (2x)
Ac 9:11 For, behold, he·prays,
1Co 14:14 in·a·bestowed·tongue, my spirit prays, but my
G4336.1 V-PNI-3P προσεύχονται (1x)
Lk 20:47 of·the widows, and pray lengthy *prayers* for·an·
G4336.1 V-PNM-2P προσεύχεσθε (12x)
Lk 6:28 ·ones cursing yeu, and pray on·behalf of·the·ones
Heb 13:18 Pray concerning us, for we·have·confidence that
Mt 5:44 ·ones hating yeu, and pray on·behalf of·the·ones
Mt 6:9 "So·then, yeu·yeurselves pray in·this·manner: 'Our
Mt 24:20 "But pray that yeur fleeing should·not happen in·
Mt 26:41 Yeu·must·keep·alert and pray, in·order·that yeu·
Mk 13:18 "But pray that yeur fleeing should·not be in·winter
Mk 13:33 "Look·out, stay·alert and pray, for yeu·do·not
Mk 14:38 Yeu·must·keep·alert and pray, in·order·that yeu·
1Th 5:17 Pray unceasingly.
1Th 5:25 Brothers, pray concerning us.
2Th 3:1 remaining, brothers: Pray concerning us in·order·
G4336.1 V-PNM-3S προσευχέσθω (2x)
Jac 5:13 among yeu suffering·hardship? Let·him·pray. *Is*
1Co 14:13 in·a·bestowed·tongue must·pray that he·may·
G4336.1 V-PNN προσεύχεσθαι (6x)
Lk 9:29 And with him praying, the aspect of·his countenance
Lk 11:1 "Lord, instruct us to·pray, just·as John also
Lk 18:1 it·is·to·be·mandatory always to·pray and not to·be·
Mt 6:5 the corners of·the broad·streets to·pray so·that they·
1Co 11:13 ·for·a·woman to·pray to·God not·fully·veiled?
1Ti 2:8 I·resolve *for* the men to·pray in every place, lifting·
G4336.1 V-PNP-ASM προσευχόμενον (2x)
Lk 9:18 his *usual time* to·be praying alone·by·himself, *that*
Lk 11:1 as he·himself was praying in·a·certain place, *that*
G4336.1 V-PNP-GSM προσευχομένου (1x)
Lk 3:21 then with·Jesus being·immersed and praying, the
G4336.1 V-PNP-NSN προσευχόμενον (1x)
Lk 1:10 multitude of·the people were praying outside at·the
G4336.1 V-PNP-NSF προσευχομένη (1x)
1Co 11:5 But every woman who·is·praying or prophesying
G4336.1 V-PNP-NSM προσευχόμενος (5x)
Lk 5:16 ·retreating into the wildernesses and was·praying.
Ac 10:30 at·the ninth hour while·praying in my house, yet
Ac 11:5 was in *the* city *of* Joppa praying, and in a·trance I·
Mt 26:39 ·bit, he·fell on his face, praying and saying, "O·
1Co 11:4 Every man praying or prophesying, having *his*
G4336.1 V-PNP-NPM προσευχόμενοι (12x)
Ac 12:12 having·been·mustered·together and *were* praying.
Ac 16:25 and Silas, while·praying, were·singing·praise·to
Mt 6:7 "But while·yeu·are·praying, yeu·should·not talk·
Mt 23:13 and for·a·pretense are·praying lengthy *prayers*.
Mk 11:24 ·as yeu·would request as·yeu·are·praying, trust
Mk 11:25 yeu·should·stand·fast while·yeu·are·praying, if
Mk 12:40 and for·a·pretense praying lengthy *prayers*.
Jud 1:20 holy trust, *yeu* who·are·praying by Holy Spirit,
Eph 6:18 prayer and petition, be·presently·praying in Spirit
Col 1:3 Lord Jesus Anointed, praying always concerning
Col 1:9 ·heard *of·it*) do·not cease praying on·yeur behalf and
Col 4:3 at·the·same·time praying also concerning us, that
G4336.1 V-PNS-1S προσεύχωμαι (1x)
1Co 14:14 For if I·should·pray in·a·bestowed·tongue, my
G4336.1 V-PNS-2S προσεύχῃ (2x)
Mt 6:5 "And whenever you·should·pray, you·shall·not be
Mt 6:6 "But you, whenever you·should·pray, enter into your
G4336.1 V-PNS-2P προσεύχησθε (1x)
Lk 11:2 to·them, "Whenever yeu·should·pray, say, 'Our
G4336.1 V-INI-3S προσηύχετο (5x)
Lk 18:11 ·being·settled, was·praying these·things toward
Lk 22:41 a·stone's cast, and bowing the knees, he·prayed,
Lk 22:44 ·strenuous·agony, he·was·praying more·earnestly.
Mk 1:35 into a·desolate place, and he·was·praying there.
Mk 14:35 ·bit, he·fell on the soil and prayed that, if·it·were
G4336.1 V-ADI-1P προσηυξάμεθα (1x)
Ac 21:5 And bowing the knees on the shore, we·prayed.
G4336.1 V-ADI-3S προσηύξατο (7x)
Ac 9:40 bowing his knees, he·prayed. And turning·back·
Ac 20:36 bowing the knees, he·prayed together with·them
Mt 26:42 a·second·time, after·going·off, he·prayed, saying,
Mt 26:44 them, going·off again, he·prayed for·a·third·time,
Mk 14:39 again, after·going·off, he·prayed, declaring the
Jac 5:17 ·like·passions with·us, and he·prayed in·prayer *for*
Jac 5:18 And he·prayed again, and the sky gave rain, and the
G4336.1 V-ADI-3P προσηύξαντο (1x)
Ac 8:15 who, after·walking·down, prayed concerning them,
G4336.1 V-ADM-2S πρόσευξαι (1x)
Mt 6:6 and after·shutting your door, pray to·your Father,
G4336.1 V-ADM-3P προσευξάσθωσαν (1x)
Jac 5:14 Called·Out·citizenry, and let·them·pray over him,
G4336.1 V-ADN προσεύξασθαι (6x)
Lk 6:12 he·went·forth to the mountain to·pray, and he·was
Lk 9:28 Jakob, he·walked·up upon the mountain to·pray.
Lk 18:10 walked·up to the Sanctuary·Atrium to·pray, the one
Ac 10:9 walked·up upon the rooftop to·pray *at·midday* about
Mt 14:23 the mountain in private to·pray, and with·early·
Mk 6:46 ·of them, he·went·off to the mountain to·pray.
G4336.1 V-ADP-NSM προσευξάμενος (1x)
Ac 28:8 ·in alongside him, and after·praying *and* laying his
G4336.1 V-ADP-NPM προσευξάμενοι (4x)
Ac 1:24 And praying, they·declared, "You, O·Lord,
Ac 6:6 ·the ambassadors, and after·praying, they·laid·forth
Ac 13:3 Then after·fasting and praying, and after·laying·
Ac 14:23 Called·Out·citizenry, after·praying with fasting,
G4336.1 V-ADS-1S προσεύξωμαι (2x)
Mt 26:36 where going·aside, I·should·pray *over* there."
Mk 14:32 "Yeu·sit·down here, until I·should·pray."
G4336.1 V-ADS-1P προσευξώμεθα (1x)
Rm 8:26 what we·should·pray·for according·to·what is·
G4336.1 V-ADS-3S προσεύξηται (1x)
Mt 19:13 ·lay his hands on them and pray. And the disciples
EG4336.1 (1x)
Phm 1:6 *praying* that the fellowship of·your trust may·
G4336.2 V-PNM-2P προσεύχεσθε (2x)
Lk 22:40 ·declared to·them, "Be·in·prayer *in·order·for yeu*
Lk 22:46 yeu·sleep? Rising·up, be·in·prayer, in·order·that
G4336.2 V-PNP-GSM προσευχομένου (1x)
Ac 22:17 to JeruSalem, even with·me being·in·prayer in the

G4337 προσ•έχω **prôséchō** *v.* (25x)
Roots:G4314 G2192 Compare:G1896 G5219 G1907 See:G3563
G4337.1 V-PAM-2S πρόσεχε (1x)
1Ti 4:13 Until I·come, give·attention to·the reading·aloud
G4337.1 V-RAI-3S προσέσχηκεν (1x)
Heb 7:13 which not·even·one·man has·given·attention at·the
G4337.2 V-PAM-2P προσέχετε (5x)
Lk 12:1 "First·of·all, beware among·yeurselves of·the
Lk 20:46 "Beware of·the scribes, the·ones delighting to·
Mt 7:15 "And beware of·the false·prophets, who·do·come to
Mt 10:17 But beware of·the men·of·clay†, for they·shall·
Mt 16:6 "Clearly·see·to·it also *that* yeu·beware of·the leaven
G4337.2 V-PAN προσέχειν (2x)
Mt 16:11 not concerning bread, *but·rather* to·beware of·the
Mt 16:12 that he·did·not declare *to·them* to·beware of·the
G4337.3 V-PAM-2P προσέχετε (5x)
Lk 17:3 Take·heed to·yeurselves. "But if your brother
Lk 21:34 "And take·heed to·yeurselves, lest·at·any·time yeur
Ac 5:35 "Men, Israelites, take·heed to·yeurselves what yeu·
Ac 20:28 "So·then take·heed to·yeurselves, and to·the entire
Mt 6:1 "Take·heed not to·do yeur merciful·act before the
G4337.3 V-PAN προσέχειν (3x)
Ac 16:14 her heart to·give·heed to·the·things being·spoken
Heb 2:1 more·abundantly to·give·heed to·the·things being·
1Ti 1:4 nor·even to·give·heed to·myths and to·endless
G4337.3 V-PAP-APM προσέχοντας (1x)
1Ti 3:8 ambiguous·of·word, not giving·heed to·much wine,
G4337.3 V-PAP-NPM προσέχοντες (3x)
2Pe 1:19 to·which yeu·do well taking·heed as to·a·lantern
Tit 1:14 not giving·heed to·Jewish myths and
1Ti 4:1 ·from the trust, giving·heed to·impostrous spirits
G4337.3 V-IAI-3P προσεῖχον (3x)
Ac 8:6 were·giving·heed to·the·things being·said by
Ac 8:10 to·this they·all were·giving·heed, from *the* least unto
Ac 8:11 And to·him they·were·giving·heed, on·account·of
EG4337.3 (1x)
Rm 11:21 *take·heed* lest·perhaps he·should·not·even spare

G4338 προσ•ηλόω **prôsēlóō** *v.* (1x)
Roots:G4314 G2247-1 Compare:G4362 G1574 G4078 G1335-2 G2520-1 xLangAlso:H8628
G4338.2 V-AAP-NSM προσηλώσας (1x)
Col 2:14 of·the midst *of·us*, already·firmly·nailing it to·the

G4339 προσ•ήλυτος **prôsēlytôs** *n.* (4x)
Roots:G4334 xLangAlso:H1616
G4339.2 N-NPM προσήλυτοι (1x)
Ac 2:10 ·from Rome, also Jews and converts·to·Judaism,
G4339.2 N-ASM προσήλυτον (2x)
Ac 6:5 and NicoLaos, a·convert·to·Judaism of·Antioch;
Mt 23:15 ·ground to·make one convert·to·Judaism, and
G4339.2 N-GPM προσηλύτων (1x)
Ac 13:43 who·are·being·reverent converts·to·Judaism Paul

G4340 πρόσ•καιρος **prôskairôs** *adj.* (4x)
Roots:G4314 G2540
G4340.1 A-NSM πρόσκαιρος (1x)
Mt 13:21 in himself, but·rather he·is just·for·a·season, and
G4340.1 A-NPM πρόσκαιροι (1x)
Mk 4:17 but·rather they·are just·for·a·season. Afterward,
G4340.1 A-NPN πρόσκαιρα (1x)
2Co 4:18 being·looked·upon *are* just·for·a·season, but the·
G4340.1 A-ASF πρόσκαιρον (1x)
Heb 11:25 full·enjoyment of·moral·failure just·for·a·season,

G4341 προσ•καλέομαι **prôskaléômai** *v.* (30x)
Roots:G4314 G2564 Compare:G3333 G1573-1 G4779 G4867
G4341.2 V-PNI-3S προσκαλεῖται (1x)
Mk 3:13 the mountain, and he·summons those·whom he
G4341.2 V-PNI-3S@ προσκαλεῖται (1x)
Mk 6:7 Then he·summoned the twelve, and he·began to·
G4341.2 V-ADM-3S προσκαλεσάσθω (1x)
Jac 5:14 sick among yeu? Let·him·summon the elders of·the
G4341.2 V-ADP-NSM προσκαλεσάμενος (22x)
Lk 7:19 And John, summoning a·certain two of·his disciples
Lk 15:26 And summoning one of·his servant·boys, he·
Lk 16:5 "And summoning each one of·his lord's needy·
Lk 18:16 But Jesus, summoning them, declared, "Allow the
Ac 13:7 man. This·man, summoning for·BarNabas and Saul
Ac 20:1 ceased, Paul, after·summoning the disciples and
Ac 23:17 So after·summoning one of·the centurions, Paul
Ac 23:18 and replied, "After·summoning me, Paul, the
Ac 23:23 And summoning a·certain two of·the centurions,
Mt 10:1 And summoning his twelve disciples, he·gave to·
Mt 15:10 And upon·summoning the crowd, he·declared to·
Mt 15:32 And after·summoning his disciples, YeShua
Mt 18:2 And YeShua, summoning a·little·child, set him in
Mt 18:32 Then after·summoning him, his lord says to·him,

Mt 20:25 But YeShua, upon·summoning them, declared,
Mk 3:23 And after·summoning them, he·was·saying to·them
Mk 7:14 And upon·summoning all the crowd, he·was·saying
Mk 8:1 they·may·eat), after·summoning his disciples, Jesus
Mk 8:34 And after·summoning the crowd *to·him* along·with
Mk 10:42 But Jesus, upon·summoning them, says to·them,
Mk 12:43 And summoning his disciples, he·says to·them,
Mk 15:44 ·has·died. And summoning the Roman·centurion,

G4341.2 V-ADP-NPM προσκαλεσάμενοι (2x)
Ac 5:40 by·him. And after·summoning the ambassadors *and*
Ac 6:2 But the twelve, after·summoning the multitude of·the

G4341.2 V-RNI-1S προσκέκλημαι (1x)
Ac 13:2 for the work to·which I·have·summoned them."

G4341.2 V-RNI-3S προσκέκληται (1x)
Ac 16:10 Lord has·summoned us to·proclaim·the·good·news

G4341.3 V-ADS-3S προσκαλέσηται (1x)
Ac 2:39 ·as Yahweh our God would call·forth·unto·himself."

G4342 προσ•καρτερέω prôskartêrĕō *v.* (10x)
Roots:G4314 G2594

G4342.2 V-FAI-1P προσκαρτερήσομεν (1x)
Ac 6:4 we·ourselves shall·diligently·continue in·the prayer

G4342.2 V-PAM-2P προσκαρτερεῖτε (1x)
Col 4:2 Diligently·continue in·the prayer, keeping·alert in it

G4342.2 V-PAP-NSM προσκαρτερῶν (1x)
Ac 8:13 he·was diligently·continuing·on with·Philippe. *And*

G4342.2 V-PAP-NPM προσκαρτεροῦντες (5x)
Ac 1:14 all were diligently·continuing with·the·same· in·the
Ac 2:42 they·were diligently·continuing in·the instruction
Ac 2:46 both while·diligently·continuing with·the·same· in
Rm 12:12 in·the prayer, by·diligently·continuing;
Rm 13:6 God's public·servants, diligently·continuing in this

G4342.3 V-PAP-GPM προσκαρτερούντων (1x)
Ac 10:7 soldier of·the·ones diligently·attending to·him,

G4342.3 V-PAS-3S προσκαρτερῇ (1x)
Mk 3:9 that a·small·boat should·diligently·attend to·him on·

G4343 προσ•καρτέρησις prôskartérēsis *n.* (1x)
Roots:G4342 Compare:G3115 G4710 G5281

G4343 N-DSF προσκαρτερήσει (1x)
Eph 6:18 ·staying·alert with all perseverance— even with·

G4344 προσ•κεφάλαιον prôskêphálaiôn *n.* (1x)
Roots:G4314 G2776

G4344 N-ASN προσκεφάλαιον (1x)
Mk 4:38 ·boat, sleeping on the pillow. And they·thoroughly·

G4345 προσ•κληρόω prôsklērŏō *v.* (1x)
Roots:G4314 G2820 Compare:G2853 G4820

G4345.3 V-API-3P προσεκληρώθησαν (1x)
Ac 17:4 were·convinced and joined·alongside with·Paul and

G4346 πρόσ•κλισις prósklisis *n.* (1x)
Roots:G4314 G2827

G4346.2 N-ASF πρόσκλισιν (1x)
1Ti 5:21 doing not·even·one·thing according·to favoritism.

G4347 προσ•κολλάω prôskôllá̄ō *v.* (4x)
Roots:G4314 G2853 xLangAlso:H1695

G4347.2 V-FPI-3S προσκολληθήσεται (3x)
Mt 19:5 the mother and shall·be·tightly·bonded to·his wife,
Mk 10:7 and mother, and shall·be·tightly·bonded to his wife
Eph 5:31 and mother, and shall·be·tightly·bonded to his

G4347.2 V-API-3S προσεκολλήθη (1x)
Ac 5:36 a·number of·men tightly·bonded·themselves, about

G4348 πρόσ•κομμα prŏskômma *n.* (6x)
Roots:G4350 Compare:G4625 See:G4349
xLangEquiv:H5063

G4348.2 N-GSN προσκόμματος (3x)
Rm 9:32 For they·stumbled at·the stumbling stone,
Rm 9:33 in Tsiyon a·stone of·stumbling and a·solid·rock of·
1Pe 2:8 and "'a·stone of·stumbling and a·solid·rock of·

G4348.3 N-NSN πρόσκομμα (1x)
1Co 8:9 ·yeurs should·become a·stumbling·block to·the·ones

G4348.3 N-ASN πρόσκομμα (1x)
Rm 14:13 *purpose* not to·place a·stumbling·block or a·trap

G4348.3 N-GSN προσκόμματος (1x)
Rm 14:20 for·the·one *being* a·stumbling·block *to·his brother*

G4349 προσ•κοπή prôskôpḗ *n.* (1x)
Roots:G4350 Compare:G4625 See:G4348 G0677

G4349.1 N-ASF προσκοπήν (1x)
2Co 6:3 not·one·bit·of an·instance·of·stumbling in not·even·

G4350 προσ•κόπτω prôskóptō *v.* (8x)
Roots:G4314 G2875 Compare:G4624

G4350.2 V-AAI-3P προσέκοψαν (1x)
Mt 7:27 the winds blew, and they·surged·against that home,

G4350.3 V-AAS-2S προσκόψῃς (2x)
Lk 4:11 palms, lest·at·any·time you·should·stub your foot
Mt 4:6 palms, lest·at·any·time you·should·stub your foot

G4350.4 V-PAI-3S προσκόπτει (3x)
Jn 11:9 the daylight, he·does·not stumble, because he·looks·
Jn 11:10 ·walk·along in the night, he·stumbles, because the
Rm 14:21 by which your brother stumbles, or is·enticed, or

G4350.4 V-PAI-3P προσκόπτουσιν (1x)
1Pe 2:8 they·who presently·stumble at·the Redemptive-word,

G4350.4 V-AAI-3P προσέκοψαν (1x)
Rm 9:32 of·Torah-Law. For they·stumbled at·the stumbling

G4351 προσ•κυλίω prôskylíō *v.* (2x)
Roots:G4314 G2947

G4351 V-AAI-3S προσεκύλισεν (1x)
Mk 15:46 out of·solid·rock, and he·rolled a·stone over the

G4351 V-AAP-NSM προσκυλίσας (1x)
Mt 27:60 in the solid·rock, and after·rolling a·great stone to·

G4352 προσ•κυνέω prôskynéō *v.* (60x)
Roots:G2952-1 G4314 Compare:G4576 G2151
G2125 See:G4353
xLangEquiv:H7812 xLangAlso:H5456 A5457

G4352.2 V-FAI-2S προσκυνήσεις (2x)
Lk 4:8 "'You·shall·fall·prostrate *directly·before* Yahweh
Mt 4:10 "'You·shall·fall·prostrate *directly·before* Yahweh

G4352.2 V-FAI-2P προσκυνήσετε (1x)
Jn 4:21 in JeruSalem, shall·yeu·fall·prostrate to·the Father.

G4352.2 V-FAI-3S προσκυνήσει (1x)
1Co 14:25 ·down on *his* face, he·shall·fall·prostrate to·God,

G4352.2 V-FAI-3P προσκυνήσουσιν (3x)
Jn 4:23 true ones·that·fall·prostrate shall·fall·prostrate to·the
Rv 13:8 residing upon the earth shall·fall·prostrate to·it,
Rv 15:4 ·come and shall·fall·prostrate in·the·sight of·you,"

G4352.2 V-FAP-NSM προσκυνήσων (2x)
Ac 8:27 *and* who had·come to JeruSalem to·fall·prostrate.
Ac 24:11 since I·walked·up to JeruSalem to·fall·prostrate.

G4352.2 V-PAI-1P προσκυνοῦμεν (1x)
Jn 4:22 ·*before* whom we·ourselves fall·prostrate, because

G4352.2 V-PAI-2P προσκυνεῖτε (1x)
Jn 4:22 Yeu·yeurselves fall·prostrate *directly·before* whom

G4352.2 V-PAI-3S προσκυνεῖ (1x)
Rv 14:9 voice, "If any·man falls·prostrate *directly·before* the

G4352.2 V-PAI-3P προσκυνοῦσιν (1x)
Rv 4:10 the throne, and they·fall·prostrate to·the·one living

G4352.2 V-PAN προσκυνεῖν (3x)
Jn 4:20 is the place where it·is·mandatory to·fall·prostrate."
Jn 4:24 *directly·before* him to·fall·prostrate in spirit and in·
Ac 7:43 which yeu·made *in·order* to·fall·prostrate to·them.

G4352.2 V-PAP-APM προσκυνοῦντας (5x)
Jn 4:23 such·as·these falling·prostrate *directly·before* him.
Jn 4:24 ·for the·ones falling·prostrate *directly·before* him to·
Rv 11:1 Sacrifice·Altar, and the·ones falling·prostrate in it.
Rv 16:2 *upon* the·ones falling·prostrate to·its derived·image.
Rv 19:20 and the·ones falling·prostrate to·its derived·image

G4352.2 V-PAP-NSF προσκυνοῦσα (1x)
Mt 20:20 *John), and she·was* falling·prostrate *to·him* and

G4352.2 V-PAP-NPM προσκυνοῦντες (1x)
Rv 14:11 and the·ones falling·prostrate *directly·before* the

G4352.2 V-IAI-3S προσεκύνει (4x)
Mt 8:2 ·coming *toward·him*, was·falling·prostrate to·him,
Mt 9:18 ·coming *to·YeShua*, was·falling·prostrate to·him,
Mt 15:25 coming *anyway*, she·was·falling·prostrate to·him,
Mt 18:26 ·down, the slave was·falling·prostrate to·him,

G4352.2 V-IAI-3P προσεκύνουν (1x)
Mk 15:19 their knees, they·were·falling·prostrate to·him.

G4352.2 V-AAI-3S προσεκύνησεν (3x)
Jn 9:38 And he·fell·prostrate to·him.
Ac 10:25 *And* falling at his feet, he·fell·prostrate *to·him.*
Mk 5:6 from a·distance, he·ran and fell·prostrate to·him.

G4352.2 V-AAI-3P προσεκύνησαν (12x)
Jn 4:20 Our fathers fell·prostrate on this mountain; and yeu
Mt 2:11 And falling·down, they·fell·prostrate to·him. Then
Mt 14:33 after·coming *alongside*, fell·prostrate to·him,
Mt 28:9 they·securely·held his feet and fell·prostrate to·him.
Mt 28:17 And upon·seeing him, they·fell·prostrate to·him,
Rv 5:14 fell·down and fell·prostrate to·the·one·living into
Rv 7:11 ·sight of·the throne. And they·fell·prostrate to·God,
Rv 11:16 fell upon their faces, and fell·prostrate to·God,
Rv 13:4 And they·fell·prostrate *directly·before* the Dragon
Rv 13:4 ·Beast, and they·fell·prostrate *directly·before* the
Rv 19:4 living·beings fell·down and fell·prostrate to·God,
Rv 20:4 ·who did·not fall·prostrate to·the Daemonic·Beast nor

G4352.2 V-AAM-2S προσκύνησον (2x)
Rv 19:10 the testimony of·Jesus. Fall·prostrate to·God, for
Rv 22:9 words of·this official·scroll. Fall·prostrate to·God."

G4352.2 V-AAM-2P προσκυνήσατε (1x)
Rv 14:7 did·come! And fall·prostrate to·the·one ·having·

G4352.2 V-AAM-3P προσκυνησάτωσαν (1x)
Heb 1:6 he·says, "' And fall·prostrate to·him, all angels of·

G4352.2 V-AAN προσκυνῆσαι (3x)
Mt 2:2 in the east, and we·came to·fall·prostrate to·him."
Rv 19:10 I·fell before his feet to·fall·prostrate to·him. And
Rv 22:8 and looked, I·fell·down to·fall·prostrate before the

G4352.2 V-AAP-NPM προσκυνήσαντες (1x)
Lk 24:52 after·falling·prostrate *directly·before* him,

G4352.2 V-AAS-1S προσκυνήσω (1x)
Mt 2:8 that upon·coming, I·also may·fall·prostrate to·him."

G4352.2 V-AAS-2S προσκυνήσῃς (2x)
Lk 4:7 if you should·fall·prostrate in·the·sight of·me, all
Mt 4:9 upon·falling·down, you·should·fall·prostrate to·me."

G4352.2 V-AAS-3P προσκυνήσωσιν (5x)
Jn 12:20 ·up in·order·that they·may·fall·prostrate at the
Rv 3:9 ·come and should·fall·prostrate in·the·sight of·your
Rv 9:20 that they·should·not fall·prostrate *directly·before* the
Rv 13:12 that they·should·fall·prostrate *directly·before* the
Rv 13:15 ·as would not fall·prostrate to·the derived·image

G4352.3 V-AAI-3S προσεκύνησεν (1x)
Heb 11:21 Sons of·Joseph, and he·leaned·prostrate upon the

G4353 προσ•κυνητής prôskynētḗs *n.* (1x)
Roots:G4352

G4353 N-NPM προσκυνηταί (1x)
Jn 4:23 true ones·that·fall·prostrate shall·fall·prostrate to·the

G4354 προσ•λαλέω prôslaléō *v.* (2x)
Roots:G4314 G2980

G4354.2 V-PAP-NPM προσλαλοῦντες (1x)
Ac 13:43 BarNabas, who, speaking·alongside with·them,

G4354.2 V-AAN προσλαλῆσαι (1x)
Ac 28:20 to·see *yeu* and to·speak·alongside *with·yeu*, for *it*·

G4355 προσ•λαμβάνω prôslambánō *v.* (14x)
Roots:G4314 G2983 Compare:G3880 G3858

G4355.2 V-2AMI-3P προσελάβοντο (1x)
Ac 18:26 Aquila and Little·Prisca purposely·took him and

G4355.2 V-2AMP-NSM προσλαβόμενος (2x)
Mt 16:22 And Peter, purposely·taking him *aside*, began to·
Mk 8:32 ·clarity·of·speech. And purposely·taking him *aside*

G4355.2 V-2AMP-NPM προσλαβόμενοι (1x)
Ac 17:5 even purposely·taking·to·themselves certain evil

G4355.3 V-2AMI-3S προσελάβετο (2x)
Rm 14:3 the·one eating, for God purposely·received him.
Rm 15:7 also the Anointed-One purposely·received us into

G4355.3 V-2AMM-2S προσλαβοῦ (2x)
Phm 1:12 *to·you.* So you·yourself purposely·receive him,
Phm 1:17 ·hold me *to·be* a·partner, purposely·receive him as

G4355.4 V-2AAN προσλαβεῖν (1x)
Ac 27:34 I·implore yeu to·each·take *some* nourishment, for

G4355.4 V-2AMI-3P προσελάβοντο (1x)
Ac 27:36 ·outlook, and they·each·took nourishment.

G4355.4 V-2AMP-NPM προσλαβόμενοι (1x)

Ac 27:33 ·of·food, each·taking·to·yeurselves not·one·thing.
G4355.5 V-PMM-2P προσλαμβάνεσθε (2x)
Rm 14:1 Now yeu·each·must·receive the·one being·weak in·
Rm 15:7 Therefore yeu·must·each·receive one·another, just·
G4355.5 V-2AMI-3P προσελάβοντο (1x)
Ac 28:2 kindling a·fire, they·each·received everyone of·us,

G4356 πρόσ•ληψις prôslēpsis *n.* (1x)
Roots:G4355 Compare:G0594
G4356 N-NSF πρόσληψις (1x)
Rm 11:15 what *shall* the personal·reception *of·them be,*

G4357 προσ•μένω prôsmĕnō *v.* (6x)
Roots:G4314 G3306
G4357.1 V-PAI-3S προσμένει (1x)
1Ti 5:5 upon God, and continues·on in·the petitions and in·
G4357.1 V-PAI-3P προσμένουσιν (2x)
Mt 15:32 because even·now they·continue·on with·me *for*
Mk 8:2 because even·now they·continue·on with·me *for*
G4357.1 V-PAN προσμένειν (1x)
Ac 11:23 ·purpose of·heart to·continue·on with·the Lord,
G4357.1 V-AAN προσμεῖναι (1x)
1Ti 1:3 Just·as I·implored you to·continue·on at Ephesus
G4357.1 V-AAP-NSM προσμείνας (1x)
Ac 18:18 And Paul, still continuing·on *there* a·sufficient

G4358 προσ•ορμίζω prôsôrmízō *v.* (1x)
Roots:G4314 G3730 Compare:G1831
G4358.2 V-API-3P προσωρμίσθησαν (1x)
Mk 6:53 ·came to the land of·Gennesaret and landed·ashore.

G4359 προσ•οφείλω prôsôphĕílō *v.* (1x)
Roots:G4314 G3784
G4359.2 V-PAI-2S προσοφείλεις (1x)
Phm 1:19 even you·yourself are·particularly·indebted to·me.

G4360 προσ•οχθίζω prôsôchthízō *v.* (2x)
Roots:G4314 Compare:G1848 G3949 See:G4360-1
xLangAlso:H6962 H6973 H1602 H8262 H3988
G4360.1 V-AAI-1S προσώχθισα (1x)
Heb 3:10 I·was·specifically·vexed with·that generation and
G4360.1 V-AAI-3S προσώχθισεν (1x)
Heb 3:17 with·whom was·he·specifically·vexed forty years?

G4361 πρόσ•πεινος prôspĕinôs *adj.* (1x)
Roots:G4314 G3983 xLangAlso:H7457
G4361.2 A-NSM πρόσπεινος (1x)
Ac 10:10 And he·became intensely·hungry and was·wanting

G4362 προσ•πήγνυμι prôspḗgnymi *v.* (1x)
Roots:G4314 G4078 Compare:G4717 G4338
G4362.2 V-AAP-NPM προσπήξαντες (1x)
Ac 2:23 hands. *And* after·directly·pegging *him to·a·cross,*

G4363 προσ•πίπτω prôspíptō *v.* (8x)
Roots:G4314 G4098
G4363.2 V-IAI-3S προσέπιπτεν (1x)
Mk 3:11 him, it·was·falling·down·before him and was·
G4363.2 V-2AAI-3S προσέπεσεν (5x)
Lk 5:8 after·seeing *it,* Simon Peter fell·down·at Jesus' knees,
Lk 8:28 and·then screaming·out, he·fell·down·before him,
Ac 16:29 ·with·trembling, he·fell·down·before Paul and
Mk 5:33 her, came and fell·down·before him and declared
Mk 7:25 spirit, upon·coming, she·fell·down toward his feet.
G4363.2 V-2AAP-NSF προσπεσοῦσα (1x)
Lk 8:47 came trembling; and falling·down·before him, she·
G4363.3 V-2AAI-3P προσέπεσον (1x)
Mt 7:25 winds blew, and they·fell·directly·against that home

G4364 προσ•ποιέομαι prôspôiĕómai *v.* (1x)
Roots:G4314 G4160 Compare:G5271
G4364.2 V-IMI-3S προσεποιεῖτο (1x)
Lk 24:28 and he·himself made·as·though he·would·traverse

G4365 προσ•πορεύομαι prôspôrĕúômai *v.* (1x)
Roots:G4314 G4198 Compare:G4313
G4365.2 V-PNI-3P προσπορεύονται (1x)
Mk 10:35 the Sons of·Zebedee, approach·close to·him,

G4366 προσ•ρήγνυμι prôsrḗgnymi *v.* (2x)
Roots:G4314 G4486 See:G2608
G4366.2 V-AAI-3S προσέρρηξεν (2x)
Lk 6:48 the stream burst·directly·against that home, but
Lk 6:49 earth, which the stream burst·directly·against, and

G4367 προσ•τάσσω prôstássō *v.* (8x)
Roots:G4314 G5021 Compare:G2004 G2753
See:G1299
EG4367 (1x)
Lk 3:23 And upon·beginning *his specific·assignment,* Jesus
G4367.2 V-AAI-3S προσέταξεν (6x)
Lk 5:14 purification, just·as Moses specifically·assigned, for
Ac 10:48 And he·specifically·assigned for·them to·be·
Mt 1:24 as the angel of·Yahweh specifically·assigned him,
Mt 8:4 the present that Moses specifically·assigned, for a·
Mt 21:6 doing just·as YeShua specifically·assigned to·them,
Mk 1:44 those·things·which Moses specifically·assigned, for
G4367.2 V-RPP-APN προστεταγμένα (1x)
Ac 10:33 the·things having·been·specifically·assigned to· by

G4368 προ•στάτις prôstátis *n.* (1x)
Roots:G4291 xLangAlso:H5833
G4368 N-NSF προστάτις (1x)
Rm 16:2 for she·herself did·become a·patroness of·many,

G4369 προσ•τίθημι prôstíthēmi *v.* (20x)
Roots:G4314 G5087 Compare:G0837 G4052 G4121
xLangAlso:H3254
EG4369 (1x)
Rv 11:2 the courtyard, the·one *proceeding* inwardly *toward*
EG4369.- (1x)
Rv 11:2 the·one *proceeding* inwardly *toward* the Temple,
G4369.2 V-IAI-3S προσετίθει (1x)
Ac 2:47 And the Lord was·placing the·ones being·saved
G4369.2 V-IPI-3P προσετίθεντο (1x)
Ac 5:14 even·more were·being·placed·alongside *the Called·*
G4369.2 V-API-3S προσετέθη (2x)
Ac 11:24 an·ample crowd was·placed·alongside the Lord.
Gal 3:19 *Torah-Law* was·placed·alongside *the promise*
G4369.2 V-API-3P προσετέθησαν (1x)
Ac 2:41 three·thousand souls were·placed·alongside *them.*
G4369.3 V-FPI-3S προστεθήσεται (2x)
Lk 12:31 of·God, and all these·things shall·be·added to·yeu.
Mt 6:33 and all these·things shall·be·added to·yeu.
G4369.3 V-AAI-3S προσέθηκεν (1x)
Lk 3:20 he·added even this upon all·*these*·things— that he·
G4369.3 V-2AAM-2S πρόσθες (1x)
Lk 17:5 declared to·the Lord, "Add trust to·us."
G4369.3 V-2AAN προσθεῖναι (2x)
Lk 12:25 yeu by·being·anxious is·able to·add one half·step
Mt 6:27 yeu by·being·anxious is·able to·add one half·step to
G4369.4 V-FPI-3S προστεθήσεται (1x)
Mk 4:24 ·with·comprehension, it·shall·be·augmented.
G4369.4 V-2AAP-NSM προσθείς (1x)
Lk 19:11 with·them hearing these·things, augmenting *it,*
G4369.5 V-2AMI-3S προσέθετο (3x)
Lk 20:11 And he·further·proceeded to·send another slave.
Lk 20:12 And he·further·proceeded to·send a·third. But also
Ac 12:3 to·the Judeans, he·further·proceeded to·arrest Peter
G4369.6 V-APN προστεθῆναι (1x)
Heb 12:19 *for* a·word not to·be·further *spoken* to·them.
G4369.7 V-API-3S προσετέθη (1x)
Ac 13:36 was·laid·to·rest, and was·laid alongside his

G4370 προσ•τρέχω prôstrĕchō *v.* (3x)
Roots:G4314 G5143
G4370.1 V-PAP-NPM προστρέχοντες (1x)
Mk 9:15 were·utterly·amazed, and running·toward *him,*
G4370.1 V-2AAP-NSM προσδραμών (1x)
Ac 8:30 And running·toward *him,* Philippe heard him
G4370.2 V-2AAP-NSM προσδραμών (1x)
Mk 10:17 after·running·forward and kneeling·down·to him,

G4371 προσ•φάγιον prôsphágiôn *n.* (1x)
Roots:G4314 G5315 Compare:G3795
G4371.1 N-ASN προσφάγιον (1x)
Jn 21:5 ¿! do·yeu·have anything for·eating?" They·

G4372 πρό•σφατος prôsphatôs *adj.* (1x)
Roots:G4253 G4969 See:G4373
G4372.2 A-ASF πρόσφατον (1x)
Heb 10:20 (a·freshly·carved and living way which he·

G4373 προ•σφάτως prôsphátōs *adv.* (1x)
Roots:G4372
G4373 ADV προσφάτως (1x)
Ac 18:2 (of·Pontus by·birth, recently having·come from

G4374 προσ•φέρω prôsphĕrō *v.* (49x)
Roots:G4314 G5342
G4374.1 V-PAP-DPM προσφέρουσιν (1x)
Mk 10:13 were·reprimanding the·ones bringing *them.*
G4374.1 V-PAS-2S προσφέρῃς (1x)
Mt 5:23 "So·then, if you·should·bring your present to the
G4374.1 V-PAS-3P προσφέρωσιν (1x)
Lk 12:11 "And whenever they·should·bring yeu before the
G4374.1 V-IAI-3P προσέφερον (3x)
Lk 18:15 Now they·were also bringing the babies to·him in·
Mt 9:2 behold, they·were·bringing to·him a·paralyzed·man
Mk 10:13 And they·were·bringing little·children to·him, that
G4374.1 V-AAI-1S προσήνεγκα (1x)
Mt 17:16 And I·brought him to·your disciples, and they·
G4374.1 V-AAI-2P προσηνέγκατε (1x)
Lk 23:14 to them, "Yeu·brought this man·of·clay† to·me as
G4374.1 V-AAI-3S προσήνεγκεν (1x)
Mt 25:20 the five talants·of·silver brought another five
G4374.1 V-AAI-3P προσήνεγκαν (7x)
Jn 19:29 and putting·it·on hyssop, brought *it* to·his mouth.
Mt 2:11 their treasures, they·brought·forth to·him presents:
Mt 4:24 into all Syria. And they·brought to·him all the·ones
Mt 8:16 ·evening occurring, they·brought to·him many
Mt 9:32 behold, *men* brought to·him a·certain·man·of·clay†,
Mt 14:35 all that surrounding·region and brought to·him all
Mt 22:19 ·tribute." And they·brought to·him a·denarius.
G4374.1 V-API-3S προσηνέχθη (3x)
Mt 12:22 one·being·possessed·with·a·demon was·brought,
Mt 18:24 beginning to·tally·up, there·was·brought to·him,
Mt 19:13 little·children were·brought to·him in·order·that
EG4374.1 (1x)
1Th 3:6 yeu to·us, *he·brings tidings* even with·he·himself·
G4374.2 V-PAI-3S προσφέρει (1x)
Heb 9:7 ·from blood, which he·offered on·behalf of·himself,
G4374.2 V-PAI-3P προσφέρουσιν (1x)
Heb 10:1 same sacrifices (which they·offer each year into
G4374.2 V-PAM-2S πρόσφερε (1x)
Mt 5:24 ·your brother, and then coming, offer your present.
G4374.2 V-PAN προσφέρειν (3x)
Jn 16:2 yeu might·presume to·offer a·ritual·ministry to·God.
Heb 5:3 , he·is·obligated to·offer *sacrifices* on·behalf of·
Heb 8:3 high·priest is·fully·established to·offer both presents
G4374.2 V-PAP-GPM προσφερόντων (1x)
Heb 8:4 ·that·offer·sacrifices, the·ones offering the presents
G4374.2 V-PAP-NSM προσφέρων (1x)
Heb 10:11 day publicly·serving and offering many·times the
G4374.2 V-PAP-NPM προσφέροντες (1x)
Lk 23:36 ·alongside *him* and offering wine·vinegar to·him
G4374.2 V-PAS-3S προσφέρῃ (2x)
Heb 5:1 ·to God, in·order·that he·may·offer both presents
Heb 9:25 in·order·that he·should·offer himself many·times,
G4374.2 V-PPI-3P προσφέρονται (2x)
Heb 9:9 both presents and sacrifices were·offered, not being·
Heb 10:8 ·*them*⁼ (which·things are·offered according·to the
G4374.2 V-PPP-NPF προσφερόμεναι (1x)
Heb 10:2 not have·ceased being·offered through the·ones
G4374.2 V-IAI-3S προσέφερεν (1x)
Heb 11:17 the promises was·offering·up his only·begotten
G4374.2 V-AAI-2P προσηνέγκατε (1x)
Ac 7:42 O·house of·IsraEl, ¿! did·yeu·offer to·me sacrifices
G4374.2 V-AAI-3S προσήνεγκεν (3x)
Ac 8:18 ·the ambassadors' hands, he·offered them valuables,
Heb 9:14 *the* eternal Spirit offered himself without·blemish
Heb 11:4 By·trust, Abel offered to·God a·much·better
G4374.2 V-2AAM-2S προσένεγκε (3x)
Lk 5:14 priest·that·offers·sacrifices, and offer concerning your
Mt 8:4 to·the priest·that·offers·sacrifices, and offer the present

Mk 1:44 ·that·offers·sacrifices, and offer concerning your
G4374.2 V-AAP-NSM προσενέγκας (2x)
Heb 5:7 days of·his flesh, *was* offering·up both petitions and
Heb 10:12 But he·himself, after·offering one sacrifice on·
G4374.2 V-AAS-3S προσενέγκῃ (1x)
Heb 8:3 this·man to·have something also that he·may·offer.
G4374.2 V-API-3S προσηνέχθη (1x)
Ac 21:26 the offering should·be·offered on·behalf of·each
G4374.2 V-APP-NSM προσενεχθείς (1x)
Heb 9:28 the Anointed-One, after·being·offered only·once
G4374.2 V-2RAI-3S-ATT προσενήνοχεν (1x)
Heb 11:17 when·being·tried, had·offered·up YiTsaq, and
G4374.3 V-PPI-3S προσφέρεται (1x)
Heb 12:7 ·discipline, God is·bearing·alongside yeu as *his*·

G4375 προσ•φιλής prôsphilḗs *adj.* (1x)
Roots:G4314 G5368
G4375.3 A-NPN προσφιλῆ (1x)
Php 4:8 ·things·as *are* of·kind·sentiment, as·many·things·as

G4376 προσ•φορά prôsphôrá *n.* (9x)
Roots:G4374 Compare:G2378 G5498-1 G0399-1
G4376.1 N-NSF προσφορά (3x)
Ac 21:26 *time* the offering should·be·offered on·behalf of·
Heb 10:18 ·*is* no·longer an·offering concerning moral·failure
Rm 15:16 ·God, in·order·that the offering·up of·the Gentiles
G4376.1 N-ASF προσφοράν (3x)
Heb 10:5 says, '" Sacrifice and offering you·did·not want,
Heb 10:8 that "Sacrifice and offering and burnt·offerings,
Eph 5:2 over on·our behalf, an·offering and a·sacrifice to·
G4376.1 N-APF προσφοράς (1x)
Ac 24:17 merciful·acts for my nation, and *making* offerings;
G4376.1 N-DSF προσφορᾷ (1x)
Heb 10:14 For by·one offering, he·has·made·fully·complete
G4376.1 N-GSF προσφορᾶς (1x)
Heb 10:10 through the offering, upon·one·occasion·only, of·

G4377 προσ•φωνέω prôsphōnéō *v.* (7x)
Roots:G4314 G5455 See:G5456
G4377.2 V-IAI-3S προσεφώνει (1x)
Ac 22:2 upon·hearing that he·was·addressing them in·the
G4377.2 V-AAI-3S προσεφώνησεν (3x)
Lk 13:12 And seeing her, Jesus addressed *her* and declared
Lk 23:20 to·fully·release Jesus, Pilate addressed *them* again.
Ac 21:40 ·large silence occurring, he·addressed *them* in·the
G4377.3 V-PAP-DPM προσφωνοῦσιν (2x)
Lk 7:32 in·a·marketplace and hollering·out to·one·another,
Mt 11:16 marketplaces and hollering·out to·their associates,
G4377.4 V-AAI-3S προσεφώνησεν (1x)
Lk 6:13 when it·was day, he·hailed his disciples *to·himself*

G4378 πρόσ•χυσις prôschysis *n.* (1x)
Roots:G4314 G5502-5 Compare:G1632 G0130 See:G4377-2
G4378.2 N-ASF πρόσχυσιν (1x)
Heb 11:28 and the pouring·out·and·application of·the blood,

G4379 προσ•ψαύω prôspsaúō *v.* (1x)
Roots:G4314 Compare:G2185
G4379.2 V-PAI-2P προσψαύετε (1x)
Lk 11:46 and yeu·yeurselves do·not reach·for the loads

G4380 προσ•ωπο•ληπτέω prôsōpôlēptéō *v.* (1x)
Roots:G4381
G4380.2 V-PAI-2P προσωποληπτεῖτε (1x)
Jac 2:9 But if yeu·show·partiality, yeu·work moral·failure,

G4381 προσ•ωπο•λήπτης prôsōpôlḗptēs *n.* (1x)
Roots:G4383 G2983 See:G0678
G4381.2 N-NSM προσωπολήπτης (1x)
Ac 10:34 In truth, I·grasp that God is not one·who·is·partial,

G4382 προσ•ωπο•ληψία prôsōpôlēpsía *n.* (4x)
Roots:G4381
G4382 N-NSF προσωποληψία (3x)
Rm 2:11 For there·is no partiality with God.
Eph 6:9 in *the* heavens, and there·is not partiality with him.
Col 3:25 ·for·which he·did·wrong, and there·is no partiality.
G4382 N-DPF προσωποληψίαις (1x)
Jac 2:1 Yeshua Anointed (*the Lord* of·Glory) with partiality.

G4383 πρόσ•ωπον prôsōpôn *n.* (80x)
Roots:G4314 G3700 Compare:G3952 G3799 G2397 xLangAlso:H6440
G4383.1 N-ASN πρόσωπον (3x)
Lk 2:31 which you·made·ready in front of·all the peoples;
Ac 3:13 and yeu·denied him in front of·Pilate, with·that·one
2Co 8:24 ·*so* in front of·the convened·Called·Out·assemblies
G4383.1 N-DSN προσώπῳ (1x)
2Co 2:10 ·account·of yeu *I·did·it* in front of·Anointed-One,
G4383.1 N-GSN προσώπου (1x)
Ac 5:41 from in·front of·the joint·council·of·Sanhedrin,
G4383.2 N-NSN πρόσωπον (4x)
Lk 9:53 him, because his face was *as* one·who·is·traversing
Mt 17:2 before them. And his face radiated·brightly as the
1Pe 3:12 to their petitions, but *the* face of·Yahweh *is* against
Rv 10:1 *was* upon his head, and his face *was* as the sun, and
G4383.2 N-NPN πρόσωπα (2x)
Rv 9:7 like gold, and their faces *were* as faces of·men·of·
Rv 9:7 gold, and their faces *were* as faces of·men·of·clay†.
G4383.2 N-ASN πρόσωπον (34x)
Lk 5:12 Jesus *and* falling on *his* face, he·petitioned him,
Lk 9:51 ·up, that he·himself firmly·set his face to·traverse to
Lk 12:56 ·how to·examine·and·verify the face of·the sky and
Lk 17:16 and he·fell·down on *his* face directly·at his feet,
Lk 21:35 ·ones who·are·sitting·down on *the* face of·all the
Lk 22:64 him, they·were·pummeling his face, and were·
Lk 24:5 alarmed and drooping the face toward the earth, *the*
Ac 6:15 joint·council·of·Sanhedrin saw his face as·if *it·was*
Ac 6:15 ·Sanhedrin saw his face as·if *it·was* an·angel's face.
Ac 17:26 ·of·clay† residing upon all the face of·the earth,
Ac 20:25 of·God, shall·gaze·upon my face no·longer.
Ac 20:38 no·longer would·they·*be·able* to·observe his face.
Ac 25:16 ·holds the legal·accusers face·to·face, and·also
Gal 2:11 I·withstood him in *his* face, because he·was
Mt 6:17 ·fasting, rub·oil·on your head and wash your face,
Mt 16:3 in·fact yeu·know to·discern the face of·the sky, but
Mt 17:6 disciples fell on their faces and were tremendously
Mt 18:10 in *the* heavens look·upon the face of·my Father,
Mt 26:39 a·little·bit, he·fell on his face, praying and saying,
Mt 26:67 Then they·spat in his face and buffeted him, and
Mk 14:65 and upon·putting·a·hood·over his face, even to·
Jac 1:23 fully·observing his natural face in a·reflected·image
1Th 2:17 the·more·abundantly to·see yeur face with much
1Th 3:10 for this·thing: to·see yeur face, and to·completely·
1Co 13:12 with an·obscured·view, but then face to face. At·
1Co 13:12 but then face to face. At·this·moment, I·know
1Co 14:25 falling·down on *his* face, he·shall·fall·prostrate
2Co 3:7 ·gaze·intently into the face of·Moses on·account·of
2Co 3:13 *did*, who·was·placing a·veil over his face, *which·is*
2Co 11:20 exalts·himself, if anyone thrashes yeu to *the* face.
Col 2:1 as·many·as have·not clearly·seen my face in flesh,
Rv 4:7 living·being *is* having the face as a·man·of·clay†, and
Rv 7:11 and they·fell on their faces in·the·sight of·the throne
Rv 22:4 And they·shall·gaze·upon his face, and his name
G4383.2 N-APN πρόσωπα (2x)
Mt 6:16 their faces in·such·a·manner·so·that they·may·be·
Rv 11:16 thrones, fell upon their faces, and fell·prostrate to·
G4383.2 N-DSN προσώπῳ (3x)
Gal 1:22 ·unknown by·the face to·the Called·Out·citizenries
2Co 3:18 all— with·a·face having·been·unveiled
2Co 4:6 of·the glory of·God in *the* face of·Jesus Anointed.
G4383.2 N-GSN προσώπου (4x)
Ac 7:45 whom God thrust·out from *the* face of·our fathers.
Rv 6:16 us from *the* face of·the·one who·is·sitting·down on
Rv 12:14 half·a·season, away·from *the* face of·the Serpent.
Rv 20:11 ·down on it, from whose face the earth and the
EG4383.2 (1x)
Mt 18:14 "In·this·manner, before *the face* of·yeur Father,
G4383.3 N-ASN πρόσωπον (1x)
Mt 22:16 ·do·not look to *the* countenance of·men·of·clay†.
G4383.3 N-GSN προσώπου (4x)
Lk 9:29 the aspect of·his countenance became different, and
Ac 2:28 ·fill me *full* of·euphoria with your countenance."
Jac 1:11 the beauty of·its countenance completely·perishes.
2Co 3:7 on·account·of the glory of·his countenance (the
G4383.4 N-ASN πρόσωπον (1x)
2Co 10:7 ·look·at things according·to surface·appearance? If
G4383.4 N-DSN προσώπῳ (1x)
2Co 5:12 who·are·boasting in a·surface·appearance and not
G4383.5 N-ASN πρόσωπον (3x)
Lk 20:21 and do·not receive *the* personal·appearance *of·any*,
Gal 2:6 receive *the* personal·appearance of·a·man·of·clay†,
Mk 12:14 look to *the* personal·appearance of·men·of·clay†,
G4383.5 N-GSN προσώπου (1x)
Ac 13:24 ·IsraEl, prior·to *the* personal·appearance of *Jesus'*
G4383.6 N-ASN πρόσωπον (1x)
2Co 10:1 (*I*, who in personal·presence *am* in·fact lowly
G4383.6 N-DSN προσώπῳ (2x)
Heb 9:24 in·the personal·presence of·God on·our behalf.
1Th 2:17 just·for a·short season (in·personal·presence, not
G4383.6 N-GSN προσώπου (8x)
Lk 1:76 *the* personal·presence of·*the*·Lord to·make·ready his
Lk 7:27 my messenger before your personal·presence, who
Lk 9:52 messengers before his personal·presence. And
Lk 10:1 up by·twos before his personal·presence, into every
Ac 3:19 ·come from *the* personal·presence of·Yahweh,
Mt 11:10 my messenger before your personal·presence, who
Mk 1:2 my messenger before your personal·presence, who
2Th 1:9 ·termination from *the* personal·presence of·the Lord,
G4383.7 N-APN πρόσωπα (1x)
Jud 1:16 while·admiring persons of·profitable·advantage
G4383.7 N-GPN προσώπων (1x)
2Co 1:11 birthed·from·out of·many persons, in·order·that
EG4383.7 (1x)
2Co 1:11 upon us through many *persons*, *such·that* thanks·

G4384 προ•τάσσω prôtássō *v.* (1x)
Roots:G4253 G5021
G4384 V-RPP-APM προτεταγμένους (1x)
Ac 17:26 specifically·determining prearranged seasons and

G4385 προ•τείνω prôtéínō *v.* (1x)
Roots:G4253 G5037-1 Compare:G1614
G4385 V-AAI-3S προέτεινεν (1x)
Ac 22:25 And as they·prestretched him with·the straps, Paul

G4386 πρότερον prôtêrôn *adj.* (10x)
Roots:G4387 Compare:G3819 G4218 G4413
G4386.1 A-ASN πρότερον (2x)
Heb 10:32 recall·to·mind·and·consider the previous days in
1Pe 1:14 ·presently·conforming to·the previous longings in
G4386.2 A-NSN πρότερον (1x)
Jn 6:62 ·Clay·Man† ascending to·where he·was previously?
G4386.2 A-ASN πρότερον (1x)
Jn 9:8 (and the·ones observing him previously that he·was
G4386.2 ADV πρότερον (3x)
Heb 4:6 and the·ones previously being·proclaimed·the·good·
2Co 1:15 to yeu previously in·order·that yeu·may·have a·
1Ti 1:13 the·one previously being a·reviler, and a·persecutor,
G4386.3 ADV πρότερον (1x)
Jn 7:51 it·should·hear directly·from him beforehand, and
G4386.4 A-ASN πρότερον (1x)
Gal 4:13 I·proclaimed·the·good·news to·yeu at·the first.
G4386.4 ADV πρότερον (1x)
Heb 7:27 sacrifices *to·the altar*, first on·behalf of·their·own

G4387 πρότερος prôtêrôs *adj.* (1x)
Roots:G4253 See:G4386 xLangAlso:H7223
G4387 A-ASF προτέραν (1x)
Eph 4:22 ·of·clay† according·to the previous manner·of·life

G4388 προ•τίθεμαι prôtíthêmai *v.* (3x)
Roots:G4253 G5087 See:G4286
G4388.4 V-2AMI-1S προεθέμην (1x)
Rm 1:13 many·times I·personally·determined to·come to yeu
G4388.4 V-2AMI-3S προέθετο (2x)
Rm 3:25 whom God personally·determined *to·be* an·atoning·
Eph 1:9 which he·personally·determined within himself

G4389 προ•τρέπομαι prôtrĕpômai *v.* (1x)
Roots:G4253 G5157 Compare:G2292 G3888
G4389.2 V-AMP-NPM προτρεψάμενοι (1x)
Ac 18:27 the brothers wrote, encouraging the disciples *there*

G4390 προ•τρέχω prôtrĕchō *v.* (2x)
Roots:G4253 G5143 See:G4274
G4390.ª V-2AAI-3S προέδραμεν (1x)
Jn 20:4 the other disciple more·swiftly outran Peter and came
G4390.ª V-2AAP-NSM προδραμών (1x)
Lk 19:4 And running·on ahead, he·climbed·up upon a·

G4391 προ•ϋπ•άρχω prôÿpárchō *v.* (2x)
Roots:G4253 G5225
G4391.2 V-IAI-3S προϋπῆρχεν (1x)
Ac 8:9 man by·the·name·of Simon was·previously in the
G4391.2 V-IAI-3P προϋπῆρχον (1x)
Lk 23:12 one·another, for they·were·previously being in

G4392 πρό•φασις prôphasis *n.* (7x)
Roots:G4253 G5316 Compare:G1942
G4392.1 N-DSF προφάσει (1x)
Lk 20:47 and pray lengthy *prayers* for·an·outward·showing.
G4392.2 N-ASF πρόφασιν (1x)
Jn 15:22 now they·do·not have a·pretense concerning their
G4392.2 N-DSF προφάσει (4x)
Ac 27:30 into the sea under·a·pretense as·though intending
Mt 23:13 ·the widows and for·a·pretense are·praying lengthy
Mk 12:40 of·the widows, and for·a·pretense praying lengthy
Php 1:18 in·every manner, whether in·pretense or in·truth,
G4392.3 N-DSF προφάσει (1x)
1Th 2:5 ·know), nor with a·pretext for·covetousness (God

G4393 προ•φέρω prôphĕrō *v.* (2x)
Roots:G4253 G5342 Compare:G4254 G4160
G4393.2 V-PAI-3S προφέρει (2x)
Lk 6:45 of·his heart, brings·forth the beneficially·good. And
Lk 6:45 ·the evil treasure of·his heart, brings·forth the evil.

G4394 προ•φητεία prôphētĕía *n.* (20x)
Roots:G4396
G4394 N-NSF προφητεία (5x)
Mt 13:14 in them is·utterly·fulfilled the prophecy of·IsaIah,
2Pe 1:20 this first, that every prophecy of·Scripture does·not
2Pe 1:21 ·of·clay† *was* prophecy carried·forth in·times·past.
1Co 12:10 of·miracles, to·another prophecy, to·another
1Co 14:22 non-trusting·ones, but the prophecy *is* not for·the
G4394 N-NPF προφητεῖαι (1x)
1Co 13:8 *there·are* prophecies, they·shall·be·fully·rendered·
G4394 N-ASF προφητείαν (2x)
Rm 12:6 *we·must·use them*: if prophecy, *then* according·to
1Co 13:2 ·have *the gracious·bestowment of* prophecy, and
G4394 N-APF προφητείας (2x)
1Th 5:20 Do·not utterly·disdain prophecies.
1Ti 1:18 according·to the preceding prophecies over you,
G4394 N-DSF προφητείᾳ (1x)
1Co 14:6 or by knowledge, or by prophesying, or by
G4394 N-GSF προφητείας (8x)
1Ti 4:14 which was·given to·you through prophecy, with *the*
Rv 1:3 the words of·the prophecy and observantly·keeping
Rv 11:6 rain in *the* days of·their prophecy. And they·have
Rv 19:10 the testimony of·Jesus is the spirit of·prophecy."
Rv 22:7 the words of·the prophecy of·this official·scroll."
Rv 22:10 ·up the words of·the prophecy of·this official·scroll
Rv 22:18 the words of·the prophecy of·this official·scroll, if
Rv 22:19 the words of·*the*·scroll of·this prophecy, God shall·
EG4394 (1x)
Mt 8:17 ·so·that *the prophecy* may·be·completely·fulfilled,

G4395 προ•φητεύω prôphētĕúō *v.* (28x)
Roots:G4396 Compare:G5537 G3132 G2813-1
xLangEquiv:H5012 A5013
G4395.1 V-FAI-3P προφητεύσουσιν (3x)
Ac 2:17 sons and yeur daughters shall·prophesy, and yeur
Ac 2:18 ·forth from my Spirit, and they·shall·prophesy.
Rv 11:3 and they·shall·prophesy a·thousand two·hundred
G4395.1 V-PAI-1P προφητεύομεν (1x)
1Co 13:9 ·*the whole*, and we·prophesy from·out of·a·portion
G4395.1 V-PAN προφητεύειν (2x)
1Co 14:31 each one, all to·prophesy, in·order·that all may·
1Co 14:39 brothers, be·zealous to·prophesy, and do·not
G4395.1 V-PAP-NSF προφητεύουσα (1x)
1Co 11:5 who·is·praying or prophesying with·her head not·
G4395.1 V-PAP-NSM προφητεύων (4x)
1Co 11:4 Every man praying or prophesying, having *his*
1Co 14:3 But the·one prophesying speaks to·men·of·clay†
1Co 14:4 the·one prophesying edifies a·convened·Called·
1Co 14:5 for greater *is* the·one prophesying than the·one
G4395.1 V-PAP-NPF προφητεύουσαι (1x)
Ac 21:9 had daughters, four virgin·daughters prophesying.
G4395.1 V-PAS-2P προφητεύητε (2x)
1Co 14:1 but more·especially that yeu·may·prophesy.
1Co 14:5 more·especially that yeu·should·prophesy, for
G4395.1 V-PAS-3P προφητεύωσιν (1x)
1Co 14:24 But if all should·prophesy, and someone should·
G4395.1 V-IAI-3P προεφήτευον (1x)
Ac 19:6 with·bestowed·tongues and were·prophesying.
G4395.1 V-AAI-1P προεφητεύσαμεν (1x)
Mt 7:22 Lord, Lord, ¿!·Did·we·not prophesy in·your name,
G4395.1 V-AAI-3S προεφήτευσεν (5x)
Jn 11:51 ·high·priest that year, he·prophesied that Jesus
Lk 1:67 was·filled with·Holy Spirit and prophesied, saying,
Mt 15:7 ·hypocrites! IsaIah did·prophesy well concerning
Mk 7:6 to·them, "IsaIah prophesied well concerning yeu, the
Jud 1:14 seventh from Adam, prophesied of·these, saying,
G4395.1 V-AAI-3P προεφήτευσαν (1x)
Mt 11:13 prophets and the Torah-Law prophesied until John.
G4395.1 V-AAM-2S προφήτευσον (3x)
Lk 22:64 ·of him, saying, "Prophesy, who is the·one
Mt 26:68 saying, "Prophesy to·us, O·Anointed-One, who is
Mk 14:65 him and to·say to·him, "Prophesy!" And the
G4395.1 V-AAN προφητεῦσαι (1x)
Rv 10:11 "It·is·mandatory·for you to·prophesy again over
G4395.1 V-AAP-NPM προφητεύσαντες (1x)
1Pe 1:10 diligently·searched *for·it* after·prophesying to yeu

G4396 προ•φήτης prôphḗtēs *n.* (150x)
Roots:G4253 G5346 See:G4395
xLangEquiv:H5030
EG4396 (1x)
1Co 14:30 sitting·down, the first *prophet* must·stay·silent.
G4396.1 N-NSM προφήτης (25x)
Jn 1:23 of·Yahweh,"ⁿ just·as IsaIah the prophet declared."
Jn 4:19 "Sir, I·observe that you·yourself are a·prophet.
Jn 4:44 already·testified that, "A·prophet has no honor in
Jn 7:40 "Truly this is the Prophet."
Jn 7:52 and see! Because a·prophet has·not been·awakened
Jn 9:17 And he·declared, "He·is a·prophet!"
Lk 1:76 ·child, shall·be·called a·prophet of·the·Most·High,
Lk 4:24 to·yeu, that not·even·one prophet is acceptable in
Lk 7:16 "A·great prophet has·been·awakened among us;"
Lk 7:28 there·is not·even·one prophet greater·than John the
Lk 7:39 "If this·man were a·prophet, he·would·be knowing
Lk 9:8 by·others that one of·the ancient prophets rose·up.
Lk 9:19 and others *say* that some prophet of·the ancient·ones
Lk 24:19 who became a·man, a·prophet powerful in deed
Ac 2:30 inherently·being a·prophet and having·seen that
Ac 7:48 in temples made·by·hands, just·as the prophet says,
Ac 8:34 you, concerning whom·does the prophet say this?
Ac 21:10 ·more days, a·certain prophet came·down from
Mt 13:57 declared to·them, "A·prophet is not without·honor
Mt 21:11 "This is YeShua the prophet, the·one from
Mk 6:4 ·saying to·them, "A·prophet is not without·honor,
Mk 6:15 others were·saying, "It·is a·prophet, or as one of·
Mk 11:32 were·holding John, that he·was really a·prophet.)
Tit 1:12 from·among themselves, a·prophet of·their own,
1Co 14:37 supposes·himself to·be a·prophet or spiritual, let·
G4396.1 N-NPM προφῆται (21x)
Jn 1:45 in the Torah-Law, and·also the prophets: Jesus from
Jn 8:52 is·dead, and the prophets; and you·yourself say, 'If
Jn 8:53 who is·dead? And the prophets are·dead. Whom·do
Lk 10:24 I·say to·yeu, that many prophets and kings wanted
Lk 16:16 "The Torah-Law and the prophets *were* until John.
Lk 24:25 in·the heart to·trust on all that the prophets spoke.
Ac 3:24 And even all the prophets from SamuEl and the·ones
Ac 10:43 "To·this·one, all the prophets do·testify— *that*
Ac 11:27 And in those days, prophets came·down from
Ac 13:1 being in Antioch, prophets and instructors as·
Ac 15:32 Judas and Silas, being prophets also themselves,
Ac 26:22 those·things·which both the prophets and Moses
Mt 7:12 to·them, for this is the Torah-Law and the prophets.
Mt 11:13 For all the prophets and the Torah-Law prophesied
Mt 13:17 ·say to·yeu, that many prophets and righteous·men
Mt 22:40 is·hung all the Torah-Law and the prophets."
1Pe 1:10 this Salvation, the prophets sought·*it*·out and
1Co 12:29 Not all *are* prophets. Not all *are* instructors.
1Co 14:29 Now *let* prophets speak two or three, and *let* the
Rv 11:10 because these two prophets tormented the·ones
Rv 18:20 holy ambassadors and the prophets, because God
G4396.1 N-ASM προφήτην (11x)
Lk 7:26 what have·yeu·gone·forth to·see? A·prophet? Yes,
Lk 13:33 *that* a·prophet should·completely·perish outside of·
Lk 20:6 having·been·persuaded *for* John to·be a·prophet."
Ac 7:37 God shall·raise·up a·prophet to·yeu from·among
Ac 8:28 and he·was·reading·aloud IsaIah the prophet.
Ac 8:30 heard him reading·aloud IsaIah the prophet, and he·
Mt 10:41 The·one who·is·accepting a·prophet in a·prophet's
Mt 11:9 what·did yeu·go·forth to·see? A·prophet? Yes, I·
Mt 14:5 because they·were·holding him as a·prophet.
Mt 21:26 we·fear the crowd, for all hold John as a·prophet."
Mt 21:46 *crowds* were·holding him *with·regard* as a·prophet.
G4396.1 N-APM προφήτας (14x)
Lk 11:49 'I·shall·dispatch to them prophets and ambassadors
Lk 13:28 Jacob, and all the prophets in the kingdom of·God,
Lk 13:34 the·one killing the prophets and casting·stones·at
Lk 16:29 'They·have Moses and the prophets. Let·them·hear
Mt 5:12 ·this·manner they·persecuted the prophets, the·ones
Mt 5:17 the Torah-Law or the prophets. I·did·not come to·
Mt 23:31 ·are the·Sons of·the·ones murdering the prophets.
Mt 23:34 I·myself dispatch to yeu prophets and wise·men
Mt 23:37 the·one killing the prophets and casting·stones·at
Rm 11:3 your prophets and completely·broke·down·and·
Jac 5:10 and the long-suffering of·the prophets who spoke
1Th 2:15 the Lord YeShua and their·own prophets, and
1Co 12:28 first ambassadors, second prophets, third
Eph 4:11 ·forth the ambassadors, and the prophets, and the
G4396.1 N-DPM προφήταις (12x)
Jn 6:45 "It·is having·been·written in the prophets, "And
Lk 6:23 their fathers were·doing *this* to·the prophets.
Lk 24:44 Torah-Law of·Moses, *the* Prophets, and *the* Psalms
Ac 13:40 the·thing having·been·declared in the prophets,
Ac 24:14 ·been·written in the Torah-Law and the prophets;
Ac 26:27 do·you·trust the prophets? I·personally·know that
Heb 1:1 long·ago to·the fathers by the prophets, God
Mk 1:2 As it·has·been·written in the prophets, "Behold, I·
1Co 14:32 *the* spirits of·prophets are·subject to·prophets.
Eph 3:5 to·his holy ambassadors and prophets by *the* Spirit):
Rv 10:7 as he·proclaimed to·his slaves the prophets.
Rv 11:18 ·of·service to·your slaves the prophets, and·also to·
G4396.1 N-GSM προφήτου (30x)
Jn 12:38 of·IsaIah the prophet may·be·completely·fulfilled,
Lk 3:4 in·a·scroll of·the·words of·IsaIah the prophet, saying,
Lk 4:17 ·scroll of·IsaIah the prophet was·handed to·him.
Lk 4:27 in IsraEl in·the·days of·EliSha the prophet, yet not·
Lk 7:26 Yes, I·say to·yeu, and much·more than·a·prophet.
Lk 11:29 ·given to·it, except the sign of·Jonah the prophet.
Ac 2:16 having·been·declared through JoEl the prophet:
Ac 3:23 soul who would not hear that prophet,'' "shall·be·
Ac 13:20 he·gave *to·them* judges, until SamuEl the prophet.
Ac 28:25 spoke well through IsaIah the prophet to our fathers
Mt 1:22 ·uttered by Yahweh through the prophet, saying,
Mt 2:5 ·this·manner it·has·been·written through the prophet,
Mt 2:15 ·uttered by Yahweh through the prophet, saying,
Mt 2:17 being·uttered by JeremIah the prophet, saying,
Mt 3:3 ·one being·uttered *of* by IsaIah the prophet, saying, "

Mt 4:14 being·uttered through IsaIah the prophet, saying,
Mt 8:17 being·uttered through IsaIah the prophet, saying,
Mt 10:41 a·prophet in a·prophet's name shall·receive a·
Mt 10:41 name shall·receive a·prophet's payment·of·service;
Mt 11:9 Yes, I·say to·yeu, and much·more·than a·prophet.
Mt 12:17 being·uttered through IsaIah the prophet, saying,
Mt 12:39 to·her, except the sign of·Jonah the prophet.
Mt 13:35 the·thing being·uttered through the prophet, saying,
Mt 16:4 except the sign of·Jonah the prophet." And leaving
Mt 21:4 the·thing being·uttered through the prophet, saying,
Mt 24:15 being·uttered through DaniEl the prophet, standing
Mt 27:9 being·uttered through JeremIah the prophet, saying,
Mt 27:35 the·thing being·uttered by the prophet, "They·
Mk 13:14 ·one being·uttered by DaniEl the prophet, standing
2Pe 2:16 ·clay† forbade the irrational·conduct of·the prophet.

G4396.1 N-GPM προφητῶν (32x)

Lk 1:70 *the* mouth of·his holy prophets, the·ones from a·
Lk 11:47 yeu·build the chamber·tombs of·the prophets, and
Lk 11:50 ·order·that the blood of·all the prophets, the *blood*
Lk 16:31 hear Moses and the prophets, neither shall·they·be·
Lk 18:31 ·been·written through the prophets *concerning* the
Lk 24:27 and all the prophets, he·was·expounding to·them in
Ac 3:18 through *the* mouth of·all his prophets, *for* the
Ac 3:21 mouth of·all his holy prophets since *the* beginning·
Ac 3:25 Yeu·yeurselves are the·Sons of·the prophets, and of·
Ac 7:42 ·as it·has·been·written in a·scroll of·the prophets,
Ac 7:52 Which of·the prophets did yeur fathers not persecute
Ac 13:15 of·the Torah-Law and the prophets, the directors·
Ac 13:27 ·man nor·even the voices of·the prophets (the·ones
Ac 15:15 the words of·the prophets do·mutually·agree, just·
Ac 28:23 Torah-Law of·Moses and the prophets, from dawn
Heb 11:32 and also David, SamuEl, and the prophets,
Mt 2:23 the·thing being·uttered through the prophets, "He·
Mt 16:14 *yet* others *say* JeremIah, or one of·the prophets."
Mt 23:29 yeu·build the graves of·the prophets and decorate
Mt 23:30 partners with·them in the blood of·the prophets.'
Mt 26:56 of·the prophets may·be·completely·fulfilled." Then
Mk 6:15 "It·is a·prophet, or as one of·the prophets."
Mk 8:28 *say*, EliJah, and others, one of·the prophets."
Rm 1:2 he·promised·beforehand through his prophets in *the*
Rm 3:21 ·attested·to by the Torah-Law and the prophets.
2Pe 3:2 ·been·already·stated by the holy prophets and of·the
1Co 14:32 And *the* spirits of·prophets are·subject to·prophets
Eph 2:20 of·the ambassadors and prophets, with·Jesus
Rv 16:6 *the* blood of·holy·ones and prophets, and you·gave
Rv 18:24 her was·found *the* blood of·prophets, and of·holy·
Rv 22:6 Yahweh, God of·the holy prophets, dispatched his
Rv 22:9 and of·your brothers the prophets, and of·the·ones

G4396.2 N-NSM προφήτης (3x)

Jn 1:21 "Are you·yourself the Prophet?" And he·answered,
Jn 1:25 not the Anointed-One, nor EliJah, nor the Prophet?"
Jn 6:14 "This is truly the Prophet, the·one who·is·coming

G4396.2 N-ASM προφήτην (1x)

Ac 3:22 God shall·raise·up a·Prophet unto·yeu from·among

G4397 προ•φητικός prôphētikốs *adj.* (2x)

Roots:G4396

G4397 A-ASM προφητικόν (1x)

2Pe 1:19 Also, we·have more·firmly the prophetic word, to·

G4397 A-GPM προφητικῶν (1x)

Rm 16:26 — also through prophetic Scriptures, according·to

G4398 προ•φῆτις prôphễtis *n.* (2x)

Roots:G4396
xLangEquiv:H5031

G4398 N-NSF προφῆτις (1x)

Lk 2:36 And there·was a·prophetess, Hanna, daughter of·

G4398 N-ASF προφῆτιν (1x)

Rv 2:20 ·one referring·to herself *as* a·prophetess, to·instruct

G4399 προ•φθάνω prôphthánō *v.* (1x)

Roots:G4253 G5348 xLangAlso:H6923

G4399.2 V-AAI-3S προέφθασεν (1x)

Mt 17:25 into the home, YeShua preempted him, saying,

G4400 προ•χειρίζομαι prôchêirízômai *v.* (2x)

Roots:G4253 G5495

G4400.2 V-ADI-3S προεχειρίσατο (1x)

Ac 22:14 'The God of·our fathers handpicked you to·know

G4400.2 V-ADN προχειρίσασθαι (1x)

Ac 26:16 to·you for this·purpose, to·handpick you *to·be* an·

G4401 προ•χειρο•τονέω prôchêirôtônếō *v.* (1x)

Roots:G4253 G5500

G4401 V-RPP-DPM προκεχειροτονημένοις (1x)

Ac 10:41 to·witnesses having·been·elected·beforehand by

G4402 Πρό•χορος Prốchôrôs *n/p.* (1x)

Roots:G4253 G5525 Compare:G4736 See:G1675

G4402.2 N/P-ASM Πρόχορον (1x)

Ac 6:5 ·Holy Spirit, and·also PhilIppe, ProChorus, Nicanor,

G4403 πρύμνα prýmna *n.* (3x)

G4403.1 N-NSF πρύμνα (1x)

Ac 27:41 unshakable, but the stern was·broken by the force

G4403.1 N-GSF πρύμνης (1x)

Ac 27:29 out of·*the*·stern, they·were·well-wishing·for *it* to·

G4403.2 N-DSF πρύμνῃ (1x)

Mk 4:38 he·himself was in the stern·of·the·boat, sleeping on

G4404 πρωΐ prōΐ *adv.* (12x)

Roots:G4253 Compare:G0219 G3722 G3721 G3317 G3796 See:G4405 G4407 G4405-1 G4406

G4404.1 ADV πρωΐ (5x)

Ac 28:23 ·Moses and the prophets, from dawn until evening.
Mt 16:3 And at·dawn, '*There·shall·be* stormy·weather today
Mt 20:1 went·out at·the·same·time as·dawn to·hire workmen
Mk 11:20 And at·dawn, as·they·were·traversing·directly·by
Mk 15:1 And immediately upon the dawn, the chief·priests,

EG4404.1 (2x)

Mt 28:1 ·it·growing·light toward the first *dawn* of·the·week,
Mk 15:25 *the* third hour *after dawn* that they·crucified him.

G4404.2 ADV πρωΐ (5x)

Jn 20:1 *day* of·the week at·the·watch·of·dawn (while·being
Mk 1:35 And at·the·watch·of·dawn, after·already·rising·up
Mk 13:35 or at·rooster-crow, or at·the·watch·of·dawn—
Mk 16:2 And very·early, at·the·watch·of·dawn of·the first
Mk 16:9 after·rising·up at·the·watch·of·dawn on·*the*·first

G4405 πρωΐα prōΐa *n.* (4x)

Roots:G4404 Compare:G0827 G3722 See:G4407 G4406

G4405 N-NSF πρωΐα (1x)

Jn 18:28 the Praetorian·hall, and it·was break·of·dawn. And

G4405 N-GSF πρωΐας (3x)

Jn 21:4 even·now with·it·becoming the·break·of·dawn, Jesus
Mt 21:18 the City with·the·break·of·dawn, he·was·hungry.
Mt 27:1 And with·the·break·of·dawn occurring, all the chief·

G4406 πρώϊμος prṓïmôs *adj.* (1x)

Roots:G4404 Compare:G3797 See:G4405 G4407 xLangEquiv:H3138

G4406.2 A-ASM πρώϊμον (1x)

Jac 5:7 he·should·receive early·autumn and latter·spring rain

G4407 πρωϊνός prōïnốs *adj.* (1x)

Roots:G4404 Compare:G5459 G3720 G3721 G3722 See:G4405 G4406

G4407.3 A-ASM πρωϊνόν (1x)

Rv 2:28 And I·shall·give him the Early·Morning star.

G4408 πρῴρα prṓra *n.* (2x)

Roots:G4253 See:G4408-1

G4408 N-NSF πρῷρα (1x)

Ac 27:41 aground; and in·fact, the bow, after·getting·stuck,

G4408 N-GSF πρῴρας (1x)

Ac 27:30 intending to·extend anchors out of·*the*·bow,

G4409 πρωτεύω prōtêúō *v.* (1x)

Roots:G4413

G4409.2 V-PAP-NSM@ πρωτεύων (1x)

Col 1:18 ·things he·himself may·come to·be·foremost·of·all,

G4410 πρωτο•καθ•εδρία prōtôkathêdría *n.* (4x)

Roots:G4413 G2515

G4410 N-ASF πρωτοκαθεδρίαν (1x)

Lk 11:43 Because yeu·love the first·row·seat in the

G4410 N-APF πρωτοκαθεδρίας (3x)

Lk 20:46 in the marketplaces, and first·row·seats in the
Mt 23:6 at the festive·suppers, and the first·row·seats in the
Mk 12:39 and first·row·seats in the gatherings, and foremost·

G4411 πρωτο•κλισία prōtôklisía *n.* (5x)

Roots:G4413 G2828

G4411.2 N-ASF πρωτοκλισίαν (2x)

Lk 14:8 ·not fully·recline·back in the foremost·place, lest a·
Mt 23:6 Also, they·are·fond·of the foremost·places at the

G4411.2 N-APF πρωτοκλισίας (3x)

Lk 14:7 how they·were·selecting the foremost·places, saying
Lk 20:46 the gatherings, and foremost·places at the festive·
Mk 12:39 the gatherings, and foremost·places at the festive·

G4412 πρῶτον prỗtôn *adj.* (62x)

Roots:G4413 G3588

G4412.2 A-NSN πρῶτον (1x)

Jn 10:40 the place where John was first immersing; and there

G4412.2 A-ASM πρῶτον (1x)

2Ti 2:6 man·that·works·the·soil to·partake first of·the fruits.

G4412.2 A-ASN πρῶτον (2x)

Jn 12:16 did·not know these·things at·the first, but·rather
Jn 19:39 also, the·one coming at·the first to Jesus by·night,

G4412.2 ADV πρῶτον (54x)

Jn 2:10 ·him, "Every man·of·clay† first places·out the good
Jn 15:18 ·know that it·has·hated me first·before *it·hated* yeu.
Jn 18:13 Then they·led him away first to HannAs *the proper*
Lk 6:42 "O·stage·acting·hypocrite, first cast·out the beam
Lk 9:59 freely·permit me to·go·off first to·bury my father.
Lk 9:61 I·shall·follow you, but first, freely·permit me to·
Lk 10:5 whatever home yeu·should·enter, first say, 'Peace
Lk 11:38 Pharisee marveled that he·did·not first immerse *his*
Lk 14:28 *does* not·indeed sit·down first *and* calculates the
Lk 14:31 *does* not·indeed sit·down first *and* takes·counsel
Lk 17:25 "But first, it·is·mandatory·for him to·suffer many·
Lk 21:9 for it·is·mandatory·for these·things to·occur first.
Ac 3:26 Jesus, dispatched him to·yeu first, blessing yeu in
Ac 7:12 in Egypt, Jacob dispatched·forth our fathers first.
Ac 11:26 *it·was* first to·be·imparted·as·a·divine·message in
Ac 13:46 Redemptive-word of·God first to·be·spoken to·yeu,
Ac 26:20 But·rather announcing first to·the·ones in
Heb 7:2 a·tenth *part* from all·things. First, in·fact, being·
Mt 5:24 head·on·out. First be·thoroughly·reconciled to·your
Mt 6:33 But seek·yeu first the kingdom of·God and his
Mt 7:5 O·stage·acting·hypocrite, first cast the beam from·
Mt 8:21 "Lord, freely·permit me first to·go·off and to·bury
Mt 12:29 his belongings, unless first he·should·bind the
Mt 13:30 "Collect the darnel·weeds first and bind them in
Mt 17:10 say that it·is·mandatory·for EliJah to·come first?"
Mt 17:11 In·fact EliJah does·come first and shall·reconstitute
Mt 17:27 a·hook and take·up the first fish ascending *on·the*
Mt 23:26 "O·blind Pharisee, first purify the interior of·the
Mk 3:27 unless he·should·bind the strong·man first, and then
Mk 4:28 earth automatically bears·fruit; first a·blade, then a·
Mk 7:27 But Jesus declared to·her, "First, allow the children
Mk 9:11 say that it·is·mandatory·for EliJah to·come first?"
Mk 9:12 in·fact, after·coming first, does·reconstitute all·
Mk 13:10 the good·news first to·be·officially·proclaimed to
Mk 16:9 ·week, *Jesus* did·appear first to·Mariam Magdalene
Rm 1:8 First in·fact, I·give·thanks to·my God through Jesus
Rm 1:16 trusting, both to·Jew first, and·also to·Greek.
Rm 2:9 performing the wrong, of·Jew first, and also of·
Rm 2:10 beneficially·good, both to·Jew first, then·also to·
Rm 15:24 yeu *from* there·to *Spain*, if first I·should·be partly
Jac 3:17 But the wisdom *that·is* from·above is first, in·fact,
1Pe 4:17 And if *it* first *begins* with us, what *is* the end of·the·
2Pe 1:20 while·knowing this first, that every prophecy of·
2Pe 3:3 while·knowing this first, that there·shall·come in the
1Th 4:16 the dead·ones in Anointed-One shall·rise·up first.
2Th 2:3 unless there·should·come the Defection first, and the
1Co 12:28 the Called·Out·citizenry: first ambassadors,
1Co 15:46 the spiritual *was* not first, but·rather the soulish,
2Co 8:5 but·rather first they·gave their·own·selves to·the

Eph 4:9 that also he·descended first into the lowermost parts
1Ti 2:1 Now·then, I·exhort first of·all *for* petitions, prayers,
1Ti 3:10 these·men must·be·tested·and·proven first; then
1Ti 5:4 they·must·learn first at·their·own house to·show·
2Ti 1:5 in you, which indwelt first in your grandmother Lois
G4412.3 ADV πρῶτον (3x)
Lk 12:1 disciples, "First·of·all, beware among·yeurselves of
Rm 3:2 For in·fact, first·of·all, they·are·entrusted·with the
1Co 11:18 For in·fact first·of·all, as·yeu are·coming·together
G4412.4 ADV πρῶτον (1x)
Ac 15:14 recounted·in·detail *that* just·as at·the·first, God

G4413 πρῶτος prōtôs *adj.* (98x)
Roots:G4253 Compare:G3391 G4386 G2570
See:G4409
G4413.1 A-NSM πρῶτος (5x)
Jn 1:15 ahead·of·me, because he·was foremost·before me.'"
Jn 1:30 ahead·of·me, because he·was foremost·before me.'
Mt 20:27 whoever should·want to·be foremost among yeu,
Mk 10:44 of·yeu should·want to·become foremost, shall·be
1Ti 1:15 ·disqualified·ones, of·whom I·myself am foremost.
G4413.1 A-NSF πρώτη (5x)
Ac 16:12 Philippi, which is a·foremost city of·the province
Mt 22:38 This is *the* foremost and greatest commandment.
Mk 12:28 "Which commandment is foremost of·all?
Mk 12:29 him, "*The* foremost of·all the commandments *is*,
Mk 12:30 ' This commandment *is* foremost.
G4413.1 A-NPM πρῶτοι (2x)
Lk 19:47 the scribes and the foremost of·the people were·
Ac 25:2 ·high·priest and the foremost of·the Judeans made·
G4413.1 A-APM πρώτους (2x)
Ac 13:50 ·ones), and·also the foremost·men of·the city *of*·
Ac 28:17 ·together the·ones being foremost of·the Jews. And
G4413.1 A-DSM πρώτῳ (2x)
Ac 28:7 *belonging* to·the foremost·man of·the island, *a·man*
1Ti 1:16 in·order·that, in me foremost, Jesus Anointed may·
G4413.1 A-DPM πρώτοις (1x)
Mk 6:21 ·commanders and the foremost·men of·Galilee,
G4413.1 A-GPF πρώτων (1x)
Ac 17:4 Greek·men and not a·few of·the foremost women.
G4413.2 A-NSM πρῶτος (28x)
Jn 1:41 This·man *Andrew* first finds his·own brother Simon
Jn 5:4 So·then, the first·one stepping·in after the agitation
Jn 8:7 without·moral·failure, let·him·cast the first stone at
Jn 20:4 outran Peter and came first to·the chamber·tomb.
Jn 20:8 also, the·one coming first to·the chamber·tomb.
Lk 14:18 to·excuse·themselves. The first declared to·him,
Lk 19:16 "Then the first came·close, saying, 'Lord, your
Lk 20:29 brothers. And the first·one, after·taking a·wife,
Ac 26:23 that *he·is·to·be* first of·a·resurrection from·among
Mt 10:2 twelve ambassadors are these: first, Simon (the·one
Mt 21:31 They·say to·him, "The first·one." YeShua says
Mt 22:25 brothers, and the first·one, upon·marrying *a·wife*,
Mk 9:35 "If any·man wants to·be first, *the same* shall·be last
Mk 12:20 seven brothers, and the first·one took a·wife, and·
Rm 10:19 ¿!·Did IsraEl not know? First Moses says, "'I·
1Co 14:30 sitting·down, the first *prophet* must·stay·silent.
1Co 15:45 ·been·written, "The first man·of·clay†, Adam,
1Co 15:47 The first man·of·clay† *was* from·out·of soil, *as*
1Ti 2:13 For Adam was·molded first, then Eve.
1Jn 4:19 should·love him, because he·himself first loved us.
Rv 1:11 the Alpha and the Omega, the First and the Last,"
Rv 1:17 "Do·not be·afraid; I AM the First and the Last.
Rv 2:8 'These·things says the First and the Last, who became
Rv 8:7 The first angel sounded, and there·happened hail and
Rv 16:2 And the first went·off and poured·out his vial upon
Rv 21:1 a·brand-new earth, for the first heaven and the first
Rv 21:19 precious stones. The first foundation *was* jasper;
Rv 22:13 Omega, beginning and end, the First and the Last.
G4413.2 A-NSF πρώτη (9x)
Lk 2:2 (*And* this enrollment first occurred with·Cyrenius
Heb 8:7 For if that first *covenant* was faultless, then no place
Heb 9:1 Accordingly in·fact, the first Tabernacle also was·
Heb 9:2 was·planned·and·constructed; the first, in which
Heb 9:18 not·even the first *covenant* has·been·inaugurated
Eph 6:2 ' (which is *the* first commandment with a·promise),
Rv 4:1 in the heaven and the first voice which I·heard *was* as
Rv 20:5 This *is* the First Resurrection. But the rest of·the
Rv 21:1 the first heaven and the first earth passed·away; and
G4413.2 A-NSN πρῶτον (1x)
Rv 4:7 And the first living·being *is* like a·lion, and the
G4413.2 A-NPM πρῶτοι (9x)
Lk 13:30 there·are last who shall·be first, and there·are first
Lk 13:30 shall·be first, and there·are first who shall·be last.
Mt 19:30 "But many *who·are* first shall·be last, and *the* last
Mt 19:30 many *who·are* first shall·be last, and *the* last first.
Mt 20:10 But the first·ones *hired*, upon·coming *forward*,
Mt 20:16 "In·this·manner, the last shall·be first, and the first
Mt 20:16 last shall·be first, and the first last; for many are
Mk 10:31 "But many *who·are* first shall·be last, and the last
Mk 10:31 *who·are* first shall·be last, and the last first."
G4413.2 A-ASM πρῶτον (1x)
Ac 1:1 In·fact, the first account I·made, O TheoPhilus, *was*
G4413.2 A-ASF πρώτην (5x)
Ac 12:10 And going·through a·first and second watch-station
Heb 8:13 he·has·made·obsolete the first *covenant with·the*
Heb 9:6 continually entered into the first Tabernacle, further·
1Ti 5:12 ·in judgment, because they·set·aside the first trust.
Rv 2:4 I·have *this* against you, that you·left your first love.
G4413.2 A-ASN πρῶτον (2x)
Heb 10:9 ·eliminates the first in·order·that he·may·establish
Rv 13:12 ·prostrate *directly·before* the first Daemonic·Beast,
G4413.2 A-APM πρώτους (1x)
Ac 27:43 to·swim, after·jumping·far·overboard first, to·get
G4413.2 A-APN πρῶτα (1x)
Rv 2:5 and repent, and do the first works; but·if·not, I·come
G4413.2 A-DSM πρώτῳ (1x)
Lk 16:5 needy·debtors, he·was·saying to·the first, 'How·
G4413.2 A-DSF πρώτῃ (6x)
Heb 9:15 ·the violations *that·were* under the first covenant),
Mt 26:17 Now on·the first *day* of·the *Sacred·Feast·of*
Mk 14:12 Now on·the first day of·the *Sacred·Feast·of*
Mk 16:9 at·the·watch·of·dawn on·*the*·first *day* of·*the*·week,
2Ti 4:16 At my first defense, not·even·one·man appeared·
Rv 20:6 *is* the·one having part in the First Resurrection. Over
G4413.2 A-DSN πρώτῳ (1x)
Mt 21:28 and coming·alongside the first, he·declared,
G4413.2 A-GSM πρώτου (1x)
Jn 19:32 broke·apart the legs of·the first, and·then *the·legs*
G4413.2 A-GSF πρώτης (4x)
Ac 20:18 are·fully·acquainted, from that first day since I·
Heb 9:8 ·been·made·apparent with·the first Tabernacle still
Mt 27:64 and the last error shall·be worse·than the first."
Php 1:5 in the good·news from *the* first day even·unto the
G4413.2 A-GSN πρώτου (1x)
Rv 13:12 authority of·the first Daemonic·Beast in·the·sight
G4413.2 A-GPM πρώτων (2x)
Mt 20:8 ·of·service, beginning from the last unto the first.'
Mt 21:36 other slaves more·than at·the first, and they·did to·
G4413.2 A-GPN πρώτων (4x)
Lk 11:26 man·of·clay† become worse·than the first·ones."
Mt 12:45 man·of·clay† become worse·than the first·ones.
2Pe 2:20 have·become worse for·them than·the first·ones.
Rv 2:19 even the last·ones *are* more·than the first·ones.
G4413.3 A-DPM πρώτοις (1x)
1Co 15:3 I·handed·down to·yeu, first-of-all, that·which also
G4413.4 A-ASF πρώτην (1x)
Lk 15:22 'Bring·out the most·prestigious long·robe, and
G4413.5 A-NPN πρῶτα (1x)
Rv 21:4 any·longer, because the former·things went·away."

G4414 πρωτο•στάτης prōtôstátēs *n.* (1x)
Roots:G4413 G2476
G4414 N-ASM πρωτοστάτην (1x)
Ac 24:5 The Land, and *being* a·champion of·the sect of·the

G4415 πρωτο•τόκια prōtôtókia *n.* (1x)
Roots:G4416
G4415.2 N-APN πρωτοτόκια (1x)
Heb 12:16 one full·meal gave·away his rights·as·first-born.

G4416 πρωτό•τοκος prōtôtókôs *adj.* (9x)
Roots:G4413 G5088 See:G4415
xLangEquiv:H1060
G4416.2 A-NSM πρωτότοκος (3x)
Col 1:15 of·the invisible God, *the* firstborn of·all creation.
Col 1:18 is *the* beginning, *the* firstborn from·out·of·the dead,
Rv 1:5 witness, *and* the firstborn from·out·of·the dead, and
G4416.2 A-ASM πρωτότοκον (4x)
Lk 2:7 And she·reproduced·and·birthed her firstborn son,
Heb 1:6 whenever he·should·bring the Firstborn into The
Mt 1:25 until she·reproduced·and·birthed her firstborn son.
Rm 8:29 in·order·for his *Son* to·be firstborn among many
G4416.2 A-APN πρωτότοκα (1x)
Heb 11:28 the firstborn should·lay·a·finger·on them.
G4416.2 A-GPM πρωτοτόκων (1x)
Heb 12:23 ·citizenry of·firstborn having·been·enrolled in

G4417 πταίω ptaíō *v.* (5x)
Roots:G4098 Compare:G4350 See:G0679 G3900
G4417.2 V-FAI-3S πταίσει (1x)
Jac 2:10 the whole Torah-Law, but shall·slip·up in one *point*
G4417.2 V-PAI-1P πταίομεν (1x)
Jac 3:2 in·many·things, absolutely·all *of·us* slip·up. If any·
G4417.2 V-PAI-3S πταίει (1x)
Jac 3:2 If any·man does·not slip·up in word, the·same *is* a·
G4417.2 V-AAI-3P ἔπταισαν (1x)
Rm 11:11 ¿!·Did they·slip·up in·order·that they·should·fall
G4417.2 V-AAS-2P πταίσητε (1x)
2Pe 1:10 these·things, no, yeu·should·not ever slip·up.

G4418 πτέρνα ptérna *n.* (1x)
See:G4419
G4418 N-ASF πτέρναν (1x)
Jn 13:18 the bread with me lifted·up his heel against me.'

G4419 πτερύγιον ptêrýgiôn *n.* (2x)
Roots:G4420 See:G4418
G4419.2 N-ASN πτερύγιον (2x)
Lk 4:9 ·set him on the topmost·ledge of·the Sanctuary·Estate
Mt 4:5 sets him on the topmost·ledge of·the Sanctuary·Estate

G4420 πτέρυξ ptéryx *n.* (5x)
Roots:G4072 Compare:G3505-1 See:G4420-2
xLangAlso:H3671 A1611
G4420 N-NPF πτέρυγες (1x)
Rv 12:14 And to·the woman, two wings of·the great eagle
G4420 N-APF πτέρυγας (3x)
Lk 13:34 *gathers* her brood under *her* wings, and yeu·did·not
Mt 23:37 her chicks under her wings, yet yeu·did·not want *it*
Rv 4:8 itself, was·having six wings apiece overflowing of·
G4420 N-GPF πτερύγων (1x)
Rv 9:9 and the sound of·their wings *was* as the·sound of·

G4421 πτηνόν ptēnón *adj.* (1x)
Roots:G4071
G4421 A-GPN πτηνῶν (1x)
1Co 15:39 of·beasts, another of·fish, and another of·birds.

G4422 πτοέω ptôéō *v.* (2x)
Compare:G5399 G4426 See:G4098 G4072 G4423
G4422 V-APP-NPM πτοηθέντες (1x)
Lk 24:37 But being·terrified and becoming alarmed, they·
G4422 V-APS-2P πτοηθῆτε (1x)
Lk 21:9 and chaos, yeu·should·not be·terrified, for it·is·

G4423 πτόησις ptóēsis *n.* (1x)
Roots:G4422 Compare:G5401
G4423 N-ASF πτόησιν (1x)
1Pe 3:6 ·good and not being·afraid *of* not·even·one terror.

G4424 Πτολεμαΐς Ptôlêmaís *n/l.* (1x)
G4424 N/L-ASF Πτολεμαΐδα (1x)
Ac 21:7 from Tyre, arrived at Ptolemais; and after·greeting

G4425 πτύον ptýôn *n.* (2x)
Roots:G4429
G4425 N-NSN πτύον (2x)

Lk 3:17 whose winnowing·fork *is* in his hand, and he·shall·
Mt 3:12 whose winnowing·fork *is* in his hand, and he·shall·

G4426 πτύρω ptýrō *v.* (1x)
Compare:G4422 G5399 G5425 G5141 See:G4429 xLangAlso:H1089

G4426 V-PPP-NPM πτυρόμενοι (1x)
Php 1:28 and not being·scared (in not·even·one·thing) by

G4427 πτύσμα ptýsma *n.* (1x)
Roots:G4429

G4427 N-GSN πτύσματος (1x)
Jn 9:6 and made clay out of·the saliva, and he·smeared the

G4428 πτύσσω ptýssō *v.* (1x)
Compare:G3961 See:G4072 G4429

G4428.2 V-AAP-NSM πτύξας (1x)
Lk 4:20 And rolling·up the official·scroll *and* giving·*it*·back

G4429 πτύω ptýō *v.* (3x)
Compare:G1692 G4428 See:G4427 G4425

G4429 V-AAI-3S ἔπτυσεν (1x)
Jn 9:6 these·things, he·spat down·on·the·open·ground and

G4429 V-AAP-NSM πτύσας (2x)
Mk 7:33 into his ears, and after·spitting, he·laid·hold of·his
Mk 8:23 of·the village. And after·spitting into his eyes *and*

G4430 πτῶμα ptō̃ma *n.* (5x)
Roots:G4098 Compare:G2966 G2347-1 See:G4431

G4430.2 N-NSN πτῶμα (1x)
Mt 24:28 "For wherever the corpse should·be, there the

G4430.2 N-NPN πτώματα (1x)
Rv 11:8 And their corpses *shall·lay* in the broad·street of·the

G4430.2 N-ASN πτῶμα (1x)
Mk 6:29 they·came and took·away his corpse and laid it in

G4430.2 N-APN πτώματα (2x)
Rv 11:9 they·shall·look·upon their corpses three and a·half
Rv 11:9 and shall·not allow their corpses to·be·placed in

G4431 πτῶσις ptō̃sis *n.* (2x)
Roots:G4098 See:G4430 xLangAlso:H4658

G4431 N-NSF πτῶσις (1x)
Mt 7:27 that home, and it·fell; and great was its downfall."

G4431 N-ASF πτῶσιν (1x)
Lk 2:34 *child* is·laid·out for a·downfall and a·raising·again

G4432 πτωχεία ptōchéîa *n.* (3x)
Roots:G4433 Compare:G5304 G5303

G4432 N-NSF πτωχεία (1x)
2Co 8:2 joy and their deep down poverty abounded to the

G4432 N-ASF πτωχείαν (1x)
Rv 2:9 the tribulation, and the poverty (but you·are wealthy

Ππ

G4432 N-DSF πτωχείᾳ (1x)
2Co 8:9 ·yeurselves by·this poverty may·become·wealthy.

G4433 πτωχεύω ptōchêúō *v.* (1x)
Roots:G4434 Compare:G5302 See:G4432 G3993

G4433.1 V-AAI-3S ἐπτώχευσεν (1x)
2Co 8:9 yeu, he·became·helplessly·poor in·order·that yeu·

G4434 πτωχός ptōchṓs *adj.* (36x)
Compare:G3993 G3998 G1189 See:G4422 G4098 xLangEquiv:H1800 H1803 xLangAlso:H6041 H6035

G4434.1 A-NSM πτωχός (1x)
Rv 3:17 ·one miserable, pitiable, helplessly·poor, blind, and

G4434.1 A-NSF πτωχή (3x)
Lk 21:3 I·say to·yeu, that this helplessly·poor widow cast *in*
Mk 12:42 ·coming, a·certain helplessly·poor widow cast·in
Mk 12:43 to·yeu, that this helplessly·poor widow has·cast·in

G4434.1 A-NPM πτωχοί (5x)
Lk 6:20 "Supremely·blessed *are* the helplessly·poor, because
Lk 7:22 *the* helplessly·poor are·proclaimed·the·good·news.'
Mt 5:3 ·blessed *are* the helplessly·poor in·the spirit, because
Mt 11:5 and *the* helplessly·poor are·*hearing*·the·good·news·.
2Co 6:10 rejoicing, as helplessly·poor yet making·wealthy

G4434.1 A-ASM πτωχόν (1x)
Jac 2:6 But yeu·yeurselves dishonored the helplessly·poor.

G4434.1 A-APM πτωχούς (8x)
Jn 12:8 always have the helplessly·poor among yeurselves.
Lk 14:13 call·forth helplessly·poor·ones, totally·maimed·
Lk 14:21 and bring·in here the helplessly·poor, and totally·
Mt 26:11 always have the helplessly·poor among yeurselves,
Mk 14:7 always have the helplessly·poor among yeurselves.
Rm 15:26 ·fund for the helplessly·poor of·the holy·ones,
Jac 2:5 God *that* selected the helplessly·poor of·this world
Rv 13:16 also the wealthy and the helplessly·poor, even the

G4434.1 A-DSM πτωχῷ (1x)
Jac 2:3 and should·declare to·the helplessly·poor, "You·

G4434.1 A-DPM πτωχοῖς (9x)
Jn 12:5 ·hundred denarii and given to·the·helplessly·poor?"
Jn 13:29 he·should·give something to·the helplessly·poor.
Lk 4:18 to·proclaim·the·good·news to·the·helplessly·poor.
Lk 18:22 thoroughly·dole·*it*·out to·*the*·helplessly·poor, and
Lk 19:8 of·my holdings I·give to·the helplessly·poor; and if
Mt 19:21 holdings and give to·*the* helplessly·poor, and you·
Mt 26:9 for·much, and to·be·given to·*the*·helplessly·poor."
Mk 10:21 and give to·the helplessly·poor, and you·shall·
Mk 14:5 and to·be·given to·the helplessly·poor·ones." And

G4434.1 A-GPM πτωχῶν (2x)
Jn 12:6 to·him concerning the helplessly·poor, but·rather
Gal 2:10 that we·should·remember the helplessly·poor, also

EG4434.1 (1x)
2Co 9:13 ·fund for them and for all *the helplessly·poor*.

G4434.2 A-NSM πτωχός (2x)
Lk 16:20 a·certain helpless·beggar by·the·name·of Lazarus
Jac 2:2 there·should·enter also a·helpless·beggar in filthy

G4434.2 A-ASM πτωχόν (1x)
Lk 16:22 *as·such, for* the helpless·beggar to·die, and *for* him

EG4434.2 (1x)
1Co 13:3 ·some·food·for *the helpless·beggars using* all my

G4434.4 A-APN πτωχά (1x)
Gal 4:9 to the weak and pitifully·poor principles— to·which

G4435 πυγμή pygmḗ *n.* (1x)
Compare:G2159 See:G4438 G4437 xLangEquiv:H0106

G4435.3 N-DSF πυγμῇ (1x)
Mk 7:3 unless they·should·wash their hands rigorously,

G4436 Πύθων Pýthōn *n/p.* (1x)
Compare:G5540-2 G3131-2 G2973

G4436.3 N/P-GSM Πύθωνος (1x)
Ac 16:16 a·spirit of·Pythonic·divination approached·and·met

G4437 πυκνός pyknṓs *adj.* (3x)
See:G4435

G4437.2 A-APF πυκνάς (1x)
1Ti 5:23 ·of your stomach and your frequent sicknesses.

G4437.3 A-APN πυκνά (1x)
Lk 5:33 ·that the disciples of·John fast frequently, and make

G4437.4 A-ASN-C πυκνότερον (1x)
Ac 24:26 ·for him more·frequently and was·conversing with·

G4438 πυκτέω pyktéō *v.* (1x)
Roots:G4435 Compare:G5299 G2852

G4438 V-PAI-1S πυκτεύω (1x)
1Co 9:26 as uncertainly; in·this·manner I·do·box, *but* not as

G4439 πύλη pýlē *n.* (10x)
Compare:G2374 See:G4440 xLangEquiv:H8179 xLangAlso:H1817

G4439 N-NSF πύλη (2x)
Mt 7:13 gate, because broad *is* the gate, and spacious *is* the
Mt 7:14 "How obstructed·and·narrow *is* the gate, and the

G4439 N-NPF πύλαι (1x)
Mt 16:18 and Hades' gates shall·not overpower it.

G4439 N-ASF πύλην (1x)
Ac 12:10 they·came to the iron gate, the·one leading to the

G4439 N-APF πύλας (1x)
Ac 9:24 they·were·meticulously·watching the gates both day

G4439 N-DSF πύλῃ (2x)
Lk 7:12 Now as he·drew·near to·the gate of·the city, behold,
Ac 3:10 at the Stately·and·Elegant Gate of·the Sanctuary·

G4439 N-GSF πύλης (3x)
Lk 13:24 through the obstructed·and·narrow gate, because
Heb 13:12 through his·own blood, suffered outside the gate.
Mt 7:13 ·in through the obstructed·and·narrow gate, because

G4440 πυλών pylṓn *n.* (20x)
Roots:G4439 Compare:G2374 See:G4440-1

G4440.1 N-NPM πυλῶνες (6x)
Rv 21:13 On *the* east *are* three gates; on *the* north *are* three
Rv 21:13 on *the* north *are* three gates; on *the* south *are*
Rv 21:13 gates; on *the* south *are* three gates; *and* on *the* west
Rv 21:13 *are* three gates; *and* on *the* west *are* three gates.
Rv 21:21 And the twelve gates *were* twelve pearls; again,
Rv 21:25 And no, its gates may·not be·shut at·day's·end, for

G4440.1 N-ASM πυλῶνα (4x)
Lk 16:20 his gate, having·been·afflicted·with·pus·sores,
Ac 10:17 for·Simon's home, they·stood·over at the gate.
Ac 12:14 voice, she·did·not open·up the gate due·to her joy,
Mt 26:71 And with·him going·out to the gate·*area*, another

G4440.1 N-APM πυλῶνας (3x)
Ac 14:13 bulls and garlands to the gates, he·was·wanting to·
Rv 21:12 and high, having twelve gates, and twelve angels
Rv 21:15 ·measure the CITY, and its gates, and its wall.

G4440.1 N-DPM πυλῶσιν (2x)
Rv 21:12 and twelve angels upon the gates, and names
Rv 22:14 of·Life·above and may·enter by·the gates into the

G4440.1 N-GSM πυλῶνος (2x)
Ac 12:13 knocking *at* the door of·the gate, a·servant·girl
Ac 12:14 "Peter is·standing before the gate!"

G4440.1 N-GPM πυλώνων (1x)
Rv 21:21 again, each one of·the gates was *made* out of·one

EG4440.1 (2x)
Ac 11:11 three men were·standing·over *the gate* at the home
Ac 12:16 And opening·up *the gate*, they·saw him and were·

G4441 πυνθάνομαι pynthánômai *v.* (12x)
πύθω pýthō [an alternate in certain tenses]
Compare:G1833 G1905 G2065 G0154 G2212 G1189 G0198

G4441.1 V-PNI-1S πυνθάνομαι (1x)
Ac 10:29 ·opposition. Accordingly, I·inquire, for·what

G4441.1 V-PNN πυνθάνεσθαι (1x)
Ac 23:20 ·though intending to·inquire more·precisely *about*

G4441.1 V-INI-3S ἐπυνθάνετο (5x)
Lk 15:26 of·his servant·boys, he·inquired what might·be
Lk 18:36 a·crowd traversing·through, he·inquired what this
Ac 21:33 ·two chains, and·then he·inquired *of·them* who he·
Ac 23:19 and departing privately, was·inquiring, "What is·
Mt 2:4 of·the people, he·was·inquiring directly·from them

G4441.1 V-INI-3P ἐπυνθάνοντο (2x)
Ac 4:7 them in the middle, they·inquired, "By what·kind·of
Ac 10:18 hollering·out, they·were·inquiring whether Simon,

G4441.1 V-2ADI-3S ἐπύθετο (1x)
Jn 4:52 So·then he·inquired personally·from them the hour

G4441.1 V-2ADN πυθέσθαι (1x)
Jn 13:24 Simon Peter beckoned to·him to·inquire who it·

G4441.2 V-2ADP-NSM πυθόμενος (1x)
Ac 23:34 he·was birthed. And ascertaining that *he·was* from

G4442 πῦρ pŷr *n.* (74x)
Compare:G5395 See:G4443 xLangEquiv:H0784 A0785

G4442.1 N-NSN πῦρ (11x)
Heb 12:29 for even our God *is* a·fully·consuming fire.
Mk 9:44 ·not completely·die, and the fire is·not quenched.'
Mk 9:46 ·not completely·die, and the fire is·not quenched.'
Mk 9:48 ·does·not die, and the fire is·not quenched.'
Jac 3:5 Behold, a·little fire kindles *something* as·big·as a·
Jac 3:6 And the tongue *is* a·fire; *it·is* the world of·
1Co 3:13 fire, and the fire shall·test·and·prove each·man's
Rv 8:7 hail and fire having·been·mixed with·blood, and
Rv 9:17 out of·their mouths proceeds·forth fire and smoke
Rv 11:5 to·bring·harm·to them, fire proceeds·forth from·out
Rv 20:9 having·been·loved. And fire descended from God

G4442.1 N-ASN πῦρ (18x)
Jn 15:6 and cast *them* into fire, and they·are·set·ablaze.
Lk 3:9 good fruit is·chopped·down and is·cast into fire."
Lk 9:54 ·want *that* we·should·declare fire to·descend from
Lk 12:49 "I·came to·cast fire upon the earth.
Lk 17:29 from Sodom, it·showered fire and sulfur from

Lk 22:55 And with·them igniting a·fire in *the* midst of·the
Ac 2:19 down·below: blood and fire and vapor of·smoke.
Ac 28:5 ·off the venomous·beast into the fire, *Paul* suffered
Mt 3:10 good fruit is·chopped·down and is·cast into fire.
Mt 7:19 good fruit is·chopped·down and is·cast into fire.
Mt 17:15 ·fallen many·times into the fire and many·times
Mt 18:8 hands or two feet *and* to·be·cast into the eternal fire.
Mt 25:41 into the eternal fire, the·one having·been·made·
Mk 9:22 ·times it·cast him even into fire and into waters in·
Mk 9:43 into the Hell·Canyon, into the inextinguishable fire,
Mk 9:45 into the Hell·Canyon, into the inextinguishable fire,
Jac 5:3 shall·eat yeur flesh as fire. Yeu·stored·up·treasure in
Rv 13:13 so that it·should·make fire to·descend from·out

G4442.1 N-DSN πυρί (16x)
Lk 3:16 shall·immerse yeu in Holy Spirit and in·fire,
Lk 3:17 he·shall·completely·burn with·fire inextinguishable.
Heb 12:18 ·touch, nor having·been·set·ablaze with·fire, nor
Mt 3:11 shall·immerse yeu in Holy Spirit and in·fire,
Mt 3:12 ·burn the chaff with·inextinguishable fire."
Mt 13:40 and are·completely·burned in·fire, in·this·manner
Mk 9:49 "For everyone shall·be·salted with·fire, and every
2Pe 3:7 having·been·stored·up, being·reserved for·fire, for
2Th 1:8 *then* in blazing fire, giving retribution to·the·ones
1Co 3:13 ·*it*·plain, because it·is·revealed by fire, and the fire
Rv 8:8 mountain being·set·ablaze with·fire was·cast into the
Rv 14:10 and he·shall·be·tormented with fire and sulfur in·
Rv 15:2 ·glassy sea having·been·mixed with·fire, and·also
Rv 17:16 her flesh, and shall·completely·burn her with fire.
Rv 18:8 she·shall·be·completely·burned with fire, because
Rv 21:8 Lake, the·one being·set·ablaze with·fire and sulfur,

G4442.1 N-GSN πυρός (27x)
Ac 2:3 tongues as of·fire were·made·visible to·them, and it·
Ac 7:30 ·Mount Sinai, in a·blaze of·fire in·the·burning·bush.
Heb 1:7 his angels spirits and his attendants a·blaze of·fire."
Heb 11:34 quenched *the* power of·fire, escaped *the* edge of·
Mt 5:22 shall·be held·liable unto the Hell·Canyon of·fire.
Mt 13:42 into the furnace of·the fire, where there·shall·be
Mt 13:50 into the furnace of·the fire, where there·shall·be
Mt 18:9 eyes *and* to·be·cast into the Hell·Canyon of·fire.
Mk 9:47 eyes *and* to·be·cast into the Hell·Canyon of·fire,
Rm 12:20 this, you·shall·stack burning·coals of·fire on his
Jud 1:7 ·example, undergoing a·justice of·eternal fire.
Jud 1:23 while·snatching *them* from·out of·the fire, hating
1Pe 1:7 ·being·tested·and·proven through fire) may·be·found
1Co 3:15 ·be·saved, but in·this·manner, as through fire.
Rv 1:14 white as snow), and his eyes *are* as a·blaze of·fire,
Rv 2:18 having his eyes as a·blaze of·fire and his feet like
Rv 3:18 having·been·refined from·among fire, in·order·that
Rv 4:5 ·*are* seven lamps of·fire being·set·ablaze in·the·sight
Rv 8:5 overfilled it from·out of·the fire of·the Sacrifice·Altar
Rv 9:18 were·killed, as·a·result of·the fire, and as·a·result
Rv 10:1 face *was* as the sun, and his feet as pillars of·fire.
Rv 14:18 having authority over the fire; and he·hollered·out
Rv 19:12 His eyes *were* as a·blaze of·fire, and on his head
Rv 19:20 into the Lake of·the Fire, the·one being·set·ablaze
Rv 20:10 was·cast into the Lake of·the Fire and sulfur, where
Rv 20:14 were·cast into the Lake of·the Fire. This is the
Rv 20:15 life-above, he·was·cast into the Lake of·the Fire.

G4442.2 N-GSN πυρός (1x)
Heb 10:27 of·Tribunal·judgment and a·fiery indignation,

G4442.3 N-DSN πυρί (1x)
Rv 16:8 ·him to·burn the men·of·clay† with solar·radiation.

G4443 πυρά pyrá *n.* (2x)
Roots:G4442 See:G4445

G4443 N-ASF πυράν (2x)
Ac 28:2 ·the·mark. For kindling a·fire, they·each·received
Ac 28:3 and putting *them* on the fire, a·viper, coming·forth

G4444 πύργος pýrgôs *n.* (4x)
Compare:G3093 See:G4443-1
xLangEquiv:H4026

G4444 N-NSM πύργος (1x)
Lk 13:4 eighteen, upon whom the tower in Siloam fell and

G4444 N-ASM πύργον (3x)
Lk 14:28 yeu, wanting to·build a·tower, *does* not·indeed sit·
Mt 21:33 a·winepress in it and·also built a·tower," and·then
Mk 12:1 dug a·vat·for·a·winepress, and built a·tower," and

G4445 πυρέσσω pyréssō *v.* (2x)
Roots:G4443 See:G4448

G4445.2 V-PAP-ASF πυρέσσουσαν (1x)
Mt 8:14 ·been·cast *on·a·couch* and burning·with·fever.

G4445.2 V-PAP-NSF πυρέσσουσα (1x)
Mk 1:30 was·laying·ill, burning·with·fever, and

G4446 πυρετός pyrêtôs *n.* (6x)
Roots:G4445

G4446.3 N-NSM πυρετός (3x)
Jn 4:52 "Yesterday at·the·seventh hour the fever left him."
Mt 8:15 he·laid·hold of·her hand, and the fever left her, and
Mk 1:31 her hand, and immediately the fever left her, and

G4446.3 N-DSM πυρετῷ (2x)
Lk 4:38 was being·clenched with·a·high fever, and they·
Lk 4:39 over her, he·reprimanded the fever, and it·left her.

G4446.3 N-DPM πυρετοῖς (1x)
Ac 28:8 being·clenched with·*recurring*·fevers and dysentery.

G4447 πύρινος pýrinôs *adj.* (1x)
Roots:G4443

G4447.1 A-APM πυρίνους (1x)
Rv 9:17 full·chest·armor, fiery, like·deep·blue·hyacinth, and

G4448 πυρόω pyróō *v.* (6x)
Roots:G4442 Compare:G2545 G2741 See:G4445
G4451 G4451-1 xLangAlso:H6884 H6338

G4448.2 V-PPP-NPM πυρούμενοι (1x)
2Pe 3:12 *the* heavens, being·set·on·fire, shall·be·dissolved,

G4448.3 V-RPP-APN πεπυρωμένα (1x)
Eph 6:16 ·be·able to·extinguish all the fiery arrows of·the

G4448.5 V-RPP-ASN πεπυρωμένον (1x)
Rv 3:18 ·from me gold having·been·refined from·among fire

G4448.5 V-RPP-NPM πεπυρωμένοι (1x)
Rv 1:15 like fine·brass (as having·been·refined in a·furnace),

G4448.6 V-PPN πυροῦσθαι (1x)
1Co 7:9 ·is significantly·better to·marry than to·be·inflamed.

G4448.7 V-PPI-1S πυροῦμαι (1x)
2Co 11:29 ·failure, and I·myself am·not being·incensed?

G4449 πυρράζω pyrrházō *v.* (2x)
Roots:G4450 See:G2063

G4449 V-PAI-3S πυρράζει (2x)
Mt 16:2 '*It·shall·be* fine·weather, for the sky is·fiery·red.'
Mt 16:3 today, for the sky is·fiery·red *and* glowering.' O·

G4450 πυρρός pyrrhôs *adj.* (2x)
Roots:G4442 Compare:G2063 G2847
xLangAlso:H8320

G4450.2 A-NSM πυρρός (2x)
Rv 6:4 ·came·forth another horse *that·was* fiery·red. And it·
Rv 12:3 and behold a·great fiery·red Dragon, having seven

G4451 πύρωσις pýrōsis *n.* (3x)
Roots:G4448 Compare:G3986 G2738 G2347

G4451.3 N-GSF πυρώσεως (2x)
Rv 18:9 ·should·look·upon the smoke of·her fiery·burning,
Rv 18:18 ·seeing the smoke of·her fiery·burning, saying,

G4451.4 N-DSF πυρώσει (1x)
1Pe 4:12 ·strangely·surprised at the fiery·trial *that·has·come*

G4453 πωλέω pōléō *v.* (22x)
Compare:G4097 G1710 xLangAlso:H4376

G4453 V-PAI-3S πωλεῖ (1x)
Mt 13:44 of·it, he·heads·on·out and sells all (as·much·as

G4453 V-PAP-APM πωλοῦντας (5x)
Jn 2:14 Sanctuary·Atrium, he·found the·ones selling oxen,
Lk 19:45 he·began to·cast·out the·ones selling and buying
Mt 21:12 and cast·out all the·ones selling and buying in the
Mt 25:9 traverse rather toward the·ones selling *oil* and buy
Mk 11:15 began to·cast·out the·ones selling and buying in

G4453 V-PAP-DPM πωλοῦσιν (1x)
Jn 2:16 And he·declared to·the·ones selling the doves,

G4453 V-PAP-GPM πωλούντων (2x)
Mt 21:12 and the seats of·the·ones selling the doves,
Mk 11:15 and the seats of·the·ones selling the doves,

G4453 V-PAP-NPM πωλοῦντες (1x)
Ac 4:34 of·open·fields or homes, upon·selling *them*, they·

G4453 V-PPI-3S πωλεῖται (2x)
Lk 12:6 five little·sparrows sold for·two assarion·coins?
Mt 10:29 two little·sparrows sold for·an·assarion·coin?

G4453 V-PPP-ASN πωλούμενον (1x)
1Co 10:25 Every thing being·sold in a·meat·market, eat *it*,

G4453 V-IAI-3P ἐπώλουν (1x)
Lk 17:28 ·buying, they·were·selling, they·were·planting,

G4453 V-AAI-3S ἐπώλησεν (1x)
Ac 5:1 together with·Sapphira his wife, sold a·possession,

G4453 V-AAM-2S πώλησον (3x)
Lk 18:22 one·thing remains·left·undone. Sell all·things, as·
Mt 19:21 ·be complete, head·on·out, sell your holdings and
Mk 10:21 you lack, head·on·out, sell as·much·as you·have,

G4453 V-AAM-2P πωλήσατε (1x)
Lk 12:33 "Sell yeur holdings and give a·merciful·act·of·

G4453 V-AAM-3S πωλησάτω (1x)
Lk 22:36 not having a·dagger, let·him·sell his garment and

G4453 V-AAN πωλῆσαι (1x)
Rv 13:17 anyone should·be·able to·buy or to·sell, except the·

G4453 V-AAP-NSM πωλήσας (1x)
Ac 4:37 by·himself on·a·plot·of·land. After·selling *it*, he·

G4454 πῶλος pōlôs *n.* (12x)
Compare:G5207

G4454.1 N-ASM πῶλον (12x)
Jn 12:15 comes *to·you*, sitting·down upon a·donkey's colt.
Lk 19:30 ·in, yeu·shall·find a·colt having·been·tied, on
Lk 19:33 And as·they were·loosing the colt, its owners
Lk 19:33 "Why·do yeu·loose the colt?"
Lk 19:35 their·own garments upon the colt, they·mounted
Mt 21:2 a·donkey having·been·tied·up, and a·colt with her.
Mt 21:5 upon a·donkey even *upon* a·colt, a·foal of·a·mated·
Mt 21:7 brought the donkey and the colt, and they·put their
Mk 11:2 into it, yeu·shall·find a·colt having·been·tied, on
Mk 11:4 ·away and found the colt outside having·been·tied
Mk 11:5 "What·are yeu·doing, loosening the colt?"
Mk 11:7 And they·brought the colt to Jesus, and they·threw

G4455 πώ•πο•τε pṓpôtê *adv.* (6x)
Roots:G4452 G4218

G4455 ADV πώποτε (6x)
Jn 1:18 ·man has·clearly·seen God ever·at·any·time. The
Jn 5:37 ·even yeu·have·heard his voice ever·at·any·time, nor
Jn 6:35 in me, no, he·should·not thirst ever·at·any·time.
Jn 8:33 ·at·all, ever·at·any·time, have·we·been·enslaved.
Lk 19:30 ·one man·of·clay† sat ever·at·any·time. Loosing it,
1Jn 4:12 ·man has·distinctly·viewed God ever·at·any·time. If

G4456 πωρόω pōróō *v.* (5x)
Compare:G4645 See:G4457

G4456.1 V-API-3S ἐπωρώθη (1x)
2Co 3:14 mental·dispositions were·petrified·hard·as·stone.

G4456.1 V-API-3P ἐπωρώθησαν (1x)
Rm 11:7 ·obtain *it*, and the rest were·petrified·hard·as·stone,

G4456.1 V-RAI-3S πεπώρωκεν (1x)
Jn 12:40 heart he·has·petrified·hard·as·stone in·order·that

G4456.1 V-RPP-ASF πεπωρωμένην (1x)
Mk 8:17 your heart still having·been·petrified·hard·as·stone?

G4456.1 V-RPP-NSF πεπωρωμένη (1x)
Mk 6:52 their heart was having·been·petrified·hard·as·stone.

G4457 πώρωσις pṓrōsis *n.* (3x)
Roots:G4456 Compare:G4643

G4457.2 N-NSF πώρωσις (1x)
Rm 11:25 *the* stony·hardness has·happened to·IsraEl *only* in

G4457.2 N-ASF πώρωσιν (1x)
Eph 4:18 on·account·of the stony·hardness of·their heart,

G4457.2 N-DSF πωρώσει (1x)
Mk 3:5 ·grieved over the stony·hardness of·their hearts, he·

G4458 πώς -pṓs *adv.* (1x)
Roots:G4225 Compare:G4459 See:G1513 G3381

G4458 PRT-I πως (1x)
Rm 11:14 so·that somehow I·may·provoke·to·jealousy *them*

G4459 πῶς pôs *adv.* (103x)
Roots:G4226
G4459.ª ADV πῶς (1x)
Ac 20:18 into Asia, with·what·manner I·have·been with you
G4459.ª ADV-I πῶς (1x)
Mt 12:29 "Or how·else·is anyone able to·enter into the
G4459.1 ADV-I πῶς (3x)
Mt 12:34 being evil, in·what·way are·yeu·able to·speak
Mt 23:33 of·vipers, in·what·way should·yeu·escape from
1Jn 4:20 he·has·clearly·seen, in·what·way is·he·able to·love
G4459.2 ADV πῶς (24x)
Jn 11:36 were·saying, "See how fond·he·was·of him!"
Lk 8:18 Accordingly, look·out·for how *well* yeu·listen·with·
Lk 12:27 "Fully·observe how the lilies grow.
Lk 12:50 to·be·immersed·in, and how am·I·clenched until
Lk 14:7 paying·close·attention how they·were·selecting the
Lk 18:24 declared, "How impossibly·difficult *it·is, that*
Ac 9:27 and gave·an·account to·them how *Saul* saw the Lord
Ac 9:27 to·him, and how he·boldly·spoke·with·clarity at
Ac 11:13 And he·announced to·us how he·saw the angel in
Ac 12:17 ·silent, he·gave·an·account to·them how the Lord
Mt 6:28 the lilies of·the field, how they·grow; they·do·not
Mt 12:4 How he·entered into the house of·God and ate the
Mk 2:26 How he·entered into the house of·God in·the·days
Mk 5:16 ·an·account to·them of·how it·happened to·the·one
Mk 10:23 to·his disciples, "How impossibly·difficult *it·is*
Mk 10:24 "Children, how exceedingly·difficult it·is for·
Mk 12:41 ·room, Jesus was·observing how the crowd cast
1Th 1:9 to yeu, and how yeu·turned·back·around to God
1Th 4:1 from us, *remember* how it·is·mandatory·for yeu to·
2Th 3:7 have·seen how it·is·necessary to·attentively·imitate
1Co 3:10 But each·man must·look·out how he·builds·upon *it*
Eph 5:15 look·out *then for* precisely how yeu·walk, not as
Col 4:6 ·for yeu to·personally·know how to·answer each
1Ti 3:15 you·may·personally·know how it·is·necessary to·
G4459.2 ADV-I πῶς (71x)
Jn 3:4 says to him, "How·is a·man·of·clay† able to·be·born,
Jn 3:9 and declared to·him, "How·are these·things able to·
Jn 3:12 and yeu·do·not trust, how shall·yeu·trust if I·should·
Jn 4:9 woman says to·him, "How·is·it *that* you, being a·Jew,
Jn 5:44 How·are yeu·yeurselves able to·trust, receiving glory
Jn 5:47 trust those *Sacred*·Writings, how shall·yeu·trust my
Jn 6:42 personally·know? So·then how·is·it *that* he·says
Jn 6:52 one·another, saying, "How·is this·man able to·give
Jn 7:15 saying, "How·does this·man personally·know *the*
Jn 8:33 have·we·been·enslaved. How·do you·yourself say,
Jn 9:10 they·were·saying to·him, "How·are your eyes
Jn 9:15 also were·asking·of him how he·received·his·sight.
Jn 9:16 Others were·saying, "How·is a·man·of·clay†, full·
Jn 9:19 So·then at·this·moment, how does·he·look·about?
Jn 9:26 "What·did he·do to·you? How·did he·open·up your
Jn 12:34 to the coming·age, and how·do you·yourself say,
Jn 14:5 ·out, so·then how are·we·able to·personally·know
Jn 14:9 ·seen the Father; so·then how·do you·yourself say,
Lk 1:34 declared to the angel, "How shall this be, since I·
Lk 6:42 Or how are·you·able to·say to·your brother,
Lk 10:26 ·written in the Torah-Law? How·do you·read *it*?
Lk 11:18 ·thoroughly·divided against himself, how shall his
Lk 12:11 authorities, do·not be·anxious·about how or what
Lk 12:56 but how·is·it that·yeu·do·not examine·and·verify
Lk 20:41 to them, "How·do they·say *it·is·mandatory·for* the
Lk 20:44 'Lord'; how is·he also his Son?
Lk 22:2 scribes were·seeking how they·may·eliminate him,
Lk 22:4 and the wardens, how he·may·hand him over to·
Ac 2:8 And how·do we·ourselves each hear our own·distinct
Ac 4:21 not·even·one·thing of·how they·should·sternly·
Ac 8:31 he·declared, "For how·is·it *that* I·might be·able *to·*
Ac 15:36 of·the Lord, *and see* how they·are."
Heb 2:3 how·shall we·ourselves utterly·escape after·
Gal 4:9 being·known by God, how·is·it *that* yeu·return
Mt 7:4 Or how shall·you·declare to·your brother, 'Give·way
Mt 10:19 yeu·should·not be·anxious·about how or what
Mt 12:26 against himself. So·then, how shall his kingdom
Mt 16:11 How·is·it that yeu·do·not understand that·I·
Mt 21:20 saying, "How·is the fig·tree withered·away *all*
Mt 22:12 to·him, 'O·associate, how did·you·enter here not
Mt 22:43 ·says to·them, "So·then how·does David in Spirit
Mt 22:45 'Lord,' how is·he his Son?
Mt 26:54 But·then how·should the Scriptures be·completely·
Mk 3:23 to·them in parables, "How·is·it possible *for·the*
Mk 4:13 this parable? How·else then shall·yeu·know all the
Mk 4:40 timid in·this·manner? How·is·it *that* yeu·do·not
Mk 8:21 ·saying to·them, "How do·yeu·not comprehend?
Mk 9:12 "Yet how it·has·been·written concerning the Son
Mk 11:18 were·seeking how they·shall·completely·destroy
Mk 12:35 Jesus was·saying, "How·do the scribes say that
Mk 14:1 scribes were·seeking how, after·taking·secure·hold
Mk 14:11 he·was·seeking how he·should·conveniently hand
Rm 3:6 ·it·never happen! Otherwise how·does God judge
Rm 4:10 So·then how was·it·reckoned?
Rm 6:2 ·who died to·Moral·Failure; how shall·we·live in it
Rm 8:32 over on·behalf·of·us all, how shall·he·not·indeed,
Rm 10:14 So·then, how shall·they·call·upon *him* in whom
Rm 10:14 they·did·not trust? And how shall·they·trust *him*
Rm 10:14 ·not hear? And how shall·they·hear apart·from
Rm 10:15 And how shall·they·officially·proclaim, unless
1Co 7:32 of·the Lord, how he·shall·accommodate the Lord.
1Co 7:33 of·the world, how he·shall·accommodate his wife.
1Co 7:34 of·the world, how she·shall·accommodate the
1Co 14:7 in·the·musical·notes, how shall·it·be·known *what*
1Co 14:9 a·clearly·discernible word, how shall·it·be·known,
1Co 14:16 ·the spirit, how·shall the·one utterly·occupying
1Co 15:12 from·among dead·men, how·do some among you
1Co 15:35 someone shall·declare, "How·are the dead·men
2Co 3:8 indeed, how·much more shall the Service of·the
1Ti 3:5 how shall·he·take·care of·a·Called·Out·citizenry
1Jn 3:17 inward·affections from him, how·does the love of·
G4459.3 ADV πῶς (2x)
Lk 8:36 to·them by·what·means the·one being·possessed·
Rv 3:3 remember by·what·means you·have·received and
G4459.3 ADV-I πῶς (1x)
Jn 9:21 But now by·what·means he·looks·about, we·do·not

Ρρ - Rho

G4461 ῥαββί rhabbí *heb.* (17x)
רַבִּי rạḇıy [Hebrew]
Roots:H7240-2 Compare:G2519 G4166 G2819-2 See:G4462 xLangAlso:H7473
G4461.2 HEB ῥαββί (17x)
Jn 1:38 They·declared to·him, "Rabbi" (which, when·
Jn 1:49 answered and says to·him, "Rabbi, you·yourself are
Jn 3:2 and declared to·him, "Rabbi, we·have·seen that you·
Jn 3:26 John and declared to·him, "Rabbi, he·who was with
Jn 4:31 were·imploring·of him, saying, "Rabbi, eat!"
Jn 6:25 they·declared to·him, "Rabbi, when did·you·come
Jn 9:2 asked·of him, saying, "Rabbi, who morally·failed,
Jn 11:8 The disciples say to·him, "Rabbi, the Judeans now
Mt 23:7 by the men·of·clay†, 'Rabbi, Rabbi' *(meaning, my·*
Mt 23:7 ·clay†, 'Rabbi, Rabbi' *(meaning, my·Superior,·my·*
Mt 23:8 But yeu·yeurselves should·not be·called 'Rabbi,' for
Mt 26:25 him over) declared, "Rabbi, is·it·I myself?
Mt 26:49 he·declared, "Be·well, Rabbi," and earnestly·
Mk 9:5 Peter says to·Jesus, "Rabbi, it·is good for·us to·be
Mk 11:21 *it*, Peter says to·him, "Rabbi, see, the fig·tree
Mk 14:45 going·toward him, he·says, "Rabbi, Rabbi," and
Mk 14:45 he·says, "Rabbi, Rabbi," and he·earnestly·kissed

G4462 ῥαββονί rhabbôní *aram.* (2x)
ῥαββουνί rhabbôuní
רַבּוּנִי rạḇûniy [Aramaic]
Roots:A7240-1 See:G4461 xLangEquiv:H7240-2
G4462 ARAM ῥαββουνι (2x)
Jn 20:16 says to·him *in·Aramaic*, "Rabboni!" (which is·to·
Mk 10:51 declared to·him, "Rabboni, that I·may·receive·

G4463 ῥαβδίζω rhabdízō *v.* (2x)
Roots:G4464
G4463.1 V-PAN ῥαβδίζειν (1x)
Ac 16:22 ·ordered *for·Paul and Silas* to·be·beaten·with·rods.
G4463.1 V-API-1S ἐρραβδίσθην (1x)
2Co 11:25 I·was·beaten·with·rods three·times, I·was·stoned

G4464 ῥάβδος rhábdôs *n.* (12x)
Roots:G4474 Compare:G0902-1 G3586 xLangAlso:H4294 H7626 H4938
G4464.1 N-NSF ῥάβδος (1x)
Heb 9:4 the manna, and Aaron's staff (the·one blossoming),
G4464.1 N-ASF ῥάβδον (2x)
Mt 10:10 tunics, nor·even shoes, nor·even a·staff, for the
Mk 6:8 *saying*, "… except a·staff merely. No knapsack, no
G4464.1 N-APF ῥάβδους (1x)
Lk 9:3 ·thing for the journey, neither staffs, nor knapsack,
G4464.1 N-GSF ῥάβδου (1x)
Heb 11:21 and he·leaned·prostrate upon the tip of·his staff.
G4464.2 N-DSF ῥάβδῳ (5x)
1Co 4:21 Should·I·come toward you with a·rod or with love,
Rv 2:27 "" And he·shall·shepherd them with a·rod of·iron, as
Rv 11:1 And he·gave to·me a·reed like a·rod, saying,
Rv 12:5 to·shepherd all the nations with a·rod of·iron; and
Rv 19:15 he·himself shall·shepherd them with a·rod of·iron,
G4464.3 N-NSF ῥάβδος (2x)
Heb 1:8 *is* to the age of·ages; a·scepter of·straightness *is* the
Heb 1:8 of·straightness *is* the scepter of·your kingdom.

G4465 ῥαβδο•ῦχος rhabdôûchôs *n.* (2x)
Roots:G4464 G2192
G4465.2 N-NPM ῥαβδοῦχοι (1x)
Ac 16:38 the enforcement·officers reported·in·detail these
G4465.2 N-APM ῥαβδούχους (1x)
Ac 16:35 dispatched the enforcement·officers, saying,

G4466 Ῥαγαῦ Rhagaû *n/p.* (1x)
רְעוּ rᵉʻû [Hebrew]
Roots:H7466
G4466.2 N/P-PRI Ῥαγαῦ (1x)
Lk 3:35 *son* of·Serug, *son* of·Reu, *son* of·Peleg, *son* of·Eber

G4467 ῥᾳδιο•ύργημα rhadiôúrgēma *n.* (1x)
Roots:G2041 Compare:G2556 See:G4468
G4467.2 N-NSN ῥᾳδιούργημα (1x)
Ac 18:14 or an·evil, mischievous·deed according·to reason,

G4468 ῥᾳδιο•υργία rhadiôurgía *n.* (1x)
Roots:G2041 See:G4467
G4468.2 N-GSF ῥᾳδιουργίας (1x)
Ac 13:10 of·all guile and all mischief, O·Son of·Slanderer!

G4469 ῥακά rhaká *aram.* (1x)
ῥακά rhaqá [Greek, Octuagint]
רֵק req [Hebrew]
Roots:H7386 Compare:G0955 G4550
G4469.1 ARAM ῥακά (1x)
Mt 5:22 to·his brother, 'Raqa·*(Worthless·One)*,' shall·be

G4470 ῥάκος rhákôs *n.* (2x)
Roots:G4486 See:G4485
G4470.1 N-GSN ῥάκους (2x)
Mt 9:16 throws a·patch of·unprocessed cloth onto an·old
Mk 2:21 ·man sews a·patch of·unprocessed cloth on an·old

G4471 Ῥαμᾶ Rhamâ *n/l.* (1x)
רָמָה ramah
Roots:H7414 Compare:G0707
G4471.2 N/L-PRI Ῥαμά (1x)
Mt 2:18 "A·voice was·heard in Ramah— a·woeful·wailing

G4472 ῥαντίζω rhantízō *v.* (4x)
Roots:G4468-3 Compare:G0907 G2708 G4365-1
See:G4473 G1975-1 G4047-5
xLangEquiv:H2236
G4472 V-PAP-NSF ῥαντίζουσα (1x)
Heb 9:13 ·red·cow) sprinkling the·ones having·been·defiled
G4472 V-AAI-3S ἐρράντισεν (2x)
Heb 9:19 wool, and hyssop, he·sprinkled both the·official·
Heb 9:21 Moreover likewise, he·sprinkled the Tabernacle
G4472 V-RPP-NPM ἐρραντισμένοι (1x)
Heb 10:22 the hearts having·been·sprinkled from an·evil

G4473 ῥαντισμός rhantismós *n.* (2x)
Roots:G4472
G4473.1 N-ASM ῥαντισμόν (1x)
1Pe 1:2 ·attentive·obedience and a·sprinkling of·the·blood
G4473.2 N-GSM ῥαντισμοῦ (1x)
Heb 12:24 ·new covenant, and to·sprinkled blood speaking

G4474 ῥαπίζω rhapízō *v.* (2x)
Compare:G5180 See:G4475
G4474 V-FAI-3S ῥαπίσει (1x)
Mt 5:39 evil·person, but·rather whoever shall·slap you on
G4474 V-AAI-3P ἐρράπισαν (1x)
Mt 26:67 his face and buffeted him, and they·slapped *him*,

G4475 ῥάπισμα rhápisma *n.* (3x)
Roots:G4474
G4475 N-ASN ῥάπισμα (1x)
Jn 18:22 ·the assistants standing·nearby gave a·slap to·Jesus,
G4475 N-APN ῥαπίσματα (1x)
Jn 19:3 And they·were·giving him slaps.
G4475 N-DPN ῥαπίσμασιν (1x)
Mk 14:65 And the assistants were·casting slaps at·him.

G4476 ῥαφίς rhaphís *n.* (3x)
See:G1976 G5168 G5169
G4476 N-GSF ῥαφίδος (3x)
Lk 18:25 to·enter·in through a·tiny·inlet of·a·needle, than *for*
Mt 19:24 to·go through *the* tiny·hole of·a·needle than *for* a·
Mk 10:25 through the tiny·inlet of·the needle, than for·a·

G4477 Ῥαχάβ Rachab *n/p.* (3x)
רָחָב Raçhab [Hebrew]
Ῥαάβ Rhaáb [Greek, Septuagint]
Roots:H7343 See:G4460 G4503 xLangAlso:H7294
G4477.2 N/P-PRI Ῥαχάβ (3x)
Heb 11:31 By·trust, Rachav the prostitute did·not
Mt 1:5 Salmon begot BoAz (birthed·from·out of·Rachav), and
Jac 2:25 And likewise also Rachav the prostitute, was·she·

G4478 Ῥαχήλ Rhachēl *n/p.* (1x)
רָחֵל raçhel [Hebrew]
Roots:H7354 Compare:G0286
G4478.2 N/P-PRI Ῥαχήλ (1x)
Mt 2:18 and much distressing; *it·was* Rachel weeping *for* her

G4479 Ῥεβέκκα Rhêbékka *n/p.* (1x)
רִבְקָה Ribqah [Hebrew]
Ρεβέκα Rêbéqa [Greek, Octuagint]
Roots:H7259
G4479.2 N/P-NSF Ρεβέκα (1x)
Rm 9:10 merely *this*. Moreover with·Rebeqah also, having

G4480 ῥέδα rhéda *n.* (1x)
Compare:G0716
G4480.1 N-GPF ῥεδῶν (1x)
Rv 18:13 sheep, horses, and carriages, "and bodies and

G4481 Ῥεμφάν Rhêmphán *n/p.* (1x)
Ῥειφάν Rhêiphán [Septuagint]
כִּיּוּן kiyûn [Hebrew]
Roots:H3594
G4481 N/P-PRI Ῥεμφάν (1x)
Ac 7:43 and the star·constellation of·yeur god Remphan, the

G4482 ῥέω rhéō *v.* (1x)
ῥεύω rhêúō
[a prolonged form for some tenses]
See:G4483 G4511 G4480-1 G2674-4
xLangAlso:H2100
G4482 V-FAI-3P ῥεύσουσιν (1x)
Jn 7:38 "from·out of·his belly shall·flow rivers of·living

G4483 ῥέω rhéō *v.* (26x)
ἐρέω êréō
[prolonged form; used for certain tenses]
Compare:G2036 G3004 G5346 G2980 G5350
See:G4487 G2046 G4490 G4482
xLangEquiv:H0559 A0560
G4483 V-API-3S ἐρρέθη (10x)
Mt 5:21 "Yeu·heard that it·was·uttered to·the ancient·ones,
Mt 5:27 "Yeu·heard that it·was·uttered to·the ancient·ones,
Mt 5:31 "It·was·uttered, 'Whoever should·divorce his wife
Mt 5:33 yeu·heard that it·was·uttered to·the ancient·ones,
Mt 5:38 "Yeu·heard that it·was·uttered, "An·eye for an·eye
Mt 5:43 "Yeu·heard that it·was·uttered, "You·shall·love
Rm 9:12 because it·was·uttered to·her, "The greater shall·
Rm 9:26 *that* in the place where it·was·uttered to·them,
Rv 6:11 ·each·one·of·them, and it·was·uttered to·them that
Rv 9:4 And it·was·uttered to·them that they·should·not
G4483 V-API-3P ἐρρήθησαν (1x)
Gal 3:16 Now the promises were·uttered to·AbRaham and
G4483 V-APP-ASN ῥηθέν (3x)
Mt 22:31 read·aloud of·the·thing being·uttered to·yeu by
Mt 24:15 ' the·one being·uttered through DaniEl the
Mk 13:14 of·Desolation," the·one being·uttered by DaniEl
G4483 V-APP-NSN ῥηθέν (11x)
Mt 1:22 ·fulfilled, the·thing being·uttered by Yahweh
Mt 2:15 ·fulfilled, the·thing being·uttered by Yahweh
Mt 2:17 ·fulfilled, the·thing being·uttered by JeremIah the
Mt 2:23 ·fulfilled, the·thing being·uttered through the
Mt 4:14 ·fulfilled, the·thing being·uttered through IsaIah the
Mt 8:17 ·fulfilled, the·one being·uttered through IsaIah the
Mt 12:17 ·fulfilled, the·thing being·uttered through IsaIah
Mt 13:35 ·fulfilled, the·thing being·uttered through the
Mt 21:4 ·fulfilled, the·thing being·uttered through the
Mt 27:9 ·fulfilled the·thing being·uttered through JeremIah
Mt 27:35 ·fulfilled, the·thing being·uttered by the prophet,
G4483 V-APP-NSM ῥηθείς (1x)
Mt 3:3 For this is·he, the·one being·uttered *of* by IsaIah the

G4484 Ῥήγιον Rhḗgiôn *n/l.* (1x)
G4484 N/L-ASN Ῥήγιον (1x)
Ac 28:13 from·there, we·arrived in Rhegium. And after one

G4485 ῥῆγμα rhēgma *n.* (1x)
Roots:G4486 Compare:G4938 G2679 See:G4470
G4485.2 N-NSN ῥῆγμα (1x)
Lk 6:49 it·fell. And the wreckage of·that home became great

G4486 ῥήγνυμι rhḗgnymi *v.* (7x)
ῥήσσω rhḗssō
ῥήκω rhḗkō [appears only in certain forms]
Compare:G2352 G2806 G3089 G4682 G4952
See:G2608 G4366 xLangAlso:H1234
G4486.2 V-FAI-3S ῥήξει (1x)
Lk 5:37 ·if·so, the fresh·new wine shall·burst the wineskins,
G4486.2 V-PAI-3S ῥήσσει (1x)
Mk 2:22 But·if·so, the fresh·new wine bursts the wineskins,
G4486.2 V-PPI-3P ῥήγνυνται (1x)
Mt 9:17 But·if·so, the wineskins are·burst, and the wine
G4486.3 V-AAM-2S ῥῆξον (1x)
Gal 4:27 ·and·giving·birth. Burst·forth and cry·out, the·one
G4486.4 V-PAI-3S ῥήσσει (1x)
Mk 9:18 *spirit* should·grasp him, he·mangles him, and he·
G4486.4 V-AAI-3S ἔρρηξεν (1x)
Lk 9:42 yet coming·alongside, the demon mangled him and
G4486.4 V-AAS-3P ῥήξωσιν (1x)
Mt 7:6 their feet, then turning·around, should·mangle yeu.

G4487 ῥῆμα rhēma *n.* (70x)
Roots:G4483 Compare:G3051 G3056 G5538
See:G4488-1
xLangEquiv:H0561 H0562
G4487.1 N-NSN ῥῆμα (11x)
Lk 1:37 because any utterance directly·from God shall·not
Lk 3:2 *the* high·priests— an·utterance of·God came to John
Lk 18:34 also, this utterance was having·been·hidden from
Mt 12:36 to·yeu, that for·every idle utterance, which if the
Mt 18:16 witnesses every utterance may·be·established."
Rm 10:8 what·does it·say? "The utterance is near you, *even*
Rm 10:8 heart" (that is, the utterance of·the trust which we·
1Pe 1:25 but the utterance of·Yahweh endures to the coming·
1Pe 1:25 ' And this is the utterance, the good·news·already·
2Co 13:1 witnesses shall every utterance be·established."
Eph 6:17 dagger of·the Spirit, which is an·utterance of·God.
G4487.1 N-NPN ῥήματα (7x)
Jn 6:63 not·even·one·thing. The utterances that I·myself
Jn 10:21 the utterances *of·one* who·is·being·possessed·with·
Jn 15:7 ·abide in me and my utterances should·abide in yeu,
Lk 1:65 And all these utterances were·conveyed among the
Lk 24:11 And their utterances appeared in·the·sight of·them
Rm 10:18 the earth, and their utterances to the utmost·parts
Rv 17:17 ·until the utterances of·God should·be·completed.
G4487.1 N-ASN ῥῆμα (11x)
Lk 1:38 May·it·happen to·me according·to your utterance."
Lk 2:15 so we·may·see this utterance, the·one having·
Lk 2:29 your slave in peace, according·to your utterance,
Lk 2:50 did·not comprehend the utterance which he·spoke
Lk 9:45 But they·were·not·understanding this utterance, and
Ac 10:37 personally·know the utterance occurring in all
Ac 28:25 ·themselves, with·Paul declaring one utterance,
Heb 6:5 and after·tasting a·good utterance of·God, and·also
Mt 5:11 ·declare all·manner·of evil utterance against yeu,
Mt 27:14 answer to him not·even one utterance, such·for the
Mk 9:32 ·not·understanding the utterance and were·afraid to·
G4487.1 N-APN ῥήματα (21x)
Jn 3:34 God dispatched speaks the utterances of·God, for *to*·
Jn 6:68 ·we·go? You·have utterances of·eternal life-above.
Jn 8:20 These utterances Jesus spoke at the treasury·room,
Jn 8:47 birthed·from·out of·God hears the utterances of·God.
Jn 12:48 me and not receiving my utterances, has *this* one
Jn 14:10 in me? "The utterances that I·myself speak to·yeu,
Jn 17:8 ·given to·them the utterances which you·have·given
Lk 2:19 ·closely·guarding all these utterances, ruminating
Lk 2:51 was·thoroughly·guarding all these utterances in her
Lk 7:1 *Jesus* fully·finished all his utterances in the hearing
Ac 2:14 be this known to·yeu and give·ear to·my utterances.
Ac 5:20 to·the people all the utterances of·this life-above."
Ac 6:11 him speaking reviling utterances against Moses and

Ac 6:13 ·not cease speaking reviling utterances against this
Ac 10:22 house, and to·hear utterances personally·from you.
Ac 10:44 As·Peter was·yet speaking these utterances, the
Ac 11:14 who shall·speak to you utterances by which you·
Ac 13:42 for·these utterances to·be·spoken to·them at the
Ac 16:38 ·in·detail these utterances to·the court·officers, and
Ac 26:25 I·clearly·enunciate utterances of·truth and·also
2Co 12:4 and heard inexpressible utterances, which is·not
G4487.1 N-DSN ῥήματι (6x)
Lk 4:4 alone, but·rather upon every utterance of·Yahweh.'"
Lk 5:5 But at your utterance, I·shall·lower the net.
Heb 1:3 upholding all·things by·the utterance of·his power)
Heb 11:3 to·have·been·completely·formed by·an·utterance,
Mt 4:4 upon every utterance that·is·proceeding·forth through
Eph 5:26 her with·the bathing of·the water by an·utterance—
G4487.1 N-DPN ῥήμασιν (1x)
Jn 5:47 ·Writings, how shall·yeu·trust my utterances?"
G4487.1 N-GSN ῥήματος (7x)
Lk 2:17 ·it·known·to·all concerning the utterance, the·one
Lk 9:45 ·were·afraid to·ask him concerning this utterance.
Lk 20:26 ·hold of·his utterances in·the·direct·presence of·the
Ac 11:16 "Then I·recalled·to·mind the utterance of·*the*·Lord,
Mt 26:75 was·*suddenly*·mindful of·the utterance *that* YeShua
Mk 14:72 ·to·mind·and·considered the utterance which Jesus
Rm 10:17 and the hearing through an·utterance of·God.
G4487.1 N-GPN ῥημάτων (6x)
Jn 12:47 someone should·hear my utterances and should·not
Lk 24:8 And they·recalled·to·mind his utterances.
Ac 5:32 are his witnesses of·these utterances; and so·also *is*
Heb 12:19 and to·a·voice of·utterances, of·which the·ones
Jud 1:17 beloved, recall·to·mind the utterances, the·ones
2Pe 3:2 of·the utterances having·been·already·stated by the

G4488 Ῥησά Rhēsá *n/p.* (1x)
רְפָיָה rᵉphayah
Roots:H7509
G4488.2 N/P-PRI Ῥησά (1x)
Lk 3:27 *son* of·Johannes, *son* of·RhesaYah, *son* of·

G4489 ῥήτωρ rhḗtōr *n.* (1x)
Roots:G4483
G4489.1 N-GSM ῥήτορος (1x)
Ac 24:1 elders, and *with* a·certain orator *named* Tertullus,

G4490 ῥητῶς rhētō̂s *adv.* (1x)
Roots:G4483
G4490 ADV ῥητῶς (1x)
1Ti 4:1 Now the Spirit expressly says that in later seasons

G4491 ῥίζα rhíza *n.* (17x)
See:G4492
xLangEquiv:H8328 A8330
G4491 N-NSF ῥίζα (7x)
Heb 12:15 lest any root of·bitterness sprouting upward
Rm 11:16 And if the root *is* holy, so *are* the branches.
Rm 11:18 bears the root, but·rather the root *that bears* you
Rm 15:12 '" There·shall·be the root of·Jesse, and the·one
1Ti 6:10 For one·root of·all the moral·wrongs is the
Rv 5:5 ·among the tribe of·Judah (the Root of·David)! He·
Rv 22:16 I AM the root and the kindred of·David, the star,
G4491 N-ASF ῥίζαν (8x)
Lk 3:9 the ax is·laid·out to the root of·the trees. Accordingly,
Lk 8:13 yet these have no root, who trust just·for a·season,
Mt 3:10 ·now also, the ax is·laid·out to the root of·the trees.
Mt 13:6 ·of it not having root, it·is·already·withered·away.
Mt 13:21 But he·does·not have root in himself, but·rather he·
Mk 4:6 on·account·of it·not having root, it·withered·away.
Mk 4:17 Yet they·do·not have root in themselves, but·rather
Rm 11:18 not you·yourself *that* bears the root, but·rather the
G4491 N-GSF ῥίζης (1x)
Rm 11:17 and became a·partner·together of·the root and the
G4491 N-GPF ῥιζῶν (1x)
Mk 11:20 ·tree having·been·withered from·out of·*the*·roots.

G4492 ῥιζόω rhizóō *v.* (2x)
Roots:G4491 See:G4492-1
xLangEquiv:H8327
G4492.1 V-RPP-NPM ἐρριζωμένοι (2x)
Eph 3:17 having·been·rooted and having·been·founded in
Col 2:7 having·been·rooted and being·built·up in him, and

G4493 ῥιπή rhipḗ *n.* (1x)
Roots:G4496
G4493.2 N-DSF ῥιπῇ (1x)
1Co 15:52 in an·instant, in a·twinkling of·an·eye, at the last

G4494 ῥιπίζω rhipízō *v.* (1x)
Roots:G4496 Compare:G2831
G4494.3 V-PPP-DSM ῥιπιζομένῳ (1x)
Jac 1:6 ·driven·by·the·wind and being·tossed·to·and·fro.

G4495 ῥιπτέω rhiptéō *v.* (1x)
Roots:G4496 Compare:G0641
G4495 V-PAP-GPM ῥιπτούντων (1x)
Ac 22:23 ·them yelling·out, and flinging·off the garments,

G4496 ῥίπτω rhíptō *v.* (7x)
Compare:G0906 See:G4474 G1614
G4496.1 V-AAI-1P ἐρρίψαμεν (1x)
Ac 27:19 with·our·own·hands, we·flung the sailing·ship's
G4496.1 V-AAP-NSN ῥίψαν (1x)
Lk 4:35 And the demon, flinging him in the midst, came·
G4496.1 V-AAP-NSM ῥίψας (1x)
Mt 27:5 And flinging the pieces·of·silver at the Temple, he·
G4496.1 V-AAP-NPM ῥίψαντες (1x)
Ac 27:29 rough,·jagged places, after·flinging four anchors
G4496.1 V-RPI-3S ἔρριπται (1x)
Lk 17:2 his neck, and *that* it·has·been·flung into the sea,
G4496.1 V-RPP-NPM ἐρριμμένοι (1x)
Mt 9:36 having·been·faint, and having·been·flung·about, as
G4496.2 V-AAI-3P ἔρριψαν (1x)
Mt 15:30 and they·quickly·deposited them directly·at the

G4496-1 ρμδ rho mu delta *n.* (1x)
See:G5516 G2395-1
G4496-1.1 N-NUI-ABB ρμδ (1x)
Rv 7:4 ·been·officially·sealed: "Rho·Mu·Delta Chiliad,"

G4497 Ῥοβο•άμ Rhôbôám *n/p.* (2x)
רְחַבְעָם rᵉchaβʻam [Hebrew]
Roots:H7346 xLangAlso:H0029 H0609 H3092 H3141 H0274 H3101 H0558 H5838 H3147 H0271 H2396 H4519 H0526 H2977 H3059 H3079 H3078 H6667
G4497.2 N/P-PRI Ῥοβοάμ (2x)
Mt 1:7 Then Solomon begot RehoboAm, and RehoboAm
Mt 1:7 begot RehoboAm, and RehoboAm begot AbiYah,

G4498 Ῥόδη Rhódē *n/p.* (1x)
Compare:G2924-3 G2918 G4677
G4498.2 N/P-NSF Ῥόδη (1x)
Ac 12:13 of·the gate, a·servant·girl (Rhoda by·name) came·

G4499 Ῥόδος Rhódôs *n/l.* (1x)
G4499 N/L-ASF Ῥόδον (1x)
Ac 21:1 and on·the next·day to Rhodes, and·from·there to

G4500 ῥοιζηδόν rhôizēdón *adv.* (1x)
G4500 ADV ῥοιζηδόν (1x)
2Pe 3:10 shall·pass·away with·a·whirring·noise ·*like*·a·, and

G4501 ῥομφαία rhômphaía *n.* (7x)
Compare:G3162 G3584-1 xLangAlso:H2719
G4501.1 N-NSF ῥομφαία (3x)
Lk 2:35 (and a·straight·sword shall·go·through your own
Rv 1:16 double-edged straight·sword is·proceeding·forth,'
Rv 19:15 ·his mouth proceeds·forth a·sharp straight·sword,'
G4501.1 N-ASF ῥομφαίαν (1x)
Rv 2:12 ·one having the sharp, double-edged straight·sword:
G4501.1 N-DSF ῥομφαίᾳ (3x)
Rv 2:16 against them with the straight·sword of·my mouth.
Rv 6:8 of·the earth, to·kill with a·straight·sword, and with
Rv 19:21 the straight·sword of·the·one who·is·sitting·down

G4502 Ῥου•βήν Rhôubḗn *n/p.* (1x)
רְאוּבֵן rᵉʼûβen [Hebrew]
Roots:H7205
G4502.3 N/P-PRI Ῥουβήν (1x)
Rv 7:5 *the* tribe of·ReuBen having·been·officially·sealed,

G4503 Ῥούθ Rhôúth *n/p.* (1x)
רוּת rûth [Hebrew]
Roots:H7327 See:G4477 G1003
G4503.2 N/P-PRI Ῥούθ (1x)
Mt 1:5 and BoAz begot Obed (birthed·from·out of·Ruth), and

G4504 Ῥοῦφος Rhôûphôs *n/p.* (2x)
See:G0223 G4613
G4504.2 N/P-ASM Ῥοῦφον (1x)
Rm 16:13 Greet Rufus, the One-Selected in *the* Lord, and his
G4504.2 N/P-GSM Ῥούφου (1x)
Mk 15:21 (the father of·AlexAnder and Rufus), in·order·that

G4505 ῥύμη rhýmē *n.* (4x)
Roots:G4506 Compare:G4113 G1353-1 G0296 G3938 See:G4512
xLangEquiv:H2351 xLangAlso:H7339
G4505.1 N-ASF ῥύμην (1x)
Ac 9:11 ·up, traverse on the avenue, the·one being·called
G4505.1 N-DPF ῥύμαις (1x)
Mt 6:2 the gatherings and in the avenues, that they·may·be·
G4505.2 N-ASF ῥύμην (1x)
Ac 12:10 going·forth, they·went·onward one alleyway, and
G4505.2 N-APF ῥύμας (1x)
Lk 14:21 into the broad·streets and alleyways of·the city, and

G4506 ῥύομαι rhýômai *v.* (18x)
Compare:G1807 G0726 G4982 See:G4511 G4511-1 G4482
xLangEquiv:H5337 A5338 xLangAlso:H2020
G4506.2 V-FDI-3S ῥύσεται (3x)
Rm 7:24 ·miserable man·of·clay†! Who shall·snatch me out
2Co 1:10 ·expectation that even yet he·shall·snatch·*us*·up—
2Ti 4:18 And the Lord shall·snatch me away·from every evil
G4506.2 V-PNI-3S ῥύεται (1x)
2Co 1:10 ·vast a·death, and does·presently·snatch·away, in
G4506.2 V-PNN ῥύεσθαι (1x)
2Pe 2:9 does·personally·know·how to·snatch devoutly· out
G4506.2 V-PNP-ASM ῥυόμενον (1x)
1Th 1:10 YeShua, the·one who·is·snatching us away·from
G4506.2 V-ADM-2S ῥῦσαι (2x)
Lk 11:4 us into a·proof·trial, but·rather snatch us away·from
Mt 6:13 us into a·proof·trial, but·rather snatch us away from
G4506.2 V-ANI-3S ἐρρύσατο (3x)
2Co 1:10 *It·is* he·who already·snatched us from·out of·so·
Col 1:13 *It·is* he·who has·already·snatched us from·out of·
2Ti 3:11 but the Lord snatched me from·out of·all *of·them*.
G4506.2 V-API-1S ἐρρύσθην (1x)
2Ti 4:17 may·hear. And·thus I·was·snatched out of·a·lion's
G4506.2 V-APP-APM ῥυσθέντας (1x)
Lk 1:74 to·grant to·us (after·being·snatched out of·*the*·hand
G4506.2 V-APS-1S ῥυσθῶ (1x)
Rm 15:31 in·order·that I·may·be·snatched away·from the·
G4506.2 V-APS-1P ῥυσθῶμεν (1x)
2Th 3:2 in·order·that we·may·be·snatched away·from the
G4506.3 V-PNP-NSM ῥυόμενος (1x)
Rm 11:26 from·out of·Tsiyon, the·one who·is·rescuing, and
G4506.3 V-ADM-3S ῥυσάσθω (1x)
Mt 27:43 ·has·confidence in God. Let·him·rescue him now,
G4506.3 V-ANI-3S ἐρρύσατο (1x)
2Pe 2:7 and *if* he·rescued righteous Lot being·worn·down·in·

G4507 ῥυπαρία rhyparía *n.* (1x)
Roots:G4508 Compare:G0167 G2549 G3393 See:G4509 G4510
G4507 N-ASF ῥυπαρίαν (1x)
Jac 1:21 ·away all filthiness and any·remaining·excess of·

G4508 ῥυπαρός rhyparṓs *adj.* (1x)
Roots:G4509 Compare:G0169 G2513 See:G4507 G4510 xLangAlso:H6674
G4508.1 A-DSF ῥυπαρᾷ (1x)

Jac 2:2 ·enter also a·helpless·beggar in filthy clothing,

G4509 ῥύπος rhýpôs *n.* (1x)
Compare:G0168 G2549 See:G4507 G4508 G4510
xLangAlso:H6675

G4509.1 N-GSM ῥύπου (1x)
1Pe 3:21 of·flesh *by* a·putting·away of·filth, but·rather an·

G4510 ῥυπόω rhypóō *v.* (2x)
Roots:G4509 See:G4508 G4507

G4510.1 V-PAP-NSM ῥυπῶν (1x)
Rv 22:11 still; and the·one being·filthy, let·him·be·filthy

G4510.1 V-AAM-3S ῥυπωσάτω (1x)
Rv 22:11 and the·one being·filthy, let·him·be·filthy still;

G4511 ῥύσις rhýsis *n.* (3x)
Roots:G4506 G4482

G4511 N-NSF ῥύσις (1x)
Lk 8:44 garment, and at·once her flow of·blood stood·still.

G4511 N-DSF ῥύσει (2x)
Lk 8:43 And a·woman being with a·flow of·blood for twelve
Mk 5:25 a·certain woman being with a·flow of·blood *for*

G4512 ῥυτίς rhytís *n.* (1x)
Roots:G4506

G4512.2 N-ASF ῥυτίδα (1x)
Eph 5:27 not having stain, or wrinkle, or any such·thing,

G4513 Ῥωμαϊκός Rhōmaïkós *adj/g.* (1x)
Roots:G4514 See:G4515

G4513.2 A/G-DPN Ῥωμαϊκοῖς (1x)
Lk 23:38 with·letters in·Greek, Roman·Latin, and Hebrew:

G4514 Ῥωμαῖος Rhōmaîôs *adj/g.* (13x)
Roots:G4516 See:G4515

EG4514 (1x)
Jn 19:32 Accordingly, the ***Roman*** soldiers came and in·fact

G4514.1 A/G-NPM Ῥωμαῖοι (1x)
Ac 2:10 the·ones temporarily·residing·here·from Rome, also

G4514.2 A/G-NSM Ῥωμαῖος (4x)
Ac 22:26 ·about to·do, for this man·of·clay† is a·Roman."
Ac 22:27 *it* to·me whether you·yourself are a·Roman!" And
Ac 22:29 ·afraid after·realizing that he·was a·Roman, and
Ac 23:27 him out, upon·learning that he·was a·Roman.

G4514.2 A/G-NPM Ῥωμαῖοι (2x)
Jn 11:48 in him, and the Romans shall·come and shall·take·
Ac 16:38 ·were·afraid after·hearing that they·were Romans.

G4514.2 A/G-ASM Ῥωμαῖον (1x)
Ac 22:25 a·man·of·clay† *who·is* a·Roman and uncondemned

G4514.2 A/G-APM Ῥωμαίους (1x)
Ac 16:37 ·clay†, *though* inherently·being Romans, they·cast

G4514.2 A/G-DPM Ῥωμαίοις (2x)
Ac 16:21 ·personally·accept, neither to·do, being Romans."
Ac 25:16 manner of·the·Romans to·gratuitously·hand·over

G4514.2 A/G-GPM Ῥωμαίων (1x)
Ac 28:17 out of·JeruSalem into the hands of·the Romans,

G4515 Ῥωμαϊστί Rhōmaïstí *adv/g.* (1x)
Roots:G4516 Compare:G1447 G1676 G4947-6
See:G4513

G4515.2 ADV Ῥωμαϊστί (1x)
Jn 19:20 in·Hebrew, in·Greek, *and* in·Roman·Latin.

G4516 Ῥώμη Rhṓmē *n/l.* (8x)
Roots:G4517 Compare:G4988 See:G4514 G4515

G4516.2 N/L-ASF Ῥώμην (4x)
Ac 19:21 there, it·is·mandatory·for me also to·see Rome."
Ac 23:11 it·is·mandatory·for you to·testify also to Rome."
Ac 28:14 And in·this·manner we·went toward Rome *on·foot.*
Ac 28:16 And when we·came to Rome, the centurion

G4516.2 N/L-DSF Ῥώμῃ (3x)
Rm 1:7 To·all the·ones being in Rome, beloved of·God,
Rm 1:15 ·the·good·news to·yeu, to·the·ones in Rome.
2Ti 1:17 But·rather, coming·to·be in Rome, he·sought·for

G4516.2 N/L-GSF Ῥώμης (1x)
Ac 18:2 ·for all the Jews to·be·deported out of·Rome). *And*

G4517 ῥώννυμι rhṓnnymi *v.* (2x)
Compare:G5463 See:G4506

G4517.3 V-RPM-2S ἔρρωσο (1x)
Ac 23:30 *they·have* specifically·against him. Farewell."

G4517.3 V-RPM-2P ἔρρωσθε (1x)
Ac 15:29 yeurselves, yeu·shall·practice well. Farewell."

Σσ - Sigma

G4518 σαβαχθάνι sabachtháni *aram.* (2x)
ὁαβακ̧θάνι shabaqtháni [Greek, Octuagint]
שְׁבַקְתַּנִי śhëɓa̭qta̭ni [Aramaic]
Roots:A7662

G4518.2 ARAM σαβαχθανί (2x)
Mt 27:46 "'Eli, Eli, lama shebaq-thani?'" That·is *to·say,*
Mk 15:34 "'Eloi, Eloi, lama shebaq-thani?'" Which, when·

G4519 σαβαώθ sabaṓth *heb.* (2x)
Τσαβαώθ Tsabaṓth [Greek, Octuagint]
צְבָאוֹת tsëɓa̦'ôth [Hebrew]
Roots:H6635 Compare:G4753 G1611-2

G4519.3 HEB Τσαβαώθ (2x)
Rm 9:29 "'Except Yahweh of·Hosts left·behind offspring†
Jac 5:4 have·entered 'into the ears of·Yahweh of·Hosts.'

G4520 σαββατισμός sabbatismós *n.* (1x)
Roots:G4521 Compare:G2663 G0372
xLangEquiv:H7677

G4520.2 N-NSM σαββατισμός (1x)
Heb 4:9 there·is·still·remaining a·Sabbath·Rest for·the

G4521 σάββατον sábbatôn *n.* (68x)
שַׁבָּת śha̭ḅa̦th [Hebrew]
שַׁבָּתוֹן śha̭ḅa̦thôn̮
Roots:H7676 Compare:G1439-1 See:G4520
xLangEquiv:H7677

G4521.1 N-NSN σάββατον (1x)
Mk 2:27 to·them, "The Sabbath came·to·be on·account·of

G4521.1 N-ASN σάββατον (9x)
Jn 5:18 not merely was·he·breaking the Sabbath— moreover
Jn 9:16 because he·does·not observantly·keep the Sabbath."
Lk 23:56 they·kept·still *over* the Sabbath according·to the
Ac 13:27 ·ones being·read·aloud each and·every Sabbath),
Ac 13:42 to·be·spoken to·them at the next Sabbath.
Ac 15:21 ·aloud in the gatherings each and·every Sabbath."
Ac 18:4 in the gathering each and·every Sabbath, and was·
Mt 12:5 in the Sanctuary·Courtyard profane the Sabbath, and
Mk 2:27 not the Clay·Man† on·account·of the Sabbath.

G4521.1 N-APN σάββατα (1x)
Ac 17:2 three Sabbaths he·was·having·discussions with·

G4521.1 N-DSN σαββάτῳ (9x)
Jn 19:31 upon the cross on the Sabbath (for that Sabbath
Lk 6:1 on the·first Sabbath after·the·second·day·of·the·feast
Lk 6:6 And it·occurred also on another Sabbath, *for* him to·
Lk 6:7 he·shall·both·relieve·and·cure on the Sabbath, that
Lk 13:14 ·relieved·and·cured on·the Sabbath, was·saying to·
Lk 13:15 does·not each·one of·yeu on·the Sabbath loosen his
Lk 14:1 ·the chief Pharisees to·eat bread on·the·Sabbath, *that*
Lk 14:3 ·it·proper to·both·relieve·and·cure on the Sabbath?"
Ac 13:44 And on·the coming Sabbath, almost all the city *of·*

G4521.1 N-DPN σάββασιν (1x)
Lk 13:10 in one of·the gatherings on *one·of* the Sabbaths.

G4521.1 N-GSN σαββάτου (9x)
Jn 19:31 on the Sabbath (for that Sabbath was the great day),
Lk 6:5 "The Son of·Clay·Man† is Lord also of·the Sabbath."
Lk 13:14 ·relieved·and·cured, and not on·the Sabbath day."
Lk 13:16 to·be·loosed from this bond on·the Sabbath day?
Lk 14:5 ·not immediately draw him up on the Sabbath day?
Mt 12:8 the Son of·Clay·Man† is Lord even of·the Sabbath."
Mk 2:28 the Son of·Clay·Man† is Lord also of·the Sabbath."
Mk 6:2 And with·Sabbath occurring, he·began to·instruct in
Mk 16:1 And with·the Sabbath already·elapsing, Mariam

G4521.1 N-GPN σαββάτων (1x)
Col 2:16 ·a·Sacred·Feast or of·a·new·moon or of·Sabbaths,

G4521.1 N-GPN@ σαββάτων (3x)
Lk 4:16 gathering on the day of·Sabbath, and he·stood·up to·
Ac 13:14 the gathering on·the day of·Sabbath, they·sat·down
Ac 16:13 Also on·the day of·Sabbath, we·went·forth outside

G4521.3 N-NSN σάββατον (4x)
Jn 5:9 was·walking, and on the same day was a·Sabbath.
Jn 5:10 ·both·relieved·and·cured, "It·is a·Sabbath. It·is·not

Jn 9:14 And it·was a·Sabbath when Jesus made the clay and
Lk 23:54 ·day, and a·Sabbath was·quickly·drawing·near.
G4521.3 N-DSN σαββάτῳ (6x)
Jn 5:16 because he·was·doing these·things on a·Sabbath.
Jn 7:22 , and on a·Sabbath, yeu·circumcise a·man-child·of·
Jn 7:23 receives circumcision on a·Sabbath in·order·that the
Jn 7:23 man·of·clay† healthy·and·sound on a·Sabbath?
Mt 12:2 do that·which it·is·not proper to·do on a·Sabbath."
Mt 24:20 ·not happen in·winter, nor·even on a·Sabbath.
G4521.3 N-DPN σάββασιν (4x)
Lk 6:2 ·which it·is·not proper to·do on the Sabbath·days?"
Mt 12:12 it·is·proper to·do good on·the Sabbath·days."
Mk 2:24 ·do they·do on the Sabbath·days that·which is·not
Mk 3:2 ·and·cure him on·the Sabbath·days, in·order·that
G4521.3 N-GSN σαββάτου (1x)
Ac 1:12 which is near JeruSalem, being a·Sabbath's journey.
G4521.4 N-GSN σαββάτου (2x)
Lk 18:12 I·fast twice in·the week, I·tithe all·things, *on* as·
Mk 16:9 ·watch·of·dawn on·*the*·first *day* of·*the*·week, *Jesus*
G4521.4 N-GPN σαββάτων (7x)
Jn 20:1 on·the first *day* of·the week at·the·watch·of·dawn
Jn 20:19 day, the first *day* of·the week, and with·the doors
Lk 24:1 on·the first *day* of·the week, with·*the*·sunrise deep
Ac 20:7 And on the first *day* of·the week, with·the disciples
Mt 28:1 ·light toward the first *dawn* of·the·week, Mariam
Mk 16:2 ·of·dawn of·the first *day* of·*the*·week, they·went to
1Co 16:2 Each first *day* of·the·week, let each·one of·yeu lay
G4521.6 N-DPN σάββασιν (9x)
Lk 4:31 he·was instructing them on the various·Sabbaths.
Lk 6:9 on·the various·Sabbaths: to·beneficially·do·good or
Mt 12:1 YeShua traversed on·the various·Sabbaths through
Mt 12:5 in the Torah-Law, that on·the various·Sabbaths the
Mt 12:10 to·both·relieve·and·cure on·the various·Sabbaths?"
Mt 12:11 into a·pit on·the various·Sabbaths, shall·not·indeed
Mk 1:21 he·was·instructing on·the various·Sabbaths.
Mk 2:23 the grain·fields on the various·Sabbaths, and his
Mk 3:4 to·beneficially·do·good on·the various·Sabbaths, or
G4521.7 N-GPN σαββάτων (1x)
Mt 28:1 And after·the·close of·the·joint·Sabbaths, with·it·

G4522 σαγήνη sagḗnē *n.* (1x)
Compare:G0293 G1350
xLangEquiv:H4365 xLangAlso:H2764
G4522 N-DSF σαγήνῃ (1x)
Mt 13:47 ·the heavens is like a·dragnet after·being·cast into

G4523 Σαδδουκαῖος Saddôukaîos *n/g.* (14x)
צְדוּקִים tsạdûqim [Hebrew]
Roots:G4524 Compare:G5330
xLangEquiv:H6659-1
G4523.2 N/G-NPM Σαδδουκαῖοι (5x)
Ac 4:1 ·the Sanctuary·Estate and the Sadducees stood·over
Ac 23:8 For in·fact, *the* Sadducees say *that* there·is not a·
Mt 16:1 the Pharisees and Sadducees inquired·of him to·
Mt 22:23 same day, *some* Sadducees came·alongside him,
Mk 12:18 Then *the* Sadducees come to him, who say *that*
G4523.2 N/G-APM Σαδδουκαίους (1x)
Mt 22:34 him, after·hearing that he·muzzled the Sadducees.
G4523.2 N/G-GPM Σαδδουκαίων (8x)
Lk 20:27 coming·alongside *him*, certain of·the·Sadducees
Ac 5:17 (being the denomination of·the Sadducees), they·
Ac 23:6 that the one part were Sadducees and the other
Ac 23:7 *between* the Pharisees and the Sadducees, and the
Mt 3:7 many of·the Pharisees and Sadducees are·coming to
Mt 16:6 of the leaven of·the Pharisees and Sadducees."
Mt 16:11 of the leaven of·the Pharisees and Sadducees?"
Mt 16:12 of the instruction of·the Pharisees and Sadducees.

G4525 σαίνω saínō *v.* (1x)
Compare:G0660 G1621 G5182 G4013 G5015 G2360
See:G4579
G4525.2 V-PPN σαίνεσθαι (1x)
1Th 3:3 *for* no·one to·be·woefully·shaken by these

G4526 σάκκος sákkôs *n.* (4x)
שַׂק ṡaq [Hebrew]
Roots:H8242
G4526 N-NSM σάκκος (1x)
Rv 6:12 sun became *as* black as sackcloth made·of·hair, and
G4526 N-APM σάκκους (1x)
Rv 11:3 sixty days, having·been·arrayed·with sackcloth."
G4526 N-DSM σάκκῳ (2x)
Lk 10:13 repented, sitting·down in sackcloth and ashes.
Mt 11:21 they·would·have repented in sackcloth and ashes.

G4527 Σαλά Salá *n/p.* (1x)
מְתוּשֶׁלַח ṡhẹlacн [Hebrew]
Σέλαχ Shélach [Greek, Octuagint]
Roots:H7974 See:G3103 G2627
G4527.2 N/P-PRI Σέλαχ (1x)
Lk 3:35 of·Reu, *son* of·Peleg, *son* of·Eber, *son* of·Shelach,

G4528 Σαλαθι•ήλ Salathiḗl *n/p.* (3x)
Σεαλτι•ήλ Shêaltiḗl [Greek, Octuagint]
שְׁאַלְתִּיאֵל ṡhᵉʼạl·ṭiy'ẹl [Hebrew]
שְׁאַלְתִּיאֵל ṡhᵉʼạl·ṭiy'ẹl [Aramaic]
Roots:H7597
xLangEquiv:A7598
G4528.2 N/P-PRI Σεαλτιήλ (2x)
Mt 1:12 exile, YeKonYah begot ShealtiEl, and ShealtiEl
Mt 1:12 begot ShealtiEl, and ShealtiEl begot ZerubBabel.
G4528.3 N/P-PRI Σεαλτιήλ (1x)
Lk 3:27 *son* of·ZorubBabel, *son* of·ShealtiEl, *son* of·

G4529 Σαλαμίς Salamís *n/l.* (1x)
Roots:G4535
G4529.2 N/L-DSF Σαλαμῖνι (1x)
Ac 13:5 ·to·be at Salamis, they·were·fully·proclaiming the

G4530 Σαλείμ Salêím *n/l.* (1x)
Roots:G4535 See:G4531 G4529
G4530 N/L-PRI Σαλείμ (1x)
Jn 3:23 immersing in Ainon near to·Salim because there·was

G4531 σαλεύω salêúō *v.* (15x)
Roots:G4535 Compare:G4787 G5015
G4531.1 V-FPI-3P σαλευθήσονται (3x)
Lk 21:26 for the powers of·the heavens shall·be·shaken.
Mt 24:29 and the powers of·the heavens shall·be·shaken.
Mk 13:25 powers, the·ones in the heavens, shall·be·shaken.
G4531.1 V-PPP-ASM σαλευόμενον (2x)
Lk 7:24 to·distinctly·view? A·reed being·shaken by a·wind?
Mt 11:7 to·distinctly·view? A·reed being·shaken by a·wind?
G4531.1 V-PPP-GPN σαλευομένων (1x)
Heb 12:27 ·and·removal of·the·things being·shaken, as *of*·
G4531.1 V-PPP-NPN σαλευόμενα (1x)
Heb 12:27 ·that the·things not being·shaken may·remain.
G4531.1 V-AAI-3S ἐσάλευσεν (1x)
Heb 12:26 whose *own* voice shook the earth at·that·time.
G4531.1 V-AAN σαλεῦσαι (1x)
Lk 6:48 home, but did·not have·strength to·shake it, for it·
G4531.1 V-API-3S ἐσαλεύθη (1x)
Ac 4:31 petitioning, the place was·shaken in which they·
G4531.1 V-APN σαλευθῆναι (2x)
Ac 16:26 the foundations of·the dungeon to·be·shaken. And
2Th 2:2 for yeu not quickly to·be·shaken in the mind, nor to·
G4531.1 V-APS-1S σαλευθῶ (1x)
Ac 2:25 my right·hand in·order·that I·should·not be·shaken.
G4531.1 V-RPP-ASN@ σεσαλευμένον (1x)
Lk 6:38 good measure, packed·down, shaken *together*, and
G4531.3 V-PAP-NPM σαλεύοντες (1x)
Ac 17:13 they·came there·also, stirring·up the crowds.

G4532 Σαλήμ Salḗm *n/l.* (2x)
שָׁלֵם ṡhạlẹṃ [Hebrew]
Roots:H8004
G4532.2 N/L-PRI Σαλήμ (2x)
Heb 7:1 For this MalkiTsedeq (King of·Salem, Priest of·God
Heb 7:2 and after·that also "King of·Salem," which is,

G4533 Σαλμών Salmṓn *n/p.* (3x)
שַׂלְמוֹן ṡạlmôṇ [Hebrew]
Roots:H8012
G4533.2 N/P-PRI Σαλμών (3x)
Lk 3:32 *son* of·BoAz, *son* of·Salmon, *son* of·Nachshon,
Mt 1:4 begot Nachshon, and Nachshon begot Salmon.
Mt 1:5 Then Salmon begot BoAz (birthed·from·out of·

G4534 Σαλμώνη Salmṓnē *n/l.* (1x)
Roots:G4529
G4534 N/L-ASF Σαλμώνην (1x)
Ac 27:7 ·sailed·leeward·near·to Crete, adjacent·to Salmone.

G4535 σάλος sálôs *n.* (1x)
Roots:G4525
G4535.3 N-GSM σάλου (1x)
Lk 21:25 a·perplexity of·*the*·reverberating and billowing sea,

G4536 σάλπιγξ sálpinx *n.* (10x)
Roots:G4535 Compare:G2768-4 G4992-1 See:G4537
xLangEquiv:H2689 xLangAlso:H7782
G4536 N-NSF σάλπιγξ (1x)
1Co 14:8 also, if·ever a·trumpet should·give an·indistinct
G4536 N-NPF σάλπιγγες (1x)
Rv 8:2 of·God; and to·them were·given seven trumpets.
G4536 N-ASF σάλπιγγα (1x)
Rv 9:14 sixth angel who was·holding the trumpet, "Loosen
G4536 N-APF σάλπιγγας (1x)
Rv 8:6 angels having the seven trumpets made themselves
G4536 N-DSF σάλπιγγι (2x)
1Th 4:16 voice, and with God's trumpet, and the dead·ones
1Co 15:52 of·an·eye, at the last trumpet, for it·shall·sound,
G4536 N-GSF σάλπιγγος (4x)
Mt 24:31 his angels with a·great sound of·a·trumpet, and
Rv 1:10 right·behind me a·great voice, as of·a·trumpet,
Rv 4:1 which I·heard *was* as a·trumpet speaking with me,
Rv 8:13 of·the remaining voices of·the trumpet of·the three

G4537 σαλπίζω salpízō *v.* (12x)
Roots:G4536 See:G4538
G4537.1 V-AAS-2S σαλπίσῃς (1x)
Mt 6:2 ·act, you·should·not sound·a·trumpet before you,
G4537.2 V-FAI-3S σαλπίσει (1x)
1Co 15:52 the last trumpet, for it·shall·sound, and the dead
G4537.2 V-PAN σαλπίζειν (2x)
Rv 8:13 of·the three angels, the·ones about to·sound!"
Rv 10:7 angel, whenever he·should·intend to·sound, even
G4537.2 V-AAI-3S ἐσάλπισεν (7x)
Rv 8:7 The first angel sounded, and there·happened hail and
Rv 8:8 And the second angel sounded, and *something* as a·
Rv 8:10 And the third angel sounded, and there·fell a·great
Rv 8:12 And the fourth angel sounded, and the third·part of·
Rv 9:1 And the fifth angel sounded, and I·saw a·star having·
Rv 9:13 And the sixth angel sounded, and I·heard one voice
Rv 11:15 And the seventh angel sounded, and there·became
G4537.2 V-AAS-3P σαλπίσωσιν (1x)
Rv 8:6 themselves ready in·order·that they·should·sound.

G4538 σαλπιστής salpistḗs *n.* (1x)
Roots:G4537
G4538 N-GPM σαλπιστῶν (1x)
Rv 18:22 and of·flute·players, and trumpeters, no, should·

G4539 Σαλώμη Salṓmē *n/p.* (2x)
שָׁלוֹם ṡhạlôṃ [Hebrew]
Roots:H7965
G4539.2 N/P-NSF Σαλώμη (2x)
Mk 15:40 mother of·little Jacob and of·Joses), and Salome;
Mk 16:1 of·*little*·Jacob) and Salome bought aromatic·spices,

G4540 Σαμάρεια Samárêia *n/l.* (11x)
שֹׁמְרוֹן ṡhómᵉrôṇ [Hebrew]
שָׁמְרַיִן ṡhọmrạyiṇ [Aramaic]
Roots:H8111 See:G4541
xLangEquiv:A8115
G4540.2 N/L-NSF Σαμάρεια (1x)
Ac 8:14 after·hearing that Samaria had·accepted the
G4540.2 N/L-ASF Σαμάρειαν (1x)

Σσ

Ac 15:3 and Samaria, giving·a·thorough·account·of the
G4540.2 N/L-DSF Σαμαρείᾳ (1x)
Ac 1:8 and in all Judea, and in·Samaria, and as·far·as·to *the*
G4540.2 N/L-GSF Σαμαρείας (8x)
Jn 4:4 And it·was·necessary·for him to·go through Samaria.
Jn 4:5 to·a·city of·Samaria being·referred·to·as Sychar *(or·*
Jn 4:7 a·woman from·out of·Samaria to·draw·out water.
Lk 17:11 went through *the* midst of·Samaria and Galilee.
Ac 8:1 pervasively·into·all the regions of·Judea and Samaria.
Ac 8:5 to·a·city of·Samaria, was·officially·proclaiming the
Ac 8:9 and astonishing the Gentiles of·Samaria, saying
Ac 9:31 of·Judea, Galilee and Samaria were·having peace,

G4541 Σαμαρείτης Samarěítēs *n/g.* (9x)
Roots:G4540 See:G4542
G4541.2 N/G-NSM Σαμαρείτης (3x)
Jn 8:48 say well that you·yourself are a·Samaritan, and have
Lk 10:33 "But some Samaritan, while·traveling, came
Lk 17:16 And he·himself was a·Samaritan.
G4541.2 N/G-NPM Σαμαρεῖται (1x)
Jn 4:40 So·then *just* as·soon·as the Samaritans came toward
G4541.2 N/G-DPM Σαμαρείταις (1x)
Jn 4:9 woman?" (for Jews do·not interact with·Samaritans).
G4541.2 N/G-GPM Σαμαρειτῶν (4x)
Jn 4:39 And many of·the Samaritans from·among that city
Lk 9:52 ·entered into a·village of·the·Samaritans, as·such to·
Ac 8:25 ·the·good·news in·many villages of·the Samaritans.
Mt 10:5 ·should·not enter into *any* city of·the·Samaritans,

G4542 Σαμαρεῖτις Samarěîtis *n/g.* (2x)
Roots:G4541
G4542.2 N/G-NSF Σαμαρεῖτις (1x)
Jn 4:9 Accordingly, the Samaritan woman says to·him,
G4542.2 N/G-GSF Σαμαρείτιδος (1x)
Jn 4:9 personally·from me, being a·Samaritan woman?

G4543 Σαμο•θρᾴκη Samŏthrákē *n/l.* (1x)
Roots:G4544
G4543 N/L-ASF Σαμοθρᾴκην (1x)
Ac 16:11 Troas, we·sailed·straight to Samos·of·Thrace, also

G4544 Σάμος Sámŏs *n/l.* (1x)
G4544 N/L-ASF Σάμον (1x)
Ac 20:15 *day of·sailing*, we·drew·alongside to Samos. And

G4545 Σαμου•ήλ Samŏuél *n/p.* (3x)
שְׁמוּאֵל shᵉmûʼel [Hebrew]
Roots:H8050
G4545.2 N/P-PRI Σαμουήλ (3x)
Ac 3:24 even all the prophets from SamuEl and the·ones of·
Ac 13:20 he·gave *to·them* judges, until SamuEl the prophet.
Heb 11:32 and also David, SamuEl, and the prophets,

G4546 Σαμψών Sampsṓn *n/p.* (1x)
שִׁמְשׁוֹן shimshôn [Hebrew]
Roots:H8123
G4546.2 N/P-PRI Σαμψών (1x)
Heb 11:32 Gideon, also Baraq, Samson, and Yiphtach; and

G4547 σανδάλιον sandáliŏn *n.* (2x)
Compare:G5266 xLangAlso:H5275
G4547 N-APN σανδάλια (2x)
Ac 12:8 ·about and shod·yourself·with your sandals." And
Mk 6:9 but·rather having·been·shod with·sandals *only*, and

G4548 σανίς sanís *n.* (1x)
G4548 N-DPF σανίσιν (1x)
Ac 27:44 in·fact, some·men on planks, and some·men on

G4549 Σαούλ Saŏúl *n/p.* (9x)
Σαούλ Shaŏúl [Greek, Octuagint]
שָׁאוּל shaʼûl [Hebrew]
Roots:H7586 Compare:G4569 See:G3972
G4549.2 N/P-PRI Σαούλ (9x)
Ac 9:4 he·heard a·voice saying to·him, "Saul, Saul, why·do
Ac 9:4 to·him, "Saul, Saul, why·do you·persecute me?
Ac 9:17 on him, he·declared, "Brother Saul, the Lord, Jesus
Ac 13:21 and God gave to·them Saul son of·Qish, a·man
Ac 22:7 heard a·voice saying to·me, 'Saul, Saul, why·do
Ac 22:7 to·me, 'Saul, Saul, why·do you persecute me?
Ac 22:13 he·declared to·me, 'Brother Saul, look·up!' And·
Ac 26:14 in·the Hebrew language, 'Saul, Saul, why·do you·
Ac 26:14 language, 'Saul, Saul, why·do you·persecute me?

G4550 σαπρός saprŏ́s *adj.* (8x)
Roots:G4595 Compare:G4190 G0995 G4524-1
See:G4549-1
G4550.2 A-NSM σαπρός (1x)
Eph 4:29 Do·not·let any rotten conversation proceed·forth
G4550.2 A-NSN σαπρόν (3x)
Lk 6:43 rotten fruit, neither *is* a·rotten tree producing good
Mt 7:17 good fruit, but the rotten tree produces evil fruit.
Mt 7:18 evil fruit, neither *is* a·rotten tree *able* to·produce
G4550.2 A-ASM σαπρόν (2x)
Lk 6:43 a·good tree is not producing rotten fruit, neither *is* a·
Mt 12:33 tree rotten, and its fruit rotten. For out of·the fruit,
G4550.2 A-ASN σαπρόν (1x)
Mt 12:33 good; or make the tree rotten, and its fruit rotten.
G4550.2 A-APN σαπρά (1x)
Mt 13:48 the good into containers but cast out the rotten.

G4551 Σαπφείρη Sapphěírē *n/p.* (1x)
Roots:G4552 See:G0367
G4551.2 N/P-DSF Σαπφείρῃ (1x)
Ac 5:1 AnanIas by·name, together with·Sapphira his wife,

G4552 σάπφειρος sápphěirŏs *n.* (1x)
סַפִּיר çappiyr [Hebrew]
Roots:H5601
G4552 N-NSF σάπφειρος (1x)
Rv 21:19 *was* jasper; the second, sapphire; the third,

G4553 σαργάνη sargánē *n.* (1x)
שְׂרַג sarag [Hebrew]
Roots:H8276 Compare:G2894 G4711
G4553 N-DSF σαργάνῃ (1x)
2Co 11:33 a·window, in a·large·basket, I·was·lowered

G4554 Σάρδεις Sárděis *n/l.* (3x)
xLangAlso:H3865
G4554 N/L-APF Σάρδεις (1x)
Rv 1:11 and to Thyatira, and to Sardis, and to PhilAdelphia,
G4554 N/L-DPF Σάρδεσιν (2x)
Rv 3:1 angel of·the Called·Out·citizenry in Sardis write,
Rv 3:4 a·few names even in Sardis which did·not tarnish

G4555 σάρδινος sárdinŏs *n.* (1x)
See:G3037 G4556
G4555 N-DSM σαρδίνῳ (1x)
Rv 4:3 in·clear·appearance like a·jasper and a·sardius stone,

G4556 σάρδιος sárdiŏs *n.* (1x)
Compare:G4555 See:G3037
G4556 N-NSM σάρδιος (1x)
Rv 21:20 the fifth, sardonyx; the sixth, sardius; the seventh,

G4557 σαρδ•όνυξ sardŏ́nyx *n.* (1x)
Roots:G4556
G4557 N-NSF σαρδόνυξ (1x)
Rv 21:20 the fifth, sardonyx; the sixth, sardius; the seventh,

G4559 σαρκικός sarkikŏ́s *adj.* (11x)
Roots:G4561 See:G4560
G4559.1 A-NSM σαρκικός (1x)
Rm 7:14 but I·myself am fleshly, having·been·sold·off
G4559.1 A-NPM σαρκικοί (3x)
1Co 3:3 for yeu·are yet fleshly. For where *there·is* among
1Co 3:3 dissensions, are·yeu not·indeed fleshly, and walk
1Co 3:4 "I *am* of·Apollos," are·yeu not·indeed fleshly?
G4559.1 A-NPN σαρκικά (1x)
2Co 10:4 of·our strategic·warfare *are* not fleshly, but·rather
G4559.1 A-APN σαρκικά (1x)
1Co 9:11 if we·ourselves shall·reap yeur fleshly·things?
G4559.1 A-DSF σαρκικῇ (1x)
2Co 1:12 before·God (not with fleshly wisdom, but·rather by
G4559.1 A-DPM σαρκικοῖς (1x)
1Co 3:1 as to·spiritual·ones, but·rather as to·fleshly·ones, as
G4559.1 A-DPN σαρκικοῖς (1x)
Rm 15:27 ·work·charity to·them in the fleshly·things.
G4559.1 A-GSF σαρκικῆς (1x)
Heb 7:16 ·to a·Torah-Law of·a·fleshly commandment, but·
G4559.1 A-GPF σαρκικῶν (1x)
1Pe 2:11 ·residents to·abstain·from the fleshly longings,

G4560 σάρκινος sárkinŏs *adj.* (1x)
Roots:G4561 See:G4559
G4560.1 A-DPF σαρκίναις (1x)
2Co 3:3 of·stone, but·rather on fleshy tablets of·heart.

G4561 σάρξ sárx *n.* (151x)
Roots:G4525-1 See:G4559 G4560 G4563
xLangEquiv:H1320 A1321
G4561.1 N-NSF σάρξ (26x)
Jn 1:14 And the Word became flesh and encamped among us
Jn 3:6 ·been·born from·out of·the flesh is flesh; and the·one
Jn 6:51 that I·myself shall·give is my flesh, which I·myself
Jn 6:55 For my flesh truly is a·full·meal, and my blood truly
Jn 6:63 the·one giving·life·above. The flesh does·not benefit
Lk 3:6 and all flesh shall·gaze·upon the custodial·Salvation
Ac 2:26 ·joy, and yet even my flesh shall·fully·encamp in
Ac 2:31 ·behind in Hades, neither did·his flesh see decay.'
Gal 2:16 ·that all flesh shall·not be·regarded·as·righteous
Gal 5:17 For the flesh longs against the Spirit, and the Spirit
Mt 16:17 Simon BarJonah, because flesh and blood did·not
Mt 19:6 no·longer two, but·rather one flesh. Accordingly,
Mt 24:22 be·cut·short, not any flesh would be·saved *to·*
Mt 26:41 In·fact, the spirit *is* eager, but the flesh *is* weak."
Mk 10:8 ·such, they·are no·longer two, but·rather one flesh.
Mk 13:20 the Days, not any flesh would be·saved; but·yet
Mk 14:38 In·fact, the spirit *is* eager, but the flesh *is* weak."
Rm 3:20 ·regarded·as·righteous any flesh in·the·sight·of·him
1Pe 1:24 on·account·that '" All flesh *is* as grass, and every
1Co 1:29 so·that all flesh may·not boast in·the·sight·of·him.
1Co 15:39 All flesh *is* not the same flesh, but·rather in·fact
1Co 15:39 All flesh *is* not the same flesh, but·rather in·fact
1Co 15:39 in·fact *there·is* one *kind·of* flesh of·men·of·clay†,
1Co 15:39 *·of* flesh of·men·of·clay†, another flesh of·beasts,
1Co 15:50 I·disclose, brothers, that flesh and blood is·not
2Co 7:5 into Macedonia, our flesh has·had no relaxation at·
G4561.1 N-ASF σάρκα (39x)
Jn 6:52 "How·is this·man able to·give us the flesh to·eat?
Jn 6:53 unless yeu·should·eat the flesh of·the Son of·Clay·
Jn 6:54 "The·one chewing my flesh, and drinking my blood,
Jn 6:56 The·one chewing my flesh, and drinking my blood,
Jn 8:15 ·yeurselves judge according·to the flesh; I·myself
Lk 24:39 because a·spirit does·not have flesh and bones,
Ac 2:17 ·forth from my Spirit upon all flesh, and yeur sons
Ac 2:30 loins, according·to the flesh, he·would·raise·up the
Gal 4:23 maidservant has·been·born according·to flesh, but
Gal 4:29 ·born according·to flesh was·persecuting the·one
Gal 5:24 they·crucified the flesh together with·the intense·
Gal 6:8 the·one sowing into his flesh, shall·reap corruption
Mt 19:5 ·his wife, and the two shall·be distinctly one flesh'"?
Mk 10:8 and the two shall·be distinctly one flesh.' As·such,
Rm 1:3 birthed·from·out of·David's Seed according·to flesh,
Rm 4:1 our father to·have·found, according·to flesh?
Rm 8:1 *·the·ones* walking not according·to flesh, but·rather
Rm 8:4 the·ones walking not according·to flesh, but·rather
Rm 8:5 being according·to flesh contemplate the·things of·
Rm 8:12 *but* not to·the flesh, to·live according·to the flesh.
Rm 8:13 For if yeu·live according·to flesh, yeu·are·about to·
Rm 9:3 of·my brothers, my kinsmen according·to flesh,
Rm 9:5 and from·out of·whom, according·to the flesh, *is* the
Rm 11:14 ·to·jealousy *them who·are* my flesh and may·save
Jud 1:8 dreamers, in·fact, contaminate flesh, ignore
1Co 1:26 many *are* wise·men according·to flesh, not many
1Co 6:16 two,'' he·replies, '"shall·be distinctly one flesh."'
1Co 10:18 Look·upon IsraEl according·to flesh. Are not·
2Co 1:17 I·purpose, do·I·purpose according·to flesh, that
2Co 5:16 ·know no·one·at·all according·to flesh. And even if
2Co 5:16 ·have·known Anointed-One according·to flesh, yet
2Co 10:2 of·us as presently·walking according·to flesh.
2Co 10:3 we·do·not strategically·war according·to flesh.
2Co 11:18 many boast according·to the flesh, I·also shall·

Eph 5:29 ·even·one·man ever hated his·own flesh, but·rather
Eph 5:31 wife, and the two shall·be distinctly one flesh."
Eph 6:5 lords (*the·ones* according·to flesh) with reverent·fear
Eph 6:12 specifically·against blood and flesh, but·rather:
Col 3:22 *who·are yeur* lords according·to flesh, not with
G4561.1 N-APF σάρκας (7x)
Jac 5:3 testimony against yeu and shall·eat yeur flesh as fire.
Rv 17:16 and shall·eat her flesh, and shall·completely·burn
Rv 19:18 that yeu·may·eat flesh of·kings, and flesh of·
Rv 19:18 flesh of·kings, and flesh of·regiment·commanders,
Rv 19:18 ·regiment·commanders, and flesh of·strong·men,
Rv 19:18 and flesh of·strong·men, and flesh of·horses, and
Rv 19:18 sitting·down on them, and flesh of·all·men, *both*
G4561.1 N-DSF σαρκί (40x)
Gal 1:16 I·did·not immediately confer with·flesh and blood,
Gal 2:20 And that·which now I·live in flesh, I·live in the
Gal 3:3 ·Spirit, are·yeu·finishing·further now in·*the*·flesh?
Gal 4:14 ·trial, the·one in my flesh, nor did·yeu·spit·*me*·out,
Gal 5:13 in·order·for an·impromptu·occasion to·the flesh.
Gal 6:12 ·project·a·good·appearance in the·flesh, these·men
Gal 6:13 in·order·that they·may·boast in yeur flesh.
Rm 2:28 ·appearance, *that·is*, with a·circumcision in·flesh.
Rm 7:5 For when we·were in the flesh, the intense·cravings
Rm 7:18 (that·is, in my flesh) dwells no beneficially·good·
Rm 7:25 Royal-Law, but with·the flesh, *a·slave* to·Moral·
Rm 8:3 ·failure, condemned Moral·Failure in the flesh,
Rm 8:8 And the·ones being in flesh are·not able to·satisfy
Rm 8:9 But yeu are not in flesh, but·rather in Spirit, if·
Rm 8:12 *but* not to·the flesh, to·live according·to the flesh.
Php 1:22 *I·continue·on* to·live in *bodily* flesh, this *continues*
Php 1:24 But to·continue·on in the flesh *is* necessary on·
Php 3:3 Jesus, and not having·confidence in flesh,
Php 3:4 *was once* also having confidence in flesh. If any
Php 3:4 *a·reason* to·have·confidence in flesh, I·myself *have*
1Pe 3:18 in·fact having·been·put·to·death in·flesh, but
1Pe 4:1 already·suffering on·behalf·of·us in·flesh, even yeu·
1Pe 4:1 in flesh has·been·restrained from·moral·failure,
1Pe 4:2 ·of *his* time in flesh to·the·longings of·men·of·clay†,
1Pe 4:6 in·fact according·to men·of·clay† in·*the*·flesh, but
1Co 7:28 such·ones shall·have tribulation in·the flesh, but I·
2Co 4:11 should·be·made·apparent in our mortal flesh.
2Co 10:3 For while·strolling·about in *bodily* flesh, we·do·not
2Co 12:7 to·me a·burly·thorn to·the flesh, a·messenger of·
Eph 2:11 *were* at·one·time the nations among flesh, the·ones
Eph 2:11 *the* Circumcision, *which·is* made·by·hand in flesh.
Eph 2:15 after·fully·rendering·inert in his flesh the hostility
Col 1:24 of·the Anointed-One in my flesh on·behalf·of·his
Col 2:1 as·many·as have·not clearly·seen my face in flesh,
Col 2:5 even though I·am·absent in·the flesh, but·yet I·am
Phm 1:16 more to·you, both in *the* flesh and in *the* Lord?
1Ti 3:16 is·made·apparent in flesh, is·regarded·as·righteous
1Jn 4:2 Jesus Anointed having·come in flesh is from·out of·
1Jn 4:3 Anointed-One, having·come in flesh is not from·out
2Jn 1:7 affirming Jesus Anointed as·coming in flesh. This is
G4561.1 N-GSF σαρκός (38x)
Jn 1:13 nor from·out of·*the*·will of·flesh, nor from·out of·
Jn 3:6 ·one having·been·born from·out of·the flesh is flesh;
Jn 17:2 you·gave him authority over·all flesh, in·order·that
Heb 2:14 have·a·common·fellowship of·flesh and blood,
Heb 5:7 who in the days of·his flesh, *was* offering·up both
Heb 9:10 ·washings, and in·regulations of·flesh, imposed
Heb 9:13 ·one·holy just·for the purification of·the flesh,
Heb 10:20 for·us through the curtain, that·is, his flesh),
Heb 12:9 fathers of·our flesh, educators·and·disciplinarians,
Gal 4:13 sickness of·the flesh, I·proclaimed·the·good·news
Gal 5:16 and no, yeu·would·not finish a·longing of·flesh.
Gal 5:17 and the Spirit against the flesh. And these are·fully·
Gal 5:19 But the works of·the flesh are apparent, which are
Gal 6:8 shall·reap corruption from·out of·the flesh; but the·
Rm 6:19 on·account·of the weakness of·yeur flesh. For just·
Rm 8:3 in that it·was·being·weak through the flesh, God,
Rm 8:3 resemblance of·morally·failing flesh and concerning
Rm 8:5 ·to flesh contemplate the·things of·the flesh, but the·
Rm 8:6 For the disposition of·the flesh *is* death, but the
Rm 8:7 ·account·that the disposition of·the flesh *is* hostility
Rm 9:8 not these children of·the flesh *that·are* children of·
Rm 13:14 do·not make provision for longings of·the flesh.
Jud 1:7 *·end* of·different flesh, are·presently·set·forth·as a·
Jud 1:23 even the tunic having·been·stained by the flesh.
1Pe 3:21 — (not *merely* of·flesh *by* a·putting·away of·filth,
2Pe 2:10 *falling·in* right·behind flesh, who·are·traversing in
2Pe 2:18 *it·is* by longings of·flesh *and* by·debaucheries *that*
1Co 5:5 for a·savage·termination of·the flesh, in·order·that
2Co 7:1 ourselves from all tarnishing of·flesh and spirit,
Eph 2:3 in·times·past in the longings of·our flesh, doing the
Eph 2:3 the determinations·of·the·will of·the flesh and of·the
Eph 5:30 of·his Body, from·out of·his flesh, and from·out
Col 1:22 in the body of·his flesh through the death, to·
Col 2:11 from·the body the moral·failures of·the flesh by the
Col 2:13 of·yeur flesh, he·made·*yeu*·alive·together along·
Col 2:18 being·puffed·up for·no·reason by his mind of·flesh,
Col 2:23 specifically·against an·indulgence of·the flesh.
1Jn 2:16 the world, the longing of·the flesh, and the longing
G4561.1 N-GPF σαρκῶν (1x)
Rv 19:21 the fowls were·stuffed·full from·among their flesh.

G4562 Σαρούχ Saroûch *n/p.* (1x)

שְׂרוּג śᵉrûg [Hebrew]
Roots:H8286 xLangAlso:H3999
G4562.2 N/P-PRI Σαρούχ (1x)
Lk 3:35 *son* of·Serug, *son* of·Reu, *son* of·Peleg, *son* of·Eber,

G4563 σαρόω sarôō *v.* (3x)

Roots:G4525-1 See:G4951
G4563 V-PAI-3S σαροῖ (1x)
Lk 15:8 ·not·indeed ignite a·lantern, and sweep the home,
G4563 V-RPP-ASM σεσαρωμένον (2x)
Lk 11:25 *it* having·been·swept and having·been·put·in·
Mt 12:44 having·been·swept and having·been·put·in·

G4564 Σάρρα Sárrha *n/p.* (4x)

שָׂרָה śạrạh [Hebrew]
Roots:H8283 xLangAlso:H8297
G4564.2 N/P-NSF Σάρρα (2x)
Heb 11:11 By·trust also, Sarah herself received a·miracle
1Pe 3:6 even·as Sarah, *who* listened·to·and·obeyed
G4564.2 N/P-DSF Σάρρᾳ (1x)
Rm 9:9 I·shall·come, and there·shall·be to·Sarah, a·son."
G4564.2 N/P-GSF Σάρρας (1x)
Rm 4:19 ·of·age, nor the deadness of·Sarah's primal·womb.

G4565 Σάρων Sárōn *n/l.* (1x)

Σάρων Shárōn [Greek, Octuagint]
שָׁרוֹן śhạrôṉ [Hebrew]
Roots:H8289
G4565.2 N/L-ASM Σαρωνᾶν (1x)
Ac 9:35 all the·ones residing·in Lod and Sharon saw him,

G4566 Σατᾶν Satân *n/p.* (1x)

שָׂטָן śạṭạṉ [Hebrew]
Roots:H7854 Compare:G0476 G3789 See:G4567
G4566.1 N/P-PRI Σατᾶν (1x)
2Co 12:7 a·messenger of·*The*·Adversary in·order·that he·

G4567 Σατανᾶς Satanâs *n/p.* (36x)

שָׂטָן śạṭạṉ [Hebrew]
Roots:H7854 Compare:G3789 G1228 G1404
See:G4566
G4567.1 N/P-NSM Σατανᾶς (17x)
Jn 13:27 the morsel, the Adversary-Accuser entered into that·
Lk 11:18 if the Adversary-Accuser is·thoroughly·divided
Lk 13:16 of·AbRaham, whom the Adversary-Accuser bound,
Lk 22:3 Then the Adversary-Accuser entered into Judas, the·
Lk 22:31 behold, the Adversary-Accuser demanded yeu·*all*,
Ac 5:3 why *has* the Adversary-Accuser completely·filled your
Mt 12:26 And if the Adversary-Accuser casts·out the
Mk 3:23 ·is·it possible *for·the* Adversary-Accuser to·cast·out
Mk 3:26 And if the Adversary-Accuser rose·up against
Mk 4:15 ·hear, the Adversary-Accuser comes immediately,
1Th 2:18 and again, but the Adversary-Accuser hindered us.
1Co 7:5 in·order·that the Adversary-Accuser may·not tempt
2Co 11:14 for the Adversary-Accuser himself is·disguised as
Rv 2:13 ·among yeu, where the Adversary-Accuser resides.
Rv 12:9 ·called Slanderer and the Adversary-Accuser, the·one
Rv 20:2 who is Slanderer and Adversary-Accuser, and bound
Rv 20:7 the Adversary-Accuser shall·be·loosened from·out
G4567.1 N/P-VSM Σατανᾶ (4x)
Lk 4:8 Get·yourself·back behind me, Adversary-Accuser. For
Mt 4:10 "Head·on·out, Adversary-Accuser! For it·has·been·
Mt 16:23 ·back behind me, Adversary-Accuser! You·are a·
Mk 8:33 ·back behind me, Adversary-Accuser! Because you·
G4567.1 N/P-ASM Σατανᾶν (4x)
Lk 10:18 "I·was·observing the Adversary-Accuser falling as
Mt 12:26 casts·out the Adversary-Accuser, he·is·divided
Mk 3:23 Adversary-Accuser to·cast·out Adversary-Accuser?
Rm 16:20 shall·shatter the Adversary-Accuser under yeur feet
G4567.1 N/P-DSM Σατανᾷ (2x)
1Co 5:5 to·the Adversary-Accuser for a·savage·termination
1Ti 1:20 to·the Adversary-Accuser in·order·that they·may·be·
G4567.1 N/P-GSM Σατανᾶ (9x)
Ac 26:18 *from* the authority of·the Adversary-Accuser to God
Mk 1:13 being·tried by the Adversary-Accuser. And he·was
2Th 2:9 ·to an·operation of·the Adversary-Accuser with all
2Co 2:11 ·not be·swindled by the Adversary-Accuser, for we·
1Ti 5:15 *falling·in* right·behind the Adversary-Accuser.
Rv 2:9 but·rather *are* a·gathering of·the Adversary-Accuser.
Rv 2:13 where the throne of·the Adversary-Accuser *is*, and
Rv 2:24 "the depths of·the Adversary-Accuser," as they·say),
Rv 3:9 the gathering of·the Adversary-Accuser (the·ones

G4568 σάτον sátôn *n.* (2x)

סְאָה çᵉʼạh [Hebrew]
Roots:H5429 Compare:G3634-1 G5518 G3358
G4568 N-APN σάτα (2x)
Lk 13:21 *and* incorporated into three seah·measures of·flour
Mt 13:33 incorporated *it* into three seah·measures of·flour,

G4569 Σαῦλος Saûlôs *n/p.* (19x)

שָׁאוּל śhạʼûl
Roots:H7586 Compare:G4549 See:G3972
G4569.2 N/P-NSM Σαῦλος (10x)
Ac 8:1 Now Saul was gladly·consenting to·his execution.
Ac 8:3 But Saul was·brutally·ravaging the Called·Out·
Ac 9:1 Now Saul, still seething with·menace and murder
Ac 9:8 And Saul was·roused from the earth, but with·his
Ac 9:19 he·was·strengthened. Now Saul was among the
Ac 9:22 But Saul was·enabled *all* the·more, and was·
Ac 9:26 Saul was·intently·trying to·tightly·join·himself to·
Ac 12:25 And BarNabas and Saul returned·back *to·Antioch*
Ac 13:1 with·HerOd·AntiPas the tetrarch), and Saul.
Ac 13:9 Then Saul (the·one also *called* Paul), being·filled
G4569.2 N/P-ASM Σαῦλον (4x)
Ac 9:11 home for a·man·of·Tarsus, Saul by·name. For,
Ac 11:25 went·forth to Tarsus, to·diligently·seek·out Saul.
Ac 13:2 ·detach for·me both BarNabas and Saul for the work
Ac 13:7 summoning for·BarNabas and Saul, sought to·hear
G4569.2 N/P-DSM Σαύλῳ (1x)
Ac 9:24 Now their plot was·known to·Saul. And they·were·
G4569.2 N/P-GSM Σαύλου (2x)
Ac 7:58 ·at the feet of·a·young·man being·called Saul.
Ac 11:30 the elders through *the* hands of·BarNabas and Saul.
EG4569.2 (2x)
Ac 9:27 and gave·an·account to·them how *Saul* saw the Lord
Ac 9:29 boldly·speaking·with·clarity, *Saul* was·speaking in

G4570 σβέννυμι sbénnymi *v.* (8x)

See:G0762 xLangAlso:H3518 H1846
G4570.1 V-PPI-3P σβέννυνται (1x)
Mt 25:8 of·yeur oil, because our lamps are·extinguished.'
G4570.1 V-AAN σβέσαι (1x)
Eph 6:16 (with which yeu·shall·be·able to·extinguish all the
G4570.2 V-FAI-3S σβέσει (1x)
Mt 12:20 flax, being·smoldering, he·shall·not quench, until
G4570.2 V-PAM-2P σβέννυτε (1x)

1Th 5:19 Do·not quench the Spirit.

G4570.2 V-PPI-3S σβέννυται (3x)

Mk 9:44 ·not completely·die, and the fire is·not quenched."

Mk 9:46 ·not completely·die, and the fire is·not quenched."

Mk 9:48 ·does·not die, and the fire is·not quenched."

G4570.2 V-AAI-3P ἔσβεσαν (1x)

Heb 11:34 quenched *the* power of·fire, escaped *the* edge of·

G4571 σέ sê *p:p.* (203x)

Roots:G4771

(abbreviated listing for G4571)

G4571 P:P-2AS σέ (197x)

(list for G4571:P:P-2AS excluded)

EG4571 (6x)

(list for EG4571: excluded)

G4572 σε•αυτοῦ sêautôû *p:f.* (39x)

σε•αυτῷ sêautȭ [dative case]

σε•αυτόν sêautőn [accusative case]

σ•αυτοῦ sautôû [genitive contracted]

σ•αυτῷ sautȭ [dative contracted]

σ•αυτόν sautőn [accusative contracted]

Roots:G4571 G0846

G4572 P:F-3ASM σεαυτόν (29x)

Jn 7:4 If you·do these·things, make yourself apparent to·the

Jn 8:53 Whom·do you·yourself make yourself *out to·be*?

Jn 10:33 you, being a·man·of·clay†, make yourself God."

Jn 14:22 that you·intend to·manifest yourself to·us, and not·

Jn 21:18 you·were younger, you·were·girding yourself, and

Lk 4:9 ·are the Son of·God, cast yourself down from·here.

Lk 4:23 bring·both·relief·and·cure·to yourself. As·many·

Lk 5:14 ·off, show yourself to·the priest·that·offers·sacrifices,

Lk 10:27 ·mind," and "your neighbor as yourself.""

Lk 23:37 ·yourself are the king of·the Jews, save yourself."

Lk 23:39 are the Anointed-One, save yourself and us."

Gal 6:1 of·gentleness, keeping·a·watch·of yourself, lest you·

Mt 4:6 *the* Son of·God, cast yourself down. For it·has·been·

Mt 8:4 ·out, show yourself to·the priest·that·offers·sacrifices,

Mt 19:19 and ""You·shall·love your neighbor as yourself.""

Mt 22:39 it, "You·shall·love your neighbor as yourself."

Mt 27:40 *it* in three days, save yourself. If you·are a·son of·

Mk 1:44 ·out, show yourself to·the priest·that·offers·sacrifices,

Mk 12:31 You·shall·love your neighbor as yourself." There·

Mk 15:30 save yourself, and descend from the cross!"

Rm 2:1 ·judge the other, you·condemn yourself; for the·one

Rm 2:19 you·have·confidence within·yourself to·be a·guide

Rm 2:21 ·else, do·you·not instruct yourself? The·one

Jac 2:8 ""You·shall·love your neighbor as yourself,"" yeu·do

Phm 1:19 even you·yourself are·particularly·indebted·to·me.

1Ti 4:7 myths, and train yourself *rather* to·devout·reverence.

1Ti 4:16 this you·shall·save both yourself and the·ones

1Ti 5:22 moral·failures. Fully·keep yourself morally·clean!

2Ti 2:15 to·present yourself verifiably·approved·to·God, an·

G4572 P:F-3ASM-C σαυτόν (1x)

Rm 14:22 *the good·benefit* for·yourself *just* in·the·sight·of·

G4572 P:F-3DSM σεαυτῷ (5x)

Jn 17:5 glorify me (*along* with yourself) with·the glory

Ac 9:34 Rise·up and toss·aside your *mat*." And immediately

Ac 16:28 You·should·inflict on·yourself not·one·bit·of harm

Rm 2:5 heart, you·store·up Wrath for·yourself in·a·Day of·

1Ti 4:16 Pay·close·attention to·yourself, and·also to·the

G4572 P:F-3GSM σεαυτοῦ (4x)

Jn 1:22 sending us, what·do you·say concerning yourself?"

Jn 8:13 "You testify concerning yourself; your testimony is

Ac 26:1 ·permitted for·you to·discourse on·your·own behalf.

2Ti 4:11 ·up *John*·Mark, bring·him with you, for he·is

G4573 σεβάζομαι sêbázômai *v.* (1x)

Roots:G4576 See:G0764 G4575

G4573.1 V-ADI-3P ἐσεβάσθησαν (1x)

Rm 1:25 the lie, and reverenced and ritually·ministered to·

G4574 σέβασμα sébasma *n.* (2x)

Roots:G4573

G4574.1 N-ASN σέβασμα (1x)

2Th 2:4 ·*is* being·referred·to·as God or that·is·reverenced,'

G4574.2 N-APN σεβάσματα (1x)

Ac 17:23 and observing·again yeur objects·of·reverence, I·

G4575 σεβαστός sêbastős *adj.* (3x)

Roots:G4573 Compare:G2541

G4575.3 A-ASM σεβαστόν (1x)

Ac 25:25 appealing this to the Revered·Emperor, I·decided

G4575.3 A-GSM σεβαστοῦ (1x)

Ac 25:21 of·the Revered·Emperor, I·commandingly·ordered

G4575.3 A-GSF σεβαστῆς (1x)

Ac 27:1 by·name, from·*the*·Revered·Emperor's battalion.

G4576 σέβομαι sébômai *v.* (10x)

Compare:G0764 G2151 G2126 G2357 G4352 G5399
See:G4573 G4586 G4587
xLangEquiv:H2043-1 H4633-1 xLangAlso:H3372

G4576.1 V-PNI-3S σέβεται (1x)

Ac 19:27 whom all Asia and The Land reverences."

G4576.1 V-PNI-3P σέβονται (2x)

Mt 15:9 But futilely do·they·reverence me, teaching *the*

Mk 7:7 And futilely do·they·reverence me, teaching *the*

G4576.1 V-PNN σέβεσθαι (1x)

Ac 18:13 men·of·clay† to·reverence God contrary·to the

G4576.1 V-PNP-GSM σεβομένου (1x)

Ac 18:7 by·the·name·of Justus, who·is·reverencing God,

G4576.1 V-PNP-NSF σεβομένη (1x)

Ac 16:14 ·purple·cloth, *a·woman* who·is·reverencing God,

G4576.2 V-PNP-APF σεβομένας (1x)

Ac 13:50 ·stirred·up the women being·reverent (even the

G4576.2 V-PNP-DPM σεβομένοις (1x)

Ac 17:17 with·the·ones who·are·being·reverent, and·also in

G4576.2 V-PNP-GPM σεβομένων (2x)

Ac 13:43 and the·ones who·are·being·reverent converts·to·

Ac 17:4 of·the·ones who·are·being·reverent Greek·men and

G4577 σειρά sêirá *n.* (1x)

Roots:G4951 Compare:G0254 G1199 See:G0138
xLangAlso:H2256

G4577 N-DPF σειραῖς (1x)

2Pe 2:4 *them* over into·drag·chains of·a·deep·murky·shroud,

G4578 σεισμός sêismős *n.* (14x)

Roots:G4579 Compare:G2978 G5494
xLangAlso:H5492

G4578.2 N-NSM σεισμός (1x)

Mt 8:24 And behold, a·great tempest occurred in the sea,

G4578.3 N-NSM σεισμός (8x)

Ac 16:26 ·warning there·was a·great earthquake, such·for

Mt 28:2 And behold, there·occurred a·great earthquake. For

Rv 6:12 and behold, there·was a·great earthquake; and the

Rv 8:5 and thunderings, and lightnings, and an·earthquake.

Rv 11:13 in that hour there·happened a·great earthquake, and

Rv 11:19 and thunderings, and an·earthquake, and great

Rv 16:18 And there·was a·great earthquake, such·as did·not

Rv 16:18 upon the earth, so·vast an·earthquake, *and* so great

G4578.3 N-NPM σεισμοί (3x)

Lk 21:11 And great earthquakes shall·be pervasive·in·all

Mt 24:7 and earthquakes shall·be pervasive·in·all places.

Mk 13:8 And earthquakes shall·be pervasive·in·all places,

G4578.3 N-ASM σεισμόν (1x)

Mt 27:54 him, upon·seeing the earthquake and the·things

G4578.3 N-DSM σεισμῷ (1x)

Rv 11:13 And in the earthquake were·killed seven thousand

G4579 σείω sêíō *v.* (5x)

Compare:G0660 G1621 G5015 G5098-2 See:G1286
G4525

G4579.1 V-PAI-1S σείω (1x)

Heb 12:26 Yet once·more I·myself do·shake not merely the

G4579.1 V-PPP-NSF σειομένη (1x)

Rv 6:13 its unripe·green·figs while·being·shaken by·a·great

G4579.1 V-API-3S ἐσείσθη (2x)

Mt 21:10 into JeruSalem, all the City was·shaken, saying,

Mt 27:51 And the earth is·shaken, and the solid·rocks are·

G4579.1 V-API-3P ἐσείσθησαν (1x)

Mt 28:4 the·ones keeping·guard are·shaken and became as·

G4580 Σεκοῦνδος Sêkôûndôs *n/p.* (1x)

G4580.2 N/P-NSM Σεκοῦνδος (1x)

Ac 20:4 *both* AristArchus and Secundus of·ThessaloNica,

G4581 Σελεύκεια Sêlêukêia *n/l.* (1x)

G4581 N/L-ASF Σελεύκειαν (1x)

Ac 13:4 these·men went·down to Seleucia. Also from·there,

G4582 σελήνη sêlḗnē *n.* (9x)

See:G4583 G0138

G4582 N-NSF σελήνη (5x)

Ac 2:20 ·be·distorted into darkness and the moon into blood,

Mt 24:29 ·be·darkened, and the moon shall·not give·forth

Mk 13:24 ·be·darkened, and the moon shall·not give·forth

Rv 6:12 made·of·hair, and the moon became as blood,

Rv 12:1 ·with the sun, and the moon beneath her feet, and

G4582 N-DSF σελήνῃ (1x)

Lk 21:25 signs in *the* sun, moon, and constellations·of·stars.

G4582 N-GSF σελήνης (3x)

1Co 15:41 ·sun, and another glory of·*the*·moon, and another

Rv 8:12 and the third·part of·the moon, and the third·part

Rv 21:23 ·the sun, neither of·the moon, in·order·that it·may·

G4583 σεληνιάζομαι sêlēniázômai *v.* (2x)

Roots:G4582

G4583 V-PNI-3S σεληνιάζεται (1x)

Mt 17:15 on·my son, because he·is·lunatic and suffers badly

G4583 V-PNP-APM σεληνιαζομένους (1x)

Mt 4:24 ·with·demons, and those·being·lunatic, and those·

G4584 Σεμεΐ Sêmêḯ *n/p.* (1x)

שִׁמְעִי śhımᵉʿıy [Hebrew]

Roots:H8096

G4584.2 N/P-PRI Σεμεΐ (1x)

Lk 3:26 *son* of·MattathIas, *son* of·Shimei, *son* of·Joseph,

G4585 σεμίδαλις sêmídalis *n.* (1x)

Compare:G0224
xLangEquiv:H5560 xLangAlso:H7058

G4585 N-ASF σεμίδαλιν (1x)

Rv 18:13 "and wine, oil, fine·flour, and wheat, "and

G4586 σεμνός sêmnős *adj.* (4x)

Roots:G4576 Compare:G0703 G1784 G2158 G2412
G5093 See:G4587

G4586.2 A-NPN σεμνά (1x)

Php 4:8 *are* morally·worthy·of·reverent·respect, as·many·

G4586.2 A-APM σεμνούς (2x)

Tit 2:2 morally·worthy·of·reverent·respect, self-controlled,

1Ti 3:8 *must·be* morally·worthy·of·reverent·respect, not

G4586.2 A-APF σεμνάς (1x)

1Ti 3:11 *must·be* morally·worthy·of·reverent·respect, not

G4587 σεμνότης sêmnőtēs *n.* (3x)

Roots:G4586 Compare:G0703 G0298 G0423

G4587.3 N-ASF σεμνότητα (1x)

Tit 2:7 impeccable·integrity·worthy·of·reverent·respect,

G4587.3 N-DSF σεμνότητι (1x)

1Ti 2:2 in·impeccable·integrity·worthy·of·reverent·respect.

G4587.3 N-GSF σεμνότητος (1x)

1Ti 3:4 all impeccable·integrity·worthy·of·reverent·respect

G4588 Σέργιος Sérgiôs *n/p.* (1x)

G4588 N/P-DSM Σεργίῳ (1x)

Ac 13:7 co-opting the proconsul, Sergius Paulus, *who·was*

G4588-3 σερίφω sêríphō *v.* (2x)

Roots:G4588-2 Compare:G2919
xLangEquiv:H1777

G4588-3 V-FAI-1S σεριφῶ (1x)

Ac 7:7 they·should·be·enslaved, I·myself shall·sheriff,'

G4588-3 V-FAI-3S σεριφεί (1x)

Heb 10:30 And again, ""Yahweh shall·sheriff his People.""

G4589 Σήθ Séth *n/p.* (1x)

῾Σήθ Shḗth [Hebrew]

שֵׁת śheth

Roots:H8352

G4589.2 N/P-PRI ῾Σήθ (1x)

Lk 3:38 *son* of·Enosh, *son* of·Sheth, *son* of·Adam, *son* of·

G4590 Σήμ Sḗm *n/p.* (1x)
Ἑήμ Shḗm [Greek, Octuagint]
שֵׁם s̆hḗm [Hebrew]
Roots:H8035
G4590.2 N/P-PRI Ἑήμ (1x)
Lk 3:36 *son* of·Arphaxad, *son* of·Shem, *son* of·Noach, *son*

G4591 σημαίνω sēmaínō *v.* (6x)
Roots:G4590-1 Compare:G3506 G1770 See:G4592 G4591-1
G4591 V-PAP-NSM σημαίνων (3x)
Jn 12:33 he·was·saying this, signifying what·kind·of death
Jn 18:32 which he·declared, signifying what·kind·of death
Jn 21:19 This he·declared, signifying by·what·kind·of death
G4591 V-AAI-3S ἐσήμανεν (2x)
Ac 11:28 Agabus, after·standing·up, signified through the
Rv 1:1 through his angel, he·signified *it* to·his slave John,
G4591 V-AAN σημᾶναι (1x)
Ac 25:27 *and* not also to·signify the legal·charge *laid*

G4592 σημεῖον sēmeîôn *n.* (77x)
Roots:G4590-1 Compare:G4973 See:G4591 G4593 xLangEquiv:H0226 A0852
G4592.1 N-NSN σημεῖον (9x)
Lk 2:12 And this *shall·be* the sign to·yeu: Yeu·shall·find a·
Lk 11:29 be·given to·it, except the sign of·Jonah the prophet
Lk 11:30 For just·as Jonah was a·sign to·the Ninevites, in·
Mt 16:4 ·given to·her, except the sign of·Jonah the prophet.
Mt 24:3 what *shall·be* the sign of·your returning·Presence,
Mt 24:30 "And at·that·time, the sign of·the Son of·Clay·
Mk 13:4 be? And what *shall·be* the sign whenever all these·
Rv 12:1 And a·great sign was·made·visible in the heaven: a·
Rv 12:3 And another sign was·made·visible in the heaven;
G4592.1 N-NPN σημεῖα (6x)
Lk 21:11 ·be frightening·things and great signs from heaven.
Lk 21:25 "And there·shall·be signs in *the* sun, moon, and
Ac 2:43 and many wonders and signs were·done through the
Ac 5:12 hands of·the ambassadors, many signs and wonders
Mk 16:17 "And these signs shall·closely·follow the·ones
2Co 12:12 the signs of·an·ambassador were·performed
G4592.1 N-ASN σημεῖον (15x)
Lk 2:34 in IsraEl, and for a·sign being·spoken·against,
Lk 11:16 personally·from him a·sign from·out of·heaven.
Lk 11:29 is an·evil generation. It·seeks·for a·sign, and a·
Mt 12:38 "Mentor, we·want to·see a·sign from you."
Mt 12:39 (*who·is* also an·adulteress) seeks·for a·sign, and a·
Mt 12:39 ·given to·her, except the sign of·Jonah the prophet
Mt 16:1 him to·fully·exhibit for·them a·sign from·out of·the
Mt 16:4 (*who·is* also an·adulteress) seeks·for a·sign, and a·
Mt 26:48 ·one handing him over gave them a·sign, saying,
Mk 8:11 ·him, seeking personally·from him a·sign from the
Mk 8:12 Why·does this generation seek·for a·sign? Certainly
Rm 4:11 And he·received *the* sign of·circumcision, an·
1Co 1:22 And whereas Jews request a·sign, and·also Greeks
1Co 14:22 the bestowed·tongues are for a·sign, not to·the·
Rv 15:1 And I·saw another sign in the heaven, great and
G4592.1 N-APN σημεῖα (9x)
Jn 4:48 him, "Unless yeu·*all*·should·see signs and wonders,
Jn 20:30 Jesus also did many other signs in·the·sight of·his
Ac 2:19 in the heaven up·above and signs on the earth down·
Ac 7:36 out, after·doing wonders and signs in *the* land of·
Ac 8:13 ·astonished upon·observing both signs and great
Mt 16:3 but are·not able *to·discern* the signs of·the seasons?
Mt 24:24 and they·shall·give great signs and wonders,
Mk 13:22 ·be·awakened and shall·give signs and wonders to
Rv 13:13 And it·does great signs, so that it·should·make fire
G4592.1 N-DPN σημείοις (3x)
Ac 2:22 with·miracles and wonders and signs, which God
Heb 2:4 ·testifying·jointly, both with·signs and wonders,
2Th 2:9 with all power and signs and lying wonders,
G4592.1 N-GPN σημείων (2x)
Mk 16:20 through the signs following·afterward. So·be·it,·
Rm 15:19 with power of·signs and wonders, with *the* power
G4592.2 N-NSN σημεῖον (6x)
Lk 11:29 a·sign, and a·miraculous·sign shall·not be·given
Lk 21:7 be? And what *is* the miraculous·sign *that shall·be*
Ac 4:16 a·notable miraculous·sign has·been·done through
Ac 4:22 whom this miraculous·sign of·healing had·happened
Mt 12:39 a·sign, and a·miraculous·sign shall·not be·given
Mt 16:4 a·sign, and a·miraculous·sign shall·not be·given to·
G4592.2 N-NPN σημεῖα (1x)
Ac 4:30 healing, and *for* miraculous·signs and wonders to·
G4592.2 N-ASN σημεῖον (8x)
Jn 2:18 to·him, "What miraculous·sign do·you·show to·us,
Jn 4:54 *is* again *the* second miraculous·sign *that* Jesus did,
Jn 6:14 seeing that Jesus did a·miraculous·sign, the men·of·
Jn 6:30 "So·then what miraculous·sign *do* you·yourself do,
Jn 10:41 in·fact, did not·even·one miraculous·sign, but all·
Jn 12:18 they·heard him to·have·done this miraculous·sign.
Lk 23:8 ·expecting to·see some miraculous·sign occurring by
Mk 8:12 'As·if a·miraculous·sign shall·*ever*·be·given to·this
G4592.2 N-APN σημεῖα (15x)
Jn 2:23 observing his miraculous·signs which he·was·doing
Jn 3:2 is·able to·do these miraculous·signs that you·yourself
Jn 6:2 ·seeing his miraculous·signs which he·was·doing
Jn 6:26 not because yeu·saw miraculous·signs, but·rather
Jn 7:31 ¿! shall·he·do more miraculous·signs than these
Jn 9:16 ·moral·failure, able to·do such miraculous·signs?"
Jn 11:47 this man·of·clay† does many miraculous·signs?
Jn 12:37 having·done so·many miraculous·signs before them
Ac 6:8 great wonders and miraculous·signs among the
Ac 8:6 ·upon the miraculous·signs which he·was·doing.
Ac 14:3 grace and granting miraculous·signs and wonders
Ac 15:12 ·detail what·many miraculous·signs and wonders
Rv 13:14 through *the means·of* the miraculous·signs which it
Rv 16:14 ·demons, doing miraculous·signs, to·traverse·forth
Rv 19:20 ·one doing the miraculous·signs in·the·sight of·it,
G4592.2 N-DPN σημείοις (1x)
2Co 12:12 all patient·endurance, by miraculous·signs, and
G4592.2 N-GPN σημείων (1x)
Jn 2:11 Jesus did this initiating of·miraculous·signs in Qanah
G4592.3 N-NSN σημεῖον (1x)
2Th 3:17 ·my·own hand, which is a·signature in every letter.

G4593 σημειόω sēmeiôō *v.* (1x)
Roots:G4592
G4593.3 V-PMM-2P σημειοῦσθε (1x)
2Th 3:14 this·letter, yeu·must·personally·note that·man and

G4594 σ•ήμερον sḗmêrôn *adv.* (41x)
Roots:G3588 G2250
G4594.1 ADV σήμερον (11x)
Lk 2:11 Because to·yeu this·day, in *the* city of·David, a·
Lk 22:34 no, it·shall·not crow this·day before you·shall·
Ac 4:9 if we·ourselves this·day are·scrutinized over *the*
Ac 22:3 ·being a·zealot of·God, just·as yeu all are this·day.
Ac 24:21 I·myself am·called·into·judgment by yeu this·day.'
Ac 26:2 I·am·about to·make·my·defense this·day before you
Ac 26:29 also all the·ones hearing me this·day, both among
Ac 27:33 saying, "This·day is·the·fourteenth day of·
Mt 6:11 'Give us this·day our sustaining bread.
Mt 27:19 many·things this·day according·to a·vision·in·a·
Mk 14:30 "Certainly I·say to·you, that this·day, *even* in this
G4594.2 ADV σήμερον (23x)
Lk 4:21 to·say to them, "Today, this Scripture has·been·
Lk 5:26 "We·saw things·way·beyond·believable today."
Lk 12:28 ·this·manner enrobes the grass, today being in the
Lk 13:32 and I·further·finish healing today and tomorrow,
Lk 13:33 it·is·necessary·for me to·traverse today, and
Lk 19:5 drop·down. For today, it·is·necessary·for me to·
Lk 19:9 declared to him, "Today, Salvation did·come to·this
Lk 23:43 "Certainly I·say to·you, today, you·shall·be with
Lk 24:21 together with·all these·things, today marks this
Ac 13:33 are my Son. Today, I·myself have·begotten you.
Ac 19:40 to·be·called·to·account concerning today's uproar,
Heb 1:5 are my Son. Today, I·myself have·begotten you"?
Heb 3:7 Spirit says, "'Today if yeu·should·hear his voice,
Heb 3:13 even·for·as·along·as it·is·called "Today," lest any
Heb 3:15 Explicitly it·is·said, "'Today, if yeu·should·hear
Heb 4:7 a·certain day, *namely* "Today," saying *it* by David
Heb 4:7 it·has·been·declared, "'Today, if yeu·should·hear
Heb 5:5 are my Son. Today, I·myself have·begotten you.
Heb 13:8 *is* the same yesterday, and today, and into the
Mt 6:30 enrobes the grass of·the field, today being *here*, and
Mt 16:3 '*There·shall·be* stormy·weather today, for the sky
Mt 21:28 'Child, head·on·out. Work today in my vineyard.
Jac 4:13 the·ones saying, "Today or tomorrow we·should·
G4594.3 ADV σήμερον (7x)
Ac 20:26 Therefore I·attest to·yeu in the present day, that I·
Mt 11:23 ·would·have remained as·long·as·unto the present.
Mt 27:8 "Field of·Blood", even·unto the present.
Mt 28:15 ·among Judeans so·far·as·unto the present·day.
Rm 11:8 and ears *for·them* not to·hear unto the present day.⇒
2Co 3:14 For even·unto the·present·day the same veil
2Co 3:15 But·yet unto the·present·day, whenever Moses is·

G4595 σήπω sḗpō *v.* (1x)
Compare:G1311 G5351 See:G4550 G4549-1
G4595.2 V-2RAI-3S σέσηπεν (1x)
Jac 5:2 Yeur wealth has·rotted, and yeur garments have·

G4596 σηρικός sērikós *adj.* (1x)
Compare:G1040
G4596.2 A-GSN σηρικοῦ (1x)
Rv 18:12 "and of·fine·linen, and purple, silk, and scarlet,

G4597 σής sḗs *n.* (3x)
סָס çaç [Hebrew]
Roots:H5580
G4597 N-NSM σής (3x)
Lk 12:33 draws·near, neither·does moth thoroughly·ruin.
Mt 6:19 upon the earth, where moth and corrosion obliterate
Mt 6:20 heaven, where neither moth nor corrosion obliterate

G4598 σητό•βρωτος sētóbrōtôs *adj.* (1x)
Roots:G4597 G0977
G4598 A-NPN σητόβρωτα (1x)
Jac 5:2 ·rotted, and yeur garments have·become moth-eaten.

G4599 σθενόω sthênóō *v.* (1x)
Roots:G4598-2 Compare:G1765 G1840 G2902 G2476 See:G4599-1 G0772
G4599.1 V-AAO-3S σθενώσαι (1x)
1Pe 5:10 may·he firmly·establish, may·he·invigorate, may·

G4600 σιαγών siagṓn *n.* (3x)
xLangEquiv:H3895
G4600.2 N-ASF σιαγόνα (2x)
Lk 6:29 ·the·one pummeling you on the cheek, hold·forth the
Mt 5:39 shall·slap you on your right cheek, turn·back to·him
EG4600.2 (1x)
Lk 6:29 on the cheek, hold·forth the other *cheek* also, and of

G4601 σιγάω sigáō *v.* (9x)
Roots:G4602 Compare:G4623 xLangAlso:H2790
G4601.1 V-PAM-3S σιγάτω (2x)
1Co 14:28 he·must·stay·silent in a·convened·Called·Out·
1Co 14:30 sitting·down, the first *prophet* must·stay·silent.
G4601.1 V-PAM-3P σιγάτωσαν (1x)
1Co 14:34 Yeur women must·stay·silent in the convened·
G4601.1 V-PAN σιγᾶν (1x)
Ac 12:17 with·his hand to·stay·silent, he·gave·an·account to·
G4601.1 V-AAI-3S ἐσίγησεν (1x)
Ac 15:12 all the multitude stayed·silent and were·listening·to
G4601.1 V-AAI-3P ἐσίγησαν (2x)
Lk 9:36 alone. And they·themselves stayed·silent, and they·
Lk 20:26 And marveling at his answer, they·stayed·silent.
G4601.1 V-AAN σιγῆσαι (1x)
Ac 15:13 And with them staying·silent, Jacob *(the*
G4601.2 V-RPP-GSN σεσιγημένου (1x)
Rm 16:25 of·*the*·Mystery having·been·intentionally·silent

G4602 σιγή sigḗ *n.* (2x)
Compare:G4623 G2974 G1769 See:G4601
G4602 N-NSF σιγή (1x)
Rv 8:1 official·seal, there·was silence in the heaven *for*
G4602 N-GSF σιγῆς (1x)

Ac 21:40 people. And with·a·large silence occurring, he·

G4603 σιδήρεος sidḗrêôs *adj.* (5x)
Roots:G4604

G4603 A-ASF σιδηρᾶν (1x)
Ac 12:10 watch-station, they·came to the iron gate, the·one

G4603 A-APM σιδηροῦς (1x)
Rv 9:9 full·chest·armor, as full·chest·armor of·iron; and the

G4603 A-DSF σιδηρᾷ (3x)
Rv 2:27 he·shall·shepherd them with a·rod of·iron, as the
Rv 12:5 all the nations with a·rod of·iron; and her child was·
Rv 19:15 shall·shepherd them with a·rod of·iron, and he·

G4604 σίδηρος sídērôs *n.* (1x)
Compare:G5557 G0696 G5475 G3432-1 G2595-3
See:G4603
xLangEquiv:H1270 A6523

G4604 N-GSM σιδήρου (1x)
Rv 18:12 "and of·bronze, iron, and marble,

G4607 σικάριος sikáriôs *n.* (1x)
Compare:G5406 G0409 G0443

G4607 N-GPM σικαρίων (1x)
Ac 21:38 the four·thousand men of·the Assassins out into the

G4608 σίκερα síkêra *n.* (1x)
שֵׁכָר śhe̱kar [Hebrew]
Roots:H7941 Compare:G3182-1

G4608.2 N-OI σίκερα (1x)
Lk 1:15 he·should·not drink wine nor intoxicating·drink, and

G4609 Σίλας Sílas *n/p.* (14x)
Roots:G4610

G4609 N/P-NSM Σίλας (4x)
Ac 15:32 Both Judas and Silas, being prophets also
Ac 16:25 And at midnight Paul and Silas, while·praying,
Ac 17:14 sea, but both Silas and TimoThy were·remaining·
Ac 18:5 And as·soon·as both Silas and TimoThy came·down

G4609 N/P-ASM Σίλαν (6x)
Ac 15:22 being·surnamed BarSabas, and Silas, men who·
Ac 15:27 we·have·dispatched Judas and Silas, themselves
Ac 15:40 And Paul, picking Silas, went·forth after·being·
Ac 16:19 ·grabbing Paul and Silas, they·drew·*them*·along
Ac 17:10 sent·forth both Paul and Silas through the night to
Ac 17:15 *with·them* a·commandment to Silas and TimoThy,

G4609 N/P-DSM Σιλᾷ (3x)
Ac 15:34 it·seemed·good to·Silas to·still·stay·over at·this·
Ac 16:29 ·trembling, he·fell·down·before Paul and Silas.
Ac 17:4 and joined·alongside with·Paul and Silas, both a·

EG4609 (1x)
Ac 16:22 ·ordered *for·Paul and Silas* to·be·beaten·with·rods.

G4610 Σιλουανός Silôuanós *n/p.* (4x)
Compare:G4609

G4610.2 N/P-NSM Σιλουανός (2x)
1Th 1:1 Paul, Silvanus, and TimoThy.
2Th 1:1 Paul, Silvanus, and TimoThy.

G4610.2 N/P-GSM Σιλουανοῦ (2x)
1Pe 5:12 Through Silvanus (the trustworthy brother as·how
2Co 1:19 yeu through us (through Silvanus, TimoThy and me

G4611 Σιλωάμ Silōám *n/l.* (3x)
שִׁלֹחַ śhıló̱ach [Hebrew]
Roots:H7975

G4611.2 N/L-PRI Σιλωάμ (3x)
Jn 9:7 wash in the pool of·Siloam" (which *from·Hebrew* is·
Jn 9:11 'Head·on·out to the pool of·Siloam and wash.' And
Lk 13:4 upon whom the tower in Siloam fell and killed them,

G4612 σιμικίνθιον simikínthiôn *n.* (1x)

G4612 N-APN σιμικίνθια (1x)
Ac 19:12 even such·for sweat·towels or aprons from his

G4613 Σίμων Símōn *n/p.* (77x)
שִׁמְעוֹן śhım'ô̱n [Hebrew]
Roots:H8095 Compare:G4826

G4613.2 N/P-NSM Σίμων (19x)
Jn 1:42 declared, "You·yourself are Simon, the son of·Jonah
Jn 6:68 Accordingly, Simon Peter answered him, "Lord, to
Jn 13:9 Simon Peter says to·him, "Lord, not my feet merely
Jn 13:24 So·then, Simon Peter beckoned to·him to·inquire
Jn 13:36 Simon Peter says to·him, "Lord, where·do you·
Jn 18:10 Now·then, having a·dagger, Simon Peter drew it
Jn 18:15 And Simon Peter was·following Jesus, and *so was*
Jn 18:25 Now Simon Peter was standing·by and warming·
Jn 20:6 So·then, Simon Peter comes following him, and he·
Jn 21:2 *Now* at·the·same·place, there·was Simon Peter, and
Jn 21:3 Simon Peter says to·them, "I·head·on·out to·fish.
Jn 21:7 that it·was the Lord, Simon Peter tightly·girded *his*
Jn 21:11 Simon Peter walked·up and drew the net upon the
Lk 5:5 And answering, Simon declared to·him, "O·Captain,
Lk 5:8 And after·seeing *it*, Simon Peter fell·down·at Jesus
Ac 10:18 ·out, they·were·inquiring whether Simon, the·one
Mt 10:2 these: first, Simon (the·one being·referred·to·as
Mt 16:16 And answering, Simon Peter declared, "You·
Mk 1:36 And Simon and the·ones with him tracked him

G4613.2 N/P-VSM Σίμων (8x)
Jn 21:15 says to·Simon Peter, "Simon, *son* of·Jonah, do·
Jn 21:16 to·him again a·second·time, "Simon, *son* of·Jonah,
Jn 21:17 to·him the third·time, "Simon, *son* of·Jonah, do·
Lk 22:31 Then the Lord declared, "Simon, Simon, behold,
Lk 22:31 the Lord declared, "Simon, Simon, behold, the
Mt 16:17 "Supremely·blessed are·you, Simon BarJonah,
Mt 17:25 "What·do you suppose, Simon? From whom·do
Mk 14:37 And he·says to·Peter, "Simon, do·you·sleep?

G4613.2 N/P-ASM Σίμωνα (11x)
Jn 1:41 first finds his·own brother Simon and says to·him,
Jn 13:6 So·then he·comes to Simon Peter, and that·one says
Jn 20:2 So·then she·runs and comes to Simon Peter and to
Lk 5:4 ·ceased speaking, he·declared to Simon, "Head·off
Lk 5:10 And Jesus declared to Simon, "Do·not be·afraid.
Lk 6:14 Simon (whom also he·named Peter), and Andrew
Ac 10:5 men to Joppa and send·for Simon, who is·surnamed
Ac 10:32 to Joppa and summarily·call·for Simon, who is·
Ac 11:13 to Joppa and send·for Simon being·surnamed Peter
Mt 4:18 saw two brothers, Simon (the·one being·referred·
Mk 1:16 the Sea of·Galilee, he·saw Simon and his brother

G4613.2 N/P-DSM Σίμωνι (3x)
Jn 21:15 when they·had·dined, Jesus says to·Simon Peter,
Lk 5:10 of·Zebedee, who were partners with·Simon. And
Mk 3:16 *these are the twelve*: on·Simon, he·laid a·name

G4613.2 N/P-GSM Σίμωνος (7x)
Jn 1:40 Andrew, Simon Peter's brother, was one from·
Jn 6:8 his disciples, Andrew, Simon Peter's brother, says to·
Lk 4:38 ·the gathering, he·entered into Simon's home. And
Lk 4:38 into Simon's home. And Simon's mother-in-law was
Lk 5:3 of·the sailboats, which was Simon's, *Jesus* asked·of
Mk 1:29 they·went into the home of·Simon and Andrew,
Mk 1:30 But Simon's mother-in-law was·laying·ill, burning·

G4613.3 N/P-NSM Σίμων (2x)
Ac 1:13 ; (Jakob *son* of·Alphaeus, Simon the Zealot, and
Mt 10:4 Simon the Zealot, and Judas IsCariot, the·one also

G4613.3 N/P-ASM Σίμωνα (2x)
Lk 6:15 of·Alphaeus), and Simon, the·one being·called
Mk 3:18 *called Lebbaeus* Thaddaeus, and Simon the Zealot;

G4613.4 N/P-NSM Σίμων (1x)
Mt 13:55 his brothers, *little*·Jacob, Joses, Simon and Jude,

G4613.4 N/P-GSM Σίμωνος (1x)
Mk 6:3 ·Jacob, Joses, Jude, and Simon? And are not his

EG4613.4 (2x)
Lk 22:32 petitioned concerning you, *Simon*, in·order·that
Lk 22:33 And *Simon* declared to·him, "Lord, I·am ready to·

G4613.5 N/P-ASM Σίμωνα (2x)
Mt 27:32 a·man·of·clay†, a·Cyrenian, Simon by·name, *and*
Mk 15:21 ·man who·was·passing·by, Simon, a·Cyrenian,

G4613.6 N/P-GSM Σίμωνος (4x)
Jn 6:71 Judas IsCariot, *the son* of·Simon, for *it·was* this·man
Jn 12:4 disciples (Judas IsCariot, Simon's *son*, the·one about
Jn 13:2 of·Judas IsCariot, *son* of·Simon, that he·should·hand
Jn 13:26 he·gave *it* to·Judas IsCariot, *the son* of·Simon.

G4613.7 N/P-GSM Σίμωνος (3x)
Lk 23:26 *in* from *the* countryside, Simon, a·Cyrenian, they·
Mt 26:6 ·to·be in BethAny, in Simon the leper's home,
Mk 14:3 in BethAny in the home of·Simon the leper, as·he

G4613.8 N/P-NSM Σίμων (4x)
Ac 8:9 man by·the·name·of Simon was·previously in the
Ac 8:13 And Simon himself also trusted.
Ac 8:18 And Simon, after·distinctly·viewing that the Holy
Ac 8:24 Then answering, Simon declared, "Yeu·yeurselves

G4613.9 N/P-DSM Σίμωνι (2x)
Ac 9:43 ·of days in Joppa with a·certain Simon, a·tanner.
Ac 10:6 *staying* with a·certain·man, Simon a·tanner, whose

G4613.9 N/P-GSM Σίμωνος (2x)
Ac 10:17 after·making·a·thorough·inquiry for·Simon's home
Ac 10:32 ·man is·a·guest in *the* home of·Simon, a·tanner,

G4613.10 N/P-NSM Σίμων (1x)
Lk 7:43 And answering, Simon declared, "I·assume that *it*·

G4613.10 N/P-VSM Σίμων (1x)
Lk 7:40 Jesus declared to him, "Simon, I·have something to·

G4613.10 N/P-DSM Σίμωνι (1x)
Lk 7:44 the woman, he·replied to·Simon, "Do·you·look·

G4613.11 N/P-DSM Σίμωνι (1x)
Lk 24:34 is·awakened and was·gazed·upon by·Simon."

G4614 Σινᾶ Sinâ *n/l.* (4x)
סִינַי çıyna̱y [Hebrew]
Roots:H5514 xLangAlso:H2722

G4614.2 N/L-PRI Σινᾶ (4x)
Ac 7:30 to·him in the wilderness of·Mount Sinai, in a·blaze
Ac 7:38 speaking with·him on Mount Sinai, and with·our
Gal 4:24 in·fact *is* from Mount Sinai, bearing·children for
Gal 4:25 For *this* Hagar is Mount Sinai in Arabia, and

G4615 σίναπι sínapi *n.* (5x)
Compare:G4690

G4615.2 N-GSN σινάπεως (5x)
Lk 13:19 "It·is like a·kernel of·mustard·seed, which a·man·
Lk 17:6 trust *that·grows* as a·kernel of·mustard·seed *does*,
Mt 13:31 heavens is like a·kernel of·mustard·seed (which
Mt 17:20 trust *that·grows* as a·kernel of·mustard·seed *does*,
Mk 4:31 "*It·is* as a·kernel of·mustard·seed, which, whenever

G4616 σινδών sindṓn *n.* (6x)
Compare:G1039

G4616 N-ASF σινδόνα (3x)
Mk 14:51 him *with* a·linen·cloth having·been·arrayed over
Mk 14:52 But abandoning the linen·cloth, he·fled from them
Mk 15:46 And after·buying a·linen·cloth and lowering *Jesus*

G4616 N-DSF σινδόνι (3x)
Lk 23:53 it down, he·swathed it in·a·linen·cloth, and laid it
Mt 27:59 the body, Joseph swathed it in·a·pure linen·cloth
Mk 15:46 ·enwrapped him in·the linen·cloth and fully·laid

G4617 σινιάζω siniázō *v.* (2x)

G4617 V-AAN σινιάσαι (1x)
Lk 22:31 demanded yeu·*all*, to·sift *yeu·all* as the wheat.

EG4617 (1x)
Ac 2:23 *And* after·directly·pegging *him to·a·cross*, yeu·

G4618 σιτευτός sitêutós *adj.* (3x)
Roots:G4621 See:G4619

G4618 A-ASM σιτευτόν (3x)
Lk 15:23 And bringing the fattened calf, sacrifice *it*.
Lk 15:27 your father sacrificed the fattened calf, because he·
Lk 15:30 you·sacrificed for·him the fattened calf.'

G4619 σιτιστός sitistós *adj.* (1x)
Roots:G4621 See:G4618

G4619.2 A-NPN σιτιστά (1x)
Mt 22:4 My bulls and fatlings *are* having·been·sacrificed,

G4620 σιτό•μετρον sitómêtrôn *n.* (1x)
Roots:G4621 G3358 Compare:G1033 G1035 G1305
G5160 G5315

G4620.2 N-ASN σιτομέτριον (1x)
Lk 12:42 *them their* ration·of·food·staples in due·season?

G4621 σῖτος sîtôs *n.* (14x)
σῖτα sîta [plural irregular neuter]
Compare:G4447-1 G5504-3 G4719 See:G4618
xLangAlso:H1715 H7668

G4621.1 N-ASM σῖτον (1x)

Mk 4:28 ·of·grain, after·that, fully·ripe grain in the head.

G4621.1 N-APM σῖτα (1x)

Ac 7:12 But after·hearing·of there·being grain in Egypt,

G4621.2 N-ASM σῖτον (7x)

Lk 3:17 ·floor and shall·gather·together the wheat into his
Lk 22:31 demanded yeu·*all*, to·sift *yeu·all* as the wheat.
Ac 27:38 sailing·ship, *by* casting·out the wheat into the sea.
Mt 3:12 and shall·gather·together his wheat into the barn,
Mt 13:29 ·uproot the wheat at·the·same·time with·them.
Mt 13:30 them, but gather·together the wheat into my barn.
Rv 18:13 wine, oil, fine·flour, and wheat, "and livestock,

G4621.2 N-GSM σίτου (5x)

Jn 12:24 to·yeu, unless the kernel of·wheat, falling into the
Lk 16:7 'A·hundred kor·measures of·wheat.' And he·says
Mt 13:25 up *in·the* midst of·the wheat, and he·went·away.
1Co 15:37 whether it·may·happen·to·be of·wheat or some
Rv 6:6 saying, "A·dry·measure of·wheat for·a·denarius,

G4623 σιωπάω siōpáō *v.* (11x)

Compare:G4601 G2974 See:G4602

G4623.1 V-PAM-2S σιώπα (1x)

Mk 4:39 to·the sea, "Keep·silent, having·been·muzzled!"

G4623.1 V-PAP-NSM σιωπῶν (1x)

Lk 1:20 And behold, you·shall·be keeping·silent, and not

G4623.1 V-IAI-3S ἐσιώπα (2x)

Mt 26:63 But YeShua was·keeping·silent. And responding,
Mk 14:61 But he·was·keeping·silent and answered not·even·

G4623.1 V-IAI-3P ἐσιώπων (2x)

Mk 3:4 a·soul, or to·kill?" But they·were·keeping·silent.
Mk 9:34 But they·were·keeping·silent, for along the way

G4623.1 V-AAS-2S σιωπήσῃς (1x)

Ac 18:9 but·rather speak, and you·should·not keep·silent,

G4623.1 V-AAS-3S σιωπήσῃ (2x)

Lk 18:39 ·reprimanding him, that he·should·keep·silent. But
Mk 10:48 ·reprimanding him that he·should·keep·silent, but

G4623.1 V-AAS-3P σιωπήσωσιν (2x)

Lk 19:40 to·yeu that if these should·keep·silent, the stones
Mt 20:31 reprimanded them that they·should·keep·silent, but

G4624 σκανδαλίζω skandalízō *v.* (30x)

Roots:G4625 Compare:G3802 G4350

G4624.1 V-PAI-3S σκανδαλίζει (4x)

Mt 5:29 "So if your right eye entraps you, pluck it out and
Mt 5:30 And if your right hand entraps you, chop it off and
Mt 18:8 So if your hand or your foot entraps you, chop it off
Mt 18:9 And if your eye entraps you, pluck it out and cast *it*

G4624.1 V-PAS-3S σκανδαλίζῃ (3x)

Mk 9:43 "So if your hand should·entrap you, chop it off.
Mk 9:45 And if your foot should·entrap you, chop it off.
Mk 9:47 "And if your eye should·entrap you, cast it out.

G4624.2 V-IPI-3P ἐσκανδαλίζοντο (2x)

Mt 13:57 And they·were·tripped·up by him. But YeShua
Mk 6:3 alongside us?" And they·were·tripped·up by him.

G4624.2 V-AAS-1P σκανδαλίσωμεν (1x)

Mt 17:27 But, in·order·that we·should·not trip them up,

G4624.2 V-APS-3S σκανδαλισθῇ (2x)

Lk 7:23 ·blessed is·he who should·not be·tripped·up by me."
Mt 11:6 *he·is*, if he·should·not be·tripped·up by me."

G4624.3 V-FPI-1S σκανδαλισθήσομαι (1x)

Mt 26:33 ·at·any·time shall·be·tripped·up·and·fall·away."

G4624.3 V-FPI-2P σκανδαλισθήσεσθε (2x)

Mt 26:31 "All yeu shall·be·tripped·up by me and·shall·fall·
Mk 14:27 "All yeu·shall·be·tripped·up by me and·shall·

G4624.3 V-FPI-3P σκανδαλισθήσονται (3x)

Mt 24:10 then many shall·be·tripped·up·and·fall·away, and
Mt 26:33 "Even if all·men shall·be·tripped·up by you and·
Mk 14:29 if all shall·be·tripped·up·and·fall·away, but·yet

G4624.3 V-PAI-3S σκανδαλίζει (1x)

Jn 6:61 to·them, "Does·this trip yeu up·to·fall·away?

G4624.3 V-API-3P ἐσκανδαλίσθησαν (1x)

Mt 15:12 *this* saying, are·tripped·up·and·fallen·away?"

G4624.3 V-APS-2P σκανδαλισθῆτε (1x)

Jn 16:1 ·that yeu·should·not be·tripped·up·and·fall·away.

G4624.4 V-PPI-3S σκανδαλίζεται (1x)

Rm 14:21 brother stumbles, or is·enticed, or is·made·weak.

G4624.5 V-PAI-3S σκανδαλίζει (1x)

1Co 8:13 Therefore·indeed, if food entices my brother unto·

G4624.5 V-PPI-3S σκανδαλίζεται (1x)

2Co 11:29 Who is·being·enticed·into·moral·failure, and I·

G4624.5 V-AAS-1S σκανδαλίσω (1x)

1Co 8:13 lest I·should·cause·the·moral·failure·of my brother

G4624.5 V-AAS-3S σκανδαλίσῃ (3x)

Lk 17:2 that he·should·cause·the·moral·failure·of one of·
Mt 18:6 would entice·or·cause·the·moral·failure·of one of·
Mk 9:42 would entice·or·cause·the·moral·failure·of one of·

G4624.7 V-PPI-3S σκανδαλίζεται (1x)

Mt 13:21 straight·away he·is·recaptured·into·moral·failure.

G4624.7 V-PPI-3P σκανδαλίζονται (1x)

Mk 4:17 immediately they·are·recaptured·into·moral·failure.

G4625 σκάνδαλον skándalôn *n.* (15x)

Roots:G2578 Compare:G3803 G4348 G4349
See:G4624 xLangAlso:H1848 H4383

G4625.2 N-ASN σκάνδαλον (4x)

Mt 16:23 me, Adversary-Accuser! You·are a·trap to·me,
Rm 11:9 and into a·hunting·pit, and into a·trap, and into a·
Rm 14:13 a·stumbling·block or a·trap in·a·brother's *way*.
Rv 2:14 ·*the·Annihilator* to·cast a·trap in·the·sight·of·the

G4625.2 N-APN σκάνδαλα (2x)

Mt 13:41 ·out·of·his kingdom all the traps, and·also the·ones
Rm 16:17 the dissensions and the traps contrary·to the

G4625.3 N-NSN σκάνδαλον (1x)

Gal 5:11 ·by·inference, the scandalous·offense of·the cross

G4625.3 N-ASN σκάνδαλον (1x)

1Co 1:23 *which·is* in·fact a·scandalous·offense to·Jews and

G4625.3 N-GSN σκανδάλου (2x)

Rm 9:33 and a·solid·rock of·scandalous·offense, and any
1Pe 2:8 ·stumbling and a·solid·rock of·scandalous·offense."

G4625.4 N-NSN σκάνδαλον (2x)

Mt 18:7 ·of·clay† through whom the scandalous·trap comes!
1Jn 2:10 in the light, and there·is no scandalous·trap in him.

G4625.4 N-APN σκάνδαλα (2x)

Lk 17:1 not·permissible *for* the scandalous·traps not to·come
Mt 18:7 for it·is a·necessity *for* scandalous·traps to·come!

G4625.4 N-GPN σκανδάλων (1x)

Mt 18:7 to·the world due·to its scandalous·traps, for it·is a·

G4626 σκάπτω skáptō *v.* (3x)

xLangAlso:H5737

G4626 V-PAN σκάπτειν (1x)

Lk 16:3 I·do·not have·strength to·dig; I·am·ashamed to·

G4626 V-AAI-3S ἔσκαψεν (1x)

Lk 6:48 building a·home, who also dug deeply and laid a·

G4626 V-AAS-1S σκάψω (1x)

Lk 13:8 also, until such·time *that* I·should·dig around it and

G4627 σκάφη skáphē *n.* (3x)

Roots:G4626 Compare:G3491 G4142 G4143

G4627 N-ASF σκάφην (1x)

Ac 27:30 and with·*them*·lowering the skiff into the sea

G4627 N-GSF σκάφης (2x)

Ac 27:16 ·strength to·make the skiff mighty·secure.
Ac 27:32 chopped·off the small·ropes of·the skiff, and they·

G4628 σκέλος skélôs *n.* (4x)

Compare:G3382 G2833-1 See:G4646
xLangEquiv:H7785 xLangAlso:H3767

G4628 N-NPN σκέλη (1x)

Jn 19:31 ·of Pilate that their legs should·be·broken·apart, and

G4628 N-APN σκέλη (2x)

Jn 19:32 came and in·fact broke·apart the legs of·the first,
Jn 19:33 having·died, they·did·not break·apart his legs.

EG4628 (1x)

Jn 19:32 legs of·the first, and·then *the·legs* of·the other one

G4629 σκέπασμα sképasma *n.* (1x)

See:G4649

G4629.2 N-APN σκεπάσματα (1x)

1Ti 6:8 ·nourishment and *the* essential·coverings, with·these

G4630 Σκευᾶς Skêuâs *n/p.* (1x)

G4630.2 N/P-GSM Σκευᾶ (1x)

Ac 19:14 this·thing: the·seven Sons of·Sceva, a·Jewish

G4631 σκευή skêuḗ *n.* (1x)

Roots:G4632

G4631.2 N-ASF σκευήν (1x)

Ac 27:19 we·flung the sailing·ship's tackle *overboard*.

G4632 σκεῦος skêûôs *n.* (23x)

Compare:G0030 G3582 G2765 G5473 See:G4631
G0643 G0384 xLangAlso:H3627

G4632.1 N-NSN σκεῦος (5x)

Jn 19:29 there·was·set·out a·vessel exceedingly·full of·wine·
Ac 9:15 Because this·man is my vessel of·Selection to·bear
Ac 10:16 three·times, and the vessel was·taken·up again
Ac 11:5 I·saw a·clear·vision. A·certain vessel descending,
2Ti 2:21 from these·things, he·shall·be a·vessel unto honor,

G4632.1 N-NPN σκεύη (2x)

2Ti 2:20 there·are not merely vessels made·of·gold and of·
Rv 2:27 as the earthenware vessels are·shattered *by·its·maker*

G4632.1 N-ASN σκεῦος (5x)

Ac 10:11 ·opened·up, and a·certain vessel descending to
Rm 9:21 to·make, in·fact, one vessel to honor and another
1Th 4:4 his·own *earthenware* vessel in renewed·holiness and
Rv 18:12 "and every *type·of* ivory vessel, and every *type·of*
Rv 18:12 and every *type·of* vessel *made* out of·*the*·most·

G4632.1 N-APN σκεύη (3x)

Heb 9:21 blood, and all the vessels of·the public·service.
Rm 9:22 *the* vessels of·wrath having·been·completely·
Rm 9:23 of·his glory upon *the* vessels of·mercy, which he·

G4632.1 N-DSN σκεύει (2x)

Lk 8:16 a·lantern, covers it with·a·vessel or places *it*
1Pe 3:7 ·to knowledge, as with·a·weaker vessel, while·

G4632.1 N-DPN σκεύεσιν (1x)

2Co 4:7 this treasure in earthenware vessels, in·order·that the

G4632.3 N-NPN σκεύη (1x)

Lk 17:31 upon the rooftop, with his belongings in the home,

G4632.3 N-APN σκεύη (2x)

Mt 12:29 and to·thoroughly·plunder his belongings, unless
Mk 3:27 ·plunder the strong·man's belongings, not·even·one

G4632.4 N-ASN σκεῦος (2x)

Ac 27:17 after·lowering the sail, they·were·carried·along
Mk 11:16 anyone should·carry *any* merchandise through the

G4633 σκηνή skēnḗ *n.* (1x)

Compare:G2570-2 G4639 G4632 See:G4633-1
G4636 G4635 xLangAlso:H0168 H5521 H4908

G4633.1 N-DPF σκηναῖς (1x)

Heb 11:9 ·foreign *land*, residing in tents with YiTsaq and

G4633-1 ὁκηνή shkēnḗ *n.* (21x)

'Σκηνή Shkēnḗ [as a proper noun]

מִשְׁכָּן mísh·kạn [Hebrew]

Roots:G4633 Compare:G1980-3
xLangEquiv:H4908

G4633-1.2 N-ASF ὁκηνήν (2x)

Ac 7:43 Also, yeu·took·up the tabernacle of·Molek, and the
Ac 15:16 ·return and shall·rebuild the tabernacle of·David,

G4633-1.2 N-APF ὁκηνάς (4x)

Lk 9:33 and we·should·make three tabernacles; one·for you
Lk 16:9 they·may·accept yeu into the eternal tabernacles.
Mt 17:4 you·want, we·should·make three tabernacles here:
Mk 9:5 And we·should·make three tabernacles: one·for·you,

G4633-1.3 N-NSF 'Σκηνή (5x)

Ac 7:44 "The Tabernacle of·Testimony was with our fathers
Heb 9:1 in·fact, the first Tabernacle also was·having
Heb 9:2 For a·Tabernacle was·planned·and·constructed; the
Heb 9:3 second curtain, *a·second* Tabernacle, the·one being·
Rv 21:3 "Behold, the Tabernacle of·God *is* with the men·

G4633-1.3 N-ASF 'Σκηνήν (4x)

Heb 8:5 ·he·was·about to·further·finish the Tabernacle:
Heb 9:6 entered into the first Tabernacle, further·finishing
Heb 9:21 likewise, he·sprinkled the Tabernacle also with·the
Rv 13:6 to·revile his name, and his Tabernacle, and the·ones

G4633-1.3 N-DSF 'Σκηνῇ (1x)

Heb 13:10 ·ritually·ministering in·the Tabernacle have no

G4633-1.3 N-GSF 'Σκηνῆς (4x)

Heb 8:2 ·things and of·the true Tabernacle, which Yahweh
Heb 9:8 ·made·apparent with·the first Tabernacle still being
Heb 9:11 the greater and more·complete Tabernacle not
Rv 15:5 the Temple of·the Tabernacle of·the Testimony in
EG4633-1.3 (1x)
Heb 9:7 But into the second *Tabernacle*, once per year, the

G4635 σκηνο•ποιός skēnôpôiós *n.* (1x)
Roots:G4633 G4160
G4635 N-NPM σκηνοποιοί (1x)
Ac 18:3 was·working, for they·were tentmakers *by* trade.

G4636 σκῆνος skēnôs *n.* (2x)
Roots:G4633 See:G4638
G4636.2 N-DSN σκήνει (1x)
2Co 5:4 the·ones being in the bodily·tent do·groan, being·
G4636.2 N-GSN σκήνους (1x)
2Co 5:1 home of·the bodily·tent should·be·demolished, we·

G4637 σκηνόω skēnôō *v.* (5x)
Roots:G4636
G4637.1 V-FAI-3S σκηνώσει (2x)
Rv 7:15 ·down on the throne shall·encamp among them.
Rv 21:3 the men·of·clay†, and he·shall·encamp with them,
G4637.1 V-PAP-APM σκηνοῦντας (1x)
Rv 13:6 Tabernacle, and the·ones encamping in the heaven.
G4637.1 V-PAP-NPM σκηνοῦντες (1x)
Rv 12:12 the heavens and the·ones encamping in them.
G4637.1 V-AAI-3S ἐσκήνωσεν (1x)
Jn 1:14 the Word became flesh and encamped among us, and

G4638 σκήνωμα skēnōma *n.* (3x)
Roots:G4637
G4638.2 N-ASN σκήνωμα (1x)
Ac 7:46 requested to·find a·suitable·Tabernacle for·the God
G4638.3 N-DSN σκηνώματι (1x)
2Pe 1:13 in this bodily·tabernacle, to·thoroughly·awaken you
G4638.3 N-GSN σκηνώματος (1x)
2Pe 1:14 the putting·away of·my bodily·tabernacle is abrupt,

G4639 σκιά skiá *n.* (8x)
Compare:G0644 G4610-1 See:G4654
xLangAlso:H6738 H6754
G4639.1 N-ASF σκιάν (1x)
Mk 4:32 birds of·the sky to·be·able to·nest under its shade."
G4639.2 N-NSF σκιά (2x)
Ac 5:15 ·by, if·even his shadow may·overshadow some of·
Col 2:17 which·things are a·shadow of·the·things impending
G4639.2 N-ASF σκιάν (1x)
Heb 10:1 the Torah-Law, having a·shadow of·the impending
G4639.2 N-DSF σκιᾷ (3x)
Lk 1:79 ·are·sitting·down in darkness and shadow of·death,
Heb 8:5 ·explicit·pattern and shadow of·the heavenly·things,
Mt 4:16 in *the* region and shadow of·death, upon·them a·
EG4639.2 (1x)
Col 2:17 *is* the Anointed-One's body *which cast the shadow*.

G4640 σκιρτάω skirtáō *v.* (3x)
Compare:G0021 G0242 G0641 G1814
xLangEquiv:H7540
G4640.1 V-AAI-3S ἐσκίρτησεν (2x)
Lk 1:41 ·Mariam, *that* the babe skipped·about in her womb,
Lk 1:44 in my ears, the babe skipped·about in my womb in
G4640.1 V-AAM-2P σκιρτήσατε (1x)
Lk 6:23 "Rejoice in that day and skip·about, for, behold,

G4641 σκληρο•καρδία sklērôkardía *n.* (3x)
Roots:G4642 G2588
G4641.1 N-ASF σκληροκαρδίαν (3x)
Mt 19:8 pertaining·to your hardness·of·heart *that* Moses
Mk 10:5 "Pertaining·to your hardness·of·heart, he·wrote
Mk 16:14 ·their lack·of·trust and hardness·of·heart, because

G4642 σκληρός sklērós *adj.* (6x)
Roots:G4628 Compare:G4457 G0840 G0972 G3120
See:G4646 xLangAlso:H7186
G4642.2 A-NSM σκληρός (2x)
Jn 6:60 declared, "This is a·hard saying; who is·able to·
Mt 25:24 I·knew you that you·are a·hard man·of·clay†,
G4642.2 A-NSN σκληρόν (2x)
Ac 9:5 persecute. *It·is* hard for·you to·kick·the·heel·back
Ac 26:14 me? *It·is* hard for·you to·kick·the·heel·back
G4642.3 A-GPM σκληρῶν (1x)
Jac 3:4 and *are* being·driven by harsh winds, *and·yet* they·
G4642.3 A-GPN σκληρῶν (1x)
Jud 1:15 and concerning all the harsh·things which irreverent

G4643 σκληρότης sklērótēs *n.* (1x)
Roots:G4642 Compare:G4457
G4643.1 N-ASF σκληρότητα (1x)
Rm 2:5 But according·to your hardness and *your* unrepentant

G4644 σκληρο•τράχηλος sklērôtráchēlôs *adj.* (1x)
Roots:G4642 G5137 Compare:G0545
G4644.1 A-VPM σκληροτράχηλοι (1x)
Ac 7:51 "Yeu·stiff-necked and uncircumcised in·the heart

G4645 σκληρύνω sklērýnō *v.* (6x)
Roots:G4642 Compare:G4456
G4645.1 V-PAI-3S σκληρύνει (1x)
Rm 9:18 ·mercy, and on·whom he·determines, he·hardens.
G4645.1 V-PAS-2P σκληρύνητε (3x)
Heb 3:8 yeu·should·not harden yeur hearts, as in the Direct·
Heb 3:15 ·hear his voice, yeu·should·not harden yeur hearts,
Heb 4:7 ·hear his voice, yeu·should·not harden yeur hearts.
G4645.2 V-IPI-3P ἐσκληρύνοντο (1x)
Ac 19:9 ·as some were·hardened and were·being·obstinate,
G4645.2 V-APS-3S σκληρυνθῇ (1x)
Heb 3:13 yeu should·be·hardened through the·delusional·

G4646 σκολιός skôliós *adj.* (4x)
Roots:G4628 Compare:G5147
G4646.1 A-DPM σκολιοῖς (1x)
1Pe 2:18 and fair·ones, but·rather also to·the warped·ones.
G4646.1 A-GSF σκολιᾶς (2x)
Ac 2:40 "Save·yeurselves from this warped generation."
Php 2:15 in the·midst of·a·warped and perverse generation,
G4646.2 A-NPN σκολιά (1x)
Lk 3:5 ·be·made·low; and the winding·paths shall·be *made*

G4647 σκόλ•οψ skólôps *n.* (1x)
Roots:G4628 G3700 Compare:G0173 G0920-1
See:G4646-3 xLangAlso:H6796 H6791 H1303
G4647.3 N-NSM σκόλοψ (1x)
2Co 12:7 there·was·given to·me a·burly·thorn to·the flesh,

G4648 σκοπέω skôpéō *v.* (6x)
Roots:G4649 Compare:G3700 G2300
xLangAlso:H6822
G4648.1 V-PAM-2S σκόπει (1x)
Lk 11:35 So·then, keep·a·watch *that* the light, the·one in
G4648.1 V-PAM-2P σκοπεῖτε (2x)
Php 2:4 Yeu·must·keep·a·watch, *but* not each·man of·his·
Php 3:17 brothers, and keep·a·watch·of the·ones walking
G4648.1 V-PAN σκοπεῖν (1x)
Rm 16:17 brothers, to·keep·a·watch·of the·ones producing
G4648.1 V-PAP-GPM σκοπούντων (1x)
2Co 4:18 not with·us keeping·a·watch·of the·*external*·things
G4648.1 V-PAP-NSM σκοπῶν (1x)
Gal 6:1 a·spirit of·gentleness, keeping·a·watch·of yourself,

G4649 σκοπός skôpós *n.* (2x)
Compare:G4629 See:G4648 G4626
xLangAlso:H6822
G4649.2 N-ASM σκοπόν (1x)
Php 3:14 according·to *that* set·aim, I·pursue *it* toward the
EG4649.2 (1x)
Php 2:5 For contemplate *and set·aim·for* this·thing among

G4650 σκορπίζω skôrpízō *v.* (5x)
Compare:G1289 See:G1287 G4651
xLangEquiv:H6327
G4650.1 V-AAI-3S ἐσκόρπισεν (1x)
2Co 9:9 "*The·righteous·man* dispersed; he·gave to·the
G4650.2 V-PAI-3S σκορπίζει (3x)
Jn 10:12 and the wolf snatches them and scatters the sheep.
Lk 11:23 the·one not gathering·together with me scatters.
Mt 12:30 the·one not gathering·together with me scatters.
G4650.2 V-APS-2P σκορπισθῆτε (1x)
Jn 16:32 has·come that yeu·should·be·scattered, each·man to

G4651 σκορπίος skôrpíôs *n.* (5x)
Roots:G4649 See:G4650
xLangEquiv:H6137
G4651 N-NPM σκορπίοι (1x)
Rv 9:3 was·given to·them, as the scorpions of·the earth have
G4651 N-ASM σκορπίον (1x)
Lk 11:12 ·request an·egg, ¿! shall·he·hand him a·scorpion?
G4651 N-DPM σκορπίοις (1x)
Rv 9:10 And they·have tails like scorpions, and there·were
G4651 N-GSM σκορπίου (1x)
Rv 9:5 *was* as *the* torment of·a·scorpion, whenever he·
G4651 N-GPM σκορπίων (1x)
Lk 10:19 to·trample upon serpents and scorpions, and upon

G4652 σκοτεινός skôtêinós *adj.* (3x)
Roots:G4655 Compare:G4653 G0850 G1104-1
G4652.1 A-NSN σκοτεινόν (2x)
Lk 11:34 should·be evil, your body *is* also opaquely·dark.
Mt 6:23 your whole body shall·be opaquely·dark. So·then,
G4652.1 A-ASN σκοτεινόν (1x)
Lk 11:36 not having any part opaquely·dark, *the* whole

G4653 σκοτία skôtía *n.* (16x)
Roots:G4655 Compare:G4652 G0850 G0266
G4653.1 N-DSF σκοτίᾳ (2x)
Lk 12:3 ·as yeu·declared in the darkness, they·shall·be·heard
Mt 10:27 "What I·say to·yeu in the darkness, declare in the
G4653.2 N-NSF σκοτία (5x)
Jn 1:5 in the darkness, and the darkness did·not grasp it.
Jn 12:35 yeu·have the light, lest darkness should·grab yeu.
1Jn 1:5 is light, and in him there·is not darkness, none·at·all.
1Jn 2:8 in yeu, because the darkness is·passing·away, and
1Jn 2:11 he·is·heading, because the darkness blinded his
G4653.2 N-DSF σκοτίᾳ (7x)
Jn 1:5 the light shines·forth in the darkness, and the darkness
Jn 8:12 he·shall·not stroll·about in the darkness, but·rather
Jn 12:35 walking in the darkness does·not personally·know
Jn 12:46 trusting in me, should·not abide in the darkness.
1Jn 2:9 brother, is in the darkness even·unto this·moment.
1Jn 2:11 his brother is in the darkness, and strolls·about in
1Jn 2:11 and strolls·about in the darkness, and does·not
G4653.3 N-NSF σκοτία (1x)
Jn 6:17 And even·now it·had·become dark, and Jesus had·
G4653.3 N-GSF σκοτίας (1x)
Jn 20:1 week at·the·watch·of·dawn (while·being still dark),

G4654 σκοτίζω skôtízō *v.* (8x)
Roots:G4655 Compare:G4656 See:G4951-5 G4651-1
G4654.1 V-FPI-3S σκοτισθήσεται (2x)
Mt 24:29 of·those days, the sun shall·be·darkened, and the
Mk 13:24 the sun shall·be·darkened, and the moon shall·
G4654.1 V-API-3S ἐσκοτίσθη (3x)
Lk 23:45 Then the sun was·darkened, and the curtain of·the
Rm 1:21 their uncomprehending heart was·already·darkened.
Rv 9:2 sun and the air were·darkened from·out of·the smoke
G4654.1 V-APM-3P σκοτισθήτωσαν (1x)
Rm 11:10 "" Let their eyes be·darkened, *such·for them* not
G4654.1 V-APS-3S σκοτισθῇ (1x)
Rv 8:12 ·that the third·part of·them should·be·darkened, and
G4654.1 V-RPP-NPM εσκοτισμενοι (1x)
Eph 4:18 innermost·understanding having·been·darkened,

G4655 σκότος skótôs *n.* (32x)
Roots:G4639 Compare:G2217 See:G4652 G4653
G4654 G4651-1
xLangEquiv:H2822
G4655.1 N-NSN σκότος (4x)
Lk 23:44 hour, and there·was a·darkness over all the land
Ac 13:11 him dimness·of·sight, then darkness; and moving·
Mt 27:45 sixth hour, there·was darkness over all the land
Mk 15:33 hour occurring, darkness came·to·be over all the
G4655.1 N-ASN σκότος (1x)
Ac 2:20 The sun shall·be·distorted into darkness and the
G4655.1 N-DSM σκότῳ (1x)
Heb 12:18 nor to·stormy·gloom, and to·darkness, and to·
G4655.2 N-NSN σκότος (4x)
Lk 11:35 *that* the light, the·one in you, is not darkness.

Mt 6:23 light, the·one in you, is darkness, how·dense *is* the
Mt 6:23 in you, is darkness, how·dense *is* the darkness!
Eph 5:8 For yeu·were once darkness, but now *yeu·are* light
G4655.2 N-ASN σκότος (5x)
Jn 3:19 the men·of·clay† loved the darkness rather than the
Mt 8:12 shall·be·cast·out into the outer darkness, where
Mt 22:13 cast·*him*·out into the outer darkness, where there·
Mt 25:30 useless slave into the outer darkness,' where there·
2Co 6:14 And what fellowship has·light alongside darkness?
G4655.2 N-DSN σκότει (5x)
Lk 1:79 ·ones who·are·sitting·down in darkness and shadow
Mt 4:16 ·ones who·are·fully·sitting in darkness, they·did·see
Rm 2:19 of·blind·men, a·light for·the·ones in darkness,
1Th 5:4 brothers, are not in darkness, in·order·that the Day
1Jn 1:6 yet should·stroll·about in the darkness, we·do·lie,
G4655.2 N-GSN σκότους (12x)
Lk 22:53 this is yeur hour, and the jurisdiction of·darkness."
Ac 26:18 to·turn·*them*·back·around from darkness to light,
Rm 13:12 we·should·put·away the works of·darkness, and
Jud 1:13 the deep·murky·shroud of·darkness into the coming·
1Pe 2:9 already·calling yeu forth out of·darkness into his
2Pe 2:17 deep·murky·shroud of·darkness has·been·reserved
1Th 5:5 We·are not of·night nor·even of·darkness.
1Co 4:5 ·things of·the darkness and shall·make·apparent the
2Co 4:6 *for* light to·radiate·brightly out of·darkness, who
Eph 5:11 with·the unfruitful works of·the darkness, but
Eph 6:12 ·world·powers of·the darkness of·this present·age,
Col 1:13 from·out of·the authority of·darkness and relocated

G4656 σκοτόω skôtóō *v.* (1x)
Roots:G4655 Compare:G4654
G4656.4 V-RPP-NSF@ ἐσκοτωμένη (1x)
Rv 16:10 his kingdom became plunged·into·darkness. And

G4657 σ•κύ•βαλον skýbalôn *n.* (1x)
Roots:G1519 G2965 G0906
G4657 N-APN σκύβαλα (1x)
Php 3:8 *them* to·be as·things·thrown·to·dogs, in·order·that I·

G4658 Σκύθης Skýthēs *n/g.* (1x)
Compare:G0915
G4658.2 N/G-NSM Σκύθης (1x)
Col 3:11 and uncircumcision, Barbarian, Scythian, slave *or*

G4659 σκυθρ•ωπός skythrōpós *adj.* (2x)
Roots:G3700
G4659 A-NPM σκυθρωποί (2x)
Lk 24:17 while·walking·along, and *why* are·yeu sullen?"
Mt 6:16 ·fast, do·not become sullen-looking just·as the

G4660 σκύλλω skýllō *v.* (3x)
Compare:G4813 See:G4661
G4660.2 V-PAI-2S σκύλλεις (1x)
Mk 5:35 daughter is·dead. Why harass the Mentor any·
G4660.2 V-PAM-2S σκύλλε (1x)
Lk 8:49 Your daughter has·died; do·not harass the Mentor."
G4660.2 V-PPM-2S σκύλλου (1x)
Lk 7:6 "Lord, do·not be·harassed. For I·am not fit that you·

G4661 σκῦλον skŷlôn *n.* (1x)
Roots:G4660 Compare:G0725 G4813 G4307-2 xLangAlso:H7998
G4661.2 N-APN σκῦλα (1x)
Lk 11:22 ·had·confided and thoroughly·doles·out his spoils.

G4662 σκωληκό•βρωτος skōlēkóbrōtôs *adj.* (1x)
Roots:G4663 G0977
G4662 A-NSM σκωληκόβρωτος (1x)
Ac 12:23 to·God. And becoming worm-eaten, he·expired.

G4663 σκώληξ skṓlēx *n.* (3x)
G4663 N-NSM σκώληξ (3x)
Mk 9:44 where "their worm does·not completely·die, and
Mk 9:46 where "their worm does·not completely·die, and
Mk 9:48 where "their worm completely·does·not die, and

G4664 σμαράγδινος smarágdinôs *adj.* (1x)
Roots:G4665
G4664 A-DSM σμαραγδίνῳ (1x)
Rv 4:3 the throne, in·clear·appearance like an·emerald.

G4665 σμάραγδος smáragdôs *n.* (1x)
G4665 N-NSM σμάραγδος (1x)
Rv 21:19 the third, chalcedony; the fourth, emerald;

G4666 σμύρνα smýrna *n.* (2x)
Roots:G3464 xLangEquiv:H4753
G4666 N-ASF σμύρναν (1x)
Mt 2:11 presents: *being* gold, frankincense, and myrrh.
G4666 N-GSF σμύρνης (1x)
Jn 19:39 ·night, bringing a·mixture of·myrrh and aloeswood

G4667 Σμύρνα Smýrna *n/l.* (1x)
Roots:G4666
G4667.2 N/L-ASF Σμύρναν (1x)
Rv 1:11 Asia: to Ephesus, and to Smyrna, and to Pergamos,

G4668 Σμυρναῖος Smyrnaîos *n/g.* (1x)
Roots:G4667
G4668.2 N/G-GPM Σμυρναίων (1x)
Rv 2:8 angel of·the Called·Out·citizenry in·Smyrna write,

G4669 σμυρνίζω smyrnízō *v.* (1x)
Roots:G4667
G4669 V-RPP-ASM ἐσμυρνισμένον (1x)
Mk 15:23 to·drink having·been·mingled·with·myrrh, but he·

G4670 Σόδομα Sódôma *n/l.* (10x)
סְדֹם çᵉdôm [Hebrew]
Roots:H5467 Compare:G1116
G4670.2 N/L-NPN Σόδομα (3x)
Rm 9:29 ·us, we·would·have become as Sodom, and would
Jud 1:7 manner to·these *angels*, Sodom and Gomorrah and
Rv 11:8 which spiritually is·called Sodom and Egypt,
G4670.2 N/L-DPN Σοδόμοις (3x)
Lk 10:12 more·tolerable at·that Day for·Sodom, than for·that
Mt 11:23 in you had·happened in Sodom, it·would·have
Mk 6:11 it·shall·be more·tolerable for·Sodom or Gomorrah
G4670.2 N/L-GPN Σοδόμων (4x)
Lk 17:29 *when* Lot went·forth from Sodom, it·showered fire
Mt 10:15 ·tolerable for·the·land of·Sodom and Gomorrah in
Mt 11:24 ·be more·tolerable for·the·land of·Sodom in *the*
2Pe 2:6 after·incinerating *the* cities of·Sodom and Gomorrah

G4671 σοί sôí *p:p.* (222x)
Roots:G4771
(abbreviated listing for G4671)
G4671.1 P:P-2DS σοί (179x)
(list for G4671.1:P:P-2DS excluded)
EG4671.1 (1x)
(list for EG4671.1: excluded)
G4671.2 P:P-2DS σοί (24x)
(list for G4671.2:P:P-2DS excluded)
G4671.3 P:P-2DS σοί (12x)
(list for G4671.3:P:P-2DS excluded)
G4671.4 P:P-2DS σοί (1x)
(list for G4671.4:P:P-2DS excluded)
G4671.5 P:P-2DS σοί (1x)
(list for G4671.5:P:P-2DS excluded)
G4671.6 P:P-2DS σοί (3x)
(list for G4671.6:P:P-2DS excluded)
G4671.7 P:P-2DS σοί (1x)
(list for G4671.7:P:P-2DS excluded)

G4672 Σολομών Sôlômṓn *n/p.* (12x)
שְׁלֹמֹה shᵉlômôh [Hebrew]
Roots:H8010 xLangAlso:H1339
G4672.2 N/P-NSM Σολομών (4x)
Lk 12:27 and·yet I·say to·yeu, not·even Solomon in all his
Ac 7:47 "And *it·was* Solomon *who* built a·house for·him.
Mt 1:7 Then Solomon begot RehoboAm, and RehoboAm
Mt 6:29 And·yet I·say to·yeu, not·even Solomon, in all his
G4672.2 N/P-ASM Σολομῶντα (1x)
Mt 1:6 and King David begot Solomon (birthed·from·out of·
G4672.2 N/P-GSM Σολομῶντος (7x)
Jn 10:23 in the Sanctuary·Atrium at Solomon's Colonnade.
Lk 11:31 earth to·hear the wisdom of·Solomon; and behold,
Lk 11:31 behold, one·of·larger·stature·than Solomon *is* here
Ac 3:11 in the colonnade being·called Solomon's, *being*
Ac 5:12 ·the·same·determination in Solomon's Colonnade.
Mt 12:42 earth to·hear the wisdom of·Solomon; and behold,
Mt 12:42 one·of·a·larger·stature·than Solomon *is* here.

G4673 σορός sôrós *n.* (1x)
See:G4987 xLangAlso:H0727
G4673.1 N-GSF σοροῦ (1x)
Lk 7:14 coming·alongside, he·laid·hold of·the coffin, and

G4674 σός sôs *p:s.* (26x)
Roots:G4771 Compare:G5212
G4674.1 P:S-2NSM σός (1x)
Jn 17:17 holy in your truth. Your Redemptive-word is truth.
G4674.1 P:S-2NSN σόν (1x)
Lk 22:42 not my will, but·rather yours be·done."
G4674.1 P:S-2NPM σοί (3x)
Jn 17:6 the world. They·were yours, and you·have·given
Lk 5:33 the·ones of·the Pharisees, but yours eat and drink?
Mk 2:18 of·the Pharisees fast, but your disciples do·not fast?
G4674.1 P:S-2NPN σά (3x)
Jn 17:10 "So·then, all my·things are yours, and your·things
Jn 17:10 my·things are yours, and your·things *are* mine, and
Lk 15:31 and all the·things *that·are* mine, they·are yours.
G4674.1 P:S-2ASF σήν (1x)
Jn 4:42 "No·longer do·we·trust on·account·of your speech,
G4674.1 P:S-2ASN σόν (2x)
Mt 20:14 Take·up the·thing *that·is* yours and head·on·out.
Mt 25:25 See, you·have *what is* yours.'
G4674.1 P:S-2APM σούς (1x)
Mk 5:19 to your house, to your *kinsfolk*, and report·in·detail
G4674.1 P:S-2APN σά (1x)
Lk 6:30 you, and of·the·one taking·away your things, do·not
G4674.1 P:S-2DSF σῇ (2x)
1Co 8:11 and by your knowledge shall the weak brother
1Co 14:16 ·it,·Amen" at your expression·of·thankfulness,
G4674.1 P:S-2DSM σῷ (4x)
Mt 7:22 Lord, ¿!·Did·we·not prophesy in·your name, and
Mt 7:22 in·your name, and in·your name cast·out demons,
Mt 7:22 name cast·out demons, and in·your name do many
Mt 13:27 did·you·not·indeed sow good seed in your field?
G4674.1 P:S-2GSF σῆς (3x)
Ac 24:2 in·this nation on·account·of your providence,
Mt 24:3 what *shall·be* the sign of·your returning·Presence,
Phm 1:14 to·do not·even·one·thing apart·from your input,
G4674.2 P:S-2NSN σόν (1x)
Jn 18:35 "¿! Am·I myself a·Jew? Your·own nation and the
G4674.2 P:S-2DSF σῇ (2x)
Ac 5:4 inherently·was·it *not·indeed* in your·own authority?
Ac 24:4 you, I·implore you in·your·own fairness to·hear of·
G4674.2 P:S-2DSM σῷ (1x)
Mt 7:3 but do·not fully·observe the beam in your·own eye?

G4675 σοῦ sôû *p:p.* (502x)
Roots:G4771
(abbreviated listing for G4675)
G4675.1 P:P-2GS σοῦ (72x)
(list for G4675.1:P:P-2GS excluded)
EG4675.1 (1x)
(list for EG4675.1: excluded)
G4675.2 P:P-2GS σοῦ (10x)
(list for G4675.2:P:P-2GS excluded)
G4675.3 P:P-2GS σοῦ (1x)
(list for G4675.3:P:P-2GS excluded)
G4675.4 P:P-2GS σοῦ (344x)
(list for G4675.4:P:P-2GS excluded)
EG4675.4 (4x)
(list for EG4675.4: excluded)
G4675.5 P:P-2GS σοῦ (45x)
(list for G4675.5:P:P-2GS excluded)
G4675.6 P:P-2GS σοῦ (11x)
(list for G4675.6:P:P-2GS excluded)
G4675.7 P:P-2GS σοῦ (12x)
(list for G4675.7:P:P-2GS excluded)
G4675.8 P:P-2GS σοῦ (2x)

(list for G4675.8:P:P-2GS excluded)

G4676 σουδάριον sôudáriôn *n.* (4x)
Compare:G3012

G4676 N-ASN σουδάριον (1x)
Jn 20:7 and the sweat·towel that was upon his head, *that* it·

G4676 N-APN σουδάρια (1x)
Ac 19:12 even such·for sweat·towels or aprons from his

G4676 N-DSN σουδαρίῳ (2x)
Jn 11:44 had·been·bound·about with·a·sweat·towel. Jesus
Lk 19:20 ·holding *for·you*, laying·*it*·away in a·sweat·towel.

G4677 Σουσάννα Sôusánna *n/p.* (1x)
Ἑσουσάν Shôushán [masculine, Octuagint]
שׁוֹשַׁנָּה shôshaṇạh [Hebrew]
Roots:H7799 Compare:G2918 G2924-3

G4677.2 N/P-NSF Σουσάννα (1x)
Lk 8:3 of·HerOd·AntiPas), and Susanna, and many others,

G4678 σοφία sôphía *n.* (52x)
Roots:G4680 Compare:G1253 See:G4679
xLangEquiv:H2451 A2452 xLangAlso:H0802

G4678.1 N-NSF σοφία (10x)
Lk 11:49 "On·account·of that, the wisdom of·God also
Mt 13:54 *does* this·man *have* this wisdom and·also *do these*
Mk 6:2 And what *is* the wisdom, the·one being·given to·
Jac 3:15 This wisdom is not *that* which·is·coming·down
Jac 3:17 But the wisdom *that·is* from·above is first, in·fact,
1Co 1:30 Jesus, who is·made to·us wisdom from God, also
1Co 3:19 For the wisdom of·this world is foolishness with
Eph 3:10 the extensively·manifold wisdom of·God may·be·
Rv 7:12 and the glory, and the wisdom, and the thanks, and
Rv 13:18 Here is the wisdom. The·one having the

G4678.1 N-ASF σοφίαν (14x)
Lk 11:31 of·the earth to·hear the wisdom of·Solomon; and
Lk 21:15 shall·give yeu a·mouth and wisdom, which all the·
Ac 7:10 and wisdom in·the·direct·presence of·Pharaoh king
Mt 12:42 of·the earth to·hear the wisdom of·Solomon; and
2Pe 3:15 ·yeu (according·to the wisdom being·given to·him).
1Co 1:19 I·shall·completely·destroy the wisdom of·the wise
1Co 1:20 not·indeed make·foolish the wisdom of·this world?
1Co 1:22 Jews request a·sign, and·also Greeks seek wisdom,
1Co 1:24 Anointed-One *is* God's power and God's wisdom,
1Co 2:6 But we·do·speak wisdom among the·ones *being*
1Co 2:6 ·mature, and not *the* wisdom of·this present·age, nor
1Co 2:7 But·rather we·speak God's wisdom in a·Mystery,
Rv 5:12 the power and wealth and wisdom and strength and
Rv 17:9 mind·*(or·understanding)*, the·one having wisdom.

G4678.1 N-DSF σοφίᾳ (12x)
Lk 2:52 was·continually·advancing in·wisdom, maturity, and
Ac 6:10 having·strength to·withstand the wisdom and the
Ac 7:22 ·and·disciplined in·all *the* wisdom of·the·Egyptians,
1Co 1:17 ·the·good·news, not with wisdom of·reasoning,
1Co 1:21 For whereas (by the wisdom of·God) the world
1Co 2:5 should·not be in *the* wisdom of·men·of·clay†, but·
2Co 1:12 before·God (not with fleshly wisdom, but·rather by
Eph 1:8 to us in all wisdom and thoughtful·insight,
Col 1:9 of·his will in all wisdom and spiritual comprehension
Col 1:28 every man·of·clay† in all wisdom, in·order·that we·
Col 3:16 yeu abundantly in all wisdom, instructing and
Col 4:5 Walk in wisdom toward the·ones outside *the Called·*

G4678.1 N-GSF σοφίας (12x)
Lk 2:40 in·spirit, being·completely·filled with·wisdom. And
Ac 6:3 full of·Holy Spirit and wisdom, whom we·shall·fully·
Rm 11:33 of·wealth, both of·*the*·wisdom and knowledge of·
Jac 1:5 if any of·yeu is·deficient of·wisdom, let·him·request
Jac 3:13 ·show his works with a·calm·mildness of·wisdom.
1Co 1:21 the world through the wisdom did·not know God,
1Co 2:1 or of·wisdom while·fully·proclaiming to·yeu the
1Co 2:4 persuasive words of·mankind's† wisdom, but·rather
1Co 2:13 words of·mankind's† wisdom, but·rather with
1Co 12:8 ·given through the Spirit a·word of·wisdom, but to·
Eph 1:17 may·give to·yeu a·spirit of·wisdom and revelation
Col 2:23 are in·fact a·rationalization of·wisdom, having

EG4678.1 (1x)
1Co 1:25 of·God is wiser·than the *wisdom* of·men·of·clay†,

G4678.2 N-NSF σοφία (2x)
Lk 7:35 "But Wisdom is·regarded·as·righteous by all her
Mt 11:19 ·men.' But Wisdom is·regarded·as·righteous by

G4678.2 N-GSF σοφίας (1x)
Col 2:3 ·away all the treasures of·Wisdom and Knowledge.

G4679 σοφίζω sôphízō *v.* (2x)
Roots:G4680 See:G2686

G4679.1 V-AAN σοφίσαι (1x)
2Ti 3:15 the·ones being·able to·make you wise to Salvation

G4679.4 V-RPP-DPM σεσοφισμένοις (1x)
2Pe 1:16 ·out myths having·been·skillfully·devised *that* we·

G4680 σοφός sôphốs *adj.* (22x)
Compare:G5429 G4908 See:G4678 G4679 G4680-2

G4680 A-NSM σοφός (6x)
Jac 3:13 Who *is* wise and fully·informed among yeu?
1Co 1:20 Where *is the* wise? Where *is the* scribe?
1Co 3:10 to·me, as a·wise chief·construction·architect, I·
1Co 3:18 among yeu seems to·be wise in this present·age, let·
1Co 3:18 a·fool, in·order that he·may·become wise.
1Co 6:5 In·this·manner, is·there not a·wise·man among yeu

G4680 A-NSN-C σοφώτερον (1x)
1Co 1:25 the foolishness of·God is wiser·than the *wisdom* of·

G4680 A-NPM σοφοί (3x)
Rm 1:22 to·be wise, they·already·became·foolish,
1Co 1:26 ·that not many *are* wise·men according·to flesh,
Eph 5:15 how yeu·walk, not as unwise, but·rather as wise,

G4680 A-APM σοφούς (4x)
Mt 23:34 dispatch to yeu prophets and wise·men and scribes,
Rm 16:19 in·fact, to·be wise in·regard·to the·thing *which·*
1Co 1:27 in·order·that he·may·put·to·shame the wise; and
1Co 3:19 "'*He·is* the·one entrapping the wise in their·own

G4680 A-DSM σοφῷ (3x)
Rm 16:27 to·*the*·only wise God, to·him *be* the glory through
Jud 1:25 to·*the*·only wise God our Savior, *be* glory and
1Ti 1:17 incorruptible, invisible, to·*the*·only wise God, *be*

G4680 A-DPM σοφοῖς (1x)
Rm 1:14 to·Barbarians, also to·wise·ones and to·stupid·ones

G4680 A-GPM σοφῶν (4x)
Lk 10:21 ·away these·things from wise and intelligent·men,
Mt 11:25 ·away these·things from wise and intelligent·men,
1Co 1:19 the wisdom of·the wise and shall·invalidate the
1Co 3:20 knows the deliberations of·the wise, that they·are

G4681 Σπανία Spanía *n/l.* (3x)

G4681 N/L-ASF Σπανίαν (2x)
Rm 15:24 ·soon·as I·should·traverse for Spain, I·shall·come
Rm 15:28 this fruit, I·shall·go·aside through yeu into Spain.

EG4681 (1x)
Rm 15:24 ·sent·onward by yeu *from* there·to *Spain*, if first I·

G4682 σπαράσσω sparássō *v.* (4x)
Roots:G4685 Compare:G4486 See:G4952

G4682.2 V-PAI-3S σπαράσσει (1x)
Lk 9:39 he·yells·out; and it·convulses him along·with foam,

G4682.2 V-AAI-3S ἐσπάραξεν (1x)
Mk 9:20 immediately the spirit convulsed *the little·child.*

G4682.2 V-AAP-NSN σπαράξαν (2x)
Mk 1:26 the impure spirit, after·convulsing him and yelling·
Mk 9:26 after·yelling·out and convulsing him repeatedly, *the*

G4683 σπαργανόω sparganốō *v.* (2x)
Roots:G4682

G4683 V-AAI-3S ἐσπαργάνωσεν (1x)
Lk 2:7 her firstborn son, and swaddled him, and leaned him

G4683 V-RPP-ASN ἐσπαργανωμένον (1x)
Lk 2:12 a·baby having·been·swaddled·*in·cloths*, laying·out

G4684 σπαταλάω spataláō *v.* (2x)
Roots:G4684-1 Compare:G4763 G5171 G2691

G4684 V-PAP-NSF σπαταλῶσα (1x)
1Ti 5:6 the·one presently·living·luxuriously has·died while·

G4684 V-AAI-2P ἐσπαταλήσατε (1x)
Jac 5:5 the earth, and lived·luxuriously. Yeu·nourished yeur

G4685 σπάω spáō *v.* (2x)
See:G0645

G4685 V-AMP-NSM σπασάμενος (2x)
Ac 16:27 having·been·opened·up, drawing his·dagger, he·
Mk 14:47 ·ones standing·nearby, upon·drawing the dagger,

G4686 σπεῖρα spêîra *n.* (8x)
Roots:G0138 Compare:G2223 G3003 G3925 G4753
See:G4711 G1507 G5506

G4686.3 N-NSF σπεῖρα (1x)
Jn 18:12 And·then the battalion, the regiment·commander,

G4686.3 N-ASF σπεῖραν (3x)
Jn 18:3 after·receiving the battalion and·also assistants
Mt 27:27 gathered·together the whole battalion against him.
Mk 15:16 And they·call·together the whole battalion.

G4686.3 N-GSF σπείρης (3x)
Ac 10:1 a·centurion from·among a·battalion being·called the
Ac 21:31 to·the regiment·commander of·the battalion that all
Ac 27:1 by·name, from·*the*·Revered·Emperor's battalion.

EG4686.3 (1x)
Ac 10:1 a·battalion being·called the Italian *Battalion*,

G4687 σπείρω spêírō *v.* (55x)
Roots:G4685 See:G4690 G4701
xLangEquiv:H2232

EG4687 (1x)
2Co 9:7 *Let* each·man *sow* just·as he·is·preinclined in·*his·*

EG4687.- (1x)
2Co 9:7 *Let* each·man *sow* just·as he·is·preinclined in·*his·*

G4687.1 V-PAI-2S σπείρεις (3x)
1Co 15:36 ·one, that·which you sow is·not giving·life,
1Co 15:37 And that·which you·sow, you·sow not the body
1Co 15:37 And that·which you·sow, you·sow not the body

G4687.1 V-PAI-3S σπείρει (1x)
Mk 4:14 "The·one sowing sows the Redemptive·word.

G4687.1 V-PAI-3P σπείρουσιν (2x)
Lk 12:24 because they·do·not sow nor·even do·they·reap.
Mt 6:26 sky, because they·do·not sow, neither do·they·reap,

G4687.1 V-PAN σπείρειν (4x)
Lk 8:5 "And as he·himself sowed, *there·was* that·which in·
Mt 13:3 "Behold, the·one sowing went·forth to·sow.
Mt 13:4 And when he·himself *went·forth* to·sow, in·fact,
Mk 4:4 And it·happened, as he *began* to·sow, that, in·fact,

G4687.1 V-PAP-DSM σπείροντι (2x)
Mt 13:24 is·likened to·a·man·of·clay† sowing good seed in
2Co 9:10 ·one fully·supplying seed to·the·one sowing, and

G4687.1 V-PAP-GSM σπείροντος (1x)
Mt 13:18 yeu·yeurselves hear the parable of·the·one sowing.

G4687.1 V-PAP-NSM σπείρων (11x)
Jn 4:36 in·order·that both the·one sowing and the·one
Jn 4:37 'One is the·one sowing, and another *is* the·one
Lk 8:5 "The·one sowing went·out to·sow his scattering·of·
Gal 6:8 Because the·one sowing into his flesh, shall·reap
Gal 6:8 ·out·of·the flesh; but the·one sowing into the Spirit,
Mt 13:3 "Behold, the·one sowing went·forth to·sow.
Mt 13:37 ·declared to·them, "The·one sowing the good seed
Mk 4:3 Behold, the·one sowing went·forth to·sow.
Mk 4:14 "The·one sowing sows the Redemptive·word.
2Co 9:6 But this *I·say*, the·one sowing sparingly also shall·
2Co 9:6 and the·one sowing toward beneficial·blessings

G4687.1 V-PAS-3S σπείρῃ (1x)
Gal 6:7 for whatever a·man·of·clay† should·sow, that also

G4687.1 V-PPI-3S σπείρεται (6x)
Mk 4:15 where the Redemptive·word is·sown: and whenever
Jac 3:18 And the fruit of·righteousness is·sown in peace by·
1Co 15:42 resurrection of·the dead. It·is·sown in corruption;
1Co 15:43 It·is·sown in dishonor; it·is·awakened in glory.
1Co 15:43 it·is·awakened in glory. It·is·sown in weakness;
1Co 15:44 It·is·sown a·soulish body; it·is·awakened a·

G4687.1 V-AAI-1S ἔσπειρα (2x)
Lk 19:22 ·not lay·down, and reaping what I·did·not sow.
Mt 25:26 that I·reap where I·did·not sow and gather·together

G4687.1 V-AAI-1P ἐσπείραμεν (1x)
1Co 9:11 If we·ourselves sowed to·yeu the spiritual·things,

G4687.1 V-AAI-2S ἔσπειρας (3x)

Lk 19:21 ·not lay·down, and reap what you·did·not sow.'
Mt 13:27 'Sir, did·you·not·indeed sow good seed in your
Mt 25:24 where you·did·not sow and gathering·together
G4687.1 V-AAI-3S ἔσπειρεν (2x)
Mt 13:25 enemy came and sowed *poisonous* darnel·weeds up
Mt 13:31 (which after·taking, a·man·of·clay† sowed in his
G4687.1 V-AAN σπεῖραι (2x)
Lk 8:5 ·one sowing went·out to·sow his scattering·of·seed.
Mk 4:3 Behold, the·one sowing went·forth to·sow.
G4687.1 V-AAP-NSM σπείρας (1x)
Mt 13:39 The enemy, the·one sowing them, is the Slanderer.
G4687.1 V-2APS-3S σπαρῇ (2x)
Mk 4:31 which, whenever it·should·be·sown in the earth,
Mk 4:32 But whenever it·should·be·sown, it·springs·up and
G4687.1 V-RPP-ASN ἐσπαρμένον (1x)
Mt 13:19 and snatches·up the *seed* having·been·sown in his
G4687.1 V-RPP-ASM ἐσπαρμένον (1x)
Mk 4:15 the·one having·been·sown in their hearts.
G4687.2 V-PPP-NPM σπειρόμενοι (2x)
Mk 4:16 the·ones being·permeated·with·seed among the
Mk 4:18 who·are being·permeated·with·seed among the
G4687.2 V-2APP-NSM σπαρείς (4x)
Mt 13:19 is the·one already·being·permeated·with·seed the
Mt 13:20 the·one already·being·permeated·with·seed among
Mt 13:22 the·one already·being·permeated·with·seed among
Mt 13:23 the·one already·being·permeated·with·seed among
G4687.2 V-2APP-NPM σπαρέντες (1x)
Mk 4:20 the·ones already·being·permeated·with·seed among

G4688 σπεκουλάτωρ spêkôulátōr *n.* (1x)
Compare:G2892
G4688.2 N-ASM σπεκουλάτωρα (1x)
Mk 6:27 And immediately dispatching a·bodyguard, the king

G4689 σπένδω spéndō *v.* (2x)
Compare:G3004-1 See:G4700-2 G4700-1
xLangAlso:H5258
G4689.2 V-PPI-1S σπένδομαι (2x)
Php 2:17 even if I·am·poured·forth·as·a·devotion upon the
2Ti 4:6 ·now, I·myself am·poured·forth·as·a·devotion, and

G4690 σπέρμα spérma *n.* (68x)
זֶרַע zera' [Hebrew]
Roots:G4687 Compare:G1074 G5207 G4615
See:G4703 G4690-1 G4690-2
xLangEquiv:H2233 A2234
G4690.1 N-DSN σπέρματι (1x)
Gal 3:16 as upon one, "And to·your single·seed," which is
G4690.1 N-GSN σπέρματος (1x)
Heb 11:11 for an·ovulation of·a·single·seed *from her·ovaries*
EG4690.1 (12x)
Mt 13:8 were·giving fruit, in·fact some *seed* a·hundredfold,
Mt 13:8 *seed* a·hundredfold, some *seed* sixtyfold, and some
Mt 13:8 some *seed* sixtyfold, and some *seed* thirtyfold.
Mt 13:23 produces, in·fact, some *seed* a·hundredfold, some
Mt 13:23 *seed* a·hundredfold, some *seed* sixtyfold, and some
Mt 13:23 some *seed* sixtyfold, and some *seed* thirtyfold."
Mk 4:8 and it·was·bearing *fruit*: one *seed* thirtyfold, and one
Mk 4:8 one *seed* thirtyfold, and one *seed* sixtyfold, and one
Mk 4:8 one *seed* sixtyfold, and one *seed* a·hundredfold."
Mk 4:20 *it*, and bear·fruit: one *seed* thirtyfold, and one *seed*
Mk 4:20 one *seed* thirtyfold, and one *seed* sixtyfold, and one
Mk 4:20 one *seed* sixtyfold, and one *seed* a·hundredfold."
G4690.2 N-DPN σπέρμασιν (1x)
Gal 3:16 He·does·not say, "And to·the seeds," as upon
EG4690.2 (2x)
Mt 13:4 to·sow, in·fact, some *seeds* fell directly·by the
Mt 13:5 But other *seeds* fell upon the rocky·places, where it·
G4690.3 N-GPN σπερμάτων (3x)
Mt 13:32 in·fact is smaller·than all the variety·of·seeds. But
Mk 4:31 *is* least of·all the variety·of·seeds that·are in the
1Co 15:38 ·determined, and to·each variety·of·seed, its·own
EG4690.3 (1x)
Mt 13:19 and snatches·up the *seed* having·been·sown in his
G4690.4 N-NSN σπέρμα (1x)
Mt 13:38 is the world, and the good seed, these are the Sons

G4690.4 N-ASN σπέρμα (4x)
Mt 13:24 ·likened to·a·man·of·clay† sowing good seed in his
Mt 13:27 did·you·not·indeed sow good seed in your field?
Mt 13:37 "The·one sowing the good seed is the Son of·Clay·
2Co 9:10 the·one fully·supplying seed to·the·one sowing,
EG4690.4 (7x)
Lk 8:6 "And other *seed* fell upon the solid·rock, and once·
Lk 8:7 "And other *seed* fell in *the* midst of·the thorns; and
Lk 8:8 "And other *seed* fell on the beneficially·good soil, and
Lk 8:14 "And the *seed* falling among the thorns, these are
Lk 8:15 "But the *seed* in the good soil, these are *the·ones*
Mk 4:4 ·sow, that, in·fact, *seed* fell directly·by the roadway
Mk 4:5 But other *seed* fell upon the rocky·ground, where it·
EG4690.5 (2x)
Heb 11:12 *many offspring†* were·born from·him·having·
Gal 3:16 as upon many *offspring†*, but·rather as upon one,
G4690.7 N-NSN σπέρμα (6x)
Jn 8:33 "We·are AbRaham's offspring†, and to·no·one·at·all
Jn 8:37 ·know that yeu·are AbRaham's offspring†, but·yet
Ac 7:6 that his "offspring† shall·be a·sojourner in an·
Rm 4:18 "'In·this·manner shall·be your offspring†.'"
Rm 9:7 Neither because they·are offspring† of·AbRaham,
2Co 11:22 So·*am*·I. Are·they *the* offspring† of·AbRaham?
G4690.7 N-ASN σπέρμα (9x)
Lk 20:28 and should·fully·raise·up offspring† to·his brother.
Mt 22:24 his wife and shall·raise·up offspring† to·his brother
Mt 22:25 And·so not having offspring†, he·left his wife to·
Mk 12:19 should·fully·raise·up offspring† for·his brother.
Mk 12:20 and·then dying, he·did·not leave offspring†.
Mk 12:21 neither *did* he·himself leave offspring†. And the
Mk 12:22 her, and they·did·not leave offspring†. Last of·all,
Rm 9:8 children of·the promise are·reckoned for offspring†.
Rm 9:29 Yahweh of·Hosts left·behind offspring† for·us, we·
G4690.7 N-DSN σπέρματι (3x)
Lk 1:55 to·AbRaham and to·his offspring† into the coming·
Ac 7:5 a·territorial·possession and to·his offspring† after him
Rm 4:16 promise to·be steadfast to·all the offspring†, not to·
G4690.7 N-GSN σπέρματος (2x)
Rm 11:1 ·Israelite, from·among AbRaham's offspring†, *from*
Rv 12:17 ·make war with the rest of·her offspring†, the·ones
G4690.8 N-NSN σπέρμα (5x)
Heb 11:18 "'In YiTsaq, a·Seed shall·be·called·forth to·you,
Gal 3:19 *promise* only·until the Seed should·come for·whom
Gal 3:29 ·by·inference, yeu·are of·AbRaham's Seed and *are*
Rm 9:7 "'In YiTsaq, a·Seed shall·be·called·forth to·you.'"
1Jn 3:9 moral·failure, because his Seed remains in him.
G4690.8 N-DSN σπέρματι (3x)
Ac 3:25 "And in·your Seed all the paternal·lineages of·the
Gal 3:16 were·uttered to·AbRaham and to·his Seed. He·
Rm 4:13 Torah-Law to·AbRaham or to·his Seed (the·one
G4690.8 N-GSN σπέρματος (5x)
Jn 7:42 comes birthed·from·out of·the Seed of·David, and
Ac 13:23 From this·man's Seed, according·to promise, God
Heb 2:16 — but·rather he·grabs·hold 'of·AbRaham's Seed.'
Rm 1:3 birthed·from·out of·David's Seed according·to flesh,
2Ti 2:8 Jesus Anointed, birthed·from·out of·David's Seed, *is*

G4691 σπερμο•λόγος spêrmôlǒgôs *adj.* (1x)
Roots:G4690 G3004 Compare:G5397 G3151 G2637
G4691.3 A-NSM σπερμολόγος (1x)
Ac 17:18 *that* this two-bit·peddler actually·supposes to·relate

G4692 σπεύδω spêúdō *v.* (6x)
Roots:G4228
G4692.1 V-PAP-APM σπεύδοντας (1x)
2Pe 3:12 ·anticipating and hastening the imminent·arrival of·
G4692.1 V-IAI-3S ἔσπευδεν (1x)
Ac 20:16 ·away in Asia. For he·was·hastening, if it·were
G4692.1 V-AAM-2S σπεῦσον (1x)
Ac 22:18 saying to·me, 'Make·haste and go·forth in haste
G4692.1 V-AAP-NSM σπεύσας (2x)
Lk 19:5 to him, "Zacchaeus, making·haste, drop·down. For
Lk 19:6 And hastening, he·dropped·down; and rejoicing, he·
G4692.2 V-AAP-NPM σπεύσαντες (1x)

Lk 2:16 And they·came with·haste and diligently·found both

G4693 σπήλαιον spḗlaiôn *n.* (6x)
Compare:G3692 G4978-1
xLangEquiv:H4631 xLangAlso:H4247
G4693.1 N-NSN σπήλαιον (1x)
Jn 11:38 the chamber·tomb. Now it·was a·cave, and a·stone
G4693.1 N-APN σπήλαια (1x)
Rv 6:15 hid themselves in the caves and among the solid·
G4693.1 N-DPN σπηλαίοις (1x)
Heb 11:38 *in* mountains, and *in* caves and in·the caverns of·
G4693.2 N-ASN σπήλαιον (3x)
Lk 19:46 " but yeu·yeurselves made it "a·den of·robbers.'"
Mt 21:13 " but yeu·yeurselves made it "a·den of·robbers.'"
Mk 11:17 But yeu·yeurselves made it "a·den of·robbers'".

G4694 σπιλάς spilás *n.* (1x)
See:G4696
G4694.2 N-NPF σπιλάδες (1x)
Jud 1:12 These are dangerous·sea·reefs at yeur love·feasts,

G4695 σπιλόω spilôō *v.* (2x)
Roots:G4696 Compare:G3435
G4695 V-PAP-NSF σπιλοῦσα (1x)
Jac 3:6 our members, the·one staining the whole body, and
G4695 V-RPP-ASM ἐσπιλωμένον (1x)
Jud 1:23 hating even the tunic having·been·stained by the

G4696 σπίλος spílôs *n.* (2x)
Compare:G3470 See:G4695
G4696.1 N-NPM σπίλοι (1x)
2Pe 2:13 a·delicate·luxury. *They·are* stains and blemishes,
G4696.1 N-ASM σπίλον (1x)
Eph 5:27 the entire·Called·Out·Citizenry not having stain, or

G4697 σπλαγχνίζομαι splanchnízômai *v.* (12x)
Roots:G4698
G4697.2 V-PNI-1S σπλαγχνίζομαι (2x)
Mt 15:32 YeShua declared, "I·empathize over the crowd,
Mk 8:2 "I·empathize over the crowd, because even·now
G4697.2 V-AOI-3S ἐσπλαγχνίσθη (6x)
Lk 7:13 And seeing her, the Lord empathized over her and
Lk 10:33 And after·seeing him, he·empathized.
Lk 15:20 saw him, and he·empathized. And·then running,
Mt 9:36 ·seeing the crowds, he·empathized concerning them
Mt 14:14 saw a·large crowd, and he·empathized over them,
Mk 6:34 saw a·large crowd, and he·empathized over them,
G4697.2 V-AOP-NSM σπλαγχνισθείς (4x)
Mt 18:27 So empathizing, the lord of·that slave fully·
Mt 20:34 And empathizing, YeShua laid·hold of·their eyes,
Mk 1:41 And Jesus, empathizing, stretching·out his hand,
Mk 9:22 you·are·able *to·do* something, empathizing over us,

G4698 σπλάγχνον splánchnôn *n.* (11x)
G4698.1 N-NPN σπλάγχνα (1x)
Ac 1:18 in·the·middle, and all his intestines poured·out.
G4698.2 N-NPN σπλάγχνα (4x)
Php 2:1 of·Spirit, if any inward·affections and compassions,
2Co 7:15 And his inward·affections are more·abundant
Phm 1:7 because the inward·affections of·the holy·ones
Phm 1:12 ·receive him, that·is, my·own inward·affections,
G4698.2 N-APN σπλάγχνα (4x)
Lk 1:78 through *the* inward·affections of·our God's mercy, in
Col 3:12 ·with compassionate inward·affections, kindness,
Phm 1:20 *the* Lord; refresh my inward·affections in *the* Lord
1Jn 3:17 and should·shut·up his inward·affections from him
G4698.2 N-DPN σπλάγχνοις (2x)
Php 1:8 ·after yeu all in inward·affections of·Jesus Anointed.
2Co 6:12 ·constricted by yeur·own inward·affections.

G4699 σπόγγος spǒngôs *n.* (3x)
G4699 N-ASM σπόγγον (3x)
Jn 19:29 after·filling a·sponge with·wine·vinegar and
Mt 27:48 after·running and taking a·sponge and filling *it*
Mk 15:36 and overfilling a·sponge of·wine·vinegar and

G4700 σποδός spôdǒs *n.* (3x)
xLangEquiv:H0665
G4700 N-NSF σποδός (1x)

Heb 9:13 and of·adult·male·goats (and ashes of·a·red·cow)

G4700 N-DSM σποδῷ (2x)

Lk 10:13 repented, sitting·down in sackcloth and ashes.

Mt 11:21 they·would·have repented in sackcloth and ashes.

G4701 σπορά spôrá *n.* (2x)

Roots:G4687 Compare:G4703

G4701.1 N-GSF σπορᾶς (1x)

1Pe 1:23 birthed·from·out of·a·corruptible sowing·of·seed,

EG4701.1 (1x)

1Pe 1:23 of·an·incorruptible *sowing·of·seed* through *the*

G4702 σπόριμος spŏrimŏs *adj.* (3x)

Roots:G4703

G4702.2 A-GPM σπορίμων (3x)

Lk 6:1 *for* him to·traverse through the grain·fields, and his

Mt 12:1 various·Sabbaths through the grain·fields, and *when*

Mk 2:23 ·traversing·directly through the grain·fields on the

G4703 σπόρος spŏrŏs *n.* (5x)

Roots:G4687 Compare:G4701 See:G4690

G4703.1 N-NSM σπόρος (2x)

Lk 8:11 this: The scattering·of·seed is the Redemptive-word

Mk 4:27 how the scattering·of·seed should·germinate and

G4703.1 N-ASM σπόρον (3x)

Lk 8:5 ·one sowing went·out to·sow his scattering·of·seed.

Mk 4:26 ·clay† should·cast the scattering·of·seed upon the

2Co 9:10 ·supply and multiply yeur scattering·of·seed, and

G4704 σπουδάζω spôudázō *v.* (11x)

Roots:G4710

G4704.2 V-FAI-1S σπουδάσω (1x)

2Pe 1:15 also, I·shall·quickly·endeavor for·yeu to·have at·

G4704.2 V-AAM-2S σπούδασον (4x)

Tit 3:12 you, or Tychicus, quickly·endeavor to·come to me

2Ti 2:15 Quickly·endeavor to·present yourself verifiably·

2Ti 4:9 Quickly·endeavor to·come to me promptly,

2Ti 4:21 Quickly·endeavor to·come before winter.

G4704.2 V-AAM-2P σπουδάσατε (2x)

2Pe 1:10 all·the·more quickly·endeavor to·make yeur

2Pe 3:14 these·things, quickly·endeavor to·be·found by·him

G4704.2 V-AAS-1P σπουδάσωμεν (1x)

Heb 4:11 we·should·quickly·endeavor to·enter into that

G4704.3 V-PAP-NPM σπουδάζοντες (1x)

Eph 4:3 diligently·endeavoring to·fully·keep the oneness of·

G4704.3 V-AAI-1S ἐσπούδασα (1x)

Gal 2:10 this very·thing which I·diligently·endeavored to·do.

G4704.3 V-AAI-1P ἐσπουδάσαμεν (1x)

1Th 2:17 diligently·endeavored the·more·abundantly to·see

G4705 σπουδαῖος spôudaîŏs *adj.* (1x)

Roots:G4710 Compare:G4289

G4705 A-ASM σπουδαῖον (1x)

2Co 8:22 ·proved many·times being diligent in many·things,

G4706 σπουδαιότερον spôudaiótêrôn *adj.* (2x)

Roots:G4707

G4706 A-ASM-C σπουδαιότερον (1x)

2Ti 1:17 he·sought·for me more·diligently·than *others*, and

G4706 ADV σπουδαιότερον (1x)

2Co 8:22 but even·now much more·diligent, with·much

G4707 σπουδαιότερος spôudaiótêrôs *adj.* (1x)

Roots:G4705 See:G4708

G4707 A-NSM-C σπουδαιότερος (1x)

2Co 8:17 inherently·being more·diligent, of·his·own·choice,

G4708 σπουδαιοτέρως spôudaiôtérōs *adv.* (1x)

Roots:G4707 Compare:G1619

G4708 ADV-C σπουδαιοτέρως (1x)

Php 2:28 I·sent him more·diligently, in·order·that seeing

G4709 σπουδαίως spôudaiōs *adv.* (2x)

Roots:G4705

G4709.1 ADV σπουδαίως (1x)

Tit 3:13 Diligently send Zenas the lawyer and Apollos

G4709.2 ADV σπουδαίως (1x)

Lk 7:4 to Jesus, they·were·imploring him earnestly, saying,

G4710 σπουδή spôudḗ *n.* (12x)

Roots:G4692 Compare:G4343 G5281 G3115 G4288

G4710.1 N-GSF σπουδῆς (2x)

Lk 1:39 into the mountainous·region with haste, into a·city

Mk 6:25 And upon·entering·in immediately with haste to the

G4710.2 N-ASF σπουδήν (4x)

Heb 6:11 of·yeu to·indicate the same diligence toward the

Jud 1:3 Beloved, while·making all diligence to·write to·yeu

2Pe 1:5 this, applying all diligence, yeu·must·fully·supply

2Co 7:11 *see* how·much diligence it·did·accomplish in·yeu,

G4710.2 N-DSF σπουδῇ (3x)

Rm 12:8 *a·group·or·group·effort, conducting* with diligence;

Rm 12:11 in·the diligence, *by* not *being* slothful; in·the spirit,

2Co 8:7 and in·knowledge, and in·all diligence, and (as·a·

G4710.2 N-GSF σπουδῆς (1x)

2Co 8:8 ·rather on·account·of the diligence of·others *in·the*

G4710.3 N-ASF σπουδήν (2x)

2Co 7:12 ·rather because·of yeur earnest·care on·our behalf

2Co 8:16 the·one giving the same earnest·care into the heart

G4711 σπυρίς spyrís *n.* (5x)

Roots:G4687 Compare:G2894 G4553

G4711 N-APF σπυρίδας (3x)

Mt 15:37 And they·took·up seven woven·baskets full *of* the

Mt 16:10 *men*, and how·many woven·baskets yeu·took·up?

Mk 8:8 ·abundance of·fragments, seven woven·baskets *full*.

G4711 N-DSF σπυρίδι (1x)

Ac 9:25 *by* lowering *him* through the wall in a·woven·basket.

G4711 N-GPF σπυρίδων (1x)

Mk 8:20 *men*, how·many woven·baskets completely·full of·

G4712 στάδιον stádiôn *n.* (6x)
στάδιος stádiôs [masculine]

Roots:G2476

G4712.1 N-APN σταδίους (2x)

Jn 6:19 about twenty·five or thirty stadia, they·observe Jesus

Lk 24:13 ·a·distance from JeruSalem *of·about* sixty stadia.

G4712.1 N-GPN σταδίων (3x)

Jn 11:18 was near to·JeruSalem, about fifteen stadia away.

Rv 14:20 bridles, for a·thousand *and* six·hundred stadia.

Rv 21:16 the CITY at twelve thousand stadia. The length

G4712.3 N-DSN σταδίῳ (1x)

1Co 9:24 that the·ones running in a·stadium·race in·fact all

G4713 στάμνος stámnôs *adj.* (1x)

Roots:G2476 Compare:G3582 G5201
xLangAlso:H1228 H6803

G4713 A-NSM στάμνος (1x)

Heb 9:4 ·gold, in which *was* a·golden urn having the manna,

G4714 στάσις stásis *n.* (9x)

Roots:G2476 Compare:G1370 G0485 See:G3904-1

G4714.1 N-ASF στάσιν (1x)

Heb 9:8 with·the first Tabernacle still being standing.

G4714.3 N-NSF στάσις (1x)

Ac 23:7 that, there·occurred a·controversy *between* the

G4714.3 N-ASF στάσιν (1x)

Ac 24:5 ·pestilence, and stirring controversy among·all the

G4714.3 N-GSF στάσεως (2x)

Ac 15:2 ·it·becoming of·no little controversy to·Paul and

Ac 23:10 So·now with·a·large controversy occurring, the

G4714.4 N-GSF στάσεως (1x)

Ac 19:40 today's uproar, with·there·inherently·being not·

G4714.6 N-ASF στάσιν (2x)

Lk 23:19 on·account·of a·certain insurrection occurring in

Lk 23:25 the prison on·account·of insurrection and murder,

G4714.6 N-DSF στάσει (1x)

Mk 15:7 who had·committed murder in the insurrection.

G4715 στατήρ statḗr *n.* (1x)

Roots:G2476 Compare:G4608-2 G5069-1 See:G1323
G1406 G1220 xLangAlso:H8255 H7192

G4715.2 N-ASM στατῆρα (1x)

Mt 17:27 you·shall·find a·silver·stater·coin *(worth four*

G4716 σταυρός staurŏs *n.* (28x)

Roots:G2476 Compare:G3586 See:G2247
xLangEquiv:H6741-1

G4716.2 N-NSM σταυρός (1x)

1Co 1:17 of·reasoning, lest the cross of·the Anointed-One

G4716.2 N-ASM σταυρόν (11x)

Jn 19:17 And bearing his·own cross, he·went·forth unto the

Lk 9:23 ·utterly·deny himself and take·up his cross each day,

Lk 14:27 whoever does·not bear his cross and come right·

Lk 23:26 a·Cyrenian, they·placed the cross on·him, *for·him*

Heb 12:2 ·before him, patiently·endured a·cross of·shame,

Mt 10:38 whoever does·not take his cross and follow right·

Mt 16:24 ·deny himself, take·up his cross, and follow me.

Mt 27:32 ·upon this·man that he·should·lift·*up* his cross.

Mk 8:34 ·deny himself, and take·up his cross, and follow me

Mk 10:21 come·over·here! Upon·taking·up the cross, follow

Mk 15:21 Rufus), in·order·that he·should·take·up his cross.

G4716.2 N-DSM σταυρῷ (4x)

Jn 19:25 *these women* stood near the cross of·Jesus: *Mariam*

Gal 6:12 be·persecuted for·the cross of·the Anointed-One.

Gal 6:14 to·boast, except in the cross of·our Lord YeShua

Col 2:14 midst *of·us*, already·firmly·nailing it to·the cross.

G4716.2 N-GSM σταυροῦ (12x)

Jn 19:19 and placed *it* on the cross. And having·been·written

Jn 19:31 should·not remain upon the cross on the Sabbath

Gal 5:11 ·offense of·the cross has·been·fully·nullified.

Mt 27:40 If you·are a·son of·God, descend from the cross."

Mt 27:42 let·him·descend now from the cross, and we·shall·

Mk 15:30 save yourself, and descend from the cross!"

Mk 15:32 now from the cross in·order·that we·may·see and

Php 2:8 as·far·as·unto death, even of·death on·a·cross.

Php 3:18 *·are* the enemies of·the cross of·the Anointed-One,

1Co 1:18 the reasoning (the·one of·the cross) is foolishness,

Eph 2:16 in one body through the cross, in himself already·

Col 1:20 the blood of *Anointed-One's* cross, *now·also he·*

G4717 σταυρόω staurŏō *v.* (46x)

Roots:G4716 Compare:G4362 G4957 G4338
xLangEquiv:H6739-1

G4717.2 V-FAI-1S σταυρώσω (1x)

Jn 19:15 Pilate says to·them, "Shall·I·crucify yeur King?

G4717.2 V-FAI-2P σταυρώσετε (1x)

Mt 23:34 ·among them yeu·shall·kill and shall·crucify, and

G4717.2 V-PAI-3P σταυροῦσιν (1x)

Mk 15:27 And together with·him, they·crucify two robbers:

G4717.2 V-PPI-3P σταυροῦνται (1x)

Mt 27:38 two robbers being·crucified together with·him, one

G4717.2 V-AAI-2P ἐσταυρώσατε (2x)

Ac 2:36 this same Jesus, whom yeu crucified, both Lord and

Ac 4:10 of·Natsareth, whom yeu crucified, whom God

G4717.2 V-AAI-3P ἐσταύρωσαν (7x)

Jn 19:18 where they·crucified him, and·also two others with

Jn 19:23 Now·then, when they·crucified Jesus, the soldiers

Lk 23:33 being·called Skull, there they·crucified him, and·

Lk 24:20 over to a·judgment of·death, and crucified him.

Gal 5:24 *·are* of·the Anointed-One, they·crucified the flesh

Mk 15:25 *the* third hour *after dawn* that they·crucified him.

1Co 2:8 *it*, they·would·have not crucified the Lord of·glory.

G4717.2 V-AAM-2S σταύρωσον (7x)

Jn 19:6 they·yelled·out, saying, "Crucify *him*, crucify *him*!

Jn 19:6 "Crucify *him*, crucify *him*!" Pilate says to·them,

Jn 19:15 "Take·*him*·away, take·*him*·away, crucify him!"

Lk 23:21 ·exclaiming, saying, "Crucify *him*, crucify him!"

Lk 23:21 "Crucify *him*, crucify him!"

Mk 15:13 And they·yelled·out again, "Crucify him!"

Mk 15:14 ·yelled·out the more·abundantly, "Crucify him!"

G4717.2 V-AAM-2P σταυρώσατε (1x)

Jn 19:6 "Yeu·yourselves take him and crucify *him*, for I·

G4717.2 V-AAN σταυρῶσαι (3x)

Jn 19:10 ·know that I·have authority to·crucify you, and I·

Mt 20:19 and to·flog, and to·crucify *him*. And on·the third

Mt 27:31 And·then they·led him away to crucify *him*.

G4717.2 V-AAP-NPM σταυρώσαντες (2x)

Mt 27:35 And after·crucifying him, they·thoroughly·divided·

Αα Ββ Γγ Δδ Εε Ζζ Ηη Θθ Ιι Κκ Λλ Μμ Νν Ξξ Οο Ππ Ρρ Σσ Ττ Υυ Φφ Χχ Ψψ Ωω

Mk 15:24 And after·crucifying him, they·were·thoroughly·

G4717.2 V-AAS-3P σταυρώσωσιν (1x)

Mk 15:20 led him out in·order·that they·should·crucify him.

G4717.2 V-API-3S ἐσταυρώθη (5x)

Jn 19:20 the place where Jesus was·crucified was near to·the

Jn 19:41 in the place where he·was·crucified, there·was an·

1Co 1:13 ·divided? ¿!·Was Paul crucified on·yeur behalf?

2Co 13:4 even though he·is·crucified as·a·result of·weakness

Rv 11:8 and Egypt, where also our Lord was·crucified.

G4717.2 V-APM-3S σταυρωθήτω (2x)

Mt 27:22 They·all say to·him, "Let·him·be·crucified!"

Mt 27:23 more·abundantly, saying, "Let·him·be·crucified!"

G4717.2 V-APN σταυρωθῆναι (3x)

Lk 23:23 voices, requesting·for him to·be·crucified. And the

Lk 24:7 ·disqualified men·of·clay†, and to·be·crucified, and

Mt 26:2 Son of·Clay·Man† is·handed·over to·be·crucified."

G4717.2 V-APS-3S σταυρωθῇ (3x)

Jn 19:16 him over to·them that he·should·be·crucified. And

Mt 27:26 ·*him*·over in·order·that he·may·be·crucified.

Mk 15:15 ·*him*·over in·order·that he·should·be·crucified.

G4717.2 V-RPI-3S ἐσταύρωται (1x)

Gal 6:14 whom *the* world has·been·crucified to·me, and·I

G4717.2 V-RPP-ASM ἐσταυρωμένον (4x)

Mt 28:5 yeu·seek YeShua, the·one having·been·crucified.

Mk 16:6 the·one having·been·crucified. He·was·awakened.

1Co 1:23 Anointed-One having·been·crucified, *which·is* in·

1Co 2:2 Anointed and this *Jesus* having·been·crucified.

G4717.2 V-RPP-NSM ἐσταυρωμένος (1x)

Gal 3:1 ·written among yeu *as* having·been·crucified?

G4718 σταφυλή staphylḗ *n.* (3x)

Roots:G4735

G4718 N-NPF σταφυλαί (1x)

Rv 14:18 ·the earth, because her clusters·of·grapes are·ripe.

G4718 N-ASF σταφυλήν (2x)

Lk 6:44 do·they·collect a·cluster·of·grapes for·vintage.

Mt 7:16 "¿!·Do men·collect a·cluster·of·grapes from thorns,

G4719 στάχυς stáchys *n.* (5x)

Roots:G2476 Compare:G4621 See:G4720

G4719 N-ASM στάχυν (1x)

Mk 4:28 first a·blade, then a·head·of·grain, after·that,

G4719 N-APM στάχυας (3x)

Lk 6:1 his disciples were·plucking the heads·of·grain, and

Mt 12:1 they·also began to·pluck heads·of·grain and to·eat.

Mk 2:23 to·make a·pathway, plucking the heads·of·grain.

G4719 N-DSM στάχυϊ (1x)

Mk 4:28 ·of·grain, after·that, fully·ripe grain in·the head.

G4720 Στάχυς Stáchys *n/p.* (1x)

Roots:G4719

G4720.2 N/P-ASM Στάχυν (1x)

Rm 16:9 in Anointed-One, and my well-beloved Stachys.

G4721 στέγη stégē *n.* (3x)

See:G4722

G4721 N-ASF στέγην (3x)

Lk 7:6 For I·am not fit that you·should·enter under my roof.

Mt 8:8 ·that you·should·enter under my roof, but·rather

Mk 2:4 the crowd, they·pulled·apart the roof where he·was,

G4722 στέγω stégō *v.* (4x)

Roots:G4721

G4722.3 V-PAI-1P στέγομεν (1x)

1Co 9:12 privilege, but·rather we·quietly·bear all·things,

G4722.3 V-PAI-3S στέγει (1x)

1Co 13:7 It·quietly·bears all·things, trusts all·things,

G4722.3 V-PAP-NSM στέγων (1x)

1Th 3:5 ·of this, when·I could·quietly·bear·it no·longer, I·

G4722.3 V-PAP-NPM στέγοντες (1x)

1Th 3:1 Therefore, when·we·could·quietly·bear *it* no·longer

G4723 στεῖρος stêirôs *n.* (4x)

Roots:G4731 xLangAlso:H6135

G4723 N-NSF στεῖρα (1x)

Lk 1:7 because·indeed EliSabeth was barren, and both were

G4723 N-NPF στεῖραι (1x)

Lk 23:29 'Supremely·blessed *are* the barren, and *the* wombs

G4723 N-VSF στεῖρα (1x)

Gal 4:27 '" Be·merry, O·barren·woman, the·one not

G4723 N-DSF στείρᾳ (1x)

Lk 1:36 ·*pregnancy* for·her (the·woman being·called barren),

G4724 στέλλω stéllō *v.* (2x)

Roots:G2476 Compare:G0567 G0868 G5563 G2967 G3992 See:G4749 G0649

G4724.2 V-PMP-NPM στελλόμενοι (1x)

2Co 8:20 we·are·deliberately·preempting this·thing: *that* not

G4724.4 V-PMN στέλλεσθαι (1x)

2Th 3:6 to·deliberately·abstain·and·withdraw yeurselves

G4725 στέμμα stémma *n.* (1x)

Roots:G4735

G4725.2 N-APN στέμματα (1x)

Ac 14:13 city, after·bringing bulls and garlands to the gates,

G4726 στεναγμός stênagmós *n.* (2x)

Roots:G4727 xLangAlso:H5009

G4726 N-DPM στεναγμοῖς (1x)

Rm 8:26 on·our behalf with·groanings unspeakable.

G4726 N-GSM στεναγμοῦ (1x)

Ac 7:34 *who·are* in Egypt, and I·heard their groaning,' 'and

G4727 στενάζω stênázō *v.* (6x)

Roots:G4728 Compare:G3600 See:G0389

G4727.3 V-PAP-NPM στενάζοντες (1x)

Heb 13:17 this with joy, and not sighing·heavily, for that *is*

G4727.3 V-AAI-3S ἐστέναξεν (1x)

Mk 7:34 to the heaven, he·sighed·heavily and says to·him,

G4727.4 V-PAI-1P στενάζομεν (3x)

Rm 8:23 Spirit, even we·ourselves groan within ourselves,

2Co 5:2 For even in this we·groan, greatly·yearning to·fully·

2Co 5:4 in the bodily·tent do·groan, being·weighed·down,

G4727.4 V-PAM-2P στενάζετε (1x)

Jac 5:9 Do·not groan against one·another, brothers, lest yeu·

G4728 στενός stênós *adj.* (3x)

Roots:G2476 Compare:G4116 G2149 G2347 See:G4729

G4728 A-NSF στενή (1x)

Mt 7:14 "How obstructed·and·narrow *is* the gate, and the

G4728 A-GSF στενῆς (2x)

Lk 13:24 to·enter through the obstructed·and·narrow gate,

Mt 7:13 ·enter·in through the obstructed·and·narrow gate,

G4729 στενο•χωρέω stênôchōréō *v.* (3x)

Roots:G4728 G5561 Compare:G4912 G2352 G4846 G4580-1 G2600-1 G0194-1 See:G4730

G4729.2 V-PPI-2P στενοχωρεῖσθε (2x)

2Co 6:12 Yeu·are·not narrowly·constricted by us, but yeu·

2Co 6:12 us, but yeu·are·narrowly·constricted by yeur·own

G4729.2 V-PPP-NPM στενοχωρούμενοι (1x)

2Co 4:8 ·yet not being·narrowly·constricted; being·at·a·loss,

G4730 στενο•χωρία stênôchōría *n.* (4x)

Roots:G4728 G5561

G4730.2 N-NSF στενοχωρία (2x)

Rm 2:9 tribulation and calamity, upon every soul of·a·man·

Rm 8:35 *Shall* tribulation, or calamity, or persecution, or

G4730.2 N-DPF στενοχωρίαις (2x)

2Co 6:4 in tribulations, in necessities, in calamities,

2Co 12:10 in calamities on·behalf of·Anointed-One, for

G4731 στερεός stêrêós *adj.* (4x)

Roots:G2476 Compare:G0949 See:G4733

G4731.1 A-NSM στερεός (1x)

2Ti 2:19 However·in·fact, the solid foundation of·God

G4731.1 A-NSF στερεά (1x)

Heb 5:14 But the solid nourishment is *for* the completely·

G4731.1 A-NPF στερεοί (1x)

1Pe 5:9 whom yeu·must·stand·up·against, solid in·the trust,

G4731.1 A-GSF στερεᾶς (1x)

Heb 5:12 ·having need of·milk and not of·solid nourishment,

G4732 στερεόω stêrêóō *v.* (3x)

Roots:G4731 Compare:G0950 G5080 See:G4733

G4732.1 V-IPI-3P ἐστερεοῦντο (1x)

Ac 16:5 Called·Out·citizenries were·made·solid in·the trust

G4732.2 V-AAI-3S ἐστερέωσεν (1x)

Ac 3:16 of·his name, *this·trust* stabilized this·man whom

G4732.2 V-API-3P ἐστερεώθησαν (1x)

Ac 3:7 at·once, his feet and ankle·joints were·stabilized.

G4733 στερέωμα stêréōma *n.* (1x)

Roots:G4732 Compare:G4740 G1476 G0804 G0951 G0181

G4733.2 N-ASN στερέωμα (1x)

Col 2:5 orderly·arrangement and the stability of·yeur trust in

G4734 Στεφανᾶς Stêphanâs *n/p.* (3x)

Roots:G4737 See:G4736

G4734.2 N/P-GSM Στεφανᾶ (3x)

1Co 1:16 also the household of·Stephanas. Finally, I·do·not

1Co 16:15 ·know the household of·Stephanas, that it·is a·

1Co 16:17 upon the arrival of·Stephanas and Fortunatus and

G4735 στέφανος stéphanôs *n.* (18x)

Compare:G1238 See:G4737 G4725 xLangEquiv:H5850

G4735 N-NSM στέφανος (5x)

Php 4:1 my joy and victor's·crown) in·this·manner stand·

1Th 2:19 expectation, or joy, or victor's·crown of·boasting?

2Ti 4:8 ·away for·me the victor's·crown of·righteousness,

Rv 6:2 a·bow. And a·victor's·crown was·given to·him, and

Rv 12:1 and upon her head a·victor's·crown of·twelve stars.

G4735 N-NPM στέφανοι (1x)

Rv 9:7 heads *were something* as victor's·crowns like gold,

G4735 N-ASM στέφανον (10x)

Jn 19:2 after·braiding a·victor's·crown out of·thorns, they·

Jn 19:5 outside bearing the thorny victor's·crown and the

Mt 27:29 And after·braiding a·victor's·crown out of·thorns,

Mk 15:17 a·thorny victor's·crown, it·is·placed·around his

Jac 1:12 he·shall·receive the victor's·crown of·life-above,

1Pe 5:4 ·obtain the undiminishable victor's·crown of·glory.

1Co 9:25 they·may·receive a·corruptible victor's·crown, but

Rv 2:10 I·shall·give you a·victor's·crown of·the life-above.

Rv 3:11 not·even·one·man should·take your victor's·crown.

Rv 14:14 having on his head a·golden victor's·crown, and in

G4735 N-APM στεφάνους (2x)

Rv 4:4 they·had on their heads victor's·crowns made·of·gold.

Rv 4:10 and cast their victor's·crowns in·the·sight of·the

G4736 Στέφανος Stéphanôs *n/p.* (9x)

Roots:G4735 Compare:G5376 G4402 G3527 G5096 G3937 G3532 See:G4734 G1675

G4736.2 N/P-NSM Στέφανος (1x)

Ac 6:8 Now Stephen, full of·trust and power, was·doing

G4736.2 N/P-ASM Στέφανον (3x)

Ac 6:5 multitude. And they·selected Stephen, a·man full of·

Ac 7:59 they·were·casting·stones·at Stephen while·he·is· *the*

Ac 8:2 went·in·procession·together·to·bury Stephen, and

G4736.2 N/P-DSM Στεφάνῳ (2x)

Ac 6:9 mutually·questioning·and·discussing with·Stephen.

Ac 11:19 the·one occurring over Stephen, went·throughout

G4736.2 N/P-GSM Στεφάνου (1x)

Ac 22:20 the blood of·your martyr Stephen was·poured·out,

EG4736.2 (2x)

Ac 7:2 And *Stephen* replied, "Men, brothers and fathers,

Ac 7:55 But *Stephen*, inherently·being full of·Holy Spirit,

G4737 στεφανόω stêphanóō *v.* (3x)

Roots:G4735 xLangEquiv:H5849

G4737 V-PPI-3S στεφανοῦται (1x)

2Ti 2:5 he·is·not victoriously·crowned unless he·should·

G4737 V-AAI-2S ἐστεφάνωσας (1x)

Heb 2:7 ·angels; you·did·victoriously·crown him with·glory

G4737 V-RPP-ASM ἐστεφανωμένον (1x)

Heb 2:9 *but·now* having·been·victoriously·crowned with·

G4738 στῆθος stē̂thôs *n.* (5x)

Roots:G2476 Compare:G2859 G2382 G3149 See:G4737-1

G4738 N-ASN στῆθος (3x)

Jn 13:25 ·one, falling·back upon Jesus' chest, says to·him,

Jn 21:20 who also sat·back upon his chest at the supper and

Lk 18:13 but·rather was·beating at his chest, saying, 'God,

G4738 N-APN στήθη (2x)

Lk 23:48 their·own chests, they·were·returning·back *from*·
Rv 15:6 ·about·with golden bands around *their* chests.

G4739 στήκω stḗkō *v.* (8x)
Roots:G2476
G4739.1 V-PAI-2P στήκετε (1x)
Php 1:27 concerning yeu— that yeu·stand·fast in one spirit,
G4739.1 V-PAI-3S στήκει (1x)
Rm 14:4 ·servant? To·his·own lord he·stands·fast or falls.
G4739.1 V-PAM-2P στήκετε (4x)
Gal 5:1 Accordingly, stand·fast in·the liberty with·which
Php 4:1 and victor's·crown) in·this·manner stand·fast in *the*
2Th 2:15 brothers, stand·fast and securely·hold·to the
1Co 16:13 Keep·alert! Stand·fast in the trust! '" Be·manly!
G4739.1 V-PAS-2P στήκητε (2x)
Mk 11:25 whenever yeu·should·stand·fast while·yeu·are·, if
1Th 3:8 now we·live, if yeu should·stand·fast in *the* Lord.

G4740 στηριγμός stērigmós *n.* (1x)
Roots:G4741 Compare:G4733 G1476 G0949 G0804 G0951 G0181
G4740.2 N-GSM στηριγμοῦ (1x)
2Pe 3:17 yeu·should·fall·from your·own firm·steadfastness.

G4741 στηρίζω stērízō *v.* (13x)
Roots:G2476 G4731 Compare:G0950 G4599 G1765 G2480 See:G1991 G4740
G4741.1 V-AAI-3S ἐστήριξεν (1x)
Lk 9:51 being·taken·up, that he·himself firmly·set his face
G4741.1 V-RPI-3S ἐστήρικται (1x)
Lk 16:26 us and yeu there·has·been·firmly·set a·great chasm
G4741.2 V-FAI-3S στηρίξει (1x)
2Th 3:3 the Lord, who shall·firmly·establish yeu and shall·
G4741.2 V-AAM-2S στήριξον (2x)
Lk 22:32 return, you·must·firmly·establish your brothers."
Rv 3:2 ·alert, and firmly·establish the·things remaining that
G4741.2 V-AAM-2P στηρίξατε (1x)
Jac 5:8 ·be·patient. Yeu·must·firmly·establish yeur hearts,
G4741.2 V-AAN στηρίξαι (3x)
Rm 16:25 being·able to·firmly·establish yeu according·to
1Th 3:2 ·Anointed-One, in·order to·firmly·establish yeu and
1Th 3:13 in·order to·firmly·establish yeur hearts blameless
G4741.2 V-AAO-3S στηρίξαι (2x)
1Pe 5:10 completely·reform yeu, may·he·firmly·establish,
2Th 2:17 ·he·comfort yeur hearts and firmly·establish yeu in
G4741.2 V-APN στηριχθῆναι (1x)
Rm 1:11 spiritual, in·order·for yeu to·be·firmly·established;
G4741.2 V-RPP-APM ἐστηριγμένους (1x)
2Pe 1:12 and *are* having·been·firmly·established in the

G4742 στίγμα stígma *n.* (1x)
Compare:G5480 See:G4743
G4742.1 N-APN στίγματα (1x)
Gal 6:17 bear in my body the marks of·the Lord YeShua.

G4743 στιγμή stigmḗ *n.* (2x)
Roots:G4742 Compare:G0823
G4743.2 N-DSF στιγμῇ (1x)
Lk 4:5 all the kingdoms of·The Land in a·moment of·time.
EG4743.2 (1x)
Lk 7:45 but she·herself since that *moment* I·entered·in, did·

G4744 στίλβω stílbō *v.* (1x)
Compare:G1823
G4744 V-PAP-NPN στίλβοντα (1x)
Mk 9:3 And his garments became glistening, exceedingly

G4745 στοά stôá *n.* (5x)
Roots:G2476
G4745 N-APF στοάς (1x)
Jn 5:2 there·is a·pool having five colonnades; in·Hebrew, *it*·
G4745 N-DSF στοᾷ (3x)
Jn 10:23 in the Sanctuary·Atrium at Solomon's Colonnade.
Ac 3:11 them in the colonnade being·called Solomon's,
Ac 5:12 ·the·same·determination in Solomon's Colonnade.
EG4745 (1x)
Jn 5:3 Among these *colonnades*, a·large multitude of·the·

G4746 στοιβάς stôibás *n.* (1x)
G4746.2 N-APF στοιβάδας (1x)
Mk 11:8 and others were·chopping limbs out of·the trees,

G4747 στοιχεῖον stôichêîon *n.* (7x)
Roots:G4748
G4747.3 N-NPN στοιχεῖα (1x)
Heb 5:12 the initial fundamental·principles of·the eloquent·
G4747.4 N-NPN στοιχεῖα (2x)
2Pe 3:10 ·*of·wind*, and *the* elements shall·be·dissolved—
2Pe 3:12 and *the* elements, being·consumed·in·a·blazing·fire
G4747.4 N-APN στοιχεῖα (3x)
Gal 4:3 ·been·enslaved under the principles of·the world.
Gal 4:9 to the weak and pitifully·poor principles— to·which
Col 2:8 *that·is*, according·to the principles of·the world,
G4747.4 N-GPN στοιχείων (1x)
Col 2:20 with·Anointed-One from the principles of·the world

G4748 στοιχέω stôichéō *v.* (5x)
Compare:G3877 G4964 See:G4747
G4748.2 V-FAI-3P στοιχήσουσιν (1x)
Gal 6:16 as·many·as shall·conform·and·march·orderly by·
G4748.2 V-PAI-2S στοιχεῖς (1x)
Ac 21:24 also conform·and·march·orderly, vigilantly·
G4748.2 V-PAN στοιχεῖν (1x)
Php 3:16 let·us·conform·and·march·orderly by·the same
G4748.2 V-PAP-DPM στοιχοῦσιν (1x)
Rm 4:12 to·the·ones conforming·and·marching·orderly in·
G4748.2 V-PAS-1P στοιχῶμεν (1x)
Gal 5:25 we·should·conform·and·march·orderly also in·

G4749 στολή stôlḗ *n.* (9x)
Roots:G4724 Compare:G2689 G4158 G2440 xLangAlso:H0899 H8278
G4749.2 N-NPF στολαί (1x)
Rv 6:11 white long·robes were·given to·each·one·of·them,
G4749.2 N-ASF στολήν (2x)
Lk 15:22 'Bring·out the most·prestigious long·robe, and
Mk 16:5 having·been·arrayed·with a·white long·robe, and
G4749.2 N-APF στολάς (4x)
Rv 7:9 ·arrayed·with white long·robes and palm·branches in
Rv 7:13 ·been·arrayed·with the white long·robes? And from·
Rv 7:14 and they·laundered their long·robes, and they·
Rv 7:14 and they·whitened their long·robes in the blood of·
G4749.2 N-DPF στολαῖς (2x)
Lk 20:46 ·ones delighting to·stroll·about in long·robes, and
Mk 12:38 the·ones wanting to·stroll·about in long·robes, and

G4750 στόμα stóma *n.* (80x)
Roots:G5114 Compare:G3790 xLangEquiv:H6310 A6433
G4750.1 N-NSN στόμα (10x)
Lk 1:64 And his mouth was·opened·up at·once, and his
Lk 6:45 of·the abundance of·the heart, his mouth speaks.
Mt 12:34 of·the abundance of·the heart the mouth speaks.
Rm 3:14 "Whose mouth overflows of·evil·prayer and of·
Rm 3:19 in·order·that every mouth may·be·stopped·up, and
Jud 1:16 And their mouth speaks outrageous·things, while·
2Co 6:11 we·have·opened·up our mouth to yeu; our heart
Rv 13:2 *feet* of·a·bear, and its mouth as a·mouth of·a·lion.
Rv 13:2 ·a·bear, and its mouth as a·mouth of·a·lion. And the
Rv 13:5 there·was·given to·it a·mouth speaking great·things
G4750.1 N-ASN στόμα (18x)
Lk 21:15 For I·myself shall·give yeu a·mouth and wisdom,
Ac 8:32 him, in·this·manner he·did·not open·up his mouth.
Ac 8:35 Philippe, opening·up his mouth and beginning from
Ac 10:34 Then Peter, opening·up his mouth, declared, "In
Ac 11:8 did anything defiled or impure enter into my mouth.'
Ac 18:14 ·Paul was·intending to·open·up his mouth, Gallio
Ac 23:2 ·ones standing·nearby him to·pummel his mouth.
Mt 5:2 And opening·up his mouth, he·was·instructing them,
Mt 13:35 "I·shall·open·up my mouth in parables; I·shall·
Mt 15:11 the·thing entering into the mouth *that* defiles the
Mt 15:17 thing traversing into the mouth passes·through into
Mt 17:27 and upon·opening·up his mouth, you·shall·find a·
2Jn 1:12 to·come to yeu, and to·speak mouth to mouth, in·
2Jn 1:12 and to·speak mouth to mouth, in·order·that our
3Jn 1:14 straight·away, and we·shall·speak mouth to mouth.
3Jn 1:14 ·away, and we·shall·speak mouth to mouth. Peace
Rv 12:16 the earth opened·up her mouth, and swallowed·up
Rv 13:6 And it·opened·up its mouth in revilement toward
G4750.1 N-APN στόματα (2x)
Heb 11:33 promises, stopped·up *the* mouths of·lions,
Jac 3:3 the bits in the horses' mouths specifically to·persuade
G4750.1 N-DSN στόματι (11x)
Jn 19:29 and putting·it·on hyssop, brought *it* to·his mouth.
Mt 15:8 ·near to·me with·their mouth and deeply·honors me
Rm 10:8 is near you, *even* in your mouth, and in your heart'"
Rm 10:9 If you·should·affirm with your mouth, "Jesus *is*
Rm 10:10 and with·the·mouth affirmation·is·made unto
Rm 15:6 *and* with one mouth, yeu·may·glorify the God and
1Pe 2:22 ·failure, neither was guile found in his mouth";
Rv 9:19 their authorities are in their mouth *and in their tails*,
Rv 10:9 but·yet it·shall·be in your mouth sweet as honey.
Rv 10:10 it; and it·was in my mouth sweet as honey.
Rv 14:5 And in their mouth was·found no guile, for they·are
G4750.1 N-GSN στόματος (34x)
Lk 1:70 just·as he·spoke through *the* mouth of·his holy
Lk 4:22 the·ones proceeding·forth out of·his mouth. And·
Lk 11:54 of·his mouth in·order·that they·may·legally·accuse
Lk 19:22 'From·out of·your·own mouth shall·I·judge you,
Lk 22:71 For we·ourselves heard *it* from his·own mouth."
Ac 1:16 ·declared through David's mouth concerning Judas
Ac 3:18 ·announced·beforehand through *the* mouth of·all his
Ac 3:21 ·which God spoke through *the* mouth of·all his holy
Ac 4:25 ·*are* the·one, through *the* mouth of·your servant·boy
Ac 15:7 of·the good·news through my mouth, and to·trust.
Ac 22:14 ·One, and to·hear *his* voice from·out of·his mouth.
Mt 4:4 ·is·proceeding·forth through *the* mouth of·Yahweh.'"
Mt 15:11 ·thing proceeding·forth out of·the mouth; *indeed*,
Mt 15:18 ·forth out of·the mouth come·forth from·out of·the
Mt 18:16 more, that "at *the* mouth of·two or three witnesses
Mt 21:16 " From·out *of·the* mouth of·infants and sucklings
Jac 3:10 From·out of·the same mouth come·forth blessing
2Th 2:8 of·his mouth and shall·fully·render·inoperative
2Co 13:1 "At *the* mouth of·two or three witnesses shall
Eph 4:29 proceed·forth from·out of·yeur mouth, but·rather
Eph 6:19 an·opening·up of·my mouth with clarity·of·speech,
Col 3:8 *and* shameful·conversation from·out of·yeur mouth.
2Ti 4:17 And·thus I·was·snatched out of·a·lion's mouth.
Rv 1:16 And 'out of·his mouth, a·sharp double-edged
Rv 2:16 against them with the straight·sword of·my mouth.
Rv 3:16 ·hot, I·intend to·vomit you out of·my mouth,
Rv 11:5 proceeds·forth from·out of·their mouth and devours
Rv 12:15 the Serpent cast out of·his mouth water as a·flood·
Rv 12:16 ·water which the Dragon cast out of·his mouth.
Rv 16:13 like frogs *come* out of·the mouth of·the Dragon,
Rv 16:13 and out of·the mouth of·the Daemonic·Beast, and
Rv 16:13 and out of·the mouth of·the Fiendish·False·Prophet.
Rv 19:15 'out of·his mouth proceeds·forth a·sharp straight·
Rv 19:21 which·is·proceeding·forth out of·his mouth; and all
G4750.1 N-GPN στομάτων (2x)
Rv 9:17 and out of·their mouths proceeds·forth fire and
Rv 9:18 ·one which·is·proceeding·forth out of·their mouths.
EG4750.1 (1x)
1Ti 5:19 "except at *the mouth* of·two or three witnesses.
G4750.4 N-APN στόματα (1x)
Heb 11:34 of·fire, escaped *the* edge of·*the*·dagger, from
G4750.4 N-DSN στόματι (1x)
Lk 21:24 And they·shall·fall by·the·edge of·a·dagger, and

G4751 στόμαχος stómachôs *n.* (1x)
Roots:G4750 Compare:G2836 G1064
G4751.2 N-ASM στόμαχον (1x)
1Ti 5:23 a·little wine on·account·of your stomach and your

G4752 στρατεία stratêía *n.* (2x)
Roots:G4754
G4752.2 N-ASF στρατείαν (1x)
1Ti 1:18 ·may·strategically·war the good strategic·warfare,
G4752.2 N-GSF στρατείας (1x)
2Co 10:4 For the weapons of·our strategic·warfare *are* not

G4753 στράτευμα strátêuma *n.* (8x)
Roots:G4754 Compare:G5069 G4686 G1543 See:G4757 G4756
G4753.2 N-APN στρατεύματα (1x)
Mt 22:7 and sending his troops, he·completely·destroyed
G4753.2 N-DPN στρατεύμασιν (1x)
Lk 23:11 him, HerOd·AntiPas (along·with his troops), after·
G4753.2 N-GPN στρατευμάτων (1x)
Rv 9:16 And the number of·troops of·the cavalry *was* twice
G4753.3 N-NPN στρατεύματα (1x)
Rv 19:14 And the armies in the heaven were·following him
G4753.3 N-APN στρατεύματα (1x)
Rv 19:19 and their armies, having·been·gathered·together
G4753.3 N-GSN στρατεύματος (1x)
Rv 19:19 ·sitting·down on the horse, and against his army.
G4753.4 N-ASN στράτευμα (1x)
Ac 23:10 ·ordered the squad·of·soldiers, upon·walking·down
G4753.4 N-DSN στρατεύματι (1x)
Ac 23:27 *him* together with·the squad·of·soldiers, I·snatched

G4754 στρατεύομαι stratêúômai *v.* (7x)
Roots:G4760-1 Compare:G4170 G4753 G3164 See:G0497 G4752 G4757
G4754.2 V-PMI-1P στρατευόμεθα (1x)
2Co 10:3 we·do·not strategically·war according·to flesh.
G4754.2 V-PMI-2S στρατεύῃ (1x)
1Ti 1:18 ·that by them, you·may·strategically·war the good
G4754.2 V-PMI-3P στρατεύονται (1x)
1Pe 2:11 longings, which strategically·war against the soul.
G4754.2 V-PMP-GPF στρατευομένων (1x)
Jac 4:1 the·ones which·are·strategically·warring in yeur
G4754.3 V-PMI-3S στρατεύεται (1x)
1Co 9:7 Who strategically·goes·to·war at·any·time with·his·
G4754.3 V-PMP-NSM στρατευόμενος (1x)
2Ti 2:4 Not·even·one·man who·is·strategically·going·to·war
G4754.6 V-PMP-NPM στρατευόμενοι (1x)
Lk 3:14 And army·officers also were·inquiring·of him,

G4755 στρατ•ηγός stratēgós *n.* (10x)
Roots:G4760-1 G0071 G2233 Compare:G1988 G1985 G0746 G0758 See:G0751-2 G4756 xLangAlso:H2951 H6346 H5633
G4755.4 N-APM στρατηγούς (1x)
Lk 22:52 chief·priests, *the* wardens of·the Sanctuary·Estate,
G4755.4 N-DPM στρατηγοῖς (1x)
Lk 22:4 with·the chief·priests and the wardens, how he·may·
G4755.5 N-NSM στρατηγός (3x)
Ac 4:1 and the high·warden of·the Sanctuary·Estate and the
Ac 5:24 priest and the high·warden of·the Sanctuary·Estate
Ac 5:26 after·going·off, the high·warden along·with the
G4755.6 N-NPM στρατηγοί (3x)
Ac 16:22 the court·officers, after·completely·tearing·away
Ac 16:35 occurring, the court·officers dispatched the
Ac 16:36 "The court·officers have·dispatched that yeu·
G4755.6 N-DPM στρατηγοῖς (2x)
Ac 16:20 escorting them to·the court·officers, they·declared,
Ac 16:38 ·in·detail these utterances to·the court·officers, and

G4756 στρατιά stratiá *n.* (2x)
Roots:G4760-1 Compare:G4753 See:G4760 G4757 G1611-2 xLangAlso:H6635
G4756.2 N-DSF στρατιᾷ (1x)
Ac 7:42 over to·ritually·minister to·the host of·the heaven,
G4756.2 N-GSF στρατιᾶς (1x)
Lk 2:13 ·to·be a·multitude of·*the*·heavenly host praising God

G4757 στρατιώτης stratiṓtēs *n.* (29x)
Roots:G4760-1 Compare:G4753 G1543 See:G4961 G4754
G4757.1 N-NSM στρατιώτης (1x)
2Ti 2:3 ·endure·hardship as a·good soldier of·Jesus Anointed
G4757.1 N-NPM στρατιῶται (9x)
Jn 19:2 And the soldiers, after·braiding a·victor's·crown out
Jn 19:23 they·crucified Jesus, the soldiers took his outer·
Jn 19:24 ·fact, in·due·course, the soldiers did these·things.
Jn 19:32 Accordingly, the *Roman* soldiers came and in·fact
Lk 23:36 And the soldiers also were·mocking him, coming·
Ac 23:31 So·then in·fact, the soldiers, according·to the
Ac 27:32 Then the soldiers chopped·off the small·ropes of·
Mt 27:27 Then the soldiers of·the governor, after·personally·
Mk 15:16 And the soldiers led him away inside the courtyard
G4757.1 N-ASM στρατιώτην (1x)
Ac 10:7 a·devoutly·reverent soldier of·the·ones diligently·
G4757.1 N-APM στρατιώτας (5x)
Lk 7:8 under authority, having soldiers under my·own·self,
Ac 21:32 to them, personally·taking soldiers and centurions.
Ac 21:32 regiment·commander and the soldiers, they·ceased
Ac 23:23 "Make·ready two·hundred soldiers, with seventy
Mt 8:9 under authority, having soldiers under my·own·self,
G4757.1 N-DSM στρατιώτῃ (2x)
Jn 19:23 four parts, a·part for·each soldier, and·also the
Ac 28:16 together with·the soldier keeping·watch·over him.
G4757.1 N-DPM στρατιώταις (3x)
Ac 12:18 no little disturbance among the soldiers as·to what
Ac 27:31 to·the centurion and to·the soldiers, "Unless these
Mt 28:12 ·gave a·significant·sum·of money to·the soldiers,
G4757.1 N-GPM στρατιωτῶν (5x)
Jn 19:34 But·rather one of·the soldiers jabbed his side with·
Ac 12:4 squads·of·four soldiers to·keep·watch·over him,
Ac 12:6 ·to·sleep between two soldiers, having·been·bound
Ac 21:35 ·and·carried by the soldiers on·account·of the force
Ac 27:42 And the soldiers' counsel was that they·should·kill
EG4757.1 (3x)
Jn 19:29 And the *soldiers*, after·filling a·sponge with·wine·
Ac 23:32 On·the next·day, *the soldiers* returned·back to the
Mt 2:16 And dispatching *soldiers*, he·eliminated all the

G4758 στρατο•λογέω stratôlôgéō *v.* (1x)
Roots:G4760-1 G3004 See:G4757
G4758.2 V-AAP-DSM στρατολογήσαντι (1x)
2Ti 2:4 ·comply with·the·one enlisting·him·to·be·a·soldier.

G4759 στρατο•πεδ•άρχης stratôpêdárchēs *n.* (1x)
Roots:G4760 G0757 See:G4232 G4686
G4759.2 N-DSM στρατοπεδάρχῃ (1x)
Ac 28:16 to·the captain·of·the·Praetorian·battalion, but Paul

G4760 στρατό•πεδον stratópêdôn *n.* (1x)
Roots:G4760-1 G3977 Compare:G3925
G4760.1 N-GPN στρατοπέδων (1x)
Lk 21:20 JeruSalem being·surrounded by army·camps, then

G4761 στρεβλόω strêblóō *v.* (1x)
Roots:G4762 Compare:G1294 See:G4760-2
G4761.3 V-PAI-3P στρεβλοῦσιν (1x)
2Pe 3:16 which *the* unlearned and unstable distort, as *they·do*

G4762 στρέφω strḗphō *v.* (19x)
Roots:G5157 See:G1994
G4762.2 V-PAN στρέφειν (1x)
Rv 11:6 authority over the waters to·turn them into blood,
G4762.2 V-PPI-1P στρεφόμεθα (1x)
Ac 13:46 life-above, behold, we·are·turned·around to the
G4762.2 V-AAI-3S ἔστρεψεν (1x)
Ac 7:42 Then God turned·around and handed them over to·
G4762.2 V-2APP-NSM στραφείς (9x)
Jn 1:38 But Jesus, turning·around and distinctly·viewing
Lk 7:9 marveled·at him. And turning·around, he·declared
Lk 7:44 And turning·around toward the woman, he·replied
Lk 9:55 But turning·around, he·reprimanded them and
Lk 10:22 And turning·around toward the disciples, he·
Lk 14:25 with·him, and turning·around, he·declared to them
Lk 22:61 And turning·around, the Lord looked·clearly·at
Lk 23:28 But turning·around toward them, Jesus declared,
Mt 16:23 But turning·around, he·declared to·Peter, "Get·
G4762.2 V-2APP-NPM στραφέντες (1x)
Mt 7:6 their feet, then turning·around, should·mangle yeu.
G4762.3 V-AAM-2S στρέψον (1x)
Mt 5:39 on your right cheek, turn·back to·him the other also.
G4762.3 V-2API-3S ἐστράφη (1x)
Jn 20:14 ·things, she·is·turned·around toward the·things
G4762.3 V-2API-3P ἐστράφησαν (1x)
Ac 7:39 in·their hearts, they·turned·back·around to Egypt,
G4762.3 V-2APP-NSF στραφεῖσα (1x)
Jn 20:16 That·woman, being·turned·back·around, says to·
G4762.3 V-2APS-2P στραφῆτε (1x)
Mt 18:3 ·yeu, unless yeu·should·be·turned·back and should·
G4762.4 V-2APP-NSM στραφείς (1x)
Lk 10:23 Then turning·himself *to·be* alongside his disciples,

G4763 στρηνιάω strēniáō *v.* (2x)
Roots:G4764 Compare:G4684 See:G2691 xLangAlso:H5727
G4763 V-AAI-3S ἐστρηνίασεν (1x)
Rv 18:7 herself and lived·in·voluptuous·luxury, give to·her
G4763 V-AAP-NPM στρηνιάσαντες (1x)
Rv 18:9 and living·in·voluptuous·luxury with her, shall·

G4764 στρῆνος strễnôs *n.* (1x)
Compare:G0970 G2902 G4516 G4988 See:G4763 G4731
G4764.2 N-GSN στρήνους (1x)
Rv 18:3 out of·the power of·her voluptuous·luxuries."

G4765 στρουθίον strôuthíôn *n.* (4x)
Roots:G2444-3 xLangEquiv:H6833
G4765 N-NPN στρουθία (2x)
Lk 12:6 "Are·not·indeed five little·sparrows sold for·two
Mt 10:29 two little·sparrows sold for·an·assarion·coin?
G4765 N-GPN στρουθίων (2x)
Lk 12:7 Yeu·surpass·the·value of·many little·sparrows.
Mt 10:31 surpass·the·value of·many little·sparrows.

G4766 στρώννυμι strṓnnymi *v.* (7x)
στρωννύω strōnnýō [simpler]
στρόω strṓō
[prolongation from a still simpler form (used as an alternate in certain tenses)]
Compare:G2693 G5291 See:G0792 G4731 G4765-7
G4766.2 V-IAI-3P ἐστρώννυον (2x)
Mt 21:8 from the trees, and they·were·spreading *them* out in
Mk 11:8 of·the trees, and they·were·spreading *them* out in
G4766.2 V-AAI-3P ἔστρωσαν (2x)
Mt 21:8 the very·large crowd spread·out their·own garments
Mk 11:8 And many spread·out their garments in the roadway
G4766.2 V-RPP-ASN ἐστρωμένον (2x)
Lk 22:12 ·big upper·room having·been·spread·out *for·guests.*
Mk 14:15 upper·room having·been·spread·out *for·guests and*
G4766.3 V-AAM-2S στρῶσον (1x)
Ac 9:34 heals you. Rise·up and toss·aside your *mat.*" And

G4767 στυγνητός stygnētós *adj.* (1x)
Roots:G4768-2 Compare:G0947 G2190 See:G0655 G4768
G4767 A-NPM στυγητοί (1x)
Tit 3:3 malice and envy, detestable·men hating one·another.

G4768 στυγνάζω stygnázō *v.* (2x)
Roots:G4768-2 Compare:G3076 G3710 G0546 G0916 See:G4767 G4768-1
G4768.2 V-PAP-NSM στυγνάζων (1x)
Mt 16:3 the sky is·fiery·red *and* glowering.' O·stage·acting·
G4768.2 V-AAP-NSM στυγνάσας (1x)
Mk 10:22 And after·glowering at the saying, he·went·away

G4769 στῦλος stŷlôs *n.* (4x)
Compare:G1477 See:G2476 xLangAlso:H5982
G4769.1 N-NSM στύλος (1x)
1Ti 3:15 ·citizenry of·the·living God, a·pillar and a·support
G4769.1 N-NPM στύλοι (2x)
Gal 2:9 the·ones seeming to·be pillars, they·gave to·me and
Rv 10:1 face *was* as the sun, and his feet as pillars of·fire.
G4769.1 N-ASM στύλον (1x)
Rv 3:12 the·one overcoming, I·shall·make a·pillar in the

G4770 Στωϊκός Stōïkós *adj/g.* (1x)
Roots:G4745 Compare:G1946
G4770 A/G-GPM Στωϊκῶν (1x)
Ac 17:18 Epicureans and of·the Stoics were·engaging him.

G4771 σύ sý *p:p.* (178x)
See:G4571 G4671 G4675 G5209 G5210 G5213 G5216
xLangEquiv:H0859 xLangAlso:H0859-1
(abbreviated listing for G4771)

Σσ

G4771.1 P:P-2NS σύ (56x)
(list for G4771.1:P:P-2NS excluded)
G4771.2 P:P-2NS σύ (122x)
(list for G4771.2:P:P-2NS excluded)

G4772 συγγένεια syngénêia *n.* (4x)
Roots:G4773 Compare:G1085
G4772.2 N-ASF συγγένειαν (1x)
Ac 7:14 his father Jacob and all his kinsfolk, in *all*, seventy
G4772.2 N-DSF συγγενείᾳ (1x)
Lk 1:61 ·is not·even·one among your kinsfolk that is·called
G4772.2 N-GSF συγγενείας (1x)
Ac 7:3 and from·among your kinsfolk, and come·over·here
EG4772.2 (1x)
Mk 3:21 And the·ones near *of·kin·to* him, hearing *of·it*, went·

G4773 συγ•γενής syngenếs *adj.* (14x)
Roots:G4862 G1085 Compare:G5546 See:G4772 xLangAlso:H1350
G4773.1 A-NSM συγγενής (1x)
Jn 18:26 ·priest, being a·kinsman of·him·whose earlobe
G4773.1 A-APM συγγενεῖς (2x)
Lk 14:12 your brothers, nor·even your kinsmen, nor·even
Ac 10:24 was calling·together his kinsmen and very·close
G4773.1 A-DPM συγγενέσιν (1x)
Mk 6:4 fatherland, and among his kinsmen, and in his·own
G4773.1 A-GPM συγγενῶν (2x)
Lk 21:16 parents, and brothers, and kinsmen, and friends;
Rm 9:3 of·my brothers, my kinsmen according·to flesh,
G4773.2 A-NPM συγγενεῖς (1x)
Lk 1:58 ·surrounding·neighbors and her kinsfolk heard that
G4773.2 A-DPM συγγενέσιν (1x)
Lk 2:44 ·seeking him among the kinsfolk and among the
EG4773.2 (1x)
Mk 5:19 to your house, to your *kinsfolk*, and report·in·detail
G4773.3 A-NSF συγγενής (1x)
Lk 1:36 "And behold, your cousin EliSabeth, she·herself *is*
G4773.5 A-NPM συγγενεῖς (1x)
Rm 16:21 and SosiPater, my Redeemed·Kinsmen, greet yeu.
G4773.5 A-ASM συγγενῆ (1x)
Rm 16:11 Greet HerOdion, my Redeemed·Kinsman. Greet
G4773.5 A-APM συγγενεῖς (1x)
Rm 16:7 and Junianus, my Redeemed·Kinsmen and my
EG4773.5 (1x)
Eph 1:12 to·be us, *his Redeemed-Kinsmen*, for a·high·praise

G4774 συγ•γνώμη syngnṓmē *n.* (1x)
Roots:G4862 G1097 Compare:G2011 G1849
G4774.2 N-ASF συγγνώμην (1x)
1Co 7:6 But I·say this in concession *concerning becoming*

G4775 συγ•κάθ•ημαι synkáthēmai *v.* (2x)
Roots:G4862 G2521
G4775.2 V-PNP-NSM συγκαθήμενος (1x)
Mk 14:54 ·high·priest. And he·was sitting·together with the
G4775.2 V-PNP-NPM συγκαθήμενοι (1x)
Ac 26:30 and the·ones *who·were* sitting·together with·them.

G4776 συγ•καθ•ίζω synkathízō *v.* (2x)
Roots:G4862 G2523
G4776.2 V-AAI-3S συνεκάθισεν (1x)
Eph 2:6 ·*us*·together and sat·*us*·down·together in the
G4776.2 V-AAP-GPM συγκαθισάντων (1x)
Lk 22:55 of·the courtyard and sitting·down·together, Peter

G4777 συγ•κακο•παθέω synkakôpathéō *v.* (1x)
Roots:G4862 G2553
G4777 V-AAM-2S συγκακοπάθησον (1x)
2Ti 1:8 but·rather you·must·endure·hardship·together in·the

G4778 συγ•κακο•υχέω synkakôuchéō *v.* (1x)
Roots:G4862 G2558
G4778.2 V-PNN συγκακουχεῖσθαι (1x)
Heb 11:25 rather to·be·maltreated·together with·the People

G4779 συγ•καλέω synkaléō *v.* (8x)
Roots:G4862 G2564 Compare:G1573-1 G4341
G4779 V-PAI-3S συγκαλεῖ (1x)
Lk 15:6 to the house, he·calls·together the friends and the
G4779 V-PAI-3P συγκαλοῦσιν (1x)
Mk 15:16 Praetorian·hall. And they·call·together the whole
G4779 V-PMI-3S συγκαλεῖται (1x)
Lk 15:9 ·then after·finding *it*, she·calls·together the friends
G4779 V-AAI-3P συνεκάλεσαν (1x)
Ac 5:21 they·called·together the joint·council·of·Sanhedrin
G4779 V-AMN συγκαλέσασθαι (1x)
Ac 28:17 ·happened *that* Paul called·together the·ones being
G4779 V-AMP-NSM συγκαλεσάμενος (3x)
Lk 9:1 And calling·together his twelve disciples, he·gave
Lk 23:13 And after·calling·together the chief·priests, the
Ac 10:24 them, Cornelius was calling·together his kinsmen

G4780 συγ•καλύπτω synkalýptō *v.* (1x)
Roots:G4862 G2572
G4780 V-RPP-NSN συγκεκαλυμμένον (1x)
Lk 12:2 ·even·one·thing having·been·altogether·concealed

G4781 συγ•κάμπτω synkámptō *v.* (1x)
Roots:G4862 G2578
G4781.2 V-AAM-2S σύγκαμψον (1x)
Rm 11:10 their back continually *be* altogether·bent·over."

G4782 συγ•κατα•βαίνω synkatabaínō *v.* (1x)
Roots:G4862 G2597
G4782 V-2AAP-NPM συγκαταβάντες (1x)
Ac 25:5 able *to·do so*, after·walking·down·together *with·me*,

G4783 συγ•κατά•θεσις synkatáthêsis *n.* (1x)
Roots:G4784 Compare:G4857 G4859
G4783.2 N-NSF συγκατάθεσις (1x)
2Co 6:16 And what mutual·compact has·a·temple of·God

G4784 συγ•κατα•τίθεμαι synkatatíthêmai *v.* (1x)
Roots:G4862 G2698 Compare:G2702 See:G4783
G4784.2 V-RNP-NSM συγκατατεθειμένος (1x)
Lk 23:51 was not having·voted·together with·the counsel

G4785 συγ•κατα•ψηφίζω synkatapsēphízō *v.* (1x)
Roots:G4862 G2596 G5585 Compare:G2674
G4785 V-API-3S συγκατεψηφίσθη (1x)
Ac 1:26 And he·was·fully·counted·together with the eleven

G4786 συγ•κεράννυμι synkêránnymi *v.* (2x)
Roots:G4862 G2767 Compare:G4830-3 G1470 G4797 G4822 G4854
G4786.1 V-AAI-3S συνεκέρασεν (1x)
1Co 12:24 need, but·yet God blended·together the Body,
G4786.2 V-RPP-NSM συγκεκραμένος (1x)
Heb 4:2 not having·been·combined·together with·the Trust

G4787 συγ•κινέω synkinéō *v.* (1x)
Roots:G4862 G2795 See:G3334
G4787.1 V-AAI-3P συνεκίνησαν (1x)
Ac 6:12 And they·jointly·stirred·up the people, the elders,

G4788 συγ•κλείω synklêíō *v.* (4x)
Roots:G4862 G2808
G4788.2 V-AAI-3S συνέκλεισεν (2x)
Gal 3:22 the Scripture jointly·confined all·things under
Rm 11:32 For God jointly·confined all the *peoples* to an·
G4788.2 V-RPP-NPM συγκεκλεισμένοι (1x)
Gal 3:23 having·been·jointly·confined in·order·for the
G4788.3 V-AAI-3P συνέκλεισαν (1x)
Lk 5:6 ·doing this, they·tightly·enclosed a·large multitude

G4789 συγ•κληρο•νόμος synklērônómôs *adj.* (4x)
Roots:G4862 G2818
G4789.1 A-NPM συγκληρονόμοι (2x)
Rm 8:17 in·fact of·God and co-heirs with·Anointed-One,
1Pe 3:7 as also *being* co-heirs of·*the*·grace of·life-above, in·
G4789.1 A-APN συγκληρονόμα (1x)
Eph 3:6 *as·for* the Gentiles to·be co-heirs, co-members, and
G4789.1 A-GPM συγκληρονόμων (1x)
Heb 11:9 and Jacob, the co-heirs of·the same promise,

G4790 συγ•κοινωνέω synkôinōnéō *v.* (3x)
Roots:G4862 G2841
G4790.1 V-AAP-NPM συγκοινωνήσαντες (1x)
Php 4:14 yeu·did well sharing·together in·my tribulation.
G4790.1 V-AAS-2P συγκοινωνήσητε (1x)
Rv 18:4 yeu·may·not share·together in·her moral·failures,
G4790.2 V-PAM-2P συγκοινωνεῖτε (1x)
Eph 5:11 And do·not fellowship·together with·the unfruitful

G4791 συγ•κοινωνός synkôinōnós *adj.* (4x)
Roots:G4862 G2844 Compare:G4830 G4805
G4791.2 A-NSM συγκοινωνός (3x)
Rm 11:17 them and became a·partner·together of·the root
1Co 9:23 ·order·that I·may·become a·partner·together of·it.
Rv 1:9 I, John, also yeur brother and partner·together in the
G4791.2 A-APM συγκοινωνούς (1x)
Php 1:7 yeu all are·being partners·together with·me of·the

G4792 συγ•κομίζω synkômízō *v.* (1x)
Roots:G4862 G2865 Compare:G2290 See:G1580
G4792.2 V-AAI-3P συνεκόμισαν (1x)
Ac 8:2 men went·in·procession·together·to·bury Stephen,

G4793 συγ•κρίνω synkrínō *v.* (5x)
Roots:G4862 G2919 Compare:G3354 See:G0799
G4793.2 V-PAP-NPM συγκρίνοντες (2x)
1Co 2:13 comparing spiritual·things with·spiritual·things.
2Co 10:12 and comparing themselves to·themselves, do·not
G4793.2 V-AAN συγκρῖναι (1x)
2Co 10:12 ·those, or to·compare ourselves with·some *who·*
EG4793.2 (2x)
Rm 8:18 season *are* not worthy *to·be·compared* alongside the
1Co 4:6 ·up over the *other*, *comparing* one against the other.

G4794 συγ•κύπτω synkýptō *v.* (1x)
Roots:G4862 G2955
G4794 V-PAP-NSF συγκύπτουσα (1x)
Lk 13:11 years, and was altogether·stooping·over, and not

G4795 συγ•κυρία synkyría *n.* (1x)
Roots:G4862 G2962
G4795 N-ASF συγκυρίαν (1x)
Lk 10:31 "And by coincidence, a·certain priest·that offers·

G4796 συγ•χαίρω synchaírō *v.* (7x)
Roots:G4862 G5463
G4796 V-PAI-1S συγχαίρω (1x)
Php 2:17 ·rejoice and·also do·rejoice·together with·yeu all.
G4796 V-PAI-3S συγχαίρει (2x)
1Co 12:26 is·glorified, all the members rejoice·together.
1Co 13:6 the injustice, but it·rejoices·together with·the truth
G4796 V-PAM-2P συγχαίρετε (1x)
Php 2:18 must·rejoice and must·rejoice·together with·me.
G4796 V-IAI-3P συνέχαιρον (1x)
Lk 1:58 with her, and they·were·rejoicing·together with·her.
G4796 V-2AOM-2P συγχάρητε (2x)
Lk 15:6 saying to·them, 'Rejoice·together with·me, because
Lk 15:9 close·neighbors saying, 'Rejoice·together with·me,

G4797 συγ•χέω synchéō *v.* (5x)
συγ•χύνω synchýnō
Roots:G4862 G5502-5 Compare:G1280 See:G4799
G4797.2 V-IAI-3P συνέχεον (1x)
Ac 21:27 Sanctuary·Courtyard, they·were·stirring·up all the
G4797.2 V-RPI-3S συγκέχυται (1x)
Ac 21:31 all JeruSalem has·been·stirred·up·into·an·uproar,
G4797.3 V-IAI-3S συνέχυνεν (1x)
Ac 9:22 *all* the·more, and was·confounding the Jews, the·
G4797.4 V-API-3S συνεχύθη (1x)
Ac 2:6 came·together and was·greatly·confused, because
G4797.4 V-RPP-NSF συγκεχυμένη (1x)
Ac 19:32 ·citizens was having·been·greatly·confused. And

G4798 συγ•χράομαι synchráômai *v.* (1x)
Roots:G4862 G5530
G4798.2 V-PNI-3P συγχρῶνται (1x)
Jn 4:9 woman?" (for Jews do·not interact with·Samaritans).

G4799 σύγ•χυσις sýnchysis *n.* (1x)
Roots:G4797 Compare:G4792-2 See:G0897 xLangAlso:H0894
G4799.2 N-GSF συγχύσεως (1x)
Ac 19:29 whole city was·filled with·mass·confusion. And

G4800 συ•ζάω syzáō *v.* (3x)
Roots:G4862 G2198
G4800 V-FAI-1P συζήσομεν (2x)
Rm 6:8 we·trust also that we·shall·live·together with·him,
2Ti 2:11 *with·him*, also we·shall·live·together *with·him*.
G4800 V-PAN συζῆν (1x)

2Co 7:3 for *us* to·die·together and to·live·together *with·yeu.*

G4801 συ•ζεύγνυμι syzeúgnymi *v.* (5x)
Roots:G4862 G2201 See:G4805
G4801.1 V-AAI-3S συνέζευξεν (2x)
Mt 19:6 what God yoked·together, a·man·of·clay† must·not
Mk 10:9 what God yoked·together, a·man·of·clay† must·
EG4801.1 (3x)
Rm 7:2 the wife *yoked·together* under·a·husband has·been·
Rm 7:3 by·becoming *yoked·together* with·another man.
Rm 7:4 *such* for yeu to·become *yoked·together* with·another,

G4802 συ•ζητέω syzētéō *v.* (10x)
Roots:G4862 G2212 Compare:G1252 G0350 G0426 See:G2214 G4804
G4802.2 V-PAI-2P συζητεῖτε (1x)
Mk 9:16 "What·do yeu·mutually·question·and·discuss
G4802.2 V-PAN συζητεῖν (2x)
Mk 1:27 ·for *them* to·mutually·question·and·discuss among
Mk 8:11 began to·mutually·question·and·discuss with·him,
G4802.2 V-PAP-APM συζητοῦντας (1x)
Mk 9:14 and scribes mutually·questioning·and·discussing *a·*
G4802.2 V-PAP-NPM συζητοῦντες (1x)
Ac 6:9 mutually·questioning·and·discussing with·Stephen.
G4802.2 V-IAI-3S συνεζήτει (1x)
Ac 9:29 also he·was·mutually·questioning·and·discussing
G4802.3 V-PAN συζητεῖν (2x)
Lk 22:23 began to·question·and·discuss among themselves,
Lk 24:15 then questioning·and·discussing *these·things,*
G4802.3 V-PAP-GPM συζητούντων (1x)
Mk 12:28 of·them questioning·and·discussing·together, one
G4802.3 V-PAP-NPM συζητοῦντες (1x)
Mk 9:10 questioning·and·discussing·with·one·another what

G4803 συ•ζήτησις syzḗtēsis *n.* (3x)
Roots:G4802
G4803 N-ASF συζήτησιν (1x)
Ac 28:29 having a·large questioning·and·discussion among
G4803 N-GSF συζητήσεως (2x)
Ac 15:2 and with·mutual·questioning·and·discussion
Ac 15:7 And with·much mutual·questioning·and·discussion,

G4804 συ•ζητητής syzētētḗs *n.* (1x)
Roots:G4802 Compare:G5386 G1261 See:G2214 G2213
G4804.2 N-NSM συζητητής (1x)
1Co 1:20 scribe? Where *is the* disputer of·this present·age?

G4805 σύ•ζυγος sýzygôs *adj.* (1x)
Roots:G4801 Compare:G3353 G4791 G4830
G4805.2 A-VSM σύζυγε (1x)
Php 4:3 you also, a·genuine yokefellow, assist these·same·

G4806 συ•ζωοποιέω syzōôpôiéō *v.* (2x)
Roots:G4862 G2227
G4806.2 V-AAI-3S συνεζωοποίησεν (2x)
Eph 2:5 he·made·*us*·alive·together in·the Anointed-One
Col 2:13 flesh, he·made·*yeu*·alive·together along·with him,

G4807 συκά•μινος sykáminôs *adj.* (1x)
שָׁקָם shaqam [Hebrew]
Roots:H8256 Compare:G4808 See:G4809 G4806-1
G4807.1 A-DSM συκαμίνῳ (1x)
Lk 17:6 *does,* yeu·might say to·this mulberry-fig·tree, 'Be·

G4808 συκῆ sykē̂ *n.* (16x)
Roots:G4810 Compare:G4809 G4807 See:G4808-1
G4808 N-NSF συκῆ (5x)
Mt 21:19 And at·once the fig·tree is·withered·away.
Mt 21:20 "How·is the fig·tree withered·away *all* at·once?
Mk 11:21 see, the fig·tree which you·did·curse has·been·
Jac 3:12 ¿!·Is a·fig·tree able, my brothers, to·produce olives?
Rv 6:13 earth, as *when* a·fig·tree casts its unripe·green·figs
G4808 N-ASF συκῆν (6x)
Jn 1:48 ·out·for you, I·saw you being under the fig·tree."
Lk 13:6 was·holding·onto a·fig·tree having·been·planted in
Lk 21:29 ·them a·parable: "See the fig·tree, and all the trees.
Mt 21:19 And seeing one fig·tree by the roadway, he·came
Mk 11:13 And after·seeing a·fig·tree in·the·distance having
Mk 11:20 ·saw the fig·tree having·been·withered from·out
G4808 N-DSF συκῇ (1x)
Lk 13:7 I·come seeking fruit on this fig·tree and find none.
G4808 N-GSF συκῆς (4x)
Jn 1:50 'I·saw you beneath the fig·tree,' do·you·trust?
Mt 21:21 the·thing *that is·done* to·the fig·tree, but·yet also·if
Mt 24:32 "Now from the fig·tree, yeu·must·learn the parable
Mk 13:28 "Now from the fig·tree, yeu·must·learn the parable

G4809 συκο•μωραία sykômōraía *n.* (1x)
Roots:G4810 Compare:G4808 See:G4807 xLangEquiv:H8256
G4809.1 N-ASF συκομωραίαν (1x)
Lk 19:4 upon a·mulberry-fig·tree in·order·that he·may·see

G4810 σῦκον sŷkôn *n.* (4x)
Compare:G3653 See:G4808 G4808-1
G4810 N-APN σῦκα (3x)
Lk 6:44 For not from·out of·thorns do·men·collect figs, nor
Mt 7:16 ·of·grapes from thorns, or figs from spear·thistles?
Jac 3:12 olives? Or a·vine, figs? In·this·manner, not·even·
G4810 N-GPN σύκων (1x)
Mk 11:13 except leaves, for it·was not *the* season for·figs.

G4811 συκο•φαντέω sykôphantéō *v.* (2x)
Roots:G4810 G5316 See:G4811-1 G4811-2
G4811.3 V-AAI-1S ἐσυκοφάντησα (1x)
Lk 19:8 and if I·extorted·by·false·charges anything *from*
G4811.3 V-AAS-2P συκοφαντήσητε (1x)
Lk 3:14 nor·even should·yeu·extort·by·false·charges, and

G4812 συλ•αγωγέω sylagōgéō *v.* (1x)
Roots:G4813 G0071
G4812.2 V-PAP-NSM συλαγωγῶν (1x)
Col 2:8 lest any·man shall·be the·one seducing yeu through

G4813 συλάω syláō *v.* (1x)
Compare:G0650 G4661 See:G4812 G2417 G0138
G4813.2 V-AAI-1S ἐσύλησα (1x)
2Co 11:8 I·despoiled other Called·Out·citizenries, taking

G4814 συ•λλαλέω syllaléō *v.* (6x)
Roots:G4862 G2980
G4814 V-PAP-NPM συλλαλοῦντες (2x)
Mt 17:3 ·made·visible to·them, speaking·together with him.
Mk 9:4 and they·were speaking·together with·Jesus.
G4814 V-IAI-3P συνελάλουν (2x)
Lk 4:36 and they·were·speaking·together among one·another
Lk 9:30 behold, two men were·speaking·together with·him,
G4814 V-AAI-3S συνελάλησεν (1x)
Lk 22:4 going·off, he·spoke·together with·the chief·priests
G4814 V-AAP-NSM συλλαλήσας (1x)
Ac 25:12 Then Festus, speaking·together with the council,

G4815 συ•λλαμβάνω syllambánō *v.* (16x)
Roots:G4862 G2983 Compare:G4084
G4815.2 V-2AAI-3P συνέλαβον (1x)
Jn 18:12 and the assistants of·the Judeans arrested Jesus and
G4815.2 V-2AAN συλλαβεῖν (3x)
Ac 12:3 Judeans, he·further·proceeded to·arrest Peter also.
Mt 26:55 ·robber with daggers and staffs to·arrest me?
Mk 14:48 ·robber, with daggers and staffs to·arrest me?
G4815.2 V-2AAP-DPM συλλαβοῦσιν (1x)
Ac 1:16 ·one becoming a·guide to·the·ones arresting Jesus),
G4815.2 V-2AAP-NPM συλλαβόντες (1x)
Lk 22:54 And arresting him, they·led *him* and brought him
G4815.2 V-2AMP-NPM συλλαβόμενοι (1x)
Ac 26:21 ·things, the Judeans, upon·arresting me in the
G4815.2 V-APP-ASM συλληφθέντα (1x)
Ac 23:27 This man *was* already·being·arrested by the
G4815.3 V-FDI-2S συλλήψῃ (1x)
Lk 1:31 And behold, you·shall·conceive in your·uterus and
G4815.3 V-2AAI-3S συνέλαβεν (1x)
Lk 1:24 wife EliSabeth conceived and was·entirely·hiding
G4815.3 V-2AAP-NSF συλλαβοῦσα (1x)
Jac 1:15 ·the longing conceiving, it·reproduces·and·births
G4815.3 V-APN συλληφθῆναι (1x)
Lk 2:21 the angel prior·to him being·conceived in the womb.
G4815.3 V-RAP-NSF συνειληφυῖα (1x)
Lk 1:36 she·herself *is* also having·conceived a·son in her
G4815.4 V-PMM-2S συλλαμβάνου (1x)
Php 4:3 ·genuine yokefellow, assist these·same·women who
G4815.4 V-2AMN συλλαβέσθαι (1x)
Lk 5:7 other sailboat *that·was* already·coming to·assist them.
G4815.5 V-2AAI-3P συνέλαβον (1x)
Lk 5:9 ·him) over the catch of·the fish which they·caught.

G4816 συ•λλέγω syllégō *v.* (8x)
Roots:G4862 G3004 Compare:G0270 G4863 G1865 G4962 See:G3048
G4816.3 V-FAI-3P συλλέξουσιν (1x)
Mt 13:41 his angels, and they·shall·collect from·out of·his
G4816.3 V-PAI-3P συλλέγουσιν (2x)
Lk 6:44 For not from·out of·thorns do·men·collect figs, nor
Mt 7:16 "¿!·Do men·collect a·cluster·of·grapes from thorns,
G4816.3 V-PAP-NPM συλλέγοντες (1x)
Mt 13:29 'No, lest while·collecting the darnel·weeds, yeu·
G4816.3 V-PPI-3S συλλέγεται (1x)
Mt 13:40 the darnel·weeds are·collected and are·completely·
G4816.3 V-AAI-3P συνέλεξαν (1x)
Mt 13:48 shore and sitting·down, they·collected the good
G4816.3 V-AAM-2P συλλέξατε (1x)
Mt 13:30 to·the reapers, "Collect the darnel·weeds first and
G4816.3 V-AAS-1P συλλέξωμεν (1x)
Mt 13:28 ·want *us* to·go·off *so·that* we·may·collect them?

G4817 συ•λλογίζομαι syllôgízômai *v.* (1x)
Roots:G4862 G3049
G4817 V-ADI-3P συνελογίσαντο (1x)
Lk 20:5 And they·reckoned·together alongside themselves,

G4818 συ•λλυπέω syllypéō *v.* (1x)
Roots:G4862 G3076
G4818.1 V-PNP-NSM συλλυπούμενος (1x)
Mk 3:5 with wrath, while·being·jointly·grieved over the

G4819 συμ•βαίνω symbaínō *v.* (8x)
Roots:G4862 G0901-3
G4819.2 V-PAN συμβαίνειν (1x)
Mk 10:32 to·them the impending·things·about to·befall him,
G4819.2 V-PAP-GSN συμβαίνοντος (1x)
1Pe 4:12 , as·though *it·is* a·strange·new·thing befalling yeu.
G4819.2 V-IAI-3P συνέβαινον (1x)
1Co 10:11 these impressive·examples were·befalling them,
G4819.2 V-2AAI-3S συνέβη (1x)
Ac 21:35 stairs, *the need* befell him to·be·lifted·and·carried
G4819.2 V-2AAP-GPM συμβάντων (1x)
Ac 20:19 and with·proof·trials, the·ones befalling me by the
G4819.2 V-RAI-3S συμβέβηκεν (1x)
2Pe 2:22 But it·has·befallen them *according·to* the true
G4819.2 V-RAP-DSN συμβεβηκότι (1x)
Ac 3:10 and astonishment at the·thing having·befallen him.
G4819.2 V-RAP-GPN συμβεβηκότων (1x)
Lk 24:14 all these·things having·befallen *in·JeruSalem.*

G4820 συμ•βάλλω symbállō *v.* (6x)
Roots:G4862 G0906 Compare:G2853 G4345 G1260 G5426
G4820.2 V-2AAI-3P συνέβαλον (1x)
Ac 4:15 they·rigorously·conferred among one·another,
G4820.3 V-PAP-NSF συμβάλλουσα (1x)
Lk 2:19 all these utterances, ruminating *on·them* in her heart.
G4820.4 V-2AAI-3S συνέβαλεν (1x)
Ac 20:14 And as he·joined·on with·us at Assos, after·taking
G4820.5 V-2AMI-3S συνεβάλετο (1x)
Ac 18:27 ·publicly, joined·in·and·helped *them* much, the·
G4820.6 V-IAI-3P συνέβαλλον (1x)
Ac 17:18 Epicureans and of·the Stoics were·engaging him.
G4820.7 V-2AAN συμβαλεῖν (1x)
Lk 14:31 king, who·is·traversing to·engage·in war against

G4821 συμ•βασιλεύω symbasileúō *v.* (2x)
Roots:G4862 G0936
G4821.1 V-FAI-1P συμβασιλεύσομεν (1x)
2Ti 2:12 ·endure, we·also shall·reign·together *with·him.* "If
G4821.1 V-AAS-1P συμβασιλεύσωμεν (1x)
1Co 4:8 we·ourselves also may·reign·together with·yeu!

G4822 συμ•βιβάζω symbibázō *v.* (6x)
Roots:G4862 G0973-1 Compare:G1246 G4786 G4854 G2919 G1011 G4907-3 See:G1688 G2601 xLangAlso:H8505

G4822.2 V-PPP-NSN συμβιβαζόμενον (1x)
Col 2:19 and being·knit·together with·the maturing·growth

G4822.2 V-APP-GPM συμβιβασθέντων (1x)
Col 2:2 may·be·comforted, being·knit·together in love, and

G4822.3 V-PPP-NSN συμβιβαζόμενον (1x)
Eph 4:16 and is·being·united·together through every amply·

G4822.4 V-FAI-3S συμβιβάσει (1x)
1Co 2:16 that he·shall·conclusively·weigh·a·matter·for him?

G4822.4 V-PAP-NPM συμβιβάζοντες (1x)
Ac 16:10 to·go·forth into Macedonia, concluding that the

G4822.5 V-PAP-NSM συμβιβάζων (1x)
Ac 9:22 in Damascus, *by* conclusively·proving that this is

G4823 συμ•βουλεύω symbôulêúō *v.* (5x)
Roots:G4862 G1011

G4823.1 V-PAI-1S συμβουλεύω (1x)
Rv 3:18 'I·jointly·give·counsel to·you to·buy personally·

G4823.1 V-AAP-NSM συμβουλεύσας (1x)
Jn 18:14 was the·one jointly·giving·counsel to·the Judeans,

G4823.2 V-AMI-3P συνεβουλεύσαντο (3x)
Jn 11:53 they·took·counsel·among·themselves in·order·that
Ac 9:23 Jews took·counsel·among·themselves to·eliminate
Mt 26:4 and they·took·counsel·among·themselves in·order·

G4824 συμ•βούλιον symbôúliôn *n.* (8x)
Roots:G4825

G4824.1 N-ASN συμβούλιον (7x)
Mt 12:14 upon·going·forth, took consultation against him,
Mt 22:15 took consultation on·specifically·how they·should·
Mt 27:1 of·the people took consultation against YeShua
Mt 27:7 And after·taking consultation, from·out of·the·same
Mt 28:12 the elders and taking consultation, they·gave a·
Mk 3:6 immediately were·making consultation with the
Mk 15:1 the chief·priests, after·making consultation with the

G4824.2 N-GSN συμβουλίου (1x)
Ac 25:12 speaking·together with the council, answered,

G4825 σύμ•βουλος sýmbôulôs *n.* (1x)
Roots:G4862 G1012 See:G1010 xLangAlso:H3289

G4825 N-NSM σύμβουλος (1x)
Rm 11:34 Yahweh's mind? Or who became his counselor?"'

G4826 Συμεών Symeṓn *n/p.* (7x)
שִׁמְעוֹן shim'ôn [Hebrew]
Roots:H8095 Compare:G4613

G4826.3 N/P-PRI Συμεών (1x)
Rv 7:7 *the* tribe of·Shimon having·been·officially·sealed,

G4826.5 N/P-PRI Συμεών (2x)
Ac 15:14 Shimon *Peter* recounted·in·detail *that* just·as at·
2Pe 1:1 Shimon Peter, a·slave and an·ambassador of·

G4826.6 N/P-PRI Συμεών (2x)
Lk 2:25 JeruSalem, whose name *was* Simeon, and the·same
Lk 2:34 And Simeon blessed them, and he·declared to

G4826.7 N/P-PRI Συμεών (1x)
Lk 3:30 *son* of·Shimeon, *son* of·Yehudah, *son* of·Yoseph,

G4826.8 N/P-PRI Συμεών (1x)
Ac 13:1 as·follows: BarNabas, Simeon (the·one being·

G4827 συμ•μαθητής symmathētḗs *n.* (1x)
Roots:G4862 G3101 See:G3102

G4827.2 N-DPM συμμαθηταῖς (1x)
Jn 11:16 ·as Twin) declared to·the fellow·disciples, "We·

G4828 συμ•μαρτυρέω symmartyréō *v.* (4x)
Roots:G4862 G3140

G4828 V-PAI-3S συμμαρτυρεῖ (1x)
Rm 8:16 The Spirit himself jointly·testifies with·our spirit

G4828 V-PAP-GSF συμμαρτυρούσης (2x)
Rm 2:15 hearts, with·their conscience jointly·testifying, and
Rm 9:1 lie, with·my conscience jointly·testifying with·me in

G4828 V-PNI-1S συμμαρτυροῦμαι (1x)
Rv 22:18 For I·jointly·testify to·everyone hearing the words

G4829 συμ•μερίζομαι symmerízômai *v.* (1x)
Roots:G4862 G3307

G4829 V-PNI-3P συμμερίζονται (1x)
1Co 9:13 to·the Sacrifice·Altar participate·together in·the

G4830 συμ•μέτοχος symmétôchôs *adj.* (2x)
Roots:G4862 G3353 Compare:G4791 G4805

G4830 A-NPM συμμέτοχοι (1x)
Eph 5:7 do·not become co-participants with·them.

G4830 A-APN συμμέτοχα (1x)
Eph 3:6 co-members, and co-participants of·his promise in

G4831 συμ•μιμητής symmimētḗs *n.* (1x)
Roots:G4862 G3401

G4831 N-NPM συμμιμηταί (1x)
Php 3:17 Become co-imitators of·me, brothers, and keep·a·

G4832 σύμ•μορφος sýmmôrphôs *adj.* (2x)
Roots:G4862 G3444 Compare:G4964

G4832.2 A-ASN σύμμορφον (1x)
Php 3:21 to·become fundamentally·in·nature·like the body

G4832.2 A-APM συμμόρφους (1x)
Rm 8:29 *to·become* fundamentally·in·nature·like the

G4833 συμ•μορφόω symmôrphóō *v.* (1x)
Roots:G4832 Compare:G3339 G3345 G3666

G4833.1 V-PPP-NSM συμμορφούμενος (1x)
Php 3:10 becoming·fundamentally·like·him in·his death—

G4834 συμ•παθέω sympathéō *v.* (2x)
Roots:G4835

G4834.2 V-AAI-2P συνεπαθήσατε (1x)
Heb 10:34 For even yeu·sympathized with·my bonds, and

G4834.2 V-AAN συμπαθῆσαι (1x)
Heb 4:15 ·not being·able to·sympathize with·our weaknesses

G4835 συμ•παθής sympathḗs *adj.* (1x)
Roots:G4841

G4835.2 A-NPM συμπαθεῖς (1x)
1Pe 3:8 sympathetic·toward·one·another, affectionate·as·

G4836 συμ•παρα•γίνομαι symparagínômai *v.* (2x)
Roots:G4862 G3854 Compare:G4867 G4871 G4863

G4836.3 V-2ADP-NPM συμπαραγενόμενοι (1x)
Lk 23:48 And all the crowds convening·publicly upon that

G4836.4 V-2ADI-3S συμπαρεγένετο (1x)
2Ti 4:16 not·even·one·man appeared·publicly·together with·

G4837 συμ•παρα•καλέω symparakaléō *v.* (1x)
Roots:G4862 G3870

G4837 V-APN συμπαρακληθῆναι (1x)
Rm 1:12 that is, to·be·comforted·together among yeu

G4838 συμ•παρα•λαμβάνω symparalambánō *v.* (4x)
Roots:G4862 G3880

G4838 V-2AAN συμπαραλαβεῖν (2x)
Ac 15:37 resolutely·purposed to·personally·take·along John,
Ac 15:38 considering·it·appropriate to·personally·take·along

G4838 V-2AAP-NSM συμπαραλαβών (1x)
Gal 2:1 with BarNabas, personally·taking·along Titus also.

G4838 V-2AAP-NPM συμπαραλαβόντες (1x)
Ac 12:25 the service (and·also personally·taking·along John,

G4839 συμ•παρα•μένω symparaménō *v.* (1x)
Roots:G4862 G3887

G4839.2 V-FAI-1S συμπαραμενῶ (1x)
Php 1:25 ·abide and shall·continue·together with·yeu all for

G4840 συμ•πάρειμι sympárêimi *v.* (1x)
Roots:G4862 G3918

G4840.2 V-PXP-NPM συμπαρόντες (1x)
Ac 25:24 and all the men being·present·together with·us,

G4841 συμ•πάσχω sympáschō *v.* (2x)
Roots:G4862 G3958

G4841.1 V-PAI-1P συμπάσχομεν (1x)
Rm 8:17 since we·suffer·together *with·him* in·order·that

G4841.1 V-PAI-3S συμπάσχει (1x)
1Co 12:26 all the members suffer·together *with·it*; or·if one

G4842 συμ•πέμπω sympémpō *v.* (2x)
Roots:G4862 G3992

G4842 V-AAI-1P συνεπέμψαμεν (2x)
2Co 8:18 But·also, we·sent·together with him the brother,
2Co 8:22 And we·sent·together with·them our brother,

G4843 συμ•περι•λαμβάνω sympêrilambánō *v.* (1x)
Roots:G4862 G4012 G2983 Compare:G0782 G1968 G4023 See:G2638 G1949

G4843.1 V-2AAP-NSM συμπεριλαβών (1x)
Ac 20:10 him, and after·altogether·enclosing·about *him*, he·

G4844 συμ•πίνω sympínō *v.* (1x)
Roots:G4862 G4095 See:G4849

G4844 V-2AAI-1P συνεπίομεν (1x)
Ac 10:41 who ate·together and drank·together with·him after

G4845 συμ•πληρόω symplēróō *v.* (3x)
Roots:G4862 G4137

G4845.2 V-IPI-3P συνεπληροῦντο (1x)
Lk 8:23 the lake, and they·were·swamped *with·water* and

G4845.4 V-PPN συμπληροῦσθαι (2x)
Lk 9:51 days to·be·completely·fulfilled for·his being·taken·
Ac 2:1 of·Pentecost to·be·completely·fulfilled, they·were

G4846 συμ•πνίγω sympnígō *v.* (5x)
Roots:G4862 G4155 Compare:G4729 See:G0638

G4846.1 V-PAI-3S συμπνίγει (1x)
Mt 13:22 of·wealth altogether·choke the Redemptive-word,

G4846.1 V-PAI-3P συμπνίγουσιν (1x)
Mk 4:19 — they·altogether·choke the Redemptive-word, and

G4846.1 V-PPI-3P συμπνίγονται (1x)
Lk 8:14 while·traversing, are·altogether·choked by anxieties

G4846.1 V-AAI-3P συνέπνιξαν (1x)
Mk 4:7 the thorns sprung·up and altogether·choked it, and it·

G4846.4 V-IAI-3P συνέπνιγον (1x)
Lk 8:42 ·out, the crowds were·altogether·constricting him.

G4847 συμ•πολίτης sympôlítēs *n.* (1x)
Roots:G4862 G4177 Compare:G4175 G1577

G4847.2 N-NPM συμπολῖται (1x)
Eph 2:19 ·rather *yeu·are* fellow-citizens with·the holy·ones

G4848 συμ•πορεύομαι sympôrêúômai *v.* (4x)
Roots:G4862 G4198

G4848.1 V-PNI-3P συμπορεύονται (1x)
Mk 10:1 again, crowds were·traversing·together toward him

G4848.1 V-INI-3S συνεπορεύετο (1x)
Lk 24:15 drawing·near, traversed·together with·them.

G4848.1 V-INI-3P συνεπορεύοντο (2x)
Lk 7:11 of·his disciples were·traversing·together with·him,
Lk 14:25 large crowds were·traversing·together with·him,

G4849 συμ•πόσιον sympósiôn *n.* (2x)
Roots:G4844

G4849.3 N-APN συμπόσια (2x)
Mk 6:39 them to·make everyone recline, party *by* party,
Mk 6:39 everyone recline, party *by* party, upon the green

G4850 συμ•πρεσβύτερος symprêsbýtêrôs *n.* (1x)
Roots:G4862 G4245 See:G4244

G4850 N-NSM συμπρεσβύτερος (1x)
1Pe 5:1 yeu, I·exhort *as* the fellow-elder, and a·witness of·

G4851 συμ•φέρω symphérō *v.* (18x)
συνενέγκω synênénkō [alternate]
Roots:G4862 G5342 Compare:G5624 G3786 G4050 G5622

EG4851 (1x)
1Co 10:33 advantage, but·rather the *advantage* of·the many

G4851.1 V-2AAP-NPM συνενέγκαντες (1x)
Ac 19:19 ·in·dark·arts, after·bringing·together the scrolls,

G4851.4 V-PAI-3S συμφέρει (7x)
Mt 5:29 *it* from you, for it·is·advantageous for·you that one
Mt 5:30 *it* from you, for it·is·advantageous for·you that one
Mt 19:10 with his wife, it·is·not advantageous to·marry."
1Co 6:12 but·yet not all·things are·advantageous. All·things
1Co 10:23 but·yet not all·things are·advantageous. All·things
2Co 8:10 ·give advice, for this is·advantageous for·yeu, who
2Co 12:1 Now·then, it·is·not advantageous for·me to·boast,

G4851.4 V-PAP-GPN συμφερόντων (1x)
Ac 20:20 ·thing of·the·things being·advantageous *to·yeu*,

G4851.5 V-PAI-3S συμφέρει (4x)
Jn 11:50 ponder that it·is·more·advantageous for·us that one

Jn 16:7 ·yeu the truth; it·is·more·advantageous for·yeu that
Jn 18:14 how·that it·was·more·advantageous *for* one man·
Mt 18:6 trusting in me, it·is·more·advantageous for·him that
G4851.6 V-PAP-ASN συμφέρον (4x)
Heb 12:10 but he *does·so* to *our* advantage, in·order·for *us*
1Co 7:35 this specifically·for yeur own advantage; not that I·
1Co 10:33 not seeking my·own advantage, but·rather the
1Co 12:7 to·each·man specifically·for the advantage *of·all.*

G4852 σύμ•φημι sýmphēmi *v.* (1x)
Roots:G4862 G5346
G4852 V-PXI-1S σύμφημι (1x)
Rm 7:16 which I·do·not want, I·concur with·the Torah-Law

G4852-2 συμφοράζω symphôrázō *v.* (1x)
Compare:G1839 See:G0799-2 xLangAlso:H8539
G4852-2 V-AAM-2P συμφοράσατε (1x)
Ac 13:41 and intently·look, and be·disconcerted. Because I·

G4853 συμ•φυλέτης symphylétēs *n.* (1x)
Roots:G4862 G5443
G4853.2 N-GPM συμφυλετῶν (1x)
1Th 2:14 suffered under yeur·own fellow·countrymen, even

G4854 σύμ•φυτος sýmphytôs *adj.* (1x)
Roots:G4862 G5453 Compare:G4822 G4786 G4797 See:G1631 G5449
G4854.2 A-NPM σύμφυτοι (1x)
Rm 6:5 if we·have·been congenitally·fused·together in·the

G4855 συμ•φύω symphýō *v.* (1x)
Roots:G4862 G5453
G4855 V-2APP-NPF συμφυεῖσαι (1x)
Lk 8:7 being·sprung·up·together·with·it, utterly·choked it.

G4856 συμ•φωνέω symphōnéō *v.* (6x)
Roots:G4859 Compare:G4909 G4934 See:G4857
G4856.3 V-PAI-3S συμφωνεῖ (1x)
Lk 5:36 *garment,* does·not mutually·agree with·the old·one.
G4856.3 V-PAI-3P συμφωνοῦσιν (1x)
Ac 15:15 words of·the prophets do·mutually·agree, just·as it·
G4856.3 V-AAI-2S συνεφώνησας (1x)
Mt 20:13 Did·you·not·indeed mutually·agree with·me for·a·
G4856.3 V-AAP-NSM συμφωνήσας (1x)
Mt 20:2 And after·mutually·agreeing with the workmen *to·*
G4856.3 V-AAS-3P συμφωνήσωσιν (1x)
Mt 18:19 that if two of·yeu should·mutually·agree on the
G4856.3 V-API-3S συνεφωνήθη (1x)
Ac 5:9 yeu are·mutually·agreed·together to·try Yahweh's

G4857 συμ•φώνησις symphṓnēsis *n.* (1x)
Roots:G4856 Compare:G4783
G4857 N-NSF συμφώνησις (1x)
2Co 6:15 And what mutual·agreement has·Anointed-One

G4858 συμ•φωνία symphōnía *n.* (1x)
Roots:G4859
G4858.3 N-GSF συμφωνίας (1x)
Lk 15:25 *and* heard instrumental·music and circle·dancing.

G4859 σύμ•φωνος sýmphōnôs *adj.* (1x)
Roots:G4862 G5456 See:G4856 G4857 G4858
G4859.3 A-GSN συμφώνου (1x)
1Co 7:5 as·a·result of·a·mutual·agreement specifically·for a·

G4860 συμ•ψηφίζω sympsēphízō *v.* (1x)
Roots:G4862 G5585
G4860 V-AAI-3P συνεψήφισαν (1x)
Ac 19:19 of·all *men.* And they·jointly·calculated the price

G4861 σύμ•ψυχος sýmpsychôs *adj.* (1x)
Roots:G4862 G5590 Compare:G3675 See:G2473
G4861.2 A-NPM σύμψυχοι (1x)
Php 2:2 love, contemplating the one jointly·common·soul.

G4862 σύν sýn *prep.* (132x)
συγ- syg- [alternate prefix]
συμ- sym- [soft prefix]
συ- sy- [rare]
Compare:G3326 G3844
G4862.1 PREP σύν (119x)
Jn 18:1 ·things, Jesus went·forth together with·his disciples
Jn 21:3 "We·ourselves also go together with·you." *And* they·
Lk 1:56 And Mariam abided together with·her about three
Lk 2:5 to·be·enrolled·in·the·census together with·Mariam,
Lk 2:13 And suddenly together with·the angel, there·came·
Lk 5:9 him (and all the·ones together with·him) over the
Lk 5:19 down through the tiles together with·the pallet into
Lk 7:6 And Jesus was·traversing together with·them. And
Lk 7:12 ·significant crowd of·the city *was* together with·her.
Lk 8:1 And the twelve *were* together with·him,
Lk 8:38 ·out was·petitioning him to·be together with·him,
Lk 9:32 Now Peter and the·ones together with·him were
Lk 19:23 ·have reclaimed my·own together with·interest?
Lk 20:1 the scribes stood·over *him* together with·the elders,
Lk 22:14 twelve ambassadors *did·likewise* together with·him.
Lk 22:56 "This·man was also together with·him."
Lk 23:32 were·led together with·him to·be·executed.
Lk 23:35 the rulers also together with·them were·sneering·at
Lk 24:1 and certain·women *were* together with·them.
Lk 24:10 and the rest *that·were* together with·them, who
Lk 24:21 IsraEl. Moreover together with·all these·things,
Lk 24:24 And some of·the·ones together with·us went·off to
Lk 24:29 And he·entered·in to·abide together with·them.
Lk 24:33 ·together, and the·ones together with·them,
Lk 24:44 I·spoke to yeu, while·still being together with·yeu:
Ac 1:14 and the petition, together with·women and Mariam
Ac 1:14 mother of·Jesus, and·also together with·his brothers
Ac 1:17 ·was having·been·fully·numbered together with·us,
Ac 1:22 *for* one to·become a·witness together with·us of·his
Ac 2:14 Peter, after·being·settled together with·the eleven,
Ac 3:4 Peter, gazing·intently upon him together with·John,
Ac 3:8 ·walking; then he·entered together with·them into the
Ac 4:13 them, that they·were together with·Jesus.
Ac 4:14 ·relieved·and·cured standing together with·them,
Ac 4:27 and Pontius Pilate, together with·Gentiles and with·
Ac 5:1 AnanIas by·name, together with·Sapphira his wife,
Ac 5:17 rising·up, and all the·ones together with·him (being
Ac 5:21 ·high·priest and the·ones together with·him, after·
Ac 8:20 "May your silver, together with·you, be *handed·*
Ac 8:31 ·he·would·climb·up to·sit·down together with·him.
Ac 10:2 and one·reverently·fearing God together with·all his
Ac 10:20 ·up, walk·down and traverse together with·them,
Ac 10:23 next·day, Peter went·forth together with·them, and
Ac 11:12 these six brothers also came together with·me, and
Ac 13:7 who was co-opting the proconsul, Sergius Paulus,
Ac 14:4 in·fact, the·one *part* was together with·the Jews,
Ac 14:4 and the·one *part was* together with·the ambassadors.
Ac 14:5 ·the Gentiles and *the* Jews together with·their rulers)
Ac 14:13 ·was·wanting to·sacrifice together with·the crowds.
Ac 14:20 next·day he·went·forth together with·BarNabas to
Ac 14:28 ·were·lingering there together with·the disciples.
Ac 15:22 and the elders, together with·all the Called·Out·
Ac 15:22 themselves to Antioch together with·Paul and
Ac 15:25 selected men to yeu together with·our beloved
Ac 16:3 Paul wanted this·man to·go·forth together with·him.
Ac 17:34 ·name·of Damaris, and others together with·them.
Ac 18:8 trusted on·the Lord together with·all his house; and
Ac 18:18 Little·Prisca and Aquila *were* together with·him—
Ac 19:38 and the craftsmen together with·him have a·matter
Ac 20:36 the knees, he·prayed together with·them all.
Ac 21:5 seeing us off (together with·wives and children)
Ac 21:18 *day,* Paul had·entered together with·us *to·come*
Ac 21:24 be·ceremonially·cleansed together with·them, and
Ac 21:26 being·ceremonially·cleansed together with·them,
Ac 21:29 ·seen Trophimus the Ephesian together with·him in
Ac 22:9 "And the·ones being together with·me, in·fact, did·
Ac 23:15 yeu·yeurselves together with·the joint·council·of·
Ac 23:27 ·over *him* together with·the squad·of·soldiers, I·
Ac 23:32 horsemen to·traverse *onward* together with·him.
Ac 24:24 days, after·arriving·publicly together with·his wife
Ac 25:23 formal·hearing·chamber, together with·both the
Ac 26:13 me and the·ones traversing together with·me.
Ac 27:2 of·ThessaloNica) being together with·us.
Ac 28:16 to·abide by·himself together with·the soldier
Gal 1:2 and all the·brothers together with·me. To·the Called·
Gal 2:3 not·even Titus (the·one together with·me being a·
Gal 3:9 ·out of·trust are·blessed together with·the trusting of·
Gal 5:24 the flesh together with·the intense·cravings and the
Mt 25:27 ·obtaining my·own together with·interest.
Mt 26:35 ·be·necessary·for me to·die together with·you, no,
Mt 27:38 two robbers being·crucified together with·him, one
Mk 2:26 he·gave also to·the·ones being together with·him?
Mk 4:10 in·company·with him (together with·the twelve)
Mk 9:4 they·gazed·upon them, EliJah together with·Moses,
Mk 15:27 And together with·him, they·crucify two robbers:
Rm 6:8 Now if we·died together with·Anointed-One, we·
Rm 8:32 how shall·he·not·indeed, together with·him, also
Rm 16:14 Hermes, and the brothers together with·them.
Rm 16:15 and all the holy·ones together with·them.
Jac 1:11 rose·above·the·horizon together with·the blazing·
Php 1:1 ·ones being at Philippi, together with·overseers and
Php 1:23 ·camp and to·be together with·Anointed-One,
Php 2:22 that as a·child together with·a·father, he·has·been·
Php 4:21 Jesus. The brothers together with·me greet yeu.
2Pe 1:18 ·out of·heaven, while·being together with·him on
1Th 4:14 also God shall·bring together with·him the·ones
1Th 4:17 ·up at·the·same·time together with·them in *the*
1Th 4:17 we·shall·be always together with·*the*·Lord.
1Th 5:10 we·should·live at·the·same·time together with·him.
1Co 1:2 called·forth *to·be* holy·ones, together with·all *those*
1Co 5:4 also with·my spirit, together with·the power of·our
1Co 10:13 ·are·able, but·rather together with·the proof·trial,
1Co 11:32 ·not be·condemned together with·the world.
1Co 15:10 the Grace of·God, the·one together with·me.
1Co 16:4 to·traverse, they·shall·traverse together with·me.
1Co 16:19 *the* Lord, together with·the Called·Out·citizenry
2Co 1:1 being at Corinth, together with·all the holy·ones,
2Co 1:21 ·one presently·confirming us together with·yeu in
2Co 4:14 Jesus, and shall·present *us* together with·yeu.
2Co 9:4 Macedonians should·come together with·me and
2Co 13:4 yet we·shall·live together with·him as·a·result of·
Eph 3:18 ·have·full·strength to·grasp together with·all the
Eph 4:31 be·expunged from yeu, together with·all malice.
Col 2:5 flesh, but·yet I·am together with·yeu in·the spirit,
Col 2:20 if yeu·did·die together with·Anointed-One from
Col 3:3 has·been·hidden together with·the Anointed-One in
Col 3:4 also shall·be·made·apparent together with·him in
Col 3:9 ·off the old man·of·clay† together with·his practices
Col 4:9 together with·Onesimus, the trustworthy and
EG4862.1 (4x)
Jn 10:16 my voice, and *together* it·shall·become one flock
Lk 6:38 packed·down, shaken *together*, and overflowing
Ac 4:32 absolutely·all·belongings *together in* common.
Ac 8:6 crowds, *being together* with·the·same·determination,
G4862.2 PREP σύν (6x)
Lk 23:11 him, HerOd·AntiPas (along·with his troops), after·
Ac 5:26 ·off, the high·warden along·with the assistants,
Ac 21:16 from Caesarea also went·together along·with us,
Mk 8:34 the crowd *to·him* along·with his disciples, *Jesus*
2Co 8:19 with·us along·with this gracious·benevolence (the·
Col 2:13 flesh, he·made·*yeu*·alive·together along·with him,
EG4862.2 (2x)
Jn 13:27 And at·that·time, *along* with the morsel, the
Jn 17:5 O·Father, glorify me (*along* with yourself) with·the
EG4862.5 (1x)
Ac 7:24 he·forcefully·defended *his fellow Israelite* and

G4863 συν•άγω synágō *v.* (61x)
Roots:G4862 G0071 Compare:G4867 G0119-1 G4896 See:G4864 G1996 xLangEquiv:H6950 xLangAlso:H6960
G4863.2 V-FAI-1S συνάξω (2x)
Lk 12:17 no place·where I·shall·gather·together my fruits?
Lk 12:18 ·ones; and there I·shall·gather·together all my
G4863.2 V-FAI-3S συνάξει (2x)
Lk 3:17 threshing·floor and shall·gather·together the wheat
Mt 3:12 threshing·floor, and shall·gather·together his wheat
G4863.2 V-FPI-3S συναχθήσεται (1x)
Mt 25:32 the nations shall·be·gathered·together before him,

Σσ

G4863.2 V-FPI-3P συναχθήσονται (2x)
Lk 17:37 *is*, there the eagles shall·be·gathered·together."
Mt 24:28 ·be, there the eagles shall·be·gathered·together.
G4863.2 V-PAI-1S συνάγω (1x)
Mt 25:26 ·not sow and gather·together from·where I·did·not
G4863.2 V-PAI-3S συνάγει (2x)
Jn 4:36 payment·of·service and gathers·together fruit into
Rv 13:10 If any·man gathers·together *another into* war·
G4863.2 V-PAI-3P συνάγουσιν (1x)
Jn 15:6 ·already·withered, and they·do·gather them together
G4863.2 V-PAP-NSM συνάγων (3x)
Lk 11:23 me, and the·one not gathering·together with me
Mt 12:30 me, and the·one not gathering·together with me
Mt 25:24 and gathering·together from·where you·did·not
G4863.2 V-PPI-3P συνάγονται (2x)
Mk 6:30 ambassadors gathered·themselves·together Jesus
Mk 7:1 of·the scribes gathered·together alongside him, after·
G4863.2 V-PPM-2P συνάγεσθε (1x)
Rv 19:17 "Come·here! And be·gathered·together for the
G4863.2 V-2AAI-3S συνήγαγεν (1x)
Rv 16:16 And he·gathered them together into the place, the·
G4863.2 V-2AAI-3P συνήγαγον (4x)
Jn 6:13 Accordingly, they·gathered·together and overfilled
Jn 11:47 Pharisees gathered·together a·joint·council·of· and
Mt 22:10 into the roadways, gathered·together all, as·many·
Mt 27:27 the Praetorian·hall, gathered·together the whole
G4863.2 V-2AAM-2P συναγάγετε (2x)
Jn 6:12 disciples, "Gather·together the remaining·excess
Mt 13:30 ·burn them, but gather·together the wheat into my
G4863.2 V-2AAN συναγαγεῖν (2x)
Rv 16:14 and of·all The Land, to·gather them together to the
Rv 20:8 earth, Gog and Magog, to·gather them together into
G4863.2 V-2AAP-DSF συναγαγούσῃ (1x)
Mt 13:47 the sea and gathering·together from·among every
G4863.2 V-2AAP-NSM συναγαγών (2x)
Lk 15:13 the younger son, gathering·together absolutely·all,
Mt 2:4 And after·gathering·together all the chief·priests and
G4863.2 V-2AAP-NPM συναγαγόντες (2x)
Ac 14:27 and gathering·together the Called·Out·citizenry,
Ac 15:30 and after·gathering·together the multitude, they·
G4863.2 V-2AAS-3S συναγάγῃ (1x)
Jn 11:52 ·order·that also he·should·gather·together into one,
G4863.2 V-API-3S συνήχθη (5x)
Jn 18:2 because many·times Jesus did·gather there together
Lk 22:66 ·elders of·the people were·gathered·together (both
Ac 13:44 the city *of·Antiochia* did·gather·together to·hear the
Mk 4:1 And a·large crowd was·gathered·together to him,
Mk 5:21 a·large crowd is·already·gathered·together to him,
G4863.2 V-API-3P συνήχθησαν (9x)
Ac 4:26 the rulers were·gathered·together in·unison against
Ac 4:27 in truth, they·were·gathered·together against your
Ac 15:6 and the elders gathered·together to·see concerning
Mt 13:2 And large crowds were·gathered·together to him,
Mt 22:34 But the Pharisees gathered·together against him,
Mt 26:3 elders of·the people were·gathered·together in the
Mt 26:57 the scribes and the elders were·gathered·together.
Mt 27:62 and the Pharisees gathered·together to Pilate,
Mk 2:2 immediately, many were·gathered·together, such·for
G4863.2 V-APN συναχθῆναι (1x)
Ac 11:26 *such·for* them to·be·gathered·together a·whole year
G4863.2 V-APP-GPM συναχθέντων (1x)
1Co 5:4 Anointed, with·yeu being·gathered·together, also
G4863.2 V-APP-NPM συναχθέντες (1x)
Mt 28:12 And after·being·gathered·together with the elders
G4863.2 V-RPP-APN συνηγμένα (1x)
Rv 19:19 having·been·gathered·together to·make war
G4863.2 V-RPP-GPM συνηγμένων (3x)
Ac 20:7 disciples having·been·gathered·together to·break
Mt 22:41 Pharisees having·been·gathered·together, YeShua
Mt 27:17 with·them having·been·gathered·together, Pilate
G4863.2 V-RPP-NPM συνηγμένοι (4x)
Jn 20:19 were having·been·gathered·together on·account·of
Ac 4:31 they·were having·been·gathered·together; and
Ac 20:8 where they·were having·been·gathered·together.
Mt 18:20 or three are having·been·gathered·together in my
G4863.3 V-PAI-3P συνάγουσιν (1x)
Mt 6:26 do·they·reap, nor·even do·they·gather into barns,
G4863.3 V-2AAI-1P συνηγάγομεν (1x)
Mt 25:38 you a·stranger, and gathered·*you*·in? Or naked,
G4863.3 V-2AAI-2P συνηγάγετε (2x)
Mt 25:35 I·was a·stranger, and yeu·gathered me in,
Mt 25:43 I·was a·stranger, and yeu·did·not gather me in,

G4864 συν•αγωγή synagōgḗ *n.* (59x)

קָהָל qahal [Hebrew]
Roots:G4863 Compare:G1577 G1218 G4866-1 G2959-1 G2959-2 See:G1997 G0656 G0752 xLangEquiv:H6951 xLangAlso:H5712 H4744

G4864.1 N-NSF συναγωγή (1x)
Rv 2:9 but·rather *are* a·gathering of·the Adversary-Accuser.
G4864.1 N-ASF συναγωγήν (11x)
Lk 4:16 custom, he·entered into the gathering on the day of·
Lk 6:6 *for* him to·enter into the gathering and to·instruct. Yet
Ac 13:14 And entering into the gathering on·the day of·
Ac 14:1 *for* them to·enter into the gathering of·the Jews, and
Ac 17:10 *there*, went·off into the gathering of·the Jews.
Ac 18:19 into the gathering, was·having·discussions with·the
Ac 19:8 the gathering, he·was·boldly·speaking·with·clarity
Mt 12:9 ·on from·there, he·went into their gathering.
Mk 1:21 after·entering into the gathering, he·was·instructing
Mk 3:1 he·entered again into the gathering, and there·was a·
Jac 2:2 if there·should·enter into yeur gathering a·man *with*
G4864.1 N-APF συναγωγάς (6x)
Lk 12:11 they·should·bring yeu before the gatherings, the
Lk 21:12 handing *yeu* over to gatherings and prisons, being·
Ac 9:2 for Damascus pertaining·to the gatherings, that if·
Ac 22:19 and thrashing in·each·of the gatherings, the·ones
Ac 26:11 many·times in all the gatherings, I·was·compelling
Mk 13:9 and yeu·shall·be·thrashed in gatherings, and yeu·
G4864.1 N-DSF συναγωγῇ (11x)
Jn 6:59 these·things in a·gathering, while·instructing in
Jn 18:20 always instructed in the gathering and in the
Lk 4:20 that·were in the gathering gazing·intently at·him.
Lk 4:28 everyone in the gathering was·filled with·rage.
Lk 4:33 And in the gathering, there·was a·man·of·clay†
Ac 17:17 ·having·discussions in the gathering with·the Jews
Ac 18:4 And he·discussed in the gathering each·and·every
Ac 18:26 to·boldly·speak·with·clarity in the gathering. But
Mt 13:54 ·instructing them in their gathering, as·such·for
Mk 1:23 But in their gathering, there·was a·man·of·clay†
Mk 6:2 he·began to·instruct in the gathering, and many
G4864.1 N-DPF συναγωγαῖς (17x)
Lk 4:15 was·instructing in their gatherings, being·glorified
Lk 4:44 officially·proclaiming in the gatherings of·Galilee.
Lk 11:43 ·love the first·row·seat in the gatherings, and the
Lk 20:46 and first·row·seats in the gatherings, and foremost·
Ac 9:20 the Anointed-One in the gatherings, *saying*, "This is
Ac 13:5 of·God in the gatherings of·the Jews, and they·were·
Ac 15:21 being·read·aloud in the gatherings each·and·every
Ac 24:12 of·a·crowd, neither in the gatherings, nor in the
Mt 4:23 instructing in their gatherings, and officially·
Mt 6:2 stage·acting·hypocrites do in the gatherings and in the
Mt 6:5 they·are·fond·of standing in the gatherings and in the
Mt 9:35 instructing in their gatherings, and officially·
Mt 10:17 and they·shall·flog yeu in their gatherings.
Mt 23:6 ·suppers, and the first·row·seats in the gatherings,
Mt 23:34 ·shall·flog in yeur gatherings and shall·persecute
Mk 1:39 officially·proclaiming in their gatherings among all
Mk 12:39 and first·row·seats in the gatherings, and foremost·
G4864.1 N-GSF συναγωγῆς (8x)
Lk 4:38 And rising·up out·of·the gathering, he·entered into
Lk 8:41 ·subsisting *as* an·executive·director of·the gathering.
Ac 6:9 ·up certain·men from·among the gathering, the·one
Ac 13:42 ·the Jews getting out·of·the gathering, the Gentiles
Ac 13:43 And with·the gathering being·let·loose, many of·
Heb 2:12 In *the* midst of·the·gathering, I·shall·splendidly·
Mk 1:29 after·coming·forth out·of·the gathering, they·went
Rv 3:9 from·among the gathering of·the Adversary-Accuser
G4864.1 N-GPF συναγωγῶν (1x)
Lk 13:10 instructing in one of·the gatherings on *one·of* the
EG4864.1 (1x)
Ac 6:9 ·one being·referred·to·as *the Gathering* of·Freedmen,
G4864.2 N-NSF συναγωγή (1x)
Ac 17:1 ThessaloNica where the gathering·place of·the Jews
G4864.2 N-ASF συναγωγήν (1x)
Lk 7:5 and he·himself built the gathering·place for·us."
G4864.2 N-DSF συναγωγῇ (1x)
Ac 18:7 whose home was·adjoining the gathering·place.

G4865 συν•αγωνίζομαι synagōnízômai *v.* (1x)

Roots:G4862 G0075

G4865.1 V-ADN συναγωνίσασθαι (1x)
Rm 15:30 love of·the Spirit, to·strive·together with·me in

G4866 συν•αθλέω synathlḗō *v.* (2x)

Roots:G4862 G0118

G4866.1 V-PAP-NPM συναθλοῦντες (1x)
Php 1:27 with·one soul struggling·together for·the trust of·
G4866.1 V-AAI-3P συνήθλησαν (1x)
Php 4:3 ·same·women who struggled·together with·me in the

G4867 συν•αθροίζω synathrôízō *v.* (3x)

Roots:G4862 G0119-1 Compare:G4871 G4863 G4836 See:G1865 G4866-1 xLangEquiv:H6908

G4867 V-AAP-NSM συναθροίσας (1x)
Ac 19:25 After·mustering·together these·men, and·also the
G4867 V-RPP-APM συνηθροισμένους (1x)
Lk 24:33 the eleven having·been·mustered·together, and the·
G4867 V-RPP-NPM συνηθροισμένοι (1x)
Ac 12:12 were having·been·mustered·together and *were*

G4868 συν•αίρω synaírō *v.* (3x)

Roots:G4862 G0142 Compare:G3049

G4868.2 V-PAI-3S συναίρει (1x)
Mt 25:19 slaves comes and tally·ups an·accounting with
G4868.2 V-PAN συναίρειν (1x)
Mt 18:24 with·him beginning to·tally·up, there·was·brought
G4868.2 V-AAN συνᾶραι (1x)
Mt 18:23 who wanted to·tally·up an·accounting among his

G4869 συν•αιχμάλωτος synaichmálôtôs *adj.* (3x)

Roots:G4862 G0164 Compare:G1198 G1202

G4869 A-NSM συναιχμάλωτος (2x)
Col 4:10 AristArchus, my fellow·prisoner·of·war, greets
Phm 1:23 you: EpAphras, my fellow·prisoner·of·war in
G4869 A-APM συναιχμαλώτους (1x)
Rm 16:7 ·Kinsmen and my fellow·prisoners·of·war, who are

G4870 συν•α•κολουθέω synakôlôuthḗō *v.* (2x)

Roots:G4862 G0190 Compare:G4902

G4870.1 V-AAN συνακολουθῆσαι (1x)
Mk 5:37 allow not·even·one·man to·follow·along with·him,
G4870.1 V-AAP-NPF συνακολουθήσασαι (1x)
Lk 23:49 and the women following·along with·him from

G4871 συν•αλίζω synalízō *v.* (1x)

Roots:G4862 Compare:G4867

G4871.2 V-PNP-NSM συναλιζόμενος (1x)
Ac 1:4 And being·huddled·close·together, *Jesus* charged

G4872 συν•ανα•βαίνω synanabaínō *v.* (2x)

Roots:G4862 G0305

G4872.1 V-2AAP-DPM συναναβᾶσιν (1x)
Ac 13:31 by·the·ones walking·up·together with·him from
G4872.1 V-2AAP-NPF συναναβᾶσαι (1x)
Mk 15:41 the·ones walking·up·together with·him to

G4873 συν•ανά•κειμαι synanákêimai *v.* (9x)

Roots:G4862 G0345

G4873 V-PNP-APM συνανακειμένους (2x)
Mt 14:9 oath and the·ones reclining·together·at·the·meal, he·
Mk 6:26 the·ones reclining·together·at·the·meal, he·did·not
G4873 V-PNP-DPM συνανακειμένοις (1x)
Mk 6:22 and the·ones reclining·together·at·the·meal, the
G4873 V-PNP-GPM συνανακειμένων (3x)
Jn 12:2 of·the·ones reclining·together·at·the·meal with·him.
Lk 14:10 of·the·ones reclining·together·at·the·meal with·you

Αα Ββ Γγ Δδ Εε Ζζ Ηη Θθ Ιι Κκ Λλ Μμ Νν Ξξ Οο Ππ Ρρ Σσ Ττ Υυ Φφ Χχ Ψψ Ωω

Lk 14:15 of·the·ones reclining·together·at·the·meal hearing
G4873 V-PNP-NPM συνανακείμενοι (1x)
Lk 7:49 the·ones reclining·together·at·the·meal began·to·say
G4873 V-INI-3P συνανέκειντο (2x)
Mt 9:10 They·were·reclining·together·at·the·meal with·
Mk 2:15 also reclined·together·at·the·meal with·Jesus and

G4874 συν•ανα•μίγνυμι synanamígnymi *v.* (3x)
Roots:G4862 G0303 G3396
G4874.2 V-PMM-2P συναναμίγνυσθε (1x)
2Th 3:14 that·man and do·not associate·with him, in·order·
G4874.2 V-PMN συναναμίγνυσθαι (2x)
1Co 5:9 not to·associate·with sexually·immoral·people,
1Co 5:11 I·wrote to·yeu not to·associate·with *such·as·these*:

G4875 συν•ανα•παύομαι synanapaúômai *v.* (1x)
Roots:G4862 G0373
G4875.2 V-ADS-1S συναναπαύσωμαι (1x)
Rm 15:32 will and may·be·refreshed·together with·yeu.

G4876 συν•αντάω synantáō *v.* (6x)
Roots:G4862 G0470-2 Compare:G0528 G2658 G5221 See:G4877
G4876.1 V-FAI-3S συναντήσει (1x)
Lk 22:10 bearing a·pitcher of·water shall·meet·up with·yeu;
G4876.1 V-AAI-3S συνήντησεν (2x)
Lk 9:37 from the mountain, a·large crowd met·up with·him.
Heb 7:10 of·*his*·father when MalkiTsedeq met·up with·him.
G4876.1 V-AAP-NSM συναντήσας (2x)
Ac 10:25 happened to·enter, Cornelius met·up with·him.
Heb 7:1 *is* the·one meeting·up with·AbRaham returning·back
G4876.2 V-FAP-APN συναντήσοντα (1x)
Ac 20:22 having·seen the·things that·shall·befall me *once* in

G4877 συν•άντησις synántēsis *n.* (1x)
Roots:G4876 Compare:G0529 G5222 xLangAlso:H7125
G4877.2 N-ASF συνάντησιν (1x)
Mt 8:34 entire city came·out to meet·up with·YeShua. And

G4878 συν•αντι•λαμβάνομαι synantilambánômai *v.* (2x)
Roots:G4862 G0482
G4878.3 V-PNI-3S συναντιλαμβάνεται (1x)
Rm 8:26 also is·helpful·and·works·together·alongside *us* in·
G4878.3 V-2ADS-3S συναντιλάβηται (1x)
Lk 10:40 she·should·be·helpful·and·work·together·alongside

G4879 συν•απ•άγω synapágō *v.* (3x)
Roots:G4862 G0520
G4879.2 V-API-3S συναπήχθη (1x)
Gal 2:13 also was·led·away·together with·their hypocrisy.
G4879.2 V-APP-NPM συναπαχθέντες (1x)
2Pe 3:17 Lest after·being·led·away·together with·the error
G4879.3 V-PMP-NPM συναπαγόμενοι (1x)
Rm 12:16 but·rather leading·yeurselves·together with·the

Σσ

G4880 συν•απο•θνήσκω synapôthnḗskō *v.* (3x)
Roots:G4862 G0599
G4880.1 V-2AAI-1P συναπεθάνομεν (1x)
2Ti 2:11 "For if we·died·together *with·him*, also we·shall·
G4880.1 V-2AAN συναποθανεῖν (2x)
Mk 14:31 ·be·necessary·for me to·die·together with·you, no,
2Co 7:3 our hearts for *us* to·die·together and to·live·together

G4881 συν•απ•όλλυμι synapóllymi *v.* (1x)
Roots:G4862 G0622
G4881.2 V-2AMI-3S συναπώλετο (1x)
Heb 11:31 did·not completely·perish·together with·the·ones

G4882 συν•απο•στέλλω synapôstéllō *v.* (1x)
Roots:G4862 G0649 See:G1821
G4882 V-AAI-1S συναπέστειλα (1x)
2Co 12:18 and I·dispatched·*him*·together·with the brother.

G4883 συν•αρμο•λογέω synarmôlôgéō *v.* (2x)
Roots:G4862 G0719 G3004
G4883.2 V-PPP-NSN συναρμολογούμενον (1x)
Eph 4:16 Body is·being·fitly·framed·together and is·being·
G4883.2 V-PPP-NSF συναρμολογουμένη (1x)
Eph 2:21 entire structure, being·fitly·framed·together, grows

G4884 συν•αρπάζω synarpázō *v.* (4x)
Roots:G4862 G0726
G4884.1 V-AAI-3P συνήρπασαν (1x)
Ac 6:12 standing·over *him*, together·they·seized him and
G4884.1 V-AAP-NPM συναρπάσαντες (1x)
Ac 19:29 with·mass·confusion. And seizing·both Gaius and
G4884.2 V-APP-GSN συναρπασθέντος (1x)
Ac 27:15 ·the sailing·ship being·snatched·up·together *in·it*,
G4884.3 V-LAI-3S συνηρπάκει (1x)
Lk 8:29 for many times it·had·altogether·seized him. And

G4885 συν•αυξάνω synauxánō *v.* (1x)
Roots:G4862 G0837
G4885 V-PPN συναυξάνεσθαι (1x)
Mt 13:30 both to·be·grown·together so·long·as·unto the

G4886 σύν•δεσμος sýndêsmôs *n.* (4x)
Roots:G4862 G1199 Compare:G0860
G4886.1 N-ASM σύνδεσμον (1x)
Ac 8:23 of·bitterness and a·joint·bond of·unrighteousness."
G4886.1 N-DSM συνδέσμῳ (1x)
Eph 4:3 the oneness of·the Spirit in the joint·bond of·peace.
G4886.2 N-NSM σύνδεσμος (1x)
Col 3:14 which is a·ligament·*(a·uniting·principle)* of·the
G4886.2 N-GPM συνδέσμων (1x)
Col 2:19 ·joints and ligaments being·fully·supplied and

G4887 συν•δέω syndéō *v.* (1x)
Roots:G4862 G1210
G4887.1 V-RPP-NPM συνδεδεμένοι (1x)
Heb 13:3 as having·been·bound·together *with·them, and*

G4888 συν•δοξάζω syndôxázō *v.* (1x)
Roots:G4862 G1392
G4888 V-APS-1P συνδοξασθῶμεν (1x)
Rm 8:17 ·that also we·may·be·glorified·together *with·him*.

G4889 σύν•δουλος sýndôulôs *n.* (10x)
Roots:G4862 G1401
G4889 N-NSM σύνδουλος (4x)
Mt 18:29 at his feet, his fellow·slave was·imploring him,
Col 4:7 a·trustworthy attendant, and a·fellow·slave in the
Rv 19:10 ·do·not *do·it*. I·am your fellow·slave, and of·your
Rv 22:9 ·not *do·it*; for I·am your fellow·slave, and of·your
G4889 N-NPM σύνδουλοι (2x)
Mt 18:31 "And his fellow·slaves, after·seeing the·things
Rv 6:11 time, until also their fellow·slaves and their brothers
G4889 N-ASM σύνδουλον (1x)
Mt 18:33 you also to·show·mercy on·your fellow·slave, even
G4889 N-APM συνδούλους (1x)
Mt 24:49 should·begin to·beat the fellow·slaves and to·eat
G4889 N-GSM συνδούλου (1x)
Col 1:7 *it* from EpAphras, our dear fellow·slave, who is a·
G4889 N-GPM συνδούλων (1x)
Mt 18:28 found one of·his fellow·slaves who was·owing

G4890 συν•δρομή syndrômḗ *n.* (1x)
Roots:G4936
G4890.1 N-NSF συνδρομή (1x)
Ac 21:30 and the people came running·together. And

G4891 συν•εγείρω synêgêírō *v.* (3x)
Roots:G4862 G1453
G4891 V-AAI-3S συνήγειρεν (1x)
Eph 2:6 *God* awakened·*us*·together and sat·*us*·down·together
G4891 V-API-2P συνηγέρθητε (2x)
Col 2:12 also yeu·are·already·awakened·together *with·him*
Col 3:1 if yeu·are·already·awakened·together with·the

G4892 συν•έδριον synédriôn *n.* (23x)
סַנְהֶדְרִין çan·hedriyn
[Hebrew transliteration]
Roots:G4862 G1476 Compare:G4244 xLangAlso:H5475
G4892.2 N-NSN συνέδριον (3x)
Mt 26:59 the joint·council·of·Sanhedrin were·seeking false·
Mk 14:55 all the joint·council·of·Sanhedrin were·seeking
Mk 15:1 and the whole joint·council·of·Sanhedrin, *and*
G4892.2 N-ASN συνέδριον (7x)
Jn 11:47 gathered·together a·joint·council·of·Sanhedrin and
Lk 22:66 into their·own joint·council·of·Sanhedrin, saying,
Ac 5:21 ·together the joint·council·of·Sanhedrin and all the
Ac 6:12 and brought *him* to the joint·council·of·Sanhedrin,
Ac 22:30 and all their joint·council·of·Sanhedrin to·come.
Ac 23:20 into the joint·council·of·Sanhedrin, as·though
Ac 23:28 him down into their joint·council·of·Sanhedrin,
G4892.2 N-APN συνέδρια (2x)
Mt 10:17 ·hand yeu over to joint·councils·of·Sanhedrin, and
Mk 13:9 ·hand yeu over to joint·councils·of·Sanhedrin, and
G4892.2 N-DSN συνεδρίῳ (7x)
Ac 5:27 they·set *them* in the joint·council·of·Sanhedrin. And
Ac 5:34 ·up in the joint·council·of·Sanhedrin, a·certain·man,
Ac 6:15 ·down in the joint·council·of·Sanhedrin saw his face
Ac 23:1 ·intently at·the joint·council·of·Sanhedrin, declared,
Ac 23:6 he·yelled·out in the joint·council·of·Sanhedrin,
Ac 23:15 with·the joint·council·of·Sanhedrin, make·it·clear
Mt 5:22 held·liable to·the joint·council·of·Sanhedrin. But
G4892.2 N-GSN συνεδρίου (3x)
Ac 4:15 of·the joint·council·of·Sanhedrin, they·rigorously·
Ac 5:41 in·front·of·the joint·council·of·Sanhedrin, rejoicing
Ac 24:20 standing·still before the joint·council·of·Sanhedrin,
EG4892.2 (1x)
Ac 5:35 And *then* he·declared to *the joint·council*, "Men,

G4893 συν•είδησις synêídēsis *n.* (32x)
Roots:G4894 xLangAlso:H4709-1
G4893.2 N-ASF συνείδησιν (1x)
Heb 10:2 further a·moral·consciousness of·moral·failures?
G4893.3 N-NSF συνείδησις (3x)
Tit 1:15 their mind and conscience has·been·contaminated.
1Co 8:7 sacrificing·to·an·idol; and their conscience (being
1Co 8:10 shall not·indeed the conscience of·him who·is
G4893.3 N-ASF συνείδησιν (15x)
Ac 24:16 continually a·conscience void·of·offense toward
Heb 9:9 ·to *the* conscience of·the·one ritually·ministering;
Heb 9:14 to·God, purify yeur conscience from dead works
Heb 13:18 that we·have a·good conscience in all·things,
Rm 13:5 but·rather also on·account·of the conscience.
1Pe 2:19 if someone on·account·of conscience *toward* God
1Pe 3:16 having a·beneficially·good conscience— in·order·
1Co 8:12 beating their weak conscience, yeu·morally·fail
1Co 10:25 not·even·one·thing on·account·of the conscience.
1Co 10:27 not·even·one·thing on·account·of the conscience.
1Co 10:28 ·it·to·*yeur*·attention, and the conscience, for
1Co 10:29 "Conscience," I·say, not·indeed your·own, but·
2Co 4:2 every man·of·clay's† conscience in·the·sight·of·God
1Ti 1:19 holding trust and a·beneficially·good conscience.
1Ti 4:2 their·own conscience having·been·seared *as·with a·*
G4893.3 N-DSF συνειδήσει (4x)
Ac 23:1 beneficially·good conscience before·God even·up·to
1Co 8:7 some, with·the conscience *still·accustomed·to* the
1Ti 3:9 the Mystery of·the trust in a·pure conscience.
2Ti 1:3 *my* forebears' *example* with a·pure conscience), how
G4893.3 N-DPF συνειδήσεσιν (1x)
2Co 5:11 to·have·been·made·manifest in yeur consciences.
G4893.3 N-GSF συνειδήσεως (8x)
Jn 8:9 by *their·own* conscience, they·were·going·forth one·
Heb 10:22 ·been·sprinkled from an·evil conscience, and the
Rm 2:15 hearts, with·their conscience jointly·testifying, and
Rm 9:1 lie, with·my conscience jointly·testifying with·me in
1Pe 3:21 of·a·beneficially·good conscience toward God)—
1Co 10:29 unduly·judged by another *man's* conscience?
2Co 1:12 the testimony of·our conscience— how·that with
1Ti 1:5 heart, and of·a·beneficially·good conscience, and of·

G4894 συν•είδω synêídō *v.* (4x)
Roots:G4862 G1492 See:G4893
G4894.2 V-RAP-GSF συνειδυίας (1x)
Ac 5:2 with·his wife also having·mutually·known *of·it*. And
G4894.3 V-2AAP-NSM συνιδών (1x)
Ac 12:12 And after·becoming·completely·aware, he·came to
G4894.3 V-2AAP-NPM συνιδόντες (1x)
Ac 14:6 after·becoming·completely·aware·of *it, the*

G4894.4 V-RAI-1S σύνοιδα (1x)
1Co 4:4 For I·am·conscious·of not·even·one·thing against·

G4895 σύν•ειμι synêimi *v.* (2x)
Roots:G4862 G1510
G4895 V-PXP-GPM συνόντων (1x)
Ac 22:11 ·by·the·hand by the·ones being·together with·me,
G4895 V-IXI-3P συνῆσαν (1x)
Lk 9:18 ·himself, *that* the disciples were·together with·him.

G4896 σύν•ειμι synêimi *v.* (1x)
Roots:G4862 G1510-1 Compare:G1573-1 G1577 G4341 G4863 G1996 G4867
G4896 V-PXP-GSM συνιόντος (1x)
Lk 8:4 with·a·large crowd being·assembled·together, and

G4897 συν•εισέρχομαι synêisérchômai *v.* (2x)
Roots:G4862 G1525
G4897 V-2AAI-3S συνεισῆλθεν (2x)
Jn 6:22 that Jesus did·not enter·together with·his disciples
Jn 18:15 ·priest, and he·entered·together with·Jesus into the

G4898 συν•έκ•δημος synékdēmôs *n.* (2x)
Roots:G4862 G1553
G4898.2 N-NSM συνέκδημος (1x)
2Co 8:19 *to·be* a·traveling·companion with·us along·with
G4898.2 N-APM συνεκδήμους (1x)
Ac 19:29 Paul's traveling·companions, they·impulsively·

G4899 συν•εκ•λεκτός synêklêktós *adj.* (1x)
Roots:G4862 G1586
G4899.1 A-NSF συνεκλεκτή (1x)
1Pe 5:13 ·*citizenry* in Babylon, selected·together *with·yeu*,

G4900 συν•ελαύνω synêlaúnō *v.* (1x)
Roots:G4862 G1643 See:G0556
G4900.2 V-AAI-3S συνήλασεν (1x)
Ac 7:26 ·were·fighting, and sternly·exhorted them *to·be* at

G4901 συν•επι•μαρτυρέω synêpimartyréō *v.* (1x)
Roots:G4862 G1957
G4901 V-PAP-GSM συνεπιμαρτυροῦντος (1x)
Heb 2:4 with·God also·further·testifying·jointly, both with·

G4902 συν•έπομαι synépômai *v.* (1x)
Roots:G4902-5 Compare:G4311 G4870
G4902.3 V-INI-3S συνείπετο (1x)
Ac 20:4 (a·Berean *Jew*), was·accompanying him. Now

G4903 συν•εργέω synêrgéō *v.* (5x)
Roots:G4904 Compare:G2872
G4903.1 V-PAI-3S συνεργεῖ (1x)
Rm 8:28 God, all·things work·together to good·benefit for·
G4903.1 V-PAP-GSM συνεργοῦντος (1x)
Mk 16:20 with·the Lord working·together *alongside* and
G4903.1 V-PAP-NPM συνεργοῦντες (1x)
2Co 6:1 Then working·together *with·him*, *it·is* not for nothing
G4903.1 V-IAI-3S συνήργει (1x)
Jac 2:22 how the trust was·working·together with·his works,
G4903.2 V-PAP-DSM συνεργοῦντι (1x)
1Co 16:16 ·everyone, the·one coworking and laboring·hard.

G4904 συν•εργός synêrgós *adj.* (13x)
Roots:G4862 G2041
G4904 A-NSM συνεργός (2x)
Rm 16:21 TimoThy, my coworker, and·also Lucius, Jason,
2Co 8:23 *he·is* my partner and coworker in·regard·to yeu,
G4904 A-NPM συνεργοί (5x)
1Co 3:9 For we·are coworkers with·God; yeu·are God's
2Co 1:24 yeur trust, but·rather are coworkers of·yeur joy—
Col 4:11 Justus). Only these coworkers for the kingdom of·
Phm 1:24 AristArchus, Demas, Luke, *these* my coworkers.
3Jn 1:8 in·order·that we·may·be coworkers with·the truth.
G4904 A-ASM συνεργόν (3x)
Rm 16:9 Greet Urbanus, our coworker in Anointed-One, and
Php 2:25 my brother, coworker, and fellow·soldier (but
1Th 3:2 of·God, and our coworker in the good·news of·
G4904 A-APM συνεργούς (1x)
Rm 16:3 and Aquila, my coworkers in Anointed-One Jesus,
G4904 A-DSM συνεργῷ (1x)
Phm 1:1 To·Philemon our dearly·beloved and coworker,
G4904 A-GPM συνεργῶν (1x)
Php 4:3 and *with* the rest of·my coworkers, the names of·

G4905 συν•έρχομαι synérchômai *v.* (32x)
Roots:G4862 G2064 xLangAlso:H0622
G4905.1 V-PNI-2P συνέρχεσθε (1x)
1Co 11:17 applaud *yeu*, because yeu·come·together not for
G4905.1 V-PNI-3S συνέρχεται (1x)
Mk 3:20 And a·crowd was·coming·together again, such·for
G4905.1 V-PNI-3P συνέρχονται (2x)
Jn 18:20 where the Judeans always come·together. And I·
Mk 14:53 the elders and the scribes come·together with·him.
G4905.1 V-PNP-GPM συνερχομένων (2x)
1Co 11:18 ·of·all, as·yeu are·coming·together among the
1Co 11:20 Now·then, as·yeu are·coming·together in·unison,
G4905.1 V-PNP-NPM συνερχόμενοι (1x)
1Co 11:33 as·yeu·are·coming·together in·order·to·eat, wait·
G4905.1 V-PNS-2P συνέρχησθε (3x)
1Co 7:5 prayer, and should·come·together in·unison again,
1Co 11:34 lest yeu·should·come·together into·judgment.
1Co 14:26 Whenever yeu·should·come·together, each·one
G4905.1 V-INI-3S συνήρχετο (1x)
Ac 5:16 There·came·together also a·multitude *out* of·the
G4905.1 V-INI-3P συνήρχοντο (1x)
Lk 5:15 him, and large crowds came·together to·hear *him*,
G4905.1 V-2AAI-3S συνῆλθεν (1x)
Ac 2:6 multitude came·together and was·greatly·confused,
G4905.1 V-2AAI-3P συνῆλθον (2x)
Ac 10:45 ·astonished, as·many·as came·together with·Peter,
Mk 6:33 before them, and together, they·came toward him.
G4905.1 V-2AAN συνελθεῖν (2x)
Ac 21:22 ·for a·multitude entirely to·come·together, for
Mt 1:18 prior·to them coming·together, she·was·found
G4905.1 V-2AAP-APM συνελθόντας (1x)
Jn 11:33 and the weeping Judeans coming·together with·her,
G4905.1 V-2AAP-DPF συνελθούσαις (1x)
Ac 16:13 ·speaking to·the women coming·together *there*.
G4905.1 V-2AAP-GPM συνελθόντων (2x)
Ac 25:17 "Accordingly, with·them coming·together here
Ac 28:17 And with·them coming·together, he·was·saying
G4905.1 V-2AAP-NPM συνελθόντες (1x)
Ac 1:6 ·fact, after·coming·together, they·were·inquiring·of
G4905.1 V-2AAS-3S συνέλθῃ (1x)
1Co 14:23 Called·Out·citizenry should·come·together in·,
G4905.1 V-RAP-APM συνεληλυθότας (1x)
Ac 10:27 ·entered·in and found many having·come·together.
G4905.1 V-RAP-NPF συνεληλυθυῖαι (1x)
Lk 23:55 who were having·come·together with·him from·out
G4905.1 V-LAI-3P συνεληλύθεισαν (1x)
Ac 19:32 ·known for·what cause they·had·come·together.
G4905.2 V-2AAI-3S συνῆλθεν (1x)
Ac 9:39 And rising·up, Peter went·together with·them.
G4905.2 V-2AAI-3P συνῆλθον (2x)
Ac 10:23 of·the brothers from Joppa went·together with·him.
Ac 21:16 from Caesarea also went·together along·with us,
G4905.2 V-2AAN συνελθεῖν (1x)
Ac 11:12 the Spirit declared to·me to·go·together with·them,
G4905.2 V-2AAP-ASM συνελθόντα (1x)
Ac 15:38 PamPhylia and not going·together with·them to the
G4905.2 V-2AAP-GPM συνελθόντων (1x)
Ac 1:21 of·the men going·together with·us during all *the*

G4906 συν•εσθίω synêsthíō *v.* (5x)
Roots:G4862 G2068
G4906 V-PAI-3S συνεσθίει (1x)
Lk 15:2 ·disqualified·men and eats·together with·them."
G4906 V-PAN συνεσθίειν (1x)
1Co 5:11 no,·not·even to·eat·together with·such·a·man.
G4906 V-IAI-3S συνήσθιεν (1x)
Gal 2:12 from Jacob, he·was·eating·together with the
G4906 V-2AAI-1P συνεφάγομεν (1x)
Ac 10:41 by God, to·us who ate·together and drank·together
G4906 V-2AAI-2S συνέφαγες (1x)
Ac 11:3 uncircumcised, and you·ate·together with·them."

G4907 σύν•εσις sýnêsis *n.* (9x)
Roots:G4920 Compare:G1108 G1253 G3563 G1271 xLangAlso:H0995
G4907.1 N-ASF σύνεσιν (2x)
Eph 3:4 yeu·are·able to·understand my comprehension in the
2Ti 2:7 the Lord give to·you comprehension in all·things.
G4907.1 N-DSF συνέσει (2x)
Lk 2:47 were·astonished at his comprehension and answers.
Col 1:9 ·his will in all wisdom and spiritual comprehension,
G4907.1 N-GSF συνέσεως (2x)
Mk 12:33 and from·out of·all the comprehension, and from·
Col 2:2 wealth of·the full·assurance of·comprehension, into
EG4907.1 (3x)
Lk 8:18 for whoever should·have *comprehension*, to·him
Lk 8:18 to·him *comprehension* shall·be·given; and whoever
Mk 4:24 *comprehension* shall·be·measured·out to·yeu. And

G4908 συν•ετός synêtós *adj.* (4x)
Roots:G4920 Compare:G5429 G4680
G4908.1 A-DSM συνετῷ (1x)
Ac 13:7 Sergius Paulus, *who·was* an·intelligent man. This·
G4908.1 A-GPM συνετῶν (3x)
Lk 10:21 these·things from wise and intelligent·men, and
Mt 11:25 these·things from wise and intelligent·men, and
1Co 1:19 shall·invalidate the discernment of·the intelligent."

G4909 συν•ευ•δοκέω synêudôkéō *v.* (6x)
Roots:G4862 G2106 Compare:G1962 G4856
G4909.2 V-PAI-2P συνευδοκεῖτε (1x)
Lk 11:48 yeu·testify and gladly·consent to·the deeds of·
G4909.2 V-PAP-NSM συνευδοκῶν (2x)
Ac 8:1 Now Saul was gladly·consenting to·his execution.
Ac 22:20 ·over, also gladly·consenting to·his execution, and
G4909.3 V-PAI-3S συνευδοκεῖ (2x)
1Co 7:12 and she·herself gives·glad·consent to·dwell with
1Co 7:13 — *if* he·himself gives·glad·consent to·dwell with
G4909.3 V-PAI-3P συνευδοκοῦσιν (1x)
Rm 1:32 also give·glad·consent to·the·ones practicing *them*.

G4910 συν•ευ•ωχέω synêuōchéō *v.* (2x)
Roots:G4862 G2095 G2192 Compare:G1792
G4910.2 V-PNP-NPM συνευωχούμενοι (2x)
Jud 1:12 ·feasts, presently·indulging·themselves·among *yeu*,
2Pe 2:13 delusions while·indulging·themselves·among yeu;

G4911 συν•εφ•ίστημι synêphístēmi *v.* (1x)
Roots:G4862 G2186
G4911.2 V-2AAI-3S συνεπέστη (1x)
Ac 16:22 And the crowd rose·up·together against them, and

G4912 συν•έχω synéchō *v.* (12x)
Roots:G4862 G2192 Compare:G4084 G5420 G4729 G2600-1 See:G4928 G3804
G4912.2 V-2AAI-3P συνέσχον (1x)
Ac 7:57 ·out with·a·loud voice, they·stopped·up their ears
G4912.3 V-FAI-3P συνέξουσιν (1x)
Lk 19:43 you, and shall·confine you on·every·side,
G4912.3 V-PAI-3P συνέχουσιν (1x)
Lk 8:45 "Captain, the crowds confine you and press·against
G4912.3 V-PAP-NPM συνέχοντες (1x)
Lk 22:63 the men, the·ones confining Jesus, were·mocking
G4912.4 V-PAI-3S συνέχει (1x)
2Co 5:14 the love of·the Anointed-One constrains us, after·
G4912.5 V-PPI-1S συνέχομαι (2x)
Lk 12:50 to·be·immersed·in, and how am·I·clenched until
Php 1:23 For I·am·clenched as·a·result of·the two *choices*,
G4912.5 V-PPP-ASM συνεχόμενον (1x)
Ac 28:8 lay·ill, being·clenched with·*recurring*·fevers and
G4912.5 V-PPP-APM συνεχομένους (1x)
Mt 4:24 ·ill, those·being·clenched by·a·diversity·of illnesses
G4912.5 V-PPP-NSF συνεχομένη (1x)
Lk 4:38 mother-in-law was being·clenched with·a·high fever
G4912.5 V-IPI-3S συνείχετο (1x)
Ac 18:5 from Macedonia, Paul was·clenched in·the spirit
G4912.5 V-IPI-3P συνείχοντο (1x)
Lk 8:37 them, because they·were·clenched with·great fear.

Αα Ββ Γγ Δδ Εε Ζζ Ηη Θθ Ιι Κκ Λλ Μμ Νν Ξξ Οο Ππ Ρρ Σσ Ττ Υυ Φφ Χχ Ψψ Ωω

G4913 συν•ήδομαι synḗdômai *v.* (1x)
Roots:G4862 G2237
G4913 V-PNI-1S συνήδομαι (1x)
Rm 7:22 For I·also·take·pleasure in·the Torah-Law of·God

G4914 συν•ήθεια synḗthêia *n.* (2x)
Roots:G4862 G2239
G4914 N-NSF συνήθεια (1x)
Jn 18:39 "Now it·is a·custom for·yeu that I·should·fully·
G4914 N-ASF συνήθειαν (1x)
1Co 11:16 do·not have *any·other* such custom, neither *do* the

G4915 συν•ηλικιώτης synēlikiṓtēs *n.* (1x)
Roots:G4862 G2244
G4915.2 N-APM συνηλικιώτας (1x)
Gal 1:14 in Judaism above many my·own·age among my

G4916 συν•θάπτω syntháptō *v.* (2x)
Roots:G4862 G2290
G4916.1 V-2API-1P συνετάφημεν (1x)
Rm 6:4 we·are·already·buried·together with·him through
G4916.1 V-2APP-NPM συνταφέντες (1x)
Col 2:12 already·being·buried·together with·him in the

G4917 συν•θλάω synthláō *v.* (2x)
Roots:G4862 Compare:G4919 G4937
G4917.2 V-FPI-3S συνθλασθήσεται (2x)
Lk 20:18 upon that stone shall·be·dashed·to·pieces; but upon
Mt 21:44 falling on this stone shall·be·dashed·to·pieces, but

G4918 συν•θλίβω synthlíbō *v.* (2x)
Roots:G4862 G2346
G4918.2 V-PAP-ASM συνθλίβοντα (1x)
Mk 5:31 "You·look·at the crowd pressing·in·around you and
G4918.2 V-IAI-3P συνέθλιβον (1x)
Mk 5:24 him, and they·were·pressing·in·around him.

G4919 συν•θρύπτω synthrýptō *v.* (1x)
Roots:G4862 G2362-3 Compare:G4917
G4919.2 V-PAP-NPM συνθρύπτοντες (1x)
Ac 21:13 ·continue weeping and jointly·crushing my heart?

G4920 συν•ίημι syníēmi *v.* (26x)
Roots:G4862 G2423-1 Compare:G0191 G0143 G1252 G1492 G3539 See:G4907 G4908 xLangAlso:H0995
G4920.2 V-FXI-3P συνήσουσιν (1x)
Rm 15:21 and those·that have·not heard shall·comprehend."
G4920.2 V-PAI-2P συνίετε (2x)
Mk 8:17 ·yeu·not·yet understand, nor·even comprehend? Is
Mk 8:21 ·saying to·them, "How do·yeu·not comprehend?"
G4920.2 V-PAI-3P συνίουσιν (2x)
Mt 13:13 they·do·not hear, neither do·they·comprehend.
2Co 10:12 themselves to·themselves, do·not comprehend.
G4920.2 V-PAM-2P συνίετε (2x)
Mt 15:10 he·declared to·them, "Hear and comprehend!
Mk 7:14 "Listen·to me, everyone, and comprehend!
G4920.2 V-PAN συνιέναι (2x)
Lk 24:45 their understanding to·comprehend the Scriptures.
Ac 7:25 ·assuming *for* his brothers to·comprehend that God,
G4920.2 V-PAP-GSM συνιέντος (1x)
Mt 13:19 of·the kingdom yet not comprehending *it*, the Evil·
G4920.2 V-PAP-NSM συνίων (2x)
Mt 13:23 hearing the Redemptive-word and comprehending *it*,
Rm 3:11 "There·is not one comprehending; there·is not one
G4920.2 V-PAP-NPM συνιέντες (1x)
Eph 5:17 ·ones, but·rather ones·comprehending what the
G4920.2 V-PAS-3P συνιῶσιν (2x)
Lk 8:10 look·upon, and hearing they·may·not comprehend.'
Mk 4:12 ·hear, and should·not comprehend, lest·at·any·time
G4920.2 V-AAI-2P συνήκατε (1x)
Mt 13:51 to·them, "Did·yeu·comprehend all these·things?
G4920.2 V-AAI-3P συνῆκαν (6x)
Lk 2:50 they·themselves did·not comprehend the utterance
Lk 18:34 they·themselves comprehended not·even·one of·
Ac 7:25 salvation to·them, but they·did·not comprehend.
Mt 16:12 Then they·comprehended that he·did·not declare
Mt 17:13 Then the disciples comprehended that he·declared
Mk 6:52 for they·did·not comprehend concerning the loaves·
G4920.2 V-2AAS-3P συνῶσιν (2x)
Ac 28:27 ·the ears, and should·comprehend with·the heart,
Mt 13:15 ·the ears, and should·comprehend with·the heart,
G4920.2 V-2AXS-2P συνῆτε (2x)
Ac 28:26 and no, should·not comprehend; and looking
Mt 13:14 and no, yeu·should·not comprehend; and looking

G4921 συν•ιστάω synistáō *v.* (16x)
συν•ιστάνω synistánō [strengthened]
συν•ίστημι synístēmi [also]
Roots:G4862 G2476 Compare:G3936 G0584 G1731 See:G0585
G4921.1 V-RAP-APM συνεστῶτας (1x)
Lk 9:32 two men, the·ones having·stood·together with·him.
G4921.2 V-PAI-1S συνίστημι (1x)
Rm 16:1 And I·commend to·yeu Phoebe, our sister, being
G4921.2 V-PAI-1P συνιστάνομεν (1x)
2Co 5:12 For not again do·we·commend ourselves to·yeu,
G4921.2 V-PAI-3S συνίστησιν (2x)
Rm 3:5 our unrighteousness commends God's righteousness
2Co 10:18 ·approved, but·rather whom the Lord commends.
G4921.2 V-PAN συνιστάνειν (1x)
2Co 3:1 Do·we·begin again to·commend ourselves?
G4921.2 V-PAP-GPM συνιστανόντων (1x)
2Co 10:12 with·some *who·are* commending themselves. But·
G4921.2 V-PAP-NSM συνιστῶν (1x)
2Co 10:18 For *it·is* not that·one commending himself *that* is
G4921.2 V-PAP-NPM συνιστῶντες (2x)
2Co 4:2 of·the truth, commending ourselves to every man·
2Co 6:4 *we·are* presently·commending ourselves as
G4921.2 V-PPN συνίστασθαι (1x)
2Co 12:11 for I·myself was·due to·be·commended by yeu,
G4921.3 V-RAI-3S συνέστηκεν (1x)
Col 1:17 all·things, and by him all·things have·consisted.
G4921.3 V-RAP-NSF συνεστῶσα (1x)
2Pe 3:5 and *there·was* an·earth having·consisted, *being·made*
G4921.4 V-PAI-1S συνίστημι (1x)
Gal 2:18 I·demolished, I·demonstrate my·own·self *to·be* a·
G4921.4 V-PAI-3S συνίστησιν (1x)
Rm 5:8 But God demonstrates his love toward us, how·that
G4921.4 V-AAI-2P συνεστήσατε (1x)
2Co 7:11 In all *things* yeu·demonstrated yeurselves to·be

G4922 συν•οδεύω synôdêúō *v.* (1x)
Roots:G4862 G3593
G4922 V-PAP-NPM συνοδεύοντες (1x)
Ac 9:7 And the men traveling·together with·him stood in·

G4923 συν•οδία synôdía *n.* (1x)
Roots:G4862 G3598
G4923.2 N-DSF συνοδίᾳ (1x)
Lk 2:44 him to·be in the caravan, they·went a·day's journey,

G4924 συν•οικέω synôikêō *v.* (1x)
Roots:G4862 G3611
G4924 V-PAP-NPM συνοικοῦντες (1x)
1Pe 3:7 *be* dwelling·together *with·them* according·to

G4925 συν•οικοδομέω synôikôdômêō *v.* (1x)
Roots:G4862 G3618
G4925.1 V-PPI-2P συνοικοδομεῖσθε (1x)
Eph 2:22 in whom yeu also are·built·together for a·residence

G4926 συν•ομιλέω synômilêō *v.* (1x)
Roots:G4862 G3656
G4926 V-PAP-NSM συνομιλῶν (1x)
Ac 10:27 And while·conversing·together with·him, he·

G4927 συν•ομ•ορέω synômôrêō *v.* (1x)
Roots:G4862 G3674 G3725
G4927.2 V-PAP-NSF συνομοροῦσα (1x)
Ac 18:7 whose home was adjoining the gathering·place.

G4928 συν•οχή synôchḗ *n.* (2x)
Roots:G4912 Compare:G3308
G4928.2 N-NSF συνοχή (1x)
Lk 21:25 the earth *shall·be the* anguished·anxiety of·nations,
G4928.2 N-GSF συνοχῆς (1x)
2Co 2:4 tribulation and anguished·anxiety of·heart I·wrote

G4929 συν•τάσσω syntássō *v.* (2x)
Roots:G4862 G5021 Compare:G2720 G1781 See:G2003 G2004
G4929.2 V-AAI-3S συνέταξεν (2x)
Mt 26:19 the disciples did as YeShua appointed them, and
Mt 27:10 the potter's field, just·as Yahweh appointed me."

G4930 συν•τέλεια syntéléia *n.* (6x)
Roots:G4931 See:G4286 xLangAlso:H0614
G4930.1 N-NSF συντέλεια (1x)
Mt 13:39 The harvest is *the* entire·completion of·the age, and
G4930.1 N-DSF συντελείᾳ (2x)
Mt 13:40 shall·it·be at the entire·completion of·this age.
Mt 13:49 shall·it·be at the entire·completion of·the age. The
G4930.1 N-GSF συντελείας (2x)
Mt 24:3 ·Presence, and of·the entire·completion of·the age?
Mt 28:20 days, even·unto the entire·completion of·the age."
G4930.2 N-DSF συντελείᾳ (1x)
Heb 9:26 ·once, at *the* complete·consummation of·the ages,

G4931 συν•τελέω syntêlêō *v.* (7x)
Roots:G4862 G5055 Compare:G0658 G1842 See:G4930 xLangAlso:H3615
G4931.1 V-PAP-NSM συντελῶν (1x)
Rm 9:28 For *Yahweh is* entirely·completing *the* matter and
G4931.1 V-PPN συντελεῖσθαι (2x)
Ac 21:27 days were·about to·be·entirely·completed, the Jews
Mk 13:4 these·things are·about to·be·entirely·completed?"
G4931.1 V-AAI-3S συνετέλεσεν (1x)
Mt 7:28 *that* when YeShua entirely·completed these sayings,
G4931.1 V-AAP-NSM συντελέσας (1x)
Lk 4:13 And after·entirely·completing *the* entire proof·trial,
G4931.1 V-APP-GPF συντελεσθεισῶν (1x)
Lk 4:2 ·the·same *days* being·entirely·completed, eventually
G4931.2 V-FAI-1S συντελέσω (1x)
Heb 8:8 'and I·shall·completely·consummate a·brand-new

G4932 συν•τέμνω syntémnō *v.* (2x)
Roots:G4862 G5114 Compare:G3973 xLangAlso:H2782
G4932.2 V-PAP-NSM συντέμνων (1x)
Rm 9:28 *the* matter and cutting·*it*·short in righteousness,
G4932.4 V-RPP-ASM συντετμημένον (1x)
Rm 9:28 shall·make a·concise·working·of *the* matter upon

G4933 συν•τηρέω syntērêō *v.* (4x)
Roots:G4862 G5083
G4933.1 V-IAI-3S συνετήρει (2x)
Lk 2:19 But Mariam was·closely·guarding all these
Mk 6:20 holy man, and he·was·closely·guarding him. And
G4933.2 V-PPI-3P συντηροῦνται (2x)
Lk 5:38 into brand-new wineskins, and both are·preserved.
Mt 9:17 into brand-new wineskins, and both are·preserved."

G4934 συν•τίθεμαι syntíthêmai *v.* (4x)
Roots:G4862 G5087 Compare:G4856 See:G0802
G4934.2 V-2AMI-3P συνέθεντο (3x)
Lk 22:5 ·glad and agreed·among·themselves to·give him
Ac 23:20 Judeans agreed·among·themselves to·ask·of you
Ac 24:9 Judeans also agreed·among·themselves, professing
G4934.2 V-LMI-3P συνετέθειντο (1x)
Jn 9:22 the Judeans had·agreed·among·themselves even·now

G4935 συν•τόμως syntómōs *adv.* (1x)
Roots:G4932
G4935 ADV συντόμως (1x)
Ac 24:4 you in·your·own fairness to·hear of·us concisely.

G4936 συν•τρέχω syntrḗchō *v.* (3x)
Roots:G4862 G5143 See:G4890
G4936 V-PAP-GPM συντρεχόντων (1x)
1Pe 4:4 of·yeu not *to·be* running·together *with·them* into the
G4936 V-2AAI-3S συνέδραμεν (1x)
Ac 3:11 John, all the people ran·together toward them in the
G4936 V-2AAI-3P συνέδραμον (1x)
Mk 6:33 him. Then they·ran·together on·foot from all the

G4937 συν•τρίβω syntríbō *v.* (8x)
Roots:G4862 G5147 Compare:G2352 G2608
See:G4936-1
xLangEquiv:H7665

G4937.2 V-FAI-3S συντρίψει (1x)
Rm 16:20 God of·peace shall·shatter the Adversary-Accuser

G4937.2 V-2FPI-3S συντριβήσεται (1x)
Jn 19:36 ·fulfilled, "'A·bone of·him shall·not be·shattered.'"

G4937.2 V-PAP-NSN συντρῖβον (1x)
Lk 9:39 and hardly does·it·depart from him, shattering him.

G4937.2 V-PPI-3S συντρίβεται (1x)
Rv 2:27 the earthenware vessels are·shattered *by·its·maker*,"

G4937.2 V-AAP-NSF συντρίψασα (1x)
Mk 14:3 spikenard. And upon·shattering the alabaster·flask,

G4937.2 V-RPN συντετρῖφθαι (1x)
Mk 5:4 and the shackles to·have·been·shattered. And not·

G4937.2 V-RPP-ASM συντετριμμένον (1x)
Mt 12:20 A·reed having·been·shattered he·did·not break·

G4937.2 V-RPP-APM συντετριμμένους (1x)
Lk 4:18 heart having·been·shattered, to·officially·proclaim

G4938 σύν•τριμμα sýntrimma *n.* (1x)
Roots:G4937 Compare:G4485 See:G4936-1
xLangAlso:H7667

G4938.2 N-NSN σύντριμμα (1x)
Rm 3:16 Shattered·ruin and misery *are* in their ways.

G4939 σύν•τροφος sýntrôphôs *adj.* (1x)
Roots:G4862 G5162

G4939.2 A-NSM σύντροφος (1x)
Ac 13:1 (*who·was* nursed·and·reared·together with·HerOd·

G4940 συν•τυγχάνω syntynchánō *v.* (1x)
Roots:G4862 G5177 Compare:G4876 See:G4941

G4940.2 V-2AAN συντυχεῖν (1x)
Lk 8:19 yet were·not able to·encounter him on·account·of

G4941 Συν•τύχη Syntýchē *n/p.* (1x)
Roots:G4940

G4941.2 N/P-ASF Συντύχην (1x)
Php 4:2 EuOdia and I·implore SynTyche to·contemplate the

G4942 συν•υπο•κρίνομαι synypôkrínômai *v.* (1x)
Roots:G4862 G5271 See:G5273

G4942 V-API-3P συνυπεκρίθησαν (1x)
Gal 2:13 ·*the* Jews also were·hypocritical·together with·him,

G4943 συν•υπο•υργέω synypôurgéō *v.* (1x)
Roots:G4862 G5259 G2041

G4943.2 V-PAP-GPM συνυπουργούντων (1x)
2Co 1:11 with·yeu also assisting·together by·the petition on·

G4944 συν•ωδίνω synōdínō *v.* (1x)
Roots:G4862 G5605

G4944.1 V-PAI-3S συνωδίνει (1x)
Rm 8:22 and jointly·experiences·birthing·pain even·up·to

G4945 συν•ωμοσία synōmôsía *n.* (1x)
Roots:G4862 G3660 Compare:G1999

G4945.3 N-ASF συνωμοσίαν (1x)
Ac 23:13 forty·men having·made this sworn·conspiracy.

G4946 Συράκουσαι Syrákôusai *n/l.* (1x)

G4946 N/L-APF Συρακούσας (1x)
Ac 28:12 after·being·moored at Syracuse, we·stayed·over *for*

G4947 Συρία Syría *n/l.* (8x)
Roots:H6865 See:G4947-6 xLangAlso:H0758

G4947.2 N/L-ASF Συρίαν (6x)
Ac 15:23 the·ones in Antioch and Syria and Cilicia, the·
Ac 15:41 And he·went·throughout Syria and Cilicia,
Ac 18:18 was·sailing·away *from·there* into Syria, and
Ac 20:3 Jews as·he·was·about to·sail into Syria, he·made·a·
Ac 21:3 on·the·left·side, we·were·sailing into Syria, and
Mt 4:24 his fame went·off into all Syria. And they·brought

G4947.2 N/L-GSF Συρίας (2x)
Lk 2:2 occurred with·Cyrenius being·governor of·Syria).
Gal 1:21 I·came into the vicinities of·Syria and Cilicia,

G4948 Σύρος Sýrôs *n/g.* (1x)
Roots:H6865 See:G4947

G4948 N/G-NSM Σύρος (1x)
Lk 4:27 of·them was·purified, except Naaman the Syrian."

G4949 Συρο•φοίνισσα Syrôphôínissa *n/g.* (1x)
Roots:G4948 G5403

G4949 N/G-NSF Συροφοινίσσα (1x)
Mk 7:26 woman was·a·Greek, a·Syro-Phoenician by·birth,

G4950 σύρτις sýrtis *n.* (2x)
Roots:G4951 Compare:G0285

G4950.2 N-ASF σύρτιν (1x)
Ac 27:17 they·should·fall into the sand·bars, after·lowering

EG4950.2 (1x)
Ac 27:41 ·seas·met *producing a·broad sand·bar*, they·ran the

G4951 σύρω sýrō *v.* (5x)
Compare:G1670 G4563 See:G2694 G4950

G4951 V-PAI-3S σύρει (1x)
Rv 12:4 And his tail dragged the third·part of·the stars of·the

G4951 V-PAP-NSM σύρων (2x)
Jn 21:8 came in·the small·boat, while·dragging the net of·
Ac 8:3 each *of* the houses *and* dragging·off both men and

G4951 V-IAI-3P ἔσυρον (2x)
Ac 14:19 and stoning Paul, they·were·dragging *him* outside
Ac 17:6 not finding them, they·were·dragging Jason and

G4952 συ•σπαράσσω sysparássō *v.* (1x)
Roots:G4862 G4682 Compare:G4486

G4952.2 V-AAI-3S συνεσπάραξεν (1x)
Lk 9:42 demon mangled him and violently·convulsed *him*.

G4953 σύ•σσημον sýssēmôn *n.* (1x)
Roots:G4862 G4591

G4953.2 N-ASN σύσσημον (1x)
Mk 14:44 over had·given them a·prearranged·signal, saying,

G4954 σύ•σσωμος sýssōmôs *adj.* (1x)
Roots:G4862 G4983

G4954.2 A-APN σύσσωμα (1x)
Eph 3:6 to·be co-heirs, co-members, and co-participants of·

G4955 συ•στασιαστής systasiastḗs *n.* (1x)
Roots:G4862 G4714

G4955 N-GPM συστασιαστῶν (1x)
Mk 15:7 ·been·bound with the fellow-insurrectionists, who

G4956 συ•στατικός systatikós *adj.* (2x)
Roots:G4921

G4956.2 A-GPM συστατικῶν (2x)
2Co 3:1 as some *do*, of·letters of·recommendation to yeu, or
2Co 3:1 or *of·letters* of·recommendation from·among yeu.

G4957 συ•σταυρόω systauróō *v.* (5x)
Roots:G4862 G4717 Compare:G4362

G4957 V-API-3S συνεσταυρώθη (1x)
Rm 6:6 man·of·clay† is·already·crucified·together *with·him*,

G4957 V-APP-GSM συσταυρωθέντος (1x)
Jn 19:32 of·the other one being·crucified·together with·him.

G4957 V-APP-NPM συσταυρωθέντες (1x)
Mt 27:44 (the·ones being·crucified·together with·him) were·

G4957 V-RPI-1S συνεσταύρωμαι (1x)
Gal 2:20 I·have·been·crucified·together with·Anointed-One,

G4957 V-RPP-NPM συνεσταυρωμένοι (1x)
Mk 15:32 the·ones having·been·crucified·together with·him

G4958 συ•στέλλω systéllō *v.* (2x)
Roots:G4862 G4724

G4958.2 V-AAI-3P συνέστειλαν (1x)
Ac 5:6 the younger·men, rising·up, tightly·wrapped him up,

G4958.4 V-RPP-NSM συνεσταλμένος (1x)
1Co 7:29 *is* having·been·drawn·tight·and·shortened in·order·

G4959 συ•στενάζω systênázō *v.* (1x)
Roots:G4862 G4727

G4959.1 V-PAI-3S συστενάζει (1x)
Rm 8:22 creation groans·together and jointly·experiences·

G4960 συ•στοιχέω systôichéō *v.* (1x)
Roots:G4862 G4748 Compare:G1526

G4960.2 V-PAI-3S συστοιχεῖ (1x)
Gal 4:25 in Arabia, and corresponds·to JeruSalem at·the

G4961 συ•στρατιώτης systratiṓtēs *n.* (2x)
Roots:G4862 G4757

G4961.1 N-ASM συστρατιώτην (1x)
Php 2:25 brother, coworker, and fellow·soldier (but yeur

G4961.1 N-DSM συστρατιώτῃ (1x)
Phm 1:2 and ArchIppus our fellow·soldier, and to·the

G4962 συ•στρέφω systréphō *v.* (1x)
Roots:G4862 G4762 Compare:G4816 G5166
See:G4963

G4962.2 V-AAP-GSM συστρέψαντος (1x)
Ac 28:3 *was* bundling·together a·multitude of·kindling·sticks

G4963 συ•στροφή systrôphḗ *n.* (2x)
Roots:G4962 Compare:G5016

G4963.2 N-GSF συστροφῆς (1x)
Ac 19:40 ·be·able to·render an·account of·this riotous·mob."

G4963.3 N-ASF συστροφήν (1x)
Ac 23:12 Judeans, making a·secret·mob, vowed·and·bound

G4964 συ•σχηματίζω syschēmatízō *v.* (3x)
Roots:G4862 G4976 Compare:G3445 G3877 G4748

G4964.2 V-PEM-2P συσχηματίζεσθε (1x)
Rm 12:2 And do·not be·conformed to·this present·age, but·

G4964.2 V-PEP-NPM συσχηματιζόμενοι (1x)
1Pe 1:14 do·not be·presently·conforming to·the previous

EG4964.2 (1x)
1Pe 1:15 but·rather, *conforming* according·to·the·one

G4965 Συχάρ Sychár *n/l.* (1x)
שֵׁכָר shekar [Hebrew]
Roots:H7941

G4965.2 N/L-PRI Συχάρ (1x)
Jn 4:5 ·Samaria being·referred·to·as Sychar *(or·intoxicating)*,

G4966 Συχέμ Sychém *n/l.* (2x)
שְׁכֶם shekem [Hebrew]
Roots:H7927

G4966.2 N/L-PRI Συχέμ (1x)
Ac 7:16 And they·were·transferred into Shekem and laid in

G4966.3 N/L-PRI Συχέμ (1x)
Ac 7:16 near the Sons of·Chamor *the father* of·Shekem.

G4967 σφαγή sphagḗ *n.* (3x)
Roots:G4969 See:G2695 xLangAlso:H2874

G4967.2 N-ASF σφαγήν (1x)
Ac 8:32 He·was·driven as a·sheep to *the* butchering; and as

G4967.2 N-GSF σφαγῆς (2x)
Rm 8:36 ·long; we·are·reckoned as sheep for·butchering."
Jac 5:5 ·nourished yeur hearts, as in a·day of·butchering.

G4969 σφάζω spházō *v.* (10x)
Compare:G2380 G0615 G5407 See:G4967 G2695
xLangAlso:H7819 H2873

G4969.1 V-AAI-3S ἔσφαξεν (2x)
1Jn 3:12 ·out of·the Evil·One and slaughtered his brother.
1Jn 3:12 for·what self-gratifying·cause did·he·slaughter him?

G4969.1 V-AAS-3P σφάξωσιν (1x)
Rv 6:4 the earth, and that they·should·slaughter one·another.

G4969.1 V-2API-2S ἐσφάγης (1x)
Rv 5:9 its official·seals, because you·were·slaughtered, and

G4969.1 V-RPP-ASF ἐσφαγμένην (1x)
Rv 13:3 heads as·though having·been·slaughtered to death,

G4969.1 V-RPP-GSN ἐσφαγμένου (1x)
Rv 13:8 of·the Lamb having·been·slaughtered from *the*

G4969.1 V-RPP-GPM ἐσφαγμένων (2x)
Rv 6:9 of·the·ones having·been·slaughtered on·account·of
Rv 18:24 of·all the·ones having·been·slaughtered upon the

G4969.1 V-RPP-NSN ἐσφαγμένον (2x)
Rv 5:6 a·Lamb standing as having·been·slaughtered, having
Rv 5:12 Lamb (the·one having·been·slaughtered) to·receive

G4970 σφόδρα sphódra *adv.* (11x)
Compare:G3029 See:G4971 xLangAlso:H3966

G4970 ADV σφόδρα (11x)
Lk 18:23 ·grieved, for he·was tremendously wealthy.
Ac 6:7 were·multiplied in JeruSalem tremendously; also a·
Mt 2:10 they·rejoiced *with* tremendously great joy.
Mt 17:6 fell on their faces and were tremendously afraid.
Mt 17:23 And they·were tremendously grieved.
Mt 18:31 that·were·happening, were tremendously grieved,
Mt 19:25 *this*, his disciples were tremendously astounded,
Mt 26:22 And being tremendously grieved, each·one of·them

Mt 27:54 happening, they·feared tremendously, saying,
Mk 16:4 ·been·rolled·away, for it·was tremendously great.
Rv 16:21 its punishing·blow was tremendously great.

G4971 σφοδρῶς sphôdrỗs *adv.* (1x)
Compare:G3029 See:G4970
G4971.1 ADV σφοδρῶς (1x)
Ac 27:18 with·us tremendously being·tossed·by·the·storm,

G4972 σφραγίζω sphragízō *v.* (26x)
Roots:G4973 See:G2696 xLangAlso:H2856
G4972.1 V-PAS-1P σφραγίζωμεν (1x)
Rv 7:3 trees, even·until we·should·officially·seal the slaves
G4972.1 V-AAI-3S ἐσφράγισεν (1x)
Jn 6:27 ·yeu, for God the Father officially·sealed this·one."
G4972.1 V-AAP-NPM σφραγίσαντες (1x)
Mt 27:66 sentinel·guard *and·by* officially·sealing the stone.
G4972.1 V-API-2P ἐσφραγίσθητε (2x)
Eph 1:13 yeu·are·already·officially·sealed with·the Holy
Eph 4:30 by whom yeu·are·already·officially·sealed to *the*
G4972.1 V-RPP-GPM ἐσφραγισμένων (1x)
Rv 7:4 number of·the·ones having·been·officially·sealed:
G4972.1 V-RPP-NPM ἐσφραγισμένοι (13x)
Rv 7:4 *thousand* having·been·officially·sealed from·among
Rv 7:5 *the* tribe of·Judah having·been·officially·sealed,
Rv 7:5 *the* tribe of·ReuBen having·been·officially·sealed,
Rv 7:5 *the* tribe of·Gad having·been·officially·sealed, twelve
Rv 7:6 *the* tribe of·Asher having·been·officially·sealed,
Rv 7:6 *the* tribe of·Naphtali having·been·officially·sealed,
Rv 7:6 *the* tribe of·MaNasseh having·been·officially·sealed,
Rv 7:7 *the* tribe of·Shimon having·been·officially·sealed,
Rv 7:7 *the* tribe of·Levi having·been·officially·sealed,
Rv 7:7 *the* tribe of·IsSakar having·been·officially·sealed,
Rv 7:8 *the* tribe of·Zebulun having·been·officially·sealed,
Rv 7:8 tribe of·Joseph having·been·officially·sealed, twelve
Rv 7:8 *the* tribe of·BenJamin having·been·officially·sealed,
G4972.2 V-AAI-3S ἐσφράγισεν (1x)
Rv 20:3 shut him up, and set·an·official·seal upon him, in·
G4972.3 V-AAI-3S ἐσφράγισεν (1x)
Jn 3:33 his testimony did·stamp·his·own·seal that God is
G4972.4 V-AMP-NSM σφραγισάμενος (2x)
Rm 15:28 and after·personally·and·officially·sealing to·them
2Co 1:22 also already·personally·and·officially·sealing us
G4972.5 V-FDI-3S σφραγίσεται (1x)
2Co 11:10 that this boasting shall·not be·sealed·up in me
G4972.5 V-AAM-2S σφράγισον (1x)
Rv 10:4 saying to·me, "Seal·up those·things·which the
G4972.5 V-AAS-2S σφραγίσῃς (1x)
Rv 22:10 to·me, "You·should·not seal·up the words of·the

G4973 σφραγίς sphragís *n.* (16x)
Roots:G5420 Compare:G4592 G0656-2 See:G4972 xLangAlso:H2368
G4973.2 N-NSF σφραγίς (1x)
1Co 9:2 ·yeurselves are the official·seal of·my commission
G4973.2 N-ASF σφραγῖδα (10x)
Rm 4:11 ·circumcision, an·official·seal of·the righteousness
2Ti 2:19 of·God stands, having this official·seal, "' Yahweh
Rv 6:3 when he·opened·up the second official·seal, I·heard
Rv 6:5 *Lamb* opened·up the third official·seal, I·heard the
Rv 6:7 when he·opened·up the fourth official·seal, I·heard
Rv 6:9 *Lamb* opened·up the fifth official·seal, I·saw beneath
Rv 6:12 I·saw when he·opened·up the sixth official·seal, and
Rv 7:2 eastern sun, having an·official·seal of·the·living God
Rv 8:1 *the Lamb* opened·up the seventh official·seal, there·
Rv 9:4 ·of·clay† who do·not have the official·seal of·God in
G4973.2 N-APF σφραγῖδας (3x)
Rv 5:2 ·up the official·scroll and to·loosen its official·seals?"
Rv 5:5 official·scroll and to·loosen its seven official·seals."
Rv 5:9 ·scroll and to·open·up its official·seals, because you·
G4973.2 N-DPF σφραγῖσιν (1x)
Rv 5:1 having·been·fully·sealed·up with·seven official·seals.
G4973.2 N-GPF σφραγίδων (1x)
Rv 6:1 *the* first from·among the official·seals, and I·heard

G4974 σφυρόν sphyrṓn *n.* (1x)
G4974 N-NPN σφυρά (1x)
Ac 3:7 at·once, his feet and ankle·joints were·stabilized.

G4975 σχεδόν schêdṓn *adv.* (3x)
Roots:G2192
G4975 ADV σχεδόν (3x)
Ac 13:44 And on·the coming Sabbath, almost all the city *of*·
Ac 19:26 at·Ephesus, but·yet almost throughout·all Asia,
Heb 9:22 And almost all·things, according·to the Torah-Law,

G4976 σχῆμα schễma *n.* (2x)
Roots:G2192 Compare:G3444 See:G4964
G4976.1 N-NSN σχῆμα (1x)
1Co 7:31 *it …* for the schematic·layout of·this world passes·
G4976.1 N-DSN σχήματι (1x)
Php 2:8 being·found in·a·schematic·layout as a·man·of·clay†

G4977 σχίζω schízō *v.* (10x)
See:G4978 G4058-7 xLangEquiv:H1234
G4977.1 V-PPP-APM σχιζομένους (1x)
Mk 1:10 water, he·saw the heavens being·split·open, and the
G4977.1 V-API-3P ἐσχίσθησαν (1x)
Mt 27:51 earth is·shaken, and the solid·rocks are·split·open,
G4977.2 V-PAI-3S σχίζει (1x)
Lk 5:36 then the brand-new *patch* makes·a·tear; and·also *the*
G4977.2 V-AAS-1P σχίσωμεν (1x)
Jn 19:24 one·another, "We·should·not tear it, but·rather we·
G4977.2 V-API-3S ἐσχίσθη (6x)
Jn 21:11 ·being so·vast·a·quantity, the net was·not torn.
Lk 23:45 and the curtain of·the Temple was·torn *down the*
Ac 14:4 the multitude of·the city was·torn·in·two. And in·
Ac 23:7 the Sadducees, and the multitude was·torn·in·two.
Mt 27:51 the curtain of·the Temple is·torn in two from top
Mk 15:38 the curtain of·the Temple was·torn in two from top

G4978 σχίσμα schísma *n.* (8x)
Roots:G4977 Compare:G1267 G1370 G5545-1
G4978.2 N-NSN σχίσμα (2x)
Mt 9:16 from the garment, and *the* tear becomes worse.
Mk 2:21 ·fullness from·the old, and *the* tear becomes worse.
G4978.3 N-NSN σχίσμα (4x)
Jn 7:43 there·was a·severing·schism among the crowd on·
Jn 9:16 And there·was a·severing·schism among them.
Jn 10:19 there·was a·severing·schism again among the
1Co 12:25 ·that there·should·not be a·severing·schism in the
G4978.3 N-NPN σχίσματα (1x)
1Co 1:10 *that* there·may·not be severing·schisms among yeu
G4978.3 N-APN σχίσματα (1x)
1Co 11:18 I·hear *for* severing·schisms to·subsist among yeu

G4979 σχοινίον schôiníôn *n.* (2x)
Roots:G2444-3 Compare:G2572-1 xLangAlso:H2256
G4979.2 N-GPN σχοινίων (1x)
Jn 2:15 And making a·lash out of·small·cords, he·cast·out
G4979.3 N-APN σχοινία (1x)
Ac 27:32 soldiers chopped·off the small·ropes of·the skiff,

G4980 σχολάζω schôlázō *v.* (2x)
Roots:G4981
G4980.2 V-PAS-2P σχολάζητε (1x)
1Co 7:5 in·order·that yeu·may·hold·off·and·give·yeurselves
G4980.3 V-PAP-ASM σχολάζοντα (1x)
Mt 12:44 *to·it*, it·finds *it* being·vacant, having·been·swept

G4981 σχολή schôlḗ *n.* (1x)
Roots:G2192 See:G4980
G4981.2 N-DSF σχολῇ (1x)
Ac 19:9 in·the school·auditorium of·a·certain·man *named*

G4982 σώζω sṓzō *v.* (111x)
Compare:G4506 xLangAlso:H3467
G4982.1 V-FAI-2S σώσεις (3x)
1Co 7:16 O·wife, whether you·shall·save the husband?
1Co 7:16 O·husband, whether you·shall·save the wife?
1Ti 4:16 for in·doing this you·shall·save both yourself and
G4982.1 V-FAI-3S σώσει (5x)
Lk 9:24 soul's·desire for·my cause, the·same shall·save it.
Mt 1:21 ·*Saves),* for he·himself shall·save his People from
Mk 8:35 *for·that* of·the good·news, the·same shall·save it.
Jac 5:15 trust shall·save the·one becoming·sickly·fatigued,
Jac 5:20 of·*the*·error of·his way shall·save a·soul from·out
G4982.1 V-FAP-NSM σώσων (1x)
Mt 27:49 we·should·see whether EliJah comes to·save him."
G4982.1 V-FPI-1P σωθησόμεθα (2x)
Rm 5:9 blood, so·much more·so we·shall·be·saved from the
Rm 5:10 after·being·reconciled, we·shall·be·saved by his
G4982.1 V-FPI-2S σωθήσῃ (3x)
Ac 11:14 to you utterances by which you·shall·be·saved, you
Ac 16:31 Jesus Anointed, and you·shall·be·saved, you and
Rm 10:9 him from·among dead·men, you·shall·be·saved.
G4982.1 V-FPI-3S σωθήσεται (11x)
Jn 10:9 should·enter·in through me, he·shall·be·saved, and
Ac 2:21 ·call·upon the name of·Yahweh shall·be·saved."
Mt 10:22 ·enduring to *the* end, this·one shall·be·saved.
Mt 24:13 ·enduring to *the* end, the·same shall·be·saved.
Mk 13:13 ·enduring to *the* end, the·same shall·be·saved.
Mk 16:16 and already·being·immersed shall·be·saved, but
Rm 9:27 sand of·the sea, the small·remnant shall·be·saved.
Rm 10:13 call·upon the name of·*the*·Lord shall·be·saved.'"
Rm 11:26 in·this·manner all IsraEl shall·be·saved; just·as it·
1Co 3:15 ·and·loss, but he·himself shall·be·saved, but in·
1Ti 2:15 Now she·shall·be·saved through the bearing·of·
G4982.1 V-PAI-3S σώζει (1x)
1Pe 3:21 corresponding·pattern, which even now saves us, *is*
G4982.1 V-PAM-2P σώζετε (1x)
Jud 1:23 And others save with a·fear while·snatching *them*
G4982.1 V-PAN σώζειν (2x)
Heb 5:7 toward the·one being·able to·save him from·out of·
Heb 7:25 ·which·place he·is·able also to·save·them to the
G4982.1 V-PPI-2P σώζεσθε (1x)
1Co 15:2 through which also yeu·are·saved, if yeu·fully·
G4982.1 V-PPI-3S σώζεται (1x)
1Pe 4:18 If the righteous·man scarcely is·saved, where shall·
G4982.1 V-PPN σώζεσθαι (1x)
Ac 27:20 for·us to·be·saved was·entirely·removed.
G4982.1 V-PPP-APM σωζομένους (1x)
Ac 2:47 the Lord was·placing the·ones being·saved each day
G4982.1 V-PPP-DPM σωζομένοις (2x)
1Co 1:18 ·perishing; but to·us who·are·being·saved, it·is the
2Co 2:15 ·Anointed-One, among the·ones being·saved, and
G4982.1 V-PPP-GPM σωζομένων (1x)
Rv 21:24 the nations, of·the·ones being·saved, shall·walk in
G4982.1 V-PPP-NPM σωζόμενοι (1x)
Lk 13:23 "Lord, *is·it so* that the·ones being·saved *are* few?
G4982.1 V-AAI-3S ἔσωσεν (4x)
Lk 23:35 ·at *him*, saying, "He·saved others, let·him·save
Mt 27:42 "He·saved others, *yet* he·is·not able to·save himself
Mk 15:31 with the scribes, "He·saved others; himself, he·is·
Tit 3:5 did), but·rather he·saved us according·to his mercy,
G4982.1 V-AAM-2S σῶσον (7x)
Jn 12:27 should·I·declare? 'Father, save me out of·this hour
Lk 23:37 ·yourself are the king of·the Jews, save yourself."
Lk 23:39 are the Anointed-One, save yourself and us.
Mt 8:25 saying, "Lord, save us! We·completely·perish.
Mt 14:30 ·down, he·yelled·out, saying, "Lord, save me."
Mt 27:40 building *it* in three days, save yourself. If you·are
Mk 15:30 save yourself, and descend from the cross!"
G4982.1 V-AAM-3S σωσάτω (1x)
Lk 23:35 "He·saved others, let·him·save himself— if this·
G4982.1 V-AAN σῶσαι (16x)
Lk 6:9 ·beneficially·do·good or to·do·bad, to·save a·soul or
Lk 9:24 For whoever should·want to·save his soul's·desire
Lk 9:56 *the* souls of·men·of·clay†, but·rather to·save *them.*"
Lk 17:33 "Whoever should·seek to·save his soul's·desire
Lk 19:10 and to·save the·one having·been·completely·lost."
Mt 16:25 For whoever should·want to·save his soul's·desire
Mt 18:11 came to·save the·one having·completely·perished.
Mt 27:42 others, *yet* he·is·not able to·save himself. If he·is
Mk 3:4 various·Sabbaths, or to·do·bad? To·save a·soul, or
Mk 8:35 For whoever should·want to·save his soul's·desire
Mk 15:31 "He·saved others; himself, he·is·not able to·save.

Jac 1:21 the·one being·able to·save yeur souls.
Jac 2:14 have works? ¿! Is the trust not able to·save him?
Jac 4:12 ·one being·able to·save and to·completely·destroy.
1Co 1:21 of·official·proclamation to·save the·ones trusting.
1Ti 1:15 into the world to·save morally·disqualified·ones,

G4982.1 V-AAP-GSM σώσαντος (1x)
2Ti 1:9 the·one saving us and calling·*us*·forth with·a·holy

G4982.1 V-AAP-NSM σώσας (1x)
Jud 1:5 this: that Yahweh, after·*first*·saving a·People out of·

G4982.1 V-AAS-1S σώσω (3x)
Jn 12:47 but·rather in·order·that I·may·save the world.
Rm 11:14 *who·are* my flesh and may·save some from·among
1Co 9:22 things in·order·that by·all·means I·may·save some.

G4982.1 V-API-1P ἐσώθημεν (1x)
Rm 8:24 For in·the Expectation, we·are·saved, but an·

G4982.1 V-API-3S ἐσώθη (3x)
Lk 8:36 ·one being·possessed·with·the·demons was·saved.
Mt 24:22 not any flesh would be·saved *to·continue living*;
Mk 13:20 not any flesh would be·saved; but·yet on·account·

G4982.1 V-APM-2P σώθητε (1x)
Ac 2:40 saying, "Save·yeurselves from this warped

G4982.1 V-APN σωθῆναι (10x)
Lk 18:26 "Who then is·able to·be·saved?"
Ac 4:12 ·clay† by which it·is·necessary·for us to·be·saved."
Ac 14:9 at·him and seeing that he·has trust to·be·saved,
Ac 15:1 manner of·Moses, yeu·are·not able to·be·saved."
Ac 15:11 ·*the*·Lord Jesus Anointed to·be·saved; according·to
Ac 27:31 the sailing·ship, yeu are·not able to·be·saved."
Mt 19:25 "Who then is·able to·be·saved?"
Mk 10:26 "Then who is·able to·be·saved?"
2Th 2:10 the love of·the truth, such·for them to·be·saved.
1Ti 2:4 who wants all men·of·clay† to·be·saved and to·come

G4982.1 V-APS-1S σωθῶ (1x)
Ac 16:30 ·for me to·do in·order·that I·may·be·saved?"

G4982.1 V-APS-2P σώθητε (1x)
Jn 5:34 but·rather I·say these·things that yeu may·be·saved.

G4982.1 V-APS-3S σωθῇ (3x)
Jn 3:17 in·order·that the world through him may·be·saved.
Mk 5:23 on·her, so·that she·may·be·saved and shall·live."
1Co 5:5 in·order·that the spirit may·be·saved in the Day of·

G4982.1 V-APS-3P σωθῶσιν (3x)
Lk 8:12 their hearts, lest trusting, they·should·be·saved.
1Th 2:16 in·order·that they·may·be·saved, in·order·for *these*
1Co 10:33 of·the many in·order·that they·may·be·saved.

G4982.1 V-RAI-3S σέσωκεν (2x)
Lk 7:50 the woman, "Your trust has·saved you; traverse in
Lk 18:42 "Receive·your·sight. Your trust has·saved you."

G4982.1 V-RPP-NPM σεσωσμένοι (2x)
Eph 2:5 (by·grace, yeu·are having·been·saved).
Eph 2:8 grace, yeu·are having·been·saved through the trust.

EG4982.1 (1x)
Ac 15:11 according·to that manner, they·also *are·saved*."

G4982.2 V-FAI-3S σώσει (1x)
2Ti 4:18 And *me*, he·shall·keep·safe·and·sound into his

G4982.3 V-FPI-1S σωθήσομαι (2x)
Mt 9:21 of·his garment, I·shall·be·made·safe·and·well."
Mk 5:28 of·his garments, I·shall·be·made·safe·and·well."

G4982.3 V-FPI-3S σωθήσεται (2x)
Jn 11:12 ·has·been·laid·asleep, he·shall·be·safe·and·well."
Lk 8:50 Merely trust, and she·shall·be·made·safe·and·well."

G4982.3 V-IPI-3P ἐσῴζοντο (1x)
Mk 6:56 ·hold of·him, they·were·made·safe·and·well.

G4982.3 V-API-3S ἐσώθη (1x)
Mt 9:22 And the woman was·made·safe·and·well from that

G4982.3 V-RAI-3S σέσωκεν (5x)
Lk 8:48 Your trust has·made you safe·and·well; depart in
Lk 17:19 Your trust has·made you safe·and·well."
Mt 9:22 your trust has·made you safe·and·well." And the
Mk 5:34 your trust has·made you safe·and·well. Head·on·out
Mk 10:52 ·out, your trust has·made you safe·and·well." And

G4982.3 V-RPI-3S σέσωσται (1x)
Ac 4:9 what·means this·man has·been·made·safe·and·well—

G4983 σῶμα sō̃ma *n.* (147x)

Roots:G4982 Compare:G5559 G5590 G4598-2
See:G4984

EG4983 (1x)
1Co 12:17 placed? If *the* whole *body is* hearing, where·is the

G4983.1 N-NSN σῶμα (22x)
Lk 11:34 clear·and·focused, your whole body is also full·of·
Lk 11:34 should·be evil, your body *is* also opaquely·dark.
Lk 11:36 "Now·then, if your whole body *is* full·of·light, not
Lk 12:23 physical·nourishment, and the body *is more·than*
Lk 17:37 to·them, "Wherever the body *is*, there the eagles
Mt 5:29 not *that* your whole body should·be·cast into Hell·
Mt 5:30 not *that* your whole body should·be·cast into Hell·
Mt 6:22 ·and·focused, your whole body shall·be full·of·light
Mt 6:23 ·be evil, your whole body shall·be opaquely·dark.
Mt 6:25 physical·nourishment, and the body *more·than* the
Rm 6:6 the body of·moral·failure may·be·fully·rendered·
Rm 8:10 *is* in yeu, in·fact, the body *is* dead through moral·
Jac 2:26 For just·as the body apart·from spirit is dead, in·
1Th 5:23 soul, and body be·fully·kept blamelessly unto the
1Co 6:13 this and these·things. But the body *is* not for·the
1Co 6:16 ·tightly·joined·to·the prostitute is one body? For
1Co 6:19 ·not personally·know that yeur body is a·temple of·
1Co 12:12 For exactly·as the body is one and has many
1Co 12:12 (being many) are one body, in·this·manner also *is*
1Co 12:17 If the whole body *is* an·eye, where·is the sense·
1Co 15:44 It·is·sown a·soulish body; it·is·awakened a·
1Co 15:44 body. There·is a·soulish body, and there·is a·

G4983.1 N-NPN σώματα (6x)
Jn 19:31 ·day, in·order·that the bodies should·not remain
Heb 13:11 For the bodies of·these animals, whose blood is·
Mt 27:52 are·opened·up, and many bodies of·holy·ones
1Co 6:15 Have·yeu·not seen that yeur bodies are members
1Co 15:40 *There·are* also celestial bodies and terrestrial
1Co 15:40 celestial bodies and terrestrial bodies, but·yet in·

G4983.1 N-ASN σῶμα (16x)
Lk 12:4 ·not be·afraid of·the·ones killing the body, and after
Ac 9:40 And turning·back·around to·the body, he·declared,
Mt 10:28 ·not be·afraid of·the·ones killing the body, but not
Mt 10:28 ·destroy both soul and body in Hell·Canyon.
Mt 14:12 ·coming·alongside, took·away the body and buried
Rm 4:19 he·did·not fully·observe his·own body, even·now
Jac 3:2 ·mature man, able also to·bridle the whole body.
Jac 3:3 them to·our *will*, and we·steer their whole body.
Jac 3:6 the·one staining the whole body, and setting·aflame
Php 3:21 who shall·transform the body of·our humble·estate
1Co 6:18 ·immorality morally·fails against his·own body.
1Co 9:27 ·down my body and bring·*it*·more·into·subjection,
1Co 13:3 ·over my body in·order·that I·should·be·set·ablaze,
1Co 15:37 you·sow not the body that·shall·be, but·rather a·
1Co 15:38 but God gives it a·body just·as he·determined,
1Co 15:38 and to·each variety·of·seed, its·own body.

G4983.1 N-ASN@ σῶμα (1x)
Heb 10:22 and the bodies having·been·bathed with·pure

G4983.1 N-APN σώματα (4x)
Rm 1:24 to·dishonor their·own bodies among themselves,
Rm 8:11 give·life·above· to yeur mortal bodies through his
Rm 12:1 of·God, to·present yeur bodies *as* a·living sacrifice,
Eph 5:28 ·love their·own wives as their·own bodies. The·one

G4983.1 N-DSN σώματι (18x)
Lk 12:22 yeu·should·eat, nor·even for·yeur body, what yeu·
Heb 13:3 as yeurselves also being *with·them* in body.
Gal 6:17 for I·myself bear in my body the marks of·the Lord
Mt 6:25 ·should·drink, nor·even for·yeur body, with·what
Mk 5:29 and she·knew in·her body that she·has·been·healed
Rm 6:12 ·Failure reign in yeur mortal body, such·for *yeu* to·
Rm 12:4 ·as we·have many members in one body, but all the
Php 1:20 shall·be·magnified in my body, whether through
1Co 5:3 ·though being·absent in·the body but being·present
1Co 6:13 but·rather for·the Lord, and the Lord for·the body.
1Co 6:20 ·then, glorify God in yeur body and in yeur spirit,
1Co 7:34 ·that she·may·be holy, both in·body and in·spirit.
1Co 15:35 And in·what·kind·of body do·they·come?
2Co 4:10 carrying·about in the body the mortal·deadness of·
2Co 4:10 of·Jesus may·be·made·apparent in our body.
2Co 5:6 that while·being·at·home in the body, *indeed*, we·
2Co 12:2 ago (whether in body, I·do·not personally·know;
2Co 12:3 ·man·of·clay†, (whether in body, or on·the·outside

G4983.1 N-GSN σώματος (21x)
Lk 11:34 "The lantern of·the body is the eye.
Mt 6:22 "The lantern of·the body is the eye.
Rm 7:24 Who shall·snatch me out of·this body of·death?
Rm 8:13 ·to·death the practices of·the body, yeu·shall·live.
Rm 8:23 ·as·sons, *that·is*, the full·redemption of·our body.
Jac 2:16 give to·them the requisite·needs of·the body— what
Jud 1:9 (he·was·discussing about *the* body of·Moses), did·
1Co 6:18 *it*, is on·the·outside of·the body; but the·one
1Co 7:4 does·not have·control·over her·own body, but·rather
1Co 7:4 does·not have·control·over his·own body, but·rather
1Co 12:12 all the members of·the one body (being many)
1Co 12:15 a·hand, I·am not from·among the body," ¿! from
1Co 12:15 this *reasoning*, is·it not from·among the body?
1Co 12:16 an·eye, I·am not from·among the body," ¿! from
1Co 12:16 this *reasoning*, is·it not from·among the body?
1Co 12:23 those *members* of·the body, which·we·presume
2Co 5:8 ·abroad from·among the body and to·be·at·home
2Co 5:10 the·things *done* through the body, pertaining·to
2Co 12:2 or·whether on·the·outside of·the body, I·do·not
2Co 12:3 in body, or on·the·outside of·the body, I·do·not
Col 2:11 the stripping·off from·the body the moral·failures

G4983.1 N-GPN σωμάτων (1x)
Rv 18:13 carriages, "and bodies and souls of·men·of·clay†.

G4983.2 N-GSN σώματος (1x)
2Co 10:10 and strong, but his bodily presence *is* weak, and

G4983.3 N-GSN σώματος (1x)
Col 2:23 an·unsparingly·harsh·treatment of·body, *although*

G4983.4 N-NSN σῶμα (10x)
Rm 12:5 we (the many) are one Body in Anointed-One, and
1Co 10:17 we·are one bread *and* one Body. For all *of·us*
1Co 12:14 For even the Body is not one member, but·rather
1Co 12:19 ·were all one member, where·is the Body placed?
1Co 12:20 in·fact *they·are* many members, but one Body.
1Co 12:27 are Anointed-One's Body and members from·
Eph 1:23 which is his Body, the complete·fullness of·the·one
Eph 4:4 *There·is* one Body, and one Spirit— just·as also yeu·
Eph 4:16 all the Body is·being·fitly·framed·together and is·
Col 2:19 from·out of·which all the Body grows·up through

G4983.4 N-ASN σῶμα (2x)
1Co 12:13 were all immersed into one Body, whether Jews
1Co 12:24 but·yet God blended·together the Body, giving

G4983.4 N-DSN σώματι (3x)
1Co 12:18 each one of·them, in the Body just·as he·wanted.
1Co 12:25 be a·severing·schism in the Body, but·rather *that*
Col 3:15 also yeu·were·called·forth in one Body; and be

G4983.4 N-GSN σώματος (7x)
1Co 12:22 ·much more *those* members of·the Body, the·ones
Eph 4:12 an·edification of·the Body of·the Anointed-One—
Eph 4:16 the maturing·growth of·the Body for its·own
Eph 5:23 And he·himself is Savior of·the Body.
Eph 5:30 because we·are members of·his Body, from·out of·
Col 1:18 is the head of·the Body (the entire·Called·Out·
Col 1:24 in my flesh on·behalf·of·his Body, which is the

G4983.5 N-NSN σῶμα (6x)
Jn 20:12 the feet, where the body of·Jesus was·lain·out.
Lk 22:19 "This is my body, the·one being·given on·yeur
Lk 23:55 the chamber·tomb and how his body was·laid.
Mt 26:26 This is my body."
Mk 14:22 This is my body."
1Co 11:24 This is my body, the·one being·broken over yeu.

G4983.5 N-ASN σῶμα (14x)
Jn 19:38 Pilate that he·may·take·away the body of·Jesus, and
Jn 19:38 So he·came and took·away the body of·Jesus.
Jn 19:40 So·then they·took the body of·Jesus and bound it
Lk 23:52 ·alongside Pilate, requested the body of·Jesus.
Lk 24:3 they·did·not find the body of·the Lord Jesus.
Lk 24:23 and not finding his body, they·came, saying also

Heb 10:5 want, but you·completely·formed a·body for·me.
Mt 27:58 Pilate, requested the body of·YeShua. Then Pilate
Mt 27:58 commandingly·ordered the body to·be·given·back.
Mt 27:59 And after·taking the body, Joseph swathed it in·a·
Mk 14:8 ·beforehand to·apply·ointment·to my body for the
Mk 15:43 ·went·in to Pilate and requested the body of·Jesus.
Mk 15:45 he·voluntarily·presented the body to·Joseph.
1Co 11:29 to·himself, not discerning the Lord's body.

G4983.5 N-DSN σώματι (3x)

1Pe 2:24 ·up our moral·failures in his·own body upon the
Eph 2:16 the both to·God in one body through the cross, in
Col 1:22 in the body of·his flesh through the death, to·

G4983.5 N-GSN σώματος (6x)

Jn 2:21 ·was·saying this concerning the temple of·his body.
Heb 10:10 ·occasion·only, of·the body of·YeShua Anointed.
Mt 26:12 ·herself, casting this ointment on my body, did *it*
Rm 7:4 Torah-Law through the body of·the Anointed-One
1Co 10:16 fellowship of·the body of·the Anointed-One?
1Co 11:27 shall·be held·liable of·the body and blood of·the

G4983.6 N-NSN σῶμα (2x)

1Co 15:44 body; it·is·awakened a·spiritual body. There·is a·
1Co 15:44 ·is a·soulish body, and there·is a·spiritual body.

G4983.7 N-NSN σῶμα (1x)

Col 2:17 *reality is* the Anointed-One's body *which cast the*

G4983.7 N-DSN σώματι (1x)

Php 3:21 fundamentally·in·nature·like the body of·his glory,

G4984 σωματικός sōmatikṓs *adj.* (4x)

Roots:G4983 See:G4985

G4984 A-NSF σωματική (1x)

1Ti 4:8 "For the *way·of* bodily training is profitable just·for

G4984 A-DSN σωματικῷ (1x)

Lk 3:22 the Holy Spirit descended in·a·bodily shape like a·

EG4984 (2x)

Php 1:22 But if *I·continue·on* to·live in *bodily* flesh, this
2Co 10:3 For while·strolling·about in *bodily* flesh, we·do·not

G4985 σωματικῶς sōmatikṓs *adv.* (1x)

Roots:G4984

G4985 ADV σωματικῶς (1x)

Col 2:9 all the complete·fullness of·Godhood resides bodily.

G4986 Σώ•πατρος Sṓpatrôs *n/p.* (1x)

Roots:G4982 G3962 Compare:G4989

G4986.2 N/P-NSM Σώπατρος (1x)

Ac 20:4 And even·as·far·as Asia, SoPater (a·Berean *Jew*),

G4987 σωρεύω sōrêúō *v.* (2x)

Roots:G4673 Compare:G4867 G4816 See:G2002

G4987.1 V-FAI-2S σωρεύσεις (1x)

Rm 12:20 doing this, you·shall·stack burning·coals of·fire

G4987.2 V-RPP-APN σεσωρευμένα (1x)

2Ti 3:6 silly·lesser·women having·been·stacked·high with·,

G4988 Σω•σθένης Sōsthénēs *n/p.* (2x)

Roots:G4982 G4599 Compare:G4516

G4988.2 N/P-NSM Σωσθένης (1x)

1Co 1:1 through God's will, and SoSthenes *our* brother.

G4988.2 N/P-ASM Σωσθένην (1x)

Ac 18:17 Then, after·grabbing SoSthenes, the director·of·

G4989 Σωσί•πατρος Sōsípatrôs *n/p.* (1x)

Roots:G4986 See:G4989

G4989 N/P-NSM Σωσίπατρος (1x)

Rm 16:21 Jason, and SosiPater, my Redeemed·Kinsmen,

G4990 σωτήρ sōtḗr *n.* (24x)

Roots:G4982 xLangAlso:H3467

G4990.3 N-NSM σωτήρ (4x)

Jn 4:42 ·know that this is truly the Savior of·the world, the
Lk 2:11 of·David, a·Savior is·reproduced·and·birthed who
Eph 5:23 And he·himself is Savior of·the Body.
1Ti 4:10 ·living God, who is *the* Savior of·all men·of·clay†,

G4990.3 N-ASM σωτῆρα (4x)

Ac 5:31 ·*the life-above*, *this* Savior with·his·own right·hand,
Ac 13:23 promise, God awakened a·Savior for·IsraEl, Jesus,
Php 3:20 which also we·fully·await *the* Savior, *the* Lord
1Jn 4:14 has·dispatched the Son *to·be* Savior of·the world.

G4990.3 N-DSM σωτῆρι (2x)

Lk 1:47 and my spirit leaped·for·joy in God my Savior.
Jud 1:25 to·*the*·only wise God our Savior, *be* glory and

G4990.3 N-GSM σωτῆρος (14x)

2Pe 1:1 of·our God and Savior YeShua Anointed.
2Pe 1:11 kingdom of·our Lord and Savior YeShua Anointed.
2Pe 2:20 of·the Lord and Savior YeShua Anointed, and *they*
2Pe 3:2 ·*stated* by·our ambassadors of·the Lord and Savior—
2Pe 3:18 of·our Lord and Savior YeShua Anointed. To·him
Tit 1:3 according·to a·full·appointment of·God our Savior.
Tit 1:4 Father God and *the* Lord Jesus Anointed our Savior.
Tit 2:10 ·*with* the instruction of·God our Savior in all·things.
Tit 2:13 glory of·our great God and Savior, Jesus Anointed
Tit 3:4 the kindness of·God our Savior and *his* affection·for·
Tit 3:6 on us abundantly through Jesus Anointed our Savior,
1Ti 1:1 ·to a·full·appointment of·God our Savior, and Lord
1Ti 2:3 and fully·acceptable in·the·sight of·God our Savior,
2Ti 1:10 ·appearing of·our Savior Jesus Anointed, *who·is*, in·

G4991 σωτηρία sōtēría *n.* (43x)

Roots:G4990 Compare:G4992
xLangEquiv:H3468

G4991.3 N-ASF σωτηρίαν (3x)

Ac 7:25 through his hand, would·give salvation to·them, but
Heb 11:7 a·floating·ark for *the* salvation of·his house;
Php 1:19 that this shall·result in salvation for·me through

G4991.3 N-GSF σωτηρίας (1x)

Ac 27:34 for this is·inherently specific·for yeur salvation, for

G4991.4 N-NSF σωτηρία (8x)

Jn 4:22 fall·prostrate, because the Salvation is from·out·of·
Lk 19:9 to him, "Today, Salvation did·come to·this house,
Ac 4:12 And the Salvation is not in not·even·one other.
Rm 11:11 ·their trespass, the Salvation *is·come* to·the
Rm 13:11 ·heavy·sleep, for now our Salvation *is* nearer than
Rv 7:10 saying, "The Salvation of·our God! To·the·one
Rv 12:10 "At·this·moment did·come the Salvation, and the
Rv 19:1 ·praise·Yahweh,·HalleluYah! The Salvation, and

G4991.4 N-ASF σωτηρίαν (13x)

Lk 1:71 "Salvation from·among our enemies and from·
Heb 1:14 on·account·of the·ones about to·inherit Salvation?
Heb 9:28 ·ones who·are·fully·awaiting him for Salvation.
Rm 1:16 it·is God's power to Salvation to·everyone trusting,
Rm 10:1 petition to God on·behalf of·IsraEl is for Salvation.
Rm 10:10 ·*the*·mouth affirmation·is·made unto Salvation.
Php 2:12 the *determined·purpose* of·yeur·own Salvation!
1Pe 1:5 through trust for a·Salvation ready to·be·revealed in
1Pe 1:9 the end of·yeur trust, *the* Salvation of·*yeur*·souls.
2Pe 3:15 long-suffering of·our Lord *as* Salvation— just·as
2Th 2:13 God chose yeu for Salvation in renewed·holiness
2Co 7:10 repentance unto Salvation without·regret, but the
2Ti 3:15 ·able to·make you wise to Salvation through a·trust,

G4991.4 N-GSF σωτηρίας (17x)

Lk 1:69 "And he·awakened a·horn of·Salvation for·us in the
Lk 1:77 to·give knowledge of·Salvation to·his People unto a·
Ac 13:26 of·this Salvation is·already·dispatched.
Ac 16:17 who fully·proclaim to·us *the* way of·Salvation."
Heb 2:3 utterly·escape after·neglecting so·vast a·Salvation?
Heb 2:10 of·their Salvation completely·mature through
Heb 5:9 initiating·cause of·eternal Salvation to·all the·ones
Heb 6:9 *of·the* things·following·in·line with·Salvation, even
Jud 1:3 to·yeu concerning the common Salvation, I·had
Php 1:28 ·destruction for·them, but of·Salvation for·yeu,
1Pe 1:10 Concerning this Salvation, the prophets sought·*it*·
1Th 5:8 and *with·the* Expectation of·Salvation for·a·helmet.
1Th 5:9 but·rather for acquisition of·Salvation through our
2Co 1:6 of·yeur comforting and Salvation, or·whether we·
2Co 1:6 ·behalf of·yeur comforting and Salvation (the·one
Eph 1:13 truth, the good·news of·yeur Salvation— in whom
2Ti 2:10 ·order·that they also may·obtain Salvation, the·one

EG4991.4 (1x)

Heb 2:3 a·Salvation? *This Salvation*, which after·receiving

G4992 σωτήριος sōtḗriôs *adj.* (8x)

σωτήριον sōtḗriôn [neuter]

Roots:G4991 Compare:G5083
xLangEquiv:H3444

G4992.4 A-NSM σωτήριος (1x)

Tit 2:11 of·God, the Custodial·Salvation, became·apparent

G4992.4 A-NSN σωτήριον (1x)

Ac 28:28 known to·yeu that the custodial·Salvation of·God

G4992.4 A-ASN σωτήριον (2x)

Lk 2:30 because my eyes saw your custodial·Salvation,
Lk 3:6 flesh shall·gaze·upon the custodial·Salvation of·God.'

G4992.4 A-GSN σωτηρίου (1x)

Eph 6:17 accept the helmet of·custodial·Salvation and the

G4992.4 N-ASF σωτηρίον (1x)

Ac 13:47 *for* you *to·be* for custodial·Salvation unto *the*

G4992.4 N-GSN σωτηρίου (2x)

2Co 6:2 in a·day of·custodial·Salvation I·swiftly·helped you.
2Co 6:2 Behold, now *is the* day of·custodial·Salvation!

G4993 σω•φρονέω sōphrônéō *v.* (6x)

Roots:G4998 Compare:G1467 See:G4994

G4993.1 V-PAI-1P σωφρονοῦμεν (1x)

2Co 5:13 *it·is* for·God; or·if we·are·of·sound·mind, *it·is* for·

G4993.1 V-PAP-ASM σωφρονοῦντα (2x)

Lk 8:35 having·been·attired and being·of·sound·mind, and
Mk 5:15 ·been·attired and being·of·sound·mind, the·one

G4993.2 V-PAN σωφρονεῖν (2x)

Rm 12:3 *moderately* in·order to·be·self-controlled, seeing·as
Tit 2:6 exhort the younger·men to·be·self-controlled.

G4993.2 V-AAM-2P σωφρονήσατε (1x)

1Pe 4:7 Accordingly, be·self-controlled, and be·sensible to

G4994 σω•φρονίζω sōphrônízō *v.* (1x)

Roots:G4998 See:G4993

G4994.3 V-PAS-3P σωφρονίζωσιν (1x)

Tit 2:4 in·order·that they·may·correctly·moderate·and·train

G4995 σω•φρονισμός sōphrônismṓs *n.* (1x)

Roots:G4994

G4995.2 N-GSM σωφρονισμοῦ (1x)

2Ti 1:7 and of·love, and of·a·sound·and·disciplined·mind.

G4996 σω•φρόνως sōphrṓnōs *adv.* (1x)

Roots:G4998

G4996.2 ADV σωφρόνως (1x)

Tit 2:12 we·should·live moderately·with·self-control,

G4997 σω•φροσύνη sōphrôsýnē *n.* (3x)

Roots:G4998 Compare:G0192

G4997.2 N-GSF σωφροσύνης (1x)

Ac 26:25 utterances of·truth and·also with·a·sound·mind.

G4997.3 N-GSF σωφροσύνης (2x)

1Ti 2:9 ·apparel with modesty·of·conduct and self-control.
1Ti 2:15 and love and renewed·holiness with self-control.

G4998 σώ•φρων sṓphrōn *adj.* (4x)

Roots:G4982 G5424 Compare:G1468

G4998.2 A-ASM σώφρονα (2x)

Tit 1:8 ·doing·beneficially·good, self-controlled, righteous,
1Ti 3:2 of·one wife, sober-minded, self-controlled, orderly,

G4998.2 A-APM σώφρονας (1x)

Tit 2:2 ·reverent·respect, self-controlled, healthy·and·sound

G4998.2 A-APF σώφρονας (1x)

Tit 2:5 *to·be* self-controlled, *sexually·and*·morally·clean,

Ττ - Tau

G4999 Ταβέρναι Tabérnai *n/l.* (1x)

G4999.2 N/L-GPF Ταβερνῶν (1x)

Ac 28:15 of·Appius and *the* Three Taverns, which upon·

G5000 Ταβιθά Tabithá *n/p.* (2x)

צְבִיָּה tsᵉbiyah [Hebrew]

Roots:H6646 Compare:G1393

G5000.2 N/P-PRI Ταβιθά (2x)

Ac 9:36 female·disciple by·the·name·of Tabitha, who (by·
Ac 9:40 to the body, he·declared, "Tabitha, rise·up." And

G5001 τάγμα tágma *n.* (1x)

Roots:G5021 See:G1297 G4928-2 G4366-2

G5001.2 N-DSN τάγματι (1x)

1Co 15:23 but each in one's·own sequence: Anointed-One, a·

G5002 τακτός taktós *adj.* (1x)

Roots:G5021 See:G0813

G5002.2 A-DSF τακτῇ (1x)

Ac 12:21 And upon·an·assigned day, after·dressing·himself

G5003 ταλαι•πωρέω talaipōréō *v.* (1x)

Roots:G5005

G5003 V-AAM-2P ταλαιπωρήσατε (1x)

Jac 4:9 Be·miserable, also mourn and weep.

G5004 ταλαι•πωρία talaipōría *n.* (2x)

Roots:G5005

G5004 N-NSF ταλαιπωρία (1x)

Rm 3:16 Shattered·ruin and misery *are* in their ways.

G5004 N-DPF ταλαιπωρίαις (1x)

Jac 5:1 howling over yeur miseries, the·ones coming·upon

G5005 ταλαί•πωρος talaípōrôs *adj.* (2x)

Roots:G5007 G3984 Compare:G5011

G5005 A-NSM ταλαίπωρος (2x)

Rm 7:24 I·myself *am* a·miserable man·of·clay†! Who shall·
Rv 3:17 that you·yourself are the·one miserable, pitiable,

G5006 ταλαντιαῖος talantiaîôs *adj.* (1x)

Roots:G5007

G5006.2 A-NSF ταλαντιαία (1x)

Rv 16:21 *the* weight·of·a·talant·*(or·fifty·pounds)*) descends

G5007 τάλαντον tálantôn *n.* (16x)

Compare:G1220 G3046 G5342
xLangEquiv:H3603 A3604

G5007.3 N-ASN τάλαντον (3x)

Mt 25:24 having·received the one talant·of·silver, declared,
Mt 25:25 upon·going·off, I·hid your talant·of·silver in the
Mt 25:28 So·then, take·away the talant·of·silver from him

G5007.3 N-APN τάλαντα (11x)

Mt 25:15 in·fact, to·one he·gave five talants·of·silver, and
Mt 25:16 receiving the five talants·of·silver worked with *the*
Mt 25:16 same, and produced another five talants·of·silver.
Mt 25:20 receiving the five talants·of·silver brought another
Mt 25:20 ·silver brought another five talants·of·silver, saying
Mt 25:20 you·handed·over to·me five talants·of·silver. See,
Mt 25:20 I·gained another five talants·of·silver upon them.'
Mt 25:22 the·one receiving the two talants·of·silver, declared
Mt 25:22 you·handed·over to·me two talants·of·silver. See,
Mt 25:22 I·gained another two talants·of·silver upon them.'
Mt 25:28 and give *it* to·the·one having ten talants·of·silver.'

G5007.3 N-GPN ταλάντων (1x)

Mt 18:24 ·man delinquent of·ten·thousand talants·of·silver.

EG5007.3 (1x)

Mt 25:18 the·one receiving the one *talant·of·silver* dug in the

G5008 ταλιθά talithá *aram.* (1x)

Compare:G2877 See:G0721 xLangAlso:H2924

G5008.3 ARAM ταλιθά (1x)

Mk 5:41 ·the hand, he·says to·her, "Talitha qumi," which,

G5009 ταμεῖον tameîôn *n.* (4x)

Compare:G0596 G4693 G2964-4 See:G5058-2
xLangAlso:H0618

G5009.2 N-NSN ταμεῖον (1x)

Lk 12:24 there·is not a·dispensary nor·even a·barn, yet God

G5009.3 N-NSN ταμιεῖον (1x)

Mt 6:6 enter into your private·chamber, and after·shutting

G5009.3 N-DPN ταμείοις (2x)

Lk 12:3 the private·chambers shall·be·officially·proclaimed
Mt 24:26 *he·is* in the private·chambers,' yeu·should·not

G5010 τάξις táxis *n.* (10x)

Roots:G5021 See:G1297-1 G4928-3 G1343-1

G5010.1 N-ASF τάξιν (1x)

Col 2:5 and looking·upon yeur orderly·arrangement and the

G5010.2 N-ASF τάξιν (8x)

Heb 5:6 ·to the assigned·order of·MalkiTsedeq·*(King·of·*,"
Heb 5:10 "according·to the assigned·order of·MalkiTsedeq.
Heb 6:20 according·to the assigned·order of·MalkiTsedeq.
Heb 7:11 ·to the assigned·order of·MalkiTsedeq and not to·
Heb 7:11 ·related according·to the assigned·order of·Aaron?
Heb 7:17 according·to the assigned·order of·MalkiTsedeq."
Heb 7:21 according·to the assigned·order of·MalkiTsedeq"")
1Co 14:40 must·be·done decently and in assigned·order.

G5010.2 N-DSF τάξει (1x)

Lk 1:8 of·God in the assigned·order of·his daily·rotation)

G5011 ταπεινός tapêinós *adj.* (9x)

Compare:G4239 G5005 See:G5013 G5012 G5014

G5011.2 A-NSM ταπεινός (2x)

Mt 11:29 because I·am gentle and lowly in·the heart, and
2Co 10:1 in personal·presence *am* in·fact lowly among yeu,

EG5011.2 (1x)

2Co 11:12 they·may·be·found *to·be lowly* even just·as we·

G5011.3 A-NSM ταπεινός (1x)

Jac 1:9 So let the brother of·the low·estate boast in his high·

G5011.3 A-APM ταπεινούς (1x)

Lk 1:52 *their* thrones and elevated *the·ones* of·low·estate.

G5011.3 A-DPM ταπεινοῖς (1x)

Rm 12:16 ·yeurselves·together with·the men·of·low·estate.

G5011.4 A-DPM ταπεινοῖς (2x)

Jac 4:6 haughty·men, but gives grace to·humble·men."
1Pe 5:5 haughty·men but gives grace to·humble·men."

G5011.5 A-APM ταπεινούς (1x)

2Co 7:6 comforting the·ones *that·are* feeling·low, comforted

G5012 ταπεινο•φροσύνη tapêinôphrôsýnē *n.* (7x)

Roots:G5011 G5424

G5012.2 N-ASF ταπεινοφροσύνην (1x)

1Pe 5:5 ·servant's·work·apron *with* the humbleness·of·mind.

G5012.2 N-DSF ταπεινοφροσύνῃ (1x)

Php 2:3 in·the humbleness·of·mind resolutely·considering

G5012.3 N-ASF ταπεινοφροσύνην (1x)

Col 3:12 ·affections, kindness, humility·of·mind, gentleness

G5012.3 N-GSF ταπεινοφροσύνης (2x)

Ac 20:19 to·the Lord with all humility·of·mind, and with·
Eph 4:2 with all humility·of·mind and gentleness, with

G5012.4 N-DSF ταπεινοφροσύνῃ (2x)

Col 2:18 in a·rigidly·imposed·humility·of·mind and in·a·
Col 2:23 and a·rigidly·imposed·humility·of·mind, and an·

G5013 ταπεινόω tapêinóō *v.* (14x)

Roots:G5011

G5013.1 V-FPI-3S ταπεινωθήσεται (1x)

Lk 3:5 every mountain and hill shall·be·made·low; and the

G5013.2 V-AAS-3S ταπεινώσῃ (1x)

2Co 12:21 again, my God may·humble me among yeu, and

G5013.3 V-FPI-3S ταπεινωθήσεται (3x)

Lk 14:11 the·one elevating himself shall·be·humbled, and
Lk 18:14 "The·one elevating himself shall·be·humbled, and
Mt 23:12 ·that shall·elevate himself shall·be·humbled, and

G5013.3 V-PPN ταπεινοῦσθαι (1x)

Php 4:12 I·have·seen·how to·be·humbled, and I·have·seen·

G5013.3 V-APM-2P ταπεινώθητε (2x)

Jac 4:10 Be·humbled in·the·sight of·the Lord, and he·shall·
1Pe 5:6 Accordingly, be·humbled under the mighty hand of·

G5013.4 V-FAI-3S ταπεινώσει (1x)

Mt 23:12 any·that shall·humble himself shall·be·elevated.

G5013.4 V-PAP-NSM ταπεινῶν (3x)

Lk 14:11 and the·one humbling himself shall·be·elevated."
Lk 18:14 and the·one humbling himself shall·be·elevated."
2Co 11:7 a·moral·failure in·humbling my·own·self that yeu·

G5013.4 V-AAI-3S ἐταπείνωσεν (1x)

Php 2:8 ·layout as a·man·of·clay†, he·humbled himself,

G5013.4 V-AAS-3S ταπεινώσῃ (1x)

Mt 18:4 Accordingly, whoever should·humble himself as

G5014 ταπείνωσις tapêínōsis *n.* (4x)

Roots:G5013 Compare:G5004

G5014.1 N-DSF ταπεινώσει (2x)

Ac 8:33 In his humiliation, his verdict was·taken·away.
Jac 1:10 but the wealthy in his·own humiliation, because as

G5014.2 N-ASF ταπείνωσιν (1x)

Lk 1:48 ·looked upon the humble·estate of·his female·slave,'

G5014.2 N-GSF ταπεινώσεως (1x)

Php 3:21 ·transform the body of·our humble·estate into the

G5015 ταράσσω tarássō *v.* (17x)

Compare:G0387 G2360 G2795 G4531 G5182
See:G1298 G5016 G5017

G5015.2 V-PAP-NSM ταράσσων (1x)

Gal 5:10 otherwise, but the·one troubling yeu shall·bear the

G5015.2 V-PAP-NPM ταράσσοντες (1x)

Gal 1:7 there·are some·men troubling yeu and willing to·

G5015.2 V-PPM-3S ταρασσέσθω (2x)

Jn 14:1 "Do·not be·troubled *in* yeur heart.
Jn 14:27 give to·yeu. Do·not be·troubled in·yeur heart, nor·

G5015.2 V-IAI-3S ἐτάρασσεν (1x)

Jn 5:4 ·descending on the pool and was·troubling the water.

G5015.2 V-AAI-3S ἐτάραξεν (1x)

Jn 11:33 in·the spirit; yet he·troubled himself *to·grieve*,

G5015.2 V-AAI-3P ἐτάραξαν (2x)

Ac 15:24 going·out from·among us troubled yeu with·words
Ac 17:8 And they·troubled the crowd and the rulers·of·the·

G5015.2 V-API-3S ἐταράχθη (3x)

Jn 13:21 these·things, Jesus was·troubled in·the spirit, and
Lk 1:12 And ZacharIas was·troubled after·seeing *him*, and
Mt 2:3 *this*, King HerOd·the·Great was·troubled, and all

G5015.2 V-API-3P ἐταράχθησαν (2x)

Mt 14:26 upon the sea, the disciples were·troubled, saying,
Mk 6:50 For they·all saw him and were·troubled. And

G5015.2 V-APS-2P ταραχθῆτε (1x)

1Pe 3:14 of·their fear, nor·even should·yeu·be·troubled."

G5015.2 V-APS-3S ταραχθῇ (1x)

Jn 5:7 whenever the water should·be·troubled, in·order·that

G5015.2 V-RPI-3S τετάρακται (1x)

Jn 12:27 "Now my soul has·been·troubled, and what should·

G5015.2 V-RPP-NPM τεταραγμένοι (1x)

Lk 24:38 "Why are·yeu having·been·troubled? And why·do

G5016 ταραχή tarachḗ *n.* (2x)

Roots:G5015 Compare:G4963 See:G5017

G5016.1 N-NPF ταραχαί (1x)

Mk 13:8 and there·shall·be famines and agitations. These *are*

G5016.1 N-ASF ταραχήν (1x)

Jn 5:4 first·one stepping·in after the agitation of·the water

G5017 τάραχος tárachôs *n.* (2x)

Roots:G5015 See:G5016

G5017.2 N-NSM τάραχος (2x)

Ac 12:18 there·was no little disturbance among the soldiers
Ac 19:23 there·occurred no little disturbance about The

G5018 Ταρσεύς Tarsêús *n/g.* (2x)

Roots:G5019

G5018 N/G-NSM Ταρσεύς (1x)

Ac 21:39 am a·man·of·clay† *who·is* a·Jew of·Tarsus, *a·city*

G5018 N/G-ASM Ταρσέα (1x)

Ac 9:11 in Judas' home for a·man·of·Tarsus, Saul by·name.

G5019 Ταρσός Tarsós *n/l.* (3x)

See:G5018

G5019.2 N/L-ASF Ταρσόν (2x)

Ac 9:30 to Caesarea and dispatched him forth to Tarsus.
Ac 11:25 went·forth to Tarsus, to·diligently·seek·out Saul.

G5019.2 N/L-DSF Ταρσῷ (1x)

Ac 22:3 a·Jew, having·been·born in Tarsus, *a·city* in·Cilicia,

G5020 ταρταρόω tartaróō *v.* (1x)

Compare:G1067 G2978-1 See:G0012 G0086

G5020.a V-AAP-NSM ταρταρώσας (1x)

2Pe 2:4 but·rather after·incarcerating *them* in·the·Abyss of·

G5021 τάσσω tássō *v.* (9x)
Compare:G2885 G1299 G4367 See:G5010 G5001 G5002

G5021.1 V-AAI-3P ἔταξαν (2x)
Ac 15:2 *occurring* alongside them, they·arranged *for* Paul
1Co 16:15 of·Achaia, and *how* they·arranged themselves for

G5021.1 V-AMP-NPM ταξάμενοι (1x)
Ac 28:23 And after·arranging a·day for·him, many·more

G5021.2 V-PPP-NSM τασσόμενος (1x)
Lk 7:8 am a·man·of·clay† being·assigned under authority,

G5021.2 V-AMI-3S ἐτάξατο (1x)
Mt 28:16 to the mountain where YeShua assigned them.

G5021.2 V-RPI-3S τέτακται (1x)
Ac 22:10 all·things which have·been·assigned for·you to·do.

G5021.2 V-RPP-NPF τεταγμέναι (1x)
Rm 13:1 authorities, they·are having·been·assigned by God.

G5021.2 V-RPP-NPM τεταγμένοι (1x)
Ac 13:48 (as·many·as were having·been·assigned to eternal

EG5021.2 (1x)
Rm 15:16 *it·has·been·assigned* for me to·be a·public·servant

G5022 ταῦρος taûros *n.* (4x)
Compare:G3439-2 xLangEquiv:A8450 xLangAlso:H7794

G5022 N-NPM ταῦροι (1x)
Mt 22:4 I·made·ready my banquet. My bulls and fatlings *are*

G5022 N-APM ταύρους (1x)
Ac 14:13 their city, after·bringing bulls and garlands to the

G5022 N-GMP ταύρων (2x)
Heb 9:13 For if the blood of·bulls and of·adult·male·goats
Heb 10:4 *for·the* blood of·bulls and of·adult·male·goats to·

G5023 τ•αῦτα taûta *p:d.* (249x)
Roots:G3778 Compare:G1565

EG5023 (1x)
Mt 21:45 *it·was* concerning them *that* he·says *these·things*.

G5023.1 P:D-NPN ταῦτα (36x)
Jn 1:28 These·things happened in BethAbara across the
Jn 3:9 to·him, "How·are these·things able to·happen?
Jn 6:9 ·fish, but·yet what are these·things among so·many?
Jn 10:21 Others were·saying, "These·things are not the
Jn 10:25 my Father's name, these·things testify concerning
Jn 12:16 ·to·mind that these·things were having·been·written
Jn 19:36 For these·things were·done that the Scripture
Jn 20:31 But these·things have·been·written in·order·that
Lk 1:20 even·until *the* day that these·things should·occur,
Lk 12:31 of·God, and all these·things shall·be·added to·yeu.
Lk 15:26 he·inquired what might·be *meant·by* these·things.
Lk 21:7 "So·then Mentor, when shall these·things be?
Lk 21:7 whenever these·things should·be·about to·happen?
Lk 21:9 for it·is·mandatory·for these·things to·occur first.
Lk 24:21 marks this third day since these·things were·done.
Ac 7:1 designated·high·priest declared, "Are these·things so?
Ac 17:11 ·*to* whether these·things might·actually·be in·this·
Ac 17:20 to·know what these·things are·actually·supposed
Ac 19:21 And as these·things were·completely·fulfilled, Paul
Heb 7:13 *priest*, concerning whom these·things are·said,
Mt 6:33 and all these·things shall·be·added to·yeu.
Mt 13:56 ·what·source *does* this·man *do* all these·things?"
Mt 23:36 I·say to·yeu, all these·things shall·come upon this
Mt 24:3 "Declare to·us, when shall these·things be?
Mt 24:34 pass·away, until all these·things should·happen.
Mk 6:2 ·what·source *does* this·man *do* these·things? And
Mk 13:4 "Declare to·us, when·shall these·things be?
Mk 13:30 so·long·as·until all these·things should·happen.
Jac 3:10 kindly·needed·for these·things to·be in·this·manner.
2Pe 1:8 For *with* these·things subsisting in·yeu and
2Pe 1:10 Selection firm. For in·doing these·things, no, yeu·
Tit 3:8 good works. These·things are the good·things and
1Co 6:8 and rob, and these·things *yeu·do to·yeur* brothers.
1Co 6:11 And some *of* yeu·were these·things, but·rather yeu·
1Co 10:6 Now these·things were our imprinted·examples,
1Co 10:11 all these impressive·examples were·befalling

G5023.1 P:D-APN ταῦτα (191x)
Jn 2:16 doves, "Take·away these·things from·here. Do·not
Jn 2:18 ·you·show to·us, *seeing* that you·do these·things?"
Jn 3:10 of·IsraEl, and you·do·not know these·things?
Jn 3:22 After these·things, Jesus and his disciples came into
Jn 5:1 After these·things, there·was a·Sacred·Feast of·the
Jn 5:14 After these·things, Jesus finds him in the Sanctuary·
Jn 5:16 because he·was·doing these·things on a·Sabbath.
Jn 5:19 that *the Father* should·do, these·things also the Son
Jn 5:34 ·man·of·clay†, but·rather I·say these·things that yeu
Jn 6:1 After these·things, Jesus went·off *to·the* other·side of·
Jn 6:59 He·declared these·things in a·gathering, while·
Jn 7:1 And after these·things, Jesus was·walking in Galilee,
Jn 7:4 *publicly*. If you·do these·things, make yourself
Jn 7:9 And after·declaring these·things to·them, he·remained
Jn 7:32 the crowd grumbling these·things concerning him,
Jn 8:26 and·I say to the world these·things which I·heard
Jn 8:28 ·as my Father instructed me, I·speak these·things.
Jn 8:30 With·him speaking these·things, many trusted in him
Jn 9:6 After·declaring these·things, he·spat down·on·the·
Jn 9:22 His parents declared these·things, because they·
Jn 9:40 ·among the Pharisees heard these·things, the·ones
Jn 11:11 These·things he·declared, and after that he·says to·
Jn 11:28 And after·declaring these·things, she·went·off and
Jn 11:43 And after·declaring these·things, he·yelled·out
Jn 12:16 his disciples did·not know these·things at·the first,
Jn 12:16 him, and *that* they·did these·things to·him.
Jn 12:36 the·Sons of·Light." These·things Jesus spoke, and
Jn 12:41 IsaIah declared these·things when he·saw his glory
Jn 13:7 ·moment, but you·shall·know after these·things."
Jn 13:17 "If yeu·personally·know these·things, supremely·
Jn 13:21 After·declaring these·things, Jesus was·troubled in·
Jn 14:25 "These·things have·I·spoken to·yeu, while·abiding
Jn 15:11 "These·things have·I·spoken to·yeu in·order·that
Jn 15:17 "These·things I·command yeu, in·order·that yeu·
Jn 15:21 "But·yet all these·things shall·they·do to·yeu on·
Jn 16:1 "These·things I·have·spoken to·yeu, in·order·that
Jn 16:3 And these·things shall·they·do to·yeu, because they·
Jn 16:4 "But·rather these·things have·I·spoken to·yeu, that
Jn 16:4 to·yeu of·them. And these·things I·did·not declare
Jn 16:6 ·rather because I·have·spoken these·things to·yeu,
Jn 16:25 "These·things I·have·spoken to·yeu in proverbs.
Jn 16:33 "I·have·spoken these·things to·yeu, in·order·that in
Jn 17:1 Jesus spoke these·things and lifted·up his eyes to the
Jn 17:13 now I·come to you, and these·things I·speak in the
Jn 18:1 After·declaring these·things, Jesus went·forth
Jn 18:22 And upon·him declaring these·things, one of·the
Jn 19:24 ·fact, in·due·course, the soldiers did these·things.
Jn 19:38 And after these·things, Joseph (the·one from
Jn 20:14 after·declaring these·things, she·is·turned·around
Jn 20:18 the Lord, and *that* he·declared these·things to·her.
Jn 21:1 After these·things, Jesus made himself apparent
Jn 21:24 these·things and writing these·things, and we·
Lk 1:19 and to·proclaim·good·news to·you of·these·things.
Lk 4:28 And hearing these·things, everyone in the gathering
Lk 5:27 And after these·things, he·went·forth and distinctly·
Lk 7:9 Now after·hearing these·things, Jesus marveled·at
Lk 8:8 While·saying these·things, he·was·hollering·out,
Lk 9:34 But with·him saying these·things, there·came a·
Lk 10:1 After these·things, the Lord expressly·indicated
Lk 10:21 earth, that you·hid·away these·things from wise
Lk 11:27 as he was·saying these·things, *that* a·certain
Lk 11:42 of·God. It·is·mandatory to·do these·things, and
Lk 11:45 *when* saying these·things, you·abusively·mistreat
Lk 11:53 And with·him saying these·things to them, the
Lk 12:4 the body, and after these·things not having anything
Lk 12:30 For all these·things, the nations of·the world seek·
Lk 13:17 And with·him saying these·things, all the·ones
Lk 14:6 to·contradict him pertaining·to these·things.
Lk 14:15 ·together·at·the·meal hearing these·things, declared
Lk 14:21 that slave announced these·things to·his lord.
Lk 16:14 also were·hearing all these·things, and they·were·
Lk 17:8 ·drink; and·then after these·things, you·yourself
Lk 18:4 "But after these *persistent appeals*, he·declared
Lk 18:11 ·settled, was·praying these·things toward himself,
Lk 18:21 "All these·things I·vigilantly·kept from·among
Lk 18:22 But Jesus, hearing these·things, declared to·him,
Lk 18:23 And after·hearing these·things, he·became
Lk 19:11 And with·them hearing these·things, augmenting *it*,
Lk 19:28 And after·declaring these·things, *Jesus* traversed·
Lk 20:2 what·kind·of authority do·you·do these·things? Or
Lk 20:8 to·yeu by what·kind·of authority I·do these·things."
Lk 21:6 "*As·for* these·things which yeu·observe, days shall·
Lk 21:31 whenever yeu·should·see these·things happening,
Lk 21:36 ·worthy to·utterly·escape all these·things, the·ones
Lk 23:31 "Because if they·do these·things to the arbor·tree
Lk 23:46 after·declaring these·things, he·breathed·his·last.
Lk 23:49 stood at·a·distance, clearly·seeing these·things.
Lk 24:9 they·announced all these·things to·the eleven and
Lk 24:10 with·them, who were·saying these·things to the
Lk 24:26 ·for the Anointed-One to·suffer these·things, and
Lk 24:36 And with·them speaking these·things, Jesus
Ac 1:9 And after·declaring these·things, with·them looking·
Ac 5:5 ·fear came upon all the·ones hearing these·things.
Ac 5:11 and upon all the·ones hearing these·things.
Ac 7:7 "And after these·things, they·shall·come·forth and
Ac 7:50 Did·not·indeed my hand make all these·things?"
Ac 7:54 upon·hearing these·things, they·were·thoroughly·
Ac 11:18 And after·hearing these·things, they·kept·still, and
Ac 12:17 he·declared, "Go·announce these·things to·Jacob,
Ac 13:20 "And after these·things, *which·took* about four·
Ac 14:15 "Men, why·do yeu·do these·things? We·ourselves
Ac 14:18 while·saying these·things, they·fully·restrained the
Ac 15:16 " After these·things, I·shall·return and shall·
Ac 15:17 says Yahweh, the·one doing all these·things."
Ac 17:8 the rulers·of·the·city *that·were* hearing these·things.
Ac 18:1 And after these·things, Paul came to Corinth, being·
Ac 19:41 And after·declaring these·things, he·dismissed the
Ac 20:36 And after·declaring these·things, with·him bowing
Ac 21:12 And as·soon·as we·heard these·things, both we·
Ac 23:22 "to·no·one that you·made these·things clear to·me.
Ac 24:9 ·themselves, professing these·things to·hold *true* in·
Ac 24:22 Felix, after·hearing these·things *and* having·seen
Ac 26:24 Festus replied *to* these·things with·a·loud voice,
Ac 26:30 And with·him declaring these·things, the king rose·
Ac 27:35 And after·declaring these·things and taking bread,
Ac 28:29 And with·him declaring these·things, the Jews
Heb 4:8 have·spoken after these·things concerning another
Gal 2:18 if I·build again these·things which I·demolished, I·
Gal 5:17 ·that yeu·may·not do these·things which yeu·might
Mt 1:20 But with·him cogitating these·things, behold, an·
Mt 4:9 he·says to·him, "All these·things I·shall·give to·you,
Mt 6:32 (For all these·things the Gentiles seek·after) for yeur
Mt 9:18 With·him speaking these·things to·them, behold, a·
Mt 11:25 earth, that you·hid·away these·things from wise
Mt 13:34 YeShua spoke all these·things to·the crowds in
Mt 13:51 "Did·yeu·comprehend all these·things?" They·say
Mt 19:20 ·him, "All these·things I·vigilantly·kept from·out
Mt 21:23 ·kind·of authority do·you·do these·things? And
Mt 21:24 to·yeu by what·kind·of authority I·do these·things.
Mt 21:27 to·yeu by what·kind·of authority I·do these·things.
Mt 23:23 "It·is·mandatory to·do these·things, and not to·
Mt 24:2 "Do·not look·for all these·things. Certainly I·say to·
Mt 24:33 yeu·should·see all these·things, yeu·must·know
Mk 2:8 "Why·do yeu·ponder these·things in yeur hearts?
Mk 10:20 Mentor, all these·things I·vigilantly·kept from·out
Mk 11:28 ·kind·of authority do·you·do these·things? And
Mk 11:28 in·order·that you·should·do these·things?"
Mk 11:29 to·yeu by what·kind·of authority I·do these·things.
Mk 11:33 ·yeu by what·kind·of authority I·do these·things."
Mk 13:4 all these·things are·about to·be·entirely·completed?
Mk 13:29 whenever yeu·should·see these·things happening,
Mk 16:12 And after these·things, he·was·made·apparent to·
Rm 8:31 what shall·we·state toward these·things? If God
Php 3:7 these·things I·have·resolutely·considered a·total·
Php 4:8 any high·praise, take·a·reckoning·of these·things.
Php 4:9 These·things, which also yeu·learned, and

1Pe 1:11 and the glories *to·come* after these·things.
2Pe 3:14 while·intently·awaiting these·things, quickly·
2Th 2:5 alongside yeu, I·was·relating these·things to·yeu?
Tit 2:15 Speak these·things, and exhort and reprove with all
1Co 4:6 And these·things, brothers, I·portrayed·as·an·
1Co 4:14 yeu do·I·write these·things, but·rather, as my
1Co 6:13 ·render·inoperative even this and these·things. But
1Co 9:8 I·speak these·things according·to·a·man·of·clay†?
1Co 9:8 ·not·indeed the Torah-Law say these·things also?
1Co 9:15 did·I·write these·things in·order·that it·should·be·
1Co 12:11 But all these·things operate by·the one and the
2Co 2:16 And who *is* sufficient specifically·for these·things?
2Co 13:10 ·of that, I·write these·things while·being·absent,
Eph 5:6 words, for on·account·of these·things the wrath of·
1Ti 3:14 These·things I·write to·you, expecting to·come to
1Ti 4:6 When·you·put·forth·the·hazard·of these·things to·
1Ti 4:11 You·must·charge and instruct these·things.
1Ti 4:15 Meditate·upon these·things; be in these·things in·
1Ti 5:7 And charge *them with* these·things, in·order·that
1Ti 6:2 of·the good·deed. These·things instruct and exhort.
1Ti 6:11 O clay·man† of·God, flee from·these·things, and
2Ti 1:12 ·of which cause also I·suffer these·things. But·yet I·
2Ti 2:2 place·the·direct·care·of these·things to·trustworthy
2Ti 2:14 Quietly·remind *them concerning* these·things—
1Jn 1:4 And these·things we·write to·yeu, in·order·that our
1Jn 2:1 My dear·children, these·things I·write to·yeu, in·
1Jn 2:26 These·things I·already·wrote to·yeu concerning the·
1Jn 5:13 These·things I·wrote to·yeu, to·the·ones trusting in
Rv 1:19 the·things·which are·about to·be after these·things.
Rv 4:1 After these·things I·saw, and behold, a·door having·
Rv 4:1 ·which it·is·mandatory to·happen after these·things."
Rv 7:1 And after these·things, I·saw four angels standing on
Rv 7:9 After these·things I·saw, and behold, a·large crowd
Rv 9:12 behold, there·come two woes still after these·things.
Rv 10:4 spoke, and you·may·not write these·things."
Rv 15:5 And after these·things, I·saw, and behold, the
Rv 16:5 divinely·holy, because you·judged these·things.
Rv 18:1 And after these·things I·saw an·angel descending
Rv 19:1 And after these·things, I·heard a·great voice of·a·
Rv 20:3 And after these·things, it·is·mandatory·for him to·
Rv 22:8 *am* the·one looking·upon these·things and hearing
Rv 22:8 feet of·the angel, the·one showing me these·things.
Rv 22:16 angel to·testify to·yeu these·things concerning the
Rv 22:18 *anything additional* alongside these·things, God
Rv 22:20 The·one testifying these·things says, "Yes, I·come

EG5023.1 (1x)
Mk 2:8 that they·are·pondering *these·things* in·this·manner

G5023.2 P:D-NPN ταῦτα (11x)
Lk 1:65 them. And all these utterances were·conveyed
Heb 11:12 from one·man, even these *many offspring†* were·
Gal 5:17 And these are·fully·set·opposed to·one·another,
Mt 10:2 the names of·the twelve ambassadors are these: first,
Mt 15:20 These are the·things defiling the man·of·clay†.
Mt 24:8 But all these *are the* beginning of·birth·pangs.
Mk 7:23 All these evil·things proceed·forth from·inside, and
Mk 13:8 famines and agitations. These *are the* beginnings
Mk 16:17 "And these signs shall·closely·follow the·ones
Rm 9:8 That·is, *it·is* not these children of·the flesh *that·are*
1Co 13:13 And right·now, these three·things continue: Trust

G5023.2 P:D-APN ταῦτα (9x)
Jn 3:2 ·one·man is·able to·do these miraculous·signs that
Jn 8:20 These utterances Jesus spoke at the treasury·room,
Lk 2:19 Mariam was·closely·guarding all these utterances,
Lk 2:51 was·thoroughly·guarding all these utterances in her
Ac 10:44 As·Peter was·yet speaking these utterances, the
Ac 13:42 were·imploring for·these utterances to·be·spoken
Ac 16:38 ·officers reported·in·detail these utterances to·the
2Pe 1:9 For in·whom these *qualities* are·not present, he·is
1Ti 5:21 you·should·vigilantly·observe these *instructions*

G5024 τ•αυτά tautá *p:d.* (5x)
Roots:G3588 G0846

G5024 P:D-APN ταυτά (4x)
Lk 6:23 in the heaven, for in the·same·manner, their fathers
Lk 6:26 of·yeu! For in the·same·manner their fathers were·
Lk 17:30 "In the·same·manner shall·it·be in·that day *when*
1Th 2:14 Because *in* the·same·manner yeu also suffered

EG5024 (1x)
Col 2:6 *in the·same·manner* as yeu·personally·received the

G5025 τ•αύταις taútais *n.* (20x)
τ•αύτας taútas
Roots:G3778 See:G5026 G5126

G5025.1 P:D-APF ταύτας (8x)
Lk 1:24 And after these days, his wife EliSabeth conceived
Ac 3:24 also fully·announced·beforehand these days.
Ac 21:15 And after these days, after·packing·up·our·
Heb 9:23 with·significantly·better sacrifices than these.
Mt 13:53 *that* when YeShua finished these parables, he·
Mk 13:2 to·him, "Do·you·look·upon these great structures?
2Co 7:1 Accordingly, having these promises, dearly·beloved
Rv 16:9 ·one having authority over these punishing·blows.

G5025.1 P:D-DPF ταύταις (9x)
Jn 5:3 Among these *colonnades*, a·large multitude of·the·
Lk 1:39 And Mariam, rising·up in these days, traversed into
Lk 23:7 himself being also at JeruSalem in these days.
Lk 24:18 the·things occurring among her in these days?
Ac 1:15 And in these days, in *the* midst of·the disciples (and
Ac 6:1 And in these days of·the disciples multiplying, there·
Mt 22:40 On these two commandments is·hung all the
1Th 3:3 no·one to·be·woefully·shaken by these tribulations.
Rv 9:20 ·not killed by these punishing·blows did·not·even

G5025.2 P:D-DPF ταύταις (3x)
Lk 6:12 And it·happened in those days *that* he·went·forth to
Lk 13:14 Accordingly, coming on those *days*, be·both·
Ac 11:27 And in those days, prophets came·down from

G5026 τ•αύτῃ taútēi *n.* (123x)
τ•αύτην taútēn
τ•αύτης taútēs
Roots:G3778 See:G5025

G5026.1 P:D-ASF ταύτην (54x)
Jn 2:11 Jesus did this initiating of·miraculous·signs in Qanah
Jn 7:8 Yeu·yeurselves walk·up to this Sacred·Feast. I·myself
Jn 7:8 I·myself do·not·yet walk·up to this Sacred·Feast,
Jn 10:6 Jesus declared this proverb to·them, but those
Jn 10:18 to·take it again. This commandment I·received
Jn 12:27 But·rather on·account·of this, I·came to this hour.
Lk 4:6 "To·you I·shall·give absolutely·all this authority and
Lk 4:23 "Entirely, yeu·shall·declare to·me this adage, 'O·
Lk 7:44 ·replied to·Simon, "Do·you·look·upon this woman?
Lk 12:41 "Lord, do·you·say this parable to us, or even to all
Lk 13:6 And he·was·relaying this parable, "A·certain·man
Lk 13:16 And this·one, being a·daughter of·AbRaham,
Lk 15:3 And he·declared this parable to them, saying,
Lk 18:5 yet on·account·of this widow personally·presenting
Lk 18:9 And he·declared also this parable to certain ones
Lk 20:2 Or who is the·one giving you this authority?
Lk 20:9 Then he·began to·relay this parable to the people,
Lk 20:19 that he·declared this parable specifically·against
Lk 24:21 ·all these·things, today marks this third day since
Ac 1:16 brothers, it·was·mandatory·for this Scripture to·be·
Ac 3:16 to·this·same·man this perfect·soundness fully·in·
Ac 7:4 *God* transferred·and·settled him into this land in
Ac 7:60 ·should·not establish this moral·failure against·them
Ac 8:19 saying, "Give·me·also this authority, in·order·that
Ac 22:4 "*It·is·I* who persecuted this Way even·unto *their*
Ac 22:28 with·a·large sum, procured this citizenship." And
Ac 23:13 forty·men having·made this sworn·conspiracy.
Ac 27:21 from Crete nor·also to·gain this battering and
Ac 28:20 Accordingly, on·account·of this cause, I·
Ac 28:20 of·IsraEl *that* I·am·entirely·bound·with this chain."
Heb 5:3 And on·account·of this (just·as concerning the
Mt 11:16 "But to·what shall·I·liken this generation?
Mt 15:15 declared to·him, "Explain this parable to·us."
Mt 21:23 these·things? And who gave you this authority?
Mt 23:36 shall·come upon this generation·of·offspring.
Mk 4:13 ·them, "Do·yeu·not personally·know this parable?
Mk 10:5 ·of·heart, he·wrote yeu this commandment.
Mk 11:28 And who gave you this authority in·order·that
Mk 12:10 "Did·yeu·not·even read·aloud this Scripture?
Rm 5:2 the embraceable·access by·the trust into this grace in
1Pe 5:12 exhorting and further·testifying this to·be *the* true
2Pe 1:18 And·also we·ourselves heard this voice being·
2Pe 3:1 This second letter, beloved, even·now I·write to·yeu,
1Co 6:13 ·fully·render·inoperative even this and these·things
2Co 4:1 On·account·of that, having this Service *of·the Spirit*
2Co 8:6 ·finish among yeu this gracious·benevolence also.
2Co 12:13 of·yeu? Graciously·forgive me this injustice.
1Ti 1:18 I·place·the·direct·care·of this charge to·you, *my*
2Ti 2:19 of·God stands, having this official·seal, "' Yahweh
1Jn 3:3 And any one having this Expectation in him cleanses
1Jn 4:21 And this commandment we·presently·have from
2Jn 1:10 and does·not bring this instruction, yeu·must·not
Rv 2:24 (as·many·as do·not have this instruction *of·JeZebel*
Rv 12:15 in·order·that he·may·cause this *woman to·be*

G5026.1 P:D-DSF ταύτῃ (28x)
Lk 11:30 the Son of·Clay·Man† shall·be to·this generation.
Lk 12:20 to·him, 'O·impetuous·one! This night, they·are·
Lk 13:7 I·come seeking fruit on this fig·tree and find none.
Lk 16:24 my tongue, because I·am·distressed in this blaze.'
Lk 17:6 *does*, yeu·might say to·this mulberry-fig·tree, 'Be·
Lk 19:42 even you, at·least in this your day, the·things
Ac 18:10 ·that I·have for·myself many people in this city."
Ac 22:3 but having·been·reared in this city personally·at
Ac 27:23 For there·stood·by me this night an·angel of·God,
Heb 11:2 For in this, the elders·of·old are·attested·to.
Mt 10:23 whenever they·should·persecute yeu in this city,
Mt 12:45 ·this·manner shall·it·be also to·this evil generation.
Mt 16:18 "But upon this Solid·Rock I·shall·build my
Mt 26:31 ·up by me and·shall·fall·away on this night. For it·
Mt 26:34 I·say to·you, that in this night, prior·to a·rooster
Mk 8:12 ·sign shall·*ever*·be·given to·this generation.'"
Mk 8:38 me and of·my Redemptive-words in this generation
Mk 14:27 by me and·shall·fall·away on this night, because
Mk 14:30 that this·day, *even* in this night, prior·to a·rooster
1Co 7:20 he·was·called·forth, in this he·must·remain.
1Co 9:12 But·yet we·did·not use this privilege, but·rather
1Co 15:19 having·placed·our·expectation in this life† in
2Co 1:15 And in·this confidence, I·was·definitely·willing to·
2Co 8:7 love, *see* that yeu·should·abound in this grace also.
2Co 8:19 with·us along·with this gracious·benevolence (the·
2Co 8:20 us in this bountiful·benevolence being·attended·to
2Co 9:4 ·be·put·to·shame in this firm·assurance of·boasting.
2Co 11:17 impulsiveness, in this firm·assurance of·boasting.

G5026.1 P:D-GSF ταύτης (32x)
Jn 10:16 which are not from·among this yard·pen. It·is·
Jn 12:27 'Father, save me out of·this hour?
Jn 15:13 "A·love greater·than this, has not·even·one·man,
Lk 7:31 shall·I·liken the men·of·clay† of·this generation?
Lk 11:31 Final·Tribunal with the men of·this generation, and
Lk 11:32 ·up in the Final·Tribunal with this generation, and
Lk 11:50 may·be·sought·out from this generation,
Lk 11:51 to·yeu, it·shall·be·sought·out of this generation.
Lk 17:25 and to·be·rejected·as·unfit by this generation.
Ac 1:17 ·clearly·obtained the allotted·portion of·this service.
Ac 1:25 to·take the allotted·portion of·this service and
Ac 2:6 Now while·this sound was·happening, the multitude
Ac 2:29 buried, and his tomb is with us even·unto this day.
Ac 2:40 "Save·yeurselves from this warped generation."
Ac 5:20 to·the people all the utterances of·this life-above."
Ac 6:3 whom we·shall·fully·establish over this need.
Ac 8:22 Now·then, repent of this depravity of·yours, and
Ac 13:26 the Redemptive-word of·this Salvation is·already·
Ac 19:25 that our prosperity is as·a·result of·this occupation.
Ac 19:40 ·be·able to·render an·account of·this riotous·mob."
Ac 23:1 ·good conscience before·God even·up·to this day."
Ac 24:21 other·than concerning this one address that I·
Ac 26:22 God, I·stand even·unto this day, being·a·witness
Ac 28:22 for in·fact, as·concerning this sect, it·is known
Heb 9:11 made·by·human·hand, that·is, not of·this creation.

Heb 12:15 should·firmly·harass *yeu* and through this, many
Heb 13:2 ·to·strangers, for through this some are·hosting
Mt 12:41 in the Final·Tribunal with this generation and shall·
Mt 12:42 in the Final·Tribunal with this generation, and shall·
2Co 9:12 Because the service of·this public·charity, not
2Co 9:13 On·account·of the proof of·this service, they·are·
Rv 22:19 from the words of·*the*·scroll of·this prophecy, God

EG5026.1 (1x)

1Th 4:8 the·one presently·ignoring *this calling·forth, it·is*

G5026.2 P:D-ASF ταύτην (1x)

Lk 23:48 convening·publicly upon that distinct·spectacle,

G5026.2 P:D-DSF ταύτῃ (3x)

Lk 13:32 "Traversing, yeu·declare to·that fox, 'Behold, I·
Lk 17:34 "I·say to·yeu, in·that night there·shall·be two
Ac 16:12 and we·were in that city lingering·awhile·for

G5026.3 P:D-ASF ταύτην (2x)

Ac 13:33 because God has·entirely·fulfilled the·same to·us,
2Co 9:5 ·announced·beforehand, *for* the·same to·be ready

G5026.3 P:D-GSF ταύτης (2x)

Ac 8:35 and beginning from the same Scripture, proclaimed·
Ac 10:30 ago I·was fasting so·far·as·unto this·same hour;

G5027 ταφή taphḗ *n.* (1x)

Roots:G2290 See:G5028
xLangEquiv:H6900

G5027.2 N-ASF ταφήν (1x)

Mt 27:7 the potter's field as a·burial·place for·the foreigners.

G5028 τάφος táphôs *n.* (7x)

Roots:G2290 Compare:G3419 See:G5027
xLangAlso:H6913 H6900

G5028 N-NSM τάφος (1x)

Rm 3:13 "Their throat *is* a·grave having·been·opened·up;

G5028 N-ASM τάφον (3x)

Mt 27:64 ·order *for* the grave to·be·made·secure until the
Mt 27:66 And traversing, they·secured the grave with the
Mt 28:1 and the other Mariam came to·observe the grave.

G5028 N-APM τάφους (1x)

Mt 23:29 Because yeu·build the graves of·the prophets and

G5028 N-DPM τάφοις (1x)

Mt 23:27 yeu·resemble graves having·been·whitewashed,

G5028 N-GSM τάφου (1x)

Mt 27:61 other Miryam, sitting·down fully·before the grave.

G5029 τάχα tácha *adv.* (2x)

Roots:G5036

G5029.2 ADV τάχα (2x)

Rm 5:7 anyone die, for perhaps over the beneficially·good·
Phm 1:15 For perhaps on·account·of that, he·departed just·

G5030 ταχέως tachéōs *adv.* (10x)

Roots:G5036 See:G5035

G5030.1 ADV ταχέως (6x)

Jn 11:31 seeing that Mary rose·up quickly and went·out,
Lk 14:21 to·his slave, 'Go·out quickly into the broad·streets
Lk 16:6 your bill, and sitting·down quickly, write fifty.
Gal 1:6 that so quickly yeu·are·transferring away·from the·
2Th 2:2 for yeu not quickly to·be·shaken in the mind, nor to·
1Ti 5:22 Lay·forth hands on·not·one·man quickly, nor·even

Tτ

G5030.2 ADV ταχέως (4x)

Php 2:19 Lord Jesus, to·send TimoThy promptly to·yeu, that
Php 2:24 in *the* Lord that also I·myself shall·come promptly.
1Co 4:19 But I·shall·come to yeu promptly, if the Lord
2Ti 4:9 Quickly·endeavor to·come to me promptly,

G5031 ταχινός tachinós *adj.* (2x)

Roots:G5029 See:G5034

G5031.2 A-NSF ταχινή (1x)

2Pe 1:14 ·away of·my bodily·tabernacle is abrupt, even just·

G5031.2 A-ASF ταχινήν (1x)

2Pe 2:1 bringing·upon themselves abrupt total·destruction.

G5032 τάχιον táchiôn *adv.* (5x)

Roots:G5036

G5032.1 ADV-C τάχιον (4x)

Jn 13:27 "What you·do, do more·swiftly."
Jn 20:4 yet the other disciple more·swiftly outran Peter and
Heb 13:19 ·that I·may·be·restored to·yeu more·swiftly.
Heb 13:23 I·shall·gaze·upon yeu, if he·should·come swiftly.

G5032.2 ADV-C τάχιον (1x)

1Ti 3:14 to·you, expecting to·come to you more·promptly.

G5033 τάχιστα táchista *adv.* (1x)

Roots:G5036 See:G5613

G5033.2 ADV-S τάχιστα (1x)

Ac 17:15 they·should·come to him as quickly·as·possible.

G5034 τάχος táchôs *n.* (8x)

Roots:G5036 See:G1722

G5034.4 N-DSN τάχει (8x)

Lk 18:8 that he·shall·make retribution for·them in haste.
Ac 12:7 him, saying, "Rise·up in haste." And his chains
Ac 22:18 'Make·haste and go·forth in haste out of·JeruSalem
Ac 25:4 he·himself was·about to·depart *for·there* in haste.
Rm 16:20 Adversary-Accuser under yeur feet in haste. The
Rv 1:1 slaves what is·mandatory to·happen in haste. And
Rv 2:5 but·if·not, I·come to·you with·haste, and shall·stir
Rv 22:6 ·*of*·which it·is·mandatory to·be·done in haste.

G5035 ταχύ tachý *adv.* (12x)

Roots:G5036 See:G5030 G5035-1

G5035.1 ADV ταχύ (12x)

Jn 11:29 *sister* heard *it*, she·is·roused swiftly and goes to
Mt 5:25 with·your legal·adversary swiftly, for·as·long·as
Mt 28:7 Then traversing swiftly, declare to·his disciples that
Mt 28:8 And coming·forth swiftly from the chamber·tomb,
Mk 9:39 *that* also shall·be·able to·swiftly speak·ill·of me.
Mk 16:8 [(And going·forth swiftly, they·fled from the
Rv 2:16 But·if·not, I·come to·you swiftly, and I·shall·wage·
Rv 3:11 'Behold, I·come swiftly. Securely·hold that·which
Rv 11:14 went·away; behold, the third woe comes swiftly.
Rv 22:7 "Behold, I·come swiftly! Supremely·blessed *is* the·
Rv 22:12 "And behold, I·come swiftly, and my payment·of·
Rv 22:20 "Yes, I·come swiftly." So·be·it,·Amen.

G5036 ταχύς tachýs *adj.* (1x)

See:G5032 G5029

G5036.1 A-NSM ταχύς (1x)

Jac 1:19 brothers, every man·of·clay† must·be swift to·hear,

G5037 τέ tê *prt.* (213x)

Compare:G2532

G5037.1 PRT τέ (62x)

Lk 2:16 with·haste and diligently·found both Mariam and
Lk 22:66 were·gathered·together (both chief·priests and
Lk 23:12 in the same day, both Pilate and HerOd·AntiPas
Ac 1:1 all that Jesus began both to·do and to·instruct,
Ac 1:8 and yeu·shall·be witnesses to·me both in JeruSalem,
Ac 2:46 both while·diligently·continuing with·the·same·
Ac 4:27 you·anointed, *they·being* both HerOd·AntiPas and
Ac 5:14 *Called·Out·citizenry*, multitudes both of·men and
Ac 8:3 *of* the houses *and* dragging·off both men and women,
Ac 8:12 Anointed, they·were·immersed, both men and
Ac 8:13 he·was·astonished upon·observing both signs and
Ac 8:38 walked·down into the water, both PhilIppe and the
Ac 9:24 ·were·meticulously·watching the gates both day and
Ac 10:2 with·all his house, both doing many merciful·acts
Ac 10:39 witnesses of·all·the·things which he·did both in the
Ac 13:2 ·then, specially·detach for·me both BarNabas and
Ac 14:1 such·for·a·large multitude both of·Jews and·also
Ac 14:5 ·became a·violent·attempt (both from·the Gentiles
Ac 14:12 In·fact, both they·were·calling BarNabas, Zeus,
Ac 15:9 ·not·even make·one·distinction between both us and
Ac 15:32 Both Judas and Silas, being prophets also
Ac 17:4 with·Paul and Silas, both a·large multitude of·the·
Ac 17:10 immediately the brothers sent·forth both Paul and
Ac 17:14 toward the sea, but both Silas and TimoThy were·
Ac 18:5 And as·soon·as both Silas and TimoThy came·down
Ac 19:10 of·the Lord Jesus, both Jews and Greeks.
Ac 19:17 ·all the·ones residing·in Ephesus, to·both Jews and
Ac 20:21 thoroughly·testifying to·both Jews and Greeks, a·
Ac 21:12 ·as we·heard these·things, both we·ourselves and
Ac 22:4 and handing·over into prisons both men and women.
Ac 24:3 all·manner·of thanksgiving both everywhere and in·
Ac 24:15 of·dead·men, both of·righteous·ones and
Ac 25:23 together with·both the regiment·commanders and
Ac 25:24 Judeans conferred with·me, both at JeruSalem, and
Ac 26:16 and a·witness, both of·the·things·which you·saw
Ac 26:22 this day, being·a·witness to·both small and great,
Ac 26:22 aside·from those·things·which both the prophets
Ac 27:1 for Italy, they·were·handing both Paul and certain
Ac 28:23 them concerning Jesus, both from the Torah-Law
Heb 2:4 also·further·testifying·jointly, both with·signs and
Heb 2:11 For both the·one making·holy and the·ones being·
Heb 5:1 God, in·order·that he·may·offer both presents and
Heb 5:7 days of·his flesh, *was* offering·up both petitions and
Heb 5:14 habit toward having discernment of·both good and
Heb 6:19 as an·anchor of·the soul, both immovably·sure and
Heb 8:3 ·priest is·fully·established to·offer both presents and
Heb 9:9 then·currently·standing, in which both presents and
Heb 9:19 hyssop, he·sprinkled both the official·scroll itself
Heb 10:33 ·yeu·were·being·made·a·public·spectacle both
Mt 22:10 all, as·many·as they·found, both *the* evil and *the*
Rm 1:12 yeu through the mutual trust, both of·yeu and me.
Rm 1:14 I·am under·an·obligation both to·Greeks and to·
Rm 1:16 to Salvation to·everyone trusting, both to·Jew first,
Rm 1:20 ·him are·quite·clearly·seen, both his supra-eternal
Rm 2:10 ·is·working the beneficially·good, both to·Jew first
Rm 3:9 for we·already·legally·charged both Jews and
Rm 14:8 For both, whether we·should·live, we·live to·the
Rm 14:8 Accordingly, both whether we·should·live, or·also
Php 1:7 yeu in my heart. Both in my bonds and in·the
1Co 1:2 of·our Lord Jesus Anointed— both their *Lord* and
1Co 1:24 to·the·ones *who·are* called·forth, to·both Jews and
Eph 1:10 things in the Anointed-One, both the·things in the

EG5037.1 (2x)

Jac 3:11 at the same narrow·opening *with·both* the fresh
Jac 3:12 ·one wellspring *is·able* to·produce *both* salt water

G5037.2 PRT τέ (49x)

Jn 2:15 from·among the Sanctuary·Atrium, also the sheep
Jn 4:42 Also they·were·saying to·the woman, "No·longer
Jn 6:18 Also, the sea was·thoroughly·roused *due·to* a·great
Lk 24:20 And·also specifically·how the chief·priests and our
Ac 2:10 also *in* Phrygia and PamPhylia, *in* Egypt and *in* the
Ac 2:10 ·residing·here·from Rome, also Jews and converts·
Ac 2:33 to·the right·hand of·God and·also receiving the
Ac 5:19 ·up the prison doors; and·also leading them out, he·
Ac 6:7 in JeruSalem tremendously; also a·large crowd of·the
Ac 7:26 Also the following day, he·made·himself·visible to·
Ac 8:25 they·did also proclaim·the·good·news in·many
Ac 8:28 Also, he·was returning·back and sitting·down in his
Ac 9:15 of·Gentiles and kings, and·also the·Sons of·IsraEl.
Ac 11:26 an·ample crowd. Also *it·was* first to·be·imparted·
Ac 13:1 Lucius of·Cyrene, Manaen also (*who·was* nursed·
Ac 13:4 ·men went·down to Seleucia. Also from·there, they·
Ac 16:11 ·straight to Samos·of·Thrace, also the following
Ac 16:13 Also on·the day of·Sabbath, we·went·forth outside
Ac 16:34 Also bringing them up into his house, he·placed·
Ac 17:26 "Also, from·out·of·one blood he·made every nation
Ac 19:11 And·also God, through the hands of·Paul, was·
Ac 19:12 to·be·removed from them, and·also *for* the evil
Ac 19:18 Also, many of·the·ones having·trusted were·*now*·
Ac 20:3 continuing *there* also *for* three lunar·months.
Ac 21:11 taking·up Paul's belt, and·also binding his·own
Ac 23:24 Also *be certain* to·provide beasts *for·them* in·order·
Ac 24:23 the centurion to·keep Paul, and·also to·hold *him·at*
Ac 25:16 face·to·face, and·also may·receive a·place to·
Ac 26:11 *Jesus*; and·also maniacally·raging·against them
Ac 27:3 we·moored at Tsidon. And·also treating Paul
Ac 27:21 to·be·sailing·away from Crete nor·also to·gain this
Ac 28:23 ·to the kingdom of·God, and·also persuading them
Heb 1:3 ·imprint of·his very·essence, also *the·one* upholding
Heb 6:5 utterance of·God, and·also *the* miraculous·powers
Heb 9:1 of·ritual·ministry *to·God*, and·also the worldly
Heb 9:2 the first, in which also *was* the Menorah·Lampstand
Heb 11:32 ·an·account concerning Gideon, also Baraq,
Heb 11:32 Samson, and Yiphtach; and also David, SamuEl,
Mt 23:6 Also, they·are·fond·of the foremost·places at the

Rm 1:14 to·Greeks and to·Barbarians, also to·wise·ones and
Rm 7:7 Torah-Law, for also I·had·not personally·known the
Rm 14:8 we·live to·the Lord; or·also whether we·should·die
Rm 14:8 we·should·live, or·also whether we·should·die,
Rm 16:26 ·being·made·apparent— also through prophetic
Jac 3:7 For every species of·wild·beasts, also of·birds, and
Jud 1:6 Also the angels, not observantly·keeping their·own
1Co 1:30 wisdom from God, also righteousness, renewed·
1Co 4:21 a·rod or with love, also in·a·spirit of·gentleness?
Rv 21:12 also having a·wall great and high, having twelve

EG5037.2 (1x)

Ac 23:8 there·is not a·resurrection, *also* not·even an·angel

G5037.3 PRT τέ (92x)

Lk 12:45 ·boys and the servant·girls, and to·eat and to·drink
Lk 21:11 And great earthquakes shall·be pervasive·in·all
Lk 21:11 ·pestilences, and there·shall·be frightening·things
Ac 1:15 midst of·the disciples (and it·was a·crowd of·names
Ac 2:3 ·fire were·made·visible to·them, and it·settled upon
Ac 2:9 and the·ones residing·in MesoPotamia and *in* Judea
Ac 2:37 ·fully·jabbed in·the heart, and they·declared to
Ac 2:40 And with·many other words, he·was·thoroughly·
Ac 2:43 ·awe came upon·every soul, and many wonders and
Ac 2:46 in the Sanctuary·Atrium and breaking bread in·each
Ac 3:10 And they·were·recognizing that he·himself was the·
Ac 4:13 ·were·marveling; and they·were·recognizing them,
Ac 4:33 resurrection of·the Lord Jesus, and great grace was
Ac 5:35 And *then* he·declared to *the joint·council*, "Men,
Ac 5:42 And every day in the Sanctuary·Atrium, and in·each
Ac 6:12 And they·jointly·stirred·up the people, the elders,
Ac 6:13 and they·set·up false witnesses saying, "This man·
Ac 8:1 ·citizenry, the·one in JeruSalem; and all besides the
Ac 8:6 And the crowds, *being together* with·the·same·
Ac 8:31 should·guide me?" And he·implored Philippe that·
Ac 9:6 And trembling and being·amazed, he·declared,
Ac 9:18 ·off from his eyes. And he·received·sight at·once.
Ac 9:24 to·Saul. And they·were·meticulously·watching the
Ac 9:29 Jesus, and also he·was·mutually·questioning·and·
Ac 10:22 ·is·reverently·fearing God and being·attested·to by
Ac 10:28 And he·replied to them, "Yeu·yeurselves are·
Ac 10:33 ·this·same·hour I·sent to you, and you did well in·
Ac 10:48 And he·specifically·assigned for·them to·be·
Ac 11:13 And he·announced to·us how he·saw the angel in
Ac 11:21 was with them, and a·large number turned·back·
Ac 12:6 ·bound with·two chains, and sentries were·guarding
Ac 12:8 And the angel declared to him, "Gird·yourself·
Ac 12:12 And after·becoming·completely·aware, he·came to
Ac 14:21 And after·proclaiming·the·good·news to·that city
Ac 15:4 and they·reported·in·detail what·many·things *that*
Ac 15:5 ·mandatory·to·circumcise them and to·charge *them*
Ac 15:39 ·separated from one·another; and *for* BarNabas,
Ac 16:12 and from·there to Philippi, which is a·foremost city
Ac 16:23 And after·placing many punishing·blows upon·
Ac 16:26 of·the dungeon to·be·shaken. And at·once, all the
Ac 17:4 who·are·being·reverent Greek·men and not a·few
Ac 17:5 ·a·commotion·in the city. And assaulting the home
Ac 17:19 And grabbing·hold of·him, they·brought·him to
Ac 18:4 each and·every Sabbath, and was·persuading Jews
Ac 18:11 And he·settled *there* a·year and six lunar·months,
Ac 18:26 And this·man began to·boldly·speak·with·clarity in
Ac 19:3 And he·declared to them, "So·then into what were·
Ac 19:6 and they·were·speaking with·bestowed·tongues
Ac 19:29 with·mass·confusion. And seizing·both Gaius and
Ac 20:7 on·the next·day; and he·was·prolonging the
Ac 20:11 and after·having·a·bite·to·eat and conversing over
Ac 20:35 ·and·supportive of·the weak, and to·remember the
Ac 21:18 with·us *to·come* alongside Jacob; and all the elders
Ac 21:20 the Lord. And·then they·declared to·him, "Do·
Ac 21:28 and this place. And furthermore, he also brought
Ac 21:30 And the whole City was·stirred, and the people
Ac 21:37 And as Paul was·about to·be·brought into the
Ac 22:7 And I·fell to the hard·ground and heard a·voice
Ac 22:8 'Who are·you, Lord?' And he·declared to me, 'It·
Ac 22:28 And the regiment·commander answered, "I·myself
Ac 23:5 And Paul replied, "I·had·not seen, brothers, that he·
Ac 23:10 ·among *the* midst of·them, and to·bring *him* into
Ac 23:35 ·publicly." And he·commandingly·ordered him
Ac 24:5 Jews in The Land, and *being* a·champion of·the sect
Ac 24:23 And he·thoroughly·arranged·for the centurion to·
Ac 24:27 took succession *after* Felix. And Felix, wanting to·
Ac 26:10 the chief·priests. And with·them being·executed,
Ac 26:16 you·saw and of·the·things·in·which I·shall·be·
Ac 26:20 Damascus, and·then in·JeruSalem and unto all the
Ac 26:30 and·also the governor, and BerNiki, and the·ones
Ac 27:3 And with another *day of·sailing*, we·moored at
Ac 27:5 And after·sailing·through the open·sea adjacent·to
Ac 27:8 And sailing·near it with·difficulty, we·came to some
Ac 27:17 undergirding the sailing·ship. And, fearing lest
Ac 27:20 over many·more days, and with·no little wintry·
Ac 27:29 And fearing lest·somehow they·should·fall into
Ac 27:43 ·the resolve, and commandingly·ordered the·ones
Heb 4:12 even·unto a·dividing of·soul and spirit, and even
Heb 4:12 of·soul and spirit, and even of·the·joints and
Heb 6:2 of·ceremonial·washings, and of·laying·on of·hands,
Heb 6:2 ·on of·hands, and of·the·resurrection of·the·dead,
Heb 6:4 once being·enlightened, and after·tasting of·the
Heb 12:2 of·shame, despising *it*, and sat·down at *the* right·
Mt 27:48 after·running and taking a·sponge and filling *it*
Mt 28:12 ·together with the elders and taking consultation,
Mk 15:36 a·sponge of·wine·vinegar and putting·it·on a·reed,
Rm 1:27 And likewise also the males, leaving the natural
Rm 2:9 the wrong, of·Jew first, and also of·Greek.
Rm 2:19 And you·have·confidence within·yourself to·be a·
Jac 3:7 also of·birds, and of·creeping·things, and of·
Eph 3:19 and to·absolutely·know the surpassing knowledge
Rv 1:2 of·Jesus Anointed, and *to* as·many·things·as he·saw.

G5037.4 PRT τέ (3x)

Ac 1:13 where they·were continuing·to·abide as·follows:
Ac 13:1 prophets and instructors as·follows: BarNabas,
Ac 21:25 ·keep themselves *from* the·following: *from* the·

G5037.7 PRT τέ (1x)

Rm 1:26 burning·passions, for even their females exchanged

G5037.8 PRT τέ (1x)

Rm 10:12 For there·is no distinction between Jew and Greek

G5037.9 PRT τέ (1x)

Ac 9:2 any *disciples* of·The Way, whether being men or

G5037.10 PRT τέ (1x)

Ac 5:24 Now as·soon·as the high priest and the high·warden

G5038 τεῖχος têîchôs *n.* (9x)

See:G5088 G5109 xLangAlso:H2346

G5038 N-NSN τεῖχος (1x)

Rv 21:14 And the wall of·the CITY *is* having twelve

G5038 N-NPN τείχη (1x)

Heb 11:30 By·trust, the walls of·Jericho fell·down, being·

G5038 N-ASN τεῖχος (3x)

Rv 21:12 also having a·wall great and high, having twelve
Rv 21:15 ·measure the CITY, and its gates, and its wall.
Rv 21:17 And he·measured its wall, a·hundred *and* forty four

G5038 N-GSN τείχους (4x)

Ac 9:25 *by* lowering *him* through the wall in a·woven·basket.
2Co 11:33 ·lowered through the wall and utterly·escaped his
Rv 21:18 And the construction of·its wall was *of* jasper.
Rv 21:19 And the foundations of·the wall of·the CITY *were*

G5039 τεκμήριον têkmḗriôn *n.* (1x)

Compare:G1732

G5039 N-DPN τεκμηρίοις (1x)

Ac 1:3 by many positive·proofs, while·being·gazed·upon by·

G5040 τεκνίον têkníôn *n.* (9x)

Roots:G5043 G2444-3 Compare:G3504 G3813 G4168

G5040.2 N-VPN τεκνία (9x)

Jn 13:33 "Dear·children, yet a·little·while I·am with yeu.
Gal 4:19 My dear·children, for·whom I·experience·
1Jn 2:1 My dear·children, these·things I·write to·yeu, in·
1Jn 2:12 I·write to·yeu, dear·children, because the moral·
1Jn 2:28 And now, dear·children, abide in him, in·order·that
1Jn 3:7 Dear·children, let not·even·one·man deceive yeu.
1Jn 3:18 My dear·children, we·should·not love in·word, nor·
1Jn 4:4 are birthed·from·out of·God, dear·children, and
1Jn 5:21 Dear·children, vigilantly·keep yeurselves from the

G5041 τεκνο•γονέω têknôgônéō *v.* (1x)

Roots:G5043 G1096

G5041 V-PAN τεκνογονεῖν (1x)

1Ti 5:14 to·bear·children, to·attend·to·the·operations·of·

G5042 τεκνο•γονία têknôgônía *n.* (1x)

Roots:G5043 G1096 See:G5041 G5042-1

G5042.1 N-GSF τεκνογονίας (1x)

1Ti 2:15 through the bearing·of·children— provided·that

G5043 τέκνον têknôn *n.* (100x)

Roots:G5088 Compare:G3816 G3813 G5207 xLangAlso:H3206 H1121

G5043 N-NSN τέκνον (4x)

Lk 1:7 Yet there·was·not a·child *born* to·them, because·
Php 2:22 proof of·him, that as a·child together with·a·father,
1Co 4:17 who is my beloved child, and trustworthy in *the*
Rv 12:5 a·rod of·iron; and her child was·snatched·up to God

G5043 N-NPN τέκνα (28x)

Jn 1:12 ·them he·gave privilege to·become children of·God,
Jn 8:39 "If yeu·were AbRaham's children, yeu·would do the
Gal 4:27 ·woman has·many more children than the·one
Gal 4:28 according·to YiTsaq, are children of·promise.
Gal 4:31 brothers, we·are not children of·a·maidservant,
Mt 10:21 *·hand·over* child, and children shall·rise·up against
Mk 13:12 *·over* child; and children shall·rise·up against
Rm 8:16 with·our spirit that we·are children of·God,
Rm 8:17 and if *we·are* children, then·also *we·are* heirs, heirs
Rm 9:7 of·AbRaham, *are* they·all *his* children. But·rather
Rm 9:8 That·is, *it·is* not these children of·the flesh *that·are*
Rm 9:8 children of·the flesh *that·are* children of·God, but·
Rm 9:8 of·God, but·rather the children of·the promise are·
Php 2:15 ·may·be blameless and untainted, children of·God,
1Pe 1:14 As attentively·obedient children, do·not be·
2Pe 2:14 ·acts·of·coveting. *They·are* children of·*the*·curse,
1Co 4:14 but·rather, as my beloved children, I·admonish *yeu*
1Co 7:14 husband; otherwise yeur children are impure, but
2Co 12:14 yeu; for the children are·not obligated to·store·up
Eph 2:3 And we·were by·nature children of·wrath, even as
Eph 5:1 attentive·imitators of·God, as beloved children,
Eph 5:8 Walk as children of·light
Eph 6:1 *Now* the children: Listen·to·and·obey yeur parents in
Col 3:20 *Now* the children: Yeu·must·listen·to·and·obey the
1Jn 3:2 Beloved, now we·are children of·God, and it·is·not·
1Jn 3:10 In this the children of·God are apparent, also the
1Jn 3:10 are apparent, also the children of·the Slanderer.
2Jn 1:13 The children of·your Selected sister greet you

G5043 N-VSN τέκνον (8x)

Lk 2:48 mother declared to him, "Child, why·did you·do us
Lk 15:31 "And he·declared to·him, 'Child, you·yourself are
Lk 16:25 But AbRaham declared, 'Child, recall·to·mind that
Mt 9:2 to·the paralyzed·man, "Child, be·of·good·courage.
Mt 21:28 the first, he·declared, 'Child, head·on·out. Work
Mk 2:5 to·the paralyzed·man, "Child, your moral·failures
1Ti 1:18 this charge to·you, *my* child TimoThy, according·to
2Ti 2:1 Accordingly, you, my child, be·enabled in the grace

G5043 N-VPN τέκνα (1x)

Mk 10:24 again, says to·them, "Children, how exceedingly·

G5043 N-ASN τέκνον (3x)

Mt 10:21 and father *shall·hand·over* child, and children
Mk 13:12 and father *shall·hand·over* child; and children
Rv 12:4 her child whenever she·should·produce·birth.

G5043 N-APN τέκνα (34x)

Jn 11:52 ·together into one, the children of·God, the·ones
Lk 1:17 hearts back·around toward *the* children," and *to*·
Lk 3:8 ·out of·these stones to·awaken children to·AbRaham.
Lk 13:34 I·wanted to·completely·gather your children, as a·
Lk 14:26 mother, and wife, and children, and brothers, and
Lk 18:29 or wife, or children, for·the·cause·of the kingdom
Lk 19:44 ·to·the·hard·ground and your children within you;
Lk 20:31 also; they·left·behind no children, and they·died.
Lk 23:28 weep over yeurselves and over yeur children.

Ac 21:21 for·them not to·circumcise the children, nor·even
Mt 2:18 Rachel weeping *for* her children. And she·was·not
Mt 3:9 ·out of·these stones to·awaken children to·AbRaham.
Mt 18:25 even his wife and children and all·things as·much·
Mt 19:29 or mother or wife or children or plots·of·land, for·
Mt 21:28 ·man·of·clay† was·having two children, and
Mt 22:24 if a·certain·man should·die not having children, his
Mt 23:37 I·wanted to·completely·gather your children as a·
Mt 27:25 "His blood *be* on us and on our children."
Mk 7:27 "First, allow the children to·be·stuffed·full. For it·
Mk 10:29 or mother or wife or children or plots·of·land, for·
Mk 10:30 sisters and mothers and children and plots·of·land,
Mk 12:19 a·wife, and should·not leave children, that his
1Pe 3:6 *It·is* of·her·whom yeu·did·become children, while·
1Th 2:7 would cherishingly·brood·over her·own children.
1Th 2:11 how as a·father *does·for* his children, exhorting and
Tit 1:6 of·one wife, having trustworthy children not in legal·
Eph 6:4 Do·not personally·anger yeur children, but·rather
Col 3:21 ·must·not contentiously·irritate yeur children, lest
1Ti 3:4 house well, having his·children in subjection with all
1Ti 5:4 But if any widow has children or grandchildren,
1Jn 3:1 to·us, that we·should·be·called children of·God. On·
1Jn 5:2 we·know that we·love the children of·God, whenever
3Jn 1:4 ·things, that I·hear·of my children walking in truth.
Rv 2:23 And I·shall·kill her children with death; and all the

G5043 N-DSN τέκνῳ (3x)
Tit 1:4 To·Titus, a·genuine child according·to a·shared trust.
1Ti 1:2 To·TimoThy, a·genuine child in trust. Grace, mercy,
2Ti 1:2 To·TimoThy, a·dearly·beloved child. Grace, mercy,

G5043 N-DPN τέκνοις (8x)
Lk 11:13 beneficially·good gifts to·yeur children, how·much
Ac 2:39 is for·yeu, and for·yeur children, and for·all the·
Ac 13:33 the·same to·us, their children, by·raising·up Jesus;
Ac 21:5 off (together with·wives and children) until *we·were*
Mt 7:11 beneficially·good gifts to·yeur children, how·much
2Co 6:13 (I·say *this* as to·my·children): Yeu·yeurselves,
2Co 12:14 parents, but·rather the parents for·the children.
2Jn 1:1 To·a·Selected lady and her children— whom I·

G5043 N-GSN τέκνου (2x)
Ac 7:5 him, *even* with·there·not being a·child *born* to·him.
Phm 1:10 I·implore you concerning my child Onesimus,

G5043 N-GPN τέκνων (8x)
Lk 7:35 is·regarded·as·righteous by all her children."
Gal 4:25 at·the present, and is·enslaved with her children.
Mt 11:19 Wisdom is·regarded·as·righteous by her children."
Mt 15:26 ·is not good to·take the children's bread and to·cast
Mk 7:27 ·is not good to·take the children's bread and to·cast
Rm 8:21 into the glorious liberty of·the children of·God.
1Ti 3:12 ·one wife, conducting their·children and their·own
2Jn 1:4 ·found from·among your children *those* walking in

EG5043 (1x)
Lk 1:35 On·account·of·which also, the *child*, being·born

G5044 τεκνο•τροφέω têknôtrôphéō *v.* (1x)
Roots:G5043 G5142

G5044 V-AAI-3S ἐτεκνοτρόφησεν (1x)
1Ti 5:10 good works (if she·nurtured·and·reared·children, if

G5045 τέκτων téktōn *n.* (2x)
Roots:G5088 Compare:G5079 See:G0753

G5045.2 N-NSM τέκτων (1x)
Mk 6:3 Is this not the carpenter, the son of·Mariam, and a·

G5045.2 N-GSM τέκτονος (1x)
Mt 13:55 ¿!·Is this not the carpenter's son?

G5046 τέλειος têlêiôs *adj.* (19x)
Roots:G5056 Compare:G3651 G5050 See:G3588

G5046.1 A-NSM τέλειος (2x)
Mt 5:48 yeur Father, the·one in the heavens, is complete.
Mt 19:21 "If you·want to·be complete, head·on·out, sell your

G5046.1 A-NSN τέλειον (2x)
Rm 12:2 ·good, most·satisfying, and complete will of·God.
Jac 1:17 act·of·giving and every complete endowment is

G5046.1 A-NPM τέλειοι (2x)
Mt 5:48 yeu·yeurselves shall·be complete *in·this·manner*,
Jac 1:4 work, that yeu·may·be complete and entirely·whole,

G5046.1 A-ASM τέλειον (3x)
Jac 1:25 ·near·to·peer into the complete Law of·Liberty, and
Eph 4:13 of·the Son of·God, into a·complete man, into a·
Col 1:28 every man·of·clay† complete in Anointed-One

G5046.1 A-ASN τέλειον (2x)
Jac 1:4 the patient·endurance have *her* complete work, that
1Co 13:10 But whenever the complete should·come, then

G5046.1 A-GSF-C τελειοτέρας (1x)
Heb 9:11 through the greater and more·complete Tabernacle

G5046.2 A-NSM τέλειος (1x)
Jac 3:2 in word, the·same *is* a·completely·mature man, able

G5046.2 A-NSF τελεία (1x)
1Jn 4:18 Love, but·rather the completely·mature love casts

G5046.2 A-NPM τέλειοι (3x)
Php 3:15 ·as *would·become* completely·mature, we·should·
1Co 14:20 But in·the contemplations be completely·mature.
Col 4:12 completely·mature and having·been·completely·

G5046.2 A-DPM τελείοις (1x)
1Co 2:6 wisdom among the·ones *being* completely·mature,

G5046.2 A-GPM τελείων (1x)
Heb 5:14 nourishment is *for* the completely·mature, *their*

G5047 τελειότης têlêiótēs *n.* (2x)
Roots:G5046

G5047.2 N-ASF τελειότητα (1x)
Heb 6:1 ·on toward the completeness·of·maturity; not

G5047.2 N-GSF τελειότητος (1x)
Col 3:14 *·uniting·principle)* of·the completeness·of·maturity.

G5048 τελειόω têlêióō *v.* (24x)
Roots:G5046 Compare:G5055 G0535 G4137 xLangAlso:H8552 H6213

G5048.1 V-PPI-3S τελειοῦται (1x)
2Co 12:9 for my power is·made·fully·complete in weakness

G5048.1 V-AAI-1S ἐτελείωσα (1x)
Jn 17:4 you on the earth. I·fully·completed the work, which

G5048.1 V-AAN τελειῶσαι (1x)
Ac 20:24 ·myself, as·so to·fully·complete my running·race

G5048.1 V-AAP-GPM τελειωσάντων (1x)
Lk 2:43 and after·fully·completing the days, *then* at their

G5048.1 V-AAS-1S τελειώσω (2x)
Jn 4:34 sending me, and *that* I·may·fully·complete his work.
Jn 5:36 gave me (in·order·that I·should·fully·complete them)

G5048.1 V-APS-3S τελειωθῇ (1x)
Jn 19:28 in·order·that the Scripture may·be·fully·completed,

G5048.1 V-APS-3P τελειωθῶσιν (1x)
Heb 11:40 ·from us, should·they·be·made·fully·complete.

G5048.1 V-RAI-3S τετελείωκεν (1x)
Heb 10:14 he·has·made·fully·complete into perpetuity the·

G5048.1 V-RPI-3S τετελείωται (1x)
1Jn 4:17 with us has·been·fully·completed, in·order·that we·

G5048.2 V-AAI-3S ἐτελείωσεν (1x)
Heb 7:19 made not·even·one·thing completely·mature, but

G5048.2 V-AAN τελειῶσαι (3x)
Heb 2:10 Salvation completely·mature through afflictions.
Heb 9:9 being·able to·make·completely·mature according·to
Heb 10:1 to·make·completely·mature the·ones coming·

G5048.2 V-API-3S ἐτελειώθη (1x)
Jac 2:22 of·the works, the trust is·made·completely·mature.

G5048.2 V-APP-NSM τελειωθείς (1x)
Heb 5:9 And being·made·completely·mature, he·became *the*

G5048.2 V-RPI-1S τετελείωμαι (1x)
Php 3:12 even·now have·been·made·completely·mature, but

G5048.2 V-RPI-3S τετελείωται (2x)
1Jn 2:5 love of·God has·been·made·completely·mature. In
1Jn 4:18 ·afraid has·not been·made·completely·mature in the

G5048.2 V-RPP-ASM τετελειωμένον (1x)
Heb 7:28 having·been·made·completely·mature to the

G5048.2 V-RPP-GPM τετελειωμένων (1x)
Heb 12:23 ·men having·been·made·completely·mature,

G5048.2 V-RPP-NSF τετελειωμένη (1x)
1Jn 4:12 love is having·been·made·completely·mature in us.

G5048.2 V-RPP-NPM τετελειωμένοι (1x)
Jn 17:23 they·may·be having·been·made·completely·mature

G5048.3 V-PPI-1S τελειοῦμαι (1x)
Lk 13:32 and on·the third *day* I·am·completely·finished.'

G5049 τελείως têléíōs *adv.* (1x)
Roots:G5046

G5049.1 ADV τελείως (1x)
1Pe 1:13 ·sober, place·yeur·expectation completely upon the

G5050 τελείωσις têlêíōsis *n.* (2x)
Roots:G5048 Compare:G5056 See:G4930

G5050.1 N-NSF τελείωσις (1x)
Lk 1:45 there·shall·be a·completion of·the·things having·

G5050.2 N-NSF τελείωσις (1x)
Heb 7:11 Accordingly in·fact, if perfection was through the

G5051 τελειωτής têlêiōtḗs *n.* (1x)
Roots:G5048

G5051.2 N-ASM τελειωτήν (1x)
Heb 12:2 the Initiator and Complete·Finisher of·the Trust—

G5052 τελεσ•φορέω têlêsphôréō *v.* (1x)
Roots:G5056 G5342

G5052.3 V-PAI-3P τελεσφοροῦσιν (1x)
Lk 8:14 ·life, and they·do·not bring·fruit·to·perfection.

G5053 τελευτάω têlêutáō *v.* (12x)
Roots:G5055 Compare:G1634 G2348 G0599 G1606 G3855 See:G0979 G5054

G5053.2 V-PAI-3S τελευτᾷ (3x)
Mk 9:44 "their worm does·not completely·die, and the fire
Mk 9:46 "their worm does·not completely·die, and the fire
Mk 9:48 "their worm completely·does·not die, and the fire

G5053.2 V-PAM-3S τελευτάτω (2x)
Mt 15:4 ·of father or mother must·completely·die *the* death."
Mk 7:10 ·of father or mother must·completely·die *the* death.

G5053.2 V-PAN τελευτᾶν (1x)
Lk 7:2 ·valued by·him, was·about to·completely·die, being

G5053.2 V-PAP-NSM τελευτῶν (1x)
Heb 11:22 (as·he·was·completely·dying) remembered

G5053.2 V-AAI-3S ἐτελεύτησεν (4x)
Ac 2:29 David, that also he·is·completely·dead and buried,
Ac 7:15 ·down into Egypt, and he·completely·died, he and
Mt 9:18 "My daughter just·completely·died at·this·moment,
Mt 22:25 upon·marrying *a·wife*, completely·died. And·so

G5053.2 V-AAP-GSM τελευτήσαντος (1x)
Mt 2:19 But upon·HerOd the·Great completely·dying, behold,

G5054 τελευτή têlêutḗ *n.* (1x)
Roots:G5053

G5054 N-GSF τελευτῆς (1x)
Mt 2:15 he·was there until the demise of·HerOd the·Great, in·

G5055 τελέω têléō *v.* (26x)
Roots:G5056 Compare:G5048 G4137 G0535 G5099

G5055.2 V-PAI-2P τελεῖτε (1x)
Jac 2:8 If however, yeu·complete *the* Royal Law according·

G5055.2 V-PAP-NSF τελοῦσα (1x)
Rm 2:27 And *if* completing the Torah-Law, *shall·not* the·one

G5055.2 V-AAI-3P ἐτέλεσαν (1x)
Ac 13:29 as·soon·as they·completed absolutely·all the·things

G5055.2 V-API-3S ἐτελέσθη (1x)
Rv 15:1 because in them the Rage of·God is·completed.

G5055.2 V-APS-3S τελεσθῇ (3x)
Rv 17:17 ·until the utterances of·God should·be·completed.
Rv 20:3 ·until the thousand years should·be·completed. And
Rv 20:7 the thousand years should·be·completed, the

G5055.2 V-APS-3P τελεσθῶσιν (1x)
Rv 15:8 ·blows of·the seven angels should·be·completed.

G5055.3 V-FPI-3S τελεσθήσεται (1x)
Lk 18:31 the Son of·Clay·Man† shall·be·finished.

G5055.3 V-AAI-3S ἐτέλεσεν (4x)
Mt 11:1 YeShua finished thoroughly·assigning *these·things*
Mt 13:53 *that* when YeShua finished these parables, he·
Mt 19:1 ·happened *that* when YeShua finished these sayings,
Mt 26:1 it·happened *that* when YeShua finished all these

G5055.3 V-AAI-3P ἐτέλεσαν (1x)
Lk 2:39 And after they·finished absolutely·all the·things

G5055.3 V-AAS-2P τελέσητε (2x)
Gal 5:16 and no, yeu·would·not finish a·longing of·flesh.

Mt 10:23 to·yeu, no, yeu·may·not finish the cities of·IsraEl,
G5055.3 V-AAS-3P τελέσωσιν (1x)
Rv 11:7 And whenever they·should·finish their testimony,
G5055.3 V-APN τελεσθῆναι (1x)
Lk 22:37 this thing having·been·written to·be·finished in me,
G5055.3 V-APS-3S τελεσθῇ (3x)
Lk 12:50 and how am·I·clenched until it·should·be·finished!
Rv 10:7 even the Mystery of·God should·be·finished, as he·
Rv 20:5 ·again until the thousand years should·be·finished.
G5055.3 V-RAI-1S τετέλεκα (1x)
2Ti 4:7 the good striving; I·have·finished the race·course; I·
G5055.3 V-RPI-3S τετέλεσται (2x)
Jn 19:28 ·now everything has·been·finished, in·order·that the
Jn 19:30 wine·vinegar, he·declared, "It·has·been·finished!"
G5055.4 V-PAI-2P τελεῖτε (1x)
Rm 13:6 For on·account·of that, yeu·fully·pay tributes also.
G5055.4 V-PAI-3S τελεῖ (1x)
Mt 17:24 mentor, does·he·not fully·pay the two·drachmas?

G5056 τέλος tĕlôs *n.* (45x)

Compare:G2778 G5411 See:G5046 G5050 G3838

G5056.1 N-NSN τέλος (17x)
Lk 1:33 ·ages, and of·his kingdom there·shall·be no end."
Lk 21:9 "Moreover, the end does·not *occur* immediately.
Heb 6:8 and *is* close to·being·cursed, whose end *is* for
Mt 24:6 *these·things* to·happen, but·still the end is not·yet.
Mt 24:14 to·all the nations, and then the end shall·come.
Mk 13:7 *such·things* to·happen, but·rather the end *is* not·yet.
Rm 6:21 yeu·are·ashamed? For the end of·those·things *is*
Rm 6:22 unto renewed·holiness, and at·the end, *unto* eternal
Rm 10:4 For Anointed-One *is the* end of·Torah-Law for
Php 3:19 whose end *is* total·destruction, whose god *is* the
1Pe 4:7 But the end of·all·things has·drawn·near.
1Pe 4:17 what *is* the end of·the·ones being·obstinate to·the
1Co 15:24 after·that, the end, whenever he·should·hand·
2Co 11:15 ·righteousness, whose end shall·be according·to
Rv 1:8 and the Omega, beginning and end," says the Lord,
Rv 21:6 the beginning and the end. I·myself shall·give to·
Rv 22:13 and the Omega, beginning and end, the First and
G5056.1 N-NPN τέλη (1x)
1Co 10:11 for whom the ends of·the ages are·attained.
G5056.1 N-ASN τέλος (10x)
Jn 13:1 the·ones in the world, he·loved them to *the* end.
Lk 22:37 ' for even the·things concerning me have an·end."
Heb 7:3 neither beginning of·days, nor end of·life†, but
Mt 10:22 But the·one patiently·enduring to *the* end, this·one
Mt 24:13 But the·one patiently·enduring to *the* end, the·same
Mt 26:58 he·sat·down with the assistants to·see the end.
Mk 3:26 able to·remain·established, but·rather has an·end.
Mk 13:13 the·one patiently·enduring to *the* end, the·same
1Pe 1:9 subsequently·obtaining the end of·yeur trust, *the*
2Co 3:13 ·IsraEl not gazing·intently for the end, with·the *veil*
G5056.1 N-GSN τέλους (6x)
Heb 3:6 Expectation *being* steadfast as·long·as·unto *the* end.
Heb 3:14 *being* steadfast as·long·as·unto *the* end.
Heb 6:11 ·assurance of·the Expectation, even·up·to *the* end,
1Co 1:8 shall·confirm yeu unto *the* end, *being* not·called·to·
2Co 1:13 that yeu·shall·acknowledge *this* even unto *the* end,
Rv 2:26 my works even·unto *the* end, to·him I·shall·give
G5056.3 N-ASN τέλος (1x)
1Th 2:16 already·anticipated upon them *is* for termination.
G5056.4 N-ASN τέλος (2x)
Lk 18:5 me as an·end·result *of·her·persistently* coming *to·me*.
Jac 5:11 of·Job and saw the end·result of·Yahweh, that
EG5056.4 (1x)
1Pe 2:8 being·obstinate. To which *end·result*, they·are also
G5056.5 N-NSN τέλος (1x)
1Ti 1:5 Now the end·purpose of·the charge is love out of·a·
EG5056.5 (1x)
1Pe 4:6 to this *end·purpose* was·the·good·news·already· also
G5056.6 N-ASN τέλος (2x)
Rm 13:7 ·one *due* the tribute, the tax to·the·one *due* the tax,
Rm 13:7 the tax to·the·one *due* the tax, the reverent·fear to·
G5056.6 N-APN τέλη (1x)
Mt 17:25 kings of·the earth take taxes or a·census·tribute?
EG5056.6 (1x)
Mt 17:24 the two·drachma *tax* came·alongside Peter and
G5056.7 N-NSN τέλος (1x)
1Pe 3:8 Now finally all *of·yeu*: *be* of·the·same·mind,

G5057 τελ•ώνης tĕlōnēs *n.* (22x)

Roots:G5056 G5608

G5057 N-NSM τελώνης (5x)
Lk 18:10 one *being* a·Pharisee and the other a·tax·collector.
Lk 18:11 ·men, adulterers, or even as this tax·collector.
Lk 18:13 "And the tax·collector, standing at·a·distance, was·
Mt 10:3 and MattHew the tax·collector *(the·one of·Alphaeus)*
Mt 18:17 ·be to·you just·as the Gentile and the tax·collector.
G5057 N-NPM τελῶναι (9x)
Lk 3:12 Then tax·collectors also came to·be·immersed, and
Lk 7:29 of·John (even the tax·collectors) regarded God as·
Lk 15:1 And all the tax·collectors and the morally·
Mt 5:46 Do·not·indeed even the tax·collectors do the same
Mt 5:47 ·indeed even the tax·collectors *greet* in·this·manner?
Mt 9:10 many tax·collectors and morally·disqualified·men
Mt 21:31 I·say to·yeu that the tax·collectors and the
Mt 21:32 "But the tax·collectors and the prostitutes did·trust
Mk 2:15 many tax·collectors and morally·disqualified·men
G5057 N-ASM τελώνην (1x)
Lk 5:27 ·forth and distinctly·viewed a·tax·collector, Levi by·
G5057 N-GPM τελωνῶν (7x)
Lk 5:29 there·was a·large crowd of·tax·collectors and others
Lk 5:30 with tax·collectors and morally·disqualified·men?
Lk 7:34 a·friend of·tax·collectors and morally·disqualified·
Mt 9:11 with the tax·collectors and morally·disqualified·men
Mt 11:19 a·friend of·tax·collectors and morally·disqualified·
Mk 2:16 the tax·collectors and morally·disqualified·men,
Mk 2:16 the tax·collectors and morally·disqualified·men?

G5058 τελ•ώνιον tĕlōniôn *n.* (3x)

Roots:G5057

G5058 N-ASN τελώνιον (3x)
Lk 5:27 sitting·down in the tax·booth. And he·declared to·
Mt 9:9 who·is·sitting·down in the tax·booth. And he·says
Mk 2:14 sitting·down in the tax·booth, and he·says to·him,

G5059 τέρας tĕras *n.* (16x)

Compare:G2295 G2297 G3634-4 G3634-5
See:G5059-1
xLangEquiv:H4159 xLangAlso:H6382

G5059.1 N-NPN τέρατα (3x)
Ac 2:43 soul, and many wonders and signs were·done
Ac 4:30 miraculous·signs and wonders to·be·done through
Ac 5:12 many signs and wonders occurred among the
G5059.1 N-APN τέρατα (8x)
Jn 4:48 "Unless yeu·*all*·should·see signs and wonders, no,
Ac 2:19 And I·shall·give wonders in the heaven up·above
Ac 6:8 was·doing great wonders and miraculous·signs
Ac 7:36 brought them out, after·doing wonders and signs in
Ac 14:3 miraculous·signs and wonders to·be·done through
Ac 15:12 what·many miraculous·signs and wonders God did
Mt 24:24 they·shall·give great signs and wonders, such·as, if
Mk 13:22 shall·give signs and wonders to utterly·lead·astray,
G5059.1 N-DPN τέρασιν (4x)
Ac 2:22 God for yeu with·miracles and wonders and signs,
Heb 2:4 both with·signs and wonders, and with·a·diversity·
2Th 2:9 with all power and signs and lying wonders,
2Co 12:12 by miraculous·signs, and wonders, and miracles
G5059.1 N-GPN τεράτων (1x)
Rm 15:19 with power of·signs and wonders, with *the* power

G5060 Τέρτιος Tĕrtiôs *n/p.* (1x)

G5060.2 N/P-NSM Τέρτιος (1x)
Rm 16:22 I, Tertius, the·one writing the letter, greet yeu in

G5061 Τέρτυλλος Tĕrtyllôs *n/p.* (2x)

G5061.2 N/P-NSM Τέρτυλλος (1x)
Ac 24:2 being·called·for, Tertullus began to·legally·accuse
G5061.2 N/P-GSM Τερτύλλου (1x)
Ac 24:1 *with* a·certain orator *named* Tertullus, who made·it·

G5062 τεσσαρά•κοντα tĕssarákônta *n.* (21x)

See:G5064

G5062 N-NUI τεσσαράκοντα (21x)
Jn 2:20 ·then the Judeans declared, "*In* forty six years, this
Lk 4:2 being·tried *for* forty days by the Slanderer.
Ac 1:3 ·being·gazed·upon by·them throughout forty days,
Ac 4:22 the man·of·clay† was more·than forty years·of·age,
Ac 7:30 "And with·forty years being·completely·fulfilled,
Ac 7:36 in *the* Red Sea, and in the wilderness forty years.
Ac 7:42 sacrifices and respect·offerings *for* forty years in the
Ac 13:21 from·among *the* tribe of·BenJamin, *for* forty years.
Ac 23:13 there·were more·than forty·men having·made this
Ac 23:21 who·lay·in·wait·for him *are* more·than forty men,
Heb 3:9 ·and·proved me, and saw my works *for* forty years.
Heb 3:17 with·whom was·he·specifically·vexed forty years?
Mt 4:2 And after·fasting forty days and forty nights,
Mt 4:2 after·fasting forty days and forty nights, eventually
Mk 1:13 ·was there in the wilderness forty days, being·tried
2Co 11:24 by *the* Jews I·received forty *stripes* minus one.
Rv 11:2 ·shall·trample the Holy City forty two lunar·months.
Rv 13:5 ·given to·it to·do *this for* forty two lunar·months.
Rv 14:1 and with him a·hundred *and* forty four thousand,
Rv 14:3 the song except the hundred *and* forty four thousand,
Rv 21:17 its wall, a·hundred *and* forty four cubits,

G5063 τεσσαρα•κοντα•ετής tĕssarakôntaĕtēs *adj.* (2x)

Roots:G5062 G2094

G5063 A-NSM τεσσαρακονταετής (1x)
Ac 7:23 "And as forty·years time was·completely·fulfilled
G5063 A-ASM τεσσαρακονταετῆ (1x)
Ac 13:18 And *for* about a·time of·forty·years, he·bore·with

G5064 τέσσαρες tĕssarês *n.* (39x) τέσσαρα tĕssara [neuter]

See:G5067

G5064 N-NPM τέσσαρες (6x)
Ac 21:23 ·say to·you. With·us are four men having a·vow
Rv 4:4 the throne *were·set·out* twenty four thrones. And upon
Rv 4:10 the twenty four Elders shall·fall in·the·sight·of·the·
Rv 9:15 And the four angels were·loosened, the·ones having·
Rv 11:16 And the twenty four Elders, the·ones sitting·down
Rv 19:4 And the twenty four Elders and the four living·
G5064 N-NPF τέσσαρες (3x)
Ac 21:9 had daughters, four virgin·daughters prophesying.
Rv 14:1 with him a·hundred *and* forty four thousand, having
Rv 14:3 the hundred *and* forty four thousand, the·ones
G5064 N-NPN τέσσαρα (5x)
Rv 4:6 the throne, *are* four living·beings overflowing of·
Rv 4:8 And *the* four living·beings, each one itself, was·
Rv 5:8 the official·scroll, the four living·beings and the
Rv 5:14 And the four living·beings were·saying, "So·be·it,·
Rv 19:4 four Elders and the four living·beings fell·down and
G5064 N-APM τέσσαρας (4x)
Rv 4:4 I·saw the twenty four Elders sitting·down, having·
Rv 7:1 And after these·things, I·saw four angels standing on
Rv 7:1 earth, securely·holding the four winds of·the earth,
Rv 9:14 trumpet, "Loosen the four angels, the·ones having·
G5064 N-APF τέσσαρας (3x)
Jn 11:17 ·*to·rest* in the chamber·tomb four days even·now.
Ac 27:29 ·jagged places, after·flinging four anchors out of·
Rv 7:1 four angels standing on the four corners of·the earth,
G5064 N-APN τέσσαρα (1x)
Jn 19:23 took his outer·garments and made four parts, a·part
G5064 N-DPM τέσσαρσιν (1x)
Rv 7:2 he·yelled·out with·a·loud voice to·the four angels, to·
G5064 N-DPF τέσσαρσιν (3x)
Ac 10:11 ·sheet having·been·tied at·the·four corners and
Ac 11:5 ·sent·down from·out of·the heaven by·four corners,
Rv 20:8 nations, the·ones in the four corners of·the earth,
G5064 N-DPN τέσσαρσιν (1x)
Ac 12:4 handing *him* over to·four squads·of·four soldiers
G5064 N-GPM τεσσάρων (4x)
Mt 24:31 his Selected-Ones from·among the four winds,

Αα Ββ Γγ Δδ Εε Ζζ Ηη Θθ Ιι Κκ Λλ Μμ Νν Ξξ Οο Ππ Ρρ Σσ Ττ Υυ Φφ Χχ Ψψ Ωω

Mk 2:3 a·paralyzed·man being·carried by four·men.
Mk 13:27 his Selected-Ones from·out of·the four winds,
Rv 21:17 wall, a·hundred *and* forty four cubits, *according·*
G5064 N-GPN τεσσάρων (7x)
Rv 5:6 midst of·the throne and of·the four living·beings, and
Rv 6:1 I·heard one from·among the four living·beings (as a·
Rv 6:6 a·voice in *the* midst of·the four living·beings saying,
Rv 7:11 and the Elders and the four living·beings, and they·
Rv 9:13 one voice from·among the four horns of·the golden
Rv 14:3 and in·the·sight of·the four living·beings, and of·
Rv 15:7 And one from·among the four living·beings gave to·
EG5064 (1x)
Mt 17:27 ·find a·silver·stater·coin *(worth four drachmas).*

G5065 τεσσαρεσ•και•δέκατος têssarêskaidékatôs *adj.* (2x)
Roots:G5064 G2532 G1182
G5065 A-NSF τεσσαρεσκαιδεκάτη (1x)
Ac 27:27 Now as·soon·as the·fourteenth night was·come,
G5065 A-ASF τεσσαρεσκαιδεκάτην (1x)
Ac 27:33 "This·day is·the·fourteenth day of·anticipating,

G5066 τεταρταῖος têtartaîôs *adj.* (1x)
Roots:G5064
G5066 A-NSM τεταρταῖος (1x)
Jn 11:39 even·now he·smells·bad, for it·is *the* fourth·day."

G5067 τέταρτος tétartôs *adj.* (10x)
Roots:G5064
G5067 A-NSM τέταρτος (3x)
Rv 8:12 And the fourth angel sounded, and the third·part of·
Rv 16:8 And the fourth angel poured·out his vial upon the
Rv 21:19 the third, chalcedony; the fourth, emerald;
G5067 A-NSN τέταρτον (1x)
Rv 4:7 as a·man·of·clay†, and the fourth living·being *is* like
G5067 A-ASF τετάρτην (2x)
Mk 6:48 And about *the* fourth watch of·the night, he·comes
Rv 6:7 And when he·opened·up the fourth official·seal, I·
G5067 A-ASN τέταρτον (1x)
Rv 6:8 was·given to·them over the fourth·part of·the earth,
G5067 A-DSF τετάρτῃ (1x)
Mt 14:25 And in·*the*·fourth watch of·the night, YeShua
G5067 A-GSF τετάρτης (1x)
Ac 10:30 And Cornelius replied, "Four days ago I·was
G5067 A-GSN τετάρτου (1x)
Rv 6:7 I·heard *the* voice of·the fourth living·being saying,

G5068 τετρά•γωνος têtrágōnôs *adj.* (1x)
Roots:G5064 G1137
xLangEquiv:H7251
G5068.2 A-NSF τετράγωνος (1x)
Rv 21:16 And the CITY lays·out foursquare, and its length is

G5069 τετράδιον têtrádiôn *n.* (1x)
Roots:G5064 Compare:G4753 G4686
G5069 N-DPN τετραδίοις (1x)
Ac 12:4 to·four squads·of·four soldiers to·keep·watch·over

G5070 τετρακισ•χίλιοι têtrakischíliôi *n.* (5x)
Roots:G5064 G5507
G5070 N-NPM τετρακισχίλιοι (2x)
Mt 15:38 And the·ones eating were four·thousand men,
Mk 8:9 the·ones eating were about four·thousand *men*, and
G5070 N-APM τετρακισχιλίους (2x)
Ac 21:38 ·uprising and leading the four·thousand men of·the
Mk 8:20 *loaves·of·bread* among the four·thousand *men*, how·
G5070 N-GPM τετρακισχιλίων (1x)
Mt 16:10 seven loaves·of·bread of·the four·thousand *men*,

G5071 τετρα•κόσιοι têtrakósiôi *n.* (4x)
τετρα•κόσια têtrakósia [neuter]
Roots:G5064 G1540
G5071 N-APN τετρακόσια (2x)
Ac 7:6 them and shall·harm *them* four·hundred years.
Gal 3:17 (the·one having·occurred four·hundred and thirty
G5071 N-DPN τετρακοσίοις (1x)
Ac 13:20 ·things, *which·took* about four·hundred and fifty
G5071 N-GPN τετρακοσίων (1x)
Ac 5:36 tightly·bonded·themselves, about four·hundred),

G5072 τετρά•μηνον têtrámēnôn *adj.* (1x)
Roots:G5064 G3376
G5072 A-NSN τετράμηνον (1x)
Jn 4:35 'There·are yet four·lunar·months, and *then* comes

G5073 τετρα•πλόος têtraplóôs *adj.* (1x)
Roots:G5064 G4118
G5073 A-ASN τετραπλοῦν (1x)
Lk 19:8 *from* any·man, I·give·back *to·him* fourfold."

G5074 τετρά•πους têtrápôus *adj.* (3x)
Roots:G5064 G4228 xLangAlso:H0929
G5074 A-NPN τετράποδα (1x)
Ac 10:12 in which all the four-footed·animals of·the earth
G5074 A-APN τετράποδα (1x)
Ac 11:6 and I·saw the four-footed·animals of·the earth, and
G5074 A-GPN τετραπόδων (1x)
Rm 1:23 and·also of·birds, and four-footed·animals, and

G5075 τετρ•αρχέω têtrarchéō *v.* (3x)
Roots:G5076
G5075 V-PAP-GSM τετραρχοῦντος (3x)
Lk 3:1 and with·Herod·AntiPas being·the·ruling·tetrarch of·
Lk 3:1 brother Philippus·II being·the·ruling·tetrarch of·Jetur
Lk 3:1 with·Lysanias being·the·ruling·tetrarch of·Abilene)—

G5076 τετρ•άρχης têtrárchēs *n.* (4x)
Roots:G5064 G0757
G5076 N-NSM τετράρχης (3x)
Lk 3:19 But Herod·AntiPas the tetrarch, being·reproved by
Lk 9:7 Now Herod·AntiPas the tetrarch heard all the·things
Mt 14:1 that season, Herod·AntiPas the tetrarch heard of·the
G5076 N-GSM τετράρχου (1x)
Ac 13:1 ·reared·together with·Herod·AntiPas the tetrarch),

G5077 τεφρόω têphrôō *v.* (1x)
G5077 V-AAP-NSM τεφρώσας (1x)
2Pe 2:6 and *if* after·incinerating *the* cities of·Sodom and

G5078 τέχνη téchnē *n.* (4x)
Roots:G5088
G5078.1 N-GSF τέχνης (1x)
Ac 17:29 silver or stone etched by·*the*·art and *the* cogitation
G5078.2 N-ASF τέχνην (1x)
Ac 18:3 was·working, for they·were tentmakers *by* trade.
G5078.2 N-GSF τέχνης (1x)
Rv 18:22 And any craftsman of·any trade, no, should·not be·
EG5078.2 (1x)
Ac 19:25 the workmen concerning the *trades* such·as·these,

G5079 τεχνίτης têchnítēs *n.* (4x)
Roots:G5078 Compare:G0753 G2040 G2939 G5045
G5079.2 N-NSM τεχνίτης (1x)
Rv 18:22 ·longer in you. And any craftsman of·any trade, no
G5079.2 N-NPM τεχνῖται (1x)
Ac 19:38 if Demetrius and the craftsmen together with·him
G5079.2 N-DPM τεχνίταις (1x)
Ac 19:24 ·furnished no little income for·the craftsmen.
G5079.3 N-NSM τεχνίτης (1x)
Heb 11:10 whose architectural·designer and civil·engineer *is*

G5080 τήκω tḗkō *v.* (1x)
Compare:G4732 See:G1300-1
xLangEquiv:H4549 xLangAlso:H4743
G5080 V-PPI-3S τήκεται (1x)
2Pe 3:12 being·consumed·in·a·blazing·fire, are·liquefied.

G5081 τηλ•αυγῶς tēlaugōs *adv.* (1x)
Roots:G5056 G0827
G5081.3 ADV τηλαυγῶς (1x)
Mk 8:25 ·upon absolutely·all·men with·complete·clarity.

G5082 τ•ηλικ•οῦτος tēlikôûtôs *p:d.* (4x)
τ•ηλικ•αύτη tēlikaútē [feminine]
Roots:G3588 G2245 G3778
G5082.2 P:D-NSM τηλικοῦτος (1x)
Rv 16:18 were upon the earth, so·vast an·earthquake, *and* so
G5082.2 P:D-NPN τηλικαῦτα (1x)
Jac 3:4 also the sailing·ships, being so·vast, and *are* being·
G5082.2 P:D-GSM τηλικούτου (1x)
2Co 1:10 already·snatched us from·out of·so·vast a·death,
G5082.2 P:D-GSF τηλικαύτης (1x)
Heb 2:3 utterly·escape after·neglecting so·vast a·Salvation?

G5083 τηρέω tērêō *v.* (75x)
Compare:G5442 G2892 G4933 G1301 G5432
See:G5084 G2334 G3906
G5083.3 V-FAI-3S τηρήσει (2x)
Jn 14:23 me, he·shall·observantly·keep my Redemptive-word
Jac 2:10 For whoever shall·observantly·keep the whole
G5083.3 V-FAI-3P τηρήσουσιν (1x)
Jn 15:20 my word, they·shall·observantly·keep yeurs also.
G5083.3 V-PAI-1S τηρῶ (1x)
Jn 8:55 I·have·seen him, and I·observantly·keep his word.
G5083.3 V-PAI-1P τηροῦμεν (1x)
1Jn 3:22 because we·observantly·keep his commandments
G5083.3 V-PAI-3S τηρεῖ (3x)
Jn 9:16 because he·does·not observantly·keep the Sabbath."
Jn 14:24 ·loving me does·not observantly·keep my sayings.
1Jn 5:18 ·being·begotten from·out of·God guards himself,
G5083.3 V-PAM-2S τηρεῖ (1x)
Rv 3:3 and heard, so·then observantly·keep *it* and repent.
G5083.3 V-PAM-2P τηρεῖτε (1x)
Mt 23:3 ·keep, yeu·must·observantly·keep *that·thing* and do
G5083.3 V-PAN τηρεῖν (5x)
Ac 15:5 to·charge *them* to·observantly·keep the Torah-Law
Ac 15:24 and to·observantly·keep the Torah-Law,' to·whom
Ac 21:25 for·them to·observantly·keep not·even·one such·
Mt 23:3 to·yeu to·observantly·keep, yeu·must·observantly·
Mt 28:20 them to·observantly·keep all·things as·much·as I·
G5083.3 V-PAP-GPM τηρούντων (2x)
Rv 12:17 the·ones observantly·keeping the commandments
Rv 22:9 and of·the·ones observantly·keeping the words of·
G5083.3 V-PAP-NSM τηρῶν (5x)
Jn 14:21 my commandments, and observantly·keeping them,
1Jn 2:4 yet not observantly·keeping his commandments is
1Jn 3:24 the·one observantly·keeping his commandments
Rv 16:15 *is* the·one keeping·alert and guarding his garments,
Rv 22:7 ·blessed *is* the·one observantly·keeping the words
G5083.3 V-PAP-NPM τηροῦντες (2x)
Rv 1:3 and observantly·keeping the·things having·been·
Rv 14:12 the·ones observantly·keeping the commandments
G5083.3 V-PAS-1P τηρῶμεν (3x)
1Jn 2:3 if we·should·observantly·keep his commandments.
1Jn 5:2 and should·observantly·keep his commandments.
1Jn 5:3 that we·should·observantly·keep his commandments,
G5083.3 V-PAS-3S τηρῇ (1x)
1Jn 2:5 should·observantly·keep his Redemptive-word, in him
G5083.3 V-IAI-3P ἐτήρουν (1x)
Ac 12:6 chains, and sentries were·guarding the prison·cell,
G5083.3 V-AAI-2S ἐτήρησας (2x)
Rv 3:8 power, and observantly·kept my Redemptive-word,
Rv 3:10 'Because you·observantly·kept the Redemptive-word
G5083.3 V-AAI-3P ἐτήρησαν (1x)
Jn 15:20 yeu also. If they·observantly·kept my word, they·
G5083.3 V-AAM-2S τήρησον (1x)
Mt 19:17 life-above, observantly·keep the commandments."
G5083.3 V-AAM-2P τηρήσατε (1x)
Jn 14:15 ·love me, observantly·keep my commandments.
G5083.3 V-AAN τηρῆσαι (1x)
1Ti 6:14 *for* you to·observantly·keep the commandment
G5083.3 V-AAP-APM τηρήσαντας (1x)
Jud 1:6 not observantly·keeping their·own principality, but·
G5083.3 V-AAS-2P τηρήσητε (2x)
Jn 15:10 If yeu·should·observantly·keep my commandments,
Mk 7:9 in·order·that yeu·may·observantly·keep yeur·own
G5083.3 V-AAS-3S τηρήσῃ (2x)
Jn 8:51 anyone should·observantly·keep my Redemptive-word
Jn 8:52 say, 'If someone should·observantly·keep my
G5083.3 V-RAI-1S τετήρηκα (1x)
Jn 15:10 just·as I·myself have·observantly·kept my Father's
G5083.3 V-RAI-3P τετηρήκασιν (1x)
Jn 17:6 them to·me, and they·have·observantly·kept your
G5083.4 V-PPN τηρεῖσθαι (1x)
Ac 24:23 ·arranged·for the centurion to·keep Paul, and·also

G5083.4 V-IPI-3S ἐτηρεῖτο (1x)
Ac 12:5 Accordingly in·fact, Peter was·kept in the prison·
G5083.5 V-PAN τηρεῖν (1x)
Ac 16:23 charging the prison·warden to·keep them securely
G5083.5 V-PAP-NPM τηροῦντες (2x)
Mt 27:54 and the·ones keeping·guard·over YeShua with him,
Mt 28:4 fear of·him, the·ones keeping·guard are·shaken and
G5083.5 V-PPN τηρεῖσθαι (2x)
Ac 25:4 Festus answered *for* Paul to·be·kept in Caesarea,
Ac 25:21 I·commandingly·ordered him to·be·kept until I·
G5083.5 V-IAI-3P ἐτήρουν (1x)
Mt 27:36 ·down, they·were·keeping·guard·over him there.
G5083.6 V-IAI-1S ἐτήρουν (1x)
Jn 17:12 in the world, I·myself was·guarding them in your
G5083.6 V-AAM-2S τήρησον (1x)
Jn 17:11 "Holy Father, guard by your·own name these
G5083.6 V-AAS-2S τηρήσῃς (1x)
Jn 17:15 ·rather that you·should·guard them beyond·reach
G5083.7 V-FAI-1S τηρήσω (2x)
2Co 11:9 to·yeu, and I·shall·purposefully·keep *it·so*.
Rv 3:10 I·also shall·purposefully·keep you from·out of·the
G5083.7 V-PAN τηρεῖν (1x)
Jac 1:27 *and* to·purposefully·keep oneself unstained from
G5083.7 V-AAI-1S ἐτήρησα (1x)
2Co 11:9 I·purposefully·kept my·own·self from·being·
G5083.7 V-AAM-2P τηρήσατε (1x)
Jud 1:21 purposefully·keep yeurselves in God's love, *yeu*
G5083.7 V-RAI-2S τετήρηκας (1x)
Jn 2:10 *but* you·yourself have·purposefully·kept the good
G5083.7 V-RAI-3S τετήρηκεν (1x)
Jn 12:7 "Leave her *alone*. She·has·purposefully·kept it for
G5083.8 V-PAN τηρεῖν (1x)
2Pe 2:9 of·proof·trials, and to·reserve unrighteous·men to a·
G5083.8 V-PPP-NPM τηρούμενοι (1x)
2Pe 3:7 are having·been·stored·up, being·reserved for·fire,
G5083.8 V-APN τηρηθῆναι (1x)
Ac 25:21 "But with·Paul appealing to·be·reserved for the
G5083.8 V-RAI-3S τετήρηκεν (1x)
Jud 1:6 ·place, he·has·reserved *them* in·supra-lasting bonds
G5083.8 V-RPI-3S τετήρηται (2x)
Jud 1:13 — for·whom have·been·reserved the deep·murky·
2Pe 2:17 ·shroud of·darkness has·been·reserved for an·age.
G5083.8 V-RPP-ASF τετηρημένην (1x)
1Pe 1:4 shrivel-proof inheritance having·been·reserved in *the*
G5083.8 V-RPP-APM τετηρημένους (1x)
2Pe 2:4 having·been·reserved for a·Tribunal·judgment;
G5083.9 V-PAM-2S τήρει (1x)
1Ti 5:22 moral·failures. Fully·keep yourself morally·clean!
G5083.9 V-PAN τηρεῖν (1x)
Eph 4:3 diligently·endeavoring to·fully·keep the oneness of·
G5083.9 V-PAP-NSM τηρῶν (1x)
Rv 2:26 overcoming and the·one fully·keeping my works
G5083.9 V-APO-3S τηρηθείη (1x)
1Th 5:23 soul, and body be·fully·kept blamelessly unto the
G5083.9 V-RAI-1S τετήρηκα (1x)
2Ti 4:7 ·finished the race·course; I·have·fully·kept the trust.
G5083.9 V-RPP-DPM τετηρημένοις (1x)
Jud 1:1 and having·been·fully·kept in·YeShua Anointed, *to*·
G5083.11 V-PAN τηρεῖν (1x)
1Co 7:37 in his heart to·keep·unmarried his virgin·daughter,

G5084 τήρησις tḗrēsis *n.* (3x)
Roots:G5083 Compare:G5438 G2334
G5084.2 N-NSF τήρησις (1x)
1Co 7:19 *is* a·proper·observance of·God's commandments.
G5084.3 N-ASF τήρησιν (1x)
Ac 4:3 on·them and placed *them* in custody for the next·day,
G5084.3 N-DSF τηρήσει (1x)
Ac 5:18 the ambassadors and placed them in public custody.

G5085 Τιβεριάς Tibēriás *n/l.* (3x)
Roots:G5086
G5085 N/L-GSF Τιβεριάδος (3x)
Jn 6:1 of·the Sea of·Galilee, *which·is the Sea* of·Tiberias.
Jn 6:23 other small·boats came out·from Tiberias near to·the
Jn 21:1 to·the disciples at the Sea of·Tiberias; and he·made

G5086 Τιβέριος Tibḗriōs *n/p.* (1x)
See:G2804 G3505
G5086.2 N/P-GSM Τιβερίου (1x)
Lk 3:1 year of·the governing·term of·Tiberius Caesar—

G5087 τίθημι títhēmi *v.* (98x)
θέω thḗō [an alternate in certain tenses]
Compare:G1120 G2476 G2598 G2749 G2578
See:G2330-3 G2007 xLangAlso:H7896 H8371
G5087.1 V-FAI-1S θήσω (1x)
Mt 12:18 my soul takes·delight. I·shall·place my Spirit upon
G5087.1 V-PAI-3S τίθησιν (3x)
Jn 2:10 "Every man·of·clay† first places·out the good wine,
Lk 8:16 covers it with·a·vessel or places *it* beneath a·couch,
Lk 11:33 ·man, after·igniting a·lantern, places *it* in hiding,
G5087.1 V-PAI-3P τιθέασιν (1x)
Mt 5:15 do·they·set·ablaze a·lantern and place it under the
G5087.1 V-PAN τιθέναι (1x)
Rm 14:13 ·more: *purpose* not to·place a·stumbling·block or
G5087.1 V-PAP-NSM τιθείς (1x)
Mk 10:16 taking them in·his·arms, while·placing his hands
G5087.1 V-IAI-3S ἐτίθει (1x)
2Co 3:13 exactly·as Moses *did*, who·was·placing a·veil over
G5087.1 V-AAI-3S ἔθηκεν (3x)
Jn 19:19 Pilate also wrote a·title and placed *it* on the cross.
Heb 1:2 by *his* Son, whom he·placed *as* heir of·all·things,
Rv 10:2 having·been·opened·up. And he·placed his right
G5087.1 V-2AAS-3S θῇ (1x)
1Co 15:25 him to·reign, even·until he·should·place all the
G5087.1 V-2AMI-2S ἔθου (1x)
Ac 5:4 authority? How *is·it* that you·placed this action in
G5087.1 V-2AMI-2P ἔθεσθε (1x)
Ac 5:25 the men whom yeu·placed in the prison·cell are
G5087.1 V-2AMI-3S ἔθετο (7x)
Ac 1:7 seasons which the Father placed in his·own authority.
Ac 12:4 ·apprehending *Peter*, *HerOd·Agrippa* placed *him* in
Ac 19:21 ·things were·completely·fulfilled, Paul placed *it* in
Ac 20:28 among which the Holy Spirit has·placed yeu *to·be*
Mt 14:3 ·of John, bound him and placed *him* in prison on·
1Th 5:9 Because God did·not place us for Wrath, but·rather
1Co 12:18 But even·now, God himself·placed the members,
G5087.1 V-2AMI-3P ἔθεντο (3x)
Ac 4:3 their hands on·them and placed *them* in custody for
Ac 5:18 upon the ambassadors and placed them in public
Ac 27:12 ·in, the majority placed counsel to·sail·away from·
G5087.1 V-2AMM-2P θέσθε (1x)
Lk 9:44 must·let these sayings be·placed into yeur ears—
G5087.1 V-2AMP-NSM θέμενος (2x)
2Co 5:19 trespasses to·them, and·also already·placing in us
1Ti 1:12 me trustworthy, placing·me into service,
G5087.1 V-API-1S ἐτέθην (2x)
1Ti 2:7 which I·myself was·placed *as* an·official·proclaimer
2Ti 1:11 I·myself was·placed *as* an·official·proclaimer, and
G5087.1 V-API-3P ἐτέθησαν (1x)
1Pe 2:8 To which *end·result*, they·are also placed.
G5087.1 V-APN τεθῆναι (1x)
Rv 11:9 shall·not allow their corpses to·be·placed in tombs.
G5087.1 V-APS-3S τεθῇ (1x)
Mk 4:21 *forth* in·order·that it·should·be·placed under the
G5087.1 V-RAI-1S τέθεικα (2x)
Ac 13:47 *by* the Lord, "I·have·placed you to·be a·light for
Rm 4:17 ·has·been·written, "I·have·placed you *as* a·father
EG5087.1 (1x)
Lk 11:33 the measuring·basket, but·rather *places it* on the
G5087.2 V-FAI-1S θήσω (1x)
Jn 13:37 you at·this·moment? I·shall·lay·down my soul on·
G5087.2 V-FAI-2S θήσεις (1x)
Jn 13:38 answered him, "Shall·you·lay·down your soul on·
G5087.2 V-FAI-3S θήσει (2x)
Lk 12:46 shall·cut him in·two, and shall·lay his portion with
Mt 24:51 he·shall·cut him in·two and shall·lay his portion
G5087.2 V-PAI-1S τίθημι (5x)
Jn 10:15 know the Father, and I·lay·down my soul on·behalf
Jn 10:17 me, because I·myself lay·down my soul in·order·
Jn 10:18 from me, but·rather I·myself lay it down of·my·
Rm 9:33 "Behold, I·lay in Tsiyon a·stone of·stumbling
1Pe 2:6 "Behold, I·lay in Tsiyon a·chief·corner stone,
G5087.2 V-PAI-3S τίθησιν (2x)
Jn 10:11 The good shepherd lays·down his·own soul on·
Jn 13:4 from·among the supper and lays·aside the garments.
G5087.2 V-PAM-3S τιθέτω (1x)
1Co 16:2 let each·one of·yeu lay *aside* personally·from
G5087.2 V-PAN τιθέναι (2x)
Ac 5:15 ·of the broad·streets, and to·lay *them* on simple·
1Jn 3:16 ·ourselves are·indebted to·lay·down *our·own* souls
G5087.2 V-PPI-3S τίθεται (1x)
Mk 15:47 ·nearby, were·observing *where* he·was·laid.
G5087.2 V-IAI-3P ἐτίθουν (3x)
Ac 3:2 ·lifted·and·carried, whom they·were·laying each day
Ac 4:35 and they·were·laying·*them*·down directly·at the
Mk 6:56 cities, or countrysides, they·were·laying the sick in
G5087.2 V-AAI-1S ἔθηκα (1x)
Lk 19:22 taking·up what I·did·not lay·down, and reaping
G5087.2 V-AAI-2S ἔθηκας (2x)
Jn 20:15 him away, declare to·me where you·laid him, and·I
Lk 19:21 You·take·up what you·did·not lay·down, and reap
G5087.2 V-AAI-3S ἔθηκεν (6x)
Lk 6:48 who also dug deeply and laid a·foundation on the
Lk 23:53 he·swathed it in·a·linen·cloth, and laid it in a·tomb
Ac 4:37 *it*, he·brought the value and laid *it* directly·at the
Ac 5:2 bringing a·certain portion, he·laid *it* directly·at the
Mt 27:60 and laid it in his·own brand-new chamber·tomb,
1Jn 3:16 *of·God*, because that·one laid·down his·own soul
G5087.2 V-AAI-3P ἔθηκαν (7x)
Jn 19:42 So they·laid Jesus there on·account·of the Judeans
Jn 20:2 ·tomb, and we·have·not seen where they·laid him."
Jn 20:13 Lord, and I·have·not seen where they·laid him."
Ac 9:37 And after·bathing her, they·laid *her* in an·upper·
Ac 13:29 from the arbor·tree, they·laid *him* in a·chamber·
Mk 6:29 and took·away his corpse and laid it in the chamber·
Mk 16:6 See the place where they·laid him!
G5087.2 V-2AAN θεῖναι (3x)
Jn 10:18 of my·own·self. I·have authority to·lay it down,
Lk 5:18 *a·way* to·carry him in and to·lay *him* in·the·sight of
1Co 3:11 not·even·one·man is·able to·lay another foundation
G5087.2 V-2AAP-GSM θέντος (1x)
Lk 14:29 Lest·perhaps, with·him laying *the* foundation, and
G5087.2 V-2AAS-1S θῶ (5x)
Lk 20:43 until I·should·lay·out your enemies *as* your foot
Ac 2:35 until I·should·lay·out your enemies *as* your foot
Heb 1:13 right·hand, until I·should·lay·out your enemies *as*
Mt 22:44 my right·hand until I·should·lay·out your enemies
Mk 12:36 my right·hand until I·should·lay·out your enemies
G5087.2 V-AAS-1S θήσω (1x)
1Co 9:18 ·the·good·news, I·may·lay·out the good·news of·
G5087.2 V-2AAS-3S θῇ (1x)
Jn 15:13 ·one·man, that someone should·lay·down his soul
G5087.2 V-2AMI-3S ἔθετο (1x)
1Co 12:28 some·of·whom *which* God laid·out among the
G5087.2 V-2AMI-3P ἔθεντο (1x)
Lk 1:66 all the·ones hearing *them* laid·*them*·up in their hearts
G5087.2 V-API-3S ἐτέθη (2x)
Jn 19:41 which, not·even·yet, not·even·one *man* was·laid.
Lk 23:55 the chamber·tomb and how his body was·laid.
G5087.2 V-API-3P ἐτέθησαν (1x)
Ac 7:16 they·were·transferred into Shekem and laid in the
G5087.2 V-APS-3P τεθῶσιν (1x)
Heb 10:13 until his enemies should·be·laid·out *as* his foot
G5087.2 V-RAI-1S τέθεικα (1x)
1Co 3:10 ·construction·architect, I·have·laid a·foundation,
G5087.2 V-RAI-2P τεθείκατε (1x)
Jn 11:34 and he·declared, "Where have·yeu·laid him?
G5087.2 V-RAP-NSM τεθεικώς (1x)
2Pe 2:6 *them*, having·laid·out an·explicit·example for those·
EG5087.2 (1x)

Rv 11:8 And their corpses shall·lay in the broad·street of·the
G5087.3 V-PAP-NPM τιθέντες (1x)
Mk 15:19 were·spitting·on him. And bowing their knees,
G5087.3 V-2AAP-NSM θείς (4x)
Lk 22:41 about a·stone's cast, and bowing the knees, he·
Ac 7:60 And bowing the knees, he·yelled·out with·a·loud
Ac 9:40 ·casting everyone forth outside, bowing his knees,
Ac 20:36 these·things, with·him bowing the knees, he·
G5087.3 V-2AAP-NPM θέντες (1x)
Ac 21:5 outside of·the city. And bowing the knees on the
G5087.4 V-AAI-1S ἔθηκα (1x)
Jn 15:16 I·myself selected yeu and laterally·positioned yeu,
G5087.5 V-2AMM-2P θέσθε (1x)
Lk 21:14 "Accordingly, firmly·settle *it* in yeur hearts, not

G5088 τίκτω tíktō *v.* (19x)
τέκω têkō [an alternate in certain tenses]
Compare:G1080 G0616 G1627 G1631
G5088.1 V-PAP-NSF τίκτουσα (1x)
Heb 6:7 it many·times and producing grain·stalk well-suited
G5088.2 V-FDI-2S τέξῃ (1x)
Lk 1:31 in your·uterus and shall·reproduce·and·birth a·son,
G5088.2 V-FDI-3S τέξεται (2x)
Mt 1:21 And she·shall·reproduce·and·birth a·son, and you·
Mt 1:23 in pregnancy and shall·reproduce·and·birth a·son,
G5088.2 V-PAI-3S τίκτει (1x)
Jac 1:15 conceiving, it·reproduces·and·births moral·failure,
G5088.2 V-PAP-NSF τίκτουσα (1x)
Gal 4:27 ·one not reproducing·and·giving·birth. Burst·forth
G5088.2 V-PAS-3S τίκτῃ (1x)
Jn 16:21 woman should·reproduce·and·give·birth, she·has
G5088.2 V-2AAI-3S ἔτεκεν (5x)
Lk 2:7 And she·reproduced·and·birthed her firstborn son,
Heb 11:11 and she·reproduced·and·gave·birth well·after· *the*
Mt 1:25 her until she·reproduced·and·birthed her firstborn
Rv 12:5 And she·reproduced·and·birthed a·son, a·male who
Rv 12:13 the woman who reproduced·and·birthed the male.
G5088.2 V-2AAN τεκεῖν (2x)
Lk 1:57 ·fulfilled for·her to·reproduce·and·give·birth, and
Lk 2:6 for·her to·reproduce·and·give·birth were·fulfilled.
G5088.2 V-API-3S ἐτέχθη (1x)
Lk 2:11 ·David, a·Savior is·reproduced·and·birthed who is
G5088.2 V-APP-NSM τεχθείς (1x)
Mt 2:2 is the·one being·reproduced·and·born King of·the
G5088.3 V-2AAN τεκεῖν (2x)
Rv 12:2 ·birthing·pain and being·tormented to·produce·birth.
Rv 12:4 the·one about to·produce·birth, in·order·that he·
G5088.3 V-2AAS-3S τέκῃ (1x)
Rv 12:4 her child whenever she·should·produce·birth.

G5089 τίλλω tíllō *v.* (3x)
See:G4951 G0138
G5089 V-PAN τίλλειν (1x)
Mt 12:1 they·also began to·pluck heads·of·grain and to·eat.
G5089 V-PAP-NPM τίλλοντες (1x)
Mk 2:23 to·make a·pathway, plucking the heads·of·grain.
G5089 V-IAI-3P ἔτιλλον (1x)
Lk 6:1 and his disciples were·plucking the heads·of·grain,

G5090 Τιμαῖος Timaîôs *n/p.* (1x)
xLangEquiv:H2931
G5090.2 N/P-GSM Τιμαίου (1x)
Mk 10:46 the blind (a·son of·Timaeus) was·sitting·down

G5091 τιμάω timáō *v.* (21x)
Roots:G5093 Compare:G1392 xLangAlso:H3513
G5091.1 V-AMI-3P ἐτιμήσαντο (1x)
Mt 27:9 ·been·appraised, who was·appraised by·the·Sons
G5091.1 V-RPP-GSM τετιμημένου (1x)
Mt 27:9 the price of·the·one having·been·appraised, who
G5091.2 V-PAM-2S τίμα (1x)
1Ti 5:3 Honor widows *that·are* really solitary·widows.
G5091.2 V-PAM-2P τιμᾶτε (1x)
1Pe 2:17 Reverently·fear God. Honor the king.
G5091.2 V-AAI-3P ἐτίμησαν (1x)
Ac 28:10 these also honored us with·many honors.
G5091.2 V-AAM-2P τιμήσατε (1x)
1Pe 2:17 Honor all·men. Love the brotherhood.
G5091.3 V-FAI-3S τιμήσει (1x)
Jn 12:26 ·attend to·me, the Father shall·deeply·honor him.
G5091.3 V-PAI-1S τιμῶ (1x)
Jn 8:49 have a·demon, but·rather I·deeply·honor my Father,
G5091.3 V-PAI-3S τιμᾷ (3x)
Jn 5:23 the Son, does·not deeply·honor the Father, the·one
Mt 15:8 with·their mouth and deeply·honors me with·their
Mk 7:6 " This People deeply·honors me with·*their*·lips, but
G5091.3 V-PAI-3P τιμῶσιν (1x)
Jn 5:23 ·honor the Son, just·as they·deeply·honor the Father.
G5091.3 V-PAM-2S τίμα (6x)
Lk 18:20 ·witness,'' "Deeply·honor your father and your
Mt 15:4 saying, "Deeply·honor your father and mother,"
Mt 19:19 "'Deeply·honor your father and mother,'" and
Mk 7:10 Moses declared, "Deeply·honor your father and
Mk 10:19 rob,'' "Deeply·honor your father and mother.
Eph 6:2 "'Deeply·honor your father and mother'" (which is
G5091.3 V-PAP-NSM τιμῶν (1x)
Jn 5:23 the Father. The·one not deeply·honoring the Son,
G5091.3 V-PAS-3P τιμῶσιν (1x)
Jn 5:23 in·order·that all *men* should·deeply·honor the Son,
G5091.3 V-AAS-3S τιμήσῃ (1x)
Mt 15:6 then no, he·should·not deeply·honor his father or

G5092 τιμή timế *n.* (43x)
Roots:G5099 Compare:G1391 xLangAlso:H3366 A3367
G5092.1 N-NSF τιμή (1x)
Mt 27:6 the Temple·Treasury, since it·is *the* price of·blood."
G5092.1 N-ASF τιμήν (1x)
Mt 27:9 ·silver, the price of·the·one having·been·appraised,
G5092.1 N-APF τιμάς (1x)
Ac 19:19 And they·jointly·calculated the price of·them and
G5092.1 N-GSF τιμῆς (5x)
Ac 5:2 and he·pilfered *part* of the price, with·his wife also
Ac 5:3 and to·pilfer *part* of the price of·the open·field?
Ac 7:16 *Jacob* purchased for·a·price of·silver·pieces near the
1Co 6:20 For yeu·are·kinsman·redeemed with·a·price. Now·
1Co 7:23 Yeu·are·kinsman·redeemed with·a·price. Do·not
G5092.2 N-APF τιμάς (1x)
Ac 4:34 ·bringing the values of·the·things being·sold·off,
G5092.2 N-DSF τιμῇ (1x)
Col 2:23 with any value specifically·against an·indulgence
G5092.4 N-NSF τιμή (7x)
Rm 2:10 But glory, honor, and peace, to·every·man, the·one
1Pe 2:7 So·then the honor *is* to·yeu, to·the·ones presently·
1Ti 1:17 to·*the*·only wise God, *be* honor and glory to the
1Ti 6:16 to·see), to·whom *be* honor and might eternal.
Rv 5:13 *be* the blessing and the honor and the glory and the
Rv 7:12 and the thanks, and the honor, and the power, and
Rv 19:1 and the glory, and the honor, and the power *are* to·
G5092.4 N-ASF τιμήν (19x)
Jn 4:44 "A·prophet has no honor in his·own fatherland.
Heb 3:3 the house has more honor *than the house* itself.
Heb 5:4 ·himself *does* anyone take the honor, but·rather *it·is*
Rm 2:7 seeking glory, honor, and eternal·incorruptibility,
Rm 9:21 in·fact, one vessel to honor and another to dishonor
Rm 13:7 *due* the reverent·fear, the honor to·the·one *due* the
Rm 13:7 reverent·fear, the honor to·the·one *due* the honor.
1Pe 1:7 may·be·found in high·praise and honor and glory at
1Pe 3:7 vessel, while·prescribing honor to·the feminine as
2Pe 1:17 personally·from Father God honor and glory, with·
1Co 12:23 we·place·around *them* more·abundant honor; and
1Co 12:24 more·abundant honor to·the·one being·lacking,
2Ti 2:20 and some *are·set·out* in·fact unto honor, and some
2Ti 2:21 ·be a·vessel unto honor, having·been·made·holy,
Rv 4:9 living·beings shall·give glory and honor and thanks
Rv 4:11 to·receive the glory and the honor and the power,
Rv 5:12 and wisdom and strength and honor and glory and
Rv 21:24 of·the earth bring their glory and honor into it.
Rv 21:26 ·bring the glory and the honor of·the nations into it.
G5092.4 N-DSF τιμῇ (4x)
Heb 2:7 ·victoriously·crown him with·glory and honor, and
Heb 2:9 ·victoriously·crowned with·glory and honor, that
Rm 12:10 ·another; in·the honor, by·showing·deference·to
1Th 4:4 *earthenware* vessel in renewed·holiness and honor,
G5092.4 N-DPF τιμαῖς (1x)
Ac 28:10 these also honored us with·many honors. And
G5092.4 N-GSF τιμῆς (2x)
1Ti 5:17 ·considered·deserving of·double honor, especially
1Ti 6:1 their·own masters worthy of·all honor, in·order·that

G5093 τίμιος tímiôs *adj.* (14x)
τιμιώτερος timiṓtêrôs [comparative]
τιμιώτατος timiṓtatôs [superlative]
Roots:G5092 Compare:G0514 G4185 See:G1784 xLangEquiv:H3368
G5093.3 A-NSM τίμιος (2x)
Ac 5:34 ·of·Torah-Law, *being* highly·valued among·all the
Heb 13:4 Highly·valued *is* the wedding in all *cultures*, and
G5093.4 A-NSN-C τιμιώτερον (1x)
1Pe 1:7 trust (*being* much more·precious·than gold *which* is·
G5093.4 A-NPN τίμια (1x)
2Pe 1:4 to·us the most·greatest and precious pledges, in·
G5093.4 A-ASM τίμιον (1x)
Jac 5:7 ·that·works·the·soil waits·for the precious fruit of·the
G5093.4 A-ASF τιμίαν (1x)
Ac 20:24 do·I·hold my soul *as* precious to·myself, as·so to·
G5093.4 A-APM τιμίους (1x)
1Co 3:12 *with* gold, silver, precious stones, wood, hay,
G5093.4 A-DSM τιμίῳ (3x)
Rv 17:4 ·been·gilded with·gold and precious stones and
Rv 18:16 ·been·gilded with gold, and precious stones, and
Rv 21:19 ·been·adorned·with all·manner·of precious stones.
G5093.4 A-DSM-S τιμιωτάτῳ (1x)
Rv 21:11 her brilliance *was* like a·precious stone, even·as a·
G5093.4 A-DSN τιμίῳ (1x)
1Pe 1:19 but·rather *it·was* with·precious blood, as of·a·
G5093.4 A-GSF τιμίου (1x)
Rv 18:12 "cargo of·gold, silver, precious stones, and pearls,
G5093.5 A-GSN-S τιμιωτάτου (1x)
Rv 18:12 *type·of* vessel *made* out of·*the*·most·precious wood,

G5094 τιμιότης timiótēs *n.* (1x)
Roots:G5093
G5094.1 N-GSF τιμιότητος (1x)
Rv 18:19 ·wealthy as·a·result of·her valuableness! Because

G5095 Τιμό•θεος Timóthêôs *n/p.* (25x)
Roots:G5092 G2316 See:G2131 G3090
G5095.2 N/P-NSM Τιμόθεος (12x)
Ac 16:1 disciple was there, TimoThy by·name, a·son of·a·
Ac 17:14 Silas and TimoThy were·remaining·behind there.
Ac 18:5 ·soon·as both Silas and TimoThy came·down from
Ac 20:4 and Gaius of·Derbe, and TimoThy, and *both*
Rm 16:21 TimoThy, my coworker, and·also Lucius, Jason,
Php 1:1 Paul and TimoThy, slaves of·Jesus Anointed.
1Th 1:1 Paul, Silvanus, and TimoThy. To·the Called·Out·
2Th 1:1 Paul, Silvanus, and TimoThy. To·the Called·Out·
1Co 16:10 Now if TimoThy should·come, look·out that he·
2Co 1:1 through God's will, and TimoThy *our* brother. To·
Col 1:1 through God's will, and TimoThy *our* brother.
Phm 1:1 of·Jesus Anointed, and TimoThy *our* brother. To·
G5095.2 N/P-VSM Τιμόθεε (2x)
1Ti 1:18 charge to·you, *my* child TimoThy, according·to the
1Ti 6:20 O TimoThy, vigilantly·keep the charge·fully·
G5095.2 N/P-ASM Τιμόθεον (6x)
Ac 17:15 a·commandment to Silas and TimoThy, that they·
Ac 19:22 to·him into Macedonia, TimoThy and Erastus, he·
Heb 13:23 brother TimoThy *is* having·been·fully·released,
Php 2:19 *the* Lord Jesus, to·send TimoThy promptly to·yeu,
1Th 3:2 and we·sent TimoThy, our brother, and attendant of·
1Co 4:17 On·account·of that, I·sent to·yeu TimoThy, who is
G5095.2 N/P-DSM Τιμοθέῳ (2x)
1Ti 1:2 To·TimoThy, a·genuine child in trust.
2Ti 1:2 To·TimoThy, a·dearly·beloved child.
G5095.2 N/P-GSM Τιμοθέου (2x)

1Th 3:6 But at·this·moment, with·TimoThy coming from
2Co 1:19 us (through Silvanus, TimoThy and me), did·not
EG5095.2 (1x)
Ac 16:3 with·him. And taking *TimoThy*, he·circumcised him

G5096 Τίμων Tímōn *n/p.* (1x)
Roots:G5092 Compare:G4736 See:G1675
G5096.2 N/P-ASM Τίμωνα (1x)
Ac 6:5 ProChorus, Nicanor, Timon, ParMenas, and

G5097 τιμ•ωρέω timōréō *v.* (2x)
Roots:G5092 See:G5098
G5097.2 V-PAP-NSM τιμωρῶν (1x)
Ac 26:11 And avenging·honor·by·punishing them many·
G5097.2 V-APS-3P τιμωρηθῶσιν (1x)
Ac 22:5 ·that they·should·be·punished·to·avenge·honor.

G5098 τιμ•ωρία timōría *n.* (1x)
Roots:G5097
G5098.1 N-GSF τιμωρίας (1x)
Heb 10:29 of·a·worse vengeance·of·honor, the·one

G5099 τίνω tínō *v.* (1x)
τίω tíō [an alternate in certain tenses]
Compare:G3409 See:G0661 G5055
G5099 V-FAI-3P τίσουσιν (1x)
2Th 1:9 who shall·pay justice with·an·eternal savage·

G5100 τὶς tìs *p:i.* (546x)
Compare:G3754 G1170 See:G3739
G5100.ª P:X-NSM τίς (2x)
Rm 8:24 for what man expectantly·awaits that·which also
1Th 5:15 Clearly·see·to·it *that* no one should·render wrong
G5100.ª P:X-ASN τί (2x)
Ac 5:34 to·make the ambassadors *stay* outside a short·while.
2Co 10:8 I·should·boast somewhat excessively concerning
G5100.ª P:X-GPM τινῶν (1x)
Jn 20:23 ·are·forgiven to·them; *and* whose *moral·failures*
G5100.2 P:I-NSF τίς (1x)
Lk 8:46 And Jesus declared, "Someone laid·hold of·me, for
G5100.2 P:X-NSM τίς (6x)
Lk 9:19 and others *say* that some prophet of·the ancient·ones
Lk 10:33 "But some Samaritan, while·traveling, came
Ac 11:29 So some of·the disciples, each of·them just·as he·
Ac 16:9 night: there·was some man of·Macedonia standing
Tit 1:12 Someone from·among themselves, a·prophet of·
Eph 4:29 *let·it·be* some beneficially·good *conversation*,
G5100.2 P:X-NSN τί (1x)
Ac 18:14 in·fact, if it·were some wrong·doing or an·evil,
G5100.2 P:X-NPM τινές (54x)
Jn 6:64 "But·yet there·are some from·among yeu that do·not
Jn 7:25 So·then, some from·among the·men of·JeruSalem
Jn 7:44 And some from·among them were·wanting to·
Jn 9:16 So·then some from·among the Pharisees were·saying
Jn 11:37 But some from·among them declared, "Was·not
Jn 11:46 But some from·among them went·off to the
Jn 13:29 For some *of·them* were·presuming, since Judas was·
Lk 6:2 And some of·the Pharisees declared to·them, "Why·
Lk 9:27 to·yeu truly, there·are some of·the·ones standing
Lk 11:15 But some from·among them declared, "He·casts·
Lk 19:39 And some of·the Pharisees from among·the crowd
Lk 24:24 And some of·the·ones together with·us went·off to
Ac 10:23 together with·them, and some of·the brothers from
Ac 11:20 And some from·among them were men of·Cyprus
Ac 17:4 And some from·among them were·convinced and
Ac 17:18 were·engaging him. And some were·saying,
Ac 19:9 But as·soon·as some were·hardened and were·
Ac 23:12 And with·it·becoming day, some of·the Judeans,
Heb 3:16 For after·hearing, some did·directly·provoke, but·
Heb 13:2 for through this some are·hosting angels, being·
Mt 12:38 Then some of·the scribes and Pharisees answered,
Mt 16:28 I·say to·yeu, there·are some of·the·ones standing
Mt 27:47 Now some of·the·ones standing there, after·hearing
Mt 28:11 ·traversing, behold, some of·the sentinel·guard,
Mk 2:6 Now some of·the scribes were there, sitting·down yet
Mk 8:3 on the way, for some of·them have·come *from* a·
Mk 9:1 to·yeu, that there·are some of·the·ones standing here

Mk 11:5 And some of·the·ones standing there were·saying
Mk 14:4 there·were some being·greatly·displeased alongside
Mk 14:65 And some began to·spit·on him, and upon·putting·
Mk 15:35 And some of·the·ones standing·nearby, after·
Rm 3:3 What if some did·not·trust?
Rm 3:8 we·are·vilified, and just·as some reply for·us to·say)
Rm 11:17 And if some of·the branches were·broken·off, and
Jud 1:4 For some men·of·clay† crept·into·place·unawares,
Php 1:15 In·fact, some officially·proclaim the Anointed-One
Php 1:15 and strife, and some also through good·purpose.
1Co 4:18 Now some are·puffed·up, as·though *it·is* not me
1Co 6:11 And some *of* yeu·were these·things, but·rather yeu·
1Co 8:7 *is* not in every·man. And some, with·the conscience
1Co 10:7 be idolaters, just·as *were* some of·them; as it·has·
1Co 10:8 just·as some of·them committed·sexual·immorality
1Co 10:9 the Anointed-One, just·as some of·them also tried
1Co 10:10 ·not·even grumble, just·as some of·them also
1Co 15:6 unto this·moment, but some also are·laid·to·rest.
1Co 15:12 from·among dead·men, how·do some among yeu
1Co 15:34 do·not morally·fail; for some are ignorant of·God
2Co 3:1 Yet·not·even do·we·have·need, as some *do*, of·
1Ti 1:6 from·which, some are·already·turned·aside to idle·
1Ti 1:19 concerning the trust, some, after·shoving·*it*·away,
1Ti 4:1 that in later seasons some shall·withdraw·from the
1Ti 5:15 For even·now some are·turned·aside, *falling·in*
1Ti 6:10 which some are·longingly·stretching·themselves·.
1Ti 6:21 which some, who·are·making·a·profession *of·trust*,
G5100.2 P:X-ASM τινά (5x)
Ac 18:23 And after·continuing *there for* some time, he·went·
Ac 27:8 with·difficulty, we·came to some place being·called
Mt 8:28 such·that *it·caused* some not to·have·strength to·
Rm 1:13 , in·order·that I·may·have some fruit among yeu
1Co 16:7 *instead*, I·expect to·stay·over some time alongside
G5100.2 P:X-ASF τινά (2x)
Ac 27:26 ·for us to·be·cast·away upon some island."
Ac 27:27 for·them to·be·heading·toward some country.
G5100.2 P:X-ASN τί (7x)
Jn 6:7 that each·one of·them may·take some small·piece."
Lk 23:8 ·expecting to·see some miraculous·sign occurring by
Ac 8:36 the roadway, they·came to some water. And the
Rm 1:11 ·give to·yeu some gracious·bestowment *which·is*
1Co 11:18 ·subsist among yeu; and I·partly trust some *of·it*.
2Co 1:17 ·planning that, ¿!·did perhaps I·use some levity?
2Co 11:16 ·that, *for* a·little·while, even·I may·boast some.
G5100.2 P:X-APM τινάς (9x)
Ac 12:1 ·forth his hands to·harm some of·the·ones from the
Ac 19:1 And finding some disciples,
Heb 4:6 since it·is·still·remaining *for* some to·enter into it,
Mk 7:2 And after·seeing some of·his disciples eating bread
Mk 12:13 And they·dispatched to him some of·the Pharisees
Rm 11:14 my flesh and may·save some from·among them.
2Th 3:11 For we·hear *that there·are* some walking among
1Co 9:22 things in·order·that by·all·means I·may·save some.
2Co 10:2 to·be·daringly·bold against some— the·ones
G5100.2 P:X-APF τινάς (5x)
Ac 9:19 was among the disciples at Damascus *for* some days.
Ac 10:48 Then they·asked him to·stay·over some days.
Ac 15:36 Now after some days, Paul declared to BarNabas,
Ac 16:12 ·were in that city lingering·awhile·for some days.
Ac 24:24 And after some days, after·arriving·publicly
G5100.2 P:X-DSM τινί (1x)
Ac 5:15 if·even his shadow may·overshadow some of·them.
G5100.2 P:X-DSN τινί (1x)
Gal 6:1 ·man·of·clay† should·be·overtaken in some trespass,
G5100.2 P:X-DPM τισίν (4x)
Heb 10:25 just·as *is* a·habit of·some, but·rather exhorting
2Co 10:12 ourselves with·some *who·are* commending
1Ti 1:3 ·that you·may·charge some not to·instruct·differently
1Ti 5:24 ·judgment; and also for·some *men·of·clay†*, they·
G5100.2 P:X-GSM τινός (2x)
Heb 3:4 house is·planned·and·constructed by some *man*; but
1Co 15:37 it·may·happen·to·be of·wheat or some of·the rest;
G5100.2 P:X-GPM τινῶν (5x)

Lk 9:7 on·account·of *that* it·was·said by some that John has·
Lk 9:8 and by some that EliJah appeared, and by·others that
Lk 21:5 And with·some saying concerning the Sanctuary·
1Ti 5:24 The moral·failures of·some men·of·clay† are
2Ti 2:18 ·occurred, and they·overturn the trust of·some.
G5100.2 P:X-GPF τινῶν (1x)
Ac 25:13 Now with·some days already·elapsing, King
G5100.2 P:X-GPN τινῶν (1x)
Ac 27:44 and some·men on some of·the *broken·pieces* from
EG5100.2 (2x)
Jn 16:17 Accordingly, *some* from·among his disciples
1Ti 5:25 the good works *of·some* are obvious·beforehand;
G5100.3 P:X-NSM τίς (43x)
Jn 3:3 to·you, unless someone should·be·born from·above,
Jn 3:5 ·say to·you, unless someone should·be·born from·out
Jn 4:33 one·another, "¿!·Did someone bring him *something*
Jn 6:50 heaven, in·order·that someone may·eat from·out·of·
Jn 8:52 say, 'If someone should·observantly·keep my
Jn 10:9 the door. If someone should·enter·in through me,
Jn 10:28 the coming·age, and someone shall·not snatch them
Jn 12:47 "And if someone should·hear my utterances and
Jn 15:6 "If someone should·not remain in me, he·is·already·
Jn 15:13 ·even·one·man, that someone should·lay·down his
Lk 8:49 speaking, there·comes someone directly·from *the*
Lk 12:13 And someone from·among the crowd declared to·
Lk 13:23 Then someone declared to·him, "Lord, *is·it so* that
Lk 14:15 And someone, of·the·ones reclining·together·at·
Lk 16:30 AbRaham! But·yet if someone should·traverse to
Lk 16:31 though someone should·rise·up from·among
Lk 22:59 one hour, someone else was·strongly·asserting,
Ac 2:45 ·to any·particular need someone was·having.
Ac 4:35 ·to any·particular need someone was·having.
Ac 5:25 Then coming·close, someone reported to·them,
Ac 8:31 *to·know them*, unless some·man should·guide me?
Ac 13:41 though someone should·give·a·thorough·account
Ac 19:24 For someone by·the·name·of Demetrius, a·
Heb 2:6 But somewhere, someone thoroughly·testified,
Mt 12:47 And someone declared to·him, "Behold, your
Mk 8:4 "From·what·source shall·someone be·able to·stuff
Mk 14:47 But someone, one of·the·ones standing·nearby,
Rm 5:7 beneficially·good·man, someone also would·dare
Jac 2:14 my brothers, though someone should·say he·has
Jac 2:18 But·yet, someone shall·declare, "You have trust,
Jac 5:19 from the truth, and someone should·turn him back·
1Pe 2:19 graciousness, if someone on·account·of conscience
2Pe 2:19 — for that·by·which someone has·been·defeated,
1Co 3:4 For whenever someone should·say, "In·fact, I·
1Co 14:24 should·prophesy, and someone should·enter·in,
1Co 14:37 If someone supposes·himself to·be a·prophet or
1Co 15:35 But·yet someone shall·declare, "How·are the
2Co 8:12 ·acceptable according·to·what someone may·have,
2Co 11:21 whatever *manner* someone may·be·daringly·bold,
1Ti 1:8 *is* good, if someone should·use it legitimately
2Ti 2:5 if someone should·contend *in·athletic·competition*,
1Jn 4:20 If someone should·declare, "I·love God," and he·
1Jn 5:16 If someone should·see his brother morally·failing a·
G5100.3 P:X-NPM τινές (4x)
Lk 13:1 same occasion, some·men were·present *who·were*
Gal 1:7 However, there·are some·men troubling yeu and
Mk 14:57 ·up, someone was·falsely·testifying against him,
2Pe 3:9 promise, as some·men resolutely·consider tardiness,
G5100.3 P:X-ASM τινά (5x)
Lk 9:49 "O·Captain, we·saw someone casting·out the
Ac 5:36 saying himself to·be someone (to·whom a·number
Ac 7:24 And seeing someone being·wronged, he·forcefully·
Ac 8:9 of·Samaria, saying himself to·be someone great;
Mk 9:38 "Mentor, we·saw someone casting·out demons in·
G5100.3 P:X-ASF τινά (1x)
1Co 5:1 the Gentiles, such·for someone to·have the father's
G5100.3 P:X-GSM τινός (3x)
Ac 8:34 Concerning himself, or concerning someone else?
Ac 18:7 into a·home of·someone by·the·name·of Justus,
Ac 25:19 ·religion, and concerning some·man *named* Jesus,

G5100.4 P:X-NSN τί (3x)
Jn 5:14 ·fail no·longer, lest something worse should·happen
Gal 2:6 ·for the·ones seeming to·be something *important*—
Gal 6:3 if any·man supposes·himself to·be something, being
G5100.4 P:X-NPN τινά (1x)
2Pe 3:16 which are some·things *that·are* hard·to·understand
G5100.4 P:X-ASN τί (18x)
Jn 13:29 he·should·give something to·the helplessly·poor.
Jn 14:14 If yeu·should·request something in my name, I·
Lk 7:40 "Simon, I·have something to·declare to·you." And
Lk 11:54 and seeking to·hunt·for something from·out of·his
Ac 3:5 to·receive something personally·from them.
Ac 17:21 *attempting* to·say or to·hear something brand-new).
Ac 21:37 "Is·it·proper for·me to·declare something to you?
Ac 23:18 ·man to you, having something to·speak to·you."
Ac 23:20 more·precisely *about* something concerning him.
Ac 25:26 I·do·not have something absolutely·certain to·write
Ac 25:26 occurring, I·may·have something to·write.
Heb 8:3 necessary *for* this·man to·have something also that
Heb 11:40 previously·looking·at something significantly·
Mt 20:20 and requesting something personally·from him.
Mk 9:22 ·yet if you·are·able *to·do* something, empathizing
Mk 16:18 and·if they·should·drink something deadly, no,
Rm 14:14 to·the·one reckoning something to·be·defiled. For·
1Co 8:2 to·personally·know something *from·experience*, he·
EG5100.4 (3x)
Jn 8:6 they·may·have *something* to·legally·accuse him·of.
Gal 2:6 for the·ones seeming *to·be something important*—
Mk 6:37 "Yeu·yeurselves give them *something* to·eat." And
G5100.5 P:X-NSM τίς (21x)
Jn 7:48 ¿! Did any from·among the rulers or from·among the
Ac 28:21 you, neither *have* any of·the brothers arriving·
Heb 3:13 "Today," lest any from·among yeu should·be·
Heb 4:1 we·should·be·alarmed, lest any from·among yeu
Heb 12:16 lest *there·be* any sexually·immoral or profane·
Jac 1:5 So, if any of·yeu is·deficient of·wisdom, let·him·
Jac 1:23 Because if any is a·hearer of·*the*·Redemptive-word,
Jac 5:13 *Is* any among yeu suffering·hardship?
Jac 5:13 Let·him·pray. *Is* any in·a·cheerful·mood?
Jac 5:14 *Is* any sick among yeu?
Php 3:4 in flesh. If any other·man presumes *a·reason* to·
Php 4:8 and if *there·is* any high·praise, take·a·reckoning·of
1Pe 4:15 For do·not·let any of·yeu suffer as a·murderer, or
1Co 1:15 lest any should·declare that I·immersed in my·own
1Co 7:12 not the Lord— if any brother has a·non-trusting
1Co 7:18 Any·man *that* is·called·forth, having·been·
1Co 7:18 be·uncircumcised. Any·man *that* is·called·forth in
1Co 7:36 Now if any *father* deems to·have·improper·
1Co 10:27 But if any of·the non-trusting·ones call·for yeu,
Eph 2:9 ·out of·works, in·order·that not any may·boast.
1Ti 5:4 But if any widow has children or grandchildren,
G5100.5 P:X-NSF τίς (6x)
Heb 12:15 of·God; lest any root of·bitterness sprouting
Rm 8:39 nor depth, nor any other created·thing shall·be·able
Rm 13:9 ' And if *there·is* any other commandment, it·is·
Php 2:1 Accordingly, if *there·is* any exhortation in
Php 2:1 ·consolation of·love, if any fellowship of·Spirit, if
Php 4:8 if *there·is* any courageous·moral·excellence, and if
G5100.5 P:X-NSN τί (2x)
Ac 25:5 ·accuse this man, if there·is any *wrong* in him.
Php 2:1 Anointed-One, if any personal·consolation of·love,
G5100.5 P:X-NPN τινά (1x)
Php 2:1 fellowship of·Spirit, if any inward·affections and
G5100.5 P:X-ASM τινά (6x)
Ac 25:16 to·gratuitously·hand·over any man·of·clay† to
Jac 5:12 nor by·the earth, nor by·any other oath. But yeur
1Th 2:9 (specifically not to·be·a·burden·upon any of·yeu),
2Th 3:8 ·for *us* not to·be·a·burden·upon any of·yeu.
1Co 1:16 I·do·not personally·know if I·immersed any other.)
2Co 12:17 ¿! Did I·swindle yeu through any of·them whom
G5100.5 P:X-ASF τινά (1x)
1Co 9:12 ·things, lest we·should·give any hindrance to·the
G5100.5 P:X-ASN τί (8x)
Lk 11:36 *is* full·of·light, not having any part opaquely·dark,
Ac 4:32 not·even one was·saying *for* any of·his holdings to·
Ac 24:20 let·them·declare if they·found any wrong·doing in
Ac 28:21 ·publicly announced or spoken any evil concerning
Gal 5:6 circumcision nor uncircumcision has·any strength,
Gal 6:15 circumcision nor uncircumcision has·any strength,
Rm 15:18 to·speak of·any of·such·things except·what
Eph 5:27 stain, or wrinkle, or any such·thing, but·rather that
G5100.5 P:X-APM τινάς (2x)
Ac 9:2 that if·ever he·should·find any *disciples* of·The Way
2Pe 3:9 being·resolved for·any to·completely·be·destroyed,
G5100.5 P:X-DSM τινί (3x)
Heb 3:12 lest there·shall·be in any of·yeu an·evil heart of·
Mt 18:12 "If it·should·happen *that* any man·of·clay† *has* a·
1Th 5:15 should·render wrong for wrong to·any *man*; but·
G5100.5 P:X-DSF τινί (1x)
Col 2:23 *although* not with any value specifically·against
G5100.5 P:X-GSM τινός (1x)
Lk 14:8 Whenever you·should·be·called·forth by any *man* to
G5100.5 P:X-GPM τινῶν (1x)
Jn 20:23 Any·of·those·whose moral·failures yeu·should·
G5100.6 P:X-NSM τίς (109x)
Jn 2:25 no need that anyone should·testify concerning the
Jn 6:46 Not that any·man has·clearly·seen the Father, except
Jn 6:51 "If any·man should·eat from·out of·this bread, he·
Jn 7:17 If any·man should·want to·do his will, he·shall·know
Jn 7:37 saying, "If any·man should·thirst, let·him·come to
Jn 8:51 I·say to·yeu, if anyone should·observantly·keep my
Jn 9:22 ·themselves even·now that if any·man should·affirm
Jn 9:31 but·rather if any·man may·be reverent·of·God, and
Jn 9:32 it·is·not been·heard that any·man opened·up eyes
Jn 11:9 of·the daylight? If any·man should·walk·along in
Jn 11:10 But if any·man should·walk·along in the night, he·
Jn 11:57 that if any·man should·know where he·is, he·
Jn 12:26 "If any·man should·attend to·me, let·him·follow me
Jn 12:26 shall·be. And if any·man should·attend to·me, the
Jn 14:23 declared to·him, "If anyone should·love me, he·
Jn 16:30 and have no need that any·man should·ask·of you.
Lk 9:23 all, "If any·man wants to·come right·behind me, he·
Lk 14:26 "If any·man comes to me and does·not
Lk 19:31 And if any·man should·ask·of yeu, 'Why do·yeu·
Ac 4:34 For neither was anyone subsisting among them in·a·
Ac 10:47 "Is any·man able to·forbid water *such·for* these not
Heb 4:11 that complete·rest, lest any·man should·fall by the
Heb 5:4 And not unto·himself *does* anyone take the honor,
Heb 10:28 Anyone setting·aside Moses' Torah-Law died
Heb 12:15 ·overseeing: lest any·man *is·found* falling·short
Gal 1:9 again, if any·man proclaims·a·good·news to·yeu
Gal 6:3 For if any·man supposes·himself to·be something,
Mt 11:27 the Father; nor·even·does anyone fully·know the
Mt 12:19 shall·he·yell·out, nor·even·shall any·man hear his
Mt 12:29 "Or how·else·is anyone able to·enter into the
Mt 16:24 disciples, "If any·man wants to·come right·behind
Mt 21:3 And if any·man should·declare anything to·yeu,
Mt 22:46 him a·word, nor·even·did anyone dare any·longer
Mt 24:4 "Look·out *that* not anyone should·deceive yeu.
Mt 24:23 "At·that·time, if any·man should·declare to·yeu,
Mk 4:23 "If any·man has ears to·hear, let·him·hear.
Mk 7:16 If any·man has ears to·hear, let·him·hear.
Mk 9:30 he·was·not willing that any·man should·know *it*.
Mk 9:35 and says to·them, "If any·man wants to·be first, *the*
Mk 11:3 And if any·man should·declare to·yeu, 'Why·do
Mk 11:16 he·was·not allowing that anyone should·carry *any*
Mk 13:5 to·say, "Look·out lest anyone should·deceive yeu.
Mk 13:21 at·that·time, if any·man should·declare to·yeu,
Rm 5:7 scarcely over a·righteous·man shall anyone die, for
Rm 8:9 yeu. But if any·man does·not have Anointed-One's
Jac 1:26 If any·man among yeu seems to·be religious, *yet* not
Jac 2:16 and anyone from·among yeu should·declare to·them
Jac 3:2 ·all *of·us* slip·up. If any·man does·not slip·up in
Jac 5:19 Brothers, if anyone among yeu should·be·led·astray
1Pe 4:11 If any·man speaks *to·others*, *let·him·be* as *one*·
1Pe 4:11 ·words of·God; if any·man attends *to·others*, *let*·
2Th 2:3 Yeu·should·not·let anyone thoroughly·delude yeu in
2Th 3:10 yeu, that if anyone does·not want to·work, nor·
2Th 3:14 Now if anyone does·not listen·to·and·obey our
Tit 1:6 if any·man is without·any·charge·of·wrong·doing, a·
1Co 3:12 And if any·man builds upon this foundation *with*
1Co 3:17 If anyone corrupts the temple of·God, this·one God
1Co 3:18 thoroughly·delude himself. If any·man among yeu
1Co 4:2 that each·man should·be·found trustworthy.
1Co 5:11 *such·as·these*: if any·man being·named a·brother
1Co 6:1 Dare anyone of·yeu, having a·matter·of·
1Co 8:2 And if anyone presumes to·personally·know
1Co 8:3 But if anyone loves God, the·same has·been·
1Co 8:10 For if any·man should·see you (the·one having
1Co 9:15 ·die rather than that anyone should·make·void my
1Co 10:28 But if any·man should·declare to·yeu, "This is
1Co 11:16 But if any·man seems to·be contentious, we·
1Co 11:34 And if any·man is·hungry, let·him·eat at home,
1Co 14:27 And·if any·man does·speak in·a·bestowed·tongue
1Co 14:38 But if any·man is·ignoring *this*, let·him·be·
1Co 16:11 not anyone should·utterly·disdain him, but send
1Co 16:22 If any·man does·not have·affection·for the Lord
2Co 2:5 But if any·man has·caused·grief, *it·is* not me *that*
2Co 5:17 As·such, IF any·man *is* in Anointed-One, *he·is* a·
2Co 8:20 this·thing: *that* not anyone should·blame us in this
2Co 10:7 If any·man has·confidence in·himself to·be of·
2Co 11:16 Again I·say, not anyone should·suppose me to·be
2Co 11:20 yeu·bear·with·it, if anyone utterly·enslaves yeu,
2Co 11:20 utterly·enslaves yeu, if anyone devours *yeu*, if
2Co 11:20 anyone devours *yeu*, if anyone takes *from·yeu*, if
2Co 11:20 takes *from·yeu*, if anyone exalts·himself, if
2Co 11:20 anyone exalts·himself, if anyone thrashes yeu to
2Co 12:6 *in·how I·boast*, lest any·man should·reckon to me
Col 2:4 this I·say, lest any·man should·defraud yeu with
Col 2:8 Look·out lest any·man shall·be the·one seducing yeu
Col 2:16 Accordingly, do·not·let anyone judge yeu
Col 3:13 to·one·another. If any·man should·hold a·fault
1Ti 3:1 "If any·man longingly·stretches·himself·toward an·
1Ti 3:5 (but if any·man has·not seen·how to·conduct his·
1Ti 5:8 Now if anyone does·not maintain·provision·for his·
1Ti 5:16 If anyone (a·man·that·trusts or a·woman·that·trusts
1Ti 6:3 If any·man instructs·differently and does·not come·
2Ti 2:21 if anyone should·entirely·purify himself from
1Jn 2:1 And if anyone should·morally·fail, we·have a·
1Jn 2:15 in the world. If any·man should·love the world, the
1Jn 2:27 yeu·have no need that anyone should·instruct yeu,
2Jn 1:10 If any·man comes to yeu *all*, and does·not bring this
Rv 3:20 and knock. If anyone should·hear my voice and
Rv 11:5 And if any·man should·determine to·bring·harm·to
Rv 11:5 And if any·man should·determine to·bring·harm·to
Rv 13:9 If any·man has an·ear, let·him·hear.
Rv 13:10 If any·man gathers·together *another into* war·
Rv 13:10 into war·captivity. If any·man kills with a·dagger,
Rv 13:17 in·order·that not anyone should·be·able to·buy or
Rv 14:9 voice, "If any·man falls·prostrate *directly·before* the
Rv 14:11 or night, nor·does anyone receiving the etching of·
Rv 20:15 And if anyone is·not found having·been·written in
Rv 22:18 official·scroll, if anyone should·place *anything*
Rv 22:19 And if anyone should·remove *anything* from the
G5100.6 P:X-NPM τινές (1x)
1Pe 3:1 in·order·that also, if some are·obstinate to·the
G5100.6 P:X-ASM τινά (4x)
Jn 13:20 the·one receiving anyone I·may·send, receives me;
Ac 19:38 have a·matter specifically·against any·man, *the*
Ac 24:12 discussing *anything* alongside anyone, or making
Col 3:13 ·hold a·fault specifically·against anyone, just·as
G5100.6 P:X-ASN τί (2x)
Lk 19:8 ·false·charges anything *from* any·man, I·give·back
Ac 26:26 for I·am·persuaded *for* not any·one of·these·things,
G5100.6 P:X-DSM τινί (2x)
Lk 12:15 from·out of·one's holdings *does* anyone's life† itself
Mk 8:26 nor·even should·you·declare *this* to·anyone in the
G5100.6 P:X-GSM τινός (6x)
Lk 20:28 wrote to·us, if any·man's brother should·die while·

Mk 11:25 if yeu·have anything against anyone, forgive, in·
Mk 12:19 wrote for·us that if any·man's brother should·die,
2Th 3:8 ·present did·we·eat personally·from anyone's bread,
1Co 3:14 If any·man's work shall·remain which he·built·
1Co 3:15 If any·man's work shall·be·completely·burned, he·
EG5100.6 (1x)
Mt 23:9 "And yeu·should·not call *anyone* yeur father upon
G5100.7 P:I-NSN τί (1x)
Jn 1:46 "Is·it·possible *for* anything beneficially·good to·be
G5100.7 P:X-NSN τί (7x)
Mk 4:22 For there·is not anything hidden, which should·not
1Co 3:7 neither is the·one planting anything, nor the·one
1Co 10:19 what do·I·reply? That an·idol is anything, or that
1Co 10:19 or that *which·is* sacrificed·to·idols is anything?
1Co 14:35 they·want to·learn anything, they·must·inquire·of
2Co 7:14 if I·have·boasted anything to·him concerning yeu,
1Ti 1:10 and if *there·is* anything else fully·set·opposed to·the
G5100.7 P:X-ASN τί (33x)
Jn 6:12 in·order·that not anything may·be·completely·lost."
Jn 7:4 *there·is* not·even·one·man *that* does anything in secret
Jn 14:13 And anything that yeu·should·request in my name,
Jn 21:5 Little·children, ¿! do·yeu·have anything for·eating?
Lk 12:4 these·things not having anything much·more to·do.
Lk 24:41 to·them, "Do·yeu·have anything edible here?
Ac 19:39 "But if yeu·seek anything concerning other·matters
Ac 24:19 they·may·actually·have anything specifically· me.
Ac 25:8 against Caesar, did·I·morally·fail *in* anything."
Ac 25:11 or have·practiced anything worthy of·death, I·do·
Ac 28:19 not·as having anything *of·which* to·legally·accuse
Mt 5:23 ·to·mind that your brother has anything against you,
Mt 21:3 And if any·man should·declare anything to·yeu,
Mt 24:17 ·not walk·down to·take·away anything out of·his
Mk 8:23 was·inquiring·of him if he·looked·upon anything.
Mk 11:13 *it to·see* if perhaps he·shall·find anything on it.
Mk 11:25 ·are·praying, if yeu·have anything against anyone,
Mk 13:15 enter *it*, to·take·away anything out of·his home.
Rm 9:11 nor·even practicing anything beneficially·good or
Jac 1:7 that he·shall·receive anything personally·from the
Php 3:15 And if *in* anything yeu·contemplate differently,
1Th 1:8 such·for us not to·have need to·speak anything.
1Co 2:2 not to·personally·know anything among yeu, except
1Co 4:5 yeu·must·not presently·judge anything before *the*
1Co 10:31 yeu·eat, or drink, or anything *that* yeu·do, do all
2Co 2:10 ·whom yeu·graciously·forgive anything, I·myself
2Co 2:10 have·graciously·forgiven anything (for·whom I·
2Co 3:5 by ourselves to·reckon anything as from·among
2Co 12:18 ¿!·Did Titus swindle anything from·yeu?
2Co 13:8 For we·are·not able *to·do* anything against the truth
Phm 1:18 you, or owes *you* anything, impute that to·me;
1Ti 6:7 plain that we·are·not·even able to·carry anything out.
1Jn 5:14 that if we·should·request anything according·to his
G5100.7 P:X-GSM τινός (1x)
Lk 19:8 I·extorted·by·false·charges anything *from* any·man,
G5100.7 P:X-GSN τινός (3x)
Lk 22:35 or shoes, ¿!·Did yeu·lack anything?" And they·
Ac 17:25 *·though* being·in·a·bind·for anything, with·himself
1Co 6:12 I·myself shall·not be·controlled under anything.
EG5100.7 (7x)
Lk 8:17 "For there·is not *anything* hidden, that shall·not
Lk 8:17 become apparent; neither *anything* hidden·away,
Ac 23:5 "You·shall·not declare *anything* badly of·a·ruler
Ac 24:12 ·Courtyard discussing *anything* alongside anyone,
Mk 4:22 neither·did *anything* become hidden·away, other·
Rv 22:18 anyone should·place *anything additional* alongside
Rv 22:19 And if anyone should·remove *anything* from the
G5100.8 P:X-NSM τίς (44x)
Jn 4:46 And there·was a·certain royal·official, whose son
Jn 5:5 And a·certain man·of·clay† was there, being in the
Jn 11:1 Now a·certain·man was sick, *named* Lazarus, from
Jn 11:49 And a·certain one from·among them, *named*
Lk 1:5 there·was a·certain priest·that·offers·sacrifices by·the·
Lk 7:36 And a·certain·one of·the Pharisees was·asking·of
Lk 8:27 there·came·and·met him a·certain man from·out
Lk 9:57 the roadway, *that* a·certain·man declared to him,
Lk 10:25 behold, a·certain expert·in·Torah-Law stood·up,
Lk 10:30 "A·certain man·of·clay† was·walking·down from
Lk 10:31 a·certain priest·that·offers·sacrifices was·walking·
Lk 11:1 as·soon·as he·ceased, a·certain·one of·his disciples
Lk 11:37 *Jesus* was·speaking, a·certain Pharisee was·asking
Lk 11:45 a·certain·one of·the experts·in·Torah-Law says
Lk 13:6 parable, "A·certain·man was·holding·onto a·fig·tree
Lk 14:2 behold, there·was a·certain man·of·clay† before
Lk 14:16 to·him, "A·certain man·of·clay† made a·great
Lk 15:11 he·declared, "A·certain man·of·clay† had two sons
Lk 16:1 "There·was a·certain wealthy man·of·clay† who
Lk 16:19 "There·was a·certain wealthy man·of·clay†, and
Lk 16:20 there·was a·certain helpless·beggar by·the·name·of
Lk 18:2 saying, "In a·certain city there·was a·certain judge
Lk 18:18 And a·certain ruler inquired·of him, saying,
Lk 18:35 drawing·near to Jericho, a·certain blind·man sat·
Lk 19:12 "A·man·of·clay†, a·certain nobleman, traversed
Lk 20:9 people, "A·certain man·of·clay† planted a·vineyard
Lk 22:50 And a·certain one from·among them smote the
Ac 3:2 And a·certain man inherently·being lame from·out
Ac 5:1 But a·certain man, Ananias by·name, together with·
Ac 5:34 ·council·of·Sanhedrin, a·certain·man, a·Pharisee
Ac 8:9 But a·certain man by·the·name·of Simon was·
Ac 9:10 And there·was a·certain disciple at Damascus,
Ac 9:36 there·was a·certain female·disciple by·the·name·of
Ac 10:1 Now there·was a·certain man in Caesarea, Cornelius
Ac 14:8 at Lystra, *there·was* a·certain man disabled in·his
Ac 16:1 And behold, a·certain disciple was there, TimoThy
Ac 18:24 Now a·certain Jew arrived in Ephesus (Apollos
Ac 20:9 And a·certain young·man by·the·name·of EuTychus
Ac 21:10 *for* many·more days, a·certain prophet came·down
Ac 22:12 "And a·certain Ananias, a·devoutly·reverent man
Ac 25:14 "There·is a·certain man having·been·left·behind
Mt 21:33 "There·was a·certain man·of·clay†, a·master·of·
Mt 22:24 Moses declared, if a·certain·man should·die not
Mk 14:51 (But·also a certain young·man was·following him
G5100.8 P:X-NSF τίς (6x)
Lk 10:38 village, and a·certain woman by·the·name·of
Lk 11:27 these·things, *that* a·certain woman from·among
Lk 22:56 ·intently at·him, a·certain servant·girl declared,
Ac 16:14 And a·certain·woman was·listening, a·woman by·
Heb 10:27 but a·certain frightful apprehension of·Tribunal·
Mk 5:25 And *there·was* a·certain woman being with a·flow
G5100.8 P:X-NSN τί (3x)
Ac 11:5 I·saw a·clear·vision. A·certain vessel descending,
Ac 19:32 some were·yelling·out a·certain·thing, *and some*
2Co 3:14 old covenant; *it·is the* certain *veil* which is·fully·
G5100.8 P:X-NPM τινές (18x)
Jn 12:20 And there·were certain Greeks, from·among the·
Lk 13:31 same day, there·came·alongside certain Pharisees,
Lk 20:27 coming·alongside *him*, certain of·the·Sadducees
Lk 20:39 And responding, certain of·the scribes declared,
Ac 6:9 But there·rose·up certain·men from·among the
Ac 13:1 Now there·were certain·men among the Called·Out·
Ac 15:1 And certain·men coming·down from Judea were·
Ac 15:5 But there·fully·rose·up certain·men from the
Ac 15:24 we·heard that certain·men going·out from·among
Ac 17:18 Now certain philosophers of·the Epicureans and
Ac 17:28 have·existence. As also certain of·yeur very·own
Ac 17:34 But certain men, being·tightly·joined to·him,
Ac 19:13 Then certain of·the itinerant Jews, *being* exorcists,
Ac 19:14 Now there·were certain·men *who·were* doing this·
Ac 19:31 And also certain·men of·the chiefs·of·Asia, being
Ac 24:18 "But *there·were* certain Jews from Asia,
Mt 9:3 And behold, certain of·the scribes declared within
Mk 7:1 Then the Pharisees and certain of·the scribes
G5100.8 P:X-NPF τινές (3x)
Lk 8:2 and·also certain women who were having·been·both·
Lk 24:1 they·made·ready, and certain·women *were* together
Lk 24:22 Moreover *still*, certain women also from·among us
G5100.8 P:X-ASM τινά (5x)
Ac 9:33 And there he·found a·certain man·of·clay†, Aeneas
Ac 13:6 ·as Paphos, they·found a·certain Jewish occultist, a·
Ac 18:2 and he·found a·certain Jew by·the·name·of Aquila
Ac 27:39 but they·were·fully·observing a·certain bay having
Mk 15:21 they·pressed·and·imposed·upon a·certain·man,
G5100.8 P:X-ASF τινά (8x)
Lk 10:38 that he·himself entered into a·certain village, and
Lk 17:12 And upon·him entering into a·certain village, there·
Lk 21:2 And he·saw also a·certain needy widow casting two
Lk 23:19 on·account·of a·certain insurrection occurring in
Ac 16:16 to prayer, *that* a·certain servant·girl having a·spirit
Heb 4:7 again he·specifically·determined a·certain day,
Rm 15:26 to·make a·certain common·welfare·fund for the
Jac 1:18 for us to·be a·certain firstfruit of·his creatures.
G5100.8 P:X-ASN τί (7x)
Ac 5:2 ·known *of·it*. And bringing a·certain portion, he·laid
Ac 10:11 ·been·opened·up, and a·certain vessel descending
Ac 21:34 And some were·crying·out a·certain·thing, *and*
Ac 23:17 for he·has a·certain·thing to·report to·him."
Ac 27:16 And running·leeward·near·to a·certain small·island
Heb 2:7 "*By* a·certain small·degree, you·made him lesser
Heb 2:9 *by* a·certain small·degree having·been·made·lesser
G5100.8 P:X-APM τινάς (8x)
Lk 7:19 And John, summoning a·certain two of·his disciples
Lk 18:9 also this parable to certain ones having·confidence
Ac 15:2 and BarNabas, and certain others from·among them,
Ac 17:5 purposely·taking·to·themselves certain evil men of·
Ac 17:6 they·were·dragging Jason and certain brothers to
Ac 23:23 And summoning a·certain two of·the centurions,
Ac 27:1 ·were·handing both Paul and certain other prisoners
Gal 2:12 For prior·to certain·men coming from Jacob, he·
G5100.8 P:X-APN τινά (2x)
Ac 17:20 For you·carry certain strange·things to our ears.
Ac 25:19 they·were·having certain issues specifically·against
G5100.8 P:X-DSM τινί (6x)
Lk 7:41 "There·was a·certain lender *having* two needy·
Lk 11:1 as he·himself was praying in a·certain place, *that* as·
Ac 9:43 ·of days in Joppa with a·certain Simon, a·tanner.
Ac 10:6 ·man is·a·guest *staying* with a·certain·man, Simon
Ac 21:16 us, bringing with *them* a·certain·man, Mnason of·
1Co 15:2 yeu·fully·hold·onto that·certain Redemptive-word I·
G5100.8 P:X-DSF τινί (1x)
Lk 18:2 "In a·certain city there·was a·certain judge— *one*
G5100.8 P:X-GSM τινός (6x)
Lk 7:2 Now a·certain centurion's slave, who was dearly·
Lk 12:16 agricultural·region of·a·certain wealthy man·of·
Lk 14:1 him going into a·house of·a·certain·man of·the chief
Lk 23:26 upon·grabbing·hold of·a·certain·man who·was· *in*
Ac 19:9 in the school·auditorium of·a·certain·man *named*
Ac 24:1 the elders, and *with* a·certain orator *named* Tertullus
G5100.8 P:X-GSF τινός (1x)
Ac 16:1 by·name, a·son of·a·certain Jewish woman (one·
EG5100.8 (1x)
Ac 14:19 And *certain* Jews came·up from Antiochia and
G5100.9 P:X-ASN τί (2x)
Jn 5:19 by himself, but·only what he·should·look·upon the
2Co 12:6 me *to·be*, or *above* what he·hears from·out of·me.
G5100.10 P:X-ASN τί (2x)
Col 3:17 And anything what soever yeu·should·do in word
Col 3:23 And anything what soever *that* yeu·should·do, be·

G5101 τίς tís *p:i.* (537x)
Roots:G5100
G5101.1 P:I-NSM τίς (19x)
Jn 7:36 What *manner·of* saying is this that he·declared,
Lk 4:36 one·another, saying, "What a·word *is* this! Because
Lk 8:25 saying among one·another, "What *manner·of man* is
Lk 14:31 "Or what king, who·is·traversing to·engage·in war
Lk 15:4 "What man·of·clay† from·among yeu, having a·
Ac 7:49 for·me, says Yahweh? Or what *is the* place of·my
Ac 17:19 "Are·we·able to·know what this brand-new
Ac 19:35 Ephesians, for what man·of·clay† is·there that
Heb 12:7 as *his·own* sons, for what son is·he whom a·father
Gal 4:15 So·then, what was the supreme·blessedness yeu
Mt 7:9 "Or what man·of·clay† is·there from·among yeu, who

Mt 12:11 to·them, "What man·of·clay† shall·there·be from·
Mk 1:27 "What is this? What *is* this brand-new instruction?
Rm 8:35 What shall·separate us from the love of·the
1Co 2:11 For what man·of·clay† personally·knows the·
1Co 9:18 the payment·of·service: What is *the voluntary*
Eph 1:18 of·his calling·forth, and what *is* the wealth of·the
Eph 3:9 and to·illuminate for·all what *is* the fellowship of·
Col 1:27 ·whom God determined to·make·known what *is* the

G5101.1 P:I-NSF τίς (15x)
Lk 8:9 him, saying, "What might·be *meant·by* this parable?
Lk 15:8 "Or what woman, having ten drachma·coins·*of*·
Ac 10:21 ·I myself whom yeu·seek. What *is* the motivation
Heb 7:11 had·the·Torah-Law·enacted), what further need
Mk 6:2 this·man *do* these·things? And what *is* the wisdom,
Rm 3:1 the Jew's superior·benefit? Or what *is* the profit of·
Rm 11:15 *is* reconciliation for·*the*·world, what *shall* the
1Th 2:19 For what *is* our expectation, or joy, or victor's·
2Co 6:14 ·ones, for what participation has·righteousness
2Co 6:14 with lawlessness? And what fellowship has·light
2Co 6:15 And what mutual·agreement has·Anointed-One
2Co 6:15 *·Ruin)*? Or what portion has·one·that·trusts with a·
2Co 6:16 And what mutual·compact has·a·temple of·God
Eph 1:18 — for yeu to·have·seen what is the expectation of·
Rv 18:18 of·her fiery·burning, saying, 'What *city is* like the

G5101.1 P:I-NSN τί (54x)
Jn 1:22 to·the·ones sending us, what·do you·say concerning
Jn 2:25 ·clay†, for he·himself was·knowing what was in the
Jn 6:9 two small·broiled·fish, but·yet what are these·things
Jn 16:17 declared among one·another, "What is this that he·
Jn 16:18 So·then they·were·saying, "What is this·thing that
Jn 18:38 Pilate says to·him, "What is truth?
Jn 21:21 "Lord, and what *about* this·man?
Lk 1:66 hearts, saying, "What then shall this little·child be?
Lk 8:30 Jesus inquired·of him, saying, "What is your name?
Lk 15:26 servant·boys, he·inquired what might·be *meant·by*
Lk 16:2 ·for him, he·declared to·him, 'What *is* this I·hear
Lk 18:36 traversing·through, he·inquired what this might·be
Lk 20:17 "So·then, what is this having·been·written, "*The*
Lk 21:7 these·things be? And what *is* the miraculous·sign
Lk 23:31 *which·is* green·with·sap, what should·be·done to
Ac 5:24 about them as·to what would·come of·this.
Ac 7:40 ·do·not personally·know what has·happened to·him.
Ac 8:36 *here·is* water. What prevents me to·be·immersed?
Ac 10:4 becoming alarmed, he·declared, "What is·it, Lord?
Ac 10:17 ·perplexed in himself *as·to* what might·be *meant·by*
Ac 12:18 among the soldiers as·to what was·become of·Peter
Ac 21:22 Now·then, why is *this*?
Ac 21:33 he·might·be, and what *it·was* he·was having·done.
Ac 23:19 was·inquiring, "What is·it that you·have to·
Heb 2:6 ·testified, saying, "What is mortal·man†, that you·
Gal 3:19 So·then, *for* what *purpose is* the Torah-Law?
Mt 9:13 But upon·departing, learn what it·means, "I·want
Mt 12:7 But if yeu·had·known what it·means, "I·want
Mt 19:27 all and followed you. What then shall·be for·us?
Mt 22:42 saying, "What·do yeu suppose concerning the
Mk 1:27 ·discuss among themselves, saying, "What is this?
Mk 5:9 And he·was·inquiring·of him, "What *is* your name?
Mk 5:14 And they·went·out to·see what it·was, the·thing
Mk 9:10 questioning·and·discussing·with·one·another what
Mk 13:4 ·shall these·things be? And what *shall·be* the sign
Rm 3:1 So·then what *is* the Jew's superior·benefit?
Rm 3:3 What if some did·not·trust?
Rm 3:9 So·then what, are·we *Jews* any·better·off?
Rm 6:15 So·then, what? Shall·we·morally·fail, because we·
Rm 8:27 the hearts personally·knows what the disposition
Rm 11:7 So·then, what *happened*?
Rm 12:2 in·order·for yeu to·examine·and·verify what *is* the
Jac 2:14 What *is* the advantage, my brothers, though
Jac 2:16 requisite·needs of·the body— what *is* the advantage
Php 1:18 For *then* what·does *it·matter*?
1Pe 4:17 *it* first *begins* with us, what *is* the end of·the·ones
1Co 15:32 I·fought·with·wild·beasts at Ephesus, what *is* the
2Co 12:13 For what is·it in·which yeu·were·inferior beyond
Eph 1:19 and what *is* the surpassing greatness of·his power
Eph 3:18 together with·all the holy·ones what *is* the breadth,
Eph 4:9 "He·ascended:" what is·it except that also he·
Eph 5:10 examining·and·verifying what is most·satisfying
Eph 5:17 but·rather ones·comprehending what the will of·
1Jn 3:2 and it·is·not·yet made·apparent what we·shall·be.

G5101.1 P:I-NPM τίνες (1x)
Lk 24:17 he·declared to·them, "What sayings *are* these that

G5101.1 P:I-ASM τίνα (2x)
Mt 5:46 loving yeu, what payment·of·service do·yeu·have?
Rm 6:21 Accordingly, what fruit were·yeu·having then in

G5101.1 P:I-ASF τίνα (2x)
Jn 18:29 and declared, "What legal·accusation do·yeu·bring
1Th 3:9 For what thanks are·we·able to·recompense to·God

G5101.1 P:I-ASN τί (153x)
Jn 1:38 them following, says to·them, "What·do yeu·seek?
Jn 2:18 to·him, "What miraculous·sign do·you·show to·us,
Jn 4:27 not·even·one·man declared, "What·do you·seek?
Jn 6:6 had·personally·known what he·was·about to·do.
Jn 6:28 to·him, "What·do we·do in·order·that we·may·work
Jn 6:30 to·him, "So·then what miraculous·sign *do* you·
Jn 6:30 and should·trust in·you? What·thing do·you·work?
Jn 7:51 beforehand, and should·know what *it·is that* he·does
Jn 8:5 such·women. Accordingly, what·do you·yourself say
Jn 9:17 to·the·blind·man again, "What·do you·yourself say
Jn 9:26 ·declared to·him again, "What·did he·do to·you?
Jn 11:47 and were·saying, "What·do we·do, because this
Jn 11:56 one·another, "What·do yeu·yourselves suppose,
Jn 12:27 soul has·been·troubled, and what should·I·declare?
Jn 12:49 *concerning* what I·should·declare and what I·
Jn 12:49 what I·should·declare and what I·should·speak.
Jn 13:12 ·them, "Yeu·must·know what I·have·done for·yeu.
Jn 15:15 the slave does·not personally·know what his lord
Jn 16:18 We·do·not personally·know what *it·is* he·speaks.
Jn 18:21 ·of the·ones having·heard what I·spoke to·them.
Jn 18:35 ·priests handed you over to·me. What·did you·do?
Lk 1:62 to·his father, *for* what he·might actually·want him
Lk 3:10 ·of him, saying, "So·then what shall·we·do?
Lk 3:12 they·declared to·him, "Mentor, what shall·we·do?
Lk 3:14 ·of him, saying, "And what·shall we·ourselves do?
Lk 6:11 alongside one·another what they·might do to·Jesus.
Lk 7:24 John, "What have·yeu·gone·forth into the
Lk 7:25 But·rather what have·yeu·gone·forth to·see?
Lk 7:26 "But·rather what have·yeu·gone·forth to·see?
Lk 10:25 ·said, "Mentor, what should·I·do to·inherit eternal
Lk 10:26 He·declared to·him, "What has·been·written in·the
Lk 12:11 be·anxious·about how or what yeu·should·plead or
Lk 12:11 what yeu·should·plead or what yeu·should·declare.
Lk 12:17 himself, saying, 'What should·I·do, because I·
Lk 12:22 be·anxious·about yeur soul, what yeu·should·eat,
Lk 12:22 body, what yeu·should·dress·yeurselves·with.
Lk 12:29 yeu·yeurselves, do·not seek what yeu·should·eat,
Lk 12:29 what yeu·should·eat, or what yeu·should·drink,
Lk 12:49 earth. Even·so, what·do I·*actually*·want, though
Lk 16:3 declared within himself, 'What should·I·do?
Lk 16:4 I·know what I·shall·do, in·order·that, whenever I·
Lk 18:6 the Lord declared, "Hear what the unjust judge says.
Lk 18:18 ·good Mentor, what should·I·be·doing to·inherit
Lk 18:41 saying, "What·do you·want *that* I·should·do for·
Lk 20:13 of·the vineyard declared, 'What should·I·do?
Lk 20:15 "So·then what shall the owner of·the vineyard do
Lk 22:71 And they·declared, "What need do·we·have of·
Lk 23:22 to·them, "For what crime did this·one commit?
Lk 23:34 for they·do·not personally·know what they·do."
Ac 2:12 to another, "What·is this·thing actually·supposed
Ac 2:37 "Men, brothers, what shall·we·do?
Ac 4:16 saying, "What shall·we·do to·these men·of·clay†?
Ac 5:35 ·heed to·yeurselves what yeu·intend to·accomplish
Ac 9:6 he·declared, "Lord, what·do you·want me to·do?
Ac 9:6 it·shall·be·spoken to·you what is·mandatory·for you
Ac 10:6 ·man shall·speak to·you what is·necessary·for you
Ac 16:30 he·replied, "Sirs, what is·necessary·for me to·do
Ac 17:18 some were·saying, "What·is·it *that* this two-bit·
Ac 17:20 we·resolve to·know what these·things are·
Ac 19:3 to them, "So·then into what were·yeu·immersed?
Ac 22:10 And I·declared, 'What should·I·do, Lord?
Ac 22:16 And now, what·is·it *that* you·are·about *to·do*?
Ac 22:26 saying, "Clearly·see what you·are·about to·do,
Heb 11:32 And what more should·I·say?
Heb 13:6 ·not be·afraid of·what a·man·of·clay† shall·do to·
Gal 4:30 But·yet what·does the Scripture say?
Mt 5:47 ·greet yeur brothers merely, what·do yeu·do *that·is*
Mt 6:3 do·not·let your left·hand know what your right·hand
Mt 6:25 be·anxious·about yeur soul, what yeu·should·eat,
Mt 6:25 what yeu·should·eat, even what yeu·should·drink,
Mt 6:25 ·yeur body, with·what yeu·should·dress·yeurselves.
Mt 6:31 ·not be·anxious, saying, 'what should·we·eat?
Mt 6:31 'what should·we·eat?' or, 'What should·we·drink?
Mt 6:31 or, '*with* what *clothing* should·we·be·arrayed?
Mt 10:19 be·anxious·about how or what yeu·should·speak,
Mt 10:19 ·be·given to·yeu in that hour what yeu·shall·speak.
Mt 11:7 concerning John, "What·did yeu·go·forth into the
Mt 11:8 But·rather what·did yeu·go·forth to·see?
Mt 11:9 But·rather what·did yeu·go·forth to·see?
Mt 12:3 to·them, "Did·yeu·not read·aloud what David did,
Mt 16:26 "For what·is a·man·of·clay† being·benefited, if he·
Mt 16:26 of·his·own soul? Or what *is·it that* a·man·of·clay†
Mt 17:25 him, saying, "What·do you suppose, Simon?
Mt 18:12 "What·do yeu·yeurselves suppose?
Mt 19:16 Mentor, what beneficially·good·thing should·I·do
Mt 19:20 from·out·of·my youth, yet what more·do·I·lack?
Mt 20:21 And he·declared to·her, "What·do you·want?
Mt 20:22 ·do·not personally·know what yeu·are·requesting.
Mt 20:32 and declared, "What·do yeu·want *that* I·should·do
Mt 21:16 to·him, "Do·you·hear what these *boys* are·saying?
Mt 21:28 "But what·do yeu suppose?
Mt 21:40 vineyard should·come, what shall·he·do to·those
Mt 22:17 So·then declare to·us, what·do you suppose?
Mt 24:3 shall these·things be? And what *shall·be* the sign
Mt 26:8 saying, "To what·purpose *is* this total·ruin?
Mt 26:15 declared, "What·do yeu·want to·give to·me?
Mt 26:62 ·you·answer nothing·at·all? What *are* these·things
Mt 26:65 "He·reviled·God! What further need have·we of·
Mt 26:66 What·do yeu·yeurselves suppose?
Mt 26:70 "I·do·not personally·know what you·are·saying."
Mt 27:22 to·them, "So·then what shall·I·do with·YeShua,
Mt 27:23 was·replying, "For what crime did·he·commit?
Mk 2:25 ·not·even·at·any·time read·aloud what David did,
Mk 6:24 she·declared to·her mother, "What shall·I·request?
Mk 8:37 Or what·is·it *that* a·man·of·clay† shall·give in·
Mk 9:6 he·had·not personally·known what he·should·speak,
Mk 9:16 "What·do yeu·mutually·question·and·discuss
Mk 9:33 ·of them, "What·was·it *that* yeu·deliberated among
Mk 10:3 he·declared to·them, "What did·Moses command
Mk 10:17 "Beneficially·good Mentor, what should·I·do that
Mk 10:36 he·declared to·them, "What·do yeu·want me to·
Mk 10:38 ·do·not personally·know what yeu·are·requesting.
Mk 10:51 says to·him, "What·do you·want *that* I·should·do
Mk 11:5 there were·saying to·them, "What·are yeu·doing,
Mk 12:9 "So·then, what·shall the owner of·the vineyard do?
Mk 13:11 be·anxious·beforehand what yeu·should·speak,
Mk 14:36 away·from me. But·yet not what I·myself will,
Mk 14:36 not what I·myself will, but·rather what you *will*."
Mk 14:40 personally·known what they·should·answer to·him
Mk 14:60 ·thing? What·are these·things they·testify·against
Mk 14:63 says, "What need do·we·have of·any·further
Mk 14:68 am·I·fully·acquainted·with what you·yourself are·
Mk 15:12 "So·then, what·do yeu·want *that* I·should·do *to*·
Mk 15:14 ·saying to·them, "For what crime did·he·commit?
Mk 15:24 upon them, *as·to* who should·take·away what.
Rm 3:5 God's righteousness—" What shall·we·state?
Rm 4:1 Accordingly, what shall·we·state *for* AbRaham our
Rm 4:3 For what·does the Scripture say?
Rm 6:1 So·then, what shall·we·state?
Rm 7:7 So·then, what shall·we·state?
Rm 8:26 ·do·not personally·know what we·should·pray·for

Rm 8:31 So·then, what shall·we·state toward these·things?
Rm 9:14 Accordingly, what shall·we·state?
Rm 9:30 So·then, what shall·we·state?
Rm 10:8 But·yet what·does it·say?
Rm 11:2 Or do·yeu·not personally·know what the Scripture
Rm 11:4 But·rather what says the response·of·Yahweh to·
Php 1:22 Even·so, I·do·not really·know what I·shall·choose.
1Co 4:7 you *one·from·another*? And what·do you·have that
1Co 4:21 What·do yeu·want?
1Co 7:16 For what do·you·personally·know, O·wife,
1Co 7:16 the husband? Or what do·you·personally·know, O·
1Co 10:19 So·then, what do·I·reply?
1Co 11:22 ·ones not having? What should·I·declare to·yeu?
1Co 14:16 ·now he·does·not personally·know what you·say?
1Co 15:29 Otherwise what shall·they·do, the·ones being·
Rv 2:7 ·one having an·ear, let·him·hear what the Spirit says
Rv 2:11 having an·ear, let·him·hear what the Spirit says to·
Rv 2:17 having an·ear, let·him·hear what the Spirit says to·
Rv 2:29 having an·ear, let·him·hear what the Spirit says to·
Rv 3:6 ·one having an·ear, let·him·hear what the Spirit says
Rv 3:13 having an·ear, let·him·hear what the Spirit says to·
Rv 3:22 having an·ear, let·him·hear what the Spirit says to·

G5101.1 P:I-APF τίνας (1x)

1Th 4:2 For yeu·personally·know what charges we·gave yeu

G5101.1 P:I-DSM τίνι (6x)

Lk 6:47 doing them, I·shall·indicate to·yeu what he·is like.
Lk 13:18 But he·was·saying, "To·what is the kingdom of·
Lk 13:18 of·God like? And to·what shall·I·liken it?
Ac 4:9 by what·means this·man has·been·made·safe·and·
Ac 10:29 I·inquire, for·what reason did·yeu·send·for me?
Mk 4:30 And he·was·saying, "To·what should·we·liken the

G5101.1 P:I-DSN τίνι (7x)

Lk 7:31 declared, "So·then to·what shall·I·liken the men·of·
Lk 7:31 of·this generation? And to·what are·they like?
Lk 13:20 And again he·declared, "To·what shall·I·liken the
Lk 14:34 ·bland, in what·manner shall·it·be·seasoned?
Mt 5:13 ·become·bland, in what·manner shall·it·be·salted?
Mt 11:16 "But to·what shall·I·liken this generation?
Mk 9:50 ·become unsalty, with what shall·yeu·season it?

G5101.1 P:I-GSN τίνος (2x)

Ac 19:32 personally·known for·what cause they·had·come·
1Jn 3:12 And for·what self-gratifying·cause did·he·slaughter

G5101.2 P:I-NSM τίς (104x)

Jn 1:19 ·that they·may·ask·of him, "Who are you·yourself?
Jn 1:22 Accordingly, they·declared to·him, "Who are·you?
Jn 4:10 voluntary·present of·God, and who is the·one saying
Jn 5:12 ·then they·asked·of him, "Who is the man·of·clay†,
Jn 5:13 being·healed had·not personally·known who it·was,
Jn 6:60 "This is a·hard saying; who is·able to·hear it?
Jn 6:64 not trusting, and who was the·one to·be·handing him
Jn 7:20 "You·have a·demon! Who seeks to·kill you?
Jn 8:25 they·were·saying to·him, "Who are you·yourself?
Jn 8:46 Who from·among yeu convicts me concerning
Jn 9:2 saying, "Rabbi, who morally·failed, this·man or his
Jn 9:21 we·do·not personally·know; or who opened·up his
Jn 9:36 That·one answered and declared, "Who is·he, Lord,
Jn 12:34 to·be·elevated'? "Who is this Son of·Clay·Man†?
Jn 12:38 "O·Yahweh, who trusted *that·which* we·ourselves
Jn 13:24 Peter beckoned to·him to·inquire who it·might·be,
Jn 13:25 upon Jesus' chest, says to·him, "Lord, who is·it?
Jn 21:12 ·by·inquiring·of him, "Who are you·yourself?
Jn 21:20 and declared, "Lord, who is the·one handing you
Lk 3:7 ·offspring of·vipers, who gave·any·indication to·yeu
Lk 4:34 us? I·personally·know you *and* who you·are, the
Lk 5:21 began to·ponder, saying, "Who is this who speaks
Lk 5:21 speaks revilements of God? Who is·able to·forgive
Lk 7:39 he·would·be knowing who and what·manner *is* the
Lk 7:49 to·say within themselves, "Who is this that also
Lk 9:9 "I·myself beheaded John, but who is this, concerning
Lk 10:22 And not·even·one·man knows who the Son is,
Lk 10:22 except the Father, and who the Father is, except
Lk 10:29 declared to Jesus, "And who is my neighbor?
Lk 12:14 ·him, "Man·of·clay†, who fully·established me *as*
Lk 12:25 "And who from·among yeu by·being·anxious is·
Lk 12:42 the Lord declared, "Who then is the trustworthy
Lk 16:11 material·wealth, who shall·entrust to·yeu the true
Lk 16:12 ·man's *material·wealth*, who shall·give to·yeu
Lk 17:7 "Now who·is·there from·among yeu having a·slave
Lk 18:26 *this*, they·declared, "Who then is·able to·be·saved
Lk 19:3 And he·was·seeking to·see who Jesus was, and was·
Lk 20:2 do·you·do these·things? Or who is the·one giving
Lk 22:27 For who *is* greater, the·one reclining·at·the·meal,
Lk 22:64 saying, "Prophesy, who is the·one striking you?
Ac 7:27 declaring, "Who fully·established you *as* ruler
Ac 7:35 declaring, "Who fully·established you *as* ruler
Ac 8:33 ·taken·away. And who shall·give·an·account of·his
Ac 9:5 And he·declared, "Who are·you, Lord?
Ac 11:17 on the Lord Jesus Anointed), then who *am* I?
Ac 21:33 and·then he·inquired *of·them* who he·might·be,
Ac 22:8 And I·myself answered, 'Who are·you, Lord?
Ac 26:15 And I·myself declared, 'Who are·you, Lord?
Gal 3:1 O stupid Galatians, who cast·an·evil·eye·on yeu to·
Gal 5:7 ·were·running well. Who cut·into·yeur·path *such·for*
Mt 3:7 ·offspring of·vipers, who gave·any·indication to·yeu
Mt 6:27 And who from·among yeu by·being·anxious is·able
Mt 10:11 yeu·should·enter, verify·by·inquiring who in it is
Mt 12:48 *this* to·him, he·declared, "Who is my mother?
Mt 18:1 ·alongside YeShua, saying, "Who then is greater in
Mt 19:25 astounded, saying, "Who then is·able to·be·saved
Mt 21:10 all the City was·shaken, saying, "Who is this?
Mt 21:23 do·you·do these·things? And who gave you this
Mt 24:45 "Who then is the trustworthy and prudent slave
Mt 26:68 to·us, O·Anointed-One, who is the·one striking
Mk 1:24 us? I·personally·know you, who you·are, the
Mk 2:7 speak revilements of God? Who is·able to·forgive
Mk 3:33 he·answered them, saying, "Who is my mother, or
Mk 4:41 they·were·saying to one·another, "Who then is this,
Mk 9:34 among one·another who *would·be* greater.
Mk 10:26 themselves, "Then who is·able to·be·saved?
Mk 11:28 do·you·do these·things? And who gave you this
Mk 15:24 upon them, *as·to* who should·take·away what.
Mk 16:3 among themselves, "Who shall·roll·away for·us the
Rm 7:24 a·miserable man·of·clay†! Who shall·snatch me
Rm 8:31 *does·this* on·our behalf, who *is·able to·be* against
Rm 8:33 Who shall·call·to·account against God's
Rm 8:34 Who·is the·one *that* shall·be·condemning?
Rm 9:19 still does·he·find·fault? For who has·withstood his
Rm 9:20 ·of·fact, O man·of·clay†, who are you·yourself,
Rm 10:6 in your heart, "Who shall·ascend into heaven?
Rm 10:7 or, "Who shall·descend into the bottomless·pit?
Rm 10:16 says, "O·Yahweh, who trusted *that·which* we·
Rm 11:34 " For who knew Yahweh's mind?
Rm 11:34 Yahweh's mind? Or who became his counselor?"
Rm 11:35 "Or who first·gave to·him that it·shall·be·
Rm 14:4 Who are you·yourself, the·one unduly·judging
Jac 3:13 Who *is* wise and fully·informed among yeu?
Jac 4:12 and to·completely·destroy. Who are you·yourself
1Pe 3:13 And who *is* the·one *that* shall·harm yeu, if yeu·
1Co 2:16 For "who knew Yahweh's mind that he·shall·
1Co 3:5 So·then, who is Paul, and who *is* Apollos, other
1Co 3:5 ·then, who is Paul, and who *is* Apollos, other than
1Co 4:7 For who distinguishes you *one·from·another*?
1Co 9:7 Who strategically·goes·to·war at·any·time with·his·
1Co 9:7 ·time with·his·own wages? Who plants a·vineyard,
1Co 9:7 from·out of·its fruit? Or who shepherds a·flock, and
1Co 14:8 an·indistinct sound, who shall·prepare·himself for
2Co 2:2 grieve yeu, then who would·be the·one making me
2Co 2:16 unto life-above. And who *is* sufficient specifically·
2Co 11:29 Who is·weak, and I·am·not weak?
2Co 11:29 weak? Who is·being·enticed·into·moral·failure,
1Jn 2:22 Who is the liar, if·not the·one who·contradicts·by·
1Jn 5:5 Who is the·one overcoming the world, if·not the·one
Rv 5:2 with·a·loud voice, "Who is worthy to·open·up the
Rv 6:17 is·come, and who is·able to·remain·established?
Rv 13:4 Daemonic·Beast, saying, "Who *is* like the Daemonic·
Rv 13:4 like the Daemonic·Beast? Who is·able to·wage·war
Rv 15:4 ¿! Who should·not reverently·fear you, O·Yahweh,

G5101.2 P:I-NSF τίς (4x)

Lk 8:45 Jesus declared, "Who·is the·one laying·hold of·me?
Lk 8:45 and you·say, 'Who·is the·one laying·hold of·me?
Mk 5:30 was·saying, "Who laid·hold of·my garments?
Mk 5:31 ·in·around you and say, 'Who laid·hold of·me?

G5101.2 P:I-NSN τί (1x)

Jn 1:21 ·of him, "So·then, who are you·yourself, EliJah?

G5101.2 P:I-NPM τίνες (4x)

Jn 6:64 ·known from·among *the* beginning who they·are,
Ac 19:15 Paul I·am·fully·acquainted·with, but who are yeu?
Mt 12:48 "Who is my mother? And who are my brothers?
Rv 7:13 answered, saying to·me, "Who are these, the·ones

G5101.2 P:I-ASM τίνα (15x)

Jn 6:68 "Lord, to whom shall·we·go?
Jn 8:53 the prophets are·dead. Whom·do you·yourself make
Jn 18:4 ·forth, he·declared to·them, "Whom·do yeu·seek?
Jn 18:7 he·inquired·of them again, "Whom·do yeu·seek?
Jn 20:15 "Woman, why do·you·weep? Whom·do you·seek?
Lk 9:18 ·of them, saying, "Who·do the crowds say me to·be
Lk 9:20 to·them, "And who·do yeu·yourselves say me to·be
Lk 12:5 But I·shall·indicate to·yeu whom yeu·should·fear.
Ac 13:25 he·was·saying, 'Whom·do yeu·surmise me to·be
Mt 16:13 disciples, saying, "Who·do the men·of·clay† say
Mt 16:15 "But yeu·yeurselves, who·do yeu·say me to·be?
Mt 27:17 declared to·them, "Whom·do yeu·want *that* I·
Mk 8:27 saying to·them, "Who·do the men·of·clay† say
Mk 8:29 says to·them, "But who·do yeu·yeurselves say me
1Pe 5:8 as a·roaring lion seeking whom he·may·swallow·up,

G5101.2 P:I-DSM τίνι (4x)

Jn 12:38 we·ourselves heard? And to·whom is·revealed the
Lk 11:19 the demons, by whom·do yeur sons cast·*them*·out?
Lk 12:20 you. Now to·whom shall·be those·things·which
Mt 12:27 the demons, by whom·do yeur sons cast·*them*·out?

G5101.2 P:I-DPM τίσιν (2x)

Heb 3:17 But with·whom was·he·specifically·vexed forty
Heb 3:18 And to·whom did·he·swear *that* 'they·were·not

G5101.2 P:I-GSM τίνος (11x)

Jn 13:22 being·at·a·loss concerning who he·is·referring·to.
Jn 19:24 ·determine·by·lot concerning it, whose it·shall·be,"
Lk 20:24 for·me a·denarius. Whose derived·image and
Lk 20:33 in the resurrection, whose wife of·them does·she·
Ac 8:34 "I·petition you, concerning whom·does the prophet
Mt 22:20 And he·says to·them, "Whose derived·image and
Mt 22:28 in the resurrection whose wife shall·she·be of·the
Mt 22:42 concerning the Anointed-One? Whose son is·he?
Mk 12:16 he·says to·them, "Whose *is* this derived·image
Mk 12:23 they·should·rise·up, whose wife shall·she·be of·
2Ti 3:14 ·personally·known from whom you·learned *them*,

G5101.2 P:I-GPM τίνων (1x)

Mt 17:25 suppose, Simon? From whom·do the kings of·the

EG5101.2 (1x)

Mt 18:4 little·child, this·one is the·one *who·is* greater in the

G5101.3 P:I-NSN τί (8x)

Jn 1:25 declared to·him, "So·then why·do you·immerse, if
Jn 18:21 Why·do you·inquire·of me?
Jn 20:15 Jesus says to·her, "Woman, why do·you·weep?
Lk 6:46 "And why·do yeu·call me, 'Lord, Lord,' and do·not
Mt 8:26 And he·says to·them, "Why are·yeu timid, O·yeu·
Mt 17:10 him, saying, "So·then why·do the scribes say that
Mk 4:40 he·declared to·them, "Why are·yeu timid in·this·
Mk 8:12 spirit, he·says, "Why·does this generation seek·for

G5101.3 P:I-ASN τί (63x)

Jn 4:27 ·do you·seek?" or, "Why·do you·speak with her?
Jn 7:19 does the Torah-Law. Why·do yeu·seek to·kill me?
Jn 9:27 and yeu·did·not listen. Why·do yeu·want to·hear *it*
Jn 10:20 and is·raving·mad; why·do yeu·listen·to him?
Jn 13:28 ·at·the·meal knew particularly why he·declared this
Jn 18:23 But if *I·spoke* well, why do·you·thrash me?
Jn 20:13 *angels* say to·her, "Woman, why do·you·weep?
Lk 2:48 to him, "Child, why·did you·do us in·this·manner?
Lk 5:22 declared to·them, "Why·do yeu·ponder in yeur
Lk 6:2 declared to·them, "Why·do yeu·do that·which it·is·

Αα Ββ Γγ Δδ Εε Ζζ Ηη Θθ Ιι Κκ Λλ Μμ Νν Ξξ Οο Ππ Ρρ Σσ Ττ Υυ Φφ Χχ Ψψ Ωω

Lk 6:41 “And why do·you·look·at the speck·of·dust, the·one
Lk 12:26 ·which·is·least, why are·yeu·anxious concerning
Lk 12:57 “Now, why·do yeu·not judge what·is·right even
Lk 18:19 declared·to·him, “Why·do you·refer·to me *as*
Lk 19:33 declared to them, “Why·do yeu·loose the colt?
Lk 20:23 he·declared to them, “Why·do yeu·try me?
Lk 22:46 and he·declared to·them, “Why·do yeu·sleep?
Lk 24:5 to them, “Why among the dead do·yeu·seek the·one
Lk 24:38 to·them, “Why are·yeu having·been·troubled?
Ac 1:11 “Yeu·men of·Galilee, why·do yeu·still·stand *there*
Ac 3:12 “Men, Israelites, why do·yeu·marvel at this?
Ac 3:12 ·marvel at this? Or why·do yeu·gaze·intently at·us,
Ac 9:4 “Saul, Saul, why·do you·persecute me?
Ac 14:15 and saying, “Men, why·do yeu·do these·things?
Ac 15:10 “Now, accordingly, why·do yeu·try God, to·put a·
Ac 21:13 Paul answered, “Why·do yeu·continue weeping
Ac 22:7 ‘Saul, Saul, why·do you·persecute me?
Ac 22:30 *as·to* why he·is·legally·accused personally·by the
Ac 26:8 Why is·it·judged *to·be* incredible with yeu, that God
Ac 26:14 ‘Saul, Saul, why·do you·persecute me?
Gal 2:14 and not as·a·Jew, why do·you·compel the Gentiles
Gal 5:11 ·proclaim circumcision, why·am I·still persecuted?
Mt 6:28 “And why are·yeu·anxious concerning apparel?
Mt 7:3 “And why do·you·look·at the speck·of·dust, the·one
Mt 14:31 “O·you·of·little·trust, why·did you·waver?
Mt 16:8 “O·yeu·of·little·trust, why·do yeu·deliberate among
Mt 19:7 ·say to·him, “So·then why·did Moses command *us*
Mt 19:17 declared to·him, “Why·do you·refer·to me *as*
Mt 20:6 idle and says to·them, ‘Why·do yeu·stand here the
Mt 22:18 evil, declared, “Why·do yeu·try me, O·stage·
Mt 26:10 “Why·do yeu·personally·present wearisome·
Mk 2:7 “Why in·this·manner, does this·man speak
Mk 2:8 ·declared to·them, “Why·do yeu·ponder these·things
Mk 2:24 to·him, “See, why·do they·do on the Sabbath·days
Mk 5:35 “Your daughter is·dead. Why harass the Mentor
Mk 5:39 ·says to·them, “Why are·yeu·in·a·commotion and
Mk 8:17 says to·them, “Why·do yeu·deliberate *that it·is*
Mk 10:18 declared to·him, “Why·do you·refer·to me *as*
Mk 11:3 ·man should·declare to·yeu, ‘Why·do yeu·do this?
Mk 12:15 he·declared to·them, “Why·do yeu·try me?
Mk 14:4 and saying, “Why·has this total·ruin of·the
Mk 14:6 *alone*. Why·do yeu·personally·present wearisome·
Mk 15:34 “My God, my God, why did·you·forsake me?
Rm 3:7 abounded to his glory, why am I·also still judged as
Rm 9:19 ·shall·declare to·me, “Why still does·he·find·fault?
Rm 9:20 already·molding *it*, “Why did·you·make me in·
Rm 14:10 But why·do you·yourself unduly·judge your
Rm 14:10 Or also, why·do you·yourself utterly·disdain
1Co 4:7 if also you·did·receive *it*, why do·you·boast, as *if*
1Co 10:30 participate·neighborly, why am·I·reviled over
1Co 15:29 awakened at·all? Why then are·they·immersed
1Co 15:30 And why·do we·ourselves risk·danger every hour
Col 2:20 the principles of·the world, why, as·though living

G5101.4 P:I-NSM τίς (9x)
Lk 7:42 So·then declare *to·me*, which of·them shall·love
Lk 9:46 entered·in among them *as·to* which of·them would·
Lk 10:36 “So·then, which of·these three·men seems to·you
Lk 11:5 to·them, “Which from·among yeu shall·have a·
Lk 14:28 “For which from·among yeu, wanting to·build a·
Lk 22:23 ·discuss among themselves, which from·among
Lk 22:24 among them, *concerning* which of·them is·reputed
Mt 21:31 Out of·the two, which one·did the will of·the
Mt 23:17 O·fools and blind·men! For which is greater, the

G5101.4 P:I-NSN τί (6x)
Lk 5:23 Which is easier, to·declare, ‘Your moral·failures
Lk 6:9 “I·shall·inquire·of yeu. Which·thing is·proper on·the
Mt 9:5 For which is easier?
Mt 23:19 O·fools and blind·men! For which *is* greater, the
Mk 2:9 Which is easier to·declare to·the paralyzed·man,
1Co 14:15 So·then, which is·it?

G5101.4 P:I-ASM τίνα (5x)
Lk 11:11 “Now which father among·yeu, *if* the son shall·
Ac 7:52 Which of·the prophets did yeur fathers not persecute
Heb 1:13 But to which of·the angels has·he·declared at·any·
Mt 27:21 governor declared to·them, “Which of the two do·
1Pe 1:11 while·searching for which or what·kind·of season

G5101.4 P:I-ASN τί (6x)
Lk 17:8 ‘Make·ready *food* which I·may·eat·for·supper, and
Mt 15:32 they·do·not have *anything* which they·may·eat,
Mk 6:36 for they·do·not have that·which they·may·eat.”
Mk 8:1 immense and not having that·which they·may·eat),
Mk 8:2 three days and do·not have that·which they·may·eat.
Rm 8:24 expectantly·awaits that·which also he·looks·upon?

G5101.4 P:I-DSM τίνι (1x)
Heb 1:5 For to·which of·the angels did·he·declare at·any·

G5101.4 P:I-GSM τίνος (1x)
Lk 14:5 he·declared, “Which of·yeu shall·have a·donkey

G5101.5 P:I-NSN τί (5x)
Jn 14:22 ·him, “Lord, how has·it·happened that you·intend
Lk 2:49 ·declared to them, “How *is·it* that yeu·were·seeking
Ac 5:9 declared to her, “How *is·it* that yeu are·mutually·
Mk 2:16 ·saying to·his disciples, “How·is·it that he·eats and
1Co 14:26 Accordingly, how is·it *to·be*, brothers?

G5101.5 P:I-ASN τί (10x)
Lk 1:18 to the angel, “How shall·I·know this for·certain?
Lk 9:25 “For how·is a·man·of·clay† benefited, after·gaining
Lk 19:15 ·that he·may·know how·much each·man had·
Lk 19:48 yet they·were·not finding how they·may·do *it*, for
Ac 5:4 in your·own authority? How *is·it* that you·placed this
Mk 4:24 to·them, “Look·out·for how *well* yeu·listen·with·
Mk 8:36 “For how shall·it·benefit a·man·of·clay†, if he·
Mk 14:64 the revilement·of·God! How·does it·appear to·yeu
1Co 14:6 with·bestowed·tongues, how shall·I·benefit yeu,
Eph 6:21 the·things against me *and* how I·fare, Tychicus

G5101.6 P:I-NSM τίς (1x)
Lk 19:15 ·may·know how·much each·man had·thoroughly·.

G5101.7 P:I-NSN-HEB τί (7x)
Jn 2:4 “Woman, what·does·this·have to·do·with·me and
Lk 4:34 “Let·*us*·be! What·does·this·have to·do·with·us and
Lk 8:28 ·declared, “What·does·this·have to·do·with·me and
Mt 8:29 saying, “What·does·this·have to·do·with·us and
Mk 1:24 “Let·*us*·be! What·does·this·have to·do·with·us and
Mk 5:7 ·declared, “What·does·this·have to·do·with·me and
1Co 5:12 For what·does·this·have to·do·with·me, to also

G5101.8 P:I-NSN τί (3x)
Jn 21:22 him to·remain until I·come, what·is·that to you?
Jn 21:23 him to·remain until I·come, what·is·that to you?
Mt 27:4 And they·declared, “What·is·that to us?

G5101.9 P:I-NPN τίνα (2x)
Jn 10:6 did·not know what·*sort·of*·things it·was that he·was·
Heb 5:12 yeu again *about* certain·things·which *are* the initial

G5101.9 P:I-GPN τίνων (1x)
1Ti 1:7 concerning certain·things·which they·so·thoroughly·.

G5102 τίτλος títlôs *n.* (2x)

G5102 N-ASM τίτλον (2x)
Jn 19:19 And Pilate also wrote a·title and placed *it* on the
Jn 19:20 of·the Judeans read·aloud this title because the

G5103 Τίτος Títôs *n/p.* (13x)

G5103.2 N/P-NSM Τίτος (3x)
Gal 2:3 But·yet not·even Titus (the·one together with·me
2Co 12:18 the brother. ¿!·Did Titus swindle anything from·
2Ti 4:10 Crescens to Galatia, *and* Titus to Dalmatia.

G5103.2 N/P-ASM Τίτον (4x)
Gal 2:1 with BarNabas, personally·taking·along Titus also.
2Co 2:13 in·my spirit, *for* me not to·find Titus, my brother.
2Co 8:6 such·for us to·exhort Titus, in·order·that just·as he·
2Co 12:18 I·exhorted Titus, and I·dispatched·*him*·together·

G5103.2 N/P-DSM Τίτῳ (1x)
Tit 1:4 To·Titus, a·genuine child according·to a·shared trust.

G5103.2 N/P-GSM Τίτου (5x)
2Co 7:6 feeling·low, comforted us by the arrival of·Titus,
2Co 7:13 we·rejoiced over the joy of·Titus, because his
2Co 7:14 (the·one *we·made* before Titus) has·now·become
2Co 8:16 earnest·care into the heart of·Titus on·yeur behalf.
2Co 8:23 If *any·should·inquire* concerning Titus, *he·is* my

G5105 τοι•γαρ•οῦν tôigarôûn *prt.* (2x)
Roots:G5104 G1063 G3767 Compare:G0686

G5105 PRT τοιγαροῦν (2x)
Heb 12:1 Consequently, we·ourselves, also having so·vast a·
1Th 4:8 Consequently, the·one presently·ignoring *this*

G5106 τοί•νυν tôínyn *prt.* (4x)
Roots:G5104 G3568 Compare:G3767 G2543

G5106.2 PRT τοίνυν (4x)
Lk 20:25 he·declared to·them, “Now·then, give·back the·
Heb 13:13 Now·then, we·should·go·forth to him outside the
Jac 2:24 Now·then yeu·clearly·see that as·a·result of·works,
1Co 9:26 Now·then, in·this·manner I·myself do·run, *but* not

G5107 τοιόσ•δε tôiốsdê *p:d.* (1x)
τοιᾶσ•δε tôiâsdê [feminine singular genitive]
Roots:G5104 G1161 See:G5108

G5107 P:D-GSF τοιᾶσδε (1x)
2Pe 1:17 with·a·voice as·such being·carried·forth to·him

G5108 τοι•οῦτος tôiôûtôs *p:d.* (65x)
τοι•οῦτ- tôiôût-
[base for the other inflections]
Roots:G5104 G3778 Compare:G3697 See:G5107

G5108.2 P:D-NPM τοιοῦτοι (1x)
1Co 7:28 morally·fail. But such·ones shall·have tribulation

G5108.3 P:D-NSM τοιοῦτος (2x)
2Co 2:7 lest·perhaps such·a·man should·be·swallowed·up
2Co 10:11 Let such·a·man reckon this, “Such·as we·are in·

G5108.3 P:D-ASM τοιοῦτον (4x)
Ac 22:22 saying, “Away·with such·a·man from the earth,
Gal 6:1 must·completely·reform such·a·man in·a·spirit of·
1Co 5:5 to·hand·over such·a·man to·the Adversary-Accuser
2Co 12:2 ·knows), such·a·man being·snatched·up unto *the*

G5108.3 P:D-DSM τοιούτῳ (2x)
1Co 5:11 no,·not·even to·eat·together with·such·a·man.
2Co 2:6 Sufficient to·such·a·man *is* this public·penalty, the·

G5108.3 P:D-GSM τοιούτου (1x)
2Co 12:5 On·behalf of·such·a·man, I·shall·boast; but on·

G5108.4 P:D-NPM τοιοῦτοι (1x)
2Co 11:13 For such·men·as·these *are* false·ambassadors,

G5108.4 P:D-APM τοιούτους (2x)
Php 2:29 *the* Lord with all joy, and hold such·men in·honor,
3Jn 1:8 to·fully·receive·and·host such·men, in·order·that we·

G5108.4 P:D-APF τοιαύτας (1x)
Jn 8:5 for·us to·cast·stones·at such·women. Accordingly,

EG5108.4 (1x)
1Ti 2:15 — provided·that *such women* should·continue in

G5108.5 P:D-NSM τοιοῦτος (1x)
Tit 3:11 that the·one such·as·this has·been·subverted and

G5108.5 P:D-NPM τοιοῦτοι (1x)
Rm 16:18 (For such·as·these are·not slaves to·our Lord Jesus

G5108.5 P:D-APM τοιούτους (2x)
Jn 4:23 the·ones such·as·these falling·prostrate *directly*·
1Co 16:18 acknowledge the·ones such·as·these.

G5108.5 P:D-APN τοιαῦτα (1x)
Ac 19:25 concerning the *trades* such·as·these, he·declared,

G5108.5 P:D-DPM τοιούτοις (2x)
2Th 3:12 Now the·ones such·as·these, we·charge and exhort
1Co 16:16 ·be·submitted·to·the·ones such·as·these, and to·

EG5108.5 (2x)
Mk 7:8 of·men·of·clay†, *such·as the* ceremonial·washings
1Co 5:11 ·wrote·to·yeu not to·associate·with *such·as·these*: if

G5108.6 P:D-ASN τοιοῦτον (1x)
Ac 21:25 ·observantly·keep not·even·one such·thing, except

G5108.6 P:D-APN τοιαῦτα (7x)
Lk 9:9 concerning whom I·myself hear such·things?” And
Lk 13:2 Galileans, because they·have·suffered such·things?
Heb 11:14 For the·ones saying such·things make·it·clear that
Gal 5:21 that the·ones practicing such·things shall·not inherit
Rm 1:32 (that the·ones practicing such·things are worthy of·
Rm 2:2 ·to truth against the·ones practicing such·things.
Rm 2:3 ·judging the·ones practicing such·things, and·yet

G5108.6 P:D-GPN τοιούτων (2x)
Gal 5:23 self-restraint— against such·things there·is no law.

Eph 5:27 or wrinkle, or any such·thing, but·rather that she·
EG5108.6 (1x)
Ac 15:24 ·whom we·did·not thoroughly·charge *such·things*),
G5108.7 N-ASF τοιούτων (1x)
1Ti 6:5 a·means·of·gain. From such *men*, withdraw·yourself
G5108.7 P:D-NSM τοιοῦτος (2x)
Heb 7:26 For such a·High·Priest was·befitting·for us, *who·is*
Phm 1:9 *I* Paul, being such as an·old·man and now also a·
G5108.7 P:D-NSF τοιαύτη (3x)
Mk 13:19 shall·be a·Tribulation, such as has·not happened
Jac 4:16 ·boast in yeur bragging. All such boasting is evil.
1Co 5:1 among yeu, and such sexual·immorality which is·
G5108.7 P:D-NPM τοιοῦτοι (3x)
1Co 15:48 As *was* the dusty·clay·man, such also *are* the
1Co 15:48 and as *is* the heavenly·man, such also *shall·be* the
2Co 10:11 letters while·being·absent, such *shall·we·be* also
G5108.7 P:D-NPF τοιαῦται (1x)
Mk 6:2 to·him, that even such miracles happen through his
G5108.7 P:D-ASM τοιοῦτον (2x)
Heb 8:1 *the* summary: we·do·have such a·High·Priest who
2Co 12:3 And I·personally·know such a·man·of·clay†,
G5108.7 P:D-ASF τοιαύτην (6x)
Ac 16:24 who, upon·having·received such a·charge, cast
Heb 12:3 having·patiently·endured such hostile·grumbling
Mt 9:8 God, the·one giving such authority to·men·of·clay†.
1Co 11:16 we·ourselves do·not have *any·other* such custom,
2Co 3:4 And such confidence we·have through the
2Co 3:12 So·then, having such an·expectation, we·use
G5108.7 P:D-ASN τοιοῦτον (1x)
Mt 18:5 whoever should·accept one such little·child in my
G5108.7 P:D-APM τοιούτους (1x)
Ac 26:29 among *the* large, to·become such as even·I am,
G5108.7 P:D-APN τοιαῦτα (3x)
Jn 9:16 ·of·moral·failure, able to·do such miraculous·signs?
Mk 7:8 cups, and many other such similar·things do·yeu·do.
Mk 7:13 ·down. And many such similar·things do·yeu·do."
G5108.7 P:D-DPF τοιαύταις (2x)
Heb 13:16 ·welfare·fund, for with·such sacrifices God is·
Mk 4:33 And with·many such parables, he·was·speaking the
G5108.7 P:D-DPN τοιούτοις (1x)
1Co 7:15 sister has·not been·enslaved in such·cases, but God
G5108.7 P:D-GPN τοιούτων (4x)
Lk 18:16 do·not forbid them, for of·such is the kingdom of·
Mt 19:14 to·come to me, for of·such is the kingdom of·the
Mk 9:37 one of·the little·children such·as·these in my name
Mk 10:14 do·not forbid them, for of·such is the kingdom of·

G5109 τοῖχος tôichôs *n.* (1x)
Roots:G5038 xLangAlso:H3796 H7023
G5109 N-VSM τοῖχε (1x)
Ac 23:3 to·pummel you, O·wall having·been·whitewashed!

G5110 τόκος tŏkôs *n.* (2x)
Roots:G5088 xLangAlso:H5392
G5110 N-DSM τόκῳ (2x)
Lk 19:23 ·have reclaimed my·own together with·interest?'
Mt 25:27 ·obtaining my·own together with·interest.

G5111 τολμάω tôlmáō *v.* (16x)
Compare:G2292 G2293 See:G5112 G5113 G0662 G5056
G5111.1 V-PAI-1P τολμῶμεν (1x)
2Co 10:12 we·do·not dare to·count·ourselves·among·those,
G5111.1 V-PAI-3S τολμᾷ (2x)
Rm 5:7 ·good·man, someone also would·dare to·die.
1Co 6:1 Dare anyone of·yeu, having a·matter·of·
G5111.1 V-IAI-3S ἐτόλμα (4x)
Jn 21:12 disciples was·daring to·verify·by·inquiring·of him,
Ac 5:13 not·even·one was·daring to·tightly·join·himself to·
Ac 7:32 ·with·trembling, was·not daring to·fully·observe.
Mk 12:34 not·even·one was·daring any·longer to·inquire·of
G5111.1 V-IAI-3P ἐτόλμων (1x)
Lk 20:40 And no·longer were·they·daring to·inquire·of him
G5111.1 V-AAI-3S ἐτόλμησεν (2x)
Mt 22:46 nor·even·did anyone dare any·longer to·inquire·of
Jud 1:9 of·Moses), did·not dare to·bring·up a·verdict·of·
G5111.2 V-FAI-1S τολμήσω (1x)
Rm 15:18 For I·shall·not venture to·speak of·any of·such·
G5111.3 V-PAI-1S τολμῶ (1x)
2Co 11:21 *this* in impulsiveness), I·also am·daringly·bold.
G5111.3 V-PAN τολμᾶν (1x)
Php 1:14 bonds, *are* all·the·more daringly·bold to·speak the
G5111.3 V-PAS-3S τολμᾷ (1x)
2Co 11:21 *manner* someone may·be·daringly·bold, (I·say
G5111.3 V-AAN τολμῆσαι (1x)
2Co 10:2 ·which I·reckon to·be·daringly·bold against some
G5111.3 V-AAP-NSM τολμήσας (1x)
Mk 15:43 kingdom of·God. Being·daringly·bold, he·went·in

G5112 τολμηρότερον tôlmērŏtêrôn *adv.* (1x)
Roots:G5111
G5112.2 ADV τολμηρότερον (1x)
Rm 15:15 But with·more·daring·boldness, brothers, I·wrote

G5113 τολμητής tôlmētḗs *n.* (1x)
Roots:G5111
G5113.2 N-NPM τολμηταί (1x)
2Pe 2:10 ·lordship. *They·are* audacious *and* self-pleasing;

G5114 τομώτερος tômŏtêrôs *adj.* (1x)
Roots:G5058-2 Compare:G0664
G5114 A-NSM-C τομώτερος (1x)
Heb 4:12 active, and *he·is* sharper, above·and·beyond any

G5115 τόξον tŏxôn *n.* (1x)
Roots:G5088 Compare:G5329-1 G3505-3 See:G5114-1 xLangEquiv:H7198
G5115.1 N-ASN τόξον (1x)
Rv 6:2 ·one who·is·sitting·down on it having a·bow. And a·

G5116 τοπάζιον tôpáziôn *n.* (1x)
xLangAlso:H6357
G5116 N-NSN τοπάζιον (1x)
Rv 21:20 beryl; the ninth, topaz; the tenth, chrysoprase;

G5117 τόπος tŏpôs *n.* (94x)
Compare:G5561 See:G0824 xLangAlso:H4725
G5117.1 N-NSM τόπος (15x)
Jn 4:20 in JeruSalem is the place where it·is·mandatory to·
Jn 19:20 ·aloud this title because the place where Jesus was·
Lk 2:7 on·account·that there·was no place for·them at the
Lk 14:22 as you·ordered, and yet there·is place *for·more*.'
Ac 4:31 And with·them petitioning, the place was·shaken in
Ac 7:33 from·your feet, for the place in which you·stand is
Ac 7:49 Yahweh? Or what *is the* place of·my complete·rest?
Heb 8:7 then no place would·be·sought for·the·second.
Mt 14:15 him, saying, "The place is desolate, and the hour
Mt 27:33 that is being·referred·to·as, *the* Place of·a·Skull,
Mk 6:35 him, say, "The place is desolate, and even·now *it*·
Mk 15:22 ·interpreted *from·Hebrew*, is *the* Place of·a·Skull.
Mk 16:6 He·is not here. See the place where they·laid him!
Rv 12:8 neither was their place found any·longer in the
Rv 20:11 And there·is·not found a·place for·them.
G5117.1 N-ASM τόπον (45x)
Jn 10:40 beyond the Jordan into the place where John was
Jn 11:48 and shall·take·away both our place and nation."
Jn 14:2 to·yeu. I·traverse to·make·ready a·place for·yeu.
Jn 14:3 ·traverse and should·make·ready a·place for·yeu, I·
Jn 18:2 over, also had·personally·known the place, because
Jn 19:13 in a·place being·referred·to·as Stone·Pavement, but
Jn 19:17 the *place* being·referred·to·as *the* Place of·a·Skull,
Jn 20:7 having·been·swathed in one place completely·apart.
Lk 4:17 the official·scroll, he·found the place where it·was
Lk 4:37 ·forth into every place in·the surrounding·region.
Lk 4:42 ·forth, he·traversed into a·desolate place. And the
Lk 9:10 privately into a·desolate place *belonging·to* the·city
Lk 10:1 into every city and place where he·himself was·
Lk 10:32 a·Levite, happening by the place, coming and
Lk 14:9 ·declare to·you, 'Give this·man place,' and then
Lk 14:9 with shame to·fully·hold·onto the very·last place.
Lk 14:10 sit·back·to·eat in the very·last place, in·order·that
Lk 16:28 also should·come into this place of·torment.'
Lk 19:5 as·soon·as Jesus came to the place, looking·up, he·
Lk 23:33 when they·went·off to the place, the·one being·
Ac 1:25 ·to, *in·order* to·traverse into his·own place."
Ac 6:14 shall·demolish this place and shall·change the
Ac 12:17 And going·forth, he·traversed into another place.
Ac 21:28 ·Courtyard and has·defiled this holy place."
Ac 25:16 may·receive a·place to·defend·himself concerning
Ac 27:8 we·came to some place being·called Good Harbors
Ac 27:41 into a·place where·two·seas·met *producing a*·
Ac 28:7 Now in about the same place, there·were *some* open·
Heb 11:8 to·go·forth into the place which he·was·about to·
Heb 12:17 for he·found no place for·repentance, even·
Mt 14:13 ·there in a·sailboat into a·desolate place in private.
Mt 26:52 "Return·back your dagger into its place, for all the·
Mt 27:33 coming to a·place being·referred·to·as GolGotha,
Mt 28:6 Come·here! See the place where the Lord was·laid·
Mk 1:35 ·out and went·off into a·desolate place, and he·was·
Mk 6:31 aside privately into a·desolate place, and rest a·
Mk 6:32 they·went·off to a·desolate place in·the sailboat in
Mk 15:22 him to *the* place *being·referred·to·as* GolGotha,
Rm 12:19 but·rather yeu·must·give place to·the wrath *of*·
Rm 15:23 no·longer having a·place *to·publicly·work* in
1Co 14:16 ·one utterly·occupying the place of·the untrained
Eph 4:27 nor·even give place to·the Slanderer.
Rv 12:6 where she·has a·place having·been·made·ready by
Rv 12:14 wilderness, into her place, where she·is·nourished
Rv 16:16 them together into the place, the·one in·Hebrew
G5117.1 N-APM τόπους (5x)
Lk 21:11 earthquakes shall·be pervasive·in·all places, also
Ac 27:2 to·sail adjacent·to the *coastal* places of·Asia, with·
Ac 27:29 ·fall into rough,·jagged places, after·flinging four
Mt 24:7 and earthquakes shall·be pervasive·in·all places.
Mk 13:8 earthquakes shall·be pervasive·in·all places, and
G5117.1 N-DSM τόπῳ (15x)
Jn 5:13 ·slipped·away, with·a·crowd being in the place.
Jn 6:10 there·was much grass in the place. Accordingly, the
Jn 11:6 two days still in *the same* place where he·was.
Jn 11:30 but·rather was in the place where Martha went·and·
Jn 19:41 Now in the place where he·was·crucified, there·was
Lk 9:12 ·of·food, because we·are here in a·desolate place."
Lk 11:1 was praying in a·certain place, *that* as·soon·as he·
Ac 7:7 ·forth and shall·ritually·minister to·me in this place.
Mt 24:15 the prophet, standing in *the* holy place," (the·one
Rm 9:26 ·be, *that* in the place where it·was·uttered to·them,
2Pe 1:19 to·a·lantern shining·forth in a·murky place— until
1Th 1:8 but·rather also in every place yeur trust toward God
1Co 1:2 ·all *those* in every place who·are·calling·upon the
2Co 2:14 aroma of·his knowledge in every place through us.
1Ti 2:8 men to·pray in every place, lifting·up divinely·holy
G5117.1 N-DPM τόποις (2x)
Ac 16:3 the·ones being in those places, for absolutely·all
Mk 1:45 was outside in desolate places, and they·came to
G5117.1 N-GSM τόπου (7x)
Jn 6:23 out·from Tiberias near to·the place where they·ate
Lk 6:17 them, he·stood·still in a·level place, and·also the
Lk 22:40 And coming·to·be at the place, he·declared to·
Ac 6:13 utterances against this holy place and *against* the
Ac 21:28 the Torah-Law, and this place. And furthermore,
Mt 14:35 him, the men of·that place dispatched into all that
Rv 2:5 your Lampstand out of·its place, unless you·should·
G5117.1 N-GPM τόπων (3x)
Lk 11:24 it·goes through waterless places, seeking a·rest·
Mt 12:43 it·goes through waterless places, seeking a·rest·
Rv 6:14 mountain and island was·stirred out of·their places.
EG5117.1 (2x)
Jn 11:41 the stone *from the place* where the·one having·died
Jn 19:17 ·went·forth unto the *place* being·referred·to·as *the*

G5118 τ•οσ•οῦτος tôsôûtôs *p:d.* (21x)
Roots:G3588 G3739 G3778
G5118.1 P:D-ASM τοσοῦτον (3x)
Jn 14:9 Jesus says to·him, "Am·I so·vast a·time with yeu,
Heb 4:7 saying *it* by David (after so·vast a·time), just·as it·
Mt 15:33 ·wilderness, such·as to·stuff·full so·vast a·crowd?
G5118.1 P:D-ASF τοσαύτην (2x)

Lk 7:9 to·yeu, not·even in IsraEl did·I·find so·vast a·trust."
Mt 8:10 to·yeu, not·even in IsraEl did·I·find so·vast a·trust.
G5118.1 P:D-ASN τοσοῦτον (2x)
Heb 7:22 According·to so·vast *an·oath*, YeShua has·become
Heb 12:1 also having so·vast a·cloud of·witnesses that·is·
G5118.2 P:D-GPM τοσούτων (1x)
Jn 21:11 ; and·yet with·there·being so·vast·a·quantity, the
G5118.3 P:D-NPM τοσοῦτοι (1x)
Mt 15:33 ·*find* for·ourselves such·a·vast·quantity·of bread in
G5118.3 P:D-ASN τοσοῦτον (1x)
Rv 18:7 give to·her such·a·vast·quantity·of torment and
G5118.4 P:D-NSM τοσοῦτος (1x)
Rv 18:17 Because in·one hour such·vast wealth is·desolated.
G5118.5 P:D-NSN τοσοῦτον (1x)
Rv 21:16 and its length is as·vast and as·long·as the breadth
G5118.6 P:D-NPN τοσαῦτα (1x)
1Co 14:10 ·are, as·it·may·be, so·many kinds of·voices in
G5118.6 P:D-APM τοσούτους (1x)
Jn 6:9 ·fish, but·yet what are these·things among so·many?"
G5118.6 P:D-APN τοσαῦτα (3x)
Jn 12:37 ·him having·done so·many miraculous·signs before
Lk 15:29 'Behold, *these* so·many years I·am·a·slave to·you,
Gal 3:4 Did·yeu·suffer so·many·things for·no·reason— if·
G5118.7 P:D-DSM τοσούτῳ (1x)
Heb 1:4 being·made so·much significantly·better·than the
G5118.7 P:D-DSN τοσούτῳ (1x)
Heb 10:25 exhorting *one·another*, and so·much the·more,
G5118.7 P:D-GSN τοσούτου (2x)
Ac 5:8 whether yeu·sold·off the open·field for·so·much?"
Ac 5:8 ·so·much?" And she·declared, "Yes, for·so·much."

G5119 τ•ό•τε tótê *adv.* (157x)
Roots:G3753 G3588 xLangAlso:A0116

G5119.2 ADV τότε (16x)
Jn 13:27 And at·that·time, *along* with the morsel, the
Heb 10:7 At·that·time I·declared, 'Behold, I·come— on *the*
Heb 12:26 *own* voice shook the earth at·that·time. But now
Mt 3:13 At·that·time, YeShua comes·directly from Galilee to
Mt 9:14 At·that·time, the disciples of·John came·alongside
Mt 12:22 At·that·time, one·being·possessed·with·a·demon
Mt 24:23 "At·that·time, if any·man should·declare to·yeu,
Mt 24:30 "And at·that·time, the sign of·the Son of·Clay·
Mt 24:30 ·be·apparent in the heaven. And at·that·time, 'all
Mt 26:3 At·that·time, the chief·priests, and the scribes, and
Mt 27:16 And at·that·time, they·were·holding a·notable
Mt 27:38 At·that·time, *there·were* two robbers being·
Mk 13:21 "And at·that·time, if any·man should·declare to·
Mk 13:26 And at·that·time, they·shall·gaze·upon 'the Son
Mk 13:27 And at·that·time, he·shall·dispatch his angels and
2Pe 3:6 the world at·that·time was·completely·destroyed,
G5119.3 ADV τότε (135x)
Jn 2:10 they·should·be·drunk, then the lesser·quality, *but*
Jn 7:10 his brothers walked·up, then he·himself walked·up
Jn 8:28 Then accordingly, Jesus declared to·them,
Jn 11:14 Then accordingly, Jesus declared to·them with·
Jn 12:16 Jesus was·glorified, then they·recalled·to·mind that
Jn 19:1 Then accordingly, Pilate took Jesus and flogged *him*.
Jn 19:16 Then accordingly, he·handed him over to·them that
Jn 20:8 Then accordingly, the other disciple entered also,
Lk 5:35 But days shall·come, and then, whenever the
Lk 6:42 and then you·shall·thoroughly·look·about to·cast·
Lk 11:26 "Then it·traverses and personally·takes *to·itself*
Lk 13:26 "Then yeu·shall·begin to·say, 'We·ate and drank
Lk 14:9 place,' and then you·should·begin with shame to·
Lk 14:10 walk·further·up higher.' Then glory shall·be with·
Lk 14:21 these·things to·his lord. Then being·angry, the
Lk 21:10 Then he·was·saying to·them, "Nation shall·be·
Lk 21:20 being·surrounded by army·camps, then know that
Lk 21:21 Then the·ones in Judea must·flee into the
Lk 21:27 "And then they·shall·gaze·upon 'the Son of·Clay·
Lk 23:30 Then shall·they·begin "to·say to·the mountains,
Lk 24:45 Then he·thoroughly·opened·up their understanding
Ac 1:12 Then they·returned·back to JeruSalem from *the*
Ac 4:8 Then Peter, being·filled with·Holy Spirit, declared to
Ac 5:26 Then after·going·off, the high·warden along·with
Ac 6:11 Then they·secretly·induced men to·say, "We·have·
Ac 7:4 Then coming·forth from·among *the* land of·the·
Ac 8:17 Then they·were·laying *their* hands on them, and
Ac 10:46 and magnifying God. Then Peter responded,
Ac 10:48 name of·the Lord. Then they·asked him to·stay·
Ac 13:3 Then after·fasting and praying, and after·laying·
Ac 13:12 Then after·seeing the·thing having·happened, the
Ac 15:22 Then it·seemed·good to·the ambassadors and the
Ac 17:14 And then immediately the brothers dispatched·
Ac 21:26 Then Paul, after·personally·taking the men on·the
Ac 21:33 Then drawing·near, the regiment·commander
Ac 23:3 Then Paul declared to him, "God is·about to·
Ac 25:12 Then Festus, speaking·together with the council,
Ac 26:1 on·your·own behalf." Then Paul, after·stretching·
Ac 27:32 Then the soldiers chopped·off the small·ropes of·
Ac 28:1 being·thoroughly·saved, then they·realized that the
Heb 10:9 he·has then declared, " Behold, I·come, *I·am* the·
Gal 4:29 Moreover, just·as then, the·one being·born
Gal 6:4 his·own work, and then he·shall·have the boasting
Mt 2:7 Then HerOd·the·Great, after·privately calling·for the
Mt 2:16 Then HerOd·the·Great, after·seeing that he·was·
Mt 2:17 Then was·completely·fulfilled, the·thing being·
Mt 3:5 Then JeruSalem was·traversing·out to him, and all
Mt 3:15 ·fulfill all righteousness." Then he·allows him.
Mt 4:1 Then YeShua was·led·up into the wilderness by the
Mt 4:5 Then the Slanderer personally·takes him up into the
Mt 4:10 Then YeShua says to·him, "Head·on·out,
Mt 4:11 Then the Slanderer leaves him, and behold, angels
Mt 5:24 ·reconciled to·your brother, and then coming, offer
Mt 7:5 and then you·shall·thoroughly·look·about to·cast the
Mt 7:23 And then I·shall·affirm to·them, 'Not·even·at·any·
Mt 8:26 ·of·little·trust?" Then already·being·awakened, he·
Mt 9:6 moral·failures," (then he·says to·the·paralyzed·man)
Mt 9:15 ·be·lifted·away from them, and then they·shall·fast.
Mt 9:29 Then he·laid·hold of·their eyes, saying,
Mt 9:37 Then he·says to·his disciples, "In·fact, the harvest
Mt 11:20 Then he·began to·reproach the cities in which the
Mt 12:13 Then he·says to·the man·of·clay†, "Stretch·out
Mt 12:29 ·man? And then he·shall·thoroughly·plunder his
Mt 12:38 Then some of·the scribes and Pharisees answered,
Mt 12:44 Then it·says, 'I·shall·return into my house from·
Mt 12:45 Then he·traverses and personally·takes with
Mt 13:26 and produced fruit, then the darnel·weeds
Mt 13:36 Then after·sending·away the crowds, YeShua went
Mt 13:43 Then the righteous shall·brilliantly·radiate·forth as
Mt 15:1 Then the scribes and Pharisees from JeruSalem
Mt 15:12 Then his disciples, after·coming·alongside,
Mt 15:28 Then answering, YeShua declared to·her, "O
Mt 16:12 Then they·comprehended that he·did·not declare
Mt 16:20 Then he·thoroughly·charged his disciples in·order·
Mt 16:24 Then YeShua declared to·his disciples, "If any·
Mt 16:27 with his angels, and then 'he·shall·give·back to·
Mt 17:13 Then the disciples comprehended that he·declared
Mt 17:19 Then after·coming·alongside YeShua in private,
Mt 18:21 Then Peter, coming·alongside him, declared,
Mt 18:32 Then after·summoning him, his lord says to·him,
Mt 19:13 Then little·children were·brought to·him in·order·
Mt 19:27 Then responding, Peter declared to·him, "Behold,
Mt 20:20 Then the mother of·the·Sons of·Zebedee came·
Mt 21:1 the Mount of·Olives), then YeShua dispatched two
Mt 22:8 "Then he·says to·his slaves, 'In·fact the wedding is
Mt 22:13 "Then the king declared to·the attendants, 'After·
Mt 22:15 Then traversing, the Pharisees took consultation
Mt 22:21 "Caesar's." Then he·says to·them, "Well·then,
Mt 23:1 Then YeShua spoke to·the crowds and to·his
Mt 24:9 "Then they·shall·hand yeu over for tribulation and
Mt 24:10 And then many shall·be·tripped·up·and·fall·away,
Mt 24:14 to·all the nations, and then the end shall·come.
Mt 24:16 "then the·ones in Judea must·flee to the mountains.
Mt 24:21 "For then there·shall·be a·Great Tribulation, such·
Mt 24:40 Then two shall·be in the field; the one is·
Mt 25:1 "Then the kingdom of·the heavens shall·be·likened
Mt 25:7 Then all those virgins are·awakened, and they·
Mt 25:31 holy angels with him, then he·shall·sit upon his
Mt 25:34 "Then the King shall·declare to·the·ones at his
Mt 25:37 "Then the righteous shall·answer him, saying,
Mt 25:41 "Then he·shall·declare also to·the·ones at *the* left·
Mt 25:44 "Then they also shall·answer him, saying, 'Lord,
Mt 25:45 Then he·shall·answer them, saying, 'Certainly I·
Mt 26:14 Then one of·the twelve, the·one being·referred·to·
Mt 26:31 Then YeShua says to·them, "All yeu shall·be·
Mt 26:36 Then YeShua comes with them to an·open·field
Mt 26:38 Then he·says to·them, "My soul is exceedingly·
Mt 26:45 Then he·comes to his disciples and says to·them,
Mt 26:50 for·which you·are·here!" Then going·alongside,
Mt 26:52 Then YeShua says to·him, "Return·back your
Mt 26:56 may·be·completely·fulfilled." Then leaving him,
Mt 26:65 Then the designated·high·priest tore·apart his
Mt 26:67 Then they·spat in his face and buffeted him, and
Mt 26:74 Then he·began to·take·an·irrevocable·vow·of·
Mt 27:3 Then after·seeing that *YeShua* was·condemned,
Mt 27:9 Then was·completely·fulfilled the·thing being·
Mt 27:13 Then Pilate says to·him, "Do·you·not hear how·
Mt 27:26 Then he·fully·released BarAbbas to·them, and
Mt 27:27 Then the soldiers of·the governor, after·personally·
Mt 27:58 of·YeShua. Then Pilate commandingly·ordered the
Mt 28:10 Then YeShua says to·them, "Do·not be·afraid!
Mk 2:20 ·away from them, and then they·shall·fast in those
Mk 3:27 first, and then he·shall·thoroughly·plunder his
Mk 13:14 must·understand), "then the·ones in Judea must·
Rm 6:21 fruit were·yeu·having then in those·things·of·which
1Th 5:3 security," then an·unexpected savage·termination
2Th 2:8 And then the Lawless·One shall·be·revealed, whom
1Co 4:5 of·the hearts. And then the high·praise from God
1Co 13:10 complete should·come, then the·thing from·out
1Co 13:12 with an·obscured·view, but then face to face.
1Co 13:12 of·a·portion, but then I·shall·fully·know just·as
1Co 15:28 should·be·made·subject to·him, then also the Son
1Co 15:54 ·itself·with immortality, then shall·occur the
2Co 12:10 for whenever I·may·be·weak, then I·am able.
Col 3:4 life·above, should·be·made·apparent, then yeu also
G5119.4 ADV τότε (4x)
Lk 16:16 *were* until John. From then·on, the kingdom of·
Mt 4:17 From then·on, YeShua began to·officially·proclaim
Mt 16:21 From then·on, YeShua began to·show to·his
Mt 26:16 And from then·on, he·was·seeking a·good·
G5119.6 ADV τότε (1x)
Gal 4:8 Moreover in·fact, when not having·seen God, yeu·
G5119.7 ADV τότε (1x)
Jn 11:6 in·fact he·remained two days still in *the same* place

G5121 το•ὐν•αντίον tônantíôn *adv.* (3x)
Roots:G3588 G1726

G5121 ADV-C τοὐναντίον (3x)
Gal 2:7 But·rather on·the·contrary, after·seeing that the
1Pe 3:9 for defamation, but on·the·contrary, a·blessing,
2Co 2:7 As·such, on·the·contrary, yeu *ought* rather to·

G5122 το•ὔνομα tôúnôma *adv.* (1x)
Roots:G3588 G3686

G5122 ADV-C τοὔνομα (1x)
Mt 27:57 ·of·clay† of Arimathaea, by·the·name·of Joseph,

G5123 τουτ•έστι tôutésti *v.* (13x)
Roots:G2076 G5124

G5123 V-PXI-C τουτέστιν (13x)
Ac 1:19 own language, AqelDama, that·is, an·open·field of·
Ac 19:4 in the·one who·is·coming after him, that·is, in the
Heb 2:14 having the might of·Death, that·is, the Slanderer;
Heb 7:5 People according·to the Torah-Law, that·is, of·their
Heb 9:11 not made·by·human·hand, that·is, not of·this
Heb 10:20 for·us through the curtain, that·is, his flesh),
Heb 11:16 ·better *fatherland*, that·is, a·heavenly·one.
Heb 13:15 of·praise to·God continually, that·is, a·fruit of·
Mt 27:46 Eli, lama shebaq-thani?" That·is *to·say*, "My
Rm 7:18 I·personally·know that in me (that·is, in my flesh)
Rm 9:8 That·is, *it·is* not these children of·the flesh *that·are*

1Pe 3:20 in which a·few (that·is eight souls) were·
Phm 1:12 ·yourself purposely·receive him, that·is, my·own

G5124 τ•οῦτο tôûtô *p:d.* (323x)

Roots:G3778

G5124.1 P:D-NSN τοῦτο (80x)

Jn 6:29 and declared to·them, "This is the work of·God, that
Jn 6:39 "And this is the Father's will, the·one sending me,
Jn 6:40 And this is the will of·the·one sending me, that
Jn 6:61 to·them, "Does·this trip yeu up·to·fall·away?
Jn 12:5 "This ointment, why was·it·not sold·off for·three·
Jn 16:17 one·another, "What is this that he·says to·us, 'A·
Jn 16:18 they·were·saying, "What is this·thing that he·says,
Jn 21:14 This *is* even·now a·third·time *that* Jesus is·made·
Lk 1:34 the angel, "How shall this be, since I·do·not have·
Lk 1:43 And from·what·source *is* this *granted* to·me, that the
Lk 1:66 "What then shall this little·child be?
Lk 2:12 And this *shall·be* the sign to·yeu: Yeu·shall·find a·
Lk 16:2 to·him, 'What *is* this I·hear concerning you?
Lk 18:34 of·these·things; also, this utterance was having·
Lk 18:36 ·through, he·inquired what this might·be *about*.
Lk 20:17 "So·then, what is this having·been·written, "*The*
Lk 22:19 gave *it* to·them, saying, "This is my body, the·one
Lk 22:20 eating·supper, saying, "This cup *is* the brand-new
Ac 2:14 residing·in JeruSalem, be this known to·yeu and
Ac 2:16 But·rather this is the·thing having·been·declared
Ac 4:22 ·of·age, on whom this miraculous·sign of·healing
Ac 5:24 about them as·to what would·come of·this.
Ac 5:38 if this counsel or this work should·be birthed·from·
Ac 10:16 Now this occurred three·times, and the vessel was·
Ac 11:10 And this occurred three·times, and absolutely·all
Ac 19:10 And this happened for·a·span·of two years, such·
Ac 19:17 And this was known to·all the·ones residing·in
Ac 19:27 So *that* not merely this our occupation is·in·danger
Ac 26:26 to·be·hidden from·him; for this·thing was not
Ac 27:34 nourishment, for this is·inherently specific·for
Heb 9:20 saying, "This *is* the blood of·the covenant which
Heb 10:33 this *was*, in·fact, while·yeu·were·being·made·a·
Mt 1:22 And all this has·happened, in·order·that it·may·be·
Mt 12:11 one sheep, that if this *sheep* should·fall into·a·pit
Mt 15:11 mouth; *indeed*, this·thing defiles the man·of·clay†
Mt 16:22 to·you, Lord. No, this shall·not be *so* with·you!"
Mt 17:21 "But this kind does·not depart except by prayer and
Mt 18:4 whoever should·humble himself as this little·child,
Mt 19:26 to·them, "With men·of·clay† this is impossible,
Mt 21:4 But all this has·happened in·order·that it·may·be·
Mt 24:14 And this good·news of·the kingdom shall·be·
Mt 26:9 For this ointment was·able to·be·sold·off for·much,
Mt 26:13 this good·news should·be·officially·proclaimed in
Mt 26:26 "Take, eat! This is my body.
Mt 26:28 for this is my blood, the·one of·the brand-new
Mt 26:42 "O·My Father, if this cup is·not able to·pass·away
Mt 26:56 "But all this has·happened in·order·that the
Mt 28:14 And if this should·be·heard by the governor, we·
Mk 1:27 saying, "What is this? What *is* this brand-new
Mk 9:21 a·time has·it·been *that* this has·happened to·him?
Mk 9:29 "By not·even·one·thing is this kind able to·come·
Mk 14:9 this good·news should·be·officially·proclaimed in
Mk 14:22 "Take, eat! This is my body.
Mk 14:24 And he·declared to·them, "This is my blood, the·
Rm 13:11 *know* that even·now, this *is the* hour for·us to·
Php 1:19 For I·have·seen that this shall·result in salvation
Php 1:22 ·live in *bodily* flesh, this *continues* a·fruit·of·work
1Pe 1:25 ' And this is the utterance, the good·news·already·
1Pe 2:19 For this *is* graciousness, if someone on·account·of
1Pe 2:20 for·beneficially·doing·good, this *is* graciousness
2Pe 1:5 Now also *besides* this, applying all diligence, yeu·
2Pe 3:5 For this is·oblivious·to them (willingly) that by·the
2Pe 3:8 But *in* this one·thing, do·not be·oblivious, O·yeu
1Th 4:3 For this is God's will, yeur renewed·holiness: for·
1Th 5:18 everything give·thanks, for this *is* the·will of·God
1Co 10:28 should·declare to·yeu, "This is sacrificed·to·idols
1Co 11:24 "Take, eat! This is my body, the·one being·
1Co 11:25 cup after eating·supper, saying, "This cup is the
1Co 15:53 For it·is·necessary·for this corruptible *being* to·
1Co 15:53 and *for* this mortal to·dress·itself·with
1Co 15:54 So whenever this corruptible *being* should·dress·
1Co 15:54 and this mortal should·dress·itself·with
2Co 7:11 For behold this very·same·thing (to·grieve yeu
2Co 8:10 I·give advice, for this is·advantageous for·yeu,
2Co 9:6 But this *I·say*, the·one sowing sparingly also shall·
Eph 5:5 For yeu·are knowing this·thing, that every sexually·
Eph 5:32 This is a·great mystery, but I·myself do·say *this* in·
Eph 6:1 ·and·obey yeur parents in *the* Lord, for this is right.
Col 3:20 according·to all·things, for this is most·satisfying
1Ti 2:3 For this *is* good and fully·acceptable in·the·sight·of·

G5124.1 P:D-ASN τοῦτο (150x)

Jn 2:12 After this, he·walked·down to CaperNaum (he and
Jn 2:22 recalled·to·mind that he·was·saying this to·them.
Jn 4:15 "Sir, give me this water, in·order·that I·may·not
Jn 4:18 is not your husband. This·thing you·have·declared *is*
Jn 4:54 This *is* again *the* second miraculous·sign *that* Jesus
Jn 6:6 And he·was·saying this, trying him, for he·himself
Jn 7:39 (But he·declared this concerning the Spirit, which
Jn 8:6 But they·were·saying this, trying him in·order·that
Jn 8:40 AbRaham did·not do this.
Jn 11:26 ·not die to the coming·age. Do·you·trust this?"
Jn 11:51 And he·did·not declare this from his·own·self, but·
Jn 12:6 Now he·declared this, not because it·was·mattering
Jn 12:18 they·heard him to·have·done this miraculous·sign.
Jn 12:27 hour?' But·rather on·account·of this, I·came to
Jn 12:33 And he·was·saying this, signifying what·kind·of
Jn 13:28 knew particularly why he·declared this to·him.
Jn 15:19 ·among the world. On·account·of this, the world
Jn 18:34 From yourself, do·you say this·thing, or did·others
Jn 18:37 I AM a·king, *for* to this I·myself have·been·born.
Jn 18:37 have·been·born. Also to this I·have·come into the
Jn 18:38 And after·declaring this, he·went·out again to
Jn 19:28 After this, Jesus, having·seen that even·now
Jn 20:20 And after·declaring this, he·showed to·them his
Jn 20:22 And after·declaring this, he·puffed·on *them*.
Jn 21:19 This he·declared, signifying by·what·kind·of death
Jn 21:19 God. And after·declaring this, he·says to·him,
Lk 1:18 to the angel, "How shall·I·know this for·certain?
Lk 2:15 BethLechem, so we·may·see this utterance, the·one
Lk 3:20 he·added even this upon all·*these*·things— that he·
Lk 5:6 And after·doing this, they·tightly·enclosed a·large
Lk 6:3 "Did·yeu·not·even read·aloud this·thing that David
Lk 7:4 worthy for·whom this shall·be·personally·furnished,
Lk 7:8 he·comes; and to·my slave, 'Do this,' and he·does *it*.
Lk 9:21 *them* to·declare not·even·to·one·man this·thing,
Lk 9:45 But they·were·not·understanding this utterance, and
Lk 9:48 "Whoever should·accept this little·child in my name
Lk 10:11 Moreover, know this, that the kingdom of·God
Lk 10:28 "You·answered uprightly. Do this, and you·shall·
Lk 12:18 ·*man* declared, 'This shall·I·do, I·shall·demolish
Lk 12:39 "And know this, that if the master·of·the·house
Lk 13:8 'Lord, leave it this year also, until such·time *that* I·
Lk 22:15 "With·longing, I·longed to·eat this Passover with
Lk 22:17 he·declared, "Take this, and thoroughly·distribute
Lk 22:19 on·yeur behalf. Do this as my continual·reminder.
Lk 22:23 it·might·be intending to·accomplish this·thing.
Lk 22:37 it·is·mandatory·for this thing having·been·written
Lk 22:42 ·willing to·personally·carry this cup from me …
Lk 24:40 And after·declaring this·thing, he·fully·exhibited
Ac 2:12 another, "What·is this·thing actually·supposed to·
Ac 2:33 ·from the Father, he·poured·forth this, which yeu
Ac 4:7 by what·kind·of name, did yeu·yourselves do this?"
Ac 5:4 How *is·it* that you·placed this action in your heart?
Ac 7:60 And after·declaring this, he·was·laid·to·rest *in*
Ac 8:34 whom·does the prophet say this? Concerning
Ac 9:21 ·ones in JeruSalem who·are·calling·upon this name,
Ac 16:18 And this she·did over many days.
Ac 19:14 certain·men *who·were* doing this·thing: the·seven
Ac 20:29 For I·myself personally·know this, that after my
Ac 21:23 "So·then do this·thing which we·say to·you.
Ac 24:14 "But this I·affirm to·you, that according·to The
Heb 6:3 And this we·shall·do, if·ever God should·freely·
Heb 7:27 People, for he·did this upon·one·occasion·only,
Heb 9:8 with·the Holy Spirit making·plain this·thing: *that*
Heb 9:15 And on·account·of this, he·is *the* mediator of·a·
Heb 13:17 — in·order·that they·may·do this with joy, and
Heb 13:19 ·implore *yeu* all·the·more to·do this, in·order·that
Gal 2:10 helplessly·poor, also *being* this very·thing which I·
Gal 3:2 This merely I·want to·learn from yeu, did·yeu·
Gal 3:17 And this I·say, Torah-Law (the·one having·
Mt 8:9 he·comes; and to·my slave, 'Do this,' and he·does *it*.
Mt 9:28 "Do·yeu·trust that I·am·able to·do this?" They·say
Mt 13:28 'A·hostile man·of·clay† did this.' Then the slaves
Mt 26:12 For she·herself, casting this ointment on my body,
Mt 26:39 if·it·is possible, let this cup pass·away from me.
Mk 5:32 ·looking·all·around to·see the·one doing this·thing.
Mk 5:43 them repeatedly that no·one should·know this, and
Mk 11:3 to·yeu, 'Why·do yeu·do this?' Yeu·declare 'The
Mk 12:24 on·account·of this·thing *that* yeu·are·led·astray, *in*
Mk 14:36 to·you. Personally·carry this cup away·from me.
Rm 2:3 And do·you·reckon this, O man·of·clay† (the·one
Rm 5:12 *a·reconciliation needed* on·account·of this: *that*
Rm 6:6 knowing this, that our old man·of·clay† is·already·
Rm 9:17 "For this same·purpose *for affliction* I·fully·
Rm 11:25 brothers, to·be·ignorant of·this mystery, lest
Rm 12:20 for *by* doing this, you·shall·stack burning·coals
Rm 13:6 ·servants, diligently·continuing in this very·thing.
Rm 14:9 For to this *determined·purpose* Anointed-One also
Rm 14:13 but·rather yeu·must·judge this all·the·more:
Rm 15:28 after·further·finishing this *consequential·matter of·*
Jac 4:15 then we·should·live, and should·do this or that."
Jud 1:4 ·written·about of·antiquity to this judgment,
Jud 1:5 yeu, *due·to* yeu once having·seen this: that Yahweh,
Php 1:6 having·confidence of·this very·thing— that the·one
Php 1:7 it·is right for·me to·contemplate this on·behalf·of·all
Php 1:9 And this I·pray, that yeur love may·abound yet more
Php 1:25 And having·this confidence, I·have·seen that I·
Php 2:5 *and set·aim·for* this·thing among yeurselves, which
Php 3:15 differently, God shall·reveal even this to·yeu.
1Pe 2:21 For toward this yeu·were·called·forth, because
1Pe 3:9 ·called·forth to this in·order·that yeu·should·inherit
1Pe 4:6 For to this *end·purpose* was·the·good·news·already·
2Pe 1:20 while·knowing this first, that every prophecy of·
2Pe 3:3 while·knowing this first, that there·shall·come in the
1Th 2:13 On·account·of this also, we·ourselves give·thanks
1Th 3:3 personally·know that we·are·laid·out to this.
1Th 3:5 On·account·of this, when·I could·quietly·bear·it no·
1Th 4:15 For this we·say to·yeu by *the* Lord's word, that we·
2Th 2:11 And on·account·of this, God shall·send them an·
2Th 3:10 we·were alongside yeu, this we·were·charging yeu
1Co 1:12 Now I·say this, that each·one of·yeu says, "In·fact,
1Co 5:2 committing this deed should·be·entirely·expelled
1Co 5:3 the·one performing this·thing in·this·manner:
1Co 7:6 But I·say this in concession *concerning becoming*
1Co 7:26 I·deem for·this to·inherently·be good on·account·
1Co 7:29 But this I·disclose, brothers, *that* the season *is*
1Co 7:35 And I·say this specifically·for yeur own advantage;
1Co 7:37 his·own will, and has·judged this·thing in his heart
1Co 9:17 For if I·practice this·thing voluntarily, I·have a·
1Co 9:23 And this I·do on·account·of the good·news, in·
1Co 11:17 Now in·this charging, I·do·not applaud *yeu*,
1Co 11:24 over yeu. Do this as my continual·reminder.
1Co 11:25 in my blood. Do this, as·often·as yeu·would·
1Co 11:26 this bread, and should·drink this cup, yeu·fully·
1Co 12:15 the body," ¿! from this *reasoning*, is·it not from·
1Co 12:16 the body," ¿! from this *reasoning*, is·it not from·
1Co 15:50 Now this I·disclose, brothers, that flesh and blood
2Co 2:1 But I·decided this for·my·own·self, not again to·
2Co 2:3 And I·wrote this same·thing to·yeu, lest coming *to·*
2Co 2:9 For to this *end* also I·wrote, that I·may·know yeur
2Co 5:5 ·one already·accomplishing for us this very·thing *is*
2Co 5:14 after·already·*conclusively*·judging this·thing: that
2Co 8:20 we·are·deliberately·preempting this·thing: *that* not
2Co 10:7 ·be of·Anointed-One, let·him·reckon this again for

2Co 10:11 Let such·a·man reckon this, "Such·as we·are in·
2Co 13:1 This *is the* third·time I·am·coming to yeu.
2Co 13:9 should·be powerful. And this also we·well-wish,
Eph 4:17 Accordingly, I·say this and attest *to·it* in *the* Lord:
Eph 5:17 On·account·of this, do·not become impetuous·ones
Eph 6:8 this he·shall·subsequently·obtain personally·from
Eph 6:18 Spirit in every season, and·also in this same *Spirit*,
Eph 6:22 whom I·sent to yeu for this very·purpose, that yeu·
Col 2:4 And this I·say, lest any·man should·defraud yeu with
1Ti 1:9 while·having·seen this: that Torah-Law is·not laid·
1Ti 1:16 But·yet on·account·of this, I·was·shown·mercy in·
1Ti 4:10 For to this also we·labor·hard and are·reproached,
1Ti 4:16 in·them, for in·doing this you·shall·save both
2Ti 1:15 This you·personally·know, that all the·ones in Asia
2Ti 3:1 But know this, that in *the* last days perilous seasons
1Jn 3:8 *the* beginning. For this *determined·purpose* the Son
Rv 2:6 But·yet you·have this, that you·hate the deeds of·the

EG5124.1 (3x)

Mk 8:30 ·to·one·man should·they·relate *this* concerning him.
2Co 8:21 *We·do this* while·maintaining·ourselves·in
Rv 2:4 'But·yet I·have *this* against you, that you·left your

G5124.2 P:D-NSN τοῦτο (11x)

Heb 13:17 not sighing·heavily, for that *is* not·a·better·end
Mk 7:2 bread with·defiled hands, that is, with·unwashed
Rm 1:12 that is, to·be·comforted·together among yeu
Rm 10:6 into heaven?" (that is, to·bring Anointed-One
Rm 10:7 bottomless·pit?" (that is, to·bring Anointed-One
Rm 10:8 and in your heart" (that is, the utterance of·the
Php 1:28 but of·Salvation for·yeu, and that from God.
1Co 6:6 against a·brother, and that before non-trusting·ones.
Eph 2:8 through the trust. And this *is* not birthed·from·out
1Ti 5:4 compensations to·their·forebears, for that is good
1Jn 4:3 not from·out of·God. And that·thing is the *spirit* of·

G5124.2 P:D-ASN τοῦτο (75x)

Jn 1:31 ·apparent to·IsraEl, on·account·of that, I·myself
Jn 3:32 ·has·clearly·seen and heard, that·thing he·testifies;
Jn 5:16 And on·account·of that, the Judeans were·
Jn 5:18 Accordingly, on·account·of that, the Judeans were·
Jn 5:28 "Do·not marvel at·that, because an·hour is·coming in
Jn 6:65 he·was·saying, "On·account·of that, I·have·declared
Jn 7:22 "On·account·of that Moses has·given to·yeu the
Jn 8:47 of·God. On·account·of that, yeu·yeurselves do·not
Jn 9:23 On·account·of that, his parents declared, "He·is of·
Jn 10:17 "On·account·of that, the Father loves me, because I·
Jn 11:7 Then after that he·says to·the disciples, "We·should·
Jn 11:11 ·things he·declared, and after that he·says to·them,
Jn 12:18 On·account·of that, the crowd *from JeruSalem* also
Jn 12:39 On·account·of that, they·were·not able to·trust,
Jn 13:11 handing him over. On·account·of that, he·declared,
Jn 14:13 ·request in my name, that·thing shall·I·do, that the
Jn 16:15 has, are mine. On·account·of that, I·declared that
Jn 19:11 to·you from·above. On·account·of that, the·one
Lk 11:19 sons cast·*them*·out? On·account·of that, they shall·
Lk 11:49 "On·account·of that, the wisdom of·God also
Lk 12:22 to his disciples, "On·account·of that, I·say to·yeu,
Lk 14:20 a·wife, and on·account·of that, I·am·not able to·
Ac 2:26 On·account·of that, my heart is·made·merry, and
Ac 3:6 ·not subsist with·me, but that·thing which I·do·have,
Ac 9:21 and·also had·come here for that *same·purpose*, in·
Ac 23:7 And with·him speaking that, there·occurred a·
Heb 1:9 hated lawlessness. On·account·of that, God, your
Heb 2:1 On·account·of that, it·is·necessary·for us more·
Heb 9:27 *to·have* a·Final·Tribunal·judgment after that—
Gal 6:7 a·man·of·clay† should·sow, that also shall·he·reap.
Mt 6:25 "On·account·of that, I·say to·yeu, do·not be·
Mt 12:27 sons cast·*them*·out? On·account·of that, they shall·
Mt 12:31 "On·account·of that, I·say to·yeu, all·manner·of
Mt 13:13 "On·account·of that, I·speak to·them in parables,
Mt 13:52 to·them, "On·account·of that, every scribe
Mt 14:2 the dead, and on·account·of that, miracles operate
Mt 18:23 "On·account·of that, the kingdom of·the heavens
Mt 21:43 "On·account·of that, I·say to·yeu, the kingdom of·
Mt 23:13 "On·account·of that, yeu·shall·receive more·
Mt 23:34 "On·account·of that, behold, I·myself dispatch to
Mt 24:44 On·account·of that, yeu·yeurselves become ready
Mk 6:14 dead·men, and on·account·of that, the miracles
Mk 11:24 On·account·of that, I·say to·yeu, all·things, as·
Mk 13:11 ·be·given to·yeu in that hour, that speak, for it·is
Mk 14:5 For that·thing was·able to·be·sold·off for·upwards·
Rm 1:26 On·account·of that, God handed them over to
Rm 4:16 On·account·of that, *righteousness is* as·a·result of·
Rm 7:15 For I·do·not practice that·thing which I·want *to·do*,
Rm 7:15 ·want *to·do*, but·rather I·do that·thing which I·hate.
Rm 7:16 But if I·do that which I·do·not want, I·concur with·
Rm 7:19 which I·do·not want, that·thing *is what* I·practice.
Rm 7:20 I·myself do·not want, *if* that·thing I·do, *it·is* no·
Rm 13:6 For on·account·of that, yeu·fully·pay tributes also.
Rm 15:9 "'On·account·of that, I·shall·explicitly·affirm you
Php 3:15 ·mature, we·should·contemplate that·thing. And if
1Th 3:7 On·account·of that, brothers, in all our tribulation
1Co 4:17 On·account·of that, I·sent to·yeu TimoThy, who is
1Co 11:10 On·account·of that, the woman is·obligated to·
1Co 11:30 On·account·of that, many *are* weak and unhealthy
2Co 1:17 Now·then, in·purposefully·planning that, ¿!·did
2Co 4:1 On·account·of that, having this Service *of·the Spirit*,
2Co 7:13 On·account·of that, we·have·been·comforted in
2Co 13:10 On·account·of that, I·write these·things while·
Eph 1:15 On·account·of that, I·also, after·hearing·of the trust
Eph 6:13 On·account·of that, take·up the whole·armor of·
Col 1:9 On·account·of that, we·ourselves also (since that
Phm 1:15 For perhaps on·account·of that, he·departed just·
Phm 1:18 you, or owes *you* anything, impute that to·me;
2Ti 2:10 On·account·of that, I·patiently·endure all·things on·
1Jn 3:1 children of·God. On·account·of that, the world does·
1Jn 4:5 world, on·account·of that they·speak from·among
3Jn 1:10 On·account·of that, if I·should·come, I·shall·
Rv 7:15 On·account·of that, they·are in·the·sight of·the
Rv 12:12 "On·account·of that, be·merry, the heavens and
Rv 18:8 On·account·of that, her punishing·blows shall·come

G5124.3 P:D-ASN τοῦτο (4x)

Lk 4:43 because I·have·been·dispatched for this·purpose."
Ac 26:16 ·made·visible to·you for this·purpose, to·handpick
Mk 1:38 there·also. For to this·purpose I·have·come·forth."
Col 4:8 whom I·sent to yeu for this same purpose, in·order·

G5125 τ•ούτοις tôútôis *p:d.* (19x)

Roots:G3778

G5125 P:D-DPM τούτοις (6x)

Ac 4:16 saying, "What shall·we·do to·these men·of·clay†?
Ac 5:35 to·accomplish concerning these men·of·clay†.
Jud 1:7 As *in* like manner to·these *angels*, Sodom and
Jud 1:14 seventh from Adam, prophesied of·these, saying,
1Th 4:18 As·such, comfort one·another with these words.
3Jn 1:10 And not being·satisfied with these·things, neither

G5125 P:D-DPN τούτοις (13x)

Lk 16:26 And on·top·of all these·things, between us and yeu
Lk 24:21 Moreover together with·all these·things, today
Heb 9:23 the heavens) to·be·purified with·these *sacrifices*,
Gal 5:21 revelries, and things like these … of·which I·
Rm 8:37 all these·things we·gain·a·decisive·victory through
Rm 14:18 ·enslaved in these·things to·the Anointed-One *is*
Rm 15:23 having a·place *to·publicly·work* in these vicinities,
Jud 1:10 animals), in these·things they·are·corrupted.
2Pe 2:20 ·again are·being·entangled in·these·things *and* are·
1Co 12:23 less·honorable, upon·these we·place·around *them*
Col 3:14 And over all these·things, *dress·yeurselves·with* the
1Ti 4:15 these·things; be in these·things in·order·that your
1Ti 6:8 essential·coverings, with·these we·shall·be·satisfied.

G5126 τ•οῦτον tôûtôn *p:d.* (66x)

Roots:G3778 See:G5025

G5126 P:D-ASM τοῦτον (64x)

Jn 2:19 declared to·them, "Tear·down this temple, and in
Jn 5:6 Jesus, seeing this·man laying·ill and knowing that he·
Jn 6:27 ·yeu, for God the Father officially·sealed this·one."
Jn 6:34 "Lord, always give us this bread."
Jn 6:58 and died. The·one chewing this bread shall·live into
Jn 7:27 But·yet we·personally·know this·man, *and* from·
Jn 9:29 ·spoken to·Moses. But *as·for* this *man*, we·do·not
Jn 9:39 I·myself did·come into this world in·order·that the·
Jn 18:40 again, saying, "Not this·one, but·rather BarAbbas.
Jn 19:8 Now·then, when Pilate heard this saying, he·was all·
Jn 19:12 "If you·should·fully·release this·man, you·are not
Jn 19:13 Accordingly, after·hearing this saying, Pilate
Jn 19:20 many of·the Judeans read·aloud this title because
Jn 21:21 Upon·seeing this·man, Peter says to·Jesus, "Lord,
Lk 9:13 we·ourselves should·buy food for all these people."
Lk 9:26 shall·be·ashamed·of that·man whenever he·should·
Lk 12:5 Yes, I·say to·yeu, fear this·one.
Lk 12:56 ·it that·yeu·do·not examine·and·verify this season?
Lk 16:28 also should·come into this place of·torment.'
Lk 19:14 saying, 'We·do·not want this·man to·reign over us
Lk 20:12 But also wounding this·man, they·cast·*him*·out.
Lk 20:13 after·seeing this·one, they·shall·be·respectful·of
Lk 23:2 saying, "We·found this·man perverting the nation,
Lk 23:14 to them, "Yeu·brought this man·of·clay† to·me as
Lk 23:18 saying, "Away·with this·man, and fully·release
Ac 2:23 this·man (by·the specifically·determined counsel
Ac 2:32 God raised·up this Jesus, of·which we·ourselves all
Ac 2:36 must·know securely that God made this same Jesus,
Ac 3:16 *this·trust* stabilized this·man whom yeu·observe
Ac 5:31 God elevated this Initiator *of·the life-above*, *this*
Ac 5:37 After this·man, Judas of·Galilee rose·up in the days
Ac 6:14 ·have·heard him saying that this Jesus of·Natsareth
Ac 7:35 "This Moses whom they·renounced, declaring,
Ac 7:35 and executive·justice?" this·man God dispatched
Ac 10:40 This·one, God awakened on·the third day and gave
Ac 13:27 their rulers, not·knowing this·man nor·even the
Ac 15:38 to·personally·take·along this·man, the·one
Ac 16:3 Paul wanted this·man to·go·forth together with·him.
Ac 17:23 *him*, I·myself fully·proclaim this *God* to·yeu.
Ac 21:28 ·Courtyard and has·defiled this holy place."
Ac 23:17 Paul was·replying, "Lead this young·man to the
Ac 23:18 asked *me* to·bring this young·man to you, having
Ac 23:25 he·wrote a·letter containing this particular·pattern:
Ac 23:27 This man *was* already·being·arrested by the
Ac 24:5 "For after·finding this man *to·be* a·viral·pestilence,
Ac 25:24 ·present·together with·us, observe this·man, about
Ac 28:26 saying, "Traverse toward this People, and declare,
Heb 8:3 *it·is* necessary *for* this·man to·have something also
Mt 19:11 "Not all·men have·room·for this saying, but·rather
Mt 21:44 ·one falling on this stone shall·be·dashed·to·pieces,
Mt 27:32 they·pressed·and·imposed·upon this·man that he·
Mk 7:29 to·her, "On·account·of this saying, head·on·out.
Mk 14:58 'I·myself shall·demolish this Temple, the·one
Mk 14:71 ·not personally·know this man·of·clay† to·whom
Rm 9:9 ·promise, "'According·to this season I·shall·come,
Rm 15:28 ·and·officially·sealing to·them this fruit, I·shall·
Php 2:23 to·send this·man from·this·same·hour as·soon·as I·
2Th 3:14 yeu·must·personally·note that·man and do·not
1Co 2:2 Jesus Anointed and this *Jesus* having·been·crucified
1Co 3:12 if any·man builds upon this foundation *with* gold,
1Co 3:17 the temple of·God, this·one God shall·corrupt. For
1Co 11:26 For as·often·as yeu·should·eat this bread, and
1Co 11:27 whoever should·eat this bread or should·drink
2Co 4:7 But we·have this treasure in earthenware vessels, in·

EG5126 (2x)

Ac 5:31 Initiator *of·the life-above*, *this* Savior with·his·own
Mt 15:12 how the Pharisees, after·hearing *this* saying, are·

G5127 τ•ούτου tôútôu *p:d.* (77x)

Roots:G3778

G5127.1 P:D-GSM τούτου (53x)

Jn 6:51 "If any·man should·eat from·out of·this bread, he·
Jn 6:61 his disciples are·grumbling about this, declared to·
Jn 6:66 As·a·result of·this, many of·his disciples went·off to
Jn 8:23 Yeu·yeurselves are from·among this world; I·myself
Jn 8:23 this world; I·myself am not from·among this world.
Jn 9:31 ·of·God, and should·do his will, this·man he·hears.
Jn 10:41 ·as John declared concerning this·man were true."
Jn 11:9 stumble, because he·looks·at the light of·this world.

Tτ

Jn 12:31 “There·is now a·Tribunal·judgment of·this world.
Jn 12:31 of·this world. The prince of·this world shall now
Jn 13:1 that he·should·walk·on from·among this world to
Jn 14:30 with yeu, for the prince of·this world comes, and
Jn 16:11 because the prince of·this world has·been·judged.
Jn 16:19 one·another concerning this·thing which I·declared,
Jn 18:17 also from·among the disciples of·this man·of·clay†?
Jn 18:29 ·accusation do·yeu·bring against this man·of·clay†?
Jn 18:36 “My kingdom is not from·among this world. If my
Jn 18:36 If my kingdom was from·among this world, my
Lk 13:16 binding·for *her* to·be·loosed from this bond on·the
Lk 16:8 Because the Sons of·this present·age are more·
Lk 20:34 “The descendants of·this present·age marry and
Ac 5:28 to·bring the blood of·this man·of·clay† upon us.
Ac 6:13 speaking reviling utterances against this holy place
Ac 9:13 I·have·heard of many·things concerning this man,
Ac 13:17 The God of·this People IsraEl selected our fathers,
Ac 13:23 From this·man's Seed, according·to promise, God
Ac 13:38 ·it known to·yeu that through this·man, *the* pardon
Ac 15:6 gathered·together to·see concerning this matter.
Ac 21:28 the Torah-Law, and this place. And furthermore,
Ac 22:22 they·were·listening·to him even·until this word,
Ac 25:20 being·at·a·loss concerning this disputable·question,
Ac 25:25 and also with·he·himself appealing this to the
Ac 28:27 the heart of·this People became·thickly·calloused,
Mt 13:15 the heart of·this People became·thickly·calloused,
Mt 13:22 and·yet the anxiety of·this present·age and the
Mt 13:40 shall·it·be at the entire·completion of·this age.
Mt 27:24 blameless of the blood of·this righteous·man. Yeu·
Mk 4:19 yet the anxieties of·this present·age— and the
Rm 7:24 Who shall·snatch me out of·this body of·death?
Jac 1:26 deluding his·own heart, this·man's religion *is* futile.
Jac 2:5 *that* selected the helplessly·poor of·this world *to·be*
1Co 1:20 scribe? Where *is the* disputer of·this present·age?
1Co 1:20 not·indeed make·foolish the wisdom of·this world?
1Co 2:6 and not *the* wisdom of·this present·age, nor of·the
1Co 2:6 ·age, nor of·the rulers of·this present·age, the·ones
1Co 2:8 ·even·one of·the rulers of·this present·age has·known
1Co 3:19 For the wisdom of·this world is foolishness with
1Co 5:10 with·the sexually·immoral·people of·this world, or
1Co 7:31 for the schematic·layout of·this world passes·away.
2Co 4:4 in whom the god of·this present·age blinded the
2Co 12:8 Over this·matter, I·implored the Lord three·times
Eph 2:2 ·walked according·to the present·age of·this world,
Eph 6:12 ·world·powers of·the darkness of·this present·age,

G5127.1 P:D-GSN τούτου (22x)

Jn 4:13 “Anyone drinking from·out of·this water shall·thirst
Jn 19:12 As·a·result of·this, Pilate was·seeking to·fully·
Lk 2:17 being·spoken to·them concerning this little·child.
Lk 9:45 ·were·afraid to·ask him concerning this utterance.
Lk 22:51 “*Stop!* Yeu·must·let·it·be, even·unto this!” And
Lk 24:4 with them thoroughly·perplexing about this, behold
Ac 15:2 to the ambassadors and elders concerning this issue.
Ac 17:32 “We·shall·hear you again concerning this *matter*.”
Ac 28:9 In·due·course, with·this happening, the rest also,
Mt 19:5 declared, “For·this cause a·man·of·clay† shall·
Mt 26:29 this·moment·on from·out of·this produce of·the
Mk 10:7 “For·this cause a·man·of·clay† shall·leave·behind
Tit 1:5 For·this, on·account·of·grace, I·left you behind in
Eph 3:1 For·this, on·account·of·grace, I, Paul, *am* the
Eph 3:14 For·this gracious·cause, I·bow my knees to the
Eph 5:31 “‘Because of·this, a·man·of·clay† shall·leave·
Col 1:27 the wealth of·the glory of·this Mystery among the
1Jn 4:6 does·not hear us. As·a·result of·this, we·know the
Rv 22:7 the words of·the prophecy of·this official·scroll.”
Rv 22:9 observantly·keeping the words of·this official·scroll.
Rv 22:10 the words of·the prophecy of·this official·scroll,
Rv 22:18 the words of·the prophecy of·this official·scroll, if

G5127.2 P:D-GSN τούτου (1x)

Rm 11:7 did·not obtain that which it·still·anxiously·seeks,

G5127.3 P:D-GSN τούτου (1x)

Rv 19:20 and with it the Fiendish·False·Prophet, the·one

G5128 τ•ούτους tôútôus *p:d.* (28x)

Roots:G3778

G5128 P:D-APM τούτους (27x)

Jn 10:19 among the Judeans on·account·of these sayings.
Jn 18:8 if yeu·seek me, allow these·men to·head·on·out,”
Lk 9:28 about eight days after these sayings, that·also
Lk 9:44 “Yeu·yeurselves must·let these sayings be·placed
Lk 19:15 that he·declared *for* these slaves to·be·hailed to·
Lk 20:16 and shall·completely·destroy these tenant·farmers,
Ac 2:22 “Men, Israelites, hear these words: Jesus of·
Ac 5:5 And upon·hearing these words, Ananias fell·down
Ac 5:24 and the chief·priests heard these words, they·were·
Ac 10:47 to·forbid water *such·for* these not to·be·immersed,
Ac 16:36 And the prison·warden announced this saying to
Ac 19:37 For yeu·brought these men *here*, *who·are* neither
Ac 21:24 after·personally·taking these·men, be·
Heb 2:15 and *that* he·may·release them, as·many·as·who
Mt 7:24 anyone that hears these sayings of·mine and does
Mt 7:26 “And everyone hearing these sayings of·mine, and
Mt 7:28 *that* when YeShua entirely·completed these sayings,
Mt 10:5 These twelve YeShua dispatched, after·charging
Mt 19:1 *that* when YeShua finished these sayings, he·moved·
Mt 26:1 when YeShua finished all these sayings, he·declared
Mk 8:4 ·someone be·able to·stuff these·men full with·bread,
Rm 8:30 he·predetermined, these also he·called·forth; and
Rm 8:30 he·called·forth, these also he·regarded·as·righteous
Rm 8:30 he·regarded·as·righteous, these also he·glorified.
1Co 6:4 do·yeu·seat these *unrighteous·ones as·judges*, the·
1Co 16:3 through *yeur* letters, these I·shall·send to·carry
2Ti 3:5 So·then, turn·yourself·away·and·avoid these *people*!

EG5128 (1x)

Ac 10:47 these not to·be·immersed, *these* who received the

G5129 τ•ούτῳ tôútō *p:d.* (89x)

Roots:G3778

G5129 P:D-DSM τούτῳ (41x)

Jn 4:27 And his disciples came upon this, and they·marveled
Jn 4:37 For in this *case*, the saying is true, ‘One is
Jn 5:38 whom he·dispatched, him yeu·yeurselves do·not
Jn 10:3 To·him, the doorkeeper opens·up, and the sheep hear
Jn 12:25 ·hating his soul in this world shall·vigilantly·keep it
Jn 13:24 ·then, Simon Peter beckoned to·him to·inquire who
Lk 4:3 a·son of·God, declare to·this stone that it·should·
Lk 7:8 under my·own·self, and I·say to·this·man, ‘Traverse
Lk 10:5 yeu·should·enter, first say, ‘Peace to·this house.’
Lk 14:9 shall·declare to·you, ‘Give this·man place,’ and
Lk 18:30 ·in·full many·times·over in this *present* season, and
Lk 19:9 “Today, Salvation did·come to·this house, because·
Lk 19:19 And he·declared likewise to·him, ‘Be you also
Lk 21:23 ·need upon the land and WRATH on this people.
Lk 23:4 “I·find not·even·one fault in this man·of·clay†.”
Lk 23:14 ·even·one fault in this man·of·clay† according·to
Ac 1:6 “Lord, do·you at this time restore the kingdom to·
Ac 7:7 ·forth and shall·ritually·minister to·me in this place.”
Ac 7:29 Then Moses fled at this saying, and was·a·sojourner
Ac 8:21 nor·even a·small·chance for·you in this matter, for
Ac 10:43 “To·this·one, all the prophets do·testify— *that*
Ac 13:39 And by him, everyone trusting is·regarded·as·
Ac 21:9 And this·man had daughters, four virgin·daughters
Ac 23:9 “We·find not·even·one wrong in this man·of·clay†,
Ac 25:5 ·accuse this man, if there·is any *wrong* in him.”
Heb 4:5 And in this *passage* again, “‘As·if they·shall·*ever*·
Gal 6:16 shall·conform·and·march·orderly by·this standard,
Mt 8:9 under my·own·self, and I·say to·this *man*, ‘Traverse,
Mt 12:32 be·forgiven him, neither in this present·age, nor in
Mt 13:54 to·say, “From·what·source *does* this·man *have* this
Mt 13:56 us? So·then from·what·source *does* this·man *do* all
Mt 20:14 ‘But I·want to·give to·this last·one, even as *I·gave*
Mk 6:2 “From·what·source *does* this·man *do* these·things?
Mk 10:30 receive a·hundred·times·over now in this season,
Rm 12:2 And do·not be·conformed to·this present·age, but·
Rm 13:9 commandment, it·is·summed·up in this saying,
1Co 3:18 yeu seems to·be wise in this present·age, let·him·
1Co 7:31 and the·ones using this world, as not abusing *it* …
1Co 14:21 and in other lips I·shall·speak to·this People; and
Eph 1:21 ·named, not merely in this present·age, but·rather
1Jn 4:17 that·one is, so·also are we·ourselves in this world.

G5129 P:D-DSN τούτῳ (48x)

Jn 4:20 Our fathers fell·prostrate on this mountain; and yeu
Jn 4:21 is·coming when, neither on this mountain, nor·even
Jn 9:30 to·them, “For in this is a·marvelous·thing, that yeu·
Jn 13:35 By this, everyone shall·know that yeu·are disciples
Jn 15:8 “In this my Father is·glorified, that yeu·may·bear
Jn 16:30 “By this, we·trust that you·came·forth from God.
Jn 20:30 are not having·been·written in this official·scroll.
Lk 1:61 among your kinsfolk that is·called by·this name.”
Lk 10:20 “Moreover, do·not rejoice in this, that the spirits
Ac 3:12 Israelites, why do·yeu·marvel at this? Or why·do
Ac 4:10 from·among dead·men, by this *name* does this·man
Ac 4:17 ·longer to·not·even·one man·of·clay† in this name.”
Ac 5:28 charge a·charge to·yeu not to·instruct in this name?
Ac 8:29 “Go·alongside and be·tightly·joined to·this chariot.”
Ac 15:15 And to·this, the words of·the prophets do·
Ac 24:2 ·reforms occurring in·this nation on·account·of your
Ac 24:10 years of·you being a·judge to·this nation, with·
Ac 24:16 And in this, I·exert myself: to·have continually a·
Mt 17:20 ·seed *does*, yeu·shall·declare to·this mountain,
Mt 21:21 but·yet also·if yeu·should·declare to·this mountain,
Mk 11:23 that whoever should·declare to·this mountain,
Php 1:18 is·being·fully·proclaimed, and in this I·do·rejoice.
1Pe 4:16 ·ashamed, but let·him·glorify God in this portion.
2Pe 1:13 for as·long·as I·am in this bodily·tabernacle, to·
2Pe 2:19 ·been·defeated, even by·this he·has·been·enslaved.
1Co 4:4 ·yet not by this have·I·been·regarded·as·righteous.
1Co 7:24 brothers, in that·*state* he·must·continue with God
1Co 11:22 Should·I·applaud yeu in this? I·do·not applaud
2Co 3:10 ·not·even been·glorified in this particular·aspect:
2Co 5:2 For even in this we·groan, greatly·yearning to·fully·
2Co 8:10 And in this, I·give advice, for this is·advantageous
2Co 9:3 on·yeur behalf should·be·made·empty on this part;
1Jn 2:3 And in this we·do·know that we·have·known him, if
1Jn 2:4 commandments is a·liar, and the truth is not in him.
1Jn 2:5 ·keep his Redemptive-word, in him truly the love of·
1Jn 2:5 ·been·made·completely·mature. In this, we·do·know
1Jn 3:10 In this the children of·God are apparent, also the
1Jn 3:16 By this we·have·known the love *of·God*, because
1Jn 3:19 And by this we·know that we·are birthed·from·out
1Jn 3:24 him. And by this we·know that he·presently·abides
1Jn 4:2 By this yeu·presently·know the Spirit of·God: every
1Jn 4:9 In this, the love of·God is·made·apparent among us,
1Jn 4:10 In this, is the love: not that we·ourselves loved God,
1Jn 4:13 By this we·know that we·abide in him, and he·
1Jn 4:17 In this, the Love with us has·been·fully·completed,
1Jn 5:2 By this we·know that we·love the children of·God,
Rv 22:18 ·blows having·been·written in this official·scroll.
Rv 22:19 ·things having·been·written in this official·scroll.

G5130 τ•ούτων tôútōn *p:d.* (71x)

Roots:G3778

G5130 P:D-GPM τούτων (25x)

Jn 17:20 “But not concerning these·men merely do·I·ask,
Lk 3:8 that God is·able from·out of·these stones to·awaken
Lk 10:36 “So·then, which of·these three·men seems to·you
Lk 17:2 ·cause·the·moral·failure·of one of·these little·ones.
Lk 21:28 “And with·these·things beginning to·happen, pull·
Ac 1:22 from us, *it·is·mandatory* of·these·men *for* one to·
Ac 1:24 which one from·among these two you·selected
Ac 5:38 to·yeu: Withdraw from these men·of·clay† and let
Ac 14:15 to·yeu to·turn·back·around from these futilities to
Ac 26:29 ·I am, *though* personally·aside·from these bonds.”
Heb 9:6 Now with·these·things having·been·fully·prepared
Mt 3:9 that God is·able from·out of·these stones to·awaken
Mt 5:37 ·thing in·excess of·these·things is birthed·from·out
Mt 10:42 should·give to·one of·these little·ones a·cup of·
Mt 11:7 And as·these·men were·departing, YeShua began to·
Mt 18:6 ·cause·the·moral·failure·of one of·these little·ones,
Mt 18:10 yeu·should·not despise one of·these little·ones, for

Αα Ββ Γγ Δδ Εε Ζζ Ηη Θθ Ιι Κκ Λλ Μμ Νν Ξξ Οο Ππ Ρρ Σσ Ττ Υυ Φφ Χχ Ψψ Ωω

Mt 18:14 one of·these little·ones should·completely·perish.
Mt 25:40 yeu·did *it* to·one of·the least of·these my brothers,
Mt 25:45 ·not do *it* to·one of·the least of·these *my brothers*,
Rm 11:30 ·shown·mercy by·the obstinate·attitude of·these,
1Th 4:6 *is* avenger concerning all these·matters, just·as also
2Ti 3:6 For from·among these *types* are the·ones
Rv 9:18 By these three, the third·part of·the men·of·clay†
Rv 20:6 in the First Resurrection. Over these, the Second

G5130 P:D-GPF τούτων (7x)
Ac 5:36 For before these days, Theudas rose·up, saying
Ac 21:38 ·*one* before these days already·making·an·uprising
Heb 1:2 spoke to·us in these last days by *his* Son, whom he·
Heb 10:18 where *there·is* pardon of·these·things, *there·is*
Mt 5:19 should·break one of·these least commandments and
Mk 12:31 ·is no other commandment greater·than these."
1Co 13:13 *and* Love; but *the* greater of·these *is* the Love.

G5130 P:D-GPN τούτων (37x)
Jn 1:50 You·shall·gaze·upon greater·things·than these."
Jn 5:20 he·shall·show him works greater·than these, that yeu
Jn 7:31 ·do more miraculous·signs than these which this·man
Jn 14:12 And greater *works* than·these shall·he·do, because
Jn 21:15 ·Jonah, do·you·love me more·than these·things?"
Jn 21:24 ·one testifying concerning these·things and writing
Lk 7:18 reported·to him concerning all these·things.
Lk 12:27 in all his glory was·arrayed as one of·these.
Lk 12:30 ·knows that yeu·have·need of·these·things.
Lk 18:34 comprehended not·even·one of·these·things; also,
Lk 21:12 before absolutely·all these·things, they·shall·throw
Lk 24:14 all these·things having·befallen *in·JeruSalem*.
Lk 24:48 "And yeu·yeurselves are witnesses of·these·things.
Ac 5:32 we·ourselves are his witnesses of·these utterances;
Ac 15:28 a·larger burden besides these·things of·necessity:
Ac 18:15 ·definitely·not willing to·be judge of·these·things."
Ac 18:17 not·even·one of·these·things was·mattering to·
Ac 19:36 Now·then, with·these·things being indisputable, it·
Ac 24:8 concerning all these·things of·which we·ourselves
Ac 25:9 to·be·judged concerning these·things before me?
Ac 25:20 and·there to·be·judged concerning these·matters.
Ac 26:21 "Because·of these·things, the Judeans, upon·
Ac 26:26 king is·fully·acquainted concerning these·things, to
Ac 26:26 *for* not any·one of·these·things, not·even·one·thing
Heb 13:11 For the bodies of·these animals, whose blood is·
Mt 6:29 in all his glory, was·arrayed as one of·these.
Mt 6:32 that yeu·have·need of·absolutely·all these·things.
2Pe 1:4 in·order·that through these, yeu·may·become
2Pe 1:12 yeu always concerning these·things, even·though
2Pe 1:15 *the ability* to·make recollection of·these·things.
2Pe 3:11 Accordingly, with·all these·things being·dissolved,
2Pe 3:16 speaking in them concerning these·things, in which
Tit 3:8 And concerning these·things, I·resolve for·you to·
1Co 9:15 I·myself used not·even·one of·these·things, and
2Ti 2:21 ·purify himself from these·things, he·shall·be a·
3Jn 1:4 I·have no joy even·greater·than these·things, that I·
Rv 18:15 "The merchants of·these·things, the·ones

EG5130 (2x)
Lk 12:29 and do·not be·in·suspense *concerning these·things*.
2Pe 1:12 *already* personally·knowing *these·things* and *are*

G5131 τράγος trágôs *n.* (4x)
Roots:G5176 Compare:G0122 G2055 G2056 xLangEquiv:H6260

G5131 N-GPM τράγων (4x)
Heb 9:12 ·not through blood of·adult·male·goats and calves,
Heb 9:13 if the blood of·bulls and of·adult·male·goats (and
Heb 9:19 the blood of·calves and of·adult·male·goats, with
Heb 10:4 and of·adult·male·goats to·remove moral·failures.

G5132 τρά•πεζα trápêza *n.* (15x)
Roots:G5064 G3979 xLangEquiv:H7979

G5132.1 N-NSF τράπεζα (2x)
Heb 9:2 the Menorah·Lampstand, and the Table, and the
Rm 11:9 says, "Let their table be·made into a·snare, and

G5132.1 N-APF τραπέζας (3x)
Jn 2:15 moneychangers' money and overturned the tables.
Mt 21:12 and he·overturned the tables of·the moneychangers
Mk 11:15 he·overturned the tables of·the moneychangers

G5132.1 N-GSF τραπέζης (7x)
Lk 16:21 falling from the wealthy·man's table. Moreover,
Lk 22:21 of·the·one handing me over *is* with me on the table.
Lk 22:30 ·may·eat and may·drink at my table in my kingdom
Mt 15:27 the·ones falling from the table of·their owners."
Mk 7:28 For even the puppies beneath the table eat from the
1Co 10:21 ·belong to·*the*·Lord's table and·also to·*the*·table
1Co 10:21 ·*the*·Lord's table and·also to·*the*·table of·demons.

G5132.2 N-ASF τράπεζαν (1x)
Ac 16:34 he·placed·forth a·meal·table and leaped·for·joy,

G5132.2 N-DPF τραπέζαις (1x)
Ac 6:2 the Redemptive-word of·God to·attend to·meal·tables.

G5132.3 N-ASF τράπεζαν (1x)
Lk 19:23 my money over *to* the bank, that at·my·coming, I·

G5133 τρα•πεζίτης trapêzítēs *n.* (1x)
Roots:G5132

G5133 N-DPM τραπεζίταις (1x)
Mt 25:27 ·for you to·cast my money to·the bankers, and *then*

G5134 τραῦμα traûma *n.* (1x)
Roots:G5103-1 Compare:G4127 G1668 See:G2352 G5147 G5149 G1626

G5134 N-APN τραύματα (1x)
Lk 10:34 *him*, he·bound·up his wounds, pouring·in oil and

G5135 τραυματίζω traumatízō *v.* (2x)
Roots:G5134

G5135 V-AAP-NPM τραυματίσαντες (1x)
Lk 20:12 a·third. But also wounding this·man, they·cast·

G5135 V-RPP-APM τετραυματισμένους (1x)
Ac 19:16 of·that house naked and having·been·wounded.

G5136 τραχηλίζω trachēlízō *v.* (1x)
Roots:G5137

G5136.2 V-RPP-NPN τετραχηλισμένα (1x)
Heb 4:13 and having·been·vulnerably·exposed to·his eyes, to

G5137 τράχηλος tráchēlōs *n.* (7x)
Roots:G5143 Compare:G0979 G2222 See:G4644 G5136 xLangAlso:H6677

G5137.1 N-ASM τράχηλον (7x)
Lk 15:20 ·fell upon his neck and earnestly·kissed him.
Lk 17:2 millstone be·set around his neck, and *that* it·has·
Ac 15:10 God, to·put a·yoke upon the neck of·the disciples,
Ac 20:37 upon Paul's neck, they·were·earnestly·kissing him,
Mt 18:6 millstone should·be·hung upon his neck, and *that*
Mk 9:42 a·mill stone be·set around his neck, and *that* it·has·
Rm 16:4 who risked their·own necks on·behalf·of·my soul,

G5138 τραχύς trachýs *adj.* (2x)
Roots:G4486 Compare:G3006

G5138 A-NPF τραχεῖαι (1x)
Lk 3:5 *path*, and the rough,·jagged roadways *shall·be made*

G5138 A-APM τραχεῖς (1x)
Ac 27:29 they·should·fall into rough,·jagged places, after·

G5139 Τραχωνῖτις Trachōnîtis *n/l.* (1x)
Roots:G5138

G5139.2 N/L-GSF Τραχωνίτιδος (1x)
Lk 3:1 of·Jetur and the·region of·Trachonitis, and with·

G5140 τρεῖς treîs *n.* (67x)
τρία tría [neuter]
See:G5151

G5140 N-NPM τρεῖς (15x)
Lk 12:52 having·been·thoroughly·divided, three against two
Ac 10:19 declared to·him, "Behold, three men seek you.
Ac 11:11 ·this·same·hour, three men were·standing·over *the*
Mt 18:20 two or three are having·been·gathered·together in
1Co 14:27 ·*it·be* two or at·the most three·men, and a·portion
1Co 14:29 Now *let* prophets speak two or three, and *let* the
1Jn 5:7 Because there·are three, the·ones testifying in the
1Jn 5:7 Word, and the Holy Spirit. And these three are one.
1Jn 5:8 And there·are three, the·ones testifying on the earth:
1Jn 5:8 water, and the blood. And the three are in the one.
Rv 6:6 for·a·denarius, and three dry·measures of·barley
Rv 21:13 On *the* east *are* three gates; on *the* north *are* three
Rv 21:13 gates; on *the* north *are* three gates; on *the* south
Rv 21:13 gates; on *the* south *are* three gates; *and* on *the* west
Rv 21:13 *are* three gates; *and* on *the* west *are* three gates.

G5140 N-NPN τρία (1x)
1Co 13:13 And right·now, these three·things continue: Trust

G5140 N-APM τρεῖς (8x)
Jn 2:6 ·room·for two or three ten·gallon·measures apiece.
Lk 1:56 together with·her about three lunar·months and·then
Lk 11:5 'Friend, kindly·lend me three loaves·of·bread,
Ac 7:20 ·nurtured in his father's house three lunar·months.
Ac 19:8 ·with·clarity for·a·span·of three lunar·months,
Ac 20:3 continuing *there* also *for* three lunar·months. *But*
Ac 28:11 on the island *for* three lunar·months, we·sailed·
Jac 5:17 ·not shower·rain on the earth *for* three years and six

G5140 N-APF τρεῖς (19x)
Lk 2:46 And after three days, it·happened *that* they·found
Lk 9:33 here, and we·should·make three tabernacles; one·
Ac 9:9 And he·was three days not looking·about, and neither
Ac 25:1 Now·then, three days after walking·over into·the
Ac 28:7 He·hosted *us for* three days courteously.
Ac 28:12 at Syracuse, we·stayed·over *for* three days.
Ac 28:17 And after three days, it·happened *that* Paul called·
Mt 12:40 For just·as Jonah was three days and three nights in
Mt 12:40 Jonah was three days and three nights in the belly
Mt 12:40 the Son of·Clay·Man† shall·be three days and three
Mt 12:40 ·Man† shall·be three days and three nights in the
Mt 15:32 even·now they·continue·on with·me *for* three days,
Mt 17:4 If you·want, we·should·make three tabernacles here
Mt 27:63 still living, 'After three days, I·am·awakened.
Mk 8:2 ·now they·continue·on with·me *for* three days and
Mk 8:31 to·be·killed, and·then after three days to·rise·up.
Mk 9:5 here. And we·should·make three tabernacles: one
Rv 11:9 they·shall·look·upon their corpses three and a·half
Rv 11:11 And after the three and a·half days, *the* Spirit of·

G5140 N-APN τρία (8x)
Lk 4:25 heaven was·shut·up for·a·span·of three years and six
Lk 13:7 'Behold, *for* three years, I·come seeking fruit on
Lk 13:21 took *and* incorporated into three seah·measures of·
Ac 17:2 and over three Sabbaths he·was·having·discussions
Gal 1:18 Then after three years, I·went·up to JeruSalem to·
Mt 13:33 a·woman incorporated *it* into three seah·measures
Rv 16:13 And I·saw three impure spirits like frogs *come* out
Rv 16:19 And the Great City became three parts, and the

G5140 N-DPM τρισίν (2x)
Lk 12:52 ·divided, three against two, and two against three.
Heb 10:28 ·from compassion upon two or three witnesses.

G5140 N-DPF τρισίν (4x)
Jn 2:19 this temple, and in three days I·shall·awaken it.
Jn 2:20 was·built, and you, in three days, shall·awaken it?
Mt 27:40 Temple and building *it* in three days, save yourself.
Mk 15:29 the Temple and building *it* in three days,

G5140 N-GPM τριῶν (6x)
Lk 10:36 "So·then, which of·these three·men seems to·you
Mt 18:16 that "at *the* mouth of·two or three witnesses every
2Co 13:1 At *the* mouth of·two or three witnesses shall every
1Ti 5:19 "'except at *the mouth* of·two or three witnesses.'"
Rv 8:13 voices of·the trumpet of·the three angels, the·ones
Rv 9:18 By these three, the third·part of·the men·of·clay†

G5140 N-GPF τριῶν (4x)
Ac 5:7 And it·was about an·interval of·three hours, and his
Ac 28:15 *the* Forum of·Appius and *the* Three Taverns, which
Mt 26:61 Temple of·God and to·build it after three days.'"
Mk 14:58 made·by·hand, and after three days I·shall·build

G5141 τρέμω trĕmō *v.* (4x)
Compare:G5425 G5399

G5141 V-PAI-3P τρέμουσιν (1x)
2Pe 2:10 they·do·not tremble·with·fear while·reviling

G5141 V-PAP-NSF τρέμουσα (2x)
Lk 8:47 she·was·not hidden, came trembling; and falling·
Mk 5:33 ·fearing and·also trembling, personally·knowing

G5141 V-PAP-NSM τρέμων (1x)
Ac 9:6 And trembling and being·amazed, he·declared,

G5142 τρέφω trĕphō *v.* (8x)
Roots:G5157 See:G1625 G2353
G5142.2 V-PAI-3S τρέφει (2x)
Lk 12:24 nor·even a·barn, yet God nourishes them. "By·
Mt 6:26 yet yeur heavenly Father nourishes them. Are·not
G5142.2 V-PAS-3P τρέφωσιν (1x)
Rv 12:6 ·ready by God, that they·should·nourish her there a·
G5142.2 V-PPI-3S τρέφεται (1x)
Rv 12:14 her place, where she·is·nourished there a·season,
G5142.2 V-PPN τρέφεσθαι (1x)
Ac 12:20 ·of their country *needed* to·be·nourished by the
G5142.2 V-AAI-1P ἐθρέψαμεν (1x)
Mt 25:37 did·we·see you hungering, and nourished *you*?
G5142.2 V-AAI-2P ἐθρέψατε (1x)
Jac 5:5 and lived·luxuriously. Yeu·nourished yeur hearts,
G5142.3 V-RPP-NSM τεθραμμένος (1x)
Lk 4:16 he·was having·been·nurtured·and·reared. And

G5143 τρέχω trĕchō *v.* (20x)
δρέμω drĕmō
[(base G1408) in certain tenses]
τράχω trăchō [Doric/Dorian Greek]
Compare:G1408 G3908-1 See:G0665-1 G1532 G1998 G4063 G4370 G4890 G4936 G1303-6 G2359 xLangEquiv:H7323
G5143.1 V-PAI-1S τρέχω (1x)
1Co 9:26 Now·then, in·this·manner I·myself do·run, *but* not
G5143.1 V-PAI-3S τρέχει (1x)
Jn 20:2 So·then she·runs and comes to Simon Peter and to
G5143.1 V-PAI-3P τρέχουσιν (1x)
1Co 9:24 running in a·stadium·race in·fact all run, but *that*
G5143.1 V-PAM-2P τρέχετε (1x)
1Co 9:24 the prize? In·this·manner run, in·order·that yeu·
G5143.1 V-PAP-GSM τρέχοντος (1x)
Rm 9:16 *it*, nor·even on·the·one running *for·it·as·a·prize*,
G5143.1 V-PAP-GPM τρεχόντων (1x)
Rv 9:9 ·sound of·chariots, of·many horses running to battle.
G5143.1 V-PAP-NPM τρέχοντες (1x)
1Co 9:24 ·know that the·ones running in a·stadium·race in·
G5143.1 V-PAS-1S τρέχω (1x)
Gal 2:2 being·of·reputation, lest·somehow I·should·run, or
G5143.1 V-PAS-1P τρέχωμεν (1x)
Heb 12:1 moral·failure— we·should·run (through patient·
G5143.1 V-IAI-2P ἐτρέχετε (1x)
Gal 5:7 Yeu·were·running well. Who cut·into·yeur·path
G5143.1 V-IAI-3P ἔτρεχον (1x)
Jn 20:4 But the two·men were·running at·the·same·time, yet
G5143.1 V-2AAI-1S ἔδραμον (2x)
Gal 2:2 lest·somehow I·should·run, or did·run, for naught.
Php 2:16 day of·Anointed-One that I·did·not run for naught
G5143.1 V-2AAI-3S ἔδραμεν (2x)
Lk 24:12 But rising·up, Peter ran to the chamber·tomb, and
Mk 5:6 Jesus from a·distance, he·ran and fell·prostrate to·
G5143.1 V-2AAI-3P ἔδραμον (1x)
Mt 28:8 and with·great joy, they·ran to·announce *it* to·his
G5143.1 V-2AAP-NSM δραμών (3x)
Lk 15:20 And·then running, he·affectionately·fell upon his
Mt 27:48 one from·among them, after·running and taking a·
Mk 15:36 And one·man, after·running and overfilling a·
G5143.2 V-PAS-3S τρέχῃ (1x)
2Th 3:1 ·the Lord may·run·unhindered and may·be·glorified,

G5144 τριά•κοντα triákŏnta *n.* (11x)
See:G5140 G5144-9
G5144.1 N-NUI τριάκοντα (6x)
Jn 6:19 having·rowed about twenty·five or thirty stadia,
Lk 3:23 Jesus himself was about thirty years·of·age, being
Gal 3:17 having·occurred four·hundred and thirty years after
Mt 26:15 they·settled·with·him for·thirty pieces·of·silver.
Mt 27:3 returned·back the thirty pieces·of·silver to·the
Mt 27:9 "And they·took the thirty pieces·of·silver, the price
G5144.2 N-NUI τριάκοντα (4x)
Mt 13:8 some *seed* sixtyfold, and some *seed* thirtyfold.
Mt 13:23 some *seed* sixtyfold, and some *seed* thirtyfold."
Mk 4:8 and it·was·bearing *fruit*: one *seed* thirtyfold, and one
Mk 4:20 *it*, and bear·fruit: one *seed* thirtyfold, and one *seed*
G5144.3 N-NUI τριακονταοκτώ (1x)
Jn 5:5 was there, being in the sickness thirty-eight years.

G5145 τρια•κόσιοι triakŏsiŏi *n.* (2x)
Roots:G5140 G1540
G5145 N-GPM τριακοσίων (2x)
Jn 12:5 why was·it·not sold·off for·three·hundred denarii
Mk 14:5 ·be·sold·off for·upwards·of three·hundred denarii

G5146 τρί•βολος trĭbŏlŏs *n.* (2x)
Roots:G5140 G1002-1 Compare:G0173 xLangEquiv:H1863 xLangAlso:H2757
G5146.2 N-APM τριβόλους (1x)
Heb 6:8 ·forth 'thorns and spear·thistles' *is* disqualified, and
G5146.2 N-GPM τριβόλων (1x)
Mt 7:16 ·of·grapes from thorns, or figs from spear·thistles?

G5147 τρίβος trĭbŏs *n.* (1x)
Compare:G5163 G1353-1 G3598 G4646 G3961 G0824-2 See:G5131 G5134 G2161-1 G1625-3 xLangAlso:H5410 H0734 H4546
EG5147.1 (1x)
Lk 3:5 ·paths shall·be *made* into a·straight *path*, and the

G5148 τρι•ετία triĕtía *n.* (1x)
Roots:G5140 G2094
G5148.2 N-ASF τριετίαν (1x)
Ac 20:31 ·alert, remembering that for·three·years, I·did·not

G5149 τρίζω trízō *v.* (1x)
Compare:G0229 G3039
G5149.2 V-PAI-3S τρίζει (1x)
Mk 9:18 and he·foams·at·the·mouth and grates his teeth

G5150 τρί•μηνον trímēnŏn *adj.* (1x)
Roots:G5140 G3376
G5150 A-ASN τρίμηνον (1x)
Heb 11:23 (being·born) was·hid three·lunar·months by his

G5151 τρίς trís *adv.* (12x)
Roots:G5140 Compare:G1810-1
G5151 ADV τρίς (12x)
Jn 13:38 crow, until you·shall·utterly·deny me three·times.
Lk 22:34 before you·shall·utterly·deny three·times, *saying*
Lk 22:61 crowing, you·shall·utterly·deny me three·times."
Ac 10:16 Now this occurred three·times, and the vessel was·
Ac 11:10 And this occurred three·times, and absolutely·all
Mt 26:34 crowing, you·shall·utterly·deny me three·times."
Mt 26:75 crowing, you·shall·utterly·deny me three·times."
Mk 14:30 twice, you·shall·utterly·deny me three·times."
Mk 14:72 twice, you·shall·utterly·deny me three·times."
2Co 11:25 I·was·beaten·with·rods three·times, I·was·stoned
2Co 11:25 ·stoned once, I·was·shipwrecked three·times, *and*
2Co 12:8 Lord three·times in·order·that it·should·withdraw

G5152 τρί•στεγον trístĕgŏn *n.* (1x)
Roots:G5140 G4721
G5152.2 N-GSN τριστέγου (1x)
Ac 20:9 he·fell down from the third·story and was·taken·up

G5153 τρισ•χίλιοι trischíliŏi *n.* (1x)
Roots:G5151 G5507
G5153 N-NPF τρισχίλιαι (1x)
Ac 2:41 about three·thousand souls were·placed·alongside

G5154 τρίτος trítŏs *adj.* (57x)
Roots:G5140
xLangEquiv:H7992
G5154.1 A-NSM τρίτος (7x)
Lk 20:31 And the third took her, and in·like·manner, the
Mt 22:26 second also, and the third, even·unto the seventh.
Mk 12:21 ·himself leave offspring†. And the third likewise.
Rv 8:10 And the third angel sounded, and there·fell a·great
Rv 14:9 And a·third angel followed them, saying with a·loud
Rv 16:4 And the third angel poured·out his vial into the
Rv 21:19 the second, sapphire; the third, chalcedony; the
G5154.1 A-NSF τρίτη (3x)
Ac 2:15 yeu assume, for it·is *but the* third hour of·the·day.
Mk 15:25 And it·was *at the* third hour *after dawn* that they·
Rv 11:14 went·away; behold, the third woe comes swiftly.
G5154.1 A-NSN τρίτον (1x)
Rv 4:7 *is* like a·calf, and the third living·being *is* having the
G5154.1 A-ASM τρίτον (1x)
Lk 20:12 And he·further·proceeded to·send a·third. But also
G5154.1 A-ASF τρίτην (3x)
Lk 24:21 ·all these·things, today marks this third day since
Mt 20:3 "And going·forth *midmorning* about the third hour,
Rv 6:5 *the Lamb* opened·up the third official·seal, I·heard
G5154.1 A-DSF τρίτῃ (15x)
Jn 2:1 And on·the third day, there·was a·wedding in Qanah
Lk 9:22 to·be·killed, and to·be·awakened on·the third day."
Lk 12:38 or should·come in the third watch, and should·
Lk 13:32 and on·the third *day* I·am·completely·finished.'
Lk 18:33 ·kill him. And on·the third day, he·shall·rise·up.
Lk 24:7 and to·be·crucified, and on·the third day to·rise·up.'
Lk 24:46 to·rise·up from·among dead·men on·the third day.
Ac 10:40 ·one, God awakened on·the third day and gave
Ac 27:19 And on·the third *day*, with·our·own·hands, we·
Mt 16:21 to·be·killed, and to·be·awakened on·the third day.
Mt 17:23 him, and on·the third day he·shall·be·awakened."
Mt 20:19 *him*. And on·the third day, he·shall·rise·up.
Mk 9:31 after·being·killed, he·shall·rise·up on·the third day.
Mk 10:34 ·kill him, and on·the third day he·shall·rise·up."
1Co 15:4 ·has·been·awakened on·the third day according·to
G5154.1 A-GSM τρίτου (1x)
2Co 12:2 ·a·man being·snatched·up unto *the* third heaven.
G5154.1 A-GSF τρίτης (2x)
Ac 23:23 ·traverse unto Caesarea from *the* third hour of·the
Mt 27:64 the grave to·be·made·secure until the third day, lest
G5154.1 A-GSN τρίτου (1x)
Rv 6:5 official·seal, I·heard the third living·being saying,
G5154.1 ADV τρίτον (1x)
1Co 12:28 second prophets, third instructors, after·that *the*·
G5154.2 A-NSN τρίτον (10x)
Rv 8:7 earth; and the third·part of·the trees was·completely·
Rv 8:8 the sea, and the third·part of·the sea became blood;
Rv 8:9 and the third·part of·the creatures (the·ones in the sea
Rv 8:9 died; and the third·part of·the ships were·thoroughly·
Rv 8:11 ·to·as Wormwood, and the third·part *of·the waters*
Rv 8:12 sounded, and the third·part of·the sun was·pounded,
Rv 8:12 sun was·pounded, and the third·part of·the moon,
Rv 8:12 ·part of·the moon, and the third·part of·the stars, in·
Rv 8:12 ·that the third·part of·them should·be·darkened, and
Rv 9:18 these three, the third·part of·the men·of·clay† were·
G5154.2 A-ASN τρίτον (4x)
Rv 8:10 and it·fell upon the third·part of·the rivers, and
Rv 8:12 day should·not shine·forth for·the third·part of·it,
Rv 9:15 they·should·kill the third·part of·the men·of·clay†.
Rv 12:4 And his tail dragged the third·part of·the stars of·the
G5154.3 A-ASN τρίτον (7x)
Jn 21:14 This *is* even·now a·third·time *that* Jesus is·made·
Jn 21:17 He·says to·him the third·time, "Simon, *son* of·
Jn 21:17 because he·declared to·him the third·time, "Do·
Lk 23:22 And *for* the third·time, he·declared to·them, "For
Mk 14:41 And he·comes the third·time, and *sternly* says to·
2Co 12:14 I·am at·the·ready *for* a·third·time to·come to yeu
2Co 13:1 This *is the* third·time I·am·coming to yeu.
G5154.3 A-GSN τρίτου (1x)
Mt 26:44 again, he·prayed for a·third·time, declaring the

G5155 τρίχινος tríchinŏs *adj.* (1x)
Roots:G2359 Compare:G2053
G5155.1 A-NSM τρίχινος (1x)
Rv 6:12 became *as* black as sackcloth made·of·hair, and the

G5156 τρόμος trŏmŏs *n.* (5x)
Roots:G5141
G5156 N-NSM τρόμος (1x)
Mk 16:8 were·having trembling·of·fear and astonishment.
G5156 N-DSM τρόμῳ (1x)
1Co 2:3 and in reverent·fear, and in much trembling.
G5156 N-GSM τρόμου (3x)
Php 2:12 , with reverent·fear and trembling, accomplish the
2Co 7:15 with reverent·fear and trembling yeu·accepted him.
Eph 6:5 flesh) with reverent·fear and trembling, with fidelity

G5157 τροπή trôpḗ *n.* (1x)
See:G5158 G4762
G5157.1 N-GSF τροπῆς (1x)
Jac 1:17 an·alteration, nor *the* slightest·shadow of·turning.

G5158 τρόπος trốpôs *n.* (13x)
See:G5157
G5158.1 N-ASM τρόπον (1x)
Ac 27:25 ·manner, it·shall turn·out according·to that·which
G5158.1 N-DSM τρόπῳ (1x)
2Th 3:16 throughout every *matter* at every turn. The Lord *be*
G5158.2 N-ASM τρόπον (4x)
Ac 15:11 to·be·saved; according·to that manner, they·also
Rm 3:2 Much in·each and·every manner. For in·fact, first·of·
Jud 1:7 As *in* like manner to·these *angels*, Sodom and
2Th 2:3 ·delude yeu in not·even·one manner, because *that*
G5158.2 N-DSM τρόπῳ (1x)
Php 1:18 *Just that* moreover, in·every manner, whether in·
G5158.3 N-NSM τρόπος (1x)
Heb 13:5 *Let·yeur* lifestyle *be* without·fondness·of·money,
G5158.4 N-ASM τρόπον (5x)
Lk 13:34 ·gather your children, as a·hen *gathers* her brood
Ac 1:11 ·come in·this·manner as yeu·distinctly·viewed him
Ac 7:28 want to·execute me, as you·executed the Egyptian
Mt 23:37 ·gather your children as a·hen completely·gathers
2Ti 3:8 Now as Jannes and Jambres stood·opposed·to Moses

G5159 τροπο•φορέω trôpôphôréō *v.* (1x)
Roots:G5158 G5409
G5159 V-AAI-3S ἐτροποφόρησεν (1x)
Ac 13:18 a·time of·forty·years, he·bore·with their lifestyle

G5160 τροφή trôphḗ *n.* (16x)
Roots:G5142 Compare:G1033 G1035 G1305 G4620 G5315 See:G5162
G5160.1 N-NSF τροφή (2x)
Heb 5:14 But the solid nourishment is *for* the completely·
Mt 3:4 his loins, and his nourishment was locusts and wild
G5160.1 N-ASF τροφήν (1x)
Ac 9:19 after·receiving nourishment, he·was·strengthened.
G5160.1 N-GSF τροφῆς (8x)
Lk 12:23 soul is more·than the physical·nourishment, and the
Ac 2:46 they·were·partaking of·nourishment in exuberant·
Ac 27:33 ·all·of·them to·partake of·nourishment, saying,
Ac 27:34 I·implore yeu to·each·take *some* nourishment, for
Ac 27:36 ·outlook, and they·each·took nourishment.
Ac 27:38 after·being·stuffed·full·to·excess with·nourishment
Heb 5:12 ·having need of·milk and not of·solid nourishment,
Mt 6:25 the soul more·than the physical·nourishment, and
G5160.2 N-GSF τροφῆς (1x)
Ac 14:17 filling·up our hearts with·nurturing and euphoria.
G5160.3 N-ASF τροφήν (1x)
Mt 24:45 to·give them the provision·of·food in due·season?
G5160.3 N-APF τροφάς (1x)
Jn 4:8 city in·order·that they·may·buy provisions·of·food).
G5160.3 N-GSF τροφῆς (2x)
Mt 10:10 the workman is deserving of·his provision·of·food.
Jac 2:15 ·be being·deficient of·the daily provision·of·food,

G5161 Τρόφιμος Trốphimôs *n/p.* (3x)
Roots:G5160
G5161.2 N/P-NSM Τρόφιμος (1x)
Ac 20:4 and *both* Tychicus and Trophimus of·Asia,
G5161.2 N/P-ASM Τρόφιμον (2x)
Ac 21:29 previously·having·clearly·seen Trophimus the
2Ti 4:20 remained at Corinth, but Trophimus, being·sick, I·

G5162 τροφός trôphốs *n.* (1x)
Roots:G5142 See:G5160
G5162.3 N-NSF τροφός (1x)
1Th 2:7 even·as a·nurturing·mother would cherishingly·

G5163 τροχιά trôchiá *n.* (1x)
Roots:G5164 Compare:G5147 G3598
G5163.1 N-APF τροχιάς (1x)
Heb 12:13 and make level tracks for·yeur feet, lest the lame

G5164 τροχός trôchốs *n.* (2x)
Roots:G5143 xLangAlso:H0212
G5164.3 N-ASM τροχόν (1x)
Jac 3:6 and setting·aflame the regular·course of·nature, and
EG5164.3 (1x)
Ac 9:3 And in the *regular·course·of* traversing, it·occurred

G5165 τρύβλιον trýbliôn *n.* (2x)
Compare:G3953 G4094
G5165 N-ASN τρύβλιον (1x)
Mk 14:20 the·one who·is·dipping with me in the dish.
G5165 N-DSN τρυβλίῳ (1x)
Mt 26:23 hand with me in the dish, the·same shall·hand me

G5166 τρυγάω trygáō *v.* (3x)
See:G1625-5
G5166 V-PAI-3P τρυγῶσιν (1x)
Lk 6:44 do·they·collect a·cluster·of·grapes for·vintage.
G5166 V-AAI-3S ἐτρύγησεν (1x)
Rv 14:19 the earth, and collected·for·vintage the vine of·the
G5166 V-AAM-2S τρύγησον (1x)
Rv 14:18 sharp sickle and collect·for·vintage the clusters of·

G5167 τρυγών trygốn *n.* (1x)
Compare:G4058 See:G5149
xLangEquiv:H8449
G5167 N-GPF τρυγόνων (1x)
Lk 2:24 "'a·braced·pair of·turtledoves or two of·the·

G5168 τρυμαλιά trymaliá *n.* (2x)
Compare:G5169 G3788 See:G5134 G5147 G5176
xLangEquiv:H5345 xLangAlso:H5357 H5347
G5168.4 N-GSF τρυμαλιᾶς (2x)
Lk 18:25 a·camel to·enter·in through a·tiny·inlet of·a·needle,
Mk 10:25 ·camel to·enter through the tiny·inlet of·the needle

G5169 τρύπημα trýpēma *n.* (1x)
Compare:G5168 G3659 G3692
G5169.4 N-GSN τρυπήματος (1x)
Mt 19:24 ·camel to·go through *the* tiny·hole of·a·needle than

G5170 Τρύφαινα Trýphaina *n/p.* (1x)
Roots:G5172
G5170.2 N/P-ASF Τρύφαιναν (1x)
Rm 16:12 Greet Tryphaena and Tryphosa, the·ones laboring·

G5171 τρυφάω trypháō *v.* (1x)
Roots:G5172 Compare:G4684 G4763 See:G1792
G5171-1 xLangAlso:H6026
G5171 V-AAI-2P ἐτρυφήσατε (1x)
Jac 5:5 Yeu·indulged·in·delicate·luxury on the earth, and

G5172 τρυφή tryphḗ *n.* (2x)
Roots:G2362-3 Compare:G4684-1 G4764 G3045
See:G5171 xLangAlso:H4574
G5172 N-ASF τρυφήν (1x)
2Pe 2:13 in the daytime *to·be* a·delicate·luxury. *They·are*
G5172 N-DSF τρυφῇ (1x)
Lk 7:25 attire, also subsisting in·delicate·luxury, are in the

G5173 Τρυφῶσα Tryphỗsa *n/p.* (1x)
Roots:G5172
G5173.2 N/P-ASF Τρυφῶσαν (1x)
Rm 16:12 Greet Tryphaena and Tryphosa, the·ones laboring·

G5174 Τρωάς Trōás *n/l.* (6x)
G5174 N/L-ASF Τρωάδα (3x)
Ac 16:8 And passing·by Mysia, they·walked·down to Troas.
Ac 20:6 and we·came to them in Troas in·only five days,
2Co 2:12 Now after·coming to Troas for the good·news of·
G5174 N/L-DSF Τρωάδι (2x)
Ac 20:5 ·beforehand, these·men were·awaiting us at Troas.
2Ti 4:13 The cape that I·left·behind at Troas with Carpus, *as*
G5174 N/L-GSF Τρωάδος (1x)
Ac 16:11 sailing from Troas, we·sailed·straight to Samos·

G5175 Τρωγύλλιον Trōgýlliōn *n/l.* (1x)
G5175 N/L-DSN Τρωγυλλίῳ (1x)
Ac 20:15 And after·abiding in Trogyllium, the following *day*

G5176 τρώγω trṓgō *v.* (6x)
Roots:G5167 G5149 G5134 G5147 Compare:G3145
G5176.1 V-PAP-NSM τρώγων (5x)
Jn 6:54 "The·one chewing my flesh, and drinking my blood,
Jn 6:56 The·one chewing my flesh, and drinking my blood,
Jn 6:57 the Father, so the·one chewing me, he·likewise
Jn 6:58 and died. The·one chewing this bread shall·live into
Jn 13:18 ·fulfilled, "The·one chewing the bread with me
G5176.1 V-PAP-NPM τρώγοντες (1x)
Mt 24:38 the Deluge, *they·were* chewing *a·full·meal* and

G5176-1 Τσαδώκ Tsadốq *n/p.* (2x)
Σαδώκ Sadṓk [Greek, Septuagint]
צָדוֹק tsạdôq [Hebrew]
Roots:H6659 See:G4524 G4523
G5176-1.2 N/P-PRI Τσαδώκ (2x)
Mt 1:14 Now Azzur begot Tsadoq, and Tsadoq begot Achim,
Mt 1:14 Azzur begot Tsadoq, and Tsadoq begot Achim, and

G5176-3 Τσαρεφάθ Tsarêpháth *n/p.* (1x)
Σάρεπτα Sárêpta [Greek, Septuagint]
צָרְפַת tsarᵉphath [Hebrew]
Roots:H6886 See:G4558
G5176-3.2 N/L-HEB Τσαρεφάθ (1x)
Lk 4:26 sent, except into *the city* Tsarephath of·Tsidon, to a·

G5176-5 Τσιδών Tsidṓn *n/l.* (11x)
Σιδών Sidṓn [Greek, Septuagint]
צִידוֹן tsiydôn [Hebrew]
Roots:H6721 Compare:G5403 See:G5176-6 G4605
G5176-5.2 N/L-ASF Τσιδῶνα (2x)
Ac 27:3 *of·sailing*, we·moored at Tsidon. And·also treating
Mk 3:8 *from* around Tyre and Tsidon— after·hearing what·
G5176-5.2 N/L-DSF Τσιδῶνι (4x)
Lk 10:13 happened in Tyre and Tsidon, the·ones happening
Lk 10:14 ·shall·be more·tolerable for·Tyre and Tsidon at the
Mt 11:21 had·occurred in Tyre and Tsidon, long·ago they·
Mt 11:22 ·shall·be more·tolerable for·Tyre and Tsidon in *the*
G5176-5.2 N/L-GSF Τσιδῶνος (5x)
Lk 4:26 into *the city* Tsarephath of·Tsidon, to a·woman *who*
Lk 6:17 from·the sea·coast of·Tyre and Tsidon, who came
Mt 15:21 departed into the district of·Tyre and Tsidon.
Mk 7:24 into the common·borders of·Tyre and Tsidon. And
Mk 7:31 ·among the borders of·Tyre and Tsidon, he·came to

G5176-6 Τσιδώνιος Tsidṓniôs *adj/g.* (1x)
Roots:G5176-5 See:G4606
G5176-6 A/G-DPF Τσιδωνίοις (1x)
Ac 12:20 ·quarreling with·them·of·Tyre and Tsidon, but

G5176-7 Τσιών Tsiṓn *n/l.* (7x)
Σιών Siṓn [Greek, Septuagint]
צִיּוֹן tsiyôn [Hebrew]
Roots:H6726 See:G4622
G5176-7.2 N/L-PRI Τσιών (7x)
Jn 12:15 "Do·not be·afraid, O·Daughter of·Tsiyon!"
Heb 12:22 ·come·alongside Mount Tsiyon and the·living
Mt 21:5 ""Declare·yeu to·the daughter of·Tsiyon,"
Rm 9:33 "Behold, I·lay in Tsiyon a·stone of·stumbling and
Rm 11:26 shall·come from·out of·Tsiyon, the·one who·is·
1Pe 2:6 "Behold, I·lay in Tsiyon a·chief·corner stone,
Rv 14:1 a·Lamb standing on the Mount Tsiyon, and with him

G5177 τυγχάνω tyncháno̅ *v.* (13x)
τύχω týchō
τεύχω têúchō
Compare:G4940 G4046 G5180 See:G5088 G1487 G3756
G5177.3 V-PAP-NPM τυγχάνοντες (1x)
Ac 24:2 saying, "While·obtaining much peace on·account·
G5177.3 V-2AAN τυχεῖν (2x)
Lk 20:35 ·ones being·accounted·fully·worthy to·obtain that
Ac 27:3 ·traverse to his·friends to·obtain caring·hospitality.
G5177.3 V-2AAP-NSM τυχών (1x)
Ac 26:22 So·then after·obtaining assistance personally·from
G5177.3 V-2AAS-3P τύχωσιν (2x)
Heb 11:35 in·order·that they·may·obtain a·significantly·
2Ti 2:10 in·order·that they also may·obtain Salvation, the·
G5177.3 V-RAI-3S τέτευχεν (1x)

Tτ

Heb 8:6 ·fact, he·has·obtained a·more·superb public·service
G5177.4 V-2AAO-3S τύχοι (1x)
1Co 15:37 kernel, whether it·may·happen·to·be of·wheat or
G5177.5 V-2AAO-3S τύχοι (1x)
1Co 14:10 There·are, as·it·may·be, so·many kinds of·voices
G5177.5 V-2AAP-ASN τυχόν (1x)
1Co 16:6 And it·may·be·that I·shall·abide·nearby or even
G5177.6 V-2AAP-APF τυχούσας (1x)
Ac 19:11 ·doing miracles (*and* not the·ones being·typical),
G5177.7 V-2AAP-ASF τυχοῦσαν (1x)
Ac 28:2 an·affection·for·mankind† way·beyond·the·mark.
G5177.8 V-PAP-ASM τυγχάνοντα (1x)
Lk 10:30 ·*him*, went·off, leaving *him* more·than half·dead.

G5178 τυμπανίζω tympanízō *v.* (1x)
Roots:G5180
G5178.2 V-API-3P ἐτυμπανίσθησαν (1x)
Heb 11:35 And others were·torturously·beaten·to·death, not

G5179 τύπος týpôs *n.* (16x)
Roots:G5180 Compare:G1165 G5262 G5261 G4610-1 G1504 See:G0499 G5296 xLangAlso:H8403
G5179.3 N-ASM τύπον (2x)
Jn 20:25 “Unless I·may·see the imprint of·the nails in his
Jn 20:25 may·cast my finger into the imprint of·the nails, and
G5179.4 N-NSM τύπος (1x)
Rm 5:14 violation, who is a·figure of·the·one impending.
G5179.4 N-APM τύπους (1x)
Ac 7:43 god Remphan, the figures which yeu·made *in·order*
G5179.5 N-ASM τύπον (6x)
Ac 7:44 ·to the particular·pattern which he·had·clearly·seen.
Ac 23:25 he·wrote a·letter containing this particular·pattern:
Heb 8:5 ·things according·to the particular·pattern, the·one
Rm 6:17 of·*the*·heart *to·that* particular·pattern of·instruction
Php 3:17 ·as yeu·hold us *as* a·particular·pattern *of·conduct*.
Tit 2:7 ·yourself·forth *as* a·particular·pattern of·good works
G5179.6 N-NPM τύποι (1x)
1Co 10:11 these impressive·examples were·befalling them,
G5179.7 N-NPM τύποι (1x)
1Co 10:6 these·things were our imprinted·examples, for us
G5179.8 N-NSM τύπος (1x)
1Ti 4:12 become a·model·example of·the·ones·that·trust, in
G5179.8 N-NPM τύποι (1x)
1Pe 5:3 but·rather being model·examples to·the·little·flock.
G5179.8 N-ASM τύπον (1x)
2Th 3:9 ·give ourselves *to·be* a·model·example for·yeu·to·
G5179.8 N-APM τύπους (1x)
1Th 1:7 ·for yeu·to·become model·examples to·all·the·ones

G5180 τύπτω týptō *v.* (14x)
Compare:G3817 G3960 G4141 G4474 G5177 See:G5179
G5180.2 V-PAN τύπτειν (2x)
Lk 12:45 and should·begin to·beat the servant·boys and
Mt 24:49 and should·begin to·beat the fellow·slaves and·to·
G5180.2 V-PAP-NPM τύπτοντες (3x)
Lk 23:48 ·things happening, while·beating their·own chests,
Ac 21:32 and the soldiers, they·ceased beating Paul.
1Co 8:12 the brothers, and beating their weak conscience,
G5180.2 V-IAI-3S ἔτυπτεν (1x)
Lk 18:13 to the heaven, but·rather was·beating at his chest,
G5180.2 V-IAI-3P ἔτυπτον (3x)
Ac 18:17 all the Greeks were·beating *him* before the Bema·
Mt 27:30 they·took the reed and were·beating at his head.
Mk 15:19 And they·were·beating his head with·a·reed and
G5180.3 V-PAN τύπτειν (2x)
Ac 23:2 ·the·ones standing·nearby him to·pummel his mouth
Ac 23:3 him, “God is·about to·pummel you, O·wall having·
G5180.3 V-PAP-DSM τύπτοντι (1x)
Lk 6:29 “To·the·one pummeling you on the cheek, hold·
G5180.3 V-PPN τύπτεσθαι (1x)
Ac 23:3 *for* me to·be·pummeled contrary·to·Torah-Law?
G5180.3 V-IAI-3P ἔτυπτον (1x)
Lk 22:64 ·a·hood·over him, they·were·pummeling his face,

G5181 Τύραννος Týrannôs *n/p.* (1x)
Roots:G2962
G5181.2 N/P-GSM Τυράννου (1x)
Ac 19:9 ·auditorium of·a·certain·man *named* Tyrannus.

G5182 τυρβάζω tyrbázō *v.* (1x)
Compare:G2360 G4049 G5015 G4525 See:G2351
G5182 V-PPI-2S τυρβάζῃ (1x)
Lk 10:41 ·are·anxious and are·disturbed about many·things.

G5183 Τύριος Týriôs *n/g.* (1x)
Roots:G5184
G5183 N/G-DPM Τυρίοις (1x)
Ac 12:20 furiously·quarreling with·them·of·Tyre and Tsidon

G5184 Τύρος Týrôs *n/l.* (11x)
צֹר tsór [Hebrew]
Roots:H6865
G5184.2 N/L-ASF Τύρον (2x)
Ac 21:3 Syria, and we·moored at Tyre, for the sailing·ship
Mk 3:8 Jordan, and *from* around Tyre and Tsidon— after·
G5184.2 N/L-DSF Τύρῳ (4x)
Lk 10:13 if these miracles happened in Tyre and Tsidon, the·
Lk 10:14 it·shall·be more·tolerable for·Tyre and Tsidon at
Mt 11:21 occurring in yeu had·occurred in Tyre and Tsidon,
Mt 11:22 it·shall·be more·tolerable for·Tyre and Tsidon in
G5184.2 N/L-GSF Τύρου (5x)
Lk 6:17 and from·the sea·coast of·Tyre and Tsidon, who
Ac 21:7 ·accomplishing the voyage from Tyre, arrived at
Mt 15:21 departed into the district of·Tyre and Tsidon.
Mk 7:24 ·off into the common·borders of·Tyre and Tsidon.
Mk 7:31 ·forth from·among the borders of·Tyre and Tsidon,

G5185 τυφλός typhlós *adj.* (54x)
Roots:G5187 Compare:G2974 See:G5186
G5185.2 A-NSM τυφλός (16x)
Jn 9:2 his parents, in·order·that he·should·be·born blind?”
Jn 9:8 him previously that he·was blind) were·saying, “Is
Jn 9:18 him that he·was blind and received·his·sight, until
Jn 9:19 who yeu say was·born blind? So·then at·this·moment
Jn 9:20 ·know that this is our son, and that he·is·born blind.
Jn 9:24 the man·of·clay† that was blind, and they·declared
Jn 9:25 ·know, how·that being blind, at·this·moment, I·
Lk 6:39 “Is·it possible·for *the* blind to·guide *the* blind?
Lk 18:35 to Jericho, a·certain blind·man sat·down directly·
Ac 13:11 against you, and you·shall·be blind, not looking·at
Mt 12:22 ·demon was·brought·to·him, *being* blind and mute,
Mt 15:14 And if a·blind·man should·guide a·blind·man,
Mk 10:46 crowd, BarTimaeus the blind (a·son of·Timaeus)
Mk 10:51 for·you?” Then the blind·man declared·to·him,
2Pe 1:9 present, he·is blind, being·dangerously·nearsighted,
Rv 3:17 pitiable, helplessly·poor, blind, and naked.
G5185.2 A-NPM τυφλοί (10x)
Jn 9:39 and the·ones looking·about may·become blind.”
Jn 9:40 “¿! Are we·ourselves also blind?”
Jn 9:41 to·them, “If yeu·were blind, yeu·would not have
Lk 7:22 heard, that ·the·blind receive·their·sight, lame·men
Mt 9:27 passing·on from·there, two blind·men followed him
Mt 9:28 into the home, the blind·men came·alongside him.
Mt 11:5 blind·men receive·their·sight and lame·men walk,
Mt 15:14 Leave them. They·are blind guides of·blind·men.
Mt 20:30 behold, two blind·men are·sitting·down beside the
Mt 21:14 And blind·men and lame·men came·alongside him
G5185.2 A-VSM τυφλέ (1x)
Mt 23:26 “O·blind Pharisee, first purify the interior of·the
G5185.2 A-VPM τυφλοί (4x)
Mt 23:16 “Woe to·yeu, *yeu* blind guides, the·ones saying,
Mt 23:17 O·fools and blind·men! For which is·greater, the
Mt 23:19 O·fools and blind·men! For which *is* greater, the
Mt 23:24 O·blind guides, the·ones thoroughly·filtering·out
G5185.2 A-ASM τυφλόν (7x)
Jn 9:1 a·man·of·clay† who·was·blind from·out of·*his*·birth.
Jn 9:13 ·man to the Pharisees, the·one formerly *being* blind.
Lk 6:39 *the* blind to·guide *the* blind? Shall·they·not·indeed
Mt 12:22 ·cured him, such·for the blind and mute·man both
Mt 15:14 And if a·blind·man should·guide a·blind·man, both
Mk 8:22 BethSaida. And they·bring a·blind·man to·him and
Mk 10:49 And they·hollered·out·for the blind·man, saying
G5185.2 A-APM τυφλούς (4x)
Lk 14:13 totally·maimed·ones, lame·ones, blind·ones.
Lk 14:21 ·maimed·ones, and lame·ones, and blind·ones.’
Mt 15:30 themselves *those that·were* lame, blind, mute,
Mt 15:31 lame·ones walking, and blind·ones looking·about.
G5185.2 A-DSM τυφλῷ (1x)
Jn 9:17 They·say to·the blind·man again, “What·do you·
G5185.2 A-DPM τυφλοῖς (2x)
Lk 4:18 and recovery·of·sight to·the·blind, to·set·apart with
Lk 7:21 to·many *that·were* blind, he·graciously·bestowed the
G5185.2 A-GSM τυφλοῦ (4x)
Jn 9:6 he·smeared the clay over the eyes of·the blind·man,
Jn 9:32 ·man opened·up eyes of·one·having·been·born blind.
Jn 11:37 ·one opening·up the eyes of·the blind, able to·make
Mk 8:23 after·grabbing·hold of·the blind·man by·the hand,
G5185.2 A-GPM τυφλῶν (4x)
Jn 5:3 ·the·ones being·feeble were·laying·ill— blind, lame,
Jn 10:21 ¿!·Is a·demon able to·open·up blind eyes?
Mt 15:14 They·are blind guides of·blind·men. And if a·
Rm 2:19 within·yourself to·be a·guide of·blind·men, a·light
EG5185.2 (1x)
Mk 8:22 him in·order·that he·may·lay·hold *of·the* blind·man.

G5186 τυφλόω typhlóō *v.* (3x)
Roots:G5185
G5186.2 V-AAI-3S ἐτύφλωσεν (2x)
2Co 4:4 of·this present·age blinded the mental·perceptions of·
1Jn 2:11 ·is·heading, because the darkness blinded his eyes.
G5186.2 V-RAI-3S τετύφλωκεν (1x)
Jn 12:40 “He·has·blinded their eyes, and their heart he·has·

G5187 τυφόω typhóō *v.* (3x)
Roots:G5188 Compare:G2755
G5187.2 V-APP-NSM τυφωθείς (1x)
1Ti 3:6 lest being·inflated·with·self-conceit he·should·fall to
G5187.2 V-RPI-3S τετύφωται (1x)
1Ti 6:4 *then* he·has·been·inflated·with·self-conceit while·
G5187.2 V-RPP-NPM τετυφωμένοι (1x)
2Ti 3:4 rash, having·been·inflated·with·self-conceit, fond·

G5188 τύφω týphō *v.* (1x)
G5188.2 V-PPP-ASN τυφόμενον (1x)
Mt 12:20 and flax, being·smoldering, he·shall·not quench,

G5189 τυφωνικός typhōnikós *adj.* (1x)
Roots:G5188
G5189.2 A-NSM τυφωνικός (1x)
Ac 27:14 But not long after, a·typhoon-like wind slammed

G5190 Τυχικός Tychikós *n/p.* (5x)
Roots:G5177
G5190.2 N/P-NSM Τυχικός (3x)
Ac 20:4 TimoThy, and *both* Tychicus and Trophimus of·
Eph 6:21 how I·fare, Tychicus shall·make·known to·yeu all·
Col 4:7 Tychicus shall·make·known to·yeu all the·things
G5190.2 N/P-ASM Τύχικον (2x)
Tit 3:12 to you, or Tychicus, quickly·endeavor to·come to
2Ti 4:12 And Tychicus I·dispatched to Ephesus.

Υυ - Upsilon

G5191 ὑακίνθινος hyakínthinôs *adj.* (1x)
Roots:G5192 Compare:G4209 G2847 xLangAlso:H8504
G5191 A-APM ὑακινθίνους (1x)
Rv 9:17 ·chest·armor, fiery, like·deep·blue·hyacinth, and

G5192 ὑάκινθος hyákinthôs *n.* (1x)
xLangAlso:H8504
G5192 N-NSM ὑάκινθος (1x)
Rv 21:20 the eleventh, deep·blue·hyacinth; the twelfth,

G5193 ὑάλινος hyálinôs *adj.* (3x)
Roots:G5194
G5193 A-NSF ὑαλίνη (1x)
Rv 4:6 ·sight of·the throne *there·is* a·transparent,·glassy sea,
G5193 A-ASF ὑαλίνην (2x)
Rv 15:2 as a·transparent,·glassy sea having·been·mixed
Rv 15:2 — standing on the transparent,·glassy sea, having

G5194 ὕαλος hyálôs *n.* (2x)
See:G5205 G5193
G5194.2 N-NSM ὕαλος (1x)
Rv 21:21 CITY *was* pure gold, as nearly·transparent glass.
G5194.2 N-DSM ὑάλῳ (1x)
Rv 21:18 And the CITY *was* pure gold, like pure glass.

G5195 ὑβρίζω hybrízō *v.* (5x)
Roots:G5196 See:G5197 G1796
G5195 V-FPI-3S ὑβρισθήσεται (1x)
Lk 18:32 ·mocked, and shall·be·abusively·mistreated, and
G5195 V-PAI-2S ὑβρίζεις (1x)
Lk 11:45 saying these·things, you·abusively·mistreat us also
G5195 V-AAI-3P ὕβρισαν (1x)
Mt 22:6 ·hold of·his slaves, abusively·mistreated *them* and
G5195 V-AAN ὑβρίσαι (1x)
Ac 14:5 ·their rulers) to·abusively·mistreat *the ambassadors*
G5195 V-APP-NPM ὑβρισθέντες (1x)
1Th 2:2 and being·abusively·mistreated in Philippi, just·as

G5196 ὕβρις hýbris *n.* (3x)
Roots:G5228 Compare:G0984 G1796 G0983 See:G5195
G5196.2 N-DPF ὕβρεσιν (1x)
2Co 12:10 in weaknesses, in mistreatments, in dire·needs, in
G5196.3 N-ASF ὕβριν (1x)
Ac 27:21 Crete nor·also to·gain this battering and damage.
G5196.3 N-GSF ὕβρεως (1x)
Ac 27:10 voyage shall·be with a·battering and much

G5197 ὑβριστής hybristḗs *n.* (2x)
Roots:G5195
G5197.2 N-ASM ὑβριστήν (1x)
1Ti 1:13 and a·persecutor, and an·abusively·insolent·man.
G5197.2 N-APM ὑβριστάς (1x)
Rm 1:30 detesters·of·God, abusively·insolent, haughty,

G5198 ὑγιαίνω hygiaínō *v.* (12x)
Roots:G5199 See:G5199-1
G5198.1 V-PAN ὑγιαίνειν (1x)
3Jn 1:2 you to·prosper and to·be·healthy·and·sound, just·as
G5198.1 V-PAP-ASM ὑγιαίνοντα (2x)
Lk 7:10 being·sent found the sick slave healthy·and·sound.
Lk 15:27 because he·fully·received him healthy·and·sound.'
G5198.1 V-PAP-APM ὑγιαίνοντας (1x)
Tit 2:2 self-controlled, healthy·and·sound in·the trust, in·
G5198.1 V-PAP-DSF ὑγιαινούσῃ (3x)
Tit 1:9 to·exhort by the healthy·and·sound instruction and to·
Tit 2:1 is·suitable·for the healthy·and·sound instruction:
1Ti 1:10 ·set·opposed to·the healthy·and·sound instruction,
G5198.1 V-PAP-DPM ὑγιαίνουσιν (1x)
1Ti 6:3 does·not come·alongside having·healthy·and·sound
G5198.1 V-PAP-GSF ὑγιαινούσης (1x)
2Ti 4:3 ·not bear·with the healthy·and·sound instruction.
G5198.1 V-PAP-GPM ὑγιαινόντων (1x)
2Ti 1:13 Retain *the* primary·model of·healthy·and·sound,
G5198.1 V-PAP-NPM ὑγιαίνοντες (1x)
Lk 5:31 them, "The·ones being·healthy·and·sound have no
G5198.1 V-PAS-3P ὑγιαίνωσιν (1x)
Tit 1:13 in·order·that they·may·be·healthy·and·sound in the

G5199 ὑγιής hygiḗs *adj.* (14x)
Roots:G0837 See:G5198 G5199-1
G5199.1 A-NSM ὑγιής (5x)
Jn 5:4 was·made healthy·and·sound from·whatever ailment
Jn 5:6 ·him, "Do·you·want to·be·made healthy·and·sound?"
Jn 5:9 the man·of·clay† was healthy·and·sound. And he·
Jn 5:14 you·have·become healthy·and·sound; morally·fail
Ac 4:10 ·nearby in·the·sight of·yeu, healthy·and·sound.
G5199.1 A-NSF ὑγιής (4x)
Lk 6:10 his hand was·restored as·healthy·and·sound as the
Mt 12:13 and it·was·restored as·healthy·and·sound as the
Mk 3:5 his hand was·restored as·healthy·and·sound as the
Mk 5:34 in peace and be healthy·and·sound away·from your
G5199.1 A-ASM ὑγιῆ (4x)
Jn 5:11 "The·one making me healthy·and·sound, that·man
Jn 5:15 ·was Jesus, the·one making him healthy·and·sound.
Jn 7:23 man·of·clay† healthy·and·sound on a·Sabbath?
Tit 2:8 healthy·and·sound reasoning *that·is* faultless in·order·
G5199.1 A-APM ὑγιεῖς (1x)
Mt 15:31 crippled·ones healthy·and·sound, lame·ones

G5200 ὑγρός hygrós *adj.* (1x)
Roots:G5205 Compare:G5515 See:G5199-3
G5200.2 A-DSN ὑγρῷ (1x)
Lk 23:31 to the arbor·tree *which·is* green·with·sap, what

G5201 ὑδρία hydría *n.* (3x)
Roots:G5204 xLangAlso:H3537
G5201.2 N-ASF ὑδρίαν (1x)
Jn 4:28 the woman left her water·jar and went·off into the
G5201.3 N-NPF ὑδρίαι (1x)
Jn 2:6 laying·out there six ceremonial·water·basins of·stone,
G5201.3 N-APF ὑδρίας (1x)
Jn 2:7 "Overfill the ceremonial·water·basins with·water."

G5202 ὑδρο•ποτέω hydrôpôtéō *v.* (1x)
Roots:G5204 G4095 Compare:G4095
G5202.2 V-PAM-2S ὑδροπότει (1x)
1Ti 5:23 No·longer drink·water·only, but·rather use a·little

G5203 ὑδρ•ωπικός hydrōpikós *adj.* (1x)
Roots:G5204 G3700
G5203 A-NSM ὑδρωπικός (1x)
Lk 14:2 man·of·clay† before him swollen·with·dropsy.

G5204 ὕδωρ hýdōr *n.* (83x)
ὕδατος hýdatôs [genitive case]
Roots:G5205 xLangAlso:H4325
G5204.2 N-NSN ὕδωρ (6x)
Jn 4:14 coming·age, but·rather the water that I·shall·give him
Jn 5:7 ·of·clay†, whenever the water should·be·troubled, in·
Jn 19:34 and straight·away blood and water came·out.
Ac 8:36 "Behold, *here·is* water. What prevents me to·be·
1Jn 5:8 the earth: the Spirit, and the water, and the blood.
Rv 16:12 EuPhrates, and its water was·dried·up, in·order·
G5204.2 N-NPN ὕδατα (2x)
Jn 3:23 to·Salim because there·was much water there. And
Rv 17:15 ·says to·me, "The *Many* Waters which you·saw,
G5204.2 N-ASN ὕδωρ (18x)
Jn 2:9 ·the·banquet tasted the water having·been·made wine,
Jn 2:9 the attendants having·drawn·out the water had·seen),
Jn 4:7 a·woman from·out of·Samaria to·draw·out water.
Jn 4:10 ·of him, and he·would·have given you living water."
Jn 4:11 from·what·source do·you·have the living water?
Jn 4:15 Sir, give me this water, in·order·that I·may·not thirst
Jn 4:46 of·Galilee, where he·made the water *into* wine. And
Jn 5:4 on the pool and was·troubling the water. So·then, the
Jn 13:5 After·that, he·casts water into the wash·basin; then
Lk 7:44 into your home, you·gave·me no water for my feet,
Ac 8:36 roadway, they·came to some water. And the eunuch
Ac 8:38 they·both walked·down into the water, both Philippe
Ac 10:47 "Is any·man able to·forbid water *such·for* these not
Mt 17:15 ·times into the fire and many·times into the water.
Mt 27:24 ·being·made, taking water, he·washed·off·his·own
Jac 3:12 *is·able* to·produce *both* salt water and fresh.
Rv 12:15 cast out of·his mouth water as a·flood·water right·
Rv 22:17 ·him·take the water of·life-above as·a·free·present.
G5204.2 N-APN ὕδατα (3x)
Mt 14:28 ·order me to·come to you upon the water."
Mt 14:29 Peter walked upon the water to·go to YeShua.
Mk 9:22 and into waters in·order·that it·should·completely·
G5204.2 N-DSN ὕδατι (13x)
Jn 1:26 "I·myself immerse in water, but one·stands *in·the*
Jn 1:31 ·of that, I·myself came immersing in the water."
Jn 1:33 sending me to·immerse in water, that·one declared
Lk 3:16 "In·fact, I·myself immerse yeu in·water, but the·one
Lk 8:25 the winds and the water, and they·listen·to·and·obey
Ac 1:5 Because in·fact, John immersed in·water, but yeu
Ac 11:16 'John in·fact immersed in·water, but yeu shall·be·
Heb 10:22 the bodies having·been·bathed with·pure water.
Mt 3:11 I·myself immerse yeu in water for repentance, but
Mk 1:8 I·myself immersed yeu in water, but he·himself
2Pe 3:6 ·completely·destroyed, being·deluged with·water.
1Jn 5:6 *and* not by the water merely, but·rather by the water
1Jn 5:6 water merely, but·rather by the water and the blood.
G5204.2 N-DPN ὕδασιν (1x)
Mt 8:32 steep·overhang into the sea and died in the waters.
G5204.2 N-GSN ὕδατος (24x)
Jn 2:7 "Overfill the ceremonial·water·basins with·water."
Jn 3:5 should·be·born from·out of·water and of·Spirit, he·is·
Jn 4:13 drinking from·out of·this water shall·thirst again.
Jn 4:14 should·drink from·out of·the water that I·myself
Jn 4:14 ·be in him a·wellspring of·water springing·up into
Jn 5:3 — *all·of·them* waiting·for the stirring of·the water.
Jn 5:4 agitation of·the water was·made healthy·and·sound
Jn 7:38 ·out of·his belly shall·flow rivers of·living water."
Lk 8:24 the wind and the surge of·water. And they·ceased,
Lk 16:24 the tip of·his finger in·water and may·cool·down
Lk 22:10 bearing a·pitcher of·water shall·meet·up with·yeu;
Ac 8:39 when they·walked·up out of·the water, Yahweh's
Heb 9:19 and of·adult·male·goats, with water, scarlet wool,
Mt 3:16 walked·up straight·away from the water. And
Mk 1:10 immediately walking·up from the water, he·saw the
Mk 9:41 should·give yeu a·cup of·water to·drink in my name
Mk 14:13 a·pitcher of·water shall·approach·and·meet yeu.
1Pe 3:20 eight souls) were·thoroughly·saved through water.
2Pe 3:5 *being·made* from·out of·water and through water—
2Pe 3:5 *being·made* from·out of·water and through water—
Eph 5:26 her with·the bathing of·the water by an·utterance—
1Jn 5:6 This is the·one coming through water and blood,
Rv 21:6 of·the water of·life-above as·a·free·present.
Rv 22:1 he·showed me a·pure river of·water of·life-above,
G5204.2 N-GPN ὑδάτων (11x)
Rv 1:15 , and his voice as *the* sound of·many waters,
Rv 7:17 shall·guide them to living wellsprings of·waters. '
Rv 8:10 of·the rivers, and upon the wellsprings of·waters;
Rv 8:11 men·of·clay† died as·a·result of·the waters, because
Rv 11:6 they·have authority over the waters to·turn them into
Rv 14:2 heaven, as a·voice of·many waters, and as a·voice
Rv 14:7 and the earth, and sea,' and wellsprings of·waters!"
Rv 16:4 and into the wellsprings of·waters, and they·became
Rv 16:5 And I·heard the angel of·the waters saying, "You·
Rv 17:1 ·one who·is·sitting·down upon the Many Waters,
Rv 19:6 and as a·voice of·many waters, and as a·voice of·
EG5204.2 (5x)
Jn 4:15 nor·even should·come here to·draw·out *water*."
Lk 8:23 they·were·swamped *with·water* and were·in·danger.
Mt 10:42 little·ones a·cup of·cold *water* to·drink merely in a·
Jac 3:11 narrow·opening *with·both* the fresh *water* and the
Rv 8:11 and the third·part *of·the waters* become wormwood

G5205 ὑετός hyêtós *n.* (6x)
Compare:G1028 G3655 xLangEquiv:H4306 xLangAlso:H1653
G5205.1 N-NSM ὑετός (1x)
Rv 11:6 in·order·that it·should·not shower rain in *the* days
G5205.1 N-ASM ὑετόν (4x)
Ac 28:2 on·account·of the assaulting rain, and on·account·
Heb 6:7 soil, after·drinking the rain which·is·coming upon it

Jac 5:7 ·should·receive early·autumn and latter·spring rain.
Jac 5:18 ·prayed again, and the sky gave rain, and the earth
G5205.2 N-APM ὑετούς (1x)
Ac 14:17 ·good, giving us seasons·of·rain from·the·sky and

G5206 υἱο•θεσία huiôthêsía *n.* (6x)

Roots:G5207 G5087
G5206.2 N-NSF υἱοθεσία (1x)
Rm 9:4 — of·whom *are* the adoption·as·sons, and the glory,
G5206.2 N-ASF υἱοθεσίαν (3x)
Gal 4:5 that we·may·receive·in·full the adoption·as·sons.
Rm 8:23 who·are·fully·awaiting the·adoption·as·sons, *that·is*
Eph 1:5 ·predetermining us for adoption·as·sons into himself
G5206.2 N-GSF υἱοθεσίας (1x)
Rm 8:15 yeu·received a·Spirit of·adoption·as·sons, by which
EG5206.3 (1x)
Mt 1:1 ·*paternal* origin *(via·adoption)* of·YeShua Anointed,

G5207 υἱός huiós *n.* (423x)

בֵּן ben [Hebrew]
Compare:G1074 G4690 G5043 G2094 See:G5207-1
xLangEquiv:H1121 A1123 xLangAlso:H1121-1
A1123-1
G5207.1 N-NSM υἱός (152x)
Jn 1:18 ever·at·any·time. The only·begotten Son, the·one
Jn 1:34 and have·testified, that this is the Son of·God."
Jn 1:42 ·yourself are Simon, the son of·Jonah. You·yourself
Jn 1:49 you·yourself are the Son of·God; you·yourself are
Jn 3:13 out·of·the heaven, the Son of·Clay·Man†, the·one
Jn 4:46 ·was·a·certain royal·official, whose son was·sick at
Jn 4:50 "Depart, your son lives." And the man·of·clay†
Jn 4:53 Jesus declared to·him, "Your son lives." And he·
Jn 5:19 I·say to·yeu, the Son is·not able to·do not·even·
Jn 5:19 should·do, these·things also the Son does likewise.
Jn 5:21 in·this·manner the Son gives·life-above·to whom he·
Jn 5:27 Tribunal·judgment, because he·is a·son of·clay†.
Jn 6:27 life-above, which the Son of·Clay·Man† shall·give
Jn 6:42 Is this not Jesus, the son of·Joseph, whose father and
Jn 6:69 are the Anointed-One, the Son of·the living God.
Jn 8:35 coming·age, *but* the Son continues·*to·remain* into the
Jn 8:36 So·then, if the Son should·set yeu free, yeu·shall
Jn 9:19 "Is this yeur son, who yeu say was·born blind?
Jn 9:20 We·personally·know that this is our son, and that he·
Jn 10:36 ·God,' because I·declared, 'I·am God's Son.'
Jn 11:4 ·God, in·order·that the Son of·God may·be·glorified
Jn 11:27 are the Anointed-One, the Son of·God, the·one
Jn 12:23 that the Son of·Clay·Man† should·be·glorified.
Jn 12:34 "Who is this Son of·Clay·Man†?
Jn 13:31 says, "Now the Son of·Clay·Man† is·glorified, and
Jn 17:1 your Son in·order·that your Son also may·glorify you
Jn 17:12 ·lost except the Son of·Total·Destruction, in·order·
Jn 19:26 "Woman, behold your son!"
Jn 20:31 is the Anointed-One, the Son of·God; and that
Lk 3:22 "You·yourself are my beloved Son; in you I·take·
Lk 3:23 about thirty years·of·age, being a·son of·Joseph
Lk 4:3 to·him, "If you·are a·son of·God, declare to·this
Lk 4:9 "If you·are the Son of·God, cast yourself down from·
Lk 4:22 "Is not this Joseph's son?"
Lk 4:41 are the Anointed-One, the Son of·God." And
Lk 5:24 ·personally·know that the Son of·Clay·Man† has
Lk 6:5 ·saying to·them, "The Son of·Clay·Man† is Lord also
Lk 7:12 ·for one·having·died, an·only son of·his mother,
Lk 7:34 The Son of·Clay·Man† has·come eating and
Lk 9:26 the Son of·Clay·Man† shall·be·ashamed·of that·
Lk 9:35 "This is my beloved Son. Listen·to him!"
Lk 9:44 "for the Son of·Clay·Man† is·about to·be·handed·
Lk 9:56 For the Son of·Clay·Man† did·not come to·
Lk 9:58 *have* nests, but the Son of·Clay·Man† does·not have
Lk 10:6 And, in·fact, if a·son of·peace should·be there,
Lk 10:22 not·even·one·man knows who the Son is, except
Lk 10:22 the Father is, except the Son, and *he* to·whomever
Lk 10:22 *he* to·whomever the Son should·resolve to·reveal
Lk 11:11 father among·yeu, *if* the son shall·request bread, ¿!
Lk 11:30 in·this·manner also the Son of·Clay·Man† shall·be
Lk 12:8 the men·of·clay†, the Son of·Clay·Man† also shall·
Lk 12:40 also, because the Son of·Clay·Man† comes in·that
Lk 12:53 ·divided against son, and son against father;
Lk 15:13 days after, the younger son, gathering·together
Lk 15:19 no·longer worthy to·be·called your son; make me
Lk 15:21 "But the son declared to·him, 'Father, I·morally·
Lk 15:21 and I·am no·longer worthy to·be·called your son.'
Lk 15:24 Because this son of·mine was dead and came·alive·
Lk 15:25 "Now his older son was in a·field, and as he·was·
Lk 15:30 But when this son of·yours came *home*, the·one
Lk 17:24 ·this·manner also shall·be the Son of·Clay·Man† in
Lk 17:30 in·that day *when* the Son of·Clay·Man† is·revealed.
Lk 18:8 "Nevertheless, the Son of·Clay·Man†, upon·
Lk 19:9 ·indeed he·himself also is a·son of·AbRaham.
Lk 19:10 For the Son of·Clay·Man† came to·seek and to·
Lk 22:22 And in·fact, the Son of·Clay·Man† departs
Lk 22:69 From now·on, the Son of·Clay·Man† shall·be
Lk 22:70 "So·then, you·yourself are the Son of·God?
Ac 4:36 ·interpreted *from·Aramaic*, is Son of·Consoling),
Ac 9:20 "This is the Son of·God!"
Ac 13:33 "You·yourself are my Son. Today, I·myself
Ac 16:1 there, TimoThy by·name, a·son of·a·certain Jewish
Ac 23:6 I·myself am a·Pharisee, a·son of·a·Pharisee; *it·is*
Ac 23:16 And the son of·Paul's sister, coming·directly after·
Heb 1:5 "'You·yourself are my Son. Today, I·myself have·
Heb 2:6 ·are·actively·mindful of·him? Or a·son of·clay†,
Heb 3:6 but Anointed-One as a·son over his·own house, of·
Heb 5:5 "'You·yourself are my Son. Today, I·myself have·
Heb 5:8 Even·though being a·Son, he·learned the attentive·
Heb 11:24 being·referred·to·as son of·Pharaoh's daughter,
Heb 12:7 as *his·own* sons, for what son is·he whom a·father
Gal 4:7 you·are no·longer a·slave, but·rather a·son; and if a·
Gal 4:7 but·rather a·son; and if a·son, *then* also an·heir of·
Gal 4:30 and her son, for the son of·the maidservant, no,
Mt 3:17 "This is my beloved Son, in whom I·take delight.
Mt 4:3 ·One declared, "If you·are a·son of·God, declare that
Mt 4:6 "If you·are *the* Son of·God, cast yourself down.
Mt 7:9 ·among yeu, who if his son should·request bread, ¿!
Mt 8:20 *have* nests, but the Son of·Clay·Man† does·not have
Mt 9:6 ·may·personally·know that the Son of·Clay·Man† has
Mt 10:23 of·IsraEl, until the Son of·Clay·Man† should·come
Mt 11:19 The Son of·Clay·Man† came eating and drinking,
Mt 11:27 the Father, except the Son, and to·whomever the
Mt 11:27 and to·whomever the Son should·resolve to·reveal
Mt 12:8 For the Son of·Clay·Man† is Lord even of·the
Mt 12:40 in·this·manner the Son of·Clay·Man† shall·be
Mt 13:37 sowing the good seed is the Son of·Clay·Man†.
Mt 13:41 The Son of·Clay·Man† shall·dispatch his angels,
Mt 13:55 ¿!·Is this not the carpenter's son? Is·not·indeed his
Mt 14:33 "Truly you·are God's Son."
Mt 16:16 are the Anointed-One, the Son of·the living God.
Mt 16:27 "For the Son of·Clay·Man† is·about to·come in the
Mt 17:5 "This is my beloved Son, in whom I·take·delight.
Mt 17:9 until the Son of·Clay·Man† should·rise·up from·
Mt 17:12 ·this·manner also, the Son of·Clay·Man† is·about
Mt 17:22 "The Son of·Clay·Man† is·about to·be·handed·
Mt 18:11 For the Son of·Clay·Man† came to·save the·one
Mt 19:28 whenever the Son of·Clay·Man† should·sit upon
Mt 20:18 and the Son of·Clay·Man† shall·be·handed·over
Mt 20:28 just·as the Son of·Clay·Man† did·not come to·be·
Mt 22:42 concerning the Anointed-One? Whose son is·he?
Mt 24:44 also, because the Son of·Clay·Man† comes at·an·
Mt 25:13 the hour in which the Son of·Clay·Man† comes.
Mt 25:31 "But whenever the Son of·Clay·Man† should·come
Mt 26:2 and·then the Son of·Clay·Man† is·handed·over to·
Mt 26:24 "In·fact, the Son of·Clay·Man† heads·on·out just·
Mt 26:24 whom the Son of·Clay·Man† is·handed·over! It·
Mt 26:45 ·near, and the Son of·Clay·Man† is·handed·over
Mt 26:63 ·yourself are the Anointed-One, the Son of·God."
Mt 27:40 save yourself. If you·are a·son of·God, descend
Mt 27:43 him," for he·declared, 'I·am a·son of·God.'"
Mt 27:54 "Truly this was God's Son."
Mk 1:11 You·yourself are my beloved Son, in whom I·take·
Mk 2:10 ·personally·know that the Son of·Clay·Man† has
Mk 2:28 As·such, the Son of·Clay·Man† is Lord also of·the
Mk 3:11 "You·yourself are the Son of·God."
Mk 6:3 not the carpenter, the son of·Mariam, and a·brother
Mk 8:38 morally·disqualified), the Son of·Clay·Man† also
Mk 9:7 "This is my beloved Son. Listen·to him.
Mk 9:9 whenever the Son of·Clay·Man† should·rise·up
Mk 9:31 ·them, "The Son of·Clay·Man† is·handed·over into
Mk 10:33 and the Son of·Clay·Man† shall·be·handed·over
Mk 10:45 For even the Son of·Clay·Man† did·not come to·
Mk 10:46 BarTimaeus the blind (a·son of·Timaeus) was·
Mk 13:32 ·ones in heaven, neither the Son, except the Father
Mk 14:21 "In·fact, the Son of·Clay·Man† heads·on·out,
Mk 14:21 whom the Son of·Clay·Man† is·handed·over! It·
Mk 14:41 Behold, the Son of·Clay·Man† is·handed·over
Mk 14:61 the Anointed-One, the Son of·the Blessed-One?
Mk 15:39 "Truly this man·of·clay† was a·son of·God."
Rm 9:9 I·shall·come, and there·shall·be to·Sarah, a·son."
1Pe 5:13 ·*yeu*, greets yeu, and *so·does John*·Mark, my son.
2Pe 1:17 "This is my beloved Son, in whom I·myself take·
2Th 2:3 should·be·revealed, the Son of·Total·Destruction,
1Co 15:28 then also the Son himself shall·be·subject to·the·
2Co 1:19 For the Son of·God, Jesus Anointed, the·one being·
1Jn 3:8 ·*purpose* the Son of·God was·made·apparent: that
1Jn 4:15 should·affirm that Jesus is the Son of·God, God
1Jn 5:5 if·not the·one trusting that Jesus is the Son of·God?
1Jn 5:20 we·personally·know that the Son of·God comes,
Rv 2:18 'These·things says the Son of·God, the·one having
Rv 21:7 ·himself shall·be my·very·own— the *distinct* son.
G5207.1 N-NPM υἱοί (8x)
Jn 4:12 drank out·of·it, and his sons, and his prized·cattle.
Lk 11:19 the demons, by whom·do yeur sons cast·*them*·out?
Ac 2:17 all flesh, and yeur sons and yeur daughters shall·
Heb 12:8 then·by·inference, yeu·are bastards and not sons.
Gal 4:6 And because yeu·are sons, God dispatched·forth the
Mt 12:27 the demons, by whom·do yeur sons cast·*them*·out?
Mt 17:26 was·replying to·him, "So the sons are free.
Mt 20:21 "Declare that these two sons of·mine may·sit, one
G5207.1 N-VSM υἱέ (3x)
Ac 13:10 and all mischief, O·Son of·Slanderer! O·Enemy
Heb 12:5 with·sons, "'My son, do·not have·little·respect of·
Mt 8:29 to·do·with·us and you, YeShua, O·Son of·God?
G5207.1 N-ASM υἱόν (81x)
Jn 1:45 prophets: Jesus from Natsareth, the son of·Joseph."
Jn 1:51 and descending' upon the Son of·Clay·Man†."
Jn 3:14 ·mandatory·for the Son of·Clay·Man† to·be·elevated
Jn 3:16 such·that he·gave his only·begotten Son, in·order·
Jn 3:17 "For God did·not dispatch his Son into the world in·
Jn 3:35 The Father loves the Son and has·given all·things
Jn 3:36 "The·one trusting in the Son has eternal life-above,
Jn 4:47 he·may·walk·down and may·heal his son, for he·
Jn 5:20 For the Father is·a·friend·to the Son and shows him
Jn 5:23 all *men* should·deeply·honor the Son, just·as they·
Jn 5:23 The·one not deeply·honoring the Son, does·not
Jn 6:40 anyone, the·one observing the Son, and trusting in
Jn 6:62 yeu·should·observe the Son of·Clay·Man† ascending
Jn 8:28 Whenever yeu·should·elevate the Son of·Clay·Man†,
Jn 9:35 "You·yourself, do·you·trust in the Son of·God?
Jn 12:34 ·for the Son of·Clay·Man† to·be·elevated'?
Jn 17:1 has·come. Glorify your Son in·order·that your Son
Jn 19:7 ·die, because he·made himself *out·to·be* God's Son."
Lk 1:13 wife EliSabeth shall·bear you a·son, and you·shall·
Lk 1:31 your·uterus and shall·reproduce·and·birth a·son, and
Lk 1:36 she·herself *is* also having·conceived a·son in her
Lk 1:57 ·and·give·birth, and she·gave·birth·to a·son.
Lk 2:7 she·reproduced·and·birthed her firstborn son, and
Lk 3:2 of·God came to·John the son of·ZacharIas in the
Lk 9:22 "It·is·mandatory·for the Son of·Clay·Man† to·suffer
Lk 9:38 you, kindly·look·upon my son, because he·is my
Lk 9:41 and shall·put·up·with yeu? Escort your son here!"
Lk 12:10 shall·declare a·word against the Son of·Clay·Man†,
Lk 20:13 ·I·do? I·shall·send my beloved son. *It·is* likely *that*
Lk 21:27 ·shall·gaze·upon 'the Son of·Clay·Man† coming in

Αα Ββ Γγ Δδ Εε Ζζ Ηη Θθ Ιι Κκ Λλ Μμ Νν Ξξ Οο Ππ Ρρ Σσ Ττ Υυ Φφ Χχ Ψψ Ωω

Lk 22:48 ·you·hand·over the Son of·Clay·Man† with·a·kiss?
Lk 24:7 ·for the Son of·Clay·Man† to·be·handed·over into
Ac 7:21 took him up and nurtured him for her·own son.
Ac 7:56 ·opened·up, and the Son of·Clay·Man† standing at
Ac 8:37 "I·trust Jesus Anointed to·be the Son of·God."
Ac 13:21 and God gave to·them Saul son of·Qish, a·man
Heb 1:5 and he·himself shall·be my·own distinct Son"?
Heb 1:8 But unto the Son *he·says*, "'Your throne, O·God, *is*
Heb 4:14 heavens, YeShua the Son of·God, we·should·take·
Heb 6:6 ·re-crucifying for·themselves the Son of·God and
Heb 7:28 , *fully·establishes the* Son *as high·priest*, having·
Heb 10:29 the·one trampling·down the Son of·God, and
Heb 12:6 he·whips every son whom he·personally·accepts."
Gal 1:16 to·reveal his Son in me in·order·that I·may·
Gal 4:4 God dispatched·forth his Son, coming·to·be birthed·
Gal 4:30 "Cast·out the maidservant and her son, for the son
Mt 1:21 And she·shall·reproduce·and·birth a·son, and you·
Mt 1:23 pregnancy and shall·reproduce·and·birth a·son, and
Mt 1:25 she·reproduced·and·birthed her firstborn son. And
Mt 2:15 "From·out of·Egypt I·called·forth my son.'"
Mt 10:37 and the·one affectionately·favoring son or daughter
Mt 11:27 and no·one·at·all fully·knows the Son, except the
Mt 16:13 ·clay† say me to·be— *me*, the Son of·Clay·Man†?
Mt 16:28 they·should·see the Son of·Clay·Man† coming in
Mt 17:15 "Lord, show·mercy on·my son, because he·is·
Mt 21:37 "But eventually, he·dispatched his son to them,
Mt 21:37 saying, 'They·shall·be·respectful·of my son.'
Mt 21:38 "But upon·seeing the son, the tenant·farmers
Mt 23:15 twice·as·much a·son of·Hell·Canyon as·yeurselves
Mt 24:30 ' and they·shall·gaze·upon 'the Son of·Clay·Man†
Mt 26:64 ·gaze·upon 'the Son of·Clay·Man† sitting·down at
Mk 8:31 it·is·mandatory·for the Son of·Clay·Man† to·suffer
Mk 9:12 ·been·written concerning the Son of·Clay·Man†,
Mk 9:17 I·brought to you my son, having a·mute spirit,
Mk 12:6 "So·then, yet having one son, his well-beloved, he·
Mk 12:6 saying, 'They·shall·be·respectful·of my son.'
Mk 13:26 they·shall·gaze·upon 'the Son of·Clay·Man†
Mk 14:62 ·gaze·upon the Son of·Clay·Man† sitting·down at
Rm 8:3 God, after·sending his·own Son in *the* resemblance
Jac 2:21 ·righteous, after·carrying·up his son YiTsaq upon
1Th 1:10 and to·patiently·await his Son from·out of·the
1Jn 2:22 the·one who·is·denying the Father and the Son.
1Jn 2:23 one who·is·denying the Son does·not·even have the
1Jn 4:9 God has·dispatched his only·begotten Son into the
1Jn 4:10 loved us and dispatched his Son *to·be the* atonement
1Jn 4:14 the Father has·dispatched the Son *to·be* Savior of·
1Jn 5:10 The·one trusting in the Son of·God has the
1Jn 5:12 The·one having the Son has the life-above; the·one
1Jn 5:12 the·one not having the Son of·God does·not have
2Jn 1:9 this·one has both the Father and the Son.
Rv 12:5 And she·reproduced·and·birthed a·son, a·male who

G5207.1 N-APM υἱούς (5x)
Lk 15:11 "A·certain man·of·clay† had two sons.
Ac 7:29 in *the* land of·Midian, where he·begot two sons.
Heb 2:10 *exist*), in·bringing many sons to glory, to·make
Gal 4:22 that AbRaham had two sons, one birthed·from·out
2Co 6:18 shall·be my·own distinct sons and daughters,"

G5207.1 N-DSM υἱῷ (15x)
Jn 3:36 ·one being·obstinate to·the Son shall·not gaze·upon
Jn 4:5 to·the open·field that Jacob gave to·his son Joseph.
Jn 5:22 he·has·given all the Tribunal·judgment to·the Son,
Jn 5:26 he·gave also to·the Son to·have life-above in himself
Jn 14:13 ·I·do, that the Father may·be·glorified in the Son.
Lk 12:53 Father shall·be·thoroughly·divided against son, and
Lk 18:31 *concerning* the Son of·Clay·Man† shall·be·finished
Heb 1:2 ·us in these last days by *his* Son, whom he·placed *as*
Heb 7:3 but having·been·made·similar to·the Son of·God,
Mt 22:2 a·king, who made a·wedding·banquet for·his son
1Jn 2:24 yeu also shall·remain in the Son, and in the Father.
1Jn 5:11 eternal life-above, and this life-above is in his Son.
1Jn 5:20 ·one *who·is* true, in his Son Jesus Anointed. This is
Rv 1:13 Lampstands, *one* like a·son of·clay·man†, having·
Rv 14:14 *one* who·is·sitting·down like a·son of·clay·man†,

G5207.1 N-DPM υἱοῖς (2x)
Heb 12:5 which thoroughly·relates to·yeu as with·sons,
Heb 12:7 is·bearing·alongside yeu as *his·own* sons, for what

G5207.1 N-GSM υἱοῦ (34x)
Jn 3:18 in the name of·the only·begotten Son of·God.
Jn 5:25 ·ones shall·hear the voice of·the Son of·God, and
Jn 6:53 yeu·should·eat the flesh of·the Son of·Clay·Man†,
Lk 6:22 name as evil, because·of the Son of·Clay·Man†.
Lk 17:22 ·see one of·the days of·the Son of·Clay·Man†, and
Lk 17:26 ·it·be also in the days of·the Son of·Clay·Man†.
Lk 21:36 to·be·established before the Son of·Clay·Man†."
Gal 2:20 I·live in the trust of·the Son of·God, the·one loving
Gal 4:6 dispatched·forth the Spirit of·his Son into yeur hearts
Gal 4:30 should·not be·heir with the son of·the free·woman.
Mt 1:1 Anointed, *the* Son of·David, *the* son of·AbRaham.
Mt 12:32 ·declare a·word against the Son of·Clay·Man†, it·
Mt 24:27 the returning·Presence of·the Son of·Clay·Man†.
Mt 24:30 the sign of·the Son of·Clay·Man† shall·be·apparent
Mt 24:37 the returning·Presence of·the Son of·Clay·Man†.
Mt 24:39 the returning·Presence of·the Son of·Clay·Man†.
Mt 28:19 of·the Father, and of·the Son, and of·the Holy
Mk 1:1 of·the good·news of·Jesus Anointed, God's Son.
Rm 1:4 ·specifically·determined *to·be the* Son of·God in
Rm 1:9 spirit in the good·news of·his Son, how unceasingly
Rm 5:10 through the death of·his Son, so·much more·so,
Rm 8:29 ·like the derived·image of·his Son, in·order·for his
Rm 8:32 ·that did·not spare his·own Son, but·rather handed
1Co 1:9 into *the* fellowship of·his Son Jesus Anointed our
Eph 4:13 recognition·and·full·knowledge of·the Son of·God,
Col 1:13 *us* into the kingdom of·the Son of·his love,
1Jn 1:3 with the Father, and with his Son Jesus Anointed.
1Jn 1:7 blood of·Jesus Anointed, his Son, purifies us from
1Jn 3:23 ·trust on·the name of·his Son Jesus Anointed; and
1Jn 5:9 of·God which he·has·testified concerning his Son.
1Jn 5:10 testimony that God has·testified concerning his Son.
1Jn 5:13 in the name of·the Son of·God, in·order·that yeu·
1Jn 5:13 ·that yeu·may·trust in the name of·the Son of·God.
2Jn 1:3 *the* Lord Jesus Anointed, the Son of·the Father, in

G5207.1 N-GPM υἱῶν (2x)
Mt 17:25 a·census·tribute? From their·own sons or from the
Mt 20:20 ·alongside him, with her sons *(Jakob and John)*,

EG5207.1 (92x)
Jn 6:71 ·referring·to Judas IsCariot, *the* son of·Simon, for *it*·
Jn 12:4 (Judas IsCariot, Simon's son, the·one about to·hand
Jn 13:2 the heart of·Judas IsCariot, son of·Simon, that he·
Jn 13:26 he·gave *it* to·Judas IsCariot, *the* son of·Simon.
Jn 21:2 Qanah in·Galilee, and the sons of·Zebedee, and two
Jn 21:15 Peter, "Simon, son of·Jonah, do·you·love me
Jn 21:16 ·time, "Simon, son of·Jonah, do·you·love me?
Jn 21:17 "Simon, son of·Jonah, do·you·have·affection·for
Lk 3:24 son of·Matthat, son of·Levi, son of·Malki, son
Lk 3:24 son of·Matthat, son of·Levi, son of·Malki, son of·
Lk 3:24 of·Matthat, son of·Levi, son of·Malki, son of·Janna
Lk 3:24 of·Levi, son of·Malki, son of·Janna, son of·Joseph,
Lk 3:24 ·Levi, son of·Malki, son of·Janna, son of·Joseph,
Lk 3:25 son of·MattathIas, son of·Amots, son of·Nachum,
Lk 3:25 son of·MattathIas, son of·Amots, son of·Nachum,
Lk 3:25 son of·Amots, son of·Nachum, son of·Esli, son of·
Lk 3:25 son of·Amots, son of·Nachum, son of·Esli, son of·
Lk 3:25 son of·Nachum, son of·Esli, son of·Naggai,
Lk 3:26 son of·Maath, son of·MattathIas, son of·Shimei, son
Lk 3:26 son of·Maath, son of·MattathIas, son of·Shimei, son
Lk 3:26 of·Maath, son of·MattathIas, son of·Shimei, son of·
Lk 3:26 son of·Shimei, son of·Joseph, son of·Jehudah,
Lk 3:26 son of·Shimei, son of·Joseph, son of·Jehudah,
Lk 3:27 son of·Johannes, son of·RhesaYah, son of·
Lk 3:27 son of·Johannes, son of·RhesaYah, son of·
Lk 3:27 son of·RhesaYah, son of·ZorubBabel, son of·
Lk 3:27 son of·ZorubBabel, son of·ShealtiEl, son of·
Lk 3:27 of·ZorubBabel, son of·ShealtiEl, son of·NeriYah,
Lk 3:28 son of·Malki, son of·Addi, son of·Qosam, son
Lk 3:28 son of·Malki, son of·Addi, son of·Qosam, son of·
Lk 3:28 son of·Addi, son of·Qosam, son of·ElModam, son
Lk 3:28 of·Addi, son of·Qosam, son of·ElModam, son of·Er
Lk 3:28 ·Addi, son of·Qosam, son of·ElModam, son of·Er,
Lk 3:29 son of·Yose, son of·EliEzer, son of·JoRim, son
Lk 3:29 son of·Yose, son of·EliEzer, son of·JoRim, son of·
Lk 3:29 son of·Yose, son of·EliEzer, son of·JoRim, son of·
Lk 3:29 son of·JoRim, son of·Matthat, son of·Levi,
Lk 3:29 son of·JoRim, son of·Matthat, son of·Levi,
Lk 3:30 son of·Shimeon, son of·Yehudah, son of·Yoseph,
Lk 3:30 son of·Shimeon, son of·Yehudah, son of·Yoseph,
Lk 3:30 of·Shimeon, son of·Yehudah, son of·Yoseph, son
Lk 3:30 of·Yehudah, son of·Yoseph, son of·Yonan, son of·
Lk 3:30 son of·Yoseph, son of·Yonan, son of·ElYaQim,
Lk 3:31 son of·Melea, son of·Mainan, son of·Mattatha, son
Lk 3:31 son of·Melea, son of·Mainan, son of·Mattatha, son
Lk 3:31 son of·Mainan, son of·Mattatha, son of·Nathan,
Lk 3:31 of·Mainan, son of·Mattatha, son of·Nathan, son of·
Lk 3:32 son of·Jesse, son of·Obed, son of·BoAz, son of·
Lk 3:32 son of·Jesse, son of·Obed, son of·BoAz, son of·
Lk 3:32 of·Jesse, son of·Obed, son of·BoAz, son of·Salmon
Lk 3:32 son of·Obed, son of·BoAz, son of·Salmon, son of·
Lk 3:32 son of·BoAz, son of·Salmon, son of·Nachshon,
Lk 3:33 son of·AmmiNadab, son of·Ram, son of·Chetsron,
Lk 3:33 son of·AmmiNadab, son of·Ram, son of·Chetsron,
Lk 3:33 son of·Ram, son of·Chetsron, son of·Perets, son
Lk 3:33 son of·Chetsron, son of·Perets, son of·Judah,
Lk 3:33 son of·Chetsron, son of·Perets, son of·Judah,
Lk 3:34 son of·Jacob, son of·YiTsaq, son of·AbRaham, son
Lk 3:34 son of·Jacob, son of·YiTsaq, son of·AbRaham, son
Lk 3:34 of·Jacob, son of·YiTsaq, son of·AbRaham, son of·
Lk 3:34 son of·AbRaham, son of·Terach, son of·Nachor,
Lk 3:34 son of·AbRaham, son of·Terach, son of·Nachor,
Lk 3:35 son of·Serug, son of·Reu, son of·Peleg, son of·Eber
Lk 3:35 son of·Serug, son of·Reu, son of·Peleg, son of·Eber
Lk 3:35 of·Serug, son of·Reu, son of·Peleg, son of·Eber,
Lk 3:35 of·Reu, son of·Peleg, son of·Eber, son of·Shelach,
Lk 3:35 of·Reu, son of·Peleg, son of·Eber, son of·Shelach,
Lk 3:36 son of·Qainan, son of·Arphaxad, son of·Shem,
Lk 3:36 son of·Qainan, son of·Arphaxad, son of·Shem, son
Lk 3:36 son of·Arphaxad, son of·Shem, son of·Noach, son
Lk 3:36 son of·Shem, son of·Noach, son of·Lemek,
Lk 3:36 son of·Shem, son of·Noach, son of·Lemek,
Lk 3:37 son of·MethuShelach, son of·Enoch, son of·Jared,
Lk 3:37 son of·MethuShelach, son of·Enoch, son of·Jared,
Lk 3:37 of·MethuShelach, son of·Enoch, son of·Jared, son
Lk 3:37 of·Enoch, son of·Jared, son of·MahalalEl, son of·
Lk 3:37 son of·Jared, son of·MahalalEl, son of·Qeinan,
Lk 3:38 son of·Enosh, son of·Sheth, son of·Adam, son
Lk 3:38 son of·Enosh, son of·Sheth, son of·Adam, son of·
Lk 3:38 of·Enosh, son of·Sheth, son of·Adam, son of·God.
Lk 3:38 of·Enosh, son of·Sheth, son of·Adam, son of·God.
Lk 6:16 *and* Judas son of·Jacobus·*Thaddaeus*, and Judas
Ac 1:13 and MattHew); (Jakob son of·Alphaeus, Simon the
Ac 1:13 the Zealot, and Judas son of·Jacobus *Thaddaeus*).
Ac 7:16 the tomb that AbRaham's son *Jacob* purchased for·a·
Ac 13:22 "I·found David, the son of·Jesse, *to·be* a·man
Heb 1:3 *His* Son (being *the* radiant·offshoot of·*his*·glory and
Heb 11:17 promises was·offering·up his only·begotten son,
Mt 20:22 YeShua declared *to·her sons*, "Yeu·do·not
Mk 13:34 "*For the* Son *of·Clay·Man†* is as·a·man·of·clay†
Rm 8:29 ·his Son, in·order·for his Son to·be firstborn among
Col 1:15 *It·is the* Son who is *the* derived·image of·the

EG5207.2 (1x)
Lk 3:23 , *as·well·as being a·grandson of·Mariam's father*,

G5207.5 N-ASM υἱόν (1x)
Mt 21:5 even *upon* a·colt, a·foal of·a·mated·donkey.""

EG5207.5 (1x)
Mt 22:42 is·he?" They·say to·him, "*The* Son of·David."

G5207.6 N-NPM υἱοί (1x)
Lk 20:34 ·them, "The descendants of·this present·age marry

G5207.6 N-GSM υἱοῦ (1x)
Mt 23:35 the blood of·ZecharYah, descendant of·BerekYah,

EG5207.6 (1x)
Lk 3:31 son of·Mattatha, son of·Nathan, son of·David,

G5207.7 N-NSM υἱός (10x)
Lk 1:32 great and shall·be·called *the* Son of·the·Most·High,
Lk 1:35 *child*, being·born holy, shall·be·called God's Son.
Lk 20:44 'Lord'; how is·he also his Son?"
Mt 12:23 "Could this be the Son of·David?
Mt 20:30 "Show·mercy on·us, O·Lord, Son of·David."
Mt 20:31 "Show·mercy on·us, O·Lord, Son of·David."
Mt 22:45 'Lord,' how is·he his Son?"
Mk 10:47 "O·Jesus, the Son of·David, show·mercy on·me.
Mk 12:35 say that the Anointed-One is a·Son of·David?
Mk 12:37 'Lord,' so from·what·source is his Son?" And the
G5207.7 N-VSM υἱέ (7x)
Lk 8:28 ·with·me and you Jesus, O·Son of·God Most·High?
Lk 18:38 "Jesus, O·Son of·David, show·mercy on·me.
Lk 18:39 *the* more— "O·Son of·David, show·mercy on·me!
Mt 9:27 ·out and saying, "O·Son of·David, show·mercy on·
Mt 15:22 Show·mercy on·me, O·Lord, O·Son of·David; my
Mk 5:7 ·me and you, Jesus, O·Son of·God Most·High?
Mk 10:48 the more— "O·Son of·David, show·mercy on·me
G5207.7 N-ASM υἱόν (1x)
Lk 20:41 ·*for* the Anointed-One to·be David's Son?
G5207.7 N-DSM υἱῷ (2x)
Mt 21:9 saying, "Hosanna to·the Son of·David! "Having·
Mt 21:15 ·Atrium, saying, "Hosanna to·the Son of·David!"
G5207.7 N-GSM υἱοῦ (2x)
Mt 1:1 of·YeShua Anointed, *the* Son of·David, *the* son of·
Rm 1:3 concerning his Son: the·one coming·to·be birthed·
G5207.8 N-NSM υἱός (1x)
Mt 1:20 saying, "Joseph, son of·David, you·should·not be·

G5207-1 Υἱοί Huiôí *n.* (53x)

בְּנֵי bĕney [Hebrew]
Roots:G5207
xLangEquiv:H1121-1 A1123-1

G5207-1.1 N-NPM Υἱοί (10x)
Lk 20:36 ·are equal·to·the·angels, and are the·Sons of·God,
Ac 3:25 "Yeu·yeurselves are the·Sons of·the prophets, and
Ac 19:14 doing this·thing: the·seven Sons of·Sceva, a·
Gal 3:7 ·out of·trust, the·same are the·Sons of·AbRaham.
Gal 3:26 For yeu·are all the·Sons of·God through the trust in
Mt 5:9 they·themselves shall·be·called the·Sons of·God.
Mt 5:45 so·that yeu·may·become the·Sons of·yeur Father,
Mk 10:35 and John, the Sons of·Zebedee, approach·close to·
Rm 8:14 are·led by·God's Spirit, these are the·Sons of·God.
Rm 9:26 they·shall·be·called the·Sons of·the·living God."
G5207-1.1 N-VPM Υἱοί (1x)
Ac 13:26 "Men, brothers, the·Sons of·AbRaham by·birth,
G5207-1.1 N-APM Υἱούς (5x)
Lk 5:10 *were* Jakob and John, the·Sons of·Zebedee, who
Ac 7:23 his heart to·visit his brothers, the Sons of·IsraEl.
Mt 26:37 ·*him* Peter and the two Sons of·Zebedee, he·began
2Co 3:7 in glory— such·for the Sons of·IsraEl not to·be·able
2Co 3:13 face, *which·is* pertaining·to the Sons of·IsraEl not
G5207-1.1 N-DPM Υἱοῖς (4x)
Ac 7:37 Moses is the·one declaring to·the Sons of·IsraEl,
Ac 10:36 Word which *God* dispatched to·the Sons of·IsraEl,
Mk 3:28 moral·failings shall·be·forgiven the Sons of·clay†,
Eph 3:5 was·not made·known to·the Sons of·clay†, as it·is
G5207-1.1 N-GPM Υἱῶν (15x)
Lk 1:16 ·shall·turn many of·the Sons of·IsraEl back·around
Ac 5:21 all the council·of·aged·men of·the Sons of·IsraEl.
Ac 7:16 ·price of·silver·pieces near the Sons of·Chamor *the*
Ac 9:15 of·Gentiles and kings, and·also the·Sons of·IsraEl.
Heb 7:5 the·ones from·among the Sons of·Levi receiving
Heb 11:21 ·dying) blessed each of·the Sons of·Joseph, and
Heb 11:22 concerning the exodus of·the Sons of·IsraEl, and
Mt 20:20 the mother of·the·Sons of·Zebedee came·alongside
Mt 27:9 who was·appraised by·the·Sons of·IsraEl,
Mt 27:56 and Joses, and the mother of·the·Sons of·Zebedee.
Rm 8:19 fully·awaits the revealing of·the Sons of·God.
Rm 9:27 Although the number of·the Sons of·IsraEl may·be
Rv 2:14 to·cast a·trap in·the·sight of·the Sons of·IsraEl,
Rv 7:4 from·among all *the* tribes of·the·Sons of·IsraEl.
Rv 21:12 *names* of·the twelve tribes of·the Sons of·IsraEl.
G5207-1.2 N-NPM Υἱοί (13x)
Jn 12:36 light, in·order·that yeu·may·be the·Sons of·Light."
Lk 6:35 ·be large, and yeu·shall·be Sons of·the Most·High,
Lk 16:8 prudently. Because the Sons of·this present·age are
Lk 20:36 ·Sons of·God, being the·Sons of·the Resurrection.
Mt 8:12 But the Sons of·the kingdom shall·be·cast·out into
Mt 9:15 ·them, "¿!·Are the Sons of·the bride-chamber able
Mt 13:38 good seed, these are the Sons of·the kingdom. But
Mt 13:38 But the darnel·weeds are the Sons of·the Evil·One.
Mt 23:31 that yeu·are the·Sons of·the·ones murdering the
Mk 2:19 ·them, "¿!·Are the Sons of·the bride-chamber able
Mk 3:17 a·name: BoanErges, which is, "Sons of·Thunder;"
1Th 5:5 Yeu·yeurselves are all the·Sons of·Light and the·
1Th 5:5 all the·Sons of·Light and the·Sons of·Day. We·are
G5207-1.2 N-APM Υἱούς (4x)
Lk 5:34 yeu·able to·make the Sons of·the bride-chamber to·
Lk 16:8 ·prudent— above·and·beyond the Sons of·the Light
Eph 5:6 wrath of·God comes upon the Sons of·the obstinate.
Col 3:6 the wrath of·God comes on the Sons of·the obstinate,
G5207-1.2 N-DPM Υἱοῖς (1x)
Eph 2:2 spirit now operating in the Sons of·the obstinate.

G5208 ὕλη hýlē *n.* (1x)

Compare:G1409-1 G0068 See:G3586
G5208.1 N-ASF ὕλην (1x)
Jac 3:5 a·little fire kindles *something* as·big·as a·forest!

G5209 ὑμᾶς hymâs *p:p.* (444x)

Roots:G5210
(abbreviated listing for G5209)
G5209.ª P:P-2AP ὑμᾶς (1x)
(list for G5209.ª:P:P-2AP excluded)
G5209.1 P:P-2AP ὑμᾶς (428x)
(list for G5209.1:P:P-2AP excluded)
G5209.1 T-GSM ὑμᾶς (1x)
(list for G5209.1:T-GSM excluded)
EG5209.1 (9x)
(list for EG5209.1: excluded)
G5209.2 P:P-2AP ὑμᾶς (5x)
(list for G5209.2:P:P-2AP excluded)

G5210 ὑμεῖς hymêîs *p:p.* (244x)

Roots:G4771 See:G5209
xLangEquiv:H0859-1
(abbreviated listing for G5210)
G5210.1 P:P-2NP ὑμεῖς (98x)
(list for G5210.1:P:P-2NP excluded)
EG5210.1 (2x)
(list for EG5210.1: excluded)
G5210.2 P:P-2NP ὑμεῖς (144x)
(list for G5210.2:P:P-2NP excluded)

G5211 Ὑμεναῖος Hymênaîos *n/p.* (2x)

Compare:G5372 G1361
G5211.2 N/P-NSM Ὑμέναιος (2x)
1Ti 1:20 of·whom are Hymenaeus and AlexAnder, whom I·
2Ti 2:17 ·as·pasture, of·whom is Hymenaeus and Philetus,

G5212 ὑμέτερος hymétêros *p:s.* (9x)

Roots:G5210 Compare:G4674
G5212.1 P:S-2NPF ὑμετέρα (1x)
Lk 6:20 the helplessly·poor, because yeurs is the kingdom
G5212.1 P:S-2NPM ὑμέτερος (1x)
Jn 7:6 "My season is·not·yet here, but yeur season is always
G5212.1 P:S-2APM ὑμέτερον (1x)
Jn 15:20 my word, they·shall·observantly·keep yeurs also.
G5212.1 P:S-2DPF ὑμετέρᾳ (1x)
Gal 6:13 in·order·that they·may·boast in yeur flesh.
G5212.1 P:S-2DPM ὑμετέρῳ (2x)
Jn 8:17 also, it·has·been·written in yeur Torah-Law that the
Rm 11:31 now are·obstinate in·order·that by·yeur mercy,
G5212.1 P:S-2GPF ὑμετέρας (1x)
2Co 8:8 and to·test·and·prove the genuineness of·yeur love.
G5212.2 P:S-2APN ὑμέτερον (1x)
Lk 16:12 who shall·give to·yeu *wealth of* yeur·own?
G5212.2 P:S-2GPF ὑμετέρας (1x)
Ac 27:34 for this is·inherently·specific·for yeur salvation, for

G5213 ὑμῖν hymîn *p:p.* (623x)

Roots:G5210
(abbreviated listing for G5213)
EG5213 (3x)
(list for EG5213: excluded)
G5213.1 P:P-2DP ὑμῖν (617x)
(list for G5213.1:P:P-2DP excluded)
G5213.2 P:P-2DP ὑμῖν (3x)
(list for G5213.2:P:P-2DP excluded)

G5214 ὑμνέω hymnéō *v.* (3x)

Roots:G5215 Compare:G0103 G5567
G5214.1 V-AAP-NPM ὑμνήσαντες (2x)
Mt 26:30 And after·singing·a·psalm, they·went·out to·the
Mk 14:26 And after·singing·a·psalm, they·went·out to·the
G5214.2 V-IAI-3P ὕμνουν (1x)
Ac 16:25 Silas, while·praying, were·singing·praise·to God,

G5215 ὕμνος hýmnôs *n.* (2x)

Compare:G5603 G5568 G5567 See:G0103
G5215 N-DPM ὕμνοις (2x)
Eph 5:19 to·yeurselves in·psalms and hymns and spiritual
Col 3:16 yeurselves in·psalms and hymns and spiritual songs

G5216 ὑμῶν hymō̂n *p:p.* (589x)

Roots:G5210
(abbreviated listing for G5216)
G5216.1 P:P-2GP ὑμῶν (202x)
(list for G5216.1:P:P-2GP excluded)
EG5216.1 (1x)
(list for EG5216.1: excluded)
G5216.2 P:P-2GP ὑμῶν (2x)
(list for G5216.2:P:P-2GP excluded)
G5216.4 P:P-2GP ὑμῶν (296x)
(list for G5216.4:P:P-2GP excluded)
G5216.4 P:P-2GP@ ὑμῶν (1x)
(list for G5216.4:P:P-2GP@ excluded)
EG5216.4 (3x)
(list for EG5216.4: excluded)
G5216.5 P:P-2GP ὑμῶν (54x)
(list for G5216.5:P:P-2GP excluded)
EG5216.5 (1x)
(list for EG5216.5: excluded)
G5216.6 P:P-2GP ὑμῶν (24x)
(list for G5216.6:P:P-2GP excluded)
G5216.7 P:P-2GP ὑμῶν (3x)
(list for G5216.7:P:P-2GP excluded)
G5216.8 P:P-2GP ὑμῶν (1x)
(list for G5216.8:P:P-2GP excluded)
G5216.9 P:P-2GP ὑμῶν (1x)
(list for G5216.9:P:P-2GP excluded)

G5217 ὑπ•άγω hypágō *v.* (82x)

Roots:G5259 G0071 Compare:G4254 G0868 G1826
See:G4013
G5217.2 V-PAI-1S ὑπάγω (15x)
Jn 7:33 ·I with yeu, and·then I·head·on·out toward the·one
Jn 8:14 ·what·source I·came and where I·head·on·out. But
Jn 8:14 from·what·source I·come and where I·head·on·out.
Jn 8:21 to·them, "I·myself head·on·out, and yeu·shall·seek
Jn 8:21 moral·failures. Where I·myself head·on·out, yeu
Jn 8:22 he·says, 'Where I·myself head·on·out, yeu are·not
Jn 13:33 'Where I·myself head·on·out, yeu are·not able to·
Jn 13:36 him, "Where I·head·on·out, you·are·not able to·
Jn 14:4 ·know to·where *it·is that* I·myself head·on·out, and
Jn 14:28 declared to·yeu, 'I·head·on·out, and I·come *back* to
Jn 16:5 "But now I·head·on·out toward the·one sending me,
Jn 16:10 righteousness, because I·head·on·out toward my
Jn 16:16 ·upon me, because I·myself head·on·out toward the
Jn 16:17 and 'I·myself head·on·out toward the Father'?
Jn 21:3 Peter says to·them, "I·head·on·out to·fish." They·
G5217.2 V-PAI-2S ὑπάγεις (5x)
Jn 11:8 to·stone you, and do·you·head·on·out there again?
Jn 13:36 "Lord, where·do you·head·on·out?" Jesus
Jn 14:5 ·know to·where *it·is that* you·head·on·out, so·then

Αα Ββ Γγ Δδ Εε Ζζ Ηη Θθ Ιι Κκ Λλ Μμ Νν Ξξ Οο Ππ Ρρ Σσ Ττ Υυ Φφ Χχ Ψψ Ωω

Jn 16:5 you asks·of me, 'Where·do you·head·on·out?'
Lk 12:58 For as you·head·on·out with your legal·adversary
G5217.2 V-PAI-3S ὑπάγει (8x)
Jn 3:8 from·what·source it·comes or where it·heads·on·out.
Jn 11:31 saying, "She·heads·on·out to the chamber·tomb
Jn 13:3 ·forth from God and was·heading·on·out to God),
Mt 13:44 from the joy of·it, he·heads·on·out and sells all
Mt 26:24 of·Clay·Man† heads·on·out just·as it·has·been·
Mk 14:21 the Son of·Clay·Man† heads·on·out, just·as it·
Rv 13:10 ·captivity, *he·himself also* heads into war·captivity
Rv 17:11 the seven, and it·heads·on·out to total·destruction.
G5217.2 V-PAM-2S ὕπαγε (22x)
Jn 4:16 Jesus says to·her, "Head·on·out, holler·out·for your
Jn 7:3 "Walk·on from·here and head·on·out into Judea, that
Jn 9:7 and he·declared to·him, "Head·on·out, wash in the
Jn 9:11 and he·declared to·me, 'Head·on·out to the pool of·
Mt 4:10 says to·him, "Head·on·out, Adversary-Accuser! For
Mt 5:24 before the Sacrifice·Altar and head·on·out. First be·
Mt 5:41 *to·head·out·for* one mile, head·on·out with him two.
Mt 8:4 *this* to·no·one. But·rather head·on·out, show yourself
Mt 8:13 declared to·the centurion, "Head·on·out; and as
Mt 9:6 take·up your simple·couch and head·on·out to your
Mt 18:15 ·morally·fail against you, head·on·out and reprove
Mt 19:21 If you·want to·be complete, head·on·out, sell your
Mt 20:14 Take·up the·thing *that·is* yours and head·on·out.
Mt 21:28 he·declared, 'Child, head·on·out. Work today in
Mk 1:44 ·not·even·one·man. But·rather head·on·out, show
Mk 2:11 take·up your mat, and head·on·out to your house.
Mk 5:19 but·rather says to·him, "Head·on·out to your house
Mk 5:34 has·made you safe·and·well. Head·on·out in peace
Mk 7:29 "On·account·of this saying, head·on·out. The
Mk 10:21 "One·thing you lack, head·on·out, sell as·much·as
Mk 10:52 Jesus declared to·him, "Head·on·out, your trust
Rv 10:8 and saying, "Head·on·out! Take the tiny·official·
G5217.2 V-PAM-2P ὑπάγετε (14x)
Lk 10:3 Head·on·out. Behold, I·myself dispatch yeu as
Lk 19:30 declaring, "Head·on·out into the village directly·
Mt 8:32 And he·declared to·them, "Head·on·out." And
Mt 20:4 ·declared, 'Yeu also head·on·out into the vineyard,
Mt 20:7 'Also yeu·yeurselves head·on·out into the vineyard
Mt 26:18 And he·declared, "Head·on·out into the City to a·
Mt 27:65 a·sentinel·guard. Head·on·out. Make·*it*·as·secure
Mt 28:10 be·afraid! Yeu·must·head·on·out *and* announce
Mk 6:38 loaves·of·bread do·yeu·have? Head·on·out and see
Mk 11:2 and says to·them, "Head·on·out into the village
Mk 14:13 and says to·them, "Head·on·out into the City, and
Mk 16:7 Moreover, head·on·out! Declare to·his disciples
Jac 2:16 yeu should·declare to·them, "Head·on·out in peace,
Rv 16:1 to·the seven angels, "Head·on·out and pour·out the
G5217.2 V-PAN ὑπάγειν (6x)
Jn 6:67 "And *do* yeu·yeurselves not want to·head·on·out?"
Jn 11:44 "Loose him, and allow·him to·head·on·out."
Jn 18:8 if yeu·seek me, allow these·men to·head·on·out,"
Lk 8:42 But with him heading·on·out, the crowds were·
Lk 17:14 it·happened, with them heading·on·out, *that* they·
Rv 17:8 ·pit, and to·head·on·out to total·destruction. And
G5217.2 V-PAP-APM ὑπάγοντας (1x)
Mk 6:33 Yet the crowds saw them heading·on·out, and many
G5217.2 V-PAP-NPM ὑπάγοντες (1x)
Mk 6:31 there·were many coming and heading·on·out, and
G5217.2 V-PAS-2P ὑπάγητε (1x)
Jn 15:16 yeu·yeurselves should·head·on·out and should·bear
G5217.2 V-PAS-3S ὑπάγῃ (1x)
Rv 14:4 the Lamb wherever he·may·head·on·out. These
G5217.2 V-IAI-3P ὑπῆγον (1x)
Jn 12:11 ·the Judeans were·heading·on·out and were·trusting
EG5217.2 (1x)
Mt 5:41 ·and·impose·upon you *to·head·out·for* one mile,
G5217.3 V-PAI-3S ὑπάγει (2x)
Jn 12:35 does·not personally·know where he·is·heading.
1Jn 2:11 ·not personally·know where he·is·heading, because
G5217.3 V-IAI-3P ὑπῆγον (1x)
Jn 6:21 upon the dry·ground for which they·were·heading.

G5217.4 V-PAM-2S ὕπαγε (3x)
Lk 4:8 declared to·him, "Get·yourself·back behind me,
Mt 16:23 ·declared to·Peter, "Get·yourself·back behind me,
Mk 8:33 Peter, saying, "Get·yourself·back behind me,

G5218 ὑπ•ακοή hypakôḗ *n.* (15x)
Roots:G5219 Compare:G3876 See:G5255
G5218.3 N-NSF ὑπακοή (2x)
Rm 16:19 yeur attentive·obedience is·already·broadcast to
2Co 10:6 yeur attentive·obedience should·be·completely·.
G5218.3 N-ASF ὑπακοήν (8x)
Heb 5:8 the attentive·obedience from the·things·which he·
Rm 1:5 for an·attentive·obedience of·trust among all the
Rm 6:16 yeurselves *as* slaves in attentive·obedience? *Yeu·*
Rm 15:18 me for an·attentive·obedience among·Gentiles,
Rm 16:26 Gentiles— for an·attentive·obedience of·trust),
1Pe 1:2 ·Spirit— to an·attentive·obedience and a·sprinkling
2Co 7:15 ·and·considering the attentive·obedience of·yeu all,
2Co 10:5 unto the attentive·obedience of·Anointed-One—
G5218.3 N-DSF ὑπακοῇ (2x)
1Pe 1:22 yeur souls in the attentive·obedience of·the truth
Phm 1:21 ·confidence in·your attentive·obedience, I·wrote
G5218.3 N-GSF ὑπακοῆς (3x)
Rm 5:19 ·manner through the attentive·obedience of·the one,
Rm 6:16 to death, or of·attentive·obedience to righteousness
1Pe 1:14 As attentively·obedient children, do·not be·

G5219 ὑπ•ακούω hypakôúō *v.* (21x)
Roots:G5259 G0191 Compare:G4337 See:G5218 G5219 xLangAlso:H8085 A8086
G5219.1 V-AAN ὑπακοῦσαι (1x)
Ac 12:13 by·name) came·alongside to·listen·attentively.
G5219.3 V-PAI-2P ὑπακούετε (1x)
Rm 6:16 to·whom yeu·listen·and·obey, indeed·whether of·
G5219.3 V-PAI-3S ὑπακούει (1x)
2Th 3:14 if anyone does·not listen·to·and·obey our word
G5219.3 V-PAI-3P ὑπακούουσιν (4x)
Lk 8:25 and the water, and they·listen·to·and·obey him."
Mt 8:27 even the winds and the sea listen·to·and·obey him!"
Mk 1:27 impure spirits, and they·listen·to·and·obey him."
Mk 4:41 even the wind and the sea listen·to·and·obey him?
G5219.3 V-PAM-2P ὑπακούετε (4x)
Eph 6:1 *Now* the children: Listen·to·and·obey yeur parents
Eph 6:5 *Now* the slaves: Listen·to·and·obey the lords (*the·*
Col 3:20 children: Yeu·must·listen·to·and·obey the parents
Col 3:22 slaves: Yeu·must·listen·to·and·obey in all·things
G5219.3 V-PAN ὑπακούειν (1x)
Rm 6:12 body, such·for *yeu* to·listen·to·and·obey her in its
G5219.3 V-PAP-DPM ὑπακούουσιν (2x)
Heb 5:9 to·all the·ones listening·to·and·obeying him,
2Th 1:8 ·ones not listening·to·and·obeying the good·news
G5219.3 V-IAI-3P ὑπήκουον (1x)
Ac 6:7 ·that·offer·sacrifices were·listening·to·and·obeying
G5219.3 V-AAI-2P ὑπηκούσατε (2x)
Rm 6:17 but yeu·listened·and·obeyed from·out of·*the·*heart
Php 2:12 beloved, just·as yeu·listened·and·obeyed always
G5219.3 V-AAI-3S ὑπήκουσεν (3x)
Lk 17:6 in the sea,' and it·would listen·to·and·obey yeu.
Heb 11:8 for an·inheritance, listened·and·obeyed; and he·
1Pe 3:6 ·as Sarah, *who* listened·to·and·obeyed AbRaham,
G5219.3 V-AAI-3P ὑπήκουσαν (1x)
Rm 10:16 ·yet not all listened·to·and·obeyed the good·news.

G5220 ὕπ•ανδρος hýpandrôs *adj.* (1x)
Roots:G5259 G0435 See:G4801
G5220.2 A-NSF ὕπανδρος (1x)
Rm 7:2 *yoked·together* under·a·husband has·been·bound by·

G5221 ὑπ•αντάω hypantáō *v.* (5x)
Roots:G5259 G0470-2 Compare:G4876 See:G5222
G5221.2 V-AAI-3S ὑπήντησεν (3x)
Jn 11:20 that Jesus was·coming, went·and·met him, but
Jn 11:30 was in the place where Martha went·and·met him.
Jn 12:18 the crowd *from JeruSalem* also went·and·met him,
G5221.3 V-AAI-3S ὑπήντησεν (1x)
Lk 8:27 the dry·ground, there·came·and·met him a·certain

G5221.3 V-AAI-3P ὑπήντησαν (1x)
Mt 8:28 ·the Girgashites, there·came·and·met him two·men

G5222 ὑπ•άντησις hypántēsis *n.* (1x)
Roots:G5221 Compare:G0529 G4877 See:G1519
G5222.2 N-ASF ὑπάντησιν (1x)
Jn 12:13 of·palm·trees, and went·forth to meet him, and

G5223 ὕπ•αρξις hýparxis *n.* (2x)
Roots:G5225
G5223.1 N-ASF ὕπαρξιν (1x)
Heb 10:34 ·significantly·better and an·enduring subsistence.
G5223.2 N-APF ὑπάρξεις (1x)
Ac 2:45 the possessions and the items·of·subsistence, and

G5224 ὑπ•άρχοντα hypárchônta *v.* (14x)
Roots:G5225 Compare:G2186-3 xLangAlso:H5233 A5232
G5224.2 V-PAP-APN ὑπάρχοντα (5x)
Lk 12:33 "Sell yeur holdings and give a·merciful·act·of·
Lk 16:1 as·though thoroughly·squandering his holdings.
Mt 19:21 head·on·out, sell your holdings and give to·*the*
Mt 25:14 ·own slaves and handed·over his holdings to·them.
1Co 13:3 *helpless·beggars using* all my holdings, and though
G5224.2 V-PAP-DPN ὑπάρχουσιν (3x)
Lk 12:44 he·shall·fully·establish him over all his holdings.
Lk 14:33 orderly·take·leave·of all his holdings, he·is·not
Mt 24:47 he·shall·fully·establish him over all his holdings.
G5224.2 V-PAP-GPN ὑπαρχόντων (5x)
Lk 8:3 who were·attending to·him from their·own holdings.
Lk 12:15 from·out of·one's holdings *does* anyone's life† itself
Lk 19:8 the half of·my holdings I·give to·the helplessly·
Ac 4:32 was·saying *for* any of·his holdings to·be his·own;
Heb 10:34 joy the plundering of·yeur holdings, knowing for
G5224.2 V-PAP-NPN ὑπάρχοντα (1x)
Lk 11:21 ·over his·own mansion, his holdings are at peace.

G5225 ὑπ•άρχω hypárchō *v.* (49x)
Roots:G5259 G0756 Compare:G1511 G5607 See:G5223 G5224 xLangEquiv:H3426 A0383
G5225.2 V-PAI-3S ὑπάρχει (1x)
Ac 3:6 Silver and gold, it·does·not subsist with·me, but that·
G5225.2 V-PAN ὑπάρχειν (4x)
Ac 19:36 yeu to·subsist having·been·fully·quieted·down and
Ac 28:18 on·account·of there not subsisting even·one cause
2Pe 3:11 what·manner is·necessary·for yeu to·subsist in *all*
1Co 11:18 I·hear *for* severing·schisms to·subsist among yeu
G5225.2 V-PAP-GSF ὑπαρχούσης (1x)
Ac 27:21 *soul* subsisting a·long·while without·a·bite·of·food
G5225.2 V-PAP-GSM ὑπάρχοντος (1x)
Ac 4:37 *and was* subsisting by·himself on·a·plot·of·land.
G5225.2 V-PAP-NSM ὑπάρχων (3x)
Lk 16:23 ·lifting·up his eyes while·subsisting in torments,
Rm 4:19 subsisting somewhere·near a·hundred·years·of·
Php 2:6 who, subsisting in *the* fundamental·nature of·God,
G5225.2 V-PAP-NPN ὑπάρχοντα (1x)
2Pe 1:8 For *with* these·things subsisting in·yeu and
G5225.2 V-PAP-NPM ὑπάρχοντες (1x)
Lk 7:25 in glorious attire, also subsisting in·delicate·luxury,
G5225.2 V-PAS-3P ὑπάρχωσιν (1x)
Jac 2:15 if a·brother or sister should·subsist *being* naked and
G5225.2 V-IAI-3S ὑπῆρχεν (4x)
Lk 8:41 he·himself was·subsisting *as* an·executive·director
Ac 4:34 For neither was anyone subsisting among them in·a·
Ac 10:12 ·animals of·the earth were·subsisting, and the wild·
Ac 28:7 about the same place, there·were *some* open·fields
G5225.2 V-IAI-3P ὑπῆρχον (2x)
Ac 4:34 for as·many·as were·subsisting *being* possessors
Ac 8:16 but they·were·subsisting merely having·been·
EG5225.2 (1x)
2Co 11:27 *subsisting* in weariness and travail, in
G5225.3 V-PAI-3S ὑπάρχει (2x)
Ac 27:34 for this is·inherently specific·for yeur salvation,
Php 3:20 For our communal·citizenship inherently·is in *the*
G5225.3 V-PAI-3P ὑπάρχουσιν (1x)
Ac 21:20 having·trusted? And they·inherently·are all zealots

G5225.3 V-PAN ὑπάρχειν (2x)
1Co 7:26 ·deem for·this to·inherently·be good on·account·of
1Co 12:22 the·ones seeming to·inherently·be more·feeble,
G5225.3 V-PAP-ASM ὑπάρχοντα (1x)
Ac 17:27 though·indeed inherently·being not at·a·distance
G5225.3 V-PAP-APM ὑπάρχοντας (1x)
Ac 16:37 men·of·clay†, *though* inherently·being Romans,
G5225.3 V-PAP-GSN ὑπάρχοντος (1x)
Ac 19:40 with·there·inherently·being not·even·one cause
G5225.3 V-PAP-GSM ὑπάρχοντος (1x)
Ac 27:12 And with·the harbor inherently·being unsuitable,
G5225.3 V-PAP-NSM ὑπάρχων (13x)
Lk 9:48 me, for the·one inherently·being least among yeu all
Lk 23:50 a·counselor inherently·being a·beneficially·good
Ac 2:30 Accordingly, inherently·being a·prophet and
Ac 3:2 And a·certain man inherently·being lame from·out
Ac 7:55 But *Stephen*, inherently·being full of·Holy Spirit,
Ac 14:8 ·was·sitting·down, inherently·being lame from·out
Ac 17:24 it, the·same·one inherently·being Lord of·heaven
Ac 22:3 esteemed·father, inherently·being a·zealot of·God,
Gal 1:14 inherently·being more·exceedingly a·zealot of·my
Gal 2:14 "If you, inherently·being a·Jew, live as·a·Gentile
1Co 11:7 his head, inherently·being God's derived·image
2Co 8:17 exhortation; but inherently·being more·diligent,
2Co 12:16 *·reckon that*, inherently·being shrewdly·cunning,
G5225.3 V-PAP-NPM ὑπάρχοντες (5x)
Lk 11:13 if yeu, inherently·being evil, personally·know·
Lk 16:14 the Pharisees, inherently·being fond·of·money,
Ac 16:20 "These men·of·clay†, inherently·being Jews, do·
Ac 17:29 Accordingly, inherently·being kindred of·God,
2Pe 2:19 *are* themselves inherently·being slaves of·the
G5225.3 V-IAI-3S ὑπῆρχεν (2x)
Ac 5:4 And being·sold·off, inherently·was·it *not·indeed* in
Ac 16:3 ·all had·seen that his father inherently·was a·Greek.

G5226 ὑπ•είκω hypêíkō *v.* (1x)
Roots:G5259 G1502 Compare:G3980 G5255 G5293
G5226 V-PAM-2P ὑπείκετε (1x)
Heb 13:17 ·governing among·yeu, and yield·yeurselves—

G5227 ὑπ•εν•αντίος hypênantíôs *adj.* (2x)
Roots:G5259 G1727 Compare:G0436 G0496 G2190
G5227.2 A-NSN ὑπεναντίον (1x)
Col 2:14 (the decrees which were sternly·opposed to·us), and
G5227.2 A-APM ὑπεναντίους (1x)
Heb 10:27 *·is* about 'to·devour the·ones sternly·opposed.'

G5228 ὑπέρ hypér *prep.* (163x)
Compare:G0507 G5259 G1909 See:G4012
xLangAlso:H5921
G5228.1 PREP ὑπέρ (20x)
Ac 12:5 But earnest prayer over him was being·made to God
Mt 10:37 affectionately·favoring father or mother over me is
Mt 10:37 affectionately·favoring son or daughter over me is
Rm 5:7 For scarcely over a·righteous·man shall anyone die,
Rm 5:7 die, for perhaps over the beneficially·good·man,
Rm 8:27 *is*, how he·makes·intercession over *the* holy·ones
Jac 5:16 and well-wish *to·God* on·behalf of·one·another,
Php 4:10 yeur·earnest·concern over me has·flourished·again,
1Co 10:30 why am·I·reviled over that·for·which I·myself
1Co 11:24 my body, the·one being·broken over yeu. Do this
1Co 12:25 should·be·anxious the same over one·another.
2Co 1:8 yeu to·be·ignorant, brothers, over our tribulation,
2Co 5:12 yeu an·impromptu·occasion for·boasting over us,
2Co 8:24 of·yeur love and of·our boasting over yeu, and *do·*
2Co 9:2 for·which I·boast over yeu to·*the*·Macedonians,
2Co 12:8 Over this·matter, I·implored the Lord three·times
Eph 1:22 feet' and gave him *to·be* head over all *things* in·the
Eph 3:13 not to·be·despondent in my tribulations over yeu,
Col 4:13 ·him, that he·has much zeal over yeu, and the·ones
1Ti 2:1 ·of·thankfulness to·be·made over all men·of·clay†,
G5228.2 PREP ὑπέρ (9x)
Lk 6:40 "A·disciple is not above his instructor, but everyone
Gal 1:14 ·advancing in Judaism above many my·own·age
Mt 10:24 "A·disciple is not above the instructor, nor·even a·
Mt 10:24 the instructor, nor·even a·slave above his lord.
Php 2:9 on·him a·name, the·one above every name,
1Co 4:6 *of·men* above that·which has·been·written, in·order·
1Co 10:13 ·not let yeu to·be·tried above what yeu·are·able,
2Co 12:6 ·reckon to me above that·which he·looks·upon me
Phm 1:16 as a·slave, but·rather above a·slave, a·brother
EG5228.2 (1x)
2Co 12:6 ·upon me *to·be*, or *above* what he·hears from·out
G5228.3 PREP ὑπέρ (3x)
Ac 26:13 the way a·light from·heaven beyond the brilliance
2Co 1:8 we·were·weighed·down beyond *our·own* ability *to·*
2Co 12:13 is·it in·which yeu·were·inferior beyond the rest
G5228.4 PREP ὑπέρ (9x)
Lk 16:8 are more·prudent— above·and·beyond the Sons of·
Heb 4:12 *he·is* sharper, above·and·beyond any double-edged
1Th 3:10 petitioning *him* above·and·beyond for this·thing:
1Th 5:13 with love above·and·beyond, on·account·of their
2Co 8:3 I·testify, even above·and·beyond *their* power, of·
2Co 11:23 I·speak— I·myself *am* above·and·beyond! … in
Eph 3:20 who·is·being·able, above·and·beyond all·things,
Eph 3:20 to·do above·and·beyond from·out of·an·abundance
Phm 1:21 ·shall·do also above·and·beyond that·which I·say.
G5228.5 PREP ὑπέρ (112x)
Jn 6:51 which I·myself shall·give on·behalf of·the life† of·
Jn 10:11 lays·down his·own soul on·behalf of·the sheep.
Jn 10:15 and I·lay·down my soul on·behalf of·the sheep.
Jn 11:4 toward death, but·rather on·behalf of·the glory of·
Jn 11:50 man·of·clay† should·die on·behalf of·the People,
Jn 11:51 that Jesus was·about to·die on·behalf of·the nation;
Jn 11:52 and not on·behalf of·the nation merely, but·rather
Jn 13:37 I·shall·lay·down my soul on·behalf of·you."
Jn 13:38 "Shall·you·lay·down your soul on·behalf of·me?
Jn 15:13 should·lay·down his soul on·behalf of·his friends.
Jn 17:19 "And on·behalf of·them, I·myself make my·own·
Jn 18:14 to·be·completely·destroyed on·behalf of·the People
Lk 6:28 pray on·behalf of·the·ones abusively·threatening
Lk 9:50 for whoever is not against us is on·behalf of·us."
Lk 22:19 body, the·one being·given on·yeur behalf. Do this
Lk 22:20 blood, the *blood* being·poured·out on·yeur behalf.
Ac 5:41 to·be·dishonorably·treated on·behalf of·his name.
Ac 8:24 petition to the Lord on·my behalf, that not·even·one
Ac 9:16 ·mandatory·for him to·suffer on·behalf of·my name.
Ac 15:26 ·handed·over their souls on·behalf of·the name of·
Ac 21:13 also to·die at JeruSalem on·behalf of·the name of·
Ac 21:26 offering should·be·offered on·behalf of·each one
Ac 26:1 for·you to·discourse on·your·own behalf." Then
Heb 2:9 ·grace of·God he·should·taste death on·behalf of·all.
Heb 5:1 is·fully·established on·behalf of·men·of·clay† in·
Heb 5:1 presents and sacrifices on·behalf of·moral·failures,
Heb 5:3 to·offer *sacrifices* on·behalf of·moral·failures.
Heb 6:20 where a·forerunner entered on·behalf of·us—
Heb 7:25 always living to·make·intercession on·their behalf.
Heb 7:27 *altar*, first on·behalf of·their·own moral·failures,
Heb 9:7 blood, which he·offered on·behalf of·himself, and
Heb 9:24 in·the personal·presence of·God on·our behalf.
Heb 10:12 one sacrifice on·behalf of·moral·failures into
Heb 13:17 they·themselves stay·alert on·behalf of·yeur souls
Gal 1:4 ·one giving himself on·behalf of·our moral·failures,
Gal 2:20 and already·handing himself over on·my behalf.
Gal 3:13 becoming a·curse on·our behalf— for it·has·been·
Mt 5:44 pray on·behalf of·the·ones abusively·threatening
Mk 9:40 For whoever is not against yeu is on·behalf of·yeu.
Rm 1:8 God through Jesus Anointed on·behalf of·all of·yeu,
Rm 5:6 Anointed-One died on·behalf of·irreverent·men
Rm 5:8 ·of·moral·failure, Anointed-One died on·our behalf.
Rm 8:26 on·our behalf with·groanings unspeakable.
Rm 8:31 If God *does·this* on·our behalf, who *is·able to·be*
Rm 8:32 but·rather handed him over on·behalf of·us all,
Rm 8:34 who also makes·intercession on·behalf of·us.
Rm 9:3 from the Anointed-One on·behalf of·my brothers,
Rm 10:1 and petition to God on·behalf of·IsraEl is for
Rm 14:15 ·your food, on·behalf of·whom Anointed-One
Rm 15:8 of·*the*·Circumcision on·behalf of·God's truth, in·
Rm 15:9 the Gentiles to·glorify God on·behalf *of·his* mercy,
Rm 15:30 with·me in the prayers to God on·my behalf,
Rm 16:4 who risked their·own necks on·behalf of·my soul,
Php 1:4 in every petition of·mine on·behalf of·yeu all while·
Php 1:7 for·me to·contemplate this on·behalf of·all of·yeu,
Php 1:29 ·bestowed to·yeu, on·behalf of·Anointed-One, not
Php 1:29 in him, but·rather also to·suffer on·behalf of·him,
Php 2:13 and to·operate on·behalf of·*his*·good·purpose.
1Pe 2:21 also suffered on·our behalf, leaving·behind a·
1Pe 3:18 a·righteous·one on·behalf of·unrighteous·ones, in·
1Pe 4:1 already·suffering on·behalf of·us in·flesh, even yeu·
1Th 5:10 the·one dying on·our behalf in·order·that, whether
2Th 1:4 of·God on·behalf of·yeur patient·endurance and
2Th 1:5 of·the kingdom of·God, on·behalf of·which also
2Th 2:1 yeu, brothers, on·behalf of·the·returning·Presence
Tit 2:14 who gave himself on·our behalf in·order·that 'he·
1Co 1:13 ¿!·Was Paul crucified on·yeur behalf? Or were·
1Co 4:6 not one *of* yeu·may·be·puffed·up over the *other*,
1Co 5:7 Passover·lamb, is·already·sacrificed on·our behalf.
1Co 15:3 Anointed-One died on·behalf of·our moral·failures
1Co 15:29 the·ones being·immersed on·behalf of·the dead,
1Co 15:29 then are·they·immersed on·behalf of·the dead?
2Co 1:6 ·are·hard-pressed, *it·is* on·behalf of·yeur comforting
2Co 1:6 ·are·comforted, *it·is* on·behalf of·yeur comforting
2Co 1:7 And our expectation on·yeur behalf *is* steadfast,
2Co 1:11 by·the petition on·our behalf, birthed·from·out·of·
2Co 1:11 *such·that* thanks·may·be·given on·our behalf.
2Co 5:14 that if one died on·behalf of·all, then·by·inference
2Co 5:15 Also, he·died on·behalf of·all in·order·that the·
2Co 5:15 ·dying on·their behalf and already·being·awakened
2Co 5:20 Now·then, we·are·elder·spokesmen on·behalf of·,
2Co 5:20 We·petition *yeu* on·behalf of·Anointed-One, be·
2Co 5:21 a·reparation·for·moral·failure on·behalf of·us, in·
2Co 7:7 distressing, yeur fervency on·behalf of·me, such·for
2Co 7:12 because·of·yeur earnest·care on·our behalf— for·it
2Co 8:16 earnest·care into·the heart of·Titus on·yeur behalf.
2Co 9:3 boasting on·yeur behalf should·be·made·empty on
2Co 9:14 And by·their petition on·behalf of·yeu, they·are·
2Co 12:5 On·behalf of·such·a·man, I·shall·boast; but on·
2Co 12:5 I·shall·boast; but on·behalf of·my·own·self, I·
2Co 12:10 in calamities on·behalf of·Anointed-One, for
2Co 12:15 and shall·be·utterly·spent on·behalf of·yeur souls,
2Co 12:19 dearly·beloved, on·behalf of·yeur edification.
2Co 13:8 against the truth, but·rather on·behalf of·the truth.
Eph 1:16 I·do·not cease giving·thanks on·behalf of·yeu,
Eph 3:1 of·Jesus, the Anointed-One, on·behalf of·yeu, the
Eph 5:2 handed himself over on·our behalf, an·offering and
Eph 5:20 giving·thanks always on·behalf of·all·things *to·our*
Eph 5:25 ·Citizenry and handed himself over on·her behalf,
Eph 6:19 and·also on·my behalf in·order·that *a·thoroughly·*
Eph 6:20 on·behalf of·which I·am·an·elder·spokesman in a·
Col 1:7 attendant on·yeur behalf of·the Anointed-One,
Col 1:9 do·not cease praying on·yeur behalf and requesting
Col 1:24 in my afflictions on·yeur behalf, and additionally·
Col 1:24 Anointed-One in my flesh on·behalf of·his Body,
Col 4:12 yeu, always striving on·yeur behalf in·the prayers,
Phm 1:13 in·order·that on·your behalf, he·may·attend to·
1Ti 2:2 on·behalf of·kings and all the·ones being in superior·
1Ti 2:6 *as* a·substitutionary·ransom on·behalf of·all— the
1Jn 3:16 that·one laid·down his·own soul on·behalf of·us,
1Jn 3:16 ·lay·down *our·own* souls on·behalf of·the brothers.
3Jn 1:7 For on·behalf of·the name, they·went·forth, taking
EG5228.5 (2x)
Heb 7:27 *and* then·afterward *on·behalf* of·the·ones of·the
Heb 9:7 of·himself, and *on·behalf* of·the ignorant·errors of·
G5228.6 PREP ὑπέρ (5x)
Rm 1:5 of·trust among all the Gentiles concerning his name,
Rm 9:27 But IsaIah yells·out concerning IsraEl, '" Although
2Co 7:4 large *is* my boasting concerning yeu. I·have·been·
2Co 7:14 if I·have·boasted anything to·him concerning yeu,
2Co 8:23 If *any·should·inquire* concerning Titus, *he·is* my
G5228.7 PREP ὑπέρ (2x)
2Co 11:5 ·fallen·short·of the very highest of·ambassadors.
2Co 12:11 ·I·fall·short·of the very highest of·ambassadors,

Αα Ββ Γγ Δδ Εε Ζζ Ηη Θθ Ιι Κκ Λλ Μμ Νν Ξξ Οο Ππ Ρρ Σσ Ττ Υυ Φφ Χχ Ψψ Ωω

G5229 ὑπερ•αίρομαι hypêraírômai *v.* (3x)
Roots:G5228 G0142 Compare:G1869 G5312
G5229.2 V-PPP-NSM ὑπεραιρόμενος (1x)
2Th 2:4 and 'is·arrogantly·exalting·himself over all *that·is*
G5229.2 V-PPS-1S ὑπεραίρωμαι (2x)
2Co 12:7 ·that I·should·not arrogantly·exalt·myself for·the
2Co 12:7 me, that I·should·not arrogantly·exalt·myself.

G5230 ὑπέρ•ακμος hypérakmôs *adj.* (1x)
Roots:G5228 G0188
G5230.2 A-NSM ὑπέρακμος (1x)
1Co 7:36 if she·should·be past·her·prime and financial·need

G5231 ὑπερ•άνω hypêránō *adv.* (3x)
Roots:G5228 G0507
G5231.2 ADV ὑπεράνω (1x)
Heb 9:5 And up·over it *were* kerubim of·glory fully·
G5231.3 ADV ὑπεράνω (2x)
Eph 1:21 high·above all principality and authority, power
Eph 4:10 is himself also the·one ascending high·above all the

G5232 ὑπερ•αυξάνω hypêrauxánō *v.* (1x)
Roots:G5228 G0837
G5232 V-PAI-3S ὑπεραυξάνει (1x)
2Th 1:3 because yeur trust grows·exceedingly, and the love

G5233 ὑπερ•βαίνω hypêrbaínō *v.* (1x)
Roots:G5228 G0901-3
G5233.2 V-PAN ὑπερβαίνειν (1x)
1Th 4:6 *for·yeu* not to·overstep and to·swindle his brother in

G5234 ὑπερ•βαλλόντως hypêrballóntōs *adv.* (1x)
Roots:G5235 Compare:G3357 G0280
G5234.2 ADV ὑπερβαλλόντως (1x)
2Co 11:23 in punishing·blows beyond·measure, in

G5235 ὑπερ•βάλλω hypêrbállō *v.* (6x)
Roots:G5228 G0906 Compare:G4052 G5242
G5235.2 V-PAP-ASF ὑπερβάλλουσαν (2x)
2Co 9:14 yeu, on·account·of the surpassing grace of·God
Eph 3:19 ·absolutely·know the surpassing knowledge of·the
G5235.2 V-PAP-ASM ὑπερβάλλοντα (1x)
Eph 2:7 in the upcoming ages the surpassing wealth of·his
G5235.2 V-PAP-GSF ὑπερβαλλούσης (1x)
2Co 3:10 because·of the surpassing glory *of·the Service of·*
G5235.2 V-PAP-NSN ὑπερβάλλον (1x)
Eph 1:19 and what *is* the surpassing greatness of·his power
EG5235.2 (1x)
2Co 3:11 glory, so·much more *surpassing is* the·one *of·the*

G5236 ὑπερ•βολή hypêrbôlḗ *n.* (8x)
Roots:G5235 Compare:G5247 See:G1519 G2596
G5236.3 N-NSF ὑπερβολή (1x)
2Co 4:7 in·order·that the surpassing·excellence of·the power
G5236.3 N-DSF ὑπερβολῇ (1x)
2Co 12:7 for·the surpassing·excellence of·the revelations,
G5236.4 N-ASF ὑπερβολήν (2x)
1Co 12:31 to·yeu *the* most surpassingly·excellent way.
2Co 4:17 "a·most surpassingly·excellent unto phenomenal"
G5236.5 N-ASF ὑπερβολήν (1x)
2Co 4:17 surpassingly·excellent unto phenomenal" eternal
G5236.6 N-ASF ὑπερβολήν (3x)
Gal 1:13 that most exceedingly I·was·persecuting the
Rm 7:13 ·become most exceedingly full·of·moral·failure.
2Co 1:8 that most exceedingly, we·were·weighed·down

Yυ

G5237 ὑπερ•είδω hypêréídō *v.* (1x)
Roots:G5228 G1492
G5237 V-AAP-NSM ὑπεριδών (1x)
Ac 17:30 in·fact, after·previously·overlooking the times of·

G5238 ὑπερ•έκεινα hypêrékêina *adv.* (1x)
Roots:G5228 G1565
G5238.2 ADV ὑπερέκεινα (1x)
2Co 10:16 into the *regions* further·beyond yeu *for·us* to·

G5239 ὑπερ•εκ•τείνω hypêrêktêínō *v.* (1x)
Roots:G5228 G1614
G5239.1 V-PAI-1P ὑπερεκτείνομεν (1x)
2Co 10:14 *even* to yeu. We·stretch·well·beyond ourselves,

G5240 ὑπερ•εκ•χύνω hypêrêkchýnō *v.* (1x)
Roots:G5228 G1632
G5240.2 V-PPP-ASN@ ὑπερεκχυνόμενον (1x)
Lk 6:38 *together*, and overflowing shall·they·give into *the*

G5241 ὑπερ•εν•τυγχάνω hypêrêntynchánō *v.* (1x)
Roots:G5228 G1793 xLangAlso:H6419
G5241 V-PAI-3S ὑπερεντυγχάνει (1x)
Rm 8:26 ·rather the Spirit himself intercedes on·our behalf

G5242 ὑπερ•έχω hypêréchō *v.* (7x)
Roots:G5228 G2192 Compare:G4052 G5235 G0511 G2519 G5308 See:G5247 xLangAlso:H7227
G5242.2 V-PAP-NSF ὑπερέχουσα (1x)
Php 4:7 of·God, the·one extending·itself·above·and·over all
G5242.3 V-PAP-APM ὑπερέχοντας (1x)
Php 2:3 one·another as·excelling·above·and·beyond their·.
G5242.4 V-PAP-DSM ὑπερέχοντι (1x)
1Pe 2:13 the Lord, whether to·a·king, as having·superiority,
EG5242.4 (1x)
Rm 13:7 render the dues to·all·ones *in·superior authority*:
G5242.5 V-PAP-ASN ὑπερέχον (1x)
Php 3:8 through the superiority of·the absolute·knowledge
G5242.6 V-PAP-DPF ὑπερεχούσαις (1x)
Rm 13:1 ·every soul submit·itself to·the·superior authorities.
EG5242.6 (1x)
Mt 23:7 Rabbi' *(meaning, my·Superior, my·Superior)*.

G5243 ὑπερ•ηφανία hypêrēphanía *n.* (1x)
Roots:G5244 Compare:G5450 G2754
G5243 N-NSF ὑπερηφανία (1x)
Mk 7:22 eye, revilement, haughtiness, *and* impulsiveness.

G5244 ὑπερ•ήφανος hypêréphanôs *adj.* (5x)
Roots:G5228 G5316 Compare:G5448 See:G5243
G5244.2 A-NPM ὑπερήφανοι (1x)
2Ti 3:2 fond·of·money, braggers, haughty, revilers,
G5244.2 A-APM ὑπερηφάνους (2x)
Lk 1:51 he·thoroughly·scattered haughty·men in·*the·* of·their
Rm 1:30 ·of·God, abusively·insolent, haughty, braggers,
G5244.2 A-DPM ὑπερηφάνοις (2x)
Jac 4:6 '" God arranges·himself·against haughty·men, but
1Pe 5:5 God arranges·himself·against haughty·men but gives

G5245 ὑπερ•νικάω hypêrnikáō *v.* (1x)
Roots:G5228 G3528
G5245.2 V-PAI-1P ὑπερνικῶμεν (1x)
Rm 8:37 all these·things we·gain·a·decisive·victory through

G5246 ὑπέρ•ογκος hypérônkôs *adj.* (2x)
Roots:G5228 G3591 Compare:G3827
G5246.2 A-APN ὑπέρογκα (2x)
Jud 1:16 mouth speaks outrageous·things, while·admiring
2Pe 2:18 when·they·are·enunciating outrageous·things of·,

G5247 ὑπερ•οχή hypêrôchḗ *n.* (2x)
Roots:G5242 Compare:G2519 G5236 G4053
G5247.2 N-ASF ὑπεροχήν (1x)
1Co 2:1 came not according·to superiority of·discourse or
G5247.3 N-DSF ὑπεροχῇ (1x)
1Ti 2:2 and all the·ones being in superior·rank, in·order·that

G5248 ὑπερ•περισσεύω hypêrpêrissêúō *v.* (2x)
Roots:G5228 G4052 See:G4050
G5248 V-PMI-1S ὑπερπερισσεύομαι (1x)
2Co 7:4 I·am·abounding·above·and·beyond with·the joy in
G5248 V-AAI-3S ὑπερεπερίσσευσεν (1x)
Rm 5:20 ·more, Grace did·abound·above·and·beyond,

G5249 ὑπερ•περισσῶς hypêrpêrissṓs *adv.* (1x)
Roots:G5228 G4057
G5249 ADV ὑπερπερισσῶς (1x)
Mk 7:37 they·were·astounded above·and·beyond·excess,

G5250 ὑπερ•πλεονάζω hypêrplêônázō *v.* (1x)
Roots:G5228 G4121
G5250.1 V-AAI-3S ὑπερεπλεόνασεν (1x)
1Ti 1:14 Lord increased·evermore·above·and·beyond with

G5251 ὑπερ•υψόω hypêrypsóō *v.* (1x)
Roots:G5228 G5312
G5251.3 V-AAI-3S ὑπερύψωσεν (1x)
Php 2:9 Therefore God also elevated him above·all·others

G5252 ὑπερ•φρονέω hypêrphrônéō *v.* (1x)
Roots:G5228 G5426
G5252 V-PAN ὑπερφρονεῖν (1x)
Rm 12:3 ·*him* not to·overly·esteem·himself more·than what

G5253 ὑπερῷον hypêrôôn *n.* (4x)
Roots:G5228 Compare:G2646
G5253.2 N-ASN ὑπερῷον (2x)
Ac 1:13 they·walked·up into the upper·chamber, where
Ac 9:39 they·led·*him*·up into the upper·chamber, and all the
G5253.2 N-DSN ὑπερῷῳ (2x)
Ac 9:37 ·bathing her, they·laid *her* in an·upper·chamber.
Ac 20:8 ·number·of lamps in the upper·chamber, where

G5254 ὑπ•έχω hypéchō *v.* (1x)
Roots:G5259 G2192
G5254.2 V-PAP-NPF ὑπέχουσαι (1x)
Jud 1:7 a·public·example, undergoing a·justice of·eternal

G5255 ὑπ•ήκοος hypḗkôôs *adj.* (3x)
Roots:G5219 Compare:G2138 G5293 See:G5218
G5255 A-NSM ὑπήκοος (1x)
Php 2:8 becoming attentively·obedient as·far·as·unto death,
G5255 A-NPM ὑπήκοοι (2x)
Ac 7:39 ·not want to·become attentively·obedient, but·rather
2Co 2:9 whether yeu·are attentively·obedient in all·things.

G5256 ὑπ•ηρετέω hypērêtéō *v.* (3x)
Roots:G5257 Compare:G1247
G5256.4 V-PAN ὑπηρετεῖν (1x)
Ac 24:23 not·one of·his own·company to·tend *to·him* or to·
G5256.4 V-AAI-3P ὑπηρέτησαν (1x)
Ac 20:34 know that these hands tended to·my needs and to·
G5256.4 V-AAP-NSM ὑπηρετήσας (1x)
Ac 13:36 "For in·fact David, after·tending to·the counsel of·

G5257 ὑπ•ηρέτης hypērétēs *n.* (20x)
Roots:G5259 Compare:G3492 G1249 G3411 See:G5256 xLangEquiv:H6686-1
G5257.3 N-NPM ὑπηρέται (9x)
Jn 7:45 So·then the assistants came to the chief·priests and
Jn 7:46 The assistants answered, "Never·at·any·time in·this·
Jn 18:12 and the assistants of·the Judeans arrested Jesus
Jn 18:18 And the slaves and the assistants stood *there*,
Jn 18:36 my assistants then·would strenuously·struggle in·
Jn 19:6 when the chief·priests and the assistants saw him,
Lk 1:2 ·becoming eyewitnesses and assistants of·the Word),
Ac 5:22 But the assistants, coming·directly *to·the dungeon*,
Mk 14:65 And the assistants were·casting slaps at·him.
G5257.3 N-ASM ὑπηρέτην (2x)
Ac 13:5 they·were·having also John·*Mark as·their* assistant.
Ac 26:16 to·handpick you *to·be* an·assistant and a·witness,
G5257.3 N-APM ὑπηρέτας (3x)
Jn 7:32 dispatched assistants in·order·that they·should·
Jn 18:3 the battalion and·also assistants from·among the
1Co 4:1 in·this·manner: as assistants of·Anointed-One and
G5257.3 N-DSM ὑπηρέτῃ (2x)
Lk 4:20 *and* giving·*it*·back to·the assistant, he·sat·down, also
Mt 5:25 should·hand you over to·the assistant, and you·shall·
G5257.3 N-DPM ὑπηρέταις (1x)
Ac 5:26 the high·warden along·with the assistants, brought
G5257.3 N-GPM ὑπηρετῶν (3x)
Jn 18:22 ·things, one of·the assistants standing·nearby gave
Mt 26:58 he·sat·down with the assistants to·see the end.
Mk 14:54 ·together with the assistants and warming·himself

G5258 ὕπνος hýpnôs *n.* (6x)
See:G5258-1 G5258-2 G0069 G1853 G5259 xLangEquiv:H8142 A8139
G5258.1 N-DSM ὕπνῳ (2x)
Lk 9:32 having·been·weighed·down with·heavy·sleep, but
Ac 20:9 becoming·weighed·down with·a·deep heavy·sleep.
G5258.1 N-GSM ὕπνου (4x)
Jn 11:13 the outstretched·resting of·the heavy·sleep.
Ac 20:9 after·being·weighed·down with heavy·sleep, he·fell
Mt 1:24 ·thoroughly·awakened from the heavy·sleep, did as

Rm 13:11 for·us to·be·awakened out of·heavy·sleep, for now
G5259 ὑπό hypó *prep.* (232x)
ὑπ- hyp- [shortened prefix]
Compare:G5228 See:G5270 xLangAlso:H8478
G5259.1 PREP ὑπό (54x)
Jn 1:48 ·out·for you, I·saw you being under the fig·tree."
Lk 7:6 For I·am not fit that you·should·enter under my roof.
Lk 7:8 am a·man·of·clay† being·assigned under authority,
Lk 7:8 authority, having soldiers under my·own·self, and I·
Lk 11:33 *it* in hiding, nor·even under the measuring·basket,
Lk 13:34 as a·hen *gathers* her brood under *her* wings, and
Lk 17:24 flashing from·out of·the·one *part* under heaven,
Lk 17:24 radiates·brightly to the *other·part* under heaven, in·
Ac 2:5 devout men from every nation under the heaven.
Ac 4:12 For there·is not·even another name under the heaven
Gal 3:10 of·works of·Torah-Law, they·are under a·curse—
Gal 3:22 all·things under moral·failure in·order·that, as·a·
Gal 3:23 to·come, we·were·dutifully·kept under Torah-Law,
Gal 3:25 no·longer under a·strict·elementary·school·teacher.
Gal 4:2 but·rather is under executive·guardians and estate·
Gal 4:3 were having·been·enslaved under the principles of·
Gal 4:4 ·out of·a·woman, coming·to·be under Torah-Law,
Gal 4:5 ·utterly·kinsman·redeem the·ones under Torah-Law,
Gal 4:21 the·ones wanting to·be under Torah-Law, do·yeu·
Gal 5:18 ·are·led by·Spirit, yeu·are not under Torah-Law.
Mt 5:15 a·lantern and place it under the measuring·basket,
Mt 8:8 not fit in·order·that you·should·enter under my roof,
Mt 8:9 For even I·myself am a·man·of·clay† under authority,
Mt 8:9 authority, having soldiers under my·own·self, and I·
Mt 14:24 sea, being·tormented under the breaking·waves,
Mt 17:12 Son of·Clay·Man† is·about to·suffer under them."
Mt 23:37 completely·gathers her chicks under her wings, yet
Mk 4:21 it·should·be·placed under the measuring·basket or
Mk 4:21 under the measuring·basket or under the couch,
Mk 4:32 birds of·the sky to·be·able to·nest under its shade."
Mk 5:26 many·things under many practitioners·of·healing
Rm 3:9 both Jews and Greeks, all to·be under moral·failure.
Rm 3:13 ' "*The* venom of·asps *is* under their lips."'
Rm 6:14 yeu, for yeu·are not under Torah-Law, but·rather
Rm 6:14 ·are not under Torah-Law, but·rather under grace.
Rm 6:15 because we·are not under Torah-Law, but·rather
Rm 6:15 ·are not under Torah-Law, but·rather under grace?
Rm 7:14 fleshly, having·been·sold·off under Moral·Failure.
Rm 16:20 shall·shatter the Adversary-Accuser under yeur feet
Jac 2:3 over·there," or "Sit·down here under my footstool,"
Jud 1:6 ·supra-lasting bonds under a·deep·murky·shroud for
1Pe 5:6 Accordingly, be·humbled under the mighty hand of·
1Th 2:14 also suffered under yeur·own fellow·countrymen,
1Th 2:14 just·as they·themselves *suffered* under the Judeans
1Co 6:12 I·myself shall·not be·controlled under anything.
1Co 9:20 Jews; to·the·ones *that* are·under Torah-Law, as
1Co 9:20 are·under Torah-Law, as under Torah-Law, that I·
1Co 9:20 I·may·gain the·ones *that* are·under *the* Torah-Law;
1Co 10:1 that all our fathers were under the cloud, and all
1Co 15:25 ·should·place all the enemies under his·own feet.
1Co 15:27 For *God* '" subjugated all·things under his feet."'
Eph 1:22 And 'he·subjugated all *things* under his feet' and
Col 1:23 ·proclaimed to every creature under the heaven), of·
1Ti 6:1 ·many slaves as are under a·yoke resolutely·consider
EG5259.1 (2x)
1Th 2:15 (even *under* the *Judeans* killing the Lord YeShua
2Co 11:32 the national·magistrate *under* Aretas the king
G5259.2 PREP ὑπό (1x)
2Co 11:24 Five·times by *the* Jews I·received forty *stripes*
G5259.3 PREP ὑπό (172x)
Jn 8:9 *this*, and being·convicted by *their·own* conscience,
Jn 10:14 and I·know my *sheep*, and am·known by mine.
Jn 14:21 the·one loving me shall·be·loved by my Father, and
Lk 1:26 the angel GabriEl was·dispatched by God to·a·city
Lk 2:18 ·that were·being·spoken to them by the shepherds.
Lk 2:21 the *name* being·called·forth by the angel prior·to
Lk 2:26 ·imparted·as·a·divine·message to·him by the Holy
Lk 3:7 ·the crowds traversing·forth to·be·immersed by him,
Lk 3:19 the tetrarch, being·reproved by him concerning
Lk 4:2 being·tried *for* forty days by the Slanderer. And in
Lk 4:15 in their gatherings, being·glorified by all.
Lk 5:15 *him*, and to·be·both·relieved·and·cured by him of
Lk 6:18 also the·ones being·harassed by impure spirits. And
Lk 7:24 to·distinctly·view? A·reed being·shaken by a·wind?
Lk 7:30 for themselves, not already·being·immersed by him.
Lk 8:14 ·traversing, are·altogether·choked by anxieties and
Lk 8:29 ·apart the bonds, he·was·driven by the demon into
Lk 8:43 be·cured·or·brought·relief, by not·even·one·man.
Lk 9:7 heard all the·things which·are·happening by him, and
Lk 9:7 on·account·of *that* it·was·said by some that John
Lk 9:8 and by some that EliJah appeared, and by·others that
Lk 10:22 "All·things are·handed·over to·me by my Father.
Lk 13:17 all the glorious·things, the·ones happening by him.
Lk 14:8 "Whenever you·should·be·called·forth by any *man*
Lk 14:8 ·than you may·be having·been·called·forth by him;
Lk 16:22 and *for* him to·be·carried·away by the angels to
Lk 17:20 Now after·being·inquired·of by the Pharisees *as·to*
Lk 21:16 "But yeu·shall·be·handed·over both by parents,
Lk 21:17 And yeu·shall·be being·hated by all on·account·of
Lk 21:20 ·see JeruSalem being·surrounded by army·camps,
Lk 21:24 JeruSalem shall·be being·trampled by Gentiles,
Lk 23:8 to·see some miraculous·sign occurring by him.
Ac 2:24 not possible *for·Jesus* to·be·securely·held by him.
Ac 4:11 "the stone being·disdainfully·rejected by yeu, the·
Ac 4:36 being·properly·called BarNabas by the ambassadors
Ac 5:16 *the* sick and *those* being·harassed by impure spirits.
Ac 8:6 ·giving·heed to·the·things being·said by PhilIppe in
Ac 10:22 ·fearing God and being·attested·to by the whole
Ac 10:22 ·the Jews, was·divinely·instructed by a·holy angel
Ac 10:33 having·been·specifically·assigned to·you by God."
Ac 10:38 all the·ones being·dominated by the Slanderer,
Ac 10:41 having·been·elected·beforehand by God, to·us who
Ac 10:42 having·been·specifically·determined by God *to·be*
Ac 12:5 was·being·made to God by the Called·Out·citizenry.
Ac 13:4 in·fact, after·being·sent·forth by the Holy Spirit,
Ac 13:45 were·contradicting the·things being·said by Paul,
Ac 15:3 being·sent·onward·on·their·journey by the Called·
Ac 15:4 they·were·fully·accepted by the Called·Out·
Ac 15:40 ·handed to·the grace of·God by the brothers.
Ac 16:2 This *disciple* was·attested·to by the brothers in
Ac 16:4 the·ones having·been·decided by the ambassadors
Ac 16:6 of·Galatia, they·were·being·forbidden by the Holy
Ac 16:14 to·give·heed to·the·things being·spoken by Paul.
Ac 17:13 also was·fully·proclaimed in Berea by Paul, they·
Ac 17:19 instruction *is*, *which·is* being·spoken by you?
Ac 17:25 nor·even is·waited·upon by *the* hands of·men·of·
Ac 20:3 *But* with·a·plot being·made against·him by the Jews
Ac 21:35 befell him to·be·lifted·and·carried by the soldiers
Ac 22:11 being·led·by·the·hand by the·ones being·together
Ac 22:12 ·to the Torah-Law, being·attested·to by all the
Ac 23:10 Paul should·be·thoroughly·drawn·apart by them)—
Ac 23:27 man *was* already·being·arrested by the Judeans
Ac 23:27 and·also *was* about to·be·eliminated by them, *but*
Ac 23:30 *which·was* about to·be *carried·out* by the Judeans,
Ac 24:21 I·myself am·called·into·judgment by yeu this·day
Ac 24:26 that valuables shall·be·given to·him by Paul, that
Ac 25:14 ·been·left·behind *as* a·chained·prisoner by Felix,
Ac 26:2 for·which I·am·called·to·account by *the* Judeans,
Ac 26:6 expectation of·the promise being·made by God to
Ac 26:7 AgrIppa, I·am·called·to·account by the Judeans.
Ac 27:11 rather than by·the·things being·said by Paul.
Ac 27:41 but the stern was·broken by the force of·the
Heb 2:3 it·was·confirmed to us by the·ones already·hearing
Heb 3:4 house is·planned·and·constructed by some *man*; but
Heb 5:4 but·rather *it·is* the·one being·called·forth by God,
Heb 5:10 being·specifically·designated by God a·High·Priest
Heb 7:7 contradiction, the lesser is·blessed by the mightier.
Heb 9:19 Torah-Law already·being·spoken by Moses to·all
Heb 11:23 ·born) was·hid three·lunar·months by his parents,
Heb 12:3 hostile·grumbling by the morally·disqualified·men
Heb 12:5 nor·even be·faint *when* being·reproved by him.
Gal 1:11 good·news, the·one being·proclaimed by me is not
Gal 3:17 having·been·previously·ratified by God in
Gal 4:9 God, or rather being·known by God, how·is·it *that*
Gal 5:15 ·out *that* yeu·may·not be·consumed by one·another.
Mt 1:22 the·thing being·uttered by Yahweh through the
Mt 2:15 the·thing being·uttered by Yahweh through the
Mt 2:16 that he·was·mocked by the Magian·astrologists,
Mt 2:17 ·fulfilled, the·thing being·uttered by JeremIah the
Mt 3:3 is·he, the·one being·uttered *of/by* IsaIah the prophet,
Mt 3:6 and they·were·immersed by him in the Jordan,
Mt 3:13 the Jordan, directly·to John to·be·immersed by him.
Mt 3:14 "I·myself have need to·be·immersed by you, and
Mt 4:1 was·led·up into the wilderness by the Spirit to·be·
Mt 4:1 wilderness by the Spirit to·be·tried by the Slanderer.
Mt 5:13 out and to·be·trampled·down by the men·of·clay†.
Mt 6:2 that they·may·be·glorified by the men·of·clay†.
Mt 8:24 the sailboat to·be·covered by the breaking·waves,
Mt 10:22 And yeu·shall·be being·hated by all *men* on·
Mt 11:7 to·distinctly·view? A·reed being·shaken by a·wind?
Mt 11:27 "All·things are·handed·over to·me by my Father,
Mt 14:8 And after·being·urged·on by her mother, she·replied
Mt 19:12 ·are eunuchs, some castrated by the men·of·clay†.
Mt 20:23 for·whom it·has·been·made·ready by my Father."
Mt 22:31 ·aloud of·the·thing being·uttered to·yeu by God,
Mt 23:7 marketplaces, and to·be·called by the men·of·clay†,
Mt 24:9 yeu, and yeu·shall·be being·hated by all the nations
Mt 27:12 when he·was·legally·accused by the chief·priests
Mt 27:35 ·fulfilled, the·thing being·uttered by the prophet,
Mk 1:5 of·JeruSalem, and all were·immersed by him in the
Mk 1:9 of·Galilee and was·immersed by John in the Jordan.
Mk 1:13 forty days, being·tried by the Adversary-Accuser.
Mk 2:3 bringing a·paralyzed·man being·carried by four·men.
Mk 5:4 chains to·have·been·thoroughly·drawn·apart by him,
Mk 13:13 And yeu·shall·be being·hated by all *men* on·
Mk 13:14 ' the·one being·uttered by DaniEl the prophet,
Mk 16:11 that he·lives and was·distinctly·viewed by her,
Rm 3:21 ·apparent, being·attested·to by the Torah-Law and
Rm 12:21 Do·not be·overcome by the bad, but·rather
Rm 13:1 authorities, they·are having·been·assigned by God.
Rm 15:15 ·account·of the grace being·given to·me by God,
Rm 15:24 ·through, and to·be·sent·onward by yeu *from*
Jac 1:14 is·tempted, being·drawn·forth by his·own longing
Jac 2:9 moral·failure, being·convicted by the Torah-Law as
Jac 3:4 so·vast, and *are* being·driven by harsh winds, *and·*
Jac 3:4 *and·yet* they·are·steered by a·very·small rudder,
Jac 3:6 of·nature, and being·set·aflame by the Hell·Canyon.
Jud 1:12 without·water being·carried·about by winds, late·
Jud 1:17 having·been·already·stated by the ambassadors of·
Php 1:28 by the·ones who·are·being·fully·set·opposed—
Php 3:12 ·for·which also I·am·grasped by the Anointed-One
1Pe 2:4 having·been·rejected·as·unfit by men·of·clay†, but
2Pe 1:17 ·such being·carried·forth to·him by the magnificent
2Pe 1:21 But·rather, while·being·carried·along by *the* Holy
2Pe 2:7 Lot being·worn·down·in·labored·anguish by the
2Pe 2:17 ·water, thick·clouds being·driven by a·whirlwind,
2Pe 3:2 utterances having·been·already·stated by the holy
1Th 1:4 having·seen, O·brothers having·been·loved by God,
1Th 2:4 ·as we·have·been·tested·and·proven by God to·be·
2Th 2:13 yeu (O·brothers having·been·loved by *the* Lord),
1Co 1:11 yeu, my brothers, by the·ones *of·the house* of·
1Co 2:12 ·things being·graciously·bestowed to·us by God.
1Co 2:15 but he·himself is·scrutinized by not·even·one·man.
1Co 4:3 ·small·thing that I·should·be·scrutinized by yeu, or
1Co 4:3 ·be·scrutinized by yeu, or by mankind's† daylight.
1Co 8:3 God, the·same has·been·absolutely·known by him.
1Co 10:9 they·were·completely·destroyed by the serpents.
1Co 10:10 they·were·completely·destroyed by the savage·
1Co 10:29 ·is my liberty unduly·judged by another *man's*
1Co 11:32 we·are·correctively·disciplined by *the* Lord, in·
1Co 14:24 or an·untrained·man, he·is·convicted by all, he·
1Co 14:24 he·is·convicted by all, he·is·scrutinized by all.
2Co 1:4 with·which we·ourselves are·comforted by God.

Αα Ββ Γγ Δδ Εε Ζζ Ηη Θθ Ιι Κκ Λλ Μμ Νν Ξξ Οο Ππ Ρρ Σσ Ττ Υυ Φφ Χχ Ψψ Ωω

2Co 1:16 to yeu, and by yeu to·be·sent·onward into Judea.
2Co 2:6 public·penalty, the·one *inflicted* by the majority.
2Co 2:11 ·should·not be·swindled by the Adversary-Accuser,
2Co 3:2 ·known and being·read·aloud by all men·of·clay†,
2Co 3:3 a·letter of·Anointed-One being·attended·to by us,
2Co 5:4 the mortality may·be·swallowed·up by the life-above
2Co 8:19 after·him·being·elected by the convened·Called·
2Co 8:19 ·benevolence (the·one being·attended·to by us to
2Co 8:20 this bountiful·benevolence being·attended·to by us.
2Co 12:11 for I·myself was·due to·be·commended by yeu,
Eph 2:11 *the* Uncircumcision by the·one being·referred·to·as
Eph 5:13 being·refuted are·made·apparent by the light, for
Col 2:18 ·seen, being·puffed·up for·no·reason by his mind
2Ti 2:26 snare, having·been·captured·alive by him at his
3Jn 1:12 Demetrius has·been·attested·to by all·men, and by
3Jn 1:12 ·been·attested·to by all·men, and by the truth itself.
Rv 6:8 and with viral·death, and by the wild·beasts of·the
Rv 6:13 ·green·figs while·being·shaken by a·great wind.
Rv 9:18 By these three, the third·part of·the men·of·clay†

G5259.5 PREP ὑπό (1x)
Ac 5:21 ·entered into the Sanctuary·Atrium at the sunrise

G5259.8 PREP ὑπό (1x)
1Co 7:25 as one·having·been·shown·mercy from *the* Lord

G5259.9 PREP ὑπ΄ (1x)
Eph 5:12 ·things which·are·occurring among them secretly.

G5260 ὑπο•βάλλω hypôbállō *v.* (1x)
Roots:G5259 G0906 Compare:G1964

G5260.2 V-2AAI-3P ὑπέβαλον (1x)
Ac 6:11 Then they·secretly·induced men to·say, "We·have·

G5261 ὑπο•γραμμός hypôgrammós *n.* (1x)
Roots:G5259 G1125

G5261.2 N-ASM ὑπογραμμόν (1x)
1Pe 2:21 leaving·behind a·written·example for·us in·order·

G5262 ὑπό•δειγμα hypódêigma *n.* (6x)
Roots:G5263 Compare:G1165 G5296 xLangAlso:H1825

G5262.2 N-APN ὑποδείγματα (1x)
Heb 9:23 (in·fact, *the* explicit·patterns of·the·things in the

G5262.2 N-DSN ὑποδείγματι (1x)
Heb 8:5 who ritually·minister unto·an·explicit·pattern and

G5262.3 N-ASN ὑπόδειγμα (3x)
Jn 13:15 For I·gave an·explicit·example to·yeu in·order·that
Jac 5:10 Take *for* an·explicit·example, my brothers, the ill·
2Pe 2:6 having·laid·out an·explicit·example for·those· to·be·

G5262.3 N-DSN ὑποδείγματι (1x)
Heb 4:11 ·fall by the same explicit·example of·the obstinate.

G5263 ὑπο•δείκνυμι hypôdêíknymi *v.* (6x)
Roots:G5259 G1166

G5263.2 V-FAI-1S ὑποδείξω (3x)
Lk 6:47 and doing them, I·shall·indicate to·yeu what he·is
Lk 12:5 But I·shall·indicate to·yeu whom yeu·should·fear.
Ac 9:16 For I·myself shall·indicate to·him what·many·things

G5263.3 V-AAI-3S ὑπέδειξεν (2x)
Lk 3:7 of·vipers, who gave·any·indication to·yeu to·flee
Mt 3:7 of·vipers, who gave·any·indication to·yeu to·flee

G5263.4 V-AAI-1S ὑπέδειξα (1x)
Ac 20:35 I·exemplified to·yeu *in* all·things, that in·this·

G5264 ὑπο•δέχομαι hypôdéchômai *v.* (4x)
Roots:G5259 G1209 Compare:G3580

G5264.2 V-ADI-3S ὑπεδέξατο (2x)
Lk 10:38 ·the·name·of Martha hospitably·received him into
Lk 19:6 ·down; and rejoicing, he·hospitably·received him.

G5264.2 V-ADP-NSF ὑποδεξαμένη (1x)
Jac 2:25 of·works, hospitably·receiving the messengers and

G5264.2 V-RNI-3S ὑποδέδεκται (1x)
Ac 17:7 whom Jason has·hospitably·received, and all these·

G5265 ὑπο•δέω hypôdéō *v.* (3x)
Roots:G5259 G1210

G5265.2 V-RPP-APM ὑποδεδεμένους (1x)
Mk 6:9 but·rather having·been·shod with·sandals *only*, and

G5265.3 V-AMM-2S ὑπόδησαι (1x)
Ac 12:8 ·yourself·about and shod·yourself·with your sandals

G5265.3 V-AMP-NPM ὑποδησάμενοι (1x)
Eph 6:15 and shodding·yeur·own feet in a·state·of·readiness

G5266 ὑπό•δημα hypódēma *n.* (10x)
Roots:G5265 Compare:G4547

G5266 N-ASN ὑπόδημα (2x)
Ac 7:33 "Loosen the shoes from·your feet, for the place in
Ac 13:25 ·comes·one after me, the shoes of·whose feet I·am

G5266 N-APN ὑποδήματα (4x)
Lk 10:4 nor a·knapsack, nor·even shoes, and yeu·should·
Lk 15:22 give *him* a·ring for his hand and shoes for his feet.
Mt 3:11 is stronger·than me, whose shoes I·am not fit to·lift·
Mt 10:10 ·even two tunics, nor·even shoes, nor·even a·staff,

G5266 N-GSN ὑποδήματος (1x)
Jn 1:27 not *even* worthy that I·may·loosen his shoe strap."

G5266 N-GPN ὑποδημάτων (3x)
Lk 3:16 the strap of·whose shoes I·am not fit to·loose.
Lk 22:35 ·any pouch, knapsack, or shoes, ¿!·Did yeu·lack
Mk 1:7 after·stooping·down, to·loose the strap of·his shoes.

G5267 ὑπό•δικος hypódikôs *adj.* (1x)
Roots:G5259 G1349 Compare:G1777

G5267.2 A-NSM ὑπόδικος (1x)
Rm 3:19 may·become liable·under·justice before·God—

G5268 ὑπο•ζύγιον hypôzýgiôn *n.* (2x)
Roots:G5259 G2218 Compare:G3688 xLangEquiv:H0860

G5268.3 N-GSN ὑποζυγίου (1x)
Mt 21:5 even *upon* a·colt, a·foal of·a·mated·donkey.""

G5268.4 N-NSN ὑποζύγιον (1x)
2Pe 2:16 a·voiceless female·donkey enunciating with *the*

G5269 ὑπο•ζώννυμι hypôzṓnnymi *v.* (1x)
Roots:G5259 G2224

G5269.1 V-PAP-NPM ὑποζωννύντες (1x)
Ac 27:17 emergency·cables, undergirding the sailing·ship.

G5270 ὑπο•κάτω hypôkátō *adv.* (9x)
Roots:G5259 G2736

G5270.2 ADV ὑποκάτω (9x)
Jn 1:50 I·declared to·you, 'I·saw you beneath the fig·tree,'
Lk 8:16 with·a·vessel or places *it* beneath a·couch, but·rather
Heb 2:8 You·subjugated all·things beneath his feet." For in
Mk 6:11 ·there, shake·off the loose·dirt beneath yeur feet for
Mk 7:28 For even the puppies beneath the table eat from the
Rv 5:3 upon the earth, nor·even beneath the earth, was·able
Rv 5:13 and on the earth, and beneath the earth, and such·as
Rv 6:9 fifth official·seal, I·saw beneath the Sacrifice·Altar
Rv 12:1 the sun, and the moon beneath her feet, and upon

G5271 ὑπο•κρίνομαι hypôkrínômai *v.* (1x)
Roots:G5259 G2919 Compare:G4364 See:G4942 G5272 G5273

G5271.2 V-PNP-APM ὑποκρινομένους (1x)
Lk 20:20 ·dispatched ambushers pretending themselves to·be

G5272 ὑπό•κρισις hypókrisis *n.* (7x)
Roots:G5271 See:G5273

G5272.1 N-ASF ὑπόκρισιν (1x)
Mk 12:15 ·seen their stage·acting·hypocrisy, he·declared to·

G5272.1 N-GSF ὑποκρίσεως (1x)
Mt 23:28 ·are exceedingly·full of·stage·acting·hypocrisy and

G5272.2 N-NSF ὑπόκρισις (1x)
Lk 12:1 of the leaven of·the Pharisees, which is hypocrisy.

G5272.2 N-ASF ὑπόκρισιν (1x)
Jac 5:12 "No, No," lest yeu·should·fall into hypocrisy.

G5272.2 N-APF ὑποκρίσεις (1x)
1Pe 2:1 and all guile, and hypocrisies, and envies, and all

G5272.2 N-DSF ὑποκρίσει (2x)
Gal 2:13 also was·led·away·together with·their hypocrisy.
1Ti 4:2 in hypocrisy with·false·words, their·own conscience

G5273 ὑπο•κριτής hypôkritḗs *n.* (20x)
Roots:G5271 See:G5272 G4942

G5273.2 N-NPM ὑποκριταί (3x)
Mt 6:2 you, just·as the stage·acting·hypocrites do in the
Mt 6:5 ·shall·not be·just·as the stage·acting·hypocrites *are*,
Mt 6:16 just·as the stage·acting·hypocrites, for they·disfigure

G5273.2 N-VSM ὑποκριτά (3x)
Lk 6:42 own·eye? "O·stage·acting·hypocrite, first cast·out
Lk 13:15 and declared, "O·stage·acting·hypocrite, does·not
Mt 7:5 O·stage·acting·hypocrite, first cast the beam from·out

G5273.2 N-VPM ὑποκριταί (12x)
Lk 11:44 and Pharisees, O·stage·acting·hypocrites! Because
Lk 12:56 O·stage·acting·hypocrites, yeu·personally·know·
Mt 15:7 "O·stage·acting·hypocrites! IsaIah did·prophesy
Mt 16:3 *and* glowering.' O·stage·acting·hypocrites, in·fact
Mt 22:18 "Why·do yeu·try me, O·stage·acting·hypocrites?
Mt 23:13 and Pharisees, O·stage·acting·hypocrites! Because
Mt 23:14 and Pharisees, O·stage·acting·hypocrites! Because
Mt 23:15 and Pharisees, O·stage·acting·hypocrites! Because
Mt 23:23 and Pharisees, O·stage·acting·hypocrites! Because
Mt 23:25 and Pharisees, O·stage·acting·hypocrites! Because
Mt 23:27 and Pharisees, O·stage·acting·hypocrites! Because
Mt 23:29 and Pharisees, O·stage·acting·hypocrites! Because

G5273.2 N-GPM ὑποκριτῶν (2x)
Mt 24:51 his portion with the stage·acting·hypocrites, where
Mk 7:6 concerning yeu, the stage·acting·hypocrites; as it·

G5274 ὑπο•λαμβάνω hypôlambánō *v.* (4x)
Roots:G5259 G2983 Compare:G3543 G1380 G2309 See:G4033-2

G5274.2 V-2AAI-3S ὑπέλαβεν (1x)
Ac 1:9 he·was·lifted·up, and a·thick·cloud received him up

G5274.3 V-2AAP-NSM ὑπολαβών (1x)
Lk 10:30 And taking·up *the question*, Jesus declared, "A·

G5274.4 V-PAI-1S ὑπολαμβάνω (1x)
Lk 7:43 Simon declared, "I·assume that *it·is the·one* to·

G5274.4 V-PAI-2P ὑπολαμβάνετε (1x)
Ac 2:15 these·men are·not drunk as yeu assume, for it·is *but*

G5275 ὑπο•λείπω hypôlêípō *v.* (1x)
Roots:G5259 G3007 See:G5277

G5275.2 V-API-1S ὑπελείφθην (1x)
Rm 11:3 sacrifice·altars, and·I alone am·all·that·is·left, and

G5276 ὑπο•λήνιον hypôlḗniôn *n.* (1x)
Roots:G5259 G3025 Compare:G3025

G5276.2 N-ASN ὑπολήνιον (1x)
Mk 12:1 around *it*, and dug a·vat·for·a·winepress, and built

G5277 ὑπο•λιμπάνω hypôlimpánō *v.* (1x)
Roots:G5275 Compare:G2641 G1303

G5277 V-PAP-NSM ὑπολιμπάνων (1x)
1Pe 2:21 behalf, leaving·behind a·written·example for·us in·

G5278 ὑπο•μένω hypôménō *v.* (17x)
Roots:G5259 G3306 Compare:G5297 G2594 G2553 G4777 See:G5281

G5278.2 V-IAI-3P ὑπέμενον (1x)
Ac 17:14 Silas and TimoThy were·remaining·behind there.

G5278.2 V-AAI-3S ὑπέμεινεν (1x)
Lk 2:43 ·back, the boy Jesus remained·behind in JeruSalem.

G5278.3 V-PAI-1S ὑπομένω (1x)
2Ti 2:10 ·of that, I·patiently·endure all·things on·account·of

G5278.3 V-PAI-1P ὑπομένομεν (1x)
2Ti 2:12 If we·patiently·endure, we·also shall·reign·together

G5278.3 V-PAI-2P ὑπομένετε (1x)
Heb 12:7 If yeu·patiently·endure corrective·discipline, God

G5278.3 V-PAI-3S ὑπομένει (2x)
Jac 1:12 *is* a·man that patiently·endures a·proof·trial,
1Co 13:7 ·awaits all·things, patiently·endures all·things.

G5278.3 V-PAP-APM ὑπομένοντας (1x)
Jac 5:11 ·blessed, the·ones patiently·enduring. Yeu·heard

G5278.3 V-PAP-NPM ὑπομένοντες (1x)
Rm 12:12 in·the tribulation, by·patiently·enduring; in·the

G5278.3 V-AAI-2P ὑπεμείνατε (1x)
Heb 10:32 yeu·patiently·endured a·large struggle of·

G5278.3 V-AAI-3S ὑπέμεινεν (1x)
Heb 12:2 ·before him, patiently·endured a·cross of·shame,

G5278.3 V-AAP-NSM ὑπομείνας (3x)
Mt 10:22 name. But the·one patiently·enduring to *the* end,
Mt 24:13 "But the·one patiently·enduring to *the* end, the·
Mk 13:13 "But the·one patiently·enduring to *the* end, the·

G5278.3 V-RAP-ASM ὑπομεμενηκότα (1x)
Heb 12:3 ·of the·one having·patiently·endured such hostile·

G5278.4 V-FAI-2P ὑπομενεῖτε (2x)

1Pe 2:20 for·morally·failing, yeu·shall·bear·it·patiently?
1Pe 2:20 ·rather if yeu·shall·bear·it·patiently when suffering

G5279 ὑπο•μιμνήσκω hypômimnḗskō *v.* (7x)
Roots:G5259 G3403
G5279.1 V-FAI-3S ὑπομνήσει (1x)
Jn 14:26 all·things, and shall·quietly·remind yeu *concerning*
G5279.1 V-PAM-2S ὑπομίμνησκε (2x)
Tit 3:1 Quietly·remind them to·submit·themselves to·
2Ti 2:14 Quietly·remind *them concerning* these·things—
G5279.1 V-PAN ὑπομιμνήσκειν (1x)
2Pe 1:12 I·shall·not neglect to·quietly·remind yeu always
G5279.1 V-AAN ὑπομνῆσαι (1x)
Jud 1:5 So I·resolve to·quietly·remind yeu, *due·to* yeu once
G5279.2 V-FAI-1S ὑπομνήσω (1x)
3Jn 1:10 if I·should·come, I·shall·quietly·recollect his deeds
G5279.3 V-AAI-3S ὑπεμνήσθη (1x)
Lk 22:61 Peter. And Peter quietly·recalled the word of·the

G5280 ὑπό•μνησις hypómnēsis *n.* (3x)
Roots:G5279
G5280.1 N-DSF ὑπομνήσει (2x)
2Pe 1:13 to·thoroughly·awaken yeu with a·reminder,
2Pe 3:1 yeur sincere innermost·minds with a·reminder:
G5280.2 N-ASF ὑπόμνησιν (1x)
2Ti 1:5 while·taking recollection of·the trust without·

G5281 ὑπο•μονή hypômonḗ *n.* (32x)
Roots:G5278 Compare:G3115 G4343 G4710
G5281 N-NSF ὑπομονή (4x)
Rm 5:4 and the patient·endurance *fully·cultivates* proven·
Jac 1:4 But let the patient·endurance have *her* complete work
Rv 13:10 Here is the patient·endurance and the trust of·the
Rv 14:12 Here is a·patient·endurance of·the holy·ones. Here
G5281 N-ASF ὑπομονήν (11x)
Rm 2:7 according·to a·patient·endurance of·beneficially·
Rm 5:3 the tribulation fully·cultivates patient·endurance,
Jac 1:3 ·testing of·yeur trust accomplishes patient·endurance.
Jac 5:11 Yeu·heard of·the patient·endurance of·Job and saw
2Pe 1:6 ·with *yeur* self-restraint, Patient·Endurance; and
2Th 3:5 and into *the* patient·endurance of·the Anointed-One.
Col 1:11 glory into all patient·endurance and long-suffering
1Ti 6:11 trust, love, patient·endurance, *and* gentleness.
Rv 2:2 wearisome·labor, and your patient·endurance, and
Rv 2:3 ·and·carried, and you·have patient·endurance, and
Rv 2:19 the trust, even your patient·endurance), also *that*
G5281 N-DSF ὑπομονῇ (9x)
Lk 8:15 ·hold·onto *it* and bear·fruit with patient·endurance.
Lk 21:19 "In yeur patient·endurance, yeu·procure yeur souls.
2Pe 1:6 ·with *yeur* patient·endurance, Devout·Reverence;
Tit 2:2 in·the trust, in·the love, in·the patient·endurance;
2Co 1:6 along·with a·patient·endurance of·the same
2Co 6:4 of·God: in much patient·endurance, in tribulations,
2Co 12:12 among yeu with all patient·endurance, by
2Ti 3:10 *my* long-suffering, *my* love, *my* patient·endurance,
Rv 1:9 the kingdom and patient·endurance of·Jesus Anointed
G5281 N-GSF ὑπομονῆς (8x)
Heb 10:36 yeu·have need of·patient·endurance in·order·that,
Heb 12:1 — we·should·run (through patient·endurance) the
Rm 8:25 *then* through patient·endurance we·fully·await *it*.
Rm 15:4 Expectation through the patient·endurance and the
Rm 15:5 may the God of·the patient·endurance and of·the
1Th 1:3 love, and the patient·endurance of·the Expectation,
2Th 1:4 ·God on·behalf of·yeur patient·endurance and trust
Rv 3:10 the Redemptive-word of·my patient·endurance, I·also

G5282 ὑπο•νοέω hypônôéō *v.* (3x)
Roots:G5259 G3539
G5282 V-PAI-2P ὑπονοεῖτε (1x)
Ac 13:25 he·was·saying, 'Whom·do yeu·surmise me to·be?
G5282 V-IAI-1S ὑπενόουν (1x)
Ac 25:18 of·such·things *as* I·myself was·surmising.
G5282 V-IAI-3P ὑπενόουν (1x)
Ac 27:27 the sailors were·surmising for·them to·be·heading·

G5283 ὑπό•νοια hypónôia *n.* (1x)
Roots:G5282
G5283 N-NPF ὑπόνοιαι (1x)
1Ti 6:4 becomes envy, strife, revilements, evil suspicions,

G5284 ὑπο•πλέω hypôpléō *v.* (2x)
Roots:G5259 G4126 Compare:G5295
G5284.2 V-AAI-1P ὑπεπλεύσαμεν (2x)
Ac 27:4 ·on from·there, we·sailed·leeward·near·to Cyprus,
Ac 27:7 progress·forward, we·sailed·leeward·near·to Crete,

G5285 ὑπο•πνέω hypôpnéō *v.* (1x)
Roots:G5259 G4154
G5285.2 V-AAP-GSM ὑποπνεύσαντος (1x)
Ac 27:13 And with·the·south·wind blowing·softly, *and*

G5286 ὑπο•πόδιον hypôpódiôn *n.* (9x)
Roots:G5259 G4228 xLangAlso:H1916 H3534
G5286 N-NSN ὑποπόδιον (2x)
Ac 7:49 the earth *is* my foot stool. What·kind·of house shall·
Mt 5:35 by the earth, because it·is his foot stool, nor toward
G5286 N-ASN ὑποπόδιον (7x)
Lk 20:43 I·should·lay·out your enemies *as* your foot stool."'
Ac 2:35 I·should·lay·out your enemies *as* your foot stool."'
Heb 1:13 I·should·lay·out your enemies *as* your foot stool"?
Heb 10:13 his enemies should·be·laid·out *as* his foot stool.
Mt 22:44 I·should·lay·out your enemies *as* your foot stool"?
Mk 12:36 ·should·lay·out your enemies *as* your foot stool."'
Jac 2:3 "Sit·down here under my footstool,"

G5287 ὑπό•στασις hypóstasis *n.* (6x)
Roots:G5259 G2476 Compare:G4006 G4136
G5287.2 N-GSF ὑποστάσεως (1x)
Heb 1:3 and *the* exact·imprint of·his very·essence, also *the*·
EG5287.2 (1x)
Jac 4:14 For what·kind·of *essence is* yeur life†?
G5287.3 N-NSF ὑπόστασις (1x)
Heb 11:1 is a·firm·assurance of·things·being·expectantly·, a·
G5287.3 N-DSF ὑποστάσει (2x)
2Co 9:4 ·be·put·to·shame in this firm·assurance of·boasting.
2Co 11:17 impulsiveness, in this firm·assurance of·boasting.
G5287.3 N-GSF ὑποστάσεως (1x)
Heb 3:14 ·onto the beginning of·the firm·assurance, *being*

G5288 ὑπο•στέλλω hypôstéllō *v.* (4x)
Roots:G5259 G4724 Compare:G0879-1 G4732-1 G5083
G5288.ª V-AMI-1S ὑπεστειλάμην (1x)
Ac 20:20 how I·kept·back not·even·one·thing of·the·things
G5288.2 V-IAI-3S ὑπέστελλεν (1x)
Gal 2:12 ·came, he·was·shrinking·back and was·distinctly·
G5288.2 V-AMI-1S ὑπεστειλάμην (1x)
Ac 20:27 For ¿!·did I·shrink·back *as* not·to·report·in·detail
G5288.2 V-AMS-3S ὑποστείληται (1x)
Heb 10:38 of·trust, and if he·should·shrink·back, my soul

G5289 ὑπο•στολή hypôstôlḗ *n.* (1x)
Roots:G5288 Compare:G0646 G2692
G5289.2 N-GSF ὑποστολῆς (1x)
Heb 10:39 not of·one·who·shrinks·back to total·destruction,

G5290 ὑπο•στρέφω hypôstréphō *v.* (35x)
Roots:G5259 G4762 Compare:G0344
G5290.2 V-FAI-1S ὑποστρέψω (1x)
Lk 11:24 *any*, it·says, 'I·shall·return·back to my house
G5290.2 V-PAM-2S ὑπόστρεφε (1x)
Lk 8:39 "Return·back to your·own house and give·an·
G5290.2 V-PAN ὑποστρέφειν (3x)
Lk 2:43 the days, *then* at their returning·back, the boy Jesus
Ac 13:34 ·men, no·longer intending to·return·back to decay,
Ac 20:3 he·made a·plan to·return·back through Macedonia.
G5290.2 V-PAP-DSM ὑποστρέφοντι (1x)
Heb 7:1 meeting·up with·AbRaham returning·back from the
G5290.2 V-PAP-NSM ὑποστρέφων (1x)
Ac 8:28 Also, he·was returning·back and sitting·down in his
G5290.2 V-IAI-3P ὑπέστρεφον (1x)
Lk 23:48 they·were·returning·back *from·where they·came.*
G5290.2 V-AAI-1S ὑπέστρεψα (1x)
Gal 1:17 into Arabia, and again returned·back to Damascus.
G5290.2 V-AAI-3S ὑπέστρεψεν (6x)
Lk 1:56 lunar·months and·then returned·back to her·own
Lk 4:1 full of·Holy Spirit, returned·back from the Jordan
Lk 4:14 And Jesus returned·back in the power of·the Spirit
Lk 8:37 ·him embarking into the sailboat, he·returned·back.
Lk 17:15 that he·was·healed, returned·back with a·loud
Ac 13:13 from them, John·*Mark* returned·back to JeruSalem
G5290.2 V-AAI-3P ὑπέστρεψαν (11x)
Lk 2:39 of·Yahweh, they·returned·back into Galilee to their·
Lk 2:45 not finding him, they·returned·back to JeruSalem,
Lk 10:17 And the seventy returned·back with joy, saying,
Lk 24:33 the same hour, they·returned·back to JeruSalem.
Lk 24:52 *directly·before* him, returned·back to JeruSalem
Ac 1:12 Then they·returned·back to JeruSalem from *the*
Ac 8:25 *as Peter and John* returned·back to JeruSalem,
Ac 12:25 and Saul returned·back *to·Antioch* from·among
Ac 14:21 a·significant·number, they·returned·back to Lystra
Ac 21:6 and those *disciples* returned·back to their·own
Ac 23:32 On·the next·day, *the soldiers* returned·back to the
G5290.2 V-AAN ὑποστρέψαι (2x)
Lk 8:40 *that*, when Jesus returned·back, the crowd fully·
Lk 19:12 ·receive for·himself a·kingdom and to·return·back.
G5290.2 V-AAP-DSM ὑποστρέψαντι (1x)
Ac 22:17 it·happened, with·me returning·back to JeruSalem,
G5290.2 V-AAP-NSM ὑποστρέψας (1x)
Mk 14:40 And upon·returning·back, he·found them sleeping
G5290.2 V-AAP-NPF ὑποστρέψασαι (2x)
Lk 23:56 And returning·back, they·made·ready aromatic·
Lk 24:9 And after·returning·back from the chamber·tomb,
G5290.2 V-AAP-NPM ὑποστρέψαντες (3x)
Lk 7:10 And upon·returning·back to the house, the·ones
Lk 9:10 ambassadors, after·returning·back, gave·an·account
Lk 17:18 They·are·not found returning·back to·give glory to·

G5291 ὑπο•στρώννυμι hypôstrṓnnymi *v.* (1x)
Roots:G5259 G4766
G5291.2 V-IAI-3P ὑπεστρώννυον (1x)
Lk 19:36 *other disciples* were·spreading·out their garments

G5292 ὑπο•ταγή hypôtagḗ *n.* (4x)
Roots:G5293 Compare:G1396
G5292 N-DSF ὑποταγῇ (4x)
Gal 2:5 ·hour, did·we·yield to·the subjection, in·order·that
2Co 9:13 over the affirmation of·yeur subjection to the good·
1Ti 2:11 A·woman must·learn in stillness with all subjection.
1Ti 3:4 house well, having his·children in subjection with all

G5293 ὑπο•τάσσω hypôtássō *v.* (41x)
Roots:G5259 G5021 Compare:G1396 G2610 G2902
See:G5292 G0506
G5293.1 V-AAI-2S ὑπέταξας (1x)
Heb 2:8 You·subjugated all·things beneath his feet.
G5293.1 V-AAI-3S ὑπέταξεν (3x)
Heb 2:5 *it·is* not to·angels *that* he·subjugated the impending
1Co 15:27 For *God* '" subjugated all·things under his feet."'
Eph 1:22 And 'he·subjugated all *things* under his feet' and
G5293.1 V-AAP-GSM ὑποτάξαντος (1x)
1Co 15:27 the·one already·subjugating all·things to
G5293.1 V-RPI-3S ὑποτέτακται (1x)
1Co 15:27 ·declare that "all·things have·been·subjugated,"
G5293.2 V-AAN ὑποτάξαι (1x)
Heb 2:8 ' For in making·subordinate to·him all things, not·
G5293.2 V-RPP-APN ὑποτεταγμένα (1x)
Heb 2:8 all things having·been·made·subordinate to·him.
G5293.3 V-2FPI-1P ὑποταγησόμεθα (1x)
Heb 12:9 more·especially be·in·subjection to·the Father of·
G5293.3 V-2FPI-3S ὑποταγήσεται (1x)
1Co 15:28 Son himself shall·be·subject to·the·one subjecting
G5293.3 V-PPI-3S ὑποτάσσεται (5x)
Lk 10:17 "Lord, even the demons are·subject to·us in your
Lk 10:20 in this, that the spirits are·subject to·yeu, but rather
Rm 8:7 God, for it·is·not subject to·the Law-of-Liberty of·
1Co 14:32 *the* spirits of·prophets are·subject to·prophets.
Eph 5:24 ·as the entire·Called·Out·Citizenry is·subject to·the
G5293.3 V-PPP-NSM ὑποτασσόμενος (1x)
Lk 2:51 Natsareth, and was being·subject to·them. And his

G5293.3 V-PPP-NPF ὑποτασσόμεναι (1x)
1Pe 3:5 while·being·in·subjection to·their·own husbands,
G5293.3 V-AAN ὑποτάξαι (1x)
Php 3:21 *within* himself to·be·able even to·subject all things
G5293.3 V-AAP-ASM ὑποτάξαντα (1x)
Rm 8:20 but·rather through the·one subjecting *it* in
G5293.3 V-AAP-DSM ὑποτάξαντι (1x)
1Co 15:28 ·be·subject to·the·one subjecting all·things in·him
G5293.3 V-2API-3S ὑπετάγη (1x)
Rm 8:20 For the creation was·made·subject to·the futility,
G5293.3 V-2APP-GPM ὑποταγέντων (1x)
1Pe 3:22 and powers already·being·made·subject to·him.
G5293.3 V-2APS-3S ὑποταγῇ (1x)
1Co 15:28 all·things should·be·made·subject to·him, then
EG5293.3 (1x)
Col 2:22 which all are *subject* to perishing with·usage)—
G5293.4 V-PMM-2P ὑποτάσσεσθε (2x)
Eph 5:22 wives: Yeu·must·submit·yeurselves to·yeur·own
Col 3:18 wives: Yeu·must·submit·yeurselves to·yeur·own
G5293.4 V-PMM-3S ὑποτασσέσθω (1x)
Rm 13:1 ·every soul submit·itself to·the·superior authorities.
G5293.4 V-PMN ὑποτάσσεσθαι (4x)
Rm 13:5 Therefore *it·is* a·necessity to·submit·oneself, not
Tit 2:9 slaves to·submit·themselves to·their·own masters *and*
Tit 3:1 them to·submit·themselves to·jurisdictions and
1Co 14:34 to·speak, but·rather to·submit·themselves, just·as
G5293.4 V-2API-3P ὑπετάγησαν (1x)
Rm 10:3 they·did·not submit·themselves to·the
G5293.4 V-2APM-2P ὑποτάγητε (2x)
Jac 4:7 Accordingly, submit·yeurselves to·God. Stand·up·
1Pe 2:13 submit·yeurselves to·every created·governance of·
G5293.5 V-PPP-APF ὑποτασσομένας (1x)
Tit 2:5 ·good, *and* being·submitted to·their·own husbands
G5293.5 V-PPP-NPF ὑποτασσόμεναι (1x)
1Pe 3:1 be·submitting·yeurselves to·yeur·own husbands,
G5293.5 V-PPP-NPM ὑποτασσόμενοι (3x)
1Pe 2:18 ·servants: be·submitting·yeurselves to·the masters
1Pe 5:5 And all *of·yeu*, being·submitted to·one·another, put·
Eph 5:21 being·submitted to·one·another in·a·reverent·fear·
G5293.5 V-PPS-2P ὑποτάσσησθε (1x)
1Co 16:16 also should·be·submitted to·the·ones such·as·
G5293.5 V-2APM-2P ὑποτάγητε (1x)
1Pe 5:5 *yeu* younger·men, be·submitted *to·yeur* elders. And

G5294 ὑπο•τίθημι hypôtíthēmi *v.* (2x)
Roots:G5259 G5087
G5294.2 V-AAI-3P ὑπέθηκαν (1x)
Rm 16:4 who risked their·own necks on·behalf of·my soul,
G5294.4 V-PMP-NSM ὑποτιθέμενος (1x)
1Ti 4:6 When·you·put·forth·the·hazard·of these·things to·

G5295 ὑπο•τρέχω hypôtréchō *v.* (1x)
Roots:G5259 G5143 Compare:G5284
G5295.2 V-2AAP-NPM ὑποδραμόντες (1x)
Ac 27:16 And running·leeward·near·to a·certain small·island

G5296 ὑπο•τύπωσις hypôtýpōsis *n.* (2x)
Roots:G5259 G5179 Compare:G5262 See:G0499
G5296.3 N-ASF ὑποτύπωσιν (1x)
1Ti 1:16 specifically·for a·primary·example for·the·ones
G5296.4 N-ASF ὑποτύπωσιν (1x)
2Ti 1:13 Retain *the* primary·model of·healthy·and·sound

G5297 ὑπο•φέρω hypôphérō *v.* (4x)
Roots:G5259 G5342 Compare:G5278 G2594
G5297.1 V-2AAN ὑπενεγκεῖν (1x)
1Co 10:13 the exit·out, for·yeu to·be·able to·bear·under *it*.
EG5297.1 (1x)
2Co 1:8 ·weighed·down beyond *our·own* ability *to·bear* it,
G5297.2 V-PAI-3S ὑποφέρει (1x)
1Pe 2:19 ·of conscience *toward* God undergoes grief,
G5297.2 V-AAI-1S ὑπήνεγκα (1x)
2Ti 3:11 at Lystra; what persecutions I·underwent, but the

G5298 ὑπο•χωρέω hypôchōréō *v.* (2x)
Roots:G5259 G5562 Compare:G0868
G5298.2 V-PAP-NSM ὑποχωρῶν (1x)
Lk 5:16 So he·himself was quietly·retreating into the
G5298.2 V-AAI-3S ὑπεχώρησεν (1x)
Lk 9:10 ·taking them, he·quietly·retreated privately into a·

G5299 ὑπ•ωπιάζω hypōpiázō *v.* (2x)
Roots:G5259 G3700 Compare:G2852 G4438
G5299.2 V-PAI-1S ὑπωπιάζω (1x)
1Co 9:27 But·rather I·knock·down my body and bring·*it*·
G5299.4 V-PAS-3S ὑπωπιάζῃ (1x)
Lk 18:5 ·avenge her, lest she·should·greatly·pester me as

G5300 ὗς hŷs *n.* (1x)
Compare:G5519 xLangAlso:H2386
G5300 N-NSF ὗς (1x)
2Pe 2:22 ·up,'" and "a·sow *keeps·on* bathing·herself in a·

G5301 ὕσσωπος hýssōpôs *n.* (2x)
אֵזוֹב 'ezôb [Hebrew]
Roots:H0231
G5301 N-DSM ὑσσώπῳ (1x)
Jn 19:29 ·wine·vinegar and putting·it·on hyssop, brought *it*
G5301 N-GSM ὑσσώπου (1x)
Heb 9:19 scarlet wool, and hyssop, he·sprinkled both the

G5302 ὑστερέω hysteréō *v.* (16x)
Roots:G5306 Compare:G3007 G4433 See:G5303 G5304 G0879-1
G5302.3 V-PPI-1P ὑστερούμεθα (1x)
1Co 8:8 nor·even if we·should·not eat, are·we·inferior.
G5302.4 V-PAP-NSM ὑστερῶν (1x)
Heb 12:15 lest any·man *is·found* falling·short from the grace
G5302.4 V-AAI-1S ὑστέρησα (1x)
2Co 12:11 *in* not·even·one·thing did·I·fall·short of·the very
G5302.4 V-RAN ὑστερηκέναι (2x)
Heb 4:1 ·among yeu should·seem to·have·fallen·short *of·it*.
2Co 11:5 ·reckon not·one·bit to·have·fallen·short of·the very
G5302.5 V-PAI-1S-C ὑστερῶ (1x)
Mt 19:20 from·out of·my youth, yet what more·do·I·lack?"
G5302.5 V-PAI-3S ὑστερεῖ (1x)
Mk 10:21 to·him, "One·thing you lack, head·on·out, sell as·
G5302.5 V-PPN ὑστερεῖσθαι (2x)
Php 4:12 to·be·hungry, even to·abound and to·be·lacking.
1Co 1:7 ·for yeu not to·be·presently·lacking in not·even·one
G5302.5 V-PPP-DSM ὑστερούντι (1x)
1Co 12:24 more·abundant honor to·the·one being·lacking,
G5302.5 V-AAI-2P ὑστερήσατε (1x)
Lk 22:35 knapsack, or shoes, ¿!·Did yeu·lack anything?
G5302.5 V-AAP-GSM ὑστερήσαντος (1x)
Jn 2:3 And lacking wine, the mother of·Jesus says to him,
G5302.6 V-PPI-3P ὑστεροῦνται (1x)
Rm 3:23 For all morally·failed and are·destitute of·the glory
G5302.6 V-PPN ὑστερεῖσθαι (1x)
Lk 15:14 that country, and he·himself began to·be·destitute.
G5302.6 V-PPP-NPM ὑστερούμενοι (1x)
Heb 11:37 ·goat hides, being·destitute, being·hard-pressed,
G5302.6 V-APP-NSM ὑστερηθείς (1x)
2Co 11:9 yeu and already·being·destitute, I·was·not a·

G5303 ὑστέρημα hystérēma *n.* (9x)
Roots:G5302 Compare:G4432 See:G5304 G5302
G5303.1 N-ASN ὑστέρημα (4x)
1Co 16:17 because the·thing *which was* lacking on·yeur *part*,
2Co 8:13 yeur abundance *may·be a·supply* for their lacking,
2Co 8:14 may·be *a·supply* for yeur lacking, that there·may·
2Co 11:9 For *that·which was* lacking to·me, the brothers
G5303.1 N-APN ὑστερήματα (3x)
1Th 3:10 and to·completely·reform the lackings of·yeur trust
2Co 9:12 ·in·particular the lackings of·the holy·ones, but·
Col 1:24 additionally·fill·up the lacking of·the tribulations
G5303.2 N-ASN ὑστέρημα (1x)
Php 2:30 ·should·utterly·supply yeur lack of·public·service,
G5303.3 N-GSN ὑστερήματος (1x)
Lk 21:4 from·out of·her destitution cast in·absolutely·all the

G5304 ὑστέρησις hystérēsis *n.* (2x)
Roots:G5302 Compare:G4432 See:G5303 G5302
G5304.1 N-ASF ὑστέρησιν (1x)
Php 4:11 I·say *this* according·to *a·particular* lacking; for I·
G5304.2 N-GSF ὑστερήσεως (1x)
Mk 12:44 from·out of·her destitution cast·in all·things, as·

G5305 ὕστερον hýsterôn *adv.* (12x)
Roots:G5306
G5305.1 ADV ὕστερον (1x)
Jn 13:36 ·follow me now, but you·shall·follow me later·on."
G5305.2 ADV ὕστερον (9x)
Lk 4:2 being·entirely·completed, eventually he·hungered.
Heb 12:11 ·rather grievous. But eventually, it·yields·forth a·
Mt 4:2 forty days and forty nights, eventually he·hungered.
Mt 21:29 not.' But eventually having·regret, he·went·off.
Mt 21:32 after·seeing *this*, did·not eventually have·regret,
Mt 21:37 "But eventually, he·dispatched his son to them,
Mt 25:11 "But eventually, the rest *of·the* virgins came also,
Mt 26:60 ·found none. But eventually, two false·witnesses
Mk 16:14 Eventually he·was·made·apparent to·the eleven,
G5305.3 ADV ὕστερον (2x)
Lk 20:32 So last of·all, the wife died also.
Mt 22:27 And last of·all, the wife died also.

G5306 ὕστερος hýsterôs *adj.* (2x)
Roots:G5259 See:G5302
G5306 A-DPM ὑστέροις (1x)
1Ti 4:1 Spirit expressly says that in later seasons some shall·
EG5306 (1x)
Ac 16:16 Now *later*, it·happened with·us traversing to prayer

G5307 ὑφαντός hyphantôs *adj.* (1x)
G5307.1 A-NSM ὑφαντός (1x)
Jn 19:23 of·it *being woven continuously* from·the·start

G5308 ὑψηλός hypsēlôs *adj.* (11x)
Roots:G5311 Compare:G0511 G5242 See:G5313 xLangAlso:H1364
G5308.1 A-NSM-C ὑψηλότερος (1x)
Heb 7:26 ·men, and becoming higher·than the heavens;
G5308.1 A-ASN ὑψηλόν (6x)
Lk 4:5 after·bringing him up upon a·high mountain, showed
Mt 4:8 ·takes him up to a·very high mountain and shows him
Mt 17:1 he·brings them up upon a·high mountain in private.
Mk 9:2 and brings them up upon a·high mountain in private,
Rv 21:10 in spirit to a·great and high mountain, and showed
Rv 21:12 also having a·wall great and high, having twelve
G5308.1 A-APN ὑψηλά (1x)
Rm 12:16 contemplating not the high·things, but·rather
G5308.1 A-DPN ὑψηλοῖς (1x)
Heb 1:3 at *the* right·hand of·the Divine·Majesty on high,
G5308.1 A-GSM ὑψηλοῦ (1x)
Ac 13:17 of·Egypt, and with a·high arm he·brought them
G5308.2 A-NSN ὑψηλόν (1x)
Lk 16:15 the·thing highly·esteemed among men·of·clay† is

G5309 ὑψηλο•φρονέω hypsēlôphrônéō *v.* (2x)
Roots:G5308 G5424
G5309 V-PAM-2S ὑψηλοφρόνει (1x)
Rm 11:20 in·the trust. Do·not·be arrogant, but·rather be·
G5309 V-PAN ὑψηλοφρονεῖν (1x)
1Ti 6:17 not to·be·arrogant nor·even to·have·placed·their·

G5310 ὕψιστος hýpsistôs *adj.* (14x)
Roots:G5311 xLangEquiv:H5945 A5946
G5310.1 A-DPN ὑψίστοις (4x)
Lk 2:14 "Glory to·God in *the* highest, and on earth, peace!
Lk 19:38 ' Peace in heaven and glory in *the* highest!"
Mt 21:9 ' Hosanna in the highest!"
Mk 11:10 Hosanna in the highest!"
G5310.2 A-NSM ὕψιστος (1x)
Ac 7:48 "But·yet the Most·High does·not reside in temples
G5310.2 A-GSM ὑψίστου (8x)
Lk 1:32 and shall·be·called *the* Son of·the·Most·High, and
Lk 1:35 *the* power of·the·Most·High shall·overshadow you.
Lk 1:76 shall·be·called a·prophet of·the·Most·High, for
Lk 6:35 and yeu·shall·be Sons of·the Most·High, because
Lk 8:28 you Jesus, O·Son of·God Most·High? I·petition you
Ac 16:17 men·of·clay† are slaves of·God Most·High, who
Heb 7:1 Priest of·God Most·High that·offers·a·sacrifice) *is*

Mk 5:7 Jesus, O·Son of·God Most·High? On·oath,·I·charge
EG5310.2 (1x)
Col 1:19 complete·fullness *of·God Most·High* takes·delight

G5311 ὕψος hýpsôs *n.* (6x)
Roots:G5228 Compare:G5313 See:G5312
G5311.1 N-NSN ὕψος (2x)
Eph 3:18 breadth, and length, and depth, and height *of·it*,
Rv 21:16 The length and the breadth and its height are equal.
G5311.3 N-ASN ὕψος (1x)
Eph 4:8 "After·ascending on·high, by·war,·he·captured
G5311.3 N-GSN ὕψους (2x)
Lk 1:78 ·over·the·horizon from·out of·on·high has·visited us
Lk 24:49 ·yeurselves·with power from·out of·on·high."
G5311.4 N-DSN ὕψει (1x)
Jac 1:9 the brother of·the low·estate boast in his high·stature,

G5312 ὑψόω hypsôō *v.* (20x)
Roots:G5311 Compare:G0450 G0461 G1817 G1869 G5229 See:G5313 G5251
G5312 V-FAI-3S ὑψώσει (2x)
Mt 23:12 any·that shall·elevate himself shall·be·humbled,
Jac 4:10 in·the·sight of·the Lord, and he·shall·elevate yeu.
G5312 V-FPI-3S ὑψωθήσεται (3x)
Lk 14:11 and the·one humbling himself shall·be·elevated."
Lk 18:14 and the·one humbling himself shall·be·elevated."
Mt 23:12 any·that shall·humble himself shall·be·elevated.
G5312 V-PAP-NSM ὑψῶν (2x)
Lk 14:11 the·one elevating himself shall·be·humbled, and
Lk 18:14 "The·one elevating himself shall·be·humbled, and
G5312 V-AAI-3S ὕψωσεν (4x)
Jn 3:14 "So just·as Moses elevated the serpent *upon a·sign·*
Lk 1:52 *their* thrones and elevated *the·ones* of·low·estate.
Ac 5:31 God elevated this Initiator *of·the life-above, this*
Ac 13:17 selected our fathers, and elevated the People in the
G5312 V-AAS-2P ὑψώσητε (1x)
Jn 8:28 to·them, "Whenever yeu·should·elevate the Son of·
G5312 V-AAS-3S ὑψώσῃ (1x)
1Pe 5:6 hand of·God, in·order·that he·may·elevate yeu in
G5312 V-APN ὑψωθῆναι (2x)
Jn 3:14 ·for the Son of·Clay·Man† to·be·elevated *also*,
Jn 12:34 ·for the Son of·Clay·Man† to·be·elevated'?
G5312 V-APP-NSF ὑψωθεῖσα (2x)
Lk 10:15 CaperNaum, the·one being·elevated·up unto the
Mt 11:23 you, CaperNaum, the·one being·elevated unto the
G5312 V-APP-NSM ὑψωθείς (1x)
Ac 2:33 So·then, after·being·elevated to·the right·hand of·
G5312 V-APS-1S ὑψωθῶ (1x)
Jn 12:32 And·I, if I·should·be·elevated from·among the
G5312 V-APS-2P ὑψωθῆτε (1x)
2Co 11:7 that yeu·yeurselves may·be·elevated? Because

G5313 ὕψωμα hýpsōma *n.* (2x)
Roots:G5312 Compare:G5308 G3349-2 See:G5251
G5313.1 N-ASN ὕψωμα (1x)
2Co 10:5 and every elevated·thing *that* is·lifting·itself·up
G5313.2 N-NSN ὕψωμα (1x)
Rm 8:39 nor height, nor depth, nor any other created·thing

Φφ - Phi

G5314 φάγος phágôs *n.* (2x)
Roots:G5315 Compare:G3630
G5314 N-NSM φάγος (2x)
Lk 7:34 ·of·clay†, a·glutton and an·excessive·wine-drinker,
Mt 11:19 ·of·clay†, a·glutton and an·excessive·wine-drinker

G5315 φάγω phágō *v.* (97x)
Compare:G0977 G1089 See:G2068
xLangAlso:H0398
G5315 V-FDI-2S φάγεσαι (1x)
Lk 17:8 these·things, you·yourself shall·eat and shall·drink'
G5315 V-FDI-3S φάγεται (2x)
Lk 14:15 "Supremely·blessed *is·he* that shall·eat bread in the
Jac 5:3 ·be testimony against yeu and shall·eat yeur flesh as
G5315 V-2FDI-3P φάγονται (1x)
Rv 17:16 her desolate and naked, and shall·eat her flesh, and
G5315 V-2AAI-1S ἔφαγον (1x)
Rv 10:10 sweet as honey. And when I·ate it, my belly was·
G5315 V-2AAI-1S@ ἔφαγον (1x)
Ac 10:14 never·at·any·time have·I·eaten anything defiled or
G5315 V-2AAI-1P ἐφάγομεν (2x)
Lk 13:26 yeu·shall·begin to·say, 'We·ate and drank in·the·
2Th 3:8 Neither as·a·free·present did·we·eat personally·from
G5315 V-2AAI-2P ἐφάγετε (1x)
Jn 6:26 ·signs, but·rather because yeu·ate from·out of·the
G5315 V-2AAI-3S ἔφαγεν (6x)
Lk 4:2 in those days, he·did·not eat not·even·one·thing. And
Lk 6:4 of·God and took and ate the Intended·Show bread,
Lk 24:43 And taking *it*, he·ate in·the·sight of·them.
Ac 9:9 not looking·about, and neither ate nor·even drank.
Mt 12:4 the house of·God and ate the Intended·Show bread,
Mk 2:26 the high·priest and ate the Intended·Show bread,
G5315 V-2AAI-3P ἔφαγον (10x)
Jn 6:23 Tiberias near to·the place where they·ate the bread,
Jn 6:31 Our fathers ate the manna in the wilderness, just·as
Jn 6:49 Yeur fathers ate the manna in the wilderness, and
Jn 6:58 ·as *the time when* yeur fathers ate the manna and died
Lk 9:17 And they·all ate and were·stuffed·full. And the
Mt 14:20 And they·all ate and were·stuffed·full. And they·
Mt 15:37 And all ate and were·stuffed·full. And they·took·
Mk 6:42 And they·all ate and were·stuffed·full.
Mk 8:8 So they·ate and were·stuffed·full. And they·took·up
1Co 10:3 And all ate the same spiritual food,
G5315 V-2AAM-2S φάγε (4x)
Jn 4:31 were·imploring·of him, saying, "Rabbi, eat!"
Lk 12:19 for many years. Rest, eat, drink, *and* be·merry.
Ac 10:13 "Peter, after·standing·up, make·sacrifice and eat."
Ac 11:7 'Peter, after·standing·up, sacrifice and eat.'
G5315 V-2AAM-2P φάγετε (3x)
Mt 26:26 and he·declared, "Take, eat! This is my body.
Mk 14:22 and he·declared, "Take, eat! This is my body.
1Co 11:24 *it* and declared, "Take, eat! This is my body, the·
G5315 V-2AAN φαγεῖν (35x)
Jn 4:32 "I·myself have a·full·meal to·eat that yeu·yeurselves
Jn 4:33 "¿!·Did someone bring him *something* to·eat?"
Jn 6:31 He·gave them bread from·out of·the heaven to·eat."
Jn 6:52 "How·is this·man able to·give us the flesh to·eat?"
Lk 6:4 which it·is·not proper to·eat except alone *for* the
Lk 8:55 ·assigned·for *something* to·be·given to·her to·eat.
Lk 9:13 "Yeu·yeurselves give them *something* to·eat." And
Lk 14:1 of·the chief Pharisees to·eat bread on·the·Sabbath,
Lk 22:15 "With·longing, I·longed to·eat this Passover with
Ac 23:12 ·to·destruction, saying neither to·eat nor to·drink
Ac 23:21 over·to·destruction, neither to·eat nor to·drink
Heb 13:10 in·the Tabernacle have no privilege to·eat.
Mt 12:4 was not being·proper for·him to·eat, neither for·the·
Mt 14:16 ·off; yeu·yeurselves give them *something* to·eat."
Mt 15:20 "But to·eat with·unwashed hands does·not defile
Mt 25:35 ·hungry, and yeu·gave me to·eat. I·was·thirsty,
Mt 25:42 yeu·did·not give me *anything* to·eat. I·was·thirsty,
Mt 26:17 ·we·should·make·ready for·you to·eat the Passover
Mk 2:26 which it·is·not proper to·eat except for·the priests·
Mk 3:20 ·for them not to·be·able so·much·as to·eat bread.
Mk 5:43 declared *for·something* to·be·given to·her to·eat.
Mk 6:31 and they·were·not·even having·opportunity to·eat.
Mk 6:37 "Yeu·yeurselves give them *something* to·eat." And
Mk 6:37 of·bread, and should·we·give *it* to·them to·eat?"
Rm 14:2 In·fact, one trusts that·he·may·eat all·things, but
Rm 14:21 *It·is* morally·good neither to·eat meat, nor·even to·
1Co 9:4 ¿!·Do we·not have privilege to·eat and to·drink?
1Co 10:7 "The People sat·down to·eat and to·drink, and
1Co 11:20 in·unison, it·is not to·eat *the* Lord's supper.
1Co 11:21 For in eating, each·one takes his·own supper
1Co 11:33 ·yeu·are·coming·together in·order to·eat, wait·for
Rv 2:7 I·shall·give to·him to·eat from·out of·the arbor·tree
Rv 2:14 ·IsraEl, *which was* to·eat things·sacrificed·to·idols,
Rv 2:17 overcoming, I·shall·give to·him to·eat from the
Rv 2:20 ·immorality and to·eat things·sacrificed·to·idols.
G5315 V-2AAO-3S φάγοι (1x)
Mk 11:14 "May no·one any·longer eat fruit from·out of·you
G5315 V-2AAP-NPM φαγόντες (3x)
Lk 15:23 sacrifice *it*. And eating *it*, we·should·be·merry!
Mk 6:44 And the·ones eating of·the loaves·of·bread were
Mk 8:9 And the·ones eating were about four·thousand *men*,
G5315 V-2AAS-1S φάγω (5x)
Lk 17:8 attend to·me until I·should·eat and should·drink;
Lk 22:11 local·travel·lodge, where I·may·eat the Passover
Lk 22:16 that no, I·should·not eat any·longer from·out of·it
Mk 14:14 local·travel·lodge where I·may·eat the Passover
1Co 8:13 *then* no, I·should·not eat meat unto the coming·
G5315 V-2AAS-1P φάγωμεν (5x)
Lk 22:8 ·ready for·us the Passover, that we·may·eat *it*."
Mt 6:31 be·anxious, saying, 'what should·we·eat?' or,
1Co 8:8 For neither if we·should·eat, do·we·excel, nor·even
1Co 8:8 nor·even if we·should·not eat, are·we·inferior.
1Co 15:32 awakened? "We·should·eat and should·drink,
G5315 V-2AAS-2S φάγῃς (1x)
Mk 14:12 ·ready in·order·that you·may·eat the Passover?
G5315 V-2AAS-2P φάγητε (5x)
Jn 6:53 I·say to·yeu, unless yeu·should·eat the flesh of·the
Lk 12:22 yeur soul, what yeu·should·eat, nor·even for·yeur
Lk 12:29 do·not seek what yeu·should·eat, or what yeu·
Mt 6:25 ·about yeur soul, what yeu·should·eat, even what
Rv 19:18 that yeu·may·eat flesh of·kings, and flesh of·
G5315 V-2AAS-3S φάγῃ (4x)
Jn 6:50 in·order·that someone may·eat from·out of·it, and
Jn 6:51 "If any·man should·eat from·out of·this bread, he·
Lk 7:36 was·asking·of him that he·should·eat with him. And
Rm 14:23 has·been·condemned if he·should·eat, because *it·*
G5315 V-2AAS-3P φάγωσιν (6x)
Jn 6:5 shall·we·buy bread in·order·that these may·eat?"
Jn 18:28 but·rather that they·may·eat the Passover.
Mt 15:32 ·do·not have *anything* which they·may·eat, and I·
Mk 6:36 for they·do·not have that·which they·may·eat."
Mk 8:1 and not having that·which they·may·eat), after·
Mk 8:2 three days and do·not have that·which they·may·eat.

G5316 φαίνω phaínō *v.* (31x)
Roots:G5337-2 Compare:G5461 G2989 G1166 G3700 See:G0398 G2014 G5322 G5457
G5316.ª V-2APS-3S φανῇ (1x)
Rm 7:13 in·order·that it·may·be·shown *to·be* moral·failure,
G5316.1 V-PAI-3S φαίνει (3x)
Jn 1:5 And the·light shines·forth in the darkness, and the
1Jn 2:8 ·away, and the true Light even·now shines·forth.
Rv 1:16 *is* as the sun *that* shines·forth in its power.
G5316.1 V-PAP-NSM φαίνων (1x)
Jn 5:35 the·one being·set·ablaze and shining·forth, and yeu
G5316.1 V-PAS-3S φαίνῃ (1x)
Rv 8:12 and the·day should·not shine·forth for·the·third·part
G5316.1 V-PAS-3P φαίνωσιν (1x)
Rv 21:23 of·the moon, in·order·that it·may·shine·forth in it,
G5316.1 V-PEI-3S φαίνεται (1x)
Mt 24:27 from *the* east and shines·forth as·far·as·to *the* west,
G5316.1 V-PEP-DSM φαίνοντι (1x)
2Pe 1:19 taking·heed as to·a·lantern shining·forth in a·murky

Ββ Γγ Δδ Εε Ζζ Ηη Θθ Ιι Κκ Λλ Μμ Νν Ξξ Οο Ππ Ρρ Σσ Ττ Υυ Φφ Χχ Ψψ Ωω

G5316.1 V-2APS-3S φανῇ (1x)
Rv 18:23 no should·not·ever shine·forth any·longer in you;
G5316.3 V-FDI-3S φανεῖται (1x)
1Pe 4:18 scarcely is·saved, where shall·appear the irreverent
G5316.3 V-PEI-3S φαίνεται (3x)
Mt 2:13 an·angel of·Yahweh appears to·Joseph according·to
Mt 2:19 ·to a·vision·in·a·dream) appears to·Joseph in Egypt,
Mk 14:64 revilement·of·God! How·does it·appear to·yeu?
G5316.3 V-PEI-3P φαίνονται (1x)
Mt 23:27 which in·fact outwardly appear stately·and·elegant,
G5316.3 V-PEP-GSM φαινομένου (1x)
Mt 2:7 personally·from them the time of·the appearing star.
G5316.3 V-PEP-NSF φαινομένη (1x)
Jac 4:14 it·is a·vapor, one·appearing just·for a·brief·moment
G5316.3 V-PPI-2P φαίνεσθε (1x)
Mt 23:28 yeu also outwardly appear righteous to·the men·
G5316.3 V-2API-3S ἐφάνη (5x)
Lk 9:8 and by some that EliJah appeared, and by·others that
Mt 1:20 an·angel of·Yahweh appeared to·him according·to
Mt 9:33 "Never·at·any·time did·it·appear in·this·manner in
Mt 13:26 fruit, then the darnel·weeds appeared also.
Mk 16:9 *day* of·*the*·week, *Jesus* did·appear first to·Mariam
G5316.3 V-2API-3P ἐφάνησαν (1x)
Lk 24:11 And their utterances appeared in·the·sight of·them
G5316.3 V-2APS-1P φανῶμεν (1x)
2Co 13:7 we·ourselves should·appear verifiably·approved,
G5316.3 V-2APS-2S φανῇς (1x)
Mt 6:18 ·that you·may·not be·appearing to·the men·of·clay†
G5316.3 V-2APS-3P φανῶσιν (1x)
Mt 6:16 in·such·a·manner·so·that they·may·be·appearing to·
G5316.4 V-2FPI-3S φανήσεται (1x)
Mt 24:30 of·the Son of·Clay·Man† shall·be·apparent in the
G5316.4 V-PEP-GPN φαινομένων (1x)
Heb 11:3 ·be not from·out of·things·being·apparent, *that·is*,
G5316.4 V-PPI-2P φαίνεσθε (1x)
Php 2:15 among whom yeu·are·apparent as brilliant·lights
G5316.4 V-2APS-3P φανῶσιν (1x)
Mt 6:5 so·that they·may·be·apparent to·the men·of·clay†.

G5317 Φάλεκ Phálêk *n/p.* (1x)

פֶּלֶג p̊eleg [Hebrew]
Φαλέγ Phálêg [Greek, Octuagint]
Roots:H6389
G5317.2 N/P-PRI Φαλέγ (1x)
Lk 3:35 of·Serug, *son* of·Reu, *son* of·Peleg, *son* of·Eber,

G5318 φανερός phanerôs *adj.* (21x)

Roots:G5316 Compare:G1552 G1854 G5457 See:G5320
G5318.1 A-NSF φανερά (1x)
1Ti 4:15 continual·advancement may·be apparent among all.
G5318.1 A-NSN φανερόν (5x)
Lk 8:17 that shall·not become apparent; neither *anything*
Ac 4:16 ·been·done through them *is* apparent to·all the·ones
Ac 7:13 and Joseph's kindred became apparent to·Pharaoh.
Rm 1:19 *which·is* known of·God, it·is apparent among them,
1Co 3:13 each·man's work shall·become apparent, for the
G5318.1 A-NPM φανεροί (1x)
1Co 11:19 ·approved may·become apparent among yeu.
G5318.1 A-NPN φανερά (3x)
Gal 5:19 the works of·the flesh are apparent, which are *these*:
1Co 14:25 secrets of·his heart become apparent; and in·this·
1Jn 3:10 In this the children of·God are apparent, also the
G5318.1 A-APM φανερούς (1x)
Php 1:13 in *the* Anointed-One to·become apparent to·all in
G5318.2 A-DSN φανερῷ (2x)
Rm 2:28 with an·outward·appearance *of·vigilantly·keeping*
Rm 2:28 neither the·one with an·outward·appearance, *that·is*,
G5318.3 A-DSN φανερῷ (3x)
Mt 6:4 ·on in private, shall himself give·back to·you openly.
Mt 6:6 looking·on in private, shall·give·back to·you openly.
Mt 6:18 ·on in private, shall·give·back to·you openly.
G5318.4 A-ASM φανερόν (3x)
Mt 12:16 ·that they·should·not make him openly·known,
Mk 3:12 ·that they·should·not make him openly·known.
Mk 4:22 other·than that it·may·come to *be* openly·known.
G5318.4 A-ASN φανερόν (1x)
Lk 8:17 ·not be·known and may·come to *be* openly·known.
G5318.5 A-NSN φανερόν (1x)
Mk 6:14 for his name was openly·well·known. And he·was·

G5319 φανερόω phanerôō *v.* (49x)

Roots:G5318 See:G5321 G1717
G5319.1 V-FAI-3S φανερώσει (1x)
1Co 4:5 ·the darkness and shall·make·apparent the counsels
G5319.1 V-FPI-2P φανερωθήσεσθε (1x)
Col 3:4 yeu also shall·be·made·apparent together with·him
G5319.1 V-PAP-DSM φανεροῦντι (1x)
2Co 2:14 the Anointed-One and making·apparent the aroma
G5319.1 V-PPI-3S φανεροῦται (1x)
Eph 5:13 all·things being·refuted are·made·apparent by the
G5319.1 V-PPP-NSN φανερούμενον (1x)
Eph 5:13 light, for any thing being·made·apparent is light.
G5319.1 V-PPP-NPM φανερούμενοι (1x)
2Co 3:3 being·made·apparent that yeu·are a·letter of·
G5319.1 V-AAI-1S ἐφανέρωσα (1x)
Jn 17:6 "I·made your name apparent to·the men·of·clay†
G5319.1 V-AAI-3S ἐφανέρωσεν (5x)
Jn 2:11 of·Galilee and made his glory apparent. And his
Jn 21:1 Jesus made himself apparent again to·the disciples
Jn 21:1 and he·made *himself* apparent in·this·manner.
Rm 1:19 among them, for God made·*it*·apparent to·them.
Tit 1:3 Redemptive-word apparent by official·proclamation,
G5319.1 V-AAM-2S φανέρωσον (1x)
Jn 7:4 ·do these·things, make yourself apparent to·the world.
G5319.1 V-AAS-1S φανερώσω (1x)
Col 4:4 in·order·that I·may·make it apparent, as it·is·
G5319.1 V-API-3S ἐφανερώθη (11x)
Jn 21:14 ·time *that* Jesus is·made·apparent to·his disciples,
Mk 16:12 he·was·made·apparent to·two·men from·among
Mk 16:14 Eventually he·was·made·apparent to·the eleven,
Col 1:26 but now·in·fact is·made·apparent to·his holy·ones
1Ti 3:16 ·Devout·Reverence. God is·made·apparent in flesh,
1Jn 1:2 (and the life-above is·made·apparent, and we·have·
1Jn 1:2 alongside the Father, and is·made·apparent to·us).
1Jn 3:2 and it·is·not·yet made·apparent what we·shall·be.
1Jn 3:5 that·one was·made·apparent in·order·that he·should·
1Jn 3:8 *purpose* the Son of·God was·made·apparent: that
1Jn 4:9 In this, the love of·God is·made·apparent among us,
G5319.1 V-API-3P ἐφανερώθησαν (1x)
Rv 15:4 ' because your righteous·acts are·made·apparent."
G5319.1 V-APN φανερωθῆναι (1x)
2Co 7:12 on·our behalf— for·it to·become·apparent to yeu
G5319.1 V-APP-ASF φανερωθεῖσαν (1x)
2Ti 1:10 but now being·made·apparent through the
G5319.1 V-APP-GSM φανερωθέντος (3x)
Rm 16:26 but now with·him·already·being·made·apparent—
1Pe 1:20 but with·him·already·being·made·apparent in the
1Pe 5:4 ·the chief·Shepherd being·made·apparent, yeu·shall·
G5319.1 V-APP-NPM φανερωθέντες (1x)
2Co 11:6 *we·are* already·being·made·apparent unto yeu in
G5319.1 V-APS-3S φανερωθῇ (10x)
Jn 1:31 in·order·that he·should·be·made·apparent to·IsraEl,
Jn 3:21 in·order·that his deeds may·be·made·apparent, that
Jn 9:3 the works of·God should·be·made·apparent in him.
Mk 4:22 which should·not be·made·apparent, neither·did
2Co 4:10 life-above of·Jesus may·be·made·apparent in our
2Co 4:11 also of·Jesus should·be·made·apparent in our
Col 3:4 *who·is* our life-above, should·be·made·apparent, then
1Jn 2:28 whenever he·should·be·made·apparent, we·may·
1Jn 3:2 ·know that, when he·should·be·made·apparent, '
Rv 3:18 of·your nakedness may·not be·made·apparent. Also,
G5319.1 V-APS-3P φανερωθῶσιν (1x)
1Jn 2:19 in·order·that they·may·be·made·apparent that they·
G5319.1 V-RPI-3S πεφανέρωται (2x)
Heb 9:26 he·has·been·made·apparent for a·cancellation of·
Rm 3:21 ·from Torah-Law has·been·made·apparent, being·
G5319.1 V-RPN πεφανερῶσθαι (1x)
Heb 9:8 not·yet to·have·been·made·apparent with·the first
G5319.2 V-APN φανερωθῆναι (1x)
2Co 5:10 every one of·us to·be·made·manifest before the
G5319.2 V-RPI-1P πεφανερώμεθα (1x)
2Co 5:11 ·clay†. But we·have·been·made·manifest to·God,
G5319.2 V-RPN πεφανερῶσθαι (1x)
2Co 5:11 I·expect also to·have·been·made·manifest in yeur

G5320 φανερῶς phanerôs *adv.* (3x)

Roots:G5318
G5320 ADV φανερῶς (3x)
Jn 7:10 also to the Sacred·Feast, not openly, but·rather as in
Ac 10:3 He·saw openly in a·clear·vision, about *the* ninth
Mk 1:45 no·longer to·be·able to·enter openly into a·city, but·

G5321 φανέρωσις phanérōsis *n.* (2x)

Roots:G5319 Compare:G2015 G0602 G0584 See:G1717
G5321.1 N-NSF φανέρωσις (1x)
1Co 12:7 But the manifestation of·the Spirit is·given to·
G5321.1 N-DSF φανερώσει (1x)
2Co 4:2 ·guile, but·rather by·the manifestation of·the truth,

G5322 φανός phanós *n.* (1x)

Roots:G5316 Compare:G2985 G3088
G5322.4 N-GPM φανῶν (1x)
Jn 18:3 Judas comes there with searchlights and torches and

G5323 Φανου•ήλ Phanôuḗl *n/p.* (1x)

פְּנוּאֵל p̊ĕnû'ēl [Hebrew]
Roots:H6439
G5323.2 N/P-PRI Φανουήλ (1x)
Lk 2:36 Hanna, daughter of·PhanuEl, from·among *the*

G5324 φαντάζω phantázō *v.* (1x)

Roots:G5316
G5324.1 V-PPP-NSN φανταζόμενον (1x)
Heb 12:21 the·thing being·made·apparent was frightful,

G5325 φαντασία phantasía *n.* (1x)

Roots:G5324
G5325.2 N-GSF φαντασίας (1x)
Ac 25:23 BerNiki coming with much pomp and entering into

G5326 φάντασμα phántasma *n.* (2x)

Roots:G5324 xLangEquiv:H8544 xLangAlso:H7496
G5326.2 N-NSN φάντασμα (2x)
Mt 14:26 saying, "It·is a·phantom!" and they·yelled·out
Mk 6:49 sea, they·supposed *it* to·be a·phantom, and they·

G5327 φάραγξ pháranx *n.* (1x)

φαράγγι pharángi [Modern Greek]
Roots:G4486 G4008 Compare:G2835-1 G4480-2 G5493 G5479-1 G0836-1 See:G1448 xLangEquiv:H1516 xLangAlso:H5158 H6010
G5327.2 N-NSF φάραγξ (1x)
Lk 3:5 Every canyon shall·be·completely·filled, and every

G5328 Φαραώ Pharaṓ *n/p.* (6x)

פַּרְעֹה p̊ar'ōh [Hebrew spelling]
Roots:H6547
G5328 N/P-PRI Φαραώ (5x)
Ac 7:10 in·the·direct·presence of·Pharaoh king of·Egypt,
Ac 7:13 and Joseph's kindred became apparent to·Pharaoh.
Ac 7:21 himself being·put·out, the Pharaoh's daughter took
Heb 11:24 being·referred·to·as son of·Pharaoh's daughter,
Rm 9:17 For the Scripture says to·Pharaoh, "For this same·
EG5328 (1x)
Ac 7:10 king of·Egypt, and *Pharaoh* fully·established him,

G5329 Φάρες Phárês *n/p.* (3x)

פֶּרֶץ p̊ereṣ [Hebrew]
Roots:H6557
G5329.2 N/P-PRI Φαρές (3x)
Lk 3:33 *son* of·Chetsron, *son* of·Perets, *son* of·Judah,
Mt 1:3 Then Judah begot Perets and Zarach (birthed·from·
Mt 1:3 ·from·out of·Tamar), and Perets begot Chetsron, and

G5330 Φαρισαῖος Pharisaîos *n/g.* (102x)
פָּרוּשׁ phąrûsh [Hebrew]
Roots:H6567 Compare:G4523
xLangEquiv:H6517-1 xLangAlso:H6659-1
G5330.2 N/G-NSM Φαρισαῖος (9x)
Lk 7:39 Now seeing *this*, the Pharisee, the·one calling·for
Lk 11:37 was·speaking, a·certain Pharisee was·asking him
Lk 11:38 seeing *this*, the Pharisee marveled that he·did·not
Lk 18:10 to·pray, the one *being* a·Pharisee and the other a·
Lk 18:11 "The Pharisee, after·being·settled, was·praying
Ac 5:34 a·certain·man, a·Pharisee by·the·name·of GamaliEl,
Ac 23:6 "Men, brothers, I·myself am a·Pharisee, a·son of·a·
Ac 26:5 denomination of·our religion, I·lived a·Pharisee.
Php 3:5 Hebrews; according·to Torah-Law, a·Pharisee;
G5330.2 N/G-NPM Φαρισαῖοι (44x)
Jn 4:1 ·as the Lord knew that the Pharisees *had* heard *it said*
Jn 7:32 The Pharisees heard the crowd grumbling these·
Jn 7:32 him, and the Pharisees and the chief·priests
Jn 7:47 Then the Pharisees answered them, "¿!·Have even
Jn 8:3 Then the scribes and the Pharisees brought to him a·
Jn 8:13 Accordingly, the Pharisees declared to·him, "You
Jn 9:15 Now·then, the Pharisees again also were·asking·of
Jn 11:47 the Pharisees gathered·together a·joint·council·of·
Jn 11:57 and the Pharisees had·given a·commandment, that
Jn 12:19 So·then the Pharisees declared among themselves,
Lk 5:17 there·were Pharisees and teachers·of·Torah-Law
Lk 5:21 And the scribes and the Pharisees began to·ponder,
Lk 5:30 scribes and Pharisees among·them were·grumbling
Lk 6:7 and the Pharisees were·meticulously·watching him,
Lk 7:30 But the Pharisees and the experts·in·Torah-Law
Lk 11:39 him, "Now yeu Pharisees purify the outside of·the
Lk 11:53 the scribes and the Pharisees began to·besiege *him*
Lk 13:31 there·came·alongside certain Pharisees, saying to·
Lk 15:2 And the Pharisees and the scribes were·murmuring,
Lk 16:14 Now the Pharisees, inherently·being fond·of·
Ac 23:8 nor a·spirit, but *the* Pharisees affirm both·things.
Mt 9:11 And upon·seeing *it*, the Pharisees declared to·his
Mt 9:14 "Why·do we·ourselves and the Pharisees fast often,
Mt 9:34 But the Pharisees were·saying, "He·casts·out the
Mt 12:2 But the Pharisees seeing *it*, declared to·him,
Mt 12:14 But the Pharisees, upon·going·forth, took
Mt 12:24 But upon·hearing *this*, the Pharisees declared,
Mt 15:1 Then the scribes and Pharisees from JeruSalem
Mt 15:12 "Have·you·seen how the Pharisees, after·hearing
Mt 16:1 to·tempt *YeShua*, the Pharisees and Sadducees
Mt 19:3 The Pharisees also came·alongside him, trying him
Mt 21:45 the chief·priests and the Pharisees knew that *it·was*
Mt 22:15 Then traversing, the Pharisees took consultation
Mt 22:34 But the Pharisees gathered·together against him,
Mt 23:2 "The scribes and the Pharisees sat·down upon the
Mt 27:62 chief·priests and the Pharisees gathered·together to
Mk 2:16 And the scribes and the Pharisees, upon·seeing him
Mk 2:24 And the Pharisees were·saying to·him, "See, why·
Mk 3:6 going·forth, the Pharisees immediately were·making
Mk 7:1 Then the Pharisees and certain of·the scribes
Mk 7:3 For the Pharisees and all the Judeans, unless they·
Mk 7:5 Then the Pharisees and the scribes inquired·of him,
Mk 8:11 And the Pharisees came·forth and began to·
Mk 10:2 to·try him, the Pharisees inquired·of him, "Is·it·
G5330.2 N/G-VSM Φαρισαῖε (1x)
Mt 23:26 "O·blind Pharisee, first purify the interior of·the
G5330.2 N/G-VPM Φαρισαῖοι (8x)
Lk 11:44 scribes and Pharisees, O·stage·acting·hypocrites!
Mt 23:13 Scribes and Pharisees, O·stage·acting·hypocrites!
Mt 23:14 Scribes and Pharisees, O·stage·acting·hypocrites!
Mt 23:15 Scribes and Pharisees, O·stage·acting·hypocrites!
Mt 23:23 Scribes and Pharisees, O·stage·acting·hypocrites!
Mt 23:25 Scribes and Pharisees, O·stage·acting·hypocrites!
Mt 23:27 Scribes and Pharisees, O·stage·acting·hypocrites!
Mt 23:29 Scribes and Pharisees, O·stage·acting·hypocrites!
G5330.2 N/G-APM Φαρισαίους (5x)
Jn 7:45 came to the chief·priests and Pharisees, and those
Jn 9:13 *the* same·man to the Pharisees, the·one formerly
Jn 11:46 them went·off to the Pharisees and declared to·them
Jn 12:42 ·account·of the Pharisees they·were·not affirming
Lk 14:3 to the experts·in·Torah-Law and Pharisees, saying,
G5330.2 N/G-DPM Φαρισαίοις (2x)
Lk 11:42 ·rather, woe to·yeu, Pharisees! Because yeu·tithe
Lk 11:43 "Woe to·yeu, Pharisees! Because yeu·love the
G5330.2 N/G-GSM Φαρισαίου (3x)
Lk 7:36 And entering into the Pharisee's home, *Jesus*
Lk 7:37 he·was·reclining·at·a·meal in the Pharisee's home,
Ac 23:6 am a·Pharisee, a·son of·a·Pharisee; *it·is* concerning
G5330.2 N/G-GPM Φαρισαίων (28x)
Jn 1:24 ·been·dispatched were from·among the Pharisees.
Jn 3:1 ·man·of·clay† from·among the Pharisees, NicoDemus
Jn 7:48 the rulers or from·among the Pharisees trust in him?
Jn 9:16 ·then some from·among the Pharisees were·saying,
Jn 9:40 *some* from·among the Pharisees heard these·things,
Jn 18:3 from·among the chief·priests and Pharisees, Judas
Lk 5:33 and likewise the·ones of·the Pharisees, but yours
Lk 6:2 And some of·the Pharisees declared to·them, "Why·
Lk 7:36 a·certain·one of·the Pharisees was·asking·of him
Lk 12:1 ·yeurselves of the leaven of·the Pharisees, which is
Lk 14:1 of·a·certain·man of·the chief Pharisees to·eat bread
Lk 17:20 after·being·inquired·of by the Pharisees *as·to* when
Lk 19:39 And some of·the Pharisees from among·the crowd
Ac 15:5 the denomination of·the Pharisees having·trusted,
Ac 23:6 Sadducees and the other Pharisees, he·yelled·out in
Ac 23:7 a·controversy *between* the Pharisees and the
Ac 23:9 the scribes *that·were* of·the Pharisees' part, upon·
Mt 3:7 ·seeing *that* many of·the Pharisees and Sadducees
Mt 5:20 more·than *that* of·the scribes and Pharisees, no, yeu·
Mt 12:38 some of·the scribes and Pharisees answered, saying
Mt 16:6 of the leaven of·the Pharisees and Sadducees."
Mt 16:11 of the leaven of·the Pharisees and Sadducees?
Mt 16:12 of the instruction of·the Pharisees and Sadducees.
Mt 22:41 with·the Pharisees having·been·gathered·together,
Mk 2:18 and the *disciples* of·the Pharisees were fasting. And
Mk 2:18 of·John and the *disciples* of·the Pharisees fast, but
Mk 8:15 for the leaven of·the Pharisees and of·the leaven of·
Mk 12:13 to him some of·the Pharisees and HerOdians, in·
EG5330.2 (2x)
Jn 7:45 and Pharisees, and those *Pharisees* declared to·them,
Jn 10:6 to·them, but those *Pharisees* did·not know what·

G5331 φαρμακεία pharmakêía *n.* (3x)
Roots:G5332 Compare:G5333 G3095
G5331.1 N-NSF φαρμακεία (1x)
Gal 5:20 making·and·supplying·of·poisonous·drugs,
G5331.1 N-DSF φαρμακείᾳ (1x)
Rv 18:23 your making·and·supplying·of·poisonous·drugs,
G5331.1 N-GPF φαρμακειῶν (1x)
Rv 9:21 of·their making·and·supplying·of·poisonous·drugs,

G5332 φαρμακεύς pharmakêús *n.* (1x)
Roots:G5332-2 Compare:G5333 G5331
G5332.1 N-DPM φαρμακεῦσιν (1x)
Rv 21:8 ·persons, and makers·of·poisonous·drugs, and

G5333 φαρμακός pharmakós *n.* (1x)
Roots:G5332-2 Compare:G2395-1 G2322 G1883-3
See:G5332 G5331 G5332-1
G5333.1 N-NPM φαρμακοί (1x)
Rv 22:15 dogs, and the·ones utilizing·poisonous·drugs, and

G5334 φάσις phásis *n.* (2x)
Roots:G5346 See:G5316
G5334.2 N-NSF φάσις (1x)
Ac 21:31 ·were·seeking·to·kill him, news ascended to·the
EG5334.3 (1x)
1Th 3:6 *he·brings* *tidings* even with·he·himself·proclaiming·

G5335 φάσκω pháskō *v.* (4x)
Roots:G5337-2 Compare:G5346 G1861 See:G0940
G5335 V-PAP-APM φάσκοντας (1x)
Rv 2:2 *that* you·tried the·ones professing to·be ambassadors
G5335 V-PAP-NPM φάσκοντες (2x)
Ac 24:9 ·among·themselves, professing these·things to·hold
Rm 1:22 Professing·themselves to·be wise, they·already·
G5335 V-IAI-3S ἔφασκεν (1x)
Ac 25:19 ·died, whom Paul was·professing to·be·alive.

G5336 φάτνη phátnē *n.* (4x)
אֵבוּס 'ębûç [Hebrew]
xLangEquiv:H0018
G5336 N-DSF φάτνῃ (3x)
Lk 2:7 him back in the feeding·trough, on·account·that there·
Lk 2:12 ·*in·cloths*, laying·out in the feeding·trough."
Lk 2:16 and·also the baby laying·out in the feeding·trough.
G5336 N-GSF φάτνης (1x)
Lk 13:15 *his* donkey from the feeding·trough, even leading·

G5337 φαῦλος phaûlôs *adj.* (4x)
Compare:G5513 G2556 G2839 G0952 G4469 G4190
G1808-1 See:G2274 G3972
G5337.1 A-NSN φαῦλον (1x)
Jac 3:16 *is*, there *is* instability and every mediocre activity.
G5337.1 A-ASN φαῦλον (1x)
Tit 2:8 having not·even·one mediocre thing to·say
G5337.2 A-APN φαῦλα (2x)
Jn 3:20 For any one practicing mediocrity hates the light,
Jn 5:29 and the·ones already·practicing the mediocrity, into

G5338 φέγγος phéngôs *n.* (3x)
Roots:G5337-2 Compare:G5458 See:G5350
G5338 N-ASN φέγγος (3x)
Lk 11:33 traversing·in may·look·about by·the brightness.
Mt 24:29 moon shall·not give·forth her brightness, and the
Mk 13:24 and the moon shall·not give·forth her brightness,

G5339 φείδομαι phêídômai *v.* (10x)
See:G5340 xLangAlso:H2820
G5339.1 V-FDI-1S φείσομαι (1x)
2Co 13:2 ·come into the *vicinity* again, I·shall·not spare *yeu*,
G5339.1 V-PNI-1S φείδομαι (1x)
2Co 12:6 ·declare truth. But I·am·sparing *in·how I·boast*,
G5339.1 V-PNP-NSM φειδόμενος (1x)
2Co 1:23 upon my soul, that to·spare yeu, I·did·not·yet
G5339.1 V-PNP-NPM φειδόμενοι (1x)
Ac 20:29 among yeu, who·are·not sparing the little·flock.
G5339.1 V-ADI-3S ἐφείσατο (4x)
Rm 8:32 He·that did·not spare his·own Son, but·rather
Rm 11:21 For if God did·not spare the fully natural branches,
2Pe 2:4 if God— did·not spare morally·failing angels, but·
2Pe 2:5 and *if* he·did·not spare *the* ancient world, but·rather
G5339.1 V-ADS-3S φείσηται (1x)
Rm 11:21 ·*heed* lest·perhaps he·should·not·even spare you.
G5339.2 V-PNI-1S φείδομαι (1x)
1Co 7:28 in·the flesh, but I·myself am·lenient·with yeu.

G5340 φειδομένως phêidôménōs *adv.* (2x)
Roots:G5339
G5340 ADV φειδομένως (2x)
2Co 9:6 the·one sowing sparingly also shall·reap sparingly
2Co 9:6 sparingly also shall·reap sparingly, and the·one

G5341 φελόνης phêlónēs *n.* (1x)
Roots:G5316
G5341 N-ASM φαιλόνην (1x)
2Ti 4:13 The cape that I·left·behind at Troas with Carpus, *as*

G5342 φέρω phérō *v.* (64x)
οἴω ôíō
ἐνέγκω ênénkō [alternate]
Compare:G0071 See:G5409
G5342.1 V-FAI-3P οἴσουσιν (1x)
Rv 21:26 And they·shall·bring the glory and the honor of·the
G5342.1 V-PAI-2P φέρετε (1x)
Jn 18:29 "What legal·accusation do·yeu·bring against this
G5342.1 V-PAI-3S φέρει (1x)
2Jn 1:10 to yeu *all*, and does·not bring this instruction, yeu·
G5342.1 V-PAI-3P φέρουσιν (5x)
Mk 7:32 And they·bring to·him a·deaf·man *with* a·speech·
Mk 8:22 to BethSaida. And they·bring a·blind·man to·him
Mk 15:22 Then they·bring him to *the* place *being·referred·to·*
2Pe 2:11 and power, do·not bring against themselves a·

Rv 21:24 and the kings of·the earth bring their glory and
G5342.1 V-PAM-2S φέρε (3x)
Jn 20:27 Then he·says to·Thomas, "Bring your finger here,
Jn 20:27 and see my hands. And bring your hand, and cast
2Ti 4:13 Carpus, *as* you·are·coming, bring *it·with·you*, and
G5342.1 V-PAM-2P φέρετε (5x)
Jn 2:8 "Draw·*it*·out now and bring *it* to·the director·of·the·
Mt 14:18 But he·declared, "Bring them here to·me.
Mt 17:17 How·long shall·I·put·up·with yeu? Bring him here
Mk 9:19 How·long shall·I·put·up·with yeu? Bring him to
Mk 12:15 "Why·do yeu·try me? Bring me a·denarius that I·
G5342.1 V-PAP-NSM φέρων (1x)
Jn 19:39 to Jesus by·night, bringing a·mixture of·myrrh and
G5342.1 V-PAP-NPF φέρουσαι (1x)
Lk 24:1 to the tomb, bringing aromatic·spices which they·
G5342.1 V-PAP-NPM φέροντες (3x)
Ac 5:16 cities all·around JeruSalem, bringing *the* sick and
Ac 25:7 stood·around, also bringing many burdensome
Mk 2:3 to him, bringing a·paralyzed·man being·carried by
G5342.1 V-PPP-ASF φερομένην (1x)
1Pe 1:13 completely upon the grace being·brought to·yeu at
G5342.1 V-IAI-3P ἔφερον (2x)
Ac 4:34 upon·selling *them*, they·were·bringing the values
Mk 1:32 the sun sank·down, they·were·bringing to him all
G5342.1 V-AAI-1S ἤνεγκα (1x)
Mk 9:17 declared, "Mentor, I·brought to you my son,
G5342.1 V-AAI-3S ἤνεγκεν (4x)
Jn 4:33 "¿!·Did someone bring him *something* to·eat?
Ac 4:37 After·selling *it*, he·brought the value and laid *it*
Mt 14:11 to·the young·girl, and she·brought *it* to·her mother
Mk 6:28 and brought his head on a·platter, and he·gave it to·
G5342.1 V-AAI-3P ἤνεγκαν (3x)
Jn 2:8 to·the director·of·the·banquet." And they·brought *it*.
Mk 9:20 And they·brought *the little·child* to him, and upon·
Mk 12:16 And they·brought *it*. And he·says to·them,
G5342.1 V-AAM-2P ἐνέγκατε (1x)
Jn 21:10 Jesus says to·them, "Bring of the small·fry which
G5342.1 V-AAP-NSM ἐνέγκας (2x)
Ac 5:2 ·known *of·it*. And bringing a·certain portion, he·laid
Ac 14:13 before their city, after·bringing bulls and garlands
G5342.1 V-AAP-NPM ἐνέγκαντες (1x)
Lk 15:23 And bringing the fattened calf, sacrifice *it*.
G5342.1 V-API-3S ἠνέχθη (1x)
Mt 14:11 And his head was·brought on a·platter and was·
G5342.1 V-APN ἐνεχθῆναι (1x)
Mk 6:27 king ordered for·his head to·be·brought. But·then
G5342.2 V-FAI-3S οἴσει (1x)
Jn 21:18 shall·gird you, and shall·carry *you* where you·do·
G5342.2 V-PAN φέρειν (1x)
Lk 23:26 the cross on·him, *for·him* to·carry *it* behind Jesus.
G5342.2 V-PAP-NPM φέροντες (1x)
Lk 5:18 And behold, men carrying a·man·of·clay† upon a·
G5342.2 V-PPN φέρεσθαι (1x)
Heb 9:16 *for* death to·be·carrying·away the·one who·is·
G5342.2 V-PPP-NPM φερόμενοι (1x)
2Pe 1:21 But·rather, while·being·carried·along by *the* Holy
G5342.2 V-PPS-1P φερώμεθα (1x)
Heb 6:1 we·should·be·carrying·on toward the
G5342.2 V-IPI-1P ἐφερόμεθα (1x)
Ac 27:15 handing *her to·the wind*, we·were·carried·*along*.
G5342.2 V-IPI-3P ἐφέροντο (1x)
Ac 27:17 the sail, they·were·carried·along in·this·manner.
G5342.2 V-API-3S ἠνέχθη (1x)
2Pe 1:21 ·of·clay† *was* prophecy carried·forth in·times·past.
G5342.2 V-APP-ASF ἐνεχθεῖσαν (1x)
2Pe 1:18 this voice being·carried·forth from·out of·heaven,
G5342.2 V-APP-GSF ἐνεχθείσης (1x)
2Pe 1:17 with·a·voice as·such being·carried·forth to·him by
G5342.3 V-PAI-3S φέρει (2x)
Jn 12:24 But if it·should·die, it·bears much fruit.
Jn 15:5 me and·I in him, the·same bears much fruit, because
G5342.3 V-PAN φέρειν (1x)
Jn 15:4 ·as the vine·sprout is·not able to·bear fruit of itself
G5342.3 V-PAP-ASN φέρον (2x)
Jn 15:2 Every vine·sprout in me not bearing fruit, *the* same
Jn 15:2 ·away; and any *vine·sprout* bearing the *proper* fruit,
G5342.3 V-PAP-NPM φέροντες (1x)
Heb 13:13 the arrayed·encampment, bearing his reproach.
G5342.3 V-PAS-2P φέρητε (2x)
Jn 15:8 Father is·glorified, that yeu·may·bear much fruit,
Jn 15:16 should·head·on·out and should·bear fruit and yeur
G5342.3 V-PAS-3S φέρῃ (1x)
Jn 15:2 ·and·purifies it, in·order·that it·may·bear more fruit.
G5342.3 V-IAI-3S ἔφερεν (1x)
Mk 4:8 ·up and growing·more, and it·was·bearing *fruit*: one
G5342.3 V-AAI-3S ἤνεγκεν (1x)
Rm 9:22 and to·make·known his power, bore with much
G5342.4 V-PEP-GSF φερομένης (1x)
Ac 2:2 of·the heaven, just·as of·a·rushing forceful wind, and
G5342.5 V-PAP-ASF φέρουσαν (1x)
Ac 12:10 to the iron gate, the·one leading to the City, which
G5342.6 V-PAP-NSM φέρων (1x)
Heb 1:3 ·essence, also *the·one* upholding all·things by·the
G5342.6 V-IAI-3P ἔφερον (1x)
Heb 12:20 they·were·not bearing·with·and·upholding the·

G5343 φεύγω phêúgō *v.* (31x)

Compare:G0590-2 G5159-1 See:G1628 G5436
G5343.1 V-FDI-3S φεύξεται (2x)
Jac 4:7 ·against the Slanderer, and he·shall·flee from yeu.
Rv 9:6 ·shall·long to·die, and Death shall·flee from them.
G5343.1 V-FDI-3P φεύξονται (1x)
Jn 10:5 ·should·not follow, but·rather shall·flee from him,
G5343.1 V-PAI-3S φεύγει (2x)
Jn 10:12 coming and leaves the sheep and flees; and the wolf
Jn 10:13 And the hired·worker flees, because he·is a·hired·
G5343.1 V-PAM-2S φεῦγε (3x)
Mt 2:13 little·child and his mother, and flee into Egypt, and
1Ti 6:11 O clay·man† of·God, flee from·these·things, and
2Ti 2:22 So flee the youthful longings, but pursue
G5343.1 V-PAM-2P φεύγετε (3x)
Mt 10:23 ·persecute yeu in this city, flee into the other, for
1Co 6:18 Flee the sexual·immorality. Every moral·failing,
1Co 10:14 my dearly·beloved, flee from the idolatry.
G5343.1 V-PAM-3P φευγέτωσαν (3x)
Lk 21:21 Then the·ones in Judea must·flee into the
Mt 24:16 "then the·ones in Judea must·flee to the mountains.
Mk 13:14 "then the·ones in Judea must·flee into the
G5343.1 V-2AAI-3S ἔφυγεν (5x)
Ac 7:29 Then Moses fled at this saying, and was a·sojourner
Mk 14:52 But abandoning the linen·cloth, he·fled from them
Rv 12:6 And the woman fled into the wilderness, where she·
Rv 16:20 And every island fled·away, and mountains were·
Rv 20:11 earth and the heaven fled·away. And there·is·not
G5343.1 V-2AAI-3P ἔφυγον (6x)
Lk 8:34 ·seeing the·thing having·happened, they·fled; and
Mt 8:33 And the·ones feeding *them* fled, and going·off into
Mt 26:56 Then leaving him, all the disciples fled.
Mk 5:14 feeding the pigs fled and gave·a·detailed·report in
Mk 14:50 Then leaving him, everyone fled.
Mk 16:8 [(And going·forth swiftly, they·fled from the
G5343.1 V-2AAN φυγεῖν (3x)
Lk 3:7 who gave·any·indication to·yeu to·flee from the
Ac 27:30 But with·the sailors seeking to·flee out·from the
Mt 3:7 who gave·any·indication to·yeu to·flee from the
G5343.1 V-2AAS-2P φύγητε (1x)
Mt 23:33 ·vipers, in·what·way should·yeu·escape from the
G5343.2 V-2AAI-3P ἔφυγον (2x)
Heb 11:34 *the* power of·fire, escaped *the* edge of·*the*·dagger
Heb 12:25 For if those·men did·not escape, *the·ones* already·

G5344 Φῆλιξ Phēlix *n/p.* (9x)

G5344.2 N/P-NSM Φῆλιξ (5x)
Ac 24:22 And Felix, after·hearing these·things *and* having·
Ac 24:24 (herself·being a·Judean), Felix sent·for Paul, and
Ac 24:25 judgment *that* shall·be, Felix, becoming alarmed,
Ac 24:27 Festus took succession *after* Felix. And Felix,
Ac 24:27 *after* Felix. And Felix, wanting to·store·up
G5344.2 N/P-VSM Φῆλιξ (1x)
Ac 24:3 everywhere and in·every·way, most·noble Felix.
G5344.2 N/P-ASM Φήλικα (1x)
Ac 23:24 ·bring·*him*·thoroughly·safe to Felix the governor."
G5344.2 N/P-DSM Φήλικι (1x)
Ac 23:26 Lysias, to·the most·noble governor Felix, be·well.
G5344.2 N/P-GSM Φήλικος (1x)
Ac 25:14 ·been·left·behind *as* a·chained·prisoner by Felix,

G5345 φήμη phḗmē *n.* (2x)

Roots:G5346 Compare:G0189 G2811 See:G2162 G2163 G0989
G5345.1 N-NSF φήμη (1x)
Mt 9:26 And the disclosure of·this *awakening* went·forth
G5345.2 N-NSF φήμη (1x)
Lk 4:14 to Galilee, and a·reputation went·forth concerning

G5346 φημί phēmí *v.* (59x)

Roots:G5337-2 Compare:G3004 G2036 G4483 G2980 See:G0989 G2163 G5345
G5346.1 V-PXI-1S φημί (3x)
1Co 7:29 But this I·disclose, brothers, *that* the season *is*
1Co 10:15 ·men; yeu·yeurselves judge what I·disclose:
1Co 15:50 Now this I·disclose, brothers, that flesh and blood
G5346.1 V-PXI-3S φησίν (3x)
Ac 8:36 And the eunuch disclosed, "Behold, *here·is* water.
Ac 10:31 and he·disclosed, 'Cornelius, your prayer is·heard,
Ac 25:24 Festus then disclosed, "King Agrippa, and all the
G5346.1 V-IXI-3S ἔφη (2x)
Lk 22:58 someone·else seeing him, was·disclosing, "You·
Mt 26:61 declared, "This·man was·disclosing, 'I·am·able
G5346.2 V-PXI-1S φημί (1x)
1Co 10:19 So·then, what do·I·reply? That an·idol is
G5346.2 V-PXI-3S φησίν (11x)
Lk 7:40 to·declare to·you." And he·replies, "Mentor,
Ac 19:35 ·down the crowd, the town·clerk replied, "Men,
Ac 22:2 they·personally·held more still). And he·replies,
Ac 23:18 to the regiment·commander and replied, "After·
Ac 25:5 "Now·then," he·replies, "the·ones among yeu
Ac 25:22 "Then tomorrow," he·replied, "You·shall·hear
Ac 26:25 But he·replied, "I·am·not raving·mad, most·noble
Heb 8:5 "'For clearly·see·to·it,'" he·replies, "'*that* you·
Mt 14:8 ·being·urged·on by her mother, she·replied, "Give
1Co 6:16 "'the two,'" he·replies, "'shall·be distinctly one
2Co 10:10 in·fact, *the·one wrongly reckoning* replies, "His
G5346.2 V-PXI-3P φασίν (1x)
Rm 3:8 we·are·vilified, and just·as some reply for·us to·say)
G5346.2 V-IXI-3S ἔφη (37x)
Jn 1:23 He·replied, "I·myself *am* "a·voice of·one·crying·
Jn 9:38 And he·replied, "Lord, I·trust.
Lk 7:44 ·around toward the woman, he·replied to·Simon,
Lk 22:70 So they·all replied, "So·then, you·yourself are the
Lk 23:3 And answering him, he·replied, "You·yourself
Ac 2:38 And Peter replied to them, "Repent, and each·one
Ac 7:2 And *Stephen* replied, "Men, brothers and fathers,
Ac 10:28 And he·replied to them, "Yeu·yeurselves are·
Ac 10:30 And Cornelius replied, "Four days ago I·was
Ac 16:30 And bringing them outside, he·replied, "Sirs,
Ac 16:37 But Paul replied to them, "After publicly thrashing
Ac 17:22 ·settled in *the* midst of·Mars'·Hill, replied, "Men,
Ac 21:37 And *Lysias* the *regiment·commander* replied, "Do·
Ac 22:27 ·yourself are a·Roman!" And he·replied, "Yes.
Ac 22:28 And Paul replied, "But I·myself, also, *am*
Ac 23:5 And Paul replied, "I·had·not seen, brothers, that he·
Ac 23:17 one of·the centurions, Paul was·replying, "Lead
Ac 23:35 he·replied, "I·shall·thoroughly·hear you whenever
Ac 25:22 Then Agrippa replied to Festus, "I·resolve also to·
Ac 26:1 Then Agrippa replied to Paul, "It·is·freely·
Ac 26:24 ·making·his·defense, Festus replied *to* these·things
Ac 26:28 But Agrippa replied to Paul, "In *such* a·brief·
Ac 26:32 Then Agrippa replied to·Festus, "This man·of·
Mt 4:7 YeShua was·replying to·him, "Again, it·has·been·
Mt 8:8 And answering, the centurion was·replying, "Lord,
Mt 13:28 He·replied to·them, 'A·hostile man·of·clay† did

Φφ

Mt 13:29 "But he·replied, 'No, lest while·collecting the
Mt 17:26 YeShua was·replying to·him, "So the sons are
Mt 19:21 YeShua replied to·him, "If you·want to·be
Mt 21:27 And he·himself replied to·them, "Neither do I·
Mt 25:21 His lord replied to·him, 'Well·done, O·
Mt 25:23 His lord replied to·him, 'Well·done, O·
Mt 26:34 YeShua replied to·him, "Certainly I·say to·you,
Mt 27:11 Jews?" And YeShua was·replying to·him, "You·
Mt 27:23 And the governor was·replying, "For what crime
Mt 27:65 So Pilate replied to·them, "Yeu·have a·sentinel·
Mk 14:29 But Peter replied to·him, "Even if all shall·be·
EG5346.2 (1x)
1Co 10:20 *No,* but·rather *I·reply* that those·things *which* the

G5347 Φῆστος Phēstôs *n/p.* (14x)

G5347.2 N/P-NSM Φῆστος (7x)
Ac 25:1 ·over into·the province, Festus walked·up from
Ac 25:4 Now·then in·fact, Festus answered *for* Paul to·be·
Ac 25:9 But Festus, wanting to·store·up influential·favor
Ac 25:12 Then Festus, speaking·together with the council,
Ac 25:14 *for* many·more days, Festus set·forth the·things
Ac 25:24 Festus then disclosed, "King Agrippa, and all the
Ac 26:24 *Paul* still·making·his·defense, Festus replied *to*
G5347.2 N/P-VSM Φῆστε (1x)
Ac 26:25 ·am·not raving·mad, most·noble Festus, but·rather
G5347.2 N/P-ASM Φῆστον (3x)
Ac 24:27 two·years, Porcius Festus took succession *after*
Ac 25:13 and BerNiki arrived in Caesarea to·greet Festus.
Ac 25:22 Then Agrippa replied to Festus, "I·resolve also to·
G5347.2 N/P-DSM Φήστῳ (1x)
Ac 26:32 Then Agrippa replied to·Festus, "This man·of·
G5347.2 N/P-GSM Φήστου (1x)
Ac 25:23 city, and with·Festus commandingly·ordering *that*
EG5347.2 (1x)
Ac 25:6 ·judgment·seat, *Festus* commandingly·ordered *for*

G5348 φθάνω phthánō *v.* (7x)

Compare:G4254 G4328 G2658 See:G4399
G5348.2 V-AAS-1P φθάσωμεν (1x)
1Th 4:15 should·not precede the·ones already·being·laid·to·
G5348.3 V-AAI-3S ἔφθασεν (1x)
1Th 2:16 So, the wrath already·anticipated upon them *is* for
G5348.4 V-AAI-1P ἐφθάσαμεν (1x)
2Co 10:14 for we·previously·came even·as·far·as yeu also,
G5348.6 V-AAI-3S ἔφθασεν (2x)
Lk 11:20 the kingdom of·God has·already·come upon yeu.
Mt 12:28 the kingdom of·God has·already·come upon yeu.
G5348.7 V-AAI-1P ἐφθάσαμεν (1x)
Php 3:16 for what we·already·attained, let·us·conform·and·
G5348.7 V-AAI-3S ἔφθασεν (1x)
Rm 9:31 of·righteousness, did·not already·attain to *the*

G5349 φθαρτός phthartós *adj.* (6x)

Roots:G5351 Compare:G0862
G5349.2 A-NSN φθαρτόν (2x)
1Co 15:53 ·for this corruptible *being* to·dress·itself·with
1Co 15:54 this corruptible *being* should·dress·itself·with
G5349.2 A-ASM φθαρτόν (1x)
1Co 9:25 they·may·receive a·corruptible victor's·crown, but
G5349.2 A-DPN φθαρτοῖς (1x)
1Pe 1:18 that *it·was* not with·corruptible·things *such·as* silver
G5349.2 A-GSM φθαρτοῦ (1x)
Rm 1:23 of·a·derived·image of·corruptible Clay·Man†, and·
G5349.2 A-GSF φθαρτῆς (1x)
1Pe 1:23 birthed·from·out of·a·corruptible sowing·of·seed,

G5350 φθέγγομαι phthéngômai *v.* (3x)

Compare:G4483 See:G5353 G5346 G5338
G5350.2 V-PDP-NPM φθεγγόμενοι (1x)
2Pe 2:18 For when·they·are·enunciating outrageous·things
G5350.2 V-PNN φθέγγεσθαι (1x)
Ac 4:18 ·charged them not to·enunciate nor·even to·instruct
G5350.2 V-ANP-NSN φθεγξάμενον (1x)
2Pe 2:16 a·voiceless female·donkey enunciating with *the*

G5351 φθείρω phthêírō *v.* (8x)

Compare:G4595 See:G5349 G5356 G1311
G5351.3 V-FAI-3S φθερεῖ (1x)
1Co 3:17 temple of·God, this·one God shall·corrupt. For the
G5351.3 V-PAI-3S φθείρει (1x)
1Co 3:17 If anyone corrupts the temple of·God, this·one God
G5351.3 V-PAI-3P φθείρουσιν (1x)
1Co 15:33 "Bad influences corrupt fine moral·habits."
G5351.3 V-PPI-3P φθείρονται (1x)
Jud 1:10 animals), in these·things they·are·corrupted.
G5351.3 V-PPP-ASM φθειρόμενον (1x)
Eph 4:22 manner·of·life (the·one being·corrupted by the
G5351.3 V-IAI-3S ἔφθειρεν (1x)
Rv 19:2 Great Prostitute, who was·corrupting the earth with
G5351.3 V-AAI-1P ἐφθείραμεν (1x)
2Co 7:2 ·wronged no·one·at·all, we·corrupted no·one·at·all,
G5351.3 V-2APS-3S φθαρῇ (1x)
2Co 11:3 mental·disposition should·be·corrupted from the

G5352 φθιν•οπ•ωρινός phthinôpōrinós *adj.* (1x)

Roots:G3703 See:G5351
G5352 A-NPN φθινοπωρινά (1x)
Jud 1:12 ·about by winds, late·autumn trees without·fruit,

G5353 φθόγγος phthôngôs *n.* (3x)

Roots:G5350
G5353.2 N-NSM φθόγγος (1x)
Rm 10:18 '" Their clear·articulation went·forth into all the
G5353.3 N-DPM φθόγγοις (1x)
1Co 14:7 ·not give a·distinction in·the musical·notes, how
EG5353.3 (1x)
1Co 14:7 how shall·it·be·known *what tune* is·being·piped or

G5354 φθονέω phthônéō *v.* (1x)

Roots:G5355 Compare:G5351
G5354 V-PAP-NPM φθονοῦντες (1x)
Gal 5:26 challenging one·another, envying one·another.

G5355 φθόνος phthônôs *n.* (9x)

Compare:G2205 See:G5354 G5351
G5355.2 N-NSM φθόνος (1x)
1Ti 6:4 ·of·words, from·out of·which becomes envy, strife,
G5355.2 N-NPM φθόνοι (1x)
Gal 5:21 envyings, murders, intoxications, revelries, and
G5355.2 N-ASM φθόνον (4x)
Mt 27:18 ·known that on·account·of envy they·handed him
Mk 15:10 chief·priests had·handed him over through envy.
Jac 4:5 that resides in us greatly·yearns *even* unto envy"?
Php 1:15 the Anointed-One even through envy and strife,
G5355.2 N-APM φθόνους (1x)
1Pe 2:1 and hypocrisies, and envies, and all backbitings,
G5355.2 N-DSM φθόνῳ (1x)
Tit 3:3 ·through·life in malice and envy, detestable·men
G5355.2 N-GSM φθόνου (1x)
Rm 1:29 malice; *being* exceedingly·full of·envy, murder,

G5356 φθορά phthôrá *n.* (9x)

Roots:G5351
G5356.2 N-NSF φθορά (1x)
1Co 15:50 kingdom; neither does the corruption inherit the
G5356.2 N-ASF φθοράν (2x)
Gal 6:8 his flesh, shall·reap corruption from·out of·the flesh;
2Pe 2:12 ·born into capture and corruption, while·reviling in
G5356.2 N-DSF φθορᾷ (2x)
2Pe 2:12 , they·shall·be·fully·corrupted in their corruption.
1Co 15:42 dead. It·is·sown in corruption; it·is·awakened in
G5356.2 N-GSF φθορᾶς (3x)
Rm 8:21 ·be·set·free from the slavery of·corruption into the
2Pe 1:4 already·escaping·from the corruption *caused* by
2Pe 2:19 inherently·being slaves of·the corruption— for that·
G5356.3 N-ASF φθοράν (1x)
Col 2:22 which all are *subject* to perishing with·usage)—

G5357 φιάλη phiálē *n.* (12x)

G5357 N-ASF φιάλην (7x)
Rv 16:2 first went·off and poured·out his vial upon the earth,
Rv 16:3 the second angel poured·out his vial into the sea,
Rv 16:4 the third angel poured·out his vial into the rivers and
Rv 16:8 the fourth angel poured·out his vial upon the sun,
Rv 16:10 the fifth angel poured·out his vial upon the throne
Rv 16:12 the sixth angel poured·out his vial upon the great
Rv 16:17 the seventh angel poured·out his vial into the air,
G5357 N-APF φιάλας (5x)
Rv 5:8 harps and golden vials overflowing with·incense,
Rv 15:7 seven angels seven golden vials overflowing of·the
Rv 16:1 "Head·on·out and pour·out the vials of·the Rage of·
Rv 17:1 of·the·one having the seven vials, and he·spoke
Rv 21:9 angels (of·the·ones having the seven vials, the·ones

G5358 φιλ•άγαθος philágathôs *adj.* (1x)

Roots:G5384 G0018
G5358 A-ASM φιλάγαθον (1x)
Tit 1:8 fond·of·doing·beneficially·good, self-controlled,

G5359 Φιλ•α•δέλφεια Philadélphêia *n/l.* (2x)

Roots:G5361
G5359.2 N/L-ASF Φιλαδέλφειαν (1x)
Rv 1:11 and to Sardis, and to PhilAdelphia, and to LaoDicea
G5359.2 N/L-DSF Φιλαδελφείᾳ (1x)
Rv 3:7 of·the Called·Out·citizenry in PhilAdelphia write,

G5360 φιλ•α•δελφία philadêlphía *n.* (6x)

Roots:G5361
G5360 N-NSF φιλαδελφία (1x)
Heb 13:1 The brotherly·affection must·continue.
G5360 N-ASF φιλαδελφίαν (2x)
1Pe 1:22 Spirit unto a·brotherly·affection without·hypocrisy,
2Pe 1:7 ·with *yeur* devout·reverence, Brotherly·Affection;
G5360 N-DSF φιλαδελφίᾳ (2x)
Rm 12:10 in the brotherly·affection, *by·showing* family·
2Pe 1:7 and along·with *yeur* brotherly·affection, Love.
G5360 N-GSF φιλαδελφίας (1x)
1Th 4:9 But concerning the brotherly·affection, yeu·have no

G5361 φιλ•ά•δελφος philádêlphôs *adj.* (1x)

Roots:G5384 G0080
G5361 A-NPM φιλάδελφοι (1x)
1Pe 3:8 ·another, affectionate·as·brothers, tender-hearted,

G5362 φίλ•ανδρος phílandrôs *n.* (1x)

Roots:G5384 G0435
G5362 N-APF φιλάνδρους (1x)
Tit 2:4 to·be affectionate·to·their·husbands *and* affectionate·

G5363 φιλ•ανθρ•ωπία philanthrōpía *n.* (2x)

Roots:G5384 G0444 See:G5364
G5363.1 N-NSF φιλανθρωπία (1x)
Tit 3:4 and *his* affection·for·mankind† became·apparent,
G5363.1 N-ASF φιλανθρωπίαν (1x)
Ac 28:2 to·us an·affection·for·mankind† way·beyond·the·.

G5364 φιλ•ανθρ•ώπως philanthrṓpōs *adv.* (1x)

Roots:G5384 G0444
G5364 ADV φιλανθρώπως (1x)
Ac 27:3 And·also treating Paul humanely, Julius freely·

G5365 φιλ•αργυρία philargyría *n.* (1x)

Roots:G5366
G5365.1 N-NSF φιλαργυρία (1x)
1Ti 6:10 the moral·wrongs is the fondness·of·money, which

G5366 φιλ•άργυρος philárgyrôs *adj.* (2x)

Roots:G5384 G0696 See:G5365
G5366.2 A-NPM φιλάργυροι (2x)
Lk 16:14 Pharisees, inherently·being fond·of·money, also
2Ti 3:2 selfish·and·self-centered, fond·of·money, braggers,

G5367 φίλ•αυτος phílautôs *adj.* (1x)

Roots:G5384 G0846
G5367.2 A-NPM φίλαυτοι (1x)
2Ti 3:2 the men·of·clay† shall·be: selfish·and·self-centered,

G5368 φιλέω philéō *v.* (25x)

Roots:G5384 Compare:G0025 G2037-1 G2309 G1014 See:G5370 G5363 G2705 G5371 G5372 xLangAlso:H5401
G5368.1 V-PAI-2S φιλεῖς (1x)
Jn 11:3 "Lord, see, he·whom you·are·fond·of is·sick."
G5368.1 V-PAI-3P φιλοῦσιν (2x)
Mt 6:5 ·hypocrites *are,* because they·are·fond·of standing in
Mt 23:6 Also, they·are·fond·of the foremost·places at the

G5368.1 V-PAP-GPM φιλούντων (1x)
Lk 20:46 in long·robes, and being·fond·of greetings in the
G5368.1 V-PAP-NSM φιλῶν (1x)
Rv 22:15 and everyone being·fond·of and committing a·lie.
G5368.1 V-IAI-3S ἐφίλει (2x)
Jn 11:36 were·saying, "See how fond·he·was·of him!"
Jn 20:2 other disciple whom Jesus was·fond·of, and she·says
G5368.2 V-PAI-1S φιλῶ (3x)
Jn 21:15 personally·know that I·have·affection·for you." He·
Jn 21:16 personally·know that I·have·affection·for you." He·
Jn 21:17 absolutely·know that I·have·affection·for you."
G5368.2 V-PAI-2S φιλεῖς (2x)
Jn 21:17 *son* of·Jonah, do·you·have·affection·for me?
Jn 21:17 the third·time, "Do·you·have·affection·for me?
G5368.2 V-PAI-3S φιλεῖ (1x)
1Co 16:22 If any·man does·not have·affection·for the Lord
G5368.2 V-PAP-APM φιλοῦντας (1x)
Tit 3:15 you. Greet the·ones having·affection·for us in the
G5368.2 V-PAS-1S φιλῶ (1x)
Rv 3:19 'As·many·as I·may·have·affection·for, I·myself
G5368.3 V-PAI-3S φιλεῖ (2x)
Jn 5:20 For the Father is·a·friend·to the Son and shows him
Jn 16:27 For the Father himself is·a·friend·to yeu, because
G5368.3 V-RAI-2P πεφιλήκατε (1x)
Jn 16:27 because yeu·yeurselves have·been·a·friend·to me,
G5368.4 V-PAP-NSM φιλῶν (3x)
Jn 12:25 The·one affectionately·favoring his soul *(and·its·*
Mt 10:37 The·one affectionately·favoring father or mother
Mt 10:37 of·me, and the·one affectionately·favoring son or
G5368.4 V-IAI-3S ἐφίλει (1x)
Jn 15:19 the world would affectionately·favor its·own, but
G5368.5 V-AAN φιλῆσαι (1x)
Lk 22:47 them, and he·drew·near to·Jesus to·kiss him.
G5368.5 V-AAS-1S φιλήσω (2x)
Mt 26:48 saying, "Whomever I·should·kiss, that·is him.
Mk 14:44 saying, "Whomever I·should·kiss, it·is him.

G5369 φιλ•ήδονος philḗdônôs *adj.* (1x)
Roots:G5384 G2237
G5369 A-NPM φιλήδονοι (1x)
2Ti 3:4 ·with·self-conceit, fond·of·sensual·pleasures rather

G5370 φίλημα phílēma *n.* (7x)
Roots:G5368 See:G2705
xLangEquiv:H5390
G5370 N-ASN φίλημα (1x)
Lk 7:45 "You·did·not give me a·kiss, but she·herself since
G5370 N-DSN φιλήματι (6x)
Lk 22:48 ·hand·over the Son of·Clay·Man† with·a·kiss?"
Rm 16:16 Greet one·another with a·holy kiss. The Called·
1Pe 5:14 Greet·yeu one·another with a·kiss of·love. Peace
1Th 5:26 Greet all the brothers with a·holy kiss.
1Co 16:20 Greet one·another with a·holy kiss.
2Co 13:12 Greet one·another with a·holy kiss.

G5371 Φιλήμων Philḗmōn *n/p.* (1x)
Roots:G5368 See:G5371
G5371.2 N/P-DSM Φιλήμονι (1x)
Phm 1:1 *our* brother. To·Philemon our dearly·beloved and

G5372 Φίλητος Philētôs *n/p.* (1x)
Roots:G5368 Compare:G5211 G1361 See:G5371
G5372.2 N/P-NSM Φίλητος (1x)
2Ti 2:17 ·as·pasture, of·whom is Hymenaeus and Philetus,

G5373 φιλία philía *n.* (1x)
Roots:G5384
G5373.2 N-NSF φιλία (1x)
Jac 4:4 ·not personally·know that the friendship of·the world

G5374 Φιλ•ιππήσιος Philippḗsiôs *n/g.* (1x)
Roots:G5375
G5374 N/G-VPM Φιλιππήσιοι (1x)
Php 4:15 Now yeu Philippians personally·know also, that at

G5375 Φίλ•ιπποι Phílippôi *n/l.* (4x)
Roots:G5376 See:G5374
G5375 N/L-ASM Φιλίππους (1x)
Ac 16:12 and from·there to Phillppi, which is a·foremost city
G5375 N/L-DPM Φιλίπποις (2x)
Php 1:1 Jesus, to·the·ones being at Phillppi, together with·
1Th 2:2 and being·abusively·mistreated in Phillppi, just·as
G5375 N/L-GSM Φιλίππων (1x)
Ac 20:6 we·ourselves sailed·away from Phillppi after the

G5376 Φίλ•ιππος Phílippôs *n/p.* (38x)
Roots:G5384 G2462 Compare:G4736 See:G1675 G2099 G1249 G5076
G5376.2 N/P-GSM Φιλίππου (2x)
Mt 16:13 the district of·Caesarea Phillppi, was·asking·of his
Mk 8:27 into the villages of·Caesarea Phillppi. And along
G5376.3 N/P-NSM Φίλιππος (9x)
Jn 1:44 Now Phillp was from BethSaida, from·among the
Jn 1:45 Phillp finds NathaniEl and says to·him, "We·have·
Jn 1:46 to·be from·out of·Natsareth?" Phillp says to·him,
Jn 6:7 Phillp answered him, "Two·hundred denarii *worth*
Jn 12:22 Phillp comes and relays *this* to·Andrew, and again
Jn 12:22 and again Andrew and Phillp relay *it* to·Jesus.
Jn 14:8 Phillp says to·him, "Lord, show us the Father,
Ac 1:13 Jakob, John, and Andrew); (Phillp and Thomas);
Mt 10:3 Phillp and BarTholomew; Thomas and MattHew the
G5376.3 N/P-VSM Φίλιππε (1x)
Jn 14:9 have·you·not known me, Phillp? The·one having·
G5376.3 N/P-ASM Φίλιππον (5x)
Jn 1:43 into Galilee, and he·finds Phillp and says to·him,
Jn 1:48 to·him, "Before Phillp hollered·out·for you, I·saw
Jn 6:5 him, Jesus says to Phillp, "From·what·source shall·
Lk 6:14 Jakob and John, and·Phillp and BarTholomew,
Mk 3:18 and Andrew, and Phillp, and BarTholomew, and
G5376.3 N/P-DSM Φιλίππῳ (1x)
Jn 12:21 the·same *Greeks* came·alongside Phillp, the·one
G5376.4 N/P-NSM Φίλιππος (6x)
Ac 8:5 And Phillppe, after·coming·down to a·city of·
Ac 8:30 And running·toward *him*, Phillppe heard him
Ac 8:35 And Phillppe, opening·up his mouth and beginning
Ac 8:37 And Phillppe declared, "If you·trust from·out of·all
Ac 8:38 ·down into the water, both Phillppe and the eunuch.
Ac 8:40 But Phillppe was·found in Ashdod, and going·
G5376.4 N/P-ASM Φίλιππον (4x)
Ac 6:5 and of·Holy Spirit, and·also Phillppe, ProChorus,
Ac 8:26 And the·angel of·Yahweh spoke to Phillppe, saying,
Ac 8:31 he·implored Phillppe that·he·would·climb·up to·sit·
Ac 8:39 Yahweh's Spirit snatched Phillppe, and the eunuch
G5376.4 N/P-DSM Φιλίππῳ (4x)
Ac 8:12 they·trusted Phillppe as·he·was·proclaiming the·
Ac 8:13 he·was diligently·continuing·on with·Phillppe. *And*
Ac 8:29 And the Spirit declared to·Phillppe, "Go·alongside
Ac 8:34 And answering Phillppe, the eunuch declared, "I·
G5376.4 N/P-GSM Φιλίππου (2x)
Ac 8:6 ·heed to·the·things being·said by Phillppe in their
Ac 21:8 And entering into the house of·Phillppe (the
G5376.5 N/P-GSM Φιλίππου (3x)
Lk 3:19 (the wife of·his brother Phillppus) and concerning
Mt 14:3 ·of HerOdias, the wife of·Phillppus, his brother.
Mk 6:17 the wife of·his brother Phillppus, because he·
G5376.6 N/P-GSM Φιλίππου (1x)
Lk 3:1 brother Phillppus·II being·the·ruling·tetrarch of·Jetur

G5377 φιλό•θεος philốthêos *adj.* (1x)
Roots:G5384 G2316
G5377 A-NPM φιλόθεοι (1x)
2Ti 3:4 ·of·sensual·pleasures rather than *being* fond·of·God,

G5378 Φιλό•λογος Philốlôgôs *n/p.* (1x)
Roots:G5384 G3056
G5378.2 N/P-ASM Φιλόλογον (1x)
Rm 16:15 Greet PhiloLogus, and Julia, Nereus, and his sister

G5379 φιλο•νεικία philônêikía *n.* (1x)
Roots:G5380 Compare:G2054 G3163 See:G3534
G5379 N-NSF φιλονεικία (1x)
Lk 22:24 And there·was also a·fond·contention among them,

G5380 φιλό•νεικος philốnêikôs *adj.* (1x)
Roots:G5384 See:G3534 G5379
G5380.2 A-NSM φιλόνεικος (1x)
1Co 11:16 if any·man seems to·be contentious, we·ourselves

G5381 φιλο•νεξία philônêxía *n.* (2x)
Roots:G5382 See:G3578
G5381.1 N-ASF φιλοξενίαν (1x)
Rm 12:13 ·sharing·with·others, by·pursuing the hospitality.
G5381.2 N-GSF φιλοξενίας (1x)
Heb 13:2 Do·not forget the hospitality·to·strangers, for

G5382 φιλό•ξενος philốxênôs *adj.* (3x)
Roots:G5384 G3581 Compare:G3580 See:G5381
G5382.2 A-NPM φιλόξενοι (1x)
1Pe 4:9 *Be* hospitable to one·another without grumbling.
G5382.2 A-ASM φιλόξενον (2x)
Tit 1:8 but·rather hospitable, fond·of·doing·beneficially·
1Ti 3:2 self-controlled, orderly, hospitable, instructive,

G5383 φιλο•πρωτεύω philôprōtêúō *v.* (1x)
Roots:G5384 G4413 Compare:G2519
G5383.1 V-PAP-NSM φιλοπρωτεύων (1x)
3Jn 1:9 the·one being·fond·of·being·foremost among·them,

G5384 φίλος phílôs *adj.* (29x)
Compare:G0026 G0027 G2064-3 G2083 See:G5368 G5373
G5384.4 A-NSM φίλος (7x)
Jn 3:29 is a·bridegroom. But the friend of·the bridegroom,
Jn 11:11 to·them, "Our friend Lazarus has·been·laid·to·rest.
Jn 19:12 ·man, you·are not Caesar's friend. Anyone making
Lk 7:34 ·wine-drinker, a·friend of·tax·collectors and
Lk 11:6 since·just·now a·friend of·mine came·directly to me
Mt 11:19 ·wine-drinker, a·friend of·tax·collectors and
Jac 4:4 be·definitely·willing to·be a·friend of·the world is·
G5384.4 A-NPM φίλοι (4x)
Jn 15:14 Yeu·yeurselves are my friends, if yeu·should·do as·
Lk 23:12 and HerOd·AntiPas became friends with one·another
Ac 19:31 of·the chiefs·of·Asia, being friends with·him,
3Jn 1:14 Peace *be* to·you. The friends greet you. Greet the
G5384.4 A-ASM φίλον (2x)
Lk 11:5 "Which from·among yeu shall·have a·friend, and
Lk 11:8 on·account·of *him* being his friend, yet on·account·
G5384.4 A-APM φίλους (8x)
Jn 15:15 but I·have·declared yeu *to·be* friends, because all·
Lk 7:6 the home, the centurion sent friends to him, saying
Lk 14:12 do·not holler·out·for your friends, nor·even your
Lk 15:6 house, he·calls·together the friends and the close·
Lk 16:9 to·yeu: Make friends for·yeurselves from·out of·the
Ac 10:24 ·together his kinsmen and very·close friends.
Ac 27:3 to·traverse to his·friends to·obtain caring·hospitality
3Jn 1:14 friends greet you. Greet the friends each·by name.
G5384.4 A-DPM φίλοις (1x)
Lk 12:4 "And I·say to·yeu, my friends, do·not be·afraid of
G5384.4 A-GPM φίλων (3x)
Jn 15:13 should·lay·down his soul on·behalf of·his friends.
Lk 15:29 in·order·that I·may·be·merry with my friends.
Lk 21:16 and kinsmen, and friends; and they·shall·put·to·
G5384.4 N-VSM φίλε (2x)
Lk 11:5 and should·declare to·him, 'Friend, kindly·lend me
Lk 14:10 he·may·declare to·you, 'Friend, walk·further·up
G5384.4 N-APF φίλας (1x)
Lk 15:9 *it*, she·calls·together the friends and the close·
G5384.5 A-NSM φίλος (1x)
Jac 2:23 ' And he·was·called God's "'Close·Friend."'

G5385 φιλο•σοφία philôsôphía *n.* (1x)
Roots:G5386 See:G4678
G5385.1 N-GSF φιλοσοφίας (1x)
Col 2:8 you through the *use·of* philosophy and an·empty

G5386 φιλό•σοφος philốsôphôs *n.* (1x)
Roots:G5384 G4680 Compare:G4804 See:G5385
G5386 N-GPM φιλοσόφων (1x)
Ac 17:18 Now certain philosophers of·the Epicureans and

G5387 φιλό•στοργος philốstôrgôs *adj.* (1x)
Roots:G5384
G5387.1 A-NPM φιλόστοργοι (1x)
Rm 12:10 *by·showing* family·affection to·one·another; in·

G5388 φιλό•τεκνος philŏtêknŏs *adj.* (1x)
Roots:G5384 G5043
G5388 A-APF φιλοτέκνους (1x)
Tit 2:4 ·to·their·husbands *and* affectionate·to·their·children,
G5389 φιλο•τιμέομαι philŏtiméŏmai *v.* (3x)
Roots:G5384 G5092
G5389.2 V-PNI-1P φιλοτιμούμεθα (1x)
2Co 5:9 Therefore we·aspire also, whether being·at·home or
G5389.2 V-PNN φιλοτιμεῖσθαι (1x)
1Th 4:11 and to·aspire to·keep·still, and to·accomplish yeur·
G5389.2 V-PNP-ASM φιλοτιμούμενον (1x)
Rm 15:20 *I·am* aspiring to·proclaim·the·good·news, *but* not
G5390 φιλο•φρόνως philŏphrŏnōs *adv.* (1x)
Roots:G5391 Compare:G5382 G5264
G5390.2 ADV φιλοφρόνως (1x)
Ac 28:7 He·hosted *us for* three days courteously.
G5391 φιλό•φρων philŏphrōn *adj.* (1x)
Roots:G5384 G5424 See:G5390
G5391 A-NPM φιλόφρονες (1x)
1Pe 3:8 ·as·brothers, tender-hearted, thoughtfully·kind—
G5392 φιμόω phimŏō *v.* (8x)
Compare:G1993 G5420 G4912 G2777-4
G5392.1 V-FAI-2S φιμώσεις (2x)
1Co 9:9 "'You·shall·not muzzle an·ox *that·is* treading·out·
1Ti 5:18 "'You·shall·not muzzle an·ox *that·is* treading·out·
G5392.1 V-PAN φιμοῦν (1x)
1Pe 2:15 beneficially·doing·good, to·muzzle the ignorance
G5392.1 V-AAI-3S ἐφίμωσεν (1x)
Mt 22:34 him, after·hearing that he·muzzled the Sadducees.
G5392.1 V-API-3S ἐφιμώθη (1x)
Mt 22:12 having wedding apparel?' And he·was·muzzled.
G5392.1 V-APM-2S φιμώθητι (2x)
Lk 4:35 him, saying, "Be·muzzled! And come·forth out of·
Mk 1:25 him, saying, "Be·muzzled! And come·forth out of·
G5392.1 V-RPM-2S πεφίμωσο (1x)
Mk 4:39 sea, "Keep·silent, having·been·muzzled!" And the
G5393 Φλέγων Phlégōn *n/p.* (1x)
Roots:G5395
G5393.2 N/P-ASM Φλέγοντα (1x)
Rm 16:14 Greet ASynkritus, Phlegon, Hermas, PatroBas,
G5394 φλογίζω phlŏgízō *v.* (2x)
Roots:G5395 Compare:G2545 G4448
G5394.1 V-PAP-NSF φλογίζουσα (1x)
Jac 3:6 whole body, and setting·aflame the regular·course
G5394.1 V-PPP-NSF φλογιζομένη (1x)
Jac 3:6 of·nature, and being·set·aflame by the Hell·Canyon.
G5395 φλόξ phlŏx *n.* (7x)
Compare:G4442 G2740 See:G5393 xLangAlso:H3851
G5395.1 N-NSF φλόξ (3x)
Rv 1:14 white as snow), and his eyes *are* as a·blaze of·fire,
Rv 2:18 the·one having his eyes as a·blaze of·fire and his
Rv 19:12 His eyes *were* as a·blaze of·fire, and on his head
G5395.1 N-ASF φλόγα (1x)
Heb 1:7 his angels spirits and his attendants a·blaze of·fire."'
G5395.1 N-DSF φλογί (2x)
Lk 16:24 my tongue, because I·am·distressed in this blaze.'
Ac 7:30 ·Mount Sinai, in a·blaze of·fire in·the·burning·bush.
G5395.2 N-GSF φλογός (1x)
2Th 1:8 *then* in blazing fire, giving retribution to·the·ones
G5396 φλυαρέω phlyarĕō *v.* (1x)
Roots:G5397
G5396.2 V-PAP-NSM φλυαρῶν (1x)
3Jn 1:10 which he·does, gossiping·against us with·evil
G5397 φλύαρος phlýarŏs *adj.* (1x)
Compare:G2637 G4691 See:G5396
G5397.2 A-NPF φλύαροι (1x)
1Ti 5:13 merely idle, but·rather gossipers also and meddlers,
G5398 φοβερός phŏbêrŏs *adj.* (3x)
Roots:G5401 Compare:G1169 xLangAlso:H3372
G5398.1 A-NSF φοβερά (1x)
Heb 10:27 but a·certain frightful apprehension of·Tribunal·
G5398.1 A-NSN φοβερόν (1x)
Heb 12:21 being·made·apparent was frightful, *such·that*
G5398.2 A-NSN φοβερόν (1x)
Heb 10:31 *It·is* a·frightful·thing to·fall into *the* hands of·the·
G5399 φοβέω phŏbĕō *v.* (93x)
Roots:G5401 Compare:G4422 G4426 G1788 G4576 G5141 G5425 See:G1629 G5401 G5400 xLangAlso:H3372 H6206
G5399.2 V-AOI-3P ἐφοβήθησαν (2x)
Lk 2:9 ·around them. And they·were·frightened *with* great
Mk 4:41 And they·were·frightened *with* a·great reverent·
G5399.3 V-FOI-1S φοβηθήσομαι (1x)
Heb 13:6 and I·shall·not be·afraid of·what a·man·of·clay†
G5399.3 V-PNI-1S φοβοῦμαι (3x)
Lk 18:4 'Even though I·am·not afraid·of God, and I·am·not
2Co 11:3 But I·fear, lest·somehow, as the Serpent
2Co 12:20 For I·fear, lest·somehow after·coming, I·should·
G5399.3 V-PNI-1P φοβούμεθα (1x)
Mt 21:26 'From·out of·men·of·clay†,' we·fear the crowd,
G5399.3 V-PNI-2S φοβῇ (1x)
Lk 23:40 "Are·not·even you·yourself afraid·of God, *seeing*
G5399.3 V-PNM-2S φοβοῦ (13x)
Jn 12:15 "Do·not be·afraid, O·Daughter of·Tsiyon!
Lk 1:13 him, "Do·not be·afraid, Zacharias, on·account·that
Lk 1:30 declared to·her, "Do·not be·afraid, Mariam, for
Lk 5:10 to Simon, "Do·not be·afraid. From now·on, you·
Lk 8:50 him, saying, "Do·not be·afraid. Merely trust, and
Lk 12:32 "Do·not be·afraid, Little Flock, because yeur
Ac 18:9 ·vision at night, "Do·not be·afraid, but·rather speak,
Ac 27:24 saying *to·me*, 'Do·not be·afraid, Paul. It·is·
Mk 5:36 ·of·the·gathering, "Do·not be·afraid, merely trust.
Rm 11:20 Do·not·be arrogant, but·rather be·afraid.
Rm 13:4 if you·should·do the bad·thing, be·afraid. For *it·is*
Rv 1:17 saying to·me, "Do·not be·afraid; I AM the First
Rv 2:10 'Fear not·one·bit·of which·things you·are·about to·
G5399.3 V-PNM-2P φοβεῖσθε (8x)
Jn 6:20 "It·is·I Myself. Do·not be·afraid."
Lk 2:10 declared to·them, "Do·not be·afraid, for behold, I·
Lk 12:7 do·not be·afraid. Yeu·surpass·the·value of·many
Mt 14:27 ·good·courage, it·is·I Myself! Do·not be·afraid."
Mt 17:7 "Be·roused·already, and do·not be·afraid."
Mt 28:5 "Yeu·yeurselves do·not be·afraid, for I·have·seen
Mt 28:10 to·them, "Do·not be·afraid! Yeu·must·head·on·out
Mk 6:50 It·is·I Myself. Do·not be·afraid."
G5399.3 V-PNP-NSM φοβούμενος (2x)
Gal 2:12 ·detaching himself, fearing the·ones from·among
1Jn 4:18 But the·one being·afraid has·not been·made·
G5399.3 V-PNP-NPF φοβούμεναι (1x)
1Pe 3:6 ·doing·good and not being·afraid *of* not·even·one
G5399.3 V-PNP-NPM φοβούμενοι (2x)
Ac 27:17 the sailing·ship. And, fearing lest they·should·fall
Ac 27:29 And fearing lest·somehow they·should·fall into
G5399.3 V-INI-3P ἐφοβοῦντο (8x)
Jn 9:22 these·things, because they·feared the Judeans. For
Lk 9:45 ·not perceive it. And they·were·afraid to·ask him
Lk 22:2 they·may·eliminate him, for they·feared the people.
Ac 5:26 *but* not with force, for they·feared the people, lest
Ac 9:26 to·the disciples, but they·were all afraid of·him, not
Mk 10:32 And·yet while·following, they·were·afraid. And
Mk 11:32 (*They·stopped, for* they·were·afraid·of the people
Mk 16:8 ·declare not·even·one·thing, for they·were·afraid)].
G5399.3 V-AOI-3S ἐφοβήθη (2x)
Jn 19:8 Pilate heard this saying, he·was all·the·more afraid,
Mt 14:5 while·wanting to·kill him, he·feared the crowd,
G5399.3 V-AOI-3P ἐφοβήθησαν (11x)
Jn 6:19 coming near to·the sailboat. And they·were·afraid.
Lk 8:35 and being·of·sound·mind, and they·were·afraid.
Lk 9:34 with these·things, they·were·afraid to·enter into the
Lk 20:19 ·against them, yet they·feared the people.
Ac 16:38 ·officers, and they·were·afraid after·hearing that
Heb 11:23 little·child; and they·were·not afraid of·the king's
Mt 17:6 fell on their faces and were tremendously afraid.
Mt 21:46 to·securely·hold him, they·feared the crowds,
Mt 27:54 the·things happening, they·feared tremendously,
Mk 5:15 ·*was* having·held the legion. And they·were·afraid.
Mk 12:12 ·secure·hold·of him, yet they·feared the crowd,
G5399.3 V-AOM-2P φοβήθητε (7x)
Lk 12:4 my friends, do·not be·afraid of·the·ones killing the
Lk 12:5 to·yeu whom yeu·should·fear. Fear the·one, *that*
Lk 12:5 Yes, I·say to·yeu, fear this·one.
Mt 10:26 Accordingly, do·not fear them. For there·is·not·
Mt 10:31 Accordingly, do·not be·afraid; yeu·yeurselves
1Pe 3:14 And "'Do·not be·afraid of·their fear, nor·even
Rv 14:7 saying with a·loud voice, "Fear God and give glory
G5399.3 V-AOP-NSM φοβηθείς (2x)
Heb 11:27 he·forsook Egypt (not fearing the rage of·the
Mt 25:25 And being·afraid, upon·going·off, I·hid your
G5399.3 V-AOP-NPM φοβηθέντες (1x)
Lk 8:25 is·yeur trust?" And being·afraid, they·marveled,
G5399.3 V-AOS-2S φοβηθῇς (1x)
Mt 1:20 you·should·not be·afraid to·personally·take Mariam
G5399.3 V-AOS-2P φοβήθητε (1x)
Lk 12:5 I·shall·indicate to·yeu whom yeu·should·fear. Fear
G5399.4 V-PNI-1S φοβοῦμαι (1x)
Gal 4:11 I·am·afraid·for yeu, lest·somehow I·have·labored·
G5399.4 V-PNN φοβεῖσθαι (1x)
Rm 13:3 But do·you·want not to·be·afraid·of the authority?
G5399.4 V-INI-1S ἐφοβούμην (1x)
Lk 19:21 For I·was·afraid·of you, because you·are an·
G5399.4 V-INI-3S ἐφοβεῖτο (1x)
Mk 6:20 for HerOd·AntiPas was·afraid·of John, having·seen
G5399.4 V-INI-3P ἐφοβοῦντο (2x)
Mk 9:32 the utterance and were·afraid to·inquire·of him.
Mk 11:18 ·destroy him, for they·were·afraid·of him,
G5399.4 V-AOI-3S ἐφοβήθη (3x)
Ac 22:29 ·commander also was·afraid after·realizing that he·
Mt 2:22 ·the·Great, *Joseph* was·afraid to·go·aside there. So
Mt 14:30 ·at the strong wind, he·was·afraid, and beginning
G5399.4 V-AOM-2P φοβήθητε (2x)
Mt 10:28 And do·not be·afraid of·the·ones killing the body,
Mt 10:28 soul. But rather be·afraid·of the·one being·able to·
G5399.5 V-AOS-1P φοβηθῶμεν (1x)
Heb 4:1 into his complete·rest, we·should·be·alarmed, lest
G5399.6 V-PNM-2P φοβεῖσθε (1x)
1Pe 2:17 Love the brotherhood. Reverently·fear God. Honor
G5399.6 V-PNP-DPM φοβουμένοις (2x)
Lk 1:50 his mercy *is* to·the·ones reverently·fearing him *unto*
Rv 11:18 to·the·ones who·are·reverently·fearing your name,
G5399.6 V-PNP-NSM φοβούμενος (4x)
Lk 18:2 judge— *one* who·is·not reverently·fearing God and
Ac 10:2 *man* and one·reverently·fearing God together with·
Ac 10:22 a·righteous man who·is·reverently·fearing God and
Ac 10:35 nation, the·one who·is·reverently·fearing him and
G5399.6 V-PNP-NPM φοβούμενοι (4x)
Ac 13:16 Israelites and the·ones reverently·fearing God,
Ac 13:26 and the·ones among yeu reverently·fearing God,
Col 3:22 with fidelity of·heart, reverently·fearing God.
Rv 19:5 and the·ones who·are·reverently·fearing him, both
G5399.6 V-PNS-3S φοβῆται (1x)
Eph 5:33 , in·order·that she·should·reverently·fear *her·own*
G5399.6 V-AOP-NSF φοβηθεῖσα (1x)
Mk 5:33 the woman, reverently·fearing and·also trembling,
G5399.6 V-AOS-3S φοβηθῇ (1x)
Rv 15:4 ¿! Who should·not reverently·fear you, O·Yahweh,
G5400 φόβητρον phŏbētrŏn *n.* (1x)
Roots:G5399 See:G1629
G5400 N-NPN φόβητρα (1x)
Lk 21:11 and there·shall·be frightening·things and great
G5401 φόβος phŏbŏs *n.* (47x)
Roots:G5337-3 Compare:G4423 G2150 G2317 G4574 See:G5399 xLangAlso:H3374 H6343
G5401.3 N-NSM φόβος (6x)
Lk 1:12 ·troubled after·seeing *him*, and fear fell upon him.
Rm 3:18 "'There·is no fear of·God fully·before their eyes.
Rm 13:3 are not *a·cause·of* fear for the beneficially·good
1Jn 4:18 There·is not fear in the Love, but·rather the

1Jn 4:18 fear, because the fear has a·tormenting·punishment
Rv 11:11 upon their feet, and great fear fell upon the·ones
G5401.3 N-NPM φόβοι (1x)
2Co 7:5 Outwardly *are* quarrels, inwardly *are* fears.
G5401.3 N-ASM φόβον (10x)
Jn 7:13 him, on·account·of the fear of·the Judeans.
Jn 19:38 ·under·cover on·account·of the fear of·the Judeans,
Jn 20:19 ·together on·account·of the fear of·the Judeans,
Lk 2:9 And they·were·frightened *with* great fear.
Rm 8:15 a·spirit of·slavery again to fear, but·rather yeu·
1Pe 3:14 "Do·not be·afraid of·their fear, nor·even should·
2Co 5:11 So·then, having·seen the fear of·the Lord, we·
1Jn 4:18 ·mature love casts out the fear, because the fear has
Rv 18:10 a·distance on·account·of the fear of·her torment,
Rv 18:15 a·distance on·account·of the fear of·her torment,
G5401.3 N-DSM φόβῳ (3x)
Lk 8:37 because they·were·clenched with·great fear. And
Heb 2:15 as·many·as·who (through fear of·death) were all
Jud 1:23 And others save with a·fear while·snatching *them*
G5401.3 N-GSM φόβου (3x)
Lk 21:26 with·men·of·clay† fainting for fear, and for·
Mt 14:26 and they·yelled·out from the fear.
Mt 28:4 And for fear of·him, the·ones keeping·guard are·
G5401.4 N-ASM φόβον (1x)
2Co 7:11 ·displeasure, moreover, *what* alarm, moreover,
G5401.5 N-NSM φόβος (4x)
Lk 1:65 And a·reverent·fear·and·awe happened on all the·
Lk 7:16 And a·reverent·fear·and·awe took·hold·of
Ac 2:43 And reverent·fear·and·awe came upon·every soul,
Ac 19:17 and Greeks. And reverent·fear·and·awe fell upon
G5401.5 N-ASM φόβον (1x)
Mk 4:41 ·frightened *with* a·great reverent·fear·and·awe, and
G5401.5 N-DSM φόβῳ (5x)
Ac 9:31 ·traversing in·the reverent·fear·and·awe of·the Lord
1Pe 1:17 of·yeur sojourning *here* in reverent·fear·and·awe—
1Pe 3:2 ·clean behavior *coupled* with reverent·fear·and·awe),
2Co 7:1 devoted·holiness in a·reverent·fear·and·awe of·God.
Eph 5:21 to·one·another in a·reverent·fear·and·awe of·God.
G5401.5 N-GSM φόβου (3x)
Lk 5:26 and were·filled with·reverent·fear·and·awe, saying,
Mt 28:8 ·tomb, with reverent·fear·and·awe and with·great
1Pe 3:15 with a·calm·mildness and a·reverent·fear·and·awe,
G5401.6 N-NSM φόβος (2x)
Ac 5:5 *and* expired. And great reverent·fear came upon all
Ac 5:11 And great reverent·fear came upon all the Called·
G5401.6 N-ASM φόβον (3x)
Rm 13:7 *due* the tax, the reverent·fear to·the·one *due* the
Rm 13:7 reverent·fear to·the·one *due* the reverent·fear, the
1Ti 5:20 in·order·that the rest also may·have reverent·fear.
G5401.6 N-DSM φόβῳ (2x)
1Pe 2:18 to·the masters with all reverent·fear, not merely to·
1Co 2:3 yeu in weakness, and in reverent·fear, and in much
G5401.6 N-GSM φόβου (3x)
Php 2:12 in my absence), with reverent·fear and trembling,
2Co 7:15 all, how with reverent·fear and trembling yeu·
Eph 6:5 according·to flesh) with reverent·fear and trembling

G5402 Φοίβη Phôíbē *n/p.* (1x)
See:G5457
G5402.2 N/P-ASF Φοίβην (1x)
Rm 16:1 And I·commend to·yeu Phoebe, our sister, being

G5403 Φοινίκη Phôiníkē *n/l.* (3x)
Roots:G5404 Compare:G5176-5 G4605 See:G5405
G5403.2 N/L-ASF Φοινίκην (2x)
Ac 15:3 they·were·going·throughout Phoenicia and Samaria,
Ac 21:2 ·ship sailing·over to Phoenicia, once·embarking,
G5403.2 N/L-GSF Φοινίκης (1x)
Ac 11:19 went·throughout as·far·as·to Phoenicia, Cyprus,

G5404 φοῖνιξ phôînix *n.* (2x)
Compare:G2566-4 See:G5405 G5403
xLangAlso:H8558
G5404.1 N-GPM φοινίκων (1x)
Jn 12:13 they·took the boughs of·palm·trees, and went·forth
G5404.2 N-NPM φοίνικες (1x)
Rv 7:9 ·with white long·robes and palm·branches in their

G5405 Φοῖνιξ Phôînix *n/l.* (1x)
Roots:G5404 See:G5403
G5405.2 N/L-ASM Φοίνικα (1x)
Ac 27:12 ·might·be·able to·arrive at Phenice to·winter *there*,

G5406 φονεύς phônéús *n.* (7x)
Roots:G5408 Compare:G0443 G0409 G4607
See:G5407 G5406-1 G3390-1 G3970-1
xLangAlso:H7523
G5406 N-NSM φονεύς (2x)
Ac 28:4 "This man·of·clay† is entirely a·murderer, whom,
1Pe 4:15 do·not·let any of·yeu suffer as a·murderer, or *as* a·
G5406 N-NPM φονεῖς (2x)
Ac 7:52 ·whom, yeu have·become betrayers and murderers,
Rv 22:15 sexually·immoral·persons, and the murderers, and
G5406 N-ASM φονέα (1x)
Ac 3:14 a·man, a·murderer, to·be·graciously·given to·yeu.
G5406 N-APM φονεῖς (1x)
Mt 22:7 ·completely·destroyed those murderers and torched
G5406 N-DPM φονεῦσιν (1x)
Rv 21:8 ones·having·been·abhorrent, and murderers, and

G5407 φονεύω phônéúō *v.* (12x)
Roots:G5406 Compare:G0615 G0337 G4969
xLangAlso:H7523
G5407 V-FAI-2S φονεύσεις (4x)
Mt 5:21 to·the ancient·ones, "You·shall·not murder," and '
Mt 19:18 YeShua declared, "'You·shall·not murder,'"
Rm 13:9 ·adultery. You·shall·not murder. You·shall·not
Jac 2:11 ·adultery, but you·shall·murder, you·have·become
G5407 V-PAI-2P φονεύετε (1x)
Jac 4:2 and do·not have. Yeu·murder and jealously·desire,
G5407 V-AAI-2P ἐφονεύσατε (2x)
Mt 23:35 of·BerekYah, whom yeu·murdered between the
Jac 5:6 ·pronounced·guilty *and* murdered the Righteous·One,
G5407 V-AAP-GPM φονευσάντων (1x)
Mt 23:31 ·are the·Sons of·the·ones murdering the prophets.
G5407 V-AAS-2S φονεύσῃς (3x)
Lk 18:20 commit·adultery,' 'You·may·not murder,'
Mk 10:19 commit·adultery,' 'You·may·not murder,'
Jac 2:11 ' also declared, "You·may·not murder." Now if
G5407 V-AAS-3S φονεύσῃ (1x)
Mt 5:21 and "whoever should·murder shall·be held·liable to·

G5408 φόνος phônôs *n.* (10x)
See:G5406 G5407
G5408 N-NPM φόνοι (3x)
Gal 5:21 envyings, murders, intoxications, revelries, and
Mt 15:19 comes·forth evil deliberations, murders, adulteries,
Mk 7:21 ·forth: adulteries, sexual·immoralities, murders,
G5408 N-ASM φόνον (3x)
Lk 23:19 occurring in the City and·also for·murder).
Lk 23:25 on·account·of insurrection and murder, whom
Mk 15:7 who had·committed murder in the insurrection.
G5408 N-DSM φόνῳ (1x)
Heb 11:37 ·tempted, they·died by murder with·a·dagger.
G5408 N-GSM φόνου (2x)
Ac 9:1 still seething with·menace and murder against the
Rm 1:29 *being* exceedingly·full of·envy, murder, strife,
G5408 N-GPM φόνων (1x)
Rv 9:21 did·they·repent out·from·among their murders, nor

G5409 φορέω phôréō *v.* (6x)
Roots:G5411 Compare:G1737 See:G2164
G5409.2 V-FAI-1P φορέσομεν (1x)
1Co 15:49 ·clay·man, we also shall·bear the derived·image
G5409.2 V-PAI-3S φορεῖ (1x)
Rm 13:4 For *it·is* not without·reason *that* he·bears the sword,
G5409.2 V-PAP-NSM φορῶν (1x)
Jn 19:5 So Jesus came·forth outside bearing the thorny
G5409.2 V-AAI-1P ἐφορέσαμεν (1x)
1Co 15:49 And just·as we·have·borne the derived·image of·
G5409.3 V-PAP-ASM φοροῦντα (1x)
Jac 2:3 ·look upon the·one prominently·wearing the splendid
G5409.3 V-PAP-NPM φοροῦντες (1x)
Mt 11:8 Behold, the·ones prominently·wearing the soft

G5410 Φόρον Phórôn *n/l.* (1x)
Compare:G0675
G5410.1 N/L-GSN Φόρου (1x)
Ac 28:15 ·meet us even·as·far·as *the* Forum of·Appius and

G5411 φόρος phôrôs *n.* (5x)
Roots:G5342 Compare:G2778 G5056 G0733-1
G3579-1 G5498-1
G5411.2 N-ASM φόρον (3x)
Lk 20:22 Is·it·proper for·us to·give tribute to·Caesar or not?
Rm 13:7 *in·superior authority*: the tribute to·the·one *due* the
Rm 13:7 the tribute to·the·one *due* the tribute, the tax to·the·
G5411.2 N-APM φόρους (2x)
Lk 23:2 and forbidding *others* to·give tributes to·Caesar,
Rm 13:6 on·account·of that, yeu·fully·pay tributes also. For

G5412 φορτίζω phôrtízō *v.* (2x)
Roots:G5414 See:G5413
G5412.1 V-PAI-2P φορτίζετε (1x)
Lk 11:46 Because yeu·load·up the men·of·clay† with·
G5412.2 V-RPP-NPM πεφορτισμένοι (1x)
Mt 11:28 laboring·hard and having·been·overloaded, and·I

G5413 φορτίον phôrtíôn *n.* (5x)
Roots:G5414 G2444-3 See:G5412
G5413.1 N-NSN φορτίον (1x)
Mt 11:30 For my yoke *is* kind, and my load is lightweight."
G5413.1 N-ASN φορτίον (1x)
Gal 6:5 For each·man shall·bear his·own load.
G5413.1 N-APN φορτία (2x)
Lk 11:46 ·up the men·of·clay† with·oppressive loads, and
Mt 23:4 ·bind weighty and oppressive loads and put *them* on
G5413.1 N-DPN φορτίοις (1x)
Lk 11:46 do·not reach·for the loads with·one of·yeur fingers.

G5414 φόρτος phôrtôs *n.* (1x)
Roots:G5342 See:G5413
G5414.2 N-GSM φόρτου (1x)
Ac 27:10 not merely of·the cargo and of·the sailing·ship,

G5415 Φορτουνάτος Phôrtôunátôs *n/p.* (1x)
G5415.2 N/P-GSM Φουρτουνάτου (1x)
1Co 16:17 arrival of·Stephanas and Fortunatus and Achaicus

G5416 φραγέλλιον phragélliôn *n.* (1x)
Roots:G5417 Compare:G3148
G5416 N-ASN φραγέλλιον (1x)
Jn 2:15 And making a·lash out of·small·cords, he·cast·out

G5417 φραγελλόω phragêllôō *v.* (2x)
Compare:G1194 G3146 See:G5416
G5417 V-AAP-NSM φραγελλώσας (2x)
Mt 27:26 BarAbbas to·them, and after·lashing YeShua, he·
Mk 15:15 BarAbbas to·them, and after·lashing Jesus, he·

G5418 φραγμός phragmôs *n.* (4x)
Roots:G5420 Compare:G3320 xLangAlso:H1447
H4881
G5418.2 N-ASM φραγμόν (2x)
Mt 21:33 "planted a·vineyard and placed a·hedge around it,
Mk 12:1 "planted a·vineyard, and placed a·hedge around *it*,
G5418.2 N-APM φραγμούς (1x)
Lk 14:23 'Go·out into the roadways and hedges, and compel
G5418.2 N-GSM φραγμοῦ (1x)
Eph 2:14 ·down the middle·wall of·hedging *between us*,

G5419 φράζω phrázō *v.* (2x)
Compare:G1285 G1834 See:G5420
G5419.2 V-AAM-2S φράσον (2x)
Mt 13:36 him, saying, "Explain to·us the parable of·the
Mt 15:15 Peter declared to·him, "Explain this parable to·us.

G5420 φράσσω phrássō *v.* (2x)
Roots:G5424 Compare:G5392 G4912 See:G5418
G5420.3 V-AAI-3P ἔφραξαν (1x)
Heb 11:33 obtained promises, stopped·up *the* mouths of·
G5420.3 V-2APS-3S φραγῇ (1x)
Rm 3:19 in·order·that every mouth may·be·stopped·up, and

G5421 φρέαρ phréar *n.* (7x)
Compare:G0012
xLangEquiv:H0875
G5421.2 N-NSN φρέαρ (1x)

Jn 4:11 a·bucket·for·drawing·water, and the well is deep.

G5421.2 N-ASN φρέαρ (3x)

Jn 4:12 Jacob, who gave us the well? Even he·himself drank

Lk 14:5 a·donkey or an·ox fallen into a·well, and shall·not

Rv 9:2 And he·opened·up the well of·the bottomless·pit, and

G5421.2 N-GSN φρέατος (3x)

Rv 9:1 the key of·the well of·the bottomless·pit·*(the·Abyss)*.

Rv 9:2 and there·ascended smoke out of·the well, as smoke

Rv 9:2 air were·darkened from·out of·the smoke of·the well.

G5422 φρεν•απατάω phrênapatáō *v.* (1x)

Roots:G5423 Compare:G0538

G5422 V-PAI-3S φρεναπατᾷ (1x)

Gal 6:3 being not·even·one·thing, he·deludes his·own mind.

G5423 φρεν•απάτης phrênapátēs *n.* (1x)

Roots:G5424 G0539 xLangAlso:H5377

G5423 N-NPM φρεναπάται (1x)

Tit 1:10 ·talkers and those·that·delude·the·mind, especially

G5424 φρήν phrḗn *n.* (2x)

Compare:G5420 G3563 G1270 See:G5426 G0878

G5424.4 N-DPF φρεσίν (2x)

1Co 14:20 little·children in·the contemplations, but·rather

1Co 14:20 But in·the contemplations be completely·mature.

G5425 φρίσσω phríssō *v.* (1x)

Compare:G5141 G5399

G5425.2 V-PAI-3P φρίσσουσιν (1x)

Jac 2:19 The demons also trust *that*, and they·shudder.

G5426 φρονέω phrônéō *v.* (30x)

Roots:G5424 Compare:G1260 G1380 G1760 G3049 G4820 G2233 G1011 G3191 See:G5427 G5428 G5431

G5426.1 V-FAI-2P φρονήσετε (1x)

Gal 5:10 Lord, that yeu·shall·contemplate not·even·one·bit

G5426.1 V-PAI-2S φρονεῖς (3x)

Ac 28:22 ·from you what·things you·contemplate, for in·fact

Mt 16:23 because you·do·not contemplate the·things of·God,

Mk 8:33 Because you·do·not contemplate the·things of·God,

G5426.1 V-PAI-2P φρονεῖτε (1x)

Php 3:15 And if *in* anything yeu·contemplate differently,

G5426.1 V-PAI-3P φρονοῦσιν (1x)

Rm 8:5 according·to flesh contemplate the·things of·the

G5426.1 V-PAM-2P φρονεῖτε (2x)

2Co 13:11 be·comforted, contemplate the same·thing, be·

Col 3:2 Contemplate the·things up·above, not the·things

G5426.1 V-PAN φρονεῖν (7x)

Rm 12:3 is·necessary to·contemplate *concerning himself*,

Rm 12:3 ·rather *for·him* to·contemplate *moderately* in·order

Rm 15:5 ·yeu the same, to·contemplate among one·another

Php 1:7 ·as it·is right for·me to·contemplate this on·behalf

Php 3:16 ·the same standard, to·contemplate the same·thing.

Php 4:2 I·implore SynTyche to·contemplate the same·thing

1Co 4:6 ·may·learn in us not to·contemplate *of·men* above

G5426.1 V-PAP-NPM φρονοῦντες (4x)

Rm 12:16 contemplating the same·thing for one·another;

Rm 12:16 same·thing for one·another; contemplating not the

Php 2:2 having the same love, contemplating the one jointly·

Php 3:19 *These are* the ones contemplating the earthly·things

G5426.1 V-PAS-1P φρονῶμεν (1x)

Php 3:15 ·mature, we·should·contemplate that·thing. And if

G5426.1 V-PAS-2P φρονῆτε (1x)

Php 2:2 my joy, that yeu·should·contemplate the same·thing

G5426.1 V-PPM-3S φρονείσθω (1x)

Php 2:5 For contemplate *and set·aim·for* this·thing among

G5426.1 V-IAI-1S ἐφρόνουν (1x)

1Co 13:11 as an·infant, I·was·contemplating as an·infant, I·

EG5426.1 (1x)

Rm 8:5 according·to Spirit *contemplate* the·things of·the

G5426.4 V-IAI-2P ἐφρονεῖτε (1x)

Php 4:10 in which also yeu·were·earnestly·concerned, but

G5426.5 V-PAN φρονεῖν (1x)

Php 4:10 that even·now at·last yeur·earnest·concern over me

G5426.6 V-PAI-3S φρονεῖ (2x)

Rm 14:6 the day, earnestly·regards *it* unto·*the*·Lord; and

Rm 14:6 day, unto·*the*·Lord he·does·not earnestly·regard *it*.

G5426.6 V-PAP-NSM φρονῶν (2x)

Rm 14:6 The·one earnestly·regarding the day, earnestly·

Rm 14:6 ·Lord; and the·one not earnestly·regarding the day,

G5427 φρόνημα phrónēma *n.* (5x)

Roots:G5426 Compare:G2307

G5427 N-NSN φρόνημα (4x)

Rm 8:6 For the disposition of·the flesh *is* death, but the

Rm 8:6 *is* death, but the disposition of·the Spirit *is* life-above

Rm 8:7 (on·account·that the disposition of·the flesh *is*

Rm 8:27 personally·knows what the disposition of·the Spirit

EG5427 (1x)

Jn 8:44 he·speaks from·out of·his·own *disposition*, because

G5428 φρόνησις phrónēsis *n.* (2x)

Roots:G5426 xLangAlso:H2451

G5428.2 N-DSF φρονήσει (2x)

Lk 1:17 by *the* thoughtful·insight of·the·righteous·ones— to·

Eph 1:8 to us in all wisdom and thoughtful·insight,

G5429 φρόνιμος phrónimôs *adj.* (14x)

Roots:G5424 Compare:G4680 G4908

G5429.2 A-NSM φρόνιμος (2x)

Lk 12:42 then is the trustworthy and prudent estate·manager,

Mt 24:45 then is the trustworthy and prudent slave whom his

G5429.2 A-NPM φρόνιμοι (3x)

Mt 10:16 Accordingly, become prudent as the serpents and

1Co 4:10 but yeu *are* prudent in Anointed-One. We·

2Co 11:19 with·pleasure, *yeurselves* being prudent.

G5429.2 A-NPM-C φρονιμώτεροι (1x)

Lk 16:8 present·age are more·prudent— above·and·beyond

G5429.2 A-NPF φρόνιμοι (3x)

Mt 25:2 five *virgins* from·among them were prudent, and the

Mt 25:4 But the prudent took oil in their containers with their

Mt 25:9 But the prudent answered, saying, '*Not·so*, lest

G5429.2 A-DSM φρονίμῳ (1x)

Mt 7:24 them, I·shall·liken him to·a·prudent man who built

G5429.2 A-DPM φρονίμοις (1x)

1Co 10:15 I·say *this* as to·prudent·men; yeu·yeurselves

G5429.2 A-DPF φρονίμοις (1x)

Mt 25:8 And the foolish declared to·the prudent, 'Give to·us

G5429.3 A-NPM φρόνιμοι (2x)

Rm 11:25 lest yeu·should·be full·of·notions personally·about

Rm 12:16 Do·not become full·of·notions personally·about

G5430 φρονίμως phrônímôs *adv.* (1x)

Roots:G5429 Compare:G3562

G5430 ADV φρονίμως (1x)

Lk 16:8 estate·manager, because he·did prudently. Because

G5431 φροντίζω phrôntízō *v.* (1x)

Roots:G5424 Compare:G3308 G3525 See:G5426

G5431.2 V-PAS-3P φροντίζωσιν (1x)

Tit 3:8 in·God may·have·a·considerable·care to·conduct

G5432 φρο•υρέω phrôuréō *v.* (4x)

Roots:G4253 G3708 Compare:G5083

G5432.2 V-FAI-3S φρουρήσει (1x)

Php 4:7 all understanding, shall·dutifully·keep yeur hearts

G5432.2 V-PPP-APM φρουρουμένους (1x)

1Pe 1:5 the·ones being·dutifully·kept by God's power

G5432.2 V-IAI-3S ἐφρούρει (1x)

2Co 11:32 Aretas the king was·dutifully·keeping the city of·

G5432.2 V-IPI-1P ἐφρουρούμεθα (1x)

Gal 3:23 to·come, we·were·dutifully·kept under Torah-Law,

G5433 φρυάσσω phryássō *v.* (1x)

Compare:G2372 G3709 G3950 G5532-1 See:G1031 G1032 xLangAlso:H7283

G5433.3 V-AAI-3P ἐφρύαξαν (1x)

Ac 4:25 ·did nations tumultuously·snort·and·prance, and *did*

G5434 φρύγανον phrýganôn *n.* (1x)

See:G5395

G5434.2 N-GPN φρυγάνων (1x)

Ac 28:3 ·together a·multitude of·kindling·sticks and putting

G5435 Φρυγία Phrygía *n/l.* (3x)

G5435 N/L-ASF Φρυγίαν (3x)

Ac 2:10 also *in* Phrygia and PamPhylia, *in* Egypt and *in* the

Ac 16:6 But going·throughout Phrygia and the country of·

Ac 18:23 of·Galatia and Phrygia in·consecutive·order,

G5436 Φύγελλος Phýgêllôs *n/p.* (1x)

Roots:G5343

G5436.2 N/P-NSM Φύγελλος (1x)

2Ti 1:15 me, of·whom *also* are Phygellus and HermoGenes.

G5437 φυγή phygḗ *n.* (2x)

Roots:G5343 See:G2707-1

G5437 N-NSF φυγή (2x)

Mt 24:20 "But pray that yeur fleeing should·not happen in·

Mk 13:18 "But pray that yeur fleeing should·not be in·winter

G5438 φυλακή phylakḗ *n.* (49x)

Roots:G5442 Compare:G5084 G3796 G3317 G0219 G4404 G2978-1 G1201 See:G5441 G5439 G5440 xLangEquiv:H3608 xLangAlso:H0953 H7585 H4931 H4929

G5438.2 N-ASF φυλακήν (1x)

Mk 6:48 And about *the* fourth watch of·the night, he·comes

G5438.2 N-APF φυλακάς (1x)

Lk 2:8 and vigilantly·keeping the night watches over their

G5438.2 N-DSF φυλακῇ (4x)

Lk 12:38 if he·should·come in the second watch, or should·

Lk 12:38 or should·come in the third watch, and should·find

Mt 14:25 And in·*the*·fourth watch of·the night, YeShua

Mt 24:43 had·personally·known in·which watch *of·the night*

G5438.4 N-NSF φυλακή (1x)

Rv 18:2 ·residence of·demons, and a·prison of·every impure

G5438.4 N-ASF φυλακήν (13x)

Jn 3:24 for John had·not·yet been·cast into the prison.

Lk 12:58 ·officer should·cast you into *debtors'* prison.

Lk 22:33 with you, even unto prison and unto death.

Lk 23:19 ·been·cast into prison on·account·of a·certain

Lk 23:25 ·cast into the prison on·account·of insurrection and

Ac 8:3 and women, he·was·handing·*them*·over to prison.

Ac 12:4 *HerOd·Agrippa* placed *him* in prison, handing *him*

Ac 12:10 a·first and second watch-station, they·came to the

Ac 16:23 ·them, they·cast *them* into prison, charging the

Ac 16:37 Romans, they·cast *us* into prison. And now do·

Mt 5:25 assistant, and you·shall·be·cast into *debtors'* prison.

Mt 18:30 going·off, he·cast him into prison, until he·should·

Rv 2:10 yeu into prison in·order·that yeu·may·be·tried, and

G5438.4 N-APF φυλακάς (2x)

Lk 21:12 *yeu* over to gatherings and prisons, being·brought

Ac 22:4 ·binding and handing·over into prisons both men

G5438.4 N-DSF φυλακῇ (10x)

Lk 3:20 — that he·permanently·shut John up in the prison.

Mt 14:3 and placed *him* in prison on·account·of HerOdias,

Mt 14:10 ·sending·word, he·beheaded John in the prison.

Mt 25:36 yeu·visited me. I·was in prison, and yeu·came to

Mt 25:39 did·we·see you sick, or in prison, and came to you

Mt 25:43 *with·clothing*, sick and in prison, and yeu·did·not

Mt 25:44 or sick, or in prison, and did·not attend to·you?

Mk 6:17 he·bound him in the prison on·account·of HerOdias,

Mk 6:27 ·off, *HerOd·AntiPas* beheaded him in the prison

1Pe 3:19 to·the spirits in prison, he·officially·proclaimed

G5438.4 N-DPF φυλακαῖς (1x)

Ac 26:10 I·myself permanently·shut·up in·prisons, receiving

G5438.4 N-GSF φυλακῆς (4x)

Ac 5:19 the night, opened·up the prison doors; and·also

Ac 12:17 brought him out of·the prison. And he·declared,

Ac 16:27 and seeing the prison doors having·been·opened·up

Ac 16:40 And going·forth out of·the prison, they·entered

EG5438.4 (2x)

Mt 4:12 that John was·handed·over *into prison*, YeShua

Mk 1:14 John already·being·handed·over *to·prison*, Jesus

G5438.5 N-ASF φυλακήν (2x)

Ac 12:6 and sentries were·guarding the prison·cell, *standing*

Ac 16:24 them into the innermost prison·cell and secured

G5438.5 N-DSF φυλακῇ (3x)

Ac 5:22 did·not find them in the prison·cell. And returning,

Ac 5:25 whom yeu·placed in the prison·cell are standing in

Ac 12:5 ·fact, Peter was·kept in the prison·cell. But earnest

G5438.5 N-GSF φυλακῆς (1x)

Rv 20:7 shall·be·loosened from·out of·his prison,

G5438.6 N-NSF φυλακή (1x)
Rv 18:2 impure spirit, and a·prison·cell of·every impure and
G5438.6 N-DPF φυλακαῖς (2x)
2Co 6:5 in punishing·blows, in imprisonments, in chaos, in
2Co 11:23 ·measure, in imprisonments more·abundantly,
G5438.6 N-GSF φυλακῆς (1x)
Heb 11:36 and furthermore, of·bonds and imprisonment.

G5439 φυλακίζω phylakízō *v.* (1x)
Roots:G5441 See:G5438
G5439 V-PAP-NSM φυλακίζων (1x)
Ac 22:19 that I·myself was imprisoning and thrashing in·

G5440 φυλακτήριον phylaktḗriôn *n.* (1x)
Roots:G5442 Compare:G2899 See:G5441 G5438 xLangEquiv:H8600-1 xLangAlso:H6734
G5440.1 N-APN φυλακτήρια (1x)
Mt 23:5 "They·broaden their tefillin and enlarge the fringes

G5441 φύλαξ phýlax *n.* (3x)
Roots:G5442 Compare:G2892 See:G5438 G5440
G5441 N-NPM φύλακες (1x)
Ac 12:6 with·two chains, and sentries were·guarding the
G5441 N-APM φύλακας (2x)
Ac 5:23 all security and the sentries standing outside before
Ac 12:19 the sentries, he·commandingly·ordered *for·them* to·

G5442 φυλάσσω phylássō *v.* (32x)
Roots:G5443 Compare:G5083 G5432 G4337 See:G5438 G5441 G1314 xLangAlso:H8104
G5442.1 V-PAN φυλάσσειν (1x)
Ac 12:4 squads·of·four soldiers to·keep·watch·over him,
G5442.1 V-PAP-DSM φυλάσσοντι (1x)
Ac 28:16 together with·the soldier keeping·watch·over him.
G5442.1 V-PAP-NSM φυλάσσων (1x)
Ac 22:20 execution, and keeping·watch·over the garments
G5442.1 V-PAS-3S φυλάσσῃ (1x)
Lk 11:21 ·armed, should·keep·watch·over his·own mansion,
G5442.2 V-PMM-2S φυλάσσου (1x)
2Ti 4:15 of·whom also you·yourself must·be·vigilant, for
G5442.2 V-PMM-2P φυλάσσεσθε (2x)
Lk 12:15 "Yeu·clearly·see·to·it, and be·vigilant due·to the
2Pe 3:17 while·foreknowing *these·things*, be·vigilant! Lest
G5442.3 V-FAI-3S φυλάξει (2x)
Jn 12:25 his soul in this world shall·vigilantly·keep it unto
2Th 3:3 ·establish yeu and shall·vigilantly·keep *yeu* from the
G5442.3 V-PAI-3P φυλάσσουσιν (1x)
Gal 6:13 being·circumcised, vigilantly·keep Torah-Law,
G5442.3 V-PAN φυλάσσειν (1x)
Ac 16:4 to·them the decrees to·vigilantly·keep, the·ones
G5442.3 V-PAP-NSM φυλάσσων (1x)
Ac 21:24 ·march·orderly, vigilantly·keeping the Torah-Law.
G5442.3 V-PAP-NPM φυλάσσοντες (2x)
Lk 2:8 camping·in·the·field and vigilantly·keeping the night
Lk 11:28 Redemptive-word of·God and vigilantly·keeping it."
G5442.3 V-PAS-3S φυλάσσῃ (1x)
Rm 2:26 uncircumcised should·vigilantly·keep the righteous·
G5442.3 V-PMN φυλάσσεσθαι (2x)
Ac 21:25 ·thing, except to·vigilantly·keep themselves *from*
Ac 23:35 him to·be·vigilantly·kept in HerOd·Agrippa's
G5442.3 V-PPP-NSM φυλασσόμενος (1x)
Lk 8:29 with·chains, even being·vigilantly·kept in·shackles.
G5442.3 V-AAI-1S ἐφύλαξα (1x)
Jn 17:12 name. "I·vigilantly·kept those·that you·have·given
G5442.3 V-AAI-2P ἐφυλάξατε (1x)
Ac 7:53 ·institution of·angels and did·not vigilantly·keep *it*."
G5442.3 V-AAI-3S ἐφύλαξεν (1x)
2Pe 2:5 ancient world, but·rather vigilantly·kept Noach, *the*
G5442.3 V-AAM-2S φύλαξον (2x)
1Ti 6:20 vigilantly·keep the charge·fully·consigned·to·
2Ti 1:14 ·your·care, you·must·vigilantly·keep through Holy
G5442.3 V-AAM-2P φυλάξατε (1x)
1Jn 5:21 Dear·children, vigilantly·keep yeurselves from the
G5442.3 V-AAN φυλάξαι (2x)
Jud 1:24 being·able to·vigilantly·keep yeu without·moral·
2Ti 1:12 that he·is able to·vigilantly·keep my trust·deposit
G5442.3 V-AMI-1S ἐφυλαξάμην (3x)
Lk 18:21 "All these·things I·vigilantly·kept from·among my
Mt 19:20 "All these·things I·vigilantly·kept from·out of·my
Mk 10:20 all these·things I·vigilantly·kept from·out of·my
EG5442.3 (2x)
Rm 2:28 an·outward·appearance *of·vigilantly·keeping* that·is
Rm 2:29 But·rather, the·one *vigilantly·keeping* in private,
G5442.4 V-AAS-2S φυλάξῃς (1x)
1Ti 5:21 angels, that you·should·vigilantly·observe these

G5443 φυλή phylḗ *n.* (31x)
Roots:G5453 Compare:G5444 G5336-3 G2840-1 xLangAlso:H4294
G5443.2 N-NPF φυλαί (2x)
Mt 24:30 'all the tribes of·the earth shall·vividly·lament,'
Rv 1:7 ' 'and all the tribes of·the earth shall·vividly·lament
G5443.2 N-ASF φυλήν (3x)
Heb 7:14 Judah, in·regard·to which tribe Moses spoke not·
Rv 13:7 was·given to·it over all tribes, and native·tongues,
Rv 14:6 and to·every nation, and tribe, and native·tongue,
G5443.2 N-APF φυλάς (2x)
Lk 22:30 ·sit on thrones judging the twelve tribes of·IsraEl."
Mt 19:28 twelve thrones, judging the twelve tribes of·IsraEl.
G5443.2 N-DPF φυλαῖς (1x)
Jac 1:1 To·the twelve tribes, to·the·ones in the Diaspora
G5443.2 N-GSF φυλῆς (20x)
Lk 2:36 of·PhanuEl, from·among *the* tribe of·Asher, herself
Ac 13:21 a·man from·among *the* tribe of·BenJamin, *for*
Heb 7:13 ·with·and·belongs·to another tribe, from which
Rm 11:1 AbRaham's offspring†, *from the* tribe of·BenJamin.
Php 3:5 *the* kindred of·IsraEl, *of·the* tribe of·BenJamin, a·
Rv 5:5 the·one being from·among the tribe of·Judah (the
Rv 5:9 blood— from·out of·every tribe, and native·tongue,
Rv 7:4 from·among all *the* tribes of·the·Sons of·IsraEl.
Rv 7:5 From·among *the* tribe of·Judah having·been·
Rv 7:5 From·among *the* tribe of·ReuBen having·been·
Rv 7:5 From·among *the* tribe of·Gad having·been·officially·
Rv 7:6 From·among *the* tribe of·Asher having·been·
Rv 7:6 From·among *the* tribe of·Naphtali having·been·
Rv 7:6 From·among *the* tribe of·MaNasseh having·been·
Rv 7:7 From·among *the* tribe of·Shimon having·been·
Rv 7:7 From·among *the* tribe of·Levi having·been·officially·
Rv 7:7 From·among *the* tribe of·IsSakar having·been·
Rv 7:8 From·among *the* tribe of·Zebulun having·been·
Rv 7:8 From·among *the* tribe of·Joseph having·been·
Rv 7:8 From·among *the* tribe of·BenJamin having·been·
G5443.2 N-GPF φυλῶν (3x)
Rv 7:9 from·among all nations, and tribes, and peoples, and
Rv 11:9 ·among the peoples and tribes and native·tongues
Rv 21:12 *the names* of·the twelve tribes of·the Sons of·IsraEl

G5444 φύλλον phýllôn *n.* (6x)
Roots:G5453 See:G5443 xLangEquiv:H5929 xLangAlso:A6074
G5444 N-NPN φύλλα (1x)
Rv 22:2 one's month. And the leaves of·the arbor·tree *were*
G5444 N-APN φύλλα (5x)
Mt 21:19 ·thing on it, except merely leaves, and he·says to·it
Mt 24:32 tender and should·sprout·forth the leaves, yeu·
Mk 11:13 a·fig·tree in·the·distance having leaves, he·came
Mk 11:13 he·found nothing·at·all except leaves, for it·was
Mk 13:28 tender and should·sprout·forth the leaves, yeu·

G5445 φύραμα phýrama *n.* (6x)
See:G5453
EG5445. [a] (1x)
Rm 11:16 Now if the *portion of·dough offered as·a* firstfruit
G5445.2 N-GSN φυράματος (1x)
Rm 9:21 from·out of·the same lump·of·clay to·make, in·fact
G5445.3 N-NSN φύραμα (2x)
Rm 11:16 *is* holy, the *whole* lump·of·dough *is* also *holy*.
1Co 5:7 yeu·may·be a·fresh·new lump·of·dough, just·as
G5445.3 N-ASN φύραμα (2x)
Gal 5:9 A·little leaven leavens the whole lump·of·dough.
1Co 5:6 a·little leaven leavens the whole lump·of·dough?

G5446 φυσικός physikôs *adj.* (3x)
Roots:G5449 Compare:G5591 G4152 G0979 See:G5447
G5446.1 A-NPN φυσικά (1x)
2Pe 2:12 these *false·teachers* (as natural, irrational animals,
G5446.1 A-ASF φυσικήν (2x)
Rm 1:26 exchanged the natural sexual·intercourse for the·
Rm 1:27 males, leaving the natural sexual·intercourse of·the

G5447 φυσικῶς physikôs *adv.* (1x)
Roots:G5446
G5447.1 ADV φυσικῶς (1x)
Jud 1:10 ·as they·are·fully·acquainted·with naturally (as

G5448 φυσιόω physiôō *v.* (7x)
Roots:G5449 Compare:G5244 G5445-5 See:G5450
G5448.2 V-PAI-3S φυσιοῖ (1x)
1Co 8:1 have knowledge. The knowledge puffs·up, but the
G5448.2 V-PPI-3S φυσιοῦται (1x)
1Co 13:4 The Love does·not brag. It·is·not puffed·up,
G5448.2 V-PPP-NSM φυσιούμενος (1x)
Col 2:18 ·not clearly·seen, being·puffed·up for·no·reason by
G5448.2 V-PPS-2P φυσιοῦσθε (1x)
1Co 4:6 ·that not one *of* yeu·may·be·puffed·up over the
G5448.2 V-API-3P ἐφυσιώθησαν (1x)
1Co 4:18 Now some are·puffed·up, as·though *it·is* not me
G5448.2 V-RPP-GPM πεφυσιωμένων (1x)
1Co 4:19 of·the·ones having·been·puffed·up, but·rather the
G5448.2 V-RPP-NPM πεφυσιωμένοι (1x)
1Co 5:2 And yeu are having·been·puffed·up, and did·not·

G5449 φύσις phýsis *n.* (14x)
Roots:G5453 Compare:G1078 G1085 See:G5448 G4854
G5449.2 N-ASF φύσιν (1x)
Rm 11:21 did·not spare the fully natural branches, *take·heed*
G5449.3 N-NSF φύσις (1x)
Jac 3:7 For every species of·wild·beasts, also of·birds, and
G5449.4 N-NSF φύσις (1x)
1Co 11:14 Or does·not·even the nature itself instruct yeu, in·
G5449.4 N-ASF φύσιν (4x)
Rm 1:26 sexual·intercourse for the·one contrary·to nature.
Rm 11:24 ·tree·which·is·wild according·to nature, and·yet
Rm 11:24 ·yet contrary·to nature, you·are·already·grafted
Rm 11:24 shall·these, according·to nature, be·grafted·into
G5449.4 N-DSF φύσει (5x)
Gal 2:15 We·ourselves *are* Jews by·nature, and not from·
Gal 4:8 to·the·ones who·are not by·nature gods *at·all*.
Rm 2:14 should·do by·nature the·things *contained* in·the
Jac 3:7 and has·been·tamed by·the nature of·mankind†.
Eph 2:3 And we·were by·nature children of·wrath, even as
G5449.4 N-GSF φύσεως (2x)
Rm 2:27 birthed·from·out of·natural uncircumcision *indeed*
2Pe 1:4 yeu·may·become partners of·divine nature, already·

G5450 φυσίωσις physiôsis *n.* (1x)
Roots:G5448 Compare:G5243 G2754
G5450.3 N-NPF φυσιώσεις (1x)
2Co 12:20 backbitings, whisperings, puffed·up·minds, *and*

G5451 φυτεία phytêía *n.* (1x)
Roots:G5452 Compare:G3001 See:G5451-1 G2707-2
G5451.2 N-NSF φυτεία (1x)
Mt 15:13 he·declared, "Every plant which my heavenly

G5452 φυτεύω phytêúō *v.* (11x)
Roots:G5453 See:G5451 G5451-1 G2707-3 xLangEquiv:H5193
G5452.1 V-PAI-3S φυτεύει (1x)
1Co 9:7 with·his·own wages? Who plants a·vineyard, and
G5452.1 V-PAP-NSM φυτεύων (2x)
1Co 3:7 As·such, neither is the·one planting anything, nor
1Co 3:8 But the·one planting and the·one watering are one,
G5452.1 V-IAI-3P ἐφύτευον (1x)
Lk 17:28 ·selling, they·were·planting, they·were·building;
G5452.1 V-AAI-1S ἐφύτευσα (1x)
1Co 3:6 I·myself planted, Apollos watered, but·yet God was·
G5452.1 V-AAI-3S ἐφύτευσεν (4x)

Lk 20:9 “A·certain man·of·clay† planted a·vineyard and
Mt 15:13 heavenly Father did·not plant shall·be·uprooted.
Mt 21:33 ·the·house, who planted a·vineyard and placed
Mk 12:1 “A·certain·man·of·clay† “planted a·vineyard, and
G5452.1 V-APM-2S φυτεύθητι (1x)
Lk 17:6 ‘Be·uprooted, and be·planted in the sea,’ and it·
G5452.1 V-RPP-ASF πεφυτευμένην (1x)
Lk 13:6 ·holding·onto a·fig·tree having·been·planted in his

G5453 φύω phýō *v.* (3x)
Compare:G0985 G1816 G4261 G0305 See:G1631 G4854 G5449
G5453 V-PAP-NSF φύουσα (1x)
Heb 12:15 of·bitterness sprouting upward should·firmly·
G5453 V-2APP-NSN φυέν (2x)
Lk 8:6 ·rock, and once·being·sprouted, it·withered·away on·
Lk 8:8 ·good soil, and once·being·sprouted, it·produced

G5454 φωλεός phōlēós *n.* (2x)
Compare:G3692
G5454 N-APM φωλεούς (2x)
Lk 9:58 “The foxes have burrows, and the birds of·the sky
Mt 8:20 “The foxes have burrows, and the birds of·the sky

G5455 φωνέω phōnéō *v.* (42x)
Roots:G5456 See:G0400 xLangAlso:H7768
G5455.3 V-PAI-3S φωνεῖ (5x)
Jn 2:9 , the director·of·the·banquet hollered·out·for the
Jn 11:28 “The Mentor is·near, and he·hollers·out·for you.”
Mt 27:47 were·saying, “This·man hollers·out·for EliJah.”
Mk 10:49 ·courage, rouse·yourself; he·hollers·out·for you.”
Mk 15:35 were·saying, “Behold, he·hollers·out·for EliJah.”
G5455.3 V-PAI-3P φωνοῦσιν (1x)
Mk 10:49 ·for him. And they·hollered·out·for the blind·man
G5455.3 V-PAM-2S φώνει (1x)
Lk 14:12 or a·supper, do·not holler·out·for your friends,
G5455.3 V-PAP-NPM φωνοῦντες (1x)
Mk 3:31 they·dispatched to him while·hollering·out·for him.
G5455.3 V-IAI-3S ἐφώνει (1x)
Lk 8:8 While·saying these·things, he·was·hollering·out,
G5455.3 V-AAI-3S ἐφώνησεν (8x)
Jn 11:28 ·things, she·went·off and hollered·out·for Mary her
Jn 12:17 him when he·hollered·out·for Lazarus from·among
Jn 18:33 the Praetorian·hall again and hollered·out·for Jesus.
Lk 8:54 ·hold of·her by·the hand, hollered·out, saying,
Ac 16:28 But Paul hollered·out with·a·loud voice, saying,
Mt 20:32 ·standing·still, YeShua hollered·out·for them and
Mk 9:35 after·sitting·down, he·hollered·out·for the twelve
Rv 14:18 the fire; and he·hollered·out with·a·loud yell to·
G5455.3 V-AAI-3P ἐφώνησαν (2x)
Jn 9:18 until such·time *that* they·hollered·out·for the parents
Jn 9:24 a·second·time they·hollered·out·for the man·of·clay†
G5455.3 V-AAM-2S φώνησον (1x)
Jn 4:16 to·her, “Head·on·out, holler·out·for your husband,
G5455.3 V-AAN φωνῆσαι (1x)
Jn 1:48 to·him, “Before Philip hollered·out·for you, I·saw
G5455.3 V-AAP-NSM φωνήσας (5x)
Lk 16:2 And hollering·out·for him, he·declared to·him,
Lk 16:24 “And hollering·out, he·himself declared, ‘Father
Lk 23:46 And hollering·out with·a·loud voice, Jesus
Ac 9:41 her up; and hollering·out·for the holy·ones and the
Ac 10:7 went·away, after·hollering·out·for two of·his
G5455.3 V-AAP-NPM φωνήσαντες (1x)
Ac 10:18 And hollering·out, they·were·inquiring whether
G5455.3 V-APN φωνηθῆναι (1x)
Mk 10:49 Jesus declared *to·them* to·holler·out·for him. And
G5455.4 V-PAI-2P φωνεῖτε (1x)
Jn 13:13 “Yeu·yeurselves hail me Mentor and Lord, and yeu·
G5455.4 V-APN φωνηθῆναι (1x)
Lk 19:15 he·declared *for* these slaves to·be·hailed to·him
G5455.6 V-FAI-3S φωνήσει (2x)
Jn 13:38 a·rooster, no, shall·not crow, until you·shall·
Lk 22:34 a·rooster, no, it·shall·not crow this·day before
G5455.6 V-AAI-3S ἐφώνησεν (5x)
Jn 18:27 denied *it* again, and immediately a·rooster crowed.
Lk 22:60 ·once, with·him still speaking, the rooster crowed.
Mt 26:74 And immediately a·rooster crowed.
Mk 14:68 entryway·of·the·courtyard, and a·rooster crowed.
Mk 14:72 And for a·second·time, a·rooster crowed. And
G5455.6 V-AAN φωνῆσαι (5x)
Lk 22:61 “Prior·to a·rooster crowing, you·shall·utterly·deny
Mt 26:34 prior·to a·rooster crowing, you·shall·utterly·deny
Mt 26:75 “Prior·to a·rooster crowing, you·shall·utterly·deny
Mk 14:30 night, prior·to a·rooster crowing twice, you·shall·
Mk 14:72 “Prior·to a·rooster crowing twice, you·shall·

G5456 φωνή phōnḗ *n.* (141x)
Roots:G5337-2 See:G5316
xLangEquiv:H6963
G5456.1 N-NSF φωνή (6x)
Lk 1:44 For, behold, as·soon·as the sound of·your greeting
Rv 1:15 , and his voice as *the* sound of·many waters,
Rv 9:9 ·armor of·iron; and the sound of·their wings *was* as
Rv 9:9 of·their wings *was* as the·sound of·chariots, of·many
Rv 18:22 “And a·sound of·harpists, and musicians, and of·
Rv 18:22 any·longer in you. And a·sound of·a·millstone, no,
G5456.1 N-ASF φωνήν (4x)
Jn 3:8 it·wants, and you·hear the sound of·it, but·yet you·
1Co 14:7 soulless,·inanimate·things giving sound, whether
1Co 14:8 a·trumpet should·give an·indistinct sound, who
Rv 14:2 thunder. And I·heard a·sound of·harpists harping
G5456.1 N-GSF φωνῆς (5x)
Ac 2:6 Now while·this sound was·happening, the multitude
Ac 9:7 ·silence, in·fact hearing the sound·of·the·voice, but
Mt 24:31 his angels with a·great sound of·a·trumpet, and
Rv 6:1 four living·beings (as a·voice of·a·thunder) saying,
Rv 10:7 ·rather in the days of·the sound of·the seventh angel,
G5456.2 N-NSF φωνή (25x)
Jn 1:23 “I·myself *am* a·voice of·one·crying·out in the
Jn 12:28 Accordingly, there·came a·voice from·out of·the
Jn 12:30 and declared, “This voice has·happened not on·
Lk 3:4 saying, “A·voice of·one·crying·out in the wilderness
Lk 9:35 And there·came a·voice from·out of·the thick·cloud,
Ac 7:31 to·fully·observe *it*, *the* voice of·Yahweh came·to·be
Ac 10:13 And there·came a·voice to him, *saying*, “Peter,
Ac 10:15 And a·voice *spoke* to him again for a·second·time,
Ac 11:9 But *the* voice answered me for a·second·time from·
Ac 12:22 public was·exclaiming, “*It·is* a·voice of·a·god, and
Ac 19:34 ·was a·Jew, there·came one voice from·out of·all
Heb 12:26 whose *own* voice shook the earth at·that·time.
Mt 2:18 ““A·voice was·heard in Ramah— a·woeful·wailing
Mt 3:3 prophet, saying, “A·voice of·one·crying·out in the
Mt 3:17 And behold, a·voice from·out of·the heavens,
Mt 17:5 And behold, a·voice from·out of·the thick·cloud,
Mk 1:3 “A·voice of·one·crying·out in the wilderness,
Mk 1:11 And there·came a·voice from·out of·the heavens,
Mk 9:7 overshadowing them, and a·voice came out of·the
Rv 1:15 in a·furnace), and his voice as *the* sound of·many
Rv 4:1 in the heaven and the first voice which I·heard *was* as
Rv 10:8 And the voice which I·heard from·out of·the heaven
Rv 16:17 air, and there·came·forth a·great voice from the
Rv 18:23 in you; and a·voice of·bridegroom and of·bride, no
Rv 19:5 Then a·voice came·forth out of·the throne, saying,
G5456.2 N-NPF φωναί (6x)
Lk 23:23 to·be·crucified. And the voices of·them and of·the
Rv 4:5 lightnings and thunderings and voices proceed·forth;
Rv 8:5 the earth; and there·were voices, and thunderings,
Rv 11:15 and there·became great voices in the heaven,
Rv 11:19 And there·occurred lightnings, and voices, and
Rv 16:18 And there·happened voices, and thunders, and
G5456.2 N-ASF φωνήν (37x)
Jn 3:29 on·account·of the bridegroom's voice. Accordingly,
Jn 5:37 Not·even yeu·have·heard his voice ever·at·any·time,
Jn 10:4 follow him, because they·personally·know his voice.
Jn 10:5 they·do·not personally·know the voice of·interlopers.
Lk 3:22 upon him, and a·voice occurred from·out of·heaven
Lk 9:36 And with the voice occurring, Jesus was·found alone
Lk 11:27 the crowd, lifting·up her·voice, declared to·him,
Lk 17:13 and they·themselves lifted·*up their* voices, saying,
Ac 2:14 eleven, lifted·up his voice and clearly·enunciated
Ac 4:24 ·hearing *it*, they·lifted·*up* their·voice toward God
Ac 9:4 upon the earth, he·heard a·voice saying to·him,
Ac 12:14 And after·recognizing Peter's voice, she·did·not
Ac 14:11 Paul did, they·lifted·up their voices, saying in·the·
Ac 22:9 but they·did·not *distinctly*·hear the voice of·the·one
Ac 22:14 ·One, and to·hear *his* voice from·out of·his mouth.
Ac 22:22 and *then* they·lifted·up their voices, saying,
Ac 26:14 upon the earth, I·heard a·voice speaking to me,
Mt 12:19 nor·even·shall any·man hear his voice in the broad·
Mk 15:37 *his spirit with* a·loud voice, breathed·his·last.
2Pe 1:18 we·ourselves heard this voice being·carried·forth
Rv 1:10 heard right·behind me a·great voice, as of·a·trumpet
Rv 1:12 And I·turned·about to·look·at the voice that spoke
Rv 5:11 and I·heard *the* voice of·many angels all·around
Rv 6:6 And I·heard a·voice in *the* midst of·the four living·
Rv 6:7 official·seal, I·heard *the* voice of·the fourth living·
Rv 9:13 and I·heard one voice from·among the four horns
Rv 10:4 to·write. And I·heard a·voice from·out of·the
Rv 11:12 And they·heard a·great voice from·out of·the
Rv 12:10 And I·heard a·loud voice saying in the heaven,
Rv 14:2 And I·heard a·voice from·out of·the heaven, as a·
Rv 14:2 from·out of·the heaven, as a·voice of·many waters,
Rv 14:2 of·many waters, and as a·voice of·a·great thunder.
Rv 18:4 And I·heard another voice from·out of·the heaven,
Rv 19:1 these·things, I·heard a·great voice of·a·large crowd
Rv 19:6 And I·heard as a·voice of·a·large crowd, and as a·
Rv 19:6 of·a·large crowd, and as a·voice of·many waters,
Rv 19:6 ·many waters, and as a·voice of·strong thunderings,
G5456.2 N-APF φωνάς (3x)
Ac 13:27 this·man nor·even the voices of·the prophets (the·
Rv 10:3 ·out, the Seven Thunders spoke their·own voices.
Rv 10:4 Thunders spoke their·own voices, I·was·about to·
G5456.2 N-DSF φωνῇ (32x)
Jn 11:43 these·things, he·yelled·out with·a·loud voice,
Lk 1:42 And she·exclaimed with·a·loud voice, and declared,
Lk 4:33 demon, and he·screamed·out with·a·loud voice,
Lk 8:28 ·before him, and with·a·loud voice he·declared,
Lk 19:37 praising God with·a·loud voice concerning all *the*
Lk 23:46 And hollering·out with·a·loud voice, Jesus
Ac 7:57 Then yelling·out with·a·loud voice, they·stopped·up
Ac 7:60 the knees, he·yelled·out with·a·loud voice, “Lord,
Ac 8:7 crying·out with·a·loud voice, were·coming·out of·
Ac 14:10 *Paul* declared with·a·loud voice, “Stand upright
Ac 16:28 But Paul hollered·out with·a·loud voice, saying,
Ac 26:24 replied *to* these·things with·a·loud voice, “Paul,
Heb 12:19 blast, and to·a·voice of·utterances, of·which the·
Mt 27:46 hour YeShua shouted·out with·a·loud voice, saying
Mt 27:50 ·yelling·out again with·a·loud voice, sent·away his
Mk 1:26 him and yelling·out with·a·loud voice, came·forth
Mk 5:7 And yelling·out with·a·loud voice, he·declared,
Mk 15:34 hour, Jesus cried·out with·a·loud voice, saying,
2Pe 2:16 with *the* voice of·a·man·of·clay† forbade the
1Th 4:16 battle·cry, with a·chief·angel's voice, and with
Rv 5:2 angel officially·proclaiming with·a·loud voice,
Rv 5:12 saying with·a·loud voice, “Worthy is the Lamb
Rv 6:10 And they·were·yelling·out with·a·loud voice, saying
Rv 7:2 God, and he·yelled·out with·a·loud voice to·the four
Rv 7:10 and yelling·out with·a·loud voice, saying, “The
Rv 8:13 in mid-heaven, saying with·a·loud voice, “Woe,
Rv 10:3 and he·yelled·out with·a·loud voice, just·as *when* a·
Rv 14:7 saying with a·loud voice, “Fear God and give glory
Rv 14:9 followed them, saying with a·loud voice, “If any·
Rv 14:15 ·out in a·loud voice to·the·one who·is·sitting·down
Rv 18:2 he·yelled·out in strength, a·great voice, saying,
Rv 19:17 and he·yelled·out with·a·loud voice, saying to·all
G5456.2 N-DPF φωναῖς (1x)
Lk 23:23 ·were·insisting with·loud voices, requesting·for
G5456.2 N-GSF φωνῆς (18x)
Jn 5:25 the dead·ones shall·hear the voice of·the Son of·God,
Jn 5:28 the·ones in the chamber·tombs shall·hear his voice.
Jn 10:3 and the sheep hear his voice, and he·calls·forth his·
Jn 10:16 ·also, and they·shall·hear my voice, and *together*
Jn 10:27 “My sheep listen·to my voice, and·I know them,

Jn 18:37 birthed·from·out of·the truth listens·to my voice."
Lk 17:15 returned·back with a·loud voice glorifying God,
Ac 11:7 And I·heard a·voice saying to·me, 'Peter, after·
Ac 22:7 to the hard·ground and heard a·voice saying to·me,
Heb 3:7 Spirit says, "Today if yeu·should·hear his voice,
Heb 3:15 if yeu·should·hear his voice, yeu·should·not
Heb 4:7 Today, if yeu·should·hear his voice, yeu·should·not
2Pe 1:17 God honor and glory, with·a·voice as·such being·
1Co 14:11 the power·*(the·meaning)* of·the voice, I·shall·be
Rv 3:20 If anyone should·hear my voice and should·open·up
Rv 14:13 And I·heard a·voice from·out of·the heaven saying
Rv 16:1 And I·heard a·great voice from·out of·the Temple
Rv 21:3 And I·heard a·great voice from·out of·the heaven

G5456.2 N-GPM φωνῶν (2x)
1Co 14:10 as·it·may·be, so·many kinds of·voices in *the*
Rv 8:13 — from·out of·the remaining voices of·the trumpet

G5456.3 N-ASF φωνήν (1x)
Gal 4:20 at·this·moment and to·change my tone, because I·

G5456.4 N-GSF φωνῆς (1x)
Ac 24:21 ·than concerning this one address that I·yelled·out

G5457 φῶς phỗs *n.* (71x)
Roots:G5337-2 Compare:G0827 G5316 G5346 G5461 See:G5462 xLangAlso:H0216

G5457.1 N-NSN φῶς (5x)
Ac 9:3 to·Damascus, and·then suddenly a·light from the
Ac 12:7 stood·over *him*, and a·light radiated·brightly in the
Ac 22:6 *for* a·significant light to·flash·all·around about me.
Mt 17:2 the sun, and his garments became white as the light.
Rv 18:23 and a·light of·a·lantern, no should·not·ever shine·

G5457.1 N-ASN φῶς (4x)
Jn 11:9 stumble, because he·looks·at the light of·this world.
Lk 8:16 ·are·traversing·in should·look·about·by the light.
Ac 22:9 ·me, in·fact, did·distinctly·view the light and were
Ac 26:13 I·saw in the way a·light from·heaven beyond the

G5457.1 N-APN φῶτα (1x)
Ac 16:29 So requesting lights, he·rushed·in, and being

G5457.1 N-DSN φωτί (2x)
Lk 12:3 they·shall·be·heard in the light; and that·which
Mt 10:27 darkness, declare in the light; and what yeu·hear in

G5457.1 N-GSN φωτός (2x)
Ac 22:11 ·to the glory of·that light, being·led·by·the·hand by
Rv 22:5 of·a·lantern, nor·even of·sun light, because Yahweh

EG5457.1 (1x)
Jn 1:10 *This Light* was in the world, and the world came·to·

G5457.2 N-NSN φῶς (19x)
Jn 1:4 and the life-above was the light of·the men·of·clay†.
Jn 1:5 And the light shines·forth in the darkness, and the
Jn 1:8 He·was not that Light, but·rather *he·was·dispatched*
Jn 1:9 *This* was the true Light which illuminates every child·
Jn 3:19 is the verdict, that the Light has·come into the world
Jn 8:12 "I AM the light of·the world. The·one following me,
Jn 9:5 I·should·be in the world, I·am a·light of·the world."
Jn 11:10 night, he·stumbles, because the light is not in him.
Jn 12:35 "Yet a·short time is the light with yeu. Walk for·as·
Lk 2:32 a·light for a·revelation of·Gentiles and *for the* glory
Lk 11:35 So·then, keep·a·watch *that* the light, the·one in
Mt 4:16 upon·them a·light did·rise·above·the·horizon.
Mt 5:14 "Yeu·yeurselves are the light of·the world. A·city
Mt 5:16 In·this·manner, *let* yeur light radiate·brightly before
Mt 6:23 So·then, if the light, the·one in you, is darkness,
Eph 5:8 once darkness, but now *yeu·are* light in *the* Lord.
Eph 5:13 light, for any thing being·made·apparent is light.
1Jn 1:5 ·in·detail to·yeu, that God is light, and in him there·
1Jn 2:8 ·away, and the true Light even·now shines·forth.

G5457.2 N-ASN φῶς (17x)
Jn 3:19 the darkness rather than the light, for their deeds
Jn 3:20 mediocrity hates the light, and does·not come
Jn 3:20 and does·not come toward the light, lest his deeds
Jn 3:21 the truth comes to the light, in·order·that his deeds
Jn 8:12 but·rather shall·have the light of·the life-above."
Jn 12:35 Walk for·as·long·as yeu·have the light, lest
Jn 12:36 For·as·long·as yeu·have the light, trust in the light,
Jn 12:36 light, trust in the light, in·order·that yeu·may·be
Jn 12:46 "I·myself *being* a·light, have·come into the world,
Ac 13:47 "I·have·placed you to·be a·light for Gentiles, *for*
Ac 26:18 ·turn·*them*·back·around from darkness to light, and
Ac 26:23 *and* is·about to·fully·proclaim light to·the People
Mt 4:16 in darkness, they·did·see a·great light. And to·the·
Rm 2:19 to·be a·guide of·blind·men, a·light for·the·ones in
1Pe 2:9 yeu forth out of·darkness into his marvelous light.
2Co 4:6 already·declaring *for* light to·radiate·brightly out of·
1Ti 6:16 *in* unapproachable light which no·one·at·all sees

G5457.2 N-DSN φωτί (7x)
Jn 5:35 just·for a·short·while to·leap·for·joy in his light.
Col 1:12 of·the allotted·heritage of·the holy·ones in the light.
1Jn 1:7 But if we·should·walk in the light as he·himself is in
1Jn 1:7 as he·himself is in the light, we·have fellowship with
1Jn 2:9 ·one saying *himself* to·be in the light, and hating his
1Jn 2:10 loving his brother abides in the light, and there·is no
Rv 21:24 being·saved, shall·walk in its light, and the kings

G5457.2 N-DSN-HEB φωτί (1x)
2Co 6:14 And what fellowship has·light alongside darkness?

G5457.2 N-GSN φωτός (9x)
Jn 1:7 he·may·testify concerning the Light, in·order·that
Jn 1:8 in·order·that he·may·testify concerning the Light.
Jn 12:36 light, in·order·that yeu·may·be the·Sons of·Light."
Lk 16:8 ·and·beyond the Sons of·the Light in their·own
Rm 13:12 ·ourselves·with the weapons·and·armor of·light.
1Th 5:5 ·yeurselves are all the·Sons of·Light and the·Sons
2Co 11:14 himself is·disguised as an·angel of·light.
Eph 5:8 Walk as children of·light
Eph 5:13 ·refuted are·made·apparent by the light, for any

G5457.2 N-GPN φώτων (1x)
Jac 1:17 descending from the Father of·lights— with whom

G5457.3 N-ASN φῶς (2x)
Lk 22:56 ·down toward the firelight and after·gazing·intently
Mk 14:54 and warming·himself alongside the firelight.

G5458 φωστήρ phōstḗr *n.* (2x)
Roots:G5457 Compare:G0796 G2987 G5338

G5458.3 N-NSM φωστήρ (1x)
Rv 21:11 of·God (even her brilliance *was* like a·precious

G5458.4 N-NPM φωστῆρες (1x)
Php 2:15 whom yeu·are·apparent as brilliant·lights in *the*

G5459 φωσ•φόρος phōsphṓrôs *adj.* (1x)
Roots:G5457 G5342 Compare:G2193-1 G3720 G4407 G2986 xLangAlso:H1966

G5459.2 A-NSM φωσφόρος (1x)
2Pe 1:19 *the* Light·Bearer should·rise·above·the·horizon in

G5460 φωτεινός phōtêinṓs *adj.* (5x)
Roots:G5457 See:G5461

G5460.2 A-NSF φωτεινή (1x)
Mt 17:5 a·thick·cloud full·of·light overshadowed them.

G5460.2 A-NSN φωτεινόν (4x)
Lk 11:34 your whole body is also full·of·light; but whenever
Lk 11:36 if your whole body *is* full·of·light, not having any
Lk 11:36 ·dark, *the* whole shall·be full·of·light, as whenever
Mt 6:22 ·focused, your whole body shall·be full·of·light.

G5461 φωτίζω phōtízō *v.* (11x)
Roots:G5457 Compare:G5316 G2989 G5337-2 See:G5460 G5462 xLangAlso:H0215 H3384

G5461.2 V-FAI-3S φωτίσει (1x)
1Co 4:5 ·come, who also shall·illuminate the hidden·things

G5461.2 V-PAI-3S φωτίζει (2x)
Jn 1:9 the true Light which illuminates every child·of·clay†
Rv 22:5 light, because Yahweh God illuminates them, and

G5461.2 V-PAS-3S φωτίζῃ (1x)
Lk 11:36 radiant·shimmer of·a·lantern may·illuminate you."

G5461.2 V-AAI-3S ἐφώτισεν (1x)
Rv 21:23 in it, for the glory of·God illuminated it, and the

G5461.2 V-AAN φωτίσαι (1x)
Eph 3:9 and to·illuminate for·all what *is* the fellowship of·

G5461.2 V-AAP-GSM φωτίσαντος (1x)
2Ti 1:10 ·nullifying Death, and illuminating life-above and

G5461.2 V-API-3S ἐφωτίσθη (1x)
Rv 18:1 and the earth was·illuminated as·a·result of·his

G5461.4 V-APP-APM φωτισθέντας (1x)
Heb 6:4 for·the·ones after once being·enlightened, and after·

G5461.4 V-APP-NPM φωτισθέντες (1x)
Heb 10:32 after·being·enlightened, yeu·patiently·endured

G5461.4 V-RPP-APM πεφωτισμένους (1x)
Eph 1:18 ·understanding having·been·enlightened— for yeu

G5462 φωτισμός phōtismṓs *n.* (2x)
Roots:G5461 Compare:G5337-1 See:G5457

G5462 N-ASM φωτισμόν (2x)
2Co 4:4 ·directly on·them, the illumination of·the glorious
2Co 4:6 ·for *the* illumination of·the absolute·knowledge of·

Χχ - Chi

G5463 χαίρω chaírō *v.* (74x)
Compare:G2436 G2165 G0782 G5059-6 See:G5485 G5487-1 G5487-2 xLangAlso:H7965

G5463.1 V-PAI-1S χαίρω (1x)
Jn 11:15 And I·am·glad on·account·of yeu that I·was not

G5463.1 V-PAI-1P χαίρομεν (1x)
2Co 13:9 For we·are·glad, whenever we·ourselves should·

G5463.1 V-PAM-2P χαίρετε (1x)
2Co 13:11 brothers, be·glad. Be·completely·reformed, be·

G5463.1 V-2AOI-3S ἐχάρη (3x)
Jn 8:56 he·should·see my day, and he·saw *it* and was·glad."
Lk 23:8 Jesus, HerOd·AntiPas was·exceedingly glad, for he·
Ac 11:23 the grace of·God, was·glad. And he·was·exhorting

G5463.1 V-2AOI-3P ἐχάρησαν (3x)
Jn 20:20 the disciples were·glad after·seeing the Lord.
Lk 22:5 And they·were·glad and agreed·among·themselves
Mk 14:11 after·hearing *this*, they·were·glad and promised

G5463.1 V-2AON χαρῆναι (1x)
Lk 15:32 *for·us* to·be·merry and to·be·glad, because this

G5463.2 V-FAI-3P χαροῦσιν (1x)
Rv 11:10 residing upon the earth shall·rejoice over them and

G5463.2 V-2FOI-1S χαρήσομαι (1x)
Php 1:18 Moreover also, I·shall·rejoice.

G5463.2 V-2FOI-3S χαρήσεται (2x)
Jn 16:20 shall·bewail, but the world shall·rejoice, and yeu
Jn 16:22 and yeur heart shall·rejoice, and not·even·one·man

G5463.2 V-2FOI-3P χαρήσονται (1x)
Lk 1:14 ·leaping·of·joy, and many shall·rejoice at his birth.

G5463.2 V-PAI-1S χαίρω (7x)
Rm 16:19 Accordingly, I·rejoice over yeu. But·yet I·want
Php 1:18 and in this I·do·rejoice. Moreover also, I·shall·
Php 2:17 trust, I·do·rejoice and·also do·rejoice·together
1Co 16:17 I·rejoice upon the arrival of·Stephanas and
2Co 7:9 *But* right·now I·do·rejoice, not that yeu·were·
2Co 7:16 I·rejoice that in everything, I·am·more·encouraged
Col 1:24 Now, I·rejoice in my afflictions on·yeur behalf,

G5463.2 V-PAI-1P χαίρομεν (1x)
1Th 3:9 all the joy with·which we·rejoice on·account·of yeu

G5463.2 V-PAI-3S χαίρει (3x)
Jn 3:29 listening·for him, rejoices with·joy on·account·of
Mt 18:13 I·say to·yeu, he·rejoices more over that·same
1Co 13:6 It·does·not rejoice over the injustice, but it·

G5463.2 V-PAM-2P χαίρετε (10x)
Lk 6:23 "Rejoice in that day and skip·about, for, behold,
Lk 10:20 "Moreover, do·not rejoice in this, that the spirits
Lk 10:20 to·yeu, but rather rejoice because yeur names are·
Mt 5:12 "Rejoice and leap·for·joy, because yeur payment·of·
Php 2:18 also yeu·yeurselves must·rejoice and must·rejoice·
Php 3:1 ·thing remaining, my brothers: Rejoice in *the* Lord!
Php 4:4 Rejoice in *the* Lord always, *and* again I·shall·declare
Php 4:4 Lord always, *and* again I·shall·declare, "Rejoice!"
1Pe 4:13 But·rather rejoice, according·to·what *portion* yeu·
1Th 5:16 Rejoice always.

G5463.2 V-PAN χαίρειν (2x)
Rm 12:15 *Love is* to·rejoice with those·rejoicing, and to·
2Co 2:3 ·was·necessary·for me to·rejoice, having·confidence

G5463.2 V-PAP-GPM χαιρόντων (1x)
Rm 12:15 *Love is* to·rejoice with those·rejoicing, and to·

G5463.2 V-PAP-NSM χαίρων (4x)
Lk 15:5 ·finding *it*, he·puts *it* upon his shoulders, rejoicing.
Lk 19:6 ·down; and rejoicing, he·hospitably·received him.
Ac 8:39 any·longer, for he·traversed on·his way rejoicing.
Col 2:5 with·yeu in·the spirit, rejoicing and looking·upon

G5463.2 V-PAP-NPM χαίροντες (6x)
Lk 19:37 multitude of·the disciples began rejoicing, praising
Ac 5:41 rejoicing that they·were·accounted·fully·worthy to·
Rm 12:12 in·the Expectation, by·rejoicing; in·the tribulation
1Co 7:30 weeping; and the·ones rejoicing, as not rejoicing;
1Co 7:30 the·ones rejoicing, as not rejoicing; and the·ones
2Co 6:10 as being·grieved yet always rejoicing, as

G5463.2 V-PAS-1P χαίρωμεν (1x)
Rv 19:7 We·should·rejoice, and should·leap·for·joy, and

G5463.2 V-PAS-3S χαίρῃ (1x)
Jn 4:36 and the·one reaping may·rejoice at·the·same·time.

G5463.2 V-IAI-3S ἔχαιρεν (1x)
Lk 13:17 And all the crowd was·rejoicing over all the

G5463.2 V-IAI-3P ἔχαιρον (1x)
Ac 13:48 the Gentiles were·rejoicing and were·glorifying

G5463.2 V-2AOI-1S ἐχάρην (3x)
Php 4:10 Now I·rejoiced in *the* Lord greatly, that even·now
2Jn 1:4 I·rejoiced very·much that I·have·found from·among
3Jn 1:3 For I·rejoiced very·much, with·*the*·brothers coming

G5463.2 V-2AOI-1P ἐχάρημεν (1x)
2Co 7:13 ·exceedingly *all* the·more, we·rejoiced over the

G5463.2 V-2AOI-2P ἐχάρητε (1x)
Jn 14:28 ·were·loving me, yeu·would rejoice that I·declared,

G5463.2 V-2AOI-3P ἐχάρησαν (2x)
Ac 15:31 And reading·*it*·aloud, they·rejoiced over the
Mt 2:10 the star *stationary*, they·rejoiced *with* tremendously

G5463.2 V-2AON χαρῆναι (1x)
2Co 7:7 on·behalf·of me, such·for me to·rejoice more.

G5463.2 V-2AOS-2P χαρῆτε (1x)
Php 2:28 ·that seeing him again, yeu·may·rejoice, and·*that*·I

G5463.3 V-2AOS-2P χαρῆτε (1x)
1Pe 4:13 of·his glory, yeu·may·be·joyful, leaping·for·joy.

G5463.4 V-PAM-2S χαῖρε (1x)
Lk 1:28 "Be·of·good·cheer, O·woman·having·been·

G5463.4 V-PAM-2P χαίρετε (1x)
Mt 28:9 them, saying, "Be·of·good·cheer." And coming·

G5463.5 V-PAM-2S χαῖρε (4x)
Jn 19:3 "*Ah*! Be·well, O·King of·the Jews!" And they·
Mt 26:49 ·toward YeShua, he·declared, "Be·well, Rabbi,"
Mt 27:29 "*Ah*! Be·well, O·King of·the·Jews!"
Mk 15:18 "*Ah*! Be·well, O·King of·the Jews!"

G5463.5 V-PAN χαίρειν (5x)
Ac 15:23 Cilicia, the·ones from·among Gentiles, be·well.
Ac 23:26 Lysias, to·the most·noble governor Felix, be·well.
Jac 1:1 the Diaspora *dispersed·among·the·Gentiles*: Be·well.
2Jn 1:10 a·home, and yeu·must·not say to·him, "Be·well."
2Jn 1:11 For the·one saying to·him, "Be·well," shares in·his

G5464 χάλαζα chálaza *n.* (4x)
Roots:G5465
xLangEquiv:H1259

G5464 N-NSF χάλαζα (3x)
Rv 8:7 sounded, and there·happened hail and fire having·
Rv 11:19 thunderings, and an·earthquake, and great hail.
Rv 16:21 And great hail (*each hailstone* about *the* weight·

G5464 N-GSF χαλάζης (1x)
Rv 16:21 ·a·result of·the punishing·blow of·the hail, because

G5465 χαλάω chaláō *v.* (7x)
Roots:G5490 Compare:G2507 G2524

G5465 V-FAI-1S χαλάσω (1x)
Lk 5:5 But at your utterance, I·shall·lower the net."

G5465 V-PAI-3P χαλῶσιν (1x)
Mk 2:4 and after·digging·through, they·lowered the mat on

G5465 V-AAM-2P χαλάσατε (1x)
Lk 5:4 Head·off into the deep and lower yeur nets for·a·catch

G5465 V-AAP-GPM χαλασάντων (1x)
Ac 27:30 the sailing·ship, and with·*them*·lowering the skiff

G5465 V-AAP-NPM χαλάσαντες (2x)
Ac 9:25 by·night, sent·*him*·down *by* lowering *him* through
Ac 27:17 ·fall into the sand·bars, after·lowering the sail,

G5465 V-API-1S ἐχαλάσθην (1x)
2Co 11:33 in·a·large·basket, I·was·lowered through the

G5466 Χαλδαῖος Chaldaîôs *n/g.* (1x)
Καλδαῖος Kaldaîôs [Greek, Octuagint]
כַּשְׂדִּי kaśdıy [Hebrew]
Roots:H3778
xLangEquiv:A3779

G5466 N/G-GPM Καλδαίων (1x)
Ac 7:4 from·among *the* land of·the·Kaldeans, he·resided in

G5467 χαλεπός chalêpós *adj.* (2x)
Roots:G5465

G5467.1 A-NPM χαλεποί (1x)
2Ti 3:1 that in *the* last days perilous seasons shall·settle·in.

G5467.2 A-NPM χαλεποί (1x)
Mt 8:28 of·the chamber·tombs, exceedingly fierce, such·that

G5468 χαλιν•αγωγέω chalinagōgéō *v.* (2x)
Roots:G5469 G0071

G5468.1 V-PAP-NSM χαλιναγωγῶν (1x)
Jac 1:26 to·be religious, *yet* not bridling his tongue, but·

G5468.1 V-AAN χαλιναγωγῆσαι (1x)
Jac 3:2 ·mature man, able also to·bridle the whole body.

G5469 χαλινός chalinós *n.* (2x)
Roots:G5465

G5469.2 N-GPM χαλινῶν (1x)
Rv 14:20 even·up·to the horses' bridles, for a·thousand *and*

G5469.3 N-APM χαλινούς (1x)
Jac 3:3 Behold, we·cast the bits in the horses' mouths

G5470 χάλκεος chálkêôs *adj.* (1x)
Roots:G5475

G5470.2 A-APN χαλκᾶ (1x)
Rv 9:20 idols made·of·gold, silver, bronze, stone, and wood

G5471 χαλκεύς chalkêús *n.* (1x)
Roots:G5475

G5471 N-NSM χαλκεύς (1x)
2Ti 4:14 AlexAnder, the coppersmith, pointedly·did me

G5472 χαλκ•ηδών chalkēdṓn *n.* (1x)
Roots:G5475 G1491

G5472.2 N-NSM χαλκηδών (1x)
Rv 21:19 sapphire; the third, chalcedony; the fourth,

G5473 χαλκίον chalkíôn *n.* (1x)
Roots:G5475 G2444-3 Compare:G0030 G3582 G2765 G4632

G5473 N-GPN χαλκίων (1x)
Mk 7:4 of·cups and pots and of·copper·vessels and couches.

G5474 χαλκο•λίβανον chalkôlíbanôn *n.* (2x)
Roots:G5475 G3030 Compare:G2240-1 xLangAlso:H5178

G5474 N-DSN χαλκολιβάνῳ (2x)
Rv 1:15 and his feet like fine·brass (as having·been·refined
Rv 2:18 eyes as a·blaze of·fire and his feet like fine·brass:

G5475 χαλκός chalkós *n.* (5x)
Roots:G5465 Compare:G5557 G0696 G4604 G3432-1 G2595-3 See:G5470 G5474 G5471 G5473 xLangEquiv:H5154

G5475 N-GSM χαλκοῦ (1x)
Rv 18:12 ·most·precious wood, "and of·bronze, iron, and

G5475.2 N-ASM χαλκόν (3x)
Mt 10:9 nor·even silver, nor·even copper·coinage in yeur
Mk 6:8 no bread, *and* no copper·coinage in the pouch,
Mk 12:41 how the crowd cast copper·coinage into the

G5475.4 N-NSM χαλκός (1x)
1Co 13:1 *as* a·reverberating bronze·gong or a·clanging

G5476 χαμαί chamaí *adv.* (2x)
Roots:G5490

G5476.1 ADV χαμαί (2x)
Jn 9:6 ·things, he·spat down·on·the·open·ground and made
Jn 18:6 ·off backwards and fell down·on·the·open·ground.

G5477 Χαναάν Chanaán *n/l.* (2x)
Καναάν Kanaán [Greek, Octuagint]
כְּנַעַן kĕna'an [Hebrew]
Roots:H3667 See:G5478

G5477.4 N/L-PRI Καναάν (2x)
Ac 7:11 over all the land of·Egypt and Kenaan, and a·great
Ac 13:19 seven nations in *the* land of·Kenaan, he·fully·

G5478 Χαναναῖος Chanaanaîôs *adj/g.* (1x)
Καναναῖος Kanaanaîôs [Octuagint]
Roots:G5477 Compare:G2581 G5466

G5478.1 A/G-NSF Καναναία (1x)
Mt 15:22 And behold, a·Kenaanite woman from those

G5479 χαρά chará *n.* (59x)
Roots:G5463 Compare:G2431 See:G5487-1 G5485
G5479.1 N-GSF χαρᾶς (1x)
Mk 4:16 immediately receive it with gladness.
G5479.2 N-NSF χαρά (17x)
Jn 3:29 this (my joy) has·been·completely·fulfilled.
Jn 15:11 ·spoken to·yeu in·order·that my joy may·remain in
Jn 15:11 in yeu, and *that* yeur joy may·be·completely·filled.
Jn 16:24 yeur joy may·be having·been·completely·filled.
Lk 1:14 to·you shall·be joy and exuberant·leaping·of·joy,
Lk 15:7 that in·this·manner, there·shall·be *such* joy in the
Lk 15:10 ·say to·yeu, *that such* joy occurs in·the·sight of·the
Ac 8:8 And there·was great joy in that city.
Gal 5:22 fruit of·the Spirit is love, joy, peace, long-suffering
Rm 14:17 righteousness, peace, and joy in Holy Spirit.
Jac 4:9 ·distorted into mourning, and *yeur* joy into dejection.
Php 4:1 and greatly·yearned·for, my joy and victor's·crown)
1Th 2:19 *is* our expectation, or joy, or victor's·crown of·
1Th 2:20 For yeu are our glory and joy.
2Co 2:3 in yeu all that my joy is *preferred* by·all of·yeu.
1Jn 1:4 our joy should·be having·been·completely·filled.
2Jn 1:12 our joy may·be having·been·completely·fulfilled.
G5479.2 N-ASF χαράν (13x)
Jn 16:20 but·yet yeur grief shall·become a·distinct joy.
Jn 16:21 longer on·account·of·the joy that a·child·of·clay†
Jn 16:22 not·even·one·man takes·away yeur joy from yeu.
Jn 17:13 ·have my joy having·been·completely·fulfilled in
Lk 2:10 I·proclaim·good·news to·yeu of·great joy, which
Ac 15:3 And they·were·causing great joy for·all the brothers.
Mt 2:10 they·rejoiced *with* tremendously great joy.
Mt 25:21 Enter into the joy of·your lord.'
Mt 25:23 Enter into the joy of·your lord.'
Jac 1:2 ·it all joy whenever yeu·should·entirely·fall·into
Php 1:25 for yeur continual·advancement and joy of·the trust
Php 2:2 completely·fulfill my joy, that yeu·should·
3Jn 1:4 I·have no joy even·greater·than these·things, that I·
G5479.2 N-DSF χαρᾷ (6x)
Jn 3:29 ·for him, rejoices with·joy on·account·of·the
Rm 15:32 I·may·come toward yeu with joy through God's
1Pe 1:8 *him*, yeu·leap·for·joy with·joy quite·unspeakable,
1Th 3:9 over all the joy with·which we·rejoice on·account·
2Co 7:4 ·abounding·above·and·beyond with·the joy in all
2Co 7:13 ·more, we·rejoiced over the joy of·Titus, because
G5479.2 N-GSF χαρᾶς (20x)
Lk 8:13 *are those* who with joy accept the Redemptive-word;
Lk 10:17 And the seventy returned·back with joy, saying,
Lk 24:41 not·trusting themselves for the joy and marveling,
Lk 24:52 him, returned·back to JeruSalem with great joy.
Ac 12:14 open·up the gate due·to her joy, but running·in,
Ac 13:52 were·completely·filled with·joy and with·Holy
Ac 20:24 to·fully·complete my running·race with joy, and
Heb 10:34 and yeu·welcomed with joy the plundering of·
Heb 12:2 who, because of·the joy being·laid·out·before him,
Heb 13:17 in·order·that they·may·do this with joy, and not
Mt 13:20 and straight·away *is* receiving it with joy.
Mt 13:44 And from the joy of·it, he·heads·on·out and sells
Mt 28:8 reverent·fear·and·awe and with·great joy, they·ran
Rm 15:13 completely·fill yeu with·all joy and peace in the·
Php 1:4 ·behalf of·yeu all while·making the petition with joy
Php 2:29 him in *the* Lord with all joy, and hold such·men in·
1Th 1:6 ·with much tribulation *and* with joy of·Holy Spirit,
2Co 1:24 but·rather are coworkers of·yeur joy— for by·the
2Co 8:2 the superabundance of·their joy and their deep
2Ti 1:4 in·order·that I·may·be·completely·filled with·joy—
G5479.3 N-GSF χαρᾶς (1x)
Col 1:11 ·endurance and long-suffering with joyfulness—
G5479.5 N-GSF χαρᾶς (1x)
Heb 12:11 does·not seem to·be joyous, but·rather grievous.

G5480 χάρ•αγμα cháragma *n.* (9x)
Roots:G5482-1 Compare:G5482 G1449 G1795 G1924 G4742 See:G5481 G1125 G5489
G5480.1 N-ASN χάραγμα (7x)
Rv 13:16 to·them they·should·be·given an·etching on their
Rv 13:17 except the·one having the etching, or the name of·
Rv 14:9 ·image, and receives *its* etching in his forehead, or
Rv 14:11 nor·does anyone receiving the etching of·its name.
Rv 16:2 the·ones having the etching of·the Daemonic·Beast,
Rv 19:20 ·ones receiving the etching of·the Daemonic·Beast,
Rv 20:4 and did·not receive the etching upon their foreheads,
G5480.1 N-DSN χαράγματι (1x)
Ac 17:29 gold or silver or stone etched by·*the*·art and *the*
G5480.1 N-GSN χαράγματος (1x)
Rv 15:2 and out·from·among its etching, *and* out·from·

G5481 χαρακτήρ charaktḗr *n.* (1x)
Roots:G5482-1 Compare:G1125 G1504 G1382 See:G5480 G5489
G5481.4 N-NSM χαρακτήρ (1x)
Heb 1:3 ·*his*·glory and *the* exact·imprint of·his very·essence,

G5482 χάραξ chárax *n.* (1x)
Roots:G5482-1 Compare:G5480 G5481 See:G1125
G5482.2 N-ASM χάρακα (1x)
Lk 19:43 and your enemies shall·cast a·palisade around you,

G5483 χαρίζομαι charízômai *v.* (24x)
Roots:G5485 Compare:G0863 G2436 G1943 See:G5486 G2170 G0884 xLangAlso:H2064
EG5483 (1x)
2Co 1:11 the gracious·bestowment *may·be·bestowed* upon us
G5483.2 V-PNI-2P χαρίζεσθε (1x)
2Co 2:10 For·whom yeu·graciously·forgive anything, I·
G5483.2 V-PPP-NPM χαριζόμενοι (2x)
Eph 4:32 being·graciously·forgiving to·one·another, also
Col 3:13 and being·graciously·forgiving to·one·another. If
G5483.2 V-ADI-3S ἐχαρίσατο (4x)
Lk 7:42 *ability* to·repay, he·graciously·forgave them·both.
Lk 7:43 ·*is the·one* to·whom he·graciously·forgave the more.
Eph 4:32 also just·as God graciously·forgave yeu in *the*
Col 3:13 ·as also the Anointed-One graciously·forgave yeu,
G5483.2 V-ADM-2P χαρίσασθε (1x)
2Co 12:13 a·freeloader of·yeu? Graciously·forgive me this
G5483.2 V-ADN χαρίσασθαι (1x)
2Co 2:7 yeu *ought* rather to·graciously·forgive *him*, and to·
G5483.2 V-ADP-NSM χαρισάμενος (1x)
Col 2:13 along·with him, graciously·forgiving us all the
G5483.2 V-RNI-1S κεχάρισμαι (2x)
2Co 2:10 if I·myself have·graciously·forgiven anything (for·
2Co 2:10 anything (for·whom I·have·graciously·forgiven *it*),
G5483.4 V-FDI-3S χαρίσεται (1x)
Rm 8:32 together with·him, also graciously·bestow to·us all
G5483.4 V-ADI-3S ἐχαρίσατο (2x)
Lk 7:21 *that·were* blind, he·graciously·bestowed the *ability*
Php 2:9 ·all·others and graciously·bestowed on·him a·name,
G5483.4 V-API-3S ἐχαρίσθη (1x)
Php 1:29 Because it·is·graciously·bestowed to·yeu, on·
G5483.4 V-APP-APN χαρισθέντα (1x)
1Co 2:12 the·things being·graciously·bestowed to·us by God
G5483.4 V-RNI-3S κεχάρισται (1x)
Gal 3:18 But God has·graciously·bestowed *the inheritance*
G5483.5 V-FPI-1S χαρισθήσομαι (1x)
Phm 1:22 yeur prayers I·shall·be·graciously·given to·yeu.
G5483.5 V-APN χαρισθῆναι (1x)
Ac 3:14 a·man, a·murderer, to·be·graciously·given to·yeu.
G5483.5 V-RNI-3S κεχάρισται (1x)
Ac 27:24 and behold, God has·graciously·given you all the·
G5483.6 V-PNN χαρίζεσθαι (1x)
Ac 25:16 of·the·Romans to·gratuitously·hand·over any man·
G5483.6 V-ADN χαρίσασθαι (1x)
Ac 25:11 no·one·at·all is·able to·gratuitously·hand me over

G5484 χάριν chárin *adv.* (9x)
Roots:G5485
G5484.1 ADV χάριν (5x)
Lk 7:47 "As·such, on·account·of·grace I·say to·you, her
Gal 3:19 the Torah-Law? On·account·of·grace, *because* of·
Tit 1:5 For·this, on·account·of·grace, I·left you behind in
Eph 3:1 For·this, on·account·of·grace, I, Paul, *am* the
1Ti 5:14 Accordingly, on·account·of·grace, I·resolve *for*
G5484.2 ADV χάριν (2x)
Jud 1:16 ·advantage through·gracious·sounding·words.
Tit 1:11 through·gracious·sounding·words for·shameful gain.
G5484.3 ADV χάριν (1x)
Eph 3:14 For·this gracious·cause, I·bow my knees to·the
G5484.4 ADV χάριν (1x)
1Jn 3:12 for·what self-gratifying·cause did·he·slaughter him?

G5485 χάρις cháris *n.* (161x)
Roots:G5463 Compare:G5543 G0018 G1656 See:G5479 G5484 G5487-1 xLangAlso:H2587
G5485.1 N-NSF χάρις (2x)
1Pe 2:19 For this *is* graciousness, if someone on·account·of
1Pe 2:20 ·good, this *is* graciousness personally·before God.
G5485.1 N-DSF χάριτι (1x)
Lk 2:52 maturity, and graciousness personally·before God
G5485.2 N-NSF χάρις (51x)
Jn 1:17 was·given through Moses, the grace and the truth
Lk 2:40 with·wisdom. And God's grace was upon him.
Lk 6:32 ·ones loving yeu, what·kind·of grace is·it to·yeu?
Lk 6:33 ·doing·good to·yeu, what·kind·of grace is·it to·yeu?
Lk 6:34 to·receive·in·full, what·kind·of grace is·it yeu?
Ac 4:33 ·the Lord Jesus, and great grace was upon them all.
Heb 13:25 The grace *be* with yeu all.
Gal 1:3 Grace *be* to·yeu and peace from Father God, and
Gal 6:18 Brothers, the grace of·our Lord YeShua Anointed
Rm 1:7 called·forth *as* holy·ones. Grace to·yeu and peace
Rm 5:15 so·much more did·abound the grace of·God and the
Rm 6:1 ·Failure in·order·that Grace may·increase·more?
Rm 11:6 of·works, otherwise the grace becomes no·longer
Rm 11:6 otherwise the grace becomes no·longer grace. But if
Rm 11:6 of·works, *then* it·is no·longer grace, otherwise the
Rm 16:20 in haste. The grace of·our Lord Jesus Anointed *be*
Rm 16:24 The grace of·our Lord Jesus Anointed *be* with yeu
Php 1:2 Grace *be* to·yeu, and peace, from God our Father
Php 4:23 The grace of·our Lord Jesus Anointed *be* with yeu
1Pe 1:2 Anointed. May grace and peace be·multiplied to·
2Pe 1:2 May grace and peace be·multiplied to·yeu in *the*
1Th 1:1 and *in* Lord YeShua Anointed. Grace *be* to·yeu, and
1Th 5:28 The grace of·our Lord YeShua Anointed *be* with
2Th 1:2 Grace to·yeu, and peace, from God our Father and
2Th 3:18 The grace of·our Lord YeShua Anointed *be* with
Tit 1:4 child according·to a·shared trust. Grace, mercy, *and*
Tit 2:11 For the grace of·God, the Custodial·Salvation,
Tit 3:15 ·for us in the trust. The grace *be* with yeu all.
1Co 1:3 Grace *be* to·yeu, and peace, from God our Father,
1Co 15:10 what I·am, and his grace, the·one *bestowed* upon
1Co 16:23 The grace of·the Lord Jesus Anointed *be* with yeu
2Co 1:2 Grace to·yeu, and peace, from God our Father and
2Co 4:15 *by* the ever·increasing grace through the many·
2Co 12:9 ·declared to·me, "My grace is·sufficient for·you,
2Co 13:14 The grace of·the Lord Jesus Anointed, and the
Eph 1:2 Grace *be* to·yeu, and peace, from God our Father
Eph 3:8 ·the·least of·all holy·ones, this grace was·given: to·
Eph 4:7 But the Grace is·given to·each one of·us according·
Eph 6:24 The Grace *be* with all the·ones loving our Lord
Col 1:2 brothers in Anointed-One. Grace *be* to·yeu, and
Col 4:18 Remember my bonds. The Grace *be* with yeu.
Phm 1:3 Grace to·yeu, and peace, from God our Father and
Phm 1:25 The grace of·our Lord Jesus Anointed *be* with yeur
1Ti 1:2 a·genuine child in trust. Grace, mercy, *and* peace
1Ti 1:14 And the grace of·our Lord increased·evermore·
1Ti 6:21 ·the·mark concerning the trust. Grace *be* with you.
2Ti 1:2 a·dearly·beloved child. Grace, mercy, *and* peace,
2Ti 4:22 Anointed *be* with your spirit. Grace *be* with yeu.
2Jn 1:3 Grace shall·be with us, mercy, *and* peace,
Rv 1:4 to·the·ones in Asia. Grace *be* to·yeu, and peace,
Rv 22:21 The grace of·our Lord Jesus Anointed *be* with yeu
G5485.2 N-ASF χάριν (34x)
Jn 1:16 all received even grace in·addition·to grace.
Lk 1:30 Mariam, for you·found grace personally·before God
Ac 2:47 ·praising God, and having grace alongside all the
Ac 7:46 who found grace in·the·sight of·God and requested
Ac 11:23 after·coming·directly and seeing the grace of·God,
Heb 4:16 ·receive mercy and should·find grace for timely

Xx

Heb 12:28 kingdom, we·may·have grace through which we·
Gal 2:9 so·then after·knowing the grace being·given to·me,
Gal 2:21 "I·do·not set·aside the grace of·God, for if
Rm 1:5 through whom we·received grace and commission
Rm 4:4 is·not reckoned according·to grace, but·rather
Rm 4:16 ·that *it·may·be* according·to grace, in·order·for the
Rm 5:2 ·access by·the trust into this grace in which we·stand
Rm 6:14 ·are not under Torah-Law, but·rather under grace.
Rm 6:15 Torah-Law, but·rather under grace? May·it·never
Rm 12:6 according·to the grace being·given to·us, *we·must·*
Rm 15:15 yeu, on·account·of the grace being·given to·me
Jac 4:6 But he·gives greater grace. Therefore he·says, '" God
Jac 4:6 haughty·men, but gives grace to·humble·men."'
Jud 1:4 irreverent·men transferring the grace of·our God
1Pe 1:13 completely upon the grace being·brought to·yeu at
1Pe 5:5 haughty·men but gives grace to·humble·men."'
1Pe 5:12 ·testifying this to·be *the* true grace of·God in which
2Th 1:12 him, according·to the grace of·our God and of·*the·*
1Co 3:10 According·to the grace of·God, the·one being·
2Co 1:15 in·order·that yeu·may·have a·second grace,
2Co 6:1 ·implore also *for* yeu to·accept the grace of·God—
2Co 8:1 we·make·known to·yeu the grace of·God, the·one
2Co 8:9 For yeu·know the grace of·our Lord Jesus Anointed,
2Co 9:8 God *is* able *to·cause* all grace to·abound toward yeu,
2Co 9:14 on·account·of the surpassing grace of·God upon
Eph 4:29 in·order·that it·may·give grace to·the·ones hearing
Col 1:6 yeu·heard *it* and recognized the grace of·God in truth
2Ti 1:9 ·to his·own determined·purpose and grace, the·one

G5485.2 N-DSF χάριτι (21x)
Ac 13:43 them to·continue·on in·the grace of·God.
Ac 14:26 having·been·directly·handed to·the grace of·God,
Ac 15:40 after·being·directly·handed to·the grace of·God by
Heb 2:9 and honor, that by·the·grace of·God he·should·taste
Heb 13:9 *for* the heart to·be·made·steadfast by·grace, not by·
Gal 1:6 yeu forth in *the* grace of·Anointed-One unto another
Rm 3:24 as·a·free·present by·his grace through the ransom·
Rm 5:15 the voluntary·present by·the grace of·the one man·
Rm 11:6 And if *it·is* by·grace, *it·is* no·longer as·a·result of·
2Pe 3:18 But grow in grace and in·*the·*knowledge of·our
2Th 2:16 and a·beneficially·good expectation in grace,
Tit 3:7 ·as·righteous by·his grace, we·should·become heirs
1Co 1:4 always concerning yeu for the grace of·God, the·one
1Co 15:10 But by·the·grace of·God I·am what I·am, and his
2Co 1:12 but·rather by God's grace), we·conducted·
2Co 8:7 love, *see* that yeu·should·abound in this grace also.
Eph 2:5 ·together in·the Anointed-One (by·grace, yeu·are
Eph 2:8 For by·the grace, yeu·are having·been·saved
Col 3:16 songs, singing with grace in yeur hearts to·the
Col 4:6 *is to·be* with grace having·been·seasoned with·salt,
2Ti 2:1 you, my child, be·enabled in the grace, the·one in

G5485.2 N-GSF χάριτος (25x)
Jn 1:14 directly·from *the* Father), full of·grace and truth.
Jn 1:16 all received even grace in·addition·to grace.
Ac 14:3 to·the Redemptive-word of·his grace and granting
Ac 15:11 we·trust through the grace of·*the·*Lord Jesus
Ac 18:27 much, the·ones having·trusted through the grace.
Ac 20:24 ·testify the good·news of·the grace of·God.
Ac 20:32 and to·the Redemptive-word of·his grace, the·one
Heb 4:16 ·of·speech to·the Throne of·Grace, in·order·that
Heb 10:29 and abusively·insulting the Spirit of·Grace?
Heb 12:15 ·man *is·found* falling·short from the grace of·God;
Gal 1:15 womb and calling·*me·*forth through his grace)
Gal 5:4 from the Anointed-One. Yeu·fell·from the grace.
Rm 5:17 receiving the superabundance of·grace and of·the
Rm 11:5 ·to·be a·remnant according·to a·Selection of·grace.
Rm 12:3 For through the grace being·given to·me, I·say to·
Php 1:7 all are·being partners·together with·me of·the grace.
1Pe 1:10 to yeu concerning the grace *to·come*—
1Pe 3:7 as also *being* co-heirs of·*the·*grace of·life-above, in·
1Pe 4:10 it as good estate·managers of·God's manifold grace.
1Pe 5:10 But the God of·all grace, the·one already·calling us
Eph 1:6 for a·glorious high·praise of·his grace— in which
Eph 1:7 of·trespasses according·to the wealth of·his grace.
Eph 2:7 ages the surpassing wealth of·his grace, *indicated* in
Eph 3:2 of·the estate·management of·the grace of·God, the·
Eph 3:7 ·to the voluntary·present of·the grace of·God, the·

G5485.2 N/P-NSF χάρις (3x)
Rm 5:20 ·more, Grace did·abound·above·and·beyond,
Rm 5:21 even in·this·manner Grace may·reign through
1Co 15:10 not I·myself but·rather the Grace of·God, the·one

EG5485.2 (2x)
1Co 9:17 an·estate·management *of·the grace of·God* has
Eph 1:8 *Yes, the wealth of·his grace* which he·abounded to

G5485.3 N-NSF χάρις (1x)
Rm 6:17 Now to·God *be* gratitude, that *formerly* yeu·were

G5485.3 N-ASF χάριν (4x)
Lk 17:9 "¿!·Does he·have gratitude *toward* that slave
Phm 1:7 For we·have much gratitude and comfort in your
1Ti 1:12 And I·have gratitude to·Anointed-One Jesus our
2Ti 1:3 I·have gratitude to·God (to·whom I·ritually·minister

G5485.3 N-DSF χάριτι (1x)
1Co 10:30 Now if by·gratitude, I·myself participate·

G5485.4 N-NSF χάρις (4x)
1Co 15:57 But thanks *be* to·God, the·one giving us the
2Co 2:14 Now thanks *be* to·God— the·one always causing
2Co 8:16 But thanks *be* to·God, the·one giving the same
2Co 9:15 Thanks *be* to·God for his indescribable voluntary·

G5485.5 N-GSF χάριτος (1x)
Lk 4:22 and they·were·marveling at the gracious words, the·

EG5485.5 (1x)
1Pe 3:15 always to *present a·gracious* defense to·every·man

G5485.6 N-ASF χάριν (3x)
1Co 16:3 ·send to·carry yeur gracious·benevolence away to
2Co 8:4 entreaty for·us to·accept the gracious·benevolence,
2Co 8:6 ·finish among yeu this gracious·benevolence also.

G5485.6 N-DSF χάριτι (1x)
2Co 8:19 ·us along·with this gracious·benevolence (the·one

EG5485.6 (2x)
Rm 15:28 *consequential·matter of·gracious·benevolence*, and
2Co 8:8 *consequential·matter of·gracious·benevolence*, and

G5485.7 N-ASF χάριν (3x)
Ac 7:10 and he·gave him influential·favor and wisdom in·
Ac 25:3 requesting an·influential·favor against *Paul*, that he·
Ac 25:9 to·store·up influential·favor with·the Judeans,

G5485.7 N-APF χάριτας (1x)
Ac 24:27 to·store·up influential·favors with·the Judeans, left

G5486 χάρισμα chárisma *n.* (21x)
Roots:G5483 Compare:G1755 G1390 G1435
See:G0884 G2170 xLangAlso:H2065

G5486.2 N-NSN χάρισμα (4x)
Rm 5:15 The gracious·bestowment *is* also in·this·manner
Rm 5:16 but the gracious·bestowment *is* as·a·result of·
Rm 6:23 *is* death, but the gracious·bestowment of·God *is*
2Co 1:11 the gracious·bestowment *may·be·bestowed* upon us

G5486.2 N-NPN χαρίσματα (3x)
Rm 11:29 For the gracious·bestowments and the calling of·
1Co 12:9 to·another, gracious·bestowments of·healing by
1Co 12:30 Not all have gracious·bestowments of·healing.

G5486.2 N-ASN χάρισμα (4x)
Rm 1:11 to·yeu some gracious·bestowment *which·is* spiritual
1Pe 4:10 each·man received a·gracious·bestowment, among
1Co 7:7 has his·own gracious·bestowment from·out of·God,
2Ti 1:6 you to·rekindle the gracious·bestowment of·God,

G5486.2 N-APN χαρίσματα (3x)
Rm 12:6 various gracious·bestowments according·to the
1Co 12:28 miracles, then gracious·bestowments of·healing,
1Co 12:31 the significantly·better gracious·bestowments.

G5486.2 N-DSN χαρίσματι (1x)
1Co 1:7 not·even·one gracious·bestowment while·fully· the

G5486.2 N-GSN χαρίσματος (1x)
1Ti 4:14 Do·not neglect the gracious·bestowment in you,

G5486.2 N-GPN χαρισμάτων (1x)
1Co 12:4 there·are varieties of·gracious·bestowments, but

EG5486.2 (4x)
1Co 12:1 concerning the spiritual *bestowments*, brothers, I·
1Co 13:2 ·should·have *the gracious·bestowment of* prophecy,
1Co 14:1 and zealously·desire the spiritual *bestowments*, but
1Co 14:12 Since yeu·are zealots of·spiritual *bestowments*,

G5487 χαριτόω charitóō *v.* (2x)
Roots:G5485

G5487.2 V-AAI-3S ἐχαρίτωσεν (1x)
Eph 1:6 — in which he·graciously·favored us in·the·one

G5487.2 V-RPP-NSF κεχαριτωμένη (1x)
Lk 1:28 ·cheer, O·woman·having·been·graciously·favored.

G5488 Χαρράν Charrhán *n/l.* (2x)
חָרָן ChARaN [Hebrew]
Roots:H2771

G5488.2 N/L-PRI Χαρράν (2x)
Ac 7:2 ·still in MesoPotamia, before he resided in Charan,
Ac 7:4 ·the·Kaldeans, he·resided in Charan. And·from·there

G5489 χάρτης chártēs *n.* (1x)
Roots:G5482-1 Compare:G3200 G5482 See:G1125
G5480 G5489-1

G5489.2 N-GSM χάρτου (1x)
2Jn 1:12 willing *to·do so* through a·sheet·of·paper and ink,

G5490 χάσμα chásma *n.* (1x)
See:G5465 G5503

G5490 N-ASN χάσμα (1x)
Lk 16:26 there·has·been·firmly·set a·great chasm, so·that

G5491 χεῖλος chêîlôs *n.* (7x)
Roots:G5490 Compare:G0123 See:G5512
xLangEquiv:H8193 xLangAlso:H6596

G5491.1 N-APN χείλη (2x)
Rm 3:13 ' "*The* venom of·asps *is* under their lips."'
1Pe 3:10 tongue from wrong and his lips not to·speak guile.

G5491.1 N-DPN χείλεσιν (3x)
Mt 15:8 and deeply·honors me with·their lips, but their heart
Mk 7:6 " This People deeply·honors me with·*their·*lips, but
1Co 14:21 ·tongues and in other lips I·shall·speak to·this

G5491.1 N-GPN χειλέων (1x)
Heb 13:15 that·is, a·fruit of·lips giving·affirmation to·his

G5491.4 N-ASN χεῖλος (1x)
Heb 11:12 innumerable sand beside the shoreline of·the sea.

G5492 χειμάζω chêimázō *v.* (1x)
Roots:G5502-5 See:G5490 G5494

G5492.2 V-PPP-GPM χειμαζομένων (1x)
Ac 27:18 ·us tremendously being·tossed·by·the·storm, the

G5493 χείμα•ρρος chêímarrhôs *n.* (1x)
Roots:G5494 G4482 Compare:G4480-2 G4215
G4132 G5327 xLangAlso:H5158

G5493 N-GSM χειμάρρου (1x)
Jn 18:1 ·his disciples to·the·other·side of·the Brook Qidron,

G5494 χειμών chêimṓn *n.* (6x)
Roots:G5502-5 Compare:G2366 G2978 G4578
G5464 See:G5490 G5492

G5494.1 N-NSM χειμών (1x)
Mt 16:3 at·dawn, '*There·shall·be* stormy·weather today, for

G5494.2 N-NSM χειμών (1x)
Jn 10:22 occurred in JeruSalem, and it·was winter.

G5494.2 N-GSM χειμῶνος (3x)
Mt 24:20 yeur fleeing should·not happen in·winter, nor·even
Mk 13:18 But pray that yeur fleeing should·not be in·winter.
2Ti 4:21 Quickly·endeavor to·come before winter. EuBulus

G5494.3 N-GSM χειμῶνος (1x)
Ac 27:20 and with·no little wintry·storm laying·upon *us*, all

G5495 χείρ chêír *n.* (180x)
Roots:G5494 G5490 Compare:G3822-5 See:G1471-6
xLangEquiv:A3028 H3027

G5495.1 N-NSF χείρ (13x)
Lk 1:66 little·child be?" And Yahweh's hand was with him.
Lk 6:6 man·of·clay† there and his right hand was withered.
Lk 6:10 so, and his hand was·restored as·healthy·and·sound
Lk 22:21 behold, the hand of·the·one handing me over *is*
Ac 4:28 to·do as·many·things·as your hand and your counsel
Ac 7:50 Did·not·indeed my hand make all these·things?
Ac 11:21 And *the* hand of·Yahweh was with them, and a·
Ac 13:11 And now behold, the Lord's hand *is* against you,
Mt 5:30 And if your right hand entraps you, chop it off and

Αα Ββ Γγ Δδ Εε Ζζ Ηη Θθ Ιι Κκ Λλ Μμ Νν Ξξ Οο Ππ Ρρ Σσ Ττ Υυ Φφ Χχ Ψψ Ωω

Mt 18:8 "So if your hand or your foot entraps you, chop it
Mk 3:5 and his hand was·restored as·healthy·and·sound as
Mk 9:43 "So if your hand should·entrap you, chop it off.
1Co 12:15 "Because I·am not a·hand, I·am not from·among

G5495.1 N-NPF χεῖρες (2x)

Ac 20:34 yeu·yeurselves know that these hands tended to·my
1Jn 1:1 ·distinctly·viewed, and our hands verified·by·touch,

G5495.1 N-ASF χεῖρα (32x)

Jn 7:30 him, but not·even·one·man threw his hand on him,
Jn 20:25 of·the nails, and may·cast my hand into his side, no
Jn 20:27 And bring your hand, and cast *it* into my side.
Lk 5:13 And stretching·out his hand, he·laid·hold of·him,
Lk 6:8 the·one having the withered hand, "Rouse·yourself
Lk 6:10 man·of·clay†, "Stretch·forth your hand." And he·
Lk 9:62 ·even·one·man, upon·throwing his hand to·a·plow
Lk 15:22 And give *him* a·ring for his hand and shoes for his
Ac 4:30 for you to·stretch·forth your hand for healing, and
Ac 9:12 laying *his* hand on·him in·such·a·manner·so·that he·
Ac 9:41 And giving her a·hand, he·raised her up; and
Ac 19:33 AlexAnder, motioning with·his hand, was·wanting
Ac 26:1 ·stretching·forth his hand, was·making·his·defense:
Mt 8:3 YeShua, stretching·out his hand, laid·hold of·him
Mt 9:18 coming *with·me*, you·must·lay your hand upon her,
Mt 12:10 ·was a·man·of·clay† having the hand withered.
Mt 12:13 man·of·clay†, "Stretch·out your hand." And he·
Mt 12:49 And stretching·forth his hand over his disciples,
Mt 14:31 upon·stretching·forth his hand, grabbed·hold of·
Mt 26:23 "The·one dipping his hand with me in the dish, the·
Mt 26:51 YeShua, upon·stretching·out his hand, drew·out
Mk 1:41 empathizing, stretching·out his hand, he·laid·hold
Mk 3:1 ·was a·man·of·clay† there having the withered hand.
Mk 3:3 the·one having the withered hand, "Rouse·yourself
Mk 3:5 ·the man·of·clay†, "Stretch·out your hand!" And he·
Mk 7:32 him in·order·that he·should·lay his hand on·him.
1Pe 5:6 be·humbled under the mighty hand of·God, in·order·
Rv 1:17 And he·laid his right hand upon me, saying to·me,
Rv 10:5 sea and upon the earth lifted his hand to the heaven,
Rv 14:9 receives *its* etching in his forehead, or in his hand,
Rv 20:1 of·the bottomless·pit and a·great chain in his hand.
Rv 20:4 foreheads, *nor* even in their hands— and they·lived

G5495.1 N-APF χεῖρας (59x)

Jn 7:44 him, but·yet not·even·one·man threw hands on him.
Jn 11:44 ·died came·forth, having·been·bound hand and foot
Jn 13:3 to·him, *directly* into his hands, and that he·came·
Jn 13:9 feet merely, but·rather also my hands and my head.
Jn 20:20 this, he·showed to·them his hands and his side.
Jn 20:27 your finger here, and see my hands. And bring your
Jn 21:18 ·agedly·old, you·shall·stretch·out your hands, and
Lk 4:40 ·*present*; and laying his hands on·each one of·them,
Lk 9:44 to·be·handed·over into *the* hands of·men·of·clay†."
Lk 13:13 And he·laid his hands on·her, and at·once she·is·
Lk 20:19 same hour sought to·throw *their* hands on him, for
Lk 21:12 these·things, they·shall·throw their hands on yeu
Lk 22:53 yeu·did·not stretch·forth yeur hands against me.
Lk 23:46 into your hands I·shall·place·the·direct·care·of my
Lk 24:7 into *the* hands of·morally·disqualified men·of·clay†,
Lk 24:39 See my hands and my feet, that I AM myself.
Lk 24:40 he·fully·exhibited for·them his hands and his feet.
Lk 24:50 BethAny, and lifting·up his hands, he·blessed them
Ac 4:3 And they·threw their hands on·them and placed *them*
Ac 5:18 and they·threw their hands upon the ambassadors
Ac 6:6 and after·praying, they·laid·forth hands on·them.
Ac 8:17 Then they·were·laying *their* hands on them, and
Ac 8:19 ·whomever I·should·lay *my* hands, he·may·receive
Ac 9:17 And after·laying his hands on him, he·declared,
Ac 12:1 violently·threw·forth his hands to·harm some of·the·
Ac 13:3 praying, and after·laying·forth hands on·them, they·
Ac 19:6 And with·Paul laying his hands on·them, the Holy
Ac 21:11 belt, and·also binding his·own hands and feet, he·
Ac 21:11 ·shall·hand *him* over into *the* hands of·Gentiles.'"
Ac 21:27 into·an·uproar, and they·threw their hands on him
Ac 28:8 and after·praying *and* laying his hands on·him, he·
Ac 28:17 out of·JeruSalem into the hands of·the Romans,
Heb 10:31 ·thing to·fall into *the* hands of·the·living God.
Heb 12:12 Therefore raise·upright the limp hands and the
Mt 15:2 ·do·not wash their hands whenever they·should·eat
Mt 17:22 to·be·handed·over into *the* hands of·men·of·clay†.
Mt 18:8 crippled, rather·than having two hands or two feet
Mt 19:13 to·him in·order·that he·may·lay his hands on them
Mt 19:15 And after·laying his hands on·them, he·traversed·
Mt 22:13 attendants, 'After·binding him hand and foot, take
Mt 26:45 ·over into *the* hands of·morally·disqualified·men.
Mt 26:50 ·alongside, they·threw their hands on YeShua and
Mt 27:24 he·washed·off·his·own hands fully·in·front of·the
Mk 5:23 ·*me* in·order·that you·may·lay your hands on·her,
Mk 6:5 except laying his hands upon·a·few unhealthy·ones
Mk 7:3 unless they·should·wash their hands rigorously,
Mk 8:23 his eyes *and* laying his hands upon·him, *Jesus* was·
Mk 8:25 ·that, *Jesus* again laid his hands upon his eyes and
Mk 9:31 is·handed·over into *the* hands of·men·of·clay†, and
Mk 9:43 than having the two hands *and* to·go·off into the
Mk 10:16 in·his·arms, while·placing his hands upon them,
Mk 14:41 ·over into the hands of·morally·disqualified·men.
Mk 14:46 And they·threw their hands on him and securely·
Mk 16:18 they·shall·lay *their* hands on unhealthy·ones, and
Rm 10:21 day·long I·spread·out my hands toward a·People
Jac 4:8 Purify *yeur* hands, *yeu* morally·disqualified, and
2Co 11:33 through the wall and utterly·escaped his hands.
1Ti 2:8 ·up divinely·holy hands, completely·apart·from
1Ti 5:22 Lay·forth hands on·not·one·man quickly, nor·even

G5495.1 N-DSF χειρί (20x)

Jn 3:35 loves the Son and has·given all·things into his hand.
Lk 3:17 whose winnowing·fork *is* in his hand, and he·shall·
Ac 7:35 and a·ransomer by *the* hand of·*the*·angel, the·one
Ac 12:17 But motioning to·them with·his hand to·stay·silent,
Ac 13:16 standing·up and motioning with·his hand, declared,
Ac 21:40 the stairs, motioned with·his hand to·the people.
Gal 3:19 ·assigned through angels in *the* hand of·a·mediator.
Gal 6:11 ·sizable letters I·write to·yeu by·my·own hand.
Mt 3:12 whose winnowing·fork *is* in his hand, and he·shall·
2Th 3:17 The salutation of·Paul by·my·own hand, which is
1Co 12:21 eye is·not able to·declare to·the hand, "I·have no
1Co 16:21 The salutation of·Paul by·my·own hand.
Col 4:18 *This·is* the salutation by·my·own hand, Paul:
Phm 1:19 wrote *this* by·my·own hand; I·myself shall·fully·
Rv 1:16 and having in his right hand seven stars. And 'out
Rv 6:5 ·down on it having a·balance·scale in his hand.
Rv 10:2 his hand a·tiny·official·scroll having·been·opened·
Rv 10:8 having·been·opened·up in the hand of·*the*·angel,
Rv 14:14 victor's·crown, and in his hand a·sharp sickle.
Rv 17:4 cup in her hand overflowing of·abominations and

G5495.1 N-DPF χερσίν (9x)

Jn 20:25 imprint of·the nails in his hands, and may·cast my
Lk 6:1 and they·were·eating by·rubbing *them* in·their hands.
Mt 15:20 "But to·eat with·unwashed hands does·not defile
Mk 7:2 ·his disciples eating bread with·defiled hands, that is,
Mk 7:5 but·rather eat the bread with·unwashed hands?"
1Th 4:11 and to·work·with yeur own hands, just·as we·
1Co 4:12 and we·labor·hard, working with·our·own hands.
Eph 4:28 the beneficially·good with·his hands, in·order·that
Rv 7:9 white long·robes and palm·branches in their hands,

G5495.1 N-GSF χειρός (25x)

Jn 10:28 shall·not snatch them from·out of·my hand.
Jn 10:29 ·able to·snatch *them* from·out of·my Father's hand.
Jn 10:39 But he·came·forth out of·their hand.
Lk 1:71 enemies and from·among *the* hand of·all the·ones
Lk 1:74 after·being·snatched out of·*the*·hand of·our enemies
Lk 8:54 taking·secure·hold of·her by·the hand, hollered·out,
Ac 3:7 ·gripping him by·the right hand, he·pulled·him·up.
Ac 7:25 that God, through his hand, would·give salvation
Ac 11:30 the elders through *the* hands of·BarNabas and Saul.
Ac 12:11 me out from·among HerOd·Agrippa's hand and *from*
Ac 15:23 *this letter of* these·things through their·own hand:
Ac 23:19 ·grabbing·hold of·him by·the hand and departing
Ac 28:3 out of·the warmth, fully·fastened·onto his hand.
Ac 28:4 ·beast hanging out·from his hand, they·were·saying
Heb 8:9 ·grabbing·hold of·them by·my hand to·lead them
Mt 8:15 And he·laid·hold of·her hand, and the fever left her,
Mt 9:25 ·entering, he·took·secure·hold of·her hand, and the
Mk 1:31 her, after·taking·secure·hold·of her hand, and
Mk 5:41 ·secure·hold of·the little·child by·the hand, he·says
Mk 8:23 ·hold of·the blind·man by·the hand, he·led him
Mk 9:27 But after·securely·holding him by·the hand, Jesus
Rv 8:4 in·the·sight of·God from·out of·the angel's hand.
Rv 10:10 ·scroll out of·the angel's hand and devoured it; and
Rv 13:16 ·given an·etching on their right hand or upon their
Rv 19:2 the blood of·his slaves *poured·out* at her hand."

G5495.1 N-GPF χειρῶν (17x)

Ac 2:23 being·taken through lawless hands. *And* after·
Ac 5:12 Then through the hands of·the ambassadors, many
Ac 7:41 they·were·merry in the works of·their·own hands.
Ac 8:18 the laying·on of·the ambassadors' hands, he·offered
Ac 12:7 And his chains fell·away from·among his hands.
Ac 14:3 ·signs and wonders to·be·done through their hands).
Ac 17:25 is·waited·upon by *the* hands of·men·of·clay†, *as*·
Ac 19:11 ·also God, through the hands of·Paul, was·doing
Ac 19:26 the *gods* being·made through hands are not gods.
Ac 24:7 with much force, led·*him*·away out of·our hands,
Heb 1:10 earth; and the heavens are works of·your hands.
Heb 2:7 fully·established him over the works of·your hands..
Heb 6:2 ·washings, and of·laying·on of·hands, and of·the·
Mk 6:2 that even such miracles happen through his hands?
1Ti 4:14 *the* laying·on of·the hands of·the council·of·elders.
2Ti 1:6 which is in you through the laying·on of·my hands.
Rv 9:20 out·from·among the works of·their hands, that they·

EG5495.1 (3x)

Lk 11:38 that he·did·not first immerse *his hands* before the
Mk 7:2 that is, with·unwashed *hands*, they·found·fault.
Mk 7:4 unless they·should·immerse *their hands*, they·do·not

G5496 χειρ•αγωγέω chêiragōgéō *v.* (2x)

Roots:G5497

G5496.2 V-PAP-NPM χειραγωγοῦντες (1x)

Ac 9:8 ·upon no·one·at·all. And leading him by·the·hand,

G5496.3 V-PPP-NSM χειραγωγούμενος (1x)

Ac 22:11 of·that light, being·led·by·the·hand by the·ones

G5497 χειρ•αγωγός chêiragōgós *n.* (1x)

Roots:G5495 G0071 See:G5496

G5497.2 N-APM χειραγωγούς (1x)

Ac 13:11 he·was·seeking others·to·lead·him·by·the·hand.

G5498 χειρό•γραφον chêirógraphôn *n.* (1x)

Roots:G5495 G1125

G5498.1 N-ASN χειρόγραφον (1x)

Col 2:14 after·rubbing·out the handwriting against us (the

G5498-1 χειρονομία chêirônômía *n.* (1x)

Compare:G1435 G2378 G3579-1 G3126-2 G4376 G4700-2 xLangAlso:H4503 A4504

G5498-1.3 N-APN χειρονομίας (1x)

Ac 7:42 to·me sacrifices and respect·offerings *for* forty years

G5499 χειρο•ποίητος chêirôpôíētôs *adj.* (6x)

Roots:G5495 G4160

G5499.1 A-ASM χειροποίητον (1x)

Mk 14:58 this Temple, the·one made·by·hand, and after

G5499.1 A-APN χειροποίητα (1x)

Heb 9:24 enter into holy·places made·by·hands, *which·are*

G5499.1 A-DPM χειροποιήτοις (2x)

Ac 7:48 does·not reside in temples made·by·hands, just·as
Ac 17:24 and earth, resides not in temples made·by·hands,

G5499.1 A-GSF χειροποιήτου (1x)

Eph 2:11 *the* Circumcision, *which·is* made·by·hand in flesh.

G5499.2 A-GSF χειροποιήτου (1x)

Heb 9:11 Tabernacle not made·by·human·hand, that·is, not

G5500 χειρο•τονέω chêirôtônéō *v.* (2x)

Roots:G5495 G5037-1 Compare:G0138 G1586 See:G4401

G5500.2 V-AAP-NPM χειροτονήσαντες (1x)

Ac 14:23 And electing for·them elders for·each Called·Out·

G5500.2 V-APP-NSM χειροτονηθείς (1x)

2Co 8:19 — but·rather also after·him·being·elected by the

G5501 χείρων chêírōn *adj.* (11x)
Roots:G2556 Compare:G2276 See:G2560

G5501.1 A-NSM-C χείρων (1x)
1Ti 5:8 the trust and is worse·than a·non-trusting·heathen.

G5501.1 A-NSF-C χείρων (1x)
Mt 27:64 and the last error shall·be worse·than the first."

G5501.1 A-NSN χεῖρον (3x)
Jn 5:14 ·longer, lest something worse should·happen to·you.
Mt 9:16 from the garment, and *the* tear becomes worse.
Mk 2:21 ·fullness from·the old, and *the* tear becomes worse.

G5501.1 A-NPN χείρονα (3x)
Lk 11:26 man·of·clay† become worse·than the first·ones."
Mt 12:45 man·of·clay† become worse·than the first·ones.
2Pe 2:20 final·states have·become worse for·them than·the

G5501.1 A-GSF χείρονος (1x)
Heb 10:29 shall·he·be·considered·deserving of·a·worse,

G5501.2 A-ASN χεῖρον (1x)
2Ti 3:13 ·advance toward the more·wicked·thing, deceiving

G5501.3 A-ASN χεῖρον (1x)
Mk 5:26 but·yet *with·her* coming rather to the more·harm.

G5502 χερουβίμ chêrôubím *n.* (1x)
κερουβίμ kêrôubím [Greek, Octuagint]
כְּרוּב kĕrûb [Hebrew]
Roots:H3742 Compare:G4587-1 G0032 See:G5501-4
xLangAlso:H8314 H4397

G5502.2 N-PRI χερουβίμ (1x)
Heb 9:5 ·over it *were* kerubim of·glory fully·overshadowing

G5503 χήρα chḗra *n.* (29x)
Roots:G5490 Compare:G3443 See:G5465 G5503-1
G5503-2 G5503-3
xLangEquiv:H0490

EG5503 (2x)
Lk 2:36 in many days, *being a·widow* after·living with a·
1Ti 5:14 I·resolve *for* younger widows to·marry, to·bear·

G5503.2 N-NSF χήρα (2x)
1Ti 5:5 Now the·one *that·is* really a·solitary·widow, and
1Ti 5:9 Let a·solitary·widow be·registered *if·she·is* not less·

G5503.2 N-APF χήρας (2x)
1Ti 5:3 Honor widows *that·are* really solitary·widows.
1Ti 5:16 ·trusts) has solitary·widows, let·them·give·relief

G5503.2 N-DPF χήραις (1x)
1Ti 5:16 ·relief to·the·ones *that·are* really solitary·widows.

G5503.3 N-NSF χήρα (8x)
Lk 2:37 and she *was* a·widow for·about eighty·four years,
Lk 7:12 and she·herself was a·widow. And a·significant
Lk 18:3 And there·was a·widow in that city, and she·was·
Lk 21:3 that this helplessly·poor widow cast *in* more·than
Mk 12:42 a·certain helplessly·poor widow cast·in two bits,
Mk 12:43 this helplessly·poor widow has·cast·in more·than
1Ti 5:4 But if any widow has children or grandchildren,
Rv 18:7 'I·sit·down a·queen, and I·am not a·widow, and no,

G5503.3 N-NPF χῆραι (3x)
Lk 4:25 I·say to·yeu in truth, many widows were in IsraEl in
Ac 6:1 because their widows were·intentionally·neglected in
Ac 9:39 upper·chamber, and all the widows stood·by him,

G5503.3 N-ASF χήραν (3x)
Lk 4:26 of·Tsidon, to·a·woman *who was* a·widow.
Lk 18:5 on·account·of this widow personally·presenting *her*
Lk 21:2 he·saw also a·certain needy widow casting two bits

G5503.3 N-APF χήρας (4x)
Ac 9:41 ·for the holy·ones and the widows, he·presented her
Jac 1:27 to·visit *the* orphans and widows in their tribulation,
1Ti 5:3 Honor widows *that·are* really solitary·widows.
1Ti 5:11 But decline *to·register* younger widows, for

G5503.3 N-DPF χήραις (1x)
1Co 7:8 I·say to·the unmarried and to·the widows, it·is good

G5503.3 N-GPF χηρῶν (3x)
Lk 20:47 who devour the homes of·the widows, and pray
Mt 23:13 the homes of·the widows and for·a·pretense are·
Mk 12:40 devouring the homes of·the widows, and for·a·

G5504 χθές chthés *adv.* (3x)

G5504.1 ADV χθές (3x)
Jn 4:52 ·declared to·him, "Yesterday at·the·seventh hour
Ac 7:28 me, as you·executed the Egyptian yesterday?"
Heb 13:8 Yeshua Anointed *is* the same yesterday, and today,

G5505 χιλιάς chiliás *n.* (25x)
Roots:G5507
xLangEquiv:H0505

G5505 N-NPF χιλιάδες (19x)
Ac 4:4 and the number of·the men was about five thousand.
1Co 10:8 ·immorality, and twenty·three thousand fell in one
Rv 5:11 ·beings and the Elders, and thousands of·thousands,
Rv 7:4 ·been·officially·sealed: "Rho·Mu·Delta Chiliad,"
Rv 7:5 having·been·officially·sealed, twelve thousand.
Rv 7:5 having·been·officially·sealed, twelve thousand.
Rv 7:5 ·Gad having·been·officially·sealed, twelve thousand.
Rv 7:6 having·been·officially·sealed, twelve thousand.
Rv 7:6 having·been·officially·sealed, twelve thousand.
Rv 7:6 having·been·officially·sealed, twelve thousand.
Rv 7:7 having·been·officially·sealed, twelve thousand.
Rv 7:7 having·been·officially·sealed, twelve thousand.
Rv 7:7 having·been·officially·sealed, twelve thousand.
Rv 7:8 having·been·officially·sealed, twelve thousand.
Rv 7:8 having·been·officially·sealed, twelve thousand.
Rv 7:8 having·been·officially·sealed, twelve thousand.
Rv 11:13 were·killed seven thousand names of·men·of·clay†
Rv 14:1 him a·hundred *and* forty four thousand, having the
Rv 14:3 hundred *and* forty four thousand, the·ones having·

G5505 N-DPF χιλιάσιν (1x)
Lk 14:31 with ten thousand to·approach·and·meet the·one

G5505 N-GPF χιλιάδων (3x)
Lk 14:31 who·is·coming against him with twenty thousand?
Rv 5:11 ·beings and the Elders, and thousands of·thousands,
Rv 21:16 he·measured the CITY at twelve thousand stadia.

EG5505 (2x)
Ac 19:19 pieces·of·silver *(which·is fifty thousand drachmas)*.
Rv 7:4 *one·hundred·and·forty·four thousand* having·been·

G5506 χιλί•αρχος chilíarchôs *n.* (23x)
Roots:G5507 G0757 Compare:G4686

G5506.2 N-NSM χιλίαρχος (11x)
Jn 18:12 ·then the battalion, the regiment·commander, and
Ac 21:33 the regiment·commander grabbed·hold of·him
Ac 22:24 the regiment·commander commandingly·ordered
Ac 22:27 *Paul*, the regiment·commander declared to·him,
Ac 22:28 And the regiment·commander answered, "I·myself
Ac 22:29 him, and the regiment·commander also was·afraid
Ac 23:10 the regiment·commander (being·moved·with·
Ac 23:19 And the regiment·commander, after·grabbing·hold
Ac 23:22 in·fact, the regiment·commander dismissed the
Ac 24:7 Lysias the regiment·commander, after·coming·near
Ac 24:22 the regiment·commander should·walk·down, I·

G5506.2 N-NPM χιλίαρχοι (1x)
Rv 6:15 wealthy·men, and the regiment·commanders, and

G5506.2 N-ASM χιλίαρχον (3x)
Ac 21:32 And upon·seeing the regiment·commander and the
Ac 23:17 this young·man to·the regiment·commander, for
Ac 23:18 *him* to·the regiment·commander and replied,

G5506.2 N-DSM χιλιάρχῳ (4x)
Ac 21:31 to·the regiment·commander of·the battalion that all
Ac 21:37 barracks, he·says to·the regiment·commander,
Ac 22:26 he·announced to·the regiment·commander, saying
Ac 23:15 to·the regiment·commander that he·should·bring

G5506.2 N-DPM χιλιάρχοις (2x)
Ac 25:23 with·both the regiment·commanders and the most
Mk 6:21 greatest·men and the regiment·commanders and the

G5506.2 N-GPM χιλιάρχων (1x)
Rv 19:18 of·kings, and flesh of·regiment·commanders, and

EG5506.2 (1x)
Ac 21:37 And *Lysias* the *regiment·commander* replied,

G5507 χίλιοι chíliôi *n.* (11x)
See:G5505

G5507 N-NPN χίλια (5x)
2Pe 3:8 *is* with *the* Lord as a·thousand years, and a·thousand
2Pe 3:8 as a·thousand years, and a·thousand years as one
Rv 20:3 even·until the thousand years should·be·completed.
Rv 20:5 ·again until the thousand years should·be·finished.
Rv 20:7 whenever the thousand years should·be·completed,

G5507 N-APF χιλίας (2x)
Rv 11:3 they·shall·prophesy a·thousand two·hundred *and*
Rv 12:6 ·nourish her there a·thousand two·hundred *and* sixty

G5507 N-APN χίλια (3x)
Rv 20:2 and bound him a·thousand years,
Rv 20:4 and reigned with Anointed-One the thousand years.
Rv 20:6 and they·shall·reign with him a·thousand years.

G5507 N-GPM χιλίων (1x)
Rv 14:20 the horses' bridles, for a·thousand *and* six·hundred

G5508 Χίος Chíôs *n/l.* (1x)

G5508 N/L-GSF Χίου (1x)
Ac 20:15 the following *day* opposite Chios; and with·another

G5509 χιτών chitṓn *n.* (11x)
כְּתֹנֶת kĕthôneth [Hebrew]
Roots:H3801 xLangAlso:H0899

G5509.1 N-ASM χιτῶνα (1x)
Jud 1:23 hating even the tunic having·been·stained by the

G5509.1 N-APM χιτῶνας (5x)
Lk 3:11 ·one having two tunics must·kindly·give to·the·one
Lk 9:3 neither money; neither to·have two tunics apiece.
Mt 10:10 *yeur* journey, nor·even two tunics, nor·even shoes,
Mk 6:9 yeu·should·not dress·yeurselves·with two tunics."
Mk 14:63 ·priest, after·tearing·apart his·own tunics, says,

G5509.2 N-NSM χιτών (1x)
Jn 19:23 inner·tunic. But the inner·tunic was without·seam,

G5509.2 N-ASM χιτῶνα (3x)
Jn 19:23 for·each soldier, and·also the inner·tunic. But the
Lk 6:29 prevent *him from taking·away your* inner·tunic also.
Mt 5:40 ·to·be·judged and to·take your inner·tunic, leave

G5509.2 N-APM χιτῶνας (1x)
Ac 9:39 what·many inner·tunics and outer·garments Dorcas

G5510 χιών chiṓn *n.* (3x)
See:G5490 G5465 G5494
xLangEquiv:H7950 A8517

G5510 N-NSF χιών (3x)
Mt 28:3 was as lightning, and his apparel white as snow.
Mk 9:3 exceedingly white as snow, such·as a·cloth-fuller
Rv 1:14 white like wool (*as* white as snow), and his eyes *are*

G5511 χλαμύς chlamýs *n.* (2x)

G5511 N-ASF χλαμύδα (2x)
Mt 27:28 they·placed a·scarlet military·cloak around him.
Mt 27:31 him, they·stripped the military·cloak *from* him and

G5512 χλευάζω chlêuázō *v.* (2x)
Roots:G5491 Compare:G1592 G1702

G5512.2 V-PAP-NPM χλευάζοντες (1x)
Ac 2:13 And while·jeering, others were·saying, "These·

G5512.2 V-IAI-3P ἐχλεύαζον (1x)
Ac 17:32 ·resurrection of·dead·men, they·were·jeering. And

G5513 χλιαρός chliarós *adj.* (1x)
Compare:G5337

G5513 A-NSM χλιαρός (1x)
Rv 3:16 *then*, because you·are lukewarm, and neither cold

G5514 Χλόη Chlóē *n/p.* (1x)
See:G5515

G5514.2 N/P-GSF Χλόης (1x)
1Co 1:11 by the·ones *of·the house* of·Chloe, that there·are

G5515 χλωρός chlōrós *adj.* (4x)
Roots:G5514 Compare:G5200

G5515.1 A-NSM χλωρός (1x)
Rv 8:7 ·up, and all green grass was·completely·burned·up.

G5515.1 A-ASN χλωρόν (1x)
Rv 9:4 ·the earth (not·even any green·thing nor·even any tree

G5515.1 A-DSM χλωρῷ (1x)
Mk 6:39 recline, party *by* party, upon the green grass.

G5515.2 A-NSM χλωρός (1x)
Rv 6:8 I·saw, and behold, a·pale horse and the·one who·is·

G5516 χξς chi xi stigma *n.* (2x)
Roots:G4742 See:G4496-1 G2395-1

G5516.1 N-NUI-ABB χξς (1x)

Rv 13:18 *clay·man's*† number *is* Chi·Xi·Stigma, *which·is*
EG5516.2 (1x)
Rv 13:18 ·Stigma, *which·is* six·hundred·and·sixty·and·six.

G5517 χοϊκός chôïkôs *adj.* (4x)
Roots:G5522
G5517.2 A-NSM χοϊκός (2x)
1Co 15:47 *was* from·out of·soil, *as* dusty·clay. The second
1Co 15:48 As *was* the dusty·clay·man, such also *are* the
G5517.2 A-NPM χοϊκοί (1x)
1Co 15:48 ·man, such also *are* the dusty·clay·men; and as *is*
G5517.2 A-GSM χοϊκοῦ (1x)
1Co 15:49 the derived·image of·the dusty·clay·man, we also

G5518 χοῖνιξ chôînix *n.* (2x)
Compare:G3634-1 G4568 xLangAlso:H0374
G5518 N-NSM χοῖνιξ (1x)
Rv 6:6 saying, "A·dry·measure of·wheat for·a·denarius,
G5518 N-NPM χοίνικες (1x)
Rv 6:6 and three dry·measures of·barley for·a·denarius;

G5519 χοῖρος chôîrôs *n.* (15x)
Compare:G5300 xLangAlso:H2386
G5519 N-NPM χοῖροι (1x)
Lk 15:16 with the carob-pods that the pigs were·eating, yet
G5519 N-APM χοίρους (5x)
Lk 8:33 the demons entered into the pigs, and the herd
Lk 15:15 and *the citizen* sent him into his fields to·feed pigs.
Mk 5:12 "Send us into the pigs, in·order·that we·may·enter
Mk 5:13 the impure spirits entered into the pigs, and the herd
Mk 5:14 And the·ones feeding the pigs fled and gave·a·
G5519 N-GPM χοίρων (8x)
Lk 8:32 there of·a·significant·number of·pigs being·fed on
Mt 7:6 yeur pearls before the pigs, lest they·should·trample
Mt 8:30 ·distance from them a·herd of·many pigs being·fed.
Mt 8:31 freely·permit us to·go·away into the herd of·pigs."
Mt 8:32 they·went·off into the herd of·pigs. And behold,
Mt 8:32 the entire herd of·pigs impulsively·dashed down
Mk 5:11 ·of the mountains, a·great herd of·pigs being·fed.
Mk 5:16 ·possessed·with·demons, and concerning the pigs.
EG5519 (1x)
Lk 8:32 ·permit them to·enter into those *pigs*. And he·freely·

G5520 χολάω chôláō *v.* (1x)
Roots:G5521
G5520.2 V-PAI-2P χολᾶτε (1x)
Jn 7:23 ·not be·broken, are·yeu·irritated with·me because I·

G5521 χολή chôlḗ *n.* (2x)
See:G5520 G5514
G5521.1 N-ASF χολήν (1x)
Ac 8:23 I·clearly·see you being in a·gall of·bitterness and a·
G5521.1 N-GSF χολῆς (1x)
Mt 27:34 ·vinegar to·drink having·been·mixed with gall, and

G5522 χόος chốôs *n.* (2x)
Roots:G5494 Compare:G1093 G2868 G5515-2
See:G5517 xLangAlso:H6083
G5522.2 N-ASM χοῦν (2x)
Mk 6:11 from·there, shake·off the loose·dirt beneath yeur
Rv 18:19 "And they·cast loose·dirt on their heads, and were·

G5523 Χοραζίν Chôrazín *n/l.* (2x)
G5523 N/L-PRI Χωραζίν (2x)
Lk 10:13 "Woe to·you, Chorazin! Woe to·you, BethSaida!
Mt 11:21 "Woe to·you, Chorazin! Woe to·you, BethSaida!

G5524 χορ•ηγέω chôrēgéō *v.* (2x)
Roots:G5525 G0071 Compare:G2186-2 See:G2023
G5524.2 V-PAI-3S χορηγεῖ (1x)
1Pe 4:11 from·out of·strength which God supplies, in·order·
G5524.2 V-AAO-3S χορηγήσαι (1x)
2Co 9:10 for feeding·upon, may·he·supply and multiply

G5525 χορός chôrôs *n.* (1x)
Compare:G3738
xLangEquiv:H4234 xLangAlso:H4246
G5525.2 N-GPM χορῶν (1x)
Lk 15:25 *and* heard instrumental·music and circle·dancing.

G5526 χορτάζω chôrtázō *v.* (15x)
Roots:G5528 See:G5527 xLangAlso:H7646
G5526.3 V-FPI-2P χορτασθήσεσθε (1x)
Lk 6:21 hungering now, because yeu·shall·be·stuffed·full.
G5526.3 V-FPI-3P χορτασθήσονται (1x)
Mt 5:6 because they·themselves shall·be·stuffed·full.
G5526.3 V-PPM-2P χορτάζεσθε (1x)
Jac 2:16 in peace, be·yeu·warmed and be·stuffed·full," but
G5526.3 V-PPN χορτάζεσθαι (1x)
Php 4:12 ·how also to·be·stuffed·full and to·be·hungry, even
G5526.3 V-AAN χορτάσαι (2x)
Mt 15:33 ·wilderness, such·as to·stuff·full so·vast a·crowd?
Mk 8:4 ·source shall·someone be·able to·stuff these·men full
G5526.3 V-API-2P ἐχορτάσθητε (1x)
Jn 6:26 ·out of·the loaves·of·bread and were·stuffed·full.
G5526.3 V-API-3P ἐχορτάσθησαν (6x)
Lk 9:17 And they·all ate and were·stuffed·full. And the
Mt 14:20 And they·all ate and were·stuffed·full. And they·
Mt 15:37 And all ate and were·stuffed·full. And they·took·
Mk 6:42 And they·all ate and were·stuffed·full.
Mk 8:8 So they·ate and were·stuffed·full. And they·took·up
Rv 19:21 all the fowls were·stuffed·full from·among their
G5526.3 V-APN χορτασθῆναι (2x)
Lk 16:21 and longing to·be·stuffed·full with the little·crumbs
Mk 7:27 First, allow the children to·be·stuffed·full. For it·is

G5527 χόρτασμα chốrtasma *n.* (1x)
Roots:G5526
G5527 N-APN χορτάσματα (1x)
Ac 7:11 and our fathers were·not finding sustenance.

G5528 χόρτος chốrtôs *n.* (15x)
See:G5526 xLangAlso:H6212 H2682
G5528.3 N-ASM χόρτον (1x)
Rv 9:4 ·should·not bring·harm·to the vegetation of·the earth
G5528.4 N-NSM χόρτος (4x)
Jn 6:10 Now there·was much grass in the place.
1Pe 1:24 " All flesh *is* as grass, and every man·of·clay's†
1Pe 1:24 ' " The grass is·withered, and its flower already·
Rv 8:7 ·up, and all green grass was·completely·burned·up.
G5528.4 N-ASM χόρτον (3x)
Lk 12:28 God in·this·manner enrobes the grass, today being
Mt 6:30 if God in·this·manner enrobes the grass of·the field,
Jac 1:11 and 'it·withered the grass, and its flower fell·away,
G5528.4 N-APM χόρτους (1x)
Mt 14:19 the crowds to·recline on the grass, and upon·taking
G5528.4 N-DSM χόρτῳ (1x)
Mk 6:39 recline, party *by* party, upon the green grass.
G5528.4 N-GSM χόρτου (2x)
Jac 1:10 because as·a·flower of·grass, he·shall·pass·away.
1Pe 1:24 man·of·clay's† glory *is* as *the* flower of·grass."'
G5528.5 N-NSM χόρτος (1x)
Mt 13:26 And when the blade blossomed and produced fruit,
G5528.5 N-ASM χόρτον (1x)
Mk 4:28 automatically bears·fruit; first a·blade, then a·head·
G5528.6 N-ASM χόρτον (1x)
1Co 3:12 silver, precious stones, wood, hay, stubble—

G5529 Χουζᾶς Chôuzâs *n/p.* (1x)
See:G2489
G5529 N/P-GSM Χουζᾶ (1x)
Lk 8:3 and Joanna, wife of·Chuza (personal·administrator

G5530 χράομαι chráômai *v.* (15x)
Roots:G5495 Compare:G5531 See:G5540
EG5530.- (1x)
Gal 5:13 are·called·forth to liberty; merely *do* not *use* the
G5530.2 V-PNI-1P χρώμεθα (1x)
2Co 3:12 we·use much boldness·of·speech·with·clarity.
G5530.2 V-PNM-2S χρῶ (1x)
1Ti 5:23 drink·water·only, but·rather use a·little wine on·
G5530.2 V-PNP-NPM χρώμενοι (1x)
1Co 7:31 and the·ones using this world, as not abusing *it* …
G5530.2 V-PNS-3S χρῆται (1x)
1Ti 1:8 *is* good, if someone should·use it legitimately
G5530.2 V-INI-3P ἐχρῶντο (1x)
Ac 27:17 after·taking·*it*·up, they·used emergency·cables,
G5530.2 V-ADI-1S ἐχρησάμην (2x)
1Co 9:15 But I·myself used not·even·one of·these·things,
2Co 1:17 ·planning that, ¿!·did perhaps I·use some levity?
G5530.2 V-ADI-1P ἐχρησάμεθα (1x)
1Co 9:12 more? But·yet we·did·not use this privilege, but·
G5530.2 V-ADM-2S χρῆσαι (1x)
1Co 7:21 if·also you·are·able to·become free, use *it* rather.
G5530.2 V-ADS-1S χρήσωμαι (1x)
2Co 13:10 ·that I·should·not treat *yeu* with·abrupt·sharpness
EG5530.2 (3x)
Gal 5:13 to liberty; merely *do* not *use* the liberty in·order·for
Rm 12:6 the grace being·given to·us, *we·must·use them*: if
1Co 13:3 ·some·food·for *the helpless·beggars using* all my
G5530.3 V-ADP-NSM χρησάμενος (1x)
Ac 27:3 at Tsidon. And·also treating Paul humanely, Julius

G5531 χράω chráō *v.* (1x)
Roots:G5530 Compare:G1155 G5541 See:G5543
G5533 G5534
G5531 V-AAM-2S χρῆσον (1x)
Lk 11:5 'Friend, kindly·lend me three loaves·of·bread,

G5532 χρεία chrêía *n.* (52x)
Roots:G5534 G5530
EG5532 (1x)
Mt 6:8 yeu·yeurselves have the *need* to·request·of him.
G5532.2 N-NSF χρεία (2x)
Lk 10:42 But one·thing is needed, and Mary selected the
Heb 7:11 ·enacted), what further need *was·there for* another
G5532.2 N-ASF χρείαν (41x)
Jn 2:25 and because he·was·having no need that anyone
Jn 13:10 having·been·bathed has no need other·than to·wash
Jn 13:29 "Buy *those·things* that we·have need·of for the
Jn 16:30 and have no need that any·man should·ask·of you.
Lk 5:31 ·sound have no need of·a·practitioner·of·healing,
Lk 9:11 the·ones having need of·therapeutic·relief·and·cure.
Lk 15:7 righteous·men who have no need of·repentance.
Lk 19:31 'Because the Lord has need of·it.'"
Lk 19:34 "The Lord has need of·it."
Lk 22:71 ·declared, "What need do·we·have of·any·further
Ac 2:45 ·to any·particular need someone was·having.
Ac 4:35 ·to any·particular need someone was·having.
Ac 28:10 they·supplied *us* the·things pertaining·to the need.
Heb 5:12 instructors, *yeu·still* have need *for·one* to·instruct
Heb 5:12 yeu·have·become ones·having need of·milk and
Heb 10:36 yeu·have need of·patient·endurance in·order·that,
Mt 3:14 saying, "I·myself have need to·be·immersed by you
Mt 6:8 ·seen what·things *are* needed before yeu·yeurselves
Mt 9:12 ·well have no need of·a·practitioner·of·healing, but·
Mt 14:16 "They·have no need to·go·off; yeu·yeurselves
Mt 21:3 'The Lord has need of·them,' and immediately he·
Mt 26:65 ·God! What further need have·we of·witnesses?
Mk 2:17 ·well have no need of·a·practitioner·of·healing, but·
Mk 2:25 David did, when he·had need and was·hungry, he
Mk 11:3 'The Lord has need of·him.' And immediately, he·
Mk 14:63 says, "What need do·we·have of·any·further
Php 4:16 yeu·sent also once and again to my need.
Php 4:19 ·completely·fulfill yeur every need according·to his
1Th 1:8 such·for us not to·have need to·speak anything.
1Th 4:9 ·affection, yeu·have no need *for·me* to·write to·yeu,
1Th 4:12 and *that* yeu·may·have need of·not·one·thing.
1Th 5:1 brothers, yeu·have no need *for·me* to·be·writing to·
1Co 12:21 to·the hand, "I·have no need of·you," nor again
1Co 12:21 the head to·the feet, "I·have no need of·yeu."
1Co 12:24 our decent·parts have no *such* need, but·yet God
Eph 4:28 *·enough* to·kindly·give to·the·one having need.
1Jn 2:27 and yeu·have no need that anyone should·instruct
1Jn 3:17 ·presently·observe his brother having need, and
Rv 3:17 ·wealthy and have need of·not·even·one·thing," yet
Rv 21:23 And the CITY has no need of·the sun, neither of·
Rv 22:5 Also, they·do·not have need of·a·lantern, nor·even
G5532.2 N-DPF χρείαις (2x)
Ac 20:34 these hands tended·to·my needs and to·the·ones
Rm 12:13 in·the needs of·the holy·ones, by·sharing·with·

G5532.2 N-GSF χρείας (3x)
Ac 6:3 whom we·shall·fully·establish over this need.
Php 2:25 and public·servant *concerning* my needs),
Eph 4:29 particularly·for the needed edification, in·order·
EG5532.2 (2x)
Ac 12:20 ·of their country *needed* to·be·nourished by the
Ac 21:35 to the stairs, *the need* befell him to·be·lifted·and·
G5532.4 N-APF χρείας (1x)
Tit 3:14 for the necessary needful·occasions, in·order·that

G5533 χρε•ωφειλέτης chrēōphêilétēs *n.* (2x)
Roots:G5531 G3781 Compare:G3781 See:G5535 G5532
G5533 N-NPM χρεωφειλέται (1x)
Lk 7:41 a·certain lender *having* two needy·debtors; the one
G5533 N-GPM χρεωφειλετῶν (1x)
Lk 16:5 each one of·his lord's needy·debtors, he·was·saying

G5534 χρή chrḗ *v.* (1x)
Roots:G5531 Compare:G1163 G3784 G0316 G2520 G4241 G1832 G0433 See:G5530 G5532 G5541
G5534.1 V-PQI-3S χρή (1x)
Jac 3:10 it·is·not kindly·needed·for these·things to·be in·

G5535 χρῄζω chrḗizō *v.* (5x)
Roots:G5532 Compare:G3784
G5535 V-PAI-1P χρῄζομεν (1x)
2Co 3:1 ourselves? Yet·not·even do·we·have·need, as some
G5535 V-PAI-2P χρῄζετε (2x)
Lk 12:30 ·knows that yeu·have·need of·these·things.
Mt 6:32 that yeu·have·need of·absolutely·all these·things.
G5535 V-PAI-3S χρῄζει (1x)
Lk 11:8 ·awakened shall·give him as·much·as he·has·need.
G5535 V-PAS-3S χρῄζῃ (1x)
Rm 16:2 matter·of·consequence she·may·have·need of·yeu,

G5536 χρῆμα chrēma *n.* (7x)
Roots:G5530 Compare:G0694 G2772 G3126 G4149 See:G5537
G5536.1 N-ASN χρῆμα (1x)
Ac 4:37 After·selling *it*, he·brought the value and laid *it*
G5536.2 N-APN χρήματα (4x)
Lk 18:24 *that* the·ones holding the valuables shall·enter into
Ac 8:18 ·the ambassadors' hands, he·offered them valuables,
Ac 24:26 ·*was* expecting that valuables shall·be·given to·him
Mk 10:23 *that* the·ones having the valuables shall·enter into
G5536.2 N-DPN χρήμασιν (1x)
Mk 10:24 having·confidence in the valuables to·enter into
G5536.2 N-GPN χρημάτων (1x)
Ac 8:20 ·present of·God may·be·procured through valuables.

G5537 χρηματίζω chrēmatízō *v.* (10x)
Roots:G5536 Compare:G5530 G5532 G4395 G3132 G5540-1 See:G5538 G3051 xLangAlso:H5001
G5537.1 V-PAP-ASM χρηματίζοντα (1x)
Heb 12:25 the·one imparting·divine·instruction on the earth,
EG5537.1 (1x)
Heb 12:25 the·one *imparting·divine·instruction* from *the*
G5537.2 V-API-3S ἐχρηματίσθη (1x)
Ac 10:22 of·the Jews, was·divinely·instructed by a·holy
G5537.2 V-APP-NSM χρηματισθείς (2x)
Heb 11:7 after·being·divinely·instructed·by·Yahweh the·
Mt 2:22 So after·being·divinely·instructed according·to a·
G5537.2 V-APP-NPM χρηματισθέντες (1x)
Mt 2:12 And after·being·divinely·instructed according·to a·
G5537.2 V-RPI-3S κεχρημάτισται (1x)
Heb 8:5 Moses had·been·divinely·instructed·by·Yahweh to·
G5537.3 V-AAN χρηματίσαι (1x)
Ac 11:26 *it·was* first to·be·imparted·as·a·divine·message in
G5537.3 V-RPP-NSN κεχρηματισμένον (1x)
Lk 2:26 it·was having·been·imparted·as·a·divine·message
G5537.5 V-FAI-3S χρηματίσει (1x)
Rm 7:3 she·shall·bear·the·public·title·of an·adulteress. But

G5538 χρηματισμός chrēmatismós *n.* (1x)
Roots:G5537 Compare:G4487 G5540-2 See:G3051
G5538.2 N-NSM χρηματισμός (1x)
Rm 11:4 ·rather what says the response·of·Yahweh to·him?

G5539 χρήσιμος chrḗsimôs *adj.* (1x)
Roots:G5540
G5539.1 A-ASN χρήσιμον (1x)
2Ti 2:14 ·words for not·even·one·thing useful, *for·this·leads*

G5540 χρῆσις chrēsis *n.* (2x)
Roots:G5530
G5540.2 N-ASF χρῆσιν (2x)
Rm 1:26 the natural sexual·intercourse for the·one contrary·
Rm 1:27 leaving the natural sexual·intercourse of·the female,

G5541 χρηστεύομαι chrēstêúômai *v.* (1x)
Roots:G5543
G5541.2 V-PNI-3S χρηστεύεται (1x)
1Co 13:4 is·long-suffering *and* is·beneficially·kind. The

G5542 χρηστο•λογία chrēstôlôgía *n.* (1x)
Roots:G5543 G3004 Compare:G2129
G5542 N-GSF χρηστολογίας (1x)
Rm 16:18 the fine·accommodating·speech and pleasant·

G5543 χρηστός chrēstós *adj.* (7x)
Roots:G5530 Compare:G5485 G0018 See:G0888
G5543.2 A-NSM χρηστός (3x)
Lk 6:35 ·High, because he·himself is kind to the·ungrateful
Mt 11:30 For my yoke *is* kind, and my load is lightweight.
1Pe 2:3 if·ever "yeu·tasted that Yahweh *is* kind."
G5543.2 A-NPM χρηστοί (1x)
Eph 4:32 And become kind to one·another, tender-hearted,
G5543.3 A-NSN χρηστόν (1x)
Rm 2:4 not·knowing that the kindness of·God leads you to
G5543.4 A-NSM-C χρηστότερος (1x)
Lk 5:39 'The old is finer *wine*.'"
G5543.4 A-APN χρῆσθ´ (1x)
1Co 15:33 "Bad influences corrupt fine moral·habits."

G5544 χρηστότης chrēstótēs *n.* (10x)
Roots:G5543 See:G0663
G5544.2 N-NSF χρηστότης (2x)
Gal 5:22 long-suffering, kindness, beneficial·goodness,
Tit 3:4 But when the kindness of·God our Savior and *his*
G5544.2 N-ASF χρηστότητα (1x)
Col 3:12 inward·affections, kindness, humility·of·mind,
G5544.2 N-DSF χρηστότητι (2x)
2Co 6:6 by long-suffering, by kindness, by Holy Spirit, by
Eph 2:7 of·his grace, *indicated* in *his* kindness toward us in
G5544.2 N-GSF χρηστότητος (1x)
Rm 2:4 Or do·you·despise the wealth of·his kindness,
G5544.3 N-ASF χρηστότητα (3x)
Rm 3:12 there·is none doing benevolent·kindness; there·is
Rm 11:22 see *both* a·benevolent·kindness and a·severe·
Rm 11:22 toward you *personally*, a·benevolent·kindness, if
G5544.3 N-DSF χρηστότητι (1x)
Rm 11:22 if you·should·persist in·the benevolent·kindness.

G5545 χρῖσμα chrîsma *n.* (3x)
Roots:G5548 See:G5547
G5545.2 N-NSN χρίσμα (2x)
1Jn 2:27 But the anointing which yeu·yeurselves already·
1Jn 2:27 ·rather as the same anointing presently·instructs yeu
G5545.2 N-ASN χρίσμα (1x)
1Jn 2:20 But yeu·yeurselves do·have an·anointing from the

G5546 Χριστ•ιανός Christianós *n/g.* (6x)
Χριστ•ιανοί Christianôí [plural]
מָשִׁיחָן mąshiyuchąn [Hebrew]
מָשִׁיחָנִים mąshiyuchąniym [Hebrew, plural]
Roots:G5547 G2389-1 Compare:G4773 G3480 G3479 See:G5546-1 xLangEquiv:H4899-1 xLangAlso:H1350
EG5546.3 (3x)
Ac 11:26 'Christians,' Little·Siblings·of·Anointed-One."
Ac 26:28 'a·Christian,' a·Little·Sibling·of·Anointed-One?"
1Pe 4:16 a·Little·Sibling·of·Anointed-One, do·not let·him·
G5546.7 N/G-NSM Χριστιανός (1x)
1Pe 4:16 *any·man suffers* as "a·Christian," a·Little·Sibling·of·
G5546.7 N/G-ASM Χριστιανόν (1x)
Ac 26:28 do·you·persuade me to·become 'a·Christian,' a·
G5546.8 N/G-APM Χριστιανούς (1x)
Ac 11:26 "The disciples *are* 'Christians,' Little·Siblings·of·

G5547 Χριστός Christós *n/p.* (579x)
מָשִׁיחַ mąshiyach [Hebrew]
Μεσσίας Mêssías [Greek transliteration]
Roots:G5548 Compare:G3323 See:G5545 G5546 xLangEquiv:H4899 xLangAlso:H4899-1
G5547.1 N/P-NSM Χριστός (11x)
Heb 13:8 YeShua Anointed *is* the same yesterday, and today,
Gal 3:1 YeShua Anointed was·previously·written among yeu
Php 2:11 should·explicitly·affirm that Jesus Anointed *is* Lord
2Pe 1:14 ·as our Lord YeShua Anointed made·plain to·me.
1Th 3:11 and our Lord YeShua Anointed, fully·direct our
2Th 2:16 Now our Lord YeShua Anointed himself, and God,
1Co 8:6 and one Lord, Jesus Anointed (through whom *are*
2Co 1:19 the Son of·God, Jesus Anointed, the·one being·
2Co 13:5 *for* yeur·own·selves that Jesus Anointed is in yeu,
1Ti 1:16 in me foremost, Jesus Anointed may·indicate the
2Ti 4:22 The Lord Jesus Anointed *be* with your spirit.
G5547.1 N/P-ASM Χριστόν (19x)
Jn 17:3 true God, and Jesus Anointed, whom you·dispatched
Ac 3:20 and *that* he·should·dispatch Jesus Anointed, the·one
Ac 8:37 he·declared, "I·trust Jesus Anointed to·be the Son
Ac 11:17 already·trusting on the Lord Jesus Anointed), then
Ac 16:31 on the Lord Jesus Anointed, and you·shall·be·
Ac 20:21 a·trust (the·one toward our Lord Jesus Anointed).
Rm 6:3 are·immersed into Jesus Anointed are·immersed into
Rm 13:14 ·yeurselves·with the Lord Jesus Anointed, and do·
Rm 15:8 ·*for* Jesus Anointed to·have·become an·attendant
Jud 1:4 only Master, God and our Lord YeShua Anointed.
Php 3:20 ·fully·await *the* Savior, *the* Lord Jesus Anointed,
1Co 2:2 among yeu, except Jesus Anointed and this *Jesus*
1Co 9:1 ·I·not·indeed clearly·seen Jesus Anointed our Lord?
1Co 16:22 ·affection·for the Lord Jesus Anointed, let·him·be
Eph 6:24 our Lord Jesus Anointed with incorruptibility. So·
2Ti 2:8 Remember *that* Jesus Anointed, birthed·from·out·of·
1Jn 2:1 the Father, Jesus Anointed, *the* righteous·one.
1Jn 4:2 spirit which affirms Jesus Anointed having·come in
2Jn 1:7 the·ones not affirming Jesus Anointed as·coming in
G5547.1 N/P-DSM Χριστῷ (13x)
Gal 3:14 for the Gentiles in YeShua Anointed— in·order·that
Gal 5:6 For in YeShua Anointed, neither circumcision nor
Rm 3:24 the ransom·in·full, the·one in Jesus Anointed—
Rm 6:11 but alive to·God in Jesus Anointed our Lord.
Rm 6:23 *is* eternal life·above in Jesus Anointed our Lord.
Rm 15:17 in Jesus Anointed in·the·things pertaining·to God.
Rm 16:18 slaves to·our Lord Jesus Anointed, but·rather to·
Jud 1:1 having·been·fully·kept in·YeShua Anointed, *to·yeu*,
Php 1:26 in me may·abound in Jesus Anointed through my
1Th 1:1 Father God and *in* Lord YeShua Anointed. Grace *be*
2Th 1:1 in God our Father and *the* Lord YeShua Anointed.
1Co 1:4 ·one already·being·given to·yeu in Jesus Anointed,
1Jn 5:20 ·*is* true, in his Son Jesus Anointed. This is the true
G5547.1 N/P-GSM Χριστοῦ (148x)
Jn 1:17 and the truth came·to·be through Jesus Anointed.
Ac 2:38 in the name of·Jesus Anointed for pardon of·moral·
Ac 3:6 In the name of·Jesus Anointed of·Natsareth, be·
Ac 4:10 by the name of·Jesus Anointed of·Natsareth, whom
Ac 8:12 the name of·Jesus Anointed, they·were·immersed,
Ac 10:36 ·news of·peace through Jesus Anointed— This·one
Ac 15:11 the grace of·*the*·Lord Jesus Anointed to·be·saved;
Ac 15:26 on·behalf·of·the name of·our Lord Jesus Anointed.
Ac 16:18 in the name of·Jesus Anointed to·come·out from
Ac 28:31 concerning the Lord Jesus Anointed— with all
Heb 10:10 ·occasion·only, of·the body of·YeShua Anointed.
Heb 13:21 of·him, through YeShua Anointed— to·whom *be*
Gal 1:1 but·rather through YeShua Anointed and Father
Gal 1:3 Father God, and *from* our Lord YeShua Anointed,
Gal 1:12 *it* through a·revelation of·YeShua Anointed.
Gal 2:16 through a·trust of·YeShua Anointed, we·ourselves
Gal 3:22 ·that, as·a·result of·trust in·YeShua Anointed, the
Gal 6:14 cross of·our Lord YeShua Anointed, through whom

Gal 6:18 grace of·our Lord YeShua Anointed *be* with yeur
Mt 1:1 origin *(via·adoption)* of·YeShua Anointed, *the* Son
Mt 1:18 the birth of·YeShua Anointed was in·this·manner.
Mk 1:1 of·the good·news of·Jesus Anointed, God's Son.
Rm 1:1 Paul, a·slave of·Jesus Anointed, called·forth *to·be*
Rm 1:4 of·the·dead; *specifically*, Jesus Anointed our Lord,
Rm 1:6 are *the* called·forth·ones of·Jesus Anointed).
Rm 1:7 from God our Father and *the* Lord Jesus Anointed.
Rm 1:8 to·my God through Jesus Anointed on·behalf of·all
Rm 2:16 ·to my good·news, *this·is* through Jesus Anointed).
Rm 3:22 righteousness through trust of·Jesus Anointed *is* for
Rm 5:1 peace toward God through our Lord Jesus Anointed,
Rm 5:11 through our Lord Jesus Anointed, through whom
Rm 5:15 of·the one man·of·clay†, Jesus Anointed, to the
Rm 5:17 in life-above through the one·man, Jesus Anointed.
Rm 5:21 eternal life-above through Jesus Anointed our Lord.
Rm 7:25 ·thanks to·God through Jesus Anointed our Lord.
Rm 15:6 the God and Father of·our Lord Jesus Anointed.
Rm 15:16 me to·be a·public·servant of·Jesus Anointed to the
Rm 15:30 on·account·of our Lord Jesus Anointed, and on·
Rm 16:20 The grace of·our Lord Jesus Anointed *be* with yeu.
Rm 16:24 The grace of·our Lord Jesus Anointed *be* with yeu
Rm 16:25 and the official·proclamation of·Jesus Anointed
Rm 16:27 the glory through Jesus Anointed into the coming·
Jac 1:1 of·God and of·*the*·Lord YeShua Anointed. To·the
Jac 2:1 the trust of·our Lord YeShua Anointed (*the Lord* of·
Jud 1:1 Jude, a·slave of·YeShua Anointed and a·brother of·
Jud 1:17 by the ambassadors of·our Lord YeShua Anointed,
Jud 1:21 mercy of·our Lord YeShua Anointed unto eternal
Php 1:1 and TimoThy, slaves of·Jesus Anointed. To·all the
Php 1:2 from God our Father and *from* Lord Jesus Anointed.
Php 1:6 ·finish *it* even·unto *the* day of·Jesus Anointed—
Php 1:8 ·after yeu all in inward·affections of·Jesus Anointed.
Php 1:11 of·the·ones through Jesus Anointed, to *the* glory
Php 1:19 an·ample·supply of·the Spirit of·Jesus Anointed
Php 4:23 The grace of·our Lord Jesus Anointed *be* with yeu
1Pe 1:1 Peter, an·ambassador of·YeShua Anointed. To·
1Pe 1:2 ·sprinkling of·the·blood of·YeShua Anointed. May
1Pe 1:3 and Father of·our Lord YeShua Anointed, the·one
1Pe 1:3 of·YeShua Anointed from·among dead·men—
1Pe 1:7 and glory at the·revealing of·YeShua Anointed—
1Pe 1:13 to·yeu at *the* revealing of·YeShua Anointed.
1Pe 2:5 well·acceptable to·God through YeShua Anointed.
1Pe 3:21 — through *the* resurrection of·YeShua Anointed,
1Pe 4:11 may·be·glorified through YeShua Anointed, to·
2Pe 1:1 a·slave and an·ambassador of·YeShua Anointed. To·
2Pe 1:1 of·our God and Savior YeShua Anointed.
2Pe 1:8 ·acknowledgment of·our Lord YeShua Anointed.
2Pe 1:11 kingdom of·our Lord and Savior YeShua Anointed.
2Pe 1:16 initial·arrival of·our Lord YeShua Anointed. But·
2Pe 2:20 of·the Lord and Savior YeShua Anointed, and *they*
2Pe 3:18 of·our Lord and Savior YeShua Anointed. To·him
1Th 1:1 God our Father, and *the* Lord YeShua Anointed.
1Th 1:3 of·the Expectation, of·our Lord YeShua Anointed),
1Th 2:19 before our Lord YeShua Anointed at his returning·
1Th 3:13 ·Presence of·our Lord YeShua Anointed with all
1Th 5:9 of·Salvation through our Lord YeShua Anointed,
1Th 5:23 returning·Presence of·our Lord YeShua Anointed.
1Th 5:28 grace of·our Lord YeShua Anointed *be* with yeu.
2Th 1:2 from God our Father and *the* Lord YeShua Anointed.
2Th 1:8 the good·news of·our Lord YeShua Anointed,
2Th 1:12 of·our Lord YeShua Anointed may·be·glorified in
2Th 1:12 of·our God and of·*the*·Lord YeShua Anointed.
2Th 2:1 ·Presence of·our Lord YeShua Anointed, and of·our
2Th 2:14 of·the·glory of·our Lord YeShua Anointed.
2Th 3:6 YeShua Anointed, to·deliberately·abstain·and·
2Th 3:12 through our Lord YeShua Anointed, in·order·that
2Th 3:18 grace of·our Lord YeShua Anointed *be* with yeu all
Tit 1:1 of·God and an·ambassador of·Jesus Anointed—
Tit 1:4 Father God and *the* Lord Jesus Anointed our Savior.
Tit 2:13 of·our great God and Savior, Jesus Anointed—
Tit 3:6 on us abundantly through Jesus Anointed our Savior,
1Co 1:1 *·be* an·ambassador of·Jesus Anointed through God's
1Co 1:2 the name of·our Lord Jesus Anointed— both their
1Co 1:3 from God our Father, and Lord Jesus Anointed.
1Co 1:7 ·awaiting the revealing of·our Lord Jesus Anointed,
1Co 1:8 ·to·account in the Day of·our Lord Jesus Anointed.
1Co 1:9 *the* fellowship of·his Son Jesus Anointed our Lord.
1Co 1:10 name of·our Lord Jesus Anointed, in·order·that yeu
1Co 5:4 name of·our Lord Jesus Anointed, with·yeu being·
1Co 5:4 together with·the power of·our Lord Jesus Anointed,
1Co 15:57 us the victory through our Lord Jesus Anointed.
1Co 16:23 The grace of·the Lord Jesus Anointed *be* with yeu
2Co 1:1 an·ambassador of·Jesus Anointed through God's
2Co 1:2 from God our Father and *from* Lord Jesus Anointed.
2Co 1:3 and Father of·our Lord Jesus Anointed, the Father
2Co 4:6 of·the glory of·God in *the* face of·Jesus Anointed.
2Co 5:18 us to·himself through Jesus Anointed, and giving
2Co 8:9 grace of·our Lord Jesus Anointed, how·that being
2Co 11:31 Father of·our Lord Jesus Anointed, the·one being
2Co 13:14 The grace of·the Lord Jesus Anointed, and the
Eph 1:1 an·ambassador of·Jesus Anointed through God's
Eph 1:2 from God our Father and *our* Lord Jesus Anointed.
Eph 1:3 Father of·our Lord Jesus Anointed, the·one already·
Eph 1:5 into himself through Jesus Anointed, according·to
Eph 1:17 the God of·our Lord Jesus Anointed, the Father of·
Eph 2:20 and prophets, with·Jesus Anointed himself being
Eph 3:9 the·one creating all things through Jesus Anointed—
Eph 3:14 my knees to the Father of·our Lord Jesus Anointed,
Eph 5:20 and Father in *the* name of·our Lord Jesus Anointed,
Eph 6:23 trust from Father God and *the* Lord Jesus Anointed.
Col 1:1 an·ambassador of·Jesus Anointed through God's
Col 1:2 from God our Father and *the* Lord Jesus Anointed.
Col 1:3 Father of·our Lord Jesus Anointed, praying always
Phm 1:1 Paul, a·chained·prisoner of·Jesus Anointed, and
Phm 1:3 from God our Father and *the* Lord Jesus Anointed.
Phm 1:9 and now also a·chained·prisoner of·Jesus Anointed.
Phm 1:25 The grace of·our Lord Jesus Anointed *be* with yeur
1Ti 1:1 of·Jesus Anointed according·to a·full·appointment
1Ti 1:1 Savior, and Lord Jesus Anointed, our Expectation.
1Ti 1:2 from God our Father and Jesus Anointed our Lord.
1Ti 4:6 you·shall·be a·good attendant of·Jesus Anointed—
1Ti 5:21 of·God, and of·Lord Jesus Anointed, and of·the
1Ti 6:3 (the·ones of·our Lord Jesus Anointed) and with·the
1Ti 6:14 ·appearing of·our Lord Jesus Anointed—
2Ti 1:1 an·ambassador of·Jesus Anointed through God's
2Ti 1:10 ·appearing of·our Savior Jesus Anointed, *who·is*, in·
2Ti 2:3 ·hardship as a·good soldier of·Jesus Anointed.
2Ti 4:1 of·God and the Lord Jesus Anointed (the·one about
1Jn 1:3 with the Father, and with his Son Jesus Anointed.
1Jn 1:7 ·another, and the blood of·Jesus Anointed, his Son,
1Jn 3:23 name of·his Son Jesus Anointed; and we·should·
2Jn 1:3 personally·from *the* Lord Jesus Anointed, the Son of·
Rv 1:1 *The* Revelation of·Jesus Anointed, which God gave
Rv 1:2 and *to* the testimony of·Jesus Anointed, and *to* as·
Rv 1:5 and from Jesus Anointed, *who·is* the trustworthy
Rv 1:9 and patient·endurance of·Jesus Anointed, came·to·be
Rv 1:9 and on·account·of the testimony of·Jesus Anointed.
Rv 12:17 ·God and having the testimony of·Jesus Anointed.
Rv 22:21 The grace of·our Lord Jesus Anointed *be* with yeu

EG5547.1 *(1x)*

Mk 13:6 'I AM *the Anointed-One*,' and shall·deceive many.

G5547.2 N/P-NSM Χριστός (106x)

Jn 1:20 "I·myself am not the Anointed-One."
Jn 1:25 if you·yourself are not the Anointed-One, nor EliJah,
Jn 1:41 ·interpreted *from·Hebrew*, is the Anointed-One.
Jn 3:28 'I·myself am not the Anointed-One,' but·rather that
Jn 4:25 ·one being·referred·to·as Anointed-One. Whenever
Jn 4:29 Could this be the Anointed-One?"
Jn 4:42 is truly the Savior of·the world, the Anointed-One."
Jn 6:69 that you·yourself are the Anointed-One, the Son of·
Jn 7:26 truly do·know that this truly is the Anointed-One.
Jn 7:27 Now whenever the Anointed-One should·come, not·
Jn 7:31 "Whenever the Anointed-One should·come, ¿!
Jn 7:41 "This is the Anointed-One." But others were·saying,
Jn 7:41 from·out of·Galilee *that* the Anointed-One comes?
Jn 7:42 that the Anointed-One comes birthed·from·out of·
Jn 10:24 If you·yourself are the Anointed-One, declare *it*
Jn 11:27 that you·yourself are the Anointed-One, the Son of·
Jn 12:34 of·the Torah-Law that the Anointed-One abides to
Jn 20:31 ·may·trust that Jesus is the Anointed-One, the Son
Lk 2:11 ·and·birthed who is *the* Anointed-One, *the* Lord.
Lk 3:15 if·perhaps he·himself might·be the Anointed-One.
Lk 4:41 "You·yourself are the Anointed-One, the Son of·
Lk 22:67 Are you·yourself the Anointed-One? Declare to·us.
Lk 23:35 if this·man is the Anointed-One, the Selected-One
Lk 23:39 If you·yourself are the Anointed-One, save yourself
Ac 9:22 conclusively·proving that this is the Anointed-One.
Ac 9:34 "Aeneas, Jesus the Anointed-One heals you. Rise·
Ac 17:3 fully·proclaim to·yeu) is the Anointed-One."
Ac 26:23 the Anointed-One *is·to·be* subjected·to·suffering,
Heb 3:6 but Anointed-One as a·son over his·own house, of·
Heb 5:5 In·this·manner also, Anointed-One did·not glorify
Heb 9:11 But Anointed-One, *the* High·Priest of·the
Heb 9:24 For the Anointed-One did·not enter into holy·
Heb 9:28 ·manner, the Anointed-One, after·being·offered
Gal 2:17 would·this·then·make Anointed-One an·attendant
Gal 2:20 No·longer I·myself, but Anointed-One lives in me.
Gal 2:21 then·by·inference, Anointed-One died, offered·
Gal 3:13 Anointed-One utterly·kinsman·redeemed us out of·
Gal 3:16 And to·your single·seed,=" which is Anointed-One.
Gal 4:19 Anointed-One should·be·fundamentally·formed in
Gal 5:1 ·fast in·the liberty with·which Anointed-One set us
Gal 5:2 ·be·circumcised, Anointed-One shall·benefit yeu
Mt 1:16 the·one being·referred·to·as Anointed-One.
Mt 2:4 directly·from them where the Anointed-One is·born.
Mt 16:16 "You·yourself are the Anointed-One, the Son of·
Mt 16:20 ·one that he·himself is YeShua, the Anointed-One.
Mt 23:8 Preeminent·Leader, *that·is* the Anointed-One, and
Mt 23:10 yeur Preeminent·Leader, *that·is* the Anointed-One.
Mt 24:5 'I AM the Anointed-One,' and shall·deceive many.
Mt 24:23 'Behold, here *is* the Anointed-One!' or 'There *he*·
Mt 26:63 ·us whether you·yourself are the Anointed-One, the
Mk 8:29 "You·yourself are the Anointed-One."
Mk 12:35 the scribes say that the Anointed-One is a·Son of·
Mk 13:21 'Behold, here *is* the Anointed-One!' or, 'Behold,
Mk 14:61 "Are you·yourself the Anointed-One, the Son of·
Mk 15:32 The Anointed-One, the King of·IsraEl, let·him·
Rm 5:6 ·to due·season, Anointed-One died on·behalf of·
Rm 5:8 full·of·moral·failure, Anointed-One died on·our
Rm 6:4 just·as Anointed-One is·already·awakened from·
Rm 6:9 ·among dead·men, Anointed-One no·longer dies.
Rm 8:10 Now if Anointed-One *is* in yeu, in·fact, the body *is*
Rm 8:34 shall·be·condemning? *It·is* Anointed-One, the·one
Rm 9:5 the flesh, *is* the Anointed-One, the·one being God
Rm 10:4 For Anointed-One *is the* end of·Torah-Law for
Rm 14:9 to this *determined·purpose* Anointed-One also died
Rm 14:15 food, on·behalf of·whom Anointed-One died.
Rm 15:3 For even the Anointed-One did·not accommodate
Rm 15:7 ·as also the Anointed-One purposely·received us
Rm 15:18 except·what Anointed-One already·accomplished
Rm 15:20 *but* not where Anointed-One is·already·named,
Php 1:18 in·truth, Anointed-One is·being·fully·proclaimed,
Php 1:20 *so* now also), Anointed-One shall·be·magnified in
Php 1:21 For me to·live *is* Anointed-One, and to·die *is* gain.
1Pe 2:21 ·called·forth, because Anointed-One also suffered
1Pe 3:18 Because Anointed-One also suffered only·once
1Co 1:13 The Anointed-One, has·he·been·divided?
1Co 1:17 For Anointed-One did·not dispatch me to·immerse,
1Co 3:11 being·laid·out, which is Jesus the Anointed-One.
1Co 3:23 *are* of·Anointed-One, and Anointed-One *is* of·God
1Co 5:7 For even Anointed-One, our Passover·lamb, is·
1Co 8:11 ·perish, on·account·of whom Anointed-One died?
1Co 10:4 *them*, and the Solid·Rock was the Anointed-One.
1Co 11:3 of·every man is the Anointed-One, and woman's
1Co 12:12 body, in·this·manner also *is* the Anointed-One.
1Co 15:3 ·received, that Anointed-One died on·behalf of·
1Co 15:12 if Anointed-One is·officially·proclaimed that he·
1Co 15:13 not·even Anointed-One has·been·awakened.

1Co 15:14 And if Anointed-One has·not been·awakened,
1Co 15:16 not·even Anointed-One has·been·awakened.
1Co 15:17 And if Anointed-One has·not been·awakened,
1Co 15:20 Anointed-One has·been·awakened from·among
1Co 15:23 one's·own sequence: Anointed-One, a·firstfruit—
Eph 4:15 in him who is the head, *namely* the Anointed-One,
Eph 5:2 in love, just·as the Anointed-One also loved us and
Eph 5:14 dead, and the Anointed-One shall·give·light to·you
Eph 5:23 ·the wife, even as the Anointed-One *is* head of·the
Eph 5:25 wives, just·as the Anointed-One also loved the
Col 1:27 the Gentiles, which is Anointed-One in yeu (the
Col 3:1 up·above, where Anointed-One is sitting·down at
Col 3:4 Whenever the Anointed-One, *who·is* our life-above,
Col 3:11 slave *or* free, but·rather Anointed-One *is* all, and
Col 3:13 ·as also the Anointed-One graciously·forgave yeu,
1Ti 1:15 of·all full·acceptance: Anointed-One Jesus came
1Ti 2:5 men·of·clay†: a·man·of·clay†, Anointed-One Jesus,
1Jn 2:22 that Jesus is not the Anointed-One? This·one is the
1Jn 5:1 Jesus is the Anointed-One has·been·born from·out
1Jn 5:6 and blood, Jesus the Anointed-One, *and* not by the
G5547.2 N/P-VSM Χριστέ (1x)
Mt 26:68 "Prophesy to·us, O·Anointed-One, who is the·one
G5547.2 N/P-ASM Χριστόν (56x)
Jn 9:22 *Jesus to·be the* Anointed-One, he·should·be cut·off·
Lk 2:26 death before he·should·see Yahweh's Anointed-One.
Lk 4:41 ·had·personally·known him to·be the Anointed-One.
Lk 9:20 Peter declared, "The Anointed-One of·God."
Lk 20:41 *it·is·mandatory·for* the Anointed-One to·be David's
Lk 23:2 saying himself to·be *the* Anointed-One, a·King."
Lk 24:26 ·for the Anointed-One to·suffer these·things, and
Lk 24:46 it·was·mandatory·for the Anointed-One to·suffer
Ac 2:30 flesh, he·would·raise·up the Anointed-One to·sit on
Ac 2:36 whom yeu crucified, both Lord and Anointed-One."
Ac 3:18 *for* the Anointed-One to·suffer in·this·manner, he·
Ac 5:42 ·the·good·news: Jesus *is* the Anointed-One.
Ac 8:5 ·officially·proclaiming the Anointed-One to·them.
Ac 9:20 ·was·officially·proclaiming the Anointed-One in the
Ac 17:3 ·was·mandatory·for the Anointed-One to·suffer and
Ac 18:5 to·the Jews *that* Jesus *is* the Anointed-One.
Ac 18:28 the Scriptures, *for* Jesus to·be the Anointed-One.
Ac 19:4 after him, that·is, in the Anointed-One Jesus."
Ac 24:24 ·heard him concerning the trust in Anointed-One.
Heb 3:1 ·Priest of·our affirmation, Anointed-One YeShua,
Gal 2:16 also trusted in Anointed-One YeShua in·order·that
Gal 3:17 ·ratified by God in Anointed-One, such·for it to·
Gal 3:24 ·teacher *to·bring·us* to Anointed-One, in·order·that
Gal 3:27 *the* Anointed-One, yeu·did·dress·yeurselves·with
Gal 3:27 yeu·did·dress·yeurselves·with *the* Anointed-One.
Gal 4:14 as an·angel of·God, *even* as Anointed-One YeShua.
Mt 27:17 the·one being·referred·to·as Anointed-One?"
Mt 27:22 the·one being·referred·to·as Anointed-One?"
Rm 8:11 the Anointed-One from·among dead·men shall also
Rm 10:6 heaven?" (that is, to·bring Anointed-One down),
Rm 10:7 ⇒" (that is, to·bring Anointed-One up from·among
Rm 15:5 one·another according·to Anointed-One Jesus,
Rm 16:5 who is a·firstfruit of·Achaia to Anointed-One.
Php 1:15 officially·proclaim the Anointed-One even through
Php 1:16 they·fully·proclaim Anointed-One out of·being·
Php 3:7 ·considered a·total·loss through Anointed-One.
Php 3:8 ·to·dogs, in·order·that I·may·gain Anointed-One—
1Pe 1:11 the afflictions *to·come* upon Anointed-One and the
1Co 1:23 officially·proclaim Anointed-One having·been·,
1Co 1:24 Jews and Greeks, Anointed-One *is* God's power
1Co 4:10 *are* fools on·account·of Anointed-One, but yeu *are*
1Co 8:12 yeu·morally·fail toward Anointed-One.
1Co 10:9 ·we·thoroughly·try the Anointed-One, just·as some
1Co 15:15 God that he·awakened the Anointed-One, whom
2Co 1:21 us together with·yeu in Anointed-One, and·also
2Co 4:5 ·proclaim, but·rather Anointed-One Jesus *the* Lord,
2Co 5:16 we·have·known Anointed-One according·to flesh,
2Co 11:3 from the fidelity, the·one in the Anointed-One.
Eph 3:17 for·the Anointed-One to·reside in yeur hearts
Eph 4:20 *that* yeu·yeurselves learned Anointed-One,
Eph 5:32 I·myself do·say *this* in·regard·to Anointed-One and
Col 2:5 and the stability of·yeur trust in Anointed-One.
Col 2:6 as yeu·personally·received the Anointed-One, Jesus
Col 2:8 of·the world, and not according·to Anointed-One,
Phm 1:6 ·good·thing among yeu in Anointed-One Jesus.
1Jn 4:3 ·not affirm Jesus, the Anointed-One, having·come in
G5547.2 N/P-DSM Χριστῷ (91x)
Gal 2:4 liberty which we·have in Anointed-One YeShua—
Gal 2:17 ·as·righteous in Anointed-One) we·ourselves also
Gal 2:20 I·have·been·crucified·together with·Anointed-One,
Gal 3:26 of·God through the trust in Anointed-One YeShua.
Gal 3:28 for yeu are all one in Anointed-One YeShua.
Gal 6:15 For in Anointed-One YeShua, neither circumcision
Rm 6:8 if we·died together with·Anointed-One, we·trust also
Rm 8:1 ·condemnation for·the·ones in Anointed-One Jesus,
Rm 8:2 Spirit of·the life-above in Anointed-One Jesus set me
Rm 8:39 us from the love of·God in Anointed-One, Jesus our
Rm 9:1 I·say *the* truth in Anointed-One, I·do·not lie, with·
Rm 12:5 are one Body in Anointed-One, and each one the
Rm 14:18 ·things to·the Anointed-One *is* most·satisfying to·
Rm 16:3 and Aquila, my coworkers in Anointed-One Jesus,
Rm 16:7 also have·come·to·be in Anointed-One before me.
Rm 16:9 Urbanus, our coworker in Anointed-One, and my
Rm 16:10 the·one verifiably·approved in Anointed-One.
Php 1:1 To·all the holy·ones in Anointed-One Jesus, to·the·
Php 1:13 my bonds in *the* Anointed-One to·become apparent
Php 1:23 and to·be together with·Anointed-One, *which·is*
Php 2:1 if *there·is* any exhortation in Anointed-One, if any
Php 2:5 yeurselves, which *was* also in Anointed-One Jesus
Php 3:3 in·spirit, and boasting in Anointed-One Jesus, and
Php 3:14 ·the upward calling of·God in Anointed-One Jesus.
Php 4:7 and yeur mental·dispositions in Anointed-One Jesus.
Php 4:13 ·things in the·one enabling me, *the* Anointed-One.
Php 4:19 ·to his wealth in glory in Anointed-One Jesus.
Php 4:21 Greet every holy·one in Anointed-One Jesus. The
1Pe 3:16 yeur beneficially·good behavior in Anointed-One.
1Pe 5:10 into his eternal glory by Anointed-One YeShua—
1Pe 5:14 to·all the·ones in Anointed-One YeShua. So·be·
1Th 2:14 the·ones in Judea being in Anointed-One YeShua.
1Th 4:16 the dead·ones in Anointed-One shall·rise·up first.
1Th 5:18 *is* the·will of·God in Anointed-One YeShua for yeu
1Co 1:2 ·having·been·made·holy in Anointed-One Jesus,
1Co 1:30 *God*, yeu are in Anointed-One Jesus, who is·made
1Co 3:1 as to·fleshly·ones, as to·infants in Anointed-One.
1Co 4:10 yeu *are* prudent in Anointed-One. We·ourselves
1Co 4:15 ·school·teachers in Anointed-One, but·yet *yeu·have*
1Co 4:15 many fathers, for in Anointed-One Jesus, I·myself
1Co 4:17 ways, the·ones in Anointed-One, just·as I·instruct
1Co 9:21 but·yet *I·am* lawfully·subject to·Anointed-One),
1Co 15:18 ·rest in Anointed-One, they·completely·perished.
1Co 15:19 in this life† in Anointed-One, we·are of·all men·
1Co 15:22 the Anointed-One shall·be·given·life-above,
1Co 15:31 which I·have in Anointed-One Jesus our Lord.
1Co 16:24 *be* with yeu all in Anointed-One Jesus. So·be·it,·
2Co 2:14 ·triumph in the Anointed-One and making·apparent
2Co 2:17 ·the·sight of·God, we·speak in *the* Anointed-One.
2Co 3:14 is·fully·rendered·inoperative in Anointed-One.
2Co 5:17 IF any·man *is* in Anointed-One, *he·is* a·brand-new
2Co 5:19 was in Anointed-One presently·reconciling *the*
2Co 11:2 *yeu as* a·morally·clean virgin to·the Anointed-One.
2Co 12:2 a·man·of·clay† in Anointed-One fourteen years
2Co 12:19 directly·in·the·sight of·God in Anointed-One, but
Eph 1:1 and to·those·that·trust in Anointed-One Jesus.
Eph 1:3 blessing by the heavenly·things in·Anointed-One,
Eph 1:10 all things in the Anointed-One, both the·things in
Eph 1:12 ·placed·our·expectation in the Anointed-One—
Eph 1:20 he·operated in the Anointed-One, after·awakening
Eph 2:5 ·*us*·alive·together in·the Anointed-One (by·grace,
Eph 2:6 in the heavenly·places in Anointed-One Jesus,
Eph 2:7 in *his* kindness toward us in Anointed-One Jesus.
Eph 2:10 already·being·created in Anointed-One Jesus for
Eph 2:13 But right·now in Anointed-One Jesus, yeu·
Eph 3:6 of·his promise in the Anointed-One through the
Eph 3:11 ages which he·made in Anointed-One, Jesus our
Eph 3:21 ·Called·Out·Citizenry, by Anointed-One Jesus,
Eph 4:32 God graciously·forgave yeu in *the* Anointed-One.
Eph 5:24 is·subject to·the Anointed-One, in·this·manner also
Eph 6:5 with fidelity of·yeur heart, as to·the Anointed-One,
Col 1:2 and trustworthy brothers in Anointed-One. Grace *be*
Col 1:4 *both* of·yeur trust in Anointed-One Jesus and *of·yeur*
Col 1:28 man·of·clay† complete in Anointed-One Jesus—
Col 2:20 if yeu·did·die together with·Anointed-One from the
Col 3:1 ·awakened·together with·the Anointed-One, seek
Col 3:3 ·been·hidden together with·the Anointed-One in God
Col 3:24 for yeu·are·slaves to·the Lord Anointed-One.
Phm 1:8 freeness·of·speech in Anointed-One to·order you *to·*
Phm 1:23 fellow·prisoner·of·war in Anointed-One Jesus,
1Ti 1:12 And I·have gratitude to·Anointed-One Jesus our
1Ti 1:14 with trust and love, the·one in Anointed-One Jesus.
1Ti 2:7 (I·relate *the* truth in Anointed-One *and* do·not lie)—
1Ti 3:13 ·clarity in *the* trust, the·one in Anointed-One Jesus.
2Ti 1:1 of·life-above, the·one in Anointed-One Jesus.
2Ti 1:9 already·being·given to·us in *the* Anointed-One, Jesus
2Ti 1:13 and love, the·one *that·is* in Anointed-One Jesus.
2Ti 2:1 in the grace, the·one in Anointed-One Jesus.
2Ti 2:10 Salvation, the·one in Anointed-One Jesus with
2Ti 3:12 in Anointed-One Jesus shall·be·persecuted.
2Ti 3:15 through a·trust, the·one in Anointed-One Jesus.
G5547.2 N/P-DSM-HEB Χριστῷ (1x)
2Co 6:15 mutual·agreement has·Anointed-One alongside
G5547.2 N/P-GSM Χριστοῦ (122x)
Ac 2:31 the resurrection of·the Anointed-One, that his soul '
Ac 4:26 against Yahweh and against his Anointed-One.''
Heb 3:14 partaking·companions of·Anointed-One, provided·
Heb 6:1 of·the Anointed-One, we·should·be·carrying·on
Heb 9:14 shall the blood of·the Anointed-One, who through
Heb 11:26 the reproach of·the Anointed-One *to·be* greater
Gal 1:6 yeu forth in *the* grace of·Anointed-One unto another
Gal 1:7 to·distort the good·news of·the Anointed-One.
Gal 1:10 ·of·clay†, I·would not be a·slave of·Anointed-One.
Gal 2:16 as·a·result of·trust of·Anointed-One and not as·a·
Gal 3:29 And if yeu *are* of·Anointed-One, then·by·inference,
Gal 4:7 *then* also an·heir of·God through Anointed-One.
Gal 5:4 ·nullified from the Anointed-One. Yeu·fell·from the
Gal 5:24 ·ones *that·are* of·the Anointed-One, they·crucified
Gal 6:2 ·fulfill the Law-of-Liberty of·the Anointed-One.
Gal 6:12 be·persecuted for·the cross of·the Anointed-One.
Mt 1:17 exile until the Anointed-One *are* fourteen
Mt 11:2 *of* the works of·the Anointed-One *and* sending·word
Mt 22:42 yeu suppose concerning the Anointed-One? Whose
Mk 9:41 name, because yeu·are of·Anointed-One, certainly
Rm 1:16 ·of the good·news of·the Anointed-One, for it·is
Rm 7:4 through the body of·the Anointed-One *such* for yeu
Rm 8:9 But if any·man does·not have Anointed-One's Spirit,
Rm 8:17 ·fact of·God and co-heirs with·Anointed-One, since
Rm 8:35 us from the love of·the Anointed-One? *Shall*
Rm 9:3 *cut·off* from the Anointed-One on·behalf of·my
Rm 14:10 ·at the Bema·judgment·seat of·the Anointed-One.
Rm 15:19 the good·news of·the Anointed-One (from
Rm 15:29 ·blessing of·the good·news of·the Anointed-One.
Rm 16:16 ·Out·citizenries of·the Anointed-One greet yeu.
Php 1:10 and without·offense in *the* day of·Anointed-One,
Php 1:27 (as·is·worthy of·the good·news of·Anointed-One),
Php 1:29 ·bestowed to·yeu, on·behalf of·Anointed-One, not
Php 2:16 by·me in *the* day of·Anointed-One that I·did·not
Php 2:21 ·own, not the·things·of the Anointed-One, Jesus.
Php 2:30 ·of the work of·Anointed-One, he·was·drawn·near
Php 3:8 of·the absolute·knowledge of·Anointed-One, Jesus
Php 3:9 ·rather the·one through a·trust of·Anointed-One (the
Php 3:12 also I·am·grasped by the Anointed-One Jesus.
Php 3:18 *are* the enemies of·the cross of·the Anointed-One,
1Pe 1:11 ·kind·of season the Spirit of·Anointed-One in them
1Pe 1:19 and without·stain, *the·blood* of·Anointed-One.
1Pe 4:1 with·Anointed-One already·suffering on·behalf of·
1Pe 4:13 yeu·share in·the afflictions of·the Anointed-One, so
1Pe 4:14 ·reproached for *the* name of·Anointed-One, *yeu·are*

1Pe 5:1 of·the afflictions of·the Anointed-One, and·also a·
1Th 2:6 to·be a·burden as ambassadors of·Anointed-One.
1Th 3:2 in the good·news of·Anointed-One, in·order to·
2Th 2:2 of·the Anointed-One is·currently·standing *at·the·*
2Th 3:5 and into *the* patient·endurance of·the Anointed-One.
1Co 1:6 testimony of·the Anointed-One was·confirmed in
1Co 1:12 ·*(called·Peter),*" and "I *am* of·Anointed-One."
1Co 1:17 of·the Anointed-One should·be·made·void *with·*
1Co 2:16 ' But we·ourselves have Anointed-One's mind.
1Co 3:23 and yeu *are* of·Anointed-One, and Anointed-One *is*
1Co 4:1 as assistants of·Anointed-One and estate·managers
1Co 6:15 bodies are members of·Anointed-One? Now·then,
1Co 6:15 ·up the members of·Anointed-One, should·I·make
1Co 7:22 *though being* free, is slave of·Anointed-One.
1Co 9:12 hindrance to·the good·news of·the Anointed-One.
1Co 9:18 good·news of·the Anointed-One without·charge,
1Co 10:16 of·the blood of·the Anointed-One? The bread
1Co 10:16 fellowship of·the body of·the Anointed-One?
1Co 11:1 of·me, just·as I·also *am* of·Anointed-One.
1Co 11:3 head *is* the man, and Anointed-One's head *is* God.
1Co 12:27 yeu·yeurselves are Anointed-One's Body and
1Co 15:23 — afterward, the·ones of·Anointed-One, at his
2Co 1:5 ·as the afflictions of·the Anointed-One abound in us,
2Co 1:5 our comforting also abounds through Anointed-One.
2Co 2:10 ·account·of yeu *I·did·it* in front of·Anointed-One,
2Co 2:12 for the good·news of·the Anointed-One (also with·
2Co 2:15 ·are to·God a·sweet·scent of·Anointed-One, among
2Co 3:3 ·are a·letter of·Anointed-One being·attended·to by
2Co 3:4 we·have through the Anointed-One toward God.
2Co 4:4 of·the glorious good·news of·the Anointed-One—
2Co 5:10 ·judgment·seat of·the Anointed-One in·order·that
2Co 5:14 For the love of·the Anointed-One constrains us,
2Co 5:20 ·elder·spokesmen on·behalf of·Anointed-One, as
2Co 5:20 *yeu* on·behalf of·Anointed-One, be·reconciled to·
2Co 8:23 ·Out·citizenries *and the* glory of·Anointed-One.
2Co 9:13 to the good·news of·Anointed-One, and·also in·
2Co 10:1 the gentleness and fairness of·Anointed-One (*I,*
2Co 10:5 unto the attentive·obedience of·Anointed-One—
2Co 10:7 in·himself to·be of·Anointed-One, let·him·reckon
2Co 10:7 because just·as he *is* of·Anointed-One, even in·
2Co 10:7 in·this·manner *are* we·ourselves of·Anointed-One.
2Co 10:14 ·*proclaiming* the good·news of·the Anointed-One.
2Co 11:10 *The* truth of·Anointed-One is in me, *such* that this
2Co 11:13 ·themselves as ambassadors of·Anointed-One.
2Co 11:23 ·they attendants of·Anointed-One? Being·beyond·
2Co 12:9 the power of·Anointed-One may·encamp upon me.
2Co 12:10 in calamities on·behalf of·Anointed-One, for
2Co 13:3 yeu·seek a·proof of·the Anointed-One speaking in
Eph 2:12 apart·from Anointed-One, having·been·utterly·
Eph 2:13 are·made near by the blood of·the Anointed-One.
Eph 3:1 ·prisoner of·Jesus, the Anointed-One, on·behalf of·
Eph 3:4 in the Mystery of·the Anointed-One).
Eph 3:8 the untraceable wealth of·the Anointed-One,
Eph 3:19 knowledge of·the love of·the Anointed-One— in·
Eph 4:7 measure of·the voluntary·present of·Anointed-One.
Eph 4:12 an·edification of·the Body of·the Anointed-One—
Eph 4:13 of·the complete·fullness of·the Anointed-One—
Eph 5:5 in the kingdom of·the Anointed-One and of·God.
Eph 6:6 but·rather as slaves of·the Anointed-One, doing the
Col 1:7 attendant on·yeur behalf of·the Anointed-One,
Col 1:24 of·the tribulations of·the Anointed-One in my flesh
Col 2:2 of·God and Father, and of·the Anointed-One,
Col 2:11 flesh by the circumcision of·the Anointed-One—
Col 2:17 *the reality is* the Anointed-One's body *which cast*
Col 3:16 Redemptive-word of·Anointed-One indwell among
Col 4:3 Mystery of·the Anointed-One on·account·of which
Col 4:12 from·among yeu, a·slave of·Anointed-One, greets
1Ti 5:11 ·contrary·to the Anointed-One, they·want to·marry,
1Ti 6:13 and *in·the·sight* of·Anointed-One Jesus (the·one
2Ti 1:2 from Father God and Anointed-One Jesus our Lord.
2Ti 2:19 naming the name of·Anointed-One, must·withdraw
2Jn 1:9 abiding in the instruction of·Anointed-One, does·not
2Jn 1:9 abiding in the instruction of·Anointed-One, this·one

Rv 11:15 of·our Lord and of·his Anointed-One, and he·shall·
Rv 12:10 and the authority of·his Anointed-One, because the
Rv 20:4 and reigned with Anointed-One the thousand years.
Rv 20:6 of·God and of·Anointed-One that·offer·sacrifices, and

G5547.2 T-GSM Χριστῷ (1x)
Gal 1:22 ·citizenries of·Judea, the·ones in Anointed-One.

EG5547.2 (9x)
Jn 18:13 *the Anointed-One having·been·bound to·Caiaphas,*
Ac 7:60 this, he·was·laid·to·rest *in Anointed-One.*
1Co 9:19 I·may·gain *all* the more *brothers in·Anointed-One.*
1Co 15:27 already·subjugating all·things to *Anointed-One.*
2Co 3:16 ·around to Yahweh *through Anointed-One,* the veil
Col 1:18 ·Out·Citizenry); *it·is Anointed·One himself* who is
Col 1:20 through the blood of *Anointed-One's* cross, *now·*
Col 1:20 to himself, through *Anointed-One, I·say,* whether
Col 2:9 because in *Anointed-One* all the complete·fullness

G5548 χρίω chríō *v.* (5x)
Compare:G0218 G1472 G3462 See:G5547 G5545 G5530
xLangEquiv:H4886 xLangAlso:A4887

G5548.2 V-AAI-2S ἔχρισας (1x)
Ac 4:27 servant·boy Jesus whom you·anointed, *they·being*

G5548.2 V-AAI-3S ἔχρισεν (3x)
Lk 4:18 upon me for·the·cause·of which he·anointed me, to·
Ac 10:38 how God anointed Jesus *who·was* from Natsareth
Heb 1:9 that, God, your God, anointed you *with·the* oil of·

G5548.2 V-AAP-NSM χρίσας (1x)
2Co 1:21 in Anointed-One, and·also already·anointing us, *is*

G5549 χρονίζω chrônízō *v.* (5x)
Roots:G5550 Compare:G1019 G3635 See:G5551

G5549.2 V-FAI-3S χρονιεῖ (1x)
Heb 10:37 who·is·coming shall·come and shall·not linger.

G5549.2 V-PAN χρονίζειν (1x)
Lk 1:21 at him *that he·would·presume* to·linger in the

G5549.2 V-PAP-GSM χρονίζοντος (1x)
Mt 25:5 Now with·the bridegroom lingering, all nodded·off

G5549.3 V-PAI-3S χρονίζει (2x)
Lk 12:45 in his heart, 'My lord is·delayed in·coming *back,*'
Mt 24:48 in his heart, 'My lord is·delayed in·coming *back,*'

G5550 χρόνος chrốnôs *n.* (61x)
Compare:G2540 G0165 See:G2198

G5550.1 N-NSM χρόνος (6x)
Lk 1:57 Now ElisabetH's time was·fulfilled for·her to·
Ac 7:17 "But just·as the time of·the promise was·drawing·
Ac 7:23 as forty·years time was·completely·fulfilled in·him,
Heb 11:32 For the time shall·be·totally·deficient·for me in·
Mk 9:21 "About how·long a·time has·it·been *that* this has·
1Pe 4:3 the time of·*our*·natural·life already·having·passed·

G5550.1 N-ASM χρόνον (27x)
Jn 5:6 *in·the sickness* even·now a·long time, says to·him,
Jn 7:33 declared to·them, "Yet a·short time am·I with yeu,
Jn 12:35 declared to·them, "Yet a·short time is the light with
Jn 14:9 says to·him, "Am·I so·vast a·time with yeu, and
Lk 18:4 And for a·time, he·did·not want·to.
Ac 13:18 And *for* about a·time of·forty·years, he·bore·with
Ac 14:3 a·sufficient time, boldly·speaking·with·clarity in the
Ac 14:28 And *it·was* no little time *that* they·were·lingering
Ac 15:33 after·continuing *there* a·time, they·were·dismissed
Ac 18:20 asking *him* to·abide a·longer time with them, he·
Ac 18:23 after·continuing *there for* some time, he·went·forth
Ac 19:22 Erastus, he·himself held·back in Asia for·a·time.
Ac 20:18 ·what·manner I·have·been with yeu at·all time,
Heb 4:7 by David (after so·vast a·time), just·as it·has·been·
Heb 5:12 For even after the time being·due *for·yeu* to·be
Gal 4:1 *that* the heir, for·a·span·of time (as·long·as he·is
Mt 2:7 personally·from them the time of·the appearing star.
Mt 2:16 ·to the time which he·precisely·ascertained
Mt 25:19 "Now after a·long time, the lord of·those slaves
Mk 2:19 with them? *For* as·long a·time as they·do·have the
Rm 7:1 ·over the man·of·clay† for·a·span·of time, *that·is, for*
1Pe 1:17 ·yeurselves *during* the time of·yeur sojourning *here*
1Pe 4:2 to·live·naturally the remainder·of *his* time in flesh
1Co 16:7 I·expect to·stay·over some time alongside yeu, if

Rv 2:21 And I·gave her time in·order·that she·should·repent
Rv 6:11 that they·should·rest yet *for* a·short time, until also
Rv 20:3 it·is·mandatory·for him to·be·loosed a·short time.

G5550.1 N-APM χρόνους (3x)
Lk 20:9 and·then he·journeyed·abroad for·a·significant time.
Ac 1:7 "It·is not for·yeu to·know times or seasons which the
Ac 17:30 ·previously·overlooking the times of·ignorance,

G5550.1 N-DSM χρόνῳ (4x)
Ac 1:6 "Lord, do·you at this time restore the kingdom to·
Ac 1:21 ·together with·us during all *the* time in which the
Ac 8:11 *for* the longest time with·the dark·occult·powers.
Jud 1:18 ·be mockers in *the* last time, who·are·traversing

G5550.1 N-DPM χρόνοις (2x)
Lk 8:29 ·clay†, for many times it·had·altogether·seized him.
Rm 16:25 having·been·intentionally·silent from·time eternal,

G5550.1 N-GSM χρόνου (3x)
Lk 4:5 all the kingdoms of·The Land in a·moment of·time.
Ac 27:9 Now with·significant·span of·time already·elapsing,
Gal 4:4 But when the complete·fullness of·time was·come,

G5550.1 N-GPM χρόνων (6x)
Lk 8:27 ·having demons for a·significant·span of·time, and
Ac 3:21 even·until *the* times of·a·reconstitution of·all·things,
1Pe 1:20 ·made·apparent in the last times on·account·of yeu
1Th 5:1 Now concerning the times and the seasons, brothers,
Tit 1:2 without·falsehood) promised before time eternal,
2Ti 1:9 in *the* Anointed-One, Jesus— before time eternal—

EG5550.1 (8x)
Jn 6:58 *It·is* not just·as *the time when* yeur fathers ate the
Lk 9:18 in his *usual time* to·be praying alone·by·himself,
Lk 13:35 me, until *the time* should·come when yeu·should·
Ac 21:1 And as·soon·as it·became *time for* us to·be·sailing·
Heb 9:5 which, now is not *the time for·us* to·say *anything* in
Mt 1:11 his brothers, upon *the time* of·the Babylonian exile.
Mt 13:25 But at the *time for* the men·of·clay† to·sleep, his
1Co 7:29 ·and·shortened in·order·that *with* the *time which* is

G5550.3 N-NSM χρόνος (1x)
Rv 10:6 in it') that there·shall·not be any·further delay.

G5550.4 N-ASM χρόνον (1x)
1Co 7:39 by·Torah-Law over a·lifetime as·long·as her

G5551 χρονο•τριβέω chrônôtribếō *v.* (1x)
Roots:G5550 G5147 See:G5549

G5551.2 V-AAN χρονοτριβῆσαι (1x)
Ac 20:16 it·should·not happen to·him to·linger·away in Asia

G5552 χρύσεος chrýsêôs *adj.* (18x)
Roots:G5557

G5552.1 A-NPN χρυσᾶ (1x)
2Ti 2:20 ·are not merely vessels made·of·gold and of·silver,

G5552.1 A-APM χρυσοῦς (1x)
Rv 4:4 they·had on their heads victor's·crowns made·of·gold.

G5552.1 A-APN χρυσᾶ (1x)
Rv 9:20 demons, and 'the idols made·of·gold, silver, bronze

G5552.2 A-NSF χρυσῆ (1x)
Heb 9:4 with·gold, in which *was* a·golden urn having the

G5552.2 A-ASM χρυσοῦν (3x)
Rv 8:3 ·Altar, having a·golden censer·for·frankincense; and
Rv 14:14 having on his head a·golden victor's·crown, and
Rv 21:15 with me was·holding a·golden reed in·order·that

G5552.2 A-ASF χρυσῆν (1x)
Rv 1:13 and having·been·girded·about·with a·golden band

G5552.2 A-ASN χρυσοῦν (3x)
Heb 9:4 having a·golden censer and the Ark of·the covenant
Rv 8:3 holy·ones upon the golden Sacrifice·Altar, the·one
Rv 17:4 and pearls, *and* having a·golden cup in her hand

G5552.2 A-APF χρυσᾶς (5x)
Rv 1:12 turning·about, I·saw seven Golden Lampstands,
Rv 1:20 right·hand, and the seven Golden Lampstands: the
Rv 5:8 ·*Elders* having harps and golden vials overflowing
Rv 15:6 having·been·girded·about·with golden bands around
Rv 15:7 to·the seven angels seven golden vials overflowing

G5552.2 A-GSN χρυσοῦ (1x)
Rv 9:13 the four horns of·the golden Sacrifice·Altar, the·one

G5552.2 A-GPF χρυσῶν (1x)

Rv 2:1 ·about in *the* midst of·the seven Golden Lampstands:

G5553 χρυσίον chrysíôn *n.* (9x)
Roots:G5557 G2444-3
xLangEquiv:H2091 A1722

G5553.1 N-GPN χρυσίων (1x)
1Pe 3:3 ·braiding of·hair and a·draping of·golden·articles, or

G5553.2 N-NSN χρυσίον (2x)
Rv 21:18 And the CITY *was* pure gold, like pure glass.
Rv 21:21 of·the CITY *was* pure gold, as nearly·transparent

G5553.2 N-ASN χρυσίον (2x)
Ac 3:6 declared, "Silver and gold, it·does·not subsist with·
Rv 3:18 ·from me gold having·been·refined from·among fire

G5553.2 N-DSN χρυσίῳ (2x)
Heb 9:4 having·been·overlaid on·all·sides with·gold, in
1Pe 1:18 *such·as* silver or gold *that* yeu·were·ransomed

G5553.2 N-GSN χρυσίου (2x)
Ac 20:33 ·for not·even·one·man's silver or gold or attire.
1Pe 1:7 much more·precious·than gold *which* is·completely·

G5554 χρυσο•δακτύλιος chrysôdaktýliôs *adj.* (1x)
Roots:G5557 G1146

G5554.2 A-NSM χρυσοδακτύλιος (1x)
Jac 2:2 yeur gathering a·man *with* a·prominent·gold·ring, in

G5555 χρυσό•λιθος chrysólithôs *n.* (1x)
Roots:G5557 G3037 See:G5556

G5555 N-NSM χρυσόλιθος (1x)
Rv 21:20 sardius; the seventh, chrysolite; the eighth, beryl;

G5556 χρυσό•πρασος chrysóprasôs *n.* (1x)
Roots:G5557 See:G5555

G5556 N-NSM χρυσόπρασος (1x)
Rv 21:20 topaz; the tenth, chrysoprase; the eleventh, deep·

G5557 χρυσός chrysós *n.* (13x)
Roots:G5530 Compare:G0696 G5475 G4604 G3432-1 G2595-3 See:G5553 G5558

G5557.1 N-NSM χρυσός (2x)
Mt 23:17 For which is greater, the gold, or the Temple, the·
Jac 5:3 Yeur gold and silver have·been·fully·rusted·down,

G5557.1 N-ASM χρυσόν (4x)
Mt 2:11 ·forth to·him presents: *being* gold, frankincense,
Mt 10:9 Yeu·should·not procure gold, nor·even silver, nor·
Mt 23:17 or the Temple, the·one making the gold holy?
1Co 3:12 ·man builds upon this foundation *with* gold, silver,

G5557.1 N-DSM χρυσῷ (6x)
Ac 17:29 *for* the divine to·be like gold or silver or stone
Mt 23:16 should·swear "by the gold of·the Temple," he·is·
1Ti 2:9 Not with braids·of·hair, or gold, or pearls, or
Rv 9:7 *were something* as victor's·crowns like gold, and their
Rv 17:4 and having·been·gilded with·gold and precious
Rv 18:16 and having·been·gilded with gold, and precious

G5557.1 N-GSM χρυσοῦ (1x)
Rv 18:12 "cargo of·gold, silver, precious stones, and pearls,

G5558 χρυσόω chrysóō *v.* (2x)
Roots:G5557

G5558.1 V-RPP-NSF κεχρυσωμένη (2x)
Rv 17:4 and scarlet, and having·been·gilded with·gold and
Rv 18:16 and scarlet, and having·been·gilded with gold,

G5559 χρώς chrṓs *n.* (1x)
Compare:G1192 G4983 See:G5530

G5559 N-GSM χρωτός (1x)
Ac 19:12 aprons from his skin's·surface to·be·brought upon

G5560 χωλός chōlós *adj.* (15x)
χωλόν chōlón [neuter]
Compare:G0376 G2948
xLangEquiv:H6455

G5560 A-NSM χωλός (2x)
Ac 3:2 a·certain man inherently·being lame from·out of·his
Ac 14:8 ·down, inherently·being lame from·out of·his

G5560 A-NSN χωλόν (1x)
Heb 12:13 feet, lest the lame *limb* should·be·turned·aside,

G5560 A-NPM χωλοί (4x)
Lk 7:22 that 'the·blind receive·their·sight, lame·men walk,
Ac 8:7 ·paralyzed and lame were·both·relieved·and·cured.
Mt 11:5 blind·men receive·their·sight and lame·men walk,
Mt 21:14 And blind·men and lame·men came·alongside him

G5560 A-ASN χωλόν (2x)
Mt 18:8 for·you to·enter into the life-above lame or crippled,
Mk 9:45 It·is better for·you to·enter lame into the life-above,

G5560 A-APM χωλούς (4x)
Lk 14:13 totally·maimed·ones, lame·ones, blind·ones.
Lk 14:21 and totally·maimed·ones, and lame·ones, and
Mt 15:30 among themselves *those that·were* lame, blind,
Mt 15:31 ·ones healthy·and·sound, lame·ones walking, and

G5560 A-GPM χωλοῦ (2x)
Jn 5:3 ·feeble were·laying·ill— blind, lame, withered— *all·*
Ac 3:11 And with·the lame·man who·was·healed securely·

G5561 χώρα chṓra *n.* (31x)
Roots:G5490 Compare:G5117 G4116 G3714 G2149 G1093

G5561.2 N-APF χώρας (2x)
Jn 4:35 and distinctly·view the wide·open·fields, because
Jac 5:4 ·and·bundling·up yeur wide·open·fields, the·one

G5561.2 N-DPF χώραις (1x)
Lk 21:21 and the·ones in the wide·open·fields must·not enter

G5561.3 N-NSF χώρα (2x)
Lk 12:16 "The agricultural·region of·a·certain wealthy
Mk 1:5 And all the region of·Judea was·traversing·out to

G5561.3 N-ASF χώραν (5x)
Jn 11:54 ·rather went·away from·there to·the region near the
Lk 8:26 they·sailed·down to the region of·the Gadarenes,
Ac 26:20 and unto all the region of·Judea, then·also to·the
Mt 8:28 to the other·side into the region of·the Girgashites,
Mk 5:1 ·side of·the sea, into the region of·the Gadarenes.

G5561.3 N-APF χώρας (1x)
Ac 8:1 pervasively·into·all the regions of·Judea and Samaria.

G5561.3 N-DSF χώρᾳ (3x)
Lk 2:8 shepherds in the same region, camping·in·the·field
Ac 10:39 which he·did both in the region of·the Judeans and
Mt 4:16 ·ones who·are·fully·sitting in *the* region and shadow

G5561.3 N-GSF χώρας (4x)
Jn 11:55 many walked·up out of·the region to JeruSalem
Lk 3:1 ·tetrarch of·Jetur and the·region of·Trachonitis, and
Ac 13:49 ·thoroughly·carried throughout the whole region.
Mk 5:10 he·should·not dispatch them outside of·the region.

EG5561.3 (4x)
Ac 8:4 went·throughout *the regions* proclaiming the
Ac 8:40 *the region*, he·proclaimed·the·good·news in·all the
Ac 9:32 while·going throughout all *the regions*, it·happened
2Co 10:16 into the *regions* further·beyond yeu *for·us* to·

G5561.4 N-ASF χώραν (8x)
Lk 15:13 journeyed·abroad into a·distant country, and there
Lk 15:14 a·strong famine in that country, and he·himself
Lk 19:12 into a·distant country to·receive for·himself a·
Ac 12:20 on·account·of their country *needed* to·be·nourished
Ac 16:6 ·throughout Phrygia and the country of·Galatia,
Ac 18:23 going·throughout *the* country of·Galatia and
Ac 27:27 for·them to·be·heading·toward some country.
Mt 2:12 ·departed into their·own country through another

G5561.4 N-GSF χώρας (1x)
Lk 15:15 to·one of·the citizens of·that country, and *the*

G5562 χωρέω chōréō *v.* (10x)
Roots:G5561 Compare:G0700

G5562.1 V-PAI-3S χωρεῖ (1x)
Jn 8:37 my Redemptive-word does·not have·room in yeu.

G5562.1 V-PAI-3P χωροῦσιν (1x)
Mt 19:11 to·them, "Not all·men have·room·for this saying,

G5562.1 V-PAN χωρεῖν (1x)
Mk 2:2 such·for *them* no·longer to·have·room, not·even

G5562.1 V-PAP-NPF χωροῦσαι (1x)
Jn 2:6 of·the Judeans, having·room·for two or three ten·

G5562.1 V-AAM-2P χωρήσατε (1x)
2Co 7:2 Have·room·for us *in yeur hearts*; we·wronged no·

G5562.1 V-AAN χωρῆσαι (2x)
Jn 21:25 the world itself to·have·room·for the official·scrolls
2Pe 3:9 but·rather for·all to·have·room for repentance.

G5562.2 V-PAI-3S χωρεῖ (1x)
Mt 15:17 traversing into the mouth passes·through into the

G5562.3 V-PAM-3S χωρείτω (1x)
Mt 19:12 ·able to·accommodate *it*, let·him·accommodate *it*.

G5562.3 V-PAN χωρεῖν (1x)
Mt 19:12 heavens. The·one being·able to·accommodate *it*,

G5563 χωρίζω chōrízō *v.* (13x)
Roots:G5561 Compare:G0873 G3307 G0630 G4198 See:G0673 G1316

G5563.2 V-FAI-3S χωρίσει (1x)
Rm 8:35 What shall·separate us from the love of·the

G5563.2 V-PAM-3S χωριζέτω (2x)
Mt 19:6 yoked·together, a·man·of·clay† must·not separate."
Mk 10:9 yoked·together, a·man·of·clay† must·not separate."

G5563.2 V-PPM-3S χωριζέσθω (1x)
1Co 7:15 ·one departs, he·must·be·separated. The brother or

G5563.2 V-AAN χωρίσαι (1x)
Rm 8:39 created·thing shall·be·able to·separate us from the

G5563.2 V-API-3S-M χωρισθῇ (1x)
1Co 7:11 But even if she·is·separated, she·must·remain

G5563.2 V-APN-M χωρισθῆναι (1x)
1Co 7:10 a·wife *is* not to·be·separated from *her* husband.

G5563.2 V-RPP-NSM κεχωρισμένος (1x)
Heb 7:26 uncontaminated, having·been·separated from the

G5563.3 V-PMI-3S χωρίζεται (1x)
1Co 7:15 the non-trusting·one departs, he·must·be·separated.

G5563.3 V-PPN χωρίζεσθαι (1x)
Ac 1:4 them, "*Yeu·are* not to·be·departing from JeruSalem,

G5563.3 V-API-3S ἐχωρίσθη (1x)
Phm 1:15 ·of that, he·departed just·for a·short·while in·

G5563.4 V-PPN χωρίζεσθαι (1x)
Ac 18:2 ·for all the Jews to·be·deported out of·Rome).

G5563.4 V-APP-NSM-M χωρισθείς (1x)
Ac 18:1 came to Corinth, being·deported out of·Athens,

G5564 χωρίον chōríôn *n.* (10x)
Roots:G5561 G2444-3 Compare:G0068 G3977-1

G5564.2 N-NPN χωρία (1x)
Ac 28:7 there·were *some* open·fields inherently *belonging*

G5564.2 N-ASN χωρίον (6x)
Ac 1:18 in·fact, this·man procured an·open·field out of·the
Ac 1:19 such·for this open·field to·be·called in·their own
Ac 1:19 AqelDama, that·is, an·open·field of·blood.)
Ac 5:8 ·me whether yeu·sold·off the open·field for·so·much?
Mt 26:36 to an·open·field being·referred·to·as GethSemane,
Mk 14:32 Then they·come to an·open·field of·which the

G5564.2 N-GSN χωρίου (2x)
Jn 4:5 *(or·intoxicating)*, near·by to·the open·field that Jacob
Ac 5:3 and to·pilfer *part* of the price of·the open·field?

G5564.2 N-GPN χωρίων (1x)
Ac 4:34 ·subsisting *being* possessors of·open·fields or homes

G5565 χωρίς chōrís *adv.* (39x)
Roots:G5561 Compare:G1622 G4133

G5565.1 ADV χωρίς (29x)
Jn 1:3 through him, and apart·from him not·even one·thing
Jn 15:5 much fruit, because apart·from me, yeu·are·not able
Lk 6:49 ·clay† building a·home apart·from a·foundation on
Heb 7:7 And apart·from any contradiction, the lesser is·
Heb 7:20 ·*priest, but* not apart·from a·swearing·of·oath.
Heb 7:21 ·become *priests* apart·from a·swearing·of·oath, but
Heb 9:7 *went* alone, *but* not apart·from blood, which he·
Heb 9:18 *covenant* has·been·inaugurated apart·from blood.
Heb 9:22 blood. And apart·from a·pouring·out·of·blood,
Heb 11:6 But apart·from trust, *it·is* impossible to·fully·
Heb 11:40 us: that not apart·from us, should·they·be·made·
Heb 12:14 ·holiness, apart·from which not·even·one·man
Mt 13:34 in parables. And apart·from a·parable, he·was·not
Mt 14:21 about five·thousand men, apart·from women and
Mt 15:38 were four·thousand men, apart·from women and
Mk 4:34 he·was·not speaking to·them apart·from a·parable.
Rm 3:21 righteousness apart·from Torah-Law has·been·
Rm 3:28 by·a·trust apart·from works of·Torah-Law.
Rm 4:6 ·whom God reckons righteousness apart·from works,
Rm 7:8 all·manner·of longing. For apart·from Torah-Law,
Rm 7:9 And I·myself was·living apart·from Torah-Law once
Rm 10:14 how shall·they·hear apart·from one·officially·?

Jac 2:26 For just·as the body apart·from spirit is dead, in·
Jac 2:26 ·this·manner also, the trust apart·from the works is
1Co 11:11 neither *is* man apart·from woman, neither *is*
1Co 11:11 woman, neither *is* woman apart·from man, in *the*
2Co 11:28 *And* apart·from the·things *that·are* externally·
Eph 2:12 in that season yeu·were apart·from Anointed-One,
Phm 1:14 to·do not·even·one·thing apart·from your input,
G5565.2 ADV χωρίς (10x)
Jn 20:7 having·been·swathed in one place completely·apart.
Heb 4:15 *to·us, yet* completely·apart·from moral·failure.
Heb 9:28 (completely·apart·from a·reparation·for·moral·),
Heb 10:28 died completely·apart·from compassion upon two
Heb 12:8 But if yeu·are completely·apart·from corrective·
Jac 2:20 that the trust, completely·apart·from the works, is
Php 2:14 all·things completely·apart·from grumblings and
1Co 4:8 Yeu·reigned *as·kings* completely·apart·from us.
1Ti 2:8 ·holy hands, completely·apart·from wrath and
1Ti 5:21 these *instructions* completely·apart·from prejudice,

G5566 χῶρος chōrôs *n.* (1x)
See:G3047
G5566.2 N-ASM χῶρον (1x)
Ac 27:12 looking·out toward *the* southwest and northwest.

Ψψ - Psi

G5567 ψάλλω psállō *v.* (5x)
Compare:G0103 G5603 G5214 See:G5568 G5597 xLangEquiv:H2167
G5567.3 V-PAP-NPM ψάλλοντες (1x)
Eph 5:19 songs, singing and making·melody in yeur heart
G5567.4 V-FAI-1S ψαλῶ (3x)
Rm 15:9 *O·Yahweh,* and shall·make·song to·your name.
1Co 14:15 understanding also. I·shall·make·song with·the
1Co 14:15 and I·shall·make·song with·the understanding
G5567.4 V-PAM-3S ψαλλέτω (1x)
Jac 5:13 *Is* any in·a·cheerful·mood? Let·him·make·song.

G5568 ψαλμός psalmôs *n.* (8x)
Roots:G5567 Compare:G5603 G5215 xLangEquiv:H4210 xLangAlso:H2172
G5568.2 N-ASM ψαλμόν (1x)
1Co 14:26 ·together, each·one of·yeu has a·psalm, has an·
G5568.2 N-DPM ψαλμοῖς (2x)
Eph 5:19 speaking to·yeurselves in·psalms and hymns and
Col 3:16 and admonishing yeurselves in·psalms and hymns
G5568.3 N-DSM ψαλμῷ (1x)
Ac 13:33 as also it·has·been·written in the second Psalm,
G5568.3 N-DPM ψαλμοῖς (1x)
Lk 24:44 of·Moses, *the* Prophets, and *the* Psalms."
G5568.3 N-GPM ψαλμῶν (2x)
Lk 20:42 And David himself says in a·scroll of·Psalms,
Ac 1:20 "For it·has·been·written in a·scroll of·Psalms, "Let
EG5568.3 (1x)
Ac 13:35 Therefore he·says also in another *Psalm*, "You·

G5569 ψευδ•ά•δελφος psêudádêlphôs *n.* (2x)
Roots:G5571 G0080
G5569 N-APM ψευδαδέλφους (1x)
Gal 2:4 false·brothers who came·in·with·ulterior·motives
G5569 N-DPM ψευδαδέλφοις (1x)
2Co 11:26 at sea, *and in* dangers among false·brothers,

G5570 ψευδ•από•στολος psêudapóstôlôs *n.* (1x)
Roots:G5571 G0652
G5570 N-NPM ψευδαπόστολοι (1x)
2Co 11:13 ·men·as·these *are* false·ambassadors, workmen

G5571 ψευδής psêudḗs *adj.* (3x)
Roots:G5574 See:G5579 xLangAlso:H8267
G5571.1 A-APM ψευδεῖς (2x)
Ac 6:13 and they·set·up false witnesses saying, "This man·
Rv 2:2 and are not, and you·found them *to·be* false·ones.
G5571.1 A-DPM ψευδέσιν (1x)
Rv 21:8 and all the·ones *who·are* false, their portion *is* in

G5572 ψευδο•διδάσκαλος psêudôdidáskalôs *n.* (4x)
Roots:G5571 G1320 Compare:G1703 See:G0903 G2403
G5572.1 N-NPM ψευδοδιδάσκαλοι (1x)
2Pe 2:1 even as there·shall·be false·teachers among yeu,
EG5572.1 (3x)
2Pe 2:3 sayings, *false·teachers* for·whom judgment from·
2Pe 2:12 But these *false·teachers* (as natural, irrational
2Pe 2:19 *These false·teachers* who·are·promising liberty to·

G5573 ψευδο•λόγος psêudôlôgôs *adj.* (1x)
Roots:G5571 G3056
G5573.1 A-GPM ψευδολόγων (1x)
1Ti 4:2 in hypocrisy with·false·words, their·own conscience

G5574 ψεύδομαι psêúdômai *v.* (12x)
Compare:G0538 G4105 See:G5579 G5573 G5583
G5574.1 V-PMM-2P ψεύδεσθε (1x)
Jac 3:14 do·not boast·over and utter·lies against the truth.
G5574.2 V-PEI-1P ψευδόμεθα (1x)
1Jn 1:6 ·stroll·about in the darkness, we·do·lie, and do·not
G5574.2 V-PEI-3P ψεύδονται (1x)
Rv 3:9 Jews and are not, but·rather do·lie), behold, I·shall·
G5574.2 V-PEP-NPM ψευδόμενοι (1x)
Mt 5:11 should·persecute *yeu*, and by·lying, should·declare
G5574.2 V-PMM-2P ψεύδεσθε (1x)
Col 3:9 Do·not lie to one·another, after·having·already·
G5574.2 V-PNI-1S ψεύδομαι (4x)
Gal 1:20 ·yeu— Behold, in·the·sight of·God, I·do·not lie.)
Rm 9:1 in Anointed-One, I·do·not lie, with·my conscience
2Co 11:31 blessed to the ages, he·has·seen that I·do·not lie.
1Ti 2:7 truth in Anointed-One *and* do·not lie)— an·instructor
G5574.2 V-ADI-2S ἐψεύσω (1x)
Ac 5:4 in your heart? You·did·not lie to·men·of·clay†, but·
G5574.2 V-ADN ψεύσασθαι (2x)
Ac 5:3 completely·filled your heart for·you to·lie to·the Holy
Heb 6:18 *it·was* impossible for·God to·lie, we·may·have a·

G5575 ψευδο•μάρτυρ psêudómártyr *n.* (3x)
Roots:G5571 G3144 See:G5576
G5575 N-NPM ψευδομάρτυρες (2x)
Mt 26:60 eventually, two false·witnesses coming·alongside,
1Co 15:15 also, we·are·found *to·be* false·witnesses of·God,
G5575 N-GPM ψευδομαρτύρων (1x)
Mt 26:60 And with·many false·witnesses coming·alongside,

G5576 ψευδο•μαρτυρέω psêudômartyréō *v.* (6x)
Roots:G5575
G5576.1 V-IAI-3P ἐψευδομαρτύρουν (2x)
Mk 14:56 For many were·falsely·testifying against him, and·
Mk 14:57 ·up, someone was·falsely·testifying against him,
G5576.2 V-FAI-2S ψευδομαρτυρήσεις (2x)
Mt 19:18 ·not steal,'" "'You·shall·not bear·false·witness,'"
Rm 13:9 You·shall·not bear·false·witness. You·shall·not
G5576.2 V-AAS-2S ψευδομαρτυρήσῃς (2x)
Lk 18:20 ·not steal,' "You·may·not bear·false·witness,'
Mk 10:19 steal,' "You·may·not bear·false·witness,'

G5577 ψευδο•μαρτυρία psêudômartyría *n.* (2x)
Roots:G5575
G5577 N-NPF ψευδομαρτυρίαι (1x)
Mt 15:19 sexual·immoralities, thefts, false·testimonies, *and*
G5577 N-ASF ψευδομαρτυρίαν (1x)
Mt 26:59 were·seeking false·testimony against YeShua, that

G5578 ψευδο•προ•φήτης psêudôprôphḗtēs *n.* (11x)
Roots:G5571 G4396 Compare:G1114 G2215 G4108 G2342
G5578.1 N-NPM ψευδοπροφῆται (5x)
Mt 24:11 And many false·prophets shall·be·awakened and
Mt 24:24 shall·be·awakened, and false·prophets, and they·
Mk 13:22 and false·prophets shall·be·awakened and shall·
2Pe 2:1 But there·came·to·be false·prophets also among the
1Jn 4:1 because many false·prophets have·gone·out into the
G5578.1 N-ASM ψευδοπροφήτην (1x)
Ac 13:6 a·certain Jewish occultist, a·false·prophet, whose
G5578.1 N-DPM ψευδοπροφήταις (1x)
Lk 6:26 their fathers were·doing to·the false·prophets.
G5578.1 N-GPM ψευδοπροφητῶν (1x)
Mt 7:15 "And beware of the false·prophets, who do·come to
G5578.2 N-NSM ψευδοπροφήτης (2x)
Rv 19:20 and with it the Fiendish·False·Prophet, the·one
Rv 20:10 ·Beast and the Fiendish·False·Prophet *were·cast*,
G5578.2 N-GSM ψευδοπροφήτου (1x)
Rv 16:13 out of·the mouth of·the Fiendish·False·Prophet.

G5579 ψεῦδος psêûdôs *n.* (9x)
Roots:G5574 See:G5582
G5579.1 N-NSN ψεῦδος (2x)
1Jn 2:21 it, and that any lie is not birthed·from·out of·the
1Jn 2:27 (and is true, and is not a·lie, even just·as it·already·
G5579.1 N-ASN ψεῦδος (3x)
Jn 8:44 in him. Whenever he·should·speak a·lie, he·speaks
Rv 21:27 or committing an·abomination or a·lie; *none shall·*
Rv 22:15 and everyone being·fond·of and committing a·lie.
G5579.1 N-DSN ψεύδει (2x)
Rm 1:25 the truth of·God with the lie, and reverenced and
2Th 2:11 *from·truth* in·order·for them to·trust the lie,
G5579.2 N-ASN ψεῦδος (1x)
Eph 4:25 Therefore, putting·away the lying, "Each·man
G5579.2 N-GSN ψεύδους (1x)
2Th 2:9 with all power and signs and lying wonders,

G5580 ψευδό•χριστος pseûdóchristôs *n.* (2x)
Roots:G5571 G5547
G5580 N-NPM ψευδόχριστοι (2x)
Mt 24:24 For false·Anointed-Ones shall·be·awakened, and
Mk 13:22 For false·Anointed-Ones and false·prophets shall·

G5581 ψευδώ•νυμος pseûdṓnymôs *adj.* (1x)
Roots:G5571 G3686
G5581 A-GSF ψευδωνύμου (1x)
1Ti 6:20 ·theories of·the falsely·named knowledge—

G5582 ψεῦσμα pseûsma *n.* (1x)
Roots:G5574 See:G5579
G5582 N-DSN ψεύσματι (1x)
Rm 3:7 "For if by my lie, the truth of·God abounded to his

G5583 ψεύστης pseústēs *n.* (10x)
Roots:G5574
G5583 N-NSM ψεύστης (6x)
Jn 8:44 ·own *disposition*, because he·is a·liar and the father
Jn 8:55 ·not seen him,' I·shall·be a·liar like yeurselves. But·
Rm 3:4 but every man·of·clay† a·liar; just·as it·has·been·
1Jn 2:4 observantly·keeping his commandments is a·liar, and
1Jn 2:22 Who is the liar, if·not the·one who·contradicts·by·
1Jn 4:20 he·should·hate his brother, he·is a·liar, for the·one
G5583 N-NPM ψεῦσται (1x)
Tit 1:12 "Cretans *are* always liars, wicked wild·beasts, lazy
G5583 N-ASM ψεύστην (2x)
1Jn 1:10 ·not morally·failed, we·make him a·liar, and his
1Jn 5:10 God has·made *God* himself a·liar, because he·has·
G5583 N-DPM ψεύσταις (1x)
1Ti 1:10 ·with·men, for·kidnappers, for·liars, for·perjurers,

G5584 ψηλαφάω psēlapháō *v.* (4x)
Roots:G5567 Compare:G2345 See:G5586
G5584.2 V-PPP-DSN ψηλαφωμένῳ (1x)
Heb 12:18 a·mountain being·verified·by·touch, nor having·
G5584.2 V-AAI-3P ἐψηλάφησαν (1x)
1Jn 1:1 and our hands verified·by·touch, concerning the
G5584.2 V-AAM-2P ψηλαφήσατε (1x)
Lk 24:39 that I AM myself. Verify·by·touching me and see,
G5584.3 V-AAO-3P ψηλαφήσειαν (1x)
Ac 17:27 perhaps they·might·feel·around·and·about·for him

G5585 ψηφίζω psēphízō *v.* (2x)
Roots:G5586
G5585.2 V-PAI-3S ψηφίζει (1x)
Lk 14:28 ·indeed sit·down first *and* calculates the expense,
G5585.2 V-AAM-3S ψηφισάτω (1x)
Rv 13:18 the understanding, let·him·calculate the number

G5586 ψῆφος psēphôs *n.* (3x)
Roots:G5567 Compare:G3037 G0121-2 G1347
See:G5585 G5584 G2702
G5586.2 N-ASF ψῆφον (2x)
Rv 2:17 and I·shall·give him a·white pebble, also on the
Rv 2:17 pebble, also on the pebble, a·brand-new name
G5586.3 N-ASF ψῆφον (1x)
Ac 26:10 ·executed, I·voted a·black·pebble *against·them*.

G5587 ψιθυρισμός psithyrismós *n.* (1x)
Roots:G5586-1 See:G5574 G5588
G5587.1 N-NPM ψιθυρισμοί (1x)
2Co 12:20 backbitings, whisperings, puffed·up·minds, *and*

G5588 ψιθυριστής psithyristḗs *n.* (1x)
Roots:G5586-1 Compare:G1228 See:G5587
G5588 N-APM ψιθυριστάς (1x)
Rm 1:29 guile, *and* mischievousness; *being* whisperers,

G5589 ψιχίον psichíôn *n.* (3x)
Roots:G5567 G2444-3 Compare:G5596
G5589 N-GPN ψιχίων (3x)
Lk 16:21 to·be·stuffed·full with the little·crumbs, the·ones
Mt 15:27 puppies eat from the little·crumbs, the·ones falling
Mk 7:28 table eat from the young·children's little·crumbs."

G5590 ψυχή psychḗ *n.* (109x)
Roots:G5594 Compare:G4151 G4157 G0979 G0981
G2222 G4983 G2372 G3563 G1271 See:G5591
xLangEquiv:H5315 xLangAlso:H7307 H2416
EG5590.1 (3x)
Ac 27:21 Now with *every soul* subsisting a·long·while
2Pe 2:5 vigilantly·kept Noach, *the* eighth *soul on-board*,
2Pe 2:14 *unrighteous souls* having eyes exceedingly·full of·
G5590.2 N-NSF ψυχή (16x)
Jn 12:27 "Now my soul has·been·troubled, and what should·
Lk 1:46 Mariam declared, "My soul does·magnify Yahweh,
Lk 12:23 "The soul is more·than the physical·nourishment,
Ac 2:31 of·the Anointed-One, that his soul 'was·not left·
Ac 3:23 And it·shall·be *that* every soul who would·not hear
Ac 4:32 trusting, the heart and the soul was one. And not·
Ac 20:10 "Do·not be·in·a·commotion, for his soul is in him.
Heb 10:38 ·shrink·back, my soul does·not take·delight in
Mt 6:25 Is not·indeed the soul more·than the physical·
Mt 12:18 in whom my soul takes·delight. I·shall·place my
Mt 26:38 to·them, "My soul is exceedingly·grieved unto
Mk 14:34 to·them, "My soul is exceedingly·grieved unto
Rm 13:1 Let·every soul submit·itself to·the·superior
1Th 5:23 every·single·part of·yeur spirit, soul, and body be·
3Jn 1:2 to·be·healthy·and·sound, just·as your soul prospers.
Rv 16:3 And every living soul in the sea died.
G5590.2 N-NPF ψυχαί (3x)
Ac 2:41 three·thousand souls were·placed·alongside *them*.
Ac 27:37 *told*, we·were two·hundred *and* seventy·six souls.
1Pe 3:20 a·few (that·is eight souls) were·thoroughly·saved
G5590.2 N-VSF ψυχή (1x)
Lk 12:19 I·shall·declare to·my soul, "Soul, you·have many
G5590.2 N-ASF ψυχήν (31x)
Jn 10:11 shepherd lays·down his·own soul on·behalf of·the
Jn 10:15 and I·lay·down my soul on·behalf of·the sheep.
Jn 10:17 I·myself lay·down my soul in·order·that I·may·take
Jn 10:24 "How·long are·you·keeping our soul in·suspense?
Jn 12:25 his soul *(and·its·desires)* shall·completely·lose it;
Jn 12:25 it; and the·one considerately·hating his soul in this
Jn 13:37 I·shall·lay·down my soul on·behalf of·you."
Jn 13:38 "Shall·you·lay·down your soul on·behalf of·me?
Jn 15:13 someone should·lay·down his soul on·behalf of·his
Lk 2:35 ·straight·sword shall·go·through your·own soul also)
Lk 6:9 or to·do·bad, to·save a·soul or to·completely·destroy
Lk 12:20 they·are·demanding·back your soul from you.
Lk 14:26 sisters, and yet his·own soul also, he·is·not able to·
Ac 2:27 because you·shall·not forsake my soul in Hades,
Ac 20:24 neither do·I·hold my soul *as* precious to·myself,
Mt 2:20 the·ones seeking the little·child's soul have·died."
Mt 10:28 but not being·able to·kill the soul. But rather be·
Mt 10:28 ·able to·completely·destroy both soul and body in
Mt 16:26 ·suffer·the·damage·and·loss of·his·own soul? Or
Mt 20:28 to·attend, and to·give his soul *to·be* a·ransom for
Mk 3:4 ·Sabbaths, or to·do·bad? To·save a·soul, or to·kill?
Mk 8:36 ·suffer·the·damage·and·loss of·his·own soul?
Mk 10:45 to·attend, and to·give his soul *to·be* a·ransom for
Rm 2:9 upon every soul of·a·man·of·clay† performing the
Rm 11:3 alone am·all·that·is·left, and they·seek my soul."
Jac 5:20 of·his way shall·save a·soul from·out of·death, and·
2Pe 2:8 by day was·tormenting *his* righteous soul *over their*
1Co 15:45 Adam, came·into·being as a·living soul." The
2Co 1:23 God *for* a·witness upon my soul, that to·spare yeu,
1Jn 3:16 that·one laid·down his·own soul on·behalf of·us,
Rv 12:11 and they·did·not love their souls even·unto death.
G5590.2 N-APF ψυχάς (16x)
Lk 9:56 to·completely·destroy *the* souls of·men·of·clay†,
Lk 21:19 In yeur patient·endurance, yeu·procure yeur souls.
Ac 14:2 ·up and harmfully·affected the souls of·the Gentiles
Ac 14:22 reaffirming the souls of·the disciples, exhorting
Ac 15:24 (dislodging·and·disturbing yeur souls, saying, '*It*·
Ac 15:26 having·handed·over their souls on·behalf of·the
Jac 1:21 the·one being·able to·save yeur souls.
1Pe 1:22 *As·such*, having·cleansed yeur souls in the
1Pe 4:19 ·place·the·direct·care·of their·own souls *to·him* in
2Pe 2:14 ·failure, while·beguiling unstable souls, having a·
1Th 2:8 but·rather also our·own souls, on·account·that yeu·
1Jn 3:16 to·lay·down *our·own* souls on·behalf of·the
Rv 6:9 ·Altar the souls of·the·ones having·been·slaughtered
Rv 8:9 ·ones in the sea, the·ones having souls) died; and the
Rv 18:13 "and bodies and souls of·men·of·clay†.
Rv 20:4 *I·saw* the souls of·the·ones having·been·beheaded
G5590.2 N-DSF ψυχῇ (7x)
Lk 12:19 Then I·shall·declare to·my soul, "Soul, you·have
Lk 12:22 ·yeu, do·not be·anxious·about yeur soul, what yeu·
Ac 2:43 reverent·fear·and·awe came upon·every soul, and
Mt 6:25 ·yeu, do·not be·anxious·about yeur soul, what yeu·
Mt 22:37 heart, and with all your soul, and with all your
Php 1:27 spirit, with·one soul struggling·together for·the
Php 2:30 ·the·personal·warning·of the soul, in·order·that he·
G5590.2 N-DPF ψυχαῖς (3x)
Ac 7:14 and all his kinsfolk, in *all*, seventy five souls.'
Heb 12:3 ·become·fatigued, being·faint in·yeur souls.
Mt 11:29 and yeu·shall·find a·rest·break for·yeur souls.
G5590.2 N-GSF ψυχῆς (12x)
Lk 10:27 and from·out of·all your soul, and from·out of·all
Ac 27:22 ·be not·even·one loss of·soul from·among yeu,
Heb 4:12 ·penetrating even·unto a·dividing of·soul and spirit
Heb 6:19 we·have as an·anchor of·the soul, both immovably·
Heb 10:39 but·rather of·a·trust to a·preservation *of·the·*soul.
Mt 16:26 ·man·of·clay† shall·give in·exchange for·his soul?
Mk 8:37 a·man·of·clay† shall·give in·exchange for·his soul?
Mk 12:30 and from·out of·all your soul, and from·out of·all
Mk 12:33 and from·out of·all the soul, and from·out of·all
Rm 16:4 their·own necks on·behalf of·my soul, for·whom
1Pe 2:11 longings, which strategically·war against the soul.
Rv 18:14 ·fruit of·the longing of·your soul went·away from
G5590.2 N-GPF ψυχῶν (5x)
Ac 27:10 and of·the sailing·ship, but·yet also of·our souls."
Heb 13:17 ·themselves stay·alert on·behalf of·yeur souls, as
1Pe 1:9 the end of·yeur trust, *the* Salvation of·*yeur·*souls.
1Pe 2:25 to·the Shepherd and Overseer of·yeur souls.
2Co 12:15 ·spent on·behalf of·yeur souls, even·though the·
G5590.3 N-ASF ψυχήν (9x)
Lk 9:24 to·save his soul's·desire shall·completely·lose it, but
Lk 9:24 ·completely·lose his soul's·desire for·my cause, the·
Lk 17:33 to·save his soul's·desire shall·completely·lose it;
Mt 10:39 finding his soul's·desire shall·completely·lose it,
Mt 10:39 the·one completely·losing his soul's·desire, for·my
Mt 16:25 to·save his soul's·desire shall·completely·lose it,
Mt 16:25 should·completely·lose his soul's·desire, for·my
Mk 8:35 to·save his soul's·desire shall·completely·lose it, but
Mk 8:35 ·completely·lose his soul's·desire for·my cause and
G5590.3 N-GSF ψυχῆς (2x)
Eph 6:6 doing the will of·God out of·a·soul's·desire
Col 3:23 be·working *it* out of·a·soul's·desire as to·the Lord
EG5590.3 (1x)
Lk 17:33 ·completely·lose his *soul's·desire* shall·preserve it.

G5591 ψυχικός psychikós *adj.* (6x)
Roots:G5590 Compare:G4152 G5446
G5591.1 A-NSM ψυχικός (1x)
1Co 2:14 But a·soulish man·of·clay† does·not accept the·
G5591.1 A-NSF ψυχική (1x)
Jac 3:15 from·above, but·rather *is* earthly, soulish, demonic.
G5591.1 A-NSN ψυχικόν (3x)
1Co 15:44 It·is·sown a·soulish body; it·is·awakened a·
1Co 15:44 a·spiritual body. There·is a·soulish body, and
1Co 15:46 first, but·rather the soulish, then·afterward the
G5591.1 A-NPM ψυχικοί (1x)
Jud 1:19 ·along·sectarian·or·partisan·lines, soulish, not

G5592 ψῦχος psŷchôs *n.* (3x)
Roots:G5594 See:G5593
G5592 N-NSN ψῦχος (1x)
Jn 18:18 ·made a·fire·of·coals because it·was cold, and they·
G5592 N-ASN ψῦχος (1x)
Ac 28:2 ·of the assaulting rain, and on·account·of the cold.
G5592 N-DSN ψύχει (1x)
2Co 11:27 in fastings many·times, in cold and nakedness.

G5593 ψυχρός psychrós *adj.* (4x)
Roots:G5592
G5593 A-NSM ψυχρός (3x)
Rv 3:15 works, that you·are neither cold nor fervently·hot.

Rv 3:15 ·hot. Oh·that you·would·be cold or fervently·hot!
Rv 3:16 ·are lukewarm, and neither cold nor fervently·hot,
G5593 A-GSN ψυχροῦ (1x)
Mt 10:42 of·these little·ones a·cup of·cold *water* to·drink

G5594 ψύχω psýchō *v.* (1x)
Compare:G4154 G0108-2 G5445-5 See:G5590 G5592
G5594.1 V-2FPI-3S ψυγήσεται (1x)
Mt 24:12 the love of·the many shall·be·chilled.

G5595 ψωμίζω psōmízō *v.* (2x)
Roots:G5596
G5595.2 V-PAM-2S ψώμιζε (1x)
Rm 12:20 should·hunger, provide·some·food·for him; if he·
G5595.2 V-AAS-1S ψωμίσω (1x)
1Co 13:3 And if·ever I·should·provide·some·food·for *the*

G5596 ψωμίον psōmíôn *n.* (4x)
Roots:G5597 G2444-3 Compare:G5589
G5596 N-ASN ψωμίον (4x)
Jn 13:26 that·man to·whom I·shall·hand the morsel, *with* I·
Jn 13:26 And dipping the morsel, he·gave *it* to·Judas
Jn 13:27 ·time, *along* with the morsel, the Adversary-Accuser
Jn 13:30 Accordingly, after·receiving the morsel, that·one

G5597 ψώχω psṓchō *v.* (1x)
Compare:G2352 G3039 See:G5567 G1813
G5597.2 V-PAP-NPM ψώχοντες (1x)
Lk 6:1 ·grain, and they·were·eating by·rubbing *them* in·their

Ωω - Omega

G5598 Ω Ō *n.* (4x)
ת ṯav [Hebrew last letter]
Compare:G5586 G0001 xLangAlso:H8419-1
G5598.1 N-LI Ω (4x)
Rv 1:8 "I AM the Alpha and the Omega, beginning and end,"
Rv 1:11 "I AM the Alpha and the Omega, the First and the
Rv 21:6 I AM the Alpha and the Omega, the beginning and
Rv 22:13 I AM the Alpha and the Omega, beginning and end

G5599 ὦ ō̂ *inj.* (17x)
xLangAlso:H1929
G5599 INJ ὦ (17x)
Lk 9:41 Jesus declared, "O distrusting and perverse
Lk 24:25 declared to them, "O stupid·ones, and slow in·the
Ac 1:1 In·fact, the first account I·made, O TheoPhilus, *was*
Ac 13:10 declared, "O *you·are* full of·all guile and all
Ac 18:14 mischievous·deed according·to reason, O Jews, I·
Ac 27:21 ·them, declared, "O Men, in·fact it·was·necessary
Gal 3:1 O stupid Galatians, who cast·an·evil·eye·on yeu to·
Mt 15:28 YeShua declared to·her, "O woman, great *is* your
Mt 17:17 YeShua declared, "O distrusting and perverse
Mk 9:19 answering him, he·says, "O distrusting generation,
Rm 2:1 — you·are without·exoneration, O man·of·clay†!
Rm 2:3 And do·you·reckon this, O man·of·clay† (the·one
Rm 9:20 As·a·matter·of·fact, O man·of·clay†, who are you·
Rm 11:33 O *the* depth of·wealth, both of·*the*·wisdom and
Jac 2:20 But do·you·want to·know, O empty man·of·clay†,
1Ti 6:11 But you, O clay·man† of·God, flee from·these·
1Ti 6:20 O TimoThy, vigilantly·keep the charge·fully·

G5600 ὦ ō̂ *v.* (67x)
ᾖς ē̂s [oblique forms]
ᾖ ē̂
ἦτε ē̂tê [2nd plural]
Roots:G1510 See:G2268-1
G5600.1 V-PXS-1S ὦ (1x)
Jn 9:5 Inasmuch·as I·should·be in the world, I·am a·light of·
G5600.1 V-PXS-1P ὦμεν (1x)
2Co 1:9 in·order·that we·may·not be having·reliance upon
G5600.1 V-PXS-2P ἦτε (2x)
Rm 11:25 lest yeu·should·be full·of·notions personally·about
2Co 13:9 ·be·weak, but yeu·yeurselves should·be powerful.
G5600.1 V-PXS-3S ᾖ (21x)
Jn 3:2 that you·yourself do unless God should·be with him."
Jn 6:65 to me, unless it·should·be having·been·given to·him
Lk 10:6 ·fact, if a·son of·peace should·be there, yeur peace
Lk 11:34 whenever your eye should·be clear·and·focused,
Lk 11:34 but whenever *your eye* should·be evil, your body
Ac 5:38 work should·be birthed·from·out of·men·of·clay†, it·
Mt 6:22 if your eye should·be clear·and·focused, your
Mt 6:23 But if your eye should·be evil, your whole body
Mt 10:13 And if, in·fact the home should·be worthy, *let* yeur
Mt 10:13 upon it, but if it·should·not be worthy, *let* yeur
Mt 24:28 For wherever the corpse should·be, there the eagles
1Co 1:10 and *that* there·may·not be severing·schisms among
1Co 2:5 in·order·that yeur trust should·not be in *the* wisdom
1Co 7:36 ·daughter, if she·should·be past·her·prime and
1Co 12:25 ·order·that there·should·not be a·severing·schism
1Co 14:28 But if there·should·not be one·who·thoroughly·,
1Co 16:4 And if it·should·be appropriate *for* me·also to·
2Co 1:17 ·to flesh, that with me there·should·be the "Yes,
Eph 5:27 such·thing, but·rather that she·should·be holy and
Phm 1:14 ·good·response should·not be as·according·to a·
1Jn 1:4 our joy should·be having·been·completely·filled.
G5600.1 V-PXS-3P ὦσιν (4x)
Mk 3:14 twelve *ambassadors*, that they·should·be with him,
Jac 2:15 *being* naked and should·be being·deficient of·the
Tit 3:14 ·occasions, in·order·that they·may·not be unfruitful.
1Co 7:29 … even the·ones having wives should·be as not
EG5600.1 (2x)
Mt 15:5 as·a·result of·me, whatever *it·should·be*, *it·is now* a·
Mk 7:11 as·a·result of·me, whatever *it·should·be*, that·thing

G5600.2 V-PXS-1S ὦ (1x)
Php 2:28 yeu·may·rejoice, and·*that*·I may·be less·grieved.
G5600.2 V-PXS-1P ὦμεν (2x)
2Co 13:7 *that* we·ourselves may·be as·though disqualified.
Eph 4:14 in·order·that we·may no·longer be infants, who·
G5600.2 V-PXS-2P ἦτε (6x)
Jn 14:3 ·that where I AM, *there* yeu·yeurselves also may·be.
Jac 1:4 *her* complete work, that yeu·may·be complete and
Php 1:10 , in·order·that yeu·may·be judged·sincere and
1Co 1:10 *that* yeu·may·be having·been·completely·reformed
1Co 5:7 in·order·that yeu·may·be a·fresh·new lump·of·
2Co 9:3 yeu·may·be having·been·personally·prepared.
G5600.2 V-PXS-3S ᾖ (19x)
Jn 3:27 ·thing, unless it·may·be having·been·given to·him
Jn 9:31 but·rather if any·man may·be reverent·of·God, and
Jn 16:24 yeur joy may·be having·been·completely·filled.
Jn 17:26 the love with·which you·loved me may·be in them,
Lk 14:8 ·man·than you may·be having·been·called·forth by
Gal 5:10 yeu shall·bear the judgment, whoever he·may·be.
Mt 6:4 so·that your merciful·act may·be in private. And your
Mt 20:4 and whatever may·be right I·shall·give to·yeu.
Mt 20:7 the vineyard, and whatever may·be right, *that* yeu·
Mk 5:18 was·imploring him that he·may·be with him.
Rm 9:27 number of·the Sons of·IsraEl may·be as the sand of·
Jac 5:15 and·if he·may·be having·committed moral·failures
Tit 1:9 ·to the instruction in·order·that he·may·be able also
1Co 7:34 ·things of·the Lord in·order·that she·may·be holy,
1Co 15:28 in·him, in·order·that God may·be all in all.
2Co 4:7 surpassing·excellence of·the power may·be of·God,
1Ti 4:15 continual·advancement may·be apparent among all.
2Ti 3:17 ·that the clay·man† of·God may·be fully·developed,
2Jn 1:12 our joy may·be having·been·completely·fulfilled.
G5600.2 V-PXS-3P ὦσιν (8x)
Jn 17:11 ·have·given to·me, in·order·that they·may·be one,
Jn 17:19 ·themselves also may·be having·been·made·holy in
Jn 17:21 "in·order·that they·all may·be one, just·as you,
Jn 17:21 "in·order·that they also may·be one in us— "in·
Jn 17:22 to·them— "in·order·that they·may·be one, just·as
Jn 17:23 "in·order·that they·may·be having·been·made· in
Jn 17:24 to·me, I·want that they·also may·be with me where
1Ti 5:7 in·order·that they·may·be above·all·blame·and·.

G5601 Ὠβήδ Ōbḗd *n/p.* (3x)
עוֹבֵד ʻôḇeḏ [Hebrew]
Roots:H5744
G5601.2 N/P-PRI Ὠβήδ (3x)
Lk 3:32 *son* of·Jesse, *son* of·Obed, *son* of·BoAz, *son* of·
Mt 1:5 , and BoAz begot Obed (birthed·from·out of·Ruth),
Mt 1:5 (birthed·from·out of·Ruth), and Obed begot Jesse.

G5602 ὧ•δε hō̂dê *adv.* (61x)
Roots:G3592 xLangAlso:H6311
G5602.1 ADV ὧδε (59x)
Jn 6:9 "There·is a·little·boy here, who has five barley loaves·
Jn 6:25 "Rabbi, when did·you·come here?"
Jn 11:21 "Lord, if you·were here, my brother would not
Jn 11:32 "Lord, if you·were here, my brother would not
Jn 20:27 "Bring your finger here, and see my hands.
Lk 4:23 in CaperNaum, do also here in your·own fatherland.
Lk 9:12 ·of·food, because we·are here in a·desolate place.
Lk 9:27 there·are some of·the·ones standing here, who no,
Lk 9:33 it·is good for·us to·be here, and we·should·make
Lk 9:41 and shall·put·up·with yeu? Escort your son here!"
Lk 11:31 one·of·larger·stature·than Solomon *is* here.
Lk 11:32 behold, one·of·larger·stature·than Jonah *is* here.
Lk 14:21 of·the city, and bring·in here the helplessly·poor,
Lk 17:21 ·even shall·they·declare, 'Behold, here *it·is*!' or,
Lk 17:23 they·shall·declare to·yeu, 'Behold, here *he·is*!' or
Lk 19:27 over them, bring *them* here, and fully·slaughter
Lk 22:38 "Lord, behold, here *are* two daggers.
Lk 23:5 in all Judea, beginning from Galilee unto here."
Lk 24:6 He·is not here, but·rather is·awakened.
Ac 9:14 And here, he·has authority personally·from the
Ac 9:21 this name, and·also had·come here for that *same*·

Heb 7:8 And here and·now, in·fact, are tithes that dying
Heb 13:14 For here we·have no continuing city, but·rather
Mt 8:29 O·Son of·God? Did·you·come here to·torment us
Mt 12:6 one·greater·than the Sanctuary·Courtyard is here.
Mt 12:41 behold, one·of·larger·stature·than Jonah is here.
Mt 12:42 one·of·a·larger·stature·than Solomon is here.
Mt 14:8 she·replied, "Give me here the head of·John the
Mt 14:17 "We·do·not have anything here except five loaves·
Mt 14:18 But he·declared, "Bring them here to·me."
Mt 16:28 there·are some of·the·ones standing here who, no,
Mt 17:4 "Lord, it·is good for·us to·be here. If you·want, we·
Mt 17:4 we·should·make three tabernacles here: one for·
Mt 17:17 shall·I·put·up·with yeu? Bring him here to·me."
Mt 20:6 to·them, 'Why·do yeu·stand here the whole day idle
Mt 22:12 'O·associate, how did·you·enter here not having
Mt 24:2 no, there·should·not be·left here a·stone upon a·
Mt 24:23 to·yeu, 'Behold, here is the Anointed-One!' or
Mt 26:38 unto death. Yeu·remain here and keep·alert with
Mt 28:6 He·is not here, for he·is·awakened, just·as he·
Mk 6:3 Simon? And are not his sisters here alongside us?
Mk 8:4 ·men full with·bread, here in a·barren·wilderness?
Mk 9:1 that there·are some of·the·ones standing here, who,
Mk 9:5 it·is good for·us to·be here. And we·should·make
Mk 11:3 And immediately, he·shall·dispatch him here."
Mk 13:21 to·yeu, 'Behold, here is the Anointed-One!' or,
Mk 14:32 disciples, "Yeu·sit·down here, until I·should·pray.
Mk 14:34 unto death. Yeu·remain here and keep·alert."
Mk 16:6 He·was·awakened. He·is not here. See the place
Jac 2:3 "You·yourself must·sit·down here in·a·good·place,"
Jac 2:3 over·there," or "Sit·down here under my footstool,"
Col 4:9 ·known to·yeu all·things, the·ones occurring here.
Rv 4:1 me, saying, "Walk·up here, and I·shall·show you
Rv 11:12 heaven saying to·them, "Walk·up here." And they·
Rv 13:10 with a·dagger. Here is the patient·endurance and
Rv 13:18 Here is the wisdom.
Rv 14:12 Here is a·patient·endurance of·the holy·ones.
Rv 14:12 of·the holy·ones. Here are the·ones observantly·
Rv 17:9 "Here is the mind·(or·understanding), the·one

EG5602.1 (1x)

Ac 16:37 way, but·rather coming ***here*** themselves, let·them·

G5602.2 ADV ὧδε (1x)

Mt 24:23 or 'There he·is!' yeu·should·not trust it.

G5603 ᾠδή ōdḗ *n.* (7x)

Roots:G0103 Compare:G5215 G5568 G0779-1 xLangEquiv:H7892

G5603.2 N-ASF ᾠδήν (5x)

Rv 5:9 And they·sing a·brand-new song, saying, "You·are
Rv 14:3 as singing a·brand-new song in·the·sight of·the
Rv 14:3 ·even·one·man was·able to·learn the song except the
Rv 15:3 And they·sing the song of·Moses, a·slave of·God,
Rv 15:3 a·slave of·God, and the song of·the Lamb, saying,

G5603.2 N-DPF ᾠδαῖς (2x)

Eph 5:19 in·psalms and hymns and spiritual songs, singing
Col 3:16 in·psalms and hymns and spiritual songs, singing

G5604 ὠδίν ōdín *n.* (4x)

See:G3601 xLangAlso:H2256

G5604.1 N-APF ὠδῖνας (1x)

Ac 2:24 raised·up, loosing the pangs of·Death, because·

G5604.2 N-NSF ὠδίν (1x)

1Th 5:3 them, just·as having the birth·pang, the·one in

G5604.2 N-GPF ὠδίνων (2x)

Mt 24:8 But all these are the beginning of·birth·pangs.
Mk 13:8 These are the beginnings of·birth·pangs.

G5605 ὠδίνω ōdínō *v.* (3x)

Roots:G5604 Compare:G3449

G5605 V-PAI-1S ὠδίνω (1x)

Gal 4:19 for·whom I·experience·birthing·pain again even·

G5605 V-PAP-NSF ὠδίνουσα (2x)

Gal 4:27 the·one not experiencing·birthing·pain, because
Rv 12:2 she·yelled·out experiencing·birthing·pain and being·

G5606 ὦμος ṓmôs *n.* (2x)

Roots:G5342 Compare:G5606-1 xLangEquiv:H3802 xLangAlso:H4546

G5606 N-APM ὤμους (2x)

Lk 15:5 ·finding it, he·puts it upon his shoulders, rejoicing.
Mt 23:4 and put them on the shoulders of·the men·of·clay†,

G5607 ὤν ṓn *v.* (159x)

οὖσα ôûsa [feminine]

ὄν ṓn [neuter]

Roots:G1510 Compare:G5225 See:G2071-2

G5607.1 V-PXP-ASF οὖσαν (5x)

Lk 13:16 And this·one, being a·daughter of·AbRaham,
Ac 13:1 among the Called·Out·citizenry being in Antioch,
Ac 17:16 upon·observing the city being utterly·idolatrous.
Ac 19:35 of·the Ephesians is·being temple·custodian of·the
Rm 16:1 our sister, being an·attendant of·the Called·Out·

G5607.1 V-PXP-ASM ὄντα (11x)

Jn 1:48 ·out·for you, I·saw you being under the fig·tree.
Lk 12:28 ·manner enrobes the grass, today being in the field,
Lk 22:3 being·surnamed IsCariot, being from·among the
Lk 23:7 to HerOd·AntiPas, himself being also at JeruSalem in
Ac 8:23 For I·clearly·see you being in a·gall of·bitterness
Ac 24:10 ·among many years of·you being a·judge to·this
Ac 26:3 especially with·you being an·expert in·all customs
Heb 3:2 being trustworthy to·the·one producing him, as also
Mt 6:30 grass of·the field, today being here, and tomorrow
2Co 8:22 we·tested·and·proved many·times being diligent in
1Ti 1:13 the·one previously being a·reviler, and a·persecutor,

G5607.1 V-PXP-APN ὄντα (1x)

Ac 7:12 But after·hearing·of there·being grain in Egypt,

G5607.1 V-PXP-APM ὄντας (9x)

Ac 9:2 disciples of·The Way, whether being men or women,
Ac 16:3 ·of the Jews, the·ones being in those places, for
Ac 22:5 Damascus, bringing the·ones being there, having·
Ac 28:17 Paul called·together the·ones being foremost of·the
Rm 16:11 the household of·Narcissus, the·ones being in the
Php 1:7 ·news, yeu all are·being partners·together with·me
Eph 2:5 even with us being dead in·the trespasses, he·made·
Col 2:13 although yeu were dead, being in the trespasses
2Ti 2:19 "" Yahweh already·knows the·ones being his."' And

G5607.1 V-PXP-DSF οὔσῃ (4x)

Lk 2:5 his espoused wife, being swellingly·pregnant.
Ac 24:24 with·his wife Drusilla (herself·being a·Judean),
1Co 1:2 ·Out·citizenry of·God, the·one being in Corinth—
2Co 1:1 ·Out·citizenry of·God, the·one being at Corinth,

G5607.1 V-PXP-DSM ὄντι (3x)

Rm 4:10 was·it·reckoned? With·him being in circumcision,
Rm 7:23 to·the Law of·Moral·Failure, the·one being in my
Rm 12:3 ·given to·me, I·say to·every·man being among yeu,

G5607.1 V-PXP-DPM οὖσιν (8x)

Ac 16:21 ·personally·accept, neither to·do, being Romans."
Ac 20:34 tended to·my needs and to·the·ones being with me.
Mk 2:26 he·gave also to·the·ones being together with·him?
Rm 1:7 To·all the·ones being in Rome, beloved of·God,
Rm 8:28 for·the·ones being called·forth according·to his
Php 1:1 Anointed-One Jesus, to·the·ones being at Philippi,
2Co 1:1 with·all the holy·ones, the·ones being in all Achaia:
Eph 1:1 To·the holy·ones being in Ephesus, and to·those·

G5607.1 V-PXP-GSN ὄντος (1x)

Ac 7:5 him, even with·there·not being a·child born to·him.

G5607.1 V-PXP-GSF οὔσης (5x)

Jn 4:9 ·drink personally·from me, being a·Samaritan woman
Jn 20:1 week at·the·watch·of·dawn (while·being still dark),
Jn 20:19 In·due·course, with·it·being almost early·evening
Ac 9:38 Now being as Lod was near to·Joppa, and after·
Mk 11:11 even·now with·the hour being late, he·went·out

G5607.1 V-PXP-GSM ὄντος (12x)

Jn 5:13 carefully·slipped·away, with·a·crowd being in the
Lk 14:32 And·if·not, with·the·other being yet far·away,
Lk 22:53 With·me being each day with yeu in the Sanctuary·
Ac 14:13 that·offers·sacrifices, the·one being before their city,
Ac 21:8 ·good·news·of·redemption, being from·among the
Ac 27:2 of·ThessaloNica) being together with·us.
Ac 27:9 and with·the voyage being even·now precarious
Mk 8:1 those days (with·the·crowd being immense and not
Mk 14:3 And with·him being in BethAny in the home of·
Mk 14:66 Now with·Peter being down·below in the
Rm 5:13 ·failure is·not imputed with·there being no law.
Eph 2:20 with·Jesus Anointed himself being the chief·corner

G5607.1 V-PXP-GPN ὄντων (1x)

Ac 19:36 Now·then, with·these·things being indisputable, it·

G5607.1 V-PXP-GPF οὐσῶν (1x)

1Th 2:14 the·ones in Judea being in Anointed-One YeShua.

G5607.1 V-PXP-GPM ὄντων (5x)

Jn 21:11 ; and·yet with·there·being so·vast·a·quantity, the
Heb 8:4 be a·priest·that·offers·a·sacrifice, being that there·are
Rm 5:6 of·irreverent·men (with·us being without·vigor).
Rm 5:8 how·that yet, with·us being full·of·moral·failure,
1Ti 2:2 of·kings and all the·ones being in superior·rank, in·

G5607.1 V-PXP-NSF οὖσα (4x)

Lk 8:43 And a·woman being with a·flow of·blood for twelve
Ac 5:17 the·ones together with·him (being the denomination
Mk 5:25 And there·was a·certain woman being with a·flow
1Co 8:7 and their conscience (being weak) is·tarnished.

G5607.1 V-PXP-NSM ὤν (48x)

Jn 1:18 only·begotten Son, the·one being in the bosom of·
Jn 3:4 ·of·clay† able to·be·born, being an·agedly·old·man?
Jn 3:13 the Son of·Clay·Man†, the·one being in the heaven.
Jn 3:31 up·above all. The·one being birthed·from·out·of·the
Jn 4:9 "How·is·it that you, being a·Jew, request some to·
Jn 6:46 Father, except the·one being personally·from God;
Jn 6:71 ·about·to·hand him over, being one from·among the
Jn 7:50 Jesus by·night and being one from·among them)
Jn 8:47 The·one being birthed·from·out·of·God hears the
Jn 9:25 ·thing I·do·personally·know, how·that being blind,
Jn 10:12 not even being a·shepherd over·that·which are not
Jn 10:33 And because you, being a·man·of·clay†, make
Jn 11:49 named Caiaphas, being the designated·high·priest
Jn 11:51 ·self, but·rather being the designated·high·priest that
Jn 12:17 BethAny was·testifying, the·one being with him
Jn 18:26 ·high·priest, being a·kinsman of·him·whose
Jn 18:37 to·the·truth. Everyone being birthed·from·out·of·the
Jn 19:38 the·one from Arimathaea) being a·disciple of·Jesus
Lk 3:23 about thirty years·of·age, being a·son of·Joseph
Lk 11:23 "The·one not being with me is against me, and the·
Lk 24:6 how he·spoke to·yeu while·still being in Galilee,
Lk 24:44 I·spoke to yeu, while·still being together with·yeu:
Ac 18:24 by·birth), an·eloquent man being powerful in the
Heb 1:3 His Son (being the radiant·offshoot of·his·glory and
Heb 5:8 Even·though being a·Son, he·learned the attentive·
Gal 2:3 Titus (the·one together with·me being a·Greek) was·
Gal 4:1 ·one·thing from·a·slave, though being lord of·all,
Gal 6:3 ·himself to·be something, being not·even·one·thing,
Mt 1:19 Joseph her husband, being a·righteous man and not
Mt 12:30 "The·one not being with me is against me, and the·
Mk 13:16 And the·one being in the field must·not return to
Mk 14:43 Judas comes·openly, being one of·the twelve,
Rm 9:5 is the Anointed-One, the·one being God over all,
Rm 11:17 and you personally, being a·wild·olive·tree, were·
2Th 2:5 ·yeu·not remember, that while·being yet alongside
Tit 3:11 ·subverted and morally·fails, being self-condemned.
1Co 9:19 For though being free from·among all men·of·clay†
1Co 9:21 (not being without·Torah-Law to·God, but·yet I·
2Co 8:9 Lord Jesus Anointed, how·that being wealthy, on·
2Co 11:31 Lord Jesus Anointed, the·one being blessed to·the
Eph 2:4 But God, being wealthy in mercy, on·account·of his
Phm 1:9 you, I Paul, being such as an·old·man and now
Rv 1:4 from the·one (the·one being, and the·one who·was,
Rv 1:8 says the Lord, "the·one being, and the·one who·was,
Rv 4:8 the·one who·was, and the·one being, and the·one
Rv 5:5 Behold the Lion, the·one being from·among the tribe
Rv 11:17 God Almighty, the·one being, and the·one that·
Rv 16:5 righteous, O·Yahweh, the·one being, and the·one

G5607.1 V-PXP-NPN ὄντα (2x)

Jac 3:4 Behold also the sailing·ships, being so·vast, and are

1Co 12:12 members of·the one body (being many) are one
G5607.1 V-PXP-NPF οὖσαι (1x)
Rm 13:1 from God; and the·ones being authorities, they·are
G5607.1 V-PXP-NPM ὄντες (25x)
Jn 9:40 heard these·things, the·ones being with him, and
Jn 11:31 So·then the Judeans, the·ones being with her in the
Lk 6:3 ·was·hungry, him and·also the·ones being with him;
Lk 20:36 and are the·Sons of·God, being the·Sons of·the
Lk 23:12 for they·were·previously being in hostility among
Ac 11:1 and the brothers, the·ones being in Judea, heard that
Ac 15:32 Judas and Silas, being prophets also themselves,
Ac 19:31 ·men of·the chiefs·of·Asia, being friends with·him
Ac 22:9 "And the·ones being together with·me, in·fact, did·
Ac 28:25 And being discordant among one·another, they·
Heb 13:3 as yeurselves also being *with·them* in body.
Mt 7:11 if yeu·yeurselves, being evil, personally·know·
Mt 12:34 O·offspring of·vipers, being evil, in·what·way are·
Rm 5:10 For if, while·being enemies, we·are·reconciled to·
Rm 8:5 For the·ones being according·to flesh contemplate
Rm 8:8 And the·ones being in flesh are·not able to·satisfy
2Pe 1:18 from·out of·heaven, while·being together with·him
2Pe 2:11 whereas angels, being greater·in strength and
1Th 5:8 But we·ourselves, being of·day, should·be·sober,
Tit 1:16 works they·deny *him*, being abhorrent, obstinate,
2Co 5:4 For even the·ones being in the bodily·tent do·groan,
2Co 11:19 with·pleasure, *yeurselves* being prudent.
Eph 2:13 yeu·yeurselves, once being at·a·distance, are·
Col 4:11 of·God *are* the·ones being from·among *the*
1Ti 3:10 then while·being without·any·charge·of·wrong· let·
EG5607.1 (1x)
Lk 3:23 ·by·law), *as·well·as being a·grandson of·Mariam's*
G5607.2 V-PXP-ASF οὖσαν (1x)
Eph 4:18 of·God through the ignorance existing in them, on·
G5607.2 V-PXP-APN ὄντα (4x)
Rm 4:17 ·forth the·things not existing as·though existing),
Rm 4:17 ·forth the·things not existing as·though existing),
1Co 1:28 even the·things not existing, in·order·that he·
1Co 1:28 he·should·fully·render·inert the·things existing,
G5607.2 V-PXP-APM ὄντας (1x)
Col 1:21 once existing *as·those* having·been·utterly·alienated
G5607.2 V-PXP-NPM ὄντες (1x)
Eph 4:18 existing *while* having·been·utterly·alienated from·
G5607.3 V-PXP-DSM ὄντι (1x)
Ac 7:2 father AbRaham while·he·was·still in MesoPotamia,
G5607.3 V-PXP-NSF οὖσα (1x)
Ac 9:39 Dorcas was·making while·she·was·still with them.
G5607.4 V-PXP-APM ὄντας (1x)
Eph 2:1 And yeu·yeurselves were·once dead in·the
G5607.6 V-PXP-DPM οὖσιν (1x)
Gal 4:8 ·were·enslaved to·the·ones who·are not by·nature
G5607.6 V-PXP-GSM ὄντος (1x)
1Co 8:10 the conscience of·him who·is weak be·reinforced

G5608 ὠνέομαι ōnéômai *v.* (1x)
Compare:G0059 G2932 G4046 See:G5092
G5608 V-ADI-3S ὠνήσατο (1x)
Ac 7:16 *son Jacob* purchased for·a·price of·silver·pieces

G5609 ὠόν ōón *n.* (1x)
xLangAlso:H1000
G5609 N-ASN ὠόν (1x)
Lk 11:12 also, if he·should·request an·egg, ¿! shall·he·hand

G5610 ὥρα hṓra *n.* (111x)
Compare:G2250 See:G3317
G5610.1 N-NSF ὥρα (33x)
Jn 1:39 day, for it·was *late·afternoon* about *the* tenth hour.
Jn 2:4 to·do·with·me and you? My hour has·not·yet come."
Jn 4:6 It·was *midday* about *the* sixth hour, *and*
Jn 4:21 trust me, because an·hour is·coming when, neither
Jn 4:23 "But·yet an·hour comes, and now is, when the true
Jn 5:25 ·certainly, I·say to·yeu, an·hour is·coming, and now
Jn 5:28 marvel at·that, because an·hour is·coming in which
Jn 7:30 his hand on him, because his hour had·not·yet come.
Jn 8:20 him, because his hour had·not·yet come.
Jn 12:23 them, saying, "The hour has·come, that the Son of·
Jn 13:1 personally·knowing that his hour has·come, that he·
Jn 16:2 ·the·gatherings. Moreover, an·hour is·come that
Jn 16:4 ·yeu, that whenever the hour should·come, yeu·may·
Jn 16:21 ·birth, she·has grief because her hour is·come, but
Jn 16:25 to·yeu in proverbs. But·yet an·hour comes, when
Jn 16:32 "Behold, an·hour comes, and now has·come that
Jn 17:1 "Father, the hour has·come. Glorify your Son in·
Jn 19:14 and *it·was midday* about *the* sixth hour, and he·says
Lk 22:14 And when the hour came, *Jesus* sat·back·to·eat,
Lk 22:53 "But·yet this is yeur hour, and the jurisdiction of·
Lk 23:44 it·was *midday* about *the* sixth hour, and there·was
Ac 2:15 yeu assume, for it·is *but the* third hour of·the day.
Mt 14:15 desolate, and the hour even·now *has* passed·away.
Mt 26:45 Behold, the hour has·drawn·near, and the Son
Mk 6:35 place is desolate, and even·now *it·is* a·late hour.
Mk 14:35 if it·were possible, the hour may·pass·away from
Mk 14:41 It·is·enough,·no·more! The hour is·come!
Mk 15:25 And it·was *at the* third hour *after dawn* that they·
Rm 13:11 ·now, this *is the* hour for·us to·be·awakened out
1Jn 2:18 Little·children, it·is *the* last hour. And just·as yeu·
1Jn 2:18 by·which we·know that it·is *the* last hour.
Rv 14:7 to·him, because the hour of·his Tribunal·judgment
Rv 14:15 and reap, because the hour is·come for·you to·reap
G5610.1 N-NPF ὧραι (1x)
Jn 11:9 "Are·there not·indeed twelve hours of·the daylight?
G5610.1 N-ASF ὥραν (21x)
Jn 4:52 he·inquired personally·from them the hour in which
Jn 4:52 ·him, "Yesterday at·the·seventh hour the fever left
Jn 12:27 But·rather on·account·of this, I·came to this hour.
Ac 3:1 Sanctuary·Courtyard at the *afternoon* hour of·prayer,
Ac 10:3 in·a·clear·vision, about *the* ninth hour of·the day,
Ac 10:9 the rooftop to·pray *at·midday* about *the* sixth hour.
Ac 10:30 and *midafternoon* at·the ninth hour while·praying
Gal 2:5 to·them, not·even just·for an·hour, did·we·yield to·
Mt 20:3 ·forth *midmorning* about the third hour, he·saw
Mt 20:5 about *the* sixth and ninth hour, he·did likewise.
Mt 20:6 Now going·forth about the eleventh hour, he·found
Mt 20:9 *hired* about the eleventh hour received a·denarius
Mt 20:12 'These last·ones did one hour, and you·made them
Mt 25:13 ·know the day nor·even the hour in which the Son
Mt 26:40 have·strength to·keep·alert with me *for* one hour?
Mt 27:46 And about the ninth hour YeShua shouted·out
Mk 14:37 ·you·not have·strength to·keep·alert *for* one hour?
1Co 15:30 why·do we·ourselves risk·danger every hour?
Rv 3:3 you·should·not know which hour I·shall·come upon
Rv 9:15 the·ones having·been·made·ready for the hour, day
Rv 17:12 as kings *for* one hour with the Scarlet·Beast.
G5610.1 N-APF ὥρας (1x)
Ac 19:34 for·a·span·of about two hours— yelling·out,
G5610.1 N-DSF ὥρᾳ (28x)
Jn 4:53 father knew that *it·was* at that hour, in which Jesus
Lk 1:10 people were praying outside at·the hour of·incense.
Lk 2:38 in·the same hour, responded·likewise·in·affirmation
Lk 7:21 in the same hour he·both·relieved·and·cured many
Lk 10:21 In that·same hour, Jesus leaped·for·joy in·the Spirit
Lk 12:12 yeu in the same hour what is·necessary to·declare.
Lk 12:39 had·personally·known in·which hour the thief
Lk 12:40 ·Clay·Man† comes in·that hour you·do·not suppose
Lk 12:46 *him*, and at an·hour when he·does·not know, and
Lk 14:17 he·dispatched his slave at·the hour of·the supper
Lk 20:19 the scribes in the same hour sought to·throw *their*
Lk 24:33 And rising·up the same hour, they·returned·back to
Ac 16:18 And he·came·out the same hour.
Ac 16:33 ·taking them in the same hour of·the night, he·
Ac 22:13 And·I, in·the same hour, looked·up at him.
Mt 8:13 his servant·boy was·healed in the *very* same hour.
Mt 10:19 ·be·given to·yeu in that hour what yeu·shall·speak.
Mt 18:1 In the same hour, the disciples came·alongside
Mt 24:42 ·do·not personally·know in·which hour yeur Lord
Mt 24:44 of·Clay·Man† comes at·an·hour which yeu·do·not
Mt 24:50 *him*, and at an·hour that he·does·not know,
Mt 26:55 In that·same hour, YeShua declared to·the crowds,
Mk 13:11 should·be·given to·yeu in that hour, that speak, for
Mk 15:34 And at·the ninth hour, Jesus cried·out with·a·loud
Rv 11:13 And in that hour there·happened a·great earthquake
Rv 18:10 Because in one hour your Tribunal·judgment came.
Rv 18:17 Because in·one hour such·vast wealth is·desolated.
Rv 18:19 Because in·one hour, she·is·desolated.'
G5610.1 N-GSF ὥρας (19x)
Jn 12:27 save me out of·this hour?' But·rather on·account·
Jn 19:27 And from that hour, the disciple took her into his·
Lk 22:59 And with·an·interval·of about one hour, someone
Lk 23:44 a·darkness over all the land until *the* ninth hour.
Ac 10:30 I·was fasting so·far·as·unto this·same hour; and
Ac 23:23 unto Caesarea from *the* third hour of·the night.
Mt 9:22 the woman was·made·safe·and·well from that hour.
Mt 15:28 And her daughter was·healed from that·very hour.
Mt 17:18 was·both·relieved·and·cured from that·very hour.
Mt 24:36 that day and hour no·one·at·all personally·knows,
Mt 27:45 from *midday*, *the* sixth hour, there·was darkness
Mt 27:45 darkness over all the land until the·ninth hour.
Mk 6:35 And even·now with·it·becoming a·late hour, his
Mk 11:11 all·things, even·now with·the hour being late, he·
Mk 13:32 that day and hour no·one·at·all personally·knows,
Mk 15:33 And *at·midday*, with·*the*·sixth hour occurring,
Mk 15:33 came·to·be over all the land until *the* ninth hour.
1Co 4:11 Even·up·to the very·present hour, also we·hunger,
Rv 3:10 ·keep you from·out of·the hour of·the proof·trial,
G5610.1 N-GPF ὡρῶν (1x)
Ac 5:7 And it·was about an·interval of·three hours, and his
EG5610.1 (3x)
Ac 3:1 the *afternoon* hour of·prayer, *being* the ninth *hour*.
Mt 26:32 "But after *it·is* the *hour* for·me to·be·awakened, I·
Mk 14:28 But·yet after *it·is* the *hour* for·me to·be·awakened,
G5610.2 N-ASF ὥραν (3x)
Jn 5:35 yeu wanted just·for a·short·while to·leap·for·joy in
2Co 7:8 yeu, even·though *it·was* just·for a·short·while.
Phm 1:15 ·departed just·for a·short·while in·order·that you·
G5610.2 N-GSF ὥρας (1x)
1Th 2:17 ·removed from yeu just·for a·short season (in·

G5611 ὡραῖος hōraîôs *adj.* (4x)
Roots:G5610 Compare:G2570 G2143 G2157 G0809 See:G5610-1
G5611.1 A-NPM ὡραῖοι (1x)
Rm 10:15 ·written, "How timely·and·elegant *are* the feet
G5611.3 A-NPM ὡραῖοι (1x)
Mt 23:27 in·fact outwardly appear stately·and·elegant, but
G5611.3 A-ASF ὡραίαν (1x)
Ac 3:2 being·referred·to·as Stately·and·Elegant, to·request
G5611.3 A-DSF ὡραίᾳ (1x)
Ac 3:10 ·act·of·charity at the Stately·and·Elegant Gate of·the

G5612 ὠρύομαι ōrýômai *v.* (1x)
G5612 V-PNP-NSM ὠρυόμενος (1x)
1Pe 5:8 Slanderer, strolls·about as a·roaring lion seeking

G5613 ὡς hōs *adv.* (496x)
Roots:G3739 Compare:G2505 G5619
G5613.ª ADV ὡς (4x)
Lk 2:15 And it·happened, after the angels went·away from
Lk 2:39 And after they·finished absolutely·all the·things
Ac 20:24 *as* precious to·myself, as·so to·fully·complete my
1Co 7:17 to·each·man, each·one according·as the Lord has·
G5613.1 ADV ὡς (376x)
Jn 1:14 glory (*the* glory as of·the·only·begotten directly·from
Jn 6:12 But as they·are·filled·up, he·says to·his disciples,
Jn 6:16 Now as early·evening occurred, his disciples walked·
Jn 7:10 the Sacred·Feast, not openly, but·rather as in secret.
Jn 7:46 ·this·manner *has* a·man·of·clay† spoken as *does* this
Jn 8:7 But as they·were·persisting·in asking·of him, after·
Jn 15:6 in me, he·is·already·cast out as the *unfruitful* vine·
Jn 20:11 Now·then, as she·was·weeping, she·stooped·near·
Jn 21:9 So·then, as they·disembarked upon the dry·ground,
Lk 3:4 As it·has·been·written in a·scroll of·the·words of·
Lk 3:23 being a·son of·Joseph (as deemed·by·law), *as·well·*
Lk 4:25 and six lunar·months, as great famine occurred over

Lk 6:10 hand was·restored as·healthy·and·sound as the other
Lk 6:22 and should·cast·out yeur name as evil, because·of
Lk 6:40 ·been·completely·reformed shall·be as his instructor.
Lk 7:12 Now as he·drew·near to·the gate of·the city, behold,
Lk 9:54 heaven and to·consume them, even as EliJah did?
Lk 10:3 I·myself dispatch yeu as adolescent·male·lambs in
Lk 10:18 the Adversary-Accuser falling as lightning from·out
Lk 10:27 ·mind,” and “your neighbor as yourself.’”
Lk 11:2 Your will be·done, as in heaven, so·also on the
Lk 11:36 *the* whole shall·be full·of·light, as whenever the
Lk 11:44 Because yeu·are as the chamber·tombs, the
Lk 12:27 in all his glory was·arrayed as one of·these.
Lk 12:58 For as you·head·on·out with your legal·adversary
Lk 14:22 ‘Lord, it·has·happened as you·ordered, and yet
Lk 15:19 your son; make me as one of·your hired·men.
Lk 15:25 in a·field, and as he·was·going·*along*, he·drew·
Lk 17:6 ·having trust *that·grows* as a·kernel of·mustard·seed
Lk 17:28 “Likewise, *it·shall·be* also as it·was in the days of·
Lk 18:11 ·men, adulterers, or even as this tax·collector.
Lk 18:17 ·not accept the kingdom of·God as a·little·child, no
Lk 19:41 And as he·drew·near, upon·seeing the City, he·
Lk 21:35 “For as a·snare it·shall·come upon all the·ones
Lk 22:26 greater among yeu, let·him·be as the younger, and
Lk 22:26 and the·one governing, as the·one attending.
Lk 22:27 am in *the* midst of·yeu as the·one attending.
Lk 22:31 demanded yeu·*all*, to·sift *yeu·all* as the wheat.
Lk 22:52 “Have·yeu·come·out, as against an·armed·robber,
Lk 22:66 Now as it·became day, the council·of·elders of·the
Lk 23:14 this man·of·clay† to·me as one·turning·away the
Lk 23:26 And as they·led him away, upon·grabbing·hold of·
Lk 24:32 ·set·ablaze within us, as he·was·speaking with·us
Lk 24:32 the way, and as he·was·thoroughly·opening·up the
Ac 1:10 And as they·were gazing·intently toward the heaven
Ac 2:15 For these·men are·not drunk as yeu assume, for it·is
Ac 3:22 unto·yeu from·among yeur brothers, as myself; him
Ac 7:23 “And as forty·years time was·completely·fulfilled
Ac 7:37 to·yeu from·among yeur brothers, as *he·did* myself;
Ac 7:51 ·oppose the Holy Spirit. As yeur fathers *are*, so·also
Ac 8:32 this, “ He·was·driven as a·sheep to *the* butchering;
Ac 8:32 *the* butchering; and as a·sacrificial·lamb *is* voiceless
Ac 8:36 And as they·traversed down the roadway, they·came
Ac 10:11 descending to him, as *being* a·great linen·sheet
Ac 10:17 But as Peter was·thoroughly·perplexed in himself
Ac 11:5 A·certain vessel descending, as a·great linen·sheet
Ac 11:17 equally·same voluntary·present (as also *he·gave* to·
Ac 13:25 And as John was·completely·fulfilling his·own
Ac 13:33 by·raising·up Jesus; as also it·has·been·written in
Ac 16:4 And as they·traversed·throughout the cities, they·
Ac 17:14 dispatched·forth Paul to·traverse as toward the sea,
Ac 17:15 they·should·come to him as quickly·as·possible.
Ac 17:28 are·stirred and have·existence. As also certain of·
Ac 19:21 And as these·things were·completely·fulfilled, Paul
Ac 20:14 And as he·joined·on with·us at Assos, after·taking
Ac 22:5 As *to·such*, the designated·high·priest *HananIah* is
Ac 22:11 “And as I·was·not looking·clearly·about due·to the
Ac 22:25 And as they·prestretched him with·the straps, Paul
Ac 23:11 Paul. For as you·thoroughly·testified concerning
Ac 23:15 tomorrow, as intending to·thoroughly·ascertain
Ac 25:10 *of* the·Judeans, even as you·yourself realize better·
Ac 25:14 And as they·were·lingering there *for* many·more
Heb 1:11 shall·become·old·and·worn·out as *does* a·garment.
Heb 3:2 to·the·one producing him, as also Moses *was*
Heb 3:5 in all his house as a·domestic·attendant (for a·
Heb 3:6 but Anointed-One as a·son over his·own house, of·
Heb 3:8 harden yeur hearts, as in the Direct·Provocation, in
Heb 3:15 harden yeur hearts, as in the Direct·Provocation.
Heb 4:3 *the obstinate·ones*, “As I·swore in my flared·anger
Heb 6:19 Which *Expectation* we·have as an·anchor of·the
Heb 7:9 And *so* as to·make a·declaration, even Levi, the·one
Heb 11:9 in the land of·promise as *in* an·estranged·foreign
Heb 11:27 for he·mightily·endured as one·clearly·seeing the
Heb 11:29 ·crossed the Red Sea as through parched·ground,
Heb 12:5 which thoroughly·relates to·yeu as with·sons,
Heb 12:7 God is·bearing·alongside yeu as *his·own* sons, for
Heb 12:16 any sexually·immoral or profane·person as Esau,
Heb 12:27 being·shaken, as *of·things* having·been·made, in·
Heb 13:3 as having·been·bound·together *with·them, and*
Heb 13:3 *and* the·ones being·maltreated, as yeurselves also
Heb 13:17 as ones·that·shall·be·giving·forth an·account—
Gal 1:9 As we·have·already·stated, so at·this·moment I·say
Gal 3:16 “And to·the·seeds,” as upon many *offspring†*, but·
Gal 3:16 as upon many *offspring†*, but·rather as upon one, “
Gal 4:12 I·petition yeu, be as I·myself *am*, because I·also
Gal 4:12 *am*, because I·also *am* as yeu *are*. Not·at·all did·
Gal 4:14 ·out, but·rather accepted me as an·angel of·God,
Gal 4:14 as an·angel of·God, *even* as Anointed-One YeShua.
Gal 5:14 ·one, “You·shall·love your neighbor as yourself.”
Gal 6:10 Accordingly, as we·have opportunity, we·should·
Mt 1:24 from the heavy·sleep, did as the angel of·Yahweh
Mt 6:10 Your will be·done— as in heaven, so·also on the
Mt 6:12 us our moral·debts, also as we·ourselves forgive our
Mt 6:29 in all his glory, was·arrayed as one of·these.
Mt 7:29 for he·was instructing them as *one* having authority,
Mt 7:29 them as *one* having authority, and not as the scribes.
Mt 8:13 “Head·on·out; and as you·trusted, *so* be·it·done to·
Mt 10:16 “Behold, I·myself dispatch yeu as sheep in *the*
Mt 10:16 Accordingly, become prudent as the serpents and
Mt 10:16 prudent as the serpents and untainted as the doves.
Mt 10:25 disciple that he·should·become as his instructor,
Mt 10:25 as his instructor, and the slave as his lord. If they·
Mt 12:13 it·was·restored as·healthy·and·sound as the other.
Mt 13:43 righteous shall·brilliantly·radiate·forth as the sun in
Mt 14:5 because they·were·holding him as a·prophet.
Mt 15:28 your trust! It·is·done for·you as you·wanted.” And
Mt 17:2 And his face radiated·brightly as the sun, and his
Mt 17:2 the sun, and his garments became white as the light.
Mt 17:20 ·have trust *that·grows* as a·kernel of·mustard·seed
Mt 18:3 ·back and should·become as the little·children, no,
Mt 18:4 whoever should·humble himself as this little·child,
Mt 18:33 fellow·slave, even as I·myself showed·mercy on·
Mt 19:19 and “You·shall·love your neighbor as yourself.”
Mt 20:14 to·give to·this last·one, even as *I·gave* to·you.
Mt 21:26 we·fear the crowd, for all hold John as a·prophet.”
Mt 21:46 *crowds* were·holding him *with·regard* as a·prophet.
Mt 22:30 ·in·marriage, but·rather they·are as God's angels in
Mt 22:39 it, “You·shall·love your neighbor as yourself.”
Mt 26:19 And the disciples did as YeShua appointed them,
Mt 26:39 from me. Nevertheless not as I·myself will, but·
Mt 26:39 not as I·myself will, but·rather as you *will*.”
Mt 26:55 “Did·yeu·come·out as against an·armed·robber
Mt 27:65 Make·*it*·as·secure as yeu·personally·know·how.”
Mt 28:3 His outline·appearance was as lightning, and his
Mt 28:9 And as they·were·traversing to·announce *it* to·his
Mt 28:15 the money, they·did as they·were·instructed. And
Mk 1:2 As it·has·been·written in the prophets, “Behold, I·
Mk 1:22 for he·was instructing them as one·having authority,
Mk 1:22 as one·having authority, and not as the scribes.
Mk 3:5 hand was·restored as·healthy·and·sound as the other.
Mk 4:26 of·God: “*It·is* as though a·man·of·clay† should·cast
Mk 4:31 “*It·is* as a·kernel of·mustard·seed, which, whenever
Mk 6:15 “It·is a·prophet, or as one of·the prophets.
Mk 6:34 them, because they·were “as sheep not having a·
Mk 7:6 the stage·acting·hypocrites; as it·has·been·written,
Mk 8:24 ·upon the men·of·clay† as how I·clearly·envision
Mk 9:3 glistening, exceedingly white as snow, such·as a·
Mk 10:1 and again, as he·had·been·accustomed, he·was·
Mk 12:25 are·given·in·marriage, but·rather are as angels,
Mk 12:31 it, “You·shall·love your neighbor as yourself.”
Mk 12:33 and to·love one's neighbor as himself, is more·
Mk 13:34 *is* as a·man·of·clay† taking·a·long·journey·abroad,
Mk 14:48 “Did·yeu·come·forth, as against an·armed·robber,
Rm 1:21 they·neither glorified *him* as God nor gave·*him*·
Rm 3:7 why am I·also still judged as morally·disqualified?
Rm 5:15 *is* also in·this·manner (but·yet not as the trespass).
Rm 5:16 endowment *is* not as through one already·morally·
Rm 5:18 So consequently, as through one trespass, *judgment*
Rm 6:13 to·God, as those·that·are·alive from·among dead·
Rm 8:36 day·long; we·are·reckoned as sheep for·butchering
Rm 9:25 As he·says also in Hosea, “I·shall·call *them* ‘My
Rm 9:27 of·the Sons of·IsraEl may·be as the sand of·the sea,
Rm 9:29 for·us, we·would·have become as Sodom, and
Rm 9:29 as Sodom, and would be·likened as Gomorrah.”
Rm 12:3 to·be·self-controlled, seeing·as God imparted to·
Rm 13:9 “You·shall·love your neighbor as yourself.”
Rm 13:13 We·should·walk decently, as in daylight, not in·
Rm 15:15 ·wrote to·yeu in part as once·again·reminding yeu,
Jac 1:10 his·own humiliation, because as a·flower of·grass,
Jac 2:8 “You·shall·love your neighbor as yourself,” yeu·do
Jac 2:9 being·convicted by the Torah-Law as transgressors.
Jac 2:12 and so do: as ones·about to·be·judged through *the*
Jac 5:3 yeu and shall·eat yeur flesh as fire. Yeu·stored·up·
Jac 5:5 Yeu·nourished yeur hearts, as in a·day of·butchering
Jud 1:7 As *in* like manner to·these *angels*, Sodom and
Jud 1:10 ·acquainted·with naturally (as irrational animals), in
Php 1:20 but·rather with all clarity·of·speech (as always, *so*
Php 2:8 ·found in·a·schematic·layout as a·man·of·clay†, he·
Php 2:12 ·as yeu·listened·and·obeyed always (not as in my
Php 2:15 among whom yeu·are·apparent as brilliant·lights in
Php 2:22 proof of·him, that as a·child together with·a·father,
1Pe 1:14 As attentively·obedient children, do·not be·
1Pe 1:19 blood, as of·a·sacrificial·lamb without·blemish and
1Pe 1:24 on·account·that “ All flesh *is* as grass, and every
1Pe 1:24 every man·of·clay's† glory *is* as *the* flower of·grass.
1Pe 2:2 as newborn babies, eagerly·crave the rational milk
1Pe 2:5 And yeu·yeurselves, as living stones, are·built·up,
1Pe 2:11 Dearly·beloved, I·implore *yeu* as sojourners and
1Pe 2:12 though they·speak·against yeu as criminals, as·a·
1Pe 2:13 the Lord, whether to·a·king, as having·superiority,
1Pe 2:14 or to·governors, as being·sent through him, in·fact,
1Pe 2:16 *Exist* as free·men, yet not retaining the liberty as a·
1Pe 2:16 yet not retaining the liberty as a·cover-up for·the
1Pe 2:16 ·the depravity, but·rather *behave* as slaves of·God.
1Pe 2:25 For yeu·were as sheep being·led·astray, but·yet are
1Pe 3:7 according·to knowledge, as with·a·weaker vessel,
1Pe 3:7 ·prescribing honor to·the feminine as also *being*
1Pe 3:16 they·should·speak·against yeu as of·criminals,
1Pe 4:10 *let·them·be* attending·to it as good estate·managers
1Pe 4:11 ·*others, let·him·be* as *one·speaking* eloquent·words
1Pe 4:11 *to·others, let·him·be* as *one·attending* from·out of·
1Pe 4:15 For do·not·let any of·yeu suffer as a·murderer, or
1Pe 4:15 or as one·interloping·in·civic·matters·as·an·.
1Pe 4:16 But if *any·man suffers* as “a·Christian,” a·Little·
1Pe 4:19 beneficial·well·doing, as to·a·trustworthy Creator.
1Pe 5:3 nor·even as exercising·lordship·against the ones·
1Pe 5:8 Slanderer, strolls·about as a·roaring lion seeking
2Pe 1:3 As with·his divine power, all·things pertaining·to
2Pe 1:19 ·do well taking·heed as to·a·lantern shining·forth in
2Pe 2:1 the People, even as there·shall·be false·teachers
2Pe 2:12 But these *false·teachers* (as natural, irrational
2Pe 3:8 one day *is* with *the* Lord as a·thousand years, and a·
2Pe 3:8 a·thousand years, and a·thousand years as one day.”
2Pe 3:9 the promise, as some·men resolutely·consider
2Pe 3:10 But the Day of·*the*·Lord shall·come as a·thief, in a·
2Pe 3:16 unlearned and unstable distort, as *they·do* also the
1Th 2:4 ·manner we·speak, not as satisfying men·of·clay†,
1Th 2:6 to·be a·burden as ambassadors of·Anointed-One.
1Th 2:11 one of·yeu), how as a·father *does·for* his children,
1Th 5:2 ·Yahweh, in·this·manner, comes as a·thief at·night.
1Th 5:4 in·order·that the Day should·grab yeu as a·thief.
1Th 5:6 we·should·not fall·asleep, as even *do* the rest, but·
2Th 2:4 ’such·for him to·sit·down as God in the Temple of·
2Th 3:15 ·so, resolutely·consider *him* not as an·enemy, but·
2Th 3:15 an·enemy, but·rather admonish *him* as a·brother.
Tit 1:5 elders in·each city, as I·myself thoroughly·assigned
Tit 1:7 without·any·charge·of·wrong·doing as an·estate· of·
1Co 3:1 am·not able to·speak to·yeu as to·spiritual·ones, but·
1Co 3:1 as to·spiritual·ones, but·rather as to·fleshly·ones, as
1Co 3:1 ·ones, but·rather as to·fleshly·ones, as to·infants in
1Co 3:5 through whom yeu·trusted, even as the Lord gave

1Co 3:10 to·me, as a·wise chief·construction·architect, I·
1Co 3:15 ·be·saved, but in·this·manner, as through fire.
1Co 4:1 us in·this·manner: as assistants of·Anointed-One
1Co 4:7 ·receive *it*, why do·you·boast, as *if* not receiving *it*?
1Co 4:9 the ambassadors) last, as doomed·to·death, because
1Co 4:13 we·entreat. We·have·now·become as scum of·the
1Co 4:14 these·things, but·rather, as my beloved children,
1Co 7:7 I·want all men·of·clay† to·be also as myself. But·yet
1Co 7:17 Except *to·personally·know that* as God imparted to·
1Co 7:25 *my* advice, as one·having·been·shown·mercy from
1Co 7:29 the·ones having wives should·be as not having *any*;
1Co 7:30 and the·ones weeping as not weeping; and the·ones
1Co 7:30 and the·ones rejoicing, as not rejoicing; and the·
1Co 7:30 and the·ones buying, as not fully·holding·onto *it*;
1Co 7:31 and the·ones using this world, as not abusing *it* …
1Co 8:7 unto this·moment, eat as sacrificing·to·an·idol; and
1Co 9:20 And to·the Jews I·became as a·Jew, in·order·that I·
1Co 9:20 *that* are·under Torah-Law, as under Torah-Law,
1Co 9:21 *·are* without·Torah-Law, as without·Torah-Law,
1Co 9:22 To·the weak, I·became as weak in·order·that I·
1Co 9:26 do·run, *but* not as uncertainly; in·this·manner I·
1Co 9:26 in·this·manner I·do·box, *but* not as thrashing air.
1Co 10:7 ·as *were* some of·them; as it·has·been·written,
1Co 10:15 I·say *this* as to·prudent·men; yeu·yeurselves
1Co 13:11 I·was an·infant, I·was·speaking as an·infant, I·
1Co 13:11 as an·infant, I·was·contemplating as an·infant, I·
1Co 13:11 as an·infant, I·was·reckoning as an·infant. But
1Co 14:33 *God* of·chaos, but·rather of·peace, as in all the
1Co 16:10 ·works the work of·*the*·Lord, as also I·myself *do*.
2Co 2:17 For we·are not as the many, shortchanging·and·
2Co 2:17 But·rather, as from·out of·sincerity, moreover as
2Co 2:17 of·sincerity, moreover as birthed·from·out of·God
2Co 3:1 Yet·not·even do·we·have·need, as some *do*, of·
2Co 3:5 to·reckon anything as from·among ourselves, but·
2Co 5:20 on·behalf of·Anointed-One, as God imploring *yeu*
2Co 6:4 ·commending ourselves as attendants of·God: in
2Co 6:8 and good·reputation, as impostors and·yet true,
2Co 6:9 as being·unknown and·yet being·recognized, as
2Co 6:9 ·unknown and·yet being·recognized, as dying and
2Co 6:9 — we·live, as being·correctively·disciplined and
2Co 6:10 as being·grieved yet always rejoicing, as
2Co 6:10 always rejoicing, as helplessly·poor yet making·
2Co 6:10 ·wealthy many, as having not·even·one·thing and·
2Co 6:13 due·reciprocation (I·say *this* as to·*my*·children):
2Co 7:14 put·to·shame; but·rather as we·spoke all·things to·
2Co 9:5 ready in·this·manner: as a·beneficial·blessing, and
2Co 10:2 reckoning of·us as presently·walking according·to
2Co 10:9 in·order·that I·may·not seem as if *I·intended* to·
2Co 11:3 But I·fear, lest·somehow, as the Serpent
2Co 11:15 also are·disguised as attendants of·righteousness,
2Co 11:16 then·also accept me as impetuous in·order·that,
2Co 11:17 ·to *the* Lord, but·rather as in impulsiveness, in
Eph 2:3 ·were by·nature children of·wrath, even as the rest.
Eph 3:5 ·known to·the Sons of·clay†, as it·is now revealed
Eph 5:1 attentive·imitators of·God, as beloved children,
Eph 5:8 *yeu·are* light in *the* Lord. Walk as children of·light
Eph 5:15 precisely how yeu·walk, not as unwise, but·rather
Eph 5:15 how yeu·walk, not as unwise, but·rather as wise,
Eph 5:22 ·yeurselves to·yeur·own husbands, as to·the Lord,
Eph 5:23 is head of·the wife, even as the Anointed-One *is*
Eph 5:28 to·love their·own wives as their·own bodies. The·
Eph 6:5 with fidelity of·yeur heart, as to·the Anointed-One,
Eph 6:6 not according·to eyeservice as men-pleasers†, but·
Eph 6:6 as men-pleasers†, but·rather as slaves of·the
Eph 6:20 I·may·boldly·speak·with·clarity as it·is·mandatory·
Col 2:6 *in the·same·manner* as yeu·personally·received the
Col 3:12 Accordingly, as Selected-Ones of·God (holy and
Col 3:18 to·yeur·own husbands, as is·appropriate in *the*
Col 3:22 not with eyeservice as men-pleasers†, but·rather
Col 3:23 be·working *it* out of·a·soul's·desire as to·the Lord
Col 4:4 I·may·make it apparent, as it·is·mandatory·for me
Phm 1:9 *I* Paul, being such as an·old·man and now also a·
Phm 1:14 should·not be as according·to a·compulsion, but·
Phm 1:16 no·longer as a·slave, but·rather above a·slave, a·
Phm 1:17 *to·be* a·partner, purposely·receive him as myself.
1Ti 5:1 ·man, but·rather exhort *him* as a·father, *likewise*
1Ti 5:1 *him* as a·father, *likewise* younger·men as brothers,
1Ti 5:2 older·women as mothers, younger·women as sisters,
1Ti 5:2 ·women as mothers, younger·women as sisters, with
2Ti 2:3 you·yourself must·endure·hardship as a·good soldier
2Ti 2:9 in which I·suffer·hardship, as a·criminal, *even* as·
2Ti 2:17 And their word, as gangrene, shall·have a·
2Ti 3:9 shall·be obvious to·all, as it·was also with·these·
1Jn 1:7 if we·should·walk in the light as he·himself is in the
1Jn 2:27 anyone should·instruct yeu, but·rather as the same
Rv 1:10 right·behind me a·great voice, as of·a·trumpet,
Rv 1:14 *are* white like wool (*as* white as snow), and his eyes
Rv 1:14 white as snow), and his eyes *are* as a·blaze of·fire,
Rv 1:15 his feet like fine·brass (as having·been·refined in a·
Rv 1:15 , and his voice as *the* sound of·many waters,
Rv 1:16 ’ and his appearance *is* as the sun *that* shines·forth
Rv 1:17 ·saw him, I·fell toward his feet as dead. And he·laid
Rv 2:18 the·one having his eyes as a·blaze of·fire and his
Rv 2:24 depths of·the Adversary-Accuser,” as they·say), I·
Rv 2:27 them with a·rod of·iron, as the earthenware vessels
Rv 2:27 are·shattered *by·its·maker*,’” as I·also have·received
Rv 3:3 ·keep·alert, I·shall·come upon you as a·thief, and no,
Rv 4:1 voice which I·heard *was* as a·trumpet speaking with
Rv 4:7 living·being *is* having the face as a·man·of·clay†, and
Rv 5:6 Elders, a·Lamb standing as having·been·slaughtered,
Rv 6:1 the four living·beings (as a·voice of·a·thunder)
Rv 6:11 about to·be·killed also as they·themselves *were*.
Rv 6:12 the sun became *as* black as sackcloth made·of·hair,
Rv 6:12 made·of·hair, and the moon became as blood,
Rv 6:13 heaven fell to the earth, as *when* a·fig·tree casts its
Rv 6:14 was·utterly·separated as an·official·scroll being·
Rv 8:8 sounded, and *something* as a·great mountain being·
Rv 8:10 ·out of·the heaven, being·set·ablaze as a·torch, and
Rv 9:2 smoke out of·the well, as smoke of·a·great furnace,
Rv 9:3 authority was·given to·them, as the scorpions of·the
Rv 9:5 And their torment *was* as *the* torment of·a·scorpion,
Rv 9:7 on their heads *were something* as victor's·crowns like
Rv 9:7 gold, and their faces *were* as faces of·men·of·clay†.
Rv 9:8 And they·were·having hair as hair of·women, and
Rv 9:8 hair of·women, and their teeth were as *teeth* of·lions.
Rv 9:9 ·having full·chest·armor, as full·chest·armor of·iron;
Rv 9:9 the sound of·their wings *was* as the·sound of·chariots,
Rv 9:17 the heads of·the horses *were* as heads of·lions, and
Rv 10:1 his head, and his face *was* as the sun, and his feet as
Rv 10:1 face *was* as the sun, and his feet as pillars of·fire.
Rv 10:7 of·God should·be·finished, as he·proclaimed to·his
Rv 10:9 but·yet it·shall·be in your mouth sweet as honey.”
Rv 10:10 and it·was in my mouth sweet as honey. And when
Rv 12:15 cast out of·his mouth water as a·flood·water right·
Rv 13:2 a·leopard, and its feet *were* as *the feet* of·a·bear,
Rv 13:2 of·a·bear, and its mouth as a·mouth of·a·lion. And
Rv 13:11 ·male·lamb, and it·was·speaking as a·dragon.
Rv 14:2 from·out of·the heaven, as a·voice of·many waters,
Rv 14:2 of·many waters, and as a·voice of·a·great thunder.
Rv 14:3 And they·do·sing, as *singing* a·brand-new song in·
Rv 15:2 And I·saw *something* as a·transparent,·glassy sea
Rv 16:3 the sea, and it·became as blood of·a·dead·man. And
Rv 16:15 “Behold, I·come as a·thief. Supremely·blessed *is*
Rv 17:12 but·yet they·do·receive authority as kings *for* one
Rv 18:6 ·give·back to·her even as she·herself gave·back to·
Rv 18:21 strong angel took·up a·stone as a·great millstone,
Rv 19:6 And I·heard as a·voice of·a·large crowd, and as a·
Rv 19:6 of·a·large crowd, and as a·voice of·many waters,
Rv 19:6 as a·voice of·many waters, and as a·voice of·strong
Rv 19:12 His eyes *were* as a·blaze of·fire, and on his head
Rv 20:8 battle, the number of·whom *is* as the sand of·the sea
Rv 21:2 having·been·made·ready as a·bride having·been·
Rv 21:21 CITY *was* pure gold, as nearly·transparent glass.
Rv 22:1 ·pure river of·water of·life-above, radiant as crystal,
Rv 22:12 me, to·give·back to·each·man as his work shall·be
EG5613.1 (3x)
Gal 2:16 “*As Jews*, having·seen that a·man·of·clay† is·not
1Pe 4:15 of·yeu suffer as a·murderer, or *as* a·thief, or *as* a·
1Pe 4:15 or *as* a·thief, or *as* a·criminal, or as one·
G5613.2 ADV ὡς (10x)
Heb 3:11 Even·as I·swore in my flared·anger, ‘As·if they·
1Pe 3:6 even·as Sarah, *who* listened·to·and·obeyed
2Pe 3:16 Even·as *he·does* also in all his letters, speaking in
1Th 2:7 *the* midst of·yeu, even·as a·nurturing·mother would
1Co 7:8 for·them if they·should·remain even·as I·also *am*.
1Co 9:5 a·wife (a·sister *in·the Trust*) even·as also *do* the rest
1Co 12:2 Gentiles being·led·away, even·as yeu·were·led
Eph 5:33 must·love his·own wife even·as himself, and *so*·
Rv 3:21 me on my throne, even·as I·also overcame and did·
Rv 21:11 *was* like a·precious stone, even·as a·jasper stone,
G5613.3 ADV ὡς (24x)
Lk 6:4 how he·entered into the house of·God and took and
Lk 8:47 she·laid·hold of·him, and how at·once, she·was·
Lk 22:61 the word of·the Lord, how he·declared to·him,
Lk 23:55 ·view the chamber·tomb and how his body was·
Lk 24:6 is·awakened. Recall·to·mind how he·spoke to·yeu
Lk 24:35 along the way, and how he·was·known to·them in
Ac 10:28 are·fully·acquainted·with how it·is a·statutory·
Ac 10:38 how God anointed Jesus *who·was* from Natsareth
Ac 11:16 the utterance of·*the*·Lord, how he·was·saying,
Ac 17:22 “Men, Athenians, I·observe how in·all·things yeu
Ac 20:20 *And* how I·kept·back not·even·one·thing of·the·
Mk 4:27 and day, but how the scattering·of·seed should·
Mk 12:26 in the scroll of·Moses, how (at the burning·bush)
Rm 1:9 the good·news of·his Son, how unceasingly I·make
Rm 10:15 ·has·been·written, “How timely·and·elegant *are*
Rm 11:2 says by EliJah? How he·confers with·God against
Rm 11:33 and knowledge of·God! How inexplorable *are* his
Php 1:8 God is my witness, how I·greatly·yearn·after yeu all
1Pe 5:12 (the trustworthy brother as·how I·reckon *it*), I·
1Th 2:10 and God *also*, how in·a·divinely·holy·manner and
1Th 2:11 (each one of·yeu), how as a·father *does·for* his
2Co 5:19 how that God was in Anointed-One presently·
2Co 7:15 ·obedience of·yeu all, how with reverent·fear and
2Ti 1:3 a·pure conscience), how without·ceasing I·have a·
G5613.4 ADV ὡς (16x)
Jn 1:39 day, for it·was *late·afternoon* about *the* tenth hour.
Jn 6:19 In·due·course, having·rowed about twenty·five or
Jn 11:18 was near to·JeruSalem, about fifteen stadia away.
Jn 21:8 the dry·ground, but·rather about two·hundred cubits
Lk 2:37 and she *was* a·widow for·about eighty·four years,
Lk 8:42 ·child, a·daughter of·about twelve years·of·age, and
Ac 1:15 a·crowd of·names in·unison *of* about a·hundred *and*
Ac 5:7 And it·was about an·interval of·three hours, and his
Ac 13:18 And *for* about a·time of·forty·years, he·bore·with
Ac 13:20 these·things, *which·took* about four·hundred and
Ac 19:34 of·all *present*, for·a·span·of about two hours—
Mk 5:13 sea. Now there·were about two·thousand *of·them*,
Mk 8:9 And the·ones eating were about four·thousand *men*,
Mk 9:21 ·of his father, “About how·long a·time has·it·been
Rv 8:1 ·was silence in the heaven *for* about half·an·hour.
Rv 16:21 *hailstone* about *the* weight·of·a·talent·*(or·fifty*·
G5613.5 ADV ὡς (42x)
Jn 2:9 Now as·soon·as the director·of·the·banquet tasted the
Jn 2:23 And as·soon·as he·was in JeruSalem at the Passover
Jn 4:1 Accordingly, as·soon·as the Lord knew that the
Jn 4:40 So·then *just* as·soon·as the Samaritans came toward
Jn 7:10 But *just* as·soon·as his brothers walked·up, then he·
Jn 11:6 Now·then, as·soon·as he·heard that he·was·sick, in·
Jn 11:20 Accordingly, Martha, as·soon·as she·heard that
Jn 11:29 As·soon·as that *sister* heard *it*, she·is·roused swiftly
Jn 11:32 So as·soon·as Mary came where Jesus was, upon·
Jn 11:33 Now as·soon·as Jesus saw her weeping, and the
Jn 18:6 Now·then, as·soon·as he·declared to·them, “I AM,”
Jn 19:33 coming to Jesus, as·soon·as they·saw him even·
Lk 1:23 And it·happened, as·soon·as the days of·his public·
Lk 1:41 And it·happened, as·soon·as ElisSabeth heard the
Lk 1:44 For, behold, as·soon·as the sound of·your greeting
Lk 5:4 Now as·soon·as he·ceased speaking, he·declared to

Lk 11:1 a·certain place, *that* as·soon·as he·ceased, a·certain·
Lk 19:5 And as·soon·as Jesus came to the place, looking·up,
Lk 19:29 And it·happened, as·soon·as he·drew·near to
Lk 20:37 the burning·bush, *just* as·soon·as he says Yahweh,
Ac 5:24 Now as·soon·as the high priest and the high·warden
Ac 9:23 And as·soon·as a·significant·number·of days were·
Ac 10:7 And as·soon·as the angel (the·one speaking to·
Ac 10:25 And as·soon·as Peter happened to·enter, Cornelius
Ac 13:29 And as·soon·as they·completed absolutely·all the·
Ac 14:5 And as·soon·as there·became a·violent·attempt
Ac 16:10 And as·soon·as he·saw the clear·vision,
Ac 16:15 And as·soon·as she·was·immersed, and·also her
Ac 17:13 But as·soon·as the Jews from ThessaloNica knew
Ac 18:5 And as·soon·as both Silas and TimoThy came·down
Ac 19:9 But as·soon·as some were·hardened and were·
Ac 20:18 And as·soon·as they·came·close to him, he·
Ac 21:1 And as·soon·as it·became *time for* us to·be·sailing·
Ac 21:12 And as·soon·as we·heard these·things, both we·
Ac 21:27 And as·soon·as the seven days were·about to·be·
Ac 27:1 And as·soon·as it·was·decided for us to·set·sail for
Ac 27:27 Now as·soon·as the·fourteenth night was·come,
Ac 28:4 And as·soon·as the barbarians saw the venomous·
Mk 4:36 they·personally·took him as·soon·as he·was in the
Rm 15:24 just as·soon·as I·should·traverse for Spain, I·shall·
Php 2:23 from·this·same·hour as·soon·as I·should·fully·see
1Co 11:34 into judgment. And as·soon·as I·may·come, I·

G5613.6 ADV ὡς (21x)

Lk 16:1 to·him as·though thoroughly·squandering his
Ac 3:12 ·gaze·intently at·us, as·though by·our·own power
Ac 23:20 ·of·Sanhedrin, as·though intending to·inquire
Ac 27:30 sea under·a·pretense as·though intending to·extend
Ac 28:19 to·appeal·to Caesar, though not·as having
Mk 10:15 the kingdom of·God as·though *he·is* a·little·child,
Rm 4:17 ·forth the·things not existing as·though existing),
Rm 9:32 of·trust, but·rather as·though *it·were* as·a·result of·
1Pe 4:12 among·yeu), as·though *it·is* a·strange·new·thing
2Th 2:2 word, nor through letter as·though through us) as·
2Th 2:2 letter as·though through us) as·though the Day of·
1Co 4:18 Now some are·puffed·up, as·though *it·is* not me
1Co 5:3 I, in·fact, even·though being·absent in·the body but
1Co 5:3 spirit, even·now, as·though being·present, I·have·
2Co 10:14 *it·is* not as·though we·are·not actually·reaching
2Co 11:21 *·charge·of* dishonor, as·though that we·ourselves
2Co 13:2 I·do·presently·forewarn as·though being·present
2Co 13:7 *that* we·ourselves may·be as·though disqualified.
Col 2:20 of·the world, why, as·though living in *the* world,
2Jn 1:5 you, my·Lady, not as·though I·wrote a·brand-new
Rv 13:3 of·its heads as·though having·been·slaughtered to

G5614 ὡσα•ννά hōsanná *heb.* (6x)

Roots:H3467 H4994

G5614 HEB ὡσαννά (6x)

Jn 12:13 and were·yelling·out, "Hosanna! "Having·been·
Mt 21:9 ·out, saying, "Hosanna to·the Son of·David!
Mt 21:9 in *the* name of·Yahweh!" Hosanna in the highest!"
Mt 21:15 ·Atrium, saying, "Hosanna to·the Son of·David!"
Mk 11:9 following were·yelling·out, saying, "Hosanna!
Mk 11:10 in *the* name of·Yahweh. Hosanna in the highest!"

G5615 ὡσ•αύτως hōsaútōs *adv.* (18x)

Roots:G5613 G0846

G5615.2 ADV ὡσαύτως (6x)

Lk 20:31 third took her, and in·like·manner, the seven also;
Mt 21:36 at·the first, and they·did to·them in·like·manner.
Mk 14:31 And also, all were·saying likewise.
1Co 11:25 In·like·manner also, *he·took* the cup after eating·
1Ti 2:9 In·like·manner also, *I·resolve for* the women to·
1Ti 3:11 In·like·manner *also, the* wives *must·be* morally·

G5615.3 ADV ὡσαύτως (11x)

Lk 13:3 ·repent, yeu·shall all likewise completely·perish.
Lk 22:20 Likewise also the cup after eating·supper, saying,
Mt 20:5 about *the* sixth and ninth hour, he·did likewise.
Mt 21:30 the second, he·declared likewise. And answering,
Mt 25:17 And likewise, the·one *having·received* the two, he
Mk 12:21 And the third likewise.
Rm 8:26 Likewise the Spirit also is·helpful·and·works·
Tit 2:3 *for* old·women likewise, *that they·be* in a·demeanor
Tit 2:6 Likewise, exhort the younger·men to·be·
1Ti 3:8 Likewise, stewards *must·be* morally·worthy·of·
1Ti 5:25 Likewise, also, the good works *of·some* are

EG5615.3 (1x)

1Ti 5:25 able to·be·hidden, *likewise following·afterward.*

G5616 ὡσ•εί hōsêí *adv.* (34x)

Roots:G5613 G1487

G5616.1 ADV ὡσεί (2x)

Ac 6:15 ·of·Sanhedrin saw his face as·if *it·was* an·angel's
Mt 28:4 keeping·guard are·shaken and became as·if dead.

G5616.2 ADV ὡσεί (18x)

Jn 4:6 on the well. It·was *midday* about *the* sixth hour, *and*
Jn 6:10 ·to·eat; the number *was* about five·thousand *men.*
Jn 19:14 Passover, and *it·was midday* about *the* sixth hour,
Jn 19:39 and aloeswood, about *a·weight* of·a·hundred
Lk 1:56 abided together with·her about three lunar·months
Lk 3:23 Jesus himself was about thirty years·of·age, being
Lk 9:14 For there·were about five·thousand men. And he·
Lk 9:28 And it·happened about eight days after these sayings
Lk 22:41 ·himself drew·away from them about a·stone's cast,
Lk 22:59 And with·an·interval·of about one hour, someone
Lk 23:44 Now it·was *midday* about *the* sixth hour, and
Ac 2:41 and in·that·one day, about three·thousand souls
Ac 4:4 and the number of·the men was about five thousand.
Ac 5:36 tightly·bonded·themselves, about four·hundred),
Ac 10:3 ·saw openly in a·clear·vision, about *the* ninth hour
Ac 19:7 And there·were about twelve men *in* all.
Mt 14:21 And the·ones eating were about five·thousand men,
Mk 6:44 ·the loaves·of·bread were about five·thousand men.

G5616.3 ADV ὡσεί (7x)

Lk 24:11 appeared in·the·sight of·them as idle·chatter, and
Ac 2:3 ·differing tongues as of·fire were·made·visible to·
Heb 1:12 And as a·mantle, you·shall·roll them up, and they·
Heb 11:12 multitude *of·them,* and as the innumerable sand
Mt 9:36 and having·been·flung·about, as sheep not having
Mt 28:3 was as lightning, and his apparel white as snow.
Mk 9:26 came·forth, and he·became as one·dead— such·for

G5616.4 ADV ὡσεί (7x)

Jn 1:32 the Spirit descending out of·heaven like a·dove, and
Lk 3:22 Spirit descended in·a·bodily shape like a·dove upon
Lk 22:44 And his heavy·sweat became like clots of·blood
Ac 9:18 And immediately, *something* like scales fell·off
Mt 3:16 ·saw the Spirit of·God descending like a·dove and
Mk 1:10 ·split·open, and the Spirit like a·dove descending
Rv 1:14 head and *his* hairs *are* white like wool (*as* white as

G5617 Ὡσηέ Hōsēé *n/p.* (1x)

הוֹשֵׁעַ hôshẹaʿ [Hebrew]

Roots:H1954

G5617.6 N/P-PRI Ὡσηέ (1x)

Rm 9:25 As he·says also in Hosea, "I·shall·call *them* 'My

G5618 ὥσ•περ hṓspêr *adv.* (42x)

Roots:G5613 G4007

G5618.1 ADV ὥσπερ (41x)

Jn 5:21 "For just·as the Father awakens the dead and gives·
Jn 5:26 For just·as the Father has life-above in himself, in·
Lk 17:24 For just·as the lightning, the·one flashing from·out
Lk 18:11 ·thanks to·you that I·am not just·as the rest of·the
Ac 2:2 from·out of·the heaven, just·as of·a·rushing forceful
Ac 3:17 *the killing* according·to ignorance, just·as also yeur
Ac 11:15 Holy Spirit fell upon them, just·as also upon us at
Heb 4:10 ·ceased from his·own works, just·as God *did* from
Heb 7:27 a·necessity each day, just·as the high·priests *do,*
Heb 9:25 ·offer himself many·times, just·as the high·priest
Gal 4:29 Moreover, just·as then, the·one being·born
Mt 5:48 ·be complete *in·this·manner,* just·as yeur Father,
Mt 6:2 before you, just·as the stage·acting·hypocrites do in
Mt 6:5 you·shall·not be just·as the stage·acting·hypocrites
Mt 6:7 ·with·tedious·babblings, just·as the Gentiles *do,* for
Mt 6:16 sullen-looking just·as the stage·acting·hypocrites,
Mt 12:40 For just·as Jonah was three days and three nights in
Mt 13:40 "Accordingly, just·as the darnel·weeds are·
Mt 18:17 ·assembly, let·him·be to·you just·as the Gentile
Mt 20:28 just·as the Son of·Clay·Man† did·not come to·be·
Mt 24:27 For just·as the lightning comes·forth from *the* east
Mt 24:37 "But just·as *were* the days of·Noach, in·this·
Mt 24:38 For just·as in the days, the·ones that·were before
Mt 25:14 *is* just·as a·man·of·clay† journeying·abroad, *who*
Mt 25:32 one from another, just·as the shepherd distinctly·
Rm 5:12 on·account·of this: *that* just·as through one man·
Rm 5:19 For just·as through the inattentive·disregard of·one
Rm 5:21 in·order·that just·as Moral·Failure reigned in Death
Rm 6:4 in·order·that just·as Anointed-One is·already·
Rm 6:19 flesh. For just·as yeu·presented yeur members *as*
Rm 11:30 For just·as yeu·yeurselves also once were·
Jac 2:26 For just·as the body apart·from spirit is dead, in·
1Th 5:3 savage·termination assaults them, just·as having the
1Co 8:5 or upon the earth (just·as there·are many gods, and
1Co 11:12 For just·as the woman *is* from·out of·the man, in·
1Co 15:22 For just·as all within Adam die, even in·this·
1Co 16:1 the holy·ones, just·as I·thoroughly·assigned to·the
2Co 1:7 steadfast, having·seen that just·as yeu·are partners
2Co 8:7 Moreover, just·as yeu·abound in everything, in·
Eph 5:24 Moreover, just·as the entire·Called·Out·Citizenry
Rv 10:3 he·yelled·out with·a·loud voice, just·as *when* a·lion

G5618.2 ADV ὥσπερ (1x)

2Co 9:5 not as·though·some act·of·coveting *was·occurring.*

G5619 ὡσ•περ•εί hōspêrêí *adv.* (1x)

Roots:G5618 G1487

G5619 ADV ὡσπερεί (1x)

1Co 15:8 ·gazed·upon by·me·also, just·as·if by·the *babe*

G5620 ὥσ•τε hṓstê *conj.* (91x)

Roots:G5613 G5037

G5620.1 CONJ ὥστε (36x)

Lk 9:52 of·the·Samaritans, as·such to·make·ready for·him.
Gal 3:9 As·such, the·ones birthed·from·out of·trust are·
Gal 3:24 As·such, the Torah-Law has·become our strict·
Gal 4:7 As·such, you·are no·longer a·slave, but·rather a·son;
Gal 4:16 As·such, have·I·become yeur enemy, being·truthful
Mt 12:12 surpass·the·value of·a·sheep? As·such, it·is·proper
Mt 15:33 a·barren·wilderness, such·as to·stuff·full so·vast
Mt 19:6 As·such, they·are no·longer two, but·rather one
Mt 23:31 "As·such, yeu·testify against·yeurselves that yeu·
Mt 24:24 ·give great signs and wonders, such·as, if possible,
Mk 2:28 As·such, the Son of·Clay·Man† is Lord also of·the
Mk 10:8 distinctly one flesh." As·such, they·are no·longer
Rm 7:4 As·such, my brothers, yeu·yeurselves also were·put·
Rm 7:12 As·such, in·fact, the Torah-Law *is* holy, and the
Rm 13:2 As·such, the·one arranging·himself·against the
Jac 1:19 As·such, my beloved brothers, every man·of·clay†
Php 2:12 As·such, my beloved, just·as yeu·listened·and·
Php 4:1 As·such, my brothers (dearly·beloved and greatly·
1Pe 4:19 As·such, even the·ones suffering according·to the
1Th 4:18 As·such, comfort one·another with these words.
1Co 3:7 As·such, neither is the·one planting anything, nor
1Co 3:21 As·such, do·not·let·one boast in men·of·clay†, for
1Co 4:5 As·such, yeu·must·not presently·judge anything
1Co 5:8 As·such, we·should·purposefully·observe the·
1Co 7:38 As·such, even the *father* giving·away·in·marriage
1Co 10:12 As·such, the·one presuming to·stand must·look·
1Co 11:27 As·such, whoever should·eat this bread or should·
1Co 11:33 As·such, my brothers, as·yeu·are·coming·together
1Co 13:2 ·have all the trust, as·such to·relocate mountains,
1Co 14:22 As·such, the bestowed·tongues are for a·sign, not
1Co 14:39 As·such, brothers, be·zealous to·prophesy, and
1Co 15:58 As·such, my beloved brothers, become
2Co 2:7 As·such, on·the·contrary, yeu *ought* rather to·
2Co 4:12 As·such in·fact, the death operates in us, but the
2Co 5:16 As·such, from now·on, we·ourselves personally·
2Co 5:17 As·such, IF any·man *is* in Anointed-One, *he·is* a·

EG5620.1 (1x)

1Pe 1:22 *As·such,* having·cleansed yeur souls in the

G5620.2 CONJ ὥστε (42x)
Lk 5:7 filled both the sailboats, such·for them to·be·sinking.
Ac 1:19 residing·in JeruSalem, such·for this open·field to·
Ac 5:15 such·for *the people* to·bear·forth the sick in·each·of
Ac 14:1 in·this·manner to·speak, such·for a·large multitude
Ac 15:39 occurred, such·for them to·be·utterly·separated
Ac 16:26 ·was a·great earthquake, such·for the foundations
Ac 19:10 for·a·span·of two years, such·for all the·ones
Ac 19:12 even such·for sweat·towels or aprons from his
Ac 19:16 ·strength against them such·for *them* to·utterly·flee
Heb 13:6 Such·for us to·say, while·exercising·courage,
Mt 8:24 in the sea, such·for the sailboat to·be·covered by
Mt 10:1 *over* impure spirits, such·for them to·cast·out and
Mt 12:22 he·both·relieved·and·cured him, such·for the blind
Mt 13:2 ·gathered·together to him, such·for him to·embark
Mt 13:32 and becomes a·tree, such·for the birds of·the sky
Mt 13:54 their gathering, as·such·for them to·be·astounded,
Mt 15:31 such·for the crowds to·marvel, while·looking·at
Mt 27:1 against YeShua such·for him to·be·put·to·death.
Mt 27:14 not·even one utterance, such·for the governor to·
Mk 1:27 such·for *them* to·mutually·question·and·discuss
Mk 1:45 to·widely·promote the matter, such·for *Jesus* no·
Mk 2:2 were·gathered·together, such·for *them* no·longer to·
Mk 2:12 in·front of·them·all, such·for all to·be·astonished
Mk 3:10 ·and·cured many, such·for as·many *of·them* as
Mk 3:20 was·coming·together again, such·for them not to·
Mk 4:32 it·produces great branches, such·for the birds of·
Mk 4:37 into the sailboat, such·for it even·now to·be·
Mk 9:26 he·became as one·dead— such·for many to·say
Mk 15:5 not·even·one·thing, such·for Pilate to·marvel.
Rm 7:6 ·which we·were·fully·held, such·for us to·be·slaves
Rm 15:19 Spirit, such·for me to·have·completely·fulfilled
Php 1:13 such·for my bonds in *the* Anointed-One to·become
1Pe 1:21 and giving glory to·him)— such·for yeur trust and
1Th 1:7 such·for yeu to·become model·examples to·all the·
1Th 1:8 toward God has·gone·forth, such·for us not to·have
2Th 1:4 such·for we ourselves to·boast in yeu among the
2Th 2:4 or that·is·reverenced,' 'such·for him to·sit·down as
1Co 1:7 such·for yeu not to·be·presently·lacking in not·
1Co 5:1 among the Gentiles, such·for someone to·have the
2Co 1:8 ability *to·bear it*, such·for us to·be·at·an·utter·loss
2Co 3:7 ·into·being in glory— such·for the Sons of·IsraEl
2Co 7:7 fervency on·behalf of·me, such·for me to·rejoice
EG5620.2 (7x)
Lk 24:16 their eyes were·securely·held, *such·for them* not
Heb 11:5 By·trust, Enoch was·transferred *such·for* him not
Heb 12:19 hearing shunned *it*, *such·for them to·request for*
Gal 5:7 well. Who cut·into·yeur·path *such·for* yeu to·not be·
Eph 4:22 *such·for* yeu to·put·off the old man·of·clay†
Eph 4:23 and *such·for yeu* to·be·rejuvenated in·the spirit of·
Col 1:10 *such·for* yeu to·walk worthily of·the Lord into all
G5620.3 CONJ ὥστε (5x)
Jn 3:16 loved the world, such·that he·gave his only·begotten
Lk 12:1 such·that they·trampled·down one·another, *Jesus*
Gal 2:13 ·together with·him, such·that BarNabas also was·
Mt 8:28 exceedingly fierce, such·that *it·caused* some not
Mk 4:1 was·gathered·together to him, such·that he *was*

G5621 ὠτίον ōtíôn *n.* (5x)
Roots:G3775 G2444-3
G5621.2 N-ASN ὠτίον (4x)
Jn 18:10 and he·chopped·off his right earlobe. And the
Jn 18:26 a·kinsman of·him·whose earlobe Peter chopped·off,
Mt 26:51 ·the designated·high·priest, he·removed his earlobe.
Mk 14:47 designated·high·priest and removed his earlobe.
G5621.2 N-GSN ὠτίου (1x)
Lk 22:51 And laying·hold of·his earlobe, he·healed him.

G5622 ὠφέλεια ōphḗlêia *n.* (2x)
Roots:G5624 Compare:G2039 G2771
G5622.1 N-NSF ὠφέλεια (1x)
Rm 3:1 ·benefit? Or what *is* the profit of·the circumcision?
G5622.2 N-GSF ὠφελείας (1x)
Jud 1:16 persons of·profitable·advantage through·gracious·.

G5623 ὠφελέω ōphêlḗō *v.* (15x)
Roots:G5624 Compare:G0018 See:G5622
xLangAlso:H3276
G5623.2 V-FAI-1S ὠφελήσω (1x)
1Co 14:6 with·bestowed·tongues, how shall·I·benefit yeu,
G5623.2 V-FAI-3S ὠφελήσει (2x)
Gal 5:2 Anointed-One shall·benefit yeu not·even·one·bit.
Mk 8:36 "For how shall·it·benefit a·man·of·clay†, if he·
G5623.2 V-PAI-2P ὠφελεῖτε (1x)
Jn 12:19 how yeu·do·not benefit not·even·one·thing?
G5623.2 V-PAI-3S ὠφελεῖ (2x)
Jn 6:63 The flesh does·not benefit not·even·one·thing. The
Rm 2:25 ·fact, circumcision benefits if you·should·practice
G5623.2 V-PPI-1S ὠφελοῦμαι (1x)
1Co 13:3 ·not have love, it·benefits not·even·one·thing.
G5623.2 V-PPI-3S ὠφελεῖται (2x)
Lk 9:25 "For how·is a·man·of·clay† benefited, after·gaining
Mt 16:26 "For what·is a·man·of·clay† being·benefited, if he·
G5623.2 V-AAI-3S ὠφέλησεν (1x)
Heb 4:2 *through* hearing did·not benefit them, not having·
G5623.2 V-APS-2S ὠφεληθῇς (2x)
Mt 15:5 "Although you·should·have·benefited as·a·result of·
Mk 7:11 Although you·should·have·benefited as·a·result of·
G5623.3 V-PAI-3S ὠφελεῖ (1x)
Mt 27:24 that *reasoning with·them* benefits nothing·at·all,
G5623.3 V-API-3P ὠφελήθησαν (1x)
Heb 13:9 which·were·not beneficial·to the·ones walking in
G5623.3 V-APP-NSF ὠφεληθεῖσα (1x)
Mk 5:26 with not·one·bit *of·it* being·beneficial, but·yet *with·*

G5624 ὠφέλιμος ōphḗlimôs *adj.* (4x)
Roots:G3786 Compare:G4851 See:G5623 G5622
G5624 A-NSM ὠφέλιμος (3x)
1Ti 4:8 bodily training is profitable just·for a·brief·moment,
1Ti 4:8 ·Reverence is profitable specifically·for all·things,
2Ti 3:16 ·God, and *is* profitable particularly·for instruction,
G5624 A-NPN ὠφέλιμα (1x)
Tit 3:8 ·things and profitable·things for·the men·of·clay†.

NOTES

NOTES

NOTES

Ingram Content Group UK Ltd.
Milton Keynes UK
UKHW050817020523
421098UK00013B/364